ANNUAL STATEMENT STUDIES

2003 2004

RMA
Annual Statement Studies
Copyright, Ordering, Licensing, and Use of Data Information

All of the information contained herein is obtained from sources believed to be accurate and reliable. All representations contained herein are believed by RMA to be as accurate as the data and methodologies will allow. However, because of the possibilities of human and mechanical error, as well as unforeseen factors beyond RMA's control, the information herein is provided "as is" without warranty of any kind and RMA makes no representations or warranties express or implied to a subscriber or licensee or any other person or entity as to the accuracy, timeliness, completeness, merchantability or fitness for any particular purpose of any of the information contained herein. Moreover, information is supplied without warranty on the understanding that any person who acts upon it or otherwise changes position in reliance thereon does so entirely at such person's own risk.

The Statement Studies is not intended to provide loan advice or recommendations of any kind. The Statement Studies and the information contained therein are intended for educational, informational, and research purposes only. Accordingly, RMA does not offer any advice regarding the suitability of any loan, of any debtor or of any other business determination made by you, and it assumes no responsibility or liability for any advice or other guidance that you may take from the Statement Studies. Prior to making any business decisions, you are advised to conduct all necessary due diligence as may be appropriate under the circumstances, and RMA assumes no responsibility or liability for any business decisions, including but not limited to loan decision, or other services rendered by you based upon the Statement Studies or results obtained therefrom.

**The Annual Statement Studies is a copyrighted product of RMA.
All rights reserved. No part of this product may be copied, reproduced, replicated, disseminated, or distributed in any form or by any means, electronic or mechanical, without the express written permission of RMA.**

To **obtain permission** to copy, quote, reproduce, replicate, disseminate, or distribute the Statement Studies please prepare a brief letter outlining at minimum who you are and what your intended use of the data is, and fax it to RMA—Information Products at 215-446-4101 or e-mail it to the following address: studies@rmahq.org. Depending on the use described, there may be a royalty fee due to RMA.

To **purchase** a copy, or additional copies, of the Statement Studies in book, disk, or CD-ROM format, you should contact RMA's Customer Relations at 1-800-677-7621. Regional data presented in the same fashion as you see in this book is available in either disk or CD-ROM format.

If the data are going to be used with or incorporated into other products that will in turn be sold to others—this typically refers to software-oriented or derived products—a **license agreement** will need to be executed. In these cases please prepare a brief letter outlining at minimum who you are and what your intended use of the data is, including information on the product that Statement Studies will be used with, and fax that to RMA—Information Products at 215-446-4101 or e-mail this to the following address: studies@rmahq.org.

If you have a **question regarding the data,** please reference the detailed explanatory notes provided in the help section of the enclosed product. If you are unable to find the answer to your question, please contact us by e-mail at the following address studies@rmahq.org. Be sure to include your detailed question along with your telephone number, fax number, and e-mail address in any correspondence with RMA.

RMA
One Liberty Place
Philadelphia, PA 19103-7398
© 2003 by RMA
ISBN 1-57070-304-3

TABLE OF CONTENTS

*General Industries Format means that a valid construction NAICS was assigned to the subject companies contained in the sample; however, the financial statements were prepared using a general or traditional manufacturing or service industries presentation of results versus using a Percentage of Completion method of accounting. Industries found in the Percentage of Completion presentation follow the presentation used by RMA in the past.

RMA—THE RISK MANAGEMENT ASSOCIATION

Founded in 1914—The Risk Management Association is a member-driven professional association whose sole purpose is to advance the use of soound risk principles in the financial services industry. RMA promotes an enterprise-wide approach to risk management that focuses on credit risk, market risk, and operational risk.

Headquartered in Philadelphia, RMA has 3,000 institutional members that include banks of all sizes as well as nonbank institutions. They are represented in the Association 16,000 commercial loan, credit, and risk management professionals in the 50 states, Puerto Rico, Canada, and numerous foreign cities, including Hong Kong, Singapore, Melbourne and London.

RMA has taken a leadership role in providing industry input to regulators as they reform the Basel Capital Accord, first instituted in 1988. This input from RMA provides regulators with information about how the Accord's proposals would impact bank capital and overall operations.

RMA's strong relationship with members and regulators helps us develop new risk management techniques and innovative products. Our education and training programs are geared to risk management professionals at every stage of their careers. Over 70% of the Association's revenue is derived from providing products and services to members.

RMA ACKNOWLEDGES AND THANKS THE FOLLOWING MEMBER INSTITUTIONS, CONTRIBUTORS TO THE 2003 RECORD-BREAKING STATEMENT STUDIES DATA SUBMISSIONS PROGRAM.

Centier Bank
Intergra Bank
Irwin Union Bank & Trust Co.
Lafayette Bank & Trust Co.
Lake City Bank
Mercantile National Bank of Indiana
National City Bank Indiana
STAR Financial Bank

IOWA
American Trust & Savings Bank
Dubuque Bank & Trust Co.
F&M Bank Iowa Central
Farmers State Bank
First National Bank of Akron
Security National Bank
Wells Fargo Bank Iowa N.A.

KANSAS
Bank of Blue Valley
Central Bank & Trust Co.
Citizens National Bank
Commerce Bank N.A.
Cornerstone Bank
Emporia State Bank and Trust
   Company
Emprise Bank
Emprise Bank N.A.
Fidelity Bank
First Bank
First National Bank
Intrust Bank
Legacy Bank
Midland National Bank
Mulvane State Bank
Silver Lake Bank
Sunflower Bank

KENTUCKY
Central Bank & Trust Co.
Community Trust Bank, N.A.
National City Bank Kentucky

LOUISIANA
Business Bank of Baton Rouge
Hibernia National Bank
Jeff Davis Bank & Trust Co.
Omni Bank
Progressive Bank
South Louisiana Bank
Whitney National Bank

MAINE
Bangor Savings Bank
Bank North Group Inc.
First Citizens Bank
First National Bank Damariscotta
Gardiner Savings Institution FSB
Gorham Savings Bank
Kennebunk Savings Bank
Norway Savings Bank

MARYLAND
Annapolis Banking & Trust Co.
Bank of Glen Burnie
Bank of Southern Maryland
Calvert Bank & Trust Co.
Chesapeake Bank of Maryland
Chevy Chase Bank FSB
Citizens National Bank
County Banking & Trust Co.
F&M Bank
Farmers & Mechanics National Bank
Frederick County Bank
Fredericktown Bank & Trust Co.
Hagerstown Trust Company
Key Bank and Trust
M & T Bank
Mercantile-Safe Deposit & Trust
Peninsula Bank
Potomac Valley Bank
Provident Bank of Maryland
Queenstown Bank of Maryland
Sandy Spring National Bank
Sequoia Bank
Westminster Union Bank

MASSACHUSETTS
Bank of Western Massachusetts
Beverly National Bank
Boston Private Bank & Trust Co.
Bristol County Savings Bank
Canton Institution for Savings
Cape Cod Bank & Trust Co.
Cape Cod Five Cents Svgs Bank
Central Co-Operative Bank
Commonwealth National Bank
Community Bank
Community National Bank
Eastern Bank
Enterprise Bank and Trust Co.
Fall River Five Cents Svgs Bank
Fleet Boston Corporation
Lawrence Savings Bank
Legacy Banks
Nantucket Bank
North Middlesex Savings Bank
Peoples Savings Bank
Slade's Ferry Trust Co.
The Milford National Bank and Trust
Webster Five Cents Savings Bank
Westbank
Westfield Bank
Winchester Savings Bank

MICHIGAN
Capitol National Bank
Century Bank & Trust
Chemical Bank Shoreline
Citizens Bank
Citizens National Bank
Comerica Bank
Commercial Bank

CSB Bank
First National Bank in Howell
FirstBank
FirstBank - Alma
Honor State Bank
Huron Community Bank
Independent Bank
Mercantile Bank of West Michigan
Metrobank
Midwest Guaranty Bank
Peoples State Bank
Southern Michigan Bank & Trust
Standard Federal Bank N.A.
State Bank
State Bank of Caledonia
United Bank & Trust
United Bank of Michigan
Valley Ridge Bank

MINNESOTA
AgriBank FCB
American Bank of St. Paul
Anchor Bank
Anchor Bank St. Paul
Beacon Bank
Bremer Bank, N.A.
Cherokee State Bank of St. Paul
Citizens Independent Bank
Community Bank Chaska
Community National Bank
Crown Bank
Excel Bank
Fidelity Bank
First Minnetonka City Bank
First National Bank Montevideo
First National Bank of Waconia
First National Bank Cannon Falls
Heritage National Bank
Home Federal Savings Bank
Merchants Bank, N.A.
Northeast Bank of Minneapolis
Northern National Bank
Roundbank
StearnsBank, N.A.
TCF National Bank
The Business Bank
US Bank National Association
Wells Fargo Bank Minnesota N.A.
Western Bank
Woodlands National Bank

MISSISSIPPI
BanCorp South Bank
Merchants & Farmers Bank
Peoples Bank & Trust Co.
Trustmark National Bank
Union Planters Bank of Mississippi
Union Planters Bk Central MS

MISSOURI
Boone County National Bank
Cass Commercial Bank
Central Trust Bank
Commerce Bank N.A.
Empire Bank
Exchange National Bank Jeff City
First Bank
First National Bank of St. Louis
Jefferson Bank of Missouri
Midwest Bank Centre
Missouri State Bank
Ozark Mountain Bank
Royal Banks of Missouri
UMB Bank N.A.
UMB Bank of St. Louis N.A.

MONTANA
American Bank
First Interstate Bank
First Interstate Bank

NEBRASKA
First National Bank & Trust Co.
First National Bank of North Platte
First National Bank of Omaha
Security National Bank Omaha
Union Bank & Trust Company
Washington County Bank

NEVADA
BankWest of Nevada
Sun West Bank

NEW HAMPSHIRE
Connecticut River Bank
Ledyard National Bank

NEW JERSEY
Commerce Bank N.A.
Hudson United Bank
OceanFirst Bank
Peapack-Gladstone Bank
Somerset Valley Bank
Sun National Bank
The Bank
Trust Company of New Jersey
Two River Community Bank
Union Center National Bank
United Trust Bank
Yardville National Bank

NEW MEXICO
Charter Bank
Citizens Bank of Clovis
Lea County State Bank
Western Commerce Bank

NEW YORK
Adirondack Bank N.A.
Adirondack Trust Company
Alliance Bank
Bank Leumi USA
BSB Bank & Trust
Canandaigua National Bank
Champlain National Bank
Chemung Canal Trust Co.
Community Bank N.A.
First Tier Bank & Trust
Fulton Savings Bank
Glens Falls National Bank
HSBC Bank USA
JP Morgan Chase
Long Island Commercial Bank
National Union Bank of Kinderhook
NBT Bank, N.A.
North Fork Bank
Saratoga National Bank
Savannah Bank N.A.
SBU Bank
State Bank of Long Island
Steuben Trust Co.
Suffolk County National Bank
Tioga State Bank
Tompkins Trust Co.

NORTH CAROLINA
Bank of America
BB&T
Capital Bank
Central Carolina Bank
East Carolina Bank
First Charter Bank
First Citizens Bank & Trust Co.
First National Bank & Trust Co.
Lexington State Bank
Wachovia Corporation

NORTH DAKOTA
Alerus Financial, N.A.
Bank of North Dakota
Bremer Bank, N.A.
Community National Bank
State Bank of Fargo

OHIO
Belmont National Bank
Charter One Bank FSB
Fifth Third Bank Northwestern OH
First Financial Bancorp
FirstMerit Bank, N.A.
Huntington National Bank
Key Bank
Liberty Savings Bank FSB
National City Bank
National City Bank Dayton
North Side Bank & Trust Co.
Provident Bank

Second National Bank
Sky Bank

UNIZAN BANK
Oklahoma
Bank of Oklahoma N.A.
Local Oklahoma Bank
Regent Bank
Stillwater National Bank

OREGON
Albina Community Bank
Centennial Bank
Pacific Continental Bank
West Coast Bank

PENNSYLVANIA
AmeriServ Bank
Blue Ball National Bank
Bryn Mawr Trust Co.
Citizens National Bank
Clearfield Bank & Trust Co.
Commerce Bank of Harrisburg
Commercial National Bank
Community Bank
County National Bank
CSB Bank
Dollar Bank
East Penn Bank
Ephrata National Bank
Fidelity Bank Pa SB
First Columbia Bank & Trust Co.
First Commonwealth Bank
First Federal Bank
First Liberty Bank & Trust
First National Bank of Slippery Rock
First National Bank Pennsylvania
First Natl Bank of County Chester
Firstrust Bank
FNB Bank
Fulton Bank
Harleysville National Bank
Honesdale National Bank
Jersey Shore State Bank
Lafayette Ambassador Bank
Lebanon Valley Farmers Bank
Luzerne National Bank
Madison Bank
Marion Center National Bank
Mellon Bank N.A.
National City Bank of PA
National Penn Bank
Northwest Savings Bank
Orrstown Bank
Pennstar Bank
Peoples Bank
PNC Bank
Portage National Bank
Roxborough-Manayunk Bank
Somerset Trust Company

Sterling Financial
Swineford National Bank
Third Federal Savings Bank
Univest National Bank & Trust Co.
Washington Federal Savings
West Milton State Bank
Woodlands Bank

RHODE ISLAND
Bank Rhode Island
Citizens Trust Company
Washington Trust Company

SOUTH CAROLINA
Bank of South Carolina
Carolina First Bank
Community FirstBank
Conway National Bank
First Citizens Bank
First National Bank of the Carolinas
Greer State Bank

SOUTH DAKOTA
American State Bank
BankWest
First National Bank Brookings
First National Bank Sioux Falls
First National Bank South Dakota
Home Federal Bank
Wells Fargo

TENNESSEE
Bank of Nashville
First Farmers and Merchants
    National Bank
First Tennessee Bank N.A.
INSOUTH Bank
Mountain National Bank

TEXAS
Amarillo National Bank
American Bank of Texas
Bank of the West
Broadway National Bank
Coastal Banc SSB
Extraco Banks N.A.
Frost National Bank

Liberty Bank SSB
MetroBank N.A.
Southside Bank
Southwest Bank of Texas N.A.
Texas Gulf Bank
Wells Fargo-El Paso
Wells Fargo-East

UTAH
Bank of Utah
Brighton Bank
First Utah Bank
State Bank of Southern Utah
Zions First National Bank

VERMONT
Community National Bank
Factory Point National Bank
Lyndonville Savings B&T Co.
National Bank of Middlebury
Passumpsic Savings Bank

VIRGINIA
Bank of Lancaster
Chesapeake Bank
Consolidated Bank & Trust Co.
Farmers & Merchants Bk E. Shore
First Community Bank, N.A.
First National Bank
First Virginia Bank
First Virginia Bank Colonial
First Virginia Bank - Hampton Rd.
First Virginia Bank Southwest
Freedom Bank of Virginia
Harbor Bank
Monarch Bank
Old Point National Bank
Virginia Bank & Trust Co.
Virginia Commerce Bank N.A.
Virginia National Bank

WASHINGTON
Bank of the Pacific
Banner Bank
City Bank
Columbia Bank
Evergreen Bank

First Heritage Bank Snohomish
Northwest Farm Credit Services
    (ACA)
Pacifica Bank
Security State Bank
Washington First International Bank
Washington Mututal
Washington Trust Bank
Whidbey Island Bank

WEST VIRGINIA
First Century Bank N.A.
Progressive Bank N.A.
United National Bank

WISCONSIN
Anchor Bank, FSB
Associated Bank Green Bay N.A.
Bank of Elmwood
Blackhawk State Bank
Bremer Bank
Citizens Bank of Mukwonago
Community Business Bank
Coulee State Bank
First Bank Financial Centre
First Banking Center
First National Bank & Trust
First National Bank Fox Valley
First National Bank of Baldwin
First National Bank of Hudson
Grafton State Bank c/o Merchants &
    Manufacturers Bancorp
Johnson Bank
M&I Bank
M&I Marshall & Ilsley Bank
Park Bank of Madison
Park Bank of Brookfield
Southport Bank
St. Francis Bank, FSB
TCF National Bank
The Business Bank of the Fox River
    Valley

WYOMING
Jackson State Bank

Introduction to

Annual Statement Studies: Financial Ratio Benchmarks, 2003-2004

and

General Organization of Content

Below are some notes about the *Annual Statement Studies: Financial Ratio Benchmarks* that we hope will explain its **presentation**, clarify its **organization**, and answer **frequently asked questions**.

- The statements that go into producing the composites presented herein are supplied by RMA member institutions and represent the financials on their commercial customers and prospects. The names of the individual entities are not known to RMA for confidentiality purposes; they are removed before the data is delivered to RMA. The raw data making up each composite is not available to any third party.

- The *Statement Studies: Financial Ratio Benchmarks* contains composite financial data. Financial statements on each industry are shown in common size, accompanied by widely used ratios. Balance sheets and income statements are shown in common size, with each item a percentage of total assets and sales (or revenues), respectively. Common size statements are computed for each individual statement in an industry group, and all the figures are then added and averaged. In some cases, because of computer rounding, the figures to the right of the decimal point do not balance exactly with the totals shown. Credits and losses are indicated by a minus sign beside the value.

- The 2003-2004 *Annual Statement Studies: Financial Ratio Benchmarks* book is organized according to the North American Industry Classification System (NAICS), a product of the U.S. Office of Management and Budget. At the top of each page of data, you will see both the NAICS and the Standard Industrial Classification (SIC) codes. An NAICS code may correspond to more than one SIC, so you may see several SICs listed. If an NAICS code maps to more than three SIC codes, only the first three SICs will be listed at the top of the page. All codes can be found in the description index and the SIC table found in the following pages. To provide further delineation, the book is broken down into 17 sections that outline major types of businesses. If you know the NAICS number you are looking for, a NAICS-page guide is provided in front of this book. If you know the SIC number you are looking for, an SIC-page guide is provided in the front of the book. In general, the book is arranged in ascending NAICS numerical order. A text-based index is provided near the end of the book. Full descriptions of each NAICS presented in the book are provided in the table of contents.

- **If you do not know the precise industry NAICS/SIC** you are looking for, contact the Census Bureau at 1-888-75NAICS or naics@census.gov. Describe the activity of the establishment for which you need an industry code and you will receive a reply. Another source to help you assign the correct NAICS/SIC industry name and number can be found at www.census.gov/epcd/www/naics.html.

- **If you cannot find the industry you are looking for** (i.e., you know you need industry xxxxxx but it is not in the product) that means that, unfortunately, we do not have it available. Many times, we have information on an industry, but because the sample size was too small or there were significant questions concerning the data, we chose not to publish it. In other instances, we simply do not have the data. Generally, we publish most of what we receive, and if it's not in the book we simply don't have it. Generally, when there are fewer than 10 financial statements in a particular size category, the composite data is not shown because such a small sample is not considered representative and could be misleading. However, all the data for that industry is shown in the All Sizes column. The total number of statements for each size category is shown in bold print at the top of each page.

- In general, the data for a particular industry appears on both the right and left pages. The heading Current Data Sorted by Assets is on the far left. The center section of the double page presentation contains the Comparative Historical Data, with the All Sizes column for the current year shown under the heading 4/1/xx-3/31/xx. Comparable data from past editions of the *Annual Statement Studies: Financial Ratio Benchmarks* also appears in this section. To the far right is the display Current Data Sorted by Sales.

- Except for contractors who use the percentage-of-completion method of accounting, companies having less than $250 million in total assets were used in our presentation regardless of the way the data was sorted. **The section for contractors using the percentage-of-completion method of accounting contains only data sorted by revenue.** Size categories are determined only by contract revenues with no upper limit placed on revenue size.

- The information shown at the top of each page includes the following: 1) the identity of the industry group; 2) its North American Industry Classification System (NAICS) number; its Standard Industrial Classification (SIC) number; 3) a breakdown by size categories of the types of financial statements reported; 4) the number of statements in each category; 5) the dates of the statements used; and 6) the size categories. For instance, 16 (4/1-9/30/xx) means that 16 statements with fiscal dates between April 1 and September 30, xxxx, make up part of the sample.

- At the bottom of each page, the sum of the sales (or revenues) and total assets for all the financial statements in each size category are shown. The data is provided to allow recasting the common size statements into dollar amounts. To do this, divide the number at the bottom of the page by the number of statements in that size category. Then multiply the result by the percentages in the common size statement.

- We appreciate the cooperation of the Construction Financial Management Association (CFMA) in permitting us to reproduce excerpts from its *Construction Industry Annual Financial Survey*. This data complements our own contractor industry data. Comparative ratios on consumer finance companies are provided in this section to assist in the analysis of the industry. These ratios were prepared by Bank One. RMA is grateful to Bank One for its contribution.

- The Sources Section of alternative information regarding certain industries is no longer included in this product.

- RMA recommends that *Annual Statement Studies: Financial Ratio Benchmarks* data be regarded only as general guidelines and not as absolute industry norms. There are several reasons why the data may not be fully representative of a given industry:

  1. The financial statements used in the *Annual Statement Studies: Financial Ratio Benchmarks* are not selected by any random or statistically reliable method. RMA member banks voluntarily submit the raw data they have available each year with no limitation on company size.

  2. Many companies have varied product lines; however, the *Annual Statement Studies: Financial Ratio Benchmarks* categorizes them by their primary product NAICS/SIC number only.

  3. Some of our industry samples are rather small in relation to the total number of firms in a given industry. A relatively small sample can increase the chances that some of our composites do not fully represent an industry.

  4. There is the chance that an extreme statement can be present in a sample, causing a disproportionate influence on the industry composite. This is particularly true in a relatively small sample.

  5. Companies within the same industry may differ in their method of operations, which in turn can directly influence their financial statements. Since they are included in our sample, these statements can significantly affect our composite calculations.

  6. Other considerations that can result in variations among different companies engaged in the same general line of business are different labor markets; geographical location; different accounting methods; quality of products handled; sources and methods of financing; and terms of sale.

For these reasons, RMA does not recommend that the Annual Statement Studies: Financial Ratio Benchmarks *figures be considered as absolute norms for a given industry. Rather, the figures should be used only as general guidelines and as a supplement to the other methods of financial analysis. RMA makes no claim as to the representativeness of the figures printed in this book.*

DEFINITION OF RATIOS
INTRODUCTION

Below the common size balance sheet and income statement presented on each data page are a series of ratios that have been computed from the financial statement data. Each ratio has three values: the upper quartile, median, and lower quartile. For any given ratio, these figures are calculated by first computing the value of the ratio for each financial statement in the sample. These values are then arrayed (listed) in an order from the strongest to the weakest. (We acknowledge that, for certain ratios, there may be differences of opinion concerning what is a strong or a weak value. RMA has resolved this problem by following general banking guidelines consistent with sound credit practice in its presentation of data.)

The array of values is then divided into four groups of equal size. The three points that divide the array are called quartiles: the upper quartile, second quartile (or median), and lower quartile. The upper quartile is that point at which one-quarter of the array of ratios falls between the strongest ratio and the upper-quartile point. The median is the middle value, and the lower quartile is that point at which three-quarters of the array falls between the strongest ratio and the lower-quartile point. In many cases we take the average of two values to arrive at the quartile value. The median and quartile values will be shown on all *Statement Studies* data pages in the order indicated below. A sample is shown below for illustrative purposes.

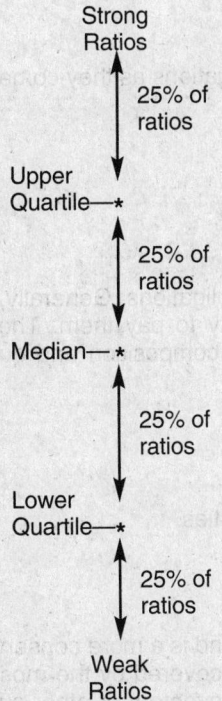

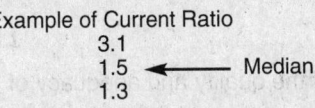

Example of Current Ratio
3.1
1.5 ←——— Median
1.3

There are several reasons for using medians and quartiles instead of an average. One is to eliminate the influence that values in an "unusual" statement would have on an average. The method used more accurately reflects the ranges of ratio values than would a straight averaging method.

It is important to understand that the spread (range) between the upper and lower quartiles represents the middle 50% of all the companies in a sample. Ratio values greater than the upper or less than the lower quartiles, therefore, begin to approach "unusual" values.

For some ratio values, you will occasionally see an entry that is other than a conventional number. These unusual entries are defined as follows:

(1) UND—This stands for "undefined," the result of the denominator in a ratio calculation approaching zero.

(2) NM—This may occasionally appear as a quartile or median for the ratios sales/working capital, debt/worth, and fixed/worth. It stands for "no meaning" in cases where the dispersion is so small that any interpretation is meaningless.

(3) 999.8—When a ratio value equals 1,000 or more, it also becomes an "unusual" value and is given the "999.8" designation. This is considered to be a close enough approximation to the actual unusually large value.

Important Notes:

Throughout the *Statement Studies,* the ratio values have been omitted whenever there were fewer than 10 statements in a sample. Occasionally, the number of statements used in a ratio array will differ from the number of statements in a sample because certain elements of data may not be present in all financial statements. **In these cases, the number of statements used is shown in parentheses to the left of the array.**

For certain ratios (sales/receivables, cost of sales/inventory, cost of sales/payables) you will see two numbers, one in **BOLD** and one in regular type. These ratios are generally called turnover ratios. The number in **BOLD** represents **the number of days** and the number in regular type is **the number of times**. Please see the definition of sales/receivables on the following pages for an excellent description of the two types of calculations and what each means.

In interpreting ratios, the "strongest" or "best" value is not always the largest numerical value, nor is the "weakest" always the lowest numerical value. The following description of each ratio appearing in the *Statement Studies* will provide details regarding the arraying of the values. The ratios in the *Statement Studies* are grouped into five principal categories: liquidity, coverage, leverage, operating, and specific expense items.

Inventory presentations are based on fiscal year-end point-in-time balances, not averages. In addition, our data capture does not permit us to know what method of inventory accounting (LIFO or FIFO, for instance) was used.

The following ratios are contained in the *Statement Studies*:

LIQUIDITY RATIOS

Liquidity is a measure of the quality and adequacy of current assets to meet current obligations as they come due.

1. Current Ratio

Computation: Total current assets divided by total current liabilities.

$$\frac{\text{Total Current Assets}}{\text{Total Current Liabilities}}$$

Interpretation: This ratio is a rough indication of a firm's ability to service its current obligations. Generally, the higher the current ratio, the greater the "cushion" between current obligations and a firm's ability to pay them. The stronger ratio reflects a numerical superiority of current assets over current liabilities. However, the composition and quality of current assets is a critical factor in the analysis of an individual firm's liquidity.

The ratio values are arrayed from the highest positive to the lowest positive.

2. Quick Ratio

Computation: Cash and equivalents plus trade receivables divided by total current liabilities.

$$\frac{\text{Cash \& Equivalents + Trade Receivables (net)}}{\text{Total Current Liabilities}}$$

Interpretation: Also known as the "acid test" ratio, it is a refinement of the current ratio and is a more conservative measure of liquidity. The ratio expresses the degree to which a company's current liabilities are covered by the most liquid current assets. Generally, any value of less than 1 to 1 implies a reciprocal "dependency" on inventory or other current assets to liquidate short-term debt.

The ratio values are arrayed from the highest positive to the lowest positive.

3. Sales/Receivables

Computation: Net sales are divided by trade receivables.

$$\frac{\text{Net Sales}}{\text{Trade Receivables (net)}}$$

In the contractor section, both accounts receivable-progress billings and accounts receivable-current retention are included in the receivables figure used in calculating the revenues/receivables and receivables/payables ratios.

Interpretation: This ratio measures the number of times trade receivables turn over during the year. The higher the turnover of receivables, the shorter the time between sale and cash collection. For example, a company with sales of $720,000 and receivables of $120,000 would have a sales/receivables ratio of 6.0, which means receivables turn over six times a year. If a company's receivables appear to be turning more slowly than the rest of the industry, further research is needed and the quality of the receivables should be examined closely.

A problem with this ratio is that it compares one day's receivables, shown at statement date, to total annual sales and does not take into consideration seasonal fluctuations. An additional problem in interpretation may arise when there is a large proportion of cash sales to total sales.

When the receivables figure is zero, the quotient will be undefined (UND) and represents the best possible ratio. The ratio values are therefore arrayed starting with undefined (UND) and then from the numerically highest value to the numerically lowest value. The only time a zero will appear in the array is when the sales figure is low and the quotient rounds off to zero. By definition, this ratio cannot be negative.

Days' Receivables: The sales/receivables ratio will have a figure printed in bold type directly to the left of the array. This figure is the days' receivables.

Computation: The sales/receivables ratio divided into 365 (the number of days in one year).

$$\frac{365}{\text{Sales/Receivables ratio}}$$

Interpretation: This figure expresses the average time in days that receivables are outstanding. Generally, the greater number of days outstanding, the greater the probability of delinquencies in accounts receivable. A comparison of a company's daily receivables may indicate the extent of a company's control over credit and collections. The terms offered by a company to its customers, however, may differ from terms within the industry and should be taken into consideration.

In the example above, 365 ÷ 6 = 61 (i.e., the average receivable is collected in 61 days).

4. Cost of Sales/Inventory

Computation: Cost of sales divided by inventory.

$$\frac{\text{Cost of Sales}}{\text{Inventory}}$$

Interpretation: This ratio measures the number of times inventory is turned over during the year. High inventory turnover can indicate better liquidity or superior merchandising. Conversely, it can indicate a shortage of needed inventory for sales. Low inventory turnover can indicate poor liquidity, possible overstocking, obsolescence, or, in contrast to these negative interpretations, a planned inventory buildup in the case of material shortages. A problem with this ratio is that it compares one day's inventory to cost of goods sold and does not take seasonal fluctuations into account. When the inventory figure is zero, the quotient will be undefined (UND) and represents the best possible ratio. The ratio values are arrayed starting with undefined (UND) and then from the numerically highest value to the numerically lowest value. The only time a zero will appear in the array is when the figure for cost of sales is very low and the quotient rounds off to zero.

Some service industries report data for cost of sales, while others do not. Note that in cases where the sample reporting it was insufficient, we have adjusted the data for cost of sales by putting it into operating expenses. Please be aware, too, that our data collection process does not provide for differentiating the method of inventory valuation.

Days' Inventory
The cost of sales/inventory ratio will have a figure printed in bold type directly to the left of the array. This figure is the days' inventory.

Computation: The cost of sales/inventory ratio divided into 365 (the number of days in one year).

$$\frac{365}{\text{Cost of Sales/Inventory ratio}}$$

Interpretation: Division of the inventory turnover ratio into 365 days yields the average length of time units are in inventory.

5. Cost of Sales/Payables

Computation: Cost of sales divided by trade payables.

$$\frac{\text{Cost of Sales}}{\text{Trade Payables}}$$

In the contractor section, both Accounts Payable-Trade and Accounts Payable-Retention are included in the payables figure used in calculating the Cost of Revenues/Payables and Receivables/Payables ratios.

Interpretation: This ratio measures the number of times trade payables turn over during the year. The higher the turnover of payables, the shorter the time between purchase and payment. If a company's payables appear to be turning more slowly than the industry, then the company may be experiencing cash shortages, disputing invoices with suppliers, enjoying extended terms, or deliberately expanding its trade credit. The ratio comparison of company to industry suggests the existence of these or other possible causes. If a firm buys on 30-day terms, it is reasonable to expect this ratio to turn over in approximately 30 days.

A problem with this ratio is that it compares one day's payables to cost of goods sold and does not take seasonal fluctuations into account. When the payables figure is zero, the quotient will be undefined (UND) and represents the best possible ratio. The

ratio values are arrayed starting with undefined (UND) and then from the numerically highest to the numerically lowest value. The only time a zero will appear in the array is when the cost of sales figure is very low and the quotient rounds off to zero.

Days' Payables

The cost of sales/payables ratio will have a figure printed in bold type directly to the left of the array. This figure is the days' payables.

Computation: The cost of sales/payables ratio divided into 365 (the number of days in one year).

$$\frac{365}{\text{Cost of Sales/Payables ratio}}$$

Interpretation: Division of the payables turnover ratio into 365 days yields the average length of time trade debt is outstanding.

6. Sales/Working Capital

Computation: Net sales divided by net working capital (current assets less current liabilities equals net working capital).

$$\frac{\text{Net Sales}}{\text{Net Working Capital}}$$

Interpretation: Working capital is a measure of the margin of protection for current creditors. It reflects the ability to finance current operations. Relating the level of sales arising from operations to the underlying working capital measures how efficiently working capital is employed. A low ratio may indicate an inefficient use of working capital while a very high ratio often signifies overtrading—a vulnerable position for creditors.

If working capital is zero, the quotient is undefined (UND). If working capital is negative, the quotient is negative. The ratio values are arrayed from the lowest positive to the highest positive, to undefined (UND), and then from the highest negative to the lowest negative.

COVERAGE RATIOS

Coverage ratios measure a firm's ability to service debt.

1. Earnings Before Interest and Taxes (EBIT)/Interest

Computation: Earnings (profit) before annual interest expense and taxes divided by annual interest expense.

$$\frac{\text{Earnings Before Interest \& Taxes}}{\text{Annual Interest Expense}}$$

Interpretation: This ratio is a measure of a firm's ability to meet interest payments. A high ratio may indicate that a borrower would have little difficulty in meeting the interest obligations of a loan. This ratio also serves as an indicator of a firm's capacity to take on additional debt.

Only those statements that reported annual interest expense were used in the calculation of this ratio. The ratio values are arrayed from the highest positive to the lowest positive and then from the lowest negative to the highest negative.

2. Net Profit + Depreciation, Depletion, Amortization/Current Maturities Long-Term Debt

Computation: Net profit plus depreciation, depletion, and amortization expenses, divided by the current portion of long-term debt.

$$\frac{\text{Net Profit + Depreciation, Depletion, Amortization Expenses}}{\text{Current Portion of Long-Term Debt}}$$

Interpretation: This ratio expresses the coverage of current maturities by cash flow from operations. Since cash flow is the primary source of debt retirement, this ratio measures the ability of a firm to service principal repayment and is an indicator of additional debt capacity. Although it is misleading to think that all cash flow is available for debt service, the ratio is a valid measure of the ability to service long-term debt.

Only data for corporations that have the following items were used:

(1) Profit or loss after taxes (positive, negative, or zero)
(2) A positive figure for depreciation/depletion/amortization expenses
(3) A positive figure for current maturities of long-term debt

Ratio values are arrayed from the highest to the lowest positive and then from the lowest to the highest negative.

LEVERAGE RATIOS

Highly leveraged firms (those with heavy debt in relation to net worth) are more vulnerable to business downturns than those with lower debt-to-worth positions. While leverage ratios help measure this vulnerability, it must be remembered that they vary greatly depending on the requirements of particular industry groups.

1. Fixed/Worth

Computation: Fixed assets (net of accumulated depreciation) divided by tangible net worth (net worth minus intangibles).

$$\frac{\text{Net Fixed Assets}}{\text{Tangible Net Worth}}$$

Interpretation: This ratio measures the extent to which owner's equity (capital) has been invested in plant and equipment (fixed assets). A lower ratio indicates a proportionately smaller investment in fixed assets in relation to net worth and a better "cushion" for creditors in case of liquidation. Similarly, a higher ratio would indicate the opposite situation. The presence of substantial leased fixed assets (not shown on the balance sheet) may deceptively lower this ratio.

Fixed assets may be zero, in which case the quotient is zero. If tangible net worth is zero, the quotient is undefined (UND). If tangible net worth is negative, the quotient is negative. The ratio values are arrayed from the lowest positive to the highest positive, undefined, and then from the highest negative to the lowest negative.

2. Debt/Worth

Computation: Total liabilities divided by tangible net worth.

$$\frac{\text{Total Liabilities}}{\text{Tangible Net Worth}}$$

Interpretation: This ratio expresses the relationship between capital contributed by creditors and that contributed by owners. It expresses the degree of protection provided by the owners for the creditors. The higher the ratio, the greater the risk being assumed by creditors. A lower ratio generally indicates greater long-term financial safety. A firm with a low debt/worth ratio usually has greater flexibility to borrow in the future. A more highly leveraged company has a more limited debt capacity.

Tangible net worth may be zero, in which case the ratio is undefined (UND). Tangible net worth may also be negative, which results in the quotient being negative. The ratio values are arrayed from the lowest to highest positive, undefined, and then from the highest to lowest negative.

OPERATING RATIOS

Operating ratios are designed to assist in the evaluation of management performance.

1. % Profits Before Taxes/Tangible Net Worth

Computation: Profit before taxes divided by tangible net worth and multiplied by 100.

$$\frac{\text{Profit Before Taxes}}{\text{Tangible Net Worth}} \times 100$$

Interpretation: This ratio expresses the rate of return on tangible capital employed. While it can serve as an indicator of management performance, the analyst is cautioned to use it in conjunction with other ratios. A high return, normally associated with effective management, could indicate an undercapitalized firm. Meanwhile, a low return, usually an indicator of inefficient management performance, could reflect a highly capitalized, conservatively operated business.

This ratio has been multiplied by 100 since it is shown as a percentage.

Profit before taxes may be zero, in which case the ratio is zero. Profits before taxes may be negative, resulting in negative quotients. Firms with negative tangible net worth have been omitted from the ratio arrays. Negative ratios will therefore only result in the case of negative profit before taxes. If the tangible net worth is zero, the quotient is undefined (UND). If there are fewer than 10 ratios for a particular size class, the result is not shown. The ratio values are arrayed starting with undefined (UND), then from the highest to the lowest positive values, and from the lowest to the highest negative values.

2. % Profit Before Taxes/Total Assets

Computation: Profit before taxes divided by total assets and multiplied by 100.

$$\frac{\text{Profit Before Taxes}}{\text{Total Assets}} \times 100$$

Interpretation: This ratio expresses the pre-tax return on total assets and measures the effectiveness of management in employing the resources available to it. If a specific ratio varies considerably from the ranges found in this book, the analyst will need to examine the makeup of the assets and take a closer look at the earnings figure. A heavily depreciated plant and a large amount of intangible assets or unusual income or expense items will cause distortions of this ratio.

This ratio has been multiplied by 100 since it is shown as a percentage. If profit before taxes is zero, the quotient is zero. If profit before taxes is negative, the quotient is negative. These ratio values are arrayed from the highest to the lowest positive and then from the lowest to the highest negative.

3. Sales/Net Fixed Assets

Computation: Net sales divided by net fixed assets (net of accumulated depreciation).

$$\frac{\text{Net Sales}}{\text{Net Fixed Assets}}$$

Interpretation: This ratio is a measure of the productive use of a firm's fixed assets. Largely depreciated fixed assets or a labor-intensive operation may cause a distortion of this ratio.

If the net fixed figure is zero, the quotient is undefined (UND). The only time a zero will appear in the array will be when the net sales figure is low and the quotient rounds off to zero. These ratio values cannot be negative.

They are arrayed from undefined (UND) and then from the highest to the lowest positive values.

4. Sales/Total Assets

Computation: Net sales divided by total assets.

$$\frac{\text{Net Sales}}{\text{Total Assets}}$$

Interpretation: This ratio is a general measure of a firm's ability to generate sales in relation to total assets. It should be used only to compare firms within specific industry groups and in conjunction with other operating ratios to determine the effective employment of assets.

The only time a zero will appear in the array will be when the net sales figure is low and the quotient rounds off to zero. The ratio values cannot be negative. They are arrayed from the highest to the lowest positive values.

EXPENSE TO SALES RATIOS

The following two ratios relate specific expense items to net sales and express this relationship as a percentage. Comparisons are convenient because the item, net sales, is used as a constant. Variations in these ratios are most pronounced between capital- and labor-intensive industries.

1. % Depreciation, Depletion, Amortization/Sales

Computation: Annual depreciation, amortization, and depletion expenses divided by net sales and multiplied by 100.

$$\frac{\text{Depreciation, Amortization, Depletion Expenses}}{\text{Net Sales}} \times 100$$

2. % Officers', Directors', Owners' Compensation/Sales

Computation: Annual officers', directors', owners' compensation divided by net sales and multiplied by 100. Included here are total salaries, bonuses, commissions, and other monetary remuneration to all officers, directors, and/or owners of the firm during the year covered by the statement. This includes drawings of partners and proprietors.

$$\frac{\text{Officers', Directors', Owners' Compensation}}{\text{Net Sales}} \times 100$$

Only statements showing a positive figure for each of the expense categories shown above were used. The ratios are arrayed from the lowest to highest positive values.

Explanation of Noncontractor Balance Sheet and Income Data

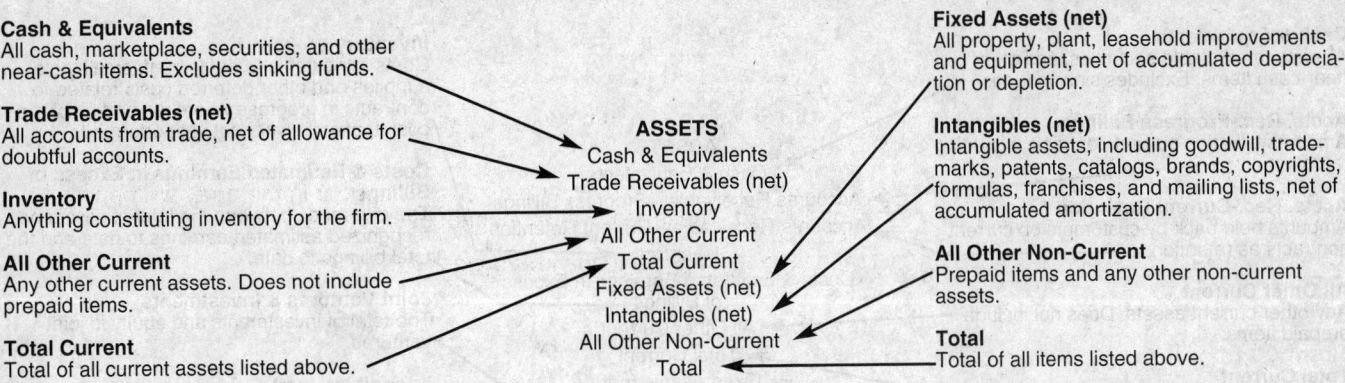

Cash & Equivalents
All cash, marketplace, securities, and other near-cash items. Excludes sinking funds.

Trade Receivables (net)
All accounts from trade, net of allowance for doubtful accounts.

Inventory
Anything constituting inventory for the firm.

All Other Current
Any other current assets. Does not include prepaid items.

Total Current
Total of all current assets listed above.

ASSETS
Cash & Equivalents
Trade Receivables (net)
Inventory
All Other Current
Total Current
Fixed Assets (net)
Intangibles (net)
All Other Non-Current
Total

Fixed Assets (net)
All property, plant, leasehold improvements and equipment, net of accumulated depreciation or depletion.

Intangibles (net)
Intangible assets, including goodwill, trademarks, patents, catalogs, brands, copyrights, formulas, franchises, and mailing lists, net of accumulated amortization.

All Other Non-Current
Prepaid items and any other non-current assets.

Total
Total of all items listed above.

Notes Payable—Short Term
All short term note obligations, including bank and commercial paper. Does not include trade notes payable.

Current Maturities—L/T/D
That portion of long term obligations that is due within the next fiscal year.

Trade Payables
Open accounts due to the trade.

Income Taxes Payable
Income taxes including current portion of deferred taxes.

All Other Current
Any other current liabilities, including bank overdrafts and accrued expenses.

LIABILITIES
Notes Payable-Short Term
Cur. Mat.-L/T/D
Trade Payables
Income Taxes Payable
All Other Current
Total Current
Long Term Debt
Deferred Taxes
All Other Non-Current
Net Worth
Total Liabilities & Net Worth

Total Current
Total of all current liabilities listed above.

Long Term Debt
All senior debt, including bonds, debentures, bank debt, mortgages, deferred portions of long term debt, and capital lease obligations.

Deferred Taxes
All deferred taxes.

All Other Non-Current
Any other non-current liabilities, including subordinated debt, and liability reserves.

Net Worth
Difference between Total Liabilities and Total Assets. Minority interest is included here.

Total Liabilities & Net Worth
Total of all items listed above.

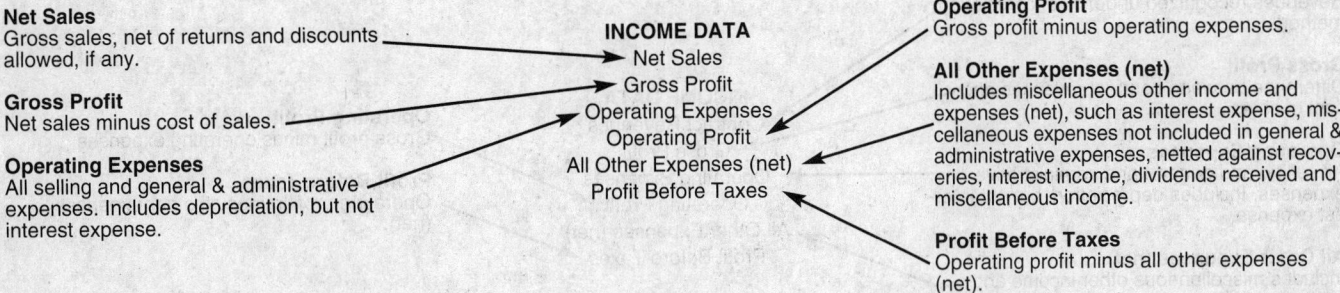

Net Sales
Gross sales, net of returns and discounts allowed, if any.

Gross Profit
Net sales minus cost of sales.

Operating Expenses
All selling and general & administrative expenses. Includes depreciation, but not interest expense.

INCOME DATA
Net Sales
Gross Profit
Operating Expenses
Operating Profit
All Other Expenses (net)
Profit Before Taxes

Operating Profit
Gross profit minus operating expenses.

All Other Expenses (net)
Includes miscellaneous other income and expenses (net), such as interest expense, miscellaneous expenses not included in general & administrative expenses, netted against recoveries, interest income, dividends received and miscellaneous income.

Profit Before Taxes
Operating profit minus all other expenses (net).

Explanation of Contractor Percentage-of-Completion Basis of Accounting
Balance Sheet and Income Data

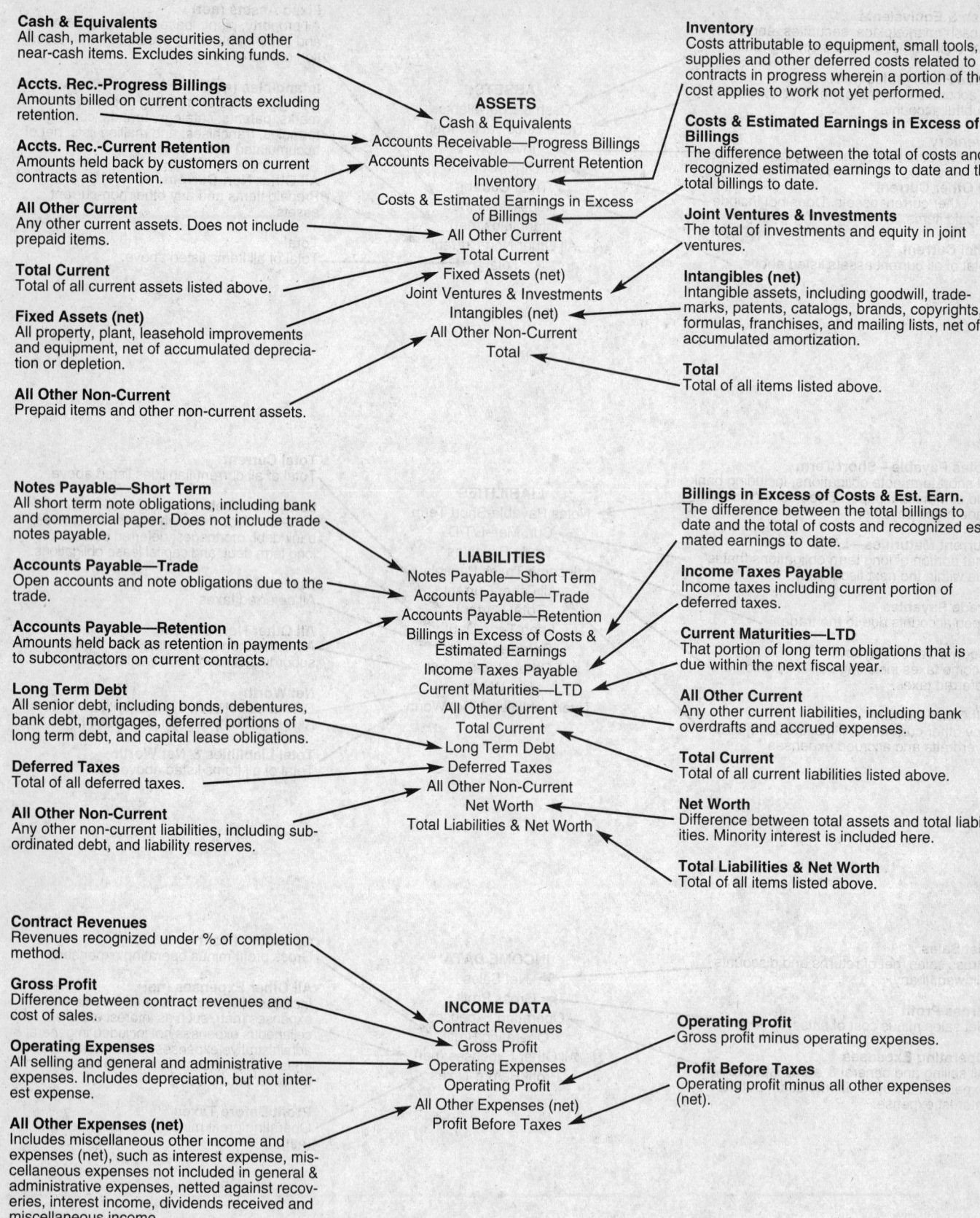

Cash & Equivalents
All cash, marketable securities, and other near-cash items. Excludes sinking funds.

Accts. Rec.-Progress Billings
Amounts billed on current contracts excluding retention.

Accts. Rec.-Current Retention
Amounts held back by customers on current contracts as retention.

All Other Current
Any other current assets. Does not include prepaid items.

Total Current
Total of all current assets listed above.

Fixed Assets (net)
All property, plant, leasehold improvements and equipment, net of accumulated depreciation or depletion.

All Other Non-Current
Prepaid items and other non-current assets.

Inventory
Costs attributable to equipment, small tools, supplies and other deferred costs related to contracts in progress wherein a portion of the cost applies to work not yet performed.

Costs & Estimated Earnings in Excess of Billings
The difference between the total of costs and recognized estimated earnings to date and the total billings to date.

Joint Ventures & Investments
The total of investments and equity in joint ventures.

Intangibles (net)
Intangible assets, including goodwill, trademarks, patents, catalogs, brands, copyrights, formulas, franchises, and mailing lists, net of accumulated amortization.

Total
Total of all items listed above.

ASSETS
Cash & Equivalents
Accounts Receivable—Progress Billings
Accounts Receivable—Current Retention
Inventory
Costs & Estimated Earnings in Excess of Billings
All Other Current
Total Current
Fixed Assets (net)
Joint Ventures & Investments
Intangibles (net)
All Other Non-Current
Total

Notes Payable—Short Term
All short term note obligations, including bank and commercial paper. Does not include trade notes payable.

Accounts Payable—Trade
Open accounts and note obligations due to the trade.

Accounts Payable—Retention
Amounts held back as retention in payments to subcontractors on current contracts.

Long Term Debt
All senior debt, including bonds, debentures, bank debt, mortgages, deferred portions of long term debt, and capital lease obligations.

Deferred Taxes
Total of all deferred taxes.

All Other Non-Current
Any other non-current liabilities, including subordinated debt, and liability reserves.

Billings in Excess of Costs & Est. Earn.
The difference between the total billings to date and the total of costs and recognized estimated earnings to date.

Income Taxes Payable
Income taxes including current portion of deferred taxes.

Current Maturities—LTD
That portion of long term obligations that is due within the next fiscal year.

All Other Current
Any other current liabilities, including bank overdrafts and accrued expenses.

Total Current
Total of all current liabilities listed above.

Net Worth
Difference between total assets and total liabilities. Minority interest is included here.

Total Liabilities & Net Worth
Total of all items listed above.

LIABILITIES
Notes Payable—Short Term
Accounts Payable—Trade
Accounts Payable—Retention
Billings in Excess of Costs & Estimated Earnings
Income Taxes Payable
Current Maturities—LTD
All Other Current
Total Current
Long Term Debt
Deferred Taxes
All Other Non-Current
Net Worth
Total Liabilities & Net Worth

Contract Revenues
Revenues recognized under % of completion method.

Gross Profit
Difference between contract revenues and cost of sales.

Operating Expenses
All selling and general and administrative expenses. Includes depreciation, but not interest expense.

All Other Expenses (net)
Includes miscellaneous other income and expenses (net), such as interest expense, miscellaneous expenses not included in general & administrative expenses, netted against recoveries, interest income, dividends received and miscellaneous income.

Operating Profit
Gross profit minus operating expenses.

Profit Before Taxes
Operating profit minus all other expenses (net).

INCOME DATA
Contract Revenues
Gross Profit
Operating Expenses
Operating Profit
All Other Expenses (net)
Profit Before Taxes

NAICS CODES APPEARING IN THE STATEMENT STUDIES

If more than three SIC codes map to one NAICS code, then only the first three SIC will appear at the top of the page listed above. For a complete listing of the SIC codes, see the Description of Industries beginning on page 29.

NAICS CODES APPEARING IN THE STATEMENT STUDIES

NAICS Codes	Page	NAICS Codes	Page	NAICS Codes	Page
327320	424-425	333314	536-537	336370	648-649
327331	426-427	333315	538-539	336399	650-651
327390	428-429	333319	540-541	336412	652-653
327910	430-431	333412	542-543	336413	654-655
327991	432-433	333414	544-545	336510	656-657
331111	434-435	333415	546-547	336611	658-659
331210	436-437	333511	548-549	336612	660-661
331221	438-439	333512	550-551	336999	662-663
331222	440-441	333513	552-553	337110	664-665
331316	442-443	333514	554-555	337121	666-667
331422	444-445	333515	556-557	337122	668-669
331491	446-447	333518	558-559	337127	670-671
331492	448-449	333612	560-561	337211	672-673
331511	450-451	333613	562-563	337214	674-675
331513	452-453	333911	564-565	337215	676-677
331521	454-455	333922	566-567	337910	678-679
331522	456-457	333923	568-569	337920	680-681
331524	458-459	333924	570-571	339112	682-683
331528	460-461	333992	572-573	339113	684-685
332111	462-463	333993	574-575	339114	686-687
332116	464-465	333994	576-577	339115	688-689
332211	466-467	333999	578-579	339116	690-691
332212	468-469	334111	580-581	339911	692-693
332311	470-471	334119	582-583	339914	694-695
332312	472-473	334210	584-585	339920	696-697
332313	474-475	334220	586-587	339932	698-699
332321	476-477	334290	588-589	339950	700-701
332322	478-479	334310	590-591	339991	702-703
332323	480-481	334411	592-593	339992	704-705
332510	482-483	334412	594-595	339994	706-707
332612	484-485	334413	596-597	339999	708-709
332618	486-487	334416	598-599	423110	712-713
332710	488-489	334417	600-601	423120	714-715
332721	490-491	334419	602-603	423130	716-717
332722	492-493	334510	604-605	423140	718-719
332811	494-495	334511	606-607	423210	720-721
332812	496-497	334512	608-609	423220	722-723
332813	498-499	334513	610-611	423310	724-725
332911	500-501	334514	612-613	423320	726-727
332912	502-503	334515	614-615	423330	728-729
332913	504-505	334516	616-617	423390	730-731
332919	506-507	334519	618-619	423410	732-733
332991	508-509	335121	620-621	423420	734-735
332996	510-511	335122	622-623	423430	736-737
332999	512-513	335129	624-625	423440	738-739
333111	514-515	335311	626-627	423450	740-741
333112	516-517	335312	628-629	423460	742-743
333120	518-519	335313	630-631	423490	744-745
333131	520-521	335314	632-633	423510	746-747
333132	522-523	335931	634-635	423520	748-749
333220	524-525	335999	636-637	423610	750-751
333291	526-527	336111	638-639	423620	752-753
333292	528-529	336211	640-641	423690	754-755
333293	530-531	336212	642-643	423710	756-757
333294	532-533	336214	644-645	423720	758-759
333298	534-535	336360	646-647	423730	760-761

If more than three SIC codes map to one NAICS code, then only the first three SIC will appear at the top of the page listed above. For a complete listing of the SIC codes, see the Description of Industries beginning on page 29.

NAICS CODES APPEARING IN THE STATEMENT STUDIES

If more than three SIC codes map to one NAICS code, then only the first three SIC will appear at the top of the page listed above. For a complete listing of the SIC codes, see the Description of Industries beginning on page 29.

NAICS CODES APPEARING IN THE STATEMENT STUDIES

If more than three SIC codes map to one NAICS code, then only the first three SIC will appear at the top of the page listed above. For a complete listing of the SIC codes, see the Description of Industries beginning on page 29.

SIC NUMBERS APPEARING IN THE STATEMENT STUDIES

SIC No.	Page
0111	86-87
0115	88-89
0119	88-89,90-91
0131	106-107
0134	92-93
0139	90-91, 94-95, 108-109
0161	94-95
0172	100-101
0173	102-103
0174	96-97
0175	98-99
0181	104-105
0191	108-109
0211	112-113
0212	110-111
0213	116-117
0241	110-111, 114-115
0252	118-119
0711	130-131
0721	130-131
0723	132-133, 212-213
0724	128-129
0741	1192-1193
0742	1192-1193
0751	134-135, 232-233
0752	134-135
0781	1148-1149
0782	1232-1233
0783	1232-1233
0811	104-105, 120-121
0831	108-109
0912	124-125
0913	126-127
0919	126-127
1221	140-141
1311	138-139
1381	148-149
1382	150-151, 1444
1389	150-151, 1444
1422	142-143
1429	144-145
1442	146-147
1499	144-145
1521	162-163, 1445
1522	164-165, 1446
1531	166-167, 168-169, 170-171, 1447, 1448
1541	168-169, 170-171, 1447, 1448
1542	170-171, 1448
1611	176-177, 1451
1622	176-177, 178-179, 1451, 1452
1623	172-173, 1449
1629	168-169, 172-173, 178-179, 206-207, 1447, 1449, 1452, 1464
1711	190-191, 192-193, 1458, 1459

SIC No.	Page
1721	176-177, 198-199, 1451, 1462
1731	190-191, 1458
1741	184-185, 1455
1742	196-197, 1461
1743	196-197, 202-203, 1461
1751	204-205
1752	200-201, 1463
1761	188-189, 1457
1771	180-181, 184-185, 1453, 1455
1781	172-173, 1449
1791	182-183, 192-193, 1454, 1459
1793	186-187, 1456
1794	206-207, 1464
1795	206-207, 1464
1796	192-193, 194-195, 1459, 1460
1799	178-179, 186-187, 194-195, 198-199, 204-205, 208-209, 1236-1237, 1452, 1456, 1460, 1462, 1465
2011	232-233
2013	234-235, 236-237
2015	238-239
2021	228-229
2022	230-231
2023	226-227
2026	226-227
2032	256-257
2033	222-223
2034	214-215, 224-225, 256-257
2035	222-223, 254-255
2037	218-219
2038	220-221
2041	214-215
2048	212-213, 232-233
2051	244-245
2052	244-245, 246-247, 248-249
2064	216-217
2066	216-217
2077	236-237, 240-241
2082	262-263
2084	264-265
2085	264-265
2086	258-259, 260-261
2087	250-251, 252-253
2092	240-241
2095	250-251
2096	248-249
2099	224-225, 250-251, 254-255, 256-257
2211	268-269
2221	268-269
2231	268-269
2241	270-271
2253	284-285
2259	284-285

SIC No.	Page
2261	272-273
2262	272-273
2269	272-273
2273	276-277
2281	266-267
2295	274-275
2298	266-267
2299	266-267, 270-271, 282-283
2311	286-287, 288-289
2321	286-287
2326	286-287
2329	290-291
2331	292-293
2335	294-295
2337	296-297
2339	298-299, 302-303
2353	300-301
2361	292-293, 294-295
2369	288-289, 290-291, 296-297, 298-299
2385	288-289, 290-291, 296-297, 298-299
2387	302-303
2389	302-303
2392	278-279, 706-707
2394	280-281
2395	282-283
2396	646-647
2399	282-283, 646-647
2411	122-123
2421	306-307, 316-317, 318-319, 326-327
2426	306-307, 316-317, 318-319
2429	306-307, 326-327
2431	314-315, 318-319
2434	664-665
2435	310-311
2439	312-313
2441	320-321
2448	320-321
2449	320-321
2451	322-323
2452	324-325
2491	308-309
2499	326-327, 708-709
2511	668-669
2512	666-667
2514	666-667
2515	666-667, 678-679
2521	672-673
2522	674-675
2531	670-671
2541	664-665, 676-677
2542	670-671, 676-677
2591	680-681

See pages 19-22 for corresponding NAICS look-up table.

SIC NUMBERS APPEARING IN THE STATEMENT STUDIES

SIC No.	Page	SIC No.	Page	SIC No.	Page
2599	670-671	3089	402-403, 404-405, 410-411	3519	650-651
2611	328-329, 330-331	3111	304-305	3523	480-481, 514-515, 566-567
2621	328-329	3172	694-695	3524	516-517
2631	330-331	3231	422-423	3531	518-519, 568-569, 656-657
2652	336-337	3251	420-421, 426-427	3532	520-521
2653	332-333	3271	426-427	3533	522-523
2657	334-335	3272	428-429	3535	566-567
2671	338-339	3273	424-425	3536	568-569
2672	340-341	3281	432-433	3537	570-571
2673	342-343	3291	430-431	3541	550-551
2675	346-347	3312	434-435, 438-439	3542	552-553
2677	344-345	3315	440-441, 486-487	3544	548-549, 554-555
2679	332-333, 340-341, 346-347	3316	438-439	3545	468-469, 556-557
2711	1026-1027	3317	436-437	3548	572-573, 626-627
2721	1028-1029	3321	450-451	3549	558-559
2731	1030-1031	3322	450-451	3552	528-529
2732	356-357	3325	452-453	3554	526-527
2741	1028-1029, 1030-1031, 1032-1033, 1034-1035	3341	448-449	3555	530-531
2752	348-349, 352-353	3354	442-443	3556	532-533
2759	350-351, 352-353, 358-359	3356	446-447	3559	514-515, 524-525, 534-535, 540-541
2761	354-355	3357	444-445, 446-447		
2771	348-349, 350-351, 358-359	3363	454-455	3561	564-565
2782	354-355	3364	456-457	3562	508-509
2789	360-361	3365	458-459	3564	542-543
2791	362-363	3369	460-461	3565	574-575
2796	362-363	3398	494-495	3566	560-561
2819	370-371, 398-399	3399	434-435, 438-439, 448-449, 486-487, 498-499	3567	576-577
2821	376-377			3568	562-563
2833	384-385	3421	466-467, 468-469	3569	544-545, 578-579
2834	386-387	3423	468-469	3571	580-581
2835	386-387	3429	482-483, 492-493, 512-513, 568-569	3577	582-583
2841	392-393	3432	504-505, 506-507	3578	582-583
2842	394-395	3433	544-545	3585	546-547
2844	392-393, 396-397	3441	472-473	3589	540-541
2851	388-389	3442	476-477	3599	488-489, 498-499, 540-541, 578-579, 618-619
2861	372-373	3443	474-475, 546-547		
2869	370-371, 374-375, 398-399	3444	476-477, 478-479, 546-547	3612	626-627
2873	378-379	3446	480-481	3613	630-631
2875	380-381	3448	470-471	3621	628-629
2879	382-383	3449	472-473, 480-481	3625	632-633
2891	390-391	3451	490-491	3629	636-637
2899	374-375, 388-389, 398-399	3452	492-493	3634	544-545, 708-709
2911	364-365	3462	462-463	3639	534-535
2951	366-367	3465	648-649	3643	634-635
2992	368-369	3469	464-465	3645	620-621
3052	414-415	3471	498-499	3646	622-623
3053	702-703	3479	496-497, 692-693, 694-695	3648	624-625
3061	416-417	3491	500-501	3651	590-591
3069	274-275, 418-419, 696-697, 698-699	3492	502-503	3661	584-585
3081	400-401	3494	506-507, 512-513	3663	586-587
3082	402-403	3495	484-485	3669	588-589
3083	406-407	3496	486-487, 570-571	3671	592-593
3084	404-405	3498	510-511	3672	594-595
3086	408-409	3499	482-483, 506-507, 512-513, 646-647, 676-677	3674	596-597
				3677	598-599
				3678	600-601

See pages 19-22 for corresponding NAICS look-up table.

SIC NUMBERS APPEARING IN THE STATEMENT STUDIES

SIC No.	Page	SIC No.	Page	SIC No.	Page
3679	586-587, 590-591, 602-603	4226	1016-1017, 1018-1019, 1022-1023	5048	742-743
3699	572-573, 624-625, 636-637	4231	1006-1007	5049	744-745
3711	638-639, 640-641	4449	974-975	5051	746-747
3713	640-641	4489	994-995	5052	748-749
3714	640-641, 650-651	4491	998-999	5063	750-751
3715	642-643	4492	1000-1001	5064	752-753, 874-875, 876-877
3721	1172-1173	4493	1342-1343	5065	754-755
3724	652-653	4499	974-975, 1000-1001, 1002-1003	5072	756-757, 886-887
3728	502-503, 654-655	4512	968-969	5074	758-759
3731	658-659, 1002-1003	4513	1014-1015	5075	760-761
3732	660-661	4522	970-971	5078	762-763
3743	564-565, 656-657	4581	996-997	5082	764-765
3792	644-645	4724	1218-1219	5083	766-767
3799	570-571, 644-645, 650-651, 662-663	4725	1220-1221	5084	768-769
3812	606-607	4729	1012-1013, 1222-1223	5085	768-769, 770-771
3822	608-609	4731	1008-1009, 1168-1169	5087	772-773, 908-909
3823	610-611	4783	1010-1011	5088	774-775
3824	612-613	4785	1006-1007	5091	776-777, 930-931
3825	612-613, 614-615	4789	1012-1013	5092	778-779, 932-933
3826	616-617	4812	1054-1055	5093	780-781
3827	536-537	4813	1052-1053	5094	782-783, 928-929
3829	612-613, 618-619, 682-683	4822	1052-1053	5099	784-785, 932-933
3841	682-683	4832	1046-1047	5111	786-787
3842	604-605, 684-685	4833	1048-1049	5112	788-789, 944-945
3843	686-687	4841	1050-1051	5113	790-791
3845	604-605	4899	986-987, 1054-1055, 1056-1057	5122	792-793, 906-907, 908-909
3851	684-685, 688-689	4911	154-155	5131	794-795
3861	538-539	4923	156-157	5136	776-777, 796-797, 916-917
3911	692-693	4924	156-157	5137	776-777, 798-799, 918-919
3914	466-467	4925	156-157	5139	800-801, 926-927
3931	704-705	4931	154-155	5141	802-803, 892-893
3944	698-699	4939	154-155	5142	804-805
3949	696-697	4941	158-159	5143	806-807
3961	694-695	4953	1242-1243, 1244-1245	5144	808-809, 896-897
3991	706-707	4959	996-997, 1228-1229, 1236-1237, 1246-1247	5145	810-811, 900-901
3993	350-351, 700-701	4971	158-159	5146	812-813
3999	304-305, 410-411, 466-467, 496-497, 620-621, 698-699, 708-709	5012	712-713	5147	814-815, 896-897
4011	972-973	5013	714-715, 864-865	5148	816-817, 898-899
4111	992-993	5014	716-717, 866-867	5149	818-819
4119	988-989, 992-993	5015	718-719, 864-865	5153	820-821
4121	986-987	5021	720-721, 868-869	5154	822-823
4141	990-991	5023	722-723, 870-871	5159	824-825
4142	990-991	5031	724-725, 882-883	5162	826-827
4151	988-989	5032	726-727, 888-889	5169	828-829
4173	1006-1007	5033	728-729, 888-889	5171	830-831, 960-961, 962-963
4212	976-977, 982-983, 1240-1241	5039	724-725, 730-731, 888-889	5172	832-833
4213	978-979, 980-981, 984-985	5043	732-733	5181	834-835, 904-905
4214	976-977, 982-983	5044	734-735, 944-945	5182	836-837, 904-905
4215	1014-1015	5045	736-737, 878-879	5191	838-839, 890-891
4221	1020-1021	5046	738-739	5192	840-841, 936-937
4222	1018-1019	5047	740-741	5193	842-843, 890-891
4225	1016-1017, 1108-1109			5194	844-845, 952-953
				5198	846-847
				5199	794-795, 800-801, 826-827, 848-849, 946-947, 952-953

See pages 19-22 for corresponding NAICS look-up table.

SIC NUMBERS APPEARING IN THE STATEMENT STUDIES

SIC No.	Page	SIC No.	Page	SIC No.	Page
5211	882-883	5984	962-963	7215	1394-1395
5231	884-885	5992	942-943	7216	1396-1397
5251	886-887	5993	952-953	7217	1234-1235
5261	890-891	5995	910-911	7219	1398-1399
5271	950-951	5999	908-909, 954-955	7221	1188-1189
5311	938-939	6019	1070-1071	7231	1388-1389
5331	940-941	6091	1084-1085	7251	1404-1405
5399	940-941	6099	1074-1075	7261	1390-1391, 1392-1393
5411	892-893, 894-895, 912-913, 964-965	6111	1068-1069	7299	1194-1195, 1238-1239, 1402-1403, 1404-1405
5421	896-897	6141	1064-1065, 1066-1067	7311	1174-1175
5431	898-899, 964-965	6153	1064-1065, 1070-1071, 1078-1079	7312	1178-1179
5441	900-901	6159	1064-1065, 1068-1069, 1070-1071	7319	1178-1179, 1182-1183, 1184-1185
5451	902-903	6162	1068-1069, 1074-1075	7322	1214-1215
5461	242-243	6163	1072-1073	7331	1032-1033, 1180-1181
5499	902-903	6211	1076-1077, 1078-1079	7334	352-353, 1212-1213
5511	852-853	6282	1080-1081, 1082-1083	7335	1190-1191
5521	854-855	6289	1084-1085	7336	1156-1157
5531	864-865, 866-867, 940-941	6321	1086-1087	7342	1228-1229, 1230-1231
5541	912-913, 914-915	6324	1086-1087	7349	1230-1231, 1236-1237
5551	860-861	6331	1088-1089, 1092-1093	7352	1128-1129, 1134-1135
5561	856-857	6351	1088-1089, 1092-1093	7353	1130-1131
5571	858-859	6361	1090-1091	7359	1124-1125, 1130-1131, 1132-1133, 1134-1135
5599	862-863	6371	1080-1081, 1100-1101	7361	1166-1167, 1208-1209
5611	916-917, 922-923	6399	1092-1093	7363	1210-1211
5621	918-919, 924-925	6411	1094-1095	7371	1158-1159
5632	922-923, 924-925	6512	1106-1107	7372	1036-1037
5651	920-921	6513	1104-1105	7373	1160-1161
5661	926-927	6514	1104-1105	7374	1060-1061
5699	922-923, 924-925	6515	1110-1111	7375	1058-1059
5712	868-869	6517	1110-1111	7377	1132-1133
5713	870-871	6519	1110-1111	7378	878-879, 1380-1381
5719	872-873	6531	1104-1105, 1112-1113, 1114-1115, 1116-1117, 1392-1393	7379	1060-1061, 1160-1161, 1162-1163
5722	874-875	6541	1142-1143	7381	1224-1225
5731	876-877	6552	174-175, 1449	7382	1226-1227
5734	878-879	6553	1392-1393	7384	1400-1401
5736	934-935	6712	1198-1199	7389	1044-1045, 1060-1061, 1152-1153, 1182-1183, 1184-1185, 1194-1195, 1212-1213, 1214-1215, 1216-1217, 1222-1223, 1238-1239
5812	1322-1323, 1358-1359, 1360-1361	6719	1200-1201	7513	1122-1123
5813	1362-1363	6722	1096-1097	7514	1118-1119
5912	906-907	6726	1100-1101	7515	1120-1121
5921	904-905	6733	1080-1081, 1084-1085	7519	1122-1123
5932	948-949	6792	1136-1137	7521	1402-1403
5941	930-931	6794	1136-1137	7532	1372-1373
5942	936-937	6798	1098-1099	7533	1368-1369
5943	944-945	6799	1078-1079	7534	412-413, 1378-1379
5944	928-929	7011	1352-1353	7536	1374-1375
5945	932-933	7032	1356-1357	7538	1366-1367
5946	880-881	7033	1354-1355	7539	1370-1371, 1378-1379
5947	946-947	7041	1352-1353		
5961	956-957	7211	1396-1397		
5962	958-959	7212	1396-1397		
5963	964-965	7213	1398-1399		
5983	960-961				

See pages 19-22 for corresponding NAICS look-up table.

SIC NUMBERS APPEARING IN THE STATEMENT STUDIES

SIC No.	Page	SIC No.	Page	SIC No.	Page
7542	1376-1377	8221	1254-1255		
7549	1004-1005, 1374-1375, 1378-1379	8222	1252-1253		
		8243	1256-1257		
7622	876-877	8249	1256-1257		
7623	1384-1385, 1386-1387	8299	1256-1257, 1258-1259, 1260-1261		
7629	1380-1381, 1382-1383, 1386-1387	8322	1312-1313, 1314-1315		
7631	928-929	8331	1316-1317		
7692	1384-1385	8351	1318-1319		
7694	628-629, 1384-1385	8361	1304-1305, 1308-1309, 1310-1311		
7699	930-931, 1380-1381, 1382-1383, 1386-1387	8399	1408-1409, 1410-1411		
7812	1038-1039	8412	1332-1333		
7819	1042-1043, 1134-1135	8611	1414-1415		
7822	784-785	8621	1416-1417		
7829	1042-1043	8631	1418-1419		
7832	1040-1041	8641	1410-1411, 1412-1413, 1420-1421		
7841	1126-1127	8661	1406-1407		
7911	1258-1259	8699	1222-1223, 1412-1413, 1414-1415, 1420-1421		
7922	1322-1323, 1330-1331				
7929	1324-1325	8711	1150-1151		
7933	1346-1347	8712	1146-1147		
7941	1326-1327, 1330-1331	8713	1152-1153		
7948	1328-1329	8721	1144-1145		
7991	1344-1345	8731	1172-1173		
7992	1340-1341	8732	1186-1187		
7993	1336-1337, 1348-1349	8733	1172-1173		
7996	1334-1335	8734	1154-1155, 1192-1193		
7997	1340-1341, 1344-1345, 1348-1349	8741	1204-1205		
		8742	1164-1165, 1166-1167, 1168-1169		
7999	1330-1331, 1338-1339, 1344-1345, 1348-1349	8743	1176-1177		
		8744	1206-1207		
8011	1264-1265, 1282-1283	8748	1148-1149, 1150-1151, 1170-1171, 1260-1261		
8021	1266-1267				
8031	1264-1265	8811	1422-1423		
8041	1268-1269	8999	1194-1195		
8042	1270-1271	9111	1426-1427		
8049	1272-1273, 1274-1275, 1276-1277	9199	1428-1429		
		9224	1430-1431		
8051	1302-1303, 1306-1307	9411	1432-1433		
8052	1302-1303, 1306-1307	9511	1434-1435		
8059	1302-1303, 1306-1307	9531	1436-1437		
8062	1294-1295, 1296-1297	9532	1438-1439		
8063	1298-1299	9611	1440-1441		
8069	1298-1299, 1300-1301				
8071	1286-1287				
8072	690-691				
8082	1288-1289				
8092	1280-1281				
8093	1276-1277, 1278-1279, 1284-1285				
8099	1278-1279, 1290-1291, 1292-1293				
8111	1140-1141				
8211	1250-1251				

See pages 19-22 for corresponding NAICS look-up table.

DESCRIPTION OF INDUSTRIES INCLUDED IN THE STATEMENT STUDIES

AGRICULTURE, FORESTRY, FISHING AND HUNTING

MINING

MINING

CONSTRUCTION—GENERAL

UTILITIES

CONSTRUCTION—GENERAL

CONSTRUCTION—GENERAL

NAICS #   **Page**

CONSTRUCTION—GENERAL

MANUFACTURING

MANUFACTURING

MANUFACTURING

MANUFACTURING

MANUFACTURING

MANUFACTURING

MANUFACTURING

MANUFACTURING

MANUFACTURING

MANUFACTURING

MANUFACTURING

MANUFACTURING

MANUFACTURING

MANUFACTURING

NAICS #   **Page**

333924   **Industrial Truck, Tractor, Trailer, and Stacker Machinery Manufacturing.** This U.S. industry comprises establishments primarily engaged in manufacturing industrial trucks, tractors, trailers, and stackers (i.e., truck-type), such as forklifts, pallet loaders and unloaders, and portable loading docks. (SIC: 3496, 3537, 3799) 570-571

333992   **Welding and Soldering Equipment Manufacturing.** This U.S. industry comprises establishments primarily engaged in manufacturing welding and soldering equipment and accessories (except transformers), such as arc, resistance, gas, plasma, laser, electron beam, and ultrasonic welding equipment; welding electrodes; coated or cored welding wire; and soldering equipment (except handheld). (SIC: 3548, 3699) 572-573

333993   **Packaging Machinery Manufacturing.** This U.S. industry comprises establishments primarily engaged in manufacturing packaging machinery, such as wrapping, bottling, canning, and labeling machinery. (SIC: 3565) 574-575

333994   **Industrial Process Furnace and Oven Manufacturing.** This U.S. Industry comprises establishments primarily engaged in manufacturing industrial process furnaces, ovens, induction and dielectric heating equipment, and kilns (except cement, chemical, wood). (SIC: 3567) 576-577

333999   **All Other Miscellaneous General Purpose Machinery Manufacturing.** This U.S. industry comprises establishments primarily engaged in manufacturing general purpose machinery (except ventilating, heating, air-conditioning, and commercial refrigeration equipment; metal working machinery; engines, turbines, and power transmission equipment; pumps and compressors; material handling equipment; power-driven handtools; welding and soldering equipment; packaging machinery; industrial process furnaces and ovens; fluid power cylinders and actuators; fluid power pumps and motors; and scales and balances). (SIC: 3569, 3599) 578-579

334111   **Electronic Computer Manufacturing.** This U.S. industry comprises establishments primarily engaged in manufacturing and/or assembling electronic computers, such as mainframes, personal computers, workstations, laptops, and computer servers. Computers can be analog, digital, or hybrid. Digital computers, the most common type, are devices that do all of the following: (1) store the processing program or programs and the data immediately necessary for the execution of the program; (2) can be freely programmed in accordance with the requirements of the user; (3) perform arithmetical computations specified by the user; and (4) execute, without human intervention, a processing program that requires the computer to modify its execution by logical decision during the processing run. Analog computers are capable of simulating mathematical models and contain at least analog, control, and programming elements. The manufacture of computers includes the assembly or integration of processors, coprocessors, memory, storage, and input/output devices into a user-programmable final product. (SIC: 3571) 580-581

334119   **Other Computer Peripheral Equipment Manufacturing.** This U.S. industry comprises establishments primarily engaged in manufacturing computer peripheral equipment (except storage devices and computer terminals). (SIC: 3577, 3578) 582-583

334210   **Telephone Apparatus Manufacturing.** This industry comprises establishments primarily engaged in manufacturing wire telephone and data communications equipment. These products may be standalone or board-level components of a larger system. Examples of products made by these establishments are central office switching equipment, cordless telephones (except cellular), PBX equipment, telephones, telephone answering machines, LAN modems, multi-user modems, and other data communications equipment, such as bridges, routers, and gateways. (SIC: 3661) 584-585

334220   **Radio and Television Broadcasting and Wireless Communications Equipment Manufacturing.** This industry comprises establishments primarily engaged in manufacturing radio and television broadcast and wireless communications equipment. Examples of products made by these establishments are: transmitting and receiving antennas, cable television equipment, GPS equipment, pagers, cellular phones, mobile communications equipment, and radio and television studio and broadcasting equipment. (SIC: 3663, 3679) 586-587

334290   **Other Communications Equipment Manufacturing.** This industry comprises establishments primarily engaged in manufacturing communications equipment (except telephone apparatus, and radio and television broadcast, and wireless communications equipment). (SIC: 3669) ... 588-589

MANUFACTURING

MANUFACTURING

MANUFACTURING

MANUFACTURING

WHOLESALE TRADE

WHOLESALE TRADE

WHOLESALE TRADE

WHOLESALE TRADE

WHOLESALE TRADE

WHOLESALE TRADE

RETAIL TRADE

RETAIL TRADE

RETAIL TRADE

RETAIL TRADE

RETAIL TRADE

TRANSPORTATION AND WAREHOUSING

TRANSPORTATION AND WAREHOUSING

TRANSPORTATION AND WAREHOUSING

INFORMATION

INFORMATION

INFORMATION

FINANCE AND INSURANCE

FINANCE AND INSURANCE

REAL ESTATE AND RENTAL AND LEASING

REAL ESTATE AND RENTAL AND LEASING

PROFESSIONAL, SCIENTIFIC, AND TECHNICAL SERVICES

PROFESSIONAL, SCIENTIFIC, AND TECHNICAL SERVICES

PROFESSIONAL, SCIENTIFIC, AND TECHNICAL SERVICES

PROFESSIONAL, SCIENTIFIC, AND TECHNICAL SERVICES

MANAGEMENT OF COMPANIES AND ENTERPRISES

551111   **Offices of Bank Holding Companies.** This U.S. industry comprises legal entities known as bank holding companies primarily engaged in holding the securities of (or other equity interests in) companies and enterprises for the purpose of owning a controlling interest or influencing the management decisions of these firms. The holding companies in this industry do not adminis-ter, oversee, and manage other establishments of the company or enterprise whose securities they hold. (SIC: 6712) 1198-1199

551112   **Offices of Other Holding Companies.** This U.S. industry comprises legal entities known as holding companies (except bank holding) primarily engaged in holding the securities of (or other equity interests in) companies and enterprises for the purpose of owning a controlling interest or influencing the management decisions of these firms. The holding companies in this industry do not administer, oversee, and manage other establishments of the company or enter-prise whose securities they hold. (SIC: 6719) 1200-1201

ADMINISTRATIVE AND SUPPORT AND WASTE MANAGEMENT AND REMEDIATION SERVICES

561110   **Office Administrative Services.** This industry comprises establishments primarily engaged in providing a range of day-to-day office administrative services, such as financial planning; billing and recordkeeping; personnel; and physical distribution and logistics for others on a contract or fee basis. These establishments do not provide operating staff to carry out the complete opera-tions of a business. (SIC: 8741) 1204-1205

561210   **Facilities Support Services.** This industry comprises establishments primarily engaged in providing operating staff to perform a combination of support services within a client's facilities. Establishments in this industry typically provide a combination of services, such as janitorial; maintenance; trash disposal; guard and security; mail routing; reception; laundry; and related services to support operations within facilities. These establishments provide operating staff to carry out these support activities; but, are not involved with or responsible for the core business or activities of the client. Establishments providing facilities (except computer and/or data pro-cessing) operation support services and establishments operating correctional facilities (i.e., jails) on a contract or fee basis are included in this industry. (SIC: 8744) 1206-1207

561310   **Employment Placement Agencies.** This industry comprises establishments primarily engaged in listing employment vacancies and in referring or placing applicants for employment. The indi-viduals referred or placed are not employees of the employment agencies. (SIC: 7361) 1208-1209

561320   **Temporary Help Services.** This industry comprises establishments primarily engaged in sup-plying workers to clients' businesses for limited periods of time to supplement the working force of the client. The individuals provided are employees of the temporary help service establish-ment. However, these establishments do not provide direct supervision of their employees at the clients' work sites. (SIC: 7363) 1210-1211

561439   **Other Business Service Centers (including Copy Shops).** This U.S. industry comprises (1) establishments generally known as copy centers or shops primarily engaged in providing photocopying, duplicating, blueprinting, and other document copying services, without also pro-viding printing services (e.g., offset printing, quick printing, digital printing, prepress services) and (2) establishments (except private mail centers) engaged in providing a range of office sup-port services (except printing services), such as document copying services, facsimile services, word processing services, on-site PC rental services, and office product sales. (SIC: 7334, 7389) 1212-1213

561440   **Collection Agencies.** This industry comprises establishments primarily engaged in collecting payments for claims and remitting payments collected to their clients. (SIC: 7322, 7389) 1214-1215

561499   **All Other Business Support Services.** This U.S. industry comprises establishments primarily engaged in providing business support services (except secretarial and other document prepa-ration services; telephone answering and telemarketing services; private mail services or doc-ument copying services conducted as separate activities or in conjunction with other office sup-port services; monetary debt collection services; credit reporting services; repossession services; and court reporting and stenotype recording services). (SIC: 7389) 1216-1217

ADMINISTRATIVE AND SUPPORT AND WASTE MANAGEMENT

EDUCATIONAL SERVICES

HEALTH CARE AND SOCIAL ASSISTANCE

HEALTH CARE AND SOCIAL ASSISTANCE

HEALTH CARE AND SOCIAL ASSISTANCE

ARTS, ENTERTAINMENT, AND RECREATION

ARTS, ENTERTAINMENT, AND RECREATION

ARTS, ENTERTAINMENT, AND RECREATION

ACCOMMODATION AND FOOD SERVICES

721110   Hotels (except Casino Hotels) and Motels. This industry comprises establishments primarily engaged in providing short-term lodging in facilities known as hotels, motor hotels, resort hotels, and motels. The establishments in this industry may offer food and beverage services, recreational services, conference rooms and convention services, laundry services, parking, and other services. (SIC: 7011, 7041) 1352-1353

721211   RV (Recreational Vehicle) Parks and Campgrounds. This U.S. industry comprises establishments primarily engaged in operating sites to accommodate campers and their equipment, including tents, tent trailers, travel trailers, and RVs (recreational vehicles). These establishments may provide access to facilities, such as washrooms, laundry rooms, recreation halls and playgrounds, stores, and snack bars. (SIC: 7033) 1354-1355

721214   Recreational and Vacation Camps (except Campgrounds). This U.S. industry comprises establishments primarily engaged in operating overnight recreational camps, such as children's camps, family vacation camps, hunting and fishing camps, and outdoor adventure retreats that offer trail riding, white-water rafting, hiking, and similar activities. These establishments provide accommodation facilities, such as cabins and fixed campsites, and other amenities, such as food services, recreational facilities and equipment, and organized recreational activities. (SIC: 7032) 1356-1357

722110   Full-Service Restaurants. This industry comprises establishments primarily engaged in providing food services to patrons who order and are served while seated (i.e. waiter/waitress service) and pay after eating. These establishments may provide this type of food services to patrons in combination with selling alcoholic beverages, providing carry out services, or presenting live nontheatrical entertainment. (SIC: 5812) 1358-1359

722211   Limited-Service Restaurants. This U.S. industry comprises establishments primarily engaged in providing food services (except snack and nonalcoholic beverage bars) where patrons generally order or select items and pay before eating. Food and drink may be consumed on premises, taken out, or delivered to the customer's location. Some establishments in this industry may provide these food services in combination with selling alcoholic beverages. (SIC: 5812) 1360-1361

722410   Drinking Places (Alcoholic Beverages). This industry comprises establishments known as bars, taverns, nightclubs, or drinking places primarily engaged in preparing and serving alcoholic beverages for immediate consumption. These establishments may also provide limited food services. (SIC: 5813) 1362-1363

OTHER SERVICES
(EXCEPT PUBLIC ADMINISTRATION)

811111   General Automotive Repair. This U.S. industry comprises establishments primarily engaged in providing (1) a wide range of mechanical and electrical repair and maintenance services for automotive vehicles, such as passenger cars, trucks, and vans, and all trailers or (2) engine repair and replacement. (SIC: 7538) 1366-1367

811112   Automotive Exhaust System Repair. This U.S. industry comprises establishments primarily engaged in replacing or repairing exhaust systems of automotive vehicles, such as passenger cars, trucks, and vans. (SIC: 7533) 1368-1369

811118   Other Automotive Mechanical and Electrical Repair and Maintenance. This U.S. industry comprises establishments primarily engaged in providing specialized mechanical or electrical repair and maintenance services (except engine repair and replacement, exhaust systems repair, and transmission repair) for automotive vehicles, such as passenger cars, trucks, and vans, and all trailers. (SIC: 7539) 1370-1371

811121   Automotive Body, Paint, and Interior Repair and Maintenance. This U.S. industry comprises establishments primarily engaged in repairing or customizing automotive vehicles, such as passenger cars, trucks, and vans, and all trailer bodies and interiors; and/or painting automotive vehicles and trailer bodies. (SIC: 7532) 1372-1373

OTHER SERVICES (EXCEPT PUBLIC ADMINISTRATION)

OTHER SERVICES (EXCEPT PUBLIC ADMINISTRATION)

PUBLIC ADMINISTRATION

CONSTRUCTION—PERCENTAGE OF COMPLETION

CONSTRUCTION—PERCENTAGE OF COMPLETION

CONSTRUCTION—PERCENTAGE OF COMPLETION

CONSTRUCTION—PERCENTAGE OF COMPLETION

AGRICULTURE, FORESTRY, FISHING AND HUNTING

Current Data Sorted By Assets

Comparative Historical Data

						Type of Statement		
	1	3	1		2	Unqualified	1	2
	2	4				Reviewed		2
4	4	5	1			Compiled	33	5
4	5	3				Tax Returns	2	3
6	16	10	2			Other	19	3
	14 (4/1-9/30/02)			59 (10/1/02-3/31/03)			4/1/98-3/31/99	4/1/99-3/31/00
0-500M	500M-2MM	2-10MM	10-50MM	50-100MM	100-250MM		ALL	ALL
14	28	25	4		2	NUMBER OF STATEMENTS	55	15
%	%	%	%	%	%	ASSETS	%	%
21.3	7.3	7.5				Cash & Equivalents	2.2	3.7
13.0	8.5	14.3				Trade Receivables (net)	5.1	6.1
13.3	13.2	17.2		D		Inventory	10.8	12.3
8.3	6.2	2.3		A		All Other Current	4.6	9.6
55.8	35.3	41.4		T		Total Current	22.7	31.7
22.6	38.3	43.9		A		Fixed Assets (net)	61.8	49.7
2.4	4.5	3.9		N		Intangibles (net)	2.2	.8
19.1	21.8	10.9		O		All Other Non-Current	13.4	17.8
100.0	100.0	100.0		T		Total	100.0	100.0
				A		LIABILITIES		
22.3	9.0	11.1		V		Notes Payable-Short Term	13.2	38.6
1.8	3.8	4.2		A		Cur. Mat.-L/T/D	3.5	2.4
9.9	7.5	11.4		I		Trade Payables	2.4	8.1
.0	.4	.1		L		Income Taxes Payable	.0	.4
8.9	5.4	13.0		A		All Other Current	2.6	4.9
42.9	26.0	39.8		B		Total Current	21.7	54.3
11.4	40.6	44.0		L		Long Term Debt	24.7	22.1
.0	.0	.0		E		Deferred Taxes	.3	3.2
2.3	3.2	1.9				All Other Non-Current	3.1	6.8
43.5	30.2	14.3				Net Worth	50.1	13.6
100.0	100.0	100.0				Total Liabilities & Net Worth	100.0	100.0
						INCOME DATA		
100.0	100.0	100.0				Net Sales	100.0	100.0
						Gross Profit		
92.6	86.1	90.0				Operating Expenses	93.9	91.8
7.4	13.9	10.0				Operating Profit	6.1	8.2
2.0	5.2	7.3				All Other Expenses (net)	3.8	-1.0
5.4	8.7	2.7				Profit Before Taxes	2.3	9.1
						RATIOS		
7.4	2.0	2.0					2.4	1.6
1.4	1.5	1.0				Current	1.1	1.0
.4	1.1	.7					.8	.4
2.6	1.2	.9					.4	.7
.8	.5	.6				Quick	.2	.3
.2	.1	.4					.1	.0
0 UND	0 UND	0 UND					0 UND	0 UND
0 UND	10 36.4	31 11.9				Sales/Receivables	4 83.3	5 68.6
21 17.0	33 11.0	49 7.5					48 7.5	21 17.7
						Cost of Sales/Inventory		
						Cost of Sales/Payables		
6.2	3.8	8.5					4.1	5.8
17.5	8.6	185.4				Sales/Working Capital	11.4	-421.2
-16.5	89.3	-11.7					-9.9	-1.9
	8.3	4.0					2.8	10.3
(23)	2.3	(21) 1.3				EBIT/Interest	(52) 1.5	(10) 2.2
	1.0	.5					.5	-.3
						Net Profit + Depr., Dep., Amort./Cur. Mat. L/T/D		
.1	.3	.6					.8	.7
.6	.7	2.2				Fixed/Worth	1.2	1.3
UND	1.7	-33.1					1.5	43.1
.2	.5	.7					.5	.8
1.1	1.2	7.5				Debt/Worth	.7	1.4
UND	14.1	-37.2					1.0	44.3
56.9	13.5	21.1				% Profit Before Taxes/Tangible Net Worth	9.1	23.6
(12) 4.6	(23) 6.2	(18) 7.4					(50) 2.7	(12) 14.8
-10.9	-1.0	-.8					-1.1	1.9
19.6	6.3	4.6				% Profit Before Taxes/Total Assets	4.8	12.4
3.1	4.3	1.0					1.2	1.3
-3.9	.2	-1.1					-3.2	.0
793.1M	21.5	11.5				Sales/Net Fixed Assets	1.0	6.0
29.4	1.1	3.2					.4	1.9
2.3	.8	.5					.3	.5
13.0	2.6	2.2				Sales/Total Assets	.4	2.7
4.8	.5	1.0					.3	.4
.5	.3	.3					.2	.3
	2.2	1.5				% Depr., Dep., Amort./Sales	5.7	2.7
(25)	8.4	(23) 3.2					(50) 9.2	8.7
	14.9	11.3					16.2	11.8
						% Officers', Directors', Owners' Comp/Sales		
12975M	53053M	125995M	196291M		909540M	Net Sales ($)	121694M	36950M
3166M	33665M	90287M	141945M		344008M	Total Assets ($)	147494M	51131M

M = $ thousand   MM = $ million
See Pages 11 through 18 for Explanation of Ratios and Data

Comparative Historical Data | | | Current Data Sorted By Sales

			Type of Statement						
3	1	7	Unqualified		2		1	1	3
1	1	6	Reviewed		1		3	2	
6	7	14	Compiled	4	6	3	1		
2	1	12	Tax Returns	7	3		1	1	
11	14	34	Other	20	5	4	2	1	2
4/1/00-3/31/01	4/1/01-3/31/02	4/1/02-3/31/03		14 (4/1-9/30/02)			59 (10/1/02-3/31/03)		
ALL	ALL	ALL		0-1MM	1-3MM	3-5MM	5-10MM	10-25MM	25MM & OVER
23	24	73	NUMBER OF STATEMENTS	31	17	7	8	5	5
%	%	%	ASSETS	%	%	%	%	%	%
8.3	11.1	9.9	Cash & Equivalents	8.9	11.8				
6.0	7.0	11.5	Trade Receivables (net)	4.5	11.3				
14.9	14.1	14.8	Inventory	6.7	15.4				
10.7	9.8	6.3	All Other Current	7.9	4.2				
39.9	42.0	42.5	Total Current	28.0	42.7				
47.4	31.3	37.1	Fixed Assets (net)	43.6	41.8				
3.9	5.5	3.9	Intangibles (net)	1.3	3.1				
8.8	21.2	16.5	All Other Non-Current	27.0	12.4				
100.0	100.0	100.0	Total	100.0	100.0				
			LIABILITIES						
31.7	21.8	12.2	Notes Payable-Short Term	11.6	15.6				
3.1	2.4	3.4	Cur. Mat.-L/T/D	1.4	4.0				
11.4	11.0	9.3	Trade Payables	3.7	6.7				
.2	.1	.2	Income Taxes Payable	.4	.2				
7.4	6.3	8.7	All Other Current	6.1	10.3				
53.8	41.6	33.8	Total Current	23.1	36.7				
22.1	11.4	33.9	Long Term Debt	33.1	44.2				
.7	1.5	.0	Deferred Taxes	.0	.0				
2.1	4.7	2.6	All Other Non-Current	4.3	.8				
21.2	40.7	29.6	Net Worth	39.5	18.2				
100.0	100.0	100.0	Total Liabilities & Net Worth	100.0	100.0				
			INCOME DATA						
100.0	100.0	100.0	Net Sales	100.0	100.0				
			Gross Profit						
83.7	82.6	89.1	Operating Expenses	83.1	89.5				
16.3	17.4	10.9	Operating Profit	16.9	10.5				
6.1	5.2	4.9	All Other Expenses (net)	7.3	6.6				
10.2	12.2	6.0	Profit Before Taxes	9.6	3.9				
			RATIOS						
1.8	3.2	2.5		3.3	1.9				
1.0	1.4	1.2	Current	1.6	1.0				
.7	.9	.8		.5	.6				
.6	1.3	1.0		.9	1.0				
.4	.2	.7	Quick	.4	.7				
.2	.0	.2		.1	.3				
0 UND	0 UND	0 UND		0 UND	0 UND				
20 18.0	1 251.0	18 20.4	Sales/Receivables	0 UND	9 38.5				
36 10.1	32 11.2	42 8.8		22 16.9	52 7.0				
			Cost of Sales/Inventory						
			Cost of Sales/Payables						
5.0	2.1	5.1		3.4	6.3				
-70.0	8.7	30.4	Sales/Working Capital	8.5	-256.7				
-5.4	-11.8	-18.8		-18.7	-8.9				
4.9	7.1	5.5		6.7	3.0				
(21) 1.1	(21) 3.2	(58) 1.8	EBIT/Interest	(23) 2.3	(14) 1.0				
-.1	-.5	.7		.7	-.4				
			Net Profit + Depr., Dep., Amort./Cur. Mat. L/T/D						
.8	.3	.3		.4	.3				
1.4	.7	.9	Fixed/Worth	.7	1.1				
6.6	1.1	14.5		2.2	16.7				
.6	.5	.5		.3	.9				
1.6	.8	1.4	Debt/Worth	.8	6.1				
16.6	14.4	23.1		1.4	21.8				
22.3	25.8	20.1	% Profit Before Taxes/Tangible Net Worth	12.0	13.5				
(19) 6.8	(20) 15.3	(59) 5.7		(26) 5.3	(14) -.1				
-17.0	2.8	-2.8		-1.7	-8.7				
8.4	12.5	6.8	% Profit Before Taxes/Total Assets	6.4	5.4				
3.1	8.7	2.8		3.4	.3				
-6.3	.0	-.4		-2.0	-2.7				
5.1	7.0	25.8		2.9	22.5				
1.4	1.7	4.0	Sales/Net Fixed Assets	.8	3.7				
.5	.9	.7		.5	.9				
1.6	1.5	3.2		.6	2.7				
.5	.5	1.2	Sales/Total Assets	.3	1.4				
.3	.2	.3		.2	.5				
2.8	1.1	1.5	% Depr., Dep., Amort./Sales	5.4	1.2				
(21) 6.1	(21) 4.9	(60) 5.2		(25) 8.9	(13) 9.1				
8.2	9.8	12.4		14.9	14.6				
		3.2	% Officers', Directors', Owners' Comp/Sales						
	(20)	7.8							
		13.3							
106131M	234987M	1297854M	Net Sales ($)	13417M	33006M	25621M	56346M	67600M	1101864M
136266M	136825M	613071M	Total Assets ($)	31986M	39120M	26142M	28309M	17543M	469971M

M = $ thousand   MM = $ million
See Pages 11 through 18 for Explanation of Ratios and Data

Current Data Sorted By Assets   **Comparative Historical Data**

0-500M	500M-2MM	2-10MM	10-50MM	50-100MM	100-250MM	Type of Statement	4/1/98-3/31/99 ALL	4/1/99-3/31/00 ALL
	1	1				Unqualified	3	1
						Reviewed	2	2
	3	3				Compiled	2	2
2			2			Tax Returns	8	1
2	7	7	1			Other	36	6
	1 (4/1-9/30/02)		28 (10/1/02-3/31/03)					
4	11	11	3			NUMBER OF STATEMENTS	51	12
%	%	%	%	%	%	**ASSETS**	%	%
	7.2	5.9				Cash & Equivalents	3.3	2.4
	5.0	6.1				Trade Receivables (net)	2.2	2.8
	12.6	18.9	D	D		Inventory	12.3	26.9
	3.4	6.0	A	A		All Other Current	5.3	3.5
	28.2	36.8	T	T		Total Current	23.1	35.6
	46.8	50.8	A	A		Fixed Assets (net)	51.7	49.7
	.1	.0				Intangibles (net)	.1	.2
	24.9	12.4	N	N		All Other Non-Current	25.1	14.5
	100.0	100.0	O	O		Total	100.0	100.0
			T	T		**LIABILITIES**		
	14.8	17.3				Notes Payable-Short Term	19.2	25.2
	1.4	1.9	A	A		Cur. Mat.-L/T/D	2.6	3.9
	3.3	5.3	V	V		Trade Payables	1.4	3.8
	.4	.1	A	A		Income Taxes Payable	.5	.0
	5.0	1.6	I	I		All Other Current	4.7	10.1
	24.9	26.2	L	L		Total Current	28.3	43.0
	16.3	18.0	A	A		Long Term Debt	20.1	21.3
	.1	.0	B	B		Deferred Taxes	.4	.8
	4.9	2.2	L	L		All Other Non-Current	6.3	1.0
	53.9	53.5	E	E		Net Worth	44.9	33.9
	100.0	100.0				Total Liabilities & Net Worth	100.0	100.0
						INCOME DATA		
	100.0	100.0				Net Sales	100.0	100.0
						Gross Profit		
	84.2	89.8				Operating Expenses	85.0	86.8
	15.8	10.2				Operating Profit	15.0	13.2
	1.2	4.7				All Other Expenses (net)	11.9	8.7
	14.5	5.4				Profit Before Taxes	3.1	4.5
						RATIOS		
	1.6	1.7					2.0	1.6
	1.3	1.5				Current	1.2	1.1
	.8	.9					.9	.1
	.5	.6					.5	.2
	.2	.4				Quick	.2	.1
	.0	.2					.1	.0
	0 UND	4 83.1					0 UND	0 UND
	0 UND	16 23.4				Sales/Receivables	0 UND	0 UND
	6 57.0	72 5.1					20 17.9	10 36.0
						Cost of Sales/Inventory		
						Cost of Sales/Payables		
	5.0	2.8					3.0	3.6
	9.9	8.6				Sales/Working Capital	14.8	NM
	-5.8	-28.7					-16.2	-1.6
	7.3	2.7					3.7	4.5
	(10) 4.0	2.3				EBIT/Interest	(42) 1.9	(10) 1.9
	2.5	.9					.9	.6
						Net Profit + Depr., Dep., Amort./Cur. Mat. L /T/D		
	.6	.7					.6	.6
	.8	1.0				Fixed/Worth	.9	1.0
	1.5	1.3					1.6	NM
	.3	.4					.4	.6
	1.0	.8				Debt/Worth	.8	1.4
	1.1	1.8					1.5	NM
	19.9	7.8					9.4	
	8.1	2.2				% Profit Before Taxes/Tangible Net Worth	(45) 2.8	
	5.4	-.7					-2.0	
	9.0	3.6					5.8	7.6
	4.7	1.3				% Profit Before Taxes/Total Assets	2.0	3.6
	3.8	-.2					-1.1	-1.6
	3.1	3.7					1.8	4.0
	.7	.5				Sales/Net Fixed Assets	.6	1.2
	.5	.3					.3	.4
	1.0	1.2					.4	1.0
	.3	.3				Sales/Total Assets	.3	.5
	.2	.2					.2	.2
	4.1	4.2					3.9	4.2
	6.1	(10) 7.1				% Depr., Dep., Amort./Sales	(50) 9.3	(11) 6.5
	15.4	16.4					12.9	11.8
						% Officers', Directors', Owners' Comp/Sales		
3517M	10148M	23807M	23248M			Net Sales ($)	96398M	44324M
1051M	13451M	35665M	49418M			Total Assets ($)	211622M	66617M

Comparative Historical Data   ## Current Data Sorted By Sales

				Type of Statement						
1	2			Unqualified						
3	2	4		Reviewed		1		2	1	
1	8	6		Compiled		3	3			
2	3	2		Tax Returns	1	1				
11	15	17		Other	13	4				
4/1/00-3/31/01	4/1/01-3/31/02	4/1/02-3/31/03			1 (4/1-9/30/02)			28 (10/1/02-3/31/03)		
ALL	ALL	ALL			0-1MM	1-3MM	3-5MM	5-10MM	10-25MM	25MM & OVER
18	30	29		**NUMBER OF STATEMENTS**	14	9	3	2	1	
%	%	%		**ASSETS**	%	%	%	%	%	%
7.1	7.3	7.5		Cash & Equivalents	4.5					D
3.4	8.8	5.1		Trade Receivables (net)	.9					A
12.7	17.8	16.8		Inventory	11.0					T
.5	5.7	4.8		All Other Current	2.6					A
23.6	39.6	34.1		Total Current	19.0					
56.5	47.5	44.4		Fixed Assets (net)	48.2					N
1.8	.0	.0		Intangibles (net)	.0					O
18.1	12.9	21.5		All Other Non-Current	32.8					T
100.0	100.0	100.0		Total	100.0					
				LIABILITIES						A
28.1	23.8	25.3		Notes Payable-Short Term	7.7					V
.6	3.5	1.4		Cur. Mat.-L/T/D	.8					A
1.1	9.5	4.3		Trade Payables	1.0					I
1.4	.7	.4		Income Taxes Payable	.2					L
4.6	3.8	8.5		All Other Current	12.2					A
35.8	41.3	39.8		Total Current	21.9					B
19.1	17.1	16.8		Long Term Debt	13.5					L
.9	.5	.0		Deferred Taxes	.0					E
4.9	3.5	3.9		All Other Non-Current	7.3					
39.2	37.6	39.4		Net Worth	57.3					
100.0	100.0	100.0		Total Liabilities & Net Worth	100.0					
				INCOME DATA						
100.0	100.0	100.0		Net Sales	100.0					
				Gross Profit						
76.7	91.3	86.5		Operating Expenses	82.6					
23.3	8.7	13.5		Operating Profit	17.4					
9.0	4.3	3.1		All Other Expenses (net)	2.8					
14.3	4.4	10.5		Profit Before Taxes	14.6					
				RATIOS						
1.4	2.2	1.7			1.5					
1.1	1.3	1.3		Current	1.1					
.6	.8	.9			.8					
.8	.8	.5			.4					
.4	.3	.3		Quick	.3					
.0	.1	.1			.0					
0 UND	0 UND	0 UND			0 UND					
2 200.4	12 30.6	6 57.0		Sales/Receivables	0 UND					
29 12.4	43 8.6	34 10.8			12 29.6					
				Cost of Sales/Inventory						
				Cost of Sales/Payables						
5.2	2.7	3.1			4.5					
NM	7.4	9.4		Sales/Working Capital	36.3					
−10.6	−27.6	−22.9			−11.3					
6.4	2.9	4.3			3.6					
(13) 2.0	(28) 2.0	(26) 2.7		EBIT/Interest	(12) 2.3					
−.7	1.0	1.6			1.3					
				Net Profit + Depr., Dep., Amort./Cur. Mat. L/T/D						
.6	.6	.6			.6					
1.0	1.0	1.0		Fixed/Worth	.8					
1.5	1.3	1.3			1.0					
.5	.4	.5			.3					
.7	.8	1.0		Debt/Worth	.7					
2.7	3.5	2.0			1.0					
24.1	17.1	14.6		% Profit Before Taxes/Tangible Net Worth	10.6					
(17) 3.2	(28) 3.4	(27) 7.2			(13) 5.1					
−12.3	.8	1.5			1.1					
17.0	6.0	8.9		% Profit Before Taxes/Total Assets	5.2					
1.8	1.8	3.8			2.6					
−3.7	.3	1.1			1.0					
2.1	3.6	5.1		Sales/Net Fixed Assets	.9					
.9	1.5	1.2			.5					
.5	.3	.4			.3					
1.0	1.0	1.2		Sales/Total Assets	.3					
.4	.6	.4			.3					
.3	.2	.2			.2					
3.4	3.8	4.2		% Depr., Dep., Amort./Sales	4.5					
(17) 7.0	(28) 5.7	(26) 5.9			(12) 11.5					
16.8	11.3	15.3			18.6					
				% Officers', Directors', Owners' Comp/Sales						
61244M	102581M	60720M		Net Sales ($)	5576M	14680M	11141M	16752M	12571M	
82860M	113567M	99585M		Total Assets ($)	22453M	32472M	8009M	15945M	20706M	

Current Data Sorted By Assets | Comparative Historical Data

0-500M	500M-2MM	2-10MM	10-50MM	50-100MM	100-250MM	Type of Statement	4/1/98-3/31/99 ALL	4/1/99-3/31/00 ALL
		1	3	1	1	Unqualified		4
1	2	3	1			Reviewed		3
	1	4				Compiled		5
4	3					Tax Returns		7
1	3	2	2	1	2	Other		31
							4/1/98-3/31/99 ALL	4/1/99-3/31/00 ALL
6	9	10	6	2	3	NUMBER OF STATEMENTS		50
%	%	%	%	%	%	ASSETS	%	%
		4.0				Cash & Equivalents	D	5.5
		15.4				Trade Receivables (net)	A	6.5
		18.8				Inventory	T	18.4
		5.4				All Other Current	A	4.9
		43.7				Total Current		35.3
		45.1				Fixed Assets (net)	N	43.4
		1.2				Intangibles (net)	O	1.5
		9.9				All Other Non-Current	T	19.8
		100.0				Total		100.0
						LIABILITIES	A	
		15.1				Notes Payable-Short Term	V	32.9
		6.5				Cur. Mat.-L/T/D	A	6.5
		4.2				Trade Payables	I	5.7
		.4				Income Taxes Payable	L	.1
		3.6				All Other Current	A	4.8
		29.8				Total Current	B	50.0
		24.4				Long Term Debt	L	18.8
		.0				Deferred Taxes	E	.3
		1.5				All Other Non-Current		2.6
		44.3				Net Worth		28.3
		100.0				Total Liabilities & Net Worth		100.0
						INCOME DATA		
		100.0				Net Sales		100.0
						Gross Profit		
		100.5				Operating Expenses		88.1
		-.5				Operating Profit		11.9
		2.6				All Other Expenses (net)		5.0
		-3.1				Profit Before Taxes		7.0
						RATIOS		
		2.5				Current		1.5
		1.0						1.0
		.9						.5
		1.3				Quick		.4
		.5					(48)	.2
		.2						.1
		11 32.6				Sales/Receivables	0 UND	
		34 10.8					4 99.8	
		116 3.2					19 19.3	
						Cost of Sales/Inventory		
						Cost of Sales/Payables		
		13.4				Sales/Working Capital		8.3
		66.0						92.9
		-15.1						-5.2
						EBIT/Interest		4.3
							(47)	2.0
								1.1
						Net Profit + Depr., Dep., Amort./Cur. Mat. L/T/D		
		.6				Fixed/Worth		.4
		1.3						.9
		3.7						2.0
		.5				Debt/Worth		.5
		1.3						1.0
		6.3						4.6
		14.5				% Profit Before Taxes/Tangible Net Worth		18.7
		.8					(44)	10.3
		-34.7						2.6
		6.8				% Profit Before Taxes/Total Assets		8.2
		.6						2.8
		-9.4						.0
		30.2				Sales/Net Fixed Assets		7.6
		1.4						1.2
		.5						.6
		3.6				Sales/Total Assets		2.2
		.7						.7
		.3						.3
		1.8				% Depr., Dep., Amort./Sales		2.3
		5.9					(44)	5.8
		11.3						9.8
						% Officers', Directors', Owners' Comp/Sales		
5400M	27872M	75600M	182090M	70504M	943885M	Net Sales ($)		468372M
1685M	9554M	48410M	130205M	134270M	593087M	Total Assets ($)		411714M

M = $ thousand   MM = $ million
See Pages 11 through 18 for Explanation of Ratios and Data

Comparative Historical Data | **Current Data Sorted By Sales**

4/1/00-3/31/01 ALL	4/1/01-3/31/02 ALL	4/1/02-3/31/03 ALL	Type of Statement	0-1MM	1-3MM	3-5MM	5-10MM	10-25MM	25MM & OVER
4	2	6	Unqualified				1	2	3
1	5	7	Reviewed	1	3		2	1	
10	8	5	Compiled		3			2	
8	6	7	Tax Returns	4	3				
10	17	11	Other	3	2			2	4
				8 (4/1-9/30/02)		28 (10/1/02-3/31/03)			
33	38	36	**NUMBER OF STATEMENTS**	8	11	3	7	7	7

00-01 ALL	01-02 ALL	02-03 ALL		0-1MM	1-3MM	3-5MM	5-10MM	10-25MM	25MM & OVER
%	%	%	**ASSETS**	%	%	%	%	%	%
8.0	8.2	8.1	Cash & Equivalents		8.8				
8.5	8.9	19.2	Trade Receivables (net)		12.4				
21.2	23.0	18.0	Inventory		12.5	D			
4.7	3.6	3.9	All Other Current		2.7	A			
42.5	43.7	49.2	Total Current		36.4	T			
44.9	42.9	39.3	Fixed Assets (net)		48.6	A			
4.1	.5	1.2	Intangibles (net)		2.6				
8.5	12.9	10.4	All Other Non-Current		12.4	N			
100.0	100.0	100.0	Total		100.0	O			
			LIABILITIES			T			
20.8	21.3	14.7	Notes Payable-Short Term		12.0				
6.2	7.1	4.3	Cur. Mat.-L/T/D		9.5	A			
9.2	5.0	12.4	Trade Payables		10.1	V			
1.0	.9	1.0	Income Taxes Payable		.4	A			
12.1	6.4	10.3	All Other Current		7.8	I			
49.4	40.7	42.6	Total Current		39.8	L			
22.9	16.8	40.6	Long Term Debt		27.1	A			
1.6	.7	.0	Deferred Taxes		.1	B			
3.6	1.4	1.8	All Other Non-Current		5.1	L			
22.5	40.4	15.0	Net Worth		28.0	E			
100.0	100.0	100.0	Total Liabilities & Net Worth		100.0				
			INCOME DATA						
100.0	100.0	100.0	Net Sales		100.0				
			Gross Profit						
90.8	94.1	94.6	Operating Expenses		96.5				
9.2	5.9	5.4	Operating Profit		3.5				
4.7	2.7	2.2	All Other Expenses (net)		.5				
4.6	3.2	3.1	Profit Before Taxes		3.1				

RATIOS

00-01 ALL	01-02 ALL	02-03 ALL	Ratio	0-1MM	1-3MM	3-5MM	5-10MM	10-25MM	25MM & OVER
1.2	2.3	2.0	Current		1.6				
1.0	1.1	1.1			.9				
.6	.8	.8			.6				
.6	1.0	1.6	Quick		.7				
.3	(37) .4	.6			.5				
.2	.1	.3			.3				
0 UND	0 UND	6 65.2	Sales/Receivables	0 UND					
14 25.5	15 24.0	30 12.3		55 6.7					
46 8.0	39 9.3	99 3.7		145 2.5					
			Cost of Sales/Inventory						
			Cost of Sales/Payables						
9.6	5.4	8.4	Sales/Working Capital		38.4				
-91.9	40.8	37.2			-169.0				
-8.5	-19.1	-17.2			-15.8				
2.6	3.8	3.8	EBIT/Interest		4.1				
(27) 1.2	(35) 1.9	(31) 2.2		(10)	3.0				
.5	.9	.9			-.1				
			Net Profit + Depr., Dep., Amort./Cur. Mat. L/T/D						
.7	.5	.3	Fixed/Worth		.8				
1.4	1.1	1.1			1.9				
NM	1.7	2.1			10.3				
1.0	.4	.6	Debt/Worth		.8				
2.3	1.2	1.8			2.3				
-7.5	3.2	6.7			12.8				
14.8	22.6	17.1	% Profit Before Taxes/Tangible Net Worth						
(23) 3.8	(35) 5.4	(33) 5.1							
-.6	.8	-1.7							
6.2	7.8	8.8	% Profit Before Taxes/Total Assets		9.4				
1.0	2.5	2.9			3.5				
-2.6	.0	-.1			-1.7				
7.6	6.4	13.4	Sales/Net Fixed Assets		7.0				
3.5	2.7	4.8			4.0				
.7	1.3	.9			.6				
3.0	2.4	2.7	Sales/Total Assets		4.0				
1.1	1.3	1.3			1.8				
.4	.5	.4			.3				
1.3	1.9	1.6	% Depr., Dep., Amort./Sales		2.8				
(28) 4.7	(35) 4.5	(33) 4.8			5.6				
11.5	10.5	9.8			10.0				
2.5	.9	1.3	% Officers', Directors', Owners' Comp/Sales						
(10) 5.1	(18) 2.1	(14) 3.4							
9.1	5.2	21.2							
340867M	305923M	1305351M	Net Sales ($)	3302M	17696M		25782M	121000M	1137571M
261175M	236499M	917211M	Total Assets ($)	7692M	24218M		33934M	96657M	754710M

M = $ thousand   MM = $ million
See Pages 11 through 18 for Explanation of Ratios and Data

Current Data Sorted By Assets   **Comparative Historical Data**

0-500M	500M-2MM	2-10MM	10-50MM	50-100MM	100-250MM	Type of Statement	4/1/98-3/31/99 ALL	4/1/99-3/31/00 ALL
			2			Unqualified		
	2	1	3			Reviewed		
	5	7	1	1		Compiled		
1	1	1		1		Tax Returns		
	1	2	3		2	Other		
	7 (4/1-9/30/02)		26 (10/1/02-3/31/03)					
1	8	11	9	2	2	NUMBER OF STATEMENTS		
%	%	%	%	%	%	**ASSETS**	%	%
		8.2				Cash & Equivalents	D	D
		13.9				Trade Receivables (net)	A	A
		22.0				Inventory	T	T
		10.0				All Other Current	A	A
		54.2				Total Current		
		43.5				Fixed Assets (net)	N	N
		.0				Intangibles (net)	O	O
		2.2				All Other Non-Current	T	T
		100.0				Total		
						LIABILITIES	A	A
		20.8				Notes Payable-Short Term	V	V
		3.1				Cur. Mat.-L/T/D	A	A
		2.1				Trade Payables	I	I
		1.3				Income Taxes Payable	L	L
		9.4				All Other Current	A	A
		36.7				Total Current	B	B
		24.6				Long Term Debt	L	L
		.4				Deferred Taxes	E	E
		.2				All Other Non-Current		
		38.1				Net Worth		
		100.0				Total Liabilities & Net Worth		
						INCOME DATA		
		100.0				Net Sales		
						Gross Profit		
		89.8				Operating Expenses		
		10.2				Operating Profit		
		1.8				All Other Expenses (net)		
		8.3				Profit Before Taxes		
						RATIOS		
		4.3						
		2.2				Current		
		.7						
		1.7						
		.7				Quick		
		.0						
	0	UND						
	19	19.5				Sales/Receivables		
	34	10.6						
						Cost of Sales/Inventory		
						Cost of Sales/Payables		
		2.2						
		5.8				Sales/Working Capital		
		−6.2						
		12.1						
	(10)	3.3				EBIT/Interest		
		2.7						
						Net Profit + Depr., Dep., Amort./Cur. Mat. L /T/D		
		.6						
		1.2				Fixed/Worth		
		27.5						
		.6						
		1.4				Debt/Worth		
		47.1						
		147.7						
	(10)	34.3				% Profit Before Taxes/Tangible Net Worth		
		8.1						
		9.4						
		8.1				% Profit Before Taxes/Total Assets		
		3.4						
		8.3						
		2.6				Sales/Net Fixed Assets		
		1.4						
		1.9						
		1.0				Sales/Total Assets		
		.8						
		1.5						
		4.6				% Depr., Dep., Amort./Sales		
		5.7						
						% Officers', Directors', Owners' Comp/Sales		
620M	12901M	60990M	356783M	50416M	213997M	Net Sales ($)		
305M	7598M	39481M	166653M	120789M	338460M	Total Assets ($)		

M = $ thousand   MM = $ million
See Pages 11 through 18 for Explanation of Ratios and Data

Comparative Historical Data | Current Data Sorted By Sales

		Type of Statement						
3	2	Unqualified					1	1
4	6	Reviewed	2	1	1	1	1	1
8	9	Compiled	2		5	1	1	1
7	8	Tax Returns	3	3	1	1	1	
9	8	Other	2		1			5
			3	7 (4/1-9/30/02)		26 (10/1/02-3/31/03)		
4/1/00-3/31/01 ALL	4/1/01-3/31/02 ALL	4/1/02-3/31/03 ALL	0-1MM	1-3MM	3-5MM	5-10MM	10-25MM	25MM & OVER
31	33	NUMBER OF STATEMENTS	3	9	2	7	4	8
%	%	ASSETS	%	%	%	%	%	%
7.1	5.8	Cash & Equivalents						
12.0	13.6	Trade Receivables (net)						
14.4	16.0	Inventory						
8.8	6.9	All Other Current						
42.4	42.3	Total Current						
45.9	49.9	Fixed Assets (net)						
1.4	.3	Intangibles (net)						
10.3	7.5	All Other Non-Current						
100.0	100.0	Total						
		LIABILITIES						
23.0	17.8	Notes Payable-Short Term						
2.5	9.6	Cur. Mat.-L/T/D						
3.6	4.3	Trade Payables						
.1	.7	Income Taxes Payable						
5.8	11.1	All Other Current						
35.0	43.4	Total Current						
33.9	40.3	Long Term Debt						
1.6	1.6	Deferred Taxes						
2.9	1.4	All Other Non-Current						
26.6	13.3	Net Worth						
100.0	100.0	Total Liabilities & Net Worth						
		INCOME DATA						
100.0	100.0	Net Sales						
		Gross Profit						
93.8	90.9	Operating Expenses						
6.2	9.1	Operating Profit						
4.7	2.6	All Other Expenses (net)						
1.4	6.5	Profit Before Taxes						
		RATIOS						
3.1	2.4	Current						
1.3	1.1							
.8	.7							
1.7	1.0	Quick						
.5	.6							
.2	.1							
0 UND	0 UND	Sales/Receivables						
36 10.2	25 14.9							
78 4.7	48 7.6							
		Cost of Sales/Inventory						
		Cost of Sales/Payables						
4.1	4.2	Sales/Working Capital						
7.5	25.3							
-5.2	-5.8							
5.5	6.5	EBIT/Interest						
(27) 1.6	(32) 3.0							
.1	1.5							
		Net Profit + Depr., Dep., Amort./Cur. Mat. L/T/D						
.5	.7	Fixed/Worth						
1.5	1.6							
4.7	46.8							
.6	.8	Debt/Worth						
1.7	2.1							
7.4	73.7							
46.2	49.2	% Profit Before Taxes/Tangible Net Worth						
(28) 6.8	(27) 19.5							
-4.7	6.0							
9.8	13.2	% Profit Before Taxes/Total Assets						
1.3	8.1							
-5.6	1.8							
6.0	5.1	Sales/Net Fixed Assets						
2.1	2.6							
1.2	1.4							
1.2	2.0	Sales/Total Assets						
.8	1.1							
.4	.7							
2.0	2.5	% Depr., Dep., Amort./Sales						
3.5	(32) 4.5							
8.3	6.2							
		% Officers', Directors', Owners' Comp/Sales						
247749M	695707M	Net Sales ($)	1072M	16280M	8265M	44296M	78782M	547012M
388586M	673286M	Total Assets ($)	1569M	16057M	5057M	47471M	101480M	501652M

M = $ thousand   MM = $ million
See Pages 11 through 18 for Explanation of Ratios and Data

Current Data Sorted By Assets   Comparative Historical Data

Type of Statement	0-500M	500M-2MM	2-10MM	10-50MM	50-100MM	100-250MM		4/1/98-3/31/99 ALL	4/1/99-3/31/00 ALL
Unqualified		2	2	6	1	1		11	11
Reviewed		3	12	10	1			28	29
Compiled	2	7	13	1				41	26
Tax Returns	6	5	3					17	12
Other	1	2	6	5	3			28	28
		27 (4/1-9/30/02)		65 (10/1/02-3/31/03)					
NUMBER OF STATEMENTS	9	19	36	22	5	1		125	106
	%	%	%	%	%	%		%	%
ASSETS									
Cash & Equivalents		6.8	6.7	4.1				10.1	6.3
Trade Receivables (net)		10.9	18.8	15.2				12.1	14.8
Inventory		12.0	14.2	15.2				12.4	14.3
All Other Current		11.8	5.8	7.6				6.3	5.2
Total Current		41.5	45.5	45.7				40.9	40.5
Fixed Assets (net)		47.9	44.2	37.8				46.8	45.7
Intangibles (net)		2.6	.4	.6				1.9	3.5
All Other Non-Current		8.0	9.9	15.8				10.4	10.3
Total		100.0	100.0	100.0				100.0	100.0
LIABILITIES									
Notes Payable-Short Term		10.0	12.4	17.8				16.9	19.4
Cur. Mat.-L/T/D		4.8	3.2	3.1				2.5	3.7
Trade Payables		10.7	9.0	8.6				7.3	11.6
Income Taxes Payable		1.1	.5	.1				.5	.2
All Other Current		12.5	6.9	3.9				5.5	3.9
Total Current		39.1	32.1	33.6				32.7	38.8
Long Term Debt		27.5	19.2	23.0				21.2	18.4
Deferred Taxes		.0	.6	.7				1.4	1.2
All Other Non-Current		.9	3.8	.9				3.6	6.6
Net Worth		32.6	44.3	41.8				41.1	34.9
Total Liabilities & Net Worth		100.0	100.0	100.0				100.0	100.0
INCOME DATA									
Net Sales		100.0	100.0	100.0				100.0	100.0
Gross Profit									
Operating Expenses		91.9	91.7	94.9				91.2	97.6
Operating Profit		8.1	8.3	5.1				8.8	2.4
All Other Expenses (net)		4.3	3.0	.6				.7	.4
Profit Before Taxes		3.8	5.3	4.5				8.1	2.0
RATIOS									
Current		2.0 / 1.1 / .4	3.1 / 1.4 / .8	2.6 / 1.5 / .8				2.8 / 1.3 / .7	2.0 / 1.1 / .5
Quick		1.1 / .3 / .1	1.5 / .7 / .4	1.4 / .7 / .2				2.0 / .7 / .1	1.1 / .6 / .2
Sales/Receivables	0 UND / 4 85.7 / 26 14.0		8 43.9 / 31 11.6 / 55 6.6	9 42.9 / 37 9.8 / 90 4.0				0 UND / 13 28.0 / 45 8.2	0 UND / 24 15.2 / 56 6.5
Cost of Sales/Inventory									
Cost of Sales/Payables									
Sales/Working Capital		11.8 / 71.6 / -12.2	5.6 / 16.3 / -19.8	4.1 / 9.1 / -42.7				5.1 / 25.0 / -16.4	6.6 / 32.0 / -7.6
EBIT/Interest		(15) 7.0 / 3.4 / 1.2	(33) 12.8 / 3.4 / 1.3	(21) 7.7 / 2.5 / 1.2				(112) 10.2 / 3.2 / .8	(90) 4.9 / 1.6 / -.8
Net Profit + Depr., Dep., Amort./Cur. Mat. L /T/D								(28) 7.9 / 3.2 / 1.5	(29) 9.3 / 3.1 / 1.0
Fixed/Worth		.3 / 1.4 / 4.1	.5 / .9 / 1.8	.5 / .9 / 2.0				.5 / .9 / 2.7	.6 / 1.0 / 2.7
Debt/Worth		.5 / 1.3 / 5.0	.6 / 1.3 / 3.1	.5 / 1.7 / 4.1				.4 / 1.1 / 3.6	.6 / 1.3 / 4.5
% Profit Before Taxes/Tangible Net Worth		(18) 110.2 / 9.3 / .0	(34) 40.3 / 28.1 / 3.1	(21) 22.5 / 13.5 / 4.4				(113) 44.3 / 14.7 / .3	(89) 23.4 / 7.7 / -1.4
% Profit Before Taxes/Total Assets		9.9 / 3.4 / -2.2	19.8 / 7.4 / 1.3	9.1 / 4.4 / 1.0				17.4 / 5.7 / -.4	10.4 / 2.6 / -5.7
Sales/Net Fixed Assets		13.3 / 3.2 / .8	12.3 / 4.1 / 2.4	7.9 / 3.9 / 1.9				9.7 / 3.5 / 1.8	9.5 / 3.2 / 1.5
Sales/Total Assets		4.2 / .9 / .6	2.9 / 1.9 / .7	2.0 / 1.1 / .7				2.6 / 1.4 / .8	2.3 / 1.4 / .8
% Depr., Dep., Amort./Sales		(16) .8 / 3.8 / 6.2	1.5 / 3.1 / 4.8	(21) 2.1 / 3.0 / 4.2				(112) 1.7 / 3.3 / 6.1	(93) 1.5 / 3.3 / 7.6
% Officers', Directors', Owners' Comp/Sales			(11) 2.5 / 4.3 / 9.1					(35) 2.4 / 4.0 / 10.7	(24) 1.8 / 5.3 / 9.5
Net Sales ($)	10043M	57228M	418149M	744602M	531566M	334464M		2101682M	1420609M
Total Assets ($)	2074M	19654M	189731M	462589M	401191M	178211M		1594831M	1096004M

Comparative Historical Data | Current Data Sorted By Sales

			Type of Statement						
9	9	12	Unqualified	1			2	3	6
24	15	26	Reviewed		3	2	5	6	10
25	11	23	Compiled	6	6	2	4	4	1
9	10	14	Tax Returns	6	5		1	2	
38	21	17	Other	1	2	2	3	4	5
4/1/00-3/31/01 ALL	4/1/01-3/31/02 ALL	4/1/02-3/31/03 ALL		27 (4/1-9/30/02)			65 (10/1/02-3/31/03)		
				0-1MM	1-3MM	3-5MM	5-10MM	10-25MM	25MM & OVER
105	66	92	**NUMBER OF STATEMENTS**	14	16	6	15	19	22
%	%	%	**ASSETS**	%	%	%	%	%	%
6.3	4.7	7.4	Cash & Equivalents	11.8	5.0		7.2	8.7	5.8
15.6	19.3	15.5	Trade Receivables (net)	4.9	10.2		19.8	19.4	20.1
12.3	15.0	12.8	Inventory	7.2	11.3		15.2	14.4	16.0
6.0	6.1	7.2	All Other Current	6.7	4.7		11.5	8.0	6.8
40.3	45.1	42.9	Total Current	30.5	31.2		53.8	50.5	48.7
46.2	44.4	44.5	Fixed Assets (net)	66.1	54.3		37.3	34.8	36.1
2.5	2.3	.9	Intangibles (net)	.4	1.0		3.0	.1	.8
11.1	8.2	11.6	All Other Non-Current	3.0	13.5		5.9	14.6	14.5
100.0	100.0	100.0	Total	100.0	100.0		100.0	100.0	100.0
			LIABILITIES						
16.8	18.4	16.6	Notes Payable-Short Term	25.7	24.7		12.3	15.7	10.0
3.9	3.0	5.3	Cur. Mat.-L/T/D	6.6	9.6		4.5	3.3	3.3
7.8	11.7	9.7	Trade Payables	8.9	6.6		13.2	7.8	13.2
.2	.2	.5	Income Taxes Payable	1.3	.0		.1	1.0	.1
6.2	7.6	7.1	All Other Current	8.7	10.9		7.8	7.7	3.5
34.9	40.8	39.0	Total Current	51.2	51.9		37.9	35.5	30.1
27.7	18.4	32.1	Long Term Debt	45.9	69.2		23.4	16.9	17.9
1.3	1.6	.7	Deferred Taxes	.0	.0		.1	1.2	1.8
3.1	2.6	2.0	All Other Non-Current	1.0	3.8		3.9	1.6	.4
32.9	36.6	26.1	Net Worth	1.8	-24.9		34.7	44.8	49.7
100.0	100.0	100.0	Total Liabilities & Net Worth	100.0	100.0		100.0	100.0	100.0
			INCOME DATA						
100.0	100.0	100.0	Net Sales	100.0	100.0		100.0	100.0	100.0
			Gross Profit						
94.2	95.5	92.7	Operating Expenses	83.3	95.2		95.2	93.8	94.8
5.8	4.5	7.3	Operating Profit	16.7	4.8		4.8	6.2	5.2
1.9	2.3	2.5	All Other Expenses (net)	11.0	2.2		.6	.7	-.1
3.9	2.2	4.8	Profit Before Taxes	5.6	2.6		4.1	5.5	5.3
			RATIOS						
2.7	2.0	2.4		1.4	2.5		2.9	3.2	2.7
1.3	1.2	1.3	Current	.4	1.2		1.3	1.6	1.5
.7	.7	.7		.1	.1		.7	.9	1.2
1.4	1.1	1.3		.3	1.5		1.3	2.0	1.5
.8	.7	.6	Quick	.1	.5		.6	1.1	.8
.2	.1	.2		.0	.0		.3	.4	.4
0 UND	5 79.6	1 313.9		0 UND	0 UND		7 52.8	6 58.5	14 25.3
25 14.3	31 11.8	27 13.3	Sales/Receivables	0 UND	17 21.8		34 10.8	32 11.5	35 10.3
55 6.6	65 5.6	48 7.5		5 66.7	73 5.0		56 6.5	46 7.9	48 7.5
			Cost of Sales/Inventory						
			Cost of Sales/Payables						
5.3	5.8	5.8		9.4	4.1		3.1	7.7	5.9
18.1	18.3	19.2	Sales/Working Capital	-9.1	20.3		20.1	18.9	10.2
-21.8	-14.2	-16.0		-1.0	-10.1		-14.8	-27.4	36.1
(90) 4.8	(60) 5.4	(84) 11.0		(10) 9.5	(15) 7.6		5.4	(17) 50.4	(21) 17.5
2.4	2.0	3.5	EBIT/Interest	2.8	3.2		2.4	6.5	5.7
-.8	.7	1.3		-8.7	.6		1.2	2.4	2.3
(18) 4.7	(10) 6.3	(17) 7.6	Net Profit + Depr., Dep.,						
2.7	2.1	1.5	Amort./Cur. Mat. L/T/D						
.7	1.3	.5							
.5	.5	.5		1.1	.5		.4	.3	.5
1.1	1.1	.9	Fixed/Worth	6.4	1.4		.9	.7	.8
2.9	3.8	2.6		-5.4	-1.1		5.2	1.7	1.4
.5	.6	.6		.7	.6		.7	.5	.5
1.2	1.5	1.3	Debt/Worth	19.9	1.6		2.2	1.0	1.0
4.1	6.5	4.5		-7.0	-2.6		6.8	3.3	2.5
(90) 24.6	18.9	32.1	% Profit Before Taxes/Tangible	(10) 137.8	(11) 27.9		(14) 34.8	(18) 62.4	25.8
8.1	(57) 7.7	(81) 14.2	Net Worth	8.0	2.2		10.5	29.5	15.9
-3.5	-1.1	3.6		-13.0	-2.2		4.7	11.9	8.7
12.2	11.8	13.2	% Profit Before Taxes/Total	14.8	13.5		11.2	26.5	12.6
4.1	2.6	6.1	Assets	3.0	1.4		2.7	9.4	7.6
-3.7	-.9	1.2		-7.1	-10.7		.5	4.6	3.0
9.1	13.0	9.1		4.0	10.2		15.5	13.3	11.7
3.8	4.0	4.2	Sales/Net Fixed Assets	2.8	2.5		5.4	5.6	5.8
1.6	1.8	2.2		.1	.8		2.8	3.6	3.5
2.4	2.4	3.1		2.4	4.2		3.2	5.3	3.2
1.4	1.4	1.7	Sales/Total Assets	.7	.9		1.9	2.1	1.8
.8	.7	.7		.1	.6		1.4	1.2	1.1
(88) 1.6	(62) 1.5	(88) 1.6	% Depr., Dep., Amort./Sales	(12) 4.1	(15) 2.5		1.2	1.3	1.3
3.4	3.1	3.2		6.5	3.6		2.6	2.1	2.4
6.3	5.5	5.1		8.8	8.0		4.4	3.5	3.4
(26) 1.4	(11) 1.1	(25) 1.3	% Officers', Directors',						
2.5	3.0	3.2	Owners' Comp/Sales						
6.3	4.7	7.1							
2804038M	1777679M	2096052M	Net Sales ($)	6722M	28853M	24465M	116965M	306965M	1612082M
2107249M	1166343M	1253450M	Total Assets ($)	14309M	33644M	45107M	81088M	163648M	915654M

M = $ thousand   MM = $ million
See Pages 11 through 18 for Explanation of Ratios and Data

Current Data Sorted By Assets   Comparative Historical Data

0-500M	500M-2MM	2-10MM	10-50MM	50-100MM	100-250MM	Type of Statement	4/1/98-3/31/99 ALL	4/1/99-3/31/00 ALL
		6	3	4	3	Unqualified	28	24
	1	10	3	1		Reviewed	11	12
	8	9	2			Compiled	26	23
4	9	9	1			Tax Returns	17	7
	4	3	1			Other	22	10
	37 (4/1-9/30/02)		44 (10/1/02-3/31/03)					
4	22	37	10	5	3	**NUMBER OF STATEMENTS**	104	76
%	%	%	%	%	%	**ASSETS**	%	%
	7.7	8.8	4.5			Cash & Equivalents	9.5	7.9
	6.7	7.7	5.5			Trade Receivables (net)	5.6	7.1
	3.4	6.6	11.3			Inventory	10.3	11.6
	4.4	6.3	1.1			All Other Current	3.9	3.1
	22.3	29.3	22.4			Total Current	29.3	29.7
	60.1	57.4	62.7			Fixed Assets (net)	59.3	57.1
	3.1	1.3	.7			Intangibles (net)	1.2	2.3
	14.6	12.0	14.3			All Other Non-Current	10.2	10.9
	100.0	100.0	100.0			Total	100.0	100.0
						LIABILITIES		
	9.9	13.2	7.5			Notes Payable-Short Term	10.9	10.9
	6.5	2.9	2.5			Cur. Mat.-L/T/D	4.5	2.9
	4.1	4.3	2.2			Trade Payables	4.7	5.4
	.1	.0	.1			Income Taxes Payable	.2	.1
	18.3	11.9	6.4			All Other Current	9.5	10.3
	38.9	32.4	18.8			Total Current	29.9	29.7
	35.2	34.3	30.6			Long Term Debt	37.9	34.7
	.0	.5	.6			Deferred Taxes	1.3	1.3
	6.4	3.6	3.6			All Other Non-Current	2.7	2.4
	19.5	29.1	46.4			Net Worth	28.2	32.0
	100.0	100.0	100.0			Total Liabilities & Net Worth	100.0	100.0
						INCOME DATA		
	100.0	100.0	100.0			Net Sales	100.0	100.0
						Gross Profit		
	98.9	92.4	95.7			Operating Expenses	105.8	90.5
	1.1	7.6	4.3			Operating Profit	-5.8	9.5
	2.6	5.6	3.5			All Other Expenses (net)	.9	5.4
	-1.5	1.9	.8			Profit Before Taxes	-6.7	4.1
						RATIOS		
	1.9	2.0	3.0				2.8	2.6
	.7	1.0	1.4			Current	1.4	1.3
	.1	.3	.7				.4	.7
	1.6	1.1	1.2				2.0	1.2
	.3	.5	.9			Quick	.4	.4
	.1	.1	.2				.1	.1
	0 UND	0 UND	4 85.0				0 UND	0 UND
	0 UND	3 141.0	20 18.7			Sales/Receivables	7 55.5	4 82.7
	18 19.9	18 20.0	51 7.2				32 11.4	29 12.5
						Cost of Sales/Inventory		
						Cost of Sales/Payables		
	13.0	9.3	4.0				4.5	3.4
	-15.2	-480.4	16.6			Sales/Working Capital	20.6	26.8
	-5.0	-5.6	-5.0				-8.2	-13.4
	3.3	9.3					9.4	6.9
	(20) 1.5	(28) 2.1				EBIT/Interest	(79) 3.0	(66) 2.1
	.6	-.8					1.1	.6
							5.6	3.9
						Net Profit + Depr., Dep., Amort./Cur. Mat. L /T/D	(13) 3.3	(10) 2.7
							1.0	1.5
	1.0	.8	.9				.7	.9
	2.8	1.2	1.4			Fixed/Worth	1.6	1.4
	-6.2	UND	3.0				7.3	7.4
	.5	.5	.3				.4	.6
	4.2	1.5	1.3			Debt/Worth	1.9	1.7
	-9.2	UND	4.2				13.4	8.9
	35.5	24.4	14.7			% Profit Before Taxes/Tangible Net Worth	24.6	26.5
	(14) 4.5	(28) 13.4	6.9				(79) 9.4	(62) 7.8
	-4.9	.1	-3.7				.8	-3.1
	8.9	10.0	6.0			% Profit Before Taxes/Total Assets	11.6	11.9
	1.6	2.1	1.8				3.3	2.7
	-2.6	-2.4	-1.3				-4.3	-2.1
	6.8	6.5	2.0				4.6	5.5
	4.4	1.9	.9			Sales/Net Fixed Assets	1.4	1.3
	.9	.5	.3				.5	.6
	3.5	2.3	1.1				1.9	1.8
	1.7	1.2	.5			Sales/Total Assets	.8	.8
	.7	.3	.2				.3	.3
	2.9	2.8	4.9				2.2	3.0
	4.1	(32) 6.3	7.1			% Depr., Dep., Amort./Sales	(97) 5.5	(75) 5.4
	8.2	14.6	20.2				11.2	11.6
							1.9	1.6
						% Officers', Directors', Owners' Comp/Sales	(25) 3.8	(16) 2.3
							8.4	11.9
8376M	67720M	325632M	116478M	281359M	172202M	Net Sales ($)	2090530M	1592361M
1353M	30055M	185620M	222921M	340190M	526538M	Total Assets ($)	2939641M	2578712M

M = $ thousand   MM = $ million
See Pages 11 through 18 for Explanation of Ratios and Data

	Comparative Historical Data				Type of Statement	Current Data Sorted By Sales					
	6	10	16		Unqualified		1		1	5	9
	5	6	15		Reviewed	1	1	2	5	5	1
	34	21	19		Compiled		9	2	6	1	1
	3	14	23		Tax Returns	8	7	5	2		1
	7	8	8		Other	2	2	2	1	1	
	4/1/00-	4/1/01-	4/1/02-				37 (4/1-9/30/02)		44 (10/1/02-3/31/03)		
	3/31/01	3/31/02	3/31/03								
	ALL	ALL	ALL			0-1MM	1-3MM	3-5MM	5-10MM	10-25MM	25MM & OVER
	55	59	81		NUMBER OF STATEMENTS	11	20	11	15	12	12
	%	%	%		ASSETS	%	%	%	%	%	%
	4.3	7.1	8.5		Cash & Equivalents	7.6	8.0	13.4	8.4	6.8	7.7
	8.5	10.7	6.5		Trade Receivables (net)	.4	6.4	5.0	6.9	11.0	8.9
	6.1	8.6	6.5		Inventory	.8	4.8	3.9	5.2	15.9	9.3
	17.1	7.8	4.5		All Other Current	2.6	6.1	.7	7.3	2.3	6.2
	35.9	34.2	26.1		Total Current	11.3	25.3	23.0	27.7	36.0	32.0
	49.4	54.6	58.4		Fixed Assets (net)	79.8	57.1	66.8	52.0	50.4	49.2
	2.1	.8	1.6		Intangibles (net)	.4	3.3	.3	1.0	1.0	2.6
	12.6	10.4	13.9		All Other Non-Current	8.4	14.4	9.9	19.4	12.5	16.1
	100.0	100.0	100.0		Total	100.0	100.0	100.0	100.0	100.0	100.0
					LIABILITIES						
	15.1	11.1	10.8		Notes Payable-Short Term	3.2	11.6	18.9	16.7	10.7	1.5
	6.7	3.2	4.4		Cur. Mat.-L/T/D	5.8	5.7	4.6	3.7	2.8	3.2
	7.0	5.0	3.8		Trade Payables	2.6	3.0	1.7	3.2	6.2	6.7
	.1	.1	.1		Income Taxes Payable	.0	.1	.0	.0	.1	.2
	12.9	8.9	12.4		All Other Current	9.5	20.8	4.3	8.7	9.7	15.4
	41.8	28.3	31.4		Total Current	21.2	41.3	29.5	32.4	29.5	26.9
	35.7	34.7	32.6		Long Term Debt	56.2	35.4	45.2	19.6	25.3	18.1
	.9	.7	.8		Deferred Taxes	.0	1.0	.0	.0	.5	3.4
	2.8	6.2	4.2		All Other Non-Current	7.9	5.5	4.0	.5	3.5	3.9
	18.9	30.1	31.0		Net Worth	14.6	16.9	21.3	47.5	41.3	47.7
	100.0	100.0	100.0		Total Liabilities & Net Worth	100.0	100.0	100.0	100.0	100.0	100.0
					INCOME DATA						
	100.0	100.0	100.0		Net Sales	100.0	100.0	100.0	100.0	100.0	100.0
					Gross Profit						
	92.0	96.1	94.4		Operating Expenses	81.0	98.6	95.6	97.5	95.5	93.8
	8.0	3.9	5.6		Operating Profit	19.0	1.4	4.4	2.5	4.5	6.2
	4.0	5.9	4.0		All Other Expenses (net)	14.6	3.6	1.2	3.4	.4	1.7
	4.0	-2.0	1.6		Profit Before Taxes	4.3	-2.2	3.2	-.9	4.1	4.6
					RATIOS						
	2.0	2.2	2.1			.8	3.8	4.5	2.0	2.1	2.4
	1.0	1.2	1.0		Current	.1	.8	1.0	1.0	1.5	1.2
	.3	.6	.4			.1	.1	.1	.6	.7	1.0
	.6	1.2	1.1			.8	2.5	1.7	.8	1.4	1.6
	.2	.5	.5		Quick	.1	.3	.9	.4	.9	.7
	.0	.2	.1			.1	.0	.1	.2	.4	.3
	0 UND	0 UND	0 UND			0 UND	0 UND	0 UND	1 387.9	11 32.4	3 120.3
	0 999.8	12 29.4	3 133.7		Sales/Receivables	0 UND	0 UND	0 UND	9 41.0	20 18.2	12 29.8
	18 20.7	38 9.5	22 17.0			2 243.0	8 47.4	18 20.5	23 15.8	29 12.6	27 13.6
					Cost of Sales/Inventory						
					Cost of Sales/Payables						
	5.2	5.2	8.1			-12.0	3.1	3.9	10.2	8.6	5.1
	-252.2	32.0	-480.9		Sales/Working Capital	-5.1	-51.8	-523.3	-480.9	24.3	47.3
	-4.5	-6.7	-5.9			-.7	-2.7	-9.7	-6.8	-32.9	-173.4
	4.2	5.2	5.8				4.0	5.4	6.8	11.0	7.4
(46)	1.7	(44) .9	(67) 2.1		EBIT/Interest	(18) 2.0	(10) 2.5	(12) 5.0	(10) 2.6	(10) 2.1
	.6	-.1	.5				-4.3	.1	-.4	-.2	1.2
			4.3		Net Profit + Depr., Dep.,						
			(12) 3.5		Amort./Cur. Mat. L/T/D						
			.1								
	.5	.7	.8			1.2	.9	.7	.9	.7	.6
	1.6	1.6	1.3		Fixed/Worth	6.5	2.0	1.3	1.1	1.3	.8
	-9.7	-525.0	16.4			-19.4	-1.7	-4.8	2.3	3.6	1.6
	.5	.5	.5			1.1	.4	.3	.4	.3	.7
	2.4	1.6	1.4		Debt/Worth	6.3	12.2	1.3	1.1	1.3	1.0
	-15.0	-529.0	23.0			-20.6	-4.1	-5.9	4.8	6.0	3.4
	26.0	33.0	25.3		% Profit Before Taxes/Tangible		10.5		33.2	28.7	30.9
(40)	7.6	(43) .5	(63) 9.3		Net Worth	(12) 4.5		12.5	(10) 14.7	9.2
	.0	-5.1	.1				-6.7		.0	1.9	.5
	8.8	9.6	9.2		% Profit Before Taxes/Total	2.1	7.2	7.4	13.6	12.6	12.6
	1.4	.0	1.9		Assets	1.7	1.4	2.5	2.4	4.1	3.3
	-3.0	-3.6	-1.3			-1.0	-4.6	-2.0	-1.1	-2.0	.2
	8.2	7.0	5.9			.6	4.5	6.3	12.0	6.9	11.7
	3.1	1.8	2.0		Sales/Net Fixed Assets	.3	1.7	4.8	5.6	2.7	2.0
	.8	.7	.6			.1	.5	1.0	1.6	1.7	.7
	2.5	2.0	2.4			.3	1.5	5.3	3.4	2.2	5.2
	.9	.8	1.1		Sales/Total Assets	.2	.8	2.3	2.3	1.6	1.1
	.4	.4	.3			.1	.3	.7	1.2	1.1	.3
	.1	.7	3.1			7.9	3.5	2.5	2.4	2.7	1.6
(52)	1.0	(52) 3.4	(76) 6.1		% Depr., Dep., Amort./Sales	(10) 19.6	(19) 5.5	7.4	(14) 4.0	(11) 4.8	(11) 4.6
	7.5	11.0	11.3			33.9	15.5	9.1	6.1	6.6	11.5
	1.5	1.0	1.5		% Officers', Directors',						
(22)	2.7	(15) 2.8	(20) 2.5		Owners' Comp/Sales						
	7.0	8.5	5.4								
	1302393M	1763565M	971767M		Net Sales ($)	4761M	40635M	41962M	104678M	163063M	616668M
	828361M	1228327M	1306677M		Total Assets ($)	23116M	81638M	35020M	119531M	154065M	893307M

M = $ thousand   MM = $ million
See Pages 11 through 18 for Explanation of Ratios and Data

Current Data Sorted By Assets   **Comparative Historical Data**

0-500M	500M-2MM	2-10MM	10-50MM	50-100MM	100-250MM	Type of Statement	4/1/98-3/31/99 ALL	4/1/99-3/31/00 ALL
						Unqualified		4
1		9	1			Reviewed	10	7
1	4	2	2		2	Compiled	20	10
4	2	2	2			Tax Returns	4	6
		1	1			Other	14	9
	10 (4/1-9/30/02)			24 (10/1/02-3/31/03)				
6	6	14	6		2	NUMBER OF STATEMENTS	48	36
%	%	%	%	%	%		%	%
		9.6				Cash & Equivalents	3.4	8.7
		18.4				Trade Receivables (net)	8.3	7.9
		9.8				Inventory	17.7	12.6
		4.5				All Other Current	3.8	2.7
		42.2				Total Current	33.2	31.9
		52.7				Fixed Assets (net)	53.2	57.7
		.2		DATA NOT AVAILABLE		Intangibles (net)	.4	.7
		4.8				All Other Non-Current	13.2	9.7
		100.0				Total	100.0	100.0
						LIABILITIES		
		14.8				Notes Payable-Short Term	23.4	20.2
		5.0				Cur. Mat.-L/T/D	3.1	4.8
		9.1				Trade Payables	5.4	5.0
		.2				Income Taxes Payable	.1	.2
		3.4				All Other Current	11.6	13.9
		32.5				Total Current	43.6	44.0
		26.5				Long Term Debt	25.6	32.8
		1.0				Deferred Taxes	.8	.5
		3.0				All Other Non-Current	3.0	15.7
		37.0				Net Worth	15.0	7.0
		100.0				Total Liabilities & Net Worth	100.0	100.0
						INCOME DATA		
		100.0				Net Sales	100.0	100.0
						Gross Profit		
		95.7				Operating Expenses	122.4	100.3
		4.3				Operating Profit	−22.4	−.3
		1.9				All Other Expenses (net)	9.0	.2
		2.4				Profit Before Taxes	−31.4	−.5

RATIOS

2-10MM	Ratio	4/1/98-3/31/99	4/1/99-3/31/00
2.9 / 2.0 / 1.0	Current	2.3 / 1.0 / .5	2.4 / .9 / .3
2.3 / 1.1 / .6	Quick	1.0 / .3 / .0	1.0 / .4 / .1
1 / 264.2 30 / 12.3 62 / 5.9	Sales/Receivables	0 UND 10 / 38.2 48 / 7.6	0 UND 2 / 186.9 33 / 11.0
	Cost of Sales/Inventory		
	Cost of Sales/Payables		
5.4 / 9.3 / NM	Sales/Working Capital	4.4 / UND / −2.7	5.3 / −97.4 / −7.2
(13) 4.9 / 2.4 / .7	EBIT/Interest	(36) 4.3 / 2.0 / −.8	(30) 2.3 / 1.4 / −.8
	Net Profit + Depr., Dep., Amort./Cur. Mat. L /T/D		
.6 / .9 / NM	Fixed/Worth	.7 / 1.5 / 6.3	.9 / 1.6 / −14.6
.5 / 1.0 / NM	Debt/Worth	.7 / 2.0 / 6.4	.7 / 2.3 / −25.5
(11) 33.2 / 13.5 / −.2	% Profit Before Taxes/Tangible Net Worth	(38) 24.2 / 8.0 / −18.8	(25) 24.6 / 7.9 / −2.5
9.3 / 6.0 / −.7	% Profit Before Taxes/Total Assets	11.3 / .6 / −11.0	7.1 / 1.9 / −7.5
4.0 / 2.3 / 1.2	Sales/Net Fixed Assets	2.6 / 1.2 / .7	2.7 / 1.6 / .8
1.8 / 1.2 / 1.0	Sales/Total Assets	.9 / .6 / .4	1.6 / .8 / .5
(13) 3.3 / 4.3 / 8.1	% Depr., Dep., Amort./Sales	(44) 4.0 / 8.2 / 13.3	2.8 / 6.0 / 12.0
	% Officers', Directors', Owners' Comp/Sales		

0-500M	500M-2MM	2-10MM	10-50MM	50-100MM	100-250MM		4/1/98-3/31/99	4/1/99-3/31/00
5022M	9824M	105713M	123776M		157792M	Net Sales ($)	206120M	239563M
1795M	8226M	69656M	129920M		251760M	Total Assets ($)	326687M	355076M

M = $ thousand   MM = $ million
See Pages 11 through 18 for Explanation of Ratios and Data

Comparative Historical Data

Current Data Sorted By Sales

			Type of Statement						
3	2	2	Unqualified	1					1
9	14	13	Reviewed		1	3	4	3	2
12	7	9	Compiled	1	3	2	1	1	1
7	3	8	Tax Returns	5	1		2		
7	4	2	Other		1		1		
4/1/00- 3/31/01 ALL	4/1/01- 3/31/02 ALL	4/1/02- 3/31/03 ALL		10 (4/1-9/30/02)			24 (10/1/02-3/31/03)		
				0-1MM	1-3MM	3-5MM	5-10MM	10-25MM	25MM & OVER
38	30	34	NUMBER OF STATEMENTS	7	6	5	8	4	4
%	%	%	ASSETS	%	%	%	%	%	%
10.1	5.6	12.9	Cash & Equivalents						
8.6	12.3	12.4	Trade Receivables (net)						
9.6	11.9	7.2	Inventory						
3.6	5.3	4.5	All Other Current						
32.0	35.1	36.9	Total Current						
56.6	56.6	53.5	Fixed Assets (net)						
.6	1.0	.4	Intangibles (net)						
10.9	7.3	9.2	All Other Non-Current						
100.0	100.0	100.0	Total						
			LIABILITIES						
17.8	22.9	13.1	Notes Payable-Short Term						
2.5	4.6	4.2	Cur. Mat.-L/T/D						
3.8	5.6	5.7	Trade Payables						
.1	.7	.1	Income Taxes Payable						
8.0	6.3	7.8	All Other Current						
32.1	40.1	30.9	Total Current						
29.7	34.3	35.2	Long Term Debt						
.8	.4	.4	Deferred Taxes						
3.6	4.1	4.7	All Other Non-Current						
33.7	21.2	28.8	Net Worth						
100.0	100.0	100.0	Total Liabilities & Net Worth						
			INCOME DATA						
100.0	100.0	100.0	Net Sales						
			Gross Profit						
95.2	94.8	93.7	Operating Expenses						
4.8	5.2	6.3	Operating Profit						
5.3	8.1	8.2	All Other Expenses (net)						
−.5	−2.9	−1.9	Profit Before Taxes						
			RATIOS						
1.9	1.7	2.5							
1.3	1.0	1.5	Current						
.7	.6	.7							
1.2	.9	2.1							
.5	.4	.8	Quick						
.2	.2	.3							
0 UND	0 UND	0 UND							
27 13.4	30 12.0	26 14.1	Sales/Receivables						
46 8.0	73 5.0	52 7.1							
			Cost of Sales/Inventory						
			Cost of Sales/Payables						
5.5	12.0	4.4							
16.8	UND	9.3	Sales/Working Capital						
−6.7	−6.6	−10.2							
2.7	2.4	3.1							
(33) 1.0	(26) 1.4	(31) 1.1	EBIT/Interest						
−.4	−.6	.1							
			Net Profit + Depr., Dep., Amort./Cur. Mat. L/T/D						
.8	.9	.7							
1.6	2.0	1.4	Fixed/Worth						
5.1	42.7	9.8							
.8	.9	.8							
1.6	2.3	1.3	Debt/Worth						
5.7	63.4	13.8							
15.5	10.9	21.6	% Profit Before Taxes/Tangible						
(33) 1.9	(24) 3.2	(29) 2.4	Net Worth						
−9.5	−12.9	−7.7							
6.3	4.1	7.6							
.9	−.2	.7	% Profit Before Taxes/Total						
−4.8	−7.7	−2.9	Assets						
3.5	3.2	5.0							
1.2	1.5	1.9	Sales/Net Fixed Assets						
.8	.9	1.0							
1.5	1.4	2.2							
.7	.8	1.2	Sales/Total Assets						
.5	.5	.6							
3.0	3.2	3.6							
6.1	(29) 4.9	(32) 5.2	% Depr., Dep., Amort./Sales						
10.1	9.1	9.9							
		1.2	% Officers', Directors',						
	(11)	2.4	Owners' Comp/Sales						
		10.8							
394812M	352860M	402127M	Net Sales ($)	2580M	11821M	20143M	63090M	58322M	246171M
537157M	471106M	461357M	Total Assets ($)	4458M	10299M	31747M	73731M	39680M	301442M

M = $ thousand   MM = $ million
See Pages 11 through 18 for Explanation of Ratios and Data

Current Data Sorted By Assets   Comparative Historical Data

0-500M	500M-2MM	2-10MM	10-50MM	50-100MM	100-250MM	Type of Statement	4/1/98-3/31/99 ALL	4/1/99-3/31/00 ALL
		1		2	2	Unqualified	3	3
1	3	8	5	1		Reviewed	4	13
2	3	8	2			Compiled	9	13
3	5	4	3			Tax Returns	5	3
	6	9	10	2		Other	14	31
	8 (4/1-9/30/02)		72 (10/1/02-3/31/03)					
6	17	30	20	5	2	NUMBER OF STATEMENTS	35	63
%	%	%	%	%	%	ASSETS	%	%
	6.1	4.6	5.4			Cash & Equivalents	6.4	3.1
	11.7	14.2	10.8			Trade Receivables (net)	7.7	13.6
	3.4	6.3	7.6			Inventory	6.0	9.7
	1.7	5.5	2.1			All Other Current	2.0	5.1
	23.0	30.6	25.9			Total Current	22.1	31.6
	69.8	63.3	55.3			Fixed Assets (net)	66.4	57.2
	.2	2.0	.7			Intangibles (net)	1.6	.5
	7.1	4.1	18.1			All Other Non-Current	9.8	10.7
	100.0	100.0	100.0			Total	100.0	100.0
						LIABILITIES		
	18.0	11.1	14.0			Notes Payable-Short Term	8.4	14.8
	7.1	3.8	3.2			Cur. Mat.-L/T/D	2.0	3.6
	2.2	3.8	4.2			Trade Payables	4.1	2.9
	.0	.6	.2			Income Taxes Payable	.1	.4
	11.4	4.7	2.1			All Other Current	4.4	4.0
	38.7	23.9	23.7			Total Current	19.0	25.6
	32.9	47.6	49.5			Long Term Debt	35.7	30.8
	.0	.0	.0			Deferred Taxes	1.3	.8
	8.6	3.9	3.3			All Other Non-Current	10.2	7.2
	19.8	24.6	23.5			Net Worth	33.8	35.7
	100.0	100.0	100.0			Total Liabilities & Net Worth	100.0	100.0
						INCOME DATA		
	100.0	100.0	100.0			Net Sales	100.0	100.0
						Gross Profit		
	81.2	85.5	90.8			Operating Expenses	80.5	84.9
	18.8	14.5	9.2			Operating Profit	19.5	15.1
	6.4	8.6	9.6			All Other Expenses (net)	−16.7	7.0
	12.4	5.9	−.4			Profit Before Taxes	36.2	8.1
						RATIOS		
	1.9	3.1	2.0				3.8	2.7
	1.0	1.2	1.4			Current	1.2	1.3
	.3	.5	.8				.5	.8
	1.5	1.5	1.5				1.9	1.5
	.5	.7	.8			Quick	(34) .8	.7
	.1	.2	.5				.3	.2
0 UND	0 UND	0 UND	0 UND				0 UND	0 UND
13 28.6	41 8.9	67 5.4				Sales/Receivables	18 19.8	47 7.8
122 3.0	161 2.3	173 2.1					97 3.8	127 2.9
						Cost of Sales/Inventory		
						Cost of Sales/Payables		
	15.8	3.1	3.6				3.5	2.6
	−486.0	9.6	26.1			Sales/Working Capital	11.9	13.8
	−2.2	−7.6	−6.6				−13.0	−9.9
	(15) 9.4	(26) 5.1	(13) 6.9				(27) 4.6	(42) 5.9
	2.9	2.4	4.5			EBIT/Interest	1.5	1.6
	−.6	.8	1.0				.0	1.0
						Net Profit + Depr., Dep., Amort./Cur. Mat. L/T/D		
	1.2	.9	.8				1.1	.8
	3.0	2.5	1.6			Fixed/Worth	1.8	1.5
	NM	NM	6.0				3.8	4.1
	.8	1.0	.8				1.0	.8
	2.2	3.0	2.3			Debt/Worth	1.8	1.6
	NM	NM	10.1				3.1	6.1
	(13) 57.7	(23) 42.5	(16) 26.4			% Profit Before Taxes/Tangible Net Worth	(30) 53.5	(54) 25.5
	23.3	8.1	5.5				8.7	9.3
	7.6	−8.3	−13.3				−4.5	−.8
	17.3	16.9	13.1			% Profit Before Taxes/Total Assets	9.8	11.5
	7.3	2.6	.9				1.5	2.0
	−4.8	−2.5	−4.4				−2.2	−.8
	3.9	2.1	4.3				1.9	2.3
	1.1	.8	1.0			Sales/Net Fixed Assets	.8	1.0
	.6	.4	.3				.3	.5
	2.3	1.1	1.4				.8	.9
	.7	.4	.5			Sales/Total Assets	.5	.5
	.4	.3	.2				.3	.3
	(13) 3.3	(28) 5.2	(17) 3.7			% Depr., Dep., Amort./Sales	(29) 3.9	(54) 4.4
	6.0	9.5	11.2				8.6	8.9
	12.1	17.0	22.8				15.4	14.4
						% Officers', Directors', Owners' Comp/Sales	(10) 1.0 / 5.0 / 7.2	
6074M	24845M	120828M	473934M	306771M	76655M	Net Sales ($)	320939M	490686M
2230M	20171M	141655M	433620M	349211M	218555M	Total Assets ($)	533508M	796679M

M = $ thousand   MM = $ million
See Pages 11 through 18 for Explanation of Ratios and Data

Comparative Historical Data — Current Data Sorted By Sales

4/1/00-3/31/01 ALL 74	4/1/01-3/31/02 ALL 63	4/1/02-3/31/03 ALL 80	Type of Statement	0-1MM	1-3MM	3-5MM	5-10MM	10-25MM	25MM & OVER
				8 (4/1-9/30/02)			72 (10/1/02-3/31/03)		
3	5	5	Unqualified				1	2	2
15	13	18	Reviewed	4	3	1	4	3	3
16	14	15	Compiled	4	8	6	1		
5	9	15	Tax Returns	4	8	1		1	1
35	22	27	Other	6	10	3	2	1	5
74	63	80	**NUMBER OF STATEMENTS**	18	25	11	8	7	11
%	%	%	**ASSETS**	%	%	%	%	%	%
6.1	4.2	6.1	Cash & Equivalents	4.4	6.5	8.0			9.3
12.5	12.3	12.1	Trade Receivables (net)	14.2	7.6	17.7			14.8
5.9	6.0	6.6	Inventory	2.6	7.9	4.0			7.5
5.0	5.7	3.8	All Other Current	.4	2.5	4.6			8.3
29.5	28.1	28.5	Total Current	21.7	24.5	34.2			40.0
60.1	62.6	61.4	Fixed Assets (net)	72.3	67.7	63.1			40.1
.7	.4	1.0	Intangibles (net)	.6	.2	.2			.0
9.7	8.9	9.2	All Other Non-Current	5.3	7.6	2.4			19.9
100.0	100.0	100.0	Total	100.0	100.0	100.0			100.0
			LIABILITIES						
15.8	12.9	14.3	Notes Payable-Short Term	17.5	12.8	15.8			14.4
3.4	3.5	4.0	Cur. Mat.-L/T/D	4.1	4.8	3.5			4.5
2.9	3.0	3.9	Trade Payables	.4	3.2	3.3			12.1
.3	.5	.3	Income Taxes Payable	.0	.6	.0			.5
4.2	6.0	5.8	All Other Current	3.9	3.9	19.3			4.7
26.6	25.9	28.3	Total Current	25.9	25.4	41.9			36.1
40.2	36.6	42.2	Long Term Debt	48.4	45.8	41.2			40.2
.1	.3	.2	Deferred Taxes	.0	.0	.0			.8
4.2	5.6	4.4	All Other Non-Current	2.5	6.9	4.2			2.6
28.8	31.6	24.9	Net Worth	23.2	21.9	12.7			20.3
100.0	100.0	100.0	Total Liabilities & Net Worth	100.0	100.0	100.0			100.0
			INCOME DATA						
100.0	100.0	100.0	Net Sales	100.0	100.0	100.0			100.0
			Gross Profit						
83.3	83.2	86.2	Operating Expenses	78.6	81.4	97.0			96.1
16.7	16.8	13.8	Operating Profit	21.4	18.6	3.0			3.9
4.8	9.6	7.9	All Other Expenses (net)	11.5	8.4	9.3			.0
11.9	7.2	5.9	Profit Before Taxes	9.9	10.2	−6.3			3.9
			RATIOS						
2.7	2.1	2.3	Current	3.1	2.8	1.7			2.5
1.2	1.2	1.2		1.1	1.0	.8			1.1
.4	.7	.6		.5	.3	.6			.7
1.8	1.6	1.6	Quick	3.1	1.3	1.4			1.8
.6	.8	.8		1.1	.5	.8			.9
.2	.2	.2		.3	.1	.3			.4
0 UND	0 UND	0 UND	Sales/Receivables	0 UND	0 UND	23 15.9			0 UND
24 15.3	35 10.4	36 10.2		122 3.0	3 115.8	45 8.2			28 13.2
160 2.3	134 2.7	124 2.9		237 1.5	104 3.5	271 1.3			65 5.6
			Cost of Sales/Inventory						
			Cost of Sales/Payables						
3.0	2.9	4.1	Sales/Working Capital	2.1	5.5	8.5			8.4
11.4	17.7	41.2		73.6	−49.4	−10.3			41.2
−5.6	−8.9	−7.8		−1.9	−5.8	−4.1			−8.2
5.3	6.8	5.7	EBIT/Interest	5.7	11.1				
(50) 3.3	(47) 2.4	(63) 2.7		(15) 2.2	(19) 2.8				
1.8	.7	.9		.3	.5				
	4.0	1.8	Net Profit + Depr., Dep., Amort./Cur. Mat. L/T/D						
	(13) 1.6	(15) .5							
	.2	−1.8							
.8	.8	.9	Fixed/Worth	1.6	1.0	1.3			.7
1.8	1.8	2.1		2.7	4.0	4.5			.9
9.2	6.4	12.7		45.9	NM	−3.8			2.0
1.0	.9	.9	Debt/Worth	1.3	.7	.7			.9
2.0	1.6	2.2		2.2	5.8	5.0			1.6
16.6	6.3	15.6		57.2	NM	−6.8			3.5
37.1	29.8	42.5	% Profit Before Taxes/Tangible Net Worth	49.8	52.9				36.8
(61) 18.5	(51) 10.5	(65) 10.2		(15) 21.7	(19) 8.8			(10)	18.5
6.7	.9	−4.2		4.9	−9.7				−4.4
12.1	11.6	14.6	% Profit Before Taxes/Total Assets	9.6	18.3	7.9			13.4
6.3	3.4	3.2		3.2	1.2	.0			9.5
.8	−1.7	−3.7		−2.4	−5.4	−4.5			−2.2
2.8	2.4	4.3	Sales/Net Fixed Assets	.9	2.6	6.2			13.3
.9	1.1	1.1		.5	1.0	2.0			5.0
.5	.5	.5		.3	.4	.4			3.4
1.0	1.0	1.4	Sales/Total Assets	.5	1.3	3.1			2.5
.5	.6	.6		.4	.5	1.2			1.5
.3	.3	.3		.3	.3	.3			1.0
4.3	4.5	3.8	% Depr., Dep., Amort./Sales	10.7	4.1	4.1			1.4
(64) 7.8	(53) 7.9	(71) 8.1		(13) 13.4	(24) 9.5	5.5		(10)	2.4
17.1	13.9	15.9		19.7	18.6	18.0			4.4
1.6		3.0	% Officers', Directors', Owners' Comp/Sales						
(10) 7.2		(13) 4.6							
13.1		11.6							
885028M	991351M	1009107M	Net Sales ($)	10880M	44710M	45170M	54017M	105360M	748970M
1214302M	1381432M	1165442M	Total Assets ($)	32799M	114304M	103226M	149559M	247375M	518179M

Current Data Sorted By Assets   **Comparative Historical Data**

0-500M	500M-2MM	2-10MM	10-50MM	50-100MM	100-250MM	Type of Statement	4/1/98-3/31/99 ALL	4/1/99-3/31/00 ALL
1						Unqualified		
		2	1			Reviewed		
	4	1	1			Compiled		
1	3	1	1			Tax Returns		
	3	5		1		Other		
	6 (4/1-9/30/02)			18 (10/1/02-3/31/03)				
2	10	9	3			NUMBER OF STATEMENTS		
%	%	%	%	%	%	**ASSETS**	%	%
	1.6			DATA NOT AVAILABLE	DATA NOT AVAILABLE	Cash & Equivalents	DATA NOT AVAILABLE	DATA NOT AVAILABLE
	3.5					Trade Receivables (net)		
	.8					Inventory		
	10.8					All Other Current		
	16.7					Total Current		
	69.7					Fixed Assets (net)		
	.2					Intangibles (net)		
	13.3					All Other Non-Current		
	100.0					Total		
						LIABILITIES		
	26.4			DATA NOT AVAILABLE	DATA NOT AVAILABLE	Notes Payable-Short Term	DATA NOT AVAILABLE	DATA NOT AVAILABLE
	2.2					Cur. Mat.-L/T/D		
	1.8					Trade Payables		
	1.8					Income Taxes Payable		
	7.8					All Other Current		
	40.0					Total Current		
	36.4					Long Term Debt		
	.0					Deferred Taxes		
	21.5					All Other Non-Current		
	2.2					Net Worth		
	100.0					Total Liabilities & Net Worth		
						INCOME DATA		
	100.0					Net Sales		
						Gross Profit		
	97.8					Operating Expenses		
	2.2					Operating Profit		
	7.7					All Other Expenses (net)		
	−5.5					Profit Before Taxes		
						RATIOS		
	.6					Current		
	.1							
	.0							
	.2					Quick		
	.0							
	.0							
0 UND						Sales/Receivables		
0 UND								
0 UND								
						Cost of Sales/Inventory		
						Cost of Sales/Payables		
	NM					Sales/Working Capital		
	−4.2							
	−2.9							
						EBIT/Interest		
						Net Profit + Depr., Dep., Amort./Cur. Mat. L /T/D		
	1.6					Fixed/Worth		
	NM							
	−2.3							
	1.3					Debt/Worth		
	NM							
	−4.8							
						% Profit Before Taxes/Tangible Net Worth		
	7.4					% Profit Before Taxes/Total Assets		
	1.8							
	−9.5							
	4.4					Sales/Net Fixed Assets		
	.6							
	.4							
	1.8					Sales/Total Assets		
	.5							
	.3							
						% Depr., Dep., Amort./Sales		
						% Officers', Directors', Owners' Comp/Sales		
224M	10515M	55987M	23696M			Net Sales ($)		
58M	12550M	53105M	40409M			Total Assets ($)		

M = $ thousand   MM = $ million
See Pages 11 through 18 for Explanation of Ratios and Data

Comparative Historical Data   Current Data Sorted By Sales

4/1/00-3/31/01 ALL	4/1/01-3/31/02 ALL	4/1/02-3/31/03 ALL	Type of Statement	0-1MM	1-3MM	3-5MM	5-10MM	10-25MM	25MM & OVER
	2	1	Unqualified	1					
	2	3	Reviewed			2		1	
D	7	6	Compiled	2	2	1	1		
A	3	5	Tax Returns	4	1				
T	8	9	Other	2	4	1	1		1
A				6 (4/1-9/30/02)			18 (10/1/02-3/31/03)		
	22	24	**NUMBER OF STATEMENTS**	9	7	4	2	1	1
N	%	%		%	%	%	%	%	%
O			**ASSETS**						
T	7.6	5.5	Cash & Equivalents						
	12.8	10.4	Trade Receivables (net)						
A	16.1	7.2	Inventory						
V	7.2	8.9	All Other Current						
A	43.8	32.0	Total Current						
I	50.0	58.2	Fixed Assets (net)						
L	1.4	.2	Intangibles (net)						
A	4.8	9.5	All Other Non-Current						
B	100.0	100.0	Total						
L			**LIABILITIES**						
E	19.7	19.0	Notes Payable-Short Term						
	1.2	1.7	Cur. Mat.-L/T/D						
	8.8	1.5	Trade Payables						
	.1	1.0	Income Taxes Payable						
	5.6	12.4	All Other Current						
	35.4	35.6	Total Current						
	45.8	30.4	Long Term Debt						
	.3	1.5	Deferred Taxes						
	2.6	9.3	All Other Non-Current						
	15.9	23.2	Net Worth						
	100.0	100.0	Total Liabilities & Net Worth						
			INCOME DATA						
	100.0	100.0	Net Sales						
			Gross Profit						
	95.8	92.7	Operating Expenses						
	4.2	7.3	Operating Profit						
	6.4	6.0	All Other Expenses (net)						
	-2.2	1.3	Profit Before Taxes						
			RATIOS						
	2.0 / 1.1 / .8	1.8 / 1.0 / .1	Current						
	1.6 / .5 / .2	1.0 / .3 / .0	Quick						
	0 UND / 33 11.0 / 77 4.7	0 UND / 4 85.4 / 66 5.6	Sales/Receivables						
			Cost of Sales/Inventory						
			Cost of Sales/Payables						
	3.4 / 54.6 / -18.0	3.2 / NM / -3.6	Sales/Working Capital						
	(20) 4.0 / 1.4 / -.4	(21) 4.0 / 1.2 / -.5	EBIT/Interest						
			Net Profit + Depr., Dep., Amort./Cur. Mat. L/T/D						
	.4 / 1.4 / 16.3	.9 / 1.9 / -56.6	Fixed/Worth						
	1.0 / 3.8 / 30.6	.7 / 2.1 / -65.9	Debt/Worth						
	(18) 19.3 / 9.4 / -18.3	(17) 22.0 / .9 / -4.5	% Profit Before Taxes/Tangible Net Worth						
	7.1 / 2.3 / -7.0	12.1 / 1.2 / -3.9	% Profit Before Taxes/Total Assets						
	7.6 / 2.6 / .7	6.3 / .7 / .5	Sales/Net Fixed Assets						
	1.8 / .9 / .4	1.8 / .6 / .3	Sales/Total Assets						
	(19) 3.0 / 4.9 / 9.0	(20) 4.3 / 7.9 / 17.5	% Depr., Dep., Amort./Sales						
			% Officers', Directors', Owners' Comp/Sales						
	251763M	90422M	Net Sales ($)	4026M	12602M	14286M	16275M	14811M	28422M
	213942M	106122M	Total Assets ($)	9082M	34533M	20938M	20116M	11766M	9687M

M = $ thousand   MM = $ million
See Pages 11 through 18 for Explanation of Ratios and Data

Current Data Sorted By Assets   Comparative Historical Data

Type of Statement	0-500M	500M-2MM	2-10MM	10-50MM	50-100MM	100-250MM	4/1/98-3/31/99 ALL	4/1/99-3/31/00 ALL
Unqualified		1		6	5		18	17
Reviewed	1	2	10	3		1	25	29
Compiled	7	5	15	1			29	35
Tax Returns	6	7	5				6	11
Other	2	12	12	4			36	34
	30 (4/1-9/30/02)			75 (10/1/02-3/31/03)		1		
NUMBER OF STATEMENTS	16	27	42	14	5	1	114	126
	%	%	%	%	%	%	%	%
ASSETS								
Cash & Equivalents	15.9	8.6	5.0	8.6			7.5	6.5
Trade Receivables (net)	5.1	10.5	17.0	13.8			16.8	14.5
Inventory	20.0	25.5	36.1	39.4			25.8	26.6
All Other Current	1.3	2.6	2.0	1.2			2.2	2.5
Total Current	42.3	47.1	60.1	63.0			52.3	50.2
Fixed Assets (net)	50.1	41.0	31.3	32.4			39.8	39.1
Intangibles (net)	1.5	.1	1.4	1.3			1.6	2.6
All Other Non-Current	6.1	11.7	7.2	3.3			6.2	8.1
Total	100.0	100.0	100.0	100.0			100.0	100.0
LIABILITIES								
Notes Payable-Short Term	38.6	13.1	13.2	14.5			13.6	15.9
Cur. Mat.-L/T/D	8.5	3.0	3.1	4.0			2.9	4.2
Trade Payables	6.8	9.1	7.0	11.2			10.2	9.8
Income Taxes Payable	.4	.1	.5	4.9			1.0	.6
All Other Current	13.5	2.8	8.9	11.9			8.0	6.4
Total Current	67.8	28.1	32.6	46.5			35.8	37.0
Long Term Debt	14.5	24.7	12.1	17.2			18.3	18.6
Deferred Taxes	.0	1.2	1.6	.9			1.8	1.0
All Other Non-Current	12.2	7.2	6.9	3.5			5.1	9.8
Net Worth	5.5	38.8	46.8	32.0			39.0	33.7
Total Liabilities & Net Worth	100.0	100.0	100.0	100.0			100.0	100.0
INCOME DATA								
Net Sales	100.0	100.0	100.0	100.0			100.0	100.0
Gross Profit	55.6	40.7	31.9	39.5			36.5	39.1
Operating Expenses	54.8	38.0	26.0	32.6			31.2	33.4
Operating Profit	.8	2.7	5.9	6.9			5.4	5.7
All Other Expenses (net)	2.6	.7	.6	3.5			1.5	1.8
Profit Before Taxes	-1.8	2.1	5.3	3.4			3.9	3.9
RATIOS								
Current	2.2	6.0	4.2	3.0			3.4	2.6
	1.0	1.5	2.1	1.5			1.5	1.4
	.4	1.0	1.4	.9			1.0	.9
Quick	.7	3.0	1.1	.8			1.3	1.1
	.4	.9	(41) .7	.3			.7	.6
	.2	.2	.4	.1			.4	.2
Sales/Receivables	0 UND	0 UND	19 19.3	16 22.8			11 34.6	5 73.9
	0 UND	11 34.4	37 10.0	25 14.4			29 12.5	27 13.4
	7 51.0	30 12.1	57 6.4	56 6.5			54 6.7	54 6.8
Cost of Sales/Inventory	0 UND	0 UND	27 13.5	94 3.9			13 27.2	11 32.5
	26 14.0	35 10.4	154 2.4	193 1.9			66 5.5	76 4.8
	123 3.0	161 2.3	326 1.1	426 .9			165 2.2	205 1.8
Cost of Sales/Payables	0 UND	0 UND	6 65.0	22 16.3			4 101.1	3 116.2
	7 51.1	15 24.7	17 21.4	50 7.3			23 16.0	25 14.7
	20 18.6	57 6.4	41 8.8	103 3.5			48 7.6	58 6.3
Sales/Working Capital	20.1	6.8	2.2	1.9			3.3	3.8
	NM	24.1	3.7	7.5			11.2	14.9
	-6.5	157.5	18.4	-17.3			748.1	-105.2
EBIT/Interest	2.1	5.5	10.5	5.4			5.8	5.9
	(12) 1.3	(25) 1.8	(40) 3.5	2.3			(105) 2.6	(114) 2.5
	-4.8	-.6	2.3	.7			.8	1.1
Net Profit + Depr., Dep., Amort./Cur. Mat. L/T/D			15.6				6.6	5.6
			(10) 3.5				(35) 2.5	(38) 2.1
			1.0				.9	1.1
Fixed/Worth	.9	.5	.3	.7			.5	.4
	2.6	1.0	.5	1.2			.9	.9
	-1.4	1.8	1.2	3.6			1.9	2.7
Debt/Worth	.7	.5	.5	.9			.5	.6
	4.2	1.7	1.0	2.2			1.3	1.6
	-6.7	4.0	2.6	15.0			3.4	5.3
% Profit Before Taxes/Tangible Net Worth	20.3	43.5	22.5	40.6			28.4	29.7
	(10) 8.9	(24) 7.6	(38) 12.6	(13) 14.7			(101) 11.7	(107) 12.0
	-13.7	-5.7	6.1	-2.7			1.7	3.6
% Profit Before Taxes/Total Assets	11.9	7.8	10.9	11.2			12.0	10.0
	.5	1.3	5.3	5.8			5.2	4.7
	-7.8	-3.5	2.1	-1.0			-.8	-.4
Sales/Net Fixed Assets	21.6	12.8	8.0	9.4			8.6	8.8
	8.5	6.6	5.4	4.9			4.2	4.5
	5.2	4.3	3.4	1.9			2.7	3.1
Sales/Total Assets	5.0	3.0	2.1	1.6			2.8	2.7
	3.5	2.3	1.2	1.1			1.5	1.7
	2.7	1.4	.8	.7			.9	.9
% Depr., Dep., Amort./Sales	1.4	2.6	2.2	3.1			1.7	2.0
	(14) 3.7	(22) 3.2	(41) 3.1	(13) 4.3			(107) 3.3	(115) 3.2
	8.2	4.4	4.9	6.0			4.8	4.7
% Officers', Directors', Owners' Comp/Sales	7.9	2.7	1.8				2.4	2.2
	(11) 12.0	(16) 3.7	(18) 2.7				(39) 4.3	(49) 3.4
	16.4	5.1	5.9				5.8	6.0
Net Sales ($)	14333M	80005M	308764M	292514M	270917M	172943M	1755652M	2126505M
Total Assets ($)	3922M	31722M	200894M	270278M	299533M	113740M	1277889M	1421611M

M = $ thousand   MM = $ million
See Pages 11 through 18 for Explanation of Ratios and Data

Comparative Historical Data   **Current Data Sorted By Sales**

	Hist 1	Hist 2	Hist 3		0-1MM	1-3MM	3-5MM	5-10MM	10-25MM	25MM & OVER
Type of Statement										
Unqualified	16	15	12		1				4	7
Reviewed	22	19	16			2	2	8	2	2
Compiled	33	39	28		4	10	4	3	7	
Tax Returns	15	12	18		6	6	3	2	1	
Other	42	31	31		2	13	3	5	6	2
	4/1/00-3/31/01 ALL	4/1/01-3/31/02 ALL	4/1/02-3/31/03 ALL		30 (4/1-9/30/02)			75 (10/1/02-3/31/03)		
NUMBER OF STATEMENTS	128	116	105		13	31	12	18	20	11
ASSETS	%	%	%		%	%	%	%	%	%
Cash & Equivalents	7.7	5.8	8.1		16.0	8.1	3.2	5.4	10.7	3.3
Trade Receivables (net)	14.7	15.0	12.7		2.6	10.5	16.0	13.9	20.7	10.9
Inventory	28.6	28.1	31.6		18.4	32.3	44.7	36.8	24.4	35.4
All Other Current	3.9	3.4	1.9		.1	1.1	7.4	1.0	2.3	1.1
Total Current	54.8	52.4	54.3		37.1	52.0	71.3	57.1	58.2	50.7
Fixed Assets (net)	37.3	38.7	36.7		55.8	35.1	23.4	31.2	38.2	39.3
Intangibles (net)	2.4	1.6	1.4		.6	1.4	.1	.9	1.6	4.1
All Other Non-Current	5.6	7.4	7.6		6.5	11.5	5.2	10.7	2.0	5.9
Total	100.0	100.0	100.0		100.0	100.0	100.0	100.0	100.0	100.0
LIABILITIES										
Notes Payable-Short Term	11.4	11.3	17.3		26.4	16.3	28.7	8.5	14.5	16.8
Cur. Mat.-L/T/D	4.4	3.8	4.2		9.6	3.1	2.4	4.4	1.9	6.5
Trade Payables	11.9	10.3	8.1		3.5	7.2	9.4	6.6	12.9	8.4
Income Taxes Payable	.9	1.2	1.2		.3	.1	.0	2.1	1.3	5.4
All Other Current	9.4	6.5	8.2		16.8	5.3	5.1	4.7	13.3	6.2
Total Current	38.0	33.0	39.1		56.6	32.1	45.6	26.4	44.0	43.1
Long Term Debt	18.1	22.0	16.7		19.5	20.8	14.0	13.3	13.9	15.2
Deferred Taxes	1.1	1.7	1.1		.0	1.5	.0	3.0	.4	.7
All Other Non-Current	4.5	3.8	7.2		15.9	8.9	2.0	8.2	2.2	5.3
Net Worth	38.2	39.5	35.9		7.9	36.7	38.4	49.0	39.5	35.7
Total Liabilities & Net Worth	100.0	100.0	100.0		100.0	100.0	100.0	100.0	100.0	100.0
INCOME DATA										
Net Sales	100.0	100.0	100.0		100.0	100.0	100.0	100.0	100.0	100.0
Gross Profit	39.3	38.5	39.2		63.5	39.4	35.1	27.2	36.8	38.0
Operating Expenses	34.0	32.4	34.4		61.1	35.9	28.5	24.6	30.2	28.8
Operating Profit	5.3	6.1	4.8		2.5	3.5	6.6	2.6	6.6	9.2
All Other Expenses (net)	.3	1.8	1.7		3.7	1.0	1.0	-.6	1.9	5.6
Profit Before Taxes	5.0	4.3	3.0		-1.2	2.5	5.6	3.2	4.7	3.5
RATIOS										
Current	2.9	3.3	3.5		6.9	6.0	2.3	4.3	4.0	1.9
	1.5	1.5	1.6		1.1	1.6	1.7	2.4	1.5	1.5
	1.0	.9	1.0		.2	1.0	1.1	1.1	1.0	.7
Quick	1.1	1.1	1.1		3.6	1.4	.8	1.0	1.8	.5
	(127) .6	(115) .6	(104) .6		.3	(30) .7	.4	.8	.8	.4
	.2	.2	.2		.1	.2	.1	.5	.3	.2
Sales/Receivables	7 51.5	6 63.1	2 173.2		0 UND	2 214.8	13 28.1	0 UND	13 27.5	22 16.6
	26 14.0	25 14.5	25 14.9		0 UND	12 31.3	38 9.6	35 10.5	25 14.3	30 12.2
	55 6.6	53 6.9	44 8.2		9 41.8	30 12.1	70 5.2	58 6.3	54 6.7	52 7.0
Cost of Sales/Inventory	9 41.9	8 44.8	10 38.3		0 UND	0 UND	64 5.7	45 8.1	23 15.9	149 2.4
	90 4.0	92 4.0	123 3.0		48 7.5	148 2.5	169 2.2	128 2.9	49 7.4	192 1.9
	240 1.5	222 1.6	241 1.5		138 2.6	300 1.2	394 .9	235 1.6	166 2.2	251 1.5
Cost of Sales/Payables	8 45.6	5 72.2	3 134.7		0 UND	1 543.5	0 UND	0 UND	7 50.2	18 20.2
	26 14.2	23 16.1	19 19.6		6 64.0	19 19.6	25 14.5	14 25.4	37 9.8	37 9.8
	54 6.8	55 6.7	47 7.8		14 25.4	39 9.3	75 4.9	30 12.3	77 4.8	83 4.4
Sales/Working Capital	3.1	3.4	2.9		7.0	2.4	2.1	2.4	4.8	3.7
	11.7	9.7	9.7		68.6	12.6	6.1	5.2	13.6	9.7
	388.0	-168.7	419.2		-4.3	999.8	85.1	41.5	NM	-18.4
EBIT/Interest	7.3	6.0	5.6			3.9	6.0	9.3	19.8	4.1
	(116) 2.9	(113) 2.8	(97) 2.5		(30) 1.0	(11) 2.5	(17) 2.9	(19) 4.9		3.4
	1.5	1.4	1.0		-1.2		2.5	1.8	2.5	2.1
Net Profit + Depr., Dep., Amort./Cur. Mat. L/T/D	5.5	4.2	4.3							
	(33) 2.7	(33) 3.0	(24) 3.0							
	1.3	1.1	1.0							
Fixed/Worth	.4	.4	.4		.5	.4	.2	.3	.5	.7
	.9	1.0	.8		2.3	1.1	.5	.5	.7	1.2
	2.5	2.0	2.3		-1.5	4.4	.9	.9	3.2	1.9
Debt/Worth	.6	.6	.7		.5	.6	.8	.5	.7	1.4
	1.3	1.6	1.4		1.4	1.3	1.6	.9	1.1	1.7
	5.0	3.4	4.1		-4.7	13.9	3.7	2.2	10.0	2.9
% Profit Before Taxes/Tangible Net Worth	37.0	34.1	23.1			21.7	44.3	14.0	36.3	37.2
	(112) 17.1	(105) 12.9	(90) 12.6		(24) 3.2	12.7	(17) 9.4	(19) 19.7	(10) 19.9	
	5.4	5.3	1.7		-5.4	2.3	5.6	10.0	7.6	
% Profit Before Taxes/Total Assets	13.6	11.7	10.9		13.4	10.2	11.5	7.1	15.7	10.5
	5.9	5.5	5.1		.9	.5	5.9	4.4	7.2	6.8
	1.5	1.7	-.3		-4.5	-2.5	1.2	1.8	4.2	2.3
Sales/Net Fixed Assets	10.9	8.8	9.2		8.5	10.3	12.6	8.3	9.9	6.1
	4.5	4.9	5.9		6.1	5.5	8.8	6.3	7.1	3.3
	2.9	3.0	3.3		.7	3.1	3.5	3.9	5.1	2.1
Sales/Total Assets	2.7	2.7	2.8		4.9	2.7	2.4	2.2	2.8	1.5
	1.7	1.7	1.5		2.8	2.0	1.4	1.5	1.9	1.2
	.9	.9	.8		.5	.9	.7	1.0	1.3	.8
% Depr., Dep., Amort./Sales	1.5	1.7	2.3		1.7	2.3	2.7	2.1	2.2	2.9
	(117) 2.9	(111) 2.7	(95) 3.5		(12) 4.6	(27) 4.1	(10) 3.4	(17) 3.2	(19) 2.9	(10) 4.0
	4.7	4.9	5.1		8.8	5.1	5.3	4.6	4.2	6.0
% Officers', Directors', Owners' Comp/Sales	2.0	1.9	2.4			3.0				
	(50) 3.4	(53) 3.7	(47) 4.4			(18) 4.6				
	5.2	6.9	8.8			10.9				
Net Sales ($)	1802128M	1640816M	1139476M		5583M	62988M	45554M	117095M	288455M	619801M
Total Assets ($)	1550855M	1363896M	920089M		4718M	53905M	39692M	95002M	198041M	528731M

M = $ thousand   MM = $ million
See Pages 11 through 18 for Explanation of Ratios and Data

Current Data Sorted By Assets | **Comparative Historical Data**

0-500M	500M-2MM	2-10MM	10-50MM	50-100MM	100-250MM		4/1/98-3/31/99 ALL	4/1/99-3/31/00 ALL
						Type of Statement		
						Unqualified	1	5
						Reviewed	12	23
4	7	14	2			Compiled	16	18
5	5	3				Tax Returns	7	2
5	5	5	2		2	Other	15	9
7 (4/1-9/30/02)			52 (10/1/02-3/31/03)					
14	17	22	4		2	**NUMBER OF STATEMENTS**	51	57
%	%	%	%	%	%	**ASSETS**	%	%
21.2	7.1	4.4		DATA NOT AVAILABLE		Cash & Equivalents	8.7	8.7
17.2	13.9	15.1				Trade Receivables (net)	17.1	25.5
5.7	12.3	8.0				Inventory	9.2	11.1
6.8	5.4	8.0				All Other Current	3.6	9.4
50.9	38.6	35.5				Total Current	38.6	54.7
40.1	49.2	52.3				Fixed Assets (net)	45.4	34.7
.1	4.3	4.8				Intangibles (net)	.3	.5
9.0	7.9	7.3				All Other Non-Current	15.7	10.1
100.0	100.0	100.0				Total	100.0	100.0
						LIABILITIES		
122.6	15.0	27.6				Notes Payable-Short Term	34.6	48.6
8.9	3.8	4.9				Cur. Mat.-L/T/D	3.7	3.7
2.7	7.8	5.2				Trade Payables	4.1	3.8
.3	.0	.1				Income Taxes Payable	.1	.1
22.5	2.1	4.3				All Other Current	28.6	11.3
157.0	28.8	42.0				Total Current	71.2	67.4
12.7	20.9	20.6				Long Term Debt	17.6	16.3
.0	.0	.4				Deferred Taxes	.0	1.1
.6	2.1	5.9				All Other Non-Current	2.7	9.9
-70.4	48.2	31.0				Net Worth	8.5	5.2
100.0	100.0	100.0				Total Liabilities & Net Worth	100.0	100.0
						INCOME DATA		
100.0	100.0	100.0				Net Sales	100.0	100.0
						Gross Profit		
91.5	82.7	81.7				Operating Expenses	94.0	91.6
8.5	17.3	18.3				Operating Profit	6.0	8.4
1.8	5.8	3.8				All Other Expenses (net)	-.7	.6
6.7	11.5	14.4				Profit Before Taxes	6.6	7.8
						RATIOS		
13.7	3.0	2.1					2.9	2.0
.8	1.3	1.2				Current	1.3	1.2
.2	.6	.7					.5	.6
13.7	2.5	1.5					1.5	1.4
.6	.8	.7				Quick	.8	.6
.1	.1	.2					.2	.2
0 UND	0 UND	0 UND					0 UND	2 201.3
1 453.7	6 64.5	70 5.2				Sales/Receivables	13 27.0	39 9.3
15 23.6	57 6.4	153 2.4					128 2.8	121 3.0
						Cost of Sales/Inventory		
						Cost of Sales/Payables		
7.4	3.1	3.8					4.0	5.3
-18.2	7.1	9.1				Sales/Working Capital	27.1	47.6
-3.8	-8.2	-4.3					-6.7	-5.2
14.2	13.3	5.5					5.6	6.0
(12) 4.2	(15) 6.1	(21) 3.5				EBIT/Interest	(40) 2.7	(55) 1.8
-.8	1.9	1.6					-2.1	.6
						Net Profit + Depr., Dep., Amort./Cur. Mat. L /T/D		
.0	.4	1.0					.1	.2
NM	1.2	1.5				Fixed/Worth	1.1	1.1
-.5	2.2	5.7					1.5	9.3
.4	.5	.9					.3	.8
NM	1.7	1.8				Debt/Worth	.9	3.0
-1.8	3.2	14.5					4.5	NM
	47.5	62.6					20.3	57.1
	(16) 23.1	(18) 21.5				% Profit Before Taxes/Tangible Net Worth	(44) 6.6	(43) 15.1
	2.5	7.7					-13.9	-2.6
51.6	29.0	10.6					11.2	18.3
15.4	9.9	6.7				% Profit Before Taxes/Total Assets	2.2	3.9
-33.4	1.4	2.4					-15.0	-1.4
UND	9.9	2.1					38.2	83.5
21.6	2.4	1.0				Sales/Net Fixed Assets	1.9	7.1
5.2	.9	.9					.9	1.5
6.4	1.5	.9					1.8	3.2
4.0	.9	.5				Sales/Total Assets	1.0	1.6
1.4	.6	.4					.4	.7
.8	2.2	3.5					3.1	1.1
(10) 4.0	(14) 5.4	(21) 4.8				% Depr., Dep., Amort./Sales	(35) 9.6	(46) 2.7
7.7	11.2	8.2					15.3	7.1
						% Officers', Directors', Owners' Comp/Sales		
15816M	20380M	51304M	77068M		310005M	Net Sales ($)	110831M	397604M
4194M	19447M	73812M	62342M		336953M	Total Assets ($)	155443M	297730M

M = $ thousand MM = $ million

See Pages 11 through 18 for Explanation of Ratios and Data

Comparative Historical Data   **Current Data Sorted By Sales**

	4/1/00-3/31/01 ALL	4/1/01-3/31/02 ALL	4/1/02-3/31/03 ALL	Type of Statement	0-1MM	1-3MM	3-5MM	5-10MM	10-25MM	25MM & OVER
				Unqualified						
	6	1		Reviewed						
		2								
	9	13	27	Compiled	5	16	5		1	
	1	3	13	Tax Returns	6	7				
	10	10	19	Other	8	7		1		3
					7 (4/1-9/30/02)		52 (10/1/02-3/31/03)			
	26	29	59	**NUMBER OF STATEMENTS**	19	30	5	1	1	3
	%	%	%	**ASSETS**	%	%	%	%	%	%
	2.7	3.5	9.2	Cash & Equivalents	12.0	9.2				
	19.5	12.1	15.3	Trade Receivables (net)	6.6	19.9				
	10.5	18.2	10.1	Inventory	7.7	9.1				
	9.6	4.0	6.7	All Other Current	11.2	4.9				
	42.3	37.7	41.4	Total Current	37.5	43.0				
	37.7	48.7	47.9	Fixed Assets (net)	54.3	43.5				
	.0	.4	3.1	Intangibles (net)	.5	5.1				
	19.9	13.2	7.6	All Other Non-Current	7.7	8.4				
	100.0	100.0	100.0	Total	100.0	100.0				
				LIABILITIES						
	39.9	33.7	45.4	Notes Payable-Short Term	85.5	31.6				
	6.0	3.2	5.1	Cur. Mat.-L/T/D	3.5	7.3				
	4.2	24.4	5.6	Trade Payables	2.3	7.6				
	.1	.2	.1	Income Taxes Payable	.2	.0				
	3.2	7.7	8.4	All Other Current	8.4	9.2				
	53.4	69.2	64.6	Total Current	100.0	55.7				
	24.9	52.0	18.2	Long Term Debt	22.5	15.2				
	.0	.0	.3	Deferred Taxes	.0	.0				
	2.4	2.0	4.8	All Other Non-Current	2.6	4.2				
	19.3	-23.3	12.1	Net Worth	-25.1	24.9				
	100.0	100.0	100.0	Total Liabilities & Net Worth	100.0	100.0				
				INCOME DATA						
	100.0	100.0	100.0	Net Sales	100.0	100.0				
				Gross Profit						
	86.9	93.5	84.7	Operating Expenses	81.5	86.4				
	13.1	6.4	15.3	Operating Profit	18.5	13.6				
	2.0	4.7	4.3	All Other Expenses (net)	6.7	2.5				
	11.1	1.7	10.9	Profit Before Taxes	11.8	11.0				
				RATIOS						
	1.5 / .9 / .6	1.4 / 1.0 / .3	2.3 / 1.3 / .5	Current	2.8 / .8 / .2	2.1 / 1.3 / 1.0				
	(25) 1.1 / .6 / .1	.8 / .3 / .1	1.6 / .7 / .2	Quick	1.9 / .2 / .1	1.6 / .8 / .3				
	0 UND / 41 8.8 / 192 1.9	0 UND / 35 10.5 / 100 3.7	0 UND / 23 15.7 / 108 3.4	Sales/Receivables	0 UND / 0 757.0 / 42 8.7	0 UND / 44 8.3 / 146 2.5				
				Cost of Sales/Inventory						
				Cost of Sales/Payables						
	8.1 / -74.5 / -6.2	5.7 / -113.9 / -5.0	4.0 / 18.7 / -5.8	Sales/Working Capital	4.7 / -6.3 / -2.1	3.8 / 9.1 / -345.0				
	(25) 8.0 / 1.9 / .6	2.9 / 1.5 / .2	(54) 9.0 / 4.2 / 1.6	EBIT/Interest	(15) 6.1 / 3.7 / 1.1	(29) 11.4 / 4.2 / 1.6				
				Net Profit + Depr., Dep., Amort./Cur. Mat. L/T/D						
	.5 / 1.4 / -16.5	.8 / 1.4 / 25.0	.6 / 1.5 / 5.5	Fixed/Worth	1.2 / 2.7 / -1.9	.5 / 1.2 / 4.3				
	.7 / 4.0 / -29.7	.7 / 3.7 / 41.3	.6 / 1.8 / 12.8	Debt/Worth	.6 / 2.6 / -8.8	.6 / 2.1 / 8.6				
	(17) 59.8 / 10.5 / -11.1	(23) 16.5 / 5.4 / -6.8	(46) 57.5 / 25.3 / 9.4	% Profit Before Taxes/Tangible Net Worth	(13) 54.1 / 27.4 / 4.9	(24) 75.2 / 28.4 / 6.8				
	21.4 / 5.7 / -3.4	7.2 / 2.0 / -2.0	17.7 / 9.0 / 1.4	% Profit Before Taxes/Total Assets	16.5 / 9.7 / .1	19.7 / 8.3 / 1.3				
	15.3 / 4.6 / 1.2	3.9 / 1.6 / .8	13.9 / 2.0 / .9	Sales/Net Fixed Assets	8.8 / 1.2 / .8	14.2 / 2.6 / 1.0				
	2.1 / .9 / .6	1.3 / .7 / .5	1.8 / .9 / .5	Sales/Total Assets	1.4 / .8 / .3	2.2 / .9 / .5				
	(21) 1.9 / 3.0 / 8.7	(27) 1.9 / 3.9 / 7.5	(50) 2.1 / 4.8 / 9.5	% Depr., Dep., Amort./Sales	(16) 3.9 / 6.6 / 11.1	(25) 1.6 / 4.1 / 8.0				
				% Officers', Directors', Owners' Comp/Sales						
	97135M	187669M	474573M	Net Sales ($)	10984M	53495M	19961M	8019M	11269M	370845M
	146792M	153597M	496748M	Total Assets ($)	17574M	62072M	41209M	19629M	5185M	351079M

M = $ thousand   MM = $ million
See Pages 11 through 18 for Explanation of Ratios and Data

AGRICULTURE—All Other Miscellaneous Crop Farming NAICS 111998 (SIC 0139, 0191, 0831)

Current Data Sorted By Assets							Comparative Historical Data		

							Type of Statement		
			5	6	2	5	Unqualified	20	12
1	11		25	9	2	1	Reviewed	38	50
12	25		30	5	1		Compiled	121	74
21	39		8	1			Tax Returns	51	37
11	17		29	12	3	2	Other	82	85
	50 (4/1–9/30/02)			233 (10/1/02–3/31/03)				4/1/98–3/31/99	4/1/99–3/31/00
0-500M	500M-2MM		2-10MM	10-50MM	50-100MM	100-250MM		ALL	ALL
45	92		97	33	8	8	NUMBER OF STATEMENTS	312	258
%	%		%	%	%	%	ASSETS	%	%
18.3	4.2		5.6	5.8			Cash & Equivalents	5.9	5.7
7.2	8.1		14.3	13.9			Trade Receivables (net)	8.5	9.8
7.2	17.2		14.1	18.9			Inventory	11.7	12.7
7.6	4.5		7.1	4.9			All Other Current	5.7	4.4
40.3	33.9		41.1	43.5			Total Current	31.7	32.5
52.0	57.6		48.0	45.6			Fixed Assets (net)	53.6	52.5
.2	.3		1.6	.8			Intangibles (net)	2.1	2.0
7.4	8.2		9.3	10.0			All Other Non-Current	12.6	13.0
100.0	100.0		100.0	100.0			Total	100.0	100.0
							LIABILITIES		
52.1	19.4		19.7	11.2			Notes Payable-Short Term	28.0	23.5
2.9	5.8		5.3	2.7			Cur. Mat.-L/T/D	5.7	5.3
5.4	4.2		5.9	5.9			Trade Payables	3.2	4.1
.1	.1		.2	.2			Income Taxes Payable	.2	.2
36.1	5.4		6.6	4.2			All Other Current	4.6	24.9
96.6	34.9		37.7	24.1			Total Current	41.8	58.0
36.9	33.0		23.9	20.9			Long Term Debt	27.4	28.4
.0	.2		.9	.5			Deferred Taxes	1.0	.9
2.4	3.9		2.5	2.0			All Other Non-Current	6.8	9.3
−36.0	28.0		34.9	52.4			Net Worth	23.0	3.4
100.0	100.0		100.0	100.0			Total Liabilities & Net Worth	100.0	100.0
							INCOME DATA		
100.0	100.0		100.0	100.0			Net Sales	100.0	100.0
							Gross Profit		
95.6	91.6		89.0	89.0			Operating Expenses	97.7	92.7
4.4	8.4		11.0	11.0			Operating Profit	2.3	7.3
3.1	5.9		3.2	1.4			All Other Expenses (net)	5.0	2.3
1.3	2.5		7.9	9.7			Profit Before Taxes	−2.7	4.9
							RATIOS		
1.7	1.8		1.8	2.9				1.9	1.8
.9	1.1		1.1	1.5			Current	1.0	1.0
.3	.5		.7	1.2				.5	.5
1.5	.7		1.0	1.9				.9	.9
.3	.2		.5	.8			Quick	.3	.3
.1	.0		.1	.4				.1	.1

0	UND	0	UND	0	UND	26	14.2	Sales/Receivables	0	UND	0	UND
0	UND	0	UND	21	17.5	44	8.2		5	68.2	20	18.3
0	UND	22	17.0	64	5.7	74	4.9		47	7.8	60	6.1

							Cost of Sales/Inventory		
							Cost of Sales/Payables		
17.3	6.3		5.4	3.2			Sales/Working Capital	5.6	4.3
−22.7	55.2		30.4	6.9				203.0	128.8
−3.8	−4.2		−11.3	41.0				−4.6	−5.0

	10.3		4.9		5.7		9.9	EBIT/Interest		4.5		3.5
(41)	1.4	(84)	1.9	(89)	2.5	(28)	3.0		(259)	2.0	(228)	1.7
	−1.2		.1		1.1		1.4			.2		.4

			6.3		4.5	Net Profit + Depr., Dep., Amort./Cur. Mat. L /T/D		3.4		5.6
	(21)	3.2	(11)	1.9			(40)	1.4	(38)	1.7
		1.1		1.3				.4		.6

.4	.9		.7	.4			Fixed/Worth	.7	.7
2.2	1.7		1.2	.8				1.3	1.4
−3.3	9.5		5.1	1.5				3.3	3.9
1.0	.8		.6	.2			Debt/Worth	.5	.7
2.1	2.3		1.6	.9				1.3	1.6
−3.3	13.8		9.1	2.3				5.0	9.0

	75.6		24.3		31.6		20.8	% Profit Before Taxes/Tangible Net Worth		23.6		21.7
(27)	20.5	(78)	5.1	(84)	11.2	(31)	11.9		(263)	6.8	(211)	5.9
	−4.8		−3.3		1.8		3.5			−1.6		−1.3

40.7	8.8		11.5	10.3			% Profit Before Taxes/Total Assets	8.8	8.8
2.2	1.3		4.9	4.4				2.5	2.6
−6.5	−1.7		1.8	1.2				−2.9	−2.0
28.6	6.8		7.0	4.3			Sales/Net Fixed Assets	4.7	4.1
5.8	1.7		2.7	2.2				1.7	1.5
1.0	.4		.9	1.1				.5	.7
5.2	1.6		2.0	1.5			Sales/Total Assets	1.6	1.4
2.8	1.1		.8	.7				.8	.7
.7	.3		.5	.5				.3	.4

	1.1		3.4		2.0		2.6	% Depr., Dep., Amort./Sales		2.9		3.0
(32)	5.3	(79)	7.7	(88)	4.0		4.2		(274)	6.2	(230)	5.7
	8.2		12.0		9.9		7.7			10.3		9.5

	1.9		2.0		2.4	% Officers', Directors', Owners' Comp/Sales		1.9		2.2
(12)	5.1	(32)	3.6	(26)	5.5		(62)	3.8	(61)	4.7
	7.0		6.3		8.0			9.1		8.4

40612M	154723M		545628M	615585M	609364M	1823786M	Net Sales ($)	2615298M	1770962M
11556M	107259M		420437M	626460M	568513M	1282825M	Total Assets ($)	2725147M	1923633M

M = $ thousand   MM = $ million
See Pages 11 through 18 for Explanation of Ratios and Data

Comparative Historical Data					Current Data Sorted By Sales					
10	1	18	**Type of Statement** Unqualified			2	2	4	10
35	34	49	Reviewed	7	11	6	11	10	4
73	57	73	Compiled	15	29	11	13	4	1
46	28	69	Tax Returns	47	15	2	3	2	
60	59	74	Other	19	19	10	11	8	7
4/1/00-3/31/01 ALL	4/1/01-3/31/02 ALL	4/1/02-3/31/03 ALL		50 (4/1-9/30/02) 0-1MM	1-3MM	233 (10/1/02-3/31/03) 3-5MM	5-10MM	10-25MM	25MM & OVER
224	179	283	**NUMBER OF STATEMENTS**	88	74	31	40	28	22
%	%	%	**ASSETS**	%	%	%	%	%	%
5.9	5.9	7.2	Cash & Equivalents	9.0	8.2	4.2	6.6	3.2	6.2
9.8	10.0	11.3	Trade Receivables (net)	4.9	8.4	16.6	17.0	18.0	20.0
13.9	14.5	14.6	Inventory	9.5	13.2	20.1	16.4	21.5	20.3
4.3	5.0	6.1	All Other Current	3.8	4.1	10.3	11.2	9.7	2.7
33.9	35.3	39.2	Total Current	27.2	34.0	51.2	51.2	52.5	49.2
52.3	52.2	51.3	Fixed Assets (net)	64.7	56.3	41.5	34.8	36.9	42.8
1.5	1.5	.8	Intangibles (net)	.1	.6	.4	1.5	2.6	1.1
12.3	10.9	8.7	All Other Non-Current	8.0	9.1	6.9	12.4	8.0	6.9
100.0	100.0	100.0	Total	100.0	100.0	100.0	100.0	100.0	100.0
			LIABILITIES						
28.2	28.1	23.3	Notes Payable-Short Term	28.5	24.9	26.7	19.3	15.5	9.2
4.6	4.8	4.6	Cur. Mat.-L/T/D	2.9	6.7	5.3	3.9	6.1	2.9
5.3	4.3	5.5	Trade Payables	3.6	2.6	4.3	10.7	9.0	11.4
.1	.4	.2	Income Taxes Payable	.2	.1	.2	.2	.2	.7
6.8	10.0	11.0	All Other Current	10.1	12.8	12.4	12.6	6.6	9.7
45.1	47.5	44.7	Total Current	45.2	47.1	48.8	46.7	37.3	34.0
31.1	29.2	28.5	Long Term Debt	39.0	28.3	22.1	22.5	18.3	19.8
.9	.9	.5	Deferred Taxes	.3	.3	1.4	.8	.2	.5
7.6	4.7	2.9	All Other Non-Current	2.9	3.0	3.6	3.3	1.9	2.3
15.3	17.6	23.4	Net Worth	12.6	21.2	24.1	26.7	42.2	43.4
100.0	100.0	100.0	Total Liabilities & Net Worth	100.0	100.0	100.0	100.0	100.0	100.0
			INCOME DATA						
100.0	100.0	100.0	Net Sales	100.0	100.0	100.0	100.0	100.0	100.0
			Gross Profit						
99.0	92.3	91.2	Operating Expenses	87.6	91.3	91.0	95.6	92.8	95.3
1.0	7.7	8.8	Operating Profit	12.4	8.7	9.0	4.4	7.2	4.6
-4.4	4.5	3.7	All Other Expenses (net)	8.5	2.3	.6	2.0	.6	.0
5.4	3.2	5.2	Profit Before Taxes	3.9	6.5	8.4	2.4	6.6	4.7
			RATIOS						
1.6	1.7	1.9		1.6	1.9	2.2	1.9	2.1	2.1
1.0	1.0	1.2	Current	1.0	1.0	1.2	1.2	1.4	1.5
.5	.4	.6		.4	.3	.8	.9	1.0	1.1
.9	.7	1.0		.8	.8	1.1	1.2	1.2	1.3
(223) .3	.3	.4	Quick	.3	.3	.5	.6	.7	.7
.1	.1	.1		.1	.1	.2	.2	.2	.5
0 UND	0 UND	0 UND		0 UND	0 UND	10 35.7	10 38.0	17 21.6	29 12.7
11 33.8	12 30.2	12 29.2	Sales/Receivables	0 UND	0 UND	36 10.3	22 16.3	29 12.7	38 9.6
47 7.8	46 8.0	49 7.4		4 88.1	28 13.1	72 5.1	49 7.5	55 6.6	69 5.3
			Cost of Sales/Inventory						
			Cost of Sales/Payables						
5.0	6.2	5.9		5.9	6.0	4.8	8.1	4.6	4.8
64.8	-236.3	31.2	Sales/Working Capital	233.7	-597.2	73.8	18.0	15.6	10.3
-5.2	-5.2	-6.7		-4.9	-3.2	-12.7	-36.9	121.1	102.7
4.3	4.3	5.6		3.9	5.4	8.0	5.0	19.3	10.3
(197) 1.8	(160) 1.7	(254) 2.2	EBIT/Interest	(75) 1.3	(70) 2.2	(28) 3.6	(37) 2.5	(27) 2.8	(17) 3.1
.7	.5	.9		-.2	.1	.6	1.2	1.5	1.5
5.0	5.0	5.2	Net Profit + Depr., Dep.,		6.3		4.6		
(47) 2.6	(29) 1.2	(47) 2.6	Amort./Cur. Mat. L/T/D		(13) 4.4		(10) 2.4		
.9	.2	1.2			1.0		.5		
.8	.9	.7		1.1	.8	.5	.3	.4	.5
1.5	1.5	1.4	Fixed/Worth	1.8	2.2	1.2	1.1	.8	1.0
6.8	8.3	5.7		6.7	16.6	5.4	2.6	1.6	1.8
.8	.7	.7		.7	.7	.7	.9	.5	.5
2.2	1.9	1.8	Debt/Worth	1.7	2.4	1.7	1.9	1.2	1.5
10.0	12.2	12.6		26.0	21.5	22.4	7.9	5.3	3.6
23.3	29.9	29.9	% Profit Before Taxes/Tangible	15.9	42.9	48.0	28.1	40.7	22.9
(185) 7.6	(142) 7.6	(236) 10.0	Net Worth	(69) 1.9	(59) 12.0	(25) 16.1	(36) 7.0	(26) 15.8	(21) 19.0
-.1	.1	.4		-3.2	-3.8	.2	4.0	6.0	9.4
7.5	8.2	11.2	% Profit Before Taxes/Total	8.7	9.9	16.6	8.3	16.4	15.2
3.0	2.2	3.5	Assets	.8	4.8	6.6	3.3	7.1	7.3
-1.1	-3.8	-.4		-2.2	-2.4	-1.5	.8	2.3	1.9
5.0	6.4	7.0		3.8	5.9	16.8	17.4	12.0	5.8
1.8	2.2	2.4	Sales/Net Fixed Assets	.6	1.8	4.0	6.2	5.5	3.8
.7	.8	.8		.2	.9	1.5	1.8	1.8	2.3
1.6	1.8	2.0		1.2	1.6	2.3	3.6	3.8	1.8
.8	1.0	1.1	Sales/Total Assets	.4	1.1	1.2	2.1	1.5	1.5
.4	.5	.5		.2	.5	.7	.7	.7	1.3
2.4	2.5	2.3		4.1	2.4	2.2	1.8	1.8	2.3
(201) 5.3	(159) 5.4	(246) 5.2	% Depr., Dep., Amort./Sales	(77) 7.9	(65) 6.6	(26) 3.7	(33) 3.5	(25) 3.4	(20) 3.3
8.7	8.8	10.2		13.1	11.8	8.2	6.2	5.2	4.6
1.2	1.7	1.9	% Officers', Directors',	1.8	2.7		2.3		
(49) 3.6	(58) 4.2	(80) 3.7	Owners' Comp/Sales	(24) 4.9	(28) 6.8	(10)	4.2		
9.1	8.2	6.9		6.2	9.1		6.0		
1990111M	2612002M	3789698M	Net Sales ($)	37455M	134530M	120925M	282819M	472757M	2741212M
2080186M	1745138M	3017050M	Total Assets ($)	87368M	231970M	134926M	279657M	462129M	1821000M

M = $ thousand   MM = $ million
See Pages 11 through 18 for Explanation of Ratios and Data

Current Data Sorted By Assets   Comparative Historical Data

			2	3	1		Type of Statement		6	7
		1	8	3	2		Unqualified		6	7
	2	5	4	3			Reviewed		19	18
	7	9	3	1			Compiled		28	30
	1	13	15	11			Tax Returns		19	20
							Other		38	26
		19 (4/1-9/30/02)		75 (10/1/02-3/31/03)					4/1/98-3/31/99	4/1/99-3/31/00
	0-500M	500M-2MM	2-10MM	10-50MM	50-100MM	100-250MM			ALL	ALL
	10	28	32	21	3		NUMBER OF STATEMENTS		110	101
	%	%	%	%	%	%	ASSETS		%	%
	9.1	7.3	4.4	3.1			Cash & Equivalents		4.3	5.6
	6.0	2.1	4.9	4.7			Trade Receivables (net)		4.6	7.8
	21.8	38.2	34.2	47.1			Inventory		32.2	36.1
	6.4	3.6	6.8	1.9			All Other Current		2.9	5.8
	43.2	51.2	50.4	56.9			Total Current		43.9	55.3
	44.6	37.8	37.4	28.0			Fixed Assets (net)		42.5	37.5
	.1	.9	.1	.3			Intangibles (net)		1.9	.8
	12.1	10.0	12.1	14.8			All Other Non-Current		11.7	6.3
	100.0	100.0	100.0	100.0			Total		100.0	100.0
							LIABILITIES			
	74.2	34.1	37.9	41.1			Notes Payable-Short Term		30.8	40.3
	7.6	2.6	2.3	5.8			Cur. Mat.-L/T/D		3.1	3.1
	5.0	2.1	2.7	2.2			Trade Payables		3.0	3.8
	.0	.0	.6	.5			Income Taxes Payable		.1	.1
	16.2	5.0	2.9	3.0			All Other Current		8.0	5.6
	103.0	43.7	46.5	52.5			Total Current		45.0	52.8
	34.1	12.9	8.6	14.2			Long Term Debt		20.4	20.9
	.0	.1	.0	.2			Deferred Taxes		.5	1.1
	2.2	6.5	4.6	5.5			All Other Non-Current		4.9	4.3
	-39.3	36.8	40.3	27.5			Net Worth		29.1	20.8
	100.0	100.0	100.0	100.0			Total Liabilities & Net Worth		100.0	100.0
							INCOME DATA			
	100.0	100.0	100.0	100.0			Net Sales		100.0	100.0
							Gross Profit			
	95.6	102.6	99.5	99.4			Operating Expenses		121.0	96.0
	4.4	-2.6	.5	.6			Operating Profit		-21.0	4.0
	2.9	3.4	4.3	1.0			All Other Expenses (net)		-8.4	-1.0
	1.5	-6.0	-3.8	-.4			Profit Before Taxes		-12.6	5.0
							RATIOS			
	3.8	2.8	1.6	1.2					1.9	2.0
	.9	1.3	1.1	1.1			Current		1.1	1.1
	.1	.8	.9	.9					.6	.8
	1.5	.9	.4	.3					.6	.5
	.1	.1	.2	.1			Quick	(105)	.1	(97) .2
	.0	.0	.0	.0					.0	.0
	0 UND	0 UND	0 UND	0 UND				0 UND	0 UND	
	0 UND	0 UND	3 136.6	5 79.5			Sales/Receivables	0 999.8	0 881.0	
	0 UND	0 UND	12 30.8	16 22.9				15 23.6	20 18.1	
							Cost of Sales/Inventory			
							Cost of Sales/Payables			
	4.8	5.4	4.3	8.1					2.4	6.3
	UND	9.8	17.3	48.0			Sales/Working Capital		27.2	82.1
	-.8	-32.5	-10.3	-14.4					-6.1	-7.9
	5.1	1.5	1.9	2.7					2.6	2.9
	.9	(27) -1.4	.0	(20) 1.0			EBIT/Interest	(80)	.9	(93) 1.2
	-1.2	-4.0	-2.2	-2.4					-.7	.3
							Net Profit + Depr., Dep., Amort./Cur. Mat. L /T/D			9.4
									(12)	2.6
										.8
	.1	.0	.5	.4					.5	.4
	8.0	.7	.8	.8			Fixed/Worth		1.1	1.2
	-14.7	1.3	1.3	2.7					6.3	3.3
	.2	.4	.5	1.2					.6	.9
	9.6	1.4	1.2	2.3			Debt/Worth		1.9	2.9
	-29.5	NM	4.0	8.1					15.9	9.9
		9.3	7.8	7.8					13.4	29.3
	(21) -2.4	(28) -1.0	(18) 1.3				% Profit Before Taxes/Tangible Net Worth	(88)	-.5	(82) 5.1
		-22.8	-21.1	-27.6					-17.2	-3.2
	9.3	2.5	2.5	2.5					4.0	7.5
	-.1	-3.5	-2.0	-.3			% Profit Before Taxes/Total Assets		-.8	1.2
	-8.2	-14.6	-9.0	-9.9					-9.1	-2.9
	UND	195.3	8.2	9.7					16.2	24.7
	14.7	3.6	1.7	3.8			Sales/Net Fixed Assets		1.6	3.4
	.7	.7	1.0	2.0					.4	.9
	2.8	2.2	1.6	1.5					1.7	2.2
	1.8	1.4	.8	1.2			Sales/Total Assets		.6	1.2
	.6	.4	.4	.7					.2	.4
		1.2	1.3	1.5					1.9	1.1
	(21) 8.1	(28) 3.3	(17) 2.3				% Depr., Dep., Amort./Sales	(87)	5.4	(84) 2.9
		18.0	5.9	5.8					13.5	6.6
		1.2					% Officers', Directors', Owners' Comp/Sales		.8	.9
		8.1						(23)	2.3	(30) 2.9
									6.5	7.7
	3960M	91168M	208834M	547748M	156250M		Net Sales ($)		760373M	1981112M
	2511M	32192M	156431M	412610M	170012M		Total Assets ($)		742531M	708800M

M = $ thousand   MM = $ million
See Pages 11 through 18 for Explanation of Ratios and Data

Comparative Historical Data				**Current Data Sorted By Sales**					
6	5	6	**Type of Statement**				2	2	2
14	10	14	Unqualified		2	3	1	4	4
25	27	14	Reviewed	2	6	2	2		2
17	17	20	Compiled	14	2	2	1		1
31	37	40	Tax Returns	12	9	3	3	9	4
4/1/00- 3/31/01	4/1/01- 3/31/02	4/1/02- 3/31/03	Other		19 (4/1-9/30/02)		75 (10/1/02-3/31/03)		
ALL	ALL	ALL		0-1MM	1-3MM	3-5MM	5-10MM	10-25MM	25MM & OVER
93	96	94	**NUMBER OF STATEMENTS**	28	19	10	9	15	13
%	%	%	**ASSETS**	%	%	%	%	%	%
5.0	5.8	5.4	Cash & Equivalents	7.3	4.0	4.5		4.2	4.9
6.1	4.5	4.1	Trade Receivables (net)	2.4	.8	.1		7.2	7.1
32.5	37.8	37.7	Inventory	13.9	45.3	54.0		48.8	50.8
5.7	5.4	4.6	All Other Current	4.9	5.3	3.8		6.2	1.6
49.4	53.5	51.8	Total Current	28.4	55.4	62.4		66.5	64.4
38.1	33.7	36.0	Fixed Assets (net)	51.8	32.8	27.5		28.5	27.3
1.0	.8	.4	Intangibles (net)	.1	.0	.0		.4	2.1
11.5	12.0	11.8	All Other Non-Current	19.7	11.9	10.1		4.6	6.2
100.0	100.0	100.0	Total	100.0	100.0	100.0		100.0	100.0
			LIABILITIES						
33.9	35.8	41.3	Notes Payable-Short Term	34.7	49.3	32.8		43.1	47.4
1.4	2.0	3.7	Cur. Mat.-L/T/D	4.2	2.1	9.2		4.6	1.1
3.3	2.6	2.7	Trade Payables	1.9	1.8	4.7		2.3	4.0
.2	.3	.4	Income Taxes Payable	.0	.1	.0		.6	.9
7.6	5.4	5.0	All Other Current	6.9	3.5	7.9		3.6	2.2
46.4	46.2	53.1	Total Current	47.8	56.7	54.6		54.2	55.7
19.3	14.1	13.9	Long Term Debt	22.9	4.7	15.1		9.8	15.7
1.2	.5	.1	Deferred Taxes	.0	.1	.0		.4	.0
6.2	5.4	5.0	All Other Non-Current	5.2	4.1	10.8		5.3	3.9
26.9	33.8	27.9	Net Worth	24.1	34.4	19.5		30.4	24.7
100.0	100.0	100.0	Total Liabilities & Net Worth	100.0	100.0	100.0		100.0	100.0
			INCOME DATA						
100.0	100.0	100.0	Net Sales	100.0	100.0	100.0		100.0	100.0
			Gross Profit						
95.4	94.9	99.7	Operating Expenses	95.5	101.6	103.5		100.6	101.0
4.6	5.1	.3	Operating Profit	4.5	−1.6	−3.5		−.6	−1.0
−.1	3.2	3.1	All Other Expenses (net)	4.2	4.7	4.2		.7	.9
4.7	1.9	−2.8	Profit Before Taxes	.3	−6.4	−7.7		−1.3	−1.9
			RATIOS						
1.8	2.1	1.7		3.3	1.5	1.7		1.4	1.4
1.2	1.2	1.2	Current	1.2	1.0	1.1		1.2	1.1
.8	.8	.8		.5	.8	.8		1.1	.9
.5	.4	.4		.8	.2	.2		.4	.7
(90) .1	(92) .1	.1	Quick	.2	.0	.1		.1	.1
.0	.0	.0		.0	.0	.0		.0	.0
0 UND	0 UND	0 UND		0 UND	0 UND	0 UND	1 285.0		0 UND
0 UND	0 UND	0 UND	Sales/Receivables	0 UND	0 UND	0 UND	9 38.9		0 999.8
17 21.4	11 32.9	10 35.8		6 58.1	9 41.7	1 509.3	12 29.6		19 19.4
			Cost of Sales/Inventory						
			Cost of Sales/Payables						
3.7	3.8	5.0		3.5	6.7	7.2		5.3	9.2
21.2	20.2	18.0	Sales/Working Capital	15.2	279.8	20.7		11.0	75.7
−10.9	−11.3	−12.0		−3.7	−5.4	−7.3		43.0	−26.0
2.7	3.2	1.9		1.6	1.6	1.4		3.2	3.7
(83) 1.3	(90) 1.4	(92) .6	EBIT/Interest	(27) 1.0	−.4	−1.7	(14)	1.3	.9
.6	.0	−2.5		−2.2	−3.1	−5.7		−2.3	−2.7
5.7		2.5	Net Profit + Depr., Dep.,						
(12) 1.9		(11) .9	Amort./Cur. Mat. L/T/D						
1.4		−1.7							
.4	.3	.4		.5	.2	.0		.5	.6
1.1	.8	.8	Fixed/Worth	.8	.8	.9		.7	.8
3.1	3.0	1.8		11.7	1.5	2.3		1.3	35.4
1.1	.7	.5		.2	.4	1.9		1.0	1.5
2.7	1.9	1.8	Debt/Worth	.6	2.4	3.6		2.0	5.0
8.2	7.3	9.7		13.5	−54.1	NM		5.1	170.8
16.2	18.5	8.8	% Profit Before Taxes/Tangible	1.7	9.4			11.8	27.3
(81) 5.3	(86) 3.8	(77) −.5	Net Worth	(23) −.3	(14) 1.2		(13)	2.7	(11) 1.2
−2.5	−12.8	−22.8		−5.5	−19.1			−17.8	−42.9
4.2	6.5	2.7	% Profit Before Taxes/Total	4.0	2.1	1.5		6.1	7.4
1.1	1.1	−.9	Assets	−.1	−3.8	−9.3		.8	−.4
−1.4	−4.1	−10.4		−3.9	−23.8	−17.7		−8.3	−14.1
7.0	17.9	15.5		4.5	14.1	UND		9.8	49.8
2.9	2.9	3.7	Sales/Net Fixed Assets	.8	4.3	5.1		5.5	8.7
.9	1.2	1.0		.6	1.1	1.6		2.8	3.0
1.5	1.8	1.9		1.2	2.0	2.3		1.8	4.3
.7	1.1	1.0	Sales/Total Assets	.5	.8	1.7		1.5	1.5
.4	.5	.5		.3	.4	.6		1.0	1.1
1.3	1.1	1.6		4.9	1.2			1.1	.4
(77) 3.5	(78) 3.7	(77) 3.4	% Depr., Dep., Amort./Sales	(25) 12.8	(15) 3.9		(13)	1.6	(10) 1.8
8.6	7.6	9.5		18.9	6.9			4.1	2.5
.8	.7	1.2	% Officers', Directors',						
(27) 1.8	(24) 1.2	(24) 2.4	Owners' Comp/Sales						
5.4	3.3	7.1							
1418205M	998243M	1007960M	Net Sales ($)	12846M	34899M	38132M	59131M	256486M	606466M
1113443M	702747M	773756M	Total Assets ($)	39673M	66162M	38112M	57442M	196580M	375787M

© RMA 2003

M = $ thousand   MM = $ million
See Pages 11 through 18 for Explanation of Ratios and Data

Current Data Sorted By Assets   Comparative Historical Data

0-500M	500M-2MM	2-10MM	10-50MM	50-100MM	100-250MM	Type of Statement	4/1/98-3/31/99 ALL	4/1/99-3/31/00 ALL
1	2	13	17	4	2	Unqualified	38	39
	2	11	12	1		Reviewed	31	35
1	12	18	9			Compiled	42	43
2	6	4	1	1		Tax Returns	10	8
2	10	30	23	8	3	Other	49	47
	41 (4/1-9/30/02)		154 (10/1/02-3/31/03)					
6	32	76	62	14	5	NUMBER OF STATEMENTS	170	172
%	%	%	%	%	%	**ASSETS**	%	%
	6.8	4.9	1.8	1.9		Cash & Equivalents	4.1	4.1
	17.3	20.8	14.4	14.9		Trade Receivables (net)	19.3	16.5
	35.6	35.3	38.2	46.4		Inventory	33.2	36.3
	3.5	9.5	15.1	8.0		All Other Current	5.1	7.5
	63.2	70.4	69.7	71.2		Total Current	61.7	64.4
	31.4	23.3	24.0	21.9		Fixed Assets (net)	28.5	27.7
	.1	.1	.3	.0		Intangibles (net)	1.6	.4
	5.2	6.2	6.1	6.9		All Other Non-Current	8.2	7.4
	100.0	100.0	100.0	100.0		Total	100.0	100.0
						LIABILITIES		
	41.0	39.8	39.8	52.1		Notes Payable-Short Term	34.4	30.9
	1.7	1.8	2.5	1.1		Cur. Mat.-L/T/D	1.6	2.4
	9.9	7.1	6.4	4.9		Trade Payables	6.6	6.1
	.0	.0	.4	.8		Income Taxes Payable	.2	.2
	11.2	6.2	6.7	7.0		All Other Current	6.0	8.0
	63.9	55.0	55.7	65.9		Total Current	48.9	47.5
	19.8	11.1	10.3	9.7		Long Term Debt	12.5	12.8
	.7	.2	1.1	1.4		Deferred Taxes	1.1	1.2
	16.0	3.9	1.6	8.3		All Other Non-Current	2.4	2.9
	-.4	29.8	31.2	14.7		Net Worth	35.0	35.6
	100.0	100.0	100.0	100.0		Total Liabilities & Net Worth	100.0	100.0
						INCOME DATA		
	100.0	100.0	100.0	100.0		Net Sales	100.0	100.0
						Gross Profit		
	101.5	95.3	100.1	99.7		Operating Expenses	98.6	99.1
	-1.5	4.7	-.1	.3		Operating Profit	1.4	.9
	1.1	1.6	.7	-.2		All Other Expenses (net)	-3.8	-3.8
	-2.6	3.1	-.8	.5		Profit Before Taxes	5.3	4.7
						RATIOS		
	3.1	1.7	1.4	1.7			1.9	1.9
	1.2	1.2	1.2	1.5		Current	1.3	1.3
	.7	1.0	1.0	1.3			1.0	1.1
	1.4	.9	.4	.5			1.0	.9
	.5	.4	.2	.1		Quick	(169) .4	(168) .4
	.1	.1	.1	.1			.1	.1
	0 UND	7 49.5	12 31.6	5 78.7			3 116.7	2 173.8
	11 32.3	31 11.7	28 12.9	9 41.2		Sales/Receivables	24 15.4	21 17.7
	24 15.5	75 4.9	52 7.0	122 3.0			60 6.1	54 6.7
						Cost of Sales/Inventory		
						Cost of Sales/Payables		
	5.7	4.9	6.5	3.9			6.1	4.7
	21.5	16.8	12.0	5.0		Sales/Working Capital	14.9	10.9
	-15.4	59.7	39.6	8.9			-408.1	38.1
	3.7	5.0	2.4	2.1			3.4	4.4
	(30) 1.6	(72) 1.5	(57) .9	(13) 1.5		EBIT/Interest	(156) 1.3	(159) 2.5
	-1.0	-.2	-.5	.9			.0	1.5
		1.9	1.7			Net Profit + Depr., Dep.,	3.1	8.6
		(10) .8	(13) .0			Amort./Cur. Mat. L /T/D	(38) .7	(41) 3.2
		-1.3	-2.5				-2.4	1.7
	.4	.3	.3	.3			.3	.3
	1.2	.7	.8	.7		Fixed/Worth	.8	.7
	2.3	1.9	1.5	1.1			1.7	1.4
	1.0	1.0	1.6	2.1			.9	.9
	3.0	3.0	2.7	2.5		Debt/Worth	1.9	2.1
	NM	9.0	5.1	4.2			4.4	4.4
	20.5	24.0	14.5	11.0		% Profit Before Taxes/Tangible	18.1	29.0
	(24) 3.4	(71) 8.7	.3	(12) 8.1		Net Worth	(159) 5.2	(164) 15.2
	-18.5	-10.8	-17.0	-.1			-15.9	4.7
	8.1	6.9	4.0	2.7		% Profit Before Taxes/Total	7.4	9.2
	1.0	1.6	.1	2.2		Assets	1.4	5.3
	-5.7	-3.5	-3.8	-.2			-4.4	1.4
	60.4	27.3	16.1	17.5			19.2	18.7
	11.5	8.8	7.9	7.5		Sales/Net Fixed Assets	8.6	8.4
	3.4	4.2	3.8	3.5			3.3	3.4
	4.7	2.6	1.9	1.6			2.9	2.4
	2.3	1.8	1.5	1.3		Sales/Total Assets	1.8	1.6
	1.1	1.2	.9	.9			1.0	1.0
	1.0	.9	.8	1.4			.9	.9
	(24) 3.4	(66) 1.6	(56) 2.0	(11) 1.7		% Depr., Dep., Amort./Sales	(143) 1.9	(148) 1.8
	6.2	2.5	2.8	2.9			3.2	3.7
	2.0	.6	.4			% Officers', Directors',	.5	.5
	(16) 3.0	(23) 1.7	(12) 1.7			Owners' Comp/Sales	(41) 1.5	(38) 1.7
	5.6	4.1	4.3				3.8	3.8
4951M	143193M	963147M	1890460M	1368105M	1624172M	Net Sales ($)	7132769M	8691436M
1448M	37847M	428665M	1354107M	1041434M	815507M	Total Assets ($)	2473584M	3745149M

© RMA 2003   M = $ thousand   MM = $ million
See Pages 11 through 18 for Explanation of Ratios and Data

Comparative Historical Data / Current Data Sorted By Sales

Comparative Historical Data			Type of Statement	Current Data Sorted By Sales					
28	43	39	Unqualified	1			1	5	16	16
35	41	26	Reviewed					6	15	5
42	38	40	Compiled	5	6	5	12	6	6
12	10	14	Tax Returns	3	7		2	1	1
74	79	76	Other	4	9	8	8	21	26
4/1/00-3/31/01 ALL	4/1/01-3/31/02 ALL	4/1/02-3/31/03 ALL		41 (4/1-9/30/02)			154 (10/1/02-3/31/03)		
				0-1MM	1-3MM	3-5MM	5-10MM	10-25MM	25MM & OVER
191	211	195	**NUMBER OF STATEMENTS**	13	22	14	33	59	54
%	%	%	**ASSETS**	%	%	%	%	%	%
6.4	3.5	3.8	Cash & Equivalents	4.1	5.5	3.1	4.6	3.8	2.7
16.2	19.1	17.6	Trade Receivables (net)	20.4	10.7	22.6	16.9	19.7	16.6
36.1	37.6	36.6	Inventory	21.6	35.8	35.3	33.5	38.8	40.5
7.7	9.4	10.1	All Other Current	4.6	6.9	14.0	9.0	10.2	12.2
66.4	69.7	68.2	Total Current	50.6	58.9	75.1	64.1	72.6	72.0
24.9	22.4	25.4	Fixed Assets (net)	40.9	34.5	20.1	27.3	22.0	21.7
2.5	1.5	.2	Intangibles (net)	.0	.2	.0	.3	.0	.3
6.2	6.4	6.3	All Other Non-Current	8.4	6.5	4.8	8.3	5.3	6.0
100.0	100.0	100.0	Total	100.0	100.0	100.0	100.0	100.0	100.0
			LIABILITIES						
32.7	36.5	41.0	Notes Payable-Short Term	19.2	68.4	41.9	33.5	39.6	40.9
2.4	2.7	1.9	Cur. Mat.-L/T/D	2.0	2.1	1.8	1.5	2.6	1.2
7.3	7.3	7.2	Trade Payables	3.2	5.5	2.8	4.9	10.3	7.9
.2	.4	.2	Income Taxes Payable	.0	.0	.1	.0	.4	.3
9.0	7.8	7.1	All Other Current	6.5	3.6	10.2	7.1	7.3	7.6
50.7	54.7	57.4	Total Current	30.9	79.7	56.7	47.1	60.2	58.0
11.8	11.9	12.7	Long Term Debt	29.2	20.4	6.6	10.9	11.4	9.6
.8	.7	.6	Deferred Taxes	.3	.0	.2	.9	.3	1.2
1.6	2.3	5.5	All Other Non-Current	.6	20.9	5.2	1.3	4.0	4.6
35.1	30.4	23.9	Net Worth	38.6	−20.9	31.3	39.8	24.2	26.6
100.0	100.0	100.0	Total Liabilities & Net Worth	100.0	100.0	100.0	100.0	100.0	100.0
			INCOME DATA						
100.0	100.0	100.0	Net Sales	100.0	100.0	100.0	100.0	100.0	100.0
			Gross Profit						
91.9	96.2	98.1	Operating Expenses	91.2	96.5	97.6	99.8	99.2	98.4
8.1	3.8	1.9	Operating Profit	8.8	3.5	2.4	.2	.8	1.6
1.9	1.1	1.0	All Other Expenses (net)	2.2	1.9	2.0	.4	1.2	.4
6.2	2.7	.8	Profit Before Taxes	6.6	1.6	.3	−.2	−.4	1.2
			RATIOS						
1.7	1.5	1.7		18.3	1.5	2.1	2.8	1.5	1.6
1.2	1.2	1.2	Current	1.9	1.0	1.1	1.3	1.2	1.3
1.1	1.1	1.0		1.0	.4	1.0	1.0	1.0	1.1
.8	.7	.7		2.3	.4	.9	.8	.7	.5
.3	.4	.3	Quick	.8	.1	.3	.3	.4	.2
.1	.1	.1		.2	.0	.1	.1	.1	.1
0 999.8	7 55.7	6 58.7		0 UND	0 UND	6 58.5	8 48.4	12 31.1	5 72.1
17 21.1	29 12.8	23 15.6	Sales/Receivables	88 4.2	0 UND	38 9.7	18 20.7	26 13.8	22 16.9
53 6.9	77 4.7	63 5.8		249 1.5	44 8.3	97 3.8	60 6.1	54 6.8	43 8.6
			Cost of Sales/Inventory						
			Cost of Sales/Payables						
4.3	5.9	5.4		1.5	5.2	7.5	4.4	7.1	5.4
10.8	11.8	12.2	Sales/Working Capital	3.6	NM	11.0	12.6	16.9	11.3
61.8	44.6	60.1		57.3	−3.9	−55.0	206.6	60.1	23.7
4.2	3.1	2.9		2.4	2.0	4.7	2.9	3.7	2.9
(167) 2.2	(192) 1.8	(182) 1.4	EBIT/Interest	(10) 1.1	(20) 1.7	(31) 1.3	(58) 1.0	(49) 1.0	1.9
1.4	.9	−.2		−5.0	−2.3	.0	−.6	−.9	.5
12.2	6.5	2.2						1.5	4.0
(37) 3.9	(41) 3.0	(36) 1.3	Net Profit + Depr., Dep., Amort./Cur. Mat. L/T/D				(12) .1	(14) 1.7	
1.9	1.4	.0						−1.9	1.2
.2	.3	.3		.3	.3	.3	.3	.3	.3
.7	.6	.8	Fixed/Worth	1.0	1.4	.9	.6	.9	.7
1.3	1.3	1.7		2.0	−1.0	2.2	1.7	1.8	1.1
1.0	1.3	1.3		.4	1.1	.7	.5	1.9	1.5
2.2	2.6	2.7	Debt/Worth	2.5	35.0	5.4	2.1	3.4	2.5
4.6	5.5	7.2		6.7	−3.4	14.0	5.5	7.1	3.9
29.4	22.7	21.0		31.7	32.5	23.6	15.5	22.1	18.6
(178) 13.9	(198) 8.7	(177) 5.0	% Profit Before Taxes/Tangible Net Worth	(12) .6	(13) 8.8	(13) 9.5	(32) .3	(56) 3.1	(51) 8.6
5.3	−1.2	−9.7		−23.0	−1.5	−13.6	−20.3	−18.9	−1.3
9.2	6.5	6.2		9.2	9.6	6.4	5.5	6.6	5.5
4.8	2.3	.9	% Profit Before Taxes/Total Assets	.1	1.4	1.3	.7	.1	2.2
1.4	−.6	−3.5		−5.8	−4.7	−3.7	−3.5	−5.3	−1.7
22.5	21.4	23.2		5.6	177.3	22.4	20.0	24.6	24.2
8.7	9.3	8.6	Sales/Net Fixed Assets	1.3	5.4	11.5	7.8	10.1	11.9
3.5	4.4	4.2		.5	2.2	3.9	3.9	5.0	5.3
2.1	2.2	2.5		.8	2.7	2.3	2.4	2.7	2.7
1.4	1.5	1.6	Sales/Total Assets	.3	1.5	1.4	1.6	1.6	1.8
.8	1.1	1.1		.2	.8	.6	1.0	1.3	1.3
.8	.8	.9		3.5	2.4	1.0	1.0	.7	.8
(165) 2.0	(184) 1.7	(166) 1.8	% Depr., Dep., Amort./Sales	(10) 5.0	(15) 5.6	(11) 2.1	(28) 1.7	(55) 1.6	(47) 1.4
3.4	2.7	3.1		16.4	12.7	3.5	3.9	2.4	2.6
.7	.7	.9					1.1	.6	
(35) 2.4	(40) 1.4	(56) 2.3	% Officers', Directors', Owners' Comp/Sales				(14) 2.0	(17) 1.4	
5.4	4.2	4.3					5.0	3.7	
5570311M	8148865M	5994028M	Net Sales ($)	5225M	40670M	58548M	234368M	1023473M	4631744M
3646601M	5104929M	3679008M	Total Assets ($)	22979M	83546M	60753M	219902M	684331M	2607497M

© RMA 2003

M = $ thousand   MM = $ million
See Pages 11 through 18 for Explanation of Ratios and Data

Current Data Sorted By Assets | Comparative Historical Data

0-500M	500M-2MM	2-10MM	10-50MM	50-100MM	100-250MM	Type of Statement	4/1/98-3/31/99 ALL	4/1/99-3/31/00 ALL
	1	1	2			Unqualified	9	8
2	10	160	81	3		Reviewed	211	194
	11	43	10			Compiled	55	48
3	9	7				Tax Returns	17	8
	8	16	9	3		Other	72	27
	27 (4/1-9/30/02)		352 (10/1/02-3/31/03)					
5	39	227	102	6		NUMBER OF STATEMENTS	364	285
%	%	%	%	%	%	**ASSETS**	%	%
	3.1	1.2	1.1			Cash & Equivalents	2.2	1.5
	6.5	6.9	8.7			Trade Receivables (net)	7.7	8.2
	8.5	14.0	13.6			Inventory	14.0	15.6
	4.5	3.4	3.0			All Other Current	2.5	1.9
	22.5	25.5	26.4			Total Current	26.4	27.3
	63.4	63.0	63.0			Fixed Assets (net)	55.8	56.9
	.2	.7	.4			Intangibles (net)	.8	.8
	13.8	10.8	10.2			All Other Non-Current	17.0	14.9
	100.0	100.0	100.0			Total	100.0	100.0
						LIABILITIES		
	16.4	19.8	18.0			Notes Payable-Short Term	16.5	20.5
	6.4	6.0	5.4			Cur. Mat.-L/T/D	5.0	4.6
	3.2	3.2	2.7			Trade Payables	2.4	2.5
	.0	.1	.0			Income Taxes Payable	.1	.1
	8.0	3.3	1.8			All Other Current	1.9	2.5
	34.1	32.2	27.9			Total Current	25.8	30.3
	46.9	34.8	35.3			Long Term Debt	31.8	29.0
	.3	.2	.1			Deferred Taxes	.3	.3
	3.6	2.1	1.6			All Other Non-Current	4.3	2.6
	15.0	30.7	35.1			Net Worth	37.8	37.8
	100.0	100.0	100.0			Total Liabilities & Net Worth	100.0	100.0
						INCOME DATA		
	100.0	100.0	100.0			Net Sales	100.0	100.0
						Gross Profit		
	96.1	96.1	94.6			Operating Expenses	82.8	82.7
	3.9	3.9	5.4			Operating Profit	17.2	17.3
	4.7	6.2	6.2			All Other Expenses (net)	−.3	3.4
	−.8	−2.4	−.9			Profit Before Taxes	17.5	13.9
						RATIOS		
	1.1	1.1	1.2			Current	1.6	1.5
	.7	.8	.9				1.1	1.0
	.4	.6	.7				.8	.7
	.4	.4	.4			Quick	.6	.5
	.2	.2	.3				.4	.3
	.1	.1	.2				.2	.2
	0 UND	16 23.0	20 18.4			Sales/Receivables	16 22.4	17 21.8
	14 25.8	28 12.9	35 10.5				34 10.7	28 12.8
	27 13.7	54 6.8	84 4.4				44 8.3	53 6.9
						Cost of Sales/Inventory		
						Cost of Sales/Payables		
	27.4	17.8	15.7			Sales/Working Capital	8.3	9.3
	−12.1	−11.4	−18.4				37.8	−152.8
	−5.3	−5.1	−6.4				−16.1	−10.4
	2.3	2.0	2.5			EBIT/Interest	5.9	8.6
	(36) .8	(220) .6	.9				(351) 3.7	(272) 4.0
	−.9	−1.0	−.1				2.1	2.1
						Net Profit + Depr., Dep.,	11.2	16.7
						Amort./Cur. Mat. L /T/D	(23) 3.9	(15) 4.7
							2.0	3.5
	1.5	1.2	1.4			Fixed/Worth	.8	.8
	3.0	2.3	2.2				1.4	1.3
	−3.5	4.0	3.1				2.6	2.4
	1.4	1.3	1.2			Debt/Worth	.7	.7
	3.3	2.5	2.1				1.6	1.4
	−6.0	4.9	3.6				3.3	2.7
	11.6	7.0	7.1			% Profit Before Taxes/Tangible	41.8	34.1
	(27) .6	(213) −1.7	−.6			Net Worth	(338) 26.2	(269) 21.7
	−15.4	−20.5	−12.8				11.1	12.0
	4.3	2.2	2.5			% Profit Before Taxes/Total	15.7	14.4
	.0	−.9	−.2			Assets	10.1	9.0
	−6.0	−5.6	−3.3				4.4	3.8
	2.9	1.5	1.2			Sales/Net Fixed Assets	2.2	2.1
	1.3	1.1	.8				1.5	1.4
	1.0	.8	.6				1.0	.9
	1.4	.8	.7			Sales/Total Assets	1.1	1.0
	.9	.6	.5				.8	.7
	.7	.5	.4				.6	.6
	6.2	8.7	8.6			% Depr., Dep., Amort./Sales	5.2	5.4
	(38) 9.4	(217) 12.0	(99) 11.8				(351) 7.2	(278) 7.6
	14.1	15.4	13.7				9.8	10.2
	2.6	1.1	.6			% Officers', Directors',	.6	.7
	(10) 3.7	(61) 2.6	(36) 1.4			Owners' Comp/Sales	(100) 1.5	(86) 1.4
	12.8	7.3	6.2				3.3	3.0
4069M	63906M	916775M	1296202M	221692M		Net Sales ($)	2277150M	1879543M
1950M	52111M	1239227M	1742419M	426202M		Total Assets ($)	2738681M	2220943M

(The right-hand portion of the current-data columns is marked vertically: DATA NOT AVAILABLE)

M = $ thousand   MM = $ million
See Pages 11 through 18 for Explanation of Ratios and Data

Comparative Historical Data / Current Data Sorted By Sales

1	10	4	Type of Statement					2	
			Unqualified		2				2
279	265	256	Reviewed	9	64	74	75	30	4
70	80	64	Compiled	5	25	18	11	4	1
9	19	19	Tax Returns	7	7	3	2		
61	49	36	Other	9	5	5	9	4	4
4/1/00-3/31/01 ALL	4/1/01-3/31/02 ALL	4/1/02-3/31/03 ALL		27 (4/1-9/30/02) 0-1MM	1-3MM	3-5MM	352 (10/1/02-3/31/03) 5-10MM	10-25MM	25MM & OVER
420	423	379	**NUMBER OF STATEMENTS**	30	103	100	97	38	11
%	%	%	**ASSETS**	%	%	%	%	%	%
1.6	1.6	1.3	Cash & Equivalents	3.2	1.1	1.0	.7	.7	9.6
7.4	9.0	7.5	Trade Receivables (net)	3.6	7.6	6.2	7.8	9.7	19.5
16.0	15.5	13.2	Inventory	4.5	13.2	14.2	14.5	14.3	11.4
2.2	2.3	3.6	All Other Current	8.6	3.0	2.3	3.8	3.2	8.9
27.2	28.4	25.7	Total Current	19.9	24.9	23.7	26.7	27.8	49.4
60.7	60.4	62.6	Fixed Assets (net)	66.0	61.2	65.2	61.9	62.6	48.2
.5	.8	.6	Intangibles (net)	.3	.3	1.0	.8	.1	.4
11.7	10.4	11.2	All Other Non-Current	13.8	13.6	10.1	10.6	9.4	2.1
100.0	100.0	100.0	Total	100.0	100.0	100.0	100.0	100.0	100.0
			LIABILITIES						
18.3	18.9	19.3	Notes Payable-Short Term	13.8	20.2	19.0	19.5	20.0	23.6
5.4	4.9	5.9	Cur. Mat.-L/T/D	4.2	6.5	5.3	7.0	5.0	2.8
2.4	2.5	3.1	Trade Payables	1.5	3.3	2.2	2.9	3.3	15.9
.1	.1	.0	Income Taxes Payable	.0	.0	.1	.0	.0	.0
3.4	3.8	3.3	All Other Current	7.8	3.2	4.2	1.9	.9	4.2
29.6	30.1	31.6	Total Current	27.3	33.2	30.9	31.3	29.3	46.4
31.9	33.4	36.1	Long Term Debt	45.7	34.6	37.9	35.6	33.4	21.4
.2	.1	.2	Deferred Taxes	.4	.0	.5	.0	.1	.0
3.3	2.8	2.3	All Other Non-Current	3.8	2.9	1.7	1.9	2.6	.2
34.9	33.5	29.8	Net Worth	22.7	29.3	29.1	31.2	34.5	31.9
100.0	100.0	100.0	Total Liabilities & Net Worth	100.0	100.0	100.0	100.0	100.0	100.0
			INCOME DATA						
100.0	100.0	100.0	Net Sales	100.0	100.0	100.0	100.0	100.0	100.0
			Gross Profit						
88.6	84.2	95.7	Operating Expenses	87.0	98.2	96.6	95.3	94.8	94.2
11.4	15.8	4.3	Operating Profit	13.0	1.8	3.4	4.7	5.2	5.8
6.5	5.6	6.1	All Other Expenses (net)	10.8	4.3	6.6	6.6	5.3	2.4
4.9	10.1	-1.7	Profit Before Taxes	2.2	-2.6	-3.1	-1.9	-.2	3.4
			RATIOS						
1.2	1.4	1.1		2.3	1.1	1.1	1.1	1.3	1.7
.9	1.0	.8	Current	.8	.7	.8	.8	.9	.9
.7	.7	.6		.3	.5	.6	.7	.7	.7
.4	.6	.4		.5	.3	.4	.4	.5	1.5
(419) .3	.3	.2	Quick	.2	.2	.2	.3	.3	.4
.2	.2	.1		.1	.1	.1	.1	.1	.2
19 19.4	18 20.5	16 23.0		0 UND	14 25.8	16 23.0	19 19.7	19 19.2	15 25.0
33 11.1	30 12.1	28 12.8	Sales/Receivables	3 131.1	27 13.5	29 12.8	31 11.9	35 10.4	30 12.0
59 6.2	58 6.3	56 6.5		47 7.8	51 7.1	54 6.8	81 4.5	70 5.2	64 5.7
			Cost of Sales/Inventory						
			Cost of Sales/Payables						
13.6	9.9	20.0		4.3	37.9	42.2	17.7	12.5	19.0
-17.5	-105.2	-11.9	Sales/Working Capital	-5.7	-9.8	-11.0	-13.4	-18.4	-32.2
-6.6	-10.3	-5.3		-3.5	-4.6	-5.4	-6.7	-5.1	-8.4
3.3	5.2	2.1		2.2	2.3	1.5	1.9	3.8	56.9
(398) 1.7	(412) 3.2	(368) .7	EBIT/Interest	(22) .9	(101) .7	.7	.7	.6	(10) 2.8
.8	1.7	-.7		-.9	-.7	-.8	-.9	.0	1.3
3.7	5.8	2.5	Net Profit + Depr., Dep.,						
(29) 1.9	(25) 1.7	(16) 1.4	Amort./Cur. Mat. L/T/D						
.9	1.1	.0							
1.0	1.1	1.2		1.2	1.1	1.3	1.3	1.4	.7
1.8	1.8	2.3	Fixed/Worth	2.5	2.3	2.7	2.3	2.2	2.3
3.1	3.3	3.9		NM	3.6	4.7	3.4	3.4	6.4
1.0	1.1	1.3		1.0	1.3	1.4	1.3	1.2	.6
1.9	1.9	2.5	Debt/Worth	2.4	2.4	2.5	2.5	2.0	2.9
3.6	3.9	4.6		-19.6	4.5	5.1	4.0	3.9	6.3
16.3	32.9	7.4	% Profit Before Taxes/Tangible	6.6	8.2	6.6	5.7	7.7	36.3
(392) 7.7	(393) 21.1	(350) -1.2	Net Worth	(22) .7	(94) -2.7	(94) -1.7	(93) -2.1	(37) -2.4	(10) 18.5
-2.3	10.3	-16.7		-7.0	-18.0	-21.8	-19.8	-13.8	7.3
7.2	11.9	2.5	% Profit Before Taxes/Total	3.4	2.2	1.5	2.3	3.8	16.8
2.4	7.5	-.6	Assets	.3	-1.0	-.8	-1.5	-1.1	5.6
-1.0	3.1	-5.0		-4.3	-5.6	-5.3	-5.7	-3.3	1.2
1.6	1.8	1.5		1.1	1.6	1.4	1.4	1.6	12.1
1.1	1.3	1.0	Sales/Net Fixed Assets	.6	1.1	.9	1.0	.9	5.7
.7	.9	.7		.2	.9	.7	.8	.7	1.2
.9	1.0	.8		.6	.9	.8	.8	.8	4.5
.6	.7	.6	Sales/Total Assets	.3	.7	.6	.6	.6	1.4
.5	.6	.5		.1	.5	.5	.5	.5	.7
7.6	6.7	8.3		7.8	9.2	8.0	8.6	6.5	1.1
(401) 9.9	(407) 9.3	(364) 11.7	% Depr., Dep., Amort./Sales	(28) 14.8	(100) 11.9	(95) 11.7	(94) 11.6	(37) 10.9	(10) 2.0
12.4	11.6	14.8		22.3	15.1	14.4	14.3	13.6	10.4
1.0	.9	1.0			2.0	1.1	.7	.6	
(128) 1.6	(138) 1.6	(109) 2.2	% Officers', Directors', Owners' Comp/Sales	(25) 3.7	(27) 2.0	(34) 1.1	(14) 1.7		
3.9	3.2	6.9			9.1	4.2	4.3	8.0	
2208436M	3300139M	2502644M	Net Sales ($)	15932M	217342M	389276M	666496M	518923M	694675M
3663263M	4452046M	3461909M	Total Assets ($)	73836M	348898M	653135M	1103426M	871254M	411360M

M = $ thousand   MM = $ million
See Pages 11 through 18 for Explanation of Ratios and Data

Current Data Sorted By Assets   **Comparative Historical Data**

Period coverage: **11 (4/1-9/30/02)** and **56 (10/1/02-3/31/03)**

0-500M	500M-2MM	2-10MM	10-50MM	50-100MM	100-250MM	Type of Statement	4/1/98-3/31/99 ALL	4/1/99-3/31/00 ALL
	4	5	5		1	Unqualified	15	18
	1	3				Reviewed	13	17
1	6	9				Compiled	10	7
3	4	2				Tax Returns	9	8
	5	7	5	1	5	Other	34	25
4	20	26	10	1	6	**NUMBER OF STATEMENTS**	81	75
%	%	%	%	%	%	**ASSETS**	%	%
	5.4	1.4	1.4			Cash & Equivalents	3.4	2.9
	4.5	5.5	4.2			Trade Receivables (net)	3.6	5.6
	23.5	34.8	36.2			Inventory	31.3	27.8
	2.6	3.1	4.9			All Other Current	3.4	3.9
	36.0	44.9	46.7			Total Current	41.7	40.2
	56.3	47.1	45.9			Fixed Assets (net)	47.9	47.4
	.0	1.5	.2			Intangibles (net)	1.4	3.4
	7.7	6.5	7.2			All Other Non-Current	9.0	9.0
	100.0	100.0	100.0			Total	100.0	100.0
						LIABILITIES		
	26.7	19.1	28.1			Notes Payable-Short Term	21.9	21.5
	4.5	4.8	3.9			Cur. Mat.-L/T/D	5.4	5.6
	3.3	6.1	5.3			Trade Payables	5.0	5.6
	.0	.0	.0			Income Taxes Payable	.2	.0
	7.6	5.5	2.5			All Other Current	7.4	6.0
	42.1	35.6	39.8			Total Current	39.9	38.7
	28.9	28.2	27.5			Long Term Debt	31.1	40.6
	.1	.0	1.5			Deferred Taxes	.7	.7
	4.1	.1	4.7			All Other Non-Current	4.4	5.9
	24.8	36.1	26.4			Net Worth	23.9	14.2
	100.0	100.0	100.0			Total Liabilities & Net Worth	100.0	100.0
						INCOME DATA		
	100.0	100.0	100.0			Net Sales	100.0	100.0
						Gross Profit		
	91.3	98.8	100.1			Operating Expenses	108.4	97.8
	8.7	1.2	-.1			Operating Profit	-8.4	2.2
	7.7	3.4	3.6			All Other Expenses (net)	4.7	7.4
	1.0	-2.2	-3.6			Profit Before Taxes	-13.1	-5.2
						RATIOS		
	3.8	2.0	1.5			Current	1.8	1.6
	1.1	1.3	1.2				1.1	1.0
	.4	.7	1.0				.7	.7
	1.7	.3	.3			Quick	.2	.4
	.1	(25) .1	.1				(79) .1	(74) .2
	.0	.0	.0				.0	.0
	0 UND	0 UND	4 92.3			Sales/Receivables	0 UND	0 999.8
	0 UND	4 84.3	8 43.6				3 126.3	6 63.2
	0 UND	15 23.9	16 22.7				10 35.9	19 19.1
						Cost of Sales/Inventory		
						Cost of Sales/Payables		
	7.8	5.8	7.0			Sales/Working Capital	7.8	9.1
	NM	15.0	13.5				31.6	279.3
	-4.3	-8.9	NM				-6.7	-10.5
	2.6	4.1	2.1			EBIT/Interest	1.2	1.9
	(19) 1.3	(25) 1.4	-.6				(74) -1.1	(69) -.1
	-1.2	-.7	-2.4				-4.8	-1.9
						Net Profit + Depr., Dep., Amort./Cur. Mat. L/T/D	.9	
							(10) .0	
							-5.1	
	.9	.5	1.1			Fixed/Worth	.9	1.0
	2.5	1.5	1.9				1.5	2.4
	-17.0	4.1	2.9				10.4	-3.9
	.4	.7	1.5			Debt/Worth	1.1	1.6
	4.3	1.9	3.3				2.7	5.6
	-32.2	5.2	5.2				27.7	-9.0
	41.3	6.0				% Profit Before Taxes/Tangible Net Worth	6.5	27.0
	(13) 8.2	(22) .8					(64) -11.4	(50) 2.7
	-.4	-27.5					-66.7	-47.9
	8.7	4.2	4.4			% Profit Before Taxes/Total Assets	1.0	4.9
	.5	.4	-3.5				-7.2	-4.5
	-3.4	-7.4	-8.1				-27.8	-14.7
	5.2	11.2	2.9			Sales/Net Fixed Assets	5.6	4.8
	1.8	2.2	2.2				2.0	2.5
	.7	.8	1.5				.9	1.0
	1.9	1.5	1.2			Sales/Total Assets	1.8	1.7
	.9	1.0	1.0				1.0	1.0
	.6	.6	.7				.6	.6
	2.8	2.2				% Depr., Dep., Amort./Sales	3.3	3.7
	(19) 5.0	(22) 6.2					(71) 6.0	(64) 5.7
	24.0	11.8					12.8	9.4
						% Officers', Directors', Owners' Comp/Sales		
2150M	40762M	141951M	237782M	39212M	1068799M	Net Sales ($)	1368880M	1650831M
815M	22734M	134580M	244965M	59355M	1000862M	Total Assets ($)	1362050M	1470382M

M = $ thousand   MM = $ million
See Pages 11 through 18 for Explanation of Ratios and Data

Comparative Historical Data | Current Data Sorted By Sales

			Type of Statement						
12	10	15	Unqualified		4	1	3	4	3
8	8	4	Reviewed	1		2		1	
12	11	16	Compiled	2	8	3	2	1	
8	8	9	Tax Returns	6	2	1			
21	30	23	Other	2	4	1	5	2	9
4/1/00-3/31/01	4/1/01-3/31/02	4/1/02-3/31/03			11 (4/1-9/30/02)		56 (10/1/02-3/31/03)		
ALL	ALL	ALL		0-1MM	1-3MM	3-5MM	5-10MM	10-25MM	25MM & OVER
61	67	67	NUMBER OF STATEMENTS	11	18	8	10	8	12
%	%	%	ASSETS	%	%	%	%	%	%
4.8	3.0	3.4	Cash & Equivalents	7.0	2.5		2.6		1.5
5.4	4.9	4.4	Trade Receivables (net)	.0	1.5		10.1		3.9
31.9	28.4	30.3	Inventory	11.6	25.8		43.1		32.3
2.6	4.2	2.8	All Other Current	.5	2.9		4.4		1.1
44.7	40.6	41.0	Total Current	19.1	32.8		60.3		38.6
45.6	48.0	51.2	Fixed Assets (net)	75.0	58.7		32.3		54.7
4.1	3.7	.8	Intangibles (net)	.5	.3		.0		.7
5.6	7.7	7.0	All Other Non-Current	5.4	8.1		7.4		6.0
100.0	100.0	100.0	Total	100.0	100.0		100.0		100.0
			LIABILITIES						
20.7	19.6	25.6	Notes Payable-Short Term	10.1	43.1		16.1		16.5
5.0	5.8	6.5	Cur. Mat.-L/T/D	6.5	5.9		5.7		12.1
6.2	4.0	5.4	Trade Payables	5.3	3.4		6.9		5.2
.0	.3	.0	Income Taxes Payable	.0	.1		.0		.0
7.7	6.7	5.5	All Other Current	7.2	5.9		7.5		3.8
39.5	36.4	43.0	Total Current	29.1	58.3		36.2		37.6
32.7	36.3	35.6	Long Term Debt	49.4	45.9		25.4		33.2
.2	.1	.3	Deferred Taxes	.0	.0		.3		.2
6.3	6.5	6.3	All Other Non-Current	1.6	12.5		.0		12.7
21.3	20.7	14.8	Net Worth	19.9	−16.8		38.2		16.4
100.0	100.0	100.0	Total Liabilities & Net Worth	100.0	100.0		100.0		100.0
			INCOME DATA						
100.0	100.0	100.0	Net Sales	100.0	100.0		100.0		100.0
			Gross Profit						
86.2	88.2	97.5	Operating Expenses	90.5	98.8		99.7		98.9
13.8	11.8	2.5	Operating Profit	9.5	1.2		.3		1.1
5.0	4.8	5.4	All Other Expenses (net)	14.5	3.6		.7		6.4
8.8	7.1	−2.9	Profit Before Taxes	−5.0	−2.4		−.4		−5.3
			RATIOS						
2.1	2.1	1.9		2.0	2.4		3.1		1.5
1.2	1.3	1.2	Current	.5	.9		1.9		1.3
.8	.7	.7		.2	.3		1.2		.9
.7	.3	.3		.6	.3		.7		.2
.2	.1 (66)	.1	Quick	.1 (17)	.1		.2		.1
.0	.0	.0		.0	.0		.1		.1
0 UND	0 999.8	0 UND		0 UND	0 UND		4 96.9		8 46.7
6 62.5	6 56.6	4 95.5	Sales/Receivables	0 UND	0 UND		9 40.5		9 42.1
15 24.2	19 18.7	11 33.5		0 UND	5 72.3		25 14.5		12 29.6
			Cost of Sales/Inventory						
			Cost of Sales/Payables						
5.9	4.9	6.6		9.0	7.4		3.5		6.7
25.8	16.7	22.3	Sales/Working Capital	−4.0	−21.8		7.5		27.2
−16.3	−6.4	−8.5		−1.1	−4.5		36.7		NM
4.1	5.0	2.6			2.4		6.4		2.5
(54) 2.8	(63) 2.6	(63) 1.1	EBIT/Interest		.9		2.4	(10)	1.6
1.6	1.5	−1.5			−1.3		−.2		−1.3
			Net Profit + Depr., Dep., Amort./Cur. Mat. L/T/D						
1.0	.7	.9		1.0	1.0		.2		1.1
2.8	1.8	1.9	Fixed/Worth	2.1	3.0		1.2		2.8
−26.6	−10.4	−45.1		5.5	−2.0		NM		−4.2
1.3	1.0	.9		.9	.5		.4		1.3
6.1	2.5	2.5	Debt/Worth	2.3	6.0		1.4		3.9
−30.1	−17.3	−92.5		−12.0	−14.8		NM		−10.3
66.4	43.9	15.1	% Profit Before Taxes/Tangible Net Worth		15.9				
(43) 27.6	(50) 20.3	(49) .6			(11) 1.9				
14.2	8.5	−17.3			−.7				
13.2	15.2	6.2	% Profit Before Taxes/Total Assets	3.1	4.7		11.6		6.5
7.7	6.5	.0		−.8	−.2		1.1		−1.2
1.6	2.4	−8.6		−10.6	−13.3		−4.7		−8.3
7.7	5.1	4.3		1.2	4.0		21.0		3.2
3.0	2.3	2.0	Sales/Net Fixed Assets	.5	1.8		3.1		1.8
1.3	1.2	1.0		.2	1.0		2.2		1.1
1.8	1.5	1.5		.8	1.7		1.9		1.2
1.2	1.1	1.0	Sales/Total Assets	.3	.9		1.1		1.0
.7	.7	.7		.1	.7		.9		.7
2.0	1.4	2.5		6.9	2.0		1.6		
(52) 5.0	(56) 3.9	(57) 6.4	% Depr., Dep., Amort./Sales	(10) 25.9	(17) 4.8		2.6		
7.1	7.1	10.9		34.5	12.2		6.7		
.8	1.0	1.1	% Officers', Directors', Owners' Comp/Sales						
(15) 2.7	(17) 3.3	(19) 2.5							
5.0	8.9	8.1							
1366144M	1529708M	1530656M	Net Sales ($)	4858M	29417M	33634M	75076M	108142M	1279529M
1042419M	1575541M	1463311M	Total Assets ($)	13538M	33143M	39426M	63387M	90479M	1223338M

M = $ thousand   MM = $ million
See Pages 11 through 18 for Explanation of Ratios and Data

Current Data Sorted By Assets   Comparative Historical Data

Type of Statement (current period groupings: 16 (4/1-9/30/02); 28 (10/1/02-3/31/03))

0-500M	500M-2MM	2-10MM	10-50MM	50-100MM	100-250MM	Type of Statement	4/1/98-3/31/99 ALL	4/1/99-3/31/00 ALL
	1	4	8	4	1	Unqualified	8	14
		1	1			Reviewed	6	7
	2	2	2			Compiled	5	6
	4					Tax Returns	1	2
1	1	2	7	3		Other	5	8
1	8	9	18	7	1	**NUMBER OF STATEMENTS**	25	37
%	%	%	%	%	%		%	%
						ASSETS		
			4.2			Cash & Equivalents	9.6	5.7
			13.4			Trade Receivables (net)	10.6	12.3
			17.3			Inventory	18.7	16.2
			7.1			All Other Current	8.8	7.0
			41.9			Total Current	47.6	41.2
			44.6			Fixed Assets (net)	45.4	49.5
			1.9			Intangibles (net)	.3	1.8
			11.6			All Other Non-Current	6.7	7.6
			100.0			Total	100.0	100.0
						LIABILITIES		
			10.8			Notes Payable-Short Term	7.3	5.7
			3.4			Cur. Mat.-L/T/D	5.1	3.9
			7.1			Trade Payables	7.1	9.6
			.8			Income Taxes Payable	.6	.6
			7.2			All Other Current	7.6	5.8
			29.3			Total Current	27.6	25.6
			22.1			Long Term Debt	16.0	26.1
			1.6			Deferred Taxes	1.6	2.3
			.4			All Other Non-Current	8.2	1.2
			46.6			Net Worth	46.6	44.7
			100.0			Total Liabilities & Net Worth	100.0	100.0
						INCOME DATA		
			100.0			Net Sales	100.0	100.0
						Gross Profit		
			94.7			Operating Expenses	93.4	98.1
			5.3			Operating Profit	6.6	1.9
			2.1			All Other Expenses (net)	.1	.3
			3.3			Profit Before Taxes	6.5	1.6
						RATIOS		
			2.8				2.9	2.9
			1.5			Current	1.7	1.8
			.8				1.0	1.2
			1.2				1.5	1.3
			.5			Quick	.5	.6
			.3				.4	.3
			22 17.0				8 43.9	12 30.1
			24 15.0			Sales/Receivables	16 23.4	18 20.5
			35 10.4				27 13.3	28 13.2
						Cost of Sales/Inventory		
						Cost of Sales/Payables		
			4.0				4.3	6.2
			16.0			Sales/Working Capital	9.6	13.5
			−29.7				NM	54.0
			11.5				(22) 9.3	8.0
			(15) 2.5			EBIT/Interest	5.3	(33) 2.1
			−.9				2.7	−1.2
						Net Profit + Depr., Dep., Amort./Cur. Mat. L /T/D		
			.5				.5	.5
			.8			Fixed/Worth	.9	1.2
			2.2				1.4	2.9
			.4				.5	.4
			1.1			Debt/Worth	1.1	1.3
			2.9				1.9	3.4
			20.0				(24) 33.3	(35) 25.5
			(17) 5.1			% Profit Before Taxes/Tangible Net Worth	18.3	13.7
			−20.0				10.0	−16.7
			12.4				16.3	13.4
			2.9			% Profit Before Taxes/Total Assets	9.8	3.7
			−4.7				4.7	−6.5
			7.2				15.1	8.4
			3.7			Sales/Net Fixed Assets	4.1	3.6
			1.6				2.4	2.1
			2.3				3.2	2.6
			1.6			Sales/Total Assets	1.8	1.7
			1.0				1.3	1.2
			3.5				(21) 1.5	(33) 2.0
			(15) 5.9			% Depr., Dep., Amort./Sales	3.0	3.6
			11.2				5.7	10.8
						% Officers', Directors', Owners' Comp/Sales		
423M	25250M	98960M	622438M	707520M	326171M	Net Sales ($)	962853M	1381603M
236M	10393M	53617M	366336M	467249M	229654M	Total Assets ($)	526402M	891921M

© RMA 2003

M = $ thousand   MM = $ million

See Pages 11 through 18 for Explanation of Ratios and Data

Comparative Historical Data | Current Data Sorted By Sales

			Type of Statement	0-1MM	1-3MM	3-5MM	5-10MM	10-25MM	25MM & OVER
10	9	18	Unqualified		1		1	7	9
2	4	3	Reviewed				1	1	1
6	9	5	Compiled		1		2	1	
	4	5	Tax Returns		1	1			
9	10	13	Other	2	1	2	1	2	8
4/1/00-3/31/01 ALL	4/1/01-3/31/02 ALL	4/1/02-3/31/03 ALL		16 (4/1-9/30/02)			28 (10/1/02-3/31/03)		
27	36	44	**NUMBER OF STATEMENTS**	2	4	4	5	11	18
%	%	%	**ASSETS**	%	%	%	%	%	%
2.6	6.1	4.3	Cash & Equivalents					7.5	3.8
9.9	13.3	14.1	Trade Receivables (net)					11.4	15.2
22.5	18.4	17.5	Inventory					20.2	16.5
4.7	6.6	5.9	All Other Current					5.7	7.2
39.7	44.5	41.8	Total Current					44.8	42.7
46.3	46.9	44.6	Fixed Assets (net)					37.5	45.1
.9	1.8	4.1	Intangibles (net)					1.2	5.5
13.1	6.8	9.6	All Other Non-Current					16.5	6.7
100.0	100.0	100.0	Total					100.0	100.0
			LIABILITIES						
14.3	14.0	12.5	Notes Payable-Short Term					5.8	11.3
5.0	3.5	4.5	Cur. Mat.-L/T/D					6.2	3.3
6.3	10.4	9.3	Trade Payables					8.9	8.8
.7	.1	.6	Income Taxes Payable					1.2	.8
9.8	5.8	7.5	All Other Current					6.9	8.3
36.1	33.8	34.6	Total Current					29.1	32.6
19.7	24.5	23.3	Long Term Debt					16.2	20.6
2.3	1.3	1.6	Deferred Taxes					1.0	2.8
1.7	4.2	3.0	All Other Non-Current					3.4	.0
40.2	36.2	37.6	Net Worth					50.3	43.9
100.0	100.0	100.0	Total Liabilities & Net Worth					100.0	100.0
			INCOME DATA						
100.0	100.0	100.0	Net Sales					100.0	100.0
			Gross Profit						
98.2	90.4	97.3	Operating Expenses					98.3	98.0
1.8	9.6	2.7	Operating Profit					1.7	2.0
.6	3.2	1.6	All Other Expenses (net)					.7	-.2
1.2	6.4	1.1	Profit Before Taxes					1.1	2.2
			RATIOS						
1.9 / 1.1 / .7	3.7 / 1.5 / .9	2.1 / 1.3 / .7	Current					2.8 / 1.9 / .9	2.1 / 1.5 / .8
.7 / .3 / .2	1.5 / .5 / .2	1.1 / .5 / .3	Quick					1.3 / .5 / .3	1.3 / .5 / .3
12 30.8 / 21 17.7 / 34 10.7	16 22.9 / 21 17.5 / 28 13.2	20 18.1 / 25 14.8 / 33 10.9	Sales/Receivables					21 17.6 / 22 16.7 / 29 12.5	23 16.1 / 27 13.5 / 35 10.4
			Cost of Sales/Inventory						
			Cost of Sales/Payables						
7.8 / 23.2 / -10.3	5.5 / 15.3 / -33.1	7.9 / 23.5 / -20.7	Sales/Working Capital					3.0 / 9.3 / -31.3	7.0 / 18.8 / -29.7
(23) 6.9 / 1.5 / -.2	(32) 4.9 / 1.6 / -.3	(41) 3.8 / 1.3 / -1.7	EBIT/Interest					(10) 8.5 / .5 / -1.7	(17) 9.4 / 2.5 / -1.0
		(12) 6.5 / 2.7 / -.7	Net Profit + Depr., Dep., Amort./Cur. Mat. L/T/D						
.5 / 1.1 / 2.5	.6 / 1.1 / 3.9	.6 / 1.2 / 2.7	Fixed/Worth					.3 / .7 / 1.6	.5 / 1.6 / 2.2
.5 / 1.7 / 3.2	.6 / .9 / 23.8	.8 / 1.7 / 4.4	Debt/Worth					.6 / 1.0 / 2.5	.7 / 1.6 / 3.1
(23) 14.3 / .7 / -14.3	(30) 20.5 / 5.1 / -13.5	(38) 17.5 / 3.7 / -20.4	% Profit Before Taxes/Tangible Net Worth					17.4 / 5.1 / -23.0	(17) 36.3 / 4.9 / -13.6
8.0 / .4 / -6.9	10.5 / 2.5 / -3.0	10.7 / 1.5 / -6.0	% Profit Before Taxes/Total Assets					11.2 / 2.3 / -7.8	11.8 / 5.4 / -5.3
6.2 / 3.2 / 1.9	6.7 / 3.6 / 1.5	8.4 / 4.0 / 1.9	Sales/Net Fixed Assets					8.2 / 5.1 / 3.1	8.7 / 4.4 / 2.3
1.8 / 1.4 / 1.0	2.0 / 1.6 / .9	2.7 / 1.7 / 1.1	Sales/Total Assets					2.2 / 1.6 / 1.1	2.7 / 1.7 / 1.3
(20) 1.5 / 5.7 / 11.3	(29) 1.3 / 4.7 / 9.8	(39) 1.9 / 3.7 / 10.1	% Depr., Dep., Amort./Sales					2.6 / 3.5 / 7.5	(15) 1.9 / 4.0 / 10.8
		(10) 1.1 / 4.4 / 10.0	% Officers', Directors', Owners' Comp/Sales						
1869821M	1124693M	1780762M	Net Sales ($)	835M	6306M	15845M	38930M	191360M	1527486M
1216302M	878710M	1127485M	Total Assets ($)	1455M	26805M	5494M	22268M	147201M	924262M

M = $ thousand   MM = $ million
See Pages 11 through 18 for Explanation of Ratios and Data

Current Data Sorted By Assets   Comparative Historical Data

						Type of Statement		
		4	1	3	1	Unqualified	4	13
1	2	11				Reviewed	8	5
2	10	12	3	1		Compiled	25	22
4	4	5				Tax Returns	9	7
	2	10	4	4		Other	12	19
	7 (4/1-9/30/02)		77 (10/1/02-3/31/03)				4/1/98-3/31/99	4/1/99-3/31/00
0-500M	500M-2MM	2-10MM	10-50MM	50-100MM	100-250MM		ALL	ALL
7	18	42	8	8	1	NUMBER OF STATEMENTS	58	66
%	%	%	%	%	%	ASSETS	%	%
	11.4	4.9				Cash & Equivalents	8.3	11.9
	12.9	8.9				Trade Receivables (net)	9.4	12.3
	34.2	31.5				Inventory	21.6	16.8
	2.0	2.6				All Other Current	6.2	4.7
	60.5	47.9				Total Current	45.5	45.7
	25.6	32.3				Fixed Assets (net)	40.8	39.4
	3.1	1.9				Intangibles (net)	.9	1.2
	10.8	17.8				All Other Non-Current	12.7	13.6
	100.0	100.0				Total	100.0	100.0
						LIABILITIES		
	18.4	23.0				Notes Payable-Short Term	19.6	16.5
	1.3	3.4				Cur. Mat.-L/T/D	7.5	4.5
	9.2	3.7				Trade Payables	4.4	6.2
	.1	.1				Income Taxes Payable	.1	.0
	5.3	8.8				All Other Current	8.9	10.6
	34.3	39.0				Total Current	40.4	37.8
	31.9	27.0				Long Term Debt	25.8	20.8
	.0	.2				Deferred Taxes	.2	1.3
	1.5	3.5				All Other Non-Current	3.8	3.6
	32.2	30.4				Net Worth	29.8	36.5
	100.0	100.0				Total Liabilities & Net Worth	100.0	100.0
						INCOME DATA		
	100.0	100.0				Net Sales	100.0	100.0
						Gross Profit		
	88.4	90.4				Operating Expenses	89.1	86.0
	11.6	9.6				Operating Profit	10.9	14.0
	1.9	5.2				All Other Expenses (net)	−11.9	1.9
	9.7	4.4				Profit Before Taxes	22.8	12.0
						RATIOS		
	4.1	3.1					1.9	2.6
	1.9	1.1				Current	1.0	1.2
	1.2	.5					.4	.7
	2.7	.8					.9	1.4
	1.0 (41)	.4				Quick	.3 (65)	.5
	.2	.1					.1	.3
0 UND	1 542.7						0 UND	0 UND
8 43.2	9 40.1					Sales/Receivables	5 80.8	11 32.5
18 20.6	24 15.2						21 17.2	37 9.9
						Cost of Sales/Inventory		
						Cost of Sales/Payables		
	3.5	5.8					5.7	5.2
	16.6	122.1				Sales/Working Capital	224.4	35.6
	68.0	−6.2					−7.7	−26.2
	8.4	6.0					7.1	7.4
(17)	4.5 (38)	1.7				EBIT/Interest	(49) 3.0	(58) 2.4
	1.9	.1					1.4	.9
						Net Profit + Depr., Dep.,		5.1
						Amort./Cur. Mat. L /T/D	(10) 2.1	2.1
								.4
	.1	.2					.5	.3
	.4	1.0				Fixed/Worth	1.4	1.0
	3.1	3.7					4.7	2.0
	.5	.7					.8	.5
	2.3	2.1				Debt/Worth	2.3	1.5
	10.3	11.7					10.4	6.5
	111.7	43.1				% Profit Before Taxes/Tangible	53.1	46.6
(17)	24.8 (37)	9.9				Net Worth	(52) 17.4	(59) 18.2
	8.1	−2.9					4.0	.6
	14.1	10.7				% Profit Before Taxes/Total	14.2	19.5
	5.8	1.4				Assets	6.6	5.8
	2.8	−2.2					1.0	−.2
	191.5	30.6					11.8	26.5
	22.2	9.6				Sales/Net Fixed Assets	4.8	5.3
	3.3	1.4					.7	2.4
	5.6	3.2					3.7	3.3
	3.5	1.4				Sales/Total Assets	1.1	1.8
	.4	.4					.4	.7
	.5	.6					.9	1.2
(12)	1.4 (34)	2.5				% Depr., Dep., Amort./Sales	(48) 3.8	(53) 3.4
	6.0	5.8					8.0	6.6
		1.3				% Officers', Directors',	1.0	1.1
	(11)	2.1				Owners' Comp/Sales	(15) 2.4	(23) 3.1
		3.0					21.2	14.0
12309M	90695M	356825M	198737M	306718M	149788M	Net Sales ($)	465137M	814763M
1588M	22989M	189074M	179478M	528950M	132800M	Total Assets ($)	427526M	573157M

© RMA 2003

Comparative Historical Data / Current Data Sorted By Sales

			Type of Statement						
5	6	9	Unqualified		2	1	2	1	3
7	6	14	Reviewed	1	2	3	2	4	2
14	18	28	Compiled	7	6	1	7	6	1
7	6	13	Tax Returns	5	3	1	4		
23	31	20	Other	2	4	2	3	3	6
4/1/00-3/31/01 ALL	4/1/01-3/31/02 ALL	4/1/02-3/31/03 ALL		0-1MM	7 (4/1-9/30/02) 1-3MM	3-5MM	5-10MM	77 (10/1/02-3/31/03) 10-25MM	25MM & OVER
56	67	84	**NUMBER OF STATEMENTS**	15	17	8	18	14	12
%	%	%	**ASSETS**	%	%	%	%	%	%
9.3	10.8	7.2	Cash & Equivalents	6.5	5.7		9.2	7.1	8.4
9.4	9.0	8.4	Trade Receivables (net)	.1	3.6		11.7	17.6	10.5
17.5	22.5	25.1	Inventory	18.6	22.6		32.3	31.0	23.1
6.4	7.0	2.6	All Other Current	1.6	1.6		2.5	2.7	4.7
42.6	49.3	43.2	Total Current	26.8	33.6		55.8	58.3	46.6
40.9	38.4	39.1	Fixed Assets (net)	54.6	41.5		28.9	34.0	38.2
.9	1.5	2.1	Intangibles (net)	1.3	3.5		4.2	.0	.3
15.6	10.8	15.7	All Other Non-Current	17.3	21.4		11.2	7.7	14.9
100.0	100.0	100.0	Total	100.0	100.0		100.0	100.0	100.0
			LIABILITIES						
18.6	16.4	17.2	Notes Payable-Short Term	5.8	13.0		23.4	25.4	20.0
5.3	5.3	3.7	Cur. Mat.-L/T/D	4.5	2.9		3.7	3.6	2.4
8.2	4.1	4.9	Trade Payables	.3	3.7		4.9	10.2	4.9
.8	.0	.1	Income Taxes Payable	.5	.2		.0	.0	.0
7.9	8.4	7.1	All Other Current	10.7	2.5		3.2	7.8	12.1
40.8	34.2	33.1	Total Current	21.7	22.2		35.2	47.0	39.4
23.9	25.6	29.9	Long Term Debt	58.1	30.3		10.6	20.6	27.0
.2	1.0	.2	Deferred Taxes	.0	.3		.1	.0	.8
2.2	3.9	2.5	All Other Non-Current	.4	7.3		2.4	1.0	1.5
32.8	35.4	34.4	Net Worth	19.8	39.9		51.7	31.4	31.2
100.0	100.0	100.0	Total Liabilities & Net Worth	100.0	100.0		100.0	100.0	100.0
			INCOME DATA						
100.0	100.0	100.0	Net Sales	100.0	100.0		100.0	100.0	100.0
			Gross Profit						
87.1	88.6	85.8	Operating Expenses	73.4	82.5		90.6	94.1	89.0
12.9	11.4	14.2	Operating Profit	26.6	17.5		9.4	5.9	10.9
-.5	5.4	3.7	All Other Expenses (net)	14.1	2.8		-.1	.9	4.3
13.5	6.0	10.5	Profit Before Taxes	12.5	14.7		9.5	4.9	6.7
			RATIOS						
1.9	3.2	3.5		7.6	3.9		3.9	2.2	3.2
1.2	1.3	1.5	Current	.8	2.4		1.9	1.3	1.3
.4	.8	.7		.1	.6		.9	.9	1.0
1.2	1.6	1.8		1.6	3.2		2.3	1.4	2.2
.3	.5	(83) .6	Quick	.5	(16) 1.3		.7	.6	.6
.1	.1	.2		.1	.1		.2	.3	.2
0 UND	0 UND	0 UND		0 UND	0 UND		5 67.7	3 142.4	9 42.3
8 46.5	10 36.8	9 41.8	Sales/Receivables	0 UND	5 68.2		13 28.9	15 24.7	15 25.0
19 18.9	31 11.9	22 16.4		4 85.1	22 16.9		32 11.5	25 14.4	28 13.1
			Cost of Sales/Inventory						
			Cost of Sales/Payables						
10.8	2.7	4.1		.9	2.7		4.7	8.6	5.3
40.1	15.1	21.0	Sales/Working Capital	-134.5	15.8		16.6	50.4	27.1
-8.0	-32.1	-16.7		-3.2	-5.3		-128.0	-70.8	765.2
8.1	3.5	8.5		7.8	5.0		15.2	8.7	25.3
(48) 3.0	(53) 1.4	(74) 3.2	EBIT/Interest	(10) 1.7	(15) 3.0	(16)	2.5	5.2	(11) 3.4
1.3	.7	1.3		.6	-.1		1.4	1.7	1.8
			Net Profit + Depr., Dep., Amort./Cur. Mat. L/T/D						
.3	.2	.2		.2	.2		.2	.3	.4
1.2	1.1	1.1	Fixed/Worth	1.3	1.6		.5	1.2	.7
3.3	2.7	3.2		58.5	5.1		1.7	2.2	1.6
.6	.7	.5		.5	.2		.4	1.2	.4
1.8	1.7	1.6	Debt/Worth	5.8	1.6		1.2	2.1	1.9
5.3	5.7	8.6		58.2	7.3		1.8	11.4	8.8
42.4	42.8	51.5	% Profit Before Taxes/Tangible	18.0	54.1		43.4	85.3	34.7
(49) 21.0	(60) 5.9	(74) 12.0	Net Worth	(12) 6.2	(16) 10.2	(17)	9.9	(13) 26.5	(11) 13.2
5.0	-5.3	3.7		-2.1	.5		1.8	6.3	6.2
15.1	8.0	12.4	% Profit Before Taxes/Total	16.9	10.2		11.8	17.9	10.9
8.7	1.9	5.4	Assets	2.0	4.2		4.5	9.4	5.9
1.1	-1.3	1.0		-.3	-1.4		1.0	2.0	3.1
34.7	12.4	27.5		9.3	16.7		34.2	79.2	71.6
4.7	5.3	8.1	Sales/Net Fixed Assets	.9	4.3		10.6	17.8	7.4
1.6	1.4	.9		.3	.5		5.1	5.4	1.0
3.7	2.3	3.9		.5	2.6		4.0	5.5	5.0
1.7	1.2	1.4	Sales/Total Assets	.4	.5		2.4	4.3	2.0
.7	.6	.4		.1	.3		1.4	2.3	.6
.8	.6	.8		4.1	1.0		.8	.3	.5
(47) 2.9	(55) 3.9	(67) 3.2	% Depr., Dep., Amort./Sales	(10) 6.3	(13) 5.6	(14)	2.2	(13) 1.2	(10) 2.6
6.0	9.2	6.9		19.0	9.6		4.3	4.4	7.8
1.7	1.4	1.3							
(16) 2.7	(19) 3.5	(22) 2.3	% Officers', Directors', Owners' Comp/Sales						
9.2	5.0	3.9							
1127277M	1269749M	1115072M	Net Sales ($)	6907M	31550M	30329M	129137M	212019M	705130M
1058695M	1225997M	1054879M	Total Assets ($)	35206M	113927M	43311M	120784M	181237M	560414M

M = $ thousand   MM = $ million
See Pages 11 through 18 for Explanation of Ratios and Data

Current Data Sorted By Assets / Comparative Historical Data

Type of Statement	0-500M	500M-2MM	2-10MM	10-50MM	50-100MM	100-250MM		4/1/98-3/31/99 ALL	4/1/99-3/31/00 ALL
		32 (4/1-9/30/02)			77 (10/1/02-3/31/03)				
Unqualified		1	2	4	1	1		17	13
Reviewed		4	11	10				33	29
Compiled	3	13	7	2				45	41
Tax Returns	17	15	4					39	20
Other	2		8	3		1		29	25
NUMBER OF STATEMENTS	22	33	32	19	1	2		163	128
ASSETS	%	%	%	%	%	%		%	%
Cash & Equivalents	12.9	5.6	8.5	4.8				8.7	9.9
Trade Receivables (net)	4.1	14.8	11.0	9.0				9.3	8.7
Inventory	5.1	21.7	16.9	14.6				16.1	13.7
All Other Current	2.0	2.2	2.7	7.5				4.0	3.4
Total Current	24.1	44.4	39.1	35.9				38.0	35.8
Fixed Assets (net)	60.9	48.6	47.3	53.0				48.3	51.1
Intangibles (net)	1.2	.1	2.9	.2				1.1	1.0
All Other Non-Current	13.7	6.9	10.6	10.9				12.5	12.1
Total	100.0	100.0	100.0	100.0				100.0	100.0
LIABILITIES									
Notes Payable-Short Term	16.4	20.4	10.6	7.0				13.1	13.3
Cur. Mat.-L/T/D	12.6	10.1	12.5	5.1				9.2	9.0
Trade Payables	4.5	7.3	6.7	6.7				5.5	5.0
Income Taxes Payable	.2	.1	.4	.1				.1	.1
All Other Current	6.3	2.2	5.1	7.0				3.7	4.8
Total Current	40.0	40.1	35.3	25.9				31.5	32.2
Long Term Debt	42.0	35.4	27.1	24.3				31.4	28.8
Deferred Taxes	.0	.2	1.4	.8				.4	.4
All Other Non-Current	12.8	7.4	2.2	2.2				2.6	3.1
Net Worth	5.2	16.9	34.0	46.7				34.0	35.5
Total Liabilities & Net Worth	100.0	100.0	100.0	100.0				100.0	100.0
INCOME DATA									
Net Sales	100.0	100.0	100.0	100.0				100.0	100.0
Gross Profit	52.6	32.2	21.1	21.5				32.5	31.7
Operating Expenses	49.7	28.4	20.8	17.4				29.9	26.4
Operating Profit	2.9	3.8	.3	4.0				2.5	5.2
All Other Expenses (net)	1.4	1.4	.8	3.6				1.1	1.4
Profit Before Taxes	1.5	2.4	-.6	.5				1.4	3.8
RATIOS									
Current	2.2	2.7	1.6	2.1				2.5	2.2
	.6	1.1	1.0	1.5				1.2	1.0
	.2	.5	.6	1.0				.6	.4
Quick	1.0	1.4	.9	1.1				1.3	1.1
	.3	.4	.3	.5			(162)	.5	(127) .5
	.0	.1	.2	.2				.2	.2
Sales/Receivables	0 UND	6 62.6	7 49.6	11 34.1				0 999.8	1 546.3
	0 UND	11 31.7	12 31.4	17 21.3				10 35.7	12 31.4
	0 UND	22 16.9	17 21.5	29 12.5				22 16.8	21 17.2
Cost of Sales/Inventory	0 UND	3 120.3	0 UND	5 72.3				0 UND	0 UND
	0 UND	28 12.8	24 15.4	19 18.8				17 21.7	11 32.2
	18 20.6	80 4.6	51 7.1	60 6.1				63 5.8	54 6.7
Cost of Sales/Payables	0 UND	0 UND	5 71.1	6 56.2				0 UND	0 UND
	0 UND	5 75.9	11 33.4	10 35.3				7 55.0	8 48.1
	11 32.8	22 16.7	28 12.9	27 13.4				23 15.6	17 21.5
Sales/Working Capital	21.4	17.6	14.8	6.1				8.0	9.2
	-26.9	64.8	NM	15.1				40.6	277.2
	-9.1	-14.1	-12.8	82.3				-16.6	-9.5
EBIT/Interest	4.0	4.2	3.7	10.3				3.8	4.8
	(20) 1.7	1.9	1.2	(16) 2.0			(152)	1.9	(123) 2.2
	.2	.5	.7	-2.9				1.0	1.1
Net Profit + Depr., Dep., Amort./Cur. Mat. L /T/D								3.6	2.3
							(29)	1.5	(22) 1.5
								.7	1.0
Fixed/Worth	1.1	.9	.7	.6				.5	.7
	3.8	2.5	1.7	1.0				1.1	1.3
	-2.4	NM	3.8	1.8				3.5	2.8
Debt/Worth	.9	1.8	1.1	.5				.8	.8
	5.1	3.5	2.2	1.2				1.8	1.7
	-4.1	-321.9	4.6	2.9				5.0	4.4
% Profit Before Taxes/Tangible Net Worth	57.3	85.0	11.4	13.5				33.6	28.4
	(13) 7.4	(24) 20.0	(28) 4.9	(18) 2.1			(147)	11.6	(112) 14.9
	-1.2	-4.8	-3.2	-11.4				.6	2.3
% Profit Before Taxes/Total Assets	20.5	10.1	6.3	6.9				10.7	9.6
	2.2	3.6	.9	.6				3.5	4.8
	-4.2	-2.6	-1.2	-3.9				.0	.2
Sales/Net Fixed Assets	10.7	18.7	15.2	5.1				9.7	10.3
	5.5	5.2	3.1	2.3				4.6	3.8
	2.4	3.4	1.9	1.3				2.3	2.0
Sales/Total Assets	4.0	4.3	3.1	2.0				3.3	3.2
	3.1	3.0	1.6	1.1				2.1	1.8
	2.0	1.9	1.1	.7				1.3	1.3
% Depr., Dep., Amort./Sales	4.6	1.7	2.3	4.8				2.7	2.6
	(18) 10.2	(31) 6.3	(30) 5.9	(17) 7.1			(157)	5.5	(120) 5.5
	17.3	10.3	11.6	13.8				10.4	9.9
% Officers', Directors', Owners' Comp/Sales	3.1	1.1	1.1					2.3	2.1
	(13) 6.4	(19) 2.6	(14) 1.6				(73)	3.8	(56) 4.8
	8.9	4.3	3.1					7.2	7.7
Net Sales ($)	20289M	130369M	324309M	631440M	28325M	1073649M		2177069M	1404790M
Total Assets ($)	6647M	39298M	149906M	420579M	61438M	381542M		1280280M	1099394M

M = $ thousand   MM = $ million
See Pages 11 through 18 for Explanation of Ratios and Data

Comparative Historical Data | Current Data Sorted By Sales

4/1/00-3/31/01 ALL	4/1/01-3/31/02 ALL	4/1/02-3/31/03 ALL	Type of Statement	0-1MM	1-3MM	3-5MM	5-10MM	10-25MM	25MM & OVER
					32 (4/1-9/30/02)		**77 (10/1/02-3/31/03)**		
14	10	9	Unqualified			1		2	6
17	17	25	Reviewed		2	3	8	9	3
28	32	25	Compiled	4	12	1	4	3	1
29	19	36	Tax Returns	12	14	4	3	3	
24	21	14	Other	1	1	1	2	4	5
112	99	109	**NUMBER OF STATEMENTS**	17	29	10	17	21	15
%	%	%	**ASSETS**	%	%	%	%	%	%
10.1	9.4	7.9	Cash & Equivalents	9.2	8.1	9.3	8.8	7.4	4.8
8.2	9.6	10.2	Trade Receivables (net)	6.9	6.0	13.1	11.3	12.2	16.1
13.2	13.3	15.1	Inventory	7.1	14.7	8.5	19.4	16.2	23.3
4.0	3.1	3.3	All Other Current	2.3	1.2	1.6	4.4	5.3	5.4
35.5	35.4	36.5	Total Current	25.5	30.0	32.5	44.0	41.1	49.6
54.1	53.4	51.3	Fixed Assets (net)	62.9	60.6	52.6	45.5	45.3	34.3
.5	.7	1.2	Intangibles (net)	1.7	.0	.1	.1	4.4	.2
9.9	10.4	11.0	All Other Non-Current	9.9	9.4	14.8	10.4	9.1	16.0
100.0	100.0	100.0	Total	100.0	100.0	100.0	100.0	100.0	100.0
			LIABILITIES						
8.7	13.8	13.8	Notes Payable-Short Term	8.9	18.2	24.8	13.6	10.2	9.1
9.5	11.4	10.2	Cur. Mat.-L/T/D	17.2	10.9	9.0	8.6	9.8	4.1
4.9	5.4	6.4	Trade Payables	5.5	6.1	2.5	6.8	7.8	8.1
.6	.3	.2	Income Taxes Payable	.3	.5	.0	.1	.2	.0
5.2	6.5	4.9	All Other Current	4.0	4.3	1.7	3.0	5.8	10.4
28.9	37.4	35.6	Total Current	35.9	39.9	38.1	32.0	33.7	31.6
27.3	29.8	32.5	Long Term Debt	40.6	45.2	18.7	31.3	22.4	23.1
.5	.6	.6	Deferred Taxes	.0	.1	2.0	.6	.8	1.0
2.5	2.1	5.9	All Other Non-Current	15.2	7.0	.9	2.2	4.7	2.6
40.8	30.1	25.5	Net Worth	8.3	7.7	40.3	33.8	38.3	41.8
100.0	100.0	100.0	Total Liabilities & Net Worth	100.0	100.0	100.0	100.0	100.0	100.0
			INCOME DATA						
100.0	100.0	100.0	Net Sales	100.0	100.0	100.0	100.0	100.0	100.0
33.8	30.7	31.6	Gross Profit	50.2	39.7	29.0	26.8	20.5	17.6
30.9	28.1	29.1	Operating Expenses	46.8	35.3	29.6	25.0	18.3	16.3
2.9	2.5	2.5	Operating Profit	3.5	4.4	-.6	1.8	2.2	1.3
.0	1.9	1.6	All Other Expenses (net)	2.8	2.2	-2.0	3.4	.9	.4
2.9	.6	.9	Profit Before Taxes	.7	2.3	1.4	-1.6	1.3	.9
			RATIOS						
2.9	1.6	1.9	Current	2.5	1.2	1.5	2.8	2.0	2.1
1.2	1.0	1.1		.9	.7	.9	1.3	1.1	1.6
.6	.5	.5		.1	.2	.6	.7	.6	1.1
1.3	.9	1.1	Quick	1.5	.5	1.3	1.6	1.0	1.2
.5	.5	.4		.4	.3	.6	.5	.4	.6
.2	.2	.2		.0	.1	.3	.3	.2	.4
0 999.8	4 102.3	0 UND	Sales/Receivables	0 UND	0 UND	5 68.4	7 55.0	8 47.9	9 42.4
9 39.1	11 34.4	11 34.7		0 UND	7 55.0	12 31.2	10 35.0	16 23.5	17 21.3
20 17.9	24 15.5	21 17.1		9 41.0	15 24.5	19 19.2	28 13.0	27 13.4	36 10.1
0 UND	0 UND	0 UND	Cost of Sales/Inventory	0 UND	0 UND	0 UND	0 UND	8 46.8	7 54.7
6 63.9	14 26.0	14 25.5		0 UND	11 32.3	11 33.4	15 24.6	13 27.2	39 9.4
43 8.5	44 8.3	57 6.4		93 3.9	63 5.8	43 8.5	79 4.6	44 8.4	57 6.4
0 UND	0 999.8	1 243.7	Cost of Sales/Payables	0 UND	0 UND	0 UND	2 190.6	7 54.1	6 59.7
8 46.3	10 36.6	9 41.9		0 UND	8 48.1	6 58.4	8 43.0	10 35.3	13 28.4
20 18.6	19 18.7	19 19.1		11 32.2	18 20.6	16 22.4	33 11.1	28 13.2	19 19.2
8.5	13.1	13.3	Sales/Working Capital	11.5	35.8	43.3	6.2	12.9	6.1
52.4	-779.1	69.2		-73.9	-26.8	-325.1	16.6	54.2	17.2
-15.8	-11.6	-13.2		-4.9	-7.8	-6.3	-46.3	-17.3	82.3
(108) 5.5	(97) 2.8	(103) 4.3	EBIT/Interest	(15) 2.6	(28) 4.5	9.9	(16) 2.9	(20) 5.1	(14) 6.9
1.8	1.4	1.6		1.2	1.9	1.6	1.0	2.1	3.0
.6	.5	.6		-.1	.6	-.2	.1	.9	-.9
(26) 3.5	(19) 1.8	(19) 1.9	Net Profit + Depr., Dep., Amort./Cur. Mat. L/T/D						
1.4	1.5	1.2							
.9	1.1	.6							
.6	.8	.8	Fixed/Worth	1.1	1.3	1.0	.5	.9	.4
1.2	1.9	1.7		3.2	7.7	1.4	1.1	1.0	.7
3.5	4.9	7.2		-2.3	-5.1	2.4	5.0	2.6	1.7
.6	1.1	1.0	Debt/Worth	.8	1.8	1.0	.9	.8	.6
1.3	2.2	2.7		4.6	14.5	1.9	2.8	2.0	1.3
3.6	14.0	13.5		-3.7	-6.2	3.8	5.2	3.7	3.2
(100) 27.3	(81) 29.1	(86) 22.6	% Profit Before Taxes/Tangible Net Worth	(11) 42.4	(16) 103.5	33.4	(16) 10.0	(19) 21.4	(14) 24.3
10.9	6.7	6.4		7.4	21.2	3.8	2.3	6.3	6.4
-.2	-.8	-3.4		-3.1	2.5	-11.2	-10.3	-3.0	-7.5
11.7	8.9	8.6	% Profit Before Taxes/Total Assets	10.2	12.5	18.6	3.0	6.5	8.5
3.6	1.9	1.4		.7	5.3	1.5	-.1	2.0	3.3
-1.2	-1.9	-2.2		-7.3	-1.7	-3.7	-3.5	-1.2	-3.6
7.5	8.2	10.9	Sales/Net Fixed Assets	6.8	7.7	5.0	14.5	22.3	19.5
3.7	3.4	4.3		2.5	4.4	3.2	7.2	3.6	5.1
2.2	2.3	2.0		1.5	2.1	1.9	1.9	1.7	2.8
3.2	3.2	3.6	Sales/Total Assets	3.7	3.2	3.5	3.4	4.1	4.8
2.0	2.0	2.3		2.0	2.7	1.5	2.0	2.0	2.3
1.4	1.4	1.2		1.0	1.6	1.0	1.2	.9	1.1
(105) 3.9	(90) 3.7	(98) 2.6	% Depr., Dep., Amort./Sales	(13) 2.0	(27) 5.6		1.4	(20) 2.1	(12) .9
6.6	7.5	6.8		11.4	9.9		10.0	5.5	3.5
11.3	10.7	11.8		21.6	13.0		11.9	9.0	6.0
(52) 2.0	(35) 1.7	(51) 1.2	% Officers', Directors', Owners' Comp/Sales	(17) .9					
3.4	3.4	2.6		3.2					
7.4	6.1	5.6		5.5					
1515766M	1788266M	2208381M	Net Sales ($)	10806M	58753M	38315M	113579M	282545M	1704383M
956380M	823322M	1059410M	Total Assets ($)	7864M	42501M	31470M	99208M	193962M	684405M

M = $ thousand   MM = $ million
See Pages 11 through 18 for Explanation of Ratios and Data

Current Data Sorted By Assets | Comparative Historical Data

	0-500M	500M-2MM	2-10MM	10-50MM	50-100MM	100-250MM	Type of Statement		4/1/98-3/31/99 ALL	4/1/99-3/31/00 ALL
			1	3	1	1	Unqualified			6
			2				Reviewed			4
	2	2	3		1		Compiled			5
	10	6		1			Tax Returns			7
	6	4	2	3			Other			13
		9 (4/1-9/30/02)		39 (10/1/02-3/31/03)						
	18	12	8	7	2	1	NUMBER OF STATEMENTS			35
	%	%	%	%	%	%	ASSETS		%	%
	19.1	12.3					Cash & Equivalents	D		14.8
	6.1	.4					Trade Receivables (net)	A		3.3
	3.5	.2					Inventory	T		5.8
	1.3	4.6					All Other Current	A		6.2
	30.0	17.5					Total Current			30.1
	51.0	62.8					Fixed Assets (net)	N		57.4
	5.7	2.1					Intangibles (net)	O		3.5
	13.3	17.6					All Other Non-Current	T		9.0
	100.0	100.0					Total			100.0
							LIABILITIES	A		
	9.4	4.6					Notes Payable-Short Term	V		5.8
	16.7	14.3					Cur. Mat.-L/T/D	A		7.6
	2.4	3.4					Trade Payables	I		6.4
	.0	.0					Income Taxes Payable	L		.0
	32.9	9.5					All Other Current	A		20.6
	61.4	31.8					Total Current	B		40.5
	50.1	83.0					Long Term Debt	L		64.2
	.0	.0					Deferred Taxes	E		.5
	7.0	13.9					All Other Non-Current			14.3
	−18.3	−28.7					Net Worth			−19.5
	100.0	100.0					Total Liabilities & Net Worth			100.0
							INCOME DATA			
	100.0	100.0					Net Sales			100.0
							Gross Profit			
	97.2	87.5					Operating Expenses			87.9
	2.8	12.5					Operating Profit			12.1
	3.1	4.4					All Other Expenses (net)			3.3
	−.3	8.2					Profit Before Taxes			8.9
							RATIOS			
	3.8	.9								2.1
	.4	.3					Current			.7
	.1	.1								.3
	3.6	.7								1.6
	.4	.3					Quick			.4
	.1	.1								.1
0	UND	0 UND						0	UND	
0	UND	0 UND					Sales/Receivables	0	UND	
0	UND	0 UND						23	15.9	
							Cost of Sales/Inventory			
							Cost of Sales/Payables			
	11.6	−178.2								9.4
	−29.5	−14.6					Sales/Working Capital			−36.6
	−6.7	−5.9								−8.7
	4.0	8.7								7.5
(16)	1.1	1.1					EBIT/Interest	(31)		3.9
	−2.1	.1								1.7
							Net Profit + Depr., Dep., Amort./Cur. Mat. L /T/D			
	1.3	NM								1.8
	−5.4	−5.6					Fixed/Worth			4.9
	−.7	−.7								−2.7
	3.9	NM								2.7
	−7.3	−9.3					Debt/Worth			8.6
	−2.3	−2.0								−6.5
							% Profit Before Taxes/Tangible Net Worth			98.2
								(20)		64.9
										28.1
	32.9	24.1					% Profit Before Taxes/Total Assets			31.6
	1.6	1.7								10.6
	−12.5	−5.2								1.6
	10.5	4.9								9.6
	6.1	2.7					Sales/Net Fixed Assets			3.1
	2.8	1.6								2.2
	5.0	3.3								3.0
	3.0	1.6					Sales/Total Assets			1.9
	1.4	1.0								1.1
	3.6	5.3								3.6
(14)	6.7	(10) 10.4					% Depr., Dep., Amort./Sales	(27)		6.0
	11.2	23.5								8.0
							% Officers', Directors', Owners' Comp/Sales			
	11050M	22125M	47725M	174680M	128518M	298573M	Net Sales ($)			441285M
	4055M	10245M	28214M	161627M	150573M	196267M	Total Assets ($)			384067M

M = $ thousand   MM = $ million
See Pages 11 through 18 for Explanation of Ratios and Data

Comparative Historical Data | | | Current Data Sorted By Sales

			Type of Statement						
6	4	6	Unqualified				1	1	4
2	1	2	Reviewed				1	1	
6	7	8	Compiled	4	1	2			1
1	5	17	Tax Returns	12	3	1	1		
18	20	15	Other	4	5	3	1		2
4/1/00-3/31/01	4/1/01-3/31/02	4/1/02-3/31/03			9 (4/1-9/30/02)		39 (10/1/02-3/31/03)		
ALL	ALL	ALL		0-1MM	1-3MM	3-5MM	5-10MM	10-25MM	25MM & OVER
33	37	48	**NUMBER OF STATEMENTS**	20	9	6	4	2	7
%	%	%	**ASSETS**	%	%	%	%	%	%
9.6	15.9	14.0	Cash & Equivalents	15.3					
5.4	8.9	7.5	Trade Receivables (net)	4.1					
7.6	6.6	6.4	Inventory	6.1					
9.4	4.6	3.7	All Other Current	3.0					
32.0	36.1	31.5	Total Current	28.4					
53.7	46.7	52.3	Fixed Assets (net)	51.3					
1.6	2.4	3.1	Intangibles (net)	5.1					
12.7	14.7	13.0	All Other Non-Current	15.2					
100.0	100.0	100.0	Total	100.0					
			LIABILITIES						
3.0	4.9	8.0	Notes Payable-Short Term	5.1					
11.7	9.6	11.6	Cur. Mat.-L/T/D	16.4					
7.0	5.7	4.5	Trade Payables	1.6					
.1	.4	.5	Income Taxes Payable	.0					
16.1	10.2	17.8	All Other Current	29.6					
37.9	30.8	42.4	Total Current	52.8					
61.5	61.5	48.3	Long Term Debt	55.4					
.6	.4	.1	Deferred Taxes	.0					
5.1	6.6	7.1	All Other Non-Current	5.9					
−5.1	.7	2.1	Net Worth	−13.9					
100.0	100.0	100.0	Total Liabilities & Net Worth	100.0					
			INCOME DATA						
100.0	100.0	100.0	Net Sales	100.0					
			Gross Profit						
88.7	87.4	90.1	Operating Expenses	96.8					
11.3	12.6	9.9	Operating Profit	3.2					
−.7	2.2	2.8	All Other Expenses (net)	4.4					
11.9	10.4	7.1	Profit Before Taxes	−1.2					
			RATIOS						
1.6	2.9	2.1		5.6					
1.0	1.4	.8	Current	.4					
.4	.6	.2		.2					
.9	2.3	1.7		1.8					
.4	.6	.5	Quick	.4					
.2	.3	.2		.1					
0 UND	0 UND	0 UND		0 UND					
7 54.0	5 78.6	0 UND	Sales/Receivables	0 UND					
18 20.6	31 11.8	19 19.0		0 UND					
			Cost of Sales/Inventory						
			Cost of Sales/Payables						
12.1	6.8	7.3		11.3					
999.8	18.1	−86.8	Sales/Working Capital	−29.5					
−7.0	−16.9	−8.2		−5.1					
11.1	9.4	10.3		4.0					
5.5 (35)	4.3 (44)	2.6	EBIT/Interest	(19) .8					
1.5	2.0	.5		−2.4					
			Net Profit + Depr., Dep., Amort./Cur. Mat. L/T/D						
1.1	.7	1.1		1.1					
2.7	2.8	4.1	Fixed/Worth	−5.3					
NM	−5.3	−3.7		−.7					
1.4	1.2	1.0		3.5					
3.3	3.6	5.6	Debt/Worth	−6.8					
NM	−20.9	−5.0		−2.7					
67.8	57.0	53.9							
33.4 (25)	39.6 (24)	20.5 (27)	% Profit Before Taxes/Tangible Net Worth						
8.9	12.5	9.8							
31.8	32.2	22.4		15.7					
15.3	17.3	4.4	% Profit Before Taxes/Total Assets	−.8					
3.9	4.5	−2.0		−17.1					
6.9	8.0	8.2		6.3					
3.2	4.5	3.2	Sales/Net Fixed Assets	2.9					
1.2	1.7	1.6		1.6					
2.7	2.5	3.6		3.4					
1.6	1.7	1.4	Sales/Total Assets	1.4					
.9	1.0	.9		.9					
4.3	3.1	3.9		4.7					
6.2 (30)	6.7 (31)	6.7 (42)	% Depr., Dep., Amort./Sales	11.1 (17)					
12.0	10.0	12.8		14.8					
		3.8	% Officers', Directors', Owners' Comp/Sales						
	(12)	5.9							
		7.9							
1084294M	547514M	682671M	Net Sales ($)	10242M	13455M	19776M	32315M	40082M	566801M
465685M	361103M	550981M	Total Assets ($)	8700M	9126M	11547M	38535M	15300M	467773M

© RMA 2003

M = $ thousand   MM = $ million
See Pages 11 through 18 for Explanation of Ratios and Data

AGRICULTURE—Shellfish Fishing NAICS 114112 (SIC 0913, 0919)

Current Data Sorted By Assets   **Comparative Historical Data**

0-500M	500M-2MM	2-10MM	10-50MM	50-100MM	100-250MM	Type of Statement	4/1/98-3/31/99 ALL	4/1/99-3/31/00 ALL
			1	1		Unqualified	2	1
1	1		3			Reviewed	6	6
2	2	5	1			Compiled	36	19
10	4	1	1			Tax Returns	11	6
2	2	1	1			Other	8	9
	10 (4/1-9/30/02)		29 (10/1/02-3/31/03)					
15	9	8	7			NUMBER OF STATEMENTS	63	41

%	%	%	%	%	%	**ASSETS**	%	%
16.0						Cash & Equivalents	8.5	13.0
5.4				D	D	Trade Receivables (net)	6.5	7.2
.5				A	A	Inventory	3.6	5.7
11.2				T	T	All Other Current	2.5	3.9
33.1				A	A	Total Current	21.0	29.8
46.6						Fixed Assets (net)	54.4	55.0
12.5				N	N	Intangibles (net)	21.5	6.0
7.6				O	O	All Other Non-Current	3.1	9.2
100.0				T	T	Total	100.0	100.0
						LIABILITIES		
18.3				A	A	Notes Payable-Short Term	41.8	6.6
6.2				V	V	Cur. Mat.-L/T/D	9.9	10.8
7.7				A	A	Trade Payables	15.8	16.9
.0				I	I	Income Taxes Payable	.2	.1
64.3				L	L	All Other Current	5.8	16.7
96.6				A	A	Total Current	73.6	51.0
19.9				B	B	Long Term Debt	57.0	42.8
.5				L	L	Deferred Taxes	.2	.1
6.7				E	E	All Other Non-Current	55.1	26.7
−23.7						Net Worth	−85.8	−20.7
100.0						Total Liabilities & Net Worth	100.0	100.0
						INCOME DATA		
100.0						Net Sales	100.0	100.0
						Gross Profit		
91.5						Operating Expenses	102.5	91.3
8.5						Operating Profit	−2.5	8.7
1.1						All Other Expenses (net)	.0	2.1
7.4						Profit Before Taxes	−2.5	6.6
						RATIOS		
1.5							1.4	1.7
.5						Current	.3	.9
.0							.1	.2
1.5							1.3	1.3
.4						Quick	.2	.5
.0							.1	.1
0 UND							0 UND	0 UND
0 UND						Sales/Receivables	1 289.7	0 UND
4 102.8							15 24.1	21 17.1
						Cost of Sales/Inventory		
						Cost of Sales/Payables		
141.7							21.2	16.8
−16.3						Sales/Working Capital	−7.2	−62.1
−2.6							−3.0	−10.1
16.4							3.8	7.8
(13) 1.5						EBIT/Interest	(57) 1.1	(38) 3.6
−1.5							−1.1	1.3
						Net Profit + Depr., Dep., Amort./Cur. Mat. L /T/D		
.0							1.5	1.1
6.9						Fixed/Worth	−19.6	2.6
−4.6							−.9	−5.7
5.2							4.8	.9
−9.7						Debt/Worth	−4.9	5.8
−3.6							−1.7	−5.2
						% Profit Before Taxes/Tangible Net Worth	100.0	88.5
							(25) 3.8	(27) 30.8
							−17.9	19.9
60.7						% Profit Before Taxes/Total Assets	16.6	31.8
4.5							2.2	14.5
−15.3							−11.0	2.6
111.7							11.4	12.0
33.1						Sales/Net Fixed Assets	2.9	4.0
3.0							1.6	2.4
5.2							2.8	3.7
3.4						Sales/Total Assets	1.6	2.3
1.8							1.0	1.4
.6							3.7	2.4
(11) 12.0						% Depr., Dep., Amort./Sales	(52) 7.8	(31) 4.4
14.4							13.2	6.6
						% Officers', Directors', Owners' Comp/Sales	(23) .9	
							3.3	
							4.3	
22145M	21964M	77917M	347823M			Net Sales ($)	291917M	275727M
3157M	8375M	31707M	160631M			Total Assets ($)	219554M	131671M

© RMA 2003

M = $ thousand   MM = $ million
See Pages 11 through 18 for Explanation of Ratios and Data

Comparative Historical Data				Current Data Sorted By Sales					
					10 (4/1-9/30/02)			29 (10/1/02-3/31/03)	
			Type of Statement						
3	1	2	Unqualified					1	1
2	2	5	Reviewed				2	1	2
7	5	10	Compiled	2	1		3	3	1
15	10	16	Tax Returns	9	5	1	1		1
8	8	6	Other	1	2	1	1		
4/1/00-3/31/01 ALL	4/1/01-3/31/02 ALL	4/1/02-3/31/03 ALL		0-1MM	1-3MM	3-5MM	5-10MM	10-25MM	25MM & OVER
35	26	39	**NUMBER OF STATEMENTS**	12	8	2	7	5	5
%	%	%	**ASSETS**	%	%	%	%	%	%
15.1	13.3	10.9	Cash & Equivalents	9.3					
10.8	14.1	12.6	Trade Receivables (net)	1.8					
11.0	17.1	14.1	Inventory	.0					
5.5	3.5	6.7	All Other Current	1.2					
42.3	48.1	44.4	Total Current	12.3					
42.0	34.5	38.3	Fixed Assets (net)	67.9					
3.3	1.7	8.2	Intangibles (net)	9.1					
12.3	15.8	9.1	All Other Non-Current	10.7					
100.0	100.0	100.0	Total	100.0					
			LIABILITIES						
56.8	13.4	13.2	Notes Payable-Short Term	13.7					
8.0	4.1	8.7	Cur. Mat.-L/T/D	9.4					
12.4	8.4	10.4	Trade Payables	5.4					
.2	.1	.0	Income Taxes Payable	.0					
95.7	4.1	27.6	All Other Current	65.2					
173.1	30.1	60.0	Total Current	93.6					
57.8	31.8	19.8	Long Term Debt	25.7					
.1	.2	.7	Deferred Taxes	.0					
12.6	5.9	3.5	All Other Non-Current	3.1					
−143.6	32.0	15.9	Net Worth	−22.5					
100.0	100.0	100.0	Total Liabilities & Net Worth	100.0					
			INCOME DATA						
100.0	100.0	100.0	Net Sales	100.0					
			Gross Profit						
91.9	93.7	91.9	Operating Expenses	87.3					
8.1	6.3	8.1	Operating Profit	12.7					
1.9	1.6	.8	All Other Expenses (net)	2.2					
6.2	4.7	7.3	Profit Before Taxes	10.4					
			RATIOS						
3.8	4.2	2.4		.8					
1.1	1.5	1.3	Current	.2					
.1	.8	.5		.0					
2.9	2.8	1.5		.5					
.7	.7	.5	Quick	.1					
.1	.2	.2		.0					
0 UND	0 UND	0 UND		0 UND					
0 UND	12 31.1	7 53.1	Sales/Receivables	0 UND					
28 13.0	29 12.5	27 13.4		0 UND					
			Cost of Sales/Inventory						
			Cost of Sales/Payables						
10.7	5.2	12.2		−69.1					
109.0	16.3	61.7	Sales/Working Capital	−4.9					
−9.6	−40.1	−16.0		−2.0					
8.5	4.5	15.3							
3.7	(25) 2.3	(35) 3.2	EBIT/Interest						
1.2	1.3	1.0							
			Net Profit + Depr., Dep., Amort./Cur. Mat. L/T/D						
.4	.5	.0		1.1					
2.1	1.0	1.0	Fixed/Worth	14.4					
34.1	1.7	6.9		−5.2					
1.2	1.2	.7		1.0					
7.3	2.3	2.8	Debt/Worth	NM					
−4.5	5.6	−9.9		−5.7					
113.9	74.7	92.9							
(25) 38.2	(24) 23.9	(28) 39.2	% Profit Before Taxes/Tangible Net Worth						
2.3	7.0	9.0							
40.0	15.2	25.2		26.5					
12.5	7.4	7.3	% Profit Before Taxes/Total Assets	2.9					
.6	.9	1.0		−1.7					
56.5	60.1	111.7		17.8					
6.0	7.8	20.6	Sales/Net Fixed Assets	3.2					
2.7	3.4	2.6		1.1					
4.6	3.4	3.7		2.7					
2.8	2.0	2.7	Sales/Total Assets	1.6					
1.7	1.4	1.4		1.0					
.6	1.4	.6							
(26) 5.0	(21) 4.8	(27) 2.9	% Depr., Dep., Amort./Sales						
9.7	7.6	12.0							
2.3		1.9							
(13) 3.8		(16) 2.5	% Officers', Directors', Owners' Comp/Sales						
24.1		9.3							
945311M	397453M	469849M	Net Sales ($)	4927M	12087M	7537M	53095M	79757M	312446M
373009M	176798M	203870M	Total Assets ($)	4963M	4252M	749M	18817M	55811M	119278M

M = $ thousand   MM = $ million
See Pages 11 through 18 for Explanation of Ratios and Data

Current Data Sorted By Assets **Comparative Historical Data**

0-500M	500M-2MM	2-10MM	10-50MM	50-100MM	100-250MM	Type of Statement	4/1/98-3/31/99 ALL	4/1/99-3/31/00 ALL
	8	28				Unqualified	12	9
	1	5				Reviewed	7	9
	4	3	1			Compiled	6	7
1	2	1				Tax Returns		1
		7				Other	5	9
	29 (4/1-9/30/02)		32 (10/1/02-3/31/03)					
1	15	44	1			NUMBER OF STATEMENTS	30	35
%	%	%	%	%	%	ASSETS	%	%
	14.4	8.9				Cash & Equivalents	7.8	10.5
	12.3	16.6				Trade Receivables (net)	13.5	14.2
	10.1	6.7				Inventory	10.8	6.5
	3.0	4.1				All Other Current	4.9	7.3
	39.8	36.4				Total Current	36.9	38.5
	49.0	52.7				Fixed Assets (net)	54.7	53.0
	.2	.2	D	D		Intangibles (net)	1.3	.7
	11.0	10.8	A	A		All Other Non-Current	7.1	7.8
	100.0	100.0	T	T		Total	100.0	100.0
			A	A		LIABILITIES		
	11.2	5.9				Notes Payable-Short Term	11.4	10.7
	3.3	4.7	N	N		Cur. Mat.-L/T/D	4.1	4.6
	7.8	5.9	O	O		Trade Payables	5.9	5.8
	.4	.1	T	T		Income Taxes Payable	.1	.2
	8.4	12.3				All Other Current	5.3	11.8
	31.0	28.9	A	A		Total Current	26.9	33.1
	20.2	16.4	V	V		Long Term Debt	25.7	21.4
	.0	.0	A	A		Deferred Taxes	1.2	.7
	.2	1.2	I	I		All Other Non-Current	1.5	2.3
	48.5	53.5	L	L		Net Worth	44.7	42.5
	100.0	100.0	A	A		Total Liabilities & Net Worth	100.0	100.0
			B	B		INCOME DATA		
	100.0	100.0	L	L		Net Sales	100.0	100.0
			E	E		Gross Profit		
	97.4	88.7				Operating Expenses	88.8	86.3
	2.6	11.3				Operating Profit	11.2	13.7
	.3	.0				All Other Expenses (net)	−.5	2.9
	2.3	11.3				Profit Before Taxes	11.7	10.8
						RATIOS		
	3.3	1.6					2.3	1.9
	1.4	1.3				Current	1.6	1.3
	.9	1.0					1.0	.7
	1.4	1.4					1.6	1.4
	.9	1.0				Quick	1.0	.7
	.4	.5					.2	.2
	2 171.3	9 40.6					8 47.7	7 53.0
	28 13.2	40 9.1				Sales/Receivables	27 13.7	18 20.2
	56 6.6	100 3.7					59 6.2	61 6.0
						Cost of Sales/Inventory		
						Cost of Sales/Payables		
	4.9	8.8					4.2	4.8
	17.6	15.9				Sales/Working Capital	11.0	11.8
	−21.7	NM					307.5	−15.2
	14.5	25.8					6.2	9.3
	(13) 2.1	(40) 10.3				EBIT/Interest	(29) 2.2	(33) 2.3
	.3	1.8					1.0	.7
		45.6				Net Profit + Depr., Dep.,		
		(11) 12.1				Amort./Cur. Mat. L /T/D		
		2.5						
	.5	.6					.7	.8
	.9	.9				Fixed/Worth	1.1	1.1
	2.7	1.6					3.3	2.7
	.2	.4					.5	.6
	.6	.7				Debt/Worth	1.4	1.4
	3.7	1.5					3.6	3.7
	25.7	49.9					37.3	35.5
	(14) 9.0	20.2				% Profit Before Taxes/Tangible	(28) 19.8	7.5
	−4.9	4.2				Net Worth	−1.6	−1.8
	15.2	26.8					14.6	24.1
	3.8	8.5				% Profit Before Taxes/Total	6.7	2.5
	−2.7	2.5				Assets	−.2	−.5
	6.8	3.9					3.9	5.2
	4.4	2.4				Sales/Net Fixed Assets	2.7	2.3
	2.0	1.0					1.3	1.1
	2.7	1.5					2.0	1.6
	2.0	1.2				Sales/Total Assets	1.4	1.1
	.9	.7					.8	.5
	1.7	4.1					2.5	2.6
	(43) 3.6	5.5				% Depr., Dep., Amort./Sales	(29) 5.4	(34) 6.2
	7.0	10.7					9.3	9.0
						% Officers', Directors', Owners' Comp/Sales		
707M	35462M	197160M	5113M			Net Sales ($)	496631M	508167M
122M	19248M	176116M	22472M			Total Assets ($)	369116M	350335M

M = $ thousand   MM = $ million
See Pages 11 through 18 for Explanation of Ratios and Data

Comparative Historical Data | Current Data Sorted By Sales

			Type of Statement	0-1MM	1-3MM	3-5MM	5-10MM	10-25MM	25MM & OVER
12	32	36	Unqualified	2	13	8	11	2	
5	3	6	Reviewed		2	2	1	1	
7	7	8	Compiled	1	4	1	2		
2	3	4	Tax Returns	1		2	1		
13	12	7	Other		5	1	1		
4/1/00-3/31/01 ALL	4/1/01-3/31/02 ALL	4/1/02-3/31/03 ALL		29 (4/1-9/30/02)			32 (10/1/02-3/31/03)		
39	57	61	**NUMBER OF STATEMENTS**	4	24	14	16	3	
%	%	%	**ASSETS**	%	%	%	%	%	%
8.6	10.0	10.9	Cash & Equivalents	9.3	8.6	11.2			D
13.7	20.4	15.2	Trade Receivables (net)	13.4	14.7	18.7			A
4.5	7.1	7.7	Inventory	6.6	10.6	7.2			T
10.4	7.5	3.8	All Other Current	1.2	5.8	4.7			A
37.2	45.0	37.5	Total Current	30.5	39.7	41.7			
51.1	43.4	51.8	Fixed Assets (net)	57.2	47.4	50.7			N
1.3	.4	.2	Intangibles (net)	.4	.0	.0			O
10.4	11.2	10.5	All Other Non-Current	11.9	12.9	7.6			T
100.0	100.0	100.0	Total	100.0	100.0	100.0			
			LIABILITIES						A
10.7	12.4	7.0	Notes Payable-Short Term	7.5	8.8	5.2			V
6.0	2.6	4.3	Cur. Mat.-L/T/D	5.2	4.2	4.2			A
5.9	7.1	6.4	Trade Payables	6.2	6.1	7.9			I
.3	.1	.2	Income Taxes Payable	.3	.0	.2			L
10.1	11.7	11.1	All Other Current	7.2	12.7	18.0			A
33.0	33.9	28.9	Total Current	26.3	31.7	35.5			B
26.0	13.6	17.5	Long Term Debt	21.1	17.1	18.5			L
.6	.2	.0	Deferred Taxes	.0	.0	.0			E
1.2	1.2	1.3	All Other Non-Current	.5	.8	.1			
39.2	51.1	52.3	Net Worth	52.1	50.3	45.8			
100.0	100.0	100.0	Total Liabilities & Net Worth	100.0	100.0	100.0			
			INCOME DATA						
100.0	100.0	100.0	Net Sales	100.0	100.0	100.0			
			Gross Profit						
88.2	87.1	90.5	Operating Expenses	93.3	90.2	84.2			
11.8	12.8	9.5	Operating Profit	6.6	9.8	15.8			
4.2	.4	.3	All Other Expenses (net)	.6	.1	.6			
7.6	12.5	9.2	Profit Before Taxes	6.0	9.8	15.2			
			RATIOS						
1.9 / 1.2 / .6	1.7 / 1.3 / 1.0	2.0 / 1.3 / 1.0	Current	1.6 / 1.2 / 1.0	2.1 / 1.2 / .6	1.6 / 1.1 / .8			
1.2 / .6 / .2	1.6 / .9 / .4	1.4 / 1.0 / .5	Quick	1.3 / 1.0 / .5	1.3 / .8 / .6	1.3 / .8 / .5			
6 64.2 / 23 16.0 / 101 3.6	10 37.5 / 39 9.5 / 90 4.0	7 52.4 / 37 9.9 / 91 4.0	Sales/Receivables	6 65.8 / 41 8.9 / 95 3.9	3 117.0 / 16 22.9 / 47 7.7	10 38.0 / 39 9.4 / 102 3.6			
			Cost of Sales/Inventory						
			Cost of Sales/Payables						
3.6 / 15.0 / -12.0	5.6 / 11.9 / 476.0	6.9 / 15.8 / -117.8	Sales/Working Capital	7.0 / 18.0 / -119.0	6.2 / 15.5 / -5.7	9.4 / 23.3 / -31.9			
(33) 12.7 / 2.5 / 1.2	(51) 25.5 / 7.1 / 1.7	(55) 21.0 / 5.4 / 1.1	EBIT/Interest	(21) 22.5 / 2.9 / -.9	(13) 28.2 / 5.4 / 1.2	(15) 22.8 / 11.2 / 4.2			
(10) 7.1 / 3.4 / 2.0	(10) 148.4 / 13.1 / 2.1	(13) 38.2 / 7.5 / 2.0	Net Profit + Depr., Dep., Amort./Cur. Mat. L/T/D						
.7 / 1.0 / 4.3	.5 / .8 / 1.3	.6 / .9 / 1.6	Fixed/Worth	.7 / 1.0 / 2.7	.5 / .7 / 2.2	.7 / 1.0 / 1.5			
.6 / 1.5 / 4.3	.4 / .8 / 2.5	.4 / .7 / 1.7	Debt/Worth	.4 / .7 / 2.8	.4 / .8 / 3.2	.6 / .9 / 1.8			
(34) 33.0 / 11.1 / 5.5	(56) 45.4 / 21.0 / 7.7	(60) 47.4 / 18.5 / 2.6	% Profit Before Taxes/Tangible Net Worth	31.7 / 11.4 / -10.3	56.9 / 20.2 / .0	(15) 50.0 / 37.0 / 9.1			
10.1 / 4.4 / 1.1	24.2 / 9.2 / 2.1	21.1 / 6.6 / 1.5	% Profit Before Taxes/Total Assets	14.5 / 4.8 / -2.3	16.1 / 5.8 / .7	29.8 / 13.3 / 5.4			
4.0 / 1.9 / 1.2	6.0 / 3.2 / 1.8	4.9 / 2.7 / 1.1	Sales/Net Fixed Assets	3.5 / 1.7 / .9	4.9 / 3.4 / 1.7	5.7 / 3.0 / 2.0			
1.5 / .9 / .5	1.8 / 1.2 / .7	1.7 / 1.2 / .7	Sales/Total Assets	1.8 / .9 / .5	1.6 / 1.2 / .8	1.8 / 1.3 / 1.2			
(36) 3.4 / 5.8 / 13.3	(53) 2.3 / 4.3 / 8.2	(60) 3.5 / 5.3 / 10.5	% Depr., Dep., Amort./Sales	(23) 4.8 / 7.9 / 14.2	3.3 / 5.3 / 8.1	3.7 / 4.7 / 8.1			
			% Officers', Directors', Owners' Comp/Sales						
406677M	389834M	238442M	Net Sales ($)	2990M	49585M	54214M	97234M	34419M	
365962M	416440M	217958M	Total Assets ($)	4279M	59852M	52212M	87947M	13668M	

M = $ thousand   MM = $ million
See Pages 11 through 18 for Explanation of Ratios and Data

Current Data Sorted By Assets							**Comparative Historical Data**		
	1	1	5			**Type of Statement**			
	2	1	3			Unqualified			5
2	3	2				Reviewed			9
2	2	1				Compiled			10
3	2	6	2			Tax Returns			7
						Other			15
	15 (4/1-9/30/02)		23 (10/1/02-3/31/03)					4/1/98-3/31/99	4/1/99-3/31/00
0-500M	500M-2MM	2-10MM	10-50MM	50-100MM	100-250MM			ALL	ALL
7	10	11	10			**NUMBER OF STATEMENTS**			46
%	%	%	%	%	%	**ASSETS**		%	%
	2.8	5.9	1.4			Cash & Equivalents			8.9
	22.9	21.6	21.3			Trade Receivables (net)			17.8
	5.7	4.9	31.0			Inventory			11.5
	3.5	7.4	4.6	D	D	All Other Current	D		4.0
	35.0	39.8	58.3	A	A	Total Current	A		42.2
	58.2	43.7	26.7	T	T	Fixed Assets (net)	T		45.5
	1.2	.9	2.8	A	A	Intangibles (net)	A		3.1
	5.6	15.7	12.2			All Other Non-Current			9.2
	100.0	100.0	100.0	N	N	Total	N		100.0
				O	O	**LIABILITIES**	O		
	11.3	6.8	19.7	T	T	Notes Payable-Short Term	T		9.8
	4.0	3.7	2.0			Cur. Mat.-L/T/D			3.9
	8.6	7.6	10.3	A	A	Trade Payables	A		9.3
	.0	.5	.6	V	V	Income Taxes Payable	V		.2
	6.5	3.8	8.2	A	A	All Other Current	A		6.1
	30.4	22.5	40.8	I	I	Total Current	I		29.3
	33.8	25.4	9.7	L	L	Long Term Debt	L		15.8
	.3	.8	2.3	A	A	Deferred Taxes	A		1.4
	.5	2.1	.9	B	B	All Other Non-Current	B		6.2
	34.9	49.3	46.3	L	L	Net Worth	L		47.4
	100.0	100.0	100.0	E	E	Total Liabilities & Net Worth	E		100.0
						INCOME DATA			
	100.0	100.0	100.0			Net Sales			100.0
						Gross Profit			
	90.9	92.4	99.3			Operating Expenses			90.6
	9.1	7.6	.7			Operating Profit			9.4
	1.3	3.2	−.4			All Other Expenses (net)			1.3
	7.8	4.4	1.2			Profit Before Taxes			8.0
						RATIOS			
	1.4	2.1	2.2						3.1
	.9	1.4	1.3			Current			1.3
	.6	.9	1.1						1.0
	1.2	1.9	1.0						1.8
	.8	1.2	.7			Quick		(45)	.7
	.4	.8	.2						.4
0 UND	0 UND	22 16.6					8	47.4	
49 7.5	33 11.1	52 7.0				Sales/Receivables		29	12.6
81 4.5	67 5.5	102 3.6					50	7.3
						Cost of Sales/Inventory			
						Cost of Sales/Payables			
	14.1	5.4	4.4						6.5
	−522.4	12.4	7.9			Sales/Working Capital			16.2
	−16.3	−83.1	72.1						−443.5
	8.2	12.2							7.0
	2.3	1.9				EBIT/Interest		(38)	2.9
	1.5	1.1							1.2
						Net Profit + Depr., Dep.,			3.6
						Amort./Cur. Mat. L./T/D		(15)	2.2
									1.1
	.9	.5	.3						.6
	1.4	.8	.3			Fixed/Worth			1.1
	NM	1.9	.8						2.0
	.6	.5	.7						.4
	1.7	1.4	1.4			Debt/Worth			1.3
	NM	2.7	2.4						2.5
		23.8	24.6			% Profit Before Taxes/Tangible			39.4
		8.3	6.3			Net Worth		(43)	19.9
		1.5	1.8						6.8
	14.1	10.4	11.0			% Profit Before Taxes/Total			14.5
	5.9	5.6	2.8			Assets			6.0
	1.6	.6	.4						.8
	5.2	5.1	15.8						9.6
	3.2	4.0	11.5			Sales/Net Fixed Assets			2.9
	1.5	2.8	1.9						1.6
	2.3	2.1	1.7						2.2
	1.5	1.6	1.5			Sales/Total Assets			1.6
	.9	1.4	1.0						.9
		2.1	1.3						2.1
		4.7	2.1			% Depr., Dep., Amort./Sales		(43)	4.7
		6.5	6.1						7.9
						% Officers', Directors',			1.4
						Owners' Comp/Sales		(14)	5.4
									11.8
5659M	19250M	74115M	336566M			Net Sales ($)			422482M
1830M	12842M	48784M	243689M			Total Assets ($)			436677M

© RMA 2003

M = $ thousand   MM = $ million
See Pages 11 through 18 for Explanation of Ratios and Data

Comparative Historical Data | Current Data Sorted By Sales

				Type of Statement						
4		6	7	Unqualified		1		1	3	2
7		4	6	Reviewed	1	1	1			3
10		10	7	Compiled	2	3	1	1		
8		11	5	Tax Returns	1	2	1	1		
13		12	13	Other	4	2	1	2	2	2
4/1/00-		4/1/01-	4/1/02-			15 (4/1-9/30/02)		23 (10/1/02-3/31/03)		
3/31/01		3/31/02	3/31/03							
ALL		ALL	ALL		0-1MM	1-3MM	3-5MM	5-10MM	10-25MM	25MM & OVER
42		43	38	**NUMBER OF STATEMENTS**	8	9	4	5	5	7
%		%	%	**ASSETS**	%	%	%	%	%	%
10.3		10.1	6.6	Cash & Equivalents						
18.3		16.5	21.5	Trade Receivables (net)						
12.6		15.9	11.8	Inventory						
4.4		4.6	5.0	All Other Current						
45.6		47.1	45.0	Total Current						
46.1		44.3	43.7	Fixed Assets (net)						
2.1		2.3	1.4	Intangibles (net)						
6.1		6.4	9.9	All Other Non-Current						
100.0		100.0	100.0	Total						
				LIABILITIES						
8.6		9.8	14.2	Notes Payable-Short Term						
6.6		5.2	3.6	Cur. Mat.-L/T/D						
9.8		7.4	8.5	Trade Payables						
.7		1.3	.3	Income Taxes Payable						
5.4		9.7	8.3	All Other Current						
31.1		33.5	34.8	Total Current						
19.5		27.2	24.7	Long Term Debt						
1.3		1.0	1.1	Deferred Taxes						
4.9		2.3	2.0	All Other Non-Current						
43.1		36.0	37.4	Net Worth						
100.0		100.0	100.0	Total Liabilities & Net Worth						
				INCOME DATA						
100.0		100.0	100.0	Net Sales						
				Gross Profit						
92.9		93.0	94.7	Operating Expenses						
7.1		7.0	5.3	Operating Profit						
1.2		2.1	1.5	All Other Expenses (net)						
5.9		4.8	3.8	Profit Before Taxes						
				RATIOS						
2.6		3.1	2.0							
1.3		1.4	1.2	Current						
1.0		1.1	.8							
1.8		2.3	1.2							
.9		1.1	.8	Quick						
.5		.4	.5							
15 24.4	0	UND	8 47.3							
35 10.3	29	12.5	41 8.9	Sales/Receivables						
60 6.1	63	5.8	80 4.5							
				Cost of Sales/Inventory						
				Cost of Sales/Payables						
5.4		5.5	7.1							
20.5		10.9	24.0	Sales/Working Capital						
−233.0		43.5	−41.4							
5.6		5.6	10.5							
(40) 2.1	(38)	1.9	(35) 2.3	EBIT/Interest						
.7		.6	1.3							
		3.4		Net Profit + Depr., Dep.,						
	(11)	3.0		Amort./Cur. Mat. L/T/D						
		1.8								
.5		.4	.5							
1.2		1.2	1.0	Fixed/Worth						
2.1		3.0	2.0							
.7		.6	.7							
1.5		1.3	1.5	Debt/Worth						
3.4		5.0	2.9							
41.0		32.8	25.8	% Profit Before Taxes/Tangible						
(39) 14.5	(38)	12.5	(32) 6.8	Net Worth						
−.6		−1.0	2.4							
16.1		13.8	10.4	% Profit Before Taxes/Total						
5.0		5.8	4.8	Assets						
−.8		−1.5	.6							
9.9		10.9	11.1							
4.1		4.5	4.4	Sales/Net Fixed Assets						
2.0		2.0	1.9							
2.3		2.2	2.2							
1.7		1.5	1.6	Sales/Total Assets						
1.1		1.1	1.2							
2.2		2.0	1.9							
(37) 6.4	(36)	5.2	(34) 4.2	% Depr., Dep., Amort./Sales						
7.8		9.1	8.2							
3.0		2.9	4.6	% Officers', Directors',						
(17) 6.6	(13)	9.3	(10) 7.1	Owners' Comp/Sales						
14.4		19.0	13.9							
700827M		530551M	435590M	Net Sales ($)	4570M	16113M	14083M	31991M	77516M	291317M
497600M		414651M	307145M	Total Assets ($)	5717M	15068M	8292M	23533M	54263M	200272M

M = $ thousand   MM = $ million
See Pages 11 through 18 for Explanation of Ratios and Data

Current Data Sorted By Assets　　　　　　　　　　　　　　Comparative Historical Data

Type of Statement	4/1/98-3/31/99 ALL	4/1/99-3/31/00 ALL
Unqualified	38	40
Reviewed	45	59
Compiled	35	41
Tax Returns	10	15
Other	29	34

Current Data column groupings:
- 83 (4/1-9/30/02): 0-500M, 500M-2MM
- 110 (10/1/02-3/31/03): 2-10MM, 10-50MM, 50-100MM, 100-250MM

	0-500M	500M-2MM	2-10MM	10-50MM	50-100MM	100-250MM		4/1/98-3/31/99 ALL	4/1/99-3/31/00 ALL
NUMBER OF STATEMENTS	19	38	67	51	7	11		157	189
	%	%	%	%	%	%	**ASSETS**	%	%
	19.9	9.7	8.2	2.6		7.8	Cash & Equivalents	10.0	8.5
	17.1	22.9	24.8	18.2		18.6	Trade Receivables (net)	21.6	19.8
	3.7	11.0	10.8	21.5		22.6	Inventory	15.2	15.0
	4.9	5.0	7.7	6.2		4.0	All Other Current	7.0	6.0
	45.6	48.5	51.4	48.5		53.0	Total Current	53.7	49.3
	50.0	43.9	40.4	40.6		35.9	Fixed Assets (net)	37.5	41.1
	.1	.3	.3	1.3		3.6	Intangibles (net)	1.1	1.1
	4.3	7.3	7.8	9.5		7.5	All Other Non-Current	7.7	8.5
	100.0	100.0	100.0	100.0		100.0	Total	100.0	100.0
							LIABILITIES		
	34.1	13.1	13.1	15.6		13.4	Notes Payable-Short Term	11.5	12.6
	5.3	5.5	3.8	4.4		2.0	Cur. Mat.-L/T/D	3.4	3.8
	19.0	9.9	14.6	11.4		8.1	Trade Payables	14.6	13.8
	.1	.1	.3	.3		.2	Income Taxes Payable	.3	.2
	11.6	5.6	10.2	9.6		10.4	All Other Current	11.1	8.6
	70.1	34.2	42.0	41.4		34.2	Total Current	40.9	39.0
	24.2	26.1	18.1	20.8		23.2	Long Term Debt	18.1	19.7
	.2	.2	.6	.6		1.3	Deferred Taxes	.9	1.0
	20.6	3.9	1.4	2.4		1.5	All Other Non-Current	4.1	3.8
	−15.1	35.5	37.9	34.8		39.8	Net Worth	35.9	36.5
	100.0	100.0	100.0	100.0		100.0	Total Liabilities & Net Worth	100.0	100.0
							INCOME DATA		
	100.0	100.0	100.0	100.0		100.0	Net Sales	100.0	100.0
							Gross Profit		
	99.2	95.6	90.0	93.9		89.3	Operating Expenses	94.5	93.3
	.8	4.4	10.0	6.1		10.7	Operating Profit	5.5	6.7
	.6	.2	1.9	1.2		.3	All Other Expenses (net)	.9	.7
	.2	4.2	8.0	4.9		10.4	Profit Before Taxes	4.6	6.0
							RATIOS		
	2.8	2.9	1.8	1.5		2.5	Current	2.2	2.0
	.9	1.6	1.3	1.1		1.6		1.3	1.3
	.5	.8	1.0	.9		1.2		1.0	.9
	2.8	1.6	1.3	.8		1.1	Quick	1.3	1.3
	.8	.9	.8	.5		.9		.8	.7
	.2	.5	.6	.3		.3		.4	.4
	0 UND	5 70.0	13 27.0	25 14.6		15 24.0	Sales/Receivables	16 22.3	14 26.7
	2 213.1	35 10.5	35 10.6	36 10.3		32 11.5		35 10.5	31 11.8
	22 17.0	62 5.8	54 6.7	51 7.1		111 3.3		56 6.6	58 6.3
							Cost of Sales/Inventory		
							Cost of Sales/Payables		
	10.6	6.0	7.6	7.2		3.9	Sales/Working Capital	6.7	6.5
	−257.5	14.9	16.4	27.0		12.3		17.0	17.5
	−14.5	−18.9	−999.8	−66.1		18.0		664.1	−73.2
	4.7	8.6	13.5	6.3		46.6	EBIT/Interest	6.2	7.0
	(17) 2.2	(35) 2.4	(62) 4.1	(50) 2.8		3.3		(140) 2.8	(171) 2.7
	−5.7	.3	1.9	1.1		1.8		1.1	1.3
			3.8	7.1			Net Profit + Depr., Dep., Amort./Cur. Mat. L/T/D	6.1	6.4
			(18) 1.9	(19) 2.7				(41) 3.4	(61) 2.1
			.9	.6				1.7	1.2
	1.2	.4	.5	.5		.4	Fixed/Worth	.5	.5
	13.7	1.2	1.0	.9		.8		1.0	1.0
	−.6	4.7	1.7	2.0		1.8		2.1	2.1
	.7	.6	.8	1.1		.9	Debt/Worth	.7	.6
	16.7	2.0	1.4	1.9		1.8		1.7	1.8
	−4.4	9.2	2.9	3.8		2.6		4.8	4.2
	60.3	51.3	28.5	33.0		50.4	% Profit Before Taxes/Tangible Net Worth	34.9	32.4
	(10) 17.5	(32) 16.9	(63) 16.2	(46) 14.8		15.4		(140) 15.3	(177) 13.5
	−6.1	.7	7.2	3.9		10.4		3.1	2.9
	9.1	14.7	11.8	11.3		19.3	% Profit Before Taxes/Total Assets	12.4	10.3
	3.6	6.6	5.1	5.1		7.9		4.5	4.6
	−21.5	−2.1	2.6	.4		2.9		.4	.7
	66.1	13.8	10.2	7.6		12.0	Sales/Net Fixed Assets	14.4	10.8
	9.3	4.4	4.7	4.6		8.7		4.8	4.3
	2.8	2.3	2.0	1.8		1.9		1.9	1.5
	11.8	2.8	3.0	2.2		2.1	Sales/Total Assets	3.0	2.7
	4.8	1.8	1.8	1.5		1.9		1.6	1.4
	2.1	1.0	.9	.8		1.5		.9	.8
	.5	1.3	1.5	1.3		1.1	% Depr., Dep., Amort./Sales	1.1	1.4
	(17) 2.7	(36) 2.3	(63) 3.0	(49) 3.2		(10) 1.5		(149) 2.5	(177) 2.9
	9.0	6.5	6.8	5.8		3.8		7.0	7.6
		1.5	1.5	.9			% Officers', Directors', Owners' Comp/Sales	1.0	1.9
		(15) 6.0	(14) 2.9	(10) 1.2				(44) 2.4	(52) 2.6
		9.4	6.3	2.8				5.1	6.3
	39694M	124476M	808562M	1882747M	674421M	3356929M	Net Sales ($)	3880659M	4294228M
	5018M	48643M	360801M	1076799M	512903M	1853820M	Total Assets ($)	2368887M	2883953M

M = $ thousand　　MM = $ million
See Pages 11 through 18 for Explanation of Ratios and Data

Comparative Historical Data   **Current Data Sorted By Sales**

			Type of Statement	0-1MM	1-3MM	3-5MM	5-10MM	10-25MM	25MM & OVER
34	26	35	Unqualified	1	4	3		7	20
39	37	58	Reviewed	3	5	8	9	17	16
41	45	45	Compiled	6	13	5	6	7	8
20	13	19	Tax Returns	8	4	3	3		1
53	51	36	Other	2	3	2	9	11	9
4/1/00-3/31/01	4/1/01-3/31/02	4/1/02-3/31/03		83 (4/1-9/30/02)			110 (10/1/02-3/31/03)		
ALL	ALL	ALL							
187	172	193	**NUMBER OF STATEMENTS**	20	29	21	27	42	54
%	%	%	**ASSETS**	%	%	%	%	%	%
8.2	9.1	8.3	Cash & Equivalents	13.2	9.3	9.7	7.7	6.4	7.0
20.9	20.4	21.4	Trade Receivables (net)	9.1	19.8	27.5	25.4	20.0	23.6
14.0	15.8	13.8	Inventory	2.8	9.5	6.5	9.6	17.3	22.3
6.9	4.8	6.1	All Other Current	8.9	5.9	6.8	7.9	5.3	4.7
50.0	50.2	49.5	Total Current	33.9	44.6	50.6	50.5	49.1	57.5
38.3	39.1	41.9	Fixed Assets (net)	62.8	47.4	37.5	40.3	40.2	35.0
1.7	1.0	.8	Intangibles (net)	.2	.3	.1	1.0	1.0	1.2
10.0	9.7	7.8	All Other Non-Current	3.1	7.7	11.8	8.1	9.7	6.3
100.0	100.0	100.0	Total	100.0	100.0	100.0	100.0	100.0	100.0
			LIABILITIES						
14.4	12.8	15.7	Notes Payable-Short Term	11.4	10.8	12.4	25.5	16.0	15.9
4.0	4.2	4.3	Cur. Mat.-L/T/D	5.7	6.2	3.9	5.0	3.7	2.9
12.7	13.6	13.3	Trade Payables	6.2	9.2	21.1	9.8	11.8	18.1
.6	.3	.2	Income Taxes Payable	.0	.0	.2	.5	.3	.2
10.9	11.0	9.2	All Other Current	6.7	10.8	8.1	11.0	9.4	8.8
42.7	41.8	42.7	Total Current	30.0	37.1	45.7	51.9	41.2	45.9
22.5	18.2	21.4	Long Term Debt	28.9	24.9	25.9	20.3	18.5	17.9
.9	.6	.6	Deferred Taxes	.3	.2	.6	.4	.6	.9
4.4	4.6	4.0	All Other Non-Current	14.4	4.2	8.9	1.0	1.2	2.0
29.4	34.8	31.3	Net Worth	26.5	33.7	19.0	26.4	38.5	33.3
100.0	100.0	100.0	Total Liabilities & Net Worth	100.0	100.0	100.0	100.0	100.0	100.0
			INCOME DATA						
100.0	100.0	100.0	Net Sales	100.0	100.0	100.0	100.0	100.0	100.0
			Gross Profit						
93.6	93.6	92.8	Operating Expenses	89.3	90.1	94.7	92.5	95.3	93.1
6.4	6.4	7.2	Operating Profit	10.7	9.9	5.3	7.4	4.7	6.9
1.2	1.9	1.2	All Other Expenses (net)	3.1	2.0	.6	1.0	.4	1.0
5.2	4.5	6.0	Profit Before Taxes	7.6	7.9	4.7	6.5	4.3	5.9
			RATIOS						
1.7	1.7	1.9	Current	2.9	2.3	1.5	1.9	1.9	1.7
1.2	1.2	1.2		.9	1.5	1.1	1.2	1.2	1.2
.9	1.0	.9		.5	.9	.7	.9	1.0	1.1
1.2	1.2	1.2	Quick	2.5	1.5	1.2	1.2	1.2	1.0
.7	.8	.7		.6	1.0	.8	.9	.6	.7
.3	.4	.4		.2	.4	.3	.4	.3	.4
15 24.9	14 26.9	13 28.4	Sales/Receivables	0 UND	4 97.0	9 40.7	12 31.5	16 23.0	25 14.8
31 11.8	31 11.7	33 11.2		0 UND	35 10.4	29 12.5	31 11.9	37 10.0	32 11.4
58 6.3	52 7.0	53 6.8		56 6.5	92 4.0	56 6.5	107 3.4	49 7.5	50 7.3
			Cost of Sales/Inventory						
			Cost of Sales/Payables						
7.5	8.1	7.6	Sales/Working Capital	5.3	4.0	9.9	7.6	9.3	7.1
27.5	20.9	20.3		-385.2	10.3	34.1	14.0	22.3	21.2
-55.2	-188.3	-63.0		-8.1	-15.4	-13.3	-98.5	-84.6	74.0
(166) 5.4	(147) 5.6	(181) 8.3	EBIT/Interest	(17) 6.4	(26) 8.0	(19) 17.9	(26) 5.9	(41) 9.2	(52) 12.1
2.2	2.6	3.2		2.8	2.4	4.4	3.3	2.9	3.3
1.0	.9	1.1		-.7	-1.9	1.2	1.2	1.1	1.4
(56) 5.6	(45) 6.6	(55) 4.4	Net Profit + Depr., Dep., Amort./Cur. Mat. L/T/D				(14) 5.1		(17) 4.9
2.0	2.2	2.5					1.8		2.6
.9	.7	1.2					.5		1.9
.5	.5	.6	Fixed/Worth	1.1	.6	.6	.5	.5	.4
1.0	1.1	1.1		1.8	1.3	1.7	1.1	1.1	.9
2.5	2.1	2.3		NM	5.1	NM	2.0	1.8	1.6
.9	1.1	.8	Debt/Worth	.6	.6	.7	.8	.9	1.2
2.0	2.0	1.8		2.0	1.3	2.2	1.3	1.6	2.2
5.4	4.8	4.0		NM	9.5	NM	3.5	2.9	3.8
(165) 29.8	(156) 31.5	(169) 39.9	% Profit Before Taxes/Tangible Net Worth	(15) 27.2	(24) 44.0	(16) 58.9	(25) 34.2	(38) 25.0	(51) 43.7
10.7	14.6	16.2		17.3	19.6	17.6	12.9	11.9	21.8
.8	1.4	4.9		8.1	3.9	4.2	3.0	.9	7.6
9.6	10.5	13.1	% Profit Before Taxes/Total Assets	12.3	15.1	18.4	9.4	11.3	14.3
3.0	4.0	5.3		5.9	6.5	5.3	5.0	3.7	6.1
-.2	.0	.4		-3.3	-5.6	.6	.5	.0	1.3
13.9	12.7	12.7	Sales/Net Fixed Assets	6.9	9.8	21.7	13.8	9.6	19.2
5.3	5.1	4.6		1.9	3.4	7.8	4.4	6.5	7.0
2.1	2.0	2.0		.8	1.2	2.9	1.8	3.2	3.4
2.9	2.9	2.8	Sales/Total Assets	2.5	2.0	3.1	3.6	3.0	3.5
1.7	1.7	1.7		.7	1.2	1.9	1.6	1.9	1.9
1.0	.9	.9		.4	.8	1.1	.8	1.2	1.4
(172) 1.1	(161) 1.2	(181) 1.3	% Depr., Dep., Amort./Sales	(16) 3.4	(28) 1.6	1.0	(25) 1.9	(41) 1.5	(50) 1.0
2.3	2.8	2.8		11.0	5.3	2.1	4.6	2.9	1.6
6.8	6.1	6.5		26.7	8.4	4.1	7.7	5.4	3.7
(47) 1.9	(41) 1.7	(48) 1.5	% Officers', Directors', Owners' Comp/Sales					(11) .9	
3.9	3.4	3.6						1.9	
6.4	4.9	7.0						4.3	
4258723M	3918141M	6886829M	Net Sales ($)	10419M	52491M	85088M	198555M	650074M	5890202M
2643617M	2329785M	3857984M	Total Assets ($)	17550M	60224M	58761M	156806M	466459M	3098184M

M = $ thousand   MM = $ million
See Pages 11 through 18 for Explanation of Ratios and Data

Current Data Sorted By Assets | **Comparative Historical Data**

0-500M	500M-2MM	2-10MM	10-50MM	50-100MM	100-250MM	Type of Statement	4/1/98-3/31/99 ALL	4/1/99-3/31/00 ALL
		7	2	1		Unqualified		
2	3	5	2			Reviewed		
4	6					Compiled		
7	4	3				Tax Returns		
3	2	1	4			Other		
10 (4/1-9/30/02)			46 (10/1/02-3/31/03)					
16	15	16	8	1		NUMBER OF STATEMENTS		
%	%	%	%	%	%	**ASSETS**	%	%
23.2	10.0	6.7			DATA NOT AVAILABLE	Cash & Equivalents	DATA NOT AVAILABLE	DATA NOT AVAILABLE
11.8	15.1	25.7				Trade Receivables (net)		
13.2	33.7	22.4				Inventory		
2.4	.9	4.5				All Other Current		
50.6	59.7	59.2				Total Current		
35.9	30.6	32.8				Fixed Assets (net)		
3.3	.8	2.7				Intangibles (net)		
10.2	8.9	5.3				All Other Non-Current		
100.0	100.0	100.0				Total		
						LIABILITIES		
13.2	13.2	14.3				Notes Payable-Short Term		
3.4	2.8	4.1				Cur. Mat.-L/T/D		
28.9	5.4	13.9				Trade Payables		
.0	.0	.0				Income Taxes Payable		
12.5	7.3	7.1				All Other Current		
58.0	28.8	39.4				Total Current		
30.1	35.4	18.5				Long Term Debt		
.0	.4	1.2				Deferred Taxes		
11.4	5.3	.1				All Other Non-Current		
.5	30.2	40.8				Net Worth		
100.0	100.0	100.0				Total Liabilities & Net Worth		
						INCOME DATA		
100.0	100.0	100.0				Net Sales		
						Gross Profit		
94.2	96.2	93.3				Operating Expenses		
5.8	3.8	6.7				Operating Profit		
.0	2.1	5.7				All Other Expenses (net)		
5.8	1.8	1.0				Profit Before Taxes		
						RATIOS		
5.2	4.0	2.9						
1.5	1.6	1.7				Current		
.4	1.3	1.1						
4.1	1.0	1.8						
1.0	.7	1.2				Quick		
.1	.4	.4						
0 UND	**5** 69.9	**26** 13.9						
0 UND	**18** 20.6	**41** 8.9				Sales/Receivables		
22 16.3	**36** 10.1	**91** 4.0						
						Cost of Sales/Inventory		
						Cost of Sales/Payables		
8.2	4.1	4.3						
32.4	10.3	11.3				Sales/Working Capital		
-28.2	27.7	28.2						
19.9	4.5	7.3						
(11) 5.4	(13) 2.1	(13) 2.1				EBIT/Interest		
-1.0	.4	.5						
						Net Profit + Depr., Dep., Amort./Cur. Mat. L/T/D		
.4	.4	.2						
3.3	.9	.6				Fixed/Worth		
-1.8	1.9	2.0						
.5	.8	.5						
5.2	2.8	1.4				Debt/Worth		
-6.8	6.7	7.8						
346.2	34.5	37.0						
(11) 76.8	(13) 6.3	9.5				% Profit Before Taxes/Tangible Net Worth		
-2.1	-9.2	-31.9						
49.8	8.4	11.8						
5.7	4.6	4.6				% Profit Before Taxes/Total Assets		
-6.8	-2.1	-1.6						
30.4	15.3	29.0						
13.2	11.9	10.9				Sales/Net Fixed Assets		
6.4	1.7	3.5						
7.3	3.1	2.5						
3.3	2.0	2.1				Sales/Total Assets		
2.2	.8	1.4						
1.4	.9	1.4						
(13) 3.2	(14) 2.0	(14) 2.2				% Depr., Dep., Amort./Sales		
4.9	11.5	7.5						
						% Officers', Directors', Owners' Comp/Sales		
12339M	64714M	131030M	260148M	97210M		Net Sales ($)		
3411M	19111M	64087M	193976M	74776M		Total Assets ($)		

M = $ thousand MM = $ million

See Pages 11 through 18 for Explanation of Ratios and Data

Comparative Historical Data | Current Data Sorted By Sales

4/1/00-3/31/01 ALL	4/1/01-3/31/02 ALL	4/1/02-3/31/03 ALL		0-1MM	1-3MM	3-5MM	5-10MM	10-25MM	25MM & OVER
			Type of Statement						
	11	10	Unqualified				1	6	3
	3	12	Reviewed	2	1	3	4	1	1
	6	10	Compiled	2	7				1
	5	14	Tax Returns	7	5	2			
	11	10	Other	4	2		1	1	2
				10 (4/1-9/30/02)		46 (10/1/02-3/31/03)			
	36	56	**NUMBER OF STATEMENTS**	15	15	5	6	8	7
%	%	%	**ASSETS**	%	%	%	%	%	%
DATA NOT AVAILABLE	8.9	11.7	Cash & Equivalents	18.3	13.3				
	24.5	18.0	Trade Receivables (net)	6.2	16.1				
	18.6	21.7	Inventory	17.4	17.2				
	1.4	4.5	All Other Current	2.5	4.4				
	53.4	55.9	Total Current	44.4	51.0				
	31.0	32.5	Fixed Assets (net)	39.3	42.4				
	3.3	3.0	Intangibles (net)	3.6	.6				
	12.3	8.5	All Other Non-Current	12.7	6.0				
	100.0	100.0	Total	100.0	100.0				
			LIABILITIES						
	17.0	15.4	Notes Payable-Short Term	10.3	15.6				
	3.1	3.4	Cur. Mat.-L/T/D	3.6	2.8				
	11.3	15.1	Trade Payables	27.0	8.1				
	.2	.0	Income Taxes Payable	.0	.0				
	7.6	9.1	All Other Current	10.6	7.8				
	39.2	43.0	Total Current	51.6	34.4				
	16.2	24.8	Long Term Debt	38.2	36.9				
	.5	.5	Deferred Taxes	.0	.4				
	1.3	5.2	All Other Non-Current	4.2	11.3				
	42.8	26.6	Net Worth	6.1	17.0				
	100.0	100.0	Total Liabilities & Net Worth	100.0	100.0				
			INCOME DATA						
	100.0	100.0	Net Sales	100.0	100.0				
			Gross Profit						
	96.7	95.1	Operating Expenses	90.8	94.4				
	3.3	4.9	Operating Profit	9.2	5.6				
	1.8	2.0	All Other Expenses (net)	5.2	1.7				
	1.4	2.9	Profit Before Taxes	4.1	3.9				
			RATIOS						
	2.1	3.2		5.4	2.5				
	1.5	1.6	Current	1.6	1.5				
	1.0	1.0		.3	1.0				
	1.5	1.5		3.2	2.2				
	1.0	.8	Quick	.6	.8				
	.4	.3		.1	.5				
	13 28.2	**3** 106.4		**0** UND	**0** UND				
	27 13.4	**27** 13.5	Sales/Receivables	**0** UND	**27** 13.7				
	44 8.4	**47** 7.8		**15** 24.1	**97** 3.8				
			Cost of Sales/Inventory						
			Cost of Sales/Payables						
	7.9	5.3		4.4	4.7				
	17.2	12.1	Sales/Working Capital	19.5	18.7				
	155.9	186.7		–24.0	49.3				
	12.5	7.0		14.5	6.3				
	(30) 3.5	(45) 2.4	EBIT/Interest	(10) 1.7	(13) 2.1				
	1.3	.5		–1.0	1.1				
			Net Profit + Depr., Dep., Amort./Cur. Mat. L/T/D						
	.3	.4		.4	.9				
	.6	.9	Fixed/Worth	1.2	1.5				
	1.3	3.5		93.9	–30.0				
	.5	.7		.4	1.2				
	1.1	1.4	Debt/Worth	3.3	2.8				
	4.6	10.0		94.9	–200.8				
	28.6	41.0		315.5	34.3				
	(33) 11.4	(49) 9.4	% Profit Before Taxes/Tangible Net Worth	(12) 39.1	(11) 1.8				
	1.2	–5.8		–7.8	–9.1				
	10.8	11.2		43.8	9.3				
	3.4	4.5	% Profit Before Taxes/Total Assets	–.4	4.8				
	.2	–2.0		–5.3	–4.2				
	31.0	20.6		17.2	15.3				
	9.8	10.5	Sales/Net Fixed Assets	8.4	6.7				
	4.1	3.0		2.5	1.3				
	4.0	3.2		3.5	5.5				
	2.3	2.1	Sales/Total Assets	2.3	2.0				
	1.6	1.3		.8	.7				
	.7	1.4		1.4	1.4				
	(31) 1.8	(50) 2.7	% Depr., Dep., Amort./Sales	(11) 4.6	3.1				
	4.8	6.2		6.5	9.0				
	3.7	4.0							
	(11) 4.8	(19) 6.2	% Officers', Directors', Owners' Comp/Sales						
	7.7	17.1							
	828772M	**565441M**	Net Sales ($)	**7629M**	**24600M**	**20092M**	**41396M**	**118029M**	**353695M**
	501172M	**355361M**	Total Assets ($)	**8323M**	**34880M**	**9660M**	**16452M**	**88268M**	**197778M**

M = $ thousand MM = $ million

See Pages 11 through 18 for Explanation of Ratios and Data

MINING

Current Data Sorted By Assets   Comparative Historical Data

0-500M	17 (4/1-9/30/02) 500M-2MM	2-10MM	171 (10/1/02-3/31/03) 10-50MM	50-100MM	100-250MM	Type of Statement	4/1/98-3/31/99 ALL	4/1/99-3/31/00 ALL
	1	13	23	11	25	Unqualified	43	38
	2	7	2			Reviewed	8	11
1	4	5	2	1		Compiled	13	14
1	1	3				Tax Returns	5	1
	14	17	38	7	10	Other	70	62
2	22	45	65	19	35	**NUMBER OF STATEMENTS**	139	126
%	%	%	%	%	%	**ASSETS**	%	%
	15.9	9.1	6.4	5.8	4.4	Cash & Equivalents	9.5	6.9
	14.9	11.7	10.5	12.2	9.7	Trade Receivables (net)	8.6	8.5
	1.8	3.5	1.7	1.4	1.7	Inventory	1.5	1.7
	10.7	4.9	2.1	2.3	1.3	All Other Current	2.1	1.9
	43.2	29.1	20.6	21.7	17.1	Total Current	21.8	19.1
	44.6	58.2	71.3	70.0	71.6	Fixed Assets (net)	61.0	67.2
	1.5	1.2	2.3	.5	1.8	Intangibles (net)	1.8	1.0
	10.7	11.4	5.8	7.7	9.5	All Other Non-Current	15.4	12.8
	100.0	100.0	100.0	100.0	100.0	Total	100.0	100.0
						LIABILITIES		
	12.8	5.0	2.1	5.6	.5	Notes Payable-Short Term	9.6	4.8
	.7	8.1	3.4	1.3	1.3	Cur. Mat.-L/T/D	3.8	4.2
	14.6	8.0	9.0	11.2	10.0	Trade Payables	7.0	7.7
	.6	.6	.1	.1	.1	Income Taxes Payable	.1	.2
	19.1	13.4	3.7	5.4	4.1	All Other Current	15.6	3.6
	47.7	35.0	18.3	23.6	16.0	Total Current	36.1	20.6
	37.8	25.2	32.9	26.6	30.0	Long Term Debt	25.0	34.4
	.1	.5	2.4	.7	3.6	Deferred Taxes	1.4	1.1
	6.7	7.7	2.8	2.9	3.9	All Other Non-Current	7.6	10.9
	7.7	31.6	43.6	46.2	46.5	Net Worth	29.9	33.0
	100.0	100.0	100.0	100.0	100.0	Total Liabilities & Net Worth	100.0	100.0
						INCOME DATA		
	100.0	100.0	100.0	100.0	100.0	Net Sales	100.0	100.0
	45.3	51.9	55.4	53.6	50.7	Gross Profit	46.1	56.3
	28.3	37.1	41.2	34.3	34.1	Operating Expenses	49.4	41.1
	17.0	14.8	14.2	19.3	16.6	Operating Profit	−3.3	15.2
	5.7	6.0	6.4	5.4	3.6	All Other Expenses (net)	−2.8	7.3
	11.3	8.8	7.9	13.9	13.0	Profit Before Taxes	−.5	7.9
						RATIOS		
	5.4	2.4	2.0	2.3	1.5		1.9	2.2
	1.3	1.1	1.1	1.2	1.0	Current	1.0	1.1
	.4	.4	.8	1.0	.8		.5	.6
	3.4	2.0	1.7	2.3	1.3		(138) 1.6	(125) 1.9
	1.0	.8	1.0	1.1	.8	Quick	.8	.9
	.2	.2	.5	.9	.6		.3	.5
0 UND	10 37.3	23 16.2	30 12.1	32 11.3			9 42.1	20 18.0
23 15.8	41 8.9	58 6.3	50 7.3	67 5.4	Sales/Receivables	39 9.3	58 6.3
71 5.1	70 5.2	88 4.1	73 5.0	111 3.3		68 5.4	87 4.2
0 UND	0 UND	0 UND	0 UND	0 UND		0 UND	0 UND
0 UND	0 UND	0 UND	0 UND	2 179.5	Cost of Sales/Inventory	0 UND	0 UND
1 411.9	8 43.7	1 282.3	2 149.4	30 12.2		10 37.6	18 20.4
0 UND	7 55.2	22 16.2	61 6.0	55 6.6		7 51.3	23 15.6
31 11.7	22 16.9	102 3.6	81 4.5	127 2.9	Cost of Sales/Payables	51 7.1	81 4.5
160 2.3	124 3.0	221 1.6	214 1.7	266 1.4		112 3.3	203 1.8
	4.6	6.6	5.7	9.3	10.2		6.3	5.5
	20.5	31.6	29.9	32.3	101.5	Sales/Working Capital	106.4	35.9
	−7.8	−7.6	−15.9	−123.5	−9.2		−4.6	−7.1
	20.0	7.7	9.1	12.6	9.9		6.3	5.6
	(17) 2.6	(36) 2.7	(58) 2.4	(16) 6.0	(30) 4.5	EBIT/Interest	(108) 1.6	(104) 2.6
	1.3	1.0	.4	4.3	1.3		−1.9	1.1
						Net Profit + Depr., Dep., Amort./Cur. Mat. L /T/D	(19) 4.5	(21) 37.9
							2.3	1.8
							.9	.6
	.4	.9	1.1	.9	1.2		.9	1.1
	1.0	1.9	1.8	1.3	1.7	Fixed/Worth	1.7	2.0
	−3.7	5.7	3.9	2.6	2.2		4.7	6.2
	.6	.5	.5	.4	.7		.5	.6
	4.6	3.0	1.6	1.0	1.3	Debt/Worth	1.4	2.1
	−5.4	11.7	4.1	2.9	2.4		5.6	7.5
	75.6	41.8	24.5	29.8	18.6		18.9	26.4
	(16) 24.3	(40) 19.7	(62) 8.0	(18) 14.0	11.1	% Profit Before Taxes/Tangible Net Worth	(114) 3.2	(107) 7.4
	5.4	2.6	−1.9	4.6	2.5		−16.7	.2
	21.0	13.2	9.7	10.5	8.8		9.9	8.3
	6.3	3.4	3.1	4.1	5.2	% Profit Before Taxes/Total Assets	1.4	3.0
	1.4	.2	−1.2	1.5	.9		−9.9	−.8
	10.1	4.3	.9	1.8	.9		1.8	1.5
	2.8	1.4	.5	.5	.4	Sales/Net Fixed Assets	.7	.6
	1.7	.6	.3	.3	.3		.5	.3
	2.5	1.4	.6	1.1	.6		.8	.7
	1.3	.7	.4	.4	.3	Sales/Total Assets	.4	.4
	.8	.4	.2	.2	.2		.3	.3
	2.2	3.9	13.6	1.8	4.3		9.6	8.8
	(15) 5.9	(40) 14.8	(60) 23.5	(14) 16.0	(20) 12.1	% Depr., Dep., Amort./Sales	(101) 18.5	(104) 17.4
	13.0	24.3	34.3	27.3	19.5		32.9	26.2
						% Officers', Directors', Owners' Comp/Sales	(11) 1.7	
							6.7	
							10.5	
1079M	41687M	229102M	1363124M	1208199M	4158443M	Net Sales ($)	2756180M	2084347M
557M	26102M	225312M	1670666M	1259200M	5518075M	Total Assets ($)	4331388M	5130428M

M = $ thousand   MM = $ million
See Pages 11 through 18 for Explanation of Ratios and Data

Comparative Historical Data | Current Data Sorted By Sales

42	65	73	Type of Statement						
42	65	73	Unqualified	1	7	8	11	15	31
9	9	11	Reviewed	1	3	2	3		2
12	15	13	Compiled	2	4	4	2	1	
5	4	5	Tax Returns	1	1	3			
75	56	86	Other	4	20	10	18	14	20
4/1/00-3/31/01 ALL	4/1/01-3/31/02 ALL	4/1/02-3/31/03 ALL			17 (4/1-9/30/02)			171 (10/1/02-3/31/03)	
				0-1MM	1-3MM	3-5MM	5-10MM	10-25MM	25MM & OVER
143	149	188	**NUMBER OF STATEMENTS**	9	35	27	34	30	53
%	%	%	**ASSETS**	%	%	%	%	%	%
9.0	9.3	7.9	Cash & Equivalents		14.3	6.7	4.1	7.0	5.7
13.5	12.1	11.3	Trade Receivables (net)		10.7	8.4	10.5	9.5	15.8
1.4	1.7	2.1	Inventory		1.3	3.0	.9	2.8	2.9
4.2	4.0	3.6	All Other Current		3.5	5.2	3.9	3.0	2.0
28.1	27.2	24.9	Total Current		29.8	23.3	19.4	22.3	26.4
60.6	61.2	64.9	Fixed Assets (net)		56.4	68.3	70.0	69.1	64.1
.6	1.5	1.6	Intangibles (net)		.9	1.5	3.9	.1	1.9
10.8	10.0	8.5	All Other Non-Current		12.8	6.8	6.7	8.5	7.5
100.0	100.0	100.0	Total		100.0	100.0	100.0	100.0	100.0
			LIABILITIES						
2.9	4.7	4.1	Notes Payable-Short Term		13.1	.9	1.6	1.2	3.6
3.2	4.2	3.7	Cur. Mat.-L/T/D		6.1	4.7	5.4	2.8	1.2
9.7	11.3	9.8	Trade Payables		11.6	6.2	8.5	6.7	14.2
.2	.4	.3	Income Taxes Payable		.3	.1	.5	.2	.2
5.4	5.2	8.0	All Other Current		10.5	14.3	5.4	3.2	5.9
21.5	25.8	25.9	Total Current		41.6	26.2	21.3	14.1	25.0
23.9	27.8	31.0	Long Term Debt		36.2	25.1	31.1	35.9	24.3
1.4	1.6	1.7	Deferred Taxes		.0	2.3	1.8	1.6	2.9
8.7	5.8	4.6	All Other Non-Current		4.2	7.9	4.5	2.3	3.4
44.6	39.0	36.8	Net Worth		17.9	38.4	41.3	46.2	44.5
100.0	100.0	100.0	Total Liabilities & Net Worth		100.0	100.0	100.0	100.0	100.0
			INCOME DATA						
100.0	100.0	100.0	Net Sales		100.0	100.0	100.0	100.0	100.0
60.0	56.6	52.2	Gross Profit		58.1	57.4	56.2	50.5	44.6
30.2	32.0	36.4	Operating Expenses		40.0	40.6	42.2	40.1	27.9
29.8	24.5	15.7	Operating Profit		18.2	16.8	13.9	10.4	16.8
1.7	4.6	5.5	All Other Expenses (net)		9.1	5.9	6.5	4.4	3.2
28.0	19.9	10.2	Profit Before Taxes		9.1	10.9	7.5	6.0	13.5
			RATIOS						
3.0	1.9	2.0	Current		2.2	2.0	1.7	2.5	2.0
1.3	1.1	1.1			1.1	1.0	1.1	1.3	1.0
.8	.6	.7			.3	.5	.6	1.0	.9
2.7	1.5	1.7	Quick		2.2	1.3	1.4	2.3	1.7
1.1	.9	.9			.9	.9	.8	1.1	.9
.6	.5	.5			.2	.3	.2	.7	.6
22 16.3	17 20.9	18 20.8	Sales/Receivables		1 299.2	15 24.7	1 302.5	34 10.8	27 13.7
61 6.0	35 10.5	51 7.1			52 7.0	41 8.8	52 5.9	62 5.9	54 6.7
86 4.3	60 6.1	84 4.3			81 4.5	90 4.1	89 4.1	91 4.0	88 4.1
0 UND	0 UND	0 UND	Cost of Sales/Inventory		0 UND	0 UND	0 UND	0 UND	0 UND
0 UND	0 UND	0 UND			0 UND	0 UND	0 UND	0 UND	0 UND
1 331.2	3 125.5	6 65.6			0 UND	3 129.3	2 206.1	19 19.7	13 28.1
20 17.8	22 16.8	17 21.8	Cost of Sales/Payables		11 32.0	10 35.2	15 24.0	30 12.2	32 11.4
72 5.1	67 5.5	78 4.7			73 5.0	100 3.7	89 4.1	97 3.8	69 5.3
208 1.8	208 1.8	213 1.7			259 1.4	384 .9	317 1.1	202 1.8	211 1.7
4.4	6.9	7.7	Sales/Working Capital		5.0	5.7	8.5	6.8	10.0
14.3	84.7	35.8			24.7	196.2	33.3	13.1	74.9
-14.6	-9.6	-9.5			-4.6	-8.0	-5.7	NM	-15.2
	12.0		14.0		9.6	EBIT/Interest		7.4	7.3	8.6	6.4	14.1
(113) 5.7	(123) 4.9	(159) 3.1	EBIT/Interest		(29) 2.0	(21) 3.8	(31) 2.9	(24) 2.6	(48) 4.9
2.9	2.3	1.0			.9	1.2	.3	.7	2.1
4.5	57.9	22.2	Net Profit + Depr., Dep., Amort./Cur. Mat. L/T/D						22.2
(14) 2.5	(21) 8.0	(21) 2.9						(10) 5.8	
1.4	3.1	1.4							1.9
.9	1.0	1.0	Fixed/Worth		.9	.9	1.1	1.0	.9
1.4	1.6	1.7			2.1	1.7	2.1	1.3	1.6
2.7	3.3	3.4			6.3	2.7	5.3	3.4	2.2
.4	.6	.5	Debt/Worth		1.2	.5	.5	.4	.6
1.4	1.6	1.6			4.7	1.5	1.8	1.0	1.3
2.9	5.2	4.9			12.7	3.5	7.3	3.8	2.9
55.0	56.5	30.9	% Profit Before Taxes/Tangible Net Worth		47.0	28.5	27.8	15.5	34.4
(136) 31.6	(136) 30.6	(172) 14.6			(29) 17.0	(25) 9.1	(32) 9.0	(28) 5.6	(52) 17.0
16.8	12.1	.9			-1.8	2.1	-2.1	-.1	7.8
25.5	20.0	11.6	% Profit Before Taxes/Total Assets		16.1	11.7	11.9	8.3	11.6
15.0	10.8	4.4			4.2	2.6	4.3	1.7	6.2
6.7	4.0	.0			-1.0	.4	-1.2	-.4	3.2
2.3	3.4	2.1	Sales/Net Fixed Assets		2.9	2.6	1.0	1.0	3.2
.9	.9	.7			1.3	.5	.5	.5	.9
.5	.6	.4			.6	.3	.3	.3	.4
.9	1.3	1.1	Sales/Total Assets		.9	1.4	.7	.6	1.6
.6	.6	.5			.6	.4	.5	.4	.6
.4	.4	.3			.3	.3	.3	.2	.3
5.1	5.6	6.5	% Depr., Dep., Amort./Sales		6.6	4.7	13.4	13.8	1.3
(107) 12.2	(112) 12.7	(151) 17.2			(28) 17.3	(25) 17.3	(31) 22.3	(27) 23.5	(33) 6.5
16.6	18.9	26.3			24.7	30.7	37.7	32.1	14.9
.7	1.9	1.2	% Officers', Directors', Owners' Comp/Sales						
(15) 3.3	(10) 4.4	(12) 3.5							
7.8	6.9	8.3							
4772866M	5347906M	7001634M	Net Sales ($)	4900M	65495M	104965M	254548M	468501M	6103225M
6722098M	7143831M	8699912M	Total Assets ($)	14275M	166553M	319984M	656575M	1598873M	5943652M

M = $ thousand   MM = $ million
See Pages 11 through 18 for Explanation of Ratios and Data

Current Data Sorted By Assets   Comparative Historical Data

Type of Statement

Type of Statement	500M-2MM	2-10MM	10-50MM	50-100MM	100-250MM	4/1/98-3/31/99 ALL	4/1/99-3/31/00 ALL
Unqualified		1	3	4	2	15	18
Reviewed		5	5			15	11
Compiled		3	1			5	7
Tax Returns	1	1					1
Other		3	5	4	2	16	15

Period groupings: 6 (4/1-9/30/02) for 0-500M / 500M-2MM; 34 (10/1/02-3/31/03) for 2-10MM / 10-50MM / 50-100MM / 100-250MM.

	0-500M	500M-2MM	2-10MM	10-50MM	50-100MM	100-250MM	4/1/98-3/31/99 ALL	4/1/99-3/31/00 ALL
NUMBER OF STATEMENTS		1	13	14	8	4	51	52

Note: Columns 0-500M, 500M-2MM, 50-100MM, and 100-250MM marked **DATA NOT AVAILABLE**.

ASSETS (%)

	2-10MM	10-50MM	4/1/98-3/31/99 ALL	4/1/99-3/31/00 ALL
Cash & Equivalents	5.6	9.0	7.6	7.1
Trade Receivables (net)	21.6	13.9	19.1	18.1
Inventory	2.9	5.9	6.9	6.4
All Other Current	5.1	3.6	2.9	2.0
Total Current	35.1	32.4	36.5	33.7
Fixed Assets (net)	53.7	53.8	50.4	49.7
Intangibles (net)	4.7	4.6	1.3	2.0
All Other Non-Current	6.5	9.1	11.7	14.6
Total	100.0	100.0	100.0	100.0

LIABILITIES

	2-10MM	10-50MM	4/1/98-3/31/99 ALL	4/1/99-3/31/00 ALL
Notes Payable-Short Term	2.9	7.0	3.4	3.7
Cur. Mat.-L/T/D	14.6	8.2	8.2	8.2
Trade Payables	19.4	8.0	12.1	12.7
Income Taxes Payable	.0	.2	.1	.2
All Other Current	9.5	7.9	10.9	8.8
Total Current	46.4	31.3	34.6	33.7
Long Term Debt	45.8	17.2	21.4	28.4
Deferred Taxes	.4	3.1	.4	.6
All Other Non-Current	.4	4.3	8.9	9.9
Net Worth	7.0	44.0	34.8	27.4
Total Liabilities & Net Worth	100.0	100.0	100.0	100.0

INCOME DATA

	2-10MM	10-50MM	4/1/98-3/31/99 ALL	4/1/99-3/31/00 ALL
Net Sales	100.0	100.0	100.0	100.0
Gross Profit	21.0	22.1	21.1	23.0
Operating Expenses	15.1	15.8	15.3	13.9
Operating Profit	5.9	6.3	5.8	9.2
All Other Expenses (net)	1.7	-.6	-.5	1.6
Profit Before Taxes	4.2	6.9	6.3	7.6

RATIOS

	2-10MM	10-50MM	4/1/98-3/31/99 ALL	4/1/99-3/31/00 ALL
Current	1.3	2.3	1.9	1.7
	.7	1.3	1.1	1.0
	.4	.8	.7	.7
Quick	1.0	1.5	1.4	1.2
	.7	.8	.8	.7
	.2	.4	.4	.4
Sales/Receivables	19 19.5	29 12.6	26 14.0	18 20.5
	28 12.9	34 10.8	37 9.9	31 11.8
	50 7.3	44 8.2	43 8.5	44 8.3
Cost of Sales/Inventory	0 UND	3 119.4	3 139.6	0 UND
	0 UND	8 45.7	13 28.5	13 27.1
	13 28.1	59 6.2	26 14.0	24 15.1
Cost of Sales/Payables	16 23.5	13 27.9	18 20.4	15 24.4
	31 11.8	27 13.6	26 14.0	21 17.3
	58 6.3	52 7.0	46 7.9	36 10.2
Sales/Working Capital	23.3	4.9	10.4	11.7
	-15.3	20.5	84.7	NM
	-7.0	-40.1	-14.8	-13.7
EBIT/Interest	38.4	(11) 18.3	(48) 9.2	(49) 10.1
	3.1	6.0	2.8	2.8
	1.6	1.3	1.1	1.3
Net Profit + Depr., Dep., Amort./Cur. Mat. L./T/D				(12) 4.8
				2.5
				1.0
Fixed/Worth	1.6	.8	.7	.8
	4.1	1.2	1.5	1.6
	-501.6	NM	5.6	4.1
Debt/Worth	2.0	.3	.6	.8
	4.3	.6	1.5	2.3
	-503.1	NM	9.2	58.0
% Profit Before Taxes/Tangible Net Worth		(11) 29.2	(41) 33.6	(40) 44.8
		3.8	17.9	25.8
		-3.7	4.2	10.0
% Profit Before Taxes/Total Assets	16.5	18.8	17.4	20.1
	10.2	8.5	5.5	7.9
	1.3	.5	.1	1.5
Sales/Net Fixed Assets	19.2	4.6	8.0	7.1
	3.1	2.5	3.0	3.4
	1.5	1.2	1.5	1.4
Sales/Total Assets	4.1	1.8	2.8	2.7
	1.7	1.1	1.6	1.6
	1.0	.9	1.0	1.0
% Depr., Dep., Amort./Sales	2.1	(13) 4.7	(40) 3.2	(38) 3.4
	7.4	6.7	5.6	6.3
	11.3	11.1	10.9	9.5
% Officers', Directors', Owners' Comp/Sales				(10) 1.0
				1.8
				7.0

	500M-2MM	2-10MM	10-50MM	50-100MM	100-250MM	4/1/98-3/31/99 ALL	4/1/99-3/31/00 ALL
Net Sales ($)	2006M	173756M	407469M	645536M	637161M	2189159M	2489032M
Total Assets ($)	1194M	73394M	353517M	567841M	711150M	1652620M	2023572M

© RMA 2003

M = $ thousand   MM = $ million
See Pages 11 through 18 for Explanation of Ratios and Data

Comparative Historical Data | Current Data Sorted By Sales

H1	H2	H3	Type of Statement	0-1MM	1-3MM	3-5MM	5-10MM	10-25MM	25MM & OVER
8	13	10	Unqualified					3	7
10	7	10	Reviewed		1	1	3	4	1
7	9	4	Compiled			1		2	1
3	1	2	Tax Returns					1	
5	12	14	Other				1	2	11
4/1/00-3/31/01	4/1/01-3/31/02	4/1/02-3/31/03			6 (4/1-9/30/02)		34 (10/1/02-3/31/03)		
ALL	ALL	ALL							
33	42	40	**NUMBER OF STATEMENTS**		2	2	4	12	20
%	%	%	**ASSETS**	%	%	%	%	%	%
10.0	11.1	8.7	Cash & Equivalents					7.1	11.1
13.9	21.1	15.5	Trade Receivables (net)					16.6	15.5
4.6	4.5	5.1	Inventory					5.5	5.6
8.2	6.2	3.9	All Other Current					4.1	4.9
36.8	42.9	33.1	Total Current					33.4	37.2
45.7	40.7	52.5	Fixed Assets (net)					55.7	44.2
2.3	4.5	3.7	Intangibles (net)					1.1	4.0
15.2	11.8	10.7	All Other Non-Current					9.8	14.6
100.0	100.0	100.0	Total					100.0	100.0
			LIABILITIES						
5.5	5.3	4.1	Notes Payable-Short Term					.9	6.8
6.8	7.6	9.6	Cur. Mat.-L/T/D					11.8	6.6
13.4	16.2	10.8	Trade Payables					13.5	8.4
.0	.2	.1	Income Taxes Payable					.0	.2
9.6	7.0	7.1	All Other Current					8.1	7.0
35.3	36.3	31.8	Total Current					34.3	29.0
23.1	19.7	30.5	Long Term Debt					16.4	33.6
.6	.3	1.5	Deferred Taxes					.4	2.6
10.2	5.8	3.8	All Other Non-Current					4.6	4.2
30.8	37.9	32.4	Net Worth					44.3	30.6
100.0	100.0	100.0	Total Liabilities & Net Worth					100.0	100.0
			INCOME DATA						
100.0	100.0	100.0	Net Sales					100.0	100.0
23.5	22.5	22.1	Gross Profit					17.0	25.3
18.4	15.3	14.9	Operating Expenses					10.4	17.6
5.2	7.2	7.1	Operating Profit					6.6	7.7
−2.8	.2	.7	All Other Expenses (net)					1.1	.2
8.0	7.0	6.4	Profit Before Taxes					5.5	7.6

RATIOS

H1	H2	H3	Ratio	10-25MM	25MM & OVER
2.1	1.8	2.2	Current	2.1	2.9
1.1	1.2	1.2		1.1	1.3
.7	.5	.6		.4	1.0
1.3	1.4	1.3	Quick	1.2	2.5
.8	1.0	.8		.7	1.1
.3	.5	.3		.4	.4
13 27.8	21 17.2	26 14.1	Sales/Receivables	27 13.4	23 15.7
32 11.5	33 10.9	36 10.0		34 10.8	38 9.6
43 8.5	48 7.6	48 7.6		46 8.0	50 7.4
0 UND	0 UND	0 UND	Cost of Sales/Inventory	2 169.5	0 UND
9 41.5	6 58.4	11 33.5		6 57.7	14 25.5
31 11.6	17 21.2	31 11.7		19 19.6	48 7.5
15 24.6	18 20.7	14 26.0	Cost of Sales/Payables	18 19.9	13 28.6
24 15.5	25 14.6	25 14.4		30 12.1	18 19.9
50 7.4	46 8.0	46 7.9		57 6.4	27 13.7
5.5	6.5	5.7	Sales/Working Capital	5.7	4.5
48.0	26.7	31.9		NM	25.2
−14.3	−10.1	−13.4		−8.9	125.7
11.8	16.5	24.8	EBIT/Interest	26.9	60.3
(31) 3.5	(38) 4.0	(36) 3.8		(11) 5.9	(17) 6.0
1.1	1.7	1.7		2.8	1.8
		2.3	Net Profit + Depr., Dep., Amort./Cur. Mat. L/T/D		
	(10) 1.4				
		.4			
.5	.4	.8	Fixed/Worth	.8	.6
1.6	1.0	1.6		1.1	1.1
55.6	4.9	25.2		3.0	83.8
.5	.6	.5	Debt/Worth	.3	.4
1.6	2.2	1.9		1.2	1.5
79.2	7.8	36.5		3.9	120.1
37.3	49.3	41.2	% Profit Before Taxes/Tangible Net Worth	31.9	63.4
(26) 26.1	(34) 19.7	(32) 15.6		(10) 9.8	(16) 16.4
8.7	4.6	.8		.0	1.2
13.5	16.6	16.6	% Profit Before Taxes/Total Assets	13.3	22.9
9.0	5.1	8.4		7.8	8.7
1.8	1.3	1.0		1.0	1.7
7.0	10.1	6.1	Sales/Net Fixed Assets	5.8	7.1
3.4	4.6	2.3		3.5	3.0
1.8	1.7	1.1		1.2	1.2
2.8	3.0	1.9	Sales/Total Assets	2.5	2.6
1.2	1.3	1.1		1.3	1.1
.7	1.0	.8		.9	.7
.6	.9	3.8	% Depr., Dep., Amort./Sales	3.4	3.1
(28) 5.6	(37) 5.1	(35) 6.8		5.6	(15) 7.0
11.0	9.6	12.0		6.7	12.0
	1.0		% Officers', Directors', Owners' Comp/Sales		
	(14) 2.0				
	3.2				

H1	H2	H3		1-3MM	3-5MM	5-10MM	10-25MM	25MM & OVER
1069295M	2529014M	1865928M	Net Sales ($)	4500M	6936M	29454M	222369M	1602669M
1001437M	1562710M	1707096M	Total Assets ($)	11156M	6171M	24894M	219099M	1445776M

M = $ thousand   MM = $ million
See Pages 11 through 18 for Explanation of Ratios and Data

Current Data Sorted By Assets   Comparative Historical Data

0-500M	500M-2MM	2-10MM	10-50MM	50-100MM	100-250MM		4/1/98-3/31/99 ALL	4/1/99-3/31/00 ALL
						Type of Statement		
		2	5	3		Unqualified	17	23
1	5	7	4			Reviewed	7	11
	2	2	2			Compiled	9	5
	1	3	1			Tax Returns	2	2
		7	5	1	2	Other	15	15
		5 (4/1-9/30/02)	48 (10/1/02-3/31/03)					
1	8	21	17	4	2	**NUMBER OF STATEMENTS**	50	56
%	%	%	%	%	%	**ASSETS**	%	%
		14.3	10.6			Cash & Equivalents	6.9	8.9
		15.2	10.2			Trade Receivables (net)	14.9	13.2
		13.2	11.7			Inventory	14.6	11.2
		2.8	4.0			All Other Current	2.2	1.5
		45.5	36.6			Total Current	38.5	34.8
		44.2	46.7			Fixed Assets (net)	49.7	52.4
		.8	2.6			Intangibles (net)	2.4	4.2
		9.5	14.1			All Other Non-Current	9.3	8.6
		100.0	100.0			Total	100.0	100.0
						LIABILITIES		
		2.4	5.3			Notes Payable-Short Term	8.4	4.2
		6.1	3.2			Cur. Mat.-L/T/D	3.5	6.1
		11.0	4.6			Trade Payables	7.6	5.6
		.0	.2			Income Taxes Payable	.3	.2
		8.8	4.9			All Other Current	6.9	5.3
		28.3	18.1			Total Current	26.7	21.5
		21.7	17.4			Long Term Debt	18.4	26.0
		.4	.0			Deferred Taxes	1.0	.8
		4.3	.7			All Other Non-Current	5.0	2.7
		45.2	63.8			Net Worth	48.9	49.0
		100.0	100.0			Total Liabilities & Net Worth	100.0	100.0
						INCOME DATA		
		100.0	100.0			Net Sales	100.0	100.0
		30.5	30.1			Gross Profit	25.7	30.9
		20.0	15.6			Operating Expenses	20.0	20.1
		10.6	14.5			Operating Profit	5.7	10.8
		1.2	−.4			All Other Expenses (net)	1.6	1.5
		9.4	14.9			Profit Before Taxes	4.1	9.3
						RATIOS		
		3.2	5.4				2.8	3.3
		1.6	2.0			Current	2.3	1.9
		1.0	1.4				.9	1.0
		1.9	3.0				1.7	2.0
		1.0	.8			Quick	1.1	1.2
		.5	.6				.5	.5
		30 12.2	31 11.6				32 11.5	30 12.3
		38 9.6	40 9.2			Sales/Receivables	43 8.6	40 9.2
		58 6.3	48 7.6				55 6.6	54 6.8
		10 36.9	17 21.0				28 13.2	12 29.5
		59 6.2	57 6.4			Cost of Sales/Inventory	47 7.8	55 6.6
		85 4.3	96 3.8				81 4.5	81 4.5
		15 24.5	14 25.4				15 24.1	17 20.9
		28 13.1	23 15.5			Cost of Sales/Payables	23 15.8	24 15.2
		54 6.8	36 10.1				36 10.1	34 10.8
		4.2	2.2				4.3	3.6
		6.7	7.9			Sales/Working Capital	7.8	7.2
		NM	13.6				−50.6	170.3
	(17)	7.2	(14) 37.9				(44) 10.7	(52) 8.7
		3.8	7.4			EBIT/Interest	4.5	4.5
		2.1	3.4				2.4	1.5
						Net Profit + Depr., Dep.,	(17) 7.9	(22) 7.9
						Amort./Cur. Mat. L /T/D	3.2	3.0
							1.9	1.5
		.4	.4				.7	.7
		1.4	.9			Fixed/Worth	1.0	1.2
		3.3	1.3				1.8	2.2
		.2	.1				.4	.5
		1.4	.7			Debt/Worth	.9	1.0
		7.8	1.0				2.2	2.5
	(19)	59.8	31.3			% Profit Before Taxes/Tangible	(47) 33.2	(53) 27.2
		13.8	14.0			Net Worth	16.8	16.4
		3.8	8.2				10.5	5.2
		13.1	19.5			% Profit Before Taxes/Total	13.3	13.2
		6.4	8.1			Assets	8.4	8.4
		2.9	4.3				5.5	2.1
		4.7	3.4				3.6	3.1
		2.4	2.4			Sales/Net Fixed Assets	2.1	2.1
		1.9	1.4				1.2	1.3
		1.5	1.2				1.6	1.5
		1.1	.9			Sales/Total Assets	1.0	1.0
		.9	.7				.8	.8
	(20)	4.6	(15) 5.2			% Depr., Dep., Amort./Sales	(40) 5.2	(47) 5.4
		7.6	7.3				7.7	7.8
		10.1	11.0				10.7	11.6
						% Officers', Directors',	(17) 1.2	(14) 1.4
						Owners' Comp/Sales	3.4	2.5
							5.4	4.7
1307M	16212M	119985M	274378M	182932M	261028M	Net Sales ($)	1250085M	1591831M
269M	10082M	104391M	311539M	322518M	262296M	Total Assets ($)	1165991M	1700798M

M = $ thousand   MM = $ million
See Pages 11 through 18 for Explanation of Ratios and Data

Comparative Historical Data | Current Data Sorted By Sales

Hist 4/1/00-3/31/01 ALL	Hist 4/1/01-3/31/02 ALL	Hist 4/1/02-3/31/03 ALL		0-1MM	1-3MM	3-5MM	5-10MM	10-25MM	25MM & OVER
					5 (4/1-9/30/02)	48 (10/1/02-3/31/03)			
			Type of Statement						
17	16	10	Unqualified			1		5	4
4	8	11	Reviewed			3	4	4	
9	12	10	Compiled		4	3	1	2	
	1	6	Tax Returns	1	1	2	1	1	
13	20	16	Other		3	2	2	5	4
43	57	53	**NUMBER OF STATEMENTS**	1	8	11	8	17	8
%	%	%	**ASSETS**	%	%	%	%	%	%
8.7	10.0	10.6	Cash & Equivalents			9.9		14.9	
12.4	12.3	13.3	Trade Receivables (net)			19.5		11.0	
11.3	10.5	11.0	Inventory			14.4		10.7	
1.8	3.7	2.8	All Other Current			1.1		1.6	
34.3	36.5	37.8	Total Current			44.9		38.2	
52.9	51.7	49.3	Fixed Assets (net)			50.9		44.6	
3.3	3.3	1.9	Intangibles (net)			3.1		2.4	
9.5	8.4	11.0	All Other Non-Current			1.1		14.8	
100.0	100.0	100.0	Total			100.0		100.0	
			LIABILITIES						
5.3	3.1	5.9	Notes Payable-Short Term			2.0		5.6	
4.0	5.6	5.8	Cur. Mat.-L/T/D			8.9		3.1	
4.8	6.5	7.7	Trade Payables			16.6		5.0	
.4	.3	.1	Income Taxes Payable			.1		.2	
5.0	3.3	6.4	All Other Current			8.8		5.1	
19.5	18.7	25.9	Total Current			36.4		18.9	
18.3	23.4	21.0	Long Term Debt			28.7		14.9	
.8	.9	.4	Deferred Taxes			.3		.0	
4.2	4.4	3.6	All Other Non-Current			3.6		2.2	
57.3	52.6	49.1	Net Worth			30.9		63.9	
100.0	100.0	100.0	Total Liabilities & Net Worth			100.0		100.0	
			INCOME DATA						
100.0	100.0	100.0	Net Sales			100.0		100.0	
30.6	32.6	29.5	Gross Profit			30.4		30.2	
19.5	21.9	19.8	Operating Expenses			24.0		16.3	
11.1	10.7	9.8	Operating Profit			6.4		13.9	
1.0	1.5	1.2	All Other Expenses (net)			1.0		−.3	
10.1	9.2	8.5	Profit Before Taxes			5.4		14.2	
			RATIOS						
3.9	5.1	3.2				2.2		5.1	
2.2	2.1	1.6	Current			1.6		2.0	
1.1	1.4	1.0				.7		1.4	
2.8	2.4	2.0				1.3		4.1	
1.2	1.2	.8	Quick			.7		1.5	
.5	.6	.5				.6		.7	
32 11.5	30 12.1	30 12.2				22 16.8		28 13.2	
41 8.8	38 9.5	40 9.1	Sales/Receivables			33 10.9		40 9.2	
57 6.4	48 7.6	51 7.2				74 4.9		50 7.3	
26 13.8	23 15.9	11 33.6				4 100.7		12 30.6	
54 6.7	52 7.1	52 7.0	Cost of Sales/Inventory			78 4.7		56 6.5	
95 3.8	76 4.8	78 4.7				109 3.3		94 3.9	
12 30.6	17 21.3	15 23.7				15 23.7		14 25.4	
24 15.2	24 15.5	26 13.8	Cost of Sales/Payables			36 10.2		23 16.2	
34 10.7	44 8.3	39 9.4				84 4.4		37 10.0	
4.1	3.5	4.0				4.5		2.9	
6.3	6.3	8.1	Sales/Working Capital			9.8		7.9	
37.2	13.7	465.8				−7.1		10.5	
13.4	15.3	9.9				13.5		25.5	
(36) 3.6	(54) 3.7	(46) 3.3	EBIT/Interest			2.9		(13) 3.9	
.9	1.4	1.9				2.1		2.9	
15.9	6.0	5.7							
(12) 5.4	(14) 2.4	(12) 3.1	Net Profit + Depr., Dep., Amort./Cur. Mat. L/T/D						
1.5	1.5	1.8							
.6	.6	.5				1.0		.4	
.8	1.1	1.1	Fixed/Worth			2.0		.9	
2.0	2.1	2.8				−4.8		1.4	
.3	.3	.2				.7		.1	
.5	.7	.9	Debt/Worth			2.5		.5	
2.5	2.8	4.5				−11.7		1.0	
26.3	28.9	41.6						45.0	
(41) 15.2	(54) 14.3	(48) 13.3	% Profit Before Taxes/Tangible Net Worth					14.0	
3.8	5.5	4.0						7.2	
16.7	12.4	12.0				9.0		19.7	
8.2	6.8	6.4	% Profit Before Taxes/Total Assets			5.1		6.1	
1.2	1.9	2.4				2.8		4.0	
3.2	3.3	3.9				5.6		3.8	
1.9	2.2	2.3	Sales/Net Fixed Assets			2.3		2.7	
1.2	1.2	1.5				1.9		1.6	
1.3	1.4	1.4				1.7		1.2	
.9	1.0	1.0	Sales/Total Assets			1.3		.9	
.7	.7	.8				1.0		.7	
5.1	5.0	5.0				6.0		5.3	
(39) 8.1	(53) 7.6	(48) 7.7	% Depr., Dep., Amort./Sales			9.1		(15) 7.6	
11.7	11.8	10.8				13.3		11.0	
		1.3							
		(13) 2.7	% Officers', Directors', Owners' Comp/Sales						
		7.2							
1171572M	1173097M	855842M	Net Sales ($)	392M	14328M	40512M	54934M	226161M	519515M
1321897M	1445457M	1011095M	Total Assets ($)	522M	11028M	32542M	70444M	259052M	637507M

M = $ thousand   MM = $ million
See Pages 11 through 18 for Explanation of Ratios and Data

Current Data Sorted By Assets   Comparative Historical Data

						Type of Statement		
		4	8	3		Unqualified		
		3	4			Reviewed		
1		1				Compiled		
1						Tax Returns		
1		5	5			Other		
	5 (4/1-9/30/02)		31 (10/1/02-3/31/03)				4/1/98-3/31/99	4/1/99-3/31/00
0-500M	500M-2MM	2-10MM	10-50MM	50-100MM	100-250MM		ALL	ALL
3		13	17	3		NUMBER OF STATEMENTS		
%	%	%	%	%	%	ASSETS	%	%
		7.4	9.9			Cash & Equivalents		
		11.2	18.0			Trade Receivables (net)		
	D	19.8	14.0		D	Inventory	D	D
	A	4.7	5.0		A	All Other Current	A	A
	T	43.1	47.0		T	Total Current	T	T
	A	46.4	47.6		A	Fixed Assets (net)	A	A
		.8	.6			Intangibles (net)		
	N	9.6	4.8		N	All Other Non-Current	N	N
	O	100.0	100.0		O	Total	O	O
	T				T	LIABILITIES	T	T
		6.8	4.0			Notes Payable-Short Term		
	A	7.7	3.8		A	Cur. Mat.-L/T/D	A	A
	V	9.0	11.4		V	Trade Payables	V	V
	A	.0	.2		A	Income Taxes Payable	A	A
	I	4.8	15.7		I	All Other Current	I	I
	L	28.4	35.2		L	Total Current	L	L
	A	24.6	14.2		A	Long Term Debt	A	A
	B	.3	.6		B	Deferred Taxes	B	B
	L	5.0	3.6		L	All Other Non-Current	L	L
	E	41.7	46.4		E	Net Worth	E	E
		100.0	100.0			Total Liabilities & Net Worth		
						INCOME DATA		
		100.0	100.0			Net Sales		
		24.4	21.0			Gross Profit		
		17.8	14.8			Operating Expenses		
		6.6	6.2			Operating Profit		
		1.9	2.3			All Other Expenses (net)		
		4.6	3.9			Profit Before Taxes		
						RATIOS		
		2.0	3.6					
		1.3	1.9			Current		
		1.2	.7					
		1.4	2.1					
		.7	1.2			Quick		
		.3	.4					
	19	19.1	33	11.0				
	30	12.1	56	6.5		Sales/Receivables		
	45	8.1	65	5.6				
	19	19.7	17	22.0				
	34	10.7	49	7.5		Cost of Sales/Inventory		
	103	3.5	105	3.5				
	13	28.1	17	20.9				
	24	15.3	28	12.9		Cost of Sales/Payables		
	40	9.0	65	5.6				
		5.0	2.8					
		14.0	5.5			Sales/Working Capital		
		26.1	–10.8					
		7.0	9.6					
		2.5 (13)	4.4			EBIT/Interest		
		1.6	–1.1					
						Net Profit + Depr., Dep., Amort./Cur. Mat. L /T/D		
		.7	.5					
		1.2	.8			Fixed/Worth		
		2.5	1.8					
		.9	.3					
		1.3	.7			Debt/Worth		
		3.9	3.1					
		39.0	18.0					
		10.6 (15)	11.6			% Profit Before Taxes/Tangible Net Worth		
		2.8	2.0					
		12.6	11.2					
		4.6	6.0			% Profit Before Taxes/Total Assets		
		1.3	–4.0					
		5.7	4.1					
		2.7	2.5			Sales/Net Fixed Assets		
		1.9	1.6					
		1.6	1.5					
		1.2	1.1			Sales/Total Assets		
		1.1	.7					
		4.5	4.2					
		7.6 (14)	7.0			% Depr., Dep., Amort./Sales		
		11.5	12.4					
						% Officers', Directors', Owners' Comp/Sales		
2013M		114110M	357673M	149390M		Net Sales ($)		
1094M		80854M	323419M	238549M		Total Assets ($)		

M = $ thousand   MM = $ million
See Pages 11 through 18 for Explanation of Ratios and Data

Comparative Historical Data | Current Data Sorted By Sales

Columns 0-1MM and 1-3MM fall under period **5 (4/1-9/30/02)**; columns 3-5MM through 25MM & OVER fall under period **31 (10/1/02-3/31/03)**.

	4/1/00-3/31/01 ALL	4/1/01-3/31/02 ALL	4/1/02-3/31/03 ALL	Type of Statement	0-1MM	1-3MM	3-5MM	5-10MM	10-25MM	25MM & OVER
		6	15	Unqualified				3	6	6
		2	7	Reviewed		2		1	3	1
		8	2	Compiled					1	
		1	1	Tax Returns	1					
		1	11	Other	1		1	2	5	2
	18	18	36	**NUMBER OF STATEMENTS**	3		3	6	15	9
		%	%	**ASSETS**	%		%	%	%	%
Data		10.8	9.8	Cash & Equivalents	Data				8.5	
Not		14.6	14.9	Trade Receivables (net)	Not				16.1	
Available		8.5	15.8	Inventory	Available				16.6	
		8.6	4.7	All Other Current					5.1	
		42.5	45.2	Total Current					46.2	
		42.9	44.8	Fixed Assets (net)					47.3	
		5.6	.9	Intangibles (net)					1.0	
		9.0	9.2	All Other Non-Current					5.4	
		100.0	100.0	Total					100.0	
				LIABILITIES						
		4.2	5.6	Notes Payable-Short Term					4.6	
		4.3	5.3	Cur. Mat.-L/T/D					4.6	
		6.1	8.9	Trade Payables					10.2	
		.2	.1	Income Taxes Payable					.2	
		5.4	9.6	All Other Current					7.9	
		20.1	29.6	Total Current					27.5	
		14.2	21.0	Long Term Debt					11.8	
		1.8	.5	Deferred Taxes					.7	
		2.6	4.3	All Other Non-Current					5.1	
		61.3	44.6	Net Worth					54.9	
		100.0	100.0	Total Liabilities & Net Worth					100.0	
				INCOME DATA						
		100.0	100.0	Net Sales					100.0	
		32.7	29.3	Gross Profit					19.3	
		20.0	22.3	Operating Expenses					14.5	
		12.7	7.1	Operating Profit					4.7	
		.5	1.7	All Other Expenses (net)					.5	
		12.2	5.3	Profit Before Taxes					4.2	
				RATIOS						
		4.4	3.0						3.0	
		2.3	1.8	Current					2.0	
		1.1	1.2						1.3	
		2.3	1.8						1.6	
		1.1	1.0	Quick					1.2	
		.7	.4						.4	
		34 10.7	28 13.0						30 12.1	
		48 7.6	37 9.7	Sales/Receivables					34 10.8	
		61 6.0	58 6.3						64 5.7	
		20 18.3	16 23.0						15 24.0	
		38 9.5	44 8.3	Cost of Sales/Inventory					49 7.5	
		64 5.7	103 3.5						107 3.4	
		11 33.3	14 26.3						15 24.8	
		28 12.9	24 15.2	Cost of Sales/Payables					28 12.9	
		38 9.7	51 7.2						53 6.9	
		2.7	3.4						3.2	
		6.0	6.6	Sales/Working Capital					4.2	
		28.5	28.6						46.6	
		14.3	7.7						8.1	
	(17)	7.0	(31) 3.2	EBIT/Interest					(13) 2.8	
		2.7	1.4						-.7	
			3.2							
		(15)	2.4	Net Profit + Depr., Dep., Amort./Cur. Mat. L/T/D						
			1.8							
		.5	.6						.6	
		.7	.9	Fixed/Worth					.8	
		1.8	1.9						1.3	
		.4	.6						.3	
		.6	.9	Debt/Worth					.7	
		1.8	2.0						1.5	
		35.7	30.3						19.3	
		16.0	(33) 10.6	% Profit Before Taxes/Tangible Net Worth					10.6	
		9.0	2.2						.9	
		18.1	11.5						11.8	
		9.3	4.3	% Profit Before Taxes/Total Assets					6.0	
		5.9	.1						.4	
		4.6	5.3						4.0	
		2.8	2.5	Sales/Net Fixed Assets					2.5	
		1.5	1.7						1.6	
		1.4	1.6						1.5	
		1.0	1.2	Sales/Total Assets					1.1	
		.8	.8						.7	
		.0	4.5						4.5	
	(17)	4.6	(33) 7.1	% Depr., Dep., Amort./Sales					(13) 7.0	
		10.2	11.9						10.7	
			1.7							
		(10)	2.7	% Officers', Directors', Owners' Comp/Sales						
			6.0							
		362265M	623186M	Net Sales ($)	2013M		11067M	43323M	221793M	344990M
		427447M	643916M	Total Assets ($)	1094M		13646M	40320M	208494M	380362M

© RMA 2003

M = $ thousand   MM = $ million

See Pages 11 through 18 for Explanation of Ratios and Data

MINING—Construction Sand and Gravel Mining NAICS 212321 (SIC 1442)

Current Data Sorted By Assets | **Comparative Historical Data**

Dating: 26 (4/1-9/30/02) covers 0-500M and 500M-2MM; 108 (10/1/02-3/31/03) covers 2-10MM through 100-250MM.

Type of Statement	0-500M	500M-2MM	2-10MM	10-50MM	50-100MM	100-250MM	4/1/98-3/31/99 ALL	4/1/99-3/31/00 ALL
Unqualified	3	4	11	13	3	2	21	13
Reviewed	2	9	18	6			35	22
Compiled	8	8	9	4			25	18
Tax Returns		8	1				7	12
Other	2		12	9		2	27	27
NUMBER OF STATEMENTS	15	29	51	32	3	4	115	92

ASSETS	%	%	%	%	%	%	%	%
Cash & Equivalents	11.4	7.6	8.7	10.7			14.1	12.6
Trade Receivables (net)	15.9	15.8	15.5	14.3			16.8	15.9
Inventory	2.5	5.0	8.1	11.6			5.9	5.5
All Other Current	1.1	6.8	1.1	3.7			4.3	2.0
Total Current	30.9	35.2	33.5	40.4			41.1	36.0
Fixed Assets (net)	62.0	57.6	54.9	42.4			51.5	54.0
Intangibles (net)	1.2	.6	5.5	2.0			1.3	1.2
All Other Non-Current	5.9	6.5	6.1	15.2			6.1	8.8
Total	100.0	100.0	100.0	100.0			100.0	100.0

LIABILITIES								
Notes Payable-Short Term	15.3	7.2	4.8	4.9			6.0	6.9
Cur. Mat.-L/T/D	7.4	6.8	6.3	3.3			5.6	6.8
Trade Payables	1.7	5.8	7.5	6.9			9.0	7.6
Income Taxes Payable	.1	.5	.1	.8			.2	.3
All Other Current	3.5	7.8	4.4	6.2			7.7	6.1
Total Current	27.8	28.0	23.0	22.2			28.6	27.8
Long Term Debt	42.8	40.5	26.8	11.9			20.2	21.7
Deferred Taxes	.0	.2	.5	1.9			.6	.9
All Other Non-Current	3.4	4.1	5.8	2.8			6.4	4.8
Net Worth	25.9	27.2	43.9	61.1			44.2	44.8
Total Liabilities & Net Worth	100.0	100.0	100.0	100.0			100.0	100.0

INCOME DATA								
Net Sales	100.0	100.0	100.0	100.0			100.0	100.0
Gross Profit	53.8	51.2	31.6	24.2			33.8	35.9
Operating Expenses	42.9	44.0	23.8	18.1			25.2	25.3
Operating Profit	11.0	7.2	7.8	6.1			8.6	10.6
All Other Expenses (net)	5.5	3.7	2.0	−.1			1.3	1.8
Profit Before Taxes	5.5	3.5	5.8	6.2			7.3	8.9

RATIOS	0-500M	500M-2MM	2-10MM	10-50MM	50-100MM	100-250MM	4/1/98-3/31/99 ALL	4/1/99-3/31/00 ALL
Current	5.1	2.2	3.0	4.1			3.4	2.8
	1.1	1.4	1.3	1.8			1.7	1.3
	.4	.6	.9	1.4			.8	.7
Quick	3.4	1.8	2.5	2.4			2.8	2.2
	.9	1.1	.9	1.0			1.2	1.1
	.4	.5	.5	.6			.6	.5
Sales/Receivables	0 UND	0 UND	27 13.6	32 11.5			26 14.1	30 12.1
	24 15.4	28 12.8	40 9.1	41 8.8			40 9.1	40 9.1
	46 7.9	61 6.0	49 7.5	54 6.8			59 6.2	56 6.5
Cost of Sales/Inventory	0 UND	0 UND	0 UND	26 14.0			0 UND	3 137.4
	0 UND	0 UND	23 16.2	45 8.1			15 24.1	17 21.1
	0 UND	56 6.5	63 5.8	83 4.4			43 8.4	54 6.8
Cost of Sales/Payables	0 UND	1 410.8	13 29.1	14 25.2			12 30.8	13 28.7
	0 UND	14 25.2	21 17.4	28 12.8			24 15.3	22 16.4
	16 22.1	48 7.6	40 9.1	43 8.5			45 8.2	39 9.3
Sales/Working Capital	5.7	5.5	4.3	2.8			3.9	5.2
	77.6	21.6	12.5	6.5			11.7	21.7
	−6.4	−10.4	−28.9	12.3			−31.4	−12.9
EBIT/Interest	4.6	6.1	9.4	20.4			8.5	8.4
	2.9	(26) 1.9	(46) 3.1	(28) 5.9			(100) 3.9	(79) 3.7
	1.0	.5	1.1	1.1			1.7	1.5
Net Profit + Depr., Dep., Amort./Cur. Mat. L/T/D			12.9	7.6			5.0	4.9
			(14) 2.6	(10) 2.3			(30) 2.5	(25) 3.3
			1.5	1.3			1.8	1.6
Fixed/Worth	.7	.8	.7	.5			.6	.6
	1.7	2.0	1.2	.7			1.1	1.1
	8.7	NM	4.4	1.2			2.7	3.1
Debt/Worth	.5	1.0	.5	.2			.4	.4
	1.4	2.9	1.2	.6			1.2	1.2
	8.0	NM	6.9	1.5			3.7	3.4
% Profit Before Taxes/Tangible Net Worth	(12) 33.4	(22) 47.7	(46) 23.4	22.8			(106) 39.0	(82) 30.1
	16.2	22.1	13.1	8.9			18.1	18.4
	2.0	−6.2	4.8	2.2			7.6	10.0
% Profit Before Taxes/Total Assets	13.6	11.9	10.9	10.6			17.5	16.9
	7.5	2.2	5.0	6.0			8.3	8.2
	.0	−3.5	.8	.9			2.3	1.7
Sales/Net Fixed Assets	8.2	6.2	4.4	3.5			5.3	4.2
	3.1	2.7	1.9	2.3			2.5	2.1
	1.9	1.2	1.6	1.3			1.5	1.4
Sales/Total Assets	5.1	2.1	1.7	1.2			1.8	1.7
	1.7	1.4	1.1	.9			1.3	1.2
	1.0	1.0	.8	.7			.9	.7
% Depr., Dep., Amort./Sales	(13) 5.9	(26) 5.3	(49) 5.2	(28) 5.8			(99) 4.6	(86) 4.9
	10.2	10.7	8.5	8.0			8.0	8.0
	15.1	16.9	14.1	10.6			11.3	11.9
% Officers', Directors', Owners' Comp/Sales		(18) 2.1	(19) 1.8				(45) 2.4	(36) 2.4
		5.1	3.0				4.4	3.8
		6.7	4.5				8.9	7.1
Net Sales ($)	10612M	54119M	340007M	756035M	291189M	444607M	1259242M	926753M
Total Assets ($)	4554M	35991M	251219M	750260M	185370M	552262M	1019392M	922801M

© RMA 2003

M = $ thousand   MM = $ million
See Pages 11 through 18 for Explanation of Ratios and Data

Comparative Historical Data / Current Data Sorted By Sales

4/1/00-3/31/01 ALL	4/1/01-3/31/02 ALL	4/1/02-3/31/03 ALL	Type of Statement	0-1MM	1-3MM	3-5MM	5-10MM	10-25MM	25MM & OVER
18	14	29	Unqualified		1	3	6	8	11
20	20	31	Reviewed	4	7	6	5	7	2
19	24	24	Compiled	4	9	2	5	2	2
11	10	17	Tax Returns	11	3	3			
25	39	33	Other	3	9	5	9	4	3
				26 (4/1-9/30/02)		108 (10/1/02-3/31/03)			
93	107	134	**NUMBER OF STATEMENTS**	22	29	19	25	21	18
%	%	%	**ASSETS**	%	%	%	%	%	%
9.0	9.7	9.4	Cash & Equivalents	8.7	5.5	10.3	9.5	16.6	7.2
16.2	16.3	15.4	Trade Receivables (net)	12.0	17.1	11.5	12.7	18.0	21.5
6.9	8.6	7.6	Inventory	2.8	9.0	4.6	11.8	7.3	8.7
3.5	2.1	3.0	All Other Current	1.0	6.9	.5	1.3	3.3	3.8
35.7	36.8	35.4	Total Current	24.5	38.5	26.9	35.3	45.2	41.2
53.9	54.2	53.2	Fixed Assets (net)	66.9	52.4	67.5	49.3	39.4	44.3
2.1	2.0	3.0	Intangibles (net)	.9	1.6	.9	6.0	6.2	1.8
8.3	6.9	8.4	All Other Non-Current	7.7	7.4	4.6	9.4	9.2	12.8
100.0	100.0	100.0	Total	100.0	100.0	100.0	100.0	100.0	100.0
			LIABILITIES						
7.1	6.0	6.5	Notes Payable-Short Term	11.9	7.2	5.7	5.1	3.7	4.6
8.1	7.1	5.6	Cur. Mat.-L/T/D	6.8	5.1	8.8	6.3	4.0	2.3
7.4	7.0	6.4	Trade Payables	1.9	5.4	5.8	8.3	7.3	10.4
.1	.2	.3	Income Taxes Payable	.0	.5	.0	.4	.2	1.0
4.9	3.6	6.2	All Other Current	2.6	7.4	6.6	3.8	6.4	10.9
27.7	23.9	24.9	Total Current	23.3	25.5	27.0	24.0	21.6	29.2
28.6	30.5	27.5	Long Term Debt	58.1	30.2	26.8	21.7	10.4	14.1
1.0	.9	1.1	Deferred Taxes	.0	.5	.6	1.1	1.0	3.8
5.4	6.6	4.3	All Other Non-Current	5.8	2.2	5.7	3.6	6.6	2.8
37.3	38.1	42.2	Net Worth	12.8	41.6	39.9	49.6	60.4	50.0
100.0	100.0	100.0	Total Liabilities & Net Worth	100.0	100.0	100.0	100.0	100.0	100.0
			INCOME DATA						
100.0	100.0	100.0	Net Sales	100.0	100.0	100.0	100.0	100.0	100.0
32.1	38.8	36.2	Gross Profit	57.8	48.1	32.0	25.7	25.1	22.3
23.6	30.0	28.4	Operating Expenses	46.8	42.6	21.9	20.3	17.6	13.7
8.5	8.9	7.8	Operating Profit	11.0	5.5	10.1	5.4	7.5	8.6
1.8	3.5	2.3	All Other Expenses (net)	7.4	3.0	1.5	.1	.5	.8
6.6	5.4	5.5	Profit Before Taxes	3.6	2.5	8.5	5.3	7.0	7.8
			RATIOS						
2.6 1.3 .8	2.5 1.6 .8	3.1 1.5 .9	Current	5.6 1.0 .4	2.5 1.6 .9	2.1 1.0 .5	3.2 1.6 .9	4.6 2.6 1.4	2.5 1.9 1.1
1.9 .9 .4	1.9 1.0 .5	2.3 1.0 .5	Quick	3.4 .9 .3	1.9 1.1 .4	1.5 .5 .4	2.1 .8 .5	4.0 2.0 .8	2.1 1.0 .7
25 14.4 40 9.0 59 6.1	26 13.8 37 9.7 60 6.1	25 14.4 40 9.2 54 6.8	Sales/Receivables	0 UND 18 19.8 44 8.4	26 13.9 44 8.3 73 5.0	18 20.1 31 11.7 44 8.4	24 15.1 28 13.2 44 8.3	37 9.9 44 8.4 54 6.8	39 9.5 55 6.6 66 5.5
1 309.9 16 22.8 61 6.0	0 999.8 32 11.5 69 5.3	0 UND 23 15.8 61 5.9	Cost of Sales/Inventory	0 UND 0 UND 6 59.5	0 UND 30 12.2 103 3.5	0 UND 8 44.5 50 7.3	7 54.8 44 8.3 83 4.4	1 299.9 29 12.6 58 6.3	12 30.7 32 11.4 55 6.7
14 25.8 24 15.1 46 7.9	13 27.6 23 15.7 41 8.9	10 35.5 20 18.1 42 8.7	Cost of Sales/Payables	0 UND 0 UND 22 16.6	11 31.8 36 10.1 51 7.2	7 53.0 14 26.1 27 13.4	12 31.0 26 13.8 42 8.8	15 24.5 22 16.5 33 11.1	18 20.5 30 12.3 49 7.5
4.8 12.7 -23.5	4.3 9.8 -33.7	4.0 12.3 -75.8	Sales/Working Capital	5.7 NM -6.9	3.3 12.9 NM	7.9 149.4 -10.5	3.7 10.3 -62.6	3.0 6.4 24.8	5.4 8.9 NM
(83) 5.5 2.6 1.1	(99) 5.6 2.5 1.2	(121) 9.5 3.1 1.0	EBIT/Interest	3.2 1.6 .6	(25) 5.4 1.9 .7	7.2 6.4 .4	(21) 9.9 1.6 .7	(17) 25.7 9.3 1.8	(17) 26.0 7.9 2.3
(20) 4.2 1.5 .7	(18) 4.0 1.9 1.0	(32) 14.6 2.6 1.5	Net Profit + Depr., Dep., Amort./Cur. Mat. L/T/D					(10) 15.8 4.3 2.1	
.8 1.5 3.6	.7 1.4 3.9	.6 1.2 4.0	Fixed/Worth	1.4 6.0 -12.0	.7 1.6 4.0	1.0 1.8 4.4	.7 1.1 2.5	.5 .6 1.3	.6 .7 1.3
.6 1.7 4.3	.6 1.5 6.3	.5 1.3 5.5	Debt/Worth	1.1 6.7 -24.1	.5 1.6 6.3	.5 1.2 5.1	.4 1.0 4.6	.3 .4 1.3	.4 1.2 2.4
(82) 27.5 13.8 1.4	(91) 31.4 14.9 4.8	(117) 29.0 13.4 3.6	% Profit Before Taxes/Tangible Net Worth	(14) 47.6 22.0 7.2	(27) 31.8 12.0 -13.7	(17) 48.5 17.9 5.4	(23) 13.8 6.2 1.9	(20) 50.6 15.5 5.6	(16) 27.1 19.2 5.6
13.0 5.9 .3	13.5 4.9 1.0	11.4 5.7 .0	% Profit Before Taxes/Total Assets	11.8 3.4 -1.3	9.3 3.4 -2.4	17.9 8.6 -2.7	8.5 2.2 .2	18.0 6.2 2.6	13.8 10.3 1.2
3.9 1.9 1.2	4.6 2.1 1.3	4.2 2.3 1.4	Sales/Net Fixed Assets	3.2 1.7 1.0	3.4 2.2 1.6	4.4 1.7 1.3	3.3 2.1 1.5	5.6 3.5 1.8	5.5 2.8 1.6
1.6 1.0 .7	1.7 1.1 .7	1.7 1.2 .8	Sales/Total Assets	1.8 1.2 .7	1.7 1.2 .8	2.2 1.3 .9	1.4 1.0 .8	1.9 1.1 .9	1.9 1.2 .7
(84) 5.6 9.2 13.0	(96) 5.3 8.8 13.1	(122) 5.3 8.5 13.2	% Depr., Dep., Amort./Sales	(20) 8.7 15.1 19.5	(26) 6.3 9.3 14.9	(17) 5.2 9.1 13.2	(23) 5.2 9.2 12.6	(20) 4.4 6.9 9.1	(16) 2.0 5.1 8.2
(29) 2.9 4.4 9.2	(41) 1.6 3.6 7.6	(51) 1.9 3.6 6.5	% Officers', Directors', Owners' Comp/Sales	(13) 4.1 6.4 8.8	(14) 3.3 5.1 7.1		(10) 1.7 2.2 3.8		
1153199M	1330787M	1896569M	Net Sales ($)	12071M	60328M	74055M	179268M	362070M	1208777M
1316651M	1177704M	1779656M	Total Assets ($)	13035M	67179M	61733M	193115M	347540M	1097054M

M = $ thousand   MM = $ million
See Pages 11 through 18 for Explanation of Ratios and Data

Current Data Sorted By Assets   Comparative Historical Data

0-500M	500M-2MM	2-10MM	10-50MM	50-100MM	100-250MM	Type of Statement	4/1/98-3/31/99 ALL	4/1/99-3/31/00 ALL
		1	7	1	2	Unqualified	6	5
		1	1			Reviewed	6	5
3	2	2				Compiled	4	3
2	1	3				Tax Returns	1	2
1	5	9	1	2	1	Other	14	11
	12 (4/1-9/30/02)			33 (10/1/02-3/31/03)				
6	8	16	9	3	3	NUMBER OF STATEMENTS	31	26
%	%	%	%	%	%		%	%
						ASSETS		
		14.0				Cash & Equivalents	13.8	9.9
		24.4				Trade Receivables (net)	23.0	19.9
		1.0				Inventory	1.0	7.0
		5.4				All Other Current	2.3	2.6
		44.8				Total Current	40.1	39.4
		43.5				Fixed Assets (net)	42.9	42.0
		4.3				Intangibles (net)	2.1	6.4
		7.4				All Other Non-Current	14.9	12.2
		100.0				Total	100.0	100.0
						LIABILITIES		
		5.2				Notes Payable-Short Term	2.9	9.4
		6.5				Cur. Mat.-L/T/D	1.9	11.3
		18.9				Trade Payables	10.0	10.9
		.3				Income Taxes Payable	.0	.0
		12.1				All Other Current	12.4	11.9
		43.0				Total Current	27.2	43.6
		19.7				Long Term Debt	26.3	14.7
		.9				Deferred Taxes	1.7	.8
		2.1				All Other Non-Current	11.6	3.5
		34.3				Net Worth	33.2	37.4
		100.0				Total Liabilities & Net Worth	100.0	100.0
						INCOME DATA		
		100.0				Net Sales	100.0	100.0
						Gross Profit		
		92.4				Operating Expenses	113.6	94.9
		7.6				Operating Profit	-13.6	5.1
		1.5				All Other Expenses (net)	17.6	-1.7
		6.1				Profit Before Taxes	-31.2	6.8
						RATIOS		
		1.2					2.9	1.8
		1.0				Current	1.5	1.2
		.8					.8	.7
		1.2					2.7	1.4
		.8				Quick	1.4	.8
		.6					.7	.6
		24 15.0					34 10.7	30 12.2
		55 6.7				Sales/Receivables	52 7.0	58 6.3
		66 5.5					61 6.0	71 5.2
						Cost of Sales/Inventory		
						Cost of Sales/Payables		
		10.9					6.6	5.2
		NM				Sales/Working Capital	15.1	28.5
		-12.2					-29.7	-10.0
		11.5					11.6	6.6
	(14)	7.2				EBIT/Interest	(21) 4.4	(24) 3.8
		1.4					.6	1.7
						Net Profit + Depr., Dep., Amort./Cur. Mat. L./T/D		
		.5					.4	.6
		1.3				Fixed/Worth	.9	1.2
		2.9					1.9	2.5
		1.2					.3	.9
		3.1				Debt/Worth	.9	1.7
		5.3					3.7	3.4
		66.1					35.4	32.9
	(15)	19.4				% Profit Before Taxes/Tangible Net Worth	(28) 8.9	(23) 14.7
		2.6					-3.8	-1.0
		17.6					21.8	12.3
		5.5				% Profit Before Taxes/Total Assets	2.3	6.4
		2.1					-2.5	1.2
		6.0					13.1	4.6
		3.6				Sales/Net Fixed Assets	3.7	2.9
		2.0					.7	.7
		2.5					2.5	1.8
		1.6				Sales/Total Assets	1.1	1.1
		.9					.4	.4
		1.7					3.0	2.3
	(13)	4.3				% Depr., Dep., Amort./Sales	(27) 7.2	(24) 9.3
		9.5					19.4	12.0
						% Officers', Directors', Owners' Comp/Sales		2.9
							(11) 5.8	
								13.4
3529M	18808M	127709M	255577M	166132M	233394M	Net Sales ($)	490954M	254937M
1597M	8898M	69137M	271188M	192379M	467335M	Total Assets ($)	692018M	473701M

M = $ thousand   MM = $ million
See Pages 11 through 18 for Explanation of Ratios and Data

Comparative Historical Data / Current Data Sorted By Sales

			Type of Statement	0-1MM	1-3MM	3-5MM	5-10MM	10-25MM	25MM & OVER
2	3	11	Unqualified		2		2	1	6
4	5	2	Reviewed		1			1	
9	7	7	Compiled	3	2		1		1
7	5	6	Tax Returns	2	2	1	1	2	
17	20	19	Other	1	7	3	2	2	4
4/1/00-3/31/01 ALL	4/1/01-3/31/02 ALL	4/1/02-3/31/03 ALL		12 (4/1-9/30/02)			33 (10/1/02-3/31/03)		
39	40	45	**NUMBER OF STATEMENTS**	6	11	4	7	6	11
%	%	%	**ASSETS**	%	%	%	%	%	%
11.4	12.0	13.4	Cash & Equivalents		13.3				15.5
22.8	24.4	18.3	Trade Receivables (net)		20.2				14.3
3.5	4.8	1.9	Inventory		3.2				2.0
3.1	4.0	3.4	All Other Current		.6				.8
40.9	45.2	37.0	Total Current		37.3				32.7
44.1	43.0	49.7	Fixed Assets (net)		44.1				52.0
5.6	3.7	1.8	Intangibles (net)		6.2				.9
9.4	8.1	11.5	All Other Non-Current		12.5				14.4
100.0	100.0	100.0	Total		100.0				100.0
			LIABILITIES						
6.1	6.6	5.1	Notes Payable-Short Term		4.0				1.5
6.8	5.5	5.3	Cur. Mat.-L/T/D		6.7				4.1
13.9	11.8	10.7	Trade Payables		9.0				15.2
.1	.7	.4	Income Taxes Payable		.0				.5
11.1	9.7	7.5	All Other Current		5.4				5.1
37.9	34.3	28.9	Total Current		25.2				26.4
19.4	15.1	21.5	Long Term Debt		35.9				9.8
.4	1.2	1.0	Deferred Taxes		.0				2.0
3.8	2.5	3.9	All Other Non-Current		4.2				4.8
38.5	46.9	44.7	Net Worth		34.7				56.9
100.0	100.0	100.0	Total Liabilities & Net Worth		100.0				100.0
			INCOME DATA						
100.0	100.0	100.0	Net Sales		100.0				100.0
			Gross Profit						
94.7	86.2	87.9	Operating Expenses		84.5				86.6
5.3	13.8	12.1	Operating Profit		15.5				13.4
−4.7	.9	1.2	All Other Expenses (net)		2.9				.3
10.0	12.9	11.0	Profit Before Taxes		12.6				13.1
			RATIOS						
2.1 1.2 .7	2.3 1.6 1.0	2.4 1.2 .8	Current		4.1 1.6 .8				2.2 1.4 .9
1.5 1.0 .6	1.7 1.2 .8	2.3 1.1 .7	Quick		4.1 1.2 .7				1.9 1.3 .8
22 16.8 46 7.9 78 4.7	34 10.8 50 7.3 72 5.1	19 19.1 48 7.6 67 5.4	Sales/Receivables		25 14.7 60 6.1 83 4.4				20 17.8 53 6.9 79 4.6
			Cost of Sales/Inventory						
			Cost of Sales/Payables						
7.1 27.1 −20.3	6.8 16.2 −236.2	7.2 18.8 −20.7	Sales/Working Capital		4.3 8.0 −7.5				7.8 49.0 −22.8
(31) 8.2 3.5 1.6	(39) 31.9 7.8 1.4	(38) 11.9 3.6 .9	EBIT/Interest		(10) 11.9 3.9 .7				
	(11) 4.5 3.1 2.1		Net Profit + Depr., Dep., Amort./Cur. Mat. L/T/D						
.6 1.5 4.5	.5 .9 2.1	.5 1.1 2.4	Fixed/Worth		.7 1.1 15.2				.5 1.1 1.5
.5 2.1 11.8	.6 1.1 3.0	.5 1.5 4.0	Debt/Worth		.8 3.0 23.2				.3 1.0 1.5
(31) 52.8 30.3 12.7	(37) 69.6 27.8 6.2	(42) 45.3 18.2 4.4	% Profit Before Taxes/Tangible Net Worth						19.6 11.4 5.0
22.3 12.5 3.4	24.9 12.3 1.7	20.4 6.2 1.1	% Profit Before Taxes/Total Assets		32.9 5.6 −.4				14.8 5.6 2.0
4.8 2.8 2.1	6.4 4.8 2.2	5.7 2.8 1.2	Sales/Net Fixed Assets		5.2 3.2 .9				5.6 1.2 .9
2.3 1.4 .7	2.4 1.8 .8	2.2 1.1 .7	Sales/Total Assets		1.6 1.0 .4				1.1 .7 .7
(34) 2.8 6.0 11.1	(35) 2.8 4.6 10.0	(37) 3.3 8.0 12.2	% Depr., Dep., Amort./Sales						
(14) 2.1 5.1 9.6	(17) 2.0 3.2 6.3	(14) 1.3 4.7 8.2	% Officers', Directors', Owners' Comp/Sales						
320339M	696815M	805149M	Net Sales ($)	3529M	22093M	16479M	49853M	84086M	629109M
360622M	621390M	1010534M	Total Assets ($)	1597M	39713M	10033M	53172M	79591M	826428M

© RMA 2003

M = $ thousand   MM = $ million
See Pages 11 through 18 for Explanation of Ratios and Data

Current Data Sorted By Assets | **Comparative Historical Data**

	0-500M	500M-2MM	2-10MM	10-50MM	50-100MM	100-250MM	Type of Statement	4/1/98-3/31/99 ALL	4/1/99-3/31/00 ALL
	1	1	10	14	8	8	Unqualified	24	30
		3	19	3					
	5	17	12	3			Reviewed	12	16
	4	6	1				Compiled	18	21
						1	Tax Returns	5	4
	9	19	25	25	2	6	Other	41	37

41 (4/1-9/30/02)　　　161 (10/1/02-3/31/03)

	0-500M	500M-2MM	2-10MM	10-50MM	50-100MM	100-250MM		ALL 100	ALL 108
	19	46	67	45	10	15	**NUMBER OF STATEMENTS**	100	108
	%	%	%	%	%	%	**ASSETS**	%	%
	17.5	11.8	9.1	9.8	6.0	4.4	Cash & Equivalents	10.8	9.6
	18.7	27.2	29.2	25.5	14.4	16.9	Trade Receivables (net)	22.8	24.9
	10.8	7.9	7.1	8.5	11.7	8.1	Inventory	6.5	7.2
	8.9	3.0	5.9	2.6	3.5	6.5	All Other Current	3.1	2.6
	56.0	49.8	51.3	46.4	35.6	35.9	Total Current	43.2	44.3
	37.4	43.4	39.7	42.2	49.1	47.2	Fixed Assets (net)	46.5	42.8
	.1	1.6	1.6	4.1	4.6	11.8	Intangibles (net)	3.6	3.2
	6.5	5.2	7.5	7.3	10.8	5.1	All Other Non-Current	6.7	9.6
	100.0	100.0	100.0	100.0	100.0	100.0	Total	100.0	100.0
							LIABILITIES		
	8.8	8.4	10.8	12.1	15.3	7.0	Notes Payable-Short Term	10.7	14.5
	23.4	6.0	6.1	4.8	26.8	2.8	Cur. Mat.-L/T/D	4.4	4.8
	5.8	11.0	11.0	10.8	7.4	11.6	Trade Payables	9.2	9.3
	3.4	.2	1.3	.3	.9	.7	Income Taxes Payable	.9	.3
	20.5	8.9	9.3	7.0	7.3	4.4	All Other Current	6.2	14.3
	62.0	34.4	38.5	34.9	57.7	26.5	Total Current	31.4	43.3
	18.6	20.0	18.0	16.5	9.1	13.5	Long Term Debt	19.4	19.0
	.0	.8	1.0	1.2	2.3	2.8	Deferred Taxes	1.7	1.0
	1.0	.8	3.5	3.7	4.0	1.3	All Other Non-Current	6.7	6.7
	18.5	43.9	39.1	43.7	26.9	55.9	Net Worth	40.8	30.0
	100.0	100.0	100.0	100.0	100.0	100.0	Total Liabilities & Net Worth	100.0	100.0
							INCOME DATA		
	100.0	100.0	100.0	100.0	100.0	100.0	Net Sales	100.0	100.0
							Gross Profit		
	87.4	96.9	95.0	90.0	90.3	88.4	Operating Expenses	96.2	96.0
	12.6	3.1	5.0	10.0	9.7	11.6	Operating Profit	3.8	4.0
	1.6	.9	1.7	1.9	7.0	2.5	All Other Expenses (net)	4.3	1.7
	11.0	2.2	3.2	8.0	2.7	9.1	Profit Before Taxes	−.5	2.3
							RATIOS		
	5.1	2.4	2.7	2.2	1.5	2.0		2.7	2.6
	2.1	1.4	1.3	1.3	.7	1.5	Current	1.4	1.5
	1.2	.8	.9	.8	.2	1.1		.9	.9
	2.8	1.7	1.7	1.6	1.3	1.3		1.9	1.9
	1.5	.9	.9	1.0	.5	1.0	Quick	1.1	1.1
	.3	.6	.6	.6	.1	.7		.5	.6
	0 UND	21 17.0	35 10.4	35 10.5	38 9.7	25 14.9		33 11.2	41 8.8
	4 103.7	48 7.6	51 7.2	57 6.4	47 7.8	56 6.5	Sales/Receivables	49 7.4	55 6.6
	35 10.3	65 5.6	67 5.4	72 5.0	59 6.2	68 5.3		71 5.1	79 4.6
							Cost of Sales/Inventory		
							Cost of Sales/Payables		
	5.3	7.2	6.3	4.5	11.9	5.9		4.8	4.0
	20.1	15.7	22.3	14.6	−16.9	8.6	Sales/Working Capital	16.6	14.9
	73.6	−44.0	−39.6	−22.9	−1.1	54.0		−30.5	−43.4
	(12) 92.0	(39) 7.8	(62) 10.3	(39) 8.9		(13) 10.2		(82) 8.0	(98) 10.0
	7.0	3.1	3.4	2.7		3.3	EBIT/Interest	2.7	1.7
	.5	.8	1.0	1.1		2.3		.7	.5
			(18) 6.1				Net Profit + Depr., Dep.,	(20) 4.4	(23) 3.3
			3.7				Amort./Cur. Mat. L /T/D	1.9	1.3
			1.4					1.1	.6
	.0	.4	.4	.3	.5	.6		.4	.4
	.6	.8	1.0	1.2	1.6	1.0	Fixed/Worth	1.1	1.1
	1.3	2.4	2.0	2.7	9.8	1.7		2.4	3.7
	.1	.6	.6	.6	.9	.4		.6	.6
	.9	1.0	1.4	1.7	1.9	1.2	Debt/Worth	1.2	1.5
	2.7	3.8	4.0	3.6	14.0	1.8		3.0	7.0
	(16) 103.0	(42) 41.3	(59) 24.0	(44) 40.6		(14) 29.8	% Profit Before Taxes/Tangible	(91) 36.2	(94) 30.4
	50.3	12.3	11.0	15.3		14.1	Net Worth	10.7	8.4
	23.9	2.6	.4	1.5		4.9		−3.6	−2.0
	60.4	14.0	10.6	14.7	11.0	13.7	% Profit Before Taxes/Total	16.0	12.7
	17.8	4.6	4.8	4.4	1.4	6.6	Assets	3.9	3.0
	8.4	−.4	.0	.6	−4.3	2.1		−1.5	−2.2
	169.0	11.1	14.3	20.5	3.7	9.7		10.8	9.4
	11.7	5.7	5.3	3.1	2.6	4.1	Sales/Net Fixed Assets	3.7	4.3
	3.5	2.2	2.8	1.3	.6	1.0		1.4	1.4
	6.0	3.1	3.0	2.2	1.4	2.5		2.3	2.9
	3.4	1.9	2.0	1.2	1.0	1.2	Sales/Total Assets	1.5	1.4
	1.9	1.0	1.2	.5	.4	.7		.8	.7
	(10) 1.4	(41) 3.1	(62) 1.5	(42) 1.0			% Depr., Dep., Amort./Sales	(84) 3.3	(94) 2.0
	7.4	4.9	3.6	5.6				7.2	4.6
	14.2	8.9	10.3	10.0				11.3	9.6
		(21) 4.3	(26) 2.3				% Officers', Directors',	(18) 2.1	(26) 2.3
		6.2	3.7				Owners' Comp/Sales	5.1	4.8
		7.6	9.8					9.6	10.0
	25282M	131047M	676331M	1572838M	588922M	3629599M	Net Sales ($)	1559661M	2452056M
	5185M	55577M	310367M	1077289M	610482M	2342168M	Total Assets ($)	2160255M	2538977M

© RMA 2003

M = $ thousand　　MM = $ million
See Pages 11 through 18 for Explanation of Ratios and Data

Comparative Historical Data | | Current Data Sorted By Sales

Comparative Historical Data			Type of Statement	Current Data Sorted By Sales					
28	41	42	Unqualified	1	4	2	2	10	23
14	16	25	Reviewed			7	8	7	3
20	33	37	Compiled	4	12	10	5	3	3
9	12	12	Tax Returns	2	6	2		1	1
42	43	86	Other	13	15	9	18	10	21
4/1/00- 3/31/01 ALL	4/1/01- 3/31/02 ALL	4/1/02- 3/31/03 ALL		41 (4/1-9/30/02) 0-1MM	1-3MM	3-5MM	161 (10/1/02-3/31/03) 5-10MM	10-25MM	25MM & OVER
113	145	202	**NUMBER OF STATEMENTS**	20	37	30	33	31	51
%	%	%	**ASSETS**	%	%	%	%	%	%
7.9	11.5	10.2	Cash & Equivalents	11.9	13.6	12.7	8.9	10.3	6.3
29.0	27.2	25.3	Trade Receivables (net)	10.1	22.8	24.5	30.2	29.0	28.0
7.4	6.9	8.2	Inventory	8.5	7.8	5.0	7.1	6.8	11.9
3.6	3.4	4.7	All Other Current	4.5	5.4	3.8	6.0	3.6	4.6
47.8	49.1	48.4	Total Current	34.9	49.6	46.0	52.3	49.7	50.8
41.6	38.5	41.9	Fixed Assets (net)	59.4	44.6	41.6	39.4	38.9	36.7
2.7	5.0	2.9	Intangibles (net)	1.7	1.4	1.6	1.8	2.0	6.6
7.8	7.3	6.8	All Other Non-Current	4.0	4.5	10.8	6.6	9.5	5.8
100.0	100.0	100.0	Total	100.0	100.0	100.0	100.0	100.0	100.0
			LIABILITIES						
12.7	11.1	10.3	Notes Payable-Short Term	6.7	7.2	5.3	8.8	14.7	15.1
4.9	5.2	8.2	Cur. Mat.-L/T/D	25.2	5.5	7.8	3.9	6.6	7.4
12.0	12.8	10.3	Trade Payables	5.1	8.5	10.2	10.7	9.0	14.3
.8	.6	.9	Income Taxes Payable	3.0	.1	.7	2.0	.2	.7
6.9	7.5	9.3	All Other Current	21.8	6.4	9.0	6.9	8.6	8.5
37.3	37.3	39.0	Total Current	61.9	27.7	33.0	32.4	39.1	46.1
21.5	22.3	17.4	Long Term Debt	28.5	22.7	18.2	20.3	14.2	8.7
1.7	1.4	1.1	Deferred Taxes	.3	.2	1.1	1.1	1.6	1.8
6.0	3.2	2.6	All Other Non-Current	5.6	1.6	1.4	2.4	4.3	1.8
33.5	35.8	39.9	Net Worth	3.7	47.7	46.3	43.8	40.8	41.6
100.0	100.0	100.0	Total Liabilities & Net Worth	100.0	100.0	100.0	100.0	100.0	100.0
			INCOME DATA						
100.0	100.0	100.0	Net Sales	100.0	100.0	100.0	100.0	100.0	100.0
			Gross Profit						
91.4	89.0	92.9	Operating Expenses	86.6	93.5	94.1	94.9	96.7	90.7
8.6	11.0	7.1	Operating Profit	13.4	6.5	5.9	5.1	3.3	9.3
1.4	2.9	1.9	All Other Expenses (net)	4.6	1.3	.9	1.3	3.5	1.2
7.2	8.1	5.2	Profit Before Taxes	8.7	5.3	5.1	3.8	-.2	8.0
			RATIOS						
2.4	2.4	2.4	Current	3.9	2.9	2.1	3.2	1.8	2.0
1.6	1.5	1.3		1.1	1.8	1.1	1.4	1.3	1.2
1.0	.9	.9		.1	1.0	.8	1.0	.9	.8
1.6	2.0	1.7	Quick	2.6	2.9	1.7	2.4	1.4	1.4
1.2	1.1	.9		.5	1.1	1.0	1.2	1.0	.9
.7	.7	.6		.0	.7	.6	1.0	.7	.5
31 11.7	31 11.8	29 12.5	Sales/Receivables	0 UND	12 31.7	21 17.0	39 9.3	33 11.2	35 10.4
54 6.8	51 7.1	50 7.4		1 305.0	47 7.7	46 7.9	61 6.0	49 7.4	50 7.3
78 4.7	72 5.1	67 5.5		68 5.4	64 5.7	89 4.1	73 5.0	66 5.5	64 5.7
			Cost of Sales/Inventory						
			Cost of Sales/Payables						
5.3	5.6	5.9	Sales/Working Capital	4.1	5.4	8.5	5.4	9.0	7.1
11.9	13.2	18.9		NM	10.0	32.5	13.2	24.3	17.0
126.9	-100.8	-32.9		-2.4	-199.0	-17.6	775.6	-56.5	-22.9
	9.2		19.9		9.3	EBIT/Interest	(14)	11.5	(33)	12.9	(25)	6.9	(30)	15.0	(29)	6.2	(43)	13.9

Net Profit + Depr., Dep., Amort./Cur. Mat. L/T/D	(23) 4.1 1.9 1.5	(39) 5.8 2.8 1.2	(38) 5.8 3.1 1.4						(11) 59.2 3.9 1.6

EBIT/Interest	(101) 9.2 3.8 1.3	(134) 19.9 4.3 2.0	(174) 9.3 3.2 1.0	(14) 11.5 1.0 -1.2	(33) 12.9 3.1 .2	(25) 6.9 2.5 1.4	(30) 15.0 4.1 1.4	(29) 6.2 2.7 1.2	(43) 13.9 3.3 1.1

Comparative Historical			Ratio	Current					
.4 / 1.2 / 2.6	.4 / 1.1 / 2.8	.4 / 1.0 / 2.1	Fixed/Worth	.5 / 1.9 / NM	.4 / .8 / 2.0	.3 / .7 / 2.3	.4 / .9 / 1.7	.3 / 1.2 / 2.1	.4 / 1.0 / 2.0
.7 / 1.9 / 4.4	.7 / 1.7 / 5.0	.6 / 1.4 / 3.5	Debt/Worth	.3 / 1.8 / -55.2	.4 / 1.0 / 3.1	.5 / 1.3 / 2.4	.5 / 1.1 / 3.8	.6 / 1.4 / 3.5	.7 / 1.5 / 3.6
(104) 49.1 / 23.3 / 7.9	(129) 62.5 / 30.8 / 10.1	(184) 38.5 / 15.0 / 2.4	% Profit Before Taxes/Tangible Net Worth	(14) 46.2 / 3.9 / -20.4	(35) 42.9 / 23.6 / .0	(28) 32.2 / 10.4 / 5.2	(31) 39.5 / 14.1 / 4.8	(28) 23.9 / 15.3 / 1.0	(48) 41.0 / 18.7 / 6.3
15.6 / 8.5 / 1.2	21.8 / 8.9 / 3.6	13.7 / 5.2 / .2	% Profit Before Taxes/Total Assets	16.2 / 1.0 / -6.5	20.3 / 8.6 / -.5	11.1 / 4.8 / 1.9	12.5 / 5.3 / -.1	10.9 / 4.2 / .5	15.2 / 7.2 / 1.0
10.8 / 4.5 / 1.8	10.7 / 5.1 / 2.5	13.4 / 5.1 / 1.8	Sales/Net Fixed Assets	5.4 / 1.2 / .5	10.6 / 4.2 / 2.0	17.3 / 6.2 / 2.2	11.6 / 5.7 / 2.7	24.7 / 4.3 / 1.6	19.5 / 6.0 / 2.9
2.9 / 1.6 / .8	3.1 / 1.9 / 1.0	2.9 / 1.8 / .9	Sales/Total Assets	1.8 / .6 / .3	2.9 / 1.9 / 1.0	3.4 / 1.8 / 1.1	3.0 / 2.1 / .8	3.0 / 2.0 / .9	3.0 / 1.8 / 1.1
(98) 2.1 / 4.4 / 7.6	(133) 1.5 / 3.6 / 7.1	(173) 1.8 / 4.8 / 10.4	% Depr., Dep., Amort./Sales	(13) 7.9 / 14.3 / 24.4	(32) 3.2 / 5.5 / 11.2	(26) 3.3 / 6.6 / 10.9	(32) 2.0 / 4.1 / 9.2	(28) 1.5 / 4.7 / 13.0	(42) .6 / 2.1 / 6.1
(28) 2.9 / 4.3 / 10.1	(44) 1.7 / 3.3 / 7.2	(59) 3.0 / 4.8 / 9.3	% Officers', Directors', Owners' Comp/Sales		(12) 3.7 / 6.0 / 7.3	(18) 3.4 / 4.7 / 8.1	(11) 1.3 / 3.0 / 6.2		
3463005M 2781985M	4269678M 3157990M	6624019M 4401068M	Net Sales ($) Total Assets ($)	10700M 38814M	67169M 74102M	117598M 158168M	236965M 218448M	480818M 544047M	5710769M 3367489M

© RMA 2003

M = $ thousand   MM = $ million
See Pages 11 through 18 for Explanation of Ratios and Data

UTILITIES

Current Data Sorted By Assets							Comparative Historical Data	

						Type of Statement		
1	4	9	14	10	21	Unqualified	92	84
1	5	8	1			Reviewed	11	14
1	5	3				Compiled	9	11
1		4				Tax Returns	8	7
2	5	11	10	1	7	Other	45	40
	29 (4/1-9/30/02)		95 (10/1/02-3/31/03)				4/1/98-3/31/99	4/1/99-3/31/00
0-500M	500M-2MM	2-10MM	10-50MM	50-100MM	100-250MM		ALL	ALL
6	19	35	25	11	28	NUMBER OF STATEMENTS	165	156
%	%	%	%	%	%	ASSETS	%	%
	15.3	11.8	13.9	10.1	5.9	Cash & Equivalents	8.0	9.4
	31.7	21.3	11.5	5.3	5.7	Trade Receivables (net)	15.6	15.9
	3.7	6.1	1.7	1.3	4.7	Inventory	5.3	4.9
	6.0	3.4	3.9	5.0	4.8	All Other Current	4.1	3.3
	56.7	42.6	31.0	21.6	21.1	Total Current	33.0	33.5
	33.4	41.1	56.9	66.0	58.2	Fixed Assets (net)	48.3	50.9
	4.6	5.9	2.1	.5	4.1	Intangibles (net)	4.7	5.3
	5.3	10.4	10.0	11.8	16.6	All Other Non-Current	14.0	10.3
	100.0	100.0	100.0	100.0	100.0	Total	100.0	100.0
						LIABILITIES		
	3.7	6.9	2.5	.2	6.0	Notes Payable-Short Term	7.6	6.1
	18.8	2.7	3.0	6.7	1.8	Cur. Mat.-L/T/D	4.9	3.4
	24.3	10.6	7.4	4.4	5.0	Trade Payables	9.7	9.4
	.0	.4	.0	.0	.1	Income Taxes Payable	.4	.4
	8.0	7.4	13.0	10.3	6.9	All Other Current	12.9	8.5
	54.8	28.0	25.9	21.5	19.8	Total Current	35.5	27.8
	37.3	34.8	17.4	30.6	42.3	Long Term Debt	33.2	25.8
	.3	1.5	1.2	.0	.9	Deferred Taxes	1.9	2.3
	6.1	10.3	8.4	3.4	7.6	All Other Non-Current	4.7	3.9
	1.5	25.3	47.1	44.4	29.4	Net Worth	24.8	40.2
	100.0	100.0	100.0	100.0	100.0	Total Liabilities & Net Worth	100.0	100.0
						INCOME DATA		
	100.0	100.0	100.0	100.0	100.0	Net Sales	100.0	100.0
						Gross Profit		
	86.5	85.2	86.3	83.5	89.0	Operating Expenses	85.3	87.3
	13.5	14.8	13.7	16.5	11.0	Operating Profit	14.7	12.7
	2.8	4.3	5.7	3.5	5.3	All Other Expenses (net)	5.6	2.2
	10.7	10.5	8.0	13.0	5.7	Profit Before Taxes	9.1	10.5
						RATIOS		
	4.8	2.4	1.8	1.3	1.5	Current	2.0	1.9
	1.7	1.4	1.1	1.1	1.1		1.2	1.2
	.5	1.1	.8	.7	.8		.7	.7
	2.6	2.4	1.7	1.0	1.3	Quick	1.6	1.6
	1.4	1.4	.9	.6	.7		.9	.9
	.3	.6	.5	.5	.4		.4	.4
	16 23.0	28 12.9	27 13.6	19 18.8	24 15.5	Sales/Receivables	21 17.4	21 17.2
	42 8.8	45 8.1	37 9.8	32 11.5	35 10.4		35 10.4	40 9.1
	64 5.7	56 6.5	62 5.8	38 9.6	45 8.1		52 7.1	59 6.2
						Cost of Sales/Inventory		
						Cost of Sales/Payables		
	3.5	4.4	6.9	10.8	9.9	Sales/Working Capital	6.1	6.4
	10.8	10.1	56.1	40.6	58.8		27.7	28.2
	-17.7	56.7	-19.4	-15.0	-23.6		-11.3	-14.7
	(16) 16.0	(29) 7.8	(20) 9.5	(10) 12.4	(27) 3.4	EBIT/Interest	(123) 6.5	(120) 7.2
	3.2	3.0	3.5	4.5	2.2		3.1	2.7
	1.6	1.3	1.9	2.0	1.5		1.8	1.7
						Net Profit + Depr., Dep., Amort./Cur. Mat. L /T/D	(42) 6.3	(28) 3.6
							2.5	2.0
							1.0	1.2
	.3	.3	.7	1.1	1.4	Fixed/Worth	.6	.7
	.7	1.1	1.1	1.4	2.5		1.8	1.3
	-3.0	3.7	2.3	2.9	8.0		4.5	2.6
	.2	.8	.5	.5	1.2	Debt/Worth	1.2	.7
	3.0	2.3	1.2	1.4	2.8		2.2	1.9
	-5.6	7.8	2.5	2.9	14.0		8.1	5.9
	(13) 61.1	(28) 29.3	(23) 23.2	32.5	(24) 20.0	% Profit Before Taxes/Tangible Net Worth	(136) 33.6	(145) 38.1
	9.5	15.9	5.4	15.5	11.0		16.7	13.7
	1.7	5.8	2.3	6.8	4.4		7.0	3.9
	21.3	12.3	8.9	16.0	5.4	% Profit Before Taxes/Total Assets	9.7	11.4
	9.0	4.9	3.2	4.2	3.1		4.6	4.3
	1.9	1.1	1.1	3.6	1.4		1.1	1.6
	61.2	45.5	2.2	1.3	2.3	Sales/Net Fixed Assets	13.2	15.3
	6.1	1.7	.8	1.0	.8		1.4	1.1
	1.3	.7	.4	.5	.5		.5	.5
	4.4	2.2	.9	.9	.6	Sales/Total Assets	1.9	2.0
	2.1	1.0	.5	.7	.5		.6	.6
	.6	.4	.3	.3	.3		.3	.3
	(15) 1.2	(30) .9	(23) 5.0		(24) 4.6	% Depr., Dep., Amort./Sales	(145) 2.2	(139) 1.9
	2.3	5.1	7.6		6.0		6.8	6.4
	8.5	14.7	12.5		8.7		10.8	11.2
		(10) 1.9				% Officers', Directors', Owners' Comp/Sales	(22) 2.7	(28) 3.6
		4.4					5.1	5.7
		6.9					8.6	11.8
4204M	53101M	226438M	488289M	566861M	2635004M	Net Sales ($)	5944212M	4574784M
1491M	19497M	162693M	557516M	798476M	4444912M	Total Assets ($)	7801849M	7283079M

M = $ thousand   MM = $ million
See Pages 11 through 18 for Explanation of Ratios and Data

Comparative Historical Data   **Current Data Sorted By Sales**

Hist 1	Hist 2	Hist 3	Type of Statement	0-1MM	1-3MM	3-5MM	5-10MM	10-25MM	25MM & OVER
57	58	59	Unqualified	2	7	6	5	8	31
14	11	15	Reviewed	2	5	2	5	1	
14	15	9	Compiled	3	2	3	1		
7	7	5	Tax Returns	1	2		2		
33	49	36	Other	4	2	1	4	10	10
4/1/00-3/31/01	4/1/01-3/31/02	4/1/02-3/31/03			29 (4/1-9/30/02)		95 (10/1/02-3/31/03)		
ALL	ALL	ALL							
125	140	124	**NUMBER OF STATEMENTS**	12	23	12	17	19	41
%	%	%	**ASSETS**	%	%	%	%	%	%
10.7	11.6	12.4	Cash & Equivalents	22.1	10.3	12.6	9.6	18.3	9.0
20.8	18.9	15.9	Trade Receivables (net)	12.4	12.3	25.0	30.7	11.4	12.2
4.7	3.9	3.8	Inventory	.9	2.7	5.9	6.1	4.2	3.6
3.8	4.3	4.2	All Other Current	4.3	3.1	2.6	3.8	3.0	6.0
40.0	38.7	36.2	Total Current	39.7	28.4	46.1	50.1	36.9	30.7
45.5	46.3	49.1	Fixed Assets (net)	44.2	56.4	44.4	36.4	46.2	54.5
4.0	4.2	3.9	Intangibles (net)	3.0	7.1	3.7	3.0	3.4	3.0
10.5	10.8	10.8	All Other Non-Current	13.1	8.2	5.8	10.5	13.6	11.8
100.0	100.0	100.0	Total	100.0	100.0	100.0	100.0	100.0	100.0
			LIABILITIES						
5.2	4.5	4.4	Notes Payable-Short Term	5.3	2.3	1.3	6.1	6.1	4.7
4.2	4.4	6.2	Cur. Mat.-L/T/D	3.9	8.0	25.2	3.9	2.3	2.9
11.1	14.1	12.3	Trade Payables	45.0	3.4	11.4	13.4	8.5	9.2
.7	.3	.1	Income Taxes Payable	.1	.1	.1	.0	.6	.0
16.8	8.8	8.7	All Other Current	4.5	6.0	4.4	12.7	13.0	9.0
38.0	32.2	31.6	Total Current	58.7	19.7	42.4	36.2	30.6	25.8
30.6	36.9	35.7	Long Term Debt	87.9	44.3	18.1	13.6	25.1	34.9
2.1	1.1	1.0	Deferred Taxes	1.1	2.3	1.4	.6	.4	.6
5.1	4.4	7.6	All Other Non-Current	7.6	7.5	6.9	11.6	5.9	7.0
24.2	25.4	24.0	Net Worth	-55.4	26.1	31.2	38.0	38.1	31.7
100.0	100.0	100.0	Total Liabilities & Net Worth	100.0	100.0	100.0	100.0	100.0	100.0
			INCOME DATA						
100.0	100.0	100.0	Net Sales	100.0	100.0	100.0	100.0	100.0	100.0
			Gross Profit						
85.6	87.3	86.1	Operating Expenses	68.0	83.2	86.8	94.8	92.1	86.3
14.4	12.7	13.9	Operating Profit	32.0	16.8	13.2	5.2	7.9	13.7
4.0	4.9	4.7	All Other Expenses (net)	9.1	5.5	3.1	4.4	2.1	4.7
10.4	7.8	9.3	Profit Before Taxes	22.9	11.3	10.2	.7	5.8	9.0
			RATIOS						
1.8	2.2	1.8		2.8	2.6	4.9	2.0	1.7	1.5
1.3	1.3	1.3	Current	1.5	1.4	1.6	1.1	1.2	1.1
.8	.8	.9		.3	.7	.9	.9	1.0	.8
1.6	1.8	1.7		2.1	2.4	4.5	1.8	1.5	1.3
.9	1.0	1.0	Quick	.8	1.4	1.6	1.1	1.0	.7
.5	.5	.4		.1	.5	.6	.7	.4	.4
27 13.6	23 16.1	25 14.4		1 259.5	16 23.0	33 11.2	33 11.1	23 15.8	26 14.1
39 9.4	35 10.4	37 10.0	Sales/Receivables	30 12.2	37 9.9	49 7.4	58 6.3	32 11.5	36 10.2
62 5.9	59 6.2	56 6.5		54 6.8	48 7.6	66 5.5	71 5.1	45 8.1	52 7.0
			Cost of Sales/Inventory						
			Cost of Sales/Payables						
7.5	6.6	6.6		2.5	5.4	2.0	6.1	10.1	11.2
23.4	18.1	20.1	Sales/Working Capital	10.9	9.1	13.9	26.4	30.4	23.2
-19.4	-24.3	-43.9		-1.8	-21.0	NM	-48.1	585.9	-25.4
(106) 7.0	(114) 6.2	(107) 7.7			3.8	10.6	(15) 7.7	4.1	(38) 8.2
3.4	2.5	2.9	EBIT/Interest	(19) 2.7	4.4	(15) 1.4	(14) 2.3	2.6	
1.6	1.5	1.5		1.2	2.6	-2.9	-.3	1.7	
(30) 4.0	(24) 2.6	(16) 4.1	Net Profit + Depr., Dep.,						
2.7	2.0	2.0	Amort./Cur. Mat. L/T/D						
1.3	.3	.8							
.6	.6	.6		.4	1.0	.4	.1	.7	1.1
1.5	1.2	1.4	Fixed/Worth	.9	2.0	1.1	.5	1.1	2.1
3.4	2.8	3.4		NM	11.5	2.4	2.3	1.8	3.8
1.0	.8	.7		.3	.4	.2	.5	.8	1.0
1.8	1.7	2.2	Debt/Worth	3.7	1.7	1.8	2.0	1.4	2.4
5.7	6.6	7.5		-8.3	44.2	3.4	6.3	2.7	9.6
(112) 37.0	(127) 31.0	(104) 31.9	% Profit Before Taxes/Tangible		27.9	66.6	(15) 33.7	15.2	(36) 54.8
14.7	10.2	13.4	Net Worth	(18) 15.2	(11) 23.2	1.9	(16) 6.1	16.0	
4.1	3.4	3.0		2.6	2.9	-6.4	2.2	8.2	
15.6	9.9	11.1	% Profit Before Taxes/Total	47.3	11.3	16.4	13.1	4.0	8.8
4.9	3.9	4.2	Assets	11.2	5.4	6.3	1.3	2.5	4.0
1.3	1.1	1.4		4.0	1.1	2.6	-3.7	-1.7	2.1
18.4	18.8	11.8		5.2	10.6	58.4	67.0	8.7	3.4
2.2	1.4	1.2	Sales/Net Fixed Assets	1.2	1.4	1.2	1.7	1.8	.9
.6	.6	.6		.6	.6	.4	.6	.6	.6
2.7	2.1	1.6		1.3	2.1	3.8	3.2	2.1	1.1
.8	.7	.6	Sales/Total Assets	.6	.7	.5	1.1	.6	.6
.4	.4	.4		.4	.4	.3	.4	.4	.4
(110) 1.7	(125) 1.4	(105) 2.1			2.1	1.7	(15) .7	2.6	(34) 3.8
4.8	4.7	5.9	% Depr., Dep., Amort./Sales	(21) 8.3	(10) 11.7	2.6	(16) 5.6	5.7	
7.9	8.0	11.4		15.7	17.1	17.0	7.3	8.3	
(22) 3.7	(22) 3.5	(20) 1.7	% Officers', Directors',						
7.4	6.1	3.5	Owners' Comp/Sales						
12.3	8.8	6.9							
3952882M	4340820M	3973897M	Net Sales ($)	6695M	40649M	46773M	122152M	298257M	3459371M
5974037M	6005087M	5984585M	Total Assets ($)	13609M	63015M	82569M	168339M	566353M	5090700M

M = $ thousand   MM = $ million
See Pages 11 through 18 for Explanation of Ratios and Data

Current Data Sorted By Assets   Comparative Historical Data

0-500M	500M-2MM	2-10MM	10-50MM	50-100MM	100-250MM	Type of Statement	4/1/98-3/31/99 ALL	4/1/99-3/31/00 ALL
	2	10	17	8	13	Unqualified	36	36
1	2	11		1		Reviewed	10	11
2	4	5				Compiled	4	13
4	2					Tax Returns	1	3
1	2	12	9	5	7	Other	20	24
	43 (4/1-9/30/02)		75 (10/1/02-3/31/03)					
8	12	38	26	14	20	**NUMBER OF STATEMENTS**	71	87
%	%	%	%	%	%	**ASSETS**	%	%
	18.9	10.2	6.9	12.1	5.4	Cash & Equivalents	8.5	8.3
	14.4	24.0	13.0	15.4	15.4	Trade Receivables (net)	14.3	19.5
	3.6	6.4	6.3	4.2	11.5	Inventory	5.8	5.8
	6.2	2.8	3.6	7.2	4.1	All Other Current	3.0	3.5
	43.2	43.4	29.9	38.9	36.5	Total Current	31.6	37.2
	43.6	46.8	54.3	47.4	50.1	Fixed Assets (net)	57.0	53.3
	7.8	2.6	8.7	4.7	5.4	Intangibles (net)	1.9	2.4
	5.4	7.2	7.1	9.0	8.0	All Other Non-Current	9.5	7.2
	100.0	100.0	100.0	100.0	100.0	Total	100.0	100.0
						LIABILITIES		
	9.9	5.2	8.0	3.2	5.9	Notes Payable-Short Term	4.3	8.6
	1.9	3.1	5.1	.6	1.9	Cur. Mat.-L/T/D	4.4	3.5
	11.2	19.6	8.4	13.6	12.4	Trade Payables	12.2	15.1
	.0	.3	.2	1.5	.3	Income Taxes Payable	.3	.3
	8.0	8.3	5.6	8.6	10.6	All Other Current	10.1	10.3
	31.0	36.4	27.4	27.5	31.1	Total Current	31.1	37.8
	27.2	22.2	25.7	28.0	24.2	Long Term Debt	24.3	21.1
	.4	1.8	.9	3.0	4.7	Deferred Taxes	4.9	3.1
	2.2	3.2	5.3	5.6	7.8	All Other Non-Current	4.0	4.8
	39.2	36.3	40.7	35.9	32.1	Net Worth	35.7	33.3
	100.0	100.0	100.0	100.0	100.0	Total Liabilities & Net Worth	100.0	100.0
						INCOME DATA		
	100.0	100.0	100.0	100.0	100.0	Net Sales	100.0	100.0
						Gross Profit		
	91.8	94.9	94.3	93.3	87.6	Operating Expenses	99.9	91.7
	8.2	5.1	5.6	6.7	12.4	Operating Profit	.1	8.3
	1.3	1.4	2.5	1.2	3.5	All Other Expenses (net)	-2.2	-.7
	6.9	3.7	3.1	5.5	9.0	Profit Before Taxes	2.2	9.0
						RATIOS		
	3.1	1.6	2.1	2.2	1.3	Current	1.5	1.4
	1.5	1.2	1.3	1.4	1.0		1.0	.9
	.9	.9	.6	1.1	.7		.7	.7
	2.4	1.3	1.8	1.7	.9	Quick	1.1	1.1
	1.1	.9	.8	1.1	.7		.6	.7
	.4	.6	.3	.4	.4		.3	.4
	1 437.0	18 20.2	16 22.5	20 17.9	23 15.6	Sales/Receivables	16 22.6	24 15.1
	26 13.9	34 10.6	26 14.0	28 12.8	39 9.4		29 12.4	37 9.9
	40 9.2	48 7.6	50 7.3	40 9.1	59 6.2		43 8.4	55 6.6
						Cost of Sales/Inventory		
						Cost of Sales/Payables		
	6.2	10.7	6.1	4.6	20.6	Sales/Working Capital	12.5	13.2
	33.0	47.9	23.0	14.7	-125.0		153.2	-100.0
	-124.4	-39.6	-12.6	NM	-15.7		-12.8	-8.8
	16.6	6.5	6.4	11.8	4.0	EBIT/Interest	4.3	6.6
	(10) 4.9	(32) 2.8	(23) 2.7	(13) 2.9	(19) 3.0		(63) 2.8	(74) 3.2
	-1.4	1.7	1.2	2.1	2.3		1.9	1.5
		5.0				Net Profit + Depr., Dep., Amort./Cur. Mat. L./T/D	24.0	15.7
		(13) 3.2					(29) 6.5	(28) 4.7
		2.1					2.2	1.9
	.3	.7	1.0	.7	.7	Fixed/Worth	.9	.8
	1.0	1.4	1.8	1.4	2.3		1.8	2.0
	59.4	2.4	3.1	2.4	2.8		2.5	3.7
	.4	.8	.5	1.5	1.6	Debt/Worth	1.2	.9
	2.2	1.8	1.9	2.2	2.8		1.9	2.2
	64.9	3.8	6.7	3.3	3.7		2.9	7.4
	82.6	27.4	25.4	38.9	48.5	% Profit Before Taxes/Tangible Net Worth	19.8	31.4
	(10) 23.5	(34) 14.6	(21) 7.8	(13) 16.2	(19) 18.6		(67) 15.1	(75) 16.4
	3.3	4.9	1.9	10.7	9.8		7.8	10.6
	27.8	9.8	7.8	9.8	11.4	% Profit Before Taxes/Total Assets	8.4	9.5
	7.7	5.1	3.7	4.5	4.4		5.1	5.4
	-.3	1.3	.8	2.7	2.8		2.8	2.2
	13.1	28.1	9.1	4.9	204.8	Sales/Net Fixed Assets	4.3	9.1
	3.2	3.5	1.2	2.1	1.0		1.4	1.8
	1.5	1.1	.7	1.1	.6		.8	.8
	2.5	4.1	2.3	1.6	2.1	Sales/Total Assets	2.0	2.7
	1.8	1.9	.8	.9	.7		.9	1.1
	.8	.8	.6	.7	.4		.6	.6
		.8	3.1	2.3	.3	% Depr., Dep., Amort./Sales	3.4	2.7
		(34) 3.4	(24) 5.9	(13) 4.9	(15) 5.3		(64) 5.0	(72) 5.7
		6.2	7.5	6.6	7.8		7.9	8.7
						% Officers', Directors', Owners' Comp/Sales		1.1
							(13)	2.9
								12.9
12685M	28431M	722186M	967151M	1570922M	4858868M	Net Sales ($)	3884590M	3692953M
2272M	14546M	180928M	638355M	1044555M	3543229M	Total Assets ($)	3710001M	3335917M

© RMA 2003

M = $ thousand   MM = $ million
See Pages 11 through 18 for Explanation of Ratios and Data

Comparative Historical Data				Current Data Sorted By Sales					
			Type of Statement	1	5		7	8	29
35	34	50	Unqualified	1	3	3	1	3	4
13	12	15	Reviewed		4	3	1	3	
14	13	11	Compiled	3	3				
5	3	6	Tax Returns	1	3	1	7	4	20
18	20	36	Other						
4/1/00- 3/31/01 ALL	4/1/01- 3/31/02 ALL	4/1/02- 3/31/03 ALL		43 (4/1-9/30/02)			75 (10/1/02-3/31/03)		
				0-1MM	1-3MM	3-5MM	5-10MM	10-25MM	25MM & OVER
85	82	118	**NUMBER OF STATEMENTS**	6	18	7	16	18	53
%	%	%	**ASSETS**	%	%	%	%	%	%
8.2	6.5	10.2	Cash & Equivalents	13.5			11.1	5.7	10.1
18.8	20.6	18.5	Trade Receivables (net)	14.7			13.2	27.6	18.8
7.7	9.7	6.7	Inventory	4.2			4.6	4.4	8.9
3.0	5.6	4.2	All Other Current	1.8			4.1	2.0	5.5
37.6	42.3	39.7	Total Current	34.3			33.0	39.8	43.4
46.5	43.9	48.1	Fixed Assets (net)	54.9			61.9	48.3	41.4
6.7	4.7	5.2	Intangibles (net)	3.0			2.5	4.9	6.7
9.2	9.1	7.0	All Other Non-Current	7.8			2.6	6.9	8.5
100.0	100.0	100.0	Total	100.0			100.0	100.0	100.0
			LIABILITIES						
9.1	11.4	9.1	Notes Payable-Short Term	12.2			4.6	6.0	7.2
3.0	4.2	3.0	Cur. Mat.-L/T/D	3.1			3.2	3.1	2.9
16.3	15.9	14.1	Trade Payables	8.8			13.1	13.4	17.0
.4	.4	.4	Income Taxes Payable	.0			.2	.5	.6
8.6	11.0	9.1	All Other Current	6.9			6.0	8.8	8.6
37.5	42.9	35.7	Total Current	30.9			26.9	31.8	36.3
19.9	22.0	24.3	Long Term Debt	28.8			26.9	19.0	24.1
2.4	2.5	2.0	Deferred Taxes	1.4			1.5	1.3	2.7
4.3	4.2	4.5	All Other Non-Current	5.3			1.8	3.3	6.2
35.8	28.4	33.5	Net Worth	33.5			42.9	44.7	30.6
100.0	100.0	100.0	Total Liabilities & Net Worth	100.0			100.0	100.0	100.0
			INCOME DATA						
100.0	100.0	100.0	Net Sales	100.0			100.0	100.0	100.0
			Gross Profit						
92.3	93.8	93.7	Operating Expenses	93.4			93.8	93.8	92.5
7.7	6.2	6.3	Operating Profit	6.6			6.1	6.2	7.5
1.7	1.5	1.8	All Other Expenses (net)	1.7			2.7	1.5	1.8
6.1	4.7	4.5	Profit Before Taxes	4.9			3.4	4.7	5.6
			RATIOS						
1.6	1.3	1.7		1.8			1.6	2.2	1.7
1.1	1.0	1.2	Current	1.1			1.3	1.2	1.2
.7	.7	.8		.8			.6	1.0	.9
1.1	1.1	1.3		1.3			1.3	1.8	1.3
.8	.5	.8	Quick	.8			.9	1.0	.8
.3	.3	.4		.5			.3	1.0	.4
16 22.6	16 22.2	17 21.3	Sales/Receivables	10 37.6			14 26.6	20 18.0	20 18.4
32 11.4	28 13.0	31 11.8		25 14.7			26 14.0	34 10.9	33 11.1
50 7.3	39 9.4	49 7.4		42 8.6			49 7.4	64 5.7	49 7.4
			Cost of Sales/Inventory						
			Cost of Sales/Payables						
11.2	21.9	7.7	Sales/Working Capital	6.8			7.4	7.5	8.9
121.9	712.0	30.7		NM			22.0	19.9	27.2
−11.8	−10.5	−34.2		−34.2			−9.6	NM	−43.4
5.1	5.1	6.3	EBIT/Interest	5.3			6.5	9.4	4.6
(73) 2.7	(72) 2.9	(104) 2.7		(16) 3.0		(14) 2.7	(17) 3.5	(47) 2.6	
1.6	1.7	1.6		1.0			1.9	1.9	1.8
24.5	5.6	6.6	Net Profit + Depr., Dep., Amort./Cur. Mat. L/T/D						72.4
(27) 6.6	(23) 2.9	(32) 2.9						(15)	5.6
2.6	.8	1.4							1.7
.7	.7	.7	Fixed/Worth	.5			.8	.8	.6
1.6	1.8	1.6		1.8			1.4	1.3	1.8
3.0	3.0	2.8		3.8			3.0	2.3	2.8
1.0	1.6	1.0	Debt/Worth	1.0			.5	.7	1.5
2.2	2.8	2.2		2.0			1.8	1.7	2.7
6.6	6.5	4.6		25.0			2.8	3.8	5.7
21.6	55.8	31.6	% Profit Before Taxes/Tangible Net Worth	25.0			15.1	31.8	40.7
(70) 13.6	(72) 17.8	(100) 13.9		(15) 8.9		(15) 6.3	(16) 12.3	(46) 17.9	
6.9	8.1	4.8		−18.5			2.7	1.5	9.7
7.0	9.3	9.4	% Profit Before Taxes/Total Assets	9.8			7.9	15.7	9.4
4.6	5.3	4.3		5.4			3.6	7.6	4.6
1.7	2.2	1.2		−4.9			1.3	1.0	2.0
13.0	37.3	19.4	Sales/Net Fixed Assets	16.4			4.1	28.0	43.8
2.6	2.5	2.7		2.2			1.3	2.8	3.4
1.1	1.5	1.0		.9			.8	.8	1.0
2.8	3.8	2.7	Sales/Total Assets	2.5			1.9	3.8	3.9
1.1	1.5	1.3		1.1			.9	1.7	1.4
.7	.9	.6		.6			.6	.6	.7
1.5	.6	1.7	% Depr., Dep., Amort./Sales	2.5			3.3	.7	.8
(77) 4.5	(72) 2.8	(100) 4.8		(14) 7.6		(15) 5.4	(17) 3.7	(43) 4.1	
6.4	5.4	7.1		9.0			6.3	6.7	6.4
.7	.7	2.0	% Officers', Directors', Owners' Comp/Sales						
(24) 2.8	(17) 2.1	(21) 4.3							
7.4	9.9	8.5							
4126664M	7835570M	8160243M	Net Sales ($)	4082M	30937M	26542M	112365M	294253M	7692064M
3365165M	4740440M	5423885M	Total Assets ($)	4632M	36888M	17928M	123525M	284624M	4956288M

© RMA 2003

M = $ thousand   MM = $ million
See Pages 11 through 18 for Explanation of Ratios and Data

Current Data Sorted By Assets   Comparative Historical Data

	0-500M	500M-2MM	2-10MM	10-50MM	50-100MM	100-250MM	Type of Statement	4/1/98-3/31/99 ALL	4/1/99-3/31/00 ALL
	1	9	23	17	6	9	Unqualified	68	54
	1	4	6	1			Reviewed	8	3
	1	6	4				Compiled	11	14
	3	3	1				Tax Returns	5	9
	4	3	11	10	3	3	Other	36	21
		33 (4/1-9/30/02)		96 (10/1/02-3/31/03)					
NUMBER OF STATEMENTS	10	25	45	28	9	12		128	101
ASSETS	%	%	%	%	%	%		%	%
Cash & Equivalents	25.6	8.6	11.1	8.0		5.6		8.7	9.3
Trade Receivables (net)	7.7	7.9	6.3	5.4		3.1		6.6	6.3
Inventory	2.2	1.7	1.7	1.4		.5		3.7	2.7
All Other Current	.7	1.9	1.1	2.0		3.2		3.5	1.3
Total Current	36.2	20.2	20.2	16.7		12.4		22.5	19.6
Fixed Assets (net)	55.3	67.1	72.4	74.3		81.4		67.1	71.8
Intangibles (net)	3.1	.5	1.0	3.5		.4		2.1	1.0
All Other Non-Current	5.4	12.2	6.3	5.5		5.8		8.2	7.7
Total	100.0	100.0	100.0	100.0		100.0		100.0	100.0
LIABILITIES									
Notes Payable-Short Term	8.4	6.3	3.0	1.7		1.6		3.1	3.2
Cur. Mat.-L/T/D	2.9	4.5	2.5	4.1		1.4		2.7	3.6
Trade Payables	.8	3.4	2.7	3.6		1.8		3.7	4.0
Income Taxes Payable	.0	.2	.0	.1		.0		.1	.1
All Other Current	5.6	2.7	2.5	2.5		1.5		3.5	3.7
Total Current	17.6	17.2	10.8	11.9		6.3		13.0	14.6
Long Term Debt	18.7	30.5	31.6	41.6		30.0		34.2	32.6
Deferred Taxes	.0	1.6	.3	.7		3.2		1.5	1.2
All Other Non-Current	8.3	5.3	6.6	3.6		12.0		6.1	7.8
Net Worth	55.4	45.4	50.7	42.2		48.6		45.1	43.9
Total Liabilities & Net Worth	100.0	100.0	100.0	100.0		100.0		100.0	100.0
INCOME DATA									
Net Sales	100.0	100.0	100.0	100.0		100.0		100.0	100.0
Gross Profit									
Operating Expenses	81.4	80.8	89.2	80.3		73.4		77.2	79.0
Operating Profit	18.6	19.2	10.8	19.7		26.6		22.8	21.0
All Other Expenses (net)	8.4	8.2	6.5	6.8		7.7		6.5	5.5
Profit Before Taxes	10.2	10.9	4.3	12.9		18.9		16.3	15.5
RATIOS									
Current	13.2	3.1	5.6	2.4		5.2		3.2	3.0
	3.8	1.4	2.5	1.1		1.3		1.4	1.5
	.2	.6	1.6	.8		.6		.7	.7
Quick	13.2	2.7	4.9	2.2		3.5		3.0	2.5
	3.1	1.2	2.5	1.0		.9		1.2	1.1
	.2	.5	1.1	.5		.4		.5	.5
Sales/Receivables	0 UND	15 25.1	27 13.4	26 13.9		27 13.7		20 18.5	17 21.7
	0 UND	35 10.4	35 10.4	32 11.4		41 8.8		31 11.8	31 11.7
	45 8.0	60 6.0	45 8.2	43 8.4		53 6.9		44 8.2	46 8.0
Cost of Sales/Inventory									
Cost of Sales/Payables									
Sales/Working Capital	1.2	4.0	1.3	1.8		1.0		2.4	2.8
	7.0	22.9	3.0	25.6		10.6		11.8	8.6
	-28.3	-11.1	9.6	-16.7		-5.9		-12.7	-15.8
EBIT/Interest		(23) 5.1	(43) 3.4	(24) 3.9		(11) 5.6		(97) 4.2	(82) 5.0
		2.8	2.0	2.3		3.1		2.8	2.9
		2.0	.6	1.6		1.7		1.8	1.4
Net Profit + Depr., Dep., Amort./Cur. Mat. L /T/D								(28) 25.3	(17) 46.0
								5.6	4.5
								2.1	2.5
Fixed/Worth	.5	1.1	1.0	1.3		1.2		1.0	1.1
	.9	1.6	1.3	2.1		2.0		1.6	1.6
	3.1	3.3	2.5	2.4		2.9		3.0	3.1
Debt/Worth	.2	.6	.4	.8		.5		.5	.4
	1.0	1.1	.9	1.3		1.4		1.3	1.2
	2.5	3.5	2.4	2.3		2.3		2.9	3.1
% Profit Before Taxes/Tangible Net Worth	207.8	20.6	10.4	10.4		20.0		19.7	18.4
	19.7	13.5	(42) 4.8	(25) 4.5		10.5		(118) 8.7	(91) 9.2
	6.8	3.5	.2	1.3		1.8		3.1	1.9
% Profit Before Taxes/Total Assets	85.7	7.0	3.8	4.6		5.4		6.4	7.9
	8.8	4.3	2.0	1.8		4.6		4.1	3.4
	3.3	1.5	-.4	.5		.9		1.5	.6
Sales/Net Fixed Assets	20.9	3.9	.6	.4		.3		2.0	.9
	6.5	.5	.3	.2		.2		.3	.3
	.3	.3	.2	.2		.1		.2	.2
Sales/Total Assets	6.6	1.0	.4	.3		.2		.6	.6
	.9	.4	.2	.2		.2		.3	.3
	.3	.3	.2	.1		.1		.2	.2
% Depr., Dep., Amort./Sales		(24) 6.5	(43) 9.5	10.5		9.8		(117) 8.3	(89) 8.5
		8.0	13.6	16.7		13.7		12.4	11.3
		13.1	20.1	21.8		24.5		20.2	16.9
% Officers', Directors', Owners' Comp/Sales								(17) 1.9	(17) 1.2
								3.6	4.2
								15.1	12.8
Net Sales ($)	9997M	18948M	96987M	263885M	158756M	395665M		997505M	979357M
Total Assets ($)	2966M	28645M	195223M	598827M	581161M	1818980M		3442928M	2859141M

M = $ thousand MM = $ million
See Pages 11 through 18 for Explanation of Ratios and Data

Comparative Historical Data | | | | | **Current Data Sorted By Sales** | | | | | |

H1	H2	H3	Type of Statement	0-1MM	1-3MM	3-5MM	5-10MM	10-25MM	25MM & OVER
38	58	65	Unqualified	23	14	7	7	7	7
3	17	12	Reviewed	7	1	1	3		
11	10	11	Compiled	5	5			1	
4	7	7	Tax Returns	1	5	1			
25	26	34	Other	12	10	1	3	3	5
4/1/00-3/31/01 ALL	4/1/01-3/31/02 ALL	4/1/02-3/31/03 ALL		33 (4/1-9/30/02)			96 (10/1/02-3/31/03)		
81	118	129	**NUMBER OF STATEMENTS**	48	35	10	13	11	12
%	%	%	**ASSETS**	%	%	%	%	%	%
7.8	7.6	10.1	Cash & Equivalents	14.2	9.6	9.3	3.4	5.7	6.6
7.6	7.2	6.0	Trade Receivables (net)	3.1	6.7	2.2	7.1	11.5	13.0
3.1	3.3	1.6	Inventory	.5	1.8	.1	3.4	1.6	4.7
2.3	2.3	1.7	All Other Current	1.4	.9	.3	1.1	1.8	6.4
20.8	20.4	19.4	Total Current	19.2	19.0	11.8	15.0	20.6	30.7
72.1	71.8	71.7	Fixed Assets (net)	71.4	74.9	80.6	73.2	66.2	59.7
1.4	2.1	1.8	Intangibles (net)	.3	1.3	4.8	3.0	1.3	6.6
5.8	5.6	7.1	All Other Non-Current	9.1	4.9	2.8	8.8	11.8	3.0
100.0	100.0	100.0	Total	100.0	100.0	100.0	100.0	100.0	100.0
			LIABILITIES						
4.5	1.9	3.4	Notes Payable-Short Term	1.9	4.2	5.2	3.8	6.3	2.7
4.2	2.2	3.6	Cur. Mat.-L/T/D	2.6	3.7	1.6	3.7	2.7	9.9
5.2	3.8	2.8	Trade Payables	1.2	2.3	1.0	4.5	3.9	9.0
.1	.1	.1	Income Taxes Payable	.1	.0	.0	.1	.1	.1
4.0	4.3	2.7	All Other Current	1.8	3.3	1.7	2.9	3.9	3.6
18.0	12.3	12.6	Total Current	7.7	13.5	9.5	15.0	16.9	25.2
32.9	30.6	32.6	Long Term Debt	30.6	31.8	43.5	32.7	40.9	26.1
1.3	1.2	.9	Deferred Taxes	.9	.3	1.3	.5	1.6	2.7
7.8	7.9	6.2	All Other Non-Current	7.4	5.0	.3	6.8	5.8	9.7
40.1	47.9	47.7	Net Worth	53.5	49.4	45.3	45.0	34.8	36.2
100.0	100.0	100.0	Total Liabilities & Net Worth	100.0	100.0	100.0	100.0	100.0	100.0
			INCOME DATA						
100.0	100.0	100.0	Net Sales	100.0	100.0	100.0	100.0	100.0	100.0
			Gross Profit						
92.5	81.9	82.8	Operating Expenses	81.6	85.7	83.2	87.5	80.5	76.4
7.5	18.1	17.2	Operating Profit	18.4	14.3	16.8	12.5	19.5	23.6
−4.9	6.0	7.5	All Other Expenses (net)	8.6	6.5	8.0	6.9	8.3	5.5
12.5	12.1	9.7	Profit Before Taxes	9.8	7.8	8.8	5.7	11.2	18.2
			RATIOS						
2.8	3.9	4.3		7.2	3.1	3.9	2.0	3.1	3.4
1.3	1.7	1.9	Current	3.1	1.7	1.2	.7	1.2	1.2
.6	.8	.7		1.2	.8	.6	.5	.9	.5
2.3	3.5	3.3		5.5	3.0	3.9	1.5	2.9	2.4
(80) .9	1.3	1.6	Quick	2.8	1.4	1.2	.5	1.1	.6
.4	.6	.5		1.2	.7	.4	.4	.8	.3
25 14.5	25 14.7	25 14.6		23 15.7	17 21.3	33 11.1	26 13.9	26 13.9	29 12.5
32 11.3	33 11.0	34 10.8	Sales/Receivables	34 10.8	32 11.4	38 9.6	38 9.7	30 12.0	41 8.8
49 7.5	48 7.7	47 7.8		45 8.2	44 8.3	49 7.5	54 6.7	58 6.3	58 6.3
			Cost of Sales/Inventory						
			Cost of Sales/Payables						
2.8	2.3	1.5		1.1	2.2	1.3	7.2	1.7	3.9
18.9	8.4	7.1	Sales/Working Capital	2.9	8.9	51.2	−20.7	18.2	20.7
−7.6	−23.8	−25.9		25.1	−23.5	−24.3	−5.1	−28.4	−5.9
4.2	4.1	4.0		3.6	5.1		3.8	2.9	8.8
(65) 2.8	(105) 2.6	(118) 2.6	EBIT/Interest	(43) 2.3	3.3	(11) 2.1	(10) 2.2	(11) 3.2	
1.6	1.4	1.5		1.5	1.0		1.4	1.7	1.9
32.1	20.6	8.6	Net Profit + Depr., Dep.,	4.5					
(15) 8.2	(26) 3.2	(28) 3.7	Amort./Cur. Mat. L/T/D	(11) 2.8					
1.8	1.4	1.6		1.3					
1.2	1.1	1.1		.9	1.1	1.3	1.2	1.0	1.0
1.7	1.7	1.6	Fixed/Worth	1.4	1.6	2.0	2.1	1.6	2.4
3.1	2.8	2.6		2.7	2.2	4.5	2.6	2.6	3.2
.6	.5	.5		.3	.5	.6	.7	.5	1.0
1.6	1.3	1.1	Debt/Worth	.7	1.0	1.1	1.4	2.0	2.2
3.3	2.6	2.5		2.2	1.7	4.2	2.7	5.8	4.1
16.8	15.6	16.1	% Profit Before Taxes/Tangible	13.5	15.5		13.8	13.3	27.3
(75) 10.4	(113) 8.3	(122) 6.3	Net Worth	(47) 6.2	(33) 6.4		2.4	(10) 8.7	(10) 19.5
2.1	2.6	1.6		1.9	.2		.7	2.1	7.7
6.1	5.5	5.1	% Profit Before Taxes/Total	4.6	6.6	5.1	3.9	4.8	18.6
3.6	3.5	3.3	Assets	3.4	3.3	1.1	1.5	3.7	5.2
1.0	.9	.5		.5	.0	.3	.4	.7	2.8
.7	.6	.7		.6	.8	.4	2.3	1.6	11.2
.3	.3	.3	Sales/Net Fixed Assets	.3	.3	.3	.2	.3	.4
.2	.2	.2		.2	.2	.2	.1	.1	.2
.5	.4	.4		.3	.5	.3	1.3	.5	2.2
.2	.2	.2	Sales/Total Assets	.3	.3	.2	.2	.3	.3
.2	.2	.2		.2	.2	.1	.1	.1	.2
8.2	7.9	8.2		8.2	9.0	7.4	7.3	2.9	2.5
(77) 12.9	(113) 14.3	(124) 12.9	% Depr., Dep., Amort./Sales	(43) 13.6	13.1	16.4	19.8	11.9	9.1
17.0	19.2	19.6		18.6	19.0	23.7	24.5	23.8	12.2
2.3	.9	1.4	% Officers', Directors',		2.3				
(13) 6.2	(15) 4.7	(16) 3.2	Owners' Comp/Sales		(10) 3.2				
20.5	11.9	9.7			9.2				
732870M	1214665M	944238M	Net Sales ($)	23382M	64059M	39190M	91793M	169141M	556673M
2458069M	3159703M	3225802M	Total Assets ($)	111306M	238537M	234377M	512526M	840147M	1288909M

M = $ thousand   MM = $ million
See Pages 11 through 18 for Explanation of Ratios and Data

CONSTRUCTION—GENERAL
INDUSTRIES FORMAT*

	Current Data Sorted By Assets							Comparative Historical Data	
2	7	27	38	23	21	**Type of Statement**			
7	43	82	52	8	7	Unqualified		84	87
33	120	139	39	1	2	Reviewed		156	198
120	183	100	16	1	2	Compiled		236	261
36	108	183	98	16	9	Tax Returns		222	275
	214 (4/1-9/30/02)		1309 (10/1/02-3/31/03)			Other		242	258
0-500M	500M-2MM	2-10MM	10-50MM	50-100MM	100-250MM			4/1/98-3/31/99 ALL	4/1/99-3/31/00 ALL
198	461	531	243	49	41	**NUMBER OF STATEMENTS**		940	1079
%	%	%	%	%	%	**ASSETS**		%	%
18.8	10.7	7.3	6.4	6.3	7.8	Cash & Equivalents		9.6	9.2
10.1	8.8	7.8	3.7	8.8	3.7	Trade Receivables (net)		11.7	11.4
31.4	53.7	61.3	69.6	61.5	53.2	Inventory		49.3	48.8
7.6	8.0	6.8	4.8	3.7	4.5	All Other Current		6.9	6.9
68.0	81.1	83.1	84.4	80.3	69.2	Total Current		77.5	76.2
19.6	10.7	9.3	7.4	12.8	13.6	Fixed Assets (net)		13.0	14.7
1.4	1.0	.8	.9	1.7	2.4	Intangibles (net)		.8	.9
11.0	7.1	6.7	7.2	5.2	14.7	All Other Non-Current		8.8	8.2
100.0	100.0	100.0	100.0	100.0	100.0	Total		100.0	100.0
						LIABILITIES			
38.1	38.1	41.1	45.5	42.6	30.0	Notes Payable-Short Term		31.0	30.9
5.1	4.4	2.3	1.7	1.7	5.5	Cur. Mat.-L/T/D		2.6	2.8
8.2	9.0	9.0	8.5	10.4	7.4	Trade Payables		12.0	12.2
.1	.3	.2	.1	.1	.1	Income Taxes Payable		.7	.2
16.6	12.9	13.2	11.1	12.7	10.2	All Other Current		15.2	17.2
68.2	64.9	65.8	66.9	67.7	53.2	Total Current		61.5	63.3
14.8	10.2	8.8	8.2	6.8	11.3	Long Term Debt		11.8	11.9
.6	.0	.2	.0	.0	.6	Deferred Taxes		.2	.2
8.2	4.2	3.1	2.3	4.4	4.1	All Other Non-Current		4.5	4.2
8.2	20.7	22.1	22.5	21.2	30.8	Net Worth		22.0	20.5
100.0	100.0	100.0	100.0	100.0	100.0	Total Liabilities & Net Worth		100.0	100.0
						INCOME DATA			
100.0	100.0	100.0	100.0	100.0	100.0	Net Sales		100.0	100.0
20.4	18.1	17.1	18.3	20.0	23.4	Gross Profit		16.8	18.2
17.0	14.5	11.9	11.9	12.6	14.2	Operating Expenses		13.4	14.1
3.5	3.5	5.2	6.4	7.4	9.2	Operating Profit		3.4	4.1
.4	.8	.5	.7	1.6	1.3	All Other Expenses (net)		.0	-.2
3.0	2.7	4.6	5.7	5.8	7.9	Profit Before Taxes		3.4	4.3
						RATIOS			
2.0	1.8	1.6	1.5	1.4	1.6			1.7	1.7
1.2	1.2	1.2	1.2	1.2	1.3	Current		1.2	1.2
.8	1.0	1.0	1.0	1.1	1.0			1.0	1.0
1.2	.7	.4	.2	.2	.6			.8	.7
(195) .4	(459) .1	(529) .1	(242) .1	.1	.1	Quick	(928)	.2	(1072) .2
.1	.0	.0	.0	.0	.1			.0	.0
0 UND	0 UND	0 UND	0 UND	0 UND	0 UND			0 UND	0 UND
0 UND	0 UND	0 999.8	1 618.7	3 106.9	1 363.4	Sales/Receivables		1 252.9	1 512.4
7 50.0	10 36.0	8 43.4	5 78.8	10 38.0	6 63.7			20 18.6	18 20.7
0 UND	6 65.9	65 5.6	125 2.9	21 17.5	76 4.8			0 999.8	0 999.8
0 UND	118 3.1	166 2.2	204 1.8	198 1.8	184 2.0	Cost of Sales/Inventory		107 3.4	111 3.3
73 5.0	221 1.7	321 1.1	304 1.2	290 1.3	287 1.3			203 1.8	210 1.7
0 UND	0 UND	3 134.9	7 48.8	14 25.5	16 23.4			1 330.8	3 116.3
0 UND	6 58.5	13 28.3	18 20.8	20 17.9	25 14.4	Cost of Sales/Payables		15 23.9	16 23.0
10 37.8	20 18.5	27 13.4	29 12.6	44 8.2	43 8.5			32 11.5	33 11.2
12.9	6.1	5.5	5.8	6.0	4.4			7.0	6.8
55.7	18.0	13.3	13.9	9.5	8.7	Sales/Working Capital		17.6	18.6
-38.6	-148.0	68.0	53.0	27.1	42.4			393.3	-671.8
13.7	12.6	19.5	21.4	10.0	32.4			11.3	13.2
(140) 4.7	(350) 3.9	(416) 6.0	(196) 7.4	(35) 4.4	(36) 6.3	EBIT/Interest	(726)	3.8	(860) 3.8
.6	1.0	1.9	2.9	2.2	2.9			1.4	1.5
	5.7	9.2	13.1			Net Profit + Depr., Dep.,		5.2	5.6
	(35) 2.1	(54) 3.4	(20) 3.9			Amort./Cur. Mat. L /T/D	(100)	2.6	(129) 2.6
	.3	1.1	1.3					.5	1.1
.0	.0	.1	.0	.0	.0			.1	.1
.5	.3	.2	.1	.1	.1	Fixed/Worth		.3	.3
18.7	1.8	.7	.4	.4	1.1			1.2	1.6
1.3	1.8	2.1	2.4	2.8	1.4			1.8	1.7
5.8	5.3	4.8	4.5	4.2	3.0	Debt/Worth		4.4	4.3
-452.5	32.5	15.5	12.7	6.9	4.7			13.7	14.9
194.7	77.0	81.3	78.2	73.7	74.2			76.4	77.1
(148) 72.2	(382) 33.5	(490) 31.5	(231) 43.6	(45) 49.6	(39) 39.8	% Profit Before Taxes/Tangible Net Worth	(836)	32.4	(955) 33.3
12.4	6.6	8.2	20.3	18.9	22.7			9.2	11.0
28.1	13.4	13.0	14.2	15.9	16.0			13.7	13.6
10.8	4.9	5.0	8.0	7.3	9.9	% Profit Before Taxes/Total Assets		5.7	5.8
.0	.3	1.1	2.9	2.4	5.7			1.2	1.3
820.9	307.5	216.4	240.3	319.7	193.1			186.7	163.4
68.1	58.0	73.7	104.5	140.6	48.5	Sales/Net Fixed Assets		56.3	52.7
24.9	20.2	20.7	27.7	34.0	11.9			15.7	13.9
8.8	3.3	2.5	2.2	2.0	1.7			3.3	3.3
4.5	2.1	1.7	1.7	1.6	1.4	Sales/Total Assets		2.1	2.1
2.7	1.3	1.1	1.1	1.0	.9			1.3	1.3
.3	.3	.2	.1	.2	.1			.2	.2
(120) 1.0	(303) .6	(375) .4	(175) .3	(30) .3	(29) .5	% Depr., Dep., Amort./Sales	(656)	.5	(783) .5
1.9	1.3	.8	.5	.6	1.0			1.1	1.1
2.7	2.1	.9	.7					1.6	1.5
(110) 4.7	(244) 3.4	(252) 2.3	(81) 2.1			% Officers', Directors', Owners' Comp/Sales	(463)	3.0	(538) 2.9
7.8	6.3	6.3						5.4	6.0
272308M	1282381M	4931310M	9059243M	5510972M	9541304M	Net Sales ($)		16304771M	16152828M
50635M	527132M	2556438M	5240360M	3478763M	6013672M	Total Assets ($)		7679953M	8867100M

M = $ thousand   MM = $ million
See Pages 11 through 18 for Explanation of Ratios and Data

Comparative Historical Data				Current Data Sorted By Sales					
			Type of Statement						
77	103	118	Unqualified	4	8	6	4	13	83
175	177	199	Reviewed	6	21	26	41	46	59
234	287	334	Compiled	32	87	68	60	64	23
321	321	422	Tax Returns	105	158	68	47	31	13
270	434	450	Other	38	110	61	65	87	89
4/1/00-3/31/01 ALL	4/1/01-3/31/02 ALL	4/1/02-3/31/03 ALL		214 (4/1-9/30/02)			1309 (10/1/02-3/31/03)		
				0-1MM	1-3MM	3-5MM	5-10MM	10-25MM	25MM & OVER
1077	1322	1523	**NUMBER OF STATEMENTS**	185	384	229	217	241	267
%	%	%	**ASSETS**	%	%	%	%	%	%
9.0	8.6	9.7	Cash & Equivalents	14.5	10.2	8.4	9.9	8.2	7.8
10.2	9.1	7.7	Trade Receivables (net)	4.2	6.3	9.6	9.4	9.8	7.0
52.3	54.6	56.2	Inventory	46.9	54.1	56.6	55.9	58.5	63.6
5.9	6.2	6.8	All Other Current	6.0	7.5	7.3	6.9	6.9	5.5
77.3	78.5	80.3	Total Current	71.6	78.0	81.9	82.1	83.4	83.9
13.1	12.5	11.0	Fixed Assets (net)	15.3	12.4	11.6	10.7	9.6	7.1
1.1	.5	1.0	Intangibles (net)	1.5	1.2	.7	.3	1.0	1.5
8.5	8.4	7.6	All Other Non-Current	11.6	8.4	5.8	7.0	6.0	7.5
100.0	100.0	100.0	Total	100.0	100.0	100.0	100.0	100.0	100.0
			LIABILITIES						
35.1	38.3	40.3	Notes Payable-Short Term	47.6	38.9	41.8	36.9	39.8	39.1
3.3	3.8	3.3	Cur. Mat.-L/T/D	4.1	5.0	2.9	2.2	2.2	2.5
10.3	10.6	8.8	Trade Payables	4.2	7.2	7.8	11.3	11.1	11.2
.2	.2	.2	Income Taxes Payable	.1	.2	.4	.3	.2	.1
14.1	13.7	13.1	All Other Current	14.5	13.2	12.4	13.2	13.6	12.1
63.0	66.7	65.7	Total Current	70.5	64.5	65.3	63.9	66.9	65.0
10.0	10.8	9.9	Long Term Debt	16.7	12.1	9.1	8.2	7.3	6.6
.2	.2	.2	Deferred Taxes	.0	.3	.0	.1	.1	.3
4.3	3.9	4.1	All Other Non-Current	9.1	4.6	3.7	2.7	2.4	2.7
22.4	18.5	20.1	Net Worth	3.7	18.5	21.9	25.0	23.3	25.4
100.0	100.0	100.0	Total Liabilities & Net Worth	100.0	100.0	100.0	100.0	100.0	100.0
			INCOME DATA						
100.0	100.0	100.0	Net Sales	100.0	100.0	100.0	100.0	100.0	100.0
18.6	18.0	18.3	Gross Profit	21.9	19.3	17.5	15.8	16.8	18.3
14.2	13.0	13.5	Operating Expenses	19.4	14.3	13.1	12.1	11.4	11.5
4.3	5.0	4.8	Operating Profit	2.5	5.1	4.4	3.7	5.4	6.8
.3	.7	.7	All Other Expenses (net)	1.9	.7	.5	.1	.4	.7
4.0	4.2	4.1	Profit Before Taxes	.6	4.4	3.8	3.6	5.0	6.1
			RATIOS						
1.7	1.6	1.7		1.9	1.9	1.7	1.6	1.6	1.5
1.2	1.2	1.2	Current	1.2	1.1	1.2	1.2	1.2	1.2
1.0	1.0	1.0		.9	.9	1.0	1.0	1.0	1.1
.6	.5	.5		.7	.5	.4	.8	.5	.3
(1068) .1	(1312) .1	(1515) .1	Quick	(183) .1	(380) .1	.1	(216) .1	.1	(266) .1
.0	.0	.0		.0	.0	.0	.0	.0	.0
0 UND	0 UND	0 UND		0 UND	0 UND	0 UND	0 UND	0 UND	0 UND
1 622.0	0 774.9	0 999.8	Sales/Receivables	0 UND	0 UND	0 UND	0 999.8	1 327.5	1 384.9
12 29.7	10 37.4	8 46.0		1 506.2	6 57.5	13 28.6	12 29.7	10 38.2	6 63.9
2 238.7	4 87.2	15 24.2		0 UND	5 74.8	26 13.8	8 48.6	40 9.1	88 4.2
119 3.1	134 2.7	140 2.6	Cost of Sales/Inventory	124 3.0	132 2.8	134 2.7	128 2.9	134 2.7	165 2.2
235 1.6	248 1.5	271 1.3		483 .8	298 1.2	275 1.5	271 1.5	241 1.5	233 1.6
1 255.4	1 374.4	0 999.8		0 UND	0 UND	1 481.5	3 141.0	7 52.6	10 36.6
13 28.1	12 29.5	11 34.4	Cost of Sales/Payables	0 UND	4 100.3	9 38.7	13 29.1	16 23.3	18 19.9
29 12.7	28 13.1	25 14.6		10 35.3	21 17.0	20 18.2	25 14.8	31 11.8	29 12.6
6.6	6.5	6.4		3.4	5.7	6.6	7.2	8.0	6.3
18.6	19.5	16.1	Sales/Working Capital	15.5	19.7	18.1	17.8	15.6	13.3
-742.0	-378.9	476.7		-21.3	-53.1	999.8	55.0	143.2	40.1
12.5	14.0	17.1		8.5	12.8	16.5	16.4	22.6	25.6
(847) 3.7	(1041) 4.2	(1173) 5.4	EBIT/Interest	(124) 2.3	(287) 4.3	(186) 4.3	(172) 5.3	(193) 7.7	(211) 8.2
1.6	1.6	1.7		-1.5	1.1	1.5	1.9	2.5	3.2
6.6	6.0	8.7			5.3	6.5	7.3	14.0	24.4
(98) 2.0	(93) 1.7	(127) 3.2	Net Profit + Depr., Dep., Amort./Cur. Mat. L/T/D		(24) 1.0	(24) 3.4	(17) 2.6	(29) 6.1	(28) 3.6
.4	.3	.9			.1	1.1	.2	1.8	1.4
.1	.0	.0		.0	.0	.1	.1	.1	.0
.3	.2	.2	Fixed/Worth	.3	.3	.3	.2	.2	.1
1.2	1.1	1.0		4.1	3.9	1.1	.7	.7	.3
1.7	2.0	2.0		2.2	2.2	1.7	1.5	2.0	2.1
4.8	5.0	4.7	Debt/Worth	8.5	6.9	4.5	4.4	4.6	3.5
17.0	18.4	19.0		UND	54.0	25.8	14.4	13.8	7.2
75.0	82.9	85.4		98.9	98.2	74.1	62.0	89.0	79.1
(953) 35.8	(1171) 37.1	(1335) 37.9	% Profit Before Taxes/Tangible Net Worth	(139) 24.2	(313) 41.0	(198) 27.6	(204) 27.6	(226) 41.0	(255) 49.5
11.2	11.3	11.0		1.1	6.6	7.2	6.9	14.5	29.4
13.6	13.7	14.9		12.1	14.8	12.7	14.3	16.0	17.4
5.7	5.8	6.3	% Profit Before Taxes/Total Assets	2.1	5.2	4.5	5.3	7.3	10.8
1.4	1.4	1.1		-4.3	.3	1.0	1.1	2.0	5.3
223.4	218.0	254.5		UND	356.6	155.2	220.2	238.7	242.6
57.7	66.5	72.5	Sales/Net Fixed Assets	49.7	53.2	60.2	80.5	96.1	106.5
17.0	17.3	21.9		11.9	18.6	19.8	21.2	32.7	34.8
3.5	3.1	3.1		2.9	3.2	3.2	3.3	3.1	2.7
2.1	1.9	1.9	Sales/Total Assets	1.2	1.8	1.9	2.1	2.2	2.0
1.3	1.2	1.2		.7	1.1	1.2	1.3	1.4	1.4
.2	.2	.2		.6	.3	.2	.2	.2	.1
(783) .5	(940) .5	(1032) .4	% Depr., Dep., Amort./Sales	(89) 1.6	(244) .7	(169) .5	(159) .4	(179) .3	(192) .3
1.1	1.1	1.1		3.3	1.5	1.1	.8	.6	.5
1.3	1.4	1.4		3.9	2.3	1.5	1.0	.8	.6
(540) 3.0	(615) 2.7	(703) 3.0	% Officers', Directors', Owners' Comp/Sales	(75) 6.7	(200) 3.8	(126) 2.6	(119) 2.6	(107) 1.4	(76) 2.2
5.8	5.2	5.8		11.4	6.2	5.4	5.0	4.2	3.9
21584023M	28279066M	30597518M	Net Sales ($)	109114M	729484M	886799M	1526974M	3710423M	23634724M
10182578M	14033297M	17867000M	Total Assets ($)	141110M	602276M	641115M	950589M	2277888M	13254022M

© RMA 2003

M = $ thousand   MM = $ million
See Pages 11 through 18 for Explanation of Ratios and Data

Current Data Sorted By Assets   **Comparative Historical Data**

0-500M	500M-2MM	2-10MM	10-50MM	50-100MM	100-250MM	Type of Statement	4/1/98-3/31/99 ALL	4/1/99-3/31/00 ALL
	2	9	15		3	Unqualified	30	32
3	2	19	7	1	1	Reviewed	29	39
3	10	7		1		Compiled	40	33
11	21	10	2		3	Tax Returns	26	35
5	10	17	2		1	Other	32	43
	22 (4/1-9/30/02)		143 (10/1/02-3/31/03)					
22	45	62	26	2	8	**NUMBER OF STATEMENTS**	157	182
%	%	%	%	%	%	**ASSETS**	%	%
22.2	11.5	11.8	11.5			Cash & Equivalents	11.1	13.9
12.1	16.0	30.8	31.4			Trade Receivables (net)	18.3	21.6
11.3	30.4	25.2	25.3			Inventory	35.6	26.7
7.3	9.6	8.1	9.8			All Other Current	9.2	11.3
53.0	67.4	75.8	78.0			Total Current	74.2	73.5
37.8	23.4	16.2	10.4			Fixed Assets (net)	14.5	16.6
3.2	.9	.3	2.0			Intangibles (net)	.7	1.0
6.0	8.4	7.7	9.6			All Other Non-Current	10.6	8.8
100.0	100.0	100.0	100.0			Total	100.0	100.0
						LIABILITIES		
15.0	20.0	19.4	15.5			Notes Payable-Short Term	21.8	19.7
10.2	15.5	3.2	1.4			Cur. Mat.-L/T/D	3.1	3.6
17.5	11.2	20.0	26.8			Trade Payables	12.8	14.7
.2	.8	.5	.2			Income Taxes Payable	3.1	.6
8.7	15.1	11.9	17.4			All Other Current	16.0	14.8
51.6	62.5	55.1	61.3			Total Current	56.7	53.4
23.5	10.9	12.5	7.8			Long Term Debt	15.4	11.2
.0	.1	.4	.4			Deferred Taxes	.3	.4
5.5	5.3	2.9	1.6			All Other Non-Current	5.2	3.5
19.5	21.3	29.2	29.0			Net Worth	22.3	31.6
100.0	100.0	100.0	100.0			Total Liabilities & Net Worth	100.0	100.0
						INCOME DATA		
100.0	100.0	100.0	100.0			Net Sales	100.0	100.0
21.2	21.8	18.2	12.4			Gross Profit	17.9	22.3
18.3	17.9	13.7	7.8			Operating Expenses	15.5	17.3
2.9	3.9	4.5	4.6			Operating Profit	2.4	5.0
.8	.1	1.0	.2			All Other Expenses (net)	1.8	.3
2.1	3.7	3.5	4.4			Profit Before Taxes	.6	4.7
						RATIOS		
1.3	1.8	2.0	1.4				1.9	2.1
1.0	1.2	1.4	1.2			Current	1.4	1.3
.6	.7	1.1	1.1				1.0	1.1
1.1	1.1	1.4	1.2				1.4	1.3
.7	(44) .3	1.0	.8			Quick	(156) .4	(181) .7
.3	.1	.2	.1				.1	.1
0 UND	0 UND	1 345.0	0 UND				0 UND	0 UND
0 UND	0 999.8	42 8.8	43 8.5			Sales/Receivables	4 95.5	15 24.6
11 32.6	29 12.5	67 5.5	57 6.4				50 7.4	51 7.2
0 UND	0 UND	0 UND	0 UND				0 UND	0 UND
0 UND	1 649.0	0 999.8	0 UND			Cost of Sales/Inventory	14 26.8	0 UND
4 91.0	116 3.1	170 2.1	188 1.9				183 2.0	141 2.6
0 UND	0 UND	5 67.4	13 27.3				0 UND	2 167.3
7 52.2	4 92.3	23 16.0	30 12.1			Cost of Sales/Payables	17 21.1	18 20.5
22 16.5	19 19.2	43 8.4	48 7.6				39 9.5	42 8.7
44.1	7.9	4.8	11.1				4.5	4.9
114.1	29.7	13.0	22.6			Sales/Working Capital	11.5	12.4
−71.8	−30.4	44.0	59.5				93.0	45.2
20.3	10.5	30.5	65.3				10.4	20.6
(19) 4.5	(36) 3.1	(50) 6.3	(19) 10.1			EBIT/Interest	(123) 3.6	(140) 5.5
−1.5	1.2	1.2	3.2				1.4	1.9
		3.5				Net Profit + Depr., Dep.,		11.1	18.0
	(13)	.8				Amort./Cur. Mat. L./T/D	(33) 2.9	(28) 5.4
		.3					.7	1.6
.2	.3	.1	.1				.1	.1
2.1	.7	.3	.1			Fixed/Worth	.2	.2
−10.7	6.6	.9	.8				.8	1.2
1.2	1.2	1.4	1.8				1.3	1.0
3.9	3.8	2.5	3.4			Debt/Worth	2.7	2.7
−13.7	26.8	6.6	5.5				8.7	7.7
152.5	93.1	49.2	71.7				50.2	62.6
(15) 67.5	(38) 30.0	(57) 14.8	(25) 30.3			% Profit Before Taxes/Tangible Net Worth	(137) 16.6	(167) 27.1
24.8	6.4	4.7	16.0				5.0	8.7
30.2	14.3	12.1	16.7				12.5	15.5
10.9	5.1	5.8	7.4			% Profit Before Taxes/Total Assets	4.2	6.4
−14.3	.8	.8	4.1				1.0	1.8
48.9	78.3	153.4	278.3				133.2	136.1
24.1	27.7	40.8	118.0			Sales/Net Fixed Assets	41.6	32.5
12.1	7.8	9.3	16.5				13.0	9.9
11.7	4.3	3.8	3.7				3.3	3.6
5.9	2.9	2.1	2.7			Sales/Total Assets	2.1	2.1
3.5	1.7	1.2	1.6				1.0	1.3
.8	.3	.2	.1				.3	.3
(16) 1.5	(35) .9	(47) .5	(22) .3			% Depr., Dep., Amort./Sales	(120) .7	(135) .8
2.9	1.9	1.2	1.0				1.6	1.7
1.8	2.3	1.4					2.4	2.2
(13) 4.0	(22) 3.9	(24) 2.0				% Officers', Directors', Owners' Comp/Sales	(62) 4.0	(78) 3.5
8.2	5.9	3.8					8.1	7.4
30028M	162658M	744871M	1510612M	187494M	5679102M	Net Sales ($)	2590394M	2757833M
5377M	51151M	291147M	577373M	152648M	1088587M	Total Assets ($)	1679940M	1908631M

Comparative Historical Data | Current Data Sorted By Sales

			Type of Statement						
32	43	29	Unqualified		4		2	3	20
56	36	33	Reviewed		2	4	7	12	8
34	41	21	Compiled	2	6	4	5	3	1
54	34	47	Tax Returns	10	13	8	10		6
46	62	35	Other	3	9	9	6	5	3
4/1/00- 3/31/01 ALL	4/1/01- 3/31/02 ALL	4/1/02- 3/31/03 ALL		22 (4/1-9/30/02)			143 (10/1/02-3/31/03)		
				0-1MM	1-3MM	3-5MM	5-10MM	10-25MM	25MM & OVER
222	216	165	NUMBER OF STATEMENTS	15	34	25	30	23	38
%	%	%	ASSETS	%	%	%	%	%	%
15.5	15.3	13.2	Cash & Equivalents	24.9	13.0	9.7	11.4	10.7	14.1
27.9	32.3	23.5	Trade Receivables (net)	2.1	12.7	11.5	24.2	41.3	38.4
20.5	16.1	24.6	Inventory	16.9	29.9	35.0	25.2	22.5	17.1
10.6	11.0	8.6	All Other Current	3.3	10.7	7.0	12.1	4.4	9.6
74.5	74.7	70.0	Total Current	47.2	66.3	63.2	73.0	78.9	79.2
17.0	16.4	20.8	Fixed Assets (net)	44.2	26.1	27.1	14.8	11.7	13.0
1.1	1.4	1.2	Intangibles (net)	4.6	1.1	.2	.2	.3	1.8
7.4	7.5	8.0	All Other Non-Current	4.2	6.5	9.5	12.0	9.0	6.0
100.0	100.0	100.0	Total	100.0	100.0	100.0	100.0	100.0	100.0
			LIABILITIES						
22.1	16.4	19.1	Notes Payable-Short Term	21.9	16.9	33.1	17.3	14.5	15.1
3.7	3.8	7.1	Cur. Mat.-L/T/D	12.1	13.4	5.4	7.3	5.2	1.6
20.6	23.8	18.3	Trade Payables	2.5	14.4	8.4	14.2	27.7	32.2
.5	.4	.5	Income Taxes Payable	.0	.2	.2	1.2	1.1	.1
19.2	14.6	15.1	All Other Current	12.1	8.4	11.9	13.6	17.2	24.4
66.0	59.0	60.1	Total Current	48.6	53.3	59.1	53.6	65.7	73.3
10.7	13.9	12.6	Long Term Debt	24.5	16.1	12.8	16.0	6.5	5.5
.3	.4	.2	Deferred Taxes	.0	.0	.0	.7	.3	.2
2.4	4.4	3.5	All Other Non-Current	5.6	8.2	2.4	3.2	.7	1.3
20.7	22.4	23.5	Net Worth	21.5	22.4	25.7	26.4	26.9	19.6
100.0	100.0	100.0	Total Liabilities & Net Worth	100.0	100.0	100.0	100.0	100.0	100.0
			INCOME DATA						
100.0	100.0	100.0	Net Sales	100.0	100.0	100.0	100.0	100.0	100.0
19.0	17.9	19.1	Gross Profit	29.5	23.9	21.6	19.0	10.8	14.0
14.5	14.4	15.0	Operating Expenses	24.5	20.2	15.9	14.6	8.6	10.1
4.5	3.5	4.1	Operating Profit	5.0	3.6	5.6	4.3	2.2	4.0
.3	.4	.4	All Other Expenses (net)	.8	1.0	.7	.3	.1	-.1
4.2	3.1	3.6	Profit Before Taxes	4.2	2.6	4.9	4.0	2.1	4.0
			RATIOS						
1.8	1.7	1.8		2.5	2.0	1.4	2.4	1.5	1.6
1.2	1.3	1.2	Current	1.0	1.2	1.1	1.6	1.2	1.2
1.0	1.1	1.0		.4	.9	.7	1.1	1.0	1.1
1.3	1.4	1.2		1.3	1.1	1.0	1.7	1.3	1.2
(221) .8	(215) 1.0	(164) .7	Quick	.4	.4	(24) .1	.8	1.0	.9
.2	.2	.1		.1	.1	.0	.2	.2	.2
0 999.8	2 232.0	0 UND		0 UND	0 UND	0 UND	1 345.0	2 152.1	1 247.6
31 11.9	39 9.4	10 37.3	Sales/Receivables	0 UND	1 278.6	0 UND	21 17.1	48 7.5	43 8.5
59 6.2	64 5.7	51 7.2		0 UND	30 12.1	3 120.3	50 7.2	84 4.4	57 6.4
0 UND	0 UND	0 UND		0 UND	0 UND	0 UND	0 UND	0 UND	0 UND
0 UND	0 UND	0 UND	Cost of Sales/Inventory	0 UND	9 42.7	72 5.1	1 717.2	0 UND	0 UND
76 4.8	18 20.0	121 3.0		147 2.5	181 2.0	194 1.9	94 3.9	107 3.4	22 17.0
3 114.6	9 42.7	1 308.7		0 UND	0 UND	0 UND	4 95.0	15 24.4	14 26.3
23 16.1	28 12.9	17 21.6	Cost of Sales/Payables	0 UND	11 32.7	5 73.3	20 18.6	27 13.6	40 9.1
47 7.7	50 7.3	40 9.0		19 19.0	26 14.1	20 18.7	30 12.3	60 6.0	57 6.4
8.0	7.6	7.3		5.5	5.2	7.5	4.4	14.6	11.3
21.2	17.8	23.5	Sales/Working Capital	116.0	37.6	33.8	13.2	24.1	23.6
275.6	82.4	-503.6		-2.2	-75.6	-68.2	33.8	-305.3	59.5
15.3	23.6	27.3		4.5	13.3	19.3	12.6	42.1	117.9
(171) 4.5	(177) 6.3	(131) 5.3	EBIT/Interest	(11) -.1	(28) 3.6	(20) 4.6	(23) 5.3	(19) 10.1	(30) 22.5
1.4	1.7	1.2		-3.0	1.1	1.8	.8	1.1	3.6
12.1	10.4	7.2	Net Profit + Depr., Dep.,						
(29) 2.7	(31) 2.9	(26) 2.0	Amort./Cur. Mat. L/T/D						
.1	1.0	.7							
.1	.1	.1		.3	.3	.1	.1	.1	.1
.3	.3	.4	Fixed/Worth	3.3	1.0	.6	.3	.3	.1
1.2	1.0	2.0		-4.6	11.0	2.5	.9	1.1	.4
1.2	1.4	1.4		1.3	1.2	1.2	1.1	1.5	1.7
3.2	3.3	3.1	Debt/Worth	3.8	4.1	3.0	2.1	2.7	3.7
13.3	10.7	10.0		-14.3	228.7	14.8	4.0	11.2	5.7
69.7	51.5	73.2	% Profit Before Taxes/Tangible	87.5	112.5	102.3	47.6	59.8	67.8
(199) 22.1	(196) 26.8	(142) 29.6	Net Worth	(11) 12.5	(27) 32.6	(22) 39.1	(26) 15.0	(21) 16.9	(35) 36.9
5.5	8.3	8.6		-17.9	6.4	11.9	7.0	3.9	13.0
13.3	12.6	15.3	% Profit Before Taxes/Total	10.5	13.7	22.1	14.4	12.3	15.5
5.7	5.5	6.4	Assets	.3	5.7	6.0	6.9	6.0	7.2
1.1	1.4	1.0		-16.3	.5	1.7	1.3	.3	3.4
151.2	134.3	126.2		28.2	54.5	62.8	117.4	166.2	244.2
54.1	45.2	38.1	Sales/Net Fixed Assets	12.3	15.8	17.4	34.5	65.6	107.7
11.4	14.7	10.5		1.0	4.2	8.3	11.2	23.5	41.2
4.2	4.3	4.3		6.1	3.9	4.0	5.4	4.3	4.9
2.7	2.8	2.6	Sales/Total Assets	1.6	2.3	2.1	2.7	3.1	3.5
1.6	1.7	1.5		.9	1.2	1.4	1.6	1.5	1.8
.3	.2	.2		1.4	.4	.3	.6	.2	.1
(166) .5	(178) .5	(127) .6	% Depr., Dep., Amort./Sales	(11) 2.5	(25) 1.5	(18) .7	(20) 1.0	(21) .3	(32) .2
1.6	1.3	1.6		4.5	3.3	1.3	1.3	.5	.5
1.7	1.5	1.6	% Officers', Directors',		2.3	1.3	3.0	1.4	.7
(104) 3.5	(100) 3.1	(70) 3.5	Owners' Comp/Sales	(18) 4.1	(10) 2.5	(15) 3.6	(10) 1.8	(11) 1.1
6.0	5.3	5.9		6.5	6.2	5.4	2.4	5.7
5853460M	6801194M	8314765M	Net Sales ($)	7894M	59020M	94825M	212091M	356192M	7584743M
2525657M	2582290M	2166283M	Total Assets ($)	8784M	48021M	51453M	105462M	273801M	1678762M

© RMA 2003   **M = $ thousand   MM = $ million**
See Pages 11 through 18 for Explanation of Ratios and Data

Current Data Sorted By Assets   Comparative Historical Data

	0-500M	500M-2MM	2-10MM	10-50MM	50-100MM	100-250MM	Type of Statement	4/1/98-3/31/99 ALL	4/1/99-3/31/00 ALL
	1	1	1	4	5	4	Unqualified	10	9
	1	2	3	1		1	Reviewed	8	11
	3	4	9	1	1		Compiled	7	12
	2	10	1	1	1		Tax Returns	6	10
	3	11	9	6	1	4	Other	11	9
	11 (4/1-9/30/02)			**79 (10/1/02-3/31/03)**					
NUMBER OF STATEMENTS	10	28	23	13	8	8		42	51
	%	%	%	%	%	%	**ASSETS**	%	%
	19.9	11.5	12.9	11.2			Cash & Equivalents	9.8	11.1
	44.8	24.2	17.3	14.0			Trade Receivables (net)	19.1	22.6
	10.7	25.9	34.8	54.7			Inventory	35.0	32.6
	13.7	14.1	9.2	8.0			All Other Current	9.0	7.1
	89.0	75.6	74.2	87.8			Total Current	72.9	73.4
	9.2	15.9	21.0	7.0			Fixed Assets (net)	20.8	19.5
	.0	1.6	.1	.2			Intangibles (net)	1.4	1.5
	1.8	6.9	4.8	4.9			All Other Non-Current	5.0	5.6
	100.0	100.0	100.0	100.0			Total	100.0	100.0
							LIABILITIES		
	79.9	34.0	24.9	29.2			Notes Payable-Short Term	23.2	18.6
	1.0	.4	11.8	5.4			Cur. Mat.-L/T/D	2.4	2.3
	16.4	12.1	13.8	18.1			Trade Payables	13.6	14.0
	.0	1.0	.0	.0			Income Taxes Payable	.2	.5
	1.8	12.7	16.4	12.0			All Other Current	16.3	17.5
	99.1	60.2	67.0	64.6			Total Current	55.7	52.9
	.8	11.1	5.2	3.7			Long Term Debt	13.2	15.4
	2.0	.1	.0	.1			Deferred Taxes	.5	.4
	1.3	7.7	4.3	4.8			All Other Non-Current	5.6	2.5
	-3.2	20.9	23.6	26.8			Net Worth	25.0	28.9
	100.0	100.0	100.0	100.0			Total Liabilities & Net Worth	100.0	100.0
							INCOME DATA		
	100.0	100.0	100.0	100.0			Net Sales	100.0	100.0
	15.8	23.8	20.2	20.3			Gross Profit	22.5	25.6
	16.7	19.3	16.6	13.6			Operating Expenses	18.6	20.5
	-.9	4.5	3.6	6.7			Operating Profit	3.9	5.0
	.4	.8	.3	.1			All Other Expenses (net)	-.5	.6
	-1.3	3.7	3.3	6.5			Profit Before Taxes	4.4	4.4
							RATIOS		
	3.0	2.1	1.3	1.9				2.2	2.2
	1.2	1.3	1.1	1.3			Current	1.3	1.4
	.9	1.0	1.0	1.1				1.1	1.1
	2.9	1.7	.9	.7				1.1	1.3
	.9	.7	.2	.1			Quick	.6	.7
	.2	.1	.0	.0				.1	.1
	0 UND	0 UND	0 UND	0 UND				0 UND	0 UND
	23 15.7	22 16.7	10 38.4	0 999.8			Sales/Receivables	9 40.3	9 42.4
	41 8.9	47 7.8	39 9.4	33 11.2				61 6.0	60 6.1
	0 UND	0 UND	0 UND	0 UND				0 UND	0 UND
	0 UND	1 295.7	0 UND	198 1.8			Cost of Sales/Inventory	78 4.7	61 6.0
	1 415.8	155 2.4	132 2.8	245 1.5				255 1.4	281 1.3
	0 UND	2 151.3	3 126.9	1 645.1				11 33.8	2 150.7
	12 29.9	21 17.2	19 19.3	21 17.6			Cost of Sales/Payables	27 13.3	19 19.5
	27 13.6	36 10.1	28 12.9	54 6.7				43 8.5	57 6.4
	5.7	6.5	13.2	4.7				3.5	3.2
	39.3	13.8	25.3	9.1			Sales/Working Capital	16.4	8.2
	-50.7	NM	184.6	27.1				63.3	36.2
		7.0	27.3	67.9				13.1	7.4
		(21) 3.2	(18) 12.4	(10) 9.8			EBIT/Interest	(34) 4.4	(38) 5.1
		-.6	1.4	8.2				2.4	2.0
							Net Profit + Depr., Dep.,		11.4
							Amort./Cur. Mat. L./T/D	(11) 5.0	
									.9
	.0	.1	.2	.1				.1	.1
	.0	.6	.7	.2			Fixed/Worth	.2	.3
	.6	5.3	3.6	.3				1.1	1.5
	.6	1.0	2.0	1.8				1.2	1.2
	5.1	3.6	6.1	3.5			Debt/Worth	3.1	2.3
	14.0	UND	13.0	7.6				7.6	5.3
		63.2	86.6	71.9			% Profit Before Taxes/Tangible	57.8	43.2
		(21) 7.4	(22) 13.7	36.9			Net Worth	(39) 22.4	(46) 22.1
		-15.9	2.6	23.3				9.2	7.5
	49.8	13.2	5.9	15.3			% Profit Before Taxes/Total	14.5	14.4
	19.4	2.8	1.2	10.1			Assets	6.0	6.0
	-5.3	-4.8	.3	6.6				1.7	1.5
	UND	98.5	66.4	179.6				96.4	78.1
	214.5	15.8	30.2	96.3			Sales/Net Fixed Assets	27.6	35.4
	27.2	10.6	11.2	11.3				5.1	6.4
	8.2	2.7	3.5	2.7				2.9	3.2
	5.5	2.1	2.5	1.9			Sales/Total Assets	1.8	1.9
	2.8	1.3	1.4	1.4				.9	.9
		.3	.2					.3	.4
		(17) .9	(19) .5				% Depr., Dep., Amort./Sales	(33) 1.0	(39) .7
		1.8	1.4					3.6	2.8
		3.0	1.1					1.7	2.2
		(16) 5.2	(12) 2.1				% Officers', Directors',	(15) 3.3	(15) 5.0
		8.8	4.9				Owners' Comp/Sales	5.5	8.0
	15140M	73190M	257471M	645363M	775309M	2265504M	Net Sales ($)	1524422M	2146814M
	3221M	34639M	108529M	281604M	633061M	1250049M	Total Assets ($)	908504M	1083957M

Comparative Historical Data | Current Data Sorted By Sales

					Type of Statement							
	11		21		16	Unqualified		1	1		2	12
	15		17		7	Reviewed		1	2	1	1	2
	12		20		18	Compiled	1	6	2	2	6	1
	8		7		15	Tax Returns	4	8	1			2
	15		28		34	Other	2	8	6	3	6	9
	4/1/00-		4/1/01-		4/1/02-			11 (4/1-9/30/02)		79 (10/1/02-3/31/03)		
	3/31/01		3/31/02		3/31/03		0-1MM	1-3MM	3-5MM	5-10MM	10-25MM	25MM & OVER
	ALL		ALL		ALL							
	61		93		90	NUMBER OF STATEMENTS	7	24	12	6	15	26
	%		%		%	ASSETS	%	%	%	%	%	%
	10.7		13.8		12.3	Cash & Equivalents		17.0	16.6		14.7	8.4
	29.4		34.1		21.3	Trade Receivables (net)		22.6	30.0		18.9	17.2
	30.9		19.5		32.0	Inventory		28.1	3.5		35.9	38.0
	5.1		9.3		10.1	All Other Current		14.6	17.4		7.2	7.2
	76.1		76.6		75.8	Total Current		82.2	67.5		76.6	70.8
	16.4		15.1		17.8	Fixed Assets (net)		13.0	30.9		16.4	21.5
	1.5		.8		.8	Intangibles (net)		1.8	.1		.0	1.0
	6.0		7.6		5.6	All Other Non-Current		2.9	1.6		6.9	6.6
	100.0		100.0		100.0	Total		100.0	100.0		100.0	100.0
					LIABILITIES						
	19.6		17.3		34.3	Notes Payable-Short Term		32.5	27.2		18.6	28.0
	3.3		2.7		4.4	Cur. Mat.-L/T/D		4.3	1.9		5.0	1.3
	21.3		23.7		13.3	Trade Payables		11.2	10.4		17.5	13.6
	1.0		.7		.3	Income Taxes Payable		1.1	.2		.0	.1
	13.5		17.4		11.0	All Other Current		8.9	16.7		18.1	10.1
	58.6		61.9		63.4	Total Current		58.0	56.4		59.3	53.1
	10.0		11.3		8.8	Long Term Debt		6.1	8.4		6.3	12.5
	.2		.1		.3	Deferred Taxes		.9	.0		.0	.2
	4.3		1.9		5.2	All Other Non-Current		6.4	2.9		3.8	4.7
	26.9		24.8		22.2	Net Worth		28.7	32.3		30.7	29.6
	100.0		100.0		100.0	Total Liabilities & Net Worth		100.0	100.0		100.0	100.0
					INCOME DATA						
	100.0		100.0		100.0	Net Sales		100.0	100.0		100.0	100.0
	19.2		19.5		20.5	Gross Profit		22.3	20.9		25.2	17.1
	16.8		13.4		16.1	Operating Expenses		19.7	16.7		19.7	10.8
	2.4		6.1		4.4	Operating Profit		2.6	4.2		5.5	6.3
	−.3		1.5		.5	All Other Expenses (net)		.4	.4		−.2	.5
	2.6		4.6		3.9	Profit Before Taxes		2.3	3.7		5.7	5.8
					RATIOS						
	1.7		1.6		1.9			2.7	2.4		1.3	1.7
	1.3		1.2		1.2	Current		1.5	1.4		1.2	1.2
	1.1		1.1		1.0			1.0	.8		1.1	1.1
	1.3		1.3		1.3			2.6	1.9		1.0	1.1
	.8		.9		.4	Quick		.7	.9		.3	.4
	.1		.3		.1			.1	.1		.0	.1
2	222.3	1	301.6	0	UND		0 UND	6 65.1	0 UND	0 UND	
24	15.1	39	9.4	10	36.9	Sales/Receivables	14 26.0	29 12.7	17 21.2	4 90.2	
64	5.7	70	5.2	45	8.2		46 7.9	46 8.0	32 11.5	50 7.3	
0	UND	0	UND	0	UND		0 UND	0 UND	0 UND	0 UND	
2	172.0	0	UND	4	85.5	Cost of Sales/Inventory	0 UND	0 UND	5 71.0	36 10.0	
177	2.1	91	4.0	199	1.8		230 1.6	0 UND	198 1.8	228 1.6	
10	35.8	14	25.3	3	118.3		2 239.0	1 298.5	7 49.4	13 28.0	
25	14.8	30	12.3	22	16.8	Cost of Sales/Payables	16 22.4	17 21.1	21 17.5	29 12.6	
48	7.6	57	6.5	36	10.1		34 10.7	35 10.5	33 11.1	47 7.7	
	5.7		7.6		6.1			5.0	7.6		7.6	4.4
	15.0		18.2		16.5	Sales/Working Capital		10.5	17.2		17.2	16.0
	62.8		66.0		128.5			764.7	NM		74.2	50.1
	15.6		23.9		25.8			22.4	27.4		83.3	79.8
(50)	6.2	(67)	5.9	(68)	5.9	EBIT/Interest	(18) 2.2	(10) 5.4	(12) 8.3	(18) 9.0	
	1.8		1.5		1.3			−5.5	3.6		1.7	2.7
			8.4									
		(16)	2.3			Net Profit + Depr., Dep., Amort./Cur. Mat. L/T/D						
			1.1									
	.1		.1		.1			.1	.1		.1	.0
	.5		.3		.3	Fixed/Worth		.4	.7		.3	.2
	.9		.9		1.4			1.1	5.2		1.4	.7
	1.4		1.4		1.2			.7	1.0		1.1	1.6
	3.0		3.4		3.9	Debt/Worth		3.3	2.7		3.5	3.4
	10.5		8.5		12.7			28.5	9.0		6.4	8.1
	52.9		48.8		78.7	% Profit Before Taxes/Tangible		74.1	65.7		98.2	80.0
(57)	27.0	(83)	21.6	(80)	24.6	Net Worth	(20) 12.3	(11) 11.4		25.6	(25) 40.0	
	6.9		5.8		3.2			−21.5	2.9		2.6	11.4
	11.6		12.9		13.6	% Profit Before Taxes/Total		20.8	18.4		13.3	13.3
	4.3		5.0		5.6	Assets		2.1	4.9		5.9	7.8
	1.6		1.1		.5			−6.1	.4		.5	4.1
	104.7		137.8		156.4			107.9	56.8		105.0	220.1
	23.2		40.5		31.1	Sales/Net Fixed Assets		31.1	15.2		25.1	65.1
	9.6		13.4		9.6			10.2	4.9		13.8	4.5
	3.7		3.6		3.1			3.0	4.1		3.5	2.7
	2.2		2.7		2.0	Sales/Total Assets		2.0	2.2		2.9	1.5
	1.2		1.3		1.3			1.3	1.7		1.9	1.0
	.4		.2		.2			.4	.1		.4	.1
(49)	1.4	(73)	.5	(56)	.6	% Depr., Dep., Amort./Sales	(14) 1.3	(10) .7	(12) .6	(14) .2	
	2.0		1.5		1.6			2.7	1.6		1.3	1.7
	1.6		1.3		1.8			2.4				
(25)	3.3	(34)	3.0	(34)	3.3	% Officers', Directors', Owners' Comp/Sales	(10) 5.4				
	7.5		6.6		6.4			8.7				
1229232M		3093365M		4031977M		Net Sales ($)	4437M	46889M	50981M	41637M	237218M	3650815M
695331M		1682443M		2311103M		Total Assets ($)	4896M	30321M	27994M	20029M	120092M	2107771M

M = $ thousand   MM = $ million
See Pages 11 through 18 for Explanation of Ratios and Data

Current Data Sorted By Assets   Comparative Historical Data

							Type of Statement			
		13	103	72	19	6	Unqualified		209	246
	14	59	127	18			Reviewed		151	196
	9	18	12	5			Compiled		44	38
	5	10	11	1			Tax Returns		18	21
	3	14	46	14	5	1	Other		92	81
		153 (4/1-9/30/02)		432 (10/1/02-3/31/03)					4/1/98-3/31/99	4/1/99-3/31/00
	0-500M	500M-2MM	2-10MM	10-50MM	50-100MM	100-250MM			ALL	ALL
	31	114	299	110	24	7	NUMBER OF STATEMENTS		514	582
	%	%	%	%	%	%	ASSETS		%	%
	22.1	20.3	21.1	21.3	24.2		Cash & Equivalents		18.8	19.6
	31.1	42.6	46.3	48.2	49.5		Trade Receivables (net)		46.9	48.6
	10.2	1.9	2.5	1.8	1.4		Inventory		3.1	2.3
	9.6	8.9	9.5	8.5	8.3		All Other Current		8.6	8.8
	73.0	73.8	79.4	79.8	83.3		Total Current		77.3	79.3
	19.0	17.1	13.2	11.9	10.4		Fixed Assets (net)		14.4	13.4
	1.6	1.0	.5	.8	.6		Intangibles (net)		.7	.7
	6.3	8.1	7.0	7.6	5.7		All Other Non-Current		7.6	6.5
	100.0	100.0	100.0	100.0	100.0		Total		100.0	100.0
							LIABILITIES			
	13.1	9.3	4.5	3.2	1.2		Notes Payable-Short Term		5.9	4.8
	5.9	2.8	1.9	1.8	1.5		Cur. Mat.-L/T/D		1.8	1.8
	20.1	23.4	33.9	39.7	43.7		Trade Payables		31.6	35.8
	.3	.6	.5	.5	.1		Income Taxes Payable		3.2	.5
	11.3	13.8	16.0	19.0	23.0		All Other Current		15.2	15.7
	50.8	50.0	56.9	64.1	69.6		Total Current		57.7	58.6
	8.0	8.8	5.4	5.2	5.3		Long Term Debt		5.6	6.1
	.0	.4	.4	.2	.2		Deferred Taxes		.6	.6
	6.2	2.0	1.3	1.3	.9		All Other Non-Current		1.6	2.2
	34.8	38.8	36.1	29.1	23.9		Net Worth		34.4	32.6
	100.0	100.0	100.0	100.0	100.0		Total Liabilities & Net Worth		100.0	100.0
							INCOME DATA			
	100.0	100.0	100.0	100.0	100.0		Net Sales		100.0	100.0
	26.6	18.9	13.6	10.3	6.4		Gross Profit		14.2	14.0
	23.9	17.7	12.1	8.2	4.8		Operating Expenses		11.4	11.8
	2.7	1.2	1.5	2.1	1.6		Operating Profit		2.7	2.2
	−.5	.0	−.1	.1	−.3		All Other Expenses (net)		−.4	−.5
	3.2	1.2	1.6	2.0	1.9		Profit Before Taxes		3.1	2.7
							RATIOS			
	2.8	2.3	1.8	1.5	1.2				1.7	1.7
	1.4	1.5	1.4	1.2	1.2		Current		1.3	1.3
	1.0	1.2	1.2	1.1	1.1				1.1	1.1
	2.1	1.9	1.5	1.2	1.1				1.4	1.5
	1.0	1.3	1.2	1.1	1.1		Quick		1.2	1.2
	.5	.9	1.0	.9	.9				1.0	1.0

8	46.0	26	13.9	38	9.7	42	8.7	43	8.4			Sales/Receivables	37	9.8	38	9.5
18	20.8	48	7.6	52	7.0	58	6.3	54	6.7				54	6.8	55	6.7
39	9.5	61	6.0	69	5.3	69	5.3	66	5.5				71	5.1	72	5.1
0	UND	0	UND	0	UND	0	UND	0	UND			Cost of Sales/Inventory	0	UND	0	UND
0	UND	0	UND	0	UND	0	UND	0	UND				0	UND	0	UND
2	220.2	0	781.8	0	999.8	0	835.8	1	528.0				0	819.7	0	971.7
4	85.1	13	27.9	27	13.5	31	11.6	40	9.2			Cost of Sales/Payables	23	16.2	25	14.7
18	19.9	27	13.4	40	9.1	50	7.4	51	7.1				40	9.1	44	8.3
29	12.7	49	7.5	60	6.1	66	5.5	65	5.6				57	6.4	62	5.9
	9.7		7.3		8.9		11.4		17.1			Sales/Working Capital		10.2		9.2
	40.0		13.4		14.9		25.0		32.5					18.1		18.4
	269.4		34.6		33.0		50.5		54.1					38.9		36.0
	21.2		10.2		24.4		60.4		61.8			EBIT/Interest		28.5		27.4
(20)	7.3	(91)	2.3	(231)	6.7	(85)	11.2	(19)	25.2				(399)	7.8	(460)	8.7
	.2		−6.3		1.3		2.7		4.0					2.3		2.2
			4.0		5.5		14.0					Net Profit + Depr., Dep.,		12.2		7.2
		(30)	1.7	(82)	2.2	(29)	3.6					Amort./Cur. Mat. L /T/D	(150)	3.3	(160)	3.1
			−.7		.9		1.1							1.6		1.4
	.1		.1		.1		.1		.1			Fixed/Worth		.1		.1
	.6		.3		.2		.2		.2					.3		.3
	56.3		.8		.5		.5		.6					.6		.6
	.4		.7		1.1		1.4		2.6			Debt/Worth		1.1		1.2
	1.5		1.5		2.0		3.3		3.8					2.2		2.3
	147.3		3.5		3.6		5.7		5.5					4.0		4.3
	96.0		31.8		29.8		34.9		35.9			% Profit Before Taxes/Tangible		43.4		42.4
(24)	51.8	(101)	9.1	(292)	11.5	(109)	18.9	(23)	24.2			Net Worth	(494)	22.4	(556)	20.4
	8.2		−7.0		1.6		7.0		15.3					7.7		7.9
	35.2		13.2		9.4		9.5		9.4			% Profit Before Taxes/Total		13.7		11.9
	12.2		3.4		3.2		4.7		4.6			Assets		6.1		5.8
	.0		−4.2		.4		2.1		2.4					2.1		1.9
	130.6		81.6		103.4		144.8		160.8			Sales/Net Fixed Assets		85.5		97.3
	29.2		45.1		43.3		63.8		95.5					42.0		41.9
	12.0		9.7		19.3		21.5		27.5					15.0		18.9
	6.8		4.5		4.1		4.0		4.0			Sales/Total Assets		4.2		4.3
	4.3		3.4		3.1		3.2		3.0					3.3		3.3
	2.9		2.2		2.4		2.3		2.4					2.4		2.4
	.3		.5		.3		.2		.1			% Depr., Dep., Amort./Sales		.3		.3
(27)	.8	(94)	.9	(275)	.5	(102)	.4	(20)	.2				(470)	.6	(542)	.6
	2.2		1.7		1.2		1.1		.5					1.4		1.2
	2.2		1.6		1.1		.5					% Officers', Directors',		1.1		1.3
(15)	4.1	(51)	2.6	(146)	2.1	(32)	1.1					Owners' Comp/Sales	(227)	2.5	(235)	2.6
	11.4		4.8		4.3		2.1							4.5		4.4

						Net Sales ($)			
56477M	493012M	4763291M	7422384M	5465134M	2945571M	Net Sales ($)		17857106M	23125552M
9540M	137421M	1453297M	2378390M	1728605M	1070794M	Total Assets ($)		5742777M	7398622M

M = $ thousand   MM = $ million
See Pages 11 through 18 for Explanation of Ratios and Data

Comparative Historical Data				Current Data Sorted By Sales					
159	156	213	Type of Statement / Unqualified		4	8	24	61	116
168	141	218	Reviewed	10	26	21	56	78	27
43	60	44	Compiled	5	16	6	9	3	5
12	14	27	Tax Returns	5	6	4	6	5	1
96	108	83	Other	4	8	5	16	24	26
4/1/00- 3/31/01 ALL	4/1/01- 3/31/02 ALL	4/1/02- 3/31/03 ALL		153 (4/1-9/30/02)			432 (10/1/02-3/31/03)		
				0-1MM	1-3MM	3-5MM	5-10MM	10-25MM	25MM & OVER
478	479	585	NUMBER OF STATEMENTS	24	60	44	111	171	175
%	%	%	ASSETS	%	%	%	%	%	%
19.5	20.1	21.1	Cash & Equivalents	18.6	18.5	15.7	23.3	22.0	21.4
49.8	48.2	45.3	Trade Receivables (net)	17.6	35.0	42.6	40.7	49.3	52.2
2.3	2.7	2.6	Inventory	16.5	7.6	1.5	1.9	.8	1.5
8.0	8.5	9.1	All Other Current	6.1	9.6	9.0	9.4	10.2	8.2
79.6	79.5	78.1	Total Current	58.8	70.7	68.8	75.3	82.3	83.3
13.3	13.0	14.0	Fixed Assets (net)	30.5	20.3	20.3	16.2	10.7	9.8
.7	1.2	.7	Intangibles (net)	1.7	1.6	.6	1.0	.2	.7
6.4	6.3	7.2	All Other Non-Current	9.1	7.3	10.3	7.5	6.8	6.3
100.0	100.0	100.0	Total	100.0	100.0	100.0	100.0	100.0	100.0
			LIABILITIES						
4.4	6.8	5.5	Notes Payable-Short Term	16.7	11.0	10.2	6.8	3.3	2.2
1.7	2.3	2.3	Cur. Mat.-L/T/D	2.5	6.8	2.9	2.7	1.2	1.4
35.3	35.9	32.7	Trade Payables	6.9	18.3	25.7	27.3	36.3	42.7
.6	.5	.5	Income Taxes Payable	.3	.3	.5	1.1	.5	.2
16.2	15.4	16.2	All Other Current	16.8	7.8	12.4	15.6	16.5	20.0
58.3	61.0	57.1	Total Current	43.2	44.1	51.7	53.5	57.7	66.5
5.6	7.6	6.3	Long Term Debt	13.4	10.2	13.7	7.2	3.7	4.2
.5	.5	.3	Deferred Taxes	.0	.7	.7	.5	.2	.2
1.4	1.5	1.7	All Other Non-Current	4.5	4.8	1.1	1.5	1.1	1.0
34.1	29.4	34.6	Net Worth	38.9	40.2	32.9	37.3	37.3	28.1
100.0	100.0	100.0	Total Liabilities & Net Worth	100.0	100.0	100.0	100.0	100.0	100.0
			INCOME DATA						
100.0	100.0	100.0	Net Sales	100.0	100.0	100.0	100.0	100.0	100.0
13.0	13.1	14.4	Gross Profit	32.9	25.6	17.1	16.1	11.4	9.0
11.0	11.6	12.7	Operating Expenses	32.1	23.8	15.6	14.1	10.0	7.3
2.0	1.5	1.6	Operating Profit	.7	1.8	1.6	2.0	1.4	1.7
−.2	.1	−.1	All Other Expenses (net)	−.4	−.3	.4	.1	−.1	−.1
2.3	1.4	1.7	Profit Before Taxes	1.2	2.1	1.2	1.9	1.5	1.8
			RATIOS						
1.7	1.7	1.8	Current	4.1	2.6	1.9	2.1	1.8	1.4
1.3	1.3	1.3		1.6	1.6	1.4	1.5	1.4	1.2
1.1	1.1	1.1		.7	1.2	1.1	1.2	1.2	1.1
1.5	1.5	1.5	Quick	3.3	2.0	1.5	1.8	1.5	1.2
1.2	1.2	1.2		.5	1.3	1.2	1.3	1.2	1.1
1.0	1.0	1.0		.2	.8	.8	1.0	1.0	1.0
39 9.3	36 10.0	35 10.6	Sales/Receivables	0 UND	18 20.2	33 11.0	31 11.6	38 9.6	42 8.7
54 6.8	54 6.8	52 7.1		17 21.2	42 8.6	54 6.8	47 7.8	54 6.8	54 6.7
72 5.1	70 5.2	66 5.5		57 6.4	72 5.1	64 5.7	70 5.2	69 5.3	64 5.7
0 UND	0 UND	0 UND	Cost of Sales/Inventory	0 UND	0 UND	0 UND	0 UND	0 UND	0 UND
0 UND	0 UND	0 UND		0 UND	0 UND	0 UND	0 UND	0 UND	0 UND
0 999.8	0 999.8	0 888.6		58 6.3	5 66.4	0 UND	1 726.0	0 999.8	0 999.8
26 14.3	27 13.8	24 15.3	Cost of Sales/Payables	9 38.8	9 38.7	19 19.0	15 23.6	27 13.7	31 11.8
42 8.7	43 8.5	39 9.3		17 21.7	26 14.2	38 9.7	37 9.7	43 8.4	48 7.6
58 6.3	60 6.0	59 6.2		36 10.3	44 8.2	52 7.0	57 6.4	63 5.8	62 5.9
10.1	9.6	9.1	Sales/Working Capital	3.7	5.9	8.2	7.5	9.4	14.3
18.6	19.3	17.4		22.6	10.2	17.8	11.4	15.8	25.3
42.4	43.1	40.7		−3.1	31.6	70.7	27.1	32.4	49.9
34.7	28.7	26.6	EBIT/Interest	6.0	14.5	8.0	18.0	24.8	60.4
(379) 8.9	(371) 7.3	(452) 5.9		(15) 1.0	(47) 2.4	(36) 2.0	(92) 5.3	(126) 5.5	(136) 16.5
2.5	1.4	1.2		−3.1	−1.0	−2.2	−1.0	1.4	3.0
9.1	10.9	7.1	Net Profit + Depr., Dep., Amort./Cur. Mat. L/T/D		6.1	3.7	5.1	5.8	14.8
(127) 3.5	(113) 3.2	(149) 2.6			(13) 3.3	(12) 1.1	(36) 2.1	(48) 2.6	(39) 5.9
1.4	1.0	.8			.4	−.5	.4	1.2	1.0
.1	.1	.1	Fixed/Worth	.1	.1	.1	.1	.1	.1
.3	.3	.3		.7	.4	.4	.3	.2	.2
.5	.6	.5		−3.7	1.0	1.5	.7	.4	.5
1.2	1.2	1.1	Debt/Worth	.3	.6	.9	1.0	1.1	1.7
2.4	2.4	2.3		.8	1.2	1.8	1.8	2.1	3.3
4.3	4.5	4.4		−13.3	4.7	5.6	3.1	3.6	5.2
43.7	37.8	33.9	% Profit Before Taxes/Tangible Net Worth	18.8	47.4	35.1	39.4	25.3	35.9
(470) 19.1	(451) 14.4	(555) 14.2		(15) 3.8	(54) 11.7	(40) 12.6	(104) 15.3	(171) 8.8	20.7
6.3	3.4	2.2		.0	−5.0	1.0	.2	2.6	6.6
11.9	9.9	10.2	% Profit Before Taxes/Total Assets	12.4	19.6	12.4	11.6	9.4	9.8
5.6	4.0	3.9		1.5	2.7	2.6	5.3	3.0	4.7
1.5	.7	.5		−3.1	−4.4	−3.8	−1.3	.8	1.7
106.2	112.1	106.2	Sales/Net Fixed Assets	36.3	61.7	72.9	79.0	118.3	161.8
48.8	45.4	46.5		10.5	19.2	31.1	39.1	51.1	83.1
19.6	18.6	17.8		1.6	8.7	7.1	12.5	22.5	28.6
4.3	4.4	4.2	Sales/Total Assets	2.9	4.0	4.1	4.0	4.5	4.3
3.4	3.3	3.2		1.3	2.5	2.9	3.0	3.4	3.6
2.6	2.6	2.4		.3	1.9	1.9	2.1	2.7	2.9
.2	.2	.3	% Depr., Dep., Amort./Sales	.5	.7	.5	.4	.2	.2
(430) .5	(425) .6	(524) .6		(18) 1.6	(51) 1.6	(38) .9	(94) .7	(162) .5	(161) .3
1.2	1.3	1.4		3.8	2.6	2.0	1.9	1.1	.7
1.0	1.2	1.1	% Officers', Directors', Owners' Comp/Sales		2.2	2.1	1.5	.9	.5
(209) 2.3	(211) 2.4	(248) 2.1			(25) 4.0	(25) 3.7	(50) 2.3	(90) 1.9	(49) 1.1
4.4	4.6	4.3			8.2	5.3	3.7	3.8	1.9
20500024M	16037820M	21145869M	Net Sales ($)	14854M	122510M	177394M	831131M	2780157M	17219823M
6516409M	5036669M	6778047M	Total Assets ($)	30848M	62946M	77108M	352895M	884658M	5369592M

Current Data Sorted By Assets | Comparative Historical Data

						Type of Statement		
5	20	111	100	16	8	Unqualified	163	168
12	85	141	20	1	1	Reviewed	135	159
10	23	17	3	1		Compiled	43	40
11	26	17	1		1	Tax Returns	15	21
8	24	55	32	7	7	Other	60	85
	163 (4/1-9/30/02)		599 (10/1/02-3/31/03)				4/1/98-3/31/99	4/1/99-3/31/00
0-500M	500M-2MM	2-10MM	10-50MM	50-100MM	100-250MM		ALL	ALL
46	178	341	156	24	17	NUMBER OF STATEMENTS	416	473
%	%	%	%	%	%	ASSETS	%	%
23.3	16.0	19.2	22.0	22.1	29.4	Cash & Equivalents	19.8	20.4
37.5	42.5	48.2	50.6	51.6	41.3	Trade Receivables (net)	46.3	47.1
3.3	4.6	3.3	2.0	1.5	1.4	Inventory	4.0	3.2
5.6	10.2	10.2	9.3	8.6	11.4	All Other Current	8.5	8.3
69.8	73.4	80.8	83.9	83.8	83.5	Total Current	78.6	79.0
16.7	17.9	12.1	8.9	8.2	10.4	Fixed Assets (net)	14.4	13.1
.5	.9	1.0	1.3	.1	1.0	Intangibles (net)	.7	1.2
12.8	7.8	6.1	5.9	7.9	5.1	All Other Non-Current	6.3	6.7
100.0	100.0	100.0	100.0	100.0	100.0	Total	100.0	100.0
						LIABILITIES		
9.7	10.5	5.4	3.7	3.4	5.4	Notes Payable-Short Term	5.6	5.1
1.5	3.4	1.8	1.2	.3	1.3	Cur. Mat.-L/T/D	2.2	1.6
29.8	27.7	37.5	43.2	47.1	39.6	Trade Payables	33.8	35.3
.2	.8	.7	.2	.1	2.7	Income Taxes Payable	1.6	.6
24.4	14.4	15.4	18.4	22.0	21.3	All Other Current	14.9	16.1
65.7	56.9	60.8	66.8	72.9	70.4	Total Current	58.1	58.7
9.5	8.8	5.2	4.2	2.8	8.4	Long Term Debt	6.5	6.2
.0	.5	.5	.1	.0	.3	Deferred Taxes	.8	.8
19.5	2.0	2.6	1.4	2.9	1.0	All Other Non-Current	1.3	1.3
5.0	31.9	30.9	27.6	21.4	19.9	Net Worth	33.4	33.0
100.0	100.0	100.0	100.0	100.0	100.0	Total Liabilities & Net Worth	100.0	100.0
						INCOME DATA		
100.0	100.0	100.0	100.0	100.0	100.0	Net Sales	100.0	100.0
19.7	19.0	12.6	9.6	9.5	10.9	Gross Profit	14.6	14.4
17.2	17.1	10.8	7.4	6.1	7.4	Operating Expenses	11.3	11.9
2.4	1.9	1.7	2.2	3.4	3.5	Operating Profit	3.2	2.4
.3	.6	.2	.0	1.1	.1	All Other Expenses (net)	.1	−.3
2.1	1.4	1.6	2.2	2.3	3.4	Profit Before Taxes	3.1	2.8
						RATIOS		
1.8	1.9	1.6	1.4	1.2	1.3		1.7	1.7
1.4	1.4	1.3	1.2	1.1	1.3	Current	1.3	1.3
.9	1.0	1.1	1.1	1.0	1.1		1.1	1.1
1.6	1.6	1.4	1.2	1.1	1.2		1.5	1.5
1.2 (177)	1.1	1.1	1.1	1.0	1.1	Quick	(415) 1.2	1.1
.7	.8	.9	.9	1.0	.9		.9	.9
9 41.4	27 13.5	38 9.5	48 7.7	43 8.6	40 9.2		36 10.0	34 10.7
26 14.1	44 8.2	55 6.6	60 6.1	56 6.5	59 6.1	Sales/Receivables	54 6.7	53 6.9
51 7.2	65 5.6	73 5.0	73 5.0	75 4.9	68 5.4		68 5.3	72 5.1
0 UND	0 UND	0 UND	0 UND	0 UND	0 UND		0 UND	0 UND
0 UND	0 UND	0 UND	0 UND	0 UND	0 UND	Cost of Sales/Inventory	0 UND	0 UND
0 UND	1 420.0	0 999.8	0 999.8	0 UND	3 107.2		0 999.8	0 988.8
10 38.3	17 21.9	28 12.9	39 9.5	40 9.2	38 9.5		22 16.6	24 15.0
24 15.1	34 10.6	45 8.2	57 6.4	52 7.0	60 6.1	Cost of Sales/Payables	45 8.1	43 8.5
58 6.3	51 7.2	64 5.7	71 5.1	75 4.9	66 5.5		62 5.9	62 5.9
12.9	8.7	9.9	11.5	20.3	12.0		9.8	9.3
30.4	17.7	20.0	21.2	39.0	18.2	Sales/Working Capital	16.9	18.6
−148.4	403.3	43.8	38.5	80.8	62.6		36.1	52.8
16.0	12.2	29.8	33.4	156.7	56.4		26.3	28.0
(27) 5.3	(155) 3.9	(262) 6.6	(118) 9.7	(17) 22.3	(13) 39.4	EBIT/Interest	(320) 8.6	(358) 7.9
−2.4	−1.1	1.5	3.3	10.1	7.4		2.9	2.2
	10.3	8.2	16.1		33.4	Net Profit + Depr., Dep.,	10.8	9.9
	(45) 3.2	(91) 2.4	(42) 6.2		(10) 13.4	Amort./Cur. Mat. L /T/D	(128) 4.0	(119) 3.8
	−3.6	.1	2.7		6.7		1.9	1.7
.1	.2	.1	.1	.1	.1		.1	.1
.3	.5	.3	.2	.3	.3	Fixed/Worth	.3	.3
1.3	1.0	.6	.5	.4	.8		.6	.6
.9	.9	1.3	1.8	2.9	2.7		1.2	1.2
2.0	1.8	2.5	3.5	4.8	4.1	Debt/Worth	2.2	2.5
6.6	5.2	5.2	5.7	7.2	7.4		4.0	5.1
77.5	40.7	35.5	35.9	46.9	60.2	% Profit Before Taxes/Tangible	45.6	46.4
(41) 32.2	(156) 14.2	(328) 13.6	(153) 17.6	29.4	(15) 28.4	Net Worth	(402) 21.7	(450) 23.6
3.6	−2.0	2.2	6.8	20.2	21.1		8.5	8.1
19.1	11.6	10.4	8.8	8.5	11.4	% Profit Before Taxes/Total	12.6	12.7
8.7	3.4	3.6	4.1	5.0	5.9	Assets	6.4	6.1
−1.8	−3.4	.5	1.5	2.9	3.9		2.3	1.7
472.9	67.9	113.6	158.5	218.7	107.3		104.8	120.0
60.2	31.7	53.1	72.5	92.9	58.4	Sales/Net Fixed Assets	40.6	52.5
21.6	11.4	20.8	31.5	44.3	23.9		18.2	20.7
8.3	4.7	4.3	3.8	4.3	3.5		4.2	4.4
4.7	3.2	3.3	3.2	3.4	3.1	Sales/Total Assets	3.3	3.3
3.3	2.3	2.4	2.5	2.4	2.6		2.4	2.4
.5	.5	.2	.2	.1	.2		.2	.2
(32) .8	(153) 1.1	(314) .5	(143) .3	(21) .2	(15) .4	% Depr., Dep., Amort./Sales	(380) .5	(414) .5
1.7	1.9	1.1	.7	.4	.6		1.3	1.2
1.2	2.2	1.0	.9			% Officers', Directors',	1.3	1.2
(17) 3.3	(81) 4.2	(152) 1.9	(40) 1.4			Owners' Comp/Sales	(179) 2.6	(202) 2.6
9.2	6.5	3.2	2.2				5.5	4.9
58457M	792369M	5721010M	10749217M	5442846M	12331143M	Net Sales ($)	16440187M	17575248M
10844M	222541M	1685205M	3394936M	1672243M	2998069M	Total Assets ($)	4604237M	5769539M

M = $ thousand   MM = $ million
See Pages 11 through 18 for Explanation of Ratios and Data

Comparative Historical Data | | | Current Data Sorted By Sales

			Type of Statement						
153	160	260	Unqualified	4	7	9	25	67	148
177	175	259	Reviewed	5	31	38	66	82	37
76	79	54	Compiled	6	18	8	13	6	3
28	24	56	Tax Returns	9	12	10	13	9	3
82	113	133	Other	6	14	12	19	30	52
4/1/00- 3/31/01 ALL	4/1/01- 3/31/02 ALL	4/1/02- 3/31/03 ALL		163 (4/1-9/30/02)			599 (10/1/02-3/31/03)		
				0-1MM	1-3MM	3-5MM	5-10MM	10-25MM	25MM & OVER
516	551	762	**NUMBER OF STATEMENTS**	30	82	77	136	194	243
%	%	%	**ASSETS**	%	%	%	%	%	%
18.6	18.9	19.6	Cash & Equivalents	27.2	15.1	15.5	16.5	20.8	22.4
47.1	47.7	46.6	Trade Receivables (net)	32.4	30.3	41.3	46.6	48.8	53.9
3.4	3.9	3.2	Inventory	3.4	9.1	5.4	3.9	2.3	.9
9.5	9.7	9.7	All Other Current	3.3	8.3	12.7	9.5	10.4	9.6
78.6	80.2	79.2	Total Current	66.3	62.7	75.0	76.4	82.2	86.9
13.5	12.3	12.9	Fixed Assets (net)	23.1	22.9	17.6	14.6	10.9	7.4
1.5	1.2	1.0	Intangibles (net)	.5	1.8	1.3	1.0	1.0	.7
6.3	6.3	6.9	All Other Non-Current	9.8	12.6	6.1	8.0	5.8	5.1
100.0	100.0	100.0	Total	100.0	100.0	100.0	100.0	100.0	100.0
			LIABILITIES						
5.6	6.2	6.4	Notes Payable-Short Term	4.1	14.7	11.2	7.8	5.5	2.4
2.4	2.4	2.0	Cur. Mat.-L/T/D	.4	3.4	2.5	3.3	2.0	.8
35.7	37.4	36.3	Trade Payables	25.5	16.7	27.0	32.5	38.6	47.4
.6	.4	.6	Income Taxes Payable	.2	.4	1.1	.8	.6	.5
15.8	16.8	16.7	All Other Current	32.6	11.5	13.8	15.0	15.0	19.6
60.1	63.1	62.0	Total Current	62.8	46.7	55.5	59.4	61.7	70.7
5.8	5.9	6.1	Long Term Debt	13.7	11.9	10.6	6.7	3.5	3.5
.6	.6	.4	Deferred Taxes	.0	.6	.6	.6	.4	.1
2.3	1.6	3.2	All Other Non-Current	4.9	3.7	11.3	1.2	2.3	2.1
31.1	28.8	28.3	Net Worth	18.2	37.1	22.1	32.1	32.0	23.6
100.0	100.0	100.0	Total Liabilities & Net Worth	100.0	100.0	100.0	100.0	100.0	100.0
			INCOME DATA						
100.0	100.0	100.0	Net Sales	100.0	100.0	100.0	100.0	100.0	100.0
15.2	14.0	13.8	Gross Profit	27.1	24.1	17.0	15.9	11.7	8.1
13.0	11.7	11.7	Operating Expenses	23.7	20.6	15.3	14.1	9.9	6.3
2.2	2.3	2.0	Operating Profit	3.4	3.5	1.7	1.8	1.8	1.8
.3	.2	.3	All Other Expenses (net)	2.5	1.3	.3	.1	.1	-.1
2.0	2.1	1.7	Profit Before Taxes	.9	2.2	1.4	1.7	1.7	1.9
			RATIOS						
1.7	1.6	1.6		2.4	2.4	1.9	1.6	1.6	1.4
1.3	1.2	1.2	Current	1.4	1.4	1.4	1.3	1.3	1.2
1.1	1.1	1.1		.9	.9	1.1	1.1	1.1	1.1
1.4	1.3	1.4		1.8	1.7	1.5	1.5	1.5	1.2
1.1 (550)	1.1 (761)	1.1	Quick	1.2 (81)	1.2	1.2	1.1	1.2	1.1
.9	.9	.9		.8	.5	.8	.8	.9	1.0
32 11.3	34 10.6	36 10.1		18 19.8	12 31.7	25 14.4	34 10.7	36 10.1	42 8.6
51 7.2	52 7.0	53 6.8	Sales/Receivables	40 9.0	44 8.3	43 8.5	50 7.3	57 6.4	56 6.5
72 5.1	69 5.3	70 5.2		57 6.4	76 4.8	67 5.4	69 5.3	75 4.9	69 5.3
0 UND	0 UND	0 UND		0 UND	0 UND	0 UND	0 UND	0 UND	0 UND
0 UND	0 UND	0 UND	Cost of Sales/Inventory	0 UND	0 UND	0 UND	0 UND	0 UND	0 UND
0 999.8	0 999.8	0 999.8		0 UND	8 44.8	0 874.7	1 566.1	0 999.8	0 UND
24 15.1	26 14.2	27 13.5		6 66.2	12 29.5	16 22.5	20 18.1	30 12.1	37 10.0
41 8.9	44 8.4	44 8.2	Cost of Sales/Payables	38 9.6	29 12.6	34 10.6	41 9.0	48 7.6	54 6.8
61 6.0	63 5.8	63 5.8		72 5.0	51 7.1	54 6.8	59 6.2	67 5.5	68 5.3
9.8	11.1	10.0		5.9	5.8	8.7	10.1	9.5	15.6
21.5	23.3	20.7	Sales/Working Capital	21.1	9.6	17.3	20.4	18.0	24.8
56.5	68.5	50.4		-243.8	-50.0	63.9	68.7	38.4	47.6
29.3	32.0	25.7		14.3	12.8	12.2	17.0	30.8	44.1
(400) 7.2	(434) 6.6	(592) 6.4	EBIT/Interest	(12) 7.6	(67) 3.6	(67) 3.0	(118) 3.6	(147) 8.1	(181) 14.0
1.8	1.6	1.5		3.5	-3.4	-1.3	.9	1.8	4.2
12.0	11.4	10.9			7.1	5.6	8.4	7.7	20.1
(127) 4.3	(110) 4.4	(194) 4.0	Net Profit + Depr., Dep., Amort./Cur. Mat. L/T/D		(21) 1.2	(21) 1.5	(35) 2.4	(49) 2.3	(67) 8.2
1.7	1.4	.3			-6.1	-4.0	1.2	-1.9	3.6
.1	.1	.1		.0	.1	.2	.2	.1	.1
.3	.3	.3	Fixed/Worth	.3	.4	.4	.4	.2	.2
.7	.7	.7		1.5	1.2	1.4	.9	.5	.5
1.2	1.4	1.3		.9	.7	.9	1.1	1.2	2.1
2.6	3.0	2.7	Debt/Worth	1.8	1.5	2.0	2.2	2.3	3.8
5.6	5.6	5.5		7.1	5.8	5.5	5.0	4.8	5.9
41.7	48.3	40.3		66.0	43.7	43.5	38.9	31.8	44.4
(482) 19.4	(520) 20.4	(717) 16.5	% Profit Before Taxes/Tangible Net Worth	(27) 23.4	(71) 14.8	(66) 14.5	(127) 12.2	(188) 12.4	(238) 22.3
5.7	6.3	3.4		.0	-11.8	1.6	2.0	1.4	7.9
11.9	11.7	10.6		15.6	12.2	11.0	12.8	9.8	9.4
5.0	5.2	4.0	% Profit Before Taxes/Total Assets	7.9	3.8	2.6	3.5	3.8	4.4
1.2	1.4	.5		-1.1	-7.4	-3.8	.2	.5	1.6
121.6	133.6	118.3		UND	44.9	70.0	79.0	108.3	196.0
51.5	50.2	48.3	Sales/Net Fixed Assets	45.4	17.4	34.0	34.4	56.0	89.1
20.0	22.0	19.2		5.5	5.9	12.0	16.1	27.0	39.4
4.5	4.5	4.3		5.1	3.3	4.1	4.5	4.4	4.3
3.4	3.4	3.3	Sales/Total Assets	3.2	2.2	3.1	3.3	3.3	3.5
2.5	2.6	2.5		1.3	1.2	2.2	2.5	2.5	3.0
.2	.2	.2		.6	.8	.4	.5	.2	.2
(438) .5	(461) .5	(678) .6	% Depr., Dep., Amort./Sales	(18) 1.5	(66) 1.6	(67) .9	(122) .9	(181) .5	(224) .3
1.1	1.0	1.2		5.1	3.5	2.2	1.5	.8	.6
1.1	1.2	1.1			2.6	2.2	1.5	.9	.8
(204) 2.5	(218) 2.7	(298) 2.2	% Officers', Directors', Owners' Comp/Sales		(39) 5.1	(33) 3.5	(71) 2.6	(76) 1.8	(71) 1.3
4.8	4.7	4.5			10.1	5.5	4.5	3.0	2.2
17244172M	21481319M	35095042M	Net Sales ($)	14821M	160930M	305539M	1001866M	3061351M	30550535M
5383686M	6728957M	99838838M	Total Assets ($)	17295M	108688M	123391M	340531M	1123226M	8270707M

M = $ thousand   MM = $ million
See Pages 11 through 18 for Explanation of Ratios and Data

Current Data Sorted By Assets   Comparative Historical Data

						Type of Statement		
1	8	45	41	5	3	Unqualified	92	102
6	40	77	5			Reviewed	98	96
4	13	14	6			Compiled	27	29
10	5	6				Tax Returns	19	13
2	6	28	15	4	2	Other	40	51
	76 (4/1-9/30/02)		264 (10/1/02-3/31/03)				4/1/98-3/31/99	4/1/99-3/31/00
0-500M	500M-2MM	2-10MM	10-50MM	50-100MM	100-250MM		ALL	ALL
23	72	170	61	9	5	NUMBER OF STATEMENTS	276	291
%	%	%	%	%	%	ASSETS	%	%
14.0	16.5	13.6	12.4			Cash & Equivalents	12.9	12.9
19.6	33.7	38.7	39.4			Trade Receivables (net)	35.0	37.1
4.1	2.0	1.9	1.7			Inventory	3.0	3.4
5.9	8.9	7.9	10.1			All Other Current	6.4	7.1
43.6	61.1	62.1	63.6			Total Current	57.3	60.5
42.7	31.1	30.7	29.7			Fixed Assets (net)	34.0	32.3
3.6	.2	.7	1.4			Intangibles (net)	1.7	1.6
10.1	7.6	6.6	5.4			All Other Non-Current	7.1	5.6
100.0	100.0	100.0	100.0			Total	100.0	100.0
						LIABILITIES		
19.2	6.2	6.3	4.6			Notes Payable-Short Term	4.4	5.3
6.1	6.9	5.5	5.2			Cur. Mat.-L/T/D	5.5	5.8
5.7	17.1	18.2	21.8			Trade Payables	16.2	18.1
.9	.5	1.5	.3			Income Taxes Payable	1.6	.8
7.5	9.4	10.9	12.6			All Other Current	12.2	11.2
39.4	40.1	42.4	44.6			Total Current	39.9	41.2
30.2	13.0	12.1	10.5			Long Term Debt	14.6	13.1
.2	.7	1.1	1.7			Deferred Taxes	1.4	1.5
3.6	2.8	2.0	1.7			All Other Non-Current	3.2	2.7
26.6	43.4	42.4	41.6			Net Worth	40.8	41.5
100.0	100.0	100.0	100.0			Total Liabilities & Net Worth	100.0	100.0
						INCOME DATA		
100.0	100.0	100.0	100.0			Net Sales	100.0	100.0
46.4	24.9	22.7	16.3			Gross Profit	25.8	24.4
43.6	23.1	19.0	12.4			Operating Expenses	21.3	19.0
2.8	1.8	3.7	3.8			Operating Profit	4.5	5.4
1.0	.2	.3	.4			All Other Expenses (net)	.0	−.1
1.8	1.6	3.3	3.4			Profit Before Taxes	4.5	5.5
						RATIOS		
2.3	2.7	2.1	1.9				2.3	2.2
1.3	1.7	1.4	1.3			Current	1.6	1.4
.3	1.2	1.1	1.1				1.1	1.1
1.6	1.9	1.9	1.5				2.0	1.8
1.1	1.4	1.2	1.1			Quick	1.3	1.2
.3	.9	.9	.8				.9	.9
0 UND	26 14.2	41 8.9	51 7.1				38 9.6	42 8.7
15 23.9	42 8.6	60 6.1	67 5.5			Sales/Receivables	56 6.5	59 6.2
57 6.4	75 4.9	78 4.7	82 4.4				77 4.8	76 4.8
0 UND	0 UND	0 UND	0 UND				0 UND	0 UND
0 UND	0 UND	0 UND	0 UND			Cost of Sales/Inventory	0 UND	0 UND
0 UND	0 UND	3 121.7	2 164.9				6 60.3	7 50.3
0 UND	13 28.0	15 23.9	24 15.0				17 20.9	21 17.1
2 197.0	26 14.1	35 10.5	38 9.7			Cost of Sales/Payables	31 11.8	31 11.9
16 23.0	42 8.7	49 7.4	59 6.1				48 7.6	50 7.3
8.4	7.2	6.5	7.0				6.5	6.6
26.7	12.4	11.9	13.8			Sales/Working Capital	11.2	13.7
−19.1	21.7	48.0	46.6				35.8	36.0
4.5	10.6	13.8	17.4				15.1	15.3
(21) 1.6	(65) 2.5	(157) 4.6	(56) 5.8			EBIT/Interest	(249) 5.4	(267) 5.4
−2.1	1.1	.6	2.1				1.9	2.4
	4.4	4.0	10.7			Net Profit + Depr., Dep.,		3.9	4.7
	(25) 1.7	(64) 2.3	(20) 4.5			Amort./Cur. Mat. L /T/D	(102) 2.6	(111) 2.1
	.8	1.4	1.6				1.4	1.4
.7	.4	.4	.4				.5	.4
1.5	.6	.7	.7			Fixed/Worth	.8	.8
−6.9	1.4	1.3	1.1				1.5	1.3
.8	.6	.7	.9				.7	.7
2.2	1.2	1.7	1.6			Debt/Worth	1.4	1.6
−10.7	3.2	2.6	2.8				3.0	3.1
32.7	34.0	38.2	30.6			% Profit Before Taxes/Tangible	42.7	43.2
(15) 11.1	(67) 12.5	(169) 15.6	(60) 17.6			Net Worth	(262) 20.8	(279) 21.3
−45.1	1.4	.2	4.1				7.0	7.1
18.0	11.3	14.3	12.3			% Profit Before Taxes/Total	17.7	15.7
1.4	4.7	5.4	6.2			Assets	7.9	8.2
−11.9	.4	−.1	2.3				2.6	3.0
14.6	14.8	14.7	11.7				11.9	12.7
7.3	9.7	7.3	6.5			Sales/Net Fixed Assets	7.3	7.6
5.1	5.4	5.0	4.8				4.1	4.8
3.8	3.4	3.0	2.6				2.8	2.9
2.9	2.5	2.2	2.1			Sales/Total Assets	2.2	2.2
1.7	1.9	1.8	1.6				1.6	1.7
2.1	1.5	1.9	2.0				2.0	1.8
(19) 4.4	(70) 3.7	(163) 3.6	(57) 3.4			% Depr., Dep., Amort./Sales	(261) 3.5	(264) 3.4
10.5	5.7	5.9	5.3				5.8	5.2
6.0	3.6	1.4	1.0				2.0	1.7
(14) 8.7	(37) 4.8	(78) 3.1	(15) 1.4			% Officers', Directors',	(125) 3.8	(140) 4.0
11.8	8.5	6.0	3.1			Owners' Comp/Sales	6.9	7.0
21432M	241782M	1799975M	2607946M	1066261M	1915119M	Net Sales ($)	4863365M	6533640M
6896M	86084M	736670M	1216577M	566687M	950486M	Total Assets ($)	2930107M	3717737M

M = $ thousand   MM = $ million
See Pages 11 through 18 for Explanation of Ratios and Data

Comparative Historical Data / Current Data Sorted By Sales

4/1/00-3/31/01 ALL	4/1/01-3/31/02 ALL	4/1/02-3/31/03 ALL		0-1MM	1-3MM	3-5MM	5-10MM	10-25MM	25MM & OVER
			Type of Statement						
81	81	103	Unqualified	1	4	3	19	35	41
84	94	128	Reviewed	3	29	26	39	28	3
41	44	31	Compiled	1	14	3	9	4	
13	18	21	Tax Returns	7	5	1	6	2	
63	75	57	Other	1	7	6	9	12	22
				76 (4/1-9/30/02)			264 (10/1/02-3/31/03)		
282	312	340	**NUMBER OF STATEMENTS**	13	59	39	82	81	66
%	%	%	**ASSETS**	%	%	%	%	%	%
13.4	12.5	13.9	Cash & Equivalents	18.2	13.9	14.4	13.0	15.7	11.7
35.4	35.5	35.8	Trade Receivables (net)	13.7	26.5	38.0	38.4	40.7	38.1
2.8	2.0	2.0	Inventory	3.3	2.6	2.1	2.4	1.4	1.6
6.7	7.1	8.5	All Other Current	2.2	9.8	8.0	7.3	7.8	11.2
58.2	57.2	60.3	Total Current	37.3	52.8	62.5	61.0	65.5	62.7
33.7	34.9	31.6	Fixed Assets (net)	41.5	38.5	30.1	31.9	27.4	29.3
1.6	1.1	1.2	Intangibles (net)	4.5	.5	.2	.7	.7	3.2
6.6	6.8	6.9	All Other Non-Current	16.7	8.2	7.2	6.4	6.4	4.8
100.0	100.0	100.0	Total	100.0	100.0	100.0	100.0	100.0	100.0
			LIABILITIES						
8.0	9.7	6.7	Notes Payable-Short Term	24.3	8.1	4.7	7.0	5.9	3.8
7.1	7.2	5.8	Cur. Mat.-L/T/D	5.0	8.7	4.8	5.6	5.2	4.9
16.9	16.7	17.4	Trade Payables	3.3	12.1	17.8	15.3	23.0	20.3
.7	.8	1.0	Income Taxes Payable	1.1	.6	1.2	1.6	1.3	.2
10.3	11.1	10.7	All Other Current	4.9	7.7	9.3	12.4	9.8	14.3
43.0	45.6	41.5	Total Current	38.5	37.2	37.8	41.8	45.0	43.6
13.9	13.4	13.2	Long Term Debt	31.8	16.4	12.4	13.2	11.2	9.5
1.3	1.8	1.0	Deferred Taxes	.4	.4	.6	1.3	1.3	1.3
1.7	4.0	2.3	All Other Non-Current	5.3	3.0	2.7	1.6	2.3	1.8
40.0	35.3	41.9	Net Worth	23.9	42.9	46.4	42.0	40.3	43.9
100.0	100.0	100.0	Total Liabilities & Net Worth	100.0	100.0	100.0	100.0	100.0	100.0
			INCOME DATA						
100.0	100.0	100.0	Net Sales	100.0	100.0	100.0	100.0	100.0	100.0
24.1	23.2	23.3	Gross Profit	54.1	32.9	25.0	22.0	19.2	14.4
20.6	19.5	20.0	Operating Expenses	49.7	32.5	18.9	18.2	15.9	11.1
3.5	3.7	3.3	Operating Profit	4.4	.4	6.1	3.8	3.3	3.3
.1	.9	.4	All Other Expenses (net)	1.5	.3	.1	.8	.0	.5
3.3	2.8	2.9	Profit Before Taxes	2.9	.0	6.0	3.0	3.3	2.8
			RATIOS						
2.1	2.0	2.1		2.0	2.6	3.1	2.0	2.0	2.1
1.4	1.4	1.5	Current	1.1	1.7	1.7	1.5	1.4	1.3
1.1	1.1	1.1		.2	1.0	1.3	1.1	1.1	1.1
1.8	1.8	1.8		1.9	1.9	1.9	1.8	1.8	1.6
1.2	1.2	1.2	Quick	1.1	1.3	1.5	1.2	1.2	1.1
.9	.8	.9		.2	.7	1.0	1.0	.9	.8
41 9.0	**38** 9.6	**37** 9.9		**0** UND	**16** 23.5	**35** 10.5	**40** 9.2	**44** 8.3	**42** 8.8
57 6.4	**56** 6.5	**57** 6.4	Sales/Receivables	**16** 23.1	**44** 8.3	**55** 6.6	**58** 6.3	**60** 6.1	**59** 6.1
77 4.7	**81** 4.5	**76** 4.8		**66** 5.5	**77** 4.7	**89** 4.1	**77** 4.7	**73** 5.0	**72** 5.1
0 UND	**0** UND	**0** UND		**0** UND	**0** UND	**0** UND	**0** UND	**0** UND	**0** UND
0 UND	**0** UND	**0** UND	Cost of Sales/Inventory	**0** UND	**0** UND	**0** UND	**0** UND	**0** UND	**0** UND
3 104.6	**4** 98.5	**2** 159.8		**0** UND	**5** 73.0	**1** 259.9	**6** 66.3	**1** 401.3	**2** 150.9
16 22.4	**16** 23.5	**15** 25.2		**0** UND	**9** 42.0	**16** 22.2	**15** 25.0	**21** 17.5	**18** 20.1
32 11.4	**31** 11.6	**29** 12.4	Cost of Sales/Payables	**2** 197.0	**27** 13.4	**33** 11.2	**27** 13.3	**37** 9.9	**29** 12.6
47 7.8	**48** 7.5	**48** 7.5		**35** 10.4	**45** 8.2	**44** 8.2	**46** 7.9	**53** 6.8	**50** 7.3
7.2	7.3	7.0		6.0	5.0	5.2	7.2	8.1	7.7
15.6	16.2	12.9	Sales/Working Capital	26.7	10.1	10.5	12.7	14.6	13.8
47.2	72.1	47.0		−6.9	253.5	19.3	59.8	41.2	46.2
10.4	10.7	12.9		13.4	4.3	29.4	12.5	14.1	18.6
(258) 3.6	(287) 3.6	(312) 4.1	EBIT/Interest	(11) 1.1	(53) 2.1	(37) 6.4	(79) 3.7	(74) 6.3	(58) 5.3
1.2	.9	1.0		−2.8	.0	2.0	.1	2.1	1.8
3.4	4.2	5.0			3.8	11.7	5.7	3.8	11.4
(97) 1.7	(98) 2.2	(112) 2.3	Net Profit + Depr., Dep., Amort./Cur. Mat. L/T/D		(16) 1.8	(13) 4.1	(31) 2.2	(33) 2.1	(17) 4.6
.9	1.1	1.3			.1	1.4	1.2	1.5	1.7
.4	.5	.4		.7	.4	.3	.4	.4	.3
.8	.8	.7	Fixed/Worth	8.2	.8	.6	.8	.7	.7
1.5	1.6	1.4		−4.7	1.6	1.2	1.3	1.1	1.3
.8	.9	.7		.8	.6	.5	.8	.8	.7
1.7	1.6	1.6	Debt/Worth	9.8	.9	1.2	1.6	1.8	1.5
3.0	2.9	2.9		−9.3	3.4	2.1	2.6	3.0	2.5
33.2	37.6	33.9			17.7	42.8	31.3	42.4	30.0
(266) 16.8	(291) 16.8	(325) 13.9	% Profit Before Taxes/Tangible Net Worth		(53) 5.1	(38) 19.0	9.0	(80) 16.5	(65) 17.3
3.3	2.3	1.2			−16.6	6.7	−8.1	2.8	2.3
14.7	13.5	13.3		24.1	10.5	23.3	11.4	14.0	12.1
6.0	5.9	5.1	% Profit Before Taxes/Total Assets	.8	3.7	7.5	4.8	6.2	5.4
.7	.0	.2		−20.6	−5.2	2.4	−2.4	1.6	1.2
13.1	12.3	14.1		10.0	12.0	16.0	14.4	15.5	14.5
7.4	6.6	7.4	Sales/Net Fixed Assets	5.1	6.4	8.2	6.8	9.5	7.4
4.4	4.2	4.9		2.8	3.4	6.1	4.9	5.9	5.1
2.9	2.8	3.0		2.5	3.1	3.0	2.8	3.2	2.8
2.2	2.2	2.3	Sales/Total Assets	1.7	2.2	2.4	2.2	2.6	2.3
1.7	1.6	1.7		1.4	1.4	1.7	1.9	1.9	1.9
1.8	1.9	1.9		5.0	2.1	1.5	1.9	1.8	1.9
(262) 3.5	(297) 3.5	(318) 3.6	% Depr., Dep., Amort./Sales	(10) 9.5	(57) 5.0	(38) 3.3	(79) 3.9	(78) 2.8	(56) 3.2
5.8	5.7	5.8		13.4	8.8	5.9	5.6	4.4	4.4
1.4	1.8	1.9			5.1	2.5	2.0	1.2	.4
(132) 3.5	(139) 4.0	(145) 3.6	% Officers', Directors', Owners' Comp/Sales		(26) 6.9	(24) 4.0	(45) 3.2	(32) 2.9	(12) 1.0
6.5	7.5	6.8			10.2	7.0	5.6	4.7	1.4
5571972M	**6854762M**	**7652515M**	Net Sales ($)	**6048M**	**116520M**	**155454M**	**607257M**	**1233376M**	**5533860M**
2814113M	**3535463M**	**3563400M**	Total Assets ($)	**3598M**	**68647M**	**76909M**	**277297M**	**548104M**	**2588845M**

M = $ thousand MM = $ million

See Pages 11 through 18 for Explanation of Ratios and Data

Current Data Sorted By Assets | **Comparative Historical Data**

0-500M	500M-2MM	2-10MM	10-50MM	50-100MM	100-250MM	Type of Statement	4/1/98-3/31/99 ALL	4/1/99-3/31/00 ALL
	3	19	40	20	22	Unqualified	138	127
3	8	30	28	6	7	Reviewed	127	114
15	41	58	14			Compiled	236	183
36	80	94	14	3	1	Tax Returns	285	236
19	46	106	55	6	11	Other	333	286
92 (4/1-9/30/02)			693 (10/1/02-3/31/03)					
73	178	307	151	35	41	NUMBER OF STATEMENTS	1119	946
%	%	%	%	%	%	ASSETS	%	%
14.9	8.1	5.8	6.8	4.5	7.5	Cash & Equivalents	6.9	7.4
4.9	5.3	4.6	4.4	7.4	4.5	Trade Receivables (net)	4.8	5.5
25.1	33.9	37.1	30.6	31.6	32.0	Inventory	29.9	31.1
7.6	7.0	6.1	5.5	2.3	2.0	All Other Current	4.2	5.2
52.5	54.3	53.5	47.3	45.8	46.0	Total Current	45.8	49.2
29.7	31.6	32.2	31.9	37.9	40.8	Fixed Assets (net)	37.2	31.9
2.1	2.2	.8	1.6	.6	1.6	Intangibles (net)	1.4	1.4
15.7	11.8	13.5	19.2	15.7	11.6	All Other Non-Current	15.6	17.5
100.0	100.0	100.0	100.0	100.0	100.0	Total	100.0	100.0
						LIABILITIES		
17.0	22.5	20.9	17.4	11.4	11.1	Notes Payable-Short Term	18.3	19.8
6.9	3.4	3.2	3.7	7.8	2.1	Cur. Mat.-L/T/D	3.9	3.9
4.9	4.6	4.6	5.6	3.8	5.9	Trade Payables	4.0	5.6
.1	.1	.2	.2	.1	.2	Income Taxes Payable	.1	.2
12.9	11.5	10.1	9.9	8.3	6.9	All Other Current	8.4	10.0
41.8	42.0	38.9	36.9	31.4	26.2	Total Current	34.6	39.4
31.2	31.1	29.9	28.9	25.8	29.4	Long Term Debt	33.8	29.9
.0	.2	.0	.3	1.1	.2	Deferred Taxes	.2	.1
26.0	4.3	4.6	5.3	3.7	4.6	All Other Non-Current	8.0	7.2
.9	22.4	26.6	28.6	38.0	39.6	Net Worth	23.4	23.4
100.0	100.0	100.0	100.0	100.0	100.0	Total Liabilities & Net Worth	100.0	100.0
						INCOME DATA		
100.0	100.0	100.0	100.0	100.0	100.0	Net Sales	100.0	100.0
						Gross Profit		
77.8	81.3	79.9	82.7	77.8	82.1	Operating Expenses	85.1	82.5
22.1	18.7	20.1	17.3	22.2	17.9	Operating Profit	14.9	17.5
5.1	7.6	7.4	5.3	4.1	6.2	All Other Expenses (net)	8.8	4.0
17.0	11.1	12.6	12.0	18.1	11.6	Profit Before Taxes	6.1	13.5
						RATIOS		
5.3	3.6	3.2	2.5	2.4	3.3		3.8	2.4
1.2	1.2	1.3	1.2	1.3	1.4	Current	1.3	1.2
.4	.6	.7	.8	.5	.9		.5	.6
1.3	1.0	.9	1.0	.5	1.1		1.3	1.0
.4	.2	(304) .2	.3	.2	.5	Quick	(1114) .2	(944) .2
.1	.0	.0	.0	.1	.1		.0	.0
0 UND	0 UND	0 UND	0 UND	2 233.0	1 374.1		0 UND	0 UND
0 UND	0 UND	0 UND	2 149.4	7 55.7	6 56.7	Sales/Receivables	0 UND	0 999.8
0 UND	6 58.5	6 62.9	17 20.9	30 12.3	32 11.2		12 29.5	15 23.6
						Cost of Sales/Inventory		
						Cost of Sales/Payables		
4.0	2.0	1.8	3.0	1.8	1.7		2.0	2.3
46.4	13.4	7.7	9.4	7.2	7.6	Sales/Working Capital	12.0	13.9
-18.2	-8.2	-10.7	-19.8	-3.5	-44.3		-5.7	-7.6
(39) 11.7	(115) 12.6	(188) 12.3	(112) 15.5	(22) 13.4	(30) 13.0		(608) 10.0	(574) 9.3
7.2	3.8	3.8	4.6	3.5	4.4	EBIT/Interest	3.7	3.2
1.6	1.1	1.4	2.0	1.3	1.6		1.4	1.4
	(10) 10.7	(14) 2.8	(16) 7.1				(67) 3.9	(56) 4.8
	3.5	2.0	3.0			Net Profit + Depr., Dep., Amort./Cur. Mat. L /T/D	1.4	.9
	2.9	.0	.6				.3	.2
.0	.0	.0	.1	.0	.1		.0	.0
.5	.5	.4	.7	.6	.5	Fixed/Worth	.8	.5
-8.0	5.6	4.5	4.3	1.9	2.6		6.7	4.1
.4	.9	1.2	1.3	.8	.9		1.1	1.2
3.4	3.8	3.3	4.0	1.9	1.9	Debt/Worth	3.9	3.6
-17.0	24.8	21.4	11.0	4.6	3.7		23.7	16.9
(52) 182.8	(142) 53.8	(260) 59.0	(136) 48.0	(32) 34.7	(39) 35.1		(918) 54.8	(795) 55.9
59.0	20.3	19.9	24.0	20.2	9.9	% Profit Before Taxes/Tangible Net Worth	21.4	21.9
6.1	4.1	3.6	6.3	5.4	2.1		4.4	4.9
43.8	14.3	12.6	9.5	10.8	11.9		11.1	11.9
11.9	3.9	4.2	4.8	4.9	4.1	% Profit Before Taxes/Total Assets	4.3	4.5
.7	.0	.3	.7	1.0	.8		.3	.5
UND	UND	559.5	63.3	159.0	44.2		147.9	261.6
42.9	10.3	14.3	6.1	2.6	1.4	Sales/Net Fixed Assets	5.2	11.0
1.6	.8	.5	.5	.4	.2		.3	.5
4.5	1.5	1.1	1.1	.6	1.1		1.1	1.3
1.4	.7	.5	.5	.4	.4	Sales/Total Assets	.4	.6
.4	.3	.2	.2	.2	.2		.2	.2
(31) 1.3	(98) .8	(190) .5	(104) .4	(23) .5	(32) .6		(710) .7	(604) .6
3.4	4.2	2.4	2.0	6.0	6.2	% Depr., Dep., Amort./Sales	4.3	2.3
7.8	14.7	12.3	11.2	16.8	17.1		15.5	12.5
(15) 2.2	(36) 2.3	(49) 2.0	(24) 1.7				(210) 2.1	(189) 1.8
11.4	5.6	6.5	3.4			% Officers', Directors', Owners' Comp/Sales	4.8	4.1
21.9	15.3	12.4	4.3					10.7
54767M	251203M	1309434M	2750584M	1530661M	4622743M	Net Sales ($)	9331714M	10623220M
21560M	217598M	1454623M	3320968M	2689671M	6666493M	Total Assets ($)	15262123M	14350473M

M = $ thousand   MM = $ million
See Pages 11 through 18 for Explanation of Ratios and Data

Comparative Historical Data | Current Data Sorted By Sales

4/1/00-3/31/01 ALL	4/1/01-3/31/02 ALL	4/1/02-3/31/03 ALL	Type of Statement	0-1MM	1-3MM	3-5MM	5-10MM	10-25MM	25MM & OVER
					92 (4/1-9/30/02)			693 (10/1/02-3/31/03)	
102	108	104	Unqualified	5	9	7	23	19	41
94	83	82	Reviewed	12	16	5	12	18	19
191	196	128	Compiled	53	42	11	10	12	
242	238	228	Tax Returns	107	61	29	15	10	6
321	323	243	Other	61	77	32	27	20	26
950	948	785	**NUMBER OF STATEMENTS**	238	205	84	87	79	92
%	%	%	**ASSETS**	%	%	%	%	%	%
6.9	6.8	7.4	Cash & Equivalents	7.3	4.7	10.6	9.5	6.9	9.1
5.0	5.2	4.9	Trade Receivables (net)	2.8	3.1	7.6	7.4	6.1	8.3
31.2	30.9	33.5	Inventory	26.5	35.3	34.3	34.2	40.7	39.7
6.7	6.9	5.9	All Other Current	5.2	6.9	9.8	5.5	3.3	4.7
49.9	49.9	51.7	Total Current	41.8	50.1	62.3	56.6	57.0	61.8
33.5	33.7	32.5	Fixed Assets (net)	44.1	31.1	24.1	25.3	28.6	23.3
1.5	1.3	1.4	Intangibles (net)	1.7	1.8	2.5	.2	.4	1.1
15.1	15.1	14.4	All Other Non-Current	12.4	17.1	11.1	17.9	14.1	13.8
100.0	100.0	100.0	Total	100.0	100.0	100.0	100.0	100.0	100.0
			LIABILITIES						
20.7	18.5	19.3	Notes Payable-Short Term	17.9	20.9	24.0	14.6	20.1	18.5
4.2	4.6	3.8	Cur. Mat.-L/T/D	4.6	3.2	3.1	3.5	5.8	2.7
6.1	5.0	4.8	Trade Payables	1.6	3.2	8.7	6.9	5.8	10.6
.2	.2	.2	Income Taxes Payable	.1	.1	.0	.8	.1	.1
10.3	11.6	10.4	All Other Current	9.3	11.9	10.3	10.0	10.2	10.5
41.5	39.9	38.5	Total Current	33.5	39.3	46.2	35.8	41.9	42.5
30.7	31.9	29.9	Long Term Debt	39.5	32.3	21.0	22.0	23.5	20.6
.1	.1	.2	Deferred Taxes	.0	.1	.2	.5	.1	.6
6.7	5.9	6.6	All Other Non-Current	9.9	7.3	3.0	3.7	4.7	4.2
21.0	22.2	24.8	Net Worth	17.1	21.0	29.8	38.0	29.8	32.1
100.0	100.0	100.0	Total Liabilities & Net Worth	100.0	100.0	100.0	100.0	100.0	100.0
			INCOME DATA						
100.0	100.0	100.0	Net Sales	100.0	100.0	100.0	100.0	100.0	100.0
			Gross Profit						
80.4	80.0	80.6	Operating Expenses	73.0	80.9	83.9	83.1	87.5	88.1
19.6	20.0	19.4	Operating Profit	26.9	19.1	16.1	16.9	12.5	11.9
6.2	8.6	6.6	All Other Expenses (net)	12.9	5.8	3.3	3.8	2.7	1.3
13.4	11.5	12.8	Profit Before Taxes	14.0	13.3	12.8	13.1	9.7	10.7
			RATIOS						
2.8	3.0	3.3		4.3	3.4	3.1	3.5	1.9	2.5
1.2	1.3	1.3	Current	1.1	1.2	1.4	1.5	1.3	1.4
.6	.7	.7		.4	.6	.8	1.0	1.0	1.0
.9	1.1	1.0		.9	.7	1.1	2.1	1.1	1.0
(944) .2	(946) .2	(782) .2	Quick	.2	(203) .1	(83) .3	.3	.2	.3
.0	.0	.0		.0	.0	.0	.0	.1	.1
0 UND	0 UND	0 UND		0 UND	0 UND	0 UND	0 UND	0 UND	1 478.6
0 999.8	0 UND	0 UND	Sales/Receivables	0 UND	0 UND	0 999.8	1 249.9	1 401.2	6 57.9
15 24.5	12 31.0	10 38.0		1 251.4	5 75.5	13 27.2	19 18.7	17 22.1	32 11.3
			Cost of Sales/Inventory						
			Cost of Sales/Payables						
2.1	2.2	2.3		1.2	1.9	2.7	2.7	3.8	3.1
12.8	10.8	10.3	Sales/Working Capital	27.9	11.7	6.8	6.0	11.5	9.1
-6.8	-9.9	-12.2		-2.7	-6.5	-23.8	-128.2	-83.5	86.9
9.0	10.5	12.7		8.1	11.0	13.3	64.0	18.0	17.9
(575) 3.2	(590) 3.4	(506) 4.1	EBIT/Interest	(109) 3.4	(133) 3.1	(65) 6.2	(68) 20.4	(60) 4.3	(71) 5.9
1.3	1.3	1.5		1.1	1.1	1.8	2.2	1.7	2.6
2.7	5.9	4.9			6.0				29.7
(59) 1.2	(50) 2.0	(50) 2.7	Net Profit + Depr., Dep., Amort./Cur. Mat. L/T/D		(10) 1.4			(14) 2.3	
.5	.5	.7			.2				1.2
.0	.0	.0		.0	.0	.0	.0	.0	.1
.7	.6	.5	Fixed/Worth	1.4	.4	.3	.2	.5	.3
5.3	5.1	4.4		16.6	6.1	2.6	1.7	2.4	1.3
1.3	1.3	1.0		1.0	1.0	1.0	.7	1.3	1.2
4.0	4.1	3.2	Debt/Worth	4.4	4.0	2.8	1.9	3.5	2.5
25.2	16.3	15.6		107.8	42.4	21.6	5.4	10.2	5.6
57.3	64.9	57.3		43.7	51.3	64.0	58.6	83.2	48.9
(787) 23.1	(812) 22.3	(661) 21.3	% Profit Before Taxes/Tangible Net Worth	(183) 11.5	(166) 18.0	(72) 31.8	(81) 24.0	(73) 34.8	(86) 27.1
5.4	4.2	4.9		.7	4.3	8.7	5.1	8.5	9.3
11.5	11.9	13.0		9.4	12.6	19.2	17.8	14.9	14.0
4.2	4.2	4.8	% Profit Before Taxes/Total Assets	2.2	3.9	5.8	6.6	5.8	7.9
.6	.3	.4		-.5	.1	1.9	.7	2.1	3.2
297.0	297.3	299.2		409.6	999.8	299.8	445.0	226.8	120.2
7.2	9.0	10.7	Sales/Net Fixed Assets	1.4	10.7	29.8	14.8	22.9	28.6
.5	.5	.6		.2	.6	3.1	1.2	1.0	1.7
1.2	1.3	1.3		.5	1.1	1.8	1.8	2.3	1.9
.5	.6	.5	Sales/Total Assets	.3	.5	.9	.7	1.0	1.1
.2	.2	.2		.1	.3	.5	.4	.4	.5
.6	.4	.6		3.0	.6	.4	.3	.4	.2
(589) 2.4	(573) 2.1	(478) 3.1	% Depr., Dep., Amort./Sales	(142) 11.8	(114) 3.1	(45) 1.7	(59) 1.6	(54) 1.3	(64) .8
11.7	10.2	13.2		20.9	11.3	5.6	4.5	7.0	5.5
2.1	1.8	2.1		5.8	3.7	1.6	1.4	1.0	
(189) 4.6	(198) 4.4	(128) 5.1	% Officers', Directors', Owners' Comp/Sales	(31) 11.4	(33) 7.0	(16) 4.4	(21) 3.1	(19) 2.1	
9.8	10.1	11.9		25.1	13.1	14.1	6.8	5.5	
10538615M	14917650M	10519392M	Net Sales ($)	104010M	368618M	329800M	635629M	1274886M	7806449M
14816284M	16547225M	14370913M	Total Assets ($)	477730M	1059245M	770631M	1286232M	2650602M	8126473M

M = $ thousand   MM = $ million
See Pages 11 through 18 for Explanation of Ratios and Data

Current Data Sorted By Assets   Comparative Historical Data

0-500M	500M-2MM	2-10MM	10-50MM	50-100MM	100-250MM	Type of Statement	4/1/98-3/31/99 ALL	4/1/99-3/31/00 ALL
2	16	126	138	29	23	Unqualified	271	276
1	32	75	16			Reviewed	98	101
8	12	9	4			Compiled	39	34
11	6	4				Tax Returns	8	11
5	15	41	39	9	8	Other	77	77
	108 (4/1-9/30/02)		521 (10/1/02-3/31/03)					
27	81	255	197	38	31	**NUMBER OF STATEMENTS**	493	499
%	%	%	%	%	%	**ASSETS**	%	%
14.4	18.1	15.8	17.2	14.1	12.3	Cash & Equivalents	14.7	14.8
20.0	24.9	32.5	29.8	26.1	25.6	Trade Receivables (net)	31.9	31.6
3.0	2.7	2.7	3.7	4.3	4.4	Inventory	3.6	2.9
1.7	4.5	7.7	9.3	9.3	9.8	All Other Current	5.9	7.1
39.1	50.2	58.7	59.9	53.7	52.1	Total Current	56.1	56.4
52.4	43.8	34.9	31.5	30.7	35.3	Fixed Assets (net)	35.8	34.3
3.2	.6	.7	1.0	3.5	3.6	Intangibles (net)	.9	1.1
5.3	5.3	5.8	7.6	12.1	8.9	All Other Non-Current	7.3	8.2
100.0	100.0	100.0	100.0	100.0	100.0	Total	100.0	100.0
						LIABILITIES		
14.4	6.0	4.0	4.0	3.2	2.1	Notes Payable-Short Term	5.1	4.9
6.4	6.9	6.0	4.9	5.0	4.2	Cur. Mat.-L/T/D	5.3	5.6
6.7	13.5	18.5	18.4	16.6	15.4	Trade Payables	16.1	16.9
.1	.3	.7	.3	.2	.4	Income Taxes Payable	1.5	.8
7.7	8.6	9.1	11.8	11.0	15.4	All Other Current	9.7	9.5
35.2	35.2	38.3	39.5	36.1	37.6	Total Current	37.8	37.7
39.8	18.5	13.7	14.1	20.4	15.0	Long Term Debt	14.2	15.0
.3	.7	1.6	1.2	1.5	1.8	Deferred Taxes	1.2	1.5
4.0	4.3	2.7	1.7	1.7	1.7	All Other Non-Current	2.5	2.2
20.7	41.3	43.8	43.5	40.3	44.0	Net Worth	44.4	43.7
100.0	100.0	100.0	100.0	100.0	100.0	Total Liabilities & Net Worth	100.0	100.0
						INCOME DATA		
100.0	100.0	100.0	100.0	100.0	100.0	Net Sales	100.0	100.0
44.6	23.6	16.7	12.8	12.4	13.1	Gross Profit	18.2	18.0
40.5	21.6	13.7	9.2	7.5	9.1	Operating Expenses	13.8	13.5
4.1	2.0	3.0	3.6	4.9	4.0	Operating Profit	4.4	4.4
.9	.3	.4	.2	.5	.4	All Other Expenses (net)	.3	.0
3.2	1.7	2.6	3.4	4.4	3.6	Profit Before Taxes	4.1	4.4
						RATIOS		
2.8	2.5	2.3	2.0	2.0	1.8		2.1	2.1
1.0	1.4	1.6	1.5	1.5	1.5	Current	1.5	1.5
.5	1.0	1.2	1.2	1.2	1.0		1.1	1.2
1.9	2.3	2.0	1.7	1.5	1.6		1.8	1.7
1.0	1.2	1.3	1.1	1.0	.9	Quick	1.2	1.2
.5	.7	.9	.9	.9	.7		.9	.9
3 134.2	18 20.5	31 11.7	34 10.9	31 11.7	32 11.2		32 11.4	34 10.6
17 21.2	37 9.9	50 7.3	49 7.4	47 7.7	55 6.6	Sales/Receivables	51 7.1	53 6.9
30 12.1	64 5.7	65 5.6	65 5.6	65 5.6	61 6.0		75 4.9	75 4.9
0 UND	0 UND	0 UND	0 UND	1 631.4	1 526.7		0 UND	0 UND
0 UND	0 UND	0 UND	2 237.6	6 57.1	8 47.3	Cost of Sales/Inventory	1 550.4	0 799.0
1 279.9	4 96.9	4 85.7	8 43.7	16 22.7	16 22.2		9 39.8	8 47.8
0 UND	8 46.5	18 20.6	21 17.2	20 18.2	24 15.3		16 22.5	19 19.2
8 47.2	22 16.8	29 12.5	33 11.2	32 11.4	33 11.2	Cost of Sales/Payables	30 12.3	32 11.5
27 13.6	49 7.4	44 8.3	47 7.7	44 8.2	41 8.9		46 7.9	45 8.0
8.9	6.6	6.4	6.2	6.1	5.9		7.0	7.0
537.0	17.2	11.6	11.8	14.4	13.1	Sales/Working Capital	13.0	11.8
-15.1	-999.8	34.1	24.9	37.7	146.1		41.4	28.0
9.8	8.8	15.3	12.6	5.2	20.5		13.3	14.0
(26) 3.2	(74) 2.0	(235) 5.2	(177) 4.5	(34) 3.3	(30) 4.2	EBIT/Interest	(446) 4.8	(468) 4.8
1.3	-.5	1.4	2.0	1.9	1.7		1.9	2.1
	3.9	3.9	2.9	5.4		Net Profit + Depr., Dep.,	3.8	4.1
	(15) 1.8	(95) 1.8	(66) 2.1	(14) 2.3		Amort./Cur. Mat. L/T/D	(187) 2.1	(200) 2.1
	1.2	1.1	1.2	1.0			1.3	1.2
.8	.6	.4	.5	.5	.6		.5	.5
2.3	.9	.8	.7	1.0	.9	Fixed/Worth	.8	.8
-41.0	2.0	1.3	1.2	1.3	1.3		1.3	1.3
.8	.6	.7	.7	1.1	.7		.7	.7
2.4	1.5	1.3	1.4	2.1	1.5	Debt/Worth	1.4	1.3
-72.2	3.8	2.2	2.8	2.9	2.4		2.6	2.6
83.0	28.6	32.9	27.8	22.1	23.1	% Profit Before Taxes/Tangible	33.6	31.2
(20) 23.4	(75) 9.4	(246) 14.1	(196) 14.8	(37) 12.1	(30) 11.9	Net Worth	(475) 19.1	(488) 17.8
-2.4	-1.8	4.1	3.6	5.9	6.2		7.3	6.8
29.7	10.2	14.2	9.9	9.5	9.2	% Profit Before Taxes/Total	14.9	13.7
10.6	3.4	5.7	5.3	3.8	4.8	Assets	8.1	7.1
2.4	-1.4	1.1	1.4	1.5	1.7		2.5	2.6
11.9	10.3	12.9	11.9	12.5	8.8		10.6	10.6
9.0	5.5	7.3	7.0	6.6	4.8	Sales/Net Fixed Assets	6.4	6.5
4.3	3.2	4.4	4.4	3.8	3.7		4.1	4.1
6.0	3.0	3.0	2.6	2.6	2.1		2.8	2.7
3.1	2.3	2.4	2.0	2.0	1.9	Sales/Total Assets	2.1	2.1
2.1	1.7	1.7	1.6	1.5	1.4		1.6	1.6
2.3	2.9	2.3	2.0	1.7	2.4		2.3	2.1
(24) 5.2	(79) 4.7	(241) 3.5	(176) 3.3	(34) 3.0	(19) 4.3	% Depr., Dep., Amort./Sales	(456) 3.6	(460) 3.7
9.2	8.1	5.5	4.7	4.3	5.0		5.2	5.4
3.9	2.0	1.3	.8			% Officers', Directors',	1.3	1.5
(15) 4.5	(43) 3.4	(102) 2.3	(44) 1.4			Owners' Comp/Sales	(174) 2.4	(199) 3.1
6.9	5.5	4.8	2.2				4.7	5.6
30416M	233091M	3124204M	9233741M	5281291M	8292920M	Net Sales ($)	17065311M	17942230M
8200M	94516M	1283731M	4359063M	2565232M	4498224M	Total Assets ($)	8649645M	9332939M

M = $ thousand   MM = $ million
See Pages 11 through 18 for Explanation of Ratios and Data

Comparative Historical Data | Current Data Sorted By Sales

4/1/00-3/31/01 ALL	4/1/01-3/31/02 ALL	4/1/02-3/31/03 ALL	Type of Statement	0-1MM	1-3MM	3-5MM	5-10MM	10-25MM	25MM & OVER
219	249	334	Unqualified	3	10	11	45	89	176
83	103	124	Reviewed	5	18	19	26	41	15
47	65	33	Compiled	8	10	1	8	2	4
15	15	21	Tax Returns	5	7	3	4	2	
96	121	117	Other	3	14	7	22	20	51
				108 (4/1-9/30/02)			521 (10/1/02-3/31/03)		
460	553	629	**NUMBER OF STATEMENTS**	24	59	41	105	154	246
%	%	%	**ASSETS**	%	%	%	%	%	%
15.5	15.0	16.2	Cash & Equivalents	17.6	15.4	21.9	14.3	17.0	15.6
31.6	32.2	29.4	Trade Receivables (net)	11.9	25.6	23.4	31.7	31.3	30.9
3.5	3.3	3.2	Inventory	2.7	2.8	2.1	3.4	3.7	3.1
7.0	7.1	7.7	All Other Current	2.7	4.6	4.3	5.8	8.8	9.7
57.6	57.6	56.5	Total Current	34.9	48.4	51.8	55.1	60.7	59.3
34.1	34.6	35.5	Fixed Assets (net)	52.0	47.1	39.3	38.7	32.3	31.1
1.3	1.3	1.2	Intangibles (net)	3.3	.9	.8	.6	1.0	1.5
7.0	6.5	6.8	All Other Non-Current	9.8	3.6	8.0	5.6	6.0	8.1
100.0	100.0	100.0	Total	100.0	100.0	100.0	100.0	100.0	100.0
			LIABILITIES						
6.2	5.4	4.5	Notes Payable-Short Term	7.8	7.4	6.6	3.8	4.5	3.5
5.4	5.2	5.6	Cur. Mat.-L/T/D	6.4	7.3	7.1	5.9	5.9	4.7
16.9	18.2	17.1	Trade Payables	5.2	10.7	14.3	15.8	19.6	19.2
.7	.6	.5	Income Taxes Payable	.0	.3	.6	.9	.4	.4
8.7	9.8	10.3	All Other Current	6.7	8.5	7.2	8.3	10.0	12.5
38.0	39.2	38.0	Total Current	26.0	34.1	35.7	34.8	40.4	40.2
14.8	15.2	16.0	Long Term Debt	37.9	22.9	16.8	14.9	12.0	15.1
1.3	1.2	1.3	Deferred Taxes	.3	.8	2.3	1.5	1.1	1.4
2.7	1.8	2.5	All Other Non-Current	3.0	3.9	3.9	3.8	2.3	1.5
43.2	42.6	42.2	Net Worth	32.8	38.2	41.2	45.0	44.2	41.7
100.0	100.0	100.0	Total Liabilities & Net Worth	100.0	100.0	100.0	100.0	100.0	100.0
			INCOME DATA						
100.0	100.0	100.0	Net Sales	100.0	100.0	100.0	100.0	100.0	100.0
16.4	17.0	17.1	Gross Profit	41.7	28.5	23.0	17.8	15.3	11.8
13.5	13.6	13.8	Operating Expenses	43.1	24.3	19.4	14.7	12.0	8.3
3.0	3.4	3.3	Operating Profit	-1.4	4.2	3.6	3.2	3.3	3.5
.0	.3	.3	All Other Expenses (net)	-.6	1.3	.3	.4	.2	.3
3.0	3.0	2.9	Profit Before Taxes	-.8	2.9	3.2	2.8	3.0	3.2
			RATIOS						
2.2	2.1	2.2	Current	2.7	3.0	2.7	2.6	2.2	1.9
1.5	1.4	1.5		1.4	1.5	1.6	1.8	1.5	1.4
1.1	1.1	1.1		.5	.9	1.0	1.2	1.1	1.2
1.9	1.7	1.8	Quick	2.3	2.8	2.5	2.2	1.8	1.6
1.2	1.2	1.2		1.0	1.1	1.6	1.3	1.3	1.1
.8	.9	.8		.5	.7	.8	.9	.8	.8
33 11.2	32 11.2	30 12.2	Sales/Receivables	3 123.7	21 17.8	17 21.4	37 9.8	29 12.6	34 10.8
51 7.1	52 7.0	47 7.7		15 23.7	37 10.0	38 9.5	54 6.8	47 7.7	48 7.5
69 5.3	73 5.0	64 5.7		60 6.1	63 5.8	61 6.0	76 4.8	63 5.8	62 5.9
0 UND	0 UND	0 UND	Cost of Sales/Inventory	0 UND	0 UND	0 UND	0 UND	0 UND	0 UND
1 384.2	1 699.2	0 918.5		0 UND	0 UND	0 UND	0 999.8	0 UND	2 215.2
9 38.8	8 47.1	8 48.5		2 164.8	5 72.1	1 270.7	12 30.2	4 84.7	9 40.2
17 21.5	17 21.4	17 21.1	Cost of Sales/Payables	3 105.8	7 51.0	8 44.5	16 23.5	21 17.7	21 17.5
30 12.2	31 11.6	29 12.4		12 30.5	20 18.5	28 13.0	26 13.9	31 11.9	32 11.6
46 8.0	47 7.7	45 8.1		30 12.1	41 8.9	48 7.6	46 7.9	45 8.1	45 8.1
6.4	6.7	6.4	Sales/Working Capital	3.4	7.2	5.4	5.8	6.7	7.4
12.4	13.1	12.8		14.8	17.2	10.9	8.7	12.4	13.3
41.9	35.6	38.1		-15.8	-34.4	NM	26.9	35.1	27.3
(418) 9.8	(500) 9.7	(576) 13.6	EBIT/Interest	(22) 5.3	(56) 9.1	(35) 13.2	(98) 15.1	(140) 14.6	(225) 13.3
3.2	3.6	4.1		1.8	2.7	2.1	4.4	5.7	4.1
1.0	1.5	1.5		-1.8	1.2	-.7	1.1	1.6	2.1
(154) 3.9	(172) 3.4	(202) 3.7	Net Profit + Depr., Dep., Amort./Cur. Mat. L/T/D		(11) 4.2	(15) 3.7	(38) 3.2	(49) 4.9	(85) 3.4
1.8	1.9	2.0			1.3	1.7	1.8	2.6	2.1
1.0	1.0	1.2			.7	.9	1.2	1.1	1.2
.4	.4	.5	Fixed/Worth	.6	.7	.4	.5	.4	.5
.8	.8	.8		1.1	1.1	.9	.8	.7	.8
1.4	1.4	1.4		7.3	5.6	1.9	1.5	1.2	1.2
.7	.7	.7	Debt/Worth	.5	.6	.5	.6	.7	.9
1.4	1.4	1.4		1.1	1.8	1.5	1.1	1.2	1.6
2.9	2.9	2.7		8.6	7.5	3.2	2.2	2.3	2.7
(441) 27.6	(535) 32.0	(604) 28.8	% Profit Before Taxes/Tangible Net Worth	(19) 25.0	(54) 34.4	(38) 30.9	(100) 28.0	(150) 33.9	(243) 25.8
12.2	14.6	13.9		2.5	15.6	9.0	13.9	16.8	13.9
.9	4.0	3.6		-17.8	3.1	-3.0	2.7	4.4	5.0
11.2	11.9	12.0	% Profit Before Taxes/Total Assets	12.5	16.2	15.7	12.3	14.8	9.3
4.7	5.4	5.3		2.9	4.3	4.0	5.5	6.5	5.0
.1	1.4	1.1		-7.9	1.1	-1.8	.4	1.4	1.5
12.3	11.6	12.0	Sales/Net Fixed Assets	10.7	10.1	10.8	9.2	14.4	13.1
6.9	6.8	6.8		3.3	5.2	5.5	6.1	7.5	7.3
4.2	4.1	4.2		1.6	2.8	3.9	3.3	5.0	4.7
2.9	2.8	2.8	Sales/Total Assets	2.3	3.1	2.9	2.7	3.0	2.8
2.2	2.2	2.2		1.2	2.3	2.2	2.1	2.4	2.2
1.6	1.6	1.6		.8	1.4	1.6	1.5	1.8	1.7
(414) 2.0	(504) 1.9	(573) 2.2	% Depr., Dep., Amort./Sales	(22) 4.0	(58) 2.8	(39) 2.1	(101) 3.0	(139) 2.2	(214) 1.9
3.3	3.5	3.6		9.1	5.2	3.9	4.2	3.2	3.2
5.0	5.2	5.5		12.7	8.1	6.5	6.1	4.9	4.4
(168) 1.2	(180) 1.3	(209) 1.1	% Officers', Directors', Owners' Comp/Sales		(29) 2.9	(23) 2.2	(39) 1.1	(65) 1.4	(45) .6
2.5	2.8	2.4			4.1	4.4	2.5	2.3	1.1
4.1	5.0	4.5			7.2	7.7	4.2	4.4	2.0
18603770M	23486068M	26195663M	Net Sales ($)	15347M	111863M	163177M	780721M	2450890M	22673665M
8636240M	11446375M	12808966M	Total Assets ($)	17407M	62752M	82713M	428889M	1182157M	11035048M

M = $ thousand   MM = $ million
See Pages 11 through 18 for Explanation of Ratios and Data

Current Data Sorted By Assets   **Comparative Historical Data**

								Type of Statement			
		5	29	37	6	6		Unqualified		43	62
	4	17	36	13				Reviewed		36	39
	2	6	7	1	1			Compiled		11	15
	4	5	4					Tax Returns		6	7
	1	8	21	8		1		Other		33	23
		48 (4/1-9/30/02)			174 (10/1/02-3/31/03)					4/1/98-3/31/99	4/1/99-3/31/00
	0-500M	500M-2MM	2-10MM	10-50MM	50-100MM	100-250MM				ALL	ALL
	11	41	97	59	7	7		NUMBER OF STATEMENTS		129	146
	%	%	%	%	%	%		ASSETS		%	%
	11.7	11.0	12.0	14.0				Cash & Equivalents		11.8	14.4
	27.3	35.6	32.2	34.4				Trade Receivables (net)		34.7	33.2
	5.2	7.3	2.8	4.6				Inventory		4.6	3.2
	4.7	5.0	10.0	8.0				All Other Current		6.8	6.7
	49.0	59.0	57.0	61.0				Total Current		58.0	57.4
	42.6	28.3	36.3	30.6				Fixed Assets (net)		32.3	33.0
	4.1	2.5	1.4	1.0				Intangibles (net)		1.4	1.4
	4.3	10.3	5.2	7.4				All Other Non-Current		8.4	8.2
	100.0	100.0	100.0	100.0				Total		100.0	100.0
								LIABILITIES			
	9.2	12.0	6.3	4.7				Notes Payable-Short Term		6.8	4.7
	7.8	5.4	5.0	4.2				Cur. Mat.-L/T/D		4.3	6.0
	14.0	13.4	16.6	19.5				Trade Payables		16.4	14.8
	1.6	.6	.9	.6				Income Taxes Payable		.8	.3
	18.2	7.2	9.9	16.1				All Other Current		9.7	11.1
	50.8	38.7	38.7	45.0				Total Current		38.1	36.9
	21.0	12.3	14.2	14.2				Long Term Debt		14.6	15.1
	.4	.7	1.7	1.2				Deferred Taxes		1.2	.7
	2.5	3.6	4.0	3.3				All Other Non-Current		4.2	4.4
	25.2	44.7	41.4	36.2				Net Worth		41.9	42.8
	100.0	100.0	100.0	100.0				Total Liabilities & Net Worth		100.0	100.0
								INCOME DATA			
	100.0	100.0	100.0	100.0				Net Sales		100.0	100.0
	37.9	31.4	23.6	16.1				Gross Profit		24.2	25.4
	32.1	27.6	19.7	11.2				Operating Expenses		19.1	20.5
	5.8	3.8	3.9	4.9				Operating Profit		5.0	4.9
	2.4	.3	.9	.5				All Other Expenses (net)		–.1	.1
	3.5	3.5	3.0	4.4				Profit Before Taxes		5.1	4.8
								RATIOS			
	1.6	3.1	1.8	1.7						2.4	2.3
	1.0	1.6	1.4	1.4				Current		1.4	1.5
	.7	1.1	1.1	1.1						1.1	1.1
	1.3	2.5	1.5	1.4						2.0	1.9
	1.0	1.3	1.2	1.1				Quick		1.2	1.2
	.5	.8	.8	.8						.8	.9

0	UND	34	10.6	38	9.7	40	9.2			Sales/Receivables	38	9.6	31	11.6
38	9.6	48	7.6	54	6.8	62	5.9				54	6.8	56	6.5
66	5.5	65	5.6	77	4.8	83	4.4				70	5.2	77	4.7
0	UND	0	UND	0	UND	0	UND			Cost of Sales/Inventory	0	UND	0	UND
2	198.8	0	UND	0	UND	1	281.6				0	UND	0	UND
28	13.0	14	26.8	6	60.9	14	25.9				9	42.0	6	59.8
0	910.0	11	34.4	20	18.5	23	15.7			Cost of Sales/Payables	15	23.8	17	21.3
28	12.9	20	17.9	37	9.7	34	10.8				34	10.8	31	11.7
66	5.5	41	9.0	52	7.0	54	6.7				48	7.6	51	7.2

	15.3	6.9	6.8	7.1			Sales/Working Capital	5.8	6.0
	999.8	12.5	14.5	13.1				13.7	13.1
	–16.1	194.9	39.6	35.2				41.8	40.1

		7.3		10.7		25.0		EBIT/Interest		10.2		11.3
	(37)	3.4	(87)	4.4	(51)	6.0			(120)	4.4	(132)	3.9
		.1		1.3		2.5				2.0		1.7
		4.9		3.0		5.2		Net Profit + Depr., Dep.,		5.9		4.0
	(13)	2.4	(37)	2.0	(22)	2.4		Amort./Cur. Mat. L /T/D	(47)	3.1	(46)	1.9
		.2		1.3		1.3				1.7		1.1

.8	.2	.5	.4			Fixed/Worth	.4	.4
2.3	.7	.9	.7				.7	.8
–2.0	1.6	1.6	1.4				1.3	1.4
.8	.6	.9	.9			Debt/Worth	.8	.7
3.5	1.2	1.4	1.8				1.6	1.4
–20.4	2.9	2.7	3.8				2.8	2.6

		31.5		28.7		26.4		% Profit Before Taxes/Tangible		39.6		38.6
	(38)	17.0	(95)	14.6	(53)	16.4		Net Worth	(124)	20.7	(138)	19.1
		.0		2.0		5.6				7.0		5.5

20.7	16.8	10.4	9.2			% Profit Before Taxes/Total	15.1	14.7
4.0	4.4	4.1	4.8			Assets	8.7	8.2
–30.1	–.4	.4	2.5				2.0	2.1
142.0	26.9	12.6	13.5			Sales/Net Fixed Assets	15.2	13.7
7.3	7.7	6.4	7.5				7.9	6.7
3.0	5.2	2.5	3.8				3.8	3.7
3.8	3.4	2.8	2.6			Sales/Total Assets	3.0	2.7
2.7	2.3	1.8	1.9				2.1	1.9
1.7	1.7	1.2	1.4				1.5	1.5

		2.1		1.8		1.7		% Depr., Dep., Amort./Sales		1.3		1.6
	(36)	4.4	(91)	4.3	(56)	3.2			(117)	3.3	(132)	3.7
		7.6		7.8		6.0				6.2		5.9
		2.1		1.9				% Officers', Directors',		1.8		1.9
	(22)	3.9	(39)	3.3				Owners' Comp/Sales	(52)	3.9	(47)	4.6
		5.5		7.9						7.9		8.4

9998M	130926M	991087M	3034141M	940352M	2392879M	Net Sales ($)	4242837M	5748406M
3237M	50319M	489606M	1448449M	428302M	987728M	Total Assets ($)	2081087M	2442610M

M = $ thousand   MM = $ million
See Pages 11 through 18 for Explanation of Ratios and Data

Comparative Historical Data				Current Data Sorted By Sales					
			Type of Statement						
43	56	83	Unqualified		5	3	6	24	45
43	40	70	Reviewed	3	14	11	17	19	6
16	24	17	Compiled	2	4	4	2	3	2
8	5	13	Tax Returns	4	4	3	2		
45	54	39	Other	3	5	7	9	9	6
4/1/00-3/31/01 ALL	4/1/01-3/31/02 ALL	4/1/02-3/31/03 ALL		48 (4/1-9/30/02) 0-1MM	1-3MM	3-5MM	174 (10/1/02-3/31/03) 5-10MM	10-25MM	25MM & OVER
155	179	222	**NUMBER OF STATEMENTS**	12	32	28	36	55	59
%	%	%	**ASSETS**	%	%	%	%	%	%
12.5	13.3	12.3	Cash & Equivalents	6.7	9.4	10.9	13.5	14.0	13.2
32.9	36.2	33.4	Trade Receivables (net)	23.9	27.6	29.0	34.4	33.7	39.5
6.8	3.4	4.2	Inventory	7.9	6.0	4.7	4.7	3.4	2.6
7.0	7.5	8.3	All Other Current	8.8	4.4	11.1	7.8	8.2	9.5
59.3	60.5	58.1	Total Current	47.3	47.3	55.7	60.5	59.3	64.8
31.4	30.6	33.4	Fixed Assets (net)	33.1	42.3	35.1	31.8	34.4	27.8
1.7	2.2	1.7	Intangibles (net)	5.4	2.9	.6	1.6	1.3	1.1
7.6	6.8	6.8	All Other Non-Current	14.2	7.5	8.6	6.2	5.0	6.2
100.0	100.0	100.0	Total	100.0	100.0	100.0	100.0	100.0	100.0
			LIABILITIES						
7.1	5.4	6.9	Notes Payable-Short Term	12.8	10.6	10.2	5.6	6.4	3.2
5.4	5.2	4.9	Cur. Mat.-L/T/D	3.4	7.7	4.9	5.2	4.7	3.7
16.4	16.9	16.9	Trade Payables	7.7	12.3	11.5	17.0	18.9	21.9
.5	1.0	.7	Income Taxes Payable	1.8	.6	1.1	.7	.6	.6
11.8	13.9	12.0	All Other Current	19.4	3.6	6.7	10.6	10.4	20.0
41.3	42.5	41.4	Total Current	45.1	34.8	34.5	39.1	40.9	49.4
14.2	14.2	14.2	Long Term Debt	17.0	22.3	11.9	13.4	12.9	11.9
1.5	1.3	1.2	Deferred Taxes	1.2	.6	.4	2.5	1.3	1.2
2.4	2.7	3.6	All Other Non-Current	7.5	4.2	2.5	3.5	2.0	4.5
40.5	39.2	39.6	Net Worth	29.2	38.1	50.8	41.5	42.8	33.0
100.0	100.0	100.0	Total Liabilities & Net Worth	100.0	100.0	100.0	100.0	100.0	100.0
			INCOME DATA						
100.0	100.0	100.0	Net Sales	100.0	100.0	100.0	100.0	100.0	100.0
22.6	21.4	22.9	Gross Profit	47.4	34.9	29.6	20.3	20.4	12.3
18.0	16.9	18.7	Operating Expenses	41.8	28.7	25.8	17.6	14.9	9.4
4.6	4.5	4.2	Operating Profit	5.6	6.1	3.7	2.7	5.4	2.8
.3	.6	.7	All Other Expenses (net)	3.7	1.2	.4	.8	.6	.2
4.2	3.9	3.4	Profit Before Taxes	1.9	5.0	3.3	1.9	4.9	2.6
			RATIOS						
1.9 / 1.4 / 1.1	1.9 / 1.4 / 1.1	1.9 / 1.4 / 1.1	Current	3.7 / 1.2 / .7	2.7 / 1.3 / 1.0	3.0 / 1.6 / 1.0	1.9 / 1.5 / 1.1	2.0 / 1.5 / 1.1	1.6 / 1.3 / 1.1
1.5 / 1.1 / .7	1.5 / 1.1 / .9	1.5 / 1.1 / .8	Quick	1.3 / .8 / .3	2.0 / 1.1 / .7	1.7 / 1.2 / .6	1.4 / 1.2 / .7	1.5 / 1.2 / .8	1.3 / 1.1 / .9
35 10.3 / 55 6.6 / 70 5.2	44 8.2 / 59 6.1 / 78 4.7	37 9.9 / 55 6.7 / 75 4.8	Sales/Receivables	6 60.5 / 61 6.0 / 80 4.6	33 11.2 / 47 7.8 / 71 5.2	37 10.0 / 56 6.6 / 67 5.4	36 10.1 / 55 6.7 / 76 4.8	36 10.1 / 51 7.2 / 77 4.7	46 7.9 / 60 6.1 / 75 4.8
0 UND / 0 UND / 12 31.3	0 UND / 0 UND / 6 57.1	0 UND / 0 966.0 / 9 41.3	Cost of Sales/Inventory	0 UND / 0 UND / 36 10.0	0 UND / 0 UND / 13 28.3	0 UND / 0 UND / 11 32.7	0 UND / 1 523.9 / 14 50.3	0 UND / 1 510.9 / 14 25.6	0 UND / 0 793.3 / 5 74.6
15 24.6 / 30 12.3 / 49 7.5	14 26.5 / 29 12.4 / 48 7.6	18 20.1 / 33 11.2 / 50 7.3	Cost of Sales/Payables	5 73.5 / 32 11.6 / 86 4.2	8 47.4 / 32 11.2 / 50 7.4	16 23.4 / 27 13.3 / 56 6.5	17 21.1 / 26 13.9 / 53 6.9	22 16.6 / 34 10.7 / 50 7.4	24 15.2 / 33 11.0 / 46 7.9
6.9 / 14.2 / 80.3	7.5 / 14.1 / 41.2	7.4 / 15.0 / 47.8	Sales/Working Capital	8.1 / 78.0 / −7.9	7.0 / 14.1 / −168.5	5.3 / 8.9 / NM	7.5 / 16.7 / 45.6	7.0 / 14.1 / 36.1	8.8 / 16.8 / 38.2
(142) 8.7 / 2.9 / 1.5	(163) 17.7 / 5.1 / 2.0	(197) 12.6 / 4.4 / 1.4	EBIT/Interest		(28) 6.6 / 3.7 / 1.2	(24) 5.5 / 3.1 / −.3	(35) 8.9 / 3.1 / 1.3	(49) 15.9 / 7.2 / 2.2	(53) 26.2 / 5.2 / 1.7
(49) 4.4 / 2.6 / 1.2	(56) 6.7 / 3.4 / 1.5	(78) 3.7 / 2.2 / 1.3	Net Profit + Depr., Dep., Amort./Cur. Mat. L/T/D				(18) 3.0 / 2.2 / .8	(21) 3.8 / 2.4 / 1.6	(23) 7.2 / 2.5 / 1.4
.4 / .8 / 1.4	.3 / .8 / 1.4	.4 / .8 / 1.6	Fixed/Worth	.3 / 1.7 / −1.9	.7 / 1.3 / 2.6	.4 / .6 / 1.4	.3 / .8 / 1.6	.4 / .8 / 1.5	.4 / .7 / 1.3
.9 / 1.7 / 3.0	.8 / 1.6 / 3.0	.8 / 1.6 / 3.0	Debt/Worth	.7 / 2.9 / −5.2	.7 / 1.8 / 5.6	.6 / .9 / 1.9	.8 / 1.4 / 2.5	.9 / 1.5 / 3.0	1.1 / 2.1 / 3.1
(150) 31.2 / 14.5 / 4.9	(170) 40.0 / 20.6 / 7.4	(208) 29.1 / 16.2 / 2.5	% Profit Before Taxes/Tangible Net Worth		(28) 57.5 / 15.3 / 1.6	21.9 / 7.5 / −2.7	30.5 / 13.3 / 1.1	29.7 / 20.0 / 4.7	(53) 25.4 / 16.0 / 4.0
11.3 / 5.2 / 1.3	14.9 / 7.1 / 2.5	10.8 / 4.6 / .8	% Profit Before Taxes/Total Assets	16.6 / .2 / −23.7	19.2 / 4.5 / .3	9.6 / 4.1 / −1.1	9.3 / 4.0 / .5	13.1 / 8.2 / 1.8	9.0 / 4.8 / 1.3
16.5 / 8.3 / 3.5	21.3 / 8.6 / 4.2	13.9 / 7.2 / 3.4	Sales/Net Fixed Assets	12.5 / 5.0 / 2.4	12.6 / 5.2 / 1.7	11.2 / 6.4 / 2.2	16.1 / 7.6 / 3.4	13.5 / 7.4 / 3.5	17.2 / 10.3 / 5.4
2.8 / 2.1 / 1.5	3.1 / 2.3 / 1.6	2.9 / 2.0 / 1.4	Sales/Total Assets	2.5 / 1.4 / 1.0	2.8 / 1.7 / 1.1	2.5 / 1.9 / 1.3	3.0 / 1.9 / 1.5	2.8 / 1.9 / 1.6	3.1 / 2.3 / 1.8
(143) 1.0 / 2.8 / 6.1	(160) 1.3 / 2.8 / 5.6	(202) 1.7 / 3.9 / 6.9	% Depr., Dep., Amort./Sales		(28) 2.5 / 6.3 / 11.4	(25) 2.4 / 5.7 / 8.3	(33) 1.8 / 4.3 / 7.2	(52) 1.3 / 3.3 / 6.7	(55) 1.2 / 2.4 / 4.7
(50) 1.9 / 3.2 / 6.1	(49) 1.6 / 3.1 / 6.4	(76) 1.9 / 3.0 / 5.7	% Officers', Directors', Owners' Comp/Sales		(18) 4.0 / 5.2 / 8.5	(12) 1.7 / 3.0 / 7.6	(17) 1.9 / 2.5 / 3.6	(15) 1.5 / 2.0 / 4.9	(10) .8 / 1.5 / 3.3
4462097M	5789441M	7499383M	Net Sales ($)	7545M	67722M	108048M	263275M	886287M	6166506M
2412704M	2842349M	3407641M	Total Assets ($)	8632M	65216M	77341M	172744M	516249M	2567459M

Current Data Sorted By Assets | Comparative Historical Data

Type of Statement	0-500M	500M-2MM	2-10MM	10-50MM	50-100MM	100-250MM	4/1/98-3/31/99 ALL	4/1/99-3/31/00 ALL
Unqualified		3	27	15	1	2	40	41
Reviewed	3	29	42	11			80	80
Compiled	12	23	15	1		1	49	50
Tax Returns	9	10	2	1		3	21	13
Other	9	27	20	6		2	41	41
	44 (4/1-9/30/02)			230 (10/1/02-3/31/03)				
NUMBER OF STATEMENTS	33	92	106	34	1	8	231	225

	0-500M %	500M-2MM %	2-10MM %	10-50MM %	50-100MM %	100-250MM %	ALL %	ALL %
ASSETS								
Cash & Equivalents	12.8	11.6	9.5	16.2			12.4	12.3
Trade Receivables (net)	31.9	38.5	40.2	42.4			40.6	40.5
Inventory	1.0	3.3	3.7	2.0			2.4	4.0
All Other Current	6.1	4.8	6.9	5.5			5.3	5.2
Total Current	51.7	58.1	60.4	66.1			60.7	61.9
Fixed Assets (net)	35.7	33.8	32.1	27.6			32.6	31.5
Intangibles (net)	.7	1.7	1.5	1.3			1.1	1.1
All Other Non-Current	11.8	6.4	5.9	5.0			5.6	5.5
Total	100.0	100.0	100.0	100.0			100.0	100.0
LIABILITIES								
Notes Payable-Short Term	14.7	12.5	8.3	4.5			7.4	8.9
Cur. Mat.-L/T/D	13.5	6.3	6.0	4.1			4.9	5.1
Trade Payables	11.0	15.5	18.4	18.1			18.8	19.1
Income Taxes Payable	.1	.7	.8	.3			1.3	.7
All Other Current	12.0	6.3	9.8	15.7			10.5	10.8
Total Current	51.3	41.3	43.3	42.7			42.9	44.6
Long Term Debt	31.9	19.3	14.8	12.9			14.4	14.6
Deferred Taxes	.1	.8	.4	1.1			1.0	1.1
All Other Non-Current	4.4	3.8	2.6	1.4			3.2	2.9
Net Worth	12.3	34.9	38.9	41.9			38.5	36.8
Total Liabilities & Net Worth	100.0	100.0	100.0	100.0			100.0	100.0
INCOME DATA								
Net Sales	100.0	100.0	100.0	100.0			100.0	100.0
Gross Profit	31.1	30.5	22.3	19.1			25.1	24.5
Operating Expenses	26.5	26.9	19.0	14.4			20.1	20.1
Operating Profit	4.6	3.7	3.2	4.7			5.1	4.4
All Other Expenses (net)	.5	.5	.8	1.1			.5	.3
Profit Before Taxes	4.1	3.2	2.5	3.6			4.6	4.2
RATIOS								
Current	2.4	2.6	2.1	2.4			1.9	2.2
	1.0	1.3	1.4	1.4			1.4	1.5
	.7	1.0	.9	1.2			1.1	1.1
Quick	2.1	2.3	1.7	2.0			1.7	1.9
	(32) 1.0	1.2	1.2	1.2			1.2	1.3
	.4	.9	.7	1.1			.9	.9
Sales/Receivables	0 UND	32 11.5	40 9.0	50 7.3			30 12.1	31 11.7
	26 13.8	48 7.7	54 6.7	73 5.0			53 6.9	55 6.7
	56 6.5	69 5.3	75 4.9	89 4.1			73 5.0	76 4.8
Cost of Sales/Inventory	0 UND	0 UND	0 UND	0 UND			0 UND	0 UND
	0 UND	0 UND	0 UND	1 616.4			0 UND	0 999.8
	0 UND	4 89.1	9 39.0	8 45.6			4 84.7	5 74.3
Cost of Sales/Payables	0 UND	11 33.9	14 26.3	19 19.5			10 35.4	15 25.1
	7 51.0	27 13.4	27 13.5	32 11.4			30 12.2	27 13.3
	22 16.2	44 8.4	46 7.9	50 7.3			46 8.0	48 7.5
Sales/Working Capital	13.4	7.6	8.2	4.9			10.3	7.4
	701.0	22.9	14.7	11.4			16.3	14.1
	−22.8	436.9	−83.0	19.8			66.1	87.8
EBIT/Interest	10.5	10.9	11.2	39.2			12.8	15.6
	(27) 5.0	(83) 2.6	(96) 3.4	(28) 4.2			(199) 5.0	(203) 4.5
	1.3	1.0	1.4	2.2			2.1	1.8
Net Profit + Depr., Dep., Amort./Cur. Mat. L /T/D		2.5	4.2	8.0			5.2	4.1
		(21) 1.4	(29) 2.0	(12) 2.9			(79) 2.3	(62) 2.2
		.9	1.2	1.0			1.3	1.5
Fixed/Worth	.5	.5	.3	.3			.3	.3
	1.5	1.1	.7	.5			.7	.7
	−6.4	2.6	2.0	1.5			1.4	1.6
Debt/Worth	1.0	.7	.8	.6			.8	.7
	6.9	2.3	1.4	1.7			1.7	1.7
	−12.8	6.4	4.2	3.8			3.4	3.6
% Profit Before Taxes/Tangible Net Worth	200.0	56.2	32.7	23.8			58.2	47.2
	(23) 48.6	(80) 24.9	(97) 15.4	(33) 15.6			(224) 29.3	(207) 25.6
	14.7	1.7	4.2	4.4			11.2	9.5
% Profit Before Taxes/Total Assets	31.0	19.8	11.5	9.8			21.6	18.1
	14.6	5.7	6.1	5.2			8.9	7.8
	2.8	.3	1.0	1.8			3.8	2.6
Sales/Net Fixed Assets	47.1	17.9	22.6	23.1			26.0	25.2
	17.5	9.0	9.8	10.3			11.6	11.3
	10.9	5.3	4.6	3.5			5.8	5.7
Sales/Total Assets	7.1	3.8	3.3	2.5			3.8	3.7
	5.4	2.8	2.5	2.0			2.9	2.8
	3.2	2.1	1.8	1.5			2.2	2.1
% Depr., Dep., Amort./Sales	1.4	2.0	1.3	.9			1.2	1.2
	(24) 2.1	(85) 3.7	(105) 3.1	(32) 2.1			(208) 2.4	(208) 2.7
	3.9	5.3	5.1	4.3			4.0	4.5
% Officers', Directors', Owners' Comp/Sales	3.4	2.2	2.0	.9			2.2	2.5
	(19) 4.6	(63) 4.5	(48) 3.4	(14) 3.4			(116) 4.5	(114) 4.5
	10.2	7.7	5.6	4.5			8.0	6.6
Net Sales ($)	45073M	291043M	1255266M	1277364M	131892M	5226081M	3241683M	4309462M
Total Assets ($)	8525M	99971M	502886M	599245M	58837M	1204262M	1482578M	1548546M

M = $ thousand   MM = $ million
See Pages 11 through 18 for Explanation of Ratios and Data

Comparative Historical Data | | Current Data Sorted By Sales

			Type of Statement	0-1MM	1-3MM	3-5MM	5-10MM	10-25MM	25MM & OVER
43	36	48	Unqualified		1	3	9	21	14
79	69	85	Reviewed	2	17	9	26	23	8
58	43	52	Compiled	4	23	9	6	8	2
19	21	25	Tax Returns	4	10	5	1	1	4
51	72	64	Other	7	10	18	12	10	7
4/1/00-3/31/01 ALL	4/1/01-3/31/02 ALL	4/1/02-3/31/03 ALL		44 (4/1-9/30/02)			230 (10/1/02-3/31/03)		
250	241	274	**NUMBER OF STATEMENTS**	17	61	44	54	63	35
%	%	%	**ASSETS**	%	%	%	%	%	%
10.6	10.5	11.7	Cash & Equivalents	14.3	11.8	10.1	9.0	11.2	17.2
40.1	40.0	38.2	Trade Receivables (net)	26.8	33.4	37.5	38.1	43.8	43.3
3.2	3.2	3.0	Inventory	2.6	2.3	2.7	4.4	3.5	1.7
5.0	4.9	5.9	All Other Current	3.4	6.2	5.2	5.2	7.4	5.8
58.9	58.6	58.8	Total Current	47.0	53.9	55.6	56.7	65.9	68.0
33.3	33.9	33.1	Fixed Assets (net)	31.8	38.5	36.5	35.1	28.5	24.9
1.6	2.1	1.4	Intangibles (net)	2.5	1.1	2.1	1.9	.5	1.6
6.3	5.4	6.6	All Other Non-Current	18.6	6.6	5.8	6.2	5.1	5.4
100.0	100.0	100.0	Total	100.0	100.0	100.0	100.0	100.0	100.0
			LIABILITIES						
9.6	8.8	9.8	Notes Payable-Short Term	16.8	13.0	11.6	10.3	5.6	5.6
4.7	5.7	6.8	Cur. Mat.-L/T/D	8.0	9.8	6.7	6.4	5.5	4.4
18.5	18.7	16.1	Trade Payables	7.8	12.2	16.5	16.6	20.3	18.0
.5	.6	.6	Income Taxes Payable	.0	.6	.9	.8	.6	.3
26.9	10.5	9.6	All Other Current	14.9	6.3	5.8	7.1	11.6	18.0
60.2	44.2	43.0	Total Current	47.5	41.9	41.5	41.3	43.6	46.3
16.6	19.0	18.4	Long Term Debt	39.4	23.7	20.4	13.1	13.6	13.4
1.0	.7	.6	Deferred Taxes	.1	1.1	.3	.5	.5	.8
3.6	3.7	3.0	All Other Non-Current	4.0	3.9	3.7	4.2	1.3	1.6
18.6	32.4	34.9	Net Worth	9.0	29.4	34.1	40.9	41.0	37.9
100.0	100.0	100.0	Total Liabilities & Net Worth	100.0	100.0	100.0	100.0	100.0	100.0
			INCOME DATA						
100.0	100.0	100.0	Net Sales	100.0	100.0	100.0	100.0	100.0	100.0
24.7	26.6	26.1	Gross Profit	38.5	29.9	31.1	25.1	19.2	21.3
20.6	22.2	22.1	Operating Expenses	34.5	25.8	27.4	22.3	15.6	14.5
4.1	4.5	4.0	Operating Profit	4.0	4.2	3.8	2.8	3.6	6.7
.6	.9	.7	All Other Expenses (net)	.4	.7	.4	1.0	.7	1.1
3.5	3.6	3.3	Profit Before Taxes	3.7	3.4	3.4	1.8	2.9	5.6
			RATIOS						
2.0	2.1	2.3	Current	2.4	2.6	2.5	2.0	2.3	2.0
1.3	1.3	1.4		1.0	1.4	1.2	1.5	1.4	1.4
1.0	1.0	1.0		.7	.7	.9	1.0	1.2	1.2
1.7	1.8	1.9	Quick	1.9	2.3	1.9	1.6	2.1	1.6
1.2	1.2 (273)	1.2		1.0	1.0 (60)	1.1	1.2	1.2	1.2
.8	.8	.8		.4	.7	.8	.8	.8	1.0
33 10.9	35 10.5	35 10.4	Sales/Receivables	0 UND	20 18.1	34 10.6	38 9.5	42 8.7	50 7.2
52 7.0	58 6.2	51 7.1		31 11.7	48 7.7	46 8.0	53 6.9	54 6.7	64 5.7
72 5.1	83 4.4	73 5.0		68 5.4	65 5.6	64 5.7	73 5.0	76 4.8	87 4.2
0 UND	0 UND	0 UND	Cost of Sales/Inventory	0 UND	0 UND	0 UND	0 UND	0 UND	0 UND
0 UND	0 UND	0 UND		0 UND	0 UND	0 UND	0 959.5	1 291.0	0 999.8
5 72.2	5 71.1	5 67.7		0 UND	0 UND	0 UND	6 60.1	8 45.2	7 49.1
14 26.7	11 34.6	11 33.5	Cost of Sales/Payables	0 UND	5 80.3	11 32.1	13 27.4	17 21.9	17 21.0
29 12.5	28 13.2	25 14.3		7 51.0	15 24.9	27 13.4	19 18.8	29 12.5	27 13.4
47 7.7	51 7.2	44 8.3		35 10.3	39 9.3	38 9.6	43 8.4	48 7.6	47 7.8
7.9	7.7	7.9	Sales/Working Capital	9.2	7.8	10.2	9.1	7.1	7.0
18.1	17.4	16.7		197.3	26.5	26.9	15.3	15.6	11.6
-282.5	-380.3	-800.0		-37.4	-35.2	-314.8	-581.7	42.8	46.8
10.4	12.7	11.5	EBIT/Interest	4.5	10.4	14.3	10.5	17.7	21.3
(227) 3.9	(222) 3.7	(242) 4.0		(15) 1.5	(53) 4.3	(38) 3.8	(53) 2.9	(55) 4.9	(28) 5.1
1.4	1.4	1.3		1.0	1.0	.4	1.3	2.1	2.1
3.8	4.6	3.9	Net Profit + Depr., Dep., Amort./Cur. Mat. L/T/D		1.5		3.1	9.4	
(60) 2.1	(57) 2.2	(65) 1.9			(14) 1.1		(19) 2.0	(18) 3.9	
1.4	1.2	1.1			.7		.6	1.9	
.3	.5	.4	Fixed/Worth	.3	.4	.6	.5	.3	.2
.9	.9	.8		2.2	1.2	1.1	.8	.5	.6
2.0	2.2	2.6		-3.7	8.5	3.6	2.0	1.6	1.1
1.0	.9	.7	Debt/Worth	.6	.8	.9	.7	.6	.7
1.8	2.0	1.7		10.4	2.5	2.3	1.4	1.4	1.9
4.0	5.0	5.3		-6.7	16.5	6.4	3.7	3.1	3.7
42.9	51.0	41.6	% Profit Before Taxes/Tangible Net Worth	166.7	59.9	61.5	33.9	31.7	40.0
(224) 21.9	(217) 24.2	(242) 18.2		(10) 18.3	(52) 29.9	(38) 27.6	(50) 14.5	(58) 15.8	(34) 21.0
6.7	6.3	4.1		-32.7	.1	-1.6	1.1	7.3	9.0
16.0	20.1	17.2	% Profit Before Taxes/Total Assets	18.6	21.6	26.1	13.4	11.5	20.5
7.3	7.0	6.4		7.2	6.5	7.5	4.4	5.8	7.3
1.2	1.1	1.2		.5	.1	.7	.4	2.5	2.2
23.8	18.7	21.4	Sales/Net Fixed Assets	35.0	18.3	18.9	16.8	26.9	29.7
9.8	9.4	10.4		13.8	9.2	9.1	8.7	12.5	13.6
5.4	5.0	5.2		6.8	5.1	5.2	4.5	5.8	8.3
3.5	3.5	3.6	Sales/Total Assets	5.7	4.5	4.1	3.4	3.4	3.4
2.8	2.5	2.6		2.6	2.6	2.8	2.5	2.6	2.2
2.0	1.9	1.9		1.2	2.0	1.9	1.8	2.0	1.9
1.0	1.4	1.4	% Depr., Dep., Amort./Sales	1.5	2.5	1.9	2.0	1.0	.8
(227) 2.6	(221) 2.9	(248) 2.9		(12) 3.6	(53) 3.8	(42) 3.6	(53) 3.7	(62) 2.4	(26) 1.5
4.5	5.5	5.1		12.9	7.0	5.8	5.1	4.3	2.3
2.2	2.0	2.2	% Officers', Directors', Owners' Comp/Sales	4.0	3.3	2.1	1.9	2.3	.9
(137) 3.9	(117) 4.0	(148) 3.9		(10) 5.6	(41) 4.5	(25) 3.0	(32) 3.0	(26) 3.8	(14) 1.7
7.2	7.4	6.6		14.4	7.8	6.7	6.6	5.7	4.0
5009229M	3282950M	8226719M	Net Sales ($)	10003M	118431M	167734M	371564M	1000280M	6558707M
1776116M	1588105M	2473726M	Total Assets ($)	5632M	47841M	70444M	182723M	424569M	1742517M

M = $ thousand   MM = $ million
See Pages 11 through 18 for Explanation of Ratios and Data

Current Data Sorted By Assets   Comparative Historical Data

						Type of Statement		
1	1	9	12	1	1	Unqualified	10	10
3	14	27	1			Reviewed	43	44
2	11	6	1			Compiled	18	25
3	2	1				Tax Returns	3	9
4	7	5	1			Other	20	12
	23 (4/1-9/30/02)		89 (10/1/02-3/31/03)				4/1/98-3/31/99	4/1/99-3/31/00
0-500M	500M-2MM	2-10MM	10-50MM	50-100MM	100-250MM		ALL	ALL
13	35	48	14	1	1	**NUMBER OF STATEMENTS**	94	100
%	%	%	%	%	%	**ASSETS**	%	%
7.3	8.8	9.7	8.3			Cash & Equivalents	10.2	8.7
40.4	46.7	43.6	48.4			Trade Receivables (net)	50.3	48.2
4.4	2.9	2.7	5.0			Inventory	4.4	4.5
10.9	9.7	12.1	9.7			All Other Current	7.7	8.3
63.0	68.0	68.3	71.4			Total Current	72.5	69.7
33.8	23.3	19.6	22.6			Fixed Assets (net)	18.9	21.9
1.1	1.3	1.5	.0			Intangibles (net)	1.6	3.1
2.2	7.3	10.7	6.0			All Other Non-Current	7.0	5.2
100.0	100.0	100.0	100.0			Total	100.0	100.0
						LIABILITIES		
23.9	11.3	10.5	7.6			Notes Payable-Short Term	9.9	10.5
12.2	3.1	3.6	3.5			Cur. Mat.-L/T/D	3.3	3.3
12.0	17.4	17.0	14.7			Trade Payables	19.3	15.4
.0	.7	1.0	1.3			Income Taxes Payable	.6	.4
7.1	12.9	17.5	19.3			All Other Current	12.8	13.5
55.2	45.4	49.6	46.4			Total Current	45.9	43.0
25.5	12.9	10.8	11.3			Long Term Debt	8.6	10.7
.0	.8	.9	.3			Deferred Taxes	1.4	.7
.0	3.0	2.5	4.1			All Other Non-Current	1.8	4.1
19.4	37.9	36.3	37.8			Net Worth	42.2	41.5
100.0	100.0	100.0	100.0			Total Liabilities & Net Worth	100.0	100.0
						INCOME DATA		
100.0	100.0	100.0	100.0			Net Sales	100.0	100.0
42.9	22.6	19.3	18.9			Gross Profit	26.2	27.0
40.0	19.5	18.9	14.1			Operating Expenses	20.6	20.8
2.9	3.1	.5	4.8			Operating Profit	5.5	6.2
1.8	.7	.6	.6			All Other Expenses (net)	.2	.5
1.1	2.4	-.1	4.1			Profit Before Taxes	5.3	5.7
						RATIOS		
2.4	2.2	1.9	2.0			Current	2.3	2.5
1.8	1.5	1.4	1.6				1.5	1.5
.5	1.2	1.0	1.3				1.2	1.3
1.7	1.9	1.5	1.7			Quick	2.1	2.1
1.1	1.2	1.2	1.2				1.3	1.3
.2	.9	.8	.9				1.0	.9
0 UND	39 9.4	45 8.2	69 5.3			Sales/Receivables	49 7.4	44 8.3
48 7.6	57 6.4	61 5.9	78 4.7				69 5.3	65 5.6
95 3.8	77 4.7	91 4.0	118 3.1				92 4.0	88 4.2
0 UND	0 UND	0 UND	0 UND			Cost of Sales/Inventory	0 UND	0 UND
0 UND	0 UND	0 UND	2 153.4				0 999.8	0 UND
0 UND	9 40.1	6 57.5	16 22.2				16 22.3	14 26.4
2 169.9	8 46.0	11 32.3	15 23.8			Cost of Sales/Payables	12 30.0	7 49.2
35 10.4	23 16.1	16 22.3	27 13.6				29 12.6	21 17.7
95 3.8	37 9.8	46 7.9	48 7.6				51 7.1	42 8.8
6.1	9.3	6.3	4.0			Sales/Working Capital	6.2	6.2
15.7	13.4	14.4	9.3				11.4	10.2
-16.8	41.2	129.3	20.7				23.5	17.8
	(32) 8.7	(43) 6.6	11.2			EBIT/Interest	(83) 23.6	(90) 16.2
	2.9	1.1	4.1				5.5	5.4
	-1.0	-3.3	2.3				2.3	1.9
		(16) 6.2				Net Profit + Depr., Dep., Amort./Cur. Mat. L /T/D	(34) 9.4	(37) 5.7
		1.5					2.6	3.6
		-.1					1.0	1.9
.1	.1	.2	.4			Fixed/Worth	.2	.2
.5	.5	.5	.5				.4	.5
2.4	1.0	1.4	.8				.8	1.0
.6	.7	.9	1.0			Debt/Worth	.6	.8
1.2	1.5	1.9	1.7				1.7	1.7
3.7	2.7	3.7	3.1				2.9	3.3
(11) 40.8	(32) 79.9	(42) 24.6	29.6			% Profit Before Taxes/Tangible Net Worth	(90) 56.2	(92) 58.3
3.8	10.8	4.4	18.7				29.1	26.8
-1.2	-.9	-14.9	9.3				9.2	10.1
18.7	14.9	10.6	13.8			% Profit Before Taxes/Total Assets	20.9	20.6
1.8	3.7	.3	5.3				8.4	10.4
-4.3	-2.8	-9.2	2.3				2.9	3.2
91.5	49.9	54.9	15.7			Sales/Net Fixed Assets	40.2	34.6
45.7	19.0	15.9	9.6				19.7	17.0
8.2	8.5	7.7	6.6				9.1	9.3
5.9	4.2	3.0	2.7			Sales/Total Assets	3.2	3.5
3.6	2.9	2.3	2.0				2.6	2.8
2.2	2.5	1.6	1.3				1.9	2.0
(10) .6	(31) .8	(46) .5	(13) 1.5			% Depr., Dep., Amort./Sales	(81) .6	(92) .7
1.7	1.2	1.7	2.7				1.2	1.5
4.6	3.1	3.5	4.1				1.8	3.0
	(15) 3.2	(25) .9				% Officers', Directors', Owners' Comp/Sales	(46) 1.5	(51) 1.8
	5.1	2.7					3.3	3.8
	5.8	7.2					6.9	10.3
13314M	142374M	500642M	564355M	96843M	230985M	Net Sales ($)	1052662M	1368209M
2786M	42836M	217766M	299997M	74268M	148345M	Total Assets ($)	486219M	730847M

© RMA 2003   M = $ thousand   MM = $ million
See Pages 11 through 18 for Explanation of Ratios and Data

Comparative Historical Data   Current Data Sorted By Sales

4/1/00-3/31/01 ALL	4/1/01-3/31/02 ALL	4/1/02-3/31/03 ALL	Type of Statement	0-1MM	1-3MM	3-5MM	5-10MM	10-25MM	25MM & OVER
14	13	25	Unqualified	1			4	8	12
35	27	45	Reviewed	1	6	11	15	11	1
29	24	19	Compiled	2	7	4	5	1	
2	8	6	Tax Returns	1	2	1	2		
22	28	17	Other	3	4	5	1	3	1
					23 (4/1-9/30/02)		89 (10/1/02-3/31/03)		
102	100	112	**NUMBER OF STATEMENTS**	8	19	21	27	23	14
%	%	%	**ASSETS**	%	%	%	%	%	%
10.5	11.1	8.9	Cash & Equivalents		7.8	6.8	10.5	10.6	8.1
47.0	47.5	44.8	Trade Receivables (net)		44.4	40.7	45.7	47.9	48.2
5.5	4.7	3.2	Inventory		1.6	4.3	2.3	2.1	5.2
6.8	8.3	10.9	All Other Current		10.3	4.2	12.6	13.0	11.1
69.8	71.7	67.8	Total Current		64.1	56.0	71.1	73.7	72.7
22.1	21.7	22.7	Fixed Assets (net)		27.0	27.7	20.8	18.3	18.3
3.3	1.7	1.7	Intangibles (net)		.3	4.0	.0	1.3	3.8
4.9	4.9	7.9	All Other Non-Current		8.5	12.3	8.1	6.7	5.1
100.0	100.0	100.0	Total		100.0	100.0	100.0	100.0	100.0
			LIABILITIES						
13.6	13.2	11.8	Notes Payable-Short Term		17.5	12.1	10.4	8.4	6.9
2.9	3.9	4.4	Cur. Mat.-L/T/D		11.1	3.0	2.1	4.0	3.0
16.6	20.4	16.1	Trade Payables		14.2	19.4	13.7	19.5	15.4
.5	.4	.8	Income Taxes Payable		.1	1.8	.4	1.1	.9
15.3	13.0	15.1	All Other Current		11.9	9.3	15.2	21.1	21.5
48.8	50.9	48.1	Total Current		54.8	45.6	41.8	54.2	47.6
13.1	13.1	13.6	Long Term Debt		29.8	15.2	7.4	8.6	13.2
.7	.6	.7	Deferred Taxes		.4	.3	2.0	.1	.6
1.6	2.4	2.5	All Other Non-Current		3.5	1.7	1.4	2.7	5.9
35.7	33.0	35.0	Net Worth		11.4	37.1	47.3	34.5	32.7
100.0	100.0	100.0	Total Liabilities & Net Worth		100.0	100.0	100.0	100.0	100.0
			INCOME DATA						
100.0	100.0	100.0	Net Sales		100.0	100.0	100.0	100.0	100.0
24.2	26.8	22.9	Gross Profit		26.3	28.2	21.2	12.0	16.8
20.4	22.9	20.8	Operating Expenses		24.6	25.7	19.0	10.6	13.7
3.9	3.9	2.2	Operating Profit		1.8	2.5	2.1	1.4	3.1
.7	.8	.8	All Other Expenses (net)		1.2	.6	.5	.5	.8
3.2	3.0	1.4	Profit Before Taxes		.6	1.9	1.6	.9	2.3
			RATIOS						
2.3	2.1	2.1			1.8	1.8	2.5	2.1	1.9
1.5	1.5	1.5	Current		1.3	1.4	1.6	1.4	1.6
1.2	1.1	1.1			.9	1.0	1.3	1.1	1.3
2.0	1.9	1.6			1.8	1.4	2.2	1.8	1.4
1.2	1.2	1.2	Quick		1.2	1.2	1.3	1.2	1.2
1.0	.8	.9			.7	.7	1.0	.9	.9
45 8.2	45 8.2	43 8.5			45 8.1	31 11.7	39 9.4	53 6.8	64 5.7
71 5.2	70 5.2	61 5.9	Sales/Receivables		60 6.1	58 6.3	57 6.4	66 5.6	84 4.3
91 4.0	89 4.1	93 3.9			94 3.9	99 3.7	77 4.7	76 4.8	112 3.2
0 UND	0 UND	0 UND			0 UND	0 UND	0 UND	0 UND	0 UND
1 371.0	0 UND	0 UND	Cost of Sales/Inventory		0 UND	1 375.4	0 UND	0 UND	5 74.3
16 22.2	8 45.0	7 52.4			1 401.0	16 22.2	0 999.8	6 59.0	16 22.2
12 30.9	16 23.3	11 32.3			8 46.0	10 35.0	3 140.3	12 30.2	16 22.7
26 14.3	33 10.9	22 16.3	Cost of Sales/Payables		21 17.2	27 13.4	16 23.1	22 16.6	27 13.7
47 7.8	55 6.7	47 7.7			48 7.6	63 5.8	37 9.8	44 8.3	43 8.6
5.8	5.8	6.4			10.3	9.2	6.0	5.7	4.0
11.7	13.6	12.9	Sales/Working Capital		14.6	17.4	12.8	10.6	9.3
27.0	40.2	40.8			−48.8	NM	21.9	68.6	20.7
12.5	9.6	6.9			6.0	8.9	7.8	7.7	11.1
(94) 3.8	(94) 3.8	(99) 2.3	EBIT/Interest	(18) 1.5	(19) 3.0	(24) 2.8	(21) .4	3.4
1.5	1.6	−1.3			−1.5	−3.3	.1	−9.4	1.9
4.8	6.6	5.0							
(29) 2.5	(29) 3.2	(31) 1.8	Net Profit + Depr., Dep., Amort./Cur. Mat. L/T/D						
1.4	1.7	.3							
.3	.3	.2			.1	.4	.1	.2	.4
.6	.6	.5	Fixed/Worth		.6	.5	.5	.5	.5
1.1	1.1	1.0			4.2	2.7	1.0	.9	1.4
.8	1.0	.8			.8	1.0	.5	1.1	1.4
1.7	1.8	1.6	Debt/Worth		1.8	1.6	.9	2.0	2.1
4.5	4.3	3.5			8.6	6.2	2.1	3.8	4.5
50.5	46.1	26.8			66.3	87.5	24.5	28.1	24.6
(94) 27.7	(91) 19.9	(100) 10.5	% Profit Before Taxes/Tangible Net Worth	(16) 3.7	(18) 10.1	(25) 6.3	(22) 14.6	(12) 15.5
6.8	6.7	−1.8			−8.9	−1.6	−.5	−31.3	7.5
18.2	14.2	11.4			11.5	12.4	10.9	13.2	9.1
7.0	5.2	2.5	% Profit Before Taxes/Total Assets		1.8	3.5	2.3	2.1	4.3
1.5	1.4	−2.7			−4.6	−3.3	−.7	−12.5	.6
31.8	29.4	48.5			50.8	19.4	61.2	57.2	24.9
14.5	15.1	15.3	Sales/Net Fixed Assets		12.2	11.4	18.4	18.0	10.4
7.8	7.8	7.9			6.8	7.5	11.5	7.8	8.2
3.5	3.3	3.6			4.0	3.8	4.0	3.6	2.9
2.6	2.6	2.6	Sales/Total Assets		2.8	2.5	2.8	2.5	2.1
2.0	2.0	1.9			2.0	1.6	2.0	2.1	1.3
.8	.7	.7			.9	1.0	.6	.3	.6
(88) 1.5	(92) 1.7	(101) 1.7	% Depr., Dep., Amort./Sales	(17) 3.5	(19) 1.8	(26) 1.2	(22) 1.4	(12) 2.1
2.9	3.2	3.4			6.5	3.6	2.3	3.1	2.8
2.3	2.3	1.4			3.9		2.1	.7	
(39) 5.0	(49) 5.0	(49) 4.4	% Officers', Directors', Owners' Comp/Sales	(10) 5.3		(14) 3.7	(10) 1.0	
10.8	7.6	7.2			12.0		7.1	2.2	
1625665M	1579733M	1548513M	Net Sales ($)	3582M	40389M	82739M	206686M	346943M	868174M
816866M	828014M	785998M	Total Assets ($)	999M	15888M	37170M	88435M	154577M	488929M

M = $ thousand   MM = $ million
See Pages 11 through 18 for Explanation of Ratios and Data

Current Data Sorted By Assets   Comparative Historical Data

							Type of Statement		
1		2		14		4	Unqualified	11	13
2		22		36		2	Reviewed	35	45
12		12		2			Compiled	15	18
6		8				1	Tax Returns	8	14
1		3		15		4	Other	13	21

	37 (4/1-9/30/02)			110 (10/1/02-3/31/03)				4/1/98-3/31/99	4/1/99-3/31/00
0-500M	500M-2MM	2-10MM	10-50MM	50-100MM	100-250MM			ALL	ALL
22	47	67	11			NUMBER OF STATEMENTS		82	111

%	%	%	%	%	%		ASSETS	%	%
15.3	12.4	11.2	15.0	D	D	Cash & Equivalents		12.8	14.2
28.6	44.7	52.4	44.8	A	A	Trade Receivables (net)		46.3	49.0
.6	5.4	3.2	4.0	T	T	Inventory		3.2	3.7
6.8	8.8	8.7	11.3	A	A	All Other Current		7.7	6.3
51.3	71.2	75.5	75.1			Total Current		70.0	73.2
38.7	22.3	17.9	17.8	N	N	Fixed Assets (net)		21.6	18.2
.7	1.1	2.2	.5	O	O	Intangibles (net)		1.0	1.3
9.2	5.4	4.4	6.6	T	T	All Other Non-Current		7.4	7.3
100.0	100.0	100.0	100.0			Total		100.0	100.0

				A	A	LIABILITIES			
19.0	8.4	9.6	8.5	V	V	Notes Payable-Short Term		10.0	11.5
7.7	3.0	2.8	2.5	A	A	Cur. Mat.-L/T/D		2.7	2.3
15.7	16.4	17.4	29.4	I	I	Trade Payables		16.6	16.6
.1	1.5	.7	.3	L	L	Income Taxes Payable		.8	.7
16.0	12.7	17.3	15.3	A	A	All Other Current		14.8	15.0
58.4	42.0	47.7	55.9	B	B	Total Current		45.0	46.1
35.7	11.0	6.7	14.9	L	L	Long Term Debt		8.2	8.0
.0	.5	.7	.2	E	E	Deferred Taxes		1.3	1.5
13.9	.6	3.1	2.4			All Other Non-Current		2.0	3.2
−8.1	45.9	41.7	26.7			Net Worth		43.6	41.1
100.0	100.0	100.0	100.0			Total Liabilities & Net Worth		100.0	100.0

						INCOME DATA			
100.0	100.0	100.0	100.0			Net Sales		100.0	100.0
30.3	27.0	19.6	24.7			Gross Profit		21.9	25.0
31.5	25.3	16.8	18.1			Operating Expenses		17.9	20.3
−1.2	1.7	2.8	6.6			Operating Profit		3.9	4.7
.8	.0	.0	.6			All Other Expenses (net)		.1	.5
−2.0	1.6	2.8	6.0			Profit Before Taxes		3.9	4.2

						RATIOS			
1.7	2.5	2.3	2.1					2.3	2.5
1.2	1.6	1.5	1.3			Current		1.6	1.7
.6	1.3	1.2	1.2					1.2	1.2

1.5	2.2	1.8	1.7					1.9	2.2
.8	1.4	1.3	1.1			Quick		1.5	1.5
.4	.9	1.0	.8					1.0	1.0

0	UND	37	9.8	57	6.4	42	8.7			46	7.9	42	8.8
24	15.0	60	6.1	70	5.2	68	5.3	Sales/Receivables		62	5.9	64	5.7
57	6.4	79	4.6	89	4.1	74	4.9			83	4.4	85	4.3

0	UND	0	UND	0	UND	0	UND			0	UND	0	UND
0	UND	0	UND	0	UND	0	UND	Cost of Sales/Inventory		0	UND	0	UND
0	UND	2	166.8	4	90.1	2	148.2			2	202.9	3	107.6

0	UND	8	44.8	13	27.5	12	29.8			12	29.4	10	37.2
11	33.0	19	18.8	22	16.3	30	12.0	Cost of Sales/Payables		23	16.0	22	16.8
44	8.3	34	10.8	39	9.3	77	4.7			35	10.4	40	9.0

19.0	6.6	5.8	12.6					6.9	6.4
118.7	10.4	10.8	17.6			Sales/Working Capital		11.1	9.9
−17.4	28.3	19.5	188.3					21.4	28.0

	6.8		21.0		25.8						14.0		21.3
(19)	4.4	(41)	5.1	(64)	5.6			EBIT/Interest		(71)	5.8	(97)	7.3
	−2.3		−.4		2.0						2.6		2.1

			3.9		16.8						9.5		8.0
		(10)	1.9	(19)	5.6			Net Profit + Depr., Dep., Amort./Cur. Mat. L /T/D		(26)	3.3	(26)	3.4
			.8		2.5						1.3		2.0

.9	.2	.2	.1					.2	.2
1.5	.4	.4	.5			Fixed/Worth		.4	.4
−.6	.9	.7	.8					.7	.7

1.1	.5	.8	1.5					.7	.6
4.9	1.1	1.4	4.6			Debt/Worth		1.2	1.3
−3.5	2.7	3.1	7.5					2.9	2.4

	64.2		31.4		35.4		66.8				45.9		49.0
(14)	20.0	(45)	11.3	(65)	14.9	(10)	33.5	% Profit Before Taxes/Tangible Net Worth		(81)	19.7	(105)	27.2
	−5.3		−5.1		4.1		17.2				7.7		6.0

19.3	15.3	15.7	20.9					15.6	19.3
5.0	3.7	4.3	17.5			% Profit Before Taxes/Total Assets		7.8	10.0
−14.8	−2.0	1.4	4.7					3.1	2.7

25.7	23.7	29.2	62.1					29.1	36.0
15.4	14.9	16.6	36.7			Sales/Net Fixed Assets		14.8	20.6
7.8	8.9	10.6	13.6					11.0	12.4

6.6	3.9	3.2	3.6					3.4	3.7
4.2	2.9	2.8	2.8			Sales/Total Assets		2.8	3.0
2.6	2.1	2.2	1.7					2.4	2.2

	1.5		.8		.9						.9		.6
(18)	3.5	(44)	2.4	(66)	1.5			% Depr., Dep., Amort./Sales		(78)	1.6	(100)	1.3
	4.4		4.5		2.5						2.5		2.5

	3.6		3.1		1.4						2.6		2.5
(12)	7.2	(33)	4.7	(29)	3.1			% Officers', Directors', Owners' Comp/Sales		(46)	5.6	(61)	4.2
	14.3		6.9		6.4						10.1		8.0

25743M	184663M	801771M	1580315M			Net Sales ($)		649323M	1152131M
5539M	54466M	294320M	195560M			Total Assets ($)		231516M	396948M

Comparative Historical Data | Current Data Sorted By Sales

Comp 1	Comp 2	Comp 3	Type of Statement	0-1MM	1-3MM	3-5MM	5-10MM	10-25MM	25MM & OVER
14	15	21	Unqualified	1	1		6	7	6
48	58	62	Reviewed	3	6	13	19	18	3
27	30	26	Compiled	6	10	7	2	1	
17	13	15	Tax Returns	2	8	2	1	1	1
23	25	23	Other	2	1	3	5	9	3
4/1/00-3/31/01 ALL	4/1/01-3/31/02 ALL	4/1/02-3/31/03 ALL		37 (4/1-9/30/02)			110 (10/1/02-3/31/03)		
129	141	147	**NUMBER OF STATEMENTS**	14	26	25	33	36	13
%	%	%	**ASSETS**	%	%	%	%	%	%
12.3	12.5	12.5	Cash & Equivalents	21.8	11.8	14.6	10.2	10.5	11.1
45.7	47.5	45.8	Trade Receivables (net)	30.5	31.5	43.6	52.9	54.0	54.3
2.7	5.0	3.6	Inventory	.3	9.3	2.7	2.2	2.6	3.4
8.2	7.0	8.6	All Other Current	4.5	5.2	10.4	9.2	10.6	9.9
69.0	72.0	70.5	Total Current	57.1	57.9	71.3	74.4	77.7	78.7
23.8	21.3	22.4	Fixed Assets (net)	41.0	28.2	20.4	18.6	17.8	17.0
1.3	1.9	1.5	Intangibles (net)	.1	.5	4.7	1.7	.4	.8
5.8	4.8	5.6	All Other Non-Current	1.8	13.4	3.6	5.3	4.0	3.4
100.0	100.0	100.0	Total	100.0	100.0	100.0	100.0	100.0	100.0
			LIABILITIES						
10.9	10.3	10.5	Notes Payable-Short Term	18.9	10.6	13.0	9.7	6.9	8.6
4.8	3.7	3.6	Cur. Mat.-L/T/D	7.0	4.9	2.9	2.9	2.8	2.4
14.6	15.8	17.7	Trade Payables	16.6	11.5	17.1	14.7	21.6	29.3
1.4	.6	.8	Income Taxes Payable	.1	1.5	1.0	1.1	.1	1.2
16.5	17.9	15.5	All Other Current	21.4	6.2	15.2	15.5	20.2	15.0
48.1	48.2	48.1	Total Current	64.0	34.6	49.2	43.8	51.7	56.7
9.9	9.1	13.1	Long Term Debt	41.2	18.0	5.2	8.8	8.0	12.6
1.1	.7	.5	Deferred Taxes	.0	.3	1.1	.2	.7	.4
2.5	2.0	3.9	All Other Non-Current	20.2	1.4	.9	1.5	2.9	5.6
38.3	39.9	34.5	Net Worth	−25.4	45.7	43.4	45.6	36.8	24.7
100.0	100.0	100.0	Total Liabilities & Net Worth	100.0	100.0	100.0	100.0	100.0	100.0
			INCOME DATA						
100.0	100.0	100.0	Net Sales	100.0	100.0	100.0	100.0	100.0	100.0
26.1	24.6	24.0	Gross Profit	33.0	34.4	20.2	21.2	19.5	19.8
21.0	21.2	21.8	Operating Expenses	35.3	32.9	21.1	17.5	15.4	15.7
5.1	3.3	2.1	Operating Profit	−2.3	1.5	−.9	3.7	4.2	4.2
.0	.4	.2	All Other Expenses (net)	.4	.8	−.4	−.3	.3	.5
5.1	2.9	1.9	Profit Before Taxes	−2.7	.7	−.5	4.0	3.8	3.7
			RATIOS						
2.3	2.2	2.3	Current	2.3	3.4	2.2	2.3	2.1	1.8
1.6	1.5	1.5		1.2	1.6	1.6	1.6	1.5	1.5
1.2	1.2	1.2		.5	1.2	1.1	1.2	1.1	1.2
2.0	2.1	1.8	Quick	2.3	2.5	1.7	2.0	1.8	1.6
1.3	1.3	1.3		1.2	1.3	1.3	1.3	1.3	1.2
.9	.9	.9		.4	.6	.8	1.1	.9	.9
42 8.7	39 9.3	41 8.8	Sales/Receivables	0 UND	13 28.7	40 9.1	52 7.0	47 7.7	53 6.9
58 6.3	66 5.5	63 5.8		42 8.7	52 7.0	65 5.6	67 5.5	66 5.5	68 5.3
83 4.4	83 4.4	79 4.6		69 5.3	72 5.1	85 4.3	92 4.0	75 4.9	74 4.9
0 UND	0 UND	0 UND	Cost of Sales/Inventory	0 UND	0 UND	0 UND	0 UND	0 UND	0 UND
0 UND	0 UND	0 UND		0 UND	0 UND	0 UND	0 UND	0 UND	0 UND
1 369.9	5 79.5	2 172.9		0 UND	6 56.5	0 UND	5 80.2	1 387.9	2 160.6
9 39.7	11 31.9	10 36.8	Cost of Sales/Payables	0 UND	2 226.3	13 29.1	13 27.6	10 35.0	13 27.7
18 19.7	21 17.6	21 17.1		18 20.9	15 24.8	29 12.6	20 18.5	24 15.4	30 12.1
32 11.3	33 11.2	42 8.6		44 8.3	43 8.5	43 8.6	33 11.2	46 8.0	60 6.1
6.4	6.8	6.6	Sales/Working Capital	8.3	5.4	6.3	6.4	6.6	9.9
11.6	13.0	13.9		NM	11.5	10.8	10.2	15.0	16.1
40.7	27.5	38.2		−7.5	71.4	41.2	23.8	44.5	27.7
15.8	14.9	14.2	EBIT/Interest	6.6	19.7	10.4	11.2	51.7	14.3
(114) 6.7	(125) 5.1	(133) 5.2		(12) .2	(23) 4.7	(22) 1.4	(31) 5.6	(33) 6.6	(12) 5.9
3.0	1.9	1.3		−5.9	1.5	−3.0	1.9	2.8	2.7
20.3	6.7	12.4	Net Profit + Depr., Dep., Amort./Cur. Mat. L/T/D						
(27) 5.9	(37) 3.8	(35) 4.2							
3.1	1.3	1.9							
.2	.2	.3	Fixed/Worth	1.0	.3	.3	.2	.3	.2
.4	.4	.5		NM	.5	.4	.4	.5	.5
1.2	.9	1.2		−.3	1.3	.9	.9	.8	.9
.7	.7	.7	Debt/Worth	.8	.4	.8	.7	1.0	1.4
1.5	1.6	1.5		NM	1.1	1.2	1.4	1.8	4.6
3.5	3.6	4.6		−3.1	3.5	3.3	2.4	5.3	10.5
51.0	43.0	42.9	% Profit Before Taxes/Tangible Net Worth		29.7	18.6	39.2	51.1	52.9
(117) 25.3	(131) 21.8	(134) 15.8		(24) 13.3	(23) 4.4	13.8	30.9	(11) 21.4	
14.6	9.3	3.2			−3.0	−11.3	4.1	12.8	6.2
20.1	16.4	17.5	% Profit Before Taxes/Total Assets	19.3	17.5	7.4	16.3	19.9	19.0
10.2	7.4	4.5		−2.2	4.5	.1	4.7	9.9	7.4
4.8	2.4	.1		−37.1	−.5	−3.4	2.6	2.8	1.9
31.0	33.1	29.2	Sales/Net Fixed Assets	23.5	16.6	22.5	35.6	29.1	63.3
19.2	17.4	16.2		11.4	12.6	14.1	19.6	17.5	41.5
10.2	10.4	10.0		3.8	7.3	9.4	11.4	13.2	20.8
3.8	3.6	3.7	Sales/Total Assets	5.6	3.9	3.7	3.6	3.7	3.9
3.0	2.9	2.9		2.8	2.8	2.6	2.7	3.0	3.1
2.3	2.3	2.2		2.0	2.0	1.9	2.2	2.8	2.7
.9	.9	.9	% Depr., Dep., Amort./Sales	1.9	1.8	.8	.6	.7	.6
(114) 1.5	(127) 1.6	(137) 1.8		(11) 3.9	(24) 3.4	(24) 2.5	1.3	(34) 1.4	(11) 1.0
2.5	2.9	3.3		7.0	5.2	4.0	2.6	2.0	1.5
2.4	2.1	2.2	% Officers', Directors', Owners' Comp/Sales		3.8	2.3	1.1	1.6	
(78) 4.8	(81) 4.5	(81) 4.0		(16) 5.4	(19) 4.3	(13) 3.1	(19) 3.1		
8.1	8.6	6.9		7.4	6.2	6.6	5.6		
1187189M	1618725M	2592492M	Net Sales ($)	7825M	47965M	97129M	237112M	546590M	1655871M
409264M	504125M	549885M	Total Assets ($)	3187M	21129M	43180M	88993M	186947M	206449M

M = $ thousand   MM = $ million
See Pages 11 through 18 for Explanation of Ratios and Data

Current Data Sorted By Assets							Comparative Historical Data	

Type of Statement

						Type of Statement		
1	1	2	1			Unqualified	3	5
	11	14				Reviewed	24	20
2	6	3				Compiled	12	21
13	6					Tax Returns	5	7
3	7	4	2			Other	10	12
	17 (4/1-9/30/02)			59 (10/1/02-3/31/03)			4/1/98-3/31/99	4/1/99-3/31/00
0-500M	500M-2MM	2-10MM	10-50MM	50-100MM	100-250MM		ALL	ALL
19	31	23	3			NUMBER OF STATEMENTS	54	65

%	%	%	%	%	%	ASSETS	%	%
13.2	14.6	9.6				Cash & Equivalents	10.2	9.0
29.5	50.2	53.1				Trade Receivables (net)	47.9	51.3
13.2	9.9	6.7				Inventory	9.6	9.7
4.6	2.8	7.4				All Other Current	7.5	6.4
60.5	77.5	76.8				Total Current	75.3	76.5
32.2	16.2	13.9				Fixed Assets (net)	18.0	18.4
2.1	2.0	4.2				Intangibles (net)	1.3	1.3
5.2	4.3	5.1				All Other Non-Current	5.5	3.8
100.0	100.0	100.0				Total	100.0	100.0

						LIABILITIES		
11.5	12.5	12.3				Notes Payable-Short Term	8.3	7.7
5.9	2.7	2.0				Cur. Mat.-L/T/D	3.3	3.3
21.1	21.5	21.2				Trade Payables	22.4	23.7
.2	.4	.5				Income Taxes Payable	1.8	.8
8.3	14.2	21.3				All Other Current	13.5	16.7
47.0	51.2	57.4				Total Current	49.2	52.2
34.4	7.3	5.5				Long Term Debt	13.4	12.0
.0	.3	.8				Deferred Taxes	1.0	.5
9.0	1.0	.6				All Other Non-Current	3.4	3.1
9.5	40.2	35.8				Net Worth	32.9	32.3
100.0	100.0	100.0				Total Liabilities & Net Worth	100.0	100.0

						INCOME DATA		
100.0	100.0	100.0				Net Sales	100.0	100.0
44.8	31.3	25.5				Gross Profit	30.5	30.1
40.3	28.4	23.0				Operating Expenses	25.4	26.3
4.5	2.9	2.6				Operating Profit	5.1	3.7
.6	.4	.1				All Other Expenses (net)	.6	.6
4.0	2.6	2.5				Profit Before Taxes	4.5	3.1

						RATIOS		
1.7	3.0	1.7					2.3	2.1
1.3	1.5	1.4				Current	1.5	1.4
.7	1.2	1.1					1.2	1.2
1.3	3.0	1.5					1.7	1.6
.8	1.4	1.1				Quick	1.1	1.2
.6	.7	.9					.9	.9
9 41.4	36 10.2	56 6.6					39 9.5	46 8.0
28 12.9	60 6.1	77 4.7				Sales/Receivables	54 6.7	55 6.7
38 9.6	85 4.3	101 3.6					68 5.3	80 4.6
5 74.5	0 UND	0 999.8					0 UND	0 789.3
11 32.6	7 54.7	4 98.2				Cost of Sales/Inventory	9 42.9	7 54.5
34 10.8	32 11.4	24 15.0					31 11.9	30 12.3
18 20.5	12 29.4	26 14.0					19 19.2	24 15.2
26 14.1	37 9.9	37 10.0				Cost of Sales/Payables	34 10.7	36 10.1
52 7.0	53 6.8	57 6.4					51 7.1	53 6.9
10.7	6.9	7.6					6.7	7.1
41.5	12.9	12.3				Sales/Working Capital	12.4	14.1
-43.7	24.2	20.8					27.1	28.2
12.0	34.7	15.7					12.3	12.8
(14) 3.7	(28) 6.1	(22) 5.9				EBIT/Interest	(49) 4.8	(60) 7.1
1.0	2.1	1.7					1.9	2.1
						Net Profit + Depr., Dep., Amort./Cur. Mat. L /T/D	6.4	5.2
							(17) 2.7	(22) 2.0
							1.4	1.0
.3	.2	.2					.2	.2
1.7	.3	.2				Fixed/Worth	.4	.4
-3.8	1.0	.7					.8	1.0
1.0	.5	1.1					1.0	.9
3.6	2.2	2.0				Debt/Worth	2.0	2.2
-11.5	4.9	3.0					4.2	5.4
114.8	64.1	27.2					50.3	52.0
(13) 54.3	(28) 33.0	(21) 15.6				% Profit Before Taxes/Tangible Net Worth	(51) 27.8	(59) 29.3
2.0	5.1	4.4					13.4	13.5
23.1	20.4	9.3					17.2	19.0
11.3	9.5	4.7				% Profit Before Taxes/Total Assets	9.4	7.2
.2	2.1	1.4					3.0	1.9
29.4	46.6	65.5					43.1	51.5
19.6	26.1	35.9				Sales/Net Fixed Assets	26.3	21.7
11.0	19.5	9.0					13.3	14.5
6.3	4.1	3.5					4.1	3.9
4.7	3.0	2.4				Sales/Total Assets	3.4	3.1
3.4	2.5	1.9					2.5	2.4
.8	.7	.5					.6	.6
(17) 1.9	(28) 1.2	(21) .8				% Depr., Dep., Amort./Sales	(47) .9	(61) .9
3.4	2.1	1.8					1.6	1.7
2.9	2.9	1.5					2.6	2.2
(14) 6.2	(19) 4.0	(16) 4.4				% Officers', Directors', Owners' Comp/Sales	(35) 4.0	(44) 3.5
11.4	10.7	7.3					7.7	6.4
24191M	113211M	259312M	120504M			Net Sales ($)	357251M	499620M
5483M	31372M	95260M	48251M			Total Assets ($)	115276M	180455M

In columns 50-100MM and 100-250MM the notation "DATA NOT AVAILABLE" appears vertically.

M = $ thousand   MM = $ million
See Pages 11 through 18 for Explanation of Ratios and Data

Comparative Historical Data | Current Data Sorted By Sales

Type of Statement					0-1MM	1-3MM	3-5MM	5-10MM	10-25MM	25MM & OVER
Unqualified	3	5	5			1	1	1	1	1
Reviewed	18	20	25			3	6	7	8	1
Compiled	17	17	11		1	5	1	3	1	
Tax Returns	6	12	19		5	11	2	1		
Other	17	18	16		1	7	3	3		2
	4/1/00-3/31/01 ALL	4/1/01-3/31/02 ALL	4/1/02-3/31/03 ALL			17 (4/1-9/30/02)		59 (10/1/02-3/31/03)		
NUMBER OF STATEMENTS	61	72	76		7	27	13	15	10	4

Percentages and Ratios

	H1	H2	H3		0-1MM	1-3MM	3-5MM	5-10MM	10-25MM	25MM & OVER
	%	%	%		%	%	%	%	%	%
ASSETS										
Cash & Equivalents	8.6	10.7	12.3			8.9	16.0	13.4	10.6	
Trade Receivables (net)	55.4	52.0	46.3			39.3	51.2	55.2	56.8	
Inventory	9.1	8.6	9.7			14.0	7.7	5.0	7.5	
All Other Current	4.7	7.1	5.0			2.8	4.3	5.3	10.6	
Total Current	77.8	78.4	73.3			65.0	79.2	78.9	85.5	
Fixed Assets (net)	14.4	17.1	19.3			24.8	16.5	13.2	9.6	
Intangibles (net)	2.8	1.8	2.6			3.2	.1	4.5	.8	
All Other Non-Current	4.6	2.6	4.7			6.9	4.2	3.4	4.1	
Total	100.0	100.0	100.0			100.0	100.0	100.0	100.0	
LIABILITIES										
Notes Payable-Short Term	12.0	11.3	12.3			16.7	10.0	11.3	7.4	
Cur. Mat.-L/T/D	3.2	2.8	3.2			4.8	2.2	2.1	1.5	
Trade Payables	23.0	29.3	21.5			21.7	22.2	21.5	22.5	
Income Taxes Payable	.5	.7	.4			.0	.1	1.1	.3	
All Other Current	15.7	16.3	15.0			12.0	14.4	18.9	22.4	
Total Current	54.4	60.5	52.5			55.3	48.8	54.9	54.1	
Long Term Debt	10.0	10.1	13.3			24.2	4.9	7.5	2.6	
Deferred Taxes	.5	.6	.4			.0	.8	1.0	.1	
All Other Non-Current	1.7	3.2	3.0			6.3	.0	.0	.9	
Net Worth	33.0	25.6	30.9			14.2	45.5	36.5	42.3	
Total Liabilities & Net Worth	100.0	100.0	100.0			100.0	100.0	100.0	100.0	
INCOME DATA										
Net Sales	100.0	100.0	100.0			100.0	100.0	100.0	100.0	
Gross Profit	28.6	28.3	32.4			37.1	30.9	24.1	27.2	
Operating Expenses	24.0	23.3	29.1			35.8	27.3	19.9	24.4	
Operating Profit	4.6	4.9	3.2			1.3	3.6	4.2	2.8	
All Other Expenses (net)	.7	.8	.3			.6	.1	.0	.1	
Profit Before Taxes	3.9	4.1	2.9			.8	3.5	4.2	2.7	
RATIOS										
Current	2.1	2.2	2.0			1.8	3.0	1.9	2.3	
	1.4	1.4	1.3			1.2	1.5	1.4	1.4	
	1.1	1.1	1.1			.7	1.1	1.3	1.3	
Quick	1.7	1.9	1.6			1.5	2.9	1.7	1.9	
	1.2	1.2	1.1			.8	1.4	1.3	1.1	
	.9	.8	.7			.6	.8	1.1	.9	
Sales/Receivables	50 7.4	38 9.5	32 11.2			25 14.6	43 8.6	52 7.1	44 8.4	
	67 5.5	62 5.9	56 6.5			37 9.7	72 5.0	79 4.6	64 5.7	
	87 4.2	86 4.2	84 4.3			69 5.3	93 3.9	111 3.3	80 4.6	
Cost of Sales/Inventory	1 320.8	0 999.8	0 UND			3 126.4	0 UND	0 UND	1 318.0	
	7 50.5	5 69.9	7 52.8			12 30.9	8 45.8	0 828.2	5 74.2	
	30 12.3	20 17.8	27 13.6			39 9.5	32 11.5	5 80.9	22 16.7	
Cost of Sales/Payables	22 16.9	21 17.7	17 21.0			17 21.8	19 19.3	15 24.1	14 26.5	
	39 9.4	34 10.6	33 11.1			32 11.3	45 8.0	31 11.9	38 9.6	
	57 6.4	48 7.6	53 6.9			55 6.6	60 6.1	53 6.8	44 8.4	
Sales/Working Capital	7.5	7.2	7.6			8.4	5.5	7.1	9.9	
	13.6	14.7	15.9			31.3	12.8	12.0	12.6	
	38.0	48.6	57.5			−25.7	246.6	19.6	19.6	
EBIT/Interest	17.1	17.8	19.5			7.3	38.6	25.3	33.4	
	(50) 6.6	(65) 8.7	(67) 6.4			(23) 3.1	(12) 8.8	(13) 6.5	10.3	
	2.0	2.4	1.7			−1.5	1.4	2.2	2.1	
Net Profit + Depr., Dep., Amort./Cur. Mat. L/T/D	6.1	9.4	19.4							
	(11) 4.7	(14) 4.3	(20) 4.0							
	2.9	1.0	2.8							
Fixed/Worth	.2	.2	.2			.3	.2	.1	.1	
	.3	.3	.4			.2	.2	.3	.2	
	1.5	1.3	1.1			−3.1	.6	.7	.3	
Debt/Worth	1.0	.9	1.0			1.3	.6	1.0	.9	
	2.8	2.4	2.2			3.6	1.8	1.9	2.0	
	6.6	10.4	4.8			−15.0	2.7	3.0	2.6	
% Profit Before Taxes/Tangible Net Worth	75.4	66.7	52.8			54.3	43.4	90.9	37.2	
	(53) 37.0	(58) 37.0	(65) 22.0			(19) 22.0	15.9	(14) 20.0	23.4	
	13.3	14.4	4.7			.0	3.5	8.9	3.4	
% Profit Before Taxes/Total Assets	19.4	23.7	16.0			15.5	18.2	21.3	11.3	
	9.3	9.7	6.5			4.3	6.5	5.7	6.2	
	2.9	2.7	1.6			−8.8	1.5	4.3	1.0	
Sales/Net Fixed Assets	62.8	52.1	45.6			30.1	47.6	46.6	88.4	
	26.1	28.5	25.5			21.2	20.7	29.6	60.8	
	15.5	16.4	14.3			14.2	14.0	9.2	36.4	
Sales/Total Assets	3.9	4.1	4.2			4.5	3.8	3.7	4.1	
	2.8	3.2	3.1			3.5	2.7	2.3	3.4	
	2.4	2.4	2.3			2.5	2.3	1.6	2.7	
% Depr., Dep., Amort./Sales	.5	.4	.6			.7	.8	.8		
	(51) .9	(68) .8	(69) 1.1			(25) 1.8	(12) 1.3	(14) .9		
	1.9	1.5	2.4			3.0	1.5	2.5		
% Officers', Directors', Owners' Comp/Sales	2.2	1.5	2.7			3.1	3.2	1.2		
	(40) 4.3	(39) 4.5	(50) 4.5			(16) 5.6	(10) 4.6	(11) 4.6		
	6.1	8.9	8.7			11.0	11.3	7.2		
Net Sales ($)	519059M	562376M	517218M		4775M	52082M	48164M	108076M	150975M	153146M
Total Assets ($)	187779M	190171M	180366M		1170M	15942M	18386M	45300M	44139M	55429M

M = $ thousand   MM = $ million
See Pages 11 through 18 for Explanation of Ratios and Data

Current Data Sorted By Assets   Comparative Historical Data

0-500M	500M-2MM	2-10MM	10-50MM	50-100MM	100-250MM	Type of Statement	4/1/98-3/31/99 ALL	4/1/99-3/31/00 ALL
	4	20	7	1	2	Unqualified	21	21
12	64	52	5			Reviewed	110	114
9	17	8	1			Compiled	34	44
12	10		2		1	Tax Returns	17	26
15	18	17	5			Other	39	39
55 (4/1-9/30/02)			227 (10/1/02-3/31/03)					
48	113	97	20	1	3	**NUMBER OF STATEMENTS**	221	244
%	%	%	%	%	%	**ASSETS**	%	%
20.2	10.4	10.9	13.7			Cash & Equivalents	10.8	11.1
33.8	46.6	51.6	46.2			Trade Receivables (net)	45.4	43.6
6.7	8.6	6.9	6.7			Inventory	7.6	9.1
4.2	8.3	9.5	11.4			All Other Current	7.1	7.1
64.9	73.9	78.9	78.0			Total Current	70.9	70.9
25.5	17.6	14.5	12.5			Fixed Assets (net)	21.5	20.8
2.2	1.8	1.3	2.7			Intangibles (net)	1.6	2.1
7.4	6.7	5.3	6.8			All Other Non-Current	6.0	6.2
100.0	100.0	100.0	100.0			Total	100.0	100.0
						LIABILITIES		
11.3	14.1	13.1	6.9			Notes Payable-Short Term	10.0	10.7
2.9	4.8	2.6	2.5			Cur. Mat.-L/T/D	3.1	3.9
16.2	20.9	25.2	15.1			Trade Payables	19.4	22.3
.1	.9	.8	.1			Income Taxes Payable	1.7	.5
14.2	12.1	16.5	17.5			All Other Current	13.1	12.7
44.7	52.8	58.2	42.0			Total Current	47.3	50.1
14.6	7.2	5.2	7.1			Long Term Debt	9.2	10.5
.1	.4	.2	.1			Deferred Taxes	.7	.8
5.8	1.6	1.4	1.5			All Other Non-Current	2.5	1.2
34.7	37.9	35.0	49.3			Net Worth	40.2	37.4
100.0	100.0	100.0	100.0			Total Liabilities & Net Worth	100.0	100.0
						INCOME DATA		
100.0	100.0	100.0	100.0			Net Sales	100.0	100.0
35.4	25.5	22.6	29.1			Gross Profit	27.0	26.6
33.1	23.9	20.1	24.4			Operating Expenses	23.6	23.1
2.3	1.6	2.5	4.7			Operating Profit	3.4	3.5
.3	−.1	.4	.4			All Other Expenses (net)	.3	.2
2.0	1.7	2.1	4.3			Profit Before Taxes	3.1	3.3
						RATIOS		
2.8	1.9	1.8	2.7				2.1	2.1
1.4	1.4	1.4	1.9			Current	1.5	1.5
1.0	1.1	1.1	1.4				1.2	1.2
2.5	1.5	1.6	2.0				1.7	1.6
1.1	1.1	1.1	1.4			Quick	1.2 (243)	1.1
.7	.8	.9	1.0				.9	.8
10 37.2	36 10.3	48 7.5	42 8.6				36 10.0	32 11.4
27 13.5	50 7.3	66 5.5	75 4.9			Sales/Receivables	55 6.6	48 7.6
44 8.4	72 5.1	84 4.4	89 4.1				74 5.0	69 5.3
0 UND	2 221.3	2 227.5	2 150.3				2 194.6	1 264.2
1 250.2	7 54.2	6 60.3	9 41.4			Cost of Sales/Inventory	8 46.5	8 46.2
10 35.0	19 19.6	12 31.3	22 16.7				20 18.4	20 18.4
1 432.1	16 23.3	25 14.5	10 34.9				14 26.1	16 23.0
12 31.4	27 13.3	38 9.6	27 13.8			Cost of Sales/Payables	26 13.8	30 12.2
29 12.6	43 8.4	50 7.4	38 9.7				40 9.2	48 7.5
9.7	8.9	7.0	4.4				8.0	7.9
40.3	15.7	11.5	8.4			Sales/Working Capital	14.1	13.4
620.5	100.7	35.0	12.4				31.9	38.6
18.1	11.7	13.6	70.1				12.0	13.4
(35) 4.2	(103) 4.0	(87) 3.6	(18) 15.1			EBIT/Interest	(195) 4.2	(220) 4.6
.0	−.1	1.3	3.1				1.6	1.7
	5.9	4.3					5.4	7.2
	(36) 3.2	(34) 2.1				Net Profit + Depr., Dep., Amort./Cur. Mat. L /T/D	(65) 2.8	(71) 3.0
	.8	.4					1.8	1.6
.1	.2	.2	.1				.2	.2
.6	.5	.3	.3			Fixed/Worth	.5	.5
8.8	.9	.6	.7				.9	.9
.5	.8	1.0	.8				.9	.9
1.1	1.5	2.0	1.1			Debt/Worth	1.5	1.6
22.0	3.3	3.4	2.8				3.5	3.2
66.3	41.2	39.1	45.0				41.4	50.3
(37) 26.0	(105) 17.3	(93) 13.8	16.7			% Profit Before Taxes/Tangible Net Worth	(211) 17.2	(226) 20.5
.9	−.4	.7	9.1				6.6	5.7
24.1	14.9	11.4	16.9				16.9	19.5
9.0	5.7	4.2	8.4			% Profit Before Taxes/Total Assets	6.6	6.6
−5.2	−2.2	.2	3.8				2.0	1.6
60.6	37.1	41.6	91.7				29.5	40.0
33.6	20.4	25.3	20.6			Sales/Net Fixed Assets	17.9	18.7
15.3	12.4	14.6	13.5				11.2	11.8
6.6	3.9	3.3	3.3				3.8	4.2
5.1	3.1	2.8	2.5			Sales/Total Assets	3.0	3.1
3.5	2.7	2.4	1.8				2.4	2.4
1.0	1.1	.9	.5				.9	.9
(33) 1.6	(105) 1.7	(90) 1.3	(17) 1.5			% Depr., Dep., Amort./Sales	(201) 1.5	(219) 1.5
2.9	2.6	1.9	1.7				2.4	2.3
3.7	2.5	1.7					2.0	2.1
(29) 6.4	(70) 4.2	(44) 3.3				% Officers', Directors', Owners' Comp/Sales	(112) 4.1	(129) 3.5
11.9	7.1	5.7					7.5	6.6
67050M	450444M	1287068M	1812605M	165402M	2399721M	Net Sales ($)	2655077M	3001013M
13197M	134575M	418216M	363876M	72749M	448194M	Total Assets ($)	1024917M	1162634M

M = $ thousand   MM = $ million
See Pages 11 through 18 for Explanation of Ratios and Data

Comparative Historical Data · Current Data Sorted By Sales

Type of Statement	4/1/00-3/31/01 ALL	4/1/01-3/31/02 ALL	4/1/02-3/31/03 ALL	0-1MM	1-3MM	3-5MM	5-10MM	10-25MM	25MM & OVER
Unqualified	19	27	34		1	4	7	12	10
Reviewed	95	104	133	4	26	31	34	30	8
Compiled	42	48	35	2	13	8	8	4	
Tax Returns	22	13	25	6	7	8	1		3
Other	44	50	55	6	15	7	13	10	4
	ALL	ALL	ALL	55 (4/1-9/30/02)			227 (10/1/02-3/31/03)		
NUMBER OF STATEMENTS	222	242	282	18	62	58	63	56	25
ASSETS	%	%	%	%	%	%	%	%	%
Cash & Equivalents	11.7	10.6	12.4	20.6	13.9	14.3	9.2	10.2	11.7
Trade Receivables (net)	43.1	46.1	45.8	26.2	42.7	43.2	48.1	55.5	46.0
Inventory	8.2	6.8	7.6	2.1	9.2	6.8	9.7	6.7	6.1
All Other Current	7.0	7.9	8.2	3.3	5.7	8.0	10.7	8.9	10.5
Total Current	70.0	71.4	74.0	52.2	71.4	72.4	77.8	81.3	74.3
Fixed Assets (net)	20.1	18.1	17.5	33.4	19.3	19.0	16.2	13.0	11.1
Intangibles (net)	2.2	3.0	2.0	3.6	2.4	.8	1.8	1.3	5.3
All Other Non-Current	7.6	7.5	6.5	10.7	6.9	7.8	4.2	4.4	9.3
Total	100.0	100.0	100.0	100.0	100.0	100.0	100.0	100.0	100.0
LIABILITIES									
Notes Payable-Short Term	11.7	9.7	12.6	14.2	13.6	11.1	13.1	12.3	12.4
Cur. Mat.-L/T/D	3.3	3.8	3.5	2.4	4.3	4.8	3.4	2.5	2.0
Trade Payables	20.9	20.2	21.1	13.6	19.0	20.9	23.1	24.2	19.9
Income Taxes Payable	.5	.5	.6	.1	.9	.5	1.0	.5	.1
All Other Current	12.9	14.4	14.3	10.4	13.0	13.6	10.5	18.0	23.8
Total Current	49.2	48.6	52.2	40.7	50.8	50.9	51.1	57.5	58.2
Long Term Debt	10.7	9.8	8.1	23.0	9.4	5.6	7.8	4.6	8.5
Deferred Taxes	1.0	.7	.3	.0	.1	.6	.1	.3	.2
All Other Non-Current	2.6	2.6	2.4	5.2	4.0	1.5	1.6	1.2	3.0
Net Worth	36.6	38.3	37.0	30.7	35.8	41.4	39.5	36.4	30.1
Total Liabilities & Net Worth	100.0	100.0	100.0	100.0	100.0	100.0	100.0	100.0	100.0
INCOME DATA									
Net Sales	100.0	100.0	100.0	100.0	100.0	100.0	100.0	100.0	100.0
Gross Profit	25.0	25.5	26.5	37.1	32.9	24.9	22.9	21.2	27.3
Operating Expenses	22.7	23.1	24.2	34.5	32.1	22.5	20.8	18.5	22.3
Operating Profit	2.3	2.5	2.3	2.6	.9	2.3	2.1	2.7	5.0
All Other Expenses (net)	.1	.3	.2	.5	.0	.0	.1	.4	.8
Profit Before Taxes	2.1	2.2	2.1	2.1	.9	2.4	1.9	2.3	4.2
RATIOS									
Current	2.0	2.2	2.0	3.2	2.2	2.0	2.4	1.7	2.3
	1.5	1.4	1.4	1.3	1.4	1.5	1.6	1.4	1.5
	1.1	1.1	1.1	.7	1.0	1.0	1.2	1.1	1.2
Quick	1.6	1.8	1.6	2.4	1.7	1.7	1.6	1.4	1.9
	1.1	1.2	1.1	1.2	1.1	1.1	1.1	1.1	1.4
	.8	.8	.9	.6	.7	.8	.9	.9	.9
Sales/Receivables	32 11.4	39 9.3	33 11.0	0 UND	29 12.4	31 11.8	38 9.7	51 7.1	36 10.3
	54 6.7	57 6.4	54 6.7	14 25.3	45 8.1	52 7.0	55 6.7	71 5.1	59 6.2
	73 5.0	81 4.5	78 4.7	51 7.2	67 5.5	75 4.8	79 4.6	87 4.2	84 4.3
Cost of Sales/Inventory	2 224.3	1 367.5	1 377.4	0 UND	1 305.8	0 UND	3 140.6	1 256.1	2 240.2
	7 54.9	6 60.6	6 61.2	0 UND	8 44.1	5 74.3	8 47.2	6 65.7	7 55.1
	15 24.2	13 28.8	16 23.5	10 37.9	20 18.3	13 27.8	16 22.5	11 33.9	16 22.3
Cost of Sales/Payables	17 21.6	16 22.4	16 23.5	0 UND	13 27.5	18 20.6	19 19.2	25 14.5	12 30.0
	30 12.1	29 12.8	28 12.9	10 38.4	24 15.1	30 12.0	27 13.4	38 9.7	28 13.1
	49 7.4	45 8.1	44 8.2	34 10.7	42 8.7	45 8.1	42 8.7	47 7.8	41 9.0
Sales/Working Capital	8.3	6.8	7.8	15.7	8.3	8.4	7.1	7.7	5.2
	13.4	13.0	13.9	149.1	21.7	15.3	11.5	12.8	10.9
	52.9	50.6	59.6	-12.7	374.3	183.3	31.2	25.9	37.4
EBIT/Interest	(208) 9.1	(216) 11.4	(247) 14.2	(12) 12.3	(54) 15.5	(50) 12.0	(59) 20.1	(49) 12.6	(23) 47.6
	3.1	4.0	3.8	2.0	2.8	5.0	3.6	4.9	8.1
	1.0	1.4	.7	-.8	-1.1	-.6	1.1	1.7	2.4
Net Profit + Depr., Dep., Amort./Cur. Mat. L/T/D	(66) 4.4	(61) 4.7	(81) 5.4		(11) 4.0	(19) 7.0	(18) 5.5	(22) 4.3	(10) 7.2
	2.1	2.1	2.3		2.4	3.7	2.5	1.9	1.9
	.6	.6	.8		-.1	.8	.7	-.2	1.1
Fixed/Worth	.2	.2	.2	.0	.2	.2	.2	.2	.1
	.5	.4	.4	1.3	.5	.4	.4	.3	.4
	1.1	1.1	.8	-1.6	1.9	.8	.7	.6	.8
Debt/Worth	1.0	.8	.8	.5	.6	.7	.7	1.2	.9
	1.8	1.7	1.6	1.9	1.7	1.3	1.6	2.0	2.0
	3.4	3.9	3.5	-5.7	6.9	2.5	3.6	3.3	4.0
% Profit Before Taxes/Tangible Net Worth	(203) 40.5	(219) 38.0	(257) 42.8	(12) 70.2	(55) 44.8	(54) 42.1	(59) 39.7	(55) 38.6	(22) 66.6
	17.9	17.7	17.3	23.2	17.3	19.6	18.1	13.2	19.6
	2.5	3.8	1.6	3.4	-16.7	-4.0	1.9	2.1	12.0
% Profit Before Taxes/Total Assets	13.1	15.0	14.7	21.5	14.5	17.3	13.4	11.0	21.1
	5.0	5.7	6.0	6.7	5.6	7.6	4.3	5.5	9.2
	.3	.8	-.6	-6.7	-7.0	-2.7	.4	.8	2.6
Sales/Net Fixed Assets	37.4	35.1	45.0	100.8	43.7	45.4	38.9	43.7	63.9
	19.3	20.1	23.6	24.0	21.3	17.9	23.4	27.2	28.4
	11.4	12.8	14.0	7.2	13.8	12.2	15.8	15.4	19.3
Sales/Total Assets	3.8	3.7	4.0	6.2	5.0	3.7	3.9	3.4	4.4
	2.9	2.9	3.1	4.5	3.4	3.0	3.1	2.9	2.9
	2.3	2.2	2.5	2.5	2.6	2.6	2.7	2.4	2.3
% Depr., Dep., Amort./Sales	(203) .8	(215) .9	(248) 1.0	(12) 1.0	(51) 1.2	(55) 1.1	(56) 1.0	(52) .8	(22) .5
	1.5	1.5	1.5	1.7	1.8	1.7	1.7	1.1	1.3
	2.4	2.4	2.3	3.4	2.9	2.7	2.2	1.7	1.7
% Officers', Directors', Owners' Comp/Sales	(113) 2.0	(112) 2.3	(151) 2.3	(12) 2.8	(34) 3.7	(39) 2.5	(32) 2.2	(25) 1.3	
	3.4	3.9	4.1	7.5	5.9	3.8	3.7	3.3	
	6.7	6.9	7.0	23.3	9.4	6.4	7.0	5.7	
Net Sales ($)	3647025M	3638337M	6182290M	11415M	120439M	226938M	437723M	857192M	4528583M
Total Assets ($)	1544392M	1775353M	1450807M	3571M	38125M	76710M	143148M	316576M	872677M

Current Data Sorted By Assets   **Comparative Historical Data**

						Type of Statement		
2	16	70	40	4	1	Unqualified	118	114
12	128	138	6		1	Reviewed	227	242
27	45	14	2			Compiled	120	107
25	22	10	1	1	1	Tax Returns	36	46
21	22	35	16	2	4	Other	113	89

0-500M	500M-2MM	2-10MM	10-50MM	50-100MM	100-250MM		4/1/98-3/31/99 ALL	4/1/99-3/31/00 ALL
	168 (4/1-9/30/02)		498 (10/1/02-3/31/03)					
87	233	267	65	7	7	NUMBER OF STATEMENTS	614	598
%	%	%	%	%	%	ASSETS	%	%
14.3	12.3	13.0	8.9			Cash & Equivalents	11.6	12.4
36.4	49.3	53.6	56.0			Trade Receivables (net)	51.5	51.8
8.5	6.2	3.7	3.6			Inventory	6.2	6.5
4.5	8.9	10.2	11.3			All Other Current	7.8	7.7
63.7	76.7	80.5	79.8			Total Current	77.1	78.4
26.8	18.1	13.1	11.7			Fixed Assets (net)	16.7	15.9
1.8	.8	1.0	3.8			Intangibles (net)	1.6	1.3
7.7	4.4	5.4	4.7			All Other Non-Current	4.6	4.3
100.0	100.0	100.0	100.0			Total	100.0	100.0
						LIABILITIES		
22.6	12.5	10.3	7.4			Notes Payable-Short Term	9.9	10.6
9.2	3.5	3.6	2.1			Cur. Mat.-L/T/D	2.9	2.8
19.5	18.2	19.1	17.1			Trade Payables	18.7	20.8
.4	1.2	1.4	.2			Income Taxes Payable	1.7	.9
13.6	12.9	16.9	22.3			All Other Current	16.5	16.4
65.4	48.2	51.2	49.2			Total Current	49.6	51.4
26.8	8.7	5.5	7.6			Long Term Debt	7.9	7.6
.0	.5	.6	.4			Deferred Taxes	1.0	.8
6.6	2.1	2.0	3.5			All Other Non-Current	2.6	2.1
1.2	40.6	40.7	39.3			Net Worth	38.8	38.0
100.0	100.0	100.0	100.0			Total Liabilities & Net Worth	100.0	100.0
						INCOME DATA		
100.0	100.0	100.0	100.0			Net Sales	100.0	100.0
39.1	26.4	20.3	17.8			Gross Profit	25.3	25.7
38.7	24.2	17.3	15.1			Operating Expenses	21.3	21.8
.5	2.1	3.0	2.7			Operating Profit	4.0	3.9
1.0	.5	.3	.4			All Other Expenses (net)	.4	.4
−.5	1.6	2.7	2.3			Profit Before Taxes	3.7	3.5
						RATIOS		
2.2	2.3	2.3	2.1				2.2	2.2
1.4	1.6	1.5	1.5			Current	1.6	1.5
.9	1.2	1.2	1.3				1.3	1.2
2.1	2.0	1.9	1.6				1.9	1.8
1.0	1.3	1.3	1.3			Quick	(613) 1.3	1.3
.6	.9	1.0	1.0				1.0	1.0
5 68.8	45 8.2	53 6.9	56 6.5				44 8.4	46 8.0
36 10.0	61 6.0	71 5.1	77 4.7			Sales/Receivables	62 5.9	64 5.7
52 7.0	80 4.6	86 4.2	91 4.0				80 4.5	82 4.5
0 UND	0 UND	0 UND	0 UND				0 UND	0 UND
3 117.1	3 105.6	2 206.1	2 202.8			Cost of Sales/Inventory	3 119.8	3 113.5
25 14.8	14 26.1	7 50.1	5 67.1				12 29.6	15 24.3
4 89.0	14 26.0	17 21.4	18 19.9				15 25.1	18 20.5
18 20.4	26 14.3	28 13.0	25 14.3			Cost of Sales/Payables	26 14.0	29 12.4
43 8.5	45 8.2	43 8.6	36 10.1				41 8.9	46 7.9
10.8	6.4	5.9	5.8				6.6	6.7
27.3	10.3	9.3	10.6			Sales/Working Capital	11.2	10.9
−70.6	23.2	18.4	17.0				21.4	20.9
7.7	13.4	20.5	19.7				18.0	18.3
(77) 2.7	(205) 2.8	(231) 5.0	(56) 4.8			EBIT/Interest	(547) 6.5	(522) 6.3
.5	−.8	1.8	1.8				2.1	2.3
4.1	4.4	6.4	19.0			Net Profit + Depr., Dep.,	9.2	7.6
(12) 1.3	(70) 1.8	(89) 2.5	(19) 3.4			Amort./Cur. Mat. L /T/D	(186) 4.2	(190) 4.0
.6	.2	.8	.7				1.7	2.0
.4	.2	.1	.1				.2	.1
1.0	.4	.3	.3			Fixed/Worth	.3	.3
UND	.9	.6	.5				.8	.7
1.1	.7	.8	.9				.8	.8
2.9	1.4	1.5	1.5			Debt/Worth	1.5	1.6
−12.5	3.3	3.1	3.4				3.2	3.1
92.2	31.2	35.8	41.3			% Profit Before Taxes/Tangible	46.9	46.0
(64) 23.6	(221) 10.1	(261) 14.4	(61) 14.7			Net Worth	(573) 26.0	(561) 23.0
5.9	−2.1	3.2	4.1				9.6	8.5
16.8	12.0	13.0	10.7			% Profit Before Taxes/Total	19.2	17.7
5.4	4.4	4.8	5.1			Assets	8.7	8.0
−5.8	−2.6	1.3	1.0				3.0	2.8
50.5	38.0	57.0	60.9				48.2	47.7
18.5	22.1	28.7	29.1			Sales/Net Fixed Assets	25.4	25.6
10.6	12.1	15.8	18.7				15.1	15.4
5.7	3.7	3.3	3.3				3.9	3.7
4.0	2.9	2.8	2.7			Sales/Total Assets	3.1	3.1
3.1	2.3	2.3	2.4				2.5	2.4
1.1	.9	.6	.4				.6	.6
(73) 2.0	(219) 1.5	(249) 1.0	(59) .9			% Depr., Dep., Amort./Sales	(564) 1.1	(554) 1.1
3.3	2.3	1.7	1.4				1.8	1.8
5.3	3.0	1.5	1.4				2.4	2.3
(47) 8.0	(134) 5.0	(111) 2.8	(14) 3.8			% Officers', Directors',	(333) 4.7	(317) 4.3
13.2	8.5	5.4	7.6			Owners' Comp/Sales	8.3	7.2
100764M	816404M	3428890M	3949889M	1531826M	3630251M	Net Sales ($)	8560447M	9711587M
23573M	270396M	1230639M	1314440M	501045M	1041145M	Total Assets ($)	3275791M	3347558M

M = $ thousand   MM = $ million
See Pages 11 through 18 for Explanation of Ratios and Data

Comparative Historical Data / Current Data Sorted By Sales

H: 4/1/00-3/31/01 ALL	H: 4/1/01-3/31/02 ALL	H: 4/1/02-3/31/03 ALL	Type of Statement	0-1MM	1-3MM	3-5MM	5-10MM	10-25MM	25MM & OVER
105	95	133	Unqualified		10	8	15	49	51
212	209	285	Reviewed	13	49	51	92	67	13
132	136	88	Compiled	15	36	18	13	5	1
46	42	60	Tax Returns	10	24	9	10	3	4
121	141	100	Other	7	22	13	13	23	22
				168 (4/1-9/30/02)			498 (10/1/02-3/31/03)		
616	623	666	**NUMBER OF STATEMENTS**	45	141	99	143	147	91
%	%	%	**ASSETS**	%	%	%	%	%	%
11.4	12.7	12.4	Cash & Equivalents	17.4	13.7	11.7	13.1	12.1	8.4
51.1	49.4	49.9	Trade Receivables (net)	28.6	42.7	52.2	51.8	56.3	55.8
6.2	5.3	5.2	Inventory	8.2	7.6	5.5	4.2	3.5	3.9
8.1	9.2	9.2	All Other Current	6.2	7.0	8.5	10.4	9.9	11.6
76.9	76.7	76.7	Total Current	60.3	71.0	78.0	79.5	81.7	79.7
16.5	16.4	16.5	Fixed Assets (net)	28.8	21.8	17.1	14.6	12.2	11.7
1.5	1.4	1.5	Intangibles (net)	2.8	1.2	.6	1.1	1.3	3.3
5.1	5.5	5.3	All Other Non-Current	8.1	5.9	4.3	4.9	4.8	5.4
100.0	100.0	100.0	Total	100.0	100.0	100.0	100.0	100.0	100.0
			LIABILITIES						
11.7	10.8	12.4	Notes Payable-Short Term	29.8	13.0	12.9	11.1	9.5	9.0
2.8	3.2	4.1	Cur. Mat.-L/T/D	12.8	4.0	3.3	2.9	4.6	1.9
19.3	18.6	18.5	Trade Payables	18.8	16.8	18.4	19.5	20.0	17.3
.8	.8	1.1	Income Taxes Payable	.4	.8	1.5	1.1	1.3	.9
16.3	17.5	15.7	All Other Current	7.4	13.0	14.3	15.5	18.4	21.2
50.9	50.9	51.8	Total Current	69.1	47.7	50.5	50.1	53.6	50.4
8.3	8.1	9.8	Long Term Debt	27.1	15.2	8.1	5.4	6.5	6.9
.9	.7	.4	Deferred Taxes	.2	.4	.3	.8	.4	.3
3.0	2.1	2.8	All Other Non-Current	7.5	3.1	1.8	2.3	1.8	3.6
36.8	38.2	35.2	Net Worth	-3.9	33.7	39.3	41.3	37.7	38.8
100.0	100.0	100.0	Total Liabilities & Net Worth	100.0	100.0	100.0	100.0	100.0	100.0
			INCOME DATA						
100.0	100.0	100.0	Net Sales	100.0	100.0	100.0	100.0	100.0	100.0
25.5	24.8	24.7	Gross Profit	39.5	32.7	25.2	21.3	19.1	19.0
21.9	21.8	22.4	Operating Expenses	39.5	30.9	23.0	18.1	16.6	15.8
3.6	3.0	2.3	Operating Profit	.1	1.8	2.1	3.1	2.5	3.2
.4	.4	.5	All Other Expenses (net)	1.1	.7	.7	.2	.3	.8
3.1	2.5	1.8	Profit Before Taxes	-1.0	1.1	1.4	2.9	2.2	2.4
			RATIOS						
2.2	2.2	2.2	Current	3.6	2.7	2.1	2.3	2.2	2.0
1.5	1.5	1.6		1.5	1.6	1.5	1.6	1.5	1.5
1.2	1.2	1.2		.9	1.1	1.3	1.2	1.3	1.3
1.8	1.8	1.9	Quick	2.9	2.2	1.7	1.9	1.9	1.6
(615) 1.3	(622) 1.2	1.3		.9	1.2	1.3	1.4	1.3	1.3
.9	.9	.9		.3	.9	1.0	.9	1.0	1.0
44 8.4	44 8.3	46 8.0	Sales/Receivables	0 UND	36 10.0	44 8.2	48 7.6	55 6.6	53 6.9
64 5.7	61 6.0	63 5.8		37 10.0	52 7.0	63 5.8	65 5.6	72 5.1	72 5.1
81 4.5	78 4.7	83 4.4		70 5.2	74 4.9	85 4.3	84 4.4	86 4.2	84 4.3
0 UND	0 UND	0 UND	Cost of Sales/Inventory	0 UND	0 UND	0 UND	0 UND	0 UND	0 999.8
3 137.1	3 133.8	2 173.4		4 101.2	4 104.0	2 171.3	2 174.3	2 198.2	1 248.8
14 26.6	10 35.5	10 36.2		32 11.5	20 18.0	10 37.6	9 39.0	7 49.6	5 68.6
16 23.4	15 24.4	15 24.6	Cost of Sales/Payables	0 UND	12 30.1	14 25.7	15 23.9	18 20.6	18 20.8
27 13.8	25 14.3	26 14.3		19 18.8	25 14.5	26 14.3	27 13.5	27 13.3	25 14.5
43 8.4	40 9.0	43 8.5		57 6.5	46 8.0	44 8.4	45 8.0	41 9.0	35 10.3
6.7	7.0	6.6	Sales/Working Capital	8.9	6.3	7.1	6.0	6.0	7.0
12.1	11.4	10.8		20.4	10.7	12.3	9.0	10.4	11.5
25.2	26.7	23.9		-41.4	54.3	19.2	23.6	18.6	19.3
16.1	15.7	15.9	EBIT/Interest	5.5	13.4	11.0	19.6	23.9	19.7
(561) 5.2	(545) 5.2	(582) 3.9		(36) 1.6	(125) 2.7	(90) 2.9	(123) 4.6	(126) 5.2	(82) 5.4
1.7	1.4	1.0		-2.1	-.1	-1.3	1.7	1.6	1.9
7.6	7.7	6.1	Net Profit + Depr., Dep., Amort./Cur. Mat. L/T/D		5.9	3.8	7.3	5.1	9.8
(182) 3.2	(177) 3.1	(194) 2.2			(35) 1.7	(28) 1.8	(49) 2.8	(49) 2.0	(27) 3.4
1.5	1.1	.6			-1.3	.4	.7	.3	1.3
.2	.2	.2	Fixed/Worth	.3	.2	.2	.2	.1	.1
.4	.3	.3		1.1	.5	.4	.3	.3	.3
.7	.8	.9		UND	1.6	.8	.7	.6	.5
.8	.8	.8	Debt/Worth	.8	.7	.8	.8	.9	.9
1.6	1.5	1.6		2.9	1.5	1.8	1.3	1.7	1.6
3.2	3.5	3.5		-11.4	3.8	3.3	3.5	3.5	3.3
45.0	45.3	36.6	% Profit Before Taxes/Tangible Net Worth	85.4	33.3	29.4	37.6	35.8	42.8
(577) 20.5	(587) 17.4	(618) 14.1		(33) 19.7	(123) 12.0	(97) 9.7	(138) 12.3	(142) 14.3	(85) 17.0
6.3	4.7	2.3		3.7	.8	-8.0	3.8	2.8	5.5
14.7	16.0	12.4	% Profit Before Taxes/Total Assets	9.7	13.3	9.2	13.9	12.1	14.0
7.5	6.3	4.7		4.8	4.6	4.6	4.4	5.3	5.7
1.8	1.5	.5		-18.4	-1.7	-3.0	1.2	1.3	1.4
46.4	47.3	49.5	Sales/Net Fixed Assets	27.1	38.1	34.1	50.6	60.4	67.8
25.3	26.9	25.2		13.7	18.8	21.6	30.2	30.9	32.6
14.4	14.8	14.0		7.8	10.9	12.9	16.2	17.3	21.5
3.8	3.7	3.6	Sales/Total Assets	4.0	4.2	3.7	3.6	3.6	3.5
3.0	3.1	2.9		3.1	2.9	3.0	3.0	2.8	3.0
2.4	2.5	2.3		2.1	2.1	2.5	2.3	2.4	2.6
.5	.5	.7	% Depr., Dep., Amort./Sales	1.2	1.0	1.0	.6	.6	.4
(557) 1.1	(559) 1.0	(612) 1.2		(39) 2.4	(128) 1.8	(90) 1.5	(138) 1.1	(134) 1.0	(83) .8
1.9	1.8	2.1		3.5	2.9	2.1	1.9	1.5	1.4
2.4	2.5	2.5	% Officers', Directors', Owners' Comp/Sales	6.1	4.1	2.6	2.1	1.4	1.4
(329) 4.4	(309) 4.7	(309) 4.7		(25) 10.6	(75) 5.9	(55) 5.0	(79) 3.3	(54) 2.7	(21) 4.1
7.7	8.4	8.0		15.4	9.5	8.5	6.2	5.7	6.7
9687957M	10672797M	13458024M	Net Sales ($)	30590M	267821M	372203M	1033547M	2212084M	9541779M
3501170M	3944160M	4381238M	Total Assets ($)	12503M	102554M	129047M	390909M	815800M	2930425M

M = $ thousand   MM = $ million
See Pages 11 through 18 for Explanation of Ratios and Data

Current Data Sorted By Assets | | | | | | | **Comparative Historical Data**

0-500M	500M-2MM	2-10MM	10-50MM	50-100MM	100-250MM	Type of Statement	4/1/98-3/31/99 ALL	4/1/99-3/31/00 ALL
	15	72	36	4	1	Unqualified	135	126
11	110	179	16			Reviewed	254	264
35	66	28	1			Compiled	123	117
54	33	5			1	Tax Returns	51	81
33	42	47	18	3	1	Other	107	111
207 (4/1-9/30/02)			604 (10/1/02-3/31/03)					
133	266	331	71	7	3	**NUMBER OF STATEMENTS**	670	699
%	%	%	%	%	%	**ASSETS**	%	%
12.8	12.0	12.6	13.3			Cash & Equivalents	11.7	11.5
33.7	48.4	54.4	53.0			Trade Receivables (net)	47.4	48.7
11.6	8.8	5.4	5.3			Inventory	8.7	8.4
2.8	5.7	8.3	9.1			All Other Current	6.4	6.2
61.0	75.0	80.7	80.6			Total Current	74.2	74.9
30.5	18.2	12.7	10.7			Fixed Assets (net)	19.2	18.4
1.5	1.6	1.0	1.2			Intangibles (net)	1.4	1.6
6.9	5.1	5.5	7.4			All Other Non-Current	5.3	5.1
100.0	100.0	100.0	100.0			Total	100.0	100.0
						LIABILITIES		
16.5	12.0	7.8	5.4			Notes Payable-Short Term	7.4	8.3
5.5	3.6	2.2	1.7			Cur. Mat.-L/T/D	3.4	3.4
23.7	21.0	25.7	25.8			Trade Payables	21.7	23.4
.4	.7	.8	.4			Income Taxes Payable	2.2	.7
13.5	13.3	18.3	22.3			All Other Current	14.4	16.1
59.6	50.6	54.8	55.6			Total Current	49.1	51.9
24.1	10.3	4.8	3.8			Long Term Debt	10.9	11.4
.1	.5	.4	.3			Deferred Taxes	.6	.8
5.2	2.6	2.5	2.6			All Other Non-Current	2.5	2.3
10.9	36.0	37.5	37.7			Net Worth	36.9	33.6
100.0	100.0	100.0	100.0			Total Liabilities & Net Worth	100.0	100.0
						INCOME DATA		
100.0	100.0	100.0	100.0			Net Sales	100.0	100.0
41.1	27.2	20.3	16.3			Gross Profit	26.2	26.2
39.8	25.0	17.9	12.7			Operating Expenses	22.6	23.0
1.3	2.2	2.4	3.6			Operating Profit	3.6	3.1
.6	.4	.2	.2			All Other Expenses (net)	.3	.2
.7	1.8	2.2	3.4			Profit Before Taxes	3.3	2.9
						RATIOS		
2.4	2.3	1.9	1.8				2.1	1.9
1.3	1.4	1.4	1.5			Current	1.5	1.5
.7	1.1	1.2	1.2				1.2	1.2
1.7	1.9	1.6	1.6				1.8	1.7
1.0	1.2	1.2	1.2			Quick (669)	1.2	1.2
.5	.8	1.0	1.0				.9	.9
5 78.6	36 10.2	50 7.2	56 6.5				36 10.1	37 9.7
29 12.6	54 6.7	68 5.4	69 5.3			Sales/Receivables	54 6.8	60 6.1
48 7.5	75 4.8	85 4.3	85 4.3				74 4.9	79 4.6
0 UND	0 UND	0 999.8	0 999.8				1 294.6	1 549.0
6 59.7	6 56.3	3 109.4	2 170.8			Cost of Sales/Inventory	6 56.4	5 70.7
27 13.6	21 17.4	10 38.2	8 48.6				20 18.4	18 19.9
1 359.4	17 21.3	24 15.3	25 14.8				17 20.9	21 17.6
28 13.1	29 12.7	36 10.2	38 9.6			Cost of Sales/Payables	30 12.2	32 11.3
45 8.2	45 8.1	52 7.0	51 7.1				46 7.9	50 7.3
11.3	7.4	7.5	7.6				7.4	7.9
55.6	14.4	12.4	11.4			Sales/Working Capital	12.6	13.0
−24.7	42.8	24.8	23.0				30.1	32.5
8.0	10.2	24.1	79.4				17.8	14.8
(111) 2.2	(235) 3.4	(292) 6.2	(56) 10.4			EBIT/Interest (583)	5.3	(621) 4.8
−.2	1.1	2.2	3.4				2.0	1.8
5.1	4.8	6.6	22.2				6.0	6.9
(13) 2.5	(68) 1.7	(113) 2.4	(18) 2.7			Net Profit + Depr., Dep., Amort./Cur. Mat. L./T/D (225)	2.8	(236) 2.6
.6	.2	1.2	1.2				1.5	1.4
.4	.2	.1	.1				.2	.2
1.5	.5	.3	.3			Fixed/Worth	.4	.4
−5.4	1.4	.7	.5				.9	.9
1.2	.7	1.0	.9				.9	1.0
3.6	2.0	1.7	1.9			Debt/Worth	1.8	1.9
−14.8	4.3	3.5	3.1				3.3	3.9
(95) 90.9	(241) 37.3	(322) 32.5	(70) 41.0				(625) 46.1	(640) 44.2
16.0	13.7	15.5	21.2			% Profit Before Taxes/Tangible Net Worth	22.4	21.5
−3.7	2.5	5.3	7.5				7.7	7.3
18.7	10.9	10.6	14.9				17.6	15.5
4.3	4.4	5.1	7.8			% Profit Before Taxes/Total Assets	8.0	6.8
−6.9	.4	1.9	3.0				2.3	2.0
46.3	41.4	48.2	64.6				40.9	41.9
22.8	23.5	28.0	29.6			Sales/Net Fixed Assets	21.8	22.9
12.3	13.6	16.9	16.2				13.2	13.8
6.7	4.0	3.5	3.2				4.0	3.9
4.4	3.2	3.0	2.9			Sales/Total Assets	3.2	3.1
3.2	2.5	2.5	2.3				2.6	2.5
(112) 1.4	(242) .9	(304) .6	(65) .4				(607) .7	(641) .6
2.1	1.5	1.1	.7			% Depr., Dep., Amort./Sales	1.3	1.3
3.7	2.3	1.7	1.1				2.1	2.1
(93) 4.9	(166) 2.6	(162) 1.5	(19) 1.0				(364) 2.3	(366) 2.6
8.1	4.0	2.7	1.7			% Officers', Directors', Owners' Comp/Sales	4.4	4.4
12.1	6.5	4.7	6.5				7.6	7.3
155155M	1043147M	4363767M	3938129M	1200630M	1385862M	Net Sales ($)	9530116M	10590274M
33583M	314806M	1450810M	1377767M	515458M	374525M	Total Assets ($)	3478666M	3762028M

M = $ thousand   MM = $ million
See Pages 11 through 18 for Explanation of Ratios and Data

Comparative Historical Data / Current Data Sorted By Sales

4/1/00-3/31/01 ALL	4/1/01-3/31/02 ALL	4/1/02-3/31/03 ALL	Type of Statement	0-1MM	1-3MM	3-5MM	5-10MM	10-25MM	25MM & OVER
112	109	128	Unqualified		5	10	19	48	46
229	227	316	Reviewed	6	36	54	104	94	22
155	137	130	Compiled	18	45	32	25	8	2
71	42	93	Tax Returns	36	29	12	13	2	1
139	197	144	Other	12	34	17	30	26	25
				207 (4/1-9/30/02)			604 (10/1/02-3/31/03)		
706	712	811	NUMBER OF STATEMENTS	72	149	125	191	178	96
%	%	%	ASSETS	%	%	%	%	%	%
11.1	12.0	12.5	Cash & Equivalents	12.3	13.6	12.4	12.3	11.8	13.2
49.3	49.1	48.7	Trade Receivables (net)	29.9	41.3	49.1	53.7	54.1	54.3
8.5	7.9	7.6	Inventory	12.7	8.7	9.4	6.2	6.1	5.2
6.6	7.0	6.6	All Other Current	3.5	3.8	6.0	7.2	8.9	8.5
75.5	75.9	75.5	Total Current	58.5	67.3	76.9	79.4	80.9	81.1
17.8	16.9	17.3	Fixed Assets (net)	32.7	24.1	17.2	14.5	12.0	10.8
1.9	1.9	1.5	Intangibles (net)	1.8	2.2	1.2	.8	1.4	2.2
4.7	5.4	5.7	All Other Non-Current	6.7	6.5	4.6	5.4	5.7	5.9
100.0	100.0	100.0	Total	100.0	100.0	100.0	100.0	100.0	100.0
			LIABILITIES						
8.7	9.0	10.3	Notes Payable-Short Term	19.5	12.3	12.4	9.3	7.4	5.0
3.5	3.2	3.2	Cur. Mat.-L/T/D	5.4	4.4	3.1	3.0	2.2	1.9
23.1	22.8	23.7	Trade Payables	20.5	20.9	21.1	25.3	26.4	25.9
.7	.7	.7	Income Taxes Payable	.5	.3	1.2	.6	.9	.4
16.5	16.6	16.1	All Other Current	14.5	11.9	13.4	15.4	20.0	21.9
52.4	52.3	54.0	Total Current	60.3	49.9	51.1	53.7	56.8	55.1
8.9	9.2	9.7	Long Term Debt	26.2	16.7	8.3	6.5	4.9	4.2
.7	.6	.4	Deferred Taxes	.0	.4	.7	.3	.4	.2
2.3	3.1	3.0	All Other Non-Current	5.7	3.1	2.5	3.3	2.5	2.0
35.7	34.8	32.8	Net Worth	7.7	30.0	37.4	36.2	35.4	38.5
100.0	100.0	100.0	Total Liabilities & Net Worth	100.0	100.0	100.0	100.0	100.0	100.0
			INCOME DATA						
100.0	100.0	100.0	Net Sales	100.0	100.0	100.0	100.0	100.0	100.0
26.2	25.5	25.8	Gross Profit	43.2	34.8	25.2	22.3	19.8	17.4
22.8	22.6	23.5	Operating Expenses	43.1	32.4	22.4	20.4	16.9	14.3
3.3	3.0	2.3	Operating Profit	.1	2.4	2.8	1.8	2.9	3.1
.3	.4	.3	All Other Expenses (net)	.6	.5	.6	.1	.1	.2
3.1	2.6	2.0	Profit Before Taxes	−.5	1.9	2.2	1.7	2.7	3.0
			RATIOS						
2.0	2.0	2.1	Current	2.5	2.3	2.4	2.1	1.7	1.7
1.5	1.4	1.4		1.2	1.4	1.5	1.5	1.4	1.5
1.2	1.2	1.1		.7	1.0	1.1	1.2	1.2	1.2
1.6	1.7	1.7	Quick	1.7	1.9	2.1	1.8	1.5	1.6
(704) 1.2	1.2	1.2		.9	1.2	1.2	1.2	1.2	1.2
.9	.9	.9		.4	.8	.8	.9	.9	1.0
39 9.5	38 9.5	37 9.8	Sales/Receivables	5 78.9	26 13.9	38 9.6	47 7.8	45 8.1	56 6.5
58 6.3	59 6.2	58 6.3		33 11.0	46 7.9	57 6.4	65 5.6	63 5.8	69 5.3
80 4.5	78 4.7	78 4.7		52 7.0	69 5.3	76 4.8	83 4.4	82 4.4	78 4.7
0 999.8	0 741.1	0 UND	Cost of Sales/Inventory	0 UND	0 UND	0 999.8	0 999.8	0 999.8	0 999.8
5 76.9	4 96.1	4 87.6		9 41.8	6 60.9	6 62.5	4 102.8	4 87.9	2 168.8
16 22.7	15 23.8	15 24.5		42 8.6	22 16.3	18 20.4	12 30.2	10 35.5	9 42.6
18 19.8	18 19.7	20 18.6	Cost of Sales/Payables	1 464.7	15 23.9	17 21.5	20 17.8	24 15.3	23 15.9
31 11.9	32 11.5	32 11.4		28 13.1	28 13.1	28 12.8	36 10.0	36 10.2	36 10.1
48 7.7	48 7.6	48 7.6		48 7.6	46 8.0	42 8.7	52 7.0	50 7.3	49 7.4
7.8	7.5	7.9	Sales/Working Capital	8.7	8.7	6.6	7.3	8.4	8.9
13.4	13.1	13.7		109.6	16.5	12.1	12.8	13.6	11.3
33.8	32.0	39.6		−12.4	319.5	46.1	29.6	28.0	24.1
13.4	15.1	15.8	EBIT/Interest	10.7	6.4	11.3	15.6	25.3	34.5
(625) 5.1	(629) 4.2	(701) 4.7		(55) 1.5	(133) 2.6	(104) 3.3	(172) 4.7	(160) 7.1	(77) 10.8
1.8	1.7	1.4		−2.3	.2	.7	1.7	3.0	3.2
6.5	4.6	5.9	Net Profit + Depr., Dep., Amort./Cur. Mat. L/T/D		5.5	5.8	4.7	8.4	14.4
(222) 2.3	(201) 2.5	(217) 2.4		(28) 1.7	(35) 2.1	(61) 2.1	(64) 3.4	(25) 2.3	
1.2	1.4	.9		.4	.3	.6	1.5	1.0	
.2	.2	.2	Fixed/Worth	.3	.3	.2	.2	.1	.1
.4	.4	.4		1.6	.7	.4	.4	.3	.3
.9	.9	1.0		−2.0	2.2	1.4	.8	.7	.5
.9	.9	.9	Debt/Worth	1.3	.8	.7	.8	1.1	1.0
1.8	1.9	1.9		3.6	2.1	1.7	1.8	1.9	1.8
3.7	4.0	4.2		−6.7	5.5	4.2	4.0	3.6	3.2
44.7	42.4	37.3	% Profit Before Taxes/Tangible Net Worth	84.6	39.8	47.9	27.7	36.3	40.6
(645) 21.7	(656) 18.7	(737) 15.9		(47) 22.5	(131) 11.8	(113) 11.3	(179) 14.3	(172) 18.8	(95) 21.7
5.8	5.2	−4.0		−12.6	.7	1.2	3.5	7.5	6.7
16.6	15.1	11.9	% Profit Before Taxes/Total Assets	20.5	11.4	13.4	10.6	12.6	14.9
6.9	6.1	4.8		2.2	4.8	4.3	4.2	5.9	6.6
1.8	1.3	.8		−12.1	−1.6	−.6	1.1	2.4	2.3
45.8	47.2	46.5	Sales/Net Fixed Assets	38.3	41.3	43.6	42.7	56.5	67.2
25.0	24.3	26.4		18.8	21.3	27.2	26.5	29.0	39.4
13.9	14.6	15.0		10.0	10.6	15.5	15.0	17.9	17.8
3.9	3.9	4.0	Sales/Total Assets	6.5	4.5	3.9	3.8	3.8	3.5
3.1	3.2	3.1		4.2	3.3	3.2	3.1	3.1	3.0
2.5	2.5	2.6		2.3	2.5	2.5	2.5	2.7	2.6
.6	.6	.7	% Depr., Dep., Amort./Sales	1.6	1.2	1.0	.7	.6	.4
(627) 1.1	(644) 1.2	(732) 1.3		(61) 2.6	(130) 1.9	(113) 1.5	(176) 1.3	(168) 1.0	(84) .7
1.9	2.0	2.1		4.1	3.4	2.3	1.9	1.4	1.1
2.6	2.2	2.2	% Officers', Directors', Owners' Comp/Sales	1.6	3.1	2.6	1.9	1.2	1.0
(367) 4.5	(362) 4.2	(441) 3.9		(48) 10.8	(93) 5.7	(84) 3.8	(102) 3.0	(92) 2.6	(22) 1.7
7.8	7.5	7.4		14.8	8.3	6.7	4.8	4.6	4.9
12159409M	12167621M	12086690M	Net Sales ($)	44375M	289215M	490439M	1402155M	2781806M	7078700M
3910758M	3820718M	4066949M	Total Assets ($)	14997M	93595M	170807M	479546M	944226M	2363778M

M = $ thousand   MM = $ million
See Pages 11 through 18 for Explanation of Ratios and Data

Current Data Sorted By Assets   Comparative Historical Data

							Type of Statement		
	4	2	3				Unqualified	9	8
3	11	11					Reviewed	21	19
1	7	3	1				Compiled	15	10
1	3						Tax Returns	4	2
	4	4	3	1	1		Other	9	11
	12 (4/1-9/30/02)			51 (10/1/02-3/31/03)				4/1/98-3/31/99	4/1/99-3/31/00
0-500M	500M-2MM	2-10MM	10-50MM	50-100MM	100-250MM			ALL	ALL
5	29	20	7	1	1		NUMBER OF STATEMENTS	58	50
%	%	%	%	%	%		ASSETS	%	%
	12.6	10.7					Cash & Equivalents	7.3	9.4
	45.6	47.9					Trade Receivables (net)	41.8	45.3
	8.8	7.1					Inventory	8.2	6.4
	7.0	12.3					All Other Current	8.5	8.8
	74.1	78.0					Total Current	65.8	69.8
	20.6	15.6					Fixed Assets (net)	25.9	23.0
	1.1	1.2					Intangibles (net)	1.1	2.9
	4.2	5.3					All Other Non-Current	7.3	4.3
	100.0	100.0					Total	100.0	100.0
							LIABILITIES		
	11.1	15.5					Notes Payable-Short Term	7.6	6.8
	3.5	3.0					Cur. Mat.-L/T/D	4.2	2.9
	17.3	13.2					Trade Payables	17.1	19.4
	.2	.3					Income Taxes Payable	1.7	.3
	13.5	19.4					All Other Current	17.6	14.4
	45.5	51.3					Total Current	48.1	43.7
	11.0	5.4					Long Term Debt	14.3	15.0
	.2	.6					Deferred Taxes	.8	.6
	2.2	1.7					All Other Non-Current	2.5	2.9
	41.0	40.9					Net Worth	34.2	37.8
	100.0	100.0					Total Liabilities & Net Worth	100.0	100.0
							INCOME DATA		
	100.0	100.0					Net Sales	100.0	100.0
	30.3	21.8					Gross Profit	26.5	29.2
	29.6	20.7					Operating Expenses	22.2	25.7
	.8	1.0					Operating Profit	4.4	3.5
	-.1	.2					All Other Expenses (net)	.8	.8
	.9	.8					Profit Before Taxes	3.6	2.8
							RATIOS		
	2.5	2.1						2.3	2.3
	1.6	1.4					Current	1.4	1.6
	1.3	1.2						1.1	1.2
	1.8	1.8						1.7	1.7
	1.3	1.1					Quick	1.1	1.3
	1.0	.8						.8	.9
41 8.9	52 7.0							39 9.4	43 8.5
61 6.0	73 5.0						Sales/Receivables	53 6.8	55 6.7
83 4.4	91 4.0							72 5.1	74 5.0
0 UND	0 UND							0 UND	0 UND
5 78.4	6 60.4						Cost of Sales/Inventory	2 149.1	7 51.3
42 8.7	28 13.0							21 17.2	19 19.7
14 25.2	9 42.1							16 23.0	17 22.0
23 15.5	22 16.8						Cost of Sales/Payables	26 14.3	27 13.7
58 6.3	35 10.3							40 9.1	43 8.4
	6.0	6.1						7.2	7.3
	11.0	8.6					Sales/Working Capital	13.7	10.5
	22.2	20.8						112.6	23.2
	19.2	9.3						9.9	11.6
(26)	2.6 (19)	4.2					EBIT/Interest	(51) 3.9	(45) 4.6
	-1.0	.2						1.8	1.3
	4.8						Net Profit + Depr., Dep.,	4.8	8.6
(21)	2.4 (20)						Amort./Cur. Mat. L /T/D	(21) 2.4	(20) 3.1
	1.3							1.3	1.6
	.2	.2						.2	.3
	.3	.4					Fixed/Worth	.6	.6
	1.1	.6						1.7	1.3
	.7	.9						.9	1.0
	1.4	1.7					Debt/Worth	2.0	1.6
	2.4	3.1						4.5	3.8
	22.0	33.7						42.2	56.3
(27)	10.6	4.5					% Profit Before Taxes/Tangible Net Worth	(53) 21.5	(46) 20.1
	-5.1	-5.8						8.0	3.3
	13.8	8.9						13.5	16.5
	3.6	1.9					% Profit Before Taxes/Total Assets	7.2	8.5
	-3.5	-2.9						1.9	1.3
	43.6	31.2						40.1	33.2
	16.1	23.7					Sales/Net Fixed Assets	15.7	17.9
	8.1	13.0						7.4	7.2
	3.6	3.0						3.7	3.5
	2.9	2.4					Sales/Total Assets	3.0	2.9
	2.3	1.9						2.0	2.0
	.8	1.1						.9	.8
(28)	1.4 (19)	1.7					% Depr., Dep., Amort./Sales	(48) 1.5	(47) 1.7
	4.1	2.2						3.3	3.3
	3.8							1.6	1.7
(15)	6.0						% Officers', Directors', Owners' Comp/Sales	(28) 3.3	(21) 3.3
	7.3							6.8	8.6
5227M	103435M	208783M	236476M	117383M	3291280M		Net Sales ($)	1424943M	377822M
1454M	36104M	91515M	165276M	61499M	211132M		Total Assets ($)	497676M	154585M

© RMA 2003

M = $ thousand   MM = $ million
See Pages 11 through 18 for Explanation of Ratios and Data

Comparative Historical Data

Current Data Sorted By Sales

					Type of Statement						
5		3		9	Unqualified		1	2	2	2	2
21		21		25	Reviewed	1	7	4	6	7	
14		15		12	Compiled		4	4	4		
1		2		5	Tax Returns	1	1	2			1
14		12		12	Other		2	2		6	2
4/1/00-		4/1/01-		4/1/02-			12 (4/1-9/30/02)			51 (10/1/02-3/31/03)	
3/31/01		3/31/02		3/31/03		0-1MM	1-3MM	3-5MM	5-10MM	10-25MM	25MM & OVER
ALL		ALL		ALL							
55		53		63	NUMBER OF STATEMENTS	2	15	14	12	15	5
%		%		%	ASSETS	%	%	%	%	%	%
13.2		13.2		13.9	Cash & Equivalents		11.2	16.6	14.7	7.0	
40.5		44.5		43.2	Trade Receivables (net)		47.9	38.4	48.0	46.8	
8.5		9.7		7.3	Inventory		5.4	11.9	4.5	7.2	
8.5		3.2		8.0	All Other Current		8.0	8.2	6.9	10.9	
70.7		70.6		72.3	Total Current		72.5	75.2	74.1	71.9	
21.5		22.4		20.4	Fixed Assets (net)		22.8	17.7	12.0	22.7	
2.4		2.9		1.0	Intangibles (net)		.9	1.4	.9	.8	
5.3		4.2		6.2	All Other Non-Current		3.7	5.8	13.0	4.6	
100.0		100.0		100.0	Total		100.0	100.0	100.0	100.0	
					LIABILITIES						
7.5		8.8		11.5	Notes Payable-Short Term		10.6	15.1	10.3	12.7	
3.2		4.0		3.1	Cur. Mat.-L/T/D		2.7	4.7	1.2	4.4	
14.5		20.2		15.4	Trade Payables		17.6	15.6	12.5	15.8	
.5		.8		.4	Income Taxes Payable		.1	.1	.6	.2	
13.1		13.3		15.7	All Other Current		9.0	14.4	26.2	17.1	
38.7		47.2		46.0	Total Current		40.0	49.9	50.7	50.2	
11.6		12.5		11.8	Long Term Debt		12.4	9.1	3.5	8.9	
.9		.4		.6	Deferred Taxes		.1	.2	.7	.3	
4.4		2.7		1.8	All Other Non-Current		.9	3.7	1.3	1.7	
44.4		37.2		39.9	Net Worth		46.7	37.2	43.7	39.0	
100.0		100.0		100.0	Total Liabilities & Net Worth		100.0	100.0	100.0	100.0	
					INCOME DATA						
100.0		100.0		100.0	Net Sales		100.0	100.0	100.0	100.0	
29.3		30.8		28.3	Gross Profit		31.6	32.1	24.8	21.7	
25.2		27.7		27.3	Operating Expenses		32.0	31.7	23.7	18.8	
4.2		3.1		1.0	Operating Profit		−.3	.4	1.1	2.9	
.3		.6		.1	All Other Expenses (net)		.2	−.5	−.1	.8	
3.9		2.5		.9	Profit Before Taxes		−.5	.9	1.2	2.1	
					RATIOS						
3.3		2.1		2.5			2.7	2.0	2.1	2.6	
1.8		1.5		1.6	Current		1.7	1.5	1.6	1.3	
1.4		1.1		1.2			1.3	1.1	1.4	1.1	
2.3		1.9		1.8			2.2	1.4	1.8	1.8	
1.3		1.2		1.3	Quick		1.3	1.1	1.4	1.0	
.9		.9		.9			1.1	.8	1.1	.7	
38 9.5	44 8.3	44 8.3			Sales/Receivables	43 8.4	42 8.6	44 8.3	65 5.6		
57 6.4	56 6.5	71 5.1				78 4.7	50 7.4	66 5.5	75 4.9		
70 5.2	73 5.0	86 4.2				88 4.1	82 4.5	85 4.3	94 3.9		
0 UND	0 UND	0 UND			Cost of Sales/Inventory	0 UND	0 UND	0 UND	2 223.8		
2 215.0	2 177.8	4 83.2				0 UND	30 12.3	1 355.6	6 56.9		
24 15.2	26 13.8	31 11.9				39 9.2	50 7.3	18 20.8	20 18.5		
13 27.9	17 21.7	12 29.5			Cost of Sales/Payables	17 21.0	13 27.2	5 73.0	15 24.0		
22 16.3	30 12.2	25 14.6				31 11.7	20 17.9	16 23.2	32 11.2		
36 10.0	50 7.3	46 7.9				57 6.4	61 5.9	34 10.8	38 9.5		
5.2	8.0	5.9			Sales/Working Capital	5.3	6.6	6.1	5.1		
8.2	13.5	11.0				9.4	8.9	9.8	17.5		
20.0	40.7	24.3				18.5	43.4	18.2	36.6		
16.5	10.4	12.4			EBIT/Interest	19.1	11.8	19.1	7.6		
(51) 5.1	(48) 4.2	(56) 3.7				(14) 5.2	(12) 2.6	(11) 4.9	4.2		
1.5	1.8	.3				−6.7	1.3	.2	.9		
5.9	8.3	3.7			Net Profit + Depr., Dep., Amort./Cur. Mat. L/T/D						
(14) 2.6	(12) 2.6	(17) 1.4									
1.5	2.2	.8									
.2	.2	.2			Fixed/Worth	.2	.2	.2	.4		
.5	.6	.3				.3	.3	.2	.5		
.9	1.2	1.0				1.1	1.1	.5	1.1		
.6	1.0	.7			Debt/Worth	.5	1.0	.9	.7		
1.5	1.7	1.6				1.2	1.9	1.3	2.7		
2.8	4.0	3.2				2.0	2.7	1.9	3.8		
52.7	30.5	28.1			% Profit Before Taxes/Tangible Net Worth	26.1	28.5	12.2	37.4		
(53) 20.5	(47) 17.1	(59) 9.0				(14) 9.8	(13) 10.6	(11) 3.1	7.6		
7.4	4.9	−.8				−12.8	4.3	−7.4	−.6		
18.5	12.0	9.7			% Profit Before Taxes/Total Assets	15.9	8.4	5.3	15.3		
8.0	5.7	3.3				4.3	3.7	.8	2.6		
1.6	.9	−3.1				−6.5	.3	−3.0	−.3		
32.2	34.4	39.2			Sales/Net Fixed Assets	38.1	39.5	49.5	29.3		
17.2	15.4	20.6				16.1	28.2	25.9	14.9		
8.2	8.1	8.0				6.6	8.4	19.5	4.9		
3.5	3.6	3.3			Sales/Total Assets	3.6	3.6	3.4	3.0		
2.7	3.0	2.6				2.5	2.7	3.1	2.3		
2.2	2.2	1.9				2.2	2.0	2.0	1.4		
.9	.8	.9			% Depr., Dep., Amort./Sales	1.1	1.1	.7	1.2		
(51) 1.8	(48) 1.7	(60) 1.7				(14) 1.3	2.3	1.2	(14) 2.0		
3.4	3.5	4.1				4.1	4.3	1.9	6.3		
2.6	2.7	2.8			% Officers', Directors', Owners' Comp/Sales						
(24) 5.3	(24) 4.9	(32) 4.6									
8.6	10.4	7.3									
474661M	712359M	3962584M			Net Sales ($)	685M	32165M	53599M	81448M	219508M	3575179M
223555M	332733M	566980M			Total Assets ($)	301M	12477M	24130M	47907M	114074M	368091M

M = $ thousand   MM = $ million
See Pages 11 through 18 for Explanation of Ratios and Data

Current Data Sorted By Assets | Comparative Historical Data

0-500M	500M-2MM	2-10MM	10-50MM	50-100MM	100-250MM	Type of Statement	4/1/98-3/31/99 ALL	4/1/99-3/31/00 ALL
	5	11	14	5	1	Unqualified	28	29
3	36	46	6		1	Reviewed	93	99
8	17	13	1		1	Compiled	33	48
10	9	5	5		1	Tax Returns	9	15
5	8	19	5		1	Other	30	42
50 (4/1-9/30/02)			181 (10/1/02-3/31/03)					
26	75	94	26	6	4	**NUMBER OF STATEMENTS**	193	233
%	%	%	%	%	%	**ASSETS**	%	%
17.9	9.3	9.2	8.8			Cash & Equivalents	11.8	9.5
33.8	53.4	57.6	55.5			Trade Receivables (net)	53.0	56.4
7.7	6.2	5.3	4.3			Inventory	5.8	6.5
5.2	7.8	9.8	14.7			All Other Current	7.1	6.4
64.7	76.8	81.8	83.2			Total Current	77.7	78.9
15.9	16.0	10.6	7.3			Fixed Assets (net)	14.0	13.2
10.6	1.9	1.6	1.3			Intangibles (net)	1.6	1.9
8.8	5.3	5.9	8.1			All Other Non-Current	6.7	6.0
100.0	100.0	100.0	100.0			Total	100.0	100.0
						LIABILITIES		
15.0	16.3	11.3	9.5			Notes Payable-Short Term	8.4	11.1
1.9	3.1	2.1	1.5			Cur. Mat.-L/T/D	2.6	2.5
16.0	14.7	15.0	12.4			Trade Payables	16.3	17.0
.1	1.2	.8	.2			Income Taxes Payable	1.1	1.1
20.1	14.3	16.6	25.1			All Other Current	17.3	15.5
53.2	49.6	45.8	48.6			Total Current	45.7	47.3
21.6	7.3	4.1	11.3			Long Term Debt	8.5	7.7
.1	.9	.6	.1			Deferred Taxes	.9	.8
5.7	3.2	2.9	3.2			All Other Non-Current	2.4	2.6
19.5	39.0	46.6	36.8			Net Worth	42.4	41.5
100.0	100.0	100.0	100.0			Total Liabilities & Net Worth	100.0	100.0
						INCOME DATA		
100.0	100.0	100.0	100.0			Net Sales	100.0	100.0
36.3	25.6	19.1	18.3			Gross Profit	24.3	24.3
34.2	23.3	15.5	13.9			Operating Expenses	20.0	20.1
2.1	2.3	3.6	4.4			Operating Profit	4.2	4.2
.1	.0	.3	−.3			All Other Expenses (net)	.1	.3
2.1	2.2	3.3	4.7			Profit Before Taxes	4.1	3.9
						RATIOS		
2.7	2.2	2.7	2.3				2.5	2.4
1.8	1.6	1.8	1.7			Current	1.7	1.7
.7	1.2	1.3	1.4				1.3	1.3
2.7	1.8	2.3	1.8				2.1	2.0
1.3	1.3	1.5	1.4			Quick	1.5	1.4
.5	1.0	1.0	1.0				1.1	1.0
0 UND	39 9.5	51 7.1	61 6.0				45 8.1	44 8.2
35 10.3	60 6.1	68 5.3	77 4.8			Sales/Receivables	60 6.0	65 5.6
51 7.2	76 4.8	85 4.3	88 4.2				77 4.8	82 4.4
0 UND	0 UND	0 UND	0 UND				0 UND	0 UND
0 800.2	2 164.0	3 137.3	2 151.3			Cost of Sales/Inventory	4 95.9	3 106.7
21 17.3	13 27.8	10 36.5	9 39.9				13 29.0	14 25.5
0 UND	10 36.6	12 31.3	14 25.7				11 33.9	12 29.4
14 25.2	14 26.4	17 21.0	17 21.9			Cost of Sales/Payables	19 19.1	19 19.5
29 12.6	26 13.9	29 12.4	25 14.7				31 11.7	34 10.7
12.0	7.7	5.1	5.9				6.3	6.1
32.3	14.6	9.3	8.3			Sales/Working Capital	10.0	10.4
−54.0	36.0	17.3	12.6				16.8	20.7
15.1	11.3	21.5	34.1				20.0	24.6
(18) 2.7	(70) 3.1	(82) 6.6	(23) 5.2			EBIT/Interest	(172) 7.0	(207) 7.2
−7.6	1.3	2.2	2.6				2.2	2.2
	6.3	9.5					15.9	14.4
	(19) 2.2	(26) 3.7				Net Profit + Depr., Dep., Amort./Cur. Mat. L /T/D	(62) 4.4	(60) 5.1
	.0	2.0					1.6	2.5
.2	.1	.1	.1				.1	.1
.9	.4	.2	.1			Fixed/Worth	.2	.2
−.4	1.1	.4	.4				.5	.6
.9	.8	.6	.9				.8	.8
1.9	1.7	1.1	1.7			Debt/Worth	1.4	1.4
−3.2	3.4	2.7	2.5				2.5	2.6
105.0	44.3	35.7	42.2				52.2	52.4
(16) 28.1	(69) 16.0	(93) 16.7	(25) 19.8			% Profit Before Taxes/Tangible Net Worth	(184) 23.9	(222) 25.1
−5.8	2.8	6.6	7.2				8.7	7.5
55.7	15.2	16.9	20.7				21.6	22.4
10.9	4.7	6.8	8.4			% Profit Before Taxes/Total Assets	10.0	9.3
−5.2	.6	2.2	3.0				3.0	2.5
77.7	67.6	79.1	84.5				70.6	70.9
36.7	32.9	44.1	48.8			Sales/Net Fixed Assets	35.5	37.3
19.9	15.6	20.8	29.0				19.2	19.5
8.3	4.3	3.7	3.6				4.0	4.2
4.8	3.4	3.1	2.8			Sales/Total Assets	3.3	3.3
3.5	2.7	2.5	1.9				2.7	2.5
.7	.6	.4	.3				.5	.5
(18) 1.4	(68) 1.0	(89) .8	(24) .6			% Depr., Dep., Amort./Sales	(173) .8	(207) .8
2.0	1.8	1.1	1.0				1.4	1.5
3.0	3.3	1.9					2.6	2.2
(19) 5.2	(51) 5.6	(59) 3.3				% Officers', Directors', Owners' Comp/Sales	(104) 4.3	(121) 4.3
8.5	8.0	5.1					7.7	7.2
47695M	304939M	1222366M	1410229M	961626M	2855780M	Net Sales ($)	3000247M	3394624M
7864M	85891M	385417M	509930M	391665M	633774M	Total Assets ($)	982799M	1179433M

M = $ thousand   MM = $ million
See Pages 11 through 18 for Explanation of Ratios and Data

Comparative Historical Data | Current Data Sorted By Sales

Comparative Historical Data			Type of Statement	Current Data Sorted By Sales					
			Unqualified		3	1	3	7	22
22	27	36	Unqualified		3	1	3	7	22
71	71	92	Reviewed		13	20	27	22	10
48	49	40	Compiled	3	11	6	8	9	3
20	20	25	Tax Returns	2	10	5	2	5	1
49	46	38	Other	1	9	4	6	14	4
4/1/00-3/31/01 ALL	4/1/01-3/31/02 ALL	4/1/02-3/31/03 ALL		50 (4/1-9/30/02)		181 (10/1/02-3/31/03)			
				0-1MM	1-3MM	3-5MM	5-10MM	10-25MM	25MM & OVER
210	213	231	**NUMBER OF STATEMENTS**	6	46	36	46	57	40
%	%	%	**ASSETS**	%	%	%	%	%	%
11.5	10.1	10.3	Cash & Equivalents		12.0	11.8	9.0	9.0	9.8
54.2	53.2	52.7	Trade Receivables (net)		44.4	47.2	59.7	57.3	55.5
5.5	5.3	5.8	Inventory		9.9	5.6	3.7	4.9	4.3
7.2	8.5	9.1	All Other Current		5.0	9.3	10.6	9.3	12.7
78.4	77.1	77.9	Total Current		71.2	73.9	82.9	80.5	82.2
14.8	14.2	12.7	Fixed Assets (net)		17.4	18.1	9.7	11.1	8.1
1.3	1.6	3.2	Intangibles (net)		4.2	2.5	.9	2.4	4.2
5.6	7.0	6.1	All Other Non-Current		7.2	5.5	6.5	6.1	5.5
100.0	100.0	100.0	Total		100.0	100.0	100.0	100.0	100.0
			LIABILITIES						
14.1	12.6	12.8	Notes Payable-Short Term		20.3	12.5	12.3	11.2	7.8
2.1	2.3	2.4	Cur. Mat.-L/T/D		3.3	2.5	1.0	2.8	1.8
16.1	16.3	14.8	Trade Payables		14.2	15.7	14.1	15.7	15.3
.9	.5	.8	Income Taxes Payable		.2	2.0	1.0	.7	.4
16.7	16.8	17.3	All Other Current		18.2	11.4	15.6	17.1	24.1
49.8	48.5	48.1	Total Current		56.1	44.1	43.9	47.4	49.4
7.4	8.7	8.4	Long Term Debt		10.0	9.4	4.2	4.6	10.5
.6	.8	.6	Deferred Taxes		.8	.9	.5	.6	.0
2.0	2.9	3.4	All Other Non-Current		5.3	2.7	2.4	3.7	2.8
40.1	39.2	39.6	Net Worth		27.8	42.9	48.9	43.6	37.3
100.0	100.0	100.0	Total Liabilities & Net Worth		100.0	100.0	100.0	100.0	100.0
			INCOME DATA						
100.0	100.0	100.0	Net Sales		100.0	100.0	100.0	100.0	100.0
23.4	23.5	23.3	Gross Profit		31.4	24.2	22.7	18.2	18.6
19.1	19.7	20.2	Operating Expenses		30.5	21.1	19.2	14.6	15.0
4.3	3.8	3.1	Operating Profit		.9	3.1	3.4	3.7	3.7
.4	.4	.1	All Other Expenses (net)		.0	.0	.0	.4	.0
3.9	3.4	2.9	Profit Before Taxes		.9	3.1	3.4	3.2	3.6
			RATIOS						
2.5 / 1.6 / 1.3	2.4 / 1.6 / 1.2	2.5 / 1.7 / 1.2	Current		2.3 / 1.5 / 1.0	2.3 / 1.6 / 1.2	2.8 / 1.8 / 1.3	2.7 / 1.6 / 1.2	2.1 / 1.7 / 1.4
2.1 / 1.3 / 1.0	2.1 / 1.3 / 1.0	1.9 / 1.4 / 1.0	Quick		1.8 / 1.1 / .6	1.9 / 1.5 / 1.0	2.4 / 1.5 / 1.2	2.3 / 1.3 / 1.0	1.7 / 1.4 / 1.0
44 8.4 / 61 6.0 / 82 4.5	42 8.6 / 62 5.9 / 81 4.5	42 8.8 / 64 5.7 / 81 4.5	Sales/Receivables		35 10.4 / 55 6.7 / 75 4.9	33 11.1 / 46 7.9 / 73 5.0	52 7.0 / 67 5.5 / 96 3.8	49 7.4 / 65 5.6 / 81 4.5	52 7.1 / 70 5.2 / 82 4.5
0 UND / 2 178.0 / 9 39.9	0 UND / 1 253.3 / 10 37.9	0 UND / 2 147.0 / 12 31.4	Cost of Sales/Inventory		0 UND / 5 77.8 / 33 11.0	0 UND / 2 163.6 / 10 35.5	3 142.9 / — / 10 36.9	0 UND / 3 300.1 / 8 43.7	1 651.6 / 3 145.9 / 7 50.8
12 31.4 / 17 21.0 / 29 12.4	11 32.2 / 18 20.6 / 27 13.5	10 35.1 / 17 21.5 / 26 13.9	Cost of Sales/Payables		6 66.1 / 16 23.1 / 30 12.0	11 32.0 / 19 19.5 / 29 12.4	7 53.0 / 13 28.8 / 28 13.1	12 30.2 / 17 21.0 / 25 14.4	15 24.9 / 18 20.0 / 25 14.7
6.6 / 11.4 / 27.3	6.3 / 10.5 / 27.7	6.3 / 11.7 / 30.9	Sales/Working Capital		7.6 / 15.3 / NM	6.7 / 14.5 / 21.5	4.4 / 9.5 / 17.8	6.4 / 11.5 / 30.9	6.2 / 9.1 / 13.9
(186) 25.5 / 6.2 / 1.7	(192) 19.2 / 5.4 / 1.7	(203) 19.3 / 4.7 / 2.0	EBIT/Interest		(41) 8.9 / 2.1 / -3.8	(31) 19.3 / 6.0 / 2.3	(42) 24.1 / 6.2 / 2.4	(49) 16.6 / 4.4 / 1.8	(37) 89.3 / 9.2 / 4.3
(46) 14.1 / 3.5 / 1.1	(46) 12.3 / 4.4 / 1.7	(57) 8.5 / 2.6 / 1.1	Net Profit + Depr., Dep., Amort./Cur. Mat. L/T/D					(13) 8.2 / 2.6 / 1.3	(17) 8.8 / 2.6 / 1.8	(13) 15.4 / 2.6 / 1.0
.1 / .3 / .7	.1 / .3 / .7	.1 / .2 / .7	Fixed/Worth		.2 / .7 / 3.4	.2 / .4 / 1.0	.1 / .1 / .3	.1 / .2 / .6	.1 / .1 / .4
.7 / 1.4 / 3.3	.7 / 1.5 / 3.5	.8 / 1.5 / 3.5	Debt/Worth		.9 / 2.1 / 8.5	.8 / 1.6 / 2.7	.6 / 1.1 / 2.1	.7 / 1.3 / 3.7	.9 / 1.6 / 2.5
(200) 58.3 / 26.4 / 7.1	(194) 47.3 / 17.7 / 4.4	(211) 39.8 / 16.7 / 4.6	% Profit Before Taxes/Tangible Net Worth		(36) 51.1 / 3.7 / -10.3	(34) 40.8 / 17.5 / 4.0	34.6 / 14.8 / 4.9	(56) 36.6 / 21.7 / 6.8	(37) 42.2 / 19.1 / 9.4
22.8 / 9.2 / 2.2	17.7 / 7.4 / 1.5	16.8 / 6.5 / 1.7	% Profit Before Taxes/Total Assets		13.2 / 1.9 / -6.9	19.9 / 6.6 / 1.4	17.1 / 6.1 / 2.7	16.7 / 6.8 / 2.1	17.9 / 8.7 / 3.7
67.1 / 34.3 / 18.4	65.8 / 33.8 / 17.2	73.0 / 39.2 / 19.3	Sales/Net Fixed Assets		57.8 / 21.9 / 13.1	39.1 / 27.3 / 13.0	73.8 / 53.0 / 32.9	85.2 / 42.5 / 20.7	87.8 / 54.8 / 29.6
4.3 / 3.3 / 2.6	4.0 / 3.1 / 2.5	4.1 / 3.2 / 2.6	Sales/Total Assets		4.2 / 2.9 / 2.5	4.2 / 3.5 / 2.7	4.1 / 3.1 / 2.5	4.0 / 3.3 / 2.9	3.8 / 3.0 / 2.2
(183) .4 / .8 / 1.5	(190) .4 / .9 / 1.5	(207) .5 / .9 / 1.4	% Depr., Dep., Amort./Sales		(35) .9 / 1.4 / 2.6	(35) .8 / 1.2 / 1.8	(44) .4 / .8 / 1.0	(54) .3 / .7 / 1.1	(35) .3 / .6 / 1.0
(119) 2.2 / 4.6 / 7.2	(126) 2.3 / 4.1 / 7.3	(138) 2.4 / 4.1 / 6.7	% Officers', Directors', Owners' Comp/Sales		(28) 3.2 / 5.0 / 9.0	(30) 3.0 / 5.5 / 8.1	(27) 1.9 / 3.6 / 6.2	(38) 1.8 / 2.9 / 5.1	(11) 1.2 / 2.2 / 4.0
3435895M	3507584M	6802635M	Net Sales ($)	4366M	91305M	143148M	335524M	852855M	5375437M
1185333M	1198869M	2014541M	Total Assets ($)	1387M	34486M	44212M	106531M	276163M	1551762M

M = $ thousand   MM = $ million
See Pages 11 through 18 for Explanation of Ratios and Data

Current Data Sorted By Assets							Comparative Historical Data	
						Type of Statement		
	1	11	3			Unqualified	13	18
4	24	26				Reviewed	48	42
6	18	2				Compiled	28	30
20	1				1	Tax Returns	10	10
2	5	5	2			Other	13	21
	29 (4/1-9/30/02)		102 (10/1/02-3/31/03)				4/1/98-3/31/99	4/1/99-3/31/00
0-500M	500M-2MM	2-10MM	10-50MM	50-100MM	100-250MM		ALL	ALL
32	49	44	5		1	NUMBER OF STATEMENTS	112	121
%	%	%	%	%	%	**ASSETS**	%	%
21.1	8.2	11.3		DATA NOT AVAILABLE		Cash & Equivalents	8.7	12.9
23.6	50.6	47.6				Trade Receivables (net)	45.7	45.9
7.1	5.1	2.5				Inventory	2.5	2.8
3.2	5.8	9.7				All Other Current	9.0	8.0
55.0	69.7	71.1				Total Current	66.0	69.5
30.0	22.5	20.4				Fixed Assets (net)	23.5	22.4
2.3	1.5	1.7				Intangibles (net)	3.1	.8
12.7	6.3	6.8				All Other Non-Current	7.4	7.2
100.0	100.0	100.0				Total	100.0	100.0
						LIABILITIES		
13.9	8.8	13.8				Notes Payable-Short Term	11.7	13.9
5.3	3.9	3.7				Cur. Mat.-L/T/D	3.0	3.2
10.8	14.6	15.0				Trade Payables	12.8	14.1
.2	.1	1.1				Income Taxes Payable	3.0	1.7
12.5	17.8	14.0				All Other Current	13.4	12.4
42.8	45.1	47.6				Total Current	44.0	45.3
23.1	13.0	6.0				Long Term Debt	12.5	10.1
.0	.6	.3				Deferred Taxes	1.2	1.1
14.2	2.3	2.9				All Other Non-Current	2.4	1.9
19.9	39.0	43.2				Net Worth	39.8	41.6
100.0	100.0	100.0				Total Liabilities & Net Worth	100.0	100.0
						INCOME DATA		
100.0	100.0	100.0				Net Sales	100.0	100.0
44.4	28.8	21.0				Gross Profit	29.9	29.5
43.4	26.8	18.3				Operating Expenses	27.1	24.4
1.1	2.0	2.7				Operating Profit	2.8	5.0
.9	.5	1.2				All Other Expenses (net)	.3	.2
.2	1.5	1.5				Profit Before Taxes	2.5	4.8
						RATIOS		
3.2	3.2	2.3					2.2	2.5
1.3	1.7	1.6				Current	1.6	1.7
.8	1.1	1.2					1.1	1.3
2.8	2.5	2.0					2.1	2.2
1.0	1.4	1.4				Quick	1.2	1.4
.5	.9	1.0					.8	1.0
0 UND	**46** 8.0	**51** 7.2					**37** 9.8	**36** 10.1
16 22.6	**63** 5.8	**73** 5.0				Sales/Receivables	**61** 6.0	**62** 5.9
45 8.1	**79** 4.6	**102** 3.6					**85** 4.3	**85** 4.3
0 UND	**0** UND	**0** UND					**0** UND	**0** UND
0 UND	**0** UND	**2** 224.3				Cost of Sales/Inventory	**0** 999.8	**0** UND
11 31.9	**10** 35.1	**9** 38.8					**4** 97.0	**3** 129.7
0 UND	**8** 46.2	**16** 22.2					**5** 70.8	**9** 39.9
10 37.7	**17** 21.2	**24** 15.0				Cost of Sales/Payables	**20** 18.6	**21** 17.3
25 14.7	**34** 10.7	**39** 9.5					**36** 10.2	**40** 9.0
10.9	5.9	6.3					6.1	5.8
30.2	10.2	9.0				Sales/Working Capital	10.8	8.3
−201.0	65.2	18.5					79.7	20.2
10.0	14.4	9.1					9.5	15.2
(27) 1.8	(45) 4.5	(41) 4.5				EBIT/Interest	(101) 4.2	(104) 7.1
−6.0	2.0	1.3					1.4	1.5
	6.5	12.8					7.3	13.3
	(15) 1.8	(12) 3.8				Net Profit + Depr., Dep., Amort./Cur. Mat. L/T/D	(28) 3.1	(23) 6.1
	1.0	1.8					2.0	2.3
.3	.1	.2					.2	.2
1.1	.5	.4				Fixed/Worth	.4	.4
NM	1.1	.9					1.0	.8
.8	.5	.6					.7	.6
3.4	1.3	1.2				Debt/Worth	1.7	1.3
NM	3.7	2.6					3.5	2.6
84.4	22.4	25.7					46.6	44.9
(24) 13.9	(44) 9.0	(41) 9.1				% Profit Before Taxes/Tangible Net Worth	(101) 21.9	(109) 25.7
−72.2	1.7	3.4					2.6	5.0
38.8	10.7	11.2					18.8	23.4
4.4	4.3	4.6				% Profit Before Taxes/Total Assets	7.6	7.6
−14.6	−1.2	.9					.6	.3
41.7	34.8	31.3					36.9	38.2
22.9	16.0	15.3				Sales/Net Fixed Assets	17.8	18.8
10.4	8.8	8.4					7.7	10.9
12.3	3.9	3.0					4.2	3.9
4.3	3.0	2.5				Sales/Total Assets	2.8	2.6
2.2	2.2	1.7					1.9	2.0
1.2	1.0	.7					.8	.8
(27) 2.2	(44) 1.8	(42) 1.5				% Depr., Dep., Amort./Sales	(101) 1.6	(102) 1.5
3.4	3.3	2.5					3.0	3.2
5.1	1.9	1.8					2.6	2.3
(21) 7.5	(26) 5.4	(21) 3.6				% Officers', Directors', Owners' Comp/Sales	(69) 4.8	(63) 5.9
10.4	8.6	6.9					9.5	9.9
39143M	163359M	442297M	144512M		912523M	Net Sales ($)	766481M	634452M
7935M	55550M	175591M	72857M		110348M	Total Assets ($)	342898M	252683M

M = $ thousand MM = $ million

See Pages 11 through 18 for Explanation of Ratios and Data

Comparative Historical Data | Current Data Sorted By Sales

			Type of Statement						
17	11	15	Unqualified		1	1	5	7	1
37	44	54	Reviewed	3	12	11	20	8	
35	33	26	Compiled	5	12	6	2		1
15	14	22	Tax Returns	14	5		2		1
21	29	14	Other	1	3	5	1	2	2
4/1/00-3/31/01 ALL	4/1/01-3/31/02 ALL	4/1/02-3/31/03 ALL		29 (4/1-9/30/02)			102 (10/1/02-3/31/03)		
				0-1MM	1-3MM	3-5MM	5-10MM	10-25MM	25MM & OVER
125	131	131	NUMBER OF STATEMENTS	23	33	23	30	17	5
%	%	%	ASSETS	%	%	%	%	%	%
10.9	12.0	12.8	Cash & Equivalents	24.0	8.2	12.7	11.3	8.2	
45.1	45.4	42.5	Trade Receivables (net)	17.3	47.5	43.7	50.4	50.5	
4.0	3.3	4.6	Inventory	6.1	6.1	5.0	3.7	1.9	
5.6	7.2	6.8	All Other Current	3.5	5.6	4.6	7.7	12.1	
65.5	67.9	66.7	Total Current	50.9	67.3	66.0	73.1	72.8	
24.2	21.2	23.3	Fixed Assets (net)	33.0	21.4	26.6	18.8	19.7	
1.8	2.2	2.1	Intangibles (net)	2.3	1.2	2.0	2.1	3.5	
8.5	8.6	7.9	All Other Non-Current	13.8	10.1	5.4	6.0	4.0	
100.0	100.0	100.0	Total	100.0	100.0	100.0	100.0	100.0	
			LIABILITIES						
13.8	13.5	11.7	Notes Payable-Short Term	10.0	10.6	8.6	19.0	9.1	
3.8	3.5	4.1	Cur. Mat.-L/T/D	5.8	4.2	4.2	2.4	4.8	
14.3	13.3	13.7	Trade Payables	4.9	14.5	12.3	20.9	12.4	
.7	.7	.5	Income Taxes Payable	.2	.1	.5	1.2	.3	
14.2	15.0	14.9	All Other Current	10.5	15.1	18.0	15.5	15.7	
46.7	46.0	44.8	Total Current	31.4	44.6	43.5	58.9	42.2	
10.1	10.2	13.0	Long Term Debt	25.7	16.2	12.4	5.5	6.1	
.8	.8	.3	Deferred Taxes	.0	.3	.8	.2	.3	
1.8	2.4	5.3	All Other Non-Current	19.2	1.9	1.6	2.8	4.0	
40.6	40.6	36.5	Net Worth	23.8	37.0	41.6	32.5	47.5	
100.0	100.0	100.0	Total Liabilities & Net Worth	100.0	100.0	100.0	100.0	100.0	
			INCOME DATA						
100.0	100.0	100.0	Net Sales	100.0	100.0	100.0	100.0	100.0	
34.0	30.3	29.9	Gross Profit	49.7	30.5	26.1	22.6	22.4	
31.5	25.8	27.6	Operating Expenses	49.2	29.9	23.6	19.5	17.2	
2.5	4.5	2.2	Operating Profit	.5	.7	2.5	3.0	5.3	
–.7	.6	.8	All Other Expenses (net)	1.1	.1	1.0	1.0	.9	
3.2	3.9	1.4	Profit Before Taxes	–.7	.5	1.5	2.0	4.3	
			RATIOS						
2.3	2.5	2.7		4.6	3.0	2.7	2.1	2.7	
1.6	1.6	1.6	Current	1.6	1.7	1.7	1.4	2.0	
1.1	1.1	1.1		1.0	1.0	1.1	1.0	1.2	
2.0	2.3	2.3		4.6	2.4	2.5	1.8	2.0	
1.3	(130) 1.4	1.3	Quick	1.1	1.1	1.5	1.2	1.5	
.8	.9	.9		.6	.8	.9	.9	.9	
41 9.0	38 9.7	36 10.3		0 UND	45 8.2	42 8.6	39 9.4	51 7.1	
61 5.9	67 5.5	59 6.2	Sales/Receivables	15 24.1	59 6.2	64 5.7	68 5.4	66 5.5	
88 4.1	91 4.0	82 4.5		48 7.7	79 4.6	104 3.5	87 4.2	86 4.3	
0 UND	0 UND	0 UND		0 UND	0 UND	0 UND	0 UND	0 UND	
0 999.8	0 UND	0 UND	Cost of Sales/Inventory	0 UND	0 UND	0 UND	2 198.3	2 195.1	
9 40.7	6 61.0	10 36.0		20 18.4	19 19.2	11 31.9	10 35.3	4 93.5	
11 33.4	8 44.7	8 45.3		0 UND	10 38.4	11 34.6	16 22.8	9 40.0	
23 16.1	19 19.3	19 19.6	Cost of Sales/Payables	3 110.0	23 16.0	20 17.9	24 15.0	17 21.7	
42 8.6	38 9.7	34 10.7		18 20.7	32 11.4	41 9.0	46 8.0	31 11.9	
6.0	6.0	6.2		7.2	5.5	4.9	7.0	6.6	
11.3	12.7	11.6	Sales/Working Capital	22.8	13.0	8.8	11.7	8.1	
45.5	580.5	79.9		309.0	263.8	74.8	266.4	30.3	
8.7	13.3	10.0		10.0	8.8	13.1	8.8	16.2	
(107) 3.9	(111) 4.1	(119) 3.9	EBIT/Interest	(19) –1.0	(31) 4.6	(21) 3.8	(27) 4.0	(16) 4.5	
1.5	1.2	.5		–8.0	.5	.8	1.1	1.4	
8.7	12.4	10.1	Net Profit + Depr., Dep.,						
(33) 3.8	(30) 3.0	(29) 3.0	Amort./Cur. Mat. L/T/D						
1.2	1.7	1.4							
.2	.2	.2		.6	.2	.1	.2	.2	
.5	.4	.5	Fixed/Worth	1.1	.5	.6	.3	.4	
1.1	1.2	1.3		5.1	1.2	1.1	1.5	.7	
.6	.7	.6		.7	.6	.5	.6	.6	
1.3	1.2	1.5	Debt/Worth	1.9	1.5	.9	2.0	1.2	
3.3	4.3	4.4		11.1	4.4	2.9	4.7	2.0	
40.9	56.0	27.1	% Profit Before Taxes/Tangible	122.2	27.2	21.2	25.3	44.0	
(112) 16.2	(116) 20.9	(114) 10.1	Net Worth	(18) 2.5	(30) 6.8	(20) 9.0	(25) 12.1	(16) 9.7	
5.7	6.8	1.2		–69.0	–5.8	3.8	4.1	4.1	
16.8	17.0	12.9	% Profit Before Taxes/Total	47.9	14.9	11.4	8.7	23.6	
6.0	8.0	4.5	Assets	2.7	4.5	4.5	4.3	3.8	
1.5	.8	–1.5		–18.7	–1.1	–2.8	.7	1.3	
28.0	42.7	34.3		36.4	35.2	41.6	41.4	23.8	
15.1	19.5	16.4	Sales/Net Fixed Assets	14.5	16.4	13.0	18.3	14.2	
8.3	9.1	9.0		7.6	8.8	4.7	14.6	9.0	
3.5	3.8	3.9		8.9	3.8	3.0	4.0	3.7	
2.6	2.7	2.7	Sales/Total Assets	2.4	3.0	2.4	2.7	3.0	
2.0	2.0	2.0		1.8	2.2	1.7	2.0	2.4	
.9	.7	.8		1.2	1.2	1.1	.5	1.2	
(113) 1.6	(112) 1.5	(119) 1.7	% Depr., Dep., Amort./Sales	(20) 1.7	(30) 1.8	(20) 2.9	(27) 1.0	1.7	
2.9	2.9	3.1		3.6	3.3	4.8	2.1	2.4	
3.3	2.6	2.4		6.1	2.0	2.2	2.8		
(67) 6.8	(67) 5.0	(70) 5.4	% Officers', Directors',	(16) 7.7	(17) 5.3	(13) 3.9	(15) 5.0		
11.1	7.7	8.7	Owners' Comp/Sales	10.2	10.4	6.8	8.7		
742274M	804277M	1701834M	Net Sales ($)	14283M	65427M	91016M	209573M	242882M	1078653M
312085M	324905M	422281M	Total Assets ($)	5345M	25986M	44223M	84003M	97815M	164909M

M = $ thousand   MM = $ million
See Pages 11 through 18 for Explanation of Ratios and Data

Current Data Sorted By Assets   Comparative Historical Data

19 (4/1-9/30/02)   85 (10/1/02-3/31/03)

0-500M	500M-2MM	2-10MM	10-50MM	50-100MM	100-250MM	Type of Statement	4/1/98-3/31/99 ALL	4/1/99-3/31/00 ALL
1	17	1 17	3	1		Unqualified	3	2
8	9	1			1	Reviewed	16	28
12	6	1				Compiled	20	17
8	9	1 7	2			Tax Returns	3	9
						Other	13	20
29	41	27	5	1	1	**NUMBER OF STATEMENTS**	55	76
%	%	%	%	%	%	**ASSETS**	%	%
17.7	8.5	4.7				Cash & Equivalents	6.2	7.1
29.8	55.4	59.6				Trade Receivables (net)	51.6	52.2
15.8	14.7	14.3				Inventory	14.1	15.0
3.3	4.4	8.4				All Other Current	3.6	5.0
66.5	83.0	87.0				Total Current	75.4	79.3
24.4	12.7	9.0				Fixed Assets (net)	17.1	12.8
.8	1.3	.4				Intangibles (net)	3.3	2.3
8.3	3.0	3.6				All Other Non-Current	4.2	5.6
100.0	100.0	100.0				Total	100.0	100.0
						LIABILITIES		
22.5	13.8	18.5				Notes Payable-Short Term	13.2	13.0
7.4	3.2	1.9				Cur. Mat.-L/T/D	3.8	3.9
16.3	19.7	18.9				Trade Payables	18.6	19.1
.4	.4	.4				Income Taxes Payable	2.1	.5
13.6	11.4	13.4				All Other Current	13.4	14.6
60.2	48.4	53.0				Total Current	51.2	51.1
11.6	4.5	5.6				Long Term Debt	13.3	8.9
.0	.2	.1				Deferred Taxes	.3	.3
.4	3.2	6.9				All Other Non-Current	6.1	6.7
27.8	43.8	34.4				Net Worth	29.1	33.1
100.0	100.0	100.0				Total Liabilities & Net Worth	100.0	100.0
						INCOME DATA		
100.0	100.0	100.0				Net Sales	100.0	100.0
42.8	28.2	21.5				Gross Profit	26.6	26.2
39.9	25.4	17.7				Operating Expenses	23.1	22.2
2.9	2.8	3.8				Operating Profit	3.5	4.1
.6	.4	.3				All Other Expenses (net)	.7	.6
2.3	2.4	3.5				Profit Before Taxes	2.8	3.4
						RATIOS		
2.1	2.3	2.5					2.1	2.4
1.2	1.6	1.5				Current	1.4	1.6
.7	1.3	1.4					1.1	1.2
1.3	1.8	1.5					1.7	1.9
.9	1.2	1.1				Quick	1.1	1.2
.4	.9	.9					.8	.8
0 UND	38 9.6	51 7.2					36 10.1	38 9.5
19 18.9	56 6.5	62 5.9				Sales/Receivables	48 7.5	54 6.8
44 8.3	72 5.1	78 4.7					72 5.1	79 4.6
0 UND	1 326.5	8 46.7					2 151.4	1 285.3
6 58.5	11 32.3	14 26.3				Cost of Sales/Inventory	11 32.8	16 23.0
57 6.4	41 8.9	30 12.2					34 10.6	34 10.6
0 UND	13 28.5	16 23.5					12 30.6	15 24.1
17 21.8	21 17.4	21 17.1				Cost of Sales/Payables	22 16.2	23 15.6
42 8.7	38 9.6	36 10.1					35 10.4	36 10.2
12.9	6.6	7.8					9.7	7.0
35.8	11.5	11.0				Sales/Working Capital	16.2	12.0
−43.3	20.3	13.1					43.3	34.8
15.9	11.7	14.2					8.4	13.7
(22) 7.2	(38) 3.4	(26) 4.4				EBIT/Interest	(48) 3.8	(73) 4.5
1.4	1.4	2.7					2.4	1.9
							5.4	8.7
						Net Profit + Depr., Dep., Amort./Cur. Mat. L./T/D	(16) 3.1	(22) 2.6
							1.4	.9
.2	.1	.1					.2	.1
.7	.3	.1				Fixed/Worth	.4	.3
NM	.5	.4					2.5	.8
1.0	.7	1.1					1.0	1.0
1.6	1.3	2.1				Debt/Worth	3.0	2.1
NM	3.3	3.0					9.7	4.8
122.3	43.6	57.7					92.9	75.1
(22) 36.7	(40) 18.1	(26) 25.4				% Profit Before Taxes/Tangible Net Worth	(51) 40.4	(69) 25.8
8.1	1.2	7.8					10.8	10.7
40.0	22.8	20.1					16.7	21.0
13.3	5.6	6.8				% Profit Before Taxes/Total Assets	7.8	7.9
.7	.7	2.5					3.2	3.1
55.4	98.8	171.9					107.4	88.9
25.4	41.0	59.7				Sales/Net Fixed Assets	40.5	44.2
16.5	18.1	28.1					13.7	25.9
8.1	4.8	3.9					4.7	4.2
4.6	3.5	3.2				Sales/Total Assets	3.6	3.4
3.2	2.9	2.7					2.9	2.9
.6	.3	.2					.5	.5
(27) 1.4	(37) .6	(26) .5				% Depr., Dep., Amort./Sales	(50) .8	(69) .7
2.4	1.4	.9					1.3	1.2
5.2	2.8	1.7					1.7	1.5
(22) 7.5	(28) 3.9	(13) 3.0				% Officers', Directors', Owners' Comp/Sales	(28) 4.7	(41) 3.4
10.4	5.8	4.7					7.2	5.2
44519M	192650M	395493M	235528M	132313M	999130M	Net Sales ($)	1407041M	2162923M
8051M	49451M	118369M	76655M	57356M	242707M	Total Assets ($)	248763M	389571M

© RMA 2003

M = $ thousand   MM = $ million
See Pages 11 through 18 for Explanation of Ratios and Data

Comparative Historical Data | Current Data Sorted By Sales

				Type of Statement						
	3		3	2	Unqualified				1	1
	19		23	38	Reviewed		6	4	16	9	3
	19		31	19	Compiled	4	5	5	3	1	1
	6		11	19	Tax Returns	2	10	3	4		
	14		17	26	Other	5	4	4	1	6	4
	4/1/00-3/31/01		4/1/01-3/31/02	4/1/02-3/31/03			19 (4/1-9/30/02)		85 (10/1/02-3/31/03)		
	ALL		ALL	ALL		0-1MM	1-3MM	3-5MM	5-10MM	10-25MM	25MM & OVER
	61		85	104	NUMBER OF STATEMENTS	11	27	16	24	17	9
	%		%	%	ASSETS	%	%	%	%	%	%
	7.3		9.3	10.7	Cash & Equivalents	21.1	12.8	9.9	8.3	6.8	
	55.4		53.8	48.6	Trade Receivables (net)	17.6	43.8	49.8	57.8	60.6	
	11.9		11.5	14.9	Inventory	27.4	10.3	19.5	12.0	13.2	
	6.6		4.8	5.1	All Other Current	2.0	4.3	2.1	6.4	8.5	
	81.1		79.4	79.3	Total Current	68.2	71.3	81.3	84.5	89.2	
	14.1		14.3	14.8	Fixed Assets (net)	26.2	21.6	14.0	9.1	7.6	
	.8		1.9	.8	Intangibles (net)	1.1	1.0	1.9	.4	.3	
	4.0		4.3	5.0	All Other Non-Current	4.4	6.1	2.8	6.0	2.8	
	100.0		100.0	100.0	Total	100.0	100.0	100.0	100.0	100.0	
					LIABILITIES						
	11.3		18.5	17.8	Notes Payable-Short Term	25.8	19.3	10.7	12.3	21.5	
	4.5		3.7	3.9	Cur. Mat.-L/T/D	7.6	5.5	4.9	1.4	3.1	
	20.1		20.6	17.9	Trade Payables	11.9	18.2	17.7	21.6	18.9	
	.6		.2	.4	Income Taxes Payable	.3	.3	.4	.6	.1	
	14.2		12.1	12.6	All Other Current	12.5	11.8	9.6	16.9	12.7	
	50.8		55.1	52.7	Total Current	58.2	55.1	43.2	52.9	56.3	
	7.0		8.1	7.1	Long Term Debt	14.0	8.4	5.2	3.6	6.9	
	.5		.4	.1	Deferred Taxes	.0	.0	.0	.3	.1	
	3.6		3.1	3.4	All Other Non-Current	.0	1.8	3.2	4.6	4.6	
	38.2		33.3	36.6	Net Worth	27.7	34.7	48.3	38.6	32.0	
	100.0		100.0	100.0	Total Liabilities & Net Worth	100.0	100.0	100.0	100.0	100.0	
					INCOME DATA						
	100.0		100.0	100.0	Net Sales	100.0	100.0	100.0	100.0	100.0	
	26.9		27.1	30.6	Gross Profit	53.0	35.9	28.2	23.5	22.6	
	21.1		23.3	27.5	Operating Expenses	50.6	32.0	25.7	20.8	18.8	
	5.8		3.9	3.2	Operating Profit	2.4	3.9	2.6	2.6	3.8	
	.2		.5	.4	All Other Expenses (net)	.7	.5	.4	.3	.2	
	5.6		3.4	2.7	Profit Before Taxes	1.7	3.4	2.1	2.3	3.6	
					RATIOS						
	2.2		2.3	2.3		3.6	1.8	2.7	2.3	2.5	
	1.5		1.5	1.5	Current	1.7	1.4	1.9	1.5	1.5	
	1.2		1.1	1.2		.7	1.0	1.4	1.2	1.3	
	1.8		1.7	1.7		2.4	1.6	1.7	1.7	2.1	
	1.2		1.2	1.1	Quick	.8	1.1	1.2	1.2	1.1	
	.9		.9	.8		.3	.8	1.0	.9	.9	
41	9.0	38	9.5	31	11.8		Sales/Receivables	0	UND	21	17.5	46	7.9	41	8.8	40	9.1	

Period	Lower		Mid		Upper	Ratio	0-1MM		1-3MM		3-5MM		5-10MM		10-25MM		25MM & OVER
41	9.0	38	9.5	31	11.8	Sales/Receivables	0	UND	21	17.5	46	7.9	41	8.8	40	9.1	
63	5.8	51	7.2	53	6.9		16	22.6	40	9.1	56	6.5	60	6.0	62	5.9	
78	4.7	75	4.9	71	5.1		31	11.9	61	6.0	72	5.1	78	4.7	77	4.8	
2	168.7	2	178.6	2	232.7	Cost of Sales/Inventory	0	UND	0	UND	4	88.2	0	UND	7	51.7	
9	39.1	11	33.6	11	33.2		66	5.5	6	58.5	20	18.1	2	172.3	11	34.0	
23	16.0	23	15.9	35	10.3		170	2.1	25	14.7	59	6.1	23	15.7	29	12.5	
14	25.4	14	26.6	13	29.1	Cost of Sales/Payables	0	UND	7	55.9	14	26.8	14	25.6	14	26.4	
23	15.9	25	14.7	21	17.5		25	14.7	21	17.7	19	18.8	21	17.3	21	17.4	
36	10.2	38	9.5	37	9.8		55	6.7	48	7.6	36	10.0	38	9.7	35	10.3	
	7.9		8.2		7.4	Sales/Working Capital		6.4		10.9		6.2		7.3		8.0	
	13.2		14.6		12.4			15.8		22.2		11.5		12.2		11.0	
	25.2		53.9		29.0			-6.1		-999.8		15.6		36.9		21.1	
	16.6		14.3		12.6	EBIT/Interest				11.7		12.7		13.0		16.4	
(58)	6.6	(71)	3.9	(92)	4.2			(23)	5.8	(15)	3.4	(22)	3.9	(16)	3.8	
	2.6		1.6		2.0					2.2		1.3		1.8		2.3	
			20.8		9.3	Net Profit + Depr., Dep., Amort./Cur. Mat. L/T/D											
		(18)	3.0	(18)	4.5												
			1.2		1.3												
	.1		.1		.1	Fixed/Worth		.2		.3		.1		.1		.1	
	.3		.4		.3			1.5		.4		.3		.2		.1	
	.7		1.2		.8			-.5		1.1		.5		.5		.7	
	.8		.9		.8	Debt/Worth		.3		1.1		.7		.7		.9	
	1.8		1.6		1.7			2.0		1.5		1.1		2.1		2.2	
	3.9		5.5		3.3			-4.3		4.2		2.7		3.4		3.6	
	83.1		66.3		50.6	% Profit Before Taxes/Tangible Net Worth				79.3		54.1		34.3		50.6	
(60)	42.1	(75)	24.1	(95)	21.7			(23)	40.0		17.0	(23)	15.5	(16)	25.4	
	14.6		6.6		5.4					14.1		.4		4.0		9.6	
	27.7		23.3		24.9	% Profit Before Taxes/Total Assets		52.4		31.5		25.2		17.9		19.2	
	10.4		9.7		7.0			13.3		13.3		5.9		5.4		6.7	
	4.8		1.4		1.5			-7.8		4.1		.2		.9		2.4	
	85.0		80.1		93.2	Sales/Net Fixed Assets		27.8		49.1		99.9		161.1		135.4	
	33.8		34.2		40.7			19.0		24.8		32.2		88.6		71.9	
	15.2		19.0		18.4			7.5		16.3		11.4		35.4		37.4	
	4.3		4.6		4.8	Sales/Total Assets		4.6		7.1		4.2		4.7		4.7	
	3.4		3.6		3.6			3.3		4.2		3.3		3.4		3.8	
	2.8		3.0		2.9			2.1		3.0		2.5		2.9		3.0	
	.5		.4		.4	% Depr., Dep., Amort./Sales		.7		.6		.5		.2		.2	
(48)	.9	(70)	.9	(96)	.7			1.8	(23)	1.1	(14)	.6	(23)	.4		.5	
	1.5		1.5		1.4			2.9		2.2		1.4		.9		.7	
	2.3		2.5		2.8	% Officers', Directors', Owners' Comp/Sales				3.9		2.4		2.3			
(32)	4.5	(47)	4.3	(65)	4.7			(19)	6.2	(11)	4.6	(17)	3.1			
	7.2		7.0		7.4					10.0		5.9		5.0			
	1104599M		1000366M		1999633M	Net Sales ($)	6998M	53588M	62077M	170488M	263950M	1442532M
	297029M		304653M		552589M	Total Assets ($)	2357M	12893M	19704M	46647M	80018M	390970M

M = $ thousand   MM = $ million
See Pages 11 through 18 for Explanation of Ratios and Data

Current Data Sorted By Assets   Comparative Historical Data

0-500M	500M-2MM	2-10MM	10-50MM	50-100MM	100-250MM	Type of Statement	4/1/98-3/31/99 ALL	4/1/99-3/31/00 ALL
	1	3	2			Unqualified	4	1
1	2	5	1			Reviewed	11	7
1	1					Compiled	2	3
1	4					Tax Returns	3	10
2	1	3	1			Other	6	8
	5 (4/1-9/30/02)		23 (10/1/02-3/31/03)					
4	9	11	4			**NUMBER OF STATEMENTS**	26	29
%	%	%	%	%	%	**ASSETS**	%	%
		5.4		D	D	Cash & Equivalents	9.8	8.3
		46.3		A	A	Trade Receivables (net)	48.4	49.1
		18.4		T	T	Inventory	9.2	13.3
		3.7		A	A	All Other Current	6.4	2.2
		73.8				Total Current	73.7	72.9
		16.6		N	N	Fixed Assets (net)	17.7	19.5
		1.9		O	O	Intangibles (net)	1.2	.8
		7.7		T	T	All Other Non-Current	7.4	6.9
		100.0				Total	100.0	100.0
				A	A	**LIABILITIES**		
		14.7		V	V	Notes Payable-Short Term	9.3	11.3
		1.8		A	A	Cur. Mat.-L/T/D	3.2	3.6
		11.4		I	I	Trade Payables	18.5	22.5
		.2		L	L	Income Taxes Payable	2.5	.4
		18.5		A	A	All Other Current	17.9	17.2
		46.5		B	B	Total Current	51.4	54.9
		9.4		L	L	Long Term Debt	8.1	12.1
		.0		E	E	Deferred Taxes	1.1	1.2
		2.5				All Other Non-Current	.7	2.6
		41.5				Net Worth	38.7	29.2
		100.0				Total Liabilities & Net Worth	100.0	100.0
						INCOME DATA		
		100.0				Net Sales	100.0	100.0
		33.3				Gross Profit	27.7	27.1
		26.2				Operating Expenses	22.5	26.0
		7.1				Operating Profit	5.2	1.2
		.4				All Other Expenses (net)	.6	-2.7
		6.7				Profit Before Taxes	4.6	3.8
						RATIOS		
		1.9				Current	2.3	1.8
		1.5					1.6	1.4
		1.1					1.2	1.0
		1.2				Quick	1.8	1.6
		1.0					1.1	1.0
		.8					.8	.6
65		5.6				Sales/Receivables	38 / 9.6	38 / 9.7
73		5.0					57 / 6.4	53 / 6.9
91		4.0					79 / 4.6	82 / 4.4
5		71.8				Cost of Sales/Inventory	0 / UND	0 / UND
15		23.9					2 / 181.8	10 / 36.9
125		2.9					15 / 24.9	36 / 10.1
15		24.8				Cost of Sales/Payables	7 / 52.1	20 / 18.1
27		13.5					22 / 16.3	38 / 9.6
48		7.6					41 / 8.9	56 / 6.5
		4.7				Sales/Working Capital	5.7	7.4
		13.1					14.8	15.6
		29.5					75.2	-266.8
						EBIT/Interest	(23) 32.7	(27) 12.9
							7.8	4.2
							3.1	2.1
						Net Profit + Depr., Dep., Amort./Cur. Mat. L./T/D		
		.1				Fixed/Worth	.1	.2
		.6					.6	.6
		.9					.9	1.7
		1.0				Debt/Worth	.6	.9
		2.2					1.0	2.3
		4.0					4.4	6.6
		84.2				% Profit Before Taxes/Tangible Net Worth	(25) 148.5	(26) 76.9
		19.9					48.5	30.1
		-17.0					16.1	11.0
		35.0				% Profit Before Taxes/Total Assets	35.8	20.7
		7.4					14.2	10.8
		-3.1					7.5	4.0
		60.5				Sales/Net Fixed Assets	52.1	62.9
		14.4					25.1	20.9
		10.7					16.0	9.2
		3.0				Sales/Total Assets	4.2	4.5
		2.6					3.1	3.0
		1.5					2.6	2.2
						% Depr., Dep., Amort./Sales	(23) .7	(24) .5
							1.0	1.1
							1.6	2.1
						% Officers', Directors', Owners' Comp/Sales	(11) 5.0	(16) 2.3
							6.9	4.6
							9.7	7.6
3345M	30542M	132234M	185356M			Net Sales ($)	321806M	123007M
861M	10163M	57730M	92525M			Total Assets ($)	148247M	50477M

M = $ thousand   MM = $ million
See Pages 11 through 18 for Explanation of Ratios and Data

Comparative Historical Data

Current Data Sorted By Sales

							Type of Statement						
	2		3		6		Unqualified			1	1	2	2
	6		5		9		Reviewed	1			4	3	1
	7		7		2		Compiled		2				
	1				4		Tax Returns		2	2			
	3		8		7		Other	1	2		2	1	1
	4/1/00-		4/1/01-		4/1/02-				5 (4/1-9/30/02)			23 (10/1/02-3/31/03)	
	3/31/01		3/31/02		3/31/03			0-1MM	1-3MM	3-5MM	5-10MM	10-25MM	25MM & OVER
	ALL		ALL		ALL								
	19		23		28		NUMBER OF STATEMENTS	2	6	3	7	6	4
	%		%		%		ASSETS	%	%	%	%	%	%
	8.4		10.2		11.2		Cash & Equivalents						
	43.9		48.0		38.8		Trade Receivables (net)						
	13.5		10.7		16.0		Inventory						
	4.5		4.5		6.8		All Other Current						
	70.3		73.4		72.9		Total Current						
	19.7		18.0		18.5		Fixed Assets (net)						
	2.7		2.4		1.2		Intangibles (net)						
	7.3		6.3		7.5		All Other Non-Current						
	100.0		100.0		100.0		Total						
							LIABILITIES						
	10.6		10.7		8.6		Notes Payable-Short Term						
	3.0		3.4		3.2		Cur. Mat.-L/T/D						
	17.0		17.1		14.9		Trade Payables						
	.0		1.3		.3		Income Taxes Payable						
	20.8		12.5		19.7		All Other Current						
	51.5		44.9		46.7		Total Current						
	9.8		9.3		12.1		Long Term Debt						
	.8		.5		.1		Deferred Taxes						
	6.0		8.9		4.9		All Other Non-Current						
	32.0		36.3		36.2		Net Worth						
	100.0		100.0		100.0		Total Liabilities & Net Worth						
							INCOME DATA						
	100.0		100.0		100.0		Net Sales						
	29.0		30.7		33.3		Gross Profit						
	21.5		24.7		27.9		Operating Expenses						
	7.5		5.9		5.4		Operating Profit						
	.7		.7		.7		All Other Expenses (net)						
	6.7		5.2		4.6		Profit Before Taxes						
							RATIOS						
	1.8		2.0		2.1								
	1.4		1.8		1.6		Current						
	.9		1.3		1.1								
	1.6		1.8		2.0								
	1.2		1.3		1.0		Quick						
	.7		.9		.6								
28	12.9	36	10.2	31	11.8								
50	7.3	47	7.8	59	6.2		Sales/Receivables						
91	4.0	78	4.7	79	4.6								
1	376.6	2	197.4	3	121.1								
8	44.9	11	33.9	12	29.7		Cost of Sales/Inventory						
33	11.1	21	17.4	55	6.7								
17	21.9	14	26.2	12	31.0								
31	11.8	25	14.4	27	13.3		Cost of Sales/Payables						
43	8.4	44	8.3	51	7.2								
	7.4		8.0		6.0								
	12.1		11.1		9.5		Sales/Working Capital						
	−342.3		24.3		36.1								
	15.7		17.7		14.2								
(16)	4.2	(21)	4.5	(23)	4.9		EBIT/Interest						
	1.8		1.6		−.4								
							Net Profit + Depr., Dep., Amort./Cur. Mat. L/T/D						
	.2		.2		.1								
	.5		.4		.6		Fixed/Worth						
	2.8		.8		1.8								
	1.3		.8		.8								
	1.6		1.4		1.9		Debt/Worth						
	6.5		5.5		4.7								
	71.0		101.8		79.2									
(17)	34.7	(21)	39.8	(25)	15.4		% Profit Before Taxes/Tangible Net Worth						
	9.8		5.9		.5								
	39.7		24.5		17.5									
	11.0		8.0		6.1		% Profit Before Taxes/Total Assets						
	4.0		2.2		−.4								
	41.6		34.0		58.2									
	22.6		22.1		14.6		Sales/Net Fixed Assets						
	10.7		13.2		8.0								
	3.6		4.4		3.4								
	2.9		3.6		2.7		Sales/Total Assets						
	2.2		2.4		2.2								
	.5		.6		.9								
(16)	.9	(21)	1.3	(24)	1.1		% Depr., Dep., Amort./Sales						
	2.5		1.7		1.8								
					2.6								
				(15)	7.7		% Officers', Directors', Owners' Comp/Sales						
					9.3								
	188567M		253607M		351477M		Net Sales ($)	510M	11093M	10722M	47133M	84397M	197622M
	76954M		101788M		161279M		Total Assets ($)	106M	4232M	3373M	25192M	38906M	89470M

© RMA 2003   M = $ thousand   MM = $ million
See Pages 11 through 18 for Explanation of Ratios and Data

Current Data Sorted By Assets   **Comparative Historical Data**

Type of Statement

0-500M	500M-2MM	2-10MM	10-50MM	50-100MM	100-250MM	Type of Statement	4/1/98-3/31/99 ALL	4/1/99-3/31/00 ALL
	1	4				Unqualified	3	4
1	8	12	3			Reviewed	18	21
3	10	5	1			Compiled	19	24
5	9					Tax Returns	11	17
6	10	10	1	1	1	Other	18	18
20 (4/1-9/30/02)			70 (10/1/02-3/31/03)					
15	**38**	**31**	**5**	**1**		**NUMBER OF STATEMENTS**	**69**	**84**

ASSETS (%)

0-500M	500M-2MM	2-10MM	10-50MM	50-100MM	100-250MM	ASSETS	4/1/98-3/31/99 ALL	4/1/99-3/31/00 ALL
19.8	11.1	7.3				Cash & Equivalents	10.5	10.0
19.2	38.7	49.4				Trade Receivables (net)	37.2	37.8
8.6	15.5	11.1				Inventory	14.4	13.3
.6	5.1	5.6				All Other Current	4.4	5.6
48.2	70.4	73.4				Total Current	66.6	66.8
36.3	18.3	13.6				Fixed Assets (net)	23.5	23.9
4.1	4.8	.2				Intangibles (net)	3.4	4.3
11.3	6.4	12.7				All Other Non-Current	6.5	5.0
100.0	100.0	100.0				Total	100.0	100.0

LIABILITIES

0-500M	500M-2MM	2-10MM	10-50MM	50-100MM	100-250MM	LIABILITIES	4/1/98-3/31/99 ALL	4/1/99-3/31/00 ALL
15.3	14.3	12.9				Notes Payable-Short Term	11.1	11.1
2.2	3.8	4.4				Cur. Mat.-L/T/D	9.3	3.7
11.1	17.0	18.0				Trade Payables	16.9	17.4
.0	.2	.7				Income Taxes Payable	1.0	.6
6.9	14.2	13.1				All Other Current	23.9	14.3
35.5	49.5	49.1				Total Current	62.3	47.2
24.7	10.2	5.3				Long Term Debt	13.7	15.8
.0	.2	.4				Deferred Taxes	.2	.2
4.2	6.3	5.3				All Other Non-Current	6.5	2.3
35.8	33.8	40.0				Net Worth	17.3	34.4
100.0	100.0	100.0				Total Liabilities & Net Worth	100.0	100.0

INCOME DATA

0-500M	500M-2MM	2-10MM	10-50MM	50-100MM	100-250MM	INCOME DATA	4/1/98-3/31/99 ALL	4/1/99-3/31/00 ALL
100.0	100.0	100.0				Net Sales	100.0	100.0
37.6	34.5	24.8				Gross Profit	29.7	28.0
33.9	33.1	19.7				Operating Expenses	27.0	23.7
3.7	1.4	5.1				Operating Profit	2.7	4.2
.3	.9	1.8				All Other Expenses (net)	.4	.3
3.3	.5	3.4				Profit Before Taxes	2.4	4.0

(Column 100-250MM: DATA NOT AVAILABLE)

RATIOS

0-500M	500M-2MM	2-10MM	10-50MM	50-100MM	100-250MM	RATIOS	4/1/98-3/31/99 ALL	4/1/99-3/31/00 ALL
3.6	2.7	1.9				Current	2.0	2.3
1.5	1.4	1.5					1.5	1.4
.6	1.0	1.2					1.1	1.0
2.0	2.2	1.7				Quick	1.3	1.8
1.3	1.0	1.1					1.0 (83)	1.0
.4	.5	.9					.6	.7
1 314.0	23 16.1	39 9.4				Sales/Receivables	26 14.0	27 13.7
9 41.8	39 9.3	54 6.7					45 8.2	42 8.8
22 17.0	66 5.5	71 5.1					54 6.8	58 6.3
0 UND	3 115.6	0 UND				Cost of Sales/Inventory	0 UND	0 UND
1 586.0	20 18.6	11 33.6					15 25.1	8 47.8
11 33.4	33 10.9	30 12.0					43 8.5	42 8.8
0 UND	12 30.0	10 35.8				Cost of Sales/Payables	9 38.7	12 30.4
5 66.9	22 16.7	22 16.8					22 16.2	22 16.3
24 15.5	42 8.8	32 11.4					39 9.4	38 9.7
10.8	7.0	7.8				Sales/Working Capital	9.1	9.1
17.4	17.1	12.8					15.4	16.7
-28.9	-262.3	32.3					179.4	86.8
23.9	5.9	11.1				EBIT/Interest	10.3	15.3
(11) 3.5	(32) 2.9	(28) 6.7					(62) 4.0	(76) 5.7
-.7	1.0	1.6					1.7	2.0
						Net Profit + Depr., Dep., Amort./Cur. Mat. L /T/D	6.6	9.3
							(13) 3.6	(23) 3.7
							2.3	.5
.2	.1	.2				Fixed/Worth	.2	.3
.6	.4	.3					.6	.6
3.5	2.6	.6					3.7	1.3
.5	1.0	1.0				Debt/Worth	.9	.8
2.2	2.5	2.2					2.2	2.1
7.2	11.0	3.2					14.7	6.1
97.8	48.4	53.8				% Profit Before Taxes/Tangible Net Worth	56.5	69.2
(13) 56.1	(33) 19.3	16.9					(54) 33.1	(73) 37.2
-12.3	-9.6	4.2					10.9	16.1
40.8	15.1	14.2				% Profit Before Taxes/Total Assets	22.1	22.4
18.7	4.9	8.0					8.6	11.6
-5.2	.2	1.8					3.0	4.2
43.6	72.5	64.1				Sales/Net Fixed Assets	45.5	39.7
16.4	21.2	36.3					23.9	19.8
11.9	11.3	13.2					8.3	9.3
7.6	4.2	4.3				Sales/Total Assets	4.6	4.4
4.9	3.3	3.1					3.4	3.2
3.8	2.2	2.2					2.6	2.4
.8	.5	.4				% Depr., Dep., Amort./Sales	.9	.6
(14) 2.7	(33) 1.5	(27) .8					(63) 1.3	(73) 1.1
5.2	2.6	1.6					2.5	2.2
2.9	2.2	1.6				% Officers', Directors', Owners' Comp/Sales	3.3	2.8
(10) 6.1	(22) 4.2	(16) 2.9					(36) 5.1	(39) 5.1
14.2	8.1	4.4					10.2	9.2
20408M	140239M	375870M	257608M	180528M		Net Sales ($)	516203M	874299M
3983M	42106M	106740M	87893M	52498M		Total Assets ($)	149193M	273727M

M = $ thousand   MM = $ million
See Pages 11 through 18 for Explanation of Ratios and Data

Comparative Historical Data | | | **Current Data Sorted By Sales**

			Type of Statement						
4	7	5	Unqualified		1		2	2	
28	27	24	Reviewed	1	2	2	12	3	4
24	28	19	Compiled	1	6	5	3	3	1
10	15	14	Tax Returns	4	6	3	1		
22	25	28	Other	3	9	3	6	4	3
4/1/00- 3/31/01	4/1/01- 3/31/02	4/1/02- 3/31/03			20 (4/1-9/30/02)		70 (10/1/02-3/31/03)		
ALL	ALL	ALL		0-1MM	1-3MM	3-5MM	5-10MM	10-25MM	25MM & OVER
88	102	90	NUMBER OF STATEMENTS	9	24	13	24	12	8
%	%	%	ASSETS	%	%	%	%	%.	%
12.3	11.9	11.5	Cash & Equivalents	9.1	18.2	11.8	2.3		
40.9	43.8	39.4	Trade Receivables (net)	34.0	29.5	44.4	67.1		
12.7	12.1	12.2	Inventory	15.9	18.6	14.4	7.3		
6.5	3.5	4.9	All Other Current	5.1	2.4	4.4	7.5		
72.3	71.4	67.9	Total Current	64.1	68.8	75.0	84.2		
21.7	20.2	19.5	Fixed Assets (net)	18.5	19.3	16.2	9.6		
1.4	1.1	2.9	Intangibles (net)	9.5	.1	.8	.3		
4.6	7.3	9.7	All Other Non-Current	7.9	11.8	8.0	5.9		
100.0	100.0	100.0	Total	100.0	100.0	100.0	100.0		
			LIABILITIES						
11.3	9.4	13.6	Notes Payable-Short Term	13.2	11.5	9.9	22.1		
3.6	4.2	3.6	Cur. Mat.-L/T/D	3.5	2.3	6.3	1.8		
16.7	19.0	16.5	Trade Payables	13.1	11.1	19.6	24.1		
.6	.4	.3	Income Taxes Payable	.2	.0	.9	.1		
11.2	17.4	13.0	All Other Current	11.8	17.4	11.1	17.4		
43.4	50.4	47.0	Total Current	41.8	42.3	47.7	65.5		
12.3	14.0	10.3	Long Term Debt	14.1	3.6	4.3	4.7		
.4	.3	.2	Deferred Taxes	.2	.1	.2	.5		
3.0	3.5	5.8	All Other Non-Current	9.0	3.3	3.2	5.2		
40.9	31.9	36.7	Net Worth	34.9	50.7	44.5	24.1		
100.0	100.0	100.0	Total Liabilities & Net Worth	100.0	100.0	100.0	100.0		
			INCOME DATA						
100.0	100.0	100.0	Net Sales	100.0	100.0	100.0	100.0		
30.4	31.6	30.7	Gross Profit	34.7	33.0	27.2	22.3		
25.9	26.6	27.4	Operating Expenses	34.3	28.8	23.2	18.8		
4.5	5.0	3.3	Operating Profit	.4	4.2	4.0	3.5		
.2	.5	1.1	All Other Expenses (net)	1.3	.0	2.0	.5		
4.2	4.5	2.2	Profit Before Taxes	-.9	4.2	2.0	3.0		
			RATIOS						
2.9	2.5	2.5		3.4	3.6	2.4	1.7		
1.6	1.5	1.4	Current	1.4	2.8	1.6	1.3		
1.3	1.0	1.0		1.1	1.1	1.2	1.2		
2.5	2.0	1.8		2.4	2.4	1.7	1.3		
(87) 1.2	1.1	1.1	Quick	1.0	1.9	1.1	1.0		
.8	.7	.7		.4	.6	.9	.9		
29 12.5	26 13.8	21 17.2		20 18.4	5 69.1	33 11.2	46 8.0		
43 8.4	41 9.0	40 9.2	Sales/Receivables	41 8.9	27 13.7	53 6.8	61 5.9		
57 6.5	64 5.7	66 5.5		84 4.4	35 10.3	67 5.4	73 5.0		
0 UND	0 UND	0 UND		1 718.8	6 60.1	0 790.3	0 UND		
8 45.7	8 43.7	14 25.6	Cost of Sales/Inventory	18 20.0	17 21.0	22 16.3	6 66.0		
36 10.1	32 11.4	29 12.6		59 6.2	29 12.4	31 11.6	19 19.6		
9 40.4	9 40.5	8 47.1		12 29.9	6 63.9	10 36.0	8 47.2		
20 18.5	20 18.5	20 18.2	Cost of Sales/Payables	19 19.1	10 35.8	25 14.9	21 17.6		
35 10.4	44 8.4	37 10.0		41 8.9	25 14.5	40 9.1	36 10.2		
6.9	8.1	7.9		6.0	7.8	7.8	13.3		
12.3	15.4	16.3	Sales/Working Capital	16.0	12.8	11.8	26.3		
33.2	101.6	83.6		88.4	NM	26.7	35.2		
16.9	16.6	10.8		4.7	42.7	13.2	10.4		
(68) 6.9	(88) 4.7	(77) 3.7	EBIT/Interest	(21) 1.9	(10) 10.8	(21) 4.2	4.5		
2.1	1.9	1.2		-1.3	3.1	1.8	2.2		
10.4	15.9	7.1	Net Profit + Depr., Dep.,						
(24) 3.8	(23) 4.0	(18) 1.7	Amort./Cur. Mat. L/T/D						
1.6	1.6	.4							
.2	.1	.2		.2	.1	.1	.3		
.4	.4	.4	Fixed/Worth	.5	.3	.3	.4		
.8	1.8	1.1		2.0	.5	.5	.6		
.5	.7	1.0		1.8	.3	.8	2.2		
1.3	1.8	2.3	Debt/Worth	2.5	.9	1.2	3.7		
3.9	8.6	4.6		9.8	3.1	3.1	7.0		
55.1	92.1	56.1	% Profit Before Taxes/Tangible	53.7	92.4	40.9	87.5		
(79) 29.8	(90) 33.7	(83) 21.0	Net Worth	(20) 4.6	21.0	18.7	60.4		
12.2	15.2	2.7		-28.7	4.3	1.1	19.4		
25.1	24.0	15.9	% Profit Before Taxes/Total	11.3	21.3	16.1	16.6		
11.7	11.9	7.3	Assets	2.3	14.0	8.1	11.1		
3.7	3.5	.6		-7.1	2.9	.6	2.4		
49.6	73.5	64.5		37.4	83.1	62.5	73.7		
26.6	30.7	22.8	Sales/Net Fixed Assets	16.4	59.8	22.6	58.6		
10.8	14.0	11.8		10.5	10.7	11.8	30.0		
4.6	5.0	4.5		3.4	6.0	3.9	4.6		
3.5	3.4	3.3	Sales/Total Assets	2.4	4.2	3.4	4.2		
2.7	2.8	2.4		1.7	2.5	2.7	3.3		
.5	.5	.5		.9	.3	.4	.4		
(80) 1.1	(97) 1.0	(80) 1.3	% Depr., Dep., Amort./Sales	(20) 2.3	(11) 1.3	(23) 1.2	(10) .5		
2.1	1.8	2.5		3.3	2.5	1.8	.9		
2.6	3.1	2.2		3.3		1.3			
(45) 4.1	(60) 5.4	(51) 3.8	% Officers', Directors',	(12) 4.6		(14) 3.0			
6.3	9.2	8.0	Owners' Comp/Sales	14.1		9.1			
1096557M	960820M	974653M	Net Sales ($)	5102M	44390M	52555M	162618M	200807M	509181M
299451M	281956M	293220M	Total Assets ($)	4173M	21222M	15325M	51121M	50743M	150636M

M = $ thousand   MM = $ million
See Pages 11 through 18 for Explanation of Ratios and Data

Current Data Sorted By Assets   Comparative Historical Data

Type of Statement

	0-500M	500M-2MM	2-10MM	10-50MM	50-100MM	100-250MM		4/1/98-3/31/99 ALL	4/1/99-3/31/00 ALL
Unqualified		10	36	31	1	3		79	86
Reviewed	5	45	80	10				115	124
Compiled	11	23	18	1				49	53
Tax Returns	25	10	5	1		1		24	31
Other	7	19	31	11	1			53	49
	79 (4/1-9/30/02)			306 (10/1/02-3/31/03)					
NUMBER OF STATEMENTS	48	107	170	54	2	4		320	343
ASSETS	%	%	%	%	%	%		%	%
Cash & Equivalents	11.6	12.3	10.5	8.4				9.4	10.4
Trade Receivables (net)	15.1	31.9	34.4	34.4				31.6	30.7
Inventory	2.0	2.1	3.2	3.2				2.2	2.4
All Other Current	3.8	3.3	7.6	9.4				4.8	5.2
Total Current	32.6	49.5	55.7	55.4				48.0	48.7
Fixed Assets (net)	60.2	43.9	37.8	35.9				44.9	44.2
Intangibles (net)	.9	.7	1.0	2.5				1.3	1.5
All Other Non-Current	6.4	5.8	5.5	6.2				5.8	5.6
Total	100.0	100.0	100.0	100.0				100.0	100.0
LIABILITIES									
Notes Payable-Short Term	14.7	6.5	6.0	5.2				7.0	8.7
Cur. Mat.-L/T/D	9.3	8.3	6.9	7.0				7.4	7.9
Trade Payables	7.5	11.3	15.2	18.0				14.0	13.7
Income Taxes Payable	.0	1.2	1.2	.4				1.4	.7
All Other Current	4.8	8.6	9.0	10.1				8.4	7.3
Total Current	36.4	36.0	38.2	40.8				38.1	38.3
Long Term Debt	39.3	19.4	15.4	20.0				18.6	18.6
Deferred Taxes	.0	1.1	1.9	2.0				1.5	1.5
All Other Non-Current	6.6	3.5	1.4	1.6				2.7	2.4
Net Worth	17.7	40.1	43.2	35.6				39.0	39.3
Total Liabilities & Net Worth	100.0	100.0	100.0	100.0				100.0	100.0
INCOME DATA									
Net Sales	100.0	100.0	100.0	100.0				100.0	100.0
Gross Profit	54.6	34.7	20.9	18.2				26.2	28.1
Operating Expenses	49.8	30.7	17.0	14.0				20.6	23.7
Operating Profit	4.8	4.0	3.9	4.2				5.5	4.5
All Other Expenses (net)	1.4	.9	.3	.8				.5	.3
Profit Before Taxes	3.3	3.1	3.6	3.4				5.0	4.2
RATIOS									
Current	1.4	2.1	2.1	1.7				1.9	1.8
	.8	1.3	1.4	1.4				1.3	1.3
	.4	1.0	1.1	1.1				.9	.9
Quick	1.4	1.8	1.8	1.4				1.6	1.6
	.7	1.2	1.1	1.1				1.1	1.1
	.3	.8	.8	.9				.8	.7
Sales/Receivables	0 UND	34 10.7	42 8.6	49 7.5				36 10.2	34 10.8
	17 22.0	52 7.1	63 5.8	58 6.3				57 6.4	56 6.5
	41 8.9	77 4.7	81 4.5	85 4.3				81 4.5	80 4.6
Cost of Sales/Inventory	0 UND	0 UND	0 UND	0 UND				0 UND	0 UND
	0 UND	0 UND	0 UND	0 852.9				0 UND	0 UND
	0 UND	3 118.4	5 70.2	5 72.0				3 122.4	3 120.8
Cost of Sales/Payables	0 UND	11 31.9	13 27.2	27 13.4				14 25.9	14 26.6
	0 UND	21 17.4	29 12.5	37 9.9				28 12.9	29 12.6
	24 15.2	38 9.7	51 7.1	49 7.4				46 8.0	47 7.7
Sales/Working Capital	31.5	9.0	6.0	8.1				9.2	8.2
	-74.9	21.3	14.8	14.2				21.5	19.0
	-13.4	798.0	88.6	66.1				-76.3	-65.0
EBIT/Interest	(43) 7.6	(96) 7.9	(154) 11.9	(53) 8.8				(305) 7.7	(326) 9.1
	2.6	2.9	3.9	4.2				3.9	3.6
	-.1	.3	1.2	1.6				1.7	1.3
Net Profit + Depr., Dep., Amort./Cur. Mat. L/T/D		(37) 3.3	(67) 3.0	(24) 2.3				(123) 3.2	(124) 4.3
		1.8	1.9	1.4				2.0	1.9
		1.1	1.0	1.0				1.2	1.2
Fixed/Worth	1.3	.4	.5	.7				.6	.6
	3.2	1.1	.9	1.1				1.2	1.1
	-65.1	2.0	1.6	1.6				2.0	2.0
Debt/Worth	1.9	.7	.7	1.1				.7	.7
	4.1	1.4	1.4	2.1				1.6	1.6
	-82.4	3.4	3.0	3.7				3.4	3.2
% Profit Before Taxes/Tangible Net Worth	(35) 143.2	(98) 36.1	(164) 26.7	(52) 30.4				(302) 39.4	(325) 37.2
	35.8	11.6	13.6	18.0				18.8	16.6
	5.6	-2.5	3.3	6.1				5.6	3.8
% Profit Before Taxes/Total Assets	19.1	13.8	11.5	9.6				14.3	14.8
	6.1	4.6	4.9	5.9				7.5	6.6
	-3.4	-2.5	.8	1.5				1.5	.9
Sales/Net Fixed Assets	6.8	12.0	9.2	8.8				8.4	7.9
	3.9	5.0	5.1	5.8				4.4	4.9
	2.4	2.5	3.2	3.5				2.8	2.8
Sales/Total Assets	3.0	2.7	2.4	2.2				2.6	2.5
	2.4	2.0	2.0	1.9				1.9	2.0
	1.6	1.5	1.5	1.5				1.5	1.4
% Depr., Dep., Amort./Sales	(44) 4.8	(98) 3.6	(160) 2.8	(51) 3.0				(299) 3.1	(315) 3.2
	12.3	6.1	5.6	4.4				5.4	5.6
	17.2	10.3	7.9	5.9				8.4	9.4
% Officers', Directors', Owners' Comp/Sales	(32) 3.2	(59) 2.6	(70) 1.6	(13) .5				(163) 2.0	(170) 2.3
	6.0	4.4	2.6	1.3				3.9	4.1
	10.5	7.4	3.8	2.2				7.4	7.1
Net Sales ($)	35733M	284596M	1408491M	2071009M	215143M	1360520M		5567058M	5010877M
Total Assets ($)	14256M	126659M	730375M	1087369M	128254M	612677M		2456194M	2459391M

M = $ thousand   MM = $ million
See Pages 11 through 18 for Explanation of Ratios and Data

Comparative Historical Data / Current Data Sorted By Sales

71	75	81	Type of Statement	0-1MM	1-3MM	3-5MM	5-10MM	10-25MM	25MM & OVER
71	75	81	Unqualified		8	6	16	24	27
120	114	140	Reviewed	6	32	26	47	21	8
50	64	53	Compiled	13	19	9	10	1	1
23	31	42	Tax Returns	21	8	4	7		2
74	77	69	Other	7	17	6	16	16	7

4/1/00-3/31/01 ALL	4/1/01-3/31/02 ALL	4/1/02-3/31/03 ALL		79 (4/1-9/30/02)			306 (10/1/02-3/31/03)		
				0-1MM	1-3MM	3-5MM	5-10MM	10-25MM	25MM & OVER
338	361	385	NUMBER OF STATEMENTS	47	84	51	96	62	45
%	%	%	**ASSETS**	%	%	%	%	%	%
10.0	9.6	10.8	Cash & Equivalents	11.3	10.7	12.7	10.4	12.0	7.2
31.1	30.6	31.2	Trade Receivables (net)	15.7	26.0	35.6	34.7	37.5	35.6
3.2	2.8	2.7	Inventory	2.4	2.8	1.9	3.4	1.9	3.8
5.4	5.9	6.2	All Other Current	3.0	3.8	6.2	6.0	9.4	10.1
49.8	48.9	50.9	Total Current	32.4	43.3	56.4	54.5	60.8	56.7
43.2	43.3	42.2	Fixed Assets (net)	59.7	49.2	38.1	38.2	33.6	35.5
1.2	1.0	1.2	Intangibles (net)	1.8	1.2	.4	.9	.6	2.6
5.7	6.8	5.8	All Other Non-Current	6.1	6.2	5.1	6.4	5.1	5.2
100.0	100.0	100.0	Total	100.0	100.0	100.0	100.0	100.0	100.0
			LIABILITIES						
7.3	8.3	7.1	Notes Payable-Short Term	13.7	7.2	5.0	7.0	4.9	5.5
8.0	8.0	7.6	Cur. Mat.-L/T/D	9.0	8.2	7.0	7.7	6.8	6.7
13.7	13.8	13.5	Trade Payables	3.8	10.9	13.5	14.3	19.3	18.5
.6	.8	.9	Income Taxes Payable	.2	.9	1.3	1.3	.9	.5
8.6	8.8	8.5	All Other Current	6.2	8.2	6.3	8.9	9.9	11.1
38.3	39.6	37.6	Total Current	32.8	35.5	33.1	39.4	41.8	42.3
20.1	20.5	20.4	Long Term Debt	36.3	24.5	14.1	14.3	16.7	21.7
1.4	1.4	1.5	Deferred Taxes	.3	1.4	1.6	1.5	1.6	2.3
2.2	2.7	2.6	All Other Non-Current	7.2	3.0	2.9	1.4	1.1	1.5
38.0	35.8	37.9	Net Worth	23.4	35.8	48.3	43.3	38.7	32.2
100.0	100.0	100.0	Total Liabilities & Net Worth	100.0	100.0	100.0	100.0	100.0	100.0
			INCOME DATA						
100.0	100.0	100.0	Net Sales	100.0	100.0	100.0	100.0	100.0	100.0
29.5	28.7	28.5	Gross Profit	57.4	35.8	23.5	22.4	19.2	16.0
25.3	25.0	24.4	Operating Expenses	51.8	32.0	19.8	18.4	15.1	12.1
4.2	3.8	4.1	Operating Profit	5.5	3.8	3.8	4.1	4.1	3.9
.5	.9	.7	All Other Expenses (net)	2.4	1.0	-.3	.2	.4	1.1
3.7	2.8	3.4	Profit Before Taxes	3.1	2.8	4.1	3.9	3.7	2.8
			RATIOS						
1.9	2.0	2.0	Current	2.0	1.9	2.8	2.1	1.9	1.7
1.3	1.2	1.3		.9	1.1	1.8	1.3	1.4	1.4
1.0	.9	1.0		.5	.8	1.1	1.0	1.1	1.1
1.6	1.6	1.7	Quick	1.6	1.4	2.2	1.9	1.6	1.3
1.1	1.0	1.1		.8	1.0	1.6	1.1	1.2	1.0
.8	.7	.8		.2	.6	1.0	.8	.9	.9
34 10.7	32 11.3	35 10.5	Sales/Receivables	0 UND	24 14.9	45 8.1	41 8.9	42 8.6	51 7.2
56 6.6	56 6.5	55 6.7		24 15.5	40 9.1	66 5.5	61 5.9	58 6.3	59 6.1
78 4.7	79 4.6	78 4.7		54 6.7	67 5.4	81 4.5	81 4.5	79 4.6	86 4.3
0 UND	0 UND	0 UND	Cost of Sales/Inventory	0 UND	0 UND	0 UND	0 UND	0 UND	0 UND
0 UND	0 UND	0 UND		0 UND	0 UND	0 UND	0 UND	0 UND	1 274.1
4 97.0	5 80.2	4 102.8		0 UND	5 74.0	2 171.1	5 70.1	4 81.1	8 44.5
12 30.0	12 29.5	11 32.1	Cost of Sales/Payables	0 UND	8 44.4	11 32.2	12 31.2	23 16.1	28 13.3
26 14.0	27 13.6	27 13.7		5 68.0	19 19.1	24 15.5	25 14.4	35 10.4	37 9.9
46 7.9	47 7.8	46 7.9		23 15.7	37 9.8	42 8.7	51 7.2	54 6.7	47 7.8
7.4	7.9	8.1	Sales/Working Capital	12.4	10.5	4.9	7.2	6.8	8.9
19.9	25.2	19.6		-87.6	54.1	10.0	16.5	15.5	16.3
-169.5	-66.6	NM		-8.7	-33.4	34.4	126.9	40.0	60.8
			EBIT/Interest	(41) 4.4	(78) 8.2	(45) 13.0	(88) 12.4	(55) 9.7	(44) 7.6
(315) 3.0	(343) 2.6	(351) 3.3		2.5	2.5	3.9	4.2	4.2	3.2
7.4 / 1.1	6.2 / .8	9.1 / 1.0		.6	-.6	.4	1.8	1.7	1.1
3.5	2.6	2.9	Net Profit + Depr., Dep., Amort./Cur. Mat. L/T/D		(27) 3.0	(20) 2.7	(34) 4.2	(29) 3.0	(19) 2.1
(120) 1.8	(123) 1.6	(133) 1.8			1.7	1.6	2.1	1.5	1.3
1.1	1.0	1.0			1.1	.9	1.4	.9	1.0
.5	.6	.6	Fixed/Worth	1.2	.7	.4	.5	.4	.8
1.1	1.2	1.1		2.8	1.2	.8	.9	.8	1.1
2.0	2.1	2.0		-196.0	2.3	1.3	1.8	1.6	1.7
.8	.9	.8	Debt/Worth	1.2	.9	.5	.7	.9	1.5
1.7	1.8	1.6		3.2	1.7	1.0	1.3	1.7	2.3
3.4	3.7	3.6		-203.7	3.7	2.2	3.2	3.1	4.0
39.0	34.2	32.5	% Profit Before Taxes/Tangible Net Worth	(35) 63.6	(75) 41.2	(49) 28.2	(92) 26.9	(61) 31.8	(42) 32.5
(314) 12.1	(336) 12.9	(354) 14.8		22.2	11.2	11.8	15.1	17.4	14.8
1.7	1.3	3.0		.7	-4.6	.5	3.5	6.5	4.7
13.5	11.1	12.1	% Profit Before Taxes/Total Assets	12.6	13.5	12.5	12.5	11.7	8.7
4.8	4.4	5.0		4.6	3.2	6.5	4.7	6.0	3.8
.4	-.1	.0		-3.2	-3.5	-.6	1.0	2.1	.7
9.3	8.9	9.2	Sales/Net Fixed Assets	4.7	7.4	10.5	10.2	17.6	9.2
4.9	4.6	4.9		2.6	3.9	4.7	5.2	6.2	5.8
2.9	2.9	2.9		1.7	2.4	3.1	3.3	3.9	3.2
2.6	2.6	2.5	Sales/Total Assets	2.4	2.7	2.4	2.5	2.6	2.3
2.0	1.9	2.0		1.7	1.9	1.9	2.0	2.1	1.9
1.4	1.4	1.5		1.1	1.5	1.4	1.7	1.7	1.5
3.0	2.9	3.2	% Depr., Dep., Amort./Sales	(45) 6.7	(75) 4.8	(49) 3.7	(91) 3.0	(57) 2.2	(38) 2.9
(306) 5.6	(338) 5.4	(355) 5.7		13.0	7.7	5.0	5.6	4.5	3.8
8.6	8.8	9.3		18.4	12.5	9.1	7.5	6.5	5.8
1.9	1.8	1.8	% Officers', Directors', Owners' Comp/Sales	(28) 3.3	(46) 3.1	(25) 1.8	(43) 1.6	(23) 1.3	(10) .4
(158) 4.5	(169) 3.8	(175) 4.3		8.6	5.0	3.2	2.8	1.8	1.0
8.7	7.8	6.3		13.1	8.2	4.9	4.1	3.8	1.4
3484979M	3894976M	5375492M	Net Sales ($)	26157M	168090M	199792M	675177M	952269M	3354007M
1999106M	2214714M	2699590M	Total Assets ($)	19041M	95569M	115546M	349198M	470223M	1650013M

© RMA 2003   M = $ thousand   MM = $ million
See Pages 11 through 18 for Explanation of Ratios and Data

Current Data Sorted By Assets | Comparative Historical Data

							Type of Statement			
1		10	46	22	1	2	Unqualified		49	53
10		62	77	9			Reviewed		98	104
16		44	16	1		1	Compiled		79	74
34		23	7			1	Tax Returns		29	33
21		48	32	6	3	1	Other		76	79
		87 (4/1-9/30/02)		407 (10/1/02-3/31/03)					4/1/98-3/31/99	4/1/99-3/31/00
0-500M	500M-2MM	2-10MM	10-50MM	50-100MM	100-250MM				ALL	ALL
82	187	178	38	4	5		NUMBER OF STATEMENTS		331	343

0-500M	500M-2MM	2-10MM	10-50MM	50-100MM	100-250MM				ALL	ALL
%	%	%	%	%	%		**ASSETS**		%	%
12.9	11.5	11.9	9.9				Cash & Equivalents		10.6	9.7
32.2	42.7	45.1	40.5				Trade Receivables (net)		41.0	42.2
9.6	9.4	7.6	4.8				Inventory		7.8	8.5
3.8	6.2	9.4	10.9				All Other Current		6.1	6.2
58.5	69.8	73.9	66.1				Total Current		65.4	66.6
33.2	22.6	17.4	25.9				Fixed Assets (net)		25.6	24.2
2.6	1.9	2.8	2.8				Intangibles (net)		3.0	3.2
5.7	5.7	5.9	5.1				All Other Non-Current		6.1	6.0
100.0	100.0	100.0	100.0				Total		100.0	100.0
							LIABILITIES			
15.7	12.2	6.9	6.5				Notes Payable-Short Term		8.6	9.0
7.4	4.4	3.9	3.5				Cur. Mat.-L/T/D		3.8	3.7
19.0	17.1	19.9	15.1				Trade Payables		18.3	17.3
.1	.9	.8	.7				Income Taxes Payable		1.2	.6
15.1	12.6	13.9	15.7				All Other Current		15.3	14.4
57.3	47.1	45.4	41.4				Total Current		47.2	45.0
26.3	14.2	8.3	12.7				Long Term Debt		13.8	13.2
.6	.6	.5	.9				Deferred Taxes		.7	.8
3.0	2.4	1.7	2.7				All Other Non-Current		4.1	3.6
12.9	35.7	44.0	42.2				Net Worth		34.2	37.3
100.0	100.0	100.0	100.0				Total Liabilities & Net Worth		100.0	100.0
							INCOME DATA			
100.0	100.0	100.0	100.0				Net Sales		100.0	100.0
41.7	32.5	24.5	24.3				Gross Profit		30.1	31.3
39.7	29.9	19.6	19.3				Operating Expenses		26.8	25.9
2.0	2.6	4.8	5.1				Operating Profit		3.4	5.4
.8	.7	.5	.6				All Other Expenses (net)		.5	.5
1.2	1.9	4.4	4.5				Profit Before Taxes		2.9	4.9
							RATIOS			
1.6	2.3	2.4	2.0						2.3	2.3
1.3	1.5	1.6	1.5				Current		1.5	1.5
.8	1.1	1.2	1.2						1.1	1.1
1.3	1.9	1.9	1.7						1.8	1.8
1.0	1.2	1.2	1.2				Quick		1.1	1.1
.5	.8	.9	.9						.8	.8

												Sales/Receivables				
6	64.2	30	12.1	44	8.2	43	8.5					Sales/Receivables	35	10.5	32	11.5
25	14.7	52	7.0	63	5.7	68	5.4						55	6.7	56	6.5
49	7.5	76	4.8	85	4.3	83	4.4						75	4.8	79	4.6
0	UND	0	UND	0	UND	0	UND					Cost of Sales/Inventory	0	UND	0	UND
2	146.5	5	76.2	3	132.2	6	63.1						3	110.8	3	119.9
25	14.8	28	13.2	25	14.6	16	22.2						22	16.9	23	16.2
6	56.2	12	31.7	14	25.4	16	23.2					Cost of Sales/Payables	13	27.9	14	26.8
23	15.5	26	13.9	31	11.9	23	16.2						25	14.3	27	13.4
41	8.9	47	7.8	57	6.4	44	8.3						44	8.2	46	8.0

	15.5		7.6		5.2		6.5				Sales/Working Capital		6.5	6.9
	39.9		13.3		9.2		10.5						13.0	12.7
	−37.2		53.2		24.8		25.7						84.1	68.5
	5.8		12.2		18.0		33.9				EBIT/Interest		12.0	14.4
(69)	2.2	(168)	4.0	(153)	7.5	(34)	6.6					(295) 3.7	(304) 6.0
	−1.4		.5		2.6		2.9						1.6	2.0
			4.8		6.0		10.0				Net Profit + Depr., Dep., Amort./Cur. Mat. L /T/D		6.2	7.4
		(50)	2.9	(55)	2.7	(15)	3.9					(100) 3.2	(94) 2.7
			1.2		1.5		1.3						1.4	1.4
	.6		.2		.2		.2				Fixed/Worth		.2	.3
	1.8		.6		.3		.5						.6	.5
	−7.7		1.5		.7		1.2						1.4	1.5
	1.4		.8		.7		.8				Debt/Worth		.8	.8
	3.3		1.5		1.5		1.7						1.8	1.7
	−21.8		4.1		2.9		2.6						4.1	4.3
	66.4		43.1		46.2		37.2				% Profit Before Taxes/Tangible Net Worth		49.0	63.6
(60)	20.7	(162)	15.5	(171)	20.4	(37)	21.7					(294) 21.1	(313) 30.8
	−4.2		−.1		6.8		8.9						5.6	11.6
	16.4		17.7		17.4		11.8				% Profit Before Taxes/Total Assets		18.2	19.4
	5.9		4.6		7.3		7.5						7.0	10.0
	−3.4		−.6		1.7		3.3						1.6	3.8
	36.5		31.9		42.6		27.0				Sales/Net Fixed Assets		34.3	34.5
	18.8		17.4		22.4		12.6						17.5	16.6
	7.7		8.9		10.1		5.0						7.6	7.1
	5.9		3.9		3.2		3.1				Sales/Total Assets		3.7	3.7
	3.9		3.1		2.5		2.3						2.8	2.8
	2.6		2.3		1.9		1.7						2.1	2.0
	1.0		.9		.7		1.1				% Depr., Dep., Amort./Sales		.9	.8
(66)	2.6	(166)	1.7	(167)	1.5	(37)	2.1					(293) 1.7	(310) 1.6
	5.2		3.1		2.6		3.6						3.3	3.1
	5.4		2.8		1.9		1.9				% Officers', Directors', Owners' Comp/Sales		2.8	2.7
(49)	7.4	(111)	4.8	(80)	3.0	(10)	3.3					(153) 5.4	(149) 5.8
	10.3		8.6		6.4		9.8						8.3	9.5

0-500M	500M-2MM	2-10MM	10-50MM	50-100MM	100-250MM				ALL	ALL
97814M	659990M	2034108M	1885050M	686883M	2313571M		Net Sales ($)		4064544M	5880244M
24094M	207661M	782641M	689946M	243461M	792731M		Total Assets ($)		2029662M	1954569M

M = $ thousand   MM = $ million
See Pages 11 through 18 for Explanation of Ratios and Data

Comparative Historical Data | Current Data Sorted By Sales

Hist 4/1/00-3/31/01	Hist 4/1/01-3/31/02	Hist 4/1/02-3/31/03	Type of Statement	0-1MM	1-3MM	3-5MM	5-10MM	10-25MM	25MM & OVER
67	50	82	Unqualified	2	4	8	14	25	29
113	119	158	Reviewed	4	25	37	51	35	6
94	99	78	Compiled	7	36	17	14	1	3
58	41	65	Tax Returns	15	27	9	9	4	1
109	108	111	Other	10	37	20	16	18	10
4/1/00-3/31/01 ALL	4/1/01-3/31/02 ALL	4/1/02-3/31/03 ALL		87 (4/1-9/30/02) 0-1MM	1-3MM	3-5MM	407 (10/1/02-3/31/03) 5-10MM	10-25MM	25MM & OVER
441	417	494	NUMBER OF STATEMENTS	38	129	91	104	83	49
%	%	%	**ASSETS**	%	%	%	%	%	%
10.3	11.1	11.9	Cash & Equivalents	14.6	12.1	12.3	11.0	11.1	11.4
42.8	39.9	41.2	Trade Receivables (net)	24.4	36.1	44.7	44.9	47.5	42.2
7.4	8.9	8.4	Inventory	7.3	11.4	8.1	7.2	8.0	4.9
7.0	6.4	7.4	All Other Current	7.3	3.9	6.6	9.3	8.8	12.2
67.5	66.3	68.8	Total Current	53.6	63.5	71.6	72.4	75.4	70.7
24.4	24.9	22.7	Fixed Assets (net)	35.1	27.5	21.1	19.1	18.3	19.1
2.3	2.3	2.5	Intangibles (net)	2.5	3.1	1.8	3.0	1.5	3.0
5.8	6.4	5.9	All Other Non-Current	8.8	6.0	5.5	5.5	4.7	7.2
100.0	100.0	100.0	Total	100.0	100.0	100.0	100.0	100.0	100.0
			LIABILITIES						
10.9	10.1	10.3	Notes Payable-Short Term	17.1	11.4	12.5	7.8	8.4	7.0
4.5	4.6	4.6	Cur. Mat.-L/T/D	4.9	7.3	4.1	3.6	3.1	2.7
19.7	16.8	18.1	Trade Payables	17.3	16.6	16.4	17.4	23.6	18.6
.6	.7	.7	Income Taxes Payable	.0	.4	.8	1.3	.6	.6
13.8	16.8	13.8	All Other Current	22.7	11.0	13.2	12.1	14.2	18.1
49.4	48.9	47.6	Total Current	62.1	46.7	47.0	42.2	50.0	47.0
12.9	13.0	14.3	Long Term Debt	32.5	20.7	10.1	9.2	8.5	11.2
.7	.7	.6	Deferred Taxes	.3	.7	.6	.5	.7	.4
2.9	2.9	2.3	All Other Non-Current	2.5	2.1	2.8	2.0	2.2	2.7
34.2	34.6	35.2	Net Worth	2.5	29.8	39.4	46.0	38.6	38.7
100.0	100.0	100.0	Total Liabilities & Net Worth	100.0	100.0	100.0	100.0	100.0	100.0
			INCOME DATA						
100.0	100.0	100.0	Net Sales	100.0	100.0	100.0	100.0	100.0	100.0
29.5	30.3	30.5	Gross Profit	42.9	37.9	30.2	28.1	20.4	24.1
25.5	25.3	26.9	Operating Expenses	40.0	35.3	26.7	23.7	16.6	19.4
4.0	5.0	3.6	Operating Profit	2.9	2.6	3.5	4.4	3.8	4.8
.7	1.1	.6	All Other Expenses (net)	1.1	1.2	.5	.2	.5	.4
3.4	3.9	2.9	Profit Before Taxes	1.8	1.5	3.0	4.2	3.3	4.3
			RATIOS						
2.0	2.3	2.2	Current	1.6	2.2	2.1	2.7	2.1	2.0
1.3	1.4	1.5		1.2	1.4	1.6	1.8	1.5	1.5
1.1	1.1	1.1		.7	1.0	1.1	1.2	1.1	1.1
1.6	1.8	1.8	Quick	1.3	1.7	1.8	2.2	1.8	1.6
1.1	1.1	1.2		.8	1.1	1.2	1.3	1.2	1.2
.8	.8	.8		.4	.7	.8	.9	.9	.8
35 10.3	32 11.4	31 11.7	Sales/Receivables	0 UND	20 17.9	36 10.2	40 9.1	40 9.2	37 9.9
55 6.6	54 6.7	54 6.8		24 15.5	46 7.9	57 6.4	62 5.9	58 6.3	59 6.2
79 4.6	76 4.8	79 4.6		53 6.9	76 4.8	79 4.6	82 4.5	76 4.8	77 4.7
0 UND	0 UND	0 UND	Cost of Sales/Inventory	0 UND	0 UND	0 UND	0 UND	0 UND	0 UND
3 129.8	5 72.4	3 108.5		0 UND	8 45.6	3 114.6	2 149.9	3 117.2	2 155.3
19 19.2	25 14.5	25 14.8		23 15.9	33 11.1	26 13.9	23 15.9	17 21.5	9 40.3
14 26.0	13 28.6	12 29.9	Cost of Sales/Payables	0 UND	13 28.1	10 37.0	13 27.7	16 23.1	14 27.0
29 12.5	26 14.1	27 13.6		29 12.4	27 13.7	25 14.6	27 13.4	30 12.1	22 16.5
50 7.3	47 7.8	48 7.6		62 5.9	48 7.6	41 8.9	50 7.3	56 6.6	40 9.0
7.8	6.7	6.7	Sales/Working Capital	9.6	7.7	6.2	5.1	7.3	6.8
17.5	13.8	13.1		41.8	18.8	13.0	8.5	10.9	14.5
92.3	80.3	51.3		-14.9	229.1	36.4	21.6	36.4	42.5
(395) 10.9	(373) 10.8	(433) 13.7	EBIT/Interest	(29) 4.9	(115) 6.8	(83) 13.9	(92) 16.8	(70) 19.6	(44) 31.1
4.0	4.3	4.8		1.8	2.6	5.5	6.8	6.6	6.6
1.2	1.2	1.1		-3.6	.1	.9	2.6	2.0	2.6
(110) 5.8	(99) 9.2	(125) 5.4	Net Profit + Depr., Dep., Amort./Cur. Mat. L/T/D		(22) 3.4	(25) 6.0	(32) 6.6	(29) 5.1	(15) 6.7
2.6	3.2	2.7			1.3	3.2	3.0	2.7	2.3
1.3	1.5	1.2			.1	2.2	1.8	1.5	1.3
.2	.2	.2	Fixed/Worth	.6	.3	.2	.2	.2	.2
.6	.6	.5		1.8	.8	.6	.3	.4	.5
1.7	1.6	1.5		-5.8	3.1	1.3	.8	.9	1.0
1.0	.8	.8	Debt/Worth	1.2	.9	.7	.6	.7	1.0
2.1	1.7	1.7		4.7	2.4	1.4	1.1	1.7	2.0
5.1	4.8	4.1		-12.2	10.0	3.4	2.8	3.8	2.7
(401) 54.2	(384) 53.4	(437) 46.3	% Profit Before Taxes/Tangible Net Worth	(27) 79.4	(104) 41.6	(82) 51.8	(100) 44.9	(78) 46.5	(46) 39.1
22.8	24.7	19.8		31.7	10.5	20.7	19.9	21.5	24.3
6.9	5.5	2.8		-20.5	-4.2	-.1	7.1	7.6	9.6
17.2	16.9	16.6	% Profit Before Taxes/Total Assets	13.3	15.9	19.3	17.8	15.4	14.8
6.6	7.3	6.5		4.0	3.7	8.0	7.2	7.4	7.4
1.4	1.1	.4		-11.7	-3.6	-.3	2.7	1.4	2.7
34.6	35.8	35.8	Sales/Net Fixed Assets	32.7	31.3	31.8	33.5	51.1	37.9
16.2	16.1	18.7		11.5	14.4	21.8	19.5	24.1	20.5
7.4	7.2	8.6		5.6	7.2	9.5	12.1	10.1	7.5
3.8	3.7	3.9	Sales/Total Assets	4.9	4.1	3.9	3.6	3.9	3.6
2.7	2.7	2.9		2.6	3.1	2.9	2.6	2.9	3.0
2.1	1.9	2.0		1.6	2.0	2.3	2.1	2.1	2.0
(397) .6	(370) .7	(444) .9	% Depr., Dep., Amort./Sales	(30) .9	(108) 1.2	(81) 1.1	(100) .9	(80) .6	(45) .8
1.6	1.7	1.7		2.7	2.3	1.6	1.8	1.2	1.5
3.3	3.2	3.2		5.7	4.7	2.9	2.9	2.6	2.5
(224) 2.4	(201) 2.4	(253) 2.6	% Officers', Directors', Owners' Comp/Sales	(21) 7.0	(79) 3.8	(49) 2.2	(53) 2.5	(36) 1.7	(15) 2.0
4.7	4.0	4.8		9.7	6.2	4.7	3.8	2.4	4.3
8.5	7.6	8.6		13.1	9.5	7.2	7.3	5.7	12.3
7561275M	5637188M	7677416M	Net Sales ($)	22617M	245351M	355101M	726250M	1278073M	5050024M
3100310M	2125206M	2740534M	Total Assets ($)	12794M	101019M	138016M	303465M	486813M	1698427M

© RMA 2003

M = $ thousand   MM = $ million

See Pages 11 through 18 for Explanation of Ratios and Data

MANUFACTURING

MANUFACTURING—Other Animal Food Manufacturing NAICS 311119 (SIC 0723, 2048)

Current Data Sorted By Assets | **Comparative Historical Data**

0-500M	500M-2MM	2-10MM	10-50MM	50-100MM	100-250MM	Type of Statement	4/1/98-3/31/99 ALL	4/1/99-3/31/00 ALL
	3	14	15	3	4	Unqualified	27	32
	4	9	1			Reviewed	21	21
1	2	6				Compiled	17	20
		1				Tax Returns	1	3
2	6	8	7	3	1	Other	30	35
	31 (4/1-9/30/02)		59 (10/1/02-3/31/03)					
3	15	38	23	6	5	**NUMBER OF STATEMENTS**	96	111
%	%	%	%	%	%	**ASSETS**	%	%
	9.2	7.1	11.7			Cash & Equivalents	6.7	8.5
	19.8	28.6	19.7			Trade Receivables (net)	23.5	22.7
	24.1	19.3	20.1			Inventory	21.8	21.9
	4.9	4.5	1.6			All Other Current	3.2	2.8
	58.0	59.5	53.1			Total Current	55.2	55.8
	39.2	34.7	33.8			Fixed Assets (net)	33.2	34.4
	.0	.7	2.4			Intangibles (net)	3.9	3.2
	2.7	5.0	10.7			All Other Non-Current	7.6	6.5
	100.0	100.0	100.0			Total	100.0	100.0
						LIABILITIES		
	16.2	14.9	3.8			Notes Payable-Short Term	11.5	12.1
	2.3	2.7	2.0			Cur. Mat.-L/T/D	3.1	3.1
	15.0	14.0	11.2			Trade Payables	16.7	16.7
	.9	.1	.2			Income Taxes Payable	.2	.3
	11.6	7.8	10.6			All Other Current	7.4	8.1
	46.0	39.4	27.7			Total Current	38.8	40.3
	13.9	16.8	13.7			Long Term Debt	17.0	17.8
	.2	.4	.4			Deferred Taxes	.7	.9
	1.9	2.5	3.8			All Other Non-Current	5.1	4.7
	37.9	40.8	54.4			Net Worth	38.4	36.3
	100.0	100.0	100.0			Total Liabilities & Net Worth	100.0	100.0
						INCOME DATA		
	100.0	100.0	100.0			Net Sales	100.0	100.0
	26.6	22.8	28.0			Gross Profit	24.2	24.1
	19.3	20.1	20.1			Operating Expenses	20.7	20.5
	7.3	2.7	7.9			Operating Profit	3.6	3.7
	.7	.3	-.3			All Other Expenses (net)	.6	.2
	6.6	2.4	8.2			Profit Before Taxes	3.0	3.5
						RATIOS		
	2.3	2.3	2.4				2.1	2.1
	1.4	1.6	1.6			Current	1.5	1.5
	1.0	1.0	1.5				1.1	1.1
	1.4	1.4	1.6				1.2	1.3
	.8	.8	.9			Quick	.7	.9
	.1	.5	.7				.5	.4
4 93.5	22 16.6	23 16.0					17 21.7	19 18.8
17 20.9	33 11.2	31 11.7				Sales/Receivables	30 12.3	29 12.4
39 9.3	50 7.3	39 9.4					42 8.6	44 8.3
18 20.7	19 18.9	26 14.3					18 20.7	14 25.2
35 10.3	31 11.9	39 9.4				Cost of Sales/Inventory	30 12.0	29 12.7
69 5.3	55 6.6	71 5.2					63 5.8	75 4.9
14 26.0	11 33.6	14 25.6					13 28.8	14 26.4
20 17.9	27 13.7	25 14.4				Cost of Sales/Payables	23 16.2	23 15.8
30 12.3	33 10.9	38 9.6					35 10.4	34 10.8
	7.9	7.1	6.1				9.5	7.6
	28.2	14.3	12.2			Sales/Working Capital	17.5	15.4
	-211.5	-232.1	19.3				53.2	70.8
	25.0	11.2	36.8				9.7	9.4
(14)	3.7 (36)	3.4 (21)	6.1			EBIT/Interest	(88) 3.3	(103) 3.0
	-1.7	1.6	2.7				1.4	1.2
							6.0	6.6
						Net Profit + Depr., Dep., Amort./Cur. Mat. L/T/D	(25) 2.6 (36)	2.3
							1.4	1.2
	.6	.4	.3				.4	.5
	.9	.7	.5			Fixed/Worth	.9	1.0
	2.5	2.2	1.3				2.0	2.1
	.6	.8	.4				.8	.8
	2.4	1.2	.6			Debt/Worth	1.6	2.0
	4.6	3.3	1.8				3.8	3.6
	93.5	30.3	42.2				36.9	48.4
(14)	24.7 (37)	16.0 (22)	27.0			% Profit Before Taxes/Tangible Net Worth	(88) 17.4 (100)	17.2
	-7.7	2.6	11.4				4.7	2.9
	20.5	11.4	26.7				14.6	13.5
	7.7	4.5	14.7			% Profit Before Taxes/Total Assets	6.6	5.0
	-3.4	1.2	6.2				1.5	.3
	11.4	16.5	14.4				19.5	18.2
	8.1	9.5	6.0			Sales/Net Fixed Assets	9.4	9.0
	4.5	4.6	4.7				5.2	4.0
	4.4	3.9	2.6				3.8	3.4
	3.2	2.7	2.3			Sales/Total Assets	2.7	2.5
	2.0	2.1	1.7				2.0	1.8
	.7	1.1	1.1				.9	1.0
(13)	1.1	2.0	2.2			% Depr., Dep., Amort./Sales	(81) 1.9 (100)	2.1
	2.2	2.9	3.1				2.9	3.2
		.7					.6	.6
	(14)	1.9				% Officers', Directors', Owners' Comp/Sales	(24) 1.8 (28)	1.9
		3.2					4.9	4.7
2544M	111979M	514165M	1235973M	857781M	1644613M	Net Sales ($)	2948733M	3680145M
1098M	20053M	185652M	543820M	373678M	784317M	Total Assets ($)	1286194M	1934340M

M = $ thousand   MM = $ million
See Pages 11 through 18 for Explanation of Ratios and Data

Comparative Historical Data | | | | **Current Data Sorted By Sales** | | | | | |

			Type of Statement	0-1MM	1-3MM	3-5MM	5-10MM	10-25MM	25MM & OVER
24	28	39	Unqualified			1	5	10	23
15	11	14	Reviewed		1	2	5	4	2
26	18	9	Compiled		2		4	3	
	2	1	Tax Returns				1		
33	26	27	Other	4	1	2	2	8	10
4/1/00-3/31/01 ALL	4/1/01-3/31/02 ALL	4/1/02-3/31/03 ALL			31 (4/1-9/30/02)			59 (10/1/02-3/31/03)	
98	85	90	**NUMBER OF STATEMENTS**	4	4	5	17	25	35
%	%	%	**ASSETS**	%	%	%	%	%	%
9.1	8.0	9.7	Cash & Equivalents				10.3	5.8	13.2
24.8	22.0	22.7	Trade Receivables (net)				21.5	30.3	19.4
22.3	22.5	20.2	Inventory				18.0	22.1	19.5
2.7	3.5	4.1	All Other Current				2.9	5.7	4.3
58.9	56.0	56.6	Total Current				52.7	63.9	56.3
32.3	34.9	35.5	Fixed Assets (net)				40.4	28.4	33.1
3.1	3.4	1.3	Intangibles (net)				.2	.8	2.6
5.7	5.7	6.6	All Other Non-Current				6.7	6.9	8.0
100.0	100.0	100.0	Total				100.0	100.0	100.0
			LIABILITIES						
10.0	9.5	11.0	Notes Payable-Short Term				15.4	11.6	4.9
2.6	2.5	2.6	Cur. Mat.-L/T/D				2.4	2.6	2.1
15.0	15.6	13.1	Trade Payables				13.2	15.2	12.5
.4	.5	.4	Income Taxes Payable				.2	.4	.7
10.9	8.6	9.4	All Other Current				8.6	7.0	10.9
39.0	36.7	36.6	Total Current				39.9	36.8	31.1
14.8	17.0	15.3	Long Term Debt				11.6	16.4	12.6
.7	.6	.6	Deferred Taxes				.2	.3	1.0
11.6	4.6	3.1	All Other Non-Current				3.2	2.2	4.0
33.9	41.1	44.5	Net Worth				45.1	44.2	51.3
100.0	100.0	100.0	Total Liabilities & Net Worth				100.0	100.0	100.0
			INCOME DATA						
100.0	100.0	100.0	Net Sales				100.0	100.0	100.0
24.1	24.5	26.2	Gross Profit				22.6	23.0	26.3
20.3	20.8	20.8	Operating Expenses				19.7	19.8	19.6
3.8	3.7	5.4	Operating Profit				2.9	3.2	6.8
.3	.6	.4	All Other Expenses (net)				.2	.3	.2
3.5	3.1	5.0	Profit Before Taxes				2.7	2.9	6.5
			RATIOS						
2.3	2.1	2.4	Current				2.5	2.4	2.6
1.5	1.5	1.6					1.4	1.7	1.6
1.1	1.1	1.2					.7	1.2	1.4
1.5	1.2	1.4	Quick				1.6	1.4	1.6
.9	.8	.8					.8	.8	.9
.6	.6	.6					.4	.6	.7
19 19.2	18 20.8	20 18.0	Sales/Receivables				15 23.6	22 16.7	23 16.2
33 11.2	28 13.2	29 12.7					25 14.8	34 10.7	27 13.6
43 8.5	37 10.0	40 9.0					33 11.2	48 7.6	39 9.4
19 19.0	19 19.2	22 16.7	Cost of Sales/Inventory				15 24.7	19 19.1	23 15.6
32 11.5	30 12.3	36 10.3					24 15.0	27 13.6	36 10.2
52 7.0	48 7.7	67 5.4					47 7.7	60 6.1	71 5.2
16 22.4	13 27.2	14 25.6	Cost of Sales/Payables				11 34.6	11 33.8	14 25.6
25 14.4	24 15.3	25 14.3					25 14.5	27 13.5	25 14.4
37 9.9	33 11.1	34 10.8					28 13.2	34 10.9	39 9.3
8.8	11.1	7.0	Sales/Working Capital				7.5	8.0	6.1
14.1	16.7	12.9					32.2	12.2	11.1
51.8	52.6	42.3					-24.7	36.8	19.4
(87) 8.3	(80) 8.2	(82) 15.8	EBIT/Interest		(15) 15.9	(24) 14.9			(30) 33.5
3.3	4.0	4.2			5.1	3.9			7.1
1.5	1.6	1.7			.2	1.6			2.8
(22) 3.6	(27) 12.5	(17) 8.7	Net Profit + Depr., Dep., Amort./Cur. Mat. L/T/D						
1.9	3.5	2.5							
1.1	2.1	1.9							
.4	.5	.4	Fixed/Worth				.4	.2	.3
.9	1.0	.7					.8	.6	.6
1.7	1.9	1.9					1.7	1.6	1.4
.7	.8	.6	Debt/Worth				.6	.8	.4
1.8	1.6	1.2					.8	1.1	.9
4.0	2.9	3.1					3.3	2.2	2.6
(92) 54.3	(80) 38.0	(87) 41.9	% Profit Before Taxes/Tangible Net Worth				40.3	(24) 30.4	(34) 44.2
18.4	17.0	19.5					14.2	17.1	27.0
4.5	4.9	3.6					-1.8	3.9	8.9
15.7	14.2	18.2	% Profit Before Taxes/Total Assets				16.5	12.4	21.0
6.0	6.5	7.6					4.8	5.6	10.0
1.7	1.9	1.4					-1.2	1.4	3.2
19.4	17.4	15.9	Sales/Net Fixed Assets				14.0	42.4	18.3
10.0	9.0	8.0					8.2	14.0	6.0
4.9	5.1	4.6					6.3	5.5	4.7
3.7	4.1	3.5	Sales/Total Assets				3.9	4.1	2.9
2.5	2.9	2.5					3.2	3.0	2.3
1.9	2.0	2.0					2.2	2.2	1.9
(86) 1.1	(78) .7	(84) .9	% Depr., Dep., Amort./Sales		(16) .9			1.0	(31) 1.0
1.8	1.5	2.0			2.0			1.2	2.2
3.2	3.0	3.1			2.7			3.0	3.1
(22) 1.1	(17) .9	(26) .7	% Officers', Directors', Owners' Comp/Sales						
2.0	1.4	1.9							
3.8	3.8	3.4							
4121131M	5118814M	4367055M	Net Sales ($)	2208M	6255M	20290M	120640M	408680M	3808982M
1656298M	1848971M	1908618M	Total Assets ($)	4352M	2850M	10505M	48441M	147310M	1695160M

M = $ thousand   MM = $ million
See Pages 11 through 18 for Explanation of Ratios and Data

Current Data Sorted By Assets   Comparative Historical Data

0-500M	500M-2MM	2-10MM	10-50MM	50-100MM	100-250MM	Type of Statement	4/1/98-3/31/99 ALL	4/1/99-3/31/00 ALL
		4	4	5	5	Unqualified	25	24
	1	1				Reviewed	6	9
	2	3				Compiled	8	8
1		4	5	2	1	Tax Returns	3	4
						Other	10	17
	18 (4/1-9/30/02)		20 (10/1/02-3/31/03)					
1	3	12	9	7	6	NUMBER OF STATEMENTS	52	62
%	%	%	%	%	%	ASSETS	%	%
		5.8				Cash & Equivalents	5.1	4.8
		17.9				Trade Receivables (net)	16.6	18.7
		16.7				Inventory	16.6	18.2
		1.3				All Other Current	1.5	.7
		41.8				Total Current	39.7	42.3
		48.2				Fixed Assets (net)	47.6	48.7
		1.3				Intangibles (net)	5.9	2.8
		8.7				All Other Non-Current	6.7	6.2
		100.0				Total	100.0	100.0
						LIABILITIES		
		8.1				Notes Payable-Short Term	10.9	8.6
		3.6				Cur. Mat.-L/T/D	3.2	4.2
		11.7				Trade Payables	9.4	11.3
		.4				Income Taxes Payable	.1	.5
		5.2				All Other Current	5.2	6.9
		29.0				Total Current	28.8	31.5
		30.0				Long Term Debt	27.4	29.0
		.3				Deferred Taxes	2.0	1.0
		1.8				All Other Non-Current	7.1	5.2
		38.9				Net Worth	34.7	33.2
		100.0				Total Liabilities & Net Worth	100.0	100.0
						INCOME DATA		
		100.0				Net Sales	100.0	100.0
		26.7				Gross Profit	26.2	24.3
		19.3				Operating Expenses	21.9	20.8
		7.4				Operating Profit	4.3	3.5
		.8				All Other Expenses (net)	1.7	1.4
		6.6				Profit Before Taxes	2.6	2.1
						RATIOS		
		2.1				Current	2.2	2.0
		1.4					1.4	1.4
		1.1					1.0	1.1
		1.3				Quick	1.4	1.2
		.7					.7	.8
		.6					.4	.5
		24 15.1				Sales/Receivables	22 16.9 25 14.8	
		32 11.5					29 12.6 31 11.8	
		38 9.6					37 9.8 44 8.4	
		11 32.3				Cost of Sales/Inventory	20 18.1 24 15.3	
		26 14.2					34 10.6 37 10.0	
		85 4.3					62 5.9 59 6.2	
		16 22.3				Cost of Sales/Payables	13 28.7 15 24.3	
		23 15.7					21 17.8 22 16.6	
		42 8.8					29 12.5 34 10.7	
		10.7				Sales/Working Capital	7.0	9.2
		16.7					17.0	18.2
		382.2					334.8	79.8
		10.2				EBIT/Interest	6.3	6.6
		4.2					(51) 3.0	2.8
		1.6					1.4	1.5
						Net Profit + Depr., Dep.,	6.3	6.3
						Amort./Cur. Mat. L./T/D	(23) 2.6 (18) 3.8	
							1.1	2.3
		.5				Fixed/Worth	.8	.7
		1.5					1.5	1.6
		2.8					2.9	3.5
		.9				Debt/Worth	.8	.9
		1.5					1.8	2.1
		3.4					3.6	5.5
		48.0				% Profit Before Taxes/Tangible	37.9	32.9
		23.1				Net Worth	(43) 14.3 (55) 19.8	
		5.1					4.9	7.8
		17.9				% Profit Before Taxes/Total	15.3	12.2
		7.9				Assets	6.9	6.2
		2.0					1.5	1.8
		5.6				Sales/Net Fixed Assets	7.3	7.4
		4.2					4.6	4.4
		2.3					2.7	2.4
		2.9				Sales/Total Assets	2.7	2.7
		2.3					2.1	2.1
		1.2					1.4	1.4
		2.6				% Depr., Dep., Amort./Sales	2.0	1.2
		(11) 3.4					(50) 2.9 (56) 2.4	
		5.1					4.7	4.4
						% Officers', Directors',	1.7	2.7
						Owners' Comp/Sales	(11) 3.2 (10) 4.5	
							4.9	8.8
414M	8292M	141980M	403591M	1062680M	1479603M	Net Sales ($)	2285658M	3123031M
25M	3592M	66810M	217920M	497873M	860453M	Total Assets ($)	1342531M	1575682M

M = $ thousand   MM = $ million
See Pages 11 through 18 for Explanation of Ratios and Data

Comparative Historical Data | Current Data Sorted By Sales

Type of Statement	4/1/00-3/31/01	4/1/01-3/31/02	4/1/02-3/31/03	0-1MM	1-3MM	3-5MM	5-10MM	10-25MM	25MM & OVER
Unqualified	15	16	18				2	2	14
Reviewed	5	6	1				1		
Compiled	7	7	4			1	1	1	1
Tax Returns	1	2	2						
Other	16	16	13	2	2	1	1	1	8
	ALL	ALL	ALL	18 (4/1-9/30/02)			20 (10/1/02-3/31/03)		
NUMBER OF STATEMENTS	44	47	38	2	2	2	5	4	23
ASSETS	%	%	%	%	%	%	%	%	%
Cash & Equivalents	7.5	6.7	4.7						2.8
Trade Receivables (net)	20.1	17.8	19.9						19.8
Inventory	17.1	17.7	19.2						19.0
All Other Current	1.2	1.9	2.3						2.8
Total Current	45.9	44.2	46.1						44.4
Fixed Assets (net)	44.3	47.2	45.4						47.2
Intangibles (net)	3.7	2.1	3.5						4.9
All Other Non-Current	6.1	6.6	5.0						3.5
Total	100.0	100.0	100.0						100.0
LIABILITIES									
Notes Payable-Short Term	7.2	8.1	11.3						9.8
Cur. Mat.-L/T/D	3.3	3.6	2.8						1.9
Trade Payables	12.9	10.6	11.1						9.1
Income Taxes Payable	.3	.4	.4						.3
All Other Current	4.9	6.4	5.4						7.0
Total Current	28.5	29.1	31.0						28.2
Long Term Debt	24.9	22.3	26.1						28.1
Deferred Taxes	1.1	1.5	1.7						2.2
All Other Non-Current	3.9	4.8	3.2						4.2
Net Worth	41.6	42.3	38.0						37.3
Total Liabilities & Net Worth	100.0	100.0	100.0						100.0
INCOME DATA									
Net Sales	100.0	100.0	100.0						100.0
Gross Profit	22.7	23.0	21.8						18.9
Operating Expenses	22.0	19.8	17.7						14.9
Operating Profit	.7	3.2	4.1						4.0
All Other Expenses (net)	-.7	1.5	.9						1.5
Profit Before Taxes	1.3	1.8	3.2						2.5
RATIOS									
Current	2.7	2.2	2.3						2.4
Current	1.6	1.6	1.4						1.4
Current	1.0	1.1	1.1						1.1
Quick	1.9	1.3	1.3						1.3
Quick	1.0	.9	.7						.7
Quick	.4	.5	.5						.5
Sales/Receivables	25 14.5	23 15.8	25 14.5						29 12.6
Sales/Receivables	32 11.4	31 11.7	34 10.8						37 10.0
Sales/Receivables	41 8.9	38 9.5	41 9.0						43 8.4
Cost of Sales/Inventory	19 19.2	26 14.1	16 23.1						27 13.3
Cost of Sales/Inventory	35 10.4	35 10.4	43 8.4						43 8.5
Cost of Sales/Inventory	57 6.4	62 5.9	64 5.7						57 6.4
Cost of Sales/Payables	15 24.0	13 28.6	16 23.3						15 24.8
Cost of Sales/Payables	23 16.1	18 20.3	21 17.6						19 19.5
Cost of Sales/Payables	35 10.4	35 10.6	29 12.6						25 14.7
Sales/Working Capital	6.2	6.0	6.7						6.0
Sales/Working Capital	13.8	11.8	14.1						11.8
Sales/Working Capital	218.0	121.3	51.2						39.9
EBIT/Interest	6.0	4.3	6.1						6.1
EBIT/Interest	(42) 2.6	(44) 2.3	(37) 2.4						2.4
EBIT/Interest	1.1	.8	1.2						1.2
Net Profit + Depr., Dep., Amort./Cur. Mat. L/T/D	5.9	5.8	5.9						7.3
Net Profit + Depr., Dep., Amort./Cur. Mat. L/T/D	(14) 3.1	(15) 2.5	(14) 3.2						(10) 3.1
Net Profit + Depr., Dep., Amort./Cur. Mat. L/T/D	1.8	1.7	2.8						2.5
Fixed/Worth	.6	.6	.7						.7
Fixed/Worth	1.1	1.4	1.3						1.5
Fixed/Worth	2.1	3.1	2.8						3.0
Debt/Worth	.8	.7	.9						.9
Debt/Worth	1.3	1.4	1.7						2.3
Debt/Worth	2.9	3.7	3.6						3.7
% Profit Before Taxes/Tangible Net Worth	19.4	16.8	30.6						25.2
% Profit Before Taxes/Tangible Net Worth	(40) 9.3	(44) 7.9	(35) 13.6						(20) 12.2
% Profit Before Taxes/Tangible Net Worth	1.0	-1.9	2.6						4.2
% Profit Before Taxes/Total Assets	7.8	8.1	9.2						7.9
% Profit Before Taxes/Total Assets	3.6	2.5	4.3						3.8
% Profit Before Taxes/Total Assets	.1	-.5	1.0						1.1
Sales/Net Fixed Assets	8.7	7.0	6.7						6.5
Sales/Net Fixed Assets	4.4	4.5	5.1						5.0
Sales/Net Fixed Assets	2.2	3.2	2.5						2.4
Sales/Total Assets	2.6	2.7	2.5						2.7
Sales/Total Assets	1.9	2.2	2.0						1.9
Sales/Total Assets	1.2	1.5	1.4						1.3
% Depr., Dep., Amort./Sales	2.1	1.6	2.2						1.7
% Depr., Dep., Amort./Sales	(39) 3.2	(43) 2.8	(31) 2.8						(18) 2.5
% Depr., Dep., Amort./Sales	4.4	4.5	4.9						3.5
% Officers', Directors', Owners' Comp/Sales		1.4	1.6						
% Officers', Directors', Owners' Comp/Sales		(10) 3.9	(12) 3.2						
% Officers', Directors', Owners' Comp/Sales		10.2	6.3						
Net Sales ($)	2145928M	2295264M	3096560M	1383M	5248M	6390M	41170M	61386M	2980983M
Total Assets ($)	1189207M	1336802M	1646673M	2811M	2292M	4340M	24785M	28807M	1583638M

© RMA 2003

M = $ thousand   MM = $ million
See Pages 11 through 18 for Explanation of Ratios and Data

Current Data Sorted By Assets   Comparative Historical Data

0-500M	500M-2MM	2-10MM	10-50MM	50-100MM	100-250MM	Type of Statement	4/1/98-3/31/99 ALL	4/1/99-3/31/00 ALL
	1	6	14	6	1	Unqualified	34	34
	5	8	3			Reviewed	20	15
4	8	3	1			Compiled	12	9
2	4	1	1			Tax Returns	3	2
	5	7	6		2	Other	25	26
	32 (4/1-9/30/02)		56 (10/1/02-3/31/03)					
6	23	25	25	6	3	**NUMBER OF STATEMENTS**	94	86
%	%	%	%	%	%	**ASSETS**	%	%
	9.0	9.1	6.9			Cash & Equivalents	8.2	7.3
	17.4	15.4	15.4			Trade Receivables (net)	19.3	18.7
	36.5	20.8	30.7			Inventory	28.5	27.1
	1.1	2.0	1.7			All Other Current	.8	1.4
	64.1	47.2	54.7			Total Current	56.7	54.5
	26.4	42.1	39.1			Fixed Assets (net)	33.5	34.8
	3.1	3.0	1.4			Intangibles (net)	4.7	5.3
	6.4	7.7	4.8			All Other Non-Current	5.2	5.3
	100.0	100.0	100.0			Total	100.0	100.0
						LIABILITIES		
	15.9	7.3	14.3			Notes Payable-Short Term	10.1	11.9
	5.8	4.1	2.7			Cur. Mat.-L/T/D	3.4	3.5
	12.6	11.9	10.6			Trade Payables	10.7	10.6
	.1	.2	.1			Income Taxes Payable	.2	.2
	7.4	8.4	7.8			All Other Current	6.9	6.8
	41.8	31.9	35.5			Total Current	31.4	32.9
	12.7	23.7	14.5			Long Term Debt	19.0	18.8
	.3	.6	.8			Deferred Taxes	.6	.5
	22.7	3.4	3.9			All Other Non-Current	7.4	4.2
	22.6	40.4	45.4			Net Worth	41.6	43.6
	100.0	100.0	100.0			Total Liabilities & Net Worth	100.0	100.0
						INCOME DATA		
	100.0	100.0	100.0			Net Sales	100.0	100.0
	36.5	38.5	26.2			Gross Profit	32.5	35.6
	36.5	33.3	22.0			Operating Expenses	37.1	30.1
	.0	5.3	4.2			Operating Profit	-4.7	5.5
	1.2	3.2	1.0			All Other Expenses (net)	2.0	1.3
	-1.2	2.1	3.2			Profit Before Taxes	-6.7	4.2
						RATIOS		
	2.5	3.6	2.3			Current	3.9	3.1
	1.5	1.5	1.5				1.8	1.7
	.9	.9	1.1				1.2	1.2
	1.0	1.3	1.0			Quick	1.6	1.5
	.5	.6	.4				.8	.7
	.3	.3	.3				.5	.4
	14 25.5	8 47.2	20 17.9			Sales/Receivables	20 18.6	19 19.5
	20 18.4	21 17.1	28 12.8				30 12.1	28 13.0
	40 9.2	36 10.1	41 8.9				43 8.4	51 7.1
	42 8.6	34 10.8	65 5.6			Cost of Sales/Inventory	46 8.0	45 8.2
	72 5.1	61 6.0	85 4.3				73 5.0	66 5.6
	133 2.7	96 3.8	102 3.6				103 3.6	103 3.6
	10 35.3	12 29.3	14 25.9			Cost of Sales/Payables	12 30.8	12 31.2
	22 16.6	26 14.2	21 17.7				23 16.2	24 15.1
	40 9.1	40 9.0	40 9.2				39 9.4	44 8.4
	5.1	4.8	6.4			Sales/Working Capital	5.0	4.8
	16.0	17.9	13.8				9.1	9.7
	-37.8	-42.7	59.1				37.9	39.0
	8.2	9.2	9.3			EBIT/Interest	5.1	5.3
	(20) 2.7	(23) 3.0	(24) 3.1				(81) 2.2	(79) 2.7
	.1	1.2	.9				.7	1.1
		9.4	10.0			Net Profit + Depr., Dep., Amort./Cur. Mat. L/T/D	4.9	8.1
		(11) 2.3	(11) 4.4				(29) 2.4	(29) 2.6
		1.5	1.9				1.2	1.3
	.2	.6	.5			Fixed/Worth	.4	.4
	.9	1.1	.9				.8	1.0
	2.9	2.8	1.9				2.2	2.0
	1.0	.6	.7			Debt/Worth	.5	.5
	2.2	1.4	1.3				1.6	1.5
	16.4	3.9	3.5				4.1	4.2
	21.7	34.2	30.2			% Profit Before Taxes/Tangible Net Worth	30.7	29.3
	(18) 8.9	(24) 15.0	(24) 10.7				(87) 15.7	(77) 15.2
	2.1	2.7	5.3				2.0	1.5
	7.3	18.2	12.6			% Profit Before Taxes/Total Assets	14.0	12.4
	3.9	4.3	4.6				5.0	5.0
	-2.6	.5	.1				-1.3	.5
	32.0	11.4	7.9			Sales/Net Fixed Assets	14.7	13.3
	10.4	5.9	4.5				7.0	6.2
	5.5	2.8	3.5				3.2	3.4
	3.4	2.7	2.2			Sales/Total Assets	2.9	2.7
	2.3	2.0	1.7				2.2	1.9
	1.6	1.3	1.4				1.3	1.4
	1.4	1.6	1.8			% Depr., Dep., Amort./Sales	1.4	1.7
	(22) 3.1	(24) 3.2	(22) 3.3				(86) 2.4	(75) 2.8
	4.4	5.5	4.1				3.8	4.3
	1.7					% Officers', Directors', Owners' Comp/Sales	1.8	1.4
	(15) 3.2						(38) 4.2	(23) 3.2
	6.4						6.6	4.3
6945M	69803M	241715M	963281M	674809M	571190M	Net Sales ($)	2023789M	2145278M
1562M	26323M	125469M	567573M	445935M	345517M	Total Assets ($)	1041054M	1219770M

M = $ thousand   MM = $ million
See Pages 11 through 18 for Explanation of Ratios and Data

Comparative Historical Data / Current Data Sorted By Sales

			Type of Statement					
25	17	28	Unqualified		1	2	5	20
12	8	16	Reviewed	4	1	6	3	2
12	15	16	Compiled	8	1	3	2	1
3	4	8	Tax Returns	1 3 4				1
22	23	20	Other	1 2	1	5	4	7
4/1/00-3/31/01	4/1/01-3/31/02	4/1/02-3/31/03			32 (4/1-9/30/02)		56 (10/1/02-3/31/03)	
ALL	ALL	ALL		0-1MM	1-3MM	3-5MM	5-10MM	10-25MM	25MM & OVER
74	67	88	**NUMBER OF STATEMENTS**	5	18	4	16	14	31
%	%	%	**ASSETS**	%	%	%	%	%	%
7.3	8.0	8.9	Cash & Equivalents		11.2		11.4	7.9	6.8
15.4	16.9	15.5	Trade Receivables (net)		15.2		19.3	16.4	16.2
30.0	29.7	28.7	Inventory		34.3		30.3	22.9	29.5
2.2	1.3	1.8	All Other Current		2.7		1.9	1.7	1.7
55.0	56.0	55.0	Total Current		63.4		62.8	49.0	54.3
36.2	36.2	33.7	Fixed Assets (net)		27.1		25.7	44.6	36.2
4.3	2.8	3.1	Intangibles (net)		3.8		2.1	2.2	4.0
4.5	5.0	8.2	All Other Non-Current		5.7		9.4	4.2	5.6
100.0	100.0	100.0	Total		100.0		100.0	100.0	100.0
			LIABILITIES						
12.2	12.2	12.7	Notes Payable-Short Term		21.5		8.1	12.8	11.4
3.4	3.7	3.7	Cur. Mat.-L/T/D		5.9		2.9	5.1	2.5
10.9	12.8	11.5	Trade Payables		10.0		13.9	15.9	10.4
.1	.6	.2	Income Taxes Payable		.1		.2	.2	.2
6.4	6.8	7.7	All Other Current		8.3		9.6	5.0	7.8
33.0	36.1	35.8	Total Current		45.7		34.6	39.0	32.3
19.4	16.4	16.8	Long Term Debt		15.4		11.7	20.1	15.7
.7	.6	.5	Deferred Taxes		.1		.3	.7	.7
9.0	6.9	8.7	All Other Non-Current		8.9		3.4	7.6	3.3
37.8	39.8	38.3	Net Worth		29.8		50.0	32.7	47.9
100.0	100.0	100.0	Total Liabilities & Net Worth		100.0		100.0	100.0	100.0
			INCOME DATA						
100.0	100.0	100.0	Net Sales		100.0		100.0	100.0	100.0
33.6	34.7	34.3	Gross Profit		41.9		36.5	28.5	27.3
26.7	28.0	31.1	Operating Expenses		41.0		30.8	27.3	22.3
6.9	6.8	3.2	Operating Profit		.9		5.8	1.2	5.1
2.3	1.1	1.6	All Other Expenses (net)		1.8		.7	1.6	.8
4.5	5.7	1.6	Profit Before Taxes		−.9		5.0	−.3	4.2
			RATIOS						
3.2	2.6	2.9			2.9		3.9	2.6	2.6
1.8	1.6	1.5	Current		1.6		1.8	1.2	1.6
1.2	1.2	1.0			.9		1.1	.7	1.1
1.3	1.4	1.2			1.2		1.5	1.4	1.2
.6	.6	.6	Quick		.6		.8	.5	.6
.3	.4	.3			.2		.3	.3	.4
16 23.3	12 29.9	13 28.2		4 89.1		7 55.8	17 21.2	22 16.3
25 14.5	24 15.0	24 15.0	Sales/Receivables	21 17.7		22 16.8	24 15.2	30 12.0
38 9.5	40 9.2	40 9.2		45 8.1		36 10.2	39 9.5	45 8.1
50 7.4	47 7.8	43 8.4		55 6.6		39 9.4	32 11.3	61 6.0
74 4.9	70 5.2	76 4.8	Cost of Sales/Inventory	104 3.5		68 5.4	45 8.1	82 4.4
114 3.2	100 3.6	102 3.6		135 2.7		117 3.1	72 5.1	102 3.6
14 25.8	13 28.6	13 28.8		7 53.3		17 21.7	12 30.5	15 24.5
22 17.0	22 16.2	23 15.8	Cost of Sales/Payables	20 18.7		25 14.7	21 17.6	23 16.1
41 9.0	40 9.1	40 9.2		42 8.6		34 10.8	50 7.3	40 9.1
4.7	5.6	5.3		4.0		5.1	7.5	5.3
8.9	12.6	14.1	Sales/Working Capital	15.2		7.7	33.4	10.0
21.8	26.8	129.8		−37.2		89.1	−12.7	47.0
	5.1	8.6	9.0		3.5		22.5	5.4	11.9
(70) 2.0	(60) 4.2	(79) 2.8	EBIT/Interest	(16) 1.4		(15) 9.2	2.4	(29) 4.0
1.0	1.4	1.1		−1.1		4.3	.4	1.7
4.8	6.7	9.5	Net Profit + Depr., Dep.,					11.0
(22) 2.8	(26) 3.4	(28) 2.7	Amort./Cur. Mat. L/T/D				(13) 4.4
1.1	1.3	1.4						1.9
.5	.4	.3		.3		.2	.7	.5
1.0	.9	1.0	Fixed/Worth	1.3		.6	1.7	.9
2.1	1.7	2.4		NM		1.1	5.0	1.5
.5	.7	.6		1.2		.5	.9	.7
1.8	1.5	1.5	Debt/Worth	2.2		1.2	2.2	1.3
3.2	2.6	4.5		NM		2.3	6.5	3.3
32.6	39.4	30.2		15.4		36.4	23.3	39.6
(67) 12.8	(61) 15.5	(80) 11.1	% Profit Before Taxes/Tangible Net Worth	(14) 8.0		30.8	(12) 9.8	10.5
2.8	6.3	3.0		−.1		12.0	2.4	4.3
11.5	17.8	11.2		6.7		21.9	9.8	12.0
5.1	7.9	4.2	% Profit Before Taxes/Total Assets	1.3		15.1	3.4	4.6
.1	2.0	.7		−6.6		3.0	−2.5	1.8
12.1	12.1	12.6		25.0		38.9	8.2	7.2
5.9	7.3	6.4	Sales/Net Fixed Assets	10.8		11.3	5.9	4.5
2.8	3.6	3.6		4.6		4.1	3.6	3.6
2.6	3.1	2.7		2.5		3.6	3.1	2.2
1.8	2.1	2.0	Sales/Total Assets	2.0		2.3	2.5	1.7
1.3	1.5	1.4		1.3		1.7	1.6	1.3
1.4	1.2	1.6		1.2		1.0	1.5	1.9
(64) 2.4	(60) 2.3	(80) 3.1	% Depr., Dep., Amort./Sales	3.6	(14) 2.8	(13) 2.5	(28) 3.0
3.9	3.1	4.3		4.8		5.5	3.7	4.1
1.4	1.6	2.1		3.8		1.7		
(24) 3.3	(22) 5.1	(34) 4.9	% Officers', Directors', Owners' Comp/Sales	(12) 6.3	(10) 3.0		
7.3		7.9		8.2		7.4		
2162390M	1699403M	2527743M	Net Sales ($)	2831M	32318M	17358M	113897M	210730M	2150609M
1217357M	981542M	1512379M	Total Assets ($)	4237M	20151M	9188M	55450M	97951M	1325402M

M = $ thousand   MM = $ million
See Pages 11 through 18 for Explanation of Ratios and Data

Current Data Sorted By Assets / Comparative Historical Data

0-500M	500M-2MM	2-10MM	10-50MM	50-100MM	100-250MM	Type of Statement	4/1/98-3/31/99 ALL	4/1/99-3/31/00 ALL
		2	7	2	2	Unqualified	18	21
	1	7	1			Reviewed	15	14
	1					Compiled	7	4
	1					Tax Returns		2
1		4	8	1	1	Other	12	22
	16 (4/1-9/30/02)		23 (10/1/02-3/31/03)					
1	3	13	16	3	3	**NUMBER OF STATEMENTS**	52	63
%	%	%	%	%	%	**ASSETS**	%	%
		2.0	1.9			Cash & Equivalents	4.2	5.4
		23.1	18.3			Trade Receivables (net)	16.3	16.5
		30.9	30.7			Inventory	30.7	27.0
		2.3	6.3			All Other Current	1.8	2.4
		58.3	57.2			Total Current	53.0	51.3
		28.7	37.4			Fixed Assets (net)	38.1	41.2
		5.5	.9			Intangibles (net)	3.9	2.9
		7.5	4.4			All Other Non-Current	5.1	4.6
		100.0	100.0			Total	100.0	100.0
						LIABILITIES		
		12.3	15.9			Notes Payable-Short Term	13.5	12.9
		2.8	3.0			Cur. Mat.-L/T/D	3.2	5.5
		24.5	16.6			Trade Payables	14.6	12.4
		.4	.3			Income Taxes Payable	.2	.3
		12.1	12.8			All Other Current	6.3	7.2
		52.1	48.7			Total Current	37.7	38.4
		16.1	15.8			Long Term Debt	17.9	22.5
		.4	.9			Deferred Taxes	1.4	1.5
		3.6	5.5			All Other Non-Current	3.3	2.9
		27.8	29.2			Net Worth	39.7	34.6
		100.0	100.0			Total Liabilities & Net Worth	100.0	100.0
						INCOME DATA		
		100.0	100.0			Net Sales	100.0	100.0
		20.6	15.7			Gross Profit	25.8	21.1
		17.2	14.2			Operating Expenses	18.5	15.6
		3.4	1.5			Operating Profit	7.3	5.4
		1.3	2.0			All Other Expenses (net)	2.3	2.1
		2.1	-.5			Profit Before Taxes	5.0	3.3
						RATIOS		
		1.7	1.7			Current	2.4	2.2
		1.1	1.2				1.4	1.4
		.8	1.1				1.0	1.2
		.7	.6			Quick	1.1	1.1
		.4	.4				.5	.6
		.3	.3				.3	.3
		23 15.6	28 12.9			Sales/Receivables	26 14.2	24 15.2
		35 10.4	40 9.1				31 11.7	31 11.9
		46 8.0	53 6.9				43 8.4	42 8.6
		25 14.5	37 9.8			Cost of Sales/Inventory	36 10.0	29 12.4
		37 9.9	106 3.4				89 4.1	82 4.4
		104 3.5	185 2.0				156 2.3	155 2.4
		20 18.0	18 20.0			Cost of Sales/Payables	19 18.9	19 19.7
		53 6.9	41 8.9				37 10.0	30 12.2
		69 5.3	52 7.0				52 7.0	48 7.6
		12.9	7.5			Sales/Working Capital	5.8	5.2
		64.8	19.4				11.0	11.2
		-16.3	77.8				59.9	43.8
		4.1	7.5			EBIT/Interest	(49) 7.0	(61) 6.8
		(11) 2.3	2.5				2.2	2.4
		.3	-1.3				1.0	1.3
						Net Profit + Depr., Dep., Amort./Cur. Mat. L /T/D	(19) 3.5	(20) 4.4
							3.0	2.8
							1.1	1.2
		.5	.8			Fixed/Worth	.7	.7
		1.5	1.1				1.0	1.1
		8.5	1.8				2.3	2.6
		1.4	1.5			Debt/Worth	.8	.9
		4.4	2.3				1.9	2.1
		25.0	5.5				4.4	5.4
		49.6	26.9			% Profit Before Taxes/Tangible Net Worth	(47) 24.8	(58) 27.6
		(11) 22.0	(14) 18.1				13.4	15.6
		-.3	-2.9				1.3	5.5
		18.5	7.6			% Profit Before Taxes/Total Assets	12.1	11.3
		2.2	2.6				3.8	5.0
		-1.3	-9.1				.2	1.2
		19.5	5.2			Sales/Net Fixed Assets	5.8	6.4
		7.6	3.9				3.7	4.1
		4.2	2.4				3.0	2.4
		3.1	2.2			Sales/Total Assets	1.7	2.4
		1.9	1.2				1.5	1.4
		1.5	.8				1.1	1.0
		1.3	1.9			% Depr., Dep., Amort./Sales	(46) 2.0	(58) 2.2
		(12) 2.4	(14) 3.4				3.4	3.3
		3.9	4.9				4.4	4.5
						% Officers', Directors', Owners' Comp/Sales	(13) .7	(13) .9
							1.1	2.2
							2.9	2.7
55M	11560M	163991M	600753M	559192M	634354M	Net Sales ($)	2654387M	3217862M
61M	4662M	69933M	443406M	203470M	564458M	Total Assets ($)	1927017M	2376453M

M = $ thousand   MM = $ million
See Pages 11 through 18 for Explanation of Ratios and Data

Comparative Historical Data | Current Data Sorted By Sales

Type of Statement	4/1/00-3/31/01 ALL	4/1/01-3/31/02 ALL	4/1/02-3/31/03 ALL	0-1MM	1-3MM	3-5MM	5-10MM	10-25MM	25MM & OVER
Unqualified	13	16	13				1	3	9
Reviewed	5	7	9		1		3	2	3
Compiled	7	5	1			1			
Tax Returns			1	1					
Other	19	15	15		1		3	4	7
				16 (4/1-9/30/02)			23 (10/1/02-3/31/03)		
NUMBER OF STATEMENTS	44	43	39	1	2	1	7	9	19
ASSETS	%	%	%	%	%	%	%	%	%
Cash & Equivalents	5.0	5.0	2.4						2.6
Trade Receivables (net)	18.2	17.3	19.8						22.2
Inventory	32.9	29.2	27.8						27.8
All Other Current	3.3	2.4	4.0						2.4
Total Current	59.3	53.9	54.0						55.0
Fixed Assets (net)	33.9	40.2	38.4						40.0
Intangibles (net)	2.1	2.5	2.8						1.1
All Other Non-Current	4.6	3.4	4.8						3.9
Total	100.0	100.0	100.0						100.0
LIABILITIES									
Notes Payable-Short Term	16.7	16.0	12.7						10.4
Cur. Mat.-L/T/D	3.6	4.4	3.0						4.0
Trade Payables	14.7	15.4	18.4						20.7
Income Taxes Payable	.3	.2	.4						.6
All Other Current	7.1	9.3	13.8						9.6
Total Current	42.4	45.3	48.3						45.4
Long Term Debt	21.9	19.2	17.5						16.5
Deferred Taxes	1.6	.9	1.2						1.6
All Other Non-Current	3.0	4.0	4.7						6.0
Net Worth	31.1	30.6	28.4						30.5
Total Liabilities & Net Worth	100.0	100.0	100.0						100.0
INCOME DATA									
Net Sales	100.0	100.0	100.0						100.0
Gross Profit	18.4	21.5	17.8						15.3
Operating Expenses	14.1	18.6	14.7						12.0
Operating Profit	4.3	3.0	3.2						3.3
All Other Expenses (net)	1.6	2.6	1.8						1.8
Profit Before Taxes	2.7	.3	1.4						1.6
RATIOS									
Current	2.4	1.9	1.8						1.8
	1.3	1.2	1.2						1.4
	1.1	1.0	.9						1.1
Quick	1.0	.7	.7						.7
	.5	.4	.4						.5
	.3	.3	.3						.3
Sales/Receivables	27 13.4	24 15.5	24 15.0						24 15.0
	34 10.9	35 10.5	35 10.4						33 10.9
	43 8.4	51 7.2	46 7.9						43 8.5
Cost of Sales/Inventory	41 9.0	35 10.6	31 11.9						25 14.4
	99 3.7	100 3.6	72 5.1						70 5.2
	163 2.2	170 2.2	131 2.8						117 3.1
Cost of Sales/Payables	16 22.5	18 20.2	17 21.5						16 23.5
	34 10.6	31 11.8	31 11.7						21 17.8
	45 8.0	59 6.1	56 6.5						46 7.9
Sales/Working Capital	4.5	5.8	10.1						7.3
	10.9	17.4	24.1						15.9
	31.1	635.8	−41.9						93.2
EBIT/Interest	(42) 5.0	(40) 3.5	(37) 5.6						5.7
	1.8	1.6	2.8						4.1
	1.2	.8	.4						1.4
Net Profit + Depr., Dep., Amort./Cur. Mat. L/T/D	(17) 5.6	(16) 2.7	(14) 5.7						
	2.4	1.4	2.4						
	1.5	.8	1.4						
Fixed/Worth	.6	.7	.8						.8
	1.0	1.3	1.3						1.0
	2.4	3.2	2.4						2.0
Debt/Worth	1.1	1.1	1.5						1.5
	2.7	2.4	2.9						2.1
	5.4	8.0	8.2						3.8
% Profit Before Taxes/Tangible Net Worth	(40) 28.3	(39) 16.1	(34) 45.3					(17)	47.5
	12.9	6.8	19.8						22.0
	3.4	.0	.0						9.0
% Profit Before Taxes/Total Assets	8.6	4.6	11.4						14.1
	3.2	2.1	2.5						7.8
	.9	−.9	−1.6						.7
Sales/Net Fixed Assets	8.7	6.9	7.6						5.9
	4.3	3.8	4.1						3.7
	3.0	2.3	2.8						2.8
Sales/Total Assets	1.9	2.4	2.4						2.5
	1.4	1.4	1.6						1.7
	1.1	1.1	.9						.9
% Depr., Dep., Amort./Sales	(37) .5	(38) 2.0	(35) 1.5					(16)	1.5
	2.9	3.3	3.3						3.2
	3.9	4.4	4.7						4.5
% Officers', Directors', Owners' Comp/Sales									
Net Sales ($)	3079261M	2492387M	1969905M	55M	4259M	4745M	49832M	149578M	1761436M
Total Assets ($)	2282009M	1846835M	1285990M	61M	5070M	843M	23883M	146663M	1109470M

M = $ thousand   MM = $ million
See Pages 11 through 18 for Explanation of Ratios and Data

Current Data Sorted By Assets   Comparative Historical Data

Columns in the "DATA NOT AVAILABLE" area (0-500M and 500M-2MM) carry no percentile data.

0-500M	500M-2MM	2-10MM	10-50MM	50-100MM	100-250MM		4/1/98-3/31/99 ALL	4/1/99-3/31/00 ALL
						Type of Statement		
		3	7	1	1	Unqualified	8	9
	2	4	9	1		Reviewed	7	7
	2	2	1			Compiled	5	4
						Tax Returns	1	2
	1	5	7	1	1	Other	9	15
	15 (4/1-9/30/02)		33 (10/1/02-3/31/03)					
	5	14	24	3	2	**NUMBER OF STATEMENTS**	30	37
%	%	%	%	%	%	**ASSETS**	%	%
		7.1	8.5			Cash & Equivalents	4.4	7.3
		20.4	17.7			Trade Receivables (net)	25.0	21.0
		20.0	19.9			Inventory	21.2	21.0
		1.6	1.1			All Other Current	1.9	2.3
		49.1	47.2			Total Current	52.5	51.7
		41.0	36.9			Fixed Assets (net)	35.0	34.2
		3.5	10.1			Intangibles (net)	7.3	7.9
		6.4	5.8			All Other Non-Current	5.1	6.2
		100.0	100.0			Total	100.0	100.0
						LIABILITIES		
		11.7	6.4			Notes Payable-Short Term	9.0	9.9
		7.0	3.9			Cur. Mat.-L/T/D	6.6	4.1
		19.8	11.2			Trade Payables	18.5	16.0
		.6	.5			Income Taxes Payable	.4	.4
		3.5	9.5			All Other Current	8.0	11.0
		42.6	31.5			Total Current	42.4	41.4
		18.1	20.4			Long Term Debt	20.0	19.2
		.3	.6			Deferred Taxes	.9	.2
		8.3	5.3			All Other Non-Current	7.8	14.5
		30.7	42.1			Net Worth	28.9	24.7
		100.0	100.0			Total Liabilities & Net Worth	100.0	100.0
						INCOME DATA		
		100.0	100.0			Net Sales	100.0	100.0
		28.4	26.2			Gross Profit	29.2	35.1
		24.6	20.0			Operating Expenses	25.2	26.5
		3.8	6.3			Operating Profit	3.9	8.6
		1.2	1.3			All Other Expenses (net)	2.2	1.5
		2.6	5.0			Profit Before Taxes	1.7	7.1
						RATIOS		
		1.6	2.0			Current	1.9	2.0
		1.3	1.6				1.3	1.3
		.8	1.1				1.0	1.0
		.9	1.5			Quick	1.0	1.1
		.6	.7				.7	.7
		.4	.4				.6	.4
		15 24.4	20 18.1			Sales/Receivables	28 13.1	19 19.2
		24 15.4	25 14.4				32 11.4	29 12.5
		31 11.6	32 11.4				39 9.4	37 10.0
		21 17.0	27 13.7			Cost of Sales/Inventory	26 14.1	28 13.1
		30 12.2	36 10.1				41 8.8	46 7.9
		51 7.2	63 5.8				63 5.8	59 6.2
		14 25.6	12 31.4			Cost of Sales/Payables	19 19.3	18 20.7
		35 10.5	24 15.2				32 11.5	32 11.4
		49 7.4	35 10.4				46 7.9	37 9.9
		18.7	6.9			Sales/Working Capital	11.4	10.0
		29.1	17.3				20.4	21.7
		−29.8	68.1				−794.5	−222.9
		(13) 4.2	(21) 17.5			EBIT/Interest	8.5	14.6
		3.3	5.8				(33) 3.1	6.0
		1.0	3.7				.4	1.8
						Net Profit + Depr., Dep., Amort./Cur. Mat. L/T/D	(10) 3.4	
							2.3	
							1.1	
		.8	.5			Fixed/Worth	.9	.7
		2.2	1.1				1.5	1.3
		NM	5.9				10.3	11.1
		.7	.6			Debt/Worth	1.3	1.1
		3.8	1.4				3.3	2.1
		NM	10.0				45.7	20.1
		(11) 56.4	(20) 56.5			% Profit Before Taxes/Tangible Net Worth	(24) 68.0	(29) 87.9
		29.7	42.6				34.9	48.8
		3.8	14.3				2.1	30.1
		10.4	23.5			% Profit Before Taxes/Total Assets	16.0	23.7
		4.8	8.0				7.0	10.2
		.3	5.1				−2.7	3.6
		13.4	8.8			Sales/Net Fixed Assets	19.5	14.4
		6.9	5.3				6.9	7.2
		3.2	3.8				5.0	4.9
		3.6	2.9			Sales/Total Assets	3.5	3.3
		2.9	2.3				2.5	2.6
		2.0	1.5				1.9	1.8
		(13) 1.3	(23) 1.6			% Depr., Dep., Amort./Sales	(27) 1.1	(32) 1.6
		1.6	2.7				1.9	2.2
		3.5					3.0	4.1
						% Officers', Directors', Owners' Comp/Sales		
	16581M	183389M	1279434M	236761M	396372M	Net Sales ($)	2196241M	2335115M
	5967M	67654M	557342M	214512M	330423M	Total Assets ($)	998946M	1098106M

M = $ thousand   MM = $ million
See Pages 11 through 18 for Explanation of Ratios and Data

Comparative Historical Data | Current Data Sorted By Sales

			Type of Statement	0-1MM	1-3MM	3-5MM	5-10MM	10-25MM	25MM & OVER
9	10	12	Unqualified					3	9
5	10	16	Reviewed	1		3		3	9
3	8	5	Compiled	1		2		1	1
2	2		Tax Returns						
9	19	15	Other	1		3		4	7
4/1/00-3/31/01 ALL	4/1/01-3/31/02 ALL	4/1/02-3/31/03 ALL			15 (4/1-9/30/02)		33 (10/1/02-3/31/03)		
28	49	48	**NUMBER OF STATEMENTS**		3		8	11	26
%	%	%	**ASSETS**	%	%	%	%	%	%
7.5	8.7	7.0	Cash & Equivalents					5.4	8.9
19.2	21.4	17.3	Trade Receivables (net)					16.0	16.9
21.1	19.5	18.1	Inventory	DATA	DATA			18.7	18.7
2.8	.4	1.2	All Other Current	NOT	NOT			1.7	.9
50.5	50.0	43.6	Total Current	AVAILABLE	AVAILABLE			41.8	45.4
37.0	39.5	40.6	Fixed Assets (net)					40.4	36.2
8.7	6.2	10.4	Intangibles (net)					12.2	13.2
3.7	4.2	5.4	All Other Non-Current					5.7	5.2
100.0	100.0	100.0	Total					100.0	100.0
			LIABILITIES						
8.4	8.8	8.4	Notes Payable-Short Term					8.7	5.4
2.6	6.6	5.5	Cur. Mat.-L/T/D					3.9	4.0
16.5	13.1	13.7	Trade Payables					14.8	10.6
.5	.3	.5	Income Taxes Payable					.3	.5
10.7	12.3	7.0	All Other Current					3.4	9.1
38.7	41.1	35.0	Total Current					31.0	29.5
19.2	22.0	22.6	Long Term Debt					22.3	18.2
.1	.4	.7	Deferred Taxes					.3	1.2
10.5	6.4	7.0	All Other Non-Current					16.8	5.6
31.4	30.1	34.8	Net Worth					29.4	45.6
100.0	100.0	100.0	Total Liabilities & Net Worth					100.0	100.0
			INCOME DATA						
100.0	100.0	100.0	Net Sales					100.0	100.0
35.7	32.2	29.4	Gross Profit					30.9	26.9
30.5	28.5	24.5	Operating Expenses					27.0	20.0
5.1	3.7	4.9	Operating Profit					4.0	6.9
1.9	1.5	1.5	All Other Expenses (net)					2.0	1.3
3.3	2.2	3.3	Profit Before Taxes					1.9	5.6
			RATIOS						
1.8	2.0	1.8	Current					1.6	2.2
1.6	1.2	1.3						1.4	1.3
.9	.9	.8						1.2	1.0
1.0	1.2	1.1	Quick					1.0	1.5
.7	.7	.6						.6	.7
.5	.5	.4						.4	.4
21 17.5	19 18.8	16 22.4	Sales/Receivables					13 28.6	19 18.9
27 13.3	27 13.6	24 15.0						26 14.1	24 15.0
34 10.7	35 10.5	32 11.5						38 9.6	30 12.1
28 13.0	24 15.2	26 14.3	Cost of Sales/Inventory					25 14.9	27 13.6
46 7.9	36 10.1	37 9.8						31 11.7	38 9.5
58 6.3	55 6.6	50 7.2						59 6.2	54 6.8
19 18.8	15 23.7	13 28.4	Cost of Sales/Payables					18 20.2	11 34.0
32 11.6	22 16.6	28 13.1						34 10.6	24 15.2
44 8.4	37 9.9	42 8.6						47 7.8	33 11.0
9.6	13.1	11.7	Sales/Working Capital					12.6	7.4
19.3	36.7	27.6						21.7	24.4
NM	-78.5	-43.6						59.1	-351.5
(27) 6.5	(43) 4.3	(43) 9.3	EBIT/Interest					4.9	(21) 21.2
2.2	2.6	3.8						3.6	5.5
1.0	.4	1.1						1.2	2.8
		(15) 4.2	Net Profit + Depr., Dep., Amort./Cur. Mat. L/T/D						
		2.0							
		1.1							
.8	.7	.8	Fixed/Worth					1.1	.4
1.5	1.4	1.8						2.4	1.1
NM	NM	NM						-12.5	NM
1.3	1.1	.9	Debt/Worth					1.4	.6
2.6	2.2	3.8						4.4	1.4
NM	NM	NM						-17.0	NM
(21) 65.4	(37) 47.3	(36) 57.1	% Profit Before Taxes/Tangible Net Worth						(20) 58.0
31.3	16.4	36.2							43.0
12.3	-5.0	6.3							14.3
17.3	13.2	12.3	% Profit Before Taxes/Total Assets					8.2	25.0
5.1	5.2	7.0						3.2	10.8
.3	-3.0	.6						.6	5.3
13.5	11.4	11.6	Sales/Net Fixed Assets					12.4	10.1
8.2	5.8	4.8						4.2	5.3
4.4	4.0	3.2						2.5	3.7
3.4	3.5	3.0	Sales/Total Assets					3.4	3.0
2.6	2.5	2.3						1.9	2.3
1.9	1.9	1.5						1.2	1.6
(24) .6	(42) 1.2	(44) 1.5	% Depr., Dep., Amort./Sales					1.3	(23) 1.6
2.4	2.9	2.6						2.4	2.5
3.5	4.8	4.4						5.3	3.4
	(20) 1.2		% Officers', Directors', Owners' Comp/Sales						
	3.7								
	6.8								
1739254M	2561503M	2112537M	Net Sales ($)		4566M		59332M	178466M	1870173M
835426M	1093996M	1175898M	Total Assets ($)		2775M		22499M	104722M	1045902M

© RMA 2003

M = $ thousand   MM = $ million
See Pages 11 through 18 for Explanation of Ratios and Data

Current Data Sorted By Assets   Comparative Historical Data

						Type of Statement		
1		2	13	3	9	Unqualified	32	34
	1	8	3			Reviewed	19	19
	2	2				Compiled	6	12
			1			Tax Returns	5	1
1	3	2	9	5	4	Other	25	24
	31 (4/1-9/30/02)		38 (10/1/02-3/31/03)				4/1/98-3/31/99	4/1/99-3/31/00
0-500M	500M-2MM	2-10MM	10-50MM	50-100MM	100-250MM		ALL	ALL
2	6	14	26	8	13	NUMBER OF STATEMENTS	87	90
%	%	%	%	%	%	ASSETS	%	%
		5.8	3.7		2.4	Cash & Equivalents	5.6	6.8
		19.3	17.1		12.2	Trade Receivables (net)	17.6	17.9
		32.1	39.8		34.5	Inventory	34.6	32.3
		1.9	1.7		1.5	All Other Current	2.0	1.6
		59.2	62.3		50.6	Total Current	59.9	58.6
		35.5	29.8		43.2	Fixed Assets (net)	33.8	32.8
		1.0	2.2		2.9	Intangibles (net)	1.5	3.0
		4.3	5.7		3.3	All Other Non-Current	4.8	5.7
		100.0	100.0		100.0	Total	100.0	100.0
						LIABILITIES		
		7.2	13.6		8.3	Notes Payable-Short Term	16.0	13.9
		4.2	2.4		3.8	Cur. Mat.-L/T/D	3.0	2.3
		11.9	12.4		11.8	Trade Payables	12.8	15.7
		.3	.1		.1	Income Taxes Payable	.2	.2
		9.4	7.7		9.3	All Other Current	6.5	5.9
		32.9	36.3		33.3	Total Current	38.5	38.0
		16.8	16.0		16.5	Long Term Debt	15.0	15.8
		1.5	.6		.9	Deferred Taxes	.8	.9
		3.6	2.7		3.6	All Other Non-Current	2.7	3.1
		45.1	44.5		45.7	Net Worth	42.9	42.2
		100.0	100.0		100.0	Total Liabilities & Net Worth	100.0	100.0
						INCOME DATA		
		100.0	100.0		100.0	Net Sales	100.0	100.0
		25.1	20.7		20.3	Gross Profit	21.3	22.1
		22.0	16.0		12.3	Operating Expenses	18.8	17.1
		3.2	4.6		8.0	Operating Profit	2.6	5.0
		.5	1.3		2.2	All Other Expenses (net)	2.1	1.5
		2.6	3.4		5.8	Profit Before Taxes	.5	3.5
						RATIOS		
		2.8	3.0		1.9		2.4	2.4
		1.7	1.6		1.6	Current	1.6	1.5
		1.3	1.2		1.3		1.2	1.1
		1.7	1.0		.6		1.0	1.2
		.7	.5		.5	Quick	.5	.5
		.4	.3		.3		.3	.3
		24 15.4	24 15.5		22 16.9		21 17.1	21 17.2
		27 13.3	32 11.4		25 14.6	Sales/Receivables	29 12.4	29 12.8
		37 10.0	44 8.2		29 12.5		34 10.6	37 10.0
		32 11.4	76 4.8		70 5.2		46 7.9	40 9.1
		67 5.4	106 3.5		96 3.8	Cost of Sales/Inventory	81 4.5	73 5.0
		106 3.4	151 2.4		131 2.8		137 2.7	120 3.1
		6 57.4	14 25.5		18 19.9		13 28.2	15 24.7
		17 21.2	24 15.2		32 11.4	Cost of Sales/Payables	24 15.1	28 13.1
		31 11.6	62 5.9		52 7.0		40 9.1	52 7.1
		6.9	4.1		5.9		5.8	4.8
		9.2	5.7		8.6	Sales/Working Capital	9.9	11.0
		28.7	15.7		16.4		27.1	28.9
		18.5	5.9		4.9		(76) 5.0	(84) 6.5
		(13) 2.2	(22) 2.8		3.0	EBIT/Interest	2.7	3.5
		1.1	1.4		2.6		1.1	1.5
						Net Profit + Depr., Dep.,	(38) 5.8	(35) 7.3
						Amort./Cur. Mat. L /T/D	2.7	3.2
							1.2	1.1
		.3	.4		.8		.4	.4
		.9	.7		1.1	Fixed/Worth	.9	.8
		1.7	1.4		1.6		1.3	1.4
		.5	.7		.7		.8	.7
		1.4	1.6		1.3	Debt/Worth	1.4	1.6
		3.6	3.7		2.3		2.8	3.6
		28.1	19.7		28.4	% Profit Before Taxes/Tangible	(85) 27.4	(85) 37.1
		(13) 11.4	(25) 15.4		19.8	Net Worth	13.9	18.6
		-.1	10.6		15.7		2.3	6.8
		15.3	10.0		11.8	% Profit Before Taxes/Total	10.5	16.3
		5.2	6.3		8.2	Assets	5.0	6.4
		.7	2.1		6.5		.6	1.6
		17.3	9.9		5.9		12.9	11.4
		7.0	6.1		3.6	Sales/Net Fixed Assets	6.0	6.5
		3.5	3.7		3.0		3.9	4.4
		3.2	1.9		2.0		2.8	2.8
		2.2	1.6		1.7	Sales/Total Assets	1.9	2.0
		1.7	1.4		1.5		1.4	1.5
		1.1	1.8		2.3		(79) .9	(81) 1.6
		1.8	(25) 2.6		(11) 2.5	% Depr., Dep., Amort./Sales	2.3	2.4
		2.6	3.4		3.3		3.2	3.3
						% Officers', Directors',	(25) 1.4	(22) .9
						Owners' Comp/Sales	2.5	1.9
							5.5	3.9
249M	15336M	181075M	1141719M	794336M	3572486M	Net Sales ($)	4220912M	5549120M
109M	6741M	81429M	690552M	571908M	2116354M	Total Assets ($)	2581184M	3087185M

M = $ thousand   MM = $ million
See Pages 11 through 18 for Explanation of Ratios and Data

Comparative Historical Data				Current Data Sorted By Sales					

Type of Statement

23	17	28	Unqualified	1				5	22
14	13	12	Reviewed			1	2	7	2
8	10	4	Compiled		1	2	1		1
1		1	Tax Returns						1
23	21	24	Other	2	2			6	14
4/1/00- 3/31/01 ALL	4/1/01- 3/31/02 ALL	4/1/02- 3/31/03 ALL		31 (4/1-9/30/02) 0-1MM	1-3MM	3-5MM	38 (10/1/02-3/31/03) 5-10MM	10-25MM	25MM & OVER
69	61	69	**NUMBER OF STATEMENTS**	3	3	3	3	18	39

%	%	%	**ASSETS**	%	%	%	%	%	%
5.2	4.9	3.7	Cash & Equivalents					5.4	2.6
15.0	15.5	16.7	Trade Receivables (net)					17.8	14.7
34.0	35.4	34.8	Inventory					34.8	37.7
3.3	2.1	2.4	All Other Current					1.7	3.3
57.5	57.8	57.6	Total Current					59.8	58.3
33.4	34.0	33.5	Fixed Assets (net)					33.1	33.9
2.4	2.4	2.7	Intangibles (net)					1.1	3.2
6.8	5.9	6.2	All Other Non-Current					6.0	4.6
100.0	100.0	100.0	Total					100.0	100.0

			LIABILITIES						
17.3	15.0	11.4	Notes Payable-Short Term					8.7	14.4
2.2	2.8	3.3	Cur. Mat.-L/T/D					3.9	3.2
12.9	13.6	13.9	Trade Payables					14.3	10.9
.1	.2	.2	Income Taxes Payable					.4	.1
6.1	5.7	7.9	All Other Current					6.7	7.9
38.7	37.3	36.7	Total Current					33.9	36.5
21.3	18.2	18.7	Long Term Debt					16.9	17.3
.7	.7	.8	Deferred Taxes					1.2	.6
5.2	5.4	3.7	All Other Non-Current					3.6	3.1
34.1	38.5	40.2	Net Worth					44.4	42.4
100.0	100.0	100.0	Total Liabilities & Net Worth					100.0	100.0

			INCOME DATA						
100.0	100.0	100.0	Net Sales					100.0	100.0
20.8	23.6	21.8	Gross Profit					23.3	18.1
16.2	18.1	16.9	Operating Expenses					18.0	12.2
4.6	5.4	5.0	Operating Profit					5.3	5.9
1.7	1.7	1.6	All Other Expenses (net)					.8	1.8
2.9	3.7	3.3	Profit Before Taxes					4.5	4.1

			RATIOS						
2.4	2.5	2.6	Current					3.2	2.8
1.5	1.7	1.6						1.6	1.6
1.1	1.1	1.2						1.1	1.2
.9	1.2	.9	Quick					1.7	.8
.5	.5	.5						.7	.5
.3	.3	.3						.3	.3
22 16.5	22 16.8	24 15.4	Sales/Receivables					22 16.7	24 15.3
28 13.1	29 12.8	30 12.2						28 13.1	30 12.1
35 10.3	37 9.8	40 9.2						43 8.5	37 9.8
43 8.4	49 7.5	49 7.4	Cost of Sales/Inventory					35 10.3	69 5.3
86 4.2	90 4.1	95 3.8						98 3.7	100 3.6
147 2.5	145 2.5	137 2.7						129 2.8	153 2.4
15 24.6	17 20.9	14 25.7	Cost of Sales/Payables					18 20.7	12 29.8
29 12.7	28 13.2	27 13.3						30 12.0	23 15.7
46 7.9	52 7.0	57 6.4						64 5.7	48 7.5
5.3	4.3	5.1	Sales/Working Capital					4.1	5.1
10.6	10.0	9.0						8.5	7.7
44.0	39.3	21.7						28.7	17.6
5.0	4.1	5.1	EBIT/Interest					8.2	5.2
(67) 2.3	(57) 2.5	(63) 2.7					(16)	3.1	(37) 2.9
1.1	1.3	1.4						1.6	1.7
15.0	3.3	5.3	Net Profit + Depr., Dep., Amort./Cur. Mat. L/T/D						5.4
(24) 2.8	(21) 2.4	(29) 2.7							(16) 3.1
1.1	1.1	1.0							1.6
.5	.5	.5	Fixed/Worth					.3	.5
1.1	1.1	.9						.7	.9
2.2	2.2	1.8						1.8	1.5
1.0	.9	.8	Debt/Worth					.3	.8
2.2	1.9	1.6						1.6	1.5
4.9	5.0	3.8						3.6	3.8
35.7	27.2	24.5	% Profit Before Taxes/Tangible Net Worth					24.5	22.7
(62) 16.6	(56) 15.1	(64) 16.1					(16)	19.7	(38) 15.7
6.3	4.7	10.3						9.5	11.9
11.3	10.4	10.6	% Profit Before Taxes/Total Assets					15.3	10.1
4.1	5.0	6.2						6.6	6.9
.3	1.1	2.0						2.0	2.5
9.3	8.1	9.8	Sales/Net Fixed Assets					8.9	9.6
5.9	6.1	6.1						6.5	5.6
3.3	3.3	3.6						3.5	3.5
2.4	2.1	2.0	Sales/Total Assets					2.4	1.9
1.6	1.7	1.7						1.9	1.6
1.3	1.3	1.5						1.6	1.4
1.1	1.6	1.6	% Depr., Dep., Amort./Sales					1.7	1.7
(65) 2.5	(54) 2.5	(65) 2.4						2.2	(36) 2.6
3.5	3.3	3.3						3.2	3.5
.9	1.4	1.2	% Officers', Directors', Owners' Comp/Sales						
(13) 1.7	(11) 4.4	(12) 2.8							
2.9	6.8	3.3							

5021362M	4408263M	5705201M	Net Sales ($)	611M	7203M	12631M	22104M	321557M	5341095M
3214604M	2727747M	3467093M	Total Assets ($)	634M	3739M	9237M	7622M	174483M	3271378M

© RMA 2003

M = $ thousand   MM = $ million
See Pages 11 through 18 for Explanation of Ratios and Data

Current Data Sorted By Assets							Comparative Historical Data	
						Type of Statement		
	1	3	7	1	3	Unqualified	10	11
		2				Reviewed	3	2
	2	2	1			Compiled	4	4
	1					Tax Returns	1	1
	3	1	5	2	2	Other	8	12
	19 (4/1-9/30/02)		17 (10/1/02-3/31/03)				**4/1/98-3/31/99**	**4/1/99-3/31/00**
0-500M	**500M-2MM**	**2-10MM**	**10-50MM**	**50-100MM**	**100-250MM**		**ALL**	**ALL**
	7	8	13	3	5	**NUMBER OF STATEMENTS**	26	30
%	%	%	%	%	%	**ASSETS**	%	%
DATA NOT AVAILABLE			4.0			Cash & Equivalents	1.6	3.2
			15.3			Trade Receivables (net)	20.7	22.8
			33.6			Inventory	41.5	38.8
			3.4			All Other Current	2.1	2.9
			56.3			Total Current	65.9	67.8
			30.9			Fixed Assets (net)	24.8	22.0
			9.0			Intangibles (net)	4.5	3.7
			3.8			All Other Non-Current	4.9	6.5
			100.0			Total	100.0	100.0
						LIABILITIES		
			16.1			Notes Payable-Short Term	16.1	21.0
			8.5			Cur. Mat.-L/T/D	3.5	2.4
			8.8			Trade Payables	12.4	14.0
			.1			Income Taxes Payable	.3	.3
			4.0			All Other Current	8.6	5.7
			37.5			Total Current	40.9	43.5
			21.8			Long Term Debt	16.0	14.2
			1.7			Deferred Taxes	.6	.7
			5.7			All Other Non-Current	3.4	8.3
			33.2			Net Worth	39.1	33.3
			100.0			Total Liabilities & Net Worth	100.0	100.0
						INCOME DATA		
			100.0			Net Sales	100.0	100.0
			21.6			Gross Profit	29.0	23.0
			15.1			Operating Expenses	26.3	18.6
			6.5			Operating Profit	2.6	4.4
			2.9			All Other Expenses (net)	1.6	2.2
			3.6			Profit Before Taxes	1.0	2.2
						RATIOS		
			2.4				2.3	2.3
			1.6			Current	1.7	1.7
			1.2				1.2	1.1
			.8				1.0	1.0
			.6			Quick	.5	.6
			.3				.3	.3
			30 12.1				**30** 12.0	**31** 11.7
			37 9.9			Sales/Receivables	**40** 9.2	**41** 8.9
			43 8.5				**52** 7.0	**58** 6.3
			59 6.1				**88** 4.2	**67** 5.4
			74 4.9			Cost of Sales/Inventory	**147** 2.5	**100** 3.7
			165 2.2				**206** 1.8	**168** 2.2
			15 24.1				**13** 29.1	**9** 40.1
			22 16.9			Cost of Sales/Payables	**25** 14.8	**22** 16.8
			36 10.2				**65** 5.6	**52** 7.0
			3.9				4.2	4.0
			7.9			Sales/Working Capital	7.3	6.6
			19.3				16.4	17.5
			17.2				7.0	8.2
			2.5			EBIT/Interest	(25) 2.8	2.3
			1.0				1.2	1.1
							7.4	6.9
						Net Profit + Depr., Dep., Amort./Cur. Mat. L /T/D	(12) 2.5	(11) 2.8
							1.4	.4
			.6				.4	.2
			.8			Fixed/Worth	.6	.7
			4.2				1.0	2.1
			1.2				1.0	.9
			3.4			Debt/Worth	1.6	3.1
			6.6				4.0	9.5
			60.1				59.7	43.8
			(12) 16.9			% Profit Before Taxes/Tangible Net Worth	(24) 22.9	(26) 26.3
			4.6				2.0	5.3
			12.8				12.2	14.2
			4.6			% Profit Before Taxes/Total Assets	5.5	5.4
			.1				.7	.6
			12.9				48.3	61.9
			4.3			Sales/Net Fixed Assets	6.5	8.3
			3.6				3.6	3.2
			1.8				2.1	2.3
			1.4			Sales/Total Assets	1.5	1.7
			.9				1.1	.9
			1.5				.6	.8
			(12) 3.2			% Depr., Dep., Amort./Sales	(20) 2.1	(26) 1.8
			6.5				4.3	4.7
						% Officers', Directors', Owners' Comp/Sales		
	18419M	96348M	544599M	217955M	974483M	Net Sales ($)	1428668M	1059202M
	7829M	51791M	377989M	202099M	760510M	Total Assets ($)	984021M	731979M

M = $ thousand MM = $ million

See Pages 11 through 18 for Explanation of Ratios and Data

Comparative Historical Data				Type of Statement	Current Data Sorted By Sales					
									3	10
11		12		15	Unqualified	1			2	
2		2		2	Reviewed					
5		6		5	Compiled	2	1	1	1	
1		1		1	Tax Returns		1			
9		18		13	Other	2	1		1	9
4/1/00-		4/1/01-		4/1/02-			19 (4/1-9/30/02)		17 (10/1/02-3/31/03)	
3/31/01		3/31/02		3/31/03		0-1MM	1-3MM	3-5MM	5-10MM	10-25MM	25MM & OVER
ALL		ALL		ALL						
28		39		36	NUMBER OF STATEMENTS	2	4	2	3	6	19
%		%		%	ASSETS	%	%	%	%	%	%
2.6		5.0		5.6	Cash & Equivalents						4.3
21.3		21.1		17.2	Trade Receivables (net)						15.3
41.6		34.2		35.8	Inventory						33.4
2.6		1.3		3.3	All Other Current						2.1
68.2		61.6		61.8	Total Current						55.1
22.6		23.9		25.6	Fixed Assets (net)						31.8
5.2		7.4		5.7	Intangibles (net)						8.8
4.0		7.0		6.9	All Other Non-Current						4.3
100.0		100.0		100.0	Total						100.0
					LIABILITIES						
22.5		17.5		16.7	Notes Payable-Short Term						9.5
2.0		3.2		4.7	Cur. Mat.-L/T/D						7.6
16.6		13.5		13.8	Trade Payables						12.4
.3		.2		.1	Income Taxes Payable						.1
5.1		7.2		6.6	All Other Current						5.8
46.5		41.6		42.0	Total Current						35.3
8.9		15.8		15.9	Long Term Debt						21.5
.7		.7		.8	Deferred Taxes						1.4
12.0		9.1		11.0	All Other Non-Current						8.1
31.8		32.9		30.2	Net Worth						33.7
100.0		100.0		100.0	Total Liabilities & Net Worth						100.0
					INCOME DATA						
100.0		100.0		100.0	Net Sales						100.0
26.9		28.5		32.4	Gross Profit						31.9
24.7		24.1		26.9	Operating Expenses						24.3
2.3		4.4		5.6	Operating Profit						7.6
1.8		1.9		2.0	All Other Expenses (net)						2.7
.5		2.5		3.6	Profit Before Taxes						4.9
					RATIOS						
1.8		2.0		2.1							2.1
1.5		1.5		1.6	Current						1.7
1.1		1.2		1.2							1.3
1.0		1.0		.9							.7
.5		.6		.5	Quick						.5
.3		.4		.3							.4
31	11.7	24	14.9	27	13.5	Sales/Receivables				32	11.4
40	9.1	41	8.9	37	9.8					38	9.7
50	7.3	51	7.1	50	7.3					55	6.6
56	6.6	46	8.0	64	5.7	Cost of Sales/Inventory				70	5.2
94	3.9	93	3.9	131	2.8					144	2.5
237	1.5	166	2.2	197	1.8					194	1.9
14	25.2	14	25.6	16	22.6	Cost of Sales/Payables				16	22.8
31	11.9	24	15.3	32	11.3					26	14.2
79	4.6	46	7.9	73	5.0					79	4.6
5.1		6.2		4.8	Sales/Working Capital						4.3
9.5		8.3		7.9							6.6
17.3		41.6		16.0							12.6
	15.7		6.0		5.5	EBIT/Interest					7.3
(27)	1.4	(37)	1.7	(34)	2.0						2.6
	.2		1.0		1.1						1.5
			3.9		9.7	Net Profit + Depr., Dep.,					8.5
		(11)	1.6	(15)	2.1	Amort./Cur. Mat. L/T/D				(12)	2.3
			1.0		.3						1.6
.3		.3		.4	Fixed/Worth						.7
.5		.9		.9							1.1
2.7		1.9		4.1							2.8
.8		1.1		1.1	Debt/Worth						1.5
3.5		2.6		3.0							2.8
9.5		7.3		7.4							4.6
	33.1		46.5		56.3	% Profit Before Taxes/Tangible					58.8
(24)	14.1	(33)	11.0	(31)	14.8	Net Worth				(17)	15.5
	1.1		−2.1		5.1						7.5
12.2		10.5		10.7	% Profit Before Taxes/Total						12.2
1.9		3.0		2.5	Assets						3.3
−3.5		.0		.5							2.0
21.3		22.4		19.7	Sales/Net Fixed Assets						5.9
8.5		7.2		5.9							4.3
5.1		3.8		3.5							3.3
2.8		2.7		2.3	Sales/Total Assets						1.7
1.9		1.7		1.5							1.3
1.1		1.1		1.1							.9
	1.1		1.1		1.2	% Depr., Dep., Amort./Sales					2.5
(26)	2.0	(36)	1.9	(33)	2.3					(18)	3.1
	3.3		3.5		3.2						6.0
			.7			% Officers', Directors',					
		(10)	1.0			Owners' Comp/Sales					
			3.9								
1236480M		1611899M		1851804M	Net Sales ($)	1703M	10116M	9599M	22643M	107809M	1699934M
830068M		1058587M		1400218M	Total Assets ($)	1414M	6500M	2764M	21302M	52745M	1315493M

© RMA 2003

M = $ thousand   MM = $ million
See Pages 11 through 18 for Explanation of Ratios and Data

Current Data Sorted By Assets   Comparative Historical Data

0-500M	500M-2MM	2-10MM	10-50MM	50-100MM	100-250MM	Type of Statement	4/1/98-3/31/99 ALL	4/1/99-3/31/00 ALL
	1	4	15	8	3	Unqualified	17	16
	1	3	7			Reviewed	5	12
1	2		1	1		Compiled	3	2
						Tax Returns		
			8	1		Other	21	10

0-500M	21 (4/1-9/30/02) 500M-2MM	2-10MM	35 (10/1/02-3/31/03) 10-50MM	50-100MM	100-250MM	NUMBER OF STATEMENTS	46	40
1	4	7	31	10	3			
%	%	%	%	%	%	**ASSETS**	%	%
			6.9	7.1		Cash & Equivalents	8.6	5.3
			28.7	34.6		Trade Receivables (net)	25.9	28.1
			10.1	10.1		Inventory	11.1	12.1
			3.5	1.3		All Other Current	1.6	1.7
			49.3	53.1		Total Current	47.2	47.2
			43.1	36.5		Fixed Assets (net)	39.3	42.2
			.6	2.0		Intangibles (net)	6.4	2.2
			7.0	8.4		All Other Non-Current	7.1	8.3
			100.0	100.0		Total	100.0	100.0
						LIABILITIES		
			6.8	2.6		Notes Payable-Short Term	4.6	6.2
			2.8	1.3		Cur. Mat.-L/T/D	2.9	2.9
			19.9	26.1		Trade Payables	20.3	21.7
			.2	.1		Income Taxes Payable	.2	.4
			13.1	15.0		All Other Current	10.4	10.0
			42.7	45.0		Total Current	38.2	41.3
			11.2	13.3		Long Term Debt	16.7	17.1
			.6	.1		Deferred Taxes	.8	.6
			1.4	.6		All Other Non-Current	3.0	3.0
			44.1	41.0		Net Worth	41.3	38.1
			100.0	100.0		Total Liabilities & Net Worth	100.0	100.0
						INCOME DATA		
			100.0	100.0		Net Sales	100.0	100.0
			22.2	11.5		Gross Profit	20.3	23.2
			19.0	10.9		Operating Expenses	16.7	20.2
			3.2	.6		Operating Profit	3.6	3.1
			.1	.0		All Other Expenses (net)	.7	.2
			3.0	.5		Profit Before Taxes	2.9	2.9
						RATIOS		
			1.6	1.4			1.7	1.5
			1.2	1.1		Current	1.2	1.2
			.9	1.1			1.1	1.0
			1.1	1.1			1.4	1.0
			.9	.9		Quick	.8	.9
			.5	.7			.6	.6
			23 16.0	17 21.7			25 14.5	24 15.3
			28 13.2	22 16.7		Sales/Receivables	30 12.2	29 12.5
			32 11.5	26 14.2			34 10.6	33 10.9
			7 50.0	1 317.7			7 53.7	7 55.0
			12 31.7	8 45.3		Cost of Sales/Inventory	11 31.9	12 31.6
			17 21.4	16 23.2			17 21.4	19 18.9
			21 17.4	18 20.8			18 19.8	20 18.5
			26 13.9	21 17.6		Cost of Sales/Payables	26 13.9	24 15.5
			31 11.8	26 14.2			33 10.9	28 13.1
			15.5	39.5			11.4	20.8
			49.6	90.8		Sales/Working Capital	38.1	56.0
			-39.7	NM			166.5	NM
			23.1	22.2			(40) 8.8	(37) 9.9
		(30)	10.2	4.2		EBIT/Interest	4.9	5.8
			3.9	1.4			2.7	2.9
			9.3			Net Profit + Depr., Dep.,	(20) 5.4	(18) 6.3
		(11)	4.6			Amort./Cur. Mat. L /T/D	3.0	3.0
			2.0				1.8	1.8
			.6	.6			.6	.8
			.8	.9		Fixed/Worth	1.1	1.0
			1.8	1.2			2.0	2.3
			.6	.9			1.0	1.0
			1.3	1.5		Debt/Worth	1.7	1.6
			2.8	2.6			4.2	4.4
			36.5	18.7		% Profit Before Taxes/Tangible	(45) 53.5	(37) 34.1
			22.4	8.2		Net Worth	19.0	21.1
			11.1	2.2			8.0	12.3
			14.8	8.9		% Profit Before Taxes/Total	11.9	12.4
			9.5	2.7		Assets	7.4	7.7
			4.8	.5			3.1	3.6
			13.0	66.8			13.6	13.1
			7.8	13.0		Sales/Net Fixed Assets	8.4	8.5
			5.5	7.1			5.5	5.7
			4.4	8.2			4.3	4.8
			3.3	5.3		Sales/Total Assets	3.3	3.6
			2.8	3.3			1.9	2.4
			.9	.3			(39) 1.3	(34) 1.5
		(27)	1.9	.8		% Depr., Dep., Amort./Sales	1.7	2.0
			2.8	1.8			2.9	2.8
						% Officers', Directors', Owners' Comp/Sales		
1328M	21580M	195327M	2760098M	4451293M	1587961M	Net Sales ($)	5595763M	3571178M
499M	5525M	47032M	753411M	698657M	566098M	Total Assets ($)	1982154M	1217029M

© RMA 2003

M = $ thousand   MM = $ million
See Pages 11 through 18 for Explanation of Ratios and Data

Comparative Historical Data / Current Data Sorted By Sales

			Type of Statement		1			2	28
14	28	31	Unqualified		1			2	28
10	4	11	Reviewed				2	2	9
1	6	5	Compiled		1	1	1		2
			Tax Returns					1	
13	23	9	Other						8
4/1/00-3/31/01 ALL	4/1/01-3/31/02 ALL	4/1/02-3/31/03 ALL		0-1MM	1-3MM (4/1-9/30/02)	3-5MM	5-10MM	10-25MM (10/1/02-3/31/03)	25MM & OVER
38	61	56	NUMBER OF STATEMENTS	2	1	3	3		47
%	%	%	ASSETS	%	%	%	%	%	%
8.7	7.5	7.3	Cash & Equivalents						6.2
26.8	31.8	28.1	Trade Receivables (net)						30.2
10.5	11.9	10.8	Inventory						11.1
1.7	3.8	2.6	All Other Current						2.6
47.6	55.1	48.8	Total Current						50.0
41.8	37.7	39.1	Fixed Assets (net)						39.1
2.2	1.3	1.7	Intangibles (net)						1.0
8.3	6.0	10.4	All Other Non-Current						9.9
100.0	100.0	100.0	Total						100.0
			LIABILITIES						
3.7	6.2	5.2	Notes Payable-Short Term						5.6
3.2	2.7	2.2	Cur. Mat.-L/T/D						2.3
16.6	24.1	20.6	Trade Payables						22.3
.4	.1	.1	Income Taxes Payable						.1
13.4	11.2	13.7	All Other Current						15.1
37.3	44.3	41.8	Total Current						45.5
17.1	15.0	12.5	Long Term Debt						13.0
1.0	.4	.5	Deferred Taxes						.4
1.2	2.7	2.5	All Other Non-Current						1.3
43.3	37.6	42.7	Net Worth						39.9
100.0	100.0	100.0	Total Liabilities & Net Worth						100.0
			INCOME DATA						
100.0	100.0	100.0	Net Sales						100.0
22.9	19.1	20.6	Gross Profit						19.2
18.9	16.8	17.6	Operating Expenses						16.4
4.0	2.3	3.1	Operating Profit						2.8
.4	.1	.1	All Other Expenses (net)						.2
3.6	2.2	2.9	Profit Before Taxes						2.6
			RATIOS						
1.6	1.5	1.6							1.4
1.3	1.2	1.2	Current						1.1
1.0	1.0	1.0							.9
1.3	1.1	1.1							1.1
1.0	.9	.9	Quick						.9
.8	.6	.6							.6
22 16.9	22 16.3	21 17.2	Sales/Receivables						21 17.5
28 13.0	27 13.6	25 14.8							25 14.8
38 9.6	33 11.0	31 11.6							32 11.5
8 47.5	5 68.7	6 63.0	Cost of Sales/Inventory						6 63.3
15 25.2	10 36.0	12 30.4							11 34.0
20 18.6	26 14.3	18 20.5							17 21.5
16 23.1	18 20.2	17 21.7	Cost of Sales/Payables						18 20.8
23 15.8	24 15.0	23 15.7							24 15.1
30 12.0	33 11.0	30 12.3							30 12.1
15.3	21.5	19.6	Sales/Working Capital						24.7
33.0	52.8	48.3							74.7
NM	445.7	-287.9							-69.2
10.0	11.3	21.1	EBIT/Interest						20.8
(35) 5.7	(56) 3.8	(52) 7.6						(45)	7.1
3.5	1.9	3.0							2.9
5.0	5.1	10.8	Net Profit + Depr., Dep., Amort./Cur. Mat. L/T/D						12.3
(19) 2.7	(28) 3.5	(17) 4.7						(15)	4.7
1.8	1.8	3.0							2.9
.6	.6	.6	Fixed/Worth						.7
1.0	1.0	.9							1.0
1.6	1.8	1.6							1.7
.8	1.0	.7	Debt/Worth						.9
1.4	1.9	1.3							1.5
2.5	3.5	3.5							3.5
36.9	28.4	34.4	% Profit Before Taxes/Tangible Net Worth						36.5
20.3	(59) 17.4	(55) 18.7							18.7
12.0	9.3	8.6							7.8
15.0	11.2	14.1	% Profit Before Taxes/Total Assets						13.1
8.8	5.9	8.4							8.4
4.8	2.9	2.5							2.2
11.5	19.7	18.5	Sales/Net Fixed Assets						19.4
8.0	9.6	9.3							9.7
5.5	5.7	5.8							6.4
4.4	5.4	5.5	Sales/Total Assets						5.7
3.5	3.9	3.5							3.7
2.2	2.8	2.6							3.1
1.0	.6	.7	% Depr., Dep., Amort./Sales						.7
(36) 2.3	(56) 1.5	(52) 1.6						(43)	1.6
3.2	2.5	2.4							2.2
			% Officers', Directors', Owners' Comp/Sales						
3049054M	10837299M	9017587M	Net Sales ($)	3369M	3472M	25336M	50255M		8935155M
958408M	2419786M	2071222M	Total Assets ($)	1673M	1505M	10316M	25560M		2032168M

M = $ thousand   MM = $ million
See Pages 11 through 18 for Explanation of Ratios and Data

Current Data Sorted By Assets   Comparative Historical Data

						Type of Statement		
	1		1	4	3	1	Unqualified	14	15
			2				Reviewed	3	6
1			3				Compiled	4	5
							Tax Returns		
1			1	3			Other	9	9

							4/1/98- 3/31/99	4/1/99- 3/31/00
0-500M	6 (4/1-9/30/02) 500M-2MM	2-10MM	10-50MM	15 (10/1/02-3/31/03) 50-100MM	100-250MM		ALL	ALL
2	1	7	7	3	1	NUMBER OF STATEMENTS	30	35
%	%	%	%	%	%	ASSETS	%	%
						Cash & Equivalents	8.0	6.8
						Trade Receivables (net)	27.1	25.6
						Inventory	18.4	20.0
						All Other Current	.3	1.7
						Total Current	53.8	54.0
						Fixed Assets (net)	39.0	35.9
						Intangibles (net)	2.2	3.6
						All Other Non-Current	5.0	6.5
						Total	100.0	100.0
						LIABILITIES		
						Notes Payable-Short Term	10.1	7.8
						Cur. Mat.-L/T/D	2.3	4.0
						Trade Payables	23.7	16.4
						Income Taxes Payable	.0	.1
						All Other Current	6.0	6.0
						Total Current	42.2	34.3
						Long Term Debt	11.6	17.8
						Deferred Taxes	.5	.6
						All Other Non-Current	3.1	3.7
						Net Worth	42.6	43.6
						Total Liabilities & Net Worth	100.0	100.0
						INCOME DATA		
						Net Sales	100.0	100.0
						Gross Profit	23.4	23.8
						Operating Expenses	19.8	19.5
						Operating Profit	3.5	4.2
						All Other Expenses (net)	1.0	1.0
						Profit Before Taxes	2.5	3.2
						RATIOS		
						Current	1.7	2.8
							1.3	1.5
							1.0	1.0
						Quick	1.2	1.4
							.8	1.0
							.5	.6
						Sales/Receivables	22 16.8	24 15.1
							27 13.4	29 12.7
							34 10.7	37 9.7
						Cost of Sales/Inventory	9 40.2	17 21.2
							21 17.0	24 15.3
							35 10.4	34 10.7
						Cost of Sales/Payables	17 21.0	16 22.9
							27 13.4	22 16.3
							35 10.4	29 12.8
						Sales/Working Capital	15.0	8.7
							26.3	19.1
							NM	137.5
						EBIT/Interest	21.9	8.6
							(29) 4.5	(32) 4.2
							1.5	1.7
						Net Profit + Depr., Dep., Amort./Cur. Mat. L/T/D		
						Fixed/Worth	.5	.5
							.9	1.0
							2.0	2.0
						Debt/Worth	.6	.6
							1.7	1.7
							3.1	3.0
						% Profit Before Taxes/Tangible Net Worth	29.4	31.6
							(29) 16.2	(32) 21.0
							6.4	7.2
						% Profit Before Taxes/Total Assets	15.5	12.7
							4.8	7.6
							1.4	3.4
						Sales/Net Fixed Assets	16.3	14.7
							6.1	8.4
							4.7	5.2
						Sales/Total Assets	5.1	4.2
							3.0	2.8
							2.6	2.0
						% Depr., Dep., Amort./Sales	1.1	1.3
							(25) 1.9	(31) 1.7
							2.7	2.5
						% Officers', Directors', Owners' Comp/Sales		
1376M 359M	9327M 1347M	103491M 39282M	422296M 104186M	960373M 200570M	254553M 161854M	Net Sales ($) Total Assets ($)	3535427M 1172296M	2254698M 790784M

M = $ thousand   MM = $ million
See Pages 11 through 18 for Explanation of Ratios and Data

Comparative Historical Data | Current Data Sorted By Sales

			Type of Statement	0-1MM	1-3MM	3-5MM	5-10MM	10-25MM	25MM & OVER
6	5	10	Unqualified				1	3	6
5	2	2	Reviewed						2
6	3	4	Compiled		1			3	
		1	Tax Returns						
11	9	5	Other	1		1		1	2
4/1/00-3/31/01 ALL	4/1/01-3/31/02 ALL	4/1/02-3/31/03 ALL			6 (4/1-9/30/02)			15 (10/1/02-3/31/03)	
28	20	21	NUMBER OF STATEMENTS	1	1	1	4	4	10
%	%	%	**ASSETS**	%	%	%	%	%	%
5.6	5.2	6.5	Cash & Equivalents						7.2
21.8	22.2	21.0	Trade Receivables (net)						24.5
17.4	16.9	22.5	Inventory						25.0
1.7	1.3	.8	All Other Current						1.0
46.5	45.7	50.8	Total Current						57.7
42.3	39.6	36.8	Fixed Assets (net)						34.9
3.4	5.1	4.5	Intangibles (net)						4.6
7.7	9.7	7.9	All Other Non-Current						2.8
100.0	100.0	100.0	Total						100.0
			LIABILITIES						
10.8	4.7	7.3	Notes Payable-Short Term						9.0
6.0	6.0	5.0	Cur. Mat.-L/T/D						1.7
16.1	16.2	17.5	Trade Payables						21.9
.0	.1	.0	Income Taxes Payable						.0
9.5	8.4	8.6	All Other Current						10.7
42.5	35.5	38.5	Total Current						43.4
28.0	22.9	24.4	Long Term Debt						15.4
.5	.7	1.0	Deferred Taxes						.0
4.1	9.9	6.1	All Other Non-Current						1.4
25.0	31.0	30.1	Net Worth						39.8
100.0	100.0	100.0	Total Liabilities & Net Worth						100.0
			INCOME DATA						
100.0	100.0	100.0	Net Sales						100.0
31.5	20.0	22.1	Gross Profit						13.8
27.5	16.6	18.7	Operating Expenses						11.4
4.0	3.4	3.4	Operating Profit						2.4
2.0	1.8	1.4	All Other Expenses (net)						.4
2.0	1.7	1.9	Profit Before Taxes						2.0
			RATIOS						
2.0	2.3	3.0	Current						2.0
1.3	1.4	1.3							1.4
.8	.8	.9							.9
1.3	1.5	1.5	Quick						1.1
.9	.9	.7							.6
.4	.4	.4							.5
24 15.0	17 21.0	16 22.2	Sales/Receivables						14 25.8
30 12.0	23 16.1	23 15.6							19 18.8
39 9.4	29 12.7	26 14.0							24 15.1
17 21.5	14 26.0	16 22.7	Cost of Sales/Inventory						12 30.6
31 11.9	24 15.4	25 14.6							18 20.4
48 7.6	32 11.4	45 8.0							29 12.7
19 19.0	17 21.3	17 21.9	Cost of Sales/Payables						16 23.5
30 12.3	18 19.8	22 16.8							18 20.7
42 8.8	21 17.3	29 12.5							29 12.5
10.8	12.2	7.7	Sales/Working Capital						11.5
28.3	33.4	73.6							51.0
-37.2	-40.4	-77.6							-125.4
11.2	(19) 19.6	(18) 6.8	EBIT/Interest						
(25) 2.8	3.2	2.7							
1.4	.0	1.2							
		4.8	Net Profit + Depr., Dep., Amort./Cur. Mat. L/T/D						
	(10)	3.1							
		1.5							
.6	.6	.6	Fixed/Worth						.6
1.5	1.0	1.1							1.0
8.9	36.0	5.2							3.0
.6	.5	.7	Debt/Worth						.8
1.8	2.1	2.3							1.6
12.3	42.4	11.9							8.3
27.3	40.5	26.3	% Profit Before Taxes/Tangible Net Worth						
(22) 20.0	(16) 20.3	(17) 10.9							
3.6	-3.4	4.7							
13.9	13.9	14.4	% Profit Before Taxes/Total Assets						16.9
5.8	7.0	3.0							5.3
.5	-5.0	.7							.3
12.9	21.9	14.6	Sales/Net Fixed Assets						15.0
5.7	10.8	11.3							13.7
3.0	4.2	5.2							10.6
3.9	5.8	4.7	Sales/Total Assets						6.4
2.6	3.0	3.6							4.3
1.2	1.6	1.7							3.6
1.7	1.0	.9	% Depr., Dep., Amort./Sales						.8
(26) 2.4	(17) 1.7	1.9							1.1
3.4	3.2	2.4							2.2
			% Officers', Directors', Owners' Comp/Sales						
1843512M	3007199M	1751416M	Net Sales ($)	74M	1302M	3465M	31169M	72595M	1642811M
751889M	843007M	507598M	Total Assets ($)	24M	335M	3109M	17823M	39422M	446885M

M = $ thousand   MM = $ million
See Pages 11 through 18 for Explanation of Ratios and Data

Current Data Sorted By Assets | **Comparative Historical Data**

Type of Statement	0-500M	500M-2MM	2-10MM	10-50MM	50-100MM	100-250MM		4/1/98-3/31/99 ALL	4/1/99-3/31/00 ALL
Unqualified		2	8	6	3	2		18	19
Reviewed	1	5	6	1				4	7
Compiled	1	1	4	1	1			12	16
Tax Returns			1	1	1				
Other		3	2	5	3	4		17	17
		17 (4/1-9/30/02)		42 (10/1/02-3/31/03)					
NUMBER OF STATEMENTS	3	10	21	13	6	6		51	59
	%	%	%	%	%	%		%	%
ASSETS									
Cash & Equivalents		11.9	7.3	4.0				6.5	9.5
Trade Receivables (net)		21.1	26.9	19.5				27.7	24.7
Inventory		29.1	20.7	30.8				27.4	24.9
All Other Current		3.4	1.4	2.4				1.7	1.9
Total Current		65.5	56.3	56.7				63.4	61.0
Fixed Assets (net)		31.2	37.7	40.0				30.9	32.5
Intangibles (net)		1.1	1.9	.4				2.0	1.8
All Other Non-Current		2.2	4.1	2.9				3.7	4.7
Total		100.0	100.0	100.0				100.0	100.0
LIABILITIES									
Notes Payable-Short Term		8.9	12.9	11.1				8.2	12.8
Cur. Mat.-L/T/D		2.2	7.3	3.0				3.0	2.1
Trade Payables		17.9	17.2	12.4				24.4	19.0
Income Taxes Payable		.1	.0	.2				.5	.2
All Other Current		6.5	6.4	6.6				8.4	7.9
Total Current		35.6	43.9	33.3				44.5	42.1
Long Term Debt		14.0	20.4	20.3				13.2	14.7
Deferred Taxes		.1	.4	.8				.7	.8
All Other Non-Current		17.2	4.0	1.1				2.4	5.2
Net Worth		33.1	31.3	44.4				39.2	37.2
Total Liabilities & Net Worth		100.0	100.0	100.0				100.0	100.0
INCOME DATA									
Net Sales		100.0	100.0	100.0				100.0	100.0
Gross Profit		20.7	17.8	12.9				15.6	15.2
Operating Expenses		18.7	12.8	8.7				13.0	10.8
Operating Profit		1.9	5.0	4.2				2.6	4.4
All Other Expenses (net)		2.1	1.1	.9				.5	.8
Profit Before Taxes		−.2	3.9	3.3				2.1	3.7
RATIOS									
Current		3.8 / 2.5 / 1.3	1.9 / 1.2 / 1.0	2.8 / 2.1 / 1.2				2.3 / 1.4 / 1.0	2.7 / 1.3 / .9
Quick		1.6 / 1.2 / .5	1.1 / .6 / .5	1.9 / 1.0 / .3				1.1 / .8 / .6	1.3 / .7 / .5
Sales/Receivables		6 59.4 / 27 13.5 / 34 10.6	24 15.0 / 30 12.2 / 41 8.9	22 16.6 / 27 13.4 / 36 10.2				21 17.5 / 35 10.4 / 43 8.5	21 17.6 / 27 13.4 / 36 10.0
Cost of Sales/Inventory		18 20.3 / 56 6.5 / 84 4.4	9 41.7 / 25 14.7 / 46 7.9	18 20.6 / 28 13.2 / 101 3.6				17 22.1 / 29 12.4 / 67 5.4	13 28.0 / 22 16.3 / 49 7.5
Cost of Sales/Payables		4 90.4 / 21 17.2 / 30 12.0	14 25.4 / 26 13.9 / 32 11.5	13 27.8 / 20 17.8 / 23 15.8				19 18.8 / 32 11.5 / 42 8.6	16 22.9 / 27 13.7 / 32 11.3
Sales/Working Capital		3.8 / 7.8 / NM	12.4 / 32.0 / −372.5	8.4 / 10.3 / 17.7				9.3 / 17.6 / 138.4	6.7 / 23.5 / −101.1
EBIT/Interest			(12) 7.5 / 3.6 / 1.3	10.9 / 5.2 / 1.9				(47) 9.4 / 3.8 / 1.7	(53) 15.0 / 4.0 / 2.3
Net Profit + Depr., Dep., Amort./Cur. Mat. L /T/D			(10) 3.6 / 3.1 / .3					(17) 4.3 / 2.2 / .9	(16) 13.3 / 4.8 / 3.4
Fixed/Worth		.1 / .8 / 1.5	1.0 / 1.2 / 2.4	.6 / .9 / 1.1				.4 / .8 / 1.6	.4 / .9 / 2.5
Debt/Worth		.3 / 1.4 / 5.5	1.2 / 2.1 / 6.7	.7 / 1.2 / 3.0				.8 / 1.8 / 3.6	.9 / 1.7 / 4.3
% Profit Before Taxes/Tangible Net Worth			(18) 47.6 / 15.7 / 1.5	33.2 / 19.5 / 4.7				(49) 32.8 / 21.6 / 6.2	(54) 41.5 / 25.5 / 11.7
% Profit Before Taxes/Total Assets			11.0 / 5.7 / −4.7	14.3 / 5.7 / 1.9				14.2 / 6.7 / 2.2	15.6 / 8.7 / 3.8
Sales/Net Fixed Assets			34.5 / 8.6 / 4.1	13.6 / 11.6 / 5.3				16.1 / 9.4 / 7.4	18.8 / 11.1 / 7.2
Sales/Total Assets			3.5 / 2.1 / 1.9	3.9 / 3.3 / 2.1	4.0 / 1.9 / 1.5			4.1 / 3.0 / 2.1	4.0 / 3.2 / 2.1
% Depr., Dep., Amort./Sales			(12) 1.3 / 2.1 / 2.8	1.3 / 1.7 / 2.3				(49) .8 / 1.6 / 2.5	(53) .7 / 1.3 / 2.1
% Officers', Directors', Owners' Comp/Sales			(10) .6 / 1.3 / 3.2					(18) 1.0 / 1.4 / 4.7	(18) .7 / 1.2 / 5.2
Net Sales ($)	1510M	40311M	367723M	756979M	1063690M	2272725M		3010533M	3667855M
Total Assets ($)	386M	13042M	115798M	345314M	353270M	984788M		1075237M	1331747M

M = $ thousand   MM = $ million
See Pages 11 through 18 for Explanation of Ratios and Data

Comparative Historical Data | Current Data Sorted By Sales

4/1/00-3/31/01 ALL	4/1/01-3/31/02 ALL	4/1/02-3/31/03 ALL	Type of Statement	0-1MM	1-3MM	3-5MM	5-10MM	10-25MM	25MM & OVER
					17 (4/1-9/30/02)			42 (10/1/02-3/31/03)	
17	24	21	Unqualified	2			1	5	13
10	8	7	Reviewed		1	1		3	2
5	11	11	Compiled	1	3	3	1	2	1
	2	3	Tax Returns		1	1			1
6	13	17	Other		1	1	1	2	12
38	58	59	NUMBER OF STATEMENTS	3	6	6	3	12	29
%	%	%	**ASSETS**	%	%	%	%	%	%
5.5	4.5	7.0	Cash & Equivalents					6.0	3.8
25.9	26.6	21.6	Trade Receivables (net)					30.5	20.5
29.1	28.6	25.4	Inventory					25.8	27.0
2.1	1.7	2.1	All Other Current					.4	2.1
62.5	61.4	56.0	Total Current					62.7	53.5
31.3	33.2	37.9	Fixed Assets (net)					33.3	39.5
2.2	1.1	1.9	Intangibles (net)					1.0	2.5
4.0	4.3	4.1	All Other Non-Current					2.9	4.4
100.0	100.0	100.0	Total					100.0	100.0
			LIABILITIES						
13.4	10.9	10.4	Notes Payable-Short Term					14.1	9.8
3.0	4.5	4.1	Cur. Mat.-L/T/D					8.6	3.5
18.2	18.7	14.9	Trade Payables					22.3	13.5
.5	.3	.1	Income Taxes Payable					.1	.2
5.7	8.3	7.3	All Other Current					6.3	8.6
40.9	42.6	36.8	Total Current					51.5	35.6
14.8	16.3	19.3	Long Term Debt					17.4	20.7
.8	.4	.5	Deferred Taxes					.4	.7
2.4	5.8	5.3	All Other Non-Current					5.0	1.5
41.0	34.9	38.1	Net Worth					25.7	41.6
100.0	100.0	100.0	Total Liabilities & Net Worth					100.0	100.0
			INCOME DATA						
100.0	100.0	100.0	Net Sales					100.0	100.0
16.2	15.2	16.4	Gross Profit					14.7	14.6
11.8	12.1	12.6	Operating Expenses					10.9	10.6
4.4	3.0	3.9	Operating Profit					3.8	3.9
.8	1.4	1.1	All Other Expenses (net)					1.2	.8
3.5	1.6	2.7	Profit Before Taxes					2.6	3.2
			RATIOS						
2.1	2.3	2.3	Current					1.7	2.4
1.4	1.4	1.6						1.3	1.4
1.1	1.1	1.1						1.0	1.1
1.3	1.2	1.4	Quick					1.0	1.3
.6	.7	.8						.6	.7
.4	.4	.4						.5	.3
24 15.4	25 14.8	20 17.8	Sales/Receivables					25 14.6	22 16.5
34 10.6	32 11.5	27 13.4						29 12.4	27 13.4
45 8.1	42 8.8	33 11.2						34 10.6	32 11.4
20 18.5	17 21.6	15 23.6	Cost of Sales/Inventory					14 26.8	16 22.7
39 9.3	34 10.7	34 10.8						31 11.9	29 12.7
77 4.7	72 5.1	70 5.2						42 8.7	79 4.6
16 22.6	16 23.1	13 28.2	Cost of Sales/Payables					17 21.1	13 27.8
25 14.5	24 15.4	20 17.8						27 13.6	20 17.8
42 8.7	34 10.9	29 12.4						32 11.3	27 13.3
5.8	7.1	8.3	Sales/Working Capital					17.1	9.5
15.2	20.3	16.4						31.9	15.5
40.7	63.4	72.0						−285.8	57.5
10.4	5.8	8.7	EBIT/Interest					6.6	10.9
(36) 3.5	(53) 2.7	(54) 3.6						3.7	(28) 3.5
2.1	1.0	1.9						1.0	1.9
	9.5	8.4	Net Profit + Depr., Dep., Amort./Cur. Mat. L/T/D						
	(15) 3.4	(18) 3.6							
	1.6	2.5							
.4	.5	.6	Fixed/Worth					.7	.7
.7	1.0	1.1						1.2	1.0
1.4	1.7	1.4						NM	1.2
.7	.8	.7	Debt/Worth					1.1	.9
1.7	1.9	1.7						2.7	1.7
3.9	3.5	3.5						NM	2.9
34.6	28.4	37.8	% Profit Before Taxes/Tangible Net Worth						40.3
(35) 21.2	(54) 15.5	(55) 13.3							14.1
12.2	3.8	3.3							6.2
11.7	10.3	10.8	% Profit Before Taxes/Total Assets					10.2	13.7
7.5	5.2	4.7						6.1	4.3
3.4	.4	2.0						−1.1	2.3
15.9	13.9	12.2	Sales/Net Fixed Assets					14.5	11.4
9.4	10.6	8.0						10.7	6.8
6.4	5.9	4.2						6.1	3.5
3.4	3.9	3.7	Sales/Total Assets					4.7	3.9
2.5	3.0	2.6						3.3	2.2
2.0	1.9	1.8						2.5	1.8
.8	.8	1.3	% Depr., Dep., Amort./Sales					1.3	1.2
(36) 1.4	(55) 1.4	(55) 2.0						(11) 1.6	(26) 1.7
2.3	2.2	2.6						2.3	2.4
1.4	.8	.5	% Officers', Directors', Owners' Comp/Sales						
(12) 2.6	(12) 2.8	(16) 1.1							
4.5	4.1	3.0							
2725389M	4649900M	4502938M	Net Sales ($)	1510M	11393M	23222M	22326M	208543M	4235944M
1077892M	1747768M	1812598M	Total Assets ($)	386M	8533M	14004M	10917M	65459M	1713299M

M = $ thousand   MM = $ million
See Pages 11 through 18 for Explanation of Ratios and Data

Current Data Sorted By Assets | Comparative Historical Data

0-500M	500M-2MM	2-10MM	10-50MM	50-100MM	100-250MM	Type of Statement	4/1/98-3/31/99 ALL	4/1/99-3/31/00 ALL
		6	21	4	4	Unqualified	44	43
	1	11	4	3		Reviewed	11	14
	9	4	3			Compiled	22	15
	1	1	1			Tax Returns	6	3
1	3	12	6	1	3	Other	29	27
	28 (4/1-9/30/02)		68 (10/1/02-3/31/03)					
2	14	34	34	5	7	**NUMBER OF STATEMENTS**	112	102
%	%	%	%	%	%	**ASSETS**	%	%
	5.0	11.3	6.7			Cash & Equivalents	6.6	8.0
	22.5	26.5	24.3			Trade Receivables (net)	25.3	25.2
	25.2	21.3	22.7			Inventory	17.1	17.5
	3.6	3.8	5.7			All Other Current	1.9	1.6
	56.3	62.9	59.4			Total Current	50.8	52.4
	37.0	29.6	34.2			Fixed Assets (net)	41.6	37.6
	1.3	1.9	2.2			Intangibles (net)	2.1	3.8
	5.4	5.6	4.2			All Other Non-Current	5.5	6.2
	100.0	100.0	100.0			Total	100.0	100.0
						LIABILITIES		
	14.5	9.1	15.3			Notes Payable-Short Term	12.3	11.4
	3.7	4.0	3.3			Cur. Mat.-L/T/D	4.3	3.8
	18.9	12.2	10.8			Trade Payables	11.6	12.7
	.0	.1	.2			Income Taxes Payable	.2	.3
	5.2	8.2	10.4			All Other Current	7.5	7.7
	42.3	33.7	40.0			Total Current	35.8	35.8
	16.0	14.8	12.0			Long Term Debt	19.4	18.8
	.0	.3	.7			Deferred Taxes	.4	.4
	.9	10.2	5.1			All Other Non-Current	5.8	4.2
	40.8	41.0	42.1			Net Worth	38.6	40.6
	100.0	100.0	100.0			Total Liabilities & Net Worth	100.0	100.0
						INCOME DATA		
	100.0	100.0	100.0			Net Sales	100.0	100.0
	27.4	17.2	16.2			Gross Profit	17.0	19.1
	23.8	13.4	13.1			Operating Expenses	14.3	14.6
	3.6	3.7	3.1			Operating Profit	2.7	4.5
	.4	.2	.0			All Other Expenses (net)	.6	.7
	3.2	3.5	3.1			Profit Before Taxes	2.1	3.8
						RATIOS		
	3.2	3.3	2.6			Current	2.4	2.0
	2.1	1.9	1.5				1.5	1.5
	.9	1.4	1.3				1.0	1.1
	2.4	2.0	1.4			Quick	1.7	1.4
	.5	1.1	.8				.9	.9
	.3	.7	.5				.5	.6
	13 28.8	13 28.1	16 23.5			Sales/Receivables	14 25.6	15 24.2
	17 20.9	19 19.3	22 16.8				19 19.3	19 19.1
	29 12.4	31 11.8	32 11.4				27 13.6	24 15.5
	13 27.8	11 32.8	12 29.7			Cost of Sales/Inventory	9 38.7	8 43.1
	26 14.1	22 16.8	26 14.1				16 22.1	16 22.9
	87 4.2	29 12.5	42 8.6				25 14.6	35 10.5
	2 147.4	6 61.8	6 60.5			Cost of Sales/Payables	6 63.1	6 59.9
	12 30.6	10 36.0	10 37.1				11 33.3	11 34.7
	18 20.3	18 20.1	22 16.9				17 21.6	17 21.0
	7.8	8.9	10.1			Sales/Working Capital	15.1	14.3
	16.6	19.2	19.3				28.6	30.1
	NM	42.8	42.2				821.3	163.1
	(12) 8.1	(33) 17.3	(30) 18.6			EBIT/Interest	(103) 5.0	(97) 10.9
	3.0	4.3	5.4				2.4	4.6
	1.1	1.8	1.8				1.0	2.3
		(10) 8.6	(12) 8.0			Net Profit + Depr., Dep., Amort./Cur. Mat. L /T/D	(32) 3.3	(31) 4.3
		3.0	3.7				2.2	2.4
		.7	1.5				1.2	1.4
	.5	.3	.4			Fixed/Worth	.6	.6
	1.2	.9	.9				1.1	.9
	2.9	1.8	1.5				2.3	2.0
	.3	.7	.5			Debt/Worth	.7	.7
	1.8	2.0	1.7				1.7	1.5
	13.4	3.5	3.8				4.0	3.9
	(12) 23.5	(33) 42.3	(31) 35.2			% Profit Before Taxes/Tangible Net Worth	(103) 29.9	(94) 51.9
	12.5	16.1	14.6				13.8	23.1
	-3.5	3.9	9.9				4.0	8.6
	13.1	14.6	14.4			% Profit Before Taxes/Total Assets	11.6	17.7
	5.9	7.7	8.7				5.3	8.1
	-.9	1.8	2.0				.1	3.2
	46.7	46.1	20.0			Sales/Net Fixed Assets	20.3	22.5
	8.0	17.1	11.8				9.7	12.3
	4.3	8.4	6.5				5.0	5.8
	7.3	6.0	5.6			Sales/Total Assets	6.3	6.0
	3.0	4.4	3.6				4.0	4.3
	2.2	3.2	2.4				2.4	2.3
	(13) .6	(32) .5	(30) .7			% Depr., Dep., Amort./Sales	(101) .7	(97) .6
	1.3	1.0	1.0				1.3	1.3
	2.3	1.8	2.1				2.3	2.4
		(14) .9				% Officers', Directors', Owners' Comp/Sales	(32) 1.1	(27) .7
		2.1					1.8	1.8
		3.2					3.7	2.8
3983M	72478M	871891M	2764573M	1938633M	3460271M	Net Sales ($)	12239163M	14746333M
873M	16457M	187821M	717396M	380313M	1112026M	Total Assets ($)	2771653M	3407051M

M = $ thousand   MM = $ million
See Pages 11 through 18 for Explanation of Ratios and Data

Comparative Historical Data — **Current Data Sorted By Sales**

	4/1/00-3/31/01 ALL	4/1/01-3/31/02 ALL	4/1/02-3/31/03 ALL	Type of Statement	0-1MM	1-3MM	3-5MM	5-10MM	10-25MM	25MM & OVER
	23	20	35	Unqualified					3	32
	13	13	16	Reviewed				3	5	8
	18	15	16	Compiled		4	2	3	3	4
	3	7	3	Tax Returns	1	2				
	24	23	26	Other	1	1	1	3	4	16
	4/1/00-3/31/01 ALL	4/1/01-3/31/02 ALL	4/1/02-3/31/03 ALL		28 (4/1-9/30/02)			68 (10/1/02-3/31/03)		
	81	78	96	**NUMBER OF STATEMENTS**	2	7	3	9	15	60
	%	%	%	**ASSETS**	%	%	%	%	%	%
	6.0	6.0	8.2	Cash & Equivalents					14.1	7.0
	25.8	25.8	24.3	Trade Receivables (net)					26.2	25.2
	19.8	24.2	21.7	Inventory					27.3	21.8
	3.2	2.5	4.4	All Other Current					1.8	3.2
	54.8	58.4	58.6	Total Current					69.4	57.2
	37.2	32.6	33.0	Fixed Assets (net)					25.4	34.0
	1.9	2.7	2.3	Intangibles (net)					.2	3.0
	6.1	6.3	6.1	All Other Non-Current					5.0	5.9
	100.0	100.0	100.0	Total					100.0	100.0
				LIABILITIES						
	10.4	13.7	11.6	Notes Payable-Short Term					12.7	12.8
	4.5	5.1	4.1	Cur. Mat.-L/T/D					1.7	3.9
	13.3	13.6	11.9	Trade Payables					15.0	10.8
	.2	.2	.2	Income Taxes Payable					.2	.2
	8.4	8.3	8.5	All Other Current					6.2	9.5
	36.7	40.9	36.4	Total Current					35.8	37.2
	16.3	17.1	14.2	Long Term Debt					15.5	13.4
	.3	.6	.5	Deferred Taxes					.6	.6
	5.2	5.9	5.9	All Other Non-Current					5.4	5.6
	41.5	35.5	43.1	Net Worth					42.6	43.3
	100.0	100.0	100.0	Total Liabilities & Net Worth					100.0	100.0
				INCOME DATA						
	100.0	100.0	100.0	Net Sales					100.0	100.0
	18.0	17.8	18.1	Gross Profit					17.3	13.5
	14.4	15.1	14.6	Operating Expenses					14.2	10.8
	3.7	2.7	3.6	Operating Profit					3.1	2.7
	.8	.4	.2	All Other Expenses (net)					.2	.3
	2.9	2.3	3.4	Profit Before Taxes					2.8	2.5
				RATIOS						
	2.3	1.9	2.8	Current					3.6	2.5
	1.4	1.4	1.7						2.5	1.5
	1.2	1.1	1.3						1.3	1.3
	1.3	1.2	1.6	Quick					2.5	1.4
	.8	.7	.9						1.0	.9
	.5	.5	.6						.6	.6
	16 22.9	14 25.2	14 25.4	Sales/Receivables					11 32.4	15 23.7
	20 18.0	20 18.5	19 19.0						14 26.4	19 19.1
	29 12.5	27 13.3	31 11.9						26 13.9	29 12.6
	10 36.7	10 35.6	11 32.0	Cost of Sales/Inventory					14 25.6	10 37.3
	19 18.9	21 17.3	22 16.5						23 16.2	20 17.9
	39 9.5	38 9.7	35 10.5						30 12.0	31 11.7
	6 62.8	7 54.4	6 64.4	Cost of Sales/Payables					6 57.3	5 70.7
	11 34.6	12 30.4	10 36.3						14 26.9	9 42.4
	19 19.1	19 19.1	17 21.0						20 17.9	16 22.3
	13.3	13.8	10.6	Sales/Working Capital					7.3	12.5
	22.9	29.3	19.2						16.8	23.6
	75.8	71.6	45.8						33.2	50.8
	5.8	8.2	14.3	EBIT/Interest					13.1	14.0
	(72) 2.7	(73) 2.9	(88) 5.1						(14) 3.2	(55) 5.7
	1.0	1.0	1.8						1.3	1.7
	5.1	5.5	7.5	Net Profit + Depr., Dep., Amort./Cur. Mat. L/T/D						8.5
	(18) 3.2	(21) 2.9	(30) 3.0							(20) 3.9
	2.1	.6	1.0							1.8
	.5	.5	.4	Fixed/Worth					.2	.4
	1.0	.9	.9						.9	.9
	1.8	2.0	1.6						1.8	1.5
	.8	.9	.6	Debt/Worth					.6	.5
	1.3	1.8	1.8						1.7	1.9
	3.9	4.9	3.8						3.0	3.8
	32.3	52.6	36.7	% Profit Before Taxes/Tangible Net Worth					36.6	35.6
	(73) 12.6	(70) 13.8	(89) 16.8						13.3	(56) 17.9
	.7	2.1	6.5						2.4	8.6
	11.5	15.4	16.1	% Profit Before Taxes/Total Assets					13.4	15.2
	5.2	5.2	8.3						4.3	9.2
	.1	.1	2.1						1.6	2.1
	23.5	30.4	27.3	Sales/Net Fixed Assets					100.2	23.3
	10.7	13.3	11.8						22.7	12.5
	5.0	6.5	6.4						8.5	8.1
	5.6	7.2	5.6	Sales/Total Assets					6.9	6.1
	3.7	4.2	3.9						4.6	4.1
	2.3	2.3	2.5						3.3	2.9
	.6	.6	.6	% Depr., Dep., Amort./Sales					.2	.6
	(71) .9	(72) 1.0	(85) 1.0						.9	(52) .9
	2.4	2.1	1.9						1.8	1.4
	.2	.5	1.1	% Officers', Directors', Owners' Comp/Sales						
	(17) 1.2	(27) 1.7	(26) 2.4							
	2.9	3.9	4.3							
	7953455M	6984215M	9111829M	Net Sales ($)	1011M	16184M	11964M	63972M	250280M	8768418M
	2260341M	1655583M	2414886M	Total Assets ($)	1991M	23671M	4060M	23204M	63061M	2298899M

© RMA 2003

M = $ thousand   MM = $ million

See Pages 11 through 18 for Explanation of Ratios and Data

Current Data Sorted By Assets   Comparative Historical Data

0-500M	500M-2MM	2-10MM	10-50MM	50-100MM	100-250MM	Type of Statement	4/1/98-3/31/99 ALL	4/1/99-3/31/00 ALL
1		5	21	5	7	Unqualified	31	30
	8	18	9			Reviewed	15	22
1	7	11	2			Compiled	16	18
1	4				1	Tax Returns	3	4
	4	7	15	3	1	Other	28	22
	27 (4/1-9/30/02)		104 (10/1/02-3/31/03)					
3	23	41	47	8	9	**NUMBER OF STATEMENTS**	93	96
%	%	%	%	%	%	**ASSETS**	%	%
	9.3	8.3	8.4			Cash & Equivalents	8.0	8.2
	29.8	28.3	20.5			Trade Receivables (net)	20.4	19.6
	22.4	18.9	19.6			Inventory	17.5	17.9
	4.1	1.2	2.6			All Other Current	1.3	1.2
	65.5	56.7	51.1			Total Current	47.2	47.0
	27.5	34.1	41.6			Fixed Assets (net)	43.0	43.6
	2.3	1.5	3.8			Intangibles (net)	3.3	4.0
	4.7	7.7	3.5			All Other Non-Current	6.5	5.5
	100.0	100.0	100.0			Total	100.0	100.0
						LIABILITIES		
	15.8	10.9	7.5			Notes Payable-Short Term	8.2	7.1
	7.0	5.3	5.8			Cur. Mat.-L/T/D	4.4	3.8
	17.3	13.6	11.1			Trade Payables	13.1	12.3
	.1	.0	.6			Income Taxes Payable	.2	.3
	5.8	7.4	8.0			All Other Current	8.0	9.9
	45.9	37.2	33.0			Total Current	33.9	33.3
	16.6	14.4	21.3			Long Term Debt	21.6	19.9
	.2	.3	.5			Deferred Taxes	.3	.4
	6.6	3.1	6.0			All Other Non-Current	3.7	4.6
	30.6	45.0	39.1			Net Worth	40.5	41.8
	100.0	100.0	100.0			Total Liabilities & Net Worth	100.0	100.0
						INCOME DATA		
	100.0	100.0	100.0			Net Sales	100.0	100.0
	25.4	24.2	22.9			Gross Profit	25.1	27.9
	21.2	18.8	17.2			Operating Expenses	21.4	23.7
	4.2	5.4	5.7			Operating Profit	3.7	4.2
	.9	1.5	.8			All Other Expenses (net)	1.0	.8
	3.3	3.9	4.9			Profit Before Taxes	2.7	3.3
						RATIOS		
	2.4	2.3	2.6				2.3	2.2
	1.3	1.5	1.6			Current	1.4	1.3
	1.1	1.1	1.1				1.0	1.1
	1.3	1.8	1.6				1.5	1.2
	.8	.9	.9			Quick	.8	.8
	.5	.6	.5				.5	.5
	16 22.5	16 22.7	18 20.4				17 21.9	17 22.1
	21 17.0	21 17.5	22 16.7			Sales/Receivables	21 17.6	22 16.2
	26 14.3	29 12.5	28 12.9				30 12.4	32 11.4
	12 29.6	12 31.5	16 23.3				16 22.1	20 18.7
	21 17.7	19 19.0	22 16.5			Cost of Sales/Inventory	25 14.8	29 12.5
	37 9.8	36 10.2	37 9.8				39 9.5	45 8.2
	8 45.8	6 63.9	9 39.4				10 37.4	12 30.9
	15 23.9	14 26.3	15 24.8			Cost of Sales/Payables	16 23.1	19 19.7
	25 14.6	20 18.6	21 17.3				26 14.2	29 12.6
	11.1	9.9	7.7				10.9	9.4
	28.9	28.2	20.7			Sales/Working Capital	23.0	28.5
	127.3	90.1	77.7				881.1	79.3
	6.3	8.0	16.9				8.6	9.9
	(22) 4.9	(35) 5.5	(45) 6.1			EBIT/Interest	(84) 4.0	(87) 3.0
	2.1	1.6	3.1				1.5	1.9
		10.1	10.4				12.4	8.1
		(10) 2.2	(24) 4.6			Net Profit + Depr., Dep., Amort./Cur. Mat. L/T/D	(39) 3.2	(32) 3.3
		.3	1.5				1.8	2.0
	.5	.4	.5				.7	.7
	.8	.9	1.1			Fixed/Worth	1.2	1.2
	2.9	1.7	2.0				2.0	2.1
	1.1	.6	.7				.6	.9
	2.7	1.7	1.6			Debt/Worth	1.6	1.6
	5.5	3.1	4.6				4.0	3.1
	82.6	34.0	55.9				49.5	37.4
	(20) 45.0	15.9	(44) 26.9			% Profit Before Taxes/Tangible Net Worth	(85) 24.8	(88) 19.4
	18.1	5.0	16.2				13.1	6.8
	21.0	14.1	19.6				18.7	16.9
	9.4	6.6	11.4			% Profit Before Taxes/Total Assets	7.8	6.4
	3.9	1.7	5.2				2.5	2.1
	41.7	40.7	11.2				13.6	12.0
	19.2	10.8	7.3			Sales/Net Fixed Assets	7.5	6.1
	9.8	5.7	4.5				4.2	3.9
	6.5	5.3	4.0				4.3	3.7
	5.2	3.7	2.9			Sales/Total Assets	3.0	2.5
	3.6	2.6	2.1				2.2	2.0
	.9	.5	1.2				1.3	1.4
	(19) 1.2	(40) 1.4	(41) 2.0			% Depr., Dep., Amort./Sales	(85) 2.1	(87) 2.3
	1.9	2.7	2.9				3.1	2.8
	1.3	1.4					1.2	1.8
	(12) 2.1	(16) 2.3				% Officers', Directors', Owners' Comp/Sales	(32) 3.1	(35) 3.5
	6.3	3.7					4.7	6.5
1920M	143644M	895253M	3432763M	2304254M	5506498M	Net Sales ($)	4879842M	5613919M
463M	29466M	192920M	1051951M	559556M	1479719M	Total Assets ($)	1880571M	2349752M

M = $ thousand   MM = $ million
See Pages 11 through 18 for Explanation of Ratios and Data

Comparative Historical Data | Current Data Sorted By Sales

			Type of Statement						
20	26	39	Unqualified	1			7	4	34
20	19	35	Reviewed		1	3	7	12	12
25	27	21	Compiled	1	3	1	8	4	4
4	4	6	Tax Returns	1	1	1	2		1
28	37	30	Other		1		3	4	22
4/1/00-3/31/01 ALL	4/1/01-3/31/02 ALL	4/1/02-3/31/03 ALL		0-1MM	27 (4/1-9/30/02) 1-3MM	3-5MM	104 (10/1/02-3/31/03) 5-10MM	10-25MM	25MM & OVER
97	113	131	**NUMBER OF STATEMENTS**	3	6	5	20	24	73
%	%	%	**ASSETS**	%	%	%	%	%	%
7.7	7.1	8.1	Cash & Equivalents				14.0	12.0	5.7
22.4	20.3	24.2	Trade Receivables (net)				26.5	26.7	23.7
18.2	20.6	20.4	Inventory				22.3	15.9	20.8
2.5	1.7	2.3	All Other Current				1.6	2.2	2.3
50.8	49.8	55.1	Total Current				64.4	56.8	52.5
41.0	42.9	36.7	Fixed Assets (net)				25.8	37.0	38.0
2.1	2.1	2.7	Intangibles (net)				2.2	.8	3.7
6.0	5.1	5.6	All Other Non-Current				7.6	5.4	5.8
100.0	100.0	100.0	Total				100.0	100.0	100.0
			LIABILITIES						
9.2	9.5	11.0	Notes Payable-Short Term				11.5	7.5	10.7
4.1	4.7	6.0	Cur. Mat.-L/T/D				6.4	6.6	5.2
15.5	13.9	14.9	Trade Payables				14.7	13.6	15.5
.3	.3	.2	Income Taxes Payable				.0	.2	.4
8.5	8.3	7.7	All Other Current				7.4	9.7	7.7
37.6	36.7	39.7	Total Current				40.0	37.6	39.5
20.7	21.3	20.4	Long Term Debt				11.4	15.5	19.0
.4	.4	.3	Deferred Taxes				.0	.7	.3
3.7	3.2	6.2	All Other Non-Current				3.6	3.3	7.1
37.6	38.3	33.4	Net Worth				45.0	42.9	34.1
100.0	100.0	100.0	Total Liabilities & Net Worth				100.0	100.0	100.0
			INCOME DATA						
100.0	100.0	100.0	Net Sales				100.0	100.0	100.0
24.1	24.8	24.1	Gross Profit				31.0	23.6	20.3
20.7	20.8	19.0	Operating Expenses				26.4	19.0	15.7
3.4	4.0	5.2	Operating Profit				4.6	4.5	4.6
.9	.9	1.1	All Other Expenses (net)				.3	.7	1.0
2.5	3.1	4.1	Profit Before Taxes				4.2	3.9	3.7
			RATIOS						
2.1	2.1	2.1					3.3	2.7	2.1
1.3	1.4	1.5	Current				1.5	1.4	1.5
1.0	1.1	1.1					1.2	1.2	1.1
1.1	1.2	1.4					2.2	2.0	1.3
.7	.8	.8	Quick				1.2	.8	.8
.5	.5	.5					.6	.7	.5
18 20.8	14 25.9	16 22.5					13 27.7	17 21.1	16 23.3
24 15.3	21 17.2	22 17.0	Sales/Receivables				23 16.1	25 14.4	21 17.5
29 12.7	29 12.8	28 13.0					27 13.6	35 10.3	27 13.4
15 23.8	18 20.7	14 25.7					19 18.8	14 26.8	14 25.4
24 15.5	24 15.4	22 16.5	Cost of Sales/Inventory				29 12.5	19 18.8	22 16.7
39 9.2	44 8.3	38 9.6					53 6.9	28 13.0	36 10.2
11 34.3	10 36.7	9 41.2					9 42.9	7 51.9	9 39.3
16 22.6	16 22.6	15 23.9	Cost of Sales/Payables				16 23.2	14 25.6	16 23.4
30 12.4	27 13.4	23 15.6					25 14.5	20 18.0	24 15.5
11.6	12.6	10.2					7.6	7.2	12.9
30.8	27.2	25.5	Sales/Working Capital				21.0	26.9	25.9
629.8	73.9	100.4					59.4	61.2	139.8
7.6	8.5	10.2					26.2	6.8	17.1
(90) 3.1	(106) 3.4	(121) 5.5	EBIT/Interest	(18) 5.0		(21) 5.1			(68) 6.3
1.4	1.7	2.2					2.1	2.2	2.5
4.4	4.2	9.4	Net Profit + Depr., Dep.,						10.1
(29) 3.1	(29) 2.7	(40) 2.9	Amort./Cur. Mat. L/T/D					(25) 3.4	
1.1	1.3	1.4							1.3
.6	.6	.5					.4	.5	.5
1.1	1.1	1.0	Fixed/Worth				.6	1.0	1.0
2.4	2.4	2.0					1.2	1.9	1.9
.8	.8	.8					.3	.7	.8
1.5	1.6	1.8	Debt/Worth				2.3	1.4	1.7
4.1	4.2	4.4					3.5	3.1	4.6
37.9	33.1	50.2	% Profit Before Taxes/Tangible				71.1	38.0	47.7
(89) 17.6	(101) 18.1	(120) 27.2	Net Worth	(19) 36.1				18.9	(68) 27.2
5.5	8.1	13.3					8.2	8.6	14.7
13.0	13.8	18.0	% Profit Before Taxes/Total				26.7	13.7	18.1
5.6	5.9	9.6	Assets				13.4	7.8	10.0
1.8	2.9	3.9					3.2	4.2	5.1
14.6	13.4	19.7					37.9	22.4	19.5
6.3	7.2	8.7	Sales/Net Fixed Assets				17.2	10.5	7.7
4.6	4.5	5.5					7.7	3.2	5.6
4.5	4.3	5.1					5.9	5.0	5.2
3.0	3.0	3.5	Sales/Total Assets				3.8	3.7	3.3
2.0	2.1	2.4					2.9	2.2	2.5
.8	.9	.9					1.1	.5	.8
(87) 1.7	(98) 1.8	(113) 1.6	% Depr., Dep., Amort./Sales	(19) 1.4		(21) 1.6		(60) 1.7	
2.9	2.5	2.7					2.1	2.7	2.7
1.6	1.4	1.4					1.9		1.3
(36) 2.8	(36) 2.6	(41) 2.3	% Officers', Directors', Owners' Comp/Sales	(14) 3.4				(11) 2.0	
4.8	4.3	4.4					7.2		3.2
6006421M	6615842M	12284332M	Net Sales ($)	1920M	11782M	19846M	143840M	405210M	11701734M
2279645M	2238273M	3314075M	Total Assets ($)	463M	11468M	10043M	41309M	168787M	3082005M

M = $ thousand   MM = $ million
See Pages 11 through 18 for Explanation of Ratios and Data

Current Data Sorted By Assets

Comparative Historical Data

						Type of Statement		
		1	4	3		Unqualified		
		2	1			Reviewed		
		1				Compiled		
1	1	3	1		2	Tax Returns		
1	1					Other		
	6 (4/1-9/30/02)		16 (10/1/02-3/31/03)				4/1/98-3/31/99 ALL	4/1/99-3/31/00 ALL
0-500M	500M-2MM	2-10MM	10-50MM	50-100MM	100-250MM			
2	2	7	6	3	2	**NUMBER OF STATEMENTS**		
%	%	%	%	%	%	**ASSETS**	%	%
						Cash & Equivalents	D	D
						Trade Receivables (net)	A	A
						Inventory	T	T
						All Other Current	A	A
						Total Current		
						Fixed Assets (net)	N	N
						Intangibles (net)	O	O
						All Other Non-Current	T	T
						Total		
						LIABILITIES	A	A
						Notes Payable-Short Term	V	V
						Cur. Mat.-L/T/D	A	A
						Trade Payables	I	I
						Income Taxes Payable	L	L
						All Other Current	A	A
						Total Current	B	B
						Long Term Debt	L	L
						Deferred Taxes	E	E
						All Other Non-Current		
						Net Worth		
						Total Liabilities & Net Worth		
						INCOME DATA		
						Net Sales		
						Gross Profit		
						Operating Expenses		
						Operating Profit		
						All Other Expenses (net)		
						Profit Before Taxes		
						RATIOS		
						Current		
						Quick		
						Sales/Receivables		
						Cost of Sales/Inventory		
						Cost of Sales/Payables		
						Sales/Working Capital		
						EBIT/Interest		
						Net Profit + Depr., Dep., Amort./Cur. Mat. L /T/D		
						Fixed/Worth		
						Debt/Worth		
						% Profit Before Taxes/Tangible Net Worth		
						% Profit Before Taxes/Total Assets		
						Sales/Net Fixed Assets		
						Sales/Total Assets		
						% Depr., Dep., Amort./Sales		
						% Officers', Directors', Owners' Comp/Sales		
3466M	7443M	88363M	349866M	579287M	684004M	Net Sales ($)		
606M	2387M	46034M	149209M	263632M	283518M	Total Assets ($)		

© RMA 2003

M = $ thousand   MM = $ million
See Pages 11 through 18 for Explanation of Ratios and Data

Comparative Historical Data | Current Data Sorted By Sales

Type of Statement

Type of Statement	4/1/01-3/31/02 ALL	4/1/02-3/31/03 ALL	0-1MM	1-3MM	3-5MM	5-10MM	10-25MM	25MM & OVER
Unqualified	2	8					1	7
Reviewed	3	3				1	1	1
Compiled	2	3		1			1	1
Tax Returns	3							
Other	16	8	1	1		1	2	3

Sales band period headers: 6 (4/1-9/30/02) covers 0-1MM, 1-3MM, 3-5MM; 16 (10/1/02-3/31/03) covers 5-10MM, 10-25MM, 25MM & OVER.

Note: Data for period 4/1/00-3/31/01 ALL — DATA NOT AVAILABLE.

	4/1/01-3/31/02 ALL	4/1/02-3/31/03 ALL	0-1MM	1-3MM	3-5MM	5-10MM	10-25MM	25MM & OVER
NUMBER OF STATEMENTS	26	22	1	2	1	2	5	11
ASSETS	%	%	%	%	%	%	%	%
Cash & Equivalents	5.9	10.1						10.1
Trade Receivables (net)	18.1	20.1						16.4
Inventory	25.4	12.7						11.7
All Other Current	1.9	2.2						2.4
Total Current	51.3	45.1						40.7
Fixed Assets (net)	31.9	42.9						47.6
Intangibles (net)	4.5	3.6						6.7
All Other Non-Current	12.2	8.4						5.0
Total	100.0	100.0						100.0
LIABILITIES								
Notes Payable-Short Term	21.9	7.2						2.5
Cur. Mat.-L/T/D	2.5	2.3						2.8
Trade Payables	10.1	7.3						5.2
Income Taxes Payable	.2	.1						.1
All Other Current	11.6	15.4						9.2
Total Current	46.3	32.3						19.8
Long Term Debt	14.0	16.7						17.4
Deferred Taxes	.1	1.1						1.4
All Other Non-Current	2.5	6.4						7.3
Net Worth	37.0	43.4						54.1
Total Liabilities & Net Worth	100.0	100.0						100.0
INCOME DATA								
Net Sales	100.0	100.0						100.0
Gross Profit	24.5	38.8						28.0
Operating Expenses	21.9	31.5						19.6
Operating Profit	2.6	7.3						8.5
All Other Expenses (net)	.7	1.2						1.1
Profit Before Taxes	1.9	6.1						7.3
RATIOS								
Current	1.8	2.6						3.7
	1.2	1.9						2.1
	.7	1.2						1.4
Quick	.8	1.9						2.8
	.6	1.0						1.2
	.3	.7						.8
Sales/Receivables	17 21.8	18 20.6						18 20.5
	29 12.5	27 13.5						25 14.4
	36 10.0	35 10.5						32 11.4
Cost of Sales/Inventory	22 16.9	21 17.6						20 18.0
	49 7.5	28 13.1						24 15.1
	72 5.0	40 9.1						33 11.2
Cost of Sales/Payables	3 106.1	9 41.5						7 49.2
	14 26.5	15 24.2						11 34.0
	24 15.3	28 13.3						16 23.2
Sales/Working Capital	8.0	8.3						7.7
	26.5	14.3						12.5
	-14.4	44.3						21.0
EBIT/Interest	4.5	25.5						25.3
	2.1	10.0						12.1
	.9	3.4						6.7
Net Profit + Depr., Dep., Amort./Cur. Mat. L/T/D								
Fixed/Worth	.5	.7						.9
	.9	1.1						1.1
	1.8	2.2						1.5
Debt/Worth	1.1	.6						.6
	2.6	1.2						1.0
	5.8	2.1						1.8
% Profit Before Taxes/Tangible Net Worth	(21) 22.8	(19) 32.0						(10) 36.4
	10.9	23.8						29.1
	.3	14.7						20.6
% Profit Before Taxes/Total Assets	8.2	20.1						22.3
	5.4	12.0						15.0
	-.4	6.3						9.8
Sales/Net Fixed Assets	16.0	8.8						7.0
	7.8	5.4						4.8
	4.6	3.7						3.3
Sales/Total Assets	3.2	3.0						3.0
	2.3	2.5						2.5
	1.4	1.6						2.1
% Depr., Dep., Amort./Sales	(23) 1.2	(19) 2.2						
	1.9	3.0						
	3.2	4.5						
% Officers', Directors', Owners' Comp/Sales								
Net Sales ($)	1622049M	1712429M	983M	3743M	4549M	15376M	74621M	1613157M
Total Assets ($)	813716M	745386M	290M	1282M	2735M	4611M	40109M	696359M

M = $ thousand   MM = $ million
See Pages 11 through 18 for Explanation of Ratios and Data

Current Data Sorted By Assets | Comparative Historical Data

0-500M	500M-2MM	2-10MM	10-50MM	50-100MM	100-250MM	Type of Statement	4/1/98-3/31/99 ALL	4/1/99-3/31/00 ALL
		3	10	7	3	Unqualified	25	37
		5	2			Reviewed	3	7
		1				Compiled	1	
		2				Tax Returns	1	
	1	4	5	3	3	Other	18	12
	9 (4/1-9/30/02)		40 (10/1/02-3/31/03)					
	1	15	17	10	6	NUMBER OF STATEMENTS	48	57
%	%	%	%	%	%	**ASSETS**	%	%
		10.1	3.4	3.1		Cash & Equivalents	5.9	6.1
		27.0	17.9	12.4		Trade Receivables (net)	17.2	19.3
		23.3	20.3	21.7		Inventory	24.9	21.8
		1.4	5.9	1.3		All Other Current	2.1	4.3
		61.8	47.5	38.5		Total Current	50.1	51.5
		31.2	44.8	44.8		Fixed Assets (net)	42.9	41.6
		4.0	2.9	9.8		Intangibles (net)	1.2	1.0
		3.0	4.8	7.0		All Other Non-Current	5.8	5.9
		100.0	100.0	100.0		Total	100.0	100.0
						LIABILITIES		
		8.3	6.8	7.5		Notes Payable-Short Term	10.5	9.0
		4.3	2.0	8.1		Cur. Mat.-L/T/D	3.3	2.9
		29.1	7.6	8.2		Trade Payables	11.0	12.6
		.1	.1	.3		Income Taxes Payable	.5	.5
		7.1	11.1	8.2		All Other Current	7.9	12.7
		48.8	27.7	32.4		Total Current	33.2	37.7
		11.4	19.6	27.7		Long Term Debt	20.4	19.6
		.5	.9	1.4		Deferred Taxes	3.1	2.9
		2.2	3.3	4.6		All Other Non-Current	2.9	2.4
		37.1	48.5	34.0		Net Worth	40.4	37.4
		100.0	100.0	100.0		Total Liabilities & Net Worth	100.0	100.0
						INCOME DATA		
		100.0	100.0	100.0		Net Sales	100.0	100.0
		20.3	16.1	11.1		Gross Profit	15.1	15.1
		18.1	12.8	9.5		Operating Expenses	12.1	11.9
		2.1	3.3	1.6		Operating Profit	3.0	3.2
		.5	.2	1.1		All Other Expenses (net)	.6	.6
		1.7	3.1	.5		Profit Before Taxes	2.4	2.6
						RATIOS		
		3.3	2.8	2.1		Current	2.3	2.1
		.9	1.6	1.3			1.7	1.7
		.9	1.3	.9			1.1	1.1
		2.6	1.0	.8		Quick	1.1	1.2
		.6	.6	.6			.7	.7
		.4	.5	.3			.4	.4
		15 25.1	15 24.2	17 21.7		Sales/Receivables	13 27.1	17 21.8
		17 20.9	21 17.1	27 13.4			21 17.6	20 17.9
		31 11.7	31 11.9	33 11.0			28 13.0	27 13.7
		7 55.1	21 17.3	33 11.1		Cost of Sales/Inventory	21 17.1	20 17.8
		21 17.2	33 11.0	42 8.7			35 10.5	32 11.3
		72 5.1	59 6.2	70 5.2			57 6.4	51 7.2
		11 32.8	6 56.9	15 24.8		Cost of Sales/Payables	9 39.1	12 30.8
		26 14.0	13 27.9	18 20.0			14 25.6	15 23.7
		39 9.3	21 17.1	24 15.2			21 17.5	20 18.5
		19.1	7.2	8.2		Sales/Working Capital	7.7	8.9
		-189.2	12.5	20.0			12.2	14.7
		-69.2	35.2	-34.2			103.7	88.6
		14.1	23.2			EBIT/Interest	5.7	7.7
		(13) 4.4	(15) 8.1				(47) 2.8	(56) 3.8
		1.9	2.4				1.0	1.7
						Net Profit + Depr., Dep., Amort./Cur. Mat. L/T/D	7.5	10.8
							(22) 1.9	(26) 6.7
							1.0	2.2
		.5	.6	.9		Fixed/Worth	.6	.6
		1.2	1.1	2.2			1.2	1.1
		2.2	1.9	8.9			1.8	2.0
		.4	.5	1.4		Debt/Worth	.8	.9
		2.3	1.3	3.1			1.4	1.5
		11.0	2.6	13.0			2.6	2.8
		46.7	42.6	124.9		% Profit Before Taxes/Tangible Net Worth	27.2	30.6
		(13) 9.4	18.2	22.1			(47) 15.4	(52) 18.2
		4.2	7.1	-11.9			1.3	8.1
		16.1	14.7	10.7		% Profit Before Taxes/Total Assets	12.7	13.4
		5.2	9.1	3.9			4.0	6.7
		1.0	3.0	-5.6			.1	1.9
		31.5	9.9	6.0		Sales/Net Fixed Assets	11.2	11.3
		11.7	7.8	3.7			5.8	7.0
		5.0	3.8	2.5			3.7	4.5
		6.0	3.5	2.7		Sales/Total Assets	3.5	3.7
		3.7	2.5	1.6			2.5	2.7
		2.2	2.0	1.1			2.0	2.1
		.6	1.3	2.3		% Depr., Dep., Amort./Sales	1.2	1.2
		(14) 1.3	2.2	3.3			(41) 1.6	(44) 1.7
		2.7	3.7	5.4			2.6	2.4
						% Officers', Directors', Owners' Comp/Sales		
4475M	402309M	1160450M	1338862M	2264533M		Net Sales ($)	6276035M	9762341M
1617M	80269M	443519M	748285M	1108300M		Total Assets ($)	2843981M	4171738M

(Left columns 0-500M and 500M-2MM marked "DATA NOT AVAILABLE")

M = $ thousand   MM = $ million
See Pages 11 through 18 for Explanation of Ratios and Data

Comparative Historical Data				Current Data Sorted By Sales					
			Type of Statement						
20	27	23	Unqualified				1	2	20
7	6	7	Reviewed			1		4	2
6	5	1	Compiled						1
3	3	2	Tax Returns					2	
21	15	16	Other		1	1	1	1	12
4/1/00-3/31/01 ALL	4/1/01-3/31/02 ALL	4/1/02-3/31/03 ALL		9 (4/1-9/30/02)			40 (10/1/02-3/31/03)		
				0-1MM	1-3MM	3-5MM	5-10MM	10-25MM	25MM & OVER
57	56	49	**NUMBER OF STATEMENTS**		1	2	2	9	35
%	%	%	**ASSETS**	%	%	%	%	%	%
5.7	5.0	5.1	Cash & Equivalents	DATA NOT AVAILABLE					4.7
20.3	19.1	18.5	Trade Receivables (net)						17.0
22.9	23.2	21.7	Inventory						21.8
3.3	4.6	4.7	All Other Current						4.2
52.2	52.0	50.0	Total Current						47.6
39.1	39.7	41.3	Fixed Assets (net)						43.4
3.2	2.4	4.3	Intangibles (net)						3.8
5.5	5.9	4.4	All Other Non-Current						5.2
100.0	100.0	100.0	Total						100.0
			LIABILITIES						
10.5	5.7	7.7	Notes Payable-Short Term						7.9
4.2	4.8	4.0	Cur. Mat.-L/T/D						3.9
12.8	15.6	14.2	Trade Payables						10.2
.2	.6	.2	Income Taxes Payable						.1
11.9	13.4	8.6	All Other Current						8.9
39.5	40.1	34.6	Total Current						31.1
19.5	22.7	18.3	Long Term Debt						18.3
1.7	1.9	1.2	Deferred Taxes						1.3
1.8	1.5	2.9	All Other Non-Current						2.5
37.5	33.8	43.1	Net Worth						46.8
100.0	100.0	100.0	Total Liabilities & Net Worth						100.0
			INCOME DATA						
100.0	100.0	100.0	Net Sales						100.0
16.7	14.8	17.2	Gross Profit						15.4
13.7	11.6	14.6	Operating Expenses						12.6
3.0	3.2	2.6	Operating Profit						2.8
.4	.9	.4	All Other Expenses (net)						.2
2.6	2.3	2.1	Profit Before Taxes						2.6
			RATIOS						
2.3	2.3	2.7							2.7
1.7	1.8	1.5	Current						1.6
1.1	1.2	1.0							1.1
1.1	1.2	.9							1.0
.7	.8	.6	Quick						.6
.5	.4	.4							.4
19 19.5	17 21.1	15 23.7							16 23.1
23 15.8	21 17.4	21 17.1	Sales/Receivables						23 15.6
36 10.2	31 11.7	30 12.3							30 12.3
23 15.8	25 14.7	21 17.1							22 17.0
39 9.5	39 9.3	37 9.9	Cost of Sales/Inventory						37 9.9
49 7.5	60 6.1	70 5.2							56 6.5
10 34.9	11 32.2	10 37.4							7 51.4
14 25.6	16 22.9	16 22.7	Cost of Sales/Payables						15 24.7
23 16.0	23 15.9	27 13.4							23 16.0
8.1	9.9	8.9							9.1
16.9	16.3	19.1	Sales/Working Capital						13.8
47.9	35.7	NM							61.0
7.1	9.0	12.1							12.3
(53) 3.1	(50) 3.4	(44) 4.8	EBIT/Interest						(31) 6.5
-.4	1.2	1.5							1.5
8.9	7.7	7.0							
(11) 1.7	(15) 3.4	(14) 4.2	Net Profit + Depr., Dep., Amort./Cur. Mat. L/T/D						
.8	1.4	1.2							
.6	.6	.7							.6
1.0	1.2	1.1	Fixed/Worth						1.0
1.7	1.9	2.0							1.9
.8	.9	.7							.6
1.3	1.7	1.4	Debt/Worth						1.4
3.0	2.8	4.9							2.6
36.9	41.5	35.5							36.3
(52) 14.0	(51) 16.8	(47) 15.5	% Profit Before Taxes/Tangible Net Worth						(34) 16.5
-11.0	3.6	5.5							5.7
14.7	14.7	12.4							14.6
4.6	4.3	5.7	% Profit Before Taxes/Total Assets						9.0
-2.8	.4	1.1							2.2
13.3	10.7	12.6							9.7
6.9	6.0	6.4	Sales/Net Fixed Assets						6.0
3.8	4.0	3.7							3.4
3.7	3.9	3.5							3.8
2.2	2.4	2.3	Sales/Total Assets						2.5
1.9	1.7	1.9							2.0
.8	1.0	1.2							1.3
(43) 1.8	(40) 1.6	(43) 2.3	% Depr., Dep., Amort./Sales						(29) 2.3
2.9	2.7	3.6							3.7
.3									
(10) .8			% Officers', Directors', Owners' Comp/Sales						
2.9									
6978163M	8262227M	5170629M	Net Sales ($)		2125M	9323M	15254M	152776M	4991151M
3516281M	3945270M	2381990M	Total Assets ($)		5772M	4386M	6774M	70166M	2294892M

M = $ thousand MM = $ million

See Pages 11 through 18 for Explanation of Ratios and Data

Current Data Sorted By Assets   Comparative Historical Data

0-500M	500M-2MM	2-10MM	10-50MM	50-100MM	100-250MM	Type of Statement	4/1/98-3/31/99 ALL	4/1/99-3/31/00 ALL
	1	6	11	2	2	Unqualified	16	16
	3	7	1			Reviewed	5	8
	2					Compiled	5	6
2	5					Tax Returns	1	3
	2	8	8	1	1	Other	6	13
	10 (4/1-9/30/02)		52 (10/1/02-3/31/03)					
2	13	21	20	3	3	**NUMBER OF STATEMENTS**	33	46
%	%	%	%	%	%	**ASSETS**	%	%
	5.3	4.2	4.8			Cash & Equivalents	4.4	4.4
	24.8	31.1	17.1			Trade Receivables (net)	21.5	24.1
	25.9	31.9	29.0			Inventory	35.8	32.9
	3.7	1.1	4.0			All Other Current	5.5	2.3
	59.6	68.2	54.9			Total Current	67.2	63.7
	31.9	26.7	33.6			Fixed Assets (net)	21.0	25.7
	.3	1.3	4.3			Intangibles (net)	9.1	6.1
	8.2	3.7	7.1			All Other Non-Current	2.6	4.4
	100.0	100.0	100.0			Total	100.0	100.0
						LIABILITIES		
	19.7	29.7	17.6			Notes Payable-Short Term	21.9	21.0
	3.6	3.7	7.2			Cur. Mat.-L/T/D	3.1	4.1
	23.2	19.8	12.3			Trade Payables	14.8	16.8
	.0	.1	.0			Income Taxes Payable	.6	.2
	16.3	4.3	6.4			All Other Current	13.6	10.3
	62.8	57.5	43.4			Total Current	53.9	52.5
	28.8	9.9	18.5			Long Term Debt	12.9	14.4
	.0	.3	.4			Deferred Taxes	1.2	.2
	11.2	3.7	3.4			All Other Non-Current	5.7	3.5
	-2.9	28.6	34.3			Net Worth	26.3	29.4
	100.0	100.0	100.0			Total Liabilities & Net Worth	100.0	100.0
						INCOME DATA		
	100.0	100.0	100.0			Net Sales	100.0	100.0
	19.5	12.4	18.6			Gross Profit	16.4	19.7
	15.7	10.0	13.1			Operating Expenses	13.0	15.0
	3.8	2.4	5.5			Operating Profit	3.4	4.7
	1.0	.9	.9			All Other Expenses (net)	1.1	1.3
	2.8	1.6	4.7			Profit Before Taxes	2.3	3.3
						RATIOS		
	1.6	1.3	1.8			Current	1.6	1.6
	1.1	1.1	1.4				1.3	1.1
	.7	.9	1.1				.9	1.0
	.8	.7	.7			Quick	.8	.8
	.5	.6	.6				.4	.5
	.4	.4	.4				.3	.3
	3 104.4	24 15.4	25 14.8			Sales/Receivables	16 22.1	21 17.1
	23 16.1	27 13.5	29 12.7				27 13.3	30 12.1
	35 10.4	36 10.1	38 9.7				36 10.3	39 9.4
	7 53.5	25 14.4	26 14.2			Cost of Sales/Inventory	17 21.2	24 15.3
	16 22.4	37 9.9	51 7.1				50 7.3	51 7.2
	40 9.1	51 7.1	77 4.7				97 3.8	95 3.8
	8 46.6	8 48.4	14 26.7			Cost of Sales/Payables	6 59.2	8 43.9
	19 19.4	28 13.1	28 13.0				18 19.9	21 17.7
	50 7.3	32 11.4	34 10.6				36 10.1	35 10.4
	38.8	20.4	8.3			Sales/Working Capital	12.1	10.9
	59.7	47.7	15.0				28.9	45.8
	-39.0	-65.0	71.4				NM	-781.6
	6.8	4.6	8.2			EBIT/Interest	(31) 5.8	(44) 6.3
	1.6	(20) 1.6	3.0				2.5	2.3
	.0	1.1	1.3				.4	1.0
						Net Profit + Depr., Dep., Amort./Cur. Mat. L/T/D	(10) 4.9	(14) 5.1
							2.7	2.2
							1.3	.7
	.8	.4	.5			Fixed/Worth	.5	.5
	.9	1.4	1.1				1.1	.9
	NM	2.4	2.2				-1.7	2.9
	1.3	2.1	1.2			Debt/Worth	1.5	1.3
	2.2	2.8	2.4				4.2	3.1
	NM	6.0	5.6				-11.7	16.5
	49.2	23.3	75.6			% Profit Before Taxes/Tangible Net Worth	47.2	41.1
(10)	10.0	(20) 8.3	(19) 23.6				(22) 20.0	(37) 18.1
	-12.8	.5	.9				2.5	2.8
	17.7	6.4	13.3			% Profit Before Taxes/Total Assets	10.8	14.8
	4.3	1.7	5.0				5.3	5.0
	-4.0	.2	.8				-.5	.4
	60.3	37.2	17.4			Sales/Net Fixed Assets	45.1	26.1
	16.9	14.1	8.0				17.5	15.7
	7.8	8.4	3.7				9.4	7.9
	6.8	4.7	2.7			Sales/Total Assets	4.7	4.4
	5.2	3.2	2.3				3.0	3.1
	2.7	2.5	1.8				2.0	1.6
	.6	.4	1.1			% Depr., Dep., Amort./Sales	(32) .6	(42) .6
	1.2	1.0	(19) 1.9				.8	1.5
	2.7	2.6	3.3				1.8	3.4
		.6				% Officers', Directors', Owners' Comp/Sales		.6
		(10) 1.3					(14) 2.1	
		3.2					5.2	
1766M	83263M	442630M	1227007M	268554M	747200M	Net Sales ($)	1338939M	1910822M
367M	15771M	125804M	540575M	187946M	448741M	Total Assets ($)	626987M	1121797M

Comparative Historical Data / Current Data Sorted By Sales

4/1/00-3/31/01 ALL	4/1/01-3/31/02 ALL	4/1/02-3/31/03 ALL	Type of Statement	10 (4/1-9/30/02) 0-1MM	1-3MM	3-5MM	52 (10/1/02-3/31/03) 5-10MM	10-25MM	25MM & OVER
11	10	22	Unqualified				1	4	17
8	6	11	Reviewed		1	3	2		5
4	5	2	Compiled			1	1	1	
1		7	Tax Returns			1	1	2	
12	17	20	Other	2	1	1	2	7	9
36	38	62	**NUMBER OF STATEMENTS**	2	2	6	7	14	31
%	%	%	**ASSETS**	%	%	%	%	%	%
5.1	4.6	5.1	Cash & Equivalents					5.7	4.9
21.2	20.9	22.9	Trade Receivables (net)					26.6	21.3
34.9	28.4	29.5	Inventory					35.7	29.1
3.7	4.0	2.6	All Other Current					1.9	2.8
64.8	57.8	60.1	Total Current					69.8	58.2
23.0	32.6	30.5	Fixed Assets (net)					25.9	29.5
7.3	5.2	3.2	Intangibles (net)					.7	5.7
4.8	4.3	6.2	All Other Non-Current					3.7	6.6
100.0	100.0	100.0	Total					100.0	100.0
			LIABILITIES						
29.9	19.5	21.9	Notes Payable-Short Term					24.7	19.0
3.9	7.3	4.7	Cur. Mat.-L/T/D					2.8	5.3
16.8	16.2	16.3	Trade Payables					17.8	14.1
.8	.3	.0	Income Taxes Payable					.0	.0
8.7	13.3	7.7	All Other Current					7.4	6.5
60.0	56.5	50.8	Total Current					52.7	44.8
10.5	20.3	17.4	Long Term Debt					11.5	15.7
1.1	.6	.4	Deferred Taxes					.3	.6
4.8	9.0	5.7	All Other Non-Current					3.8	3.7
23.6	13.5	25.7	Net Worth					31.7	35.2
100.0	100.0	100.0	Total Liabilities & Net Worth					100.0	100.0
			INCOME DATA						
100.0	100.0	100.0	Net Sales					100.0	100.0
15.8	17.5	18.1	Gross Profit					12.6	17.5
13.7	15.1	13.6	Operating Expenses					11.0	11.7
2.2	2.4	4.5	Operating Profit					1.6	5.8
1.5	1.0	.9	All Other Expenses (net)					1.0	.8
.7	1.4	3.5	Profit Before Taxes					.6	4.9
			RATIOS						
1.6	1.3	1.7	Current					1.7	1.7
1.2	1.1	1.3						1.3	1.3
.8	.9	.9						1.0	1.1
.6	.7	.8	Quick					.7	.8
.4	.4	.5						.5	.6
.2	.3	.4						.4	.4
14 25.7	17 21.2	22 16.3	Sales/Receivables					23 16.1	25 14.4
25 14.5	26 13.8	27 13.4						27 13.5	30 12.3
34 10.8	33 11.2	37 9.8						38 9.6	36 10.2
20 18.5	18 20.0	22 16.6	Cost of Sales/Inventory					15 24.4	29 12.8
46 7.9	34 10.7	40 9.1						38 9.6	41 8.8
86 4.3	78 4.7	63 5.8						63 5.8	74 4.9
8 47.8	12 29.6	8 44.0	Cost of Sales/Payables					6 65.5	12 29.7
18 20.0	21 17.0	24 15.4						13 27.2	28 12.9
33 11.1	33 11.0	32 11.4						36 10.2	32 11.5
14.9	18.4	12.0	Sales/Working Capital					15.3	9.1
41.3	83.5	27.4						35.4	15.8
-20.9	-59.4	-71.7						-157.6	85.9
3.0	3.2	6.9	EBIT/Interest					5.1	7.7
(35) 1.5	1.8	(61) 2.5						1.5	(30) 3.1
.7	.4	1.1						.5	1.4
6.0	1.9	3.1	Net Profit + Depr., Dep., Amort./Cur. Mat. L/T/D						3.3
(16) 2.7	(14) 1.0	(20) 1.7							(11) 2.7
1.6	.3	.6							1.1
.5	.9	.6	Fixed/Worth					.4	.6
1.3	1.5	1.1						.9	1.0
NM	3.6	2.4						1.5	1.8
2.3	1.9	1.3	Debt/Worth					1.5	1.1
4.5	4.4	2.6						3.0	2.4
NM	11.1	6.0						4.3	5.8
52.4	54.0	40.4	% Profit Before Taxes/Tangible Net Worth					26.4	48.0
(27) 20.8	(31) 8.2	(56) 14.9						3.0	(28) 17.8
5.0	-5.0	.9						-5.4	2.8
9.1	8.5	12.3	% Profit Before Taxes/Total Assets					4.3	13.7
2.3	1.7	4.4						.8	5.4
-1.2	-2.5	.4						-1.4	.9
41.4	23.6	27.5	Sales/Net Fixed Assets					52.2	14.7
15.4	12.0	10.8						24.1	8.8
8.1	4.4	6.6						7.9	5.4
4.7	4.1	4.4	Sales/Total Assets					5.9	3.1
3.5	3.2	2.7						4.1	2.3
1.6	2.0	2.1						2.3	1.8
.6	.5	.8	% Depr., Dep., Amort./Sales					.3	.9
(34) 1.1	(36) 1.2	(60) 1.4						.9	(29) 1.5
2.2	3.2	2.5						1.3	2.4
.7		.8	% Officers', Directors', Owners' Comp/Sales						
(11) 1.8		(21) 1.3							
4.4		3.3							
1839436M	1457104M	2770420M	Net Sales ($)	1242M	3966M	25251M	56630M	245583M	2437748M
934714M	772849M	1319204M	Total Assets ($)	1057M	790M	10203M	16807M	83614M	1206733M

M = $ thousand   MM = $ million
See Pages 11 through 18 for Explanation of Ratios and Data

Current Data Sorted By Assets | Comparative Historical Data

0-500M	500M-2MM	2-10MM	10-50MM	50-100MM	100-250MM	Type of Statement	4/1/98-3/31/99 ALL	4/1/99-3/31/00 ALL
		1	4	1	1	Unqualified	8	10
1	6	4				Reviewed	17	16
29	11	1				Compiled	64	53
19	7				1	Tax Returns	32	21
1	3	5	6			Other	44	21
	13 (4/1-9/30/02)		88 (10/1/02-3/31/03)					
50	27	11	10	1	2	NUMBER OF STATEMENTS	165	121
%	%	%	%	%	%	ASSETS	%	%
10.6	8.9	13.1	8.7			Cash & Equivalents	12.5	12.7
4.1	4.5	9.5	5.2			Trade Receivables (net)	4.9	5.6
5.3	2.9	4.1	5.2			Inventory	4.7	6.4
2.7	1.2	1.3	3.7			All Other Current	2.4	2.1
22.7	17.5	28.0	22.8			Total Current	24.6	26.8
52.2	53.5	52.5	60.3			Fixed Assets (net)	51.5	56.8
9.8	15.2	12.5	13.4			Intangibles (net)	15.5	7.1
15.4	13.8	7.0	3.5			All Other Non-Current	8.4	9.3
100.0	100.0	100.0	100.0			Total	100.0	100.0
						LIABILITIES		
10.4	2.6	3.2	.2			Notes Payable-Short Term	4.5	5.0
6.4	5.6	7.4	7.0			Cur. Mat.-L/T/D	7.1	8.2
12.4	5.6	7.8	12.0			Trade Payables	10.4	12.8
.1	.0	1.7	.0			Income Taxes Payable	.2	.2
23.6	10.6	6.7	6.2			All Other Current	10.0	18.2
52.9	24.5	26.8	25.4			Total Current	32.1	44.5
48.2	38.5	38.1	41.1			Long Term Debt	36.4	36.5
.0	.6	.0	.2			Deferred Taxes	.2	.1
4.6	4.1	7.7	4.6			All Other Non-Current	14.1	13.9
-5.7	32.3	27.4	28.7			Net Worth	17.1	4.9
100.0	100.0	100.0	100.0			Total Liabilities & Net Worth	100.0	100.0
						INCOME DATA		
100.0	100.0	100.0	100.0			Net Sales	100.0	100.0
57.9	49.9	56.5	42.4			Gross Profit	49.8	54.6
54.8	41.1	46.1	34.4			Operating Expenses	44.5	49.3
3.1	8.8	10.3	7.9			Operating Profit	5.3	5.3
1.8	3.4	2.8	1.6			All Other Expenses (net)	1.5	2.1
1.2	5.4	7.5	6.3			Profit Before Taxes	3.8	3.1
						RATIOS		
1.2	1.4	1.9	1.4			Current	1.7	1.2
.4	.8	1.1	1.1				.7	.7
.1	.4	.3	.3				.3	.4
.8	1.2	1.8	1.0			Quick	1.3	1.0
.3	.6	.9	.7				(160) .5	(119) .4
.1	.2	.1	.2				.2	.2
0 UND	0 UND	0 999.8	1 483.0			Sales/Receivables	0 UND	0 UND
0 UND	0 999.8	2 163.5	3 138.1				0 UND	1 281.3
3 133.0	3 145.0	16 22.6	17 20.9				6 64.4	9 40.0
2 167.5	2 218.5	4 91.8	3 118.4			Cost of Sales/Inventory	3 104.6	5 76.0
5 72.1	3 113.6	10 38.2	8 46.4				7 51.8	11 33.8
17 21.2	12 31.0	20 18.1	28 13.1				16 22.5	22 16.6
0 UND	3 138.0	7 49.3	6 57.7			Cost of Sales/Payables	3 106.1	5 68.0
8 47.9	8 45.3	29 12.4	27 13.4				13 27.7	21 17.0
35 10.6	15 24.1	41 9.0	52 7.0				41 8.8	46 8.0
67.3	39.2	15.8	20.9			Sales/Working Capital	30.7	59.2
-29.7	-100.0	164.0	NM				-83.3	-43.7
-10.1	-23.4	-10.9	-12.3				-12.3	-12.4
5.6	12.5	22.1	12.0			EBIT/Interest	6.3	8.3
(40) 1.4	(25) 2.8	9.2	5.7				(143) 2.7	(112) 2.8
-.3	.9	2.9	1.6				.7	1.3
						Net Profit + Depr., Dep., Amort./Cur. Mat. L /T/D	3.9	3.5
							(30) 2.5	(10) 2.0
							1.4	1.3
1.1	1.0	.8	1.4			Fixed/Worth	1.3	1.0
-68.7	1.9	16.9	4.3				4.0	3.6
-1.6	-7.8	-3.4	NM				-3.9	-2.1
1.5	.8	.9	1.5			Debt/Worth	1.5	1.2
-32.9	2.8	18.5	4.7				6.8	4.0
-2.8	-17.8	-8.9	NM				-6.7	-4.1
100.0	117.0					% Profit Before Taxes/Tangible Net Worth	110.1	102.2
(23) 19.8	(19) 57.3						(103) 45.7	(78) 40.4
-5.9	13.8						13.9	15.6
18.8	31.9	29.5	27.9			% Profit Before Taxes/Total Assets	21.8	22.3
4.8	8.5	20.5	9.8				7.7	10.2
-9.7	.0	14.0	4.5				-1.3	2.1
19.8	9.7	8.9	5.5			Sales/Net Fixed Assets	10.7	12.0
8.8	5.8	5.9	4.3				5.0	6.1
4.3	4.0	2.5	2.5				3.3	3.4
6.5	4.3	4.4	2.8			Sales/Total Assets	4.2	5.6
4.4	2.9	2.3	2.2				2.7	3.4
2.6	1.6	1.8	2.0				1.7	2.2
1.9	2.3	2.7	3.8			% Depr., Dep., Amort./Sales	1.9	1.7
(47) 2.9	(25) 3.3	4.2	4.5				(151) 3.3	(110) 2.9
4.9	6.5	7.4	6.7				4.9	4.9
5.9	3.7					% Officers', Directors', Owners' Comp/Sales	3.1	3.8
(29) 7.8	(11) 5.1						(86) 4.8	(46) 7.4
10.6	17.5						10.9	12.2
42539M	91408M	129982M	366822M	116872M	1485607M	Net Sales ($)	2086554M	1163826M
9968M	28015M	53921M	155388M	62821M	274326M	Total Assets ($)	782622M	508845M

© RMA 2003

M = $ thousand   MM = $ million
See Pages 11 through 18 for Explanation of Ratios and Data

Comparative Historical Data　　　　　　　　　　　　Current Data Sorted By Sales

Type of Statement									
12	7	7	Unqualified				1		6
21	12	11	Reviewed	1	2	1	3	4	
45	37	41	Compiled	22	15	3		1	
40	30	27	Tax Returns	13	11	1	1		1
21	28	15	Other	3		1	2	2	7

4/1/00-3/31/01 ALL	4/1/01-3/31/02 ALL	4/1/02-3/31/03 ALL		13 (4/1-9/30/02) 0-1MM	1-3MM	3-5MM	88 (10/1/02-3/31/03) 5-10MM	10-25MM	25MM & OVER
139	114	101	**NUMBER OF STATEMENTS**	39	28	6	7	7	14
%	%	%	**ASSETS**	%	%	%	%	%	%
12.5	14.1	10.1	Cash & Equivalents	10.0	9.1				8.1
6.3	6.6	4.8	Trade Receivables (net)	5.1	1.1				4.1
5.9	5.4	5.0	Inventory	5.9	2.0				8.3
2.6	2.4	2.2	All Other Current	3.5	.5				3.6
27.3	28.5	22.2	Total Current	24.5	12.8				24.2
51.4	49.0	53.0	Fixed Assets (net)	53.7	50.9				57.2
10.8	12.8	12.3	Intangibles (net)	9.6	14.7				15.5
10.4	9.7	12.5	All Other Non-Current	12.3	21.7				3.1
100.0	100.0	100.0	Total	100.0	100.0				100.0
			LIABILITIES						
3.2	4.9	6.3	Notes Payable-Short Term	11.6	2.7				.5
7.4	6.7	6.3	Cur. Mat.-L/T/D	6.2	6.4				5.6
11.0	9.8	10.1	Trade Payables	14.8	3.4				13.0
.2	.2	.2	Income Taxes Payable	.1	.0				.0
12.0	12.8	16.1	All Other Current	21.3	20.0				8.1
33.8	34.3	39.0	Total Current	54.0	32.4				27.2
35.8	34.2	44.1	Long Term Debt	53.1	40.1				45.7
.1	.2	.2	Deferred Taxes	.0	.3				.2
8.1	8.8	4.9	All Other Non-Current	3.2	5.6				5.1
22.2	22.5	11.8	Net Worth	-10.3	21.6				21.9
100.0	100.0	100.0	Total Liabilities & Net Worth	100.0	100.0				100.0
			INCOME DATA						
100.0	100.0	100.0	Net Sales	100.0	100.0				100.0
49.3	53.9	54.5	Gross Profit	59.5	51.3				50.4
43.9	47.8	48.6	Operating Expenses	57.3	42.1				43.6
5.4	6.1	5.9	Operating Profit	2.2	9.1				6.8
1.2	2.1	2.4	All Other Expenses (net)	2.8	2.1				2.5
4.2	4.0	3.5	Profit Before Taxes	-.6	7.0				4.4
			RATIOS						
1.4 .8 .4	1.9 .9 .4	1.4 .7 .2	Current	1.4 .4 .1	1.4 .7 .1				1.4 .8 .4
1.0 .5 .2	1.5 .7 .2	1.0 .5 .1	Quick	.8 .4 .1	1.2 .4 .0				.8 .5 .4
0 UND / 1 477.0 / 11 34.2	0 UND / 0 849.5 / 8 46.8	0 UND / 1 519.7 / 5 67.0	Sales/Receivables	0 UND / 1 427.5 / 7 56.1	0 UND / 0 UND / 1 336.4				0 UND / 3 138.1 / 8 45.5
3 128.4 / 6 65.5 / 20 18.0	3 130.8 / 7 50.4 / 19 19.3	2 172.4 / 5 67.5 / 19 19.7	Cost of Sales/Inventory	2 157.7 / 9 42.0 / 24 14.9	1 259.7 / 3 130.8 / 5 70.3				5 78.6 / 14 26.3 / 38 9.7
5 69.7 / 15 24.1 / 31 11.9	5 73.8 / 12 29.9 / 35 10.4	2 147.0 / 10 35.3 / 37 9.8	Cost of Sales/Payables	2 165.2 / 17 21.0 / 43 8.5	0 UND / 3 117.6 / 8 44.0				12 29.7 / 29 12.4 / 61 6.0
45.1 / -68.0 / -16.1	22.5 / -145.1 / -16.8	39.9 / -75.8 / -11.6	Sales/Working Capital	40.7 / -26.1 / -9.6	110.4 / -90.9 / -12.5				21.6 / -387.7 / -12.3
(120) 11.5 / 2.8 / 1.0	(95) 6.8 / 1.9 / .3	(89) 9.6 / 2.9 / .8	EBIT/Interest	(34) 3.0 / .9 / -.8	(22) 10.0 / 5.7 / 1.1				12.0 / 5.7 / 1.1
(17) 2.5 / 1.4 / 1.0	(19) 2.0 / 1.3 / .2		Net Profit + Depr., Dep., Amort./Cur. Mat. L/T/D						
.9 / 2.8 / -4.9	.9 / 3.1 / -2.2	1.1 / 5.7 / -2.1	Fixed/Worth	1.3 / -12.5 / -1.6	.9 / 2.6 / -3.9				1.4 / 6.1 / -18.4
1.1 / 3.6 / -7.8	1.1 / 4.4 / -4.2	1.1 / 7.4 / -4.8	Debt/Worth	1.7 / -7.3 / -2.7	.7 / 6.2 / -5.9				1.5 / 6.6 / -24.2
(95) 109.7 / 55.7 / 9.0	(72) 88.6 / 36.8 / 6.4	(58) 89.0 / 42.3 / 7.4	% Profit Before Taxes/Tangible Net Worth	(16) 32.1 / 8.6 / -11.9	(19) 219.3 / 65.1 / 19.5			(10)	75.6 / 49.6 / 14.7
29.7 / 11.2 / -.3	24.2 / 5.8 / -1.4	27.9 / 7.7 / -1.6	% Profit Before Taxes/Total Assets	10.7 / -.9 / -12.7	56.4 / 13.4 / 1.1				26.4 / 9.8 / .4
13.8 / 5.9 / 3.2	13.2 / 5.2 / 3.7	13.3 / 6.2 / 4.0	Sales/Net Fixed Assets	18.7 / 5.9 / 3.0	15.4 / 8.3 / 5.0				8.0 / 4.7 / 2.5
4.8 / 2.9 / 1.9	4.3 / 3.0 / 1.9	5.2 / 3.2 / 2.1	Sales/Total Assets	5.3 / 3.0 / 2.2	6.3 / 4.3 / 2.1				3.3 / 2.2 / 1.8
(130) 1.9 / 3.0 / 4.7	(106) 1.7 / 3.1 / 5.1	(95) 2.1 / 3.4 / 5.7	% Depr., Dep., Amort./Sales	(36) 2.0 / 4.3 / 6.3	(26) 2.0 / 2.8 / 3.3			(13)	3.7 / 4.6 / 6.8
(67) 2.3 / 4.2 / 9.4	(52) 3.4 / 7.4 / 16.4	(48) 2.9 / 7.1 / 10.7	% Officers', Directors', Owners' Comp/Sales	(21) 6.4 / 8.5 / 11.3	(12) 1.8 / 5.7 / 8.3				
1113911M	1075723M	2233230M	Net Sales ($)	23912M	48085M	23827M	49191M	91886M	1996329M
626238M	508122M	584439M	Total Assets ($)	9129M	16396M	7583M	24767M	29693M	496871M

© RMA 2003

M = $ thousand　　MM = $ million
See Pages 11 through 18 for Explanation of Ratios and Data

Current Data Sorted By Assets   Comparative Historical Data

0-500M	500M-2MM	2-10MM	10-50MM	50-100MM	100-250MM	Type of Statement	4/1/98-3/31/99 ALL 165	4/1/99-3/31/00 ALL 146
1	7	12	18	7	1	Unqualified	45	36
.5	11	22	9	4		Reviewed	41	34
6	4	9	4			Compiled	23	33
						Tax Returns	12	9
3	11	5	7	5	3	Other	44	34
	38 (4/1-9/30/02)		112 (10/1/02-3/31/03)					
15	**33**	**48**	**38**	**12**	**4**	**NUMBER OF STATEMENTS**	**165**	**146**
%	%	%	%	%	%	**ASSETS**	%	%
13.3	10.2	7.9	8.4	4.6		Cash & Equivalents	9.7	9.4
14.0	24.1	20.3	15.1	15.1		Trade Receivables (net)	19.8	19.6
6.7	13.9	12.7	9.8	6.5		Inventory	9.3	10.2
1.8	2.7	1.9	2.0	3.7		All Other Current	1.6	2.1
35.7	50.9	42.8	35.3	29.9		Total Current	40.5	41.3
46.9	42.8	46.1	48.5	52.9		Fixed Assets (net)	46.4	48.0
5.5	1.6	4.3	5.5	9.9		Intangibles (net)	5.2	4.1
11.8	4.7	6.8	10.8	7.2		All Other Non-Current	8.0	6.7
100.0	100.0	100.0	100.0	100.0		Total	100.0	100.0
						LIABILITIES		
20.8	7.5	8.9	3.5	8.3		Notes Payable-Short Term	5.3	4.8
2.9	5.3	6.2	4.6	4.1		Cur. Mat.-L/T/D	5.4	5.4
14.4	14.1	17.1	9.8	10.6		Trade Payables	14.1	15.4
.0	.4	.3	.2	.0		Income Taxes Payable	.4	.2
8.7	5.1	9.6	10.5	11.8		All Other Current	8.3	7.8
46.7	32.3	42.1	28.6	34.8		Total Current	33.5	33.6
49.9	20.3	19.5	28.7	21.6		Long Term Debt	26.9	26.6
.0	.4	1.0	1.3	1.9		Deferred Taxes	.6	.8
5.2	3.2	8.5	3.1	6.1		All Other Non-Current	5.9	8.9
-1.8	43.9	28.8	38.4	35.6		Net Worth	33.1	30.0
100.0	100.0	100.0	100.0	100.0		Total Liabilities & Net Worth	100.0	100.0
						INCOME DATA		
100.0	100.0	100.0	100.0	100.0		Net Sales	100.0	100.0
48.2	37.1	30.5	34.0	40.4		Gross Profit	35.0	36.4
41.5	31.8	25.5	29.2	37.3		Operating Expenses	30.9	31.5
6.7	5.4	5.1	4.8	3.0		Operating Profit	4.1	4.9
1.2	.7	1.6	1.2	1.0		All Other Expenses (net)	.9	1.1
5.5	4.6	3.5	3.5	2.0		Profit Before Taxes	3.2	3.8
						RATIOS		
2.8	2.7	1.5	1.9	1.1		Current	1.9	1.9
.8	1.4	1.0	1.2	1.0			1.2	1.2
.5	1.1	.7	.8	.7			.9	.9
1.5	2.1	1.0	1.2	.8		Quick	1.5	1.4
.7	1.0	.6	.8	.7			.9	.8
.3	.6	.4	.4	.4			.6	.6
0 UND	10 36.8	21 17.3	20 18.7	23 15.9		Sales/Receivables	19 19.7	18 20.6
0 999.8	26 13.9	28 13.0	27 13.7	26 13.9			27 13.7	26 13.9
22 16.5	39 9.4	35 10.4	32 11.2	30 12.0			36 10.2	32 11.2
1 245.3	10 35.8	8 45.5	12 29.9	14 26.4		Cost of Sales/Inventory	9 40.0	9 42.7
6 62.0	21 17.6	20 18.0	24 15.4	17 21.7			18 19.9	15 23.8
16 22.7	31 11.9	33 10.9	39 9.3	23 16.0			29 12.7	29 12.4
1 368.0	9 39.2	21 17.1	17 21.5	22 16.5		Cost of Sales/Payables	16 22.2	15 23.9
3 114.1	23 15.6	33 11.2	24 15.5	29 12.6			28 13.1	28 13.1
35 10.5	42 8.8	43 8.5	32 11.6	42 8.8			40 9.0	42 8.7
41.0	9.6	21.5	10.9	72.0		Sales/Working Capital	11.5	12.9
-87.0	18.5	103.4	31.0	NM			42.5	37.9
-38.3	60.0	-16.7	-24.4	-53.2			-42.0	-43.4
(12) 13.5	(30) 19.8	(44) 10.0	(36) 7.8	4.0		EBIT/Interest	(152) 7.9	(141) 6.9
7.6	5.5	3.4	3.1	2.0			3.0	2.8
3.2	1.8	1.9	1.5	1.1			1.2	1.4
		(18) 10.0	(16) 3.6			Net Profit + Depr., Dep., Amort./Cur. Mat. L/T/D	(63) 7.4	(45) 3.7
		2.4	2.4				3.2	2.4
		1.5	1.5				1.7	1.3
.9	.6	.9	.8	1.4		Fixed/Worth	.8	.9
5.4	.9	1.8	1.7	1.8			1.6	1.8
-1.7	2.4	5.0	4.0	3.6			4.0	3.1
1.0	.6	1.1	.8	1.6		Debt/Worth	.9	1.2
8.9	1.3	2.8	2.7	1.8			2.1	2.2
-11.9	3.6	7.4	5.8	4.4			8.2	6.0
(10) 260.9	(30) 43.1	(39) 56.8	(35) 27.3	(10) 19.0		% Profit Before Taxes/Tangible Net Worth	(137) 39.1	(126) 42.3
151.4	25.5	23.1	16.7	10.3			19.8	24.4
25.6	7.5	13.7	5.5	1.9			4.0	7.4
43.8	21.3	16.1	11.2	5.8		% Profit Before Taxes/Total Assets	14.2	14.4
15.2	10.7	6.8	4.1	3.0			6.6	6.7
1.3	2.2	2.5	1.8	.3			.6	1.7
18.1	14.5	11.5	6.7	5.2		Sales/Net Fixed Assets	10.3	11.2
10.7	7.8	5.5	4.4	4.2			5.3	5.4
6.1	4.8	3.1	2.8	2.4			3.2	3.2
7.4	4.2	3.1	2.5	2.7		Sales/Total Assets	3.3	3.9
5.3	3.4	2.4	2.0	1.8			2.3	2.5
3.0	2.4	1.8	1.5	1.5			1.6	1.8
(13) 1.1	1.7	(44) 1.7	(37) 2.6	2.8		% Depr., Dep., Amort./Sales	(153) 1.9	(132) 1.8
1.7	2.7	2.9	3.5	4.0			3.0	3.0
3.1	3.8	4.8	5.3	4.9			4.8	4.3
	(26) 2.4	(17) 1.8	(10) 1.6			% Officers', Directors', Owners' Comp/Sales	(65) 2.0	(65) 1.8
	4.5	2.7	2.8				4.0	4.4
	7.9	5.1	7.6				6.7	10.0
16579M	139975M	570711M	1808231M	1791907M	1810061M	Net Sales ($)	5651544M	4253085M
3364M	41173M	226150M	886542M	865144M	540070M	Total Assets ($)	2522667M	2104898M

© RMA 2003

M = $ thousand   MM = $ million

See Pages 11 through 18 for Explanation of Ratios and Data

Comparative Historical Data   Current Data Sorted By Sales

			Type of Statement						
29	36	38	Unqualified		2	1	2	10	23
30	32	39	Reviewed		2	4	12	12	9
30	39	29	Compiled	2	5	4	10	4	4
8	16	10	Tax Returns	3	5	1	1		
47	60	34	Other	4	4	6	3	4	13
4/1/00-	4/1/01-	4/1/02-			38 (4/1-9/30/02)			112 (10/1/02-3/31/03)	
3/31/01	3/31/02	3/31/03							
ALL	ALL	ALL		0-1MM	1-3MM	3-5MM	5-10MM	10-25MM	25MM & OVER
144	183	150	**NUMBER OF STATEMENTS**	9	18	16	28	30	49
%	%	%	**ASSETS**	%	%	%	%	%	%
9.2	8.9	8.6	Cash & Equivalents		12.5	9.8	9.2	8.1	6.2
18.0	16.0	18.8	Trade Receivables (net)		22.4	17.6	22.6	20.3	16.9
9.3	8.8	11.1	Inventory		7.8	15.3	13.7	12.5	10.0
1.8	2.1	2.2	All Other Current		5.0	.9	.8	2.0	2.6
38.4	35.8	40.7	Total Current		47.6	43.6	46.4	42.9	35.6
48.5	50.6	46.4	Fixed Assets (net)		41.9	44.1	43.9	45.7	47.3
5.8	6.7	4.9	Intangibles (net)		3.5	4.8	2.7	5.0	7.0
7.4	6.9	7.9	All Other Non-Current		6.9	7.6	7.0	6.4	10.0
100.0	100.0	100.0	Total		100.0	100.0	100.0	100.0	100.0
			LIABILITIES						
6.0	4.3	8.1	Notes Payable-Short Term		17.8	8.6	10.0	6.4	4.8
5.3	5.2	5.1	Cur. Mat.-L/T/D		4.0	7.8	5.5	5.0	4.1
14.8	11.9	14.9	Trade Payables		15.2	11.9	17.2	16.0	15.6
.1	.2	.2	Income Taxes Payable		.1	.5	.2	.4	.2
8.4	8.7	9.1	All Other Current		10.4	5.5	9.6	6.7	12.1
34.6	30.4	37.4	Total Current		47.5	34.3	42.4	34.5	36.8
27.8	30.9	26.0	Long Term Debt		35.0	22.2	17.8	23.2	26.2
.7	.7	.9	Deferred Taxes		.0	.7	.2	1.1	1.8
5.5	11.5	5.5	All Other Non-Current		1.5	4.7	1.8	10.7	5.4
31.3	26.4	30.1	Net Worth		16.1	38.1	37.7	30.5	29.9
100.0	100.0	100.0	Total Liabilities & Net Worth		100.0	100.0	100.0	100.0	100.0
			INCOME DATA						
100.0	100.0	100.0	Net Sales		100.0	100.0	100.0	100.0	100.0
38.7	38.0	35.5	Gross Profit		39.2	39.1	30.8	29.4	35.5
33.7	32.6	30.4	Operating Expenses		33.8	33.7	26.3	24.4	30.8
5.0	5.3	5.2	Operating Profit		5.5	5.5	4.5	4.9	4.7
1.3	1.7	1.3	All Other Expenses (net)		2.4	1.5	.6	.8	1.5
3.7	3.6	3.8	Profit Before Taxes		3.1	4.0	3.8	4.2	3.1
			RATIOS						
1.8	1.9	1.8			2.7	2.5	1.8	1.7	1.5
1.2	1.1	1.1	Current		1.1	1.4	1.0	1.2	1.1
.7	.8	.7			.6	.8	.7	.8	.7
1.4	1.3	1.2			1.6	1.5	1.3	1.2	1.0
(143) .8	.8	.8	Quick		.7	.9	.7	.8	.7
.5	.5	.5			.4	.5	.4	.6	.4
19 18.9	15 24.0	18 20.1		0 999.8	5 71.4	23 16.2	20 18.6	20 18.1	
25 14.4	24 15.0	25 14.3	Sales/Receivables	18 20.7	24 15.3	29 12.5	29 12.7	25 14.3	
32 11.5	33 11.2	34 10.7		38 9.6	38 9.5	37 9.9	35 10.5	30 12.0	
9 39.7	8 45.3	10 37.3		4 99.7	11 32.9	14 26.8	8 45.8	12 29.8	
16 23.0	15 25.0	18 20.3	Cost of Sales/Inventory	10 35.6	28 13.2	21 17.3	24 15.4	18 20.3	
29 12.6	29 12.5	31 11.6		21 17.6	39 9.3	32 11.4	39 9.4	30 12.2	
19 19.4	15 24.6	17 21.5		1 299.0	16 23.2	22 16.6	18 20.8	18 19.8	
29 12.6	24 15.1	25 14.3	Cost of Sales/Payables	17 21.3	29 12.5	36 10.2	26 14.0	24 15.0	
44 8.2	40 9.2	38 9.5		42 8.6	43 8.5	43 8.5	37 9.8	35 10.5	
12.7	13.5	15.0			9.5	13.5	13.2	18.4	17.2
52.9	69.5	68.4	Sales/Working Capital		NM	30.0	96.0	49.9	76.9
−22.9	−32.0	−24.4			−40.2	NM	−24.7	−51.2	−20.8
6.8	7.7	8.9			16.0	12.0	19.8	5.5	7.3
(139) 3.2	(165) 2.6	(138) 3.6	EBIT/Interest	(16) 6.3	(15) 3.9	(26) 6.7	(27) 3.0	(47) 2.5	
1.5	1.2	1.6		1.0	2.1	1.7	1.9	1.3	
5.4	6.1	5.2	Net Profit + Depr., Dep.,					5.5	5.5
(45) 2.2	(46) 2.9	(52) 2.4	Amort./Cur. Mat. L/T/D			(11) 1.8	(25) 2.2		
1.6	1.2	1.5					1.4	1.6	
.9	1.0	.8			.6	.7	.7	.9	1.1
1.6	1.9	1.7	Fixed/Worth		1.2	1.5	1.1	1.7	1.7
6.3	7.6	4.5			−19.3	4.1	2.6	4.1	4.1
1.0	1.1	.9			.6	.8	.7	.8	1.3
2.0	2.6	2.7	Debt/Worth		2.6	2.3	1.5	3.0	2.6
9.7	13.9	6.9			−27.8	6.0	4.2	5.7	6.1
41.1	51.3	46.8	% Profit Before Taxes/Tangible		41.0	45.8	45.1	61.3	26.2
(119) 24.0	(148) 23.2	(126) 20.5	Net Worth	(13) 19.9	(13) 28.4	(24) 25.6	(25) 22.8	(43) 15.4	
7.8	6.7	7.3		−11.6	8.9	10.3	8.9	5.5	
13.1	15.1	15.6	% Profit Before Taxes/Total		32.0	13.8	22.3	16.8	10.6
6.3	7.0	6.5	Assets		7.2	8.3	8.4	6.4	3.9
1.5	1.2	1.4			−2.7	1.7	1.6	3.8	1.0
9.6	8.9	10.6			18.9	10.4	12.0	11.9	6.7
5.1	4.6	5.9	Sales/Net Fixed Assets		12.8	6.0	7.6	4.9	4.8
3.0	2.9	3.3			4.4	3.5	4.0	2.9	2.9
3.2	3.3	3.5			5.7	3.9	3.6	3.2	2.9
2.3	2.2	2.5	Sales/Total Assets		3.9	2.5	2.7	2.3	2.2
1.7	1.5	1.8			2.4	2.1	2.0	1.7	1.5
2.0	2.0	2.0			1.2	2.5	1.7	1.7	2.6
(135) 3.0	(168) 3.2	(142) 3.0	% Depr., Dep., Amort./Sales	(16) 1.9	3.3	2.8	(27) 2.9	(47) 3.4	
4.3	4.8	4.6		3.1	5.1	4.1	4.5	4.5	
2.5	2.2	1.8			1.5		1.6	2.3	1.7
(56) 4.0	(60) 3.6	(60) 3.3	% Officers', Directors',	(12) 3.2		(12) 2.2	(12) 3.0	(11) 3.0	
8.3	7.0	6.3	Owners' Comp/Sales	4.7		6.3	5.4	7.5	
4334974M	5666052M	6137464M	Net Sales ($)	5519M	35281M	60808M	206863M	475066M	5353927M
2305911M	3046846M	2562443M	Total Assets ($)	2779M	16166M	26239M	82075M	227671M	2207513M

M = $ thousand   MM = $ million
See Pages 11 through 18 for Explanation of Ratios and Data

Current Data Sorted By Assets   **Comparative Historical Data**

0-500M	500M-2MM	2-10MM	10-50MM	50-100MM	100-250MM	Type of Statement	4/1/98-3/31/99 ALL	4/1/99-3/31/00 ALL
		2	3	1	2	Unqualified	12	11
	1	2	1			Reviewed	8	5
	2	3				Compiled	9	7
2	2	1				Tax Returns	3	4
1	3	2	1			Other	11	8
		5 (4/1-9/30/02)		24 (10/1/02-3/31/03)				
3	8	10	5	1	2	**NUMBER OF STATEMENTS**	43	35
%	%	%	%	%	%	**ASSETS**	%	%
		17.1				Cash & Equivalents	7.7	8.4
		19.3				Trade Receivables (net)	19.3	20.3
		9.5				Inventory	14.2	14.5
		.2				All Other Current	2.1	3.0
		46.1				Total Current	43.3	46.2
		40.6				Fixed Assets (net)	44.9	41.2
		10.3				Intangibles (net)	7.0	7.1
		3.0				All Other Non-Current	4.8	5.5
		100.0				Total	100.0	100.0
						LIABILITIES		
		7.0				Notes Payable-Short Term	7.5	7.0
		4.0				Cur. Mat.-L/T/D	6.3	6.7
		13.3				Trade Payables	13.5	14.9
		1.0				Income Taxes Payable	.7	.7
		10.8				All Other Current	10.5	6.2
		36.2				Total Current	38.5	35.5
		17.5				Long Term Debt	24.4	27.8
		.6				Deferred Taxes	1.3	.9
		.4				All Other Non-Current	5.3	4.9
		45.3				Net Worth	30.6	30.9
		100.0				Total Liabilities & Net Worth	100.0	100.0
						INCOME DATA		
		100.0				Net Sales	100.0	100.0
		42.3				Gross Profit	38.0	37.6
		27.8				Operating Expenses	33.0	32.5
		14.5				Operating Profit	5.0	5.1
		.9				All Other Expenses (net)	1.8	1.4
		13.6				Profit Before Taxes	3.2	3.7
						RATIOS		
		4.5					2.2	2.2
		1.3				Current	1.2	1.4
		.6					.7	1.0
		3.5					1.5	1.7
		1.0				Quick	.6	.8
		.4					.4	.5
		16 23.4					16 22.5	19 19.6
		34 10.7				Sales/Receivables	26 14.3	30 12.0
		55 6.6					39 9.4	40 9.2
		15 23.7					21 17.2	27 13.7
		37 9.8				Cost of Sales/Inventory	33 11.1	35 10.3
		51 7.1					48 7.6	48 7.6
		10 35.6					13 27.6	21 17.2
		23 15.7				Cost of Sales/Payables	23 15.6	32 11.4
		50 7.3					37 9.9	46 8.0
		3.9					9.1	10.9
		26.4				Sales/Working Capital	39.9	17.8
		–18.4					–24.8	–167.1
		21.7					7.6	7.9
		11.5				EBIT/Interest	(38) 4.0	(33) 3.4
		4.5					.7	.8
						Net Profit + Depr., Dep.,	15.0	
						Amort./Cur. Mat. L /T/D	(11) 3.6	
							1.1	
		.7					1.0	.7
		.9				Fixed/Worth	1.5	1.4
		1.8					4.0	7.7
		1.0					.8	1.0
		1.3				Debt/Worth	2.0	1.5
		1.9					8.2	15.4
						% Profit Before Taxes/Tangible	74.4	41.4
						Net Worth	(36) 30.7	(28) 28.5
							.0	4.8
		38.5				% Profit Before Taxes/Total	21.3	11.5
		15.8				Assets	10.2	8.7
		7.0					–.9	–.4
		9.3					10.9	11.0
		6.3				Sales/Net Fixed Assets	5.3	5.7
		2.9					2.8	2.9
		2.8					3.5	3.1
		2.0				Sales/Total Assets	2.4	1.8
		1.5					1.6	1.4
		2.7					1.8	1.5
		3.9				% Depr., Dep., Amort./Sales	(40) 3.2	(32) 3.1
		4.5					5.4	4.8
						% Officers', Directors',	3.8	3.4
						Owners' Comp/Sales	(19) 4.6	(19) 4.3
							6.5	5.1
2269M	26190M	110860M	180452M	121573M	641866M	Net Sales ($)	1042844M	1042309M
703M	7139M	54213M	88121M	72189M	327291M	Total Assets ($)	656877M	648144M

M = $ thousand   MM = $ million
See Pages 11 through 18 for Explanation of Ratios and Data

Comparative Historical Data   Current Data Sorted By Sales

4/1/00-3/31/01 ALL	4/1/01-3/31/02 ALL	4/1/02-3/31/03 ALL		Q-1MM	1-3MM	3-5MM	5-10MM	10-25MM	25MM & OVER
			Type of Statement			5 (4/1-9/30/02)		24 (10/1/02-3/31/03)	
9	9	8	Unqualified				2	1	5
7	4	4	Reviewed			1	1	2	
5	5	5	Compiled		1		2	2	
3	3	5	Tax Returns	2	1	1	1		
12	9	7	Other	1	2	1		1	1
36	30	29	**NUMBER OF STATEMENTS**	3	4	4	6	6	6
%	%	%	**ASSETS**	%	%	%	%	%	%
7.4	9.5	16.3	Cash & Equivalents						
22.9	20.3	18.9	Trade Receivables (net)						
17.8	13.1	13.9	Inventory						
2.0	.9	.9	All Other Current						
50.2	43.7	50.0	Total Current						
39.4	45.2	41.2	Fixed Assets (net)						
6.2	6.7	5.2	Intangibles (net)						
4.2	4.3	3.5	All Other Non-Current						
100.0	100.0	100.0	Total						
			LIABILITIES						
7.8	8.0	6.7	Notes Payable-Short Term						
4.5	5.3	3.1	Cur. Mat.-L/T/D						
14.8	10.9	10.6	Trade Payables						
.2	.1	.4	Income Taxes Payable						
6.5	7.2	7.9	All Other Current						
33.8	31.7	28.7	Total Current						
18.9	25.8	21.0	Long Term Debt						
1.2	1.0	.5	Deferred Taxes						
3.9	6.8	5.6	All Other Non-Current						
42.2	34.6	44.1	Net Worth						
100.0	100.0	100.0	Total Liabilities & Net Worth						
			INCOME DATA						
100.0	100.0	100.0	Net Sales						
37.3	38.0	40.0	Gross Profit						
32.2	31.4	30.3	Operating Expenses						
5.1	6.6	9.6	Operating Profit						
1.3	1.9	1.0	All Other Expenses (net)						
3.8	4.7	8.7	Profit Before Taxes						
			RATIOS						
2.6	2.1	4.6	Current						
1.4	1.4	1.7							
1.0	1.0	1.0							
1.8	1.4	2.8	Quick						
1.0	1.0	1.1							
.6	.6	.6							
26 13.8	20 18.7	17 21.6	Sales/Receivables						
34 10.7	27 13.5	28 13.1							
42 8.7	36 10.0	36 10.2							
23 15.9	21 17.0	21 17.7	Cost of Sales/Inventory						
35 10.4	27 13.6	35 10.5							
62 5.9	49 7.5	47 7.8							
23 15.7	14 26.6	10 37.4	Cost of Sales/Payables						
31 11.8	23 16.0	23 15.9							
44 8.3	35 10.5	38 9.5							
9.0	9.7	5.6	Sales/Working Capital						
15.7	15.3	10.7							
NM	NM	NM							
8.7	13.0	16.9	EBIT/Interest						
(33) 3.3	(29) 3.3	(28) 7.6							
1.2	1.2	3.2							
		19.6	Net Profit + Depr., Dep.,						
	(10)	4.5	Amort./Cur. Mat. L/T/D						
		1.8							
.5	.7	.6	Fixed/Worth						
1.2	1.2	.9							
2.6	NM	2.0							
.5	.8	.8	Debt/Worth						
1.2	1.5	1.3							
4.1	NM	3.4							
32.7	41.3	76.9	% Profit Before Taxes/Tangible Net Worth						
(32) 19.2	(23) 19.2	(27) 32.6							
2.8	5.5	18.6							
13.3	17.7	22.8	% Profit Before Taxes/Total Assets						
6.9	7.9	15.8							
.4	1.2	6.2							
13.0	8.9	13.1	Sales/Net Fixed Assets						
6.1	5.1	6.7							
3.4	3.2	3.7							
2.9	3.2	3.1	Sales/Total Assets						
2.2	2.2	2.6							
1.8	1.7	1.6							
1.5	1.9	2.3	% Depr., Dep., Amort./Sales						
(31) 2.9	(26) 3.1	(26) 3.1							
4.8	4.4	4.2							
2.0		2.1	% Officers', Directors', Owners' Comp/Sales						
(13) 4.1		(16) 4.3							
5.9		7.0							
1433947M	1294581M	1083210M	Net Sales ($)	2269M	8271M	16490M	48140M	103574M	904466M
759160M	617190M	549656M	Total Assets ($)	703M	3051M	8660M	27020M	45562M	464660M

© RMA 2003

M = $ thousand   MM = $ million
See Pages 11 through 18 for Explanation of Ratios and Data

Current Data Sorted By Assets   Comparative Historical Data

0-500M	500M-2MM	2-10MM	10-50MM	50-100MM	100-250MM	Type of Statement	4/1/98-3/31/99 ALL	4/1/99-3/31/00 ALL
			9	3	2	Unqualified	8	11
	1	1	2			Reviewed	3	5
	2		1			Compiled	5	4
		1				Tax Returns	3	
4	3	4	3	1		Other	9	10
	11 (4/1-9/30/02)		26 (10/1/02-3/31/03)					
4	6	6	15	4	2	**NUMBER OF STATEMENTS**	28	30
%	%	%	%	%	%	**ASSETS**	%	%
			4.3			Cash & Equivalents	10.4	7.5
			23.8			Trade Receivables (net)	20.6	22.9
			14.1			Inventory	12.0	13.2
			1.8			All Other Current	1.8	1.9
			43.9			Total Current	44.9	45.5
			41.6			Fixed Assets (net)	43.8	45.9
			6.8			Intangibles (net)	5.5	2.7
			7.7			All Other Non-Current	5.9	6.0
			100.0			Total	100.0	100.0
						LIABILITIES		
			10.7			Notes Payable-Short Term	9.1	13.1
			2.3			Cur. Mat.-L/T/D	3.0	4.0
			13.4			Trade Payables	10.7	14.5
			.2			Income Taxes Payable	.1	.3
			9.1			All Other Current	6.8	12.3
			35.6			Total Current	29.8	44.3
			17.6			Long Term Debt	23.3	22.7
			.9			Deferred Taxes	1.0	1.2
			1.9			All Other Non-Current	6.0	4.0
			44.1			Net Worth	39.9	27.8
			100.0			Total Liabilities & Net Worth	100.0	100.0
						INCOME DATA		
			100.0			Net Sales	100.0	100.0
			34.0			Gross Profit	35.2	33.0
			29.4			Operating Expenses	31.1	28.7
			4.5			Operating Profit	4.1	4.3
			.5			All Other Expenses (net)	.6	1.5
			4.0			Profit Before Taxes	3.5	2.8
						RATIOS		
			2.5			Current	3.7	1.4
			1.4				1.7	1.1
			.8				1.0	.9
			1.6			Quick	2.7	1.0
			.9				1.2	.7
			.5				.6	.4
		31	11.9			Sales/Receivables	29 12.6	26 13.8
		32	11.5				32 11.6	31 12.0
		37	9.8				40 9.0	38 9.5
		16	22.9			Cost of Sales/Inventory	19 19.5	16 22.1
		32	11.5				25 14.5	28 13.3
		41	8.9				34 10.6	39 9.4
		16	23.0			Cost of Sales/Payables	12 29.8	20 18.2
		19	18.8				23 15.7	29 12.5
		43	8.6				35 10.4	46 8.0
			10.2			Sales/Working Capital	7.2	23.3
			22.2				13.4	89.1
			−22.0				NM	−37.4
			7.2			EBIT/Interest	5.5	5.4
		(13)	4.7				(24) 2.1	2.5
			.8				1.0	.8
						Net Profit + Depr., Dep., Amort./Cur. Mat. L /T/D	8.0	7.7
							(10) 4.6	(11) 2.6
							2.1	1.4
			.6			Fixed/Worth	.5	.6
			1.2				1.4	1.6
			5.0				4.1	4.6
			.4			Debt/Worth	.5	1.1
			1.1				1.2	3.1
			7.3				5.5	6.2
			52.2			% Profit Before Taxes/Tangible Net Worth	29.8	57.9
		(13)	33.2				(22) 15.0	(26) 13.5
			9.0				2.3	−.1
			11.7			% Profit Before Taxes/Total Assets	12.7	13.4
			7.5				4.7	5.5
			2.6				.0	−1.1
			9.1			Sales/Net Fixed Assets	11.3	9.5
			6.1				5.3	5.7
			4.6				2.6	2.8
			3.1			Sales/Total Assets	3.1	3.1
			2.7				2.1	2.4
			2.1				1.3	1.6
			1.9			% Depr., Dep., Amort./Sales	1.4	1.8
		(14)	2.4				(24) 3.2	(26) 3.3
			3.9				4.3	4.1
						% Officers', Directors', Owners' Comp/Sales	2.6	
							(12) 5.8	
							11.6	
5130M	23859M	84329M	984372M	621518M	493758M	Net Sales ($)	977335M	1107942M
733M	8041M	31194M	387225M	332383M	260164M	Total Assets ($)	474184M	521263M

M = $ thousand   MM = $ million
See Pages 11 through 18 for Explanation of Ratios and Data

Comparative Historical Data

Current Data Sorted By Sales

4/1/00-3/31/01 ALL	4/1/01-3/31/02 ALL	4/1/02-3/31/03 ALL		11 (4/1-9/30/02) 0-1MM	1-3MM	3-5MM	26 (10/1/02-3/31/03) 5-10MM	10-25MM	25MM & OVER
			Type of Statement						
10	9	14	Unqualified						14
	2	4	Reviewed				2		2
12	10	3	Compiled		1		1		1
		5	Tax Returns						
7	12	11	Other	1	3	3	1	3	4
29	33	37	**NUMBER OF STATEMENTS**	1	5	3	3	4	21
%	%	%	**ASSETS**	%	%	%	%	%	%
5.4	3.3	6.3	Cash & Equivalents						6.1
23.3	21.4	20.3	Trade Receivables (net)						22.9
13.0	13.8	12.4	Inventory						13.3
2.5	2.7	1.8	All Other Current						1.6
44.2	41.3	40.8	Total Current						44.0
46.6	43.2	43.7	Fixed Assets (net)						41.2
3.5	9.2	7.2	Intangibles (net)						7.2
5.7	6.3	8.3	All Other Non-Current						7.6
100.0	100.0	100.0	Total						100.0
			LIABILITIES						
8.4	8.0	7.2	Notes Payable-Short Term						8.6
4.4	6.1	3.0	Cur. Mat.-L/T/D						2.3
15.1	17.0	13.8	Trade Payables						12.3
.2	.5	.2	Income Taxes Payable						.2
8.5	10.4	10.9	All Other Current						10.2
36.7	42.1	35.1	Total Current						33.5
18.7	26.7	20.2	Long Term Debt						15.6
1.2	1.7	1.2	Deferred Taxes						1.6
7.4	11.6	2.8	All Other Non-Current						2.6
36.1	18.0	40.6	Net Worth						46.8
100.0	100.0	100.0	Total Liabilities & Net Worth						100.0
			INCOME DATA						
100.0	100.0	100.0	Net Sales						100.0
33.3	36.9	35.7	Gross Profit						35.1
29.4	31.9	31.2	Operating Expenses						30.1
3.9	4.9	4.4	Operating Profit						5.0
.0	3.5	.9	All Other Expenses (net)						.7
3.9	1.4	3.5	Profit Before Taxes						4.3
			RATIOS						
2.0 1.2 .9	1.8 1.1 .7	2.1 1.2 .8	Current						2.4 1.4 .9
1.2 .7 .5	1.1 .6 .5	1.6 .8 .5	Quick						1.6 .9 .7
26 14.2 33 11.2 39 9.5	24 15.2 32 11.3 39 9.3	24 15.2 31 11.8 36 10.1	Sales/Receivables						29 12.7 34 10.9 38 9.5
19 19.3 26 14.1 33 11.2	19 19.4 32 11.4 43 8.4	16 23.3 26 14.2 35 10.5	Cost of Sales/Inventory						19 19.2 31 12.0 40 9.1
22 16.7 30 12.2 43 8.5	20 17.8 27 13.6 41 9.0	15 24.4 22 16.5 43 8.6	Cost of Sales/Payables						17 20.9 22 16.8 43 8.6
11.4 41.4 -55.0	12.6 117.0 -28.9	10.4 71.8 -30.0	Sales/Working Capital						8.9 15.4 NM
(27) 6.3 3.5 2.4	4.3 2.7 2.0	(32) 14.1 4.5 .1	EBIT/Interest					(19)	16.2 5.2 1.8
(11) 4.8 3.5 1.6	(15) 9.3 3.1 1.6	(10) 5.5 2.4 2.2	Net Profit + Depr., Dep., Amort./Cur. Mat. L/T/D						
.6 1.5 4.2	1.1 2.5 NM	.6 1.3 3.5	Fixed/Worth						.6 1.0 3.8
.9 1.8 6.4	1.2 3.2 NM	.4 1.2 7.5	Debt/Worth						.4 1.1 5.3
(24) 41.8 23.4 11.2	(25) 48.0 25.2 12.8	(31) 60.8 26.4 7.3	% Profit Before Taxes/Tangible Net Worth					(18)	38.7 23.3 13.9
14.1 8.0 3.9	10.5 6.5 3.0	19.3 7.5 .0	% Profit Before Taxes/Total Assets						15.5 7.9 4.2
8.0 5.5 3.9	9.7 5.7 4.4	10.9 6.1 4.1	Sales/Net Fixed Assets						8.7 6.0 4.3
3.1 2.5 2.0	3.0 2.4 1.7	3.3 2.4 1.9	Sales/Total Assets						2.8 2.3 1.9
(27) 1.6 2.8 3.9	(29) 1.3 2.1 3.6	(33) 1.9 3.1 4.9	% Depr., Dep., Amort./Sales					(18)	2.0 2.7 4.5
	(10) 1.9 3.7 13.6	(11) .9 2.4 11.3	% Officers', Directors', Owners' Comp/Sales						
1563876M	2018408M	2212966M	Net Sales ($)	335M	7577M	12918M	22061M	70427M	2099648M
760047M	954167M	1019740M	Total Assets ($)	245M	2646M	5486M	5538M	26053M	979772M

M = $ thousand   MM = $ million
See Pages 11 through 18 for Explanation of Ratios and Data

Current Data Sorted By Assets

Comparative Historical Data

0-500M	500M-2MM	2-10MM	10-50MM	50-100MM	100-250MM	Type of Statement		4/1/98-3/31/99 ALL	4/1/99-3/31/00 ALL
			1	5	2	1	Unqualified		7
			3	1			Reviewed		3
	4		4	1			Compiled		4
1	1						Tax Returns		3
1	3		4	2	1	2	Other		4
	13 (4/1-9/30/02)			24 (10/1/02-3/31/03)						
2	8	12	9	3	3	**NUMBER OF STATEMENTS**			21
%	%	%	%	%	%	**ASSETS**		%	%
		10.8				Cash & Equivalents			5.6
		21.5				Trade Receivables (net)			22.7
		19.4				Inventory			26.2
		3.2				All Other Current			1.3
		54.9				Total Current			55.9
		23.5				Fixed Assets (net)			31.7
		13.9				Intangibles (net)			4.3
		7.7				All Other Non-Current			8.1
		100.0				Total			100.0
						LIABILITIES			
		5.9				Notes Payable-Short Term			11.9
		5.0				Cur. Mat.-L/T/D			4.1
		12.1				Trade Payables			14.0
		.0				Income Taxes Payable			.7
		3.7				All Other Current			11.6
		26.7				Total Current			42.2
		21.5				Long Term Debt			15.9
		.1				Deferred Taxes			.6
		17.6				All Other Non-Current			2.7
		34.0				Net Worth			38.5
		100.0				Total Liabilities & Net Worth			100.0
						INCOME DATA			
		100.0				Net Sales			100.0
		45.8				Gross Profit			44.3
		40.5				Operating Expenses			41.2
		5.3				Operating Profit			3.1
		1.5				All Other Expenses (net)			.0
		3.8				Profit Before Taxes			3.2
						RATIOS			
		4.4							2.2
		2.5				Current			1.5
		1.3							1.1
		2.7							1.3
		1.3				Quick			.8
		.8							.5
		24 15.2							22 16.6
		31 11.8				Sales/Receivables			31 11.9
		42 8.7							42 8.6
		38 9.7							51 7.2
		57 6.4				Cost of Sales/Inventory			63 5.8
		102 3.6							86 4.2
		18 20.2							18 20.3
		29 12.8				Cost of Sales/Payables			28 13.2
		57 6.4							60 6.1
		4.9							7.9
		8.3				Sales/Working Capital			17.1
		31.7							109.4
		(10) 12.3							(19) 9.0
		4.4				EBIT/Interest			3.9
		1.0							1.2
						Net Profit + Depr., Dep., Amort./Cur. Mat. L /T/D			
		.4							.4
		.7				Fixed/Worth			.7
		2.6							1.0
		.4							.7
		2.0				Debt/Worth			1.3
		44.8							2.5
		73.9							41.4
		(10) 33.3				% Profit Before Taxes/Tangible Net Worth			(19) 18.1
		13.6							6.6
		16.5							17.1
		10.5				% Profit Before Taxes/Total Assets			7.5
		1.6							1.3
		39.7							14.9
		13.8				Sales/Net Fixed Assets			8.8
		5.9							5.7
		2.6							2.9
		2.5				Sales/Total Assets			2.6
		1.7							2.2
		1.3							1.7
		(10) 2.2				% Depr., Dep., Amort./Sales			(19) 2.2
		3.1							5.1
						% Officers', Directors', Owners' Comp/Sales			
1157M	23220M	125625M	453269M	385811M	635324M	Net Sales ($)			947857M
624M	9185M	58529M	191089M	195304M	451583M	Total Assets ($)			418871M

M = $ thousand   MM = $ million
See Pages 11 through 18 for Explanation of Ratios and Data

Comparative Historical Data | Current Data Sorted By Sales

			Type of Statement	0-1MM	1-3MM	3-5MM	5-10MM	10-25MM	25MM & OVER
5	4	9	Unqualified					2	7
2	5	4	Reviewed				3		1
4	7	9	Compiled		2	3	2	1	1
1	1	2	Tax Returns	1	1				
4	1	13	Other	1	2	1	1	4	4
4/1/00-3/31/01 ALL	4/1/01-3/31/02 ALL	4/1/02-3/31/03 ALL		13 (4/1-9/30/02)			24 (10/1/02-3/31/03)		
16	18	37	**NUMBER OF STATEMENTS**	2	5	4	6	7	13
%	%	%	**ASSETS**	%	%	%	%	%	%
7.0	10.6	8.2	Cash & Equivalents						5.8
22.6	20.0	20.0	Trade Receivables (net)						17.4
21.0	20.7	23.4	Inventory						32.8
2.0	3.7	3.2	All Other Current						3.6
52.6	55.0	54.7	Total Current						59.6
33.0	29.8	29.5	Fixed Assets (net)						29.0
6.8	1.6	5.5	Intangibles (net)						1.1
7.6	13.6	10.3	All Other Non-Current						10.2
100.0	100.0	100.0	Total						100.0
			LIABILITIES						
5.7	8.5	8.7	Notes Payable-Short Term						12.9
4.0	3.5	4.2	Cur. Mat.-L/T/D						3.2
14.7	10.4	13.7	Trade Payables						15.1
1.2	1.2	.1	Income Taxes Payable						.2
5.7	6.6	8.5	All Other Current						11.7
31.5	30.2	35.3	Total Current						43.1
16.4	14.3	17.3	Long Term Debt						12.0
.4	.3	.4	Deferred Taxes						1.1
2.4	4.7	9.5	All Other Non-Current						2.6
49.4	50.5	37.4	Net Worth						41.3
100.0	100.0	100.0	Total Liabilities & Net Worth						100.0
			INCOME DATA						
100.0	100.0	100.0	Net Sales						100.0
43.3	49.2	42.9	Gross Profit						35.7
37.4	41.5	38.4	Operating Expenses						31.3
5.9	7.6	4.5	Operating Profit						4.4
.8	1.1	1.1	All Other Expenses (net)						.8
5.1	6.5	3.5	Profit Before Taxes						3.6
			RATIOS						
2.1	3.9	3.0							2.7
1.7	1.8	1.3	Current						1.3
1.4	1.3	1.1							1.1
1.3	2.2	1.9							1.1
.9	1.1	.8	Quick						.5
.7	.6	.4							.3
22 16.4	24 15.1	23 15.6							24 15.3
31 11.9	30 12.4	31 11.7	Sales/Receivables						30 12.1
50 7.3	38 9.7	39 9.4							37 9.9
39 9.5	50 7.3	38 9.6							54 6.7
53 6.8	70 5.2	61 6.0	Cost of Sales/Inventory						90 4.1
73 5.0	94 3.9	95 3.9							113 3.2
21 17.1	19 18.9	21 17.4							24 15.1
32 11.4	32 11.4	38 9.6	Cost of Sales/Payables						39 9.4
56 6.5	49 7.4	51 7.1							58 6.3
7.7	5.9	5.5							8.0
11.9	9.3	15.8	Sales/Working Capital						18.2
21.1	21.5	64.0							41.8
(13) 18.3	(16) 16.7	(32) 9.6							(12) 9.4
3.1	4.6	3.6	EBIT/Interest						5.0
1.5	2.2	1.2							1.6
		(12) 10.1	Net Profit + Depr., Dep.,						
		2.1	Amort./Cur. Mat. L/T/D						
		1.8							
.4	.4	.3							.3
.7	.6	.9	Fixed/Worth						.8
1.4	1.0	2.3							1.0
.5	.4	.7							.7
1.0	1.0	1.9	Debt/Worth						1.5
1.8	2.1	4.3							3.3
(14) 39.5	(17) 38.7	(33) 33.4	% Profit Before Taxes/Tangible						32.6
10.5	20.4	16.7	Net Worth						15.4
3.3	9.8	7.5							4.8
21.1	21.4	13.7	% Profit Before Taxes/Total						11.9
5.7	9.4	5.9	Assets						8.1
1.7	3.0	1.3							1.5
14.6	15.1	15.3							10.5
8.5	9.0	9.1	Sales/Net Fixed Assets						7.7
5.0	4.2	4.7							5.3
3.3	2.8	2.6							2.6
2.5	2.2	2.5	Sales/Total Assets						2.0
1.9	1.6	1.6							1.7
(15) 2.4	1.5	(35) 1.7	% Depr., Dep., Amort./Sales						2.0
2.8	2.9	2.6							3.2
4.7	4.7	4.0							5.1
	(10) 2.3	(15) 1.6	% Officers', Directors',						
	6.3	5.9	Owners' Comp/Sales						
	8.2	14.5							
639552M	770617M	1624406M	Net Sales ($)	1157M	9598M	15215M	41828M	125964M	1430644M
317996M	405220M	906314M	Total Assets ($)	624M	7951M	5175M	18519M	65584M	808461M

M = $ thousand   MM = $ million
See Pages 11 through 18 for Explanation of Ratios and Data

Current Data Sorted By Assets | | | | | Comparative Historical Data

0-500M	500M-2MM	2-10MM	10-50MM	50-100MM	100-250MM	Type of Statement	4/1/98-3/31/99 ALL	4/1/99-3/31/00 ALL
		1	3	2		Unqualified	11	13
	2	7	3			Reviewed	20	17
	1	3	1			Compiled	7	7
1	1					Tax Returns		
2	2	4	4	2	1	Other	10	19
		8 (4/1-9/30/02)	32 (10/1/02-3/31/03)					
3	6	15	11	4	1	**NUMBER OF STATEMENTS**	48	56
%	%	%	%	%	%	**ASSETS**	%	%
		7.0	10.2			Cash & Equivalents	5.3	6.2
		17.9	17.3			Trade Receivables (net)	18.8	16.1
		26.5	30.1			Inventory	27.5	27.5
		2.5	1.7			All Other Current	1.4	1.7
		54.0	59.2			Total Current	52.9	51.5
		36.8	29.1			Fixed Assets (net)	34.9	31.5
		2.4	7.0			Intangibles (net)	5.4	9.3
		6.9	4.6			All Other Non-Current	6.8	7.7
		100.0	100.0			Total	100.0	100.0
						LIABILITIES		
		8.4	14.8			Notes Payable-Short Term	12.9	11.0
		3.0	2.3			Cur. Mat.-L/T/D	4.6	5.9
		10.7	8.6			Trade Payables	14.1	10.9
		1.2	.6			Income Taxes Payable	.6	.1
		6.0	5.7			All Other Current	7.2	6.6
		29.2	32.0			Total Current	39.2	34.6
		21.9	14.4			Long Term Debt	16.5	20.7
		.5	.1			Deferred Taxes	.7	.6
		3.9	2.9			All Other Non-Current	8.4	15.2
		44.6	50.5			Net Worth	35.2	28.7
		100.0	100.0			Total Liabilities & Net Worth	100.0	100.0
						INCOME DATA		
		100.0	100.0			Net Sales	100.0	100.0
		29.2	32.8			Gross Profit	33.3	33.7
		26.2	25.4			Operating Expenses	28.6	27.2
		3.0	7.4			Operating Profit	4.7	6.5
		.4	1.0			All Other Expenses (net)	2.5	1.3
		2.6	6.4			Profit Before Taxes	2.2	5.2
						RATIOS		
		2.8	2.9				2.2	2.2
		1.6	2.2			Current	1.5	1.4
		1.3	1.2				1.2	1.1
		1.2	2.3				1.2	1.0
		.8	.7			Quick	.7	.6
		.5	.6				.4	.4
		20 17.8	27 13.4				26 14.2	20 18.5
		31 11.7	33 10.9			Sales/Receivables	35 10.5	28 13.2
		37 9.9	44 8.4				43 8.5	40 9.2
		47 7.7	45 8.1				51 7.2	47 7.8
		55 6.7	65 5.6			Cost of Sales/Inventory	77 4.7	59 6.2
		83 4.4	119 3.1				111 3.3	88 4.2
		16 23.1	5 75.1				20 17.9	17 21.1
		22 16.3	28 13.0			Cost of Sales/Payables	35 10.6	25 14.5
		31 11.7	32 11.5				53 6.8	32 11.5
		5.2	3.0				6.2	6.5
		14.2	7.7			Sales/Working Capital	11.9	14.3
		22.0	19.2				26.3	43.3
		7.7	8.0				9.9	7.6
		(12) 2.6	(10) 4.8			EBIT/Interest	(46) 3.4	(52) 3.0
		1.7	2.3				1.8	2.0
						Net Profit + Depr., Dep., Amort./Cur. Mat. L/T/D	3.3 / (15) 2.4 / .6	5.5 / (21) 3.3 / 1.3
		.3	.2				.5	.5
		1.0	.9			Fixed/Worth	.9	.9
		1.5	1.2				2.0	8.3
		.6	.7				.7	.7
		1.3	1.1			Debt/Worth	1.6	2.4
		2.4	1.9				4.0	11.5
		49.3	31.8				38.6	41.8
		(14) 15.1	15.8			% Profit Before Taxes/Tangible Net Worth	(40) 23.6	(44) 18.8
		5.6	9.9				9.7	9.2
		23.1	13.0				15.2	17.4
		5.3	8.8			% Profit Before Taxes/Total Assets	7.9	8.3
		1.9	4.4				3.0	3.7
		16.0	20.8				11.3	11.6
		6.6	6.4			Sales/Net Fixed Assets	6.7	6.6
		2.7	3.5				4.0	3.9
		2.9	2.3				2.7	2.6
		2.5	1.8			Sales/Total Assets	2.1	2.1
		1.6	1.4				1.3	1.4
		1.6					1.4	1.0
		(13) 2.6				% Depr., Dep., Amort./Sales	(46) 2.0	(52) 1.9
		3.9					3.8	3.5
						% Officers', Directors', Owners' Comp/Sales	1.5 / (15) 3.6 / 5.7	.9 / (14) 3.3 / 6.0
5110M	20656M	199040M	395788M	368463M	179194M	Net Sales ($)	926040M	1615393M
1239M	7139M	84967M	224361M	251796M	169409M	Total Assets ($)	586020M	1128326M

M = $ thousand   MM = $ million
See Pages 11 through 18 for Explanation of Ratios and Data

Comparative Historical Data   **Current Data Sorted By Sales**

4/1/00-3/31/01 ALL	4/1/01-3/31/02 ALL	4/1/02-3/31/03 ALL		0-1MM	1-3MM	3-5MM	5-10MM	10-25MM	25MM & OVER
			Type of Statement						
9	10	6	Unqualified		1			1	4
14	13	12	Reviewed		2	4		3	3
5	10	5	Compiled	1				4	
2		2	Tax Returns				1		
16	11	15	Other	1	2	1	2	2	7
					8 (4/1-9/30/02)			32 (10/1/02-3/31/03)	
46	44	40	NUMBER OF STATEMENTS	2	4	3	7	10	14
%	%	%	**ASSETS**	%	%	%	%	%	%
8.4	6.3	8.8	Cash & Equivalents					13.9	4.4
16.3	19.0	19.7	Trade Receivables (net)					21.0	17.0
29.3	26.9	27.5	Inventory					26.6	32.3
1.6	2.3	1.8	All Other Current					2.3	1.8
55.7	54.6	57.6	Total Current					63.8	55.5
30.9	31.2	27.6	Fixed Assets (net)					30.0	25.9
5.6	5.0	5.8	Intangibles (net)					.8	11.3
7.9	9.2	8.9	All Other Non-Current					5.3	7.4
100.0	100.0	100.0	Total					100.0	100.0
			LIABILITIES						
10.0	12.0	8.1	Notes Payable-Short Term					6.0	12.6
6.7	3.3	2.6	Cur. Mat.-L/T/D					2.0	2.2
13.1	11.7	11.8	Trade Payables					10.2	10.3
.2	.1	.7	Income Taxes Payable					1.4	.8
8.1	6.3	8.0	All Other Current					7.1	10.7
38.1	33.5	31.2	Total Current					26.6	36.5
20.3	19.8	18.4	Long Term Debt					12.9	19.3
.4	.3	.3	Deferred Taxes					.1	.3
7.6	7.1	4.0	All Other Non-Current					5.7	2.2
33.6	39.3	46.1	Net Worth					54.7	41.8
100.0	100.0	100.0	Total Liabilities & Net Worth					100.0	100.0
			INCOME DATA						
100.0	100.0	100.0	Net Sales					100.0	100.0
35.6	35.3	31.6	Gross Profit					33.9	26.3
29.6	28.8	27.2	Operating Expenses					27.2	20.9
6.0	6.4	4.4	Operating Profit					6.7	5.3
2.0	1.7	1.4	All Other Expenses (net)					.4	3.1
4.0	4.7	3.0	Profit Before Taxes					6.3	2.2
			RATIOS						
2.4	3.1	3.0	Current					3.6	2.4
1.4	1.7	2.1						2.6	1.4
.9	1.1	1.3						1.9	1.1
1.3	1.2	1.7	Quick					2.2	.8
.7	.8	.9						1.5	.6
.4	.4	.6						.9	.4
21 17.1	30 12.0	20 18.4	Sales/Receivables					24 15.5	20 18.3
35 10.3	40 9.1	32 11.3						34 10.8	35 10.5
42 8.6	48 7.6	43 8.4						38 9.6	47 7.7
36 10.1	49 7.5	39 9.4	Cost of Sales/Inventory					52 7.0	44 8.2
67 5.5	70 5.2	54 6.7						58 6.3	60 6.0
136 2.7	114 3.2	88 4.2						76 4.8	154 2.4
20 18.6	24 15.5	16 22.8	Cost of Sales/Payables					12 29.8	12 30.8
33 11.1	36 10.3	25 14.8						22 16.7	26 14.2
59 6.2	44 8.4	38 9.7						30 12.1	37 10.0
4.1	3.5	5.2	Sales/Working Capital					4.4	6.5
13.3	9.1	9.8						5.5	12.6
-56.7	109.6	19.5						15.7	34.3
(42) 5.5	(39) 6.7	(33) 6.7	EBIT/Interest						6.1
2.7	2.7	3.7						(13)	3.7
1.6	1.2	2.1							2.3
(11) 15.0	(14) 7.2	(11) 8.8	Net Profit + Depr., Dep.,						
5.4	2.8	4.2	Amort./Cur. Mat. L/T/D						
2.3	2.2	1.9							
.5	.3	.2	Fixed/Worth					.3	.3
.9	.8	.7						.5	1.0
2.0	2.4	1.5						1.0	1.9
.9	.7	.7	Debt/Worth					.5	1.0
1.9	1.3	1.3						.9	1.7
6.1	4.0	2.5						1.3	4.1
(40) 39.9	(38) 28.3	(37) 37.1	% Profit Before Taxes/Tangible					49.3	80.5
16.2	14.1	18.6	Net Worth					25.2	(13) 21.3
6.9	2.9	7.6						7.1	10.9
14.3	13.3	15.9	% Profit Before Taxes/Total					25.4	12.6
7.2	4.9	7.0	Assets					13.0	7.4
2.4	1.2	3.3						4.0	3.9
11.9	9.7	24.3	Sales/Net Fixed Assets					20.5	15.5
5.9	4.9	9.1						7.6	8.0
3.4	3.4	4.2						3.7	5.2
2.5	2.2	2.9	Sales/Total Assets					3.2	2.3
1.8	1.6	2.1						2.4	1.3
1.2	1.0	1.4						1.7	1.3
(40) .6	(39) 1.4	(31) 1.3	% Depr., Dep., Amort./Sales						.4
1.9	2.2	2.0						(11)	1.8
2.8	4.4	3.0							3.6
(13) 1.7	(11) 2.5	(11) 1.8	% Officers', Directors',						
4.0	3.6	5.1	Owners' Comp/Sales						
5.5	8.8	7.7							
1318488M	1131462M	1168251M	Net Sales ($)	941M	8294M	11277M	50997M	190653M	906089M
1014342M	837504M	738911M	Total Assets ($)	1100M	6058M	5345M	25949M	92604M	607855M

M = $ thousand   MM = $ million

Current Data Sorted By Assets   **Comparative Historical Data**

0-500M	500M-2MM	2-10MM	10-50MM	50-100MM	100-250MM	Type of Statement	4/1/98-3/31/99 ALL	4/1/99-3/31/00 ALL
		1	4	1	1	Unqualified	13	7
	2	5	1			Reviewed	1	1
1	1	3				Compiled	9	5
2						Tax Returns	1	
		1	4		1	Other	6	2
		6 (4/1-9/30/02)		23 (10/1/02-3/31/03)				
3	4	10	9	1	2	**NUMBER OF STATEMENTS**	30	15
%	%	%	%	%	%	**ASSETS**	%	%
		8.2				Cash & Equivalents	4.9	5.0
		17.9				Trade Receivables (net)	23.3	24.2
		24.2				Inventory	30.6	27.4
		2.6				All Other Current	1.4	1.1
		52.9				Total Current	60.3	57.7
		44.1				Fixed Assets (net)	31.2	35.5
		.7				Intangibles (net)	2.3	.9
		2.3				All Other Non-Current	6.2	5.9
		100.0				Total	100.0	100.0
						LIABILITIES		
		6.9				Notes Payable-Short Term	12.7	11.7
		5.9				Cur. Mat.-L/T/D	2.7	3.3
		14.6				Trade Payables	16.2	15.4
		.0				Income Taxes Payable	.2	.2
		5.3				All Other Current	12.3	9.1
		32.7				Total Current	44.1	39.7
		24.1				Long Term Debt	14.4	17.9
		.5				Deferred Taxes	1.4	.9
		2.0				All Other Non-Current	5.1	3.4
		40.7				Net Worth	35.0	38.1
		100.0				Total Liabilities & Net Worth	100.0	100.0
						INCOME DATA		
		100.0				Net Sales	100.0	100.0
		31.1				Gross Profit	30.4	28.0
		25.7				Operating Expenses	28.2	24.6
		5.4				Operating Profit	2.2	3.5
		1.5				All Other Expenses (net)	1.0	.5
		4.0				Profit Before Taxes	1.2	2.9
						RATIOS		
		2.4					2.1	2.1
		1.5				Current	1.7	1.3
		1.0					1.1	1.0
		1.5					1.1	.8
		.7				Quick	.7	.7
		.4					.4	.5
		18 20.0					23 15.9	27 13.7
		23 15.9				Sales/Receivables	29 12.6	33 11.1
		33 11.0					35 10.4	40 9.1
		23 15.8					24 15.3	23 16.1
		45 8.0				Cost of Sales/Inventory	56 6.5	49 7.4
		69 5.3					113 3.2	75 4.9
		17 21.9					19 18.8	21 17.3
		26 13.9				Cost of Sales/Payables	31 11.6	30 12.2
		39 9.3					46 7.9	35 10.3
		9.4					6.8	7.4
		16.0				Sales/Working Capital	14.1	25.7
		396.3					NM	355.0
		6.1					6.6	5.2
		4.4				EBIT/Interest	(29) 3.4	2.8
		2.0					1.2	1.5
						Net Profit + Depr., Dep., Amort./Cur. Mat. L /T/D		
		.5					.4	.5
		1.0				Fixed/Worth	.9	.9
		3.2					1.6	1.7
		.7					1.0	.7
		1.3				Debt/Worth	1.7	1.6
		5.0					3.7	4.1
		55.4					37.4	18.1
		16.5				% Profit Before Taxes/Tangible Net Worth	(27) 15.9	(14) 12.6
		3.4					7.4	7.5
		11.2					11.1	9.2
		5.7				% Profit Before Taxes/Total Assets	6.0	5.0
		2.0					.4	1.2
		14.3					19.9	16.4
		6.3				Sales/Net Fixed Assets	8.6	8.2
		3.8					5.1	3.7
		3.8					4.0	3.3
		2.7				Sales/Total Assets	2.5	2.8
		2.1					1.9	1.8
		2.0					1.5	1.3
		2.9				% Depr., Dep., Amort./Sales	(28) 2.0	2.1
		4.2					3.1	3.7
							2.2	
						% Officers', Directors', Owners' Comp/Sales	(11) 3.7	
							5.2	
2587M	16162M	128036M	453898M	29723M	388637M	Net Sales ($)	696558M	862251M
442M	5133M	48192M	235666M	57100M	242660M	Total Assets ($)	420472M	391309M

M = $ thousand   MM = $ million
See Pages 11 through 18 for Explanation of Ratios and Data

Comparative Historical Data | Current Data Sorted By Sales

Type of Statement

	4/1/00-3/31/01 ALL	4/1/01-3/31/02 ALL	4/1/02-3/31/03 ALL	Type of Statement	0-1MM	1-3MM	3-5MM	5-10MM	10-25MM	25MM & OVER
Unqualified	5	5	7	Unqualified					1	6
Reviewed	2	1	8	Reviewed		1	1	2	3	1
Compiled	5	7	5	Compiled	1	1		1	1	1
Tax Returns	2	2	2	Tax Returns	1	1				
Other	5	13	7	Other			1		2	4
					6 (4/1-9/30/02)			23 (10/1/02-3/31/03)		
NUMBER OF STATEMENTS	19	28	29	NUMBER OF STATEMENTS	2	3	2	3	7	12

ASSETS (%)

Item	4/1/00-3/31/01 ALL	4/1/01-3/31/02 ALL	4/1/02-3/31/03 ALL	0-1MM	1-3MM	3-5MM	5-10MM	10-25MM	25MM & OVER
Cash & Equivalents	7.1	7.9	6.2						5.9
Trade Receivables (net)	22.7	20.3	21.1						17.5
Inventory	33.3	29.7	24.1						24.6
All Other Current	2.4	2.1	3.5						4.9
Total Current	65.5	60.0	54.9						52.9
Fixed Assets (net)	29.2	28.3	34.9						36.0
Intangibles (net)	1.3	5.3	3.8						5.7
All Other Non-Current	4.0	6.3	6.4						5.4
Total	100.0	100.0	100.0						100.0

LIABILITIES

Item	4/1/00-3/31/01 ALL	4/1/01-3/31/02 ALL	4/1/02-3/31/03 ALL	0-1MM	1-3MM	3-5MM	5-10MM	10-25MM	25MM & OVER
Notes Payable-Short Term	16.9	10.9	9.4						9.5
Cur. Mat.-L/T/D	2.8	4.8	3.2						2.2
Trade Payables	15.4	12.7	15.7						14.2
Income Taxes Payable	.1	.7	.0						.1
All Other Current	5.5	7.2	16.3						7.3
Total Current	40.7	36.2	44.6						33.4
Long Term Debt	12.9	12.5	15.6						14.6
Deferred Taxes	.8	1.1	.7						1.3
All Other Non-Current	6.9	5.3	2.6						1.8
Net Worth	38.7	44.8	36.4						48.8
Total Liabilities & Net Worth	100.0	100.0	100.0						100.0

INCOME DATA

Item	4/1/00-3/31/01 ALL	4/1/01-3/31/02 ALL	4/1/02-3/31/03 ALL	0-1MM	1-3MM	3-5MM	5-10MM	10-25MM	25MM & OVER
Net Sales	100.0	100.0	100.0						100.0
Gross Profit	33.1	31.4	32.6						30.3
Operating Expenses	30.1	26.7	28.0						24.2
Operating Profit	3.0	4.7	4.6						6.1
All Other Expenses (net)	1.0	2.3	1.6						1.6
Profit Before Taxes	1.9	2.4	3.0						4.5

RATIOS

Ratio	4/1/00-3/31/01 ALL	4/1/01-3/31/02 ALL	4/1/02-3/31/03 ALL	25MM & OVER
Current	2.4 / 1.5 / 1.2	2.2 / 1.7 / 1.2	1.8 / 1.2 / .9	2.0 / 1.4 / 1.0
Quick	1.0 / .6 / .4	1.2 / .7 / .4	.9 / .6 / .4	1.0 / .7 / .4
Sales/Receivables	(22) 16.9 / (27) 13.7 / (37) 9.8	(24) 15.0 / (30) 12.3 / (39) 9.4	(20) 18.5 / (30) 12.2 / (37) 9.8	(23) 16.0 / (30) 12.0 / (38) 9.6
Cost of Sales/Inventory	(33) 10.9 / (85) 4.3 / (98) 3.7	(35) 10.6 / (67) 5.4 / (98) 3.7	(26) 14.2 / (41) 8.8 / (77) 4.7	(25) 14.4 / (51) 7.1 / (104) 3.5
Cost of Sales/Payables	(19) 19.1 / (29) 12.4 / (49) 7.5	(13) 28.9 / (24) 15.2 / (36) 10.2	(18) 20.1 / (27) 13.5 / (40) 9.1	(26) 14.2 / (29) 12.4 / (51) 7.2
Sales/Working Capital	7.4 / 10.2 / 21.7	7.3 / 10.4 / 28.3	9.4 / 20.5 / −131.4	6.4 / 12.5 / 204.2
EBIT/Interest	5.0 / 2.0 / 1.2	10.2 / (25) 3.0 / 1.5	7.1 / (26) 4.3 / 1.3	7.8 / (11) 6.5 / 2.5
Net Profit + Depr., Dep., Amort./Cur. Mat. L/T/D			11.6 / (12) 3.0 / 1.4	
Fixed/Worth	.4 / .7 / 3.5	.5 / .7 / 1.1	.5 / 1.0 / 3.4	.5 / .7 / 1.8
Debt/Worth	.6 / 1.3 / 4.6	.7 / 1.3 / 3.1	.7 / 1.9 / 7.4	.5 / 1.2 / 5.2
% Profit Before Taxes/Tangible Net Worth	17.8 / (17) 12.2 / 2.6	35.7 / (26) 20.2 / 1.5	44.8 / (26) 16.5 / 2.2	38.7 / (11) 21.1 / 8.3
% Profit Before Taxes/Total Assets	9.0 / 3.0 / 1.0	15.9 / 5.1 / .7	11.0 / 5.6 / 1.7	13.9 / 8.6 / 4.5
Sales/Net Fixed Assets	35.2 / 14.6 / 6.5	15.5 / 9.6 / 5.1	16.4 / 6.8 / 3.8	9.4 / 5.9 / 3.4
Sales/Total Assets	3.4 / 2.8 / 1.8	3.1 / 2.0 / 1.4	3.5 / 2.3 / 2.0	2.4 / 2.1 / 1.6
% Depr., Dep., Amort./Sales	1.4 / (18) 2.0 / 2.7	1.3 / 2.1 / 3.1	1.7 / (28) 2.5 / 3.2	1.7 / 2.5 / 3.0
% Officers', Directors', Owners' Comp/Sales			6.6 / (11) 8.6 / 10.1	

	4/1/00-3/31/01 ALL	4/1/01-3/31/02 ALL	4/1/02-3/31/03 ALL	0-1MM	1-3MM	3-5MM	5-10MM	10-25MM	25MM & OVER
Net Sales ($)	651833M	1686221M	1019043M	1368M	5281M	7731M	17612M	102863M	884188M
Total Assets ($)	260436M	970846M	589193M	291M	6115M	2230M	6738M	63418M	510401M

© RMA 2003

M = $ thousand   MM = $ million
See Pages 11 through 18 for Explanation of Ratios and Data

Current Data Sorted By Assets   Comparative Historical Data

						Type of Statement		
		13	18	5	2	Unqualified	38	34
	8	10	4	1		Reviewed	16	16
2	6	9	1			Compiled	25	19
4	3	1				Tax Returns	6	4
4	9	15	18	6	3	Other	27	35
	32 (4/1-9/30/02)			109 (10/1/02-3/31/03)			4/1/98-3/31/99	4/1/99-3/31/00
0-500M	500M-2MM	2-10MM	10-50MM	50-100MM	100-250MM		ALL	ALL
10	26	48	41	11	5	NUMBER OF STATEMENTS	112	108
%	%	%	%	%	%	ASSETS	%	%
8.3	6.2	6.7	10.1	10.7		Cash & Equivalents	7.2	9.0
21.7	24.6	22.3	18.5	22.8		Trade Receivables (net)	20.8	21.2
15.5	20.6	22.1	26.5	12.8		Inventory	21.7	22.6
.3	2.3	2.6	2.7	3.1		All Other Current	2.2	2.5
45.8	53.6	53.7	57.7	49.4		Total Current	51.9	55.3
47.0	32.4	35.2	34.0	30.5		Fixed Assets (net)	38.9	33.5
2.6	2.9	4.7	4.5	10.4		Intangibles (net)	3.6	4.3
4.6	11.1	6.5	3.8	9.7		All Other Non-Current	5.6	6.8
100.0	100.0	100.0	100.0	100.0		Total	100.0	100.0
						LIABILITIES		
10.4	10.3	10.0	12.2	.5		Notes Payable-Short Term	10.2	9.2
6.9	5.3	4.0	3.6	4.5		Cur. Mat.-L/T/D	5.1	3.7
13.1	20.0	15.6	11.2	13.0		Trade Payables	16.8	14.2
.0	.3	.9	.3	.6		Income Taxes Payable	.1	.3
3.6	5.1	9.3	7.9	19.4		All Other Current	8.6	7.4
34.0	41.0	39.8	35.2	38.0		Total Current	40.9	34.9
29.1	15.2	17.7	19.1	9.4		Long Term Debt	20.0	21.3
.0	.0	.2	.5	1.8		Deferred Taxes	.3	.4
6.1	6.4	8.7	4.2	6.1		All Other Non-Current	4.2	4.0
30.8	37.4	33.5	40.9	44.6		Net Worth	34.6	39.4
100.0	100.0	100.0	100.0	100.0		Total Liabilities & Net Worth	100.0	100.0
						INCOME DATA		
100.0	100.0	100.0	100.0	100.0		Net Sales	100.0	100.0
56.4	40.5	27.5	25.5	21.9		Gross Profit	33.5	31.6
51.9	37.4	24.3	19.3	14.9		Operating Expenses	27.7	26.7
4.4	3.1	3.2	6.2	7.0		Operating Profit	5.8	4.9
1.1	.2	.9	2.0	1.1		All Other Expenses (net)	.7	.3
3.3	2.9	2.3	4.2	5.9		Profit Before Taxes	5.1	4.6
						RATIOS		
4.2	2.5	2.0	2.4	2.6			2.1	2.5
1.7	1.4	1.3	1.6	1.9		Current	1.3	1.6
.5	.7	1.0	1.0	1.1			1.0	1.1
2.8	1.4	1.0	1.5	1.9			1.1	1.5
.9	.8	.7	.7	1.0		Quick	.6	.7
.4	.5	.4	.4	.7			.4	.5
0 UND	12 30.4	19 19.5	26 14.2	27 13.7			21 17.7	21 17.8
23 16.2	23 15.6	27 13.6	33 11.0	29 12.7		Sales/Receivables	29 12.5	29 12.5
36 10.0	35 10.4	42 8.7	41 9.0	39 9.4			39 9.4	38 9.7
3 107.2	16 23.5	14 25.3	26 14.2	5 67.3			20 18.4	23 16.2
19 19.2	40 9.0	41 8.9	67 5.5	25 14.5		Cost of Sales/Inventory	40 9.2	42 8.8
72 5.1	60 6.0	91 4.0	107 3.4	53 6.9			79 4.6	70 5.2
0 UND	12 31.2	13 27.6	16 23.2	9 41.8			18 20.4	15 23.8
21 17.7	34 10.6	25 14.3	23 15.6	13 27.8		Cost of Sales/Payables	31 11.6	25 14.5
77 4.7	65 5.6	35 10.3	36 10.1	30 12.2			51 7.2	43 8.5
13.2	9.2	9.0	4.3	6.9			9.3	6.5
21.7	23.4	32.9	13.0	15.3		Sales/Working Capital	20.7	14.5
-25.6	-27.0	NM	315.4	54.5			NM	58.9
35.9	5.7	8.7	15.3	17.5			11.3	8.6
.9	(23) 1.8	(46) 2.7	(40) 5.1	(10) 14.8		EBIT/Interest	(107) 4.1	(101) 3.8
-1.4	.1	.8	1.9	3.9			1.7	1.5
		6.1	19.4			Net Profit + Depr., Dep.,		7.0	10.2
		(12) 4.3	(21) 6.3			Amort./Cur. Mat. L /T/D	(40) 4.0	(39) 4.1
		2.2	2.0				1.8	1.5
.5	.2	.4	.4	.5			.6	.5
1.4	.9	1.2	.8	.8		Fixed/Worth	1.0	.9
-4.7	2.8	2.4	2.6	1.4			2.6	3.1
.8	1.0	1.0	.7	1.0			.8	.6
1.3	2.1	1.8	2.0	1.4		Debt/Worth	1.8	1.7
-8.6	5.1	5.2	3.9	3.0			5.4	5.7
	48.2	30.1	41.7	74.2		% Profit Before Taxes/Tangible	58.1	44.7
	(25) 21.6	(41) 16.1	(39) 21.1	(10) 41.3		Net Worth	(95) 29.3	(92) 21.6
	-4.9	5.6	9.1	10.1			14.5	7.1
71.0	16.2	12.1	17.0	17.8		% Profit Before Taxes/Total	17.5	15.9
.7	7.4	4.4	8.1	11.4		Assets	9.4	7.4
-7.1	-1.5	.1	3.1	5.3			2.9	1.8
19.6	51.7	20.1	13.5	18.5			11.8	15.0
9.0	12.4	7.9	5.7	8.7		Sales/Net Fixed Assets	6.1	7.7
5.4	6.0	3.6	3.3	3.1			3.6	3.9
5.2	4.3	3.8	2.5	3.5			3.4	3.6
4.0	3.2	2.4	1.9	2.4		Sales/Total Assets	2.5	2.5
3.2	2.4	1.7	1.4	1.2			1.8	1.6
	1.2	1.2	1.1				1.3	1.2
	(20) 2.2	(44) 2.0	(38) 2.8			% Depr., Dep., Amort./Sales	(105) 2.9	(96) 2.2
	4.6	3.7	4.4				4.2	3.3
	3.3	1.5				% Officers', Directors',		2.1	1.6
	(13) 4.0	(15) 2.2				Owners' Comp/Sales	(39) 3.8	(32) 2.5
	7.3	5.1					7.7	5.9
8936M	103089M	587222M	1862121M	1924748M	2171160M	Net Sales ($)	3749473M	5468876M
2392M	28386M	222635M	949750M	766015M	925474M	Total Assets ($)	1891030M	2804398M

M = $ thousand   MM = $ million
See Pages 11 through 18 for Explanation of Ratios and Data

Comparative Historical Data | Current Data Sorted By Sales

	4/1/00-3/31/01 ALL	4/1/01-3/31/02 ALL	4/1/02-3/31/03 ALL	32 (4/1-9/30/02)	109 (10/1/02-3/31/03)				
Type of Statement				0-1MM	1-3MM	3-5MM	5-10MM	10-25MM	25MM & OVER
Unqualified	32	32	38		1		3	10	24
Reviewed	18	22	22		4	4	4	6	4
Compiled	23	30	18	2	3	2	5	5	1
Tax Returns	14	9	8	4	1	2	1		
Other	45	62	55	4	6	4	10	10	21
NUMBER OF STATEMENTS	132	155	141	10	15	12	23	31	50
ASSETS	%	%	%	%	%	%	%	%	%
Cash & Equivalents	6.9	7.3	8.0	7.4	6.4	11.7	5.4	9.8	7.7
Trade Receivables (net)	22.1	20.1	21.7	13.3	21.2	25.7	21.9	22.6	21.9
Inventory	22.4	20.4	21.9	14.9	19.1	22.4	19.9	24.1	23.6
All Other Current	2.6	3.0	2.4	.0	4.5	1.6	2.5	1.5	3.0
Total Current	54.1	50.7	54.0	35.6	51.2	61.5	49.8	58.0	56.1
Fixed Assets (net)	33.7	37.3	34.7	53.4	38.2	26.9	38.1	32.3	31.6
Intangibles (net)	6.1	4.3	4.7	5.8	3.5	1.8	3.4	4.1	6.5
All Other Non-Current	6.1	7.6	6.6	5.2	7.1	9.7	8.7	5.5	5.8
Total	100.0	100.0	100.0	100.0	100.0	100.0	100.0	100.0	100.0
LIABILITIES									
Notes Payable-Short Term	11.1	11.7	9.8	9.0	6.9	10.7	11.8	11.7	8.4
Cur. Mat.-L/T/D	5.3	5.4	4.3	7.7	4.5	6.0	3.7	4.0	3.6
Trade Payables	18.3	14.4	14.7	11.3	13.0	23.6	13.4	16.6	13.2
Income Taxes Payable	.2	.2	.5	.0	.2	.1	1.8	.1	.5
All Other Current	13.2	23.4	8.6	14.6	4.6	5.6	5.6	7.2	11.7
Total Current	48.1	55.2	37.9	42.6	29.2	46.0	36.2	39.6	37.4
Long Term Debt	18.3	19.1	18.0	33.1	18.6	13.6	18.5	16.8	16.4
Deferred Taxes	.4	.6	.4	.0	.0	.0	.3	.3	.8
All Other Non-Current	5.8	8.8	6.5	6.1	6.0	6.9	15.0	3.4	4.6
Net Worth	27.4	16.3	37.2	18.2	46.2	33.4	30.0	39.9	40.8
Total Liabilities & Net Worth	100.0	100.0	100.0	100.0	100.0	100.0	100.0	100.0	100.0
INCOME DATA									
Net Sales	100.0	100.0	100.0	100.0	100.0	100.0	100.0	100.0	100.0
Gross Profit	33.6	33.8	31.5	58.8	44.4	26.7	30.1	26.8	26.8
Operating Expenses	29.3	28.9	26.9	55.4	41.0	25.3	27.8	22.3	19.8
Operating Profit	4.3	5.0	4.6	3.4	3.4	1.4	2.3	4.5	7.0
All Other Expenses (net)	1.2	1.7	1.2	1.6	1.2	.0	1.2	1.1	1.4
Profit Before Taxes	3.1	3.3	3.4	1.8	2.1	1.3	1.2	3.4	5.7
RATIOS									
Current	2.0	2.2	2.2	3.9	2.6	3.0	1.9	2.0	2.0
	1.3	1.3	1.4	.9	1.9	1.5	1.1	1.4	1.5
	.9	.9	1.0	.3	1.4	.9	1.0	1.2	1.1
Quick	1.0	1.2	1.2	2.1	1.5	1.7	1.1	1.4	1.1
	.6	.6	.8	.5	1.0	.8	.7	.8	.8
	.4	.4	.5	.2	.6	.4	.5	.5	.5
Sales/Receivables	21 17.6	21 17.4	20 18.0	0 UND	12 30.0	7 53.5	20 18.2	17 21.3	25 14.8
	31 11.9	30 12.1	30 12.3	23 16.1	26 14.1	31 11.6	27 13.7	27 13.7	32 11.6
	38 9.7	39 9.4	39 9.4	38 9.6	35 10.5	81 4.5	42 8.6	44 8.3	39 9.5
Cost of Sales/Inventory	24 15.5	19 18.9	20 18.5	7 51.4	25 14.5	10 34.8	18 20.7	11 32.7	25 14.7
	44 8.3	41 8.8	43 8.4	37 9.9	42 8.7	43 8.5	43 8.4	42 8.6	47 7.8
	84 4.3	85 4.3	79 4.6	75 4.9	62 5.9	97 3.8	69 5.3	87 4.2	77 4.7
Cost of Sales/Payables	17 21.0	16 22.4	13 28.2	0 UND	11 32.4	11 34.6	14 26.8	17 21.2	13 28.0
	31 12.0	25 14.6	25 14.4	39 9.5	18 20.0	39 9.3	27 13.3	28 13.0	25 14.7
	51 7.2	48 7.6	39 9.5	130 2.8	45 8.1	85 4.3	31 11.8	38 9.5	34 10.7
Sales/Working Capital	9.6	7.7	6.9	15.0	8.0	5.6	7.4	6.1	5.9
	24.2	23.5	18.0	NM	12.5	31.2	84.9	16.6	14.8
	-50.6	-32.8	218.2	-4.2	20.6	NM	-210.9	44.8	70.0
EBIT/Interest	9.6	7.7	13.5	17.6	5.7	19.8	8.0	9.9	18.6
	(121) 3.4	(142) 2.8	(134) 3.2	.9	1.5	(11) 1.8	(20) 2.5	(30) 2.6	(48) 5.8
	1.3	1.0	1.4	-3.9	.1	-1.1	-.5	1.5	2.9
Net Profit + Depr., Dep., Amort./Cur. Mat. L/T/D	7.9	7.3	7.1					7.3	15.0
	(37) 2.6	(40) 3.4	(45) 4.9				(12) 4.3	4.3	(24) 5.1
	1.1	1.1	2.3					1.6	2.8
Fixed/Worth	.5	.5	.4	.8	.5	.1	.5	.4	.4
	1.3	1.1	.9	NM	.8	.4	1.2	.8	.9
	3.6	3.5	2.5	-3.3	1.9	4.3	3.0	1.5	2.3
Debt/Worth	1.1	.9	.9	1.1	.8	.7	1.1	1.0	.9
	2.6	2.1	1.9	NM	1.2	3.9	1.9	1.8	1.8
	7.5	7.8	4.5	-5.9	4.5	42.9	5.4	3.5	4.0
% Profit Before Taxes/Tangible Net Worth	51.3	51.4	45.6		56.3	30.4	40.1	27.8	54.1
	(108) 24.5	(129) 19.9	(125) 21.1		7.1	(11) 4.5	(20) 23.9	(28) 15.7	(46) 23.8
	10.9	3.2	5.0		-3.6	-29.0	3.0	.8	11.3
% Profit Before Taxes/Total Assets	18.0	17.0	15.4	28.6	9.7	13.0	16.8	19.0	17.0
	6.5	5.5	6.0	-.6	2.4	3.9	4.3	4.9	8.1
	1.1	.0	1.5	-7.1	-2.0	-5.7	-1.4	2.3	4.7
Sales/Net Fixed Assets	18.2	14.6	20.6	9.9	28.4	322.3	22.3	20.4	19.7
	8.1	6.7	7.9	6.6	7.2	18.7	7.6	8.0	8.4
	3.9	3.3	3.7	1.6	4.2	5.6	3.2	3.8	3.7
Sales/Total Assets	3.7	3.2	3.8	4.3	4.2	4.0	4.1	3.8	3.4
	2.5	2.2	2.3	3.6	3.1	2.5	2.5	2.2	2.1
	1.6	1.5	1.6	1.2	1.8	1.8	1.4	1.7	1.4
% Depr., Dep., Amort./Sales	1.0	1.6	1.2		1.8		1.7	.8	1.1
	(106) 2.2	(134) 2.4	(121) 2.1	(14) 2.9		(20) 2.0	(29) 3.0	(44) 1.7	
	3.8	4.4	4.3	5.4		4.2	4.5	4.2	
% Officers', Directors', Owners' Comp/Sales	2.0	1.9	1.5				1.3	1.1	
	(49) 4.1	(47) 3.6	(44) 3.8			(10) 2.6	(10) 2.0		
	6.8	7.9	7.5			8.7	5.1		
Net Sales ($)	3603683M	4666410M	6657276M	6837M	33834M	47169M	157829M	503690M	5907917M
Total Assets ($)	1803632M	2478852M	2894652M	5874M	15304M	23996M	84007M	226708M	2538763M

M = $ thousand   MM = $ million
See Pages 11 through 18 for Explanation of Ratios and Data

Current Data Sorted By Assets   Comparative Historical Data

0-500M	500M-2MM	2-10MM	10-50MM	50-100MM	100-250MM	Type of Statement	4/1/98-3/31/99 ALL	4/1/99-3/31/00 ALL
	1	5	28	4	7	Unqualified	48	47
	2	3	6			Reviewed	13	13
1		1	1			Compiled	12	13
2	1		1			Tax Returns	4	1
	9	6	14	2	8	Other	31	31
	14 (4/1-9/30/02)		87 (10/1/02-3/31/03)					
3	13	14	50	6	15	NUMBER OF STATEMENTS	108	105
%	%	%	%	%	%	ASSETS	%	%
	7.4	3.2	6.4		7.7	Cash & Equivalents	8.6	7.4
	22.0	28.1	16.5		14.5	Trade Receivables (net)	18.0	16.0
	16.6	18.9	13.9		10.4	Inventory	14.2	13.4
	.3	4.0	2.8		1.3	All Other Current	2.5	3.4
	46.2	54.2	39.7		33.9	Total Current	43.3	40.2
	41.2	30.8	37.5		40.9	Fixed Assets (net)	39.1	37.5
	5.8	8.3	14.3		18.5	Intangibles (net)	11.8	13.7
	6.9	6.6	8.5		6.7	All Other Non-Current	5.7	8.6
	100.0	100.0	100.0		100.0	Total	100.0	100.0
						LIABILITIES		
	9.0	15.4	7.1		3.4	Notes Payable-Short Term	8.8	7.2
	6.2	4.5	4.2		2.1	Cur. Mat.-L/T/D	7.2	3.9
	15.7	17.3	14.7		10.3	Trade Payables	15.7	13.0
	.0	.0	.2		.3	Income Taxes Payable	.3	.2
	14.0	7.3	8.1		7.0	All Other Current	9.2	7.9
	44.9	44.5	34.3		23.2	Total Current	41.3	32.3
	20.4	10.4	20.9		29.0	Long Term Debt	25.9	24.5
	.0	.0	1.1		3.2	Deferred Taxes	1.2	1.1
	25.6	10.7	5.6		4.1	All Other Non-Current	4.7	4.4
	9.1	34.4	38.2		40.4	Net Worth	26.9	37.7
	100.0	100.0	100.0		100.0	Total Liabilities & Net Worth	100.0	100.0
						INCOME DATA		
	100.0	100.0	100.0		100.0	Net Sales	100.0	100.0
	39.6	25.7	33.3		36.2	Gross Profit	32.0	35.3
	42.2	19.9	28.0		27.2	Operating Expenses	28.3	29.9
	-2.7	5.8	5.2		9.0	Operating Profit	3.7	5.4
	1.2	.6	.8		2.4	All Other Expenses (net)	1.6	1.0
	-3.9	5.1	4.5		6.6	Profit Before Taxes	2.1	4.4
						RATIOS		
	2.3	2.1	1.8		1.9		2.1	2.1
	1.4	1.2	1.2		1.4	Current	1.3	1.2
	.7	.9	.9		1.0		.9	.9
	1.1	1.2	1.2		1.3		1.4	1.3
	.8	.7	.7		1.0	Quick	.7	.7
	.4	.4	.4		.6		.4	.4
19 19.6	15 24.3	18 20.3			29 12.8		18 20.5	20 18.0
26 13.8	21 17.7	25 14.3			31 11.7	Sales/Receivables	28 13.2	28 13.2
40 9.1	39 9.4	32 11.3			37 9.9		36 10.1	36 10.0
5 68.2	16 23.1	19 19.6			20 18.7		17 20.9	18 19.8
30 12.2	24 15.3	28 12.9			24 15.3	Cost of Sales/Inventory	25 14.7	28 13.1
68 5.4	30 12.2	38 9.5			44 8.4		37 9.7	40 9.1
18 20.8	12 30.9	17 21.0			18 20.0		15 25.0	17 21.7
21 17.8	20 18.4	27 13.5			35 10.4	Cost of Sales/Payables	27 13.4	27 13.3
37 9.8	29 12.7	47 7.7			45 8.1		46 7.9	44 8.3
	10.2	16.5	12.9		10.0		9.4	10.3
	31.6	47.2	35.2		15.5	Sales/Working Capital	22.9	34.8
	-27.8	-98.5	-60.7		305.1		-64.1	-62.4
	3.8	7.2	22.5		20.4		6.7	8.1
	(12) -3.2	(12) 3.2	(46) 4.1		(14) 4.7	EBIT/Interest	(99) 3.1	(94) 2.1
	-16.7	1.0	1.1		2.9		1.1	1.3
			6.5			Net Profit + Depr., Dep.,	4.8	3.4
			(13) 1.5			Amort./Cur. Mat. L/T/D	(40) 2.5	(40) 2.2
			.8				1.1	1.4
	.2	.4	.6		.7		.7	.7
	1.3	.9	1.1		2.3	Fixed/Worth	1.3	1.5
	NM	NM	4.0		6.7		13.7	9.5
	.8	.7	.7		1.0		1.0	.7
	2.5	1.1	1.7		3.1	Debt/Worth	2.3	1.8
	-20.6	NM	8.4		6.9		34.7	13.8
		72.5	68.2		49.6	% Profit Before Taxes/Tangible	46.4	38.4
	(11) 14.4	(43) 22.3			(12) 31.7	Net Worth	(83) 24.2	(81) 20.9
	5.4	6.6			10.7		8.9	6.9
	9.2	10.3	15.9		14.3	% Profit Before Taxes/Total	14.6	12.4
	-8.3	6.1	6.2		11.4	Assets	6.5	5.9
	-20.0	1.2	1.6		5.7		.7	1.0
	17.1	35.8	12.0		8.1		10.2	10.8
	6.8	13.8	6.1		4.1	Sales/Net Fixed Assets	5.9	5.3
	2.5	6.3	4.1		2.8		3.4	3.4
	4.1	5.4	3.0		2.4		3.0	2.9
	2.9	3.5	2.3		1.5	Sales/Total Assets	2.1	2.0
	1.4	2.7	1.5		1.2		1.3	1.3
	2.7	1.0	2.5				2.3	2.3
	(10) 6.8	(10) 2.8	(49) 3.3			% Depr., Dep., Amort./Sales	(89) 3.2	(90) 4.0
	9.4	5.5	4.4				5.0	5.4
						% Officers', Directors',	1.4	1.2
						Owners' Comp/Sales	(13) 2.9	(18) 3.7
							13.8	6.9
826M	60944M	359748M	2587469M	849588M	4377502M	Net Sales ($)	7616295M	7188842M
303M	19740M	79361M	1117391M	374784M	2646232M	Total Assets ($)	4077692M	3600490M

M = $ thousand   MM = $ million
See Pages 11 through 18 for Explanation of Ratios and Data

Comparative Historical Data / Current Data Sorted By Sales

Hist 1	Hist 2	Hist 3	Type of Statement	0-1MM	1-3MM	3-5MM	5-10MM	10-25MM	25MM & OVER
30	36	45	Unqualified				2	6	37
7	11	11	Reviewed		1		2	4	4
15	16	2	Compiled	1					1
2	1	4	Tax Returns	2	1				1
30	40	39	Other	2	1	2	5	8	21
4/1/00-3/31/01 ALL	4/1/01-3/31/02 ALL	4/1/02-3/31/03 ALL		14 (4/1-9/30/02)			87 (10/1/02-3/31/03)		
84	104	101	NUMBER OF STATEMENTS	5	3	2	9	18	64
%	%	%	**ASSETS**	%	%	%	%	%	%
7.6	7.4	6.7	Cash & Equivalents					4.1	6.9
18.1	17.3	18.5	Trade Receivables (net)					16.4	19.1
15.5	13.9	14.6	Inventory					12.5	14.4
2.7	2.9	2.5	All Other Current					2.5	2.6
43.9	41.5	42.2	Total Current					35.5	43.0
36.1	35.9	36.6	Fixed Assets (net)					38.0	35.6
13.8	14.8	13.7	Intangibles (net)					15.5	14.3
6.2	7.8	7.5	All Other Non-Current					11.0	7.0
100.0	100.0	100.0	Total					100.0	100.0
			LIABILITIES						
5.9	7.0	8.0	Notes Payable-Short Term					8.9	6.7
4.6	4.2	4.2	Cur. Mat.-L/T/D					7.4	3.7
13.0	12.3	14.6	Trade Payables					12.4	15.4
.2	.4	.3	Income Taxes Payable					.1	.3
6.5	7.9	8.6	All Other Current					7.3	8.3
30.3	31.8	35.6	Total Current					36.0	34.4
22.7	21.4	21.2	Long Term Debt					20.3	21.8
1.5	1.4	1.1	Deferred Taxes					1.0	1.5
5.4	6.7	8.8	All Other Non-Current					5.1	6.6
40.1	38.7	33.3	Net Worth					37.5	35.8
100.0	100.0	100.0	Total Liabilities & Net Worth					100.0	100.0
			INCOME DATA						
100.0	100.0	100.0	Net Sales					100.0	100.0
32.2	36.1	34.0	Gross Profit					37.4	30.9
29.0	30.4	29.3	Operating Expenses					33.9	25.4
3.2	5.8	4.6	Operating Profit					3.5	5.5
.9	1.1	1.1	All Other Expenses (net)					1.1	.8
2.2	4.7	3.5	Profit Before Taxes					2.5	4.7
			RATIOS						
1.9 1.4 1.1	1.9 1.3 .9	1.8 1.2 .9	Current					1.8 1.1 .6	1.8 1.2 .9
1.3 .9 .6	1.3 .8 .5	1.2 .7 .4	Quick					1.1 .5 .3	1.2 .8 .4
21 17.4 32 11.3 40 9.1	22 16.8 27 13.4 34 10.6	18 19.9 27 13.5 35 10.4	Sales/Receivables					18 20.4 23 16.2 34 10.9	18 20.4 28 12.8 35 10.6
18 20.8 28 12.9 43 8.6	20 18.6 28 13.2 39 9.5	19 19.3 27 13.6 39 9.4	Cost of Sales/Inventory					21 17.5 29 12.6 40 9.1	18 20.0 25 14.4 36 10.0
15 23.7 24 15.0 40 9.1	14 25.2 25 14.6 42 8.6	17 21.4 27 13.4 44 8.4	Cost of Sales/Payables					15 24.8 26 14.3 41 8.9	17 21.5 29 12.7 44 8.2
8.7 19.2 124.4	10.7 25.0 -141.8	11.9 34.8 -72.7	Sales/Working Capital					13.6 60.6 -11.1	13.2 37.1 -81.0
(78) 8.4 2.0 1.0	(100) 9.8 3.1 1.0	(92) 14.5 3.3 1.0	EBIT/Interest					(17) 8.3 2.7 .2	(59) 22.5 4.1 1.5
(24) 2.6 1.1 .6	(28) 4.3 1.9 .9	(21) 8.5 2.2 1.1	Net Profit + Depr., Dep., Amort./Cur. Mat. L/T/D						(16) 9.9 3.2 1.6
.6 1.4 10.5	.6 1.2 -17.6	.6 1.2 6.1	Fixed/Worth					.5 1.2 NM	.6 1.1 5.0
.8 1.5 17.3	.8 1.8 -28.2	.8 1.8 10.2	Debt/Worth					.7 3.0 -5.7	.8 1.6 8.6
(64) 32.3 17.4 1.2	(77) 40.2 22.0 6.3	(80) 55.8 22.3 5.5	% Profit Before Taxes/Tangible Net Worth					(13) 71.7 14.4 6.8	(53) 56.2 23.9 5.6
12.4 5.1 .3	14.1 5.2 .3	14.3 6.1 .0	% Profit Before Taxes/Total Assets					7.0 4.8 -2.0	15.5 8.0 1.9
11.6 6.2 3.8	12.5 6.4 3.7	14.4 6.6 4.1	Sales/Net Fixed Assets					15.2 6.1 2.6	14.5 7.5 4.4
3.0 2.3 1.4	3.1 2.3 1.4	3.4 2.4 1.5	Sales/Total Assets					3.5 2.1 1.3	3.3 2.5 1.8
(69) 2.2 3.4 5.1	(86) 1.6 3.3 5.0	(80) 2.3 3.1 4.5	% Depr., Dep., Amort./Sales					(14) 3.1 4.0 5.7	(51) 1.6 2.9 3.9
(17) 1.4 3.9 9.0	(16) 2.3 4.3 8.8	(17) .9 2.0 6.0	% Officers', Directors', Owners' Comp/Sales						
6188955M 3119371M	6958379M 3723808M	8236077M 4237811M	Net Sales ($) Total Assets ($)	2582M 2455M	7273M 4430M	8374M 3355M	64047M 44164M	324096M 187278M	7829705M 3996129M

M = $ thousand   MM = $ million
See Pages 11 through 18 for Explanation of Ratios and Data

Current Data Sorted By Assets   Comparative Historical Data

Type of Statement	0-500M	500M-2MM	2-10MM	10-50MM	50-100MM	100-250MM		4/1/98-3/31/99 ALL	4/1/99-3/31/00 ALL
Unqualified	1	3	8	6					
Reviewed	3	2	5						
Compiled	1	4	1	1					
Tax Returns		1	7	1	1	1			
Other									
		13 (4/1-9/30/02)		33 (10/1/02-3/31/03)					
NUMBER OF STATEMENTS	5	10	21	8	1	1			
ASSETS	%	%	%	%	%	%		%	%
Cash & Equivalents		4.4	7.0					D	D
Trade Receivables (net)		34.8	30.5					A	A
Inventory		26.5	24.0					T	T
All Other Current		2.9	1.8					A	A
Total Current		68.6	63.4						
Fixed Assets (net)		21.9	27.4					N	N
Intangibles (net)		2.2	3.4					O	O
All Other Non-Current		7.3	5.8					T	T
Total		100.0	100.0						
LIABILITIES								A	A
Notes Payable-Short Term		12.9	16.1					V	V
Cur. Mat.-L/T/D		1.3	4.4					A	A
Trade Payables		21.0	23.4					I	I
Income Taxes Payable		.4	.0					L	L
All Other Current		5.6	6.8					A	A
Total Current		41.2	50.8					B	B
Long Term Debt		10.1	20.8					L	L
Deferred Taxes		.0	.4					E	E
All Other Non-Current		.7	3.1						
Net Worth		48.1	24.8						
Total Liabilities & Net Worth		100.0	100.0						
INCOME DATA									
Net Sales		100.0	100.0						
Gross Profit		32.8	30.8						
Operating Expenses		29.6	30.4						
Operating Profit		3.3	.4						
All Other Expenses (net)		.6	.7						
Profit Before Taxes		2.7	-.3						
RATIOS									
Current		3.1	2.0						
		1.6	1.1						
		1.2	.8						
Quick		1.3	1.0						
		1.0	.7						
		.8	.4						
Sales/Receivables	14	26.6	23 15.8						
	24	15.1	36 10.2						
	37	9.9	50 7.3						
Cost of Sales/Inventory	0	UND	13 27.9						
	41	8.8	23 16.0						
	76	4.8	97 3.8						
Cost of Sales/Payables	3	136.0	21 17.7						
	20	18.4	35 10.6						
	57	6.4	70 5.2						
Sales/Working Capital		5.4	8.7						
		19.4	91.7						
		82.8	-18.3						
EBIT/Interest			1.9						
		(18)	.8						
			-1.5						
Net Profit + Depr., Dep., Amort./Cur. Mat. L./T/D									
Fixed/Worth		.1	.2						
		.2	1.1						
		.7	4.6						
Debt/Worth		.3	1.1						
		1.4	2.6						
		2.7	26.6						
% Profit Before Taxes/Tangible Net Worth		11.3	12.2						
		.4 (18)	.1						
		-9.0	-21.0						
% Profit Before Taxes/Total Assets		5.2	2.6						
		.5	-.3						
		-2.7	-8.8						
Sales/Net Fixed Assets		195.2	146.0						
		66.7	11.1						
		7.7	5.4						
Sales/Total Assets		10.2	4.1						
		3.3	2.8						
		1.9	1.7						
% Depr., Dep., Amort./Sales			.2						
		(20)	2.3						
			6.4						
% Officers', Directors', Owners' Comp/Sales									
Net Sales ($)	3021M	77735M	249312M	616785M	137778M	135651M			
Total Assets ($)	1510M	13599M	89942M	150468M	89814M	203808M			

© RMA 2003

M = $ thousand   MM = $ million
See Pages 11 through 18 for Explanation of Ratios and Data

Comparative Historical Data | Current Data Sorted By Sales

			Type of Statement						
		6	Unqualified					1	5
		12	Reviewed	1	1	2	2	6	
		10	Compiled	4		1		5	
		7	Tax Returns	1	2		1	2	1
		11	Other		2	1	2	3	3
4/1/00-3/31/01 ALL	4/1/01-3/31/02 ALL	4/1/02-3/31/03 ALL		13 (4/1-9/30/02)			33 (10/1/02-3/31/03)		
				0-1MM	1-3MM	3-5MM	5-10MM	10-25MM	25MM & OVER
		46	NUMBER OF STATEMENTS	6	5	4	5	17	9
%	%	%	ASSETS	%	%	%	%	%	%
D	D	7.5	Cash & Equivalents					3.8	
A	A	29.1	Trade Receivables (net)					37.3	
T	T	22.8	Inventory					31.4	
A	A	2.1	All Other Current					1.4	
		61.5	Total Current					73.9	
N	N	27.3	Fixed Assets (net)					17.2	
O	O	4.1	Intangibles (net)					2.7	
T	T	7.2	All Other Non-Current					6.2	
		100.0	Total					100.0	
A	A		LIABILITIES						
V	V	15.5	Notes Payable-Short Term					23.0	
A	A	3.1	Cur. Mat.-L/T/D					3.0	
I	I	20.8	Trade Payables					25.5	
L	L	.2	Income Taxes Payable					.0	
A	A	6.0	All Other Current					6.0	
B	B	45.6	Total Current					57.5	
L	L	20.0	Long Term Debt					20.1	
E	E	.5	Deferred Taxes					.3	
		2.5	All Other Non-Current					3.9	
		31.5	Net Worth					18.3	
		100.0	Total Liabilities & Net Worth					100.0	
			INCOME DATA						
		100.0	Net Sales					100.0	
		31.6	Gross Profit					23.6	
		28.3	Operating Expenses					22.0	
		3.3	Operating Profit					1.5	
		1.0	All Other Expenses (net)					.7	
		2.2	Profit Before Taxes					.8	
			RATIOS						
		2.2						1.9	
		1.3	Current					1.2	
		.9						.9	
		1.2						1.0	
		.8	Quick					.7	
		.4						.3	
	20	18.0						22	16.7
	32	11.3	Sales/Receivables					34	10.7
	43	8.5						46	8.0
	14	26.8						13	27.1
	30	12.0	Cost of Sales/Inventory					29	12.7
	80	4.6						95	3.8
	15	24.2						16	23.4
	28	13.0	Cost of Sales/Payables					27	13.4
	60	6.1						53	6.8
		7.8						11.5	
		30.4	Sales/Working Capital					87.2	
		−51.2						−45.1	
		5.3						5.3	
	(39)	1.8	EBIT/Interest				(15)	1.4	
		−.4						.4	
			Net Profit + Depr., Dep., Amort./Cur. Mat. L/T/D						
		.2						.2	
		.7	Fixed/Worth					.4	
		2.8						4.0	
		1.0						1.4	
		2.0	Debt/Worth					3.2	
		6.3						52.7	
		32.7						30.3	
	(40)	5.1	% Profit Before Taxes/Tangible Net Worth				(14)	4.4	
		−7.2						−1.2	
		11.0						4.4	
		1.5	% Profit Before Taxes/Total Assets					.8	
		−2.5						−1.9	
		164.5						186.4	
		12.2	Sales/Net Fixed Assets					28.3	
		5.0						11.1	
		4.1						5.5	
		2.6	Sales/Total Assets					3.6	
		1.7						2.4	
		.3						.2	
	(41)	1.7	% Depr., Dep., Amort./Sales					.4	
		5.0						3.0	
		1.4						1.4	
	(18)	2.7	% Officers', Directors', Owners' Comp/Sales				(10)	2.4	
		5.0						2.8	
		1220282M	Net Sales ($)	3390M	12660M	18401M	42547M	267270M	876014M
		549141M	Total Assets ($)	2028M	8479M	8250M	17778M	79875M	432731M

M = $ thousand   MM = $ million
See Pages 11 through 18 for Explanation of Ratios and Data

	Current Data Sorted By Assets						Comparative Historical Data	

Type of Statement	0-500M	500M-2MM	2-10MM	10-50MM	50-100MM	100-250MM	4/1/98-3/31/99 ALL	4/1/99-3/31/00 ALL
Unqualified			4	3	1	1	9	6
Reviewed		1	6				5	3
Compiled		2	2				10	7
Tax Returns			1				3	2
Other			3	4	1	1	19	16
		3 (4/1-9/30/02)	27 (10/1/02-3/31/03)					
NUMBER OF STATEMENTS		3	16	7	2	2	46	34

Columns marked DATA NOT AVAILABLE: 0-500M; all data presented appears under the 2-10MM column and the two Comparative Historical columns.

ASSETS	2-10MM %	4/1/98-3/31/99 ALL %	4/1/99-3/31/00 ALL %
Cash & Equivalents	9.3	10.6	15.3
Trade Receivables (net)	8.2	5.6	6.9
Inventory	10.6	11.2	11.5
All Other Current	.6	2.2	.7
Total Current	28.7	29.7	34.4
Fixed Assets (net)	58.6	60.2	56.4
Intangibles (net)	8.6	5.3	5.7
All Other Non-Current	4.1	4.9	3.5
Total	100.0	100.0	100.0
LIABILITIES			
Notes Payable-Short Term	3.0	7.4	6.2
Cur. Mat.-L/T/D	5.3	5.1	5.0
Trade Payables	7.0	9.5	8.0
Income Taxes Payable	.1	.1	.0
All Other Current	8.5	8.8	6.2
Total Current	23.9	30.9	25.3
Long Term Debt	34.9	25.9	30.0
Deferred Taxes	.5	.5	1.0
All Other Non-Current	4.7	8.7	5.8
Net Worth	36.0	33.9	37.9
Total Liabilities & Net Worth	100.0	100.0	100.0
INCOME DATA			
Net Sales	100.0	100.0	100.0
Gross Profit	47.5	44.8	43.9
Operating Expenses	41.0	44.1	39.1
Operating Profit	6.5	.7	4.9
All Other Expenses (net)	2.4	3.1	2.2
Profit Before Taxes	4.1	−2.4	2.7

RATIOS	2-10MM	4/1/98-3/31/99 ALL	4/1/99-3/31/00 ALL
Current	2.2 / 1.5 / .9	2.7 / 1.5 / .6	3.0 / 1.7 / 1.0
Quick	1.4 / .9 / .5	(45) 2.0 / .9 / .3	(33) 1.9 / 1.0 / .3
Sales/Receivables	6 60.5 / 22 16.3 / 28 12.9	3 144.7 / 12 29.8 / 25 14.5	5 72.3 / 15 24.0 / 24 15.0
Cost of Sales/Inventory	27 13.4 / 47 7.7 / 67 5.4	23 15.6 / 37 10.0 / 68 5.3	26 13.8 / 43 8.6 / 65 5.6
Cost of Sales/Payables	17 21.0 / 26 14.0 / 50 7.3	21 17.6 / 31 11.7 / 82 4.5	15 24.5 / 33 11.1 / 46 7.9
Sales/Working Capital	7.9 / 22.3 / NM	8.3 / 22.9 / −13.0	6.6 / 11.2 / NM
EBIT/Interest	4.1 / 1.9 / 1.1	(39) 3.8 / 2.1 / −.6	(29) 5.4 / 2.4 / .5
Net Profit + Depr., Dep., Amort./Cur. Mat. L./T/D			
Fixed/Worth	1.4 / 1.9 / 4.7	1.1 / 2.0 / 7.1	.8 / 1.2 / 6.9
Debt/Worth	1.3 / 1.9 / 5.0	.7 / 1.8 / 10.2	.6 / 1.2 / 10.8
% Profit Before Taxes/Tangible Net Worth	(15) 39.2 / 11.7 / 1.0	(38) 38.3 / 14.4 / .6	(30) 41.8 / 18.7 / −10.8
% Profit Before Taxes/Total Assets	13.2 / 4.0 / .2	10.4 / 2.7 / −7.5	23.7 / 4.1 / −3.5
Sales/Net Fixed Assets	3.6 / 2.1 / 1.6	6.3 / 2.6 / 1.2	5.8 / 2.3 / 1.5
Sales/Total Assets	2.2 / 1.3 / 1.0	2.1 / 1.5 / .9	2.0 / 1.4 / 1.0
% Depr., Dep., Amort./Sales	3.1 / 6.0 / 8.7	(43) 3.2 / 5.9 / 9.1	(30) 2.8 / 6.1 / 9.5
% Officers', Directors', Owners' Comp/Sales		(11) 1.6 / 3.7 / 8.9	(12) 4.0 / 7.3 / 14.2

	500M-2MM	2-10MM	10-50MM	50-100MM	100-250MM	4/1/98-3/31/99 ALL	4/1/99-3/31/00 ALL
Net Sales ($)	9416M	186020M	211189M	128157M	318729M	803341M	387086M
Total Assets ($)	3635M	102413M	175210M	159330M	223323M	650770M	353795M

M = $ thousand   MM = $ million
See Pages 11 through 18 for Explanation of Ratios and Data

Comparative Historical Data / Current Data Sorted By Sales

4/1/00-3/31/01 ALL	4/1/01-3/31/02 ALL	4/1/02-3/31/03 ALL	Type of Statement	0-1MM	1-3MM	3-5MM	5-10MM	10-25MM	25MM & OVER
9	11	9	Unqualified				2	2	5
1	3	7	Reviewed			1	4	1	1
4	4	4	Compiled	1.	1	1	1		
3	6	1	Tax Returns		1				
12	13	9	Other				1	4	4
					3 (4/1-9/30/02)			27 (10/1/02-3/31/03)	
29	37	30	**NUMBER OF STATEMENTS**	1	2	2	8	7	10
%	%	%	**ASSETS**	%	%	%	%	%	%
10.0	11.0	11.2	Cash & Equivalents						13.1
8.8	7.7	7.0	Trade Receivables (net)						8.2
11.5	13.3	10.0	Inventory						8.5
3.5	2.2	1.1	All Other Current						1.6
33.8	34.3	29.3	Total Current						31.4
49.4	52.8	58.9	Fixed Assets (net)						45.9
8.0	8.0	8.8	Intangibles (net)						19.7
8.8	5.0	2.9	All Other Non-Current						3.0
100.0	100.0	100.0	Total						100.0
			LIABILITIES						
3.3	3.4	2.4	Notes Payable-Short Term						2.4
3.9	4.5	4.1	Cur. Mat.-L/T/D						3.5
8.6	10.4	7.5	Trade Payables						7.1
.0	.2	.5	Income Taxes Payable						.4
7.1	6.5	10.7	All Other Current						10.7
22.8	25.1	25.2	Total Current						24.1
27.1	30.8	26.6	Long Term Debt						17.0
.5	.4	.6	Deferred Taxes						.4
5.9	6.6	5.0	All Other Non-Current						7.4
43.6	37.0	42.6	Net Worth						51.2
100.0	100.0	100.0	Total Liabilities & Net Worth						100.0
			INCOME DATA						
100.0	100.0	100.0	Net Sales						100.0
38.4	36.7	40.3	Gross Profit						32.8
32.1	32.5	35.1	Operating Expenses						25.8
6.2	4.2	5.1	Operating Profit						7.0
2.1	1.6	2.0	All Other Expenses (net)						1.4
4.1	2.6	3.1	Profit Before Taxes						5.6
			RATIOS						
2.8 1.6 .7	2.3 1.2 .8	2.3 1.5 .6	Current						2.3 1.5 .6
1.6 .7 .3	1.4 .6 .3	1.5 .9 .3	Quick						1.8 .8 .3
3 105.7 23 15.9 35 10.5	5 70.5 17 21.3 32 11.5	5 76.1 21 17.3 28 12.9	Sales/Receivables						3 117.0 17 21.3 27 13.5
23 15.9 32 11.3 58 6.3	27 13.3 41 9.0 62 5.9	22 16.2 39 9.2 57 6.4	Cost of Sales/Inventory						15 24.0 22 16.8 35 10.4
16 23.0 28 12.9 45 8.1	23 15.6 29 12.6 50 7.4	17 21.5 28 13.1 44 8.3	Cost of Sales/Payables						14 26.6 20 18.1 37 9.8
6.5 32.6 −18.6	6.7 46.2 −24.5	7.7 15.9 −17.6	Sales/Working Capital						7.9 19.8 −25.5
(24) 6.2 3.3 .6	(35) 7.8 1.9 .7	(29) 9.8 2.2 .7	EBIT/Interest						
			Net Profit + Depr., Dep., Amort./Cur. Mat. L/T/D						
.7 1.6 3.3	.8 2.1 6.9	1.2 1.8 3.9	Fixed/Worth						.9 1.9 −16.6
.6 2.0 5.3	.7 2.3 8.9	.9 1.8 4.5	Debt/Worth						.3 1.9 −143.9
(26) 45.1 22.4 −5.2	(32) 33.9 18.1 −3.9	(26) 40.1 8.6 .9	% Profit Before Taxes/Tangible Net Worth						
17.5 5.9 −2.0	10.5 4.8 −2.0	13.6 3.1 −.2	% Profit Before Taxes/Total Assets						15.9 4.6 .0
8.8 2.2 1.4	6.0 3.0 1.4	3.8 1.6 1.2	Sales/Net Fixed Assets						13.5 5.3 1.2
2.4 1.5 .9	2.3 1.4 1.0	1.9 1.1 .9	Sales/Total Assets						3.8 1.4 .9
(25) 1.8 4.1 8.1	2.0 4.4 7.2	(28) 2.9 6.0 8.4	% Depr., Dep., Amort./Sales						
			% Officers', Directors', Owners' Comp/Sales						
786033M	805582M	853511M	Net Sales ($)	744M	4127M	6735M	58187M	109571M	674147M
634589M	570553M	663911M	Total Assets ($)	915M	3824M	7726M	48427M	93152M	509867M

M = $ thousand   MM = $ million
See Pages 11 through 18 for Explanation of Ratios and Data

Current Data Sorted By Assets   Comparative Historical Data

						Type of Statement	17	19
		3	10	4	4	Unqualified	17	19
	2	4	5	2		Reviewed	19	16
	3	3				Compiled	8	8
3	2					Tax Returns	2	5
1	4	14	12	8	3	Other	20	27
	21 (4/1-9/30/02)		66 (10/1/02-3/31/03)				4/1/98-3/31/99	4/1/99-3/31/00
0-500M	500M-2MM	2-10MM	10-50MM	50-100MM	100-250MM		ALL	ALL
4	11	24	27	14	7	NUMBER OF STATEMENTS	66	75
%	%	%	%	%	%	**ASSETS**	%	%
	2.6	5.4	3.5	2.2		Cash & Equivalents	3.6	4.1
	8.6	8.4	6.8	12.4		Trade Receivables (net)	8.4	7.8
	53.8	46.4	39.1	36.3		Inventory	44.8	42.2
	.3	1.8	2.3	3.1		All Other Current	2.3	3.3
	65.2	62.0	51.7	54.0		Total Current	59.2	57.4
	20.2	32.3	45.7	39.4		Fixed Assets (net)	33.5	35.2
	2.6	1.4	1.0	1.0		Intangibles (net)	2.0	2.1
	12.0	4.2	1.7	5.6		All Other Non-Current	5.3	5.2
	100.0	100.0	100.0	100.0		Total	100.0	100.0
						LIABILITIES		
	6.9	14.6	13.8	21.0		Notes Payable-Short Term	12.2	17.0
	1.5	2.0	1.9	3.2		Cur. Mat.-L/T/D	2.3	1.9
	8.1	9.3	4.0	11.0		Trade Payables	9.4	8.4
	.2	.1	.1	.5		Income Taxes Payable	.2	.1
	5.7	8.4	6.0	4.2		All Other Current	4.0	4.5
	22.4	34.5	25.9	39.9		Total Current	28.0	31.9
	26.6	21.8	22.1	17.3		Long Term Debt	19.6	22.6
	.0	.6	1.0	.6		Deferred Taxes	.5	.4
	6.9	7.4	5.0	1.9		All Other Non-Current	6.4	10.8
	44.1	35.8	46.0	40.3		Net Worth	45.4	34.2
	100.0	100.0	100.0	100.0		Total Liabilities & Net Worth	100.0	100.0
						INCOME DATA		
	100.0	100.0	100.0	100.0		Net Sales	100.0	100.0
	54.1	42.7	48.3	35.1		Gross Profit	46.8	47.2
	41.3	39.3	37.9	23.3		Operating Expenses	29.9	32.4
	12.8	3.5	10.4	11.8		Operating Profit	17.0	14.8
	2.8	5.9	7.8	-3.9		All Other Expenses (net)	2.6	4.8
	10.0	-2.5	2.6	15.7		Profit Before Taxes	14.4	10.0
						RATIOS		
	5.8	3.6	3.2	2.1			4.2	3.0
	3.1	2.0	2.5	1.4		Current	2.1	1.9
	2.0	1.2	1.4	1.0			1.4	1.3
	.6	.8	.7	.7			.7	.6
	.5	.3	.4	.4		Quick	.4	.3
	.4	.2	.2	.2			.2	.2
	9 39.3	27 13.6	32 11.3	35 10.3			20 17.9	21 17.2
	27 13.5	34 10.7	47 7.7	45 8.2		Sales/Receivables	33 10.9	38 9.5
	54 6.7	41 8.9	65 5.6	62 5.9			51 7.1	52 7.0
	269 1.4	131 2.8	328 1.1	120 3.0			257 1.4	248 1.5
	384 1.0	501 .7	679 .5	297 1.2		Cost of Sales/Inventory	441 .8	450 .8
	634 .6	704 .5	956 .4	581 .6			673 .5	575 .6
	26 14.1	29 12.7	17 21.4	47 7.7			29 12.7	22 16.3
	69 5.3	50 7.3	34 10.8	86 4.2		Cost of Sales/Payables	58 6.3	58 6.3
	115 3.2	109 3.3	70 5.2	111 3.3			96 3.8	111 3.3
	1.6	1.4	1.0	1.4			1.6	1.6
	2.4	3.2	2.0	6.7		Sales/Working Capital	2.8	3.0
	3.4	13.5	4.0	-268.8			7.0	7.1
	10.6	4.6	4.8	9.2			8.1	6.3
	6.7	(22) 1.8	(25) 1.7	4.7		EBIT/Interest	(62) 4.5	(65) 4.0
	2.1	-.6	.2	2.9			2.4	1.6
			3.3			Net Profit + Depr., Dep.,	11.3	6.7
			(12) 1.5			Amort./Cur. Mat. L./T/D	(32) 6.0	(26) 4.7
			-1.5				1.9	1.8
	.1	.2	.7	.4			.4	.4
	.5	.6	1.0	.8		Fixed/Worth	.8	.8
	1.4	1.7	1.7	2.0			1.6	2.0
	.6	.6	.5	.8			.5	.7
	1.6	1.7	1.3	1.3		Debt/Worth	1.2	1.6
	2.6	3.9	2.3	2.7			2.8	4.0
	28.7	21.1	13.2	38.7		% Profit Before Taxes/Tangible	39.3	30.2
	(10) 19.5	(20) 9.2	(26) 3.2	27.0		Net Worth	(62) 21.9	(67) 17.8
	10.4	-5.0	-3.5	10.4			10.7	10.7
	14.7	6.8	6.5	12.0		% Profit Before Taxes/Total	16.4	13.0
	6.2	2.3	1.0	8.0		Assets	8.7	7.5
	5.7	-5.3	-3.5	2.3			4.6	2.5
	17.0	9.0	2.3	3.0			4.8	5.0
	8.9	2.7	1.2	1.3		Sales/Net Fixed Assets	2.5	2.8
	3.0	1.3	.5	1.0			1.7	1.3
	1.3	1.0	.7	.9			1.1	1.0
	.9	.6	.5	.7		Sales/Total Assets	.8	.7
	.7	.4	.3	.4			.6	.5
	1.6	1.5	4.9	.8			2.8	2.3
	(10) 3.4	(20) 5.3	(24) 9.1	(12) 6.7		% Depr., Dep., Amort./Sales	(59) 4.2	(67) 4.1
	6.3	9.0	12.8	8.6			6.0	7.2
								2.6
						% Officers', Directors',	(10)	5.3
						Owners' Comp/Sales		14.9
2355M	16841M	103325M	347717M	786079M	714313M	Net Sales ($)	2053687M	1892574M
1016M	16121M	122621M	632067M	951628M	1095509M	Total Assets ($)	1819186M	1933673M

M = $ thousand   MM = $ million
See Pages 11 through 18 for Explanation of Ratios and Data

Comparative Historical Data / Current Data Sorted By Sales

Current Data Sorted By Sales groupings: 21 (4/1-9/30/02) covers 0-1MM, 1-3MM, 3-5MM; 66 (10/1/02-3/31/03) covers 5-10MM, 10-25MM, 25MM & OVER.

4/1/00-3/31/01 ALL	4/1/01-3/31/02 ALL	4/1/02-3/31/03 ALL		0-1MM	1-3MM	3-5MM	5-10MM	10-25MM	25MM & OVER
			Type of Statement						
15	9	21	Unqualified			2	4	6	9
18	13	13	Reviewed	1	4	2	1	3	2
8	12	6	Compiled	1	4	1			
2	3	5	Tax Returns	4	1				
35	31	42	Other	1	11	6	8	8	8
78	68	87	**NUMBER OF STATEMENTS**	7	20	11	13	17	19
%	%	%	**ASSETS**	%	%	%	%	%	%
3.6	3.3	3.6	Cash & Equivalents		1.5	5.9	5.0	3.2	3.9
9.5	8.3	8.3	Trade Receivables (net)		7.0	6.8	7.9	6.8	13.9
46.4	47.6	43.2	Inventory		47.4	45.2	35.9	44.5	36.0
2.0	1.9	2.0	All Other Current		1.7	.6	3.4	3.1	1.7
61.6	61.0	57.1	Total Current		57.5	58.5	52.3	57.5	55.5
32.4	33.1	35.7	Fixed Assets (net)		35.0	40.2	44.8	34.6	36.2
2.3	2.9	1.5	Intangibles (net)		1.9	.1	1.2	.5	2.4
3.7	3.0	5.7	All Other Non-Current		5.6	1.2	1.7	7.3	5.8
100.0	100.0	100.0	Total		100.0	100.0	100.0	100.0	100.0
			LIABILITIES						
17.1	13.6	13.4	Notes Payable-Short Term		13.7	7.4	15.5	16.9	15.7
2.1	2.4	2.2	Cur. Mat.-L/T/D		1.6	2.3	1.8	1.9	3.5
7.6	6.5	8.2	Trade Payables		12.2	5.4	5.4	5.6	10.0
.3	.2	.2	Income Taxes Payable		.3	.0	.2	.0	.4
5.5	6.9	6.1	All Other Current		6.8	8.5	8.0	4.4	5.4
32.6	29.7	30.1	Total Current		34.5	23.6	31.0	28.9	34.9
18.9	21.8	23.9	Long Term Debt		23.1	22.2	27.9	14.3	18.6
.5	.5	.6	Deferred Taxes		.6	.3	.9	1.1	.2
3.8	5.3	6.2	All Other Non-Current		6.8	13.7	5.5	2.4	3.5
44.1	42.6	39.2	Net Worth		35.0	40.3	34.8	53.3	42.7
100.0	100.0	100.0	Total Liabilities & Net Worth		100.0	100.0	100.0	100.0	100.0
			INCOME DATA						
100.0	100.0	100.0	Net Sales		100.0	100.0	100.0	100.0	100.0
47.7	47.7	44.9	Gross Profit		47.8	46.4	46.9	40.7	35.3
31.4	33.2	36.7	Operating Expenses		42.2	39.7	37.2	32.2	23.3
16.2	14.6	8.2	Operating Profit		5.6	6.7	9.7	8.5	12.0
3.3	5.7	4.2	All Other Expenses (net)		7.2	5.8	7.5	2.8	-.8
13.0	8.9	4.0	Profit Before Taxes		-1.6	.9	2.2	5.7	12.8
			RATIOS						
3.2	3.7	3.2			3.8	5.4	2.6	3.2	2.7
2.1	2.2	2.0	Current		2.4	2.0	1.8	2.6	1.6
1.4	1.4	1.3			1.3	1.4	1.2	1.4	1.0
.6	.7	.7			.5	3.4	.6	.9	.8
.4	.3	.4	Quick		.3	.4	.3	.5	.4
.2	.2	.2			.2	.2	.2	.2	.3
25 14.7	23 15.8	27 13.3			25 14.6	25 14.7	32 11.5	30 12.3	35 10.3
43 8.5	36 10.1	38 9.5	Sales/Receivables		37 9.8	33 11.1	41 8.9	41 8.8	41 8.8
60 6.0	51 7.1	54 6.7			55 6.7	52 7.0	60 6.1	53 6.9	69 5.3
295 1.2	301 1.2	230 1.6			280 1.3	76 4.8	150 2.4	296 1.2	150 2.4
467 .8	515 .7	443 .8	Cost of Sales/Inventory		463 .8	610 .6	580 .6	523 .7	230 1.6
670 .5	813 .4	761 .5			742 .5	863 .4	982 .4	904 .4	323 1.1
24 14.9	19 19.0	26 14.1			34 10.9	20 18.2	23 16.2	32 11.5	24 15.2
49 7.4	46 8.0	51 7.1	Cost of Sales/Payables		74 4.9	25 14.3	50 7.3	47 7.8	56 6.5
117 3.1	81 4.5	108 3.4			137 2.7	51 7.1	108 3.4	87 4.2	110 3.3
1.5	1.4	1.3			1.1	1.7	1.0	1.2	2.5
2.6	2.4	2.5	Sales/Working Capital		2.2	2.4	2.0	1.9	6.1
5.0	5.4	6.1			5.8	3.6	10.6	4.4	55.3
(75) 8.4	(66) 4.5	(81) 6.8			(17) 5.4	7.9	(11) 2.0	9.7	10.9
2.9	2.9	2.3	EBIT/Interest		2.1	1.7	1.7	1.7	4.9
1.7	1.1	1.0			-.4	-.3	1.2	-.5	2.8
(32) 8.1	(20) 5.3	(34) 4.0							(12) 5.1
3.8	3.4	2.7	Net Profit + Depr., Dep., Amort./Cur. Mat. L/T/D						2.9
1.8	2.5	1.1							1.4
.5	.4	.4			.2	.5	.7	.5	.5
.7	.8	.9	Fixed/Worth		.9	1.2	1.0	.9	.9
1.6	1.6	1.6			1.7	2.5	2.7	1.0	2.0
.5	.6	.7			.8	.5	1.0	.4	.7
1.2	1.3	1.3	Debt/Worth		1.6	1.6	2.3	.7	1.3
2.7	2.5	2.9			3.1	1.8	4.2	1.8	2.8
(71) 32.8	(61) 27.0	(79) 24.9			(17) 28.2	(10) 14.4	(12) 9.3	(16) 19.6	39.7
16.1	12.7	10.5	% Profit Before Taxes/Tangible Net Worth		10.9	7.6	3.2	9.0	25.4
7.9	2.1	.7			-6.4	-3.8	.9	-5.0	6.9
15.6	10.4	8.8			7.8	7.3	2.8	9.4	13.7
6.8	5.4	3.0	% Profit Before Taxes/Total Assets		2.2	2.6	1.5	1.8	8.6
2.6	.5	-1.0			-8.0	-5.1	.5	-4.3	3.0
5.9	5.3	5.8			15.5	9.4	2.9	2.8	3.7
2.7	2.5	2.2	Sales/Net Fixed Assets		2.7	2.2	1.3	1.3	2.0
1.4	1.3	1.1			.9	.5	.5	1.0	1.2
1.0	1.0	.9			1.1	1.5	.9	.7	1.2
.7	.7	.6	Sales/Total Assets		.6	.6	.5	.5	.8
.6	.5	.4			.4	.3	.3	.5	.7
(70) 2.4	(62) 3.4	(76) 2.5			(16) 1.6	(10) 1.2	(12) 4.9	(15) 4.1	(18) 1.1
4.6	5.3	5.8	% Depr., Dep., Amort./Sales		4.2	4.8	7.9	6.5	5.8
6.6	8.9	10.1			9.6	11.2	14.3	10.9	8.6
	(12) 2.0	(12) 2.5	% Officers', Directors', Owners' Comp/Sales						
	5.6	4.7							
	8.0	6.5							
2143629M	1276105M	1970630M	Net Sales ($)	3764M	36622M	41427M	88572M	281576M	1518669M
1897871M	1613096M	2818962M	Total Assets ($)	5423M	97606M	86202M	218613M	632188M	1778930M

© RMA 2003

M = $ thousand   MM = $ million

See Pages 11 through 18 for Explanation of Ratios and Data

Current Data Sorted By Assets | Comparative Historical Data

	1	1	3	5			Type of Statement				
			3	1			Unqualified		22		18
		1	2				Reviewed		4		4
1			1				Compiled		5		2
			1	5	3	1	Tax Returns				
							Other		10		11
	7 (4/1-9/30/02)			21 (10/1/02-3/31/03)					4/1/98-		4/1/99-
									3/31/99		3/31/00
0-500M	500M-2MM	2-10MM	10-50MM	50-100MM	100-250MM				ALL		ALL
1	2	10	11	3	1	NUMBER OF STATEMENTS			41		35
%	%	%	%	%	%	ASSETS			%		%
		12.8	5.8			Cash & Equivalents			5.5		4.4
		19.5	21.0			Trade Receivables (net)			20.6		21.6
		17.3	16.0			Inventory			20.5		17.6
		4.3	3.5			All Other Current			2.2		2.1
		53.9	46.3			Total Current			48.8		45.7
		39.2	41.6			Fixed Assets (net)			45.5		47.4
		.0	.0			Intangibles (net)			.9		1.0
		6.9	12.1			All Other Non-Current			4.8		5.9
		100.0	100.0			Total			100.0		100.0
						LIABILITIES					
		2.3	11.9			Notes Payable-Short Term			7.3		6.7
		4.2	2.6			Cur. Mat.-L/T/D			4.0		4.7
		17.4	14.9			Trade Payables			15.0		12.9
		.0	.6			Income Taxes Payable			.1		.2
		4.3	5.3			All Other Current			7.9		4.8
		28.2	35.2			Total Current			34.5		29.3
		21.1	14.8			Long Term Debt			27.8		29.2
		.0	1.6			Deferred Taxes			1.5		1.6
		.8	6.0			All Other Non-Current			5.4		5.4
		49.9	42.3			Net Worth			30.8		34.5
		100.0	100.0			Total Liabilities & Net Worth			100.0		100.0
						INCOME DATA					
		100.0	100.0			Net Sales			100.0		100.0
		16.0	9.4			Gross Profit			13.3		13.8
		14.6	11.0			Operating Expenses			10.5		9.3
		1.4	-1.6			Operating Profit			2.9		4.4
		-1.9	1.1			All Other Expenses (net)			1.9		1.9
		3.3	-2.7			Profit Before Taxes			1.0		2.6
						RATIOS					
		4.4	3.1						2.7		2.3
		1.8	1.3			Current			1.6		1.6
		1.4	1.0						1.2		1.2
		2.9	1.2						1.3		1.6
		1.0	.6			Quick			.9		.8
		.2	.4						.6		.6
	6	62.0	28	13.2				27	13.4	33	11.0
	34	10.7	48	7.6		Sales/Receivables		39	9.3	43	8.4
	46	7.9	71	5.2				49	7.4	50	7.3
	0	UND	27	13.3				26	14.1	18	20.7
	29	12.5	42	8.7		Cost of Sales/Inventory		42	8.6	40	9.0
	70	5.2	63	5.8				57	6.4	63	5.8
	6	60.2	14	26.1				13	28.7	14	25.8
	15	24.1	24	15.0		Cost of Sales/Payables		26	14.0	29	12.7
	56	6.6	48	7.6				47	7.8	48	7.6
		5.1	5.1						5.6		5.4
		13.3	13.4			Sales/Working Capital			11.4		12.4
		16.2	134.5						23.5		24.6
		13.1	2.6						4.5		3.9
		5.9	(10) -.6			EBIT/Interest		(39)	2.3	(33)	1.5
		-.6	-4.6						1.0		.5
						Net Profit + Depr., Dep.,			10.7		2.2
						Amort./Cur. Mat. L./T/D		(17) 2.7		(13) 1.3	
									1.6		.5
		.2	.8						.7		.7
		.7	.9			Fixed/Worth			1.3		1.1
		1.4	1.1						3.8		4.0
		.5	.5						1.0		.8
		1.2	2.2			Debt/Worth			2.7		2.0
		2.2	2.4						5.1		5.0
		49.8	14.3			% Profit Before Taxes/Tangible			36.8		25.9
		22.2	(10) 3.3			Net Worth		(36)	19.8	(32)	13.3
		-6.7	-8.2						6.7		-3.9
		20.8	3.8			% Profit Before Taxes/Total			11.2		7.3
		8.5	.9			Assets			5.2		2.5
		-3.0	-11.5						.4		-2.6
		77.5	4.5						9.4		7.0
		6.5	3.2			Sales/Net Fixed Assets			3.9		3.4
		1.7	2.3						2.5		2.0
		2.9	2.0						2.3		2.1
		2.1	1.2			Sales/Total Assets			1.8		1.8
		1.2	1.1						1.3		1.2
			2.0						2.3		2.1
			6.4			% Depr., Dep., Amort./Sales		(38)	3.8	(28)	3.8
			6.9						5.9		6.3
						% Officers', Directors',					
						Owners' Comp/Sales					
1524M	10732M	106510M	439198M	326165M	272698M	Net Sales ($)			1973514M		2023454M
292M	3547M	54317M	306023M	186017M	214837M	Total Assets ($)			1234763M		1438332M

Comparative Historical Data / Current Data Sorted By Sales

4/1/00-3/31/01 ALL	4/1/01-3/31/02 ALL	4/1/02-3/31/03 ALL		0-1MM	1-3MM	3-5MM	5-10MM	10-25MM	25MM & OVER
			Type of Statement						
14	3	9	Unqualified				2	2	5
2	1	4	Reviewed		1		1	2	
6	5	3	Compiled		1		2		
1	1	2	Tax Returns		1			1	
13	10	10	Other					2	8
				7 (4/1-9/30/02)			21 (10/1/02-3/31/03)		
36	20	28	**NUMBER OF STATEMENTS**		3		5	7	13
%	%	%	**ASSETS**	%	%	%	%	%	%
4.1	5.5	8.0	Cash & Equivalents	DATA NOT AVAILABLE		DATA NOT AVAILABLE			5.3
19.5	17.9	20.6	Trade Receivables (net)						21.6
20.9	30.3	20.1	Inventory						16.7
2.6	2.0	3.7	All Other Current						2.4
47.0	55.7	52.3	Total Current						46.0
46.3	38.1	39.0	Fixed Assets (net)						45.1
.7	.4	.2	Intangibles (net)						.5
6.0	5.8	8.4	All Other Non-Current						8.4
100.0	100.0	100.0	Total						100.0
			LIABILITIES						
9.4	16.6	9.2	Notes Payable-Short Term						13.4
5.3	4.2	4.1	Cur. Mat.-L/T/D						5.4
11.4	12.2	18.3	Trade Payables						15.6
.7	1.0	.5	Income Taxes Payable						1.0
4.3	7.6	4.1	All Other Current						2.6
31.1	41.6	36.2	Total Current						38.1
24.7	22.6	16.8	Long Term Debt						14.2
1.4	1.5	.9	Deferred Taxes						1.8
5.6	1.4	4.4	All Other Non-Current						3.9
37.3	32.9	41.7	Net Worth						42.0
100.0	100.0	100.0	Total Liabilities & Net Worth						100.0
			INCOME DATA						
100.0	100.0	100.0	Net Sales						100.0
16.0	10.5	13.2	Gross Profit						9.2
14.0	11.0	11.9	Operating Expenses						7.6
2.0	-.5	1.3	Operating Profit						1.5
1.8	3.7	.0	All Other Expenses (net)						1.0
.2	-4.2	1.4	Profit Before Taxes						.6
			RATIOS						
3.1	3.0	2.4							2.3
1.7	1.7	1.4	Current						1.2
1.2	1.0	1.1							.8
1.5	1.4	1.2							1.2
.7	.6	.6	Quick						.6
.4	.3	.4							.4
29 12.4	**27** 13.6	**27** 13.7							**30** 12.1
37 10.0	**37** 9.8	**36** 10.2	Sales/Receivables						**45** 8.1
49 7.5	**54** 6.7	**49** 7.4							**68** 5.4
23 16.0	**42** 8.7	**24** 15.1							**19** 19.0
52 7.0	**53** 6.9	**39** 9.4	Cost of Sales/Inventory						**42** 8.7
64 5.7	**92** 4.0	**65** 5.7							**64** 5.7
16 22.4	**14** 27.0	**13** 29.1							**17** 21.7
24 15.1	**21** 17.1	**25** 14.5	Cost of Sales/Payables						**26** 13.9
37 9.9	**34** 10.7	**49** 7.4							**49** 7.5
5.4	4.5	6.7							7.0
10.6	10.3	13.8	Sales/Working Capital						24.7
21.8	NM	29.8							-44.6
3.1	2.6	10.1							3.4
(32) 1.2	(17) .2	(27) 1.8	EBIT/Interest						(12) 1.4
-.9	-3.1	-2.6							-1.9
2.1									
(11) 1.3			Net Profit + Depr., Dep., Amort./Cur. Mat. L/T/D						
.8									
.7	.5	.4							.7
1.1	.9	.8	Fixed/Worth						1.0
1.9	2.2	1.4							2.1
.7	.6	.6							.6
1.3	2.0	2.0	Debt/Worth						2.3
3.6	4.7	2.9							3.0
17.8	23.0	35.9							16.1
(33) 4.0	(18) -6.5	(26) 11.9	% Profit Before Taxes/Tangible Net Worth						(12) 5.2
-8.8	-31.9	-2.6							-1.6
5.0	7.9	10.5							5.6
1.4	-4.6	4.3	% Profit Before Taxes/Total Assets						1.9
-4.9	-10.9	-2.8							-2.2
6.3	14.3	9.1							4.7
3.7	3.3	4.0	Sales/Net Fixed Assets						3.2
2.4	2.2	2.3							2.3
2.4	2.0	2.2							2.0
1.7	1.5	1.7	Sales/Total Assets						1.4
1.3	1.2	1.2							1.1
2.1	.1	1.6							2.3
(34) 3.7	(18) 4.5	(26) 4.4	% Depr., Dep., Amort./Sales						(12) 5.3
5.8	5.8	6.9							7.1
			% Officers', Directors', Owners' Comp/Sales						
1555657M	1176923M	1156827M	Net Sales ($)		7041M		38288M	110216M	1001282M
1104182M	786133M	765033M	Total Assets ($)		5939M		22519M	64100M	672475M

M = $ thousand MM = $ million

See Pages 11 through 18 for Explanation of Ratios and Data

Current Data Sorted By Assets   Comparative Historical Data

0-500M	500M-2MM	2-10MM	10-50MM	50-100MM	100-250MM	Type of Statement	4/1/98-3/31/99 ALL	4/1/99-3/31/00 ALL
1	1	11	16	3	4	Unqualified	53	38
1	2	11	2	1		Reviewed	32	18
1	6	3	1			Compiled	11	8
1						Tax Returns	3	4
	1	8	9	1		Other	36	31
	16 (4/1-9/30/02)		67 (10/1/02-3/31/03)					
3	10	33	28	5	4	NUMBER OF STATEMENTS	135	99
%	%	%	%	%	%	ASSETS	%	%
	8.1	6.6	6.2			Cash & Equivalents	6.5	7.8
	29.8	28.1	23.5			Trade Receivables (net)	23.5	22.9
	29.1	28.3	23.8			Inventory	26.5	23.5
	7.3	1.1	3.1			All Other Current	2.5	2.4
	74.2	64.0	56.6			Total Current	59.0	56.7
	15.2	28.4	37.7			Fixed Assets (net)	33.4	35.4
	1.4	.4	.4			Intangibles (net)	2.2	2.3
	9.1	7.2	5.3			All Other Non-Current	5.4	5.6
	100.0	100.0	100.0			Total	100.0	100.0
						LIABILITIES		
	15.5	11.4	7.4			Notes Payable-Short Term	8.5	11.0
	4.7	3.2	4.0			Cur. Mat.-L/T/D	3.9	3.9
	22.8	19.4	13.3			Trade Payables	12.0	12.3
	.0	.2	.1			Income Taxes Payable	.4	.6
	5.4	6.2	6.3			All Other Current	7.9	9.9
	48.4	40.5	31.1			Total Current	32.6	37.7
	10.0	13.0	16.7			Long Term Debt	20.6	19.2
	.0	.4	2.0			Deferred Taxes	1.3	1.2
	1.2	6.2	6.7			All Other Non-Current	4.1	5.1
	40.4	39.9	43.5			Net Worth	41.4	36.8
	100.0	100.0	100.0			Total Liabilities & Net Worth	100.0	100.0
						INCOME DATA		
	100.0	100.0	100.0			Net Sales	100.0	100.0
	32.7	27.5	16.9			Gross Profit	24.9	21.1
	28.6	22.1	14.2			Operating Expenses	20.7	17.5
	4.1	5.5	2.7			Operating Profit	4.2	3.7
	.8	1.9	1.0			All Other Expenses (net)	1.7	1.8
	3.3	3.6	1.7			Profit Before Taxes	2.5	1.8

RATIOS

0-500M	500M-2MM	2-10MM	10-50MM	50-100MM	100-250MM	Ratio	4/1/98-3/31/99 ALL	4/1/99-3/31/00 ALL
	2.9	2.5	2.8			Current	3.6	2.6
	1.2	1.6	2.0				1.8	1.7
	1.1	1.1	1.2				1.2	1.2
	1.0	1.3	1.3			Quick	1.7	1.4
	.7	.8	.9				(134) 1.0	.9
	.3	.5	.6				.6	.5
9 39.4	29 12.5	32 11.3				Sales/Receivables	36 10.2	34 10.7
37 9.8	46 8.0	45 8.1					47 7.7	47 7.8
63 5.8	66 5.5	64 5.7					62 5.9	60 6.1
19 19.0	37 9.8	38 9.5				Cost of Sales/Inventory	40 9.2	43 8.5
50 7.3	66 5.6	56 6.5					67 5.4	66 5.5
91 4.0	89 4.1	92 4.0					107 3.4	94 3.9
21 17.1	18 19.9	15 24.6				Cost of Sales/Payables	16 23.1	16 23.3
32 11.5	37 9.9	24 15.0					25 14.7	28 13.1
59 6.2	58 6.3	49 7.4					37 9.8	41 9.0
	4.3	5.6	4.7			Sales/Working Capital	3.8	4.4
	20.6	11.1	6.6				6.9	7.8
	143.2	31.4	16.0				20.5	24.9
		22.3	5.8			EBIT/Interest	6.6	5.3
	(26)	6.1	(26) 2.6				(122) 2.6	(89) 2.3
		1.3	.9				1.3	.8
			2.5			Net Profit + Depr., Dep., Amort./Cur. Mat. L/T/D	4.3	7.2
			(10) 2.2				(55) 2.3	(31) 2.3
			1.7				1.4	1.0
	.0	.2	.3			Fixed/Worth	.4	.4
	.2	.6	1.0				.8	.9
	2.1	1.1	2.1				1.4	2.1
	.5	.5	.6			Debt/Worth	.6	.6
	1.1	1.3	1.5				1.4	1.8
	8.2	2.5	3.0				3.3	4.7
		47.4	35.9			% Profit Before Taxes/Tangible Net Worth	29.6	22.0
		(30) 32.0	9.8				(127) 14.8	(90) 9.8
		6.2	-2.9				5.0	-1.1
	23.7	20.9	9.3			% Profit Before Taxes/Total Assets	13.0	8.0
	17.7	9.9	2.9				5.9	4.4
	-5.4	.8	-1.1				1.6	-1.5
	366.8	95.3	8.7			Sales/Net Fixed Assets	11.9	11.2
	36.7	6.6	4.9				5.6	4.2
	9.5	4.1	2.8				3.2	2.5
	4.8	2.9	2.2			Sales/Total Assets	2.3	2.3
	2.9	2.2	1.8				1.8	1.5
	2.0	1.4	1.2				1.3	1.2
		.7	2.3			% Depr., Dep., Amort./Sales	1.5	1.6
		(28) 2.2	(25) 3.6				(117) 3.2	(84) 3.5
		4.6	6.2				4.5	5.8
		2.2				% Officers', Directors', Owners' Comp/Sales	2.0	2.2
		(15) 4.5					(32) 3.8	(17) 3.1
		7.0					6.4	5.7
4756M	43220M	393697M	1170136M	441075M	951259M	Net Sales ($)	6291587M	4639231M
627M	12734M	175495M	663539M	309098M	559088M	Total Assets ($)	4400473M	3198028M

M = $ thousand   MM = $ million
See Pages 11 through 18 for Explanation of Ratios and Data

Comparative Historical Data | **Current Data Sorted By Sales**

Hist 4/1/00-3/31/01 ALL	Hist 4/1/01-3/31/02 ALL	Hist 4/1/02-3/31/03 ALL	Type of Statement	0-1MM	1-3MM	3-5MM	5-10MM	10-25MM	25MM & OVER
32	17	35	Unqualified			2	4	9	20
18	11	17	Reviewed	1	1	1	5	6	3
11	22	11	Compiled	1	2	2	3	2	1
4	1	1	Tax Returns			1			
29	28	19	Other	1	1		5	5	7
				16 (4/1-9/30/02)			67 (10/1/02-3/31/03)		
94	79	83	**NUMBER OF STATEMENTS**	2	5	6	17	22	31
%	%	%	**ASSETS**	%	%	%	%	%	%
4.7	5.1	6.7	Cash & Equivalents				6.7	4.1	8.1
26.4	21.9	26.8	Trade Receivables (net)				20.7	29.9	25.7
25.7	26.2	26.3	Inventory				24.3	29.2	24.8
2.8	3.0	2.5	All Other Current				4.9	1.5	2.8
59.5	56.2	62.3	Total Current				56.6	64.8	61.3
32.4	37.3	30.9	Fixed Assets (net)				31.2	31.1	33.8
2.4	1.6	.6	Intangibles (net)				.6	.2	.8
5.7	4.8	6.2	All Other Non-Current				11.6	3.9	4.1
100.0	100.0	100.0	Total				100.0	100.0	100.0
			LIABILITIES						
9.5	10.0	10.9	Notes Payable-Short Term				9.0	14.3	7.6
3.4	4.2	3.4	Cur. Mat.-L/T/D				3.8	2.0	3.2
14.0	13.9	16.4	Trade Payables				11.8	24.6	11.9
.2	.2	.1	Income Taxes Payable				.0	.2	.1
7.7	6.9	6.2	All Other Current				5.1	6.1	6.8
34.8	35.1	36.9	Total Current				29.7	47.2	29.5
17.9	17.8	13.9	Long Term Debt				10.7	15.5	13.8
1.0	1.0	1.1	Deferred Taxes				.6	1.6	1.5
4.7	4.2	4.9	All Other Non-Current				6.2	6.9	4.5
41.7	41.8	43.2	Net Worth				52.8	28.8	50.6
100.0	100.0	100.0	Total Liabilities & Net Worth				100.0	100.0	100.0
			INCOME DATA						
100.0	100.0	100.0	Net Sales				100.0	100.0	100.0
24.5	22.3	23.5	Gross Profit				30.8	18.6	19.0
19.6	20.6	19.3	Operating Expenses				25.9	15.6	14.6
4.9	1.7	4.2	Operating Profit				4.9	3.0	4.3
2.2	2.1	1.4	All Other Expenses (net)				2.4	.9	1.2
2.6	-.5	2.8	Profit Before Taxes				2.5	2.1	3.1
			RATIOS						
3.0	2.9	2.5	Current				2.4	2.3	3.5
2.0	1.8	1.8					1.9	1.4	2.2
1.3	1.2	1.2					1.3	1.1	1.5
1.6	1.5	1.4	Quick				1.1	1.2	2.0
1.0	.8	.9					.8	.8	1.1
.6	.4	.6					.5	.5	.7
37 9.8	32 11.4	30 12.1	Sales/Receivables				24 15.0	30 12.3	33 11.2
46 7.9	45 8.1	44 8.2					41 9.0	45 8.2	44 8.2
60 6.1	54 6.7	64 5.7					64 5.7	60 6.1	66 5.5
37 9.9	48 7.7	38 9.7	Cost of Sales/Inventory				27 13.5	39 9.4	38 9.6
69 5.3	65 5.6	63 5.8					71 5.1	59 6.2	63 5.8
100 3.7	103 3.6	85 4.3					162 2.3	75 4.8	80 4.6
16 22.6	17 21.9	16 23.3	Cost of Sales/Payables				19 19.4	21 17.6	13 28.8
25 14.6	28 13.1	28 12.9					27 13.6	41 9.0	24 15.2
41 8.8	44 8.4	51 7.2					50 7.3	66 5.5	36 10.0
4.5	4.5	4.8	Sales/Working Capital				4.2	5.9	4.3
7.3	7.2	7.7					7.1	13.7	6.2
16.7	23.2	27.3					19.5	42.7	10.7
5.3	6.6	11.0	EBIT/Interest				(13) 16.8	(18) 8.2	(27) 10.7
(89) 2.1	(75) 1.7	(68) 3.2					5.8	2.4	3.2
1.1	-.9	1.0					1.8	.5	1.6
4.5	2.1	2.8	Net Profit + Depr., Dep., Amort./Cur. Mat. L/T/D						(10) 3.9
(35) 2.9	(24) 1.2	(23) 2.1							2.3
1.0	-.5	1.3							1.9
.5	.4	.2	Fixed/Worth				.2	.2	.3
.9	.8	.6					.6	.9	.7
1.5	2.0	1.3					1.2	1.3	1.5
.6	.4	.5	Debt/Worth				.4	.7	.4
1.3	1.3	1.3					1.2	1.6	1.1
3.8	3.5	2.4					1.8	7.8	2.1
28.4	28.6	38.7	% Profit Before Taxes/Tangible Net Worth				36.6	45.7	36.0
(84) 11.9	(73) 6.2	(79) 14.9					18.4	(20) 19.6	10.5
1.9	-6.7	.9					2.1	3.2	-2.1
11.8	7.6	14.4	% Profit Before Taxes/Total Assets				17.4	16.4	9.9
5.2	2.2	5.8					8.6	3.3	3.5
.5	-4.6	.0					.8	.3	-.8
13.7	11.1	27.7	Sales/Net Fixed Assets				59.1	125.6	9.3
4.6	4.0	5.6					4.8	6.9	5.0
3.3	2.4	3.6					3.3	3.4	3.3
2.4	2.3	2.8	Sales/Total Assets				2.6	3.2	2.7
1.8	1.6	1.9					1.7	1.9	1.8
1.2	1.1	1.4					1.2	1.3	1.4
1.2	.6	1.3	% Depr., Dep., Amort./Sales				(16) .3	(19) .6	(27) 2.1
(79) 3.3	(70) 3.0	(73) 2.8					3.5	2.1	3.6
5.5	5.6	5.3					7.4	4.7	5.4
2.2	1.2	2.2	% Officers', Directors', Owners' Comp/Sales						
(29) 3.8	(20) 3.2	(24) 4.0							
7.5	4.3	6.0							
5014873M	2601098M	3004143M	Net Sales ($)	755M	11708M	24284M	119613M	347657M	2500126M
3228664M	1924035M	1720581M	Total Assets ($)	520M	4229M	13303M	84012M	185666M	1432851M

M = $ thousand   MM = $ million
See Pages 11 through 18 for Explanation of Ratios and Data

Current Data Sorted By Assets   Comparative Historical Data

0-500M	500M-2MM	2-10MM	10-50MM	50-100MM	100-250MM		4/1/98-3/31/99 ALL	4/1/99-3/31/00 ALL
						Type of Statement		
		3	6			Unqualified	13	9
	5	7	1			Reviewed	12	9
		4	1			Compiled	6	8
1						Tax Returns	1	2
1	1	4	3		1	Other	14	7
1	6	18	11		1	**NUMBER OF STATEMENTS**	46	35
%	%	%	%	%	%	**ASSETS**	%	%
		7.2	8.4			Cash & Equivalents	5.5	5.5
		22.5	22.0			Trade Receivables (net)	25.4	26.2
		37.3	25.8			Inventory	31.4	29.1
		1.5	2.5			All Other Current	1.4	2.4
		68.5	58.8			Total Current	63.7	63.3
		19.5	20.0			Fixed Assets (net)	28.8	28.2
		3.9	14.7			Intangibles (net)	3.1	4.1
		8.0	6.5			All Other Non-Current	4.4	4.5
		100.0	100.0			Total	100.0	100.0
						LIABILITIES		
		11.3	5.1			Notes Payable-Short Term	12.3	10.9
		2.8	4.3			Cur. Mat.-L/T/D	2.2	2.7
		13.1	9.3			Trade Payables	14.6	14.2
		.4	.4			Income Taxes Payable	.5	.4
		10.5	12.6			All Other Current	7.3	7.3
		38.2	31.7			Total Current	36.7	35.4
		8.9	11.6			Long Term Debt	17.7	14.7
		.5	.9			Deferred Taxes	.7	1.0
		2.8	9.3			All Other Non-Current	5.2	9.0
		49.6	46.5			Net Worth	39.6	39.9
		100.0	100.0			Total Liabilities & Net Worth	100.0	100.0
						INCOME DATA		
		100.0	100.0			Net Sales	100.0	100.0
		24.4	25.8			Gross Profit	25.7	24.4
		20.3	18.6			Operating Expenses	20.8	19.1
		4.1	7.2			Operating Profit	4.9	5.3
		.7	.7			All Other Expenses (net)	1.5	1.8
		3.4	6.5			Profit Before Taxes	3.4	3.5
						RATIOS		
		3.0	3.8			Current	2.7	3.0
		1.9	1.6				1.6	1.8
		1.3	1.4				1.3	1.3
		1.2	2.2			Quick	1.1	1.3
		.8	.8				.8	.9
		.5	.7				.6	.6
		33 11.0	39 9.4			Sales/Receivables	35 10.4	37 9.9
		39 9.5	48 7.6				49 7.4	45 8.1
		47 7.8	61 6.0				57 6.4	54 6.7
		62 5.9	49 7.5			Cost of Sales/Inventory	37 9.8	34 10.9
		74 5.0	68 5.4				74 4.9	68 5.3
		125 2.9	97 3.8				154 2.4	92 4.0
		11 32.7	14 26.2			Cost of Sales/Payables	19 19.1	14 25.4
		27 13.4	20 18.1				31 11.8	27 13.6
		37 9.7	34 10.7				41 8.9	37 9.9
		4.4	5.7			Sales/Working Capital	3.9	4.3
		6.7	8.6				8.3	8.1
		14.0	16.0				16.5	16.7
		10.5	11.6			EBIT/Interest	6.1	8.3
		(16) 3.3	(10) 6.7				(43) 2.9	(33) 3.3
		1.5	1.4				1.2	1.1
						Net Profit + Depr., Dep., Amort./Cur. Mat. L /T/D	4.0	7.1
							(17) 2.1	(13) 2.9
							1.1	1.3
		.2	.1			Fixed/Worth	.3	.4
		.4	1.0				.7	.7
		.7	55.1				1.2	1.6
		.6	.5			Debt/Worth	.8	.8
		1.1	2.5				1.6	1.6
		3.9	132.9				3.7	3.7
		30.8				% Profit Before Taxes/Tangible Net Worth	37.6	35.1
		(17) 12.0					(44) 12.9	(32) 14.5
		2.2					4.6	.4
		11.4	20.1			% Profit Before Taxes/Total Assets	12.0	11.9
		4.5	11.7				5.7	6.6
		1.5	4.8				.9	.1
		46.6	32.2			Sales/Net Fixed Assets	16.1	17.5
		12.9	7.8				6.5	6.3
		5.1	5.6				4.2	4.6
		2.5	2.0			Sales/Total Assets	2.7	2.6
		2.1	1.7				1.8	1.9
		1.6	1.6				1.3	1.4
		1.0	1.3			% Depr., Dep., Amort./Sales	1.4	1.2
		(17) 1.9	(10) 4.0				(43) 2.5	(34) 2.5
		3.9	6.0				4.0	4.0
						% Officers', Directors', Owners' Comp/Sales	1.7	1.6
							(19) 4.4	(14) 2.7
							7.6	7.2
1664M	18687M	192941M	337140M	158419M		Net Sales ($)	1596577M	944378M
247M	8864M	91261M	201837M	118242M		Total Assets ($)	1182687M	627668M

(Columns 0-500M, 500M-2MM, 50-100MM, and 100-250MM are marked "DATA NOT AVAILABLE" across the Assets, Liabilities, and Income Data sections.)

M = $ thousand   MM = $ million
See Pages 11 through 18 for Explanation of Ratios and Data

Comparative Historical Data / Current Data Sorted By Sales

	4/1/00-3/31/01 ALL	4/1/01-3/31/02 ALL	4/1/02-3/31/03 ALL		0-1MM	1-3MM	3-5MM	5-10MM	10-25MM	25MM & OVER
Type of Statement										
Unqualified	5	3	9					2	4	3
Reviewed	4	7	13			3	3	5	2	
Compiled	13	11	5				1	1	3	
Tax Returns	1	2	1			1				
Other	5	5	9			1		1	6	1
Period						14 (4/1-9/30/02)		23 (10/1/02-3/31/03)		
NUMBER OF STATEMENTS	28	28	37			5	4	9	15	4
	%	%	%		%	%	%	%	%	%
ASSETS										
Cash & Equivalents	4.2	7.6	8.5						7.3	
Trade Receivables (net)	24.0	20.3	21.8						25.6	
Inventory	27.1	27.5	31.7						32.1	
All Other Current	3.5	4.0	1.5						2.0	
Total Current	58.8	59.4	63.6						67.0	
Fixed Assets (net)	29.0	30.8	23.7						14.9	
Intangibles (net)	4.5	5.0	6.5						8.8	
All Other Non-Current	7.7	4.8	6.2						9.3	
Total	100.0	100.0	100.0						100.0	
LIABILITIES										
Notes Payable-Short Term	7.9	9.8	9.6						10.2	
Cur. Mat.-L/T/D	3.1	5.5	3.2						3.4	
Trade Payables	12.2	9.9	12.1						15.3	
Income Taxes Payable	.3	.4	.3						.5	
All Other Current	8.5	6.9	11.4						14.1	
Total Current	32.0	32.6	36.7						43.5	
Long Term Debt	18.6	17.9	11.3						6.9	
Deferred Taxes	.9	.7	.6						.3	
All Other Non-Current	11.5	5.2	4.8						5.0	
Net Worth	37.0	43.6	46.6						44.3	
Total Liabilities & Net Worth	100.0	100.0	100.0						100.0	
INCOME DATA										
Net Sales	100.0	100.0	100.0						100.0	
Gross Profit	25.3	24.2	26.1						23.4	
Operating Expenses	20.1	21.9	22.2						19.1	
Operating Profit	5.2	2.4	3.9						4.3	
All Other Expenses (net)	1.4	1.5	.8						.2	
Profit Before Taxes	3.7	.9	3.1						4.1	
RATIOS										
Current	2.9	3.4	3.0						2.0	
	1.8	2.0	1.7						1.5	
	1.2	1.3	1.4						1.1	
Quick	1.3	1.4	1.3						1.0	
	.9	.8	.8						.7	
	.6	.6	.6						.6	
Sales/Receivables	33 11.0	28 12.9	33 11.1						35 10.5	
	43 8.4	37 9.9	41 8.8						45 8.2	
	53 6.9	46 8.0	49 7.5						59 6.2	
Cost of Sales/Inventory	41 8.8	39 9.3	53 6.9						49 7.5	
	72 5.1	76 4.8	72 5.1						65 5.6	
	96 3.8	97 3.8	119 3.1						101 3.6	
Cost of Sales/Payables	14 26.4	9 38.8	14 26.7						14 26.2	
	21 17.5	20 18.4	26 13.9						28 13.2	
	37 9.8	38 9.6	36 10.1						53 6.9	
Sales/Working Capital	4.7	4.2	4.8						5.8	
	7.5	8.0	7.5						8.6	
	24.5	12.9	16.2						22.9	
EBIT/Interest	16.7	7.3	(32) 10.4						(13) 12.2	
	3.3	2.1	4.4						5.6	
	1.9	.2	1.2						.4	
Net Profit + Depr., Dep., Amort./Cur. Mat. L/T/D	(12) 4.5		(18) 3.9							
	2.2		2.6							
	.4		1.7							
Fixed/Worth	.4	.5	.2						.2	
	.9	1.0	.5						.5	
	5.2	2.9	1.0						1.0	
Debt/Worth	.9	.4	.6						.7	
	1.6	1.3	1.2						2.1	
	9.1	6.9	6.0						6.7	
% Profit Before Taxes/Tangible Net Worth	(23) 46.7	(25) 22.7	(33) 36.9						(14) 55.7	
	12.5	3.3	12.0						14.4	
	5.1	-6.2	.9						-.3	
% Profit Before Taxes/Total Assets	12.0	9.8	13.7						20.1	
	5.4	2.9	5.4						5.4	
	2.2	-3.4	.4						.2	
Sales/Net Fixed Assets	20.3	11.6	32.7						44.1	
	6.2	5.7	8.3						17.0	
	3.9	4.2	5.2						7.8	
Sales/Total Assets	2.7	2.3	2.3						2.5	
	1.8	1.7	1.8						1.7	
	1.5	1.5	1.5						1.6	
% Depr., Dep., Amort./Sales	(26) .0	(27) .1	(34) 1.2						(13) .9	
	.9	1.6	2.2						1.9	
	4.2	4.3	4.1						5.0	
% Officers', Directors', Owners' Comp/Sales	(12) 2.3	(14) 2.4	(16) 1.8							
	3.8	4.5	3.8							
	7.9	6.9	8.5							
Net Sales ($)	937226M	554835M	708851M			10080M	16497M	63054M	279722M	339498M
Total Assets ($)	651712M	361073M	420451M			7184M	8142M	32631M	146737M	225757M

M = $ thousand   MM = $ million

See Pages 11 through 18 for Explanation of Ratios and Data

Current Data Sorted By Assets   Comparative Historical Data

						Type of Statement		
1	2	8 8 1	5 3	1 1		Unqualified Reviewed Compiled	17 12 10	21 11 4
1	3	1				Tax Returns	4	3
3 3	5 2	1 5	10		1	Other	16	14
	8 (4/1-9/30/02)		56 (10/1/02-3/31/03)				4/1/98- 3/31/99	4/1/99- 3/31/00
0-500M	500M-2MM	2-10MM	10-50MM	50-100MM	100-250MM		ALL	ALL
8	12	23	18	2	1	NUMBER OF STATEMENTS	59	53
%	%	%	%	%	%	ASSETS	%	%
	8.6	4.9	7.5			Cash & Equivalents	6.5	8.8
	46.6	30.4	20.0			Trade Receivables (net)	27.9	24.0
	2.4	32.3	34.2			Inventory	20.1	19.3
	.7	1.6	3.4			All Other Current	1.6	1.9
	58.3	69.2	65.1			Total Current	56.1	54.0
	28.2	24.5	23.3			Fixed Assets (net)	34.6	35.8
	3.9	2.3	7.6			Intangibles (net)	2.5	4.4
	9.5	4.0	4.0			All Other Non-Current	6.8	5.7
	100.0	100.0	100.0			Total	100.0	100.0
						LIABILITIES		
	9.0	19.6	10.6			Notes Payable-Short Term	14.7	9.5
	8.9	2.5	2.4			Cur. Mat.-L/T/D	5.2	6.5
	20.5	23.6	13.9			Trade Payables	14.4	15.7
	.0	.2	.2			Income Taxes Payable	.1	.3
	8.9	8.9	5.2			All Other Current	6.1	7.2
	47.2	54.7	32.3			Total Current	40.6	39.1
	28.5	8.5	19.8			Long Term Debt	17.1	14.7
	.1	.2	.7			Deferred Taxes	1.0	1.3
	1.9	3.7	.6			All Other Non-Current	2.8	4.1
	22.4	32.9	46.6			Net Worth	38.6	40.8
	100.0	100.0	100.0			Total Liabilities & Net Worth	100.0	100.0
						INCOME DATA		
	100.0	100.0	100.0			Net Sales	100.0	100.0
	41.1	26.4	28.5			Gross Profit	26.2	26.5
	36.3	21.9	20.9			Operating Expenses	21.5	20.9
	4.8	4.6	7.6			Operating Profit	4.7	5.7
	.8	1.6	2.7			All Other Expenses (net)	1.2	1.9
	4.0	3.0	4.9			Profit Before Taxes	3.5	3.8
						RATIOS		
	2.3	1.8	3.2				2.5	2.4
	1.3	1.2	2.2			Current	1.3	1.5
	.9	.9	1.5				1.0	1.0
	2.2	.9	1.4				1.4	1.5
	1.0	.7	1.2			Quick	.9	.8
	.8	.4	.5				.5	.5

	21	17.3	35	10.3	33	11.1			Sales/Receivables	33	10.9	27	13.3
	32	11.3	44	8.3	43	8.5				44	8.3	40	9.2
	54	6.8	54	6.8	54	6.8				58	6.3	52	7.0
	0	UND	26	13.8	33	11.2			Cost of Sales/Inventory	15	24.6	13	28.2
	1	260.6	63	5.8	65	5.6				46	8.0	41	9.0
	3	104.6	95	3.8	108	3.4				82	4.5	70	5.2
	1	388.9	19	18.8	20	18.5			Cost of Sales/Payables	18	20.7	16	22.9
	11	32.6	31	11.9	28	12.8				28	13.2	28	12.9
	36	10.2	52	7.0	50	7.2				45	8.1	54	6.8

	12.8	6.8	3.5			Sales/Working Capital	7.5	7.5
	48.0	15.0	5.9				20.6	13.6
	−119.1	−97.9	13.3				999.8	NM

		11.6		10.1		7.3			EBIT/Interest		7.9		8.4
	(10)	2.6		2.6	(17)	3.8				(55)	2.6	(49)	3.5
		.5		1.7		1.8					1.2		.8

							Net Profit + Depr., Dep., Amort./Cur. Mat. L /T/D		2.9		7.4
			(15)					(55)/(15)	1.4	(16)	3.4
									.4		1.5

	.4	.2	.2			Fixed/Worth	.4	.5
	2.0	.4	.4				.9	.9
	−7.2	2.3	1.1				3.0	2.1
	1.2	1.0	.7			Debt/Worth	.9	.7
	4.4	2.4	1.5				2.4	1.6
	−19.7	4.3	2.3				5.2	3.8

				56.9		47.7	% Profit Before Taxes/Tangible Net Worth		38.2		48.8
			(20)	13.8	(17)	12.9		(55)	15.3	(51)	12.7
				7.2		4.6			3.9		4.8

	19.9	13.8	12.5			% Profit Before Taxes/Total Assets	13.5	17.6
	1.5	4.6	5.1				5.9	6.8
	−3.5	3.0	1.7				.7	.2
	74.9	74.4	29.1			Sales/Net Fixed Assets	15.7	14.4
	29.7	14.0	8.8				6.6	7.3
	9.8	8.4	5.3				3.9	3.4
	5.7	3.4	2.3			Sales/Total Assets	2.8	3.0
	4.4	2.7	1.8				2.1	2.1
	3.5	1.5	1.4				1.5	1.6

		.7		.5		.6	% Depr., Dep., Amort./Sales		1.4		1.4
		1.2		1.5	(16)	1.9		(56)	2.9	(46)	3.1
		4.0		2.5		4.1			4.3		4.7

						% Officers', Directors', Owners' Comp/Sales	1.8	2.6
							(18) 5.1	(19) 4.3
							10.9	7.5

4009M	46757M	285150M	667093M	266110M	265906M	Net Sales ($)	1883589M	1400509M
1181M	9737M	113298M	343486M	143169M	113612M	Total Assets ($)	1048694M	720086M

M = $ thousand   MM = $ million
See Pages 11 through 18 for Explanation of Ratios and Data

Comparative Historical Data / Current Data Sorted By Sales

	4/1/00-3/31/01 ALL		4/1/01-3/31/02 ALL		4/1/02-3/31/03 ALL	Type of Statement	0-1MM	1-3MM	3-5MM	5-10MM		10-25MM		25MM & OVER
	10		7		14	Unqualified		1		3		7		3
	10		8		15	Reviewed	2	1		3		4		5
	9		7		5	Compiled	1	3		1				
	2		1		9	Tax Returns	3		2	1		1		
	4		7		21	Other	3	2	2	1		6		9
	4/1/00-3/31/01		4/1/01-3/31/02		4/1/02-3/31/03			8 (4/1-9/30/02)			56 (10/1/02-3/31/03)			
	ALL 35		ALL 30		ALL 64	**NUMBER OF STATEMENTS**	9	7	4	9		18		17
	%		%		%	**ASSETS**	%	%	%	%		%		%
	6.2		5.5		8.3	Cash & Equivalents						5.5		9.1
	26.5		26.9		28.0	Trade Receivables (net)						28.1		27.8
	24.0		24.0		25.3	Inventory						26.2		36.9
	2.7		1.5		1.9	All Other Current						2.7		2.6
	59.4		57.8		63.4	Total Current						62.4		76.4
	28.3		32.3		27.3	Fixed Assets (net)						25.8		18.1
	3.7		4.6		3.8	Intangibles (net)						7.4		1.3
	8.7		5.3		5.5	All Other Non-Current						4.3		4.2
	100.0		100.0		100.0	Total						100.0		100.0
						LIABILITIES								
	11.3		14.2		12.6	Notes Payable-Short Term						13.2		10.4
	4.5		4.7		4.4	Cur. Mat.-L/T/D						2.1		1.5
	15.3		15.7		17.6	Trade Payables						19.0		22.7
	.2		.1		.2	Income Taxes Payable						.2		.1
	14.4		6.8		7.3	All Other Current						6.6		7.7
	45.7		41.5		42.0	Total Current						41.1		42.3
	19.7		24.6		17.5	Long Term Debt						15.5		9.1
	.4		.6		.3	Deferred Taxes						.7		.2
	2.9		4.4		2.8	All Other Non-Current						3.1		.7
	31.3		28.8		37.4	Net Worth						39.6		47.7
	100.0		100.0		100.0	Total Liabilities & Net Worth						100.0		100.0
						INCOME DATA								
	100.0		100.0		100.0	Net Sales						100.0		100.0
	28.8		23.6		30.4	Gross Profit						25.2		21.0
	26.7		21.9		25.8	Operating Expenses						22.0		14.6
	2.0		1.7		4.6	Operating Profit						3.2		6.3
	1.8		1.8		1.6	All Other Expenses (net)						.9		1.8
	.2		-.1		3.0	Profit Before Taxes						2.3		4.6
						RATIOS								
	2.2 / 1.4 / 1.1		2.9 / 1.6 / 1.1		2.5 / 1.6 / 1.0	Current						2.7 / 1.7 / 1.2		2.9 / 1.6 / 1.4
	1.1 / .7 / .4		1.5 / 1.0 / .5		1.4 / .9 / .5	Quick						1.3 / .9 / .5		1.6 / 1.1 / .5
30 / 43 / 54	12.3 / 8.5 / 6.8	33 / 40 / 49	11.2 / 9.1 / 7.5	24 / 40 / 52	15.0 / 9.2 / 7.0	Sales/Receivables					28 / 43 / 55	13.0 / 8.5 / 6.7	37 / 48 / 55	10.0 / 7.6 / 6.7
23 / 50 / 72	15.7 / 7.3 / 5.0	22 / 46 / 73	16.4 / 7.9 / 5.0	4 / 42 / 93	104.1 / 8.6 / 3.9	Cost of Sales/Inventory					14 / 48 / 89	26.7 / 7.5 / 4.1	36 / 58 / 102	10.2 / 6.3 / 3.6
15 / 29 / 53	24.4 / 12.4 / 6.9	16 / 28 / 39	22.1 / 13.0 / 9.3	14 / 25 / 47	26.2 / 14.5 / 7.7	Cost of Sales/Payables					18 / 27 / 40	20.4 / 13.5 / 9.0	25 / 35 / 54	14.7 / 10.4 / 6.8
	6.5 / 14.1 / 80.4		6.6 / 13.2 / 142.1		5.3 / 12.7 / UND	Sales/Working Capital						4.9 / 10.9 / 36.5		4.7 / 6.5 / 17.0
(33)	6.0 / 2.2 / .2		3.1 / 1.9 / .6	(57)	9.8 / 3.1 / 1.3	EBIT/Interest					(17)	4.4 / 2.4 / .6	(16)	17.7 / 4.6 / 2.4
(10)	6.4 / 2.3 / 1.4			(12)	12.9 / 3.7 / 1.6	Net Profit + Depr., Dep., Amort./Cur. Mat. L/T/D								
	.3 / .8 / 5.2		.5 / 1.6 / NM		.2 / .5 / 1.9	Fixed/Worth						.2 / .7 / 1.6		.2 / .2 / .5
	.7 / 2.1 / 8.1		.7 / 3.5 / NM		.8 / 1.8 / 3.9	Debt/Worth						.9 / 1.5 / 4.1		.5 / 1.6 / 2.4
(29)	36.3 / 10.6 / -.3	(23)	26.5 / 6.2 / .6	(55)	35.6 / 11.7 / 4.0	% Profit Before Taxes/Tangible Net Worth					(16)	26.1 / 9.2 / -7.3		66.8 / 16.4 / 4.8
	7.5 / 4.2 / -3.0		9.1 / 2.2 / -2.0		13.6 / 4.1 / .5	% Profit Before Taxes/Total Assets						6.2 / 3.5 / 1.1		22.3 / 6.9 / 2.8
	28.8 / 10.7 / 4.7		21.6 / 9.2 / 3.7		40.6 / 13.5 / 6.7	Sales/Net Fixed Assets						38.0 / 13.0 / 6.5		35.8 / 11.9 / 7.5
	3.2 / 2.5 / 1.6		3.5 / 2.3 / 1.6		3.7 / 2.7 / 1.6	Sales/Total Assets						3.5 / 2.6 / 1.5		3.1 / 2.0 / 1.7
(33)	.7 / 2.0 / 3.4	(28)	.3 / 1.8 / 3.6	(59)	.6 / 1.5 / 3.7	% Depr., Dep., Amort./Sales						1.1 / 1.9 / 4.0	(15)	.3 / 1.1 / 2.2
(13)	1.5 / 3.4 / 6.0	(10)	2.9 / 4.3 / 6.1	(26)	2.5 / 3.8 / 7.0	% Officers', Directors', Owners' Comp/Sales								
	502588M		744869M		1535025M	Net Sales ($)	4890M	17183M	13489M	67079M		259723M		1172661M
	261769M		372686M		724483M	Total Assets ($)	6207M	6835M	5617M	36367M		131654M		537803M

M = $ thousand   MM = $ million
See Pages 11 through 18 for Explanation of Ratios and Data

Current Data Sorted By Assets · Comparative Historical Data

	0-500M	500M-2MM	2-10MM	10-50MM	50-100MM	100-250MM	Type of Statement	4/1/98-3/31/99 ALL	4/1/99-3/31/00 ALL
		8 (4/1-9/30/02)			30 (10/1/02-3/31/03)				
Unqualified			1						7
Reviewed		2	12	5		1			10
Compiled		1	1						4
Tax Returns	2	2	2	1					2
Other	1	3		3	1				9
NUMBER OF STATEMENTS	3	8	16	9	1	1			32
	%	%	%	%	%	%	ASSETS	%	%
			14.4				Cash & Equivalents		5.8
			22.1				Trade Receivables (net)		29.5
			21.3				Inventory		27.6
			2.8				All Other Current		2.3
			60.6				Total Current		65.2
			25.3				Fixed Assets (net)	DATA NOT AVAILABLE	25.7
			5.8				Intangibles (net)		4.7
			8.3				All Other Non-Current		4.4
			100.0				Total		100.0
							LIABILITIES		
			6.9				Notes Payable-Short Term		14.1
			2.4				Cur. Mat.-L/T/D		1.7
			16.1				Trade Payables		14.6
			.2				Income Taxes Payable		.2
			7.3				All Other Current		7.5
			32.9				Total Current		38.1
			13.4				Long Term Debt		19.4
			.8				Deferred Taxes		.8
			2.7				All Other Non-Current		3.2
			50.2				Net Worth		38.5
			100.0				Total Liabilities & Net Worth		100.0
							INCOME DATA		
			100.0				Net Sales		100.0
			25.5				Gross Profit		25.6
			23.8				Operating Expenses		21.3
			1.7				Operating Profit		4.2
			1.7				All Other Expenses (net)		.9
			.0				Profit Before Taxes		3.4
							RATIOS		
			2.7						3.1
			1.6				Current		1.8
			1.1						1.2
			2.0						1.3
			.9				Quick	(31)	.8
			.5						.6
			32 11.3					39 9.3	
			48 7.6				Sales/Receivables	52 7.1	
			54 6.8					63 5.8	
			28 13.1					40 9.1	
			51 7.2				Cost of Sales/Inventory	57 6.4	
			75 4.8					90 4.1	
			18 20.2					18 19.8	
			34 10.6				Cost of Sales/Payables	34 10.7	
			50 7.3					45 8.1	
			3.9						4.7
			11.2				Sales/Working Capital		8.2
			52.3						13.0
			2.4						17.8
		(13)	1.5				EBIT/Interest	(30)	4.4
			−.1						1.0
							Net Profit + Depr., Dep., Amort./Cur. Mat. L /T/D		
			.2						.3
			.6				Fixed/Worth		.6
			1.3						1.1
			.5						.7
			.9				Debt/Worth		1.6
			3.1						4.9
			7.6						42.8
		(14)	1.3				% Profit Before Taxes/Tangible Net Worth	(29)	16.4
			−5.7						−.3
			4.1						14.9
			1.2				% Profit Before Taxes/Total Assets		6.0
			−1.9						−.2
			20.4						19.0
			9.7				Sales/Net Fixed Assets		7.2
			3.7						5.0
			2.7						2.6
			1.6				Sales/Total Assets		1.9
			1.2						1.5
			1.5						.9
		(15)	2.5				% Depr., Dep., Amort./Sales	(25)	1.7
			4.9						2.5
							% Officers', Directors', Owners' Comp/Sales		1.9
								(11)	4.5
									9.4
3220M	13870M	143182M	306452M	94428M	304650M	Net Sales ($)		1282006M
1118M	5747M	81655M	166154M	88067M	139304M	Total Assets ($)		758054M

M = $ thousand   MM = $ million
See Pages 11 through 18 for Explanation of Ratios and Data

Comparative Historical Data   Current Data Sorted By Sales

			Type of Statement	0-1MM	1-3MM	3-5MM	5-10MM	10-25MM	25MM & OVER
5	4	7	Unqualified				1	1	5
6	7	16	Reviewed	1	2	1	7	5	
4	4	1	Compiled		1				
1	1	5	Tax Returns	1	4		1	3	2
4	7	9	Other		3				
4/1/00-3/31/01 ALL	4/1/01-3/31/02 ALL	4/1/02-3/31/03 ALL			8 (4/1-9/30/02)		30 (10/1/02-3/31/03)		
20	22	38	**NUMBER OF STATEMENTS**	2	10	1	9	9	7
%	%	%	**ASSETS**	%	%	%	%	%	%
8.9	5.4	9.9	Cash & Equivalents		6.6				
28.2	26.1	27.4	Trade Receivables (net)		37.2				
24.9	24.7	20.4	Inventory		18.4				
1.0	2.4	1.7	All Other Current		.5				
62.9	58.7	59.4	Total Current		62.7				
28.9	29.3	26.5	Fixed Assets (net)		24.7				
2.3	3.9	5.5	Intangibles (net)		3.5				
5.9	8.2	8.6	All Other Non-Current		9.2				
100.0	100.0	100.0	Total		100.0				
			LIABILITIES						
13.4	9.5	8.6	Notes Payable-Short Term		7.9				
2.3	3.8	3.3	Cur. Mat.-L/T/D		5.4				
13.6	14.3	16.0	Trade Payables		18.6				
.8	.3	.2	Income Taxes Payable		.1				
8.2	6.1	7.4	All Other Current		10.0				
38.3	34.0	35.5	Total Current		42.0				
16.2	17.6	18.9	Long Term Debt		19.5				
1.7	.5	.4	Deferred Taxes		.8				
2.1	4.1	15.8	All Other Non-Current		52.8				
41.6	43.7	29.4	Net Worth		−15.1				
100.0	100.0	100.0	Total Liabilities & Net Worth		100.0				
			INCOME DATA						
100.0	100.0	100.0	Net Sales		100.0				
23.6	23.3	27.6	Gross Profit		40.7				
20.1	22.6	25.9	Operating Expenses		39.9				
3.5	.7	1.7	Operating Profit		.8				
.1	1.1	1.3	All Other Expenses (net)		1.0				
3.4	−.4	.4	Profit Before Taxes		−.2				
			RATIOS						
3.1	2.3	2.7			2.5				
1.8	1.6	1.5	Current		1.6				
1.2	1.2	1.2			.9				
1.5	1.4	2.0			2.0				
.9	.9	1.0	Quick		1.1				
.7	.6	.6			.7				
37 9.9	37 9.7	38 9.7			43 8.5				
45 8.1	48 7.6	49 7.5	Sales/Receivables		51 7.2				
52 7.0	60 6.1	54 6.8			61 6.0				
32 11.5	34 10.6	25 14.5			17 20.9				
50 7.3	58 6.3	45 8.1	Cost of Sales/Inventory		41 9.0				
78 4.7	77 4.7	72 5.0			54 6.7				
12 30.3	18 20.7	19 19.4			24 15.4				
20 18.3	33 11.0	31 11.7	Cost of Sales/Payables		26 13.9				
48 7.7	46 8.0	47 7.7			55 6.6				
4.2	5.9	5.3			8.3				
8.3	9.8	11.6	Sales/Working Capital		16.0				
29.7	21.0	26.6			−44.2				
23.6	3.7	2.6							
(19) 4.9	(20) 1.9	(31) 1.5	EBIT/Interest						
2.0	−.6	−1.4							
		1.9	Net Profit + Depr., Dep.,						
		(13) 1.2	Amort./Cur. Mat. L/T/D						
		−.3							
.2	.4	.4			.4				
.5	.6	.8	Fixed/Worth		1.1				
1.9	1.6	1.9			NM				
.4	.6	.5			1.7				
1.5	1.5	2.0	Debt/Worth		3.7				
4.8	2.9	4.5			NM				
47.5	18.1	14.6	% Profit Before Taxes/Tangible		8.2				
(19) 28.0	(20) 5.9	(32) 3.1	Net Worth						
15.0	−11.1	−6.0							
22.3	7.2	6.8	% Profit Before Taxes/Total		8.2				
10.1	2.7	1.5	Assets		1.5				
3.6	−3.5	−2.2			−8.4				
45.5	16.0	19.3			37.8				
6.3	7.8	9.3	Sales/Net Fixed Assets		15.5				
3.4	3.5	3.4			5.0				
3.1	2.5	2.9			3.7				
2.4	2.2	1.9	Sales/Total Assets		3.0				
1.6	1.3	1.2			1.8				
.4	.6	1.4			1.0				
(13) 1.8	(20) 2.2	(35) 2.3	% Depr., Dep., Amort./Sales		2.1				
3.7	3.4	4.2			3.2				
		3.1	% Officers', Directors',						
		(16) 4.7	Owners' Comp/Sales						
		6.6							
946163M	809393M	865802M	Net Sales ($)	1222M	18582M	3163M	67789M	147084M	627962M
561994M	443664M	482045M	Total Assets ($)	1046M	9616M	2111M	46606M	105228M	317438M

Current Data Sorted By Assets   Comparative Historical Data

0-500M	500M-2MM	2-10MM	10-50MM	50-100MM	100-250MM	Type of Statement	4/1/98-3/31/99 ALL	4/1/99-3/31/00 ALL
1			4	7	2	1	Unqualified	21	14
1			8	3			Reviewed	12	8
2	3	2					Compiled	12	8
1							Tax Returns	3	1
	4	5	5	3	1	Other	11	9
		13 (4/1-9/30/02)		40 (10/1/02-3/31/03)				
5	7	19	15	5	2	**NUMBER OF STATEMENTS**	59	40
%	%	%	%	%	%		%	%

ASSETS

2-10MM	10-50MM		Hist 99	Hist 00
9.2	7.2	Cash & Equivalents	5.5	4.7
19.3	23.0	Trade Receivables (net)	24.4	19.6
34.0	33.3	Inventory	34.4	37.1
9.3	2.2	All Other Current	1.4	1.5
71.8	65.7	Total Current	65.6	63.0
23.0	23.9	Fixed Assets (net)	25.2	29.3
1.7	2.5	Intangibles (net)	2.7	1.9
3.5	7.9	All Other Non-Current	6.4	5.8
100.0	100.0	Total	100.0	100.0

LIABILITIES

2-10MM	10-50MM		Hist 99	Hist 00
13.5	8.5	Notes Payable-Short Term	11.5	7.7
3.4	2.5	Cur. Mat.-L/T/D	4.5	7.1
20.6	14.1	Trade Payables	22.2	19.5
.1	.5	Income Taxes Payable	.9	.3
14.9	8.2	All Other Current	7.0	6.8
52.5	33.8	Total Current	46.2	41.4
13.6	17.4	Long Term Debt	18.3	21.2
.6	.8	Deferred Taxes	.6	.7
3.3	1.6	All Other Non-Current	7.8	3.2
29.9	46.3	Net Worth	27.2	33.6
100.0	100.0	Total Liabilities & Net Worth	100.0	100.0

INCOME DATA

2-10MM	10-50MM		Hist 99	Hist 00
100.0	100.0	Net Sales	100.0	100.0
28.5	31.8	Gross Profit	27.8	26.6
24.2	23.7	Operating Expenses	23.4	23.1
4.3	8.2	Operating Profit	4.5	3.5
1.1	1.4	All Other Expenses (net)	2.2	1.7
3.2	6.8	Profit Before Taxes	2.3	1.8

RATIOS

2-10MM	10-50MM		Hist 99	Hist 00
2.3	4.4	Current	2.3	2.4
1.5	2.0		1.7	1.6
1.0	1.5		1.1	1.2
1.2	1.5	Quick	1.0	1.1
.5	.7		.7	.6
.1	.5		.4	.3
9 39.8	30 12.3	Sales/Receivables	26 13.8	15 23.6
35 10.4	44 8.2		38 9.6	31 11.6
49 7.5	68 5.3		49 7.5	40 9.2
43 8.5	56 6.5	Cost of Sales/Inventory	48 7.6	60 6.1
72 5.1	90 4.1		76 4.8	79 4.6
134 2.7	198 1.8		102 3.6	98 3.7
31 11.6	26 14.1	Cost of Sales/Payables	27 13.7	17 21.9
57 6.5	43 8.5		40 9.0	35 10.5
71 5.1	58 6.3		58 6.3	56 6.5
6.0	3.2	Sales/Working Capital	5.8	6.4
8.7	5.1		10.0	13.8
70.3	9.8		61.1	22.5
6.2	19.6	EBIT/Interest	6.0	6.4
(16) 3.3	(13) 3.9		(57) 2.9	(38) 2.9
1.4	1.7		1.6	1.0
		Net Profit + Depr., Dep., Amort./Cur. Mat. L /T/D	10.2	3.8
			(19) 3.4	(11) 2.3
			1.5	1.4
.2	.2	Fixed/Worth	.3	.5
.5	.6		.7	.8
1.1	1.2		1.9	2.1
1.7	.4	Debt/Worth	.7	.9
2.6	1.2		2.4	2.2
5.2	4.3		6.4	5.5
71.9	49.4	% Profit Before Taxes/Tangible Net Worth	33.9	38.2
(18) 27.7	21.6		(51) 18.5	(37) 20.9
11.4	10.2		9.4	-.4
10.8	13.7	% Profit Before Taxes/Total Assets	12.1	12.9
6.4	9.7		5.4	4.8
1.2	4.7		1.9	-.7
26.4	12.7	Sales/Net Fixed Assets	23.6	16.7
11.8	8.1		11.0	8.3
5.0	5.6		5.5	5.4
2.7	2.1	Sales/Total Assets	3.2	2.8
2.1	1.6		2.4	2.5
1.9	1.5		1.6	1.6
.6	1.3	% Depr., Dep., Amort./Sales	.6	1.2
(17) 2.4	(14) 2.4		(53) 1.9	(37) 1.8
3.4	3.9		2.9	2.6
		% Officers', Directors', Owners' Comp/Sales	2.2	1.6
			(14) 3.4	(12) 3.5
			5.0	7.4

0-500M	500M-2MM	2-10MM	10-50MM	50-100MM	100-250MM		Hist 99	Hist 00
9413M	14982M	228249M	603031M	593423M	426159M	Net Sales ($)	1942867M	1664172M
1774M	4861M	106596M	366422M	375346M	225628M	Total Assets ($)	1188602M	928289M

M = $ thousand   MM = $ million
See Pages 11 through 18 for Explanation of Ratios and Data

Comparative Historical Data   Current Data Sorted By Sales

4/1/00-3/31/01 ALL	4/1/01-3/31/02 ALL	4/1/02-3/31/03 ALL	Type of Statement	0-1MM	1-3MM	3-5MM	5-10MM	10-25MM	25MM & OVER
11	10	15	Unqualified	1				6	8
3	9	12	Reviewed		2	1	3	4	2
10	7	7	Compiled	1	3		2	1	
4	3	1	Tax Returns			1			
12	15	18	Other	1	3		2	5	7
					13 (4/1-9/30/02)			40 (10/1/02-3/31/03)	
40	44	53	NUMBER OF STATEMENTS	3	9	1	7	16	17
%	%	%	**ASSETS**	%	%	%	%	%	%
5.8	6.1	9.1	Cash & Equivalents					6.7	7.5
19.6	20.7	20.4	Trade Receivables (net)					21.8	24.3
32.6	30.9	28.5	Inventory					38.6	23.1
2.3	3.6	5.0	All Other Current					2.8	2.6
60.4	61.3	63.0	Total Current					69.9	57.5
29.2	30.8	26.4	Fixed Assets (net)					24.8	30.2
5.7	1.2	3.4	Intangibles (net)					.1	6.1
4.7	6.7	7.1	All Other Non-Current					5.2	6.3
100.0	100.0	100.0	Total					100.0	100.0
			LIABILITIES						
7.8	11.8	9.6	Notes Payable-Short Term					13.0	4.9
6.2	3.3	2.9	Cur. Mat.-L/T/D					4.0	2.6
14.2	15.7	17.8	Trade Payables					21.8	12.2
.3	.1	.2	Income Taxes Payable					.1	.5
7.3	9.0	12.6	All Other Current					10.5	10.2
35.7	39.8	43.2	Total Current					49.4	30.5
22.4	21.3	16.7	Long Term Debt					18.0	18.7
.6	.8	.7	Deferred Taxes					.6	1.6
3.5	2.0	4.3	All Other Non-Current					1.5	4.5
37.7	36.1	35.1	Net Worth					30.6	44.7
100.0	100.0	100.0	Total Liabilities & Net Worth					100.0	100.0
			INCOME DATA						
100.0	100.0	100.0	Net Sales					100.0	100.0
33.5	30.5	31.7	Gross Profit					31.9	27.1
28.0	24.8	25.7	Operating Expenses					25.8	17.5
5.5	5.6	6.0	Operating Profit					6.1	9.6
.8	1.4	1.4	All Other Expenses (net)					1.4	1.5
4.7	4.3	4.6	Profit Before Taxes					4.7	8.1
			RATIOS						
2.8	2.5	2.4	Current					1.9	4.2
1.8	1.8	1.7						1.5	2.0
1.2	1.1	1.0						1.1	1.3
1.1	1.3	1.2	Quick					.8	1.4
.7	(43) .8	.6						.5	1.1
.4	.5	.5						.4	.7
16 / 23.4	16 / 23.4	13 / 27.2	Sales/Receivables					18 / 20.4	31 / 11.6
33 / 10.9	34 / 10.9	34 / 10.9						36 / 10.2	44 / 8.2
54 / 6.8	55 / 6.6	49 / 7.5						49 / 7.5	64 / 5.7
24 / 15.2	38 / 9.7	37 / 9.8	Cost of Sales/Inventory					61 / 6.0	45 / 8.0
76 / 4.8	71 / 5.1	61 / 6.0						96 / 3.8	59 / 6.2
139 / 2.6	119 / 3.1	115 / 3.2						140 / 2.6	90 / 4.1
17 / 21.8	20 / 18.3	24 / 15.0	Cost of Sales/Payables					39 / 9.5	23 / 15.9
39 / 9.3	33 / 11.0	41 / 8.8						57 / 6.4	26 / 14.1
63 / 5.8	52 / 7.0	64 / 5.7						71 / 5.1	43 / 8.5
4.5	4.7	4.5	Sales/Working Capital					5.3	3.4
7.9	8.6	9.8						9.9	6.1
27.3	57.4	136.1						64.3	15.0
8.7	9.3	10.5	EBIT/Interest					7.8	20.6
(36) 3.5	(41) 3.8	(44) 3.6					(15) 3.2	(14) 9.2
1.7	1.7	1.4						1.2	1.8
		4.6	Net Profit + Depr., Dep., Amort./Cur. Mat. L/T/D						
		(15) 2.2							
		1.0							
.4	.4	.3	Fixed/Worth					.5	.3
.8	.8	.8						.9	.8
2.6	1.6	1.4						1.1	2.0
.8	.9	.8	Debt/Worth					1.3	.3
1.9	1.9	2.2						2.9	1.1
5.2	4.3	6.3						5.6	4.7
55.3	48.8	49.2	% Profit Before Taxes/Tangible Net Worth					76.3	49.4
(36) 25.3	(41) 22.0	(48) 27.7						25.5	(15) 32.6
14.0	9.6	10.7						7.1	17.1
17.6	20.0	13.9	% Profit Before Taxes/Total Assets					15.1	15.6
9.1	7.6	8.0						6.2	11.8
3.6	1.1	1.7						1.5	5.4
20.7	15.1	19.0	Sales/Net Fixed Assets					17.2	10.4
8.8	7.5	8.4						9.7	6.1
5.0	4.8	4.9						5.2	4.4
3.4	2.6	2.4	Sales/Total Assets					2.6	2.1
1.9	2.1	2.1						2.1	1.8
1.6	1.6	1.6						1.7	1.4
.7	1.1	1.3	% Depr., Dep., Amort./Sales					1.9	1.5
(34) 1.6	(41) 2.3	(46) 2.7					(15) 2.6	(16) 2.9
2.6	3.3	3.6						3.5	3.6
1.6	1.6	2.1	% Officers', Directors', Owners' Comp/Sales						
(14) 5.1	(11) 3.9	(13) 5.4							
7.2	5.6	11.7							
1959415M	1680979M	1875257M	Net Sales ($)	2089M	19322M	4442M	50091M	271069M	1528244M
984211M	967645M	1080627M	Total Assets ($)	1449M	6905M	2135M	30609M	141384M	898145M

M = $ thousand   MM = $ million
See Pages 11 through 18 for Explanation of Ratios and Data

Current Data Sorted By Assets | Comparative Historical Data

						Type of Statement		
		9	10		1	Unqualified	15	10
	2	11	1	1		Reviewed	17	19
	2	4	1		1	Compiled	8	10
1		1			1	Tax Returns		1
	3	5	5	2		Other	12	14
	13 (4/1-9/30/02)		48 (10/1/02-3/31/03)				4/1/98-3/31/99	4/1/99-3/31/00
0-500M	500M-2MM	2-10MM	10-50MM	50-100MM	100-250MM		ALL	ALL
1	7	30	17	3	3	NUMBER OF STATEMENTS	52	54
%	%	%	%	%	%	ASSETS	%	%
		10.2	8.8			Cash & Equivalents	3.2	4.1
		29.4	25.1			Trade Receivables (net)	29.0	28.3
		38.8	31.1			Inventory	36.2	38.5
		3.5	3.5			All Other Current	1.4	1.6
		81.8	68.5			Total Current	69.9	72.5
		13.1	20.6			Fixed Assets (net)	24.2	22.2
		1.8	5.1			Intangibles (net)	1.5	.9
		3.4	5.7			All Other Non-Current	4.4	4.4
		100.0	100.0			Total	100.0	100.0
						LIABILITIES		
		14.0	9.6			Notes Payable-Short Term	14.1	17.8
		4.2	3.9			Cur. Mat.-L/T/D	2.8	2.3
		23.9	15.1			Trade Payables	17.3	15.8
		.2	.1			Income Taxes Payable	.6	.4
		6.8	12.9			All Other Current	8.7	7.1
		49.1	41.5			Total Current	43.5	43.5
		8.5	16.2			Long Term Debt	15.0	11.1
		.0	.2			Deferred Taxes	.2	.3
		2.5	2.0			All Other Non-Current	7.4	10.0
		39.8	40.1			Net Worth	33.9	35.2
		100.0	100.0			Total Liabilities & Net Worth	100.0	100.0
						INCOME DATA		
		100.0	100.0			Net Sales	100.0	100.0
		30.2	24.7			Gross Profit	27.7	28.4
		26.2	18.9			Operating Expenses	24.1	23.2
		4.0	5.8			Operating Profit	3.7	5.2
		.4	1.7			All Other Expenses (net)	1.5	1.6
		3.6	4.1			Profit Before Taxes	2.1	3.6
						RATIOS		
		2.6	2.3				2.3	2.4
		1.7	1.8			Current	1.7	1.6
		1.3	1.3				1.3	1.3
		1.5	1.5				1.1	1.2
		.8	.8			Quick	.8	.7
		.5	.4				.5	.4
		32 11.5	8 43.6				34 10.9	33 11.0
		43 8.5	53 6.9			Sales/Receivables	46 7.9	45 8.2
		55 6.6	63 5.8				61 6.0	63 5.8
		37 10.0	51 7.1				47 7.7	40 9.2
		86 4.3	68 5.4			Cost of Sales/Inventory	81 4.5	85 4.3
		123 3.0	98 3.7				121 3.0	122 3.0
		27 13.6	15 24.9				19 19.3	16 22.7
		38 9.7	23 16.1			Cost of Sales/Payables	32 11.4	30 12.0
		69 5.3	53 6.9				49 7.5	53 6.9
		4.6	4.6				5.4	5.9
		9.0	8.4			Sales/Working Capital	8.6	9.4
		18.0	13.6				16.1	17.7
		12.1	7.1				5.1	7.1
	(26)	4.0	(15) 4.5			EBIT/Interest	(48) 2.7	(50) 3.0
		1.9	1.7				1.1	1.3
						Net Profit + Depr., Dep.,	10.7	22.0
						Amort./Cur. Mat. L./T/D	(13) 2.5	(12) 3.5
							1.1	.8
		.1	.2				.3	.2
		.4	.5			Fixed/Worth	.5	.4
		.7	1.6				1.1	1.1
		.8	.8				1.1	.8
		1.9	1.8			Debt/Worth	1.9	1.8
		3.7	3.5				3.7	3.0
		41.1	54.6				30.8	43.7
	(28)	21.5	(16) 31.7			% Profit Before Taxes/Tangible Net Worth	(48) 22.4	(52) 19.3
		6.6	4.6				5.5	3.2
		15.0	16.4				11.7	13.4
		8.7	10.6			% Profit Before Taxes/Total Assets	5.8	6.5
		2.7	1.0				.7	1.2
		59.0	28.7				27.5	48.6
		17.1	13.0			Sales/Net Fixed Assets	11.6	15.9
		11.2	6.3				6.7	7.5
		3.3	3.0				2.9	3.1
		2.4	2.2			Sales/Total Assets	2.2	2.3
		1.9	1.6				1.7	1.7
		.8	.6				.7	.6
	(25)	1.3	(15) 1.5			% Depr., Dep., Amort./Sales	(44) 1.2	(50) 1.1
		2.1	1.9				2.2	1.8
						% Officers', Directors',	2.2	2.1
						Owners' Comp/Sales	(20) 2.7	(21) 3.4
							5.4	5.3
3489M	16935M	350953M	866051M	465396M	2807116M	Net Sales ($)	1369585M	1276224M
360M	7579M	131881M	365514M	241295M	469216M	Total Assets ($)	705459M	653300M

M = $ thousand   MM = $ million
See Pages 11 through 18 for Explanation of Ratios and Data

Comparative Historical Data · Current Data Sorted By Sales

Type of Statement	4/1/00-3/31/01 ALL	4/1/01-3/31/02 ALL	4/1/02-3/31/03 ALL	0-1MM	1-3MM	3-5MM	5-10MM	10-25MM	25MM & OVER
Unqualified	12	11	20			1	4	7	8
Reviewed	14	7	15		2	2	6	3	2
Compiled	7	13	8	1	2		2	2	1
Tax Returns		2	3		1			1	1
Other	7	13	15			3	1	3	8
					13 (4/1-9/30/02)		**48 (10/1/02-3/31/03)**		
NUMBER OF STATEMENTS	40	46	61	1	5	6	13	16	20
ASSETS	%	%	%	%	%	%	%	%	%
Cash & Equivalents	6.5	6.0	9.0				17.5	7.0	5.8
Trade Receivables (net)	26.4	25.9	28.1				25.4	28.7	27.7
Inventory	36.0	38.9	35.5				37.3	36.6	34.3
All Other Current	1.7	1.7	3.9				.8	4.9	4.3
Total Current	70.5	72.5	76.5				81.0	77.2	72.0
Fixed Assets (net)	23.5	21.3	16.5				14.2	17.8	18.1
Intangibles (net)	1.3	1.3	2.4				1.8	.5	4.3
All Other Non-Current	4.7	5.0	4.7				3.0	4.4	5.5
Total	100.0	100.0	100.0				100.0	100.0	100.0
LIABILITIES									
Notes Payable-Short Term	15.1	17.3	12.1				17.1	8.3	11.8
Cur. Mat.-L/T/D	3.6	2.9	3.7				4.2	5.7	2.5
Trade Payables	13.8	13.8	19.8				19.3	21.4	21.3
Income Taxes Payable	.0	.0	.1				.0	.2	.1
All Other Current	12.2	8.9	9.9				8.1	9.6	10.9
Total Current	44.7	42.9	45.7				48.7	45.3	46.6
Long Term Debt	10.1	11.5	10.8				6.9	7.5	12.9
Deferred Taxes	.3	.4	.2				.0	.0	.4
All Other Non-Current	5.9	2.5	2.6				1.9	3.6	2.2
Net Worth	39.0	42.6	40.8				42.5	43.6	37.9
Total Liabilities & Net Worth	100.0	100.0	100.0				100.0	100.0	100.0
INCOME DATA									
Net Sales	100.0	100.0	100.0				100.0	100.0	100.0
Gross Profit	26.9	28.6	29.8				33.7	25.6	27.5
Operating Expenses	21.7	24.2	24.5				30.4	21.0	21.1
Operating Profit	5.1	4.4	5.3				3.3	4.6	6.3
All Other Expenses (net)	1.2	1.1	.8				1.2	.9	1.1
Profit Before Taxes	3.9	3.3	4.6				2.1	3.7	5.3
RATIOS									
Current	2.6	2.9	2.6				2.6	3.2	2.9
	1.6	2.0	1.8				1.8	1.7	1.6
	1.2	1.3	1.3				1.1	1.3	1.2
Quick	1.1	1.8	1.5				1.5	1.8	1.5
	.6	.9	.8				.8	.8	.8
	.5	.5	.5				.6	.4	.4
Sales/Receivables	31 · 11.6	33 · 11.1	25 · 14.7				33 · 11.2	18 · 20.1	19 · 19.2
	47 · 7.7	42 · 8.7	42 · 8.7				41 · 8.8	39 · 9.3	46 · 7.9
	57 · 6.4	59 · 6.2	59 · 6.2				51 · 7.2	56 · 6.5	59 · 6.1
Cost of Sales/Inventory	65 · 5.6	57 · 6.4	41 · 8.8				46 · 7.9	36 · 10.2	49 · 7.5
	86 · 4.2	93 · 3.9	75 · 4.9				94 · 3.9	88 · 4.2	65 · 5.6
	112 · 3.3	127 · 2.9	113 · 3.2				135 · 2.7	99 · 3.7	78 · 4.7
Cost of Sales/Payables	17 · 21.3	16 · 22.4	20 · 17.9				23 · 15.9	14 · 27.0	21 · 17.4
	28 · 13.0	29 · 12.6	31 · 11.9				31 · 11.9	32 · 11.6	29 · 12.7
	42 · 8.8	40 · 9.2	53 · 6.9				44 · 8.3	61 · 6.0	53 · 6.9
Sales/Working Capital	6.2	4.2	4.3				3.8	4.8	5.9
	8.9	7.2	8.0				6.9	9.2	8.8
	14.2	14.1	15.6				NM	15.1	16.9
EBIT/Interest	(37) 7.7	(40) 7.9	(51) 8.1				(10) 11.3	(14) 12.1	(17) 10.8
	3.0	2.7	3.9				2.7	4.5	6.9
	1.1	.5	2.0				-2.2	1.9	2.3
Net Profit + Depr., Dep., Amort./Cur. Mat. L/T/D	(10) 9.5	(12) 5.2	(20) 11.0						
	3.4	2.8	4.0						
	.4	.6	1.4						
Fixed/Worth	.2	.2	.1				.1	.2	.1
	.5	.5	.4				.3	.4	.5
	1.0	1.1	.7				.7	.7	1.1
Debt/Worth	.9	.5	.8				.8	.5	1.2
	2.0	1.4	1.9				1.2	1.9	2.2
	4.2	5.5	3.3				4.1	2.9	3.9
% Profit Before Taxes/Tangible Net Worth	(38) 43.3	(45) 29.2	(58) 48.4				(12) 34.8	(15) 33.8	(19) 63.0
	15.2	15.6	22.5				19.0	22.0	35.5
	2.5	-2.5	6.5				2.0	5.8	11.1
% Profit Before Taxes/Total Assets	17.6	13.2	14.1				15.3	14.5	19.9
	7.4	4.2	7.0				3.8	9.3	10.3
	.8	-1.7	2.3				.0	3.3	2.1
Sales/Net Fixed Assets	24.6	23.4	41.1				72.6	35.0	41.2
	15.4	12.2	17.3				14.0	16.4	18.0
	5.2	6.0	9.4				9.4	7.7	8.4
Sales/Total Assets	2.6	2.8	3.1				2.8	3.4	3.7
	2.0	2.1	2.3				2.4	2.3	2.3
	1.7	1.6	1.8				1.8	1.9	1.9
% Depr., Dep., Amort./Sales	(35) .8	(41) .7	(52) .8					(14) .8	(18) .6
	1.4	1.4	1.3					1.3	1.3
	2.1	2.4	1.7					2.5	1.9
% Officers', Directors', Owners' Comp/Sales	(13) 1.5	(17) 1.6	(21) 2.4						
	2.2	3.4	4.0						
	6.2	5.5	8.9						
Net Sales ($)	1360135M	1607115M	4509940M	785M	10769M	23479M	98148M	252395M	4124364M
Total Assets ($)	806076M	932311M	1215845M	651M	6476M	12244M	55524M	117852M	1023098M

© RMA 2003

M = $ thousand   MM = $ million

See Pages 11 through 18 for Explanation of Ratios and Data

Current Data Sorted By Assets — Comparative Historical Data

Type of Statement	0-500M	500M-2MM	2-10MM	10-50MM	50-100MM	100-250MM		4/1/98-3/31/99 ALL	4/1/99-3/31/00 ALL
Unqualified			1	3	1			8	4
Reviewed	2	3	5	2				12	14
Compiled	6	2	3					10	14
Tax Returns	4	2						4	3
Other	2	6	7	4				16	18
	13 (4/1-9/30/02)			40 (10/1/02-3/31/03)					
NUMBER OF STATEMENTS	14	13	16	9	1			50	53
ASSETS	%	%	%	%	%	%		%	%
Cash & Equivalents	5.7	8.4	4.6				D	9.9	10.0
Trade Receivables (net)	27.2	24.1	29.1				A	25.5	26.6
Inventory	28.4	37.6	32.6				T	32.6	28.5
All Other Current	5.6	1.5	3.3				A	1.7	1.3
Total Current	67.0	71.6	69.8					69.7	66.3
Fixed Assets (net)	22.4	20.1	21.1				N	21.2	24.2
Intangibles (net)	3.7	3.6	.9				O	3.0	2.9
All Other Non-Current	6.8	4.7	8.2				T	6.1	6.6
Total	100.0	100.0	100.0					100.0	100.0
LIABILITIES							A V		
Notes Payable-Short Term	28.1	14.3	20.2				A	13.0	11.6
Cur. Mat.-L/T/D	5.5	6.3	1.9				I	3.3	3.0
Trade Payables	15.3	16.7	14.5				L	13.7	13.3
Income Taxes Payable	.0	.2	.0				A	.2	.2
All Other Current	30.1	11.7	4.8				B	7.4	7.8
Total Current	79.0	49.1	41.4				L	37.5	35.8
Long Term Debt	15.2	10.8	8.0				E	12.0	14.5
Deferred Taxes	.0	.0	.3					.3	.2
All Other Non-Current	3.9	1.1	7.0					6.6	8.8
Net Worth	1.9	38.9	43.3					43.5	40.6
Total Liabilities & Net Worth	100.0	100.0	100.0					100.0	100.0
INCOME DATA									
Net Sales	100.0	100.0	100.0					100.0	100.0
Gross Profit	45.8	43.0	27.1					34.8	35.9
Operating Expenses	44.7	40.5	24.6					30.1	31.1
Operating Profit	1.1	2.5	2.5					4.7	4.9
All Other Expenses (net)	.6	.4	.4					.7	.6
Profit Before Taxes	.5	2.1	2.1					4.0	4.3
RATIOS									
Current	1.8	2.1	2.7					3.3	3.4
	1.1	1.7	1.7					1.9	1.8
	.8	1.1	1.3					1.3	1.3
Quick	1.1	1.1	1.4					1.7	1.9
	.5	.7	.8					.9	.9
	.3	.3	.6					.6	.6
Sales/Receivables	18 19.9	19 18.9	33 11.0					25 14.6	27 13.5
	24 15.2	31 11.8	47 7.8					35 10.5	43 8.5
	29 12.5	45 8.1	67 5.5					47 7.8	53 6.8
Cost of Sales/Inventory	19 18.9	56 6.6	45 8.0					39 9.5	33 11.0
	40 9.1	98 3.7	63 5.8					78 4.7	73 5.0
	74 4.9	124 3.0	114 3.2					108 3.4	105 3.5
Cost of Sales/Payables	16 23.1	17 21.2	16 22.5					14 26.6	16 23.3
	22 16.3	38 9.7	25 14.5					25 14.5	24 15.4
	41 9.0	52 7.1	46 8.0					45 8.1	46 7.9
Sales/Working Capital	13.9	7.6	6.5					4.5	4.4
	50.6	12.1	9.2					9.0	8.0
	-26.3	NM	16.8					15.8	17.9
EBIT/Interest	7.3	7.5	9.6					9.8	8.6
	2.0	1.8	(15) 3.9				(46) 3.1	(49) 3.5
	-5.4	.6	.6					.3	2.2
Net Profit + Depr., Dep., Amort./Cur. Mat. L/T/D								4.8	8.8
			(15)				(16) 2.8	4.6
								.6	2.5
Fixed/Worth	.5	.4	.1					.2	.2
	1.2	.5	.5					.6	.5
	-1.0	.7	1.1					1.2	1.1
Debt/Worth	.9	.7	.6					.6	.5
	2.7	1.4	1.4					1.5	1.2
	-7.0	7.2	2.8					3.6	3.8
% Profit Before Taxes/Tangible Net Worth		27.3	17.7					41.6	40.1
	(11) 2.1	(15) 4.7				(46) 16.2	(47) 19.6
		-1.9	-4.9					-4.9	5.5
% Profit Before Taxes/Total Assets	11.3	10.7	12.6					20.1	14.7
	5.8	1.3	3.6					5.7	6.6
	-12.4	-.2	-1.0					-1.7	2.7
Sales/Net Fixed Assets	27.5	25.3	57.8					26.3	27.6
	18.9	17.2	15.3					16.3	14.9
	13.9	10.4	5.5					8.2	6.8
Sales/Total Assets	5.8	3.1	2.9					2.9	2.9
	3.9	2.8	2.2					2.4	2.3
	2.9	2.3	1.8					1.8	1.7
% Depr., Dep., Amort./Sales	1.0	1.3	.7					.9	1.0
	(12) 1.3	(11) 1.7	1.2				(46) 1.7	(51) 2.0
	2.1	2.9	2.2					2.9	2.8
% Officers', Directors', Owners' Comp/Sales								2.1	2.1
							(30) 4.7	(32) 4.7
								9.4	7.1
Net Sales ($)	13975M	35293M	155939M	290601M	140412M			618267M	484962M
Total Assets ($)	3418M	12740M	62650M	191776M	77565M			329128M	247375M

M = $ thousand   MM = $ million
See Pages 11 through 18 for Explanation of Ratios and Data

Comparative Historical Data | Current Data Sorted By Sales

			Type of Statement	0-1MM	1-3MM	3-5MM	5-10MM	10-25MM	25MM & OVER
1	5	5	Unqualified				1	1	3
7	12	12	Reviewed		3	3	3	1	2
20	13	11	Compiled	2	6	1	1	1	1
5	5	6	Tax Returns	4	2		1	1	
12	15	19	Other	1	5	3	4	3	3
4/1/00-3/31/01	4/1/01-3/31/02	4/1/02-3/31/03			13 (4/1-9/30/02)		40 (10/1/02-3/31/03)		
ALL	ALL	ALL							
45	50	53	NUMBER OF STATEMENTS	7	16	6	9	6	9
%	%	%	ASSETS	%	%	%	%	%	%
11.1	7.9	6.9	Cash & Equivalents		5.6				
26.9	25.5	25.5	Trade Receivables (net)		23.9				
29.2	35.6	32.3	Inventory		38.0				
2.1	1.1	3.3	All Other Current		1.7				
69.3	70.1	68.0	Total Current		69.2				
22.5	22.1	21.9	Fixed Assets (net)		21.4				
3.4	2.2	3.7	Intangibles (net)		4.0				
4.8	5.6	6.3	All Other Non-Current		5.4				
100.0	100.0	100.0	Total		100.0				
			LIABILITIES						
10.6	15.0	18.4	Notes Payable-Short Term		20.8				
3.7	4.4	4.2	Cur. Mat.-L/T/D		6.2				
12.5	14.1	14.3	Trade Payables		15.7				
.2	.1	.0	Income Taxes Payable		.1				
14.0	17.0	13.8	All Other Current		32.5				
41.1	50.7	50.7	Total Current		75.2				
15.5	16.2	11.9	Long Term Debt		8.2				
.1	.0	.1	Deferred Taxes		.0				
3.5	4.5	4.1	All Other Non-Current		4.3				
39.8	28.6	33.2	Net Worth		12.3				
100.0	100.0	100.0	Total Liabilities & Net Worth		100.0				
			INCOME DATA						
100.0	100.0	100.0	Net Sales		100.0				
36.2	36.8	36.3	Gross Profit		41.8				
31.1	32.8	33.3	Operating Expenses		40.7				
5.1	4.0	3.0	Operating Profit		1.1				
.6	1.1	.6	All Other Expenses (net)		1.1				
4.5	2.9	2.4	Profit Before Taxes		.0				
			RATIOS						
3.6	2.8	2.6	Current		2.0				
2.1	1.5	1.7			1.5				
1.5	1.1	1.1			.8				
2.3	1.3	1.2	Quick		1.0				
1.2	.7	.7			.5				
.6	.5	.5			.3				
23 16.0	23 15.7	22 16.7	Sales/Receivables		19 19.2				
33 11.1	35 10.3	36 10.0			25 14.4				
53 6.9	50 7.2	48 7.6			37 9.9				
30 12.1	52 7.1	45 8.2	Cost of Sales/Inventory		35 10.4				
62 5.9	89 4.1	70 5.2			80 4.6				
94 3.9	125 2.9	108 3.4			104 3.5				
6 56.8	10 37.0	16 23.2	Cost of Sales/Payables		16 22.5				
21 17.1	22 16.4	26 13.8			26 14.2				
38 9.5	48 7.6	47 7.8			44 8.4				
4.5	4.9	6.3	Sales/Working Capital		8.1				
8.1	9.8	11.3			19.6				
14.9	101.4	146.8			-32.9				
11.1	7.3	8.7	EBIT/Interest		3.1				
(41) 3.1	(45) 2.6	(51) 3.0			1.6				
1.3	.2	.6			-4.9				
4.0		5.0	Net Profit + Depr., Dep., Amort./Cur. Mat. L/T/D						
(10) 2.6		(12) 2.2							
1.7		.1							
.2	.2	.3	Fixed/Worth		.4				
.4	.6	.6			.7				
1.2	2.4	1.4			NM				
.4	.6	.7	Debt/Worth		.8				
1.2	1.8	1.5			1.7				
2.8	18.5	3.7			-22.8				
40.7	35.4	26.2	% Profit Before Taxes/Tangible Net Worth		19.0				
(38) 15.7	(42) 13.8	(43) 12.2			(11) 1.5				
3.8	-1.9	-3.6			-63.6				
21.0	15.7	11.0	% Profit Before Taxes/Total Assets		7.5				
5.8	5.6	6.0			1.2				
.7	-4.9	-1.0			-5.4				
30.3	26.3	25.3	Sales/Net Fixed Assets		28.9				
18.3	16.7	14.9			18.0				
7.7	8.0	7.9			11.9				
3.3	3.3	3.5	Sales/Total Assets		4.1				
2.4	2.4	2.4			3.1				
2.0	1.7	1.9			2.5				
.7	.9	1.0	% Depr., Dep., Amort./Sales		1.0				
(43) 1.3	(46) 1.2	(49) 1.7			(15) 1.7				
2.3	2.4	2.9			2.9				
3.8	2.8	3.8	% Officers', Directors', Owners' Comp/Sales		3.4				
(25) 6.6	(27) 5.3	(29) 7.2			(11) 8.6				
10.9	12.0	12.1			13.6				
948266M	587542M	636220M	Net Sales ($)	4014M	28130M	23739M	64570M	100321M	415446M
412737M	317340M	348149M	Total Assets ($)	1120M	9101M	12136M	31437M	58420M	235935M

© RMA 2003   M = $ thousand   MM = $ million
See Pages 11 through 18 for Explanation of Ratios and Data

Current Data Sorted By Assets | Comparative Historical Data

	0-500M	500M-2MM	2-10MM	10-50MM	50-100MM	100-250MM	Type of Statement	4/1/98-3/31/99 ALL	4/1/99-3/31/00 ALL
		1	14	18	6	4	Unqualified	44	41
	2	14	13	8		1	Reviewed	27	26
	2	8	9				Compiled	36	27
	4	7	1				Tax Returns	6	6
	4	12	15	9		3	Other	32	36
		36 (4/1-9/30/02)			119 (10/1/02-3/31/03)				
NUMBER OF STATEMENTS	12	42	52	35	6	8		145	136
ASSETS	%	%	%	%	%	%		%	%
Cash & Equivalents	14.2	10.1	5.7	5.1				5.5	6.8
Trade Receivables (net)	16.0	25.9	23.9	24.9				24.6	28.0
Inventory	28.5	31.8	33.5	32.7				32.0	28.3
All Other Current	2.5	5.4	5.6	3.7				4.1	2.1
Total Current	61.2	73.1	68.7	66.4				66.2	65.1
Fixed Assets (net)	17.2	19.0	23.8	20.2				25.4	24.9
Intangibles (net)	5.9	2.2	3.2	4.4				1.8	3.3
All Other Non-Current	15.7	5.7	4.3	8.9				6.6	6.7
Total	100.0	100.0	100.0	100.0				100.0	100.0
LIABILITIES									
Notes Payable-Short Term	15.9	10.2	11.2	13.3				9.9	11.1
Cur. Mat.-L/T/D	12.4	3.2	3.5	3.0				4.2	3.2
Trade Payables	15.0	13.9	16.9	16.1				13.3	13.7
Income Taxes Payable	.9	.2	.2	.2				.4	.1
All Other Current	26.6	15.2	11.4	9.5				8.9	9.5
Total Current	70.9	42.7	43.2	42.1				36.7	37.7
Long Term Debt	15.0	14.1	14.2	12.7				16.0	14.8
Deferred Taxes	.0	.0	.2	.9				.8	.5
All Other Non-Current	10.7	4.5	8.2	5.1				5.8	6.0
Net Worth	3.5	38.7	34.2	39.3				40.7	41.0
Total Liabilities & Net Worth	100.0	100.0	100.0	100.0				100.0	100.0
INCOME DATA									
Net Sales	100.0	100.0	100.0	100.0				100.0	100.0
Gross Profit	36.3	33.2	27.3	23.4				28.9	27.9
Operating Expenses	33.0	30.6	23.5	20.1				24.8	23.5
Operating Profit	3.2	2.6	3.8	3.4				4.1	4.4
All Other Expenses (net)	.7	.9	2.1	.7				1.3	.9
Profit Before Taxes	2.5	1.7	1.6	2.7				2.9	3.5
RATIOS									
Current	1.5	3.1	2.4	3.1				2.9	3.0
	.8	2.0	1.5	1.7				2.0	1.8
	.6	1.1	1.2	1.1				1.2	1.2
Quick	.7	1.5	1.2	1.2				1.6	1.5
	.4	.8	.7	.8				.8	1.0
	.0	.4	.4	.5				.5	.6
Sales/Receivables	0 UND	16 22.5	27 13.8	27 13.7				29 12.8	33 11.0
	2 163.6	35 10.5	40 9.1	36 10.1				38 9.5	44 8.3
	24 15.4	48 7.7	56 6.5	57 6.4				52 7.0	56 6.5
Cost of Sales/Inventory	0 UND	27 13.3	44 8.4	44 8.3				35 10.5	31 11.9
	16 22.5	64 5.7	72 5.1	70 5.2				65 5.6	58 6.3
	49 7.4	112 3.3	110 3.3	106 3.5				111 3.3	100 3.6
Cost of Sales/Payables	0 UND	15 25.0	15 24.3	14 26.9				15 24.1	16 23.4
	10 36.5	24 14.9	30 12.2	24 15.1				24 15.1	27 13.7
	42 8.7	41 8.8	54 6.8	53 6.8				41 8.8	43 8.4
Sales/Working Capital	22.2	3.7	4.9	5.4				4.7	4.7
	-48.4	8.7	9.0	10.4				7.7	7.2
	-15.8	41.4	25.4	43.5				16.3	22.1
EBIT/Interest		(33) 6.8	(46) 7.6	(32) 8.8				(133) 6.2	(126) 8.6
		2.7	2.1	3.7				2.5	3.4
		.9	.5	1.8				1.0	1.2
Net Profit + Depr., Dep., Amort./Cur. Mat. L/T/D			(12) 3.1	(12) 2.4				(47) 7.0	(27) 7.6
			1.5	2.0				2.5	2.3
			.7	.8				1.0	1.5
Fixed/Worth	.2	.1	.2	.2				.2	.2
	3.5	.4	.5	.5				.5	.5
	-.4	1.2	2.5	1.9				1.3	1.2
Debt/Worth	2.4	.6	.8	.8				.7	.6
	36.1	1.7	2.1	1.8				1.3	1.6
	-3.2	4.9	10.3	6.5				3.4	3.9
% Profit Before Taxes/Tangible Net Worth		(37) 42.7	(46) 30.1	(31) 44.0				(133) 29.1	(126) 41.2
		11.2	11.8	21.9				15.9	19.8
		.7	-.6	5.9				2.8	4.6
% Profit Before Taxes/Total Assets	25.2	16.0	9.3	15.1				10.9	14.7
	4.2	4.4	3.1	6.7				4.8	7.7
	-12.9	-.1	-.8	1.9				.8	.6
Sales/Net Fixed Assets	603.0	60.8	37.7	59.2				41.5	28.9
	45.6	20.3	12.5	11.7				10.9	11.4
	16.3	9.0	6.3	5.7				4.7	4.8
Sales/Total Assets	7.3	4.0	2.9	3.0				2.9	3.0
	4.1	2.4	2.3	2.1				2.2	2.2
	1.9	1.8	1.4	1.7				1.6	1.6
% Depr., Dep., Amort./Sales		(34) .6	(43) .4	(29) .3				(125) .8	(120) .9
		1.8	1.1	1.9				1.7	1.8
		3.4	3.1	3.2				4.0	3.5
% Officers', Directors', Owners' Comp/Sales		(21) 3.3	(12) 2.5					(53) 2.6	(44) 1.8
		5.9	5.7					5.2	4.1
		9.7	7.6					8.3	7.5
Net Sales ($)	13558M	137742M	575556M	1585455M	708121M	1908823M		4139366M	3468179M
Total Assets ($)	3125M	51198M	259346M	706803M	398336M	1304052M		2385140M	2143173M

M = $ thousand   MM = $ million
See Pages 11 through 18 for Explanation of Ratios and Data

Comparative Historical Data   **Current Data Sorted By Sales**

Hist 1	Hist 2	Hist 3	Type of Statement	0-1MM	1-3MM	3-5MM	5-10MM	10-25MM	25MM & OVER
32	20	43	Unqualified		1	1	4	8	29
28	20	38	Reviewed	2	4	10	8	8	6
40	27	19	Compiled	2	4	7	2	4	
4	6	12	Tax Returns	2	6	3	1		
29	39	43	Other	5	9	3	8	10	8
4/1/00-3/31/01	4/1/01-3/31/02	4/1/02-3/31/03		36 (4/1-9/30/02)			119 (10/1/02-3/31/03)		
ALL	ALL	ALL							
133	112	155	**NUMBER OF STATEMENTS**	11	24	24	23	30	43
%	%	%	**ASSETS**	%	%	%	%	%	%
5.8	5.8	7.4	Cash & Equivalents	15.7	11.2	7.2	4.7	6.9	5.1
25.9	24.3	23.7	Trade Receivables (net)	10.6	22.2	30.9	23.0	24.4	23.8
30.3	29.6	32.5	Inventory	32.7	30.4	31.2	32.1	30.9	35.9
2.2	3.7	4.6	All Other Current	3.2	2.4	7.3	4.2	4.7	4.7
64.2	63.4	68.2	Total Current	62.3	66.2	76.6	64.0	66.9	69.5
26.8	27.2	20.6	Fixed Assets (net)	17.9	23.3	17.5	26.8	22.4	17.0
4.4	3.1	4.4	Intangibles (net)	.7	5.8	.7	6.4	2.0	7.2
4.6	6.3	6.8	All Other Non-Current	19.1	4.8	5.2	2.8	8.7	6.3
100.0	100.0	100.0	Total	100.0	100.0	100.0	100.0	100.0	100.0
			LIABILITIES						
12.5	13.8	11.7	Notes Payable-Short Term	9.3	13.1	9.6	14.6	13.6	9.8
5.1	5.2	4.0	Cur. Mat.-L/T/D	11.6	3.2	5.2	3.3	2.6	3.2
14.7	14.0	15.3	Trade Payables	14.0	12.7	15.8	16.0	14.4	17.1
.4	.2	.3	Income Taxes Payable	.1	.5	.3	.2	.1	.3
9.8	6.5	12.9	All Other Current	28.4	15.1	16.9	6.7	10.4	10.5
42.4	39.8	44.2	Total Current	63.3	44.7	47.8	40.7	41.2	40.9
16.4	14.6	14.8	Long Term Debt	21.6	20.2	8.3	11.0	14.2	16.0
.4	.6	.4	Deferred Taxes	.1	.3	.0	.1	.6	.6
8.3	3.2	6.5	All Other Non-Current	12.6	1.9	10.3	9.3	4.1	5.7
32.6	41.9	34.2	Net Worth	2.5	32.9	33.6	38.8	40.0	36.8
100.0	100.0	100.0	Total Liabilities & Net Worth	100.0	100.0	100.0	100.0	100.0	100.0
			INCOME DATA						
100.0	100.0	100.0	Net Sales	100.0	100.0	100.0	100.0	100.0	100.0
27.4	31.3	28.1	Gross Profit	32.8	34.9	30.0	30.5	24.3	23.5
23.7	27.8	24.7	Operating Expenses	32.0	30.8	27.3	26.1	23.1	18.3
3.7	3.5	3.4	Operating Profit	.8	4.1	2.6	4.3	1.2	5.2
1.4	1.0	1.4	All Other Expenses (net)	1.7	1.6	.9	1.5	1.5	1.5
2.3	2.5	2.0	Profit Before Taxes	-1.0	2.5	1.8	2.8	-.3	3.7
			RATIOS						
2.6	2.7	2.8	Current	2.6	2.9	3.1	2.4	3.2	2.6
1.8	1.7	1.7		1.0	1.6	1.5	1.7	1.6	1.9
1.2	1.1	1.1		.7	.8	1.1	1.2	1.1	1.4
1.3	1.3	1.3	Quick	1.2	1.8	1.3	1.2	1.6	1.2
.8	.8	.8		.4	.8	.8	.7	.7	.8
.6	.4	.4		.0	.4	.4	.5	.4	.4
30 12.0	30 12.3	21 17.6	Sales/Receivables	0 UND	12 29.6	20 18.6	24 15.2	25 14.4	29 12.5
41 9.0	41 8.8	37 9.9		15 23.6	30 12.0	39 9.4	38 9.6	39 9.3	38 9.5
52 7.0	53 6.9	53 6.9		33 11.2	59 6.2	55 6.6	53 6.9	61 5.9	48 7.7
38 9.6	31 11.8	35 10.6	Cost of Sales/Inventory	12 31.6	26 13.9	21 17.3	41 9.0	39 9.5	51 7.1
65 5.7	71 5.1	70 5.2		52 7.0	79 4.6	58 6.2	65 5.6	70 5.2	76 4.8
106 3.4	118 3.1	108 3.4		250 1.5	147 2.5	105 3.5	120 3.0	104 3.5	100 3.6
16 23.0	14 25.5	14 26.4	Cost of Sales/Payables	11 34.5	5 77.2	10 37.0	16 22.4	10 35.4	18 20.3
28 13.1	26 14.2	27 13.5		21 17.0	23 16.1	24 14.9	29 12.5	24 15.2	32 11.3
43 8.5	53 6.9	48 7.6		67 5.4	44 8.3	54 6.8	51 7.1	47 7.7	48 7.6
5.3	4.8	4.5	Sales/Working Capital	2.8	3.9	5.2	5.9	4.1	4.9
8.8	8.4	9.3		-68.4	7.4	10.6	10.1	10.5	8.8
28.2	29.2	41.5		-15.1	-35.7	46.6	41.4	39.7	16.6
5.9	6.3	6.8	EBIT/Interest		4.3	4.6	7.6	9.3	8.8
(123) 2.1	(99) 2.2	(133) 2.7		(18) 1.8	(21) 2.2	(20) 1.9	(26) 2.7	(40) 3.7	
1.0	.1	1.0		.2	.4	.4	.9	2.1	
4.5	6.5	5.9	Net Profit + Depr., Dep., Amort./Cur. Mat. L/T/D						7.8
(38) 1.8	(31) 1.3	(37) 2.1						(14) 2.2	
.8	.4	.8						1.5	
.3	.2	.2	Fixed/Worth	.1	.2	.1	.2	.2	.2
.8	.6	.5		1.2	.8	.3	.6	.4	.5
2.6	1.7	2.1		-.8	13.0	1.0	2.7	2.1	1.5
.9	.6	.8	Debt/Worth	1.6	.7	.6	.5	.6	1.1
2.0	1.4	2.0		59.7	2.8	1.7	3.2	1.8	1.8
6.2	4.6	8.3		-3.4	18.4	4.1	8.1	7.5	4.8
34.7	32.9	41.3	% Profit Before Taxes/Tangible Net Worth		69.7	50.2	51.5	21.2	41.3
(113) 16.1	(102) 10.7	(131) 17.9		(20) 16.5	(21) 8.0	(21) 12.2	(28) 8.5	(35) 28.7	
.8	-.7	2.0		-8.0	-.1	-1.2	-.5	17.9	
13.0	13.0	13.1	% Profit Before Taxes/Total Assets	13.1	17.4	15.1	12.9	7.6	15.3
4.5	2.9	4.7		.5	5.8	2.2	3.8	2.2	7.9
.0	-2.4	.2		-10.4	.1	-3.2	-.8	-.4	4.5
27.0	24.5	45.0	Sales/Net Fixed Assets	767.0	35.9	138.4	41.1	21.1	66.8
9.7	9.0	15.2		19.9	16.5	29.3	13.9	8.8	14.8
4.7	4.3	6.8		2.3	8.2	11.4	4.3	5.9	6.8
3.0	2.9	3.2	Sales/Total Assets	4.0	3.9	4.1	3.2	2.8	3.1
2.2	2.1	2.2		1.5	2.0	2.5	2.5	2.3	2.1
1.5	1.4	1.6		1.1	1.3	1.8	1.4	1.5	1.7
.7	.6	.5	% Depr., Dep., Amort./Sales		.9	.4	.6	.6	.3
(114) 1.8	(94) 1.6	(123) 1.5		(22) 2.1	(19) 1.2	(18) 1.1	(24) 2.0	(33) 1.2	
3.9	3.4	3.2		3.5	3.6	2.9	3.5	2.9	
2.3	1.8	2.5	% Officers', Directors', Owners' Comp/Sales		2.4				
(52) 4.5	(45) 3.2	(44) 5.4		(13) 4.6					
6.9	6.2	9.2		8.2					
4577547M	2153511M	4929255M	Net Sales ($)	7398M	46121M	98345M	165596M	487769M	4124026M
2526185M	1281000M	2722860M	Total Assets ($)	5680M	27452M	39814M	84612M	279759M	2285543M

M = $ thousand   MM = $ million
See Pages 11 through 18 for Explanation of Ratios and Data

Current Data Sorted By Assets　　　　　**Comparative Historical Data**

0-500M	500M-2MM	2-10MM	10-50MM	50-100MM	100-250MM		4/1/98-3/31/99 ALL	4/1/99-3/31/00 ALL
						Type of Statement		
		4	8		2	Unqualified	12	11
	1	4	2			Reviewed	9	5
2	2	2				Compiled	11	6
						Tax Returns	3	3
		2	3			Other	11	9
	8 (4/1-9/30/02)		24 (10/1/02-3/31/03)					
2	3	12	13		2	**NUMBER OF STATEMENTS**	46	34
%	%	%	%	%	%	**ASSETS**	%	%
		10.5	10.7			Cash & Equivalents	8.6	12.2
		33.2	22.8			Trade Receivables (net)	23.4	25.9
		32.9	37.2			Inventory	28.5	28.6
		2.9	2.8			All Other Current	3.8	4.2
		79.5	73.5			Total Current	64.3	71.0
		16.8	18.3			Fixed Assets (net)	28.7	19.0
		.1	1.2	DATA NOT AVAILABLE		Intangibles (net)	2.5	3.8
		3.6	7.0			All Other Non-Current	4.6	6.1
		100.0	100.0			Total	100.0	100.0
						LIABILITIES		
		9.4	12.6			Notes Payable-Short Term	20.4	12.5
		7.9	2.9			Cur. Mat.-L/T/D	4.6	6.0
		19.7	14.5			Trade Payables	11.6	12.9
		.1	.2			Income Taxes Payable	.0	.0
		3.6	5.0			All Other Current	15.5	5.8
		40.7	35.1			Total Current	52.2	37.2
		4.2	7.4			Long Term Debt	19.5	19.3
		.3	.6			Deferred Taxes	.4	.3
		11.0	4.7			All Other Non-Current	3.5	8.0
		43.8	52.1			Net Worth	24.5	35.2
		100.0	100.0			Total Liabilities & Net Worth	100.0	100.0
						INCOME DATA		
		100.0	100.0			Net Sales	100.0	100.0
		26.8	22.7			Gross Profit	16.5	23.6
		22.5	20.3			Operating Expenses	23.0	18.8
		4.4	2.4			Operating Profit	-6.5	4.8
		1.2	.4			All Other Expenses (net)	2.4	1.2
		3.1	2.0			Profit Before Taxes	-8.9	3.6
						RATIOS		
		3.8	6.4			Current	3.2	3.7
		1.7	3.5				1.6	2.0
		1.5	1.4				.8	1.4
		2.8	3.8			Quick	1.6	2.3
		.9	1.7				.7	1.0
		.6	.4				.3	.5
		25　14.3	15　24.0			Sales/Receivables	19　19.1	30　12.2
		53　6.9	41　9.0				42　8.6	41　9.0
		96　3.8	69　5.3				57　6.4	61　6.0
		29　12.4	55　6.7			Cost of Sales/Inventory	23　16.2	24　14.9
		54　6.8	95　3.9				68　5.4	67　5.5
		162　2.3	121　3.0				118　3.1	106　3.4
		28　12.8	14　25.4			Cost of Sales/Payables	9　42.3	11　32.1
		37　9.9	27　13.6				22　16.4	21　17.3
		48　7.6	44　8.2				41　8.9	37　9.9
		2.5	2.0			Sales/Working Capital	3.7	3.6
		6.3	3.4				7.6	5.5
		16.3	14.4				-75.9	20.4
	(11)	4.5	7.8			EBIT/Interest	(40)　6.0	(31)　4.5
		2.2	2.9				2.1	2.2
		1.9	.8				.8	1.1
						Net Profit + Depr., Dep., Amort./Cur. Mat. L/T/D	(14)　5.4	
							2.2	
							.3	
		.0	.1			Fixed/Worth	.2	.2
		.3	.2				.5	.5
		.6	.6				7.2	2.1
		.8	.2			Debt/Worth	.6	.6
		1.6	.4				1.7	2.1
		2.7	2.7				12.1	11.0
		28.9	20.5			% Profit Before Taxes/Tangible Net Worth	(39)　39.1	(29)　35.2
		10.4	(12)　2.6				10.5	11.6
		6.6	.0				1.7	2.3
		12.1	5.6			% Profit Before Taxes/Total Assets	9.4	18.5
		4.3	1.7				4.8	5.0
		1.9	.1				.0	.9
		442.8	23.4			Sales/Net Fixed Assets	28.8	28.7
		21.6	12.7				10.0	12.8
		7.9	5.7				5.1	7.1
		4.0	2.7			Sales/Total Assets	3.3	2.6
		1.9	1.8				2.0	1.9
		1.3	1.2				1.5	1.5
	(10)	.6	1.0			% Depr., Dep., Amort./Sales	(41)　1.3	(31)　1.1
		2.3	1.5				2.2	2.1
		3.8	3.1				4.4	3.2
						% Officers', Directors', Owners' Comp/Sales	(15)　2.5	
							3.8	
							9.6	
289M	11808M	159850M	543724M		655502M	Net Sales ($)	1468301M	1840585M
232M	3893M	66058M	276553M		402384M	Total Assets ($)	950555M	1200634M

© RMA 2003

M = $ thousand　　MM = $ million
See Pages 11 through 18 for Explanation of Ratios and Data

Comparative Historical Data | Current Data Sorted By Sales

						Type of Statement	0-1MM	1-3MM	3-5MM	5-10MM	10-25MM	25MM & OVER
	3		2		14	Unqualified				3	4	7
	9		7		7	Reviewed		1		3	2	1
	3		3		6	Compiled	2		2		2	2
	2					Tax Returns				1		
	5		3		5	Other		1			2	2
	4/1/00-3/31/01 ALL		4/1/01-3/31/02 ALL		4/1/02-3/31/03 ALL		8 (4/1-9/30/02)		24 (10/1/02-3/31/03)			
	22		15		32	NUMBER OF STATEMENTS	2		4	6	10	10

N	%	N	%	N	%	ASSETS	0-1MM	1-3MM	3-5MM	5-10MM	10-25MM %	25MM&OVER %
	6.9		8.9		11.1	Cash & Equivalents					16.4	8.4
	28.1		28.6		27.6	Trade Receivables (net)					21.4	24.4
	29.7		34.4		31.5	Inventory		DATA			27.1	39.9
	2.9		2.5		2.9	All Other Current		NOT			2.9	3.5
	67.5		74.3		73.1	Total Current		AVAILABLE			67.8	76.3
	21.4		15.1		18.6	Fixed Assets (net)					22.3	16.8
	3.5		.3		.7	Intangibles (net)					1.0	1.0
	6.5		8.6		7.7	All Other Non-Current					9.0	5.9
	100.0		100.0		100.0	Total					100.0	100.0

						LIABILITIES					10-25MM	25MM&OVER
	15.9		18.5		9.9	Notes Payable-Short Term					8.5	11.3
	3.2		4.5		4.8	Cur. Mat.-L/T/D					2.1	3.9
	12.1		12.9		14.8	Trade Payables					14.2	20.8
	.1		.1		.2	Income Taxes Payable					.1	.4
	6.3		5.8		4.8	All Other Current					3.3	8.2
	37.6		41.7		34.6	Total Current					28.3	44.6
	17.0		4.7		11.6	Long Term Debt					8.1	18.4
	.1		.0		.4	Deferred Taxes					.5	.3
	10.1		13.1		7.8	All Other Non-Current					.7	5.6
	35.2		40.4		45.6	Net Worth					62.4	31.2
	100.0		100.0		100.0	Total Liabilities & Net Worth					100.0	100.0

						INCOME DATA					10-25MM	25MM&OVER
	100.0		100.0		100.0	Net Sales					100.0	100.0
	26.5		24.5		25.9	Gross Profit					22.1	24.5
	22.6		25.2		22.7	Operating Expenses					20.1	18.7
	3.9		-.7		3.2	Operating Profit					2.0	5.8
	2.3		1.6		.8	All Other Expenses (net)					.2	1.4
	1.6		-2.4		2.5	Profit Before Taxes					1.8	4.4

RATIOS

N1	P1	N2	P2	N3	P3	Ratio	0-1MM	1-3MM	3-5MM	5-10MM	N	10-25MM	N	25MM&OVER
	3.2		3.0		4.6	Current						8.1		3.6
	2.1		1.8		2.5							1.9		2.3
	1.1		1.2		1.5							1.6		1.3
	1.6		1.2		2.7	Quick						5.2		2.1
	.9		.9		1.5							1.3		1.0
	.6		.6		.7							.5		.3
24	15.4	31	11.8	26	13.8	Sales/Receivables					14	26.7	17	21.6
55	6.7	45	8.2	41	8.8						39	9.2	35	10.5
66	5.5	85	4.3	74	4.9						69	5.3	45	8.1
32	11.5	20	18.6	29	12.8	Cost of Sales/Inventory					26	13.9	36	10.3
75	4.8	69	5.3	72	5.1						76	4.8	70	5.2
153	2.4	166	2.2	124	2.9						114	3.2	113	3.2
13	27.5	12	29.6	12	30.7	Cost of Sales/Payables					11	34.2	20	18.1
25	14.9	25	14.4	28	13.1						18	20.2	28	12.9
42	8.7	33	11.0	43	8.6						42	8.7	42	8.7
	3.6		3.3		2.5	Sales/Working Capital						1.7		3.4
	5.7		6.8		5.0							5.2		8.6
	21.7		13.2		14.5							11.4		19.0
(18)	4.4	(13)	5.1	(29)	5.0	EBIT/Interest						7.1		17.7
	2.1		1.5		2.3							3.6		2.8
	1.0		-1.4		1.3							1.0		1.3
				(10)	7.0	Net Profit + Depr., Dep., Amort./Cur. Mat. L/T/D								
					1.7									
					.5									
	.2		.1		.1	Fixed/Worth						.1		.0
	.5		.5		.3							.3		.2
	3.4		1.0		.6							.6		NM
	.7		.5		.3	Debt/Worth						.1		.4
	1.8		1.5		1.2							.8		1.5
	5.5		3.7		3.0							1.3		NM
(18)	24.2	(14)	16.0	(30)	19.3	% Profit Before Taxes/Tangible Net Worth						21.8		
	6.2		3.9		7.6							2.6		
	-2.8		-55.9		-.1							.6		
	9.1		7.3		9.2	% Profit Before Taxes/Total Assets						10.5		17.6
	2.2		.0		2.6							2.1		6.3
	-.6		-14.6		.1							.3		2.0
	38.7		86.9		94.9	Sales/Net Fixed Assets						22.6		130.4
	11.5		17.9		13.0							8.3		13.7
	4.2		6.2		6.0							4.9		10.7
	2.4		2.9		2.9	Sales/Total Assets						3.3		3.5
	1.7		2.2		1.9							1.7		2.6
	1.3		1.4		1.3							.9		1.8
(18)	.7	(14)	.3	(28)	.8	% Depr., Dep., Amort./Sales						1.3		
	1.4		1.6		1.7							2.4		
	4.5		4.9		3.4							4.0		
				(10)	.8	% Officers', Directors', Owners' Comp/Sales								
					3.5									
					5.9									

							0-1MM	1-3MM	3-5MM	5-10MM	10-25MM	25MM & OVER
	1345397M		185916M		1371173M	Net Sales ($)	289M		16389M	47003M	180513M	1126979M
	824362M		86563M		749120M	Total Assets ($)	232M		8143M	31736M	133464M	575545M

M = $ thousand   MM = $ million
See Pages 11 through 18 for Explanation of Ratios and Data

Current Data Sorted By Assets   Comparative Historical Data

Timeframe groups: **8 (4/1-9/30/02)** covers 0-500M, 500M-2MM, 2-10MM. **23 (10/1/02-3/31/03)** covers 10-50MM, 50-100MM, 100-250MM.

M = $ thousand   MM = $ million

Type of Statement

Type of Statement	0-500M	500M-2MM	2-10MM	10-50MM	50-100MM	100-250MM
Unqualified		1	2	3		
Reviewed		3	8	1		
Compiled	2	2	3			
Tax Returns		1				
Other			4			1
NUMBER OF STATEMENTS	2	7	17	4		1

ASSETS, LIABILITIES, INCOME & RATIOS

	0-500M %	500M-2MM %	2-10MM %	10-50MM %	50-100MM %	100-250MM %	4/1/98-3/31/99 ALL %	4/1/99-3/31/00 ALL %
ASSETS					DATA NOT AVAILABLE		DATA NOT AVAILABLE	DATA NOT AVAILABLE
Cash & Equivalents			13.9					
Trade Receivables (net)			24.8					
Inventory			38.1					
All Other Current			8.2					
Total Current			85.0					
Fixed Assets (net)			7.7					
Intangibles (net)			2.0					
All Other Non-Current			5.4					
Total			100.0					
LIABILITIES								
Notes Payable-Short Term			10.1					
Cur. Mat.-L/T/D			.8					
Trade Payables			11.2					
Income Taxes Payable			.6					
All Other Current			10.3					
Total Current			33.0					
Long Term Debt			7.0					
Deferred Taxes			.0					
All Other Non-Current			3.7					
Net Worth			56.3					
Total Liabilities & Net Worth			100.0					
INCOME DATA								
Net Sales			100.0					
Gross Profit			32.4					
Operating Expenses			27.2					
Operating Profit			5.2					
All Other Expenses (net)			−.4					
Profit Before Taxes			5.5					
RATIOS								
Current			3.5 / 2.7 / 2.1					
Quick			2.0 / 1.1 / .8					
Sales/Receivables			20 → 18.6 / 49 → 7.5 / 74 → 4.9					
Cost of Sales/Inventory			58 → 6.3 / 138 → 2.6 / 175 → 2.1					
Cost of Sales/Payables			11 → 32.3 / 24 → 15.2 / 42 → 8.8					
Sales/Working Capital			2.2 / 3.6 / 6.0					
EBIT/Interest			10.3 / (15) 5.4 / 1.8					
Net Profit + Depr., Dep., Amort./Cur. Mat. L /T/D								
Fixed/Worth			.0 / .1 / .2					
Debt/Worth			.5 / .6 / 2.3					
% Profit Before Taxes/Tangible Net Worth			33.1 / 11.9 / 3.9					
% Profit Before Taxes/Total Assets			19.2 / 7.1 / 2.3					
Sales/Net Fixed Assets			118.3 / 36.8 / 13.6					
Sales/Total Assets			2.7 / 1.6 / 1.2					
% Depr., Dep., Amort./Sales			.3 / (15) .5 / 1.5					
% Officers', Directors', Owners' Comp/Sales								
Net Sales ($)	1641M	24171M	166764M	255609M		157302M		
Total Assets ($)	480M	8266M	89589M	112651M		124267M		

M = $ thousand   MM = $ million
See Pages 11 through 18 for Explanation of Ratios and Data

Comparative Historical Data   ## Current Data Sorted By Sales

			Type of Statement		8 (4/1-9/30/02)		23 (10/1/02-3/31/03)			
		6	Unqualified		1	1			1	3
		11	Reviewed			4	4	3		
		6	Compiled	1	1	1	1	1		1
		3	Tax Returns	1	2				2	
		5	Other			1	1			1
4/1/00-3/31/01 ALL	4/1/01-3/31/02 ALL	4/1/02-3/31/03 ALL		0-1MM	1-3MM	3-5MM	5-10MM	10-25MM	25MM & OVER	
		31	**NUMBER OF STATEMENTS**	2	4	7	6	7	5	
%	%	%	**ASSETS**	%	%	%	%	%	%	
D	D	11.3	Cash & Equivalents							
A	A	25.4	Trade Receivables (net)							
T	T	37.3	Inventory							
A	A	5.6	All Other Current							
		79.6	Total Current							
N	N	14.2	Fixed Assets (net)							
O	O	1.5	Intangibles (net)							
T	T	4.7	All Other Non-Current							
		100.0	Total							
A	A		**LIABILITIES**							
V	V	12.7	Notes Payable-Short Term							
A	A	4.4	Cur. Mat.-L/T/D							
I	I	13.4	Trade Payables							
L	L	.3	Income Taxes Payable							
A	A	11.4	All Other Current							
B	B	42.3	Total Current							
L	L	10.4	Long Term Debt							
E	E	.3	Deferred Taxes							
		6.8	All Other Non-Current							
		40.2	Net Worth							
		100.0	Total Liabilities & Net Worth							
			INCOME DATA							
		100.0	Net Sales							
		32.4	Gross Profit							
		29.3	Operating Expenses							
		3.1	Operating Profit							
		.9	All Other Expenses (net)							
		2.2	Profit Before Taxes							
			RATIOS							
		2.8								
		2.0	Current							
		1.3								
		1.6								
		.9	Quick							
		.5								
	24	15.1								
	43	8.6	Sales/Receivables							
	61	6.0								
	49	7.5								
	110	3.3	Cost of Sales/Inventory							
	148	2.5								
	13	27.4								
	24	15.2	Cost of Sales/Payables							
	39	9.5								
		3.3								
		6.5	Sales/Working Capital							
		14.3								
		10.0								
	(28)	2.7	EBIT/Interest							
		1.5								
			Net Profit + Depr., Dep., Amort./Cur. Mat. L/T/D							
		.0								
		.2	Fixed/Worth							
		.7								
		.5								
		1.3	Debt/Worth							
		3.4								
		24.9	% Profit Before Taxes/Tangible							
	(27)	11.9	Net Worth							
		1.4								
		13.0	% Profit Before Taxes/Total							
		5.7	Assets							
		.6								
		106.3								
		33.8	Sales/Net Fixed Assets							
		8.3								
		3.1								
		2.2	Sales/Total Assets							
		1.3								
		.2								
	(28)	.7	% Depr., Dep., Amort./Sales							
		1.2								
		2.9	% Officers', Directors',							
	(18)	5.3	Owners' Comp/Sales							
		7.5								
		605487M	Net Sales ($)	1238M	9016M	29033M	44423M	108866M	412911M	
		335253M	Total Assets ($)	2470M	3544M	13615M	36830M	41876M	236918M	

M = $ thousand   MM = $ million
See Pages 11 through 18 for Explanation of Ratios and Data

Current Data Sorted By Assets							Comparative Historical Data	

0-500M	500M-2MM	2-10MM	10-50MM	50-100MM	100-250MM	Type of Statement	4/1/98-3/31/99 ALL	4/1/99-3/31/00 ALL
		4	7	1	2	Unqualified	9	6
	1	3	1			Reviewed	7	7
2	2					Compiled		1
1						Tax Returns		1
	5 (4/1-9/30/02)		3 / 23 (10/1/02-3/31/03)		1	Other	8	11
3	3	7	11	1	3	NUMBER OF STATEMENTS	24	26
%	%	%	%	%	%	**ASSETS**	%	%
			5.7			Cash & Equivalents	3.7	4.6
			29.3			Trade Receivables (net)	26.0	27.0
			43.6			Inventory	49.5	35.4
			2.0			All Other Current	2.0	2.9
			80.6			Total Current	81.2	69.8
			12.1			Fixed Assets (net)	13.4	18.2
			.2			Intangibles (net)	.6	2.9
			7.1			All Other Non-Current	4.8	9.1
			100.0			Total	100.0	100.0
						LIABILITIES		
			12.2			Notes Payable-Short Term	21.8	20.5
			.5			Cur. Mat.-L/T/D	2.0	1.4
			16.4			Trade Payables	14.8	12.2
			.1			Income Taxes Payable	.5	1.0
			9.4			All Other Current	5.6	8.0
			38.5			Total Current	44.8	43.2
			5.5			Long Term Debt	11.4	10.9
			.0			Deferred Taxes	.4	.4
			3.7			All Other Non-Current	2.2	3.9
			52.3			Net Worth	41.2	41.7
			100.0			Total Liabilities & Net Worth	100.0	100.0
						INCOME DATA		
			100.0			Net Sales	100.0	100.0
			20.9			Gross Profit	26.4	32.6
			18.6			Operating Expenses	23.5	33.8
			2.3			Operating Profit	3.0	-1.3
			.5			All Other Expenses (net)	1.0	-5.1
			1.8			Profit Before Taxes	1.9	3.8
						RATIOS		
			2.8 / 2.4 / 1.4			Current	2.5 / 1.8 / 1.5	2.3 / 1.8 / 1.3
			1.9 / 1.0 / .4			Quick	1.2 / .6 / .4	1.3 / .7 / .4
		34 / 52 / 70	10.6 / 7.1 / 5.2			Sales/Receivables	31 / 45 / 67 · 11.9 / 8.0 / 5.5	29 / 57 / 74 · 12.6 / 6.5 / 4.9
		60 / 118 / 164	6.1 / 3.1 / 2.2			Cost of Sales/Inventory	83 / 143 / 184 · 4.4 / 2.6 / 2.0	67 / 94 / 138 · 5.4 / 3.9 / 2.6
		18 / 35 / 41	20.3 / 10.6 / 9.0			Cost of Sales/Payables	22 / 36 / 55 · 16.5 / 10.1 / 6.6	15 / 35 / 48 · 24.7 / 10.5 / 7.6
			2.2 / 5.4 / 9.7			Sales/Working Capital	3.2 / 6.1 / 8.0	4.0 / 5.6 / 19.6
		(10)	24.7 / 3.8 / 1.2			EBIT/Interest	(21) 3.4 / 1.5 / 1.3	(23) 5.4 / 2.0 / 1.2
						Net Profit + Depr., Dep., Amort./Cur. Mat. L /T/D		
			.1 / .2 / .5			Fixed/Worth	.0 / .2 / .7	.1 / .4 / 1.3
			.5 / .9 / 2.0			Debt/Worth	.8 / 1.4 / 3.8	.8 / 1.6 / 2.2
			32.2 / 4.7 / 2.0			% Profit Before Taxes/Tangible Net Worth	22.6 / 8.7 / 2.1	28.1 / (24) 7.8 / 4.5
			9.6 / 2.3 / 1.0			% Profit Before Taxes/Total Assets	7.2 / 4.5 / .9	8.7 / 3.6 / 2.4
			53.7 / 32.3 / 8.3			Sales/Net Fixed Assets	97.5 / 29.4 / 8.5	57.1 / 14.5 / 7.3
			3.5 / 2.1 / 1.3			Sales/Total Assets	2.3 / 2.1 / 1.4	2.2 / 1.9 / 1.3
						% Depr., Dep., Amort./Sales	(20) .4 / .9 / 1.6	(24) .3 / .9 / 3.3
						% Officers', Directors', Owners' Comp/Sales		(10) 2.9 / 4.3 / 7.9
3036M	7451M	74978M	510128M	187948M	953081M	Net Sales ($)	1195068M	1601447M
746M	3178M	30578M	243311M	59736M	487010M	Total Assets ($)	650377M	850867M

© RMA 2003

M = $ thousand   MM = $ million
See Pages 11 through 18 for Explanation of Ratios and Data

Comparative Historical Data | Current Data Sorted By Sales

										Type of Statement	0-1MM	1-3MM	3-5MM	5-10MM	10-25MM	25MM & OVER
	6		7		14			2	1	11	Unqualified						
	8		3		5		2	2	1		Reviewed						
	4		6		4	3	1				Compiled						
	1		2		1						Tax Returns	1					
	4		8		4				2	2	Other		3	3	4	2	
	4/1/00-		4/1/01-		4/1/02-		5 (4/1-9/30/02)			23 (10/1/02-3/31/03)							
	3/31/01		3/31/02		3/31/03												
	ALL		ALL		ALL												
	23		26		28						NUMBER OF STATEMENTS	1	3	3	4	4	13
	%		%		%						ASSETS	%	%	%	%	%	%
	6.2		6.0		6.9						Cash & Equivalents						3.8
	31.1		25.7		25.0						Trade Receivables (net)						34.9
	42.2		43.1		45.6						Inventory						40.8
	1.3		2.8		2.0						All Other Current						1.3
	80.9		77.5		79.5						Total Current						80.8
	14.9		13.8		13.3						Fixed Assets (net)						13.5
	1.5		1.0		.5						Intangibles (net)						.5
	2.7		7.7		6.7						All Other Non-Current						5.2
	100.0		100.0		100.0						Total						100.0
											LIABILITIES						
	18.4		18.6		15.2						Notes Payable-Short Term						12.4
	1.1		6.7		2.8						Cur. Mat.-L/T/D						1.2
	16.5		17.5		15.2						Trade Payables						18.0
	.4		.6		.6						Income Taxes Payable						.4
	7.5		13.7		10.9						All Other Current						10.6
	43.9		57.2		44.7						Total Current						42.6
	11.6		12.2		18.1						Long Term Debt						5.6
	.4		.4		.3						Deferred Taxes						.0
	1.5		9.5		20.8						All Other Non-Current						3.2
	42.6		20.8		16.0						Net Worth						48.6
	100.0		100.0		100.0						Total Liabilities & Net Worth						100.0
											INCOME DATA						
	100.0		100.0		100.0						Net Sales						100.0
	25.9		28.9		28.8						Gross Profit						26.6
	22.6		28.2		26.7						Operating Expenses						22.6
	3.3		.7		2.0						Operating Profit						4.0
	1.4		2.6		1.7						All Other Expenses (net)						1.2
	1.9		−1.9		.4						Profit Before Taxes						2.8
											RATIOS						
	2.8		2.3		2.7												2.7
	1.7		1.7		1.9						Current						2.0
	1.4		1.1		1.4												1.5
	1.5		.8		1.4												1.5
	.7		.6		.7						Quick						.8
	.5		.3		.3												.5
32	11.3	25	14.5	22	16.3						Sales/Receivables					34	10.6
54	6.7	46	8.0	37	10.0											41	9.0
68	5.3	61	6.0	62	5.9											60	6.1
77	4.8	74	4.9	54	6.8						Cost of Sales/Inventory					46	8.0
95	3.8	116	3.2	115	3.2											104	3.5
146	2.5	170	2.1	160	2.3											124	2.9
24	15.5	23	15.7	14	25.8						Cost of Sales/Payables					23	15.7
39	9.3	34	10.6	35	10.5											35	10.4
63	5.8	58	6.3	45	8.2											40	9.1
	3.9		4.4		5.0						Sales/Working Capital						5.5
	6.1		5.6		6.4												6.6
	9.5		50.3		9.6												9.5
	5.8		3.9		7.1												9.3
(21)	2.3	(25)	2.0	(25)	2.2						EBIT/Interest						5.5
	1.3		−1.4		1.3												1.6
											Net Profit + Depr., Dep., Amort./Cur. Mat. L/T/D						
	.1		.1		.1						Fixed/Worth						.1
	.3		.3		.3												.3
	.6		3.2		.6												.5
	1.0		1.0		.6						Debt/Worth						.6
	1.6		1.6		1.1												.9
	2.5		NM		3.2												1.8
	24.1		22.9		23.1						% Profit Before Taxes/Tangible Net Worth						31.6
	7.8	(20)	8.9	(24)	6.2												20.5
	1.0		−7.4		2.3												5.1
	9.0		8.9		11.5						% Profit Before Taxes/Total Assets						14.3
	3.8		3.0		2.6												9.6
	.3		−10.3		.9												1.8
	54.4		68.8		63.3						Sales/Net Fixed Assets						49.6
	24.4		33.8		23.6												16.4
	6.8		9.9		11.7												9.4
	2.4		2.5		3.2						Sales/Total Assets						3.5
	1.9		2.0		2.1												2.1
	1.4		1.6		1.7												2.0
	.2		.4		.4						% Depr., Dep., Amort./Sales						.6
(22)	.7	(23)	.8	(26)	.8											(12)	1.2
	1.5		1.7		1.7												2.0
											% Officers', Directors', Owners' Comp/Sales						
	878816M		1098697M		1736622M						Net Sales ($)	429M	3862M	10274M	29589M	81406M	1611062M
	450357M		599434M		824559M						Total Assets ($)	115M	1179M	5089M	14795M	58133M	745248M

© RMA 2003

M = $ thousand   MM = $ million
See Pages 11 through 18 for Explanation of Ratios and Data

Current Data Sorted By Assets   **Comparative Historical Data**

0-500M	500M-2MM	2-10MM	10-50MM	50-100MM	100-250MM	Type of Statement	4/1/98-3/31/99 ALL	4/1/99-3/31/00 ALL
	7	9	7	1	2	Unqualified	34	21
	3	8	5			Reviewed	21	21
3	1	2				Compiled	9	11
	1					Tax Returns	3	4
	1	3	2	1	2	Other	19	22
	21 (4/1-9/30/02)		36 (10/1/02-3/31/03)					
3	12	22	14	2	4	**NUMBER OF STATEMENTS**	86	79
%	%	%	%	%	%	**ASSETS**	%	%
	6.9	10.0	18.2			Cash & Equivalents	7.4	10.4
	27.6	22.8	26.0			Trade Receivables (net)	24.7	23.7
	46.9	47.2	34.1			Inventory	39.1	40.8
	.5	3.1	2.1			All Other Current	4.5	2.0
	81.9	83.2	80.4			Total Current	75.6	76.9
	13.2	9.8	12.8			Fixed Assets (net)	16.8	16.1
	2.0	.7	1.2			Intangibles (net)	2.1	1.7
	2.9	6.4	5.6			All Other Non-Current	5.4	5.3
	100.0	100.0	100.0			Total	100.0	100.0
						LIABILITIES		
	20.9	20.1	9.5			Notes Payable-Short Term	16.8	13.4
	6.3	1.6	1.9			Cur. Mat.-L/T/D	2.5	2.7
	14.7	12.7	10.9			Trade Payables	13.9	11.9
	.0	.0	.2			Income Taxes Payable	.4	.5
	3.5	6.0	8.6			All Other Current	11.5	6.4
	45.5	40.3	31.0			Total Current	45.1	34.9
	19.9	6.2	5.9			Long Term Debt	13.3	15.2
	.0	.1	1.1			Deferred Taxes	.2	.2
	4.5	5.5	5.1			All Other Non-Current	8.2	9.2
	30.2	47.9	56.9			Net Worth	33.2	40.5
	100.0	100.0	100.0			Total Liabilities & Net Worth	100.0	100.0
						INCOME DATA		
	100.0	100.0	100.0			Net Sales	100.0	100.0
	33.2	30.5	29.4			Gross Profit	28.5	29.9
	33.4	27.5	28.7			Operating Expenses	24.8	26.2
	−.3	3.0	.8			Operating Profit	3.7	3.7
	−.3	1.1	.0			All Other Expenses (net)	.8	1.0
	.0	1.9	.8			Profit Before Taxes	2.8	2.7
						RATIOS		
	5.2	4.3	7.6			Current	3.9	5.9
	2.7	1.9	3.2				2.0	2.6
	1.1	1.5	1.3				1.4	1.5
	2.3	1.8	6.0			Quick	1.7	2.0
	.9	.7	1.5				.8	1.1
	.4	.5	.5				.5	.4
27 13.3	24 15.3	38 9.5				Sales/Receivables	29 12.6	23 16.1
47 7.8	33 11.1	48 7.7					42 8.7	43 8.6
78 4.7	44 8.3	83 4.4					57 6.4	56 6.6
119 3.1	67 5.5	62 5.9				Cost of Sales/Inventory	57 6.4	66 5.5
136 2.7	111 3.3	135 2.7					89 4.1	101 3.6
166 2.2	165 2.2	184 2.0					149 2.4	156 2.3
9 39.3	12 30.1	15 24.0				Cost of Sales/Payables	13 28.4	14 26.6
31 11.8	19 19.2	25 14.7					25 14.7	22 16.6
52 7.0	44 8.3	49 7.4					38 9.7	37 9.8
	2.3	3.7	2.3			Sales/Working Capital	3.5	3.3
	5.0	5.6	3.5				6.4	5.3
	44.9	10.4	8.9				12.8	10.7
	8.0	7.3	5.5			EBIT/Interest	7.3	7.1
	1.0	(19) 2.9	(11) 2.8				(76) 2.0	(67) 2.1
	−2.3	.7	1.5				1.1	1.0
						Net Profit + Depr., Dep., Amort./Cur. Mat. L /T/D	6.8	3.7
							(30) 2.8	(22) 2.4
							1.2	.8
	.1	.1	.1			Fixed/Worth	.1	.1
	.4	.2	.3				.4	.3
	NM	.5	.5				1.4	.8
	.5	.4	.2			Debt/Worth	.6	.4
	2.2	1.1	.8				1.7	1.3
	NM	2.5	2.4				6.2	4.5
		38.5	33.5			% Profit Before Taxes/Tangible Net Worth	33.4	38.4
	(21)	11.1	4.8				(75) 13.6	(72) 15.6
		−.9	−4.1				1.9	6.0
	7.2	10.3	10.0			% Profit Before Taxes/Total Assets	12.2	12.1
	.5	3.8	2.5				4.5	5.9
	−8.7	−2.1	−2.5				.3	1.1
	73.9	87.0	34.6			Sales/Net Fixed Assets	36.9	52.4
	38.8	22.0	20.8				16.5	14.8
	8.0	16.6	7.3				8.3	8.8
	2.5	2.9	2.1			Sales/Total Assets	3.1	2.9
	1.9	2.0	1.9				2.0	2.0
	1.5	1.8	1.3				1.5	1.6
	.4	.6	.8			% Depr., Dep., Amort./Sales	.6	.8
	.9	(20) .9	(13) 2.2				(79) 1.3	(72) 1.5
	1.5	1.6	2.9				2.1	2.1
		2.8				% Officers', Directors', Owners' Comp/Sales	1.9	1.7
	(10)	5.3					(29) 2.7	(29) 3.1
		8.0					5.7	7.4
1898M	28227M	232911M	554692M	230625M	672685M	Net Sales ($)	3609189M	4185583M
573M	14411M	105602M	329509M	168733M	439638M	Total Assets ($)	1896921M	2228632M

© RMA 2003

M = $ thousand   MM = $ million
See Pages 11 through 18 for Explanation of Ratios and Data

Comparative Historical Data

Current Data Sorted By Sales

			Type of Statement	0-1MM	1-3MM	3-5MM	5-10MM	10-25MM	25MM & OVER
18	12	19	Unqualified		6		6	4	9
10	10	20	Reviewed		3		7	3	4
16	10	5	Compiled			1	1		
2	1	4	Tax Returns	3		1			
12	15	9	Other		1	1	1	1	5
4/1/00-3/31/01 ALL	4/1/01-3/31/02 ALL	4/1/02-3/31/03 ALL			21 (4/1-9/30/02)		36 (10/1/02-3/31/03)		
58	48	57	**NUMBER OF STATEMENTS**	3	10	3	15	8	18
%	%	%	**ASSETS**	%	%	%	%	%	%
11.3	13.1	11.1	Cash & Equivalents		8.1		5.9		11.9
25.2	22.6	24.0	Trade Receivables (net)		25.0		25.3		27.2
35.7	37.9	42.6	Inventory		45.6		50.1		37.0
2.9	2.4	2.5	All Other Current		.4		2.2		3.0
75.0	76.0	80.2	Total Current		79.2		83.4		79.2
17.5	14.9	13.5	Fixed Assets (net)		15.1		8.1		15.1
2.3	2.5	1.1	Intangibles (net)		2.4		.9		1.4
5.2	6.6	5.2	All Other Non-Current		3.3		7.5		4.3
100.0	100.0	100.0	Total		100.0		100.0		100.0
			LIABILITIES						
13.4	13.4	16.3	Notes Payable-Short Term		17.9		23.0		12.6
2.6	2.5	4.2	Cur. Mat.-L/T/D		7.6		1.8		1.7
13.3	12.3	11.5	Trade Payables		13.3		14.5		9.7
.2	.4	.2	Income Taxes Payable		.0		.0		.5
9.0	8.9	6.1	All Other Current		4.1		4.6		8.7
38.6	37.6	38.2	Total Current		42.9		43.9		33.2
9.1	12.1	9.7	Long Term Debt		23.8		6.1		5.7
.4	.5	.3	Deferred Taxes		.0		.1		1.0
7.3	9.0	8.2	All Other Non-Current		5.4		6.9		14.2
44.6	40.9	43.5	Net Worth		27.9		43.0		45.9
100.0	100.0	100.0	Total Liabilities & Net Worth		100.0		100.0		100.0
			INCOME DATA						
100.0	100.0	100.0	Net Sales		100.0		100.0		100.0
28.2	31.4	32.4	Gross Profit		33.0		31.2		32.2
25.9	27.0	30.4	Operating Expenses		33.1		28.8		28.0
2.3	4.5	2.0	Operating Profit		−.1		2.4		4.2
1.1	1.6	.6	All Other Expenses (net)		−.3		.6		1.2
1.2	2.9	1.3	Profit Before Taxes		.2		1.8		3.0
			RATIOS						
4.3	3.2	5.6			5.7		3.8		4.7
1.8	2.3	2.6	Current		2.9		1.7		3.0
1.3	1.5	1.3			1.0		1.3		1.4
1.8	2.0	2.5			2.7		1.0		2.5
.9	1.0	1.0	Quick		1.0		.7		1.4
.5	.5	.5			.3		.4		.5
28 13.3	24 15.0	25 14.4		29 12.6		24 15.2		36 10.1	
43 8.4	43 8.5	43 8.6	Sales/Receivables	47 7.8		35 10.3		48 7.7	
62 5.9	57 6.4	68 5.4		83 4.4		48 7.6		88 4.1	
58 6.3	55 6.7	79 4.6		120 3.1		64 5.7		68 5.3	
83 4.4	112 3.2	129 2.8	Cost of Sales/Inventory	136 2.7		151 2.4		134 2.7	
140 2.6	155 2.4	172 2.1		165 2.2		182 2.0		185 2.0	
14 26.2	11 34.1	13 29.0		9 40.6		16 23.3		13 27.1	
23 15.6	20 18.1	24 15.3	Cost of Sales/Payables	31 11.8		23 15.8		26 14.0	
42 8.6	42 8.7	42 8.6		52 7.0		49 7.4		38 9.5	
3.6	2.8	2.6			2.3		4.6		2.4
6.3	4.7	4.6	Sales/Working Capital		5.0		5.8		3.7
13.4	10.3	10.4			NM		10.8		8.9
7.3	7.6	7.1			11.4		6.9		6.1
(51) 2.2	(42) 2.5	(50) 2.7	EBIT/Interest	1.0		(12) 2.6		(17) 3.3	
1.1	1.2	.8			−15.7		.8		1.5
4.6	7.1	18.7	Net Profit + Depr., Dep.,						19.4
(13) 2.2	(13) 1.6	(22) 3.3	Amort./Cur. Mat. L/T/D					(12) 4.7	
1.0	1.0	1.8							2.6
.2	.1	.1			.1		.1		.2
.4	.2	.2	Fixed/Worth		.6		.2		.2
.7	.6	.5			−2.1		.5		.5
.3	.5	.4			.4		.8		.3
1.3	1.1	1.1	Debt/Worth		2.2		2.3		.6
3.3	2.5	2.8			−6.1		3.7		2.2
28.4	24.7	33.4	% Profit Before Taxes/Tangible				34.5		26.9
(52) 8.2	(42) 13.0	(51) 7.2	Net Worth				12.3	(17) 11.0	
.7	1.4	−1.9					−1.9		2.6
11.6	12.8	10.1	% Profit Before Taxes/Total		11.9		10.3		10.7
3.6	4.2	3.1	Assets		.5		3.1		3.9
−.3	.0	−2.6			−10.2		−1.7		.8
33.7	58.3	50.4			60.1		83.5		34.6
13.7	17.3	20.9	Sales/Net Fixed Assets		22.6		21.9		10.0
8.6	8.2	8.4			6.2		16.1		7.2
2.9	2.6	2.4			2.4		3.1		2.0
2.0	1.8	1.9	Sales/Total Assets		1.8		2.0		1.8
1.5	1.4	1.5			1.4		1.8		1.4
.7	.6	.6			.4		.6		1.0
(48) 1.4	(36) 1.4	(53) 1.4	% Depr., Dep., Amort./Sales	1.3		(14) .7		(17) 2.4	
2.5	2.3	2.4			1.7		1.7		3.0
1.3	1.3	2.2	% Officers', Directors',						
(23) 2.2	(14) 2.1	(20) 3.7	Owners' Comp/Sales						
6.7	4.9	7.0							
1795372M	2273722M	1721038M	Net Sales ($)	1898M	19069M	11452M	127248M	125426M	1435945M
1017529M	1384919M	1058466M	Total Assets ($)	573M	11082M	8892M	68685M	70560M	898674M

M = $ thousand   MM = $ million
See Pages 11 through 18 for Explanation of Ratios and Data

Current Data Sorted By Assets   **Comparative Historical Data**

0-500M	500M-2MM	2-10MM	10-50MM	50-100MM	100-250MM	Type of Statement	4/1/98-3/31/99 ALL	4/1/99-3/31/00 ALL
		2	6	1		Unqualified	7	4
	3	5	1	1		Reviewed	1	6
	1	1				Compiled	2	3
4	6	5				Tax Returns	1	
1		3				Other	3	3
	1 (4/1-9/30/02)		39 (10/1/02-3/31/03)					
5	10	16	7	2		NUMBER OF STATEMENTS	14	16
%	%	%	%	%	%		%	%

(For 0-500M, 10-50MM, 50-100MM, 100-250MM current-data columns: DATA NOT AVAILABLE)

500M-2MM	2-10MM	Item	4/1/98-3/31/99 ALL	4/1/99-3/31/00 ALL
		ASSETS		
12.7	4.5	Cash & Equivalents	6.7	5.3
13.3	16.7	Trade Receivables (net)	27.4	34.3
60.2	48.1	Inventory	38.3	28.8
5.1	2.0	All Other Current	7.5	2.7
91.4	71.3	Total Current	79.8	71.0
4.9	18.2	Fixed Assets (net)	12.5	18.4
.0	.2	Intangibles (net)	3.0	2.2
3.7	10.4	All Other Non-Current	4.6	8.4
100.0	100.0	Total	100.0	100.0
		LIABILITIES		
21.7	27.9	Notes Payable-Short Term	21.3	14.0
10.9	.5	Cur. Mat.-L/T/D	2.3	2.4
18.0	20.7	Trade Payables	12.3	19.5
.3	.5	Income Taxes Payable	.0	.1
4.3	5.8	All Other Current	9.1	12.3
55.3	55.5	Total Current	44.9	48.2
17.1	16.0	Long Term Debt	17.5	18.9
.1	.0	Deferred Taxes	.0	.0
6.5	7.3	All Other Non-Current	5.6	7.6
21.0	21.2	Net Worth	31.9	25.3
100.0	100.0	Total Liabilities & Net Worth	100.0	100.0
		INCOME DATA		
100.0	100.0	Net Sales	100.0	100.0
22.3	20.2	Gross Profit	22.1	27.2
15.4	15.2	Operating Expenses	19.2	24.3
6.9	5.0	Operating Profit	2.8	2.9
.9	.2	All Other Expenses (net)	1.5	2.0
6.0	4.9	Profit Before Taxes	1.3	.8
		RATIOS		
4.0	1.7	Current	2.5	2.8
1.4	1.4		1.8	1.6
1.2	.8		1.5	1.1
.8	.7	Quick	.9	1.5
.3	.1		.8	.9
.0	.1		.6	.5
0 UND	0 UND	Sales/Receivables	25 14.4	27 13.5
0 UND	0 UND		35 10.4	44 8.2
10 36.8	21 17.5		46 8.0	64 5.7
30 12.3	0 UND	Cost of Sales/Inventory	39 9.5	29 12.4
89 4.1	40 9.1		61 6.0	45 8.2
444 .8	266 1.4		108 3.4	96 3.8
0 UND	0 UND	Cost of Sales/Payables	10 36.3	21 17.6
5 80.5	35 10.4		16 22.5	31 11.8
40 9.1	42 8.6		29 12.6	39 9.3
1.0	8.5	Sales/Working Capital	5.1	5.4
10.7	16.7		7.6	8.1
31.1	NM		11.5	327.4
	10.3	EBIT/Interest	(13) 3.2	3.3
(13)	5.3		1.5	(15) 1.8
	1.4		.2	.4
		Net Profit + Depr., Dep., Amort./Cur. Mat. L/T/D		
.0	.0	Fixed/Worth	.1	.1
.1	.2		.3	.3
.6	2.8		1.0	28.9
2.2	1.9	Debt/Worth	1.4	.9
5.2	4.2		1.9	2.0
8.7	11.8		5.3	48.6
81.6	96.3	% Profit Before Taxes/Tangible Net Worth	44.9	20.9
32.1	(14) 30.6		(13) 10.8	(13) 7.5
12.1	11.4		.3	-9.7
16.1	15.7	% Profit Before Taxes/Total Assets	9.8	11.6
8.7	8.2		2.6	2.5
1.4	1.0		-3.7	-4.5
UND	364.9	Sales/Net Fixed Assets	107.7	59.8
119.8	100.3		31.6	22.5
39.5	18.0		17.0	10.3
4.1	5.5	Sales/Total Assets	3.5	3.1
2.6	2.3		2.6	2.5
.8	.5		2.0	2.3
	.1	% Depr., Dep., Amort./Sales	.3	.5
(12)	.3		(13) .6	(14) .7
	1.4		1.4	2.2
		% Officers', Directors', Owners' Comp/Sales		2.2
			(10)	3.3
				8.5

0-500M	500M-2MM	2-10MM	10-50MM	50-100MM		
4461M	34204M	281969M	398976M	486777M	Net Sales ($)	792142M 732321M
945M	12363M	82415M	150619M	107395M	Total Assets ($)	325611M 345437M

M = $ thousand   MM = $ million
See Pages 11 through 18 for Explanation of Ratios and Data

Comparative Historical Data   Current Data Sorted By Sales

Type of Statement	4/1/00-3/31/01 ALL	4/1/01-3/31/02 ALL	4/1/02-3/31/03 ALL	0-1MM	1-3MM	3-5MM	5-10MM	10-25MM	25MM & OVER
Unqualified	7	4	8		1			2	6
Reviewed	3	3	9		2			1	5
Compiled	1	4	2						
Tax Returns	2	4	16	4	6	2	3	1	1
Other	5	5	5	1	2		2		1
					1 (4/1-9/30/02)		39 (10/1/02-3/31/03)		
NUMBER OF STATEMENTS	18	16	40	5	11	2	5	4	13

ASSETS (%)

	4/1/00-3/31/01	4/1/01-3/31/02	4/1/02-3/31/03	0-1MM	1-3MM	3-5MM	5-10MM	10-25MM	25MM & OVER
Cash & Equivalents	14.2	11.1	10.5		13.0				12.6
Trade Receivables (net)	26.4	33.5	17.3		9.6				31.4
Inventory	31.7	29.7	41.2		26.1				30.2
All Other Current	5.0	1.8	4.2		8.0				2.4
Total Current	77.2	76.1	73.2		56.6				76.6
Fixed Assets (net)	10.7	16.3	17.8		24.6				13.9
Intangibles (net)	4.2	.2	.2		.3				.4
All Other Non-Current	7.9	7.3	8.8		18.5				9.0
Total	100.0	100.0	100.0		100.0				100.0

LIABILITIES

	4/1/00-3/31/01	4/1/01-3/31/02	4/1/02-3/31/03	0-1MM	1-3MM	3-5MM	5-10MM	10-25MM	25MM & OVER
Notes Payable-Short Term	16.3	13.5	22.8		27.1				5.7
Cur. Mat.-L/T/D	3.7	5.3	4.3		13.4				1.2
Trade Payables	19.9	14.7	20.3		18.0				22.2
Income Taxes Payable	1.5	.1	.4		.2				.8
All Other Current	4.9	40.3	9.8		4.5				12.5
Total Current	46.2	74.0	57.6		63.3				42.4
Long Term Debt	6.1	12.5	18.9		32.3				12.0
Deferred Taxes	.4	.1	.0		.0				.0
All Other Non-Current	5.5	24.6	5.1		8.8				2.3
Net Worth	41.8	−11.2	18.4		−4.3				43.3
Total Liabilities & Net Worth	100.0	100.0	100.0		100.0				100.0

INCOME DATA

	4/1/00-3/31/01	4/1/01-3/31/02	4/1/02-3/31/03	0-1MM	1-3MM	3-5MM	5-10MM	10-25MM	25MM & OVER
Net Sales	100.0	100.0	100.0		100.0				100.0
Gross Profit	33.3	28.9	23.4		21.2				24.7
Operating Expenses	27.2	25.3	17.6		12.1				20.4
Operating Profit	6.0	3.6	5.8		9.1				4.3
All Other Expenses (net)	.5	1.4	.7		−.2				−.1
Profit Before Taxes	5.5	2.2	5.1		9.4				4.4

RATIOS

	4/1/00-3/31/01	4/1/01-3/31/02	4/1/02-3/31/03	0-1MM	1-3MM	3-5MM	5-10MM	10-25MM	25MM & OVER
Current	3.8	2.5	2.1		1.8				3.2
	1.6	1.8	1.4		1.1				2.0
	1.1	1.3	.9		.1				1.3
Quick	3.3	1.6	1.0		.6				2.1
	.6	.9	.4		.2				1.1
	.4	.4	.1		.1				.5
Sales/Receivables	33 11.0	14 25.7	0 UND	0 UND				3 125.2	
	45 8.1	31 11.8	1 268.8	0 UND				23 15.9	
	54 6.8	44 8.2	28 13.2	1 243.6				42 8.7	
Cost of Sales/Inventory	42 8.8	12 30.7	0 788.7	0 UND				16 22.9	
	63 5.8	48 7.6	41 8.8	0 UND				36 10.2	
	109 3.3	96 3.8	178 2.0	117 3.1				53 6.9	
Cost of Sales/Payables	17 21.1	5 72.7	0 UND	0 UND				16 22.4	
	36 10.3	21 17.3	18 20.0	0 978.0				22 16.9	
	72 5.0	33 11.2	40 9.2	32 11.3				37 10.0	
Sales/Working Capital	3.4	6.5	7.5		5.7				8.1
	8.9	10.5	16.4		29.9				11.4
	28.2	35.1	UND		−7.1				24.7
EBIT/Interest	(15) 6.8	(13) 4.5	(33) 12.8					(12) 32.3	
	1.4	1.4	6.6					8.5	
	.9	−.2	2.3					2.6	
Net Profit + Depr., Dep., Amort./Cur. Mat. L/T/D									
Fixed/Worth	.1	.1	.0		.0				.0
	.3	.2	.2		.6				.2
	.6	NM	3.2		7.8				.9
Debt/Worth	.4	.6	1.9		2.7				.4
	2.6	2.9	3.9		8.6				1.7
	6.5	NM	17.2		46.7				3.5
% Profit Before Taxes/Tangible Net Worth	81.3	54.0	89.1						63.0
	15.7	(12) 30.8	(35) 34.1						26.8
	−1.8	−4.4	14.5						14.3
% Profit Before Taxes/Total Assets	22.2	25.6	16.4		24.0				19.4
	7.9	3.6	9.1		2.5				14.5
	−.4	−5.7	1.4		.7				6.9
Sales/Net Fixed Assets	153.7	154.9	235.5		999.8				142.4
	22.1	79.9	91.4		99.3				107.2
	15.7	16.6	16.4		14.0				18.1
Sales/Total Assets	2.8	5.4	5.0		5.1				6.2
	2.5	3.6	2.7		1.8				3.7
	1.6	2.6	1.0		.5				2.9
% Depr., Dep., Amort./Sales	(17) .2	(14) .2	(30) .2						.2
	.5	.3	.6						.4
	2.0	1.8	1.7						1.4
% Officers', Directors', Owners' Comp/Sales			(15) .5						
			2.4						
			3.7						
Net Sales ($)	825646M	839962M	1206387M	1479M	20035M	7770M	34732M	59821M	1082550M
Total Assets ($)	420107M	365757M	353737M	4005M	24747M	2095M	14923M	20406M	287561M

© RMA 2003

M = $ thousand   MM = $ million
See Pages 11 through 18 for Explanation of Ratios and Data

Current Data Sorted By Assets   Comparative Historical Data

0-500M	500M-2MM	2-10MM	10-50MM	50-100MM	100-250MM	Type of Statement	4/1/98-3/31/99	4/1/99-3/31/00
1		4	8			Unqualified	6	6
1	2	13	3		1	Reviewed	17	10
	1	2	2			Compiled	3	2
						Tax Returns		
				2		Other	2	1
								5
		7 (4/1-9/30/02)	31 (10/1/02-3/31/03)					
2	3	19	13		1	NUMBER OF STATEMENTS	28 ALL	24 ALL
%	%	%	%	%	%		%	%

ASSETS

0-500M	500M-2MM	2-10MM	10-50MM	50-100MM	100-250MM		4/1/98-3/31/99	4/1/99-3/31/00
		8.3	6.6	D		Cash & Equivalents	12.1	8.4
		27.3	18.1	A		Trade Receivables (net)	30.3	40.7
		47.5	45.8	T		Inventory	35.5	30.4
		2.9	7.2	A		All Other Current	6.3	4.5
		86.0	77.8			Total Current	84.2	84.0
		5.2	11.2	N		Fixed Assets (net)	9.3	10.1
		2.0	5.5	O		Intangibles (net)	3.1	.3
		6.8	5.5	T		All Other Non-Current	3.4	5.6
		100.0	100.0			Total	100.0	100.0

LIABILITIES

0-500M	500M-2MM	2-10MM	10-50MM	50-100MM	100-250MM		4/1/98-3/31/99	4/1/99-3/31/00
		13.2	11.0	A		Notes Payable-Short Term	19.2	20.0
		.9	1.9	V		Cur. Mat.-L/T/D	2.3	4.6
		34.9	23.1	A		Trade Payables	21.2	25.9
		.4	1.2	I		Income Taxes Payable	.1	.8
		11.9	8.2	L		All Other Current	6.2	9.2
		61.4	45.4	A		Total Current	49.0	60.5
		.5	8.1	B		Long Term Debt	5.8	4.1
		.4	.1	L		Deferred Taxes	.1	.0
		4.8	2.4	E		All Other Non-Current	.8	2.9
		33.0	44.0			Net Worth	44.2	32.5
		100.0	100.0			Total Liabilities & Net Worth	100.0	100.0

INCOME DATA

0-500M	500M-2MM	2-10MM	10-50MM	50-100MM	100-250MM		4/1/98-3/31/99	4/1/99-3/31/00
		100.0	100.0			Net Sales	100.0	100.0
		29.8	32.6			Gross Profit	33.2	28.0
		28.2	26.1			Operating Expenses	32.0	27.5
		1.6	6.6			Operating Profit	1.2	.5
		.7	1.1			All Other Expenses (net)	.9	−1.8
		.9	5.5			Profit Before Taxes	.2	2.4

RATIOS

0-500M	500M-2MM	2-10MM	10-50MM	50-100MM	100-250MM		4/1/98-3/31/99	4/1/99-3/31/00
		1.7	2.6			Current	3.5	1.9
		1.4	1.6				1.6	1.4
		1.2	1.4				1.3	1.0
		.9	1.0			Quick	2.1	1.2
		.6	.6				.9	.8
		.3	.1				.5	.5
		0 999.8	1 344.6			Sales/Receivables	11 33.2	29 12.4
		27 13.4	13 28.8				35 10.4	50 7.3
		41 8.8	48 7.6				58 6.3	60 6.1
		46 7.9	38 9.5			Cost of Sales/Inventory	34 10.8	24 15.0
		55 6.6	113 3.2				70 5.3	41 9.0
		64 5.7	131 2.8				104 3.5	64 5.7
		24 14.9	25 14.3			Cost of Sales/Payables	21 17.0	23 15.9
		37 9.8	31 11.7				36 10.1	38 9.7
		53 6.9	44 8.2				54 6.7	45 8.2
		12.0	6.3			Sales/Working Capital	5.5	7.8
		19.8	14.0				10.2	13.0
		49.0	18.7				20.3	114.3
		8.1	16.6			EBIT/Interest	4.7	4.6
		(17) 2.0	(11) 3.6				(24) 2.4	(20) 2.1
		.1	3.1				.0	1.3
						Net Profit + Depr., Dep., Amort./Cur. Mat. L /T/D		
		.0	.1			Fixed/Worth	.1	.0
		.1	.2				.2	.1
		.7	1.2				.4	.3
		.9	.5			Debt/Worth	.4	1.0
		2.3	1.6				1.1	2.0
		8.4	7.3				4.0	4.5
		69.3	75.7			% Profit Before Taxes/Tangible Net Worth	40.3	40.1
		27.1	(12) 28.8				(25) 16.6	(23) 19.0
		1.8	8.4				2.8	5.3
		19.4	20.9			% Profit Before Taxes/Total Assets	19.9	10.7
		13.9	8.3				5.6	4.2
		.6	2.6				−.1	1.0
		441.5	81.1			Sales/Net Fixed Assets	162.4	337.5
		162.4	30.5				46.9	76.4
		55.0	18.2				20.9	27.2
		6.0	4.9			Sales/Total Assets	4.1	3.9
		4.9	3.1				3.1	3.5
		3.3	2.0				2.4	2.8
		.2	.3			% Depr., Dep., Amort./Sales	.2	.1
		(15) .3	(12) .6				(27) .5	(20) .6
		.4	1.0				1.5	1.2
						% Officers', Directors', Owners' Comp/Sales	.9	1.4
							(13) 2.1	(15) 4.0
							4.2	5.6
861M	26330M	403335M	1047100M		83052M	Net Sales ($)	1096331M	797781M
85M	4954M	95002M	338126M		116339M	Total Assets ($)	496525M	315500M

M = $ thousand   MM = $ million
See Pages 11 through 18 for Explanation of Ratios and Data

Comparative Historical Data   **Current Data Sorted By Sales**

4/1/00-3/31/01 ALL	4/1/01-3/31/02 ALL	4/1/02-3/31/03 ALL	Type of Statement	0-1MM	1-3MM	3-5MM	5-10MM	10-25MM	25MM & OVER
4	6	13	Unqualified	1			2	2	10
9	7	19	Reviewed					9	8
7	3	4	Compiled	1		1		2	
1			Tax Returns						
2	4	2	Other						2
				7 (4/1-9/30/02)			31 (10/1/02-3/31/03)		
23	20	38	**NUMBER OF STATEMENTS**	2		1	2	13	20
%	%	%	**ASSETS**	%	%	%	%	%	%
15.7	10.5	10.8	Cash & Equivalents					8.7	9.9
28.6	26.3	25.2	Trade Receivables (net)					34.4	16.7
37.5	39.1	43.9	Inventory					38.3	49.9
5.7	4.5	4.2	All Other Current		DATA			4.2	4.8
87.5	80.4	84.2	Total Current		NOT			85.7	81.4
5.0	12.2	7.1	Fixed Assets (net)		AVAILABLE			4.8	9.7
.7	2.2	2.9	Intangibles (net)					1.9	3.6
6.9	5.3	5.6	All Other Non-Current					7.6	5.3
100.0	100.0	100.0	Total					100.0	100.0
			LIABILITIES						
13.3	23.0	14.2	Notes Payable-Short Term					9.1	10.7
1.1	1.5	1.5	Cur. Mat.-L/T/D					.2	2.0
19.9	23.4	28.9	Trade Payables					35.6	26.7
.2	.3	.6	Income Taxes Payable					.6	.8
11.5	10.9	11.5	All Other Current					16.1	9.9
46.0	59.1	56.7	Total Current					61.6	50.2
5.0	8.4	5.3	Long Term Debt					.2	5.6
.0	.0	.2	Deferred Taxes					.5	.1
2.8	1.1	3.5	All Other Non-Current					4.0	3.5
46.5	31.4	34.0	Net Worth					33.6	40.7
100.0	100.0	100.0	Total Liabilities & Net Worth					100.0	100.0
			INCOME DATA						
100.0	100.0	100.0	Net Sales					100.0	100.0
38.1	35.5	31.8	Gross Profit					34.0	31.1
31.0	34.7	28.0	Operating Expenses					30.3	25.4
7.1	.8	3.8	Operating Profit					3.7	5.7
.2	1.6	.7	All Other Expenses (net)					.7	.7
6.9	-.8	3.1	Profit Before Taxes					3.0	5.0
			RATIOS						
2.7	2.5	2.0						1.9	2.2
1.9	1.6	1.5	Current					1.5	1.5
1.3	1.3	1.2						1.1	1.3
1.2	1.1	1.0						1.1	.8
1.0	.7	.6	Quick					.8	.6
.6	.5	.2						.3	.1
19 18.8	5 79.9	1 328.1						14 26.1	0 844.3
42 8.6	39 9.3	25 14.8	Sales/Receivables					31 11.9	13 28.0
58 6.3	53 6.9	46 7.9						44 8.2	40 9.1
43 8.4	40 9.2	38 9.5						23 16.0	46 7.9
64 5.7	61 6.0	56 6.5	Cost of Sales/Inventory					49 7.4	71 5.1
166 2.2	127 2.9	113 3.2						75 4.9	128 2.8
28 13.0	13 27.7	25 14.7						24 14.9	26 14.0
43 8.6	37 10.0	32 11.4	Cost of Sales/Payables					37 9.8	33 11.0
47 7.8	50 7.4	46 7.9						76 4.8	43 8.5
3.7	4.8	8.0						11.1	6.7
7.0	9.4	14.0	Sales/Working Capital					13.6	14.7
15.3	20.5	38.9						NM	26.7
7.7	5.3	8.2						8.3	8.1
(15) 2.4	(15) 1.6	(32) 4.2	EBIT/Interest			(11)		2.0	(17) 5.3
.0	-.3	1.2						-.8	2.8
			Net Profit + Depr., Dep., Amort./Cur. Mat. L/T/D						
.0	.1	.0						.0	.1
.1	.2	.2	Fixed/Worth					.1	.2
.2	.5	.7						.6	.9
.6	1.0	.8						.9	.6
1.1	1.4	1.9	Debt/Worth					2.2	1.8
2.5	3.8	8.7						7.4	10.3
60.9	25.9	69.3						67.4	78.1
(22) 24.1	(18) 6.6	(35) 27.1	% Profit Before Taxes/Tangible Net Worth			(12)		19.1	(19) 27.1
5.5	-12.2	3.8						-8.7	11.3
23.6	8.7	20.1						25.6	19.7
12.9	2.2	11.3	% Profit Before Taxes/Total Assets					15.2	11.3
.3	-12.1	.6						-1.6	3.3
231.2	94.0	367.7						646.4	100.4
99.4	32.9	85.5	Sales/Net Fixed Assets					184.9	42.3
22.7	20.0	28.3						69.3	20.6
3.8	3.8	5.4						6.2	5.1
2.8	3.0	4.0	Sales/Total Assets					4.6	4.4
2.0	2.0	2.5						2.9	2.0
.1	.2	.2							.2
(18) .3	(16) .7	(31) .3	% Depr., Dep., Amort./Sales					(19)	.5
.6	1.2	.9							1.0
	3.2	2.2							
	(10) 6.8	(14) 5.0	% Officers', Directors', Owners' Comp/Sales						
	9.8	9.0							
713332M	338403M	1560678M	Net Sales ($)	861M	3729M	12528M		203071M	1340489M
325176M	113880M	554506M	Total Assets ($)	85M	1301M	3995M		55142M	493983M

M = $ thousand   MM = $ million

See Pages 11 through 18 for Explanation of Ratios and Data

Current Data Sorted By Assets | **Comparative Historical Data**

Type of Statement	0-500M	500M-2MM	2-10MM	10-50MM	50-100MM	100-250MM		4/1/98-3/31/99 ALL	4/1/99-3/31/00 ALL
Unqualified			4	6	1			16	12
Reviewed		2	7	1				15	13
Compiled			1					7	4
Tax Returns	1							2	
Other		1		6				6	11
			6 (4/1-9/30/02)		24 (10/1/02-3/31/03)				
NUMBER OF STATEMENTS	1	3	12	13	1			46	40
	%	%	%	%	%	%		%	%
ASSETS									
Cash & Equivalents			9.0	15.5				12.2	11.5
Trade Receivables (net)			16.9	13.3		D		28.6	27.7
Inventory			52.1	30.1		A		35.9	31.3
All Other Current			4.8	12.2		T		1.5	8.1
Total Current			82.9	71.0		A		78.1	78.6
Fixed Assets (net)			4.0	9.4				11.5	12.7
Intangibles (net)			4.2	3.4		N		2.4	2.6
All Other Non-Current			8.9	16.2		O		8.0	6.1
Total			100.0	100.0		T		100.0	100.0
LIABILITIES									
Notes Payable-Short Term			19.9	7.5		A		14.3	16.2
Cur. Mat.-L/T/D			.7	1.5		V		2.9	1.5
Trade Payables			19.8	16.2		A		18.3	19.0
Income Taxes Payable			.1	1.6		I		.4	.3
All Other Current			5.3	9.7		L		7.8	8.0
Total Current			45.7	36.5		A		43.7	45.0
Long Term Debt			1.3	8.7		B		9.2	8.0
Deferred Taxes			.0	.4		L		.4	.1
All Other Non-Current			8.3	6.4		E		1.9	4.9
Net Worth			44.7	47.9				44.8	42.0
Total Liabilities & Net Worth			100.0	100.0				100.0	100.0
INCOME DATA									
Net Sales			100.0	100.0				100.0	100.0
Gross Profit			28.6	33.3				27.7	26.7
Operating Expenses			25.7	29.0				24.3	25.6
Operating Profit			3.0	4.3				3.4	1.1
All Other Expenses (net)			1.3	.9				.5	-.1
Profit Before Taxes			1.7	3.4				3.0	1.2
RATIOS									
Current			2.5 / 2.0 / 1.5	3.2 / 2.3 / 1.1				3.3 / 1.9 / 1.3	3.2 / 2.0 / 1.3
Quick			.9 / .5 / .3	1.7 / .7 / .1				1.9 / 1.1 / .5	1.9 / 1.0 / .4
Sales/Receivables			(6) 63.3 / (28) 12.9 / (53) 6.8	(2) 162.6 / (10) 35.3 / (26) 14.1				(22) 17.0 / (32) 11.3 / (54) 6.7	(19) 19.5 / (38) 9.6 / (61) 6.0
Cost of Sales/Inventory			(58) 6.3 / (96) 3.8 / (181) 2.0	(20) 18.0 / (59) 6.2 / (100) 3.6				(31) 11.7 / (66) 5.6 / (118) 3.1	(24) 15.2 / (50) 7.3 / (113) 3.2
Cost of Sales/Payables			(19) 19.3 / (39) 9.4 / (57) 6.4	(9) 39.5 / (28) 12.8 / (57) 6.4				(12) 29.9 / (23) 15.8 / (51) 7.2	(14) 27.0 / (30) 12.0 / (46) 7.9
Sales/Working Capital			3.9 / 6.7 / 10.1	4.1 / 5.5 / 64.3				5.1 / 7.5 / 21.7	4.4 / 8.8 / 24.2
EBIT/Interest			(11) 4.2 / 1.5 / 1.1	9.0 / 3.4 / .0				(40) 6.7 / 2.3 / 1.2	(31) 7.3 / 2.5 / .6
Net Profit + Depr., Dep., Amort./Cur. Mat. L /T/D								(13) 16.5 / 1.8 / .3	
Fixed/Worth			.0 / .1 / .3	.1 / .3 / .6				.1 / .2 / .6	.0 / .2 / .5
Debt/Worth			.6 / 1.1 / 3.5	.6 / 1.2 / 2.6				.6 / 1.2 / 2.9	.4 / 1.6 / 4.2
% Profit Before Taxes/Tangible Net Worth			15.4 / 3.0 / -1.0	(12) 48.8 / 25.6 / -8.1				(43) 46.5 / 21.3 / 3.6	(38) 43.3 / 15.9 / .3
% Profit Before Taxes/Total Assets			7.4 / 1.5 / -.5	17.5 / 7.1 / -4.0				19.5 / 6.5 / 1.3	11.6 / 6.9 / .0
Sales/Net Fixed Assets			256.9 / 174.4 / 41.3	63.8 / 38.5 / 12.3				74.4 / 33.0 / 15.1	253.7 / 32.4 / 12.9
Sales/Total Assets			3.3 / 2.3 / 1.5	3.8 / 2.5 / 1.8				3.7 / 2.9 / 2.1	3.4 / 2.5 / 1.9
% Depr., Dep., Amort./Sales			(10) .1 / .5 / .7	(12) .4 / .6 / 1.7				(41) .3 / .8 / 1.5	(29) .3 / .8 / 1.8
% Officers', Directors', Owners' Comp/Sales								(16) 1.6 / 3.4 / 5.8	(19) 2.3 / 3.0 / 5.9
Net Sales ($)	1229M	11327M	146801M	632918M	175694M			1680646M	1179687M
Total Assets ($)	83M	4363M	54706M	235782M	69946M			782988M	656670M

M = $ thousand   MM = $ million
See Pages 11 through 18 for Explanation of Ratios and Data

Comparative Historical Data					Current Data Sorted By Sales					

				Type of Statement						
13	6	11		Unqualified	1		1	3	6	
12	10	10		Reviewed	2	4	3	1		
3	1	1		Compiled		1				
1	2	1		Tax Returns	1					
	4	7		Other	1			6		
4/1/00-3/31/01 ALL	4/1/01-3/31/02 ALL	4/1/02-3/31/03 ALL			0-1MM	6 (4/1-9/30/02) 1-3MM	3-5MM	24 (10/1/02-3/31/03) 5-10MM	10-25MM	25MM & OVER
29	23	30		**NUMBER OF STATEMENTS**	3	3	2	6	6	13

%	%	%		**ASSETS**	%	%	%	%	%	%
11.8	16.7	13.0		Cash & Equivalents						10.1
32.5	24.5	15.5		Trade Receivables (net)						13.2
35.4	36.7	40.1		Inventory						36.5
2.7	2.9	7.2		All Other Current						12.5
82.4	80.8	75.8		Total Current						72.4
9.6	10.6	8.2		Fixed Assets (net)						8.5
2.6	1.6	5.1		Intangibles (net)						7.9
5.4	7.0	10.9		All Other Non-Current						11.2
100.0	100.0	100.0		Total						100.0

				LIABILITIES						
17.6	16.3	12.6		Notes Payable-Short Term						9.0
1.5	.7	1.0		Cur. Mat.-L/T/D						1.5
20.2	16.6	16.6		Trade Payables						18.8
.2	.6	.7		Income Taxes Payable						1.5
6.7	9.9	7.3		All Other Current						9.9
46.3	44.2	38.2		Total Current						40.7
6.2	6.1	4.4		Long Term Debt						7.3
.2	.2	.2		Deferred Taxes						.3
3.1	2.3	7.2		All Other Non-Current						6.2
44.3	47.2	50.0		Net Worth						45.5
100.0	100.0	100.0		Total Liabilities & Net Worth						100.0

				INCOME DATA						
100.0	100.0	100.0		Net Sales						100.0
29.3	28.8	32.1		Gross Profit						33.6
24.3	24.7	28.6		Operating Expenses						28.4
5.0	4.1	3.5		Operating Profit						5.1
.9	.6	1.0		All Other Expenses (net)						1.3
4.1	3.5	2.5		Profit Before Taxes						3.8

				RATIOS						
2.8	3.3	3.5								3.2
1.7	1.7	2.1		Current						2.0
1.4	1.3	1.4								1.1
1.7	2.1	1.8								1.6
.8	1.0	.6		Quick						.2
.5	.5	.3								.1
23 15.7	8 44.0	3 137.5							1	256.6
35 10.3	27 13.7	19 19.4		Sales/Receivables					8	45.9
57 6.5	40 9.2	43 8.5							20	18.2
31 11.7	20 18.0	36 10.1							37	10.0
54 6.7	66 5.5	64 5.7		Cost of Sales/Inventory					59	6.2
130 2.8	136 2.7	152 2.4							73	5.0
13 28.4	12 31.1	11 33.0							13	28.7
28 13.0	18 20.8	33 11.2		Cost of Sales/Payables					28	12.8
49 7.5	41 9.0	56 6.5							46	7.9
4.4	5.3	4.2								4.3
8.9	8.6	6.7		Sales/Working Capital						7.7
19.6	20.6	17.2								69.9
14.3	5.3	5.7								9.0
(23) 3.2	(18) 2.2	(28) 2.9		EBIT/Interest						4.0
1.0	1.0	.5								.3
				Net Profit + Depr., Dep., Amort./Cur. Mat. L/T/D						
.0	.1	.0								.1
.1	.1	.2		Fixed/Worth						.4
.6	.4	.5								.7
.6	.2	.4								.8
1.6	1.2	1.1		Debt/Worth						1.4
2.9	3.3	2.6								3.2
54.7	34.3	33.6		% Profit Before Taxes/Tangible Net Worth						50.7
17.7	(20) 12.5	(28) 7.2							(11)	26.1
4.6	8.1	-3.1								-9.3
18.5	12.8	14.2		% Profit Before Taxes/Total Assets						17.5
6.7	8.5	3.3								9.0
.7	2.1	-2.5								-3.7
146.8	195.9	232.5		Sales/Net Fixed Assets						129.2
57.0	64.0	58.8								46.0
16.4	18.0	23.4								19.3
3.8	4.3	3.6		Sales/Total Assets						4.7
2.8	2.8	2.5								2.6
2.0	2.5	1.7								2.1
.1	.1	.3		% Depr., Dep., Amort./Sales						.3
(24) .6	.6	(26) .6							(11)	.6
1.1	1.6	1.3								1.3
1.2				% Officers', Directors', Owners' Comp/Sales						
(15) 2.8										
5.1										
890412M	1023013M	967969M		Net Sales ($)		4600M	7713M	44574M	105848M	805234M
336312M	467700M	364880M		Total Assets ($)		3791M	3173M	31251M	48214M	278451M

M = $ thousand   MM = $ million
See Pages 11 through 18 for Explanation of Ratios and Data

Note in Assets/Liabilities/Income columns 0-1MM, 1-3MM, 3-5MM, 5-10MM, 10-25MM: **DATA NOT AVAILABLE**

Current Data Sorted By Assets | **Comparative Historical Data**

0-500M	500M-2MM	2-10MM	10-50MM	50-100MM	100-250MM		4/1/98-3/31/99 ALL	4/1/99-3/31/00 ALL
						Type of Statement		
		10	5	3	2	Unqualified	25	22
	9	22	8			Reviewed	28	26
	2	2				Compiled	17	10
	1					Tax Returns	3	4
		1	2	2		Other	12	11
	15 (4/1-9/30/02)		54 (10/1/02-3/31/03)					
	12	35	15	5	2	**NUMBER OF STATEMENTS**	85	73
%	%	%	%	%	%	**ASSETS**	%	%
DATA NOT AVAILABLE	5.6	5.2	11.0			Cash & Equivalents	10.0	7.0
	21.9	34.3	27.2			Trade Receivables (net)	29.2	31.3
	50.0	43.6	39.6			Inventory	37.9	38.2
	4.5	1.5	7.2			All Other Current	2.7	2.3
	82.1	84.6	85.0			Total Current	79.8	78.8
	11.9	10.5	5.6			Fixed Assets (net)	13.7	13.4
	.9	.3	2.7			Intangibles (net)	2.2	2.9
	5.1	4.6	6.7			All Other Non-Current	4.3	4.9
	100.0	100.0	100.0			Total	100.0	100.0
						LIABILITIES		
	17.2	12.0	6.3			Notes Payable-Short Term	17.6	20.1
	1.4	1.3	.6			Cur. Mat.-L/T/D	4.2	4.2
	18.4	24.2	21.5			Trade Payables	22.1	17.3
	.0	.7	.1			Income Taxes Payable	.3	.4
	12.2	12.3	12.1			All Other Current	13.6	10.0
	49.2	50.5	40.7			Total Current	57.8	51.9
	6.0	5.1	5.3			Long Term Debt	8.3	7.5
	.4	.0	.1			Deferred Taxes	.1	.4
	5.3	4.5	9.9			All Other Non-Current	12.5	5.7
	39.1	39.9	44.1			Net Worth	21.2	34.5
	100.0	100.0	100.0			Total Liabilities & Net Worth	100.0	100.0
						INCOME DATA		
	100.0	100.0	100.0			Net Sales	100.0	100.0
	34.5	30.4	26.8			Gross Profit	30.5	31.6
	32.6	27.0	22.0			Operating Expenses	26.1	28.0
	1.9	3.4	4.8			Operating Profit	4.3	3.7
	1.1	.1	.3			All Other Expenses (net)	1.4	.8
	.8	3.3	4.4			Profit Before Taxes	2.9	2.9
						RATIOS		
	2.0	2.3	3.7				2.7	2.5
	1.7	1.8	2.6			Current	1.8	1.6
	1.2	1.4	1.6				1.2	1.2
	1.0	1.3	1.9				1.4	1.4
	.4	.8	1.0			Quick	.8	.7
	.2	.5	.6				.4	.5
	0 744.0	**14** 25.9	**6** 64.5				**20** 18.3	**20** 18.0
	21 17.3	**38** 9.5	**26** 14.2			Sales/Receivables	**44** 8.2	**47** 7.8
	34 10.9	**57** 6.4	**63** 5.8				**62** 5.9	**65** 5.6
	62 5.9	**36** 10.2	**32** 11.6				**41** 9.0	**40** 9.1
	88 4.1	**56** 6.5	**45** 8.1			Cost of Sales/Inventory	**84** 4.3	**77** 4.8
	135 2.7	**111** 3.3	**114** 3.2				**127** 2.9	**153** 2.4
	17 22.0	**18** 20.1	**18** 20.2				**19** 19.3	**18** 20.7
	33 11.2	**32** 11.5	**29** 12.8			Cost of Sales/Payables	**33** 11.2	**27** 13.3
	57 6.4	**44** 8.3	**57** 6.4				**43** 8.6	**50** 7.4
	6.2	4.9	3.5				4.8	4.8
	13.3	11.5	4.9			Sales/Working Capital	8.6	8.5
	24.7	18.5	15.5				24.3	20.8
	3.6	8.5	24.7				6.5	7.4
	(10) 1.6	(33) 3.4	6.4			EBIT/Interest	(78) 3.3	(66) 2.7
	.3	1.9	1.6				1.3	1.3
							10.2	8.8
						Net Profit + Depr., Dep., Amort./Cur. Mat. L /T/D	(22) 2.3	(16) 2.7
							.8	1.1
	.2	.1	.1				.1	.1
	.4	.2	.1			Fixed/Worth	.4	.3
	.6	.5	.4				.7	1.0
	.8	.9	.4				.6	.8
	3.0	1.4	1.0			Debt/Worth	1.5	1.6
	4.7	2.3	4.5				4.7	4.8
	14.4	46.8	48.0				44.0	45.5
	10.3	(33) 20.7	(13) 29.4			% Profit Before Taxes/Tangible Net Worth	(73) 15.2	(62) 15.1
	2.1	5.1	8.9				4.3	4.0
	6.6	16.2	21.9				20.2	14.8
	2.6	6.0	9.2			% Profit Before Taxes/Total Assets	6.9	5.3
	.5	1.8	1.3				.9	1.1
	118.7	134.0	164.9				66.7	56.2
	31.9	62.5	84.4			Sales/Net Fixed Assets	29.8	24.8
	16.4	26.5	30.6				14.2	13.7
	3.4	5.4	3.3				3.5	3.4
	2.9	3.5	2.4			Sales/Total Assets	2.8	2.5
	2.4	2.2	1.8				1.8	1.9
	.3	.2	.2				.3	.6
	.8	.6	(12) .5			% Depr., Dep., Amort./Sales	(75) .8	(62) .9
	2.1	1.0	1.0				1.5	1.8
		.9					1.7	1.4
		(16) 2.0				% Officers', Directors', Owners' Comp/Sales	(37) 3.0	(34) 2.6
		4.4					5.4	5.6
	48952M	**769232M**	**965009M**	**707555M**	**753413M**	Net Sales ($)	**2528204M**	**3470520M**
	14671M	**198047M**	**348059M**	**357143M**	**368919M**	Total Assets ($)	**1181734M**	**1419967M**

M = $ thousand MM = $ million

See Pages 11 through 18 for Explanation of Ratios and Data

Comparative Historical Data				Current Data Sorted By Sales					
			Type of Statement						
10	10	20	Unqualified				2	5	13
20	19	39	Reviewed		2	6	4	9	18
15	14	4	Compiled		1			3	
		1	Tax Returns		1				
10	12	5	Other				1		4
4/1/00-3/31/01	**4/1/01-3/31/02**	**4/1/02-3/31/03**		**15 (4/1-9/30/02)**			**54 (10/1/02-3/31/03)**		
ALL	**ALL**	**ALL**		**0-1MM**	**1-3MM**	**3-5MM**	**5-10MM**	**10-25MM**	**25MM & OVER**
55	55	69	**NUMBER OF STATEMENTS**		4	6	7	17	35
%	%	%	**ASSETS**	%	%	%	%	%	%
6.1	4.6	7.4	Cash & Equivalents	**D A T A**				6.9	7.8
31.6	29.4	30.2	Trade Receivables (net)					34.4	30.5
35.2	39.0	42.1	Inventory					40.5	40.6
3.7	3.5	3.2	All Other Current					2.2	3.5
76.6	76.4	82.9	Total Current					84.0	82.5
13.9	14.5	9.7	Fixed Assets (net)	**N O T**				11.3	7.7
1.8	3.3	1.6	Intangibles (net)					.2	2.4
7.6	5.7	5.8	All Other Non-Current					4.5	7.4
100.0	100.0	100.0	Total					100.0	100.0
			LIABILITIES	**A V A I L A B L E**					
18.5	15.4	12.4	Notes Payable-Short Term					15.9	8.8
3.0	1.8	1.2	Cur. Mat.-L/T/D					1.3	.8
15.6	16.1	21.0	Trade Payables					17.3	24.7
.2	.3	.4	Income Taxes Payable					.2	.2
9.8	10.5	11.8	All Other Current					12.7	11.1
47.0	44.1	46.8	Total Current					47.5	45.6
8.4	14.6	5.4	Long Term Debt					7.9	3.6
.2	.3	.1	Deferred Taxes					.0	.1
4.2	5.0	5.5	All Other Non-Current					3.3	7.0
40.2	35.9	42.2	Net Worth					41.3	43.8
100.0	100.0	100.0	Total Liabilities & Net Worth					100.0	100.0
			INCOME DATA						
100.0	100.0	100.0	Net Sales					100.0	100.0
33.4	32.4	29.9	Gross Profit					26.3	27.4
29.5	27.5	26.6	Operating Expenses					24.4	23.4
3.8	4.8	3.3	Operating Profit					2.0	4.0
1.0	1.8	.4	All Other Expenses (net)					-1.1	.6
2.8	3.1	2.9	Profit Before Taxes					3.1	3.4
			RATIOS						
2.8	2.7	2.6						2.6	3.1
1.6	1.8	1.8	Current					2.0	1.8
1.2	1.3	1.4						1.4	1.4
1.5	1.4	1.3						1.4	1.3
.7	(54) .8	.8	Quick					.9	.9
.4	.4	.5						.6	.6
18 20.3	**12** 30.9	**12** 31.1						**27** 13.4	**7** 52.3
49 7.5	**36** 10.3	**35** 10.5	Sales/Receivables					**38** 9.5	**26** 14.2
60 6.1	**61** 6.0	**59** 6.2						**57** 6.4	**56** 6.5
35 10.5	**35** 10.4	**36** 10.1						**43** 8.6	**33** 11.2
72 5.1	**75** 4.9	**68** 5.4	Cost of Sales/Inventory					**73** 5.0	**43** 8.6
122 3.0	**108** 3.4	**112** 3.2						**110** 3.3	**84** 4.3
18 19.8	**15** 24.6	**18** 20.5						**11** 31.9	**18** 20.1
28 13.3	**22** 16.7	**31** 11.9	Cost of Sales/Payables					**31** 11.9	**28** 12.9
40 9.0	**41** 8.9	**46** 8.0						**42** 8.6	**41** 8.8
5.3	5.0	4.7						4.7	4.9
9.4	9.4	9.5	Sales/Working Capital					6.5	12.1
22.9	19.6	17.6						14.5	26.3
6.7	7.5	12.8						7.6	15.7
(50) 2.8	(51) 2.6	(64) 3.1	EBIT/Interest					2.7	(33) 6.2
1.7	1.4	1.6						1.7	2.1
	21.4	29.3							
	(12) 8.2	(16) 3.5	Net Profit + Depr., Dep., Amort./Cur. Mat. L/T/D						
	1.2	1.0							
.1	.1	.1						.1	.1
.2	.3	.2	Fixed/Worth					.1	.2
.7	.9	.5						.7	.4
.6	.8	.8						.8	.6
1.7	1.5	1.4	Debt/Worth					1.1	1.2
3.5	3.0	2.8						2.3	3.0
40.8	45.4	35.3						53.6	66.6
(48) 15.6	(50) 14.3	(64) 14.7	% Profit Before Taxes/Tangible Net Worth					(15) 7.0	(32) 29.9
5.0	4.0	6.3						4.1	10.8
13.1	17.2	16.0						11.9	22.1
5.3	6.4	6.5	% Profit Before Taxes/Total Assets					5.0	9.8
1.7	2.0	1.8						1.5	2.3
73.7	67.9	131.3						224.8	128.6
29.8	36.1	53.8	Sales/Net Fixed Assets					62.5	69.6
13.2	14.7	18.7						25.8	28.6
3.7	4.2	4.1						4.1	5.5
2.6	2.8	2.8	Sales/Total Assets					2.8	3.3
1.9	1.9	2.2						2.2	2.2
.2	.2	.3						.2	.2
(43) .7	(47) .8	(63) .6	% Depr., Dep., Amort./Sales					.4	(29) .5
1.7	1.3	1.1						1.0	1.0
1.1	1.3	1.1							
(22) 3.1	(24) 2.9	(27) 2.6	% Officers', Directors', Owners' Comp/Sales						
4.6	5.5	4.5							
2539897M	**2782580M**	**3244161M**	Net Sales ($)		**9405M**	**21877M**	**52612M**	**231816M**	**2928451M**
1164474M	**1047037M**	**1286839M**	Total Assets ($)		**3307M**	**7725M**	**29379M**	**91024M**	**1155404M**

M = $ thousand MM = $ million

See Pages 11 through 18 for Explanation of Ratios and Data

Current Data Sorted By Assets   **Comparative Historical Data**

0-500M	500M-2MM	2-10MM	10-50MM	50-100MM	100-250MM	Type of Statement	4/1/98-3/31/99 ALL	4/1/99-3/31/00 ALL
1		3			.1	Unqualified	3	4
1	3	8	1			Reviewed	12	15
	2	1	1			Compiled	4	5
	3					Tax Returns	2	2
1	3	6			1	Other	6	4
	6 (4/1-9/30/02)		30 (10/1/02-3/31/03)					
3	11	18	2	1	1	NUMBER OF STATEMENTS	27	30
%	%	%	%	%	%	ASSETS	%	%
	8.7	9.8				Cash & Equivalents	4.9	4.8
	41.7	34.3				Trade Receivables (net)	30.4	32.4
	22.9	33.3				Inventory	39.6	39.4
	6.1	4.3				All Other Current	1.5	1.6
	79.3	81.7				Total Current	76.4	78.1
	15.7	14.0				Fixed Assets (net)	15.3	15.4
	.0	.4				Intangibles (net)	2.8	1.5
	5.0	3.9				All Other Non-Current	5.5	5.0
	100.0	100.0				Total	100.0	100.0
						LIABILITIES		
	19.6	10.2				Notes Payable-Short Term	21.0	21.1
	6.4	5.1				Cur. Mat.-L/T/D	2.5	3.1
	14.5	12.5				Trade Payables	8.0	13.1
	.0	.0				Income Taxes Payable	.2	.2
	17.5	12.8				All Other Current	8.0	8.8
	58.0	40.7				Total Current	39.7	46.3
	5.4	10.0				Long Term Debt	15.9	9.9
	.0	.3				Deferred Taxes	.3	.3
	4.4	4.0				All Other Non-Current	7.0	5.7
	32.2	45.0				Net Worth	37.1	37.7
	100.0	100.0				Total Liabilities & Net Worth	100.0	100.0
						INCOME DATA		
	100.0	100.0				Net Sales	100.0	100.0
	31.2	30.9				Gross Profit	30.1	27.4
	32.0	26.6				Operating Expenses	25.5	23.6
	−.8	4.3				Operating Profit	4.6	3.8
	.3	.7				All Other Expenses (net)	2.1	1.7
	−1.1	3.6				Profit Before Taxes	2.5	2.1
						RATIOS		
	2.4	3.1					3.3	2.8
	1.4	2.1				Current	2.1	1.8
	1.1	1.4					1.5	1.3
	2.2	1.5					1.5	1.2
	.8	1.0				Quick	.9	.7
	.4	.7					.6	.5
	48 7.7	39 9.4					36 10.0	32 11.3
	57 6.4	47 7.7				Sales/Receivables	44 8.4	47 7.7
	69 5.3	61 6.0					69 5.3	62 5.9
	0 UND	16 23.5					66 5.5	55 6.6
	26 14.1	82 4.4				Cost of Sales/Inventory	89 4.1	78 4.7
	97 3.8	165 2.2					114 3.2	138 2.6
	16 23.0	7 51.9					9 38.7	10 35.1
	19 19.2	17 21.6				Cost of Sales/Payables	18 20.5	19 19.4
	40 9.1	36 10.1					30 12.2	33 10.9
	5.1	3.2					3.4	3.9
	11.7	5.4				Sales/Working Capital	5.4	6.8
	70.3	13.7					8.8	15.7
		14.9					3.8	4.9
		3.3				EBIT/Interest	2.0 (29)	1.4
		1.8					1.2	.4
						Net Profit + Depr., Dep., Amort./Cur. Mat. L /T/D		
	.2	.1					.2	.2
	.6	.3				Fixed/Worth	.3	.3
	.7	.8					1.2	.7
	1.0	.6					.6	.7
	1.7	1.2				Debt/Worth	1.7	2.0
	3.7	2.6					4.9	2.7
	26.1	28.9					30.9	32.3
	(10) 6.6	(16) 19.5				% Profit Before Taxes/Tangible Net Worth	(25) 9.7	(27) 10.8
	−94.7	8.5					3.2	.4
	15.0	14.1					10.0	14.1
	2.2	6.5				% Profit Before Taxes/Total Assets	5.1	3.3
	−6.8	1.3					.8	−.6
	32.8	61.7					35.2	43.2
	18.2	25.1				Sales/Net Fixed Assets	19.3	19.3
	10.6	10.7					7.5	9.8
	4.4	3.1					2.7	2.9
	2.5	2.4				Sales/Total Assets	2.2	2.3
	2.2	1.7					1.8	1.9
	.5	.3					.4	.6
	(17) 1.6	.8				% Depr., Dep., Amort./Sales	(25) 1.1	(27) 1.1
	2.9	1.3					3.3	2.4
							2.1	2.2
						% Officers', Directors', Owners' Comp/Sales	(15) 3.0	(16) 5.9
							5.8	10.0
1866M	42001M	233639M	40617M	73592M	139441M	Net Sales ($)	476547M	273566M
479M	14660M	90721M	24452M	55373M	143638M	Total Assets ($)	281088M	136532M

M = $ thousand   MM = $ million
See Pages 11 through 18 for Explanation of Ratios and Data

Comparative Historical Data | Current Data Sorted By Sales

					Type of Statement							
	3		3		5	Unqualified	1				1	2	1
	8		10		13	Reviewed		1	2		6	3	1
	6		2		4	Compiled		1	1			2	
	1		1		3	Tax Returns		2	1				
	6		5		11	Other	1			2	4	2	2
	4/1/00- 3/31/01 ALL		4/1/01- 3/31/02 ALL		4/1/02- 3/31/03 ALL		0-1MM	6 (4/1-9/30/02) 1-3MM	3-5MM	5-10MM	30 (10/1/02-3/31/03)	10-25MM	25MM & OVER
	24		21		36	NUMBER OF STATEMENTS	2	4	6	11		9	4
	%		%		%		%	%	%	%		%	%
						ASSETS							
	3.7		7.7		8.4	Cash & Equivalents				3.7			
	27.9		26.8		36.7	Trade Receivables (net)				43.0			
	38.2		39.7		27.2	Inventory				30.0			
	1.7		3.5		5.3	All Other Current				7.2			
	71.4		77.8		77.6	Total Current				83.9			
	16.5		15.7		15.5	Fixed Assets (net)				13.2			
	.1.8		4.0		3.0	Intangibles (net)				.0			
	10.2		2.5		3.9	All Other Non-Current				2.9			
	100.0		100.0		100.0	Total				100.0			
						LIABILITIES							
	21.9		21.5		14.3	Notes Payable-Short Term				16.8			
	5.2		2.5		6.4	Cur. Mat.-L/T/D				5.7			
	10.5		9.2		12.0	Trade Payables				15.0			
	.1		.1		.2	Income Taxes Payable				.1			
	13.7		7.9		12.8	All Other Current				7.9			
	51.5		41.3		45.6	Total Current				45.5			
	16.5		8.4		7.7	Long Term Debt				10.1			
	.2		.0		.3	Deferred Taxes				.0			
	7.9		6.2		4.8	All Other Non-Current				2.1			
	23.9		44.0		41.6	Net Worth				42.3			
	100.0		100.0		100.0	Total Liabilities & Net Worth				100.0			
						INCOME DATA							
	100.0		100.0		100.0	Net Sales				100.0			
	27.6		32.3		30.0	Gross Profit				28.0			
	24.6		29.0		26.7	Operating Expenses				25.5			
	3.0		3.3		3.3	Operating Profit				2.5			
	2.6		1.1		.8	All Other Expenses (net)				.6			
	.4		2.3		2.5	Profit Before Taxes				1.9			
						RATIOS							
	2.9		3.0		2.6					2.4			
	1.5		1.8		1.8	Current				1.8			
	1.0		1.2		1.3					1.4			
	1.1		1.2		1.6					1.2			
	.7		.7		.9	Quick				1.1			
	.4		.5		.6					.7			
26	13.9	33	11.0	41	9.0					48	7.7		
44	8.2	42	8.7	52	7.1	Sales/Receivables				56	6.5		
58	6.3	60	6.1	67	5.4					83	4.4		
46	7.9	45	8.1	7	52.0					0	UND		
88	4.2	116	3.1	65	5.6	Cost of Sales/Inventory				139	2.6		
133	2.8	149	2.5	139	2.6					181	2.0		
9	41.3	11	33.9	9	40.5					17	21.7		
21	17.2	20	17.9	17	21.1	Cost of Sales/Payables				32	11.5		
35	10.5	35	10.5	33	10.9					47	7.7		
	4.6		3.7		4.5					3.4			
	13.4		6.6		7.9	Sales/Working Capital				4.9			
	NM		14.6		20.1					12.1			
	5.2		6.5		9.7					11.6			
	1.6		2.0	(32)	2.9	EBIT/Interest				2.9			
	.4		1.0		1.0					1.0			
				(13)	11.6	Net Profit + Depr., Dep., Amort./Cur. Mat. L/T/D				1.0			
					.4					.4			
	.2		.1		.2					.2			
	1.2		.3		.4	Fixed/Worth				.3			
	3.9		.6		.9					.7			
	1.3		.6		.7					.7			
	4.7		1.4		1.7	Debt/Worth				1.7			
	25.7		2.7		3.0					2.6			
	53.7		23.5		28.1					20.9			
(21)	16.1	(18)	11.8	(32)	14.7	% Profit Before Taxes/Tangible Net Worth				(10)	9.9		
	−41.8		.6		3.7					1.6			
	15.1		12.5		14.9					5.9			
	1.6		3.1		5.8	% Profit Before Taxes/Total Assets				4.0			
	−4.3		−.1		1.0					.0			
	53.9		63.3		33.8					42.6			
	20.8		19.2		18.2	Sales/Net Fixed Assets				21.1			
	6.3		8.4		10.7					10.8			
	2.9		2.4		3.1					3.4			
	2.4		2.0		2.4	Sales/Total Assets				2.0			
	1.6		1.7		1.9					1.7			
	.5		.4		.5					.3			
(18)	1.5	(19)	1.7	(35)	1.2	% Depr., Dep., Amort./Sales				(10)	.7		
	3.5		2.8		2.4					1.6			
	1.5		2.9		2.3								
(13)	5.8	(14)	4.0	(19)	4.5	% Officers', Directors', Owners' Comp/Sales							
	8.9		5.5		7.0								
	468257M		303305M		531156M	Net Sales ($)	279M	7286M	22154M	77777M		149433M	274227M
	303154M		161510M		329323M	Total Assets ($)	96M	2500M	10412M	37506M		58792M	220017M

M = $ thousand   MM = $ million
See Pages 11 through 18 for Explanation of Ratios and Data

Current Data Sorted By Assets · Comparative Historical Data

0-500M	500M-2MM	2-10MM	10-50MM	50-100MM	100-250MM	Type of Statement	4/1/98-3/31/99 ALL	4/1/99-3/31/00 ALL
	1	7	14	6	5	Unqualified	26	18
	8	18	2			Reviewed	17	22
4	13	4	1			Compiled	14	13
6	5	1				Tax Returns	6	5
4	10	6	8	2	4	Other	24	34
	29 (4/1-9/30/02)			99 (10/1/02-3/31/03)				
14	37	36	24	8	9	NUMBER OF STATEMENTS	87	92
%	%	%	%	%	%	ASSETS	%	%
17.5	7.0	8.4	8.7			Cash & Equivalents	7.8	6.5
31.5	25.4	24.7	24.0			Trade Receivables (net)	23.0	23.9
15.9	36.4	36.4	34.9			Inventory	37.3	38.2
.5	3.7	4.9	2.7			All Other Current	2.7	1.1
65.4	72.6	74.4	70.3			Total Current	70.8	69.7
27.4	19.2	17.4	15.9			Fixed Assets (net)	17.2	17.9
3.2	1.5	2.8	2.3			Intangibles (net)	5.5	6.5
4.0	6.7	5.4	11.5			All Other Non-Current	6.5	5.8
100.0	100.0	100.0	100.0			Total	100.0	100.0
						LIABILITIES		
9.6	11.0	18.1	10.4			Notes Payable-Short Term	15.7	17.2
1.4	5.9	2.8	2.4			Cur. Mat.-L/T/D	3.4	3.2
24.9	16.8	20.1	9.8			Trade Payables	14.4	13.3
.0	.1	.2	.1			Income Taxes Payable	.6	.5
14.4	6.7	14.0	7.2			All Other Current	10.3	10.6
50.3	40.5	55.1	29.9			Total Current	44.4	44.9
27.3	12.1	7.5	5.8			Long Term Debt	14.9	15.2
.1	.8	.5	.5			Deferred Taxes	.3	.1
4.1	10.9	4.2	3.4			All Other Non-Current	7.0	4.0
18.1	35.7	32.6	60.4			Net Worth	33.4	35.8
100.0	100.0	100.0	100.0			Total Liabilities & Net Worth	100.0	100.0
						INCOME DATA		
100.0	100.0	100.0	100.0			Net Sales	100.0	100.0
45.9	35.7	30.8	34.6			Gross Profit	32.7	34.6
43.0	34.6	29.4	28.4			Operating Expenses	54.3	28.9
2.8	1.1	1.4	6.2			Operating Profit	-21.6	5.7
.2	.8	.7	.4			All Other Expenses (net)	4.0	1.8
2.6	.3	.7	5.8			Profit Before Taxes	-25.6	3.9
						RATIOS		
2.2	3.6	2.4	4.4				2.4	2.6
1.6	1.8	1.7	2.2			Current	1.6	1.5
.7	1.4	1.1	1.5				1.2	1.1
1.8	1.3	1.0	2.0				1.3	1.2
.7	.8	.7	1.0			Quick	.7	.6
.5	.5	.4	.5				.4	.4
0 UND	23 15.6	10 37.7	34 10.6				19 19.6	16 22.8
30 12.4	35 10.5	36 10.0	60 6.1			Sales/Receivables	40 9.2	35 10.4
39 9.3	51 7.2	52 7.0	71 5.1				53 6.9	57 6.3
0 UND	47 7.8	25 14.5	74 4.9				50 7.3	50 7.3
4 84.2	78 4.7	83 4.4	138 2.6			Cost of Sales/Inventory	98 3.7	87 4.2
54 6.8	156 2.3	127 2.9	183 2.0				144 2.5	146 2.5
0 UND	20 18.7	20 18.4	16 22.3				18 20.3	14 25.6
23 15.8	29 12.5	30 12.3	29 12.5			Cost of Sales/Payables	32 11.5	23 15.7
45 8.1	54 6.8	47 7.7	55 6.6				52 7.0	45 8.1
9.7	3.9	5.7	3.0				4.6	4.8
24.4	8.4	9.8	5.0			Sales/Working Capital	8.7	11.7
-38.5	16.2	54.4	8.1				21.0	55.3
	(31) 5.2	(31) 11.4	(21) 12.4				(76) 5.3	(85) 6.7
	1.9	3.8	4.5			EBIT/Interest	2.7	3.2
	-.6	1.3	2.5				1.0	1.2
							(28) 3.9	(22) 4.1
						Net Profit + Depr., Dep., Amort./Cur. Mat. L/T/D	1.7	2.1
							.8	.2
.1	.1	.2	.1				.2	.1
.8	.3	.4	.2			Fixed/Worth	.5	.5
-4.6	1.2	1.1	.4				1.7	1.9
.6	.6	.8	.3				1.1	.8
3.2	1.1	1.4	.7			Debt/Worth	2.4	2.3
-4.2	3.3	7.2	1.4				7.2	8.1
	(34) 27.3	(30) 48.5	29.0			% Profit Before Taxes/Tangible Net Worth	(75) 38.9	(81) 56.5
	6.4	17.7	14.4				23.2	23.4
	-3.2	5.6	4.8				1.7	3.7
32.7	8.7	12.6	13.7				15.6	15.5
11.6	2.6	6.0	8.3			% Profit Before Taxes/Total Assets	7.5	9.1
-4.0	-2.9	-.9	2.0				-.2	.7
139.7	46.1	46.1	36.7				31.1	51.9
30.5	21.6	20.8	13.7			Sales/Net Fixed Assets	15.7	15.8
8.4	8.8	10.1	7.2				9.3	8.9
5.8	3.4	3.4	1.9				3.1	3.0
4.7	2.5	2.7	1.7			Sales/Total Assets	2.1	2.1
2.9	1.7	1.8	1.4				1.5	1.6
	(31) .7	(34) .7	(23) 1.1				(70) .7	(68) .6
	1.4	1.0	1.9			% Depr., Dep., Amort./Sales	1.6	1.5
	2.9	1.7	2.8				2.4	2.4
	(15) 2.8	(13) 2.4					(40) 2.4	(41) 2.2
	4.2	6.0				% Officers', Directors', Owners' Comp/Sales	4.0	5.1
	9.5	9.2					9.5	10.7
16540M	122347M	460403M	999585M	1184498M	2540404M	Net Sales ($)	3774587M	3121462M
3412M	46541M	169611M	586000M	593310M	1527714M	Total Assets ($)	2227204M	1711250M

© RMA 2003

M = $ thousand   MM = $ million
See Pages 11 through 18 for Explanation of Ratios and Data

Comparative Historical Data				Current Data Sorted By Sales					
18	11	33	**Type of Statement**			1	3	9	20
18	11	28	Unqualified	1	2	5	7	10	3
15	19	21	Reviewed	1	10	5	3	3	
4	9	12	Compiled	4	6	1			1
26	30	34	Tax Returns	5	4	6	3	4	12
4/1/00-	4/1/01-	4/1/02-	Other		29 (4/1-9/30/02)		99 (10/1/02-3/31/03)		
3/31/01	3/31/02	3/31/03		0-1MM	1-3MM	3-5MM	5-10MM	10-25MM	25MM & OVER
ALL	ALL	ALL							
81	80	128	**NUMBER OF STATEMENTS**	11	22	18	16	25	36
%	%	%	**ASSETS**	%	%	%	%	%	%
8.2	7.7	8.5	Cash & Equivalents	9.9	8.9	11.6	7.3	9.4	6.3
25.4	23.1	25.6	Trade Receivables (net)	40.4	18.7	25.5	25.0	25.7	25.7
36.4	38.6	34.0	Inventory	8.9	34.6	37.7	38.0	35.0	37.1
2.9	2.4	3.4	All Other Current	.5	2.2	1.7	7.3	5.2	2.8
72.9	71.9	71.6	Total Current	59.7	64.3	76.4	77.5	75.4	71.9
14.5	19.9	18.6	Fixed Assets (net)	32.2	25.2	13.3	14.4	18.7	15.1
4.9	3.6	3.2	Intangibles (net)	4.1	1.9	3.5	.2	2.0	5.7
7.7	4.7	6.6	All Other Non-Current	3.8	8.6	6.8	7.9	3.9	7.3
100.0	100.0	100.0	Total	100.0	100.0	100.0	100.0	100.0	100.0
			LIABILITIES						
18.8	17.1	13.1	Notes Payable-Short Term	8.1	11.1	20.9	13.6	8.9	14.8
3.1	4.7	3.5	Cur. Mat.-L/T/D	.4	2.9	12.8	2.3	1.7	1.9
15.8	14.3	16.4	Trade Payables	27.5	12.8	19.1	16.9	19.4	11.7
.4	.1	.2	Income Taxes Payable	.0	.2	.0	.1	.0	.5
8.6	12.5	10.2	All Other Current	14.4	5.0	9.2	19.4	7.6	10.3
46.7	48.7	43.5	Total Current	50.4	31.9	62.0	52.3	37.8	39.2
9.1	12.0	11.0	Long Term Debt	35.9	18.3	5.7	7.1	5.4	7.2
.3	.1	.5	Deferred Taxes	.1	.3	1.4	.6	.6	.4
4.8	5.3	5.9	All Other Non-Current	2.3	15.6	5.8	5.1	2.5	3.7
39.3	33.9	39.1	Net Worth	11.2	33.9	25.2	35.0	53.6	49.5
100.0	100.0	100.0	Total Liabilities & Net Worth	100.0	100.0	100.0	100.0	100.0	100.0
			INCOME DATA						
100.0	100.0	100.0	Net Sales	100.0	100.0	100.0	100.0	100.0	100.0
31.7	33.6	34.4	Gross Profit	46.1	43.5	27.4	25.2	34.8	32.4
26.2	29.8	31.0	Operating Expenses	44.3	42.0	27.3	26.9	28.8	25.3
5.6	3.8	3.4	Operating Profit	1.8	1.4	.1	−1.7	6.0	7.1
1.4	1.4	.8	All Other Expenses (net)	.5	1.0	.7	.5	.5	1.0
4.1	2.4	2.6	Profit Before Taxes	1.3	.4	−.6	−2.3	5.5	6.1
			RATIOS						
2.5	2.6	3.1		2.6	3.8	3.4	2.2	3.2	3.4
1.7	1.7	1.8	Current	1.1	1.8	1.8	1.7	2.2	1.8
1.1	1.0	1.3		.7	1.4	.8	1.4	1.5	1.4
1.1	1.2	1.4		2.6	1.3	1.5	.9	1.8	1.4
.7	.6	.8	Quick	.8	.8	.8	.6	.8	.9
.4	.3	.5		.6	.6	.4	.4	.4	.5
22	16.9	17	21.6	26	14.2	30	12.1	5	72.6	22	16.3	9	42.0	20	18.1	34	10.8
39	9.3	37	9.8	39	9.4	Sales/Receivables	35	10.3	34	10.8	34	10.8	37	9.7	40	9.1	45	8.1
54	6.7	53	6.9	60	6.1		70	5.2	48	7.7	54	6.7	56	6.6	58	6.3	67	5.5
55	6.6	45	8.2	31	11.6		0	UND	50	7.3	23	15.7	27	13.3	25	14.5	58	6.3
82	4.5	92	4.0	85	4.3	Cost of Sales/Inventory	3	106.5	101	3.6	108	3.4	73	5.0	84	4.3	115	3.2
138	2.7	149	2.4	148	2.5		65	5.6	168	2.2	132	2.8	117	3.1	164	2.2	152	2.4
17	21.7	14	26.0	19	18.7		0	UND	19	19.4	18	20.4	14	25.5	25	14.6	20	18.2
27	13.6	26	13.8	30	12.4	Cost of Sales/Payables	29	12.5	36	10.1	32	11.5	20	18.5	30	12.0	29	12.5
42	8.7	40	9.2	46	7.9		47	7.8	60	6.1	59	6.2	44	8.3	42	8.7	39	9.3
	5.0		5.0		4.3			8.4		3.4		4.2		5.8		4.2		3.7
	9.1		8.2		7.8	Sales/Working Capital		23.4		9.0		8.6		7.8		8.5		6.8
	36.8		185.7		16.4			−31.4		16.0		−10.6		29.8		13.0		9.7
	10.0		6.8		10.0					4.5		10.0		2.9		25.1		12.4
(75)	3.6	(73)	2.2	(109)	4.0	EBIT/Interest	(20)			.7	(15)	3.5	(11)	1.3	(23)	7.5	(33)	7.8
	1.4		1.2		1.3					−2.2		−.5		−1.2		2.8		2.5
	6.4		9.1		8.9	Net Profit + Depr., Dep.,												35.3
(21)	3.7	(15)	1.5	(28)	2.8	Amort./Cur. Mat. L/T/D											(11)	6.4
	1.8		.7		1.2													2.6
	.1		.2		.1			.6		.2		.0		.1		.1		.2
	.3		.5		.3	Fixed/Worth		1.6		.4		.2		.2		.2		.3
	1.0		2.1		1.0			−5.8		2.1		NM		2.3		.6		.8
	.8		.9		.6			.8		.4		.7		.8		.4		.5
	1.6		2.1		1.2	Debt/Worth		4.7		1.3		1.2		1.3		1.0		1.3
	5.1		5.2		3.5			−3.5		3.5		NM		5.2		1.5		1.9
	40.4		34.4		40.0	% Profit Before Taxes/Tangible				30.1		32.3		48.3		45.7		30.7
(72)	20.3	(67)	12.7	(112)	15.4	Net Worth	(20)		(14)	6.0	(13)	12.4		4.9		21.4	(33)	20.0
	4.9		1.9		3.5					−6.7		5.3		−5.3		10.3		11.7
	16.4		13.2		12.6			35.2		8.6		11.1		6.1		24.4		13.8
	7.7		4.5		6.2	% Profit Before Taxes/Total		5.0		1.1		4.4		1.1		7.9		9.2
	1.3		.2		.7	Assets		−6.0		−4.9		−5.3		−6.3		3.6		5.3
	62.9		37.9		41.4			107.1		26.3		98.2		94.6		53.2		39.2
	17.7		18.7		19.4	Sales/Net Fixed Assets		8.5		12.1		26.0		39.2		17.2		16.8
	11.2		9.2		8.2			3.2		6.9		12.2		12.3		7.3		9.4
	3.0		3.5		3.3			5.6		3.5		3.4		3.3		3.7		2.5
	2.3		2.4		2.2	Sales/Total Assets		2.9		1.9		2.7		2.8		2.7		1.7
	1.6		1.7		1.6			1.4		1.6		1.8		1.7		1.8		1.6
	.4		.7		.8					1.3		.5		.3		.8		1.1
(67)	1.3	(69)	1.3	(111)	1.5	% Depr., Dep., Amort./Sales	(19)		(16)	2.0	(14)	.8	(24)	1.1	(31)	1.5		1.5
	1.9		2.6		2.6					2.9		1.3		1.9		2.8		2.4
	1.7		2.9		3.4					4.1		2.6						
(34)	3.2	(38)	5.1	(44)	5.0	% Officers', Directors',	(10)		(11)	8.3		3.5						
	6.6		8.6		9.4	Owners' Comp/Sales				11.9		4.3						
3074997M	2205997M	5323777M	Net Sales ($)	6830M	41409M	73483M	121060M	409268M	4671727M
1629230M	1185733M	2926588M	Total Assets ($)	4257M	21776M	39901M	55258M	194976M	2610420M

© RMA 2003

M = $ thousand   MM = $million
See Pages 11 through 18 for Explanation of Ratios and Data

Current Data Sorted By Assets | Comparative Historical Data

0-500M	500M-2MM	2-10MM	10-50MM	50-100MM	100-250MM	Type of Statement	4/1/98-3/31/99 ALL	4/1/99-3/31/00 ALL
	2	1	5	1	4	Unqualified	4	3
1		7	2			Reviewed	9	9
1	1	4	1			Compiled	3	5
2						Tax Returns	1	
	2	4	3			Other	10	4
4	5	16	11	1	4	**NUMBER OF STATEMENTS**	27	21
%	%	%	%	%	%	**ASSETS**	%	%
		5.7	9.0			Cash & Equivalents	8.4	7.9
		31.8	24.5			Trade Receivables (net)	27.5	28.8
		31.3	21.6			Inventory	29.9	38.0
		3.6	1.8			All Other Current	3.3	.6
		72.3	56.8			Total Current	69.1	75.4
		20.4	17.2			Fixed Assets (net)	18.6	14.8
		3.6	9.4			Intangibles (net)	3.1	2.5
		3.6	16.5			All Other Non-Current	9.2	7.2
		100.0	100.0			Total	100.0	100.0
						LIABILITIES		
		15.7	12.7			Notes Payable-Short Term	9.4	16.3
		2.3	1.7			Cur. Mat.-L/T/D	2.7	.9
		20.1	9.7			Trade Payables	13.3	20.5
		.4	.0			Income Taxes Payable	.2	.3
		11.4	9.3			All Other Current	8.8	2.4
		49.8	33.4			Total Current	34.4	40.4
		10.6	16.7			Long Term Debt	11.5	8.8
		.0	.2			Deferred Taxes	1.5	.5
		3.0	2.7			All Other Non-Current	7.1	2.2
		36.5	47.0			Net Worth	45.5	48.1
		100.0	100.0			Total Liabilities & Net Worth	100.0	100.0
						INCOME DATA		
		100.0	100.0			Net Sales	100.0	100.0
		25.9	31.1			Gross Profit	23.6	22.0
		21.9	27.7			Operating Expenses	18.5	19.6
		4.0	3.5			Operating Profit	5.1	2.4
		1.2	.5			All Other Expenses (net)	–.3	.8
		2.9	3.0			Profit Before Taxes	5.4	1.6
						RATIOS		
		2.7	3.2			Current	4.3	3.5
		1.6	1.4				2.3	1.8
		1.0	1.0				1.6	1.3
		1.7	2.6			Quick	1.9	1.6
		.7	.7				1.3	1.0
		.5	.5				.8	.7
		37 9.9	33 11.2			Sales/Receivables	30 12.0	30 12.3
		44 8.3	36 10.2				45 8.2	46 8.0
		57 6.4	66 5.5				53 6.8	53 6.9
		27 13.7	21 17.8			Cost of Sales/Inventory	32 11.4	33 11.1
		43 8.6	67 5.4				63 5.8	68 5.3
		116 3.1	142 2.6				94 3.9	139 2.6
		11 32.3	16 23.2			Cost of Sales/Payables	9 42.3	13 28.7
		21 17.3	18 20.3				17 21.2	30 12.0
		39 9.4	40 9.0				41 9.0	46 7.9
		5.2	5.2			Sales/Working Capital	3.7	4.6
		9.1	12.6				5.9	6.2
		181.3	154.6				13.8	15.7
		65.3				EBIT/Interest	13.2	7.0
		(15) 2.2					(23) 5.0	(15) 3.0
		1.7					1.8	1.4
						Net Profit + Depr., Dep., Amort./Cur. Mat. L /T/D		
		.1	.2			Fixed/Worth	.1	.1
		.6	.3				.3	.2
		6.8	1.9				.9	.4
		.5	.5			Debt/Worth	.4	.6
		2.0	1.3				.8	1.0
		18.1	3.2				7.1	2.8
		60.6				% Profit Before Taxes/Tangible Net Worth	41.0	29.0
		(13) 13.6					(24) 14.9	(20) 12.1
		8.8					4.8	4.0
		12.8	14.1			% Profit Before Taxes/Total Assets	21.7	11.9
		6.3	5.0				11.2	6.0
		2.3	1.3				3.0	.5
		57.1	33.2			Sales/Net Fixed Assets	39.8	60.2
		21.8	13.9				19.1	29.9
		4.3	10.0				7.5	8.0
		3.5	2.6			Sales/Total Assets	3.1	3.7
		2.7	1.8				2.1	2.2
		1.5	1.0				1.7	1.7
		.3				% Depr., Dep., Amort./Sales	.4	.3
		(15) 1.4					(24) 1.2	(18) .8
		2.3					1.7	1.9
						% Officers', Directors', Owners' Comp/Sales	3.2	1.5
							(11) 5.0	(10) 4.9
							16.5	8.4
2896M	20210M	217969M	467796M	182964M	1511424M	Net Sales ($)	934693M	672754M
1113M	4590M	77710M	235501M	69823M	771798M	Total Assets ($)	388587M	292413M

Date range labels: 8 (4/1-9/30/02) spans 500M-2MM / 2-10MM; 33 (10/1/02-3/31/03) spans 10-50MM.

M = $ thousand   MM = $ million
See Pages 11 through 18 for Explanation of Ratios and Data

Comparative Historical Data | Current Data Sorted By Sales

	4/1/00-3/31/01 ALL	4/1/01-3/31/02 ALL	4/1/02-3/31/03 ALL	0-1MM	1-3MM	3-5MM	5-10MM	10-25MM	25MM & OVER
Type of Statement									
Unqualified	3	8	13		1		2	3	7
Reviewed	8	6	10	1		1	2	2	4
Compiled	6	7	7		1	2		3	1
Tax Returns	2	2	2	1	1				
Other	6	6	9		1	1	1	4	2
				8 (4/1-9/30/02)			33 (10/1/02-3/31/03)		
NUMBER OF STATEMENTS	25	27	41	2	4	4	5	12	14
ASSETS	%	%	%	%	%	%	%	%	%
Cash & Equivalents	7.6	7.0	7.9					6.6	7.8
Trade Receivables (net)	34.4	25.0	25.8					30.7	29.0
Inventory	31.6	31.1	25.5					24.5	27.8
All Other Current	2.0	6.7	5.5					.6	4.0
Total Current	75.5	69.8	64.7					62.4	68.7
Fixed Assets (net)	15.0	19.2	21.9					18.4	16.1
Intangibles (net)	2.6	3.0	5.5					9.3	4.7
All Other Non-Current	6.8	8.0	8.0					9.8	10.5
Total	100.0	100.0	100.0					100.0	100.0
LIABILITIES									
Notes Payable-Short Term	16.4	17.5	16.2					21.1	5.5
Cur. Mat.-L/T/D	3.1	1.7	2.3					1.8	1.1
Trade Payables	22.8	15.6	17.2					10.8	21.9
Income Taxes Payable	.1	.1	.3					.1	.6
All Other Current	4.4	7.3	10.3					9.4	6.8
Total Current	46.7	42.3	46.3					43.2	35.9
Long Term Debt	10.2	12.6	13.5					15.0	9.9
Deferred Taxes	.0	.1	.1					.1	.1
All Other Non-Current	3.7	3.9	2.8					5.2	2.7
Net Worth	39.3	41.1	37.4					36.6	51.3
Total Liabilities & Net Worth	100.0	100.0	100.0					100.0	100.0
INCOME DATA									
Net Sales	100.0	100.0	100.0					100.0	100.0
Gross Profit	20.0	19.8	27.8					33.5	21.1
Operating Expenses	16.6	16.9	24.9					29.1	18.0
Operating Profit	3.4	2.9	2.9					4.4	3.1
All Other Expenses (net)	1.0	1.5	1.1					1.7	.0
Profit Before Taxes	2.4	1.5	1.9					2.7	3.0
RATIOS									
Current	2.4	2.6	2.6					3.1	3.8
	1.6	1.8	1.6					1.5	2.1
	1.2	1.2	1.0					1.0	1.3
Quick	1.4	1.1	1.7					2.4	2.0
	.8	.9	.7					.7	1.3
	.6	.4	.4					.5	.7
Sales/Receivables	29 12.6	31 12.0	28 13.3					37 9.8	28 12.8
	48 7.5	36 10.0	38 9.7					52 7.0	36 10.3
	56 6.5	46 8.0	56 6.5					58 6.3	61 6.0
Cost of Sales/Inventory	16 22.8	22 16.9	20 17.9					33 11.0	21 17.8
	45 8.1	51 7.1	44 8.3					66 5.5	32 11.4
	126 2.9	116 3.1	113 3.2					123 3.0	87 4.2
Cost of Sales/Payables	16 23.2	9 42.7	13 27.3					8 44.4	17 21.8
	21 17.8	19 19.2	23 15.8					20 18.6	24 15.0
	42 8.8	34 10.8	40 9.2					57 6.4	37 9.7
Sales/Working Capital	5.8	4.9	5.6					4.3	4.8
	9.2	7.5	11.4					11.3	8.9
	31.1	37.4	UND					206.0	25.0
EBIT/Interest	6.6	6.0	6.7					4.3	9.7
	(21) 2.1	(25) 1.9	(35) 2.1					(11) 1.9	(12) 5.8
	.2	1.1	.8					1.5	1.0
Net Profit + Depr., Dep., Amort./Cur. Mat. L/T/D									
Fixed/Worth	.1	.1	.2					.2	.1
	.2	.3	.4					.6	.3
	.7	1.4	5.3					-1.2	.7
Debt/Worth	.7	.6	.6					.5	.5
	1.9	1.3	1.5					1.7	1.1
	3.6	4.2	17.8					-7.4	2.0
% Profit Before Taxes/Tangible Net Worth	40.2	35.3	57.2						37.7
	(24) 11.7	(25) 21.7	(33) 16.5						(13) 17.1
	-6.7	2.0	7.0						3.6
% Profit Before Taxes/Total Assets	15.1	12.2	14.1					12.8	16.4
	3.4	2.9	6.0					2.9	8.3
	-1.2	.5	1.0					1.5	3.6
Sales/Net Fixed Assets	347.5	87.5	44.8					39.9	93.0
	39.1	17.7	13.7					16.3	12.7
	9.0	10.2	6.1					6.7	9.6
Sales/Total Assets	3.9	3.6	3.4					3.1	4.0
	2.4	2.4	2.4					1.8	2.5
	1.6	1.4	1.5					1.1	1.9
% Depr., Dep., Amort./Sales	.5	.2	.6					1.4	.3
	(21) 1.0	(22) .8	(35) 1.7					(11) 2.3	(11) .7
	3.0	2.7	2.7					3.5	2.3
% Officers', Directors', Owners' Comp/Sales	1.1		1.9						
	(13) 2.0		(12) 4.4						
	6.7		10.0						
Net Sales ($)	1258456M	1645218M	2403259M	410M	6748M	15380M	40357M	178236M	2162128M
Total Assets ($)	527912M	702744M	1160535M	253M	2970M	8147M	17672M	115040M	1016453M

© RMA 2003

M = $ thousand   MM = $ million
See Pages 11 through 18 for Explanation of Ratios and Data

Current Data Sorted By Assets   Comparative Historical Data

	0-500M	500M-2MM	2-10MM	10-50MM	50-100MM	100-250MM	Type of Statement	4/1/98-3/31/99 ALL	4/1/99-3/31/00 ALL
	1	1	10	38	14	5	Unqualified	75	77
		7	31	23	1	1	Reviewed	80	70
	6	20	24	2			Compiled	79	80
	7	12	4	2			Tax Returns	19	29
	1	6	21	23	8	1	Other	65	61
		56 (4/1-9/30/02)			213 (10/1/02-3/31/03)				
	15	46	90	88	23	7	NUMBER OF STATEMENTS	318	317
	%	%	%	%	%	%	ASSETS	%	%
	5.6	7.7	4.9	3.5	6.9		Cash & Equivalents	5.5	6.3
	5.9	13.8	11.2	8.6	10.4		Trade Receivables (net)	11.6	11.9
	25.2	25.3	26.6	28.1	23.3		Inventory	26.9	26.1
	2.4	2.1	4.3	6.5	6.9		All Other Current	3.4	3.4
	39.2	48.9	47.0	46.7	47.5		Total Current	47.5	47.7
	49.6	43.7	43.6	45.8	36.0		Fixed Assets (net)	41.4	41.6
	6.1	.7	.9	.3	1.1		Intangibles (net)	.8	.7
	5.2	6.7	8.4	7.2	15.4		All Other Non-Current	10.3	10.0
	100.0	100.0	100.0	100.0	100.0		Total	100.0	100.0
							LIABILITIES		
	8.2	14.5	16.0	12.6	9.3		Notes Payable-Short Term	14.9	12.9
	13.0	7.6	6.9	6.0	6.2		Cur. Mat.-L/T/D	5.5	4.9
	7.9	6.2	5.9	5.9	6.0		Trade Payables	6.4	6.8
	.0	.0	.1	.1	.1		Income Taxes Payable	.1	.3
	5.6	6.1	3.8	5.2	4.9		All Other Current	5.2	5.2
	34.6	34.4	32.7	29.8	26.5		Total Current	32.2	30.1
	46.5	23.7	23.2	22.2	27.8		Long Term Debt	24.6	23.2
	.6	.2	.4	1.1	.4		Deferred Taxes	.6	.6
	1.6	3.9	6.6	5.8	5.2		All Other Non-Current	3.8	4.4
	16.8	37.8	37.0	41.2	40.1		Net Worth	38.8	41.8
	100.0	100.0	100.0	100.0	100.0		Total Liabilities & Net Worth	100.0	100.0
							INCOME DATA		
	100.0	100.0	100.0	100.0	100.0		Net Sales	100.0	100.0
	27.3	28.8	20.5	11.8	16.2		Gross Profit	19.4	21.1
	23.4	27.0	19.1	10.6	9.7		Operating Expenses	16.2	15.7
	3.9	1.8	1.4	1.2	6.5		Operating Profit	3.2	5.4
	1.4	.8	1.4	.6	1.8		All Other Expenses (net)	1.5	1.3
	2.5	1.0	−.1	.6	4.7		Profit Before Taxes	1.8	4.1
							RATIOS		
	2.5	3.1	2.2	2.8	2.5			2.5	2.7
	1.7	1.6	1.4	1.7	1.6		Current	1.5	1.6
	.6	.9	1.1	1.1	1.2			1.0	1.1
	.9	1.4	.9	.8	.9			1.0	1.1
	.3	.6	.4	.4	.5		Quick	.5	.5
	.1	.2	.2	.2	.3			.3	.3
	0 869.0	8 46.2	11 33.5	10 35.3	14 26.6			13 28.5	12 29.4
	6 60.2	16 22.5	18 20.5	16 22.6	20 18.3		Sales/Receivables	18 20.1	17 21.3
	11 33.3	23 15.6	26 14.1	23 16.1	33 11.0			26 14.1	25 14.5
	11 33.9	17 21.1	23 15.9	37 10.0	41 8.9			33 11.2	28 12.8
	32 11.3	47 7.7	55 6.7	62 5.9	71 5.2		Cost of Sales/Inventory	58 6.3	54 6.7
	126 2.9	71 5.1	98 3.7	95 3.8	111 3.3			96 3.8	89 4.1
	3 128.0	1 568.2	4 94.0	7 55.1	9 42.2			5 80.2	5 74.0
	9 38.7	5 74.4	9 42.6	12 30.7	18 20.3		Cost of Sales/Payables	10 35.6	11 32.1
	20 17.9	18 20.3	21 17.0	19 18.8	26 14.1			18 20.0	19 19.1
	8.9	9.6	6.6	5.3	4.4			6.1	6.6
	36.6	19.3	15.9	9.7	9.9		Sales/Working Capital	12.1	12.2
	−28.0	−63.4	144.0	36.8	17.6			166.7	60.9
	8.0	4.3	3.7	4.0	6.8			4.0	5.8
(12) 2.2		(42) 1.8	(85) 1.5	(86) 1.9	(21) 2.8		EBIT/Interest	(306) 2.0	(305) 2.6
	−.9	.3	.2	−.5	1.2			.9	1.4
			2.0	7.2				2.8	3.1
		(27)	1.6	(23) 2.0			Net Profit + Depr., Dep., Amort./Cur. Mat. L/T/D	(85) 1.6	(72) 2.0
			.4	.4				.8	.8
	1.1	.5	.5	.7	.3			.5	.5
	3.5	.9	1.0	1.1	.9		Fixed/Worth	1.0	1.0
	−1.9	4.0	2.9	2.0	2.1			1.9	2.1
	1.6	.6	.7	.6	.8			.7	.7
	5.4	1.8	1.7	1.7	2.1		Debt/Worth	1.8	1.6
	−11.4	5.0	6.8	3.0	3.4			3.5	3.2
	29.8	36.0	16.1	18.4	39.6			24.5	33.6
(11) 7.1		(42) 10.0	(79) 5.8	(84) 5.1	11.5		% Profit Before Taxes/Tangible Net Worth	(291) 11.5	(303) 16.3
	−16.7	−6.8	−5.0	−5.0	5.2			.4	3.5
	12.3	9.1	6.6	6.9	9.0			10.1	13.3
	2.6	4.4	1.5	1.6	4.3		% Profit Before Taxes/Total Assets	4.0	6.3
	−14.3	−2.2	−2.6	−3.4	.7			−.7	1.5
	15.3	14.1	8.4	6.5	6.6			8.2	9.9
	5.1	6.0	5.0	3.4	4.9		Sales/Net Fixed Assets	4.9	5.2
	4.0	3.8	3.4	2.5	2.3			3.1	3.0
	6.1	3.7	2.9	2.3	1.7			2.6	2.8
	3.5	2.5	2.0	1.6	1.2		Sales/Total Assets	1.9	2.0
	2.1	1.8	1.4	1.1	.9			1.2	1.3
	1.9	2.5	1.9	2.3	1.9			2.2	2.0
(12) 2.7		(43) 3.7	(85) 3.5	(85) 4.0	(21) 3.3		% Depr., Dep., Amort./Sales	(296) 3.5	(291) 3.5
	5.7	5.7	5.4	5.7	5.7			5.4	5.5
		2.3	1.1	1.1				1.1	1.3
	(24)	4.2	(32) 1.8	(21) 1.8			% Officers', Directors', Owners' Comp/Sales	(114) 2.3	(110) 2.4
		6.4	3.5	2.8				4.8	5.5
	14859M	154443M	920642M	3096764M	2114600M	1426066M	Net Sales ($)	10111204M	6806789M
	4071M	53418M	445610M	1871057M	1494378M	1093205M	Total Assets ($)	5326889M	4585226M

M = $ thousand   MM = $ million
See Pages 11 through 18 for Explanation of Ratios and Data

Comparative Historical Data | Current Data Sorted By Sales

H1	H2	H3		Type of Statement	0-1MM	1-3MM	3-5MM	5-10MM	10-25MM	25MM & OVER
58	79	69		Unqualified	1		1	2	15	50
65	61	63		Reviewed	1	4	8	13	21	16
63	79	52		Compiled	5	13	14	9	11	
18	22	25		Tax Returns	6	9	4	3	3	
64	86	60		Other	2	2	5	10	15	26
4/1/00-3/31/01 ALL	4/1/01-3/31/02 ALL	4/1/02-3/31/03 ALL			56 (4/1-9/30/02)			213 (10/1/02-3/31/03)		
268	327	269		**NUMBER OF STATEMENTS**	15	28	32	37	65	92
%	%	%		**ASSETS**	%	%	%	%	%	%
5.7	5.3	5.1		Cash & Equivalents	7.0	4.2	5.1	6.6	4.9	4.5
11.7	11.8	10.3		Trade Receivables (net)	4.3	11.2	9.2	16.0	9.5	9.7
27.9	26.8	26.2		Inventory	21.3	17.8	32.1	24.2	29.8	25.8
3.9	4.8	4.8		All Other Current	1.1	3.1	2.5	3.0	5.4	6.8
49.3	48.7	46.3		Total Current	33.7	36.3	48.9	49.8	49.6	46.8
40.6	41.0	44.3		Fixed Assets (net)	53.8	50.1	46.4	42.1	41.4	43.2
1.0	.8	1.0		Intangibles (net)	5.9	.9	.7	1.5	.3	.7
9.1	9.5	8.4		All Other Non-Current	6.6	12.7	4.0	6.6	8.6	9.4
100.0	100.0	100.0		Total	100.0	100.0	100.0	100.0	100.0	100.0
				LIABILITIES						
15.4	13.1	13.3		Notes Payable-Short Term	8.3	11.1	19.4	16.1	12.0	12.3
5.4	5.4	7.0		Cur. Mat.-L/T/D	9.0	6.6	9.6	6.9	7.3	5.6
6.5	7.0	6.0		Trade Payables	4.8	7.6	3.9	6.9	6.0	6.2
.2	.1	.1		Income Taxes Payable	.0	.0	.0	.0	.2	.1
6.7	5.5	4.8		All Other Current	3.9	5.3	6.0	4.4	3.4	5.7
34.2	31.0	31.2		Total Current	26.0	30.6	38.9	34.3	28.9	29.9
22.2	25.0	25.1		Long Term Debt	60.2	27.2	21.0	24.0	19.9	24.4
.5	.6	.6		Deferred Taxes	.1	.7	.2	.3	1.0	.7
3.3	3.6	6.1		All Other Non-Current	9.1	6.2	5.3	3.9	4.3	7.9
39.8	39.8	36.9		Net Worth	4.7	35.3	34.5	37.5	45.8	37.1
100.0	100.0	100.0		Total Liabilities & Net Worth	100.0	100.0	100.0	100.0	100.0	100.0
				INCOME DATA						
100.0	100.0	100.0		Net Sales	100.0	100.0	100.0	100.0	100.0	100.0
19.5	20.3	19.0		Gross Profit	39.3	29.5	24.7	17.0	16.7	12.9
16.0	17.4	17.0		Operating Expenses	32.6	30.1	23.3	14.8	15.2	10.5
3.5	2.9	1.9		Operating Profit	6.7	-.6	1.4	2.2	1.5	2.3
1.5	1.4	1.2		All Other Expenses (net)	4.0	.5	.9	1.5	.9	1.1
2.0	1.4	.8		Profit Before Taxes	2.7	-1.1	.5	.7	.6	1.2
				RATIOS						
2.7	2.9	2.5		Current	2.8	2.2	2.9	2.0	3.0	2.5
1.5	1.7	1.6			1.7	1.3	1.5	1.4	1.7	1.6
1.0	1.1	1.1			.2	.7	.7	.9	1.1	1.1
1.0	1.0	.9		Quick	1.3	1.0	.7	1.1	1.0	.9
(266) .4	.5	.4			.2	.4	.4	.4	.5	.4
.2	.2	.2			.1	.2	.2	.3	.2	.2
11 33.0	11 34.4	10 35.4		Sales/Receivables	0 869.0	6 58.8	11 34.3	14 27.0	9 38.5	11 31.8
16 22.8	18 20.7	17 21.9			5 67.2	17 20.9	14 26.4	19 19.2	15 23.9	17 21.6
25 14.4	26 14.0	24 15.3			20 18.7	31 11.9	23 15.9	28 13.2	23 15.8	23 15.9
32 11.4	32 11.5	27 13.6		Cost of Sales/Inventory	11 33.9	11 32.9	22 16.4	17 21.2	34 10.9	34 10.6
56 6.6	56 6.5	56 6.5			59 6.1	49 7.4	65 5.6	47 7.7	67 5.5	52 7.1
94 3.9	95 3.8	91 4.0			134 2.7	79 4.6	127 2.9	71 5.1	99 5.1	81 4.5
4 86.3	4 84.7	5 80.6		Cost of Sales/Payables	0 UND	4 102.6	2 224.8	3 116.9	3 104.7	8 46.7
9 38.5	11 31.9	10 36.1			7 52.3	10 37.4	6 64.4	9 39.8	9 41.2	12 29.6
17 21.4	20 18.1	20 17.9			24 15.4	25 14.6	19 18.7	22 16.9	21 17.6	19 19.1
6.3	5.5	6.5		Sales/Working Capital	5.0	9.4	6.3	8.6	5.6	6.6
12.6	11.3	13.0			14.5	40.3	17.0	17.3	10.9	10.8
180.6	61.1	89.8			-14.0	-11.0	-12.8	-199.9	29.4	36.2
(252) 5.1	(302) 3.6	(253) 4.1		EBIT/Interest	(11) 3.8	(25) 3.3	4.1	(34) 4.3	(61) 3.5	(90) 4.8
1.8	1.5	1.7			1.4	1.4	1.3	2.0	1.6	2.1
.6	.3	.1			.0	-1.1	.4	.5	.0	.5
(66) 3.0	(81) 3.3	(66) 3.4		Net Profit + Depr., Dep., Amort./Cur. Mat. L/T/D				(11) 2.1	(20) 2.5	(25) 5.6
1.4	1.5	1.6						1.6	1.5	2.5
.7	.2	.4						.2	.6	.4
.5	.5	.6		Fixed/Worth	2.1	.6	.6	.6	.5	.6
1.0	.9	1.1			4.5	1.1	1.5	.9	.9	1.1
2.1	2.2	2.7			-1.0	4.7	3.2	2.5	1.7	2.1
.7	.6	.7		Debt/Worth	3.4	.6	.7	1.0	.5	.8
1.5	1.5	1.8			6.2	1.9	1.8	1.8	1.4	1.8
3.4	4.5	3.9			-2.4	8.5	10.9	4.0	2.8	3.3
(243) 22.6	(300) 21.0	(245) 19.0		% Profit Before Taxes/Tangible Net Worth		(24) 17.3	(28) 16.7	(34) 24.1	(62) 13.0	(88) 21.8
9.6	6.5	7.1				4.6	4.4	10.4	4.8	8.1
-1.6	-5.1	-4.4				-6.9	-.5	-1.8	-5.1	-3.9
9.7	8.5	7.1		% Profit Before Taxes/Total Assets	10.3	5.5	6.9	7.3	7.7	7.8
3.3	2.1	1.9			2.1	.7	1.2	3.2	1.9	3.0
-2.2	-2.9	-2.1			-4.5	-4.4	-3.4	-3.1	-2.2	-1.5
9.8	9.5	8.2		Sales/Net Fixed Assets	7.1	6.3	10.2	11.8	7.8	8.1
5.4	4.9	4.7			4.0	4.8	3.9	5.4	5.2	4.5
3.2	2.9	2.9			.7	3.8	2.9	3.8	2.9	2.5
2.8	2.6	2.7		Sales/Total Assets	2.7	3.3	2.9	3.4	2.7	2.4
2.0	1.8	1.8			1.7	2.2	2.1	2.3	1.7	1.7
1.4	1.3	1.2			.5	1.5	1.3	1.7	1.2	1.1
(248) 2.1	(306) 1.7	(249) 2.2		% Depr., Dep., Amort./Sales	(12) 1.5	(26) 2.4	2.8	(32) 2.0	(63) 2.4	(84) 1.8
3.3	3.3	3.7			5.3	3.9	3.6	4.4	3.7	3.6
5.5	5.5	5.5			13.3	6.5	5.0	5.9	4.9	5.7
(92) 1.2	(100) 1.3	(86) 1.1		% Officers', Directors', Owners' Comp/Sales		(15) 2.3	(11) 2.3	(18) .8	(19) 1.4	(17) .9
1.9	1.9	2.3				4.6	2.7	1.6	2.1	1.2
4.0	4.0	3.7				6.7	4.6	3.1	3.9	2.1
9489578M	7802169M	7727374M		Net Sales ($)	9018M	51738M	129368M	266721M	1087864M	6182665M
5023073M	5260892M	4961739M		Total Assets ($)	13275M	36439M	73892M	132179M	680246M	4025708M

M = $ thousand   MM = $ million
See Pages 11 through 18 for Explanation of Ratios and Data

Current Data Sorted By Assets   Comparative Historical Data

0-500M	500M-2MM	2-10MM	10-50MM	50-100MM	100-250MM	Type of Statement	4/1/98-3/31/99 ALL	4/1/99-3/31/00 ALL
		3	8	1	1	Unqualified	17	20
	1	6	2			Reviewed	12	12
1	4	2				Compiled	8	8
1	1					Tax Returns	1	3
1		5	7	1	2	Other	9	13
	10 (4/1-9/30/02)		37 (10/1/02-3/31/03)					
3	6	16	17	2	3	NUMBER OF STATEMENTS	47	56
%	%	%	%	%	%	ASSETS	%	%
		3.2	4.7			Cash & Equivalents	4.0	3.5
		17.4	18.1			Trade Receivables (net)	21.0	20.9
		37.2	36.4			Inventory	37.4	33.9
		1.3	1.2			All Other Current	1.1	1.5
		59.1	60.5			Total Current	63.4	59.7
		31.2	33.6			Fixed Assets (net)	30.0	31.3
		1.9	.8			Intangibles (net)	.6	1.7
		7.8	5.2			All Other Non-Current	6.0	7.3
		100.0	100.0			Total	100.0	100.0
						LIABILITIES		
		23.0	16.1			Notes Payable-Short Term	17.8	18.5
		4.4	3.1			Cur. Mat.-L/T/D	3.2	5.1
		8.2	6.6			Trade Payables	10.0	9.9
		.0	.1			Income Taxes Payable	.5	.2
		2.7	6.4			All Other Current	4.8	4.7
		38.3	32.3			Total Current	36.3	38.5
		15.0	19.0			Long Term Debt	16.7	17.2
		.5	.3			Deferred Taxes	.2	.6
		1.9	2.1			All Other Non-Current	3.0	2.6
		44.2	46.3			Net Worth	43.8	41.2
		100.0	100.0			Total Liabilities & Net Worth	100.0	100.0
						INCOME DATA		
		100.0	100.0			Net Sales	100.0	100.0
		19.8	17.5			Gross Profit	16.2	18.7
		16.3	13.8			Operating Expenses	11.5	13.2
		3.5	3.7			Operating Profit	4.7	5.4
		.2	1.1			All Other Expenses (net)	1.0	1.1
		3.3	2.6			Profit Before Taxes	3.7	4.3
						RATIOS		
		2.8	3.5			Current	2.7	2.2
		1.4	1.9				1.7	1.5
		1.3	1.3				1.5	1.2
		.9	1.7			Quick	1.3	1.0
		.7	.6				.6	.6
		.3	.3				.4	.4
		9 40.1	11 31.8			Sales/Receivables	14 25.2	14 26.7
		16 23.4	21 17.0				22 16.7	24 15.4
		25 14.8	34 10.8				34 10.6	34 10.8
		26 14.1	43 8.5			Cost of Sales/Inventory	27 13.8	30 12.3
		46 8.0	61 6.0				44 8.4	48 7.5
		64 5.7	81 4.5				80 4.6	74 4.9
		5 72.0	5 80.9			Cost of Sales/Payables	8 44.8	7 49.0
		9 39.4	9 39.4				11 33.3	12 30.0
		17 21.1	14 25.9				17 21.5	21 17.6
		8.7	5.9			Sales/Working Capital	7.2	9.1
		16.2	9.3				12.8	15.4
		118.3	27.2				21.7	28.1
		16.1	10.5			EBIT/Interest	6.1	5.8
		5.1	(16) 6.1				3.4 (51)	3.9
		1.8	2.1				1.7	2.2
						Net Profit + Depr., Dep., Amort./Cur. Mat. L /T/D	(11) 6.4	3.8
							2.7 (21)	2.0
							.8	.6
		.5	.3			Fixed/Worth	.4	.4
		.7	.8				.5	.9
		1.3	1.1				1.2	1.3
		.5	.7			Debt/Worth	.7	.9
		1.5	1.0				1.1	1.8
		4.5	1.6				2.6	2.8
		(15) 53.1	33.2			% Profit Before Taxes/Tangible Net Worth	(45) 33.1	(53) 39.2
		16.4	20.6				18.3	22.0
		5.4	11.0				6.8	12.4
		16.1	14.8			% Profit Before Taxes/Total Assets	15.3	12.6
		7.4	9.4				7.0	8.6
		1.7	4.3				2.8	4.0
		43.7	16.8			Sales/Net Fixed Assets	24.8	19.8
		11.8	7.6				12.0	12.0
		5.8	4.3				7.0	5.1
		4.8	4.0			Sales/Total Assets	4.4	4.2
		3.2	2.6				3.1	2.9
		2.5	2.0				2.0	1.9
		.6	.8			% Depr., Dep., Amort./Sales	.7	.7
		1.2	(15) 1.4				(46) 1.2	(49) 1.0
		2.4	2.5				2.2	2.6
						% Officers', Directors', Owners' Comp/Sales	.7	.8
							(16) 1.8	(14) 2.1
							3.8	5.6
5187M	59565M	289697M	1039956M	768525M	891144M	Net Sales ($)	1687831M	2489869M
908M	8752M	79472M	357309M	198547M	426049M	Total Assets ($)	503259M	760626M

M = $ thousand   MM = $ million
See Pages 11 through 18 for Explanation of Ratios and Data

Comparative Historical Data / Current Data Sorted By Sales

Hist 1	Hist 2	Hist 3	Type of Statement	0-1MM	1-3MM	3-5MM	5-10MM	10-25MM	25MM & OVER
6	9	13	Unqualified				1	3	9
10	6	9	Reviewed				2	4	3
6	8	7	Compiled		1	2	1	2	1
3		2	Tax Returns	1			1		
19	16	16	Other		1		1	4	10
4/1/00-3/31/01 ALL	4/1/01-3/31/02 ALL	4/1/02-3/31/03 ALL				10 (4/1-9/30/02)		37 (10/1/02-3/31/03)	
44	39	47	**NUMBER OF STATEMENTS**	1	2	2	6	13	23
%	%	%	**ASSETS**	%	%	%	%	%	%
4.1	3.7	5.1	Cash & Equivalents					2.9	5.5
17.0	21.8	20.7	Trade Receivables (net)					15.6	19.3
36.7	31.3	32.5	Inventory					41.4	33.8
2.4	2.5	1.8	All Other Current					.8	1.5
60.1	59.3	60.1	Total Current					60.7	60.1
32.0	31.0	30.0	Fixed Assets (net)					26.0	31.8
.5	.9	1.3	Intangibles (net)					.0	1.4
7.4	8.7	8.5	All Other Non-Current					13.3	6.7
100.0	100.0	100.0	Total					100.0	100.0
			LIABILITIES						
19.8	13.1	15.2	Notes Payable-Short Term					27.8	13.0
6.0	2.8	3.4	Cur. Mat.-L/T/D					2.8	3.5
7.2	8.6	9.3	Trade Payables					8.1	7.8
.1	.2	.1	Income Taxes Payable					.0	.1
9.5	3.7	7.7	All Other Current					4.3	6.8
42.5	28.4	35.7	Total Current					43.1	31.2
18.2	21.2	17.8	Long Term Debt					11.9	18.8
.2	.4	.4	Deferred Taxes					.4	.6
2.0	3.5	1.5	All Other Non-Current					1.0	1.7
37.1	46.6	44.6	Net Worth					43.6	47.7
100.0	100.0	100.0	Total Liabilities & Net Worth					100.0	100.0
			INCOME DATA						
100.0	100.0	100.0	Net Sales					100.0	100.0
18.2	19.0	19.2	Gross Profit					11.8	16.8
13.3	13.0	16.1	Operating Expenses					9.1	13.4
4.9	6.0	3.2	Operating Profit					2.7	3.4
1.3	.8	.5	All Other Expenses (net)					.6	.5
3.6	5.2	2.6	Profit Before Taxes					2.1	2.9
			RATIOS						
2.4 / 1.6 / 1.0	3.5 / 2.1 / 1.4	3.0 / 1.7 / 1.3	Current					3.1 / 1.4 / 1.0	3.1 / 1.9 / 1.5
.8 / .4 / .2	1.6 / .8 / .5	1.3 / .8 / .4	Quick					.9 / .4 / .3	1.4 / .9 / .4
8 47.6 / 14 26.1 / 26 14.1	14 26.5 / 26 14.3 / 33 11.0	12 30.8 / 21 17.0 / 30 12.0	Sales/Receivables					9 41.8 / 16 23.1 / 26 14.3	11 32.9 / 21 17.0 / 30 12.0
26 14.3 / 46 7.9 / 89 4.1	21 17.8 / 45 8.1 / 67 5.4	20 18.7 / 45 8.2 / 73 5.0	Cost of Sales/Inventory					13 27.6 / 47 7.8 / 77 4.7	23 16.1 / 52 7.0 / 77 4.7
5 79.5 / 9 41.2 / 17 21.6	6 59.7 / 9 39.8 / 16 23.2	5 72.2 / 10 35.6 / 18 20.0	Cost of Sales/Payables					4 82.0 / 7 51.1 / 13 28.3	5 79.0 / 10 36.1 / 17 21.2
7.4 / 17.4 / 90.2	6.6 / 10.4 / 21.1	6.8 / 15.7 / 29.5	Sales/Working Capital					7.3 / 21.8 / NM	6.4 / 10.2 / 21.2
(41) 5.4 / 2.6 / 1.1	(38) 7.4 / 4.2 / 1.7	(44) 11.1 / 5.3 / 2.0	EBIT/Interest					5.8 / 3.0 / 1.1	(22) 22.7 / 6.6 / 3.7
		(14) 4.2 / 2.4 / 1.1	Net Profit + Depr., Dep., Amort./Cur. Mat. L/T/D						
.4 / .8 / 1.7	.3 / .7 / 1.2	.4 / .7 / 1.1	Fixed/Worth					.3 / .6 / 1.3	.4 / .7 / 1.1
.6 / 1.7 / 3.8	.5 / 1.0 / 2.3	.7 / 1.1 / 2.2	Debt/Worth					.4 / 1.8 / 3.3	.7 / 1.0 / 2.0
(42) 34.0 / 14.2 / 4.2	(35) 38.3 / 26.1 / 10.6	(44) 33.6 / 20.1 / 7.8	% Profit Before Taxes/Tangible Net Worth				(12) 24.9 / 6.7 / 2.4		32.4 / 23.0 / 13.3
13.7 / 4.1 / .4	17.8 / 10.1 / 2.9	14.2 / 6.8 / 1.9	% Profit Before Taxes/Total Assets					11.9 / 2.9 / .3	14.6 / 8.3 / 6.1
27.8 / 12.8 / 5.3	42.3 / 12.9 / 6.2	33.2 / 10.3 / 6.1	Sales/Net Fixed Assets					59.6 / 15.8 / 7.7	16.9 / 11.0 / 6.3
5.4 / 3.3 / 1.9	4.4 / 3.1 / 1.8	4.7 / 3.2 / 2.3	Sales/Total Assets					6.7 / 3.2 / 2.5	4.7 / 3.2 / 2.3
(41) .8 / 1.2 / 2.9	(36) .4 / 1.3 / 2.6	(42) .7 / 1.2 / 2.5	% Depr., Dep., Amort./Sales				(12) .3 / .9 / 1.9		(20) .8 / 1.1 / 2.2
(11) .4 / 1.5 / 3.5	(10) .4 / .8 / 2.2	(17) .6 / 1.2 / 2.7	% Officers', Directors', Owners' Comp/Sales						
2164589M	1854996M	3054074M	Net Sales ($)	640M	3976M	8264M	47454M	239152M	2754588M
806719M	677553M	1071037M	Total Assets ($)	309M	2156M	1589M	18493M	78758M	969732M

© RMA 2003
M = $ thousand   MM = $ million
See Pages 11 through 18 for Explanation of Ratios and Data

Current Data Sorted By Assets | Comparative Historical Data

0-500M	500M-2MM	2-10MM		10-50MM		50-100MM	100-250MM	Type of Statement				
		3		11		2	2	Unqualified			22	25
		9		3				Reviewed			16	18
1	5	1						Compiled			9	9
1	1	1		1				Tax Returns			1	
		13		10		1		Other			13	18
	23 (4/1-9/30/02)			41 (10/1/02-3/31/03)							4/1/98-3/31/99 ALL	4/1/99-3/31/00 ALL
2	6	27		24		3	2	NUMBER OF STATEMENTS			61	70
%	%	%		%		%	%	ASSETS			%	%
		7.8		3.1				Cash & Equivalents			6.6	4.0
		16.8		18.5				Trade Receivables (net)			19.6	20.4
		33.2		35.3				Inventory			31.5	32.4
		1.7		4.7				All Other Current			2.5	3.2
		59.5		61.7				Total Current			60.3	59.9
		33.2		29.4				Fixed Assets (net)			31.4	31.2
		2.1		.6				Intangibles (net)			.9	1.2
		5.2		8.3				All Other Non-Current			7.4	7.7
		100.0		100.0				Total			100.0	100.0
								LIABILITIES				
		14.1		15.9				Notes Payable-Short Term			17.6	17.3
		5.8		4.9				Cur. Mat.-L/T/D			3.3	3.8
		11.6		8.5				Trade Payables			10.8	10.0
		.3		.2				Income Taxes Payable			.5	.2
		4.8		5.1				All Other Current			6.4	6.7
		36.6		34.5				Total Current			38.6	38.0
		22.3		10.7				Long Term Debt			15.0	14.1
		1.3		1.1				Deferred Taxes			.9	1.1
		2.5		1.3				All Other Non-Current			2.8	4.2
		37.3		52.3				Net Worth			42.6	42.5
		100.0		100.0				Total Liabilities & Net Worth			100.0	100.0
								INCOME DATA				
		100.0		100.0				Net Sales			100.0	100.0
		20.1		16.5				Gross Profit			16.8	17.6
		18.7		13.2				Operating Expenses			11.7	13.0
		1.5		3.3				Operating Profit			5.2	4.5
		1.3		.7				All Other Expenses (net)			.6	.3
		.2		2.6				Profit Before Taxes			4.6	4.2
								RATIOS				
		2.7		3.6							2.4	2.8
		1.5		1.6				Current			1.5	1.5
		1.2		1.2							1.2	1.1
		1.1		1.3							1.4	1.1
		.6		.8				Quick			.6	.7
		.4		.3							.4	.3
		21	17.8	23	15.6				16	22.9	23	15.9
		29	12.8	35	10.3			Sales/Receivables	26	14.2	32	11.5
		50	7.3	53	6.9				43	8.4	41	8.8
		31	11.7	62	5.9				34	10.6	35	10.4
		56	6.6	97	3.8			Cost of Sales/Inventory	56	6.5	62	5.9
		112	3.3	140	2.6				83	4.4	104	3.5
		13	28.1	10	38.0				9	40.8	10	34.9
		20	18.5	17	21.2			Cost of Sales/Payables	16	22.4	16	22.6
		39	9.4	33	11.0				29	12.6	25	14.9
		5.8		3.5							7.0	6.4
		8.7		7.1				Sales/Working Capital			12.5	11.5
		25.0		20.4							36.6	28.5
		2.7		5.2							7.5	6.5
		1.6	(22)	2.3				EBIT/Interest	(56)	3.3	(64)	3.0
		−.8		1.4							1.0	1.4
								Net Profit + Depr., Dep.,		4.6		4.3
			(24)					Amort./Cur. Mat. L /T/D	(24)	2.3	(20)	2.0
										1.3		.9
		.4		.4							.3	.3
		1.0		.7				Fixed/Worth			.8	.8
		1.7		1.0							1.4	1.5
		.9		.3							.5	.5
		1.7		1.0				Debt/Worth			1.5	1.5
		4.2		2.3							3.0	3.5
		15.2		11.3				% Profit Before Taxes/Tangible		29.7		31.9
	(26)	7.1		6.4				Net Worth	(57)	12.7	(65)	14.2
		−5.7		2.8						−1.6		5.5
		5.7		5.7							12.4	11.3
		1.5		2.7				% Profit Before Taxes/Total Assets			5.7	6.5
		−3.1		.9							−1.2	1.9
		16.2		9.7							16.5	16.7
		6.8		6.4				Sales/Net Fixed Assets			8.1	8.2
		3.2		4.5							4.5	3.7
		2.8		2.0							2.9	2.9
		1.8		1.7				Sales/Total Assets			2.0	2.1
		1.3		1.3							1.4	1.4
		.9		2.0							1.2	1.1
	(25)	2.0	(18)	2.9			% Depr., Dep., Amort./Sales	(58)	1.8	(61)	1.9
		4.4		4.6							2.9	3.4
								% Officers', Directors',		1.4		1.5
								Owners' Comp/Sales	(15)	1.9	(11)	4.0
										3.2		6.5
5456M	33474M	271379M		907480M		456558M	578518M	Net Sales ($)			1876243M	2541717M
667M	9360M	134764M		541499M		233089M	465965M	Total Assets ($)			917398M	1143534M

M = $ thousand   MM = $ million
See Pages 11 through 18 for Explanation of Ratios and Data

Comparative Historical Data | Current Data Sorted By Sales

			Type of Statement	0-1MM	1-3MM	3-5MM	5-10MM	10-25MM	25MM & OVER
20	19	18	Unqualified				1	2	15
16	16	12	Reviewed				4	5	3
11	5	7	Compiled		2			2	
1	2	3	Tax Returns	3	1		1	9	
19	13	24	Other	1	3		6		6
4/1/00- 3/31/01 ALL	4/1/01- 3/31/02 ALL	4/1/02- 3/31/03 ALL			23 (4/1-9/30/02)			41 (10/1/02-3/31/03)	
67	55	64	NUMBER OF STATEMENTS		5	6	11	18	24
%	%	%	ASSETS	%	%	%	%	%	%
7.4	5.5	5.5	Cash & Equivalents				10.1	6.8	2.0
18.1	14.6	18.0	Trade Receivables (net)				15.1	22.4	15.4
29.5	32.5	32.7	Inventory				34.4	40.5	30.7
3.2	5.3	3.2	All Other Current				1.6	2.4	4.5
58.2	58.0	59.4	Total Current				61.3	72.1	52.7
31.5	32.4	29.3	Fixed Assets (net)				36.7	20.3	31.2
1.7	.8	3.7	Intangibles (net)				.0	.4	7.5
8.5	8.8	7.6	All Other Non-Current				1.9	7.2	8.6
100.0	100.0	100.0	Total				100.0	100.0	100.0
			LIABILITIES						
14.7	15.6	14.7	Notes Payable-Short Term				11.5	19.8	12.0
3.5	5.2	4.9	Cur. Mat.-L/T/D				10.0	2.4	6.3
8.7	10.2	12.2	Trade Payables				10.1	12.2	7.7
.4	.4	.2	Income Taxes Payable				.7	.1	.2
7.0	4.1	5.8	All Other Current				3.3	5.6	4.9
34.3	35.4	37.9	Total Current				35.6	40.1	30.9
18.8	17.2	16.1	Long Term Debt				18.4	11.3	15.9
.7	.7	1.1	Deferred Taxes				1.8	.1	1.5
2.1	2.1	2.5	All Other Non-Current				1.7	3.1	3.4
44.0	44.6	42.4	Net Worth				42.4	45.4	48.3
100.0	100.0	100.0	Total Liabilities & Net Worth				100.0	100.0	100.0
			INCOME DATA						
100.0	100.0	100.0	Net Sales				100.0	100.0	100.0
19.2	18.1	18.9	Gross Profit				22.5	19.2	13.8
14.6	14.6	16.5	Operating Expenses				18.7	16.1	11.1
4.6	3.5	2.4	Operating Profit				3.8	3.1	2.7
1.1	1.2	.8	All Other Expenses (net)				.9	.7	1.2
3.5	2.3	1.6	Profit Before Taxes				2.9	2.4	1.5
			RATIOS						
2.8	3.1	2.7					3.2	2.8	2.9
1.8	1.7	1.6	Current				1.7	1.8	1.6
1.2	1.2	1.2					1.3	1.4	1.2
1.4	1.3	1.1					1.1	2.0	1.0
.8	.5	.6	Quick				.6	.8	.5
.4	.3	.4					.4	.5	.3
21 17.5	17 21.8	17 21.0					21 17.8	16 22.1	15 25.1
30 12.0	28 13.1	30 12.2	Sales/Receivables				27 13.3	36 10.2	26 14.0
45 8.1	39 9.5	50 7.3					50 7.3	52 7.0	43 8.5
32 11.6	46 8.0	33 11.0					52 7.0	43 8.4	40 9.2
67 5.4	80 4.6	68 5.4	Cost of Sales/Inventory				83 4.4	79 4.6	70 5.2
115 3.2	125 2.9	115 3.2					148 2.5	140 2.6	110 3.3
9 41.9	10 38.2	12 29.6					13 27.5	12 30.3	9 41.9
14 26.2	16 22.6	18 19.9	Cost of Sales/Payables				23 15.6	16 22.2	15 23.7
27 13.7	28 12.9	36 10.2					39 9.4	44 8.3	28 13.2
4.1	4.7	4.9					4.0	6.0	4.2
9.5	8.3	11.7	Sales/Working Capital				7.8	8.5	13.2
22.6	26.1	25.2					16.0	14.1	26.6
7.0	3.8	4.5					5.7	4.5	3.9
(63) 2.6	(54) 2.3	(61) 1.9	EBIT/Interest				1.7	2.6	(22) 1.9
1.1	1.1	1.1					1.3	1.3	.9
7.8	6.8	3.5	Net Profit + Depr., Dep.,						
(21) 2.6	(20) 3.3	(19) 1.9	Amort./Cur. Mat. L/T/D						
.9	1.6	.9							
.3	.4	.4					.5	.3	.5
.8	.8	.7	Fixed/Worth				1.2	.4	.8
1.4	1.2	1.4					1.7	1.0	1.5
.7	.7	.7					.9	.5	.6
1.1	1.2	1.4	Debt/Worth				1.2	1.3	1.4
3.1	2.8	3.6					3.1	3.3	2.5
33.0	17.4	14.2	% Profit Before Taxes/Tangible				18.5	15.6	9.5
(62) 14.4	(54) 8.1	(59) 7.5	Net Worth				8.5	9.8	(21) 5.1
3.9	1.2	1.0					2.4	1.9	-4.3
14.5	6.7	5.7	% Profit Before Taxes/Total				9.8	5.8	5.7
5.9	3.4	2.5	Assets				2.2	2.7	2.7
.7	.6	.0					1.1	1.1	-.9
12.5	11.5	15.5					9.7	34.3	10.7
7.4	6.1	7.0	Sales/Net Fixed Assets				6.7	13.0	5.7
3.9	3.6	3.9					2.7	6.1	4.1
2.5	2.2	2.6					2.2	3.2	2.3
2.0	1.8	1.8	Sales/Total Assets				1.6	1.9	1.7
1.2	1.2	1.4					1.0	1.7	1.3
1.3	1.1	1.3					1.0	1.5	1.3
(59) 2.3	(49) 2.6	(52) 2.6	% Depr., Dep., Amort./Sales				1.7	(14) 2.0	(17) 3.1
4.1	4.9	4.2					4.2	4.7	4.2
1.4		1.3	% Officers', Directors',						
(14) 3.8		(11) 3.2	Owners' Comp/Sales						
5.8		5.1							
2330461M	1758879M	2252865M	Net Sales ($)	10816M	24026M		78640M	279207M	1860176M
1295142M	1063646M	1385344M	Total Assets ($)	7554M	16196M		51456M	141639M	1168499M

M = $ thousand   MM = $ million
See Pages 11 through 18 for Explanation of Ratios and Data

Current Data Sorted By Assets | Comparative Historical Data

0-500M	500M-2MM	2-10MM	10-50MM	50-100MM	100-250MM	Type of Statement	4/1/98-3/31/99 ALL	4/1/99-3/31/00 ALL
	1	3	3	2	2	Unqualified	10	6
	3	17	2	1		Reviewed	12	19
2	8	7	1			Compiled	18	17
1	2	2				Tax Returns	3	1
1	9	5	2			Other	18	7
	6 (4/1-9/30/02)		68 (10/1/02-3/31/03)					
4	23	34	8	3	2	NUMBER OF STATEMENTS	61	50
%	%	%	%	%	%		%	%
						ASSETS		
	9.6	4.6				Cash & Equivalents	6.4	5.5
	29.8	25.1				Trade Receivables (net)	31.9	30.7
	18.7	20.5				Inventory	22.6	22.9
	2.5	3.6				All Other Current	2.0	1.5
	60.7	53.8				Total Current	63.0	60.6
	31.6	33.2				Fixed Assets (net)	29.5	29.9
	2.8	1.1				Intangibles (net)	1.3	2.6
	4.8	11.9				All Other Non-Current	6.2	6.9
	100.0	100.0				Total	100.0	100.0
						LIABILITIES		
	14.0	13.2				Notes Payable-Short Term	13.0	12.5
	4.9	4.2				Cur. Mat.-L/T/D	5.0	4.0
	9.8	7.8				Trade Payables	13.3	11.5
	.1	.0				Income Taxes Payable	.3	.1
	14.9	7.5				All Other Current	9.9	7.2
	43.7	32.8				Total Current	41.6	35.3
	24.7	24.5				Long Term Debt	17.0	17.8
	.0	.6				Deferred Taxes	.4	.4
	1.1	3.4				All Other Non-Current	4.4	3.8
	30.6	38.8				Net Worth	36.7	42.6
	100.0	100.0				Total Liabilities & Net Worth	100.0	100.0
						INCOME DATA		
	100.0	100.0				Net Sales	100.0	100.0
	36.2	28.5				Gross Profit	28.0	27.4
	30.9	24.5				Operating Expenses	22.8	21.0
	5.2	4.0				Operating Profit	5.2	6.3
	1.4	.4				All Other Expenses (net)	.8	.6
	3.8	3.7				Profit Before Taxes	4.4	5.7
						RATIOS		
	2.8	2.6					2.6	3.6
	1.6	1.8				Current	1.5	1.7
	1.0	1.2					1.1	1.1
	2.1	1.6					1.6	2.1
	1.1	1.0				Quick	.9	1.0
	.6	.6					.6	.7
	24 15.4	22 16.9					28 13.1	21 17.3
	33 11.0	32 11.6				Sales/Receivables	38 9.6	32 11.3
	45 8.1	39 9.3					51 7.1	48 7.6
	16 22.8	25 14.4					21 17.1	18 20.2
	30 12.3	34 10.7				Cost of Sales/Inventory	39 9.4	35 10.3
	49 7.4	49 7.5					60 6.0	46 8.0
	11 32.9	6 62.0					11 33.2	6 60.1
	17 21.7	10 36.9				Cost of Sales/Payables	21 17.6	13 27.9
	23 15.6	17 21.4					29 12.4	26 14.2
	8.7	7.5					7.1	7.5
	13.6	15.2				Sales/Working Capital	16.6	13.8
	709.7	34.2					52.7	69.7
	12.4	7.6					9.0	12.5
	(22) 3.4	(32) 4.3				EBIT/Interest	(54) 3.6	(45) 4.1
	.9	2.6					1.5	2.1
						Net Profit + Depr., Dep.,	3.1	5.2
						Amort./Cur. Mat. L /T/D	(13) 2.2	(13) 2.6
							1.2	2.0
	.4	.4					.4	.4
	.9	.8				Fixed/Worth	.9	.8
	5.5	1.6					1.7	1.3
	1.1	.6					.7	.6
	1.6	2.0				Debt/Worth	1.9	1.6
	18.0	3.2					5.2	3.1
	72.5	46.5				% Profit Before Taxes/Tangible	62.8	61.0
	(20) 20.3	(31) 16.1				Net Worth	(54) 32.6	(46) 31.2
	4.4	5.0					11.7	10.4
	28.8	15.2				% Profit Before Taxes/Total	24.1	28.4
	5.9	6.0				Assets	8.3	11.5
	.8	2.3					3.7	3.0
	27.1	15.0					19.2	19.8
	11.3	8.9				Sales/Net Fixed Assets	12.0	12.1
	5.7	5.8					7.1	7.2
	4.3	3.5					3.8	3.9
	2.9	2.6				Sales/Total Assets	2.9	3.0
	2.6	1.9					2.4	2.5
	1.4	1.2					1.0	1.1
	(21) 2.6	(31) 1.8				% Depr., Dep., Amort./Sales	(57) 1.5	(49) 1.7
	4.5	3.1					2.6	2.3
	1.8	1.6					1.9	2.2
	(10) 4.7	(12) 2.8				% Officers', Directors',	(21) 3.2	(21) 3.3
	7.3	7.1				Owners' Comp/Sales	6.4	5.3
4123M	90080M	463036M	260852M	387610M	762059M	Net Sales ($)	679220M	628912M
844M	27859M	154059M	126860M	212402M	452614M	Total Assets ($)	233129M	206946M

M = $ thousand   MM = $ million
See Pages 11 through 18 for Explanation of Ratios and Data

Comparative Historical Data　　Current Data Sorted By Sales

			Type of Statement						
7	3	11	Unqualified		1		2	2	6
13	11	23	Reviewed		1	1	8	8	5
16	21	18	Compiled	2	1	4	5	3	3
7	6	5	Tax Returns		2	3			
14	22	17	Other		5	5	2	2	3
4/1/00-3/31/01 ALL	4/1/01-3/31/02 ALL	4/1/02-3/31/03 ALL		0-1MM	6 (4/1-9/30/02) 1-3MM	3-5MM	68 (10/1/02-3/31/03) 5-10MM	10-25MM	25MM & OVER
57	63	74	NUMBER OF STATEMENTS	2	10	13	17	15	17
%	%	%	ASSETS	%	%	%	%	%	%
5.5	8.0	6.7	Cash & Equivalents		11.3	6.0	8.9	5.5	3.7
26.2	27.2	27.0	Trade Receivables (net)		23.4	29.1	25.2	24.2	30.7
19.8	21.0	19.7	Inventory		15.9	18.4	20.0	19.1	23.7
2.0	3.0	2.9	All Other Current		1.4	2.7	5.8	1.4	2.5
53.5	59.2	56.3	Total Current		52.1	56.2	59.9	50.2	60.6
34.5	30.7	32.7	Fixed Assets (net)		35.7	32.1	30.3	37.7	28.3
3.0	5.0	2.5	Intangibles (net)		5.9	.3	.6	2.4	4.3
9.0	5.2	8.5	All Other Non-Current		6.3	11.3	9.1	9.7	6.8
100.0	100.0	100.0	Total		100.0	100.0	100.0	100.0	100.0
			LIABILITIES						
11.6	13.6	13.8	Notes Payable-Short Term		6.5	19.8	5.1	14.0	19.8
6.0	4.4	4.5	Cur. Mat.-L/T/D		5.6	4.6	5.2	4.1	3.8
10.6	10.8	9.0	Trade Payables		5.6	9.9	8.8	7.5	10.7
.3	.6	.2	Income Taxes Payable		.1	.0	.0	.0	.6
8.7	10.8	11.1	All Other Current		12.7	12.0	10.0	6.9	11.1
37.3	40.2	38.6	Total Current		30.5	46.3	29.2	32.6	46.1
20.1	19.9	22.7	Long Term Debt		31.6	28.5	24.4	22.5	10.6
.4	.3	.4	Deferred Taxes		.0	.0	.4	.5	.9
4.2	3.5	2.8	All Other Non-Current		2.9	2.6	1.3	3.5	3.2
38.1	36.2	35.5	Net Worth		35.0	22.5	44.8	41.0	39.2
100.0	100.0	100.0	Total Liabilities & Net Worth		100.0	100.0	100.0	100.0	100.0
			INCOME DATA						
100.0	100.0	100.0	Net Sales		100.0	100.0	100.0	100.0	100.0
30.1	30.1	30.4	Gross Profit		40.7	34.0	29.5	30.7	22.7
24.6	26.2	25.9	Operating Expenses		33.5	32.0	24.3	24.8	19.1
5.5	3.9	4.5	Operating Profit		7.2	2.1	5.3	5.9	3.6
1.6	1.1	.7	All Other Expenses (net)		1.8	.9	.3	.5	.5
3.9	2.7	3.8	Profit Before Taxes		5.4	1.2	5.0	5.4	3.1
			RATIOS						
2.4	2.3	2.5			3.5	2.5	3.6	2.5	1.9
1.4	1.5	1.6	Current		1.8	1.6	2.4	1.3	1.2
1.1	1.2	1.1			1.0	1.0	1.3	1.1	1.0
1.3	1.3	1.6			2.0	1.7	2.6	1.8	1.0
.9	.9	1.0	Quick		1.2	1.2	1.5	.8	.8
.6	.6	.6			.6	.6	.8	.5	.5
22　16.6	21　17.8	23　16.1		12　30.4	28　13.1	20　18.1	22　16.5	24　14.9	
30　12.0	30　12.3	34　10.8	Sales/Receivables	30　12.3	34　10.7	28　12.9	35　10.3	39　9.3	
40　9.2	40　9.1	45　8.1		43　8.4	47　7.8	37　9.8	41　8.9	57　6.4	
19　19.5	22　16.9	23　15.7		12　31.5	26　14.0	19　19.6	22　16.7	25　14.8	
32　11.5	36　10.3	33　11.0	Cost of Sales/Inventory	36　10.2	32　11.5	35　10.5	30　12.0	45　8.1	
45　8.2	49　7.5	49　7.5		46　8.0	48　7.6	49　7.5	51　7.1	55　6.6	
6　58.4	8　47.4	6　56.5		6　64.2	8　46.0	6　58.4	6　61.7	11　34.0	
16　23.5	14　26.6	15　24.7	Cost of Sales/Payables	15　25.1	15　24.5	15　24.9	12　31.3	19　19.1	
30　12.3	27　13.4	23　16.1		19　19.0	28　13.0	19　18.9	17　21.9	27　13.7	
9.4	8.4	7.9			7.6	7.8	6.8	8.4	10.6
21.5	17.1	16.0	Sales/Working Capital		11.4	13.3	9.6	19.2	30.9
102.3	50.7	124.7			NM	NM	26.2	123.4	318.0
	7.7	6.9	9.1	EBIT/Interest			5.3	10.3	9.9	9.2
(51)　3.8	(61)　2.9	(69)　4.1	EBIT/Interest		(12)　2.7	(15)　5.0	5.6	(16)　4.1	
1.4	1.5	1.5				-.8	2.6	3.2	2.1
4.3	4.0	5.2	Net Profit + Depr., Dep.,						
(14)　1.8	(13)　2.7	(19)　3.4	Amort./Cur. Mat. L/T/D						
.3	1.2	1.5							
.6	.5	.5			.4	.6	.2	.5	.5
.9	.9	.8	Fixed/Worth		.9	.9	.6	.8	.6
2.6	2.2	2.3			NM	6.8	2.2	1.5	1.5
.9	.8	.7			.9	1.2	.3	.6	.9
2.0	1.9	1.9	Debt/Worth		1.9	2.3	1.1	1.8	2.0
3.9	6.3	4.2			NM	79.6	3.7	2.3	3.0
70.0	52.8	53.7	% Profit Before Taxes/Tangible		34.8	68.4	84.1	46.0	
(53)　33.2	(55)　21.7	(65)　18.6	Net Worth	(11)　14.7	(16)　18.1	(14)　20.5	(16)　17.5	
7.9	-.6	6.1			2.2	5.2	10.0	12.3	
21.5	17.0	15.9	% Profit Before Taxes/Total		31.5	12.0	23.0	17.2	13.2
10.0	6.4	6.7	Assets		7.7	5.9	6.8	11.9	7.1
2.7	-.5	1.7			-.3	-4.9	2.9	4.6	2.8
20.3	19.9	16.2			15.6	26.3	17.9	13.6	16.3
10.0	12.3	9.1	Sales/Net Fixed Assets		9.9	12.5	9.1	6.7	11.3
5.5	6.2	5.5			3.8	4.2	6.0	4.7	4.7
4.0	4.1	3.7			3.2	4.1	3.9	3.4	4.1
2.9	2.9	2.6	Sales/Total Assets		2.7	2.6	2.8	2.6	2.4
2.2	2.3	2.0			1.8	1.9	2.0	2.0	2.0
1.3	1.4	1.5	% Depr., Dep., Amort./Sales		1.4	1.5	1.4	1.5	
(51)　2.3	(58)　1.9	(66)　2.1		(11)　2.6	1.8	(13)　2.3	(15)　1.9	
3.2	3.4	3.2			3.4	2.9	3.1	3.4	
1.7	2.7	1.7	% Officers', Directors',						
(20)　2.6	(21)　4.0	(23)　4.5	Owners' Comp/Sales						
5.9	6.2	7.4							
835248M	729735M	1967760M	Net Sales ($)	1027M	20865M	48914M	129518M	212051M	1555385M
329287M	291776M	974638M	Total Assets ($)	210M	8566M	20604M	48702M	84830M	811726M

M = $ thousand　　MM = $ million
See Pages 11 through 18 for Explanation of Ratios and Data

Current Data Sorted By Assets — **Comparative Historical Data**

Type of Statement	0-500M	500M-2MM	2-10MM	10-50MM	50-100MM	100-250MM		ALL 4/1/98-3/31/99	ALL 4/1/99-3/31/00
Unqualified	1	1	8	13	3	3		40	33
Reviewed		25	42	6				52	68
Compiled	12	22	12			1		56	37
Tax Returns	8	5				1		14	19
Other	11	10	18	11	2	4		41	54
		37 (4/1-9/30/02)		182 (10/1/02-3/31/03)					
NUMBER OF STATEMENTS	32	63	80	30	5	9		203	211
ASSETS	%	%	%	%	%	%		%	%
Cash & Equivalents	10.7	9.0	5.7	5.1				8.0	6.8
Trade Receivables (net)	30.2	35.7	30.3	20.7				29.7	30.8
Inventory	19.7	19.2	24.7	29.4				26.3	25.5
All Other Current	.6	3.0	3.1	5.9				2.2	2.1
Total Current	61.2	66.9	63.7	61.1				66.3	65.1
Fixed Assets (net)	28.9	25.8	28.9	25.2				26.9	28.0
Intangibles (net)	3.2	.9	1.9	5.2				1.7	1.8
All Other Non-Current	6.8	6.4	5.5	8.4				5.1	5.0
Total	100.0	100.0	100.0	100.0				100.0	100.0
LIABILITIES									
Notes Payable-Short Term	13.9	10.3	13.4	15.7				13.2	13.5
Cur. Mat.-L/T/D	5.6	5.2	4.1	3.2				4.2	4.7
Trade Payables	19.5	15.2	12.9	7.4				12.3	14.1
Income Taxes Payable	.0	.4	.4	.4				.5	.3
All Other Current	10.7	8.9	9.5	9.1				9.9	9.8
Total Current	49.7	40.0	40.4	35.8				40.1	42.3
Long Term Debt	31.8	14.3	18.9	11.2				18.0	17.0
Deferred Taxes	.0	.3	.3	.8				.4	.4
All Other Non-Current	6.6	7.1	4.7	2.6				4.3	4.9
Net Worth	11.9	38.3	35.7	49.6				37.2	35.4
Total Liabilities & Net Worth	100.0	100.0	100.0	100.0				100.0	100.0
INCOME DATA									
Net Sales	100.0	100.0	100.0	100.0				100.0	100.0
Gross Profit	41.2	32.4	25.4	20.6				26.6	28.1
Operating Expenses	38.3	30.1	20.7	16.5				21.9	23.3
Operating Profit	3.0	2.2	4.7	4.2				4.7	4.8
All Other Expenses (net)	1.4	.6	1.2	.3				1.2	1.0
Profit Before Taxes	1.6	1.6	3.5	3.9				3.5	3.8
RATIOS									
Current	2.6	2.7	2.7	2.7				2.8	2.6
	1.2	1.8	1.6	1.6				1.7	1.6
	.8	1.2	1.2	1.2				1.3	1.1
Quick	1.8	2.1	1.4	1.4				1.6	1.6
	.8	1.1	1.0	.6				.9	.9
	.3	.7	.5	.4				.5	.5
Sales/Receivables	9 38.8	23 15.8	25 14.6	21 17.2				23 15.9	23 15.7
	29 12.4	38 9.7	42 8.6	34 10.8				35 10.4	38 9.7
	44 8.3	57 6.4	68 5.3	46 8.0				57 6.4	60 6.1
Cost of Sales/Inventory	7 51.0	10 37.1	19 19.7	38 9.6				29 12.6	23 15.9
	26 14.1	28 12.8	46 7.9	60 6.1				47 7.8	45 8.2
	59 6.2	44 8.3	75 4.9	96 3.8				76 4.8	70 5.2
Cost of Sales/Payables	12 31.2	12 30.5	13 27.2	9 41.4				10 35.5	11 32.7
	30 12.2	21 17.6	22 16.3	13 28.6				20 17.9	22 16.6
	57 6.4	40 9.2	38 9.7	23 15.9				34 10.8	39 9.4
Sales/Working Capital	9.0	7.0	5.8	5.7				5.9	6.5
	41.6	11.5	9.5	12.1				9.4	11.8
	-33.9	38.7	28.6	27.1				24.0	45.8
EBIT/Interest	(28) 4.8	(57) 9.1	(78) 7.7	(26) 15.6				(177) 8.0	(197) 9.3
	1.0	2.7	3.8	3.8				3.1	3.7
	-1.7	.8	1.9	2.0				1.3	1.4
Net Profit + Depr., Dep., Amort./Cur. Mat. L /T/D		(13) 3.0	(26) 4.8	(14) 14.5				(67) 7.3	(54) 7.0
		2.1	1.8	4.2				2.5	2.2
		1.0	1.1	2.3				.8	1.7
Fixed/Worth	.5	.3	.4	.4				.3	.3
	2.5	.6	1.0	.6				.7	.7
	-1.9	2.2	1.7	1.0				1.7	2.0
Debt/Worth	1.0	.6	.9	.5				1.0	.8
	5.9	1.4	1.9	1.1				1.7	1.7
	-6.4	3.7	5.0	2.8				3.9	4.2
% Profit Before Taxes/Tangible Net Worth	(19) 89.3	(55) 39.4	(74) 46.9	(29) 26.4				(185) 54.8	(188) 48.0
	44.9	15.3	21.6	13.3				22.8	24.4
	.0	.9	10.4	5.4				7.3	8.9
% Profit Before Taxes/Total Assets	20.7	14.6	14.2	12.1				20.5	17.5
	.7	5.8	6.9	5.2				7.2	7.5
	-10.8	-.4	2.5	3.3				1.9	1.9
Sales/Net Fixed Assets	45.8	26.1	16.0	17.9				28.8	20.4
	15.6	18.1	9.9	9.8				10.8	10.8
	8.4	7.3	5.6	5.6				5.7	5.8
Sales/Total Assets	4.8	4.0	3.0	2.8				3.3	3.6
	3.7	3.3	2.3	2.1				2.5	2.5
	2.5	2.3	1.9	1.6				1.8	1.9
% Depr., Dep., Amort./Sales	(28) .8	(59) 1.0	1.0	(29) 1.1				(185) 1.0	(190) 1.0
	1.7	1.7	2.0	1.7				1.9	1.9
	4.0	3.0	2.8	2.8				3.0	3.0
% Officers', Directors', Owners' Comp/Sales	(20) 2.7	(38) 3.4	(33) 1.3					(81) 2.3	(81) 2.1
	8.2	6.0	3.0					4.5	4.1
	9.8	9.5	4.7					7.4	6.9
Net Sales ($)	39585M	245592M	852175M	1325122M	928454M	3496984M		3100424M	2885506M
Total Assets ($)	9391M	73483M	345140M	602141M	317075M	1398435M		1348585M	1190775M

M = $ thousand   MM = $ million
See Pages 11 through 18 for Explanation of Ratios and Data

Comparative Historical Data   **Current Data Sorted By Sales**

			Type of Statement						
28	34	29	Unqualified	1	1		3	10	14
60	47	73	Reviewed		10	16	24	16	7
45	43	47	Compiled	7	14	10	9	6	1
9	13	14	Tax Returns	2	8	1	2		1
55	69	56	Other	5	11	6	9	9	16
4/1/00-3/31/01 ALL	4/1/01-3/31/02 ALL	4/1/02-3/31/03 ALL		37 (4/1-9/30/02)			182 (10/1/02-3/31/03)		
				0-1MM	1-3MM	3-5MM	5-10MM	10-25MM	25MM & OVER
197	206	219	NUMBER OF STATEMENTS	15	44	33	47	41	39
%	%	%	**ASSETS**	%	%	%	%	%	%
6.3	5.9	7.5	Cash & Equivalents	5.6	10.7	7.6	7.8	5.8	6.2
30.2	30.5	30.0	Trade Receivables (net)	24.7	31.6	34.1	34.5	28.6	23.0
25.1	23.7	23.2	Inventory	18.2	19.2	19.4	22.9	25.3	30.7
2.3	3.6	3.1	All Other Current	1.6	1.7	3.9	2.3	3.1	5.3
63.9	63.6	63.8	Total Current	50.2	63.2	65.0	67.5	62.9	65.2
28.7	28.5	27.4	Fixed Assets (net)	38.8	28.7	28.0	24.2	26.9	25.2
1.8	1.7	2.4	Intangibles (net)	4.3	1.4	.5	1.1	6.3	2.0
5.5	6.0	6.4	All Other Non-Current	6.7	6.6	6.5	7.2	3.9	7.5
100.0	100.0	100.0	Total	100.0	100.0	100.0	100.0	100.0	100.0
			LIABILITIES						
13.1	12.8	12.3	Notes Payable-Short Term	12.8	9.7	13.2	12.8	12.7	13.1
3.7	3.6	4.4	Cur. Mat.-L/T/D	6.7	4.9	5.5	4.8	3.4	2.7
12.4	13.0	13.6	Trade Payables	15.3	16.3	14.3	15.0	11.9	9.4
.3	.2	.4	Income Taxes Payable	.0	.0	.9	.2	.6	.4
10.2	9.4	9.8	All Other Current	8.7	9.4	9.2	10.0	9.5	11.5
39.7	39.0	40.5	Total Current	43.4	40.3	43.1	42.8	38.0	37.1
17.9	17.9	18.1	Long Term Debt	51.8	19.9	17.0	14.5	15.2	11.2
.5	.4	.3	Deferred Taxes	.0	.3	.3	.2	.4	.5
4.1	4.0	5.2	All Other Non-Current	4.7	11.1	2.3	6.2	3.0	2.0
37.9	38.5	36.0	Net Worth	-.1	28.3	37.3	36.3	43.3	49.2
100.0	100.0	100.0	Total Liabilities & Net Worth	100.0	100.0	100.0	100.0	100.0	100.0
			INCOME DATA						
100.0	100.0	100.0	Net Sales	100.0	100.0	100.0	100.0	100.0	100.0
29.0	25.8	29.3	Gross Profit	40.2	38.0	30.5	28.0	22.9	22.7
24.3	22.3	25.6	Operating Expenses	37.8	35.1	28.4	23.8	17.6	18.2
4.7	3.5	3.8	Operating Profit	2.3	2.9	2.1	4.2	5.3	4.5
1.1	1.2	.9	All Other Expenses (net)	2.7	.8	.8	.7	1.2	.2
3.6	2.3	2.9	Profit Before Taxes	-.3	2.1	1.3	3.5	4.1	4.3
			RATIOS						
2.5	2.8	2.7		3.0	3.1	2.3	2.6	2.9	2.7
1.7	1.7	1.6	Current	.9	1.4	1.6	1.5	1.8	1.9
1.2	1.2	1.1		.7	1.1	1.1	1.3	1.1	1.3
1.5	1.7	1.6		1.4	2.1	1.5	1.5	1.8	1.3
1.0	1.0	.9	Quick	.6	1.1	.9	1.0	1.0	.7
.5	.5	.5		.3	.6	.7	.7	.5	.5
25 14.8	24 14.9	23 16.0		10 37.0	26 13.9	29 12.6	25 14.5	23 16.0	21 17.2
38 9.6	38 9.6	35 10.3	Sales/Receivables	30 12.3	38 9.7	38 9.7	42 8.8	31 11.8	33 10.9
56 6.6	54 6.7	53 6.9		53 6.9	57 6.4	56 6.5	59 6.2	56 6.5	43 8.4
22 16.8	15 24.3	17 21.0		26 14.3	7 51.9	14 26.4	17 22.0	17 21.0	36 10.2
48 7.6	43 8.5	39 9.4	Cost of Sales/Inventory	47 7.8	27 13.4	29 12.5	38 9.6	44 8.4	56 6.6
70 5.2	67 5.4	68 5.4		76 4.8	67 5.5	60 6.1	55 6.6	73 5.0	88 4.1
10 35.4	10 36.2	12 31.6		8 48.1	16 22.2	13 28.1	12 29.5	8 45.6	9 40.7
19 19.1	19 19.4	20 18.0	Cost of Sales/Payables	48 7.5	29 12.7	21 17.6	18 19.9	18 20.5	14 25.2
34 10.8	33 11.1	36 10.2		63 5.7	40 9.2	38 9.7	43 8.5	26 14.0	24 15.5
6.1	6.2	6.2		7.2	6.4	6.7	7.4	5.0	5.1
11.7	11.1	11.4	Sales/Working Capital	-33.7	11.6	13.0	10.5	9.7	10.1
33.3	32.4	49.1		-14.6	72.0	47.5	27.0	53.7	19.2
10.6	7.2	10.1		2.7	5.0	5.5	14.6	13.2	17.2
(185) 3.2	(186) 2.4	(201) 3.6	EBIT/Interest	(14) .3	(36) 2.0	(31) 2.5	(39) 5.2	4.4	(34) 5.9
1.4	1.0	1.5		-1.0	-.4	1.2	2.1	2.1	2.8
4.4	5.1	6.0			2.0		4.8	7.7	26.5
(49) 2.3	(62) 2.5	(58) 2.7	Net Profit + Depr., Dep., Amort./Cur. Mat. L/T/D		(12) 1.3		(13) 2.7	(12) 4.6	(14) 4.2
1.4	1.2	1.4			.9		1.4	2.2	2.7
.3	.3	.3		.5	.3	.3	.3	.4	.3
.7	.7	.8	Fixed/Worth	4.7	1.0	.7	.8	.7	.5
1.5	1.7	2.1		-1.0	5.9	1.5	1.8	1.7	.8
.8	.7	.7		.5	.8	.7	.7	.6	.4
1.8	1.5	1.8	Debt/Worth	6.5	2.0	1.5	2.1	1.8	.9
3.5	4.7	5.4		-2.9	25.4	4.4	5.4	3.7	2.7
45.9	31.9	44.9			67.7	29.9	47.7	42.8	43.1
(175) 23.4	(186) 15.5	(191) 17.3	% Profit Before Taxes/Tangible Net Worth		(34) 12.2	(30) 14.3	(44) 25.3	(36) 20.8	16.2
8.7	3.6	6.5			1.7	4.7	6.1	11.3	7.5
18.1	14.2	14.4		6.3	17.4	11.1	14.9	15.1	16.2
8.5	5.5	6.2	% Profit Before Taxes/Total Assets	-3.2	3.2	3.5	7.0	8.7	7.1
1.5	.3	1.6		-9.9	-3.3	.9	2.7	3.5	3.5
22.0	20.2	20.5		15.2	24.0	24.3	23.5	18.4	15.3
10.1	10.6	11.3	Sales/Net Fixed Assets	8.4	16.0	9.5	15.1	11.9	10.2
5.2	6.0	6.6		4.2	6.9	5.9	6.7	6.9	6.8
3.6	3.5	3.6		3.1	4.2	3.5	3.6	3.2	3.4
2.6	2.6	2.6	Sales/Total Assets	2.4	3.3	2.9	2.6	2.5	2.4
1.9	2.0	2.0		1.8	2.1	2.1	2.1	1.9	1.9
.9	1.1	1.0		1.1	.8	.8	1.0	.9	1.3
(174) 1.7	(191) 2.0	(207) 1.8	% Depr., Dep., Amort./Sales	(14) 2.0	(37) 3.0	1.7	1.7	1.8	(35) 1.5
2.9	3.0	3.0		4.6	3.9	3.0	2.5	2.6	2.5
2.0	1.9	2.0			3.8	2.8	1.3	1.2	
(82) 4.4	(71) 4.0	(94) 4.7	% Officers', Directors', Owners' Comp/Sales		(30) 6.8	(18) 5.1	(23) 3.8	(13) 1.9	
7.0	8.0	8.5			9.0	9.5	6.2	4.1	
3762896M	5667132M	6887912M	Net Sales ($)	8755M	82856M	127605M	346395M	645599M	5676702M
1676850M	2339345M	2745665M	Total Assets ($)	5927M	33143M	51448M	133067M	283581M	2238499M

M = $ thousand   MM = $ million
See Pages 11 through 18 for Explanation of Ratios and Data

Current Data Sorted By Assets | Comparative Historical Data

Type of Statement	0-500M	500M-2MM	2-10MM	10-50MM	50-100MM	100-250MM	4/1/98-3/31/99 ALL	4/1/99-3/31/00 ALL
Unqualified			3	6	5		25	20
Reviewed			10	5			22	14
Compiled	3	2	.5	2			16	13
Tax Returns	4	4	2				2	4
Other		3	3	3	2		11	22

12 (4/1-9/30/02) (0-500M, 500M-2MM)   48 (10/1/02-3/31/03) (2-10MM, 10-50MM, 50-100MM)

NUMBER OF STATEMENTS	7	9	23	14	7		76	73
	%	%	%	%	%	%	%	%

Columns 0-500M, 500M-2MM, 50-100MM, 100-250MM: **DATA NOT AVAILABLE**

	2-10MM	10-50MM	4/1/98-3/31/99 ALL	4/1/99-3/31/00 ALL
ASSETS				
Cash & Equivalents	3.6	5.5	4.4	3.6
Trade Receivables (net)	17.8	11.4	19.2	19.5
Inventory	32.7	34.9	30.5	31.7
All Other Current	1.2	1.5	3.2	1.7
Total Current	55.4	53.3	57.2	56.5
Fixed Assets (net)	40.8	36.3	32.8	33.8
Intangibles (net)	.7	.4	2.1	4.2
All Other Non-Current	3.1	9.9	7.9	5.4
Total	100.0	100.0	100.0	100.0
LIABILITIES				
Notes Payable-Short Term	14.9	8.1	13.2	15.2
Cur. Mat.-L/T/D	6.8	2.9	4.8	4.3
Trade Payables	8.3	4.2	8.2	7.7
Income Taxes Payable	.2	.1	.4	.2
All Other Current	4.3	3.3	7.6	7.5
Total Current	34.4	18.6	34.2	34.9
Long Term Debt	26.1	15.8	18.6	25.4
Deferred Taxes	.7	.0	.6	.5
All Other Non-Current	1.3	1.4	3.5	4.0
Net Worth	37.6	64.2	43.1	35.2
Total Liabilities & Net Worth	100.0	100.0	100.0	100.0
INCOME DATA				
Net Sales	100.0	100.0	100.0	100.0
Gross Profit	18.5	15.3	21.4	20.3
Operating Expenses	16.4	12.2	15.6	15.5
Operating Profit	2.1	3.1	5.8	4.7
All Other Expenses (net)	1.2	-.6	1.3	2.1
Profit Before Taxes	.8	3.7	4.6	2.6
RATIOS				
Current	2.1	6.2	3.4	3.0
	1.7	2.6	1.8	1.6
	1.2	1.9	1.1	1.1
Quick	1.0	1.7	1.3	1.2
	.5	.8	.7	.6
	.4	.4	.4	.4
Sales/Receivables	17 21.4	14 27.0	18 19.9	21 17.2
	31 11.9	18 20.0	28 13.0	28 13.2
	41 8.9	28 13.0	40 9.0	38 9.5
Cost of Sales/Inventory	41 9.0	45 8.1	34 10.7	32 11.4
	63 5.8	77 4.7	70 5.2	69 5.3
	120 3.0	100 3.7	96 3.8	123 3.0
Cost of Sales/Payables	9 42.2	5 73.8	7 53.5	7 48.8
	12 29.3	7 50.7	13 27.6	14 26.7
	26 14.2	12 30.7	23 16.0	23 15.8
Sales/Working Capital	6.0	3.1	4.9	4.8
	7.6	6.2	10.2	11.5
	71.0	NM	31.2	30.1
EBIT/Interest	7.1	24.7	8.1	6.8
	3.4	(13) 2.1	(72) 3.1	(69) 2.5
	1.2	-7.6	1.4	1.1
Net Profit + Depr., Dep., Amort./Cur. Mat. L /T/D			3.9	3.5
			(28) 2.0	(26) 2.7
			1.1	1.5
Fixed/Worth	.6	.2	.4	.4
	1.0	.4	.8	.9
	1.5	1.5	1.6	3.5
Debt/Worth	.7	.1	.5	.8
	1.5	.4	1.7	2.1
	4.8	1.2	2.9	8.3
% Profit Before Taxes/Tangible Net Worth	24.6	25.6	40.9	31.8
	(21) 14.9	14.7	(70) 21.2	(62) 18.4
	3.3	-2.3	3.9	5.4
% Profit Before Taxes/Total Assets	10.5	17.4	15.6	13.0
	4.4	5.1	7.6	6.1
	.4	-1.4	1.9	.8
Sales/Net Fixed Assets	9.7	13.0	10.6	11.7
	4.4	7.4	6.6	6.6
	3.8	2.3	4.4	4.0
Sales/Total Assets	3.0	2.6	2.9	2.9
	2.0	1.7	2.0	1.7
	1.3	1.0	1.4	1.3
% Depr., Dep., Amort./Sales	2.1	1.3	1.5	1.5
	3.5	(11) 4.1	(68) 2.3	(64) 2.4
	5.1	6.2	3.3	4.2
% Officers', Directors', Owners' Comp/Sales			1.0	1.0
			(24) 2.9	(22) 2.2
			5.5	5.1

	0-500M	500M-2MM	2-10MM	10-50MM	50-100MM	4/1/98-3/31/99 ALL	4/1/99-3/31/00 ALL
Net Sales ($)	9570M	30313M	228172M	565841M	562270M	2175738M	2516586M
Total Assets ($)	2506M	11222M	111280M	287384M	462054M	1286820M	1304875M

M = $ thousand   MM = $ million
See Pages 11 through 18 for Explanation of Ratios and Data

Comparative Historical Data				Current Data Sorted By Sales					
			Type of Statement						
15	15	14	Unqualified				2	3	9
14	18	15	Reviewed			1	6	7	1
18	18	10	Compiled	2	3	1	3	1	1
2	4	10	Tax Returns	1	6	1	1	1	
17	17	11	Other			2	3	1	5
4/1/00-3/31/01 ALL	4/1/01-3/31/02 ALL	4/1/02-3/31/03 ALL		0-1MM	1-3MM 12 (4/1-9/30/02)	3-5MM	5-10MM	10-25MM 48 (10/1/02-3/31/03)	25MM & OVER
66	72	60	**NUMBER OF STATEMENTS**	3	9	5	15	13	15
%	%	%	**ASSETS**	%	%	%	%	%	%
8.2	6.4	5.1	Cash & Equivalents				3.1	4.4	3.8
17.5	16.8	16.4	Trade Receivables (net)				19.9	14.0	12.8
30.6	30.7	33.3	Inventory				30.2	33.4	47.0
2.6	2.2	1.2	All Other Current				1.1	1.8	1.2
58.8	56.2	55.9	Total Current				54.3	53.6	64.7
33.1	35.4	37.6	Fixed Assets (net)				43.3	39.3	25.7
2.8	2.2	.9	Intangibles (net)				.3	.9	.8
5.2	6.2	5.6	All Other Non-Current				2.1	6.2	8.9
100.0	100.0	100.0	Total				100.0	100.0	100.0
			LIABILITIES						
15.0	17.8	12.2	Notes Payable-Short Term				11.7	11.7	15.4
4.9	5.2	7.4	Cur. Mat.-L/T/D				5.1	7.3	6.8
8.8	8.3	10.3	Trade Payables				10.4	4.0	5.0
.3	.0	.2	Income Taxes Payable				.2	.2	.3
9.4	8.2	4.5	All Other Current				4.1	4.4	2.9
38.4	39.6	34.6	Total Current				31.5	27.7	30.4
21.1	23.0	25.7	Long Term Debt				28.0	18.3	15.6
.4	.3	.4	Deferred Taxes				.7	.3	.3
3.3	3.0	.9	All Other Non-Current				1.1	1.4	.5
36.8	34.2	38.4	Net Worth				38.7	52.3	53.2
100.0	100.0	100.0	Total Liabilities & Net Worth				100.0	100.0	100.0
			INCOME DATA						
100.0	100.0	100.0	Net Sales				100.0	100.0	100.0
21.0	23.2	20.7	Gross Profit				19.6	14.7	19.3
16.1	20.9	17.6	Operating Expenses				15.2	11.4	14.9
4.8	2.2	3.1	Operating Profit				4.4	3.2	4.4
1.2	2.1	1.0	All Other Expenses (net)				1.5	.1	.6
3.6	.1	2.1	Profit Before Taxes				2.9	3.1	3.8
			RATIOS						
2.8	2.5	2.7	Current				2.0	5.1	2.9
1.7	1.5	1.7					1.6	2.2	2.1
1.1	1.1	1.1					1.2	1.1	1.3
1.3	1.2	1.2	Quick				1.0	2.5	1.2
.6	.6	.6					.6	.6	.7
.3	.4	.3					.4	.3	.1
17 22.1	19 19.7	16 22.6	Sales/Receivables				17 21.2	12 30.3	16 23.0
24 15.4	24 15.0	23 15.7					34 10.8	24 15.3	21 17.7
40 9.0	35 10.3	37 9.9					45 8.0	35 10.4	26 13.9
21 17.3	33 10.9	35 10.5	Cost of Sales/Inventory				41 9.0	39 9.4	49 7.4
60 6.0	64 5.7	62 5.9					63 5.8	70 5.2	93 3.9
101 3.6	114 3.2	119 3.1					123 3.0	93 3.9	276 1.3
6 56.6	8 48.4	7 50.4	Cost of Sales/Payables				11 32.3	5 78.3	6 58.1
13 27.3	14 25.6	13 27.8					21 17.0	5 70.3	10 37.6
21 17.3	27 13.7	28 13.2					30 12.2	10 37.2	14 26.9
5.2	5.8	5.5	Sales/Working Capital				6.0	4.7	1.6
13.1	9.4	8.1					8.0	6.9	7.2
76.7	69.7	212.3					31.1	263.3	8.4
(61) 5.8	(64) 4.0	(58) 6.4	EBIT/Interest				16.6	8.0	(14) 9.4
2.1	1.5	1.9					1.6	4.0	2.0
.7	-.4	1.0					1.2	.6	1.1
(13) 5.9	(16) 1.3	(17) 3.3	Net Profit + Depr., Dep., Amort./Cur. Mat. L/T/D						
2.0	.9	1.4							
1.6	.1	1.1							
.4	.4	.3	Fixed/Worth				.7	.4	.2
1.0	1.0	.9					1.2	.7	.4
4.0	3.2	2.1					2.1	1.5	1.0
.6	.6	.5	Debt/Worth				.7	.2	.4
1.9	1.9	1.5					1.6	1.1	.9
7.6	5.3	4.7					4.8	3.9	2.4
50.9	27.9	24.9	% Profit Before Taxes/Tangible Net Worth				27.5	31.0	22.4
(61) 12.0	(66) 6.8	(52) 11.7				(14)	12.2	17.3	8.2
-.8	-8.3	1.9					1.3	3.5	1.5
17.3	10.2	10.4	% Profit Before Taxes/Total Assets				10.5	11.9	15.4
5.5	1.6	3.4					2.2	7.2	2.7
-1.0	-7.2	.1					.4	1.6	.5
17.2	14.0	12.4	Sales/Net Fixed Assets				9.5	12.6	12.7
6.5	5.7	5.2					4.3	4.6	7.3
3.9	3.0	3.4					3.3	3.2	4.9
3.4	2.6	2.8	Sales/Total Assets				2.8	3.1	2.6
2.1	1.8	2.0					1.6	2.0	1.7
1.4	1.4	1.3					1.3	1.4	1.0
1.6	1.2	1.8	% Depr., Dep., Amort./Sales				2.9	1.8	1.3
(57) 2.8	(67) 2.9	(55) 3.4				(14)	4.8	(12) 2.8	(13) 3.1
3.8	4.8	5.1					6.1	4.7	3.8
1.7	1.5	1.0	% Officers', Directors', Owners' Comp/Sales						
(30) 2.2	(27) 2.4	(20) 1.7							
4.0	8.5	2.8							
1371894M	1502117M	1396166M	Net Sales ($)	2077M	16544M	22037M	122793M	217657M	1015058M
865558M	828332M	874446M	Total Assets ($)	872M	7395M	9737M	82436M	131614M	642392M

M = $ thousand   MM = $ million
See Pages 11 through 18 for Explanation of Ratios and Data

Current Data Sorted By Assets   **Comparative Historical Data**

0-500M	500M-2MM	2-10MM	10-50MM	50-100MM	100-250MM	Type of Statement	4/1/98-3/31/99 ALL	4/1/99-3/31/00 ALL
	1	3				Unqualified		
	1	3	1			Reviewed		
	7	4				Compiled		
1	2	1				Tax Returns		
1	5	3	1			Other		
	7 (4/1-9/30/02)		27 (10/1/02-3/31/03)					
2	16	14	2			NUMBER OF STATEMENTS		
%	%	%	%	%	%	ASSETS	%	%
	7.7	7.2				Cash & Equivalents		
	29.3	14.7		D	D	Trade Receivables (net)	D	D
	20.5	26.6		A	A	Inventory	A	A
	7.1	3.6	D	T	T	All Other Current	T	T
	64.6	52.0	A	A	A	Total Current	A	A
	23.9	40.3	T			Fixed Assets (net)		
	1.1	.5	A	N	N	Intangibles (net)	N	N
	10.5	7.2		O	O	All Other Non-Current	O	O
	100.0	100.0	N	T	T	Total	T	T
			O			LIABILITIES		
	11.3	7.9	T	A	A	Notes Payable-Short Term	A	A
	3.7	6.5		V	V	Cur. Mat.-L/T/D	V	V
	18.5	7.7	A	A	A	Trade Payables	A	A
	.5	.0	V	I	I	Income Taxes Payable	I	I
	9.8	6.2	A	L	L	All Other Current	L	L
	43.7	28.2	I	A	A	Total Current	A	A
	10.4	26.5	L	B	B	Long Term Debt	B	B
	.0	.4	A	L	L	Deferred Taxes	L	L
	6.9	3.2	B	E	E	All Other Non-Current	E	E
	39.0	41.7	L			Net Worth		
	100.0	100.0	E			Total Liabilities & Net Worth		
						INCOME DATA		
	100.0	100.0				Net Sales		
	29.1	17.5				Gross Profit		
	23.5	14.8				Operating Expenses		
	5.6	2.7				Operating Profit		
	.5	−.3				All Other Expenses (net)		
	5.1	3.1				Profit Before Taxes		
						RATIOS		
	3.7	2.8				Current		
	1.4	1.8						
	.9	1.5						
	2.4	1.7				Quick		
	.9	.6						
	.5	.4						
17	21.9	16 22.3				Sales/Receivables		
28	13.1	23 15.6						
56	6.5	27 13.5						
7	52.2	25 14.6				Cost of Sales/Inventory		
38	9.7	39 9.4						
49	7.5	71 5.2						
11	32.3	5 68.1				Cost of Sales/Payables		
25	14.8	10 37.5						
40	9.1	14 25.3						
	8.2	7.2				Sales/Working Capital		
	16.6	10.1						
	NM	21.0						
	23.5	7.3				EBIT/Interest		
(12)	7.4	(12) 1.7						
	1.5	.4						
						Net Profit + Depr., Dep., Amort./Cur. Mat. L /T/D		
	.3	.5				Fixed/Worth		
	.6	1.1						
	1.2	3.0						
	.4	.5				Debt/Worth		
	2.2	1.1						
	6.4	9.2						
	78.2	40.4				% Profit Before Taxes/Tangible Net Worth		
(14)	37.3	(13) 11.0						
	9.8	.6						
	25.8	14.0				% Profit Before Taxes/Total Assets		
	14.4	5.2						
	3.6	−.6						
	24.9	9.9				Sales/Net Fixed Assets		
	17.7	5.4						
	7.6	4.1						
	4.6	3.4				Sales/Total Assets		
	3.3	2.5						
	2.4	1.6						
	.8	1.8				% Depr., Dep., Amort./Sales		
(13)	2.7	(13) 3.2						
	3.5	5.4						
		.9				% Officers', Directors', Owners' Comp/Sales		
	(11)	2.9						
		4.1						
1056M	67458M	172762M	40289M			Net Sales ($)		
384M	20472M	72790M	29445M			Total Assets ($)		

© RMA 2003

M = $ thousand   MM = $ million
See Pages 11 through 18 for Explanation of Ratios and Data

Comparative Historical Data   Current Data Sorted By Sales

			Type of Statement						
		4	Unqualified	1				3	
		5	Reviewed		1	2	2		
		11	Compiled	1	6	1		3	
		4	Tax Returns	1	1		2		
		10	Other	1	1	2	2	3	1
4/1/00-3/31/01 ALL	4/1/01-3/31/02 ALL	4/1/02-3/31/03 ALL		7 (4/1-9/30/02)			27 (10/1/02-3/31/03)		
				0-1MM	1-3MM	3-5MM	5-10MM	10-25MM	25MM & OVER
		34	NUMBER OF STATEMENTS	2	4	9	7	11	1
%	%	%	ASSETS	%	%	%	%	%	%
D	D	6.8	Cash & Equivalents					7.7	
A	A	23.1	Trade Receivables (net)					15.5	
T	T	24.3	Inventory					27.2	
A	A	4.9	All Other Current					4.1	
		59.1	Total Current					54.5	
N	N	32.1	Fixed Assets (net)					40.2	
O	O	.7	Intangibles (net)					.2	
T	T	8.1	All Other Non-Current					5.1	
		100.0	Total					100.0	
A	A		LIABILITIES						
V	V	10.7	Notes Payable-Short Term					8.9	
A	A	4.5	Cur. Mat.-L/T/D					6.0	
I	I	13.9	Trade Payables					6.0	
L	L	.2	Income Taxes Payable					.0	
A	A	7.9	All Other Current					7.2	
B	B	37.3	Total Current					28.2	
L	L	20.6	Long Term Debt					23.9	
E	E	.3	Deferred Taxes					.1	
		5.3	All Other Non-Current					1.4	
		36.5	Net Worth					46.5	
		100.0	Total Liabilities & Net Worth					100.0	
			INCOME DATA						
		100.0	Net Sales					100.0	
		24.5	Gross Profit					16.0	
		20.4	Operating Expenses					13.2	
		4.0	Operating Profit					2.8	
		.4	All Other Expenses (net)					–.6	
		3.6	Profit Before Taxes					3.4	
			RATIOS						
		3.3						2.3	
		1.6	Current					1.6	
		1.2						1.5	
		1.8						1.3	
		.7	Quick					.6	
		.5						.5	
	17	21.8					16	23.2	
	25	14.8	Sales/Receivables				20	18.0	
	41	8.8					27	13.7	
	17	21.8					21	17.6	
	39	9.4	Cost of Sales/Inventory				38	9.6	
	68	5.4					65	5.6	
	8	46.6					5	80.3	
	18	19.9	Cost of Sales/Payables				8	46.6	
	34	10.9					12	29.6	
		7.0						8.3	
		12.5	Sales/Working Capital					11.5	
		37.8						20.4	
		8.3						8.1	
	(28)	3.6	EBIT/Interest				(10)	3.2	
		1.1						.9	
			Net Profit + Depr., Dep., Amort./Cur. Mat. L/T/D						
		.5						.5	
		.8	Fixed/Worth					.8	
		2.3						2.3	
		.6						.6	
		2.2	Debt/Worth					.8	
		7.3						7.2	
		55.9	% Profit Before Taxes/Tangible Net Worth					46.6	
	(30)	27.0						11.0	
		1.1						.1	
		20.8	% Profit Before Taxes/Total Assets					19.2	
		10.8						6.8	
		.2						.1	
		20.8						10.3	
		7.6	Sales/Net Fixed Assets					7.0	
		4.6						4.3	
		4.2						4.0	
		2.7	Sales/Total Assets					2.7	
		1.8						1.9	
		1.6						1.9	
	(30)	2.8	% Depr., Dep., Amort./Sales				(10)	2.9	
		4.4						4.5	
		1.3							
	(18)	3.1	% Officers', Directors', Owners' Comp/Sales						
		4.3							
		281565M	Net Sales ($)	1056M	9962M	32555M	49183M	158063M	30746M
		123091M	Total Assets ($)	384M	4683M	12069M	28361M	60551M	17043M

M = $ thousand   MM = $ million
                        See Pages 11 through 18 for Explanation of Ratios and Data

Current Data Sorted By Assets   Comparative Historical Data

						Type of Statement		
1	1	2	4			Unqualified	10	10
5	14	15	2			Reviewed	22	26
9	22	12	1			Compiled	42	37
5	12	1		2	2	Tax Returns	8	8
	9	17				Other	33	34

0-500M	36 (4/1-9/30/02) 500M-2MM	2-10MM	99 (10/1/02-3/31/03) 10-50MM	50-100MM	100-250MM		4/1/98-3/31/99 ALL	4/1/99-3/31/00 ALL
20	58	47	8	2		NUMBER OF STATEMENTS	115	115
%	%	%	%	%	%	ASSETS	%	%
5.0	5.8	5.6			D	Cash & Equivalents	5.9	4.2
26.7	29.8	25.8			A	Trade Receivables (net)	25.4	29.2
20.6	20.1	22.4			T	Inventory	22.2	19.0
2.6	3.7	2.5			A	All Other Current	1.4	2.4
54.9	59.4	56.4				Total Current	54.9	54.8
38.1	34.6	37.3			N	Fixed Assets (net)	35.4	35.9
2.8	1.2	1.9			O	Intangibles (net)	3.0	2.2
4.3	4.8	4.5			T	All Other Non-Current	6.6	7.0
100.0	100.0	100.0				Total	100.0	100.0
					A	LIABILITIES		
13.8	13.3	14.2			V	Notes Payable-Short Term	12.7	13.9
3.9	5.7	4.7			A	Cur. Mat.-L/T/D	4.6	4.7
17.5	13.6	12.3			I	Trade Payables	10.6	10.9
.0	.1	.1			L	Income Taxes Payable	.2	.1
9.5	8.0	8.1			A	All Other Current	7.7	9.3
44.7	40.8	39.3			B	Total Current	35.9	38.9
28.4	21.4	19.7			L	Long Term Debt	20.3	18.1
.1	.2	.3			E	Deferred Taxes	.3	.4
9.5	3.9	4.3				All Other Non-Current	5.1	2.4
17.3	33.7	36.3				Net Worth	38.4	40.2
100.0	100.0	100.0				Total Liabilities & Net Worth	100.0	100.0
						INCOME DATA		
100.0	100.0	100.0				Net Sales	100.0	100.0
42.3	25.1	22.1				Gross Profit	24.1	24.4
42.3	23.8	19.1				Operating Expenses	20.2	20.8
.1	1.3	3.0				Operating Profit	3.9	3.5
.7	.7	1.1				All Other Expenses (net)	.5	1.0
–.6	.7	2.0				Profit Before Taxes	3.5	2.6
						RATIOS		
2.4	2.5	2.5					2.9	2.5
1.3	1.6	1.4				Current	1.5	1.4
.6	1.0	1.1					1.0	1.0
1.8	1.6	1.8					1.8	1.4
.5	.8	.9				Quick	(114) .9	.9
.3	.5	.5					.5	.5
10 37.2	22 16.4	30 12.3					23 15.8	25 14.3
24 15.5	35 10.6	35 10.4				Sales/Receivables	31 11.9	35 10.5
39 9.3	42 8.6	44 8.3					37 9.8	45 8.2
8 43.5	13 28.9	22 16.3					20 18.7	15 23.7
31 11.8	25 14.8	36 10.1				Cost of Sales/Inventory	31 11.7	28 13.2
60 6.0	47 7.7	65 5.6					50 7.3	45 8.1
4 92.8	8 43.4	13 28.9					5 73.0	7 52.3
18 20.0	17 21.0	18 20.0				Cost of Sales/Payables	11 32.3	13 27.5
36 10.2	29 12.4	30 12.2					28 13.2	24 15.2
11.5	7.5	7.3					8.1	9.3
92.7	16.3	13.5				Sales/Working Capital	15.5	21.1
–22.7	NM	41.2					UND	489.7
2.5	3.4	5.7					10.0	6.5
(17) .7	(54) 1.5	(41) 2.2				EBIT/Interest	(106) 3.3	(107) 2.8
–2.5	–.8	.0					1.3	1.6
		3.4				Net Profit + Depr., Dep.,	3.5	4.1
	(13)	1.9				Amort./Cur. Mat. L /T/D	(24) 1.6	(32) 2.1
		.6					.9	1.1
.9	.4	.5					.5	.5
6.1	1.1	1.2				Fixed/Worth	1.0	1.0
–2.4	4.0	2.5					2.5	1.8
1.3	.9	.9					.6	.7
18.7	2.1	1.7				Debt/Worth	1.6	1.5
–13.7	10.9	5.7					4.1	3.3
211.9	32.2	32.8				% Profit Before Taxes/Tangible	45.3	41.7
(12) 25.5	(49) 5.8	(44) 10.2				Net Worth	(99) 19.3	(105) 16.6
–6.5	–12.1	–5.7					5.5	2.9
7.5	8.7	12.1				% Profit Before Taxes/Total	18.0	15.2
–.9	2.1	4.1				Assets	7.2	5.6
–4.2	–5.1	–1.9					1.4	1.5
26.8	20.5	9.6					15.2	17.4
10.0	10.2	7.1				Sales/Net Fixed Assets	7.1	8.9
5.4	6.0	4.0					5.1	4.8
6.4	4.3	3.0					3.8	4.1
4.1	3.4	2.4				Sales/Total Assets	2.8	3.0
3.0	2.2	1.7					2.0	2.0
1.2	1.4	1.8					1.6	1.5
(17) 2.3	(56) 2.3	(43) 2.4				% Depr., Dep., Amort./Sales	(108) 2.5	(106) 2.2
5.4	3.5	3.6					3.6	3.5
4.3	1.8	1.9				% Officers', Directors',	1.7	1.6
(12) 7.0	(38) 3.1	(20) 3.2				Owners' Comp/Sales	(51) 4.0	(54) 2.2
13.5	4.9	4.9					6.9	4.5
20219M	214345M	389156M	372687M	196346M		Net Sales ($)	1285564M	1095205M
4837M	62966M	164052M	161099M	124326M		Total Assets ($)	603340M	510997M

M = $ thousand   MM = $ million
See Pages 11 through 18 for Explanation of Ratios and Data

Comparative Historical Data | Current Data Sorted By Sales

					Type of Statement						
	7		2		7	Unqualified		1			3	3
	22		15		32	Reviewed	3	1	8	12	6	2
	38		42		39	Compiled	4	14	5	14	2	
	10		11		22	Tax Returns	3	9	6	4		
	31		25		35	Other	3	7	6	11	4	4
	4/1/00-3/31/01 ALL		4/1/01-3/31/02 ALL		4/1/02-3/31/03 ALL		36 (4/1-9/30/02)			99 (10/1/02-3/31/03)		
							0-1MM	1-3MM	3-5MM	5-10MM	10-25MM	25MM & OVER
	108		95		135	NUMBER OF STATEMENTS	13	32	25	41	15	9
	%		%		%	ASSETS	%	%	%	%	%	%
	4.6		4.6		5.5	Cash & Equivalents	9.3	3.9	3.8	6.6	5.9	
	30.3		29.8		27.1	Trade Receivables (net)	18.3	29.5	24.6	30.3	29.8	
	21.1		19.8		21.0	Inventory	18.5	20.4	20.7	20.4	29.1	
	1.4		4.1		3.1	All Other Current	5.4	3.1	3.9	2.2	2.2	
	57.4		58.3		56.7	Total Current	51.4	56.8	53.0	59.5	66.9	
	33.6		33.5		36.8	Fixed Assets (net)	36.7	36.2	41.3	35.1	28.7	
	2.8		2.7		2.0	Intangibles (net)	4.3	1.6	2.6	.9	1.3	
	6.2		5.4		4.5	All Other Non-Current	7.6	5.4	3.0	4.5	3.1	
	100.0		100.0		100.0	Total	100.0	100.0	100.0	100.0	100.0	
						LIABILITIES						
	17.8		15.1		14.0	Notes Payable-Short Term	21.8	9.8	14.6	13.1	16.9	
	3.9		5.3		5.1	Cur. Mat.-L/T/D	4.2	4.5	5.0	5.6	5.6	
	12.8		13.8		13.2	Trade Payables	9.6	16.1	13.5	12.4	15.6	
	.2		.1		.1	Income Taxes Payable	.4	.0	.0	.1	.0	
	11.8		7.8		8.3	All Other Current	10.4	7.6	8.4	8.0	9.5	
	46.4		42.1		40.8	Total Current	46.5	38.0	41.5	39.1	47.6	
	18.4		19.1		22.1	Long Term Debt	18.2	29.6	24.3	19.5	9.9	
	.2		.2		.2	Deferred Taxes	.2	.1	.2	.4	.1	
	3.4		3.9		4.9	All Other Non-Current	2.2	6.4	3.7	4.8	6.4	
	31.5		34.6		32.1	Net Worth	33.0	25.8	30.3	36.2	36.0	
	100.0		100.0		100.0	Total Liabilities & Net Worth	100.0	100.0	100.0	100.0	100.0	
						INCOME DATA						
	100.0		100.0		100.0	Net Sales	100.0	100.0	100.0	100.0	100.0	
	22.5		22.8		25.7	Gross Profit	40.7	31.5	29.0	19.7	19.4	
	19.7		20.8		23.9	Operating Expenses	42.4	29.9	25.4	18.7	15.8	
	2.7		2.0		1.8	Operating Profit	-1.7	1.6	3.6	1.0	3.6	
	.6		.8		.8	All Other Expenses (net)	1.0	.9	1.2	.7	.6	
	2.1		1.2		1.0	Profit Before Taxes	-2.7	.7	2.3	.3	3.0	
						RATIOS						
	2.2		2.4		2.4		2.9	2.7	1.7	2.9	2.8	
	1.3		1.4		1.4	Current	.9	1.6	1.2	1.7	1.3	
	1.0		1.0		1.0		.5	1.1	.8	1.2	1.0	
	1.3		1.4		1.6		2.2	1.8	1.1	2.1	1.8	
	.8		.9		.8	Quick	.4	.9	.6	.9	.8	
	.5		.5		.4		.3	.5	.4	.6	.5	

23	15.9	25	14.5	23	15.7	Sales/Receivables	0 UND	23 16.1	23 16.0	27 13.4	20 17.9	
32	11.3	35	10.5	34	10.8		32 11.5	35 10.4	36 10.3	33 11.0	34 10.8	
40	9.1	42	8.7	42	8.6		52 7.0	44 8.4	42 8.7	42 8.6	42 8.8	
16	23.0	12	29.2	18	20.8	Cost of Sales/Inventory	0 UND	13 29.2	17 21.2	15 24.4	22 16.3	
29	12.8	31	11.8	32	11.5		56 6.5	30 12.3	37 9.8	32 11.5	29 12.4	
46	8.0	48	7.6	56	6.5		120 3.0	51 7.2	71 5.2	50 7.3	44 8.2	
7	51.1	10	38.1	9	42.8	Cost of Sales/Payables	5 80.5	9 41.0	13 28.3	8 43.0	11 34.1	
14	26.0	16	23.1	17	20.9		27 13.6	18 20.1	26 14.0	17 21.8	16 23.2	
25	14.5	30	12.4	29	12.6		43 8.4	37 9.8	36 10.2	26 14.3	21 17.0	
	10.4		7.6		7.5	Sales/Working Capital	6.4	7.5	11.4	7.4	9.2	
	22.4		21.7		16.7		-33.9	14.4	26.5	14.2	29.8	
	-224.4		-205.0		999.8		-6.3	761.2	-33.3	28.4	-171.5	
	5.9		3.7		3.4	EBIT/Interest	.9	3.4	6.6	2.9	9.9	
(106)	2.3	(92)	1.6	(122)	1.7		(11) .2	(31) 1.6	(23) 1.8	(35) 1.0	(13) 5.3	
	1.2		.4		-.3		-8.8	.5	.1	-1.3	.3	
	3.3		2.6		2.6	Net Profit + Depr., Dep., Amort./Cur. Mat. L/T/D				2.6		
(23)	2.2	(23)	1.1	(24)	1.3					(11) 1.2		
	1.2		.6		.4					.3		
	.5		.5		.5	Fixed/Worth	.4	.5	.9	.5	.3	
	1.1		1.2		1.3		1.2	2.0	1.8	1.0	1.2	
	2.8		2.8		3.9		-50.9	NM	3.6	1.7	4.5	
	.8		1.0		1.0	Debt/Worth	.6	.8	1.3	.8	.6	
	1.8		1.8		2.1		2.0	2.2	2.5	1.5	2.6	
	6.5		5.6		8.8		-113.7	NM	13.4	3.6	12.7	
	40.9		26.3		34.1	% Profit Before Taxes/Tangible Net Worth		47.3	46.5	30.9	56.8	
(91)	11.9	(86)	7.9	(114)	8.9			(24) 4.8	(22) 11.7	(38) 3.5	(13) 30.3	
	2.1		-4.4		-6.2			-13.1	-5.2	-7.6	12.4	
	12.7		8.0		9.5	% Profit Before Taxes/Total Assets	.7	9.2	11.7	8.1	19.0	
	4.8		2.1		2.4		-1.9	1.3	4.4	1.2	12.1	
	.9		-2.2		-3.8		-4.8	-4.0	-1.1	-5.1	.8	
	20.8		19.7		13.1	Sales/Net Fixed Assets	10.7	20.9	10.2	14.9	13.2	
	9.9		8.6		7.7		5.9	10.9	6.3	8.6	9.6	
	5.7		5.1		4.6		3.1	5.4	4.6	4.5	7.1	
	4.5		3.9		4.0	Sales/Total Assets	3.7	4.8	3.6	4.3	4.1	
	3.4		3.0		2.8		2.0	3.1	2.4	2.6	3.8	
	2.3		2.2		2.1		1.1	2.1	1.9	2.3	2.8	
	1.1		.6		1.6	% Depr., Dep., Amort./Sales	2.0	1.6	1.9	1.4	1.7	
(98)	2.0	(87)	2.1	(125)	2.4		(11) 3.3	(30) 2.3	(23) 2.9	(39) 2.1	(14) 2.2	
	2.9		3.1		3.8		6.2	4.4	4.4	3.1	3.2	
	1.3		2.0		2.2	% Officers', Directors', Owners' Comp/Sales		3.1	1.6	2.1		
(56)	2.4	(52)	2.9	(70)	3.6			(23) 5.0	(14) 2.7	(22) 3.1		
	3.9		4.3		5.6			8.1	3.7	4.9		
	2218493M		815665M		1192753M	Net Sales ($)	7182M	62289M	95000M	271128M	199152M	558002M
	921040M		368996M		517280M	Total Assets ($)	4307M	22092M	41328M	108061M	75284M	266208M

M = $ thousand   MM = $ million
See Pages 11 through 18 for Explanation of Ratios and Data

Current Data Sorted By Assets | Comparative Historical Data

						Type of Statement		
		1	4	4	2	Unqualified	12	16
		3	1			Reviewed	7	7
	4	4		4		Compiled	5	4
2						Tax Returns		
1		4	5	2	4	Other	5	7
	10 (4/1-9/30/02)		31 (10/1/02-3/31/03)				4/1/98-3/31/99	4/1/99-3/31/00
0-500M	500M-2MM	2-10MM	10-50MM	50-100MM	100-250MM		ALL	ALL
3	4	12	10	6	6	NUMBER OF STATEMENTS	29	34
%	%	%	%	%	%	ASSETS	%	%
		5.5	20.4			Cash & Equivalents	15.8	12.9
		16.5	15.7			Trade Receivables (net)	16.1	18.9
		28.9	15.8			Inventory	24.6	26.0
		7.4	8.2			All Other Current	2.6	3.7
		58.4	60.2			Total Current	59.1	61.5
		34.2	34.3			Fixed Assets (net)	26.0	27.3
		4.4	1.5			Intangibles (net)	7.5	5.1
		3.0	3.9			All Other Non-Current	7.3	6.0
		100.0	100.0			Total	100.0	100.0
						LIABILITIES		
		14.1	7.4			Notes Payable-Short Term	8.8	8.2
		4.0	4.3			Cur. Mat.-L/T/D	2.7	3.5
		10.7	8.7			Trade Payables	9.5	9.4
		.2	.0			Income Taxes Payable	.7	.3
		17.0	14.8			All Other Current	14.8	16.9
		45.9	35.1			Total Current	36.6	38.3
		11.8	13.8			Long Term Debt	15.2	15.0
		.0	2.2			Deferred Taxes	1.1	.8
		3.2	1.1			All Other Non-Current	7.0	2.8
		39.0	47.9			Net Worth	40.1	43.0
		100.0	100.0			Total Liabilities & Net Worth	100.0	100.0
						INCOME DATA		
		100.0	100.0			Net Sales	100.0	100.0
		19.8	17.9			Gross Profit	21.3	20.9
		19.6	13.7			Operating Expenses	16.3	15.4
		.1	4.1			Operating Profit	5.1	5.5
		.5	.4			All Other Expenses (net)	.9	.9
		-.4	3.8			Profit Before Taxes	4.2	4.6
						RATIOS		
		1.6	3.1				2.4	2.1
		1.5	1.5			Current	1.7	1.6
		1.0	1.0				1.2	1.2
		.8	1.9				1.4	1.5
		.5	1.0			Quick	1.0	.8
		.2	.5				.5	.4
		11 34.2	13 27.2				13 28.7	11 31.8
		16 22.1	20 18.5			Sales/Receivables	16 22.5	21 17.2
		23 15.6	25 14.7				24 15.1	32 11.3
		29 12.7	19 19.2				14 25.6	19 19.4
		40 9.1	23 15.9			Cost of Sales/Inventory	31 11.6	34 10.6
		43 8.4	33 10.9				50 7.3	55 6.6
		8 43.5	7 49.9				7 53.0	7 50.0
		12 30.6	14 26.0			Cost of Sales/Payables	14 26.4	14 26.7
		19 19.0	23 15.6				19 19.0	22 16.9
		15.3	4.9				8.8	8.3
		19.5	10.7			Sales/Working Capital	12.8	15.7
		NM	NM				41.8	45.6
		10.0					17.1	30.3
		.5				EBIT/Interest	(26) 6.4	(30) 7.0
		-1.8					1.8	3.2
						Net Profit + Depr., Dep.,	12.9	
						Amort./Cur. Mat. L./T/D	(11) 4.6	
							1.8	
		.5	.4				.3	.2
		.8	.9			Fixed/Worth	.7	.5
		3.7	1.7				1.5	1.1
		.8	.3				.7	.6
		2.0	1.9			Debt/Worth	1.3	1.2
		6.1	2.7				4.4	2.8
		26.5	48.5			% Profit Before Taxes/Tangible	34.1	44.0
	(11) -10.7	14.9				Net Worth	(24) 27.0	(30) 20.3
		-36.6	-1.6				19.9	10.4
		7.2	14.5			% Profit Before Taxes/Total	17.9	17.7
		-1.0	7.1			Assets	9.8	10.9
		-9.4	.0				3.1	4.8
		15.8	11.1				25.0	27.6
		8.1	9.7			Sales/Net Fixed Assets	17.2	13.9
		7.0	5.7				9.1	7.6
		3.7	3.5				4.1	3.6
		2.9	2.3			Sales/Total Assets	2.7	2.7
		2.4	1.4				1.8	2.1
		1.0					.7	.6
		1.2				% Depr., Dep., Amort./Sales	(26) 1.0	(29) .8
		1.4					1.8	1.3
						% Officers', Directors',		
						Owners' Comp/Sales		
2556M	20825M	212332M	480080M	780941M	1147684M	Net Sales ($)	2599800M	3307220M
829M	6691M	70038M	214032M	377630M	741495M	Total Assets ($)	1109817M	1519060M

M = $ thousand   MM = $ million
See Pages 11 through 18 for Explanation of Ratios and Data

Comparative Historical Data				Current Data Sorted By Sales					
			Type of Statement						
15	9	11	Unqualified					1	10
1	3	4	Reviewed				2	2	
6	8	8	Compiled		1		3	4	
1	1	2	Tax Returns	1	1				
10	18	16	Other	1				4	11
4/1/00-3/31/01	**4/1/01-3/31/02**	**4/1/02-3/31/03**		**10 (4/1-9/30/02)**			**31 (10/1/02-3/31/03)**		
ALL	**ALL**	**ALL**		**0-1MM**	**1-3MM**	**3-5MM**	**5-10MM**	**10-25MM**	**25MM & OVER**
33	39	41	**NUMBER OF STATEMENTS**	2	2		5	11	21
%	%	%	**ASSETS**	%	%	%	%	%	%
10.3	12.3	10.6	Cash & Equivalents			DATA NOT AVAILABLE		11.1	11.8
17.2	15.3	15.0	Trade Receivables (net)					13.1	16.0
27.8	23.9	25.3	Inventory					23.6	19.1
8.8	3.9	8.2	All Other Current					7.0	8.6
64.1	55.4	59.1	Total Current					54.8	55.5
21.8	29.6	26.5	Fixed Assets (net)					37.3	24.6
3.1	6.3	5.4	Intangibles (net)					4.7	7.4
11.1	8.7	8.9	All Other Non-Current					3.2	12.5
100.0	100.0	100.0	Total					100.0	100.0
			LIABILITIES						
12.6	9.3	13.2	Notes Payable-Short Term					12.3	6.1
3.4	2.5	3.3	Cur. Mat.-L/T/D					3.9	3.3
9.2	6.6	8.6	Trade Payables					10.8	8.7
.2	.3	.1	Income Taxes Payable					.2	.1
20.6	18.0	14.3	All Other Current					13.7	18.5
46.1	36.7	39.6	Total Current					40.9	36.8
9.2	15.9	10.3	Long Term Debt					11.8	9.3
.9	.7	1.0	Deferred Taxes					1.2	1.1
2.9	5.0	4.2	All Other Non-Current					1.5	2.4
40.9	41.8	44.9	Net Worth					44.5	50.4
100.0	100.0	100.0	Total Liabilities & Net Worth					100.0	100.0
			INCOME DATA						
100.0	100.0	100.0	Net Sales					100.0	100.0
19.1	24.3	21.6	Gross Profit					23.4	17.6
15.1	21.7	19.3	Operating Expenses					21.1	15.1
4.1	2.6	2.3	Operating Profit					2.4	2.5
.9	.9	.2	All Other Expenses (net)					.5	.3
3.2	1.7	2.1	Profit Before Taxes					1.8	2.1
			RATIOS						
2.1	2.4	1.9						1.6	1.9
1.4	1.5	1.5	Current					1.5	1.6
1.0	1.0	1.0						.7	1.2
1.4	1.3	1.1						.8	1.2
.6	.7	.6	Quick					.6	.9
.2	.4	.3						.2	.4
13 28.9	**13** 27.7	**13** 27.8						**10** 35.4	**15** 24.4
21 17.2	**22** 16.7	**18** 20.6	Sales/Receivables					**17** 21.8	**20** 18.6
32 11.3	**39** 9.4	**25** 14.9						**25** 14.3	**28** 12.9
17 20.9	**27** 13.6	**23** 15.9						**25** 14.5	**21** 17.6
30 12.3	**39** 9.5	**32** 11.5	Cost of Sales/Inventory					**29** 12.7	**28** 12.9
67 5.5	**74** 4.9	**54** 6.7						**44** 8.3	**56** 6.6
7 55.3	**7** 52.2	**7** 50.8						**8** 43.0	**7** 50.8
12 31.2	**12** 29.6	**12** 29.3	Cost of Sales/Payables					**12** 29.3	**13** 28.7
20 17.8	**17** 21.3	**20** 18.3						**25** 14.5	**24** 15.0
7.3	5.8	7.6						14.7	7.1
13.0	17.5	14.7	Sales/Working Capital					23.3	12.3
−55.9	158.2	111.8						−26.5	31.3
14.2	7.4	9.7						11.5	8.7
(30) 6.6	(33) 2.0	(39) 2.5	EBIT/Interest					(10) 3.3	(20) 2.6
1.8	1.0	−1.6						−.9	−2.8
			Net Profit + Depr., Dep., Amort./Cur. Mat. L/T/D						
.2	.4	.3						.6	.3
.4	.8	.6	Fixed/Worth					.9	.5
1.6	1.6	1.4						2.6	1.2
.6	.7	.7						.5	.6
1.2	1.8	1.3	Debt/Worth					1.8	1.1
4.1	2.7	2.7						2.9	2.3
29.5	24.1	31.5						27.3	23.6
(27) 23.3	(35) 10.0	(38) 8.6	% Profit Before Taxes/Tangible Net Worth					(10) 6.4	(20) 8.6
11.6	.5	−13.0						−21.7	−16.6
13.3	9.0	11.5						8.3	12.4
7.0	3.7	4.1	% Profit Before Taxes/Total Assets					4.1	2.6
2.8	−.1	−4.4						−4.6	−3.6
38.8	14.9	16.5						10.1	14.2
13.2	7.8	10.0	Sales/Net Fixed Assets					8.0	10.5
7.2	5.0	6.9						6.7	7.2
3.2	2.7	3.6						3.5	2.9
2.2	2.1	2.6	Sales/Total Assets					2.6	2.3
1.3	1.2	1.5						2.1	1.4
.6	.7	.9						1.0	.9
(27) 1.0	(36) 1.1	(35) 1.1	% Depr., Dep., Amort./Sales					1.1	(17) 1.1
1.5	1.6	1.6						1.4	1.6
	.9								
	(10) 2.9		% Officers', Directors', Owners' Comp/Sales						
	10.6								
3105737M	**2292838M**	**2644418M**	Net Sales ($)	**1168M**	**2727M**		**38329M**	**205432M**	**2396762M**
1677515M	**1368428M**	**1410715M**	Total Assets ($)	**510M**	**2019M**		**12494M**	**98706M**	**1296986M**

M = $ thousand MM = $ million

See Pages 11 through 18 for Explanation of Ratios and Data

Current Data Sorted By Assets / Comparative Historical Data

Type of Statement	0-500M	500M-2MM	2-10MM	10-50MM	50-100MM	100-250MM	4/1/98-3/31/99 ALL	4/1/99-3/31/00 ALL
Unqualified			7	4		1	25	14
Reviewed		2	14	2			19	20
Compiled	3	5	5				20	13
Tax Returns	1	3	2				5	7
Other	2	7	5	3		1	23	23
		10 (4/1-9/30/02)		57 (10/1/02-3/31/03)				
NUMBER OF STATEMENTS	6	17	33	9		2	92	77

(Columns 10-50MM, 50-100MM, 100-250MM: DATA NOT AVAILABLE for the percentage/ratio detail.)

ASSETS	0-500M	500M-2MM	2-10MM	4/1/98-3/31/99	4/1/99-3/31/00
	%	%	%	%	%
Cash & Equivalents		7.0	11.4	11.9	9.9
Trade Receivables (net)		27.6	19.1	23.3	21.9
Inventory		29.0	24.3	24.2	26.2
All Other Current		1.3	1.6	3.0	2.3
Total Current		64.9	56.4	62.3	60.3
Fixed Assets (net)		28.4	32.8	30.8	29.5
Intangibles (net)		2.6	3.5	2.1	4.3
All Other Non-Current		4.1	7.2	4.8	6.0
Total		100.0	100.0	100.0	100.0

LIABILITIES	500M-2MM	2-10MM	4/1/98-3/31/99	4/1/99-3/31/00
Notes Payable-Short Term	20.9	8.7	9.7	11.0
Cur. Mat.-L/T/D	3.1	2.5	3.8	3.6
Trade Payables	16.0	10.3	13.0	11.1
Income Taxes Payable	.0	.4	.3	.4
All Other Current	15.9	18.2	13.5	15.5
Total Current	55.9	40.1	40.4	41.5
Long Term Debt	17.2	13.0	18.2	16.1
Deferred Taxes	.0	.2	.4	.4
All Other Non-Current	3.4	2.4	4.8	5.0
Net Worth	23.4	44.3	36.1	37.1
Total Liabilities & Net Worth	100.0	100.0	100.0	100.0

INCOME DATA	500M-2MM	2-10MM	4/1/98-3/31/99	4/1/99-3/31/00
Net Sales	100.0	100.0	100.0	100.0
Gross Profit	30.7	28.8	26.1	26.6
Operating Expenses	27.5	23.5	20.8	21.5
Operating Profit	3.2	5.4	5.3	5.1
All Other Expenses (net)	.4	.5	.7	.4
Profit Before Taxes	2.8	4.9	4.6	4.7

RATIOS	500M-2MM	2-10MM	4/1/98-3/31/99	4/1/99-3/31/00
Current	2.0 / 1.4 / 1.0	2.6 / 1.6 / .9	2.3 / 1.5 / 1.1	2.3 / 1.7 / 1.1
Quick	1.4 / .8 / .3	1.8 / .7 / .4	1.4 / .8 / .6	1.4 / .8 / .5
Sales/Receivables	8 44.5 / 29 12.6 / 66 5.5	9 40.5 / 24 15.3 / 37 9.8	15 24.9 / 29 12.7 / 40 9.2	15 23.7 / 29 12.8 / 41 8.9
Cost of Sales/Inventory	24 15.0 / 38 9.6 / 56 6.5	30 12.1 / 55 6.7 / 71 5.1	26 14.0 / 37 9.9 / 54 6.7	29 12.8 / 46 8.0 / 64 5.7
Cost of Sales/Payables	8 44.4 / 16 22.6 / 49 7.5	10 37.7 / 16 22.5 / 35 10.6	8 45.9 / 17 21.4 / 32 11.2	9 42.5 / 14 26.3 / 27 13.5
Sales/Working Capital	10.2 / 18.9 / NM	6.0 / 14.0 / NM	7.3 / 15.2 / 48.3	6.8 / 12.7 / 44.4
EBIT/Interest	(15) 24.4 / 5.5 / 1.8	(30) 17.4 / 6.2 / 1.9	(82) 10.0 / 4.4 / 2.1	(70) 12.4 / 5.0 / 1.6
Net Profit + Depr., Dep., Amort./Cur. Mat. L/T/D		(13) 22.7 / 6.3 / 2.2	(28) 8.4 / 3.4 / 2.0	(25) 10.9 / 2.9 / 2.0
Fixed/Worth	.5 / .8 / 6.7	.3 / .7 / 1.8	.4 / 1.0 / 1.8	.4 / .7 / 1.5
Debt/Worth	1.1 / 3.1 / 20.1	.5 / 1.2 / 3.7	.8 / 1.8 / 4.0	.7 / 1.5 / 3.7
% Profit Before Taxes/Tangible Net Worth	(14) 77.7 / 47.8 / 9.9	(31) 58.2 / 39.2 / 7.6	(81) 55.9 / 29.3 / 13.6	(66) 52.8 / 29.4 / 10.6
% Profit Before Taxes/Total Assets	25.0 / 13.5 / 1.7	22.1 / 8.7 / 1.0	20.8 / 10.5 / 2.7	22.1 / 10.7 / 2.5
Sales/Net Fixed Assets	27.4 / 12.0 / 6.7	19.5 / 9.2 / 4.5	19.0 / 11.0 / 6.4	19.9 / 10.2 / 5.4
Sales/Total Assets	4.1 / 3.5 / 2.2	3.4 / 2.4 / 1.8	3.7 / 2.9 / 2.4	3.5 / 2.8 / 2.0
% Depr., Dep., Amort./Sales	1.4 / 1.9 / 2.8	(32) 1.3 / 1.9 / 3.1	(81) 1.1 / 1.6 / 2.3	(72) 1.3 / 2.0 / 3.0
% Officers', Directors', Owners' Comp/Sales		(11) 1.6 / 3.0 / 5.7	(24) 1.8 / 3.9 / 6.9	(24) 1.4 / 3.7

	0-500M	500M-2MM	2-10MM	10-50MM	100-250MM	4/1/98-3/31/99	4/1/99-3/31/00
Net Sales ($)	11199M	65369M	431163M	342006M	352214M	1614358M	1577282M
Total Assets ($)	1827M	21084M	172252M	148568M	342818M	732684M	844654M

M = $ thousand   MM = $ million
See Pages 11 through 18 for Explanation of Ratios and Data

Comparative Historical Data				Current Data Sorted By Sales					
			Type of Statement						
10	8	12	Unqualified				1	5	6
13	12	18	Reviewed			3	5	8	2
17	14	13	Compiled		1	7	4	1	
6	8	6	Tax Returns	1	2	1	2		
35	28	18	Other		5	3	1	6	3
4/1/00-	4/1/01-	4/1/02-			10 (4/1-9/30/02)		57 (10/1/02-3/31/03)		
3/31/01	3/31/02	3/31/03							
ALL	ALL	ALL		0-1MM	1-3MM	3-5MM	5-10MM	10-25MM	25MM & OVER
81	70	67	**NUMBER OF STATEMENTS**	1	8	14	13	20	11
%	%	%	**ASSETS**	%	%	%	%	%	%
10.5	11.9	12.1	Cash & Equivalents			10.9	16.5	13.0	15.5
21.7	18.7	20.2	Trade Receivables (net)			17.1	14.8	22.4	15.4
26.1	24.7	26.6	Inventory			28.8	28.1	21.1	24.2
4.3	3.8	1.6	All Other Current			1.1	.8	2.3	2.1
62.6	59.2	60.5	Total Current			57.8	60.2	58.8	57.2
26.8	31.0	28.8	Fixed Assets (net)			37.0	30.2	26.2	25.4
3.4	2.2	4.9	Intangibles (net)			1.2	2.3	7.8	9.7
7.2	7.6	5.7	All Other Non-Current			3.9	7.4	7.2	7.7
100.0	100.0	100.0	Total			100.0	100.0	100.0	100.0
			LIABILITIES						
13.2	8.4	13.2	Notes Payable-Short Term			9.1	5.0	10.5	5.3
3.7	2.5	2.4	Cur. Mat.-L/T/D			3.6	3.2	2.1	1.2
11.2	11.4	11.2	Trade Payables			14.6	8.5	11.7	8.7
.4	.0	.2	Income Taxes Payable			.0	.0	.6	.0
18.9	15.0	16.5	All Other Current			28.5	13.6	15.1	17.6
47.5	37.3	43.4	Total Current			55.7	30.3	40.0	32.8
12.5	17.5	15.1	Long Term Debt			20.5	14.7	11.0	16.3
.2	.3	.1	Deferred Taxes			.0	.0	.3	.1
4.4	5.2	3.8	All Other Non-Current			4.1	.9	2.8	10.3
35.4	39.6	37.5	Net Worth			19.6	54.2	46.0	40.5
100.0	100.0	100.0	Total Liabilities & Net Worth			100.0	100.0	100.0	100.0
			INCOME DATA						
100.0	100.0	100.0	Net Sales			100.0	100.0	100.0	100.0
25.0	29.3	30.4	Gross Profit			37.6	35.5	25.2	26.4
21.0	23.2	25.4	Operating Expenses			33.8	27.5	19.8	20.8
4.0	6.1	5.0	Operating Profit			3.8	8.0	5.3	5.6
−.1	1.7	.7	All Other Expenses (net)			.9	−.2	.9	1.4
4.1	4.4	4.3	Profit Before Taxes			2.9	8.2	4.4	4.1
			RATIOS						
2.2	2.8	2.5				2.0	6.7	2.7	2.8
1.4	1.5	1.6	Current			1.3	1.8	1.6	1.7
.9	1.0	1.1				.9	1.3	1.0	1.2
1.3	1.7	1.8				1.3	3.3	1.8	2.4
.7	.7	.8	Quick			.5	1.3	.8	.8
.3	.4	.4				.1	.4	.5	.4
12 29.6	12 31.1	9 40.4	Sales/Receivables		9 40.5	3 126.1	10 36.3	13 28.9	
23 16.1	21 17.2	24 15.3			20 18.5	10 38.0	24 15.1	20 18.5	
44 8.3	41 8.9	37 9.8			36 10.1	32 11.4	51 7.2	34 10.9	
28 12.9	31 11.8	27 13.6	Cost of Sales/Inventory		24 14.9	31 11.7	25 14.6	35 10.3	
41 9.0	39 9.3	46 8.0			51 7.2	48 7.6	36 10.1	46 7.9	
68 5.4	53 6.8	67 5.5			96 3.8	75 4.8	60 6.1	63 5.8	
10 35.7	7 51.9	9 39.0	Cost of Sales/Payables		14 26.5	4 97.8	9 38.7	10 37.5	
17 21.4	16 22.5	16 22.6			21 17.3	11 33.3	17 22.0	18 20.5	
31 11.8	26 13.9	34 10.8			39 9.3	23 16.1	38 9.7	25 14.5	
8.0	8.0	6.3	Sales/Working Capital		13.1	6.5	5.6	5.7	
17.5	15.1	14.0			24.2	12.2	13.2	8.2	
−134.3	213.4	71.0			−21.4	29.8	229.6	41.3	
14.0	13.9	20.5	EBIT/Interest		14.5	32.8	28.9	20.2	
(78) 5.1	(66) 5.6	(62) 7.0		(12) 2.2	13.1	(18) 4.8	10.0		
1.1	1.1	1.8			1.8	7.0	1.3		
15.9	18.6	20.4	Net Profit + Depr., Dep., Amort./Cur. Mat. L/T/D				34.6		
(25) 2.5	(20) 7.5	(21) 6.3				(10) 5.2			
1.4	2.6	2.4				1.9			
.3	.3	.4	Fixed/Worth		.6	.3	.2	.6	
.9	.6	.7			1.4	.6	.6	.7	
1.9	1.8	2.0			NM	1.0	1.7	1.5	
.7	.5	.6	Debt/Worth		1.4	.3	.5	.9	
1.9	1.7	1.7			3.4	1.1	1.2	1.3	
5.9	3.2	4.6			NM	2.1	4.6	3.2	
51.0	52.0	62.6	% Profit Before Taxes/Tangible Net Worth		68.6	84.2	61.1		
(72) 30.6	(63) 30.8	(58) 42.6		(11) 42.8	44.2	(18) 41.6			
10.4	6.4	10.0			4.9	31.1	7.1		
21.5	22.9	24.4	% Profit Before Taxes/Total Assets		21.9	47.3	27.8	15.4	
6.8	9.6	10.1			6.1	19.2	6.1	11.4	
1.0	.9	1.7			1.3	11.8	−2.0	1.8	
26.8	22.0	24.0	Sales/Net Fixed Assets		22.5	27.4	27.9	15.9	
11.6	10.2	10.6			10.5	9.2	13.6	8.4	
5.9	5.0	6.3			4.0	5.6	6.1	6.6	
3.4	3.7	3.6	Sales/Total Assets		5.1	4.0	3.4	3.5	
2.6	2.7	2.7			3.0	3.0	2.4	1.9	
2.0	1.8	1.8			1.8	2.3	1.9	1.7	
1.3	1.4	1.3	% Depr., Dep., Amort./Sales		1.8	1.9	1.1	1.4	
(69) 1.9	(65) 1.7	(63) 1.9		(13) 2.3	2.8	(18) 1.5	2.2		
2.8	2.8	2.8			3.7	3.1	2.0	3.1	
.9	1.2	1.3	% Officers', Directors', Owners' Comp/Sales						
(22) 1.9	(22) 2.7	(20) 2.7							
5.6	4.4	5.6							
1730443M	1244676M	1201951M	Net Sales ($)	331M	14888M	53466M	93512M	326146M	713608M
866373M	716858M	686549M	Total Assets ($)	31M	6802M	22114M	33916M	139011M	484675M

© RMA 2003   M = $ thousand   MM = $ million
See Pages 11 through 18 for Explanation of Ratios and Data

Current Data Sorted By Assets							Comparative Historical Data	
						Type of Statement		
	5	12	12	2		Unqualified	32	19
	13	17	11	1		Reviewed	36	32
4	14	14				Compiled	34	36
6	9	3	1			Tax Returns	18	20
5	4	29	6	5	1	Other	46	46
	41 (4/1-9/30/02)		133 (10/1/02-3/31/03)				4/1/98- 3/31/99	4/1/99- 3/31/00
0-500M	500M-2MM	2-10MM	10-50MM	50-100MM	100-250MM		ALL	ALL
15	45	75	30	8	1	NUMBER OF STATEMENTS	166	153
%	%	%	%	%	%	**ASSETS**	%	%
9.4	8.6	6.1	6.3			Cash & Equivalents	7.1	5.3
28.6	28.0	18.9	17.3			Trade Receivables (net)	21.1	21.8
24.5	22.2	30.1	25.5			Inventory	27.5	28.2
.6	4.1	2.1	3.6			All Other Current	2.0	2.0
63.1	62.9	57.2	52.7			Total Current	57.7	57.3
23.5	30.0	32.6	32.3			Fixed Assets (net)	31.1	32.2
1.7	3.7	2.8	4.2			Intangibles (net)	3.2	3.4
11.6	3.4	7.4	10.8			All Other Non-Current	8.0	7.0
100.0	100.0	100.0	100.0			Total	100.0	100.0
						LIABILITIES		
23.7	13.8	14.7	9.9			Notes Payable-Short Term	13.6	14.9
3.0	6.2	4.7	3.7			Cur. Mat.-L/T/D	5.6	4.3
21.1	15.6	11.6	9.7			Trade Payables	12.0	13.0
.0	.6	.3	.3			Income Taxes Payable	.5	.2
20.1	10.9	5.5	7.7			All Other Current	9.1	9.0
67.9	47.1	36.9	31.4			Total Current	40.7	41.4
25.3	23.5	18.7	17.3			Long Term Debt	20.9	20.8
.0	.0	.5	.7			Deferred Taxes	.6	.5
.1	4.1	3.2	5.7			All Other Non-Current	6.2	8.1
6.6	25.3	40.6	44.9			Net Worth	31.5	29.3
100.0	100.0	100.0	100.0			Total Liabilities & Net Worth	100.0	100.0
						INCOME DATA		
100.0	100.0	100.0	100.0			Net Sales	100.0	100.0
41.0	30.5	24.4	22.8			Gross Profit	29.5	28.9
35.6	27.6	20.1	17.2			Operating Expenses	24.4	23.7
5.4	2.9	4.4	5.6			Operating Profit	5.1	5.2
1.1	1.6	1.3	.8			All Other Expenses (net)	1.2	1.6
4.3	1.3	3.0	4.8			Profit Before Taxes	3.9	3.6
						RATIOS		
1.6	2.0	2.4	2.7			Current	2.6	2.2
1.1	1.5	1.5	1.8				1.5	1.5
.8	1.2	1.2	.9				1.1	1.1
1.6	1.3	1.2	1.3			Quick	1.3	1.1
(14) .7	.9	.7	.8				.7	.7
.1	.5	.4	.3				.4	.3
0 UND	17 21.0	19 19.7	19 18.9			Sales/Receivables	19 19.6	21 17.3
18 20.8	29 12.8	30 12.4	31 11.7				34 10.7	33 11.1
35 10.3	40 9.2	42 8.7	42 8.6				48 7.6	44 8.2
0 UND	18 20.8	37 9.8	32 11.6			Cost of Sales/Inventory	29 12.4	28 12.9
9 38.6	36 10.0	57 6.4	54 6.8				60 6.1	61 6.0
52 7.0	65 5.6	95 3.9	111 3.3				98 3.7	91 4.0
0 UND	6 58.9	9 41.0	12 30.2			Cost of Sales/Payables	11 34.5	13 27.5
24 15.1	21 17.3	18 20.1	15 24.2				21 17.5	23 16.2
57 6.5	45 8.1	36 10.1	36 10.0				40 9.1	36 10.1
12.0	9.8	6.5	5.0			Sales/Working Capital	6.2	7.2
56.2	20.3	11.9	9.5				11.2	12.3
-43.1	71.8	27.6	-42.8				131.7	119.2
6.2	9.3	9.2	15.8			EBIT/Interest	6.8	6.1
(13) 1.5	(42) 2.6	(72) 3.2	(28) 3.6				(156) 2.9	(143) 2.2
-2.9	-1.1	1.8	1.6				1.2	1.2
		3.6	4.5			Net Profit + Depr., Dep., Amort./Cur. Mat. L /T/D	5.6	5.2
	(24) 1.9	(10) 2.2					(46) 2.5	(43) 2.1
	1.0	1.1					1.1	1.6
.5	.4	.3	.4			Fixed/Worth	.4	.4
1.1	1.5	.9	.8				.9	1.1
6.2	-21.2	2.2	1.9				2.6	3.3
1.9	1.1	.6	.3			Debt/Worth	.9	1.0
6.2	2.9	1.9	1.5				2.1	2.6
-136.0	-54.8	4.7	3.8				6.5	7.5
225.0	74.5	41.8	33.0			% Profit Before Taxes/Tangible Net Worth	50.6	61.4
(11) 113.9	(32) 31.6	(70) 19.7	(28) 16.8				(144) 23.4	(134) 22.1
-22.2	-5.0	5.1	11.3				7.4	7.2
30.0	19.1	16.3	15.5			% Profit Before Taxes/Total Assets	15.4	14.9
4.3	5.9	6.7	7.0				6.1	5.2
-9.1	-5.0	1.5	2.2				1.6	1.0
95.6	37.1	14.4	8.7			Sales/Net Fixed Assets	16.8	17.6
19.3	11.5	7.6	6.2				8.1	8.8
13.2	6.2	3.7	3.9				4.1	3.9
6.1	4.6	3.1	2.2			Sales/Total Assets	3.0	3.3
4.2	3.0	2.3	1.8				2.0	2.1
3.7	2.0	1.5	1.4				1.4	1.5
	.9	1.5	1.1			% Depr., Dep., Amort./Sales	1.3	1.3
	(42) 2.3	(73) 2.6	(28) 2.3				(153) 2.2	(136) 1.9
	3.9	4.1	4.0				3.4	4.0
	1.7	1.2				% Officers', Directors', Owners' Comp/Sales	2.0	1.9
	(19) 3.3	(31) 2.7					(66) 3.6	(63) 3.5
	8.1	5.5					8.5	6.8
13494M	202961M	837575M	1131808M	604996M	613324M	Net Sales ($)	3146764M	2352421M
3059M	53702M	358830M	571597M	541042M	235466M	Total Assets ($)	1913128M	1207890M

M = $ thousand   MM = $ million
See Pages 11 through 18 for Explanation of Ratios and Data

Comparative Historical Data | Current Data Sorted By Sales

					Type of Statement						
	33		30	31	Unqualified		4	2	4	9	12
	41		41	42	Reviewed		8	6	5	14	9
	35		34	32	Compiled	2	10	6	10	3	1
	13		19	19	Tax Returns	3	7	3	3	2	1
	48		73	50	Other	3	5	2	15	17	8
	4/1/00- 3/31/01 ALL		4/1/01- 3/31/02 ALL	4/1/02- 3/31/03 ALL		0-1MM	41 (4/1-9/30/02) 1-3MM	3-5MM	5-10MM	133 (10/1/02-3/31/03) 10-25MM	25MM & OVER
	170		197	174	NUMBER OF STATEMENTS	8	34	19	37	45	31
	%		%	%	ASSETS	%	%	%	%	%	%
	4.3		6.5	6.8	Cash & Equivalents		8.7	7.3	7.8	6.1	5.7
	22.9		24.6	21.5	Trade Receivables (net)		23.9	21.7	23.2	20.7	18.2
	27.5		26.4	26.2	Inventory		16.4	25.0	31.0	27.0	26.4
	1.9		2.2	2.8	All Other Current		.6	4.8	3.5	3.6	2.5
	56.6		59.7	57.3	Total Current		49.6	58.7	65.5	57.4	52.9
	31.8		29.8	31.3	Fixed Assets (net)		35.8	38.1	25.6	30.8	32.9
	4.4		3.0	4.0	Intangibles (net)		5.8	1.2	2.5	3.6	7.2
	7.2		7.4	7.3	All Other Non-Current		8.8	2.0	6.4	8.2	7.1
	100.0		100.0	100.0	Total		100.0	100.0	100.0	100.0	100.0
					LIABILITIES						
	14.5		13.4	14.1	Notes Payable-Short Term		13.3	12.7	19.0	11.7	9.2
	4.0		4.3	4.7	Cur. Mat.-L/T/D		5.9	8.3	3.8	4.9	3.1
	12.6		12.0	12.7	Trade Payables		13.9	14.3	12.6	11.6	9.9
	.3		.2	.4	Income Taxes Payable		.2	.0	.7	.6	.4
	9.2		9.3	8.5	All Other Current		9.9	8.5	7.2	6.6	7.7
	40.6		39.2	40.4	Total Current		43.2	43.8	43.3	35.4	30.3
	24.0		19.4	21.1	Long Term Debt		29.9	20.4	16.5	16.5	22.2
	.7		.4	.4	Deferred Taxes		.0	.0	.6	.5	1.0
	5.4		4.9	3.5	All Other Non-Current		5.7	3.6	1.6	5.2	1.8
	29.3		36.1	34.5	Net Worth		21.2	32.2	38.1	42.3	44.7
	100.0		100.0	100.0	Total Liabilities & Net Worth		100.0	100.0	100.0	100.0	100.0
					INCOME DATA						
	100.0		100.0	100.0	Net Sales		100.0	100.0	100.0	100.0	100.0
	27.0		28.4	27.4	Gross Profit		30.7	29.6	27.2	23.1	23.3
	22.4		23.7	22.9	Operating Expenses		27.8	25.9	22.5	18.0	17.6
	4.6		4.7	4.5	Operating Profit		3.0	3.6	4.8	5.0	5.7
	1.7		1.4	1.3	All Other Expenses (net)		2.3	1.5	1.1	.8	1.1
	2.8		3.2	3.2	Profit Before Taxes		.7	2.1	3.6	4.2	4.6
					RATIOS						
	2.3		2.4	2.3			2.0	1.9	3.5	2.4	3.0
	1.5		1.5	1.5	Current		1.3	1.4	1.5	1.5	2.2
	1.1		1.2	1.1			.7	1.1	1.2	1.2	1.3
	1.2		1.4	1.3			1.4	1.2	1.7	1.2	1.4
(169)	.7		.8 (172)	.7	Quick		.9	.6	.8	.7 (30)	.7
	.4		.4	.4			.4	.3	.4	.4	.6
23	16.0	25	14.6 18	20.7		24 15.5	15 24.1	19 19.5	17 21.1	18 20.7
35	10.5	36	10.2 29	12.4	Sales/Receivables	32 11.5	29 12.8	29 12.8	30 12.1	32 11.6
47	7.7	48	7.6 42	8.8		49 7.5	37 9.8	37 9.9	41 8.9	42 8.6
31	11.6	30	12.2 27	13.4		7 49.8	26 14.1	37 10.0	27 13.4	40 9.1
57	6.4	56	6.6 52	7.0	Cost of Sales/Inventory	35 10.3	43 8.5	58 6.3	54 6.8	54 6.8
89	4.1	95	3.8 84	4.4		82 4.5	73 5.0	103 3.5	83 4.4	83 4.4
11	33.2	11	34.3 9	41.1		6 62.7	10 35.7	8 44.2	7 49.3	9 39.9
21	17.2	21	17.6 18	20.1	Cost of Sales/Payables	26 14.2	29 12.6	18 20.1	14 25.2	15 24.7
36	10.0	37	10.0 36	10.2		55 6.6	60 6.1	36 10.1	26 14.1	21 17.3
	6.7		6.6	7.2			9.2	9.3	4.8	7.0	5.9
	11.3		12.0	13.1	Sales/Working Capital		17.0	19.0	12.5	12.7	8.3
	65.7		39.2	63.3			-14.3	81.4	32.7	28.5	27.9
	6.7		7.3	9.2			4.3	8.0	16.7	10.3	9.2
(160)	2.2	(185)	2.8 (163)	3.1	EBIT/Interest		1.2	2.1 (34)	3.9 (42)	3.8 (28)	3.0
	.9		1.1	1.1			-2.4	.3	1.9	2.5	1.1
	3.9		3.8	3.8	Net Profit + Depr., Dep.,					4.4	3.0
(49)	2.0	(57)	2.0 (44)	1.9	Amort./Cur. Mat. L/T/D				(12)	2.4 (14)	2.2
	.8		1.2	1.0						1.3	1.1
	.5		.4	.4			.7	.5	.3	.3	.5
	1.1		.9	1.1	Fixed/Worth		2.3	1.5	.6	1.0	.9
	4.2		2.1	2.8			-94.4	7.3	2.6	2.0	2.2
	1.1		.8	.9			1.8	1.0	.5	.7	.6
	2.4		1.7	2.1	Debt/Worth		6.4	1.9	1.6	1.8	2.1
	10.3		4.4	7.7			-106.4	12.9	8.2	3.5	4.3
	45.5		46.8	50.4	% Profit Before Taxes/Tangible		116.6	43.2	44.8	51.6	38.9
(138)	20.8	(174)	21.7 (149)	20.6	Net Worth	(24) 13.8	(16) 9.6	(32) 24.5	(43) 28.2	(29) 18.7
	2.2		5.7	5.5			-18.2	-18.6	9.8	12.9	8.2
	13.9		16.4	16.7	% Profit Before Taxes/Total		11.0	11.7	18.6	18.1	16.1
	5.3		7.3	6.3	Assets		.5	3.2	7.7	8.5	6.1
	-.4		1.2	.8			-8.7	-3.5	3.7	3.4	.9
	16.0		25.9	19.9			15.4	12.1	25.8	16.3	10.1
	7.7		7.7	7.9	Sales/Net Fixed Assets		6.9	6.3	12.1	7.6	6.1
	4.8		4.7	4.7			2.7	3.6	6.4	4.6	4.6
	3.2		3.2	3.5			3.6	3.0	3.8	3.3	3.1
	2.2		2.1	2.4	Sales/Total Assets		2.1	2.2	2.7	2.4	2.0
	1.6		1.6	1.6			1.1	1.7	1.7	1.7	1.6
	1.2		1.2	1.4			1.4	2.2	1.0	1.6	.7
(150)	2.1	(177)	2.1 (160)	2.4	% Depr., Dep., Amort./Sales	(31) 3.1	3.3 (35)	2.0 (42)	2.3 (29)	2.0
	3.7		3.4	4.0			5.6	4.2	3.1	3.0	4.3
	1.6		1.9	1.5	% Officers', Directors',		2.8		1.4	.8	
(72)	3.6	(70)	3.9 (61)	3.5	Owners' Comp/Sales	(12) 4.6		(17) 2.9 (14)	2.1	
	6.9		6.7	6.7			7.8		5.2	6.3	
	4299068M		5161938M	3404158M	Net Sales ($)	3389M	70754M	75611M	260244M	750828M	2243332M
	2627764M		2526579M	1763696M	Total Assets ($)	850M	47106M	40384M	119909M	341754M	1213693M

M = $ thousand   MM = $ million
See Pages 11 through 18 for Explanation of Ratios and Data

Current Data Sorted By Assets | Comparative Historical Data

0-500M	500M-2MM	2-10MM	10-50MM	50-100MM	100-250MM		4/1/98-3/31/99 ALL	4/1/99-3/31/00 ALL
						Type of Statement		
1		1	9	1	7	Unqualified	31	23
	2	7	5			Reviewed	15	12
	3	1				Compiled	10	6
2		1				Tax Returns	1	3
	2	4	10	5	4	Other	27	21
7 (4/1-9/30/02)			58 (10/1/02-3/31/03)					
3	7	14	24	6	11	NUMBER OF STATEMENTS	84	65
%	%	%	%	%	%	**ASSETS**	%	%
		6.1	3.6		5.2	Cash & Equivalents	6.1	4.5
		30.9	19.6		12.6	Trade Receivables (net)	21.3	21.8
		22.6	20.2		8.9	Inventory	20.1	17.4
		.5	3.3		3.1	All Other Current	1.5	.8
		60.1	46.9		29.8	Total Current	48.9	44.5
		29.0	40.6		53.2	Fixed Assets (net)	44.8	48.5
		2.4	3.6		14.3	Intangibles (net)	2.0	1.9
		8.5	9.0		2.6	All Other Non-Current	4.2	5.0
		100.0	100.0		100.0	Total	100.0	100.0
						LIABILITIES		
		14.6	7.0		12.6	Notes Payable-Short Term	6.2	6.9
		5.3	4.5		2.7	Cur. Mat.-L/T/D	5.0	5.2
		20.8	13.7		7.1	Trade Payables	13.7	14.0
		.3	.0		.2	Income Taxes Payable	.2	.1
		5.6	7.1		6.9	All Other Current	9.2	7.4
		46.6	32.3		29.6	Total Current	34.3	33.7
		13.9	21.4		22.8	Long Term Debt	22.1	25.3
		.1	1.5		4.3	Deferred Taxes	1.5	1.2
		2.7	6.3		1.8	All Other Non-Current	4.9	3.6
		36.7	38.5		41.6	Net Worth	37.2	36.2
		100.0	100.0		100.0	Total Liabilities & Net Worth	100.0	100.0
						INCOME DATA		
		100.0	100.0		100.0	Net Sales	100.0	100.0
		22.6	25.2		26.6	Gross Profit	23.6	28.5
		20.8	21.0		22.9	Operating Expenses	18.4	21.7
		1.8	4.2		3.7	Operating Profit	5.2	6.7
		1.3	1.8		1.4	All Other Expenses (net)	1.7	1.3
		.5	2.4		2.2	Profit Before Taxes	3.5	5.4
						RATIOS		
		2.6	2.9		1.8	Current	2.7	2.0
		1.2	1.6		1.4		1.6	1.2
		.8	1.0		.8		1.0	.9
		1.4	1.4		1.0	Quick	1.4	1.1
		.7	.9		.8		.9	.8
		.4	.4		.6		.5	.5
		41 8.9	34 10.9		33 10.9	Sales/Receivables	30 12.3	30 12.0
		52 7.1	41 9.0		41 9.0		37 9.9	41 9.0
		62 5.9	49 7.4		52 7.0		46 7.9	47 7.8
		36 10.1	27 13.6		28 13.1	Cost of Sales/Inventory	27 13.5	22 16.6
		61 6.0	53 6.9		39 9.5		41 8.9	37 9.9
		74 4.9	88 4.2		48 7.7		73 5.0	60 6.1
		19 19.3	20 18.1		21 17.1	Cost of Sales/Payables	22 16.5	25 14.6
		38 9.7	30 12.3		31 11.8		29 12.5	35 10.6
		68 5.4	50 7.3		41 9.0		40 9.1	46 8.0
		4.8	4.8		7.9	Sales/Working Capital	5.9	9.0
		48.2	10.9		11.7		11.9	42.7
		-22.1	758.7		-21.6		-130.4	-84.7
		15.1	8.0		5.7	EBIT/Interest	10.7	8.6
		(12) 4.0	(23) 3.4		4.0		(80) 3.0	(59) 4.1
		.8	.9		-.8		1.3	2.2
						Net Profit + Depr., Dep., Amort./Cur. Mat. L /T/D	6.9	5.6
							(33) 3.1	(27) 3.2
							1.7	1.6
		.1	.5		1.2	Fixed/Worth	.7	.7
		.7	1.4		1.8		1.3	1.4
		2.0	3.9		2.8		3.0	2.6
		.4	.8		1.0	Debt/Worth	.7	.9
		1.9	2.0		2.1		2.3	2.0
		NM	6.0		3.9		3.8	3.1
		31.0	34.5			% Profit Before Taxes/Tangible Net Worth	35.6	42.7
		(11) 8.8	(21) 16.2				(77) 24.6	(62) 27.3
		1.4	.7				6.8	8.9
		10.9	12.4		7.4	% Profit Before Taxes/Total Assets	12.5	16.5
		3.5	6.6		3.3		6.9	7.0
		-.4	-.1		-1.2		1.2	3.3
		163.0	12.9		3.5	Sales/Net Fixed Assets	7.9	6.9
		8.3	3.8		1.8		4.1	3.9
		4.5	2.6		1.4		2.6	2.4
		2.5	2.1		1.4	Sales/Total Assets	2.4	2.3
		2.1	1.5		1.1		1.8	1.9
		1.6	1.2		.6		1.4	1.3
		1.2	2.2			% Depr., Dep., Amort./Sales	1.6	1.7
		(11) 1.8	(20) 3.7				(75) 3.1	(58) 3.1
		4.5	6.7				4.8	4.8
						% Officers', Directors', Owners' Comp/Sales	2.9	1.8
							(15) 5.2	(13) 3.9
							10.2	6.1
1600M	31771M	143581M	946988M	509552M	1704419M	Net Sales ($)	4235449M	2836471M
661M	8364M	65532M	574831M	422959M	1645958M	Total Assets ($)	2565983M	1962981M

© RMA 2003

M = $ thousand   MM = $ million
See Pages 11 through 18 for Explanation of Ratios and Data

Comparative Historical Data | Current Data Sorted By Sales

4/1/00-3/31/01 ALL	4/1/01-3/31/02 ALL	4/1/02-3/31/03 ALL	Type of Statement	0-1MM	1-3MM	3-5MM	5-10MM	10-25MM	25MM & OVER
26	17	19	Unqualified	1				4	14
10	4	14	Reviewed			2	2	7	3
2	7	4	Compiled		2		1	1	
	2	3	Tax Returns	1	1	1			
16	27	25	Other		2	2	1	6	14
					7 (4/1-9/30/02)		58 (10/1/02-3/31/03)		
54	57	65	**NUMBER OF STATEMENTS**	2	5	5	4	18	31
%	%	%	**ASSETS**	%	%	%	%	%	%
2.7	4.0	5.2	Cash & Equivalents					4.3	5.5
23.1	22.8	24.1	Trade Receivables (net)					28.5	19.8
21.2	15.2	18.2	Inventory					19.1	14.2
.9	2.5	2.3	All Other Current					.8	3.7
47.9	44.5	49.8	Total Current					52.6	43.1
44.0	46.9	38.8	Fixed Assets (net)					32.6	45.2
3.9	4.1	4.4	Intangibles (net)					4.0	6.2
3.6	4.5	7.0	All Other Non-Current					10.8	5.4
100.0	100.0	100.0	Total					100.0	100.0
			LIABILITIES						
9.1	8.8	10.5	Notes Payable-Short Term					14.1	8.1
7.2	7.0	4.2	Cur. Mat.-L/T/D					6.4	2.4
15.1	12.8	15.0	Trade Payables					19.3	10.7
.1	.2	.1	Income Taxes Payable					.2	.1
8.2	8.8	6.6	All Other Current					3.7	8.1
39.7	37.5	36.4	Total Current					43.7	29.5
25.2	25.1	19.2	Long Term Debt					14.0	20.8
1.6	1.1	1.4	Deferred Taxes					1.0	2.1
5.1	4.3	4.5	All Other Non-Current					2.6	5.0
28.4	31.9	38.6	Net Worth					38.8	42.5
100.0	100.0	100.0	Total Liabilities & Net Worth					100.0	100.0
			INCOME DATA						
100.0	100.0	100.0	Net Sales					100.0	100.0
21.7	24.9	24.6	Gross Profit					26.6	24.2
16.6	19.6	21.5	Operating Expenses					22.2	19.6
5.1	5.3	3.2	Operating Profit					4.4	4.6
2.1	2.5	1.5	All Other Expenses (net)					2.1	1.0
3.0	2.7	1.6	Profit Before Taxes					2.3	3.6
			RATIOS						
1.6	2.0	2.2						2.5	1.9
1.3	1.2	1.4	Current					1.2	1.6
.9	.8	1.0						.7	1.2
.9	1.3	1.4						1.6	1.2
.6	.7	1.0	Quick					.8	1.0
.5	.4	.5						.4	.7
30 12.1	31 11.7	34 10.7						35 10.4	33 10.9
39 9.4	38 9.5	44 8.3	Sales/Receivables					44 8.3	41 8.8
48 7.6	52 7.1	59 6.2						62 5.9	52 7.0
31 11.7	17 21.5	29 12.6						23 16.1	27 13.6
46 8.0	35 10.3	48 7.7	Cost of Sales/Inventory					45 8.1	39 9.5
66 5.5	68 5.4	71 5.1						80 4.6	58 6.3
22 16.8	18 20.5	21 17.4						15 24.4	21 17.1
32 11.4	29 12.7	34 10.7	Cost of Sales/Payables					34 10.7	31 11.8
39 9.4	51 7.1	54 6.8						61 6.0	40 9.1
10.1	9.9	6.5						3.9	6.7
22.3	19.1	12.8	Sales/Working Capital					31.1	10.4
-113.2	-23.0	NM						-13.4	21.5
5.3	5.9	7.8						7.5	8.1
(53) 3.1	(49) 2.1	(60) 3.3	EBIT/Interest				(16)	3.3 (29)	4.0
.1	.7	.8						1.0	1.9
3.5	2.8	4.1							8.1
(21) 1.5	(15) 1.8	(18) 2.6	Net Profit + Depr., Dep., Amort./Cur. Mat. L/T/D					(10)	3.5
.2	.9	1.4							2.1
.7	.8	.4						.1	1.0
1.5	1.3	1.2	Fixed/Worth					.7	1.2
3.5	3.3	2.7						13.6	2.0
1.0	.9	.7						.4	.8
2.3	2.1	2.0	Debt/Worth					2.0	1.9
8.8	7.1	5.9						NM	3.6
50.2	33.2	29.3						33.3	28.2
(45) 21.2	(48) 14.0	(54) 15.7	% Profit Before Taxes/Tangible Net Worth				(14)	14.2 (28)	16.9
-8.0	-1.0	1.2						4.0	2.5
13.6	12.1	10.2						10.7	11.2
8.0	5.3	4.7	% Profit Before Taxes/Total Assets					4.1	6.5
-3.6	-.8	-.8						.8	.3
8.8	6.9	15.3						230.1	6.4
4.2	3.4	4.3	Sales/Net Fixed Assets					4.4	2.9
2.6	2.5	2.3						2.6	1.8
2.6	2.2	2.2						2.4	1.8
1.8	1.7	1.6	Sales/Total Assets					1.7	1.4
1.4	1.3	1.1						1.2	1.0
1.4	1.7	1.4							1.6
(47) 2.9	(43) 3.8	(50) 3.3	% Depr., Dep., Amort./Sales					(15) 4.3	(22) 3.6
4.5	6.6	5.6						5.4	5.6
	1.5	1.3							
(11)	2.8 (18)	3.3	% Officers', Directors', Owners' Comp/Sales						
	6.3	5.9							
2906514M	2699066M	3337911M	Net Sales ($)	134M	8932M	21116M	29870M	286966M	2990893M
2066267M	1967051M	2718305M	Total Assets ($)	236M	5211M	41821M	13328M	177528M	2480181M

M = $ thousand   MM = $ million
See Pages 11 through 18 for Explanation of Ratios and Data

Current Data Sorted By Assets   Comparative Historical Data

	0-500M	500M-2MM	2-10MM	10-50MM	50-100MM	100-250MM	Type of Statement	4/1/98-3/31/99 ALL	4/1/99-3/31/00 ALL
			1	2	3	5	Unqualified	13	12
		1	3	1			Reviewed	4	4
		1					Compiled	2	1
							Tax Returns		
		2	2	1			Other	7	3
		6 (4/1-9/30/02)		16 (10/1/02-3/31/03)					
		4	6	4	3	5	NUMBER OF STATEMENTS	26	20

Current asset-size columns: DATA NOT AVAILABLE.

	%	%
ASSETS		
Cash & Equivalents	6.6	4.5
Trade Receivables (net)	18.0	22.0
Inventory	15.4	15.9
All Other Current	1.1	2.2
Total Current	41.0	44.7
Fixed Assets (net)	51.5	47.5
Intangibles (net)	1.9	2.3
All Other Non-Current	5.6	5.5
Total	100.0	100.0
LIABILITIES		
Notes Payable-Short Term	5.0	6.2
Cur. Mat.-L/T/D	4.9	5.9
Trade Payables	11.1	14.9
Income Taxes Payable	.2	.1
All Other Current	10.2	6.0
Total Current	31.3	33.0
Long Term Debt	33.2	26.6
Deferred Taxes	1.9	1.2
All Other Non-Current	2.2	.8
Net Worth	31.3	38.4
Total Liabilities & Net Worth	100.0	100.0
INCOME DATA		
Net Sales	100.0	100.0
Gross Profit	25.6	23.6
Operating Expenses	18.9	17.2
Operating Profit	6.7	6.5
All Other Expenses (net)	3.9	2.2
Profit Before Taxes	2.9	4.2

RATIOS

Ratio	4/1/98-3/31/99	4/1/99-3/31/00
Current	2.0	2.4
	1.3	1.5
	.9	.9
Quick	1.1	1.1
	.7	.9
	.5	.5
Sales/Receivables	26 14.1	32 11.5
	41 8.9	39 9.4
	52 7.0	46 7.9
Cost of Sales/Inventory	25 14.6	21 17.3
	41 9.0	45 8.1
	60 6.1	55 6.6
Cost of Sales/Payables	22 16.9	22 16.6
	30 12.3	33 11.0
	41 8.9	41 9.0
Sales/Working Capital	7.5	6.8
	19.1	15.8
	-36.1	-52.3
EBIT/Interest	(25) 4.4	(17) 5.2
	2.2	2.6
	1.4	1.1
Net Profit + Depr., Dep., Amort./Cur. Mat. L /T/D		
Fixed/Worth	1.0	.7
	1.7	1.4
	5.2	2.6
Debt/Worth	1.1	1.1
	2.6	1.6
	7.9	3.4
% Profit Before Taxes/Tangible Net Worth	(24) 37.7	(19) 29.2
	24.0	17.4
	12.0	8.1
% Profit Before Taxes/Total Assets	12.9	10.9
	5.2	6.4
	1.2	1.7
Sales/Net Fixed Assets	6.0	6.8
	2.7	3.2
	1.5	1.8
Sales/Total Assets	2.2	2.3
	1.4	1.8
	1.0	1.0
% Depr., Dep., Amort./Sales	(23) 2.1	(14) 2.1
	4.3	4.1
	6.0	6.9
% Officers', Directors', Owners' Comp/Sales		

	0-500M	500M-2MM	2-10MM	10-50MM	50-100MM	100-250MM		4/1/98-3/31/99	4/1/99-3/31/00
Net Sales ($)		18486M	92041M	130456M	230600M	1073297M		1345686M	1385544M
Total Assets ($)		4905M	38428M	80206M	223519M	1054069M		1275217M	1212795M

Comparative Historical Data | Current Data Sorted By Sales

			Type of Statement						
6	10	11	Unqualified					2	9
4	4	5	Reviewed		1			3	1
1	8	1	Compiled		1				
1			Tax Returns						
6	3	5	Other	1			1	2	1
4/1/00-3/31/01	4/1/01-3/31/02	4/1/02-3/31/03			6 (4/1-9/30/02)		16 (10/1/02-3/31/03)		
ALL	ALL	ALL		0-1MM	1-3MM	3-5MM	5-10MM	10-25MM	25MM & OVER
18	25	22	NUMBER OF STATEMENTS	1	2	1	1	7	11
%	%	%	ASSETS	%	%	%	%	%	%
5.5	3.1	7.8	Cash & Equivalents	D					5.8
25.1	23.5	26.5	Trade Receivables (net)	A					16.2
17.0	14.9	15.6	Inventory	T					14.7
.4	4.6	1.8	All Other Current	A					2.6
48.0	46.1	51.7	Total Current						39.3
39.1	42.7	38.0	Fixed Assets (net)	N					49.6
3.3	5.6	1.7	Intangibles (net)	O					.5
9.6	5.6	8.6	All Other Non-Current	T					10.6
100.0	100.0	100.0	Total						100.0
			LIABILITIES	A					
5.9	8.0	10.1	Notes Payable-Short Term	V					6.2
5.2	9.1	7.8	Cur. Mat.-L/T/D	A					5.1
21.3	14.5	18.1	Trade Payables	I					10.9
.1	.0	.0	Income Taxes Payable	L					.0
5.1	7.9	5.6	All Other Current	A					4.9
37.6	39.5	41.7	Total Current	B					27.2
20.0	25.8	19.3	Long Term Debt	L					21.2
1.1	1.7	1.3	Deferred Taxes	E					1.6
4.7	2.1	5.1	All Other Non-Current						2.6
36.6	30.8	32.6	Net Worth						47.4
100.0	100.0	100.0	Total Liabilities & Net Worth						100.0
			INCOME DATA						
100.0	100.0	100.0	Net Sales						100.0
18.3	20.0	20.3	Gross Profit						18.5
14.5	16.5	16.9	Operating Expenses						13.3
3.8	3.5	3.4	Operating Profit						5.3
-.7	.8	.4	All Other Expenses (net)						-.5
4.5	2.7	3.0	Profit Before Taxes						5.8
			RATIOS						
2.6	2.2	2.0							2.0
1.6	1.4	1.4	Current						1.7
.9	.8	.8							.8
1.3	1.1	1.2							1.2
.9	.7	.7	Quick						.6
.6	.5	.5							.5
24 14.9	32 11.4	33 11.0							28 13.0
37 9.8	41 9.0	42 8.8	Sales/Receivables						36 10.3
48 7.6	52 7.1	52 7.0							52 7.0
23 15.8	18 20.2	20 18.1							36 10.2
42 8.6	30 12.1	38 9.6	Cost of Sales/Inventory						43 8.4
55 6.7	60 6.0	59 6.2							61 6.0
21 17.2	19 18.9	17 21.5							21 17.7
27 13.4	32 11.3	37 9.8	Cost of Sales/Payables						35 10.4
48 7.7	39 9.4	54 6.7							43 8.5
7.1	5.8	7.3							7.4
13.6	15.4	24.9	Sales/Working Capital						9.3
-29.9	-20.5	-25.8							-37.2
10.6	3.3	6.2							16.3
(17) 1.9	(23) 1.9	(21) 2.2	EBIT/Interest						4.3
1.5	.8	1.3							2.0
			Net Profit + Depr., Dep., Amort./Cur. Mat. L/T/D						
.7	.9	.7							.6
1.7	1.8	1.4	Fixed/Worth						1.2
3.0	3.9	2.6							2.2
.8	1.4	.8							.5
2.3	2.8	1.9	Debt/Worth						1.1
10.6	5.8	6.2							3.1
40.7	20.1	34.5							21.7
(17) 22.4	(23) 10.3	(19) 12.3	% Profit Before Taxes/Tangible Net Worth						11.6
5.3	1.2	3.8							3.8
11.7	8.3	9.0							10.5
3.3	3.6	3.2	% Profit Before Taxes/Total Assets						4.2
1.3	-.4	1.4							2.5
12.2	6.6	11.9							4.1
5.0	4.6	4.7	Sales/Net Fixed Assets						2.6
3.1	2.6	2.6							1.6
2.8	2.3	2.9							1.8
1.9	1.8	1.8	Sales/Total Assets						1.1
1.4	1.5	1.0							.7
1.7	1.1	1.7							
(16) 2.4	(23) 2.6	(18) 3.4	% Depr., Dep., Amort./Sales						
3.8	4.2	4.6							
			% Officers', Directors', Owners' Comp/Sales						
953011M	1322170M	1544880M	Net Sales ($)		2553M	9180M	6753M	102635M	1423759M
700746M	999554M	1401127M	Total Assets ($)		1471M	2443M	991M	52061M	1344161M

© RMA 2003

M = $ thousand   MM = $ million

See Pages 11 through 18 for Explanation of Ratios and Data

Current Data Sorted By Assets   **Comparative Historical Data**

0-500M	500M-2MM	2-10MM	10-50MM	50-100MM	100-250MM	Type of Statement	4/1/98-3/31/99 ALL	4/1/99-3/31/00 ALL
1	1	11	25	2	4	Unqualified	38	47
1	11	44	16			Reviewed	61	61
2	18	15	1			Compiled	31	27
	5	1				Tax Returns	4	6
1	10	41	19	1	2	Other	72	53
	48 (4/1-9/30/02)		184 (10/1/02-3/31/03)					
5	45	112	61	3	6	NUMBER OF STATEMENTS	206	194
%	%	%	%	%	%	ASSETS	%	%
	7.4	7.8	8.3			Cash & Equivalents	8.3	6.3
	33.6	25.7	21.5			Trade Receivables (net)	26.7	28.5
	17.7	14.7	14.8			Inventory	14.2	15.6
	1.3	1.5	3.0			All Other Current	1.7	1.7
	60.1	49.7	47.6			Total Current	51.0	52.1
	32.0	41.0	41.3			Fixed Assets (net)	39.4	39.3
	1.7	2.3	2.9			Intangibles (net)	1.8	1.9
	6.3	7.0	8.2			All Other Non-Current	7.9	6.6
	100.0	100.0	100.0			Total	100.0	100.0
						LIABILITIES		
	11.5	7.0	9.4			Notes Payable-Short Term	7.2	8.1
	5.2	5.7	5.4			Cur. Mat.-L/T/D	5.0	5.1
	17.9	15.8	11.2			Trade Payables	13.9	16.3
	.2	.1	.1			Income Taxes Payable	.2	.2
	11.1	6.5	6.7			All Other Current	7.1	7.6
	45.9	35.1	32.8			Total Current	33.4	37.3
	17.5	23.6	18.8			Long Term Debt	24.0	24.6
	.3	.8	1.4			Deferred Taxes	.7	.9
	8.7	6.5	2.3			All Other Non-Current	3.5	3.8
	27.6	33.9	44.7			Net Worth	38.4	33.4
	100.0	100.0	100.0			Total Liabilities & Net Worth	100.0	100.0
						INCOME DATA		
	100.0	100.0	100.0			Net Sales	100.0	100.0
	27.6	25.5	24.8			Gross Profit	27.5	26.4
	25.8	23.7	19.7			Operating Expenses	22.4	21.9
	1.9	1.8	5.1			Operating Profit	5.1	4.5
	.1	1.0	.9			All Other Expenses (net)	1.0	1.2
	1.8	.8	4.2			Profit Before Taxes	4.2	3.3
						RATIOS		
	2.8	2.6	2.4				2.3	2.3
	1.5	1.5	1.5			Current	1.6	1.3
	.9	1.0	1.1				1.1	1.0
	2.0	1.7	1.5				1.6	1.6
	.9	1.0	1.0			Quick	1.0 (193)	.9
	.6	.6	.6				.7	.6
29 12.6	30 12.1	29 12.8					30 12.0	36 10.2
39 9.3	37 9.8	39 9.4				Sales/Receivables	37 10.0	40 9.0
46 8.0	49 7.5	49 7.5					46 7.9	48 7.6
12 29.8	19 19.5	22 16.3					18 20.4	19 18.9
25 14.8	27 13.5	31 11.7				Cost of Sales/Inventory	26 14.1	30 12.3
40 9.2	39 9.3	39 9.1					39 9.4	43 8.5
17 21.2	14 25.4	15 24.1					14 25.2	18 20.7
26 14.2	27 13.4	22 16.6				Cost of Sales/Payables	25 14.5	31 11.8
42 8.8	48 7.6	33 11.1					41 9.0	46 8.0
7.2	7.2	7.7					8.2	8.2
19.5	16.9	15.2				Sales/Working Capital	15.1	18.2
−58.0	−106.2	66.5					54.5	231.3
7.6	5.2	10.9					7.4	6.2
(41) 3.1	(108) 2.5	(60) 3.6				EBIT/Interest	(193) 3.3	(188) 3.0
.8	.9	1.5					1.6	1.3
1.6	2.5	3.3					3.7	3.6
(13) 1.0	(40) 2.0	(29) 2.4				Net Profit + Depr., Dep., Amort./Cur. Mat. L/T/D	(91) 1.8	(76) 2.1
.1	.9	1.2					1.2	1.4
.3	.7	.5					.6	.7
1.2	1.3	1.0				Fixed/Worth	1.1	1.4
13.1	3.4	1.7					2.0	3.0
.6	.8	.5					.8	.9
2.2	2.1	1.2				Debt/Worth	1.6	2.5
29.2	5.7	2.7					3.5	5.1
39.1	29.3	27.8					35.9	39.8
(36) 10.3	(100) 11.4	(55) 15.2				% Profit Before Taxes/Tangible Net Worth	(191) 18.8	(179) 17.6
−4.4	2.8	3.7					7.8	5.0
11.8	9.2	12.6					15.0	13.4
4.7	3.5	6.7				% Profit Before Taxes/Total Assets	7.1	6.0
−2.7	−.3	1.2					1.9	1.2
20.7	11.5	7.4					11.2	11.4
10.6	5.8	4.8				Sales/Net Fixed Assets	6.3	5.6
6.3	3.3	3.5					3.7	3.5
4.2	3.0	2.5					3.3	3.0
3.0	2.3	1.9				Sales/Total Assets	2.5	2.2
2.1	1.8	1.6					1.8	1.8
1.5	1.9	2.0					1.7	1.7
(44) 2.7	(107) 2.8	(58) 3.6				% Depr., Dep., Amort./Sales	(190) 2.7	(177) 2.9
3.6	3.9	4.9					3.7	3.9
2.7	1.9	.9					2.4	1.9
(22) 4.5	(49) 3.2	(18) 1.8				% Officers', Directors', Owners' Comp/Sales	(77) 3.9	(71) 3.1
7.0	5.4	3.4					6.4	6.0
4303M	180977M	1377010M	2392442M	332800M	1667821M	Net Sales ($)	4675091M	4873462M
1049M	58533M	571487M	1189741M	193331M	1225524M	Total Assets ($)	2570421M	2909236M

M = $ thousand   MM = $ million
See Pages 11 through 18 for Explanation of Ratios and Data

Comparative Historical Data | Current Data Sorted By Sales

			Type of Statement						
34	34	44	Unqualified	1		1	7	10	25
59	46	72	Reviewed	1	1	7	22	27	14
43	36	34	Compiled		9	13	7	5	
8	4	8	Tax Returns		4	3		1	
56	68	74	Other		5	5	18	27	19
4/1/00- 3/31/01 ALL	4/1/01- 3/31/02 ALL	4/1/02- 3/31/03 ALL		48 (4/1-9/30/02)			184 (10/1/02-3/31/03)		
				0-1MM	1-3MM	3-5MM	5-10MM	10-25MM	25MM & OVER
200	188	232	NUMBER OF STATEMENTS	2	19	29	54	70	58
%	%	%	ASSETS	%	%	%	%	%	%
5.7	7.2	7.8	Cash & Equivalents		10.4	8.9	7.9	7.7	6.7
29.4	26.7	25.8	Trade Receivables (net)		25.6	29.7	28.7	25.8	21.4
15.3	15.1	15.5	Inventory		19.9	16.6	15.1	13.4	16.2
2.9	1.7	1.9	All Other Current		.8	1.4	.9	1.8	3.3
53.3	50.6	51.0	Total Current		56.6	56.6	52.6	48.6	47.6
37.1	38.3	39.4	Fixed Assets (net)		33.1	36.1	39.4	40.4	42.4
2.1	3.1	2.4	Intangibles (net)		4.7	1.5	1.5	2.2	2.9
7.5	7.9	7.2	All Other Non-Current		5.6	5.8	6.6	8.8	7.1
100.0	100.0	100.0	Total		100.0	100.0	100.0	100.0	100.0
			LIABILITIES						
9.4	7.5	8.7	Notes Payable-Short Term		16.3	7.3	7.9	8.7	7.5
4.8	5.1	5.4	Cur. Mat.-L/T/D		2.0	5.2	6.6	5.9	4.9
17.3	15.3	14.9	Trade Payables		14.7	16.0	16.5	15.5	12.3
.1	.1	.1	Income Taxes Payable		.2	.2	.1	.1	.1
8.0	6.9	7.4	All Other Current		3.7	6.2	9.4	8.0	6.7
39.6	34.9	36.5	Total Current		36.8	34.9	40.4	38.2	31.5
20.9	21.0	21.1	Long Term Debt		18.4	22.1	21.6	21.9	20.0
.9	1.3	1.0	Deferred Taxes		.3	.1	.6	1.4	1.4
3.7	3.5	5.9	All Other Non-Current		3.0	9.8	10.4	3.6	3.0
34.8	39.4	35.6	Net Worth		41.4	33.0	27.0	34.9	44.1
100.0	100.0	100.0	Total Liabilities & Net Worth		100.0	100.0	100.0	100.0	100.0
			INCOME DATA						
100.0	100.0	100.0	Net Sales		100.0	100.0	100.0	100.0	100.0
24.1	24.8	25.6	Gross Profit		31.4	24.7	26.7	25.2	23.6
20.3	21.8	22.7	Operating Expenses		31.9	24.4	24.1	22.3	18.2
3.8	3.0	2.8	Operating Profit		-.4	.3	2.6	2.9	5.4
1.0	1.1	.8	All Other Expenses (net)		.2	.6	.8	1.1	1.0
2.8	1.9	2.0	Profit Before Taxes		-.6	-.3	1.8	1.9	4.4
			RATIOS						
2.2	2.6	2.5			4.3	3.6	2.8	2.0	2.3
1.3	1.4	1.5	Current		1.5	1.5	1.4	1.4	1.5
1.0	1.0	1.0			1.1	.9	.9	1.0	1.1
1.4	1.7	1.6			2.5	2.5	2.1	1.4	1.4
.9	1.0	.9	Quick		.9	1.0	.8	.9	1.0
.6	.6	.6			.6	.6	.6	.6	.5
33 11.1	31 11.9	30 12.3		26 14.1	30 12.0	32 11.2	31 11.8	27 13.6
40 9.2	37 9.9	39 9.5	Sales/Receivables	41 9.0	39 9.4	41 8.8	36 10.0	37 9.8
46 7.9	43 8.5	47 7.8		46 7.9	44 8.4	49 7.4	49 7.4	43 8.6
18 20.7	18 20.1	19 18.9		23 16.1	17 21.5	16 22.4	18 20.1	23 15.9
28 13.3	25 14.5	28 13.1	Cost of Sales/Inventory	37 9.9	27 13.5	28 13.2	23 16.2	34 10.9
39 9.4	39 9.3	40 9.1		62 5.9	40 9.2	41 8.8	36 10.2	40 9.1
16 22.2	16 23.2	16 23.0		12 29.2	15 24.2	15 23.8	15 25.1	17 21.9
28 12.9	26 14.2	25 14.4	Cost of Sales/Payables	31 11.7	26 14.2	25 14.3	27 13.5	21 17.5
42 8.7	38 9.6	42 8.6		46 7.9	38 9.6	48 7.7	47 7.8	34 10.7
9.0	7.4	7.7		6.6	5.5	6.6	9.0	8.9
20.9	17.2	15.7	Sales/Working Capital	14.4	15.5	19.2	19.9	13.9
-495.6	-158.5	-173.6		50.5	-312.7	-54.8	-108.3	53.3
5.9	6.4	6.1		6.1	9.2	4.3	5.0	11.2
(182) 2.4	(175) 2.4	(223) 2.9	EBIT/Interest	1.3 (25) 2.3	(52) 2.5	(68) 2.7	(57) 5.2
1.4	.8	1.2		-1.1	-.3	.8	1.4	1.5
3.4	3.3	2.9	Net Profit + Depr., Dep.,			2.2	2.5	6.2
(69) 2.0	(62) 1.7	(85) 2.0	Amort./Cur. Mat. L/T/D	(14) 1.6	(31) 2.1	(25) 2.7
1.3	.8	1.0				.8	1.1	1.4
.6	.5	.6		.4	.3	.5	.7	.6
1.2	1.2	1.2	Fixed/Worth	.8	1.2	1.3	1.3	1.0
2.7	2.5	3.0		2.3	20.3	4.1	3.2	1.7
.8	.6	.7		.3	.4	.8	.9	.5
2.0	1.6	1.9	Debt/Worth	2.2	1.9	2.2	1.8	1.2
6.3	5.7	5.5		7.5	44.7	7.8	6.9	2.9
33.0	25.1	29.8		28.8	30.5	34.5	27.8	28.9
(174) 16.3	(167) 9.4	(204) 11.7	% Profit Before Taxes/Tangible Net Worth	(18) 6.0	(23) 9.9	(44) 12.0	(64) 11.3	(53) 15.5
5.7	-.1	1.9		-6.3	1.7	-.2	2.8	5.5
10.9	10.0	10.3		8.1	8.3	9.7	9.3	14.3
5.3	3.5	4.2	% Profit Before Taxes/Total Assets	1.4	2.8	4.9	3.2	6.8
1.4	-.4	.2		-4.3	-8.8	-.6	1.1	1.4
12.6	12.0	11.5		29.3	18.3	13.5	9.8	8.3
7.2	6.0	6.0	Sales/Net Fixed Assets	12.6	7.0	6.3	5.7	5.0
4.0	3.6	3.6		2.6	4.3	3.2	3.6	3.5
3.3	3.2	3.0		3.9	3.3	3.3	2.9	2.7
2.4	2.3	2.3	Sales/Total Assets	2.4	2.5	2.4	2.2	2.0
1.8	1.7	1.8		1.4	2.0	1.8	1.8	1.7
1.5	1.4	1.9		1.4	2.0	2.1	1.9	1.8
(185) 2.6	(172) 2.8	(217) 3.0	% Depr., Dep., Amort./Sales	(18) 2.9	(27) 3.2	(52) 2.8	(67) 3.1	(51) 3.0
3.6	4.0	4.2		4.7	3.8	4.0	4.4	4.4
1.7	1.9	1.6			3.0	1.9	1.7	.7
(70) 3.7	(72) 3.5	(92) 3.2	% Officers', Directors', Owners' Comp/Sales	(13) 4.6	(28) 4.3	(26) 2.4	(17) 1.4
6.0	5.6	5.4		7.0	5.6	4.4	2.0
5258800M	5350003M	5955353M	Net Sales ($)	64M	38908M	115179M	404118M	1191910M	4205174M
2710940M	2678763M	3239665M	Total Assets ($)	26M	23043M	47117M	179909M	549546M	2440024M

© RMA 2003 M = $ thousand MM = $ million See Pages 11 through 18 for Explanation of Ratios and Data

Current Data Sorted By Assets | Comparative Historical Data

0-500M	500M-2MM	2-10MM	10-50MM	50-100MM	100-250MM	Type of Statement	4/1/98-3/31/99 ALL	4/1/99-3/31/00 ALL
	2	1	8	2	1	Unqualified	10	8
	2	11	3	2	1	Reviewed	8	6
	1	1				Compiled	2	2
	1					Tax Returns	1	1
	2	3	7			Other	12	9
	10 (4/1-9/30/02)		**33 (10/1/02-3/31/03)**					
	6	16	18	2	1	**NUMBER OF STATEMENTS**	33	26
%	%	%	%	%	%	**ASSETS**	%	%
		3.8	4.7			Cash & Equivalents	2.5	5.2
		24.1	15.3			Trade Receivables (net)	25.5	24.3
		25.9	19.9			Inventory	24.4	25.9
D A T A N O T		2.2	1.2			All Other Current	1.4	1.7
		56.0	41.1			Total Current	53.8	57.1
		38.3	49.7			Fixed Assets (net)	39.1	33.0
		.2	2.8			Intangibles (net)	2.8	4.6
		5.6	6.4			All Other Non-Current	4.3	5.3
		100.0	100.0			Total	100.0	100.0
						LIABILITIES		
A V A I L A B L E		9.9	8.7			Notes Payable-Short Term	14.9	10.2
		5.3	4.3			Cur. Mat.-L/T/D	5.4	5.8
		15.1	10.0			Trade Payables	14.0	13.2
		.1	.4			Income Taxes Payable	.3	.7
		9.8	8.6			All Other Current	5.7	6.1
		40.2	32.1			Total Current	40.4	36.0
		20.6	23.4			Long Term Debt	21.8	20.1
		1.1	2.5			Deferred Taxes	1.1	1.1
		4.3	3.2			All Other Non-Current	3.9	4.5
		33.8	38.8			Net Worth	32.8	38.2
		100.0	100.0			Total Liabilities & Net Worth	100.0	100.0
						INCOME DATA		
		100.0	100.0			Net Sales	100.0	100.0
		25.3	19.4			Gross Profit	24.7	24.0
		22.2	16.3			Operating Expenses	21.7	19.5
		3.1	3.1			Operating Profit	3.0	4.5
		1.6	1.3			All Other Expenses (net)	1.5	1.9
		1.5	1.8			Profit Before Taxes	1.5	2.6
						RATIOS		
		2.1 / 1.3 / 1.0	2.2 / 1.3 / 1.0			Current	1.8 / 1.3 / 1.1	2.4 / 1.7 / 1.2
		1.0 / .7 / .4	1.2 / .6 / .4			Quick	1.1 / .7 / .5	1.3 / .8 / .5
		31 11.9 / 41 8.8 / 49 7.5	28 13.2 / 31 11.8 / 40 9.0			Sales/Receivables	36 10.1 / 41 8.9 / 54 6.8	33 10.9 / 45 8.1 / 50 7.3
		38 9.7 / 54 6.7 / 91 4.0	37 9.9 / 50 7.3 / 72 5.1			Cost of Sales/Inventory	31 11.7 / 60 6.1 / 74 4.9	33 11.2 / 62 5.9 / 85 4.3
		20 17.8 / 31 11.8 / 38 9.5	16 23.4 / 25 14.5 / 40 9.1			Cost of Sales/Payables	17 21.8 / 26 14.0 / 40 9.1	19 18.7 / 26 13.8 / 36 10.0
		6.1 / 17.9 / NM	7.1 / 25.9 / NM			Sales/Working Capital	9.5 / 16.0 / 41.5	5.6 / 9.9 / 29.2
		4.9 / 2.6 / 1.0	5.4 / 2.8 / .7			EBIT/Interest	(32) 3.2 / 1.8 / .2	3.7 / 2.5 / 1.3
						Net Profit + Depr., Dep., Amort./Cur. Mat. L/T/D	(12) 3.2 / 1.9 / .7	
		.5 / 1.0 / 2.2	.9 / 1.7 / 2.4			Fixed/Worth	.7 / 1.3 / 2.5	.5 / 1.2 / 2.3
		1.0 / 2.0 / 4.7	1.1 / 1.9 / 3.4			Debt/Worth	1.1 / 1.7 / 6.0	.8 / 1.8 / 3.9
		(15) 36.7 / 10.8 / -1.3	30.1 / 9.7 / -4.2			% Profit Before Taxes/Tangible Net Worth	(27) 24.9 / 10.9 / -1.4	(24) 40.7 / 12.0 / 2.7
		11.1 / 3.9 / -.1	9.2 / 4.8 / -1.0			% Profit Before Taxes/Total Assets	7.9 / 2.4 / -2.7	8.7 / 4.3 / 1.1
		8.2 / 5.2 / 4.0	4.6 / 3.1 / 2.1			Sales/Net Fixed Assets	10.0 / 4.6 / 3.4	20.3 / 5.3 / 3.9
		2.6 / 2.2 / 1.5	2.0 / 1.6 / 1.2			Sales/Total Assets	2.8 / 2.0 / 1.6	2.4 / 2.0 / 1.6
		(15) 2.6 / 3.2 / 4.6	(17) 3.3 / 5.3 / 7.8			% Depr., Dep., Amort./Sales	(30) 2.2 / 4.3 / 6.1	(21) 1.1 / 2.5 / 4.0
						% Officers', Directors', Owners' Comp/Sales	(11) 2.2 / 3.3 / 5.1	(10) 2.9 / 3.9 / 5.0
	18714M	175785M	695173M	179758M	277444M	Net Sales ($)	121816M	1136304M
	7895M	88526M	410996M	127544M	157496M	Total Assets ($)	748085M	730804M

M = $ thousand   MM = $ million
See Pages 11 through 18 for Explanation of Ratios and Data

Comparative Historical Data | Current Data Sorted By Sales

1 4/1/00-3/31/01 ALL	6 4/1/01-3/31/02 ALL	12 4/1/02-3/31/03 ALL	Type of Statement	0-1MM	1-3MM	3-5MM	5-10MM	10-25MM	25MM & OVER
1	6	12	Unqualified				1	2	9
7	6	16	Reviewed			2	7	7	
10	6	2	Compiled	1				1	
2	3	1	Tax Returns				1		
11	10	12	Other		1	1	2	3	5
				10 (4/1-9/30/02)			33 (10/1/02-3/31/03)		
31	31	43	NUMBER OF STATEMENTS	1	1	3	11	13	14
%	%	%	**ASSETS**	%	%	%	%	%	%
4.3	2.5	3.8	Cash & Equivalents				4.7	3.5	3.7
24.8	20.3	20.3	Trade Receivables (net)				23.5	18.9	17.1
24.8	21.6	22.9	Inventory				26.4	22.3	21.1
1.7	2.0	1.5	All Other Current				1.9	1.6	1.5
55.6	46.4	48.4	Total Current				56.6	46.3	43.5
32.5	44.8	43.9	Fixed Assets (net)				36.4	48.0	47.3
4.5	2.9	1.3	Intangibles (net)				.1	1.0	3.1
7.4	5.9	6.3	All Other Non-Current				6.9	4.7	6.2
100.0	100.0	100.0	Total				100.0	100.0	100.0
			LIABILITIES						
13.4	11.4	8.5	Notes Payable-Short Term				8.8	12.3	6.2
5.1	5.1	4.7	Cur. Mat.-L/T/D				5.8	4.4	4.6
13.3	12.0	12.5	Trade Payables				17.7	10.2	11.4
.3	.2	.2	Income Taxes Payable				.0	.1	.5
6.3	7.7	8.1	All Other Current				4.6	10.2	10.7
38.4	36.3	34.0	Total Current				36.9	37.1	33.3
24.8	25.2	22.7	Long Term Debt				19.8	23.5	24.6
1.5	1.6	2.0	Deferred Taxes				1.1	2.0	3.4
8.0	2.7	4.8	All Other Non-Current				7.1	1.4	2.8
27.3	34.2	36.5	Net Worth				35.1	35.9	35.8
100.0	100.0	100.0	Total Liabilities & Net Worth				100.0	100.0	100.0
			INCOME DATA						
100.0	100.0	100.0	Net Sales				100.0	100.0	100.0
23.4	23.5	24.7	Gross Profit				25.4	20.4	19.4
20.8	20.6	20.4	Operating Expenses				24.4	17.1	15.0
2.6	3.0	4.3	Operating Profit				1.0	3.3	4.4
2.2	1.8	2.0	All Other Expenses (net)				1.2	2.0	1.1
.4	1.2	2.3	Profit Before Taxes				-.2	1.3	3.3
			RATIOS						
1.8	2.4	2.0	Current				2.3	2.1	1.6
1.5	1.2	1.3					1.5	1.1	1.3
1.2	.9	1.1					1.2	.8	1.1
1.0	1.3	1.0	Quick				1.0	1.0	.8
.7	.7	.7					.8	.5	.7
.6	.5	.5					.6	.3	.5
32 11.4	27 13.5	29 12.5	Sales/Receivables				29 12.8	25 14.8	28 13.1
39 9.2	36 10.2	34 10.6					40 9.1	32 11.6	32 11.3
47 7.7	43 8.5	47 7.8					47 7.8	47 7.7	40 9.0
32 11.3	29 12.6	37 9.9	Cost of Sales/Inventory				34 10.7	38 9.7	37 9.9
48 7.6	54 6.8	56 6.5					60 6.1	58 6.2	48 7.5
85 4.3	76 4.8	79 4.6					109 3.3	74 4.9	68 5.3
16 23.0	14 25.6	17 21.9	Cost of Sales/Payables				16 22.2	21 17.7	16 22.2
28 13.0	26 14.3	28 12.8					31 11.7	28 12.8	25 14.4
38 9.5	40 9.2	40 9.1					47 7.7	37 9.9	40 9.1
7.7	7.0	7.5	Sales/Working Capital				4.5	6.6	12.7
14.2	23.2	18.4					17.3	30.8	22.8
21.8	-43.5	30.8					21.9	-22.3	34.1
3.7	4.3	4.9	EBIT/Interest				3.3	4.9	5.4
(30) 1.7	2.1	(42) 2.8					.9	3.2	3.8
.7	.4	.8					-1.7	1.0	1.5
	3.3	2.2	Net Profit + Depr., Dep., Amort./Cur. Mat. L/T/D						
	(16) 1.9	(15) 1.7							
	.8	1.1							
.6	.7	.8	Fixed/Worth				.6	.8	.9
1.3	1.3	1.3					.8	1.9	1.5
5.5	3.4	2.2					1.9	3.2	3.1
1.3	.9	1.1	Debt/Worth				1.2	.8	1.2
2.6	2.0	1.9					1.7	2.3	1.7
27.3	6.8	4.1					4.7	5.6	4.3
38.3	23.6	21.2	% Profit Before Taxes/Tangible Net Worth				9.5	27.4	34.2
(26) 12.8	(27) 12.9	(42) 8.9				(10) -.7	10.8	14.9
-5.8	-18.6	-1.7					-23.8	1.4	5.9
7.8	9.3	7.5	% Profit Before Taxes/Total Assets				7.5	6.4	10.5
3.8	3.7	3.3					-.1	4.6	6.0
-2.2	-4.5	-.4					-6.3	.4	1.3
8.6	7.0	7.6	Sales/Net Fixed Assets				18.6	6.1	6.9
5.9	4.5	4.0					4.8	3.5	3.7
4.4	3.0	2.6					3.7	2.4	2.2
2.9	2.5	2.5	Sales/Total Assets				2.6	2.4	2.6
2.0	1.8	1.7					2.0	1.7	1.7
1.5	1.6	1.4					1.2	1.4	1.4
.5	2.0	2.7	% Depr., Dep., Amort./Sales				2.7	2.9	2.7
(27) 2.5	(29) 3.4	(39) 3.7					3.2	(12) 5.0	(12) 4.2
4.0	4.8	5.4					4.1	7.4	5.3
2.9		1.2	% Officers', Directors', Owners' Comp/Sales						
(11) 4.2		(10) 2.2							
6.1		7.2							
1170884M	1160625M	1346874M	Net Sales ($)	173M	1928M	10929M	87550M	204360M	1041934M
642061M	615805M	792457M	Total Assets ($)	1409M	1249M	4236M	58180M	119722M	607661M

© RMA 2003

M = $ thousand   MM = $ million
See Pages 11 through 18 for Explanation of Ratios and Data

Current Data Sorted By Assets   Comparative Historical Data

0-500M	500M-2MM	2-10MM	10-50MM	50-100MM	100-250MM	Type of Statement	4/1/98-3/31/99 ALL	4/1/99-3/31/00 ALL
	1	4	8		1	Unqualified	33	19
	5	19	6			Reviewed	42	39
1	7	1	1			Compiled	15	17
1	1					Tax Returns	5	2
	1	3	4	3		Other	23	23
2	15	27	19	3	1	**NUMBER OF STATEMENTS**	118	100
%	%	%	%	%	%	**ASSETS**	%	%
	7.0	8.0	6.2			Cash & Equivalents	7.2	6.6
	30.4	24.5	21.3			Trade Receivables (net)	25.7	26.6
	19.7	17.0	16.6			Inventory	19.5	18.6
	.8	1.8	2.2			All Other Current	1.1	1.0
	57.9	51.3	46.2			Total Current	53.6	52.8
	34.0	43.7	41.2			Fixed Assets (net)	38.8	39.9
	2.0	1.1	6.5			Intangibles (net)	2.6	1.6
	6.0	3.9	6.1			All Other Non-Current	5.1	5.7
	100.0	100.0	100.0			Total	100.0	100.0
						LIABILITIES		
	14.3	7.5	9.5			Notes Payable-Short Term	10.6	8.7
	6.9	6.1	4.8			Cur. Mat.-L/T/D	5.9	4.9
	11.8	12.9	12.9			Trade Payables	13.8	15.2
	.0	.1	.1			Income Taxes Payable	.4	.3
	8.2	5.6	4.1			All Other Current	7.3	7.0
	41.2	32.1	31.4			Total Current	38.0	36.0
	20.0	26.2	20.0			Long Term Debt	18.7	19.5
	.0	.9	1.1			Deferred Taxes	1.0	1.0
	9.3	4.8	4.2			All Other Non-Current	4.3	4.6
	29.4	35.9	43.3			Net Worth	38.0	38.8
	100.0	100.0	100.0			Total Liabilities & Net Worth	100.0	100.0
						INCOME DATA		
	100.0	100.0	100.0			Net Sales	100.0	100.0
	30.2	25.6	24.8			Gross Profit	25.9	26.3
	28.4	22.8	20.9			Operating Expenses	25.9	20.9
	1.8	2.8	3.9			Operating Profit	.0	5.4
	1.0	1.3	.9			All Other Expenses (net)	.4	1.0
	.8	1.5	3.0			Profit Before Taxes	-.3	4.4
						RATIOS		
	2.4	2.7	2.1				2.5	2.4
	1.3	1.9	1.6			Current	1.5	1.6
	1.1	1.2	1.2				1.1	1.0
	1.7	1.8	1.5				1.4	1.5
	.9	1.2	1.0			Quick	.9	.9
	.5	.7	.5				.6	.7
	32 11.4	30 12.0	30 12.1				31 11.8	34 10.8
	34 10.9	36 10.2	38 9.5			Sales/Receivables	39 9.4	40 9.2
	35 10.3	45 8.2	48 7.7				48 7.6	49 7.5
	12 30.1	27 13.7	24 15.3				24 15.4	22 16.6
	29 12.6	34 10.8	36 10.1			Cost of Sales/Inventory	37 9.9	36 10.0
	59 6.2	45 8.1	63 5.8				62 5.9	52 7.0
	4 98.9	14 25.6	17 21.2				14 25.7	14 25.9
	16 22.6	25 14.6	27 13.4			Cost of Sales/Payables	25 14.4	29 12.8
	28 13.1	32 11.4	44 8.3				40 9.2	39 9.4
	9.5	6.1	6.1				7.0	6.6
	35.2	9.0	12.4			Sales/Working Capital	13.0	12.8
	78.1	32.5	21.2				85.3	104.9
	3.5	4.8	4.4				7.5	8.3
	1.1	2.9	3.1			EBIT/Interest	(109) 2.9	(92) 3.4
	.0	.0	1.6				1.0	1.9
							3.9	4.3
						Net Profit + Depr., Dep., Amort./Cur. Mat. L/T/D	(51) 2.5	(37) 2.6
							.9	1.4
	.7	.7	.8				.6	.6
	1.0	1.1	1.3			Fixed/Worth	1.0	1.1
	2.9	1.6	2.1				2.3	2.2
	.8	1.0	.9				.9	.8
	3.4	1.7	1.7			Debt/Worth	1.7	1.4
	8.0	3.1	3.4				5.3	4.4
	12.0	30.5	23.6				35.4	40.9
	(14) 2.9	(25) 8.6	(17) 17.1			% Profit Before Taxes/Tangible Net Worth	(109) 17.3	(89) 23.6
	-7.7	-5.4	3.1				.6	9.5
	7.8	12.2	10.8				14.3	15.9
	.2	2.7	4.8			% Profit Before Taxes/Total Assets	6.3	8.1
	-3.8	-2.2	1.4				.1	2.8
	16.6	7.0	8.1				13.1	11.2
	14.3	4.5	4.2			Sales/Net Fixed Assets	5.8	4.9
	4.7	2.8	2.7				3.2	3.2
	3.8	2.7	2.2				2.9	2.9
	2.9	2.0	1.8			Sales/Total Assets	2.2	2.1
	2.3	1.6	1.3				1.6	1.6
	1.4	2.6	2.6				1.7	1.8
	(14) 2.5	3.4	(17) 3.8			% Depr., Dep., Amort./Sales	(106) 2.8	(91) 2.8
	5.1	6.1	5.4				4.3	4.6
		1.9					2.1	2.1
		(14) 5.6				% Officers', Directors', Owners' Comp/Sales	(53) 3.8	(37) 3.8
		12.3					8.9	9.3
1489M	70571M	325131M	702897M	444167M	183946M	Net Sales ($)	2815383M	1975692M
344M	20671M	140188M	393609M	202941M	114177M	Total Assets ($)	1508649M	1040978M

M = $ thousand   MM = $ million
See Pages 11 through 18 for Explanation of Ratios and Data

Comparative Historical Data | Current Data Sorted By Sales

			Type of Statement						
17	14	14	Unqualified				1	3	10
24	20	30	Reviewed		3	1	10	12	4
16	8	10	Compiled	1	3	1	4	1	
1		2	Tax Returns	1	1				
21	18	11	Other			1	3		7
4/1/00- 3/31/01	4/1/01- 3/31/02	4/1/02- 3/31/03			15 (4/1-9/30/02)			52 (10/1/02-3/31/03)	
ALL	ALL	ALL		0-1MM	1-3MM	3-5MM	5-10MM	10-25MM	25MM & OVER
79	60	67	**NUMBER OF STATEMENTS**	2	7	3	18	16	21
%	%	%	**ASSETS**	%	%	%	%	%	%
5.8	5.0	6.7	Cash & Equivalents				7.2	9.2	4.8
25.3	22.2	25.3	Trade Receivables (net)				27.9	22.8	23.6
20.1	18.3	17.2	Inventory				14.7	16.3	17.3
1.8	2.6	1.6	All Other Current				.7	2.2	2.6
53.1	48.0	50.9	Total Current				50.6	50.5	48.3
38.9	44.2	40.0	Fixed Assets (net)				41.6	39.9	38.6
2.4	2.2	4.2	Intangibles (net)				2.8	4.0	7.8
5.6	5.5	4.9	All Other Non-Current				5.0	5.5	5.3
100.0	100.0	100.0	Total				100.0	100.0	100.0
			LIABILITIES						
9.8	11.0	9.4	Notes Payable-Short Term				12.5	5.6	9.1
6.3	4.6	6.5	Cur. Mat.-L/T/D				4.2	8.3	4.0
14.7	12.7	12.3	Trade Payables				11.2	12.9	14.9
.2	.0	.1	Income Taxes Payable				.1	.1	.1
6.7	6.6	6.0	All Other Current				6.6	5.4	5.2
37.7	35.0	34.3	Total Current				34.6	32.3	33.2
19.2	24.9	23.7	Long Term Debt				21.5	29.8	23.0
.8	1.1	.8	Deferred Taxes				.6	.9	1.3
3.6	5.0	5.6	All Other Non-Current				13.8	.3	5.7
38.7	34.1	35.7	Net Worth				29.4	36.7	36.8
100.0	100.0	100.0	Total Liabilities & Net Worth				100.0	100.0	100.0
			INCOME DATA						
100.0	100.0	100.0	Net Sales				100.0	100.0	100.0
26.0	23.5	27.2	Gross Profit				25.3	27.2	24.1
20.6	20.7	23.8	Operating Expenses				23.2	24.3	19.4
5.4	2.8	3.4	Operating Profit				2.1	2.9	4.7
1.1	1.4	1.2	All Other Expenses (net)				1.2	1.2	1.1
4.3	1.5	2.2	Profit Before Taxes				.9	1.7	3.6
			RATIOS						
2.0 / 1.4 / 1.1	2.1 / 1.4 / 1.1	2.4 / 1.6 / 1.1	Current				2.9 / 1.4 / 1.1	2.4 / 2.0 / 1.2	2.0 / 1.5 / 1.2
1.2 / .8 / .5	1.2 / .7 / .5	1.6 / 1.0 / .6	Quick				2.3 / 1.0 / .7	1.7 / 1.2 / .6	1.4 / .9 / .6
33 11.2 / 40 9.0 / 47 7.8	27 13.4 / 38 9.6 / 49 7.4	31 11.9 / 35 10.3 / 44 8.3	Sales/Receivables				27 13.3 / 34 10.7 / 48 7.6	32 11.3 / 37 9.8 / 41 8.8	30 12.2 / 36 10.2 / 47 7.8
27 13.3 / 40 9.1 / 62 5.9	26 14.1 / 37 10.0 / 71 5.1	24 15.3 / 34 10.9 / 53 6.9	Cost of Sales/Inventory				13 27.7 / 30 12.3 / 38 9.7	24 15.5 / 31 11.9 / 42 8.7	22 16.4 / 34 10.8 / 51 7.2
15 24.9 / 28 13.0 / 42 8.7	15 23.7 / 25 14.4 / 45 8.2	14 25.8 / 25 14.7 / 33 10.9	Cost of Sales/Payables				5 67.9 / 17 21.1 / 29 12.8	17 21.1 / 26 14.3 / 30 12.2	20 18.0 / 27 13.4 / 44 8.3
8.5 / 16.2 / 77.9	6.8 / 14.1 / 82.9	7.3 / 15.2 / 50.2	Sales/Working Capital				7.0 / 26.1 / 66.4	5.9 / 9.0 / 30.5	9.9 / 14.3 / 25.9
(72) 6.3 / 2.6 / 1.3	(58) 4.0 / 1.8 / .5	(66) 4.6 / 2.5 / .8	EBIT/Interest				3.6 / 1.5 / .0	4.6 / 3.3 / .4	(20) 6.6 / 3.4 / 1.6
(30) 4.3 / 1.6 / 1.1	(22) 3.5 / 2.3 / 1.0	(24) 3.5 / 2.5 / 1.0	Net Profit + Depr., Dep., Amort./Cur. Mat. L/T/D					(10)	5.9 / 2.7 / 2.0
.6 / 1.2 / 2.3	.9 / 1.4 / 3.4	.7 / 1.1 / 2.1	Fixed/Worth				.7 / 1.1 / 3.3	.7 / 1.1 / 1.7	.8 / 1.5 / 2.4
.8 / 1.7 / 3.5	1.0 / 1.9 / 6.3	1.0 / 1.7 / 4.4	Debt/Worth				1.1 / 2.3 / 8.1	.9 / 1.6 / 3.4	1.0 / 1.8 / 3.9
(72) 40.1 / 21.0 / 5.3	(55) 21.5 / 9.0 / -3.1	(60) 21.7 / 9.8 / -2.0	% Profit Before Taxes/Tangible Net Worth	(16)		(14)	22.2 / 5.9 / -11.1	23.3 / 10.4 / -2.4	(18) 25.2 / 19.0 / 3.1
16.3 / 6.1 / 1.4	6.8 / 2.8 / -2.9	10.0 / 2.4 / -1.0	% Profit Before Taxes/Total Assets				6.3 / 2.0 / -3.9	8.8 / 3.5 / -1.4	12.5 / 5.7 / 1.4
10.9 / 5.3 / 3.2	9.2 / 3.7 / 2.8	11.5 / 5.0 / 3.5	Sales/Net Fixed Assets				14.6 / 5.1 / 3.2	7.8 / 5.0 / 3.0	9.7 / 4.7 / 3.6
2.9 / 2.0 / 1.6	2.9 / 1.9 / 1.5	2.7 / 2.1 / 1.6	Sales/Total Assets				3.9 / 2.5 / 1.8	2.7 / 2.0 / 1.6	2.5 / 1.9 / 1.5
(76) 1.6 / 2.6 / 4.0	(56) 2.3 / 3.4 / 4.7	(64) 2.3 / 3.6 / 5.3	% Depr., Dep., Amort./Sales				1.6 / 3.2 / 4.0	(15) 2.7 / 4.6 / 6.7	(20) 2.0 / 3.7 / 4.7
(32) 1.8 / 3.4 / 7.8	(19) 1.1 / 2.2 / 4.1	(28) 2.1 / 4.6 / 9.3	% Officers', Directors', Owners' Comp/Sales			(10)	4.5 / 5.8 / 13.2		
2518235M	2169118M	1728201M	Net Sales ($)	1489M	15352M	11243M	134231M	234274M	1331612M
1359178M	1291259M	871930M	Total Assets ($)	344M	9037M	4907M	56975M	122979M	677688M

© RMA 2003

M = $ thousand   MM = $ million
See Pages 11 through 18 for Explanation of Ratios and Data

Current Data Sorted By Assets / Comparative Historical Data

0-500M	500M-2MM	2-10MM	10-50MM	50-100MM	100-250MM	Type of Statement	4/1/98-3/31/99 ALL	4/1/99-3/31/00 ALL
	1	4	12		6	Unqualified	21	16
	3	7	2			Reviewed	19	20
	6	4				Compiled	12	22
1	1	1				Tax Returns		5
	2	11	5	1	1	Other	19	22
	14 (4/1-9/30/02)		54 (10/1/02-3/31/03)					
1	13	27	19	1	7	NUMBER OF STATEMENTS	71	85
%	%	%	%	%	%	**ASSETS**	%	%
	10.4	4.7	5.8			Cash & Equivalents	7.2	8.3
	26.9	31.4	18.6			Trade Receivables (net)	26.0	27.9
	21.7	23.1	20.4			Inventory	21.8	19.5
	.6	1.5	.7			All Other Current	2.1	2.2
	59.5	60.7	45.5			Total Current	57.0	57.9
	34.4	32.3	42.6			Fixed Assets (net)	35.8	33.8
	.6	1.7	5.3			Intangibles (net)	1.5	2.9
	5.6	5.3	6.5			All Other Non-Current	5.7	5.4
	100.0	100.0	100.0			Total	100.0	100.0
						LIABILITIES		
	6.0	12.2	9.2			Notes Payable-Short Term	12.0	10.3
	5.7	4.8	5.8			Cur. Mat.-L/T/D	5.4	5.5
	15.2	18.8	11.8			Trade Payables	17.6	17.8
	.0	.1	.2			Income Taxes Payable	.1	.3
	9.6	8.3	6.5			All Other Current	7.4	9.6
	36.5	44.2	33.5			Total Current	42.5	43.5
	15.7	19.9	23.4			Long Term Debt	19.6	18.9
	.2	.2	.5			Deferred Taxes	.7	.5
	3.8	3.5	3.3			All Other Non-Current	5.1	4.4
	43.9	32.3	39.2			Net Worth	32.1	32.6
	100.0	100.0	100.0			Total Liabilities & Net Worth	100.0	100.0
						INCOME DATA		
	100.0	100.0	100.0			Net Sales	100.0	100.0
	34.1	28.0	27.7			Gross Profit	27.3	30.2
	29.3	21.4	24.0			Operating Expenses	23.3	25.3
	4.9	6.5	3.7			Operating Profit	4.0	4.9
	.8	3.1	.5			All Other Expenses (net)	.8	1.6
	4.0	3.5	3.2			Profit Before Taxes	3.2	3.3
						RATIOS		
	3.3	2.1	2.0			Current	2.1	2.1
	1.7	1.4	1.4				1.3	1.4
	1.0	1.1	1.0				.9	.9
	1.9	1.2	1.2			Quick	1.1	1.5
	.8	.8	.8				.8	.9
	.6	.6	.5				.5	.5
	18 20.7	30 12.3	36 10.1			Sales/Receivables	33 11.2	29 12.4
	28 13.0	42 8.6	42 8.7				41 8.9	43 8.4
	44 8.3	57 6.4	48 7.6				50 7.3	55 6.6
	17 22.0	29 12.5	42 8.7			Cost of Sales/Inventory	34 10.8	25 14.4
	47 7.8	46 7.9	73 5.0				48 7.6	41 8.9
	62 5.9	64 5.7	102 3.6				70 5.2	66 5.5
	15 24.4	14 26.9	23 15.5			Cost of Sales/Payables	19 19.5	18 20.5
	21 17.1	37 9.9	38 9.7				34 10.8	35 10.6
	34 10.7	53 6.9	65 5.6				55 6.7	53 6.9
	7.9	8.7	8.4			Sales/Working Capital	7.4	7.2
	13.4	14.4	14.6				14.8	16.9
	NM	31.2	109.4				-49.6	-52.0
	18.9	7.8	9.5			EBIT/Interest	6.7	6.5
	6.2	(26) 3.9	(18) 4.2				(63) 2.3	(78) 2.0
	1.4	1.0	1.1				1.0	.8
		8.7				Net Profit + Depr., Dep., Amort./Cur. Mat. L./T/D	6.4	3.6
		(10) 1.9					(26) 1.8	(16) 2.8
		1.1					1.0	.8
	.2	.5	.7			Fixed/Worth	.6	.5
	.6	1.0	1.5				1.2	1.1
	1.9	1.8	2.7				2.7	6.1
	.7	1.3	1.1			Debt/Worth	1.2	.8
	1.1	2.3	2.0				2.6	2.6
	2.2	3.6	4.2				6.0	10.8
	38.4	54.8	25.9			% Profit Before Taxes/Tangible Net Worth	41.8	47.7
	(12) 12.7	(25) 19.1	16.1				(66) 21.1	(72) 17.6
	2.9	1.5	-3.4				1.0	1.0
	20.8	14.3	16.3			% Profit Before Taxes/Total Assets	11.9	14.6
	9.7	6.6	5.5				5.1	4.6
	1.4	.3	-.5				-.1	-.7
	28.1	11.7	6.0			Sales/Net Fixed Assets	12.8	17.6
	9.3	9.4	3.5				6.2	7.4
	4.9	4.7	2.2				3.5	3.7
	4.6	3.3	2.0			Sales/Total Assets	2.9	3.5
	2.9	2.4	1.6				2.0	2.2
	2.3	1.8	1.1				1.5	1.5
	.5	1.0	3.1			% Depr., Dep., Amort./Sales	1.4	1.3
	(12) 2.1	(26) 2.6	(16) 4.4				(66) 2.5	(74) 2.8
	4.0	3.7	9.2				4.0	4.3
						% Officers', Directors', Owners' Comp/Sales	1.8	2.5
							(24) 5.6	(36) 5.3
							7.5	9.7
1813M	50853M	313902M	680486M	190949M	1340550M	Net Sales ($)	1594386M	1161042M
401M	15243M	129274M	404704M	94907M	938072M	Total Assets ($)	943584M	821837M

© RMA 2003

M = $ thousand   MM = $ million
See Pages 11 through 18 for Explanation of Ratios and Data

Comparative Historical Data   Current Data Sorted By Sales

	4/1/00-3/31/01 ALL	4/1/01-3/31/02 ALL	4/1/02-3/31/03 ALL	Type of Statement	0-1MM	1-3MM	3-5MM	5-10MM	10-25MM	25MM & OVER
	12	15	23	Unqualified		1		1	9	12
	16	12	12	Reviewed		1	2	4	4	1
	16	19	10	Compiled		3	2	3	2	
	2	2	3	Tax Returns		1	1	1	1	
	24	33	20	Other	2		1	4	8	5
						14 (4/1-9/30/02)			54 (10/1/02-3/31/03)	
NUMBER OF STATEMENTS	70	81	68		2	6	6	12	24	18
	%	%	%	**ASSETS**	%	%	%	%	%	%
	6.2	5.3	5.8	Cash & Equivalents				7.5	4.1	3.8
	29.3	26.3	24.6	Trade Receivables (net)				35.1	25.2	18.7
	21.7	21.6	21.0	Inventory				20.5	24.2	20.3
	2.2	1.4	1.0	All Other Current				1.2	.8	.8
	59.3	54.7	52.4	Total Current				64.4	54.3	43.6
	29.1	35.3	35.5	Fixed Assets (net)				30.9	35.3	31.8
	5.0	5.3	6.8	Intangibles (net)				2.0	3.5	19.3
	6.6	4.7	5.3	All Other Non-Current				2.7	6.9	5.3
	100.0	100.0	100.0	Total				100.0	100.0	100.0
				LIABILITIES						
	10.9	12.0	8.7	Notes Payable-Short Term				10.1	9.5	5.4
	5.2	5.2	5.3	Cur. Mat.-L/T/D				4.5	6.8	3.6
	22.8	16.2	14.7	Trade Payables				18.3	17.3	11.2
	.2	.1	.1	Income Taxes Payable				.0	.1	.3
	6.9	6.4	7.6	All Other Current				8.8	9.0	5.1
	45.9	39.9	36.5	Total Current				41.8	42.6	25.7
	17.7	21.3	21.6	Long Term Debt				14.1	21.4	25.9
	.4	.7	.6	Deferred Taxes				.0	.4	1.3
	3.1	3.9	5.1	All Other Non-Current				2.8	3.2	9.7
	32.8	34.3	36.2	Net Worth				41.3	32.3	37.3
	100.0	100.0	100.0	Total Liabilities & Net Worth				100.0	100.0	100.0
				INCOME DATA						
	100.0	100.0	100.0	Net Sales				100.0	100.0	100.0
	27.6	27.8	28.7	Gross Profit				32.9	24.7	23.8
	23.5	22.4	23.2	Operating Expenses				29.1	21.6	16.5
	4.1	5.4	5.5	Operating Profit				3.8	3.1	7.2
	1.0	2.2	2.1	All Other Expenses (net)				.7	.9	2.7
	3.1	3.3	3.4	Profit Before Taxes				3.1	2.2	4.5
				RATIOS						
	2.2	2.4	2.1	Current				2.1	1.8	2.2
	1.3	1.3	1.4					1.5	1.3	1.7
	1.0	1.1	1.1					1.2	1.1	1.3
	1.3	1.3	1.2	Quick				1.4	1.0	1.2
	.8	.7	.8					.9	.8	.8
	.5	.5	.6					.7	.5	.6
	31 11.9	31 11.8	30 12.3	Sales/Receivables				29 12.6	30 12.0	33 11.0
	40 9.2	40 9.2	39 9.4					39 9.3	42 8.6	37 9.8
	52 7.0	49 7.4	48 7.6					61 6.0	48 7.6	44 8.3
	25 14.7	32 11.3	29 12.5	Cost of Sales/Inventory				25 14.7	31 11.9	42 8.8
	47 7.7	46 7.9	50 7.2					36 10.3	58 6.3	53 6.9
	74 5.0	66 5.6	71 5.1					71 5.1	67 5.4	78 4.7
	23 15.8	16 22.6	16 22.4	Cost of Sales/Payables				13 28.6	15 23.9	24 15.4
	35 10.3	32 11.5	30 12.1					34 10.6	37 9.9	29 12.5
	62 5.9	44 8.3	44 8.3					60 6.1	56 6.5	38 9.6
	6.8	7.3	8.8	Sales/Working Capital				7.9	9.5	8.0
	25.0	18.4	14.3					13.7	17.6	12.1
	181.8	150.2	37.0					34.0	110.4	30.7
	(67) 7.9	(78) 7.3	(66) 7.8	EBIT/Interest				(11) 24.4	6.3	8.0
	3.2	2.9	3.6					3.5	4.1	2.8
	.7	1.0	1.2					1.7	.4	1.3
	(24) 4.6	(21) 4.0	(21) 5.6	Net Profit + Depr., Dep., Amort./Cur. Mat. L/T/D						
	3.1	1.8	1.9							
	.8	.7	1.1							
	.5	.6	.5	Fixed/Worth				.4	.7	.8
	.8	1.3	1.2					.5	1.1	1.5
	2.3	2.8	2.6					1.7	2.3	−1.1
	1.1	1.0	1.1	Debt/Worth				.8	1.6	1.2
	3.2	2.4	2.1					1.4	2.7	2.9
	8.9	8.5	5.3					3.3	4.1	−3.5
	(62) 72.6	(73) 55.5	(60) 49.1	% Profit Before Taxes/Tangible Net Worth				(11) 42.1	56.3	(13) 53.4
	24.3	28.2	18.9					17.2	14.0	21.9
	2.8	7.4	2.1					8.8	−5.9	17.7
	14.9	14.3	13.2	% Profit Before Taxes/Total Assets				22.2	12.8	14.0
	4.4	7.1	6.2					6.4	6.5	5.1
	−1.5	.0	.4					2.2	−1.8	1.5
	19.1	13.5	11.0	Sales/Net Fixed Assets				15.9	11.1	7.2
	8.8	6.3	6.9					10.0	7.1	5.6
	4.1	3.5	3.6					7.9	3.2	4.1
	3.5	3.3	2.9	Sales/Total Assets				4.2	3.1	2.3
	2.2	2.1	2.1					2.7	2.1	1.7
	1.6	1.6	1.4					1.9	1.5	1.3
	(63) 1.4	(74) 1.4	(61) 1.3	% Depr., Dep., Amort./Sales				(11) 1.8	(22) 1.2	(14) 2.6
	2.6	3.0	3.0					3.0	2.8	3.7
	3.9	4.7	5.1					4.6	5.5	5.3
	(27) 2.4	(25) 2.4	(17) 1.6	% Officers', Directors', Owners' Comp/Sales						
	3.6	4.0	4.1							
	6.3	5.8	5.4							
	1435604M	2351093M	2578553M	Net Sales ($)	965M	13581M	25321M	92540M	394856M	2051290M
	901348M	1363849M	1582601M	Total Assets ($)	2798M	6569M	9998M	42772M	220046M	1300418M

M = $ thousand   MM = $ million
See Pages 11 through 18 for Explanation of Ratios and Data

Current Data Sorted By Assets   Comparative Historical Data

0-500M	500M-2MM	2-10MM	10-50MM	50-100MM	100-250MM	Type of Statement	4/1/98-3/31/99 ALL	4/1/99-3/31/00 ALL
		3	10	1	2	Unqualified	21	22
1	8	19	3			Reviewed	23	19
	3	4				Compiled	13	11
1	1					Tax Returns	5	4
2	3	6	5	2	1	Other	20	27
	15 (4/1-9/30/02)		60 (10/1/02-3/31/03)					
4	15	32	18	3	3	**NUMBER OF STATEMENTS**	82	83
%	%	%	%	%	%	**ASSETS**	%	%
	4.9	3.5	6.0			Cash & Equivalents	6.0	6.6
	31.0	31.0	21.5			Trade Receivables (net)	30.2	28.7
	18.0	27.7	19.7			Inventory	20.3	20.5
	.6	1.3	2.1			All Other Current	1.5	1.2
	54.5	63.6	49.3			Total Current	58.0	57.0
	34.9	28.1	42.0			Fixed Assets (net)	34.0	29.8
	3.1	2.1	4.8			Intangibles (net)	2.3	8.1
	7.5	6.3	3.9			All Other Non-Current	5.7	5.0
	100.0	100.0	100.0			Total	100.0	100.0
						LIABILITIES		
	6.4	11.0	9.1			Notes Payable-Short Term	8.7	6.5
	5.9	4.5	8.2			Cur. Mat.-L/T/D	5.2	4.8
	22.5	17.9	9.5			Trade Payables	16.7	17.5
	.3	.1	.2			Income Taxes Payable	.5	.2
	10.2	8.2	9.2			All Other Current	8.1	7.0
	45.2	41.8	36.3			Total Current	39.1	35.9
	16.3	11.3	18.4			Long Term Debt	16.5	17.8
	.2	.4	2.0			Deferred Taxes	.8	.8
	8.7	6.8	2.9			All Other Non-Current	2.6	6.3
	29.6	39.7	40.4			Net Worth	41.0	39.2
	100.0	100.0	100.0			Total Liabilities & Net Worth	100.0	100.0
						INCOME DATA		
	100.0	100.0	100.0			Net Sales	100.0	100.0
	35.6	29.6	30.9			Gross Profit	30.4	32.1
	31.9	27.8	24.8			Operating Expenses	24.7	25.9
	3.7	1.8	6.1			Operating Profit	5.7	6.2
	1.6	.7	4.0			All Other Expenses (net)	1.1	1.2
	2.1	1.1	2.2			Profit Before Taxes	4.6	5.0
						RATIOS		
	1.9	2.3	2.9			Current	2.3	2.7
	1.2	1.5	1.4				1.5	1.5
	.8	1.1	1.1				1.1	1.1
	1.4	1.1	1.8			Quick	1.6	1.5
	.8	.9	.9				.9	.9
	.6	.6	.6				.7	.7
	33 11.1	39 9.4	37 9.8			Sales/Receivables	36 10.0	35 10.4
	44 8.3	44 8.2	43 8.4				45 8.1	44 8.3
	52 7.1	50 7.4	49 7.4				53 6.9	58 6.3
	16 22.4	29 12.6	41 8.9			Cost of Sales/Inventory	24 15.2	32 11.4
	27 13.5	44 8.2	48 7.6				40 9.2	48 7.7
	57 6.4	84 4.3	68 5.4				62 5.9	72 5.1
	30 12.3	26 13.9	12 31.4			Cost of Sales/Payables	17 21.7	25 14.7
	42 8.7	34 10.8	24 14.9				32 11.5	34 10.9
	76 4.8	46 7.9	45 8.2				49 7.5	53 6.9
	8.7	5.3	4.8			Sales/Working Capital	6.4	7.0
	21.8	13.7	17.5				12.3	12.1
	−28.3	66.2	39.3				52.5	28.9
	9.4	5.2	8.4			EBIT/Interest	8.9	6.1
	(14) 3.8	(30) 1.9	(16) 3.6				(75) 3.9	(74) 4.1
	.9	1.3	1.1				1.2	1.9
		4.2	2.5			Net Profit + Depr., Dep.,	6.5	4.8
	(10)	2.2	(10) 1.6			Amort./Cur. Mat. L /T/D	(31) 2.7	(30) 2.2
		1.1	1.1				1.2	1.3
	.6	.5	.8			Fixed/Worth	.4	.4
	1.1	.8	1.2				.8	1.0
	2.4	1.4	2.8				1.7	2.3
	1.3	.8	.6			Debt/Worth	.7	.8
	2.7	1.7	1.4				1.6	2.0
	4.9	3.9	4.8				3.2	4.3
	30.7	24.8	24.2			% Profit Before Taxes/Tangible	44.5	38.8
	(13) 18.5	(31) 7.5	(16) 15.4			Net Worth	(76) 17.4	(69) 20.4
	4.2	1.2	9.5				4.3	4.9
	12.4	9.4	11.8			% Profit Before Taxes/Total	16.2	14.8
	3.3	1.7	7.3			Assets	6.9	8.1
	.3	.6	1.1				1.3	2.3
	13.0	19.1	6.0			Sales/Net Fixed Assets	13.7	16.1
	8.6	9.7	4.8				7.2	7.1
	5.5	5.4	3.2				3.9	4.2
	3.2	3.1	2.2			Sales/Total Assets	3.1	2.9
	2.4	2.5	1.7				2.3	2.3
	2.2	1.9	1.3				1.7	1.6
	1.4	1.7	3.5			% Depr., Dep., Amort./Sales	1.6	1.3
	2.2	(30) 2.3	(17) 4.7				(77) 2.9	(78) 2.3
	6.0	3.2	5.5				4.3	3.6
	2.8	4.4				% Officers', Directors',	2.0	1.4
	(10) 4.8	(12) 6.1				Owners' Comp/Sales	(33) 2.8	(28) 2.5
	6.6	10.5					4.3	8.0
5488M	45267M	378440M	685240M	252994M	639300M	Net Sales ($)	1975250M	3179526M
488M	16892M	151032M	376379M	161038M	476501M	Total Assets ($)	1041662M	1975107M

Comparative Historical Data | | Current Data Sorted By Sales

					Type of Statement						
15		21		16	Unqualified					7	9
21		17		31	Reviewed	1	4	6	8	10	2 -
12		10		7	Compiled		2	1	3		1
2		3		2	Tax Returns			2			
23		21		19	Other	1	3	2	2	5	6
4/1/00-		4/1/01-		4/1/02-				15 (4/1-9/30/02)		60 (10/1/02-3/31/03)	
3/31/01		3/31/02		3/31/03		0-1MM	1-3MM	3-5MM	5-10MM	10-25MM	25MM & OVER
ALL		ALL		ALL							
73		72		75	**NUMBER OF STATEMENTS**	2	9	11	13	22	18
%		%		%	**ASSETS**	%	%	%	%	%	%
8.1		5.4		5.2	Cash & Equivalents			4.6	5.8	4.9	2.2
25.8		27.7		26.6	Trade Receivables (net)			24.9	28.3	28.9	22.6
19.6		21.3		22.0	Inventory			23.2	24.5	24.8	19.1
2.2		2.1		1.5	All Other Current			2.1	1.4	1.5	1.8
55.7		56.5		55.3	Total Current			54.9	60.0	60.2	45.8
31.3		32.6		33.8	Fixed Assets (net)			35.4	31.2	30.9	38.3
5.2		3.9		4.5	Intangibles (net)			1.6	4.2	2.8	9.5
7.7		7.1		6.3	All Other Non-Current			8.2	4.6	6.1	6.4
100.0		100.0		100.0	Total			100.0	100.0	100.0	100.0
					LIABILITIES						
7.0		10.7		9.6	Notes Payable-Short Term			12.8	7.3	10.3	10.2
5.1		5.4		6.1	Cur. Mat.-L/T/D			6.0	6.7	3.7	8.0
15.5		17.6		15.5	Trade Payables			16.8	17.8	16.1	10.6
.1		.0		.2	Income Taxes Payable			.2	.3	.1	.2
6.7		6.6		8.4	All Other Current			6.8	10.4	5.7	11.1
34.3		40.4		39.9	Total Current			42.5	42.4	35.9	40.1
17.7		17.6		17.1	Long Term Debt			14.5	10.8	15.2	19.0
.5		.6		.9	Deferred Taxes			.1	.8	.4	2.5
3.7		4.4		6.5	All Other Non-Current			7.6	10.3	3.2	8.2
43.9		37.0		35.5	Net Worth			35.3	35.6	45.4	30.3
100.0		100.0		100.0	Total Liabilities & Net Worth			100.0	100.0	100.0	100.0
					INCOME DATA						
100.0		100.0		100.0	Net Sales			100.0	100.0	100.0	100.0
31.1		28.0		31.8	Gross Profit			41.8	30.3	30.0	24.6
25.0		25.3		28.1	Operating Expenses			38.1	28.5	26.5	19.6
6.1		2.7		3.7	Operating Profit			3.8	1.8	3.6	5.0
1.4		1.5		1.8	All Other Expenses (net)			1.5	.7	.9	4.7
4.7		1.3		1.9	Profit Before Taxes			2.3	1.1	2.6	.2
					RATIOS						
2.8		2.4		2.1				2.1	2.3	3.4	1.6
1.7		1.4		1.5	Current			1.2	1.2	1.5	1.3
1.0		1.0		1.1				.8	1.1	1.1	1.1
1.8		1.4		1.1				1.4	1.2	1.2	1.1
1.0		.8		.8	Quick			.7	.8	1.0	.7
.6		.5		.6				.4	.5	.7	.6
32	11.6	38	9.7	37	9.7	Sales/Receivables	19	19.0	36	10.1	40	9.2	38	9.5

Sales/Receivables:

						0-1MM	1-3MM	3-5MM	5-10MM	10-25MM	25MM & OVER
32	11.6	38	9.7	37	9.7		19	19.0	36	10.1	40	9.2	38	9.5

Sales/Receivables
- 32 11.6 | 38 9.7 | 37 9.7 | 19 19.0 | 36 10.1 | 40 9.2 | 38 9.5
- 41 8.9 | 43 8.4 | 43 8.4 | 40 9.2 | 42 8.6 | 47 7.8 | 40 9.0
- 52 7.1 | 53 6.8 | 50 7.4 | 52 7.1 | 49 7.4 | 49 7.4 | 47 7.7

Cost of Sales/Inventory
- 27 13.8 | 29 12.6 | 27 13.3 | 14 26.8 | 29 12.5 | 33 10.9 | 34 10.7
- 45 8.2 | 49 7.4 | 43 8.5 | 27 13.5 | 43 8.4 | 47 7.8 | 45 8.2
- 67 5.5 | 71 5.2 | 67 5.4 | 57 6.4 | 80 4.6 | 75 4.8 | 58 6.2

Cost of Sales/Payables
- 18 19.9 | 23 16.2 | 21 17.1 | 20 18.6 | 22 16.4 | 24 14.9 | 14 25.5
- 34 10.8 | 35 10.5 | 32 11.4 | 32 11.5 | 37 9.8 | 35 10.6 | 25 14.3
- 52 7.0 | 55 6.6 | 45 8.2 | 60 6.1 | 51 7.1 | 44 8.2 | 33 11.1

Sales/Working Capital
- 6.2 | 7.0 | 6.7 | | 6.7 | 6.2 | 4.0 | 11.9
- 11.5 | 14.5 | 17.4 | | 27.7 | 25.3 | 13.7 | 18.4
- 254.7 | 125.3 | 95.3 | | -116.6 | 81.1 | 76.6 | 45.8

EBIT/Interest
- 6.5 | 3.4 | 6.1 | | 5.4 | 7.0 | 4.4
- (66) 2.3 | (65) 1.5 | (69) 2.7 | | 2.7 | (20) 3.6 | (17) 2.5
- 1.0 | .7 | 1.3 | | 1.4 | 1.0 | 1.3

Net Profit + Depr., Dep., Amort./Cur. Mat. L/T/D
- 3.4 | 2.1 | 3.6 | | | | 2.2
- (23) 1.9 | (27) 1.4 | (27) 1.6 | | | (12) 1.6
- .9 | .7 | 1.1 | | | | .5

Fixed/Worth
- .4 | .5 | .5 | | .3 | .6 | .4 | 1.0
- .8 | 1.0 | 1.0 | | 1.1 | 1.0 | .7 | 2.0
- 1.5 | 2.3 | 2.4 | | 2.5 | 1.6 | 1.3 | NM

Debt/Worth
- .8 | .9 | .9 | | 1.3 | .8 | .9 | 1.4
- 1.4 | 2.4 | 2.0 | | 1.5 | 2.1 | 1.2 | 3.3
- 2.6 | 6.0 | 5.0 | | 6.5 | 7.1 | 2.3 | NM

% Profit Before Taxes/Tangible Net Worth
- 36.2 | 21.6 | 28.6 | | 45.7 | 19.2 | 28.7 | 44.3
- (67) 13.8 | (66) 9.1 | (66) 14.6 | (10) 21.5 | (12) 12.9 | 14.2 | (14) 15.6
- .4 | -.7 | 2.3 | | 3.1 | 2.2 | -2.2 | 9.1

% Profit Before Taxes/Total Assets
- 14.4 | 7.5 | 11.4 | | 12.4 | 11.0 | 12.4 | 8.9
- 5.6 | 1.7 | 4.2 | | 3.1 | 1.9 | 5.7 | 3.5
- .1 | -.7 | .7 | | 2.1 | .8 | -.4 | 1.1

Sales/Net Fixed Assets
- 16.9 | 15.1 | 11.4 | | 13.0 | 16.6 | 14.0 | 6.6
- 7.5 | 6.6 | 7.0 | | 8.8 | 9.2 | 8.3 | 4.9
- 4.1 | 3.9 | 4.3 | | 5.5 | 5.2 | 4.3 | 3.4

Sales/Total Assets
- 3.1 | 3.0 | 2.8 | | 4.1 | 2.8 | 3.1 | 2.3
- 2.2 | 2.1 | 2.3 | | 2.5 | 2.5 | 2.3 | 1.8
- 1.5 | 1.5 | 1.7 | | 2.2 | 2.1 | 1.4 | 1.4

% Depr., Dep., Amort./Sales
- .8 | 1.4 | 2.0 | | 1.6 | 2.0 | 1.9 | 2.4
- (65) 2.6 | (64) 2.4 | (69) 3.1 | (10) 3.0 | (12) 3.0 | (21) 2.9 | (17) 3.6
- 4.2 | 4.0 | 4.9 | | 6.7 | 3.5 | 4.4 | 5.5

% Officers', Directors', Owners' Comp/Sales
- 1.6 | 1.8 | 2.4
- (26) 2.8 | (32) 3.6 | (33) 4.4
- 6.0 | 5.5 | 6.8

2188129M	2758349M	2006729M	Net Sales ($)	422M 18723M 41650M 102347M 368514M 1475073M
1340947M	1765464M	1182330M	Total Assets ($)	98M 8930M 16013M 44440M 185912M 926937M

M = $ thousand   MM = $ million
See Pages 11 through 18 for Explanation of Ratios and Data

Current Data Sorted By Assets   Comparative Historical Data

0-500M	500M-2MM	2-10MM	10-50MM	50-100MM	100-250MM	Type of Statement	4/1/98-3/31/99 ALL	4/1/99-3/31/00 ALL
	1	6	5	2	1	Unqualified	9	12
	4	13				Reviewed	15	12
	4	6				Compiled	6	14
	1					Tax Returns	2	2
1		4	8	1	1	Other	6	11
	15 (4/1-9/30/02)		43 (10/1/02-3/31/03)					
1	10	29	13	3	2	NUMBER OF STATEMENTS	38	51
%	%	%	%	%	%	**ASSETS**	%	%
	7.4	4.4	5.7			Cash & Equivalents	5.0	5.2
	25.3	23.1	16.1			Trade Receivables (net)	24.9	24.3
	25.2	24.7	16.9			Inventory	20.0	19.5
	.6	1.5	1.5			All Other Current	2.2	1.4
	58.5	53.8	40.1			Total Current	52.0	50.4
	37.1	35.2	49.4			Fixed Assets (net)	36.8	40.3
	.4	3.3	1.8			Intangibles (net)	3.8	3.6
	4.0	7.8	8.7			All Other Non-Current	7.4	5.7
	100.0	100.0	100.0			Total	100.0	100.0
						LIABILITIES		
	8.6	12.1	7.4			Notes Payable-Short Term	14.4	13.2
	4.0	5.4	10.0			Cur. Mat.-L/T/D	3.3	4.2
	19.6	17.3	11.5			Trade Payables	14.8	17.2
	.1	.3	.8			Income Taxes Payable	.3	.3
	8.3	7.0	7.4			All Other Current	6.2	7.5
	40.6	42.1	37.1			Total Current	39.1	42.3
	33.1	14.8	16.9			Long Term Debt	20.8	23.8
	.6	1.1	2.9			Deferred Taxes	.8	.5
	11.6	15.5	8.4			All Other Non-Current	5.8	5.9
	14.2	26.5	34.7			Net Worth	33.5	27.4
	100.0	100.0	100.0			Total Liabilities & Net Worth	100.0	100.0
						INCOME DATA		
	100.0	100.0	100.0			Net Sales	100.0	100.0
	31.5	26.5	26.3			Gross Profit	23.7	26.8
	30.0	23.6	20.7			Operating Expenses	18.2	22.3
	1.5	2.9	5.6			Operating Profit	5.5	4.5
	3.5	1.3	1.6			All Other Expenses (net)	1.8	3.0
	−1.9	1.6	4.0			Profit Before Taxes	3.7	1.4
						RATIOS		
	3.1	1.8	1.8			Current	1.9	2.2
	1.3	1.2	1.1				1.5	1.3
	.9	1.0	.7				1.1	.9
	2.0	.8	1.2			Quick	1.1	1.3
	.7	.6	.4				.8	.7
	.5	.4	.3				.6	.4
	27 13.7	33 11.0	25 14.6			Sales/Receivables	34 10.6	33 10.9
	43 8.4	42 8.6	31 11.9				44 8.2	42 8.7
	49 7.4	51 7.2	48 7.6				50 7.3	49 7.4
	41 9.0	37 10.0	32 11.5			Cost of Sales/Inventory	34 10.8	32 11.3
	59 6.2	50 7.3	49 7.4				41 8.8	46 7.9
	98 3.7	88 4.1	62 5.8				54 6.8	60 6.1
	18 20.1	29 12.4	17 21.9			Cost of Sales/Payables	23 16.0	21 17.6
	47 7.7	40 9.1	30 12.1				31 11.9	40 9.1
	73 5.0	59 6.2	52 7.0				45 8.1	60 6.1
	5.8	8.1	8.4			Sales/Working Capital	7.6	7.9
	15.1	26.6	45.8				15.3	16.5
	−40.3	−533.7	−10.8				56.6	−53.8
	3.5	4.4	9.7			EBIT/Interest	4.4	7.3
	1.5	(27) 2.2	2.6				(36) 3.0	(47) 2.4
	.9	1.0	1.7				1.4	1.3
		9.3				Net Profit + Depr., Dep.,	8.6	3.9
		(11) 1.8				Amort./Cur. Mat. L /T/D	(13) 4.5	(13) 2.8
		1.4					1.7	1.6
	.5	.5	.8			Fixed/Worth	.6	.6
	1.3	1.1	1.5				1.0	1.4
	−1.4	2.3	2.8				2.5	4.8
	.6	1.2	1.0			Debt/Worth	1.0	.9
	3.8	2.1	2.2				1.8	2.2
	−4.6	5.4	3.3				4.3	9.1
		21.5	40.3			% Profit Before Taxes/Tangible	42.6	38.3
		(25) 9.0	(12) 14.4			Net Worth	(34) 12.8	(44) 16.7
		1.3	4.2				3.6	6.2
	7.3	8.3	13.3			% Profit Before Taxes/Total	13.7	12.2
	2.2	3.5	5.3			Assets	6.0	4.1
	−.6	.2	1.8				1.4	.4
	11.3	12.6	5.0			Sales/Net Fixed Assets	8.8	8.6
	7.6	5.1	3.4				5.4	5.0
	4.1	2.7	2.4				3.7	3.1
	2.8	2.7	2.0			Sales/Total Assets	2.7	2.7
	2.4	2.0	1.8				1.9	2.1
	1.7	1.2	1.5				1.6	1.5
	2.8	1.7	2.9			% Depr., Dep., Amort./Sales	1.9	1.8
	3.5	(28) 3.6	5.1				3.2	(47) 3.3
	5.0	5.3	6.0				4.8	5.1
		1.7				% Officers', Directors',	1.6	2.3
		(13) 3.1				Owners' Comp/Sales	(15) 2.7	(19) 4.1
		6.1					4.8	6.3
571M	31869M	283368M	348497M	381945M	451206M	Net Sales ($)	971327M	1000218M
222M	14337M	145549M	211270M	220284M	287187M	Total Assets ($)	537360M	518871M

M = $ thousand   MM = $ million
See Pages 11 through 18 for Explanation of Ratios and Data

Comparative Historical Data | | | | Current Data Sorted By Sales

			Type of Statement						
15	21	15	Unqualified		1	2	2	3	7
11	15	17	Reviewed		2	4	6	4	1
13	11	10	Compiled		1	3	4	2	
4	1	1	Tax Returns		1				
11	17	15	Other	1		1	2	7	4
4/1/00- 3/31/01 ALL	4/1/01- 3/31/02 ALL	4/1/02- 3/31/03 ALL			15 (4/1-9/30/02)		43 (10/1/02-3/31/03)		
				0-1MM	1-3MM	3-5MM	5-10MM	10-25MM	25MM & OVER
54	65	58	NUMBER OF STATEMENTS	1	5	10	14	16	12
%	%	%	ASSETS	%	%	%	%	%	%
5.8	3.2	5.3	Cash & Equivalents			7.1	4.2	6.3	5.2
25.6	24.2	21.7	Trade Receivables (net)			26.1	21.6	23.1	18.6
19.8	23.2	22.6	Inventory			26.8	24.4	23.2	20.1
1.3	1.0	1.2	All Other Current			1.0	.4	2.5	1.1
52.6	51.6	50.8	Total Current			61.0	50.5	55.0	45.1
36.1	37.7	38.7	Fixed Assets (net)			31.5	39.8	38.0	41.8
4.2	4.0	3.4	Intangibles (net)			3.8	1.2	.9	5.0
7.1	6.7	7.1	All Other Non-Current			3.7	8.4	6.1	8.0
100.0	100.0	100.0	Total			100.0	100.0	100.0	100.0
			LIABILITIES						
10.9	11.7	10.6	Notes Payable-Short Term			9.6	10.1	14.3	10.0
5.3	6.9	5.9	Cur. Mat.-L/T/D			4.3	7.0	4.0	10.0
14.5	17.2	16.7	Trade Payables			21.2	16.3	17.3	15.2
.2	.3	.5	Income Taxes Payable			.0	.7	.3	1.0
6.7	6.4	6.9	All Other Current			7.8	7.6	8.9	4.8
37.5	42.5	40.6	Total Current			42.9	41.7	44.7	41.1
20.1	22.1	18.5	Long Term Debt			13.2	17.5	13.9	14.0
.9	1.1	1.5	Deferred Taxes			.5	1.6	1.5	2.6
8.2	11.4	12.0	All Other Non-Current			14.0	26.6	5.7	5.2
33.3	22.9	27.4	Net Worth			29.4	12.6	34.2	37.1
100.0	100.0	100.0	Total Liabilities & Net Worth			100.0	100.0	100.0	100.0
			INCOME DATA						
100.0	100.0	100.0	Net Sales			100.0	100.0	100.0	100.0
26.2	26.5	27.4	Gross Profit			30.7	31.1	24.6	24.9
21.7	23.4	23.7	Operating Expenses			28.4	28.6	20.8	18.1
4.5	3.1	3.7	Operating Profit			2.3	2.5	3.8	6.9
2.1	2.6	1.8	All Other Expenses (net)			1.8	1.5	1.3	1.7
2.4	.6	1.9	Profit Before Taxes			.5	1.0	2.5	5.2
			RATIOS						
2.3	1.6	1.8				3.2	1.9	1.7	1.6
1.4	1.2	1.2	Current			1.3	1.1	1.2	1.3
1.0	.9	.8				.9	.8	.8	.7
1.3	.9	1.0				1.9	.7	1.2	.8
.8	.6	.6	Quick			.7	.6	.5	.6
.5	.5	.4				.5	.4	.4	.3
36 10.2	32 11.4	29 12.5				33 11.2	31 11.9	30 12.3	27 13.5
42 8.6	40 9.0	41 8.9	Sales/Receivables			47 7.7	43 8.4	37 9.8	31 11.7
52 7.1	47 7.8	50 7.3				67 5.4	49 7.5	50 7.3	51 7.2
32 11.4	36 10.3	37 9.9				29 12.6	39 9.4	38 9.7	37 9.8
43 8.5	52 7.1	53 6.9	Cost of Sales/Inventory			64 5.7	56 6.6	49 7.4	53 6.8
59 6.1	65 5.7	78 4.7				100 3.6	129 2.8	57 6.4	75 4.8
18 20.3	23 16.0	27 13.7				18 19.8	31 11.8	27 13.8	22 16.7
34 10.8	39 9.5	42 8.7	Cost of Sales/Payables			49 7.5	49 7.5	40 9.0	38 9.5
48 7.5	50 7.3	60 6.0				83 4.4	67 5.5	55 6.6	60 6.1
7.2	11.6	8.1				4.9	8.4	9.2	9.6
15.2	33.5	20.5	Sales/Working Capital			15.1	33.2	23.9	26.4
-548.6	-56.3	-30.6				-61.5	-22.4	-19.5	-17.6
	4.8		5.0		4.6				5.5		7.8		11.1
(49) 2.7	(62) 1.8	(56) 2.3	EBIT/Interest				2.3	(15) 2.5	2.6
1.0	.7	1.2					1.2	1.0	1.4
2.6	1.8	4.3	Net Profit + Depr., Dep.,						
(16) 1.5	(18) 1.2	(25) 1.6	Amort./Cur. Mat. L/T/D						
.6	.6	1.3							
.6	.8	.7				.4	.8	.9	.7
1.0	1.7	1.4	Fixed/Worth			1.3	1.6	1.3	1.0
3.3	-16.2	2.7				NM	2.2	2.2	3.5
.8	1.5	1.1				.6	1.3	1.4	.9
1.7	2.4	2.2	Debt/Worth			2.3	2.1	2.3	2.1
4.7	-43.5	6.1				NM	8.0	3.4	4.6
36.2	24.9	33.3	% Profit Before Taxes/Tangible				19.2	35.1	42.8
(44) 15.4	(48) 11.5	(50) 11.7	Net Worth			(12) 10.0	(15) 14.0	(11) 32.8
6.4	1.7	3.2					7.3	3.5	6.3
13.5	10.2	8.9	% Profit Before Taxes/Total			6.1	7.6	9.3	20.7
6.4	3.0	4.0	Assets			.5	4.0	4.5	6.2
.1	-.7	.4				-3.4	.7	.3	1.4
9.7	11.1	10.3				11.3	10.5	13.5	6.0
5.8	6.4	5.0	Sales/Net Fixed Assets			7.0	4.0	5.6	5.0
3.6	3.1	2.7				4.6	1.9	3.2	2.9
2.6	2.9	2.5				2.7	2.6	2.8	2.0
2.1	2.0	1.9	Sales/Total Assets			2.0	2.0	2.1	1.8
1.6	1.5	1.5				1.4	1.0	1.7	1.5
1.0	2.1	2.5				3.0	2.9	1.5	2.7
(52) 3.0	(56) 3.0	(57) 3.6	% Depr., Dep., Amort./Sales			3.8	3.8	(15) 2.2	3.2
4.7	4.8	5.5				6.4	5.6	3.9	6.1
2.0	2.0	1.9	% Officers', Directors',						
(23) 3.6	(23) 2.7	(24) 3.3	Owners' Comp/Sales						
5.8	3.4	6.8							
1396404M	2959276M	1497456M	Net Sales ($)	571M	10738M	37560M	106493M	277136M	1064958M
796877M	1257733M	878849M	Total Assets ($)	222M	9527M	22927M	69285M	145193M	631695M

© RMA 2003

M = $ thousand   MM = $ million
See Pages 11 through 18 for Explanation of Ratios and Data

Current Data Sorted By Assets | Comparative Historical Data

		4 (4/1-9/30/02)		26 (10/1/02-3/31/03)				
0-500M	500M-2MM	2-10MM	10-50MM	50-100MM	100-250MM	Type of Statement	4/1/98-3/31/99	4/1/99-3/31/00
		5	4	1	1	Unqualified	18	14
	1	5	3			Reviewed	8	10
	2					Compiled	4	3
						Tax Returns		1
		5	2	1		Other	11	9
	3	15	9	2	1	NUMBER OF STATEMENTS	41 ALL	37 ALL
%	%	%	%	%	%	ASSETS	%	%
		5.2				Cash & Equivalents	7.9	7.3
		31.1				Trade Receivables (net)	30.2	29.9
		13.6				Inventory	19.5	19.2
		.7				All Other Current	1.2	1.3
		50.6				Total Current	58.8	57.7
		42.8				Fixed Assets (net)	35.3	35.1
		1.6				Intangibles (net)	2.0	2.4
		5.0				All Other Non-Current	3.9	4.7
		100.0				Total	100.0	100.0
						LIABILITIES		
		16.0				Notes Payable-Short Term	9.6	14.0
		7.7				Cur. Mat.-L/T/D	3.4	5.4
		10.3				Trade Payables	15.2	14.5
		.3				Income Taxes Payable	.1	.3
		5.9				All Other Current	7.7	7.1
		40.2				Total Current	36.0	41.2
		24.4				Long Term Debt	23.0	23.3
		.7				Deferred Taxes	1.0	.8
		8.5				All Other Non-Current	1.6	3.0
		26.2				Net Worth	38.4	31.7
		100.0				Total Liabilities & Net Worth	100.0	100.0
						INCOME DATA		
		100.0				Net Sales	100.0	100.0
		24.1				Gross Profit	24.2	22.8
		24.3				Operating Expenses	20.7	18.6
		-.2				Operating Profit	3.5	4.3
		1.9				All Other Expenses (net)	1.3	1.2
		-2.1				Profit Before Taxes	2.2	3.1
						RATIOS		
		1.8				Current	2.6	2.4
		1.3					1.7	1.6
		1.0					1.3	.9
		1.2				Quick	1.8	2.2
		.9					1.0	1.0
		.7					.8	.5
		(41) 8.9				Sales/Receivables	(38) 9.7	(38) 9.6
		(47) 7.7					(45) 8.1	(45) 8.1
		(60) 6.1					(53) 6.9	(55) 6.6
		(21) 17.7				Cost of Sales/Inventory	(22) 16.6	(25) 14.8
		(30) 12.2					(39) 9.4	(38) 9.7
		(40) 9.0					(52) 7.0	(55) 6.7
		(10) 35.0				Cost of Sales/Payables	(15) 24.0	(19) 19.4
		(19) 18.9					(25) 14.3	(25) 14.5
		(28) 13.1					(37) 10.0	(35) 10.5
		11.6				Sales/Working Capital	6.6	6.4
		20.0					11.0	12.5
		-156.3					22.4	-35.5
		4.1				EBIT/Interest	(36) 6.0	(32) 6.6
		1.5					2.7	2.1
		-.3					1.4	1.1
						Net Profit + Depr., Dep., Amort./Cur. Mat. L./T/D	(13) 3.8	
							2.0	
							1.0	
		1.0				Fixed/Worth	.6	.8
		1.6					1.1	1.4
		4.4					2.0	2.9
		1.6				Debt/Worth	.7	.8
		2.7					1.5	1.9
		6.3					5.4	8.0
		32.4				% Profit Before Taxes/Tangible Net Worth	(38) 24.2	(32) 23.0
	(14)	6.5					12.8	14.2
		-41.3					4.4	5.6
		11.5				% Profit Before Taxes/Total Assets	8.9	8.7
		1.5					5.7	4.4
		-6.6					1.7	1.0
		7.9				Sales/Net Fixed Assets	14.0	12.7
		5.3					5.7	5.6
		2.4					4.1	3.7
		3.1				Sales/Total Assets	2.9	2.6
		2.1					2.3	1.9
		1.7					1.8	1.6
		3.1				% Depr., Dep., Amort./Sales	(37) 1.9	(33) 2.2
	(14)	4.4					2.7	2.9
		7.8					3.7	4.7
						% Officers', Directors', Owners' Comp/Sales	(14) 1.8	
							4.3	
							6.2	
	12133M	179967M	461617M	169369M	187653M	Net Sales ($)	1187639M	1505501M
	4291M	85527M	253361M	105641M	104688M	Total Assets ($)	608159M	795437M

(Data Not Available columns: 0-500M, 500M-2MM)

M = $ thousand   MM = $ million
See Pages 11 through 18 for Explanation of Ratios and Data

Comparative Historical Data | Current Data Sorted By Sales

Hist 1	Hist 2	Hist 3	Type of Statement	0-1MM	1-3MM	3-5MM	5-10MM	10-25MM	25MM & OVER
12	8	11	Unqualified				1	3	7
11	8	9	Reviewed		1	1	2	3	2
6	3	2	Compiled			1	1		
			Tax Returns						
			Other				2	3	3
7 4/1/00-3/31/01 ALL	9 4/1/01-3/31/02 ALL	8 4/1/02-3/31/03 ALL		4 (4/1-9/30/02)			26 (10/1/02-3/31/03)		
36	28	30	NUMBER OF STATEMENTS	1	1	2	6	9	12
%	%	%	ASSETS	%	%	%	%	%	%
6.7	7.0	5.1	Cash & Equivalents						5.6
31.0	24.7	27.0	Trade Receivables (net)						22.6
17.0	16.5	18.2	Inventory						24.1
1.0	.6	1.7	All Other Current						2.9
55.8	48.8	52.0	Total Current						55.2
36.4	41.7	41.2	Fixed Assets (net)						38.8
4.3	4.4	1.1	Intangibles (net)						1.9
4.5	5.2	5.6	All Other Non-Current						4.0
100.0	100.0	100.0	Total						100.0
			LIABILITIES						
12.5	14.8	13.2	Notes Payable-Short Term						11.4
7.6	8.2	5.8	Cur. Mat.-L/T/D						3.8
15.5	17.1	11.2	Trade Payables						11.5
.1	.0	.2	Income Taxes Payable						.0
5.6	5.7	6.5	All Other Current						8.2
41.4	45.7	36.9	Total Current						34.9
24.3	24.3	22.0	Long Term Debt						18.8
.5	.7	.7	Deferred Taxes						.8
3.4	3.7	9.5	All Other Non-Current						9.2
30.4	25.6	30.8	Net Worth						36.3
100.0	100.0	100.0	Total Liabilities & Net Worth						100.0
			INCOME DATA						
100.0	100.0	100.0	Net Sales						100.0
21.0	27.2	24.8	Gross Profit						23.6
19.4	25.6	22.3	Operating Expenses						18.7
1.6	1.6	2.5	Operating Profit						4.8
1.3	1.6	1.6	All Other Expenses (net)						1.3
.3	-.1	.9	Profit Before Taxes						3.5
			RATIOS						
2.3	1.5	2.2	Current						2.4
1.2	1.1	1.4							1.5
.9	.8	1.1							1.2
1.8	.9	1.2	Quick						1.2
.8	.7	.8							.8
.6	.5	.6							.6
38 9.7	38 9.7	38 9.6	Sales/Receivables						35 10.4
49 7.5	45 8.2	47 7.8							41 8.9
55 6.6	52 7.0	59 6.2							54 6.7
21 17.4	24 15.3	24 15.5	Cost of Sales/Inventory						38 9.5
29 12.5	32 11.4	39 9.4							49 7.4
42 8.7	43 8.5	58 6.3							91 4.0
16 23.2	18 20.2	17 22.0	Cost of Sales/Payables						19 19.5
24 15.0	31 11.7	21 17.8							21 17.8
39 9.4	52 7.0	31 12.0							24 15.0
5.6	10.4	7.0	Sales/Working Capital						6.5
33.3	48.8	14.2							7.7
-151.2	-17.6	56.0							44.5
1.9	1.9	5.2	EBIT/Interest						5.1
(31) 1.2	(27) 1.0	2.0							2.1
.3	-.2	.4							.5
2.4	1.7	3.0	Net Profit + Depr., Dep., Amort./Cur. Mat. L/T/D						
(13) 1.2	(10) 1.2	(11) 1.8							
.4	.7	1.3							
.8	1.1	.9	Fixed/Worth						.9
1.4	1.9	1.3							1.0
3.3	3.9	2.5							2.4
.9	2.1	1.2	Debt/Worth						1.1
2.1	3.5	2.2							2.0
5.7	8.1	4.7							3.9
30.8	10.1	29.0	% Profit Before Taxes/Tangible Net Worth						14.4
(31) 3.5	(26) 1.7	(28) 10.1						(11)	11.4
-2.5	-9.3	-3.8							-3.9
4.8	2.1	11.1	% Profit Before Taxes/Total Assets						8.7
1.5	.2	2.7							3.6
-2.4	-4.9	-1.1							-.8
11.2	8.1	6.9	Sales/Net Fixed Assets						4.9
5.8	4.7	4.7							4.3
3.8	2.7	3.4							3.5
2.8	2.8	2.4	Sales/Total Assets						2.3
2.0	2.0	2.0							1.8
1.7	1.3	1.7							1.6
1.6	2.2	2.4	% Depr., Dep., Amort./Sales						2.4
(33) 2.8	(27) 3.3	(28) 3.3							3.0
3.7	4.9	5.1							4.5
1.5	2.3		% Officers', Directors', Owners' Comp/Sales						
(10) 2.5	(10) 3.4								
8.6	11.0								
1216321M	479611M	1010739M	Net Sales ($)		2075M	8050M	46804M	119474M	834336M
598550M	264226M	553508M	Total Assets ($)		1162M	11282M	22938M	57343M	460783M

© RMA 2003

M = $ thousand   MM = $ million
See Pages 11 through 18 for Explanation of Ratios and Data

Current Data Sorted By Assets   **Comparative Historical Data**

0-500M	500M-2MM	2-10MM	10-50MM	50-100MM	100-250MM		4/1/98-3/31/99 ALL	4/1/99-3/31/00 ALL
						Type of Statement		
		2	12	2	3	Unqualified	17	23
	5	8	4			Reviewed	20	16
2	8	9		2		Compiled	18	15
	3		1			Tax Returns	1	2
1	3	10	10	1	1	Other	16	16
	15 (4/1-9/30/02)		70 (10/1/02-3/31/03)					
3	19	29	27	3	4	**NUMBER OF STATEMENTS**	72	72
%	%	%	%	%	%	**ASSETS**	%	%
	7.5	8.1	9.2			Cash & Equivalents	7.0	5.1
	38.2	27.5	20.7			Trade Receivables (net)	25.6	27.3
	21.8	21.9	22.0			Inventory	21.8	23.7
	1.8	.9	1.9			All Other Current	2.2	1.4
	69.3	58.5	53.8			Total Current	56.6	57.6
	26.4	25.7	31.7			Fixed Assets (net)	33.4	35.3
	.6	6.3	7.5			Intangibles (net)	3.6	2.3
	3.7	9.6	7.0			All Other Non-Current	6.3	4.9
	100.0	100.0	100.0			Total	100.0	100.0
						LIABILITIES		
	15.4	12.6	8.9			Notes Payable-Short Term	9.0	11.1
	2.5	5.5	4.1			Cur. Mat.-L/T/D	4.9	5.7
	18.8	14.9	12.6			Trade Payables	15.5	18.0
	.5	.4	.2			Income Taxes Payable	.3	.6
	11.3	6.4	4.7			All Other Current	5.8	9.6
	48.4	39.9	30.6			Total Current	35.5	45.0
	11.5	14.0	17.3			Long Term Debt	20.0	18.2
	.0	.4	.6			Deferred Taxes	.5	.7
	3.1	6.0	8.2			All Other Non-Current	4.4	3.4
	36.9	39.7	43.3			Net Worth	39.5	32.7
	100.0	100.0	100.0			Total Liabilities & Net Worth	100.0	100.0
						INCOME DATA		
	100.0	100.0	100.0			Net Sales	100.0	100.0
	24.7	27.4	27.6			Gross Profit	29.3	28.3
	23.0	22.4	21.6			Operating Expenses	24.3	23.5
	1.7	5.0	6.0			Operating Profit	5.0	4.8
	1.4	.7	1.7			All Other Expenses (net)	1.4	1.3
	.4	4.3	4.3			Profit Before Taxes	3.6	3.5
						RATIOS		
	2.4	2.4	2.9				2.5	2.0
	1.4	1.6	2.0			Current	1.7	1.4
	.9	1.1	1.1				1.1	1.0
	1.5	1.5	1.8				1.5	1.1
	1.0	1.0	1.0			Quick	.9	.7
	.6	.6	.6				.5	.5
	27 13.7	37 9.7	38 9.7				32 11.4	35 10.3
	35 10.5	45 8.2	45 8.2			Sales/Receivables	39 9.4	43 8.5
	42 8.7	51 7.2	54 6.8				53 6.9	52 7.0
	11 33.1	30 12.1	36 10.2				29 12.6	32 11.5
	28 13.2	45 8.1	51 7.2			Cost of Sales/Inventory	49 7.5	55 6.7
	79 4.6	57 6.4	88 4.2				78 4.7	85 4.3
	8 44.4	18 20.4	16 22.2				18 20.4	21 17.2
	24 15.1	26 14.3	32 11.3			Cost of Sales/Payables	30 12.2	31 11.6
	54 6.7	45 8.1	50 7.3				45 8.1	56 6.6
	7.7	6.0	3.9				6.2	7.8
	16.0	12.1	7.9			Sales/Working Capital	9.9	15.2
	-138.1	106.4	45.3				52.3	NM
	(18) 4.6	(26) 8.7	(25) 6.3				(64) 8.1	(70) 7.3
	1.2	3.9	2.4			EBIT/Interest	2.9	3.3
	-.3	1.7	1.3				1.5	1.5
			(11) 6.0			Net Profit + Depr., Dep.,	(24) 3.5	(27) 7.5
			2.2			Amort./Cur. Mat. L /T/D	2.0	2.6
			.4				1.2	.9
	.3	.2	.5				.4	.5
	.6	.7	.8			Fixed/Worth	.8	1.0
	2.0	1.5	1.6				2.1	2.5
	.7	.8	.8				.8	1.0
	1.9	1.6	1.6			Debt/Worth	1.7	2.2
	6.0	5.3	3.1				4.3	7.2
	(18) 30.0	(25) 34.3	(25) 21.1			% Profit Before Taxes/Tangible	(69) 43.9	(62) 49.3
	4.9	19.6	9.8			Net Worth	18.6	24.6
	-15.6	8.1	1.5				5.3	8.7
	8.5	13.9	10.1			% Profit Before Taxes/Total	14.7	14.9
	1.1	8.8	2.9			Assets	6.5	7.2
	-5.5	2.2	1.1				1.8	1.8
	25.2	63.2	19.6				12.7	13.5
	15.5	8.1	4.6			Sales/Net Fixed Assets	6.9	6.1
	5.8	5.3	3.0				4.0	3.4
	4.7	3.1	2.4				2.6	2.7
	3.4	2.0	1.3			Sales/Total Assets	2.1	2.0
	2.0	1.6	1.1				1.6	1.7
	(17) 1.3	(22) 1.8	(22) 1.5				(65) 1.6	(65) 1.3
	2.1	3.2	2.9			% Depr., Dep., Amort./Sales	3.0	2.9
	3.9	4.9	5.0				4.3	4.2
	(13) 2.2	(10) 1.6				% Officers', Directors',	(28) 2.6	(24) 1.5
	3.6	2.9				Owners' Comp/Sales	3.3	3.5
	7.7	4.9					4.8	4.6
4665M	94317M	329334M	993251M	442870M	992344M	Net Sales ($)	1673560M	1707790M
714M	23546M	146919M	626425M	199278M	532997M	Total Assets ($)	954225M	985489M

See Pages 11 through 18 for Explanation of Ratios and Data

Comparative Historical Data | | | | ## Current Data Sorted By Sales

4/1/00-3/31/01 ALL	4/1/01-3/31/02 ALL	4/1/02-3/31/03 ALL	Type of Statement	0-1MM	1-3MM	3-5MM	5-10MM	10-25MM	25MM & OVER
20	25	19	Unqualified				1	5	13
10	18	17	Reviewed		2		5	5	4
14	20	19	Compiled	3	3	2	5	5	1
5	4	4	Tax Returns			1	2	1	
17	27	26	Other		2	2	8	6	8
					15 (4/1-9/30/02)			70 (10/1/02-3/31/03)	
66	94	85	NUMBER OF STATEMENTS	3	7	6	21	22	26
%	%	%	ASSETS	%	%	%	%	%	%
4.1	6.1	8.9	Cash & Equivalents				7.4	8.5	6.9
25.4	26.6	27.6	Trade Receivables (net)				33.2	26.3	25.0
26.8	23.6	22.2	Inventory				17.4	22.9	25.8
1.5	1.9	1.6	All Other Current				1.7	1.2	2.1
57.8	58.1	60.2	Total Current				59.7	59.0	59.7
32.0	32.1	27.7	Fixed Assets (net)				28.1	28.1	29.7
3.6	3.5	5.5	Intangibles (net)				4.0	4.4	6.4
6.6	6.3	6.6	All Other Non-Current				8.3	8.6	4.2
100.0	100.0	100.0	Total				100.0	100.0	100.0
			LIABILITIES						
14.5	12.8	13.9	Notes Payable-Short Term				11.5	15.1	9.1
4.1	5.4	4.0	Cur. Mat.-L/T/D				2.7	5.8	3.7
16.4	15.2	15.0	Trade Payables				17.2	12.8	14.3
.5	.4	.3	Income Taxes Payable				.8	.2	.1
8.1	7.4	7.5	All Other Current				8.1	3.8	7.5
43.6	41.3	40.8	Total Current				40.5	37.7	34.8
19.7	17.2	14.3	Long Term Debt				14.3	15.4	17.1
.5	.5	.4	Deferred Taxes				.3	.3	.8
3.9	5.8	6.2	All Other Non-Current				6.4	4.5	9.8
32.3	35.2	38.3	Net Worth				38.5	42.0	37.6
100.0	100.0	100.0	Total Liabilities & Net Worth				100.0	100.0	100.0
			INCOME DATA						
100.0	100.0	100.0	Net Sales				100.0	100.0	100.0
29.0	25.6	25.8	Gross Profit				25.1	27.6	23.1
25.1	21.5	21.2	Operating Expenses				20.8	22.5	17.5
3.9	4.0	4.6	Operating Profit				4.2	5.1	5.6
−.4	1.2	1.2	All Other Expenses (net)				.7	.8	1.9
4.3	2.8	3.4	Profit Before Taxes				3.5	4.3	3.7
			RATIOS						
2.0	2.1	2.5	Current				2.3	2.9	2.5
1.3	1.4	1.6					1.5	1.6	2.1
.9	1.0	1.0					1.0	1.0	1.1
1.0	1.2	1.7	Quick				1.8	1.8	1.4
.7	.8	1.0					1.0	.9	1.0
.4	.5	.6					.7	.6	.6
32 11.3	34 10.7	33 11.1	Sales/Receivables				27 13.3	36 10.3	37 9.8
40 9.1	42 8.6	42 8.6					39 9.3	44 8.3	45 8.0
53 6.9	50 7.3	51 7.1					50 7.2	47 7.8	52 7.0
34 10.8	29 12.5	26 14.1	Cost of Sales/Inventory				13 27.3	23 16.1	39 9.5
51 7.1	45 8.2	45 8.1					31 11.8	48 7.5	52 7.0
92 4.0	78 4.7	66 5.5					47 7.8	63 5.8	88 4.1
23 16.2	17 20.9	16 23.0	Cost of Sales/Payables				15 24.7	15 24.4	19 19.6
32 11.5	30 12.4	27 13.4					24 15.1	25 14.4	31 11.6
48 7.6	44 8.3	44 8.3					40 9.1	43 8.5	41 8.8
6.8	6.4	4.8	Sales/Working Capital				9.2	4.9	4.6
15.8	14.6	11.4					14.7	10.6	8.5
−74.5	UND	215.2					NM	72.7	283.9
(63) 5.3	(89) 5.1	(78) 6.7	EBIT/Interest				(19) 7.6	(21) 6.8	(23) 6.6
2.3	2.0	2.5					3.5	4.5	2.4
1.3	.8	.9					1.5	2.1	1.3
(20) 5.4	(22) 5.9	(22) 5.3	Net Profit + Depr., Dep., Amort./Cur. Mat. L/T/D						
2.5	2.1	2.3							
1.7	.7	.4							
.5	.5	.3	Fixed/Worth				.3	.2	.5
1.0	1.0	.7					.7	.6	.7
2.2	2.3	1.6					1.4	1.4	2.2
1.1	.8	.8	Debt/Worth				.7	.9	.9
2.1	2.2	1.7					1.5	1.5	2.7
6.6	4.5	4.9					4.0	2.8	5.8
(59) 37.1	(82) 28.0	(77) 29.4	% Profit Before Taxes/Tangible Net Worth				(20) 31.2	(20) 33.0	(24) 25.6
16.3	10.0	13.1					13.0	16.1	12.4
5.3	.1	−1.0					5.5	5.0	1.2
11.7	12.6	11.3	% Profit Before Taxes/Total Assets				16.6	11.5	11.6
4.2	3.6	4.5					3.9	8.6	3.7
.9	−.7	.2					1.3	2.5	.9
16.2	19.3	23.8	Sales/Net Fixed Assets				32.4	24.7	19.6
7.6	7.6	8.1					10.0	7.3	6.9
4.0	3.8	4.0					5.3	3.7	3.5
2.9	3.0	3.3	Sales/Total Assets				4.0	3.1	2.6
2.0	2.1	2.0					3.0	1.9	1.8
1.5	1.6	1.4					1.8	1.3	1.5
(61) 1.0	(82) .9	(68) 1.3	% Depr., Dep., Amort./Sales				(16) 1.4	(19) 1.8	(19) .8
2.6	2.4	2.8					2.5	3.3	2.1
4.6	4.4	4.5					4.0	4.9	4.1
(26) 1.7	(28) 1.6	(33) 1.1	% Officers', Directors', Owners' Comp/Sales					(12) .9	
4.3	2.6	3.0						1.4	
6.8	5.5	4.4						3.2	
1988404M	2827354M	2856781M	Net Sales ($)	1977M	14952M	26274M	151684M	359393M	2302501M
991789M	1494352M	1529879M	Total Assets ($)	1050M	8966M	12375M	67260M	219089M	1221139M

M = $ thousand   MM = $ million
See Pages 11 through 18 for Explanation of Ratios and Data

Current Data Sorted By Assets   Comparative Historical Data

						Type of Statement		
1	5	41	49	8	5	Unqualified	144	135
7	41	124	34		1	Reviewed	254	236
16	76	47	5			Compiled	214	173
24	22	10				Tax Returns	40	42
14	46	77	36	3	4	Other	228	215
	180 (4/1-9/30/02)		516 (10/1/02-3/31/03)				4/1/98-3/31/99	4/1/99-3/31/00
0-500M	500M-2MM	2-10MM	10-50MM	50-100MM	100-250MM		ALL	ALL
62	190	299	124	11	10	NUMBER OF STATEMENTS	880	801
%	%	%	%	%	%	ASSETS	%	%
10.8	8.5	6.8	6.4	2.1	2.8	Cash & Equivalents	7.9	7.2
31.6	29.6	27.7	24.7	18.6	18.8	Trade Receivables (net)	29.7	29.4
10.6	8.0	10.4	10.6	8.7	11.9	Inventory	9.7	9.6
1.6	1.6	1.6	2.2	3.2	1.6	All Other Current	1.3	1.5
54.5	47.7	46.6	43.9	32.6	35.1	Total Current	48.6	47.7
36.6	41.8	46.5	47.8	57.9	36.2	Fixed Assets (net)	43.5	43.6
3.9	4.2	1.6	2.8	7.2	24.7	Intangibles (net)	2.7	3.2
5.0	6.3	5.2	5.5	2.3	4.0	All Other Non-Current	5.2	5.5
100.0	100.0	100.0	100.0	100.0	100.0	Total	100.0	100.0
						LIABILITIES		
12.4	6.4	8.0	7.6	4.6	.9	Notes Payable-Short Term	7.0	8.1
7.4	9.4	8.4	6.5	7.9	6.1	Cur. Mat.-L/T/D	7.3	7.3
22.6	13.7	13.2	11.8	6.6	7.4	Trade Payables	13.5	14.0
.0	.2	.2	.3	.0	.2	Income Taxes Payable	.3	.2
9.8	10.2	7.3	7.5	7.0	13.5	All Other Current	7.3	7.8
52.2	39.8	37.1	33.7	26.2	28.1	Total Current	35.4	37.5
37.5	32.9	29.6	26.7	40.5	24.0	Long Term Debt	27.6	29.9
.2	.4	.7	1.3	3.8	2.6	Deferred Taxes	.9	.8
5.7	6.7	3.0	2.9	6.0	8.2	All Other Non-Current	3.6	3.4
4.4	20.1	29.7	35.4	23.5	37.1	Net Worth	32.5	28.4
100.0	100.0	100.0	100.0	100.0	100.0	Total Liabilities & Net Worth	100.0	100.0
						INCOME DATA		
100.0	100.0	100.0	100.0	100.0	100.0	Net Sales	100.0	100.0
45.7	42.9	31.1	25.7	26.9	29.2	Gross Profit	33.4	33.4
45.0	40.7	28.8	22.2	21.4	19.0	Operating Expenses	28.8	29.2
.7	2.2	2.3	3.5	5.5	10.2	Operating Profit	4.6	4.1
1.2	2.0	1.8	1.4	2.6	4.9	All Other Expenses (net)	1.6	1.6
−.5	.3	.6	2.2	2.9	5.3	Profit Before Taxes	3.0	2.5
						RATIOS		
2.7	2.0	1.8	2.0	1.4	2.0		2.0	1.9
1.2	1.2	1.3	1.3	1.3	1.5	Current	1.4	1.3
.7	.9	.9	.9	1.1	1.1		1.0	1.0
2.3	1.6	1.4	1.4	1.0	1.2		1.6	1.6
1.0	1.0	.9	.8	.9	.9	Quick	1.1	1.0
.5	.7	.6	.6	.6	.7		.7	.7

												Sales/Receivables				
21	17.8	32	11.5	40	9.1	41	8.9	43	8.5	47	7.7	Sales/Receivables	37	9.9	38	9.5
33	10.9	43	8.4	49	7.4	53	6.8	47	7.7	55	6.7		49	7.5	48	7.6
46	7.9	54	6.8	60	6.1	63	5.8	55	6.7	58	6.3		60	6.1	60	6.1
3	128.6	6	56.4	13	28.6	18	19.7	16	22.5	26	13.8	Cost of Sales/Inventory	10	35.5	12	31.4
14	25.6	15	23.6	22	16.8	25	14.6	24	15.0	47	7.8		19	18.9	21	17.5
33	11.1	28	13.0	35	10.4	40	9.1	46	8.0	85	4.3		31	11.8	34	10.9
16	23.0	17	21.0	18	20.1	20	18.0	20	18.3	22	16.6	Cost of Sales/Payables	19	18.9	20	18.5
33	10.9	33	11.2	29	12.5	31	11.8	23	16.0	28	13.2		28	12.9	30	12.1
61	5.9	51	7.2	47	7.7	44	8.2	29	12.6	39	9.2		43	8.5	45	8.2

									Sales/Working Capital		
	9.9	9.5	7.9	7.7	14.4	6.9	Sales/Working Capital	8.5	9.1
	41.7	25.9	24.5	20.9	27.6	12.1		17.4	19.3
	−27.7	−92.9	−58.1	−62.2	63.3	NM		273.7	−103.0

											EBIT/Interest				
	3.6		3.5		3.2		6.2		2.5	15.1	EBIT/Interest		4.9		4.2
(54)	1.0	(179)	1.6	(291)	1.4	(120)	2.0		1.9	2.7		(846)	2.4	(776)	2.1
	−2.4		−.2		.2		.8		1.1	1.4			1.2		.9
			3.1		2.1		3.5				Net Profit + Depr., Dep., Amort./Cur. Mat. L /T/D		3.1		2.5
		(47)	1.6	(120)	1.4	(52)	1.7					(368)	1.8	(307)	1.6
			1.1		.7		1.1						1.2		1.0
	.6		.9		.9		.9		2.1	.8	Fixed/Worth		.8		.9
	3.1		2.5		1.8		1.6		2.7	2.2			1.5		1.8
	−.9		NM		3.7		2.8		17.8	−.3			3.3		4.3
	.9		1.4		1.3		1.0		2.3	.5	Debt/Worth		1.1		1.3
	6.1		3.7		2.5		2.2		3.2	2.9			2.3		2.7
	−3.2		NM		5.7		4.7		26.9	−1.8			5.3		7.8

											% Profit Before Taxes/Tangible Net Worth				
	31.7		30.2		24.5		20.3				% Profit Before Taxes/Tangible Net Worth		39.4		39.2
(36)	11.2	(143)	11.3	(273)	5.4	(115)	10.6					(799)	19.0	(703)	16.7
	−12.5		−7.7		−9.1		−.5						4.5		2.4
	10.2		7.6		6.9		7.9		5.2	13.7	% Profit Before Taxes/Total Assets		11.8		10.7
	−.3		2.1		1.3		3.4		4.1	6.2			5.6		4.4
	−12.7		−3.3		−3.1		−.2		.2	3.0			.9		−.5
	17.7		9.7		6.7		4.9		3.1	5.6	Sales/Net Fixed Assets		8.5		8.1
	11.2		5.5		4.0		3.6		2.1	4.0			5.0		4.7
	6.1		3.7		2.7		2.6		1.9	3.0			3.2		3.1
	4.5		3.1		2.4		2.1		1.6	1.7	Sales/Total Assets		2.8		2.7
	3.7		2.4		1.8		1.8		1.3	1.3			2.1		2.0
	2.7		1.8		1.5		1.3		1.2	.7			1.6		1.6

											% Depr., Dep., Amort./Sales				
	1.7		3.4		3.6		3.8		4.6		% Depr., Dep., Amort./Sales		2.8		3.0
(55)	3.5	(182)	5.2	(288)	5.3	(121)	4.8	(10)	4.9			(840)	4.2	(751)	4.5
	5.1		8.2		7.0		6.5		6.6				6.0		6.0
	5.0		4.2		2.3		2.0				% Officers', Directors', Owners' Comp/Sales		2.9		3.0
(44)	7.5	(105)	6.2	(149)	3.5	(35)	3.2					(426)	5.0	(371)	4.8
	12.1		9.1		5.6		5.5						7.9		7.7

61714M	530227M	2913118M	4182587M	1095668M	1684763M	Net Sales ($)	11339765M	13241801M
16962M	221396M	1461615M	2415301M	766041M	1352879M	Total Assets ($)	6720118M	6989197M

    M = $ thousand   MM = $ million
See Pages 11 through 18 for Explanation of Ratios and Data

Comparative Historical Data   Current Data Sorted By Sales

			Type of Statement	0-1MM	1-3MM	3-5MM	5-10MM	10-25MM	25MM & OVER
103	99	109	Unqualified	1	3	5	11	41	48
200	182	207	Reviewed		37	24	72	58	16
186	182	144	Compiled	8	55	35	33	9	4
41	39	56	Tax Returns	18	25	5	4	3	1
203	252	180	Other	11	41	23	31	39	35
4/1/00-3/31/01 ALL	4/1/01-3/31/02 ALL	4/1/02-3/31/03 ALL		180 (4/1-9/30/02)			516 (10/1/02-3/31/03)		
733	754	696	NUMBER OF STATEMENTS	38	161	92	151	150	104
%	%	%	ASSETS	%	%	%	%	%	%
7.0	6.8	7.4	Cash & Equivalents	11.7	8.8	8.1	8.0	5.5	5.3
29.0	27.5	27.8	Trade Receivables (net)	27.1	27.1	28.2	28.8	28.9	25.6
9.7	9.4	9.8	Inventory	8.9	8.3	8.6	9.6	11.5	11.3
1.3	1.8	1.7	All Other Current	1.1	1.4	2.2	1.1	2.3	2.1
47.0	45.6	46.8	Total Current	48.8	45.6	47.2	47.5	48.2	44.2
43.4	44.6	44.6	Fixed Assets (net)	39.8	43.7	45.8	45.1	44.5	46.1
3.3	3.5	3.2	Intangibles (net)	5.7	4.2	1.9	2.0	1.9	5.5
6.3	6.3	5.5	All Other Non-Current	5.8	6.5	5.2	5.4	5.4	4.1
100.0	100.0	100.0	Total	100.0	100.0	100.0	100.0	100.0	100.0
			LIABILITIES						
8.3	8.8	7.7	Notes Payable-Short Term	9.9	6.8	7.4	7.8	8.9	6.8
7.4	7.7	8.2	Cur. Mat.-L/T/D	6.1	9.9	7.9	8.9	7.4	6.9
14.2	13.5	13.7	Trade Payables	20.7	14.2	14.6	12.0	13.4	12.8
.2	.2	.2	Income Taxes Payable	.0	.2	.2	.2	.1	.3
7.6	7.7	8.4	All Other Current	9.4	8.6	8.6	7.9	8.4	8.5
37.8	37.8	38.3	Total Current	46.1	39.7	38.7	36.7	38.2	35.2
29.5	32.8	30.8	Long Term Debt	41.4	36.7	34.3	27.6	25.8	26.7
.8	.8	.7	Deferred Taxes	.1	.4	.5	.8	.9	1.3
3.1	4.5	4.3	All Other Non-Current	8.1	7.1	2.9	3.7	2.1	3.9
28.9	24.1	25.8	Net Worth	4.4	16.0	23.6	31.2	32.9	32.9
100.0	100.0	100.0	Total Liabilities & Net Worth	100.0	100.0	100.0	100.0	100.0	100.0
			INCOME DATA						
100.0	100.0	100.0	Net Sales	100.0	100.0	100.0	100.0	100.0	100.0
33.6	33.9	34.6	Gross Profit	46.6	44.0	34.6	34.9	28.4	23.9
29.7	31.3	32.0	Operating Expenses	46.1	42.0	33.5	31.8	25.7	19.7
3.9	2.7	2.5	Operating Profit	.5	2.1	1.2	3.0	2.7	4.2
1.7	1.9	1.8	All Other Expenses (net)	1.5	2.2	1.9	1.8	1.3	1.6
2.2	.8	.8	Profit Before Taxes	-1.0	-.2	-.7	1.2	1.4	2.6
			RATIOS						
1.9	1.9	2.0		3.4	1.9	1.8	2.1	1.7	1.9
1.3	1.3	1.3	Current	1.7	1.2	1.2	1.3	1.2	1.3
.9	.9	.9		.7	.8	1.0	1.0	.9	.9
1.5	1.4	1.5		3.0	1.7	1.3	1.7	1.3	1.3
1.0	.9	.9	Quick	1.3	1.0	1.0	1.0	.9	.8
.7	.6	.6		.6	.6	.7	.7	.6	.6
38 9.6	36 10.2	37 9.9		12 30.3	30 12.0	36 10.1	41 8.9	42 8.7	39 9.4
49 7.4	47 7.8	47 7.7	Sales/Receivables	40 9.2	42 8.7	46 7.9	51 7.1	50 7.3	48 7.5
60 6.1	57 6.4	59 6.2		47 7.8	53 6.9	56 6.5	60 6.0	59 6.2	60 6.1
12 31.2	11 32.9	11 32.4		0 UND	7 51.2	7 53.3	12 29.6	14 25.8	17 20.9
21 17.8	21 17.6	21 17.5	Cost of Sales/Inventory	13 27.7	16 23.0	18 20.3	19 19.0	25 14.6	24 14.9
33 11.0	32 11.3	34 10.7		35 10.4	34 10.7	27 13.3	33 11.1	35 10.3	40 9.1
20 18.2	19 19.4	18 20.1		14 25.9	17 21.4	18 19.9	18 20.4	20 18.0	19 19.6
31 11.9	30 12.0	31 11.9	Cost of Sales/Payables	30 12.1	34 10.7	34 10.8	28 13.1	31 11.8	28 13.1
47 7.8	47 7.7	47 7.7		65 5.6	53 6.9	50 7.3	49 7.4	43 8.6	40 9.2
9.2	9.9	8.5		7.6	8.9	10.1	7.1	10.2	8.4
22.2	21.7	24.5	Sales/Working Capital	25.1	31.9	26.1	18.0	24.8	22.1
-60.1	-51.8	-64.6		-35.2	-36.6	NM	-263.2	-89.9	-68.9
4.2	3.4	3.7		2.7	3.3	2.1	3.6	4.2	6.3
(699) 1.8	(721) 1.5	(665) 1.6	EBIT/Interest	(32) .9	(151) 1.3	(88) 1.2	(148) 1.7	(147) 1.9	(99) 2.2
.7	.1	.3		-3.2	-.5	.1	.7	.4	1.1
2.5	2.4	2.6			3.0	1.9	2.4	2.7	2.7
(239) 1.5	(244) 1.3	(233) 1.6	Net Profit + Depr., Dep., Amort./Cur. Mat. L/T/D		(34) 1.6	(29) 1.1	(67) 1.6	(63) 1.7	(38) 1.5
.8	.7	.9			1.0	.1	.9	.8	1.0
.9	.9	.9		.6	1.0	1.0	.9	.9	.8
1.8	1.8	1.9	Fixed/Worth	3.9	2.8	2.4	1.5	1.7	1.8
4.1	5.0	4.7		-.6	-5.8	6.6	3.2	3.0	3.4
1.3	1.2	1.3		.7	1.4	1.4	1.3	1.3	1.0
2.7	2.7	2.8	Debt/Worth	7.5	4.3	3.8	2.2	2.4	2.6
7.8	8.5	8.4		-3.2	-12.7	13.6	4.9	4.6	6.0
35.8	26.1	25.6		28.4	27.3	23.4	22.8	26.6	30.2
(636) 13.6	(630) 9.1	(583) 7.8	% Profit Before Taxes/Tangible Net Worth	(21) 3.2	(113) 6.9	(77) 2.3	(136) 7.5	(146) 8.0	(90) 14.1
1.2	-7.6	-6.9		-12.8	-13.0	-15.4	-1.1	-9.3	.1
10.3	8.2	7.5		7.9	8.2	6.0	7.3	7.1	9.2
3.5	2.2	2.1	% Profit Before Taxes/Total Assets	-1.0	1.1	.6	2.2	2.4	4.1
-1.0	-3.4	-2.7		-15.7	-6.4	-5.1	-1.1	-2.4	.2
8.3	8.3	7.9		15.5	11.0	8.0	7.5	7.5	5.5
4.6	4.5	4.4	Sales/Net Fixed Assets	8.6	5.2	4.9	4.1	4.2	3.8
3.1	2.8	3.0		3.6	3.1	2.8	2.9	2.8	3.1
2.6	2.7	2.6		4.3	3.1	2.8	2.4	2.5	2.2
2.1	2.0	2.0	Sales/Total Assets	3.3	2.2	2.1	1.9	1.9	1.9
1.6	1.5	1.5		1.9	1.5	1.5	1.5	1.5	1.5
2.8	2.9	3.5		1.9	3.5	3.1	3.5	3.3	3.7
(676) 4.3	(709) 4.5	(661) 5.1	% Depr., Dep., Amort./Sales	(32) 4.4	(155) 5.7	(87) 5.0	(144) 5.4	(147) 4.7	(96) 4.7
6.1	6.5	7.0		6.3	9.0	6.7	7.4	6.3	5.8
2.5	2.8	2.8		4.6	4.4	2.6	2.5	2.0	.6
(330) 4.2	(350) 4.7	(334) 4.7	% Officers', Directors', Owners' Comp/Sales	(26) 7.2	(91) 6.6	(53) 4.7	(85) 4.0	(65) 3.1	(14) 3.1
7.4	8.7	7.6		11.9	9.2	7.5	5.9	6.0	5.4
10180949M	11004918M	10468077M	Net Sales ($)	23907M	319158M	363881M	1065692M	2317786M	6377653M
5750166M	6543164M	6234194M	Total Assets ($)	8675M	166169M	189639M	608274M	1266429M	3995008M

© RMA 2003   M = $ thousand   MM = $ million
See Pages 11 through 18 for Explanation of Ratios and Data

Current Data Sorted By Assets   **Comparative Historical Data**

0-500M	500M-2MM	2-10MM	10-50MM	50-100MM	100-250MM	Type of Statement	4/1/98-3/31/99 ALL	4/1/99-3/31/00 ALL
		4	2			Unqualified		
	5	3	4			Reviewed		
1	3	3				Compiled		
1	2					Tax Returns		
2	4	3	1			Other		
	12 (4/1-9/30/02)			26 (10/1/02-3/31/03)				
4	14	13	7			**NUMBER OF STATEMENTS**		
%	%	%	%	%	%	**ASSETS**	%	%
	5.4	13.5				Cash & Equivalents		
	31.2	22.9	D	D		Trade Receivables (net)	D	D
	11.4	11.1	A	A		Inventory	A	A
	.1	1.2	T	T		All Other Current	T	T
	48.0	48.7	A	A		Total Current	A	A
	43.6	40.9				Fixed Assets (net)		
	2.7	6.9	N	N		Intangibles (net)	N	N
	5.7	3.5	O	O		All Other Non-Current	O	O
	100.0	100.0	T	T		Total	T	T
						LIABILITIES		
	14.6	6.1	A	A		Notes Payable-Short Term	A	A
	5.2	8.1	V	V		Cur. Mat.-L/T/D	V	V
	16.1	10.1	A	A		Trade Payables	A	A
	.3	.4	I	I		Income Taxes Payable	I	I
	6.3	10.0	L	L		All Other Current	L	L
	42.6	34.7	A	A		Total Current	A	A
	27.8	24.6	B	B		Long Term Debt	B	B
	.1	.7	L	L		Deferred Taxes	L	L
	6.2	2.5	E	E		All Other Non-Current	E	E
	23.4	37.6				Net Worth		
	100.0	100.0				Total Liabilities & Net Worth		
						INCOME DATA		
	100.0	100.0				Net Sales		
	45.1	36.0				Gross Profit		
	40.2	31.6				Operating Expenses		
	4.9	4.4				Operating Profit		
	3.2	1.6				All Other Expenses (net)		
	1.7	2.8				Profit Before Taxes		
						RATIOS		
	1.6	2.4						
	1.0	1.8				Current		
	.7	.9						
	1.2	1.6						
	.8	1.2				Quick		
	.5	.6						
36	10.1	27 13.4						
42	8.6	45 8.1				Sales/Receivables		
53	6.9	55 6.6						
6	57.9	27 13.4						
25	14.5	33 11.1				Cost of Sales/Inventory		
52	7.0	44 8.2						
28	13.1	14 25.3						
31	11.7	31 11.7				Cost of Sales/Payables		
59	6.2	37 9.8						
	11.4	7.4						
	260.5	9.9				Sales/Working Capital		
	−22.5	−25.4						
	9.4	11.0						
(13)	2.5	(12) 1.3				EBIT/Interest		
	−.3	−.6						
						Net Profit + Depr., Dep., Amort./Cur. Mat. L /T/D		
	1.0	.8						
	1.6	1.4				Fixed/Worth		
	−4.6	5.0						
	1.0	.9						
	2.8	2.1				Debt/Worth		
	−17.6	7.9						
	58.5	62.7						
(10)	13.4	(11) 22.0				% Profit Before Taxes/Tangible Net Worth		
	−4.0	−1.1						
	13.5	19.0						
	3.3	2.1				% Profit Before Taxes/Total Assets		
	−3.0	−4.5						
	11.4	9.0						
	5.4	3.9				Sales/Net Fixed Assets		
	3.3	2.9						
	3.3	2.4						
	2.2	1.7				Sales/Total Assets		
	1.6	1.4						
	1.6	3.1						
	4.4	5.0				% Depr., Dep., Amort./Sales		
	6.4	7.0						
						% Officers', Directors', Owners' Comp/Sales		
2378M	39799M	117596M	208299M			Net Sales ($)		
617M	17207M	65898M	129399M			Total Assets ($)		

M = $ thousand   MM = $ million
See Pages 11 through 18 for Explanation of Ratios and Data

Comparative Historical Data | Current Data Sorted By Sales

		Type of Statement						
	6	Unqualified				2	2	2
	12	Reviewed		3	2	2	3	2
	7	Compiled	1	2	2	1	1	
	3	Tax Returns	2	1				
	10	Other	2	4	1	2	1	

4/1/00-3/31/01 ALL	4/1/01-3/31/02 ALL	4/1/02-3/31/03 ALL		12 (4/1-9/30/02)			26 (10/1/02-3/31/03)		
				0-1MM	1-3MM	3-5MM	5-10MM	10-25MM	25MM & OVER
%	%	38 %	NUMBER OF STATEMENTS	5 %	10 %	5 %	7 %	7 %	4 %
			ASSETS						
D	D	9.9	Cash & Equivalents		5.4				
A	A	28.1	Trade Receivables (net)		26.6				
T	T	11.3	Inventory		9.1				
A	A	1.2	All Other Current		.0				
		50.6	Total Current		41.0				
N	N	39.8	Fixed Assets (net)		47.2				
O	O	4.6	Intangibles (net)		5.6				
T	T	5.1	All Other Non-Current		6.2				
		100.0	Total		100.0				
A	A		**LIABILITIES**						
V	V	11.3	Notes Payable-Short Term		13.2				
A	A	6.9	Cur. Mat.-L/T/D		6.0				
I	I	14.3	Trade Payables		16.3				
L	L	.3	Income Taxes Payable		.2				
A	A	7.0	All Other Current		4.7				
B	B	39.7	Total Current		40.3				
L	L	24.9	Long Term Debt		27.7				
E	E	.6	Deferred Taxes		.0				
		4.2	All Other Non-Current		6.0				
		30.7	Net Worth		26.0				
		100.0	Total Liabilities & Net Worth		100.0				
			INCOME DATA						
		100.0	Net Sales		100.0				
		41.0	Gross Profit		46.7				
		36.3	Operating Expenses		44.8				
		4.7	Operating Profit		1.9				
		2.3	All Other Expenses (net)		1.6				
		2.4	Profit Before Taxes		.3				
			RATIOS						
		2.2			1.9				
		1.4	Current		1.0				
		.9			.7				
		1.6			1.5				
		1.0	Quick		.8				
		.6			.5				
		34 10.7			39 9.3				
		45 8.1	Sales/Receivables		47 7.8				
		53 6.8			53 6.9				
		12 30.4			8 43.0				
		30 12.1	Cost of Sales/Inventory		34 10.8				
		48 7.6			52 7.0				
		24 15.0			28 12.9				
		31 11.6	Cost of Sales/Payables		31 11.7				
		53 6.9			70 5.2				
		7.4			11.1				
		22.2	Sales/Working Capital		260.5				
		−25.7			−11.4				
		7.8			10.6				
		(36) 2.4	EBIT/Interest		2.1				
		.1			−1.2				
		14.0	Net Profit + Depr., Dep.,						
		(18) 2.0	Amort./Cur. Mat. L/T/D						
		.8							
		.7			1.0				
		1.4	Fixed/Worth		1.6				
		NM			−2.6				
		.9			.9				
		2.1	Debt/Worth		2.8				
		NM			−4.7				
		32.1	% Profit Before Taxes/Tangible						
		(29) 14.3	Net Worth						
		.7							
		12.6	% Profit Before Taxes/Total		13.7				
		4.2	Assets		2.3				
		−2.5			−10.4				
		11.4			7.6				
		4.6	Sales/Net Fixed Assets		4.8				
		3.1			2.8				
		3.0			3.1				
		1.9	Sales/Total Assets		2.1				
		1.5			1.4				
		2.3			3.0				
		(36) 4.7	% Depr., Dep., Amort./Sales		5.0				
		6.3			10.2				
		3.2	% Officers', Directors',						
		(18) 5.6	Owners' Comp/Sales						
		8.5							
		368072M	Net Sales ($)	2627M	23050M	18731M	55383M	112135M	156146M
		213121M	Total Assets ($)	1823M	13199M	9039M	28905M	69018M	91137M

© RMA 2003

M = $ thousand   MM = $ million
See Pages 11 through 18 for Explanation of Ratios and Data

Current Data Sorted By Assets   **Comparative Historical Data**

						Type of Statement	4/1/98-3/31/99 ALL	4/1/99-3/31/00 ALL
			3	8	4	Unqualified		
	9		17	5		Reviewed		
6	17		12			Compiled		
6	3		2			Tax Returns		
4	12		11	2	2	Other		
	35 (4/1-9/30/02)			88 (10/1/02-3/31/03)				
0-500M	500M-2MM	2-10MM	10-50MM	50-100MM	100-250MM	NUMBER OF STATEMENTS		
16	41	45	15	6				
%	%	%	%	%	%	**ASSETS**	%	%
6.0	8.6	4.8	8.3			Cash & Equivalents		
34.9	26.3	27.2	28.7		D	Trade Receivables (net)	D	D
10.1	9.1	9.0	11.0		A	Inventory	A	A
5.2	1.2	1.1	2.3		T	All Other Current	T	T
56.2	45.2	42.1	50.4		A	Total Current	A	A
27.7	41.4	52.3	40.7			Fixed Assets (net)		
2.2	4.1	.8	4.0		N	Intangibles (net)	N	N
13.8	9.3	4.7	4.8		O	All Other Non-Current	O	O
100.0	100.0	100.0	100.0		T	Total	T	T
					A	**LIABILITIES**	A	A
9.6	11.2	8.9	10.7		V	Notes Payable-Short Term	V	V
5.2	7.0	9.8	7.8		A	Cur. Mat.-L/T/D	A	A
31.9	13.4	13.3	13.3		I	Trade Payables	I	I
.0	.1	.2	.2		L	Income Taxes Payable	L	L
5.4	7.0	7.0	7.0		A	All Other Current	A	A
52.1	38.8	39.2	39.0		B	Total Current	B	B
42.1	27.8	35.2	21.7		L	Long Term Debt	L	L
.8	.2	1.1	1.8		E	Deferred Taxes	E	E
4.2	6.5	4.6	5.4			All Other Non-Current		
.9	26.8	20.0	32.1			Net Worth		
100.0	100.0	100.0	100.0			Total Liabilities & Net Worth		
						INCOME DATA		
100.0	100.0	100.0	100.0			Net Sales		
						Gross Profit		
97.5	99.7	95.6	95.4			Operating Expenses		
2.5	.3	4.4	4.6			Operating Profit		
.9	.9	2.6	1.7			All Other Expenses (net)		
1.5	-.6	1.7	2.9			Profit Before Taxes		
						RATIOS		
2.5	2.2	1.4	1.9					
1.3	1.3	1.1	1.2			Current		
.7	.8	.8	1.0					
1.4	1.9	1.2	1.3					
.8	1.0	.8	1.0			Quick		
.5	.6	.6	.6					
11 34.1	33 10.9	37 9.8	44 8.3					
28 13.1	40 9.1	48 7.7	63 5.8			Sales/Receivables		
43 8.4	48 7.6	56 6.5	68 5.4					
						Cost of Sales/Inventory		
						Cost of Sales/Payables		
16.3	8.1	18.6	7.4					
40.1	19.3	81.5	31.6			Sales/Working Capital		
-42.0	-19.1	-16.3	-107.2					
10.9	4.3	2.7	7.0					
(13) 3.1	(38) 1.4	(43) 1.1	2.7			EBIT/Interest		
.4	-.9	.3	1.4					
		1.5				Net Profit + Depr., Dep.,		
		(18) 1.1				Amort./Cur. Mat. L /T/D		
		.7						
.4	.8	1.4	.9					
1.6	1.6	3.1	1.2			Fixed/Worth		
-1.3	25.1	-41.8	11.5					
1.1	1.0	1.8	1.1					
151.9	2.2	3.8	1.5			Debt/Worth		
-4.6	46.3	-79.5	19.5					
	25.2	23.2	33.9			% Profit Before Taxes/Tangible		
	(32) 10.2	(33) 4.3	(13) 12.8			Net Worth		
	-11.8	-9.7	2.4					
21.3	7.2	7.1	10.2					
5.7	1.4	.8	2.5			% Profit Before Taxes/Total		
-9.6	-5.9	-4.5	.8			Assets		
24.4	7.8	6.0	7.0					
17.7	5.2	4.0	5.0			Sales/Net Fixed Assets		
10.5	3.1	2.3	2.7					
7.3	2.9	2.6	2.1					
4.0	2.0	1.9	1.8			Sales/Total Assets		
3.3	1.6	1.5	1.5					
.7	3.9	3.8	3.2					
(14) 2.5	(39) 5.8	(43) 4.9	4.6			% Depr., Dep., Amort./Sales		
3.7	7.4	7.9	6.0					
5.4	3.4	1.6				% Officers', Directors',		
(13) 8.8	(22) 6.7	(24) 3.2				Owners' Comp/Sales		
16.7	11.1	5.6						
19468M	118895M	403294M	553581M	640916M		Net Sales ($)		
4188M	51483M	212547M	310509M	389549M		Total Assets ($)		

M = $ thousand   MM = $ million
See Pages 11 through 18 for Explanation of Ratios and Data

Comparative Historical Data | Current Data Sorted By Sales

4/1/00-3/31/01 ALL	4/1/01-3/31/02 ALL	4/1/02-3/31/03 ALL	Type of Statement	0-1MM	1-3MM	3-5MM	5-10MM	10-25MM	25MM & OVER
		15	Unqualified					4	11
		31	Reviewed		7	4	9	9	2
		35	Compiled	5	12	9	5	4	
		11	Tax Returns	3	6	1		1	
		31	Other	2	10	3	8	4	4
					35 (4/1-9/30/02)		88 (10/1/02-3/31/03)		
%	%	% 123	**NUMBER OF STATEMENTS** 10 / 35 / 17 / 22 / 22 / 17	%	%	%	%	%	%
		6.9	Cash & Equivalents	8.7	8.3	4.9	4.6	8.1	6.1
		28.0	Trade Receivables (net)	21.2	25.7	26.8	35.5	26.2	30.5
		9.4	Inventory	6.0	8.4	6.9	12.9	9.6	11.1
		1.8	All Other Current	9.9	.8	.7	1.6	.8	1.6
		46.0	Total Current	45.8	43.1	39.2	54.6	44.8	49.3
		43.5	Fixed Assets (net)	38.0	42.3	50.5	39.3	51.3	37.7
		2.8	Intangibles (net)	1.2	5.2	2.1	.3	.3	6.4
		7.6	All Other Non-Current	14.9	9.4	8.1	5.8	3.7	6.6
		100.0	Total	100.0	100.0	100.0	100.0	100.0	100.0
			LIABILITIES						
		9.6	Notes Payable-Short Term	5.3	7.3	17.6	11.9	7.4	8.4
		7.8	Cur. Mat.-L/T/D	1.0	7.6	6.9	10.2	9.9	7.1
		16.1	Trade Payables	8.7	19.1	13.5	19.3	13.3	16.3
		.1	Income Taxes Payable	.2	.1	.0	.3	.2	.0
		6.8	All Other Current	2.9	6.2	5.0	12.0	5.2	7.5
		40.4	Total Current	18.1	40.4	43.1	53.6	36.0	39.4
		31.7	Long Term Debt	29.8	41.6	30.6	26.6	30.3	21.8
		.9	Deferred Taxes	1.2	.2	.1	1.5	1.0	1.7
		5.1	All Other Non-Current	.9	3.2	6.4	10.7	3.5	5.0
		22.0	Net Worth	49.9	14.6	19.8	7.6	29.2	32.1
		100.0	Total Liabilities & Net Worth	100.0	100.0	100.0	100.0	100.0	100.0
			INCOME DATA						
		100.0	Net Sales	100.0	100.0	100.0	100.0	100.0	100.0
			Gross Profit						
		97.1	Operating Expenses	92.6	97.2	99.9	99.9	95.8	94.5
		2.9	Operating Profit	7.4	2.8	.1	.1	4.2	5.5
		1.7	All Other Expenses (net)	3.2	1.3	2.1	1.0	2.0	1.6
		1.3	Profit Before Taxes	4.2	1.5	-2.0	-.9	2.2	3.9
			RATIOS						
		1.8	Current	6.8	1.9	1.5	1.5	1.7	1.7
		1.2		3.4	1.3	.9	1.1	1.2	1.2
		.8		1.2	.7	.6	.8	1.0	1.0
		1.4	Quick	4.7	1.7	1.3	1.2	1.4	1.3
		.9		1.9	1.0	.7	.7	.9	1.0
		.6		.6	.5	.5	.6	.7	.7
34		10.7	Sales/Receivables	0 UND	25 14.5	36 10.1	40 9.1	35 10.5	50 7.3
45		8.1		34 10.7	37 10.0	45 8.2	47 7.8	46 8.0	62 5.9
56		6.5		55 6.7	45 8.2	61 6.0	55 6.6	54 6.8	67 5.4
			Cost of Sales/Inventory						
			Cost of Sales/Payables						
		10.8	Sales/Working Capital	4.1	11.0	25.8	14.8	12.1	8.2
		37.8		10.5	37.8	-36.7	66.5	29.4	31.6
		-23.8		34.4	-17.5	-13.3	-16.4	205.4	NM
		4.1	EBIT/Interest		(33) 5.7	(16) 3.4	(21) 2.0	5.0	(16) 4.9
	(114)	1.5			1.9	.6	.5	1.7	2.7
		.4			.3	-.9	-3.4	1.1	1.3
		2.2	Net Profit + Depr., Dep.,				(10) 1.6	(10) 2.1	
	(42)	1.5	Amort./Cur. Mat. L/T/D				1.2	1.3	
		.8					.4	.6	
		.9	Fixed/Worth	.3	1.0	1.1	.7	.9	.7
		1.7		.7	1.7	2.7	3.6	1.8	1.2
		208.0		2.4	-7.2	-23.9	-4.1	3.2	7.8
		1.4	Debt/Worth	.4	1.8	1.6	1.7	1.5	1.4
		3.1		.6	3.1	3.7	7.4	2.7	1.7
		-98.4		4.3	-12.1	-34.6	-9.6	7.7	29.9
		29.1	% Profit Before Taxes/Tangible		(24) 46.4	(10) 18.9	(14) 19.3	(21) 45.7	(14) 27.0
	(92)	11.3	Net Worth		18.3	-3.1	-8.2	13.2	15.2
		-3.3			-2.5	-21.6	-34.3	2.2	4.2
		9.0	% Profit Before Taxes/Total	18.7	10.1	4.6	5.1	10.4	10.5
		1.9	Assets	7.4	2.9	-1.6	-1.6	1.7	5.2
		-3.1		3.0	-6.4	-8.3	-6.0	.3	1.0
		8.2	Sales/Net Fixed Assets	18.3	10.8	7.4	15.6	4.9	7.1
		4.8		8.6	5.3	3.9	5.9	4.0	5.4
		2.8		2.2	3.2	2.2	3.8	2.6	2.9
		2.9	Sales/Total Assets	4.0	3.9	2.7	3.4	2.4	2.2
		2.1		1.8	2.2	1.9	2.7	2.0	1.8
		1.5		1.0	1.6	1.5	1.6	1.6	1.2
		2.9	% Depr., Dep., Amort./Sales		(34) 3.3	(16) 4.0	(21) 2.3	(20) 3.5	(16) 3.6
	(116)	4.7			5.8	4.8	4.5	5.0	4.6
		6.9			8.6	7.8	5.4	6.2	5.5
		2.7	% Officers', Directors',		(21) 4.2	(10) 3.1	(13) 2.1		
	(63)	5.2	Owners' Comp/Sales		7.2	6.0	3.0		
		8.8			13.4	8.4	4.8		
1736154M			Net Sales ($)	5312M	69532M	62138M	147375M	330772M	1121025M
968276M			Total Assets ($)	6173M	43118M	33808M	63044M	178558M	643575M

(Left two historical columns 4/1/00-3/31/01 ALL and 4/1/01-3/31/02 ALL: DATA NOT AVAILABLE)

M = $ thousand   MM = $ million
See Pages 11 through 18 for Explanation of Ratios and Data

Current Data Sorted By Assets   Comparative Historical Data

						Type of Statement		
		3	4			Unqualified	12	9
	5	6	3			Reviewed	15	18
1	3	2				Compiled	14	12
2						Tax Returns	7	2
1	4	11	4	2	1	Other	24	17
	12 (4/1-9/30/02)		40 (10/1/02-3/31/03)				4/1/98-3/31/99	4/1/99-3/31/00
0-500M	500M-2MM	2-10MM	10-50MM	50-100MM	100-250MM		ALL	ALL
4	12	22	11	2	1	NUMBER OF STATEMENTS	72	58
%	%	%	%	%	%	ASSETS	%	%
	8.4	5.0	10.0			Cash & Equivalents	8.1	5.4
	38.7	33.5	23.9			Trade Receivables (net)	30.3	31.3
	18.5	17.5	13.6			Inventory	15.4	15.4
	.9	4.0	2.7			All Other Current	2.4	2.5
	66.5	59.9	50.2			Total Current	56.3	54.6
	24.9	30.3	37.1			Fixed Assets (net)	33.8	36.0
	3.5	4.3	9.2			Intangibles (net)	4.0	3.3
	5.1	5.4	3.5			All Other Non-Current	5.8	6.2
	100.0	100.0	100.0			Total	100.0	100.0
						LIABILITIES		
	9.5	9.5	9.4			Notes Payable-Short Term	5.5	9.7
	2.5	5.0	5.0			Cur. Mat.-L/T/D	5.6	6.1
	21.2	19.4	12.6			Trade Payables	15.2	14.9
	1.6	.1	.0			Income Taxes Payable	.3	.7
	11.6	8.3	9.8			All Other Current	8.1	9.2
	46.4	42.4	37.0			Total Current	34.8	40.6
	5.3	24.1	10.2			Long Term Debt	23.3	19.4
	.3	.9	1.7			Deferred Taxes	.6	1.0
	.6	2.2	2.2			All Other Non-Current	3.1	4.6
	47.4	30.4	48.8			Net Worth	38.3	34.4
	100.0	100.0	100.0			Total Liabilities & Net Worth	100.0	100.0
						INCOME DATA		
	100.0	100.0	100.0			Net Sales	100.0	100.0
	38.8	25.9	31.9			Gross Profit	31.1	31.5
	35.3	24.2	26.5			Operating Expenses	26.1	26.9
	3.5	1.7	5.4			Operating Profit	5.0	4.6
	.1	1.4	.7			All Other Expenses (net)	1.1	−.2
	3.5	.3	4.7			Profit Before Taxes	3.8	4.8
						RATIOS		
	2.5	2.2	2.3				2.7	1.9
	1.6	1.6	1.4			Current	1.5	1.3
	1.2	1.1	.8				1.1	.9
	1.9	1.4	1.7				1.7	1.4
	1.2	1.0	.8			Quick	.9	.9
	.7	.6	.5				.7	.6
31 11.7	35 10.4	34 10.9				Sales/Receivables	31 11.9	33 10.9
34 10.6	41 8.9	42 8.6					40 9.2	44 8.4
40 9.1	56 6.5	46 7.9					52 7.1	60 6.1
19 18.7	19 19.6	21 17.7				Cost of Sales/Inventory	19 19.0	17 21.5
24 15.1	28 13.2	25 14.6					27 13.4	28 13.0
38 9.5	47 7.7	57 6.4					47 7.7	46 7.9
15 24.0	22 16.7	22 16.7				Cost of Sales/Payables	17 20.9	19 19.2
28 12.9	31 11.6	32 11.4					28 13.1	26 14.0
53 6.8	50 7.3	44 8.3					37 9.9	40 9.1
	10.1	8.7	5.8			Sales/Working Capital	7.3	8.9
	15.9	13.8	16.3				15.9	21.6
	53.5	77.1	−22.6				63.7	−89.9
	36.9	4.4	20.3			EBIT/Interest	7.8	13.3
(10) 6.0	(18) 2.0	3.9				(65) 2.8	(54) 3.6
	−3.9	.5	−5.1				.9	1.3
						Net Profit + Depr., Dep., Amort./Cur. Mat. L /T/D	6.0	7.4
							(23) 2.1	(24) 2.8
							1.6	1.1
	.2	.3	.5			Fixed/Worth	.5	.6
	.5	1.0	1.0				.9	1.2
	1.0	30.6	1.8				2.2	2.1
	.6	.9	.7			Debt/Worth	.7	1.2
	1.0	1.4	1.4				1.6	1.9
	2.3	45.6	2.7				4.7	4.8
	97.6	28.5	61.5			% Profit Before Taxes/Tangible Net Worth	41.0	50.4
(11) 25.8	(18) 9.0	25.6				(65) 19.8	(51) 23.5
	−7.3	−3.2	−6.4				1.8	4.9
	32.3	8.7	19.3			% Profit Before Taxes/Total Assets	16.1	13.5
	12.9	2.7	4.7				7.2	6.9
	−3.8	−2.8	−3.7				−.1	1.1
	55.4	25.1	8.3			Sales/Net Fixed Assets	13.8	12.0
	22.2	8.7	5.8				8.3	7.2
	7.9	4.6	4.0				5.1	4.9
	5.3	3.6	2.2			Sales/Total Assets	3.5	3.0
	3.4	2.7	2.1				2.6	2.5
	2.9	2.2	1.8				1.9	2.0
	1.1	1.3	2.3			% Depr., Dep., Amort./Sales	1.5	1.6
(10) 1.7	(21) 2.9	3.5				(63) 2.8	(54) 2.6
	3.5	4.0	6.2				3.8	3.8
						% Officers', Directors', Owners' Comp/Sales	3.1	2.9
							(22) 4.0	(18) 4.3
							8.3	7.6
4854M	66054M	264812M	488741M	281260M	160829M	Net Sales ($)	1761015M	1245800M
898M	15323M	99136M	243105M	145074M	138457M	Total Assets ($)	906354M	670070M

M = $ thousand   MM = $ million
See Pages 11 through 18 for Explanation of Ratios and Data

Comparative Historical Data | Current Data Sorted By Sales

Type of Statement

Type of Statement	4/1/00-3/31/01 ALL	4/1/01-3/31/02 ALL	4/1/02-3/31/03 ALL	0-1MM	1-3MM	3-5MM	5-10MM	10-25MM	25MM & OVER
Unqualified	8	8	7				1	2	4
Reviewed	8	16	14		1		6	2	3
Compiled	10	6	6		1	2		1	
Tax Returns	3	2	2	1	1	3			
Other	16	21	23	1	2	2	4	7	8
NUMBER OF STATEMENTS	45	53	52	2	5	7	11	12	15

Periods: 12 (4/1-9/30/02), 40 (10/1/02-3/31/03)

ASSETS (%)

	(45)	(53)	(52)	Item	0-1MM	1-3MM	3-5MM	5-10MM	10-25MM	25MM & OVER
	5.1	7.3	7.5	Cash & Equivalents				9.3	3.7	8.0
	33.7	34.2	34.4	Trade Receivables (net)				35.6	39.4	24.9
	16.6	16.0	16.9	Inventory				16.0	20.6	17.8
	1.5	1.4	2.6	All Other Current				2.4	4.1	2.5
	56.9	58.9	61.4	Total Current				63.4	67.7	53.2
	33.5	30.5	28.2	Fixed Assets (net)				27.9	25.8	31.8
	5.4	5.5	6.0	Intangibles (net)				1.5	2.6	11.5
	4.1	5.1	4.5	All Other Non-Current				7.3	3.9	3.5
	100.0	100.0	100.0	Total				100.0	100.0	100.0

LIABILITIES

				Item				5-10MM	10-25MM	25MM & OVER
	9.2	12.5	9.4	Notes Payable-Short Term				5.2	10.9	10.8
	5.7	5.4	4.6	Cur. Mat.-L/T/D				2.9	5.6	4.8
	15.8	17.6	18.7	Trade Payables				17.0	23.1	13.0
	.4	.4	.4	Income Taxes Payable				1.2	.1	.0
	9.2	12.5	9.6	All Other Current				13.5	8.7	10.2
	40.4	48.3	42.7	Total Current				39.7	48.4	38.8
	17.9	17.5	15.1	Long Term Debt				16.3	14.8	10.7
	.9	.7	.8	Deferred Taxes				1.0	.8	1.4
	4.5	3.6	1.9	All Other Non-Current				.4	2.6	2.8
	36.4	29.8	39.4	Net Worth				42.5	33.3	46.2
	100.0	100.0	100.0	Total Liabilities & Net Worth				100.0	100.0	100.0

INCOME DATA

				Item				5-10MM	10-25MM	25MM & OVER
	100.0	100.0	100.0	Net Sales				100.0	100.0	100.0
	29.3	29.1	31.4	Gross Profit				26.7	27.9	30.9
	25.8	26.6	27.6	Operating Expenses				22.8	25.8	25.9
	3.5	2.5	3.8	Operating Profit				3.9	2.1	5.0
	1.4	.5	.8	All Other Expenses (net)				.4	.2	.8
	2.1	2.0	3.0	Profit Before Taxes				3.4	1.9	4.2

RATIOS (upper / median / lower)

				Ratio				5-10MM	10-25MM	25MM & OVER
	1.8 / 1.5 / .9	1.9 / 1.4 / .9	2.2 / 1.6 / 1.1	Current				2.2 / 1.6 / 1.3	2.2 / 1.6 / 1.0	1.9 / 1.4 / 1.0
	1.3 / .9 / .6	1.3 / 1.0 / .6	1.5 / 1.0 / .7	Quick				1.5 / 1.1	1.3 / .9 / .7	1.5 / .8 / .5
	32 11.5 / 46 8.0 / 56 6.5	33 11.1 / 39 9.3 / 51 7.1	33 11.1 / 39 9.4 / 48 7.6	Sales/Receivables				31 11.8 / 38 9.5 / 46 7.9	36 10.1 / 48 7.7 / 61 6.0	35 10.4 / 43 8.6 / 47 7.8
	21 17.3 / 27 13.3 / 49 7.5	18 19.9 / 24 14.9 / 51 7.1	19 19.4 / 25 14.3 / 46 8.0	Cost of Sales/Inventory				18 20.1 / 20 18.3 / 34 10.7	19 18.8 / 28 13.2 / 45 8.1	21 17.7 / 29 12.5 / 79 4.6
	17 20.9 / 27 13.6 / 44 8.2	16 22.8 / 26 14.0 / 43 8.4	20 18.5 / 31 11.8 / 47 7.7	Cost of Sales/Payables				14 25.7 / 26 14.0 / 37 9.9	22 16.3 / 31 11.6 / 59 6.1	22 16.7 / 32 11.4 / 45 8.2
	10.3 / 16.0 / -70.0	10.5 / 18.0 / -44.1	8.5 / 14.1 / 63.9	Sales/Working Capital				8.9 / 14.3 / 20.6	9.4 / 13.8 / 163.6	5.8 / 11.6 / -151.2
	(42) 6.3 / 2.1 / .8	(48) 5.2 / 2.6 / .3	(45) 13.6 / 2.6 / .4	EBIT/Interest					(10) 4.4 / 2.5 / .6	18.7 / 2.9 / 1.9
	(10) 5.9 / 1.2 / .3	(19) 10.1 / 2.5 / .6	(17) 4.2 / 1.4 / .9	Net Profit + Depr., Dep., Amort./Cur. Mat. L/T/D						
	.5 / 1.2 / 4.0	.3 / .8 / 2.3	.3 / .8 / 2.4	Fixed/Worth				.2 / .7 / 2.5	.3 / .7 / 14.3	.5 / 1.0 / 1.8
	1.0 / 1.9 / 9.4	.8 / 1.6 / 4.8	.7 / 1.3 / 5.2	Debt/Worth				.5 / .9 / 5.4	1.0 / 1.4 / 24.6	.8 / 1.4 / 3.4
	(41) 32.6 / 17.2 / 3.9	(46) 45.2 / 16.7 / 2.4	(46) 40.1 / 17.8 / -2.1	% Profit Before Taxes/Tangible Net Worth				31.9 / (10) 21.5 / 3.1	47.9 / (10) 23.3 / 2.7	61.5 / 25.6 / 6.9
	12.2 / 5.4 / -.1	11.3 / 5.3 / -2.5	18.9 / 4.2 / -2.4	% Profit Before Taxes/Total Assets				20.4 / 7.5 / .5	15.3 / 3.9 / -.6	17.6 / 4.2 / 3.1
	14.3 / 7.3 / 4.2	22.4 / 8.9 / 4.5	24.5 / 8.7 / 4.9	Sales/Net Fixed Assets				39.8 / 12.6 / 7.5	55.5 / 17.1 / 5.4	8.7 / 5.9 / 4.7
	3.4 / 2.6 / 1.8	3.4 / 2.8 / 2.0	3.6 / 2.6 / 2.0	Sales/Total Assets				3.7 / 3.3 / 2.2	3.7 / 3.0 / 2.3	2.2 / 2.0 / 1.8
	(41) 1.0 / 2.7 / 4.1	(48) .9 / 2.6 / 4.4	(47) 1.4 / 2.8 / 3.9	% Depr., Dep., Amort./Sales					.7 / 2.4 / 3.2	2.2 / 2.8 / 4.3
	(10) 1.8 / 4.2 / 6.6	(18) 1.6 / 5.2 / 8.1	(16) 2.8 / 5.1 / 8.0	% Officers', Directors', Owners' Comp/Sales						
	964415M	1019125M	1266550M	Net Sales ($)	1420M	11100M	26988M	87960M	180784M	958298M
	463968M	428057M	641993M	Total Assets ($)	145M	3419M	12334M	30300M	60777M	535018M

M = $ thousand　　MM = $ million
See Pages 11 through 18 for Explanation of Ratios and Data

Current Data Sorted By Assets   Comparative Historical Data

0-500M	500M-2MM	2-10MM	10-50MM	50-100MM	100-250MM	Type of Statement	4/1/98-3/31/99 ALL	4/1/99-3/31/00 ALL
		1	6		1	Unqualified	8	8
		3	4			Reviewed	5	6
	1	1				Compiled	3	4
	1	2	3			Tax Returns	2	1
						Other	3	9
		4 (4/1-9/30/02)	20 (10/1/02-3/31/03)					
	2	7	13	1	1	**NUMBER OF STATEMENTS**	21	28
%	%	%	%	%	%	**ASSETS**	%	%
D			4.0			Cash & Equivalents	4.3	5.4
A			28.5			Trade Receivables (net)	28.3	29.6
T			8.5			Inventory	12.1	15.3
A			1.5			All Other Current	1.4	.5
			42.4			Total Current	46.1	50.8
N			48.5			Fixed Assets (net)	47.5	40.8
O			.9			Intangibles (net)	.4	2.1
T			8.1			All Other Non-Current	6.1	6.3
			100.0			Total	100.0	100.0
A						**LIABILITIES**		
V			3.7			Notes Payable-Short Term	6.6	9.8
A			3.7			Cur. Mat.-L/T/D	17.2	5.2
I			8.8			Trade Payables	11.5	16.5
L			.0			Income Taxes Payable	.5	.1
A			6.5			All Other Current	5.5	6.3
B			22.6			Total Current	41.3	37.8
L			25.5			Long Term Debt	53.3	27.6
E			.4			Deferred Taxes	1.2	1.8
			4.6			All Other Non-Current	10.2	3.3
			46.9			Net Worth	−6.1	29.6
			100.0			Total Liabilities & Net Worth	100.0	100.0
						INCOME DATA		
			100.0			Net Sales	100.0	100.0
			22.1			Gross Profit	30.3	29.2
			17.9			Operating Expenses	24.6	26.1
			4.2			Operating Profit	5.6	3.1
			1.0			All Other Expenses (net)	1.8	1.0
			3.1			Profit Before Taxes	3.9	2.2
						RATIOS		
			3.2				1.9	2.1
			2.1			Current	1.4	1.3
			1.1				1.1	1.1
			2.3				1.3	1.7
			1.5			Quick	1.0	1.1
			.8				.8	.5
			58 6.3				43 8.4	39 9.3
			64 5.7			Sales/Receivables	55 6.7	49 7.4
			72 5.1				64 5.7	67 5.5
			20 17.8				15 24.0	19 19.7
			23 16.2			Cost of Sales/Inventory	23 16.1	29 12.7
			31 11.8				34 10.7	45 8.2
			17 20.9				19 19.1	22 16.8
			20 18.1			Cost of Sales/Payables	24 15.0	31 11.6
			26 13.9				38 9.6	49 7.5
			4.9				7.4	5.4
			7.2			Sales/Working Capital	18.7	17.3
			NM				105.1	88.4
			9.2				(20) 5.3	(27) 6.2
			2.3			EBIT/Interest	2.9	3.6
			.8				1.2	1.5
						Net Profit + Depr., Dep., Amort./Cur. Mat. L /T/D		
			.7				.8	.9
			1.0			Fixed/Worth	1.7	1.4
			1.2				4.6	6.6
			.6				1.4	1.1
			.9			Debt/Worth	1.8	2.1
			1.6				10.2	12.7
			25.7				(18) 50.7	(23) 36.0
		(12)	7.6			% Profit Before Taxes/Tangible Net Worth	20.1	17.6
			1.5				7.0	6.6
			12.4				11.7	15.6
			2.8			% Profit Before Taxes/Total Assets	6.3	5.6
			−1.2				3.1	2.1
			5.4				7.8	7.5
			3.3			Sales/Net Fixed Assets	5.7	4.4
			2.5				3.1	3.3
			2.1				2.4	2.3
			1.7			Sales/Total Assets	2.0	1.8
			1.3				1.7	1.6
			3.6				(20) 3.0	(24) 3.0
		(12)	4.8			% Depr., Dep., Amort./Sales	4.2	4.3
			5.5				5.6	5.3
								1.3
						% Officers', Directors', Owners' Comp/Sales	(10)	3.6
								9.1
	2322M	73111M	515113M	95107M	202184M	Net Sales ($)	469080M	735264M
	2296M	46414M	306243M	93555M	131658M	Total Assets ($)	257467M	413291M

Comparative Historical Data | | Current Data Sorted By Sales

	4/1/00-3/31/01 ALL	4/1/01-3/31/02 ALL	4/1/02-3/31/03 ALL	Type of Statement	0-1MM	1-3MM	3-5MM	5-10MM	10-25MM	25MM & OVER
	11	7	8	Unqualified		1			1	6
	4	5	7	Reviewed		1			3	3
	5	4	2	Compiled			1		1	
				Tax Returns						
				Other	1		1		4	1
	4 (4/1/00-3/31/01)	7 (4/1/01-3/31/02)	7 (4/1/02-3/31/03)			4 (4/1-9/30/02)			20 (10/1/02-3/31/03)	
	ALL	ALL	ALL							
NUMBER OF STATEMENTS	24	23	24		1	2	2		9	10
	%	%	%	**ASSETS**	%	%	%		%	%
	5.0	6.1	3.4	Cash & Equivalents				D		5.5
	30.4	30.5	27.8	Trade Receivables (net)				A		30.3
	12.0	12.9	13.5	Inventory				T		11.6
	1.7	1.8	4.0	All Other Current				A		3.5
	49.0	51.2	48.8	Total Current						50.9
	38.2	36.5	40.0	Fixed Assets (net)				N		39.0
	5.8	4.7	3.1	Intangibles (net)				O		3.9
	7.1	7.6	8.2	All Other Non-Current				T		6.2
	100.0	100.0	100.0	Total						100.0
				LIABILITIES				A		
	4.6	9.8	9.4	Notes Payable-Short Term				V		.5
	2.8	4.9	3.4	Cur. Mat.-L/T/D				A		2.8
	16.0	14.6	11.0	Trade Payables				I		9.6
	.4	1.6	.2	Income Taxes Payable				L		.5
	8.4	9.7	8.2	All Other Current				A		7.7
	32.2	40.6	32.3	Total Current				B		21.1
	29.0	24.4	20.9	Long Term Debt				L		19.3
	1.9	3.1	1.3	Deferred Taxes				E		.8
	2.0	1.6	4.8	All Other Non-Current						6.2
	34.8	30.4	40.7	Net Worth						52.6
	100.0	100.0	100.0	Total Liabilities & Net Worth						100.0
				INCOME DATA						
	100.0	100.0	100.0	Net Sales						100.0
	25.6	29.7	28.7	Gross Profit						26.9
	21.0	23.9	25.3	Operating Expenses						21.7
	4.6	5.9	3.4	Operating Profit						5.3
	1.1	1.1	1.3	All Other Expenses (net)						.3
	3.5	4.8	2.1	Profit Before Taxes						5.0
				RATIOS						
	2.1	2.1	2.6							3.5
	1.6	1.3	1.6	Current						2.6
	1.1	1.0	1.0							2.0
	1.5	1.5	1.9							2.7
	1.0	1.0	1.0	Quick						1.8
	.8	.6	.6							1.3
	39 9.4	45 8.1	56 6.5							58 6.3
	53 6.9	58 6.3	60 6.1	Sales/Receivables						66 5.5
	68 5.4	63 5.8	76 4.8							73 5.0
	16 23.5	17 21.4	21 17.6							22 16.4
	23 16.1	25 14.8	30 12.2	Cost of Sales/Inventory						28 12.8
	37 9.8	54 6.8	52 7.0							46 8.0
	27 13.3	23 16.0	18 20.0							18 20.8
	33 10.9	35 10.5	26 13.9	Cost of Sales/Payables						21 17.8
	50 7.2	53 6.9	54 6.8							29 12.5
	6.6	6.4	4.7							3.9
	16.7	12.8	10.1	Sales/Working Capital						6.2
	41.2	88.6	-383.9							8.9
	6.5	9.0	8.5							15.4
	(22) 2.7	3.8	2.4	EBIT/Interest						5.9
	1.9	1.6	.1							1.8
			(10) 4.3	Net Profit + Depr., Dep.,						
			3.2	Amort./Cur. Mat. L/T/D						
			1.3							
	.6	.6	.6							.6
	1.3	1.0	1.1	Fixed/Worth						.8
	4.1	2.4	1.8							1.1
	1.0	.9	.6							.5
	1.6	1.4	1.3	Debt/Worth						.8
	10.2	4.4	3.6							1.5
	40.9	31.4	24.4	% Profit Before Taxes/Tangible						30.7
	(21) 18.4	(20) 19.2	(21) 6.1	Net Worth						10.9
	10.3	5.5	.0							4.1
	10.9	11.1	8.2	% Profit Before Taxes/Total						16.5
	6.6	8.9	2.4	Assets						5.5
	3.0	2.3	-2.3							2.0
	10.1	6.4	6.7							6.6
	5.0	5.4	3.7	Sales/Net Fixed Assets						5.0
	3.4	3.4	2.5							2.8
	2.7	2.4	1.9							2.3
	1.9	1.8	1.6	Sales/Total Assets						1.7
	1.4	1.4	1.0							1.2
	2.1	2.0	3.0							
	(20) 3.8	(18) 3.9	(21) 4.5	% Depr., Dep., Amort./Sales						
	4.3	4.4	5.6							
				% Officers', Directors', Owners' Comp/Sales						
	1083854M	744058M	887837M	Net Sales ($)	888M	3142M	9384M		154830M	719593M
	788498M	460788M	580166M	Total Assets ($)	801M	3992M	11882M		100767M	462724M

M = $ thousand   MM = $ million
See Pages 11 through 18 for Explanation of Ratios and Data

Current Data Sorted By Assets   Comparative Historical Data

0-500M	500M-2MM	2-10MM	10-50MM	50-100MM	100-250MM	Type of Statement	4/1/98-3/31/99 ALL	4/1/99-3/31/00 ALL
		14	27	5	3	Unqualified	63	65
2	21	49	11			Reviewed	106	95
17	36	34			1	Compiled	125	94
19	23	7				Tax Returns	51	38
10	31	42	15	2	4	Other	126	121
83 (4/1-9/30/02)			290 (10/1/02-3/31/03)					
48	111	146	53	7	8	**NUMBER OF STATEMENTS**	471	413
%	%	%	%	%	%	**ASSETS**	%	%
11.8	8.5	7.9	7.4			Cash & Equivalents	9.0	6.9
29.3	31.8	28.2	24.7			Trade Receivables (net)	29.6	28.5
6.8	11.5	11.4	14.4			Inventory	11.6	11.0
2.5	1.5	1.9	2.1			All Other Current	1.4	1.4
50.4	53.3	49.5	48.6			Total Current	51.6	47.8
36.6	37.9	42.1	42.8			Fixed Assets (net)	38.8	41.3
3.4	2.2	3.5	2.9			Intangibles (net)	3.8	4.3
9.6	6.7	4.9	5.8			All Other Non-Current	5.8	6.7
100.0	100.0	100.0	100.0			Total	100.0	100.0
						LIABILITIES		
5.3	8.5	9.3	7.1			Notes Payable-Short Term	8.5	8.3
8.7	7.6	7.6	6.8			Cur. Mat.-L/T/D	7.2	6.4
21.9	16.2	16.0	11.8			Trade Payables	14.3	13.6
.3	.4	.2	.2			Income Taxes Payable	.4	.3
7.3	7.7	9.7	8.5			All Other Current	8.9	8.4
43.6	40.4	42.8	34.5			Total Current	39.3	37.0
31.3	28.6	24.4	25.4			Long Term Debt	26.6	26.8
.0	.3	.7	1.5			Deferred Taxes	.7	.7
4.9	3.1	3.0	2.9			All Other Non-Current	4.1	4.4
20.2	27.6	29.1	35.7			Net Worth	29.3	31.1
100.0	100.0	100.0	100.0			Total Liabilities & Net Worth	100.0	100.0
						INCOME DATA		
100.0	100.0	100.0	100.0			Net Sales	100.0	100.0
46.6	40.9	34.2	27.3			Gross Profit	36.1	36.7
44.3	38.1	30.1	22.4			Operating Expenses	31.0	31.9
2.3	2.9	4.1	4.9			Operating Profit	5.1	4.8
1.1	1.5	1.5	1.6			All Other Expenses (net)	1.4	1.5
1.2	1.4	2.6	3.3			Profit Before Taxes	3.7	3.3
						RATIOS		
2.3	2.0	1.6	2.4			Current	2.2	2.1
1.3	1.3	1.2	1.3				1.4	1.3
.7	1.0	.9	.9				1.0	1.0
2.1	1.6	1.3	1.4			Quick	1.6	1.6
1.0	1.0	.9	.8				1.1	.9
.5	.7	.6	.6				.7	.7
21 17.7	34 10.6	39 9.3	39 9.4			Sales/Receivables	33 11.2	35 10.6
29 12.8	41 8.9	48 7.6	50 7.3				44 8.3	46 7.9
41 8.9	54 6.7	58 6.3	60 6.1				55 6.6	59 6.1
0 830.6	7 51.4	13 28.1	22 16.3			Cost of Sales/Inventory	11 34.2	12 29.8
5 78.9	19 19.6	25 14.8	36 10.2				23 15.9	24 15.1
24 15.4	36 10.2	42 8.7	57 6.4				38 9.6	39 9.3
15 24.8	17 21.4	23 16.1	23 16.0			Cost of Sales/Payables	18 20.0	18 20.4
36 10.2	32 11.4	37 9.9	30 12.1				28 13.1	29 12.5
59 6.2	51 7.1	54 6.7	46 8.0				45 8.1	48 7.5
13.7	8.2	9.8	6.8			Sales/Working Capital	8.1	8.2
31.2	19.4	27.5	14.4				18.0	18.3
-20.6	-90.6	-38.9	-63.9				-484.4	-77.4
(39) 4.9	(105) 4.7	(141) 5.5	(51) 5.8			EBIT/Interest	(437) 6.2	(389) 5.4
1.1	1.8	2.4	2.7				2.7	2.3
-2.4	-.4	.8	1.0				1.3	1.1
	(23) 2.7	(45) 2.3	(20) 2.3			Net Profit + Depr., Dep., Amort./Cur. Mat. L /T/D	(156) 3.8	(129) 3.4
	1.2	1.2	2.0				2.2	1.8
	.5	.4	1.2				1.2	1.1
.3	.5	.8	.6			Fixed/Worth	.6	.7
2.6	1.3	1.7	1.6				1.3	1.6
-3.6	7.2	4.2	2.7				4.2	5.0
.9	1.1	1.0	.8			Debt/Worth	1.0	1.2
3.7	2.4	2.0	2.0				2.3	2.6
-10.5	21.7	9.0	4.9				8.5	8.8
(33) 65.2	(88) 40.3	(127) 38.2	(51) 35.7			% Profit Before Taxes/Tangible Net Worth	(405) 51.4	(352) 45.1
10.5	8.9	16.3	14.6				23.9	20.3
-15.5	-10.5	2.3	4.3				9.5	2.3
25.2	12.1	10.1	8.9			% Profit Before Taxes/Total Assets	14.9	12.6
3.0	2.8	3.9	4.3				6.9	5.1
-10.3	-4.9	-.5	.2				1.5	.4
26.3	14.0	9.4	7.8			Sales/Net Fixed Assets	11.9	9.4
11.0	7.7	4.5	4.5				6.0	5.5
6.8	4.0	2.8	2.7				3.6	3.3
4.9	3.5	2.7	2.2			Sales/Total Assets	3.1	2.8
3.4	2.5	1.9	1.7				2.3	2.1
2.8	1.9	1.5	1.5				1.7	1.6
(39) 1.8	(105) 2.1	(139) 2.8	(51) 3.1			% Depr., Dep., Amort./Sales	(429) 2.3	(378) 2.4
3.9	4.5	4.4	4.7				3.6	3.8
5.7	6.9	6.8	5.6				5.6	5.7
(33) 4.4	(75) 3.5	(56) 2.0	(10) 2.7			% Officers', Directors', Owners' Comp/Sales	(220) 3.1	(175) 3.4
9.0	5.8	4.1	3.8				5.8	6.0
16.9	8.6	6.4	7.0				9.8	10.6
55279M	337054M	1414117M	1976062M	850346M	1765298M	Net Sales ($)	5662550M	7222941M
12232M	127255M	672005M	1125403M	500617M	1057673M	Total Assets ($)	3063937M	3628100M

M = $ thousand   MM = $ million
See Pages 11 through 18 for Explanation of Ratios and Data

Comparative Historical Data | Current Data Sorted By Sales

						Type of Statement													
	39		30		49	Unqualified						5		15		29			
	80		61		83	Reviewed	3		8		17	23		25		7			
	129		112		88	Compiled	12		27		25	18		5		1			
	33		39		49	Tax Returns	8		26		9	4		2					
	117		133		104	Other	8		25		12	25		18		16			
	4/1/00-3/31/01 ALL		4/1/01-3/31/02 ALL		4/1/02-3/31/03 ALL				83 (4/1-9/30/02)				290 (10/1/02-3/31/03)						
							0-1MM		1-3MM		3-5MM	5-10MM		10-25MM		25MM & OVER			
	398		375		373	NUMBER OF STATEMENTS	31		86		63	75		65		53			
	%		%		%	ASSETS	%		%		%	%		%		%			
	8.7		7.8		8.5	Cash & Equivalents	7.6		9.4		8.4	9.4		7.6		7.3			
	29.4		28.3		28.6	Trade Receivables (net)	27.0		27.0		32.2	28.0		31.5		25.3			
	12.3		11.2		11.3	Inventory	8.3		9.7		8.3	11.3		14.3		15.9			
	1.7		1.4		1.9	All Other Current	3.1		1.6		1.8	1.6		1.9		2.5			
	52.0		48.8		50.4	Total Current	46.0		47.7		50.7	50.4		55.2		51.0			
	39.8		41.5		40.1	Fixed Assets (net)	38.0		42.5		41.1	40.9		38.0		37.6			
	3.8		4.4		3.5	Intangibles (net)	4.5		3.4		2.1	3.0		2.3		6.8			
	4.5		5.3		6.0	All Other Non-Current	11.4		6.4		6.0	5.8		4.5		4.6			
	100.0		100.0		100.0	Total	100.0		100.0		100.0	100.0		100.0		100.0			
						LIABILITIES													
	8.5		8.6		7.9	Notes Payable-Short Term	6.3		7.8		6.9	9.1		9.7		6.2			
	6.3		7.4		7.7	Cur. Mat.-L/T/D	9.8		7.9		9.0	7.1		6.0		7.8			
	14.8		13.9		16.1	Trade Payables	18.8		16.8		15.0	15.4		17.4		13.7			
	.2		.2		.3	Income Taxes Payable	.4		.3		.5	.2		.3		.2			
	7.9		7.3		8.6	All Other Current	7.5		6.9		6.7	9.2		12.1		9.3			
	37.6		37.5		40.6	Total Current	42.8		39.8		38.1	41.1		45.6		37.1			
	25.3		27.5		26.7	Long Term Debt	32.2		35.5		28.2	21.1		20.2		23.4			
	.7		.5		.6	Deferred Taxes	.0		.2		.6	.8		.7		1.3			
	4.4		4.9		3.3	All Other Non-Current	2.9		3.2		2.6	4.5		3.2		2.8			
	31.9		29.6		28.8	Net Worth	22.0		21.4		30.6	32.6		30.3		35.3			
	100.0		100.0		100.0	Total Liabilities & Net Worth	100.0		100.0		100.0	100.0		100.0		100.0			
						INCOME DATA													
	100.0		100.0		100.0	Net Sales	100.0		100.0		100.0	100.0		100.0		100.0			
	35.5		36.8		36.6	Gross Profit	50.7		41.5		39.5	35.6		29.7		26.9			
	31.4		33.5		32.9	Operating Expenses	48.8		39.1		37.2	30.7		24.9		21.6			
	4.1		3.4		3.7	Operating Profit	2.0		2.4		2.3	4.9		4.9		5.2			
	1.4		2.0		1.5	All Other Expenses (net)	1.0		1.8		1.7	1.3		1.3		1.6			
	2.7		1.4		2.2	Profit Before Taxes	.9		.6		.6	3.6		3.6		3.6			
						RATIOS													
	2.3		2.1		2.0		2.3		1.9		2.2	1.8		1.7		2.3			
	1.4		1.3		1.3	Current	1.3		1.3		1.3	1.3		1.2		1.3			
	1.0		1.0		.9		.7		.8		.9	.9		1.0		1.0			
	1.8		1.6		1.5		1.9		1.6		1.7	1.4		1.3		1.3			
	1.0		.9		.9	Quick	.9		.9		1.1	1.0		.8		.8			
	.6		.6		.6		.5		.6		.7	.7		.6		.6			
34	10.6	33	11.0	35	10.5		23	15.8	28	13.2	38 9.7	36 10.1	39	9.3	39	9.4			
46	7.9	45	8.1	43	8.4	Sales/Receivables	38	9.6	39	9.3	50 7.3	45 8.1	49	7.5	46	7.9			
57	6.4	58	6.3	56	6.5		45	8.1	48	7.7	62 5.9	55 6.6	58	6.3	60	6.1			
10	34.9	10	34.9	11	33.4		4	101.5	4	97.4	6 57.7	10 37.3	19	19.6	21	17.6			
23	16.1	22	16.7	23	15.7	Cost of Sales/Inventory	22	16.6	18	20.8	15 23.8	22 16.8	30	12.1	32	11.3			
41	8.9	43	8.5	40	9.0		40	9.0	29	12.4	34 10.8	34 10.8	45	8.0	57	6.4			
18	20.1	19	19.6	20	18.6		20	18.5	16	23.0	22 16.4	18 20.0	25	14.8	16	22.3			
31	11.7	31	11.9	34	10.6	Cost of Sales/Payables	46	8.0	33	11.1	37 9.8	31 11.7	35	10.3	30	12.2			
49	7.5	48	7.6	51	7.1		69	5.3	57	6.4	58 6.3	48 7.6	48	7.6	45	8.1			
	7.5		8.4		8.7			11.6		8.7	7.4	9.8		10.0		6.8			
	17.4		18.6		21.3	Sales/Working Capital		20.4		27.8	19.9	24.9		22.7		14.4			
	UND		-116.9		-49.9			-19.5		-37.4	-51.8	-66.5		-113.0		NM			
	5.2		4.6		5.1			5.0		4.1	4.1	8.4		6.7		6.2			
(370)	2.2	(356)	1.6	(351)	2.2	EBIT/Interest	(26) 1.5	(80)	1.5	(60) 1.3	(71) 3.1	(63)	3.1	(51)	2.7			
	.8		.6		.4			-1.6		-.7	-.4	.8		1.3		1.1			
	3.6		3.0		2.3					1.4	3.2	2.2		3.0		2.3			
(100)	1.9	(95)	1.3	(98)	1.2	Net Profit + Depr., Dep., Amort./Cur. Mat. L/T/D			(14) 1.0	(17) 1.2	(23) 1.2	(16)	1.9	(25)	1.9			
	1.0		.7		.6					.6	.3	.1		1.0		.8			
	.6		.7		.6			.4		.7	.6	.7		.6		.7			
	1.4		1.7		1.5	Fixed/Worth		3.3		2.2	1.5	1.4		1.5		1.7			
	4.0		4.9		4.5			-3.1		NM	5.0	3.8		2.9		3.0			
	.9		1.0		1.0			1.1		1.1	1.1	.9		1.0		.7			
	2.5		2.7		2.6	Debt/Worth		6.4		3.0	2.6	1.8		2.6		2.5			
	7.7		8.9		10.3			-8.5		NM	9.0	6.6		5.3		6.3			
	38.0		32.0		40.8			70.0		46.3	17.9	48.1		47.6		38.7			
(337)	18.5	(316)	9.8	(310)	13.2	% Profit Before Taxes/Tangible Net Worth	(20) 9.3	(65)	7.5	(53) 4.8	(65) 19.9	(59)	26.0	(48)	15.0			
	.6		-.3		-.1			-21.6		-11.1	-20.0	3.3		5.8		4.7			
	13.7		10.2		11.7			13.2		13.6	6.5	15.1		12.6		11.8			
	4.9		2.5		3.5	% Profit Before Taxes/Total Assets		4.6		1.5	1.9	5.7		5.9		5.1			
	-.9		-1.6		-1.8			-10.5		-7.4	-5.5	-.1		1.8		.6			
	10.5		10.3		11.8			15.0		13.4	11.0	13.4		15.9		7.9			
	6.2		5.5		5.6	Sales/Net Fixed Assets		8.5		6.3	5.0	4.9		6.0		4.9			
	3.7		3.1		3.2			3.9		3.5	2.8	2.9		3.1		3.5			
	3.0		2.9		3.1			3.4		3.6	3.0	2.9		3.0		2.2			
	2.2		2.1		2.2	Sales/Total Assets		3.0		2.4	2.0	2.0		2.2		1.9			
	1.7		1.6		1.6			2.0		1.7	1.5	1.6		1.6		1.5			
	2.0		1.9		2.6			3.9		2.6	2.6	2.5		1.8		3.1			
(372)	3.6	(350)	4.0	(346)	4.4	% Depr., Dep., Amort./Sales	(25) 5.7	(81)	4.6	(59) 5.3	(72) 4.0	(61)	3.5	(48)	4.3			
	5.4		5.9		6.4			7.1		7.7	7.1	6.1		5.7		5.3			
	3.1		2.9		3.2			5.5		3.2	3.4	3.3		1.4					
(188)	5.1	(185)	5.0	(175)	5.2	% Officers', Directors', Owners' Comp/Sales	(23) 10.2	(60)	5.2	(36) 5.7	(28) 4.6	(22)	2.3					
	8.4		9.4		8.8			19.0		9.0	7.4	7.3		4.4					
	5244548M		5522774M		6398156M	Net Sales ($)	19017M		167130M		246537M	549870M		1057803M		4357799M			
	2733624M		2973728M		3495185M	Total Assets ($)	9021M		77540M		135509M	281423M		525678M		2466014M			

© RMA 2003

M = $ thousand   MM = $ million
See Pages 11 through 18 for Explanation of Ratios and Data

Current Data Sorted By Assets — Comparative Historical Data

Period groupings (Current Data): **13 (4/1-9/30/02)** · **40 (10/1/02-3/31/03)**

Type of Statement	0-500M	500M-2MM	2-10MM	10-50MM	50-100MM	100-250MM		4/1/98-3/31/99 ALL	4/1/99-3/31/00 ALL
Unqualified	1	4	9	3				8	5
Reviewed	1	8	5	2				27	25
Compiled	1	3	1	1				9	7
Tax Returns								1	
Other		7	7					15	15
NUMBER OF STATEMENTS	3	22	22	6				60	52
	%	%	%	%	%	%		%	%
ASSETS									
Cash & Equivalents		5.8	7.2					7.0	8.0
Trade Receivables (net)		32.0	24.0					31.0	27.1
Inventory		5.4	4.4					7.8	7.1
All Other Current		.9	.6					1.1	2.4
Total Current		44.0	36.3					47.0	44.6
Fixed Assets (net)		50.6	46.5					43.0	47.6
Intangibles (net)		.3	8.1		DATA	DATA		4.1	2.8
All Other Non-Current		5.1	9.1		NOT	NOT		5.9	5.0
Total		100.0	100.0		AVAILABLE	AVAILABLE		100.0	100.0
LIABILITIES									
Notes Payable-Short Term		14.8	5.7					7.7	4.6
Cur. Mat.-L/T/D		8.0	5.5					6.4	6.5
Trade Payables		11.7	6.3					10.4	7.3
Income Taxes Payable		.1	.8					.6	.3
All Other Current		9.1	7.1					8.5	7.7
Total Current		43.7	25.4					33.6	26.4
Long Term Debt		26.0	33.9					24.9	26.3
Deferred Taxes		3.6	.9					1.3	1.3
All Other Non-Current		1.7	4.7					3.8	3.8
Net Worth		25.0	35.2					36.4	42.3
Total Liabilities & Net Worth		100.0	100.0					100.0	100.0
INCOME DATA									
Net Sales		100.0	100.0					100.0	100.0
Gross Profit		40.5	31.2					38.0	32.2
Operating Expenses		39.1	28.2					32.6	26.4
Operating Profit		1.4	3.0					5.4	5.8
All Other Expenses (net)		.3	2.2					1.2	1.4
Profit Before Taxes		1.1	.9					4.2	4.4

RATIOS

Ratio	0-500M	500M-2MM	2-10MM	10-50MM	50-100MM	100-250MM	4/1/98-3/31/99	4/1/99-3/31/00
Current		1.5	2.3				2.2	2.8
		1.1	1.5				1.4	1.8
		.8	1.0				1.1	1.3
Quick		1.4	1.9				1.9	2.4
		1.0	1.2				1.2	1.4
		.6	.8				.8	.9
Sales/Receivables	38	9.7	34 10.7				41 8.9	42 8.7
	52	7.1	47 7.7				49 7.5	51 7.1
	76	4.8	58 6.3				58 6.3	61 5.9
Cost of Sales/Inventory	0	UND	0 UND				0 UND	2 187.4
	6	63.2	10 34.9				3 110.8	13 27.7
	14	25.5	17 21.5				30 12.2	24 15.0
Cost of Sales/Payables	19	19.6	9 40.9				10 34.9	12 29.9
	27	13.5	18 19.8				21 17.0	17 21.5
	36	10.1	30 12.3				39 9.4	26 14.0
Sales/Working Capital		12.7	7.3				7.7	6.7
		73.9	18.8				16.1	9.7
		-18.2	999.8				181.2	26.6
EBIT/Interest	(20)	5.6	(20) 4.8				(56) 6.2	(50) 5.7
		1.4	1.9				3.5	2.7
		-.2	.2				1.4	1.7
Net Profit + Depr., Dep., Amort./Cur. Mat. L /T/D							(22) 5.5	(26) 5.1
							2.3	1.9
							1.4	1.2
Fixed/Worth		.9	.8				.6	.8
		2.5	1.8				1.1	1.1
		8.2	4.7				2.6	2.6
Debt/Worth		1.2	.8				.7	.6
		3.9	2.9				1.8	1.5
		17.0	6.6				4.2	3.1
% Profit Before Taxes/Tangible Net Worth	(19)	32.9	(19) 73.8				(55) 52.8	(49) 35.8
		-2.5	9.7				20.6	13.0
		-18.0	.7				7.9	6.1
% Profit Before Taxes/Total Assets		9.3	14.9				19.3	11.6
		.3	4.3				6.3	5.3
		-5.6	-1.0				2.6	2.3
Sales/Net Fixed Assets		7.6	6.7				8.9	6.7
		3.7	3.8				6.6	4.1
		2.0	2.5				2.4	2.2
Sales/Total Assets		3.0	2.5				3.1	2.5
		2.2	1.7				2.2	1.7
		1.6	1.3				1.5	1.4
% Depr., Dep., Amort./Sales	(20)	3.8	3.2				(58) 2.3	(50) 3.3
		5.0	5.6				4.2	4.9
		9.9	8.6				7.3	7.9
% Officers', Directors', Owners' Comp/Sales	(16)	3.3					(36) 3.3	(26) 2.5
		4.5					7.0	5.4
		7.0					9.3	8.3
Net Sales ($)	1707M	59812M	170510M	155935M			472185M	695494M
Total Assets ($)	1052M	25041M	98236M	99178M			253072M	543515M

M = $ thousand   MM = $ million
See Pages 11 through 18 for Explanation of Ratios and Data

Comparative Historical Data				Current Data Sorted By Sales					
			Type of Statement						
3	1	3	Unqualified					1	2
16	18	15	Reviewed	1	2	4	5	3	
19	14	15	Compiled	2	7	2	4		
2	2	5	Tax Returns	1	2	1		1	
16	20	15	Other	1	3	5	4	2	
4/1/00-3/31/01	4/1/01-3/31/02	4/1/02-3/31/03			13 (4/1-9/30/02)		40 (10/1/02-3/31/03)		
ALL	ALL	ALL		0-1MM	1-3MM	3-5MM	5-10MM	10-25MM	25MM & OVER
56	55	53	**NUMBER OF STATEMENTS**	5	14	12	13	7	2
%	%	%		%	%	%	%	%	%
			ASSETS						
8.9	9.2	5.7	Cash & Equivalents		8.5	5.5	4.0		
29.8	27.6	27.1	Trade Receivables (net)		27.0	32.7	28.6		
7.0	4.7	4.5	Inventory		4.0	5.2	4.7		
1.8	2.1	.7	All Other Current		.3	1.5	.3		
47.5	43.7	38.0	Total Current		39.7	44.9	37.6		
45.6	47.2	51.6	Fixed Assets (net)		56.9	42.7	45.3		
1.6	2.8	4.1	Intangibles (net)		.0	6.4	9.0		
5.3	6.3	6.3	All Other Non-Current		3.3	6.1	8.1		
100.0	100.0	100.0	Total		100.0	100.0	100.0		
			LIABILITIES						
10.2	8.6	9.2	Notes Payable-Short Term		10.2	14.5	6.7		
7.3	7.2	6.8	Cur. Mat.-L/T/D		9.1	6.8	6.5		
10.8	7.6	8.3	Trade Payables		8.9	12.0	7.0		
.2	.3	.4	Income Taxes Payable		1.4	.0	.0		
6.2	6.5	7.4	All Other Current		8.7	8.9	5.9		
34.7	30.1	32.1	Total Current		38.3	42.4	26.2		
23.9	26.0	31.3	Long Term Debt		32.7	27.7	34.4		
.8	.7	1.9	Deferred Taxes		5.7	.0	.9		
3.4	4.2	4.4	All Other Non-Current		.1	3.5	8.0		
37.1	38.8	30.2	Net Worth		23.1	26.4	30.4		
100.0	100.0	100.0	Total Liabilities & Net Worth		100.0	100.0	100.0		
			INCOME DATA						
100.0	100.0	100.0	Net Sales		100.0	100.0	100.0		
37.1	39.1	37.8	Gross Profit		45.0	30.9	31.9		
32.8	35.6	34.5	Operating Expenses		43.0	31.1	26.2		
4.3	3.5	3.3	Operating Profit		2.0	-.2	5.7		
1.0	1.3	1.5	All Other Expenses (net)		.3	1.8	2.1		
3.3	2.2	1.9	Profit Before Taxes		1.6	-2.0	3.6		
			RATIOS						
2.0	2.8	2.0			1.6	1.8	2.5		
1.4	1.3	1.3	Current		1.2	.9	1.3		
.9	.9	.8			.8	.7	1.2		
1.7	2.7	1.7			1.5	1.4	2.1		
1.1	1.1	1.2	Quick		1.2	.9	1.2		
.8	.8	.8			.8	.5	1.2		
36 10.3	36 10.2	38 9.6		38 9.6	38 9.7	40 9.0			
48 7.6	43 8.5	51 7.1	Sales/Receivables	50 7.3	50 7.3	53 6.8			
61 5.9	57 6.4	67 5.5		76 4.8	63 5.8	73 5.0			
0 UND	0 UND	0 UND		0 UND	4 95.1	0 UND			
7 53.1	6 58.7	6 59.3	Cost of Sales/Inventory	3 111.0	8 47.0	11 33.2			
26 14.3	13 29.0	15 24.8		7 49.8	17 21.8	22 16.2			
11 33.9	4 93.7	11 34.7		16 22.6	3 124.5	9 42.5			
21 17.3	16 22.4	21 17.7	Cost of Sales/Payables	23 15.9	27 13.5	17 22.0			
36 10.2	30 12.3	30 12.3		38 9.7	41 8.9	21 17.7			
8.5	8.0	9.3			9.7	11.1	8.2		
18.7	21.9	30.0	Sales/Working Capital		51.9	NM	17.5		
-77.6	-55.8	-29.5			-31.3	-12.3	36.1		
5.2	5.4	4.4			5.2	3.8	4.6		
(54) 2.5	(53) 1.7	(49) 2.0	EBIT/Interest		(13) 1.1	(11) 1.0	(12) 2.5		
1.0	-.5	.6			-.2	-1.6	1.3		
2.3	3.3	11.4	Net Profit + Depr., Dep.,						
(15) 1.6	(18) 1.5	(11) 2.5	Amort./Cur. Mat. L/T/D						
1.0	.8	.8							
.7	.6	1.0			1.0	.6	1.0		
1.4	1.3	2.1	Fixed/Worth		2.7	3.1	2.1		
2.6	3.8	5.8			NM	5.7	11.0		
.9	.7	1.1			1.1	1.9	1.6		
2.3	1.8	3.3	Debt/Worth		4.0	4.1	4.5		
3.5	5.5	9.1			NM	10.0	13.1		
42.8	33.5	43.6	% Profit Before Taxes/Tangible		40.1	19.9	69.7		
(54) 21.4	(50) 11.0	(46) 9.3	Net Worth		(11) -1.6	(11) 4.9	(11) 11.6		
3.1	-13.7	-4.2			-18.0	-16.3	2.0		
10.8	13.0	12.0	% Profit Before Taxes/Total		16.3	6.0	12.0		
5.6	3.0	3.2	Assets		-.1	1.0	4.4		
.1	-5.6	-1.7			-5.6	-8.1	.7		
10.5	7.5	6.7			5.0	21.9	6.1		
4.8	4.4	3.6	Sales/Net Fixed Assets		3.4	3.7	4.1		
2.5	2.6	2.1			2.0	2.6	2.9		
3.1	2.9	2.4			2.3	2.9	2.6		
2.0	1.9	1.8	Sales/Total Assets		2.0	2.0	1.6		
1.6	1.5	1.3			1.4	1.6	1.3		
2.6	2.9	3.8			3.9	1.9	4.6		
(55) 4.9	(54) 5.6	(51) 5.8	% Depr., Dep., Amort./Sales		(13) 6.4	6.1	(12) 6.5		
7.1	8.0	9.0			11.7	9.2	9.6		
3.4	4.6	3.1	% Officers', Directors',		3.3				
(30) 6.3	(30) 7.5	(27) 4.4	Owners' Comp/Sales		(11) 3.7				
10.3	10.7	6.2			6.1				
294802M	465159M	387964M	Net Sales ($)	2110M	27094M	48324M	97254M	103725M	109457M
163364M	284658M	223507M	Total Assets ($)	8936M	15639M	27839M	65600M	57706M	47787M

M = $ thousand   MM = $ million
See Pages 11 through 18 for Explanation of Ratios and Data

Current Data Sorted By Assets | Comparative Historical Data

Type of Statement

	0-500M	500M-2MM	2-10MM	10-50MM	50-100MM	100-250MM	Type of Statement	4/1/98-3/31/99 ALL	4/1/99-3/31/00 ALL
			3	2		1	Unqualified	9	10
		2	7	1			Reviewed	15	25
	2	7	2				Compiled	19	14
	3	1	1				Tax Returns	7	5
	1	6	5	3		1	Other	10	16
		9 (4/1-9/30/02)		39 (10/1/02-3/31/03)					
	6	16	18	6		2	**NUMBER OF STATEMENTS**	60	70

Main Data (percentages / ratios)

Columns (left to right): 0-500M · 500M-2MM · 2-10MM · 10-50MM · 50-100MM · 100-250MM · Description · 4/1/98-3/31/99 ALL · 4/1/99-3/31/00 ALL. Middle/right asset columns marked **DATA NOT AVAILABLE**.

0-500M	500M-2MM	2-10MM	Description	98/99 ALL	99/00 ALL
%	%	%	**ASSETS**	%	%
	5.2	15.2	Cash & Equivalents	6.9	10.0
	32.3	30.1	Trade Receivables (net)	30.8	29.4
	10.9	7.7	Inventory	9.4	9.0
	3.8	3.6	All Other Current	1.2	2.2
	52.2	56.7	Total Current	48.3	50.6
	39.4	33.5	Fixed Assets (net)	41.3	38.0
	3.9	4.5	Intangibles (net)	4.1	6.6
	4.4	5.3	All Other Non-Current	6.2	4.8
	100.0	100.0	Total	100.0	100.0
			LIABILITIES		
	9.4	7.4	Notes Payable-Short Term	11.4	11.4
	6.4	4.6	Cur. Mat.-L/T/D	8.1	7.3
	12.3	10.5	Trade Payables	10.9	10.7
	.0	.1	Income Taxes Payable	.5	.4
	6.4	8.8	All Other Current	12.2	7.8
	34.4	31.5	Total Current	43.1	37.8
	31.9	21.6	Long Term Debt	24.5	21.4
	.0	.6	Deferred Taxes	1.1	.6
	4.9	.8	All Other Non-Current	2.8	5.5
	28.7	45.5	Net Worth	28.5	34.8
	100.0	100.0	Total Liabilities & Net Worth	100.0	100.0
			INCOME DATA		
	100.0	100.0	Net Sales	100.0	100.0
	39.3	39.1	Gross Profit	40.5	39.2
	38.5	32.9	Operating Expenses	37.0	34.2
	.8	6.2	Operating Profit	3.5	5.0
	1.0	1.0	All Other Expenses (net)	1.9	1.9
	-.1	5.2	Profit Before Taxes	1.6	3.1
			RATIOS		
	2.4	2.7	Current	2.1	2.7
	1.4	1.9		1.2	1.2
	1.1	1.3		.8	.9
	1.7	2.0	Quick	1.7	1.8
	.9	1.7		.9	1.0
	.5	1.0		.7	.6
	38 9.6	46 7.8	Sales/Receivables	37 9.8	39 9.4
	51 7.2	60 6.1		53 6.9	54 6.8
	64 5.7	63 5.8		69 5.3	69 5.3
	15 24.7	10 36.9	Cost of Sales/Inventory	5 79.4	6 60.7
	18 20.2	20 18.5		16 22.2	19 18.8
	42 8.7	32 11.4		31 11.8	33 11.0
	18 19.8	13 27.7	Cost of Sales/Payables	12 31.1	13 27.6
	24 15.0	24 14.9		22 16.4	25 14.8
	45 8.1	43 8.4		35 10.6	48 7.5
	6.3	5.4	Sales/Working Capital	7.1	6.1
	19.6	8.0		30.9	21.4
	143.7	32.5		-19.5	-55.4
	5.2	17.9	EBIT/Interest	3.2	6.6
	(14) 1.3	(17) 3.0		(52) 1.7	(64) 2.3
	-.5	1.6		.1	1.1
		2.4	Net Profit + Depr., Dep., Amort./Cur. Mat. L/T/D	2.4	1.8
		(17) 1.5		(17) 1.5	(20) 1.5
		1.1		1.1	1.2
	.8	.4	Fixed/Worth	.7	.6
	1.3	.9		1.6	1.3
	6.5	2.0		7.2	11.7
	1.3	.7	Debt/Worth	.9	.7
	3.3	1.4		2.2	2.5
	8.5	3.1		11.6	25.4
	54.1	42.9	% Profit Before Taxes/Tangible Net Worth	29.9	43.4
	(14) 6.9	(17) 25.8		(50) 13.4	(57) 19.9
	-14.7	11.0		-4.0	3.5
	10.8	16.7	% Profit Before Taxes/Total Assets	10.2	15.5
	.9	8.6		3.0	6.0
	-10.0	2.7		-3.1	-.1
	14.6	9.6	Sales/Net Fixed Assets	8.9	10.0
	5.8	6.3		4.6	5.6
	3.8	4.7		3.1	3.5
	2.6	2.3	Sales/Total Assets	2.6	2.8
	2.2	2.0		1.9	2.0
	1.8	1.5		1.6	1.4
	1.7	3.2	% Depr., Dep., Amort./Sales	3.6	2.4
	(14) 3.0	(17) 3.8		(54) 5.9	(66) 4.8
	7.2	6.1		8.1	7.5
	4.2		% Officers', Directors', Owners' Comp/Sales	4.4	3.4
	(10) 5.9			(26) 5.9	(35) 7.1
	14.2			8.6	12.2

Net Sales / Total Assets

	0-500M	500M-2MM	2-10MM	10-50MM	50-100MM	100-250MM		98/99 ALL	99/00 ALL
Net Sales ($)	2360M	38520M	171594M	174259M		269642M		398624M	666005M
Total Assets ($)	1376M	16496M	87227M	98900M		262266M		299394M	503638M

M = $ thousand   MM = $ million
See Pages 11 through 18 for Explanation of Ratios and Data

Comparative Historical Data / Current Data Sorted By Sales

	Comparative Historical Data			Type of Statement	0-1MM	1-3MM	3-5MM	5-10MM	10-25MM	25MM & OVER
	8	6	6	Unqualified				1	3	2
	11	12	10	Reviewed		1	3	4	2	
	14	15	11	Compiled	3	5	1	2		
	4	1	5	Tax Returns	3	1		1		
	21	11	16	Other	1	5	3	2	2	3
	4/1/00-3/31/01 ALL	4/1/01-3/31/02 ALL	4/1/02-3/31/03 ALL			9 (4/1-9/30/02)		39 (10/1/02-3/31/03)		
	58	45	48	NUMBER OF STATEMENTS	7	12	7	10	7	5
	%	%	%	ASSETS	%	%	%	%	%	%
	8.1	10.8	10.5	Cash & Equivalents		6.4		16.6		
	30.9	32.3	29.5	Trade Receivables (net)		31.9		30.7		
	7.2	7.3	9.2	Inventory		10.9		7.1		
	2.2	3.4	3.3	All Other Current		1.0		1.3		
	48.4	53.8	52.6	Total Current		50.2		55.7		
	39.2	32.0	35.1	Fixed Assets (net)		41.9		30.4		
	6.1	9.0	6.0	Intangibles (net)		4.5		6.1		
	6.4	4.6	6.4	All Other Non-Current		3.4		7.9		
	100.0	100.0	100.0	Total		100.0		100.0		
				LIABILITIES						
	11.2	7.9	7.5	Notes Payable-Short Term		11.3		5.6		
	8.6	7.0	4.9	Cur. Mat.-L/T/D		6.8		3.2		
	12.8	12.3	11.1	Trade Payables		12.5		7.8		
	.1	.2	.1	Income Taxes Payable		.0		.0		
	8.2	8.0	7.7	All Other Current		4.5		13.4		
	41.0	35.5	31.3	Total Current		35.1		30.1		
	28.5	21.4	24.0	Long Term Debt		34.6		10.7		
	.4	.4	.6	Deferred Taxes		.0		.4		
	4.5	3.0	2.9	All Other Non-Current		5.7		1.6		
	25.6	39.7	41.3	Net Worth		24.5		57.2		
	100.0	100.0	100.0	Total Liabilities & Net Worth		100.0		100.0		
				INCOME DATA						
	100.0	100.0	100.0	Net Sales		100.0		100.0		
	39.1	36.8	39.6	Gross Profit		41.9		37.8		
	34.2	31.1	36.1	Operating Expenses		41.4		29.3		
	4.9	5.6	3.5	Operating Profit		.5		8.6		
	1.7	1.7	1.2	All Other Expenses (net)		1.1		.9		
	3.2	3.9	2.2	Profit Before Taxes		-.6		7.7		
				RATIOS						
	2.3	3.2	2.7			2.4		2.4		
	1.5	1.8	1.8	Current		1.2		1.9		
	.8	1.0	1.1			.9		1.3		
	1.8	2.3	2.0			1.9		2.1		
	1.3	1.4	1.4	Quick		.9		1.6		
	.6	.8	.8			.5		1.1		
	37 9.9	41 8.9	41 8.9			45 8.1		33 11.2		
	52 7.0	55 6.6	53 6.9	Sales/Receivables		56 6.5		52 7.0		
	71 5.1	69 5.3	64 5.7			65 5.6		61 6.0		
	6 56.2	7 54.0	10 34.8			15 24.6		0 UND		
	19 19.0	14 26.4	19 19.0	Cost of Sales/Inventory		18 20.2		20 18.5		
	30 12.1	30 12.2	42 8.7			58 6.3		32 11.4		
	13 28.6	12 31.1	16 22.9			19 19.3		9 39.9		
	27 13.5	23 16.2	24 15.0	Cost of Sales/Payables		28 13.1		17 22.0		
	49 7.4	45 8.1	43 8.4			75 4.9		28 13.0		
	7.5	4.7	4.4			6.3		5.5		
	15.3	11.1	11.1	Sales/Working Capital		22.4		7.8		
	-19.5	UND	63.3			NM		32.5		
	6.9	6.3	7.6			4.6				
(54)	2.1	(40) 2.0	(44) 2.1	EBIT/Interest		1.0				
	.7	.1	.6			-1.4				
			2.7	Net Profit + Depr., Dep.,						
			(11) 2.0	Amort./Cur. Mat. L/T/D						
			1.4							
	.6	.4	.5			.9		.3		
	1.3	.9	1.1	Fixed/Worth		1.3		.5		
	7.7	4.7	2.1			14.3		.9		
	.7	.5	.7			1.3		.6		
	2.0	2.7	2.0	Debt/Worth		4.4		.8		
	12.2	8.5	4.2			19.5		2.4		
	48.0	55.9	42.0	% Profit Before Taxes/Tangible		54.1		53.7		
(45)	20.0	(36) 16.8	(43) 19.2	Net Worth	(10)	-.4		28.2		
	2.4	-3.9	-4.8			-52.2		18.4		
	15.2	17.4	13.0	% Profit Before Taxes/Total		10.7		25.2		
	4.6	3.7	3.3	Assets		-.2		14.7		
	.0	-1.8	-2.4			-12.0		8.5		
	11.4	11.7	10.2			7.5		12.9		
	6.9	7.4	5.8	Sales/Net Fixed Assets		5.1		7.0		
	3.5	4.2	3.9			3.1		4.7		
	2.8	2.6	2.4			2.3		2.9		
	2.2	2.3	2.0	Sales/Total Assets		2.1		2.1		
	1.6	1.6	1.5			1.7		1.5		
	3.3	1.7	2.7			2.1				
(53)	5.1	(41) 4.1	(42) 4.1	% Depr., Dep., Amort./Sales	(10)	4.0				
	7.0	6.9	6.6			9.2				
	4.4	2.1	3.6	% Officers', Directors',						
(29)	7.7	(22) 5.9	(18) 6.2	Owners' Comp/Sales						
	13.8	8.1	12.5							
	540316M	769987M	656375M	Net Sales ($)	3332M	23768M	30262M	71513M	130721M	396779M
	429547M	580919M	466265M	Total Assets ($)	1933M	12453M	16194M	37823M	70123M	327739M

M = $ thousand   MM = $ million
See Pages 11 through 18 for Explanation of Ratios and Data

Current Data Sorted By Assets / Comparative Historical Data

Type of Statement

	0-500M	500M-2MM	2-10MM	10-50MM	50-100MM	100-250MM		4/1/98-3/31/99 ALL	4/1/99-3/31/00 ALL
Unqualified		1	2	2	6	4		22	18
Reviewed			3	2				7	5
Compiled		1						3	4
Tax Returns	1	2						1	
Other	1		3	4	1	6		14	10
	9 (4/1-9/30/02)			30 (10/1/02-3/31/03)					
NUMBER OF STATEMENTS	2	4	8	8	7	10		47	37

100-250MM %		4/1/98-3/31/99 ALL %	4/1/99-3/31/00 ALL %
	ASSETS		
5.8	Cash & Equivalents	5.5	9.0
18.9	Trade Receivables (net)	17.6	26.0
19.9	Inventory	15.3	18.5
1.5	All Other Current	1.8	2.9
46.2	Total Current	40.1	56.2
33.9	Fixed Assets (net)	48.4	36.4
6.1	Intangibles (net)	3.0	2.2
13.8	All Other Non-Current	8.5	5.1
100.0	Total	100.0	100.0
	LIABILITIES		
2.8	Notes Payable-Short Term	7.0	7.7
1.0	Cur. Mat.-L/T/D	6.1	2.2
19.9	Trade Payables	13.3	21.4
.5	Income Taxes Payable	.1	.6
7.9	All Other Current	7.5	8.7
32.0	Total Current	34.0	40.7
7.5	Long Term Debt	20.4	12.8
2.6	Deferred Taxes	2.0	2.3
6.8	All Other Non-Current	6.0	6.8
51.1	Net Worth	37.5	37.4
100.0	Total Liabilities & Net Worth	100.0	100.0
	INCOME DATA		
100.0	Net Sales	100.0	100.0
15.9	Gross Profit	21.7	20.5
11.7	Operating Expenses	16.4	16.3
4.2	Operating Profit	5.3	4.2
-.2	All Other Expenses (net)	1.4	1.1
4.5	Profit Before Taxes	3.9	3.0
	RATIOS		
1.8 / 1.5 / 1.2	Current	1.5 / 1.2 / .9	1.8 / 1.3 / 1.0
.9 / .8 / .5	Quick	.9 / .6 / .4	1.1 / .8 / .5
18 20.1 / 25 14.9 / 47 7.7	Sales/Receivables	17 21.2 / 28 12.8 / 42 8.7	22 16.4 / 38 9.5 / 52 7.0
16 22.7 / 28 13.2 / 52 7.0	Cost of Sales/Inventory	16 22.4 / 28 13.2 / 48 7.6	10 35.2 / 32 11.3 / 55 6.7
23 15.8 / 32 11.4 / 48 7.7	Cost of Sales/Payables	16 22.2 / 26 14.2 / 38 9.6	20 18.1 / 36 10.0 / 60 6.0
11.6 / 18.9 / NM	Sales/Working Capital	14.0 / 32.1 / -78.7	10.7 / 20.7 / 134.9
5.6 / 3.2 / 1.6	EBIT/Interest	(45) 5.6 / 3.2 / 1.6	(35) 13.3 / 6.8 / 1.3
	Net Profit + Depr., Dep., Amort./Cur. Mat. L/T/D	(20) 6.7 / 3.2 / 1.5	(17) 33.4 / 4.0 / 1.8
.3 / .9 / 1.6	Fixed/Worth	.9 / 1.4 / 2.6	.6 / 1.0 / 1.9
.6 / 1.0 / 2.1	Debt/Worth	1.1 / 1.9 / 3.6	.9 / 1.7 / 3.2
	% Profit Before Taxes/Tangible Net Worth	(46) 31.4 / 17.2 / 7.1	(35) 42.0 / 23.2 / 10.0
19.9 / 9.0 / 1.5	% Profit Before Taxes/Total Assets	11.8 / 5.4 / 1.6	16.7 / 7.7 / .4
22.5 / 6.7 / 4.5	Sales/Net Fixed Assets	10.2 / 3.9 / 2.1	17.5 / 7.8 / 3.7
3.4 / 2.5 / 1.5	Sales/Total Assets	3.1 / 2.1 / 1.2	3.4 / 2.5 / 1.4
	% Depr., Dep., Amort./Sales	(42) 1.6 / 2.6 / 5.6	(34) 1.1 / 1.9 / 4.4
	% Officers', Directors', Owners' Comp/Sales		

0-500M	500M-2MM	2-10MM	10-50MM	50-100MM	100-250MM		4/1/98-3/31/99 ALL	4/1/99-3/31/00 ALL
7378M	14878M	97997M	562899M	2033428M	4070396M	Net Sales ($)	4124031M	5095024M
276M	5053M	37879M	188915M	500456M	1532570M	Total Assets ($)	1783297M	2074671M

M = $ thousand   MM = $ million
See Pages 11 through 18 for Explanation of Ratios and Data

Comparative Historical Data | Current Data Sorted By Sales

4/1/00-3/31/01 ALL	4/1/01-3/31/02 ALL	4/1/02-3/31/03 ALL	Type of Statement	0-1MM	1-3MM	3-5MM	5-10MM	10-25MM	25MM & OVER
19	16	15	Unqualified				2	1	12
6	2	5	Reviewed		1	1	1		2
7	5	1	Compiled		1				
		3	Tax Returns			2	1		
15	15	15	Other	1				1	12
				9 (4/1-9/30/02)			30 (10/1/02-3/31/03)		
47	38	39	**NUMBER OF STATEMENTS**	1	2	4	4	2	26
%	%	%	**ASSETS**	%	%	%	%	%	%
7.7	9.7	10.9	Cash & Equivalents						8.3
23.2	22.3	21.3	Trade Receivables (net)						23.3
14.9	16.7	15.9	Inventory						17.5
4.3	4.0	6.5	All Other Current						4.5
50.1	52.7	54.6	Total Current						53.6
39.4	34.8	34.3	Fixed Assets (net)						32.9
2.0	3.2	3.0	Intangibles (net)						3.0
8.5	9.3	8.2	All Other Non-Current						10.5
100.0	100.0	100.0	Total						100.0
			LIABILITIES						
6.1	7.9	6.2	Notes Payable-Short Term						4.4
2.6	3.3	3.0	Cur. Mat.-L/T/D						1.5
18.8	18.9	20.6	Trade Payables						22.9
.4	.2	.3	Income Taxes Payable						.3
7.0	7.7	9.8	All Other Current						8.1
34.8	38.0	39.9	Total Current						37.2
20.5	17.2	9.4	Long Term Debt						8.8
1.9	1.6	1.8	Deferred Taxes						2.0
2.9	3.7	5.7	All Other Non-Current						7.5
39.8	39.5	43.2	Net Worth						44.5
100.0	100.0	100.0	Total Liabilities & Net Worth						100.0
			INCOME DATA						
100.0	100.0	100.0	Net Sales						100.0
28.6	24.2	20.3	Gross Profit						13.7
19.2	15.7	14.9	Operating Expenses						10.0
9.4	8.5	5.3	Operating Profit						3.7
.1	.8	.3	All Other Expenses (net)						.2
9.3	7.7	5.1	Profit Before Taxes						3.5
			RATIOS						
2.1	2.0	1.8	Current						1.8
1.3	1.4	1.4							1.5
1.1	.9	1.0							1.1
1.3	1.2	1.1	Quick						1.0
.8	.8	.8							.9
.6	.6	.5							.5
18 20.7	14 26.5	17 21.1	Sales/Receivables						19 18.9
32 11.4	28 13.0	28 13.1							28 13.1
55 6.6	52 7.0	37 9.7							36 10.1
9 39.2	9 39.4	10 36.2	Cost of Sales/Inventory						12 31.1
20 18.0	24 15.2	21 17.6							25 14.4
58 6.3	48 7.6	38 9.7							37 9.9
22 16.4	15 23.8	19 19.5	Cost of Sales/Payables						22 16.8
37 10.0	24 15.1	31 11.6							32 11.4
57 6.4	54 6.7	45 8.1							41 9.0
8.9	9.2	8.7	Sales/Working Capital						10.9
24.9	20.8	22.8							21.8
185.5	-269.5	999.8							45.7
11.2	14.5	31.7	EBIT/Interest						23.1
(42) 4.1	(36) 8.0	(35) 7.4							(23) 8.5
1.8	2.3	2.5							2.5
12.1	12.8		Net Profit + Depr., Dep.,						
(15) 2.6	(12) 2.8		Amort./Cur. Mat. L/T/D						
.4	1.3								
.4	.2	.2	Fixed/Worth						.3
1.0	.9	.8							.8
2.0	1.9	1.5							1.5
.9	.8	.8	Debt/Worth						.8
1.6	1.7	1.6							1.3
2.9	2.9	2.6							2.0
51.1	60.3	36.1	% Profit Before Taxes/Tangible Net Worth						31.9
(46) 27.4	(34) 34.0	(37) 12.6							(25) 12.0
5.3	10.9	6.0							5.5
17.1	25.4	16.0	% Profit Before Taxes/Total Assets						12.4
8.0	12.1	6.8							5.5
2.3	5.1	1.7							1.9
19.5	35.3	29.0	Sales/Net Fixed Assets						24.0
7.5	9.4	8.1							8.3
2.9	3.9	3.9							4.7
3.7	3.8	3.7	Sales/Total Assets						3.8
2.2	2.5	2.4							2.8
1.4	1.6	1.8							1.9
.9	.6	.5	% Depr., Dep., Amort./Sales						.5
(38) 1.5	(34) 1.4	(37) 1.7							(25) 1.4
4.0	3.5	3.7							3.2
2.3			% Officers', Directors', Owners' Comp/Sales						
(10) 4.5									
9.8									
6167750M	5260492M	6786976M	Net Sales ($)	79M	4881M	15321M	28111M	32821M	6705763M
2773021M	1994066M	2265149M	Total Assets ($)	35M	4672M	8780M	10286M	17137M	2224239M

M = $ thousand   MM = $ million
See Pages 11 through 18 for Explanation of Ratios and Data

MANUFACTURING—Asphalt Paving Mixture and Block Manufacturing   NAICS 324121 (SIC 2951)

Current Data Sorted By Assets							Comparative Historical Data	

							Type of Statement		
1	1	5	11	1	2		Unqualified	17	12
	5	16	1	1			Reviewed	15	15
	3	2					Compiled	11	8
	3						Tax Returns	1	3
1	1	4	4				Other	10	15
	11 (4/1-9/30/02)		51 (10/1/02-3/31/03)					4/1/98-3/31/99	4/1/99-3/31/00
0-500M	500M-2MM	2-10MM	10-50MM	50-100MM	100-250MM			ALL	ALL
2	13	27	16	2	2		NUMBER OF STATEMENTS	54	53
%	%	%	%	%	%		ASSETS	%	%
	17.9	10.8	9.4				Cash & Equivalents	11.6	14.1
	20.2	23.7	21.3				Trade Receivables (net)	25.8	25.6
	7.9	6.1	14.9				Inventory	6.2	7.7
	8.5	5.2	3.2				All Other Current	3.5	4.0
	54.6	45.8	48.9				Total Current	47.1	51.4
	35.3	41.9	39.3				Fixed Assets (net)	37.8	39.7
	3.3	1.4	.3				Intangibles (net)	4.9	2.4
	6.8	10.9	11.4				All Other Non-Current	10.2	6.4
	100.0	100.0	100.0				Total	100.0	100.0
							LIABILITIES		
	10.9	8.2	4.8				Notes Payable-Short Term	4.2	5.5
	4.3	8.4	4.4				Cur. Mat.-L/T/D	4.6	4.6
	16.8	11.6	12.9				Trade Payables	13.4	16.4
	.4	.7	.7				Income Taxes Payable	.6	.2
	6.2	5.3	5.9				All Other Current	10.0	8.1
	38.6	34.3	28.8				Total Current	32.9	34.8
	20.2	14.3	12.7				Long Term Debt	16.3	15.8
	.7	1.7	1.4				Deferred Taxes	2.5	.4
	6.0	1.8	.7				All Other Non-Current	4.0	2.3
	34.5	47.9	56.4				Net Worth	44.4	46.7
	100.0	100.0	100.0				Total Liabilities & Net Worth	100.0	100.0
							INCOME DATA		
	100.0	100.0	100.0				Net Sales	100.0	100.0
	22.9	21.7	21.5				Gross Profit	20.4	20.6
	20.2	16.7	18.0				Operating Expenses	14.2	14.0
	2.7	5.0	3.5				Operating Profit	6.2	6.6
	.5	1.7	−.5				All Other Expenses (net)	.1	.2
	2.2	3.3	4.0				Profit Before Taxes	6.1	6.4
							RATIOS		
	2.7	2.0	2.7					2.5	2.6
	1.4	1.5	1.7				Current	1.4	1.4
	.9	.8	1.3					1.1	1.0
	1.7	1.6	1.6					1.9	2.1
	1.1	.8	1.0				Quick	1.2	1.1
	.4	.5	.5					.8	.7

											Sales/Receivables				
2	149.0	10	36.3	24	15.1						Sales/Receivables	18	20.3	19	18.9
35	10.4	31	11.8	42	8.7							38	9.5	41	8.9
54	6.7	77	4.7	68	5.3							66	5.5	56	6.5

0	UND	0	UND	9	42.3			Cost of Sales/Inventory	1	428.9	1	721.3
4	95.2	4	88.3	29	12.4				6	59.5	10	35.0
16	23.4	30	12.4	60	6.1				20	18.3	26	13.9

4	91.3	7	49.1	20	17.8			Cost of Sales/Payables	10	37.8	14	26.2
31	11.9	19	18.8	28	13.2				19	19.5	23	15.9
68	5.4	56	6.5	48	7.6				44	8.2	43	8.4

	8.0		7.5		5.8			Sales/Working Capital		6.9		5.9
	11.5		18.4		10.4					18.9		15.3
	NM		−24.0		22.1					162.8		NM

		6.1		7.7		9.3			EBIT/Interest			22.3			18.9
(12)		1.4	(21)	3.9	(15)	6.0				(48)		7.2	(44)		7.4
		−1.0		1.5		2.7						1.9			1.4

		Net Profit + Depr., Dep., Amort./Cur. Mat. L /T/D		15.1		11.4
			(21)	4.5	(11)	4.0
				1.2		1.7

	.2		.5		.4			Fixed/Worth		.5		.4
	.9		.9		.6					.9		.9
	UND		2.0		1.2					2.1		2.0

	.7		.5		.4			Debt/Worth		.5		.4
	2.2		1.2		.9					1.4		1.1
	UND		2.7		1.6					4.1		3.5

		57.8		30.6		26.8			% Profit Before Taxes/Tangible Net Worth			53.1			35.1
(11)		20.2		17.7		11.5				(49)		23.6	(49)		27.1
		−1.3		3.7		6.7						11.6			10.7

	7.8		13.8		13.3			% Profit Before Taxes/Total Assets		17.7		20.6
	2.9		6.2		7.4					10.7		8.8
	−1.6		1.2		3.3					3.6		4.5

	18.8		8.2		8.6			Sales/Net Fixed Assets		10.8		8.9
	11.5		6.4		4.3					5.5		5.4
	3.4		3.0		2.2					3.4		3.3

	2.6		2.9		2.7			Sales/Total Assets		2.9		2.7
	2.1		2.0		1.9					2.1		2.1
	1.6		1.1		1.1					1.4		1.5

		2.6		2.8		2.9			% Depr., Dep., Amort./Sales			1.9			1.9
		3.2	(24)	4.5	(15)	5.3				(50)		3.3	(43)		3.5
		5.1		6.6		6.2						5.1			4.2

		% Officers', Directors', Owners' Comp/Sales			1.6			.9
			(18)		2.5	(16)		1.8
					4.9			6.7

1332M	36575M	234859M	648486M	162447M	872196M		Net Sales ($)	829827M	1190756M
600M	16676M	122250M	361586M	116430M	356118M		Total Assets ($)	546705M	659039M

© RMA 2003

M = $ thousand   MM = $ million
See Pages 11 through 18 for Explanation of Ratios and Data

Comparative Historical Data | | | | Current Data Sorted By Sales

				Type of Statement						
	13		15	21	Unqualified	1	1	1	4	3	11
	13		17	23	Reviewed		4	4	8	6	1
	8		13	5	Compiled		1	3	1		
	6		5	3	Tax Returns	1	1	1			
	11		23	10	Other	1	1		2	3	3
	4/1/00-3/31/01 ALL		4/1/01-3/31/02 ALL	4/1/02-3/31/03 ALL		0-1MM	11 (4/1-9/30/02) 1-3MM	3-5MM	5-10MM	51 (10/1/02-3/31/03) 10-25MM	25MM & OVER
	51		73	62	NUMBER OF STATEMENTS	3	8	9	15	12	15
	%		%	%	ASSETS	%	%	%	%	%	%
	8.1		9.1	11.7	Cash & Equivalents				5.6	9.5	11.1
	25.8		25.6	22.6	Trade Receivables (net)				21.7	29.8	19.8
	6.5		8.4	8.8	Inventory				8.0	5.4	14.1
	8.6		5.8	5.2	All Other Current				1.7	6.2	2.9
	49.0		48.9	48.3	Total Current				37.0	51.0	47.8
	41.8		40.6	39.7	Fixed Assets (net)				43.2	37.8	45.9
	2.5		1.5	2.2	Intangibles (net)				3.4	1.1	1.1
	6.7		9.1	9.8	All Other Non-Current				16.4	10.1	5.2
	100.0		100.0	100.0	Total				100.0	100.0	100.0
					LIABILITIES						
	6.4		7.7	9.4	Notes Payable-Short Term				7.4	10.2	4.6
	15.7		5.8	6.1	Cur. Mat.-L/T/D				10.8	5.7	3.0
	16.1		14.7	13.7	Trade Payables				10.5	12.3	12.1
	.5		.2	.7	Income Taxes Payable				.9	.2	1.1
	9.0		8.2	5.7	All Other Current				4.2	6.1	5.8
	47.6		36.7	35.7	Total Current				33.8	34.5	26.6
	15.5		17.9	14.8	Long Term Debt				16.5	13.5	13.8
	.9		.7	1.4	Deferred Taxes				1.6	1.5	2.3
	9.7		5.8	2.6	All Other Non-Current				3.6	2.8	1.8
	26.3		38.9	45.5	Net Worth				44.6	47.7	55.4
	100.0		100.0	100.0	Total Liabilities & Net Worth				100.0	100.0	100.0
					INCOME DATA						
	100.0		100.0	100.0	Net Sales				100.0	100.0	100.0
	20.9		23.7	21.3	Gross Profit				28.3	17.0	18.2
	17.0		16.8	17.6	Operating Expenses				25.1	14.9	13.1
	3.8		7.0	3.6	Operating Profit				3.2	2.1	5.2
	.3		1.3	.7	All Other Expenses (net)				1.6	-.1	-.2
	3.6		5.6	2.9	Profit Before Taxes				1.6	2.1	5.3
					RATIOS						
	2.5		2.0	2.1					1.6	2.0	2.7
	1.4		1.3	1.5	Current				1.1	1.7	1.8
	.9		1.1	.9					.8	1.1	1.3
	1.8		1.4	1.5					1.4	1.8	1.7
	1.1		1.0	1.0	Quick				.7	1.2	1.0
	.6		.7	.5					.4	.6	.9
22	16.5	23	15.6	13 27.8				18 19.9	12 30.1	24 15.5
42	8.6	40	9.2	36 10.2	Sales/Receivables			42 8.6	36 10.1	29 12.5
65	5.6	68	5.4	58 6.3				77 4.7	86 4.2	47 7.7
0	UND	2	185.6	1 282.3				2 216.4	2 231.1	13 28.3
9	42.9	10	35.8	10 35.7	Cost of Sales/Inventory			10 36.7	7 51.9	19 19.2
20	18.1	27	13.7	30 12.2				50 7.3	19 19.2	37 9.9
16	22.3	10	35.4	11 32.1				7 53.0	7 53.5	17 21.8
25	14.7	26	14.0	24 15.3	Cost of Sales/Payables			23 15.8	19 18.8	24 15.3
42	8.6	37	9.8	52 7.0				97 3.8	45 8.1	33 11.0
	6.6		8.7	7.5					11.1	7.5	6.0
	18.1		17.4	13.9	Sales/Working Capital				110.6	12.3	10.3
	-70.2		62.7	-65.7					-11.5	113.6	23.3
	12.4		12.5	8.6					4.5	9.3	18.1
(49)	3.2	(66)	4.7	(54) 4.5	EBIT/Interest			(12) 2.1	(11) 4.5	(14) 7.3
	1.5		2.0	1.2					1.2	-1.8	4.2
	5.1		4.5	3.2	Net Profit + Depr., Dep.,						
(15)	2.2	(30)	2.2	(19) 1.5	Amort./Cur. Mat. L/T/D						
	1.2		1.5	1.0							
	.5		.5	.4					.5	.5	.5
	1.0		1.0	.9	Fixed/Worth				.9	.7	1.0
	1.9		2.0	1.6					3.3	1.3	1.3
	.5		.8	.5					.4	.5	.4
	1.4		1.5	1.2	Debt/Worth				1.5	1.1	.9
	4.3		3.4	2.7					3.6	2.4	1.6
	30.1		38.5	31.1	% Profit Before Taxes/Tangible				61.8	27.9	27.4
(46)	15.6	(68)	20.1	(59) 17.1	Net Worth			(14) 9.3	13.9	18.4
	6.5		7.3	4.9					.8	-28.6	11.2
	12.6		14.2	12.1	% Profit Before Taxes/Total				7.8	16.4	13.6
	5.3		8.2	5.8	Assets				3.8	5.5	8.9
	1.9		2.9	1.1					1.1	-1.4	4.9
	10.0		9.2	10.0					9.6	8.2	7.6
	6.3		5.8	5.8	Sales/Net Fixed Assets				3.8	7.0	4.5
	2.5		2.9	2.9					1.8	6.4	2.7
	3.2		3.0	2.8					2.3	3.0	3.2
	2.0		2.1	1.9	Sales/Total Assets				1.9	2.4	1.9
	1.5		1.4	1.3					1.0	1.8	1.4
	2.0		1.2	2.8					3.2	2.0	2.5
(47)	3.7	(69)	3.2	(56) 3.7	% Depr., Dep., Amort./Sales			5.9	(10) 3.1	(13) 3.3
	7.0		6.0	6.1					7.1	6.1	5.5
	1.4		1.6	1.6	% Officers', Directors',						
(18)	2.7	(21)	2.2	(19) 2.8	Owners' Comp/Sales						
	5.1		3.6	4.3							
	1375202M		5144906M	1955895M	Net Sales ($)	2330M	17435M	32413M	101263M	193792M	1608662M
	781389M		2080926M	973660M	Total Assets ($)	1414M	10518M	25496M	83008M	95870M	757354M

© RMA 2003   M = $ thousand   MM = $ million
See Pages 11 through 18 for Explanation of Ratios and Data

Current Data Sorted By Assets   **Comparative Historical Data**

0-500M	500M-2MM	2-10MM	10-50MM	50-100MM	100-250MM	Type of Statement	4/1/98-3/31/99 ALL	4/1/99-3/31/00 ALL
	1	7	7	2	2	Unqualified	10	12
	6	8	3			Reviewed	7	14
1	1	4	2			Compiled	6	7
1	2	4	4			Tax Returns	3	6
						Other	17	9
	7 (4/1-9/30/02)		48 (10/1/02-3/31/03)					
2	10	23	16	2	2	**NUMBER OF STATEMENTS**	43	48
%	%	%	%	%	%	**ASSETS**	%	%
	6.4	8.4	10.6			Cash & Equivalents	9.9	9.0
	34.5	28.9	20.0			Trade Receivables (net)	27.4	28.2
	25.3	29.8	15.7			Inventory	19.3	20.0
	.8	1.5	3.1			All Other Current	1.4	3.1
	67.0	68.5	49.4			Total Current	57.9	60.2
	23.6	25.5	31.4			Fixed Assets (net)	28.7	25.0
	.3	2.6	3.2			Intangibles (net)	4.0	3.8
	9.1	3.4	16.1			All Other Non-Current	9.4	11.0
	100.0	100.0	100.0			Total	100.0	100.0
						LIABILITIES		
	8.3	15.0	5.2			Notes Payable-Short Term	8.1	4.1
	3.8	3.4	2.6			Cur. Mat.-L/T/D	2.3	2.5
	13.9	21.1	11.0			Trade Payables	16.0	18.1
	.3	.4	.6			Income Taxes Payable	.3	.3
	6.2	6.9	13.7			All Other Current	9.4	12.0
	32.4	46.7	33.2			Total Current	36.1	37.0
	9.8	11.6	11.8			Long Term Debt	20.7	19.9
	.5	.7	1.8			Deferred Taxes	.3	.4
	14.8	1.5	3.6			All Other Non-Current	4.1	3.9
	42.4	39.5	49.7			Net Worth	38.7	38.8
	100.0	100.0	100.0			Total Liabilities & Net Worth	100.0	100.0
						INCOME DATA		
	100.0	100.0	100.0			Net Sales	100.0	100.0
	43.9	33.8	31.9			Gross Profit	36.9	34.4
	37.4	29.7	23.7			Operating Expenses	30.8	29.2
	6.5	4.1	8.2			Operating Profit	6.1	5.2
	1.0	.4	1.0			All Other Expenses (net)	1.0	.2
	5.5	3.7	7.2			Profit Before Taxes	5.1	5.0
						RATIOS		
	4.0	2.2	4.0				2.7	2.4
	2.0	1.4	1.3			Current	1.9	1.7
	1.3	1.1	.9				1.2	1.2
	2.0	1.4	2.9				1.7	1.5
	1.2	.6	.9			Quick	1.1	1.1
	1.0	.4	.5				.7	.8
	38 9.6	28 12.9	37 9.9				35 10.3	39 9.4
	50 7.4	45 8.1	43 8.5			Sales/Receivables	48 7.6	45 8.0
	56 6.5	59 6.2	59 6.1				59 6.1	61 6.0
	37 9.9	33 11.0	20 18.7				37 9.8	32 11.5
	56 6.5	64 5.7	46 7.9			Cost of Sales/Inventory	53 6.9	57 6.4
	69 5.3	90 4.0	77 4.8				68 5.3	79 4.6
	8 43.8	23 16.0	20 17.8				30 12.3	26 14.0
	30 12.1	36 10.1	34 10.7			Cost of Sales/Payables	38 9.7	37 10.0
	37 9.8	56 6.5	53 6.9				55 6.6	56 6.5
	5.8	6.4	4.6				6.1	5.9
	9.9	18.5	14.8			Sales/Working Capital	10.2	8.5
	15.9	65.0	−123.8				22.4	23.7
		(20) 20.8	(15) 15.2				(38) 7.5	(42) 13.7
		5.5	9.5			EBIT/Interest	3.7	3.9
		1.8	3.2				2.1	1.6
							(16) 8.5	(14) 5.8
						Net Profit + Depr., Dep., Amort./Cur. Mat. L /T/D	4.0	3.2
							1.6	1.4
	.2	.2	.3				.3	.3
	.5	.5	.6			Fixed/Worth	.8	.7
	5.0	1.5	1.9				1.8	1.3
	.2	.9	.3				.6	.9
	.8	2.5	1.2			Debt/Worth	1.7	1.6
	17.5	3.9	2.9				7.5	3.4
		53.3	43.8				(38) 57.8	(45) 56.5
		20.1	(15) 27.4			% Profit Before Taxes/Tangible Net Worth	25.5	24.6
		1.8	9.0				12.3	9.3
	21.1	15.3	18.9				14.5	16.6
	15.8	7.2	10.3			% Profit Before Taxes/Total Assets	8.0	8.1
	.0	.6	2.6				2.8	2.2
	23.9	44.9	16.6				20.9	20.1
	15.8	12.4	5.3			Sales/Net Fixed Assets	10.2	10.2
	9.4	6.5	3.6				5.0	5.0
	3.5	3.7	2.3				3.1	2.7
	2.8	2.7	1.6			Sales/Total Assets	2.4	2.2
	1.7	1.9	1.1				1.4	1.6
	.8	.7	.9				.4	.5
	1.3	(21) 1.6	2.0			% Depr., Dep., Amort./Sales	(40) 1.7	(46) 1.7
	2.5	3.0	3.1				2.5	2.7
							(15) 1.6	(19) 1.3
						% Officers', Directors', Owners' Comp/Sales	2.7	3.8
							7.8	5.4
1313M	32131M	372777M	523045M	216418M	464136M	Net Sales ($)	1066378M	1409366M
374M	11586M	139746M	293445M	140095M	344140M	Total Assets ($)	616685M	783317M

M = $ thousand   MM = $ million
See Pages 11 through 18 for Explanation of Ratios and Data

Comparative Historical Data | Current Data Sorted By Sales

						Type of Statement	0-1MM	1-3MM	3-5MM	5-10MM	10-25MM	25MM & OVER
	10		11		19	Unqualified		1	1	1	9	7
	14		10		17	Reviewed		3	2	2	6	4
	7		5		7	Compiled		1			4	2
	3		3		1	Tax Returns		1				
	6		17		11	Other	1		3	2	3	2
	4/1/00-3/31/01		4/1/01-3/31/02		4/1/02-3/31/03			7 (4/1-9/30/02)			48 (10/1/02-3/31/03)	
	ALL		ALL		ALL		0-1MM	1-3MM	3-5MM	5-10MM	10-25MM	25MM & OVER
	40		46		55	NUMBER OF STATEMENTS	1	6	6	5	22	15
	%		%		%	ASSETS	%	%	%	%	%	%
	10.6		7.2		7.9	Cash & Equivalents					8.3	6.6
	29.2		27.6		26.2	Trade Receivables (net)					22.7	25.7
	21.1		24.1		24.4	Inventory					23.3	23.1
	.9		3.3		1.9	All Other Current					2.2	2.6
	61.8		62.2		60.3	Total Current					56.5	58.0
	24.1		27.3		27.5	Fixed Assets (net)					28.4	30.1
	3.4		6.6		3.9	Intangibles (net)					3.7	6.1
	10.7		3.9		8.3	All Other Non-Current					11.4	5.8
	100.0		100.0		100.0	Total					100.0	100.0
						LIABILITIES						
	11.0		11.4		9.4	Notes Payable-Short Term					11.5	6.5
	3.4		3.1		3.2	Cur. Mat.-L/T/D					3.3	3.4
	21.0		17.5		15.9	Trade Payables					14.0	20.0
	.1		.1		.4	Income Taxes Payable					.3	.7
	9.1		6.0		10.4	All Other Current					11.1	8.4
	44.6		38.0		39.3	Total Current					40.1	39.1
	12.9		15.6		12.2	Long Term Debt					11.8	16.0
	.4		.7		1.0	Deferred Taxes					1.0	1.7
	4.4		3.5		4.8	All Other Non-Current					2.3	4.3
	37.6		42.2		42.7	Net Worth					44.7	39.0
	100.0		100.0		100.0	Total Liabilities & Net Worth					100.0	100.0
						INCOME DATA						
	100.0		100.0		100.0	Net Sales					100.0	100.0
	29.2		33.7		34.3	Gross Profit					37.1	26.8
	25.2		29.8		28.3	Operating Expenses					30.2	20.5
	4.0		3.9		5.9	Operating Profit					6.9	6.3
	.4		.8		.7	All Other Expenses (net)					.5	1.1
	3.7		3.1		5.2	Profit Before Taxes					6.4	5.2
						RATIOS						
	2.6		2.6		2.7						2.9	1.8
	1.3		1.6		1.5	Current					1.6	1.3
	.9		1.2		1.1						1.0	1.2
	1.5		1.6		1.4						1.7	1.0
	.8		.8		.9	Quick					.8	.7
	.6		.7		.5						.4	.6
37	9.9	35	10.4	31	12.0	Sales/Receivables				30	12.2	28	12.9
46	8.0	42	8.7	45	8.1					43	8.5	43	8.5
56	6.6	51	7.2	59	6.2					49	7.5	65	5.6
29	12.4	42	8.7	34	10.7	Cost of Sales/Inventory				33	11.0	33	11.2
55	6.7	59	6.2	62	5.9					64	5.7	53	6.8
74	4.9	82	4.5	73	5.0					90	4.0	72	5.1
25	14.4	24	15.4	23	16.2	Cost of Sales/Payables				28	13.0	21	17.2
40	9.2	31	11.6	35	10.5					36	10.2	39	9.5
60	6.1	56	6.5	53	6.9					54	6.7	53	6.9
	5.1		5.5		6.1	Sales/Working Capital					4.6	6.9
	19.5		9.8		12.2						13.0	14.4
	-96.9		30.0		62.7						-264.2	48.6
	8.5		9.0		17.8	EBIT/Interest					21.8	13.6
(39)	3.5	(40)	3.4	(49)	6.8					(19)	9.5	9.8
	1.6		1.0		2.0						2.7	2.7
	4.3		3.9		8.1	Net Profit + Depr., Dep., Amort./Cur. Mat. L/T/D						
(17)	3.4	(11)	2.8	(17)	5.7							
	1.2		1.3		1.3							
	.3		.3		.3	Fixed/Worth					.3	.3
	.5		.6		.6						.6	.8
	1.9		1.5		1.7						1.7	2.0
	.7		.7		.6	Debt/Worth					.4	1.0
	2.1		1.7		1.5						1.3	2.5
	4.2		5.4		3.9						4.1	3.9
	37.1		50.8		43.1	% Profit Before Taxes/Tangible Net Worth					55.5	57.5
(38)	17.5	(44)	14.9	(52)	19.8					28.8	(14)	38.5
	8.5		1.2		4.7						4.4	18.4
	12.2		15.8		19.8	% Profit Before Taxes/Total Assets					22.5	16.2
	6.8		5.2		9.1						9.9	10.5
	1.2		.1		2.2						3.0	2.6
	27.4		20.9		18.4	Sales/Net Fixed Assets					16.8	17.5
	12.3		9.9		10.6						7.7	6.0
	5.0		4.3		4.5						3.7	4.3
	3.2		3.0		3.1	Sales/Total Assets					2.9	3.4
	2.3		2.1		2.2						2.0	2.2
	1.6		1.7		1.5						1.4	1.5
	.3		.9		.9	% Depr., Dep., Amort./Sales					1.3	.9
	1.2	(41)	1.8	(52)	1.9					(20)	2.3	2.3
	2.3		3.2		2.8						3.8	3.0
	1.9		1.9		2.0	% Officers', Directors', Owners' Comp/Sales						
(17)	3.6	(11)	3.2	(17)	3.2							
	6.4		5.3		4.9							
	1747752M		1264670M		1609820M	Net Sales ($)	161M	11189M	23602M	39147M	360432M	1175289M
	716754M		687201M		929386M	Total Assets ($)	80M	5562M	10385M	20550M	198733M	694076M

© RMA 2003   M = $ thousand   MM = $ million
See Pages 11 through 18 for Explanation of Ratios and Data

Current Data Sorted By Assets | Comparative Historical Data

Type of Statement	0-500M	500M-2MM	2-10MM	10-50MM	50-100MM	100-250MM		4/1/98-3/31/99 ALL	4/1/99-3/31/00 ALL
Unqualified			9	12	4	2		28	28
Reviewed		3	8	1				13	15
Compiled		2	2					14	10
Tax Returns		4	1					4	3
Other	1	3	5	13	3	2		27	29
		16 (4/1-9/30/02)			59 (10/1/02-3/31/03)				
NUMBER OF STATEMENTS	1	12	25	26	7	4		86	85
	%	%	%	%	%	%		%	%
ASSETS									
Cash & Equivalents		12.5	7.1	8.9				8.2	6.2
Trade Receivables (net)		36.8	23.5	18.7				27.6	23.0
Inventory		24.1	19.9	14.5				17.9	18.8
All Other Current		.5	2.0	3.1				2.6	2.3
Total Current		73.9	52.4	45.2				56.3	50.4
Fixed Assets (net)		19.0	35.4	42.1				32.3	35.6
Intangibles (net)		1.0	4.5	7.9				3.7	7.5
All Other Non-Current		6.0	7.6	4.7				7.7	6.5
Total		100.0	100.0	100.0				100.0	100.0
LIABILITIES									
Notes Payable-Short Term		14.3	6.2	5.2				5.1	7.5
Cur. Mat.-L/T/D		1.9	4.2	4.2				3.2	4.0
Trade Payables		27.7	13.9	13.7				16.6	12.2
Income Taxes Payable		.7	.1	.1				.5	.6
All Other Current		10.6	12.9	8.9				9.9	9.3
Total Current		55.2	37.2	32.2				35.3	33.6
Long Term Debt		10.0	19.7	23.7				17.5	21.3
Deferred Taxes		.4	1.0	.5				.8	1.1
All Other Non-Current		1.5	7.1	5.3				5.6	4.6
Net Worth		32.9	35.1	38.4				40.8	39.4
Total Liabilities & Net Worth		100.0	100.0	100.0				100.0	100.0
INCOME DATA									
Net Sales		100.0	100.0	100.0				100.0	100.0
Gross Profit		39.2	37.6	33.0				29.9	35.0
Operating Expenses		36.1	31.1	25.4				25.1	28.3
Operating Profit		3.1	6.6	7.6				4.8	6.7
All Other Expenses (net)		.8	1.5	1.9				1.1	1.0
Profit Before Taxes		2.3	5.0	5.7				3.7	5.7
RATIOS									
Current		1.9 1.3 1.0	2.0 1.5 1.0	2.3 1.4 .9				2.5 1.7 1.1	2.4 1.6 1.0
Quick		1.4 .7 .6	1.2 .9 .6	1.5 .8 .5				1.5 1.0 .6	1.3 .8 .5
Sales/Receivables		29 12.7 44 8.3 48 7.6	30 12.0 40 9.1 53 6.8	34 10.7 45 8.2 53 6.9				37 9.8 47 7.8 59 6.2	37 10.0 47 7.8 57 6.4
Cost of Sales/Inventory		26 14.1 39 9.3 93 3.9	32 11.3 53 6.9 86 4.2	25 14.4 46 8.0 96 3.8				22 16.6 50 7.3 74 4.9	41 9.0 63 5.8 88 4.1
Cost of Sales/Payables		27 13.8 55 6.6 71 5.1	24 15.0 44 8.2 54 6.8	30 12.3 41 8.8 60 6.1				22 16.5 38 9.5 60 6.0	24 15.4 37 9.9 56 6.5
Sales/Working Capital		6.6 39.4 NM	9.1 13.9 137.5	6.0 13.0 -23.3				5.4 8.8 65.8	5.5 11.1 NM
EBIT/Interest			13.6 4.0 1.5	14.5 6.6 .8				(74) 9.6 4.4 1.7	11.9 3.9 1.2
Net Profit + Depr., Dep., Amort./Cur. Mat. L /T/D			(10) 5.9 2.5 .9	(14) 11.6 2.7 1.5				(26) 6.1 2.5 1.0	(30) 3.9 1.9 1.0
Fixed/Worth		.2 .8 1.1	.4 1.1 3.4	.6 1.3 188.8				.4 .9 1.8	.5 1.3 2.7
Debt/Worth		1.1 2.4 9.6	.8 1.5 3.8	.5 1.2 343.1				.8 1.8 3.7	.7 2.0 6.2
% Profit Before Taxes/Tangible Net Worth		(11) 32.0 13.8 3.0	(22) 57.2 20.4 2.9	(21) 33.1 20.7 2.5				(80) 41.4 25.7 6.2	(73) 41.6 20.3 5.0
% Profit Before Taxes/Total Assets		13.4 7.9 .4	22.4 7.7 .8	20.5 7.9 -.5				18.7 7.5 2.1	17.8 8.0 1.3
Sales/Net Fixed Assets		211.2 28.6 6.3	17.6 6.2 2.8	5.7 3.6 2.4				16.0 7.0 3.6	11.5 4.6 2.8
Sales/Total Assets		4.8 2.7 1.9	3.0 2.0 1.3	2.0 1.6 1.0				2.8 1.8 1.2	2.4 1.6 1.1
% Depr., Dep., Amort./Sales		(10) .5 1.6 3.2	(23) 1.1 3.7 4.9	(24) 2.2 4.1 6.5				(71) 1.2 2.3 4.6	(77) 1.5 3.1 6.0
% Officers', Directors', Owners' Comp/Sales			(10) 3.5 7.5 20.1					(23) 2.3 4.4 11.7	(24) 2.1 5.2 10.7
Net Sales ($)	1797M	43105M	264002M	1051874M	512220M	790221M		3615530M	3099180M
Total Assets ($)	459M	14509M	132304M	674940M	429972M	653940M		2807395M	2643383M

M = $ thousand   MM = $ million
See Pages 11 through 18 for Explanation of Ratios and Data

Comparative Historical Data				Current Data Sorted By Sales					
			Type of Statement						
17	15	27	Unqualified		1	1	3	8	14
12	14	12	Reviewed		1	2	4	5	
10	15	4	Compiled		1	1	2		
4	2	5	Tax Returns		2	1	2		
29	33	27	Other		2	2	3	7	13
4/1/00-3/31/01	**4/1/01-3/31/02**	**4/1/02-3/31/03**		**16 (4/1-9/30/02)**			**59 (10/1/02-3/31/03)**		
ALL	**ALL**	**ALL**		**0-1MM**	**1-3MM**	**3-5MM**	**5-10MM**	**10-25MM**	**25MM & OVER**
72	79	75	**NUMBER OF STATEMENTS**		7	7	14	20	27
%	%	%	**ASSETS**	%	%	%	%	%	%
6.9	6.5	8.5	Cash & Equivalents	DATA NOT AVAILABLE			5.0	11.3	5.3
24.5	24.5	23.5	Trade Receivables (net)				25.7	18.9	22.1
19.5	18.2	18.5	Inventory				19.6	18.3	17.3
3.4	2.7	2.2	All Other Current				2.2	2.1	3.2
54.3	51.8	52.8	Total Current				52.4	50.6	48.0
30.3	36.6	35.1	Fixed Assets (net)				37.4	35.5	37.6
6.5	4.7	5.9	Intangibles (net)				4.9	5.3	9.3
8.2	6.9	6.2	All Other Non-Current				5.3	8.6	5.1
100.0	100.0	100.0	Total				100.0	100.0	100.0
			LIABILITIES						
8.4	9.0	6.5	Notes Payable-Short Term				10.1	3.1	5.8
3.4	4.9	4.5	Cur. Mat.-L/T/D				5.2	4.1	6.1
14.6	14.5	15.7	Trade Payables				17.7	10.6	14.9
.4	.4	.2	Income Taxes Payable				.6	.1	.1
8.0	8.1	10.2	All Other Current				12.1	11.5	7.7
34.8	37.0	37.2	Total Current				45.7	29.5	34.6
18.1	20.9	18.7	Long Term Debt				18.7	19.9	18.0
.9	.8	.8	Deferred Taxes				.7	.7	1.1
7.7	8.5	5.3	All Other Non-Current				9.2	2.5	6.6
38.5	32.2	38.0	Net Worth				25.8	47.5	39.7
100.0	100.0	100.0	Total Liabilities & Net Worth				100.0	100.0	100.0
			INCOME DATA						
100.0	100.0	100.0	Net Sales				100.0	100.0	100.0
34.0	34.9	35.1	Gross Profit				44.2	36.2	29.6
27.3	31.1	28.8	Operating Expenses				36.2	29.2	22.1
6.7	3.8	6.3	Operating Profit				7.9	7.0	7.4
2.2	1.9	1.5	All Other Expenses (net)				1.5	.7	1.7
4.5	1.9	4.7	Profit Before Taxes				6.5	6.3	5.7
			RATIOS						
2.5	2.2	2.2					1.9	2.2	2.4
1.6	1.6	1.5	Current				1.1	1.6	1.5
1.0	1.0	1.0					.8	1.2	1.1
1.4	1.5	1.4					1.1	1.4	1.4
1.0	.7	.9	Quick				.9	1.1	.9
.5	.5	.5					.4	.6	.5
35 10.5	**32** 11.4	**33** 11.2					**29** 12.5	**28** 12.9	**41** 8.8
46 8.0	**42** 8.7	**44** 8.3	Sales/Receivables				**40** 9.1	**39** 9.5	**49** 7.5
59 6.2	**52** 7.0	**54** 6.8					**54** 6.8	**46** 7.9	**60** 6.0
38 9.7	**25** 14.4	**29** 12.7					**27** 13.7	**32** 11.5	**29** 12.7
54 6.8	**46** 8.0	**53** 6.8	Cost of Sales/Inventory				**50** 7.3	**69** 5.3	**53** 6.9
89 4.1	**77** 4.7	**93** 3.9					**93** 3.9	**99** 3.7	**92** 4.0
23 15.8	**23** 15.9	**27** 13.5					**24** 15.0	**17** 22.0	**30** 12.0
34 10.6	**34** 10.9	**43** 8.6	Cost of Sales/Payables				**45** 8.1	**38** 9.6	**39** 9.3
58 6.3	**59** 6.2	**64** 5.7					**54** 6.7	**54** 6.8	**62** 5.9
4.9	5.7	6.0					9.5	4.8	5.9
8.4	13.1	11.2	Sales/Working Capital				68.3	10.7	9.1
775.6	−189.6	165.9					−20.9	47.6	43.4
8.7	7.2	10.9					7.0	47.8	14.1
(62) 3.6	(75) 2.6	(72) 4.5	EBIT/Interest				(13) 3.4	5.6	7.0
1.2	1.0	1.3					1.4	1.6	1.5
10.6	7.0	5.8							10.4
(19) 1.8	(16) 2.4	(30) 1.8	Net Profit + Depr., Dep., Amort./Cur. Mat. L/T/D						(14) 1.8
1.1	1.3	.8							.7
.4	.5	.5					1.1	.2	.6
1.0	1.4	.9	Fixed/Worth				1.4	.9	1.1
2.6	5.2	2.5					NM	1.3	9.2
.8	.8	.7					1.4	.7	.6
1.9	2.3	1.5	Debt/Worth				3.0	1.0	1.5
12.8	9.7	3.9					NM	1.5	18.7
43.5	32.3	34.1					81.5	27.0	36.1
(60) 20.0	(66) 15.3	(65) 20.7	% Profit Before Taxes/Tangible Net Worth				(11) 55.6	(18) 12.1	(23) 23.4
5.4	3.2	3.0					20.1	2.4	6.5
15.2	13.3	14.1					18.8	18.8	16.5
6.8	4.9	7.4	% Profit Before Taxes/Total Assets				8.9	6.9	8.9
.4	.0	.4					1.6	1.2	2.7
16.1	14.7	11.2					15.5	18.2	5.2
5.7	4.7	4.8	Sales/Net Fixed Assets				7.1	4.3	3.5
3.3	2.7	2.7					2.0	2.2	2.8
2.7	3.1	2.6					3.2	2.8	1.9
1.7	1.9	1.6	Sales/Total Assets				2.2	1.5	1.6
1.1	1.1	1.1					1.2	1.0	1.2
1.0	1.2	1.6					2.1	.8	2.3
(57) 2.9	(69) 2.9	(67) 3.1	% Depr., Dep., Amort./Sales				(12) 3.4	(19) 4.0	(24) 3.0
4.2	4.9	4.8					4.7	5.0	5.5
2.2	2.3	2.6							
(18) 3.7	(22) 5.1	(18) 7.5	% Officers', Directors', Owners' Comp/Sales						
9.7	12.1	19.2							
3277314M	**2446249M**	**2663219M**	Net Sales ($)		**14949M**	**24813M**	**101550M**	**338638M**	**2183269M**
2732900M	**1667479M**	**1906124M**	Total Assets ($)		**8044M**	**23871M**	**58022M**	**243771M**	**1572416M**

M = $ thousand MM = $ million

See Pages 11 through 18 for Explanation of Ratios and Data

Current Data Sorted By Assets / Comparative Historical Data

0-500M	500M-2MM	2-10MM	10-50MM	50-100MM	100-250MM		4/1/98-3/31/99 ALL	4/1/99-3/31/00 ALL
	7 (4/1-9/30/02)		18 (10/1/02-3/31/03)			**Type of Statement**		
	1		6	1	4	Unqualified	24	14
	2	1				Reviewed	7	5
	1					Compiled	5	7
						Tax Returns	1	1
		1	7		1	Other	10	13
	4	2	13	1	5	**NUMBER OF STATEMENTS**	47	40
%	%	%	%	%	%	**ASSETS**	%	%
			11.6			Cash & Equivalents	6.7	9.9
			19.8			Trade Receivables (net)	23.4	23.7
			11.2			Inventory	22.4	16.0
			1.2			All Other Current	3.2	2.6
			43.9			Total Current	55.6	52.2
			42.4			Fixed Assets (net)	34.0	34.1
			9.4			Intangibles (net)	2.8	5.0
			4.4			All Other Non-Current	7.6	8.8
			100.0			Total	100.0	100.0
						LIABILITIES		
			6.1			Notes Payable-Short Term	9.4	7.2
			3.3			Cur. Mat.-L/T/D	2.8	3.3
			11.4			Trade Payables	17.4	14.4
			.2			Income Taxes Payable	.3	.7
			4.1			All Other Current	7.5	8.0
			25.1			Total Current	37.5	33.7
			18.8			Long Term Debt	15.6	20.4
			1.4			Deferred Taxes	2.1	1.2
			8.2			All Other Non-Current	3.8	6.1
			46.4			Net Worth	41.0	38.6
			100.0			Total Liabilities & Net Worth	100.0	100.0
						INCOME DATA		
			100.0			Net Sales	100.0	100.0
			40.7			Gross Profit	31.4	36.1
			31.4			Operating Expenses	28.5	30.2
			9.2			Operating Profit	2.9	5.9
			2.4			All Other Expenses (net)	.3	.0
			6.8			Profit Before Taxes	2.6	5.9
						RATIOS		
			3.9 / 1.9 / .8			Current	2.4 / 1.4 / 1.1	2.9 / 1.5 / 1.0
			3.1 / 1.2 / .5			Quick	1.2 / .8 / .5	2.0 / .9 / .6
			36 10.1 / 53 6.9 / 66 5.5			Sales/Receivables	32 11.6 / 42 8.6 / 53 6.9	35 10.3 / 50 7.3 / 59 6.2
			28 13.1 / 53 6.9 / 80 4.6			Cost of Sales/Inventory	35 10.3 / 53 6.8 / 83 4.4	28 13.0 / 50 7.4 / 72 5.1
			30 12.0 / 39 9.4 / 64 5.7			Cost of Sales/Payables	28 12.8 / 40 9.1 / 64 5.7	23 15.9 / 37 9.9 / 60 6.1
			3.0 / 7.3 / -24.2			Sales/Working Capital	6.2 / 14.1 / 41.8	5.0 / 10.9 / 136.9
			(12) 30.2 / 2.3 / 1.6			EBIT/Interest	(43) 7.3 / 3.4 / 1.1	(36) 8.8 / 4.0 / 1.6
						Net Profit + Depr., Dep., Amort./Cur. Mat. L /T/D	(23) 12.1 / 3.0 / 1.5	(14) 8.1 / 3.3 / 1.3
			.5 / .7 / 3.6			Fixed/Worth	.4 / .9 / 2.4	.5 / 1.1 / 2.9
			.4 / 1.4 / 5.4			Debt/Worth	.6 / 2.0 / 4.2	.9 / 2.4 / 7.2
			(11) 29.6 / 18.6 / 4.4			% Profit Before Taxes/Tangible Net Worth	(44) 37.6 / 21.0 / 5.1	(37) 45.6 / 16.9 / 6.9
			19.3 / 3.8 / 1.2			% Profit Before Taxes/Total Assets	12.1 / 6.9 / 1.3	15.0 / 6.6 / 1.9
			5.1 / 3.2 / 1.8			Sales/Net Fixed Assets	13.4 / 6.5 / 3.0	13.2 / 4.5 / 2.3
			1.7 / 1.2 / 1.0			Sales/Total Assets	2.5 / 2.0 / 1.1	2.3 / 1.6 / 1.1
			2.7 / 4.2 / 6.8			% Depr., Dep., Amort./Sales	(44) 1.2 / 2.6 / 5.4	(37) 1.2 / 2.8 / 5.5
						% Officers', Directors', Owners' Comp/Sales	(13) 2.5 / 3.1 / 5.3	(13) 1.7 / 4.5 / 12.5
	13945M	29189M	442577M	89554M	957593M	Net Sales ($)	1116135M	874847M
	4191M	7777M	344798M	58240M	859441M	Total Assets ($)	741018M	675518M

(Left-hand columns 0-500M, 500M-2MM, 2-10MM, 50-100MM, 100-250MM: DATA NOT AVAILABLE for the percentage and ratio sections.)

M = $ thousand   MM = $ million
See Pages 11 through 18 for Explanation of Ratios and Data

Comparative Historical Data | Current Data Sorted By Sales

			Type of Statement						
6	7	12	Unqualified	1				3	8
4	4	3	Reviewed		2			1	
4	2		Compiled						
	1		Tax Returns			1			
		1	Other				1	2	6
14	16	9			7 (4/1-9/30/02)			18 (10/1/02-3/31/03)	
4/1/00-3/31/01	4/1/01-3/31/02	4/1/02-3/31/03		0-1MM	1-3MM	3-5MM	5-10MM	10-25MM	25MM & OVER
ALL	ALL	ALL							
28	30	25	**NUMBER OF STATEMENTS**	1	3	1	1	6	14
%	%	%	**ASSETS**	%	%	%	%	%	%
10.2	7.0	9.3	Cash & Equivalents						7.0
24.2	22.7	25.5	Trade Receivables (net)						21.8
16.4	16.1	16.5	Inventory						15.9
1.9	1.4	1.6	All Other Current						1.9
52.8	47.2	52.9	Total Current						46.5
34.2	38.9	33.1	Fixed Assets (net)						36.4
5.3	7.4	8.5	Intangibles (net)						9.9
7.7	6.4	5.4	All Other Non-Current						7.2
100.0	100.0	100.0	Total						100.0
			LIABILITIES						
5.5	6.4	7.6	Notes Payable-Short Term						5.0
2.5	5.1	4.6	Cur. Mat.-L/T/D						5.4
12.3	17.4	15.4	Trade Payables						12.9
.4	.2	.2	Income Taxes Payable						.2
7.0	7.8	8.4	All Other Current						5.6
27.7	36.9	36.2	Total Current						29.2
23.6	29.5	18.6	Long Term Debt						21.7
1.1	1.1	1.8	Deferred Taxes						1.6
6.0	3.6	4.8	All Other Non-Current						5.6
41.6	28.8	38.7	Net Worth						41.9
100.0	100.0	100.0	Total Liabilities & Net Worth						100.0
			INCOME DATA						
100.0	100.0	100.0	Net Sales						100.0
34.2	37.3	38.5	Gross Profit						35.5
29.1	30.4	30.7	Operating Expenses						24.8
5.1	7.0	7.8	Operating Profit						10.7
.3	3.1	1.4	All Other Expenses (net)						1.2
4.8	3.9	6.4	Profit Before Taxes						9.5
			RATIOS						
3.5	2.0	2.6							2.9
2.0	1.3	1.5	Current						1.9
1.2	.8	1.0							1.0
2.4	1.2	1.3							1.5
1.0	.8	.9	Quick						1.0
.6	.5	.6							.5
33 11.2	33 11.0	36 10.1						42	8.8
49 7.5	42 8.6	53 6.9	Sales/Receivables					55	6.6
70 5.2	62 5.9	68 5.3						73	5.0
30 12.2	21 17.7	37 9.9						48	7.6
48 7.6	55 6.6	54 6.8	Cost of Sales/Inventory					65	5.6
98 3.7	106 3.4	86 4.2						92	4.0
18 20.2	31 11.7	33 11.0						35	10.5
37 9.8	41 8.8	40 9.0	Cost of Sales/Payables					44	8.3
53 6.9	75 4.8	64 5.7						61	6.0
4.4	6.6	3.9							3.3
8.7	17.0	8.9	Sales/Working Capital						6.7
23.3	-28.3	-173.1							-161.1
19.6	6.6	13.3							14.3
(27) 3.5	(27) 2.0	(23) 2.7	EBIT/Interest					(13)	2.7
1.6	1.0	2.0							2.1
2.5	2.9	2.5	Net Profit + Depr., Dep.,						
(11) 1.5	(12) 1.8	(13) 1.4	Amort./Cur. Mat. L/T/D						
.4	.6	.7							
.4	.7	.5							.6
.8	1.4	1.0	Fixed/Worth						1.3
3.2	7.3	2.8							2.6
.8	1.6	1.2							1.1
1.8	4.1	2.2	Debt/Worth						2.1
4.3	13.4	5.2							6.4
27.5	40.2	47.4	% Profit Before Taxes/Tangible						58.2
(25) 10.8	(25) 18.5	(22) 19.3	Net Worth					(13)	19.4
3.9	8.0	5.7							9.8
12.2	9.2	17.4	% Profit Before Taxes/Total						23.5
5.7	2.9	3.9	Assets						4.0
1.2	-1.0	1.2							2.5
11.1	8.9	9.9							6.0
4.6	4.7	4.6	Sales/Net Fixed Assets						3.6
1.7	2.4	2.8							2.9
2.2	2.2	2.2							1.6
1.4	1.5	1.4	Sales/Total Assets						1.3
.7	.9	1.1							1.1
1.2	2.2	1.8							2.6
(26) 2.5	(25) 3.3	(23) 3.2	% Depr., Dep., Amort./Sales					(12)	4.1
6.3	5.0	5.8							5.7
			% Officers', Directors', Owners' Comp/Sales						
481692M	1008047M	1532858M	Net Sales ($)	1699M	12246M	6132M	98614M		1414167M
424154M	828651M	1274447M	Total Assets ($)	681M	3510M	13705M	91244M		1165307M

© RMA 2003   M = $ thousand   MM = $ million
See Pages 11 through 18 for Explanation of Ratios and Data

Current Data Sorted By Assets   Comparative Historical Data

	0-500M	500M-2MM	2-10MM	10-50MM	50-100MM	100-250MM		4/1/98-3/31/99 ALL	4/1/99-3/31/00 ALL
Type of Statement									
Unqualified			4	15	3	4		20	22
Reviewed		2	3	4				9	14
Compiled		4	3	1				4	8
Tax Returns		1	1					1	2
Other	1	2	7	11	2			21	14
	21 (4/1-9/30/02)			47 (10/1/02-3/31/03)					
NUMBER OF STATEMENTS	1	9	18	31	5	4		55	60
	%	%	%	%	%	%		%	%
ASSETS									
Cash & Equivalents			6.5	6.8				7.7	8.9
Trade Receivables (net)			29.8	16.7				22.4	25.0
Inventory			24.0	15.4				17.8	17.7
All Other Current			2.9	6.0				2.1	1.7
Total Current			63.2	44.8				49.9	53.3
Fixed Assets (net)			29.4	45.5				36.2	32.0
Intangibles (net)			2.3	3.1				7.7	9.6
All Other Non-Current			5.0	6.6				6.1	5.1
Total			100.0	100.0				100.0	100.0
LIABILITIES									
Notes Payable-Short Term			9.9	3.9				6.7	6.7
Cur. Mat.-L/T/D			2.4	4.3				4.2	3.2
Trade Payables			16.7	7.6				11.6	14.3
Income Taxes Payable			.2	.1				.8	.4
All Other Current			17.8	7.2				7.8	7.4
Total Current			47.0	23.1				31.1	31.9
Long Term Debt			16.8	18.5				21.4	20.7
Deferred Taxes			1.6	1.0				.8	.9
All Other Non-Current			2.5	6.5				5.4	3.2
Net Worth			32.2	50.9				41.3	43.3
Total Liabilities & Net Worth			100.0	100.0				100.0	100.0
INCOME DATA									
Net Sales			100.0	100.0				100.0	100.0
Gross Profit			24.0	29.6				36.7	36.0
Operating Expenses			24.1	18.8				28.2	28.5
Operating Profit			.0	10.9				8.5	7.4
All Other Expenses (net)			1.8	.5				2.1	.8
Profit Before Taxes			−1.8	10.4				6.4	6.6
RATIOS									
Current			2.1	3.0				2.5	2.8
			1.3	1.7				1.7	1.8
			1.0	1.4				1.0	1.1
Quick			1.0	1.6				1.3	1.7
			.7	1.1				1.0	1.1
			.5	.7				.5	.7
Sales/Receivables		45	8.0	31 11.9			33	11.2	33 11.1
		54	6.7	44 8.3			44	8.3	49 7.4
		76	4.8	56 6.5			54	6.8	65 5.6
Cost of Sales/Inventory		24	15.2	19 19.6			37	9.8	35 10.4
		54	6.8	53 6.9			60	6.1	57 6.5
		93	3.9	85 4.3			94	3.9	77 4.7
Cost of Sales/Payables		27	13.6	19 19.1			20	18.4	19 19.5
		45	8.1	27 13.8			35	10.5	39 9.4
		59	6.2	34 10.6			50	7.3	59 6.2
Sales/Working Capital			5.4	3.6				6.6	4.4
			14.7	8.3				9.6	8.9
			NM	19.0				808.4	32.7
EBIT/Interest		(16)	7.1	(28) 15.6			(52)	12.0	(57) 9.9
			1.4	8.7				3.4	4.2
			−.2	3.6				1.1	1.5
Net Profit + Depr., Dep., Amort./Cur. Mat. L /T/D							(16)	16.2	(23) 19.8
								3.4	5.2
								2.3	2.2
Fixed/Worth			.2	.5				.6	.4
			.4	.7				1.0	1.0
			3.3	1.4				2.8	1.8
Debt/Worth			1.4	.5				.7	.7
			2.8	.8				1.7	1.4
			5.4	1.4				7.1	4.8
% Profit Before Taxes/Tangible Net Worth		(17)	60.3	(30) 36.5			(46)	54.0	(52) 43.6
			6.9	27.0				24.5	23.9
			−10.8	15.8				9.0	9.9
% Profit Before Taxes/Total Assets			6.5	21.0				21.4	15.7
			1.5	12.4				10.0	8.8
			−2.7	6.6				1.0	1.4
Sales/Net Fixed Assets			37.9	8.4				9.8	16.0
			13.7	2.9				4.8	6.5
			2.9	1.7				3.0	3.2
Sales/Total Assets			2.5	1.6				2.4	2.4
			1.8	1.3				1.6	1.7
			1.3	1.1				1.3	1.1
% Depr., Dep., Amort./Sales		(15)	1.1	(28) 1.7			(43)	1.4	(55) 1.2
			1.5	4.3				2.9	2.9
			4.1	5.9				4.5	5.3
% Officers', Directors', Owners' Comp/Sales							(15)	3.3	(21) 2.4
								4.9	4.8
								7.9	9.5
Net Sales ($)	1603M	34786M	177963M	1090118M	358029M	824378M		2336811M	2625260M
Total Assets ($)	418M	11805M	108628M	810696M	382380M	594301M		1638065M	1865727M

M = $ thousand   MM = $ million
See Pages 11 through 18 for Explanation of Ratios and Data

Comparative Historical Data | | Current Data Sorted By Sales

23	28	26	**Type of Statement**				1	8	17
23	28	26	Unqualified				1	8	17
10	8	9	Reviewed		2		1	4	2
7	10	8	Compiled		4		2	1	
	2	2	Tax Returns	1		1	1		
19	19	23	Other	2	2		5	6	8
4/1/00-3/31/01	4/1/01-3/31/02	4/1/02-3/31/03		0-1MM	21 (4/1-9/30/02)		47 (10/1/02-3/31/03)		
ALL	ALL	ALL		0-1MM	1-3MM	3-5MM	5-10MM	10-25MM	25MM & OVER
59	67	68	**NUMBER OF STATEMENTS**	1	3	8	10	19	27
%	%	%	**ASSETS**	%	%	%	%	%	%
8.2	6.8	7.7	Cash & Equivalents				6.9	5.4	8.1
20.9	19.5	23.4	Trade Receivables (net)				33.6	21.4	16.6
18.8	17.5	19.6	Inventory				31.4	22.1	14.8
2.4	4.5	4.1	All Other Current				.5	8.1	3.5
50.3	48.4	54.8	Total Current				72.4	57.0	43.0
35.7	37.9	34.7	Fixed Assets (net)				21.0	33.1	42.6
6.5	5.3	3.5	Intangibles (net)				2.4	1.7	5.6
7.5	8.4	7.1	All Other Non-Current				4.3	8.2	8.8
100.0	100.0	100.0	Total				100.0	100.0	100.0
			LIABILITIES						
6.3	6.4	6.2	Notes Payable-Short Term				6.5	6.6	4.3
3.2	4.5	3.2	Cur. Mat.-L/T/D				.4	3.9	4.1
12.6	12.0	12.3	Trade Payables				18.0	11.0	7.6
.3	.3	.2	Income Taxes Payable				.5	.1	.2
6.9	7.4	10.9	All Other Current				25.8	8.2	6.6
29.3	30.6	32.8	Total Current				51.0	29.8	22.8
21.0	20.7	16.7	Long Term Debt				10.0	16.5	16.6
1.3	1.0	1.2	Deferred Taxes				.2	2.0	1.2
3.7	5.3	4.8	All Other Non-Current				2.1	6.0	5.8
44.6	42.4	44.6	Net Worth				36.6	45.6	53.7
100.0	100.0	100.0	Total Liabilities & Net Worth				100.0	100.0	100.0
			INCOME DATA						
100.0	100.0	100.0	Net Sales				100.0	100.0	100.0
32.2	33.5	30.0	Gross Profit				27.6	26.9	28.2
24.0	25.9	23.3	Operating Expenses				21.4	22.2	17.8
8.2	7.7	6.7	Operating Profit				6.2	4.7	10.5
.4	1.2	.9	All Other Expenses (net)				1.5	.5	.2
7.9	6.4	5.8	Profit Before Taxes				4.7	4.2	10.2
			RATIOS						
2.5	2.6	2.8					5.8	3.0	2.9
1.8	1.8	1.7	Current				1.5	2.1	1.7
1.2	1.1	1.3					.9	1.3	1.4
1.4	1.6	1.3					3.0	1.6	1.2
1.0	.8	1.0	Quick				.9	.8	1.1
.7	.5	.6					.4	.6	.7
32 11.3	32 11.4	36 10.0					42 8.6	37 9.9	31 11.9
47 7.7	43 8.5	47 7.8	Sales/Receivables				50 7.3	47 7.8	43 8.4
57 6.4	56 6.5	62 5.9					70 5.2	62 5.9	57 6.3
26 14.1	24 15.4	22 16.8					33 11.2	36 10.0	22 16.9
57 6.4	58 6.3	51 7.2	Cost of Sales/Inventory				60 6.0	70 5.2	36 10.1
87 4.2	80 4.6	90 4.1					171 2.1	97 3.8	72 5.1
21 17.1	22 16.3	19 19.0					12 29.2	24 14.9	18 19.9
40 9.1	32 11.3	32 11.5	Cost of Sales/Payables				43 8.5	29 12.5	27 13.3
54 6.7	67 5.5	51 7.2					52 7.1	45 8.1	44 8.2
4.4	4.3	4.3					4.1	3.5	4.2
8.2	9.0	8.8	Sales/Working Capital				11.4	5.7	10.7
25.6	81.2	16.3					NM	15.2	15.5
9.9	9.1	11.3						9.4	31.5
(56) 3.8	(63) 3.1	(61) 5.9	EBIT/Interest				(17)	(25) 3.2	8.6
1.6	1.2	1.6						1.2	2.8
12.0	5.8	13.6							30.1
(20) 2.3	(21) 1.4	(20) 2.2	Net Profit + Depr., Dep., Amort./Cur. Mat. L/T/D					(10) 8.0	
1.3	1.0	.4							.4
.4	.3	.2					.2	.2	.4
1.1	1.0	.6	Fixed/Worth				.3	.7	.7
1.9	1.8	1.6					21.1	1.9	1.3
.6	.7	.6					1.0	.7	.5
1.3	1.6	1.3	Debt/Worth				2.2	1.3	.7
4.2	3.4	2.9					35.4	2.5	1.4
51.4	47.9	37.0						26.6	36.8
(53) 21.5	(62) 17.9	(64) 19.0	% Profit Before Taxes/Tangible Net Worth					12.6	(25) 27.3
10.4	1.8	4.8						.8	5.5
17.0	14.8	17.8					9.5	12.4	21.6
8.4	5.5	6.7	% Profit Before Taxes/Total Assets				5.7	5.4	12.8
1.6	.6	2.0					.9	.4	3.5
15.1	12.5	23.4					40.4	17.4	5.8
4.8	4.8	5.1	Sales/Net Fixed Assets				23.1	6.6	3.6
2.3	1.9	2.3					4.0	2.5	2.0
2.2	2.1	2.0					3.7	1.9	1.7
1.4	1.4	1.4	Sales/Total Assets				1.9	1.5	1.2
1.0	.9	1.1					1.2	1.2	1.1
1.3	1.0	1.3						.6	2.0
(49) 2.7	(58) 3.1	(58) 2.4	% Depr., Dep., Amort./Sales				(17)	2.5	(22) 3.8
5.1	5.7	5.0						5.4	5.7
2.2	1.6	1.7							
(11) 4.3	(19) 2.9	(16) 2.3	% Officers', Directors', Owners' Comp/Sales						
8.4	10.4	7.5							
2573668M	2728520M	2486877M	Net Sales ($)	930M	5119M	31231M	77253M	334239M	2038105M
1869397M	2184806M	1908228M	Total Assets ($)	813M	1829M	29446M	46785M	236785M	1592570M

M = $ thousand   MM = $ million
See Pages 11 through 18 for Explanation of Ratios and Data

Current Data Sorted By Assets   Comparative Historical Data

0-500M	500M-2MM	2-10MM	10-50MM	50-100MM	100-250MM	Type of Statement	4/1/98-3/31/99 ALL	4/1/99-3/31/00 ALL
	3	15	19	15	9	Unqualified	64	49
1	11	25	4	1		Reviewed	36	38
5	13	2	1			Compiled	30	23
1	6	3		1	1	Tax Returns	4	7
2	13	25	14	3	4	Other	53	65
	39 (4/1-9/30/02)			158 (10/1/02-3/31/03)				
9	46	70	38	20	14	**NUMBER OF STATEMENTS**	187	182
%	%	%	%	%	%	**ASSETS**	%	%
	8.1	5.4	3.4	3.2	4.2	Cash & Equivalents	6.5	6.4
	31.9	27.0	22.3	20.7	17.6	Trade Receivables (net)	26.3	27.2
	22.0	23.7	20.9	21.0	19.7	Inventory	19.9	20.2
	2.7	2.3	3.8	4.0	2.4	All Other Current	1.8	1.4
	64.8	58.4	50.3	48.9	44.0	Total Current	54.5	55.2
	30.7	35.8	42.0	38.4	37.3	Fixed Assets (net)	36.9	36.5
	.6	1.9	4.2	8.0	12.0	Intangibles (net)	3.8	3.5
	3.9	3.9	3.5	4.7	6.7	All Other Non-Current	4.8	4.8
	100.0	100.0	100.0	100.0	100.0	Total	100.0	100.0
						LIABILITIES		
	14.4	10.2	11.3	4.4	.6	Notes Payable-Short Term	11.2	9.2
	8.4	5.6	5.7	8.6	3.4	Cur. Mat.-L/T/D	4.2	4.4
	17.0	17.2	15.0	13.9	13.4	Trade Payables	15.7	15.9
	.0	.5	.4	.2	.2	Income Taxes Payable	.3	.6
	8.6	7.4	6.6	11.9	8.1	All Other Current	7.3	9.4
	48.4	40.9	38.9	39.1	25.8	Total Current	38.7	39.5
	20.3	17.7	22.5	13.4	34.4	Long Term Debt	19.8	20.5
	.4	.8	1.6	2.6	.9	Deferred Taxes	1.1	.9
	7.8	6.1	6.1	10.6	7.7	All Other Non-Current	4.9	3.1
	23.1	34.5	31.0	34.4	31.3	Net Worth	35.6	36.0
	100.0	100.0	100.0	100.0	100.0	Total Liabilities & Net Worth	100.0	100.0
						INCOME DATA		
	100.0	100.0	100.0	100.0	100.0	Net Sales	100.0	100.0
	30.2	26.6	23.1	19.8	22.1	Gross Profit	27.9	30.3
	28.1	22.7	16.1	14.8	14.7	Operating Expenses	21.8	23.6
	2.1	4.0	7.0	5.0	7.4	Operating Profit	6.1	6.8
	1.3	1.2	1.6	1.8	2.6	All Other Expenses (net)	1.4	1.6
	.8	2.8	5.4	3.1	4.8	Profit Before Taxes	4.7	5.1
						RATIOS		
	2.6	2.3	1.7	2.1	2.2	Current	2.1	2.2
	1.5	1.3	1.3	1.4	1.6		1.4	1.5
	1.1	1.0	1.0	1.0	1.3		1.0	1.0
	1.6	1.4	.9	1.2	1.2	Quick	1.4	1.5
	1.1	.7	.7	.7	.7		.8	.9
	.6	.5	.5	.4	.6		.6	.5
	33 11.1	33 11.1	42 8.7	34 10.7	24 15.0	Sales/Receivables	35 10.4	38 9.7
	44 8.3	42 8.7	49 7.5	48 7.5	48 7.5		45 8.0	48 7.5
	59 6.2	53 6.9	55 6.6	54 6.8	53 6.9		55 6.6	59 6.2
	30 12.3	29 12.4	45 8.1	41 8.8	37 9.9	Cost of Sales/Inventory	29 12.5	34 10.8
	44 8.3	45 8.1	53 6.9	49 7.4	50 7.4		48 7.6	52 7.0
	59 5.4	68 5.4	73 5.0	59 6.2	66 5.5		67 5.4	74 4.9
	19 19.3	23 15.6	21 17.1	19 19.3	27 13.7	Cost of Sales/Payables	23 15.8	26 13.9
	30 12.0	39 9.4	40 9.1	26 14.0	35 10.4		34 10.7	35 10.3
	47 7.8	50 7.4	51 7.1	39 9.3	41 9.0		52 7.1	51 7.2
	5.5	6.2	8.9	6.0	6.3	Sales/Working Capital	7.0	6.3
	11.3	18.3	16.1	12.8	10.3		14.1	11.7
	NM	−210.4	261.6	136.0	18.5		89.9	135.5
	(42) 7.7	(66) 7.0	(37) 8.2	(18) 7.9	11.9	EBIT/Interest	(169) 8.6	(159) 7.5
	1.5	2.7	4.3	4.6	3.3		3.3	3.1
	−.5	1.1	1.7	.0	1.8		1.2	1.5
		(20) 3.6	(16) 4.2			Net Profit + Depr., Dep., Amort./Cur. Mat. L /T/D	(72) 5.5	(57) 4.9
		1.9	2.1				2.6	2.5
		.7	1.1				1.2	1.3
	.3	.5	1.1	.7	.6	Fixed/Worth	.5	.6
	.8	1.1	1.8	1.3	2.2		1.1	1.1
	3.7	2.8	2.2	3.3	NM		2.7	2.4
	.6	.7	1.7	.9	1.6	Debt/Worth	.7	.8
	2.0	2.1	2.6	2.0	2.9		2.1	2.0
	19.5	6.6	4.0	7.4	NM		6.1	4.2
	(38) 44.4	(65) 48.2	(36) 39.9	(17) 29.8	(11) 84.1	% Profit Before Taxes/Tangible Net Worth	(165) 44.4	(165) 45.8
	11.8	19.6	22.1	19.6	15.2		22.6	23.4
	−4.7	5.9	10.2	8.4	4.6		7.4	8.6
	22.1	12.5	12.7	11.5	12.7	% Profit Before Taxes/Total Assets	15.9	16.8
	2.2	5.1	5.9	7.9	6.3		6.8	7.1
	−4.1	.8	1.9	−1.0	2.5		1.3	1.8
	28.6	12.0	6.1	6.6	5.5	Sales/Net Fixed Assets	10.3	11.0
	9.7	6.6	4.0	4.3	4.2		5.3	5.3
	4.6	3.5	2.5	2.5	1.9		3.3	3.3
	3.1	2.8	2.1	2.1	2.0	Sales/Total Assets	2.7	2.6
	2.7	2.2	1.9	1.7	1.3		2.0	2.0
	1.8	1.5	1.2	1.3	1.0		1.4	1.4
	(42) 1.0	(64) 1.6	(33) 2.8	(17) 2.6	(11) 1.5	% Depr., Dep., Amort./Sales	(173) 2.0	(162) 1.7
	2.4	2.7	4.2	3.3	2.8		3.2	3.2
	4.3	5.1	6.9	6.2	4.1		4.6	5.3
	(23) 2.6	(21) 2.7				% Officers', Directors', Owners' Comp/Sales	(48) 1.9	(58) 1.9
	6.0	4.6					4.4	4.8
	7.7	8.2					7.1	7.6
9306M	139406M	767308M	1482302M	2575639M	4213622M	Net Sales ($)	4759537M	4178120M
2509M	53592M	336414M	878223M	1371639M	2166408M	Total Assets ($)	2971521M	2746111M

Comparative Historical Data | Current Data Sorted By Sales

			Type of Statement	0-1MM	1-3MM	3-5MM	5-10MM	10-25MM	25MM & OVER
36	32	61	Unqualified		2	1	9	10	39
30	21	42	Reviewed	1	6	6	15	11	3
32	32	21	Compiled	3	9	6	1	2	
6	6	12	Tax Returns	1	3	2	2	2	2
40	58	61	Other	3	9	8	7	12	22
4/1/00-3/31/01 ALL	4/1/01-3/31/02 ALL	4/1/02-3/31/03 ALL			39 (4/1-9/30/02)		158 (10/1/02-3/31/03)		
144	149	197	NUMBER OF STATEMENTS	8	29	23	34	37	66
%	%	%	ASSETS	%	%	%	%	%	%
4.5	6.5	5.5	Cash & Equivalents		8.8	5.3	6.1	5.8	3.4
29.6	24.9	25.6	Trade Receivables (net)		27.5	29.4	26.6	27.2	22.7
22.3	21.4	22.3	Inventory		19.5	22.8	23.4	22.9	22.3
2.6	3.1	2.8	All Other Current		2.3	2.9	2.2	2.5	3.3
58.9	56.0	56.2	Total Current		58.2	60.4	58.3	58.4	51.7
34.2	36.0	35.9	Fixed Assets (net)		34.1	34.8	35.2	35.7	37.3
2.6	3.8	3.3	Intangibles (net)		.7	.4	2.9	2.5	6.2
4.3	4.2	4.6	All Other Non-Current		7.1	4.4	3.6	3.4	4.7
100.0	100.0	100.0	Total		100.0	100.0	100.0	100.0	100.0
			LIABILITIES						
13.3	11.8	9.9	Notes Payable-Short Term		15.1	10.8	10.4	9.9	7.2
5.3	5.1	6.3	Cur. Mat.-L/T/D		8.0	7.7	6.0	4.7	6.1
17.7	14.4	16.4	Trade Payables		16.9	13.8	14.3	19.9	15.6
.5	.2	.3	Income Taxes Payable		.1	.7	.3	.2	.3
11.6	10.9	9.9	All Other Current		23.0	8.0	6.4	7.0	8.7
48.3	42.4	42.7	Total Current		63.2	40.9	37.4	41.6	38.0
20.2	21.0	21.6	Long Term Debt		21.7	23.8	17.6	16.1	20.1
.7	.6	1.0	Deferred Taxes		.6	.5	.6	.6	1.9
7.7	5.2	7.2	All Other Non-Current		7.8	2.5	10.6	3.1	7.8
23.0	30.8	27.4	Net Worth		6.6	32.2	33.7	38.5	32.2
100.0	100.0	100.0	Total Liabilities & Net Worth		100.0	100.0	100.0	100.0	100.0
			INCOME DATA						
100.0	100.0	100.0	Net Sales		100.0	100.0	100.0	100.0	100.0
27.6	26.1	26.8	Gross Profit		31.1	28.4	28.2	26.8	20.6
22.6	22.5	22.1	Operating Expenses		32.2	25.0	25.0	19.7	14.5
5.0	3.5	4.6	Operating Profit		-1.1	3.4	3.2	7.1	6.1
1.9	1.8	1.5	All Other Expenses (net)		1.7	.5	1.5	1.2	1.7
3.1	1.7	3.1	Profit Before Taxes		-2.8	2.9	1.8	5.9	4.4
			RATIOS						
2.0 / 1.4 / 1.0	2.4 / 1.4 / .9	2.1 / 1.4 / 1.0	Current		2.3 / 1.4 / .7	2.5 / 1.5 / 1.0	2.7 / 1.6 / 1.0	2.0 / 1.2 / 1.0	2.1 / 1.4 / 1.0
1.2 / .8 / .5	1.3 / .8 / .5	1.2 / .7 / .5	Quick		1.6 / .7 / .4	1.5 / 1.0 / .6	1.6 / .8 / .5	1.1 / .7 / .6	1.2 / .7 / .5
38 9.6 / 48 7.6 / 59 6.1	35 10.5 / 45 8.2 / 54 6.7	34 10.7 / 45 8.1 / 54 6.7	Sales/Receivables		31 11.7 / 44 8.4 / 59 6.2	38 9.6 / 49 7.5 / 60 6.1	32 11.3 / 39 9.3 / 52 7.0	34 10.8 / 43 8.6 / 53 6.8	36 10.1 / 48 7.6 / 54 6.8
32 11.3 / 49 7.5 / 73 5.0	30 12.2 / 44 8.2 / 70 5.2	33 11.1 / 49 7.5 / 65 5.6	Cost of Sales/Inventory		32 11.5 / 48 7.5 / 60 6.1	27 13.6 / 40 9.2 / 80 4.6	27 13.6 / 45 8.1 / 68 5.3	29 12.7 / 41 8.9 / 65 5.6	43 8.4 / 51 7.1 / 63 5.8
21 17.0 / 34 10.6 / 54 6.8	18 20.1 / 30 12.1 / 49 7.4	21 17.0 / 36 10.1 / 48 7.6	Cost of Sales/Payables		26 14.2 / 41 8.9 / 53 6.9	15 24.0 / 30 12.3 / 47 7.7	12 30.1 / 27 13.6 / 41 8.8	28 12.9 / 43 8.5 / 53 6.9	22 16.9 / 34 10.7 / 45 8.2
7.0 / 15.4 / NM	5.7 / 14.0 / -88.3	6.6 / 12.5 / 584.7	Sales/Working Capital		5.3 / 14.1 / -17.7	6.2 / 13.3 / 192.6	5.5 / 10.7 / NM	7.5 / 23.1 / -146.7	7.4 / 11.8 / 122.0
(131) 4.8 / 2.4 / 1.0	(134) 4.7 / 2.2 / .4	(185) 7.4 / 3.0 / .8	EBIT/Interest		(26) 2.9 / -.1 / -3.7	(22) 5.9 / 3.0 / .7	(32) 5.8 / 1.6 / .7	(35) 10.3 / 5.5 / 2.6	(63) 10.8 / 3.8 / 1.6
(41) 6.0 / 2.7 / 1.4	(46) 2.7 / 1.6 / .9	(55) 4.5 / 2.1 / .8	Net Profit + Depr., Dep., Amort./Cur. Mat. L/T/D					(14) 5.9 / 2.9 / 1.3	(22) 7.7 / 1.9 / .9
.5 / 1.2 / 3.6	.5 / 1.4 / 3.1	.6 / 1.3 / 3.1	Fixed/Worth		.4 / 1.4 / 23.0	.3 / 1.2 / 2.6	.4 / .9 / 2.3	.7 / 1.2 / 2.2	.8 / 1.5 / 2.8
1.0 / 2.3 / 7.0	.9 / 2.3 / 7.9	1.1 / 2.2 / 7.5	Debt/Worth		1.0 / 2.1 / NM	.8 / 2.2 / 7.9	.7 / 2.0 / 5.5	1.1 / 1.9 / 5.6	1.4 / 2.6 / 5.5
(122) 42.5 / 26.1 / 3.8	(126) 27.5 / 11.5 / -.3	(171) 41.7 / 18.4 / 4.1	% Profit Before Taxes/Tangible Net Worth		(22) 17.9 / -2.7 / -38.6	(22) 76.5 / 23.9 / -.2	(31) 32.4 / 15.8 / -1.4	(36) 68.2 / 29.2 / 15.9	(58) 41.0 / 19.9 / 11.0
13.9 / 5.5 / .4	11.2 / 4.2 / -2.0	12.8 / 5.9 / -.2	% Profit Before Taxes/Total Assets		6.7 / -2.4 / -12.3	20.3 / 4.0 / -.2	11.0 / 3.2 / -1.1	16.2 / 10.3 / 3.4	11.8 / 6.3 / 1.9
14.3 / 6.1 / 3.6	13.0 / 5.3 / 3.1	12.7 / 5.5 / 3.3	Sales/Net Fixed Assets		21.6 / 9.2 / 2.5	15.8 / 6.1 / 3.1	25.0 / 5.8 / 3.4	11.4 / 7.0 / 3.9	6.7 / 4.5 / 3.0
2.9 / 2.1 / 1.4	2.6 / 1.9 / 1.3	2.8 / 2.1 / 1.4	Sales/Total Assets		3.1 / 2.5 / 1.6	2.8 / 2.1 / 1.7	3.1 / 2.2 / 1.4	2.8 / 2.3 / 1.7	2.2 / 1.9 / 1.3
(123) 1.1 / 2.2 / 4.2	(130) 1.3 / 2.7 / 4.7	(174) 1.6 / 3.2 / 5.3	% Depr., Dep., Amort./Sales		(26) 1.4 / 2.8 / 5.4	(20) .4 / 3.0 / 5.3	(33) 1.4 / 3.5 / 6.4	(33) 1.7 / 2.9 / 5.2	(56) 2.0 / 3.1 / 4.9
(47) 1.6 / 4.0 / 8.6	(42) 2.7 / 6.8 / 10.3	(54) 2.6 / 4.6 / 7.8	% Officers', Directors', Owners' Comp/Sales			(13) 1.9 / 3.1 / 5.0	(12) 3.0 / 6.1 / 9.0	(11) 1.8 / 4.6 / 6.0		
4510836M	5275774M	9187583M	Net Sales ($)	4819M	54990M	91459M	235467M	608857M	8191991M
2917156M	3734934M	4808785M	Total Assets ($)	3214M	30678M	45160M	126291M	316545M	4286897M

© RMA 2003   M = $ thousand   MM = $ million
See Pages 11 through 18 for Explanation of Ratios and Data

Current Data Sorted By Assets

Comparative Historical Data

		1	5	5	1		Type of Statement		14		13
	3	1	6	1		1	Unqualified		14		13
	1	1	1				Reviewed		11		9
	2						Compiled		7		8
1	1		6	1		1	Tax Returns		3		2
							Other		13		14
	12 (4/1-9/30/02)			25 (10/1/02-3/31/03)					4/1/98-		4/1/99-
									3/31/99		3/31/00
0-500M	500M-2MM	2-10MM	10-50MM	50-100MM	100-250MM				ALL		ALL
1	8	18	7	1	2		NUMBER OF STATEMENTS		48		46
%	%	%	%	%	%		ASSETS		%		%
		6.8					Cash & Equivalents		7.6		5.6
		21.3					Trade Receivables (net)		20.0		24.7
		21.9					Inventory		27.8		27.9
		.7					All Other Current		3.5		1.8
		50.7					Total Current		58.8		60.0
		41.8					Fixed Assets (net)		33.5		32.8
		.4					Intangibles (net)		3.1		2.4
		7.2					All Other Non-Current		4.6		4.7
		100.0					Total		100.0		100.0
							LIABILITIES				
		18.0					Notes Payable-Short Term		13.8		13.3
		2.4					Cur. Mat.-L/T/D		3.3		3.1
		13.2					Trade Payables		17.7		19.1
		.2					Income Taxes Payable		.3		.3
		9.6					All Other Current		7.3		7.4
		43.4					Total Current		42.4		43.1
		11.3					Long Term Debt		18.3		17.8
		1.2					Deferred Taxes		.4		.4
		.7					All Other Non-Current		6.1		4.0
		43.5					Net Worth		32.9		34.6
		100.0					Total Liabilities & Net Worth		100.0		100.0
							INCOME DATA				
		100.0					Net Sales		100.0		100.0
		35.3					Gross Profit		27.7		28.5
		33.4					Operating Expenses		22.3		23.4
		1.9					Operating Profit		5.4		5.0
		-.7					All Other Expenses (net)		2.0		1.3
		2.6					Profit Before Taxes		3.4		3.8
							RATIOS				
		1.8							2.0		2.1
		1.1					Current		1.4		1.4
		.9							1.0		1.0
		1.0							1.1		1.0
		.7					Quick		.6		.8
		.5							.3		.4
	23	16.0						20 18.0		29 12.8
	44	8.4					Sales/Receivables	35 10.4		43 8.5
	61	5.9						48 7.7		55 6.7
	50	7.3						47 7.7		37 9.9
	70	5.2					Cost of Sales/Inventory	70 5.2		63 5.7
	90	4.1						118 3.1		120 3.0
	23	16.0						22 16.3		25 14.7
	36	10.1					Cost of Sales/Payables	37 10.0		41 8.9
	81	4.5						62 5.9		64 5.7
		9.9							5.2		6.1
		26.4					Sales/Working Capital		13.8		13.8
		-28.7							NM		454.0
		5.2							6.4		5.8
		3.6					EBIT/Interest	(47)	2.6	(43)	3.2
		1.0							1.3		1.1
							Net Profit + Depr., Dep.,		6.4		3.8
							Amort./Cur. Mat. L /T/D	(15)	3.1	(10)	1.6
									.9		-.6
		.7							.7		.6
		.9					Fixed/Worth		1.2		.9
		1.6							2.3		2.2
		.8							.9		.7
		1.7					Debt/Worth		2.3		1.7
		1.9							7.3		4.6
		25.1					% Profit Before Taxes/Tangible		47.3		32.4
		11.6					Net Worth	(44)	22.0	(42)	17.8
		-.1							7.2		2.9
		9.8					% Profit Before Taxes/Total		14.8		13.1
		5.5					Assets		6.6		5.3
		.0							1.6		.3
		7.4							11.8		11.4
		4.0					Sales/Net Fixed Assets		5.4		7.0
		2.5							3.7		4.2
		2.5							2.5		2.6
		1.7					Sales/Total Assets		2.0		2.0
		1.2							1.3		1.5
		2.0							1.3		1.3
	(17)	4.5					% Depr., Dep., Amort./Sales	(43)	2.1	(37)	2.3
		7.0							4.0		3.9
							% Officers', Directors',		1.4		1.4
							Owners' Comp/Sales	(14)	3.9	(13)	2.7
									11.9		8.4
1007M	26271M	167575M	317327M	121110M	590652M		Net Sales ($)		2096667M		1903193M
356M	7873M	81974M	147412M	51736M	306865M		Total Assets ($)		1399818M		1191512M

© RMA 2003

M = $ thousand   MM = $ million
See Pages 11 through 18 for Explanation of Ratios and Data

Comparative Historical Data   Current Data Sorted By Sales

					Type of Statement						
	10		10		12	Unqualified		1		2	3	6
	7		6		11	Reviewed		2	4	2	1	2
	6		5		2	Compiled		1		1		
	1		2		2	Tax Returns		2				
	18		10		10	Other		1	3	2	1	3
	4/1/00- 3/31/01		4/1/01- 3/31/02		4/1/02- 3/31/03			12 (4/1-9/30/02)		25 (10/1/02-3/31/03)		
	ALL		ALL		ALL		0-1MM	1-3MM	3-5MM	5-10MM	10-25MM	25MM & OVER
	42		33		37	NUMBER OF STATEMENTS	7	7	7	7	5	11

					ASSETS						
	%		%		%		%	%	%	%	%	%
	4.7		6.8		7.9	Cash & Equivalents						10.5
	23.1		21.6		22.0	Trade Receivables (net)	D					23.8
	27.5		25.4		25.0	Inventory	A					23.6
	1.8		2.5		1.1	All Other Current	T					1.3
	57.1		56.3		56.0	Total Current	A					59.2
	31.5		30.1		32.8	Fixed Assets (net)						29.6
	4.9		7.0		2.7	Intangibles (net)	N					8.4
	6.5		6.6		8.5	All Other Non-Current	O					2.8
	100.0		100.0		100.0	Total	T					100.0

					LIABILITIES						
	17.2		14.5		12.1	Notes Payable-Short Term	A					3.2
	3.3		3.2		3.1	Cur. Mat.-L/T/D	V					3.1
	14.9		12.5		15.8	Trade Payables	A					16.4
	.4		.5		.6	Income Taxes Payable	I					1.6
	12.5		10.4		9.5	All Other Current	L					13.8
	48.3		41.1		41.1	Total Current	A					38.1
	10.4		14.7		13.8	Long Term Debt	B					11.3
	.5		.5		.8	Deferred Taxes	L					1.4
	4.7		5.1		3.6	All Other Non-Current	E					7.3
	36.0		38.6		40.6	Net Worth						41.9
	100.0		100.0		100.0	Total Liabilities & Net Worth						100.0

					INCOME DATA						
	100.0		100.0		100.0	Net Sales						100.0
	31.4		33.0		32.3	Gross Profit						25.1
	28.5		29.4		29.1	Operating Expenses						21.1
	3.0		3.6		3.2	Operating Profit						4.0
	.5		1.0		.2	All Other Expenses (net)						.7
	2.5		2.6		3.0	Profit Before Taxes						3.3

					RATIOS						
	2.1		2.4		2.1							2.0
	1.3		1.3		1.4	Current						1.5
	.9		1.1		1.0							1.1
	1.2		1.2		1.3							1.2
	.6		.7		.7	Quick						.9
	.3		.4		.4							.5
28	13.0	25	14.6	21	17.7						24	15.2
36	10.2	40	9.0	36	10.2	Sales/Receivables					35	10.4
56	6.5	60	6.1	60	6.1						51	7.1
39	9.4	53	6.9	46	8.0						19	19.4
60	6.1	72	5.1	60	6.1	Cost of Sales/Inventory					59	6.2
125	2.9	105	3.5	89	4.1						82	4.5
20	18.3	23	16.2	22	16.3						23	15.7
32	11.3	33	11.0	35	10.5	Cost of Sales/Payables					33	11.2
50	7.3	47	7.8	60	6.0						48	7.6
	8.2		7.6		7.7							5.3
	18.0		15.1		19.2	Sales/Working Capital						17.9
	−50.9		47.4		−84.1							44.8
	8.1		17.6		5.6							11.8
(40)	2.0	(30)	3.0	(36)	3.7	EBIT/Interest					(10)	4.1
	1.3		1.2		1.1							1.7
	5.5				6.5							
(13)	1.8			(13)	2.4	Net Profit + Depr., Dep., Amort./Cur. Mat. L/T/D						
	1.2				1.0							
	.5		.4		.5							.6
	.9		.7		.8	Fixed/Worth						.8
	2.9		1.9		1.5							1.7
	.6		.6		.6							.6
	1.7		1.5		1.4	Debt/Worth						1.7
	5.2		3.9		2.5							3.5
	30.1		38.8		31.1	% Profit Before Taxes/Tangible Net Worth						41.2
(36)	18.2	(30)	15.1	(35)	17.5						(10)	17.5
	8.8		6.0		1.1							7.4
	11.4		10.7		10.6	% Profit Before Taxes/Total Assets						11.6
	4.0		5.6		6.5							6.2
	1.2		1.5		.4							.7
	13.3		16.1		15.1	Sales/Net Fixed Assets						16.3
	6.7		6.5		7.0							7.9
	4.3		4.1		3.7							4.7
	2.5		2.1		2.8	Sales/Total Assets						2.6
	1.9		1.9		2.1							2.3
	1.7		1.4		1.5							1.8
	1.7		1.4		1.9	% Depr., Dep., Amort./Sales						1.9
(39)	2.4	(30)	2.1	(35)	2.6							2.1
	4.1		4.1		5.1							3.0
	1.6		1.6		1.8	% Officers', Directors', Owners' Comp/Sales						
(14)	3.8	(13)	4.5	(13)	3.9							
	8.6		9.2		7.7							
1550978M		806334M		1223942M		Net Sales ($)		12265M	26309M	53240M	70083M	1062045M
870549M		512544M		596216M		Total Assets ($)		6067M	16639M	28957M	32894M	511659M

© RMA 2003   M = $ thousand   MM = $ million
See Pages 11 through 18 for Explanation of Ratios and Data

Current Data Sorted By Assets   Comparative Historical Data

	0-500M	500M-2MM	2-10MM	10-50MM	50-100MM	100-250MM	Type of Statement		4/1/98-3/31/99 ALL	4/1/99-3/31/00 ALL
			1	1		1	Unqualified			9
	1	1	2	1			Reviewed			2
	1	1	4				Compiled			5
							Tax Returns			
	1	1	4	2		1	Other			9
		3 (4/1-9/30/02)		17 (10/1/02-3/31/03)						
	0-500M	500M-2MM	2-10MM	10-50MM	50-100MM	100-250MM				
NUMBER OF STATEMENTS		3	11	4	1	1				25
	%	%	%	%	%	%	**ASSETS**		%	%
			7.1				Cash & Equivalents			7.5
			19.4				Trade Receivables (net)			25.2
	D		25.0				Inventory	D		31.3
	A		2.6				All Other Current	A		1.7
	T		54.1				Total Current	T		65.7
	A		43.1				Fixed Assets (net)	A		24.8
			.2				Intangibles (net)			1.9
	N		2.6				All Other Non-Current	N		7.6
	O		100.0				Total	O		100.0
	T						**LIABILITIES**	T		
			9.1				Notes Payable-Short Term			7.0
	A		15.4				Cur. Mat.-L/T/D	A		2.8
	V		13.1				Trade Payables	V		15.5
	A		.1				Income Taxes Payable	A		.3
	I		6.0				All Other Current	I		8.6
	L		43.8				Total Current	L		34.2
	A		10.6				Long Term Debt	A		18.4
	B		1.6				Deferred Taxes	B		.5
	L		10.5				All Other Non-Current	L		4.8
	E		33.4				Net Worth	E		42.0
			100.0				Total Liabilities & Net Worth			100.0
							INCOME DATA			
			100.0				Net Sales			100.0
			34.5				Gross Profit			31.4
			28.9				Operating Expenses			25.3
			5.7				Operating Profit			6.1
			2.2				All Other Expenses (net)			.5
			3.5				Profit Before Taxes			5.6
							RATIOS			
			1.7							3.8
			1.5				Current			2.0
			1.1							1.3
			.7							1.6
			.6				Quick			1.1
			.3							.5
			16 22.9							22 16.7
			24 15.5				Sales/Receivables			42 8.7
			51 7.2							55 6.6
			26 13.8							47 7.7
			71 5.1				Cost of Sales/Inventory			75 4.9
			85 4.3							97 3.8
			19 19.1							22 16.6
			25 14.8				Cost of Sales/Payables			33 11.1
			50 7.2							43 8.6
			4.7							3.8
			14.1				Sales/Working Capital			7.5
			125.7							22.8
			5.2							5.4
			1.6				EBIT/Interest		(23)	4.0
			1.4							1.9
							Net Profit + Depr., Dep., Amort./Cur. Mat. L /T/D			
			.5							.2
			1.4				Fixed/Worth			.6
			3.9							1.4
			1.0							.7
			3.0				Debt/Worth			1.6
			7.4							3.7
			36.6							28.3
		(10)	22.4				% Profit Before Taxes/Tangible Net Worth		(23)	22.2
			3.9							8.2
			7.8							13.3
			3.9				% Profit Before Taxes/Total Assets			9.0
			.8							3.2
			11.5							14.7
			6.3				Sales/Net Fixed Assets			8.6
			2.1							7.0
			2.9							2.7
			2.3				Sales/Total Assets			2.2
			1.2							1.7
			1.2							1.2
			2.2				% Depr., Dep., Amort./Sales		(20)	1.8
			6.4							2.3
							% Officers', Directors', Owners' Comp/Sales			
		8467M	128137M	188238M	99690M	511705M	Net Sales ($)			1668429M
		3208M	56538M	109253M	57549M	203982M	Total Assets ($)			831033M

M = $ thousand   MM = $ million
See Pages 11 through 18 for Explanation of Ratios and Data

Comparative Historical Data				Current Data Sorted By Sales					

Type of Statement

7	5	3	Unqualified				1		2
2	2	4	Reviewed		1	1	1	1	1
5	4	5	Compiled		2	1	1	1	1
1			Tax Returns						
5	11	8	Other	3				2	3

4/1/00- 3/31/01 ALL	4/1/01- 3/31/02 ALL	4/1/02- 3/31/03 ALL		0-1MM	3 (4/1-9/30/02) 1-3MM	3-5MM	17 (10/1/02-3/31/03) 5-10MM	10-25MM	25MM & OVER
20	22	20	**NUMBER OF STATEMENTS**	3	3	3	3	4	7
%	%	%	**ASSETS**	%	%	%	%	%	%
11.4	4.3	5.3	Cash & Equivalents	D					
21.4	21.3	20.0	Trade Receivables (net)	A					
31.6	28.7	28.8	Inventory	T					
1.0	3.7	4.4	All Other Current	A					
65.4	58.0	58.6	Total Current						
25.6	34.5	36.6	Fixed Assets (net)	N					
2.5	2.2	1.0	Intangibles (net)	O					
6.6	5.3	3.8	All Other Non-Current	T					
100.0	100.0	100.0	Total						
			LIABILITIES	A					
14.4	15.1	11.1	Notes Payable-Short Term	V					
4.9	7.8	10.8	Cur. Mat.-L/T/D	A					
12.7	29.5	13.5	Trade Payables	I					
.3	.6	.2	Income Taxes Payable	L					
5.3	5.7	6.8	All Other Current	A					
37.6	58.8	42.3	Total Current	B					
13.1	13.9	10.1	Long Term Debt	L					
.3	1.0	1.1	Deferred Taxes	E					
6.5	.3	6.8	All Other Non-Current						
42.4	26.0	39.7	Net Worth						
100.0	100.0	100.0	Total Liabilities & Net Worth						
			INCOME DATA						
100.0	100.0	100.0	Net Sales						
30.2	25.3	33.0	Gross Profit						
24.8	23.4	27.1	Operating Expenses						
5.4	2.0	5.9	Operating Profit						
−2.1	1.3	1.4	All Other Expenses (net)						
7.5	.6	4.4	Profit Before Taxes						
			RATIOS						
4.2	2.1	2.4							
1.3	1.2	1.5	Current						
1.2	.8	1.1							
1.7	.9	.8							
.7	.6	.6	Quick						
.5	.3	.3							
23 16.0	28 13.0	17 21.5							
35 10.4	38 9.5	34 10.8	Sales/Receivables						
45 8.1	43 8.6	57 6.4							
47 7.8	36 10.3	40 9.1							
84 4.3	57 6.4	74 4.9	Cost of Sales/Inventory						
128 2.9	92 4.0	103 3.6							
19 19.3	25 14.7	18 20.4							
33 11.0	39 9.4	26 14.2	Cost of Sales/Payables						
39 9.3	70 5.2	47 7.7							
4.4	9.0	4.8							
10.1	16.7	13.0	Sales/Working Capital						
26.2	−13.7	35.5							
9.9	4.3	7.0							
(18) 3.9	(18) 1.9	3.3	EBIT/Interest						
1.9	1.3	1.5							
			Net Profit + Depr., Dep., Amort./Cur. Mat. L/T/D						
.3	.5	.4							
.9	1.2	.8	Fixed/Worth						
1.8	2.4	2.3							
.8	.9	.7							
1.4	3.2	1.3	Debt/Worth						
4.6	5.3	4.2							
54.9	26.0	35.6							
(19) 27.8	(20) 11.6	(19) 24.0	% Profit Before Taxes/Tangible Net Worth						
16.4	2.5	6.3							
18.4	11.1	15.9							
10.7	2.6	5.1	% Profit Before Taxes/Total Assets						
7.7	−.5	1.1							
14.6	10.1	14.1							
7.9	7.2	7.6	Sales/Net Fixed Assets						
6.2	4.4	3.9							
2.6	2.6	2.7							
2.0	2.0	2.1	Sales/Total Assets						
1.6	1.6	1.5							
1.4	.9	1.5							
1.8	(20) 1.8	(17) 2.2	% Depr., Dep., Amort./Sales						
3.3	3.0	4.1							
			% Officers', Directors', Owners' Comp/Sales						
501982M	632971M	936237M	Net Sales ($)		4876M	11796M	19275M	73560M	826730M
264335M	328190M	430530M	Total Assets ($)		6851M	4852M	11405M	28495M	378927M

M = $ thousand   MM = $ million
See Pages 11 through 18 for Explanation of Ratios and Data

Current Data Sorted By Assets							Comparative Historical Data	
	2	2	7	1	3	**Type of Statement** Unqualified	15	13
		2	2			Reviewed	5	
	2	2				Compiled	8	5
						Tax Returns	1	
1		1	3	1	1	Other	6	3
	7 (4/1-9/30/02)		24 (10/1/02-3/31/03)				4/1/98-3/31/99	4/1/99-3/31/00
0-500M	500M-2MM	2-10MM	10-50MM	50-100MM	100-250MM		ALL	ALL
1	4	7	12	2	5	**NUMBER OF STATEMENTS**	35	21
%	%	%	%	%	%	**ASSETS**	%	%
			5.3			Cash & Equivalents	7.1	4.4
			16.5			Trade Receivables (net)	24.4	20.1
			33.7			Inventory	26.7	38.6
			6.1			All Other Current	2.7	2.6
			61.7			Total Current	60.8	65.7
			28.1			Fixed Assets (net)	26.0	18.6
			3.3			Intangibles (net)	4.2	7.0
			6.9			All Other Non-Current	9.0	8.8
			100.0			Total	100.0	100.0
						LIABILITIES		
			11.7			Notes Payable-Short Term	13.8	14.3
			1.2			Cur. Mat.-L/T/D	3.2	4.3
			12.8			Trade Payables	21.8	16.1
			.4			Income Taxes Payable	.1	.7
			9.3			All Other Current	10.1	10.8
			35.4			Total Current	49.0	46.2
			11.4			Long Term Debt	15.2	15.9
			1.7			Deferred Taxes	.9	.3
			5.1			All Other Non-Current	4.5	7.7
			46.4			Net Worth	30.5	29.9
			100.0			Total Liabilities & Net Worth	100.0	100.0
						INCOME DATA		
			100.0			Net Sales	100.0	100.0
			28.6			Gross Profit	36.2	36.2
			22.5			Operating Expenses	45.3	29.7
			6.1			Operating Profit	-9.1	6.5
			1.3			All Other Expenses (net)	2.0	3.4
			4.8			Profit Before Taxes	-11.2	3.1
						RATIOS		
			2.3				1.9	2.2
			1.9			Current	1.2	1.3
			1.4				.8	1.0
			1.1				1.1	1.2
			.8			Quick	.6	.4
			.4				.4	.3
		30	12.2				26 14.1	21 17.3
		36	10.2			Sales/Receivables	40 9.2	42 8.8
		55	6.6				60 6.1	59 6.2
		65	5.6				44 8.3	71 5.2
		100	3.6			Cost of Sales/Inventory	80 4.5	129 2.8
		141	2.6				122 3.0	230 1.6
		23	15.8				29 12.8	30 12.4
		39	9.5			Cost of Sales/Payables	54 6.8	51 7.2
		60	6.1				96 3.8	90 4.0
			3.9				6.2	4.0
			5.5			Sales/Working Capital	15.5	11.4
			8.3				-28.3	UND
			16.0				(33) 6.6	(20) 4.0
		(11)	4.1			EBIT/Interest	2.6	2.0
			2.5				1.4	.6
							(17) 4.7	(12) 8.8
						Net Profit + Depr., Dep., Amort./Cur. Mat. L./T/D	1.9	1.8
							.8	.3
			.3				.3	.5
			.5			Fixed/Worth	.8	.9
			1.1				1.6	2.1
			.7				1.0	1.0
			1.3			Debt/Worth	2.2	3.0
			2.3				4.0	18.0
			35.1			% Profit Before Taxes/Tangible	(32) 32.7	(18) 90.5
			20.3			Net Worth	15.5	24.7
			6.1				4.9	-1.0
			12.2			% Profit Before Taxes/Total	10.8	11.5
			6.7			Assets	5.1	3.7
			2.1				.6	-2.6
			12.1				19.2	15.2
			4.5			Sales/Net Fixed Assets	12.9	10.7
			2.2				5.9	7.2
			2.1				2.7	2.1
			1.4			Sales/Total Assets	2.2	1.9
			1.0				1.7	1.0
			.9				(32) 1.1	1.4
			2.5			% Depr., Dep., Amort./Sales	2.0	2.3
			4.3				3.9	5.1
							(11) 2.7	
						% Officers', Directors', Owners' Comp/Sales	5.4	
							12.9	
1662M	11224M	100228M	401155M	211082M	1249516M	Net Sales ($)	1121888M	1101497M
395M	4470M	41760M	256907M	127053M	774409M	Total Assets ($)	651128M	841114M

M = $ thousand   MM = $ million
See Pages 11 through 18 for Explanation of Ratios and Data

Comparative Historical Data | **Current Data Sorted By Sales**

	7		12		15	**Type of Statement** Unqualified	1			2	6		6
	1		1		5	Reviewed				2			3
	10		7		4	Compiled		2		1			1
	1					Tax Returns							
	6		7		7	Other		1			2		4
	4/1/00-3/31/01		**4/1/01-3/31/02**		**4/1/02-3/31/03**		**7 (4/1-9/30/02)**			**24 (10/1/02-3/31/03)**			
	ALL		**ALL**		**ALL**		**0-1MM**	**1-3MM**	**3-5MM**	**5-10MM**	**10-25MM**		**25MM & OVER**
	25		27		31	**NUMBER OF STATEMENTS**	1	3		5	8		14
	%		%		%	**ASSETS**	%	%	%	%	%		%
	6.0		8.7		5.4	Cash & Equivalents			DATA NOT AVAILABLE				2.9
	19.8		21.5		23.1	Trade Receivables (net)							24.5
	33.7		27.4		32.1	Inventory							37.0
	1.8		2.7		4.2	All Other Current							4.7
	61.3		60.2		64.9	Total Current							69.1
	22.3		25.2		23.1	Fixed Assets (net)							17.9
	6.1		3.4		5.1	Intangibles (net)							4.8
	10.3		11.2		7.0	All Other Non-Current							8.2
	100.0		100.0		100.0	Total							100.0
						LIABILITIES							
	10.0		15.4		13.3	Notes Payable-Short Term							11.4
	1.8		2.5		2.9	Cur. Mat.-L/T/D							3.3
	12.7		12.0		15.6	Trade Payables							21.0
	.1		.4		.4	Income Taxes Payable							.6
	8.8		5.9		9.4	All Other Current							11.2
	33.4		36.3		41.6	Total Current							47.5
	16.3		13.1		11.4	Long Term Debt							7.2
	.2		.4		1.4	Deferred Taxes							1.1
	7.6		1.6		4.2	All Other Non-Current							3.4
	42.4		48.7		41.4	Net Worth							40.8
	100.0		100.0		100.0	Total Liabilities & Net Worth							100.0
						INCOME DATA							
	100.0		100.0		100.0	Net Sales							100.0
	30.3		30.0		29.8	Gross Profit							24.4
	25.5		26.1		23.6	Operating Expenses							16.6
	4.8		3.9		6.1	Operating Profit							7.7
	2.9		1.5		1.4	All Other Expenses (net)							1.9
	1.9		2.4		4.7	Profit Before Taxes							5.9
						RATIOS							
	3.7		3.5		2.1								2.2
	1.9		1.8		1.6	Current							1.4
	1.2		1.0		1.1								1.1
	1.7		2.1		1.1								.9
	.8		.7		.8	Quick							.6
	.3		.5		.4								.3
20	18.3	**34**	10.8	**31**	11.7							**33**	11.1
36	10.2	**42**	8.7	**37**	9.8	Sales/Receivables						**47**	7.7
53	6.9	**65**	5.6	**58**	6.3							**64**	5.7
53	6.9	**37**	9.9	**48**	7.7							**59**	6.2
94	3.9	**84**	4.3	**95**	3.9	Cost of Sales/Inventory						**97**	3.8
177	2.1	**164**	2.2	**131**	2.8							**146**	2.5
17	22.0	**17**	21.2	**23**	15.6							**37**	9.8
31	11.9	**37**	10.0	**37**	9.8	Cost of Sales/Payables						**42**	8.8
62	5.9	**51**	7.2	**61**	6.0							**67**	5.4
	3.8		3.8		5.1								5.3
	6.4		5.3		6.9	Sales/Working Capital							7.8
	31.9		89.1		25.5								36.6
	6.7		3.5		6.9								17.2
(23)	1.7	(21)	1.7	(27)	3.2	EBIT/Interest						(13)	4.7
	.9		1.0		1.8								2.2
					11.9								
				(13)	3.3	Net Profit + Depr., Dep., Amort./Cur. Mat. L/T/D							
					1.7								
	.2		.2		.2								.2
	.3		.4		.4	Fixed/Worth							.4
	1.5		1.2		1.0								.6
	.3		.3		.8								.9
	1.0		1.2		1.7	Debt/Worth							1.7
	4.2		2.8		3.4								3.1
	29.5		17.4		33.9								34.3
(21)	16.0	(25)	10.1	(29)	17.1	% Profit Before Taxes/Tangible Net Worth						(13)	19.9
	2.1		2.1		5.2								12.1
	13.3		10.9		12.4								13.6
	2.8		3.0		6.1	% Profit Before Taxes/Total Assets							11.3
	−.1		.9		2.3								1.9
	39.9		17.2		37.8								23.0
	11.7		11.7		11.1	Sales/Net Fixed Assets							12.4
	6.0		3.7		3.2								7.3
	2.7		2.1		2.5								2.5
	1.7		1.5		1.7	Sales/Total Assets							1.9
	1.1		1.1		1.2								1.3
	.3		1.3		1.1								.5
(24)	1.4	(24)	1.7	(26)	1.9	% Depr., Dep., Amort./Sales						(12)	1.4
	3.3		3.1		4.0								1.8
						% Officers', Directors', Owners' Comp/Sales							
	1498201M		**1479118M**		**1974867M**	Net Sales ($)	**598M**	**5508M**		**41705M**	**137177M**		**1789879M**
	1040981M		**876403M**		**1204994M**	Total Assets ($)	**700M**	**2699M**		**26521M**	**110572M**		**1064502M**

M = $ thousand MM = $ million

See Pages 11 through 18 for Explanation of Ratios and Data

Current Data Sorted By Assets   Comparative Historical Data

0-500M	500M-2MM	2-10MM	10-50MM	50-100MM	100-250MM		4/1/98-3/31/99 ALL	4/1/99-3/31/00 ALL
	13 (4/1-9/30/02)		45 (10/1/02-3/31/03)			**Type of Statement**	25	33
	2	7	7	3	1	Unqualified	25	33
1	1	1	2			Reviewed	2	6
	1	1	1			Compiled	6	10
	1	2				Tax Returns	1	3
	6	9	8	1	3	Other	25	20
1	10	21	18	4	4	**NUMBER OF STATEMENTS**	59	72
%	%	%	%	%	%	**ASSETS**	%	%
	8.8	9.6	6.3			Cash & Equivalents	11.2	8.8
	41.4	16.9	21.2			Trade Receivables (net)	21.9	23.2
	25.7	31.3	30.4			Inventory	27.1	27.6
	.3	3.1	2.4			All Other Current	2.8	3.8
	76.2	60.9	60.3			Total Current	63.0	63.4
	13.8	28.5	29.8			Fixed Assets (net)	28.5	25.6
	.2	4.0	5.4			Intangibles (net)	4.4	5.9
	9.8	6.6	4.4			All Other Non-Current	4.2	5.1
	100.0	100.0	100.0			Total	100.0	100.0
						LIABILITIES		
	8.9	7.2	10.1			Notes Payable-Short Term	9.9	8.4
	1.9	7.6	3.7			Cur. Mat.-L/T/D	2.8	3.1
	24.1	11.5	14.3			Trade Payables	12.7	15.5
	.8	.8	.4			Income Taxes Payable	.4	.3
	17.9	10.3	14.5			All Other Current	6.7	9.6
	53.6	37.3	43.0			Total Current	32.4	36.9
	10.4	10.2	11.2			Long Term Debt	16.8	14.5
	.0	.5	.3			Deferred Taxes	1.2	.3
	4.1	4.2	8.3			All Other Non-Current	3.2	3.5
	32.0	47.9	37.2			Net Worth	46.4	44.9
	100.0	100.0	100.0			Total Liabilities & Net Worth	100.0	100.0
						INCOME DATA		
	100.0	100.0	100.0			Net Sales	100.0	100.0
	46.6	41.1	45.9			Gross Profit	44.8	43.4
	43.6	33.3	39.3			Operating Expenses	36.8	34.9
	3.0	7.9	6.6			Operating Profit	8.0	8.5
	.8	1.0	3.3			All Other Expenses (net)	.8	.2
	2.2	6.8	3.3			Profit Before Taxes	7.2	8.3
						RATIOS		
	2.0	3.5	2.1				3.1	3.0
	1.5	1.6	1.3			Current	2.0	1.9
	1.0	1.1	1.0				1.3	1.2
	1.8	1.4	1.2				2.1	1.7
	.8	.6	.6			Quick	1.1	.9
	.6	.5	.4				.5	.6
	31 11.9	29 12.8	38 9.5				33 11.0	31 11.6
	55 6.7	34 10.9	52 7.0			Sales/Receivables	45 8.1	45 8.1
	81 4.5	38 9.5	67 5.5				61 6.0	60 6.1
	18 20.6	73 5.0	78 4.7				70 5.2	63 5.8
	67 5.4	106 3.4	145 2.5			Cost of Sales/Inventory	106 3.5	93 3.9
	117 3.1	127 2.9	169 2.2				151 2.4	125 2.9
	34 10.8	14 26.4	46 7.9				25 14.8	23 15.6
	42 8.7	32 11.6	52 7.1			Cost of Sales/Payables	42 8.6	44 8.3
	81 4.5	48 7.7	66 5.5				74 5.0	70 5.2
	5.2	4.3	5.4				3.8	4.0
	15.4	9.1	12.5			Sales/Working Capital	6.0	6.2
	117.7	62.9	NM				17.2	18.0
		15.6	20.5				(51) 21.8	(64) 14.1
	(18)	6.0	(17) 3.9			EBIT/Interest	6.7	4.2
		1.0	1.2				2.1	1.7
		3.9				Net Profit + Depr., Dep.,	(23) 23.7	(23) 29.1
	(10)	1.6				Amort./Cur. Mat. L /T/D	6.6	3.3
		.5					3.3	.8
	.2	.1	.2				.3	.3
	.6	.7	1.1			Fixed/Worth	.6	.6
	1.1	1.3	2.6				.9	1.1
	1.0	.6	.9				.4	.6
	2.2	1.0	1.7			Debt/Worth	.9	1.6
	7.1	2.7	6.4				2.4	3.8
	55.2	53.0	53.9			% Profit Before Taxes/Tangible	(53) 49.7	(67) 61.0
	8.6	(20) 33.6	(17) 24.2			Net Worth	32.7	24.8
	−1.9	2.0	12.3				12.3	7.3
	7.2	19.2	16.6			% Profit Before Taxes/Total	27.2	20.1
	4.2	10.0	6.6			Assets	14.6	8.5
	−.5	−.1	1.3				4.1	2.1
	74.7	17.9	16.4				15.8	21.7
	24.5	8.1	6.0			Sales/Net Fixed Assets	6.0	8.2
	12.0	4.5	3.8				3.1	4.0
	3.1	2.8	2.5				2.3	2.6
	2.7	2.0	1.6			Sales/Total Assets	1.7	1.8
	2.1	1.3	1.2				1.1	1.2
		1.3	1.3				(52) 1.4	(61) .9
	(19)	3.1	(13) 2.4			% Depr., Dep., Amort./Sales	2.5	2.2
		5.1	3.9				3.1	4.4
						% Officers', Directors',	(13) 1.1	(17) 1.9
						Owners' Comp/Sales	2.8	5.1
							6.1	9.4
3217M	29540M	262394M	800855M	361495M	993762M	Net Sales ($)	3052174M	3030563M
451M	10798M	133373M	432518M	269208M	578691M	Total Assets ($)	2030009M	2235379M

M = $ thousand   MM = $ million
See Pages 11 through 18 for Explanation of Ratios and Data

Comparative Historical Data | Current Data Sorted By Sales

Hist 1	Hist 2	Hist 3	Type of Statement	0-1MM	1-3MM	3-5MM	5-10MM	10-25MM	25MM & OVER
18	15	20	Unqualified	2	1	3	3		11
8	6	4	Reviewed		1	1	1		1
10	5	4	Compiled		1	1	1		1
2	2	3	Tax Returns	1		2			
19	22	27	Other	2	4	3	10		8
4/1/00-3/31/01 ALL	4/1/01-3/31/02 ALL	4/1/02-3/31/03 ALL		13 (4/1-9/30/02)			45 (10/1/02-3/31/03)		
57	50	58	**NUMBER OF STATEMENTS**	5	7	10	15		21
%	%	%	**ASSETS**	%	%	%	%	%	%
8.7	7.7	7.8	Cash & Equivalents				5.7	9.2	5.2
17.8	21.4	23.2	Trade Receivables (net)				16.9	14.5	23.2
26.2	25.9	27.7	Inventory				33.0	28.5	27.4
5.7	2.1	2.4	All Other Current				3.4	3.9	2.2
58.4	57.2	61.2	Total Current				58.9	56.1	58.1
29.7	29.0	26.6	Fixed Assets (net)				29.8	31.5	29.3
5.6	8.1	4.0	Intangibles (net)				3.5	8.0	3.7
6.3	5.7	8.2	All Other Non-Current				7.8	4.4	8.9
100.0	100.0	100.0	Total				100.0	100.0	100.0
			LIABILITIES						
6.2	7.0	7.8	Notes Payable-Short Term				8.0	7.5	8.0
3.2	4.9	5.3	Cur. Mat.-L/T/D				5.6	7.5	5.5
13.2	14.2	13.9	Trade Payables				13.5	9.6	13.6
.2	.3	.6	Income Taxes Payable				.2	1.1	.3
8.4	10.7	13.0	All Other Current				6.2	15.2	13.0
31.1	37.1	40.7	Total Current				33.6	41.0	40.5
21.8	15.0	10.7	Long Term Debt				7.2	12.7	10.7
.5	.4	.4	Deferred Taxes				1.1	.0	.7
4.5	4.8	5.5	All Other Non-Current				7.8	6.0	5.1
42.1	42.8	42.8	Net Worth				50.4	40.3	43.1
100.0	100.0	100.0	Total Liabilities & Net Worth				100.0	100.0	100.0

*(Columns 0-1MM, 1-3MM and 3-5MM for the ASSETS and LIABILITIES sections: **DATA NOT AVAILABLE**)*

Hist 1	Hist 2	Hist 3		0-1MM	1-3MM	3-5MM	5-10MM	10-25MM	25MM & OVER
			INCOME DATA						
100.0	100.0	100.0	Net Sales				100.0	100.0	100.0
44.1	44.1	43.4	Gross Profit				42.2	45.4	41.9
38.4	39.3	37.1	Operating Expenses				38.4	37.7	34.2
5.7	4.9	6.3	Operating Profit				3.8	7.6	7.7
.7	1.2	1.8	All Other Expenses (net)				1.2	3.7	1.4
5.0	3.7	4.5	Profit Before Taxes				2.6	4.0	6.3
			RATIOS						
2.7	2.4	2.1	Current				6.7	2.1	2.0
2.2	1.6	1.5					1.6	1.5	1.5
1.4	1.2	1.0					1.1	.9	1.0
1.3	1.3	1.3	Quick				2.8	1.3	1.1
.8	.8	.7					.5	.6	.7
.5	.6	.5					.4	.4	.4
27 13.6	31 11.9	31 11.6	Sales/Receivables				26 14.1	27 13.5	34 10.7
40 9.0	40 9.1	39 9.4					37 9.9	36 10.0	45 8.1
53 6.9	54 6.7	60 6.1					39 9.4	59 6.1	68 5.4
69 5.3	69 5.3	63 5.8	Cost of Sales/Inventory				70 5.2	75 4.9	55 6.6
104 3.5	91 4.0	90 4.0					116 3.1	117 3.1	88 4.1
135 2.7	139 2.6	144 2.5					138 2.6	179 2.0	150 2.4
27 13.5	28 13.1	28 13.2	Cost of Sales/Payables				18 20.8	25 14.7	30 12.3
43 8.4	36 10.1	41 9.0					33 11.1	46 7.9	41 9.0
67 5.4	71 5.1	64 5.7					66 5.5	64 5.7	53 6.9
4.1	4.6	5.6	Sales/Working Capital				3.8	4.4	6.8
6.2	10.2	11.1					8.2	10.5	11.7
13.2	24.8	100.7					46.7	-46.4	81.2
(52) 11.9	(45) 8.8	(51) 13.5	EBIT/Interest				38.6	(20) 15.1
2.9	2.6	3.4						4.3	3.9
1.2	.6	1.0						1.0	1.2
(23) 7.0	(18) 3.5	(20) 3.9	Net Profit + Depr., Dep., Amort./Cur. Mat. L/T/D						
2.5	1.5	1.8							
.5	.7	.6							
.4	.4	.2	Fixed/Worth				.1	.2	.3
.7	.7	.7					.8	1.2	.8
1.4	2.1	1.3					1.4	2.7	1.8
.7	.8	.8	Debt/Worth				.1	.8	.8
1.5	1.9	1.4					1.4	2.0	1.2
3.7	3.4	3.2					2.9	2.9	3.7
(52) 31.1	(45) 38.9	(56) 44.4	% Profit Before Taxes/Tangible Net Worth				(14) 59.7	52.1
14.0	19.2	22.7						33.6	24.2
4.7	.6	.6						9.2	6.7
13.5	13.2	16.4	% Profit Before Taxes/Total Assets				9.2	20.0	22.3
5.4	4.7	6.4					2.9	9.9	9.3
1.1	-1.5	.1					-3.7	.1	1.2
13.0	13.9	22.5	Sales/Net Fixed Assets				40.7	19.5	12.8
7.7	7.2	9.2					7.4	5.2	7.3
3.5	4.0	4.5					3.9	2.3	4.4
2.5	2.7	2.7	Sales/Total Assets				2.8	2.1	2.6
1.9	1.8	2.0					2.0	1.4	1.9
1.1	1.1	1.3					1.1	.9	1.5
(53) 1.5	(43) 2.0	(48) 1.2	% Depr., Dep., Amort./Sales				.4	(11) 2.3	(17) 1.9
2.8	2.8	2.5					3.2	4.6	2.5
5.0	4.2	4.4					5.3	6.5	3.7
(10) 2.4	(11) .8	(14) 2.4	% Officers', Directors', Owners' Comp/Sales						
5.7	3.2	5.7							
9.2	12.3	15.4							
3198151M	2482459M	2451263M	Net Sales ($)	10741M	26652M	80417M	254142M	2079311M
1834223M	1773070M	1425039M	Total Assets ($)	4692M	9842M	46240M	206866M	1157399M

M = $ thousand   MM = $ million
See Pages 11 through 18 for Explanation of Ratios and Data

Current Data Sorted By Assets   **Comparative Historical Data**

	0-500M	500M-2MM	2-10MM	10-50MM	50-100MM	100-250MM		4/1/98-3/31/99 ALL	4/1/99-3/31/00 ALL
Type of Statement									
Unqualified		2	13	21	7	7		46	31
Reviewed	1	2	9	3	1			9	8
Compiled		1	8	2				8	5
Tax Returns		3	3					1	6
Other	4	9	11	10	3	6		28	28
		19 (4/1-9/30/02)		107 (10/1/02-3/31/03)					
NUMBER OF STATEMENTS	5	17	44	36	11	13		92	78
ASSETS	%	%	%	%	%	%		%	%
Cash & Equivalents		10.4	13.7	12.5	18.6	11.1		11.9	11.4
Trade Receivables (net)		32.8	28.4	19.6	22.6	19.5		18.6	21.0
Inventory		18.5	20.1	21.1	12.3	17.0		21.2	20.8
All Other Current		9.5	3.9	2.7	3.4	2.4		2.6	3.8
Total Current		71.3	66.1	55.8	56.9	49.9		54.3	57.0
Fixed Assets (net)		19.2	25.0	27.8	16.7	33.5		29.5	27.7
Intangibles (net)		6.2	4.0	8.0	15.3	10.0		9.4	7.4
All Other Non-Current		3.3	4.9	8.4	11.2	6.6		6.7	7.9
Total		100.0	100.0	100.0	100.0	100.0		100.0	100.0
LIABILITIES									
Notes Payable-Short Term		13.4	4.3	9.1	3.7	2.7		8.4	7.6
Cur. Mat.-L/T/D		2.1	3.2	3.0	9.0	2.5		3.9	4.3
Trade Payables		25.3	17.6	11.9	8.0	6.4		13.1	13.7
Income Taxes Payable		.9	.3	1.1	.6	.6		.6	.5
All Other Current		6.3	8.6	9.9	17.8	21.8		10.3	8.3
Total Current		48.0	34.0	35.1	39.2	34.0		36.3	34.4
Long Term Debt		14.3	16.3	17.2	14.0	20.2		14.8	14.2
Deferred Taxes		.2	.5	.3	.4	1.0		.9	.4
All Other Non-Current		10.7	4.6	4.0	4.9	2.1		4.7	5.3
Net Worth		26.9	44.6	43.5	41.5	42.7		43.3	45.8
Total Liabilities & Net Worth		100.0	100.0	100.0	100.0	100.0		100.0	100.0
INCOME DATA									
Net Sales		100.0	100.0	100.0	100.0	100.0		100.0	100.0
Gross Profit		47.7	40.9	44.3	59.7	55.4		38.8	46.2
Operating Expenses		38.9	32.6	33.0	45.1	41.0		89.5	36.2
Operating Profit		8.7	8.4	11.4	14.6	14.4		-50.7	10.0
All Other Expenses (net)		1.6	.5	.9	3.0	2.2		3.6	.9
Profit Before Taxes		7.1	7.8	10.5	11.6	12.2		-54.3	9.1
RATIOS									
Current		2.5	3.1	2.9	3.7	3.4		2.6	3.1
		1.9	2.0	1.8	2.5	1.6		1.6	1.8
		1.1	1.6	1.2	1.0	1.0		1.1	1.2
Quick		1.5	2.1	1.6	2.3	2.1		1.5	2.0
		.9	1.3	.9	1.4	.9		.9	1.0
		.6	.8	.6	.9	.5		.5	.5
Sales/Receivables		24 15.0	31 11.9	37 9.8	51 7.2	45 8.2		34 10.9	35 10.4
		33 11.2	43 8.5	55 6.6	55 6.7	58 6.3		50 7.4	49 7.4
		45 8.1	56 6.5	61 6.0	86 4.3	92 4.0		65 5.6	66 5.5
Cost of Sales/Inventory		6 66.1	27 13.6	69 5.3	39 9.5	75 4.8		59 6.1	67 5.5
		26 13.8	61 5.9	102 3.6	104 3.5	144 2.5		106 3.4	96 3.8
		82 4.5	95 3.8	168 2.2	146 2.5	182 2.0		145 2.5	139 2.6
Cost of Sales/Payables		32 11.2	21 17.8	23 15.9	27 13.6	32 11.4		29 12.5	29 12.6
		41 9.0	31 11.7	41 8.9	48 7.5	45 8.2		52 7.0	48 7.5
		66 5.5	51 7.2	66 5.5	92 4.0	65 5.6		82 4.4	75 4.8
Sales/Working Capital		6.7	4.1	3.6	1.9	3.2		3.8	3.2
		9.8	6.6	6.0	3.5	6.6		8.2	7.4
		55.4	12.2	18.9	273.8	-39.2		41.1	18.5
EBIT/Interest		60.4	20.3	31.4	114.5	30.2		15.9	19.8
		(16) 15.2	(40) 7.1	(33) 5.2	17.1	(11) 8.0		(79) 4.0	(65) 4.1
		2.4	3.5	2.0	1.2	4.1		2.1	1.3
Net Profit + Depr., Dep., Amort./Cur. Mat. L/T/D			(11) 5.0					(37) 17.5	(25) 19.9
			3.2					5.9	7.3
			2.4					1.8	2.6
Fixed/Worth		.1	.2	.2	.3	.5		.4	.3
		.7	.7	.7	.3	1.2		.9	.6
		4.1	1.1	1.3	-3.9	3.0		2.4	1.5
Debt/Worth		1.1	.5	.5	.5	.8		.6	.6
		3.1	1.0	1.2	.9	3.2		1.5	1.2
		7.7	2.6	3.7	-14.5	6.2		5.2	2.9
% Profit Before Taxes/Tangible Net Worth		115.1	54.6	59.1		150.9		59.8	61.6
		(14) 46.1	(39) 27.8	(33) 27.8		21.5		(76) 28.7	(70) 25.2
		15.2	12.2	13.6		11.7		10.3	4.2
% Profit Before Taxes/Total Assets		28.3	25.0	23.7	30.1	16.6		20.7	22.0
		15.5	11.9	12.3	10.7	11.7		10.1	8.9
		3.9	3.7	2.4	.3	4.8		2.1	2.0
Sales/Net Fixed Assets		60.1	29.8	17.1	13.8	7.3		10.6	13.2
		32.9	8.8	4.2	5.6	3.3		4.6	5.2
		13.3	4.4	3.0	5.0	1.8		2.5	2.7
Sales/Total Assets		4.2	3.0	2.1	1.9	1.4		1.8	2.0
		3.1	2.1	1.3	1.1	1.1		1.2	1.2
		1.7	1.6	.8	.8	.6		.9	.9
% Depr., Dep., Amort./Sales		.6	1.3	2.0		2.2		1.9	1.4
		(12) 1.1	(36) 1.8	(29) 3.2		(10) 4.1		(79) 3.1	(63) 2.9
		1.9	3.7	4.3		5.4		4.4	4.9
% Officers', Directors', Owners' Comp/Sales		5.2	1.4					2.6	1.8
		(10) 17.7	(14) 4.5					(21) 4.7	(17) 4.9
		23.9	9.4					9.6	14.9
Net Sales ($)	7418M	59042M	566019M	1134743M	1109963M	2239798M		2890017M	3132574M
Total Assets ($)	1054M	20405M	238159M	834388M	758554M	2166072M		2633135M	2838248M

M = $ thousand   MM = $ million
See Pages 11 through 18 for Explanation of Ratios and Data

Comparative Historical Data

Current Data Sorted By Sales

			Type of Statement						
25	26	50	Unqualified		2	1	9	12	26
9	7	16	Reviewed	1	1	1	4	7	2
16	23	11	Compiled			1	6	4	
2	4	6	Tax Returns		1	3	1	1	
22	21	43	Other		9	3	6	8	17
4/1/00-3/31/01 ALL	4/1/01-3/31/02 ALL	4/1/02-3/31/03 ALL			19 (4/1-9/30/02)			107 (10/1/02-3/31/03)	
				0-1MM	1-3MM	3-5MM	5-10MM	10-25MM	25MM & OVER
74	81	126	NUMBER OF STATEMENTS	1	13	9	26	32	45
%	%	%	ASSETS	%	%	%	%	%	%
8.7	10.3	13.8	Cash & Equivalents		17.5		15.4	9.4	14.3
24.6	25.3	25.3	Trade Receivables (net)		25.4		23.7	27.4	23.8
22.7	21.3	18.9	Inventory		15.6		19.2	22.7	18.0
2.6	3.7	4.0	All Other Current		4.6		2.7	2.5	3.0
58.7	60.6	62.0	Total Current		63.2		61.1	62.0	59.1
28.6	23.3	25.0	Fixed Assets (net)		22.8		26.5	25.1	25.5
7.4	7.5	6.9	Intangibles (net)		8.1		8.7	5.8	7.6
5.3	8.6	6.2	All Other Non-Current		5.9		3.8	7.1	7.7
100.0	100.0	100.0	Total		100.0		100.0	100.0	100.0
			LIABILITIES						
8.0	5.0	6.5	Notes Payable-Short Term		14.8		5.3	6.4	6.0
4.6	3.1	3.4	Cur. Mat.-L/T/D		1.1		3.6	3.7	3.8
17.1	18.3	15.3	Trade Payables		20.1		14.5	14.7	13.3
.4	1.0	.7	Income Taxes Payable		1.0		.5	.0	1.2
9.1	10.0	10.5	All Other Current		1.9		8.9	11.7	14.5
39.2	37.3	36.4	Total Current		39.0		32.9	36.5	38.8
18.8	17.3	16.1	Long Term Debt		18.0		20.8	15.5	13.8
.4	.4	.4	Deferred Taxes		.3		.1	.4	.8
5.8	4.6	6.4	All Other Non-Current		17.6		6.7	3.9	3.7
35.8	40.3	40.7	Net Worth		25.1		39.5	43.7	43.0
100.0	100.0	100.0	Total Liabilities & Net Worth		100.0		100.0	100.0	100.0
			INCOME DATA						
100.0	100.0	100.0	Net Sales		100.0		100.0	100.0	100.0
42.1	46.5	45.9	Gross Profit		49.4		44.3	42.7	48.0
33.7	37.3	35.1	Operating Expenses		35.0		36.3	33.9	34.3
8.4	9.2	10.8	Operating Profit		14.4		7.9	8.7	13.7
1.3	.6	1.1	All Other Expenses (net)		1.6		.6	1.3	1.2
7.1	8.6	9.6	Profit Before Taxes		12.8		7.4	7.5	12.4
			RATIOS						
2.7	2.9	3.0	Current		3.3		3.3	2.6	2.8
1.6	1.8	1.9			2.5		1.9	1.7	1.7
1.2	1.3	1.3			1.1		1.7	1.3	1.0
1.5	1.9	2.2	Quick		2.7		2.4	1.6	2.0
.8	1.0	1.0			1.4		1.4	1.0	.9
.5	.7	.6			.7		.8	.6	.6
35 10.3	34 10.7	32 11.3	Sales/Receivables	19 19.0		26 14.3	41 9.0	39 9.3	
47 7.8	50 7.3	46 7.9		31 11.6		46 8.0	55 6.7	53 6.9	
68 5.3	68 5.4	59 6.2		39 9.4		55 6.0	60 6.0	66 5.5	
46 7.9	44 8.3	33 11.1	Cost of Sales/Inventory	11 33.2		34 10.8	50 7.4	46 7.9	
94 3.9	85 4.3	77 4.7		16 22.9		61 5.9	84 4.3	102 3.6	
135 2.7	137 2.7	129 2.8		82 4.5		90 4.1	134 2.7	172 2.1	
31 11.7	27 13.4	25 14.5	Cost of Sales/Payables	25 14.5		19 18.9	23 15.9	29 12.8	
49 7.4	45 8.1	40 9.2		29 12.5		29 12.7	40 9.2	45 8.1	
81 4.5	88 4.1	62 5.8		39 9.2		50 7.2	59 6.2	76 4.8	
4.1	4.1	3.8	Sales/Working Capital		7.7		3.5	4.8	3.7
8.2	7.4	7.5			11.4		5.9	8.3	6.6
21.1	18.4	16.3			NM		12.6	13.2	99.1
(68) 13.2	(67) 20.8	(115) 27.8	EBIT/Interest	(12) 320.0		(24) 16.9	(29) 18.0	(41) 47.4	
4.2	8.4	7.5		25.4		7.2	6.2	8.0	
1.7	3.0	2.8		1.8		1.9	3.7	2.6	
(29) 7.4	(25) 10.7	(31) 19.6	Net Profit + Depr., Dep., Amort./Cur. Mat. L/T/D					(16) 36.7	
2.9	4.5	3.5						12.0	
1.4	1.8	1.8						1.8	
.3	.3	.2	Fixed/Worth		.2		.2	.2	.3
.7	.5	.7			.7		1.0	.7	.6
1.7	1.0	1.4			-4.0		4.3	1.1	1.5
.9	.6	.5	Debt/Worth		.5		.5	.6	.5
1.9	1.2	1.4			2.0		1.5	1.2	1.4
6.6	4.1	4.7			-11.6		10.9	2.6	5.8
(66) 65.0	(72) 52.2	(110) 68.7	% Profit Before Taxes/Tangible Net Worth			(21) 55.4	(30) 64.4	(41) 72.6	
30.9	29.0	29.3				28.0	29.5	27.3	
12.0	11.5	13.6				8.3	11.1	17.6	
16.7	22.7	25.3	% Profit Before Taxes/Total Assets		92.7		29.9	20.9	26.7
8.0	10.5	13.0			27.1		7.6	12.9	12.6
2.1	3.3	3.5			6.2		2.8	4.1	4.5
14.6	25.8	30.7	Sales/Net Fixed Assets		71.7		29.6	27.4	17.5
5.2	9.2	7.1			42.4		8.8	7.1	5.2
2.8	3.6	3.8			3.9		4.5	3.6	3.5
2.5	2.6	2.6	Sales/Total Assets		6.7		2.8	2.2	2.1
1.4	1.8	1.8			2.0		2.0	2.0	1.3
1.1	1.1	1.1			1.4		1.1	1.0	.9
(64) .9	(66) .2	(96) 1.2	% Depr., Dep., Amort./Sales			(20) 1.3	(27) 1.3	(35) .9	
2.4	1.5	2.1				1.8	2.4	2.2	
4.5	3.5	3.7				4.6	3.5	4.4	
(20) 1.3	(24) 2.3	(30) 1.4	% Officers', Directors', Owners' Comp/Sales				(10) .8		
7.0	5.2	4.9					2.3		
10.1	14.2	14.1					8.7		
3058663M	2641317M	5116983M	Net Sales ($)	11M	26982M	35145M	200840M	556039M	4297966M
2702597M	2005562M	4018632M	Total Assets ($)	11M	12572M	19649M	174846M	395126M	3416428M

M = $ thousand   MM = $ million
See Pages 11 through 18 for Explanation of Ratios and Data

Current Data Sorted By Assets   Comparative Historical Data

0-500M	500M-2MM	2-10MM	10-50MM	50-100MM	100-250MM	Type of Statement	4/1/98-3/31/99 ALL	4/1/99-3/31/00 ALL
		8	12	1	1	Unqualified	32	30
	7	21	4			Reviewed	40	28
1	8	6				Compiled	19	17
1	3	1			1	Tax Returns	5	4
	4	17	7	2	1	Other	33	40
	22 (4/1-9/30/02)		84 (10/1/02-3/31/03)					
2	22	53	23	3	3	**NUMBER OF STATEMENTS**	129	119
%	%	%	%	%	%	**ASSETS**	%	%
	7.1	7.2	13.6			Cash & Equivalents	7.5	7.5
	29.5	25.7	22.9			Trade Receivables (net)	28.6	29.1
	26.2	28.4	21.4			Inventory	28.5	26.7
	1.7	2.0	2.8			All Other Current	2.7	1.8
	64.6	63.4	60.8			Total Current	67.3	65.0
	19.9	27.4	27.6			Fixed Assets (net)	23.3	25.2
	6.1	1.9	4.2			Intangibles (net)	3.6	3.6
	9.4	7.3	7.4			All Other Non-Current	5.9	6.1
	100.0	100.0	100.0			Total	100.0	100.0
						LIABILITIES		
	7.5	9.4	3.8			Notes Payable-Short Term	10.6	11.3
	11.4	5.2	2.4			Cur. Mat.-L/T/D	3.5	3.3
	17.7	15.2	12.4			Trade Payables	16.8	17.4
	.0	.2	.4			Income Taxes Payable	.3	.2
	6.3	9.3	10.2			All Other Current	8.2	8.4
	43.1	39.3	29.2			Total Current	39.4	40.6
	19.0	16.2	12.0			Long Term Debt	15.3	15.4
	.3	.3	.1			Deferred Taxes	.4	.4
	1.5	4.7	2.9			All Other Non-Current	4.1	4.3
	36.1	39.5	55.8			Net Worth	40.9	39.3
	100.0	100.0	100.0			Total Liabilities & Net Worth	100.0	100.0
						INCOME DATA		
	100.0	100.0	100.0			Net Sales	100.0	100.0
	34.1	32.4	37.1			Gross Profit	33.4	33.3
	31.5	28.8	31.9			Operating Expenses	29.4	28.7
	2.6	3.6	5.2			Operating Profit	4.0	4.6
	1.0	1.0	.1			All Other Expenses (net)	.8	1.4
	1.5	2.6	5.1			Profit Before Taxes	3.2	3.3
						RATIOS		
	3.9	3.0	3.4			Current	3.0	2.8
	1.4	1.9	2.1				1.9	1.7
	1.0	1.3	1.7				1.3	1.2
	2.5	1.4	2.1			Quick	1.6	1.6
	.7	.9	1.1				.9	.9
	.5	.6	.9				.6	.6
	(34) 10.8	(33) 11.2	(38) 9.5			Sales/Receivables	(36) 10.1	(35) 10.6
	(38) 9.5	(40) 9.1	(48) 7.6				(43) 8.5	(46) 7.9
	(68) 5.4	(49) 7.4	(59) 6.2				(52) 7.0	(54) 6.7
	(32) 11.5	(55) 6.6	(64) 5.7			Cost of Sales/Inventory	(48) 7.6	(41) 8.9
	(57) 6.4	(66) 5.5	(76) 4.8				(66) 5.5	(71) 5.2
	(90) 4.1	(91) 4.0	(88) 4.1				(96) 3.8	(96) 3.8
	(28) 13.1	(18) 20.8	(24) 15.5			Cost of Sales/Payables	(23) 16.1	(25) 14.6
	(32) 11.3	(25) 14.5	(34) 10.7				(38) 9.7	(34) 10.8
	(54) 6.7	(54) 6.8	(56) 6.5				(51) 7.2	(50) 7.3
	3.8	5.1	3.8			Sales/Working Capital	5.0	5.2
	17.4	7.8	5.7				7.4	9.0
	−63.4	21.6	10.0				18.2	31.2
	3.5	8.8	37.4			EBIT/Interest	9.4	6.3
	(20) 1.3	(47) 4.3	(21) 13.6				(113) 3.0	(104) 2.9
	.0	1.1	2.8				1.5	1.7
		(14) 6.6				Net Profit + Depr., Dep.,	8.6	8.0
		3.0				Amort./Cur. Mat. L/T/D	(47) 2.6	(35) 2.8
		1.5					.8	1.6
	.2	.3	.3			Fixed/Worth	.2	.3
	.7	.7	.5				.5	.7
	2.6	1.5	.8				1.3	1.8
	.7	.6	.4			Debt/Worth	.6	.7
	2.9	1.4	.9				1.2	1.7
	32.8	5.0	1.7				4.5	4.6
	(19) 20.5	(49) 32.0	(22) 29.8			% Profit Before Taxes/Tangible Net Worth	(118) 36.7	(110) 35.7
	3.7	9.5	19.7				17.3	17.8
	1.7	2.4	3.2				4.8	8.1
	6.5	11.9	18.4			% Profit Before Taxes/Total Assets	14.2	13.9
	1.4	4.8	8.5				7.1	7.0
	−3.1	.6	1.7				1.7	2.5
	31.4	14.1	12.1			Sales/Net Fixed Assets	22.5	17.6
	18.9	9.9	6.4				11.2	11.0
	6.3	5.4	5.0				6.3	5.2
	3.4	2.8	2.2			Sales/Total Assets	3.0	3.0
	2.3	2.2	1.7				2.4	2.4
	1.7	1.7	1.3				1.8	1.8
	(17) 1.0	(43) 1.4	(21) 1.4			% Depr., Dep., Amort./Sales	(115) 1.0	(105) 1.1
	1.5	1.9	2.0				1.6	1.6
	3.0	3.4	3.5				2.4	2.3
		(11) 1.8				% Officers', Directors', Owners' Comp/Sales	2.6	1.9
		2.4					(38) 4.7	(31) 3.9
		5.0					8.3	6.4
976M	69011M	584664M	976205M	244412M	1233952M	Net Sales ($)	3470885M	3986967M
580M	28663M	265867M	548630M	178162M	602321M	Total Assets ($)	1694679M	2016512M

M = $ thousand   MM = $ million
See Pages 11 through 18 for Explanation of Ratios and Data

Comparative Historical Data / Current Data Sorted By Sales

					Type of Statement	0-1MM	1-3MM	3-5MM	5-10MM	10-25MM	25MM & OVER
	21		21		22	Unqualified				4	3	15
	26		21		32	Reviewed		1	9	6	13	3
	21		29		15	Compiled	1	5	4	4	1	
	3		4		6	Tax Returns	1	2	1	1	1	1
	27		36		31	Other		1	4	11	8	7
	4/1/00-3/31/01 ALL		4/1/01-3/31/02 ALL		4/1/02-3/31/03 ALL		22 (4/1-9/30/02)		84 (10/1/02-3/31/03)			
	98		111		106	**NUMBER OF STATEMENTS**	2	9	18	26	25	26
	%		%		%	**ASSETS**	%	%	%	%	%	%
	6.2		8.7		8.4	Cash & Equivalents			5.9	7.0	7.4	12.7
	28.1		26.0		25.3	Trade Receivables (net)			25.5	27.7	26.3	22.3
	29.2		25.2		26.6	Inventory			32.7	25.9	29.0	22.5
	2.1		2.4		2.1	All Other Current			1.3	2.9	2.0	2.4
	65.6		62.3		62.4	Total Current			65.3	63.6	64.7	59.9
	23.6		25.0		25.8	Fixed Assets (net)			25.2	26.8	25.6	26.1
	4.9		3.9		4.2	Intangibles (net)			3.7	2.4	2.5	6.6
	5.9		8.9		7.6	All Other Non-Current			5.7	7.3	7.2	7.5
	100.0		100.0		100.0	Total			100.0	100.0	100.0	100.0
						LIABILITIES						
	10.9		7.7		7.1	Notes Payable-Short Term			9.5	7.1	11.8	2.3
	2.9		3.8		6.4	Cur. Mat.-L/T/D			8.6	5.8	4.9	2.1
	19.0		16.3		14.8	Trade Payables			14.8	19.2	13.4	12.4
	.3		.2		.2	Income Taxes Payable			.0	.3	.3	.4
	8.7		10.0		8.5	All Other Current			8.5	8.8	7.0	9.9
	41.7		38.0		37.0	Total Current			41.4	41.3	37.3	27.1
	14.1		13.4		16.6	Long Term Debt			15.9	18.0	13.6	13.8
	.4		.2		.3	Deferred Taxes			.1	.1	.6	.1
	5.5		5.0		3.6	All Other Non-Current			1.1	8.6	1.8	3.1
	38.3		43.4		42.5	Net Worth			41.5	31.9	46.7	55.8
	100.0		100.0		100.0	Total Liabilities & Net Worth			100.0	100.0	100.0	100.0
						INCOME DATA						
	100.0		100.0		100.0	Net Sales			100.0	100.0	100.0	100.0
	32.7		34.8		34.5	Gross Profit			34.7	31.6	31.1	38.8
	29.3		32.3		30.9	Operating Expenses			32.9	30.0	25.6	32.2
	3.4		2.5		3.6	Operating Profit			1.8	1.6	5.5	6.6
	1.1		1.2		.9	All Other Expenses (net)			1.4	.8	1.0	.1
	2.2		1.3		2.8	Profit Before Taxes			.4	.8	4.5	6.5
						RATIOS						
	2.7		3.4		3.2				4.6	2.9	2.5	3.3
	1.5		1.8		1.9	Current			2.1	1.8	1.9	2.1
	1.1		1.2		1.3				1.0	1.1	1.3	1.7
	1.4		1.7		1.6				2.1	1.6	1.4	2.2
	.8		1.0		.9	Quick			.8	.9	.9	1.1
	.5		.6		.6				.4	.6	.6	.9
33	11.2	34	10.7	34	10.8		34	10.8	30	12.1	34	10.7	32	11.4
41	8.9	43	8.5	42	8.7	Sales/Receivables	37	9.8	44	8.3	41	8.9	43	8.4
54	6.8	54	6.8	52	7.0		45	8.0	52	7.0	51	7.1	51	7.2
46	7.9	48	7.6	51	7.2		55	6.7	42	8.6	57	6.4	62	5.9
70	5.2	71	5.2	70	5.2	Cost of Sales/Inventory	76	4.8	58	6.3	66	5.5	73	5.0
94	3.9	91	4.0	89	4.1		105	3.5	89	4.1	89	4.1	86	4.3
25	14.6	21	17.6	21	17.0		19	18.7	17	21.4	18	20.5	25	14.9
37	10.5	35	10.5	32	11.5	Cost of Sales/Payables	29	12.6	35	10.4	27	13.5	34	10.6
55	6.7	51	7.1	48	7.6		34	10.8	64	5.7	44	8.3	46	8.0
	5.1		4.5		4.7				3.6	6.1	4.9	4.0
	10.8		7.8		7.7	Sales/Working Capital			7.4	8.0	6.8	5.7
	36.3		27.3		18.3				NM	33.5	14.9	10.0
	7.5		6.9		9.9				5.0	12.9	8.7	37.9
(93)	2.2	(93)	1.6	(95)	3.9	EBIT/Interest	(15)	2.2	(20)	3.4	4.5	(24)	10.4
	1.0		−.1		1.1			1.2		.8	1.8	3.6
	14.3		6.5		7.5	Net Profit + Depr., Dep.,						23.7
(37)	2.7	(28)	1.4	(27)	2.9	Amort./Cur. Mat. L/T/D					(10)	2.5
	.9		−.2		1.7							1.8
	.3		.3		.3				.2	.3	.3	.3
	.8		.7		.7	Fixed/Worth			.5	.8	.6	.5
	2.9		1.7		1.5				1.7	4.5	1.3	1.0
	.7		.5		.5				.5	.6	.6	.4
	1.8		1.4		1.3	Debt/Worth			2.2	1.7	1.2	.8
	7.0		4.4		4.3				4.5	22.0	2.4	1.8
	35.0		22.6		29.0	% Profit Before Taxes/Tangible			27.8	19.4	34.0	28.3
(87)	11.4	(98)	8.1	(96)	11.4	Net Worth	(16)	6.6	(22)	6.8	21.6	(25)	19.5
	1.3		−3.3		2.4			2.5		−11.2	2.2	6.6
	10.7		8.8		12.4	% Profit Before Taxes/Total			6.5	10.3	13.4	18.7
	3.9		2.2		3.6	Assets			2.7	2.7	8.3	9.0
	.4		−2.9		.2				.6	−3.4	1.3	2.9
	23.6		17.9		15.4				24.2	14.2	14.8	12.4
	11.4		9.0		9.3	Sales/Net Fixed Assets			14.7	9.8	10.7	7.0
	5.9		5.4		5.4				4.1	5.3	5.5	5.3
	3.1		2.9		2.6				3.4	2.8	2.8	2.4
	2.4		2.0		2.1	Sales/Total Assets			2.2	2.3	2.2	1.8
	1.8		1.5		1.6				1.7	1.7	1.7	1.4
	1.0		.8		1.3				1.6	1.2	1.4	1.4
(92)	1.6	(101)	1.6	(88)	1.9	% Depr., Dep., Amort./Sales	(12)	2.5	(19)	2.3	(23)	1.9	(23)	1.7
	2.6		2.8		3.4			4.2		3.4	3.4	2.7
	3.6		2.4		2.2	% Officers', Directors',						
(27)	4.7	(37)	4.5	(24)	3.8	Owners' Comp/Sales						
	8.7		7.2		6.7							
	2394571M		3150182M		3109220M	Net Sales ($)	976M	16656M	72393M	194977M	402884M	2421334M
	1247408M		1682686M		1624223M	Total Assets ($)	580M	9717M	37395M	100442M	194674M	1281415M

M = $ thousand   MM = $ million
See Pages 11 through 18 for Explanation of Ratios and Data

Current Data Sorted By Assets   **Comparative Historical Data**

0-500M	500M-2MM	2-10MM	10-50MM	50-100MM	100-250MM	Type of Statement	4/1/98-3/31/99 ALL	4/1/99-3/31/00 ALL
	5	6	10	2	1	Unqualified	29	29
		10	4	1		Reviewed	14	20
	7	1				Compiled	16	15
3	1	1				Tax Returns	1	1
1	5	9	5	1	1	Other	27	21
	15 (4/1-9/30/02)		59 (10/1/02-3/31/03)					
4	18	27	19	4	2	**NUMBER OF STATEMENTS**	87	86
%	%	%	%	%	%	**ASSETS**	%	%
	11.1	5.1	6.3			Cash & Equivalents	9.5	7.8
	30.7	28.2	21.7			Trade Receivables (net)	27.7	27.2
	25.5	25.7	20.1			Inventory	23.2	24.6
	4.9	2.7	2.7			All Other Current	1.5	1.4
	72.2	61.8	50.9			Total Current	61.9	60.9
	21.5	17.5	29.9			Fixed Assets (net)	25.0	23.7
	2.0	7.5	10.6			Intangibles (net)	6.4	7.2
	4.3	13.2	8.5			All Other Non-Current	6.7	8.2
	100.0	100.0	100.0			Total	100.0	100.0
						LIABILITIES		
	13.0	13.3	9.8			Notes Payable-Short Term	8.4	10.7
	4.8	3.3	4.4			Cur. Mat.-L/T/D	2.8	4.0
	17.4	19.2	13.1			Trade Payables	15.7	16.0
	.1	.2	.2			Income Taxes Payable	.2	.2
	9.3	7.4	6.4			All Other Current	10.2	8.4
	44.5	43.4	34.0			Total Current	37.4	39.4
	6.4	8.5	17.9			Long Term Debt	13.9	15.2
	.1	.3	1.4			Deferred Taxes	.3	.6
	5.9	7.0	3.0			All Other Non-Current	5.5	5.4
	43.1	40.8	43.8			Net Worth	42.9	39.4
	100.0	100.0	100.0			Total Liabilities & Net Worth	100.0	100.0
						INCOME DATA		
	100.0	100.0	100.0			Net Sales	100.0	100.0
	41.7	33.2	31.1			Gross Profit	34.6	35.3
	34.3	27.9	24.8			Operating Expenses	29.1	29.8
	7.4	5.4	6.2			Operating Profit	5.5	5.5
	.9	1.3	1.3			All Other Expenses (net)	.5	.2
	6.5	4.1	4.9			Profit Before Taxes	5.0	5.3
						RATIOS		
	2.4	2.0	2.4				2.7	2.3
	1.7	1.4	1.3			Current	1.7	1.5
	1.2	1.2	1.1				1.2	1.2
	1.7	1.0	1.3				1.5	1.5
	1.0	.7	.7			Quick	1.0	.9
	.6	.5	.6				.7	.6
	30 12.0	36 10.2	33 11.1				36 10.1	38 9.5
	37 9.7	46 7.9	42 8.8			Sales/Receivables	45 8.1	46 7.9
	44 8.3	54 6.7	49 7.4				56 6.6	57 6.4
	39 9.4	51 7.2	40 9.1				40 9.2	40 9.0
	46 8.0	65 5.6	55 6.7			Cost of Sales/Inventory	56 6.5	60 6.1
	69 5.3	90 4.1	75 4.9				81 4.5	90 4.1
	12 30.2	26 13.8	24 15.5				24 15.4	24 15.0
	39 9.5	41 8.9	32 11.2			Cost of Sales/Payables	33 11.1	36 10.2
	57 6.5	54 6.8	54 6.8				45 8.2	50 7.3
	6.8	6.4	5.3				5.6	6.4
	11.8	11.9	12.9			Sales/Working Capital	9.4	9.5
	22.6	22.7	73.0				30.4	23.1
	26.7	(24) 5.6	8.0				(81) 11.4	(79) 7.3
	(17) 3.1	2.2	(17) 5.0			EBIT/Interest	3.5	3.3
	.5	1.0	3.4				1.9	1.4
		3.8				Net Profit + Depr., Dep.,	8.7	7.4
		(10) 1.1				Amort./Cur. Mat. L./T/D	(30) 3.3	(31) 2.3
		.5					1.2	1.7
	.2	.2	.5				.3	.3
	.5	.5	.7			Fixed/Worth	.6	.7
	.9	1.0	1.6				1.5	1.5
	.7	.8	.7				.6	.8
	1.4	1.9	2.0			Debt/Worth	1.5	1.8
	2.7	3.5	5.2				3.3	4.3
	56.5	21.4	39.0			% Profit Before Taxes/Tangible	(77) 39.1	(77) 42.3
	(17) 28.6	(24) 6.4	(15) 20.0			Net Worth	19.3	18.3
	.5	.5	9.1				5.4	4.8
	43.4	11.0	10.8			% Profit Before Taxes/Total	16.2	16.2
	6.2	2.3	8.5			Assets	7.0	6.7
	-.7	.1	5.5				1.7	1.7
	45.2	24.7	7.6				17.4	18.6
	18.9	15.5	5.3			Sales/Net Fixed Assets	9.8	10.2
	7.5	7.0	4.4				4.9	5.6
	3.8	2.5	2.2				3.0	2.9
	2.9	1.9	1.8			Sales/Total Assets	2.3	2.2
	2.4	1.4	1.5				1.6	1.5
	.6	1.0	2.0			% Depr., Dep., Amort./Sales	(77) 1.4	(79) 1.1
	(16) 1.5	(26) 1.8	(16) 2.7				2.2	2.2
	2.4	2.5	3.7				3.4	3.3
	3.3					% Officers', Directors',	4.1	3.2
	(10) 4.7					Owners' Comp/Sales	(30) 6.6	(26) 4.3
	10.2						10.4	8.3
5907M	76386M	257420M	854542M	507231M	321808M	Net Sales ($)	2468306M	2259902M
1603M	25433M	129417M	476430M	310800M	402229M	Total Assets ($)	1772889M	1497670M

M = $ thousand   MM = $ million
See Pages 11 through 18 for Explanation of Ratios and Data

Comparative Historical Data / **Current Data Sorted By Sales**

Hist 4/1/00-3/31/01	Hist 4/1/01-3/31/02	Hist 4/1/02-3/31/03		0-1MM	1-3MM	3-5MM	5-10MM	10-25MM	25MM & OVER
			Type of Statement						
18	12	19	Unqualified			2	2	4	11
13	15	20	Reviewed			7	6	3	4
18	12	8	Compiled			5	3		
3	4	5	Tax Returns	1	4			3	
32	25	22	Other	1	1	4	2	9	5
ALL	ALL	ALL			15 (4/1-9/30/02)		59 (10/1/02-3/31/03)		
84	68	74	**NUMBER OF STATEMENTS**	2	5	18	13	16	20
%	%	%	**ASSETS**	%	%	%	%	%	%
5.7	5.6	7.3	Cash & Equivalents			7.2	9.0	4.6	7.3
26.0	28.8	26.5	Trade Receivables (net)			27.4	35.3	23.5	21.6
24.8	24.3	23.7	Inventory			22.7	25.7	30.6	16.4
1.9	2.1	3.0	All Other Current			5.0	.3	4.8	2.2
58.3	60.9	60.5	Total Current			62.3	70.2	63.5	47.6
24.3	24.1	22.2	Fixed Assets (net)			21.3	18.5	23.7	26.2
9.9	9.0	8.3	Intangibles (net)			2.7	5.6	3.2	17.9
7.4	6.0	9.1	All Other Non-Current			13.7	5.7	9.6	8.2
100.0	100.0	100.0	Total			100.0	100.0	100.0	100.0
			LIABILITIES						
9.2	10.0	10.8	Notes Payable-Short Term			13.6	14.4	12.8	8.1
5.6	4.4	4.4	Cur. Mat.-L/T/D			5.3	3.4	2.1	4.8
15.9	15.2	16.4	Trade Payables			16.7	17.9	19.3	13.2
.4	.3	.2	Income Taxes Payable			.0	.1	.4	.3
7.1	7.5	7.0	All Other Current			10.1	5.4	8.3	6.2
38.3	37.3	38.9	Total Current			45.7	41.3	43.0	32.6
13.0	13.6	10.6	Long Term Debt			8.3	7.0	8.8	18.1
.7	.7	.6	Deferred Taxes			.1	.2	.9	1.1
6.3	4.2	5.3	All Other Non-Current			5.9	7.5	2.0	4.4
41.8	44.2	44.6	Net Worth			39.9	43.9	45.3	43.8
100.0	100.0	100.0	Total Liabilities & Net Worth			100.0	100.0	100.0	100.0
			INCOME DATA						
100.0	100.0	100.0	Net Sales			100.0	100.0	100.0	100.0
36.4	35.3	35.3	Gross Profit			42.0	30.8	27.5	32.2
31.2	31.2	29.4	Operating Expenses			38.5	25.1	23.9	24.2
5.2	4.1	5.9	Operating Profit			3.5	5.8	3.7	8.0
-.4	1.6	1.2	All Other Expenses (net)			1.3	.8	.9	1.8
5.6	2.5	4.8	Profit Before Taxes			2.2	4.9	2.8	6.2
			RATIOS						
2.2	2.2	2.4	Current			1.8	2.8	2.2	2.3
1.6	1.7	1.5				1.5	1.7	1.4	1.3
1.2	1.2	1.2				1.2	1.3	1.2	1.0
1.2	1.4	1.3	Quick			1.2	1.6	1.0	1.3
.8	.9	.7				.7	1.0	.6	.7
.6	.6	.5				.5	.7	.4	.5
38 9.6	37 9.9	33 11.0	Sales/Receivables			33 11.0	33 11.0	35 10.3	33 11.0
48 7.5	48 7.5	40 9.0				42 8.8	38 9.7	41 9.0	45 8.2
59 6.2	60 6.1	50 7.3				52 7.1	56 6.6	49 7.4	49 7.4
43 8.5	43 8.6	41 8.8	Cost of Sales/Inventory			42 8.7	37 9.9	53 6.9	40 9.1
67 5.4	59 6.1	57 6.4				54 6.7	47 7.8	81 4.5	52 7.0
102 3.6	85 4.3	86 4.2				76 4.8	66 5.5	90 4.1	65 5.6
29 12.5	25 14.7	24 15.5	Cost of Sales/Payables			17 21.2	21 17.6	27 13.6	30 12.3
39 9.3	37 10.0	37 9.8				39 9.4	28 13.0	43 8.4	35 10.5
58 6.3	50 7.3	54 6.8				60 6.0	45 8.1	53 6.9	53 6.9
6.0	5.9	5.8	Sales/Working Capital			7.1	4.6	6.0	6.1
9.9	8.3	11.2				13.7	8.4	11.9	17.1
23.1	19.4	31.1				31.2	16.9	18.8	NM
6.2	5.9	6.4	EBIT/Interest			4.2	20.0	6.0	12.0
(82) 2.9	(65) 2.5	(66) 3.4				(17) 1.4	(12) 2.2	(15) 4.1	(18) 5.1
1.3	.9	1.0				.3	1.0	1.9	2.7
3.5	4.3	3.7	Net Profit + Depr., Dep., Amort./Cur. Mat. L/T/D						7.4
(24) 1.7	(27) 1.5	(27) 1.9						(10)	2.6
.7	.6	1.0							1.0
.3	.3	.2	Fixed/Worth			.2	.2	.3	.6
.8	.7	.6				.7	.5	.5	1.3
2.3	1.2	1.3				1.2	.8	.7	NM
.8	1.0	.7	Debt/Worth			.7	.7	.6	.9
1.6	1.5	1.7				1.7	1.7	1.6	2.7
4.3	3.8	3.5				3.2	3.5	2.1	NM
42.0	43.9	37.5	% Profit Before Taxes/Tangible Net Worth			30.1	38.6	29.8	42.2
(73) 15.7	(64) 10.1	(65) 15.4				(16) 5.8	(12) 8.6	9.4	(15) 25.0
4.8	-4.7	.5				-2.7	.5	2.0	16.4
12.1	15.8	14.8	% Profit Before Taxes/Total Assets			14.2	30.4	7.8	16.0
4.8	4.0	6.4				1.8	3.7	4.9	9.7
1.3	-.3	.1				-1.7	.1	1.0	5.6
19.3	21.1	24.7	Sales/Net Fixed Assets			38.2	30.4	20.2	16.6
9.9	9.7	10.3				11.4	17.0	8.5	5.4
4.9	5.1	5.2				7.5	7.0	4.4	4.0
2.6	2.8	2.7	Sales/Total Assets			3.3	3.3	2.5	2.3
2.0	2.1	2.1				2.5	2.5	1.9	1.8
1.6	1.5	1.5				1.6	1.7	1.5	1.0
1.4	1.2	1.1	% Depr., Dep., Amort./Sales			.9	1.1	.3	2.3
(74) 2.3	(63) 2.2	(66) 2.2				(16) 2.2	1.7	(15) 1.6	(17) 3.5
3.5	3.4	3.0				3.1	2.3	2.3	3.9
2.8	2.7	4.2	% Officers', Directors', Owners' Comp/Sales						
(27) 6.2	(16) 6.2	(22) 7.2							
9.0	10.7	10.0							
2122580M	2390942M	2023294M	Net Sales ($)	1861M	10480M	71450M	87822M	271820M	1579861M
1926287M	1555604M	1345912M	Total Assets ($)	707M	6824M	32077M	39553M	143583M	1123168M

M = $ thousand   MM = $ million
See Pages 11 through 18 for Explanation of Ratios and Data

Current Data Sorted By Assets | Comparative Historical Data

Type of Statement	0-500M	500M-2MM	2-10MM	10-50MM	50-100MM	100-250MM		4/1/98-3/31/99 ALL	4/1/99-3/31/00 ALL
Unqualified			4	5	3	2		16	15
Reviewed		1	6	5	3	2		12	5
Compiled	2	2	2					12	6
Tax Returns	3	1						1	2
Other	1	1	5	4				8	13
	8 (4/1-9/30/02)		34 (10/1/02-3/31/03)						
NUMBER OF STATEMENTS	6	5	17	9	3	2		49	41
ASSETS	%	%	%	%	%	%		%	%
Cash & Equivalents			5.8					7.1	8.3
Trade Receivables (net)			33.8					26.9	27.3
Inventory			26.0					26.5	23.8
All Other Current			2.9					3.2	2.5
Total Current			68.5					63.7	61.9
Fixed Assets (net)			25.8					25.6	30.3
Intangibles (net)			1.8					2.5	3.5
All Other Non-Current			3.9					8.3	4.2
Total			100.0					100.0	100.0
LIABILITIES									
Notes Payable-Short Term			7.5					10.7	8.5
Cur. Mat.-L/T/D			4.0					3.1	3.4
Trade Payables			21.5					16.6	16.0
Income Taxes Payable			.2					.6	.2
All Other Current			9.7					9.9	11.7
Total Current			43.0					41.0	39.7
Long Term Debt			12.2					16.8	18.8
Deferred Taxes			.0					.2	.4
All Other Non-Current			4.0					5.2	4.8
Net Worth			40.8					36.8	36.3
Total Liabilities & Net Worth			100.0					100.0	100.0
INCOME DATA									
Net Sales			100.0					100.0	100.0
Gross Profit			33.6					38.6	41.3
Operating Expenses			29.4					33.5	35.1
Operating Profit			4.2					5.1	6.2
All Other Expenses (net)			.4					.7	.8
Profit Before Taxes			3.8					4.5	5.4
RATIOS									
Current			2.9					2.9	2.9
			1.8					1.5	1.7
			1.1					1.0	1.1
Quick			1.6					1.5	1.9
			1.0					.8	1.0
			.5					.5	.6
Sales/Receivables			30 12.1					34 10.7	38 9.5
			45 8.2					42 8.6	47 7.7
			65 5.6					47 7.7	60 6.1
Cost of Sales/Inventory			38 9.7					49 7.4	46 7.9
			52 7.0					62 5.9	67 5.5
			71 5.2					92 4.0	97 3.8
Cost of Sales/Payables			21 17.0					18 20.1	28 12.8
			53 7.0					40 9.2	44 8.3
			72 5.1					57 6.4	59 6.2
Sales/Working Capital			5.0					5.2	4.3
			9.7					14.2	12.8
			47.2					392.8	88.4
EBIT/Interest			14.7					19.5	21.3
			(15) 4.4					(43) 4.6	(38) 4.9
			1.6					1.2	1.0
Net Profit + Depr., Dep., Amort./Cur. Mat. L./T/D								31.1	12.7
								(12) 7.2	(15) 5.9
								1.2	.9
Fixed/Worth			.1					.2	.4
			.7					.9	1.0
			1.5					2.6	2.7
Debt/Worth			.7					.6	.5
			1.1					1.9	2.1
			3.6					6.0	5.4
% Profit Before Taxes/Tangible Net Worth			37.1					52.6	42.8
			(16) 13.7					(43) 17.2	(36) 24.0
			4.3					.8	2.6
% Profit Before Taxes/Total Assets			13.2					18.5	17.7
			5.7					6.7	11.2
			.7					.2	-.7
Sales/Net Fixed Assets			36.4					20.0	13.4
			9.1					10.4	7.8
			6.2					5.5	4.5
Sales/Total Assets			2.7					3.1	2.7
			2.4					2.4	2.1
			1.9					1.7	1.4
% Depr., Dep., Amort./Sales			1.5					.8	1.5
			(15) 2.0					(46) 1.7	(38) 2.1
			2.5					2.8	3.2
% Officers', Directors', Owners' Comp/Sales								1.9	1.6
								(16) 3.0	(14) 2.6
								8.8	4.3
Net Sales ($)	8204M	17660M	187722M	371658M	562282M	250707M		1815014M	2005088M
Total Assets ($)	1559M	6107M	77968M	159169M	229698M	230613M		867315M	1143319M

M = $ thousand   MM = $ million
See Pages 11 through 18 for Explanation of Ratios and Data

Comparative Historical Data | Current Data Sorted By Sales

			Type of Statement						
13	7	14	Unqualified			1	1	4	8
8	4	7	Reviewed			1	3	3	
6	11	6	Compiled	1	2	1	2		
3	2	4	Tax Returns		3	1			
14	16	11	Other	1	1	1		4	4
4/1/00-3/31/01	4/1/01-3/31/02	4/1/02-3/31/03		8 (4/1-9/30/02)			34 (10/1/02-3/31/03)		
ALL	ALL	ALL		0-1MM	1-3MM	3-5MM	5-10MM	10-25MM	25MM & OVER
44	40	42	NUMBER OF STATEMENTS	2	6	5	6	11	12
%	%	%	ASSETS	%	%	%	%	%	%
7.6	6.3	6.5	Cash & Equivalents					4.7	5.8
23.7	26.6	28.5	Trade Receivables (net)					30.3	23.6
25.9	25.6	26.6	Inventory					28.2	25.3
3.7	2.6	4.0	All Other Current					5.4	5.9
60.9	61.1	65.7	Total Current					68.6	60.5
26.6	28.0	26.1	Fixed Assets (net)					25.0	27.5
4.9	6.3	3.2	Intangibles (net)					2.6	7.0
7.6	4.6	4.9	All Other Non-Current					3.7	4.9
100.0	100.0	100.0	Total					100.0	100.0
			LIABILITIES						
11.0	12.8	15.1	Notes Payable-Short Term					14.3	10.0
3.7	5.2	4.0	Cur. Mat.-L/T/D					2.9	4.0
16.0	16.8	18.4	Trade Payables					20.6	18.5
.4	.3	.2	Income Taxes Payable					.0	.3
8.7	19.2	9.4	All Other Current					6.3	10.5
39.9	54.3	47.1	Total Current					44.1	43.3
14.1	16.4	13.0	Long Term Debt					11.5	17.5
.4	.6	.4	Deferred Taxes					.4	.6
4.6	5.6	5.4	All Other Non-Current					6.4	5.2
40.9	23.0	34.0	Net Worth					37.6	33.4
100.0	100.0	100.0	Total Liabilities & Net Worth					100.0	100.0
			INCOME DATA						
100.0	100.0	100.0	Net Sales					100.0	100.0
40.5	41.3	35.3	Gross Profit					27.9	35.8
34.5	35.6	30.9	Operating Expenses					24.1	28.0
6.0	5.7	4.3	Operating Profit					3.8	7.8
1.3	1.8	.8	All Other Expenses (net)					.7	1.3
4.8	3.9	3.6	Profit Before Taxes					3.1	6.5
			RATIOS						
2.7 1.4 1.0	1.8 1.3 .9	2.4 1.6 1.1	Current					2.2 1.6 1.1	1.8 1.3 1.1
1.5 .6 .5	1.0 .6 .5	1.4 .8 .5	Quick					1.6 .6 .4	1.1 .6 .4
26 14.0 41 9.0 54 6.8	32 11.4 41 8.8 50 7.2	31 11.8 40 9.1 52 7.0	Sales/Receivables					31 11.6 48 7.6 54 6.7	33 11.1 41 8.9 50 7.3
46 8.0 63 5.8 92 4.0	42 8.7 58 6.3 81 4.5	38 9.6 60 6.1 78 4.7	Cost of Sales/Inventory					38 9.6 63 5.8 70 5.2	35 10.5 72 5.1 130 2.8
16 23.1 34 10.7 58 6.2	18 20.7 38 9.7 70 5.2	23 15.8 44 8.3 63 5.8	Cost of Sales/Payables					23 16.0 47 7.7 53 6.9	25 14.4 46 7.9 73 5.0
7.0 14.3 NM	8.4 18.3 -53.3	6.3 11.2 34.0	Sales/Working Capital					7.2 9.7 65.4	8.1 15.9 26.6
(38) 15.3 4.1 1.5	(37) 8.1 2.6 1.2	(37) 11.4 4.4 1.4	EBIT/Interest						(11) 11.6 4.7 2.8
		(10) 4.4 1.8 -.6	Net Profit + Depr., Dep., Amort./Cur. Mat. L/T/D						
.3 .8 2.1	.4 .9 2.7	.3 .8 1.8	Fixed/Worth					.1 .6 1.5	.4 1.3 2.0
.8 2.0 3.7	1.1 2.6 6.5	.7 1.9 3.7	Debt/Worth					.7 1.6 3.5	.7 2.3 6.9
(41) 44.9 23.0 5.9	(33) 37.8 15.8 2.6	(37) 35.5 18.3 1.7	% Profit Before Taxes/Tangible Net Worth				(10)	50.9 12.0 -4.0	(10) 53.9 25.5 21.5
17.9 9.0 .9	12.0 5.4 .8	14.1 6.2 .5	% Profit Before Taxes/Total Assets					18.6 1.7 -2.3	15.4 10.1 6.7
25.9 10.1 5.7	30.5 8.5 5.2	23.0 9.7 6.0	Sales/Net Fixed Assets					50.1 7.2 6.2	17.7 8.0 4.4
2.9 2.2 1.9	3.1 2.3 1.9	3.0 2.3 1.8	Sales/Total Assets					2.9 2.5 1.8	3.3 2.2 1.3
(36) .8 1.8 3.2	(34) 1.1 2.2 3.9	(38) 1.4 2.0 3.0	% Depr., Dep., Amort./Sales					1.5 2.1 2.5	1.2 1.9 2.9
(13) 2.5 5.2 11.1	(17) 2.9 5.4 12.9	(13) 2.6 4.3 11.8	% Officers', Directors', Owners' Comp/Sales						
2179955M	1019067M	1398233M	Net Sales ($)	739M	10618M	21020M	37387M	180278M	1148191M
1085276M	600592M	705114M	Total Assets ($)	134M	4613M	9426M	16510M	80711M	593720M

© RMA 2003

M = $ thousand   MM = $ million

See Pages 11 through 18 for Explanation of Ratios and Data

Current Data Sorted By Assets   **Comparative Historical Data**

	0-500M	500M-2MM	2-10MM	10-50MM	50-100MM	100-250MM	Type of Statement	4/1/98-3/31/99 ALL	4/1/99-3/31/00 ALL
			7	6	2		Unqualified	19	19
	2	11	4				Reviewed	14	12
	4	4					Compiled	13	12
	2	1					Tax Returns	1	2
1 / 1	5	10	10	1	2		Other	21	21
	13 (4/1-9/30/02)		60 (10/1/02-3/31/03)						
2	**13**	**33**	**20**	**3**	**2**	**NUMBER OF STATEMENTS**	**68**	**66**
%	%	%	%	%	%	%	ASSETS	%	%
	4.2	8.4	7.3			Cash & Equivalents	6.3	6.3
	30.4	27.0	26.6			Trade Receivables (net)	31.3	31.0
	26.3	23.3	21.4			Inventory	25.0	24.0
	1.7	5.0	2.2			All Other Current	1.7	1.4
	62.6	63.7	57.5			Total Current	64.3	62.7
	29.9	22.8	30.8			Fixed Assets (net)	21.1	27.8
	1.1	7.8	1.7			Intangibles (net)	4.0	3.9
	6.4	5.7	9.9			All Other Non-Current	10.6	5.6
	100.0	100.0	100.0			Total	100.0	100.0
						LIABILITIES		
	9.4	7.5	15.1			Notes Payable-Short Term	13.5	12.1
	8.9	3.0	2.9			Cur. Mat.-L/T/D	4.5	3.9
	20.0	19.2	15.1			Trade Payables	17.2	21.3
	.1	.9	.2			Income Taxes Payable	.3	.6
	13.1	8.9	7.3			All Other Current	10.1	7.8
	51.5	39.4	40.8			Total Current	45.6	45.7
	14.1	14.4	17.3			Long Term Debt	13.6	13.7
	.1	.5	.4			Deferred Taxes	.4	.4
	1.7	5.1	4.3			All Other Non-Current	4.2	3.4
	32.7	40.7	37.2			Net Worth	36.3	36.8
	100.0	100.0	100.0			Total Liabilities & Net Worth	100.0	100.0
						INCOME DATA		
	100.0	100.0	100.0			Net Sales	100.0	100.0
	46.5	40.9	31.2			Gross Profit	41.5	38.1
	45.6	35.3	27.6			Operating Expenses	37.1	32.8
	.9	5.6	3.6			Operating Profit	4.4	5.3
	1.0	1.1	1.1			All Other Expenses (net)	.8	.8
	-.1	4.6	2.6			Profit Before Taxes	3.6	4.4
						RATIOS		
	2.5	2.4	1.9				2.1	2.0
	1.3	1.5	1.5			Current	1.4	1.3
	.9	1.2	1.1				1.1	1.0
	1.3	1.2	1.1				1.3	1.2
	.7	.9	.8			Quick	.8	.8
	.4	.6	.6				.6	.5
	29 12.7	29 12.6	36 10.1				33 11.1	39 9.3
	43 8.4	39 9.3	45 8.1			Sales/Receivables	43 8.5	45 8.1
	50 7.2	47 7.8	55 6.6				56 6.5	58 6.3
	46 8.0	39 9.3	44 8.3				40 9.2	35 10.4
	52 7.0	51 7.2	61 6.0			Cost of Sales/Inventory	60 6.1	54 6.7
	91 4.0	76 4.8	77 4.7				85 4.3	91 4.0
	29 12.8	31 11.9	22 16.7				23 15.9	33 11.1
	42 8.6	43 8.4	42 8.6			Cost of Sales/Payables	36 10.1	44 8.4
	71 5.1	67 5.4	52 7.1				64 5.7	68 5.4
	9.8	5.6	7.3				6.1	6.0
	19.0	12.9	10.8			Sales/Working Capital	14.4	12.6
	-66.0	33.9	74.4				77.4	131.0
	11.6	(29) 20.5	9.0				(64) 6.0	(61) 8.9
	(11) 1.3	6.5	5.4			EBIT/Interest	3.1	2.8
	.9	3.0	1.4				1.5	1.2
		(13) 22.7				Net Profit + Depr., Dep.,	(26) 9.1	(20) 3.2
		5.2				Amort./Cur. Mat. L /T/D	2.3	1.5
		1.6					1.3	.5
	.6	.3	.5				.3	.3
	.8	.9	.9			Fixed/Worth	.6	.7
	1.9	2.9	1.3				1.1	1.4
	.9	.8	1.0				.9	.9
	2.3	2.0	2.4			Debt/Worth	2.0	1.7
	4.6	8.4	4.9				5.2	4.2
	27.0	64.4	37.2			% Profit Before Taxes/Tangible	(60) 44.7	(59) 44.5
	(12) 6.2	(31) 19.7	16.9			Net Worth	18.5	24.0
	-.9	6.8	3.8				6.5	4.4
	9.4	13.7	9.0			% Profit Before Taxes/Total	13.1	16.8
	3.2	8.8	4.4			Assets	6.1	5.9
	.0	4.3	1.3				2.5	.9
	19.5	23.7	13.3				26.0	21.0
	12.5	12.4	6.7			Sales/Net Fixed Assets	14.6	11.1
	6.7	5.8	3.8				7.3	5.4
	3.6	3.0	2.5				3.3	3.0
	2.7	2.4	2.1			Sales/Total Assets	2.6	2.4
	2.3	1.9	1.4				1.9	1.7
	1.2	1.2	1.1				1.0	1.0
	(12) 1.9	(30) 1.7	(18) 2.1			% Depr., Dep., Amort./Sales	(64) 1.6	(56) 1.6
	4.2	2.3	2.6				2.7	3.2
		2.2				% Officers', Directors',	(29) 2.2	(24) 2.6
		(11) 3.5				Owners' Comp/Sales	5.2	4.3
		4.1					8.8	6.2
1954M	43999M	399693M	861127M	395922M	498324M	Net Sales ($)	1893413M	1480983M
651M	16130M	158796M	414301M	204276M	334113M	Total Assets ($)	742793M	719726M

M = $ thousand   MM = $ million
See Pages 11 through 18 for Explanation of Ratios and Data

Comparative Historical Data | Current Data Sorted By Sales

4/1/00-3/31/01 ALL	4/1/01-3/31/02 ALL	4/1/02-3/31/03 ALL	Type of Statement	0-1MM	1-3MM	3-5MM	5-10MM	10-25MM	25MM & OVER
14	13	15	Unqualified			2		6	7
17	14	17	Reviewed		2	1	4	6	4
14	16	8	Compiled		1	5	1	1	
2	4	4	Tax Returns		1	1	2		
21	27	29	Other	2	4		5	9	9
				13 (4/1-9/30/02)			60 (10/1/02-3/31/03)		
68	74	73	NUMBER OF STATEMENTS	2	8	9	12	22	20
%	%	%	ASSETS	%	%	%	%	%	%
4.8	7.5	7.0	Cash & Equivalents				3.4	10.8	3.7
33.0	32.6	27.7	Trade Receivables (net)				26.6	27.8	29.9
24.7	23.7	23.7	Inventory				22.6	20.8	25.5
1.2	1.3	3.5	All Other Current				12.1	1.6	2.8
63.7	65.1	62.0	Total Current				64.6	61.0	61.9
22.5	20.0	26.0	Fixed Assets (net)				24.9	28.0	25.7
5.3	7.2	5.1	Intangibles (net)				4.7	3.7	4.3
8.5	7.7	6.9	All Other Non-Current				5.7	7.3	8.1
100.0	100.0	100.0	Total				100.0	100.0	100.0
			LIABILITIES						
14.6	13.2	9.7	Notes Payable-Short Term				11.0	7.1	15.1
4.8	3.3	4.1	Cur. Mat.-L/T/D				3.7	2.4	2.9
17.9	19.1	18.0	Trade Payables				19.6	18.9	16.8
.2	.2	.5	Income Taxes Payable				.9	1.0	.1
10.1	9.3	12.1	All Other Current				9.2	8.7	9.5
47.6	45.0	44.4	Total Current				44.4	38.1	44.5
11.1	13.2	16.2	Long Term Debt				13.1	16.6	18.1
.2	.3	.3	Deferred Taxes				.3	.6	.1
4.1	3.3	3.9	All Other Non-Current				2.7	4.0	3.4
36.9	38.2	35.2	Net Worth				39.4	40.6	33.8
100.0	100.0	100.0	Total Liabilities & Net Worth				100.0	100.0	100.0
			INCOME DATA						
100.0	100.0	100.0	Net Sales				100.0	100.0	100.0
39.3	41.0	38.9	Gross Profit				38.3	38.0	33.6
35.2	36.6	34.6	Operating Expenses				35.8	33.7	27.8
4.1	4.4	4.3	Operating Profit				2.4	4.2	5.8
.7	1.1	1.0	All Other Expenses (net)				.4	.2	1.9
3.4	3.3	3.2	Profit Before Taxes				2.0	4.1	3.9
			RATIOS						
1.9 / 1.3 / 1.0	2.3 / 1.4 / 1.1	2.2 / 1.4 / 1.1	Current				2.2 / 1.4 / 1.1	2.4 / 1.5 / 1.2	1.9 / 1.4 / 1.1
1.1 / .8 / .6	1.4 / .8 / .6	1.2 / .8 / .5	Quick				1.1 / .6 / .4	1.5 / .9 / .7	1.0 / .8 / .6
38 9.6 / 48 7.7 / 55 6.6	36 10.1 / 44 8.2 / 54 6.7	32 11.4 / 43 8.5 / 53 6.9	Sales/Receivables				25 14.5 / 40 9.2 / 47 7.7	28 13.2 / 38 9.7 / 52 7.0	36 10.1 / 47 7.8 / 57 6.5
42 8.7 / 58 6.3 / 87 4.2	46 7.9 / 62 5.9 / 82 4.4	43 8.5 / 55 6.6 / 79 4.6	Cost of Sales/Inventory				23 15.8 / 50 7.3 / 72 5.1	43 8.5 / 54 6.7 / 73 5.0	44 8.3 / 67 5.4 / 77 4.7
25 14.7 / 41 9.0 / 54 6.7	21 17.4 / 42 8.7 / 58 6.3	30 12.4 / 43 8.6 / 55 6.6	Cost of Sales/Payables				28 13.0 / 47 7.7 / 63 5.8	31 11.9 / 44 8.3 / 57 6.4	26 13.8 / 39 9.3 / 51 7.1
7.6 / 18.9 / 123.4	6.0 / 16.2 / 75.2	7.1 / 12.9 / 46.0	Sales/Working Capital				6.2 / 13.7 / 66.6	6.5 / 11.5 / 31.5	8.4 / 10.9 / 47.5
(63) 7.3 / 2.5 / 1.0	(65) 6.7 / 2.5 / 1.1	(66) 12.4 / 4.6 / 1.5	EBIT/Interest				(10) 12.6 / 4.1 / 3.1	(20) 20.6 / 7.5 / 4.4	8.3 / 4.1 / 1.9
(27) 7.3 / 1.8 / 1.2	(16) 3.2 / 1.3 / .6	(27) 10.6 / 2.5 / 1.3	Net Profit + Depr., Dep., Amort./Cur. Mat. L/T/D					(10) 18.9 / 2.7 / 1.3	
.3 / .6 / 1.4	.2 / .6 / 1.8	.4 / .9 / 1.8	Fixed/Worth				.5 / .8 / 1.5	.5 / .9 / 1.8	.4 / 1.0 / 1.6
1.1 / 1.8 / 4.4	.7 / 1.9 / 6.3	.9 / 2.4 / 5.7	Debt/Worth				.8 / 1.8 / 3.4	.7 / 1.8 / 5.5	1.1 / 2.5 / 6.0
(62) 35.7 / 13.8 / 1.8	(61) 32.4 / 13.6 / 2.5	(68) 47.0 / 18.8 / 3.0	% Profit Before Taxes/Tangible Net Worth				42.6 / 16.3 / 7.8	(21) 100.6 / 19.7 / 5.4	(19) 47.3 / 25.2 / 13.0
11.6 / 3.8 / .0	11.5 / 4.1 / .4	12.4 / 7.1 / 1.3	% Profit Before Taxes/Total Assets				11.0 / 5.6 / 4.0	13.5 / 9.5 / 3.9	13.3 / 7.5 / 2.3
25.4 / 15.1 / 7.3	28.5 / 16.1 / 7.2	16.0 / 10.3 / 5.8	Sales/Net Fixed Assets				18.4 / 12.0 / 5.9	21.1 / 8.1 / 4.3	14.3 / 9.6 / 6.4
3.3 / 2.5 / 1.9	3.3 / 2.5 / 1.8	2.8 / 2.4 / 1.6	Sales/Total Assets				3.4 / 2.5 / 1.9	3.2 / 2.2 / 1.4	2.8 / 2.3 / 1.9
(59) .9 / 1.5 / 3.0	(64) 1.0 / 1.6 / 2.7	(65) 1.2 / 1.9 / 2.6	% Depr., Dep., Amort./Sales				(11) 1.2 / 1.4 / 2.0	(19) 1.4 / 2.1 / 2.6	(19) .9 / 2.0 / 2.4
(22) 2.9 / 3.6 / 6.5	(27) 3.1 / 4.1 / 8.4	(24) 3.2 / 4.1	% Officers', Directors', Owners' Comp/Sales						
1832843M	1826510M	2201019M	Net Sales ($)	1033M	15708M	37815M	89636M	378478M	1678349M
951397M	912929M	1128267M	Total Assets ($)	685M	12314M	17088M	38598M	206889M	852693M

© RMA 2003

M = $ thousand   MM = $ million
See Pages 11 through 18 for Explanation of Ratios and Data

396 MANUFACTURING—Toilet Preparation Manufacturing NAICS 325620 (SIC 2844)

Current Data Sorted By Assets							Comparative Historical Data	

						Type of Statement		
1	1	9	7	7	3	Unqualified	30	36
	1	10	1			Reviewed	10	15
	4	5	2			Compiled	16	9
1	4					Tax Returns	2	4
	6	10	10	3	2	Other	21	20
	16 (4/1-9/30/02)		71 (10/1/02-3/31/03)				4/1/98-3/31/99 ALL	4/1/99-3/31/00 ALL
0-500M	500M-2MM	2-10MM	10-50MM	50-100MM	100-250MM			
2	16	34	20	10	5	**NUMBER OF STATEMENTS**	79	84
%	%	%	%	%	%	**ASSETS**	%	%
	8.3	7.6	9.2	5.8		Cash & Equivalents	7.1	6.2
	32.6	25.6	26.8	27.4		Trade Receivables (net)	27.4	26.8
	27.7	35.5	33.4	28.1		Inventory	28.3	32.6
	.4	2.7	2.1	1.8		All Other Current	2.9	2.0
	68.9	71.5	71.5	63.1		Total Current	65.7	67.6
	20.4	22.3	18.0	21.3		Fixed Assets (net)	22.0	19.3
	2.1	3.2	5.5	12.6		Intangibles (net)	6.6	6.7
	8.5	3.0	5.0	3.1		All Other Non-Current	5.7	6.4
	100.0	100.0	100.0	100.0		Total	100.0	100.0
						LIABILITIES		
	13.1	14.7	8.5	12.7		Notes Payable-Short Term	10.8	11.7
	1.5	6.7	3.1	2.2		Cur. Mat.-L/T/D	2.9	3.6
	29.7	20.3	16.4	9.9		Trade Payables	17.0	18.5
	.6	.4	1.4	.3		Income Taxes Payable	.7	.7
	10.4	9.2	9.5	15.4		All Other Current	10.1	10.0
	55.4	51.3	39.1	40.6		Total Current	41.4	44.5
	14.2	13.6	12.7	12.2		Long Term Debt	15.6	12.8
	.3	.1	.5	.5		Deferred Taxes	.5	.5
	5.5	9.1	5.6	8.5		All Other Non-Current	8.9	4.2
	24.7	25.9	42.2	38.2		Net Worth	33.6	38.0
	100.0	100.0	100.0	100.0		Total Liabilities & Net Worth	100.0	100.0
						INCOME DATA		
	100.0	100.0	100.0	100.0		Net Sales	100.0	100.0
	41.9	34.6	42.9	36.3		Gross Profit	45.3	43.0
	37.2	31.8	37.1	31.6		Operating Expenses	39.9	37.7
	4.7	2.9	5.8	4.7		Operating Profit	5.3	5.3
	.6	1.0	.4	3.4		All Other Expenses (net)	2.2	1.4
	4.1	1.8	5.3	1.4		Profit Before Taxes	3.2	3.9
						RATIOS		
	2.0	2.4	3.1	3.1		Current	2.6	2.4
	1.5	1.3	1.9	1.5			1.6	1.5
	1.0	1.0	1.3	1.3			1.2	1.1
	1.1	1.3	1.6	1.7		Quick	1.2	1.1
	.8	.7	.9	1.0		(78)	.8	.7
	.4	.4	.6	.5			.6	.5
21 17.4	32 11.5	33 11.0	47 7.7			Sales/Receivables	37 9.9	38 9.6
47 7.7	42 8.7	45 8.1	58 6.3				48 7.6	46 7.9
65 5.7	51 7.2	65 5.6	72 5.1				63 5.8	60 6.1
21 17.3	55 6.7	66 5.5	43 8.4			Cost of Sales/Inventory	53 6.8	66 5.5
71 5.2	79 4.6	92 4.0	100 3.6				97 3.8	107 3.4
135 2.7	131 2.8	143 2.6	199 1.8				148 2.5	157 2.3
23 16.1	25 14.7	25 14.6	16 23.0			Cost of Sales/Payables	34 10.9	34 10.7
45 8.0	43 8.5	40 9.1	31 11.9				55 6.6	52 7.0
97 3.8	73 5.0	85 4.3	57 6.4				76 4.8	76 4.8
	8.1	5.6	3.9	3.0		Sales/Working Capital	5.0	5.1
	15.2	14.6	6.8	7.0			8.7	8.9
	NM	NM	16.6	41.1			39.7	28.2
	9.0	7.1	15.8			EBIT/Interest	9.9	7.5
	(14) 3.7	(32) 3.2	(18) 7.2			(71)	2.4	(78) 3.1
	1.3	.7	1.2				.4	1.6
		14.4				Net Profit + Depr., Dep., Amort./Cur. Mat. L/T/D	6.4	8.5
		(14) .8				(32)	2.4	(28) 4.2
		-.1					.2	.9
	.0	.2	.2	.3		Fixed/Worth	.4	.2
	.4	1.0	.4	.7			.7	.6
	1.4	4.2	1.2	1.8			2.1	1.8
	1.5	1.4	.6	1.0		Debt/Worth	1.1	.8
	1.9	3.3	1.6	3.1			2.1	2.3
	14.0	34.8	4.8	5.4			6.6	5.5
	96.2	43.1	59.8			% Profit Before Taxes/Tangible Net Worth	53.0	48.1
	(13) 19.4	(27) 15.6	(18) 25.3			(67)	22.9	(73) 22.6
	2.3	1.1	4.4				4.1	7.8
	21.2	12.7	19.2	11.9		% Profit Before Taxes/Total Assets	17.3	12.3
	4.8	4.3	10.5	8.5			5.7	7.4
	.6	-1.6	.6	4.0			-1.1	2.6
	778.9	27.8	84.6	26.8		Sales/Net Fixed Assets	21.8	32.4
	11.4	12.3	12.5	8.5			11.4	12.9
	6.7	5.8	8.3	4.8			6.9	6.9
	3.6	2.8	2.7	2.3		Sales/Total Assets	2.6	2.5
	2.7	2.1	2.1	1.8			2.0	2.0
	1.8	1.5	1.4	1.1			1.4	1.5
	1.5	1.2	.6			% Depr., Dep., Amort./Sales	1.2	1.0
	(12) 3.0	(30) 2.0	(16) 1.8			(71)	1.9	(70) 2.0
	4.8	3.1	2.5				2.8	2.9
		1.7				% Officers', Directors', Owners' Comp/Sales	3.1	1.8
		(14) 3.7				(22)	4.3	(26) 4.2
		7.4					7.9	7.6
1472M	59969M	403431M	1206228M	1086065M	1094377M	Net Sales ($)	2954997M	3345984M
44M	19811M	180119M	550806M	665488M	848730M	Total Assets ($)	1757352M	1893940M

© RMA 2003

M = $ thousand   MM = $ million
See Pages 11 through 18 for Explanation of Ratios and Data

Comparative Historical Data | Current Data Sorted By Sales

			Type of Statement		16 (4/1-9/30/02)		71 (10/1/02-3/31/03)		
				0-1MM	1-3MM	3-5MM	5-10MM	10-25MM	25MM & OVER
22	23	28	Unqualified	1	2		2	9	14
7	7	12	Reviewed		1		5	5	1
20	19	11	Compiled		2	3	3	2	1
4	2	5	Tax Returns		3	2			
27	29	31	Other		2	3	4	8	14
4/1/00-3/31/01 ALL	4/1/01-3/31/02 ALL	4/1/02-3/31/03 ALL							
80	80	87	**NUMBER OF STATEMENTS**	1	10	8	14	24	30
%	%	%	**ASSETS**	%	%	%	%	%	%
6.3	7.7	8.2	Cash & Equivalents		17.5		11.8	5.2	6.9
29.2	26.3	26.5	Trade Receivables (net)		17.4		26.2	27.0	27.5
32.5	31.2	31.3	Inventory		25.4		30.2	34.1	30.7
1.8	1.8	2.3	All Other Current		1.1		2.4	2.5	2.7
69.8	67.0	68.3	Total Current		61.3		70.6	68.8	67.8
21.2	19.9	20.2	Fixed Assets (net)		18.8		22.5	20.5	19.1
4.8	6.8	6.8	Intangibles (net)		8.3		5.1	6.7	8.4
4.2	6.4	4.7	All Other Non-Current		11.5		1.8	4.0	4.8
100.0	100.0	100.0	Total		100.0		100.0	100.0	100.0
			LIABILITIES						
10.9	13.1	15.1	Notes Payable-Short Term		36.8		13.0	12.6	8.5
2.6	4.7	4.1	Cur. Mat.-L/T/D		2.2		3.7	9.1	1.8
19.4	17.5	19.0	Trade Payables		23.2		18.8	20.6	13.9
.3	.6	.7	Income Taxes Payable		.0		.6	.2	1.2
10.3	7.9	10.7	All Other Current		10.9		8.6	8.4	13.1
43.6	43.8	49.6	Total Current		73.3		44.7	51.0	38.5
15.7	11.4	13.6	Long Term Debt		13.9		12.1	12.8	15.1
.3	.3	.3	Deferred Taxes		.4		.1	.2	.6
7.0	8.9	7.7	All Other Non-Current		7.9		13.9	9.1	3.2
33.4	35.6	28.7	Net Worth		4.5		29.3	26.9	42.6
100.0	100.0	100.0	Total Liabilities & Net Worth		100.0		100.0	100.0	100.0
			INCOME DATA						
100.0	100.0	100.0	Net Sales		100.0		100.0	100.0	100.0
40.5	42.8	39.4	Gross Profit		46.2		40.5	34.0	41.9
34.3	38.9	35.1	Operating Expenses		49.1		33.5	29.9	35.5
6.2	3.9	4.3	Operating Profit		-2.9		7.0	4.1	6.4
1.6	1.4	1.0	All Other Expenses (net)		.9		1.3	1.9	.2
4.7	2.5	3.3	Profit Before Taxes		-3.8		5.7	2.2	6.2
			RATIOS						
2.5	2.5	2.7	Current		3.0		2.9	2.5	3.0
1.7	1.7	1.5			1.1		1.4	1.3	1.6
1.2	1.2	1.1			.6		1.1	.9	1.4
1.3	1.2	1.3	Quick		1.4		1.5	1.2	1.6
.8	.8	.8			.7		.7	.7	.9
.5	.5	.5			.3		.4	.4	.6
38 9.6	33 10.9	33 11.1	Sales/Receivables	10 37.1		31 11.9	34 10.6	38 9.6	
48 7.6	46 8.0	46 7.9		53 6.9		41 9.0	41 9.0	51 7.1	
64 5.7	62 5.9	62 5.9		65 5.6		61 6.0	47 7.8	66 5.6	
58 6.3	72 5.1	54 6.7	Cost of Sales/Inventory	11 34.7		65 5.6	53 6.9	64 5.7	
97 3.8	99 3.7	82 4.4		105 3.5		92 4.0	72 5.1	96 3.8	
156 2.3	163 2.2	143 2.5		265 1.4		131 2.8	103 3.6	143 2.5	
32 11.5	25 14.8	24 14.9	Cost of Sales/Payables	19 19.4		23 16.0	22 16.4	19 19.7	
50 7.3	43 8.4	41 8.8		66 5.6		53 6.8	38 9.6	33 10.9	
66 5.5	70 5.2	74 4.9		129 2.8		96 3.8	52 7.0	68 5.4	
4.8	4.5	4.6	Sales/Working Capital		2.0		4.2	6.8	4.2
7.8	7.2	10.7			17.2		11.4	15.9	6.8
23.2	32.5	25.2			-14.8		46.1	-56.2	12.3
(75) 6.4	(69) 9.5	(80) 9.2	EBIT/Interest				(13) 10.8	(22) 7.9	(29) 23.0
2.8	2.6	3.5					2.8	4.0	7.7
1.3	1.1	1.2					1.1	1.0	2.4
(29) 6.7	(23) 8.2	(33) 10.1	Net Profit + Depr., Dep., Amort./Cur. Mat. L/T/D						(13) 39.6
3.1	2.5	3.2							5.0
1.0	.3	.6							2.7
.3	.3	.2	Fixed/Worth		.1		.1	.3	.3
.6	.5	.7			1.0		.7	1.3	.5
1.5	1.6	3.4			-92.8		5.5	NM	1.1
1.0	.8	1.1	Debt/Worth		1.6		.7	1.4	.7
2.3	2.1	2.5			9.2		7.3	2.4	1.8
5.1	6.5	15.2			-10.1		13.9	NM	5.2
(72) 54.3	(68) 46.3	(70) 45.9	% Profit Before Taxes/Tangible Net Worth				(12) 62.8	(18) 59.5	(27) 51.1
24.6	17.0	23.6					20.2	28.0	32.0
7.8	2.2	3.8					7.3	1.9	16.3
17.1	15.7	14.9	% Profit Before Taxes/Total Assets		2.9		15.6	20.2	18.9
7.0	4.8	7.2			.1		4.9	7.1	10.9
1.8	.4	.6			-11.9		.7	-.4	4.7
24.1	24.6	38.7	Sales/Net Fixed Assets		UND		111.2	35.5	31.8
12.6	12.1	11.2			8.3		12.6	16.4	11.1
5.8	6.2	6.4			4.9		3.8	7.1	6.6
2.6	2.6	2.8	Sales/Total Assets		2.3		2.6	3.1	2.7
2.1	2.0	2.1			1.6		1.6	2.5	1.9
1.7	1.3	1.5			.8		1.4	1.7	1.4
(70) .9	(69) .9	(71) 1.2	% Depr., Dep., Amort./Sales				(11) 1.9	(23) 1.1	(25) .7
1.7	1.7	2.1					2.5	2.0	1.8
2.8	2.8	2.9					3.3	2.6	2.5
(28) 1.7	(30) 3.0	(26) 1.9	% Officers', Directors', Owners' Comp/Sales					(10) 1.7	
3.9	5.4	4.3						3.0	
7.0	11.8	9.5						7.4	
2966858M	2888523M	3851542M	Net Sales ($)	21M	18932M	30506M	100728M	381965M	3319390M
1701416M	1909431M	2264998M	Total Assets ($)	10M	13903M	11159M	66161M	240499M	1933266M

M = $ thousand   MM = $ million
See Pages 11 through 18 for Explanation of Ratios and Data

Current Data Sorted By Assets   **Comparative Historical Data**

0-500M	500M-2MM	2-10MM	10-50MM	50-100MM	100-250MM	Type of Statement	4/1/98-3/31/99 ALL	4/1/99-3/31/00 ALL
	3	12	16	3	2	Unqualified	27	34
	3	15	2			Reviewed	20	25
1	5	5				Compiled	15	15
1		1				Tax Returns	8	3
1	4	13	10	1	4	Other	28	26
	16 (4/1-9/30/02)		86 (10/1/02-3/31/03)					
3	15	46	28	4	6	**NUMBER OF STATEMENTS**	98	103
%	%	%	%	%	%	**ASSETS**	%	%
	10.7	13.9	5.9			Cash & Equivalents	7.4	8.9
	25.6	28.3	23.6			Trade Receivables (net)	29.6	28.2
	22.8	21.9	27.1			Inventory	22.2	20.8
	7.3	1.6	2.5			All Other Current	2.4	1.7
	66.4	65.7	59.1			Total Current	61.5	59.7
	24.5	26.3	30.5			Fixed Assets (net)	24.9	29.0
	2.9	3.5	7.1			Intangibles (net)	5.8	5.5
	6.2	4.4	3.2			All Other Non-Current	7.7	5.8
	100.0	100.0	100.0			Total	100.0	100.0
						LIABILITIES		
	4.6	11.5	10.5			Notes Payable-Short Term	10.0	11.4
	4.5	3.1	5.0			Cur. Mat.-L/T/D	2.4	3.8
	28.5	18.4	15.2			Trade Payables	15.4	15.8
	.0	.3	.1			Income Taxes Payable	.7	1.0
	12.2	10.3	8.2			All Other Current	8.2	7.1
	49.8	43.5	38.9			Total Current	36.7	39.1
	10.7	11.3	17.0			Long Term Debt	13.4	13.5
	.9	.2	.8			Deferred Taxes	.5	.8
	6.9	3.8	9.3			All Other Non-Current	3.3	3.9
	31.7	41.2	34.0			Net Worth	46.1	42.8
	100.0	100.0	100.0			Total Liabilities & Net Worth	100.0	100.0
						INCOME DATA		
	100.0	100.0	100.0			Net Sales	100.0	100.0
	35.5	36.3	30.1			Gross Profit	35.4	36.4
	33.6	30.0	23.8			Operating Expenses	43.4	29.2
	1.9	6.3	6.3			Operating Profit	−8.1	7.2
	1.0	.3	1.8			All Other Expenses (net)	−81.7	.8
	.9	6.1	4.5			Profit Before Taxes	73.6	6.4
						RATIOS		
	2.8	2.9	2.4			Current	2.8	2.5
	1.7	1.4	1.7				1.7	1.5
	1.3	1.0	.9				1.2	1.0
	1.3	2.1	1.1			Quick	1.8	1.7
	.8	.9	.7				1.0	.9
	.6	.5	.5				.7	.6
25 14.6	29 12.4	39 9.4				Sales/Receivables	38 9.5	38 9.7
39 9.4	44 8.2	47 7.8					46 8.0	47 7.8
51 7.2	59 6.2	56 6.5					58 6.3	63 5.8
32 11.4	24 15.5	48 7.6				Cost of Sales/Inventory	34 10.7	36 10.2
59 6.2	48 7.6	70 5.2					53 6.9	53 6.9
108 3.4	81 4.5	112 3.3					74 4.9	83 4.4
17 21.3	21 17.0	23 15.6				Cost of Sales/Payables	24 14.9	27 13.4
36 10.0	37 9.9	41 8.9					38 9.6	43 8.5
79 4.6	52 7.1	58 6.3					59 6.1	61
3.9	4.7	3.8				Sales/Working Capital	4.8	5.7
9.2	14.1	6.3					8.2	9.6
25.9	NM	NM					23.9	316.6
6.6	23.8	7.9				EBIT/Interest	19.2	12.7
(14) 2.1	(42) 4.5	(26) 3.3					(86) 3.7	(94) 3.7
−1.6	1.8	1.3					1.0	1.8
	26.8	2.7				Net Profit + Depr., Dep., Amort./Cur. Mat. L/T/D	18.9	7.1
	(17) 6.3	(11) 1.1					(31) 2.8	(31) 1.9
	.7	.6					1.6	1.1
	.2	.3	.6			Fixed/Worth	.3	.4
	.4	.7	1.1				.6	.8
	.9	1.9	5.7				1.3	1.9
	.4	.6	.8			Debt/Worth	.5	.7
	.9	1.7	3.2				1.2	1.6
	4.0	3.3	16.0				3.5	4.6
	17.5	53.6	66.3			% Profit Before Taxes/Tangible Net Worth	53.5	41.1
(13) 8.5	(42) 16.0	(24) 32.7					(90) 21.8	(93) 22.9
	.8	6.6	.8				5.7	9.6
	7.2	18.1	16.0			% Profit Before Taxes/Total Assets	19.8	17.9
	1.2	10.2	6.3				8.0	6.9
	−1.0	1.8	1.8				.9	2.8
	20.3	25.6	13.6			Sales/Net Fixed Assets	21.5	15.8
	11.5	11.0	5.5				9.5	7.3
	5.6	5.3	3.2				4.6	4.1
	3.5	3.2	2.1			Sales/Total Assets	2.8	2.8
	2.0	2.5	1.7				2.0	1.8
	1.6	1.7	1.2				1.5	1.4
	1.6	.8	1.3			% Depr., Dep., Amort./Sales	1.3	1.4
(12) 2.6	(44) 1.6	(26) 2.7					(88) 2.0	(91) 2.3
	4.9	3.3	5.3				3.5	3.5
		1.6				% Officers', Directors', Owners' Comp/Sales	1.5	1.4
	(17) 3.6						(25) 3.2	(25) 5.4
		7.2					6.7	9.3
2909M	53350M	995723M	1086727M	376126M	1502409M	Net Sales ($)	2624623M	2619274M
976M	19760M	226050M	641250M	245567M	1199115M	Total Assets ($)	1464003M	1943332M

M = $ thousand   MM = $ million
See Pages 11 through 18 for Explanation of Ratios and Data

Comparative Historical Data | Current Data Sorted By Sales

			Type of Statement	0-1MM	1-3MM	3-5MM	5-10MM	10-25MM	25MM & OVER
20	20	36	Unqualified	1	1	2	7	8	17
19	15	20	Reviewed		1	3	8	6	2
30	25	11	Compiled	1	3		5	2	
9	2	2	Tax Returns	1				1	
42	28	33	Other	1	2	1	6	12	11
4/1/00-3/31/01 ALL	4/1/01-3/31/02 ALL	4/1/02-3/31/03 ALL		16 (4/1-9/30/02)			86 (10/1/02-3/31/03)		
120	90	102	**NUMBER OF STATEMENTS**	4	7	6	26	29	30
%	%	%	**ASSETS**	%	%	%	%	%	%
6.0	8.9	10.3	Cash & Equivalents				15.3	9.6	6.1
27.1	26.7	25.9	Trade Receivables (net)				28.1	24.2	25.5
22.2	23.5	23.1	Inventory				23.8	19.6	25.8
4.0	2.7	2.9	All Other Current				3.1	1.8	3.1
59.2	61.8	62.2	Total Current				70.2	55.1	60.5
27.2	26.9	28.0	Fixed Assets (net)				22.3	34.9	27.4
6.3	5.5	5.3	Intangibles (net)				1.2	6.8	8.5
7.3	5.8	4.5	All Other Non-Current				6.4	3.1	3.5
100.0	100.0	100.0	Total				100.0	100.0	100.0
			LIABILITIES						
11.0	9.5	9.4	Notes Payable-Short Term				10.1	10.2	9.3
4.2	3.7	4.1	Cur. Mat.-L/T/D				2.5	3.9	5.9
16.5	15.9	18.5	Trade Payables				23.6	18.3	16.3
.2	.2	.2	Income Taxes Payable				.1	.3	.3
10.0	9.3	9.8	All Other Current				10.2	8.8	10.2
41.9	38.6	42.0	Total Current				46.5	41.4	42.0
16.2	12.9	15.5	Long Term Debt				8.3	14.9	20.6
.5	.4	.5	Deferred Taxes				.6	.5	.7
3.4	2.9	6.0	All Other Non-Current				5.9	6.1	5.4
37.9	45.2	36.0	Net Worth				38.7	37.1	31.2
100.0	100.0	100.0	Total Liabilities & Net Worth				100.0	100.0	100.0
			INCOME DATA						
100.0	100.0	100.0	Net Sales				100.0	100.0	100.0
34.8	37.0	34.2	Gross Profit				37.6	34.5	28.3
29.7	31.6	28.3	Operating Expenses				30.6	28.3	21.3
5.1	5.4	5.8	Operating Profit				7.1	6.1	7.0
1.2	1.1	1.1	All Other Expenses (net)				.6	.9	1.4
3.9	4.4	4.8	Profit Before Taxes				6.5	5.2	5.6
			RATIOS						
2.4 1.5 1.0	2.8 1.6 1.1	2.7 1.5 1.1	Current				4.0 1.7 1.2	2.0 1.3 1.0	2.2 1.5 .9
1.5 .8 .5	1.6 .9 .6	1.3 .8 .5	Quick				2.8 .9 .5	1.1 .9 .5	1.1 .6 .5
36 10.2 47 7.8 56 6.5	35 10.4 43 8.5 54 6.7	35 10.5 46 8.0 58 6.3	Sales/Receivables				22 16.4 42 8.7 60 6.1	37 10.0 44 8.2 53 6.8	38 9.5 48 7.6 59 6.2
35 10.3 58 6.3 85 4.3	39 9.3 59 6.2 95 3.8	32 11.3 56 6.5 90 4.1	Cost of Sales/Inventory				24 15.0 52 7.0 88 4.2	28 12.9 48 7.6 92 4.0	49 7.4 64 5.7 83 4.4
26 13.8 41 9.0 60 6.0	24 15.2 36 10.2 61 6.0	22 16.4 39 9.3 59 6.2	Cost of Sales/Payables				18 20.7 37 9.9 55 6.6	24 15.1 32 11.3 72 5.1	23 15.7 40 9.1 59 6.2
5.5 11.9 NM	4.8 9.0 43.5	4.3 9.5 126.6	Sales/Working Capital				3.5 7.8 39.9	5.2 18.8 -199.8	4.4 12.7 -35.9
(107) 10.5 2.6 1.1	(78) 14.1 2.8 1.3	(94) 10.5 3.5 1.4	EBIT/Interest	(24)			30.4 4.2 .9	(27) 10.3 4.2 1.2	(28) 10.3 5.1 2.3
(44) 6.2 1.9 .5	(30) 10.2 2.8 .8	(36) 9.6 2.7 .8	Net Profit + Depr., Dep., Amort./Cur. Mat. L/T/D					(14) 6.0 1.8 .3	(11) 3.8 2.2 .9
.3 .7 2.8	.3 .6 1.5	.4 .8 2.2	Fixed/Worth				.2 .4 .9	.7 1.0 2.5	.5 1.3 4.8
.7 1.9 7.4	.6 1.5 4.5	.7 1.9 6.9	Debt/Worth				.4 1.0 2.5	.9 2.4 5.0	1.3 4.3 15.2
(108) 43.9 17.7 2.1	(82) 39.3 18.3 4.5	(89) 49.7 16.9 4.9	% Profit Before Taxes/Tangible Net Worth	(24)			68.0 14.6 5.6	(24) 47.9 23.8 .3	(26) 81.6 38.3 14.2
13.8 5.1 .4	15.1 4.9 1.1	16.2 7.1 1.2	% Profit Before Taxes/Total Assets				21.5 7.6 .0	18.2 10.1 .5	17.9 8.7 3.8
23.1 9.3 4.3	16.4 8.3 4.9	20.4 7.7 4.8	Sales/Net Fixed Assets				25.6 13.1 7.4	12.1 5.4 3.3	21.0 6.2 5.1
2.9 2.0 1.4	2.8 2.1 1.3	2.6 1.9 1.5	Sales/Total Assets				3.4 2.5 1.7	2.8 1.9 1.5	2.4 1.9 1.4
(104) .6 1.6 3.6	(78) .6 1.4 3.2	(93) 1.0 2.3 3.7	% Depr., Dep., Amort./Sales				(23) .9 1.6 4.6	1.0 2.4 5.0	(27) .9 2.3 3.4
(38) 2.4 5.9 9.5	(32) 3.0 5.1 8.7	(29) 2.0 3.7 7.2	% Officers', Directors', Owners' Comp/Sales				(10) 2.1 3.6 6.4		
3912471M 2898928M	3688980M 2421379M	4017244M 2332718M	Net Sales ($) Total Assets ($)	3181M 2066M	14105M 7417M	24195M 14616M	201675M 95902M	481820M 287048M	3292268M 1925669M

M = $ thousand   MM = $ million
See Pages 11 through 18 for Explanation of Ratios and Data

Current Data Sorted By Assets

Comparative Historical Data

						Type of Statement		
		3	10	2	1	Unqualified	13	17
	3	12	4			Reviewed	12	17
	2	3				Compiled	5	7
1						Tax Returns		2
	6	11	5	3	5	Other	24	19
	13 (4/1-9/30/02)		58 (10/1/02-3/31/03)				4/1/98-3/31/99	4/1/99-3/31/00
0-500M	500M-2MM	2-10MM	10-50MM	50-100MM	100-250MM		ALL	ALL
1	11	29	19	5	6	NUMBER OF STATEMENTS	54	62
%	%	%	%	%	%	ASSETS	%	%
	6.4	3.9	3.6			Cash & Equivalents	6.7	5.5
	37.5	25.8	21.2			Trade Receivables (net)	23.8	29.9
	30.7	26.7	26.0			Inventory	22.1	21.6
	1.2	.5	1.8			All Other Current	2.5	1.2
	75.7	56.9	52.6			Total Current	55.0	58.2
	19.0	34.7	36.3			Fixed Assets (net)	37.2	33.5
	2.2	1.3	2.9			Intangibles (net)	1.8	2.9
	3.1	7.1	8.1			All Other Non-Current	6.1	5.4
	100.0	100.0	100.0			Total	100.0	100.0
						LIABILITIES		
	10.6	13.5	10.1			Notes Payable-Short Term	8.0	9.6
	2.1	3.8	3.7			Cur. Mat.-L/T/D	3.0	3.3
	30.8	17.1	13.4			Trade Payables	15.4	22.4
	.6	.5	.5			Income Taxes Payable	.2	.3
	11.1	10.7	6.2			All Other Current	9.6	7.1
	55.2	45.7	33.8			Total Current	36.2	42.6
	5.9	11.1	21.7			Long Term Debt	21.1	16.8
	.2	.4	1.3			Deferred Taxes	.6	.8
	4.5	4.8	3.4			All Other Non-Current	7.1	5.8
	34.3	38.0	39.8			Net Worth	34.9	34.0
	100.0	100.0	100.0			Total Liabilities & Net Worth	100.0	100.0
						INCOME DATA		
	100.0	100.0	100.0			Net Sales	100.0	100.0
	36.1	26.2	24.4			Gross Profit	23.4	24.4
	28.6	24.3	17.1			Operating Expenses	39.9	20.3
	7.5	1.8	7.2			Operating Profit	−16.6	4.1
	.1	.4	1.0			All Other Expenses (net)	2.0	1.1
	7.4	1.4	6.3			Profit Before Taxes	−18.6	3.0
						RATIOS		
	4.1	2.4	2.0				2.6	2.1
	1.5	1.2	1.6			Current	1.7	1.4
	.6	.9	1.0				1.2	1.1
	1.8	1.3	1.3				1.3	1.2
	1.1	.7	.6			Quick	.9	.9
	.5	.5	.5				.5	.6
33	10.9	32 11.2	34 10.8				33 11.0	37 9.8
44	8.3	45 8.2	40 9.2			Sales/Receivables	43 8.6	50 7.3
52	7.1	56 6.6	49 7.5				50 7.3	57 6.4
22	16.4	40 9.2	38 9.6				31 11.9	29 12.4
49	7.4	58 6.3	57 6.4			Cost of Sales/Inventory	40 9.2	42 8.6
84	4.3	104 3.5	96 3.8				65 5.6	64 5.7
23	15.7	21 17.1	18 20.0				20 17.9	28 13.0
40	9.0	42 8.6	30 12.2			Cost of Sales/Payables	32 11.3	42 8.6
67	5.4	63 5.8	53 6.9				51 7.1	63 5.8
	4.6	7.4	6.2				5.8	7.5
	15.3	14.4	9.9			Sales/Working Capital	9.5	14.6
	−15.8	−65.4	109.4				29.5	56.1
	23.8	11.1	8.7				7.4	8.5
(10)	14.2	(26) 2.5	5.1			EBIT/Interest	(48) 3.3	(60) 4.4
	7.0	−.3	2.2				1.9	1.7
						Net Profit + Depr., Dep.,	4.3	9.4
						Amort./Cur. Mat. L /T/D	(18) 2.2	(18) 4.8
							1.1	2.0
	.1	.3	.3				.5	.5
	.4	.8	1.1			Fixed/Worth	1.2	1.0
	−21.7	2.0	1.9				2.4	2.4
	.3	.6	1.0				.7	.9
	2.2	1.8	1.9			Debt/Worth	1.7	1.9
	−41.1	3.1	2.5				4.6	5.6
		46.8	44.5			% Profit Before Taxes/Tangible	34.6	48.7
	(27)	15.3	24.6			Net Worth	(45) 21.9	(56) 18.3
		1.5	8.4				7.4	3.2
	25.6	15.2	13.2				12.6	13.5
	15.7	4.5	6.8			% Profit Before Taxes/Total Assets	6.7	7.2
	6.9	.1	3.0				2.1	1.3
	85.2	17.8	13.8				12.6	19.3
	26.6	5.8	4.7			Sales/Net Fixed Assets	5.3	7.1
	9.2	2.7	2.8				2.8	3.6
	4.7	2.8	2.1				2.6	3.1
	2.9	1.9	1.9			Sales/Total Assets	2.0	2.1
	2.2	1.5	1.2				1.5	1.6
	.9	.9	1.8				1.5	1.4
(10)	1.2	2.3	3.7			% Depr., Dep., Amort./Sales	(48) 2.7	(59) 2.7
	1.8	5.8	4.7				4.7	5.0
						% Officers', Directors',	2.4	2.3
						Owners' Comp/Sales	(13) 5.2	(19) 4.3
							8.4	7.2
516M	41610M	289811M	595153M	507952M	1221115M	Net Sales ($)	1296554M	1879379M
307M	13263M	137514M	317687M	362049M	852275M	Total Assets ($)	705446M	1125114M

M = $ thousand   MM = $ million
See Pages 11 through 18 for Explanation of Ratios and Data

Comparative Historical Data   ## Current Data Sorted By Sales

			Type of Statement	0-1MM	1-3MM	3-5MM	5-10MM	10-25MM	25MM & OVER
12	10	16	Unqualified			1	2	6	7
12	13	19	Reviewed			5	4	7	3
10	13	5	Compiled			3	1	1	
3	1	1	Tax Returns	1					
19	20	30	Other		5	4	5	5	11
4/1/00-3/31/01	4/1/01-3/31/02	4/1/02-3/31/03			13 (4/1-9/30/02)		58 (10/1/02-3/31/03)		
ALL	ALL	ALL							
56	57	71	**NUMBER OF STATEMENTS**	1	5	13	12	19	21
%	%	%	**ASSETS**	%	%	%	%	%	%
3.9	5.5	4.4	Cash & Equivalents			5.8	3.1	4.8	3.9
26.3	24.8	25.1	Trade Receivables (net)			30.6	24.0	24.5	23.6
24.2	21.6	25.4	Inventory			25.9	20.4	27.6	22.9
1.5	2.2	1.6	All Other Current			1.1	.4	1.3	3.3
55.9	54.0	56.5	Total Current			63.4	47.9	58.3	53.7
35.8	39.0	32.7	Fixed Assets (net)			26.1	42.9	31.5	35.0
2.1	1.6	3.5	Intangibles (net)			2.7	.9	1.6	8.1
6.2	5.4	7.2	All Other Non-Current			7.8	8.3	8.6	3.3
100.0	100.0	100.0	Total			100.0	100.0	100.0	100.0
			LIABILITIES						
9.5	10.4	10.3	Notes Payable-Short Term			4.6	19.0	12.4	7.2
6.1	4.9	4.0	Cur. Mat.-L/T/D			.7	4.5	4.9	3.4
19.3	16.3	17.7	Trade Payables			21.7	16.8	16.3	14.3
.0	.7	.5	Income Taxes Payable			1.4	.5	.1	.5
7.3	9.4	9.0	All Other Current			24.2	3.6	6.0	7.5
42.3	41.7	41.5	Total Current			52.5	44.4	39.7	32.9
16.9	16.6	15.3	Long Term Debt			6.0	16.9	16.1	18.2
.3	.8	.7	Deferred Taxes			.6	.5	.3	1.4
4.6	5.4	8.9	All Other Non-Current			3.6	8.4	1.6	20.6
35.8	35.4	33.5	Net Worth			37.4	29.8	42.2	26.9
100.0	100.0	100.0	Total Liabilities & Net Worth			100.0	100.0	100.0	100.0
			INCOME DATA						
100.0	100.0	100.0	Net Sales			100.0	100.0	100.0	100.0
26.9	26.1	27.1	Gross Profit			35.1	26.7	24.0	23.3
21.3	21.7	22.7	Operating Expenses			33.1	21.7	19.3	18.4
5.5	4.4	4.3	Operating Profit			2.0	5.0	4.7	4.9
1.2	1.3	.8	All Other Expenses (net)			.4	.1	.9	1.8
4.3	3.1	3.5	Profit Before Taxes			1.6	4.9	3.8	3.1
			RATIOS						
1.8	2.2	2.5				3.7	1.4	2.5	2.3
1.3	1.3	1.4	Current			2.3	1.1	1.4	1.6
1.1	.9	1.0				.7	.7	1.1	1.2
1.0	1.3	1.4				2.2	.8	1.4	1.4
.7	.7	.7	Quick			1.0	.6	.7	.6
.5	.6	.5				.3	.4	.5	.5
33 11.0	37 9.8	34 10.8		34 10.6	26 14.2	33 11.2	39 9.5		
44 8.2	42 8.6	43 8.5	Sales/Receivables	46 7.9	43 8.4	40 9.2	45 8.2		
55 6.7	52 7.0	50 7.2		74 4.9	56 6.5	47 7.8	53 6.9		
34 10.9	34 10.7	40 9.2		33 11.0	23 16.0	38 9.6	48 7.5		
51 7.2	48 7.6	58 6.3	Cost of Sales/Inventory	64 5.7	46 8.0	51 7.2	57 6.4		
79 4.6	71 5.2	81 4.5		131 2.8	67 5.5	76 4.8	71 5.1		
24 15.5	21 17.1	22 16.7		19 18.9	26 14.3	22 16.9	19 19.3		
38 9.6	32 11.4	36 10.1	Cost of Sales/Payables	50 7.3	42 8.6	30 12.2	35 10.4		
56 6.5	51 7.1	62 5.9		81 4.5	54 6.7	49 7.5	62 5.9		
8.3	6.4	6.2				4.2	13.9	6.9	5.8
17.1	18.2	14.4	Sales/Working Capital			7.5	45.7	11.7	9.9
109.4	-98.2	140.9				-13.4	-12.6	87.9	25.5
7.7	5.3	10.8					16.8	14.9	7.1
(52) 2.8	(53) 2.4	(67) 3.3	EBIT/Interest				1.8	3.2	3.3
1.2	.5	1.1					-2.9	1.6	.8
5.5	3.1	8.3							31.1
(16) 2.9	(24) 2.3	(27) 3.9	Net Profit + Depr., Dep., Amort./Cur. Mat. L/T/D					(11)	8.3
.6	1.2	1.6							1.4
.5	.6	.3				.1	.8	.4	.3
1.1	1.1	1.0	Fixed/Worth			.5	2.0	.8	1.2
1.8	2.6	3.1				-.9	7.8	1.3	4.3
.9	.9	.8				.3	1.4	.9	.9
2.0	1.8	2.0	Debt/Worth			.6	2.3	1.9	2.1
4.4	4.2	4.4				-4.5	12.3	2.5	8.5
36.6	25.0	46.2				64.2	46.8		45.1
(52) 13.2	(50) 13.6	(61) 16.7	% Profit Before Taxes/Tangible Net Worth			16.8	15.3	(17)	20.6
2.3	1.0	4.1				-23.6	4.5		3.8
11.0	10.6	14.9				15.3	18.3	15.6	10.9
6.1	5.3	6.0	% Profit Before Taxes/Total Assets			8.6	4.3	3.4	6.0
1.0	-1.0	.3				-.6	-7.6	1.2	-.6
17.0	9.7	20.4				32.3	6.0	15.2	14.3
5.2	4.7	6.1	Sales/Net Fixed Assets			20.4	4.8	7.3	5.9
3.0	2.8	3.1				3.1	2.4	3.3	3.0
3.1	2.7	2.6				2.8	2.7	2.9	2.2
2.0	1.8	1.9	Sales/Total Assets			1.9	1.7	2.2	1.9
1.5	1.3	1.5				1.4	1.1	1.6	1.4
1.1	1.1	1.1				.9	.9	1.4	1.8
(53) 2.6	(53) 3.2	(68) 2.5	% Depr., Dep., Amort./Sales	(12)	1.9	4.0	1.9	(19)	3.0
4.7	5.3	5.0				5.6	5.8	4.2	4.1
2.0	1.8	2.5							
(21) 4.7	(17) 3.1	(19) 4.4	% Officers', Directors', Owners' Comp/Sales						
5.4	7.9	6.2							
1573718M	2153750M	2656157M	Net Sales ($)	516M	12784M	51350M	91993M	356245M	2143269M
869958M	1475534M	1683095M	Total Assets ($)	307M	6577M	28687M	58862M	186864M	1401798M

M = $ thousand   MM = $ million
See Pages 11 through 18 for Explanation of Ratios and Data

Current Data Sorted By Assets   Comparative Historical Data

						Type of Statement		
	3	4 5 5	3 2	1		Unqualified		5
2	4	5				Reviewed		4
2	3	1				Compiled		
		3	1	2		Tax Returns		
	11 (4/1-9/30/02)		30 (10/1/02-3/31/03)			Other	4/1/98-3/31/99	13 4/1/99-3/31/00
0-500M	500M-2MM	2-10MM	10-50MM	50-100MM	100-250MM		ALL	ALL
4	10	18	6	3		NUMBER OF STATEMENTS		22
%	%	%	%	%	%	ASSETS	%	%
	9.3	6.9			D	Cash & Equivalents	D	10.0
	22.1	25.4			A	Trade Receivables (net)	A	23.1
	14.8	19.5			T	Inventory	T	18.9
	4.3	2.4			A	All Other Current	A	1.8
	50.5	54.2				Total Current		53.8
	34.6	37.6			N	Fixed Assets (net)	N	37.1
	4.8	3.4			O	Intangibles (net)	O	1.4
	10.2	4.7			T	All Other Non-Current	T	7.6
	100.0	100.0				Total		100.0
					A	LIABILITIES	A	
	10.6	9.1			V	Notes Payable-Short Term	V	10.4
	8.2	3.9			A	Cur. Mat.-L/T/D	A	6.5
	21.6	10.7			I	Trade Payables	I	16.6
	.0	.9			L	Income Taxes Payable	L	.1
	4.3	4.9			A	All Other Current	A	9.8
	44.7	29.6			B	Total Current	B	43.4
	34.2	13.8			L	Long Term Debt	L	21.2
	.0	.8			E	Deferred Taxes	E	.6
	1.0	2.9				All Other Non-Current		5.7
	20.0	52.9				Net Worth		29.1
	100.0	100.0				Total Liabilities & Net Worth		100.0
						INCOME DATA		
	100.0	100.0				Net Sales		100.0
	35.1	30.2				Gross Profit		25.8
	34.4	25.0				Operating Expenses		22.6
	.7	5.2				Operating Profit		3.1
	2.2	1.1				All Other Expenses (net)		1.5
	−1.4	4.1				Profit Before Taxes		1.6
						RATIOS		
	3.1	3.7						2.4
	1.2	1.7				Current		1.8
	.8	1.0						.9
	2.5	2.7						1.7
	.6	1.1				Quick		.9
	.4	.6						.5
28	12.9	31 12.0					32	11.4
35	10.5	46 8.0				Sales/Receivables	44	8.3
63	5.8	58 6.3					60	6.1
0	UND	27 13.3					29	12.7
26	13.8	39 9.3				Cost of Sales/Inventory	42	8.6
67	5.5	68 5.4					68	5.4
24	15.3	14 27.0					16	22.8
54	6.8	31 11.9				Cost of Sales/Payables	40	9.0
106	3.4	40 9.1					68	5.4
	10.4	4.8						5.5
	31.5	9.2				Sales/Working Capital		9.2
	−19.3	NM						−85.0
		10.7						10.1
	(17)	4.8				EBIT/Interest	(20)	2.8
		1.5						−1.4
						Net Profit + Depr., Dep., Amort./Cur. Mat. L./T/D		
	.3	.5						.4
	2.1	.8				Fixed/Worth		1.3
	−1.6	1.4						14.8
	.9	.4						.7
	7.3	.9				Debt/Worth		1.7
	−6.0	2.7						22.2
		27.9				% Profit Before Taxes/Tangible Net Worth		46.9
	(17)	10.9					(18)	35.7
		2.2						14.9
	4.3	12.3						19.3
	.3	6.3				% Profit Before Taxes/Total Assets		9.9
	−6.4	1.0						−3.8
	19.1	7.8						14.7
	8.1	6.5				Sales/Net Fixed Assets		7.5
	3.1	4.1						2.5
	3.2	2.7						2.4
	2.2	2.3				Sales/Total Assets		1.8
	1.2	1.7						1.4
		2.5						2.0
		3.8				% Depr., Dep., Amort./Sales	(21)	3.6
		6.3						5.8
						% Officers', Directors', Owners' Comp/Sales		
3390M	25995M	202374M	159720M	269937M		Net Sales ($)		420152M
570M	12605M	99165M	105444M	177873M		Total Assets ($)		273971M

M = $ thousand   MM = $ million
See Pages 11 through 18 for Explanation of Ratios and Data

Comparative Historical Data | Current Data Sorted By Sales

Type of Statement	4/1/00-3/31/01 ALL	4/1/01-3/31/02 ALL	4/1/02-3/31/03 ALL		0-1MM	1-3MM	3-5MM	5-10MM	10-25MM	25MM & OVER
Unqualified	5	1	8						6	2
Reviewed	2	4	10			1	2	3	2	2
Compiled	1	6	9			5		1	3	
Tax Returns	1	1	6		1	1	2	1	1	
Other	7	8	8		2	1	2			3
					11 (4/1-9/30/02)			30 (10/1/02-3/31/03)		
NUMBER OF STATEMENTS	16	20	41		3	8	6	5	12	7
	%	%	%	**ASSETS**	%	%	%	%	%	%
	8.7	8.1	8.2	Cash & Equivalents					5.5	
	23.4	25.2	24.1	Trade Receivables (net)					24.8	
	15.6	18.0	18.1	Inventory					20.1	
	1.0	2.3	3.5	All Other Current					3.4	
	48.7	53.7	53.9	Total Current					53.8	
	47.4	33.7	36.0	Fixed Assets (net)					34.5	
	.1	6.6	3.0	Intangibles (net)					1.5	
	3.7	6.0	7.1	All Other Non-Current					10.2	
	100.0	100.0	100.0	Total					100.0	
				LIABILITIES						
	5.7	9.9	7.7	Notes Payable-Short Term					6.9	
	4.5	6.7	5.4	Cur. Mat.-L/T/D					2.8	
	10.9	14.3	13.5	Trade Payables					9.1	
	.1	.3	.4	Income Taxes Payable					.9	
	10.3	6.4	6.0	All Other Current					6.1	
	31.5	37.7	33.1	Total Current					25.8	
	24.1	27.5	23.7	Long Term Debt					7.6	
	.1	.1	.7	Deferred Taxes					.8	
	2.2	6.2	2.8	All Other Non-Current					4.6	
	42.1	28.5	39.7	Net Worth					61.2	
	100.0	100.0	100.0	Total Liabilities & Net Worth					100.0	
				INCOME DATA						
	100.0	100.0	100.0	Net Sales					100.0	
	28.7	26.2	33.3	Gross Profit					24.7	
	19.4	22.5	29.6	Operating Expenses					23.3	
	9.2	3.7	3.7	Operating Profit					1.4	
	1.7	2.0	1.0	All Other Expenses (net)					.0	
	7.5	1.7	2.7	Profit Before Taxes					1.4	
				RATIOS						
	3.4	3.2	3.7	Current					3.7	
	1.8	1.7	1.8						2.5	
	1.6	1.1	1.1						1.5	
	2.3	2.2	2.2	Quick					2.2	
	1.1	.8	.9						1.5	
	.7	.5	.6						.8	
	29 12.6	30 12.0	31 11.7	Sales/Receivables					32 11.6	
	37 9.9	36 10.2	37 9.9						41 9.0	
	44 8.3	52 7.1	58 6.3						57 6.3	
	25 14.4	24 15.1	21 17.4	Cost of Sales/Inventory					23 15.7	
	38 9.7	38 9.5	42 8.7						38 9.6	
	64 5.7	64 5.7	70 5.2						68 5.3	
	12 29.2	16 22.8	13 27.8	Cost of Sales/Payables					9 41.4	
	23 15.8	27 13.4	30 12.1						17 21.5	
	41 8.9	37 9.7	49 7.5						36 10.0	
	5.5	5.5	5.2	Sales/Working Capital					4.8	
	9.5	12.1	9.2						7.9	
	12.8	60.0	100.3						10.0	
	19.2	11.4	9.8	EBIT/Interest					32.0	
	(14) 5.7	(18) 2.9	(37) 2.9						(11) 8.4	
	2.6	-.3	.0						1.9	
				Net Profit + Depr., Dep., Amort./Cur. Mat. L/T/D						
	.6	.4	.4	Fixed/Worth					.3	
	.9	1.2	.9						.7	
	1.8	-4.1	2.1						1.0	
	.4	.6	.4	Debt/Worth					.3	
	1.1	1.8	1.1						.6	
	2.1	-13.7	4.4						1.0	
	48.0	27.5	24.9	% Profit Before Taxes/Tangible Net Worth					22.5	
	(15) 30.5	(13) 15.1	(33) 10.9						8.3	
	14.4	2.0	.3						-4.4	
	21.5	20.5	12.0	% Profit Before Taxes/Total Assets					11.8	
	11.1	4.6	3.9						4.7	
	5.8	-5.6	-2.7						-4.0	
	8.3	16.1	10.9	Sales/Net Fixed Assets					11.5	
	3.7	8.0	6.7						6.7	
	2.4	3.0	3.6						4.1	
	2.6	2.7	2.7	Sales/Total Assets					2.7	
	1.8	2.2	2.1						2.2	
	1.5	1.5	1.4						1.8	
	2.0	1.6	2.4	% Depr., Dep., Amort./Sales					1.4	
	(14) 3.9	(18) 3.2	(37) 3.7						3.8	
	5.2	4.6	6.1						5.8	
			3.0	% Officers', Directors', Owners' Comp/Sales						
		(12) 4.3								
		8.4								
	413917M	536051M	661416M	Net Sales ($)	1316M	17154M	21533M	39513M	183415M	398485M
	239226M	468651M	395657M	Total Assets ($)	381M	15473M	10493M	17924M	104974M	246412M

M = $ thousand   MM = $ million
See Pages 11 through 18 for Explanation of Ratios and Data

Current Data Sorted By Assets | Comparative Historical Data

0-500M	500M-2MM	2-10MM	10-50MM	50-100MM	100-250MM	Type of Statement	4/1/98-3/31/99 ALL	4/1/99-3/31/00 ALL
		10	11	3	4	Unqualified	9	6
1	4	24	6			Reviewed	4	5
2	9	6				Compiled	4	4
2	1	1				Tax Returns		
2	12	23	11	7	6	Other	8	9
	44 (4/1-9/30/02)		101 (10/1/02-3/31/03)					
7	26	64	28	10	10	**NUMBER OF STATEMENTS**	25	24
%	%	%	%	%	%	**ASSETS**	%	%
	6.1	4.7	5.5	1.9	2.2	Cash & Equivalents	6.4	10.7
	29.5	27.9	22.8	16.5	21.5	Trade Receivables (net)	23.9	22.7
	18.3	20.2	16.4	15.2	12.8	Inventory	25.4	23.3
	.1	2.0	2.3	6.1	2.5	All Other Current	1.1	3.4
	53.9	54.8	47.1	39.6	39.0	Total Current	56.8	60.2
	33.2	35.0	40.4	27.7	36.5	Fixed Assets (net)	37.2	36.7
	1.8	4.2	4.6	24.4	12.5	Intangibles (net)	1.8	.4
	11.1	6.0	8.0	8.2	12.0	All Other Non-Current	4.2	2.7
	100.0	100.0	100.0	100.0	100.0	Total	100.0	100.0
						LIABILITIES		
	15.3	13.6	9.5	13.4	1.8	Notes Payable-Short Term	8.0	7.8
	7.6	4.6	5.9	2.2	5.3	Cur. Mat.-L/T/D	3.5	3.1
	19.7	16.1	18.2	10.6	10.6	Trade Payables	16.1	18.3
	.3	.2	.3	.0	1.1	Income Taxes Payable	.2	.1
	8.6	9.5	8.5	8.2	9.1	All Other Current	6.7	8.6
	51.5	44.0	42.5	34.5	28.0	Total Current	34.6	37.9
	23.0	17.2	19.7	23.2	28.1	Long Term Debt	23.8	17.8
	1.2	.8	1.4	1.3	1.8	Deferred Taxes	1.8	1.2
	5.9	5.6	3.2	6.2	10.5	All Other Non-Current	2.1	5.0
	18.4	32.4	33.2	34.8	31.6	Net Worth	37.7	38.1
	100.0	100.0	100.0	100.0	100.0	Total Liabilities & Net Worth	100.0	100.0
						INCOME DATA		
	100.0	100.0	100.0	100.0	100.0	Net Sales	100.0	100.0
	25.7	25.7	25.5	27.7	24.3	Gross Profit	24.5	24.8
	26.0	21.1	19.4	22.7	16.7	Operating Expenses	18.2	16.3
	-.3	4.5	6.1	5.0	7.6	Operating Profit	6.2	8.5
	2.3	1.2	1.6	3.6	3.0	All Other Expenses (net)	1.5	.9
	-2.6	3.3	4.5	1.4	4.5	Profit Before Taxes	4.7	7.6
						RATIOS		
	1.3	1.8	1.8	1.3	1.7	Current	2.3	2.1
	1.0	1.3	1.2	1.2	1.5		1.7	1.6
	.8	.9	.7	1.0	1.1		1.3	1.3
	.9	1.1	1.2	.8	1.0	Quick	1.3	1.2
	.6	.7	.7	.6	.8		1.0	.9
	.4	.5	.4	.4	.6		.6	.6
	36 10.3	34 10.6	35 10.4	35 10.3	40 9.1	Sales/Receivables	33 11.0	26 14.3
	47 7.7	47 7.8	49 7.4	47 7.7	48 7.6		41 8.8	38 9.5
	56 6.5	63 5.8	58 6.3	51 7.1	61 6.0		55 6.6	60 6.1
	17 21.6	27 13.5	32 11.5	24 15.1	18 20.2	Cost of Sales/Inventory	34 10.8	41 9.0
	42 8.7	50 7.2	53 6.9	49 7.4	46 8.0		62 5.9	57 6.4
	70 5.2	66 5.6	73 5.0	104 3.5	54 6.8		85 4.3	72 5.1
	20 18.3	23 15.6	29 12.6	29 12.8	26 13.8	Cost of Sales/Payables	26 14.2	16 23.3
	39 9.4	35 10.4	45 8.1	36 10.0	30 12.3		40 9.1	36 10.2
	52 7.1	56 6.5	58 6.3	55 6.7	39 9.5		50 7.2	62 5.9
	16.9	8.9	7.3	9.7	9.0	Sales/Working Capital	6.3	5.8
	NM	15.8	21.7	31.0	13.5		9.2	9.6
	-22.7	-50.4	-12.5	NM	46.8		19.3	19.1
	4.7	14.0	12.3	3.6		EBIT/Interest	10.1	11.1
	(23) .6	(62) 2.3	4.1	2.4			3.7	(22) 4.8
	-2.2	.5	1.5	1.8			1.8	2.3
		4.3	6.1			Net Profit + Depr., Dep., Amort./Cur. Mat. L/T/D		
		(17) 1.7	(13) 3.3					
		.7	1.9					
	.5	.6	.7	1.1	.7	Fixed/Worth	.5	.5
	2.4	1.1	1.3	3.9	1.6		1.2	1.1
	NM	2.6	7.3	-3.6	-7.4		1.9	2.3
	1.1	1.0	.8	2.4	1.2	Debt/Worth	.8	.9
	4.1	2.5	1.8	7.1	2.0		2.1	2.0
	NM	13.3	11.2	-8.0	-14.7		3.4	4.0
	37.7	50.7	45.6			% Profit Before Taxes/Tangible Net Worth	43.1	59.8
	(20) 1.9	(53) 19.3	(23) 28.1				25.9	(23) 44.5
	-39.7	.9	2.6				7.0	15.5
	11.6	12.4	15.6	9.4	9.3	% Profit Before Taxes/Total Assets	18.6	18.6
	-1.1	5.3	7.7	3.3	4.4		6.1	14.4
	-10.2	-1.2	1.3	1.5	2.6		2.2	4.9
	17.2	9.2	8.1	6.8	5.9	Sales/Net Fixed Assets	11.4	12.5
	5.4	6.4	4.1	5.1	3.8		5.5	5.5
	3.9	3.7	2.9	3.8	3.3		3.1	3.8
	2.6	2.5	2.1	1.6	1.7	Sales/Total Assets	2.7	2.4
	2.1	1.9	1.7	1.3	1.4		1.9	2.0
	1.7	1.4	1.2	.9	1.2		1.6	1.5
	2.3	2.3	2.8			% Depr., Dep., Amort./Sales	1.7	1.3
	(24) 4.1	(57) 3.7	(26) 4.2				(21) 2.5	(23) 2.3
	6.4	4.9	5.8				3.1	3.2
	2.5	2.0				% Officers', Directors', Owners' Comp/Sales		
	(18) 4.6	(25) 3.1						
	7.9	4.4						
6336M	75704M	637174M	1133514M	940627M	1924248M	Net Sales ($)	1466639M	773524M
2409M	34035M	332552M	636397M	687333M	1302718M	Total Assets ($)	867990M	424300M

M = $ thousand   MM = $ million
See Pages 11 through 18 for Explanation of Ratios and Data

Comparative Historical Data | Current Data Sorted By Sales

			Type of Statement						
6	10	28	Unqualified			1	4	7	16
5	5	35	Reviewed	1	2	4	11	14	3
4	7	17	Compiled	2	6	5	1	3	
3	1	4	Tax Returns		3	1			
11	10	61	Other	2	11	7	8	12	21
4/1/00-3/31/01	4/1/01-3/31/02	4/1/02-3/31/03		44 (4/1-9/30/02)			101 (10/1/02-3/31/03)		
ALL	ALL	ALL		0-1MM	1-3MM	3-5MM	5-10MM	10-25MM	25MM & OVER
29	33	145	NUMBER OF STATEMENTS	5	22	18	24	36	40
%	%	%	ASSETS	%	%	%	%	%	%
4.5	4.9	4.8	Cash & Equivalents		7.3	3.7	5.9	3.8	4.5
21.7	22.6	26.3	Trade Receivables (net)		30.2	22.2	28.2	29.5	22.4
22.5	21.5	18.4	Inventory		18.1	22.9	16.2	20.4	15.7
.9	2.3	1.9	All Other Current		1.3	1.0	2.4	.9	3.6
49.6	51.3	51.4	Total Current		56.9	50.0	52.7	54.5	46.2
42.7	44.4	35.0	Fixed Assets (net)		33.3	30.9	39.5	35.2	34.1
2.0	1.5	5.6	Intangibles (net)		.4	8.1	2.4	4.8	10.1
5.7	2.7	7.9	All Other Non-Current		9.4	11.1	5.5	5.5	9.6
100.0	100.0	100.0	Total		100.0	100.0	100.0	100.0	100.0
			LIABILITIES						
9.4	10.9	12.4	Notes Payable-Short Term		19.5	11.4	11.9	11.8	9.3
7.2	6.4	5.3	Cur. Mat.-L/T/D		7.2	4.2	5.4	5.1	4.8
14.3	12.7	16.3	Trade Payables		20.7	14.7	16.4	14.9	16.7
.7	.1	.3	Income Taxes Payable		.1	.7	.1	.1	.5
8.2	12.8	8.9	All Other Current		8.8	8.9	8.7	10.5	8.4
39.9	42.9	43.2	Total Current		56.2	39.9	42.5	42.5	39.6
25.7	18.0	19.6	Long Term Debt		19.9	18.3	19.7	16.8	21.4
1.0	1.6	1.1	Deferred Taxes		1.4	1.1	.3	1.0	1.6
2.4	6.8	5.3	All Other Non-Current		7.1	4.3	3.8	6.1	5.6
31.1	30.6	30.9	Net Worth		15.4	36.5	33.7	33.7	31.7
100.0	100.0	100.0	Total Liabilities & Net Worth		100.0	100.0	100.0	100.0	100.0
			INCOME DATA						
100.0	100.0	100.0	Net Sales		100.0	100.0	100.0	100.0	100.0
29.5	25.8	26.0	Gross Profit		28.9	27.1	24.8	25.7	25.5
22.2	23.7	21.9	Operating Expenses		28.3	25.2	20.5	19.7	19.4
7.4	2.1	4.1	Operating Profit		.6	1.8	4.4	6.1	6.1
2.1	2.1	1.8	All Other Expenses (net)		2.2	1.4	1.1	1.5	2.3
5.3	.0	2.4	Profit Before Taxes		-1.6	.5	3.3	4.5	3.8
			RATIOS						
1.7	2.1	1.7	Current		1.3	1.8	2.0	1.8	1.7
1.1	1.2	1.2			1.0	1.1	1.3	1.4	1.2
.9	.9	.9			.8	.9	1.0	.9	.9
.8	1.0	1.0	Quick		.9	.9	1.4	1.1	1.0
.6	.6	.7			.6	.6	.9	.7	.7
.5	.4	.5			.4	.4	.4	.5	.5
30 12.1	29 12.5	36 10.2	Sales/Receivables		37 9.8	29 12.6	32 11.4	37 9.9	39 9.4
38 9.6	40 9.1	48 7.7			49 7.4	43 8.5	51 7.2	47 7.8	48 7.5
52 7.1	48 7.7	58 6.3			86 4.2	64 5.7	59 6.1	57 6.4	57 6.4
41 8.9	43 8.5	27 13.7	Cost of Sales/Inventory		22 16.3	38 9.6	23 15.9	26 13.9	25 14.9
60 6.1	49 7.5	48 7.6			57 6.4	58 6.2	39 9.4	48 7.7	47 7.8
85 4.3	77 4.7	66 5.5			87 4.2	94 3.9	59 6.1	65 5.7	59 6.2
23 15.9	15 23.6	26 14.0	Cost of Sales/Payables		22 16.8	22 16.5	27 13.5	23 16.1	29 12.5
37 10.0	25 14.4	36 10.1			49 7.5	31 11.9	34 10.6	33 11.0	41 8.9
51 7.2	44 8.3	53 6.9			77 4.8	52 7.0	56 6.6	50 7.3	51 7.2
7.3	7.2	9.3	Sales/Working Capital		10.3	8.6	8.6	9.0	9.4
27.9	22.4	18.3			272.7	81.5	17.2	15.0	22.1
-71.3	-75.1	-42.3			-22.7	-23.8	-137.4	-40.0	-120.5
6.1	4.6	8.7	EBIT/Interest		7.7	10.5	13.8	11.1	6.5
(32) 2.7	1.5	(137) 2.3		(20) 1.0	(16) 1.0	(23) 1.7	(35) 4.3	(39) 3.1	
1.5	-1.2	.6			-2.4	-.2	1.1	.9	1.6
7.5	2.2	4.1	Net Profit + Depr., Dep., Amort./Cur. Mat. L/T/D					11.3	6.5
(11) 4.7	(10) 1.7	(46) 2.5					(11) 2.2	(20) 3.3	
1.5	.5	1.1						1.6	2.0
.9	.9	.6	Fixed/Worth		.5	.3	.7	.6	.8
1.2	1.5	1.2			1.9	1.4	1.2	1.0	1.5
2.8	2.9	4.6			10.9	3.8	2.6	3.4	18.0
1.1	1.1	1.0	Debt/Worth		1.3	.6	.9	1.0	1.6
2.9	2.0	2.5			3.6	2.6	2.1	1.8	2.7
4.0	5.9	13.8			72.2	54.5	29.9	7.6	79.3
50.0	19.6	45.3	% Profit Before Taxes/Tangible Net Worth		55.6	19.3	42.7	56.7	47.3
(27) 26.9	(28) 10.9	(117) 18.9		(18) 14.5	(15) 2.0	(19) 16.1	(30) 25.7	(31) 19.8	
4.5	-.5	.8			-33.1	-30.3	1.3	12.5	5.8
19.7	6.7	12.0	% Profit Before Taxes/Total Assets		11.6	6.4	12.8	17.6	11.1
7.0	2.3	4.2			.7	.0	2.9	6.6	4.7
1.2	-5.5	-.9			-10.2	-4.7	.5	.0	1.8
7.0	6.7	8.8	Sales/Net Fixed Assets		17.2	16.9	9.5	11.6	6.7
4.7	5.3	5.6			5.1	8.6	5.5	6.4	4.8
2.3	2.7	3.5			3.9	3.1	2.4	3.7	3.6
2.3	2.4	2.4	Sales/Total Assets		2.5	2.3	2.4	2.7	2.1
1.8	2.0	1.8			1.9	1.6	1.8	2.0	1.6
1.2	1.5	1.3			1.4	1.2	1.2	1.5	1.2
2.4	2.0	2.5	% Depr., Dep., Amort./Sales		2.1	2.6	2.0	2.3	2.7
(27) 3.0	(31) 2.9	(127) 3.9		(20) 4.7	(14) 3.8	(23) 4.0	(34) 3.4	(33) 4.0	
5.3	5.0	5.0			6.8	5.1	6.9	4.3	4.9
3.9	3.0	2.0	% Officers', Directors', Owners' Comp/Sales		3.3		1.8	2.0	
(10) 5.8	(11) 5.2	(51) 3.5		(13) 4.8		(13) 2.4	(11) 3.1		
9.3	7.1	5.8			7.9		5.5	3.5	
986822M	1511989M	4717603M	Net Sales ($)	2054M	48837M	72181M	185212M	505131M	3904188M
528792M	861600M	2995444M	Total Assets ($)	1582M	32385M	48712M	115456M	267843M	2529466M

© RMA 2003

M = $ thousand   MM = $ million

See Pages 11 through 18 for Explanation of Ratios and Data

Current Data Sorted By Assets | **Comparative Historical Data**

0-500M	500M-2MM	2-10MM	10-50MM	50-100MM	100-250MM	Type of Statement	4/1/98-3/31/99 ALL	4/1/99-3/31/00 ALL
		2	5	1	2	Unqualified	16	9
		2	1		1	Reviewed	4	7
1	3	2	1			Compiled	3	4
1		1				Tax Returns	1	1
	2	4	3	1	1	Other	9	12
		10 (4/1-9/30/02)	24 (10/1/02-3/31/03)					
2	5	11	10	3	3	NUMBER OF STATEMENTS	33	33
%	%	%	%	%	%	**ASSETS**	%	%
		6.0	4.3			Cash & Equivalents	6.0	5.5
		27.9	21.4			Trade Receivables (net)	20.4	22.5
		31.1	21.4			Inventory	21.5	20.7
		.4	1.2			All Other Current	1.9	1.6
		65.5	48.2			Total Current	49.8	50.3
		29.4	36.0			Fixed Assets (net)	34.7	35.5
		.7	13.6			Intangibles (net)	8.3	4.4
		4.4	2.3			All Other Non-Current	7.2	9.8
		100.0	100.0			Total	100.0	100.0
						LIABILITIES		
		28.2	4.8			Notes Payable-Short Term	12.4	10.2
		3.5	3.0			Cur. Mat.-L/T/D	6.6	5.8
		16.2	11.8			Trade Payables	17.5	13.7
		.1	.0			Income Taxes Payable	.5	.3
		7.7	7.1			All Other Current	6.3	6.7
		55.7	26.8			Total Current	43.3	36.7
		9.5	21.0			Long Term Debt	15.6	19.0
		.6	2.2			Deferred Taxes	.7	.8
		8.0	5.8			All Other Non-Current	9.3	4.7
		26.2	44.2			Net Worth	31.2	38.8
		100.0	100.0			Total Liabilities & Net Worth	100.0	100.0
						INCOME DATA		
		100.0	100.0			Net Sales	100.0	100.0
		25.5	25.3			Gross Profit	26.3	30.8
		21.8	20.8			Operating Expenses	24.2	24.5
		3.6	4.5			Operating Profit	2.1	6.4
		1.4	2.4			All Other Expenses (net)	1.9	1.3
		2.3	2.1			Profit Before Taxes	.2	5.1
						RATIOS		
		2.3	2.4				2.0	2.3
		1.4	2.0			Current	1.2	1.4
		1.1	1.4				.8	1.1
		1.2	1.3				1.4	1.7
		.7	.9			Quick	.6	.8
		.4	.8				.3	.6
		30 12.0	35 10.4				29 12.6	39 9.4
		43 8.5	40 9.2			Sales/Receivables	37 9.8	47 7.7
		53 6.8	50 7.3				53 6.9	55 6.7
		39 9.3	36 10.2				34 10.8	33 11.2
		54 6.8	54 6.7			Cost of Sales/Inventory	52 7.0	51 7.2
		64 5.7	78 4.7				86 4.2	72 5.0
		24 15.2	22 16.6				31 11.7	23 16.0
		31 11.6	32 11.4			Cost of Sales/Payables	41 8.8	33 11.0
		38 9.7	44 8.4				58 6.3	54 6.8
		4.8	5.0				7.5	7.1
		13.5	8.4			Sales/Working Capital	17.6	11.1
		53.1	15.0				-15.6	35.5
		4.0					(30) 13.7	(31) 12.1
		1.0				EBIT/Interest	3.8	3.8
		.4					1.1	1.3
						Net Profit + Depr., Dep.,	(12) 6.3	
						Amort./Cur. Mat. L /T/D	1.9	
							1.0	
		.3	.7				.7	.5
		.8	1.1			Fixed/Worth	1.3	.8
		1.9	2.1				10.1	2.2
		.4	1.1				.7	.6
		1.6	1.3			Debt/Worth	2.6	1.9
		8.4	3.7				20.7	4.6
		43.3	(10)			% Profit Before Taxes/Tangible	(27) 44.5	(31) 28.7
		5.5				Net Worth	18.0	15.4
		-7.7					6.6	5.7
		10.0	11.5				12.9	16.7
		.0	3.1			% Profit Before Taxes/Total	7.4	6.0
		-2.8	-1.8			Assets	.5	1.7
		15.5	6.6				6.9	8.5
		12.5	4.8			Sales/Net Fixed Assets	5.1	5.1
		4.7	4.2				3.6	3.4
		3.2	2.1				2.3	2.1
		2.4	1.7			Sales/Total Assets	1.7	1.7
		1.9	1.4				1.4	1.3
		1.4	2.8				(27) 2.3	(27) 2.5
		2.3	4.1			% Depr., Dep., Amort./Sales	4.0	3.7
		4.4	6.1				4.8	5.0
						% Officers', Directors', Owners' Comp/Sales		
1861M	17252M	114269M	368872M	249804M	661669M	Net Sales ($)	1255551M	1373919M
681M	8465M	46635M	221509M	232955M	425774M	Total Assets ($)	786435M	855114M

© RMA 2003

M = $ thousand   MM = $ million
See Pages 11 through 18 for Explanation of Ratios and Data

Comparative Historical Data | **Current Data Sorted By Sales**

4/1/00-3/31/01 ALL	4/1/01-3/31/02 ALL	4/1/02-3/31/03 ALL	Type of Statement	0-1MM	1-3MM	3-5MM	5-10MM	10-25MM	25MM & OVER
						10 (4/1-9/30/02)		24 (10/1/02-3/31/03)	
5	5	10	Unqualified				1	2	7
6	8	4	Reviewed				1	1	2
7	7	7	Compiled	1	2	1	1	1	1
1	1	2	Tax Returns		1			1	
16	11	11	Other			2	2	3	4
35	32	34	NUMBER OF STATEMENTS	1	3	3	5	8	14
%	%	%	**ASSETS**	%	%	%	%	%	%
6.3	6.5	6.2	Cash & Equivalents						5.4
24.8	27.1	23.6	Trade Receivables (net)						18.9
22.7	23.0	22.6	Inventory						19.8
2.3	.9	.8	All Other Current						1.3
56.1	57.4	53.2	Total Current						45.4
31.0	28.7	37.2	Fixed Assets (net)						41.7
6.0	6.6	6.1	Intangibles (net)						9.9
6.8	7.3	3.5	All Other Non-Current						3.0
100.0	100.0	100.0	Total						100.0
			LIABILITIES						
13.1	10.3	13.6	Notes Payable-Short Term						5.5
4.3	3.3	2.8	Cur. Mat.-L/T/D						2.8
15.1	15.9	12.1	Trade Payables						11.0
.1	.2	.0	Income Taxes Payable						.0
7.3	6.6	7.4	All Other Current						8.4
39.9	36.4	36.0	Total Current						27.7
15.8	14.9	17.8	Long Term Debt						20.7
.8	.6	1.2	Deferred Taxes						2.3
5.9	2.8	7.6	All Other Non-Current						6.3
37.7	45.3	37.4	Net Worth						43.1
100.0	100.0	100.0	Total Liabilities & Net Worth						100.0
			INCOME DATA						
100.0	100.0	100.0	Net Sales						100.0
28.4	28.3	27.4	Gross Profit						24.8
22.8	24.7	23.3	Operating Expenses						20.3
5.5	3.5	4.1	Operating Profit						4.5
1.4	1.0	1.9	All Other Expenses (net)						2.4
4.1	2.6	2.2	Profit Before Taxes						2.1
			RATIOS						
2.7 1.7 1.1	3.6 1.8 1.2	2.3 1.8 1.2	Current						2.3 1.9 1.1
1.7 .9 .5	2.2 1.0 .6	1.5 .9 .6	Quick						1.3 .8 .7
40 9.2 46 7.9 54 6.8	39 9.3 47 7.7 60 6.1	34 10.8 41 9.0 50 7.3	Sales/Receivables						35 10.4 38 9.5 50 7.3
40 9.1 57 6.4 69 5.3	34 10.9 52 7.0 79 4.6	38 9.7 48 7.6 65 5.6	Cost of Sales/Inventory						39 9.3 52 7.1 77 4.7
25 14.6 38 9.5 53 6.9	22 16.4 28 12.9 48 7.6	21 17.5 29 12.4 42 8.8	Cost of Sales/Payables						25 14.8 32 11.2 44 8.4
5.6 9.8 46.8	4.7 7.5 32.6	4.9 9.1 26.4	Sales/Working Capital						5.0 9.0 29.3
7.1 (30) 3.0 1.4	10.9 (30) 2.4 .9	7.1 (29) 1.6 .4	EBIT/Interest						11.8 (10) 1.9 1.3
10.7 (10) 4.3 1.6			Net Profit + Depr., Dep., Amort./Cur. Mat. L/T/D						
.5 .8 2.2	.3 .7 1.9	.6 .9 2.2	Fixed/Worth						.8 1.1 2.8
.6 1.8 5.7	.4 1.6 4.4	.6 1.7 4.9	Debt/Worth						.6 1.3 5.6
39.8 (32) 20.5 6.1	23.6 (29) 6.5 .4	27.9 (31) 16.1 -6.4	% Profit Before Taxes/Tangible Net Worth						26.6 (12) 18.4 3.5
14.7 6.2 1.3	10.2 2.7 .1	12.2 3.2 -1.4	% Profit Before Taxes/Total Assets						11.5 3.6 1.6
11.6 6.4 3.6	14.6 5.9 3.6	10.1 4.9 3.6	Sales/Net Fixed Assets						5.2 4.6 3.0
2.6 1.9 1.4	2.8 1.8 1.3	2.4 1.9 1.6	Sales/Total Assets						1.9 1.7 1.2
2.0 (28) 3.3 4.8	.6 (25) 2.2 4.1	2.3 (31) 3.7 5.6	% Depr., Dep., Amort./Sales						3.1 (12) 4.7 6.7
		1.8 (11) 3.3 4.5	% Officers', Directors', Owners' Comp/Sales						
1256313M 804515M	858180M 644504M	1413727M 936019M	Net Sales ($) Total Assets ($)	819M 329M	6856M 3908M	11438M 4909M	36665M 14042M	120698M 67215M	1237251M 845616M

M = $ thousand   MM = $ million
See Pages 11 through 18 for Explanation of Ratios and Data

Current Data Sorted By Assets   Comparative Historical Data

Type of Statement	0-500M	500M-2MM	2-10MM	10-50MM	50-100MM	100-250MM		4/1/98-3/31/99 ALL	4/1/99-3/31/00 ALL
Unqualified		1	7	6	2	2		19	30
Reviewed		7	17	3		1		22	21
Compiled		7	1					14	13
Tax Returns	1	3	1					2	1
Other	3	4	7	5	3			28	21
	19 (4/1-9/30/02)		62 (10/1/02-3/31/03)						
NUMBER OF STATEMENTS	4	22	33	14	5	3		85	86
ASSETS	%	%	%	%	%	%		%	%
Cash & Equivalents		9.9	7.4	2.4				6.0	6.3
Trade Receivables (net)		36.0	26.2	28.0				29.7	27.7
Inventory		20.2	17.3	18.2				19.3	19.5
All Other Current		1.9	1.8	1.8				2.9	2.0
Total Current		67.9	52.6	50.5				57.9	55.6
Fixed Assets (net)		27.9	40.0	38.4				33.9	35.5
Intangibles (net)		.4	1.4	4.5				3.1	3.2
All Other Non-Current		3.7	5.9	6.6				5.1	5.7
Total		100.0	100.0	100.0				100.0	100.0
LIABILITIES									
Notes Payable-Short Term		11.7	6.8	8.3				10.8	10.3
Cur. Mat.-L/T/D		5.5	4.8	4.0				5.8	4.2
Trade Payables		23.0	15.8	15.5				19.4	17.6
Income Taxes Payable		.1	.1	.0				.5	.5
All Other Current		8.1	6.3	9.7				8.1	7.6
Total Current		48.4	33.7	37.5				44.6	40.2
Long Term Debt		13.9	18.9	26.7				20.8	21.0
Deferred Taxes		.8	.4	.2				.5	.6
All Other Non-Current		3.7	1.6	2.6				4.8	4.0
Net Worth		33.2	45.4	33.1				29.3	34.2
Total Liabilities & Net Worth		100.0	100.0	100.0				100.0	100.0
INCOME DATA									
Net Sales		100.0	100.0	100.0				100.0	100.0
Gross Profit		28.3	28.4	19.6				27.2	26.5
Operating Expenses		27.1	22.7	17.8				22.5	21.1
Operating Profit		1.2	5.7	1.8				4.7	5.4
All Other Expenses (net)		.8	.8	1.7				1.3	1.5
Profit Before Taxes		.4	4.8	.1				3.4	3.9
RATIOS									
Current		2.2	2.8	1.9				2.1	2.2
		1.3	1.6	1.5				1.2	1.3
		1.1	1.1	1.0				1.0	1.1
Quick		1.7	1.7	1.1				1.5	1.3
		.8	1.0	.8				.8	.9
		.6	.7	.7				.5	.6
Sales/Receivables		28 13.3	34 10.8	40 9.1				35 10.4	35 10.4
		40 9.2	45 8.2	48 7.6				43 8.4	43 8.4
		51 7.2	53 6.9	59 6.2				53 6.9	52 7.0
Cost of Sales/Inventory		16 23.5	26 13.9	31 11.8				24 14.9	24 15.5
		32 11.5	39 9.4	40 9.2				36 10.1	40 9.2
		64 5.7	58 6.3	44 8.2				62 5.9	54 6.7
Cost of Sales/Payables		18 19.8	21 17.5	21 17.5				25 14.7	22 17.0
		36 10.2	29 12.7	31 11.9				33 11.2	31 11.8
		49 7.5	50 7.3	40 9.1				52 7.0	45 8.1
Sales/Working Capital		7.5	5.5	8.6				7.6	8.0
		25.3	12.3	15.4				16.4	17.5
		75.5	124.6	NM				UND	75.3
EBIT/Interest		(20) 7.5	(30) 9.9	(12) 7.6				(81) 7.3	(82) 9.7
		2.9	4.5	5.8				3.1	4.2
		-4.8	1.6	.6				1.3	1.5
Net Profit + Depr., Dep., Amort./Cur. Mat. L /T/D			(10) 4.3					(35) 5.6	(30) 8.3
			1.0					2.4	2.9
			.2					1.1	1.0
Fixed/Worth		.4	.4	.8				.6	.6
		.9	1.1	1.3				1.0	1.1
		2.7	1.8	NM				2.3	2.0
Debt/Worth		1.1	.4	1.1				1.1	.8
		2.1	1.5	1.8				2.2	2.1
		6.8	2.6	NM				4.0	3.8
% Profit Before Taxes/Tangible Net Worth		(19) 26.2	(31) 60.5	(11) 22.3				(76) 57.9	(78) 43.2
		9.0	16.2	13.5				23.7	20.7
		-56.8	7.7	-4.9				6.2	6.2
% Profit Before Taxes/Total Assets		14.7	20.5	11.6				12.6	15.3
		5.1	7.9	7.4				8.1	7.6
		-10.3	2.4	-1.1				1.5	1.2
Sales/Net Fixed Assets		22.7	13.2	6.9				13.6	13.0
		12.6	5.4	5.4				6.9	6.5
		7.0	2.6	4.2				4.4	3.7
Sales/Total Assets		4.3	2.9	2.5				3.2	3.1
		3.4	2.0	2.1				2.4	2.4
		2.2	1.5	1.7				1.6	1.6
% Depr., Dep., Amort./Sales		1.1	(32) 1.7	(11) 2.7				(79) 1.4	(79) 1.5
		1.7	3.0	3.4				2.5	2.3
		2.7	4.9	5.0				4.0	4.4
% Officers', Directors', Owners' Comp/Sales		(15) 2.7	(13) 2.3					(32) 2.0	(29) 2.3
		4.1	2.6					3.4	4.0
		7.4	5.9					7.0	7.6
Net Sales ($)	4684M	81058M	351543M	651802M	699545M	808039M		2410400M	2070574M
Total Assets ($)	1003M	25206M	149721M	322039M	380072M	541044M		1273339M	1184704M

© RMA 2003

M = $ thousand   MM = $ million
See Pages 11 through 18 for Explanation of Ratios and Data

Comparative Historical Data — Current Data Sorted By Sales

4/1/00-3/31/01 ALL	4/1/01-3/31/02 ALL	4/1/02-3/31/03 ALL	Type of Statement	0-1MM	1-3MM	3-5MM	5-10MM	10-25MM	25MM & OVER
					19 (4/1-9/30/02)		62 (10/1/02-3/31/03)		
13	16	18	Unqualified			1	3	3	11
22	18	27	Reviewed		2	9	5	9	2
12	15	9	Compiled		4	2	2		1
2	2	5	Tax Returns		2	2		1	
26	25	22	Other	2	2	3	4	3	8
75	76	81	**NUMBER OF STATEMENTS**	2	10	17	14	16	22
%	%	%	**ASSETS**	%	%	%	%	%	%
3.9	5.4	6.5	Cash & Equivalents		12.6	6.3	11.7	4.4	2.2
28.6	27.9	28.7	Trade Receivables (net)		33.9	34.1	23.2	29.5	25.2
21.2	19.1	19.4	Inventory		19.7	19.6	14.9	19.1	20.4
1.8	1.8	1.8	All Other Current		2.3	2.0	.3	2.6	2.1
55.4	54.2	56.4	Total Current		68.5	62.0	50.1	55.6	50.0
33.0	35.8	35.4	Fixed Assets (net)		26.1	34.2	42.6	37.0	36.6
3.7	3.2	2.7	Intangibles (net)		.7	.2	2.1	1.0	7.3
7.9	6.7	5.5	All Other Non-Current		4.7	3.6	5.1	6.4	6.2
100.0	100.0	100.0	Total		100.0	100.0	100.0	100.0	100.0
			LIABILITIES						
12.6	13.2	8.5	Notes Payable-Short Term		8.5	12.3	5.7	8.1	6.5
6.6	3.4	4.6	Cur. Mat.-L/T/D		2.4	5.8	7.6	3.1	4.3
18.2	16.0	17.1	Trade Payables		16.2	20.1	15.4	21.6	13.5
.3	.1	.1	Income Taxes Payable		.1	.0	.0	.2	.0
11.5	12.1	18.6	All Other Current		8.2	6.2	5.3	8.5	10.1
49.2	44.9	48.9	Total Current		35.4	44.4	33.8	41.6	34.5
22.6	19.9	19.2	Long Term Debt		21.5	13.8	19.8	16.6	23.6
.6	.4	.5	Deferred Taxes		.3	1.3	.1	.0	.8
7.2	3.9	3.4	All Other Non-Current		.3	5.9	1.9	.4	3.0
20.4	30.9	28.0	Net Worth		42.6	34.5	44.3	41.4	38.2
100.0	100.0	100.0	Total Liabilities & Net Worth		100.0	100.0	100.0	100.0	100.0
			INCOME DATA						
100.0	100.0	100.0	Net Sales		100.0	100.0	100.0	100.0	100.0
28.0	26.2	27.2	Gross Profit		36.8	28.0	30.4	21.7	23.0
23.4	22.8	23.9	Operating Expenses		34.5	25.0	24.3	19.3	18.0
4.6	3.5	3.2	Operating Profit		2.3	3.0	6.1	2.3	4.9
2.2	1.9	1.0	All Other Expenses (net)		.7	1.1	1.0	1.5	.9
2.5	1.6	2.2	Profit Before Taxes		1.6	2.0	5.2	.9	4.0
			RATIOS						
1.7	2.1	2.2	Current		6.2	2.3	2.3	2.2	1.8
1.2	1.3	1.4			3.6	1.3	1.9	1.2	1.5
.9	1.0	1.0			1.1	1.1	1.1	.9	1.1
1.0	1.3	1.6	Quick		4.1	1.3	1.7	1.4	1.0
.7	.7	.8			2.0	.8	1.3	.7	.7
.5	.6	.6			.7	.6	.5	.5	.6
31 11.8	32 11.5	31 11.7	Sales/Receivables		28 12.9	36 10.1	26 14.1	24 15.0	37 10.0
42 8.8	42 8.6	44 8.3			38 9.5	45 8.2	47 7.8	36 10.1	46 7.9
53 6.9	51 7.2	53 6.9			67 5.5	58 6.3	52 7.0	50 7.3	52 7.1
24 15.3	26 13.9	26 14.1	Cost of Sales/Inventory		20 18.3	24 15.2	16 22.9	23 15.8	31 11.7
38 9.6	37 9.9	39 9.4			49 7.4	36 10.2	37 9.9	30 12.0	40 9.1
63 5.8	57 6.4	59 6.2			69 5.3	71 5.1	59 7.3	50 7.3	59 6.1
24 15.2	17 21.5	21 17.5	Cost of Sales/Payables		27 13.5	18 19.8	20 17.8	20 18.2	21 17.5
34 10.6	24 14.9	33 10.9			36 10.0	31 11.7	36 10.0	26 13.9	31 11.9
50 7.3	45 8.1	47 7.8			47 7.8	53 6.9	52 7.0	45 8.1	39 9.3
10.4	8.4	6.9	Sales/Working Capital		2.8	6.1	6.3	9.5	8.5
24.6	21.7	13.9			9.8	18.9	12.2	22.5	13.7
-30.6	-254.2	99.5			39.6	68.3	NM	-76.9	100.5
5.9	4.9	7.5	EBIT/Interest			4.7	10.3	16.6	7.6
(73) 3.3	(74) 2.8	(74) 4.0				2.3	(13) 6.9	(14) 4.3	(20) 4.7
1.2	1.0	.9				-.8	.8	1.8	2.0
5.3	6.6	5.3	Net Profit + Depr., Dep., Amort./Cur. Mat. L/T/D						
(20) 3.4	(21) 2.3	(23) 2.1							
1.1	1.4	.9							
.6	.6	.5	Fixed/Worth		.4	.4	.6	.4	.8
1.4	1.0	1.0			.6	1.0	1.0	.8	1.2
3.0	3.0	2.2			NM	2.7	1.5	2.3	2.2
1.3	1.0	.7	Debt/Worth		.2	1.0	.6	.5	1.3
2.4	2.1	1.6			1.9	1.7	1.6	1.5	1.5
8.4	7.7	5.2			NM	7.3	2.6	6.0	4.0
57.1	41.1	35.0	% Profit Before Taxes/Tangible Net Worth			17.2	77.4	62.4	22.9
(63) 21.1	(68) 15.1	(70) 13.9			(16)	10.0	(13) 26.2	(14) 19.8	(19) 14.3
5.8	2.6	5.6				-.2	11.3	6.7	.0
13.2	11.5	16.6	% Profit Before Taxes/Total Assets		21.0	8.7	25.4	21.2	11.3
7.0	5.1	6.3			7.6	3.5	14.3	6.6	7.4
1.1	.0	-.1			-11.6	-5.3	.8	2.3	1.8
18.0	15.3	14.8	Sales/Net Fixed Assets		25.6	14.4	13.2	18.3	7.4
8.2	6.1	6.5			12.7	7.2	5.5	7.2	5.7
4.3	4.4	4.1			5.1	3.8	2.5	4.9	4.1
3.3	3.3	3.2	Sales/Total Assets		3.6	4.0	3.6	3.4	2.5
2.5	2.3	2.4			2.7	2.8	1.9	2.7	2.2
1.7	1.7	1.6			1.4	1.6	1.3	2.1	1.6
1.2	1.3	1.5	% Depr., Dep., Amort./Sales		1.8	1.0	2.1	1.1	2.6
(72) 2.0	(72) 2.5	(74) 2.8			2.4	2.2	3.5	(14) 2.7	(18) 3.6
3.4	4.4	4.5			4.2	3.5	6.8	3.6	5.3
2.6	1.4	2.4	% Officers', Directors', Owners' Comp/Sales			2.9			
(24) 5.0	(26) 3.3	(28) 3.7			(12)	5.5			
7.6	7.2	6.2				6.2			
2988317M	2133729M	2596671M	Net Sales ($)	587M	19016M	68133M	93965M	245571M	2169399M
1360338M	1158113M	1419085M	Total Assets ($)	225M	9469M	29152M	52343M	107454M	1220442M

M = $ thousand   MM = $ million
See Pages 11 through 18 for Explanation of Ratios and Data

Current Data Sorted By Assets   Comparative Historical Data

0-500M	500M-2MM	2-10MM	10-50MM	50-100MM	100-250MM	Type of Statement	ALL 994 (4/1/98-3/31/99)	ALL 1009 (4/1/99-3/31/00)
2	5	49	75	20	14	Unqualified	233	225
2	36	136	30	3		Reviewed	246	277
10	44	54	5	1		Compiled	182	192
12	24	9				Tax Returns	36	29
12	53	125	77	28	12	Other	297	286
	159 (4/1-9/30/02)		679 (10/1/02-3/31/03)					
38	162	373	187	52	26	NUMBER OF STATEMENTS	994	1009
%	%	%	%	%	%	ASSETS	%	%
9.7	7.8	6.1	5.7	3.9	5.9	Cash & Equivalents	6.2	5.8
25.2	27.5	26.0	22.4	19.4	16.4	Trade Receivables (net)	25.3	26.0
22.4	22.1	22.0	19.3	16.4	13.0	Inventory	19.6	19.2
1.6	1.3	2.0	2.4	3.3	3.0	All Other Current	1.7	1.6
59.0	58.8	56.0	49.7	43.1	38.3	Total Current	52.8	52.6
32.8	33.2	35.6	39.9	39.5	39.8	Fixed Assets (net)	38.1	37.9
1.7	2.9	3.0	4.9	10.1	17.8	Intangibles (net)	3.7	3.9
6.5	5.1	5.4	5.5	7.4	4.1	All Other Non-Current	5.3	5.6
100.0	100.0	100.0	100.0	100.0	100.0	Total	100.0	100.0
						LIABILITIES		
16.1	11.6	11.0	10.0	4.3	1.2	Notes Payable-Short Term	10.7	10.1
4.7	5.8	5.9	5.4	6.4	5.1	Cur. Mat.-L/T/D	5.1	5.1
12.4	17.8	14.8	13.4	11.4	9.9	Trade Payables	14.7	15.2
.2	.1	.2	.3	.3	.3	Income Taxes Payable	.3	.3
16.9	8.2	8.5	7.5	8.9	12.1	All Other Current	8.2	7.9
50.3	43.5	40.3	36.6	31.2	28.6	Total Current	39.0	39.0
20.8	21.5	17.9	20.1	20.5	30.7	Long Term Debt	21.1	21.1
.3	.2	.6	1.0	1.6	1.8	Deferred Taxes	.8	.9
11.7	6.5	4.7	4.2	7.0	10.2	All Other Non-Current	5.1	5.1
17.0	28.3	36.5	38.1	39.6	28.6	Net Worth	34.0	33.8
100.0	100.0	100.0	100.0	100.0	100.0	Total Liabilities & Net Worth	100.0	100.0
						INCOME DATA		
100.0	100.0	100.0	100.0	100.0	100.0	Net Sales	100.0	100.0
42.0	34.0	25.8	25.5	22.4	26.9	Gross Profit	27.7	27.9
41.7	31.6	20.9	19.8	16.7	17.0	Operating Expenses	22.5	22.4
.3	2.3	4.9	5.8	5.7	9.9	Operating Profit	5.1	5.4
1.5	1.2	1.3	1.8	2.7	3.5	All Other Expenses (net)	1.6	1.6
−1.2	1.1	3.6	3.9	3.1	6.4	Profit Before Taxes	3.5	3.8
						RATIOS		
2.1	2.3	2.3	2.3	2.0	2.2	Current	2.2	2.1
1.5	1.4	1.4	1.4	1.5	1.5		1.5	1.4
.8	1.0	1.0	.9	1.1	1.1		1.0	1.0
1.2	1.4	1.5	1.3	1.3	1.1	Quick	1.3	1.3
.7	(161) .9	.8	.8	.8	.8		.8	.8
.4	.5	.5	.5	.6	.6		.5	.5
22 16.4	29 12.5	33 11.0	38 9.5	40 9.1	35 10.5	Sales/Receivables	35 10.5	38 9.7
36 10.0	42 8.7	45 8.1	48 7.6	48 7.6	44 8.3		45 8.1	48 7.6
45 8.0	55 6.6	56 6.5	57 6.4	59 6.2	51 7.1		55 6.6	58 6.3
15 23.9	26 14.2	32 11.3	36 10.1	39 9.4	33 11.2	Cost of Sales/Inventory	28 12.8	29 12.4
42 8.7	47 7.8	47 7.7	52 7.0	52 7.0	49 7.5		46 7.9	47 7.8
104 3.5	66 5.5	70 5.2	75 4.9	76 4.8	58 6.2		68 5.4	68 5.4
15 24.8	18 20.2	19 19.1	22 16.3	24 15.1	28 12.9	Cost of Sales/Payables	20 18.0	23 16.0
25 14.3	40 9.2	32 11.4	35 10.5	35 10.5	35 10.4		31 11.6	35 10.5
58 6.3	55 6.6	46 7.9	48 7.5	43 8.6	41 9.0		46 7.9	50 7.4
7.5	7.0	6.0	5.4	5.9	6.8	Sales/Working Capital	6.7	6.7
14.5	15.1	12.8	12.6	10.6	12.0		13.4	14.3
−20.5	NM	−228.1	−52.6	70.8	85.8		846.7	UND
4.5	5.5	10.1	7.5	8.7	6.0	EBIT/Interest	7.0	7.3
(26) 1.7	(146) 2.0	(358) 3.3	(177) 3.0	(50) 2.8	3.1		(924) 3.1	(951) 2.9
−1.7	−1.0	1.4	1.3	.8	1.3		1.3	1.2
	3.2	3.8	3.4	7.3	5.4	Net Profit + Depr., Dep., Amort./Cur. Mat. L /T/D	5.1	4.1
(27)	(27) 1.9	(105) 2.1	(72) 1.7	(29) 2.7	(11) 2.7		(375) 2.5	(327) 2.2
	.8	1.4	1.1	1.4	1.3		1.2	1.3
.4	.5	.5	.6	.9	1.0	Fixed/Worth	.6	.6
1.1	1.0	1.0	1.2	1.3	2.2		1.2	1.3
−12.4	3.8	2.2	2.5	3.1	−1.2		2.9	3.0
.8	.7	.9	.7	.9	1.5	Debt/Worth	.9	.9
2.2	2.0	1.9	1.8	1.8	3.4		2.0	2.2
−41.3	9.4	4.1	4.8	5.0	−6.2		5.5	6.7
74.2	45.1	41.8	35.9	28.8	58.3	% Profit Before Taxes/Tangible Net Worth	44.5	44.6
(27) 13.6	(132) 14.3	(332) 18.2	(169) 15.9	(44) 15.9	(18) 19.0		(878) 22.4	(880) 20.8
−17.1	−9.0	5.4	3.0	4.6	12.0		6.2	6.1
15.8	13.6	13.6	12.3	11.8	12.0	% Profit Before Taxes/Total Assets	15.1	14.5
2.6	3.9	6.1	5.4	5.0	8.1		6.7	6.2
−10.8	−6.6	1.1	.9	−.4	.9		1.2	.6
23.3	15.8	10.6	7.0	5.6	5.2	Sales/Net Fixed Assets	9.1	8.7
7.9	8.1	5.8	3.9	3.8	3.7		5.3	5.2
5.0	4.5	3.7	2.8	2.5	2.8		3.2	3.2
3.2	3.1	2.6	2.0	1.7	1.7	Sales/Total Assets	2.5	2.4
2.5	2.4	2.0	1.6	1.4	1.4		1.9	1.9
1.9	1.8	1.5	1.3	1.1	1.1		1.5	1.4
1.6	2.0	2.3	2.9	3.1	2.7	% Depr., Dep., Amort./Sales	2.1	2.2
(30) 4.7	(146) 3.5	(357) 3.9	(174) 4.0	(46) 4.7	(16) 4.0		(904) 3.4	(916) 3.7
6.3	5.6	5.6	5.6	5.9	5.5		5.2	5.3
1.8	2.7	2.0	1.2			% Officers', Directors', Owners' Comp/Sales	2.4	2.7
(16) 9.7	(77) 4.8	(128) 3.3	(38) 2.3				(336) 4.4	(317) 4.6
22.9	8.6	5.3	5.0				7.9	7.9
29746M	496672M	3811477M	6460956M	5431942M	5078337M	Net Sales ($)	25383719M	25016124M
11373M	195757M	1879408M	3893907M	3704030M	3717366M	Total Assets ($)	15748102M	15772669M

© RMA 2003

M = $ thousand   MM = $ million
See Pages 11 through 18 for Explanation of Ratios and Data

Comparative Historical Data | **Current Data Sorted By Sales**

			Type of Statement	0-1MM	1-3MM	3-5MM	5-10MM	10-25MM	25MM & OVER
185	159	165	Unqualified	2	2	3	22	55	81
233	208	207	Reviewed	3	28	21	65	65	25
186	172	114	Compiled	7	29	21	37	17	3
37	30	45	Tax Returns	11	14	11	7	2	
271	334	307	Other	14	31	26	72	72	92
4/1/00-3/31/01 ALL	4/1/01-3/31/02 ALL	4/1/02-3/31/03 ALL		\<—159 (4/1-9/30/02)—\>			\<—679 (10/1/02-3/31/03)—\>		
912	903	838	**NUMBER OF STATEMENTS**	37	104	82	203	211	201
%	%	%	**ASSETS**	%	%	%	%	%	%
6.1	5.9	6.4	Cash & Equivalents	9.2	5.4	9.1	7.2	6.0	4.8
26.7	25.5	24.7	Trade Receivables (net)	19.0	26.0	25.0	26.1	25.7	22.7
19.5	19.6	20.8	Inventory	18.8	21.5	22.1	21.4	21.8	18.5
1.9	1.6	2.0	All Other Current	.2	1.4	1.9	1.8	2.3	2.7
54.2	52.5	53.9	Total Current	47.3	54.3	58.0	56.5	55.8	48.7
36.3	37.7	36.3	Fixed Assets (net)	41.4	35.5	33.5	35.5	36.6	37.4
4.0	4.4	4.2	Intangibles (net)	3.0	4.2	1.8	3.7	2.2	8.1
5.5	5.5	5.5	All Other Non-Current	8.3	5.9	6.7	4.2	5.4	5.7
100.0	100.0	100.0	Total	100.0	100.0	100.0	100.0	100.0	100.0
			LIABILITIES						
10.6	10.5	10.4	Notes Payable-Short Term	12.6	12.4	12.5	10.8	10.9	7.1
5.3	6.6	5.7	Cur. Mat.-L/T/D	6.5	6.1	4.9	5.9	5.8	5.4
15.6	14.9	14.6	Trade Payables	11.5	14.6	16.1	14.7	15.1	13.8
.2	.2	.2	Income Taxes Payable	.1	.1	.3	.2	.1	.4
7.8	7.4	8.7	All Other Current	10.6	11.1	9.3	7.7	7.5	9.2
39.4	39.6	39.6	Total Current	41.3	44.2	43.0	39.4	39.4	36.0
19.7	20.8	19.8	Long Term Debt	29.9	21.1	22.7	17.5	18.5	19.8
.6	.7	.7	Deferred Taxes	.1	.6	.2	.6	.5	1.4
4.8	5.5	5.6	All Other Non-Current	10.2	7.5	4.7	5.2	4.1	6.0
35.4	33.4	34.3	Net Worth	18.5	26.6	29.3	37.4	37.5	36.8
100.0	100.0	100.0	Total Liabilities & Net Worth	100.0	100.0	100.0	100.0	100.0	100.0
			INCOME DATA						
100.0	100.0	100.0	Net Sales	100.0	100.0	100.0	100.0	100.0	100.0
27.1	26.6	27.9	Gross Profit	45.0	34.2	29.1	27.7	25.2	24.1
21.9	23.0	23.3	Operating Expenses	44.1	32.5	26.1	22.5	20.0	17.8
5.2	3.6	4.6	Operating Profit	.9	1.7	3.1	5.2	5.2	6.2
1.7	2.0	1.6	All Other Expenses (net)	2.4	1.6	.7	1.4	1.3	2.2
3.5	1.6	3.0	Profit Before Taxes	-1.5	.1	2.3	3.8	3.9	4.0
			RATIOS						
2.2	2.1	2.2	Current	1.9	2.3	2.4	2.4	2.4	2.1
1.4	1.3	1.4		1.4	1.3	1.5	1.4	1.4	1.5
1.0	1.0	1.0		.8	.8	1.0	1.0	1.0	1.0
1.4	1.3	1.4	Quick	1.5	1.2	1.5	1.5	1.5	1.2
.8	.8 (837)	.8		.7	.7 (81)	.9	.8	.8	.8
.5	.5	.5		.4	.4	.5	.5	.5	.6
36 10.1	35 10.5	34 10.8	Sales/Receivables	25 14.8	34 10.6	28 12.9	31 11.6	36 10.2	37 9.8
47 7.7	45 8.1	45 8.1		39 9.3	46 7.9	41 8.9	44 8.3	46 8.0	47 7.8
59 6.2	57 6.4	56 6.5		48 7.6	58 6.2	57 6.4	57 6.5	56 6.6	56 6.5
29 12.7	27 13.3	32 11.3	Cost of Sales/Inventory	13 27.7	33 10.9	30 12.3	30 12.0	33 11.1	34 10.9
45 8.1	46 8.0	49 7.5		39 9.5	53 6.9	48 7.6	47 7.7	47 7.7	48 7.6
67 5.5	66 5.6	72 5.1		104 3.5	99 3.7	73 5.0	69 5.3	71 5.1	71 5.1
20 17.8	20 18.5	21 17.7	Cost of Sales/Payables	17 22.1	16 22.6	18 20.8	19 19.6	19 19.1	25 14.8
34 10.9	31 11.6	34 10.8		31 11.7	39 9.3	32 11.3	31 12.0	34 10.6	35 10.5
49 7.4	48 7.7	47 7.7		71 5.1	57 6.4	47 7.8	46 8.0	46 7.9	46 7.9
6.5	6.8	6.2	Sales/Working Capital	7.4	6.5	5.8	6.3	5.5	6.7
14.0	15.7	13.2		13.6	18.0	12.8	12.1	15.7	12.5
-608.8	-88.4	-324.6		-17.4	-21.9	-353.3	198.7	-153.7	103.6
7.2	5.3	8.1	EBIT/Interest	2.1	4.6	5.4	11.3	8.7	8.8
(845) 2.6	(847) 1.9	(783) 2.9		(28) 1.2	(95) 1.9	(74) 2.3	(192) 3.4	(203) 3.2	(191) 3.4
1.1	.3	1.1		-1.5	-1.7	.0	1.4	1.3	1.5
4.2	3.2	3.9	Net Profit + Depr., Dep., Amort./Cur. Mat. L/T/D		3.0	3.6	3.6	4.1	5.4
(261) 1.9	(250) 1.5	(248) 2.1			(25) 1.9	(12) 1.7	(51) 2.1	(69) 2.0	(88) 2.7
1.0	.6	1.1			.8	1.4	1.0	1.2	1.3
.5	.6	.6	Fixed/Worth	.6	.6	.5	.5	.5	.6
1.2	1.2	1.1		1.5	1.2	1.0	1.0	1.0	1.3
2.4	2.9	2.8		-8.5	8.7	3.9	2.3	2.4	2.7
.9	1.0	.9	Debt/Worth	.7	.8	1.0	.9	.8	.9
2.0	2.0	1.9		1.5	2.8	2.0	1.8	1.8	1.9
5.0	5.7	5.5		-32.9	10.5	13.5	3.7	4.3	5.4
41.7	33.7	40.3	% Profit Before Taxes/Tangible Net Worth	74.4	31.4	40.4	43.5	41.7	36.3
(806) 18.8	(780) 12.1	(722) 16.7		(26) 1.8	(82) 13.3	(68) 9.2	(178) 18.2	(196) 18.8	(172) 19.5
4.5	-2.5	2.9		-17.3	-17.8	-1.4	4.6	4.0	6.9
14.1	10.7	12.7	% Profit Before Taxes/Total Assets	7.2	10.1	13.7	15.8	12.0	12.6
5.6	3.3	5.2		.3	3.6	3.6	5.9	6.1	6.7
.4	-2.7	.2		-9.9	-9.1	-2.5	1.0	.9	1.8
9.7	9.6	10.2	Sales/Net Fixed Assets	10.9	12.7	14.6	10.5	10.6	7.1
5.7	5.4	5.6		5.6	6.3	7.7	5.9	5.8	4.5
3.6	3.2	3.4		2.8	3.2	3.5	3.8	3.3	3.2
2.6	2.6	2.5	Sales/Total Assets	2.6	2.6	2.8	2.7	2.6	2.2
2.0	1.9	1.9		1.9	1.9	2.1	2.1	1.9	1.7
1.5	1.4	1.4		1.1	1.5	1.4	1.6	1.3	1.3
2.0	2.1	2.4	% Depr., Dep., Amort./Sales	4.6	2.4	2.2	2.5	2.2	2.6
(818) 3.5	(809) 3.7	(769) 3.9		(28) 6.3	(94) 3.5	(75) 4.2	(201) 3.9	(198) 3.8	(173) 3.7
5.2	5.4	5.6		11.2	6.3	6.0	5.3	5.5	5.3
2.1	1.8	2.0	% Officers', Directors', Owners' Comp/Sales	1.8	2.6	1.9	2.0	2.0	.8
(318) 3.7	(301) 3.3	(262) 3.7		(14) 8.6	(51) 4.7	(34) 4.5	(75) 3.2	(62) 3.4	(26) 1.4
6.1	6.0	6.8		21.6	9.3	7.4	7.0	4.8	3.7
21899571M	21677401M	21309130M	Net Sales ($)	22877M	209039M	330315M	1479384M	3379022M	15888493M
13811470M	13915511M	13401841M	Total Assets ($)	13738M	122912M	199684M	804573M	1923469M	10337465M

M = $ thousand   MM = $ million
See Pages 11 through 18 for Explanation of Ratios and Data

Current Data Sorted By Assets | Comparative Historical Data

						Type of Statement		
1	2	3	1			Unqualified		1
	1	7	2			Reviewed	13	13
4	10	2	1			Compiled	22	20
1	2					Tax Returns	3	4
	2	3	3			Other	15	8
	5 (4/1-9/30/02)		40 (10/1/02-3/31/03)				4/1/98- 3/31/99	4/1/99- 3/31/00
0-500M	500M-2MM	2-10MM	10-50MM	50-100MM	100-250MM		ALL	ALL
6	17	15	7			NUMBER OF STATEMENTS	53	46
%	%	%	%	%	%	ASSETS	%	%
	3.2	7.8				Cash & Equivalents	6.4	9.6
	23.5	26.4				Trade Receivables (net)	22.8	23.2
	33.5	23.8				Inventory	33.3	31.6
	2.4	3.4				All Other Current	1.3	1.3
	62.6	61.3	D A T A	D A T A		Total Current	63.7	65.8
	28.7	31.9				Fixed Assets (net)	31.1	28.7
	.3	3.2	N O T	N O T		Intangibles (net)	1.3	2.2
	8.3	3.6				All Other Non-Current	3.9	3.3
	100.0	100.0	A V A I L A B L E	A V A I L A B L E		Total	100.0	100.0
						LIABILITIES		
	8.6	8.5				Notes Payable-Short Term	9.4	11.4
	5.7	3.6				Cur. Mat.-L/T/D	5.2	3.9
	30.7	19.7				Trade Payables	30.7	29.3
	.0	.1				Income Taxes Payable	1.6	.3
	15.7	15.4				All Other Current	20.6	7.8
	60.8	47.3				Total Current	67.6	52.7
	17.4	17.8				Long Term Debt	15.6	16.7
	.5	.5				Deferred Taxes	.1	.2
	.1	4.2				All Other Non-Current	4.0	5.0
	21.2	30.2				Net Worth	12.7	25.3
	100.0	100.0				Total Liabilities & Net Worth	100.0	100.0
						INCOME DATA		
	100.0	100.0				Net Sales	100.0	100.0
	31.7	34.5				Gross Profit	38.2	37.4
	31.8	29.8				Operating Expenses	36.4	34.4
	−.1	4.7				Operating Profit	1.9	3.0
	−.7	.3				All Other Expenses (net)	.5	.7
	.7	4.4				Profit Before Taxes	1.3	2.3
						RATIOS		
	1.2	1.6					1.6	1.6
	1.0	1.3				Current	1.3	1.3
	.9	1.1					1.0	1.0
	.7	1.1					.8	.9
	.5	.7				Quick	.5	.7
	.2	.4					.4	.4
17 21.3	31 11.8				Sales/Receivables	16 22.6	9 40.5
36 10.3	38 9.6					27 13.6	33 11.0
45 8.0	47 7.7					41 8.8	49 7.5
37 9.8	33 11.1				Cost of Sales/Inventory	38 9.7	38 9.7
62 5.9	44 8.3					65 5.6	63 5.8
95 3.9	93 3.9					86 4.2	85 4.3
27 13.6	24 15.0				Cost of Sales/Payables	30 12.3	31 11.8
55 6.7	37 9.8					53 6.8	51 7.1
73 5.0	57 6.4					84 4.3	79 4.6
22.5	9.5				Sales/Working Capital	11.4	11.4
−121.5	24.8					20.4	16.4
−50.2	59.5					UND	NM
6.1	7.8				EBIT/Interest	6.0	8.0
2.5	(14) 3.6					(49) 2.8	(42) 3.2
−.3	2.0					1.0	1.1
					Net Profit + Depr., Dep., Amort./Cur. Mat. L /T/D		3.1	3.7
						(14) 2.0	(10) 1.9
						1.2	1.4
.7	.5				Fixed/Worth	.6	.5
1.7	1.3					.9	.8
3.5	2.3					3.2	2.2
1.3	1.5				Debt/Worth	1.3	1.5
5.8	2.8					2.1	2.3
8.5	5.2					6.5	6.8
37.3	90.9				% Profit Before Taxes/Tangible Net Worth	33.8	57.2
(15) 14.7	22.2					(44) 14.6	(41) 17.6
−2.9	8.4					2.3	3.9
9.8	13.5				% Profit Before Taxes/Total Assets	9.9	11.5
3.1	5.9					3.8	5.7
−2.4	2.4					.1	.7
16.8	14.7				Sales/Net Fixed Assets	22.5	29.2
11.5	9.3					11.4	13.0
7.3	4.5					6.0	6.6
3.7	3.3				Sales/Total Assets	3.6	4.0
3.1	2.2					3.1	2.9
2.1	1.8					2.2	2.1
1.4	1.4				% Depr., Dep., Amort./Sales	1.1	1.0
(16) 1.9	2.1					(51) 1.7	(41) 1.9
2.3	2.6					2.6	2.4
					% Officers', Directors', Owners' Comp/Sales	1.6	1.6
						(32) 4.2	(27) 3.4
						7.7	5.7
5487M	58461M	201351M	354808M			Net Sales ($)	426613M	388345M
977M	19506M	76194M	159081M			Total Assets ($)	152471M	153679M

© RMA 2003

M = $ thousand   MM = $ million
See Pages 11 through 18 for Explanation of Ratios and Data

Comparative Historical Data | Current Data Sorted By Sales

						Type of Statement	0-1MM	1-3MM	3-5MM	5-10MM	10-25MM	25MM & OVER
	2		2		7	Unqualified	1	1		3		2
	10		4		10	Reviewed			2	2	4	2
	14		17		17	Compiled	3	6	5		2	1
	6		5		3	Tax Returns	1	1		1		
	10		10		8	Other		1	1	2	2	2
	4/1/00-		4/1/01-		4/1/02-			5 (4/1-9/30/02)			40 (10/1/02-3/31/03)	
	3/31/01		3/31/02		3/31/03							
	ALL		ALL		ALL							
	42		38		45	**NUMBER OF STATEMENTS**	5	9	8	8	8	7
	%		%		%	**ASSETS**	%	%	%	%	%	%
	4.3		5.8		5.2	Cash & Equivalents						
	25.9		23.5		23.9	Trade Receivables (net)						
	30.1		32.8		29.1	Inventory						
	.9		2.3		3.3	All Other Current						
	61.3		64.4		61.5	Total Current						
	31.6		28.8		28.7	Fixed Assets (net)						
	3.4		2.5		4.5	Intangibles (net)						
	3.7		4.3		5.3	All Other Non-Current						
	100.0		100.0		100.0	Total						
						LIABILITIES						
	10.1		16.0		8.7	Notes Payable-Short Term						
	2.9		3.7		5.0	Cur. Mat.-L/T/D						
	33.1		37.0		28.1	Trade Payables						
	.0		.1		.0	Income Taxes Payable						
	14.7		8.8		12.7	All Other Current						
	60.8		65.6		54.6	Total Current						
	26.7		19.6		18.4	Long Term Debt						
	.1		.1		.4	Deferred Taxes						
	6.7		5.4		1.8	All Other Non-Current						
	5.7		9.3		24.8	Net Worth						
	100.0		100.0		100.0	Total Liabilities & Net Worth						
						INCOME DATA						
	100.0		100.0		100.0	Net Sales						
	33.6		34.3		35.8	Gross Profit						
	32.7		31.7		33.2	Operating Expenses						
	1.0		2.6		2.6	Operating Profit						
	.6		.6		.3	All Other Expenses (net)						
	.4		2.0		2.3	Profit Before Taxes						
						RATIOS						
	1.4		1.5		1.5							
	1.1		1.2		1.1	Current						
	.9		.9		1.0							
	.8		.8		.9							
	.5		.5		.5	Quick						
	.3		.3		.3							
15	24.0	12	30.1	11	32.8							
34	10.8	26	13.8	36	10.0	Sales/Receivables						
44	8.2	39	9.4	46	8.0							
31	11.6	33	11.0	34	10.9							
55	6.7	58	6.3	60	6.1	Cost of Sales/Inventory						
88	4.1	84	4.4	88	4.1							
24	15.1	30	12.0	30	12.3							
51	7.2	56	6.6	50	7.3	Cost of Sales/Payables						
89	4.1	91	4.0	69	5.3							
	17.5		12.0		12.4							
	66.1		28.3		42.8	Sales/Working Capital						
	-34.3		-60.9		-88.0							
	7.1		5.1		7.3							
(39)	2.0	(36)	2.3	(43)	3.0	EBIT/Interest						
	.9		.9		1.5							
					2.6	Net Profit + Depr., Dep.,						
				(14)	1.7	Amort./Cur. Mat. L/T/D						
					1.2							
	.7		.6		.6							
	1.4		1.5		1.3	Fixed/Worth						
	10.7		4.2		2.8							
	2.1		2.0		1.8							
	4.0		4.4		3.9	Debt/Worth						
	38.5		10.7		6.5							
	30.1		47.8		61.4	% Profit Before Taxes/Tangible						
(33)	13.5	(30)	21.1	(39)	18.6	Net Worth						
	2.6		1.1		5.2							
	9.9		12.0		10.3	% Profit Before Taxes/Total						
	1.8		3.9		3.9	Assets						
	-.3		-.5		1.2							
	20.8		26.2		20.3							
	15.0		13.2		11.3	Sales/Net Fixed Assets						
	4.8		6.8		6.3							
	4.1		4.3		3.5							
	2.8		3.1		2.7	Sales/Total Assets						
	2.0		2.2		2.1							
	.9		1.0		1.4							
(39)	1.9	(36)	1.6	(41)	2.1	% Depr., Dep., Amort./Sales						
	2.5		2.5		2.7							
	1.3		.7		.7							
(18)	3.5	(22)	1.3	(21)	2.3	% Officers', Directors',						
	6.1		5.5		4.2	Owners' Comp/Sales						
	487797M		785280M		620107M	Net Sales ($)	3260M	20105M	31663M	57801M	130876M	376402M
	174263M		305475M		255758M	Total Assets ($)	1486M	6981M	12446M	23381M	68451M	143013M

M = $ thousand   MM = $ million
See Pages 11 through 18 for Explanation of Ratios and Data

Current Data Sorted By Assets   Comparative Historical Data

						Type of Statement		
	1	4	3		1	Unqualified		
	1	2				Reviewed		
1	2	4				Compiled		
1				5		Tax Returns		
1		3				Other		
	6 (4/1-9/30/02)			25 (10/1/02-3/31/03)			4/1/98-3/31/99	4/1/99-3/31/00
0-500M	500M-2MM	2-10MM	10-50MM	50-100MM	100-250MM		ALL	ALL
3	6	13	8		1	NUMBER OF STATEMENTS		
%	%	%	%	%	%	ASSETS	%	%
		8.8				Cash & Equivalents		
		27.2				Trade Receivables (net)		
		28.0		D		Inventory	D	D
		1.1		A		All Other Current	A	A
		65.0		T		Total Current	T	T
		27.5		A		Fixed Assets (net)	A	A
		4.8				Intangibles (net)		
		2.7		N		All Other Non-Current	N	N
		100.0		O		Total	O	O
				T		LIABILITIES	T	T
		7.6				Notes Payable-Short Term		
		2.3		A		Cur. Mat.-L/T/D	A	A
		13.3		V		Trade Payables	V	V
		.1		A		Income Taxes Payable	A	A
		5.7		I		All Other Current	I	I
		29.1		L		Total Current	L	L
		16.5		A		Long Term Debt	A	A
		.4		B		Deferred Taxes	B	B
		3.3		L		All Other Non-Current	L	L
		50.7		E		Net Worth	E	E
		100.0				Total Liabilities & Net Worth		
						INCOME DATA		
		100.0				Net Sales		
		30.6				Gross Profit		
		24.2				Operating Expenses		
		6.4				Operating Profit		
		1.1				All Other Expenses (net)		
		5.3				Profit Before Taxes		
						RATIOS		
		7.5						
		2.5				Current		
		1.6						
		4.0						
		1.6				Quick		
		1.0						
	38	9.7						
	42	8.7				Sales/Receivables		
	52	7.0						
	38	9.6						
	52	7.0				Cost of Sales/Inventory		
	154	2.4						
	14	26.0						
	20	18.0				Cost of Sales/Payables		
	38	9.6						
		2.8						
		7.3				Sales/Working Capital		
		9.8						
		14.1						
	(11)	4.1				EBIT/Interest		
		2.3						
						Net Profit + Depr., Dep., Amort./Cur. Mat. L /T/D		
		.2						
		.5				Fixed/Worth		
		2.4						
		.2						
		.6				Debt/Worth		
		5.0						
		25.7				% Profit Before Taxes/Tangible		
	(11)	20.4				Net Worth		
		8.1						
		15.1						
		5.4				% Profit Before Taxes/Total		
		2.5				Assets		
		32.6						
		5.4				Sales/Net Fixed Assets		
		3.1						
		2.6						
		1.9				Sales/Total Assets		
		1.3						
		.9						
		2.8				% Depr., Dep., Amort./Sales		
		5.1						
						% Officers', Directors', Owners' Comp/Sales		
2251M	23210M	165919M	261311M		265300M	Net Sales ($)		
777M	9660M	78440M	154698M		192654M	Total Assets ($)		

© RMA 2003

M = $ thousand   MM = $ million
See Pages 11 through 18 for Explanation of Ratios and Data

Comparative Historical Data / Current Data Sorted By Sales

4/1/00-3/31/01 ALL	4/1/01-3/31/02 ALL	4/1/02-3/31/03 ALL	Type of Statement	0-1MM	1-3MM	3-5MM	5-10MM	10-25MM	25MM & OVER
3	5	9	Unqualified			2	1	3	3
3	5	3	Reviewed			1	1	1	
6	6	7	Compiled		1	3	1	1	
1		1	Tax Returns	1					
17	6	11	Other	1	1	1	1	6	1
				6 (4/1-9/30/02)			25 (10/1/02-3/31/03)		
30	22	31	NUMBER OF STATEMENTS	2	2	7	4	11	5
%	%	%	ASSETS	%	%	%	%	%	%
7.9	6.3	9.3	Cash & Equivalents					5.5	
31.7	28.5	24.0	Trade Receivables (net)					24.0	
27.4	31.0	26.3	Inventory					26.1	
2.3	.9	1.0	All Other Current					1.2	
69.1	66.6	60.5	Total Current					56.8	
23.7	24.5	28.9	Fixed Assets (net)					27.0	
.4	1.5	4.9	Intangibles (net)					7.0	
6.8	7.5	5.7	All Other Non-Current					9.2	
100.0	100.0	100.0	Total					100.0	
			LIABILITIES						
10.6	13.5	5.7	Notes Payable-Short Term					6.0	
3.2	5.0	3.9	Cur. Mat.-L/T/D					1.8	
17.7	13.8	12.9	Trade Payables					12.5	
.6	.2	.4	Income Taxes Payable					1.0	
10.2	14.4	18.1	All Other Current					6.1	
42.4	46.8	41.0	Total Current					27.3	
14.5	25.1	21.9	Long Term Debt					18.4	
.5	.8	.3	Deferred Taxes					.7	
.7	1.2	7.1	All Other Non-Current					4.5	
42.0	26.0	29.7	Net Worth					49.1	
100.0	100.0	100.0	Total Liabilities & Net Worth					100.0	
			INCOME DATA						
100.0	100.0	100.0	Net Sales					100.0	
30.5	29.9	32.8	Gross Profit					33.6	
25.0	26.6	26.6	Operating Expenses					26.0	
5.4	3.3	6.2	Operating Profit					7.6	
1.0	2.2	1.9	All Other Expenses (net)					1.6	
4.4	1.1	4.3	Profit Before Taxes					6.0	
			RATIOS						
2.8	2.4	5.1	Current					5.2	
1.8	1.6	2.1						2.1	
1.1	1.3	1.2						1.2	
1.6	1.2	2.5	Quick					2.5	
1.0	1.0	1.4						1.4	
.6	.6	.7						.6	
43 8.5	35 10.4	38 9.7	Sales/Receivables					45 8.2	
49 7.4	45 8.1	46 7.9						48 7.7	
56 6.5	50 7.4	51 7.1						59 6.2	
37 9.9	42 8.7	36 10.1	Cost of Sales/Inventory					45 8.1	
64 5.7	61 6.0	56 6.5						68 5.3	
101 3.6	105 3.5	85 4.3						132 2.8	
23 15.9	15 25.0	16 22.1	Cost of Sales/Payables					14 25.5	
32 11.3	25 14.8	27 13.3						29 12.8	
51 7.1	38 9.5	44 8.3						48 7.5	
4.2	5.2	3.6	Sales/Working Capital					3.6	
7.4	9.2	7.9						7.3	
46.7	20.6	29.1						14.7	
(29) 19.2	(19) 6.3	(28) 9.1	EBIT/Interest					(10) 17.7	
4.0	2.5	4.4						4.1	
1.8	1.0	2.2						2.0	
			Net Profit + Depr., Dep., Amort./Cur. Mat. L/T/D						
.2	.1	.3	Fixed/Worth					.3	
.5	.5	.7						.5	
1.3	2.3	2.8						−79.2	
.7	.6	.3	Debt/Worth					.4	
1.4	1.2	1.0						.6	
3.1	3.0	5.2						−217.8	
35.6	36.2	43.2	% Profit Before Taxes/Tangible Net Worth						
25.3	(20) 9.7	(25) 12.1							
8.4	.5	4.3							
18.8	11.3	17.4	% Profit Before Taxes/Total Assets					15.0	
7.3	4.4	6.6						6.9	
3.2	−.5	2.0						2.3	
34.2	37.1	17.0	Sales/Net Fixed Assets					17.0	
11.2	17.8	6.5						7.8	
5.0	4.1	4.1						4.5	
2.8	3.0	2.7	Sales/Total Assets					2.1	
2.3	2.4	1.9						1.8	
1.7	1.5	1.3						1.1	
(28) .9	(21) .5	(30) 1.1	% Depr., Dep., Amort./Sales					(10) 1.2	
1.6	1.2	2.6						2.9	
3.3	2.9	5.1						4.7	
(13) 2.4			% Officers', Directors', Owners' Comp/Sales						
4.0									
8.0									
736549M	412017M	717991M	Net Sales ($)	1176M	3965M	27528M	32742M	195248M	457332M
335566M	200074M	436229M	Total Assets ($)	693M	1287M	14004M	23412M	131219M	265614M

© RMA 2003

M = $ thousand   MM = $ million

See Pages 11 through 18 for Explanation of Ratios and Data

Current Data Sorted By Assets   Comparative Historical Data

0-500M	500M-2MM	2-10MM	10-50MM	50-100MM	100-250MM	Type of Statement	4/1/98-3/31/99 ALL	4/1/99-3/31/00 ALL
		2	1			Unqualified		6
	1	1	3			Reviewed		5
	5	3				Compiled		7
2	1					Tax Returns		1
2	7	2	1	2		Other		10
	2 (4/1-9/30/02)		28 (10/1/02-3/31/03)					
4	14	8	2	2		NUMBER OF STATEMENTS		29
%	%	%	%	%	%	ASSETS	%	%
	7.3				D	Cash & Equivalents	D	8.6
	36.3				A	Trade Receivables (net)	A	28.8
	18.6				T	Inventory	T	18.8
	3.0				A	All Other Current	A	2.6
	65.2					Total Current		58.7
	29.1				N	Fixed Assets (net)	N	31.9
	.5				O	Intangibles (net)	O	5.4
	5.2				T	All Other Non-Current	T	4.0
	100.0					Total		100.0
					A	LIABILITIES	A	
	9.7				V	Notes Payable-Short Term	V	20.1
	6.9				A	Cur. Mat.-L/T/D	A	4.1
	19.3				I	Trade Payables	I	18.4
	.1				L	Income Taxes Payable	L	.2
	13.0				A	All Other Current	A	12.1
	49.1				B	Total Current	B	54.9
	15.0				L	Long Term Debt	L	20.5
	.1				E	Deferred Taxes	E	.4
	11.0					All Other Non-Current		12.1
	24.9					Net Worth		12.1
	100.0					Total Liabilities & Net Worth		100.0
						INCOME DATA		
	100.0					Net Sales		100.0
	32.7					Gross Profit		28.6
	29.6					Operating Expenses		23.7
	3.2					Operating Profit		4.9
	.9					All Other Expenses (net)		1.3
	2.2					Profit Before Taxes		3.6
						RATIOS		
	2.0 / 1.3 / .9					Current		2.0 / 1.5 / 1.0
	1.2 / 1.0 / .6					Quick		1.4 / .9 / .6
	(29) 12.6 / (47) 7.7 / (66) 5.6					Sales/Receivables		(27) 13.5 / (44) 8.3 / (58) 6.3
	(26) 14.1 / (31) 11.6 / (49) 7.4					Cost of Sales/Inventory		(18) 20.6 / (31) 11.8 / (50) 7.3
	(20) 18.6 / (31) 12.0 / (44) 8.3					Cost of Sales/Payables		(21) 17.1 / (30) 12.1 / (42) 8.7
	10.0 / 26.1 / -50.9					Sales/Working Capital		9.0 / 13.3 / NM
	10.8 / 4.4 / .5					EBIT/Interest		(27) 9.0 / 4.2 / 1.2
						Net Profit + Depr., Dep., Amort./Cur. Mat. L/T/D		
	.4 / 1.2 / NM					Fixed/Worth		.5 / 1.2 / NM
	1.4 / 4.4 / NM					Debt/Worth		1.2 / 1.8 / -485.8
	(11) 69.2 / 21.8 / 6.5					% Profit Before Taxes/Tangible Net Worth		(21) 33.6 / 14.5 / .7
	13.3 / 7.6 / -2.6					% Profit Before Taxes/Total Assets		18.4 / 7.4 / .3
	28.1 / 13.5 / 3.8					Sales/Net Fixed Assets		24.3 / 8.0 / 4.1
	4.0 / 3.1 / 2.0					Sales/Total Assets		3.4 / 2.6 / 1.7
	(13) .8 / 1.4 / 7.3					% Depr., Dep., Amort./Sales		(24) 1.0 / 2.3 / 3.7
	(11) 2.7 / 6.0 / 9.3					% Officers', Directors', Owners' Comp/Sales		(10) 3.9 / 7.3 / 14.8
5994M	48189M	48572M	102726M	147737M		Net Sales ($)		906433M
1443M	14550M	23594M	47585M	123306M		Total Assets ($)		568866M

M = $ thousand   MM = $ million
See Pages 11 through 18 for Explanation of Ratios and Data

Comparative Historical Data				Current Data Sorted By Sales					
			Type of Statement						
7	2	3	Unqualified				2		1
5	6	2	Reviewed		2				
7	6	8	Compiled	1	1	2	3	1	
2	1	3	Tax Returns		2		1		
11	10	14	Other	2	4	3	2		3
4/1/00- 3/31/01	4/1/01- 3/31/02	4/1/02- 3/31/03			2 (4/1-9/30/02)		28 (10/1/02-3/31/03)		
ALL	ALL	ALL		0-1MM	1-3MM	3-5MM	5-10MM	10-25MM	25MM & OVER
32	25	30	**NUMBER OF STATEMENTS**	3	9	5	8	1	4
%	%	%	**ASSETS**	%	%	%	%	%	%
10.1	8.4	8.2	Cash & Equivalents						
28.3	27.3	34.2	Trade Receivables (net)						
17.4	16.7	19.0	Inventory						
2.8	4.5	3.0	All Other Current						
58.6	56.9	64.3	Total Current						
30.8	32.8	30.3	Fixed Assets (net)						
5.8	3.0	.5	Intangibles (net)						
4.8	7.2	5.0	All Other Non-Current						
100.0	100.0	100.0	Total						
			LIABILITIES						
9.3	9.5	9.1	Notes Payable-Short Term						
2.8	4.9	6.5	Cur. Mat.-L/T/D						
14.1	16.6	17.5	Trade Payables						
.2	.4	.1	Income Taxes Payable						
8.8	10.1	8.9	All Other Current						
35.1	41.5	42.0	Total Current						
13.9	26.8	18.1	Long Term Debt						
.5	.9	.3	Deferred Taxes						
4.4	4.9	6.8	All Other Non-Current						
46.1	26.0	32.8	Net Worth						
100.0	100.0	100.0	Total Liabilities & Net Worth						
			INCOME DATA						
100.0	100.0	100.0	Net Sales						
30.0	37.0	32.3	Gross Profit						
25.0	34.1	27.9	Operating Expenses						
5.0	2.9	4.4	Operating Profit						
.6	2.2	1.2	All Other Expenses (net)						
4.3	.7	3.2	Profit Before Taxes						
			RATIOS						
3.0	2.8	2.6							
2.0	1.4	1.6	Current						
1.1	.8	1.0							
2.0	2.1	1.5							
1.4	.9	1.0	Quick						
.7	.5	.8							
30 12.3	34 10.7	36 10.3							
41 9.0	49 7.4	47 7.7	Sales/Receivables						
51 7.1	56 6.5	65 5.6							
22 16.8	22 16.2	26 14.0							
32 11.4	39 9.4	36 10.0	Cost of Sales/Inventory						
61 5.9	64 5.7	49 7.4							
17 20.9	27 13.3	20 18.5							
26 13.8	35 10.5	37 9.9	Cost of Sales/Payables						
33 10.9	59 6.2	50 7.3							
5.7	7.9	6.0							
9.7	15.4	12.4	Sales/Working Capital						
56.9	−38.8	−810.1							
13.2	9.9	7.8							
(27) 3.4	(24) 2.5	(26) 2.4	EBIT/Interest						
1.5	−2.4	.7							
			Net Profit + Depr., Dep., Amort./Cur. Mat. L/T/D						
.3	.4	.4							
.7	1.2	1.2	Fixed/Worth						
2.5	NM	2.4							
.4	1.7	.7							
1.1	2.7	3.0	Debt/Worth						
6.2	NM	5.9							
28.1	72.7	69.2	% Profit Before Taxes/Tangible						
(27) 12.4	(19) 26.0	(27) 14.5	Net Worth						
3.4	−36.2	6.2							
19.2	22.3	13.3	% Profit Before Taxes/Total						
5.3	7.6	5.9	Assets						
1.4	−13.2	1.6							
16.2	14.4	22.4							
8.4	7.9	10.0	Sales/Net Fixed Assets						
4.9	3.1	3.7							
3.2	2.9	3.4							
2.2	1.9	2.7	Sales/Total Assets						
1.7	1.5	1.9							
1.2	.9	1.1							
(30) 2.2	(23) 2.5	(28) 2.5	% Depr., Dep., Amort./Sales						
4.6	4.1	5.7							
2.7	3.7	2.6							
(15) 5.3	(12) 5.0	(17) 5.1	% Officers', Directors', Owners' Comp/Sales						
9.7	10.1	6.8							
752951M	194380M	353218M	Net Sales ($)	1947M	17537M	21362M	51780M	10129M	250463M
407029M	126145M	210478M	Total Assets ($)	1558M	7684M	6039M	22391M	1915M	170891M

M = $ thousand   MM = $ million
See Pages 11 through 18 for Explanation of Ratios and Data

Current Data Sorted By Assets   Comparative Historical Data

0-500M	500M-2MM	2-10MM	10-50MM	50-100MM	100-250MM	Type of Statement	4/1/98-3/31/99 ALL	4/1/99-3/31/00 ALL
1	1	10	10	2	3	Unqualified	30	31
	7	22	3			Reviewed	41	40
	5	8	2			Compiled	24	29
1	3	2	8			Tax Returns	4	8
1	8	8	15	3	2	Other	39	42
	32 (4/1-9/30/02)			83 (10/1/02-3/31/03)				
3	24	50	28	5	5	**NUMBER OF STATEMENTS**	138	150
%	%	%	%	%	%	**ASSETS**	%	%
	9.3	7.2	6.0			Cash & Equivalents	8.2	7.4
	29.1	23.4	19.3			Trade Receivables (net)	26.6	27.2
	18.3	24.4	20.1			Inventory	20.1	22.0
	5.2	2.0	1.7			All Other Current	1.3	1.3
	61.9	57.0	47.1			Total Current	56.3	57.9
	31.9	36.9	40.4			Fixed Assets (net)	33.3	31.0
	2.8	1.9	7.8			Intangibles (net)	4.0	4.7
	3.4	4.2	4.6			All Other Non-Current	6.4	6.4
	100.0	100.0	100.0			Total	100.0	100.0
						LIABILITIES		
	12.4	9.2	8.3			Notes Payable-Short Term	11.0	9.5
	5.4	5.7	3.6			Cur. Mat.-L/T/D	4.6	5.0
	16.3	12.7	8.7			Trade Payables	12.9	14.0
	.5	.1	.3			Income Taxes Payable	.1	.4
	12.7	10.6	6.9			All Other Current	8.5	8.9
	47.3	38.4	27.8			Total Current	37.2	37.8
	18.4	18.7	20.1			Long Term Debt	19.2	19.1
	.2	.7	1.7			Deferred Taxes	.9	.6
	5.9	2.7	8.0			All Other Non-Current	7.4	5.6
	28.2	39.6	42.3			Net Worth	35.4	37.0
	100.0	100.0	100.0			Total Liabilities & Net Worth	100.0	100.0
						INCOME DATA		
	100.0	100.0	100.0			Net Sales	100.0	100.0
	33.5	27.7	27.5			Gross Profit	29.2	31.0
	30.4	24.2	21.4			Operating Expenses	25.2	25.2
	3.2	3.5	6.1			Operating Profit	4.0	5.8
	.6	1.4	1.4			All Other Expenses (net)	1.2	.6
	2.6	2.1	4.6			Profit Before Taxes	2.8	5.1
						RATIOS		
	2.6	3.3	3.0				2.8	2.6
	1.2	1.7	1.7			Current	1.7	1.6
	.9	.9	1.1				1.1	1.1
	1.8	1.9	1.7				1.8	1.5
	.8	1.0	.8			Quick	1.0	.9
	.6	.4	.5				.6	.6
36 10.0	31 11.8	39 9.4					34 10.7	38 9.7
43 8.6	43 8.5	46 7.9				Sales/Receivables	44 8.2	47 7.8
60 6.1	56 6.5	58 6.3					53 6.9	57 6.4
20 17.9	32 11.4	48 7.7					27 13.4	29 12.5
31 11.6	55 6.7	60 6.1				Cost of Sales/Inventory	42 8.8	49 7.5
87 4.2	84 4.3	75 4.9					69 5.3	96 3.8
11 31.9	17 21.6	20 18.4					15 24.6	21 17.6
31 11.9	27 13.6	26 13.9				Cost of Sales/Payables	25 14.4	33 10.9
48 7.6	45 8.2	34 10.8					41 8.9	48 7.6
	6.4	4.4	5.2				5.9	5.5
	27.1	10.1	9.2			Sales/Working Capital	10.2	10.2
	−49.3	−54.6	44.7				43.2	63.8
	5.4	9.5	13.3				6.3	7.5
(21)	1.8 (46)	4.5 (26)	2.5			EBIT/Interest	(127) 3.0	(130) 3.4
	1.2	1.4	.9				1.7	1.4
		6.3	3.3				5.0	4.3
	(17)	4.0 (12)	1.9			Net Profit + Depr., Dep., Amort./Cur. Mat. L/T/D	(52) 2.5	(42) 2.3
		1.2	.6				1.3	1.0
	.6	.4	.5				.4	.4
	1.1	.9	1.0			Fixed/Worth	.9	.9
	4.4	2.3	3.5				2.3	2.7
	1.0	.6	.7				.6	.6
	2.4	1.4	1.5			Debt/Worth	1.4	1.8
	10.9	5.6	4.0				6.4	6.6
	40.0	41.0	33.7				33.2	45.9
(19)	25.2 (45)	19.6 (24)	19.7			% Profit Before Taxes/Tangible Net Worth	(115) 17.4	(126) 21.4
	5.0	6.2	.5				6.3	7.0
	8.6	14.0	14.5				14.0	18.0
	4.0	5.1	5.7			% Profit Before Taxes/Total Assets	6.9	7.9
	.7	.0	.0				2.6	1.7
	20.1	13.4	7.2				12.1	14.2
	7.6	6.6	3.8			Sales/Net Fixed Assets	6.6	6.7
	4.7	3.2	2.1				3.5	3.9
	3.0	2.8	1.8				2.9	2.9
	2.3	1.9	1.5			Sales/Total Assets	2.0	1.9
	1.8	1.4	1.2				1.5	1.4
	1.0	1.7	3.3				1.7	1.3
(22)	2.6 (48)	2.9 (25)	4.3			% Depr., Dep., Amort./Sales	(124) 2.7	(135) 2.6
	5.1	4.2	5.1				4.0	4.4
	3.2	1.8					2.0	2.7
(13)	6.5 (21)	4.1				% Officers', Directors', Owners' Comp/Sales	(43) 4.1	(41) 4.2
	8.5	7.5					7.9	7.5
2740M	74098M	478994M	1160727M	550575M	831110M	Net Sales ($)	2927449M	2997405M
1104M	29313M	234870M	766500M	321486M	734670M	Total Assets ($)	1979125M	2073938M

© RMA 2003

M = $ thousand   MM = $ million
See Pages 11 through 18 for Explanation of Ratios and Data

Comparative Historical Data / Current Data Sorted By Sales

					Type of Statement						
	27		32	27	Unqualified	2		2	5	5	13
	40		28	32	Reviewed		4	4	10	10	4
	26		24	13	Compiled		3	4	5	1	
	2		5	6	Tax Returns	1	1	2		2	
	41		63	37	Other		7	4	3	8	15
	4/1/00-3/31/01		4/1/01-3/31/02	4/1/02-3/31/03			32 (4/1-9/30/02)			83 (10/1/02-3/31/03)	
	ALL		ALL	ALL		0-1MM	1-3MM	3-5MM	5-10MM	10-25MM	25MM & OVER
	136		152	115	NUMBER OF STATEMENTS	3	15	16	23	26	32
	%		%	%	ASSETS	%	%	%	%	%	%
	7.8		8.4	7.6	Cash & Equivalents		6.4	7.5	9.7	5.2	8.1
	24.3		26.6	23.3	Trade Receivables (net)		23.3	27.1	22.6	23.5	21.9
	24.2		23.4	21.6	Inventory		23.2	18.4	21.5	22.5	21.6
	1.8		1.7	2.7	All Other Current		5.7	2.4	3.1	1.6	2.1
	58.2		60.0	55.2	Total Current		58.6	55.3	56.9	52.8	53.7
	29.9		29.0	36.5	Fixed Assets (net)		32.8	36.2	36.5	40.7	35.5
	5.5		3.9	3.7	Intangibles (net)		4.4	3.2	1.8	4.9	4.5
	6.5		7.0	4.5	All Other Non-Current		4.2	5.4	4.8	1.6	6.3
	100.0		100.0	100.0	Total		100.0	100.0	100.0	100.0	100.0
					LIABILITIES						
	11.1		11.9	9.4	Notes Payable-Short Term		13.4	9.3	11.0	9.1	7.4
	4.2		5.0	4.8	Cur. Mat.-L/T/D		6.1	4.5	6.9	3.3	4.2
	11.5		13.9	12.7	Trade Payables		12.7	11.7	13.8	14.4	11.7
	.2		.2	.3	Income Taxes Payable		.2	.2	.5	.1	.4
	10.0		7.0	9.9	All Other Current		23.0	8.4	9.5	6.5	7.5
	37.1		38.0	37.0	Total Current		55.4	34.1	41.7	33.3	31.2
	17.1		16.2	18.2	Long Term Debt		26.8	16.7	17.7	20.3	14.4
	.7		.5	.9	Deferred Taxes		.3	.8	.4	1.0	1.5
	4.0		4.5	5.3	All Other Non-Current		4.8	8.8	3.6	4.8	5.8
	41.1		40.8	38.6	Net Worth		12.7	39.6	36.7	40.6	47.0
	100.0		100.0	100.0	Total Liabilities & Net Worth		100.0	100.0	100.0	100.0	100.0
					INCOME DATA						
	100.0		100.0	100.0	Net Sales		100.0	100.0	100.0	100.0	100.0
	28.9		31.7	29.5	Gross Profit		40.3	31.9	26.0	25.4	27.3
	23.7		26.7	25.5	Operating Expenses		40.1	28.7	22.0	20.1	21.9
	5.2		5.1	4.1	Operating Profit		.2	3.3	4.0	5.3	5.4
	1.9		1.6	1.2	All Other Expenses (net)		1.1	.2	2.2	1.6	.8
	3.3		3.5	2.9	Profit Before Taxes		−.9	3.1	1.7	3.7	4.6
					RATIOS						
	2.8		2.9	3.1			1.6	3.2	3.2	2.3	3.2
	1.5		1.6	1.7	Current		1.0	2.0	1.8	1.6	1.7
	1.1		1.1	1.0			.7	1.1	.7	1.1	1.2
	1.5		1.8	1.8			1.0	2.1	1.7	1.4	2.1
	.7		.9	.9	Quick		.6	1.5	1.0	.7	.9
	.5		.6	.5			.4	.6	.4	.5	.5
34	10.6	36	10.1	33 10.9	Sales/Receivables	32 11.4	40 9.2	28 13.0	31 11.8	37 9.8	
44	8.4	45	8.1	43 8.4		42 8.7	48 7.6	38 9.6	45 8.1	45 8.2	
53	6.9	59	6.2	58 6.3		61 6.0	59 6.2	51 7.2	56 6.5	59 6.2	
30	12.0	31	11.9	32 11.5	Cost of Sales/Inventory	20 17.8	26 14.2	29 12.7	32 11.3	41 8.8	
55	6.6	50	7.3	56 6.5		49 7.5	36 10.0	39 9.3	58 6.3	66 5.5	
90	4.1	93	3.9	83 4.4		112 3.3	64 5.7	73 5.0	84 4.3	87 4.2	
15	24.1	18	19.8	18 19.8	Cost of Sales/Payables	7 51.0	17 21.6	18 20.6	20 18.2	19 19.0	
28	13.1	29	12.6	28 12.9		32 11.3	30 12.0	29 12.8	30 12.0	26 13.9	
39	9.3	43	8.5	40 9.0		47 7.8	49 7.5	39 9.4	45 8.1	36 10.2	
	5.4		4.4	5.1	Sales/Working Capital		5.7	5.6	4.0	6.1	4.3
	9.3		9.8	9.8			−211.7	9.3	10.5	10.1	8.3
	44.4		132.0	−211.7			−8.2	22.8	−11.4	50.5	43.2
	6.0		5.8	8.1	EBIT/Interest		1.8	7.8	16.0	7.6	17.3
(116)	2.7	(134)	2.3	(103) 2.9		(12) 1.4	(15) 3.2	(20) 4.7	(25) 2.9	(28) 4.2	
	.9		1.1	1.1			−2.7	1.5	1.2	1.4	1.0
	9.8		4.8	4.3	Net Profit + Depr., Dep., Amort./Cur. Mat. L/T/D					7.0	
(43)	2.7	(50)	2.5	(44) 2.2					(17) 2.1	
	1.2		1.0	1.3						1.3	
	.5		.4	.5	Fixed/Worth		.4	.6	.5	.6	.4
	.8		.8	.9			3.9	.9	1.0	1.1	.8
	2.0		2.1	2.4			−.9	1.6	3.4	2.3	1.5
	.6		.6	.6	Debt/Worth		2.0	.9	.5	.7	.5
	1.5		1.4	1.6			9.1	1.3	2.2	2.0	1.0
	4.4		4.3	5.9			−26.0	5.9	6.1	3.8	2.3
	43.6		36.2	36.4	% Profit Before Taxes/Tangible Net Worth		52.7	33.1	41.3	33.3	33.8
(118)	12.6	(134)	12.9	(99) 17.1		(10) 35.6	(14) 10.9	(19) 22.1	(24) 22.4	(29) 13.1	
	2.3		1.5	3.4			−.8	4.3	9.0	2.4	2.1
	15.9		12.4	12.6	% Profit Before Taxes/Total Assets		6.1	12.3	19.1	13.2	17.3
	4.7		4.4	4.3			2.4	4.6	6.9	5.9	4.2
	−.7		.3	.2			−11.3	3.0	−1.6	.5	.1
	14.2		16.2	11.1	Sales/Net Fixed Assets		20.0	13.2	21.7	9.9	7.3
	7.5		8.2	5.3			6.1	5.4	6.7	5.8	4.5
	4.3		4.7	3.0			4.5	3.4	2.8	2.6	3.0
	2.6		2.9	2.5	Sales/Total Assets		3.0	2.5	2.9	2.3	1.9
	2.2		2.1	1.8			1.9	1.9	2.0	2.0	1.6
	1.5		1.4	1.3			1.3	1.2	1.4	1.4	1.2
	1.5		1.6	1.8	% Depr., Dep., Amort./Sales		.6	1.2	1.0	2.1	2.6
(122)	2.8	(145)	3.0	(105) 3.4		(13) 3.2	2.4	2.7	(22) 3.0	(29) 3.7	
	4.2		4.1	4.8			6.0	4.7	5.1	4.6	4.8
	1.9		2.4	1.9	% Officers', Directors', Owners' Comp/Sales				2.3		
(32)	3.7	(43)	4.7	(40) 4.8					(13) 4.3		
	7.9		8.3	8.0					6.5		
2637949M		4014413M		3098244M	Net Sales ($)	1785M	29221M	61502M	164450M	383181M	2458105M
1689788M		2523090M		2087943M	Total Assets ($)	1329M	18994M	36516M	83833M	250680M	1696591M

M = $ thousand   MM = $ million
See Pages 11 through 18 for Explanation of Ratios and Data

Current Data Sorted By Assets							Comparative Historical Data	

						Type of Statement		
		2	8	3	1	Unqualified	14	16
		3	3			Reviewed	8	5
		1	1			Compiled	7	4
						Tax Returns	1	
1	1	3	4	2		Other	13	8
							4/1/98-	4/1/99-
	8 (4/1-9/30/02)		25 (10/1/02-3/31/03)				3/31/99	3/31/00
0-500M	500M-2MM	2-10MM	10-50MM	50-100MM	100-250MM		ALL	ALL
1	1	9	16	5	1	NUMBER OF STATEMENTS	43	33
%	%	%	%	%	%	ASSETS	%	%
			8.9			Cash & Equivalents	10.1	12.1
			10.1			Trade Receivables (net)	18.4	17.7
			14.9			Inventory	20.3	20.6
			1.6			All Other Current	.9	3.3
			35.5			Total Current	49.7	53.8
			55.6			Fixed Assets (net)	40.8	35.2
			1.1			Intangibles (net)	2.3	2.2
			7.8			All Other Non-Current	7.2	8.8
			100.0			Total	100.0	100.0
						LIABILITIES		
			3.7			Notes Payable-Short Term	5.9	5.0
			3.7			Cur. Mat.-L/T/D	3.6	3.3
			4.5			Trade Payables	9.1	7.9
			.3			Income Taxes Payable	.3	.3
			3.2			All Other Current	6.1	9.9
			15.5			Total Current	25.1	26.3
			34.0			Long Term Debt	21.0	20.2
			3.2			Deferred Taxes	.6	1.1
			1.3			All Other Non-Current	5.3	2.4
			46.0			Net Worth	48.0	49.9
			100.0			Total Liabilities & Net Worth	100.0	100.0
						INCOME DATA		
			100.0			Net Sales	100.0	100.0
			36.3			Gross Profit	30.3	34.4
			23.8			Operating Expenses	22.8	22.1
			12.5			Operating Profit	7.5	12.3
			2.7			All Other Expenses (net)	1.3	.4
			9.8			Profit Before Taxes	6.2	11.9
						RATIOS		
			3.6				3.6	4.2
			2.4			Current	2.8	2.5
			1.6				1.3	1.5
			1.9				2.2	2.4
			1.2			Quick	1.3	1.5
			.6				.8	.7
		25	14.4				39 9.2	36 10.1
		37	9.8			Sales/Receivables	46 7.9	45 8.1
		54	6.7				54 6.8	52 7.0
		50	7.3				42 8.6	42 8.8
		88	4.1			Cost of Sales/Inventory	76 4.8	67 5.4
		128	2.9				132 2.8	123 3.0
		16	22.6				20 18.4	20 18.5
		22	16.8			Cost of Sales/Payables	29 12.6	30 12.3
		40	9.1				41 8.8	38 9.7
			2.9				3.1	3.0
			4.5			Sales/Working Capital	5.1	4.6
			7.2				14.5	10.9
			8.5				11.6	53.0
		(15)	5.0			EBIT/Interest	(39) 4.0	(29) 8.8
			2.0				1.5	3.6
						Net Profit + Depr., Dep.,	5.4	28.0
						Amort./Cur. Mat. L/T/D	(12) 3.5	(12) 3.1
							2.5	2.4
			.7				.5	.5
			1.5			Fixed/Worth	.8	.8
			2.6				1.4	1.3
			.4				.6	.4
			1.6			Debt/Worth	.9	.9
			2.6				3.3	2.4
			31.0			% Profit Before Taxes/Tangible	32.1	42.5
			19.6			Net Worth	(40) 20.4	(30) 27.1
			6.6				5.2	17.9
			14.9			% Profit Before Taxes/Total	15.8	19.9
			8.0			Assets	8.2	14.0
			2.6				1.1	7.6
			2.6				4.8	5.4
			1.4			Sales/Net Fixed Assets	3.1	3.5
			1.2				1.7	2.1
			1.0				1.6	1.7
			.9			Sales/Total Assets	1.2	1.3
			.7				.8	.9
			5.3				3.0	2.4
			7.3			% Depr., Dep., Amort./Sales	(37) 5.2	(30) 4.0
			10.0				7.8	5.3
						% Officers', Directors',	1.9	
						Owners' Comp/Sales	(14) 3.4	
							6.1	
478M	2363M	55488M	363608M	351343M	103916M	Net Sales ($)	835156M	668503M
63M	1862M	38993M	338744M	347260M	136319M	Total Assets ($)	829191M	650766M

M = $ thousand   MM = $ million
See Pages 11 through 18 for Explanation of Ratios and Data

Comparative Historical Data

Current Data Sorted By Sales

					Type of Statement						
	16		14		14	Unqualified		1	1	5	7
	4		5		6	Reviewed		1	3	1	1
	7		10		2	Compiled		1		1	1
					1	Tax Returns	1				
	11		14		10	Other	1	1	4	2	2
	4/1/00-3/31/01 ALL		4/1/01-3/31/02 ALL		4/1/02-3/31/03 ALL		0-1MM	8 (4/1-9/30/02) 1-3MM	3-5MM	25 (10/1/02-3/31/03) 5-10MM 10-25MM	25MM & OVER
	38		43		33	NUMBER OF STATEMENTS	1	4	4	8 8	11
	%		%		%	ASSETS	%	%	%	% %	%
	11.8		8.6		7.3	Cash & Equivalents					7.8
	15.3		15.6		11.8	Trade Receivables (net)					12.3
	17.0		17.5		21.3	Inventory					19.0
	2.8		2.9		1.6	All Other Current					2.2
	46.9		44.6		42.1	Total Current					41.2
	41.8		44.0		49.2	Fixed Assets (net)					44.6
	1.5		2.6		1.6	Intangibles (net)					.9
	9.8		8.9		7.0	All Other Non-Current					13.3
	100.0		100.0		100.0	Total					100.0
						LIABILITIES					
	7.1		8.3		4.1	Notes Payable-Short Term					4.1
	5.0		3.4		3.6	Cur. Mat.-L/T/D					2.3
	7.6		7.5		5.4	Trade Payables					4.5
	.2		.1		.2	Income Taxes Payable					.1
	5.8		5.5		7.3	All Other Current					7.9
	25.7		24.8		20.5	Total Current					18.9
	19.8		22.4		30.2	Long Term Debt					18.7
	1.1		2.0		1.8	Deferred Taxes					.9
	1.5		4.2		1.8	All Other Non-Current					2.3
	51.9		46.6		45.7	Net Worth					59.1
	100.0		100.0		100.0	Total Liabilities & Net Worth					100.0
						INCOME DATA					
	100.0		100.0		100.0	Net Sales					100.0
	33.1		29.6		34.5	Gross Profit					34.1
	20.4		21.8		24.6	Operating Expenses					21.8
	12.7		7.8		9.9	Operating Profit					12.3
	1.3		2.3		1.7	All Other Expenses (net)					.8
	11.3		5.5		8.2	Profit Before Taxes					11.5
						RATIOS					
	4.5		3.2		3.4						3.7
	2.3		1.9		2.5	Current					2.6
	1.4		1.2		1.6						1.4
	2.8		2.1		1.8						2.0
	1.2		.8		1.1	Quick					1.2
	.5		.5		.5						.5
32	11.6	29	12.4	25	14.5					35	10.6
39	9.5	38	9.7	35	10.4	Sales/Receivables				37	9.9
47	7.8	48	7.6	54	6.8					40	9.2
33	11.0	39	9.3	51	7.1					49	7.5
75	4.9	64	5.7	91	4.0	Cost of Sales/Inventory				87	4.2
109	3.4	105	3.5	160	2.3					158	2.3
16	22.6	17	21.2	16	23.3					16	23.2
25	14.8	25	14.5	25	14.8	Cost of Sales/Payables				25	14.8
35	10.4	34	10.8	35	10.3					29	12.5
	2.9		3.6		3.0						2.8
	5.8		8.1		4.2	Sales/Working Capital					3.9
	13.2		30.4		9.2						12.2
	15.8		12.3		9.4						56.2
(35)	3.9	(40)	2.7	(31)	5.2	EBIT/Interest				(10)	8.1
	2.3		1.4		2.3						5.0
	180.0		6.2			Net Profit + Depr., Dep.,					
(10)	6.8	(12)	3.0			Amort./Cur. Mat. L/T/D					
	2.0		1.3								
	.5		.5		.6						.5
	.7		.8		1.0	Fixed/Worth					.8
	1.1		1.6		1.9						1.3
	.4		.4		.4						.3
	.7		1.3		1.5	Debt/Worth					.7
	2.4		2.8		2.2						1.5
	36.9		26.3		27.8						28.6
(36)	25.1	(39)	15.4	(32)	17.0	% Profit Before Taxes/Tangible Net Worth					17.8
	11.3		5.8		7.3						16.1
	19.3		12.0		14.5						18.1
	13.0		5.8		6.6	% Profit Before Taxes/Total Assets					9.6
	4.6		1.1		3.2						6.3
	4.6		5.3		4.5						4.4
	3.0		3.2		2.2	Sales/Net Fixed Assets					2.8
	1.5		1.6		1.3						1.2
	1.5		1.9		1.4						1.7
	1.2		1.2		1.0	Sales/Total Assets					1.0
	.7		.8		.8						.7
	2.9		2.0		3.8						
(37)	4.1	(39)	4.0	(31)	4.8	% Depr., Dep., Amort./Sales					
	7.9		5.2		9.2						
	1.1		2.5			% Officers', Directors',					
(11)	2.2	(15)	3.7			Owners' Comp/Sales					
	3.2		5.7								
	902608M		1065160M		877196M	Net Sales ($)	478M	2363M	16373M	64965M 109859M	683158M
	975820M		1035056M		863241M	Total Assets ($)	63M	1862M	12014M	63360M 138220M	647722M

M = $ thousand   MM = $ million
See Pages 11 through 18 for Explanation of Ratios and Data

Current Data Sorted By Assets   Comparative Historical Data

Type of Statement	0-500M	500M-2MM	2-10MM	10-50MM	50-100MM	100-250MM	4/1/98-3/31/99 ALL	4/1/99-3/31/00 ALL
Unqualified	1		6	10	1	1	14	16
Reviewed		3	14	4			28	27
Compiled	3	8	6	6			20	14
Tax Returns	7	3	3	3			4	4
Other	2	10	13	7	2	1	21	27
	11 (4/1-9/30/02)			94 (10/1/02-3/31/03)				
NUMBER OF STATEMENTS	13	24	42	21	3	2	87	88
ASSETS	%	%	%	%	%	%	%	%
Cash & Equivalents	10.2	5.5	6.9	6.8			7.4	8.3
Trade Receivables (net)	28.1	29.9	23.6	25.9			27.2	29.5
Inventory	16.8	20.1	27.2	18.2			23.3	20.5
All Other Current	1.0	3.9	1.5	4.6			3.0	1.6
Total Current	56.2	59.3	59.2	55.4			60.9	60.0
Fixed Assets (net)	38.1	32.8	31.0	32.7			29.7	28.5
Intangibles (net)	1.1	2.1	3.7	6.7			4.3	5.4
All Other Non-Current	4.6	5.7	6.1	5.2			5.0	6.1
Total	100.0	100.0	100.0	100.0			100.0	100.0
LIABILITIES								
Notes Payable-Short Term	13.7	8.5	11.0	12.7			10.0	8.6
Cur. Mat.-L/T/D	4.5	3.6	5.1	5.3			4.8	4.3
Trade Payables	24.0	12.6	11.2	13.2			14.0	16.4
Income Taxes Payable	.2	.2	.2	.6			.4	.6
All Other Current	13.5	8.9	12.6	9.2			8.5	8.4
Total Current	55.9	33.9	40.0	41.1			37.7	38.4
Long Term Debt	38.5	20.0	16.9	16.7			17.2	17.4
Deferred Taxes	.7	.1	.4	1.1			.6	.8
All Other Non-Current	3.6	4.9	5.7	2.6			5.3	7.3
Net Worth	1.6	41.1	37.0	38.5			39.0	36.2
Total Liabilities & Net Worth	100.0	100.0	100.0	100.0			100.0	100.0
INCOME DATA								
Net Sales	100.0	100.0	100.0	100.0			100.0	100.0
Gross Profit	45.3	39.1	29.9	21.2			31.0	28.1
Operating Expenses	40.7	36.6	25.8	17.4			27.4	23.3
Operating Profit	4.5	2.5	4.1	3.8			3.6	4.8
All Other Expenses (net)	1.7	.9	1.7	1.2			.9	1.2
Profit Before Taxes	2.9	1.6	2.4	2.6			2.7	3.6
RATIOS								
Current	1.7	3.6	2.9	2.0			2.8	2.4
	1.0	1.7	1.6	1.4			1.8	1.6
	.6	1.1	1.0	1.1			1.1	1.1
Quick	1.4	1.7	1.3	1.2			1.7	1.5
	.9	1.1	.8	.7			.8	1.0
	.4	.7	.5	.6			.6	.6
Sales/Receivables	25 14.7	31 11.8	30 12.1	36 10.0			34 10.8	34 10.6
	31 12.0	42 8.6	43 8.5	47 7.7			43 8.4	44 8.3
	47 7.8	51 7.2	60 6.1	55 6.6			51 7.1	57 6.4
Cost of Sales/Inventory	0 UND	15 23.9	38 9.5	23 15.6			23 16.2	17 21.4
	31 11.9	31 11.7	69 5.3	45 8.1			46 7.9	42 8.7
	64 5.7	66 5.6	112 3.3	63 5.8			89 4.1	68 5.4
Cost of Sales/Payables	21 17.4	17 21.6	15 23.9	18 20.3			17 22.0	17 20.9
	42 8.8	27 13.7	27 13.8	31 11.7			25 14.7	27 13.4
	67 5.4	48 7.5	44 8.4	44 8.2			42 8.6	42 8.7
Sales/Working Capital	13.5	5.2	4.4	6.9			5.2	5.9
	UND	13.4	8.4	13.1			8.5	10.8
	-10.7	37.8	NM	63.8			36.1	35.6
EBIT/Interest	6.1	5.3	6.6	8.7			9.5	5.8
	(11) 1.3	(23) 2.8	(39) 2.8	(19) 4.0			(80) 3.7	(81) 3.5
	.0	.7	1.2	.3			1.4	1.3
Net Profit + Depr., Dep., Amort./Cur. Mat. L /T/D				(10) 2.3			10.5	3.3
				1.8			(28) 3.3	(23) 2.0
				.7			1.4	.2
Fixed/Worth	.5	.2	.3	.6			.4	.4
	11.9	.9	.7	1.1			.7	.9
	-.9	2.3	2.3	2.1			1.7	2.9
Debt/Worth	1.5	.7	.7	1.4			.7	.8
	17.6	1.5	1.4	2.0			1.7	2.3
	-3.7	5.0	4.6	3.7			4.5	6.0
% Profit Before Taxes/Tangible Net Worth		(23) 19.6	(36) 24.9	42.3			41.4	42.6
		10.8	10.2	20.9			(73) 25.0	(77) 19.3
		-1.6	2.2	1.4			8.9	4.7
% Profit Before Taxes/Total Assets	49.6	10.2	8.6	14.7			17.2	14.4
	4.1	4.1	4.5	5.6			9.5	7.1
	-1.0	-.7	.5	.6			1.6	1.3
Sales/Net Fixed Assets	24.7	24.6	12.3	12.3			18.1	21.7
	13.6	6.8	8.9	6.7			8.8	11.1
	3.8	4.3	4.1	4.4			4.7	4.7
Sales/Total Assets	4.7	2.9	2.6	2.5			2.9	3.0
	3.0	2.6	2.0	2.1			2.2	2.2
	2.2	2.1	1.5	1.5			1.6	1.6
% Depr., Dep., Amort./Sales	(10) 1.9	(23) 1.3	(40) 1.5	(19) 1.5			(79) 1.3	(74) 1.4
	3.6	3.2	2.6	2.6			2.2	2.4
	7.4	6.7	4.8	3.5			3.4	3.9
% Officers', Directors', Owners' Comp/Sales		(16) 4.0	(14) 1.8				(37) 2.2	(35) 2.0
		5.6	3.6				3.5	3.5
		7.4	6.4				6.7	11.2
Net Sales ($)	9803M	76660M	428460M	770623M	398435M	361418M	1497283M	1825562M
Total Assets ($)	3148M	30125M	219266M	412387M	222793M	303741M	832593M	983556M

© RMA 2003

M = $ thousand   MM = $ million
See Pages 11 through 18 for Explanation of Ratios and Data

MANUFACTURING—Glass Product Manufacturing Made of Purchased Glass   NAICS 327215 (SIC 3231)

Comparative Historical Data				Current Data Sorted By Sales					
12	11	19	**Type of Statement** Unqualified	1		1	1	6	10
23	17	21	Reviewed		2	4	7	6	2
17	15	17	Compiled	1	8	3	2	3	
6	2	13	Tax Returns	5	3	2	2	1	
31	29	35	Other	3	3	7	9	4	9
4/1/00-3/31/01 ALL	4/1/01-3/31/02 ALL	4/1/02-3/31/03 ALL		11 (4/1-9/30/02) 0-1MM	1-3MM	3-5MM	94 (10/1/02-3/31/03) 5-10MM	10-25MM	25MM & OVER
89	74	105	**NUMBER OF STATEMENTS**	10	16	17	21	20	21
%	%	%	**ASSETS**	%	%	%	%	%	%
8.4	6.5	6.9	Cash & Equivalents	11.2	6.3	10.6	8.9	1.5	5.4
25.5	26.1	26.0	Trade Receivables (net)	27.9	25.6	23.7	25.5	26.6	27.0
20.0	19.9	21.9	Inventory	12.1	18.5	24.9	21.4	30.7	18.9
2.3	2.1	2.7	All Other Current	4.2	1.4	2.5	1.8	1.8	4.9
56.1	54.6	57.5	Total Current	55.4	51.9	61.7	57.5	60.6	56.3
31.6	33.8	32.4	Fixed Assets (net)	43.9	34.8	29.6	36.3	26.0	29.7
6.0	5.8	4.6	Intangibles (net)	.4	4.9	2.0	1.4	5.7	10.6
6.3	5.8	5.5	All Other Non-Current	.3	8.4	6.7	4.8	7.6	3.4
100.0	100.0	100.0	Total	100.0	100.0	100.0	100.0	100.0	100.0
			LIABILITIES						
8.6	9.2	10.6	Notes Payable-Short Term	13.4	5.7	11.2	10.9	15.0	7.9
5.0	4.2	4.7	Cur. Mat.-L/T/D	5.0	3.4	3.4	7.1	5.1	4.1
12.7	13.2	13.8	Trade Payables	20.8	14.4	11.9	12.2	12.6	14.3
.4	.7	.3	Income Taxes Payable	.2	.3	.4	.4	.2	.1
7.3	8.6	11.0	All Other Current	15.5	9.2	4.7	9.1	7.3	20.7
34.0	35.9	40.4	Total Current	54.9	33.0	31.6	39.7	40.3	47.1
20.3	17.9	20.1	Long Term Debt	30.6	30.5	19.6	14.4	16.0	17.3
.5	.4	.6	Deferred Taxes	.9	.2	.3	.4	.7	1.0
9.6	6.3	5.0	All Other Non-Current	5.8	3.7	10.1	4.2	1.9	5.2
35.7	39.5	33.9	Net Worth	8.3	32.6	38.4	41.3	41.2	29.3
100.0	100.0	100.0	Total Liabilities & Net Worth	100.0	100.0	100.0	100.0	100.0	100.0
			INCOME DATA						
100.0	100.0	100.0	Net Sales	100.0	100.0	100.0	100.0	100.0	100.0
30.6	28.0	32.1	Gross Profit	48.6	38.1	37.5	27.7	26.6	24.9
25.4	25.3	28.2	Operating Expenses	44.7	34.5	32.7	24.6	25.1	18.4
5.1	2.7	3.9	Operating Profit	3.9	3.6	4.8	3.1	1.5	6.6
1.3	1.4	1.4	All Other Expenses (net)	1.9	1.2	1.2	1.8	.8	1.4
3.8	1.3	2.6	Profit Before Taxes	2.0	2.4	3.6	1.3	.7	5.2
			RATIOS						
2.8	3.1	2.6	Current	2.2	2.9	3.8	2.6	2.8	2.1
1.8	1.5	1.5		.9	1.5	1.7	1.5	1.5	1.5
1.2	1.0	1.0		.5	1.2	1.3	1.0	1.0	1.1
1.7	1.6	1.4	Quick	1.6	1.4	1.9	1.4	1.1	1.2
1.0	.9	.9		.7	1.0	1.1	.9	.7	.8
.6	.6	.6		.4	.7	.6	.6	.6	.6
32 11.3	35 10.5	30 12.1	Sales/Receivables	29 12.8	25 14.5	26 14.2	35 10.5	31 11.7	36 10.0
44 8.3	42 8.7	43 8.6		35 10.3	39 9.5	40 9.2	44 8.2	45 8.1	47 7.7
52 7.1	52 7.0	54 6.8		55 6.7	49 7.5	51 7.2	49 7.5	62 5.9	59 6.2
21 17.4	25 14.6	27 13.7	Cost of Sales/Inventory	0 UND	24 15.4	45 8.1	25 14.5	32 11.4	29 12.6
41 8.8	42 8.8	50 7.3		17 22.0	31 11.7	59 6.2	54 6.7	60 6.1	49 7.4
67 5.4	78 4.7	81 4.5		48 7.5	85 4.3	104 3.5	77 4.7	119 3.1	62 5.9
18 20.5	16 22.5	18 20.3	Cost of Sales/Payables	23 16.0	19 18.9	15 24.7	15 24.5	16 22.9	20 18.3
27 13.7	24 15.0	29 12.8		42 8.7	33 10.9	35 10.4	24 15.4	27 13.8	29 12.7
41 8.8	40 9.1	48 7.6		92 3.9	54 6.7	47 7.8	46 7.9	34 10.6	51 7.1
5.3	5.9	6.1	Sales/Working Capital	9.5	5.4	4.0	5.4	4.4	7.0
8.9	10.0	11.3		UND	12.8	8.4	10.6	10.8	10.7
27.2	NM	UND		-8.1	43.4	22.4	-245.4	NM	53.6
(82) 6.1	(67) 5.7	(97) 6.3	EBIT/Interest		(13) 5.4	(16) 6.4	(20) 6.6	(19) 5.8	(20) 9.4
2.9	2.6	2.8			3.4	2.7	2.8	2.2	3.6
1.3	.0	1.1			.7	1.3	1.1	.1	2.0
(25) 4.2	(21) 3.7	(25) 3.6	Net Profit + Depr., Dep., Amort./Cur. Mat. L/T/D						
2.2	2.3	2.1							
1.1	.8	1.0							
.4	.5	.4	Fixed/Worth	.5	.4	.2	.5	.3	.6
1.0	.9	1.0		7.1	1.1	.5	1.2	.7	1.1
3.5	3.7	2.9		-1.7	11.2	2.9	1.6	2.0	2.8
.8	.8	1.0	Debt/Worth	1.7	.5	.6	.8	1.0	1.4
2.7	2.2	1.9		10.0	2.2	1.4	1.3	1.9	2.5
6.9	7.0	8.2		-3.7	12.6	8.2	2.4	3.3	5.2
(74) 41.2	(63) 29.8	(90) 33.3	% Profit Before Taxes/Tangible Net Worth		(13) 59.4	(15) 48.2	(19) 19.3	(19) 24.9	(18) 49.0
19.2	15.4	14.6			15.8	5.8	10.9	8.6	31.4
5.8	1.0	2.2			-7.1	2.6	1.3	-1.0	13.6
14.0	12.1	11.3	% Profit Before Taxes/Total Assets	47.9	15.7	9.1	10.1	5.8	15.1
5.3	4.4	4.7		2.6	8.5	2.6	5.6	3.5	9.8
1.6	-4.0	.5		-9.8	-.5	.8	.3	-.6	2.3
15.9	13.5	14.4	Sales/Net Fixed Assets	30.9	20.4	33.6	11.7	37.3	12.3
7.6	6.8	8.0		4.9	9.2	10.0	6.7	7.9	9.0
4.2	3.7	4.1		3.1	3.5	4.1	3.4	5.3	4.9
2.8	2.7	2.7	Sales/Total Assets	3.8	3.3	2.7	3.1	2.5	2.6
2.1	2.2	2.2		2.6	2.2	2.4	2.2	2.2	2.2
1.5	1.3	1.6		1.3	1.5	1.7	1.5	1.8	1.6
(80) 1.4	(63) 1.2	(96) 1.6	% Depr., Dep., Amort./Sales		(15) 2.2	(16) 1.2	(17) 2.1	(20) 1.2	1.5
2.4	2.7	2.8			3.2	3.6	2.9	2.4	2.5
3.8	4.4	4.8			6.2	7.0	4.4	3.8	3.2
(32) 2.0	(28) 1.9	(43) 3.3	% Officers', Directors', Owners' Comp/Sales		(10) 4.0	(12) 2.8			
4.9	3.1	4.8			5.4	5.1			
9.5	6.0	7.4			7.8	7.2			
2098095M	1893841M	2045399M	Net Sales ($)	5668M	30365M	65868M	146387M	333939M	1463172M
1186134M	1280045M	1191460M	Total Assets ($)	2545M	24546M	38159M	91208M	157320M	877682M

© RMA 2003

M = $ thousand   MM = $ million
See Pages 11 through 18 for Explanation of Ratios and Data

Current Data Sorted By Assets | **Comparative Historical Data**

	0-500M	500M-2MM	2-10MM	10-50MM	50-100MM	100-250MM	4/1/98-3/31/99 ALL	4/1/99-3/31/00 ALL
Type of Statement								
Unqualified	1	3	9	19	11	7	48	52
Reviewed	2	7	33	12			57	44
Compiled	5	12	18	2	1		55	46
Tax Returns	1	8	3	1			9	6
Other	1	5	24	14	3	4	56	52
	37 (4/1-9/30/02)			169 (10/1/02-3/31/03)				
NUMBER OF STATEMENTS	10	35	87	48	15	11	225	200
	%	%	%	%	%	%	%	%
ASSETS								
Cash & Equivalents	16.7	10.6	10.3	6.2	4.0	5.5	9.4	9.7
Trade Receivables (net)	32.7	29.2	24.7	19.6	17.9	15.0	25.1	23.7
Inventory	6.5	8.0	5.9	8.3	7.5	5.8	6.6	6.4
All Other Current	3.9	2.5	2.8	1.8	2.1	1.6	2.1	1.8
Total Current	59.8	50.2	43.7	35.9	31.5	27.9	43.2	41.6
Fixed Assets (net)	37.2	40.5	47.0	56.2	57.2	56.9	47.5	48.3
Intangibles (net)	.4	1.4	1.7	1.6	3.6	8.5	2.2	2.7
All Other Non-Current	2.6	7.9	7.6	6.3	7.8	6.7	7.1	7.4
Total	100.0	100.0	100.0	100.0	100.0	100.0	100.0	100.0
LIABILITIES								
Notes Payable-Short Term	2.6	8.3	5.8	4.2	5.7	3.0	5.6	5.1
Cur. Mat.-L/T/D	3.3	6.7	6.2	6.7	6.0	2.5	6.1	5.4
Trade Payables	22.8	18.4	13.3	12.9	8.1	6.5	13.8	12.8
Income Taxes Payable	.0	.2	.2	.1	.5	.4	.4	.3
All Other Current	18.6	5.7	6.4	6.9	5.0	4.3	6.3	6.5
Total Current	47.3	39.3	31.9	30.9	25.3	16.7	32.1	30.1
Long Term Debt	16.8	20.8	17.8	22.1	23.2	23.1	21.3	22.7
Deferred Taxes	.4	.5	1.2	2.2	3.3	2.3	1.1	1.1
All Other Non-Current	25.5	3.7	4.1	2.1	3.4	4.0	2.9	3.3
Net Worth	10.0	35.7	45.0	42.7	44.8	54.0	42.5	42.8
Total Liabilities & Net Worth	100.0	100.0	100.0	100.0	100.0	100.0	100.0	100.0
INCOME DATA								
Net Sales	100.0	100.0	100.0	100.0	100.0	100.0	100.0	100.0
Gross Profit	25.6	32.1	30.3	26.9	21.3	31.5	27.6	27.8
Operating Expenses	25.6	29.7	27.4	23.7	16.7	21.5	22.4	22.1
Operating Profit	.1	2.5	2.9	3.2	4.6	9.9	5.2	5.7
All Other Expenses (net)	-1.1	.7	.0	.5	1.0	1.5	.0	-.7
Profit Before Taxes	1.1	1.8	2.9	2.7	3.6	8.4	5.2	6.3
RATIOS								
Current	2.8	2.9	2.3	2.1	2.3	3.4	2.2	2.0
	1.3	1.2	1.7	1.3	1.2	1.9	1.4	1.5
	.9	.9	1.1	.9	1.0	1.4	1.0	1.0
Quick	2.6	2.1	1.8	1.5	1.0	2.1	1.7	1.6
	1.2	1.0	1.4	.9	.9	1.2	1.1	1.1
	.6	.6	.7	.6	.6	1.0	.8	.8
Sales/Receivables	**29** 12.7	**26** 14.0	**32** 11.5	**32** 11.3	**38** 9.7	**35** 10.4	**33** 10.9	**34** 10.7
	36 10.1	**33** 11.0	**40** 9.0	**40** 9.1	**46** 8.0	**47** 7.8	**43** 8.5	**44** 8.3
	52 7.1	**46** 7.9	**52** 7.0	**48** 7.5	**58** 6.3	**61** 6.0	**54** 6.8	**56** 6.6
Cost of Sales/Inventory	**0** UND	**3** 120.7	**4** 88.3	**8** 45.3	**13** 28.8	**14** 26.9	**6** 66.3	**6** 59.9
	8 48.4	**11** 34.0	**7** 52.7	**20** 18.6	**25** 14.7	**30** 12.2	**12** 30.6	**12** 30.1
	18 19.8	**24** 15.5	**20** 18.7	**41** 8.9	**49** 7.4	**61** 5.9	**26** 14.3	**25** 14.5
Cost of Sales/Payables	**12** 29.7	**19** 19.5	**19** 19.2	**19** 19.0	**21** 17.3	**16** 23.3	**23** 15.9	**21** 17.6
	20 17.9	**30** 12.1	**27** 13.4	**29** 12.6	**27** 13.8	**23** 16.0	**31** 11.8	**31** 11.8
	51 7.1	**44** 8.3	**45** 8.0	**43** 8.6	**37** 9.7	**38** 9.5	**43** 8.5	**44** 8.2
Sales/Working Capital	11.8	7.0	7.7	8.5	6.1	4.7	8.0	8.2
	20.6	23.5	14.0	22.4	31.8	7.4	16.5	16.9
	-57.0	-50.4	65.3	-35.2	-226.3	17.4	NM	144.4
EBIT/Interest		7.3	8.5	7.5	7.6		9.9	10.2
		(31) 2.5	(81) 4.0	(44) 3.1	4.3		(206) 3.9	(188) 4.6
		1.0	1.2	1.3	1.5		2.2	2.4
Net Profit + Depr., Dep., Amort./Cur. Mat. L/T/D			2.7	2.3			4.7	3.6
			(25) 2.0	(21) 1.8			(87) 2.2	(77) 2.4
			1.2	1.2			1.3	1.5
Fixed/Worth	.1	.5	.6	.8	1.0	.8	.7	.7
	1.0	1.3	1.0	1.3	1.5	1.2	1.1	1.3
	4.7	2.9	2.1	2.2	2.3	4.6	2.2	2.3
Debt/Worth	1.0	.4	.6	.6	.3	.3	.7	.6
	3.7	1.7	1.0	1.2	1.7	.9	1.3	1.5
	NM	4.2	2.6	2.8	2.6	4.6	3.0	2.8
% Profit Before Taxes/Tangible Net Worth		29.8	32.6	21.7	28.3	34.5	39.2	41.5
		(30) 10.0	(82) 14.7	(44) 12.1	5.2	(10) 14.9	(212) 21.9	(188) 23.7
		-1.4	3.4	2.5	.2	9.8	10.7	11.4
% Profit Before Taxes/Total Assets	13.7	14.6	12.6	8.7	7.8	10.8	16.4	15.9
	3.2	3.8	6.0	4.4	3.7	8.2	8.8	8.9
	-5.2	-.1	.9	.8	.1	4.2	3.6	4.1
Sales/Net Fixed Assets	UND	14.6	7.7	4.8	3.3	2.8	6.8	5.9
	7.9	6.4	4.2	2.9	2.4	2.4	4.3	3.8
	2.8	4.4	2.8	2.4	1.7	.7	2.7	2.4
Sales/Total Assets	4.1	3.3	2.7	2.0	1.7	1.6	2.6	2.5
	3.4	2.4	2.0	1.7	1.2	1.2	1.9	1.8
	1.8	2.1	1.5	1.3	.8	.5	1.4	1.3
% Depr., Dep., Amort./Sales		3.2	3.0	2.9	4.5		3.4	3.3
		(33) 4.9	(85) 5.2	(47) 5.0	(10) 7.0		(206) 4.9	(187) 4.8
		7.4	7.2	6.7	9.9		6.2	6.2
% Officers', Directors', Owners' Comp/Sales		1.6	1.4	1.3			1.6	1.4
		(21) 2.7	(45) 2.5	(10) 1.8			(79) 2.7	(64) 3.1
		4.6	4.4	2.3			4.8	5.3
Net Sales ($)	10343M	124703M	903046M	1740290M	1624586M	1917941M	5499354M	5286016M
Total Assets ($)	3357M	45893M	418633M	1012945M	1221803M	1782190M	3827239M	3612641M

M = $ thousand MM = $ million

See Pages 11 through 18 for Explanation of Ratios and Data

Comparative Historical Data				Current Data Sorted By Sales					

Type of Statement

			Type of Statement						
37	31	50	Unqualified	1	3	1	5	8	32
47	34	54	Reviewed		6	7	19	15	7
39	43	38	Compiled	5	8	3	12	7	3
7	4	13	Tax Returns	1	3	5	2	1	1
56	59	51	Other		3	3	8	18	19
4/1/00-3/31/01 ALL	4/1/01-3/31/02 ALL	4/1/02-3/31/03 ALL		37 (4/1-9/30/02)		169 (10/1/02-3/31/03)			
				0-1MM	1-3MM	3-5MM	5-10MM	10-25MM	25MM & OVER
186	171	206	**NUMBER OF STATEMENTS**	7	23	19	46	49	62

%	%	%	**ASSETS**	%	%	%	%	%	%
8.0	9.2	9.0	Cash & Equivalents		9.5	8.9	9.7	10.4	5.7
23.4	23.1	23.6	Trade Receivables (net)		21.2	22.4	28.4	25.6	20.0
7.0	7.0	6.9	Inventory		8.8	4.3	7.0	5.4	7.9
2.1	3.0	2.5	All Other Current		1.8	3.8	2.8	2.5	1.8
40.4	42.3	42.0	Total Current		41.3	39.4	47.9	43.9	35.4
48.5	47.6	48.8	Fixed Assets (net)		46.0	56.5	42.2	47.5	54.7
2.5	3.1	2.1	Intangibles (net)		2.2	1.1	1.6	1.5	3.2
8.6	7.0	7.1	All Other Non-Current		10.5	3.0	8.3	7.1	6.7
100.0	100.0	100.0	Total		100.0	100.0	100.0	100.0	100.0

			LIABILITIES						
5.4	5.3	5.5	Notes Payable-Short Term		8.1	10.9	5.1	4.3	4.3
5.9	6.0	6.0	Cur. Mat.-L/T/D		6.9	8.6	5.4	6.7	5.3
13.5	12.2	13.8	Trade Payables		11.4	19.6	13.3	13.8	12.1
.2	.2	.2	Income Taxes Payable		.0	.0	.3	.2	.2
6.5	6.6	6.8	All Other Current		8.3	5.8	5.5	8.4	5.3
31.6	30.2	32.4	Total Current		34.7	44.9	29.5	33.4	27.3
20.8	20.7	20.0	Long Term Debt		23.1	24.6	14.5	20.0	21.2
1.3	1.3	1.5	Deferred Taxes		.6	.0	1.4	1.3	2.6
3.7	4.1	4.5	All Other Non-Current		1.0	3.8	4.8	3.6	3.0
42.6	43.6	41.6	Net Worth		40.6	26.7	49.8	41.7	45.9
100.0	100.0	100.0	Total Liabilities & Net Worth		100.0	100.0	100.0	100.0	100.0

			INCOME DATA						
100.0	100.0	100.0	Net Sales		100.0	100.0	100.0	100.0	100.0
26.9	27.9	29.0	Gross Profit		33.2	29.8	27.9	29.7	27.0
22.6	23.5	25.7	Operating Expenses		31.2	27.6	24.7	26.6	22.0
4.3	4.4	3.2	Operating Profit		1.9	2.2	3.2	3.1	5.1
.4	.7	.3	All Other Expenses (net)		.3	.4	.1	-.1	.9
3.9	3.7	2.9	Profit Before Taxes		1.7	1.9	3.1	3.2	4.1

			RATIOS						
2.0	2.2	2.3	Current		2.2	2.3	2.8	2.1	2.3
1.3	1.5	1.5			1.2	1.1	1.9	1.6	1.4
.9	1.0	.9			.8	.6	1.1	.9	1.0
1.6	1.8	1.8	Quick		1.7	1.9	2.2	1.7	1.6
.9	1.1	1.2			.8	1.0	1.4	1.3	1.0
.7	.7	.6			.6	.4	.8	.7	.7
32 11.3	34 10.8	31 11.6	Sales/Receivables	20 18.4	28 13.0	32 11.3	34 10.9	36 10.2	
42 8.6	43 8.5	40 9.1		31 11.8	35 10.3	42 8.7	39 9.4	44 8.2	
53 6.9	51 7.1	51 7.2		51 7.2	56 6.5	52 7.0	52 7.0	50 7.3	
6 60.2	5 67.8	5 72.9	Cost of Sales/Inventory	4 81.3	3 120.7	3 118.6	5 72.0	13 27.2	
15 25.0	12 29.7	13 27.1		14 25.2	7 51.5	6 56.4	9 40.8	23 15.9	
30 12.2	29 12.8	31 11.9		47 7.8	20 18.3	19 19.6	19 19.0	42 8.7	
18 20.4	18 20.7	19 19.2	Cost of Sales/Payables	15 24.8	22 16.4	17 22.0	20 18.6	21 17.3	
29 12.4	26 14.0	27 13.3		30 12.1	41 9.0	22 16.7	27 13.4	28 12.9	
45 8.0	40 9.1	43 8.5		36 10.0	68 5.4	36 10.1	47 7.8	41 9.0	
8.5	7.7	7.5	Sales/Working Capital		11.5	7.4	6.5	8.5	6.1
21.0	16.5	15.7			23.5	33.4	12.9	15.7	15.9
-42.2	145.1	-68.5			-26.5	-11.8	81.9	-35.8	NM
7.5	9.9	7.6	EBIT/Interest	(21) 4.6	(16) 5.6	(42) 7.2	(47) 11.6	(57) 7.7	
(176) 2.9	(162) 3.0	(188) 3.6		1.4	2.1	4.2	4.4	5.2	
1.3	1.4	1.3		.1	.6	.9	1.7	2.4	
3.7	4.7	3.4	Net Profit + Depr., Dep., Amort./Cur. Mat. L/T/D			(15) 4.5	(15) 2.8	(23) 4.6	
(59) 2.1	(57) 1.9	(63) 2.0				2.1	2.0	2.1	
1.3	.9	1.3				1.1	1.3	1.5	
.7	.6	.6	Fixed/Worth		.6	.8	.5	.7	.8
1.3	1.1	1.2			1.4	1.7	.9	1.0	1.3
2.4	2.1	2.4			3.5	37.2	1.7	2.5	2.1
.6	.5	.6	Debt/Worth		.3	.4	.5	.7	.7
1.4	1.5	1.2			2.4	1.7	.9	1.0	1.3
3.3	2.8	3.1			5.7	49.6	1.9	4.1	2.4
34.2	31.1	28.8	% Profit Before Taxes/Tangible Net Worth	(21) 27.1	(15) 24.2	(44) 30.2	(45) 33.3	(59) 24.6	
(174) 16.5	(160) 15.4	(189) 13.0		3.0	9.8	12.8	18.2	13.0	
4.8	4.8	2.7		-14.7	.4	1.4	7.9	3.5	
12.4	12.3	11.1	% Profit Before Taxes/Total Assets		12.5	12.3	13.6	12.3	9.7
6.3	5.8	4.9			1.0	3.2	6.5	6.2	5.6
1.4	1.7	.7			-4.0	-.1	.5	1.7	1.7
6.4	6.8	6.7	Sales/Net Fixed Assets		8.3	6.4	9.3	7.6	4.5
3.8	4.1	4.0			4.8	4.4	4.7	3.9	2.8
2.7	2.7	2.5			3.6	2.2	3.3	2.8	2.1
2.5	2.5	2.6	Sales/Total Assets		3.2	2.5	2.8	2.6	2.0
1.9	1.9	1.9			2.1	2.2	2.2	1.8	1.6
1.4	1.5	1.5			1.6	1.3	1.6	1.6	1.1
3.2	3.5	3.5	% Depr., Dep., Amort./Sales	3.7	(18) 4.6	(44) 2.6	(48) 3.5	(50) 3.1	
(176) 4.8	(157) 5.1	(188) 5.3		5.2	5.8	4.5	5.4	4.9	
6.9	6.7	7.4		7.7	7.6	7.0	7.2	6.9	
1.6	1.1	1.5	% Officers', Directors', Owners' Comp/Sales	(13) 2.5	(11) 1.7	(26) 1.4	(21) 1.6		
(71) 2.4	(53) 2.0	(80) 2.5		3.6	2.4	2.2	2.2		
4.9	3.5	4.2		6.8	4.3	5.1	3.4		
5158821M	5293258M	6320909M	Net Sales ($)	4559M	50992M	75373M	323668M	778556M	5087761M
3400893M	3396428M	4484821M	Total Assets ($)	2360M	28524M	41753M	157101M	402502M	3852581M

M = $ thousand   MM = $ million
See Pages 11 through 18 for Explanation of Ratios and Data

Current Data Sorted By Assets / Comparative Historical Data

0-500M	500M-2MM	2-10MM	10-50MM	50-100MM	100-250MM	Type of Statement	4/1/98-3/31/99 ALL	4/1/99-3/31/00 ALL
2	1	4	9	4	4	Unqualified	41	35
	7	19	4			Reviewed	41	50
1	3	5	2			Compiled	40	22
	4	3				Tax Returns	8	4
1	5	9	10		1	Other	39	53
	13 (4/1-9/30/02)		85 (10/1/02-3/31/03)					
4	20	40	25	5	4	**NUMBER OF STATEMENTS**	169	164
%	%	%	%	%	%	**ASSETS**	%	%
	6.9	8.0	9.0			Cash & Equivalents	7.5	7.5
	23.6	18.6	20.2			Trade Receivables (net)	23.1	24.1
	16.0	18.9	17.3			Inventory	18.3	17.3
	.5	1.4	2.7			All Other Current	2.2	1.4
	46.9	46.9	49.1			Total Current	51.2	50.4
	47.9	43.4	43.5			Fixed Assets (net)	40.9	41.3
	1.1	.9	1.8			Intangibles (net)	1.4	1.8
	4.0	8.8	5.6			All Other Non-Current	6.5	6.5
	100.0	100.0	100.0			Total	100.0	100.0
						LIABILITIES		
	11.3	6.8	5.2			Notes Payable-Short Term	8.2	8.3
	8.0	7.5	5.6			Cur. Mat.-L/T/D	4.4	4.5
	16.6	10.1	9.4			Trade Payables	12.9	12.3
	.6	.5	.5			Income Taxes Payable	.3	.5
	7.0	5.5	4.9			All Other Current	8.6	7.3
	43.4	30.5	25.7			Total Current	34.4	32.9
	29.0	21.2	24.5			Long Term Debt	19.4	19.9
	.9	.7	1.7			Deferred Taxes	.8	.8
	1.6	6.1	2.3			All Other Non-Current	5.7	6.1
	25.2	41.6	45.8			Net Worth	39.6	40.4
	100.0	100.0	100.0			Total Liabilities & Net Worth	100.0	100.0
						INCOME DATA		
	100.0	100.0	100.0			Net Sales	100.0	100.0
	37.0	33.3	28.0			Gross Profit	30.4	30.4
	34.1	29.2	20.4			Operating Expenses	25.3	23.8
	2.9	4.1	7.5			Operating Profit	5.1	6.7
	1.8	1.1	1.3			All Other Expenses (net)	.6	1.1
	1.1	3.0	6.2			Profit Before Taxes	4.5	5.5
						RATIOS		
	1.9	3.0	3.0			Current	2.6	2.6
	1.4	1.7	2.1				1.6	1.6
	.7	.9	1.3				1.1	1.1
	1.5	1.8	2.2			Quick	1.5	1.6
	.7	.8	.8				.9	1.0
	.3	.5	.6				.6	.7
	21 / 17.5	25 / 14.7	38 / 9.6			Sales/Receivables	31 / 11.6	33 / 11.0
	38 / 9.7	35 / 10.4	46 / 7.9				42 / 8.7	45 / 8.2
	59 / 6.2	54 / 6.8	55 / 6.7				56 / 6.5	58 / 6.3
	6 / 60.7	33 / 11.0	34 / 10.7			Cost of Sales/Inventory	25 / 14.6	25 / 14.6
	55 / 6.6	57 / 6.4	61 / 5.9				51 / 7.1	47 / 7.8
	84 / 4.4	92 / 4.0	93 / 3.9				79 / 4.6	70 / 5.2
	22 / 16.6	17 / 21.7	21 / 21.8			Cost of Sales/Payables	21 / 17.5	20 / 18.5
	36 / 10.1	24 / 14.9	31 / 11.6				31 / 11.8	31 / 11.7
	59 / 6.2	42 / 8.7	38 / 9.5				46 / 7.9	46 / 7.9
	6.7	5.2	3.9			Sales/Working Capital	5.3	5.6
	16.4	13.1	7.6				10.0	9.4
	-18.2	-34.2	16.1				37.5	38.2
	(18) 7.4	(38) 8.1	(24) 11.2			EBIT/Interest	(157) 8.1	(147) 8.5
	2.1	2.4	3.9				3.6	3.6
	1.2	.5	2.6				1.5	1.9
		(18) 4.1				Net Profit + Depr., Dep., Amort./Cur. Mat. L /T/D	(71) 6.2	(69) 4.8
		2.4					2.2	2.4
		1.0					1.2	1.6
	.5	.5	.6			Fixed/Worth	.5	.6
	2.0	1.2	1.1				1.0	1.1
	51.0	2.1	1.9				2.0	2.0
	.9	.6	.6			Debt/Worth	.6	.7
	3.4	1.7	1.1				1.5	1.4
	90.0	3.3	2.7				3.1	3.3
	(17) 39.3	(38) 24.5	(23) 28.5			% Profit Before Taxes/Tangible Net Worth	(157) 32.2	(150) 38.0
	15.5	12.5	15.3				21.7	24.4
	2.7	-.2	4.9				10.7	11.0
	9.2	14.7	13.0			% Profit Before Taxes/Total Assets	15.4	15.6
	3.4	4.1	6.6				7.3	9.6
	.2	-.6	3.2				2.5	3.3
	6.9	8.2	5.1			Sales/Net Fixed Assets	7.5	7.3
	4.1	4.2	3.3				4.4	4.6
	2.7	2.7	2.6				3.0	3.1
	2.6	2.3	1.9			Sales/Total Assets	2.3	2.3
	1.8	1.8	1.6				1.7	1.8
	1.5	1.3	1.2				1.4	1.5
	3.0	3.2	2.8			% Depr., Dep., Amort./Sales	(164) 2.5	(153) 2.3
	4.7	4.7	(24) 3.8				3.4	3.3
	8.3	7.9	4.9				4.8	4.8
		(18) 1.6				% Officers', Directors', Owners' Comp/Sales	(54) 2.0	(54) 1.8
		2.7					3.7	3.3
		5.0					6.9	6.2
1849M	55082M	319008M	842318M	592141M	689966M	Net Sales ($)	3290553M	2568931M
787M	27624M	186667M	548359M	353713M	548151M	Total Assets ($)	2005318M	1575709M

M = $ thousand   MM = $ million
See Pages 11 through 18 for Explanation of Ratios and Data

Comparative Historical Data / Current Data Sorted By Sales

				Type of Statement						
16		24	24	Unqualified	2	1		3	5	13
26		29	30	Reviewed		6	5	8	9	2
24		20	11	Compiled	1	2	2	2	2	2
11		10	7	Tax Returns		3	1	3		
29		27	26	Other		4	7	3	4	8
4/1/00-3/31/01		4/1/01-3/31/02	4/1/02-3/31/03			13 (4/1-9/30/02)		85 (10/1/02-3/31/03)		
ALL		ALL	ALL		0-1MM	1-3MM	3-5MM	5-10MM	10-25MM	25MM & OVER
106		110	98	NUMBER OF STATEMENTS	3	16	15	19	20	25
%		%	%	ASSETS	%	%	%	%	%	%
8.0		7.2	7.4	Cash & Equivalents		4.8	10.1	7.6	7.7	8.0
20.2		20.7	19.9	Trade Receivables (net)		17.4	21.5	18.8	21.2	20.7
19.0		18.7	17.9	Inventory		17.4	15.4	16.8	22.6	16.4
2.4		3.3	1.7	All Other Current		.6	.7	1.5	2.0	2.8
49.6		50.0	46.9	Total Current		40.1	47.6	44.6	53.5	48.0
42.2		43.1	44.2	Fixed Assets (net)		55.5	41.2	47.6	38.1	41.6
2.5		1.0	2.3	Intangibles (net)		1.3	.2	1.3	1.6	4.4
5.7		6.0	6.6	All Other Non-Current		3.1	10.9	6.5	6.8	6.1
100.0		100.0	100.0	Total		100.0	100.0	100.0	100.0	100.0
				LIABILITIES						
8.9		8.9	7.2	Notes Payable-Short Term		9.6	9.9	3.3	9.4	4.1
4.8		5.8	6.7	Cur. Mat.-L/T/D		8.6	8.3	6.6	6.0	5.5
10.9		12.3	11.1	Trade Payables		12.5	12.3	10.8	11.6	9.2
.3		.5	.5	Income Taxes Payable		.6	.1	1.3	.2	.4
6.4		6.5	5.8	All Other Current		5.6	7.3	4.6	5.3	6.2
31.3		33.9	31.4	Total Current		37.0	37.9	26.6	32.5	25.5
22.3		26.9	24.1	Long Term Debt		34.4	23.3	21.8	19.7	23.5
.7		.5	1.0	Deferred Taxes		.5	.8	1.6	.2	1.6
6.8		4.0	4.0	All Other Non-Current		.8	10.8	2.1	4.3	2.3
38.9		34.8	39.4	Net Worth		27.3	27.2	48.0	43.3	47.2
100.0		100.0	100.0	Total Liabilities & Net Worth		100.0	100.0	100.0	100.0	100.0
				INCOME DATA						
100.0		100.0	100.0	Net Sales		100.0	100.0	100.0	100.0	100.0
31.1		32.0	32.7	Gross Profit		37.1	35.7	31.7	32.6	28.3
25.2		26.2	27.4	Operating Expenses		36.3	33.5	25.1	26.6	19.3
5.9		5.8	5.4	Operating Profit		.7	2.2	6.5	6.0	9.0
1.0		1.3	1.2	All Other Expenses (net)		2.8	.9	1.0	.9	1.0
4.9		4.5	4.2	Profit Before Taxes		−2.1	1.3	5.5	5.1	8.0
				RATIOS						
3.1		2.3	2.7			2.8	2.0	3.0	3.1	2.4
1.7		1.5	1.6	Current		1.2	1.4	2.1	2.2	1.9
1.1		1.0	1.0			.8	.6	1.1	.9	1.5
1.9		1.5	1.7			1.6	1.5	2.1	1.8	1.6
.8		.8	.8	Quick		.6	.7	1.1	.8	.8
.5		.5	.5			.3	.4	.5	.5	.6
24	15.3	27 13.6	29 12.6		24 15.0	20 18.5	30 12.3	30 12.1	31 11.9	
39	9.4	38 9.5	39 9.3	Sales/Receivables	38 9.7	35 10.3	35 10.4	40 9.2	41 8.9	
52	7.0	51 7.2	52 7.0		58 6.3	55 6.7	54 6.8	50 7.3	53 6.8	
27	13.5	35 10.5	28 13.1		12 29.8	6 59.6	22 16.5	34 10.8	34 10.7	
55	6.6	57 6.4	56 6.5	Cost of Sales/Inventory	71 5.1	62 5.9	48 7.6	57 6.4	55 6.6	
79	4.6	82 4.4	89 4.1		98 3.7	76 4.8	80 4.5	95 3.8	85 4.3	
17	21.1	18 20.3	17 21.3		20 18.7	10 35.0	19 19.5	17 21.5	16 23.5	
29	12.6	27 13.7	28 13.0	Cost of Sales/Payables	36 10.1	26 14.1	25 14.6	32 11.6	25 14.3	
42	8.7	43 8.4	43 8.6		59 6.2	69 5.3	42 8.6	43 8.6	37 9.8	
5.4		6.2	5.7			5.7	9.4	4.1	4.2	5.5
9.4		10.8	10.1	Sales/Working Capital		NM	14.6	7.4	6.7	8.3
60.2		96.2	−264.8			−14.7	−5.7	111.6	−47.9	14.4
	7.4	7.4	9.2			3.7	3.3	12.7	8.2	20.2
(99)	2.7	(100) 3.4	(93) 3.1	EBIT/Interest	(15) 1.5	(13) 1.4	(18) 5.3	4.6	(24) 5.1	
	1.4	1.3	1.6			.7	−.1	1.7	2.2	2.9
	6.8	5.8	4.8	Net Profit + Depr., Dep.,				7.2		8.1
(32)	2.2	(36) 2.1	(38) 2.3	Amort./Cur. Mat. L/T/D			(10) 2.7		(10) 1.6	
	1.3	1.0	1.4					1.3		1.3
	.6	.6	.6			.6	.4	.7	.5	.6
	1.2	1.2	1.2	Fixed/Worth		2.8	1.3	1.2	1.1	1.2
	2.4	2.1	2.2			15.1	71.0	2.2	2.1	1.5
	.7	.7	.7			.4	1.2	.4	.5	.6
	1.7	1.7	1.6	Debt/Worth		4.2	2.6	.8	1.5	1.3
	3.8	3.7	4.4			20.4	156.5	3.3	4.0	2.2
	33.3	36.5	32.8	% Profit Before Taxes/Tangible		37.4	22.0	36.1	37.9	33.7
(93)	18.8	(101) 22.9	(89) 14.7	Net Worth	(14) 7.0	(13) 9.5	14.7	(18) 15.7	(23) 18.1	
	7.3	8.7	4.3			.3	−8.9	4.5	5.9	11.9
	15.2	16.3	13.2	% Profit Before Taxes/Total		7.7	8.6	11.9	14.7	16.1
	6.7	6.9	5.6	Assets		1.0	2.3	7.5	6.8	8.4
	2.4	2.2	1.7			−2.6	−2.5	2.6	3.5	5.4
	6.9	7.3	6.4			4.5	10.4	6.7	11.8	5.2
	4.3	4.0	3.8	Sales/Net Fixed Assets		3.7	3.7	3.0	4.7	3.7
	2.9	2.6	2.6			2.0	2.5	1.9	3.2	2.6
	2.3	2.3	2.2			2.5	2.4	2.3	2.4	2.0
	1.8	1.8	1.7	Sales/Total Assets		1.6	1.6	1.7	1.9	1.6
	1.5	1.4	1.3			1.3	1.1	1.3	1.5	1.4
	2.1	2.3	3.0			3.3	3.0	3.1	2.5	2.9
(103)	3.3	(104) 3.7	(96) 4.2	% Depr., Dep., Amort./Sales	6.6	5.5	4.4	(19) 4.1	3.7	
	5.9	6.0	7.1			9.5	10.5	8.0	4.9	4.7
	1.9	2.1	1.7	% Officers', Directors',						
(45)	3.8	(44) 3.2	(33) 3.2	Owners' Comp/Sales						
	6.5	5.0	6.2							
1534042M		2194082M	2500364M	Net Sales ($)	500M	31467M	58944M	137215M	301193M	1971045M
949047M		1268220M	1665301M	Total Assets ($)	318M	23745M	40402M	96080M	178892M	1325864M

© RMA 2003

M = $ thousand   MM = $ million
See Pages 11 through 18 for Explanation of Ratios and Data

Current Data Sorted By Assets | Comparative Historical Data

0-500M	500M-2MM	2-10MM	10-50MM	50-100MM	100-250MM		4/1/98-3/31/99 ALL	4/1/99-3/31/00 ALL
						Type of Statement		
		9	18	4	1	Unqualified	46	24
1	6	34	8			Reviewed	35	44
1	5	11	1			Compiled	23	22
4	4	3				Tax Returns	4	9
1	8	18	13	1		Other	29	40
	21 (4/1-9/30/02)		130 (10/1/02-3/31/03)					
7	23	75	40	5	1	**NUMBER OF STATEMENTS**	137	139
%	%	%	%	%	%	**ASSETS**	%	%
	7.7	7.8	4.6			Cash & Equivalents	7.3	7.3
	24.7	29.6	32.8			Trade Receivables (net)	32.5	32.1
	17.7	13.3	11.0			Inventory	13.3	13.3
	.7	3.0	7.4			All Other Current	3.1	3.4
	50.9	53.8	55.8			Total Current	56.2	56.1
	38.7	37.7	37.8			Fixed Assets (net)	37.2	36.6
	.7	2.7	1.1			Intangibles (net)	1.7	1.9
	9.7	5.8	5.4			All Other Non-Current	4.8	5.4
	100.0	100.0	100.0			Total	100.0	100.0
						LIABILITIES		
	5.3	8.2	7.7			Notes Payable-Short Term	8.6	7.3
	6.0	4.3	4.0			Cur. Mat.-L/T/D	3.9	4.4
	14.7	13.7	12.6			Trade Payables	15.5	13.6
	.3	.2	.5			Income Taxes Payable	.4	.2
	6.9	8.8	11.6			All Other Current	10.6	10.8
	33.2	35.2	36.4			Total Current	38.9	36.4
	19.9	18.0	20.1			Long Term Debt	20.7	17.3
	.5	.3	.3			Deferred Taxes	.5	.4
	7.9	4.1	1.7			All Other Non-Current	5.0	4.4
	38.5	42.4	41.5			Net Worth	34.9	41.5
	100.0	100.0	100.0			Total Liabilities & Net Worth	100.0	100.0
						INCOME DATA		
	100.0	100.0	100.0			Net Sales	100.0	100.0
	42.5	31.2	25.1			Gross Profit	27.7	31.3
	36.5	25.3	20.5			Operating Expenses	25.3	28.6
	6.0	5.8	4.6			Operating Profit	2.4	2.7
	1.1	1.1	.5			All Other Expenses (net)	.2	-2.6
	5.0	4.8	4.1			Profit Before Taxes	2.2	5.3
						RATIOS		
	2.7	2.8	2.4				2.2	2.3
	2.1	1.6	1.7			Current	1.5	1.6
	.9	1.1	1.2				1.1	1.1
	2.0	2.0	1.5				1.7	1.8
	1.1	1.1	1.2			Quick	1.1	1.1
	.6	.6	.8				.7	.7
	20 17.9	37 9.9	47 7.8				40 9.0	38 9.6
	43 8.6	49 7.4	67 5.5			Sales/Receivables	56 6.5	51 7.1
	55 6.6	73 5.0	100 3.7				76 4.8	74 4.9
	23 16.2	14 26.0	7 50.4				11 31.8	11 32.0
	59 6.1	33 11.1	24 15.1			Cost of Sales/Inventory	29 12.7	28 12.9
	102 3.6	67 5.5	58 6.3				58 6.3	54 6.8
	22 16.3	17 21.0	18 20.5				22 16.9	20 18.0
	34 10.6	29 12.4	30 12.2			Cost of Sales/Payables	37 9.8	29 12.5
	58 6.2	41 8.9	48 7.6				53 6.9	50 7.3
	5.0	5.4	5.6				5.7	6.3
	9.3	10.1	8.4			Sales/Working Capital	9.9	11.3
	-82.3	58.2	22.3				35.7	57.3
	10.1	(67) 9.0	(34) 10.5				(125) 8.8	(121) 11.1
	(20) 3.3	4.8	3.4			EBIT/Interest	3.8	4.8
	1.5	1.5	1.9				1.9	1.9
		(24) 4.5	(19) 8.8				(45) 5.6	(36) 7.7
		2.5	3.1			Net Profit + Depr., Dep., Amort./Cur. Mat. L/T/D	2.8	2.6
		1.2	1.4				1.5	1.6
	.5	.5	.6				.5	.5
	.8	.9	.9			Fixed/Worth	1.0	.9
	2.3	1.7	1.5				2.4	1.7
	.5	.6	.7				.8	.7
	1.0	1.5	1.4			Debt/Worth	1.8	1.4
	5.0	2.9	2.8				4.3	3.2
	43.7	(70) 38.2	(38) 32.0				(125) 45.3	(127) 43.7
	(21) 16.7	21.9	18.6			% Profit Before Taxes/Tangible Net Worth	23.2	27.0
	6.9	8.3	6.9				11.8	10.9
	15.3	14.8	10.9				16.5	18.7
	7.3	8.2	6.3			% Profit Before Taxes/Total Assets	7.6	8.7
	3.1	1.7	2.1				3.5	3.3
	8.6	8.8	7.5				9.3	12.8
	6.7	5.0	4.7			Sales/Net Fixed Assets	5.8	6.4
	3.7	3.1	2.8				3.4	3.8
	2.8	2.5	2.1				2.4	2.6
	1.9	2.0	1.7			Sales/Total Assets	1.9	2.1
	1.6	1.4	1.3				1.4	1.6
	2.0	(69) 2.3	(37) 2.0				(128) 1.8	(128) 1.8
	(22) 3.4	3.5	3.3			% Depr., Dep., Amort./Sales	2.9	3.0
	5.9	5.4	5.4				4.6	4.8
	2.1	(31) 1.2					(34) 1.5	(49) 2.2
	(15) 5.2	3.1				% Officers', Directors', Owners' Comp/Sales	3.3	4.2
	11.5	5.4					6.0	9.5
6735M	71257M	712103M	1485436M	414537M	384776M	Net Sales ($)	2644423M	2331757M
2044M	33780M	371692M	881584M	305015M	223421M	Total Assets ($)	1514199M	1200293M

M = $ thousand   MM = $ million
See Pages 11 through 18 for Explanation of Ratios and Data

Comparative Historical Data | Current Data Sorted By Sales

						Type of Statement						
	25		32		32	Unqualified			1	4	4	23
	34		37		49	Reviewed		4	5	19	15	6
	32		40		18	Compiled	1	4	6	3	4	
	9		8		11	Tax Returns	2	7		2		
	36		45		41	Other	1	7	6	7	10	10
	4/1/00- 3/31/01 ALL		4/1/01- 3/31/02 ALL		4/1/02- 3/31/03 ALL		0-1MM	21 (4/1-9/30/02) 1-3MM	3-5MM	130 (10/1/02-3/31/03) 5-10MM	10-25MM	25MM & OVER
	136		162		151	NUMBER OF STATEMENTS	4	22	18	35	33	39
	%		%		%	ASSETS	%	%	%	%	%	%
	9.1		6.8		7.2	Cash & Equivalents		11.6	9.5	5.7	7.7	3.8
	29.6		30.0		28.9	Trade Receivables (net)		20.6	23.4	31.3	33.1	31.4
	13.3		13.8		13.3	Inventory		16.7	14.1	13.5	12.7	11.8
	3.6		3.4		3.8	All Other Current		1.9	.4	3.2	5.2	5.8
	55.6		54.0		53.2	Total Current		50.9	47.4	53.7	58.8	52.7
	37.4		36.8		38.8	Fixed Assets (net)		37.7	44.3	39.8	31.9	40.2
	3.0		2.7		2.0	Intangibles (net)		1.4	4.2	2.7	1.0	1.8
	4.0		6.4		6.0	All Other Non-Current		10.0	4.1	3.8	8.3	5.3
	100.0		100.0		100.0	Total		100.0	100.0	100.0	100.0	100.0
						LIABILITIES						
	7.9		9.1		7.3	Notes Payable-Short Term		3.7	10.1	9.4	7.5	6.1
	4.3		4.7		4.8	Cur. Mat.-L/T/D		5.7	4.6	5.2	3.9	3.8
	14.2		15.3		14.2	Trade Payables		12.6	11.8	13.6	15.3	12.7
	.3		.2		.3	Income Taxes Payable		.0	.2	.2	.5	.5
	10.5		10.5		9.5	All Other Current		6.5	5.2	9.2	10.4	11.7
	37.3		39.8		36.0	Total Current		28.6	32.0	37.6	37.5	34.9
	22.4		21.0		22.4	Long Term Debt		22.5	25.7	16.2	13.0	23.4
	.5		.6		.3	Deferred Taxes		.5	.2	.4	.2	.4
	3.6		4.1		3.8	All Other Non-Current		6.6	4.0	4.3	4.7	1.3
	36.3		34.4		37.4	Net Worth		41.9	38.1	41.5	44.6	39.9
	100.0		100.0		100.0	Total Liabilities & Net Worth		100.0	100.0	100.0	100.0	100.0
						INCOME DATA						
	100.0		100.0		100.0	Net Sales		100.0	100.0	100.0	100.0	100.0
	30.4		28.6		31.0	Gross Profit		40.8	37.6	32.1	27.7	23.6
	23.9		24.1		25.9	Operating Expenses		34.4	30.4	28.2	21.9	18.4
	6.5		4.6		5.2	Operating Profit		6.4	7.2	4.0	5.8	5.2
	1.2		1.5		.9	All Other Expenses (net)		1.0	2.1	.9	.3	.9
	5.3		3.1		4.2	Profit Before Taxes		5.5	5.1	3.1	5.5	4.3
						RATIOS						
	2.2		2.2		2.6			4.2	3.2	2.3	2.5	2.3
	1.6		1.4		1.7	Current		2.1	1.8	1.3	1.5	1.7
	1.1		1.0		1.1			1.0	1.1	1.1	1.0	1.2
	1.6		1.4		1.7			2.2	2.1	1.8	1.6	1.4
	1.1		1.0		1.1	Quick		1.2	1.4	1.0	1.1	1.1
	.7		.6		.6			.5	.5	.6	.6	.9
32	11.3	34	10.7	33	11.0		15	23.8	30	12.2	42	8.7	35	10.4	45	8.1
47	7.8	50	7.3	52	7.1	Sales/Receivables	37	9.9	48	7.5	55	6.7	49	7.5	61	6.0
72	5.1	70	5.2	76	4.8		66	5.5	86	4.3	67	5.4	85	4.3	73	5.0
11	34.5	10	38.2	12	29.9		26	13.8	25	14.3	9	40.2	9	40.7	12	29.9
28	12.9	33	11.0	33	11.2	Cost of Sales/Inventory	70	5.2	45	8.1	32	11.3	23	16.0	26	14.2
59	6.2	63	5.8	68	5.3		116	3.2	92	4.3	65	5.6	45	8.1	59	6.2
19	19.0	22	16.9	17	20.9		17	21.9	15	24.3	21	17.1	19	19.4	17	20.9
31	11.7	33	11.1	29	12.4	Cost of Sales/Payables	28	12.9	31	11.9	29	12.4	31	11.9	27	13.3
46	8.0	49	7.4	49	7.5		59	6.2	59	6.2	51	7.2	41	8.9	46	7.9
	6.0		6.8		5.3			4.6	5.3	6.7	4.6	6.4
	9.5		14.6		9.5	Sales/Working Capital		6.2	8.0	11.3	10.7	8.6
	57.6		−421.6		46.1			UND	NM	58.2	NM	17.2
	9.1		7.1		10.0			17.0	6.4	8.9	12.2	9.3
(119)	2.9	(149)	3.0	(133)	3.5	EBIT/Interest	(20)	3.3	(16)	2.2	(30)	5.0	(29)	5.0	(34)	3.5
	1.5		1.4		1.4			1.6		−.7		1.2		1.9		2.0
	4.7		5.0		4.7						3.6	4.3	9.1
(41)	2.1	(56)	2.4	(52)	2.5	Net Profit + Depr., Dep., Amort./Cur. Mat. L/T/D			(16)	2.1	(11)	3.0	(17)	2.8
	1.3		1.3		1.4						1.0	1.7	1.6
	.5		.6		.5			.4	.5	.6	.3	.7
	1.0		1.2		.9	Fixed/Worth		.8	1.3	1.3	.8	1.1
	2.1		3.2		1.8			3.7	3.3	1.6	1.7	1.5
	.8		1.0		.6			.3	.8	.6	.5	1.0
	1.6		2.3		1.4	Debt/Worth		.9	1.6	1.6	1.3	1.6
	3.9		5.4		3.0			7.8	5.3	2.9	3.0	2.7
	44.9		40.3		38.8			38.6	62.6	37.3	38.1	36.6
(121)	24.6	(144)	19.8	(140)	20.2	% Profit Before Taxes/Tangible Net Worth	(20)	18.4	(16)	21.6	(33)	21.5	(31)	22.3	(37)	18.4
	9.4		8.3		7.2			6.8		7.6		3.2		12.3		9.7
	17.8		12.4		14.6			18.6	18.7	14.3	17.4	11.3
	7.4		6.2		7.3	% Profit Before Taxes/Total Assets		7.7	3.7	7.5	11.7	6.8
	2.2		1.4		1.5			.7	−2.6	1.3	2.8	3.4
	12.5		10.1		8.5			9.8	6.5	8.4	12.9	7.1
	5.7		6.0		4.9	Sales/Net Fixed Assets		6.6	3.6	4.7	6.9	4.5
	3.5		3.8		3.8			3.4	1.9	2.8	4.6	2.9
	2.6		2.6		2.4			2.5	2.0	2.5	2.6	2.2
	2.0		2.0		1.9	Sales/Total Assets		1.8	1.3	2.1	2.1	1.8
	1.5		1.5		1.4			1.3	1.1	1.5	1.6	1.3
	1.5		1.7		2.1			2.0	2.9	2.7	1.8	2.1
(129)	3.2	(146)	3.3	(139)	3.5	% Depr., Dep., Amort./Sales	(20)	3.6	(16)	3.4	4.1	(29)	2.6	(36)	3.1
	4.9		4.8		5.4			6.6	6.6	7.0	4.1	4.3
	2.4		1.9		1.6			2.1		1.6	1.0	
(43)	4.0	(60)	3.7	(56)	3.2	% Officers', Directors', Owners' Comp/Sales	(12)	7.0	(17)	3.0	(12)	2.3	
	6.3		8.1		7.0			11.6		6.8	4.9	
	2862304M		3283755M		3074844M	Net Sales ($)	2451M	48817M	72814M	256848M	500004M	2193910M
	1555730M		1945310M		1817536M	Total Assets ($)	1051M	36458M	54888M	166079M	255218M	1303842M

© RMA 2003   M = $ thousand   MM = $ million
See Pages 11 through 18 for Explanation of Ratios and Data

Current Data Sorted By Assets							Comparative Historical Data	
		4	3		1	Type of Statement Unqualified	12	11
	8	7	1			Reviewed	11	7
	1	2				Compiled	3	7
		1				Tax Returns	1	
	2	1	3	1		Other	8	7
	6 (4/1-9/30/02)		29 (10/1/02-3/31/03)				4/1/98-3/31/99	4/1/99-3/31/00
0-500M	500M-2MM	2-10MM	10-50MM	50-100MM	100-250MM		ALL	ALL
	11	15	7	1	1	NUMBER OF STATEMENTS	35	32
%	%	%	%	%	%	ASSETS	%	%
D A T A N O T A V A I L A B L E	4.6	6.9				Cash & Equivalents	7.0	4.3
	31.7	22.7				Trade Receivables (net)	23.8	27.1
	24.3	25.3				Inventory	32.1	34.1
	1.2	6.8				All Other Current	2.6	1.1
	61.7	61.8				Total Current	65.5	66.7
	25.2	28.6				Fixed Assets (net)	27.1	25.9
	3.4	4.1				Intangibles (net)	3.0	1.8
	9.7	5.5				All Other Non-Current	4.4	5.7
	100.0	100.0				Total	100.0	100.0
						LIABILITIES		
	18.0	8.9				Notes Payable-Short Term	7.2	14.4
	2.1	11.9				Cur. Mat.-L/T/D	3.2	2.1
	22.9	10.3				Trade Payables	15.7	16.2
	.0	.4				Income Taxes Payable	.4	.1
	5.1	6.5				All Other Current	9.1	9.2
	48.1	38.1				Total Current	35.6	42.0
	14.7	14.4				Long Term Debt	11.9	9.3
	.0	.4				Deferred Taxes	.8	.9
	1.9	1.4				All Other Non-Current	6.2	4.6
	35.3	45.7				Net Worth	45.5	43.2
	100.0	100.0				Total Liabilities & Net Worth	100.0	100.0
						INCOME DATA		
	100.0	100.0				Net Sales	100.0	100.0
	26.5	34.2				Gross Profit	31.1	32.5
	22.7	28.7				Operating Expenses	24.9	27.0
	3.8	5.5				Operating Profit	6.2	5.5
	.8	2.2				All Other Expenses (net)	.1	.9
	2.9	3.3				Profit Before Taxes	6.1	4.6
						RATIOS		
	2.8	3.6					3.0	2.7
	1.0	1.6				Current	2.0	1.4
	.8	1.1					1.3	1.1
	1.9	1.3					1.4	1.4
	.7	1.0				Quick	1.1	.8
	.3	.6					.5	.5
	33 11.1	**38** 9.6					**32** 11.5	**37** 9.7
	46 8.0	**49** 7.4				Sales/Receivables	**46** 8.0	**49** 7.5
	49 7.5	**59** 6.2					**58** 6.3	**62** 5.9
	23 15.8	**42** 8.7					**62** 5.9	**62** 5.8
	54 6.7	**74** 5.0				Cost of Sales/Inventory	**86** 4.2	**90** 4.0
	71 5.1	**84** 4.4					**147** 2.5	**138** 2.6
	15 24.0	**12** 29.9					**18** 20.7	**13** 27.9
	39 9.4	**25** 14.6				Cost of Sales/Payables	**30** 12.2	**29** 12.6
	88 4.1	**40** 9.1					**56** 6.5	**57** 6.5
	6.1	3.3					4.0	4.9
	148.9	7.3				Sales/Working Capital	6.2	7.0
	−35.2	27.2					11.6	53.0
	9.6	10.1					15.6	12.3
	2.7	2.5				EBIT/Interest	(29) 5.2	(28) 2.6
	1.7	.4					1.6	1.3
							3.4	5.9
						Net Profit + Depr., Dep., Amort./Cur. Mat. L/T/D	(15) 1.9	(10) 2.9
							.8	1.5
	.4	.3					.3	.4
	1.1	.7				Fixed/Worth	.6	.6
	3.4	1.0					1.8	1.2
	.7	.6					.5	.6
	2.4	1.1				Debt/Worth	1.2	1.8
	10.6	3.8					3.4	4.3
	80.4	37.0					45.4	34.9
	20.9	(14) 15.2				% Profit Before Taxes/Tangible Net Worth	(33) 26.9	(30) 15.0
	1.2	.8					14.1	2.3
	8.5	10.6					19.9	11.3
	3.8	5.6				% Profit Before Taxes/Total Assets	11.1	5.1
	.8	−2.0					2.5	1.3
	15.7	9.6					13.4	14.4
	9.7	6.1				Sales/Net Fixed Assets	6.6	6.5
	6.8	3.4					3.6	4.8
	3.1	2.2					2.3	2.4
	2.7	1.8				Sales/Total Assets	1.9	1.8
	1.8	1.2					1.2	1.5
	1.7	2.1					.8	1.4
	2.8	(14) 2.9				% Depr., Dep., Amort./Sales	(31) 2.2	(27) 2.2
	4.0	4.4					3.5	3.6
							2.6	3.3
						% Officers', Directors', Owners' Comp/Sales	(11) 5.0	(11) 5.5
							7.2	8.4
	28324M	129983M	266268M	113409M	97848M	Net Sales ($)	754748M	496983M
	12233M	74190M	181524M	81020M	143558M	Total Assets ($)	504511M	343704M

M = $ thousand MM = $ million

See Pages 11 through 18 for Explanation of Ratios and Data

Comparative Historical Data | Current Data Sorted By Sales

				Type of Statement						
12		9	8	Unqualified		1	1	3	3	
7		13	16	Reviewed	6	6	3	1	1	
14		26	3	Compiled	1	1		1		
1		6	1	Tax Returns				1		
7		30	7	Other	1	1		2	2	3
4/1/00-3/31/01		4/1/01-3/31/02	4/1/02-3/31/03			6 (4/1-9/30/02)		29 (10/1/02-3/31/03)		
ALL		ALL	ALL		0-1MM	1-3MM	3-5MM	5-10MM	10-25MM	25MM & OVER
41		84	35	**NUMBER OF STATEMENTS**	8	9	4	8	8	6
%		%	%	**ASSETS**	%	%	%	%	%	%
4.6		7.1	5.9	Cash & Equivalents	D					
24.9		25.4	24.7	Trade Receivables (net)	A					
25.2		25.1	24.7	Inventory	T					
3.1		3.8	4.7	All Other Current	A					
57.8		61.5	60.1	Total Current						
33.0		29.2	27.9	Fixed Assets (net)	N					
4.0		2.5	4.6	Intangibles (net)	O					
5.2		6.8	7.4	All Other Non-Current	T					
100.0		100.0	100.0	Total						
				LIABILITIES	A					
12.0		12.1	11.2	Notes Payable-Short Term	V					
3.9		5.2	7.4	Cur. Mat.-L/T/D	A					
14.0		12.2	14.2	Trade Payables	I					
.3		.2	.3	Income Taxes Payable	L					
8.3		6.4	6.0	All Other Current	A					
38.5		36.1	39.1	Total Current	B					
24.1		15.3	15.6	Long Term Debt	L					
.4		.7	.4	Deferred Taxes	E					
4.1		5.8	2.4	All Other Non-Current						
32.8		42.2	42.4	Net Worth						
100.0		100.0	100.0	Total Liabilities & Net Worth						
				INCOME DATA						
100.0		100.0	100.0	Net Sales						
30.1		29.0	30.5	Gross Profit						
25.5		26.0	24.9	Operating Expenses						
4.6		3.0	5.6	Operating Profit						
1.9		1.2	1.6	All Other Expenses (net)						
2.7		1.8	4.0	Profit Before Taxes						
				RATIOS						
2.7		3.5	2.9							
1.5		1.8	1.6	Current						
1.1		1.1	1.0							
1.8		1.8	1.7							
.8		.9	.9	Quick						
.4		.5	.5							
35	10.3	37 9.9	35 10.5							
44	8.4	47 7.8	46 7.9	Sales/Receivables						
60	6.1	60 6.1	59 6.2							
36	10.0	36 10.1	39 9.4							
60	6.1	57 6.4	68 5.3	Cost of Sales/Inventory						
89	4.1	102 3.6	84 4.4							
18	20.0	15 24.7	15 24.0							
31	11.8	24 14.9	27 13.6	Cost of Sales/Payables						
42	8.8	41 9.0	46 8.0							
6.0		4.2	4.4							
9.9		7.7	7.8	Sales/Working Capital						
42.8		38.4	148.9							
(40)	8.7	(74) 6.4	10.1							
	3.3	2.9	2.9	EBIT/Interest						
	.8	.4	1.3							
		4.6	5.5	Net Profit + Depr., Dep.,						
(28)		1.6	(11) 2.2	Amort./Cur. Mat. L/T/D						
		.5	1.3							
.6		.3	.4							
1.1		.7	.8	Fixed/Worth						
2.5		2.1	2.0							
.8		.5	.6							
2.2		1.4	1.3	Debt/Worth						
7.8		4.8	5.0							
(37)	43.8	(77) 30.9	(33) 32.3	% Profit Before Taxes/Tangible						
	25.5	14.2	20.9	Net Worth						
	2.8	-3.0	1.7							
11.8		12.3	10.6							
6.7		4.4	6.3	% Profit Before Taxes/Total Assets						
-1.2		-2.4	.8							
11.0		12.9	9.7							
6.1		7.2	6.8	Sales/Net Fixed Assets						
3.7		3.6	4.5							
2.3		2.5	2.3							
1.8		1.9	1.8	Sales/Total Assets						
1.4		1.4	1.4							
2.1		1.6	2.0							
(37)	3.1	(75) 2.5	(33) 2.9	% Depr., Dep., Amort./Sales						
	4.9	4.1	4.2							
3.6		3.5	2.0	% Officers', Directors',						
(12)	6.8	(33) 5.4	(12) 3.6	Owners' Comp/Sales						
	13.0	9.0	4.9							
992258M		1596588M	635832M	Net Sales ($)		17663M	34901M	31051M	130070M	422147M
710007M		996330M	492525M	Total Assets ($)		8502M	25229M	18344M	81505M	358945M

© RMA 2003

M = $ thousand   MM = $ million
See Pages 11 through 18 for Explanation of Ratios and Data

Current Data Sorted By Assets   Comparative Historical Data

0-500M	500M-2MM	2-10MM	10-50MM	50-100MM	100-250MM	Type of Statement	4/1/98-3/31/99 ALL	4/1/99-3/31/00 ALL
	1	6	2	1		Unqualified	14	9
	5	5	2			Reviewed	15	17
	9	3				Compiled	20	19
6	7	2			1	Tax Returns	10	10
4	10	6	3		1	Other	20	19
	11 (4/1-9/30/02)		63 (10/1/02-3/31/03)		1			
10	32	22	8		1	**NUMBER OF STATEMENTS**	79	74
%	%	%	%	%	%	**ASSETS**	%	%
8.8	5.1	3.7				Cash & Equivalents	7.0	6.9
20.5	27.2	24.8				Trade Receivables (net)	23.6	23.9
27.6	16.9	27.9				Inventory	22.4	22.8
5.0	3.8	2.0				All Other Current	1.1	1.4
61.9	53.0	58.4				Total Current	54.1	55.0
25.2	40.4	36.5				Fixed Assets (net)	35.6	36.8
.4	1.0	.9				Intangibles (net)	2.6	2.0
12.4	5.5	4.3				All Other Non-Current	7.7	6.1
100.0	100.0	100.0				Total	100.0	100.0
						LIABILITIES		
10.4	6.5	12.1				Notes Payable-Short Term	5.3	7.5
1.9	5.6	5.9				Cur. Mat.-L/T/D	5.5	4.1
15.9	17.0	21.4				Trade Payables	15.0	13.8
.2	.1	.0				Income Taxes Payable	.2	.1
17.9	8.5	8.6				All Other Current	10.4	11.1
46.3	37.8	48.1				Total Current	36.4	36.6
22.1	24.5	13.0				Long Term Debt	22.5	18.8
.5	.0	.4				Deferred Taxes	.4	.8
4.2	5.5	6.2				All Other Non-Current	5.9	2.2
26.9	32.1	32.2				Net Worth	34.9	41.7
100.0	100.0	100.0				Total Liabilities & Net Worth	100.0	100.0
						INCOME DATA		
100.0	100.0	100.0				Net Sales	100.0	100.0
43.4	37.1	31.8				Gross Profit	34.2	37.2
41.9	32.8	28.5				Operating Expenses	28.1	28.9
1.5	4.3	3.3				Operating Profit	6.1	8.3
.7	1.5	1.2				All Other Expenses (net)	1.1	.9
.8	2.8	2.0				Profit Before Taxes	5.0	7.4
						RATIOS		
2.1 1.6 .8	2.3 1.4 .9	2.0 1.5 1.1				Current	2.6 1.7 1.2	2.4 1.5 1.1
1.6 .4 .1	1.5 .8 .4	.9 .6 .3				Quick	1.7 1.0 .7	1.4 .8 .5
0 UND 14 25.7 34 10.8	22 16.7 36 10.2 52 7.1	26 14.0 37 10.0 45 8.1				Sales/Receivables	25 14.4 43 8.5 59 6.2	29 12.7 38 9.6 53 6.9
17 21.8 36 10.1 142 2.6	9 39.4 29 12.4 63 5.8	32 11.4 56 6.6 121 3.0				Cost of Sales/Inventory	27 13.6 52 7.0 88 4.1	30 12.3 64 5.7 92 3.9
1 279.6 17 21.8 61 6.0	14 26.6 27 13.5 45 8.0	14 25.6 30 12.2 52 7.0				Cost of Sales/Payables	20 18.3 31 11.9 51 7.1	21 17.5 32 11.4 47 7.8
9.6 18.0 -139.0	6.0 26.4 -81.2	8.5 14.2 37.2				Sales/Working Capital	5.4 9.7 26.1	7.1 11.9 29.6
	8.2 5.1 2.5	(20) 18.8 2.5 .2				EBIT/Interest	(76) 9.2 2.5 1.1	(69) 14.7 5.7 1.9
						Net Profit + Depr., Dep., Amort./Cur. Mat. L /T/D	(28) 6.7 3.3 1.6	(19) 7.4 2.4 1.8
.1 .5 NM	.6 1.4 25.8	.5 .8 1.9				Fixed/Worth	.4 .7 1.7	.4 .8 1.8
.7 2.7 NM	1.1 2.5 46.8	.7 1.7 11.2				Debt/Worth	.7 1.3 3.6	.8 1.5 3.0
	(27) 77.8 23.5 9.5	(18) 53.4 24.8 -.4				% Profit Before Taxes/Tangible Net Worth	(69) 26.2 16.8 6.0	(71) 54.6 22.8 9.3
32.8 8.5 -4.2	18.0 5.9 3.7	19.6 4.9 -2.7				% Profit Before Taxes/Total Assets	12.4 6.2 1.5	18.7 10.0 3.1
UND 27.1 8.7	14.2 6.9 3.7	11.4 6.3 2.1				Sales/Net Fixed Assets	13.8 6.6 3.0	17.8 7.4 2.3
6.7 4.2 1.5	3.6 2.4 1.7	3.1 2.0 1.3				Sales/Total Assets	2.7 1.9 1.4	3.0 2.1 1.3
	(30) 2.2 3.8 8.6	(19) 1.6 2.5 7.3				% Depr., Dep., Amort./Sales	(74) 1.6 2.8 4.7	(67) 1.4 2.3 4.3
	(22) 2.4 5.7 7.0	(12) 1.6 2.4 4.0				% Officers', Directors', Owners' Comp/Sales	(37) 2.8 4.9 8.1	(35) 2.2 5.2 8.9
13303M	99515M	225481M	367047M	76786M	338821M	Net Sales ($)	738542M	1163837M
3110M	37056M	101197M	171791M	67346M	112889M	Total Assets ($)	697427M	1101656M

M = $ thousand   MM = $ million
See Pages 11 through 18 for Explanation of Ratios and Data

Comparative Historical Data | Current Data Sorted By Sales

								Type of Statement						
	6		9		10			Unqualified	1	1	1	1	3	3
	10		16		12			Reviewed		4	1	3	3	1
	16		24		12			Compiled		6	1	3	2	
	14		7		16			Tax Returns	2	8	3	1	1	1
	12		19		24			Other	2	8	2	5	5	2
	4/1/00-3/31/01 ALL		4/1/01-3/31/02 ALL		4/1/02-3/31/03 ALL				0-1MM	11 (4/1-9/30/02) 1-3MM	3-5MM	63 (10/1/02-3/31/03) 5-10MM	10-25MM	25MM & OVER
	58		75		74			NUMBER OF STATEMENTS	5	27	8	13	14	7
	%		%		%			ASSETS	%	%	%	%	%	%
	8.1		11.0		5.4			Cash & Equivalents		8.5		2.9	4.9	
	22.3		22.2		24.7			Trade Receivables (net)		25.0		24.7	31.9	
	20.8		17.8		22.2			Inventory		20.7		21.7	30.5	
	1.9		2.2		3.1			All Other Current		4.1		3.9	1.4	
	53.2		53.2		55.5			Total Current		58.3		53.2	68.7	
	39.9		37.7		36.3			Fixed Assets (net)		37.3		39.7	27.5	
	1.8		3.1		2.0			Intangibles (net)		.4		.5	.7	
	5.1		6.1		6.2			All Other Non-Current		4.0		6.5	3.1	
	100.0		100.0		100.0			Total		100.0		100.0	100.0	
								LIABILITIES						
	10.0		6.8		8.4			Notes Payable-Short Term		5.5		9.1	12.8	
	4.1		7.7		4.8			Cur. Mat.-L/T/D		6.6		4.3	2.6	
	14.5		12.3		20.0			Trade Payables		14.1		19.5	25.0	
	.3		.1		.1			Income Taxes Payable		.2		.0	.0	
	6.8		9.3		9.4			All Other Current		11.4		8.5	9.9	
	35.8		36.2		42.8			Total Current		37.8		41.4	50.4	
	19.0		21.3		19.9			Long Term Debt		22.1		13.7	11.5	
	.3		.4		.3			Deferred Taxes		.0		.3	.4	
	4.0		5.6		5.4			All Other Non-Current		4.7		5.9	6.5	
	40.9		36.5		31.6			Net Worth		35.4		38.7	31.2	
	100.0		100.0		100.0			Total Liabilities & Net Worth		100.0		100.0	100.0	
								INCOME DATA						
	100.0		100.0		100.0			Net Sales		100.0		100.0	100.0	
	34.4		35.2		36.5			Gross Profit		40.5		29.1	31.0	
	27.2		27.7		32.2			Operating Expenses		35.0		24.8	25.2	
	7.2		7.5		4.3			Operating Profit		5.5		4.4	5.8	
	.3		1.7		1.2			All Other Expenses (net)		1.1		.4	.9	
	6.9		5.8		3.0			Profit Before Taxes		4.4		3.9	4.9	
								RATIOS						
	2.2		2.5		2.2					2.3		2.5	2.1	
	1.6		1.4		1.6			Current		1.9		1.7	1.6	
	1.1		1.0		1.0					1.0		1.0	1.2	
	1.3		1.5		1.2					1.8		1.3	1.7	
	.8		.8		.7			Quick		.8		.7	.7	
	.5		.5		.4					.4		.4	.4	
20	17.8	21	17.3	23	16.1				19	19.4	20	18.6	25	14.7
35	10.5	34	10.8	35	10.5		Sales/Receivables	36	10.2	36	10.3	32	11.3
47	7.8	42	8.7	45	8.1			52	7.1	45	8.0	40	9.1
20	18.3	13	27.0	17	21.8			16	22.3	18	20.1	22	16.7
53	6.9	33	11.0	44	8.2		Cost of Sales/Inventory	46	8.0	37	9.9	62	5.9
99	3.7	91	4.0	95	3.8			87	4.2	85	4.3	106	3.4
16	23.0	13	27.1	14	25.6			9	38.6	14	25.7	13	29.1
27	13.3	23	15.8	27	13.8		Cost of Sales/Payables	21	17.3	21	17.7	32	11.4
45	8.1	46	7.9	52	7.0			54	6.8	41	9.0	53	6.9
	5.8		6.8		7.0					5.6		6.1	9.0	
	10.7		14.0		13.1		Sales/Working Capital		10.6		10.1	14.2	
	44.0		747.6		UND				UND		NM	25.8	
	12.3		12.6		11.6				8.3		10.1	42.2	
(56)	4.1	(68)	2.8	(70)	4.5		EBIT/Interest		5.7	(12)	3.4	(13)	5.9
	1.7		1.2		1.2				1.2		1.1	1.9	
	9.8		4.1		5.8		Net Profit + Depr., Dep.,						
(17)	2.7	(19)	2.1	(17)	2.7		Amort./Cur. Mat. L/T/D						
	1.3		1.3		1.0								
	.4		.5		.5				.3		.7	.2	
	.9		.9		.9		Fixed/Worth		1.0		.9	.6	
	2.1		4.0		3.1				2.7		1.6	1.2	
	.6		.7		.9				.7		.9	.6	
	1.4		1.8		2.1		Debt/Worth		2.2		1.5	2.4	
	3.5		6.4		7.1				4.9		3.1	5.7	
	54.1		56.2		68.7		% Profit Before Taxes/Tangible		86.9		44.2	51.0	
(54)	24.3	(67)	28.8	(61)	24.2		Net Worth	(23)	16.7	(11)	23.5	(12)	33.7
	8.9		10.5		7.9				7.9		1.9	24.0	
	22.9		22.8		19.7		% Profit Before Taxes/Total		20.6		18.2	28.0	
	8.6		7.6		5.7		Assets		5.4		7.0	7.2	
	2.4		1.4		.7				1.5		.5	-.5	
	13.5		12.8		21.3				20.9		11.1	44.5	
	6.6		6.2		7.0		Sales/Net Fixed Assets		6.0		6.9	8.8	
	2.6		3.4		2.9				3.4		2.6	5.7	
	3.0		3.0		3.7				3.5		3.8	4.3	
	2.2		2.3		2.3		Sales/Total Assets		2.3		2.6	2.7	
	1.4		1.4		1.4				1.6		1.4	1.7	
	1.6		1.3		1.9				2.3		1.6	.7	
(51)	2.7	(68)	2.7	(64)	3.1		% Depr., Dep., Amort./Sales	(23)	4.6		2.2	(11)	2.0
	5.1		4.8		6.8				10.2		3.9	2.5	
	1.9		2.6		2.0				4.7				
(37)	4.4	(42)	4.1	(43)	4.2		% Officers', Directors',	(18)	6.2				
	6.9		6.2		6.9		Owners' Comp/Sales		7.5				
	598417M		976144M		1120953M		Net Sales ($)	1946M	56354M	30189M	85159M	216687M	730618M
	496361M		610669M		493389M		Total Assets ($)	2437M	27132M	16152M	44242M	88213M	315213M

M = $ thousand   MM = $ million
See Pages 11 through 18 for Explanation of Ratios and Data

Current Data Sorted By Assets   Comparative Historical Data

						Type of Statement		
		5	8	3	1	Unqualified	29	29
	2	8	4			Reviewed	18	10
2	6	3				Compiled	16	12
1	3					Tax Returns		1
2	4	7	6	4	2	Other	41	34
	15 (4/1-9/30/02)		56 (10/1/02-3/31/03)				4/1/98-3/31/99	4/1/99-3/31/00
0-500M	500M-2MM	2-10MM	10-50MM	50-100MM	100-250MM		ALL	ALL
5	15	23	18	7	3	**NUMBER OF STATEMENTS**	104	86
%	%	%	%	%	%	**ASSETS**	%	%
	4.6	5.5	6.0			Cash & Equivalents	5.1	6.8
	36.0	28.5	22.4			Trade Receivables (net)	26.4	26.8
	17.0	17.9	24.9			Inventory	23.7	21.7
	5.6	2.8	3.7			All Other Current	2.0	3.2
	63.2	54.7	56.9			Total Current	57.3	58.6
	26.2	34.1	33.3			Fixed Assets (net)	34.2	32.0
	.6	3.1	4.0			Intangibles (net)	1.9	2.8
	9.9	8.1	5.8			All Other Non-Current	6.5	6.5
	100.0	100.0	100.0			Total	100.0	100.0
						LIABILITIES		
	14.0	11.7	12.7			Notes Payable-Short Term	10.1	8.6
	2.9	5.2	2.8			Cur. Mat.-L/T/D	4.6	3.5
	21.2	15.9	11.8			Trade Payables	15.9	14.9
	.0	.1	1.1			Income Taxes Payable	.4	.7
	6.5	6.3	9.1			All Other Current	9.0	8.9
	44.5	39.2	37.5			Total Current	39.9	36.6
	14.4	14.0	10.2			Long Term Debt	19.4	20.1
	.3	.2	.1			Deferred Taxes	.9	1.1
	4.5	5.8	8.1			All Other Non-Current	4.8	6.7
	36.2	40.8	44.2			Net Worth	34.9	35.4
	100.0	100.0	100.0			Total Liabilities & Net Worth	100.0	100.0
						INCOME DATA		
	100.0	100.0	100.0			Net Sales	100.0	100.0
	30.6	25.1	24.8			Gross Profit	22.8	22.9
	24.2	20.7	18.8			Operating Expenses	17.1	17.4
	6.4	4.4	6.0			Operating Profit	5.7	5.5
	.2	.4	1.0			All Other Expenses (net)	1.5	1.0
	6.2	3.9	5.1			Profit Before Taxes	4.2	4.5
						RATIOS		
	3.6	2.3	3.4				2.5	2.6
	1.5	1.2	2.1			Current	1.5	1.8
	.9	.9	1.0				1.0	1.1
	1.5	1.4	1.3				1.5	1.4
	.9	.9	.9			Quick	.8	1.0
	.6	.5	.4				.5	.6
40	9.1	37 9.9	36 10.1				34 10.6	38 9.5
50	7.4	45 8.1	43 8.5			Sales/Receivables	45 8.2	48 7.6
76	4.8	52 7.0	57 6.4				57 6.4	64 5.7
2	230.3	23 15.6	28 13.2				18 19.9	28 13.1
22	16.4	46 8.0	75 4.8			Cost of Sales/Inventory	59 6.2	60 6.1
83	4.4	58 6.3	125 2.9				94 3.9	97 3.7
27	13.7	21 17.4	15 24.9				20 17.9	22 16.4
49	7.4	29 12.7	33 11.2			Cost of Sales/Payables	31 11.7	34 10.6
64	5.7	47 7.7	44 8.4				45 8.2	51 7.2
	4.9	6.0	3.3				5.5	4.2
	12.9	20.8	5.2			Sales/Working Capital	11.1	7.9
	−33.8	−45.2	−128.3				132.3	48.0
	19.4	9.0	27.3				7.5	7.7
(12)	6.0	(22) 3.6	(16) 3.7			EBIT/Interest	(95) 3.4	(71) 3.0
	2.7	1.6	−.6				1.5	1.3
						Net Profit + Depr., Dep.,	8.5	31.2
						Amort./Cur. Mat. L /T/D	(38) 3.4	(25) 3.1
							2.0	1.5
	.3	.3	.5				.4	.4
	.6	1.1	.9			Fixed/Worth	.9	.9
	2.0	2.3	1.4				2.3	3.0
	1.0	.5	.5				.9	.7
	2.4	2.8	1.6			Debt/Worth	2.0	2.1
	4.5	4.8	3.3				4.7	5.9
	65.7	39.0	53.8			% Profit Before Taxes/Tangible	42.2	47.6
(14)	38.6	22.7	(17) 25.5			Net Worth	(98) 22.1	(77) 18.9
	6.4	4.3	−10.2				6.9	4.5
	42.6	11.7	20.8			% Profit Before Taxes/Total	14.8	14.9
	7.6	6.6	7.8			Assets	6.8	5.3
	3.1	1.1	−3.7				2.0	1.0
	42.0	13.7	11.3				14.7	19.2
	13.5	6.7	5.2			Sales/Net Fixed Assets	6.6	5.2
	4.2	2.9	2.7				3.1	3.0
	3.1	2.7	2.1				2.7	2.6
	2.5	2.1	1.6			Sales/Total Assets	1.8	1.7
	1.9	1.4	1.2				1.3	1.3
	.4	1.6	1.9				1.4	1.0
(13)	1.6	(21) 2.2	(17) 4.0			% Depr., Dep., Amort./Sales	(87) 2.7	(74) 2.5
	2.6	4.4	6.3				4.3	4.6
							2.0	1.5
						% Officers', Directors',	(25) 4.3	(21) 5.0
						Owners' Comp/Sales	6.8	7.6
5704M	48461M	286443M	673200M	754546M	595132M	Net Sales ($)	5172302M	4610758M
1299M	19717M	134251M	386027M	441517M	593736M	Total Assets ($)	3553931M	3243704M

M = $ thousand   MM = $ million
See Pages 11 through 18 for Explanation of Ratios and Data

Comparative Historical Data | | | | **Current Data Sorted By Sales** | | | | | |

			Type of Statement						
23	26	17	Unqualified		2	1		4	10
15	12	14	Reviewed		2	2		6	4
8	19	11	Compiled	1	2	5	2	1	
6	1	4	Tax Returns		3	1			
28	33	25	Other	1	5	2	2	7	8
4/1/00-3/31/01	4/1/01-3/31/02	4/1/02-3/31/03			15 (4/1-9/30/02)			56 (10/1/02-3/31/03)	
ALL	ALL	ALL		0-1MM	1-3MM	3-5MM	5-10MM	10-25MM	25MM & OVER
80	91	71	**NUMBER OF STATEMENTS**	2	10	12	7	18	22
%	%	%	**ASSETS**	%	%	%	%	%	%
5.2	4.5	5.7	Cash & Equivalents		5.2	4.6		7.5	3.8
25.2	26.1	27.0	Trade Receivables (net)		23.5	32.9		27.0	27.0
20.4	22.0	20.3	Inventory		10.9	14.6		22.7	26.7
2.7	3.1	3.8	All Other Current		.3	6.8		2.6	5.6
53.4	55.6	56.8	Total Current		39.9	59.0		59.7	63.2
35.4	33.4	32.5	Fixed Assets (net)		41.0	30.0		32.1	28.7
3.5	2.6	2.6	Intangibles (net)		1.9	4.3		.3	4.5
7.7	8.4	8.0	All Other Non-Current		17.2	6.8		7.8	3.6
100.0	100.0	100.0	Total		100.0	100.0		100.0	100.0
			LIABILITIES						
9.3	11.7	11.2	Notes Payable-Short Term		5.6	12.3		9.4	14.3
4.5	4.0	4.0	Cur. Mat.-L/T/D		1.2	5.0		5.5	2.0
14.6	14.5	15.6	Trade Payables		11.6	21.9		12.5	16.3
.5	.4	.3	Income Taxes Payable		.0	.0		.8	.4
8.3	9.6	8.8	All Other Current		15.9	7.3		4.9	9.3
37.2	40.2	39.9	Total Current		34.4	46.5		33.0	42.3
21.6	17.4	16.5	Long Term Debt		33.0	12.2		11.4	13.6
.9	.7	.4	Deferred Taxes		.0	.4		.2	.9
5.9	3.5	6.1	All Other Non-Current		2.4	8.3		8.7	6.5
34.4	38.2	37.1	Net Worth		30.1	32.5		46.7	36.6
100.0	100.0	100.0	Total Liabilities & Net Worth		100.0	100.0		100.0	100.0
			INCOME DATA						
100.0	100.0	100.0	Net Sales		100.0	100.0		100.0	100.0
22.1	22.1	24.9	Gross Profit		40.4	27.8		20.0	18.2
17.6	18.4	20.3	Operating Expenses		33.2	24.5		14.3	15.4
4.5	3.7	4.7	Operating Profit		7.2	3.3		5.7	2.8
2.5	1.7	.8	All Other Expenses (net)		.9	-.7		1.2	1.1
2.0	2.0	3.8	Profit Before Taxes		6.3	3.9		4.5	1.7
			RATIOS						
2.1	2.3	2.4	Current		7.6	2.2		3.6	2.7
1.4	1.4	1.6			1.5	1.3		2.1	1.6
1.0	1.0	1.0			.2	.8		1.1	1.1
1.3	1.2	1.4	Quick		2.1	1.0		1.8	1.1
.8	.8	.9			1.1	.7		1.0	.9
.5	.4	.5			.1	.6		.6	.4
36 10.0	35 10.4	37 9.9	Sales/Receivables	0 UND	44 8.2			38 9.7	38 9.5
49 7.4	47 7.7	47 7.7		41 8.9	50 7.3			46 8.0	50 7.4
59 6.1	59 6.2	57 6.5		74 4.9	58 6.2			56 6.6	61 6.0
22 16.6	24 15.2	16 23.5	Cost of Sales/Inventory	0 UND	2 187.3			37 9.9	24 15.5
57 6.4	55 6.6	50 7.4		1 304.6	19 18.9			52 7.0	91 4.0
82 4.5	91 4.0	92 4.0		96 3.8	67 5.5			70 5.2	120 3.0
23 15.6	14 25.3	20 18.0	Cost of Sales/Payables	6 62.6	24 15.5			12 29.8	25 14.9
37 9.8	33 11.0	33 11.2		21 17.4	46 7.9			29 12.8	33 11.0
53 6.9	46 7.9	50 7.3		51 7.2	64 5.7			39 9.4	43 8.4
5.7	5.2	4.5	Sales/Working Capital		4.4	5.5		3.6	4.4
12.3	11.7	11.3			12.2	17.0		6.4	7.1
93.0	999.8	-154.9			-17.9	-15.7		NM	49.3
(71) 5.0	(81) 4.8	(65) 10.4	EBIT/Interest		6.6			24.8	15.7
2.3	2.1	3.6			(11) 5.7		(17)	2.6 (21)	3.8
.9	.6	.7			1.9			-1.2	-.5
(21) 3.4	7.9		Net Profit + Depr., Dep.,						
1.7	(18) 2.0		Amort./Cur. Mat. L/T/D						
.9	1.0								
.6	.4	.4	Fixed/Worth		.4	.4		.4	.7
1.2	.8	.9			1.9	1.3		.7	1.1
3.5	1.6	2.1			NM	2.9		1.4	1.2
.9	.9	.6	Debt/Worth		.8	1.1		.4	.8
2.2	1.9	2.2			3.5	3.6		1.2	1.6
7.8	4.5	4.6			NM	6.8		3.3	4.4
(69) 27.7	(83) 28.2	(65) 51.6	% Profit Before Taxes/Tangible		65.4			31.1	51.6
9.2	13.3	24.3	Net Worth		(11) 24.3		(17)	12.1 (21)	25.3
.0	-2.3	3.7			3.4			-2.8	-6.3
8.9	10.4	16.4	% Profit Before Taxes/Total		42.9	15.7		19.0	12.4
3.9	3.9	6.3	Assets		7.2	6.2		4.3	6.6
-.7	-1.3	-.6			2.1	2.7		-2.6	-2.7
9.6	15.8	14.4	Sales/Net Fixed Assets		28.0	17.3		10.3	18.5
5.3	6.2	6.6			7.6	11.8		5.7	7.6
2.9	3.1	3.0			1.8	2.1		3.7	2.9
2.4	2.5	2.7	Sales/Total Assets		4.2	3.0		2.3	2.7
1.7	1.9	1.9			2.8	2.4		1.6	1.9
1.2	1.2	1.3			1.0	.9		1.5	1.1
(65) 1.6	(77) 1.0	(63) 1.5	% Depr., Dep., Amort./Sales		.7			1.6	1.5
3.0	2.6	2.9			(11) 2.2		(17)	2.9 (20)	2.6
5.4	4.5	5.0			5.2			5.1	4.5
(17) 1.9	(25) 2.3	(22) 1.0	% Officers', Directors',						
4.9	3.3	1.9	Owners' Comp/Sales						
7.3	7.8	4.0							
3626800M	4549108M	2363486M	Net Sales ($)	1729M	16479M	49915M	46612M	297593M	1951158M
2874293M	3244067M	1576547M	Total Assets ($)	1315M	9318M	38870M	27312M	180614M	1319118M

M = $ thousand   MM = $ million
See Pages 11 through 18 for Explanation of Ratios and Data

Current Data Sorted By Assets   Comparative Historical Data

			4	9	6	1	Type of Statement		
		3	10				Unqualified	26	20
	1	3	3	2			Reviewed	13	7
	6	1					Compiled	5	3
	3	1	7	7	3	3	Tax Returns		3
							Other	26	24
		15 (4/1-9/30/02)		58 (10/1/02-3/31/03)				4/1/98-3/31/99	4/1/99-3/31/00
	0-500M	500M-2MM	2-10MM	10-50MM	50-100MM	100-250MM		ALL	ALL
	10	8	24	18	9	4	NUMBER OF STATEMENTS	70	57
	%	%	%	%	%	%	ASSETS	%	%
	8.3		6.0	4.6			Cash & Equivalents	4.9	6.0
	24.4		34.8	32.6			Trade Receivables (net)	26.8	26.2
	20.6		27.7	29.1			Inventory	31.4	26.5
	4.5		1.0	1.5			All Other Current	1.4	1.6
	57.9		69.5	67.8			Total Current	64.5	60.2
	31.3		24.4	25.7			Fixed Assets (net)	29.1	33.1
	.0		1.7	4.1			Intangibles (net)	2.5	3.1
	10.8		4.5	2.3			All Other Non-Current	3.8	3.6
	100.0		100.0	100.0			Total	100.0	100.0
							LIABILITIES		
	6.3		19.1	20.1			Notes Payable-Short Term	14.3	10.8
	4.5		5.6	2.1			Cur. Mat.-L/T/D	2.8	4.5
	13.0		22.2	12.8			Trade Payables	15.8	16.3
	.0		.4	.4			Income Taxes Payable	.2	.6
	10.8		6.2	7.7			All Other Current	9.7	10.0
	34.6		53.4	43.1			Total Current	42.8	42.1
	26.1		12.6	10.5			Long Term Debt	17.7	16.0
	.2		.1	.7			Deferred Taxes	.8	2.7
	5.6		4.5	9.4			All Other Non-Current	5.7	7.9
	33.6		29.4	36.4			Net Worth	33.1	31.3
	100.0		100.0	100.0			Total Liabilities & Net Worth	100.0	100.0
							INCOME DATA		
	100.0		100.0	100.0			Net Sales	100.0	100.0
	44.4		19.6	21.7			Gross Profit	18.1	17.5
	42.8		16.9	15.2			Operating Expenses	14.1	13.5
	1.6		2.6	6.5			Operating Profit	4.0	4.1
	.6		.9	.7			All Other Expenses (net)	1.0	1.1
	1.0		1.7	5.8			Profit Before Taxes	3.1	3.0
							RATIOS		
	3.3		2.1	2.4				2.8	2.4
	1.9		1.1	1.4			Current	1.6	1.6
	1.3		.9	1.1				1.1	1.1
	2.1		1.3	1.5				1.2	1.2
	.8		.8	.8			Quick	.7	.7
	.5		.5	.4				.5	.5

									Sales/Receivables				
19	19.5			37	9.9	38	9.7			33	11.1	35	10.5
41	8.8			45	8.1	52	7.0			43	8.5	46	8.0
58	6.3			66	5.5	71	5.2			53	6.8	58	6.3

									Cost of Sales/Inventory				
0	UND			28	13.0	51	7.2			44	8.4	36	10.1
62	5.9			45	8.0	65	5.6			71	5.1	62	5.9
99	3.7			89	4.1	89	4.1			99	3.7	90	4.0

									Cost of Sales/Payables				
2	195.5			25	14.6	14	27.0			18	20.8	20	18.1
36	10.1			36	10.2	27	13.7			25	14.4	32	11.3
53	6.9			58	6.3	46	7.9			44	8.3	47	7.8

6.8			4.9	4.4			Sales/Working Capital		4.4		4.9
8.5			42.9	12.2					8.9		12.7
NM			−76.8	131.6					52.7		47.6

									EBIT/Interest				
					5.3		15.6				9.6		7.4
					1.3		5.2		(65)		2.9	(54)	2.5
					.9		1.0				1.2		.9

							Net Profit + Depr., Dep., Amort./Cur. Mat. L /T/D				
									9.5		10.4
								(26)	2.6	(27)	2.7
									1.4		1.4

.2			.5	.1			Fixed/Worth		.3		.4
1.1			1.1	.8					.8		1.1
−2.8			1.8	4.1					2.1		2.2

.3			1.5	1.1			Debt/Worth		1.1		1.1
1.5			3.3	1.5					2.5		2.3
−8.2			10.5	8.0					5.3		5.9

									% Profit Before Taxes/Tangible Net Worth				
		(23)		29.4	(15)	58.8				50.1		34.4
				9.3		38.2			(62)	22.7	(51)	18.8
				−6.4		3.9				5.6		3.1

28.7			6.3	20.5			% Profit Before Taxes/Total Assets		15.7		12.2
.2			1.2	9.2					6.6		4.0
−7.4			−.5	.1					.8		−.9

31.5			38.8	30.1			Sales/Net Fixed Assets		17.1		17.3
11.7			11.5	7.8					7.3		5.2
4.0			5.7	3.6					3.7		2.9

4.2			3.1	2.5			Sales/Total Assets		2.7		2.4
2.6			2.4	1.7					1.9		1.8
1.6			2.1	1.5					1.5		1.3

									% Depr., Dep., Amort./Sales				
	1.2				.8		.8				1.3		1.1
	3.1		(23)		1.9		1.9		(57)		2.0	(48)	2.4
	8.7				2.8		3.6				2.8		3.9

									% Officers', Directors', Owners' Comp/Sales				
											3.3		1.7
									(13)		6.6	(17)	3.6
											8.4		5.5

7993M	22072M	239548M	833873M	1021167M	665328M	Net Sales ($)		4283540M	3470999M
2688M	7267M	100747M	433170M	617704M	533019M	Total Assets ($)		2648248M	2494818M

M = $ thousand   MM = $ million
See Pages 11 through 18 for Explanation of Ratios and Data

Comparative Historical Data   Current Data Sorted By Sales

			Type of Statement						
11	13	20	Unqualified				2	3	15
8	9	13	Reviewed		1	3	5	4	
8	7	9	Compiled	1	2	1	1	2	2
1	2	7	Tax Returns	4	3				
27	34	24	Other	3	2		4	4	11
4/1/00-3/31/01	4/1/01-3/31/02	4/1/02-3/31/03			15 (4/1-9/30/02)			58 (10/1/02-3/31/03)	
ALL	ALL	ALL		0-1MM	1-3MM	3-5MM	5-10MM	10-25MM	25MM & OVER
55	65	73	**NUMBER OF STATEMENTS**	8	8	4	12	13	28
%	%	%	**ASSETS**	%	%	%	%	%	%
4.1	4.0	6.2	Cash & Equivalents				5.7	3.5	4.4
28.6	26.1	30.4	Trade Receivables (net)				35.1	40.7	23.8
28.9	27.3	26.1	Inventory				27.8	27.7	30.7
1.8	2.1	1.8	All Other Current				.6	1.0	1.0
63.4	59.4	64.4	Total Current				69.2	73.0	59.8
29.1	31.7	28.7	Fixed Assets (net)				24.3	20.9	33.7
1.9	1.7	2.4	Intangibles (net)				1.2	2.9	3.7
5.5	7.1	4.4	All Other Non-Current				5.3	3.2	2.7
100.0	100.0	100.0	Total				100.0	100.0	100.0
			LIABILITIES						
12.9	13.0	14.1	Notes Payable-Short Term				19.7	20.3	13.7
3.1	3.5	3.9	Cur. Mat.-L/T/D				5.0	3.2	2.8
18.0	13.7	17.2	Trade Payables				17.7	26.0	11.8
.3	.6	.3	Income Taxes Payable				.3	.4	.3
9.5	8.8	7.6	All Other Current				6.6	6.4	7.6
43.9	39.6	43.0	Total Current				49.3	56.4	36.3
17.2	15.5	17.0	Long Term Debt				13.6	6.2	20.2
.8	.8	.7	Deferred Taxes				.1	.2	1.1
6.4	7.0	6.2	All Other Non-Current				8.1	2.9	8.3
31.7	36.4	33.0	Net Worth				28.9	34.3	34.1
100.0	100.0	100.0	Total Liabilities & Net Worth				100.0	100.0	100.0
			INCOME DATA						
100.0	100.0	100.0	Net Sales				100.0	100.0	100.0
19.4	21.2	23.5	Gross Profit				18.9	21.3	16.4
15.0	17.1	20.7	Operating Expenses				17.9	14.3	13.5
4.4	4.0	2.8	Operating Profit				1.1	7.0	3.0
1.2	1.2	.9	All Other Expenses (net)				1.0	.9	1.1
3.2	2.8	1.9	Profit Before Taxes				.1	6.1	1.8
			RATIOS						
2.3	2.4	2.3					2.2	2.1	2.4
1.6	1.5	1.7	Current				1.3	1.2	1.7
1.0	1.1	1.1					.9	1.0	1.2
1.1	1.2	1.4					1.4	1.3	1.1
.7	.8	.8	Quick				.8	.9	.8
.5	.5	.5					.6	.5	.5
37 10.0	33 11.0	36 10.1					36 10.2	39 9.3	38 9.7
47 7.8	46 7.9	46 7.9	Sales/Receivables				50 7.4	46 7.9	47 7.8
61 6.0	56 6.5	60 6.1					73 5.0	56 6.6	57 6.4
41 8.9	32 11.3	32 11.5					28 13.0	28 12.9	54 6.7
64 5.7	59 6.2	58 6.3	Cost of Sales/Inventory				46 7.9	49 7.5	68 5.4
101 3.6	92 4.0	91 4.0					100 3.6	71 5.1	93 3.9
17 21.2	18 20.1	15 23.6					18 20.0	17 21.8	15 24.0
29 12.4	29 12.6	32 11.2	Cost of Sales/Payables				31 11.9	38 9.7	30 12.3
58 6.3	46 8.0	49 7.5					47 7.8	65 5.6	40 9.0
5.2	5.0	5.1					4.1	5.2	4.7
10.6	10.5	9.9	Sales/Working Capital				81.8	38.1	7.6
197.4	115.3	67.6					−76.8	NM	20.4
8.1	9.3	6.2					2.6	15.2	8.1
(54) 3.9	(64) 2.5	(68) 2.0	EBIT/Interest				1.1	5.8	2.6
1.1	.5	.7					.4	2.3	.6
6.7	4.4	6.4							
(14) 4.3	(21) 2.4	(15) 3.1	Net Profit + Depr., Dep., Amort./Cur. Mat. L/T/D						
1.9	1.2	1.3							
.3	.4	.4					.3	.3	.5
.9	1.0	1.1	Fixed/Worth				1.3	.7	1.3
2.2	2.0	3.4					2.7	1.2	4.5
.9	.8	.9					1.6	1.0	1.1
1.9	1.9	1.9	Debt/Worth				2.6	2.7	2.6
5.8	4.3	9.7					10.5	7.7	9.1
47.2	41.0	38.9					11.7	60.2	38.2
(51) 21.2	(60) 19.8	(62) 12.4	% Profit Before Taxes/Tangible Net Worth				1.9	(12) 40.9	(23) 11.1
5.1	1.1	−.4					−23.5	11.6	−1.2
14.2	14.2	10.3					3.6	21.0	12.2
6.9	4.8	3.8	% Profit Before Taxes/Total Assets				.3	7.3	3.5
.6	−1.6	−.5					−1.3	2.8	−.5
19.2	13.3	19.2					14.5	55.0	11.2
7.0	5.8	7.9	Sales/Net Fixed Assets				11.1	18.1	4.9
4.2	3.8	4.2					7.8	5.7	3.3
2.5	2.5	3.0					2.8	4.0	2.2
2.1	2.0	2.2	Sales/Total Assets				2.4	2.3	1.7
1.6	1.5	1.5					1.9	1.8	1.5
.7	1.2	1.1					1.5	.5	1.2
(49) 1.9	(57) 2.9	(70) 2.2	% Depr., Dep., Amort./Sales			(11) 1.9		1.1	(27) 2.5
3.2	4.3	4.2					2.8	4.0	4.2
1.1	1.8	2.3							
(17) 2.8	(13) 3.9	(22) 6.6	% Officers', Directors', Owners' Comp/Sales						
7.4	8.7	11.7							
2535239M	3540742M	2789981M	Net Sales ($)	3996M	16460M	15408M	90465M	200863M	2462789M
1563464M	2159538M	1694595M	Total Assets ($)	1829M	6934M	10840M	40942M	88541M	1545509M

Current Data Sorted By Assets | Comparative Historical Data

Period labels: **14 (4/1-9/30/02)** (0-500M & 500M-2MM) • **47 (10/1/02-3/31/03)** (2-10MM through 100-250MM)

Comparative Historical periods: **4/1/98-3/31/99 ALL** and **4/1/99-3/31/00 ALL**

	0-500M	500M-2MM	2-10MM	10-50MM	50-100MM	100-250MM		4/1/98-3/31/99 ALL	4/1/99-3/31/00 ALL
Type of Statement									
Unqualified		3	3	5	2	3	Unqualified	25	17
Reviewed		4	12	6			Reviewed	10	13
Compiled	1	1	5				Compiled	4	5
Tax Returns	2						Tax Returns	1	2
Other		3	1	3	5	2	Other	17	12
NUMBER OF STATEMENTS	3	11	21	14	7	5		57	49
	%	%	%	%	%	%	**ASSETS**	%	%
		8.8	5.8	6.1			Cash & Equivalents	4.1	7.3
		28.6	28.6	22.6			Trade Receivables (net)	27.9	26.4
		20.9	27.9	32.4			Inventory	27.4	26.0
		5.6	1.9	1.4			All Other Current	1.1	1.8
		64.0	64.2	62.5			Total Current	60.5	61.4
		31.0	25.6	30.6			Fixed Assets (net)	31.6	30.0
		.0	3.6	.1			Intangibles (net)	1.8	2.1
		5.0	6.5	6.9			All Other Non-Current	6.1	6.5
		100.0	100.0	100.0			Total	100.0	100.0
							LIABILITIES		
		15.9	11.1	14.6			Notes Payable-Short Term	11.5	9.7
		4.3	3.1	2.4			Cur. Mat.-L/T/D	3.1	3.3
		19.4	17.0	14.5			Trade Payables	17.0	18.0
		.0	.2	.1			Income Taxes Payable	.1	.3
		7.0	7.5	8.2			All Other Current	8.4	9.5
		46.5	38.8	39.9			Total Current	40.1	40.7
		18.5	19.0	7.9			Long Term Debt	17.2	18.3
		.3	.2	1.9			Deferred Taxes	.9	.7
		10.4	4.7	1.0			All Other Non-Current	5.7	3.3
		24.3	37.4	49.4			Net Worth	36.0	37.0
		100.0	100.0	100.0			Total Liabilities & Net Worth	100.0	100.0
							INCOME DATA		
		100.0	100.0	100.0			Net Sales	100.0	100.0
		27.7	23.0	14.4			Gross Profit	19.3	21.4
		25.1	19.1	12.0			Operating Expenses	14.1	15.0
		2.6	3.9	2.5			Operating Profit	5.2	6.3
		2.8	.7	.5			All Other Expenses (net)	1.5	.7
		-.2	3.2	2.0			Profit Before Taxes	3.7	5.6
							RATIOS		
		2.8	2.5	2.4				2.8	3.0
		1.6	2.0	1.6			Current	1.6	1.6
		.9	1.3	1.2				1.0	1.0
		1.3	1.8	1.3				1.4	1.6
		1.0	1.0	.7			Quick	.9	.8
		.4	.5	.4				.5	.5
		28 13.2	43 8.5	36 10.2				35 10.6	35 10.5
		41 8.9	49 7.4	44 8.3			Sales/Receivables	43 8.6	47 7.8
		55 6.6	62 5.9	54 6.8				53 6.9	57 6.4
		0 UND	16 22.9	55 6.7				36 10.0	28 13.1
		36 10.1	69 5.3	73 5.0			Cost of Sales/Inventory	64 5.7	59 6.1
		58 6.3	96 3.8	98 3.7				82 4.5	90 4.1
		12 29.8	24 15.1	16 22.4				22 16.3	17 20.9
		22 16.9	44 8.4	31 11.7			Cost of Sales/Payables	34 10.7	31 11.7
		38 9.6	56 6.6	53 6.9				45 8.1	53 6.9
		3.5	4.7	3.0				5.4	4.6
		11.9	7.3	9.8			Sales/Working Capital	11.8	9.7
		-23.4	16.1	30.6				108.4	NM
		1.8	9.3	7.4				7.3	15.0
		(10) .4	(19) 3.2	(12) 2.9			EBIT/Interest	(52) 2.8	(41) 3.9
		-1.8	1.6	.8				1.6	1.7
							Net Profit + Depr., Dep.,	6.5	7.7
							Amort./Cur. Mat. L/T/D	(20) 2.9	(13) 4.6
								1.7	1.6
		.2	.3	.4				.5	.3
		.6	.6	.6			Fixed/Worth	.9	.6
		-9.8	1.6	1.3				2.2	1.7
		.4	.8	.5				.9	.5
		2.0	1.8	1.0			Debt/Worth	2.1	1.7
		-14.5	4.7	2.3				5.9	4.5
			53.7	14.0			% Profit Before Taxes/Tangible	41.6	56.4
		(19) 10.8	10.8	4.5			Net Worth	(54) 21.0	(43) 26.5
			5.4	-.3				10.7	14.9
		2.0	9.3	6.0			% Profit Before Taxes/Total	11.8	19.6
		.4	5.1	2.6			Assets	7.6	11.1
		-12.2	1.4	-.1				1.7	2.8
		20.0	16.1	12.6				19.4	17.3
		10.5	7.5	6.3			Sales/Net Fixed Assets	7.5	7.8
		5.0	4.8	3.2				3.2	3.8
		3.6	2.5	2.5				2.7	2.6
		2.4	1.8	1.9			Sales/Total Assets	2.2	2.1
		1.9	1.4	1.2				1.4	1.6
		.7	1.5	1.7				1.1	1.1
		(10) 2.0	(18) 2.5	2.4			% Depr., Dep., Amort./Sales	(49) 1.7	(43) 1.8
		5.2	3.4	3.4				3.4	3.5
							% Officers', Directors',	1.3	.8
							Owners' Comp/Sales	(12) 2.9	(12) 2.9
								4.7	3.9
Net Sales ($)	8405M	31926M	170647M	499355M	545300M	1187328M		3716793M	2221138M
Total Assets ($)	725M	13557M	89855M	283449M	407562M	829804M		2446239M	1335548M

M = $ thousand   MM = $ million
See Pages 11 through 18 for Explanation of Ratios and Data

Comparative Historical Data / Current Data Sorted By Sales

4/1/00-3/31/01 ALL	4/1/01-3/31/02 ALL	4/1/02-3/31/03 ALL	Type of Statement	0-1MM	1-3MM	3-5MM	5-10MM	10-25MM	25MM & OVER
12	10	13	Unqualified			1		3	9
12	7	21	Reviewed		2	4	5	4	6
8	8	10	Compiled	1	2	2	4	1	
1	1	3	Tax Returns	2			1		
12	13	14	Other			4	1		9
				14 (4/1-9/30/02)			47 (10/1/02-3/31/03)		
45	39	61	**NUMBER OF STATEMENTS**	3	4	11	11	8	24
%	%	%	**ASSETS**	%	%	%	%	%	%
5.8	9.0	5.9	Cash & Equivalents			9.1	5.7		4.1
28.8	24.8	24.7	Trade Receivables (net)			28.4	30.3		20.5
24.0	22.0	29.5	Inventory			23.6	25.3		31.6
1.1	4.1	2.4	All Other Current			3.4	4.1		1.1
59.7	59.9	62.5	Total Current			64.5	65.4		57.3
31.9	31.2	29.1	Fixed Assets (net)			27.4	25.1		33.1
1.6	2.9	1.6	Intangibles (net)			1.8	3.4		.7
6.8	6.0	6.7	All Other Non-Current			6.3	6.1		8.8
100.0	100.0	100.0	Total			100.0	100.0		100.0
			LIABILITIES						
15.0	9.8	14.4	Notes Payable-Short Term			13.2	11.1		13.0
5.5	3.8	4.3	Cur. Mat.-L/T/D			3.0	3.7		6.0
16.8	13.3	15.9	Trade Payables			19.6	15.7		14.3
.1	.0	.1	Income Taxes Payable			.1	.2		.1
7.2	9.9	6.8	All Other Current			9.9	6.5		6.7
44.7	37.0	41.5	Total Current			45.9	37.3		40.0
23.9	15.4	17.4	Long Term Debt			21.0	28.2		9.3
.8	.2	.8	Deferred Taxes			.1	.2		1.8
5.6	7.3	6.6	All Other Non-Current			8.3	5.0		7.2
24.8	39.8	33.7	Net Worth			24.8	29.2		41.7
100.0	100.0	100.0	Total Liabilities & Net Worth			100.0	100.0		100.0
			INCOME DATA						
100.0	100.0	100.0	Net Sales			100.0	100.0		100.0
23.6	23.7	21.9	Gross Profit			24.9	29.6		14.1
19.1	20.2	18.7	Operating Expenses			21.2	25.0		10.6
4.5	3.5	3.2	Operating Profit			3.7	4.6		3.5
.4	1.1	1.2	All Other Expenses (net)			1.6	1.0		1.1
4.1	2.4	2.0	Profit Before Taxes			2.1	3.6		2.4
			RATIOS						
3.0	3.4	2.5	Current			2.5	2.5		1.8
1.6	1.8	1.6				1.6	1.9		1.5
.9	1.1	1.1				1.2	1.2		1.1
1.7	2.1	1.2	Quick			2.0	1.6		1.1
.8	1.0	.8				1.0	.9		.6
.5	.5	.4				.5	.4		.4
29 12.4	33 11.0	36 10.2	Sales/Receivables			29 12.8	37 9.9		36 10.2
44 8.2	47 7.8	46 7.9				50 7.3	46 7.9		47 7.8
55 6.7	55 6.6	55 6.7				61 5.9	81 4.5		52 7.0
19 19.5	26 13.8	40 9.1	Cost of Sales/Inventory			0 UND	8 47.9		57 6.4
48 7.5	46 8.0	71 5.1				41 8.9	41 8.8		83 4.4
91 4.0	89 4.1	102 3.6				73 5.0	93 3.9		113 3.2
17 20.9	13 27.2	19 18.9	Cost of Sales/Payables			13 28.5	30 12.3		22 16.3
27 13.3	26 13.9	33 11.2				23 16.2	44 8.4		33 10.9
47 7.8	46 8.0	52 7.1				54 6.7	64 5.7		49 7.4
4.6	4.4	4.9	Sales/Working Capital			4.5	5.9		5.4
10.1	8.4	9.2				11.8	8.8		9.8
-88.2	44.2	27.5				27.5	25.7		39.6
(40) 4.4	(32) 4.3	(56) 8.8	EBIT/Interest	(10) 3.2		24.1		(22) 11.3	
2.5	.9	2.2		1.7		5.2		3.2	
1.3	-1.6	-.2		-1.3		1.6		.4	
(13) 7.4	(10) 4.3	(17) 7.3	Net Profit + Depr., Dep., Amort./Cur. Mat. L/T/D						
2.2	.5	2.0							
1.7	-.2	.6							
.5	.3	.4	Fixed/Worth			.1	.3		.4
1.2	.9	.7				.6	.6		.9
10.8	1.8	2.0				2.8	1.2		1.4
.6	.6	.7	Debt/Worth			.8	.7		.8
2.6	1.3	1.7				2.0	1.6		1.6
25.8	5.5	5.5				6.4	1.9		3.4
(35) 30.7	(36) 28.0	(54) 30.5	% Profit Before Taxes/Tangible Net Worth						33.9
14.4	6.1	7.3							6.7
7.7	-10.3	-4.4							-3.7
16.6	10.8	8.9	% Profit Before Taxes/Total Assets			8.9	19.1		9.3
6.1	.3	3.3				2.0	5.4		3.6
1.4	-6.0	-2.2				-5.5	1.5		-.9
19.1	12.7	13.7	Sales/Net Fixed Assets			27.4	21.3		9.7
8.6	6.9	7.5				8.2	7.5		5.7
3.9	3.5	3.8				2.9	6.3		2.5
3.0	2.5	2.5	Sales/Total Assets			2.9	2.8		2.2
2.2	1.8	1.9				1.9	2.4		1.9
1.6	1.5	1.2				1.2	1.6		1.0
(41) 1.3	(35) .9	(57) 1.4	% Depr., Dep., Amort./Sales				1.7		1.4
2.1	2.5	2.3					2.5		2.5
4.3	4.5	4.0					3.3		4.3
		(18) 1.1	% Officers', Directors', Owners' Comp/Sales						
		2.6							
		4.3							
2209475M	1179435M	2442961M	Net Sales ($)	2210M	9815M	42036M	80823M	94581M	2213496M
1097863M	726460M	1624952M	Total Assets ($)	2345M	4169M	24449M	47717M	52615M	1493657M

M = $ thousand   MM = $ million
See Pages 11 through 18 for Explanation of Ratios and Data

Current Data Sorted By Assets | **Comparative Historical Data**

	0-500M	500M-2MM	2-10MM	10-50MM	50-100MM	100-250MM	Type of Statement	4/1/98-3/31/99 ALL	4/1/99-3/31/00 ALL
			3	6	1	1	Unqualified	11	16
	1		7	4			Reviewed	8	14
	1	2	1	1			Compiled	12	6
	1	4	1				Tax Returns	1	5
	2	2	8	4	1	1	Other	18	17
			12 (4/1-9/30/02)	40 (10/1/02-3/31/03)					
NUMBER OF STATEMENTS	4	8	20	15	2	3		50	58
	%	%	%	%	%	%	**ASSETS**	%	%
			7.0	3.2			Cash & Equivalents	4.5	5.2
			26.4	22.0			Trade Receivables (net)	29.2	29.1
			37.0	34.0			Inventory	24.3	26.5
			1.2	2.1			All Other Current	1.6	1.8
			71.7	61.3			Total Current	59.7	62.7
			17.9	29.0			Fixed Assets (net)	32.9	28.9
			2.5	4.6			Intangibles (net)	2.5	3.3
			7.9	5.1			All Other Non-Current	4.9	5.1
			100.0	100.0			Total	100.0	100.0
							LIABILITIES		
			19.5	15.9			Notes Payable-Short Term	14.9	14.6
			3.3	2.2			Cur. Mat.-L/T/D	4.0	4.5
			16.2	18.2			Trade Payables	18.4	18.2
			.0	.2			Income Taxes Payable	.4	.3
			5.8	6.3			All Other Current	7.4	6.4
			44.9	42.9			Total Current	45.1	44.0
			7.3	12.4			Long Term Debt	15.6	15.7
			1.0	1.1			Deferred Taxes	.5	.1
			5.2	4.3			All Other Non-Current	5.9	4.3
			41.6	39.3			Net Worth	32.9	35.9
			100.0	100.0			Total Liabilities & Net Worth	100.0	100.0
							INCOME DATA		
			100.0	100.0			Net Sales	100.0	100.0
			24.9	14.4			Gross Profit	21.6	22.5
			22.1	12.7			Operating Expenses	15.9	17.9
			2.9	1.6			Operating Profit	5.6	4.6
			.2	.7			All Other Expenses (net)	1.5	1.3
			2.6	1.0			Profit Before Taxes	4.1	3.3
							RATIOS		
			3.9	1.6				1.8	1.7
			1.4	1.3			Current	1.3	1.3
			1.1	1.2				1.0	1.1
			1.0	1.1				.9	.9
			.7	.5			Quick	.7	.7
			.5	.3				.5	.5
			31 11.7	29 12.6				36 10.1	37 9.8
			48 7.5	44 8.4			Sales/Receivables	40 9.0	47 7.8
			55 6.6	51 7.1				54 6.7	56 6.6
			51 7.1	52 7.0				32 11.4	29 12.4
			76 4.8	75 4.9			Cost of Sales/Inventory	49 7.5	56 6.6
			146 2.5	121 3.0				70 5.2	86 4.2
			21 17.7	28 13.0				22 16.6	22 16.9
			26 14.1	40 9.1			Cost of Sales/Payables	33 11.0	37 9.8
			50 7.3	46 8.0				44 8.3	49 7.4
			4.6	9.0				8.6	7.9
			10.3	12.8			Sales/Working Capital	16.5	16.7
			58.6	18.2				122.0	58.3
			3.4	3.1				5.0	5.3
			(16) 1.8	(14) 1.7			EBIT/Interest	(47) 2.5	(54) 3.0
			-.4	-.1				1.4	1.3
							Net Profit + Depr., Dep., Amort./Cur. Mat. L /T/D	4.0	6.5
								(18) 2.0	(18) 3.5
								.8	2.2
			.1	.4				.5	.3
			.4	.8			Fixed/Worth	1.0	.9
			1.4	1.8				1.8	1.7
			.5	1.3				1.2	1.0
			2.0	1.8			Debt/Worth	1.9	2.2
			4.1	3.3				4.6	4.6
			28.3	18.3				32.8	37.2
			(19) 11.8	(14) 4.6			% Profit Before Taxes/Tangible Net Worth	(45) 16.2	(53) 18.3
			-3.1	-3.5				7.0	5.1
			7.2	4.2				13.1	11.9
			2.5	1.8			% Profit Before Taxes/Total Assets	6.1	4.9
			-2.1	-.5				1.4	1.1
			52.1	11.6				18.5	22.4
			19.1	7.4			Sales/Net Fixed Assets	6.2	7.0
			6.5	5.0				4.4	4.4
			2.4	2.2				2.7	2.8
			2.1	2.0			Sales/Total Assets	2.2	2.1
			1.4	1.6				1.8	1.6
			.5	1.4				1.4	1.2
			(18) 1.8	2.5			% Depr., Dep., Amort./Sales	(45) 2.1	(50) 2.7
			3.1	3.8				4.1	4.3
								3.6	3.9
							% Officers', Directors', Owners' Comp/Sales	(17) 4.6	(19) 4.8
								9.5	8.0
	4206M	18529M	206356M	585390M	136100M	368185M	Net Sales ($)	1862639M	1460164M
	1064M	9463M	96396M	309719M	135935M	535856M	Total Assets ($)	990294M	866927M

M = $ thousand   MM = $ million
See Pages 11 through 18 for Explanation of Ratios and Data

Comparative Historical Data | Current Data Sorted By Sales

			Type of Statement						
13	15	11	Unqualified				1	5	5
12	9	12	Reviewed		3	2	2	3	2
3	3	5	Compiled		1	2	1		1
2	4	6	Tax Returns	2	2		1		1
18	17	18	Other	2	1	1	3	5	6
4/1/00-3/31/01	4/1/01-3/31/02	4/1/02-3/31/03		0-1MM	1-3MM	3-5MM	5-10MM	10-25MM	25MM & OVER
ALL	ALL	ALL		12 (4/1-9/30/02)			40 (10/1/02-3/31/03)		
48	48	52	**NUMBER OF STATEMENTS**	4	7	5	8	13	15
%	%	%	**ASSETS**	%	%	%	%	%	%
5.7	5.7	5.9	Cash & Equivalents					4.0	5.3
25.1	27.3	25.2	Trade Receivables (net)					30.0	21.3
27.4	24.3	33.2	Inventory					34.8	30.6
2.1	1.1	1.5	All Other Current					2.0	2.2
60.2	58.4	65.8	Total Current					70.8	59.5
29.9	33.8	25.1	Fixed Assets (net)					19.1	33.9
2.2	2.9	2.5	Intangibles (net)					6.6	2.5
7.7	4.9	6.6	All Other Non-Current					3.5	4.1
100.0	100.0	100.0	Total					100.0	100.0
			LIABILITIES						
12.5	11.8	20.0	Notes Payable-Short Term					20.5	15.6
2.7	4.1	3.2	Cur. Mat.-L/T/D					1.8	2.1
15.8	17.1	16.8	Trade Payables					17.9	15.8
.2	.3	.3	Income Taxes Payable					.9	.2
6.5	8.3	5.5	All Other Current					7.3	6.9
37.8	41.7	45.7	Total Current					48.4	40.6
12.9	13.4	10.9	Long Term Debt					7.5	11.5
.3	.6	.8	Deferred Taxes					.3	1.0
5.3	6.3	5.7	All Other Non-Current					5.3	6.4
43.7	38.1	36.9	Net Worth					38.4	40.5
100.0	100.0	100.0	Total Liabilities & Net Worth					100.0	100.0
			INCOME DATA						
100.0	100.0	100.0	Net Sales					100.0	100.0
23.3	22.3	21.9	Gross Profit					18.1	16.3
18.1	19.0	19.9	Operating Expenses					17.8	12.3
5.2	3.4	2.0	Operating Profit					.3	4.0
1.3	1.3	.4	All Other Expenses (net)					.5	.9
3.9	2.0	1.5	Profit Before Taxes					-.2	3.2
			RATIOS						
2.6	2.1	1.9						1.9	1.6
1.4	1.4	1.3	Current					1.3	1.3
1.1	1.1	1.1						1.2	1.1
1.2	1.3	1.0						.8	1.1
.7	.7	.6	Quick					.6	.4
.5	.5	.4						.5	.3
34 10.8	33 10.9	35 10.4						40 9.1	35 10.4
44 8.2	41 8.8	46 7.9	Sales/Receivables					50 7.3	44 8.2
54 6.8	50 7.4	55 6.6						61 6.0	51 7.1
33 10.9	25 14.5	50 7.3						35 10.6	52 7.0
58 6.3	49 7.4	74 4.9	Cost of Sales/Inventory					77 4.7	73 5.0
87 4.2	78 4.7	121 3.0						111 3.3	121 3.0
21 17.3	17 21.1	22 16.2						24 15.4	31 11.6
32 11.6	31 11.6	38 9.6	Cost of Sales/Payables					44 8.4	38 9.5
46 7.9	46 7.9	52 7.0						53 6.9	47 7.7
5.0	8.1	5.1						4.8	7.1
13.1	16.5	12.0	Sales/Working Capital					11.0	14.0
24.9	77.8	62.3						17.3	52.7
9.1	7.0	3.0						3.6	4.0
(42) 3.0	(44) 1.8	(45) 1.5	EBIT/Interest					2.1	(13) 1.4
1.5	.1	-1.7						-5.7	-.9
9.3		49.0	Net Profit + Depr., Dep.,						
(12) 1.6		(15) 2.6	Amort./Cur. Mat. L/T/D						
.7		1.3							
.2	.3	.2						.2	.4
.6	1.0	.7	Fixed/Worth					.4	.9
1.7	3.3	1.5						1.3	1.8
.5	.7	1.0						1.2	.8
1.5	1.7	1.9	Debt/Worth					2.0	1.7
3.6	6.5	3.6						3.6	2.9
28.3	24.5	17.5	% Profit Before Taxes/Tangible					25.2	18.3
(44) 16.1	(42) 9.5	(47) 8.2	Net Worth					(12) 7.3	(14) 4.6
4.7	-3.1	-5.3						-12.6	-3.5
13.0	10.0	5.3	% Profit Before Taxes/Total					5.5	5.3
5.0	3.6	2.0	Assets					2.1	1.8
1.2	-2.7	-3.7						-3.0	-.5
22.5	14.8	25.1						26.2	10.6
7.2	6.6	8.9	Sales/Net Fixed Assets					11.6	6.0
3.6	3.9	4.5						5.5	3.1
2.3	2.6	2.3						2.6	2.2
2.0	2.1	2.0	Sales/Total Assets					1.9	2.0
1.4	1.6	1.3						1.5	1.2
1.0	1.1	.7						.5	1.4
(41) 2.2	(41) 2.9	(47) 2.0	% Depr., Dep., Amort./Sales					(12) 1.6	(14) 2.5
3.3	4.4	4.0						2.6	4.0
1.7	2.4	2.1	% Officers', Directors',						
(17) 4.1	(19) 5.5	(18) 3.9	Owners' Comp/Sales						
6.5	8.3	8.1							
2058063M	1457735M	1318766M	Net Sales ($)	2056M	14787M	17347M	55163M	239158M	990255M
1175347M	877749M	1088433M	Total Assets ($)	2216M	8812M	9327M	30174M	277921M	759983M

M = $ thousand   MM = $ million
See Pages 11 through 18 for Explanation of Ratios and Data

Current Data Sorted By Assets　　　　　　　　Comparative Historical Data

0-500M	500M-2MM	2-10MM	10-50MM	50-100MM	100-250MM	Type of Statement	4/1/98-3/31/99 ALL	4/1/99-3/31/00 ALL
1		7	4	1		Unqualified	13	12
		5	2			Reviewed	4	4
	2	1				Compiled	4	3
2	1					Tax Returns		
	1	4	3	1	1	Other	15	19
4 (4/1-9/30/02)			32 (10/1/02-3/31/03)					
3	4	17	9	2	1	NUMBER OF STATEMENTS	36	38
%	%	%	%	%	%	**ASSETS**	%	%
		3.4				Cash & Equivalents	6.8	6.7
		34.7				Trade Receivables (net)	24.8	24.1
		25.6				Inventory	21.4	24.7
		2.7				All Other Current	1.5	.6
		66.4				Total Current	54.5	56.0
		28.2				Fixed Assets (net)	36.4	34.1
		1.9				Intangibles (net)	6.3	7.4
		3.5				All Other Non-Current	2.8	2.5
		100.0				Total	100.0	100.0
						LIABILITIES		
		15.6				Notes Payable-Short Term	9.6	11.7
		2.7				Cur. Mat.-L/T/D	3.5	3.1
		18.3				Trade Payables	18.7	15.3
		.1				Income Taxes Payable	.0	.6
		8.9				All Other Current	6.3	6.8
		45.7				Total Current	38.1	37.4
		8.6				Long Term Debt	21.0	17.3
		1.2				Deferred Taxes	1.3	.7
		15.5				All Other Non-Current	3.9	2.6
		29.0				Net Worth	35.7	42.0
		100.0				Total Liabilities & Net Worth	100.0	100.0
						INCOME DATA		
		100.0				Net Sales	100.0	100.0
		19.8				Gross Profit	20.1	22.0
		15.8				Operating Expenses	13.5	15.5
		4.0				Operating Profit	6.6	6.4
		1.2				All Other Expenses (net)	1.6	.5
		2.8				Profit Before Taxes	5.0	5.9
						RATIOS		
		2.1				Current	2.2	2.9
		1.5					1.3	1.6
		1.1					.9	1.2
		1.2				Quick	1.4	1.4
		.9					.7	.8
		.7					.5	.5
		34 10.8				Sales/Receivables	35 10.3	38 9.5
		48 7.7					39 9.4	44 8.3
		61 6.0					50 7.2	52 7.0
		24 15.0				Cost of Sales/Inventory	27 13.3	36 10.1
		34 10.6					42 8.7	58 6.3
		75 4.9					65 5.6	77 4.8
		23 15.6				Cost of Sales/Payables	25 14.9	21 17.7
		32 11.5					33 11.0	32 11.4
		37 9.8					46 8.0	46 8.0
		8.1				Sales/Working Capital	6.9	6.0
		16.5					20.4	10.5
		81.5					−41.3	28.7
		10.2				EBIT/Interest	7.9	11.0
	(15)	3.6					(33) 3.9	(33) 4.6
		1.3					2.5	2.7
						Net Profit + Depr., Dep., Amort./Cur. Mat. L /T/D		20.5
							(10) 6.2	
								1.5
		.3				Fixed/Worth	.5	.6
		.8					1.2	.8
		NM					2.4	1.8
		.9				Debt/Worth	1.2	.6
		2.2					1.9	1.7
		NM					3.8	3.2
		80.5				% Profit Before Taxes/Tangible Net Worth	47.2	41.7
	(13)	10.1					(32) 25.6	(35) 27.9
		1.2					13.7	19.0
		20.3				% Profit Before Taxes/Total Assets	13.3	16.4
		4.8					9.0	10.1
		.6					5.6	6.4
		23.7				Sales/Net Fixed Assets	14.0	10.6
		8.4					6.3	6.5
		5.6					3.7	3.6
		3.4				Sales/Total Assets	2.9	2.6
		2.7					2.1	2.1
		1.8					1.5	1.5
		1.2				% Depr., Dep., Amort./Sales	1.3	1.4
	(14)	2.0					(30) 1.8	(34) 2.0
		2.7					2.8	3.9
						% Officers', Directors', Owners' Comp/Sales		
1412M	10884M	242985M	468856M	271295M	194667M	Net Sales ($)	2702768M	2110558M
432M	5571M	94431M	251340M	147876M	131542M	Total Assets ($)	1477553M	1093372M

M = $ thousand　　MM = $ million
See Pages 11 through 18 for Explanation of Ratios and Data

Comparative Historical Data | Current Data Sorted By Sales

			Type of Statement						
6	7	13	Unqualified	1			1	5	6
8	9	7	Reviewed	1			1	4	2
7	7	3	Compiled		2			1	
3	2	3	Tax Returns	2			1		
13	12	10	Other		1		1	3	5
4/1/00-3/31/01 ALL	4/1/01-3/31/02 ALL	4/1/02-3/31/03 ALL		0-1MM	1-3MM	3-5MM	5-10MM	10-25MM	25MM & OVER
				4 (4/1-9/30/02)			**32 (10/1/02-3/31/03)**		
37	37	36	**NUMBER OF STATEMENTS**	3	3		4	13	13
%	%	%	**ASSETS**	%	%		%	%	%
4.3	7.0	4.0	Cash & Equivalents					3.9	1.8
26.2	24.0	28.2	Trade Receivables (net)					31.8	24.8
25.1	22.2	24.2	Inventory					24.9	25.2
1.0	2.7	2.1	All Other Current	D				2.8	2.9
56.6	55.9	58.5	Total Current	A				63.4	54.7
33.3	34.2	34.2	Fixed Assets (net)	T				30.8	41.5
4.6	6.5	3.2	Intangibles (net)	A				1.6	.1
5.4	3.4	4.2	All Other Non-Current	N				4.2	3.7
100.0	100.0	100.0	Total	O				100.0	100.0
			LIABILITIES	T					
10.2	9.1	11.0	Notes Payable-Short Term	A				17.5	6.2
3.7	3.0	4.2	Cur. Mat.-L/T/D	V				3.1	6.3
14.9	13.4	16.3	Trade Payables	A				18.9	15.5
.3	.3	.1	Income Taxes Payable	I				.1	.1
7.7	6.0	8.8	All Other Current	L				8.7	6.7
36.8	31.8	40.3	Total Current	A				48.3	34.8
19.4	22.7	15.5	Long Term Debt	B				9.5	19.1
.5	1.0	1.1	Deferred Taxes	L				1.5	1.2
2.8	6.9	15.0	All Other Non-Current	E				17.4	9.2
40.5	37.7	28.1	Net Worth					23.3	35.6
100.0	100.0	100.0	Total Liabilities & Net Worth					100.0	100.0
			INCOME DATA						
100.0	100.0	100.0	Net Sales					100.0	100.0
20.7	22.1	20.0	Gross Profit					18.9	18.0
14.5	17.5	16.0	Operating Expenses					15.3	12.5
6.1	4.6	3.9	Operating Profit					3.6	5.5
1.0	1.3	1.5	All Other Expenses (net)					1.4	1.7
5.1	3.2	2.4	Profit Before Taxes					2.2	3.8
			RATIOS						
2.5	4.2	2.9						1.6	3.0
1.5	1.6	1.4	Current					1.3	1.5
1.1	1.1	1.2						1.0	1.3
1.3	1.5	1.3						.9	1.2
.8	.9	.8	Quick					.8	.8
.5	.6	.6						.6	.6
33 10.9	33 11.2	34 10.7						32 11.2	36 10.3
41 8.8	39 9.3	45 8.2	Sales/Receivables					42 8.6	44 8.3
53 6.9	55 6.7	61 6.0						61 6.0	48 7.7
33 11.0	29 12.6	27 13.6						28 13.1	25 14.9
50 7.4	48 7.7	40 9.2	Cost of Sales/Inventory					34 10.6	53 6.9
77 4.7	78 4.7	78 4.7						65 5.6	82 4.4
17 22.1	19 19.1	18 20.1						29 12.7	19 19.0
27 13.3	27 13.7	30 12.2	Cost of Sales/Payables					32 11.5	26 14.3
36 10.2	37 9.8	37 9.9						37 9.9	35 10.5
6.6	3.4	5.1						13.1	5.1
15.3	11.1	16.1	Sales/Working Capital					18.0	10.9
35.5	45.2	42.2						186.0	22.5
(34) 11.6	(34) 7.8	(33) 8.5						(12) 10.3	8.5
4.0	3.4	3.4	EBIT/Interest					1.8	3.9
2.2	.2	1.2						1.2	2.2
(12) 19.7	(12) 14.4	(11) 4.3	Net Profit + Depr., Dep.,						
4.9	3.6	2.8	Amort./Cur. Mat. L/T/D						
1.5	.6	1.7							
.5	.4	.5						.4	.6
1.0	1.1	1.0	Fixed/Worth					.8	1.5
2.0	3.1	3.3						NM	3.0
.8	.9	.9						1.4	.8
1.7	2.1	2.1	Debt/Worth					2.9	2.2
3.0	7.0	9.4						NM	4.3
(34) 57.6	(33) 40.5	(29) 53.9	% Profit Before Taxes/Tangible					(10) 102.2	(12) 54.1
26.3	13.6	11.3	Net Worth					28.9	15.0
10.4	-4.3	4.5						1.0	4.2
17.8	15.6	17.1	% Profit Before Taxes/Total					19.5	17.5
9.4	6.0	5.0	Assets					2.4	5.5
4.2	-2.0	.8						.3	2.8
12.2	9.8	15.4						20.5	11.7
7.7	6.7	7.0	Sales/Net Fixed Assets					8.3	3.5
4.3	3.1	3.4						4.9	2.7
2.9	2.7	3.0						3.4	2.4
2.1	1.6	2.1	Sales/Total Assets					2.7	1.9
1.6	1.4	1.5						1.8	1.5
(34) 1.4	(35) .9	(31) 1.7	% Depr., Dep., Amort./Sales					(11) 1.3	1.9
1.8	2.1	2.5						2.0	3.8
3.3	3.4	4.6						2.7	5.1
(15) 1.3		(14) 1.0	% Officers', Directors',						
4.0		1.9	Owners' Comp/Sales						
7.2		3.4							
1714174M	1651548M	1190099M	Net Sales ($)	1412M	4997M		29942M	191542M	962206M
906300M	1061044M	631192M	Total Assets ($)	432M	3737M		13659M	76432M	536932M

© RMA 2003

M = $ thousand   MM = $ million
See Pages 11 through 18 for Explanation of Ratios and Data

Current Data Sorted By Assets							Comparative Historical Data	
						Type of Statement		
		3	6		1	Unqualified	14	5
	2	9	1			Reviewed	7	11
2	1	1	1			Compiled	1	3
	1					Tax Returns	1	
		3	4		4	Other	9	7
7 (4/1-9/30/02)			32 (10/1/02-3/31/03)				**4/1/98-3/31/99**	**4/1/99-3/31/00**
0-500M	**500M-2MM**	**2-10MM**	**10-50MM**	**50-100MM**	**100-250MM**		**ALL**	**ALL**
2	4	16	12		5	**NUMBER OF STATEMENTS**	32	26
%	%	%	%	%	%	**ASSETS**	%	%
		11.8	1.2	DATA NOT AVAILABLE		Cash & Equivalents	8.8	6.1
		27.1	18.3			Trade Receivables (net)	25.0	30.2
		30.7	27.4			Inventory	31.1	31.4
		1.2	2.4			All Other Current	1.0	1.3
		70.9	49.3			Total Current	65.8	69.0
		22.8	38.2			Fixed Assets (net)	25.9	22.4
		3.9	7.5			Intangibles (net)	1.9	4.2
		2.3	4.9			All Other Non-Current	6.3	4.4
		100.0	100.0			Total	100.0	100.0
						LIABILITIES		
		17.8	7.5			Notes Payable-Short Term	14.5	14.8
		2.3	8.0			Cur. Mat.-L/T/D	1.8	2.6
		15.8	10.5			Trade Payables	14.2	19.4
		.4	.0			Income Taxes Payable	.6	.2
		4.8	4.2			All Other Current	8.1	7.1
		41.1	30.1			Total Current	39.2	44.2
		9.3	13.4			Long Term Debt	11.9	14.7
		.4	1.5			Deferred Taxes	.6	.7
		3.6	3.4			All Other Non-Current	3.1	1.7
		45.5	51.5			Net Worth	45.2	38.6
		100.0	100.0			Total Liabilities & Net Worth	100.0	100.0
						INCOME DATA		
		100.0	100.0			Net Sales	100.0	100.0
		30.4	22.5			Gross Profit	26.9	28.5
		22.8	20.7			Operating Expenses	19.7	22.1
		7.6	1.8			Operating Profit	7.2	6.4
		.8	3.7			All Other Expenses (net)	.9	-.5
		6.8	-1.9			Profit Before Taxes	6.3	6.9
						RATIOS		
		3.7	3.9				4.3	3.7
		1.7	2.0			Current	1.7	1.4
		1.1	.9				1.2	1.1
		2.3	.8				1.7	1.6
		.7	.7			Quick	.7	.8
		.6	.4				.5	.5
		37 10.0	**36** 10.0				**35** 10.3	**41** 9.0
		42 8.6	**42** 8.7			Sales/Receivables	**43** 8.5	**48** 7.6
		49 7.4	**50** 7.2				**56** 6.5	**61** 5.9
		42 8.7	**53** 6.8				**45** 8.1	**50** 7.4
		61 5.9	**102** 3.6			Cost of Sales/Inventory	**71** 5.1	**80** 4.6
		81 4.5	**130** 2.8				**111** 3.3	**104** 3.5
		21 17.4	**20** 18.3				**19** 19.3	**27** 13.4
		34 10.9	**30** 12.2			Cost of Sales/Payables	**31** 11.9	**36** 10.2
		45 8.1	**37** 9.8				**44** 8.3	**50** 7.3
		4.4	3.7				4.0	4.8
		8.3	6.9			Sales/Working Capital	9.9	10.4
		33.1	NM				21.9	276.5
		6.6	2.7				28.5	12.3
		(14) 2.4	1.7			EBIT/Interest	(30) 4.6	(22) 2.4
		1.5	-2.9				2.2	1.4
						Net Profit + Depr., Dep., Amort./Cur. Mat. L /T/D		
		.2	.7				.3	.3
		.6	.7			Fixed/Worth	.6	.6
		1.4	2.0				1.3	3.2
		.5	.2				.3	.8
		1.7	1.1			Debt/Worth	1.7	2.3
		3.1	3.7				3.9	6.9
		64.4	7.0				51.6	58.4
		19.4	(10) 1.2			% Profit Before Taxes/Tangible Net Worth	(30) 23.8	(22) 24.7
		12.2	-6.5				10.6	15.4
		16.1	5.9				19.1	20.1
		5.1	.7			% Profit Before Taxes/Total Assets	11.0	6.6
		2.4	-6.5				4.4	2.0
		44.1	7.3				18.8	26.2
		12.6	3.8			Sales/Net Fixed Assets	9.3	9.0
		6.6	2.8				4.8	4.6
		3.0	2.2				2.6	2.6
		2.6	1.4			Sales/Total Assets	2.0	1.9
		1.7	1.1				1.6	1.4
		.7	2.1				1.0	1.1
		2.0	3.8			% Depr., Dep., Amort./Sales	(30) 1.7	(24) 2.1
		2.5	6.8				2.7	3.5
							1.4	
						% Officers', Directors', Owners' Comp/Sales	(10) 4.2	
							9.5	
2599M	**13776M**	**191589M**	**458049M**		**1309620M**	Net Sales ($)	**1084409M**	**792302M**
878M	**4490M**	**81755M**	**295549M**		**826781M**	Total Assets ($)	**626431M**	**544694M**

M = $ thousand MM = $ million

See Pages 11 through 18 for Explanation of Ratios and Data

Comparative Historical Data | Current Data Sorted By Sales

			Type of Statement	0-1MM	1-3MM	3-5MM	5-10MM	10-25MM	25MM & OVER
10	9	10	Unqualified					4	6
7	9	12	Reviewed		1	1	5	5	
6	3	5	Compiled		2		2		1
		1	Tax Returns		1				
10	6	11	Other				1	4	6
4/1/00-3/31/01	4/1/01-3/31/02	4/1/02-3/31/03			7 (4/1-9/30/02)			32 (10/1/02-3/31/03)	
ALL	ALL	ALL							
33	27	39	**NUMBER OF STATEMENTS**		4	1	8	13	13
%	%	%	**ASSETS**	%	%	%	%	%	%
3.6	2.8	6.5	Cash & Equivalents					3.4	1.0
32.4	28.3	25.8	Trade Receivables (net)					27.5	22.3
28.2	26.8	29.1	Inventory					30.3	29.6
2.9	2.2	1.5	All Other Current					.5	2.5
67.0	60.2	62.9	Total Current					61.7	55.4
25.5	30.5	27.3	Fixed Assets (net)					26.0	33.8
3.9	4.8	5.5	Intangibles (net)					8.9	4.3
3.6	4.5	4.3	All Other Non-Current					3.5	6.5
100.0	100.0	100.0	Total					100.0	100.0
			LIABILITIES						
15.9	12.6	12.1	Notes Payable-Short Term					19.3	7.2
3.4	3.2	3.8	Cur. Mat.-L/T/D					8.3	1.4
22.5	16.7	13.8	Trade Payables					15.9	11.9
.3	.2	.3	Income Taxes Payable					.0	.1
4.8	4.3	5.4	All Other Current					5.7	4.4
46.8	37.0	35.4	Total Current					49.1	25.0
18.0	17.6	13.4	Long Term Debt					11.2	18.0
1.0	.7	.9	Deferred Taxes					.5	1.8
2.3	1.3	4.6	All Other Non-Current					5.9	3.6
32.0	43.4	45.8	Net Worth					33.3	51.6
100.0	100.0	100.0	Total Liabilities & Net Worth					100.0	100.0
			INCOME DATA						
100.0	100.0	100.0	Net Sales					100.0	100.0
27.4	25.8	28.9	Gross Profit					25.5	21.5
21.1	23.2	24.3	Operating Expenses					21.8	16.5
6.3	2.6	4.6	Operating Profit					3.7	4.9
1.1	2.5	1.9	All Other Expenses (net)					3.4	1.6
5.2	.2	2.8	Profit Before Taxes					.3	3.3
			RATIOS						
1.8	2.9	3.0						1.6	4.4
1.5	1.8	2.0	Current					1.1	2.4
1.1	1.1	1.1						.9	1.7
1.2	1.6	1.9						.7	1.6
.7	.9	.8	Quick					.6	.9
.5	.7	.6						.5	.7
43 8.6	38 9.7	37 9.7						40 9.1	39 9.5
54 6.8	45 8.1	42 8.6	Sales/Receivables					46 8.0	42 8.6
65 5.7	59 6.2	51 7.1						51 7.2	56 6.5
42 8.7	35 10.4	52 7.0						51 7.2	58 6.3
64 5.7	61 6.0	74 4.9	Cost of Sales/Inventory					74 4.9	103 3.6
87 4.2	113 3.2	116 3.1						86 4.2	123 3.0
32 11.3	23 15.6	20 18.5						31 11.7	18 19.8
47 7.8	38 9.6	33 11.2	Cost of Sales/Payables					34 10.6	30 12.3
60 6.1	50 7.3	43 8.5						47 7.8	35 10.4
5.6	4.7	4.2						9.1	3.9
10.3	9.4	8.0	Sales/Working Capital					34.4	4.4
97.9	32.9	28.9						-79.7	7.8
7.2	2.4	5.5						2.7	8.6
(32) 2.9	(24) 1.2	(35) 2.1	EBIT/Interest					(12) 2.3	2.0
1.7	-.9	.6						.0	-.6
7.0		12.1	Net Profit + Depr., Dep.,						
(13) 2.1		(13) 1.7	Amort./Cur. Mat. L/T/D						
.6		.4							
.4	.4	.3						.6	.5
1.0	.8	.7	Fixed/Worth					1.2	.7
2.5	2.2	1.5						10.6	1.0
1.5	.5	.5						1.7	.2
2.8	1.5	1.7	Debt/Worth					2.8	1.1
6.7	5.1	3.1						62.6	2.4
50.3	14.9	42.2	% Profit Before Taxes/Tangible					56.1	40.0
(29) 28.3	(26) 4.4	(35) 12.2	Net Worth					(11) 17.1	(12) 5.6
14.0	-5.2	.4						4.2	-1.3
14.8	5.1	9.2	% Profit Before Taxes/Total					7.2	11.0
6.9	1.3	3.1	Assets					3.6	3.1
2.2	-2.2	.0						-.4	-.5
20.1	15.8	17.9						15.5	8.4
8.3	6.6	8.5	Sales/Net Fixed Assets					10.5	5.5
6.0	2.9	3.6						4.6	3.4
2.7	3.0	2.8						2.9	2.1
2.3	2.1	2.0	Sales/Total Assets					2.2	1.6
1.6	1.4	1.4						1.5	1.4
.8	.7	.8						2.0	1.3
1.6	(26) 1.9	(38) 2.2	% Depr., Dep., Amort./Sales					2.5	(12) 3.0
2.8	3.1	3.7						4.2	3.8
		2.5	% Officers', Directors',						
		(10) 7.1	Owners' Comp/Sales						
		9.8							
1568105M	877538M	1975633M	Net Sales ($)		6949M	3575M	57768M	207110M	1700231M
936525M	559050M	1209453M	Total Assets ($)		3222M	939M	29964M	104980M	1070348M

(For columns 0-1MM through 5-10MM in the Assets, Liabilities, Income Data and upper Ratios sections: DATA NOT AVAILABLE)

© RMA 2003

M = $ thousand   MM = $ million
See Pages 11 through 18 for Explanation of Ratios and Data

Current Data Sorted By Assets / Comparative Historical Data

						Type of Statement		
		1	2	1	1	Unqualified	9	10
		2	2			Reviewed	5	2
1		2				Compiled	6	3
2						Tax Returns		
		6	3	1		Other	6	12
	6 (4/1-9/30/02)		18 (10/1/02-3/31/03)				**4/1/98-3/31/99**	**4/1/99-3/31/00**
0-500M	**500M-2MM**	**2-10MM**	**10-50MM**	**50-100MM**	**100-250MM**		**ALL**	**ALL**
3		11	7	2	1	**NUMBER OF STATEMENTS**	26	27
%	%	%	%	%	%	**ASSETS**	%	%
	D A T A N O T A V A I L A B L E	6.4				Cash & Equivalents	4.1	6.7
		27.5				Trade Receivables (net)	25.0	23.6
		22.9				Inventory	33.7	25.5
		.4				All Other Current	2.3	.9
		57.2				Total Current	65.0	56.7
		36.7				Fixed Assets (net)	25.6	29.8
		1.8				Intangibles (net)	2.5	3.7
		4.2				All Other Non-Current	6.9	9.8
		100.0				Total	100.0	100.0
						LIABILITIES		
		17.2				Notes Payable-Short Term	14.6	11.4
		9.0				Cur. Mat.-L/T/D	2.3	2.1
		17.7				Trade Payables	11.4	12.8
		.0				Income Taxes Payable	.4	.1
		7.3				All Other Current	6.4	6.2
		51.2				Total Current	35.2	32.6
		9.9				Long Term Debt	11.1	12.7
		.2				Deferred Taxes	.4	.3
		10.2				All Other Non-Current	10.1	6.0
		28.4				Net Worth	43.2	48.4
		100.0				Total Liabilities & Net Worth	100.0	100.0
						INCOME DATA		
		100.0				Net Sales	100.0	100.0
		19.3				Gross Profit	23.7	21.4
		18.5				Operating Expenses	15.5	16.0
		.8				Operating Profit	8.2	5.4
		1.1				All Other Expenses (net)	2.0	-1.0
		-.3				Profit Before Taxes	6.2	6.3
						RATIOS		
		3.0					2.7	3.2
		1.1				Current	2.0	1.9
		.8					1.4	1.2
		1.8					1.3	1.4
		.7				Quick	.9	1.0
		.3					.6	.6
		26 14.2					**37** 9.9	**31** 11.7
		40 9.1				Sales/Receivables	**43** 8.5	**38** 9.5
		51 7.1					**51** 7.1	**48** 7.6
		15 24.3					**42** 8.6	**38** 9.6
		33 11.0				Cost of Sales/Inventory	**79** 4.6	**51** 7.2
		65 5.6					**110** 3.3	**89** 4.1
		18 20.0					**13** 27.4	**16** 22.3
		27 13.3				Cost of Sales/Payables	**25** 14.4	**26** 13.9
		47 7.8					**32** 11.4	**35** 10.5
		7.3					3.6	4.3
		34.8				Sales/Working Capital	6.9	8.1
		-19.8					13.3	18.7
		6.0					16.2	13.8
		(10) 3.3				EBIT/Interest	(24) 3.9	(21) 3.8
		2.0					1.8	2.5
						Net Profit + Depr., Dep., Amort./Cur. Mat. L /T/D		
		.7					.3	.4
		1.0				Fixed/Worth	.6	.6
		-7.8					1.2	1.2
		.6					.5	.4
		2.9				Debt/Worth	1.5	1.0
		-32.4					3.3	4.1
							35.9	38.9
						% Profit Before Taxes/Tangible Net Worth	(25) 20.3	(25) 17.2
							11.2	9.0
		10.0					18.1	13.1
		3.9				% Profit Before Taxes/Total Assets	8.9	6.8
		.9					3.6	4.8
		16.6					13.0	10.4
		12.5				Sales/Net Fixed Assets	8.3	7.4
		3.8					6.7	4.9
		3.5					2.5	3.0
		2.8				Sales/Total Assets	1.9	1.9
		1.9					1.2	1.2
		.9					1.3	1.5
		2.0				% Depr., Dep., Amort./Sales	(21) 2.0	(17) 2.6
		4.4					3.1	3.9
						% Officers', Directors', Owners' Comp/Sales		
3481M		**161788M**	**208125M**	**161424M**	**174018M**	Net Sales ($)	**968380M**	**1380522M**
1004M		**57603M**	**149949M**	**121536M**	**205077M**	Total Assets ($)	**578476M**	**926353M**

M = $ thousand MM = $ million

See Pages 11 through 18 for Explanation of Ratios and Data

Comparative Historical Data   Current Data Sorted By Sales

			Type of Statement						
8	10	5	Unqualified					1	4
5	3	4	Reviewed				1	2	1
6	7	3	Compiled	1			1	1	
	1	2	Tax Returns						
12	8	10	Other		2		1	5	3
4/1/00-	4/1/01-	4/1/02-			1				
3/31/01	3/31/02	3/31/03			6 (4/1-9/30/02)		18 (10/1/02-3/31/03)		
ALL	ALL	ALL		0-1MM	1-3MM	3-5MM	5-10MM	10-25MM	25MM & OVER
31	29	24	**NUMBER OF STATEMENTS**	1	3		3	9	8
%	%	%	**ASSETS**	%	%	%	%	%	%
6.5	5.5	5.7	Cash & Equivalents			D			
22.5	25.7	24.9	Trade Receivables (net)			A			
32.1	30.4	25.5	Inventory			T			
1.7	4.6	.9	All Other Current			A			
62.9	66.1	56.9	Total Current						
26.8	26.9	35.5	Fixed Assets (net)			N			
2.7	1.5	3.1	Intangibles (net)			O			
7.7	5.5	4.4	All Other Non-Current			T			
100.0	100.0	100.0	Total						
			LIABILITIES			A			
14.5	15.2	13.4	Notes Payable-Short Term			V			
2.2	1.7	5.4	Cur. Mat.-L/T/D			A			
12.7	15.6	16.5	Trade Payables			I			
.8	1.0	.0	Income Taxes Payable			L			
6.6	6.9	6.6	All Other Current			A			
36.8	40.4	41.9	Total Current			B			
11.0	9.7	14.7	Long Term Debt			L			
1.1	.7	.2	Deferred Taxes			E			
7.4	4.8	7.3	All Other Non-Current						
43.7	44.4	35.9	Net Worth						
100.0	100.0	100.0	Total Liabilities & Net Worth						
			INCOME DATA						
100.0	100.0	100.0	Net Sales						
22.6	21.4	21.5	Gross Profit						
17.0	18.3	19.8	Operating Expenses						
5.6	3.2	1.8	Operating Profit						
2.6	1.1	1.0	All Other Expenses (net)						
3.0	2.0	.7	Profit Before Taxes						
			RATIOS						
2.8	2.7	3.1							
1.7	1.5	1.3	Current						
1.2	1.2	.9							
1.4	1.3	1.6							
.7	.8	.7	Quick						
.5	.5	.5							
35 10.4	34 10.7	31 11.9							
44 8.2	43 8.4	45 8.0	Sales/Receivables						
50 7.4	55 6.7	53 6.8							
40 9.1	31 11.8	26 13.8							
64 5.7	68 5.3	62 5.9	Cost of Sales/Inventory						
119 3.1	118 3.1	81 4.5							
14 26.8	16 23.4	17 21.5							
26 14.2	24 15.0	23 15.5	Cost of Sales/Payables						
40 9.1	51 7.2	44 8.3							
4.4	3.8	5.2							
6.3	7.6	20.6	Sales/Working Capital						
22.2	22.0	NM							
8.4	4.6	6.1							
(28) 2.7	(25) 2.2	(22) 2.3	EBIT/Interest						
1.3	1.2	1.4							
			Net Profit + Depr., Dep., Amort./Cur. Mat. L/T/D						
.4	.3	.5							
.6	.5	.8	Fixed/Worth						
.9	1.2	2.2							
.7	.6	.6							
1.2	1.1	2.0	Debt/Worth						
4.4	3.4	5.0							
24.4	18.9	23.0							
(28) 11.0	(28) 7.4	(21) 8.9	% Profit Before Taxes/Tangible Net Worth						
2.5	-.6	-5.7							
10.4	7.4	7.0							
4.3	2.6	2.9	% Profit Before Taxes/Total Assets						
.7	-.1	-1.4							
18.6	29.4	13.5							
6.8	8.4	6.8	Sales/Net Fixed Assets						
3.8	5.2	3.2							
2.4	2.4	3.4							
1.7	1.9	2.4	Sales/Total Assets						
1.2	1.3	1.1							
.9	.6	1.3							
(24) 2.3	(25) 2.1	(21) 3.0	% Depr., Dep., Amort./Sales						
4.0	3.6	4.6							
			% Officers', Directors', Owners' Comp/Sales						
1415191M	1047565M	708836M	Net Sales ($)	826M	3956M		21534M	163977M	518543M
894304M	682555M	535169M	Total Assets ($)	317M	2891M		11587M	88815M	431559M

© RMA 2003   M = $ thousand   MM = $ million
See Pages 11 through 18 for Explanation of Ratios and Data

Current Data Sorted By Assets   Comparative Historical Data

						Type of Statement		
		1	4	8		1	Unqualified	21	9
			4	4			Reviewed	8	5
		2	2			1	Compiled	3	4
1							Tax Returns	1	1
		2	3	3	1	1	Other	12	19
		13 (4/1-9/30/02)		25 (10/1/02-3/31/03)				4/1/98-3/31/99	4/1/99-3/31/00
0-500M	500M-2MM	2-10MM	10-50MM	50-100MM	100-250MM		ALL	ALL
1	5	13	15	1	3	**NUMBER OF STATEMENTS**	45	38
%	%	%	%	%	%	**ASSETS**	%	%
		1.8	9.6			Cash & Equivalents	8.2	5.1
		29.8	22.5			Trade Receivables (net)	20.6	26.6
		23.0	31.3			Inventory	27.9	26.0
		2.4	2.3			All Other Current	1.3	1.0
		56.9	65.7			Total Current	58.0	58.7
		30.1	23.1			Fixed Assets (net)	28.9	29.4
		8.1	5.1			Intangibles (net)	3.2	4.7
		4.8	6.1			All Other Non-Current	9.9	7.1
		100.0	100.0			Total	100.0	100.0
						LIABILITIES		
		14.2	9.1			Notes Payable-Short Term	14.2	13.9
		3.2	7.2			Cur. Mat.-L/T/D	3.1	3.2
		16.7	18.2			Trade Payables	13.2	17.0
		.1	1.1			Income Taxes Payable	.3	.1
		14.2	6.6			All Other Current	7.5	7.3
		48.3	42.3			Total Current	38.3	41.5
		8.5	6.5			Long Term Debt	17.6	18.2
		.9	.9			Deferred Taxes	.6	.7
		7.0	3.7			All Other Non-Current	3.9	6.1
		35.4	46.6			Net Worth	39.5	33.5
		100.0	100.0			Total Liabilities & Net Worth	100.0	100.0
						INCOME DATA		
		100.0	100.0			Net Sales	100.0	100.0
		27.8	16.7			Gross Profit	19.8	22.2
		25.2	11.8			Operating Expenses	14.8	16.8
		2.6	4.9			Operating Profit	5.1	5.4
		-.2	.6			All Other Expenses (net)	1.0	1.6
		2.8	4.3			Profit Before Taxes	4.0	3.8
						RATIOS		
		1.7	4.3				2.6	2.4
		1.2	1.8			Current	1.6	1.6
		.8	.9				1.1	1.0
		.9	2.0				1.3	1.4
		.6	1.0			Quick	.8	.9
		.5	.3				.4	.5
		31 11.9	26 13.9				10 35.3	26 14.0
		43 8.5	44 8.3			Sales/Receivables	35 10.5	45 8.1
		63 5.8	59 6.2				49 7.5	56 6.5
		7 53.2	44 8.3				19 18.9	19 19.3
		23 15.6	74 4.9			Cost of Sales/Inventory	37 9.8	42 8.6
		80 4.6	102 3.6				94 3.9	89 4.1
		21 17.5	33 11.1				7 51.5	17 21.5
		30 12.0	43 8.4			Cost of Sales/Payables	25 14.8	29 12.4
		52 7.0	50 7.3				33 11.1	43 8.6
		9.5	3.6				6.6	6.0
		23.8	7.4			Sales/Working Capital	13.8	13.1
		-20.5	-58.7				55.8	216.8
		3.9	28.3				8.4	18.1
		(12) 1.7	4.6			EBIT/Interest	(42) 3.4	(37) 3.0
		-.5	1.9				1.2	1.2
							8.6	
						Net Profit + Depr., Dep., Amort./Cur. Mat. L /T/D	(15) 3.5	
							2.4	
		.4	.2				.2	.4
		1.1	.7			Fixed/Worth	.8	.8
		2.3	2.0				1.9	4.5
		1.4	.6				.5	.8
		2.8	1.1			Debt/Worth	1.4	1.7
		4.4	4.6				4.3	9.1
		145.1	16.6				33.6	43.3
		6.9	(14) 12.1			% Profit Before Taxes/Tangible Net Worth	(36) 15.4	(31) 19.7
		-8.7	3.4				2.7	8.6
		9.0	9.1				13.6	17.7
		2.4	4.2			% Profit Before Taxes/Total Assets	6.8	6.7
		-3.1	1.8				.6	1.0
		35.8	18.8				33.0	30.2
		8.0	13.8			Sales/Net Fixed Assets	12.7	10.6
		4.8	4.1				4.4	3.8
		4.2	2.6				4.4	3.8
		2.2	1.7			Sales/Total Assets	3.2	2.3
		1.4	1.1				1.5	1.6
		.9	.7				.5	.7
		2.9	1.1			% Depr., Dep., Amort./Sales	(42) 1.3	(33) 1.8
		3.6	2.6				2.6	4.0
							1.2	1.3
						% Officers', Directors', Owners' Comp/Sales	(15) 2.1	(15) 3.4
							3.3	7.7
2457M	19481M	168372M	678537M	106522M	1661410M	Net Sales ($)	1819566M	1678647M
412M	6441M	68602M	364894M	54828M	476962M	Total Assets ($)	898486M	959145M

M = $ thousand   MM = $ million
See Pages 11 through 18 for Explanation of Ratios and Data

Comparative Historical Data				Current Data Sorted By Sales					
Type of Statement									
Unqualified	17	13	14	1	1			5	7
Reviewed	13	12	8				2	3	3
Compiled	6	5	5			1	2	1	1
Tax Returns	3	2	1		1				
Other	9	12	10		1	1	1	2	5
	4/1/00-3/31/01 ALL	4/1/01-3/31/02 ALL	4/1/02-3/31/03 ALL	\<-- 13 (4/1-9/30/02) --\>			\<-- 25 (10/1/02-3/31/03) --\>		
				0-1MM	1-3MM	3-5MM	5-10MM	10-25MM	25MM & OVER
NUMBER OF STATEMENTS	48	44	38	1	3	2	5	11	16
ASSETS	%	%	%	%	%	%	%	%	%
Cash & Equivalents	5.5	6.5	6.2					8.6	6.5
Trade Receivables (net)	24.4	24.2	25.3					26.4	29.9
Inventory	33.4	32.4	26.5					21.0	27.7
All Other Current	1.3	2.2	2.6					2.2	3.5
Total Current	64.6	65.3	60.7					58.2	67.5
Fixed Assets (net)	25.6	22.8	27.8					31.8	23.0
Intangibles (net)	2.1	2.2	5.0					3.5	3.1
All Other Non-Current	7.6	9.6	6.6					6.6	6.3
Total	100.0	100.0	100.0					100.0	100.0
LIABILITIES									
Notes Payable-Short Term	16.1	18.6	11.4					11.6	11.6
Cur. Mat.-L/T/D	4.1	4.1	6.6					2.5	8.0
Trade Payables	17.3	14.3	17.2					16.9	20.2
Income Taxes Payable	.3	.7	.5					.0	1.1
All Other Current	9.6	8.0	10.6					13.1	8.3
Total Current	47.4	45.6	46.3					44.2	49.2
Long Term Debt	15.9	27.5	10.6					7.7	11.2
Deferred Taxes	.9	.6	.9					1.1	.5
All Other Non-Current	5.9	6.1	4.9					7.4	3.9
Net Worth	30.0	20.2	37.4					39.7	35.2
Total Liabilities & Net Worth	100.0	100.0	100.0					100.0	100.0
INCOME DATA									
Net Sales	100.0	100.0	100.0					100.0	100.0
Gross Profit	23.1	20.9	21.0					26.3	15.0
Operating Expenses	19.7	17.3	18.1					22.9	11.8
Operating Profit	3.4	3.6	2.8					3.4	3.2
All Other Expenses (net)	1.2	1.6	.3					.1	.3
Profit Before Taxes	2.1	2.0	2.6					3.4	2.9
RATIOS									
Current	2.2	2.5	2.2					1.8	2.5
	1.6	1.6	1.4					1.1	1.3
	1.0	1.0	.9					.8	1.0
Quick	1.1	1.2	1.3					1.0	1.5
	.6	.7	.7					.6	1.0
	.4	.3	.4					.5	.4
Sales/Receivables	18 20.0	19 19.0	26 13.9					37 9.9	30 12.1
	36 10.0	36 10.0	42 8.7					43 8.5	40 9.0
	49 7.5	48 7.6	55 6.6					62 5.9	51 7.1
Cost of Sales/Inventory	29 12.7	27 13.4	18 20.6					14 25.3	20 18.3
	63 5.8	52 7.1	46 7.9					43 8.6	48 7.7
	80 4.6	86 4.2	86 4.3					168 2.2	84 4.4
Cost of Sales/Payables	16 22.2	14 25.4	19 19.6					30 12.0	16 23.1
	29 12.7	24 15.1	39 9.4					52 7.0	42 8.6
	43 8.6	34 10.8	50 7.3					56 6.5	44 8.2
Sales/Working Capital	6.1	6.4	4.7					3.6	4.6
	17.7	15.7	17.9					55.9	16.2
	NM	132.9	-50.0					-17.3	NM
EBIT/Interest	7.8	4.9	8.9					77.2	20.4
	(46) 3.1	(41) 1.6	(36) 2.1					3.9	4.0
	1.3	.8	.6					.7	1.7
Net Profit + Depr., Dep., Amort./Cur. Mat. L/T/D	8.4	6.3	5.1						
	(12) 4.7	(11) 2.8	(10) 1.3						
	1.5	1.1	.6						
Fixed/Worth	.3	.2	.3					.1	.3
	.7	.7	1.0					1.1	.8
	1.7	3.4	2.4					2.3	6.7
Debt/Worth	.9	.8	.7					1.1	.6
	1.5	1.6	1.7					2.3	3.1
	5.4	12.1	6.8					3.9	25.6
% Profit Before Taxes/Tangible Net Worth	25.0	27.3	25.1					48.3	25.0
	(41) 15.0	(36) 9.0	(35) 10.5					7.4	(14) 11.8
	4.6	-.1	-1.3					-.8	2.5
% Profit Before Taxes/Total Assets	10.0	7.2	9.2					12.7	9.1
	3.8	2.4	3.5					4.2	4.2
	.7	-.2	-.8					-.3	1.9
Sales/Net Fixed Assets	37.8	40.1	25.7					26.4	22.0
	12.3	15.2	12.0					8.0	14.5
	5.5	6.1	4.4					3.6	6.6
Sales/Total Assets	4.0	3.8	3.6					3.8	3.3
	2.8	2.5	2.1					2.1	2.2
	1.7	1.7	1.4					1.0	1.7
% Depr., Dep., Amort./Sales	.5	.5	.8					.9	.6
	(44) 1.2	(39) 1.0	(34) 1.7					1.8	(14) 1.0
	2.7	3.1	3.4					4.4	2.8
% Officers', Directors', Owners' Comp/Sales	1.1	1.6	2.0						
	(24) 2.7	(21) 2.8	(19) 2.9						
	6.4	7.8	4.7						
Net Sales ($)	1565928M	1655869M	2636779M	468M	7064M	9665M	31116M	167284M	2421182M
Total Assets ($)	633585M	792930M	972139M	2786M	3148M	2250M	19284M	109927M	834744M

Current Data Sorted By Assets   Comparative Historical Data

						Type of Statement		
1		4	11	1	3	Unqualified	32	27
	3	6	1			Reviewed	23	24
	8	8				Compiled	15	12
	1					Tax Returns		2
		16	8	1		Other	29	29
	14 (4/1-9/30/02)		58 (10/1/02-3/31/03)				4/1/98-3/31/99	4/1/99-3/31/00
0-500M	500M-2MM	2-10MM	10-50MM	50-100MM	100-250MM		ALL	ALL
1	12	34	20	2	3	NUMBER OF STATEMENTS	99	94
%	%	%	%	%	%	**ASSETS**	%	%
	9.1	7.6	6.3			Cash & Equivalents	7.0	8.2
	28.5	23.9	15.7			Trade Receivables (net)	24.7	24.7
	22.7	19.7	12.7			Inventory	16.4	17.2
	1.5	1.5	3.5			All Other Current	1.4	1.6
	61.7	52.7	38.2			Total Current	49.4	51.7
	36.3	35.5	52.7			Fixed Assets (net)	41.7	39.4
	.2	.5	.8			Intangibles (net)	2.3	1.8
	1.8	11.3	8.3			All Other Non-Current	6.5	7.1
	100.0	100.0	100.0			Total	100.0	100.0
						LIABILITIES		
	8.5	9.3	4.5			Notes Payable-Short Term	9.8	8.2
	4.5	5.6	6.6			Cur. Mat.-L/T/D	4.0	3.6
	19.8	13.4	9.1			Trade Payables	12.4	12.0
	1.3	.2	.3			Income Taxes Payable	.3	.1
	5.1	7.3	6.5			All Other Current	6.5	7.1
	39.1	35.8	27.0			Total Current	32.9	31.0
	16.7	19.2	22.0			Long Term Debt	24.8	19.7
	.1	.4	2.1			Deferred Taxes	.7	.7
	7.3	3.5	7.4			All Other Non-Current	2.6	3.8
	36.8	41.1	41.4			Net Worth	38.9	44.7
	100.0	100.0	100.0			Total Liabilities & Net Worth	100.0	100.0
						INCOME DATA		
	100.0	100.0	100.0			Net Sales	100.0	100.0
	30.8	25.0	16.4			Gross Profit	22.3	23.3
	31.9	23.4	14.2			Operating Expenses	16.3	18.1
	-1.1	1.6	2.1			Operating Profit	6.0	5.2
	.6	1.3	1.4			All Other Expenses (net)	1.5	1.2
	-1.7	.3	.8			Profit Before Taxes	4.4	4.0
						RATIOS		
	3.5	2.7	2.8				2.2	3.0
	1.7	1.6	1.6			Current	1.6	1.9
	.9	.9	1.1				1.1	1.1
	2.0	1.9	1.7				1.5	1.9
	1.1	.9	.9			Quick	1.0	1.2
	.6	.4	.5				.6	.7
	37 9.8	41 8.8	38 9.7				34 10.7	38 9.7
	53 6.8	53 6.9	43 8.5			Sales/Receivables	44 8.3	45 8.1
	61 6.0	67 5.5	49 7.4				55 6.6	57 6.4
	31 11.7	29 12.7	26 13.8				21 17.0	20 18.0
	41 8.8	49 7.4	35 10.5			Cost of Sales/Inventory	32 11.3	37 9.9
	88 4.1	71 5.2	52 7.0				52 7.1	64 5.7
	20 18.4	20 18.5	17 21.9				17 21.2	19 19.7
	34 10.6	34 10.9	27 13.5			Cost of Sales/Payables	26 14.2	28 13.1
	77 4.8	49 7.4	37 9.8				35 10.3	37 9.8
	3.9	5.3	5.3				6.0	4.8
	11.4	10.9	9.8			Sales/Working Capital	13.4	9.2
	NM	-37.5	93.9				62.5	40.9
	2.6	7.1	5.0				11.1	8.5
	(11) .2	(31) 1.6	(17) 1.3			EBIT/Interest	(93) 3.5	(85) 2.6
	-4.8	-.8	-1.6				1.1	.8
		2.9				Net Profit + Depr., Dep.,		6.3
		(10) 2.3				Amort./Cur. Mat. L /T/D	(44) 6.3 2.7	(36) 2.7
		1.1					1.2	1.3
	.3	.4	.7				.6	.4
	1.0	.8	1.3			Fixed/Worth	1.2	.8
	NM	1.5	2.9				2.0	1.7
	.5	.7	.7				1.0	.5
	1.4	1.3	1.1			Debt/Worth	1.7	1.4
	NM	2.6	4.6				3.7	2.9
		15.7	21.6				35.8	29.5
		(31) 5.9	(19) 3.7			% Profit Before Taxes/Tangible Net Worth	(93) 19.9	(91) 12.2
		-3.4	-13.5				4.6	.5
	2.9	9.1	8.4				15.7	12.7
	-3.3	.9	1.5			% Profit Before Taxes/Total Assets	6.6	5.3
	-15.9	-3.1	-5.7				.6	.1
	12.2	9.4	3.5				8.7	9.6
	6.5	5.2	2.8			Sales/Net Fixed Assets	4.3	4.9
	3.6	2.8	1.7				2.7	2.5
	2.6	2.1	1.6				2.6	2.5
	2.1	1.7	1.3			Sales/Total Assets	1.9	1.8
	1.6	1.4	1.0				1.3	1.3
	1.5	2.7	4.4				2.0	1.8
	(11) 2.2	(31) 4.2	(19) 6.2			% Depr., Dep., Amort./Sales	(92) 3.3	(87) 3.5
	4.5	8.0	8.2				4.8	5.3
							1.3	1.5
						% Officers', Directors', Owners' Comp/Sales	(26) 2.9	(25) 4.1
							6.6	6.6
191M	32671M	252737M	544216M	205064M	440990M	Net Sales ($)	3086057M	2411841M
163M	15078M	146444M	419874M	138979M	491446M	Total Assets ($)	2117366M	1774932M

© RMA 2003

M = $ thousand   MM = $ million
See Pages 11 through 18 for Explanation of Ratios and Data

Comparative Historical Data   Current Data Sorted By Sales

			Type of Statement						
23	21	20	Unqualified	1		1	1	8	9
19	12	10	Reviewed	2	2		4	1	1
14	14	16	Compiled		5	5	5	1	
	1	1	Tax Returns			1			
35	21	25	Other		2	1	10	8	4
4/1/00-3/31/01	4/1/01-3/31/02	4/1/02-3/31/03			14 (4/1-9/30/02)			58 (10/1/02-3/31/03)	
ALL	ALL	ALL		0-1MM	1-3MM	3-5MM	5-10MM	10-25MM	25MM & OVER
91	69	72	NUMBER OF STATEMENTS	3	9	8	20	18	14
%	%	%	ASSETS	%	%	%	%	%	%
7.4	6.9	7.9	Cash & Equivalents				8.9	6.6	8.6
24.6	22.5	21.5	Trade Receivables (net)				24.3	22.0	15.4
14.6	17.9	17.4	Inventory				19.2	18.0	13.1
1.8	2.9	2.0	All Other Current				1.7	3.4	1.8
48.3	50.1	48.8	Total Current				54.2	50.0	38.9
42.3	39.1	41.4	Fixed Assets (net)				36.0	42.4	51.3
3.3	2.7	1.5	Intangibles (net)				.9	.4	3.7
6.1	8.1	8.4	All Other Non-Current				8.9	7.2	6.1
100.0	100.0	100.0	Total				100.0	100.0	100.0
			LIABILITIES						
7.8	8.4	7.2	Notes Payable-Short Term				8.8	9.4	1.4
4.3	4.1	5.8	Cur. Mat.-L/T/D				5.2	4.6	10.1
13.4	11.1	12.9	Trade Payables				13.6	10.0	8.9
.3	.2	.4	Income Taxes Payable				.1	.4	.4
9.1	7.4	6.5	All Other Current				7.8	6.6	7.1
34.9	31.2	32.8	Total Current				35.5	31.0	28.0
21.4	18.4	19.1	Long Term Debt				17.1	17.2	19.3
.9	.8	.9	Deferred Taxes				.3	2.0	1.1
4.2	5.2	5.4	All Other Non-Current				4.1	5.1	8.3
38.7	44.4	41.8	Net Worth				43.1	44.7	43.3
100.0	100.0	100.0	Total Liabilities & Net Worth				100.0	100.0	100.0
			INCOME DATA						
100.0	100.0	100.0	Net Sales				100.0	100.0	100.0
19.8	21.3	23.4	Gross Profit				26.5	19.9	16.4
16.3	18.9	21.6	Operating Expenses				24.0	18.3	11.8
3.5	2.3	1.8	Operating Profit				2.6	1.7	4.6
1.2	1.0	1.2	All Other Expenses (net)				.4	1.2	1.4
2.3	1.3	.6	Profit Before Taxes				2.2	.5	3.2
			RATIOS						
2.3	3.0	3.2					2.6	3.9	3.7
1.4	1.8	1.6	Current				1.8	1.4	2.2
.9	1.1	1.0					1.1	1.0	.8
1.6	2.0	1.9					2.0	2.1	2.1
.9	1.0	.9	Quick				1.0	.8	1.1
.5	.5	.5					.5	.5	.6
38 9.5	36 10.2	39 9.4					31 11.9	40 9.0	37 9.7
47 7.7	44 8.3	49 7.4	Sales/Receivables				50 7.3	46 7.9	42 8.7
57 6.4	57 6.5	59 6.2					55 6.7	56 6.6	53 6.8
19 18.9	23 16.0	28 12.8					30 12.1	24 15.1	28 13.0
31 11.7	39 9.5	38 9.7	Cost of Sales/Inventory				45 8.1	36 10.3	31 11.6
52 7.0	68 5.4	66 5.6					63 5.8	65 5.6	66 5.5
17 21.9	14 26.1	18 20.5					21 17.3	17 21.0	14 25.4
27 13.4	23 16.0	31 11.7	Cost of Sales/Payables				35 10.5	25 14.4	25 14.5
41 8.9	36 10.3	43 8.6					42 8.7	36 10.1	40 9.2
6.2	4.6	4.8					5.5	3.3	4.3
14.4	9.3	10.5	Sales/Working Capital				8.5	16.2	6.6
−70.3	32.6	−360.4					61.6	NM	−21.0
5.3	4.5	4.8					7.1	2.5	6.0
(82) 2.0	(60) 1.7	(64) 1.2	EBIT/Interest		(19) 1.3	(14) .7			(13) 2.9
.5	−1.0	−1.3			.2	−1.5			−.8
4.1	3.2	3.0	Net Profit + Depr., Dep.,					2.8	
(27) 2.7	(16) 1.7	(20) 1.8	Amort./Cur. Mat. L/T/D				(10) 1.4		
1.7	.8	1.0						.7	
.6	.4	.4					.4	.4	.7
1.2	.9	1.0	Fixed/Worth				.8	1.1	1.1
2.5	1.8	2.9					1.5	1.9	10.3
.6	.5	.7					.5	.7	.6
1.7	1.1	1.3	Debt/Worth				1.1	1.2	1.0
4.3	3.6	4.1					2.5	2.9	13.6
22.5	16.2	17.2	% Profit Before Taxes/Tangible				16.1	19.3	36.3
(80) 9.8	(63) 4.0	(65) 5.7	Net Worth		(18) 8.3	(17) 3.5			(13) 14.5
.9	−11.1	−9.8			−.7	−12.1			−8.0
8.1	9.0	8.4	% Profit Before Taxes/Total				9.5	7.9	8.9
3.4	2.0	.6	Assets				.6	.6	3.1
−1.6	−4.2	−4.4					−2.2	−5.5	−2.4
7.0	7.3	6.8					8.3	6.8	3.4
4.0	4.5	3.8	Sales/Net Fixed Assets				6.0	3.4	2.2
2.9	2.7	2.5					4.0	2.7	2.0
2.2	2.1	2.0					2.4	1.8	1.6
1.7	1.8	1.6	Sales/Total Assets				1.9	1.6	1.2
1.2	1.3	1.2					1.5	1.3	1.0
2.3	2.2	2.8					2.5	2.6	4.4
(87) 3.6	(63) 4.1	(65) 4.5	% Depr., Dep., Amort./Sales		(19) 3.3			(11) 5.4	6.2
5.3	6.4	7.4					7.2	8.2	7.1
1.4	1.0	1.6	% Officers', Directors',						
(21) 3.8	(17) 2.0	(18) 3.4	Owners' Comp/Sales						
5.2	5.1	6.0							
2075006M	1420078M	1475869M	Net Sales ($)	1985M	17148M	28987M	134127M	303273M	990349M
1498381M	1108209M	1211984M	Total Assets ($)	1701M	20366M	15748M	76721M	218669M	878779M

© RMA 2003 M = $ thousand   MM = $ million
See Pages 11 through 18 for Explanation of Ratios and Data

Current Data Sorted By Assets   Comparative Historical Data

0-500M	500M-2MM	2-10MM	10-50MM	50-100MM	100-250MM	Type of Statement	4/1/98-3/31/99 ALL	4/1/99-3/31/00 ALL
	1	2	3	2	3	Unqualified	7	8
1	3	5	5			Reviewed	8	16
2	2	3	1			Compiled	6	4
	3	1				Tax Returns	3	
1	1	5	3	3	1	Other	13	11
	5 (4/1-9/30/02)		46 (10/1/02-3/31/03)					
4	10	16	12	5	4	**NUMBER OF STATEMENTS**	37	39
%	%	%	%	%	%	**ASSETS**	%	%
	15.6	5.6	5.2			Cash & Equivalents	5.4	8.7
	30.9	33.4	18.0			Trade Receivables (net)	28.9	26.4
	21.7	22.4	25.5			Inventory	21.3	21.2
	3.6	.6	4.7			All Other Current	.6	2.1
	71.7	61.9	53.4			Total Current	56.2	58.4
	25.6	34.7	35.0			Fixed Assets (net)	34.9	34.2
	.0	.9	2.9			Intangibles (net)	2.3	1.8
	2.7	2.6	8.7			All Other Non-Current	6.5	5.7
	100.0	100.0	100.0			Total	100.0	100.0
						LIABILITIES		
	14.6	16.6	11.2			Notes Payable-Short Term	11.7	7.5
	4.7	6.2	2.6			Cur. Mat.-L/T/D	3.9	5.0
	18.3	19.0	9.2			Trade Payables	16.8	16.5
	.0	.1	.2			Income Taxes Payable	.2	.2
	8.7	6.4	11.3			All Other Current	8.7	7.5
	46.4	48.4	34.6			Total Current	41.2	36.7
	10.0	19.5	10.7			Long Term Debt	14.6	12.1
	.0	.9	1.2			Deferred Taxes	.9	.8
	13.3	3.5	2.6			All Other Non-Current	8.7	7.6
	30.3	27.7	50.9			Net Worth	34.5	42.7
	100.0	100.0	100.0			Total Liabilities & Net Worth	100.0	100.0
						INCOME DATA		
	100.0	100.0	100.0			Net Sales	100.0	100.0
	31.6	25.4	19.2			Gross Profit	24.1	23.6
	26.0	21.5	14.6			Operating Expenses	16.9	19.6
	5.6	3.9	4.7			Operating Profit	7.3	3.9
	.8	1.8	1.0			All Other Expenses (net)	1.7	.7
	4.8	2.0	3.7			Profit Before Taxes	5.5	3.2
						RATIOS		
	3.4	2.4	2.0			Current	2.0	2.9
	1.5	1.3	1.6				1.5	1.8
	.9	.9	.7				.9	1.0
	2.6	1.2	1.4			Quick	1.2	1.9
	1.0	.9	.7				.9	.8
	.4	.5	.3				.5	.6
	23 15.9	40 9.1	31 11.9			Sales/Receivables	36 10.0	40 9.1
	45 8.1	53 6.9	44 8.2				48 7.6	52 7.0
	56 6.5	67 5.4	51 7.1				63 5.8	60 6.1
	0 UND	17 21.5	29 12.6			Cost of Sales/Inventory	24 15.4	29 12.6
	65 5.6	38 9.6	67 5.4				46 7.9	46 7.9
	110 3.3	98 3.7	119 3.1				77 4.7	76 4.8
	10 38.1	15 24.7	15 23.8			Cost of Sales/Payables	20 18.0	20 18.2
	22 16.6	28 12.9	32 11.5				29 12.8	29 12.7
	60 6.0	50 7.4	33 10.9				45 8.0	69 5.3
	6.8	5.7	6.4			Sales/Working Capital	6.2	4.8
	27.8	9.2	9.1				17.0	7.8
	−32.8	NM	−12.6				−49.1	77.5
		5.5	10.9			EBIT/Interest	8.9	8.4
		2.1	(10) 4.2				(35) 3.4	(34) 2.8
		.7	−.3				1.8	.8
						Net Profit + Depr., Dep., Amort./Cur. Mat. L /T/D	8.1	3.2
							(10) 2.5	(15) 2.2
							1.9	.4
	.1	.6	.3			Fixed/Worth	.5	.4
	.9	.9	.7				.9	.7
	NM	1.9	1.9				2.3	1.8
	.5	1.6	.4			Debt/Worth	.7	.5
	3.6	2.7	.9				1.8	1.3
	NM	4.4	3.4				6.3	3.2
	(15)	34.7	27.4			% Profit Before Taxes/Tangible Net Worth	(32) 65.5	(37) 35.8
		11.9	11.4				29.1	17.1
		−.9	−11.9				10.3	1.6
	34.4	12.4	14.2			% Profit Before Taxes/Total Assets	18.0	14.7
	10.4	3.0	3.9				10.4	6.7
	−.5	−.9	−3.6				2.8	.3
	160.1	11.2	7.2			Sales/Net Fixed Assets	11.9	13.0
	8.5	6.4	3.6				5.7	5.9
	6.2	4.6	2.8				3.4	3.2
	3.9	2.7	2.0			Sales/Total Assets	2.6	2.3
	2.7	2.1	1.6				2.1	2.0
	1.6	1.5	1.2				1.4	1.4
	(14)	.8	1.3			% Depr., Dep., Amort./Sales	1.7	1.2
		2.1	(11) 4.6				2.4	(37) 2.4
		4.1	7.0				3.6	4.4
						% Officers', Directors', Owners' Comp/Sales	1.6	1.1
							(10) 3.8	(12) 1.8
							6.7	
2274M	36207M	136316M	321674M	726356M	932329M	Net Sales ($)	1245012M	1259220M
1188M	12106M	60972M	236281M	380136M	578536M	Total Assets ($)	692190M	695842M

M = $ thousand   MM = $ million
See Pages 11 through 18 for Explanation of Ratios and Data

Comparative Historical Data / Current Data Sorted By Sales

		Comparative Historical Data		Type of Statement	0-1MM	1-3MM	3-5MM	5-10MM	10-25MM	25MM & OVER
	7	7	11	Unqualified			1	1	3	6
	16	8	14	Reviewed		4	1	2	6	1
	12	5	8	Compiled	2	2	1		2	1
		1	4	Tax Returns		1	1		1	
	14	12	14	Other	1	2		3	3	5
	4/1/00-3/31/01 ALL	4/1/01-3/31/02 ALL	4/1/02-3/31/03 ALL		5 (4/1-9/30/02)			46 (10/1/02-3/31/03)		
	49	33	51	**NUMBER OF STATEMENTS**	3	9	4	7	15	13
	%	%	%	**ASSETS**	%	%	%	%	%	%
	7.9	8.6	6.5	Cash & Equivalents					7.7	2.9
	29.5	24.1	27.2	Trade Receivables (net)					29.4	19.7
	21.3	21.8	21.9	Inventory					20.8	21.9
	1.2	1.7	2.2	All Other Current					2.4	3.8
	60.0	56.2	57.8	Total Current					60.4	48.3
	32.9	36.5	33.4	Fixed Assets (net)					33.3	39.6
	1.8	1.2	2.1	Intangibles (net)					1.6	5.3
	5.3	6.1	6.7	All Other Non-Current					4.7	6.8
	100.0	100.0	100.0	Total					100.0	100.0
				LIABILITIES						
	10.9	13.1	13.2	Notes Payable-Short Term					14.0	5.6
	5.9	7.6	4.5	Cur. Mat.-L/T/D					5.7	4.0
	16.5	14.9	16.9	Trade Payables					14.2	15.5
	.1	.2	.2	Income Taxes Payable					.1	.5
	10.2	6.4	8.9	All Other Current					9.3	11.9
	43.6	42.2	43.7	Total Current					43.2	37.4
	17.3	12.4	16.4	Long Term Debt					12.8	17.3
	.8	1.4	1.1	Deferred Taxes					1.6	2.0
	8.2	4.7	5.6	All Other Non-Current					3.3	4.8
	30.1	39.3	33.2	Net Worth					39.1	38.4
	100.0	100.0	100.0	Total Liabilities & Net Worth					100.0	100.0
				INCOME DATA						
	100.0	100.0	100.0	Net Sales					100.0	100.0
	24.2	19.5	24.6	Gross Profit					20.2	20.3
	19.5	18.5	19.5	Operating Expenses					16.8	13.0
	4.6	1.0	5.0	Operating Profit					3.4	7.3
	1.6	1.6	1.3	All Other Expenses (net)					.9	1.2
	3.0	−.6	3.7	Profit Before Taxes					2.4	6.2
				RATIOS						
	2.1 / 1.5 / 1.0	1.8 / 1.6 / .9	2.2 / 1.3 / .8	Current					2.1 / 1.6 / 1.2	2.9 / 1.2 / .7
	1.2 / .9 / .5	1.2 / .8 / .5	1.2 / .8 / .5	Quick					1.2 / 1.0 / .6	1.2 / .7 / .4
	39 9.4 / 47 7.8 / 66 5.6	34 10.9 / 49 7.4 / 64 5.7	39 9.5 / 46 7.9 / 58 6.3	Sales/Receivables					29 12.8 / 41 9.0 / 52 7.0	39 9.3 / 42 8.8 / 49 7.4
	23 15.8 / 50 7.3 / 73 5.0	29 12.8 / 38 9.6 / 83 4.4	24 14.9 / 54 6.8 / 99 3.7	Cost of Sales/Inventory					24 14.9 / 47 7.8 / 76 4.8	21 17.7 / 72 5.1 / 117 3.1
	20 18.4 / 30 12.3 / 49 7.4	20 18.4 / 32 11.6 / 42 8.7	18 20.7 / 33 10.9 / 51 7.2	Cost of Sales/Payables					15 24.5 / 22 17.0 / 34 10.9	23 16.1 / 34 10.7 / 51 7.1
	6.1 / 12.5 / 172.1	6.0 / 9.7 / −71.2	6.5 / 15.6 / −22.8	Sales/Working Capital					6.7 / 10.7 / 55.2	5.3 / 27.3 / −10.9
	(45) 4.5 / 1.7 / .9	(27) 3.1 / 1.6 / −1.3	(44) 8.5 / 3.0 / .8	EBIT/Interest				(13) 11.4 / 4.2 / −.4		(11) 8.6 / 3.1 / 2.0
	(12) 2.4 / 1.2 / .1			Net Profit + Depr., Dep., Amort./Cur. Mat. L/T/D						
	.4 / 1.1 / 2.7	.5 / .9 / 1.9	.5 / .9 / 2.8	Fixed/Worth					.5 / .8 / 1.9	.6 / 1.7 / 4.9
	1.0 / 2.3 / 6.5	.8 / 2.0 / 3.4	.7 / 2.9 / 6.0	Debt/Worth					.5 / 1.1 / 5.4	.8 / 3.5 / 7.7
	(45) 46.0 / 13.5 / .2	24.5 / 6.5 / −8.4	(47) 46.8 / 21.2 / −.9	% Profit Before Taxes/Tangible Net Worth					(14) 53.2 / 15.9 / −6.5	67.3 / 25.9 / 16.0
	10.5 / 2.8 / −.6	6.5 / 1.6 / −6.3	14.2 / 4.4 / −.6	% Profit Before Taxes/Total Assets					15.1 / 2.9 / −3.9	15.0 / 5.2 / 4.5
	9.3 / 6.4 / 3.6	10.6 / 5.6 / 2.4	11.1 / 6.1 / 3.1	Sales/Net Fixed Assets					12.2 / 6.5 / 2.9	6.8 / 4.5 / 2.2
	2.5 / 1.9 / 1.5	2.3 / 1.8 / 1.2	2.6 / 1.9 / 1.2	Sales/Total Assets					2.7 / 2.1 / 1.6	2.0 / 1.6 / 1.0
	(44) 1.4 / 2.8 / 4.9	(28) 2.2 / 3.7 / 5.8	(42) 1.2 / 2.4 / 4.7	% Depr., Dep., Amort./Sales					(13) .8 / 4.2 / 6.1	
	(10) 1.4 / 2.3 / 7.4		(14) 2.1 / 3.3 / 5.8	% Officers', Directors', Owners' Comp/Sales						
	1252070M	1026204M	2155156M	Net Sales ($)	876M	17600M	16515M	51652M	256325M	1812188M
	700998M	603632M	1269219M	Total Assets ($)	739M	12274M	6167M	24763M	130415M	1094861M

© RMA 2003

M = $ thousand   MM = $ million
See Pages 11 through 18 for Explanation of Ratios and Data

Current Data Sorted By Assets   Comparative Historical Data

0-500M	500M-2MM	2-10MM	10-50MM	50-100MM	100-250MM	Type of Statement	4/1/98-3/31/99 ALL	4/1/99-3/31/00 ALL
	1	4	5	2		Unqualified	22	13
	1	9	6			Reviewed	18	24
1	4	2	3			Compiled	12	11
1	2					Tax Returns	3	4
1	4	9	7	1	2	Other	20	24
	13 (4/1-9/30/02)		52 (10/1/02-3/31/03)					
3	12	24	21	3	2	**NUMBER OF STATEMENTS**	75	76
%	%	%	%	%	%	**ASSETS**	%	%
	12.2	5.5	5.6			Cash & Equivalents	7.3	7.8
	23.9	27.9	22.4			Trade Receivables (net)	26.9	26.5
	15.0	18.2	17.1			Inventory	18.7	17.6
	1.0	2.1	1.1			All Other Current	1.5	1.0
	52.0	53.7	46.1			Total Current	54.4	52.9
	32.9	36.5	46.5			Fixed Assets (net)	36.8	39.3
	5.3	2.3	1.3			Intangibles (net)	2.6	2.7
	9.8	7.5	6.1			All Other Non-Current	6.1	5.1
	100.0	100.0	100.0			Total	100.0	100.0
						LIABILITIES		
	11.5	9.5	9.2			Notes Payable-Short Term	10.2	9.2
	4.3	3.9	4.6			Cur. Mat.-L/T/D	3.7	5.1
	10.4	20.3	11.7			Trade Payables	15.0	13.1
	.0	.2	.1			Income Taxes Payable	.2	.2
	15.6	7.5	7.1			All Other Current	7.6	60.5
	41.7	41.4	32.8			Total Current	36.7	88.1
	17.5	21.7	22.8			Long Term Debt	18.7	19.1
	.6	.5	2.1			Deferred Taxes	1.2	1.1
	9.3	3.2	4.7			All Other Non-Current	3.2	5.4
	30.8	33.3	37.7			Net Worth	40.2	-13.7
	100.0	100.0	100.0			Total Liabilities & Net Worth	100.0	100.0
						INCOME DATA		
	100.0	100.0	100.0			Net Sales	100.0	100.0
	24.8	21.1	18.1			Gross Profit	25.5	24.6
	24.4	17.6	14.0			Operating Expenses	19.5	19.0
	.4	3.5	4.1			Operating Profit	6.0	5.7
	1.1	1.6	1.0			All Other Expenses (net)	1.4	1.0
	-.7	1.9	3.2			Profit Before Taxes	4.6	4.7
						RATIOS		
	3.6	1.9	2.8				2.3	2.3
	1.9	1.1	1.4			Current	1.5	1.4
	.7	.9	.8				1.0	1.0
	2.4	1.3	1.4				1.5	1.6
	1.4	.6	.8			Quick	.9	.9
	.5	.5	.5				.5	.6
31	11.9	40 9.1	39 9.3				37 9.9	41 8.9
43	8.5	54 6.8	45 8.0			Sales/Receivables	44 8.3	48 7.6
54	6.8	63 5.8	54 6.8				54 6.7	59 6.2
24	15.1	21 17.3	23 16.0				22 17.0	23 16.0
34	10.8	46 7.9	37 9.9			Cost of Sales/Inventory	36 10.2	38 9.5
38	9.6	74 5.0	69 5.3				62 5.9	64 5.7
15	23.8	24 15.3	17 21.7				21 17.3	18 20.8
20	18.2	41 8.9	25 14.4			Cost of Sales/Payables	31 12.0	29 12.4
37	9.8	65 5.6	43 8.5				43 8.4	45 8.1
	6.1	9.5	5.3				7.3	6.2
	8.2	33.9	14.2			Sales/Working Capital	11.8	15.4
	-31.5	-27.8	-26.6				219.5	-132.2
	6.2	6.5	5.9				9.2	8.7
(11)	2.5	(23) 2.5	(19) 3.6			EBIT/Interest	(67) 3.3	(72) 4.1
	-1.1	1.1	.9				1.3	2.0
			7.4			Net Profit + Depr., Dep.,	5.3	4.4
			(12) 2.1			Amort./Cur. Mat. L./T/D	(37) 2.5	(22) 2.0
			.9				1.5	1.3
	.5	.4	.9				.5	.7
	.6	1.5	1.5			Fixed/Worth	1.0	1.2
	-4.8	4.5	2.4				2.3	3.6
	.3	.9	1.3				.7	.7
	2.1	2.8	1.8			Debt/Worth	1.5	2.2
	-10.3	8.1	2.9				4.5	7.8
		42.4	27.0				41.6	67.5
		(21) 13.3	(20) 10.8			% Profit Before Taxes/Tangible Net Worth	(69) 17.5	(66) 30.5
		2.0	-1.6				6.8	11.5
	10.1	9.1	10.4				16.5	16.9
	1.9	4.0	5.3			% Profit Before Taxes/Total Assets	8.1	7.4
	-12.0	.2	-.2				1.4	2.3
	13.2	7.9	6.2				9.9	8.7
	5.8	5.1	3.7			Sales/Net Fixed Assets	5.8	4.8
	3.6	3.6	2.5				3.5	3.1
	2.4	2.5	2.0				2.6	2.4
	2.0	1.8	1.7			Sales/Total Assets	2.1	1.9
	1.4	1.3	1.5				1.6	1.5
	2.2	1.6	3.4				1.8	2.2
	3.7	(23) 3.4	(20) 4.2			% Depr., Dep., Amort./Sales	(71) 3.0	(64) 3.3
	5.2	6.3	5.3				4.3	4.9
		1.1					2.4	1.2
		(10) 2.0				% Officers', Directors', Owners' Comp/Sales	(24) 4.3	(29) 3.1
		5.2					7.7	7.8
1949M	30783M	229636M	870264M	392667M	530026M	Net Sales ($)	2142991M	1898232M
631M	14775M	123975M	499020M	233150M	343804M	Total Assets ($)	1180825M	1234771M

Comparative Historical Data | Current Data Sorted By Sales

								Type of Statement						
	15		14		12			Unqualified		1		2	2	7
	15		18		16			Reviewed			4	2	8	2
	9		16		10			Compiled	1	3	1		3	2
	7		3		3			Tax Returns	1	1	1			
	21		22		24			Other	1	2	4	1	6	10
	4/1/00-3/31/01 ALL		4/1/01-3/31/02 ALL		4/1/02-3/31/03 ALL				0-1MM 13 (4/1-9/30/02)	1-3MM	3-5MM	5-10MM 52 (10/1/02-3/31/03)	10-25MM	25MM & OVER
	67		73		65			NUMBER OF STATEMENTS	3	7	10	5	19	21
	%		%		%			ASSETS	%	%	%	%	%	%
	6.0		8.3		7.3			Cash & Equivalents			5.2		6.6	6.3
	26.1		25.3		25.5			Trade Receivables (net)			20.7		30.9	22.7
	17.4		19.9		16.3			Inventory			18.8		17.0	15.4
	1.3		2.3		1.6			All Other Current			2.1		1.6	1.7
	50.8		55.7		50.8			Total Current			46.9		56.1	46.2
	41.3		36.2		39.6			Fixed Assets (net)			44.9		32.4	46.4
	1.8		1.2		2.9			Intangibles (net)			.9		2.6	3.2
	6.1		6.9		6.8			All Other Non-Current			7.2		8.9	4.2
	100.0		100.0		100.0			Total			100.0		100.0	100.0
								LIABILITIES						
	12.7		10.6		8.8			Notes Payable-Short Term			13.8		9.9	5.7
	4.2		6.2		3.9			Cur. Mat.-L/T/D			6.2		3.6	3.5
	15.6		13.3		14.8			Trade Payables			15.0		19.8	11.9
	.1		.2		.2			Income Taxes Payable			.2		.1	.3
	8.4		7.7		11.1			All Other Current			6.1		8.1	10.3
	41.0		38.0		38.8			Total Current			41.3		41.6	31.7
	21.4		14.5		28.6			Long Term Debt			28.5		13.3	22.0
	.8		.9		1.1			Deferred Taxes			1.0		.7	1.9
	3.6		2.8		4.8			All Other Non-Current			9.6		3.4	4.8
	33.3		43.8		26.7			Net Worth			19.5		41.0	39.6
	100.0		100.0		100.0			Total Liabilities & Net Worth			100.0		100.0	100.0
								INCOME DATA						
	100.0		100.0		100.0			Net Sales			100.0		100.0	100.0
	23.2		22.4		22.3			Gross Profit			20.3		24.4	17.5
	19.4		19.4		19.1			Operating Expenses			20.8		18.5	13.1
	3.8		3.0		3.2			Operating Profit			−.5		5.9	4.4
	1.4		1.1		.8			All Other Expenses (net)			2.3		.7	1.0
	2.4		2.0		2.4			Profit Before Taxes			−2.8		5.2	3.4
								RATIOS						
	2.4		2.9		2.2						2.5		1.9	2.5
	1.4		1.6		1.3			Current			1.0		1.3	1.4
	.8		1.0		.9						.7		.9	1.0
	1.9		1.9		1.4						1.9		1.3	1.4
	.9		.9		.9			Quick			.5		.9	1.0
	.4		.5		.5						.3		.5	.6
40	9.0	37	9.8	38	9.5				25 14.4		11.4	41 9.0	39 9.5
47	7.7	50	7.3	46	7.9			Sales/Receivables	32 11.4			52 7.0	45 8.0
57	6.4	61	6.0	60	6.1				49 7.4			63 5.8	53 6.9
23	16.1	24	15.4	22	16.9				26 13.8			22 16.7	21 17.4
32	11.4	41	8.8	36	10.2			Cost of Sales/Inventory	41 8.8			39 9.3	30 12.3
63	5.8	78	4.7	58	6.3				57 6.4			59 6.2	62 5.9
17	21.0	19	19.5	18	20.7				16 23.2			18 20.5	18 19.9
33	11.0	28	13.1	29	12.7			Cost of Sales/Payables	29 12.5			36 10.0	25 14.4
47	7.8	44	8.3	46	7.9				57 6.4			66 5.5	41 9.0
	6.6		5.0		7.1						7.5		8.3	6.4
	16.8		9.8		16.7			Sales/Working Capital			−249.6		17.8	12.8
	−19.4		103.0		−28.8						−12.8		−71.3	NM
	7.7		7.5		7.5						2.8		9.4	9.5
(64)	2.1	(66)	2.0	(61)	3.5			EBIT/Interest			1.1	(17) 4.4	(20) 5.1
	.9		.3		.7						−2.0		2.1	.9
	4.1		5.5		9.8			Net Profit + Depr., Dep.,						11.0
(14)	2.9	(32)	1.9	(23)	2.4			Amort./Cur. Mat. L/T/D					(11) 2.4
	1.2		.7		.8									.8
	.6		.4		.5						.6		.4	.8
	1.1		.9		1.4			Fixed/Worth			2.8		.8	1.4
	4.4		1.7		3.2						NM		1.8	2.4
	.6		.5		.6						.6		.6	1.2
	1.6		1.3		1.9			Debt/Worth			4.0		1.6	1.7
	8.0		3.0		5.3						NM		9.1	2.9
	37.4		20.1		32.1			% Profit Before Taxes/Tangible					44.0	36.4
(56)	17.3	(68)	6.9	(56)	10.8			Net Worth				(17) 17.9	(20) 13.7
	3.6		−10.2		1.1								4.8	−1.6
	13.1		9.8		10.9			% Profit Before Taxes/Total			8.1		19.4	11.6
	3.6		2.8		4.3			Assets			.3		8.6	7.8
	−.4		−3.5		−.5						−15.9		1.9	−.2
	7.0		8.2		7.2						12.1		16.5	6.2
	4.7		4.9		4.9			Sales/Net Fixed Assets			4.7		5.7	3.7
	3.3		3.2		3.1						1.5		4.1	2.7
	2.4		2.2		2.2						2.5		2.6	2.0
	1.9		1.7		1.8			Sales/Total Assets			2.1		1.9	1.7
	1.5		1.5		1.5						1.1		1.5	1.5
	2.7		1.4		2.1						1.8		1.4	3.0
(62)	3.9	(65)	3.4	(59)	3.8			% Depr., Dep., Amort./Sales			4.6	(18) 3.5	(18) 4.1
	5.1		5.6		5.4						7.0		4.8	5.5
	2.3		1.7		1.6			% Officers', Directors',						
(24)	3.2	(28)	3.7	(23)	3.7			Owners' Comp/Sales						
	6.3		7.4		6.3									
	1472328M		1603825M		2055325M			Net Sales ($)	1712M	12416M	37649M	30895M	271951M	1700702M
	827846M		932033M		1215355M			Total Assets ($)	1245M	7242M	22308M	22538M	147655M	1014367M

M = $ thousand   MM = $ million
See Pages 11 through 18 for Explanation of Ratios and Data

Current Data Sorted By Assets — Comparative Historical Data

0-500M	500M-2MM	2-10MM	10-50MM	50-100MM	100-250MM	Type of Statement	4/1/98-3/31/99 ALL	4/1/99-3/31/00 ALL
			5	2	1	Unqualified	9	8
	2		3			Reviewed	6	7
1	4	2	1			Compiled	3	3
1		1				Tax Returns	1	
		1	1	1		Other	7	11
2	6	4	10	3	1	**NUMBER OF STATEMENTS**	26	29

Period groupings: 6 (4/1-9/30/02) ; 20 (10/1/02-3/31/03)

0-500M %	500M-2MM %	2-10MM %	10-50MM %	50-100MM %	100-250MM %	ASSETS	%	%
			9.4			Cash & Equivalents	7.6	7.3
			20.3			Trade Receivables (net)	29.1	27.3
			14.1			Inventory	15.7	19.2
			3.8			All Other Current	2.5	.8
			47.6			Total Current	54.9	54.6
			33.8			Fixed Assets (net)	35.6	37.0
			6.2			Intangibles (net)	4.2	3.6
			12.4			All Other Non-Current	5.3	4.8
			100.0			Total	100.0	100.0
						LIABILITIES		
			3.3			Notes Payable-Short Term	9.1	10.1
			2.5			Cur. Mat.-L/T/D	3.8	5.2
			9.1			Trade Payables	14.5	13.8
			.0			Income Taxes Payable	.1	.3
			9.1			All Other Current	8.3	8.8
			24.0			Total Current	35.8	38.1
			6.8			Long Term Debt	20.7	25.4
			.7			Deferred Taxes	.6	.4
			2.7			All Other Non-Current	2.5	3.8
			65.9			Net Worth	40.4	32.2
			100.0			Total Liabilities & Net Worth	100.0	100.0
						INCOME DATA		
			100.0			Net Sales	100.0	100.0
			17.9			Gross Profit	25.4	26.4
			15.4			Operating Expenses	20.4	20.5
			2.5			Operating Profit	5.0	5.9
			−1.2			All Other Expenses (net)	−2.4	1.7
			3.7			Profit Before Taxes	7.4	4.2

RATIOS

0-500M	500M-2MM	2-10MM	10-50MM	50-100MM	100-250MM	Ratio	4/1/98-3/31/99 ALL	4/1/99-3/31/00 ALL
			3.1			Current	2.4	2.0
			2.0				1.7	1.5
			1.6				1.0	1.1
			1.8			Quick	1.6	1.6
			1.4				.9	.9
			.8				.6	.6
		44	8.4			Sales/Receivables	39 9.3	35 10.4
		51	7.2				49 7.4	45 8.1
		60	6.0				54 6.8	60 6.1
		36	10.1			Cost of Sales/Inventory	22 16.7	28 13.0
		40	9.1				41 8.9	41 8.8
		49	7.4				53 6.9	79 4.6
		15	24.3			Cost of Sales/Payables	18 19.8	23 15.9
		27	13.6				30 12.0	33 11.0
		37	10.0				45 8.0	49 7.5
			3.0			Sales/Working Capital	6.7	7.8
			7.0				12.2	14.0
			11.1				NM	43.6
						EBIT/Interest	(24) 6.7	(27) 5.4
							3.0	2.5
							.9	1.8
						Net Profit + Depr., Dep., Amort./Cur. Mat. L /T/D		
			.3			Fixed/Worth	.6	.8
			.6				1.3	1.3
			.9				1.8	3.3
			.3			Debt/Worth	.8	1.5
			.5				1.9	2.4
			1.0				3.5	7.4
			26.3			% Profit Before Taxes/Tangible Net Worth	(25) 61.0	(27) 55.9
			8.3				21.1	25.2
			−1.6				4.5	9.0
			11.5			% Profit Before Taxes/Total Assets	14.6	10.8
			6.5				7.4	5.8
			−1.0				.8	3.0
			8.4			Sales/Net Fixed Assets	10.4	9.4
			4.8				5.8	4.7
			3.1				3.1	3.3
			1.8			Sales/Total Assets	3.0	2.6
			1.3				1.9	1.9
			1.0				1.4	1.4
						% Depr., Dep., Amort./Sales	(24) 2.5	(25) 2.6
							3.0	3.7
							6.2	5.2
						% Officers', Directors', Owners' Comp/Sales	(10) 4.2	(10) 2.8
							6.0	5.0
							10.8	6.6
2681M	15131M	29618M	293363M	461340M	207286M	Net Sales ($)	1161243M	858347M
833M	8551M	13110M	192883M	273515M	121640M	Total Assets ($)	679388M	495771M

© RMA 2003

M = $ thousand   MM = $ million
See Pages 11 through 18 for Explanation of Ratios and Data

Comparative Historical Data | Current Data Sorted By Sales

4/1/00-3/31/01 ALL	4/1/01-3/31/02 ALL	4/1/02-3/31/03 ALL		0-1MM	1-3MM	3-5MM	5-10MM	10-25MM	25MM & OVER
			Type of Statement						
3	2	8	Unqualified					2	6
3	6	7	Reviewed		1	2	1	2	1
7	9	7	Compiled		5			2	
	1	1	Tax Returns		1				
8	10	3	Other			1			2
				6 (4/1-9/30/02)			20 (10/1/02-3/31/03)		
21	28	26	**NUMBER OF STATEMENTS**		7	3	1	6	9
%	%	%	**ASSETS**	%	%	%	%	%	%
7.9	6.6	8.9	Cash & Equivalents	DATA NOT AVAILABLE					
29.7	25.7	21.6	Trade Receivables (net)						
17.8	17.8	16.8	Inventory						
1.7	2.4	2.6	All Other Current						
57.1	52.5	49.9	Total Current						
30.6	36.7	38.4	Fixed Assets (net)						
3.3	4.8	4.5	Intangibles (net)						
9.0	6.1	7.2	All Other Non-Current						
100.0	100.0	100.0	Total						
			LIABILITIES						
9.9	9.5	5.1	Notes Payable-Short Term						
3.0	6.2	3.6	Cur. Mat.-L/T/D						
14.7	13.3	10.5	Trade Payables						
.2	.1	.3	Income Taxes Payable						
6.7	9.8	7.7	All Other Current						
34.4	38.9	27.2	Total Current						
15.4	22.1	15.8	Long Term Debt						
.1	.3	.7	Deferred Taxes						
2.8	5.6	1.8	All Other Non-Current						
47.3	33.0	54.5	Net Worth						
100.0	100.0	100.0	Total Liabilities & Net Worth						
			INCOME DATA						
100.0	100.0	100.0	Net Sales						
28.4	24.5	23.1	Gross Profit						
20.9	19.8	21.1	Operating Expenses						
7.4	4.6	2.0	Operating Profit						
-.6	1.6	.3	All Other Expenses (net)						
8.0	3.1	1.7	Profit Before Taxes						
			RATIOS						
2.5	2.5	2.7							
1.8	1.5	1.8	Current						
1.2	1.0	1.4							
1.6	1.7	1.8							
1.2	.9	1.0	Quick						
.6	.5	.8							
37 9.7	**39** 9.3	**38** 9.7							
51 7.2	**47** 7.8	**48** 7.6	Sales/Receivables						
65 5.6	**60** 6.1	**53** 6.9							
30 12.1	**31** 11.8	**28** 13.2							
39 9.5	**42** 8.7	**43** 8.6	Cost of Sales/Inventory						
61 6.0	**73** 5.0	**63** 5.8							
18 20.3	**16** 23.2	**15** 24.3							
30 12.2	**34** 10.7	**28** 13.1	Cost of Sales/Payables						
53 6.8	**51** 7.2	**37** 10.0							
6.3	6.5	5.3							
8.7	10.2	8.2	Sales/Working Capital						
30.7	NM	14.0							
18.1	6.5	5.3							
(19) 5.4	(25) 2.2	(22) 2.7	EBIT/Interest						
2.4	.6	-1.7							
			Net Profit + Depr., Dep., Amort./Cur. Mat. L/T/D						
.3	.9	.5							
.7	1.4	.8	Fixed/Worth						
1.4	20.2	1.2							
.5	.8	.4							
1.5	2.9	1.0	Debt/Worth						
2.2	51.2	2.0							
48.6	50.8	21.1							
33.3	(22) 10.5	8.3	% Profit Before Taxes/Tangible Net Worth						
10.5	-5.0	-5.2							
22.6	10.7	10.7							
15.2	4.1	3.2	% Profit Before Taxes/Total Assets						
4.0	-1.6	-3.2							
10.5	9.5	7.6							
6.8	4.7	5.3	Sales/Net Fixed Assets						
3.9	2.7	2.9							
2.8	2.6	2.6							
1.7	1.6	1.7	Sales/Total Assets						
1.4	1.1	1.2							
1.1	2.0	3.2							
(19) 2.6	(24) 4.0	(23) 4.2	% Depr., Dep., Amort./Sales						
3.9	6.2	7.8							
	2.0								
	(11) 3.7		% Officers', Directors', Owners' Comp/Sales						
	6.2								
533759M	543396M	1009419M	Net Sales ($)		12908M	12717M	7979M	92196M	883619M
327139M	341369M	610532M	Total Assets ($)		7387M	8277M	2532M	75609M	516727M

M = $ thousand MM = $ million

See Pages 11 through 18 for Explanation of Ratios and Data

Current Data Sorted By Assets | **Comparative Historical Data**

0-500M	500M-2MM	2-10MM	10-50MM	50-100MM	100-250MM		4/1/98-3/31/99 ALL	4/1/99-3/31/00 ALL
						Type of Statement		
		4	2			Unqualified	6	10
1		5	1		1	Reviewed	12	8
3	3	2	1			Compiled	8	5
						Tax Returns	1	
	1	6	3			Other	12	15
9 (4/1-9/30/02)			24 (10/1/02-3/31/03)					
4	4	17	7		1	**NUMBER OF STATEMENTS**	39	38
%	%	%	%	%	%	**ASSETS**	%	%
		7.4		DATA NOT AVAILABLE		Cash & Equivalents	8.9	8.9
		26.0				Trade Receivables (net)	26.4	26.5
		10.6				Inventory	17.9	14.9
		1.7				All Other Current	.8	1.1
		45.8				Total Current	54.0	51.5
		48.6				Fixed Assets (net)	38.2	41.9
		.8				Intangibles (net)	1.7	1.3
		4.8				All Other Non-Current	6.0	5.3
		100.0				Total	100.0	100.0
						LIABILITIES		
		10.2				Notes Payable-Short Term	4.6	9.6
		4.9				Cur. Mat.-L/T/D	3.5	3.9
		11.8				Trade Payables	11.3	14.8
		.0				Income Taxes Payable	.2	.2
		8.2				All Other Current	9.0	8.6
		35.1				Total Current	28.7	37.1
		25.9				Long Term Debt	15.6	19.6
		.7				Deferred Taxes	.5	.6
		6.4				All Other Non-Current	11.9	7.1
		31.9				Net Worth	43.3	35.7
		100.0				Total Liabilities & Net Worth	100.0	100.0
						INCOME DATA		
		100.0				Net Sales	100.0	100.0
		19.0				Gross Profit	24.2	27.3
		19.3				Operating Expenses	19.2	20.5
		-.2				Operating Profit	5.0	6.8
		2.6				All Other Expenses (net)	2.0	1.3
		-2.8				Profit Before Taxes	3.0	5.5
						RATIOS		
		2.1					2.5	2.1
		1.2				Current	1.9	1.3
		.8					1.3	1.1
		1.7					1.7	1.5
		.8				Quick	1.4	1.0
		.5					.8	.7
		44 8.3					**34** 10.6	**34** 10.8
		49 7.5				Sales/Receivables	**43** 8.4	**44** 8.4
		70 5.2					**52** 7.0	**52** 7.0
		18 20.1					**20** 18.1	**17** 21.2
		28 13.2				Cost of Sales/Inventory	**30** 12.2	**31** 11.8
		38 9.6					**45** 8.1	**44** 8.4
		18 19.7					**14** 25.6	**20** 18.1
		31 11.8				Cost of Sales/Payables	**23** 15.8	**29** 12.6
		40 9.1					**32** 11.5	**43** 8.4
		7.8					7.6	7.8
		23.2				Sales/Working Capital	10.4	21.8
		-22.3					18.1	99.5
		2.2					19.5	7.8
		(15) 1.1				EBIT/Interest	(36) 4.5	(35) 3.6
		-1.5					1.5	1.7
							3.9	2.4
						Net Profit + Depr., Dep., Amort./Cur. Mat. L /T/D	(16) 3.0	(14) 1.5
							1.9	1.2
		1.1					.4	.6
		1.6				Fixed/Worth	.9	1.3
		3.0					1.7	2.3
		1.9					.5	.9
		2.2				Debt/Worth	1.1	2.1
		3.9					2.9	4.6
		16.4					56.0	64.0
		(16) 1.1				% Profit Before Taxes/Tangible Net Worth	(34) 21.9	(36) 29.0
		-17.5					12.3	9.7
		3.4					22.3	18.2
		.2				% Profit Before Taxes/Total Assets	8.2	9.6
		-8.0					3.3	3.1
		5.6					11.2	9.3
		3.4				Sales/Net Fixed Assets	5.2	5.3
		2.0					3.8	3.4
		2.0					2.8	2.9
		1.7				Sales/Total Assets	2.2	2.2
		1.2					1.8	1.6
		3.5					1.9	1.4
		(16) 4.1				% Depr., Dep., Amort./Sales	(36) 2.6	(34) 3.2
		6.6					4.0	5.2
		2.7					2.1	3.1
		(10) 4.7				% Officers', Directors', Owners' Comp/Sales	(16) 3.6	(17) 6.0
		6.7					6.3	7.2
3983M	11433M	147651M	220576M		89541M	Net Sales ($)	725059M	548088M
1294M	5135M	88404M	142090M		109425M	Total Assets ($)	317521M	299345M

M = $ thousand MM = $ million

See Pages 11 through 18 for Explanation of Ratios and Data

Comparative Historical Data   Current Data Sorted By Sales

			Type of Statement			0-1MM	1-3MM	3-5MM	5-10MM	10-25MM	25MM & OVER
5	4	6	Unqualified					1	2	2	1
7	10	8	Reviewed	1				1	3	2	1
7	9	9	Compiled	2	3			2	1		1
	3		Tax Returns								
17	17	10	Other					3	2	4	1
4/1/00-	4/1/01-	4/1/02-			9 (4/1-9/30/02)			24 (10/1/02-3/31/03)			
3/31/01	3/31/02	3/31/03									
ALL	ALL	ALL									
36	43	33	**NUMBER OF STATEMENTS**	3	3	7	8	8	4		
%	%	%	**ASSETS**	%	%	%	%	%	%		
6.9	4.7	7.6	Cash & Equivalents								
26.8	25.1	24.5	Trade Receivables (net)								
16.1	14.3	12.3	Inventory								
1.4	1.7	2.4	All Other Current								
51.2	45.8	46.7	Total Current								
39.7	45.2	44.7	Fixed Assets (net)								
2.4	2.6	3.2	Intangibles (net)								
6.7	6.3	5.3	All Other Non-Current								
100.0	100.0	100.0	Total								
			LIABILITIES								
8.0	11.0	8.8	Notes Payable-Short Term								
3.6	5.0	4.2	Cur. Mat.-L/T/D								
14.2	12.5	11.6	Trade Payables								
.0	.0	.1	Income Taxes Payable								
7.4	7.9	7.1	All Other Current								
33.2	36.4	31.7	Total Current								
17.9	25.5	23.1	Long Term Debt								
.3	.4	.8	Deferred Taxes								
13.7	3.3	5.1	All Other Non-Current								
34.9	34.4	39.3	Net Worth								
100.0	100.0	100.0	Total Liabilities & Net Worth								
			INCOME DATA								
100.0	100.0	100.0	Net Sales								
19.3	22.2	22.8	Gross Profit								
16.6	20.6	21.7	Operating Expenses								
2.7	1.6	1.1	Operating Profit								
1.6	1.9	1.7	All Other Expenses (net)								
1.2	-.4	-.6	Profit Before Taxes								
			RATIOS								
3.0	2.0	2.6									
1.7	1.2	1.6	Current								
1.0	.9	1.0									
1.8	1.3	1.9									
1.0	.8	1.0	Quick								
.7	.6	.6									
43 8.4	41 8.9	40 9.2									
51 7.1	53 6.9	48 7.6	Sales/Receivables								
61 6.0	62 5.9	60 6.1									
21 17.8	19 19.7	19 19.2									
33 11.0	31 11.9	28 13.2	Cost of Sales/Inventory								
60 6.1	45 8.1	39 9.4									
21 17.5	23 15.8	17 21.9									
28 13.1	31 11.8	28 13.1	Cost of Sales/Payables								
40 9.2	39 9.4	36 10.0									
5.1	8.3	6.5									
11.2	22.3	14.2	Sales/Working Capital								
119.8	-77.7	458.3									
8.4	2.9	3.2									
(33) 2.1	(40) 1.2	(29) 1.1	EBIT/Interest								
.2	-.6	-3.1									
	1.8		Net Profit + Depr., Dep.,								
	(13) 1.3		Amort./Cur. Mat. L/T/D								
	.4										
.5	.9	.6									
1.3	1.6	1.5	Fixed/Worth								
4.3	3.4	3.0									
.7	1.2	.7									
2.2	2.5	2.1	Debt/Worth								
6.2	7.2	4.0									
45.9	26.9	24.9	% Profit Before Taxes/Tangible								
(31) 13.8	(41) 2.9	(29) .8	Net Worth								
-5.5	-20.7	-9.1									
12.0	8.1	9.1	% Profit Before Taxes/Total								
3.3	.9	.2	Assets								
-3.9	-6.5	-6.3									
8.6	7.4	6.2									
5.6	4.6	4.3	Sales/Net Fixed Assets								
2.7	2.2	2.7									
2.6	2.3	2.3									
1.7	1.8	1.8	Sales/Total Assets								
1.3	1.3	1.3									
1.4	1.9	3.3									
(31) 2.7	(37) 3.5	(31) 3.9	% Depr., Dep., Amort./Sales								
4.2	6.2	5.8									
2.6	3.3	3.4	% Officers', Directors',								
(12) 3.8	(19) 5.3	(16) 5.8	Owners' Comp/Sales								
5.4	9.0	11.3									
690396M	929029M	473184M	Net Sales ($)	2640M	5514M	27478M	66716M	138399M	232437M		
513565M	870270M	346348M	Total Assets ($)	851M	2312M	24394M	41417M	86688M	190686M		

© RMA 2003   M = $ thousand   MM = $ million
See Pages 11 through 18 for Explanation of Ratios and Data

Current Data Sorted By Assets   Comparative Historical Data

0-500M	500M-2MM	2-10MM	10-50MM	50-100MM	100-250MM	Type of Statement	4/1/98-3/31/99 ALL	4/1/99-3/31/00 ALL
		3	3	1		Unqualified	8	5
1	2	5	1			Reviewed	8	9
1	6	2	1			Compiled	3	8
		1				Tax Returns		2
	3	2	2		1	Other	6	7
	6 (4/1-9/30/02)		29 (10/1/02-3/31/03)					
2	12	12	7	1	1	**NUMBER OF STATEMENTS**	25	31
%	%	%	%	%	%	**ASSETS**	%	%
	4.9	9.4				Cash & Equivalents	3.2	5.0
	26.5	29.0				Trade Receivables (net)	29.8	30.0
	18.6	16.0				Inventory	19.6	17.1
	1.7	2.8				All Other Current	1.6	2.1
	51.7	57.2				Total Current	54.2	54.2
	34.1	30.8				Fixed Assets (net)	39.0	34.6
	3.9	3.6				Intangibles (net)	2.7	2.4
	10.3	8.4				All Other Non-Current	4.2	8.9
	100.0	100.0				Total	100.0	100.0
						LIABILITIES		
	12.5	10.6				Notes Payable-Short Term	10.5	9.6
	5.1	7.7				Cur. Mat.-L/T/D	5.0	4.3
	17.0	10.0				Trade Payables	13.9	14.7
	.0	.6				Income Taxes Payable	.1	.2
	9.2	11.0				All Other Current	8.3	8.8
	43.8	40.0				Total Current	37.7	37.6
	27.2	14.4				Long Term Debt	27.6	22.5
	.1	.1				Deferred Taxes	1.5	.6
	17.8	4.2				All Other Non-Current	5.3	4.1
	11.1	41.4				Net Worth	28.0	35.2
	100.0	100.0				Total Liabilities & Net Worth	100.0	100.0
						INCOME DATA		
	100.0	100.0				Net Sales	100.0	100.0
	25.7	30.5				Gross Profit	23.1	29.3
	24.2	26.3				Operating Expenses	18.2	21.8
	1.5	4.2				Operating Profit	4.9	7.6
	2.1	1.2				All Other Expenses (net)	1.8	1.8
	−.6	3.0				Profit Before Taxes	3.1	5.8
						RATIOS		
	1.9	2.2					1.9	2.9
	1.5	1.6				Current	1.4	1.6
	.6	1.1					1.0	1.0
	1.4	1.5					1.3	2.0
	.8	1.0				Quick	1.0	1.0
	.4	.7					.5	.5
	23 15.8	50 7.2					38 9.6	36 10.0
	33 11.1	54 6.8				Sales/Receivables	55 6.7	46 8.0
	49 7.4	64 5.7					62 5.9	56 6.5
	6 65.0	21 17.2					28 13.2	17 21.5
	33 11.2	32 11.4				Cost of Sales/Inventory	44 8.2	38 9.6
	48 7.6	63 5.8					62 5.9	62 5.9
	17 21.0	13 27.5					18 19.9	18 20.3
	23 15.9	26 14.0				Cost of Sales/Payables	30 12.0	33 11.1
	45 8.1	40 9.1					44 8.2	52 7.0
	10.4	5.3					8.4	6.5
	18.2	11.7				Sales/Working Capital	15.6	18.4
	−12.6	34.8					NM	−87.2
	3.5	6.7					8.3	15.1
	(11) 1.0	(11) 1.9				EBIT/Interest	2.8	(28) 2.9
	−1.1	1.5					1.2	1.3
						Net Profit + Depr., Dep., Amort./Cur. Mat. L /T/D	(11) 1.5 1.3 .8	
	.7	.4					.6	.3
	1.9	.8				Fixed/Worth	1.8	1.3
	−2.6	2.7					5.5	59.6
	.9	.5					1.2	.5
	17.3	2.0				Debt/Worth	2.6	2.1
	−5.1	5.2					12.3	132.9
		52.4				% Profit Before Taxes/Tangible Net Worth	(22) 50.9	(24) 65.5
		21.2					28.0	27.0
		4.4					8.1	11.0
	10.4	15.4				% Profit Before Taxes/Total Assets	13.8	18.8
	.3	5.0					7.4	8.0
	−9.1	1.6					1.3	2.5
	28.9	15.8				Sales/Net Fixed Assets	11.4	11.0
	8.4	6.0					4.7	6.3
	3.3	4.3					2.7	3.5
	3.0	2.7				Sales/Total Assets	2.8	3.3
	2.2	1.9					1.8	2.0
	1.9	1.5					1.4	1.5
	(10) 1.5	1.2				% Depr., Dep., Amort./Sales	(24) 1.7	(27) 1.8
	3.6	2.8					2.6	3.0
	5.0	3.9					3.7	4.7
						% Officers', Directors', Owners' Comp/Sales		(11) 1.3
								5.8
								7.5
592M	35540M	115546M	223989M	99666M	172152M	Net Sales ($)	565689M	364247M
254M	13358M	56890M	130701M	61239M	191421M	Total Assets ($)	301626M	213832M

M = $ thousand   MM = $ million
See Pages 11 through 18 for Explanation of Ratios and Data

Comparative Historical Data   ## Current Data Sorted By Sales

				Type of Statement						
4	3		7	Unqualified	1			1	3	2
12	8		9	Reviewed	1	1	2	2	2	1
8	8		10	Compiled	1	3	2	3	1	
3	1		1	Tax Returns		1				
4	8		8	Other	2			2	2	2
4/1/00- 3/31/01 ALL	4/1/01- 3/31/02 ALL		4/1/02- 3/31/03 ALL		6 (4/1-9/30/02)			29 (10/1/02-3/31/03)		
					0-1MM	1-3MM	3-5MM	5-10MM	10-25MM	25MM & OVER
31	28		35	NUMBER OF STATEMENTS	3	7	4	8	8	5
%	%		%	ASSETS	%	%	%	%	%	%
6.4	6.7		8.3	Cash & Equivalents						
27.9	25.2		24.7	Trade Receivables (net)						
13.7	16.7		18.3	Inventory						
4.5	4.3		2.5	All Other Current						
52.5	52.8		53.8	Total Current						
41.5	35.7		31.6	Fixed Assets (net)						
1.2	5.4		6.0	Intangibles (net)						
4.7	6.1		8.6	All Other Non-Current						
100.0	100.0		100.0	Total						
				LIABILITIES						
9.3	8.6		9.1	Notes Payable-Short Term						
5.0	5.7		4.8	Cur. Mat.-L/T/D						
15.1	17.3		13.1	Trade Payables						
.3	.4		.3	Income Taxes Payable						
12.2	8.2		9.5	All Other Current						
41.9	40.2		36.9	Total Current						
19.8	16.6		20.5	Long Term Debt						
.5	.7		.4	Deferred Taxes						
2.7	2.7		8.0	All Other Non-Current						
35.0	39.8		34.2	Net Worth						
100.0	100.0		100.0	Total Liabilities & Net Worth						
				INCOME DATA						
100.0	100.0		100.0	Net Sales						
27.4	22.9		26.2	Gross Profit						
20.2	19.2		23.7	Operating Expenses						
7.2	3.7		2.5	Operating Profit						
1.2	1.6		1.8	All Other Expenses (net)						
6.0	2.1		.7	Profit Before Taxes						
				RATIOS						
2.3	2.4		2.5							
1.4	1.4		1.7	Current						
1.0	1.0		1.1							
1.4	1.5		1.5							
.9	.9		1.0	Quick						
.6	.4		.6							
32 11.3	35 10.4	28	13.2							
45 8.1	46 7.9	48	7.5	Sales/Receivables						
58 6.3	56 6.6	59	6.2							
11 34.4	18 20.6	20	18.3							
32 11.4	42 8.8	34	10.7	Cost of Sales/Inventory						
46 7.9	59 6.2	61	6.0							
18 20.4	18 20.3	14	26.0							
27 13.6	32 11.5	24	15.4	Cost of Sales/Payables						
44 8.3	47 7.8	41	8.8							
6.7	6.2		7.3							
22.9	11.7		14.1	Sales/Working Capital						
−83.7	70.4		38.1							
11.9	4.6		7.5							
(28) 2.6	(24) 1.1	(30)	1.8	EBIT/Interest						
1.0	.2		.1							
5.3	2.4		3.1							
(11) 3.6	(10) 1.1	(10)	1.3	Net Profit + Depr., Dep., Amort./Cur. Mat. L/T/D						
1.2	−.6		−.6							
.6	.5		.4							
1.2	.9		1.0	Fixed/Worth						
3.3	2.8		6.3							
.7	.6		.5							
2.0	1.7		1.8	Debt/Worth						
6.5	8.7		31.5							
61.4	20.2		25.9							
(27) 22.6	(25) 4.7	(28)	16.7	% Profit Before Taxes/Tangible Net Worth						
1.6	−10.1		5.1							
22.0	10.0		9.3							
6.3	2.6		3.8	% Profit Before Taxes/Total Assets						
.2	−2.1		.0							
10.8	9.7		14.4							
4.8	5.9		7.9	Sales/Net Fixed Assets						
3.1	2.8		3.5							
2.8	2.7		2.7							
1.9	1.9		2.1	Sales/Total Assets						
1.6	1.3		1.4							
1.1	1.5		1.4							
2.5	(26) 3.2	(31)	3.2	% Depr., Dep., Amort./Sales						
3.9	5.1		4.1							
1.4	1.3		1.3							
(11) 6.0	(10) 4.9	(10)	5.2	% Officers', Directors', Owners' Comp/Sales						
6.4	9.1		7.8							
352359M	301617M		647485M	Net Sales ($)	1532M	11995M	15750M	55574M	146051M	416583M
195449M	197525M		453863M	Total Assets ($)	3395M	6407M	8461M	23327M	95586M	316687M

© RMA 2003

M = $ thousand   MM = $ million
See Pages 11 through 18 for Explanation of Ratios and Data

Current Data Sorted By Assets | Comparative Historical Data

0-500M	500M-2MM	2-10MM	10-50MM	50-100MM	100-250MM	Type of Statement	4/1/98-3/31/99 ALL	4/1/99-3/31/00 ALL
		5	11	5	2	Unqualified	20	19
	7	10	3			Reviewed	15	14
2	3	5				Compiled	13	10
2	2	4				Tax Returns		6
	4	11	9	3		Other	30	20
	23 (4/1-9/30/02)		65 (10/1/02-3/31/03)					
4	16	35	23	8	2	**NUMBER OF STATEMENTS**	78	69
%	%	%	%	%	%	**ASSETS**	%	%
	9.2	6.0	3.2			Cash & Equivalents	4.9	6.6
	26.9	24.1	18.8			Trade Receivables (net)	25.8	24.6
	18.6	26.6	22.7			Inventory	26.3	26.3
	2.1	1.7	2.4			All Other Current	.8	1.1
	56.8	58.4	47.1			Total Current	57.8	58.6
	32.5	35.3	40.2			Fixed Assets (net)	32.4	33.2
	2.8	.3	2.7			Intangibles (net)	3.5	1.6
	7.9	5.9	10.0			All Other Non-Current	6.3	6.6
	100.0	100.0	100.0			Total	100.0	100.0
						LIABILITIES		
	22.2	12.6	11.2			Notes Payable-Short Term	10.8	9.5
	9.3	5.7	5.0			Cur. Mat.-L/T/D	5.3	5.1
	12.7	13.9	11.9			Trade Payables	13.2	13.3
	.2	.1	.1			Income Taxes Payable	.2	.2
	9.0	6.2	9.3			All Other Current	7.2	7.3
	53.3	38.4	37.5			Total Current	36.7	35.4
	20.1	22.8	13.8			Long Term Debt	14.1	19.3
	.5	.5	1.7			Deferred Taxes	.7	.6
	10.4	7.3	4.6			All Other Non-Current	5.4	6.5
	15.7	31.0	42.4			Net Worth	43.2	38.2
	100.0	100.0	100.0			Total Liabilities & Net Worth	100.0	100.0
						INCOME DATA		
	100.0	100.0	100.0			Net Sales	100.0	100.0
	28.9	25.8	17.4			Gross Profit	23.6	26.5
	29.6	23.8	16.4			Operating Expenses	16.0	21.9
	-.7	2.0	1.0			Operating Profit	7.5	4.6
	-1.0	1.9	1.7			All Other Expenses (net)	1.3	1.1
	.3	.2	-.7			Profit Before Taxes	6.2	3.5
						RATIOS		
	1.8 1.1 .9	2.5 1.7 1.1	2.0 1.1 .9			Current	2.3 1.9 1.2	2.4 1.7 1.2
	1.0 .7 .4	1.5 .7 .5	1.1 .6 .4			Quick	1.3 .9 .5	1.3 .9 .5
	31 11.9 48 7.6 59 6.1	35 10.3 47 7.7 61 6.0	42 8.8 51 7.2 58 6.3			Sales/Receivables	39 9.4 47 7.8 59 6.2	37 9.9 47 7.8 58 6.3
	15 23.9 41 8.8 82 4.4	36 10.0 70 5.2 112 3.3	36 10.1 68 5.3 83 4.4			Cost of Sales/Inventory	37 9.9 65 5.6 96 3.8	36 10.2 71 5.1 104 3.5
	17 21.6 20 18.3 52 7.1	19 19.3 35 10.6 52 7.1	24 15.0 39 9.4 45 8.0			Cost of Sales/Payables	21 17.8 29 12.4 43 8.6	17 21.1 32 11.6 48 7.7
	6.8 31.6 -26.3	5.1 7.7 95.9	5.7 39.2 -59.7			Sales/Working Capital	4.6 8.3 24.5	4.7 7.2 21.7
	(14) 3.3 1.4 .2	(32) 5.6 2.4 .8	(21) 3.7 1.8 -.3			EBIT/Interest	(72) 12.8 4.0 1.5	(65) 6.1 3.2 1.1
		(12) 3.9 2.9 1.4				Net Profit + Depr., Dep., Amort./Cur. Mat. L /T/D	(30) 7.0 2.5 1.5	(18) 3.4 2.4 .5
	.9 2.5 -3.4	.5 1.1 3.9	.5 1.0 2.0			Fixed/Worth	.4 .8 2.0	.4 1.0 2.2
	1.3 5.8 -12.6	.9 2.3 8.1	1.1 1.8 2.4			Debt/Worth	.7 1.2 4.2	.8 1.5 4.5
	(10) 26.1 7.7 2.4	(28) 29.7 10.4 -11.2	(21) 13.7 8.9 -6.9			% Profit Before Taxes/Tangible Net Worth	(71) 37.2 23.9 9.3	(64) 33.4 15.2 2.2
	6.3 2.1 -3.3	6.7 3.8 -1.2	7.2 3.3 -3.3			% Profit Before Taxes/Total Assets	14.9 8.9 2.4	12.0 5.6 .5
	13.3 5.5 3.8	10.9 4.7 3.2	8.8 3.2 2.1			Sales/Net Fixed Assets	9.8 5.9 3.7	11.9 6.5 3.6
	2.6 2.0 1.6	2.2 1.8 1.4	1.7 1.4 1.2			Sales/Total Assets	2.3 1.8 1.3	2.5 1.9 1.3
	(15) 2.1 4.2 10.1	(34) 1.9 3.3 6.1	(21) 2.4 4.6 5.3			% Depr., Dep., Amort./Sales	(68) 1.6 2.7 4.4	(59) 1.8 2.8 4.8
		(15) 2.0 5.7 8.5				% Officers', Directors', Owners' Comp/Sales	(22) 2.1 4.3 8.2	(24) 1.7 6.1 11.0
3341M	37621M	305499M	694378M	735488M	381400M	Net Sales ($)	2582199M	2247734M
905M	18715M	170644M	469819M	553546M	423817M	Total Assets ($)	1618060M	1495851M

© RMA 2003

M = $ thousand   MM = $ million
See Pages 11 through 18 for Explanation of Ratios and Data

Comparative Historical Data

Current Data Sorted By Sales

Hist 1	Hist 2	Hist 3	Type of Statement	0-1MM	1-3MM	3-5MM	5-10MM	10-25MM	25MM & OVER
23	21	23	Unqualified			1	2	6	14
16	11	20	Reviewed		6	4	3	6	1
12	15	10	Compiled	2	3	2	1	2	
2	4	8	Tax Returns	1	3	2	1	1	
29	33	27	Other		3	1	8	6	9
4/1/00-3/31/01 ALL	4/1/01-3/31/02 ALL	4/1/02-3/31/03 ALL		23 (4/1-9/30/02)		65 (10/1/02-3/31/03)			
82	84	88	NUMBER OF STATEMENTS	3	15	10	15	21	24
%	%	%	**ASSETS**	%	%	%	%	%	%
5.9	4.7	5.9	Cash & Equivalents		8.8	7.9	9.3	3.4	3.1
25.1	22.9	22.6	Trade Receivables (net)		28.2	23.5	22.4	23.6	18.2
24.8	23.9	23.3	Inventory		16.0	28.7	26.5	23.2	23.9
2.1	2.5	2.4	All Other Current		2.3	.9	2.1	1.3	2.5
57.9	53.9	54.3	Total Current		55.3	61.1	60.3	51.4	47.7
34.4	35.6	35.9	Fixed Assets (net)		34.2	30.5	32.3	42.0	37.0
2.0	3.9	2.7	Intangibles (net)		2.9	.1	.6	2.5	5.4
5.7	6.5	7.2	All Other Non-Current		7.7	8.3	6.8	4.1	9.9
100.0	100.0	100.0	Total		100.0	100.0	100.0	100.0	100.0
			LIABILITIES						
10.7	14.6	13.6	Notes Payable-Short Term		22.9	9.0	13.7	11.4	10.4
4.6	4.8	6.1	Cur. Mat.-L/T/D		6.5	8.3	4.5	7.1	4.8
15.0	14.6	12.5	Trade Payables		13.3	9.7	13.3	14.9	11.1
.4	.2	.1	Income Taxes Payable		.2	.1	.0	.1	.2
7.3	8.0	7.5	All Other Current		11.6	5.4	6.6	7.2	7.4
37.9	42.3	39.9	Total Current		54.6	32.4	38.1	40.8	33.8
16.4	21.0	20.7	Long Term Debt		19.7	24.7	20.7	19.2	14.8
.7	.7	.8	Deferred Taxes		.6	.2	.1	.9	1.7
7.7	4.3	8.6	All Other Non-Current		11.1	8.2	4.2	5.4	9.9
37.3	31.8	30.0	Net Worth		14.1	34.4	36.9	33.7	39.7
100.0	100.0	100.0	Total Liabilities & Net Worth		100.0	100.0	100.0	100.0	100.0
			INCOME DATA						
100.0	100.0	100.0	Net Sales		100.0	100.0	100.0	100.0	100.0
23.1	24.7	23.8	Gross Profit		30.2	22.9	30.7	21.9	15.5
18.3	21.3	22.4	Operating Expenses		33.1	22.9	27.3	20.5	12.0
4.9	3.4	1.4	Operating Profit		-2.9	-.1	3.4	1.4	3.5
.8	1.8	1.2	All Other Expenses (net)		-1.2	.8	1.8	2.4	1.5
4.1	1.6	.2	Profit Before Taxes		-1.7	-.9	1.6	-1.0	2.0
			RATIOS						
2.4	2.2	2.1	Current		1.8	2.5	2.9	2.1	2.0
1.5	1.3	1.4			1.1	1.7	1.8	1.4	1.3
1.1	1.0	1.0			.9	1.6	1.1	.9	1.0
1.3	1.1	1.2	Quick		1.0	1.5	1.8	1.1	.9
.7	.6	.7			.7	.9	.6	.7	.6
.5	.4	.5			.4	.6	.5	.4	.5
40 9.1	38 9.7	36 10.0	Sales/Receivables	32 11.6	37 10.0	35 10.3	36 10.2	43 8.5	
47 7.8	48 7.6	48 7.6		50 7.3	48 7.6	47 7.7	46 8.0	52 7.0	
58 6.3	58 6.3	60 6.1		67 5.4	102 3.6	49 7.4	57 6.4	62 5.9	
28 13.3	32 11.5	34 10.8	Cost of Sales/Inventory	14 25.4	10 36.1	45 8.0	34 10.7	38 9.6	
58 6.3	61 5.9	62 5.9		37 10.0	81 4.5	76 4.8	57 6.4	69 5.3	
102 3.6	89 4.1	105 3.5		89 4.1	130 2.8	116 3.1	103 3.5	92 4.0	
21 17.4	25 14.7	19 19.6	Cost of Sales/Payables	15 24.5	15 25.0	19 19.3	29 12.7	25 14.9	
33 11.2	35 10.3	32 11.3		20 17.9	19 19.5	33 10.9	39 9.3	37 10.0	
52 7.1	51 7.2	47 7.7		59 6.2	62 5.9	46 7.9	55 6.7	45 8.1	
4.6	5.6	5.7	Sales/Working Capital		8.6	3.5	4.0	6.1	4.7
9.7	13.6	11.9			60.1	7.2	7.7	13.0	15.4
39.9	NM	786.4			-20.8	8.5	30.9	-28.2	71.7
	6.4		5.1		4.5	EBIT/Interest		2.4			4.9		4.9		6.5

Hist 1	Hist 2	Hist 3		0-1MM	1-3MM	3-5MM	5-10MM	10-25MM	25MM & OVER
(72) 6.4	(79) 5.1	(80) 4.5	EBIT/Interest		(12) 2.4		(14) 4.9	(20) 4.9	(23) 6.5
2.3	1.8	1.9			.8		2.3	2.3	1.9
.8	.1	.3			-1.4		.7	.3	.4
(21) 3.1	(28) 3.2	(26) 3.3	Net Profit + Depr., Dep., Amort./Cur. Mat. L/T/D						
1.4	1.3	2.0							
.6	.7	.6							
.4	.5	.6	Fixed/Worth		.9	.2	.3	.7	.5
.9	1.2	1.2			3.3	.9	.8	1.2	.9
2.0	3.6	3.6			-2.3	NM	6.2	2.1	2.0
.9	1.1	1.1	Debt/Worth		1.3	.9	.6	1.3	.9
1.5	1.9	2.2			5.5	1.7	1.4	2.1	1.7
3.6	6.6	8.6			-11.4	NM	9.3	4.5	2.6
(73) 28.8	(69) 29.0	(69) 24.3	% Profit Before Taxes/Tangible Net Worth				(12) 33.5	(18) 25.6	(20) 24.0
15.4	15.4	10.0					9.6	9.4	11.8
1.8	-2.9	-5.0					-2.9	-5.7	2.0
11.3	9.8	7.3	% Profit Before Taxes/Total Assets		3.6	8.5	8.6	6.4	9.2
4.3	3.1	3.3			.3	4.8	3.7	3.9	3.4
-.1	-4.5	-3.2			-10.1	-7.3	-.4	-1.6	-3.2
11.8	10.6	9.5	Sales/Net Fixed Assets		8.4	20.5	14.9	7.4	8.4
5.2	5.1	4.3			4.6	5.1	4.5	4.2	4.0
3.5	3.1	2.9			3.0	3.0	3.7	2.4	2.7
2.4	2.2	2.1	Sales/Total Assets		2.5	1.9	2.3	2.2	1.8
1.6	1.6	1.7			1.9	1.6	1.8	1.7	1.5
1.3	1.3	1.3			1.5	1.2	1.4	1.3	1.1
(73) 1.3	(80) 1.5	(82) 2.0	% Depr., Dep., Amort./Sales		(14) 2.1		2.0	2.5	(20) 2.2
3.0	3.2	3.9			4.4		3.8	3.5	4.1
4.5	4.7	6.0			10.4		7.6	5.6	5.1
(20) 2.0	(19) 1.9	(28) 2.5	% Officers', Directors', Owners' Comp/Sales						
5.4	3.5	6.2							
9.9	8.4	12.0							
2589364M	2453606M	2157727M	Net Sales ($)	1816M	27577M	40221M	106274M	311716M	1670123M
1793783M	1706065M	1637446M	Total Assets ($)	619M	15549M	31091M	62969M	201026M	1326192M

M = $ thousand   MM = $ million
See Pages 11 through 18 for Explanation of Ratios and Data

Current Data Sorted By Assets　　　　　　　　　　　　　Comparative Historical Data

0-500M	500M-2MM	2-10MM	10-50MM	50-100MM	100-250MM	Type of Statement	4/1/98-3/31/99 ALL	4/1/99-3/31/00 ALL
		17	29	6	1	Unqualified	46	51
3	18	61	14			Reviewed	48	61
6	26	29	3			Compiled	58	48
3	5	1	1			Tax Returns	7	6
3	19	39	19	3	1	Other	83	75
61 (4/1-9/30/02)		246 (10/1/02-3/31/03)						
15	68	147	66	9	2	NUMBER OF STATEMENTS	242	241
%	%	%	%	%	%	ASSETS	%	%
9.7	7.8	7.1	7.2			Cash & Equivalents	7.2	6.5
24.9	27.4	26.9	21.7			Trade Receivables (net)	24.9	27.0
19.8	20.8	21.4	19.4			Inventory	20.7	19.5
.3	1.8	1.2	2.6			All Other Current	1.2	1.3
54.7	57.8	56.6	50.9			Total Current	54.0	54.3
38.6	34.6	35.4	39.9			Fixed Assets (net)	36.7	35.7
1.5	1.4	2.9	3.7			Intangibles (net)	3.7	4.1
5.2	6.2	5.1	5.4			All Other Non-Current	5.6	5.9
100.0	100.0	100.0	100.0			Total	100.0	100.0
						LIABILITIES		
20.3	9.7	9.4	11.0			Notes Payable-Short Term	7.6	7.7
13.4	6.5	5.4	5.8			Cur. Mat.-L/T/D	5.0	5.2
12.6	13.6	14.1	12.0			Trade Payables	14.5	14.2
.0	.1	.1	.2			Income Taxes Payable	.2	.3
14.2	8.5	9.1	7.9			All Other Current	8.1	17.7
60.5	38.3	38.1	36.8			Total Current	35.5	45.0
22.2	19.0	17.6	20.0			Long Term Debt	20.4	20.1
.5	.4	.6	.8			Deferred Taxes	.9	.8
8.4	4.9	6.6	3.6			All Other Non-Current	5.2	5.3
8.4	37.3	37.0	38.7			Net Worth	38.0	28.8
100.0	100.0	100.0	100.0			Total Liabilities & Net Worth	100.0	100.0
						INCOME DATA		
100.0	100.0	100.0	100.0			Net Sales	100.0	100.0
33.7	30.0	24.4	19.3			Gross Profit	26.6	27.5
35.5	28.9	22.0	17.1			Operating Expenses	20.6	22.5
−1.8	1.2	2.4	2.2			Operating Profit	5.9	5.0
.8	1.2	1.3	1.6			All Other Expenses (net)	1.0	1.0
−2.6	.0	1.1	.6			Profit Before Taxes	5.0	4.0
						RATIOS		
2.5	2.7	2.5	2.3				2.7	2.5
1.5	1.4	1.5	1.4			Current	1.7	1.6
.4	1.0	1.0	.9				1.1	1.1
1.5	1.9	1.5	1.4				1.6	1.6
1.1	.9	.8	.7			Quick	1.0	.9
.2	.5	.5	.5				.6	.6
25　14.6	32　11.3	37　9.8	38　9.6				34　10.8	37　9.9
33　11.1	44　8.4	49　7.5	50　7.4			Sales/Receivables	42　8.7	46　7.9
47　7.7	54　6.8	60　6.1	59　6.2				52　7.1	56　6.5
6　62.3	21　17.6	33　11.1	33　11.2				29　12.6	27　13.3
29　12.4	42　8.6	48　7.6	48　7.6			Cost of Sales/Inventory	46　7.9	44　8.3
88　4.2	75　4.9	78　4.7	75　4.8				66　5.5	66　5.5
5　66.5	17　22.1	21　17.3	16　22.7				18　20.7	19　19.7
26　14.0	29　12.5	31　11.9	32　11.4			Cost of Sales/Payables	26　13.8	30　12.1
35　10.5	44　8.3	46　8.0	42　8.7				40　9.2	44　8.3
6.3	5.3	6.0	5.6				6.3	5.7
33.9	13.3	11.3	12.6			Sales/Working Capital	11.3	10.6
−12.4	244.6	−998.5	−19.7				32.9	57.2
3.3	9.5	5.3	3.5				9.2	8.5
(11)　−.1	(64)　1.5	(138)　2.1	(63)　1.2			EBIT/Interest	(220)　3.9	(228)　3.5
−4.8	−.9	.4	.2				1.8	1.3
	1.9	2.9	4.7				3.9	3.5
	(16)　1.5	(48)　1.6	(25)　2.0			Net Profit + Depr., Dep., Amort./Cur. Mat. L /T/D	(87)　2.3	(88)　1.8
	−.3	.5	.7				1.2	.8
.6	.4	.5	.6				.5	.5
1.8	1.0	1.0	1.4			Fixed/Worth	1.0	1.0
−1.5	3.6	2.2	3.3				2.3	3.1
1.1	.6	.8	.6				.7	.7
3.7	1.5	2.2	2.5			Debt/Worth	1.7	2.0
−5.3	6.2	4.1	7.4				4.8	5.6
35.8	35.7	26.5	17.1				48.6	45.3
(10)　3.1	(57)　7.5	(131)　12.1	(60)　5.4			% Profit Before Taxes/Tangible Net Worth	(221)　25.0	(214)　21.9
−39.5	−12.0	−3.3	−5.7				9.4	6.5
4.8	12.4	10.8	6.8				17.4	16.2
−.9	1.7	3.0	.9			% Profit Before Taxes/Total Assets	8.3	7.2
−18.1	−4.7	−1.7	−2.1				2.8	1.2
16.5	12.5	9.2	6.6				11.1	10.3
12.0	7.2	5.6	4.0			Sales/Net Fixed Assets	5.8	6.1
4.9	4.3	4.0	2.7				3.4	3.7
4.6	3.0	2.4	1.9				2.7	2.7
2.4	2.2	2.0	1.6			Sales/Total Assets	2.0	2.1
1.8	1.6	1.6	1.2				1.6	1.6
1.1	2.0	2.5	2.8				1.9	1.7
(10)　3.3	(62)　3.8	(139)　3.8	(62)　3.7			% Depr., Dep., Amort./Sales	(222)　3.1	(219)　3.1
4.5	6.3	5.3	4.8				4.6	4.7
5.8	3.6	2.0	1.1				1.7	2.0
(10)　8.9	(41)　6.2	(72)　3.6	(14)　1.7			% Officers', Directors', Owners' Comp/Sales	(103)　4.6	(120)　4.6
11.8	9.5	6.2	4.3				7.6	7.8
11978M	190178M	1466082M	2214472M	933963M	536891M	Net Sales ($)	3763069M	3816895M
4126M	83079M	742808M	1384985M	694025M	463457M	Total Assets ($)	2201412M	2322293M

© RMA 2003

M = $ thousand　　MM = $ million
See Pages 11 through 18 for Explanation of Ratios and Data

Comparative Historical Data | | | Current Data Sorted By Sales

			Type of Statement						
36	35	53	Unqualified		1	6	16	30
74	77	96	Reviewed	3	7	19	33	26	8
62	53	64	Compiled	5	21	14	9	14	1
12	13	10	Tax Returns	3	3	2	1	1	
72	63	84	Other	4	17	8	10	33	12
4/1/00-3/31/01	4/1/01-3/31/02	4/1/02-3/31/03			61 (4/1-9/30/02)		246 (10/1/02-3/31/03)		
ALL	ALL	ALL		0-1MM	1-3MM	3-5MM	5-10MM	10-25MM	25MM & OVER
256	241	307	**NUMBER OF STATEMENTS**	15	48	44	59	90	51
%	%	%	**ASSETS**	%	%	%	%	%	%
6.2	6.8	7.7	Cash & Equivalents	7.4	8.9	7.9	7.0	7.0	8.2
26.1	24.5	25.4	Trade Receivables (net)	19.3	24.7	28.8	27.2	25.3	22.9
20.7	21.0	20.5	Inventory	24.2	17.9	21.0	20.8	21.7	19.2
1.9	1.6	1.6	All Other Current	.8	2.1	.6	1.6	2.0	1.8
55.0	53.8	55.2	Total Current	51.8	53.5	58.2	56.7	56.0	52.0
36.6	37.3	36.4	Fixed Assets (net)	39.3	37.5	35.8	35.0	35.6	38.2
3.2	3.7	2.9	Intangibles (net)	1.3	1.6	2.2	3.9	2.9	3.8
5.2	5.2	5.5	All Other Non-Current	7.6	7.4	3.8	4.5	5.4	6.0
100.0	100.0	100.0	Total	100.0	100.0	100.0	100.0	100.0	100.0
			LIABILITIES						
8.3	8.8	10.2	Notes Payable-Short Term	25.0	9.3	6.8	9.1	11.3	9.1
5.9	5.5	6.0	Cur. Mat.-L/T/D	8.6	7.0	6.3	5.6	5.7	4.8
14.1	13.1	13.3	Trade Payables	9.9	10.8	13.6	15.6	13.4	13.6
.3	.1	.1	Income Taxes Payable	.0	.1	.1	.1	.1	.3
8.7	6.7	8.9	All Other Current	14.1	8.9	9.9	8.2	8.4	8.1
37.2	34.3	38.6	Total Current	57.6	36.1	36.8	38.7	39.0	35.9
18.5	19.3	18.8	Long Term Debt	11.8	26.4	18.1	16.9	18.5	17.1
.9	.8	.6	Deferred Taxes	.7	.6	.3	.6	.7	.8
4.6	4.5	5.7	All Other Non-Current	9.0	1.8	8.6	4.1	7.0	5.3
38.7	41.2	36.3	Net Worth	21.0	34.9	36.3	39.6	34.8	40.9
100.0	100.0	100.0	Total Liabilities & Net Worth	100.0	100.0	100.0	100.0	100.0	100.0
			INCOME DATA						
100.0	100.0	100.0	Net Sales	100.0	100.0	100.0	100.0	100.0	100.0
25.6	24.4	25.0	Gross Profit	30.2	32.6	30.4	23.4	21.6	19.4
20.7	21.7	23.0	Operating Expenses	31.8	32.6	28.3	21.4	18.8	15.9
4.9	2.7	2.0	Operating Profit	-1.6	.0	2.1	1.9	2.7	3.5
1.3	1.5	1.4	All Other Expenses (net)	1.3	1.3	1.3	1.1	1.7	1.2
3.6	1.1	.6	Profit Before Taxes	-2.9	-1.4	.8	.8	1.1	2.3
			RATIOS						
2.3	2.9	2.5		2.2	2.7	3.1	2.5	2.3	2.4
1.6	1.6	1.4	Current	1.4	1.4	1.8	1.5	1.4	1.4
1.1	1.1	1.0		.8	1.0	1.0	1.0	1.0	1.1
1.4	1.7	1.5		1.4	1.9	2.1	1.5	1.5	1.5
.9	.9	.8	Quick	.7	1.0	1.0	.9	.8	.8
.6	.6	.5		.3	.4	.5	.6	.5	.6
35 10.3	34 10.9	36 10.0		33 11.1	29 12.7	38 9.6	37 9.8	37 9.9	36 10.0
46 7.9	44 8.2	47 7.7	Sales/Receivables	45 8.1	45 8.1	47 7.8	50 7.3	49 7.5	46 7.9
56 6.5	56 6.5	57 6.4		52 7.0	64 5.7	56 6.6	60 6.1	59 6.2	56 6.5
28 13.0	30 12.2	31 11.8		29 12.4	20 18.3	32 11.3	31 11.6	33 11.0	32 11.5
45 8.1	45 8.0	46 7.9	Cost of Sales/Inventory	61 5.9	42 8.7	45 8.1	49 7.4	49 7.4	45 8.2
67 5.4	73 5.0	76 4.8		111 3.3	79 4.6	81 4.5	71 5.1	78 4.7	66 5.6
19 18.8	16 22.4	19 19.7		5 66.5	15 23.8	22 16.5	23 15.9	19 19.7	16 22.6
29 12.8	26 14.1	30 12.1	Cost of Sales/Payables	31 11.6	28 12.9	29 12.7	31 11.8	32 11.4	31 11.6
41 8.9	40 9.1	43 8.5		43 8.5	38 9.5	44 8.2	48 7.7	43 8.5	41 8.9
6.2	5.6	5.8		4.8	4.8	4.9	6.1	5.7	5.9
11.1	10.0	11.6	Sales/Working Capital	15.2	16.6	9.5	11.3	11.4	11.2
62.1	46.0	-443.5		-12.2	821.1	-72.7	-443.5	-118.4	53.7
	7.4	4.5	5.3		1.9	4.3	10.4	4.6	6.0	6.8
(238) 2.9	(225) 1.8	(287) 1.7	EBIT/Interest	(12) -.2	(42) 1.3	(43) 1.9	(54) 1.6	(87) 2.0	(49) 2.5
1.2	.3	.0		-5.7	-1.8	.4	-1.1	.7	.3
3.9	3.5	3.1			2.9	2.8	2.0	5.1	4.9
(80) 2.0	(72) 1.6	(94) 1.6	Net Profit + Depr., Dep., Amort./Cur. Mat. L/T/D	(13) 1.8	(10) 1.4	(22) 1.2	(26) 2.1	(20) 2.1
1.1	.7	.5			-.6	.6	.3	.6	.9
.5	.5	.5		.4	.5	.4	.6	.6	.6
1.1	1.0	1.0	Fixed/Worth	1.0	1.0	1.4	1.1	1.0	1.1
2.1	2.0	2.9		23.9	5.9	2.9	2.3	2.9	2.8
.7	.7	.7		.6	.6	.7	.7	.8	.6
1.7	1.6	2.2	Debt/Worth	1.3	1.7	2.5	2.3	2.3	1.5
4.3	3.9	5.6		23.5	10.9	4.2	4.5	6.9	5.6
40.0	26.3	26.5		27.3	27.7	30.6	30.6	23.9	25.8
(229) 18.8	(222) 9.3	(267) 8.4	% Profit Before Taxes/Tangible Net Worth	(12) .9	(38) 2.8	(39) 7.7	(51) 8.0	(82) 9.2	(45) 10.4
3.6	-4.0	-5.8		-16.9	-13.3	-3.3	-12.0	-3.0	-4.6
14.1	8.4	9.2		3.0	7.2	9.9	9.9	9.3	9.3
6.1	2.9	2.1	% Profit Before Taxes/Total Assets	.0	.5	2.2	2.1	2.4	3.1
.7	-1.9	-2.6		-13.0	-11.5	-1.2	-4.4	-1.1	-1.4
10.0	8.9	9.4		14.4	10.2	11.8	8.8	9.8	7.7
5.6	5.6	5.3	Sales/Net Fixed Assets	4.9	5.3	7.3	5.3	5.3	4.4
3.8	3.4	3.5		2.8	3.5	4.6	3.8	3.3	3.2
2.7	2.5	2.5		2.2	2.5	3.0	2.5	2.3	2.2
2.1	2.0	1.9	Sales/Total Assets	1.8	1.8	2.2	2.0	1.9	1.8
1.5	1.5	1.4		1.0	1.3	1.7	1.5	1.4	1.3
1.9	2.2	2.5		1.1	2.3	2.0	2.6	2.4	2.5
(236) 3.1	(219) 3.5	(283) 3.7	% Depr., Dep., Amort./Sales	(11) 3.6	(42) 4.9	(42) 3.8	(55) 3.9	(85) 3.7	(48) 3.3
4.9	5.6	5.5		7.4	7.4	6.6	5.3	5.2	4.1
2.9	2.1	2.1			3.7	3.4	1.8	1.7	
(112) 5.9	(100) 4.9	(137) 4.5	% Officers', Directors', Owners' Comp/Sales	(33) 7.5	(26) 6.3	(28) 3.2	(34) 3.1	
8.8	8.4	7.8		11.1	10.0	6.0	5.6	
4253687M	4556160M	5353564M	Net Sales ($)	9493M	95433M	177049M	441009M	1390078M	3240502M
2461283M	2861080M	3372480M	Total Assets ($)	6301M	59845M	98461M	236667M	843868M	2127338M

M = $ thousand   MM = $ million
See Pages 11 through 18 for Explanation of Ratios and Data

Current Data Sorted By Assets

Comparative Historical Data

						Type of Statement		
			4		3	Unqualified	13	8
1	4	4 2	4		1	Reviewed	7	11
						Compiled	4	5
1	1	2	2	2	1	Tax Returns	3	
	6 (4/1-9/30/02)		22 (10/1/02-3/31/03)			Other	14	7
0-500M	500M-2MM	2-10MM	10-50MM	50-100MM	100-250MM		4/1/98-3/31/99 ALL	4/1/99-3/31/00 ALL
2	5	8	6	2	5	NUMBER OF STATEMENTS	41	31
%	%	%	%	%	%	ASSETS	%	%
						Cash & Equivalents	7.7	10.8
						Trade Receivables (net)	23.0	22.2
						Inventory	31.6	28.8
						All Other Current	3.2	2.3
						Total Current	65.4	64.2
						Fixed Assets (net)	27.5	26.2
						Intangibles (net)	2.2	1.1
						All Other Non-Current	4.9	8.5
						Total	100.0	100.0
						LIABILITIES		
						Notes Payable-Short Term	9.1	8.7
						Cur. Mat.-L/T/D	4.0	4.1
						Trade Payables	12.1	10.2
						Income Taxes Payable	.2	.1
						All Other Current	8.8	7.4
						Total Current	34.2	30.4
						Long Term Debt	21.5	14.8
						Deferred Taxes	.6	1.2
						All Other Non-Current	4.6	4.4
						Net Worth	39.1	49.2
						Total Liabilities & Net Worth	100.0	100.0
						INCOME DATA		
						Net Sales	100.0	100.0
						Gross Profit	37.0	32.6
						Operating Expenses	31.1	24.9
						Operating Profit	6.0	7.7
						All Other Expenses (net)	1.2	2.5
						Profit Before Taxes	4.7	5.2
						RATIOS		
						Current	3.2	3.1
							2.2	2.1
							1.2	1.4
						Quick	1.5	2.2
							.9	.8
							.6	.6
						Sales/Receivables	32 11.3	37 10.0
							47 7.8	44 8.2
							59 6.2	59 6.2
						Cost of Sales/Inventory	54 6.8	47 7.7
							100 3.7	97 3.8
							157 2.3	163 2.2
						Cost of Sales/Payables	18 20.2	11 33.9
							31 12.0	26 14.0
							46 8.0	43 8.5
						Sales/Working Capital	3.7	3.4
							5.1	5.1
							17.7	11.8
						EBIT/Interest	(38) 8.5	(29) 12.4
							2.8	3.3
							1.3	.9
						Net Profit + Depr., Dep., Amort./Cur. Mat. L /T/D	(17) 3.6	(12) 8.5
							2.6	2.3
							1.2	1.2
						Fixed/Worth	.3	.2
							.8	.4
							1.6	1.2
						Debt/Worth	.8	.5
							1.5	.9
							4.7	2.7
						% Profit Before Taxes/Tangible Net Worth	(38) 37.6	(30) 45.3
							24.4	14.3
							6.4	-1.1
						% Profit Before Taxes/Total Assets	16.2	19.3
							7.8	5.7
							.4	-.6
						Sales/Net Fixed Assets	14.2	12.1
							6.8	6.5
							3.7	4.1
						Sales/Total Assets	2.2	2.4
							1.8	1.7
							1.3	1.4
						% Depr., Dep., Amort./Sales	(35) 1.4	(29) 2.1
							2.3	3.0
							4.5	4.1
						% Officers', Directors', Owners' Comp/Sales	(14) 2.3	(15) 2.4
							5.5	3.5
							8.6	5.4
1298M	11685M	84081M	199346M	129565M	1617467M	Net Sales ($)	876603M	698273M
386M	7030M	45780M	111723M	122753M	854011M	Total Assets ($)	531694M	481420M

© RMA 2003

M = $ thousand   MM = $ million
See Pages 11 through 18 for Explanation of Ratios and Data

Comparative Historical Data				Current Data Sorted By Sales					

			Type of Statement						
5	5	7	Unqualified					2	5
9	4	4	Reviewed			1	1	2	
4	5	8	Compiled	2	2	1		2	1
1	1		Tax Returns			1			
7	14	9	Other	1	1	1		2	4
4/1/00-3/31/01	4/1/01-3/31/02	4/1/02-3/31/03			6 (4/1-9/30/02)		22 (10/1/02-3/31/03)		
ALL	ALL	ALL		0-1MM	1-3MM	3-5MM	5-10MM	10-25MM	25MM & OVER
26	29	28	**NUMBER OF STATEMENTS**	3	3	3	1	8	10
%	%	%	**ASSETS**	%	%	%	%	%	%
9.3	4.8	10.9	Cash & Equivalents						9.8
20.8	21.9	22.1	Trade Receivables (net)						26.0
30.1	40.3	27.2	Inventory						31.8
2.0	.8	1.4	All Other Current						1.9
62.3	67.8	61.6	Total Current						69.5
28.1	24.7	27.4	Fixed Assets (net)						20.8
5.3	1.3	1.5	Intangibles (net)						1.5
4.4	6.2	9.8	All Other Non-Current						8.3
100.0	100.0	100.0	Total						100.0
			LIABILITIES						
6.8	12.5	7.8	Notes Payable-Short Term						7.8
7.0	3.6	4.1	Cur. Mat.-L/T/D						2.5
8.6	11.3	7.7	Trade Payables						6.5
.3	.1	.3	Income Taxes Payable						.8
9.1	6.2	9.0	All Other Current						8.4
31.7	33.6	28.9	Total Current						26.0
18.0	14.7	14.6	Long Term Debt						14.8
.2	.5	1.2	Deferred Taxes						1.3
7.0	3.9	10.1	All Other Non-Current						7.2
43.0	47.3	45.1	Net Worth						50.7
100.0	100.0	100.0	Total Liabilities & Net Worth						100.0
			INCOME DATA						
100.0	100.0	100.0	Net Sales						100.0
32.2	35.2	35.9	Gross Profit						41.3
24.6	30.7	31.4	Operating Expenses						36.5
7.6	4.4	4.5	Operating Profit						4.8
1.8	1.9	1.7	All Other Expenses (net)						2.7
5.7	2.6	2.8	Profit Before Taxes						2.1
			RATIOS						
3.8	3.6	3.4							4.8
2.3	2.1	2.2	Current						2.3
1.6	1.4	1.5							2.1
2.4	1.6	2.1							2.7
1.1	.6	1.1	Quick						1.1
.4	.3	.6							.9
26 14.3	35 10.5	30 12.0						45	8.1
41 8.9	45 8.0	46 7.9	Sales/Receivables					58	6.3
55 6.6	59 6.2	60 6.1						76	4.8
45 8.1	75 4.9	50 7.3						93	3.9
81 4.5	135 2.7	94 3.9	Cost of Sales/Inventory					134	2.7
134 2.7	259 1.4	162 2.3						206	1.8
17 22.0	17 21.9	5 76.4						7	48.8
23 15.7	36 10.2	19 18.8	Cost of Sales/Payables					17	21.6
35 10.6	55 6.6	44 8.4						28	12.9
3.9	3.1	3.7							2.0
5.4	3.9	4.8	Sales/Working Capital						4.1
7.9	8.1	9.5							5.8
15.6	8.2	6.3							
(25) 3.1	(27) 1.9	(25) 2.9	EBIT/Interest						
1.8	.9	1.5							
6.2			Net Profit + Depr., Dep.,						
(11) 2.4			Amort./Cur. Mat. L/T/D						
1.6									
.2	.3	.2							.2
.6	.4	.6	Fixed/Worth						.4
2.3	.8	1.6							.6
.5	.6	.4							.3
.9	1.0	1.1	Debt/Worth						.9
4.3	2.4	2.3							2.1
57.3	21.5	32.9	% Profit Before Taxes/Tangible						
(23) 14.6	8.1	(26) 12.9	Net Worth						
6.3	-2.9	1.9							
15.8	13.6	12.1	% Profit Before Taxes/Total						14.8
6.5	2.7	5.0	Assets						1.0
2.1	-1.1	.6							-5.2
13.5	14.0	16.7							14.7
6.2	7.3	6.3	Sales/Net Fixed Assets						6.5
3.5	4.0	3.5							3.9
2.2	2.1	2.2							2.1
1.7	1.6	1.4	Sales/Total Assets						1.3
1.3	1.1	1.2							.9
1.4	1.8	1.1							
(25) 3.3	(28) 3.4	(24) 3.7	% Depr., Dep., Amort./Sales						
5.3	4.7	5.0							
	1.9	2.2	% Officers', Directors',						
	(12) 5.3	(11) 7.1	Owners' Comp/Sales						
	8.9	17.2							
1013633M	609065M	2043442M	Net Sales ($)	1741M	4021M	12558M	6065M	126827M	1892230M
640200M	397754M	1141683M	Total Assets ($)	1429M	5151M	6814M	4571M	69396M	1054322M

© RMA 2003

M = $ thousand   MM = $ million
See Pages 11 through 18 for Explanation of Ratios and Data

Current Data Sorted By Assets   **Comparative Historical Data**

0-500M	500M-2MM	2-10MM	10-50MM	50-100MM	100-250MM	Type of Statement	4/1/98-3/31/99 ALL	4/1/99-3/31/00 ALL
1		6	10	1	1	Unqualified	16	11
	5	6	1			Reviewed	11	9
	5	4				Compiled	4	4
3	1					Tax Returns		2
2	3	2		2	3	Other	15	13
	13 (4/1-9/30/02)		43 (10/1/02-3/31/03)					
6	14	18	11	3	4	**NUMBER OF STATEMENTS**	46	39
%	%	%	%	%	%	**ASSETS**	%	%
	8.7	7.6	6.6			Cash & Equivalents	7.2	6.1
	27.8	21.5	26.5			Trade Receivables (net)	27.8	26.8
	34.1	37.0	27.5			Inventory	35.0	33.1
	.7	2.6	2.5			All Other Current	.8	2.1
	71.3	68.7	63.1			Total Current	70.8	68.2
	25.8	18.0	22.1			Fixed Assets (net)	21.4	23.8
	.2	4.7	2.8			Intangibles (net)	2.8	3.8
	2.8	8.6	12.1			All Other Non-Current	4.9	4.2
	100.0	100.0	100.0			Total	100.0	100.0
						LIABILITIES		
	6.3	13.6	9.8			Notes Payable-Short Term	10.2	11.7
	6.6	2.8	1.6			Cur. Mat.-L/T/D	3.3	4.2
	15.9	10.4	7.7			Trade Payables	13.8	11.3
	.2	.1	.1			Income Taxes Payable	.2	.3
	9.1	7.1	8.8			All Other Current	10.4	10.3
	38.0	34.1	28.0			Total Current	38.0	37.8
	22.2	11.4	8.3			Long Term Debt	14.2	13.9
	.3	.2	.2			Deferred Taxes	.8	.3
	3.2	.7	5.3			All Other Non-Current	4.4	4.7
	36.3	53.6	58.1			Net Worth	42.6	43.4
	100.0	100.0	100.0			Total Liabilities & Net Worth	100.0	100.0
						INCOME DATA		
	100.0	100.0	100.0			Net Sales	100.0	100.0
	38.6	36.2	31.1			Gross Profit	33.2	35.1
	36.3	30.6	25.3			Operating Expenses	27.0	28.0
	2.3	5.5	5.8			Operating Profit	6.1	7.0
	1.1	.7	.4			All Other Expenses (net)	1.2	1.3
	1.2	4.8	5.4			Profit Before Taxes	4.9	5.8
						RATIOS		
	3.6	4.8	3.8			Current	3.8	3.4
	1.9	2.8	2.7				2.1	1.6
	1.4	1.5	1.4				1.3	1.2
	1.5	1.9	1.8			Quick	1.8	1.5
	.9	1.0	1.3				.9	.8
	.6	.5	1.0				.6	.6
	30 12.1	34 10.7	49 7.5			Sales/Receivables	43 8.5	36 10.1
	36 10.3	42 8.6	52 7.0				50 7.3	49 7.5
	52 7.0	66 5.5	80 4.6				66 5.5	62 5.9
	40 9.2	84 4.4	91 4.0			Cost of Sales/Inventory	77 4.7	57 6.4
	81 4.5	115 3.2	98 3.7				103 3.6	101 3.6
	148 2.5	155 2.4	105 3.5				164 2.2	137 2.7
	17 21.7	18 20.3	14 25.2			Cost of Sales/Payables	22 16.5	21 17.2
	26 14.0	33 11.1	22 16.8				31 11.9	32 11.6
	58 6.3	47 7.8	29 12.8				45 8.1	43 8.6
	3.8	2.9	3.4			Sales/Working Capital	3.9	3.4
	8.3	3.8	4.1				5.6	8.6
	17.1	11.1	9.8				14.5	15.4
	(12) 5.9	11.6	24.7			EBIT/Interest	(40) 9.9	(34) 9.8
	2.4	6.1	11.4				3.6	4.4
	.0	2.2	3.9				1.8	1.6
						Net Profit + Depr., Dep., Amort./Cur. Mat. L /T/D	(13) 10.1	(14) 3.4
							2.4	1.2
							1.3	.6
	.3	.2	.3			Fixed/Worth	.2	.2
	.8	.3	.4				.5	.6
	2.5	.6	.6				1.1	1.3
	.7	.3	.5			Debt/Worth	.5	.5
	1.8	.9	.6				1.3	1.1
	6.6	4.3	1.3				4.3	5.7
	(13) 39.2	38.1	31.0			% Profit Before Taxes/Tangible Net Worth	(43) 45.5	(36) 44.8
	6.5	13.9	15.5				18.3	20.6
	−26.2	6.3	5.0				8.6	4.3
	11.7	12.8	16.9			% Profit Before Taxes/Total Assets	14.8	22.6
	3.5	7.5	7.0				7.1	7.2
	−1.5	1.7	3.3				2.9	1.7
	25.4	24.6	13.5			Sales/Net Fixed Assets	19.0	20.7
	13.1	6.9	5.7				8.4	8.9
	5.0	5.0	5.2				5.2	5.8
	3.4	2.4	2.0			Sales/Total Assets	2.5	2.7
	2.4	1.6	1.6				1.8	1.8
	1.7	1.2	1.3				1.4	1.3
	(12) 1.6	(15) 1.8	1.9			% Depr., Dep., Amort./Sales	(38) 1.4	(36) 1.1
	3.9	2.6	2.6				2.4	2.1
	5.7	4.2	3.7				3.7	3.9
	(10) 4.4					% Officers', Directors', Owners' Comp/Sales	(13) 5.2	(16) 3.9
	8.2						8.1	7.2
	9.2						12.0	11.5
2874M	39428M	151578M	317792M	368413M	1063924M	Net Sales ($)	922327M	938519M
953M	15275M	87723M	191454M	236395M	704481M	Total Assets ($)	654274M	670315M

M = $ thousand   MM = $ million
See Pages 11 through 18 for Explanation of Ratios and Data

Comparative Historical Data | Current Data Sorted By Sales

				Type of Statement						
10	8		19	Unqualified	1	1	1	2	8	6
11	8		12	Reviewed		2	3	6		1
6	8		9	Compiled		4	2		2	1
2	3		4	Tax Returns	4		1			
6	11		12	Other	2	2	1	2		5
4/1/00-3/31/01	4/1/01-3/31/02		4/1/02-3/31/03			13 (4/1-9/30/02)			43 (10/1/02-3/31/03)	
ALL	ALL		ALL		0-1MM	1-3MM	3-5MM	5-10MM	10-25MM	25MM & OVER
35	38		56	NUMBER OF STATEMENTS	7	9	7	10	10	13
%	%		%	ASSETS	%	%	%	%	%	%
6.4	5.9		7.8	Cash & Equivalents				8.7	2.5	8.0
25.8	24.7		24.9	Trade Receivables (net)				20.7	27.1	23.0
30.7	28.2		31.9	Inventory				36.8	31.6	34.9
1.2	3.5		1.7	All Other Current				2.1	4.0	2.1
64.2	62.3		66.3	Total Current				68.3	65.3	68.0
25.6	27.9		22.4	Fixed Assets (net)				20.2	22.6	13.4
6.1	3.8		4.2	Intangibles (net)				2.3	2.1	10.0
4.2	6.0		7.1	All Other Non-Current				9.2	10.0	8.6
100.0	100.0		100.0	Total				100.0	100.0	100.0
				LIABILITIES						
12.1	15.8		8.7	Notes Payable-Short Term				8.9	14.1	8.2
4.9	4.2		4.0	Cur. Mat.-L/T/D				2.3	2.3	1.8
13.0	10.4		11.5	Trade Payables				11.4	10.8	8.9
.2	.3		.1	Income Taxes Payable				.1	.3	.1
8.2	8.1		10.4	All Other Current				5.3	11.6	12.0
38.3	38.7		34.7	Total Current				28.0	39.2	31.0
20.2	24.5		17.1	Long Term Debt				10.5	8.9	17.1
.1	.7		.2	Deferred Taxes				.3	.1	.4
5.1	3.6		4.5	All Other Non-Current				2.0	3.1	12.7
36.3	32.4		43.5	Net Worth				59.2	48.7	38.9
100.0	100.0		100.0	Total Liabilities & Net Worth				100.0	100.0	100.0
				INCOME DATA						
100.0	100.0		100.0	Net Sales				100.0	100.0	100.0
35.3	36.2		36.0	Gross Profit				36.3	35.2	30.9
31.8	35.0		31.9	Operating Expenses				31.8	32.2	22.8
3.5	1.1		4.1	Operating Profit				4.5	3.0	8.1
2.1	2.5		1.1	All Other Expenses (net)				.8	.2	1.5
1.4	−1.3		3.0	Profit Before Taxes				3.6	2.8	6.6
				RATIOS						
3.8	3.2		3.7					4.8	3.2	4.0
1.6	1.7		2.3	Current				3.1	2.3	3.0
1.1	1.1		1.4					1.9	1.2	1.4
1.8	1.5		1.6					1.8	1.6	1.7
.9	.8		1.2	Quick				1.5	1.1	1.4
.6	.5		.6					.5	.6	.7

33	11.1	38	9.5	35	10.5	Sales/Receivables				31	11.8	46	7.9	38	9.6
42	8.6	43	8.4	45	8.1					38	9.7	57	6.4	49	7.5
54	6.7	55	6.6	59	6.2					43	8.5	78	4.7	59	6.2
60	6.1	45	8.1	52	7.1	Cost of Sales/Inventory				70	5.2	96	3.8	93	3.9
91	4.0	92	4.0	99	3.7					129	2.8	109	3.4	103	3.6
119	3.1	127	2.9	139	2.6					155	2.4	142	2.6	123	3.0
19	18.9	16	23.4	15	24.4	Cost of Sales/Payables				13	27.8	21	17.3	14	25.5
31	11.9	25	14.6	28	13.2					33	11.1	26	14.3	28	13.0
42	8.6	44	8.3	47	7.8					38	9.5	40	9.0	39	9.4

4.0	4.3		3.4	Sales/Working Capital				2.9	3.5	3.4
6.4	8.5		5.4					3.8	4.6	5.4
62.6	22.7		13.6					8.9	57.1	11.8
	6.4		4.0		8.6	EBIT/Interest			6.7	22.3
(33)	2.4	(36)	1.4	(53)	4.2				4.4	4.3
	.7		−1.8		1.0				2.5	2.9
	2.3		2.4		9.9	Net Profit + Depr., Dep.,				
(10)	1.1	(11)	1.5	(17)	2.4	Amort./Cur. Mat. L/T/D				
	.8		.1		1.0					
.3	.4		.3	Fixed/Worth			.2	.3	.3
.8	.8		.4				.3	.4	.4
1.4	3.5		.9				.5	.9	.8
.8	.9		.5	Debt/Worth			.2	.5	.9
1.6	1.8		1.5				.7	.8	2.1
7.1	11.1		4.6				1.5	4.5	5.1

	35.7		21.3		37.6	% Profit Before Taxes/Tangible		15.5	39.4	44.1
(29)	14.1	(30)	9.5	(52)	12.8	Net Worth		11.1	11.0	(12) 30.8
	2.2		−25.0		1.8			−2.2	4.1	16.0
	14.9		9.6		11.7	% Profit Before Taxes/Total		11.7	6.6	18.0
	3.6		1.6		6.9	Assets		7.5	4.8	9.8
	−.8		−10.0		.6			−1.1	2.8	4.8
	15.8		16.7		21.1	Sales/Net Fixed Assets		25.8	15.5	27.1
	7.8		6.5		9.3			6.9	5.4	12.3
	5.5		3.9		5.1			5.0	4.9	10.0
	2.5		2.5		2.5	Sales/Total Assets		2.7	1.9	2.1
	2.0		1.8		1.7			1.6	1.5	1.8
	1.5		1.3		1.4			1.4	1.3	1.5

	1.2		1.5		1.5	% Depr., Dep., Amort./Sales				.7
(34)	2.3	(35)	2.6	(47)	2.6				(11)	1.4
	4.1		4.4		4.2					2.6
	3.0		4.0		3.4	% Officers', Directors',				
(20)	6.7	(16)	7.6	(19)	7.0	Owners' Comp/Sales				
	8.3		9.5		9.4					

788830M	627143M		1944009M	Net Sales ($)	3848M	18417M	28159M	67332M	166472M	1659781M
523525M	354654M		1236281M	Total Assets ($)	1708M	14826M	14165M	39744M	111031M	1054807M

© RMA 2003

M = $ thousand   MM = $ million
See Pages 11 through 18 for Explanation of Ratios and Data

Current Data Sorted By Assets   **Comparative Historical Data**

Type of Statement

Type of Statement	0-500M	500M-2MM	2-10MM	10-50MM	50-100MM	100-250MM		4/1/98-3/31/99 ALL	4/1/99-3/31/00 ALL
Unqualified			3	6		4		10	14
Reviewed		2	14	2				11	9
Compiled	1	1	2					6	9
Tax Returns	3		1	5	1	1		7	5
Other		3	1			1		11	8
	6 (4/1-9/30/02)			45 (10/1/02-3/31/03)					
NUMBER OF STATEMENTS	4	6	21	13	1	6		45	45

	0-500M %	500M-2MM %	2-10MM %	10-50MM %	50-100MM %	100-250MM %		4/1/98-3/31/99 ALL %	4/1/99-3/31/00 ALL %
ASSETS									
Cash & Equivalents			8.3	8.5				7.7	12.2
Trade Receivables (net)			30.7	28.6				26.2	24.1
Inventory			25.3	25.8				26.5	26.7
All Other Current			4.8	3.7				3.6	4.3
Total Current			69.1	66.6				64.0	67.2
Fixed Assets (net)			25.0	29.1				24.1	23.7
Intangibles (net)			1.1	.6				3.3	3.1
All Other Non-Current			4.8	3.7				8.6	6.0
Total			100.0	100.0				100.0	100.0
LIABILITIES									
Notes Payable-Short Term			9.7	10.0				9.2	8.5
Cur. Mat.-L/T/D			3.6	2.4				3.2	4.8
Trade Payables			17.5	14.6				16.2	16.5
Income Taxes Payable			.7	.0				.6	.3
All Other Current			12.0	12.6				12.4	15.2
Total Current			43.4	39.7				41.7	45.3
Long Term Debt			14.5	12.8				15.7	12.9
Deferred Taxes			.3	.9				.7	.6
All Other Non-Current			7.5	1.0				1.3	3.8
Net Worth			34.2	45.6				40.6	37.3
Total Liabilities & Net Worth			100.0	100.0				100.0	100.0
INCOME DATA									
Net Sales			100.0	100.0				100.0	100.0
Gross Profit			24.5	25.8				29.1	27.8
Operating Expenses			22.6	21.0				24.1	22.0
Operating Profit			1.9	4.8				5.0	5.8
All Other Expenses (net)			.4	.4				.5	.4
Profit Before Taxes			1.5	4.3				4.5	5.4
RATIOS									
Current			3.0	4.1				2.2	2.1
			1.8	1.5				1.5	1.6
			1.2	1.2				1.1	1.2
Quick			1.3	2.2				1.1	1.2
			.9	1.0				.9	.8
			.7	.5				.4	.5
Sales/Receivables			25 14.8	30 12.3				13 27.3	16 22.6
			43 8.5	40 9.1				33 11.1	39 9.4
			65 5.6	67 5.4				56 6.6	58 6.3
Cost of Sales/Inventory			28 12.9	34 10.7				20 18.1	29 12.7
			43 8.5	44 8.2				39 9.3	50 7.3
			68 5.3	71 5.1				69 5.3	83 4.4
Cost of Sales/Payables			18 20.9	13 27.5				15 24.2	14 26.8
			27 13.5	34 10.7				25 14.4	29 12.4
			48 7.7	42 8.7				37 9.8	45 8.0
Sales/Working Capital			4.7	5.7				6.3	6.5
			9.9	8.8				14.4	10.7
			27.8	20.4				54.8	24.3
EBIT/Interest			11.1	18.8				11.0	19.0
			(20) 2.0	6.5				(41) 4.1	(43) 5.8
			1.1	3.4				1.8	1.9
Net Profit + Depr., Dep., Amort./Cur. Mat. L/T/D								3.9	4.3
								(20) 1.5	(17) 2.3
								.9	1.2
Fixed/Worth			.2	.3				.3	.2
			.8	.5				.6	.5
			2.1	1.4				1.3	1.4
Debt/Worth			.7	.4				.9	.7
			1.7	1.8				1.8	1.7
			3.8	2.9				3.3	3.4
% Profit Before Taxes/Tangible Net Worth			44.9	28.1				41.3	58.8
			(18) 10.6	24.4				(43) 21.9	(42) 28.2
			1.3	11.6				9.6	14.2
% Profit Before Taxes/Total Assets			20.1	19.9				19.2	22.8
			2.0	6.2				7.4	11.3
			.2	4.5				3.2	2.9
Sales/Net Fixed Assets			23.6	16.8				35.7	25.9
			10.7	7.7				10.3	10.1
			7.4	5.1				6.7	6.8
Sales/Total Assets			3.3	2.8				3.8	3.5
			2.3	2.3				2.7	2.5
			1.9	1.6				2.0	1.9
% Depr., Dep., Amort./Sales			.8	1.2				.8	.9
			(19) 1.8	1.9				(41) 1.3	(41) 1.7
			3.2	2.5				2.2	2.3
% Officers', Directors', Owners' Comp/Sales			1.2					2.0	2.0
			(12) 4.1					(11) 3.1	(18) 4.2
			6.9					5.7	6.6
Net Sales ($)	5218M	25766M	273281M	559561M	222763M	2123187M		1408647M	1508667M
Total Assets ($)	822M	8379M	106302M	236554M	91111M	990951M		744562M	761510M

M = $ thousand   MM = $ million
See Pages 11 through 18 for Explanation of Ratios and Data

Comparative Historical Data | Current Data Sorted By Sales

Type of Statement	4/1/00-3/31/01	4/1/01-3/31/02	4/1/02-3/31/03	0-1MM	1-3MM	3-5MM	5-10MM	10-25MM	25MM & OVER
Unqualified	12	12	13					2	11
Reviewed	10	13	18			2	8	8	
Compiled	6	12	4		1		1	1	
Tax Returns	7	4	5	1	2			1	1
Other	11	15	11	1		3		1	7
	ALL	ALL	ALL	6 (4/1-9/30/02)			45 (10/1/02-3/31/03)		
NUMBER OF STATEMENTS	46	56	51	2	3	5	9	13	19

ASSETS	%	%	%	%	%	%	%	%	%
Cash & Equivalents	8.7	11.7	10.5					9.5	10.7
Trade Receivables (net)	26.2	26.9	29.0					24.0	24.3
Inventory	26.8	21.4	24.4					23.0	26.5
All Other Current	2.7	2.5	3.9					4.4	4.1
Total Current	64.3	62.5	67.8					61.0	65.6
Fixed Assets (net)	28.5	27.4	26.6					31.8	27.2
Intangibles (net)	3.2	3.1	1.0					1.3	1.2
All Other Non-Current	3.9	7.0	4.7					5.9	5.9
Total	100.0	100.0	100.0					100.0	100.0

LIABILITIES									
Notes Payable-Short Term	7.9	8.7	10.6					9.6	7.9
Cur. Mat.-L/T/D	4.1	5.5	2.9					5.0	1.7
Trade Payables	15.1	13.6	16.3					16.4	14.1
Income Taxes Payable	.2	.6	.4					.1	.1
All Other Current	12.6	11.3	11.1					12.6	12.6
Total Current	40.0	39.7	41.2					43.7	36.4
Long Term Debt	16.7	14.5	19.9					19.4	10.3
Deferred Taxes	.7	.4	.6					.2	1.2
All Other Non-Current	2.5	4.1	4.7					9.8	3.4
Net Worth	40.0	41.4	33.6					27.0	48.7
Total Liabilities & Net Worth	100.0	100.0	100.0					100.0	100.0

INCOME DATA									
Net Sales	100.0	100.0	100.0					100.0	100.0
Gross Profit	27.8	28.7	25.3					21.9	23.2
Operating Expenses	21.8	24.3	22.9					18.5	19.6
Operating Profit	6.0	4.4	2.3					3.4	3.7
All Other Expenses (net)	.8	.6	.4					.6	.3
Profit Before Taxes	5.2	3.8	1.9					2.8	3.4

RATIOS									
Current	2.1 1.5 1.3	2.3 1.6 1.2	3.3 1.7 1.3					2.6 1.5 1.1	3.7 1.7 1.3
Quick	1.3 .9 .6	1.4 1.0 .7	1.4 1.0 .6					1.2 .7 .7	1.3 1.0 .6
Sales/Receivables	21 17.4 44 8.4 60 6.1	28 13.0 40 9.1 50 7.3	27 13.5 38 9.6 60 6.0					25 14.7 38 9.6 61 5.9	27 13.6 31 11.9 43 8.5
Cost of Sales/Inventory	27 13.7 44 8.4 78 4.7	22 16.5 37 9.8 65 5.6	29 12.4 43 8.5 70 5.2					24 15.2 42 8.7 72 5.1	33 11.2 41 8.9 64 5.7
Cost of Sales/Payables	17 22.1 29 12.5 46 8.0	13 28.6 26 14.0 40 9.1	13 27.7 25 14.5 42 8.8					13 28.3 35 10.4 48 7.7	14 26.4 25 14.5 34 10.7
Sales/Working Capital	7.2 10.5 21.9	6.0 11.0 28.9	5.2 10.0 20.1					8.4 11.3 87.5	5.2 9.9 14.4
EBIT/Interest	(44) 13.9 5.2 2.0	(54) 15.0 4.3 .9	(48) 12.2 4.2 1.2					(12) 7.7 2.7 -.6	(18) 29.9 6.2 3.6
Net Profit + Depr., Dep., Amort./Cur. Mat. L/T/D	(20) 13.0 3.3 1.5	(20) 3.6 1.8 .7	(12) 5.7 2.0 1.0						
Fixed/Worth	.3 .8 1.4	.3 .7 1.6	.3 .6 1.5					.5 1.4 3.3	.3 .5 1.0
Debt/Worth	1.1 1.8 3.5	.8 1.7 2.9	.6 1.4 3.0					1.4 2.4 13.6	.5 1.3 2.5
% Profit Before Taxes/Tangible Net Worth	(44) 71.2 31.0 13.4	(54) 48.6 29.3 1.6	(47) 38.2 20.5 2.3					(11) 84.6 27.5 -13.9	27.5 20.5 3.5
% Profit Before Taxes/Total Assets	18.4 9.6 2.4	20.4 9.7 -.2	19.4 5.2 .5					18.9 5.2 -5.1	12.1 5.7 1.7
Sales/Net Fixed Assets	19.0 9.1 6.0	18.2 9.6 6.1	21.3 10.0 5.9					16.6 9.1 4.6	14.4 9.9 5.4
Sales/Total Assets	3.0 2.6 1.9	3.7 2.6 2.0	3.3 2.4 1.9					3.6 2.3 1.6	3.1 2.7 2.2
% Depr., Dep., Amort./Sales	(43) 1.2 1.8 2.5	(52) 1.0 1.8 3.0	(43) .9 1.8 2.8					(11) 1.2 2.1 3.6	(15) .9 1.9 2.2
% Officers', Directors', Owners' Comp/Sales	(13) 3.2 4.5 6.3	(21) 2.6 4.0 6.4	(17) 2.5 4.7 8.5						
Net Sales ($)	1596958M	1773843M	3209776M	1549M	6259M	18835M	67834M	209086M	2906213M
Total Assets ($)	756330M	1015313M	1434119M	495M	1952M	8136M	29702M	96232M	1297602M

© RMA 2003   M = $ thousand   MM = $ million
See Pages 11 through 18 for Explanation of Ratios and Data

Current Data Sorted By Assets | Comparative Historical Data

						Type of Statement		
	1	29	37	4	7	Unqualified	100	96
2	42	83	13	1		Reviewed	145	139
13	47	31	2			Compiled	107	120
10	14	4				Tax Returns	31	25
6	30	48	34	2	3	Other	111	109
	92 (4/1-9/30/02)		371 (10/1/02-3/31/03)				4/1/98-3/31/99	4/1/99-3/31/00
0-500M	500M-2MM	2-10MM	10-50MM	50-100MM	100-250MM		ALL	ALL
31	134	195	86	7	10	NUMBER OF STATEMENTS	494	489
%	%	%	%	%	%	ASSETS	%	%
11.6	9.5	10.3	8.7		8.2	Cash & Equivalents	8.4	8.3
31.7	36.2	32.9	33.1		27.0	Trade Receivables (net)	37.2	36.8
13.1	16.9	15.8	14.1		15.4	Inventory	15.9	15.3
1.9	2.5	5.6	6.0		5.6	All Other Current	4.9	4.9
58.4	65.1	64.7	61.9		56.1	Total Current	66.3	65.3
33.2	28.4	27.4	28.6		30.0	Fixed Assets (net)	27.1	28.1
1.0	1.8	1.6	3.2		8.2	Intangibles (net)	1.7	1.7
7.4	4.7	6.3	6.3		5.7	All Other Non-Current	4.9	4.8
100.0	100.0	100.0	100.0		100.0	Total	100.0	100.0
						LIABILITIES		
14.8	13.5	9.9	11.1		4.3	Notes Payable-Short Term	11.5	10.7
6.2	4.7	3.7	3.5		2.0	Cur. Mat.-L/T/D	3.7	3.9
14.8	15.5	15.2	15.5		10.9	Trade Payables	17.4	17.9
1.7	.5	.5	.2		.0	Income Taxes Payable	.6	.4
10.4	8.2	9.6	10.0		14.7	All Other Current	11.2	10.8
47.8	42.4	38.9	40.3		31.9	Total Current	44.5	43.7
21.8	15.8	14.9	14.1		13.3	Long Term Debt	15.1	16.2
.1	.5	.4	.9		1.5	Deferred Taxes	.5	.6
3.7	5.1	3.8	2.9		9.0	All Other Non-Current	3.9	3.7
26.6	36.3	42.0	41.8		44.2	Net Worth	36.0	35.8
100.0	100.0	100.0	100.0		100.0	Total Liabilities & Net Worth	100.0	100.0
						INCOME DATA		
100.0	100.0	100.0	100.0		100.0	Net Sales	100.0	100.0
45.3	30.7	26.5	20.1		16.7	Gross Profit	26.5	27.0
44.3	28.8	23.5	15.8		11.1	Operating Expenses	22.8	21.4
1.0	1.8	3.0	4.4		5.6	Operating Profit	3.7	5.5
.7	1.1	.6	1.2		2.0	All Other Expenses (net)	.8	1.1
.3	.7	2.5	3.2		3.6	Profit Before Taxes	2.9	4.5
						RATIOS		
3.4	2.4	2.7	2.3		2.9		2.2	2.5
2.0	1.6	1.6	1.5		1.7	Current	1.6	1.6
.8	1.1	1.2	1.2		1.3		1.2	1.1
2.3	1.8	1.8	1.6		2.1		1.7	1.7
1.1	(133) 1.1	1.1	.9		1.1	Quick	1.1	1.0
.4	.6	.8	.7		.7		.7	.7
12 29.7	34 10.7	38 9.7	45 8.1		45 8.1		39 9.4	38 9.6
33 11.2	49 7.5	52 7.0	61 5.9		62 5.9	Sales/Receivables	53 6.9	53 6.9
48 7.6	69 5.3	68 5.4	82 4.5		82 4.5		69 5.3	70 5.2
1 372.5	9 39.9	11 34.7	9 42.8		14 25.5		7 49.7	8 45.7
15 24.7	31 11.8	32 11.4	24 15.2		38 9.7	Cost of Sales/Inventory	26 14.0	26 14.2
56 6.5	61 6.0	64 5.7	54 6.8		66 5.5		52 7.0	52 7.0
5 68.7	18 20.6	17 21.5	22 16.3		17 21.2		19 19.3	20 18.6
19 18.9	31 11.8	29 12.7	35 10.4		31 11.8	Cost of Sales/Payables	31 11.8	32 11.3
48 7.7	48 7.7	48 7.5	49 7.4		40 9.0		43 8.4	48 7.6
8.8	5.3	5.2	5.4		4.8		6.2	6.0
14.1	10.7	8.3	8.9		6.6	Sales/Working Capital	10.8	11.3
-29.9	47.8	19.1	27.6		16.3		25.8	33.3
18.3	7.5	11.4	8.9		21.6		9.2	10.9
(27) 2.9	(122) 1.6	(187) 2.9	(79) 3.1		3.3	EBIT/Interest	(447) 4.3	(446) 3.8
-2.7	-.9	.8	1.2		1.1		1.9	1.5
	2.8	4.4	3.5			Net Profit + Depr., Dep.,	5.8	5.2
	(32) 1.2	(62) 2.3	(31) 2.0			Amort./Cur. Mat. L /T/D	(189) 3.3	(150) 2.8
	.4	1.0	.6				1.8	1.4
.3	.3	.4	.3		.5		.3	.3
.8	.7	.6	.9		.7	Fixed/Worth	.6	.7
-2.7	2.1	1.4	1.7		2.0		1.5	1.7
.5	.7	.6	.7		.8		.8	.8
1.1	1.7	1.7	1.8		1.8	Debt/Worth	1.7	1.9
-16.8	5.3	3.5	3.5		3.4		3.8	4.2
56.2	28.5	27.8	23.7			% Profit Before Taxes/Tangible	48.0	49.3
(22) 24.9	(119) 8.0	(185) 8.8	(82) 12.4			Net Worth	(464) 25.5	(446) 23.4
4.8	-14.8	.9	2.2				10.6	7.9
22.6	10.1	9.6	10.9		11.5		17.7	17.4
4.5	2.0	3.5	4.0		6.2	% Profit Before Taxes/Total Assets	8.0	7.7
-7.2	-6.7	-.2	.5		.2		3.3	1.8
65.2	23.3	18.0	12.3		10.1		20.9	20.6
13.5	10.3	8.0	7.4		6.1	Sales/Net Fixed Assets	10.6	10.0
4.7	5.2	5.1	3.9		3.7		5.9	5.1
4.7	3.1	2.7	2.4		1.9		3.2	3.1
3.7	2.4	2.0	1.8		1.7	Sales/Total Assets	2.5	2.4
2.5	1.7	1.6	1.4		1.3		1.9	1.8
.8	1.2	1.4	1.3				1.0	1.1
(23) 2.4	(125) 2.1	(187) 2.4	(79) 2.0			% Depr., Dep., Amort./Sales	(465) 1.8	(447) 1.9
4.7	3.9	4.0	3.0				2.9	2.9
5.1	2.9	1.9	.8				2.4	2.4
(21) 9.3	(72) 5.7	(85) 3.7	(16) 1.6			% Officers', Directors', Owners' Comp/Sales	(214) 4.6	(208) 4.3
14.7	8.5	6.7	5.6				7.8	8.1
35743M	388892M	1868947M	3441110M	831215M	2496730M	Net Sales ($)	9128204M	10032748M
9196M	160290M	885028M	1861533M	490332M	1538208M	Total Assets ($)	4263878M	5280342M

© RMA 2003

M = $ thousand   MM = $ million
See Pages 11 through 18 for Explanation of Ratios and Data

Comparative Historical Data | Current Data Sorted By Sales

				Type of Statement	0-1MM	1-3MM	3-5MM	5-10MM	10-25MM	25MM & OVER
	67	67	78	Unqualified		2		14	21	41
	117	108	141	Reviewed	5	20	34	33	37	12
	122	107	93	Compiled	8	37	23	20	5	
	35	24	28	Tax Returns	4	14	7	3		
	106	126	123	Other	5	26	9	26	25	32
	4/1/00-3/31/01	4/1/01-3/31/02	4/1/02-3/31/03		92 (4/1-9/30/02)			371 (10/1/02-3/31/03)		
	ALL	ALL	ALL							
	447	432	463	**NUMBER OF STATEMENTS**	22	99	73	96	88	85
	%	%	%	**ASSETS**	%	%	%	%	%	%
	8.2	8.9	9.7	Cash & Equivalents	9.6	12.1	9.4	8.8	11.7	6.4
	37.1	35.1	33.4	Trade Receivables (net)	25.1	29.9	34.8	35.6	36.3	33.2
	15.6	15.2	15.9	Inventory	17.2	15.0	17.5	15.7	14.2	17.2
	5.1	5.3	4.5	All Other Current	.8	2.8	3.5	4.9	6.4	5.8
	66.0	64.4	63.6	Total Current	52.7	59.7	65.3	65.0	68.7	62.6
	26.4	27.5	28.4	Fixed Assets (net)	38.0	30.6	27.9	28.6	25.0	27.1
	2.1	2.8	2.1	Intangibles (net)	1.2	3.1	1.5	1.1	.8	4.4
	5.6	5.2	5.9	All Other Non-Current	8.2	6.6	5.3	5.3	5.6	6.0
	100.0	100.0	100.0	Total	100.0	100.0	100.0	100.0	100.0	100.0
				LIABILITIES						
	11.1	11.5	11.4	Notes Payable-Short Term	16.4	14.0	9.7	10.0	11.0	10.4
	3.7	3.7	4.1	Cur. Mat.-L/T/D	7.2	4.9	4.4	4.6	2.7	2.9
	16.7	15.6	15.2	Trade Payables	12.3	13.3	14.5	16.9	16.0	15.8
	.3	.3	.5	Income Taxes Payable	2.0	.3	1.0	.2	.6	.2
	11.2	9.9	9.4	All Other Current	13.8	7.4	7.7	8.9	10.5	11.4
	43.0	41.1	40.5	Total Current	51.7	39.9	37.3	40.6	40.8	40.8
	15.0	15.4	15.5	Long Term Debt	32.5	17.8	15.7	13.6	12.5	13.6
	.6	.6	.5	Deferred Taxes	.0	.4	.4	.5	.5	.9
	4.3	4.9	4.2	All Other Non-Current	2.2	5.0	4.9	4.0	2.9	4.7
	37.1	38.0	39.3	Net Worth	13.6	36.9	41.7	41.2	43.3	40.0
	100.0	100.0	100.0	Total Liabilities & Net Worth	100.0	100.0	100.0	100.0	100.0	100.0
				INCOME DATA						
	100.0	100.0	100.0	Net Sales	100.0	100.0	100.0	100.0	100.0	100.0
	28.2	27.4	27.5	Gross Profit	40.3	36.5	29.0	26.5	21.9	19.5
	23.0	23.3	24.7	Operating Expenses	39.8	35.9	25.4	23.0	18.5	15.3
	5.2	4.1	2.9	Operating Profit	.5	.6	3.6	3.5	3.4	4.2
	1.1	1.1	.9	All Other Expenses (net)	2.0	.9	1.0	.4	.7	1.1
	4.1	3.0	2.0	Profit Before Taxes	-1.5	-.3	2.6	3.1	2.7	3.1
				RATIOS						
	2.4	2.6	2.6	Current	3.5	2.7	2.8	2.4	2.8	2.2
	1.5	1.6	1.6		1.2	1.6	1.9	1.6	1.6	1.5
	1.1	1.1	1.2		.7	.9	1.3	1.2	1.2	1.2
	1.6	1.8	1.8	Quick	2.6	2.1	1.8	1.5	1.9	1.3
	1.1	1.0	(462) 1.1		.7	(98) 1.1	1.3	1.1	1.2	.9
	.7	.7	.7		.4	.5	.8	.8	.8	.6
39	9.4	36 10.0	37 10.0	Sales/Receivables	27 13.5	32 11.6	37 9.9	38 9.5	40 9.1	43 8.5
53	6.9	53 6.9	51 7.1		46 7.9	45 8.0	50 7.3	52 7.1	55 6.7	55 6.6
74	4.9	70 5.2	70 5.2		60 6.1	66 5.5	73 5.0	66 5.5	80 4.5	79 4.6
8	46.4	8 46.8	9 39.9	Cost of Sales/Inventory	5 74.9	7 49.9	11 33.6	12 31.4	8 45.8	12 31.2
26	14.0	27 13.6	29 12.4		53 6.9	40 9.0	33 11.0	26 14.0	25 14.5	29 12.4
54	6.8	53 6.9	61 6.0		121 3.0	73 5.0	64 5.7	59 6.2	46 8.0	62 5.9
18	20.5	17 22.0	17 20.9	Cost of Sales/Payables	13 28.7	14 26.4	15 23.9	19 18.8	17 21.2	19 19.3
31	11.8	29 12.6	31 11.9		34 10.6	29 12.4	30 12.2	30 12.1	29 12.7	35 10.5
47	7.8	46 7.9	48 7.7		51 7.2	51 7.2	50 7.3	45 8.1	45 8.2	43 8.4
	5.7	5.2	5.4	Sales/Working Capital	4.6	5.0	4.9	6.6	4.9	5.7
	10.8	10.4	9.9		12.6	10.7	8.2	10.0	8.2	9.6
	35.7	33.0	28.8		-21.2	-48.5	15.1	23.6	17.3	26.0
	9.9	8.5	9.3	EBIT/Interest	5.3	6.9	8.4	12.8	9.6	14.8
(405)	3.8	(394) 2.5	(432) 2.7		1.3	(88) 1.2	(66) 2.9	(92) 2.9	(82) 3.9	(82) 2.7
	1.6	1.0	.5		-3.9	-1.9	1.3	.2	1.3	1.2
	7.5	6.0	3.7	Net Profit + Depr., Dep., Amort./Cur. Mat. L/T/D		4.8	3.6	4.3	3.0	5.7
(122)	3.1	(103) 2.7	(137) 1.8		(21) 1.3	(21) 2.3	(33) 1.8	(27) 1.7	(35) 2.0	
	1.5	1.2	.6		.3	1.0	.5	1.0	.6	
	.3	.3	.3	Fixed/Worth	.4	.3	.3	.4	.3	.3
	.6	.7	.7		2.2	.9	.7	.6	.5	.9
	1.5	1.8	1.6		-2.4	3.2	1.4	1.6	1.1	1.7
	.8	.7	.7	Debt/Worth	.8	.6	.7	.7	.7	1.0
	1.7	1.8	1.7		3.8	1.7	1.4	1.7	1.5	1.9
	4.4	4.5	4.0		-9.9	9.0	3.9	3.5	3.2	3.9
	49.3	37.4	28.3	% Profit Before Taxes/Tangible Net Worth	69.9	26.4	28.8	35.1	20.5	30.6
(411)	25.3	(389) 15.0	(424) 10.1		(15) 4.5	(83) 5.0	(69) 11.4	(91) 10.3	(86) 8.8	(80) 13.8
	7.3	1.7	-.9		-2.1	-15.7	2.9	-1.2	1.8	1.7
	17.6	13.5	10.6	% Profit Before Taxes/Total Assets	11.4	10.1	9.7	12.8	8.8	12.4
	8.2	5.1	3.4		1.0	1.3	4.5	3.5	4.3	4.2
	2.2	.2	-1.1		-24.8	-7.2	.6	-.8	.8	.4
	21.9	19.2	18.6	Sales/Net Fixed Assets	9.5	25.5	19.0	19.4	19.1	12.7
	10.6	9.5	8.5		4.5	9.3	8.3	8.6	9.2	8.0
	5.3	5.5	4.6		2.9	3.4	4.6	5.4	5.9	4.5
	3.2	3.0	2.9	Sales/Total Assets	2.6	3.1	2.9	3.0	2.9	2.5
	2.4	2.2	2.1		1.9	1.9	2.1	2.4	2.1	1.9
	1.8	1.7	1.6		1.0	1.4	1.6	1.7	1.7	1.6
	1.0	1.0	1.3	% Depr., Dep., Amort./Sales	2.1	1.2	1.4	1.3	1.3	1.3
(411)	1.8	(403) 1.8	(428) 2.2		(19) 3.0	(89) 2.4	(68) 2.5	(91) 2.3	(85) 1.8	(76) 2.0
	3.1	3.4	3.7		5.1	5.2	5.1	4.0	2.5	3.1
	2.3	2.0	2.3	% Officers', Directors', Owners' Comp/Sales	5.3	3.7	2.7	2.1	1.3	.6
(201)	4.9	(182) 4.1	(195) 4.7		(13) 7.6	(55) 6.0	(35) 5.1	(42) 4.0	(36) 2.3	(14) 1.6
	8.1	7.7	8.3		16.5	10.0	7.8	6.8	5.6	4.0
	10610294M	9079120M	9062637M	Net Sales ($)	14001M	194696M	281490M	700298M	1398801M	6473351M
	4964310M	5063790M	4944587M	Total Assets ($)	8956M	110786M	144850M	341362M	731259M	3607374M

M = $ thousand   MM = $ million
See Pages 11 through 18 for Explanation of Ratios and Data

Current Data Sorted By Assets　　　　　　Comparative Historical Data

0-500M	500M-2MM	2-10MM	10-50MM	50-100MM	100-250MM		4/1/98-3/31/99 ALL	4/1/99-3/31/00 ALL
						Type of Statement		
1	2	11	8	2	1	Unqualified	43	41
1	17	27	2	1		Reviewed	47	46
3	12	9	1			Compiled	33	37
3	2					Tax Returns	4	5
1	17	18			1	Other	39	34
	44 (4/1-9/30/02)		96 (10/1/02-3/31/03)					
9	50	65	11	3	2	**NUMBER OF STATEMENTS**	166	163
%	%	%	%	%	%	**ASSETS**	%	%
	7.3	10.2	5.0			Cash & Equivalents	8.8	9.5
	29.3	26.0	22.9			Trade Receivables (net)	29.9	29.0
	20.1	19.5	16.6			Inventory	21.0	18.8
	5.0	4.7	2.4			All Other Current	2.9	3.8
	61.7	60.4	47.0			Total Current	62.6	61.1
	30.1	31.7	39.5			Fixed Assets (net)	28.1	29.9
	3.3	.5	1.4			Intangibles (net)	3.2	3.0
	4.9	7.4	12.1			All Other Non-Current	6.1	6.0
	100.0	100.0	100.0			Total	100.0	100.0
						LIABILITIES		
	17.5	8.5	13.1			Notes Payable-Short Term	8.9	7.9
	4.3	4.8	4.7			Cur. Mat.-L/T/D	3.4	3.8
	16.6	12.2	10.5			Trade Payables	13.5	13.4
	.5	.2	.1			Income Taxes Payable	.5	.5
	11.4	9.9	13.4			All Other Current	11.2	11.8
	50.3	35.6	41.7			Total Current	37.4	37.3
	16.3	15.9	17.2			Long Term Debt	16.3	15.9
	.2	.7	.2			Deferred Taxes	.7	.6
	7.4	3.7	1.1			All Other Non-Current	3.6	3.6
	25.8	44.0	39.8			Net Worth	41.8	42.7
	100.0	100.0	100.0			Total Liabilities & Net Worth	100.0	100.0
						INCOME DATA		
	100.0	100.0	100.0			Net Sales	100.0	100.0
	31.4	22.9	21.0			Gross Profit	27.2	27.5
	31.3	20.0	17.8			Operating Expenses	22.1	21.9
	.1	2.9	3.3			Operating Profit	5.1	5.6
	1.6	.7	1.0			All Other Expenses (net)	.8	.9
	-1.4	2.2	2.2			Profit Before Taxes	4.3	4.7
						RATIOS		
	2.4	2.9	1.5				2.7	2.6
	1.3	1.6	1.2			Current	1.8	1.8
	.8	1.1	.9				1.2	1.1
	1.4	2.0	.9				1.8	1.7
	.7	.9	.7			Quick	1.1	1.0
	.4	.6	.4				.7	.7
32	11.4　32	11.4　34	10.6				38　9.6　37	9.9
46	8.0　44	8.4　41	9.0			Sales/Receivables	47　7.8　47	7.7
62	5.9　59	6.2　70	5.2				60　6.1　62	5.9
20	18.1　27	13.6　36	10.2				23　15.7　20	18.0
45	8.1　50	7.3　44	8.3			Cost of Sales/Inventory	46　7.9　40	9.2
74	4.9　74	4.9　63	5.8				71　5.2　76	4.8
21	17.5　14	26.9　17	21.7				16　23.0　15	24.3
31	11.8　27	13.7　26	14.2			Cost of Sales/Payables	28　13.1　28	13.2
55	6.6　44	8.3　50	7.3				44　8.2　45	8.1
	6.0	4.6	9.2				5.0	5.2
	17.6	9.3	44.2			Sales/Working Capital	8.4	9.3
	-17.7	27.9	-38.8				24.1	34.4
	7.0	5.3	6.3				12.3	11.3
	(48) .9	(59) 2.4	2.8			EBIT/Interest	(148) 4.5	(146) 3.6
	-2.8	1.1	1.4				1.4	1.4
		2.5					7.2	5.8
	(23)	1.5				Net Profit + Depr., Dep., Amort./Cur. Mat. L /T/D	(71) 2.4	(70) 2.2
		.7					1.1	1.2
	.5	.4	.9				.4	.4
	2.1	.7	1.1			Fixed/Worth	.8	.8
	-6.6	1.6	1.5				1.5	1.7
	.7	.6	1.0				.6	.6
	2.7	1.6	1.3			Debt/Worth	1.3	1.5
	-29.7	3.6	3.2				4.1	3.7
	60.3	24.8	17.0				43.0	43.1
	(37) 7.7	(64) 9.7	8.1			% Profit Before Taxes/Tangible Net Worth	(150) 21.4	(151) 19.0
	-11.6	.9	1.7				6.9	4.9
	8.6	7.8	8.3				17.4	18.7
	.6	3.6	2.9			% Profit Before Taxes/Total Assets	8.5	7.5
	-14.1	.3	1.0				1.6	1.6
	15.8	14.0	5.8				14.3	16.2
	10.2	6.3	4.1			Sales/Net Fixed Assets	7.8	7.1
	4.8	4.1	2.3				5.2	4.4
	3.1	2.3	2.2				2.8	2.8
	2.3	1.8	1.5			Sales/Total Assets	2.2	2.0
	1.6	1.5	1.1				1.6	1.5
	1.2	1.5	2.6				1.3	1.2
	(48) 2.1	(63) 2.2	3.1			% Depr., Dep., Amort./Sales	(157) 2.1	(147) 2.1
	2.8	3.8	4.7				3.3	3.6
	3.0	2.7					2.2	2.9
	(27) 5.5	(21) 3.2				% Officers', Directors', Owners' Comp/Sales	(54) 4.3	(63) 4.9
	10.1	5.9					8.1	8.0
10127M	149849M	661007M	560188M	434358M	506102M	Net Sales ($)	5114319M	3844362M
2373M	63615M	334749M	282319M	238386M	216223M	Total Assets ($)	2965061M	2292378M

M = $ thousand　　MM = $ million
See Pages 11 through 18 for Explanation of Ratios and Data

Comparative Historical Data				Current Data Sorted By Sales					

Type of Statement

					0-1MM	1-3MM	3-5MM	5-10MM	10-25MM	25MM & OVER
	34	34	25	Unqualified	1	1		6	6	11
	38	34	48	Reviewed	1	7	11	17	8	4
	42	31	25	Compiled	2	12	6	4	1	
	8	6	5	Tax Returns	1	3	1			
	37	43	37	Other	1	11	6	11	7	1
	4/1/00-3/31/01	4/1/01-3/31/02	4/1/02-3/31/03			44 (4/1-9/30/02)		96 (10/1/02-3/31/03)		
	ALL	ALL	ALL							
	159	148	140	**NUMBER OF STATEMENTS**	6	34	24	38	22	16

ASSETS

	%	%	%		%	%	%	%	%	%
	7.7	9.1	8.0	Cash & Equivalents	6.9	8.3	11.1	9.2	3.3	
	29.1	26.3	26.9	Trade Receivables (net)	27.1	28.2	26.2	26.7	30.1	
	19.9	19.6	19.4	Inventory	17.2	19.4	22.6	19.3	16.2	
	4.1	3.5	4.6	All Other Current	4.9	7.4	2.6	4.7	4.6	
	60.7	58.5	58.9	Total Current	56.1	63.3	62.5	59.8	54.3	
	31.4	31.9	32.0	Fixed Assets (net)	36.2	28.9	29.0	31.8	32.8	
	2.0	2.3	2.6	Intangibles (net)	4.2	1.3	.3	.8	4.6	
	5.8	7.3	6.4	All Other Non-Current	3.6	6.4	8.2	7.6	8.3	
	100.0	100.0	100.0	Total	100.0	100.0	100.0	100.0	100.0	

LIABILITIES

					0-1MM	1-3MM	3-5MM	5-10MM	10-25MM	25MM & OVER
	11.4	11.2	13.5	Notes Payable-Short Term	18.1	16.9	11.3	8.7	9.9	
	3.3	3.9	4.4	Cur. Mat.-L/T/D	4.8	4.0	4.2	5.1	3.9	
	13.0	12.7	13.7	Trade Payables	13.6	16.7	15.2	10.4	14.2	
	.3	.2	.3	Income Taxes Payable	.8	.1	.1	.3	.2	
	12.0	9.5	11.4	All Other Current	13.4	10.3	7.9	11.5	15.9	
	40.0	37.5	43.4	Total Current	50.7	47.9	38.7	36.0	44.1	
	17.3	17.7	16.5	Long Term Debt	23.4	13.1	13.1	15.5	14.1	
	.6	.7	.4	Deferred Taxes	.1	.2	.8	.6	.2	
	5.1	5.2	5.6	All Other Non-Current	8.4	5.7	4.9	4.7	4.2	
	37.1	38.9	34.1	Net Worth	17.4	33.0	42.5	43.1	37.4	
	100.0	100.0	100.0	Total Liabilities & Net Worth	100.0	100.0	100.0	100.0	100.0	

INCOME DATA

	100.0	100.0	100.0	Net Sales	100.0	100.0	100.0	100.0	100.0	
	26.5	27.3	26.7	Gross Profit	33.9	28.0	22.6	20.7	20.4	
	21.8	24.6	24.5	Operating Expenses	34.3	26.8	20.3	16.9	15.1	
	4.6	2.7	2.3	Operating Profit	−.4	1.2	2.4	3.7	5.3	
	1.2	1.1	1.2	All Other Expenses (net)	1.2	1.4	.6	1.1	1.3	
	3.4	1.6	1.1	Profit Before Taxes	−1.6	−.2	1.7	2.6	4.0	

RATIOS

					0-1MM	1-3MM	3-5MM	5-10MM	10-25MM	25MM & OVER
	2.4	2.6	2.4		2.4	2.6	3.0	2.6	1.7	
	1.6	1.7	1.4	Current	1.1	1.5	1.5	1.7	1.2	
	1.1	1.1	1.0		.7	1.1	1.1	1.1	1.0	
	1.5	1.8	1.4		1.3	2.1	1.9	1.6	1.0	
	.9	.9	.8	Quick	.6	.8	.8	1.0	.7	
	.6	.6	.5		.4	.6	.6	.6	.4	

36	10.0	34	10.6	31	11.7	Sales/Receivables	33	11.2	26	13.8	30	12.2	32	11.5	32	11.4
49	7.4	47	7.7	43	8.5		51	7.2	39	9.3	40	9.2	43	8.5	53	6.9
64	5.7	59	6.2	61	5.9		64	5.7	56	6.5	56	6.5	58	6.2	66	5.6
23	15.6	26	14.0	24	15.0	Cost of Sales/Inventory	23	16.1	19	19.6	29	12.8	16	22.6	18	20.1
43	8.4	47	7.7	46	7.9		45	8.1	46	8.0	49	7.4	45	8.2	44	8.4
68	5.4	72	5.1	72	5.0		71	5.1	76	4.8	77	4.8	70	5.2	59	6.2
16	23.1	17	21.1	16	23.5	Cost of Sales/Payables	21	17.2	16	23.5	14	25.5	11	32.3	18	20.6
26	14.1	26	14.1	27	13.6		32	11.3	24	15.0	27	13.3	24	15.4	28	13.0
44	8.4	41	8.8	46	8.0		57	6.4	55	6.6	47	7.7	37	10.0	41	8.9

					0-1MM	1-3MM	3-5MM	5-10MM	10-25MM	25MM & OVER
	5.1	5.1	5.6	Sales/Working Capital	5.4	7.1	4.8	5.1	9.0	
	11.2	9.0	11.2		84.1	11.1	10.3	9.6	24.2	
	54.1	37.5	283.1		−14.6	40.8	40.8	30.3	NM	

	11.7		8.1		6.3	EBIT/Interest		4.3		5.0	
(143)	2.8	(139)	2.1	(131)	2.0		(33)	1.1	(23)	1.3	
	1.4		.5		.5			−1.5		−3.7	

(continued EBIT/Interest right columns: 5.1 / 2.0 / .4 (34); 5.9 / 2.5 / 1.1 (20); 11.0 / 5.7 / 2.0)

	5.8		5.0		3.8	Net Profit + Depr., Dep., Amort./Cur. Mat. L/T/D					
(56)	2.1	(51)	2.0	(33)	1.8					
	1.3		.8		.8					

(Net Profit + Depr. right columns: (11) 3.2 / 1.7 / 1.1)

						0-1MM	1-3MM	3-5MM	5-10MM	10-25MM	25MM & OVER
	.4		.4		.5	Fixed/Worth	.6	.5	.4	.5	.8	
	.9		.9		1.1		3.6	.7	.7	.7	1.1	
	2.2		2.2		2.9		−3.0	5.0	1.9	1.2	1.5	
	.6		.6		.8	Debt/Worth	.9	.8	.4	.7	1.2	
	1.8		1.6		1.9		8.9	2.0	1.5	1.2	1.7	
	4.0		4.6		8.1		−11.9	13.8	3.8	3.8	3.8	

	38.7		25.8		28.0	% Profit Before Taxes/Tangible Net Worth		58.0		26.5		27.8
(142)	18.8	(134)	9.0	(121)	10.1		(23)	5.0	(19)	7.7	(37)	11.6
	5.8		−1.2		.3			−21.4		−1.1		−.7

(% Profit Before Taxes/Tangible Net Worth right columns: (21) 22.8 / 7.3 / 1.6; 49.8 / 22.5 / 8.4)

						0-1MM	1-3MM	3-5MM	5-10MM	10-25MM	25MM & OVER
	14.1		9.9		8.3	% Profit Before Taxes/Total Assets	8.6	7.1	8.3	9.0	11.3	
	5.9		3.4		2.9		.6	2.0	3.0	3.9	5.6	
	1.5		−1.1		−1.0		−6.8	−8.2	−.4	.4	1.9	
	15.7		13.4		14.8	Sales/Net Fixed Assets	15.1	15.0	15.0	16.8	16.0	
	7.1		6.5		7.4		7.3	9.9	8.1	7.5	4.8	
	4.1		3.7		4.1		3.5	4.3	5.0	4.1	3.3	
	2.7		2.6		2.6	Sales/Total Assets	2.7	3.0	2.7	2.4	2.9	
	2.1		2.0		2.0		1.8	2.2	2.0	2.0	1.9	
	1.5		1.4		1.5		1.4	1.6	1.6	1.6	1.4	

	1.4		1.3		1.3	% Depr., Dep., Amort./Sales		1.8	1.2	1.5	.9	1.2
(146)	2.2	(139)	2.4	(134)	2.3		(32)	2.3	2.2	2.2	1.9 (20)	2.7
	3.6		3.9		3.8			6.1	2.8	3.5	3.1	4.3

	2.5		3.2		3.0	% Officers', Directors', Owners' Comp/Sales		2.5		3.2
(60)	5.6	(51)	5.0	(55)	5.1		(17)	5.6	(13)	5.9
	8.4		7.2		9.5			9.0		11.0

(% Officers' Comp/Sales right columns: (13) 3.0 / 3.2 / 8.2)

					0-1MM	1-3MM	3-5MM	5-10MM	10-25MM	25MM & OVER
3559730M	3295283M	2321631M	Net Sales ($)	3364M	73701M	90765M	276302M	330279M	1547220M
2003210M	1922502M	1137665M	Total Assets ($)	1901M	41870M	46721M	145203M	167975M	733995M

M = $ thousand   MM = $ million
See Pages 11 through 18 for Explanation of Ratios and Data

Current Data Sorted By Assets   **Comparative Historical Data**

0-500M	500M-2MM	2-10MM	10-50MM	50-100MM	100-250MM	Type of Statement	4/1/98-3/31/99 ALL	4/1/99-3/31/00 ALL
1	9	6	11	5	6	Unqualified	25	31
4	13	25	3	1		Reviewed	42	38
1	1	5	2			Compiled	30	16
1	1	1	1			Tax Returns	8	7
3	12	19	5	4	3	Other	49	43
	28 (4/1-9/30/02)		112 (10/1/02-3/31/03)					
9	35	56	21	10	9	**NUMBER OF STATEMENTS**	154	135
%	%	%	%	%	%	**ASSETS**	%	%
	6.5	6.5	8.4	5.4		Cash & Equivalents	7.1	7.6
	31.6	34.4	21.6	19.7		Trade Receivables (net)	32.3	28.9
	33.3	27.8	26.6	16.4		Inventory	27.8	27.2
	1.8	4.5	4.8	.7		All Other Current	1.5	2.2
	73.2	73.2	61.4	42.1		Total Current	68.6	66.0
	18.1	20.2	31.3	36.2		Fixed Assets (net)	23.7	25.1
	1.3	2.4	2.9	17.3		Intangibles (net)	2.6	4.0
	7.3	4.2	4.4	4.4		All Other Non-Current	5.0	4.9
	100.0	100.0	100.0	100.0		Total	100.0	100.0
						LIABILITIES		
	12.2	13.3	12.1	4.5		Notes Payable-Short Term	9.1	9.7
	4.9	3.1	2.4	2.4		Cur. Mat.-L/T/D	3.0	3.3
	22.1	16.1	9.5	6.4		Trade Payables	13.9	12.7
	.0	.9	.3	.3		Income Taxes Payable	.3	.2
	14.2	9.9	9.1	9.5		All Other Current	13.1	10.2
	53.4	43.2	33.3	23.1		Total Current	39.5	36.2
	16.6	11.0	16.9	27.7		Long Term Debt	17.7	19.2
	.3	.2	.7	1.1		Deferred Taxes	.4	.3
	9.3	5.5	8.3	2.4		All Other Non-Current	4.7	4.7
	20.5	40.0	40.8	45.7		Net Worth	37.8	39.5
	100.0	100.0	100.0	100.0		Total Liabilities & Net Worth	100.0	100.0
						INCOME DATA		
	100.0	100.0	100.0	100.0		Net Sales	100.0	100.0
	33.5	30.6	29.9	29.6		Gross Profit	30.5	31.4
	31.8	26.5	23.2	22.5		Operating Expenses	24.8	24.7
	1.7	4.1	6.7	7.1		Operating Profit	5.7	6.8
	1.0	1.0	1.2	2.1		All Other Expenses (net)	1.2	1.5
	.8	3.1	5.5	5.0		Profit Before Taxes	4.5	5.2
						RATIOS		
	2.4	2.7	3.5	2.8		Current	3.1	2.9
	1.3	1.7	2.1	2.2			2.1	1.9
	1.1	1.3	1.2	1.3			1.3	1.3
	1.1	1.6	1.8	1.7		Quick	2.1	1.6
	.7	.9	1.1	1.2			1.1	1.0
	.5	.6	.6	1.0			.7	.6
	21 17.5	32 11.3	29 12.6	27 13.4		Sales/Receivables	32 11.6	26 13.9
	34 10.7	48 7.6	38 9.7	43 8.4			47 7.8	39 9.2
	54 6.7	65 5.6	51 7.1	59 6.2			61 5.9	61 6.0
	28 13.0	28 13.1	39 9.3	30 12.0		Cost of Sales/Inventory	34 10.7	36 10.2
	53 6.9	53 6.9	60 6.1	39 9.3			57 6.4	59 6.2
	110 3.3	85 4.3	94 3.9	79 4.6			81 4.5	80 4.6
	14 26.6	16 22.5	14 26.3	15 24.4		Cost of Sales/Payables	14 26.2	14 26.8
	37 9.9	30 12.2	21 17.5	17 21.2			28 13.2	22 16.4
	48 7.6	44 8.3	40 9.2	27 13.4			42 8.8	38 9.7
	5.6	5.9	4.3	5.0		Sales/Working Capital	4.9	5.4
	20.0	9.0	7.7	8.1			7.5	9.1
	75.0	17.1	40.3	43.1			14.1	22.4
	4.3	11.2	10.2			EBIT/Interest	11.7	11.1
	(31) 2.1	(51) 3.0	5.1				(138) 3.9	(120) 4.6
	.7	1.3	1.5				1.6	1.9
		2.9	14.1			Net Profit + Depr., Dep., Amort./Cur. Mat. L /T/D	8.6	8.0
	(20) 1.8		(10) 4.6				(39) 2.7	(40) 3.7
	.5		3.2				1.2	1.9
	.4	.3	.4	.8		Fixed/Worth	.3	.3
	.7	.5	.8	1.3			.5	.7
	-2.3	1.0	1.5	NM			1.2	1.4
	.7	.8	.9	1.0		Debt/Worth	.6	.6
	3.5	1.9	1.3	1.7			1.7	1.8
	-15.6	4.3	4.1	NM			3.2	4.8
	33.8	48.9	39.5			% Profit Before Taxes/Tangible Net Worth	43.1	63.3
	(24) 6.9	(55) 17.5	(20) 23.0				(139) 25.1	(121) 30.8
	1.6	4.2	12.1				9.5	13.7
	9.9	17.7	17.8	13.9		% Profit Before Taxes/Total Assets	19.0	22.9
	1.8	6.0	7.8	8.2			8.9	10.3
	-3.8	1.1	1.9	1.5			2.6	3.6
	34.5	32.9	12.3	6.9		Sales/Net Fixed Assets	24.5	23.6
	19.6	14.9	5.1	5.3			11.4	11.3
	13.3	8.9	4.1	3.7			6.5	6.3
	4.1	3.3	2.3	2.3		Sales/Total Assets	3.1	3.0
	3.2	2.6	2.0	1.5			2.5	2.4
	2.4	2.1	1.6	1.2			1.8	1.8
	.9	.8	1.4	1.9		% Depr., Dep., Amort./Sales	.9	1.0
	(32) 1.5	(55) 1.4	(18) 2.3	2.8			(138) 1.7	(123) 1.7
	2.2	2.0	3.0	4.2			2.6	2.6
	2.8	1.6				% Officers', Directors', Owners' Comp/Sales	1.6	1.2
	(18) 5.5	(28) 2.8					(58) 3.0	(46) 3.1
	9.9	4.5					5.4	5.4
12205M	123334M	756644M	752231M	1426434M	2509605M	Net Sales ($)	5049220M	5793065M
3043M	38118M	274391M	378345M	792676M	1436273M	Total Assets ($)	2719074M	2901311M

Comparative Historical Data | | | Current Data Sorted By Sales

			Type of Statement						
28	19	28	Unqualified				2	5	21
29	28	39	Reviewed	1	4	7	9	12	6
23	20	24	Compiled	4	4	8	4	4	
5	3	3	Tax Returns		2		1		
40	40	46	Other	1	6	4	11	11	13
4/1/00-3/31/01 ALL	4/1/01-3/31/02 ALL	4/1/02-3/31/03 ALL		0-1MM	28 (4/1-9/30/02) 1-3MM	3-5MM	112 (10/1/02-3/31/03) 5-10MM	10-25MM	25MM & OVER
125	110	140	NUMBER OF STATEMENTS	6	16	19	27	32	40
%	%	%	ASSETS	%	%	%	%	%	%
5.0	8.1	6.6	Cash & Equivalents		4.7	9.3	6.6	5.4	7.1
28.2	29.0	30.3	Trade Receivables (net)		34.7	31.6	36.8	29.8	22.9
30.1	26.5	27.3	Inventory		36.6	26.6	27.7	27.4	22.4
1.7	2.0	3.4	All Other Current		1.4	2.8	5.5	4.8	1.6
64.9	65.6	67.6	Total Current		77.4	70.3	76.5	67.4	54.1
25.2	24.3	23.4	Fixed Assets (net)		16.8	21.5	14.9	27.0	31.6
3.1	3.5	3.6	Intangibles (net)		1.4	.7	1.3	2.4	8.6
6.8	6.5	5.3	All Other Non-Current		4.4	7.5	7.3	3.2	5.7
100.0	100.0	100.0	Total		100.0	100.0	100.0	100.0	100.0
			LIABILITIES						
12.7	10.7	11.4	Notes Payable-Short Term		6.4	15.0	16.7	11.1	8.4
3.3	3.9	3.7	Cur. Mat.-L/T/D		5.5	3.9	1.9	3.8	2.9
14.4	13.4	16.9	Trade Payables		22.1	22.9	20.7	13.0	9.5
.3	.2	.5	Income Taxes Payable		.1	.3	1.2	.5	.2
8.5	10.2	10.5	All Other Current		6.3	12.7	10.8	12.8	9.7
39.2	38.4	43.0	Total Current		40.4	54.9	51.2	41.3	30.7
18.4	15.3	15.5	Long Term Debt		10.9	15.6	12.7	13.7	19.9
.4	.7	.5	Deferred Taxes		.0	.5	.1	.5	.9
4.9	5.3	6.7	All Other Non-Current		13.1	9.3	4.3	5.3	5.9
37.2	40.3	34.3	Net Worth		35.6	19.7	31.6	39.2	42.6
100.0	100.0	100.0	Total Liabilities & Net Worth		100.0	100.0	100.0	100.0	100.0
			INCOME DATA						
100.0	100.0	100.0	Net Sales		100.0	100.0	100.0	100.0	100.0
28.5	29.6	31.2	Gross Profit		31.0	33.1	31.1	30.8	31.0
23.7	24.1	26.9	Operating Expenses		29.8	30.8	28.6	25.4	24.2
4.7	5.6	4.3	Operating Profit		1.2	2.3	2.5	5.4	6.7
1.4	1.1	1.2	All Other Expenses (net)		.7	.7	1.5	1.0	1.4
3.3	4.4	3.1	Profit Before Taxes		.5	1.6	1.0	4.5	5.3
			RATIOS						
3.0	2.8	2.7			4.2	2.1	2.1	2.8	2.8
1.7	1.7	1.6	Current		2.4	1.3	1.5	1.6	2.1
1.2	1.2	1.1			1.2	1.0	1.1	1.2	1.2
1.5	1.5	1.4			2.1	1.1	1.2	1.6	1.7
.8	.9	.9	Quick		1.1	.7	.8	.9	1.1
.5	.6	.6			.6	.6	.5	.6	.7
28 12.9	29 12.6	28 13.1		19 19.3	19 19.5	37 9.9	26 13.9	30 12.2	
41 8.8	41 8.9	41 8.9	Sales/Receivables	52 7.0	29 12.7	49 7.5	39 9.4	38 9.7	
52 7.0	60 6.0	60 6.1		62 5.9	48 7.6	66 5.5	61 6.0	55 6.6	
41 8.8	37 9.8	30 12.2		33 10.9	17 21.3	30 12.2	28 13.1	36 10.2	
59 6.2	50 7.3	54 6.8	Cost of Sales/Inventory	73 5.0	36 10.3	60 6.1	52 7.0	50 7.3	
82 4.4	78 4.7	85 4.3		113 3.2	117 3.1	91 4.0	82 4.4	69 5.3	
16 22.8	13 27.9	15 24.1		14 25.3	21 17.5	30 12.2	14 25.5	13 27.6	
25 14.5	23 16.0	28 13.0	Cost of Sales/Payables	34 10.7	32 11.4	40 9.2	25 14.8	20 18.1	
40 9.0	40 9.1	43 8.5		50 7.3	55 6.6	55 6.7	34 10.8	30 12.0	
5.7	5.4	5.7			4.4	5.6	5.9	6.1	5.8
10.0	9.5	10.4	Sales/Working Capital		6.7	28.1	8.9	10.8	9.8
24.7	22.4	38.7			21.3	−645.0	42.5	26.1	35.4
9.4	8.8	9.6		2.6	6.2	20.8	9.9	11.4	
(116) 2.6	(96) 2.6	(128) 3.0	EBIT/Interest	(11) 1.6	(18) 2.3	(25) 1.9	(30) 3.5	(38) 3.9	
1.1	1.4	1.3		1.1	1.2	−.7	1.9	1.7	
7.5	3.9	6.8	Net Profit + Depr., Dep.,					2.7	15.6
(40) 2.4	(37) 2.0	(50) 2.5	Amort./Cur. Mat. L/T/D			(11) 2.3	(21) 5.0		
1.0	1.3	1.2					1.1	3.2	
.4	.3	.3			.2	.4	.2	.4	.5
.7	.6	.7	Fixed/Worth		.4	.7	.5	.7	.9
1.6	1.6	1.6			1.0	−2.3	1.2	1.9	1.6
.8	.7	.9			.5	.9	1.0	.8	1.0
1.9	1.5	2.0	Debt/Worth		1.0	3.0	2.2	2.0	1.3
5.7	4.8	5.4			3.6	−10.4	8.3	5.6	4.5
42.0	35.4	40.6	% Profit Before Taxes/Tangible	13.7	32.9	33.3	51.3	43.7	
(115) 18.7	(98) 19.0	(122) 17.6	Net Worth	(15) 4.3	(13) 13.8	(23) 12.5	(31) 31.7	(36) 21.9	
2.4	3.5	4.1		−4.2	4.4	.6	10.6	7.0	
16.0	15.5	16.0	% Profit Before Taxes/Total		6.9	10.0	17.7	17.6	18.2
6.4	5.6	5.2	Assets		.9	4.3	1.6	8.2	10.6
.2	1.1	.8			−3.1	.5	−2.5	3.3	2.9
21.6	22.3	27.8			33.5	34.2	37.6	21.1	13.4
11.1	12.3	13.4	Sales/Net Fixed Assets		18.1	18.0	23.4	10.4	6.5
5.8	5.2	6.7			13.5	9.8	10.0	5.8	3.9
3.1	3.0	3.4			3.5	4.7	3.4	3.3	2.6
2.3	2.2	2.4	Sales/Total Assets		2.9	3.4	2.3	2.7	2.0
1.9	1.8	1.9			2.0	2.0	2.0	2.2	1.5
1.0	1.2	1.0			1.2	1.0	.6	.9	1.5
(111) 1.6	(95) 1.7	(128) 1.6	% Depr., Dep., Amort./Sales	(15) 1.6	(16) 1.4	(25) 1.4	1.4	(36) 2.3	
2.5	2.7	2.5			2.2	2.3	1.9	2.5	3.0
1.2	1.5	1.8	% Officers', Directors',		1.4	2.0	1.0		
(43) 3.0	(33) 2.5	(54) 3.6	Owners' Comp/Sales	(13) 3.9	(15) 2.8	(12) 2.8			
6.6	4.9	6.8			7.2	6.7	4.1		
5309744M	4647583M	5580453M	Net Sales ($)	4552M	34537M	72643M	182318M	545188M	4741215M
2667811M	2525345M	2922846M	Total Assets ($)	2424M	13742M	24258M	76282M	230061M	2576079M

© RMA 2003

M = $ thousand   MM = $ million
See Pages 11 through 18 for Explanation of Ratios and Data

Current Data Sorted By Assets   Comparative Historical Data

	0-500M	500M-2MM	2-10MM	10-50MM	50-100MM	100-250MM	Type of Statement		4/1/98-3/31/99 ALL	4/1/99-3/31/00 ALL
	2	1	20	20	2	1	Unqualified		41	31
	2	29	51	5			Reviewed		104	113
	6	43	23	1			Compiled		62	79
	8	6	6				Tax Returns		14	14
	5	24	34	9	1	2	Other		63	64
		68 (4/1-9/30/02)		233 (10/1/02-3/31/03)						
	23	103	134	35	3	3	NUMBER OF STATEMENTS		284	301
	%	%	%	%	%	%	ASSETS		%	%
	8.7	8.2	7.8	10.1			Cash & Equivalents		8.4	9.8
	32.5	28.7	28.6	22.4			Trade Receivables (net)		29.4	31.5
	15.0	18.5	18.4	20.0			Inventory		18.5	17.0
	3.2	3.6	3.2	2.9			All Other Current		2.9	3.2
	59.3	59.0	58.1	55.4			Total Current		59.3	61.5
	31.9	34.5	33.6	31.2			Fixed Assets (net)		34.0	31.5
	4.1	1.5	3.1	6.9			Intangibles (net)		2.0	2.3
	4.4	5.1	5.3	6.4			All Other Non-Current		4.7	4.6
	100.0	100.0	100.0	100.0			Total		100.0	100.0
							LIABILITIES			
	14.6	12.3	9.4	7.9			Notes Payable-Short Term		9.1	8.9
	4.9	6.6	5.1	4.2			Cur. Mat.-L/T/D		4.9	4.2
	16.5	13.8	12.9	11.1			Trade Payables		13.7	14.0
	.1	.6	.1	.3			Income Taxes Payable		.4	.3
	5.8	7.6	10.6	8.1			All Other Current		8.2	9.6
	41.9	40.9	38.2	31.5			Total Current		36.4	36.9
	27.9	18.8	20.0	16.0			Long Term Debt		17.9	16.7
	.0	.3	.6	.5			Deferred Taxes		.5	.4
	2.4	6.0	3.2	6.1			All Other Non-Current		2.2	2.9
	27.7	33.9	38.0	46.0			Net Worth		42.9	43.0
	100.0	100.0	100.0	100.0			Total Liabilities & Net Worth		100.0	100.0
							INCOME DATA			
	100.0	100.0	100.0	100.0			Net Sales		100.0	100.0
	39.5	30.5	25.3	26.6			Gross Profit		29.1	29.0
	36.8	30.5	23.3	20.4			Operating Expenses		24.0	23.4
	2.7	.0	2.0	6.2			Operating Profit		5.1	5.6
	.5	1.0	1.5	1.7			All Other Expenses (net)		1.0	1.0
	2.2	-1.0	.5	4.5			Profit Before Taxes		4.1	4.6
							RATIOS			
	2.5	2.4	2.4	3.3					2.6	2.7
	1.5	1.5	1.6	1.7			Current		1.7	1.7
	.7	1.0	1.1	1.2					1.1	1.2
	2.4	1.8	1.6	1.8					1.7	1.9
	.9	.8	.9	.9			Quick	(283)	1.0	1.1
	.6	.5	.6	.6					.6	.7
12	31.4	32 11.4	35 10.4	34 10.8				33	11.1	36 10.2
37	10.0	40 9.1	47 7.7	49 7.4			Sales/Receivables	44	8.2	46 8.0
52	7.0	58 6.3	61 6.0	63 5.8				57	6.4	61 6.0
0	UND	15 23.9	21 17.0	38 9.7				22	16.6	16 23.2
21	17.5	35 10.5	44 8.3	55 6.6			Cost of Sales/Inventory	37	9.9	35 10.5
47	7.8	62 5.9	68 5.3	79 4.6				63	5.8	60 6.1
2	239.0	14 25.4	15 24.8	18 20.7				15	24.4	16 23.3
21	17.6	26 13.8	26 14.0	27 13.3			Cost of Sales/Payables	24	15.1	25 14.9
57	6.5	40 9.2	42 8.7	41 8.9				42	8.7	41 8.9
	8.3	6.2	5.9	5.1					5.9	5.7
	19.6	12.1	9.8	7.3			Sales/Working Capital		10.5	9.6
	-169.4	-160.9	33.4	27.1					38.0	26.2
	13.5	4.7	6.7	9.3					9.5	13.0
(16)	3.1	(90) .4	(127) 1.9	(31) 2.5			EBIT/Interest	(260)	3.5	(283) 3.8
	-.8	-3.3	.2	.7					1.6	1.4
		4.2	6.1	2.0			Net Profit + Depr., Dep.,		4.2	4.2
		(27) 1.7	(34) 1.4	(14) 1.4			Amort./Cur. Mat. L /T/D	(109)	2.4	(111) 2.5
		-.2	.5	.1					1.3	1.1
	.3	.5	.4	.4					.4	.3
	1.3	1.2	.8	.7			Fixed/Worth		.8	.7
	10.8	3.2	2.3	3.0					1.6	1.7
	.7	.7	.8	.6					.6	.5
	2.4	2.2	1.8	1.0			Debt/Worth		1.5	1.4
	22.3	8.1	4.2	4.9					3.4	3.4
	59.7	23.8	23.1	40.9			% Profit Before Taxes/Tangible		40.1	41.0
(18)	28.5	(85) 3.1	(126) 7.6	(32) 18.1			Net Worth	(270)	19.8	(280) 17.4
	-7.6	-24.8	-9.9	.5					6.7	4.4
	20.4	8.2	10.7	16.7			% Profit Before Taxes/Total		16.4	16.6
	10.7	.1	3.0	3.6			Assets		7.1	6.6
	-3.6	-12.8	-4.1	-1.2					2.0	1.2
	32.8	14.8	13.3	10.0					13.8	15.2
	17.8	7.0	6.2	6.3			Sales/Net Fixed Assets		7.4	7.6
	6.7	4.1	3.6	3.2					4.2	4.3
	5.7	2.8	2.6	2.1					3.0	2.9
	4.0	2.3	1.9	1.6			Sales/Total Assets		2.4	2.3
	1.9	1.7	1.6	1.1					1.7	1.7
	.8	1.9	1.9	2.0					1.6	1.4
(19)	2.0	(99) 3.2	(131) 3.4	(33) 3.4			% Depr., Dep., Amort./Sales	(268)	2.7	(282) 2.8
	4.7	5.6	5.8	4.6					4.2	4.4
	5.4	3.2	1.5				% Officers', Directors',		2.3	2.6
(12)	7.7	(64) 6.0	(63) 3.6				Owners' Comp/Sales	(145)	4.2	(153) 5.2
	12.1	8.8	5.7						7.2	8.3
	27937M	285170M	1142869M	1195443M	303240M	424352M	Net Sales ($)		3170297M	4984183M
	6667M	120908M	583798M	712347M	180062M	365296M	Total Assets ($)		1619940M	2424858M

M = $ thousand   MM = $ million
See Pages 11 through 18 for Explanation of Ratios and Data

Comparative Historical Data | **Current Data Sorted By Sales**

Hist 1	Hist 2	Hist 3	Type of Statement	0-1MM	1-3MM	3-5MM	5-10MM	10-25MM	25MM & OVER
25	28	46	Unqualified	2		3	11	15	15
97	78	87	Reviewed	1	18	18	29	17	4
84	75	73	Compiled	6	28	19	16	3	1
11	17	20	Tax Returns	1	12	2	4	1	
62	60	75	Other	4	19	13	18	11	10
4/1/00-3/31/01 ALL	4/1/01-3/31/02 ALL	4/1/02-3/31/03 ALL		68 (4/1-9/30/02)	233 (10/1/02-3/31/03)				
279	258	301	**NUMBER OF STATEMENTS**	14	77	55	78	47	30
%	%	%	**ASSETS**	%	%	%	%	%	%
10.2	9.2	8.3	Cash & Equivalents	9.7	8.3	9.1	6.8	8.6	9.3
32.0	29.1	28.2	Trade Receivables (net)	29.1	28.9	27.7	26.9	30.6	26.6
16.7	18.2	18.3	Inventory	13.4	17.2	17.6	19.5	18.8	20.9
2.5	2.5	3.5	All Other Current	4.5	2.2	4.4	3.9	2.5	5.8
61.5	59.0	58.4	Total Current	56.7	56.7	58.7	57.1	60.5	62.7
31.4	33.2	33.2	Fixed Assets (net)	35.0	34.1	34.7	36.4	27.8	27.7
2.4	2.8	3.1	Intangibles (net)	3.3	3.0	1.2	2.4	5.9	4.4
4.6	4.9	5.3	All Other Non-Current	4.5	6.2	5.4	4.1	5.8	5.3
100.0	100.0	100.0	Total	100.0	100.0	100.0	100.0	100.0	100.0
			LIABILITIES						
9.1	11.6	10.5	Notes Payable-Short Term	6.3	12.6	11.5	10.7	9.4	6.8
4.5	4.7	5.4	Cur. Mat.-L/T/D	4.7	6.3	6.6	4.7	5.1	3.8
14.6	13.6	13.3	Trade Payables	10.2	13.3	14.4	13.6	12.3	13.6
.4	.2	.3	Income Taxes Payable	.1	.3	.3	.1	1.0	.2
9.1	9.6	8.9	All Other Current	10.3	7.5	6.8	9.8	11.7	9.0
37.7	39.8	38.5	Total Current	31.6	39.9	39.5	38.9	39.5	33.3
18.9	19.4	19.6	Long Term Debt	21.8	21.9	18.1	24.2	11.8	15.6
.6	.5	.4	Deferred Taxes	.6	.2	.5	.4	.8	.5
3.8	4.2	4.7	All Other Non-Current	.7	5.7	5.3	3.9	4.3	6.2
39.0	36.2	36.7	Net Worth	45.2	32.3	36.6	32.6	43.6	44.4
100.0	100.0	100.0	Total Liabilities & Net Worth	100.0	100.0	100.0	100.0	100.0	100.0
			INCOME DATA						
100.0	100.0	100.0	Net Sales	100.0	100.0	100.0	100.0	100.0	100.0
29.8	27.8	28.2	Gross Profit	38.8	33.7	26.3	26.1	24.6	23.5
23.9	25.1	26.2	Operating Expenses	35.9	33.7	26.1	23.6	20.5	18.5
5.9	2.7	1.9	Operating Profit	2.9	.0	.2	2.4	4.2	5.0
.9	1.5	1.3	All Other Expenses (net)	.6	1.1	1.2	1.4	1.7	1.0
4.9	1.2	.7	Profit Before Taxes	2.3	−1.2	−1.0	1.1	2.4	4.0
			RATIOS						
2.8 / 1.7 / 1.1	2.5 / 1.5 / 1.0	2.5 / 1.6 / 1.1	Current	7.2 / 1.6 / 1.2	2.9 / 1.7 / .9	2.2 / 1.5 / 1.0	2.2 / 1.4 / 1.1	2.1 / 1.7 / 1.2	3.4 / 1.8 / 1.3
2.0 / 1.2 / .7	1.7 / 1.0 / .6	1.7 / .9 / .6	Quick	5.4 / .9 / .7	2.2 / .9 / .5	1.5 / .9 / .7	1.6 / .8 / .5	1.5 / 1.0 / .6	2.4 / 1.0 / .6
36 10.1 / 48 7.7 / 61 6.0	32 11.3 / 45 8.1 / 60 6.1	33 11.0 / 46 7.9 / 60 6.0	Sales/Receivables	42 8.6 / 53 6.9 / 94 3.9	31 11.9 / 40 9.1 / 61 6.0	31 11.8 / 42 8.6 / 59 6.2	34 10.6 / 47 7.8 / 57 6.4	32 11.3 / 45 8.1 / 64 5.7	43 8.6 / 50 7.3 / 65 5.6
15 24.1 / 32 11.3 / 54 6.7	17 21.8 / 35 10.5 / 65 5.6	20 18.0 / 41 8.8 / 68 5.4	Cost of Sales/Inventory	0 UND / 41 8.9 / 124 2.9	10 35.7 / 37 10.0 / 65 5.7	15 23.6 / 27 13.6 / 52 7.1	25 14.5 / 45 8.1 / 73 5.0	12 31.6 / 43 8.4 / 71 5.1	28 13.1 / 52 7.0 / 85 4.3
15 24.6 / 28 12.9 / 44 8.4	12 30.5 / 25 14.9 / 41 8.9	15 24.7 / 26 13.8 / 41 9.0	Cost of Sales/Payables	1 299.7 / 23 15.9 / 100 3.7	11 33.9 / 23 15.6 / 46 7.9	16 22.7 / 31 11.7 / 39 9.4	17 21.1 / 28 13.0 / 42 8.7	14 27.0 / 25 14.7 / 36 10.3	18 20.6 / 30 12.0 / 40 9.1
5.8 / 10.0 / 37.9	5.8 / 11.5 / 132.9	5.8 / 10.6 / 59.4	Sales/Working Capital	2.9 / 9.4 / 23.0	5.4 / 13.9 / −39.8	6.9 / 10.4 / 80.8	6.0 / 13.0 / 44.1	6.0 / 9.7 / 30.3	3.9 / 6.9 / 15.2
(253) 10.7 / 3.7 / 1.8	(238) 5.3 / 1.9 / .3	(269) 6.3 / 1.8 / −1.0	EBIT/Interest		(67) 4.8 / 1.3 / −2.8	(50) 3.6 / 1.0 / −2.8	(75) 5.2 / 1.9 / .2	(43) 15.5 / 4.5 / .0	(26) 11.1 / 2.9 / .6
(95) 3.6 / 1.9 / 1.2	(80) 2.9 / 1.3 / .4	(80) 3.6 / 1.4 / .1	Net Profit + Depr., Dep., Amort./Cur. Mat. L/T/D		(16) 2.2 / .2 / −.4	(14) 4.4 / 1.8 / .6	(20) 3.9 / 1.3 / .2	(18) 10.2 / 1.8 / .2	
.4 / .8 / 1.8	.4 / .9 / 2.5	.4 / .9 / 2.5	Fixed/Worth	.3 / .9 / 6.6	.4 / 1.3 / 5.7	.5 / 1.0 / 1.9	.5 / 1.2 / 2.5	.3 / .6 / 1.9	.3 / .6 / 1.8
.7 / 1.7 / 3.9	.8 / 2.0 / 5.5	.7 / 1.8 / 5.6	Debt/Worth	.2 / 1.7 / 10.9	.6 / 2.4 / 14.5	.8 / 1.9 / 5.2	.8 / 2.1 / 5.6	.6 / 1.3 / 3.4	.6 / 1.1 / 5.1
(254) 48.9 / 24.4 / 9.8	(229) 34.6 / 9.8 / −1.8	(266) 29.1 / 7.4 / −11.6	% Profit Before Taxes/Tangible Net Worth	29.5 / −7.5 / −64.0	(59) 32.5 / 7.8 / −20.2	(52) 18.7 / 1.1 / −24.4	(72) 24.6 / 6.2 / −6.4	(41) 28.0 / 20.8 / .1	(28) 50.7 / 17.5 / −2.3
17.5 / 7.9 / 3.4	10.7 / 3.4 / −3.1	11.9 / 2.6 / −5.2	% Profit Before Taxes/Total Assets	18.8 / −1.0 / −8.6	11.7 / 1.4 / −13.3	5.6 / .4 / −10.7	7.9 / 2.4 / −2.4	13.6 / 5.6 / −3.3	15.5 / 5.0 / −.6
13.9 / 7.9 / 4.6	14.5 / 7.0 / 4.0	14.6 / 6.7 / 3.9	Sales/Net Fixed Assets	19.0 / 5.7 / 3.6	16.1 / 7.2 / 3.6	16.6 / 6.7 / 4.7	11.8 / 5.6 / 3.5	16.4 / 8.5 / 4.8	12.2 / 7.0 / 4.0
3.0 / 2.3 / 1.8	2.9 / 2.2 / 1.6	2.7 / 2.1 / 1.6	Sales/Total Assets	2.3 / 1.9 / 1.0	3.0 / 2.2 / 1.6	2.8 / 2.2 / 1.9	2.7 / 2.0 / 1.6	2.7 / 2.1 / 1.4	2.3 / 1.7 / 1.4
(258) 1.4 / 2.6 / 4.1	(241) 1.5 / 2.7 / 5.0	(288) 1.9 / 3.2 / 5.3	% Depr., Dep., Amort./Sales	(11) 1.6 / 3.6 / 5.4	(72) 1.9 / 3.7 / 6.8	1.9 / 3.2 / 6.3	(74) 2.2 / 3.7 / 5.7	1.3 / 2.3 / 4.1	(29) 1.5 / 2.7 / 4.4
(135) 3.1 / 5.8 / 8.5	(124) 2.1 / 4.3 / 7.6	(143) 2.3 / 4.6 / 7.5	% Officers', Directors', Owners' Comp/Sales		(47) 4.0 / 6.5 / 10.1	(39) 2.7 / 4.9 / 7.0	(35) 1.3 / 3.7 / 6.1	(15) 1.1 / 1.7 / 3.3	
4989224M	3575184M	3379011M	Net Sales ($)	8196M	151403M	218444M	567963M	667289M	1765716M
2406908M	1833729M	1969078M	Total Assets ($)	5470M	75337M	105203M	317363M	360998M	1104707M

M = $ thousand   MM = $ million
See Pages 11 through 18 for Explanation of Ratios and Data

Current Data Sorted By Assets   Comparative Historical Data

0-500M	500M-2MM	2-10MM	10-50MM	50-100MM	100-250MM	Type of Statement	4/1/98-3/31/99 ALL	4/1/99-3/31/00 ALL
	1	5		1	2	Unqualified	11	11
	12	14				Reviewed	22	22
2	3	4	1			Compiled	17	23
3	6			1		Tax Returns	2	8
1	3	7	2	1		Other	20	18
	14 (4/1-9/30/02)			55 (10/1/02-3/31/03)				
6	25	30	3	3	2	NUMBER OF STATEMENTS	72	82
%	%	%	%	%	%	**ASSETS**	%	%
	5.4	7.3				Cash & Equivalents	8.5	9.5
	40.8	33.7				Trade Receivables (net)	33.5	31.0
	19.2	20.9				Inventory	20.5	19.2
	6.3	6.7				All Other Current	3.5	3.6
	71.7	68.7				Total Current	66.1	63.4
	22.7	23.2				Fixed Assets (net)	24.0	26.0
	1.3	3.1				Intangibles (net)	2.9	4.7
	4.4	5.0				All Other Non-Current	7.0	6.0
	100.0	100.0				Total	100.0	100.0
						LIABILITIES		
	11.5	14.0				Notes Payable-Short Term	10.6	13.8
	4.5	3.2				Cur. Mat.-L/T/D	3.4	3.8
	17.0	15.9				Trade Payables	15.2	13.9
	1.7	.4				Income Taxes Payable	.4	.4
	13.6	10.4				All Other Current	10.1	12.3
	48.4	43.9				Total Current	39.7	44.2
	17.0	16.8				Long Term Debt	15.2	16.1
	.4	.3				Deferred Taxes	1.2	.8
	2.3	3.6				All Other Non-Current	6.2	6.1
	31.9	35.4				Net Worth	37.7	32.7
	100.0	100.0				Total Liabilities & Net Worth	100.0	100.0
						INCOME DATA		
	100.0	100.0				Net Sales	100.0	100.0
	35.1	33.0				Gross Profit	33.9	34.0
	31.7	30.2				Operating Expenses	27.4	29.3
	3.4	2.8				Operating Profit	6.6	4.7
	.9	.6				All Other Expenses (net)	.9	1.1
	2.5	2.1				Profit Before Taxes	5.6	3.6
						RATIOS		
	2.2	2.3					2.8	2.4
	1.6	1.7				Current	1.6	1.5
	1.1	1.2					1.2	1.2
	1.4	1.7					1.7	1.6
	1.0	.7				Quick	1.0	.9
	.6	.6					.7	.5
	32 11.3	38 9.6					31 11.7	26 13.9
	56 6.5	53 6.8				Sales/Receivables	48 7.5	43 8.4
	71 5.1	69 5.3					68 5.4	63 5.8
	0 UND	3 145.7					14 27.0	6 58.0
	26 14.2	39 9.3				Cost of Sales/Inventory	45 8.1	34 10.7
	75 4.8	113 3.2					74 4.9	71 5.2
	13 28.8	22 16.7					15 23.8	13 28.6
	33 11.1	32 11.4				Cost of Sales/Payables	28 12.9	26 13.9
	52 7.1	53 7.0					48 7.6	44 8.4
	7.9	5.2					6.1	6.6
	9.5	8.6				Sales/Working Capital	10.4	10.6
	34.2	19.8					27.1	30.8
	13.5	7.2					14.6	8.5
	(28) 3.5	2.0				EBIT/Interest	(67) 4.5	(74) 2.3
	1.2	1.2					2.2	1.0
		4.9				Net Profit + Depr., Dep.,		
	(11)	4.3				Amort./Cur. Mat. L /T/D	(28) 8.8 / 3.6 / 1.5	(22) 7.7 / 3.5 / 1.4
		1.4						
	.3	.2					.3	.3
	.7	.6				Fixed/Worth	.7	.6
	2.0	1.7					1.3	3.5
	1.1	1.0					.8	.9
	1.8	2.0				Debt/Worth	1.8	1.8
	6.7	4.2					4.3	9.0
	44.1	34.6					59.5	54.8
	(22) 11.1	(26) 8.8				% Profit Before Taxes/Tangible Net Worth	(66) 33.7	(67) 19.0
	4.2	3.2					11.1	3.3
	16.2	8.7					23.9	14.3
	4.3	2.7				% Profit Before Taxes/Total Assets	9.2	5.1
	1.1	.6					3.4	-.2
	33.6	30.7					24.7	27.8
	15.8	10.1				Sales/Net Fixed Assets	13.8	13.3
	7.1	4.8					6.8	7.0
	3.5	2.4					3.1	3.4
	2.8	2.1				Sales/Total Assets	2.5	2.4
	2.2	1.5					1.9	1.8
	1.0	.9					1.1	.9
	(22) 1.7	(28) 1.6				% Depr., Dep., Amort./Sales	(60) 1.6	(73) 1.5
	2.6	2.4					2.6	2.8
	4.2	3.5					2.8	3.2
	(15) 9.3	(18) 5.7				% Officers', Directors', Owners' Comp/Sales	(39) 4.5	(39) 5.6
	14.4	7.0					8.3	11.7
6206M	78816M	290808M	105415M	702938M	403206M	Net Sales ($)	980481M	1480928M
1894M	28596M	140821M	55195M	213447M	240235M	Total Assets ($)	516638M	873139M

M = $ thousand   MM = $ million
See Pages 11 through 18 for Explanation of Ratios and Data

Comparative Historical Data | Current Data Sorted By Sales

						Type of Statement								
	6		9		9	Unqualified		1			2	3	3	
	18		24		26	Reviewed		4		8	7	6	1	
	20		13		10	Compiled		5		1	2	1	1	
	9		5		10	Tax Returns	2	5		2			1	
	17		16		14	Other	2	2		3	3	1	3	
	4/1/00-		4/1/01-		4/1/02-			14 (4/1-9/30/02)			55 (10/1/02-3/31/03)			
	3/31/01		3/31/02		3/31/03									
	ALL		ALL		ALL		0-1MM	1-3MM		3-5MM	5-10MM	10-25MM	25MM & OVER	
	70		67		69	**NUMBER OF STATEMENTS**	4	17		14	14	11	9	
	%		%		%	**ASSETS**	%	%		%	%	%	%	
	11.8		10.2		7.0	Cash & Equivalents		10.0		5.3	5.7	5.3		
	29.9		29.2		34.9	Trade Receivables (net)		44.0		32.0	31.9	42.1		
	20.2		18.9		19.1	Inventory		21.1		17.2	18.7	20.4		
	3.1		3.7		5.4	All Other Current		.9		9.5	6.3	11.2		
	65.0		62.0		66.4	Total Current		76.0		64.0	62.6	78.9		
	26.5		27.4		25.4	Fixed Assets (net)		18.8		29.6	27.1	15.6		
	3.4		3.4		3.0	Intangibles (net)		.8		.8	4.5	2.6		
	5.1		7.3		5.2	All Other Non-Current		4.4		5.7	5.8	2.8		
	100.0		100.0		100.0	Total		100.0		100.0	100.0	100.0		
						LIABILITIES								
	13.1		11.6		11.9	Notes Payable-Short Term		16.1		7.9	9.5	14.2		
	4.3		4.6		4.5	Cur. Mat.-L/T/D		6.3		3.5	4.3	1.8		
	13.1		14.8		15.8	Trade Payables		19.9		12.1	13.4	21.0		
	.5		.6		.9	Income Taxes Payable		.2		2.7	1.0	.0		
	13.8		9.3		10.6	All Other Current		11.9		11.9	11.0	13.6		
	44.9		40.9		43.7	Total Current		54.4		38.1	39.2	50.6		
	15.4		17.0		16.6	Long Term Debt		16.0		22.7	17.9	9.3		
	.6		.4		.5	Deferred Taxes		.8		.4	.5	.0		
	3.2		3.3		5.0	All Other Non-Current		4.0		2.5	2.8	2.3		
	36.0		38.3		34.1	Net Worth		24.8		36.2	39.6	37.8		
	100.0		100.0		100.0	Total Liabilities & Net Worth		100.0		100.0	100.0	100.0		
						INCOME DATA								
	100.0		100.0		100.0	Net Sales		100.0		100.0	100.0	100.0		
	36.6		36.0		34.7	Gross Profit		35.1		34.2	32.7	32.2		
	32.1		30.9		31.8	Operating Expenses		34.3		30.3	28.2	29.2		
	4.5		5.0		2.9	Operating Profit		.7		3.9	4.5	3.0		
	.6		.8		.9	All Other Expenses (net)		.6		1.1	1.0	.0		
	3.9		4.2		2.0	Profit Before Taxes		.2		2.8	3.5	3.0		
						RATIOS								
	2.2		2.1		2.2			2.0		2.2	2.2	2.3		
	1.5		1.6		1.6	Current		1.6		1.9	1.6	1.7		
	1.2		1.1		1.1			1.0		1.1	1.3	1.2		
	1.5		1.3		1.5			1.9		1.3	1.4	1.7		
	1.0		.9		.9	Quick		1.0		1.0	.8	.8		
	.6		.6		.6			.6		.5	.6	.6		
28	13.2	31	11.6	34	10.7		34	10.7	15	24.9	25	14.9	39	9.3
44	8.4	44	8.4	53	6.8	Sales/Receivables	46	7.9	52	7.1	54	6.8	58	6.3
62	5.8	59	6.2	68	5.3		70	5.2	62	5.8	68	5.4	86	4.2
13	28.2	10	37.8	2	151.6		0	UND	0	UND	0	UND	2	163.3
42	8.6	40	9.2	33	11.0	Cost of Sales/Inventory	33	11.0	26	13.9	29	12.5	70	5.2
81	4.5	74	4.9	80	4.6		74	4.9	74	4.9	92	4.0	124	2.9
15	24.3	16	23.3	14	26.0		18	20.8	10	36.6	13	28.8	22	16.3
28	13.2	27	13.5	32	11.3	Cost of Sales/Payables	36	10.1	21	17.5	28	13.1	31	11.9
43	8.6	46	7.9	48	7.6		54	6.8	39	9.4	44	8.4	72	5.1
	7.1		7.0		6.3			8.1		6.5	5.8	5.2		
	12.0		12.0		9.5	Sales/Working Capital		10.6		8.2	9.5	6.9		
	31.0		48.4		34.2			214.4		128.0	58.6	11.1		
	8.3		8.3		11.1			9.0		18.3	11.2	6.4		
(66)	2.9	(59)	3.9	(67)	2.5	EBIT/Interest	(16)	2.2		2.9	2.0	(10)	3.8	
	1.1		1.6		1.2			1.2		.9	1.3	1.3		
	7.0		3.6		5.3	Net Profit + Depr., Dep.,								
(22)	2.4	(19)	2.0	(21)	3.3	Amort./Cur. Mat. L/T/D								
	1.2		1.1		1.4									
	.3		.3		.3			.2		.3	.3	.1		
	.8		.7		.7	Fixed/Worth		.7		.6	.7	.5		
	2.0		2.2		2.1			NM		2.1	1.7	1.2		
	.9		.9		.8			1.5		.8	1.2	.7		
	2.2		1.7		1.9	Debt/Worth		2.1		1.5	1.8	1.4		
	4.1		4.9		4.8			NM		5.4	3.5	4.0		
	40.7		46.9		42.3	% Profit Before Taxes/Tangible		55.7		41.0	34.5	39.8		
(64)	22.0	(60)	23.9	(59)	10.5	Net Worth	(13)	11.7	(13)	9.7	(13)	9.4	(10)	12.9	
	4.7		6.6		2.8			.7		-1.0	3.0	6.2		
	14.6		17.6		11.3	% Profit Before Taxes/Total		15.8		17.5	11.1	13.3		
	5.8		7.5		3.6	Assets		2.1		3.5	3.9	3.4		
	.5		1.6		.6			.2		-.1	1.7	1.3		
	24.1		22.9		29.3			67.1		18.6	29.2	88.6		
	13.4		11.6		11.7	Sales/Net Fixed Assets		18.5		13.2	11.6	24.2		
	6.1		5.2		4.9			8.7		4.5	4.4	7.0		
	3.0		2.9		3.2			3.7		3.2	2.6	2.5		
	2.3		2.3		2.3	Sales/Total Assets		3.3		2.6	2.1	2.2		
	1.8		1.8		1.8			2.2		2.1	1.8	1.9		
	1.1		1.1		1.0			1.1		1.0	.9	.3		
(67)	1.7	(60)	2.0	(62)	2.0	% Depr., Dep., Amort./Sales	(14)	1.8	(12)	1.8	(13)	1.6	1.3	
	2.6		3.3		3.0			3.7		2.6	2.6	2.2		
	4.1		3.3		3.6	% Officers', Directors',				4.2				
(35)	6.2	(36)	5.2	(40)	5.8	Owners' Comp/Sales			(11)	10.8				
	13.1		7.6		10.4					17.9				
	1079015M		1058583M		1587389M	Net Sales ($)	2417M	39522M		56570M	100929M	148993M	1238958M	
	618485M		623389M		680188M	Total Assets ($)	1606M	19603M		25144M	48495M	67789M	517551M	

M = $ thousand   MM = $ million
See Pages 11 through 18 for Explanation of Ratios and Data

Current Data Sorted By Assets | Comparative Historical Data

Type of Statement

	0-500M	500M-2MM	2-10MM	10-50MM	50-100MM	100-250MM		4/1/98-3/31/99 ALL	4/1/99-3/31/00 ALL
Unqualified		5	7	9	3	4		24	23
Reviewed		5	13	4				23	16
Compiled	1	2	3					19	15
Tax Returns	1		1					5	2
Other	1	6	8	7	2			25	25

Current data period headers: 15 (4/1-9/30/02) [500M-2MM]; 67 (10/1/02-3/31/03) [10-50MM]

Data

0-500M	500M-2MM	2-10MM	10-50MM	50-100MM	100-250MM		4/1/98-3/31/99 ALL	4/1/99-3/31/00 ALL
3	18	32	20	5	4	**NUMBER OF STATEMENTS**	96	81
%	%	%	%	%	%	**ASSETS**	%	%
	2.0	5.6	7.6			Cash & Equivalents	9.4	9.5
	22.6	22.5	20.5			Trade Receivables (net)	25.0	24.1
	39.9	29.7	23.2			Inventory	28.0	26.3
	.7	1.3	2.6			All Other Current	1.7	2.2
	65.2	59.1	53.8			Total Current	64.1	62.3
	27.9	28.4	29.8			Fixed Assets (net)	25.9	25.1
	3.3	5.3	8.4			Intangibles (net)	5.0	5.5
	3.6	7.3	8.0			All Other Non-Current	5.0	7.1
	100.0	100.0	100.0			Total	100.0	100.0
						LIABILITIES		
	17.3	14.3	6.3			Notes Payable-Short Term	12.3	8.8
	5.7	6.1	3.7			Cur. Mat.-L/T/D	3.3	2.7
	10.2	11.5	10.0			Trade Payables	13.3	12.8
	.0	.4	.5			Income Taxes Payable	.5	.5
	4.3	7.5	9.0			All Other Current	9.0	7.0
	37.6	39.8	29.5			Total Current	38.4	31.9
	22.1	14.4	14.3			Long Term Debt	15.5	12.8
	.3	.6	.7			Deferred Taxes	.4	.7
	6.9	.6	3.7			All Other Non-Current	7.1	5.0
	33.0	44.6	51.8			Net Worth	38.7	49.7
	100.0	100.0	100.0			Total Liabilities & Net Worth	100.0	100.0
						INCOME DATA		
	100.0	100.0	100.0			Net Sales	100.0	100.0
	32.1	28.8	30.3			Gross Profit	32.9	33.7
	30.2	23.1	24.6			Operating Expenses	26.1	27.2
	1.9	5.7	5.7			Operating Profit	6.8	6.5
	1.4	.8	1.3			All Other Expenses (net)	1.2	.6
	.5	4.9	4.4			Profit Before Taxes	5.6	5.9
						RATIOS		
	2.4	2.8	3.5				3.6	3.7
	2.1	2.0	1.8			Current	1.8	2.2
	1.3	1.2	1.3				1.2	1.3
	1.1	1.3	2.0				2.2	2.2
	.7	.9	1.0			Quick	.9	1.2
	.3	.5	.6				.5	.6
	21 17.5	26 13.9	35 10.3				33 10.9	36 10.1
	37 9.7	34 10.7	39 9.3			Sales/Receivables	42 8.6	45 8.1
	47 7.7	48 7.7	46 7.9				53 6.9	54 6.8
	54 6.7	39 9.3	44 8.3				43 8.6	43 8.4
	93 3.9	69 5.3	57 6.4			Cost of Sales/Inventory	69 5.3	71 5.1
	151 2.4	111 3.3	78 4.7				99 3.7	95 3.8
	11 34.1	13 27.4	14 27.0				19 19.3	17 20.9
	25 14.5	22 16.9	27 13.7			Cost of Sales/Payables	31 11.9	28 13.2
	32 11.5	38 9.7	40 9.1				49 7.4	49 7.5
	4.1	4.8	5.9				4.3	3.6
	7.7	9.4	7.9			Sales/Working Capital	7.8	6.1
	20.0	28.3	14.2				22.1	15.1
	7.7	12.6	20.2				11.3	18.2
	(17) 1.7	3.0	(17) 7.9			EBIT/Interest	(81) 3.0	(69) 6.6
	−.3	1.0	1.7				1.4	2.6
		8.5					11.3	9.9
		(15) 3.1				Net Profit + Depr., Dep., Amort./Cur. Mat. L /T/D	(33) 3.5	(28) 5.1
		2.0					1.6	1.8
	.5	.4	.3				.3	.3
	.7	.8	.6			Fixed/Worth	.7	.6
	NM	2.8	1.1				2.3	1.4
	.7	.5	.4				.4	.4
	2.2	1.1	1.0			Debt/Worth	1.4	.9
	NM	6.2	2.0				6.4	3.2
	32.7	37.9	39.7				38.1	38.7
	(14) 9.5	(26) 16.1	(18) 17.5			% Profit Before Taxes/Tangible Net Worth	(82) 20.5	(70) 24.0
	−12.4	1.0	6.4				6.1	13.1
	8.7	16.2	18.9				17.6	17.7
	1.3	5.9	7.8			% Profit Before Taxes/Total Assets	7.3	12.5
	−7.6	.0	1.0				1.7	5.5
	16.4	20.6	10.3				19.2	15.9
	10.6	8.5	6.1			Sales/Net Fixed Assets	8.4	7.8
	6.1	4.3	4.5				4.6	4.5
	2.8	2.7	2.2				2.6	2.4
	2.3	2.1	1.8			Sales/Total Assets	1.9	1.8
	1.5	1.6	1.6				1.6	1.5
	1.1	1.1	2.2				1.4	1.3
	(17) 3.2	2.0	(19) 3.0			% Depr., Dep., Amort./Sales	(84) 2.7	(70) 2.3
	6.6	3.6	4.7				4.5	3.8
	3.2	2.5					2.0	2.0
	(10) 5.3	(13) 4.2				% Officers', Directors', Owners' Comp/Sales	(37) 4.4	(27) 4.8
	6.3	6.7					6.0	
3752M	53168M	346541M	713559M	418821M	749966M	Net Sales ($)	2551622M	2866573M
615M	24280M	162635M	399383M	335226M	601640M	Total Assets ($)	1714581M	1767445M

M = $ thousand   MM = $ million
See Pages 11 through 18 for Explanation of Ratios and Data

Comparative Historical Data | Current Data Sorted By Sales

Hist 1	Hist 2	Hist 3	Type of Statement	0-1MM	1-3MM	3-5MM	5-10MM	10-25MM	25MM & OVER
27	31	23	Unqualified			1	2	4	16
23	18	22	Reviewed		2	4	7	6	3
30	31	9	Compiled		3	4		2	
11	8	4	Tax Returns	1	1	1	1		
27	56	24	Other	1	5	2	4	5	7
4/1/00-3/31/01 ALL	4/1/01-3/31/02 ALL	4/1/02-3/31/03 ALL		15 (4/1-9/30/02)			67 (10/1/02-3/31/03)		
118	144	82	NUMBER OF STATEMENTS	2	11	12	14	17	26
%	%	%	**ASSETS**	%	%	%	%	%	%
8.2	6.8	6.0	Cash & Equivalents		3.9	2.3	5.9	8.2	7.5
24.9	22.4	21.3	Trade Receivables (net)		19.8	24.3	20.7	23.6	20.2
26.6	29.0	30.3	Inventory		40.5	35.3	28.5	26.7	23.2
1.7	2.0	2.3	All Other Current		.5	1.5	.4	2.0	4.7
61.3	60.2	59.8	Total Current		64.7	63.3	55.6	60.6	55.6
28.6	28.2	28.1	Fixed Assets (net)		30.2	27.8	26.5	29.4	29.0
5.0	7.1	5.3	Intangibles (net)		2.8	4.6	7.7	5.1	5.8
5.0	4.5	6.8	All Other Non-Current		2.3	4.3	10.2	4.9	9.6
100.0	100.0	100.0	Total		100.0	100.0	100.0	100.0	100.0
			LIABILITIES						
9.5	11.4	11.2	Notes Payable-Short Term		14.3	15.5	13.8	9.8	8.3
3.6	3.6	5.6	Cur. Mat.-L/T/D		8.0	6.0	10.1	3.3	3.7
12.7	12.4	11.2	Trade Payables		11.6	10.5	11.2	11.9	10.9
.3	.2	.3	Income Taxes Payable		.0	.0	.2	.6	.5
7.6	6.9	9.6	All Other Current		10.8	6.1	4.4	9.7	11.5
33.7	34.5	37.9	Total Current		44.6	38.1	39.7	35.3	35.0
17.7	19.1	15.9	Long Term Debt		28.2	12.9	15.4	14.0	13.9
.6	.6	.6	Deferred Taxes		.1	.4	1.0	.4	.8
3.2	4.9	3.6	All Other Non-Current		8.2	2.8	.0	1.1	5.8
44.9	41.0	41.9	Net Worth		18.8	45.7	44.0	49.2	44.5
100.0	100.0	100.0	Total Liabilities & Net Worth		100.0	100.0	100.0	100.0	100.0
			INCOME DATA						
100.0	100.0	100.0	Net Sales		100.0	100.0	100.0	100.0	100.0
32.9	31.2	30.0	Gross Profit		30.6	32.0	30.1	30.6	28.8
26.1	26.1	24.9	Operating Expenses		28.7	28.9	23.2	23.6	22.9
6.8	5.0	5.2	Operating Profit		1.9	3.1	6.9	7.0	5.9
1.1	1.6	1.3	All Other Expenses (net)		1.8	.6	.3	2.1	1.6
5.7	3.5	3.8	Profit Before Taxes		.1	2.5	6.7	4.8	4.3
			RATIOS						
3.4	3.5	2.8			3.1	2.7	3.1	2.5	2.8
2.1	1.9	1.9	Current		2.3	1.6	2.0	1.9	1.8
1.2	1.3	1.3			.9	1.3	.7	1.3	1.2
2.0	1.8	1.3			1.2	.9	1.4	1.5	1.7
1.0	1.0	.9	Quick		1.0	.7	.9	1.0	.9
.6	.5	.5			.3	.6	.4	.6	.5
36 10.3	33 11.2	29 12.6		12 29.6	22 16.2	24 15.1	29 12.5	35 10.5	
44 8.3	42 8.7	38 9.6	Sales/Receivables	39 9.5	36 10.1	35 10.5	33 11.1	41 8.9	
56 6.6	54 6.8	47 7.7		46 7.9	50 7.3	47 7.7	49 7.5	49 7.5	
37 9.9	46 8.0	46 8.0		52 7.0	55 6.6	35 10.4	41 8.9	42 8.7	
69 5.3	70 5.2	69 5.3	Cost of Sales/Inventory	115 3.2	92 4.0	70 5.2	54 6.7	63 5.8	
111 3.3	123 3.0	109 3.3		155 2.3	170 2.1	118 3.3	78 4.7	99 3.7	
19 19.4	16 23.5	13 27.9		11 34.1	11 33.0	11 31.9	14 25.4	17 21.6	
27 13.4	25 14.5	23 15.7	Cost of Sales/Payables	22 16.8	23 15.9	25 14.4	22 16.9	25 14.6	
41 8.9	46 8.0	35 10.4		30 12.2	34 10.8	36 10.0	47 7.8	40 9.1	
4.1	4.3	4.7			3.8	4.4	-4.9	7.0	4.8
6.9	7.6	8.0	Sales/Working Capital		5.1	9.3	8.8	9.5	7.1
25.0	16.5	16.0			-49.2	15.4	-14.0	14.1	18.0
19.6	9.6	13.3			5.4	10.2	12.9	14.2	20.9
(108) 4.5	(130) 2.5	(76) 3.3	EBIT/Interest	(10) .9	2.9	3.9	(16) 3.8	(23) 7.9	
1.5	1.1	1.0			-1.3	-.3	.7	2.5	1.2
5.7	4.3	4.1	Net Profit + Depr., Dep., Amort./Cur. Mat. L/T/D						3.5
(43) 2.5	(33) 2.5	(31) 2.4						(10)	1.6
1.4	1.2	1.1							1.1
.3	.3	.4			.4	.5	.2	.4	.4
.7	.7	.7	Fixed/Worth		.7	.7	.8	.7	.7
1.3	2.0	1.3			-2.5	1.0	-6.0	1.3	1.3
.4	.5	.6			.5	.7	.4	.4	.6
1.2	1.3	1.2	Debt/Worth		3.2	1.2	1.1	1.2	1.1
4.0	4.9	4.1			-3.9	2.6	-43.1	3.5	4.4
39.8	28.1	32.2			37.7	47.7		32.2	34.4
(103) 24.7	(120) 12.3	(68) 16.3	% Profit Before Taxes/Tangible Net Worth		(11) 20.3	(10) 15.0	(16) 21.8	(22) 16.8	
7.7	.8	1.2			-3.0	3.6		12.7	4.7
19.3	11.7	16.2			7.0	14.8	24.5	16.8	17.8
9.1	5.3	6.0	% Profit Before Taxes/Total Assets		-3.7	4.1	7.4	6.8	6.7
2.5	.3	-.5			-9.7	-1.8	-.5	4.6	.8
13.1	14.4	17.2			28.1	19.0	21.6	12.9	10.5
7.0	7.7	7.3	Sales/Net Fixed Assets		8.6	11.4	8.4	7.8	5.2
4.5	3.8	4.4			2.9	3.5	4.4	5.1	4.1
2.4	2.5	2.6			2.6	2.9	2.7	2.8	2.2
1.9	1.8	1.9	Sales/Total Assets		1.8	2.2	2.1	2.1	1.7
1.5	1.3	1.5			1.3	1.5	1.6	1.6	1.3
1.6	1.5	1.5				1.1	1.5	.9	2.3
(110) 2.8	(130) 2.6	(77) 3.0	% Depr., Dep., Amort./Sales			2.4	2.0	2.8	(24) 3.1
4.3	4.6	4.4				5.7	4.6	3.6	4.5
3.1	2.8	2.4							
(49) 5.6	(42) 4.5	(28) 3.9	% Officers', Directors', Owners' Comp/Sales						
12.9	10.3	6.1							
3729056M	5056870M	2285807M	Net Sales ($)	1145M	23560M	45267M	104528M	283736M	1827571M
2474253M	3432756M	1523779M	Total Assets ($)	444M	12480M	23624M	56655M	136055M	1294521M

© RMA 2003   M = $ thousand   MM = $ million
See Pages 11 through 18 for Explanation of Ratios and Data

Current Data Sorted By Assets   **Comparative Historical Data**

	0-500M	500M-2MM	2-10MM	10-50MM	50-100MM	100-250MM		4/1/98-3/31/99 ALL	4/1/99-3/31/00 ALL
Type of Statement									
Unqualified			1		1			6	7
Reviewed		3	5					8	16
Compiled	1	5	3	1		1		7	7
Tax Returns		1						1	1
Other	1	2	2	3				11	7
		7 (4/1-9/30/02)		22 (10/1/02-3/31/03)					
NUMBER OF STATEMENTS	2	11	11	4	1			33	38
	%	%	%	%	%	%		%	%
ASSETS									
Cash & Equivalents		9.0	6.7				D	5.9	7.8
Trade Receivables (net)		23.0	28.3				A	26.1	27.8
Inventory		24.2	24.4				T	23.1	19.8
All Other Current		5.5	1.8				A	2.1	.7
Total Current		61.6	61.2					57.1	56.1
Fixed Assets (net)		26.1	30.9				N	35.8	36.0
Intangibles (net)		3.5	5.6				O	2.7	3.1
All Other Non-Current		8.8	2.3				T	4.3	4.8
Total		100.0	100.0					100.0	100.0
LIABILITIES							A		
Notes Payable-Short Term		5.9	20.7				V	7.5	7.2
Cur. Mat.-L/T/D		4.5	3.1				A	2.9	4.7
Trade Payables		9.8	11.0				I	13.9	14.0
Income Taxes Payable		.1	.0				L	.3	.2
All Other Current		27.1	7.3				A	5.9	6.5
Total Current		47.4	42.1				B	30.4	32.5
Long Term Debt		25.7	8.4				L	23.0	15.9
Deferred Taxes		.0	.7				E	.9	.7
All Other Non-Current		20.4	1.7					2.7	2.0
Net Worth		6.5	47.1					42.9	48.8
Total Liabilities & Net Worth		100.0	100.0					100.0	100.0
INCOME DATA									
Net Sales		100.0	100.0					100.0	100.0
Gross Profit		40.1	32.7					30.9	31.2
Operating Expenses		31.7	23.9					21.3	22.0
Operating Profit		8.4	8.9					9.6	9.2
All Other Expenses (net)		3.8	-.2					1.3	1.5
Profit Before Taxes		4.6	9.1					8.3	7.7
RATIOS									
Current		2.9	4.3					3.0	2.9
		1.6	2.0					2.0	1.7
		1.0	1.3					1.4	1.2
Quick		1.1	1.9					1.6	2.0
		.9	1.1					1.2	1.0
		.5	.6					.7	.8
Sales/Receivables	35	10.4	41 8.9					35 10.6	36 10.1
	41	9.0	51 7.1					43 8.4	46 7.9
	59	6.2	62 5.9					55 6.7	55 6.6
Cost of Sales/Inventory	42	8.7	48 7.6					33 11.1	28 13.0
	73	5.0	64 5.7					55 6.6	49 7.4
	117	3.1	95 3.8					84 4.3	70 5.2
Cost of Sales/Payables	13	27.4	11 34.1					16 23.0	14 26.4
	29	12.7	22 16.7					28 12.9	24 15.2
	44	8.2	47 7.8					41 8.8	45 8.1
Sales/Working Capital		5.3	3.8					5.5	6.2
		6.9	7.2					8.3	8.8
		-55.9	11.3					14.8	20.9
EBIT/Interest		7.3	21.9					15.5	10.9
		1.9	(10) 5.5					(31) 7.3	(34) 4.1
		1.1	1.1					2.2	2.1
Net Profit + Depr., Dep., Amort./Cur. Mat. L /T/D								(11) 10.8	(12) 3.6
								3.2	2.3
								1.9	2.0
Fixed/Worth		.2	.3					.5	.5
		.8	.6					1.0	.9
		-.2	1.1					1.6	1.6
Debt/Worth		.7	.2					.5	.5
		1.4	1.0					1.4	1.3
		-10.6	2.8					4.1	2.8
% Profit Before Taxes/Tangible Net Worth			47.0					52.7	43.7
		(10)	11.5					(31) 32.4	23.1
			.2					14.5	10.2
% Profit Before Taxes/Total Assets		5.6	16.3					26.1	19.1
		2.5	9.8					13.9	8.3
		.2	.1					5.0	4.5
Sales/Net Fixed Assets		28.7	13.0					11.5	10.0
		7.4	8.6					6.7	6.1
		4.6	2.5					3.9	4.6
Sales/Total Assets		2.5	2.6					2.6	2.5
		2.0	1.9					2.0	2.1
		1.4	1.3					1.7	1.8
% Depr., Dep., Amort./Sales		1.8	2.3					2.1	2.4
	(10)	4.2	(10) 3.7					(28) 2.8	(32) 3.3
		5.6	4.7					4.9	5.0
% Officers', Directors', Owners' Comp/Sales								2.7	3.2
								(16) 4.1	(18) 5.9
								5.2	9.8
Net Sales ($)	2469M	25265M	92193M	65002M	97146M			271183M	329336M
Total Assets ($)	681M	12605M	43359M	57796M	73151M			129328M	168926M

M = $ thousand   MM = $ million
See Pages 11 through 18 for Explanation of Ratios and Data

Comparative Historical Data

Current Data Sorted By Sales

4/1/00-3/31/01	4/1/01-3/31/02	4/1/02-3/31/03	Type of Statement	0-1MM	1-3MM	3-5MM	5-10MM	10-25MM	25MM & OVER
3	3	2	Unqualified					1	1
12	13	9	Reviewed		2	4	1	2	
8	8	9	Compiled	1	3	2	3		
2		1	Tax Returns		1				
11	6	8	Other		3	2		2	1
ALL	ALL	ALL		7 (4/1-9/30/02)			22 (10/1/02-3/31/03)		
36	30	29	NUMBER OF STATEMENTS	1	9	8	4	5	2
%	%	%	ASSETS	%	%	%	%	%	%
5.2	6.2	8.0	Cash & Equivalents						
26.7	24.8	23.7	Trade Receivables (net)						
19.9	18.7	23.5	Inventory						
.9	2.5	3.6	All Other Current						
52.6	52.1	58.8	Total Current						
40.0	38.3	32.8	Fixed Assets (net)						
4.2	4.6	3.6	Intangibles (net)						
3.1	4.9	4.8	All Other Non-Current						
100.0	100.0	100.0	Total						
			LIABILITIES						
9.8	8.3	11.6	Notes Payable-Short Term						
4.8	4.7	4.1	Cur. Mat.-L/T/D						
13.4	10.3	10.4	Trade Payables						
.2	.2	.1	Income Taxes Payable						
9.8	11.4	14.9	All Other Current						
38.1	34.8	41.0	Total Current						
19.6	17.7	15.6	Long Term Debt						
.4	.9	.5	Deferred Taxes						
8.8	10.3	8.9	All Other Non-Current						
33.0	36.3	33.9	Net Worth						
100.0	100.0	100.0	Total Liabilities & Net Worth						
			INCOME DATA						
100.0	100.0	100.0	Net Sales						
27.6	27.6	34.2	Gross Profit						
22.3	25.0	27.2	Operating Expenses						
5.3	2.6	6.9	Operating Profit						
2.3	1.5	1.4	All Other Expenses (net)						
3.0	1.1	5.5	Profit Before Taxes						
			RATIOS						
2.2 1.6 1.1	3.6 1.5 1.2	3.3 1.7 1.2	Current						
1.3 .9 .6	1.8 .9 .6	1.4 1.0 .6	Quick						
(39) 9.3 (50) 7.3 (59) 6.2	(38) 9.6 (48) 7.6 (58) 6.3	(37) 9.7 (44) 8.3 (56) 6.6	Sales/Receivables						
(35) 10.5 (47) 7.8 (72) 5.0	(31) 11.7 (49) 7.5 (61) 6.0	(45) 8.1 (64) 5.7 (100) 3.6	Cost of Sales/Inventory						
(19) 19.6 (36) 10.2 (47) 7.8	(11) 33.6 (22) 16.5 (35) 10.3	(12) 30.5 (25) 14.5 (44) 8.3	Cost of Sales/Payables						
7.0 10.2 29.5	5.4 11.8 32.8	5.2 7.2 22.8	Sales/Working Capital						
(34) 5.2 2.0 1.2	(28) 4.0 1.3 -.4	(28) 8.0 2.5 1.1	EBIT/Interest						
(11) 4.9 2.0 1.6			Net Profit + Depr., Dep., Amort./Cur. Mat. L/T/D						
.6 1.0 1.8	.5 1.0 1.5	.4 .8 1.6	Fixed/Worth						
.7 1.4 4.3	.5 1.0 3.3	.5 1.0 3.0	Debt/Worth						
(31) 28.8 10.2 1.7	(27) 15.1 4.4 -2.8	(24) 25.0 5.4 .2	% Profit Before Taxes/Tangible Net Worth						
10.9 3.9 .6	7.2 1.2 -3.3	11.4 3.4 .1	% Profit Before Taxes/Total Assets						
9.0 5.2 2.7	8.5 6.4 2.4	13.5 7.3 2.6	Sales/Net Fixed Assets						
2.5 2.0 1.4	2.3 1.8 1.2	2.5 1.9 1.3	Sales/Total Assets						
(32) 2.4 3.8 5.9	(29) 2.6 3.9 6.6	(27) 2.3 4.4 5.2	% Depr., Dep., Amort./Sales						
(19) 2.7 5.9 8.4	(11) 2.2 2.8 7.4	(16) 3.0 6.2 12.7	% Officers', Directors', Owners' Comp/Sales						
464139M	251752M	282075M	Net Sales ($)	720M	15346M	32702M	27129M	78740M	127438M
319082M	153624M	187592M	Total Assets ($)	890M	8866M	17592M	18730M	51223M	90291M

© RMA 2003

M = $ thousand   MM = $ million
See Pages 11 through 18 for Explanation of Ratios and Data

Current Data Sorted By Assets   Comparative Historical Data

Type of Statement

0-500M	500M-2MM	2-10MM	10-50MM	50-100MM	100-250MM	Type of Statement	4/1/98-3/31/99	4/1/99-3/31/00
	1	10	18	6	2	Unqualified	42	55
3	12	33	6			Reviewed	59	50
3	10	9	3			Compiled	30	37
6	9	4				Tax Returns	18	21
7	16	25	18	2	2	Other	47	64
46 (4/1-9/30/02)			159 (10/1/02-3/31/03)				ALL	ALL
19	48	81	45	8	4	NUMBER OF STATEMENTS	196	227

ASSETS

0-500M %	500M-2MM %	2-10MM %	10-50MM %	50-100MM %	100-250MM %	ASSETS	%	%
8.4	6.2	6.9	7.4			Cash & Equivalents	6.8	6.2
30.8	30.6	24.0	21.0			Trade Receivables (net)	26.1	27.3
16.6	27.6	27.1	24.5			Inventory	24.9	25.0
2.6	1.3	3.2	2.5			All Other Current	1.6	2.0
58.4	65.7	61.1	55.4			Total Current	59.5	60.4
34.0	27.9	30.0	32.9			Fixed Assets (net)	31.7	30.6
4.2	1.7	4.7	4.9			Intangibles (net)	3.5	4.1
3.4	4.7	4.2	6.8			All Other Non-Current	5.4	4.8
100.0	100.0	100.0	100.0			Total	100.0	100.0

LIABILITIES

0-500M	500M-2MM	2-10MM	10-50MM	50-100MM	100-250MM	LIABILITIES	Hist1	Hist2
7.9	12.8	11.9	9.8			Notes Payable-Short Term	15.5	13.3
5.9	3.7	4.4	3.4			Cur. Mat.-L/T/D	4.1	3.8
16.7	18.9	14.0	9.9			Trade Payables	15.2	14.9
1.1	.3	.2	.1			Income Taxes Payable	.5	.3
11.6	8.8	7.8	7.3			All Other Current	8.5	9.1
43.1	44.6	38.2	30.4			Total Current	43.9	41.4
29.3	18.6	16.2	14.0			Long Term Debt	16.2	16.3
.0	.4	.2	.7			Deferred Taxes	.6	.5
.2	1.8	4.3	8.8			All Other Non-Current	5.1	4.8
27.6	34.6	41.0	46.1			Net Worth	34.2	36.9
100.0	100.0	100.0	100.0			Total Liabilities & Net Worth	100.0	100.0

INCOME DATA

0-500M	500M-2MM	2-10MM	10-50MM	50-100MM	100-250MM	INCOME DATA	Hist1	Hist2
100.0	100.0	100.0	100.0			Net Sales	100.0	100.0
40.4	33.4	24.7	25.0			Gross Profit	27.0	28.4
37.7	30.6	21.0	20.0			Operating Expenses	22.6	22.6
2.7	2.8	3.7	4.9			Operating Profit	4.3	5.8
1.0	1.1	1.7	2.0			All Other Expenses (net)	.9	1.4
1.7	1.7	2.0	2.9			Profit Before Taxes	3.4	4.4

RATIOS

0-500M	500M-2MM	2-10MM	10-50MM	50-100MM	100-250MM	RATIOS	Hist1	Hist2
2.9	2.2	3.0	3.3			Current	2.4	2.5
1.5	1.5	1.6	1.8				1.5	1.6
.9	1.2	1.2	1.3				1.1	1.1
1.7	1.2	1.5	1.8			Quick	1.6	1.4
.8	.9	.9	.9				.9 (226)	.9
.5	.5	.5	.5				.5	.6
19 18.7	33 11.2	32 11.6	39 9.4			Sales/Receivables	33 11.1	37 9.8
31 11.7	43 8.5	43 8.5	49 7.4				44 8.3	48 7.6
44 8.3	59 6.2	54 6.8	58 6.3				54 6.7	57 6.4
2 191.0	27 13.4	46 7.9	44 8.3			Cost of Sales/Inventory	31 11.8	35 10.4
35 10.5	77 4.7	62 5.9	64 5.7				52 7.0	56 6.5
46 8.0	107 3.4	88 4.1	100 3.7				82 4.4	88 4.2
14 25.8	20 18.2	17 21.4	18 20.7			Cost of Sales/Payables	16 22.3	20 18.6
24 15.1	30 12.2	27 13.4	30 12.3				30 12.1	30 12.1
47 7.7	65 5.6	46 7.9	38 9.7				47 7.8	48 7.6
6.5	6.1	4.6	4.0			Sales/Working Capital	6.2	5.1
13.7	11.3	10.0	6.0				11.8	10.6
−55.7	28.1	25.6	18.2				79.4	35.9
35.4	5.9	7.9	12.0			EBIT/Interest	6.5	8.3
(13) 1.9	(46) 2.3	(73) 2.1	(40) 3.2				(179) 3.3	(204) 3.1
−7.8	1.0	1.1	1.2				1.2	1.3
	3.7	3.0	6.5			Net Profit + Depr., Dep., Amort./Cur. Mat. L /T/D	6.5	5.4
	(13) 2.3	(25) 1.7	(20) 2.5				(68) 2.9	(78) 3.0
	.9	.9	.9				1.6	1.4
.3	.3	.4	.3			Fixed/Worth	.4	.4
1.7	.7	.8	.7				.8	.9
−112.0	1.9	1.8	1.7				2.6	2.1
.6	1.1	.5	.3			Debt/Worth	.8	.7
3.0	1.7	1.8	1.4				1.9	1.8
−233.0	4.5	6.5	3.9				6.1	5.9
101.6	34.3	22.4	24.7			% Profit Before Taxes/Tangible Net Worth	48.7	55.0
(14) 35.5	(43) 13.6	(73) 9.7	(40) 9.8				(170) 23.3	(202) 23.5
−3.2	.7	1.0	1.2				8.9	8.1
25.0	9.6	11.0	12.5			% Profit Before Taxes/Total Assets	13.8	17.7
4.5	4.1	3.1	5.5				7.8	7.4
−14.4	.1	.3	.6				1.2	1.4
46.7	27.7	20.9	9.1			Sales/Net Fixed Assets	16.9	17.3
15.5	12.3	7.1	4.7				6.6	7.1
5.7	5.4	4.0	3.3				4.0	3.9
5.7	3.0	2.5	1.8			Sales/Total Assets	2.9	2.6
3.4	2.3	1.9	1.6				2.0	2.0
2.2	1.7	1.4	1.3				1.6	1.5
1.4	1.0	1.2	1.7			% Depr., Dep., Amort./Sales	1.2	1.2
(13) 2.9	(44) 2.4	(74) 2.8	(41) 3.6				(175) 2.4	(218) 2.5
8.0	5.0	4.2	5.1				4.1	4.1
3.7	2.5	2.4	1.3			% Officers', Directors', Owners' Comp/Sales	2.2	2.0
(12) 5.1	(31) 5.0	(29) 3.9	(10) 5.5				(88) 4.3	(81) 4.6
9.2	9.1	6.2	13.8				6.7	8.5
16442M	157021M	807433M	1543157M	625165M	791701M	Net Sales ($)	4776825M	5319835M
4553M	63548M	402414M	980787M	544875M	591097M	Total Assets ($)	2725917M	2905403M

M = $ thousand   MM = $ million
See Pages 11 through 18 for Explanation of Ratios and Data

Comparative Historical Data | Current Data Sorted By Sales

					Type of Statement						
	40		32	37	Unqualified		2	1	2	12	20
	53		47	54	Reviewed	2	6	13	13	16	4
	37		48	25	Compiled	1	9	3	4	7	1
	19		11	19	Tax Returns	5	7	4	2	1	
	57		72	70	Other	5	14	6	18	12	15
	4/1/00-3/31/01 ALL		4/1/01-3/31/02 ALL	4/1/02-3/31/03 ALL			46 (4/1-9/30/02)		159 (10/1/02-3/31/03)		
						0-1MM	1-3MM	3-5MM	5-10MM	10-25MM	25MM & OVER
	206		210	205	NUMBER OF STATEMENTS	13	38	27	39	48	40
	%		%	%	ASSETS	%	%	%	%	%	%
	7.0		7.0	6.9	Cash & Equivalents	8.0	6.4	6.3	5.6	8.0	7.3
	27.5		25.7	25.1	Trade Receivables (net)	26.4	29.5	25.5	26.6	22.3	21.9
	24.0		23.8	25.0	Inventory	20.4	21.6	30.1	26.9	25.5	24.1
	2.4		1.3	2.6	All Other Current	.4	2.6	1.8	3.8	2.4	2.7
	60.9		57.8	59.6	Total Current	55.2	60.1	63.7	63.0	58.2	56.0
	30.2		32.9	31.6	Fixed Assets (net)	37.3	32.3	27.6	27.2	33.1	34.1
	2.6		3.5	4.0	Intangibles (net)	4.6	3.5	4.8	5.1	3.6	3.1
	6.3		5.7	4.9	All Other Non-Current	2.8	4.1	3.8	4.7	5.1	6.8
	100.0		100.0	100.0	Total	100.0	100.0	100.0	100.0	100.0	100.0
					LIABILITIES						
	12.7		11.9	10.8	Notes Payable-Short Term	9.2	11.3	8.9	14.0	11.4	8.1
	3.6		4.5	4.4	Cur. Mat.-L/T/D	2.6	5.9	3.5	4.1	3.9	5.0
	16.0		14.5	14.1	Trade Payables	16.3	14.6	14.0	14.9	15.2	11.0
	.3		.4	.3	Income Taxes Payable	.0	.9	.2	.1	.3	.1
	7.1		7.7	8.3	All Other Current	14.1	8.7	9.1	9.1	5.4	8.4
	39.7		39.0	37.9	Total Current	42.2	41.4	35.7	42.1	36.2	32.6
	17.1		17.2	18.0	Long Term Debt	29.1	25.3	15.5	9.5	19.3	15.9
	.6		.7	.5	Deferred Taxes	.0	.3	.3	.3	.4	1.4
	4.1		5.9	4.3	All Other Non-Current	.5	2.2	.9	5.4	9.0	3.3
	38.5		37.2	39.2	Net Worth	28.4	30.7	47.6	42.7	35.1	46.8
	100.0		100.0	100.0	Total Liabilities & Net Worth	100.0	100.0	100.0	100.0	100.0	100.0
					INCOME DATA						
	100.0		100.0	100.0	Net Sales	100.0	100.0	100.0	100.0	100.0	100.0
	28.7		26.4	28.4	Gross Profit	36.9	34.1	32.5	26.2	24.3	24.6
	23.3		23.7	24.6	Operating Expenses	39.2	31.1	28.7	21.4	20.5	18.8
	5.4		2.7	3.9	Operating Profit	-2.3	3.0	3.7	4.9	3.7	5.9
	1.5		1.6	1.6	All Other Expenses (net)	.9	1.6	1.2	1.6	2.5	1.2
	3.9		1.1	2.2	Profit Before Taxes	-3.2	1.4	2.5	3.3	1.3	4.7
					RATIOS						
	2.8		2.6	2.7		6.1	2.3	3.0	2.4	2.8	3.3
	1.5		1.5	1.6	Current	1.5	1.4	1.8	1.5	1.7	1.7
	1.1		1.1	1.2		.9	1.0	1.4	1.1	1.3	1.2
	1.5		1.5	1.6		2.0	1.5	2.1	1.3	1.6	1.7
	.9		.9	.9	Quick	.8	.9	1.1	.7	.9	.9
	.6		.5	.5		.5	.5	.7	.5	.5	.5
38	9.7	36	10.3	32 11.3		0 UND	31 11.7	32 11.5	35 10.3	30 12.0	39 9.4
47	7.8	43	8.4	43 8.4	Sales/Receivables	31 11.7	44 8.3	41 9.0	49 7.5	41 8.8	50 7.3
57	6.4	54	6.8	55 6.6		42 8.8	70 5.2	51 7.2	54 6.8	52 7.0	57 6.4
34	10.8	32	11.5	35 10.4		2 180.1	20 18.2	43 8.4	30 12.2	44 8.3	36 10.0
54	6.8	55	6.7	60 6.1	Cost of Sales/Inventory	42 8.8	56 6.5	77 4.8	60 6.1	61 6.0	57 6.4
83	4.4	85	4.3	93 3.9		94 3.4	104 3.5	107 3.4	85 4.3	85 4.3	92 4.0
17	21.1	16	22.2	18 20.6		12 30.6	18 20.0	13 27.4	17 21.3	18 19.9	18 19.9
30	12.1	29	12.5	28 12.9	Cost of Sales/Payables	38 9.5	26 13.9	28 13.0	25 14.6	30 12.2	30 12.1
50	7.3	48	7.7	46 8.0		56 6.5	63 5.8	53 6.9	50 7.2	42 8.7	39 9.2
	5.6		6.0	4.7		5.8	4.7	4.2	7.2	4.7	3.9
	10.4		10.9	9.2	Sales/Working Capital	12.1	11.3	7.6	11.7	7.1	7.3
	34.8		49.4	27.8		UND	-213.3	15.1	28.0	24.0	27.0
	7.0		4.6	6.8		5.1	8.1	16.0	4.9	10.3	
(177)	2.7	(190)	1.9	(183) 2.3	EBIT/Interest	(33) 1.9	(25) 3.3	(37) 2.1	(46) 1.8	(34) 3.9	
	1.2		-.2	1.0		.6	1.9	1.1	1.0	1.5	
	6.0		4.6	3.6			3.4		4.6	11.4	
(71)	2.3	(66)	1.4	(66) 2.3	Net Profit + Depr., Dep., Amort./Cur. Mat. L/T/D	(11) 1.7	(20) 2.2	(18) 2.5		
	1.4		.6	1.0		1.1	.8	1.6		
	.3		.4	.4		.5	.3	.2	.4	.4	.3
	.8		1.0	.8	Fixed/Worth	1.7	1.5	.6	.6	.9	.8
	2.0		2.3	2.1		UND	11.5	1.0	1.2	4.1	1.7
	.6		.7	.6		1.1	1.1	.6	.6	.5	.5
	2.0		1.9	1.7	Debt/Worth	3.0	2.5	1.1	1.6	2.2	1.5
	4.5		4.7	4.9		UND	31.7	2.6	3.9	8.7	2.4
	43.1		28.4	28.5		70.5	53.6	21.9	35.2	21.4	29.0
(187)	16.3	(185)	8.0	(182) 10.8	% Profit Before Taxes/Tangible Net Worth	(10) 4.7	(31) 7.5	(24) 13.3	(37) 10.8	(41) 7.3	(39) 15.2
	4.3		-7.0	.6		-29.4	-1.1	2.5	.9	.1	7.3
	15.2		9.1	11.3		14.1	8.7	11.8	15.4	10.5	12.7
	5.5		3.1	4.1	% Profit Before Taxes/Total Assets	.0	2.5	6.4	4.1	2.2	6.8
	.9		-3.3	.1		-26.3	-1.3	2.2	.1	.0	2.6
	18.2		14.3	20.4		50.4	24.4	38.8	21.0	15.0	9.8
	6.8		5.9	6.9	Sales/Net Fixed Assets	8.0	8.5	12.3	7.1	7.0	4.4
	3.8		3.5	3.7		4.2	3.2	4.1	4.3	3.4	3.3
	2.7		2.7	2.6		4.7	3.0	2.5	2.8	2.6	2.0
	2.1		2.0	1.9	Sales/Total Assets	2.7	2.0	2.3	1.9	1.9	1.7
	1.5		1.3	1.4		1.8	1.2	1.4	1.5	1.3	1.3
	1.2		1.1	1.3			2.3	.9	1.2	1.0	1.9
(190)	2.1	(189)	2.7	(179) 2.9	% Depr., Dep., Amort./Sales	(31) 3.4	(26) 1.7	(35) 2.5	(44) 2.4	(34) 3.5	
	3.7		4.4	4.9		6.2	5.2	3.9	4.2	5.0	
	2.3		2.5	2.5			2.8	3.9	2.3	1.2	
(84)	4.0	(80)	4.4	(82) 4.6	% Officers', Directors', Owners' Comp/Sales	(25) 4.5	(15) 5.6	(18) 3.8	(13) 3.1	
	7.8		8.2	9.1		8.2	11.4	6.9	7.3	
	5105111M		5050480M	3940919M	Net Sales ($)	6764M	74783M	112650M	278613M	808019M	2660090M
	3043376M		2980016M	2587274M	Total Assets ($)	2858M	46955M	63353M	156943M	510966M	1806199M

© RMA 2003

M = $ thousand   MM = $ million
See Pages 11 through 18 for Explanation of Ratios and Data

Current Data Sorted By Assets   Comparative Historical Data

						Type of Statement		
	3	24	20	3	1	Unqualified	63	64
3	41	75	10	1		Reviewed	200	198
30	93	42	2			Compiled	257	226
25	43	12	2	1		Tax Returns	64	55
12	60	60	16	4	2	Other	183	186
	122 (4/1-9/30/02)		463 (10/1/02-3/31/03)				4/1/98-3/31/99	4/1/99-3/31/00
0-500M	500M-2MM	2-10MM	10-50MM	50-100MM	100-250MM		ALL	ALL
70	240	213	50	9	3	NUMBER OF STATEMENTS	767	729
%	%	%	%	%	%	ASSETS	%	%
8.7	9.4	6.1	9.8			Cash & Equivalents	8.4	8.7
23.7	25.5	22.3	18.0			Trade Receivables (net)	25.2	25.6
8.5	18.1	20.2	17.7			Inventory	16.4	16.9
2.7	2.0	3.0	3.1			All Other Current	1.8	1.9
43.6	55.0	51.5	48.6			Total Current	51.8	53.2
48.1	38.3	39.0	41.5			Fixed Assets (net)	40.5	38.6
4.0	1.9	2.5	4.7			Intangibles (net)	2.5	3.1
4.4	4.7	7.0	5.2			All Other Non-Current	5.2	5.2
100.0	100.0	100.0	100.0			Total	100.0	100.0
						LIABILITIES		
16.9	10.5	10.0	9.0			Notes Payable-Short Term	8.8	9.3
15.0	7.0	6.4	5.3			Cur. Mat.-L/T/D	6.6	6.3
14.7	11.5	10.2	9.9			Trade Payables	11.0	11.7
.2	.2	.4	.1			Income Taxes Payable	.4	.2
9.1	7.6	7.2	9.2			All Other Current	8.6	8.3
55.8	36.8	34.1	33.5			Total Current	35.4	35.9
39.7	25.1	21.8	22.7			Long Term Debt	23.5	22.6
.3	.5	.9	1.2			Deferred Taxes	.6	.6
7.9	5.1	5.0	7.7			All Other Non-Current	3.7	4.6
-3.7	32.6	38.2	34.8			Net Worth	36.9	36.3
100.0	100.0	100.0	100.0			Total Liabilities & Net Worth	100.0	100.0
						INCOME DATA		
100.0	100.0	100.0	100.0			Net Sales	100.0	100.0
49.7	35.7	27.1	23.7			Gross Profit	34.5	32.5
48.3	33.9	24.7	19.2			Operating Expenses	28.2	27.8
1.5	1.8	2.4	4.5			Operating Profit	6.3	4.8
2.0	2.0	1.9	2.0			All Other Expenses (net)	1.5	1.6
-.5	-.3	.5	2.5			Profit Before Taxes	4.8	3.1
						RATIOS		
1.6	3.2	2.5	2.1				2.6	2.7
1.1	1.6	1.4	1.4			Current	1.5	1.5
.7	1.1	1.1	1.0				1.0	1.0
1.3	2.1	1.3	1.2				1.7	1.9
.8	.9	.8	.8			Quick	1.0	1.0
.4	.5	.5	.5				.6	.6

6	65.2	33	11.2	35	10.3	28	12.8				Sales/Receivables	30	12.2	33	11.0
31	11.8	45	8.0	49	7.5	43	8.4					42	8.6	45	8.1
45	8.1	57	6.4	61	6.0	60	6.1					56	6.5	59	6.2
0	UND	12	31.6	28	13.1	28	13.0				Cost of Sales/Inventory	13	28.9	13	27.1
4	92.9	37	9.9	55	6.6	45	8.1					35	10.3	36	10.1
21	17.5	77	4.8	97	3.7	80	4.6					66	5.5	70	5.2
5	67.5	11	31.9	16	22.7	18	20.6				Cost of Sales/Payables	12	29.9	13	27.5
24	15.3	25	14.6	26	14.1	27	13.5					23	16.1	26	14.3
39	9.4	47	7.8	41	8.9	40	9.2					39	9.4	41	8.8

17.8		5.8		5.3		5.4		Sales/Working Capital	6.2	5.9
103.6		11.0		11.4		12.1			11.7	11.6
-22.2		73.3		55.7		102.7			174.2	89.0

	4.7		4.3		3.6		7.1		EBIT/Interest		8.1		6.5
(63)	1.5	(223)	1.6	(201)	1.7	(49)	2.2		(715)	3.2	(671)	2.6
	-.9		-1.1		-.4		.6			1.4		.9

			2.3		3.5		4.8		Net Profit + Depr., Dep., Amort./Cur. Mat. L /T/D		4.7		3.5
		(57)	1.4	(69)	1.5	(18)	1.9		(270)	2.4	(233)	1.7
			.5		.8		.7			1.4		1.0

.9		.5		.5		.7		Fixed/Worth	.6	.5
2.5		1.1		1.1		1.3			1.1	1.1
-4.8		4.0		2.4		3.5			2.6	2.9
1.0		.6		.7		.9		Debt/Worth	.7	.7
5.0		1.9		1.8		1.7			1.7	1.8
-9.0		7.2		4.6		5.4			4.1	4.7

	44.1		28.3		28.0		29.4		% Profit Before Taxes/Tangible Net Worth		46.4		37.7
(47)	16.0	(200)	6.6	(194)	7.8	(43)	11.5		(682)	24.2	(640)	16.2
	-26.7		-8.2		-8.1		-3.6			7.2		1.9

15.5		9.3		7.4		10.6		% Profit Before Taxes/Total Assets	17.0	13.3
4.1		2.0		2.7		3.4			7.7	5.4
-14.2		-7.6		-3.8		-1.0			1.8	-.3
18.3		11.7		8.0		5.9		Sales/Net Fixed Assets	10.0	10.3
7.5		5.6		3.9		3.6			5.3	5.2
3.6		3.0		2.5		2.3			3.2	3.2
5.5		2.6		2.1		2.1		Sales/Total Assets	2.7	2.5
3.1		1.9		1.5		1.5			2.0	1.9
2.1		1.4		1.2		1.0			1.5	1.4

	2.4		2.6		2.7		3.0		% Depr., Dep., Amort./Sales		2.3		2.5
(63)	4.2	(229)	5.0	(207)	4.9	(48)	5.3		(717)	4.0	(679)	4.4
	6.5		8.2		7.8		8.0			6.3		6.6

	6.0		3.7		1.8		1.0		% Officers', Directors', Owners' Comp/Sales		3.1		3.4
(51)	10.2	(151)	6.5	(88)	4.0	(16)	2.2		(379)	5.7	(363)	5.9
	15.0		9.8		6.8		4.6			9.2		10.0

74004M	570563M	1528167M	1639433M	1631535M	395085M	Net Sales ($)	7289780M	9577488M
20815M	283389M	947793M	908719M	688456M	428424M	Total Assets ($)	4495469M	4451639M

M = $ thousand   MM = $ million
See Pages 11 through 18 for Explanation of Ratios and Data

Comparative Historical Data | **Current Data Sorted By Sales**

Hist 1	Hist 2	Hist 3	Type of Statement					
59	50	51	Unqualified		2	3	8	22	16
179	142	130	Reviewed	1	41	36	30	17	5
214	223	167	Compiled	18	82	38	21	7	1
72	59	83	Tax Returns	26	34	15	3	3	2
184	196	154	Other	14	48	30	30	20	12

4/1/00-3/31/01 ALL	4/1/01-3/31/02 ALL	4/1/02-3/31/03 ALL		122 (4/1-9/30/02)			463 (10/1/02-3/31/03)		
				0-1MM	1-3MM	3-5MM	5-10MM	10-25MM	25MM & OVER
708	670	585	NUMBER OF STATEMENTS	59	207	122	92	69	36
%	%	%	**ASSETS**	%	%	%	%	%	%
9.1	8.0	8.0	Cash & Equivalents	6.4	10.0	6.7	6.1	8.5	7.8
25.8	23.7	23.3	Trade Receivables (net)	20.4	22.8	24.7	25.7	23.2	19.8
17.1	17.7	17.7	Inventory	10.4	16.7	18.3	22.7	17.6	20.2
2.0	1.8	2.6	All Other Current	.8	2.2	3.3	2.8	3.8	2.5
54.0	51.2	51.5	Total Current	38.0	51.6	53.0	57.4	53.1	50.2
38.1	39.5	39.9	Fixed Assets (net)	51.2	40.7	39.8	34.5	38.4	34.0
2.8	3.3	3.0	Intangibles (net)	3.9	2.8	1.4	2.1	2.7	11.0
5.1	6.0	5.6	All Other Non-Current	7.0	4.9	5.8	6.1	5.7	4.8
100.0	100.0	100.0	Total	100.0	100.0	100.0	100.0	100.0	100.0
			LIABILITIES						
8.6	10.5	10.9	Notes Payable-Short Term	11.9	12.4	9.5	12.2	8.1	6.8
6.7	7.2	7.5	Cur. Mat.-L/T/D	15.4	7.2	7.0	5.9	6.3	4.6
11.7	10.9	11.2	Trade Payables	9.6	11.3	11.4	12.1	10.8	11.4
.3	.2	.3	Income Taxes Payable	.1	.3	.1	.3	.8	.2
8.5	7.5	7.8	All Other Current	8.1	7.7	6.1	8.2	8.4	11.4
35.7	36.3	37.6	Total Current	45.0	38.8	34.1	38.7	34.5	34.3
21.1	24.9	25.6	Long Term Debt	39.1	27.2	25.4	18.9	19.8	22.6
.7	.6	.7	Deferred Taxes	.4	.5	.6	.8	1.2	.7
4.9	5.0	5.6	All Other Non-Current	7.3	5.6	4.7	4.8	3.9	10.3
37.6	33.2	30.5	Net Worth	8.1	27.8	35.1	36.8	40.7	32.1
100.0	100.0	100.0	Total Liabilities & Net Worth	100.0	100.0	100.0	100.0	100.0	100.0
			INCOME DATA						
100.0	100.0	100.0	Net Sales	100.0	100.0	100.0	100.0	100.0	100.0
32.5	31.5	33.2	Gross Profit	53.9	34.7	32.1	27.8	23.6	26.3
27.5	28.6	30.9	Operating Expenses	53.1	32.8	30.3	25.3	19.3	21.8
5.0	2.9	2.3	Operating Profit	.7	1.8	1.8	2.5	4.2	4.4
1.6	2.0	2.0	All Other Expenses (net)	2.6	2.4	1.6	1.8	1.2	1.9
3.4	.9	.3	Profit Before Taxes	-1.9	-.6	.2	.8	3.0	2.6
			RATIOS						
2.6	2.4	2.6	Current	1.6	3.0	2.9	2.4	2.5	2.2
1.5	1.5	1.4		1.1	1.5	1.6	1.4	1.6	1.4
1.1	1.0	1.0		.6	1.0	1.1	1.1	1.2	1.2
1.7	1.5	1.6	Quick	1.3	1.9	1.6	1.3	1.4	1.0
1.0	.9	.8		.8	.9	1.0	.8	.9	.8
.6	.5	.5		.4	.5	.5	.5	.6	.6
33 11.0	30 12.0	31 11.8	Sales/Receivables	17 20.9	31 11.9	35 10.5	36 10.2	31 11.9	32 11.6
45 8.1	43 8.4	45 8.1		39 9.4	43 8.5	50 7.2	47 7.7	45 8.2	46 8.0
59 6.2	57 6.4	58 6.3		56 6.5	56 6.5	60 6.0	60 6.1	55 6.6	57 6.4
13 27.1	15 24.2	14 26.7	Cost of Sales/Inventory	0 UND	11 32.5	23 15.6	26 13.9	25 14.8	20 17.9
36 10.2	40 9.2	40 9.1		3 132.7	32 11.4	46 8.0	53 6.9	43 8.4	44 8.2
73 5.0	78 4.7	79 4.6		43 8.4	79 4.6	81 4.5	93 3.9	74 4.9	82 4.5
14 26.3	13 28.4	14 26.9	Cost of Sales/Payables	10 37.0	11 32.2	14 25.7	14 26.0	16 22.2	18 19.8
25 14.4	25 14.6	26 14.2		30 12.1	24 15.0	26 14.2	25 14.9	25 14.4	31 11.8
41 9.0	41 8.9	42 8.7		72 5.1	41 9.0	45 8.1	40 9.1	39 9.2	41 9.0
5.5	5.5	5.8	Sales/Working Capital	11.8	5.5	5.5	6.0	5.3	5.8
11.1	11.6	12.9		122.7	11.5	10.4	13.2	11.1	12.1
98.1	-131.9	391.1		-10.0	-379.7	61.5	46.8	25.9	47.9
6.3	4.4	4.3	EBIT/Interest	3.2	3.6	4.4	5.7	8.3	6.9
(643) 2.6	(627) 1.6	(548) 1.7		(52) .3	(193) 1.4	(117) 2.0	(86) 2.0	(65) 2.5	(35) 2.6
.9	-.1	-.7		-2.1	-1.3	.0	-.5	.9	.9
3.8	2.9	2.9	Net Profit + Depr., Dep., Amort./Cur. Mat. L/T/D		2.0	2.9	5.4	4.2	4.4
(206) 2.0	(190) 1.5	(156) 1.5			(42) 1.5	(41) 1.3	(30) 2.0	(23) 2.0	(16) 2.1
1.0	.6	.6			.5	.6	.8	1.0	.8
.5	.6	.6	Fixed/Worth	.9	.6	.6	.4	.6	.7
1.1	1.2	1.2		2.3	1.3	1.1	1.0	1.1	1.1
2.6	3.4	3.8		-9.0	6.9	2.1	2.2	2.4	8.6
.7	.9	.7	Debt/Worth	.8	.7	.7	.7	.7	1.1
1.7	2.0	2.0		2.9	2.4	1.9	1.8	1.6	1.8
4.8	6.4	7.1		-18.0	15.7	4.3	5.4	3.9	22.1
45.0	31.5	29.6	% Profit Before Taxes/Tangible Net Worth	40.5	30.7	22.4	32.8	33.1	27.5
(623) 18.3	(566) 9.4	(493) 7.5		(42) .2	(167) 4.8	(110) 7.8	(82) 10.4	(63) 15.0	(29) 8.8
2.5	-9.3	-8.3		-41.6	-11.9	-5.0	-.2	-2.9	-.9
15.4	10.2	9.4	% Profit Before Taxes/Total Assets	12.8	9.8	7.4	8.8	13.3	10.2
5.9	2.3	2.5		.2	1.6	2.8	3.3	3.5	3.9
.1	-4.5	-5.5		-15.5	-8.0	-2.9	-3.5	-.9	-.1
10.3	9.3	10.8	Sales/Net Fixed Assets	10.9	10.9	8.4	14.7	8.6	10.0
5.4	4.8	4.9		3.8	5.0	5.0	6.2	4.0	5.2
3.4	2.9	2.8		2.3	2.8	2.7	3.1	3.0	3.6
2.6	2.4	2.5	Sales/Total Assets	2.7	2.5	2.6	2.5	2.2	2.3
2.0	1.8	1.8		1.8	1.8	1.7	1.9	1.7	1.9
1.5	1.3	1.3		1.3	1.3	1.2	1.3	1.4	1.2
2.1	2.6	2.7	% Depr., Dep., Amort./Sales	3.5	3.1	3.2	1.7	2.2	2.4
(669) 3.8	(621) 4.5	(558) 4.9		(53) 5.8	(197) 5.4	(119) 5.0	(91) 3.5	(64) 4.6	(34) 3.3
6.3	7.0	7.8		10.6	8.7	7.5	7.2	6.7	5.6
3.0	3.1	2.9	% Officers', Directors', Owners' Comp/Sales	7.3	3.4	3.7	1.8	1.0	1.2
(371) 5.7	(346) 5.4	(309) 6.0		(39) 12.8	(129) 7.3	(71) 5.4	(35) 3.4	(25) 2.7	(10) 1.9
9.3	9.5	10.2		15.2	10.6	7.7	6.0	4.5	19.6
7183766M	7051444M	5838787M	Net Sales ($)	40233M	391216M	483517M	624869M	1054141M	3244811M
3922601M	4406821M	3277596M	Total Assets ($)	25824M	239036M	324094M	379197M	674188M	1635257M

M = $ thousand   MM = $ million
See Pages 11 through 18 for Explanation of Ratios and Data

Current Data Sorted By Assets   Comparative Historical Data

0-500M	500M-2MM	2-10MM	10-50MM	50-100MM	100-250MM		4/1/98-3/31/99 ALL	4/1/99-3/31/00 ALL
	50 (4/1-9/30/02)		120 (10/1/02-3/31/03)			**Type of Statement**		
		10	9	1		Unqualified	19	18
2	17	34	6			Reviewed	58	61
4	25	9	1			Compiled	43	49
2	5					Tax Returns	2	4
5	15	13	12			Other	43	47
13	62	66	28	1		**NUMBER OF STATEMENTS**	165	179
%	%	%	%	%	%	**ASSETS**	%	%
8.3	6.6	3.9	2.8			Cash & Equivalents	7.1	7.3
31.7	25.7	19.0	17.4			Trade Receivables (net)	23.9	24.6
20.3	20.5	24.7	17.6			Inventory	22.2	20.5
1.6	1.8	1.3	1.9			All Other Current	1.2	1.2
61.9	54.6	48.9	39.7			Total Current	54.5	53.7
34.2	37.2	40.6	48.0			Fixed Assets (net)	37.3	38.3
1.8	1.5	2.9	7.4			Intangibles (net)	2.7	2.5
2.1	6.7	7.6	4.9			All Other Non-Current	5.5	5.5
100.0	100.0	100.0	100.0			Total	100.0	100.0
						LIABILITIES		
13.2	8.6	11.2	8.2			Notes Payable-Short Term	8.9	7.6
1.5	6.8	7.8	8.7			Cur. Mat.-L/T/D	6.4	6.4
12.2	13.0	10.7	9.1			Trade Payables	12.2	12.2
.0	.1	.3	.1			Income Taxes Payable	.3	.4
4.7	7.8	5.9	7.8			All Other Current	6.2	7.9
31.7	36.4	35.8	33.9			Total Current	33.9	34.4
26.6	21.3	25.5	27.0			Long Term Debt	22.4	21.7
.2	.7	1.0	.9			Deferred Taxes	.9	.9
2.1	4.7	3.8	4.4			All Other Non-Current	4.7	5.6
39.5	36.9	33.8	33.8			Net Worth	38.0	37.3
100.0	100.0	100.0	100.0			Total Liabilities & Net Worth	100.0	100.0
						INCOME DATA		
100.0	100.0	100.0	100.0			Net Sales	100.0	100.0
42.4	30.0	22.4	19.3			Gross Profit	28.3	28.5
46.8	30.2	20.0	15.4			Operating Expenses	22.2	21.9
−4.5	−.3	2.4	3.9			Operating Profit	6.1	6.6
3.1	1.4	2.3	3.7			All Other Expenses (net)	1.5	2.1
−7.6	−1.6	.1	.2			Profit Before Taxes	4.6	4.5
						RATIOS		
4.4	2.7	2.1	1.8			Current	2.5	2.5
2.7	1.5	1.4	1.0				1.6	1.6
1.4	1.1	1.1	.8				1.1	1.1
2.6	1.4	1.0	.8			Quick	1.6	1.5
1.6	.9	.6	.6				.9	.9
.7	.6	.4	.4				.5	.6
35 10.5	38 9.6	34 10.6	38 9.5			Sales/Receivables	34 10.7	36 10.1
45 8.2	44 8.2	42 8.7	48 7.6				42 8.8	46 8.0
60 6.0	59 6.1	55 6.6	57 6.4				51 7.1	56 6.5
0 UND	23 15.8	38 9.6	29 12.8			Cost of Sales/Inventory	31 11.8	29 12.6
15 25.0	47 7.7	63 5.7	57 6.4				54 6.8	50 7.3
54 6.7	80 4.6	113 3.2	80 4.6				83 4.4	82 4.4
10 35.2	13 27.3	15 24.7	16 23.4			Cost of Sales/Payables	15 24.3	18 20.8
20 17.9	29 12.8	25 14.4	28 13.0				30 12.3	27 13.8
34 10.7	51 7.2	37 9.8	38 9.6				41 8.9	41 8.9
5.6	6.0	5.7	6.5			Sales/Working Capital	5.6	5.8
8.1	12.9	12.9	562.4				9.8	10.6
69.0	38.4	86.0	−22.0				30.6	34.6
7.9	3.9	3.2	4.0			EBIT/Interest	7.0	5.6
(11) −1.8	(56) 1.1	(65) 1.9	1.3				(154) 2.7	(173) 2.9
−5.2	−1.5	−.4	−.9				1.7	1.5
	2.9	2.4	2.7			Net Profit + Depr., Dep., Amort./Cur. Mat. L /T/D	3.4	3.9
	(18) 1.2	(28) 1.5	(11) 1.5				(70) 1.7	(57) 1.8
	.1	.9	.6				1.1	.9
.2	.4	.7	1.1			Fixed/Worth	.5	.6
.5	1.0	1.3	1.9				1.0	1.0
NM	2.5	3.1	4.1				2.3	2.1
.4	.6	.9	1.0			Debt/Worth	.8	.9
.8	1.4	1.8	3.0				1.7	1.7
NM	5.8	6.2	7.2				3.8	3.6
37.5	19.1	17.6	17.3			% Profit Before Taxes/Tangible Net Worth	32.3	34.8
(10) 4.8	(52) 2.5	(57) 7.0	(23) 13.6				(146) 16.9	(163) 16.5
−26.3	−11.7	−7.5	−5.3				7.9	5.4
17.3	6.7	5.8	6.8			% Profit Before Taxes/Total Assets	12.9	12.4
−9.0	1.0	2.4	1.7				6.3	5.9
−21.7	−5.7	−5.5	−2.6				2.8	2.0
22.4	14.9	7.0	3.3			Sales/Net Fixed Assets	10.4	9.8
11.1	5.5	3.6	2.5				5.1	5.1
3.3	2.9	2.4	2.0				3.5	3.1
4.1	2.8	2.0	1.7			Sales/Total Assets	2.6	2.4
2.5	1.8	1.5	1.3				1.9	1.9
1.5	1.4	1.2	.9				1.4	1.4
	2.5	3.0	4.6			% Depr., Dep., Amort./Sales	2.4	2.4
	(59) 4.2	(64) 5.5	(27) 5.7				(150) 3.8	(168) 3.7
	9.0	7.6	7.0				5.6	6.2
	3.8	2.0				% Officers', Directors', Owners' Comp/Sales	3.2	3.1
	(42) 5.3	(34) 4.4					(83) 6.0	(96) 6.1
	10.1	6.7					9.8	9.0
8446M	146302M	499999M	656222M	67784M		Net Sales ($)	1734370M	1800469M
3243M	71979M	322524M	521728M	59197M		Total Assets ($)	1101823M	1143727M

D A T A   N O T   A V A I L A B L E

Comparative Historical Data | Current Data Sorted By Sales

			Type of Statement						
20	23	20	Unqualified			2	4	11	3
62	49	59	Reviewed	2	9	14	21	10	3
65	49	39	Compiled	5	21	6	5	2	
7	6	7	Tax Returns	3	4				
44	49	45	Other	8	9	6	11	7	4
4/1/00-3/31/01 ALL	4/1/01-3/31/02 ALL	4/1/02-3/31/03 ALL		50 (4/1-9/30/02)			120 (10/1/02-3/31/03)		
				0-1MM	1-3MM	3-5MM	5-10MM	10-25MM	25MM & OVER
198	176	170	NUMBER OF STATEMENTS	18	43	28	41	30	10
%	%	%	ASSETS	%	%	%	%	%	%
6.6	5.2	5.0	Cash & Equivalents	8.4	5.9	7.9	3.0	1.5	6.0
23.6	22.6	22.2	Trade Receivables (net)	20.3	26.6	22.2	20.2	20.8	18.1
21.2	20.1	21.6	Inventory	20.1	16.9	26.6	25.5	23.0	10.1
1.5	1.6	1.6	All Other Current	2.3	1.7	1.1	1.3	1.6	1.7
52.9	49.5	50.3	Total Current	51.2	51.2	57.7	50.0	47.0	36.0
37.6	41.4	40.2	Fixed Assets (net)	40.9	41.5	34.8	34.5	45.7	56.5
3.5	3.2	3.0	Intangibles (net)	3.6	.7	1.0	7.3	2.8	1.1
6.0	5.9	6.4	All Other Non-Current	4.3	6.6	6.5	8.2	4.6	6.5
100.0	100.0	100.0	Total	100.0	100.0	100.0	100.0	100.0	100.0
			LIABILITIES						
8.7	10.5	9.8	Notes Payable-Short Term	8.1	7.8	9.9	12.4	10.9	8.1
6.8	7.7	7.1	Cur. Mat.-L/T/D	3.6	7.1	7.3	6.6	10.0	6.3
11.4	11.7	11.4	Trade Payables	7.9	11.7	11.9	12.8	10.8	11.0
.3	.2	.2	Income Taxes Payable	.0	.2	.1	.1	.5	.1
7.3	5.7	6.8	All Other Current	5.3	7.0	9.1	5.1	6.8	8.8
34.6	35.8	35.3	Total Current	24.9	33.7	38.2	37.0	39.0	34.4
21.6	22.5	24.3	Long Term Debt	33.3	21.8	19.4	25.2	23.8	31.0
1.0	.9	.8	Deferred Taxes	1.0	.5	.8	.7	.9	2.5
5.1	4.1	4.2	All Other Non-Current	1.3	5.1	1.5	7.1	3.5	2.4
37.8	36.6	35.4	Net Worth	39.6	38.8	40.1	30.0	32.7	29.7
100.0	100.0	100.0	Total Liabilities & Net Worth	100.0	100.0	100.0	100.0	100.0	100.0
			INCOME DATA						
100.0	100.0	100.0	Net Sales	100.0	100.0	100.0	100.0	100.0	100.0
27.3	27.0	26.1	Gross Profit	44.1	30.1	24.8	21.4	21.0	14.6
22.7	24.8	25.0	Operating Expenses	51.7	28.5	23.9	19.2	17.1	11.6
4.6	2.2	1.1	Operating Profit	−7.6	1.6	.9	2.2	3.9	3.0
2.2	2.4	2.2	All Other Expenses (net)	3.4	1.5	1.9	2.0	3.0	2.9
2.4	−.2	−1.1	Profit Before Taxes	−11.1	.0	−1.0	.3	.9	.1
			RATIOS						
2.2	2.3	2.4		5.0	2.8	2.8	1.9	1.8	1.7
1.5	1.4	1.4	Current	2.7	1.6	1.5	1.3	1.1	.9
1.1	1.0	1.0		1.4	1.1	1.1	1.1	1.0	.7
1.4	1.4	1.2		3.0	1.6	1.3	.8	.9	1.3
.8	.8	.7	Quick	1.2	1.0	1.0	.6	.6	.5
.6	.5	.5		.7	.6	.5	.4	.4	.5
33 11.0	34 10.7	37 9.8		35 10.4	38 9.5	38 9.6	29 12.4	36 10.1	41 8.9
45 8.2	44 8.3	43 8.4	Sales/Receivables	46 8.0	50 7.3	40 9.1	41 9.1	48 7.6	51 7.2
55 6.7	52 7.0	58 6.3		67 5.4	63 5.8	46 7.9	55 6.6	59 6.2	58 6.3
27 13.7	31 11.9	29 12.6		6 62.1	21 17.4	37 9.7	35 10.3	37 9.8	22 16.7
49 7.4	50 7.3	55 6.6	Cost of Sales/Inventory	39 9.3	40 9.1	70 5.2	63 5.8	65 5.7	27 13.3
83 4.4	77 4.8	89 4.1		148 2.5	68 5.3	121 4.0	103 3.5	79 4.6	52 7.0
15 24.0	15 25.1	15 24.9		9 42.3	12 30.8	14 25.8	15 24.6	22 16.3	15 24.4
23 15.6	27 13.4	26 14.1	Cost of Sales/Payables	17 20.9	25 14.7	25 14.6	28 12.9	33 11.1	29 12.7
38 9.6	39 9.3	40 9.1		43 8.4	49 7.4	36 10.0	41 9.0	39 9.4	46 8.0
5.9	6.7	5.9		3.0	6.1	4.7	6.0	8.8	11.2
11.6	13.7	13.6	Sales/Working Capital	7.9	12.9	12.8	16.8	33.4	−39.3
49.8	140.8	205.4		42.4	41.8	32.1	46.6	−62.3	−9.3
	4.8		3.0		3.7		6.5		3.9		4.6		2.6		3.6		4.2
(180) 2.3	(168) 1.5	(161) 1.4	EBIT/Interest	(15) −1.7	(39) 1.2	(26) 1.4	1.3	2.1	2.3
1.2	−.2	−1.0		−4.9	−.7	−.9	−.4	.7	−1.4
2.7	2.5	2.4	Net Profit + Depr., Dep.,		2.7	2.5	2.6	2.4	
(51) 1.4	(56) 1.3	(58) 1.4	Amort./Cur. Mat. L/T/D		(10) 1.4	(13) 1.4	(16) 1.5	(11) 1.5	
.4	.6	.7			.6	.6	.4	.8	
.5	.6	.6		.3	.5	.4	.8	1.1	1.3
1.1	1.2	1.2	Fixed/Worth	.8	1.0	.9	1.4	1.4	1.9
2.2	2.6	3.0		−10.2	2.0	2.1	56.4	2.8	3.8
.8	.8	.8		.2	.6	.8	.9	1.0	1.2
1.7	1.7	1.6	Debt/Worth	.7	1.2	1.5	3.1	2.1	2.2
3.9	4.9	5.8		−13.7	3.2	3.8	118.2	5.1	5.5
29.3	21.6	19.9		31.5	18.3	12.7	16.7	29.4	
(173) 16.1	(155) 6.4	(143) 5.4	% Profit Before Taxes/Tangible Net Worth	(13) −.6	(37) 3.0	(26) 4.5	(33) 5.4	(25) 14.8	
4.0	−15.0	−8.8		−27.5	−10.9	−12.5	−11.1	4.1	
11.8	8.0	6.6		7.4	7.1	6.5	3.9	9.2	6.6
5.0	1.9	1.5	% Profit Before Taxes/Total Assets	−16.1	1.2	1.7	.7	3.3	1.5
.7	−5.5	−5.9		−22.3	−6.9	−5.6	−4.8	−1.3	−6.1
10.0	8.1	9.2		12.3	13.0	15.9	10.5	5.4	3.0
5.3	4.4	3.7	Sales/Net Fixed Assets	3.3	4.3	6.0	6.2	3.4	2.6
3.3	2.7	2.5		1.7	2.7	3.0	2.4	2.5	1.7
2.5	2.5	2.2		2.0	2.4	2.6	2.5	1.9	1.7
1.9	1.8	1.6	Sales/Total Assets	1.4	1.7	1.8	1.6	1.6	1.3
1.4	1.3	1.2		.8	1.4	1.3	1.1	1.2	1.1
2.1	2.6	2.9		4.5	3.4	2.2	1.9	3.5	
(182) 3.9	(167) 4.6	(159) 5.1	% Depr., Dep., Amort./Sales	(12) 9.0	(40) 4.9	4.3	(40) 5.1	5.1	
5.9	6.8	7.6		24.0	8.6	7.6	7.5	6.4	
3.4	2.7	2.8		6.4	3.6	3.8	2.1	1.1	
(114) 5.8	(88) 5.0	(91) 5.2	% Officers', Directors', Owners' Comp/Sales	(11) 7.5	(31) 5.4	(18) 5.4	(18) 4.8	(11) 2.8	
9.1	8.5	8.7		14.7	10.4	7.5	8.4	3.7	
1840795M	1703405M	1378753M	Net Sales ($)	10788M	83963M	110187M	277651M	502113M	394051M
1225276M	1098324M	978671M	Total Assets ($)	9760M	49086M	68380M	199481M	335716M	316248M

M = $ thousand   MM = $ million
See Pages 11 through 18 for Explanation of Ratios and Data

Current Data Sorted By Assets   **Comparative Historical Data**

0-500M	500M-2MM	2-10MM	10-50MM	50-100MM	100-250MM	Type of Statement	4/1/98-3/31/99 ALL	4/1/99-3/31/00 ALL
	1	2	15	2	4	Unqualified	17	25
	7	25	6			Reviewed	37	32
1	9	5	3			Compiled	12	9
	2	1				Tax Returns	1	
1	5	9	8	3	2	Other	28	18
	29 (4/1-9/30/02)		82 (10/1/02-3/31/03)					
2	24	42	32	5	6	**NUMBER OF STATEMENTS**	95	84
%	%	%	%	%	%	**ASSETS**	%	%
	8.5	5.2	9.3			Cash & Equivalents	6.1	6.1
	30.5	21.8	18.2			Trade Receivables (net)	25.0	25.8
	29.7	30.0	29.7			Inventory	30.9	29.2
	.8	2.3	1.6			All Other Current	1.2	1.2
	69.5	59.4	58.7			Total Current	63.3	62.3
	24.4	32.5	31.4			Fixed Assets (net)	30.4	29.4
	1.0	3.1	4.3			Intangibles (net)	2.4	3.5
	5.1	5.0	5.6			All Other Non-Current	4.0	4.8
	100.0	100.0	100.0			Total	100.0	100.0
						LIABILITIES		
	13.3	13.2	10.5			Notes Payable-Short Term	12.5	14.6
	5.4	5.9	4.6			Cur. Mat.-L/T/D	5.6	3.7
	14.0	13.0	10.7			Trade Payables	16.1	14.5
	.0	.5	.1			Income Taxes Payable	.4	.3
	6.2	9.7	4.6			All Other Current	6.7	6.4
	38.9	42.4	30.5			Total Current	41.4	39.4
	14.9	14.0	9.0			Long Term Debt	19.0	15.8
	.3	.9	1.0			Deferred Taxes	.7	.9
	5.9	5.8	2.3			All Other Non-Current	3.7	4.5
	40.0	36.8	57.2			Net Worth	35.2	39.3
	100.0	100.0	100.0			Total Liabilities & Net Worth	100.0	100.0
						INCOME DATA		
	100.0	100.0	100.0			Net Sales	100.0	100.0
	27.8	24.4	27.8			Gross Profit	29.3	25.7
	26.2	22.7	22.2			Operating Expenses	23.2	20.9
	1.6	1.7	5.6			Operating Profit	6.0	4.8
	.3	1.9	.9			All Other Expenses (net)	1.9	.8
	1.3	-.2	4.7			Profit Before Taxes	4.2	4.0
						RATIOS		
	5.0	2.1	4.3			Current	2.3	2.6
	1.6	1.4	1.9				1.6	1.6
	1.3	1.0	1.2				1.2	1.3
	2.8	1.1	2.7			Quick	1.1	1.2
	1.0	.5	.8				.7	.8
	.7	.4	.5				.5	.6
	36 10.2	37 9.8	37 9.8			Sales/Receivables	35 10.5	40 9.1
	47 7.8	41 8.9	42 8.6				45 8.1	48 7.6
	55 6.6	51 7.1	52 7.1				53 6.9	54 6.8
	43 8.6	60 6.1	58 6.3			Cost of Sales/Inventory	45 8.2	40 9.2
	60 6.1	76 4.8	97 3.7				72 5.1	73 5.0
	92 4.0	104 3.5	142 2.6				104 3.5	110 3.3
	9 41.8	20 18.7	18 20.2			Cost of Sales/Payables	26 13.9	23 16.1
	26 13.9	28 13.0	28 12.8				36 10.1	33 10.9
	55 6.7	46 8.0	46 8.0				51 7.2	45 8.1
	5.1	5.7	2.6			Sales/Working Capital	5.8	4.9
	9.2	11.8	5.8				9.2	8.6
	16.7	-768.1	17.7				24.4	14.5
	6.2	4.9	11.2			EBIT/Interest	7.1	6.9
	(19) .6	(38) 1.6	(28) 4.9				(92) 3.4	(75) 3.1
	-.8	-1.1	2.7				1.6	1.5
		2.3	6.2			Net Profit + Depr., Dep., Amort./Cur. Mat. L /T/D	4.9	5.7
		(19) 1.5	(10) 2.9				(43) 2.3	(37) 2.7
		.6	2.4				1.5	1.9
	.2	.4	.4			Fixed/Worth	.4	.4
	.5	.8	.6				.9	.8
	2.1	3.5	1.1				2.2	1.5
	.3	.8	.3			Debt/Worth	.9	.7
	1.2	1.9	.7				1.9	1.7
	5.1	4.3	2.2				4.7	3.0
	42.2	14.1	30.2			% Profit Before Taxes/Tangible Net Worth	46.7	33.1
	(20) 1.1	(36) 6.4	17.3				(85) 21.8	(77) 19.7
	-15.1	-7.5	5.8				11.7	7.0
	11.0	6.0	12.1			% Profit Before Taxes/Total Assets	13.6	14.3
	-.7	1.5	8.4				7.3	7.2
	-5.1	-4.3	3.2				2.6	2.3
	38.0	9.4	9.7			Sales/Net Fixed Assets	15.5	15.4
	13.5	6.4	5.5				7.1	6.4
	5.7	4.5	3.3				4.6	4.0
	2.5	2.1	1.9			Sales/Total Assets	2.7	2.4
	2.2	1.8	1.4				2.1	1.8
	2.0	1.5	1.2				1.6	1.5
	1.1	2.0	2.3			% Depr., Dep., Amort./Sales	1.4	1.6
	(21) 2.6	(38) 3.5	4.1				(92) 2.6	(74) 3.2
	4.9	5.7	6.0				3.6	4.2
		2.2				% Officers', Directors', Owners' Comp/Sales	2.2	1.9
		(18) 3.0					(31) 4.6	(24) 3.8
		7.1					7.6	6.6
2296M	78314M	355791M	1000910M	545218M	835661M	Net Sales ($)	1782677M	2710769M
592M	33133M	193001M	641186M	330193M	943737M	Total Assets ($)	1092135M	1730868M

M = $ thousand   MM = $ million
See Pages 11 through 18 for Explanation of Ratios and Data

Comparative Historical Data | **Current Data Sorted By Sales**

4/1/00-3/31/01 ALL	4/1/01-3/31/02 ALL	4/1/02-3/31/03 ALL	Type of Statement	0-1MM	1-3MM	3-5MM	5-10MM	10-25MM	25MM & OVER
18	19	24	Unqualified			1	2	6	15
32	29	38	Reviewed		6	7	9	13	3
21	15	18	Compiled	1	4	5	3	5	
4	2	3	Tax Returns		1		2		
24	19	28	Other		4	3	5	7	9
					29 (4/1-9/30/02)		82 (10/1/02-3/31/03)		
99	84	111	**NUMBER OF STATEMENTS**	1	15	16	21	31	27
%	%	%	**ASSETS**	%	%	%	%	%	%
5.8	6.7	7.1	Cash & Equivalents		7.9	4.4	9.7	7.2	6.2
25.8	22.5	22.6	Trade Receivables (net)		28.7	23.9	22.6	21.8	18.7
29.6	27.1	29.1	Inventory		28.0	25.4	29.8	32.3	28.4
1.7	1.3	1.8	All Other Current		1.0	2.0	.6	2.9	1.3
62.9	57.6	60.5	Total Current		65.6	55.7	62.7	64.2	54.6
28.9	33.3	30.2	Fixed Assets (net)		27.4	37.0	28.5	27.3	32.0
2.8	3.7	4.3	Intangibles (net)		2.1	3.7	1.7	4.1	8.0
5.3	5.3	5.0	All Other Non-Current		4.9	3.6	7.0	4.4	5.4
100.0	100.0	100.0	Total		100.0	100.0	100.0	100.0	100.0
			LIABILITIES						
11.2	11.2	11.6	Notes Payable-Short Term		18.5	12.4	9.0	12.6	8.5
4.3	5.6	5.1	Cur. Mat.-L/T/D		5.8	8.0	5.3	4.8	3.5
12.5	12.2	12.2	Trade Payables		12.0	13.8	11.1	12.2	12.0
.2	.1	.2	Income Taxes Payable		.0	.1	.0	.6	.1
7.5	5.5	7.0	All Other Current		3.2	12.0	9.0	6.2	5.7
35.8	34.6	36.1	Total Current		39.5	46.3	34.5	36.5	29.8
13.9	15.7	13.3	Long Term Debt		19.3	18.6	10.3	9.6	12.9
.7	.8	.8	Deferred Taxes		.4	.4	.9	1.2	.8
2.9	2.8	5.0	All Other Non-Current		4.9	4.8	9.7	2.4	4.7
46.7	46.1	44.8	Net Worth		36.0	29.9	44.5	50.2	51.9
100.0	100.0	100.0	Total Liabilities & Net Worth		100.0	100.0	100.0	100.0	100.0
			INCOME DATA						
100.0	100.0	100.0	Net Sales		100.0	100.0	100.0	100.0	100.0
27.9	26.1	26.3	Gross Profit		28.8	21.9	27.2	26.8	25.8
22.2	22.9	23.1	Operating Expenses		28.4	20.6	24.9	23.1	19.9
5.6	3.2	3.2	Operating Profit		.5	1.3	2.3	3.7	6.0
1.1	1.9	1.2	All Other Expenses (net)		1.2	2.5	.7	1.0	.9
4.6	1.3	2.0	Profit Before Taxes		-.7	-1.2	1.5	2.7	5.1
			RATIOS						
2.8 / 1.7 / 1.3	2.6 / 1.6 / 1.3	3.0 / 1.7 / 1.3	Current		5.2 / 1.5 / .9	1.7 / 1.4 / .8	5.1 / 1.6 / 1.3	4.1 / 1.8 / 1.2	2.4 / 2.1 / 1.4
1.5 / .9 / .5	1.5 / .8 / .5	1.4 / .8 / .5	Quick		2.2 / .9 / .5	1.1 / .6 / .4	4.4 / .7 / .5	2.1 / .6 / .4	1.5 / .9 / .6
39 9.4 / 45 8.2 / 52 7.0	38 9.7 / 45 8.1 / 55 6.6	37 9.8 / 43 8.4 / 53 6.6	Sales/Receivables	41 9.0 / 46 8.0 / 55 6.6	37 9.8 / 46 9.3 / 53 6.9	32 11.3 / 39 9.3 / 42 8.6	38 9.6 / 46 8.0 / 56 6.5	38 9.5 / 47 7.8 / 55 6.6	
41 8.9 / 71 5.2 / 105 3.5	48 7.7 / 70 5.2 / 108 3.4	53 6.8 / 77 4.7 / 114 3.2	Cost of Sales/Inventory	48 7.5 / 71 5.1 / 132 2.8	31 11.6 / 61 5.9 / 78 4.7	34 10.9 / 70 5.2 / 97 3.8	63 5.8 / 95 3.9 / 138 2.7	53 6.9 / 81 4.5 / 129 2.8	
17 21.6 / 28 13.1 / 42 8.7	20 18.0 / 30 12.1 / 41 8.8	17 21.1 / 29 12.8 / 46 8.0	Cost of Sales/Payables	6 56.3 / 24 15.1 / 67 5.4	17 21.8 / 29 12.6 / 46 7.9	15 24.6 / 23 16.0 / 43 8.6	19 19.5 / 28 13.1 / 46 7.9	24 15.0 / 31 11.8 / 45 8.2	
4.9 / 8.2 / 17.2	4.7 / 8.9 / 17.8	4.6 / 7.5 / 18.8	Sales/Working Capital		5.4 / 9.5 / -48.8	7.2 / 15.4 / -22.1	4.8 / 10.9 / 15.1	4.1 / 6.3 / 23.8	3.4 / 7.0 / 14.1
(85) 9.2 / 3.4 / 1.6	(78) 4.1 / 1.9 / -.1	(96) 6.2 / 2.6 / .4	EBIT/Interest	(11) 1.6 / .4 / -1.6	5.0 / .8 / -.3	(16) 6.0 / 2.4 / -1.5	(28) 8.0 / 2.8 / -.3	(24) 24.6 / 4.9 / 2.7	
(35) 6.5 / 3.7 / 1.4	(28) 3.2 / 2.0 / .8	(39) 3.0 / 1.9 / 1.1	Net Profit + Depr., Dep., Amort./Cur. Mat. L/T/D					(15) 5.1 / 2.3 / 1.5	(10) 3.5 / 2.1 / 1.1
.4 / .6 / 1.1	.4 / .8 / 1.6	.4 / .7 / 1.9	Fixed/Worth		.1 / .8 / 3.6	.5 / 1.2 / 13.5	.3 / .7 / 2.9	.4 / .5 / 1.2	.6 / .8 / 1.5
.5 / 1.4 / 2.9	.5 / 1.4 / 3.0	.4 / 1.2 / 3.7	Debt/Worth		.5 / 2.2 / 5.5	1.0 / 2.5 / 28.3	.2 / 1.2 / 3.9	.4 / 1.3 / 2.6	.5 / .7 / 4.0
(94) 38.1 / 16.7 / 5.5	(77) 26.3 / 7.9 / -5.6	(99) 23.5 / 8.5 / -4.2	% Profit Before Taxes/Tangible Net Worth	(12) 16.3 / -7.3 / -19.0	(14) 52.8 / 3.2 / -4.4	(17) 19.2 / 12.0 / -1.5	(30) 24.0 / 8.0 / -6.2	(25) 31.5 / 15.9 / 5.3	
15.3 / 7.6 / 1.9	11.0 / 3.8 / -2.2	9.8 / 3.2 / -3.1	% Profit Before Taxes/Total Assets		3.8 / -3.3 / -5.1	7.4 / -.5 / -4.4	11.3 / 4.4 / -5.8	10.5 / 3.2 / -3.4	12.1 / 6.4 / 2.2
12.8 / 7.4 / 4.1	9.2 / 6.1 / 3.0	11.1 / 6.4 / 4.1	Sales/Net Fixed Assets		19.9 / 8.1 / 3.8	9.0 / 5.7 / 4.0	18.0 / 8.0 / 4.7	10.1 / 6.9 / 4.4	7.9 / 4.9 / 3.0
2.5 / 1.9 / 1.5	2.3 / 1.7 / 1.3	2.2 / 1.7 / 1.3	Sales/Total Assets		2.2 / 2.1 / 1.5	2.4 / 1.9 / 1.4	2.8 / 2.0 / 1.6	2.0 / 1.5 / 1.3	2.0 / 1.4 / 1.1
(89) 1.4 / 2.5 / 4.0	(81) 1.6 / 3.2 / 4.8	(101) 1.9 / 3.6 / 5.3	% Depr., Dep., Amort./Sales	(13) 1.4 / 4.3 / 7.8	(15) 2.2 / 4.5 / 6.9	(18) 1.8 / 3.1 / 4.4	(29) 2.0 / 3.5 / 5.3	(25) 2.2 / 3.6 / 5.0	
(33) 3.2 / 5.4 / 7.8	(22) 3.4 / 4.6 / 6.6	(32) 2.5 / 6.1 / 8.2	% Officers', Directors', Owners' Comp/Sales					(11) 2.2 / 3.0 / 7.5	
2548536M / 1611471M	1759116M / 1208607M	2818190M / 2141842M	Net Sales ($) / Total Assets ($)	568M / 295M	31455M / 18087M	60328M / 33188M	141152M / 84283M	483342M / 313140M	2101345M / 1692849M

M = $ thousand   MM = $ million
See Pages 11 through 18 for Explanation of Ratios and Data

Current Data Sorted By Assets   Comparative Historical Data

0-500M	500M-2MM	2-10MM	10-50MM	50-100MM	100-250MM	Type of Statement	4/1/98-3/31/99 ALL	4/1/99-3/31/00 ALL
		7	1			Unqualified	13	15
	11	7	4			Reviewed	21	21
3	5	7	1			Compiled	10	16
3	1	1				Tax Returns	2	
	5	10	1			Other	14	23
	21 (4/1-9/30/02)		**46 (10/1/02-3/31/03)**					
6	22	32	7			NUMBER OF STATEMENTS	60	75
%	%	%	%	%	%	**ASSETS**	%	%
	7.1	4.1	D	D		Cash & Equivalents	7.0	6.7
	28.4	20.2	A	A		Trade Receivables (net)	23.1	22.7
	4.3	5.8	T	T		Inventory	8.2	5.7
	.4	1.6	A	A		All Other Current	1.2	.9
	40.2	31.8				Total Current	39.5	36.0
	45.4	59.1	N	N		Fixed Assets (net)	49.1	53.7
	6.4	2.5	O	O		Intangibles (net)	2.0	4.3
	8.0	6.6	T	T		All Other Non-Current	9.4	6.0
	100.0	100.0				Total	100.0	100.0
			A	A		**LIABILITIES**		
	5.2	9.2	V	V		Notes Payable-Short Term	6.6	8.1
	7.8	7.9	A	A		Cur. Mat.-L/T/D	6.5	6.2
	10.4	8.6	I	I		Trade Payables	9.8	9.3
	.1	.1	L	L		Income Taxes Payable	.3	.1
	9.6	4.0	A	A		All Other Current	5.8	4.8
	33.2	29.9	B	B		Total Current	29.0	28.5
	17.4	31.2	L	L		Long Term Debt	28.3	24.4
	.8	1.7	E	E		Deferred Taxes	1.1	.9
	4.2	1.6				All Other Non-Current	4.1	6.2
	44.5	35.7				Net Worth	37.5	40.1
	100.0	100.0				Total Liabilities & Net Worth	100.0	100.0
						INCOME DATA		
	100.0	100.0				Net Sales	100.0	100.0
	37.4	28.9				Gross Profit	31.1	32.3
	37.4	24.3				Operating Expenses	26.3	25.5
	.0	4.5				Operating Profit	4.8	6.7
	2.0	2.0				All Other Expenses (net)	2.1	1.0
	−2.0	2.6				Profit Before Taxes	2.7	5.7
						RATIOS		
	3.4 1.7 .7	1.8 1.0 .7				Current	2.1 1.4 .9	2.3 1.1 .8
	3.4 1.6 .6	1.2 .7 .5				Quick	1.9 1.0 .7	1.6 .8 .6
	44 8.3 50 7.4 62 5.9	47 7.8 56 6.5 65 5.6				Sales/Receivables	38 9.6 48 7.6 57 6.4	43 8.4 53 6.9 59 6.1
	0 UND 0 UND 11 34.2	0 UND 2 189.0 11 33.1				Cost of Sales/Inventory	0 UND 5 70.3 30 12.3	0 UND 6 57.4 33 11.1
	12 31.5 20 17.9 35 10.4	17 21.9 25 14.5 53 6.9				Cost of Sales/Payables	13 27.4 21 17.2 41 9.0	14 25.3 29 12.5 40 9.2
	6.5 14.4 −15.2	9.7 −96.7 −9.2				Sales/Working Capital	8.7 17.9 −87.2	6.2 53.2 −18.9
	2.5 (17) .4 −3.4	3.7 (28) 1.9 .9				EBIT/Interest	8.0 (53) 3.5 1.6	4.9 (71) 2.9 1.3
		1.8 (11) 1.3 .8				Net Profit + Depr., Dep., Amort./Cur. Mat. L /T/D	5.3 (31) 2.4 1.0	4.0 (29) 1.7 .4
	.6 1.1 5.8	1.4 2.1 4.0				Fixed/Worth	.7 1.2 2.1	.8 1.7 3.6
	.3 1.0 6.9	1.1 2.2 4.5				Debt/Worth	.8 1.4 3.0	.6 1.7 5.6
	13.2 (18) −4.3 −16.9	24.6 (30) 9.9 −2.4				% Profit Before Taxes/Tangible Net Worth	37.9 (53) 21.7 6.4	42.7 (65) 21.1 2.4
	4.4 −3.8 −11.4	7.4 2.9 −.2				% Profit Before Taxes/Total Assets	17.9 7.5 2.1	15.7 6.6 1.3
	11.7 3.6 2.1	3.6 2.1 1.1				Sales/Net Fixed Assets	6.4 3.4 2.0	5.1 2.6 1.6
	2.6 2.0 1.2	2.0 1.2 .8				Sales/Total Assets	2.1 1.6 1.3	2.0 1.5 1.0
	2.6 (21) 5.8 7.9	4.2 (28) 6.8 10.2				% Depr., Dep., Amort./Sales	3.3 (56) 5.1 7.4	3.5 (72) 5.5 7.7
	4.1 (10) 5.7 8.8	1.2 (13) 3.0 5.1				% Officers', Directors', Owners' Comp/Sales	3.3 (24) 4.6 8.8	3.2 (32) 4.5 8.0
3276M	60545M	250231M	111756M			Net Sales ($)	717187M	749154M
1586M	30591M	185359M	112419M			Total Assets ($)	509321M	597319M

© RMA 2003

M = $ thousand MM = $ million
See Pages 11 through 18 for Explanation of Ratios and Data

	Comparative Historical Data			Type of Statement	Current Data Sorted By Sales					
	10	8	8	Unqualified		1	1	4	1	1
	20	16	22	Reviewed		9	4	5	4	
	25	10	16	Compiled	3	5	4	3	1	
	1	1	5	Tax Returns	2	1	2			
	15	23	16	Other		3	1	8	2	2
	4/1/00-3/31/01	4/1/01-3/31/02	4/1/02-3/31/03			21 (4/1-9/30/02)		46 (10/1/02-3/31/03)		
	ALL	ALL	ALL		0-1MM	1-3MM	3-5MM	5-10MM	10-25MM	25MM & OVER
	71	58	67	NUMBER OF STATEMENTS	5	19	12	20	8	3
	%	%	%	ASSETS	%	%	%	%	%	%
	9.8	6.6	5.2	Cash & Equivalents		4.9	4.9	6.6		
	23.8	23.9	22.8	Trade Receivables (net)		21.3	28.2	22.4		
	6.6	4.7	5.7	Inventory		1.6	12.8	4.3		
	1.7	.8	1.2	All Other Current		1.7	.4	2.0		
	41.8	36.0	34.9	Total Current		29.4	46.3	35.3		
	48.4	52.0	53.4	Fixed Assets (net)		57.8	40.0	56.4		
	2.2	4.2	3.5	Intangibles (net)		6.0	5.4	1.9		
	7.6	7.8	8.2	All Other Non-Current		6.8	8.3	6.5		
	100.0	100.0	100.0	Total		100.0	100.0	100.0		
				LIABILITIES						
	7.6	8.6	8.7	Notes Payable-Short Term		6.7	7.6	7.9		
	6.6	7.3	8.8	Cur. Mat.-L/T/D		8.5	6.0	6.7		
	10.3	10.7	10.3	Trade Payables		11.1	14.2	8.3		
	.4	.2	.1	Income Taxes Payable		.1	.3	.0		
	7.3	6.4	5.8	All Other Current		9.5	4.0	4.5		
	32.3	33.2	33.8	Total Current		35.9	32.1	27.4		
	21.0	27.4	26.6	Long Term Debt		24.8	23.5	26.9		
	1.2	.8	1.1	Deferred Taxes		.9	.9	1.6		
	5.0	3.0	3.2	All Other Non-Current		3.2	4.3	1.8		
	40.4	35.7	35.3	Net Worth		35.1	39.1	42.4		
	100.0	100.0	100.0	Total Liabilities & Net Worth		100.0	100.0	100.0		
				INCOME DATA						
	100.0	100.0	100.0	Net Sales		100.0	100.0	100.0		
	29.8	31.4	34.8	Gross Profit		35.6	28.7	32.8		
	25.6	28.2	32.4	Operating Expenses		36.1	29.3	27.8		
	4.1	3.3	2.4	Operating Profit		-.5	-.6	5.0		
	.7	2.2	2.1	All Other Expenses (net)		3.0	-.2	2.4		
	3.4	1.1	.3	Profit Before Taxes		-3.5	-.4	2.6		
				RATIOS						
	2.9	1.8	2.2			2.9	2.2	2.4		
	1.2	1.0	1.0	Current		.7	1.6	1.0		
	.8	.7	.7			.5	.8	.8		
	2.9	1.8	1.9			2.9	1.9	2.3		
	1.0	.9	.8	Quick		.6	.8	1.0		
	.6	.6	.5			.4	.5	.6		
	38 9.7	42 8.7	46 8.0			44 8.3	48 7.5	47 7.8		
	50 7.4	53 6.8	55 6.7	Sales/Receivables		52 7.0	58 6.3	55 6.6		
	56 6.5	62 5.9	63 5.8			63 5.8	67 5.4	62 5.9		
	0 UND	0 UND	0 UND			0 UND	0 UND	0 UND		
	1 292.5	3 141.6	1 281.1	Cost of Sales/Inventory		0 UND	6 56.3	6 66.2		
	11 34.7	12 31.0	11 33.0			3 131.3	33 11.0	26 14.0		
	10 34.8	16 22.2	15 24.1			8 45.2	16 22.4	16 22.3		
	22 16.5	24 15.0	24 15.4	Cost of Sales/Payables		22 16.8	28 13.3	23 16.0		
	39 9.4	40 9.2	52 7.0			50 7.3	60 6.1	52 7.0		
	6.0	8.4	8.1			6.8	6.1	8.2		
	24.6	NM	264.7	Sales/Working Capital		-12.7	10.1	-564.3		
	-27.6	-11.8	-10.1			-5.8	NM	-26.7		
	4.4	4.4	2.8			2.7	2.9	2.3		
(65)	2.2	(53) 1.5	(58) 1.6	EBIT/Interest	(15)	.4	(10) 1.4	(17) 1.6		
	.7	.0	.1			-3.7	-3.8	.8		
	2.9	2.5	2.6	Net Profit + Depr., Dep.,						
(23)	1.6	(26) 1.1	(24) 1.4	Amort./Cur. Mat. L/T/D						
	1.0	-.1	.7							
	.6	1.0	.9			.8	.5	1.0		
	1.4	1.8	2.0	Fixed/Worth		2.5	1.2	1.7		
	3.9	6.6	4.5			7.4	11.7	3.0		
	.6	.9	.9			.4	.8	.8		
	1.7	1.9	1.9	Debt/Worth		2.8	1.7	1.4		
	5.6	10.4	6.4			8.6	15.2	4.0		
	32.5	26.8	23.8	% Profit Before Taxes/Tangible		19.9	21.4	14.4		
(61)	11.5	(47) 7.0	(57) 6.0	Net Worth	(15)	-4.3	(10) -1.7	(19) 6.0		
	.8	-6.2	-4.9			-23.8	-22.5	-1.8		
	10.8	7.6	6.8	% Profit Before Taxes/Total		3.6	6.6	6.6		
	4.0	2.0	2.4	Assets		-3.9	-1.6	2.6		
	-.7	-4.8	-4.3			-11.9	-7.2	-.2		
	7.6	4.9	5.6			3.1	25.2	3.6		
	3.0	2.7	2.3	Sales/Net Fixed Assets		2.1	5.6	2.2		
	1.8	1.5	1.4			1.2	1.2	1.3		
	2.3	2.1	2.2			2.0	2.6	2.1		
	1.7	1.5	1.4	Sales/Total Assets		1.2	1.9	1.2		
	1.0	1.0	1.0			.7	.8	1.0		
	3.1	3.6	3.6			5.4	1.7	3.8		
(70)	5.6	(55) 6.3	(62) 6.6	% Depr., Dep., Amort./Sales	(18)	7.9	(11) 4.4	(17) 7.9		
	8.0	8.9	9.7			16.2	7.4	9.6		
	2.5	2.3	2.8	% Officers', Directors',						
(32)	4.7	(24) 5.1	(28) 4.5	Owners' Comp/Sales						
	7.1	7.5	8.1							
	439762M	413665M	425808M	Net Sales ($)	2225M	37084M	42569M	147018M	102327M	94585M
	297303M	377600M	329955M	Total Assets ($)	1314M	39078M	39780M	118171M	70412M	61200M

M = $ thousand   MM = $ million
See Pages 11 through 18 for Explanation of Ratios and Data

Current Data Sorted By Assets — Comparative Historical Data

Type of Statement	0-500M	500M-2MM	2-10MM	10-50MM	50-100MM	100-250MM	4/1/98-3/31/99 ALL	4/1/99-3/31/00 ALL
Unqualified		2	9	6	1	2	16	21
Reviewed	1	13	16	3			29	38
Compiled	4	12	5				22	20
Tax Returns	4	5	1				1	6
Other		16	13	9	3	2	34	26
		23 (4/1-9/30/02)		104 (10/1/02-3/31/03)				
NUMBER OF STATEMENTS	9	48	44	18	4	4	102	111
ASSETS	%	%	%	%	%	%	%	%
Cash & Equivalents		7.5	7.1	2.9			7.7	6.2
Trade Receivables (net)		29.7	23.8	24.1			29.7	28.9
Inventory		11.1	12.4	13.9			11.4	13.7
All Other Current		2.0	1.6	2.2			3.0	1.6
Total Current		50.3	44.8	43.1			51.9	50.4
Fixed Assets (net)		37.7	44.4	48.9			39.1	37.9
Intangibles (net)		4.4	3.4	3.1			3.4	3.9
All Other Non-Current		7.6	7.4	4.9			5.6	7.8
Total		100.0	100.0	100.0			100.0	100.0
LIABILITIES								
Notes Payable-Short Term		10.8	10.2	12.6			10.9	11.7
Cur. Mat.-L/T/D		4.0	6.7	5.3			4.5	5.1
Trade Payables		10.3	9.9	15.9			14.6	15.1
Income Taxes Payable		.2	.1	.1			.3	.2
All Other Current		9.5	7.7	6.4			10.0	9.1
Total Current		34.8	34.6	40.3			40.2	41.2
Long Term Debt		23.3	27.7	33.9			24.2	29.1
Deferred Taxes		.2	.4	.8			.4	.6
All Other Non-Current		5.1	4.1	4.0			4.4	4.4
Net Worth		36.5	33.1	21.1			30.7	24.6
Total Liabilities & Net Worth		100.0	100.0	100.0			100.0	100.0
INCOME DATA								
Net Sales		100.0	100.0	100.0			100.0	100.0
Gross Profit		35.7	29.6	28.1			32.7	32.9
Operating Expenses		33.8	22.4	18.2			26.1	27.1
Operating Profit		1.9	7.2	9.9			6.6	5.7
All Other Expenses (net)		1.5	2.2	2.1			1.4	1.6
Profit Before Taxes		.4	5.0	7.8			5.2	4.1
RATIOS								
Current		2.6	2.7	2.2			2.2	2.0
		1.4	1.1	1.4			1.4	1.4
		1.0	.8	.9			.9	.9
Quick		2.1	2.0	1.2			1.6	1.6
		1.0	.8	.9			.9	.9
		.6	.5	.5			.6	.5
Sales/Receivables		42 8.7	36 10.3	41 9.0			38 9.7	39 9.3
		53 6.9	43 8.6	44 8.3			47 7.8	48 7.7
		64 5.7	57 6.4	52 7.0			54 6.8	59 6.2
Cost of Sales/Inventory		8 44.4	8 44.5	15 23.7			10 36.1	13 27.2
		22 16.7	24 15.3	43 8.5			18 19.9	23 16.0
		43 8.4	46 7.9	92 4.0			42 8.7	46 8.0
Cost of Sales/Payables		14 25.5	14 25.3	18 20.6			17 21.2	19 19.7
		21 17.1	25 14.9	32 11.4			29 12.4	32 11.4
		33 10.9	36 10.2	48 7.6			39 9.5	47 7.7
Sales/Working Capital		6.5	7.1	6.0			7.6	7.9
		14.8	37.2	13.1			18.9	17.0
		-406.2	-24.6	-29.9			-77.9	-35.5
EBIT/Interest		7.8	7.2	10.6			9.1	10.0
	(45)	1.7	(42) 3.3	4.1			(94) 3.0	(104) 3.1
		-.7	.8	2.3			1.2	1.2
Net Profit + Depr., Dep., Amort./Cur. Mat. L /T/D		2.7	2.6				4.0	6.1
	(10)	1.4	(11) 1.5				(29) 1.9	(29) 3.4
		.2	.4				.9	1.3
Fixed/Worth		.6	.6	1.4			.7	.7
		.9	1.4	2.1			1.2	1.3
		3.2	7.3	4.5			3.8	13.3
Debt/Worth		.5	.9	1.4			.9	.7
		1.9	1.7	2.3			2.0	2.4
		5.2	9.9	7.8			6.4	15.7
% Profit Before Taxes/Tangible Net Worth		44.9	37.8	63.8			42.1	50.9
	(40)	13.0	(39) 19.5	(16) 30.7			(88) 16.2	(87) 24.0
		.1	.1	12.4			.9	7.3
% Profit Before Taxes/Total Assets		12.9	13.8	20.4			18.0	21.1
		3.1	5.4	11.2			7.2	6.8
		-7.6	-.8	3.8			.8	.9
Sales/Net Fixed Assets		12.4	8.0	8.2			11.5	11.7
		5.6	4.0	2.5			6.1	5.8
		3.5	2.0	1.5			2.8	2.9
Sales/Total Assets		2.5	2.3	2.5			2.9	2.7
		2.0	1.7	1.1			2.1	2.1
		1.5	1.1	.9			1.4	1.4
% Depr., Dep., Amort./Sales		2.2	2.0	2.5			1.7	1.8
	(46)	3.5	(43) 3.5	(16) 4.9			(90) 2.6	(106) 3.1
		6.1	5.6	8.1			5.2	4.7
% Officers', Directors', Owners' Comp/Sales		2.3					2.7	2.6
	(29)	4.8					(41) 4.4	(45) 4.0
		8.1					9.1	7.7
Net Sales ($)	6430M	121873M	411756M	899263M	1458508M	840757M	1970413M	1839174M
Total Assets ($)	2003M	58571M	222979M	395201M	281309M	645541M	876917M	879514M

M = $ thousand   MM = $ million
See Pages 11 through 18 for Explanation of Ratios and Data

Comparative Historical Data / Current Data Sorted By Sales

					Type of Statement						
	16		14		20	Unqualified		2	1	2	8	7
	38		29		33	Reviewed	2	4	10	8	9	
	33		24		21	Compiled	4	10	6	1		
	10		7		10	Tax Returns	4	5		1		
	37		49		43	Other	3	13	1	7	7	12
	4/1/00-3/31/01 ALL		4/1/01-3/31/02 ALL		4/1/02-3/31/03 ALL		23 (4/1-9/30/02) 0-1MM	1-3MM	104 (10/1/02-3/31/03) 3-5MM	5-10MM	10-25MM	25MM & OVER
	134		123		127	NUMBER OF STATEMENTS	13	34	18	19	24	19
	%		%		%	ASSETS	%	%	%	%	%	%
	6.8		7.0		6.9	Cash & Equivalents	12.1	6.2	7.8	10.2	5.2	2.3
	31.2		27.7		27.3	Trade Receivables (net)	25.7	25.9	27.6	30.0	23.9	32.5
	12.4		14.8		12.3	Inventory	14.6	8.9	8.7	7.3	17.8	18.6
	1.1		2.9		2.1	All Other Current	3.2	1.7	2.8	1.3	2.2	2.0
	51.5		52.4		48.6	Total Current	55.6	42.6	47.0	48.8	49.1	55.4
	38.2		37.6		41.3	Fixed Assets (net)	36.3	45.3	42.2	40.7	40.9	37.6
	3.6		3.5		3.7	Intangibles (net)	7.3	3.2	3.9	1.2	4.4	3.5
	6.7		6.5		6.4	All Other Non-Current	1.5	8.8	6.9	9.2	5.6	3.4
	100.0		100.0		100.0	Total	100.0	100.0	100.0	100.0	100.0	100.0
					LIABILITIES						
	12.0		12.9		11.6	Notes Payable-Short Term	15.4	7.3	7.1	10.5	12.8	20.6
	5.4		6.0		5.8	Cur. Mat.-L/T/D	2.3	5.9	6.1	8.4	4.2	7.0
	14.8		12.7		11.9	Trade Payables	6.7	10.2	7.6	9.2	13.0	24.0
	.4		.2		.1	Income Taxes Payable	.0	.1	.4	.1	.1	.0
	8.7		8.1		8.5	All Other Current	7.3	9.6	8.2	6.4	8.7	9.5
	41.3		40.0		38.0	Total Current	31.7	33.2	29.5	34.6	38.8	61.2
	26.6		24.9		27.3	Long Term Debt	43.9	30.9	17.5	27.3	19.9	28.1
	.5		.6		.4	Deferred Taxes	.1	.2	.5	.6	.4	.5
	7.1		6.5		5.7	All Other Non-Current	12.9	3.3	2.7	4.8	7.6	5.0
	24.6		28.0		28.8	Net Worth	12.1	31.8	49.8	32.7	33.2	5.3
	100.0		100.0		100.0	Total Liabilities & Net Worth	100.0	100.0	100.0	100.0	100.0	100.0
					INCOME DATA						
	100.0		100.0		100.0	Net Sales	100.0	100.0	100.0	100.0	100.0	100.0
	32.5		31.4		32.3	Gross Profit	46.2	33.8	36.0	33.7	28.5	19.8
	25.7		27.5		26.8	Operating Expenses	43.5	31.4	31.6	25.0	21.0	11.5
	6.8		4.0		5.5	Operating Profit	2.7	2.3	4.4	8.7	7.5	8.2
	1.7		2.1		1.9	All Other Expenses (net)	3.1	2.2	.5	1.8	1.8	2.0
	5.1		1.9		3.6	Profit Before Taxes	-.4	.2	3.9	6.9	5.7	6.2
					RATIOS						
	2.1		2.2		2.4		3.5	2.6	2.2	5.4	2.4	1.7
	1.3		1.3		1.3	Current	1.3	1.2	1.6	1.1	1.3	1.2
	.9		.9		.8		.9	.8	1.0	.8	.9	.7
	1.6		1.4		1.5		2.8	2.4	1.7	5.0	1.4	1.0
	1.0		.8		.9	Quick	1.0	.8	1.3	.9	.8	.7
	.6		.5		.6		.6	.6	.7	.7	.5	.4
39	9.4	35	10.3	37	9.8		49 7.4	36 10.1	42 8.6	37 9.8	36 10.1	35 10.4
48	7.5	46	7.9	48	7.7	Sales/Receivables	64 5.7	50 7.3	51 7.1	45 8.1	43 8.6	41 8.8
59	6.2	58	6.3	61	6.0		83 4.4	63 5.8	63 5.8	55 6.7	51 7.2	51 7.2
8	45.6	11	33.7	12	31.1		15 23.7	8 45.9	2 159.4	5 70.8	19 19.4	15 25.0
20	18.6	25	14.3	23	15.6	Cost of Sales/Inventory	23 15.6	22 16.7	19 19.7	20 18.4	44 8.3	22 16.6
40	9.1	55	6.6	47	7.8		60 6.1	46 7.9	45 8.1	35 10.3	80 4.6	44 8.2
19	19.7	13	28.0	15	24.3		15 24.8	10 29.4	12 29.4	11 32.7	20 17.9	24 15.0
27	13.3	27	13.4	25	14.7	Cost of Sales/Payables	23 16.2	21 17.2	20 18.0	20 18.0	31 11.9	34 10.8
40	9.0	41	8.9	37	10.0		39 9.5	31 11.8	31 11.6	33 11.2	45 8.1	45 8.2
	8.5		5.7		6.9		3.4	5.6	7.3	3.8	7.6	10.2
	17.6		24.4		19.7	Sales/Working Capital	9.0	29.0	12.4	67.8	19.4	24.7
	-38.9		-56.4		-28.7		NM	-19.5	NM	-24.9	-34.5	-14.2
	9.6		5.7		7.5		6.1	4.4	7.8	7.6	9.1	10.4
(126)	3.0	(116)	2.0	(120)	3.1	EBIT/Interest	(12) 1.6	(31) 1.4	3.5	4.1	(22) 3.8	(18) 5.3
	1.0		-.3		.8		-1.4	-.3	.9	1.4	1.0	2.8
	7.9		5.1		2.9	Net Profit + Depr., Dep.,						
(29)	2.5	(37)	1.5	(28)	1.5	Amort./Cur. Mat. L/T/D						
	1.3		.8		.8							
	.6		.5		.7		.3	.7	.6	.6	.6	1.3
	1.5		1.4		1.6	Fixed/Worth	9.7	2.0	.8	1.5	1.7	1.7
	6.4		5.5		9.7		-1.0	11.6	1.5	10.5	3.9	-.8
	.7		.9		.9		.8	.7	.5	.2	1.2	1.6
	2.3		2.2		2.2	Debt/Worth	11.0	2.9	1.1	2.1	2.0	6.4
	13.4		9.1		11.0		-3.4	14.9	2.0	13.6	7.3	-3.8
	55.7		34.3		44.9	% Profit Before Taxes/Tangible		53.3	26.3	36.0	48.0	81.4
(110)	23.5	(102)	13.5	(104)	20.1	Net Worth	(28) 5.4	16.4	(16) 19.7	(21) 28.5	(12) 32.9	
	6.5		-5.2		1.3		-9.6	-.2	9.2	15.0	12.4	
	21.0		12.4		16.9		13.4	8.1	13.0	19.1	16.6	32.5
	8.3		3.1		5.0	% Profit Before Taxes/Total Assets	.9	.8	4.4	5.0	10.7	18.6
	.0		-4.1		-.2		-15.5	-3.8	-.1	1.0	.3	6.8
	14.1		16.0		11.8		53.0	6.8	8.8	11.2	11.0	22.5
	7.1		6.0		5.0	Sales/Net Fixed Assets	11.4	4.4	5.0	5.6	4.5	6.0
	3.2		2.7		2.6		2.2	2.2	3.5	2.1	2.7	2.7
	3.2		2.9		2.5		3.2	2.4	2.4	2.9	2.4	5.4
	2.2		1.9		1.8	Sales/Total Assets	1.5	1.8	2.0	1.7	1.9	2.4
	1.5		1.1		1.2		.7	1.1	1.5	1.4	1.2	1.2
	1.4		1.7		2.0		.7	2.9	2.9	1.8	1.8	1.0
(126)	2.5	(114)	3.0	(117)	3.5	% Depr., Dep., Amort./Sales	(11) 3.2	(32) 4.7	3.8	3.1	3.4	(13) 1.4
	4.9		5.7		5.6		13.0	7.5	5.7	5.3	5.4	4.3
	2.6		2.7		2.4	% Officers', Directors',		2.9				
(58)	4.8	(48)	4.7	(46)	4.8	Owners' Comp/Sales	(19) 5.1					
	12.9		10.3		8.6		13.0					
2719574M		2579486M		3738587M		Net Sales ($)	8008M	65789M	65738M	134401M	350987M	3113664M
1095523M		1432425M		1605604M		Total Assets ($)	8365M	51804M	40697M	78632M	215154M	1210952M

© RMA 2003 M = $ thousand   MM = $ million
See Pages 11 through 18 for Explanation of Ratios and Data

Current Data Sorted By Assets   Comparative Historical Data

	0-500M	500M-2MM	2-10MM	10-50MM	50-100MM	100-250MM	Type of Statement	4/1/98-3/31/99 ALL	4/1/99-3/31/00 ALL
	3	14	7	8		1	Unqualified	23	29
	4	18	32	4			Reviewed	46	43
	3	9	12	1			Compiled	44	33
			3				Tax Returns	5	11
	6	14	20	7	1		Other	42	40
	33 (4/1-9/30/02)		134 (10/1/02-3/31/03)						
NUMBER OF STATEMENTS	16	55	74	20	1	1		160	156
	%	%	%	%	%	%	**ASSETS**	%	%
	9.4	9.2	8.3	9.0			Cash & Equivalents	8.1	8.4
	29.9	30.1	22.9	16.2			Trade Receivables (net)	25.8	24.9
	5.9	7.2	8.2	11.6			Inventory	8.9	8.4
	.0	1.7	1.3	2.1			All Other Current	2.1	2.0
	45.3	48.1	40.7	38.9			Total Current	44.8	43.7
	47.8	40.3	49.2	49.4			Fixed Assets (net)	44.3	47.1
	.8	2.7	1.7	3.4			Intangibles (net)	2.6	4.4
	6.1	8.9	8.4	8.4			All Other Non-Current	8.3	4.9
	100.0	100.0	100.0	100.0			Total	100.0	100.0
							LIABILITIES		
	28.2	12.7	9.4	7.9			Notes Payable-Short Term	7.5	7.6
	3.1	6.1	5.7	8.9			Cur. Mat.-L/T/D	4.4	5.3
	14.5	14.0	10.1	8.1			Trade Payables	10.2	11.7
	.0	.1	.0	.2			Income Taxes Payable	.4	.4
	5.5	12.5	6.8	7.7			All Other Current	9.5	10.8
	51.3	45.3	32.0	32.9			Total Current	32.1	35.8
	20.7	23.3	22.2	23.0			Long Term Debt	21.8	20.6
	.0	.4	.4	1.5			Deferred Taxes	.8	.7
	7.8	2.7	5.5	5.1			All Other Non-Current	5.1	5.8
	20.1	28.3	39.9	37.5			Net Worth	40.3	37.1
	100.0	100.0	100.0	100.0			Total Liabilities & Net Worth	100.0	100.0
							INCOME DATA		
	100.0	100.0	100.0	100.0			Net Sales	100.0	100.0
	37.7	38.6	29.4	25.7			Gross Profit	32.2	32.4
	36.5	37.2	25.3	17.9			Operating Expenses	26.8	26.9
	1.3	1.4	4.1	7.8			Operating Profit	5.4	5.6
	2.6	2.0	2.0	2.2			All Other Expenses (net)	2.0	1.7
	-1.3	-.7	2.1	5.7			Profit Before Taxes	3.4	3.8
							RATIOS		
	3.4	1.9	2.1	2.2			Current	2.4	2.4
	1.2	1.2	1.4	1.1				1.4	1.3
	.4	.8	1.0	.7				1.0	.8
	3.3	1.6	1.6	1.6			Quick	1.9	1.8
	1.1	1.0	1.0	.7				1.0	1.0
	.4	.5	.7	.4				.6	.6

Sales/Receivables

0-500M	500M-2MM	2-10MM	10-50MM	4/1/98-3/31/99 ALL	4/1/99-3/31/00 ALL
10 37.5	35 10.4	37 9.8	32 11.2	37 9.9	36 10.2
37 9.9	43 8.5	47 7.8	43 8.4	46 7.9	46 7.9
52 7.0	53 6.9	54 6.7	51 7.2	56 6.6	55 6.6

Cost of Sales/Inventory

0-500M	500M-2MM	2-10MM	10-50MM	4/1/98-3/31/99 ALL	4/1/99-3/31/00 ALL
0 UND	3 141.7	7 52.1	6 58.4	5 79.4	4 85.6
3 118.1	11 34.4	14 25.5	25 14.5	14 25.3	12 30.2
17 22.0	24 14.9	31 11.7	50 7.3	31 11.9	31 11.9

Cost of Sales/Payables

0-500M	500M-2MM	2-10MM	10-50MM	4/1/98-3/31/99 ALL	4/1/99-3/31/00 ALL
0 UND	15 24.1	15 25.0	16 22.9	15 23.6	14 25.5
18 19.7	24 15.5	24 15.2	22 16.4	25 14.5	24 15.2
51 7.2	45 8.0	45 8.1	28 12.8	37 10.0	37 10.0

Sales/Working Capital

0-500M	500M-2MM	2-10MM	10-50MM	4/1/98-3/31/99 ALL	4/1/99-3/31/00 ALL
11.5	9.9	8.6	7.0	7.5	7.6
58.5	31.7	20.1	NM	18.7	21.2
-9.6	-32.1	-94.8	-8.6	-134.5	-24.6

EBIT/Interest

0-500M	500M-2MM	2-10MM	10-50MM	4/1/98-3/31/99 ALL	4/1/99-3/31/00 ALL
(15) 8.3	(52) 2.9	(69) 6.3	11.7	(145) 7.2	(140) 8.4
.3	1.3	2.1	3.4	3.0	2.9
-11.1	.2	.3	.1	1.3	.9

Net Profit + Depr., Dep., Amort./Cur. Mat. L/T/D

0-500M	500M-2MM	2-10MM	10-50MM	4/1/98-3/31/99 ALL	4/1/99-3/31/00 ALL
		(25) 4.8		(56) 5.9	(47) 5.2
		2.5		2.6	2.6
		.7		1.3	1.6

Fixed/Worth

0-500M	500M-2MM	2-10MM	10-50MM	4/1/98-3/31/99 ALL	4/1/99-3/31/00 ALL
1.0	.6	.8	.7	.6	.7
2.3	1.5	1.3	1.3	1.2	1.4
-1.7	3.8	2.3	3.8	2.7	3.5

Debt/Worth

0-500M	500M-2MM	2-10MM	10-50MM	4/1/98-3/31/99 ALL	4/1/99-3/31/00 ALL
1.0	.9	.8	.6	.7	.7
2.6	2.0	1.7	2.0	1.6	1.7
-9.8	8.2	2.7	8.0	4.6	5.8

% Profit Before Taxes/Tangible Net Worth

0-500M	500M-2MM	2-10MM	10-50MM	4/1/98-3/31/99 ALL	4/1/99-3/31/00 ALL
(11) 43.3	(45) 16.8	(67) 33.5	(18) 30.8	(144) 37.0	(129) 41.9
21.1	4.1	10.7	18.3	17.8	14.7
-69.3	-5.4	-2.8	-7.0	9.1	1.4

% Profit Before Taxes/Total Assets

0-500M	500M-2MM	2-10MM	10-50MM	4/1/98-3/31/99 ALL	4/1/99-3/31/00 ALL
20.1	4.5	10.9	12.5	15.1	14.9
-1.8	1.3	3.1	6.6	6.9	6.4
-27.3	-2.2	-1.5	-3.4	1.5	-.2

Sales/Net Fixed Assets

0-500M	500M-2MM	2-10MM	10-50MM	4/1/98-3/31/99 ALL	4/1/99-3/31/00 ALL
17.8	11.8	6.2	4.3	9.1	8.1
8.9	6.8	3.4	3.1	5.0	4.0
4.3	3.8	2.2	2.0	2.4	2.3

Sales/Total Assets

0-500M	500M-2MM	2-10MM	10-50MM	4/1/98-3/31/99 ALL	4/1/99-3/31/00 ALL
5.0	3.6	2.4	1.6	2.7	2.6
3.8	2.5	1.7	1.4	1.9	1.9
2.3	1.8	1.2	1.1	1.4	1.4

% Depr., Dep., Amort./Sales

0-500M	500M-2MM	2-10MM	10-50MM	4/1/98-3/31/99 ALL	4/1/99-3/31/00 ALL
(14) 1.5	(50) 2.5	(69) 2.8	3.6	(143) 2.1	(137) 2.4
3.3	4.2	4.7	5.5	3.5	4.0
5.3	6.2	8.0	9.2		6.7

% Officers', Directors', Owners' Comp/Sales

500M-2MM	2-10MM	4/1/98-3/31/99 ALL	4/1/99-3/31/00 ALL
(41) 3.5	(29) 2.7	(71) 3.6	(67) 3.2
7.8	4.5	6.3	7.1
12.3	6.7	10.5	13.0

Dollar Data

	0-500M	500M-2MM	2-10MM	10-50MM	50-100MM	100-250MM	4/1/98-3/31/99 ALL	4/1/99-3/31/00 ALL
Net Sales ($)	17194M	177855M	551270M	638427M	124852M	108068M	1954801M	1611325M
Total Assets ($)	5159M	64279M	310010M	459339M	91726M	111226M	1187865M	1027870M

M = $ thousand   MM = $ million
See Pages 11 through 18 for Explanation of Ratios and Data

Comparative Historical Data | Current Data Sorted By Sales

Type of Statement	4/1/00-3/31/01 ALL	4/1/01-3/31/02 ALL	4/1/02-3/31/03 ALL	0-1MM	1-3MM	3-5MM	5-10MM	10-25MM	25MM & OVER
Unqualified	21	22	16		1	1		5	9
Reviewed	44	44	53	2	11	15	13	10	2
Compiled	34	46	35	4	12	9	7	1	2
Tax Returns	10	6	15	4	6	1	4		
Other	46	52	48	3	15	6	13	7	4
				33 (4/1-9/30/02)			134 (10/1/02-3/31/03)		
NUMBER OF STATEMENTS	155	170	167	13	45	32	37	23	17
ASSETS	%	%	%	%	%	%	%	%	%
Cash & Equivalents	8.2	8.8	8.8	4.3	10.4	6.8	10.0	8.8	9.7
Trade Receivables (net)	27.8	25.7	25.1	21.8	22.1	27.0	28.8	27.4	20.6
Inventory	6.7	7.6	8.1	8.2	4.9	6.4	7.9	11.6	15.8
All Other Current	1.9	2.3	1.4	.1	1.8	1.7	.8	1.4	1.8
Total Current	44.7	44.5	43.4	34.4	39.2	41.9	47.5	49.2	47.9
Fixed Assets (net)	44.1	45.0	46.1	52.7	49.6	50.3	41.4	40.1	42.0
Intangibles (net)	4.2	3.5	2.2	6.5	2.3	.3	1.3	1.7	4.5
All Other Non-Current	7.0	7.0	8.3	6.4	8.9	7.5	9.8	9.0	5.6
Total	100.0	100.0	100.0	100.0	100.0	100.0	100.0	100.0	100.0
LIABILITIES									
Notes Payable-Short Term	6.6	10.4	12.2	38.3	11.8	11.2	8.0	8.1	9.6
Cur. Mat.-L/T/D	5.8	5.5	6.2	2.5	5.0	6.8	6.3	6.1	11.0
Trade Payables	11.2	11.5	11.5	10.9	8.3	11.4	14.0	16.2	8.8
Income Taxes Payable	.1	.4	.1	.0	.0	.1	.1	.1	.3
All Other Current	9.6	9.1	8.7	9.6	8.8	8.5	8.8	7.3	9.7
Total Current	33.4	36.9	38.6	61.4	33.9	38.0	37.2	37.8	39.3
Long Term Debt	25.2	22.7	22.2	27.9	29.0	20.3	17.7	19.1	17.8
Deferred Taxes	.6	.5	.5	.0	.5	.4	.3	.6	1.2
All Other Non-Current	5.7	7.4	4.7	6.9	2.1	6.6	8.5	1.9	1.4
Net Worth	35.0	32.5	33.9	3.7	34.5	34.8	36.2	40.5	40.2
Total Liabilities & Net Worth	100.0	100.0	100.0	100.0	100.0	100.0	100.0	100.0	100.0
INCOME DATA									
Net Sales	100.0	100.0	100.0	100.0	100.0	100.0	100.0	100.0	100.0
Gross Profit	31.6	30.0	32.6	44.6	40.4	29.9	29.2	24.5	26.6
Operating Expenses	25.6	27.4	29.3	40.3	39.1	28.9	26.0	17.0	19.2
Operating Profit	6.1	2.6	3.4	4.4	1.3	1.1	3.2	7.5	7.4
All Other Expenses (net)	1.8	2.3	2.1	3.8	2.1	1.3	2.1	2.0	2.3
Profit Before Taxes	4.3	.4	1.3	.5	-.8	-.2	1.1	5.4	5.2
RATIOS									
Current	2.7	2.0	2.1	1.3	2.7	1.8	2.0	2.7	2.2
	1.5	1.4	1.3	.7	1.3	1.1	1.4	1.3	1.5
	.9	.9	.8	.3	.8	.7	1.0	.9	.7
Quick	2.1	1.7	1.6	1.2	2.6	1.4	1.6	2.3	1.6
	1.1	1.0	1.0	.4	1.1	.8	1.1	1.0	.8
	.7	.6	.6	.2	.5	.7	.6	.7	.6
Sales/Receivables	39 9.3	34 10.6	35 10.4	18 20.4	30 12.2	40 9.1	35 10.4	31 11.6	31 11.7
	47 7.8	45 8.0	45 8.1	51 7.1	41 8.9	48 7.6	48 7.6	41 9.0	41 8.8
	56 6.5	57 6.4	53 6.9	65 5.6	50 7.3	55 6.6	55 6.6	52 7.3	50 7.3
Cost of Sales/Inventory	3 120.5	4 96.9	4 84.1	0 UND	2 158.1	4 86.7	3 112.5	5 70.1	6 57.3
	8 45.4	10 36.1	14 26.8	19 19.1	12 30.1	12 31.5	11 34.3	23 16.1	23 15.6
	25 14.9	27 13.4	31 11.9	45 8.0	30 12.0	26 13.9	23 15.8	41 9.0	80 4.6
Cost of Sales/Payables	14 25.3	14 26.0	15 24.8	0 UND	11 33.7	16 22.1	13 27.3	17 21.4	12 29.6
	23 15.7	24 14.9	24 15.5	33 11.1	20 18.2	23 15.8	32 11.5	25 14.4	22 16.5
	36 10.2	40 9.1	44 8.2	78 4.7	46 8.0	43 8.4	45 8.1	43 8.5	27 13.7
Sales/Working Capital	7.5	9.8	9.7	12.0	7.2	11.7	9.7	6.3	7.1
	16.6	21.9	22.4	-16.7	19.9	75.1	17.3	30.9	13.7
	-38.5	-35.7	-26.7	-5.8	-32.2	-15.9	NM	-83.5	-12.8
EBIT/Interest	(141) 7.0	(155) 4.2	(158) 5.3	5.2	2.7	4.2	4.3	10.7	14.5
	2.5	1.2	1.7	1.0	(43) .9	(28) 1.3	(35) 2.1	(22) 4.5	6.1
	1.0	-1.5	.0	-.2	.0	-1.8	-.1	1.3	1.4
Net Profit + Depr., Dep., Amort./Cur. Mat. L/T/D	(47) 4.9	(49) 3.1	(38) 4.8		(11) 1.9		(10) 4.8	(11) 7.0	
	2.4	1.5	1.9		.6		2.5	2.0	
	1.0	.4	.6		.3		1.1	.6	
Fixed/Worth	.6	.7	.7	2.0	.9	.8	.6	.6	.4
	1.4	1.5	1.4	6.0	1.6	1.6	1.1	1.3	1.1
	5.8	3.8	3.0	-.9	2.5	2.7	3.0	2.2	5.4
Debt/Worth	.6	.7	.9	2.0	.9	.8	.8	.7	.6
	1.7	1.9	2.0	9.7	2.0	1.7	1.9	1.7	1.7
	16.6	8.3	5.3	-3.1	3.1	4.3	4.5	3.3	9.7
% Profit Before Taxes/Tangible Net Worth	(126) 42.5	(141) 28.1	(142) 28.6		13.4	13.6	32.3	51.8	60.8
	19.0	7.8	9.2	(38) 1.2	(27) 4.0	(31) 13.2	27.9	(15) 22.2	
	3.9	-15.0	-3.6		-7.1	-10.4	.2	6.5	9.4
% Profit Before Taxes/Total Assets	14.1	9.7	10.0	15.1	3.9	8.7	9.9	18.8	16.2
	5.3	1.5	2.5	-.2	.0	2.3	4.2	10.0	9.1
	.3	-7.2	-2.5	-9.8	-3.4	-6.7	-1.9	1.8	.8
Sales/Net Fixed Assets	8.7	9.0	8.5	7.6	7.6	7.2	11.8	9.1	5.9
	4.9	4.6	4.3	3.9	4.4	4.0	4.7	5.1	3.5
	2.8	2.3	2.5	1.9	2.5	2.3	2.5	3.3	2.7
Sales/Total Assets	2.8	2.7	2.8	3.8	2.8	2.5	3.1	3.0	2.6
	2.1	1.9	2.0	1.6	2.0	2.0	2.1	2.2	1.4
	1.4	1.3	1.3	1.1	1.2	1.5	1.2	1.7	1.3
% Depr., Dep., Amort./Sales	(144) 2.1	(155) 2.3	(154) 2.7	(11) 3.0	(43) 3.3	(31) 3.0	(33) 2.1	(20) 1.9	(16) 3.2
	3.6	4.2	4.2	4.7	5.3	4.5	3.5	3.0	4.8
	6.5	7.3	7.2	8.1	8.0	7.9	5.9	5.7	8.2
% Officers', Directors', Owners' Comp/Sales	(82) 3.6	(81) 2.6	(82) 2.9		(28) 4.4	(17) 3.4	(19) 2.9		
	5.8	5.3	5.4		7.5	5.2	4.9		
	9.9	7.9	10.0		17.7	9.0	9.1		
Net Sales ($)	1694964M	2418295M	1617666M	8185M	91028M	129339M	241886M	337500M	809728M
Total Assets ($)	1023064M	1212177M	1041739M	5219M	62798M	78994M	141592M	196679M	556457M

M = $ thousand   MM = $ million
See Pages 11 through 18 for Explanation of Ratios and Data

Current Data Sorted By Assets | **Comparative Historical Data**

0-500M	500M-2MM	2-10MM	10-50MM	50-100MM	100-250MM	Type of Statement	4/1/98-3/31/99 ALL	4/1/99-3/31/00 ALL
1		5	3	3		Unqualified	10	9
	5	5	1			Reviewed	7	8
1	6	1				Compiled	7	11
4	3	2				Tax Returns	1	4
1	6	8	6	1	1	Other	11	20
	16 (4/1-9/30/02)		47 (10/1/02-3/31/03)					
7	20	21	10	4	1	**NUMBER OF STATEMENTS**	36	52
%	%	%	%	%	%	**ASSETS**	%	%
	6.5	7.1	1.7			Cash & Equivalents	7.1	10.1
	30.6	25.7	22.4			Trade Receivables (net)	25.6	24.3
	28.0	34.2	34.0			Inventory	30.3	29.6
	2.0	.4	3.2			All Other Current	1.1	1.3
	67.1	67.5	61.3			Total Current	64.1	65.2
	20.8	24.4	23.7			Fixed Assets (net)	23.5	25.1
	3.2	2.2	10.7			Intangibles (net)	6.9	5.7
	8.9	5.9	4.3			All Other Non-Current	5.6	4.0
	100.0	100.0	100.0			Total	100.0	100.0
						LIABILITIES		
	15.6	11.6	18.0			Notes Payable-Short Term	11.0	11.1
	6.5	7.5	5.8			Cur. Mat.-L/T/D	3.7	3.7
	15.9	17.2	8.2			Trade Payables	14.6	10.4
	.0	.0	.0			Income Taxes Payable	.1	.2
	7.2	11.4	9.6			All Other Current	13.9	10.8
	45.2	47.7	41.5			Total Current	43.3	36.2
	10.6	14.7	12.5			Long Term Debt	14.6	17.9
	.0	.2	.2			Deferred Taxes	.3	.2
	16.6	5.3	8.6			All Other Non-Current	5.5	7.7
	27.6	32.1	37.2			Net Worth	36.3	38.0
	100.0	100.0	100.0			Total Liabilities & Net Worth	100.0	100.0
						INCOME DATA		
	100.0	100.0	100.0			Net Sales	100.0	100.0
	42.1	27.2	27.0			Gross Profit	33.8	34.2
	40.1	24.3	22.6			Operating Expenses	28.2	28.9
	2.0	2.9	4.4			Operating Profit	5.6	5.3
	.4	1.3	2.0			All Other Expenses (net)	1.0	1.4
	1.6	1.6	2.4			Profit Before Taxes	4.6	4.0
						RATIOS		
	2.7	2.4	2.5				2.8	3.1
	1.5	1.5	2.0			Current	1.9	2.2
	1.2	1.2	.9				.9	1.3
	1.3	1.3	1.2				1.4	1.6
	.9	.7	.9			Quick	.9	1.0
	.5	.5	.2				.5	.5
	38 9.7	34 10.8	42 8.8				34 10.8	35 10.3
	49 7.5	47 7.8	51 7.1			Sales/Receivables	42 8.6	52 7.0
	54 6.7	60 6.0	66 5.5				57 6.4	60 6.1
	34 10.8	49 7.5	79 4.6				43 8.4	56 6.5
	69 5.3	66 5.5	111 3.3			Cost of Sales/Inventory	98 3.7	97 3.7
	120 3.0	148 2.5	194 1.9				137 2.7	147 2.5
	24 14.9	22 16.3	17 21.9				14 25.4	16 23.1
	45 8.1	30 12.0	25 14.5			Cost of Sales/Payables	34 10.7	26 13.9
	63 5.8	63 5.8	34 10.7				44 8.3	43 8.5
	4.7	4.1	4.8				4.9	3.5
	11.4	10.1	5.6			Sales/Working Capital	8.2	6.1
	27.8	21.0	−63.2				NM	13.5
	3.7	7.7					(32) 9.3	(44) 7.3
(19)	1.8	1.7				EBIT/Interest	3.2	2.4
	−.3	−2.9					1.2	1.3
						Net Profit + Depr., Dep.,	(10) 6.0	(14) 3.5
						Amort./Cur. Mat. L/T/D	1.9	1.0
							.9	.4
	.3	.4	.4				.2	.3
	.7	.7	.7			Fixed/Worth	.7	.7
	7.0	2.0	NM				2.4	3.3
	.8	.7	.6				.7	.6
	2.2	2.2	2.2			Debt/Worth	2.0	1.6
	18.3	6.1	NM				14.6	9.3
	45.4	38.0				% Profit Before Taxes/Tangible	(31) 47.9	(43) 38.8
(17)	9.4	(19) 8.3				Net Worth	20.0	18.7
	−6.9	−7.5					3.7	7.7
	6.7	11.5	12.8				13.6	15.8
	3.4	1.0	2.5			% Profit Before Taxes/Total	4.3	6.9
	−5.8	−6.6	−.9			Assets	1.3	2.1
	29.4	21.1	11.8				28.1	23.5
	15.4	8.5	7.5			Sales/Net Fixed Assets	9.6	6.1
	5.1	4.7	3.6				4.4	4.0
	3.1	3.1	2.0				2.9	2.5
	2.2	2.1	1.5			Sales/Total Assets	2.0	1.7
	1.8	1.2	.9				1.3	1.2
	1.1	1.9					(30) .7	(46) .7
(18)	1.8	(20) 2.7				% Depr., Dep., Amort./Sales	2.6	2.3
	2.7	5.0					3.8	4.3
						% Officers', Directors',	(13) 3.9	(17) 2.3
						Owners' Comp/Sales	7.1	5.9
							13.7	10.4
3345M	54844M	264495M	293481M	335600M	155546M	Net Sales ($)	642587M	1240389M
1504M	22265M	118734M	194213M	315480M	153546M	Total Assets ($)	421095M	1018532M

M = $ thousand   MM = $ million
See Pages 11 through 18 for Explanation of Ratios and Data

Comparative Historical Data | Current Data Sorted By Sales

			Type of Statement						
8	4	12	Unqualified	1				5	6
6	10	11	Reviewed	1	2	2	3	2	1
11	8	8	Compiled	1	2	4	1		
4	4	9	Tax Returns	6	2			1	
18	21	23	Other	2	3	3	3	6	6
4/1/00-3/31/01	4/1/01-3/31/02	4/1/02-3/31/03		16 (4/1-9/30/02)			47 (10/1/02-3/31/03)		
ALL	ALL	ALL		0-1MM	1-3MM	3-5MM	5-10MM	10-25MM	25MM & OVER
47	47	63	**NUMBER OF STATEMENTS**	11	9	9	7	14	13
%	%	%	**ASSETS**	%	%	%	%	%	%
9.1	8.5	6.2	Cash & Equivalents	4.6				4.1	6.5
27.7	25.8	25.0	Trade Receivables (net)	21.6				20.9	24.6
30.6	31.8	31.3	Inventory	30.5				30.1	34.0
1.3	1.1	1.5	All Other Current	.4				2.6	.8
68.7	67.1	63.9	Total Current	57.1				57.7	65.9
23.3	22.9	26.6	Fixed Assets (net)	36.9				28.5	26.1
1.7	3.9	3.8	Intangibles (net)	2.6				8.4	3.9
6.3	6.1	5.7	All Other Non-Current	3.3				5.5	4.1
100.0	100.0	100.0	Total	100.0				100.0	100.0
			LIABILITIES						
13.5	11.5	14.3	Notes Payable-Short Term	15.9				17.9	7.2
3.0	3.9	7.1	Cur. Mat.-L/T/D	6.3				9.2	5.8
16.5	12.7	15.9	Trade Payables	25.9				10.4	13.5
.1	.2	.0	Income Taxes Payable	.0				.0	.0
11.0	10.7	8.5	All Other Current	4.8				8.4	13.7
44.1	39.1	45.8	Total Current	52.9				45.9	40.2
14.8	14.6	16.9	Long Term Debt	37.0				17.0	7.8
.5	.2	.3	Deferred Taxes	.0				.3	1.1
9.0	14.5	10.9	All Other Non-Current	22.5				6.1	12.6
31.6	31.5	26.1	Net Worth	−12.3				30.8	38.3
100.0	100.0	100.0	Total Liabilities & Net Worth	100.0				100.0	100.0
			INCOME DATA						
100.0	100.0	100.0	Net Sales	100.0				100.0	100.0
32.6	34.0	35.3	Gross Profit	48.2				27.3	27.9
26.2	31.3	32.0	Operating Expenses	46.0				23.2	20.1
6.4	2.7	3.2	Operating Profit	2.2				4.1	7.9
1.3	1.7	1.4	All Other Expenses (net)	2.4				1.3	2.7
5.1	1.0	1.8	Profit Before Taxes	−.2				2.8	5.1
			RATIOS						
3.0	2.9	2.6	Current	4.2				2.1	2.5
1.7	1.9	1.6		1.6				1.5	2.0
1.2	1.3	1.1		.7				1.1	1.2
1.6	1.3	1.3	Quick	1.5				1.0	1.4
1.0	.9	.8		.6				.7	.9
.6	.5	.5		.5				.2	.5
38 9.6	38 9.7	32 11.3	Sales/Receivables	14 25.6				32 11.6	37 9.8
48 7.6	49 7.5	49 7.5		57 6.4				46 7.9	54 6.7
61 6.0	57 6.5	58 6.2		72 5.0				53 6.8	61 6.0
37 9.8	59 6.2	51 7.1	Cost of Sales/Inventory	10 35.2				51 7.2	56 6.6
88 4.1	102 3.6	75 4.9		63 5.8				98 3.7	81 4.5
130 2.8	157 2.3	153 2.4		207 1.8				147 2.5	157 2.3
14 25.5	17 21.6	20 18.3	Cost of Sales/Payables	6 61.0				19 19.4	16 22.5
30 12.3	36 10.2	30 12.0		52 7.0				25 14.8	25 14.3
48 7.6	51 7.2	54 6.8		85 4.3				34 10.7	42 8.7
4.2	3.9	4.3	Sales/Working Capital	3.0				5.1	4.1
6.8	6.4	9.6		8.5				11.0	5.9
23.4	13.9	22.5		−6.5				NM	17.7
9.6	3.9	3.9	EBIT/Interest	3.5				7.4	10.7
(43) 3.1	(44) 1.7	(58) 1.7		(10) .2				2.4	(10) 2.3
1.2	.0	−.8		−1.1				.7	−.3
18.3	6.0	3.6	Net Profit + Depr., Dep.,						
(10) 3.3	(13) 2.0	(17) .8	Amort./Cur. Mat. L/T/D						
1.9	.4	.0							
.2	.4	.4	Fixed/Worth	.5				.6	.4
.6	.9	.9		98.0				.9	.6
2.4	5.0	2.5		−.4				NM	1.0
.7	.8	.7	Debt/Worth	1.2				.9	.5
1.7	2.4	2.2		−8.5				1.7	.8
5.5	23.9	17.6		−3.5				NM	5.6
44.7	28.6	38.0	% Profit Before Taxes/Tangible					30.6	40.8
(40) 20.7	(39) 11.7	(51) 9.2	Net Worth					(11) 12.7	(12) 18.2
3.1	2.8	−7.5						4.1	−10.6
17.7	9.2	9.7	% Profit Before Taxes/Total	3.9				10.0	23.4
6.9	2.6	1.8	Assets	−3.8				2.3	4.2
.7	−4.3	−5.5		−11.2				−2.4	−2.5
32.8	22.9	16.8	Sales/Net Fixed Assets	33.6				10.0	15.4
10.3	7.9	8.3		6.0				7.7	7.2
4.3	4.6	4.1		4.2				3.6	3.9
2.8	2.4	2.7	Sales/Total Assets	2.2				2.9	2.5
1.9	1.7	1.9		1.7				1.8	1.5
1.4	1.3	1.3		1.3				1.1	1.0
.6	1.3	1.8	% Depr., Dep., Amort./Sales					2.4	1.5
(38) 1.4	(44) 2.3	(55) 2.6						(12) 3.8	(11) 2.6
3.2	4.1	4.9						5.9	4.9
1.6	1.7	2.5	% Officers', Directors',						
(15) 2.8	(19) 5.1	(22) 6.3	Owners' Comp/Sales						
4.8	8.0	9.1							
1058863M	797805M	1107311M	Net Sales ($)	6742M	19651M	36406M	46778M	207977M	789757M
806147M	622477M	805742M	Total Assets ($)	3952M	10031M	16040M	25926M	129971M	619822M

M = $ thousand   MM = $ million
See Pages 11 through 18 for Explanation of Ratios and Data

Current Data Sorted By Assets   Comparative Historical Data

0-500M	500M-2MM	2-10MM	10-50MM	50-100MM	100-250MM	Type of Statement	4/1/98-3/31/99 ALL	4/1/99-3/31/00 ALL
		6	7	1		Unqualified	10	6
	2	8	1			Reviewed	4	3
	1	2	1			Compiled	4	4
1		1				Tax Returns	1	
	3	6	2		1	Other	9	4
	10 (4/1-9/30/02)		33 (10/1/02-3/31/03)					
1	6	23	11	2		NUMBER OF STATEMENTS	28	17
%	%	%	%	%	%	**ASSETS**	%	%
		4.9	3.5			Cash & Equivalents	7.0	10.1
		21.5	18.4			Trade Receivables (net)	27.4	26.9
		33.2	30.0			Inventory	35.8	23.9
		3.0	4.1			All Other Current	1.5	1.5
		62.6	56.1			Total Current	71.7	62.4
		31.4	29.3			Fixed Assets (net)	22.9	24.9
		2.2	5.6			Intangibles (net)	2.0	5.1
		3.8	9.0			All Other Non-Current	3.4	7.6
		100.0	100.0			Total	100.0	100.0
						LIABILITIES		
		16.4	11.4			Notes Payable-Short Term	12.2	4.1
		5.2	5.0			Cur. Mat.-L/T/D	3.1	3.8
		12.6	13.1			Trade Payables	17.7	16.4
		.1	.0			Income Taxes Payable	1.6	.2
		7.3	5.9			All Other Current	6.4	5.3
		41.7	35.3			Total Current	41.0	29.8
		12.5	16.6			Long Term Debt	15.0	18.7
		.3	.9			Deferred Taxes	.5	1.2
		3.3	6.8			All Other Non-Current	2.2	3.3
		42.3	40.3			Net Worth	41.2	47.0
		100.0	100.0			Total Liabilities & Net Worth	100.0	100.0
						INCOME DATA		
		100.0	100.0			Net Sales	100.0	100.0
		34.4	19.2			Gross Profit	29.7	29.2
		30.3	16.9			Operating Expenses	23.1	22.0
		4.1	2.3			Operating Profit	6.5	7.3
		1.5	1.5			All Other Expenses (net)	1.3	1.1
		2.6	.8			Profit Before Taxes	5.3	6.2
						RATIOS		
		2.4	2.5			Current	3.6	4.7
		1.7	1.3				1.7	2.0
		1.1	1.1				1.2	1.4
		1.0	1.2			Quick	2.2	3.1
		.6	.5				.8	1.1
		.4	.4				.5	.6
		33 11.2	34 10.7			Sales/Receivables	36 10.0	41 8.9
		49 7.4	43 8.5				48 7.6	49 7.5
		66 5.5	47 7.7				57 6.4	61 6.0
		58 6.3	50 7.4			Cost of Sales/Inventory	59 6.2	49 7.5
		111 3.3	76 4.8				96 3.8	56 6.5
		160 2.3	109 3.3				125 2.9	84 4.3
		20 18.6	23 16.1			Cost of Sales/Payables	21 17.8	19 18.8
		41 8.9	35 10.4				28 13.2	30 12.0
		72 5.1	44 8.4				68 5.4	53 6.9
		3.7	4.3			Sales/Working Capital	3.8	3.6
		8.5	10.5				7.6	6.1
		32.6	35.0				11.7	13.2
		4.7	8.6			EBIT/Interest	11.2	19.1
		(21) 2.2	(10) 5.9				(23) 3.1	(14) 5.7
		.8	1.2				.7	2.3
		5.2				Net Profit + Depr., Dep., Amort./Cur. Mat. L/T/D	4.8	
		(12) 1.5					(11) 2.8	
		.6					.8	
		.4	.3			Fixed/Worth	.1	.2
		.6	.9				.5	.8
		1.6	2.4				1.7	NM
		.8	.7			Debt/Worth	.4	.2
		1.2	1.2				1.7	.9
		2.9	7.4				4.4	NM
		18.6				% Profit Before Taxes/Tangible Net Worth	30.0	39.4
		6.0					(26) 17.1	(13) 23.8
		-2.0					-3.8	13.1
		4.5	12.0			% Profit Before Taxes/Total Assets	16.6	21.5
		3.0	5.0				10.1	12.2
		-1.1	2.6				-.7	5.1
		14.4	20.0			Sales/Net Fixed Assets	33.4	15.5
		5.7	5.2				12.3	6.5
		2.3	3.8				4.2	4.4
		2.1	2.1			Sales/Total Assets	2.6	2.3
		1.6	1.9				1.9	1.8
		1.0	1.0				1.5	1.2
		2.0				% Depr., Dep., Amort./Sales	.9	1.6
		(22) 3.5					(27) 2.1	(14) 2.5
		6.2					4.3	5.5
						% Officers', Directors', Owners' Comp/Sales	3.5	
							(10) 4.1	
							6.2	
570M	16610M	210501M	451140M	121141M		Net Sales ($)	787967M	716042M
132M	7209M	129884M	259814M	114717M		Total Assets ($)	496251M	495700M

M = $ thousand   MM = $ million
See Pages 11 through 18 for Explanation of Ratios and Data

Comparative Historical Data | Current Data Sorted By Sales

				Type of Statement						
	8	5	14	Unqualified			2	1	5	6
	1	4	11	Reviewed		1	2	6	1	1
	5	4	4	Compiled			1	1	1	1
			2	Tax Returns	1		1			
	8	3	12	Other	1	2		5	2	2
	4/1/00-3/31/01 ALL	4/1/01-3/31/02 ALL	4/1/02-3/31/03 ALL		10 (4/1-9/30/02)			33 (10/1/02-3/31/03)		
					0-1MM	1-3MM	3-5MM	5-10MM	10-25MM	25MM & OVER
	22	16	43	NUMBER OF STATEMENTS	2	5	4	13	9	10
	%	%	%	ASSETS	%	%	%	%		%
	8.3	4.8	5.1	Cash & Equivalents				5.1		4.2
	25.1	24.7	20.5	Trade Receivables (net)				23.7		18.5
	29.9	29.9	32.5	Inventory				31.0		29.0
	1.6	2.2	2.8	All Other Current				1.5		3.6
	65.0	61.6	60.9	Total Current				61.3		55.3
	23.2	30.7	29.5	Fixed Assets (net)				32.4		34.8
	5.7	2.6	3.5	Intangibles (net)				2.2		3.7
	6.0	5.1	6.2	All Other Non-Current				4.0		6.2
	100.0	100.0	100.0	Total				100.0		100.0
				LIABILITIES						
	25.8	9.3	16.3	Notes Payable-Short Term				19.7		9.3
	3.1	3.6	5.6	Cur. Mat.-L/T/D				6.2		4.4
	15.8	15.6	13.3	Trade Payables				14.8		12.8
	.1	.0	.0	Income Taxes Payable				.1		.0
	6.5	4.6	9.0	All Other Current				7.5		6.1
	51.3	33.1	44.3	Total Current				48.2		32.6
	17.1	15.4	17.8	Long Term Debt				12.5		14.3
	.4	1.1	.5	Deferred Taxes				.5		1.3
	3.8	3.1	5.4	All Other Non-Current				4.0		13.9
	27.4	47.4	32.1	Net Worth				34.8		37.9
	100.0	100.0	100.0	Total Liabilities & Net Worth				100.0		100.0
				INCOME DATA						
	100.0	100.0	100.0	Net Sales				100.0		100.0
	31.6	34.1	30.8	Gross Profit				31.3		19.6
	25.3	31.2	26.9	Operating Expenses				28.6		15.5
	6.3	2.8	3.8	Operating Profit				2.7		4.1
	1.6	.5	1.8	All Other Expenses (net)				1.6		1.6
	4.8	2.3	2.1	Profit Before Taxes				1.0		2.5
				RATIOS						
	3.7	3.1	2.4					1.7		3.9
	2.2	2.2	1.4	Current				1.3		2.1
	1.3	1.3	1.0					1.0		1.0
	1.7	1.8	1.1					1.0		1.4
	1.1	1.1	.6	Quick				.6		1.0
	.5	.4	.3					.5		.4
41	9.0	36 10.0	32 11.3	Sales/Receivables				44 8.2		32 11.4
49	7.5	46 7.9	46 7.9					55 6.6		36 10.3
63	5.8	56 6.5	58 6.3					66 5.5		44 8.3
51	7.2	52 7.1	54 6.8	Cost of Sales/Inventory				47 7.7		50 7.4
75	4.8	85 4.3	101 3.6					96 3.8		76 4.8
118	3.1	116 3.1	139 2.6					132 2.8		88 4.1
21	17.3	22 16.4	20 18.6	Cost of Sales/Payables				36 10.1		17 22.1
33	11.1	34 10.6	38 9.5					44 8.4		30 12.2
51	7.1	44 8.3	54 6.7					67 5.5		37 9.7
	3.4	4.4	4.8	Sales/Working Capital				7.4		4.1
	5.8	6.5	11.3					15.4		8.7
	17.1	17.1	-75.5					NM		NM
(18)	6.9	(14) 6.1	(40) 6.0	EBIT/Interest				4.5		
	4.1	2.8	2.6					2.7		
	1.8	1.1	.6					1.2		
			4.3	Net Profit + Depr., Dep.,						
		(17)	2.4	Amort./Cur. Mat. L/T/D						
			.9							
	.1	.4	.4	Fixed/Worth				.4		.4
	.6	.6	.9					.7		.9
	23.6	1.5	2.4					2.3		NM
	.4	.4	.9	Debt/Worth				1.1		.5
	1.1	.9	1.6					2.1		1.0
	53.4	2.6	7.4					3.0		NM
(18)	46.8	(15) 29.2	(37) 21.9	% Profit Before Taxes/Tangible Net Worth				21.9		
	21.8	11.0	7.8					6.0		
	10.3	1.8	-1.8					1.3		
	15.5	9.2	6.7	% Profit Before Taxes/Total Assets				5.2		12.0
	10.1	5.4	3.4					3.0		5.0
	4.3	.5	-1.9					.7		3.7
	29.4	11.5	20.0	Sales/Net Fixed Assets				20.8		12.4
	8.6	6.8	6.2					6.8		5.1
	4.3	4.3	3.7					2.1		3.3
	2.4	2.3	2.4	Sales/Total Assets				2.4		2.2
	2.1	1.9	1.6					1.4		1.9
	1.1	1.4	1.0					1.1		1.3
(13)	.5	(14) 1.1	(37) 2.2	% Depr., Dep., Amort./Sales			(11)	1.6		1.9
	1.4	3.2	3.4					4.8		4.0
	2.7	4.1	5.8					7.7		6.0
			1.9	% Officers', Directors', Owners' Comp/Sales						
		(12)	3.8							
			6.2							
	1268270M	535180M	799962M	Net Sales ($)	1507M	11500M	16973M	96848M	152349M	520785M
	1021785M	307364M	511756M	Total Assets ($)	1437M	13108M	13504M	66850M	101276M	315581M

© RMA 2003

M = $ thousand   MM = $ million
See Pages 11 through 18 for Explanation of Ratios and Data

Current Data Sorted By Assets   Comparative Historical Data

	0-500M	500M-2MM	2-10MM	10-50MM	50-100MM	100-250MM		4/1/98-3/31/99 ALL	4/1/99-3/31/00 ALL
Type of Statement									
Unqualified				2		1		7	10
Reviewed		2	4	3				8	6
Compiled			1	1				2	6
Tax Returns				1					1
Other		1		4	2	1		9	10
NUMBER OF STATEMENTS		2	6	11	2	2		26	33
	%	%	%	%	%	%		%	%
ASSETS									
Cash & Equivalents				4.4				3.8	6.7
Trade Receivables (net)				28.6				27.7	26.6
Inventory				38.1				30.4	33.2
All Other Current				1.8				.8	2.1
Total Current				73.0				62.7	68.6
Fixed Assets (net)				19.8				25.4	22.5
Intangibles (net)				2.0				4.6	3.2
All Other Non-Current				5.2				7.3	5.7
Total				100.0				100.0	100.0
LIABILITIES									
Notes Payable-Short Term				13.3				15.2	12.3
Cur. Mat.-L/T/D				2.4				3.4	2.4
Trade Payables				11.7				13.1	13.1
Income Taxes Payable				.3				.2	.1
All Other Current				9.7				7.4	9.8
Total Current				37.4				39.3	37.8
Long Term Debt				18.6				16.4	15.3
Deferred Taxes				.2				.3	.4
All Other Non-Current				1.4				1.6	6.0
Net Worth				42.3				42.4	40.4
Total Liabilities & Net Worth				100.0				100.0	100.0
INCOME DATA									
Net Sales				100.0				100.0	100.0
Gross Profit				31.8				31.3	31.5
Operating Expenses				28.2				24.8	24.6
Operating Profit				3.6				6.5	6.8
All Other Expenses (net)				.6				1.5	1.3
Profit Before Taxes				3.0				5.0	5.5
RATIOS									
Current				2.4				2.5	2.6
				2.1				1.8	1.9
				1.6				1.2	1.3
Quick				1.4				1.4	1.4
				.9				.8	1.0
				.7				.5	.6
Sales/Receivables			40	9.2			37	9.9 33	11.1
			49	7.4			46	7.9 45	8.2
			59	6.2			57	6.4 59	6.2
Cost of Sales/Inventory			72	5.1			51	7.2 55	6.6
			105	3.5			76	4.8 85	4.3
			139	2.6			107	3.4 119	3.1
Cost of Sales/Payables			22	16.6			19	19.6 17	21.3
			26	14.2			29	12.8 27	13.7
			32	11.5			40	9.1 44	8.3
Sales/Working Capital				4.7				5.4	4.9
				5.5				8.4	7.2
				7.7				19.1	13.9
EBIT/Interest				5.2				9.4	11.6
				4.1			(23)	2.9 (30)	5.3
				2.0				1.3	.9
Net Profit + Depr., Dep., Amort./Cur. Mat. L /T/D								11.2	
							(13)	3.8	
								1.1	
Fixed/Worth				.1				.4	.2
				.4				.7	.6
				.9				1.2	1.1
Debt/Worth				.8				.6	.8
				1.1				1.3	1.5
				1.6				5.8	5.0
% Profit Before Taxes/Tangible Net Worth				32.7				38.9	78.5
			(10)	7.3			(23)	16.5 (30)	23.4
				3.1				4.9	3.5
% Profit Before Taxes/Total Assets				12.7				20.9	21.5
				4.5				5.6	13.3
				1.8				1.0	.6
Sales/Net Fixed Assets				30.6				19.3	22.9
				10.8				7.9	9.4
				8.0				5.3	5.4
Sales/Total Assets				2.5				2.8	2.5
				2.1				2.0	2.0
				1.7				1.5	1.5
% Depr., Dep., Amort./Sales				.5				1.4	.8
				2.1			(23)	2.6 (30)	2.1
				2.4				3.4	3.0
% Officers', Directors', Owners' Comp/Sales								1.5	
							(10)	2.5	
								5.6	
Net Sales ($)	4502M	62660M	425571M	395023M	615354M			790934M	1233309M
Total Assets ($)	1721M	33306M	203418M	137795M	339568M			430355M	620138M

M = $ thousand   MM = $ million
See Pages 11 through 18 for Explanation of Ratios and Data

Comparative Historical Data | Current Data Sorted By Sales

4/1/00-3/31/01 ALL	4/1/01-3/31/02 ALL	4/1/02-3/31/03 ALL	Type of Statement	0-1MM	1-3MM (1, 4/1-9/30/02)	3-5MM	5-10MM	10-25MM	25MM & OVER
7	2	3	Unqualified						3
5	9	9	Reviewed		2		1	4	2
4	4	2	Compiled					2	
1	2	1	Tax Returns						1
8	13	8	Other		1		1	1	6
25	30	23	**NUMBER OF STATEMENTS**		2		2	7	12
%	%	%	**ASSETS**	%	%	%	%	%	%
4.0	5.0	6.7	Cash & Equivalents	D		D			7.2
24.1	22.6	30.5	Trade Receivables (net)	A		A			31.5
29.5	35.3	33.4	Inventory	T		T			33.9
3.0	2.3	2.4	All Other Current	A		A			2.2
60.6	65.3	73.0	Total Current						74.8
26.3	22.5	19.8	Fixed Assets (net)	N		N			18.8
3.0	5.3	2.9	Intangibles (net)	O		O			1.9
10.1	6.9	4.3	All Other Non-Current	T		T			4.5
100.0	100.0	100.0	Total						100.0
			LIABILITIES	A		A			
9.3	9.6	9.5	Notes Payable-Short Term	V		V			10.4
2.8	3.1	3.4	Cur. Mat.-L/T/D	A		A			3.7
10.7	14.0	13.6	Trade Payables	I		I			12.5
.1	.1	.3	Income Taxes Payable	L		L			.4
12.7	11.7	13.2	All Other Current	A		A			12.4
35.6	38.5	40.0	Total Current	B		B			39.4
16.3	16.0	12.7	Long Term Debt	L		L			17.1
.3	.2	.1	Deferred Taxes	E		E			.0
1.7	3.5	5.0	All Other Non-Current						.8
46.2	41.8	42.2	Net Worth						42.7
100.0	100.0	100.0	Total Liabilities & Net Worth						100.0
			INCOME DATA						
100.0	100.0	100.0	Net Sales						100.0
31.3	32.5	34.2	Gross Profit						33.9
25.3	29.6	29.6	Operating Expenses						27.5
6.1	3.0	4.7	Operating Profit						6.3
.8	1.3	.5	All Other Expenses (net)						.4
5.2	1.7	4.2	Profit Before Taxes						5.9
			RATIOS						
2.6 / 1.6 / 1.1	2.6 / 1.9 / 1.3	2.3 / 1.9 / 1.4	Current						2.8 / 1.9 / 1.5
1.3 / .8 / .6	1.3 / .7 / .6	1.4 / .9 / .6	Quick						1.4 / .9 / .8
35 10.5 / 43 8.6 / 51 7.1	31 11.7 / 40 9.1 / 55 6.7	40 9.1 / 49 7.4 / 66 5.6	Sales/Receivables						41 8.9 / 50 7.3 / 60 6.1
49 7.5 / 77 4.7 / 112 3.3	54 6.8 / 94 3.9 / 138 2.6	56 6.6 / 88 4.1 / 139 2.6	Cost of Sales/Inventory						42 8.6 / 85 4.3 / 107 3.4
17 21.8 / 23 15.7 / 37 9.9	18 20.0 / 27 13.4 / 64 5.7	22 16.6 / 30 12.4 / 46 7.9	Cost of Sales/Payables						17 21.9 / 27 13.7 / 43 8.5
5.2 / 11.0 / 25.8	4.1 / 6.6 / 17.9	5.0 / 6.4 / 9.3	Sales/Working Capital						5.1 / 6.9 / 9.1
10.4 / (19) 3.1 / 1.1	6.0 / (27) 1.3 / .4	18.8 / (22) 4.4 / 2.4	EBIT/Interest						25.5 / 4.9 / 2.6
	(10) 9.1 / 3.5 / 1.5		Net Profit + Depr., Dep., Amort./Cur. Mat. L/T/D						
.2 / .6 / 1.0	.2 / .5 / 1.0	.2 / .4 / .9	Fixed/Worth						.1 / .4 / .7
.7 / 1.3 / 2.5	.5 / 1.1 / 3.1	.7 / 1.1 / 2.4	Debt/Worth						.6 / 1.1 / 2.2
60.4 / 13.8 / -1.4	47.5 / (27) 9.5 / -5.8	37.7 / (21) 21.6 / 5.4	% Profit Before Taxes/Tangible Net Worth						65.7 / (11) 25.7 / 5.2
20.6 / 7.9 / -.1	16.3 / 1.0 / -2.6	18.2 / 4.9 / 2.3	% Profit Before Taxes/Total Assets						22.3 / 6.4 / 2.9
22.8 / 8.9 / 4.6	24.4 / 13.4 / 5.7	26.1 / 17.0 / 8.0	Sales/Net Fixed Assets						27.9 / 13.9 / 8.6
2.3 / 1.9 / 1.6	2.3 / 1.9 / 1.3	2.5 / 2.1 / 1.7	Sales/Total Assets						2.5 / 2.2 / 2.0
(20) 1.2 / 2.2 / 3.3	(26) 1.0 / 2.4 / 3.4	(22) .7 / 1.8 / 2.5	% Depr., Dep., Amort./Sales						(11) .5 / 1.5 / 2.4
			% Officers', Directors', Owners' Comp/Sales						
1350765M	1288201M	1503110M	Net Sales ($)		4502M		12672M	113078M	1372858M
759534M	645124M	715808M	Total Assets ($)		1721M		9136M	66832M	638119M

M = $ thousand   MM = $ million
See Pages 11 through 18 for Explanation of Ratios and Data

Current Data Sorted By Assets   Comparative Historical Data

0-500M	500M-2MM	2-10MM	10-50MM	50-100MM	100-250MM	Type of Statement	4/1/98-3/31/99 ALL	4/1/99-3/31/00 ALL
	1	9	16	4	4	Unqualified	26	30
	4	11	4	1		Reviewed	23	19
1	2	5				Compiled	6	12
	2	17	9			Tax Returns	3	2
						Other	32	39
	26 (4/1-9/30/02)		64 (10/1/02-3/31/03)					
0-500M	500M-2MM	2-10MM	10-50MM	50-100MM	100-250MM			
1	9	42	29	5	4	NUMBER OF STATEMENTS	90	102
%	%	%	%	%	%	ASSETS	%	%
		4.9	6.2			Cash & Equivalents	4.9	7.8
		27.3	20.0			Trade Receivables (net)	27.3	27.4
		33.4	32.6			Inventory	30.1	29.3
		2.0	2.3			All Other Current	3.3	.6
		67.7	61.2			Total Current	65.5	65.1
		22.7	24.9			Fixed Assets (net)	25.5	24.3
		2.1	6.0			Intangibles (net)	2.2	3.4
		7.5	7.9			All Other Non-Current	6.8	7.2
		100.0	100.0			Total	100.0	100.0
						LIABILITIES		
		15.4	12.2			Notes Payable-Short Term	8.7	10.3
		3.5	2.1			Cur. Mat.-L/T/D	2.7	3.3
		14.3	10.5			Trade Payables	15.9	13.3
		.2	.2			Income Taxes Payable	.5	.4
		8.0	6.8			All Other Current	7.8	7.7
		41.4	31.8			Total Current	35.5	35.0
		11.3	12.9			Long Term Debt	17.4	15.3
		.2	1.1			Deferred Taxes	.3	.6
		4.7	4.3			All Other Non-Current	4.5	4.7
		42.4	50.0			Net Worth	42.3	44.4
		100.0	100.0			Total Liabilities & Net Worth	100.0	100.0
						INCOME DATA		
		100.0	100.0			Net Sales	100.0	100.0
		29.5	28.3			Gross Profit	29.7	32.3
		25.0	23.3			Operating Expenses	24.0	25.9
		4.6	5.0			Operating Profit	5.7	6.4
		1.4	1.1			All Other Expenses (net)	.9	1.2
		3.1	3.9			Profit Before Taxes	4.8	5.2
						RATIOS		
		3.0	3.4			Current	3.2	3.4
		1.6	2.1				2.0	2.0
		1.1	1.3				1.4	1.4
		1.3	1.4			Quick	1.6	1.6
		.8	.8				1.0	1.0
		.5	.5				.6	.7
		37 9.9	39 9.4			Sales/Receivables	38 9.5	38 9.7
		51 7.1	46 7.9				46 7.9	46 8.0
		66 5.5	58 6.3				53 6.8	55 6.6
		63 5.8	64 5.7			Cost of Sales/Inventory	49 7.5	49 7.5
		101 3.6	88 4.2				72 5.1	80 4.5
		129 2.8	206 1.8				117 3.1	123 3.0
		16 23.3	22 16.7			Cost of Sales/Payables	19 18.8	18 20.5
		30 12.2	31 11.9				36 10.0	31 11.7
		54 6.7	45 8.1				55 6.6	48 7.6
		3.6	3.2			Sales/Working Capital	4.0	3.8
		9.1	4.8				6.8	6.1
		24.6	8.5				11.5	14.1
		16.2	14.5			EBIT/Interest	14.9	10.9
		(41) 3.0	(28) 2.7				(77) 4.8	(93) 3.4
		1.4	.9				1.3	1.0
		6.6	7.1			Net Profit + Depr., Dep., Amort./Cur. Mat. L/T/D	4.5	3.9
		(16) 1.7	(15) 2.0				(28) 2.0	(30) 2.1
		.8	.8				1.2	1.4
		.2	.3			Fixed/Worth	.3	.3
		.5	.6				.5	.5
		1.4	1.0				1.0	1.0
		.6	.5			Debt/Worth	.6	.6
		1.4	1.4				1.3	1.0
		4.0	3.2				3.3	2.7
		29.4	20.0			% Profit Before Taxes/Tangible Net Worth	33.9	36.0
		(37) 10.4	(27) 7.8				(83) 15.5	(92) 15.0
		4.2	.1				6.0	3.9
		14.3	9.4			% Profit Before Taxes/Total Assets	15.3	18.2
		5.5	3.9				6.1	6.6
		1.0	−.1				1.4	.1
		20.3	11.9			Sales/Net Fixed Assets	21.7	23.4
		10.4	5.9				7.7	9.2
		4.6	3.5				4.4	4.5
		2.5	1.9			Sales/Total Assets	2.5	2.5
		1.7	1.3				1.8	1.9
		1.3	1.0				1.4	1.4
		1.0	1.6			% Depr., Dep., Amort./Sales	.9	1.5
		(40) 2.2	(27) 3.3				(77) 2.6	(89) 2.7
		3.6	5.0				4.3	4.4
		1.5				% Officers', Directors', Owners' Comp/Sales	1.6	1.7
		(22) 3.1					(29) 2.6	(33) 4.9
		8.4					7.0	10.2
964M	28191M	420090M	1016153M	519147M	615604M	Net Sales ($)	2886065M	2156422M
188M	11676M	220368M	695535M	319737M	478925M	Total Assets ($)	1616529M	1416635M

© RMA 2003

M = $ thousand   MM = $ million
See Pages 11 through 18 for Explanation of Ratios and Data

Comparative Historical Data				Current Data Sorted By Sales					
30	33	34	**Type of Statement** Unqualified			4	1	7	22
16	14	20	Reviewed		2	4	5	7	2
17	13	8	Compiled	1	2	1	2	2	
3			Tax Returns						
28	32	28	Other		2	4	5	13	4
4/1/00-3/31/01 ALL	4/1/01-3/31/02 ALL	4/1/02-3/31/03 ALL		0-1MM	1-3MM	3-5MM	5-10MM	10-25MM	25MM & OVER
					26 (4/1-9/30/02)		64 (10/1/02-3/31/03)		
94	92	90	**NUMBER OF STATEMENTS**	1	6	13	13	29	28
%	%	%	**ASSETS**	%	%	%	%	%	%
4.7	5.5	6.2	Cash & Equivalents			6.6	1.4	7.5	6.5
29.3	27.0	25.5	Trade Receivables (net)			24.4	30.3	22.4	24.9
29.5	32.3	30.9	Inventory			30.6	34.5	31.3	30.1
2.0	1.4	2.0	All Other Current			1.6	1.4	2.8	1.9
65.5	66.1	64.5	Total Current			63.2	67.6	64.0	63.5
22.2	22.6	24.0	Fixed Assets (net)			26.4	22.7	20.8	25.7
4.0	3.7	4.3	Intangibles (net)			4.9	1.2	5.3	4.8
8.2	7.6	7.1	All Other Non-Current			5.5	8.5	9.9	6.0
100.0	100.0	100.0	Total			100.0	100.0	100.0	100.0
			LIABILITIES						
11.7	15.6	14.2	Notes Payable-Short Term			21.0	19.9	10.4	10.6
3.7	3.7	3.2	Cur. Mat.-L/T/D			3.1	4.4	2.5	3.3
14.8	15.6	13.5	Trade Payables			12.6	18.6	12.6	9.8
.3	.3	.2	Income Taxes Payable			.0	.2	.1	.1
8.6	6.8	7.6	All Other Current			7.2	4.9	8.8	8.5
39.2	41.9	38.6	Total Current			43.9	47.9	34.4	32.3
15.0	14.6	11.5	Long Term Debt			10.5	15.9	10.3	12.3
.3	.3	.5	Deferred Taxes			.0	.2	.4	1.1
4.1	2.8	4.0	All Other Non-Current			3.0	4.3	5.3	3.4
41.5	40.3	45.4	Net Worth			42.5	31.7	49.7	50.9
100.0	100.0	100.0	Total Liabilities & Net Worth			100.0	100.0	100.0	100.0
			INCOME DATA						
100.0	100.0	100.0	Net Sales			100.0	100.0	100.0	100.0
32.2	30.6	31.1	Gross Profit			39.6	25.9	29.4	29.8
26.7	25.7	26.6	Operating Expenses			33.4	22.2	23.7	24.1
5.6	4.9	4.5	Operating Profit			6.3	3.7	5.7	5.6
1.3	1.9	.9	All Other Expenses (net)			1.9	2.2	.9	.7
4.2	2.9	3.6	Profit Before Taxes			4.4	1.5	4.7	4.9
			RATIOS						
2.8	2.6	3.2				4.6	2.0	3.3	3.5
1.7	1.8	1.7	Current			1.3	1.5	2.0	1.9
1.2	1.2	1.2				.9	1.0	1.2	1.4
1.4	1.3	1.4				1.7	.9	1.4	1.4
.9	.9	.8	Quick			.8	.7	.9	1.0
.6	.5	.5				.4	.4	.5	.7
42 8.8	42 8.7	38 9.6				36 10.2	37 10.0	33 11.1	41 8.9
50 7.4	46 7.9	49 7.4	Sales/Receivables			44 8.3	54 6.7	46 7.9	53 6.9
61 6.0	54 6.7	63 5.8				56 6.5	83 4.4	56 6.5	65 5.6
55 6.6	52 7.0	59 6.2				41 8.9	52 7.0	60 6.1	62 5.9
80 4.6	90 4.1	88 4.1	Cost of Sales/Inventory			88 4.1	95 3.8	101 3.6	87 4.2
110 3.3	140 2.6	134 2.7				155 2.3	195 1.9	130 2.8	127 2.9
17 21.2	20 18.0	20 18.2				11 32.2	26 13.8	19 18.8	19 18.8
33 11.1	36 10.1	31 11.9	Cost of Sales/Payables			38 9.6	32 11.3	31 11.6	26 14.1
51 7.2	53 6.9	47 7.8				53 6.8	71 5.1	49 7.5	35 10.4
4.4	4.4	3.5				4.7	4.1	3.4	3.0
6.9	6.6	6.4	Sales/Working Capital			14.1	11.2	5.1	5.1
20.6	17.2	18.2				-81.9	NM	16.7	10.1
8.8	6.4	15.2				5.2	6.1	21.8	25.5
(88) 2.9	(87) 2.1	(87) 3.0	EBIT/Interest		(12) 2.4		2.3	(28) 4.1	(27) 3.9
1.3	.8	1.2				.8	1.1	2.2	1.5
5.2	4.7	7.1						7.7	7.3
(27) 2.3	(23) .8	(39) 1.7	Net Profit + Depr., Dep., Amort./Cur. Mat. L/T/D				(11) 5.2	(19) 2.0	
1.0	-.1	.8					1.7	.8	
.2	.2	.3				.3	.3	.2	.3
.5	.5	.5	Fixed/Worth			.9	.5	.5	.5
1.0	1.4	1.3				NM	6.6	1.2	.9
.8	.6	.5				.3	.8	.5	.4
1.5	1.7	1.4	Debt/Worth			2.2	2.2	1.2	1.3
4.4	4.1	3.5				NM	21.8	3.6	2.2
38.7	27.9	28.7				50.5	14.6	28.7	28.7
(86) 14.3	(84) 9.3	(80) 10.8	% Profit Before Taxes/Tangible Net Worth		(10) 19.0		(11) 4.6	(27) 13.3	(27) 13.2
4.9	-.5	1.7				6.4	3.1	1.1	1.5
13.1	12.0	11.0				31.9	7.8	15.7	11.6
5.5	3.7	5.0	% Profit Before Taxes/Total Assets			5.4	2.7	5.8	5.3
1.3	-.5	.3				-.4	.2	1.0	.4
28.2	20.8	18.9				37.5	19.3	21.7	11.5
9.7	9.1	8.1	Sales/Net Fixed Assets			7.9	10.1	10.2	5.9
5.0	4.5	4.7				3.1	5.6	4.1	4.8
2.7	2.4	2.2				2.4	2.3	2.6	2.1
1.9	1.8	1.6	Sales/Total Assets			1.7	1.6	1.6	1.5
1.4	1.3	1.3				1.4	1.2	1.1	1.4
.8	.8	1.2				1.2	1.4	1.0	1.6
(82) 2.1	(84) 2.3	(83) 2.9	% Depr., Dep., Amort./Sales		(11) 3.8	(12) 2.7	(28) 1.8	(27) 3.2	
3.6	3.6	4.0				9.6	3.6	3.6	4.2
1.6	1.5	1.6						1.6	
(33) 3.5	(29) 3.8	(33) 3.5	% Officers', Directors', Owners' Comp/Sales					(15) 2.6	
6.6	6.1	7.6						4.9	
2400456M	2049816M	2600149M	Net Sales ($)	964M	14075M	54335M	92824M	464964M	1972987M
1707243M	1365528M	1726429M	Total Assets ($)	188M	8920M	30389M	59757M	342867M	1284308M

© RMA 2003

M = $ thousand   MM = $ million

See Pages 11 through 18 for Explanation of Ratios and Data

Current Data Sorted By Assets   **Comparative Historical Data**

0-500M	500M-2MM	2-10MM	10-50MM	50-100MM	100-250MM	Type of Statement	4/1/98-3/31/99 ALL	4/1/99-3/31/00 ALL
	1	2	1	2	1	Unqualified	5	5
	2	2	4			Reviewed	2	7
	2	3				Compiled	4	4
						Tax Returns		
		2	4	1	1	Other	3	8
	1 (4/1-9/30/02)		25 (10/1/02-3/31/03)					
	8	9	9	3	2	NUMBER OF STATEMENTS	14	24
%	%	%	%	%	%	ASSETS	%	%

Left size columns marked: **DATA NOT AVAILABLE**

		ASSETS	4/1/98-3/31/99 ALL	4/1/99-3/31/00 ALL
		Cash & Equivalents	8.5	6.2
		Trade Receivables (net)	25.1	28.0
		Inventory	30.5	29.1
		All Other Current	2.8	2.9
		Total Current	66.8	66.2
		Fixed Assets (net)	24.6	26.5
		Intangibles (net)	1.4	1.5
		All Other Non-Current	7.1	5.7
		Total	100.0	100.0
		LIABILITIES		
		Notes Payable-Short Term	9.3	11.2
		Cur. Mat.-L/T/D	2.7	3.6
		Trade Payables	9.7	14.7
		Income Taxes Payable	.1	.2
		All Other Current	5.1	5.8
		Total Current	26.9	35.4
		Long Term Debt	16.5	16.0
		Deferred Taxes	.8	.3
		All Other Non-Current	.5	.4
		Net Worth	55.4	47.9
		Total Liabilities & Net Worth	100.0	100.0
		INCOME DATA		
		Net Sales	100.0	100.0
		Gross Profit	35.1	31.0
		Operating Expenses	27.3	25.5
		Operating Profit	7.7	5.5
		All Other Expenses (net)	.7	1.0
		Profit Before Taxes	7.0	4.5

RATIOS

Ratio		4/1/98-3/31/99		4/1/99-3/31/00
Current		5.2		4.9
		3.4		2.0
		1.5		1.1
Quick		3.6		2.9
		1.2		1.0
		.6		.6
Sales/Receivables	30	12.0	40	9.2
	46	7.9	51	7.2
	55	6.7	65	5.6
Cost of Sales/Inventory	60	6.1	42	8.8
	96	3.8	80	4.6
	130	2.8	116	3.1
Cost of Sales/Payables	14	26.5	24	15.3
	19	19.1	32	11.5
	38	9.5	51	7.2
Sales/Working Capital		3.3		2.9
		4.7		7.0
		7.8		97.3
EBIT/Interest		10.5		14.6
	(12)	4.6	(22)	5.0
		1.2		1.2
Net Profit + Depr., Dep., Amort./Cur. Mat. L /T/D				
Fixed/Worth		.2		.1
		.5		.9
		1.0		1.5
Debt/Worth		.3		.3
		.9		1.1
		1.8		3.2
% Profit Before Taxes/Tangible Net Worth		32.1		28.6
		21.8		17.5
		6.6		2.1
% Profit Before Taxes/Total Assets		20.6		14.6
		13.4		8.8
		1.6		1.4
Sales/Net Fixed Assets		37.9		23.9
		7.4		8.0
		4.0		4.3
Sales/Total Assets		2.8		2.6
		1.6		1.9
		1.3		1.3
% Depr., Dep., Amort./Sales				.8
			(20)	3.4
				5.5
% Officers', Directors', Owners' Comp/Sales				

0-500M	500M-2MM	2-10MM	10-50MM	50-100MM	100-250MM		4/1/98-3/31/99	4/1/99-3/31/00
	9672M	69001M	227358M	187390M	385215M	Net Sales ($)	479472M	639853M
	3851M	40968M	187722M	220010M	387854M	Total Assets ($)	367534M	479950M

M = $ thousand   MM = $ million
See Pages 11 through 18 for Explanation of Ratios and Data

Comparative Historical Data / Current Data Sorted By Sales

4/1/00-3/31/01 ALL	4/1/01-3/31/02 ALL	4/1/02-3/31/03 ALL	Type of Statement	0-1MM	1-3MM	3-5MM	5-10MM	10-25MM	25MM & OVER
2	6	6	Unqualified				2 2		4
3	5	7	Reviewed	1	1			1	3
6	6	5	Compiled			4		1	
	1		Tax Returns						
6	6	8	Other	1				4	3
				1 (4/1-9/30/02)		25 (10/1/02-3/31/03)			
17	24	26	**NUMBER OF STATEMENTS**	1	1	6	4	5	10
%	%	%	**ASSETS**	%	%	%	%	%	%
6.5	10.0	9.1	Cash & Equivalents						7.9
20.3	21.4	20.9	Trade Receivables (net)						18.9
29.9	30.5	26.8	Inventory						26.6
3.1	1.8	1.8	All Other Current						2.7
59.7	63.8	58.5	Total Current						56.1
33.7	28.1	28.8	Fixed Assets (net)						28.5
2.6	3.8	4.8	Intangibles (net)						4.8
4.0	4.4	7.9	All Other Non-Current						10.6
100.0	100.0	100.0	Total						100.0
			LIABILITIES						
4.0	7.1	7.5	Notes Payable-Short Term						7.9
4.0	4.5	6.0	Cur. Mat.-L/T/D						5.5
13.0	12.0	9.8	Trade Payables						8.6
.2	.3	.4	Income Taxes Payable						.3
6.6	7.1	4.9	All Other Current						5.6
27.7	31.1	28.7	Total Current						28.0
27.6	22.2	18.6	Long Term Debt						16.4
.5	.5	.5	Deferred Taxes						.7
5.1	3.2	4.2	All Other Non-Current						5.5
39.0	43.0	48.0	Net Worth						49.5
100.0	100.0	100.0	Total Liabilities & Net Worth						100.0
			INCOME DATA						
100.0	100.0	100.0	Net Sales						100.0
26.8	26.7	27.0	Gross Profit						24.8
19.3	22.7	22.9	Operating Expenses						17.9
7.5	4.0	4.1	Operating Profit						7.0
1.2	1.4	.9	All Other Expenses (net)						.8
6.3	2.6	3.2	Profit Before Taxes						6.2
			RATIOS						
3.7	4.0	4.2	Current						3.3
2.3	1.9	2.1							1.9
1.6	1.2	1.2							1.5
1.5	2.2	2.3	Quick						2.0
.9	.8	1.1							.9
.7	.7	.5							.5
41 9.0	39 9.3	42 8.8	Sales/Receivables						49 7.4
53 6.8	46 8.0	50 7.3							57 6.4
70 5.2	59 6.2	59 6.1							63 5.8
72 5.1	51 7.2	59 6.2	Cost of Sales/Inventory						59 6.2
92 4.0	84 4.3	88 4.2							98 3.7
165 2.2	138 2.6	131 2.8							180 2.0
17 21.5	16 22.5	14 25.8	Cost of Sales/Payables						18 20.4
35 10.4	25 14.4	28 12.9							26 13.8
52 7.0	42 8.7	50 7.3							58 6.3
2.6	2.3	2.6	Sales/Working Capital						2.6
5.3	6.5	4.9							4.4
8.2	18.2	11.4							9.0
10.2	5.9	8.0	EBIT/Interest						9.2
3.4	(23) 2.0	(22) 2.5							5.8
1.4	.8	.3							1.8
		7.4	Net Profit + Depr., Dep., Amort./Cur. Mat. L/T/D						
	(12)	2.4							
		.6							
.4	.3	.1	Fixed/Worth						.2
1.0	.7	.6							.6
2.1	1.8	2.4							1.5
.7	.5	.5	Debt/Worth						.5
2.7	1.8	1.5							.9
3.5	4.6	3.8							3.2
36.6	19.6	23.0	% Profit Before Taxes/Tangible Net Worth						32.1
(16) 22.2	(21) 10.8	(25) 17.0							18.9
7.0	.3	−7.4							3.0
12.0	8.2	11.5	% Profit Before Taxes/Total Assets						12.3
8.8	2.2	4.1							7.6
1.6	−1.1	−2.0							1.9
7.1	24.6	11.6	Sales/Net Fixed Assets						9.3
4.6	5.0	4.9							4.4
2.9	2.7	2.7							2.2
1.9	1.9	1.9	Sales/Total Assets						1.6
1.4	1.3	1.5							1.0
1.0	1.1	1.0							.9
.2	.5	2.1	% Depr., Dep., Amort./Sales						
(16) 3.3	(21) 1.9	(23) 3.4							
5.3	3.7	4.6							
			% Officers', Directors', Owners' Comp/Sales						
780134M	481787M	878636M	Net Sales ($)		1863M	24070M	31656M	82588M	738459M
746369M	445014M	840405M	Total Assets ($)		938M	15125M	24553M	73708M	726081M

In the current-data columns, the note "DATA NOT AVAILABLE" appears in the 0-1MM column for the Assets and Liabilities sections.

M = $ thousand   MM = $ million
See Pages 11 through 18 for Explanation of Ratios and Data

Current Data Sorted By Assets   Comparative Historical Data

	0-500M	500M-2MM	2-10MM	10-50MM	50-100MM	100-250MM	Type of Statement	4/1/98-3/31/99 ALL	4/1/99-3/31/00 ALL
			5	10		1	Unqualified	19	13
	1	16	5				Reviewed	32	38
2	10	5	2				Compiled	17	17
2	2	3					Tax Returns	2	3
1	6	8	5	1	1		Other	24	27
	24 (4/1-9/30/02)			62 (10/1/02-3/31/03)					
0-500M	500M-2MM	2-10MM	10-50MM	50-100MM	100-250MM		NUMBER OF STATEMENTS		
5	19	37	22	1	2			94	98
%	%	%	%	%	%		**ASSETS**	%	%
	9.0	4.7	6.2				Cash & Equivalents	6.9	6.3
	37.5	27.1	23.4				Trade Receivables (net)	26.6	28.3
	27.4	29.6	24.3				Inventory	23.7	24.4
	2.5	2.0	4.7				All Other Current	3.0	3.0
	76.4	63.3	58.6				Total Current	60.2	62.0
	19.8	29.3	35.8				Fixed Assets (net)	29.8	26.8
	.4	2.1	1.6				Intangibles (net)	4.3	4.2
	3.4	5.3	4.0				All Other Non-Current	5.7	7.1
	100.0	100.0	100.0				Total	100.0	100.0
							LIABILITIES		
	9.3	13.9	9.2				Notes Payable-Short Term	11.4	14.2
	7.1	3.0	3.0				Cur. Mat.-L/T/D	3.4	4.4
	25.9	16.2	10.8				Trade Payables	15.3	16.5
	.1	.3	.3				Income Taxes Payable	.3	.5
	10.9	5.9	9.0				All Other Current	9.1	7.7
	53.3	39.4	32.4				Total Current	39.6	43.3
	15.5	14.2	13.2				Long Term Debt	14.0	14.7
	.8	.9	1.0				Deferred Taxes	.6	2.0
	2.9	2.2	5.8				All Other Non-Current	4.6	5.7
	27.5	43.3	47.6				Net Worth	41.3	34.4
	100.0	100.0	100.0				Total Liabilities & Net Worth	100.0	100.0
							INCOME DATA		
	100.0	100.0	100.0				Net Sales	100.0	100.0
	30.3	25.8	22.1				Gross Profit	27.3	27.4
	26.7	22.3	17.4				Operating Expenses	21.5	23.5
	3.6	3.5	4.6				Operating Profit	5.8	4.0
	.6	1.2	1.0				All Other Expenses (net)	1.7	1.5
	2.9	2.4	3.6				Profit Before Taxes	4.0	2.4
							RATIOS		
	2.0	2.2	3.1					2.4	2.3
	1.6	1.5	1.6				Current	1.5	1.5
	1.2	1.2	1.4					1.1	1.1
	1.5	1.3	1.3					1.6	1.3
	1.0	.7	.9				Quick	.8	.8
	.5	.5	.6					.5	.5
	36 10.1	33 11.1	38 9.5					35 10.5	38 9.6
	45 8.0	49 7.4	46 8.0				Sales/Receivables	40 9.0	45 8.1
	60 6.1	60 6.0	59 6.2					52 7.0	61 6.0
	18 20.4	36 10.3	29 12.5					27 13.5	30 12.3
	37 10.0	71 5.1	67 5.5				Cost of Sales/Inventory	54 6.7	51 7.2
	107 3.4	137 2.7	125 2.9					92 4.0	102 3.6
	22 16.3	21 17.1	12 29.9					17 21.3	22 16.8
	43 8.4	33 11.0	27 13.7				Cost of Sales/Payables	34 10.8	36 10.2
	53 6.9	52 7.1	46 8.0					45 8.1	47 7.7
	5.2	3.9	4.2					5.6	6.4
	10.0	11.5	7.0				Sales/Working Capital	11.8	11.9
	38.4	18.7	11.2					52.2	62.3
	9.0	11.0	21.9					9.5	6.9
	(17) 2.2	(36) 3.8	(20) 2.1				EBIT/Interest	(89) 3.2	(94) 2.9
	-.1	.6	.7					1.2	1.2
		8.1	13.4					5.4	5.1
		(19) 3.5	(10) 4.3				Net Profit + Depr., Dep., Amort./Cur. Mat. L./T/D	(37) 2.7	(25) 1.5
		1.6	1.4					.9	.6
	.2	.2	.5					.4	.4
	.4	.6	.6				Fixed/Worth	.8	.9
	1.5	1.5	1.2					1.5	2.0
	1.0	.8	.7					.7	.9
	2.0	1.5	1.3				Debt/Worth	1.7	1.9
	6.8	3.1	1.9					3.4	4.7
	60.4	27.8	34.0					40.9	44.8
	(16) 8.8	(34) 11.0	17.1				% Profit Before Taxes/Tangible Net Worth	(87) 18.6	(83) 15.0
	-1.4	3.4	-1.3					4.8	2.8
	12.1	12.5	15.9					13.6	12.2
	2.8	5.0	4.4				% Profit Before Taxes/Total Assets	4.9	4.2
	-.9	-.4	-.5					1.4	.4
	39.1	22.3	10.6					14.9	19.5
	18.5	7.5	4.2				Sales/Net Fixed Assets	9.3	8.5
	7.1	3.7	2.8					4.0	4.4
	4.0	2.6	1.9					3.1	3.1
	2.6	2.0	1.6				Sales/Total Assets	2.0	2.1
	1.8	1.3	1.3					1.5	1.4
	.4	1.2	1.2					1.2	.9
	1.3	(35) 3.0	3.1				% Depr., Dep., Amort./Sales	(86) 2.5	(91) 2.3
	3.5	4.2	4.6					3.8	3.4
		2.0						2.1	2.4
		(18) 3.1					% Officers', Directors', Owners' Comp/Sales	(37) 5.1	(40) 4.3
		5.2						8.8	7.7
3309M	68451M	339802M	797485M	137938M	711065M		Net Sales ($)	1584132M	1649822M
1706M	22805M	170574M	502821M	86696M	339266M		Total Assets ($)	1032376M	1103634M

M = $ thousand   MM = $ million
See Pages 11 through 18 for Explanation of Ratios and Data

Comparative Historical Data / Current Data Sorted By Sales

	4/1/00-3/31/01 ALL	4/1/01-3/31/02 ALL	4/1/02-3/31/03 ALL	Type of Statement	0-1MM	1-3MM	3-5MM	5-10MM	10-25MM	25MM & OVER
	15	14	16	Unqualified		1		1	3	11
	28	24	22	Reviewed		1	2	8	9	2
	24	20	19	Compiled	2	7	3	4	3	
	3	4	7	Tax Returns	2	1	1	1	2	
	29	33	22	Other	1	4	3	4	4	6
						24 (4/1-9/30/02)			**62 (10/1/02-3/31/03)**	
	99	95	86	**NUMBER OF STATEMENTS**	5	14	9	18	21	19
	%	%	%	**ASSETS**	%	%	%	%	%	%
	7.2	7.3	6.4	Cash & Equivalents		7.1		6.5	3.8	7.1
	30.6	28.9	28.6	Trade Receivables (net)		26.0		29.0	31.7	23.0
	24.3	23.3	26.1	Inventory		31.7		31.1	25.5	21.7
	3.2	2.5	3.1	All Other Current		3.1		2.0	2.0	5.4
	65.3	62.0	64.1	Total Current		67.9		68.7	63.0	57.2
	27.0	28.0	29.5	Fixed Assets (net)		26.9		24.9	32.0	34.0
	2.3	3.1	1.6	Intangibles (net)		.5		3.2	1.0	2.2
	5.4	6.9	4.8	All Other Non-Current		4.7		3.2	4.0	6.5
	100.0	100.0	100.0	Total		100.0		100.0	100.0	100.0
				LIABILITIES						
	11.0	11.2	10.5	Notes Payable-Short Term		10.2		11.3	13.8	8.7
	3.8	4.0	4.2	Cur. Mat.-L/T/D		8.5		2.9	3.0	2.9
	18.4	17.0	16.8	Trade Payables		15.3		18.3	18.3	10.2
	.6	.4	.3	Income Taxes Payable		.0		.4	.4	.4
	9.2	7.7	9.0	All Other Current		11.3		4.5	6.6	10.7
	43.0	40.3	40.8	Total Current		45.4		37.3	42.2	32.7
	11.2	15.3	15.9	Long Term Debt		18.6		18.5	11.5	11.9
	.6	1.0	1.3	Deferred Taxes		1.3		.8	.3	3.0
	4.7	3.5	4.3	All Other Non-Current		3.3		1.5	7.0	2.9
	40.5	39.9	37.7	Net Worth		31.4		41.8	39.0	49.4
	100.0	100.0	100.0	Total Liabilities & Net Worth		100.0		100.0	100.0	100.0
				INCOME DATA						
	100.0	100.0	100.0	Net Sales		100.0		100.0	100.0	100.0
	24.5	26.8	26.1	Gross Profit		30.1		23.7	26.2	24.2
	20.7	23.4	23.1	Operating Expenses		26.6		21.8	21.5	18.3
	3.8	3.4	3.0	Operating Profit		3.5		1.8	4.7	5.8
	1.1	1.4	1.1	All Other Expenses (net)		1.2		1.2	1.0	.8
	2.7	2.0	1.9	Profit Before Taxes		2.3		.7	3.7	5.0
				RATIOS						
	2.4	2.2	2.3			2.6		3.3	2.5	2.3
	1.5	1.5	1.6	Current		1.6		1.6	1.5	1.7
	1.1	1.2	1.3			.9		1.4	1.2	1.5
	1.4	1.2	1.5			1.7		1.6	1.3	1.6
	.9	.9	.8	Quick		.6		.9	.7	.9
	.6	.6	.5			.3		.6	.6	.5
	39 9.5	35 10.5	37 9.8			34 10.7		38 9.6	31 11.6	40 9.2
	51 7.2	46 7.9	47 7.7	Sales/Receivables		48 7.6		48 7.6	49 7.4	46 7.9
	58 6.3	61 6.0	60 6.1			85 4.3		55 6.6	66 5.5	59 6.2
	23 15.7	25 14.7	26 14.0			38 9.7		26 13.8	27 13.4	28 13.2
	42 8.6	46 7.9	55 6.6	Cost of Sales/Inventory		86 4.2		58 6.3	59 6.2	55 6.6
	97 3.8	105 3.5	117 3.1			175 2.1		139 2.6	91 4.0	128 2.9
	20 17.9	18 20.4	17 21.0			14 26.1		17 21.4	25 14.9	11 34.3
	33 11.1	31 11.6	33 11.1	Cost of Sales/Payables		33 11.1		32 11.3	33 11.0	27 13.7
	48 7.5	49 7.5	51 7.1			52 7.0		49 7.5	51 7.2	44 8.2
	4.9	5.8	4.4			4.1		3.6	5.0	4.3
	9.5	9.6	9.2	Sales/Working Capital		7.9		8.9	12.6	9.3
	54.7	27.7	18.7			-231.3		14.5	25.0	11.0
	10.0	6.5	10.0			4.8		7.1	13.6	37.3
(91) 2.7	(89) 2.4	(80) 2.3	EBIT/Interest	(12) 2.0		(17) 1.2	4.8	(17) 3.2
	1.1	.3	.0			-.3		-.6	1.7	1.2
	7.4	9.2	7.3							
(32) 3.1	(30) 3.4	(35) 2.4	Net Profit + Depr., Dep., Amort./Cur. Mat. L/T/D						
	1.0	1.0	1.3							
	.4	.4	.3			.3		.2	.3	.4
	.6	.7	.6	Fixed/Worth		.8		.5	.6	.6
	1.4	1.5	1.7			1.9		1.2	1.3	1.2
	.7	.7	.8			.7		.8	1.0	.6
	1.6	1.6	1.6	Debt/Worth		2.0		2.5	1.5	1.3
	3.2	3.2	3.1			4.1		3.2	3.0	1.8
	37.5	33.1	31.1			21.1		18.1	64.8	27.7
(90) 11.8	(86) 11.9	(77) 11.3	% Profit Before Taxes/Tangible Net Worth	(12) 6.8		(16) 5.4	(20) 23.4	16.1
	2.2	-.8	-1.1			-.7		-7.4	5.4	1.8
	14.2	11.5	12.2			6.6		9.4	16.6	15.3
	4.5	4.7	3.8	% Profit Before Taxes/Total Assets		3.0		.3	8.4	7.2
	.3	-1.3	-1.9			-2.4		-5.0	1.6	.8
	18.3	15.9	21.2			29.6		39.0	21.4	10.6
	9.8	8.0	6.7	Sales/Net Fixed Assets		6.7		8.3	8.6	4.2
	4.3	4.2	3.7			3.3		4.5	4.1	2.9
	3.1	2.6	2.6			2.3		3.7	2.7	2.0
	2.1	2.0	1.9	Sales/Total Assets		1.5		2.3	2.2	1.6
	1.5	1.4	1.4			1.0		1.3	1.8	1.4
	1.0	1.1	1.0			1.0		1.0	.6	1.1
(90) 2.1	(88) 2.3	(83) 2.5	% Depr., Dep., Amort./Sales	(13) 3.2		(17) 2.5	1.9	(18) 3.1
	3.4	4.1	4.3			5.4		3.8	4.0	4.5
	1.7	1.7	2.4						1.9	
(38) 2.5	(39) 2.9	(34) 3.7	% Officers', Directors', Owners' Comp/Sales				(11) 3.1	
	8.4	5.8	7.6						4.0	
	2571143M	1744741M	2058050M	Net Sales ($)	3309M	28317M	38336M	127785M	342377M	1517926M
	1305259M	1092669M	1123868M	Total Assets ($)	1706M	21085M	20033M	67667M	170491M	842886M

M = $ thousand   MM = $ million
See Pages 11 through 18 for Explanation of Ratios and Data

Current Data Sorted By Assets | Comparative Historical Data

							Type of Statement		
		3	31	28	5	7	Unqualified	85	87
		26	81	19	1		Reviewed	127	121
	18	43	36	2			Compiled	124	135
	31	17	9	1			Tax Returns	47	41
	6	43	61	28	7	4	Other	149	170
		121 (4/1-9/30/02)		386 (10/1/02-3/31/03)				4/1/98-3/31/99	4/1/99-3/31/00
	0-500M	500M-2MM	2-10MM	10-50MM	50-100MM	100-250MM		ALL	ALL
	55	132	218	78	13	11	NUMBER OF STATEMENTS	532	554
	%	%	%	%	%	%	ASSETS	%	%
	9.9	9.0	9.8	7.7	3.1	7.6	Cash & Equivalents	7.8	8.2
	25.2	27.8	25.4	21.9	20.5	15.5	Trade Receivables (net)	27.2	28.2
	18.8	19.0	22.7	22.1	26.6	16.9	Inventory	20.3	19.9
	2.3	3.0	2.5	2.8	6.1	6.4	All Other Current	2.2	2.0
	56.2	58.8	60.3	54.5	56.3	46.3	Total Current	57.4	58.3
	33.5	35.5	32.9	35.0	36.6	31.6	Fixed Assets (net)	34.3	33.5
	5.3	2.0	2.0	5.3	2.7	16.8	Intangibles (net)	3.1	2.8
	5.0	3.7	4.7	5.2	4.4	5.2	All Other Non-Current	5.2	5.5
	100.0	100.0	100.0	100.0	100.0	100.0	Total	100.0	100.0
							LIABILITIES		
	15.3	11.3	9.9	8.3	7.1	4.3	Notes Payable-Short Term	8.8	10.1
	9.5	5.5	4.6	4.9	3.5	5.5	Cur. Mat.-L/T/D	4.8	5.3
	22.6	14.9	12.5	10.7	10.9	8.1	Trade Payables	13.3	14.1
	.2	.2	.3	.3	.6	.2	Income Taxes Payable	.5	.3
	10.0	10.5	8.4	8.2	12.8	8.3	All Other Current	8.6	8.3
	57.5	42.5	35.6	32.5	34.8	26.4	Total Current	36.0	38.1
	32.1	23.4	16.2	16.7	18.9	17.6	Long Term Debt	20.6	19.5
	.1	.3	.8	.9	.9	1.9	Deferred Taxes	.7	.7
	17.1	6.8	3.7	6.8	8.1	10.5	All Other Non-Current	3.9	4.4
	−6.7	27.1	43.7	43.2	37.2	43.7	Net Worth	38.9	37.4
	100.0	100.0	100.0	100.0	100.0	100.0	Total Liabilities & Net Worth	100.0	100.0
							INCOME DATA		
	100.0	100.0	100.0	100.0	100.0	100.0	Net Sales	100.0	100.0
	44.0	33.1	26.7	22.3	20.9	24.0	Gross Profit	31.3	31.3
	41.9	32.5	23.1	16.8	17.6	15.8	Operating Expenses	24.8	26.3
	2.1	.6	3.6	5.5	3.3	8.3	Operating Profit	6.5	5.1
	2.2	1.5	1.0	1.4	2.1	3.8	All Other Expenses (net)	1.3	1.2
	−.1	−.9	2.6	4.1	1.2	4.5	Profit Before Taxes	5.2	3.9
							RATIOS		
	2.1	2.7	2.5	2.9	2.6	3.3		2.7	2.6
	1.0	1.5	1.7	1.7	1.8	2.2	Current	1.7	1.6
	.7	.9	1.1	1.2	1.5	1.8		1.1	1.1
	1.6	1.6	1.6	1.8	1.3	1.7		1.7	1.7
	.7	.9	.9	.9	.8	1.3	Quick (530)	1.0	1.0
	.3	.6	.6	.5	.5	.6		.6	.6
15	24.2	32	11.4	33	11.1	35	10.5	32	11.6	42	8.6	Sales/Receivables	31	11.8	35	10.5

							Sales/Receivables		
15 — 24.2	32 — 11.4	33 — 11.1	35 — 10.5	32 — 11.6	42 — 8.6		31 — 11.8	35 — 10.5
28 — 13.1	43 — 8.4	44 — 8.4	50 — 7.3	42 — 8.8	45 — 8.1		43 — 8.6	45 — 8.0
46 — 8.0	59 — 6.2	57 — 6.4	57 — 6.4	65 — 5.6	59 — 6.1		56 — 6.6	58 — 6.3
10 — 37.1	11 — 34.7	28 — 13.1	36 — 10.0	47 — 7.7	42 — 8.7	Cost of Sales/Inventory	19 — 19.1	18 — 20.6
31 — 11.8	35 — 10.5	51 — 7.1	60 — 6.1	63 — 5.8	66 — 5.5		42 — 8.7	42 — 8.8
67 — 5.5	70 — 5.2	83 — 4.4	86 — 4.3	101 — 3.6	84 — 4.3		72 — 5.0	72 — 5.1
13 — 27.4	14 — 26.1	16 — 22.7	17 — 22.0	11 — 32.5	24 — 15.4	Cost of Sales/Payables	14 — 25.3	16 — 22.6
32 — 11.2	29 — 12.6	28 — 13.0	27 — 13.4	28 — 13.0	28 — 12.9		25 — 14.8	28 — 13.1
61 — 6.0	52 — 7.0	43 — 8.4	35 — 10.4	40 — 9.2	42 — 8.6		37 — 9.8	43 — 8.5
10.2	5.9	4.5	4.2	5.3	3.0	Sales/Working Capital	5.6	5.5
169.3	14.7	8.5	7.5	6.2	4.9		9.9	11.0
−16.4	−51.0	35.2	22.7	11.9	10.7		43.4	41.5
6.2	4.9	9.8	11.8	7.1	14.6	EBIT/Interest	9.7	9.6
(47) 2.2	(121) 1.2	(199) 3.2	(73) 3.9	.8	2.8	(493)	3.8	(509) 3.0
−1.2	−2.5	.9	1.2	−.3	.7		1.6	1.3
	5.4	5.1	5.8			Net Profit + Depr., Dep., Amort./Cur. Mat. L/T/D	5.9	4.6
(24) 2.2	(55) 2.7	(25) 2.3			(199)	2.6	(175) 2.3
1.1	1.0	1.2				1.3	1.2
.6	.5	.3	.5	.6	.5	Fixed/Worth	.4	.4
3.2	1.3	1.3	1.5	1.2	1.0		.9	.9
−1.7	18.6	1.8	2.3	1.9	41.4		2.1	2.3
2.0	.8	.5	.6	1.0	.6	Debt/Worth	.7	.7
7.9	2.7	1.3	1.5	2.1	1.7		1.7	1.6
−5.8	34.4	3.8	3.6	3.7	91.0		4.5	4.9
84.8	25.4	32.2	33.5	39.2		% Profit Before Taxes/Tangible Net Worth	54.1	47.0
(29) 21.6	(102) 4.9	(205) 13.4	(72) 16.3	−2.7	(486)	25.6	(492) 19.7
3.1	−15.8	.8	4.0	−11.5		8.5	5.0
20.4	7.9	12.9	13.6	15.0	10.4	% Profit Before Taxes/Total Assets	19.0	15.8
4.4	.5	5.0	5.6	−.4	3.8		8.8	6.3
−13.6	−12.2	.1	−.1	−2.3	−1.3		2.5	1.0
41.2	15.5	14.2	9.6	8.2	5.3	Sales/Net Fixed Assets	14.7	15.1
8.3	7.4	7.0	4.9	6.5	4.7		6.8	7.0
4.0	3.7	3.2	3.2	2.5	2.7		3.9	3.8
4.3	3.1	2.5	2.0	2.1	1.4	Sales/Total Assets	2.8	2.8
2.8	2.2	1.9	1.6	1.7	1.0		2.2	2.1
1.8	1.6	1.5	1.3	1.3	1.0		1.7	1.6
1.5	1.7	1.6	2.0	1.7		% Depr., Dep., Amort./Sales	1.4	1.6
(45) 3.0	(123) 3.7	(203) 2.8	(70) 3.7	(12) 2.8	(478)	2.6	(501) 3.0
6.6	6.2	5.2	5.8	4.7		4.3	5.0
4.1	2.6	2.0	2.2			% Officers', Directors', Owners' Comp/Sales	2.5	2.9
(32) 7.2	(81) 5.4	(83) 4.0	(14) 3.8		(232)	4.7	(264) 5.0
11.1	9.0	7.1	5.0			8.8	8.4
48979M	367575M	2006705M	2331584M	1523119M	2111427M	Net Sales ($)	9595396M	8180384M
15604M	156384M	1015440M	1421418M	868199M	1800586M	Total Assets ($)	5648635M	4671592M

© RMA 2003

M = $ thousand   MM = $ million
See Pages 11 through 18 for Explanation of Ratios and Data

Comparative Historical Data | **Current Data Sorted By Sales**

			Type of Statement						
67	62	74	Unqualified		3	4	14	21	32
104	99	127	Reviewed		13	30	40	34	10
141	103	99	Compiled	12	40	18	20	8	1
53	32	58	Tax Returns	26	14	8	7	3	
165	160	149	Other	7	31	22	24	37	28
4/1/00- 3/31/01	4/1/01- 3/31/02	4/1/02- 3/31/03		121 (4/1-9/30/02)			386 (10/1/02-3/31/03)		
ALL	ALL	ALL		0-1MM	1-3MM	3-5MM	5-10MM	10-25MM	25MM & OVER
530	456	507	**NUMBER OF STATEMENTS**	45	101	82	105	103	71
%	%	%	**ASSETS**	%	%	%	%	%	%
7.6	7.8	9.1	Cash & Equivalents	8.3	9.7	10.4	9.7	9.3	5.6
28.4	24.4	25.1	Trade Receivables (net)	20.1	25.5	28.2	24.1	27.2	22.5
20.8	21.2	21.2	Inventory	17.2	17.7	18.4	24.1	23.5	24.3
1.8	2.2	2.8	All Other Current	2.6	2.5	2.9	2.3	2.6	4.5
58.6	55.5	58.2	Total Current	48.2	55.4	60.0	60.2	62.6	56.9
33.3	34.7	34.0	Fixed Assets (net)	41.0	37.8	33.8	34.5	28.6	31.8
3.5	3.8	3.2	Intangibles (net)	5.9	2.6	1.9	1.3	3.6	6.0
4.7	6.0	4.6	All Other Non-Current	4.9	4.1	4.3	4.0	5.1	5.3
100.0	100.0	100.0	Total	100.0	100.0	100.0	100.0	100.0	100.0
			LIABILITIES						
13.6	9.7	10.4	Notes Payable-Short Term	13.2	11.0	12.3	9.9	9.0	8.4
4.9	5.4	5.4	Cur. Mat.-L/T/D	10.5	5.6	5.3	5.0	4.4	4.3
14.8	12.5	13.8	Trade Payables	16.2	15.8	12.9	12.8	13.5	12.4
.4	.2	.3	Income Taxes Payable	.0	.1	.4	.2	.5	.3
10.4	8.0	9.2	All Other Current	10.3	8.9	9.2	8.2	9.7	9.5
44.1	35.8	39.1	Total Current	50.2	41.4	40.0	36.0	37.2	34.8
19.3	22.1	20.0	Long Term Debt	38.0	26.0	16.8	16.4	14.3	17.0
.5	.7	.6	Deferred Taxes	.0	.1	.6	1.2	.4	1.0
4.6	4.0	6.7	All Other Non-Current	19.4	7.6	3.1	5.1	4.5	6.9
31.5	37.4	33.7	Net Worth	−7.6	24.9	39.4	41.2	43.5	40.4
100.0	100.0	100.0	Total Liabilities & Net Worth	100.0	100.0	100.0	100.0	100.0	100.0
			INCOME DATA						
100.0	100.0	100.0	Net Sales	100.0	100.0	100.0	100.0	100.0	100.0
31.1	30.5	29.4	Gross Profit	41.1	37.0	28.5	26.2	25.6	22.3
25.2	27.2	26.3	Operating Expenses	40.9	35.7	25.8	23.6	20.2	17.0
5.9	3.3	3.1	Operating Profit	.2	1.2	2.6	2.6	5.4	5.3
1.5	1.5	1.4	All Other Expenses (net)	3.5	1.5	1.2	1.0	.9	1.9
4.3	1.8	1.6	Profit Before Taxes	−3.3	−.2	1.5	1.6	4.4	3.4
			RATIOS						
2.6	2.7	2.6		2.8	2.1	2.7	2.9	2.6	2.5
1.6	1.6	1.6	Current	1.0	1.5	1.5	1.7	1.9	1.8
1.1	1.1	1.0		.6	.8	1.1	1.1	1.2	1.3
1.7	1.6	1.6		2.0	1.6	1.7	1.6	1.7	1.5
.9	(455) .9	.9	Quick	.6	.9	1.0	.9	.9	.8
.6	.6	.5		.3	.5	.6	.6	.6	.5
33 11.0	32 11.5	32 11.6		16 22.8	30 12.3	37 10.0	30 12.1	33 11.0	32 11.4
46 8.0	41 8.8	43 8.5	Sales/Receivables	29 12.6	46 8.0	46 7.9	39 9.3	45 8.1	45 8.2
60 6.1	55 6.7	57 6.4		57 6.4	58 6.3	60 6.0	50 7.4	59 6.2	58 6.3
20 18.6	22 16.6	23 15.9		6 62.7	12 29.7	18 20.7	26 14.1	35 10.3	38 9.5
43 8.4	48 7.7	46 7.9	Cost of Sales/Inventory	33 11.2	35 10.4	41 9.0	47 7.8	53 6.9	60 6.1
78 4.7	87 4.2	78 4.7		72 5.1	75 5.5	67 5.5	83 4.4	80 4.5	81 4.5
16 22.3	15 24.7	16 23.3		12 29.6	18 20.7	15 24.8	15 24.9	15 23.7	20 18.3
29 12.8	25 14.3	28 13.0	Cost of Sales/Payables	25 14.8	36 10.1	22 16.9	28 13.2	28 12.9	28 13.0
44 8.2	41 8.8	44 8.3		50 7.3	61 6.0	43 8.5	41 8.9	43 8.5	37 9.7
5.8	5.2	5.0		9.5	6.8	5.4	3.8	4.4	4.8
10.7	10.5	9.8	Sales/Working Capital	−328.0	15.0	9.6	7.8	8.3	7.9
55.7	57.5	93.9		−9.8	−31.9	68.0	51.1	20.8	17.8
(489) 8.5	(421) 6.0	(464) 7.2		(38) 4.7	(90) 3.3	(75) 7.1	(101) 7.1	(91) 17.5	(69) 10.8
3.1	2.0	2.6	EBIT/Interest	1.4	.9	2.8	2.7	4.0	4.1
1.2	.4	.1		−1.3	−2.0	.6	.8	1.5	.7
(148) 5.2	(126) 3.6	(119) 5.1	Net Profit + Depr., Dep.,		(15) 5.6	(18) 4.2	(34) 5.1	(20) 4.6	(30) 7.8
2.4	1.6	2.4	Amort./Cur. Mat. L/T/D		1.5	1.9	3.2	2.1	3.2
1.2	.8	1.1			.4	1.3	.9	1.4	1.4
.4	.4	.4		1.0	.6	.3	.3	.3	.5
1.0	.9	1.0	Fixed/Worth	3.2	1.9	.8	.8	.7	.9
2.6	2.4	3.1		−1.7	67.2	2.0	2.3	1.7	1.9
.7	.7	.7		1.7	.9	.5	.5	.5	.9
1.8	1.7	1.8	Debt/Worth	7.9	2.8	1.3	1.3	1.3	1.6
5.7	5.1	6.2		−5.1	NM	3.9	4.4	3.9	3.3
(467) 48.5	(398) 31.9	(430) 32.2	% Profit Before Taxes/Tangible	(24) 100.9	(76) 21.5	(73) 27.0	(94) 29.5	(97) 36.3	(66) 38.2
23.1	12.0	12.2	Net Worth	19.9	2.6	6.9	10.3	18.9	12.9
5.8	−.3	−3.0		−7.6	−36.6	.3	−.2	6.6	−3.2
17.7	12.0	12.6	% Profit Before Taxes/Total	13.8	8.8	10.7	10.9	16.5	13.6
7.3	3.7	4.2	Assets	.6	.2	3.9	4.8	6.4	5.3
.9	−2.3	−2.5		−15.7	−11.8	−.7	−1.0	1.5	−1.3
14.5	13.0	13.3		24.4	12.2	14.0	16.3	15.4	9.2
7.2	6.2	6.7	Sales/Net Fixed Assets	5.2	6.1	7.2	7.1	8.4	6.0
3.9	3.4	3.4		2.0	3.2	3.3	3.2	4.3	3.7
2.8	2.6	2.6		2.9	2.8	2.6	2.7	2.7	2.2
2.1	1.9	1.9	Sales/Total Assets	2.1	1.9	1.9	1.9	2.1	1.8
1.5	1.4	1.5		1.2	1.5	1.5	1.5	1.6	1.3
(481) 1.4	(416) 1.5	(459) 1.7	% Depr., Dep., Amort./Sales	(37) 2.0	(93) 2.2	(75) 1.6	(100) 1.6	(95) 1.4	(59) 1.7
2.8	2.9	3.2		6.2	3.9	3.7	3.0	2.5	2.9
4.7	5.1	5.7		12.3	6.5	6.2	4.9	5.1	3.9
(261) 2.8	(197) 2.9	(211) 2.4	% Officers', Directors',	(22) 3.4	(68) 2.9	(39) 2.9	(41) 2.4	(31) 1.7	(10) 1.3
4.8	4.5	5.1	Owners' Comp/Sales	6.7	6.1	5.7	4.4	3.4	2.5
8.1	7.9	8.4		10.6	9.2	7.9	8.7	5.4	3.7
11080584M	8383931M	8389389M	Net Sales ($)	24685M	197224M	318743M	752017M	1658032M	5438688M
5307303M	4851500M	5277631M	Total Assets ($)	14729M	119175M	176251M	431615M	895712M	3640149M

M = $ thousand   MM = $ million
See Pages 11 through 18 for Explanation of Ratios and Data

Current Data Sorted By Assets   **Comparative Historical Data**

0-500M	500M-2MM	2-10MM	10-50MM	50-100MM	100-250MM	Type of Statement	4/1/98-3/31/99 ALL	4/1/99-3/31/00 ALL
		12	12	2	7	Unqualified	49	55
	2	18	4			Reviewed	26	28
2	7	10	2			Compiled	39	33
3	3	3				Tax Returns	3	10
1	7	10	6		1	Other	54	42
	29 (4/1-9/30/02)		83 (10/1/02-3/31/03)					
6	19	53	24	2	8	NUMBER OF STATEMENTS	171	168
%	%	%	%	%	%	ASSETS	%	%
	6.4	5.6	5.4			Cash & Equivalents	6.8	6.5
	19.9	17.1	20.3			Trade Receivables (net)	19.8	20.7
	41.7	46.2	44.1			Inventory	42.7	40.7
	1.8	2.0	1.8			All Other Current	1.8	2.7
	69.7	70.9	71.7			Total Current	71.1	70.6
	20.3	20.5	23.7			Fixed Assets (net)	21.9	21.3
	3.1	3.8	.8			Intangibles (net)	2.6	2.6
	6.9	4.8	3.8			All Other Non-Current	4.4	5.5
	100.0	100.0	100.0			Total	100.0	100.0
						LIABILITIES		
	21.2	19.7	18.7			Notes Payable-Short Term	16.6	16.5
	4.4	2.5	2.9			Cur. Mat.-L/T/D	2.9	3.1
	10.3	10.2	9.2			Trade Payables	11.9	12.4
	.0	.3	.3			Income Taxes Payable	.3	.3
	10.0	12.2	10.0			All Other Current	9.6	9.8
	46.0	44.8	41.1			Total Current	41.2	42.2
	18.3	13.2	10.2			Long Term Debt	14.0	14.2
	.1	.3	.3			Deferred Taxes	.4	.4
	11.7	7.3	1.7			All Other Non-Current	4.9	3.8
	23.9	34.5	46.7			Net Worth	39.4	39.5
	100.0	100.0	100.0			Total Liabilities & Net Worth	100.0	100.0
						INCOME DATA		
	100.0	100.0	100.0			Net Sales	100.0	100.0
	33.4	27.4	21.0			Gross Profit	28.3	25.8
	29.8	24.5	19.3			Operating Expenses	22.8	21.6
	3.5	3.0	1.7			Operating Profit	5.5	4.2
	1.0	.6	1.4			All Other Expenses (net)	1.4	1.6
	2.5	2.4	.2			Profit Before Taxes	4.1	2.6
						RATIOS		
	2.9	2.9	2.8			Current	3.0	2.8
	1.6	1.6	1.8				2.0	1.7
	1.1	1.2	1.4				1.3	1.2
	1.0	.9	1.2			Quick	1.2	1.3
	.6	.6	.6				.7	(166) .7
	.2	.2	.3				.4	.3
4	96.0	22 16.6	18 19.8			Sales/Receivables	20 18.4	19 18.9
27	13.6	34 10.6	45 8.0				33 11.2	35 10.4
47	7.7	46 8.0	72 5.1				54 6.7	61 6.0
52	7.0	79 4.6	79 4.6			Cost of Sales/Inventory	71 5.1	64 5.7
80	4.6	135 2.7	115 3.2				107 3.4	110 3.3
162	2.2	200 1.8	179 2.0				170 2.1	164 2.2
9	40.8	11 32.4	15 25.2			Cost of Sales/Payables	12 30.9	15 24.8
18	19.8	25 14.9	27 13.5				22 16.6	23 15.7
46	8.0	42 8.7	40 9.2				38 9.7	40 9.1
	4.2	3.7	3.0			Sales/Working Capital	3.3	3.8
	8.5	7.0	4.9				6.0	6.0
	15.6	17.5	12.9				11.6	19.8
	9.2	6.6	5.5			EBIT/Interest	7.9	7.2
	2.0	(48) 2.1	(23) 2.4				(163) 3.1	(162) 2.2
	-1.4	.8	1.0				1.3	.9
		5.1	7.6			Net Profit + Depr., Dep., Amort./Cur. Mat. L /T/D	5.0	6.5
	(12)	2.8	(10) 3.2				(59) 2.6	(61) 2.1
		-.1	-.3				1.2	.6
	.2	.2	.3			Fixed/Worth	.2	.3
	.6	.4	.5				.5	.5
	-1.2	2.2	1.0				1.1	1.1
	.6	.6	.5			Debt/Worth	.7	.7
	1.7	2.1	1.0				1.3	1.6
	-7.1	6.2	3.3				3.9	4.5
	37.7	25.2	13.3			% Profit Before Taxes/Tangible Net Worth	34.2	24.0
(14)	9.5	(46) 8.4	(23) 4.9				(152) 16.1	(160) 10.2
	-22.6	2.7	-13.2				3.4	.2
	12.7	6.5	8.5			% Profit Before Taxes/Total Assets	14.8	9.7
	2.5	2.0	2.5				6.1	3.5
	-10.2	-.1	-4.0				.6	-.1
	23.1	26.5	10.9			Sales/Net Fixed Assets	20.3	22.3
	14.0	9.6	6.8				10.0	9.2
	9.9	5.3	5.1				5.8	5.7
	2.8	2.2	2.1			Sales/Total Assets	2.3	2.3
	2.1	1.7	1.5				1.8	1.8
	1.5	1.3	1.3				1.4	1.3
	1.4	1.0	1.7			% Depr., Dep., Amort./Sales	1.1	1.1
(16)	1.9	(46) 1.8	(22) 2.4				(151) 1.9	(148) 1.9
	3.3	3.8	3.0				2.7	3.0
	1.6	1.6				% Officers', Directors', Owners' Comp/Sales	1.3	1.3
(12)	3.0	(18) 2.3					(51) 3.2	(58) 2.7
	7.5	4.6					5.6	5.0
6126M	46104M	487216M	683340M	254493M	1764400M	Net Sales ($)	5315516M	4857858M
1781M	22183M	279769M	426318M	150303M	1377263M	Total Assets ($)	3205948M	3204710M

Comparative Historical Data						Current Data Sorted By Sales				

			Type of Statement							
36	27	33	Unqualified			2	6	11	14	
22	26	24	Reviewed		1	3	10	7	3	
30	28	21	Compiled	2	5	4	7	2	1	
5	15	9	Tax Returns	2	3	1	3			
47	38	25	Other		8	2	3	8	4	
4/1/00-3/31/01 ALL	4/1/01-3/31/02 ALL	4/1/02-3/31/03 ALL		0-1MM	29 (4/1-9/30/02) 1-3MM	3-5MM	83 (10/1/02-3/31/03) 5-10MM	10-25MM	25MM & OVER	
140	134	112	NUMBER OF STATEMENTS	4	17	12	29	28	22	
%	%	%	ASSETS	%	%	%	%	%	%	
6.7	6.1	6.1	Cash & Equivalents		10.2	3.7	7.2	3.0	6.4	
19.5	18.6	19.3	Trade Receivables (net)		23.5	10.3	15.1	23.0	23.2	
40.5	41.7	43.2	Inventory		39.4	54.1	47.2	43.8	33.2	
2.3	2.4	1.8	All Other Current		1.4	2.1	1.8	2.5	1.5	
69.0	68.8	70.4	Total Current		74.5	70.3	71.4	72.3	64.3	
22.3	20.6	20.8	Fixed Assets (net)		15.7	13.9	21.2	23.7	21.8	
3.5	4.0	4.2	Intangibles (net)		3.5	9.0	3.2	.2	9.3	
5.2	6.6	4.6	All Other Non-Current		6.4	6.7	4.2	3.8	4.5	
100.0	100.0	100.0	Total		100.0	100.0	100.0	100.0	100.0	
			LIABILITIES							
14.9	16.8	19.0	Notes Payable-Short Term		12.8	27.5	17.0	23.0	12.0	
3.0	3.3	2.8	Cur. Mat.-L/T/D		5.0	1.4	3.1	2.0	2.1	
11.3	11.0	10.4	Trade Payables		14.0	6.5	11.5	9.2	8.9	
.2	.2	.2	Income Taxes Payable		.1	.0	.3	.1	.4	
11.1	9.9	11.0	All Other Current		9.9	8.0	16.8	8.2	11.2	
40.6	41.2	43.4	Total Current		41.8	43.4	48.8	42.5	34.6	
13.8	12.9	14.0	Long Term Debt		29.8	17.6	12.9	7.7	11.7	
.6	.2	.3	Deferred Taxes		.1	.0	.4	.2	.6	
7.8	5.7	7.7	All Other Non-Current		11.7	2.2	6.4	8.0	7.2	
37.3	40.0	34.6	Net Worth		16.6	36.8	31.5	41.7	46.0	
100.0	100.0	100.0	Total Liabilities & Net Worth		100.0	100.0	100.0	100.0	100.0	
			INCOME DATA							
100.0	100.0	100.0	Net Sales		100.0	100.0	100.0	100.0	100.0	
27.4	27.1	27.2	Gross Profit		36.8	30.2	28.2	20.5	23.5	
22.7	24.2	24.1	Operating Expenses		34.4	28.2	25.3	19.3	18.4	
4.7	2.9	3.1	Operating Profit		2.4	2.0	2.9	1.3	5.1	
1.6	1.3	1.0	All Other Expenses (net)		1.1	.3	.6	1.1	1.7	
3.1	1.6	2.0	Profit Before Taxes		1.3	1.7	2.4	.2	3.4	
			RATIOS							
3.1	2.8	2.9	Current		3.2	2.7	2.9	2.9	3.3	
1.8	1.8	1.7			1.9	1.5	1.5	1.7	2.0	
1.2	1.2	1.2			1.2	1.3	1.1	1.1	1.4	
1.2	1.1	1.1	Quick		1.3	1.0	.7	1.0	2.1	
.7	.6	.6			.8	.3	.4	.6	.9	
.3	.4	.3			.4	.1	.2	.4	.4	
21 17.3	19 18.9	18 19.8	Sales/Receivables	6 66.2	7 53.2	22 16.6	24 15.3	27 13.7	
34 10.8	32 11.5	35 10.3		28 13.0	21 17.6	33 10.9	46 8.0	50 7.3	
51 7.2	52 7.0	55 6.6		47 7.7	37 10.0	44 8.3	72 5.1	86 4.3	
61 6.0	54 6.7	73 5.0	Cost of Sales/Inventory	41 9.0	77 4.7	88 4.1	66 5.5	72 5.1	
103 3.5	102 3.6	105 3.5		80 4.6	176 2.1	135 2.7	137 2.7	85 4.3	
163 2.2	162 2.2	179 2.0		173 2.1	303 1.2	181 2.0	181 2.0	107 3.4	
13 27.3	12 30.1	13 28.7	Cost of Sales/Payables	14 25.2	8 45.2	16 22.9	12 29.4	16 23.2	
23 16.0	25 14.9	23 16.2		22 16.9	10 36.2	29 12.7	22 16.8	23 16.2	
36 10.1	33 11.2	42 8.8		54 6.8	35 10.5	51 7.2	37 9.8	28 12.9	
3.5	3.9	3.5	Sales/Working Capital	4.2	2.6	3.5	3.6	3.0	
6.5	7.3	6.9		8.3	8.5	7.0	4.9	6.1	
17.2	19.2	14.5		11.7	14.3	39.5	18.3	9.6	
(131) 5.3	(125) 7.6	(103) 6.2	EBIT/Interest	(15) 6.2	8.9	(28) 3.4	(23) 11.8	(21) 5.3	
2.1	1.7	2.1		2.1	1.2	2.0	1.6	3.2	
1.0	.5	.8		-.6	-.6	.8	-.2	1.4	
(38) 5.9	(37) 6.2	(32) 9.8	Net Profit + Depr., Dep., Amort./Cur. Mat. L/T/D				(11) 12.0		
2.6	2.0	3.6					5.0		
1.2	.8	.9					3.3		
.3	.2	.3	Fixed/Worth	.2	.2	.2	.3	.3	
.6	.5	.5		.5	.2	.6	.4	.5	
1.2	1.3	2.1		-1.0	129.7	2.6	.9	2.1	
.8	.6	.6	Debt/Worth	.5	.4	.9	.6	.5	
1.5	1.4	1.7		2.8	2.2	2.2	1.1	1.4	
4.4	4.6	5.2		-5.1	250.4	6.4	3.9	3.6	
27.0	21.7	25.0	% Profit Before Taxes/Tangible Net Worth	32.4	36.6	20.5	16.1	41.4	
(128) 9.7	(117) 6.3	(96) 8.3		(12) 9.5	(10) 15.1	(25) 6.8	(26) 5.3	(20) 10.4	
.5	-1.1	1.3		-16.6	-.8	1.2	-8.5	5.1	
11.0	8.9	7.9	% Profit Before Taxes/Total Assets	14.6	9.4	4.4	8.3	11.1	
4.2	1.7	2.1		4.0	.4	1.9	2.1	4.5	
-.1	-2.1	-.4		-8.2	-2.6	-.2	-10.8	1.4	
19.5	24.8	22.8	Sales/Net Fixed Assets	26.9	38.8	29.4	13.3	10.0	
9.3	11.2	9.3		14.6	16.1	8.9	7.1	7.3	
5.5	6.3	5.7		10.7	8.7	5.2	5.1	5.8	
2.4	2.7	2.2	Sales/Total Assets	3.1	2.3	2.1	2.3	2.1	
1.8	1.9	1.6		2.1	1.5	1.8	1.6	1.5	
1.3	1.3	1.3		1.5	1.0	1.3	1.3	1.3	
(123) 1.0	(121) .8	(99) 1.3	% Depr., Dep., Amort./Sales	(15) 1.7	(10) 1.0	(25) .9	(25) 1.4	(20) 1.7	
2.0	1.9	2.0		2.0	1.4	1.9	2.4	2.0	
3.2	2.9	3.3		3.5	3.3	3.8	3.5	3.0	
(44) 1.8	(46) .9	(37) 1.6	% Officers', Directors', Owners' Comp/Sales	(12) 1.8		(11) 1.7			
3.5	2.5	2.6		4.6		2.7			
5.7	6.0	5.2		8.6		4.6			
3332209M	3265305M	3241679M	Net Sales ($)	1193M	34820M	45846M	210037M	463450M	2486333M
2236457M	2203059M	2257617M	Total Assets ($)	1111M	17292M	33124M	130381M	294659M	1781050M

M = $ thousand   MM = $ million
See Pages 11 through 18 for Explanation of Ratios and Data

Current Data Sorted By Assets

Comparative Historical Data

							Type of Statement			
	1		3		5	1	3	Unqualified		15	13
	1		1		1			Reviewed		5	6
2	3							Compiled		7	5
3	3		1					Tax Returns			
1	2		8		7	2		Other		13	10
	13 (4/1-9/30/02)				35 (10/1/02-3/31/03)					4/1/98- 3/31/99	4/1/99- 3/31/00
0-500M	500M-2MM		2-10MM		10-50MM	50-100MM	100-250MM			ALL	ALL
6	10		13		13	3	3	NUMBER OF STATEMENTS		40	34
%	%		%		%	%	%	ASSETS		%	%
	5.7		4.1		6.7			Cash & Equivalents		7.0	5.1
	19.0		17.1		23.3			Trade Receivables (net)		22.5	19.3
	46.8		48.5		34.3			Inventory		40.2	42.5
	.5		2.8		2.9			All Other Current		3.0	3.7
	72.1		72.4		67.3			Total Current		72.8	70.5
	21.7		20.5		27.6			Fixed Assets (net)		19.3	18.2
	.3		2.1		2.7			Intangibles (net)		3.7	4.4
	5.9		5.0		2.4			All Other Non-Current		4.2	6.8
	100.0		100.0		100.0			Total		100.0	100.0
								LIABILITIES			
	19.2		11.7		15.4			Notes Payable-Short Term		12.8	17.7
	1.3		3.8		2.3			Cur. Mat.-L/T/D		3.6	1.8
	23.2		15.7		12.1			Trade Payables		12.0	12.5
	.5		.5		.2			Income Taxes Payable		.4	.3
	6.0		15.2		10.9			All Other Current		8.1	7.8
	50.2		47.0		40.9			Total Current		36.9	40.2
	21.5		15.8		16.0			Long Term Debt		14.0	14.7
	.0		.1		.3			Deferred Taxes		.1	.2
	1.4		7.8		2.8			All Other Non-Current		5.6	6.6
	26.9		29.4		40.0			Net Worth		43.5	38.4
	100.0		100.0		100.0			Total Liabilities & Net Worth		100.0	100.0
								INCOME DATA			
	100.0		100.0		100.0			Net Sales		100.0	100.0
	27.7		30.8		24.8			Gross Profit		29.6	28.6
	28.3		28.2		20.9			Operating Expenses		23.7	21.9
	-.5		2.6		3.9			Operating Profit		5.9	6.7
	.2		2.1		1.2			All Other Expenses (net)		1.9	1.1
	-.7		.5		2.7			Profit Before Taxes		4.0	5.6
								RATIOS			
	5.5		4.9		3.4					3.9	3.1
	1.3		1.8		1.6			Current		2.2	2.0
	.9		1.2		1.1					1.3	1.2
	2.5		1.5		2.0					1.5	1.8
	.3		.5		.5			Quick		.7	.5
	.2		.3		.5					.4	.3

13	28.3	9	39.1	38	9.6		20	18.4	16	22.3
20	18.6	33	11.0	51	7.2	Sales/Receivables	40	9.1	35	10.5
42	8.7	59	6.2	59	6.2		56	6.6	54	6.8
47	7.7	72	5.1	65	5.6		60	6.1	64	5.7
86	4.2	93	3.9	89	4.1	Cost of Sales/Inventory	89	4.1	89	4.1
177	2.1	216	1.7	118	3.1		148	2.5	146	2.5
11	31.8	12	29.4	24	15.0		11	32.5	10	36.1
38	9.6	16	23.1	31	11.7	Cost of Sales/Payables	24	15.2	30	12.1
77	4.7	51	7.1	40	9.0		55	6.7	45	8.1

	6.4	3.1	3.4			3.3	3.5
	16.0	6.1	6.5	Sales/Working Capital		5.1	6.0
	-26.0	225.5	67.9			15.9	22.7
	7.4	6.5	11.3			5.7	4.4
	1.9	2.3	2.5	EBIT/Interest	(38) 2.2	(29) 1.9
	-2.3	.5	.7			1.3	1.3
				Net Profit + Depr., Dep., Amort./Cur. Mat. L /T/D	(12)	4.1 2.5 .9	
	.1	.3	.5			.2	.2
	.6	.4	.6	Fixed/Worth		.5	.5
	2.6	1.5	1.8			1.5	2.7
	2.0	.9	.5			.5	.7
	3.1	3.0	1.5	Debt/Worth		1.5	1.7
	9.6	6.1	6.4			4.4	8.9
	37.7	41.2	23.2			30.3	35.9
	8.1	(12) 13.8	(12) 8.8	% Profit Before Taxes/Tangible Net Worth	(39) 13.1	(29) 22.6
	-35.4	4.0	-4.6			6.8	9.1
	7.9	13.7	7.7			9.9	14.2
	1.2	2.7	3.2	% Profit Before Taxes/Total Assets		5.2	5.2
	-8.2	-2.6	-1.8			1.1	2.0
	69.1	43.2	8.4			25.1	46.5
	13.6	7.9	7.6	Sales/Net Fixed Assets		12.6	12.7
	7.5	5.3	4.4			6.7	5.9
	3.1	3.4	2.1			2.6	2.6
	2.5	2.0	1.8	Sales/Total Assets		1.9	1.8
	1.6	1.3	1.3			1.6	1.3
	1.2	1.2	1.3			.9	.7
	2.0	(12) 2.1	2.6	% Depr., Dep., Amort./Sales	(33) 1.6	(28) 1.2
	2.5	3.4	3.5			3.3	3.3
				% Officers', Directors', Owners' Comp/Sales	(12)	2.1 2.6 4.6	

6841M	30325M	218457M	455703M	405983M	735030M	Net Sales ($)	1275366M	1149390M
2112M	13453M	80022M	270924M	192460M	488674M	Total Assets ($)	712017M	730952M

© RMA 2003

M = $ thousand   MM = $ million
See Pages 11 through 18 for Explanation of Ratios and Data

Comparative Historical Data   **Current Data Sorted By Sales**

		Comparative Historical Data				13 (4/1-9/30/02)	35 (10/1/02-3/31/03)			
Type of Statement					0-1MM	1-3MM	3-5MM	5-10MM	10-25MM	25MM & OVER
Unqualified	8	13	13		1	1			2	9
Reviewed	1	1	3		1	1			1	
Compiled	5	5	5	1	3	1				
Tax Returns	4	5	7	2	4			1		
Other	11	13	20		2	2	1	7	8	
	4/1/00-3/31/01 ALL	4/1/01-3/31/02 ALL	4/1/02-3/31/03 ALL							
NUMBER OF STATEMENTS	29	37	48	3	11	5	1	11	17
ASSETS	%	%	%	%	%	%	%	%	%
Cash & Equivalents	4.0	5.1	5.5		4.7			4.6	3.7
Trade Receivables (net)	18.1	17.4	20.2		19.1			21.7	22.5
Inventory	43.4	42.1	42.5		50.6			34.8	37.7
All Other Current	1.4	1.4	1.9		.1			4.4	2.1
Total Current	66.8	66.0	70.0		74.5			65.6	66.0
Fixed Assets (net)	23.0	25.2	21.5		12.6			30.9	21.8
Intangibles (net)	4.4	3.8	3.1		1.0			.5	7.3
All Other Non-Current	5.8	5.0	5.4		11.9			3.1	4.9
Total	100.0	100.0	100.0		100.0			100.0	100.0
LIABILITIES									
Notes Payable-Short Term	13.9	18.8	16.7		22.1			10.7	15.7
Cur. Mat.-L/T/D	3.3	4.1	2.0		1.1			2.9	2.4
Trade Payables	15.7	17.8	18.5		27.4			15.7	15.4
Income Taxes Payable	.0	.0	.4		.0			.5	.3
All Other Current	7.5	10.0	10.4		4.0			18.2	12.7
Total Current	40.4	50.8	48.0		54.7			47.8	46.5
Long Term Debt	17.3	18.6	16.2		28.6			11.5	12.3
Deferred Taxes	.3	.5	.1		.0			.0	.2
All Other Non-Current	4.9	6.6	5.0		.5			6.7	6.5
Net Worth	37.1	23.5	30.8		16.3			34.0	34.5
Total Liabilities & Net Worth	100.0	100.0	100.0		100.0			100.0	100.0
INCOME DATA									
Net Sales	100.0	100.0	100.0		100.0			100.0	100.0
Gross Profit	28.5	29.4	28.3		31.5			24.7	26.5
Operating Expenses	24.0	25.6	25.5		32.3			21.6	20.6
Operating Profit	4.5	3.8	2.8		−.8			3.1	5.8
All Other Expenses (net)	1.1	1.9	1.2		.1			1.5	1.4
Profit Before Taxes	3.4	1.8	1.5		−1.0			1.6	4.4
RATIOS									
Current	2.8	2.9	2.9		5.6			3.8	2.4
	1.8	1.3	1.6		1.4			1.8	1.4
	1.1	1.0	1.0		.9			1.0	1.1
Quick	.9	1.2	1.3		1.8			2.0	.9
	.6	(36) .5	.5		.4			.5	.5
	.2	.3	.3		.3			.4	.4
Sales/Receivables	11 32.5	12 29.6	18 19.9		16 23.3			27 13.5	28 13.3
	38 9.7	34 10.9	41 8.9		34 10.9			57 6.4	43 8.4
	55 6.6	49 7.4	58 6.2		47 7.8			60 6.1	57 6.4
Cost of Sales/Inventory	64 5.7	71 5.2	65 5.6		44 8.4			59 6.2	63 5.8
	95 3.8	86 4.2	91 4.0		86 4.2			89 4.1	92 4.0
	125 2.9	140 2.6	165 2.2		277 1.3			100 3.7	119 3.1
Cost of Sales/Payables	11 34.5	11 32.5	15 24.4		6 64.3			14 25.4	26 14.2
	33 10.9	27 13.6	28 13.1		25 14.7			26 14.2	33 11.2
	47 7.7	55 6.6	47 7.8		69 5.3			73 5.0	40 9.0
Sales/Working Capital	3.8	3.8	3.9		7.3			3.4	4.4
	9.2	16.3	8.4		17.1			6.5	9.3
	27.2	NM	97.7		−14.1			−384.7	67.9
EBIT/Interest	(28) 4.5	(36) 7.9	(46) 11.0					11.0	11.3
	2.3	1.6	2.3					1.5	4.0
	1.3	1.1	.3					−1.2	1.9
Net Profit + Depr., Dep., Amort./Cur. Mat. L/T/D									
Fixed/Worth	.3	.4	.3		.1			.4	.5
	.6	.8	.5		.3			.6	.7
	1.6	4.0	1.3		.7			2.3	1.9
Debt/Worth	.8	1.1	.8		1.4			.5	1.0
	1.8	3.6	2.6		3.0			2.1	2.6
	7.0	20.6	6.2		16.0			6.1	7.2
% Profit Before Taxes/Tangible Net Worth	(27) 33.3	(29) 36.6	(44) 37.3		(10) 53.1			(10) 29.6	(15) 31.0
	14.2	20.3	17.6		6.6			6.5	23.9
	5.7	1.3	−3.3		−29.5			1.3	12.7
% Profit Before Taxes/Total Assets	9.7	11.3	9.1		18.6			9.2	9.6
	4.0	2.4	4.3		1.5			1.4	5.7
	1.1	.4	−.8		−5.8			−3.9	3.2
Sales/Net Fixed Assets	29.8	15.5	31.5		129.8			8.1	11.9
	12.3	7.7	8.6		16.6			5.6	8.6
	5.2	5.8	5.6		9.7			4.4	6.7
Sales/Total Assets	2.7	2.7	2.9		4.0			2.2	2.3
	2.1	1.8	1.9		3.1			1.9	1.8
	1.4	1.4	1.4		1.4			1.5	1.4
% Depr., Dep., Amort./Sales	(26) .6	(32) 1.3	(42) 1.4					(10) 2.1	(16) 1.0
	1.3	1.9	2.1					3.1	2.0
	2.2	3.2	3.3					4.1	2.9
% Officers', Directors', Owners' Comp/Sales	(12) 2.0	(16) 1.3	(15) 1.3						
	3.4	3.6	3.2						
	7.0	10.7	9.5						
Net Sales ($)	911445M	1653824M	1852339M	1969M	24783M	19288M	8585M	187039M	1610675M
Total Assets ($)	527907M	920384M	1047645M	1284M	14289M	9938M	2238M	101272M	918624M

M = $ thousand   MM = $ million
See Pages 11 through 18 for Explanation of Ratios and Data

Current Data Sorted By Assets   Comparative Historical Data

0-500M	500M-2MM	2-10MM	10-50MM	50-100MM	100-250MM	Type of Statement	4/1/98-3/31/99	4/1/99-3/31/00
	2	18	15	2	4	Unqualified	61	37
2	5	12	11	1		Reviewed	27	32
3	8	7	1			Compiled	17	21
2	2	1				Tax Returns	6	8
1	7	13	13	5	1	Other	39	40
	27 (4/1-9/30/02)		109 (10/1/02-3/31/03)					
0-500M	500M-2MM	2-10MM	10-50MM	50-100MM	100-250MM		ALL	ALL
8	24	51	40	8	5	NUMBER OF STATEMENTS	150	138
%	%	%	%	%	%	**ASSETS**	%	%
	7.8	4.4	6.5			Cash & Equivalents	7.1	6.7
	28.2	27.1	22.8			Trade Receivables (net)	23.3	23.9
	27.2	32.7	29.5			Inventory	35.2	34.0
	4.1	4.6	2.2			All Other Current	2.4	3.4
	67.3	68.7	61.0			Total Current	68.0	68.0
	27.0	25.1	24.5			Fixed Assets (net)	23.8	22.8
	1.1	3.1	6.0			Intangibles (net)	3.0	3.7
	4.6	3.1	8.4			All Other Non-Current	5.2	5.5
	100.0	100.0	100.0			Total	100.0	100.0
						LIABILITIES		
	12.2	13.3	12.2			Notes Payable-Short Term	12.9	13.7
	11.5	5.3	2.5			Cur. Mat.-L/T/D	3.6	3.8
	13.9	14.1	13.3			Trade Payables	13.0	14.6
	.1	.3	.3			Income Taxes Payable	.4	.4
	14.7	10.9	13.7			All Other Current	9.6	10.7
	52.4	43.9	42.1			Total Current	39.3	43.2
	19.0	14.3	13.5			Long Term Debt	15.1	14.1
	.2	.5	.6			Deferred Taxes	.4	.4
	2.6	5.3	3.7			All Other Non-Current	4.5	5.5
	25.8	36.0	40.1			Net Worth	40.7	36.9
	100.0	100.0	100.0			Total Liabilities & Net Worth	100.0	100.0
						INCOME DATA		
	100.0	100.0	100.0			Net Sales	100.0	100.0
	32.4	26.9	24.3			Gross Profit	26.9	28.1
	28.1	23.4	19.9			Operating Expenses	21.1	22.4
	4.3	3.5	4.4			Operating Profit	5.7	5.8
	1.3	.9	1.1			All Other Expenses (net)	.8	1.1
	2.9	2.6	3.2			Profit Before Taxes	5.0	4.6
						RATIOS		
	2.6	2.5	2.3				2.8	2.8
	1.3	1.6	1.6			Current	1.7	1.7
	.9	1.1	1.1				1.3	1.2
	1.5	1.4	1.2				1.3	1.3
	.8	.6	.7			Quick	(149) .8	.7
	.5	.4	.4				.5	.4
27 13.5	31 11.8	37 9.9					30 12.2	32 11.3
38 9.5	50 7.2	54 6.8				Sales/Receivables	42 8.8	43 8.4
53 6.8	71 5.2	74 5.0					55 6.6	58 6.3
22 16.7	38 9.7	56 6.5					43 8.5	43 8.6
63 5.8	86 4.2	105 3.5				Cost of Sales/Inventory	80 4.5	88 4.2
101 3.6	136 2.7	159 2.3					136 2.7	130 2.8
11 33.0	18 20.4	17 21.8					17 21.6	19 19.3
36 10.3	33 11.2	30 12.3				Cost of Sales/Payables	27 13.3	28 12.8
43 8.4	54 6.7	50 7.3					42 8.7	48 7.7
	4.9	3.9	4.6				4.2	4.4
	13.3	7.0	8.1			Sales/Working Capital	7.9	7.7
	-63.4	20.0	20.1				15.3	18.2
	5.5	9.2	11.2				9.5	7.4
	(23) 2.1	(48) 2.4	3.8			EBIT/Interest	(142) 3.5	(134) 3.5
	.6	.8	1.2				1.7	1.6
		(15) 3.4	(10) 8.0			Net Profit + Depr., Dep.,	(64) 7.5	(36) 6.4
		1.2	2.6			Amort./Cur. Mat. L /T/D	3.7	3.3
		.5	.4				1.7	1.4
	.4	.3	.3				.3	.3
	1.2	.8	.7			Fixed/Worth	.5	.5
	3.6	2.0	1.9				1.3	1.4
	1.6	.9	1.0				.8	.8
	3.8	2.2	1.5			Debt/Worth	1.6	1.8
	11.8	5.9	6.0				4.1	4.0
	33.1	36.8	32.0			% Profit Before Taxes/Tangible	39.0	34.6
	(21) 14.4	(49) 14.3	(36) 12.8			Net Worth	(143) 21.9	(124) 20.1
	-.5	-4.8	5.5				10.2	7.3
	9.2	10.1	11.2			% Profit Before Taxes/Total	14.7	13.8
	3.6	2.7	5.1			Assets	7.5	6.7
	-.9	-.8	.9				2.6	2.1
	29.2	21.5	13.4				22.9	24.6
	13.4	8.5	6.3			Sales/Net Fixed Assets	10.8	10.4
	3.1	5.5	3.4				5.3	5.3
	3.3	2.8	1.9				2.8	2.6
	2.6	1.9	1.4			Sales/Total Assets	1.9	1.9
	1.4	1.5	1.0				1.4	1.4
	1.1	1.1	1.5				.9	1.0
	(21) 1.8	(45) 1.8	(36) 2.4			% Depr., Dep., Amort./Sales	(136) 1.6	(118) 1.8
	5.4	3.3	3.5				3.1	3.4
		(13) 2.9	2.3			% Officers', Directors',	2.7	2.5
		4.0	(10) 5.4			Owners' Comp/Sales	(41) 4.8	(41) 4.0
		8.1	9.1				7.5	7.5
7561M	72717M	502193M	1276414M	515330M	1310634M	Net Sales ($)	6050151M	4088066M
2381M	29451M	267155M	823337M	547788M	787625M	Total Assets ($)	3801299M	2724927M

Comparative Historical Data | Current Data Sorted By Sales

			Type of Statement						
32	45	41	Unqualified		3	2	4	16	16
26	30	31	Reviewed	1	4	4	6	11	5
21	20	19	Compiled	3	5	3	5	3	
10	8	5	Tax Returns	1	1	2	1		
40	58	40	Other	2	3	3	6	14	12
4/1/00-3/31/01	4/1/01-3/31/02	4/1/02-3/31/03		27 (4/1-9/30/02)		109 (10/1/02-3/31/03)			
ALL	ALL	ALL		0-1MM	1-3MM	3-5MM	5-10MM	10-25MM	25MM & OVER
129	161	136	NUMBER OF STATEMENTS	7	16	14	22	44	33
%	%	%	ASSETS	%	%	%	%	%	%
6.7	5.8	6.3	Cash & Equivalents		7.1	3.7	3.2	5.8	8.0
23.0	24.5	25.3	Trade Receivables (net)		25.9	23.5	25.4	24.3	26.3
34.3	31.1	30.3	Inventory		25.6	33.4	36.9	29.5	29.2
2.5	3.8	3.7	All Other Current		2.9	4.7	2.6	5.0	3.2
66.6	65.1	65.7	Total Current		61.6	65.4	68.0	64.6	66.8
22.7	23.9	25.4	Fixed Assets (net)		33.3	27.6	23.4	25.4	21.4
3.9	4.0	3.6	Intangibles (net)		.6	3.7	2.5	4.1	5.9
6.7	7.0	5.3	All Other Non-Current		4.5	3.3	6.0	5.8	6.0
100.0	100.0	100.0	Total		100.0	100.0	100.0	100.0	100.0
			LIABILITIES						
14.2	16.4	13.3	Notes Payable-Short Term		11.4	13.2	15.7	13.6	11.0
3.6	4.7	5.5	Cur. Mat.-L/T/D		9.6	14.9	5.5	4.1	1.7
13.7	14.4	13.1	Trade Payables		10.4	14.0	13.1	12.6	15.2
.6	.5	.3	Income Taxes Payable		.2	.1	.4	.2	.4
9.1	9.8	11.8	All Other Current		9.4	13.9	14.8	12.0	11.4
41.2	45.8	44.0	Total Current		40.9	56.2	49.6	42.5	39.8
16.0	16.0	15.9	Long Term Debt		25.8	19.4	13.2	13.4	13.8
.3	.4	.5	Deferred Taxes		.7	.7	.3	.5	.4
3.5	3.8	4.5	All Other Non-Current		3.5	2.7	7.6	3.5	4.1
38.9	34.0	35.0	Net Worth		29.1	21.0	29.3	40.1	41.8
100.0	100.0	100.0	Total Liabilities & Net Worth		100.0	100.0	100.0	100.0	100.0
			INCOME DATA						
100.0	100.0	100.0	Net Sales		100.0	100.0	100.0	100.0	100.0
26.1	27.1	27.3	Gross Profit		34.7	26.2	31.4	23.5	22.1
22.4	23.7	24.1	Operating Expenses		30.6	24.6	26.5	21.7	18.7
3.7	3.4	3.2	Operating Profit		4.1	1.6	4.9	1.9	3.4
1.3	1.7	1.1	All Other Expenses (net)		1.7	1.6	.9	.8	1.1
2.4	1.7	2.1	Profit Before Taxes		2.4	.0	3.9	1.1	2.3
			RATIOS						
2.7	2.5	2.6	Current		3.2	1.6	2.4	2.7	3.1
1.7	1.5	1.6			1.6	1.3	1.6	1.6	1.7
1.2	1.1	1.1			.9	1.0	1.0	1.1	1.2
1.3	1.2	1.4	Quick		1.8	.8	1.1	1.3	1.5
.7	.7	.7			.8	.5	.6	.6	.8
.4	.4	.4			.4	.3	.3	.3	.6
30 12.1	31 11.8	34 10.7	Sales/Receivables	27 13.5	36 10.1	30 12.1	30 12.4	40 9.2	
44 8.4	48 7.6	49 7.5		38 9.5	50 7.3	44 8.3	51 7.1	58 6.3	
56 6.5	64 5.7	71 5.2		61 6.0	64 5.7	53 6.9	68 5.3	75 4.9	
52 7.1	37 9.9	36 10.1	Cost of Sales/Inventory	21 17.8	7 56.0	41 8.8	38 9.6	40 9.2	
92 4.0	86 4.2	87 4.2		65 5.6	67 5.5	97 3.7	93 3.9	103 3.5	
136 2.7	142 2.6	148 2.5		119 3.1	107 3.4	155 2.4	124 2.9	156 2.3	
15 24.1	16 22.6	17 21.8	Cost of Sales/Payables	14 26.1	8 44.5	11 31.9	17 22.1	20 17.9	
26 14.2	31 12.0	30 12.2		33 11.1	35 10.6	38 9.5	27 13.5	29 12.4	
47 7.8	52 7.0	47 7.8		43 8.4	59 6.2	52 7.0	46 7.9	49 7.5	
4.4	5.2	3.9	Sales/Working Capital		4.2	5.9	4.4	3.5	3.4
7.2	9.5	7.7			9.0	15.1	7.7	8.9	5.4
27.2	29.5	33.5			-63.4	NM	NM	24.6	19.6
(122) 7.8	(153) 5.6	(130) 6.3	EBIT/Interest		4.3	2.1	9.5	5.8	14.0
2.8	2.0	2.3			1.5	(13) 1.7	(19) 2.5	2.2	(31) 4.4
1.2	.1	.7			-.1	1.2	1.3	-1.5	1.7
(31) 4.3	(36) 5.3	(35) 3.7	Net Profit + Depr., Dep., Amort./Cur. Mat. L/T/D					(11) 6.8	
2.4	2.2	1.5						1.2	
1.5	1.1	.5						-.2	
.3	.3	.3	Fixed/Worth		.4	.6	.5	.3	.3
.5	.7	.8			.9	1.4	1.3	.7	.5
1.5	1.7	2.6			3.6	9.9	2.2	2.0	1.4
.6	.8	1.0	Debt/Worth		1.2	1.7	1.2	.5	1.0
1.6	2.0	2.3			3.1	3.7	2.2	2.4	1.4
4.2	6.0	7.3			5.4	52.2	13.8	5.9	4.6
(115) 32.0	(140) 29.2	(124) 24.9	% Profit Before Taxes/Tangible Net Worth	(14) 29.0	(13) 36.3	(20) 63.3	(42) 22.4	(30) 31.8	
17.4	11.2	11.8		8.7	16.3	22.8	7.6	11.8	
4.1	-6.7	-1.4		-4.2	2.0	-1.4	-20.3	2.3	
12.2	8.8	9.2	% Profit Before Taxes/Total Assets		6.6	3.5	13.7	7.6	10.7
5.8	2.9	3.0			.8	1.9	7.4	2.3	5.4
.9	-2.9	-.7			-2.0	.7	-.1	-5.3	1.2
21.6	20.6	20.6	Sales/Net Fixed Assets		28.7	29.7	18.7	20.6	14.0
11.0	8.2	7.9			10.1	10.2	9.9	6.9	7.6
4.7	4.7	4.1			2.7	5.1	5.4	3.6	4.7
2.4	2.4	2.6	Sales/Total Assets		3.0	3.2	3.1	2.2	1.8
1.8	1.7	1.7			2.3	1.9	2.2	1.7	1.5
1.3	1.2	1.2			1.3	1.1	1.5	1.2	1.1
(113) 1.1	(144) 1.2	(118) 1.4	% Depr., Dep., Amort./Sales		.4	(12) 1.4	(19) 1.1	(38) 1.3	(26) 1.4
1.7	2.1	2.1			1.6	3.5	1.7	2.4	2.1
4.1	4.2	3.4			4.9	6.0	3.0	3.3	2.9
(30) 2.6	(41) 2.3	(33) 2.5	% Officers', Directors', Owners' Comp/Sales						
5.1	3.5	4.8							
7.4	7.6	8.5							
4256144M	6180935M	3684849M	Net Sales ($)	3937M	31373M	57833M	158630M	662020M	2771056M
2906237M	4237544M	2457737M	Total Assets ($)	3058M	23462M	34248M	92925M	514700M	1789344M

M = $ thousand   MM = $ million
See Pages 11 through 18 for Explanation of Ratios and Data

Current Data Sorted By Assets   Comparative Historical Data

0-500M	500M-2MM	2-10MM	10-50MM	50-100MM	100-250MM	Type of Statement	4/1/98-3/31/99 ALL	4/1/99-3/31/00 ALL
	2	2	2	1	2	Unqualified	12	8
		5	2			Reviewed	8	8
	3	3	1			Compiled	6	2
1		1				Tax Returns	1	3
		2	6	1		Other	6	14
	5 (4/1-9/30/02)		29 (10/1/02-3/31/03)					
1	5	13	11	2	2	NUMBER OF STATEMENTS	33	35
%	%	%	%	%	%	ASSETS	%	%
		6.3	7.3			Cash & Equivalents	5.9	6.8
		21.5	21.8			Trade Receivables (net)	22.5	21.9
		35.7	29.0			Inventory	30.4	31.6
		1.6	3.1			All Other Current	3.5	1.3
		65.0	61.1			Total Current	62.2	61.5
		28.4	23.9			Fixed Assets (net)	28.7	28.8
		2.4	8.7			Intangibles (net)	3.9	1.0
		4.2	6.3			All Other Non-Current	5.2	8.8
		100.0	100.0			Total	100.0	100.0
						LIABILITIES		
		11.1	7.2			Notes Payable-Short Term	15.0	9.0
		4.3	1.8			Cur. Mat.-L/T/D	3.4	3.7
		12.4	11.9			Trade Payables	14.5	9.7
		.0	.5			Income Taxes Payable	.5	.2
		8.4	6.0			All Other Current	9.0	13.0
		36.2	27.4			Total Current	42.4	35.6
		25.8	11.0			Long Term Debt	18.3	21.8
		.0	.3			Deferred Taxes	-.1	.6
		1.4	.3			All Other Non-Current	.8	4.5
		36.5	60.9			Net Worth	38.7	37.5
		100.0	100.0			Total Liabilities & Net Worth	100.0	100.0
						INCOME DATA		
		100.0	100.0			Net Sales	100.0	100.0
		37.5	30.5			Gross Profit	30.5	33.7
		35.1	26.0			Operating Expenses	28.3	28.2
		2.5	4.5			Operating Profit	2.2	5.5
		.9	.4			All Other Expenses (net)	.3	1.9
		1.5	4.1			Profit Before Taxes	1.9	3.7
						RATIOS		
		3.7	4.0				3.2	3.4
		1.7	2.3			Current	1.4	1.9
		1.3	1.5				1.0	1.2
		2.1	1.9				1.8	1.5
		.8	1.1			Quick	.6	.9
		.4	.8				.4	.5
		38 9.5	38 9.6				26 14.1	30 12.2
		44 8.3	52 7.1			Sales/Receivables	38 9.7	51 7.1
		58 6.3	68 5.4				50 7.3	59 6.2
		45 8.1	40 9.2				32 11.3	45 8.1
		121 3.0	89 4.1			Cost of Sales/Inventory	75 4.9	106 3.4
		219 1.7	148 2.5				132 2.8	184 2.0
		16 23.3	19 19.6				14 26.5	18 20.9
		52 7.0	37 9.9			Cost of Sales/Payables	35 10.5	28 13.2
		62 5.9	53 6.9				54 6.8	45 8.1
		3.5	2.6				5.8	3.1
		4.3	4.8			Sales/Working Capital	17.7	8.1
		13.7	8.8				UND	20.2
		10.5	9.6				4.7	9.0
		1.9	(10) 5.9			EBIT/Interest	(28) 2.2	(33) 2.7
		.8	2.2				1.2	1.0
						Net Profit + Depr., Dep., Amort./Cur. Mat. L /T/D		(11) 6.0
								2.4
								.8
		.4	.3				.3	.3
		.7	.4			Fixed/Worth	.7	.7
		3.7	.6				2.6	1.4
		.5	.3				.4	.6
		1.6	.6			Debt/Worth	2.4	2.3
		38.1	1.2				6.6	6.0
		18.5	30.5				28.5	42.1
	(11)	12.2	17.4			% Profit Before Taxes/Tangible Net Worth	(29) 14.1	16.9
		-.6	4.7				3.6	1.4
		8.0	10.9				10.1	12.8
		2.0	5.8			% Profit Before Taxes/Total Assets	4.7	5.5
		-.7	3.3				1.1	.3
		12.3	14.2				18.7	12.2
		5.7	6.2			Sales/Net Fixed Assets	7.7	5.8
		3.6	4.1				5.5	3.0
		2.1	2.1				2.7	1.9
		1.6	1.3			Sales/Total Assets	1.7	1.5
		1.2	1.1				1.4	1.1
		1.3					1.0	1.2
		2.5				% Depr., Dep., Amort./Sales	(28) 1.9	(32) 2.1
		4.3					2.3	4.2
						% Officers', Directors', Owners' Comp/Sales		3.5
								(10) 5.8
								16.4
2210M	13980M	82748M	289944M	188534M	348460M	Net Sales ($)	1181984M	1214735M
135M	5892M	53892M	195485M	123222M	246973M	Total Assets ($)	719707M	802904M

M = $ thousand   MM = $ million
See Pages 11 through 18 for Explanation of Ratios and Data

Comparative Historical Data | Current Data Sorted By Sales

	4/1/00-3/31/01 ALL	4/1/01-3/31/02 ALL	4/1/02-3/31/03 ALL		0-1MM	1-3MM	3-5MM	5-10MM	10-25MM	25MM & OVER
				Type of Statement		5 (4/1-9/30/02)		29 (10/1/02-3/31/03)		
	7	10	9	Unqualified		1	3			5
	6	6	7	Reviewed		3	2	1		1
	7	10	7	Compiled	3	1	1	2		
	1	2	2	Tax Returns	2					
	7	7	9	Other		1		1	2	5
	28	35	34	**NUMBER OF STATEMENTS**		6	5	7	5	11
	%	%	%	**ASSETS**	%	%	%	%	%	%
	7.7	9.0	8.0	Cash & Equivalents						5.6
	23.9	22.9	23.3	Trade Receivables (net)						22.1
	28.8	25.7	30.1	Inventory						30.3
	1.7	1.1	1.8	All Other Current						1.4
	62.2	58.8	63.2	Total Current						59.4
	30.6	30.2	25.3	Fixed Assets (net)						20.6
	1.2	4.2	5.1	Intangibles (net)						10.2
	6.0	6.8	6.4	All Other Non-Current						9.8
	100.0	100.0	100.0	Total						100.0
				LIABILITIES						
	12.3	9.9	8.9	Notes Payable-Short Term						8.7
	3.8	4.4	3.4	Cur. Mat.-L/T/D						2.0
	12.5	14.7	11.8	Trade Payables						12.5
	.2	.2	.2	Income Taxes Payable						.2
	8.9	8.4	8.3	All Other Current						9.3
	37.7	37.6	32.6	Total Current						32.7
	21.0	20.2	21.9	Long Term Debt						16.6
	.3	.8	.3	Deferred Taxes						.5
	4.3	1.4	.9	All Other Non-Current						1.0
	36.6	40.1	44.3	Net Worth						49.2
	100.0	100.0	100.0	Total Liabilities & Net Worth						100.0
				INCOME DATA						
	100.0	100.0	100.0	Net Sales						100.0
	33.5	33.0	33.2	Gross Profit						28.8
	28.8	29.0	30.3	Operating Expenses						24.4
	4.7	3.9	2.9	Operating Profit						4.4
	1.6	1.7	.9	All Other Expenses (net)						1.1
	3.1	2.2	2.0	Profit Before Taxes						3.3
				RATIOS						
	2.9	2.6	3.4	Current						2.7
	1.9	1.9	2.0							2.2
	1.1	1.1	1.4							1.5
	1.6	1.6	1.6	Quick						1.7
	.8	.9	1.0							1.0
	.6	.5	.5							.5
	27 13.6	37 9.9	38 9.6	Sales/Receivables						38 9.6
	53 6.8	45 8.1	44 8.3							48 7.6
	69 5.3	67 5.5	56 6.6							68 5.4
	46 8.0	41 9.0	38 9.6	Cost of Sales/Inventory						53 6.9
	103 3.5	87 4.2	90 4.1							91 4.0
	144 2.5	150 2.4	182 2.0							134 2.7
	17 21.5	15 25.0	15 24.6	Cost of Sales/Payables						19 19.6
	34 10.8	34 10.8	36 10.0							37 9.9
	47 7.7	66 5.5	56 6.5							49 7.5
	3.7	3.4	3.7	Sales/Working Capital						4.4
	6.9	8.6	5.4							5.9
	19.4	49.7	14.2							8.8
	7.5	9.3	11.3	EBIT/Interest						16.2
	2.0	(31) 2.9	(32) 2.5						(10)	3.8
	1.2	1.8	1.2							2.2
		7.7	5.3	Net Profit + Depr., Dep., Amort./Cur. Mat. L/T/D						
	(14)	(14) 2.2	(14) 2.2							
		1.0	1.5							
	.3	.4	.3	Fixed/Worth						.2
	.9	.8	.6							.6
	2.2	2.4	1.5							1.6
	.7	.6	.4	Debt/Worth						.3
	2.5	1.4	1.2							1.2
	5.3	5.6	7.0							6.9
	37.5	34.6	25.7	% Profit Before Taxes/Tangible Net Worth						30.5
	12.8	(32) 15.1	(31) 15.8							23.2
	2.9	7.9	4.7							7.7
	7.1	12.2	9.2	% Profit Before Taxes/Total Assets						7.9
	3.8	5.2	3.4							3.7
	.9	1.8	.8							2.2
	16.0	10.0	13.1	Sales/Net Fixed Assets						14.2
	6.2	6.4	6.4							6.9
	3.2	3.8	4.2							6.2
	2.1	2.2	2.1	Sales/Total Assets						2.2
	1.5	1.5	1.5							1.6
	1.1	1.2	1.2							1.3
	.8	1.0	1.4	% Depr., Dep., Amort./Sales						1.4
	(26) 2.0	(32) 2.3	(30) 2.4						(10)	2.1
	3.1	3.2	3.6							2.9
	2.4	1.7	.7	% Officers', Directors', Owners' Comp/Sales						
	(10) 4.2	(10) 4.0	(11) 4.0							
	6.7	5.8	4.4							
	530897M	806042M	925876M	Net Sales ($)		10889M	18970M	52838M	84455M	758724M
	362443M	568042M	625599M	Total Assets ($)		7398M	10820M	33954M	66617M	506810M

M = $ thousand   MM = $ million
See Pages 11 through 18 for Explanation of Ratios and Data

Current Data Sorted By Assets **Comparative Historical Data**

	0-500M	500M-2MM	2-10MM	10-50MM	50-100MM	100-250MM	Type of Statement	4/1/98-3/31/99 ALL	4/1/99-3/31/00 ALL
		5	5	6	1	4	Unqualified	12	11
			4	2			Reviewed	6	9
			5	1			Compiled	10	5
		5	2	1			Tax Returns	1	2
		1		1	•		Other	16	26
		9	9	3	2	3			
		17 (4/1-9/30/02)		46 (10/1/02-3/31/03)					
		15	25	13	3	7	NUMBER OF STATEMENTS	45	53
	%	%	%	%	%	%	ASSETS	%	%
D		8.5	9.8	4.6			Cash & Equivalents	8.3	8.3
A		31.1	32.4	18.9			Trade Receivables (net)	23.7	23.3
T		30.5	22.6	31.2			Inventory	26.6	33.4
A		2.9	2.8	3.9			All Other Current	3.0	2.3
		73.0	67.7	58.5			Total Current	61.6	67.3
N		24.5	26.0	27.1			Fixed Assets (net)	26.5	21.1
O		.7	3.0	11.4			Intangibles (net)	5.0	5.2
T		1.8	3.4	2.9			All Other Non-Current	7.0	6.4
		100.0	100.0	100.0			Total	100.0	100.0
A							LIABILITIES		
V		12.3	13.4	7.8			Notes Payable-Short Term	8.7	13.5
A		7.4	4.0	3.7			Cur. Mat.-L/T/D	2.4	3.2
I		14.3	12.8	9.8			Trade Payables	15.4	15.1
L		.1	1.5	.3			Income Taxes Payable	.5	.1
A		5.5	7.7	5.7			All Other Current	8.2	8.3
B		39.6	39.5	27.3			Total Current	35.2	40.1
L		7.6	12.7	8.7			Long Term Debt	14.2	18.3
E		.1	1.1	1.1			Deferred Taxes	1.7	1.2
		2.1	4.4	5.9			All Other Non-Current	2.9	2.7
		50.5	42.3	56.9			Net Worth	46.0	37.6
		100.0	100.0	100.0			Total Liabilities & Net Worth	100.0	100.0
							INCOME DATA		
		100.0	100.0	100.0			Net Sales	100.0	100.0
		33.1	35.9	34.7			Gross Profit	39.4	28.9
		33.5	28.1	28.7			Operating Expenses	31.8	25.8
		-.5	7.8	6.0			Operating Profit	7.6	3.1
		1.9	1.3	2.4			All Other Expenses (net)	.1	1.1
		-2.3	6.5	3.6			Profit Before Taxes	7.5	1.9
							RATIOS		
		3.1	3.2	6.1				3.1	3.0
		1.7	1.7	2.3			Current	2.1	1.8
		1.2	1.2	1.2				1.3	1.2
		1.6	1.8	2.0				1.8	1.5
		.9	1.1	.9			Quick	.9	.9
		.6	.6	.5				.6	.4
	43	8.4	39	9.4	43	8.6	Sales/Receivables	40	9.2	28	12.9
	51	7.2	58	6.3	56	6.5		55	6.6	48	7.6
	77	4.8	75	4.9	68	5.3		68	5.3	78	4.7
	13	27.0	3	112.1	80	4.6	Cost of Sales/Inventory	46	8.0	55	6.6
	77	4.7	57	6.4	97	3.7		90	4.1	94	3.9
	135	2.7	100	3.7	203	1.8		175	2.1	143	2.5
	10	37.2	17	21.1	19	19.4	Cost of Sales/Payables	20	18.4	20	18.6
	36	10.1	38	9.6	34	10.8		40	9.1	34	10.9
	53	6.8	45	8.2	49	7.4		70	5.2	55	6.6
		3.6		4.0		2.4	Sales/Working Capital		3.5		4.0
		8.1		7.0		4.4			5.4		5.3
		27.2		14.9		12.3			17.4		18.1
		5.9		9.0		10.5	EBIT/Interest		12.6		4.8
	(14)	2.1	(23)	5.6		2.6		(37)	4.5	(48)	1.8
		-9.2		2.4		.8			1.7		.8
							Net Profit + Depr., Dep., Amort./Cur. Mat. L/T/D		10.4		8.4
								(19)	2.4	(19)	1.2
									1.2		.3
		.1		.1		.2	Fixed/Worth		.2		.3
		.3		.4		.5			.5		.6
		1.0		1.4		1.6			1.5		1.8
		.5		.7		.4	Debt/Worth		.4		.7
		1.1		1.3		1.0			1.5		2.2
		1.6		3.6		2.4			4.2		5.9
		13.4		48.9		21.4	% Profit Before Taxes/Tangible Net Worth		31.8		25.0
		6.1	(24)	22.1	(11)	14.4		(41)	18.4	(47)	6.8
		-39.7		5.5		2.0			7.7		1.4
		6.9		15.5		13.6	% Profit Before Taxes/Total Assets		16.8		8.1
		3.9		9.9		5.8			7.1		2.9
		-22.0		1.4		-.4			2.2		-.9
		58.7		42.9		10.9	Sales/Net Fixed Assets		11.0		20.9
		12.4		10.0		6.0			7.6		9.4
		5.9		4.2		3.2			3.0		4.0
		3.0		2.5		2.0	Sales/Total Assets		2.2		2.4
		1.9		1.9		1.4			1.5		1.6
		1.4		1.4		.7			.9		1.1
		1.6		.6		2.8	% Depr., Dep., Amort./Sales		1.5		1.2
	(11)	2.5	(24)	1.8	(12)	3.6		(39)	2.6	(43)	2.7
		6.8		3.9		5.1			4.7		4.2
				2.5			% Officers', Directors', Owners' Comp/Sales		2.0		2.2
			(10)	3.5				(11)	3.0	(12)	3.2
				12.8					8.2		6.0
		48865M	185478M	335080M	222376M	1500823M	Net Sales ($)	1324000M	2049818M
		21842M	95585M	258136M	217970M	1300073M	Total Assets ($)	1314021M	1655023M

M = $ thousand   MM = $ million
See Pages 11 through 18 for Explanation of Ratios and Data

Comparative Historical Data | | | | Current Data Sorted By Sales

4/1/00-3/31/01 ALL	4/1/01-3/31/02 ALL	4/1/02-3/31/03 ALL	Type of Statement	0-1MM	1-3MM	3-5MM	5-10MM	10-25MM	25MM & OVER
12	12	16	Unqualified		1		2	5	8
4	6	6	Reviewed			1	4	1	
6	8	11	Compiled		3	1	5	2	
3	4	4	Tax Returns			2		1	1
24	23	26	Other	1	6	4	7	2	6
49	53	63	**NUMBER OF STATEMENTS**	1	10	8	18	11	15
					17 (4/1-9/30/02)		**46 (10/1/02-3/31/03)**		
%	%	%	**ASSETS**	%	%	%	%	%	%
9.8	7.0	8.1	Cash & Equivalents		10.1		6.8	11.4	7.1
29.3	28.9	27.3	Trade Receivables (net)		26.5		37.9	22.7	21.5
25.3	28.6	25.2	Inventory		29.9		27.4	23.1	23.4
2.3	4.3	3.0	All Other Current		1.3		2.9	4.6	2.4
66.8	68.8	63.7	Total Current		67.8		75.0	61.9	54.3
22.8	20.0	25.6	Fixed Assets (net)		26.8		20.2	18.9	24.8
5.3	5.6	6.5	Intangibles (net)		2.8		1.6	15.8	11.8
5.1	5.5	4.2	All Other Non-Current		2.6		3.3	3.4	9.1
100.0	100.0	100.0	Total		100.0		100.0	100.0	100.0
			LIABILITIES						
9.9	13.9	10.2	Notes Payable-Short Term		10.5		17.0	6.3	4.3
2.9	2.5	4.4	Cur. Mat.-L/T/D		7.3		4.6	3.6	1.9
17.7	15.3	11.8	Trade Payables		15.6		13.8	13.1	10.1
.5	.5	.7	Income Taxes Payable		.2		1.8	.7	.3
8.9	9.0	6.8	All Other Current		7.0		7.4	7.0	7.9
40.0	41.2	34.0	Total Current		40.7		44.6	30.7	24.4
15.4	12.5	10.1	Long Term Debt		7.8		9.9	5.2	7.5
1.0	1.2	1.0	Deferred Taxes		.9		.7	1.8	1.2
1.8	3.3	5.6	All Other Non-Current		6.8		2.2	4.9	11.2
41.8	41.7	49.2	Net Worth		43.8		42.5	57.3	55.7
100.0	100.0	100.0	Total Liabilities & Net Worth		100.0		100.0	100.0	100.0
			INCOME DATA						
100.0	100.0	100.0	Net Sales		100.0		100.0	100.0	100.0
29.9	30.9	34.8	Gross Profit		37.0		34.8	34.2	30.0
25.0	24.5	29.6	Operating Expenses		38.3		28.4	27.5	25.2
4.9	6.3	5.2	Operating Profit		-1.3		6.4	6.7	4.8
.7	1.6	2.0	All Other Expenses (net)		2.6		1.4	1.9	2.0
4.2	4.7	3.2	Profit Before Taxes		-3.8		5.0	4.8	2.8
			RATIOS						
3.4	2.8	3.2			3.1		2.8	6.0	3.2
2.0	1.8	1.9	Current		1.6		1.8	2.3	2.4
1.3	1.2	1.2			.9		1.2	1.2	1.6
1.7	1.3	1.9			1.6		1.7	1.9	2.0
1.0	.8	1.0	Quick		.9		.9	1.3	1.3
.7	.5	.6			.4		.6	.5	.8
46 8.0	42 8.7	43 8.4			42 8.7		48 7.6	37 10.0	41 9.0
58 6.3	54 6.7	57 6.4	Sales/Receivables		71 5.1		63 5.8	54 6.7	58 6.3
86 4.2	76 4.8	76 4.8			86 4.3		75 4.9	58 6.3	76 4.8
35 10.5	31 11.8	23 16.2			36 10.3		15 25.0	51 7.2	41 8.9
80 4.5	60 6.1	81 4.5	Cost of Sales/Inventory		112 3.3		64 5.7	84 4.3	81 4.5
155 2.3	141 2.6	123 3.0			149 2.4		100 3.7	148 2.5	122 3.0
23 15.9	22 16.8	19 19.6			31 11.6		17 21.5	26 13.9	19 19.2
40 9.1	35 10.5	37 9.9	Cost of Sales/Payables		51 7.1		39 9.5	34 10.8	37 9.9
54 6.7	49 7.4	48 7.7			115 3.2		45 8.1	47 7.7	51 7.1
3.0	4.1	3.6			3.1		4.1	2.5	3.0
5.3	5.3	5.9	Sales/Working Capital		4.9		8.1	5.2	4.4
14.4	21.0	13.5			-26.5		14.0	18.1	10.3
9.0	8.1	8.8			6.0		7.3	62.0	22.9
(42) 2.5	(48) 4.0	(60) 4.0	EBIT/Interest		1.9	(16)	4.4	9.1	2.2
-.3	1.7	.8			-32.2		1.8	3.6	.5
6.3	5.2	6.8	Net Profit + Depr., Dep.,						
(13) 1.2	(13) 1.9	(16) 2.6	Amort./Cur. Mat. L/T/D						
.3	1.1	1.5							
.2	.2	.2			.1		.1	.1	.2
.5	.6	.5	Fixed/Worth		.4		.3	.3	.5
1.4	1.2	1.6			3.5		1.2	1.6	1.7
.3	.6	.4			.6		.6	.3	.3
1.3	1.5	1.1	Debt/Worth		1.3		1.3	1.1	.6
3.1	5.8	2.8			10.0		2.8	6.4	2.8
33.1	46.7	25.6	% Profit Before Taxes/Tangible		31.7		33.3		23.8
(44) 14.5	(47) 22.8	(58) 13.8	Net Worth		.2	(17)	14.4	(13)	8.2
-3.4	7.4	2.0			-89.0		4.8		2.6
15.0	16.9	12.9	% Profit Before Taxes/Total		12.6		10.6	20.2	7.8
4.8	6.5	5.4	Assets		.4		6.1	11.4	2.4
-1.9	1.5	-.3			-25.9		1.3	3.2	-3.6
13.0	22.0	29.6			24.2		59.6	29.6	9.1
8.9	11.0	6.7	Sales/Net Fixed Assets		9.0		22.1	9.2	6.3
4.8	5.7	3.5			4.9		4.9	3.3	3.6
2.2	2.6	2.4			1.8		3.0	2.4	2.0
1.4	1.7	1.6	Sales/Total Assets		1.5		2.3	1.6	1.2
1.1	1.3	1.1			1.2		1.7	.9	.9
1.7	1.4	1.4					.4	1.8	1.4
(33) 3.2	(45) 2.9	(53) 2.9	% Depr., Dep., Amort./Sales			(16)	1.1	(10) 3.3	(11) 2.9
4.6	3.8	4.4					2.6	4.6	3.8
2.2	1.8	2.7							
(10) 3.4	(16) 3.2	(19) 3.6	% Officers', Directors', Owners' Comp/Sales						
5.7	9.8	8.9							
1776641M	2142662M	2292622M	Net Sales ($)	334M	22300M	31470M	122604M	182805M	1933109M
1607680M	1478566M	1893606M	Total Assets ($)	1006M	17089M	20649M	80630M	142654M	1631578M

M = $ thousand   MM = $ million
See Pages 11 through 18 for Explanation of Ratios and Data

Current Data Sorted By Assets · Comparative Historical Data

0-500M	500M-2MM	2-10MM	10-50MM	50-100MM	100-250MM	Type of Statement	4/1/98-3/31/99 ALL	4/1/99-3/31/00 ALL
1		6	1			Unqualified		
	3	1	1			Reviewed		
1	2	1				Compiled		
1	1	1				Tax Returns		
	5	7	1			Other		
	7 (4/1-9/30/02)		26 (10/1/02-3/31/03)					
3	11	16	3			**NUMBER OF STATEMENTS**		
%	%	%	%	%	%	**ASSETS**	%	%
	3.7	4.8	D	D	D	Cash & Equivalents	D	D
	26.3	22.7	A	A	A	Trade Receivables (net)	A	A
	25.1	24.8	T	T	T	Inventory	T	T
	1.8	2.6	A	A	A	All Other Current	A	A
	57.0	54.9				Total Current		
	33.4	31.8	N	N	N	Fixed Assets (net)	N	N
	2.0	2.1	O	O	O	Intangibles (net)	O	O
	7.6	11.2	T	T	T	All Other Non-Current	T	T
	100.0	100.0				Total		
			A	A	A	**LIABILITIES**	A	A
	17.6	15.8	V	V	V	Notes Payable-Short Term	V	V
	4.8	6.3	A	A	A	Cur. Mat.-L/T/D	A	A
	15.7	17.5	I	I	I	Trade Payables	I	I
	.1	.6	L	L	L	Income Taxes Payable	L	L
	15.9	12.9	A	A	A	All Other Current	A	A
	53.9	53.1	B	B	B	Total Current	B	B
	15.8	17.9	L	L	L	Long Term Debt	L	L
	.0	.6	E	E	E	Deferred Taxes	E	E
	11.2	3.9				All Other Non-Current		
	19.1	24.4				Net Worth		
	100.0	100.0				Total Liabilities & Net Worth		
						INCOME DATA		
	100.0	100.0				Net Sales		
	27.2	24.5				Gross Profit		
	28.2	30.7				Operating Expenses		
	-1.0	-6.2				Operating Profit		
	1.6	1.5				All Other Expenses (net)		
	-2.5	-7.7				Profit Before Taxes		
						RATIOS		
	1.6	1.3				Current		
	1.1	1.1						
	.6	.8						
	1.0	.8				Quick		
	.7	.4						
	.3	.3						
25	14.6	21 / 17.5				Sales/Receivables		
43	8.4	46 / 8.0						
85	4.3	58 / 6.3						
21	17.3	35 / 10.5				Cost of Sales/Inventory		
56	6.6	59 / 6.1						
115	3.2	158 / 2.3						
25	14.7	26 / 14.2				Cost of Sales/Payables		
34	10.6	32 / 11.4						
51	7.2	65 / 5.6						
	7.6	10.3				Sales/Working Capital		
	43.0	29.3						
	-6.1	-15.7						
	3.2	2.2				EBIT/Interest		
(10)	1.0	(14) -.3						
	-2.3	-7.7						
						Net Profit + Depr., Dep., Amort./Cur. Mat. L /T/D		
	.5	.5				Fixed/Worth		
	1.8	1.2						
	12.1	-9.2						
	1.5	1.3				Debt/Worth		
	6.9	4.0						
	14.5	-17.8						
		28.8				% Profit Before Taxes/Tangible Net Worth		
	(11)	2.1						
		-71.6						
	3.5	2.5				% Profit Before Taxes/Total Assets		
	.8	-7.6						
	-13.0	-27.8						
	17.8	14.2				Sales/Net Fixed Assets		
	6.6	4.6						
	3.3	3.0						
	2.6	2.3				Sales/Total Assets		
	1.8	1.9						
	1.3	1.0						
	2.0	1.2				% Depr., Dep., Amort./Sales		
	4.8	4.0						
	7.1	6.3						
						% Officers', Directors', Owners' Comp/Sales		
2469M	28606M	160863M	104522M			Net Sales ($)		
649M	13784M	84847M	56131M			Total Assets ($)		

M = $ thousand   MM = $ million
See Pages 11 through 18 for Explanation of Ratios and Data

Comparative Historical Data | Current Data Sorted By Sales

4/1/00-3/31/01 ALL	4/1/01-3/31/02 ALL	4/1/02-3/31/03 ALL	Type of Statement	0-1MM	1-3MM	3-5MM	5-10MM	10-25MM	25MM & OVER
		8	Unqualified	1	1		4	1	1
		5	Reviewed		2	1		1	1
		4	Compiled	1	2		1		
		3	Tax Returns		2	1			
		13	Other		2	2	5	3	1
					7 (4/1-9/30/02)			26 (10/1/02-3/31/03)	
33		**NUMBER OF STATEMENTS**	2	9	4	10	5	3

4/1/00-3/31/01 ALL	4/1/01-3/31/02 ALL	4/1/02-3/31/03 ALL		0-1MM	1-3MM	3-5MM	5-10MM	10-25MM	25MM & OVER
%	%	%	**ASSETS**	%	%	%	%	%	%
D	D	7.7	Cash & Equivalents				4.9		
A	A	25.5	Trade Receivables (net)				21.3		
T	T	24.0	Inventory				28.2		
A	A	2.3	All Other Current				3.3		
		59.6	Total Current				57.7		
N	N	29.1	Fixed Assets (net)				34.2		
O	O	2.0	Intangibles (net)				2.6		
T	T	9.3	All Other Non-Current				5.6		
		100.0	Total				100.0		
A	A		**LIABILITIES**						
V	V	16.3	Notes Payable-Short Term				14.7		
A	A	4.9	Cur. Mat.-L/T/D				5.8		
I	I	17.5	Trade Payables				16.5		
L	L	.4	Income Taxes Payable				.9		
A	A	15.1	All Other Current				10.1		
B	B	54.3	Total Current				47.8		
L	L	15.0	Long Term Debt				21.1		
E	E	.3	Deferred Taxes				.0		
		5.6	All Other Non-Current				2.9		
		24.8	Net Worth				28.2		
		100.0	Total Liabilities & Net Worth				100.0		
			INCOME DATA						
		100.0	Net Sales				100.0		
		26.4	Gross Profit				29.0		
		29.0	Operating Expenses				36.0		
		-2.6	Operating Profit				-7.0		
		1.3	All Other Expenses (net)				1.4		
		-4.0	Profit Before Taxes				-8.4		
			RATIOS						
		1.5					1.3		
		1.1	Current				1.2		
		.8					1.0		
		1.0					.8		
		.6	Quick				.5		
		.3					.3		
23		15.5					22	16.8	
46		7.9	Sales/Receivables				46	8.0	
72		5.1					57	6.4	
32		11.3					38	9.7	
59		6.2	Cost of Sales/Inventory				66	5.6	
116		3.2					183	2.0	
25		14.7					25	14.6	
34		10.6	Cost of Sales/Payables				32	11.4	
63		5.8					61	6.0	
		8.9					9.5		
		30.7	Sales/Working Capital				26.8		
		-16.4					NM		
		4.2							
	(28)	1.2	EBIT/Interest						
		-2.4							
			Net Profit + Depr., Dep., Amort./Cur. Mat. L/T/D						
		.5					.5		
		1.2	Fixed/Worth				1.2		
		NM					NM		
		1.2					1.5		
		3.9	Debt/Worth				3.7		
		NM					NM		
		28.9							
	(25)	6.3	% Profit Before Taxes/Tangible Net Worth						
		-11.5							
		4.5					8.1		
		.0	% Profit Before Taxes/Total Assets				-7.7		
		-12.6					-26.4		
		18.6					11.1		
		6.6	Sales/Net Fixed Assets				4.6		
		3.3					2.8		
		2.3					2.5		
		1.8	Sales/Total Assets				1.9		
		1.2					1.1		
		1.2					2.6		
	(32)	3.9	% Depr., Dep., Amort./Sales				4.3		
		6.2					6.3		
		3.9							
	(12)	6.0	% Officers', Directors', Owners' Comp/Sales						
		6.5							
		296460M	Net Sales ($)	915M	14090M	14638M	69624M	86447M	110746M
		155411M	Total Assets ($)	420M	12062M	5891M	47425M	42986M	46627M

M = $ thousand   MM = $ million
See Pages 11 through 18 for Explanation of Ratios and Data

Current Data Sorted By Assets   Comparative Historical Data

0-500M	500M-2MM	2-10MM	10-50MM	50-100MM	100-250MM	Type of Statement	4/1/98-3/31/99 ALL	4/1/99-3/31/00 ALL
		2	4	1	1	Unqualified	7	11
1	5	12				Reviewed	9	12
2	2	4				Compiled	5	6
	2					Tax Returns		1
3	3	7	5		1	Other	10	11
	6 (4/1-9/30/02)		46 (10/1/02-3/31/03)					
3	12	25	9	1	2	NUMBER OF STATEMENTS	31	41
%	%	%	%	%	%	**ASSETS**	%	%
	11.8	7.0				Cash & Equivalents	9.0	7.0
	37.6	25.0				Trade Receivables (net)	20.2	24.8
	24.7	29.5				Inventory	31.4	35.0
	1.4	4.5				All Other Current	3.7	4.4
	75.6	66.1				Total Current	64.4	71.3
	21.3	22.4				Fixed Assets (net)	24.6	20.0
	.7	3.1				Intangibles (net)	2.9	2.6
	2.5	8.4				All Other Non-Current	8.1	6.1
	100.0	100.0				Total	100.0	100.0
						LIABILITIES		
	19.3	16.3				Notes Payable-Short Term	4.5	12.9
	5.0	2.6				Cur. Mat.-L/T/D	3.9	4.0
	15.7	12.4				Trade Payables	10.4	12.9
	.1	.0				Income Taxes Payable	.3	.4
	16.9	15.2				All Other Current	20.1	22.8
	57.0	46.5				Total Current	39.2	53.2
	16.8	11.1				Long Term Debt	17.3	11.1
	.0	.5				Deferred Taxes	.4	.5
	3.7	8.3				All Other Non-Current	3.2	5.4
	22.6	33.6				Net Worth	39.9	29.9
	100.0	100.0				Total Liabilities & Net Worth	100.0	100.0
						INCOME DATA		
	100.0	100.0				Net Sales	100.0	100.0
	33.8	29.3				Gross Profit	30.0	32.7
	26.8	28.2				Operating Expenses	27.5	29.3
	7.1	1.2				Operating Profit	2.5	3.3
	.6	1.3				All Other Expenses (net)	.1	.9
	6.4	-.1				Profit Before Taxes	2.4	2.5
						RATIOS		
	2.0	2.6				Current	2.7	2.1
	1.3	1.6					1.6	1.4
	1.0	1.2					1.3	1.0
	1.5	1.1				Quick	1.2	1.1
	.9	.9					.8	.5
	.5	.5					.5	.3
	30 12.3	41 8.9				Sales/Receivables	29 12.5	36 10.2
	41 8.9	59 6.2					37 9.8	49 7.4
	50 7.3	65 5.6					52 7.0	62 5.9
	18 20.2	51 7.1				Cost of Sales/Inventory	19 18.8	61 6.0
	28 12.9	112 3.3					71 5.2	87 4.2
	74 4.9	160 2.3					144 2.5	150 2.4
	9 39.1	23 16.1				Cost of Sales/Payables	13 27.1	18 20.5
	27 13.3	38 9.6					22 17.0	34 10.9
	41 8.8	52 7.0					35 10.3	48 7.6
	9.0	3.1				Sales/Working Capital	4.6	5.5
	15.4	6.3					9.6	11.6
	424.7	20.5					17.5	UND
	5.0	4.8				EBIT/Interest	14.5	3.8
	(11) 3.1	(22) 2.3					(27) 2.6	(35) 1.7
	1.2	-.9					1.0	.7
						Net Profit + Depr., Dep., Amort./Cur. Mat. L /T/D	12.3	3.8
							(12) 2.2	(16) 1.5
							.3	.7
	.5	.2				Fixed/Worth	.2	.2
	1.1	.6					.5	.7
	NM	6.2					1.6	2.8
	1.5	.7				Debt/Worth	.8	1.1
	9.7	2.2					1.6	3.0
	NM	19.9					4.8	13.5
		35.7				% Profit Before Taxes/Tangible Net Worth	29.0	38.4
		(22) 9.0					(30) 7.3	(37) 11.5
		-8.7					.0	-4.9
	20.6	8.1				% Profit Before Taxes/Total Assets	10.2	8.2
	5.6	2.5					2.9	3.1
	1.1	-7.9					.0	-1.3
	20.5	21.6				Sales/Net Fixed Assets	22.9	19.9
	16.7	8.7					10.7	12.1
	10.8	3.5					5.2	6.4
	4.0	1.8				Sales/Total Assets	2.6	2.2
	3.5	1.5					1.9	1.9
	2.1	1.1					1.6	1.5
	.6	1.6				% Depr., Dep., Amort./Sales	.8	.9
	1.9	(24) 2.2					(27) 1.8	(38) 1.8
	2.6	4.0					3.7	3.9
						% Officers', Directors', Owners' Comp/Sales	4.1	2.8
							(10) 7.4	(13) 7.2
							16.0	11.7
2760M	40211M	178411M	276030M	42821M	378741M	Net Sales ($)	900633M	633547M
1010M	14106M	111319M	185482M	66154M	305578M	Total Assets ($)	548864M	394054M

M = $ thousand   MM = $ million
See Pages 11 through 18 for Explanation of Ratios and Data

Comparative Historical Data · Current Data Sorted By Sales

4/1/00-3/31/01 ALL	4/1/01-3/31/02 ALL	4/1/02-3/31/03 ALL	Type of Statement	0-1MM	1-3MM	3-5MM	5-10MM	10-25MM	25MM & OVER
8	7	8	Unqualified		1		1	1	5
9	10	18	Reviewed	1	5	6	4	2	
4	5	8	Compiled	1	3	1	2	1	
2	2	2	Tax Returns			2			
11	13	16	Other			4	7	2	3
				6 (4/1-9/30/02)		46 (10/1/02-3/31/03)			
ALL 34	ALL 37	ALL 52	**NUMBER OF STATEMENTS**	2	9	13	14	6	8
%	%	%	**ASSETS**	%	%	%	%	%	%
7.0	6.6	8.7	Cash & Equivalents			13.9	7.2		
23.6	24.0	26.6	Trade Receivables (net)			27.0	25.8		
35.1	35.1	29.0	Inventory			27.2	31.9		
2.8	2.5	4.6	All Other Current			2.9	3.3		
68.5	68.2	69.0	Total Current			71.1	68.3		
22.8	21.6	22.1	Fixed Assets (net)			17.9	23.5		
3.1	3.1	2.6	Intangibles (net)			.2	1.9		
5.6	7.0	6.4	All Other Non-Current			10.7	6.4		
100.0	100.0	100.0	Total			100.0	100.0		
			LIABILITIES						
12.0	12.9	16.7	Notes Payable-Short Term			13.0	17.6		
2.5	5.1	3.4	Cur. Mat.-L/T/D			3.1	3.1		
12.1	15.0	16.0	Trade Payables			11.1	14.1		
.5	.1	.1	Income Taxes Payable			.0	.1		
17.0	16.4	17.9	All Other Current			15.8	14.6		
44.1	49.5	54.0	Total Current			43.0	49.6		
11.5	9.0	11.4	Long Term Debt			8.5	11.1		
.3	.3	.4	Deferred Taxes			.1	.8		
7.1	14.0	10.3	All Other Non-Current			2.9	11.8		
36.9	27.2	23.9	Net Worth			45.6	26.7		
100.0	100.0	100.0	Total Liabilities & Net Worth			100.0	100.0		
			INCOME DATA						
100.0	100.0	100.0	Net Sales			100.0	100.0		
32.1	31.9	29.8	Gross Profit			38.3	29.4		
27.4	30.1	26.8	Operating Expenses			31.1	27.5		
4.6	1.8	3.0	Operating Profit			7.1	1.9		
1.2	1.4	1.0	All Other Expenses (net)			.2	1.5		
3.5	.3	2.0	Profit Before Taxes			6.9	.5		
			RATIOS						
2.3	2.4	2.1	Current			4.4	2.3		
1.5	1.4	1.5				1.8	1.6		
1.1	1.1	1.1				1.2	1.1		
1.1	1.0	1.0	Quick			1.7	1.4		
.6	.7	.8				1.0	.9		
.4	.5	.5				.6	.5		
36 10.1	35 10.3	38 9.5	Sales/Receivables			30 12.1	41 8.8		
42 8.7	44 8.2	49 7.4				41 8.9	51 7.1		
56 6.5	57 6.4	64 5.7				63 5.8	64 5.7		
56 6.5	56 6.5	38 9.5	Cost of Sales/Inventory			28 12.9	47 7.8		
101 3.6	86 4.3	76 4.8				99 3.7	98 3.7		
146 2.5	166 2.2	153 2.4				187 1.9	158 2.3		
19 19.4	18 20.1	21 17.0	Cost of Sales/Payables			16 22.8	21 17.4		
31 11.7	30 12.0	37 9.9				29 12.4	39 9.3		
46 7.9	54 6.8	52 7.0				45 8.1	50 7.2		
4.3	4.1	5.1	Sales/Working Capital			2.7	4.0		
8.2	7.4	8.6				7.3	6.4		
38.9	48.1	34.0				23.6	NM		
9.8	3.7	5.3	EBIT/Interest			6.5	3.8		
(32) 3.7	(33) 1.0	(48) 2.4				(11) 5.0	(13) 2.2		
1.3	-2.4	-.8				2.4	-.7		
5.7		4.3	Net Profit + Depr., Dep., Amort./Cur. Mat. L/T/D						
(10) 2.9		(16) 1.3							
.3		-1.4							
.2	.2	.3	Fixed/Worth			.2	.6		
.6	.6	.7				.4	2.3		
2.9	2.4	10.3				.9	NM		
.9	.6	1.0	Debt/Worth			.3	.7		
1.4	1.6	2.2				1.6	4.8		
6.4	9.1	70.8				2.4	NM		
56.4	26.1	43.6	% Profit Before Taxes/Tangible Net Worth			54.4	45.1		
(31) 17.4	(31) 1.0	(43) 18.0				(12) 35.8	(11) 7.3		
4.2	-7.0	-5.9				-1.7	-8.1		
14.0	7.9	13.7	% Profit Before Taxes/Total Assets			23.8	5.7		
5.2	.0	3.2				15.6	.9		
.7	-4.2	-4.2				-1.2	-6.1		
26.2	19.1	19.2	Sales/Net Fixed Assets			21.8	20.9		
10.0	10.6	10.4				12.1	10.4		
6.3	6.9	5.3				5.1	4.8		
2.5	2.5	2.6	Sales/Total Assets			3.8	2.1		
1.8	1.7	1.7				1.7	1.6		
1.4	1.4	1.2				1.2	1.4		
.7	1.4	1.4	% Depr., Dep., Amort./Sales			1.2	1.4		
(32) 1.5	(35) 2.2	(49) 2.1				2.4	(13) 2.0		
3.4	3.6	3.0				3.7	2.4		
1.8	2.1	1.6	% Officers', Directors', Owners' Comp/Sales						
(14) 4.1	(16) 2.9	(18) 3.1							
7.7	6.5	6.3							
416977M	755401M	918974M	Net Sales ($)	1355M	21137M	51593M	102836M	115953M	626100M
279967M	509055M	683649M	Total Assets ($)	623M	15600M	35536M	66549M	74660M	490681M

M = $ thousand   MM = $ million
See Pages 11 through 18 for Explanation of Ratios and Data

Current Data Sorted By Assets

Comparative Historical Data

0-500M	500M-2MM	2-10MM	10-50MM	50-100MM	100-250MM	Type of Statement	4/1/98-3/31/99 ALL	4/1/99-3/31/00 ALL
	2	5	5			Unqualified	36	36
	2	11	4			Reviewed	17	23
	3	7				Compiled	19	19
	2	2				Tax Returns	6	2
	4	5	3			Other	30	31
	10 (4/1-9/30/02)		45 (10/1/02-3/31/03)					
	13	30	12			NUMBER OF STATEMENTS	108	111
%	%	%	%	%	%	ASSETS	%	%
	7.2	13.6	14.9			Cash & Equivalents	7.9	9.3
D	25.1	23.2	16.1	D	D	Trade Receivables (net)	26.2	24.2
A	27.4	33.1	28.3	A	A	Inventory	31.3	30.9
T	5.2	3.5	7.8	T	T	All Other Current	2.8	2.5
A	65.0	73.3	67.0	A	A	Total Current	68.2	66.9
	24.3	18.1	24.8			Fixed Assets (net)	21.3	21.8
N	.2	2.2	.3	N	N	Intangibles (net)	4.1	5.1
O	10.6	6.3	7.9	O	O	All Other Non-Current	6.5	6.2
T	100.0	100.0	100.0	T	T	Total	100.0	100.0
						LIABILITIES		
A	17.5	9.5	5.6	A	A	Notes Payable-Short Term	9.5	10.7
V	4.4	1.9	1.7	V	V	Cur. Mat.-L/T/D	3.0	3.4
A	14.8	13.5	5.3	A	A	Trade Payables	12.5	11.0
I	.1	.4	.0	I	I	Income Taxes Payable	.2	.3
L	10.7	18.9	11.5	L	L	All Other Current	13.0	15.8
A	47.5	44.1	24.1	A	A	Total Current	38.2	41.1
B	10.3	5.0	10.9	B	B	Long Term Debt	17.3	12.3
L	.0	.2	1.3	L	L	Deferred Taxes	.5	.4
E	6.3	4.2	1.4	E	E	All Other Non-Current	3.2	4.4
	35.9	46.4	62.3			Net Worth	40.8	41.7
	100.0	100.0	100.0			Total Liabilities & Net Worth	100.0	100.0
						INCOME DATA		
	100.0	100.0	100.0			Net Sales	100.0	100.0
	30.8	31.6	28.2			Gross Profit	30.7	32.5
	31.9	27.2	27.0			Operating Expenses	26.2	29.3
	-1.2	4.4	1.2			Operating Profit	4.5	3.2
	-.1	.9	.8			All Other Expenses (net)	1.2	1.0
	-1.0	3.5	.5			Profit Before Taxes	3.3	2.2
						RATIOS		
	2.7	3.0	8.8				3.1	2.8
	2.0	1.9	3.2			Current	1.7	1.8
	1.1	1.2	1.8				1.4	1.3
	1.7	1.4	6.6				1.4	1.5
	.9	.8	1.1			Quick	.9	.9
	.4	.5	.7				.6	.5
25	14.8	35 10.4	29 12.8				36 10.1	33 11.2
35	10.5	43 8.4	51 7.2			Sales/Receivables	48 7.7	46 8.0
51	7.1	53 6.9	63 5.8				66 5.5	65 5.7
20	18.1	34 10.8	87 4.2				49 7.5	55 6.6
66	5.5	96 3.8	138 2.6			Cost of Sales/Inventory	97 3.8	93 3.9
88	4.2	158 2.3	181 2.0				139 2.6	156 2.3
17	21.3	13 28.0	13 27.7				13 27.1	15 24.2
25	14.6	33 11.2	20 18.3			Cost of Sales/Payables	28 13.3	32 11.3
41	9.0	48 7.6	28 13.1				52 7.0	44 8.3
	4.7	3.3	1.0				3.4	3.4
	7.7	5.3	2.9			Sales/Working Capital	6.3	6.0
	NM	24.3	4.7				12.2	14.2
	6.0	8.9					6.7	7.7
(12)	-.8	(26) 4.3				EBIT/Interest	(97) 2.8	(102) 2.1
	-11.4	1.5					.6	.9
						Net Profit + Depr., Dep.,		4.2	2.6
						Amort./Cur. Mat. L /T/D	(33) 2.1	(29) 1.3
							.6	-.3
	.2	.1	.2				.2	.2
	.6	.4	.4			Fixed/Worth	.5	.5
	1.2	.8	.7				1.6	1.6
	.6	.4	.2				.8	.6
	1.3	1.0	.7			Debt/Worth	1.6	1.4
	2.4	3.8	1.2				3.7	4.6
	18.5	35.6	11.0			% Profit Before Taxes/Tangible	35.0	26.4
(12)	.1	(29) 12.5	-.5			Net Worth	(98) 13.6	(100) 9.0
	-15.7	2.0	-4.9				-.5	-.2
	11.6	9.5	8.3			% Profit Before Taxes/Total	12.3	10.2
	-1.4	5.6	.2			Assets	5.5	3.1
	-19.3	.4	-3.6				-.4	-.2
	18.4	27.1	9.2				19.1	18.2
	11.3	12.9	4.0			Sales/Net Fixed Assets	9.8	8.1
	6.6	6.6	2.7				5.6	5.0
	3.1	2.4	1.3				2.3	2.1
	2.9	1.8	1.1			Sales/Total Assets	1.8	1.7
	2.0	1.2	.7				1.3	1.3
	.9	.7	2.3				1.2	1.2
	1.9	(26) 1.6	(11) 4.2			% Depr., Dep., Amort./Sales	(93) 1.9	(99) 1.7
	3.0	3.1	5.7				3.1	3.6
	3.2					% Officers', Directors',	2.4	2.3
(12)	4.4					Owners' Comp/Sales	(35) 5.0	(35) 4.3
	9.2						6.7	7.0
	42219M	206256M	255229M			Net Sales ($)	2336936M	2708271M
	17068M	114597M	242185M			Total Assets ($)	1795000M	2146238M

Comparative Historical Data					Current Data Sorted By Sales					

20	12	12	Type of Statement		1	3	2	3	3
19	8	17	Unqualified		2	3	7	4	1
25	18	10	Reviewed		3	2	3	2	
3		4	Compiled		1	2		1	
20	24	12	Tax Returns			4	6	2	
			Other						

						10 (4/1-9/30/02)		45 (10/1/02-3/31/03)		
4/1/00-3/31/01 ALL	4/1/01-3/31/02 ALL	4/1/02-3/31/03 ALL		0-1MM	1-3MM	3-5MM	5-10MM	10-25MM	25MM & OVER
87	62	55	**NUMBER OF STATEMENTS**	7	14	18	12	4

%	%	%	**ASSETS**	%	%	%	%	%	%
9.3	10.9	12.4	Cash & Equivalents			5.1	15.8	17.1	
22.2	19.3	22.1	Trade Receivables (net)			25.7	24.1	20.0	
27.0	30.1	30.7	Inventory			34.3	31.2	29.9	
4.6	5.5	4.8	All Other Current			3.8	2.4	6.5	
63.2	65.9	70.0	Total Current			68.9	73.5	73.5	
23.9	23.5	21.0	Fixed Assets (net)			27.0	18.7	19.0	
5.6	3.1	1.3	Intangibles (net)			.2	3.1	1.0	
7.4	7.6	7.7	All Other Non-Current			3.9	4.6	6.5	
100.0	100.0	100.0	Total			100.0	100.0	100.0	

(DATA NOT AVAILABLE for 0-1MM and 1-3MM columns)

			LIABILITIES						
13.0	7.7	10.5	Notes Payable-Short Term			23.7	6.5	4.6	
3.9	2.6	2.4	Cur. Mat.-L/T/D			3.2	2.3	1.1	
10.8	11.9	12.0	Trade Payables			14.0	15.1	8.2	
.5	.5	.2	Income Taxes Payable			.0	.6	.0	
15.5	12.9	15.3	All Other Current			6.9	16.6	23.2	
43.7	35.5	40.5	Total Current			47.8	41.1	37.1	
12.6	15.6	7.6	Long Term Debt			10.2	4.2	7.1	
.4	.5	.4	Deferred Taxes			.3	.3	.5	
7.6	3.5	4.1	All Other Non-Current			7.1	3.2	2.7	
35.8	44.8	47.4	Net Worth			34.6	51.1	52.7	
100.0	100.0	100.0	Total Liabilities & Net Worth			100.0	100.0	100.0	

			INCOME DATA						
100.0	100.0	100.0	Net Sales			100.0	100.0	100.0	
32.1	33.8	30.7	Gross Profit			32.7	28.7	28.5	
29.1	29.7	28.3	Operating Expenses			29.0	26.4	26.0	
2.9	4.1	2.4	Operating Profit			3.8	2.3	2.5	
1.3	1.8	.6	All Other Expenses (net)			1.0	.1	.9	
1.7	2.3	1.8	Profit Before Taxes			2.8	2.2	1.7	

			RATIOS						
2.6	3.1	3.2				2.8	3.5	4.3	
1.6	1.9	2.1	Current			1.8	2.2	2.1	
1.1	1.3	1.2				1.3	1.2	1.4	

1.5	1.4	1.5				1.5	2.0	1.3	
.8	.9	.9	Quick			.8	1.0	.8	
.4	.7	.6				.5	.6	.7	

30	12.3	28	13.1	28	12.9			33	11.0	28	13.2	28	12.8	
42	8.7	44	8.3	43	8.5	Sales/Receivables		49	7.4	37	9.8	53	6.8	
59	6.2	57	6.4	55	6.6			61	6.0	47	7.7	63	5.8	

39	9.3	53	6.9	46	7.9			40	9.1	34	10.8	66	5.5	
78	4.7	100	3.6	86	4.3	Cost of Sales/Inventory		84	4.3	80	4.6	109	3.4	
139	2.6	133	2.8	152	2.4			151	2.4	141	2.6	165	2.2	

15	23.9	13	27.5	14	26.7			15	23.8	9	41.4	16	22.5	
27	13.5	24	15.2	27	13.7	Cost of Sales/Payables		31	11.6	30	12.1	24	15.3	
46	7.9	45	8.2	42	8.8			71	5.2	48	7.7	33	11.0	

4.1	3.5	2.8				4.0	2.9	2.5	
7.8	5.8	4.9	Sales/Working Capital			6.5	5.4	3.9	
29.2	9.8	15.8				21.6	19.7	13.2	

	9.2		9.9		7.8				7.3		12.8	
(74)	3.4	(56)	3.1	(47)	2.7	EBIT/Interest	(13)	3.4	(16)	3.7	
	.9		.4		-.8			-2.4		-.7	

	5.6		2.3		4.6	Net Profit + Depr., Dep.,			
(20)	1.5	(15)	1.0	(16)	1.7	Amort./Cur. Mat. L/T/D			
	.4		.5		.2				

.2	.2	.2				.2	.1	.1	
.5	.5	.4	Fixed/Worth			.6	.4	.3	
3.3	1.1	.9				1.2	.6	.7	

.7	.5	.4				.6	.3	.3	
1.7	1.1	.9	Debt/Worth			1.7	.6	1.1	
7.6	3.3	2.5				2.7	7.5	2.1	

	34.3		27.9		26.7	% Profit Before Taxes/Tangible		31.6		35.6	12.2
(72)	14.4	(56)	12.7	(53)	9.0	Net Worth	(13)	12.5	(17)	18.8	3.8
	2.1		.7		-3.7			-.9		-1.2	-4.8

12.6	12.0	10.1	% Profit Before Taxes/Total			11.1	9.5	8.3	
5.7	3.4	2.7	Assets			4.3	5.3	1.5	
-1.2	-1.2	-2.4				-5.4	-2.3	-3.6	

16.4	23.5	21.8				16.0	29.5	15.5	
7.9	8.5	9.5	Sales/Net Fixed Assets			8.8	17.8	8.3	
5.3	4.2	5.6				6.5	4.3	4.6	

2.3	2.1	2.6				3.0	2.7	2.3	
1.7	1.6	1.7	Sales/Total Assets			2.0	1.9	1.2	
1.2	1.2	1.1				1.1	1.4	1.1	

	1.2		.6		1.0			1.0		.7	.9
(76)	2.2	(52)	1.8	(50)	2.0	% Depr., Dep., Amort./Sales	(13)	2.4	(15)	1.7	(11) 2.5
	3.1		4.5		3.7			3.7		4.2	3.4

	3.8		3.6		2.9	% Officers', Directors',			
(30)	7.0	(18)	5.5	(21)	4.4	Owners' Comp/Sales			
	10.4		8.3		8.4				

1615526M	1751998M	503704M	Net Sales ($)		14527M	49594M	131482M	193554M	114547M
1232041M	1195473M	373850M	Total Assets ($)		12701M	29065M	91305M	162670M	78109M

M = $ thousand   MM = $ million
See Pages 11 through 18 for Explanation of Ratios and Data

Current Data Sorted By Assets   **Comparative Historical Data**

0-500M	500M-2MM	2-10MM	10-50MM	50-100MM	100-250MM		4/1/98-3/31/99 ALL	4/1/99-3/31/00 ALL
						Type of Statement		
		6	8	1	3	Unqualified	10	16
	8	10				Reviewed	16	13
	3	2				Compiled	9	12
						Tax Returns	1	
1	1	7	5	1	3	Other	16	14
	10 (4/1-9/30/02)		49 (10/1/02-3/31/03)					
1	12	25	13	2	6	**NUMBER OF STATEMENTS**	52	55
%	%	%	%	%	%		%	%
						ASSETS		
	8.3	8.8	5.8			Cash & Equivalents	10.7	9.9
	27.4	19.7	23.4			Trade Receivables (net)	26.0	24.0
	38.0	35.4	29.2			Inventory	28.5	28.5
	2.5	2.8	4.2			All Other Current	1.5	3.3
	76.1	66.8	62.7			Total Current	66.8	65.7
	14.3	24.5	19.3			Fixed Assets (net)	23.8	21.9
	7.2	1.7	13.6			Intangibles (net)	4.0	5.7
	2.4	7.0	4.4			All Other Non-Current	5.4	6.6
	100.0	100.0	100.0			Total	100.0	100.0
						LIABILITIES		
	13.8	6.7	5.2			Notes Payable-Short Term	8.3	12.3
	4.4	4.1	9.2			Cur. Mat.-L/T/D	3.3	3.3
	14.0	12.5	13.3			Trade Payables	15.2	14.7
	.0	.2	.9			Income Taxes Payable	.7	.7
	13.5	18.0	13.1			All Other Current	16.1	16.7
	45.8	41.4	41.7			Total Current	43.5	47.5
	9.0	14.2	13.7			Long Term Debt	16.1	13.6
	.0	.4	.4			Deferred Taxes	.5	.4
	10.1	3.5	5.6			All Other Non-Current	6.6	8.2
	35.1	40.4	38.6			Net Worth	33.4	30.3
	100.0	100.0	100.0			Total Liabilities & Net Worth	100.0	100.0
						INCOME DATA		
	100.0	100.0	100.0			Net Sales	100.0	100.0
	37.2	32.1	34.0			Gross Profit	34.5	34.0
	34.7	29.4	31.4			Operating Expenses	26.5	29.3
	2.5	2.7	2.5			Operating Profit	8.0	4.7
	1.9	1.3	1.4			All Other Expenses (net)	2.6	1.3
	.6	1.3	1.1			Profit Before Taxes	5.4	3.4
						RATIOS		
	3.3	3.0	2.2				2.7	2.1
	1.5	1.8	1.4			Current	1.4	1.3
	1.2	1.3	1.1				1.0	1.1
	1.5	1.4	1.3				1.4	1.2
	1.0	.8	.6			Quick	.8	.8
	.4	.4	.4				.5	.4
	37 9.9	29 12.6	37 10.0				33 11.1	26 14.2
	45 8.1	40 9.2	56 6.5			Sales/Receivables	47 7.7	49 7.4
	59 6.2	51 7.1	67 5.5				60 6.1	64 5.7
	49 7.5	56 6.5	56 6.5				44 8.3	29 12.7
	108 3.4	108 3.4	73 5.0			Cost of Sales/Inventory	70 5.2	83 4.4
	157 2.3	177 2.1	156 2.3				130 2.8	125 2.9
	20 18.6	16 22.5	29 12.8				19 19.0	19 19.0
	28 13.3	30 12.0	38 9.7			Cost of Sales/Payables	33 11.1	35 10.5
	47 7.7	43 8.4	62 5.9				60 6.1	55 6.6
	3.7	3.3	5.3				5.7	5.9
	10.1	5.6	11.0			Sales/Working Capital	10.8	12.3
	13.8	15.1	NM				131.1	61.8
	12.2	(22) 9.3	(12) 6.6				(49) 15.1	(51) 9.3
	2.2	1.8	1.4			EBIT/Interest	4.2	2.7
	.5	1.0	−1.1				1.1	1.1
						Net Profit + Depr., Dep.,	(19) 18.3	(19) 7.1
						Amort./Cur. Mat. L/T/D	3.3	3.5
							1.5	1.1
	.2	.2	.2				.3	.2
	.5	.6	.5			Fixed/Worth	.7	.8
	3.4	1.4	4.3				2.3	2.4
	.7	.7	1.3				.8	.9
	1.8	1.5	3.1			Debt/Worth	2.2	3.3
	39.6	3.2	9.0				12.2	6.6
	(10) 55.8	(22) 22.5	(12) 42.8			% Profit Before Taxes/Tangible	(45) 68.7	(44) 41.5
	18.9	10.4	8.1			Net Worth	24.6	19.4
	−7.2	−1.2	−9.3				8.3	5.0
	15.1	5.8	10.5			% Profit Before Taxes/Total	14.6	13.5
	1.8	1.9	1.7			Assets	6.1	4.6
	−3.2	−2.0	−3.4				1.4	.5
	74.3	41.8	34.8				36.7	26.6
	22.6	8.9	7.8			Sales/Net Fixed Assets	11.1	12.2
	7.8	3.7	5.4				4.9	5.3
	2.9	1.6	1.6				2.5	2.6
	2.1	1.6	1.6			Sales/Total Assets	1.9	1.8
	1.6	1.4	1.3				1.5	1.4
		(24) .8	1.2				(47) .8	(49) .9
		2.4	3.5			% Depr., Dep., Amort./Sales	2.4	1.7
		4.5	4.0				4.0	3.4
						% Officers', Directors',	(16) 1.7	(16) 1.9
						Owners' Comp/Sales	3.3	3.9
							8.0	7.5
5078M	29582M	229357M	570952M	122654M	956862M	Net Sales ($)	1507204M	1635231M
415M	13940M	128665M	370998M	134509M	753289M	Total Assets ($)	905459M	1060446M

Comparative Historical Data | Current Data Sorted By Sales

			Type of Statement	0-1MM	1-3MM	3-5MM	5-10MM	10-25MM	25MM & OVER
14	18	18	Unqualified				3	5	10
13	12	18	Reviewed	1	7	3	5	2	
11	15	5	Compiled		2	1	2		
	2		Tax Returns						
18	19	18	Other		1		4	5	8
4/1/00-3/31/01 ALL	4/1/01-3/31/02 ALL	4/1/02-3/31/03 ALL			10 (4/1-9/30/02)			49 (10/1/02-3/31/03)	
56	66	59	**NUMBER OF STATEMENTS**	1	10	4	14	12	18
%	%	%	**ASSETS**	%	%	%	%	%	%
9.1	8.2	8.4	Cash & Equivalents		8.9		11.0	4.1	7.4
24.4	24.3	22.0	Trade Receivables (net)		21.8		21.5	23.0	23.4
27.8	27.5	31.8	Inventory		38.8		30.8	38.0	25.6
1.4	4.9	4.1	All Other Current		3.0		1.5	4.8	7.1
62.8	64.9	66.3	Total Current		72.5		64.8	69.9	63.5
23.3	22.7	20.9	Fixed Assets (net)		15.9		28.6	15.1	18.6
7.3	7.0	7.2	Intangibles (net)		8.6		1.3	7.2	12.8
6.6	5.4	5.6	All Other Non-Current		3.0		5.4	7.8	5.2
100.0	100.0	100.0	Total		100.0		100.0	100.0	100.0
			LIABILITIES						
10.5	8.3	7.9	Notes Payable-Short Term		13.4		11.8	6.1	3.9
4.2	4.8	4.9	Cur. Mat.-L/T/D		4.2		3.9	7.0	5.2
14.2	14.0	12.0	Trade Payables		12.5		10.1	19.0	10.3
.8	.3	.4	Income Taxes Payable		.0		.2	.2	.9
13.6	17.7	17.6	All Other Current		12.8		19.4	17.1	21.1
43.3	45.1	42.7	Total Current		42.8		45.3	49.4	41.4
8.8	11.0	12.3	Long Term Debt		9.5		13.8	9.6	11.5
.5	.5	.4	Deferred Taxes		.0		.8	.1	.7
4.8	6.7	5.4	All Other Non-Current		12.1		2.1	10.1	2.6
42.5	36.8	39.1	Net Worth		35.6		38.0	30.8	43.8
100.0	100.0	100.0	Total Liabilities & Net Worth		100.0		100.0	100.0	100.0
			INCOME DATA						
100.0	100.0	100.0	Net Sales		100.0		100.0	100.0	100.0
36.0	32.6	33.7	Gross Profit		38.3		32.0	30.8	32.7
31.1	31.6	31.1	Operating Expenses		37.1		30.5	28.4	29.2
4.8	1.0	2.6	Operating Profit		1.2		1.5	2.5	3.5
.4	1.7	1.3	All Other Expenses (net)		2.0		1.1	1.0	.8
4.5	-.7	1.3	Profit Before Taxes		-.7		.4	1.4	2.8
			RATIOS						
2.4 1.5 1.0	2.8 1.4 1.1	2.7 1.6 1.2	Current		3.4 1.5 1.2		3.0 1.6 1.1	2.0 1.7 1.0	2.2 1.5 1.2
1.4 .8 .5	1.3 .8 .4	1.3 .8 .4	Quick		1.6 .8 .4		1.3 .9 .4	.9 .6 .3	1.4 .7 .5
30 12.3 50 7.3 67 5.4	33 11.2 49 7.5 63 5.8	33 11.0 45 8.1 62 5.9	Sales/Receivables		35 10.6 41 8.9 52 7.0		29 12.4 39 9.4 54 6.7	32 11.4 41 9.0 59 6.2	44 8.4 62 5.9 71 5.1
36 10.3 86 4.2 144 2.5	25 14.7 81 4.5 140 2.6	56 6.5 82 4.5 150 2.4	Cost of Sales/Inventory		65 5.6 126 2.9 238 1.5		14 25.8 78 4.7 157 2.3	56 6.5 77 4.7 165 2.2	63 5.8 76 4.8 93 3.9
23 15.7 35 10.4 51 7.2	22 16.4 38 9.6 53 6.9	20 18.5 32 11.3 46 7.9	Cost of Sales/Payables		19 18.8 23 15.9 51 7.2		10 37.8 28 13.1 43 8.5	33 11.1 41 8.8 60 6.1	22 16.7 32 11.4 48 7.6
4.0 11.8 72.8	4.6 10.2 50.7	4.2 7.1 17.9	Sales/Working Capital		3.4 7.5 13.7		4.1 7.1 NM	4.7 9.1 NM	4.4 7.0 15.0
10.9 (47) 3.7 1.1	5.4 (60) 1.2 -2.0	7.0 (54) 1.8 -.2	EBIT/Interest				6.4 1.7 -5.3	14.8 (11) 2.7 1.6	6.6 (16) 2.5 -1.1
21.4 (23) 2.9 1.1	5.0 (19) 1.0 -.1	5.5 (23) 1.2 .2	Net Profit + Depr., Dep., Amort./Cur. Mat. L/T/D						
.3 .6 2.1	.3 .6 4.7	.2 .6 1.4	Fixed/Worth		.2 .6 NM		.4 .8 1.2	.1 1.1 NM	.3 .5 .9
.6 1.7 5.2	.8 2.5 11.9	.8 1.9 3.7	Debt/Worth		.6 2.4 NM		1.0 1.6 2.7	1.2 3.2 NM	1.0 1.9 3.2
37.2 (47) 15.1 4.3	19.2 (53) 2.7 -15.0	28.6 (52) 9.3 -4.9	% Profit Before Taxes/Tangible Net Worth				24.4 (13) 6.7 -11.5		31.2 (17) 7.6 -6.1
15.0 6.2 1.2	6.7 1.2 -7.5	7.1 1.9 -3.2	% Profit Before Taxes/Total Assets		3.7 1.4 -6.2		7.7 2.3 -5.8	6.7 3.6 .7	10.3 2.5 -2.8
27.6 9.1 4.1	32.5 9.8 4.6	31.9 8.9 4.9	Sales/Net Fixed Assets		50.7 22.6 8.1		23.7 6.9 3.7	58.1 19.0 5.6	23.6 8.9 5.9
2.6 1.7 1.2	2.4 1.7 1.3	2.0 1.6 1.3	Sales/Total Assets		2.4 1.9 1.1		2.9 1.6 1.4	2.7 1.9 1.6	1.8 1.4 1.2
1.0 (51) 1.9 3.8	.9 (56) 2.3 4.6	1.1 (54) 2.7 4.2	% Depr., Dep., Amort./Sales				1.6 2.8 4.6	.5 (11) .9 3.6	1.3 (17) 2.8 4.0
3.1 (18) 5.4 11.0	3.8 (15) 5.6 7.8	3.9 (19) 7.5 12.0	% Officers', Directors', Owners' Comp/Sales						
2101584M 1407611M	2440456M 1674488M	1914485M 1401816M	Net Sales ($) Total Assets ($)	911M 591M	19120M 12195M	17601M 15253M	92562M 53757M	196353M 121711M	1587938M 1198309M

M = $ thousand   MM = $ million
See Pages 11 through 18 for Explanation of Ratios and Data

Current Data Sorted By Assets   Comparative Historical Data

0-500M	500M-2MM	2-10MM	10-50MM	50-100MM	100-250MM	Type of Statement	4/1/98-3/31/99 ALL	4/1/99-3/31/00 ALL
		8	9	1	3	Unqualified	24	25
	4	10	3			Reviewed	15	14
2	6	3			1	Compiled	8	7
4	2					Tax Returns	2	4
1	1	7	7	1		Other	31	18
	11 (4/1-9/30/02)		62 (10/1/02-3/31/03)					
7	13	28	19	2	4	**NUMBER OF STATEMENTS**	80	68
%	%	%	%	%	%	**ASSETS**	%	%
	20.9	13.7	10.0			Cash & Equivalents	9.9	7.5
	24.7	20.1	23.2			Trade Receivables (net)	24.5	24.5
	20.2	34.0	25.9			Inventory	34.0	35.4
	2.4	2.7	3.5			All Other Current	2.1	2.1
	68.2	70.5	62.6			Total Current	70.5	69.6
	22.7	21.1	24.6			Fixed Assets (net)	21.7	19.7
	.1	2.0	6.8			Intangibles (net)	2.8	5.7
	9.0	6.4	5.9			All Other Non-Current	5.1	5.1
	100.0	100.0	100.0			Total	100.0	100.0
						LIABILITIES		
	10.0	6.1	6.5			Notes Payable-Short Term	10.8	9.7
	1.3	5.0	3.7			Cur. Mat.-L/T/D	4.4	4.5
	13.3	10.5	9.1			Trade Payables	15.0	12.9
	.1	.5	.1			Income Taxes Payable	.4	.2
	14.8	14.8	17.4			All Other Current	14.6	16.6
	39.6	36.9	36.9			Total Current	45.2	43.9
	11.4	14.1	11.7			Long Term Debt	16.4	13.3
	.0	1.0	.8			Deferred Taxes	.5	.5
	4.3	3.3	1.5			All Other Non-Current	7.0	5.2
	44.6	44.7	49.2			Net Worth	31.0	37.0
	100.0	100.0	100.0			Total Liabilities & Net Worth	100.0	100.0
						INCOME DATA		
	100.0	100.0	100.0			Net Sales	100.0	100.0
	40.7	33.5	34.9			Gross Profit	32.8	33.0
	35.1	28.2	29.5			Operating Expenses	30.2	29.5
	5.7	5.3	5.5			Operating Profit	2.6	3.5
	1.0	1.1	.6			All Other Expenses (net)	1.3	1.1
	4.6	4.2	4.9			Profit Before Taxes	1.3	2.4
						RATIOS		
	2.9	3.4	2.8			Current	2.7	2.4
	1.7	2.1	1.5				1.6	1.7
	1.3	1.3	1.4				1.2	1.2
	2.0	1.9	1.2			Quick	1.4	1.3
	1.3	.9	.8				.8	.7
	.6	.6	.6				.5	.4
	24 14.9	28 13.0	48 7.6			Sales/Receivables	33 11.2	35 10.5
	37 10.0	35 10.5	52 7.0				46 7.9	45 8.2
	53 6.9	48 7.6	63 5.8				57 6.4	55 6.6
	9 39.9	51 7.1	84 4.3			Cost of Sales/Inventory	66 5.5	62 5.9
	43 8.4	103 3.5	95 3.8				95 3.8	101 3.6
	125 2.9	164 2.2	116 3.1				142 2.6	128 2.9
	10 35.4	19 19.2	16 22.7			Cost of Sales/Payables	21 17.6	19 19.1
	22 16.6	23 15.9	30 12.3				34 10.7	30 12.2
	93 3.9	36 10.0	50 7.3				50 7.3	48 7.6
	3.5	3.6	4.3			Sales/Working Capital	4.1	4.0
	7.8	5.7	7.5				7.9	7.1
	18.3	12.1	13.8				25.1	22.6
	12.1	13.0	13.7			EBIT/Interest	9.2	10.1
	(11) 2.7	(24) 3.5	(16) 4.2				(74) 2.6	(62) 3.2
	1.1	1.5	.7				.7	.9
		5.5				Net Profit + Depr., Dep., Amort./Cur. Mat. L /T/D	4.2	5.0
		(12) 1.8					(30) 1.5	(23) 1.4
		1.0					.3	.5
	.2	.2	.3			Fixed/Worth	.2	.2
	.4	.4	.5				.6	.5
	1.1	1.0	1.1				1.9	1.4
	.5	.4	.7			Debt/Worth	.8	.7
	1.4	1.5	1.4				1.7	1.7
	4.3	3.5	2.3				11.2	4.8
	41.4	23.6	44.6			% Profit Before Taxes/Tangible Net Worth	38.4	43.9
	10.9	(25) 12.6	(18) 14.8				(65) 17.8	(59) 18.4
	−12.7	.1	−.3				2.7	4.0
	20.3	19.7	13.5			% Profit Before Taxes/Total Assets	12.8	15.8
	6.0	5.3	6.0				5.3	5.4
	−1.7	−.4	1.4				.1	.5
	44.8	17.4	11.0			Sales/Net Fixed Assets	25.3	26.9
	19.4	11.3	8.7				9.1	11.2
	5.8	7.1	5.4				5.9	6.5
	2.7	2.4	1.9			Sales/Total Assets	2.6	2.4
	2.4	1.8	1.6				1.9	2.0
	1.8	1.2	1.2				1.4	1.4
	.8	1.2	1.5			% Depr., Dep., Amort./Sales	1.0	.8
	(10) 2.8	(26) 2.1	(18) 2.7				(72) 2.1	(57) 1.9
	4.0	3.3	4.8				2.9	3.0
						% Officers', Directors', Owners' Comp/Sales	3.1	3.3
							(18) 4.3	(17) 4.3
							6.3	8.6
9867M	43540M	274773M	673350M	277785M	505150M	Net Sales ($)	1358783M	1704425M
1868M	16633M	154515M	444971M	147325M	671457M	Total Assets ($)	858548M	1093008M

M = $ thousand   MM = $ million
See Pages 11 through 18 for Explanation of Ratios and Data

Comparative Historical Data | Current Data Sorted By Sales

Type of Statement									
Unqualified	12	9	21			1	3	6	11
Reviewed	15	13	17		2	3	4	7	1
Compiled	11	9	12		5	3	2	1	1
Tax Returns	2		6	2	3	1			
Other	15	25	17	1	2		4	4	6

	4/1/00-3/31/01 ALL	4/1/01-3/31/02 ALL	4/1/02-3/31/03 ALL	___ 11 (4/1-9/30/02) ___			___ 62 (10/1/02-3/31/03) ___		
				0-1MM	1-3MM	3-5MM	5-10MM	10-25MM	25MM & OVER
NUMBER OF STATEMENTS	55	56	73	3	12	7	14	18	19
ASSETS	%	%	%	%	%	%	%	%	%
Cash & Equivalents	8.1	8.5	12.9		18.1		19.6	9.0	9.2
Trade Receivables (net)	24.1	22.8	23.9		35.2		18.0	24.0	20.3
Inventory	30.3	33.2	26.6		26.0		31.0	32.1	21.0
All Other Current	4.1	3.8	3.5		.9		3.9	2.6	6.2
Total Current	66.6	68.3	66.8		80.3		72.5	67.7	56.7
Fixed Assets (net)	20.2	21.3	20.3		17.7		21.7	24.2	15.6
Intangibles (net)	7.2	5.9	5.9		.9		.5	3.5	17.6
All Other Non-Current	6.1	4.5	7.0		1.1		5.3	4.6	10.0
Total	100.0	100.0	100.0		100.0		100.0	100.0	100.0
LIABILITIES									
Notes Payable-Short Term	7.4	9.6	6.5		4.9		11.9	5.4	4.9
Cur. Mat.-L/T/D	6.0	5.1	3.5		.2		5.1	3.9	4.4
Trade Payables	10.9	11.8	10.5		9.9		9.9	9.8	9.7
Income Taxes Payable	.4	.2	.3		.0		.1	.7	.4
All Other Current	15.5	14.7	15.3		19.2		16.4	14.1	16.2
Total Current	40.3	41.3	36.1		34.2		43.5	34.0	35.6
Long Term Debt	13.3	14.5	13.3		9.1		10.1	14.0	12.4
Deferred Taxes	.4	.3	.8		.0		1.2	.6	1.5
All Other Non-Current	5.7	5.4	5.8		6.8		3.4	1.5	3.6
Net Worth	40.3	38.5	44.0		49.9		41.8	49.9	46.9
Total Liabilities & Net Worth	100.0	100.0	100.0		100.0		100.0	100.0	100.0
INCOME DATA									
Net Sales	100.0	100.0	100.0		100.0		100.0	100.0	100.0
Gross Profit	34.3	33.7	36.4		42.9		30.7	36.7	33.9
Operating Expenses	32.0	30.0	30.5		38.7		30.3	30.4	23.6
Operating Profit	2.3	3.7	6.0		4.2		.4	6.3	10.2
All Other Expenses (net)	.7	1.5	1.1		1.2		.0	.9	1.3
Profit Before Taxes	1.6	2.2	4.9		3.0		.4	5.3	9.0
RATIOS									
Current	2.7 / 1.7 / 1.2	3.0 / 1.5 / 1.3	3.0 / 1.8 / 1.3		3.8 / 2.7 / 1.7		3.6 / 1.8 / 1.1	3.1 / 2.0 / 1.3	2.0 / 1.4 / 1.2
Quick	1.2 / .9 / .5	1.2 / .7 / .5	1.7 / .9 / .6		2.5 / 1.3 / 1.0		2.1 / .8 / .5	1.7 / .9 / .6	1.1 / .7 / .5
Sales/Receivables	41 8.9 / 52 7.0 / 61 5.9	32 11.2 / 44 8.3 / 58 6.3	30 12.3 / 41 8.9 / 54 6.8		24 15.4 / 39 9.4 / 54 6.8		21 17.8 / 32 11.4 / 58 6.3	30 12.3 / 38 9.5 / 50 7.2	39 9.3 / 50 7.2 / 57 6.4
Cost of Sales/Inventory	63 5.8 / 102 3.6 / 145 2.5	72 5.0 / 102 3.6 / 153 2.4	43 8.4 / 92 4.0 / 125 2.9		12 31.2 / 71 5.1 / 156 2.3		29 12.7 / 84 4.3 / 138 2.6	59 6.2 / 96 3.8 / 153 2.4	66 5.5 / 93 3.9 / 109 3.3
Cost of Sales/Payables	18 20.6 / 29 12.4 / 52 7.0	16 23.4 / 27 13.3 / 43 8.6	16 22.4 / 25 14.5 / 40 9.1		3 138.9 / 17 21.3 / 33 11.1		11 32.2 / 22 16.4 / 35 10.5	18 20.3 / 23 16.2 / 28 12.8	25 14.5 / 33 11.2 / 45 8.2
Sales/Working Capital	3.6 / 6.1 / 16.7	3.3 / 8.1 / 14.8	3.8 / 7.5 / 17.5		2.8 / 6.6 / 10.8		3.1 / 5.9 / 267.3	3.7 / 6.1 / 17.0	4.8 / 9.2 / 18.3
EBIT/Interest	(53) 8.3 / 2.0 / .6	(53) 9.1 / 2.7 / -.1	(62) 11.0 / 3.1 / 1.2		(10) 3.0 / 2.0 / -.5		(10) 8.9 / 2.0 / -5.7	(16) 22.8 / 7.7 / 2.3	(16) 13.7 / 3.7 / 2.4
Net Profit + Depr., Dep., Amort./Cur. Mat. L/T/D	(19) 3.0 / 1.5 / .1	(19) 3.0 / 1.3 / .1	(25) 5.0 / 1.5 / 1.0						(10) 4.6 / 1.3 / 1.1
Fixed/Worth	.3 / .5 / 1.4	.3 / .6 / 1.4	.2 / .4 / 1.5		.0 / .2 / .7		.2 / .8 / 1.1	.3 / .4 / 1.2	.3 / .6 / -5.9
Debt/Worth	.7 / 1.6 / 6.4	1.0 / 1.8 / 4.3	.5 / 1.5 / 3.8		.4 / 1.0 / 3.0		.5 / 1.6 / 4.8	.4 / .9 / 2.0	.5 / 2.0 / -49.8
% Profit Before Taxes/Tangible Net Worth	(48) 31.7 / 11.8 / -2.7	(47) 29.7 / 15.1 / -9.0	(63) 28.3 / 11.6 / -.7		11.6 / 6.4 / -15.5		(12) 15.6 / -1.6 / -22.7	(17) 34.4 / 12.9 / 6.0	(14) 61.6 / 16.7 / 8.3
% Profit Before Taxes/Total Assets	11.9 / 3.3 / -.8	13.7 / 4.5 / -3.8	15.0 / 5.6 / -.2		9.3 / 3.6 / -3.6		7.2 / -1.1 / -8.8	22.7 / 11.4 / 3.3	11.8 / 8.7 / 4.2
Sales/Net Fixed Assets	16.3 / 8.6 / 5.2	16.1 / 10.9 / 6.6	20.6 / 10.6 / 6.9		186.2 / 51.0 / 5.7		15.0 / 11.2 / 7.0	17.6 / 10.4 / 7.2	12.2 / 9.0 / 6.6
Sales/Total Assets	2.3 / 1.7 / 1.3	2.2 / 1.8 / 1.3	2.4 / 1.8 / 1.2		5.1 / 2.4 / 1.7		2.5 / 1.8 / 1.1	3.0 / 2.0 / 1.5	1.9 / 1.5 / 1.2
% Depr., Dep., Amort./Sales	(50) 1.4 / 2.1 / 2.8	(51) .8 / 1.7 / 3.5	(65) 1.2 / 2.1 / 3.1		(10) .4 / 1.9 / 4.9		(11) 1.6 / 2.2 / 3.8	1.3 / 1.8 / 4.1	(18) 1.4 / 2.3 / 2.8
% Officers', Directors', Owners' Comp/Sales	(14) 2.6 / 4.4 / 6.9	(14) 2.7 / 3.8 / 8.2	(22) 3.5 / 5.1 / 9.6		(10) 3.1 / 4.9 / 8.6				
Net Sales ($)	1219503M	1154377M	1784465M	1788M	22589M	29725M	100622M	289074M	1340667M
Total Assets ($)	872244M	894204M	1436769M	792M	11319M	19555M	67491M	159129M	1178483M

M = $ thousand   MM = $ million
See Pages 11 through 18 for Explanation of Ratios and Data

Current Data Sorted By Assets | **Comparative Historical Data**

						Type of Statement		
	1	19	18	5	3	Unqualified	48	54
1	4	14	2	1	1	Reviewed	41	44
5	21	9				Compiled	28	36
3	6	2				Tax Returns	4	6
4	9	24	13	1	2	Other	57	66
	38 (4/1-9/30/02)		130 (10/1/02-3/31/03)				4/1/98-3/31/99 ALL	4/1/99-3/31/00 ALL
0-500M	500M-2MM	2-10MM	10-50MM	50-100MM	100-250MM			
13	41	68	33	7	6	NUMBER OF STATEMENTS	178	206
%	%	%	%	%	%	ASSETS	%	%
7.8	9.2	8.7	17.5			Cash & Equivalents	9.9	11.1
26.8	26.8	23.7	25.7			Trade Receivables (net)	26.3	27.4
27.5	29.8	33.2	19.7			Inventory	28.1	27.7
1.0	3.4	4.9	5.6			All Other Current	4.8	3.7
63.1	69.1	70.5	68.4			Total Current	69.1	69.9
22.6	22.2	21.6	22.4			Fixed Assets (net)	21.4	20.5
2.7	2.0	1.2	2.6			Intangibles (net)	2.2	3.8
11.6	6.7	6.8	6.5			All Other Non-Current	7.4	5.9
100.0	100.0	100.0	100.0			Total	100.0	100.0
						LIABILITIES		
48.7	13.3	11.9	6.8			Notes Payable-Short Term	9.6	9.0
6.3	3.6	2.7	2.8			Cur. Mat.-L/T/D	2.9	2.3
14.9	14.3	13.3	9.1			Trade Payables	13.7	13.0
.0	.1	.1	.6			Income Taxes Payable	.5	.5
16.1	11.0	13.2	19.2			All Other Current	16.2	17.6
86.1	42.3	41.2	38.5			Total Current	42.9	42.5
12.1	13.6	9.7	11.7			Long Term Debt	10.9	11.2
.0	.2	.4	1.2			Deferred Taxes	.3	.5
.3	5.2	2.7	5.5			All Other Non-Current	5.1	3.8
1.5	38.7	46.0	43.1			Net Worth	40.7	42.1
100.0	100.0	100.0	100.0			Total Liabilities & Net Worth	100.0	100.0
						INCOME DATA		
100.0	100.0	100.0	100.0			Net Sales	100.0	100.0
32.4	36.9	29.7	28.9			Gross Profit	29.5	31.1
30.6	35.4	28.5	25.3			Operating Expenses	26.4	26.6
1.8	1.5	1.3	3.5			Operating Profit	3.0	4.5
.8	.9	1.1	1.0			All Other Expenses (net)	.9	.4
1.0	.6	.2	2.6			Profit Before Taxes	2.1	4.1
						RATIOS		
2.1	2.4	2.7	2.8			Current	2.5	2.8
.9	1.5	1.8	1.7				1.7	1.7
.3	1.1	1.3	1.2				1.2	1.2
.9	1.3	1.3	1.9			Quick	1.5	1.6
.5	.8	.8	1.1				.9	.9
.3	.4	.5	.6				.5	.6
0 UND	26 14.0	31 11.6	50 7.4			Sales/Receivables	32 11.3	37 9.8
38 9.7	46 7.9	45 8.2	60 6.0				50 7.4	53 6.9
59 6.2	63 5.8	64 5.7	83 4.4				63 5.8	68 5.3
3 105.6	44 8.3	50 7.3	35 10.4			Cost of Sales/Inventory	38 9.6	39 9.3
31 11.9	72 5.1	86 4.2	89 4.1				79 4.6	73 5.0
92 4.0	129 2.8	148 2.5	118 3.1				117 3.1	118 3.1
0 UND	24 15.3	17 21.2	23 15.7			Cost of Sales/Payables	18 20.5	17 21.7
14 27.0	35 10.5	35 10.5	31 11.9				31 11.7	29 12.6
34 10.7	62 5.9	51 7.2	44 8.3				50 7.4	46 7.9
9.7	4.5	3.6	2.7			Sales/Working Capital	4.3	4.2
-59.7	8.5	6.0	4.5				7.8	6.6
-13.0	28.3	13.3	11.5				20.3	19.6
(11) 16.4	(34) 8.7	(60) 10.2	(28) 11.2			EBIT/Interest	(156) 18.5	(174) 16.8
2.0	1.6	3.4	3.3				4.4	3.6
-5.1	-.5	-2.1	1.3				1.2	1.1
		(22) 5.5	(11) 3.4			Net Profit + Depr., Dep., Amort./Cur. Mat. L /T/D	(57) 17.7	(63) 7.3
		2.1	2.6				3.9	3.5
		.6	.9				1.6	1.3
.1	.2	.1	.2			Fixed/Worth	.2	.2
1.1	.4	.5	.5				.5	.4
43.1	2.5	.9	1.3				1.1	1.2
1.0	.5	.5	.6			Debt/Worth	.6	.6
11.2	1.7	1.3	1.6				1.3	1.3
NM	6.7	3.3	3.1				4.1	3.5
(10) 318.7	(35) 18.4	(66) 31.4	(30) 20.3			% Profit Before Taxes/Tangible Net Worth	(162) 47.2	(190) 39.0
59.1	6.7	8.9	7.4				22.8	17.0
-33.2	-6.1	-11.7	.7				5.5	4.1
43.2	7.0	11.2	8.7			% Profit Before Taxes/Total Assets	18.6	15.9
4.6	1.6	4.3	4.0				8.0	6.1
-16.5	-2.7	-5.5	.2				1.2	.5
UND	20.6	21.9	10.8			Sales/Net Fixed Assets	23.1	23.3
19.1	11.3	9.4	6.7				11.1	10.5
10.6	6.1	5.5	4.8				6.0	5.8
8.8	2.6	2.2	1.6			Sales/Total Assets	2.5	2.4
3.3	1.9	1.8	1.2				1.9	1.8
1.9	1.5	1.3	.9				1.5	1.3
	(36) .8	(66) 1.3	(29) 1.6			% Depr., Dep., Amort./Sales	(155) 1.1	(180) 1.1
	2.5	2.2	2.1				1.7	1.9
	4.5	4.7	3.3				3.0	3.0
	(22) 4.1	(16) 2.7				% Officers', Directors', Owners' Comp/Sales	(50) 2.7	(55) 2.6
	6.4	4.5					5.7	5.2
	8.9	8.9					7.7	9.7
14438M	104657M	603719M	946466M	742833M	857223M	Net Sales ($)	3974278M	4739129M
3709M	51569M	333467M	732295M	501260M	900289M	Total Assets ($)	2359632M	3194486M

© RMA 2003

M = $ thousand   MM = $ million
See Pages 11 through 18 for Explanation of Ratios and Data

Comparative Historical Data   ## Current Data Sorted By Sales

			Type of Statement						
45	28	46	Unqualified		2	1	9	17	17
49	51	23	Reviewed	1	3	3	9	4	3
54	50	35	Compiled	5	16	9	3	1	1
11	11	11	Tax Returns	2	6	2	1		
64	74	53	Other	2	12	5	17	5	12
4/1/00-3/31/01	4/1/01-3/31/02	4/1/02-3/31/03			38 (4/1-9/30/02)		130 (10/1/02-3/31/03)		
ALL	ALL	ALL		0-1MM	1-3MM	3-5MM	5-10MM	10-25MM	25MM & OVER
223	214	168	NUMBER OF STATEMENTS	10	39	20	39	27	33
%	%	%	**ASSETS**	%	%	%	%	%	%
8.7	8.3	10.8	Cash & Equivalents	6.9	8.4	8.9	9.2	14.2	14.9
27.1	24.4	24.8	Trade Receivables (net)	20.8	24.8	27.2	23.7	22.9	27.5
28.1	29.6	28.4	Inventory	43.1	28.5	29.8	31.8	26.5	20.4
4.0	3.7	4.4	All Other Current	1.9	2.3	3.5	5.4	4.9	6.4
68.0	66.0	68.3	Total Current	72.6	64.1	69.4	70.1	68.5	69.3
20.8	23.9	21.8	Fixed Assets (net)	23.9	23.5	20.9	23.5	21.6	18.1
5.4	4.3	2.5	Intangibles (net)	1.0	2.6	.6	1.5	1.3	5.9
5.8	5.8	7.3	All Other Non-Current	2.5	9.9	9.1	4.9	8.6	6.7
100.0	100.0	100.0	Total	100.0	100.0	100.0	100.0	100.0	100.0
			LIABILITIES						
12.3	13.2	13.5	Notes Payable-Short Term	46.3	17.2	9.8	10.7	10.2	7.6
2.8	5.2	3.2	Cur. Mat.-L/T/D	3.2	4.1	4.4	2.5	2.7	2.5
13.6	13.8	12.3	Trade Payables	17.0	13.3	13.7	10.8	14.1	9.3
.3	.3	.2	Income Taxes Payable	.0	.1	.1	.1	.4	.6
16.2	13.7	14.6	All Other Current	7.1	11.6	13.1	15.5	13.0	21.6
45.2	46.2	43.9	Total Current	73.6	46.3	41.1	39.6	40.4	41.5
12.4	13.6	11.7	Long Term Debt	11.7	11.7	15.1	11.7	9.9	11.1
.3	.4	.5	Deferred Taxes	.0	.2	.1	.3	1.5	.4
4.0	4.5	3.9	All Other Non-Current	.3	4.6	5.5	3.5	2.3	4.7
38.1	35.4	40.1	Net Worth	14.4	37.2	38.2	44.9	45.9	42.3
100.0	100.0	100.0	Total Liabilities & Net Worth	100.0	100.0	100.0	100.0	100.0	100.0
			INCOME DATA						
100.0	100.0	100.0	Net Sales	100.0	100.0	100.0	100.0	100.0	100.0
31.3	32.6	31.7	Gross Profit	42.9	34.5	33.3	30.2	28.4	28.3
26.1	30.0	29.6	Operating Expenses	34.6	34.7	32.2	29.3	25.2	24.6
5.3	2.6	2.0	Operating Profit	8.3	-.2	1.1	.9	3.2	3.7
.9	1.3	1.0	All Other Expenses (net)	1.5	1.4	.9	1.1	.8	.6
4.4	1.3	1.0	Profit Before Taxes	6.9	-1.7	.2	-.1	2.4	3.1
			RATIOS						
2.4	2.4	2.6		2.7	2.2	3.5	2.8	2.7	2.3
1.6	1.6	1.7	Current	2.1	1.5	1.8	1.9	1.7	1.7
1.1	1.0	1.2		.6	1.0	1.2	1.3	1.1	1.3
1.2	1.2	1.4		1.2	1.1	1.3	1.4	1.7	1.7
.8	.7	.8	Quick	.4	.7	.9	1.0	.8	1.1
.5	.4	.5		.3	.3	.5	.4	.6	.6
36 10.2	32 11.4	34 10.8		11 34.1	22 16.2	27 13.6	32 11.5	34 10.9	47 7.8
51 7.2	46 8.0	50 7.4	Sales/Receivables	39 9.4	46 8.0	52 7.0	47 7.8	50 7.4	63 5.8
69 5.3	62 5.9	71 5.1		61 5.9	65 5.6	72 5.1	64 5.7	60 6.1	91 4.0
36 10.1	42 8.7	45 8.1		15 24.3	43 8.5	30 12.1	53 6.8	36 10.0	40 9.1
73 5.0	79 4.6	78 4.7	Cost of Sales/Inventory	103 3.5	68 5.4	103 3.5	84 4.3	77 4.8	78 4.7
120 3.1	150 2.4	137 2.7		313 1.2	143 2.5	152 2.4	140 2.6	136 2.7	111 3.3
19 19.0	18 20.3	17 21.3		11 34.0	14 27.0	25 14.5	12 30.1	21 17.0	24 15.1
32 11.5	31 11.7	32 11.4	Cost of Sales/Payables	24 15.4	37 9.8	34 10.6	25 14.4	37 9.9	31 11.7
50 7.2	57 6.3	49 7.5		86 4.2	69 5.3	47 7.7	49 7.5	52 7.1	40 9.1
4.4	4.2	3.5		1.9	4.3	4.1	2.9	3.8	3.0
7.9	7.7	6.6	Sales/Working Capital	8.9	8.6	7.6	7.0	6.6	5.3
29.2	67.6	20.5		-16.1	88.3	11.8	16.3	29.9	9.7
11.6	6.4	10.0			8.1	3.7	10.7	11.2	11.7
(191) 3.1	(193) 2.0	(146) 2.7	EBIT/Interest	(35) 1.7	(17) 1.5	(35) 2.9	(23) 3.7	(30) 4.4
1.3	-.3	-.1			-2.2	-3.5	.0	1.4	1.4
6.8	6.0	5.4				6.5	2.3	10.2
(52) 2.2	(52) 1.6	(47) 2.5	Net Profit + Depr., Dep., Amort./Cur. Mat. L/T/D		(14) 3.2	(10) 1.9	(11) 2.5
.5	.9	.8				1.4	.7	.9
.2	.2	.2		.0	.2	.4	.1	.2	.2
.5	.6	.5	Fixed/Worth	.2	.5	.6	.5	.5	.5
2.2	2.1	1.2		2.4	3.0	1.4	1.3	1.2	1.0
.7	.8	.5		.5	.5	.5	.5	.5	.9
1.9	1.8	1.5	Debt/Worth	1.3	2.1	2.0	1.0	1.5	1.6
6.0	6.0	4.0		NM	11.2	7.5	3.8	3.0	4.1
41.1	28.3	29.3			24.5	31.2	30.1	27.7	37.5
(192) 17.6	(182) 9.3	(153) 8.0	% Profit Before Taxes/Tangible Net Worth	(34) 7.3	(18) 15.7	(36) 7.2	9.0	(30) 9.6
3.8	-4.8	-5.7			-20.7	-13.0	-11.6	.4	.7
14.1	11.0	10.5		59.4	6.8	7.9	11.4	11.9	10.7
5.7	3.4	3.1	% Profit Before Taxes/Total Assets	1.8	1.6	2.5	2.2	4.3	4.6
1.0	-2.7	-3.1		-5.4	-8.2	-4.2	-6.8	.1	.6
26.1	21.5	20.2		UND	22.0	24.3	21.5	16.5	15.0
10.2	9.3	9.4	Sales/Net Fixed Assets	11.1	10.9	8.5	11.4	8.2	8.0
5.6	4.6	5.5		7.4	5.5	5.8	4.2	5.4	5.0
2.5	2.4	2.2		3.2	2.7	2.3	2.2	2.2	1.7
1.8	1.8	1.7	Sales/Total Assets	1.5	1.8	1.9	1.8	1.8	1.4
1.3	1.3	1.2		1.1	1.3	1.5	1.3	1.2	1.0
.8	1.2	1.4			.9	.9	1.4	1.4	1.6
(191) 1.7	(192) 2.3	(152) 2.2	% Depr., Dep., Amort./Sales	(33) 2.7	3.2	(38) 2.2	(24) 2.2	(30) 2.0
3.1	3.6	4.1			4.6	6.6	3.5	3.7	3.2
2.5	2.9	2.9			4.0		2.6		
(69) 5.7	(72) 5.0	(52) 5.1	% Officers', Directors', Owners' Comp/Sales	(21) 5.9	(11) 4.8			
10.9	8.0	8.9			9.9		8.5		
4969837M	4391542M	3269336M	Net Sales ($)	6345M	80103M	77593M	288792M	470756M	2345747M
3900478M	3310238M	2522589M	Total Assets ($)	4401M	52211M	47135M	193359M	302426M	1923057M

Current Data Sorted By Assets   Comparative Historical Data

						Type of Statement		
		3	3	1	3	Unqualified	15	19
	4	3	1			Reviewed	13	13
	4	1				Compiled	10	8
	1					Tax Returns	1	1
1	3	7	7	3		Other	14	12
	8 (4/1-9/30/02)		37 (10/1/02-3/31/03)				4/1/98-3/31/99	4/1/99-3/31/00
0-500M	500M-2MM	2-10MM	10-50MM	50-100MM	100-250MM		ALL	ALL
1	12	14	11	4	3	NUMBER OF STATEMENTS	53	53
%	%	%	%	%	%	ASSETS	%	%
	7.7	10.3	17.8			Cash & Equivalents	11.2	10.8
	31.3	17.7	22.2			Trade Receivables (net)	24.3	27.9
	24.0	24.7	31.2			Inventory	22.3	25.5
	1.4	7.4	5.8			All Other Current	2.4	1.9
	64.4	60.1	77.0			Total Current	60.2	66.1
	25.3	30.6	15.7			Fixed Assets (net)	28.4	23.9
	2.2	1.2	5.0			Intangibles (net)	4.4	3.9
	8.2	8.1	2.3			All Other Non-Current	7.0	6.1
	100.0	100.0	100.0			Total	100.0	100.0
						LIABILITIES		
	9.7	8.4	7.9			Notes Payable-Short Term	6.9	5.5
	5.2	3.3	1.1			Cur. Mat.-L/T/D	3.3	3.4
	18.4	7.1	9.4			Trade Payables	10.9	13.1
	.1	.0	.1			Income Taxes Payable	.4	.5
	7.4	6.4	14.6			All Other Current	9.6	12.0
	40.8	25.1	33.2			Total Current	31.0	34.5
	17.6	15.4	7.7			Long Term Debt	15.2	9.9
	.1	.6	.1			Deferred Taxes	.8	.4
	6.7	4.9	2.1			All Other Non-Current	6.2	6.0
	34.8	54.0	57.0			Net Worth	46.7	49.2
	100.0	100.0	100.0			Total Liabilities & Net Worth	100.0	100.0
						INCOME DATA		
	100.0	100.0	100.0			Net Sales	100.0	100.0
	42.6	37.0	38.5			Gross Profit	38.9	39.7
	38.2	31.2	33.3			Operating Expenses	42.6	33.2
	4.4	5.9	5.3			Operating Profit	-3.7	6.6
	1.5	.2	1.2			All Other Expenses (net)	1.1	.5
	2.9	5.7	4.0			Profit Before Taxes	-4.8	6.0
						RATIOS		
	2.0	5.7	4.7				2.8	3.7
	1.5	3.3	2.9			Current	2.0	1.9
	1.2	1.6	1.5				1.5	1.4
	1.7	3.7	2.5				2.1	1.8
	.7	1.3	1.1			Quick	1.1	1.1
	.5	.6	.6				.7	.8
	32 11.5	27 13.4	37 9.9				38 9.5	44 8.3
	42 8.7	45 8.0	45 8.1			Sales/Receivables	52 7.0	56 6.6
	57 6.4	55 6.6	64 5.7				62 5.9	61 5.9
	22 16.3	38 9.6	63 5.8				40 9.2	51 7.2
	54 6.8	95 3.9	134 2.7			Cost of Sales/Inventory	94 3.9	91 4.0
	132 2.8	120 3.1	173 2.1				116 3.2	125 2.9
	27 13.7	9 38.8	17 21.5				18 20.7	19 18.8
	33 10.9	17 21.1	31 11.8			Cost of Sales/Payables	32 11.3	32 11.3
	63 5.8	33 11.1	46 7.9				52 7.0	62 5.9
	8.0	3.2	2.6				3.5	3.5
	12.9	4.2	4.8			Sales/Working Capital	5.9	5.6
	26.2	8.1	7.1				14.1	14.5
	4.2	11.6					9.3	18.6
	2.8	(13) 4.4				EBIT/Interest	(45) 3.2	(45) 4.0
	1.3	.8					1.3	1.3
						Net Profit + Depr., Dep.,	10.3	10.7
						Amort./Cur. Mat. L/T/D	(24) 3.0	(21) 2.5
							1.2	1.7
	.3	.3	.1				.3	.2
	.7	.5	.4			Fixed/Worth	.6	.4
	1.2	1.3	.6				1.0	.9
	1.3	.2	.3				.5	.4
	2.3	.7	1.0			Debt/Worth	1.2	1.0
	3.4	2.9	1.9				2.6	2.1
	27.6	53.9	36.9				33.9	52.8
	(11) 19.3	22.2	(10) 12.3			% Profit Before Taxes/Tangible Net Worth	(48) 16.3	(48) 17.2
	3.0	3.5	-2.6				2.4	2.9
	9.5	19.8	12.5				13.6	24.8
	4.5	7.4	4.8			% Profit Before Taxes/Total Assets	7.1	7.5
	.7	1.6	-2.1				.7	.9
	23.4	10.6	21.9				16.2	20.6
	14.3	6.9	14.7			Sales/Net Fixed Assets	5.7	9.2
	8.3	3.5	7.0				3.3	4.5
	3.3	2.1	2.4				2.2	2.5
	2.6	1.6	1.7			Sales/Total Assets	1.8	1.9
	2.1	1.1	1.1				1.2	1.3
	1.0	1.4					1.5	1.4
	2.2	(13) 2.8				% Depr., Dep., Amort./Sales	(48) 3.2	(49) 2.7
	4.5	8.8					5.7	4.6
							2.2	4.1
						% Officers', Directors', Owners' Comp/Sales	(16) 4.2	(16) 5.3
							11.6	8.8
805M	38280M	127998M	450546M	250430M	519804M	Net Sales ($)	1692758M	1984746M
249M	14874M	81581M	281050M	244731M	539636M	Total Assets ($)	1395991M	1286875M

Comparative Historical Data | Current Data Sorted By Sales

					Type of Statement						
	14		9		10	Unqualified			1	3	6
	11		14		8	Reviewed	2	2	2	1	1
	9		8		5	Compiled	1	3	1		
	1		3		1	Tax Returns		1			
	13		15		21	Other	1	3	2	2	4	9
	4/1/00-3/31/01 ALL		4/1/01-3/31/02 ALL		4/1/02-3/31/03 ALL			8 (4/1-9/30/02)			37 (10/1/02-3/31/03)	
							0-1MM	1-3MM	3-5MM	5-10MM	10-25MM	25MM & OVER
	48		49		45	NUMBER OF STATEMENTS	1	6	8	6	8	16
	%		%		%	ASSETS	%	%	%	%	%	%
	7.8		7.1		11.2	Cash & Equivalents						13.7
	24.7		25.0		23.3	Trade Receivables (net)						21.1
	27.8		27.3		26.0	Inventory						27.2
	5.1		2.4		4.8	All Other Current						5.2
	65.3		61.8		65.3	Total Current						67.3
	23.9		24.7		23.9	Fixed Assets (net)						19.2
	4.1		4.9		3.8	Intangibles (net)						7.8
	6.6		8.6		6.9	All Other Non-Current						5.7
	100.0		100.0		100.0	Total						100.0
						LIABILITIES						
	4.8		11.9		8.1	Notes Payable-Short Term						5.3
	3.1		3.5		3.2	Cur. Mat.-L/T/D						2.0
	15.8		10.3		10.4	Trade Payables						8.6
	.7		.5		.1	Income Taxes Payable						.3
	12.3		6.9		9.3	All Other Current						12.6
	36.6		33.1		31.3	Total Current						28.8
	12.5		15.5		13.1	Long Term Debt						9.2
	.7		.3		.3	Deferred Taxes						.2
	5.1		3.3		4.3	All Other Non-Current						2.7
	45.2		47.7		51.0	Net Worth						59.0
	100.0		100.0		100.0	Total Liabilities & Net Worth						100.0
						INCOME DATA						
	100.0		100.0		100.0	Net Sales						100.0
	40.4		42.2		40.5	Gross Profit						42.7
	35.0		36.4		35.9	Operating Expenses						39.4
	5.4		5.9		4.7	Operating Profit						3.4
	1.9		1.5		.8	All Other Expenses (net)						.7
	3.5		4.3		3.8	Profit Before Taxes						2.7
						RATIOS						
	3.0		3.9		4.1							4.4
	1.7		1.9		2.1	Current						2.6
	1.3		1.4		1.5							1.7
	1.3		1.7		2.5							2.5
	1.0		1.0		1.0	Quick						1.1
	.7		.6		.6							.7
31	11.9	35	10.3	34	10.7						37	9.7
52	7.1	44	8.3	46	7.9	Sales/Receivables					53	6.9
66	5.5	72	5.1	67	5.5						71	5.1
55	6.7	54	6.7	52	7.1						76	4.8
96	3.8	105	3.5	103	3.5	Cost of Sales/Inventory					139	2.6
143	2.6	160	2.3	140	2.6						182	2.0
21	17.4	16	22.4	17	21.8						20	18.3
38	9.7	34	10.9	27	13.6	Cost of Sales/Payables					37	9.8
82	4.4	54	6.8	53	6.9						73	5.0
	3.7		3.6		3.3							2.7
	6.2		5.1		4.9	Sales/Working Capital						3.7
	14.5		16.0		9.5							6.0
	13.9		4.9		8.1							8.0
(44)	3.4	(44)	2.1	(40)	3.1	EBIT/Interest					(12)	3.4
	1.6		.8		1.2							.0
	9.9		5.5		6.5	Net Profit + Depr., Dep.,						
(17)	3.3	(21)	2.1	(11)	3.2	Amort./Cur. Mat. L/T/D						
	1.9		.8		.7							
	.2		.3		.2							.2
	.4		.6		.4	Fixed/Worth						.4
	1.0		1.0		1.0							.7
	.5		.5		.4							.4
	1.5		1.2		1.0	Debt/Worth						.7
	3.2		3.3		2.3							1.7
	42.4		36.1		30.7	% Profit Before Taxes/Tangible						28.3
(46)	14.2	(46)	12.4	(43)	14.9	Net Worth					(15)	9.8
	5.6		.3		.5							-2.4
	15.7		10.9		14.0	% Profit Before Taxes/Total						11.2
	6.5		3.0		4.8	Assets						4.5
	1.7		-.2		.0							-1.4
	21.8		18.2		18.4							15.3
	9.5		8.4		10.0	Sales/Net Fixed Assets						8.1
	4.2		4.1		5.1							4.0
	2.4		2.3		2.4							2.1
	1.8		1.8		1.7	Sales/Total Assets						1.4
	1.2		1.2		1.1							.8
	1.1		1.7		1.7							2.2
(36)	2.0	(44)	2.7	(40)	2.7	% Depr., Dep., Amort./Sales					(12)	4.5
	4.9		4.6		5.3							7.4
	4.6		2.1		3.2	% Officers', Directors',						
(14)	7.9	(12)	5.3	(15)	5.1	Owners' Comp/Sales						
	11.0		12.4		9.3							
	2203626M		1653073M		1387863M	Net Sales ($)	805M	13563M	30173M	43683M	117467M	1182172M
	1505463M		1176331M		1162121M	Total Assets ($)	249M	11480M	14959M	27147M	73187M	1035099M

© RMA 2003

M = $ thousand   MM = $ million
See Pages 11 through 18 for Explanation of Ratios and Data

Current Data Sorted By Assets — Comparative Historical Data

Type of Statement	0-500M	500M-2MM	2-10MM	10-50MM	50-100MM	100-250MM		4/1/98-3/31/99 ALL	4/1/99-3/31/00 ALL
Unqualified			2	6				20	16
Reviewed	1		3	1				4	2
Compiled	1	1	2	1				4	4
Tax Returns	1	1	1	1					1
Other		3	5	2	1	2		21	15
		10 (4/1-9/30/02)		22 (10/1/02-3/31/03)					
NUMBER OF STATEMENTS	3	4	13	9	1	2		49	38
	%	%	%	%	%	%		%	%

ASSETS

	0-500M	500M-2MM	2-10MM	10-50MM	50-100MM	100-250MM		98-99 ALL	99-00 ALL
Cash & Equivalents			7.9					5.5	6.9
Trade Receivables (net)			28.8					21.1	20.1
Inventory			24.3					31.1	34.1
All Other Current			1.0					4.5	4.5
Total Current			62.0					62.2	65.5
Fixed Assets (net)			31.9					25.0	23.4
Intangibles (net)			3.4					5.6	4.6
All Other Non-Current			2.8					7.3	6.4
Total			100.0					100.0	100.0

LIABILITIES

	2-10MM		98-99 ALL	99-00 ALL
Notes Payable-Short Term	10.8		10.9	10.4
Cur. Mat.-L/T/D	3.2		2.7	2.0
Trade Payables	15.8		12.0	12.0
Income Taxes Payable	.7		.3	.4
All Other Current	12.6		9.0	12.6
Total Current	43.1		34.8	37.4
Long Term Debt	16.4		20.2	13.1
Deferred Taxes	1.4		.8	.6
All Other Non-Current	.9		4.9	4.5
Net Worth	38.2		39.2	44.3
Total Liabilities & Net Worth	100.0		100.0	100.0

INCOME DATA

	2-10MM		98-99 ALL	99-00 ALL
Net Sales	100.0		100.0	100.0
Gross Profit	42.0		38.4	36.8
Operating Expenses	37.8		31.6	32.8
Operating Profit	4.2		6.8	4.1
All Other Expenses (net)	2.0		1.7	1.5
Profit Before Taxes	2.1		5.1	2.6

RATIOS

	500M-2MM	2-10MM		98-99 ALL	99-00 ALL
Current		2.0 / 1.3 / 1.1		3.1 / 1.7 / 1.3	3.3 / 1.8 / 1.4
Quick		1.3 / .7 / .4		1.5 / .7 / .5	1.5 / .7 / .3
Sales/Receivables		38 9.5 / 50 7.3 / 59 6.2		36 10.2 / 49 7.5 / 62 5.9	33 10.9 / 49 7.5 / 62 5.9
Cost of Sales/Inventory		23 16.1 / 72 5.1 / 120 3.0		61 6.0 / 100 3.7 / 159 2.3	54 6.7 / 139 2.6 / 194 1.9
Cost of Sales/Payables		24 15.2 / 52 7.0 / 65 5.6		20 18.0 / 40 9.1 / 52 7.0	24 15.1 / 34 10.7 / 53 6.9
Sales/Working Capital		5.8 / 12.8 / 118.6		4.1 / 6.9 / 13.7	3.2 / 5.3 / 17.6
EBIT/Interest		10.7 / 2.3 / .8		(39) 6.2 / 2.4 / .9	6.0 / 2.8 / .7
Net Profit + Depr., Dep., Amort./Cur. Mat. L/T/D				(12) 7.4 / 2.4 / .6	
Fixed/Worth		.3 / .5 / 1.9		.3 / .5 / 1.4	.2 / .4 / 1.4
Debt/Worth		.9 / 1.5 / 3.4		.8 / 1.8 / 3.9	.5 / 1.4 / 2.9
% Profit Before Taxes/Tangible Net Worth	(12)	33.0 / 4.8 / -5.9		(44) 42.5 / 17.1 / 1.6	(35) 31.2 / 13.8 / 1.9
% Profit Before Taxes/Total Assets		20.7 / 1.5 / -1.0		16.1 / 6.4 / -.4	14.4 / 6.1 / 1.2
Sales/Net Fixed Assets		21.6 / 9.5 / 3.9		15.9 / 9.4 / 3.5	21.3 / 11.1 / 3.6
Sales/Total Assets		2.8 / 2.3 / 1.4		2.1 / 1.6 / 1.2	2.2 / 1.5 / 1.0
% Depr., Dep., Amort./Sales				(40) 1.9 / 3.0 / 4.8	(30) 1.2 / 2.8 / 5.5
% Officers', Directors', Owners' Comp/Sales				(11) 2.4 / 4.4 / 7.3	

	0-500M	500M-2MM	2-10MM	10-50MM	50-100MM	100-250MM		98-99 ALL	99-00 ALL
Net Sales ($)	1012M	13575M	117267M	309418M	93515M	371148M		1268323M	797068M
Total Assets ($)	655M	3998M	60577M	177955M	56961M	378159M		858921M	630598M

M = $ thousand   MM = $ million
See Pages 11 through 18 for Explanation of Ratios and Data

Comparative Historical Data | Current Data Sorted By Sales

						Type of Statement							
	9		10		8	Unqualified				2		3	3
	4		4		5	Reviewed	1			3			1
	4		6		3	Compiled	1			1		1	
	3		2		3	Tax Returns	1	1				1	
	17		11		13	Other	1	1	1	3		3	4
	4/1/00-3/31/01 ALL		4/1/01-3/31/02 ALL		4/1/02-3/31/03 ALL		0-1MM	10 (4/1-9/30/02) 1-3MM	3-5MM	22 (10/1/02-3/31/03) 5-10MM		10-25MM	25MM & OVER
	37		33		32	**NUMBER OF STATEMENTS**	4	2	1	9		8	8
	%		%		%	**ASSETS**	%	%	%	%		%	%
	7.4		8.7		8.2	Cash & Equivalents							
	24.9		22.8		22.6	Trade Receivables (net)							
	28.0		29.2		24.1	Inventory							
	5.2		3.9		1.7	All Other Current							
	65.5		64.6		56.6	Total Current							
	20.2		24.6		33.6	Fixed Assets (net)							
	6.9		6.1		4.6	Intangibles (net)							
	7.4		5.1		5.2	All Other Non-Current							
	100.0		100.0		100.0	Total							
						LIABILITIES							
	7.0		10.3		12.6	Notes Payable-Short Term							
	8.1		7.0		5.5	Cur. Mat.-L/T/D							
	14.0		14.1		13.2	Trade Payables							
	.6		.7		.5	Income Taxes Payable							
	12.6		10.8		10.7	All Other Current							
	42.4		42.9		42.6	Total Current							
	12.7		19.0		15.8	Long Term Debt							
	.5		.6		1.6	Deferred Taxes							
	3.8		3.8		1.9	All Other Non-Current							
	40.6		33.8		38.2	Net Worth							
	100.0		100.0		100.0	Total Liabilities & Net Worth							
						INCOME DATA							
	100.0		100.0		100.0	Net Sales							
	38.1		38.2		40.8	Gross Profit							
	33.5		37.4		37.6	Operating Expenses							
	4.6		.8		3.2	Operating Profit							
	1.5		1.1		1.6	All Other Expenses (net)							
	3.2		−.3		1.6	Profit Before Taxes							
						RATIOS							
	3.1		2.1		2.0								
	2.0		1.5		1.3	Current							
	1.2		1.1		.8								
	1.5		1.2		1.0								
	.9		.8		.6	Quick							
	.5		.5		.4								
26	14.1	23	15.8	28	12.8								
45	8.1	40	9.2	45	8.1	Sales/Receivables							
63	5.8	54	6.8	59	6.1								
28	13.0	43	8.5	34	10.7								
79	4.6	87	4.2	68	5.4	Cost of Sales/Inventory							
135	2.7	143	2.5	111	3.3								
18	19.8	19	19.7	21	17.7								
29	12.7	29	12.4	38	9.5	Cost of Sales/Payables							
63	5.8	47	7.8	59	6.2								
	4.0		4.1		7.3								
	7.2		9.4		16.0	Sales/Working Capital							
	40.8		102.6		−20.5								
	13.9		4.6		9.6								
(31)	3.6	(29)	2.0	(31)	3.1	EBIT/Interest							
	1.1		−.6		.8								
			2.2		4.0	Net Profit + Depr., Dep.,							
		(10)	1.7	(11)	1.8	Amort./Cur. Mat. L/T/D							
			−1.3		.4								
	.2		.4		.5								
	.4		1.1		.9	Fixed/Worth							
	1.6		1.9		2.6								
	.6		1.3		.9								
	1.3		1.8		1.7	Debt/Worth							
	4.4		10.8		5.5								
	38.7		39.3		32.0	% Profit Before Taxes/Tangible							
(33)	21.8	(29)	12.2	(30)	11.7	Net Worth							
	6.5		−7.1		.4								
	20.2		5.8		11.9	% Profit Before Taxes/Total							
	6.0		2.5		3.1	Assets							
	.6		−4.7		−.4								
	31.8		22.5		19.4								
	10.9		8.9		8.7	Sales/Net Fixed Assets							
	6.7		4.9		2.9								
	2.9		3.1		2.8								
	2.0		1.9		1.9	Sales/Total Assets							
	1.4		1.3		1.3								
	1.1		1.0		1.4								
(29)	1.9	(30)	2.5	(27)	3.6	% Depr., Dep., Amort./Sales							
	4.0		4.9		5.4								
	2.2					% Officers', Directors',							
(10)	3.7					Owners' Comp/Sales							
	9.5												
	1116909M		838907M		905935M	Net Sales ($)	1787M	2823M	4849M	70061M		126831M	699584M
	793489M		662074M		678305M	Total Assets ($)	4762M	1435M	904M	39770M		68094M	563340M

© RMA 2003   M = $ thousand   MM = $ million
See Pages 11 through 18 for Explanation of Ratios and Data

Current Data Sorted By Assets   **Comparative Historical Data**

						Type of Statement		
		16	16	5	6	Unqualified	35	32
	8	12	2	2		Reviewed	25	24
3	9	5	1			Compiled	15	11
1	3	2	1			Tax Returns	4	5
1	6	20	7	5	1	Other	26	21
	18 (4/1-9/30/02)		114 (10/1/02-3/31/03)				4/1/98-3/31/99	4/1/99-3/31/00
0-500M	500M-2MM	2-10MM	10-50MM	50-100MM	100-250MM		ALL	ALL
5	26	55	27	12	7	NUMBER OF STATEMENTS	105	93
%	%	%	%	%	%	ASSETS	%	%
	7.2	5.7	5.3	8.2		Cash & Equivalents	7.2	8.2
	29.1	29.2	28.5	19.1		Trade Receivables (net)	30.6	27.8
	29.8	31.0	29.0	28.1		Inventory	28.0	27.9
	1.6	2.8	3.7	4.8		All Other Current	3.6	3.2
	67.7	68.7	66.6	60.2		Total Current	69.4	67.1
	24.7	20.0	19.1	22.0		Fixed Assets (net)	20.7	22.1
	1.2	5.4	7.6	9.0		Intangibles (net)	5.4	6.4
	6.4	5.9	6.6	8.8		All Other Non-Current	4.5	4.4
	100.0	100.0	100.0	100.0		Total	100.0	100.0
						LIABILITIES		
	19.1	15.3	10.0	5.7		Notes Payable-Short Term	7.7	9.5
	3.8	11.6	3.6	6.8		Cur. Mat.-L/T/D	3.6	3.6
	14.5	15.8	9.7	9.2		Trade Payables	16.2	14.8
	.0	.1	.2	.3		Income Taxes Payable	.4	.3
	8.0	13.5	14.3	10.6		All Other Current	12.2	11.7
	45.4	56.3	37.9	32.6		Total Current	40.1	40.1
	15.5	10.5	15.9	19.3		Long Term Debt	17.2	13.7
	.0	.2	.6	.2		Deferred Taxes	.6	.6
	10.2	16.3	4.1	2.5		All Other Non-Current	4.0	8.6
	28.9	16.7	41.4	45.5		Net Worth	38.0	37.0
	100.0	100.0	100.0	100.0		Total Liabilities & Net Worth	100.0	100.0
						INCOME DATA		
	100.0	100.0	100.0	100.0		Net Sales	100.0	100.0
	46.1	30.5	33.2	30.0		Gross Profit	34.6	37.4
	45.3	29.4	29.4	22.4		Operating Expenses	28.6	32.5
	.8	1.1	3.8	7.6		Operating Profit	6.0	4.9
	1.1	1.6	.6	2.9		All Other Expenses (net)	1.2	1.4
	-.3	-.5	3.2	4.6		Profit Before Taxes	4.8	3.5
						RATIOS		
	2.3	2.2	2.9	3.9			2.8	2.5
	1.5	1.6	1.8	1.9		Current	1.9	1.7
	1.3	1.1	1.3	1.6			1.3	1.2
	1.6	1.2	1.7	1.4			1.6	1.5
	.9	.8	.8	.9		Quick	1.0	.9
	.5	.5	.6	.7			.7	.6
30 12.1	34 10.8	32 11.5	33 11.2			Sales/Receivables	39 9.2	35 10.3
46 8.0	48 7.6	51 7.1	44 8.3				49 7.5	50 7.3
61 6.0	71 5.1	71 5.1	57 6.4				67 5.5	67 5.5
18 20.5	43 8.4	70 5.2	69 5.3			Cost of Sales/Inventory	37 10.0	39 9.4
61 6.0	69 5.3	91 4.0	90 4.1				72 5.1	75 4.9
163 2.2	116 3.1	134 2.7	109 3.3				112 3.3	122 3.0
16 23.2	20 18.2	19 18.8	13 28.6			Cost of Sales/Payables	23 15.9	22 16.4
38 9.7	34 10.7	27 13.7	30 12.2				37 9.8	39 9.4
61 6.0	60 6.1	46 8.0	49 7.4				52 7.0	59 6.1
	5.3	5.4	3.4	2.9			4.8	4.5
	10.5	8.7	5.3	5.2		Sales/Working Capital	6.9	7.6
	25.1	35.1	11.1	11.2			13.8	20.1
	(22) 4.9	(52) 4.9	(23) 10.5	(11) 9.0		EBIT/Interest	(98) 12.4	(83) 11.4
	1.4	2.2	3.1	2.3			3.5	3.6
	-.2	.7	.4	1.5			1.6	1.2
		(20) 2.6	(12) 7.7			Net Profit + Depr., Dep.,	(47) 8.5	(30) 7.8
		1.8	1.9			Amort./Cur. Mat. L /T/D	2.5	3.1
		1.2	.9				1.2	1.5
	.2	.2	.3	.3			.3	.3
	.6	.6	.6	.7		Fixed/Worth	.5	.6
	4.9	2.4	1.9	1.9			1.4	1.5
	1.2	1.0	.8	.5			.8	.8
	2.6	2.0	2.1	1.6		Debt/Worth	1.9	2.0
	8.1	9.7	9.1	9.3			4.6	4.5
	(24) 33.9	(47) 27.4	(25) 28.8	(11) 30.4		% Profit Before Taxes/Tangible Net Worth	(96) 39.2	(82) 44.0
	9.1	10.1	16.4	19.5			22.9	26.3
	-11.0	.4	-10.4	8.9			9.3	5.9
	8.9	8.0	13.2	12.0		% Profit Before Taxes/Total Assets	16.6	16.0
	1.8	3.4	6.3	4.5			6.5	7.8
	-4.1	-.8	-3.3	2.7			3.2	1.2
	52.4	32.7	19.3	9.9		Sales/Net Fixed Assets	26.5	22.7
	15.1	19.7	11.5	8.3			13.7	12.6
	3.5	6.1	5.8	5.3			5.9	5.7
	3.3	2.9	2.3	1.7		Sales/Total Assets	2.7	2.7
	2.2	2.1	1.7	1.6			2.1	2.0
	1.7	1.6	1.3	1.1			1.7	1.4
	(23) .8	(49) .8	(25) 1.0	(11) 1.5		% Depr., Dep., Amort./Sales	(93) .7	(83) .9
	1.6	1.5	1.9	2.5			1.4	2.2
	3.5	2.8	3.6	3.4			2.5	3.5
	(12) 2.5	(21) 1.0				% Officers', Directors', Owners' Comp/Sales	(24) 2.0	(24) 1.5
	5.6	2.5					3.7	3.7
	7.1	5.3					5.1	7.1
2464M	68373M	610555M	1045955M	1396515M	1334597M	Net Sales ($)	3392979M	2720521M
918M	27686M	289367M	605386M	867748M	923486M	Total Assets ($)	2113531M	2031633M

© RMA 2003

M = $ thousand   MM = $ million
See Pages 11 through 18 for Explanation of Ratios and Data

Comparative Historical Data | Current Data Sorted By Sales

4/1/00-3/31/01 ALL	4/1/01-3/31/02 ALL	4/1/02-3/31/03 ALL	Item	0-1MM	1-3MM	3-5MM	5-10MM	10-25MM	25MM & OVER
			Type of Statement		18 (4/1-9/30/02)		114 (10/1/02-3/31/03)		
24	31	43	Unqualified		1	1	4	15	22
22	15	24	Reviewed		6	6	2	6	4
11	14	18	Compiled	3	8		4	3	
2	1	7	Tax Returns	1	1	2	2		1
27	18	40	Other	3	4	1	6	14	12
86	79	132	**NUMBER OF STATEMENTS**	7	20	10	18	38	39
%	%	%	**ASSETS**	%	%	%	%	%	%
8.5	8.1	6.4	Cash & Equivalents		7.3	7.2	7.6	4.7	6.8
27.0	28.8	27.6	Trade Receivables (net)		28.3	25.7	26.8	31.1	26.5
28.5	26.6	29.4	Inventory		33.7	24.0	26.4	31.2	27.8
3.6	3.5	2.9	All Other Current		2.0	1.1	3.7	2.6	3.9
67.5	67.1	66.2	Total Current		71.3	58.0	64.5	69.6	64.9
19.8	19.8	22.0	Fixed Assets (net)		21.1	34.9	20.2	17.6	21.3
5.2	6.1	5.5	Intangibles (net)		1.8	1.0	4.9	7.0	7.9
7.5	7.0	6.2	All Other Non-Current		5.8	6.0	10.4	5.8	5.8
100.0	100.0	100.0	Total		100.0	100.0	100.0	100.0	100.0
			LIABILITIES						
9.7	12.3	13.3	Notes Payable-Short Term		21.3	12.4	13.0	13.2	8.5
4.7	3.4	7.3	Cur. Mat.-L/T/D		3.0	2.8	27.1	4.2	4.7
15.1	13.4	13.4	Trade Payables		13.2	12.1	16.1	16.0	10.7
.3	.2	.6	Income Taxes Payable		.0	.0	.0	.1	.2
10.7	13.2	12.0	All Other Current		9.6	11.1	14.1	12.7	13.5
40.5	42.4	46.7	Total Current		47.0	38.4	70.3	46.3	37.7
14.1	14.2	15.6	Long Term Debt		9.1	21.6	11.5	9.5	17.7
.3	.2	.2	Deferred Taxes		.0	.3	.4	.1	.4
4.8	7.7	10.3	All Other Non-Current		10.4	5.9	26.7	9.4	6.3
40.3	35.5	27.2	Net Worth		33.5	33.7	-8.9	34.7	38.0
100.0	100.0	100.0	Total Liabilities & Net Worth		100.0	100.0	100.0	100.0	100.0
			INCOME DATA						
100.0	100.0	100.0	Net Sales		100.0	100.0	100.0	100.0	100.0
33.8	34.9	35.0	Gross Profit		41.3	42.0	30.6	30.8	32.3
29.7	33.1	32.6	Operating Expenses		44.4	36.7	33.1	27.6	25.8
4.0	1.8	2.4	Operating Profit		-3.1	5.3	-2.4	3.1	6.5
1.4	1.5	1.5	All Other Expenses (net)		2.1	1.5	.7	1.2	1.4
2.6	.3	.9	Profit Before Taxes		-5.2	3.8	-3.1	1.9	5.1
			RATIOS						
2.8	2.6	2.4	Current		3.1	2.4	2.5	2.1	2.9
1.8	1.6	1.7			1.5	1.6	1.6	1.6	1.8
1.2	1.2	1.2			1.1	1.3	.9	1.2	1.2
1.5	1.3	1.4	Quick		1.6	1.7	1.6	1.3	1.5
.9	.9	.8			1.0	.9	.9	.8	.8
.6	.6	.5			.4	.5	.4	.5	.6
33 11.0	34 10.9	34 10.8	Sales/Receivables	35 10.5	29 12.8	33 11.2	34 10.9	36 10.2	
47 7.8	51 7.1	47 7.7		50 7.3	52 7.1	42 8.8	50 7.3	49 7.4	
61 6.0	71 5.2	64 5.7		70 5.2	62 5.9	51 7.2	74 4.9	64 5.7	
36 10.3	55 6.7	46 7.9	Cost of Sales/Inventory	20 18.1	21 17.6	49 7.4	45 8.1	60 6.1	
71 5.1	75 4.8	74 4.9		80 4.5	68 5.3	65 5.6	82 4.4	78 4.7	
115 3.2	126 2.9	116 3.1		184 2.0	111 3.3	94 3.9	118 3.1	110 3.3	
19 19.3	20 18.6	19 19.1	Cost of Sales/Payables	18 20.4	12 29.9	20 18.1	21 17.5	19 18.8	
38 9.6	31 11.7	34 10.7		42 8.6	29 12.5	34 10.8	35 10.4	34 10.8	
54 6.8	49 7.5	56 6.6		67 5.4	75 4.9	56 6.6	59 6.2	44 8.4	
4.4	4.0	4.5	Sales/Working Capital		4.9	4.2	5.1	5.1	3.9
8.4	7.3	8.1			8.5	10.4	9.1	8.1	7.1
33.1	15.5	20.8			48.3	40.4	-84.6	18.3	15.8
6.6	5.0	5.4	EBIT/Interest		4.8		4.6	5.1	8.4
(77) 3.6	(73) 2.0	(120) 2.4			(18) .5		(17) 2.1	(36) 2.8	(36) 3.5
.9	-.3	.5			-1.7		-.1	.5	1.9
4.6	3.8	4.0	Net Profit + Depr., Dep., Amort./Cur. Mat. L/T/D					3.0	15.2
(26) 1.4	(30) 1.9	(43) 1.8					(14)	(19) 1.8	2.8
.8	.6	1.1						-.3	1.2
.3	.2	.3	Fixed/Worth		.3	.5	.2	.2	.4
.6	.7	.7			.5	1.0	.5	.4	.8
1.4	1.7	2.6			1.4	4.0	4.2	1.5	1.9
.7	.7	.9	Debt/Worth		.8	1.1	.8	1.0	.7
1.7	2.1	2.1			2.5	1.7	2.8	2.1	2.0
6.0	5.4	9.2			6.5	7.2	27.1	7.0	9.2
41.8	29.2	30.4	% Profit Before Taxes/Tangible Net Worth		14.4	36.8	54.8	27.9	30.7
(77) 16.2	(69) 10.4	(115) 12.4			(18) .9	11.1	(15) 7.2	(35) 12.4	(34) 20.1
2.5	-3.5	-.6			-13.4	6.3	-.6	-5.8	8.4
14.5	8.5	8.8	% Profit Before Taxes/Total Assets		4.5	8.3	4.8	8.7	13.2
7.1	3.1	3.9			-.8	3.7	1.5	4.1	6.3
.1	-2.2	-1.4			-7.7	1.9	-4.8	-1.3	2.9
31.4	33.3	28.8	Sales/Net Fixed Assets		37.0	91.8	44.2	30.9	16.3
11.1	11.5	12.3			15.1	4.3	24.4	16.4	10.1
6.5	5.6	5.5			7.2	2.7	3.9	7.2	5.5
3.0	2.4	2.6	Sales/Total Assets		2.6	2.6	2.9	2.7	2.3
2.0	1.8	2.0			2.1	2.0	2.2	2.0	1.7
1.6	1.5	1.5			1.6	1.2	1.4	1.6	1.4
.9	.9	1.0	% Depr., Dep., Amort./Sales		.9	.7	.8	.8	1.2
(75) 1.7	(70) 1.7	(117) 1.8			(16) 2.1	2.0	(15) 2.1	(36) 1.5	(35) 1.9
3.0	3.1	3.4			3.4	5.5	4.6	2.4	3.4
1.9	1.9	1.5	% Officers', Directors', Owners' Comp/Sales					1.3	
(27) 4.6	(18) 4.3	(37) 3.1						(10) 3.8	
8.8	6.6							9.3	
2262400M	3584236M	4458459M	Net Sales ($)	2454M	38747M	41483M	125746M	563727M	3686302M
1408727M	2274181M	2714591M	Total Assets ($)	2969M	27310M	26351M	73759M	310440M	2273762M

Current Data Sorted By Assets   Comparative Historical Data

0-500M	500M-2MM	2-10MM	10-50MM	50-100MM	100-250MM	Type of Statement	4/1/98-3/31/99 ALL	4/1/99-3/31/00 ALL
	2	2	7		1	Unqualified	20	13
	7	11	3			Reviewed	13	17
1	2	3				Compiled	7	8
			1			Tax Returns	1	4
	1	5	6			Other	10	16
	11 (4/1-9/30/02)		41 (10/1/02-3/31/03)					
1	12	21	17		1	**NUMBER OF STATEMENTS**	51	58
%	%	%	%	%	%	**ASSETS**	%	%
	11.7	6.0	10.9			Cash & Equivalents	8.1	7.2
	32.8	29.9	22.9			Trade Receivables (net)	35.1	33.1
	19.2	26.1	13.9			Inventory	19.5	22.6
	3.0	5.8	5.3			All Other Current	3.9	2.8
	66.6	67.8	53.0			Total Current	66.5	65.8
	27.1	21.9	35.1			Fixed Assets (net)	24.4	22.8
	.4	5.4	4.0			Intangibles (net)	3.7	5.0
	5.9	4.9	7.9			All Other Non-Current	5.4	6.4
	100.0	100.0	100.0			Total	100.0	100.0
						LIABILITIES		
	5.4	16.5	9.9			Notes Payable-Short Term	9.7	8.8
	1.7	6.4	3.4			Cur. Mat.-L/T/D	2.6	2.6
	19.5	18.0	11.7			Trade Payables	20.2	18.8
	.3	.1	.1			Income Taxes Payable	.2	.1
	13.7	13.9	18.9			All Other Current	14.0	12.5
	40.6	55.0	44.0			Total Current	46.8	42.9
	6.8	9.8	15.8			Long Term Debt	12.2	14.5
	.3	.3	.3			Deferred Taxes	.4	.3
	4.8	7.5	4.0			All Other Non-Current	2.9	5.8
	47.5	27.4	35.9			Net Worth	37.7	36.5
	100.0	100.0	100.0			Total Liabilities & Net Worth	100.0	100.0
						INCOME DATA		
	100.0	100.0	100.0			Net Sales	100.0	100.0
	43.9	27.3	31.1			Gross Profit	31.1	33.6
	38.3	25.4	24.1			Operating Expenses	26.7	27.5
	5.6	1.9	7.0			Operating Profit	4.5	6.1
	.7	.9	.7			All Other Expenses (net)	1.1	1.3
	4.9	1.0	6.3			Profit Before Taxes	3.3	4.7
						RATIOS		
	3.7	2.3	2.3				2.3	2.9
	1.7	1.4	1.2			Current	1.5	1.8
	1.1	1.1	1.0				1.1	1.1
	2.7	1.4	1.9				1.4	2.0
	1.2	.8	.8			Quick	1.0	1.0
	.6	.4	.6				.7	.6
20	18.5	40 9.0	36 10.0				37 9.9	40 9.1
38	9.5	54 6.8	49 7.4			Sales/Receivables	52 7.0	56 6.5
58	6.3	73 5.0	57 6.4				65 5.6	69 5.3
21	17.6	39 9.4	20 18.1				19 19.0	25 14.4
46	7.9	59 6.2	38 9.5			Cost of Sales/Inventory	53 6.9	58 6.3
116	3.2	92 4.0	61 6.0				76 4.8	77 4.7
14	25.7	19 19.1	16 22.3				22 16.5	20 18.6
27	13.4	33 11.0	26 13.9			Cost of Sales/Payables	39 9.4	37 9.9
74	5.0	47 7.8	40 9.1				59 6.2	55 6.6
	5.5	6.4	4.6				5.2	4.7
	17.8	9.2	12.1			Sales/Working Capital	9.3	7.5
	NM	61.1	-105.5				40.1	87.4
	20.8	6.0	16.4				10.4	6.3
(11)	12.7	(20) 2.2	(13) 6.2			EBIT/Interest	(47) 3.4	(48) 2.9
	-1.1	.9	2.4				1.6	1.3
							5.2	3.7
						Net Profit + Depr., Dep., Amort./Cur. Mat. L/T/D	(20) 2.6	(19) 2.4
							1.5	.7
	.2	.3	.8				.3	.3
	.5	.6	1.3			Fixed/Worth	.7	.6
	1.7	2.1	1.8				1.3	3.0
	.4	.9	.5				.8	.6
	1.0	1.9	2.6			Debt/Worth	1.8	1.7
	4.2	15.4	12.2				4.3	6.2
	80.7	17.1	67.1				33.4	44.2
(11)	24.1	(17) 8.3	(14) 25.6			% Profit Before Taxes/Tangible Net Worth	(47) 15.9	(49) 18.3
	8.5	-.3	13.9				7.7	3.9
	26.0	8.4	17.4				12.5	14.9
	12.6	4.0	10.7			% Profit Before Taxes/Total Assets	5.6	6.9
	-3.6	-.1	5.2				1.8	.9
	24.2	25.0	8.5				21.4	24.3
	14.5	14.0	5.6			Sales/Net Fixed Assets	10.1	12.2
	7.0	6.9	3.9				6.0	5.5
	5.0	2.8	2.4				2.9	3.0
	2.6	2.1	1.7			Sales/Total Assets	2.1	2.2
	1.8	1.4	1.5				1.6	1.6
	1.4	1.7	2.1				1.1	1.2
(10)	1.9	(20) 2.1	(15) 2.4			% Depr., Dep., Amort./Sales	(48) 1.8	(53) 1.7
	3.0	3.1	4.2				2.9	2.4
							2.9	5.0
						% Officers', Directors', Owners' Comp/Sales	(14) 6.0	(17) 6.5
								9.3
722M	46909M	213512M	861773M		165606M	Net Sales ($)	1263419M	1240395M
366M	14363M	97513M	418905M		113461M	Total Assets ($)	844425M	827654M

(Center columns 0-500M, 50-100MM, and 100-250MM marked "DATA NOT AVAILABLE.")

M = $ thousand   MM = $ million
See Pages 11 through 18 for Explanation of Ratios and Data

Comparative Historical Data / Current Data Sorted By Sales

						Type of Statement					2	8
	9		9		10	Unqualified				6	2	8
	18		6		16	Reviewed		3	1	6	3	3
	7		13		10	Compiled		4	2	3	1	
	4		1		4	Tax Returns	1		1		1	1
	18		14		12	Other		1		3	4	4
	4/1/00-3/31/01 ALL		4/1/01-3/31/02 ALL		4/1/02-3/31/03 ALL		0-1MM	11 (4/1-9/30/02) 1-3MM	3-5MM	5-10MM	41 (10/1/02-3/31/03) 10-25MM	25MM & OVER
	56		43		52	NUMBER OF STATEMENTS	1	8	4	12	11	16
	%		%		%	ASSETS	%	%	%	%	%	%
	9.1		9.9		9.1	Cash & Equivalents				6.8	7.7	9.7
	30.8		25.1		28.1	Trade Receivables (net)				30.2	30.8	23.4
	20.7		20.8		20.9	Inventory				21.8	21.2	19.5
	4.6		5.0		4.8	All Other Current				2.1	2.9	5.6
	65.2		60.7		62.8	Total Current				60.9	62.7	58.2
	23.8		26.7		27.2	Fixed Assets (net)				28.6	28.3	28.5
	3.9		5.7		3.7	Intangibles (net)				3.4	6.5	4.6
	7.0		6.8		6.3	All Other Non-Current				7.2	2.5	8.7
	100.0		100.0		100.0	Total				100.0	100.0	100.0
						LIABILITIES						
	7.7		6.9		11.2	Notes Payable-Short Term				12.2	5.7	10.0
	1.8		6.2		4.3	Cur. Mat.-L/T/D				4.5	6.2	4.6
	16.8		12.6		15.8	Trade Payables				14.2	18.8	14.8
	.1		.1		.2	Income Taxes Payable				.5	.1	.2
	15.2		12.3		16.9	All Other Current				6.0	11.9	26.7
	41.6		38.0		48.3	Total Current				37.3	42.8	56.2
	11.2		12.6		11.0	Long Term Debt				12.2	8.5	15.1
	.4		.7		.3	Deferred Taxes				.1	.3	.4
	4.7		1.6		5.5	All Other Non-Current				6.6	7.2	4.3
	42.0		47.0		35.0	Net Worth				43.8	41.1	23.9
	100.0		100.0		100.0	Total Liabilities & Net Worth				100.0	100.0	100.0
						INCOME DATA						
	100.0		100.0		100.0	Net Sales				100.0	100.0	100.0
	31.4		28.9		33.5	Gross Profit				27.2	33.7	28.7
	24.5		24.3		29.1	Operating Expenses				25.0	27.1	23.6
	6.9		4.6		4.4	Operating Profit				2.2	6.6	5.1
	1.4		1.7		.8	All Other Expenses (net)				.3	.5	.8
	5.5		2.9		3.6	Profit Before Taxes				1.9	6.0	4.3
						RATIOS						
	3.1		3.0		2.3					2.4	2.0	2.4
	1.7		1.7		1.5	Current				1.9	1.5	1.1
	1.1		1.1		1.0					1.1	1.2	.9
	1.7		1.9		1.6					1.7	1.3	1.5
	1.1		1.0		.9	Quick				1.0	1.0	.7
	.6		.5		.5					.5	.7	.5
38	9.5	30	12.1	37	10.0				47 7.8	36 10.1	36 10.1
54	6.7	49	7.4	49	7.4	Sales/Receivables			53 6.8	41 8.8	49 7.4
62	5.8	58	6.2	63	5.8				67 5.4	66 5.6	59 6.2
28	12.9	31	11.6	25	14.5				34 10.7	15 23.9	19 19.0
54	6.8	62	5.9	49	7.5	Cost of Sales/Inventory			44 8.4	90 4.1	39 9.4
80	4.6	77	4.8	90	4.1				79 4.6	96 3.8	63 5.8
18	20.7	14	25.6	17	21.7				20 18.3	15 24.5	18 20.7
29	12.4	20	17.9	30	12.2	Cost of Sales/Payables			36 10.3	30 12.3	27 13.4
47	7.7	37	9.8	46	7.9				47 7.8	46 7.9	38 9.7
	4.3		3.6		5.5					5.0	6.0	5.1
	8.4		9.2		13.7	Sales/Working Capital				8.4	17.2	NM
	40.0		79.1		-151.1					75.4	25.1	-45.5
	9.2		12.9		12.4					8.7	10.3	18.9
(48)	3.8	(39)	2.9	(45)	4.7	EBIT/Interest			2.9	(10) 4.9	(12) 7.0
	1.9		.6		1.0					.9	2.3	1.5
	4.9		5.2		8.0	Net Profit + Depr., Dep.,						
(14)	3.5	(15)	1.8	(19)	4.6	Amort./Cur. Mat. L/T/D					
	.6		.5		1.6							
	.3		.3		.4					.3	.5	.6
	.5		.7		.6	Fixed/Worth				.5	.6	1.3
	1.5		1.7		1.9					1.4	1.3	NM
	.5		.4		.6					.6	.6	.8
	1.5		1.2		1.8	Debt/Worth				1.3	1.8	2.9
	3.9		6.2		8.1					2.1	4.8	NM
	34.2		21.4		58.4	% Profit Before Taxes/Tangible			20.4	25.4	70.8
(50)	17.9	(38)	13.4	(44)	15.3	Net Worth	(11) 8.1	(10) 15.1	(12) 30.7
	4.7		-4.1		2.9				-.6	8.2	14.8
	16.6		9.8		13.8	% Profit Before Taxes/Total				8.6	13.0	18.1
	6.0		5.7		7.8	Assets				4.1	7.8	10.5
	2.2		-2.1		.1					-.2	4.0	7.0
	19.2		16.2		21.8					19.5	23.8	14.7
	11.8		8.5		9.6	Sales/Net Fixed Assets				9.2	14.0	6.1
	5.0		4.7		5.0					4.5	2.4	5.0
	2.6		2.6		2.7					2.7	3.3	2.6
	2.0		1.7		1.9	Sales/Total Assets				2.0	2.1	1.9
	1.5		1.3		1.5					1.4	1.5	1.5
	1.0		1.0		1.7					1.8	1.5	2.0
(54)	1.9	(41)	2.1	(47)	2.2	% Depr., Dep., Amort./Sales			2.9	1.8	(14) 2.4
	3.3		3.2		3.1					3.2	2.0	3.6
	2.0		1.0		3.2	% Officers', Directors',						
(19)	4.2	(10)	5.6	(12)	5.7	Owners' Comp/Sales					
	7.0		11.1		10.4							
	1253298M		1548733M		1288522M	Net Sales ($)	722M	16757M	14448M	90707M	151066M	1014822M
	744218M		1082064M		644608M	Total Assets ($)	366M	12394M	4761M	47531M	87354M	492202M

© RMA 2003

M = $ thousand   MM = $ million

See Pages 11 through 18 for Explanation of Ratios and Data

Current Data Sorted By Assets   **Comparative Historical Data**

	0-500M	500M-2MM	2-10MM	10-50MM	50-100MM	100-250MM	Type of Statement	4/1/98-3/31/99 ALL	4/1/99-3/31/00 ALL
	1	8	10	2	1		Unqualified	20	18
	3	13	3				Reviewed	13	15
2	6	1	1				Compiled	9	6
1	1						Tax Returns	1	
2	2	7	5	2		Other	14	10
		16 (4/1-9/30/02)		55 (10/1/02-3/31/03)					
5	13	29	19	4	1	**NUMBER OF STATEMENTS**	57	49
%	%	%	%	%	%	**ASSETS**	%	%
	9.6	8.2	8.0			Cash & Equivalents	8.2	7.2
	26.4	24.0	27.1			Trade Receivables (net)	28.7	30.1
	23.9	32.6	29.5			Inventory	32.3	29.7
	2.8	3.1	3.1			All Other Current	1.9	1.0
	62.7	67.9	67.8			Total Current	71.0	68.1
	24.2	17.8	21.6			Fixed Assets (net)	21.4	22.2
	6.4	3.0	3.6			Intangibles (net)	2.6	4.3
	6.8	11.3	7.1			All Other Non-Current	5.0	5.3
	100.0	100.0	100.0			Total	100.0	100.0
						LIABILITIES		
	4.7	9.9	12.8			Notes Payable-Short Term	11.3	9.7
	7.4	2.2	2.6			Cur. Mat.-L/T/D	2.6	4.0
	14.1	13.7	12.9			Trade Payables	13.1	12.8
	.3	.0	.1			Income Taxes Payable	1.2	.4
	7.1	15.1	15.1			All Other Current	13.6	14.1
	33.7	40.9	43.6			Total Current	41.8	41.1
	8.4	10.7	14.1			Long Term Debt	16.6	14.7
	.3	.0	.3			Deferred Taxes	.3	.7
	5.9	7.1	6.3			All Other Non-Current	4.5	7.3
	51.7	41.2	35.8			Net Worth	36.8	36.1
	100.0	100.0	100.0			Total Liabilities & Net Worth	100.0	100.0
						INCOME DATA		
	100.0	100.0	100.0			Net Sales	100.0	100.0
	48.2	28.9	31.8			Gross Profit	32.2	30.0
	41.9	26.3	26.8			Operating Expenses	26.2	25.5
	6.4	2.6	5.0			Operating Profit	5.9	4.5
	1.1	.5	1.3			All Other Expenses (net)	1.4	1.2
	5.2	2.0	3.7			Profit Before Taxes	4.5	3.3
						RATIOS		
	3.6	2.4	2.2				2.8	2.5
	2.6	1.7	1.9			Current	1.8	2.0
	1.2	1.3	1.1				1.3	1.5
	2.2	1.1	1.2				1.4	1.4
	1.1	.8	.7			Quick	.9	1.0
	.6	.5	.6				.6	.7
	23 15.9	34 10.7	41 9.0				31 11.7	34 10.7
	45 8.1	47 7.8	53 6.9			Sales/Receivables	46 8.0	53 6.8
	59 6.2	59 6.2	73 5.0				63 5.8	68 5.3
	41 8.9	43 8.6	52 7.0				48 7.5	46 8.0
	110 3.3	98 3.7	101 3.6			Cost of Sales/Inventory	87 4.2	83 4.4
	276 1.3	134 2.7	112 3.3				114 3.2	111 3.3
	13 28.6	23 16.1	19 19.7				18 20.1	17 21.3
	38 9.7	32 11.6	43 8.6			Cost of Sales/Payables	25 14.6	34 10.8
	99 3.7	53 6.8	57 6.4				38 9.6	49 7.5
	3.9	4.4	3.6				4.5	4.3
	5.4	6.9	6.7			Sales/Working Capital	6.4	6.0
	295.7	12.4	31.1				17.7	10.5
	(10) 11.2	(27) 9.6	(17) 9.6				(50) 6.7	(48) 7.4
	5.3	1.5	3.7			EBIT/Interest	2.7	2.9
	−2.3	.4	1.2				1.5	1.4
						Net Profit + Depr., Dep., Amort./Cur. Mat. L /T/D	5.2	7.2
						(21)	2.7 (20)	2.5
							1.7	.8
	.2	.2	.2				.2	.3
	.5	.5	.7			Fixed/Worth	.5	.5
	1.5	.8	19.4				1.3	.9
	.4	.8	.5				.8	.8
	1.0	1.3	1.9			Debt/Worth	1.3	1.2
	2.8	3.5	39.9				3.3	2.9
	(12) 41.6	(26) 28.6	(15) 40.4			% Profit Before Taxes/Tangible Net Worth	(51) 42.9	(43) 45.8
	10.2	8.3	9.3				17.5	13.1
	.1	−2.9	4.1				9.1	4.8
	13.0	12.0	12.4			% Profit Before Taxes/Total Assets	13.7	12.6
	4.5	2.1	6.2				9.0	5.8
	.7	−1.8	2.2				2.4	2.2
	22.0	21.6	25.3				30.9	19.1
	7.9	12.5	6.5			Sales/Net Fixed Assets	13.7	9.6
	4.5	7.7	4.5				5.2	5.5
	2.8	2.3	2.3				2.8	2.4
	1.9	1.7	1.5			Sales/Total Assets	2.1	1.9
	1.4	1.4	1.4				1.5	1.6
	(10) 1.7	(27) 1.3	(16) 1.2			% Depr., Dep., Amort./Sales	(51) .8	(45) 1.0
	2.7	1.9	2.5				1.5	1.6
	3.3	3.3	3.4				2.5	2.8
		(10) 3.0				% Officers', Directors', Owners' Comp/Sales	(16) 2.3	(12) 2.3
		3.9					3.2	3.7
		7.6					6.3	
4220M	34121M	321471M	632409M	461829M	199739M	Net Sales ($)	1416097M	1625650M
1699M	16285M	172329M	380715M	261609M	159799M	Total Assets ($)	860835M	1009498M

Comparative Historical Data / Current Data Sorted By Sales

			Type of Statement	0-1MM	1-3MM	3-5MM	5-10MM	10-25MM	25MM & OVER
12	13	22	Unqualified		1	1	2	8	10
8	12	19	Reviewed		4	1	5	7	2
10	6	10	Compiled	1	4	1	2	1	1
	2	2	Tax Returns	1	1				
16	12	18	Other	2	2	2	1	7	4
4/1/00-3/31/01	4/1/01-3/31/02	4/1/02-3/31/03			16 (4/1-9/30/02)		55 (10/1/02-3/31/03)		
ALL	ALL	ALL							
46	45	71	**NUMBER OF STATEMENTS**	4	12	5	10	23	17
%	%	%	**ASSETS**	%	%	%	%	%	%
6.1	6.8	8.5	Cash & Equivalents		9.8		13.0	6.9	9.0
31.8	28.8	26.0	Trade Receivables (net)		30.2		21.9	26.2	26.9
28.1	28.3	30.2	Inventory		23.4		20.4	34.6	29.4
4.0	2.1	2.7	All Other Current		1.9		4.4	3.6	1.0
70.0	66.0	67.4	Total Current		65.3		59.7	71.2	66.4
20.0	23.4	20.4	Fixed Assets (net)		17.6		22.3	19.3	23.0
3.5	2.5	4.1	Intangibles (net)		5.7		1.7	4.2	4.7
6.5	8.1	8.2	All Other Non-Current		11.4		16.3	5.2	5.9
100.0	100.0	100.0	Total		100.0		100.0	100.0	100.0
			LIABILITIES						
10.8	9.6	10.4	Notes Payable-Short Term		9.6		.6	13.2	9.2
2.7	4.6	3.2	Cur. Mat.-L/T/D		7.5		3.0	2.0	2.8
14.6	10.9	13.0	Trade Payables		12.6		14.1	13.6	12.6
.1	.2	.2	Income Taxes Payable		.8		.0	.1	.3
13.7	17.6	13.2	All Other Current		6.6		15.4	17.4	12.8
42.1	42.8	40.0	Total Current		37.1		33.1	46.2	37.8
14.1	14.7	13.1	Long Term Debt		7.2		13.8	11.8	14.8
.8	.4	.3	Deferred Taxes		.3		.0	.1	1.0
6.1	2.2	6.4	All Other Non-Current		6.9		1.2	11.4	5.1
36.9	39.9	40.2	Net Worth		48.6		51.8	30.5	41.3
100.0	100.0	100.0	Total Liabilities & Net Worth		100.0		100.0	100.0	100.0
			INCOME DATA						
100.0	100.0	100.0	Net Sales		100.0		100.0	100.0	100.0
33.7	25.8	34.6	Gross Profit		45.3		26.9	27.8	31.2
27.4	22.8	30.6	Operating Expenses		44.0		25.3	24.8	25.2
6.4	3.0	4.1	Operating Profit		1.3		1.6	3.0	5.9
1.8	1.7	1.1	All Other Expenses (net)		.6		-.5	1.3	1.2
4.6	1.4	3.0	Profit Before Taxes		.7		2.1	1.7	4.7
			RATIOS						
2.9	2.5	2.7			2.8		2.7	2.0	2.9
1.8	2.0	1.9	Current		2.3		1.5	1.7	2.1
1.2	1.2	1.3			.9		1.4	1.1	1.2
1.6	1.5	1.4			2.1		1.6	1.1	1.5
.8	.9	.8	Quick		1.1		1.0	.7	.9
.6	.6	.6			.6		.6	.5	.7
39 9.4	36 10.1	37 10.0			45 8.2		26 14.1	39 9.4	38 9.5
55 6.7	51 7.2	51 7.1	Sales/Receivables		52 7.0		34 10.7	52 7.0	51 7.1
68 5.4	60 6.1	61 6.0			68 5.4		50 7.3	75 4.8	59 6.2
35 10.5	36 10.0	47 7.8			42 8.8		17 21.5	56 6.6	49 7.5
77 4.8	68 5.4	98 3.7	Cost of Sales/Inventory		63 5.8		60 6.1	101 3.6	79 4.6
121 3.0	107 3.4	133 2.7			204 1.8		107 3.4	142 2.6	108 3.4
24 15.4	11 31.9	19 19.7			12 30.3		18 20.3	20 17.9	17 21.8
32 11.2	19 19.2	32 11.4	Cost of Sales/Payables		36 10.0		27 13.7	32 11.6	39 9.4
54 6.8	32 11.4	57 6.4			98 3.7		36 10.2	60 6.1	47 7.7
4.4	5.1	4.1			3.9		5.0	4.6	3.7
6.8	7.8	6.7	Sales/Working Capital		5.7		8.6	6.9	6.7
18.3	16.7	14.8			NM		13.4	21.3	24.1
7.8	6.3	7.0			6.6			8.3	6.4
(44) 3.4	(44) 2.7	(64) 2.8	EBIT/Interest	(10) 1.4			(22) 1.7	(16) 4.3	
1.9	.2	.6			-4.6			.2	2.7
4.5	3.6	5.3	Net Profit + Depr., Dep.,						
(14) 2.9	(11) 1.4	(15) 3.3	Amort./Cur. Mat. L/T/D						
1.4	.4	1.5							
.3	.3	.2			.1		.2	.3	.2
.4	.6	.6	Fixed/Worth		.5		.3	.7	.5
1.3	1.3	1.7			1.3		1.2	2.1	2.4
.7	.6	.6			.4		.3	1.0	.5
1.5	1.3	1.3	Debt/Worth		.8		1.0	3.1	1.5
4.4	2.7	4.2			3.7		2.0	8.4	5.2
52.0	24.0	34.8	% Profit Before Taxes/Tangible		30.2		29.7	33.6	53.4
(42) 16.6	(42) 8.4	(61) 9.3	Net Worth	(11) 5.6			(18) 14.5	(15) 11.3	
7.0	-8.8	.7			-12.0		1.3	-5.5	5.8
12.9	11.0	12.1	% Profit Before Taxes/Total		9.0		6.9	12.4	13.0
7.8	4.1	4.1	Assets		2.5		3.0	3.3	7.6
2.9	-3.0	-.7			-5.7		.6	-2.6	3.5
23.7	16.0	24.3			81.5		25.3	19.0	28.3
14.7	9.0	9.1	Sales/Net Fixed Assets		10.4		11.3	10.0	6.5
5.3	5.3	5.7			5.8		4.9	7.1	4.8
2.5	2.5	2.3			3.2		2.3	2.4	2.4
2.1	2.0	1.7	Sales/Total Assets		1.8		1.7	1.7	1.8
1.6	1.6	1.4			1.3		1.3	1.4	1.5
1.0	1.3	1.3						1.5	1.2
(41) 1.6	(43) 1.9	(62) 2.0	% Depr., Dep., Amort./Sales				(20) 2.3	(16) 2.0	
2.9	3.0	3.3						4.0	2.9
2.1	1.6	2.6	% Officers', Directors',						
(10) 4.1	(10) 3.0	(20) 5.0	Owners' Comp/Sales						
8.1	5.9	8.0							
1616389M	1098731M	1653789M	Net Sales ($)	2017M	23675M	21630M	73268M	388290M	1144909M
962620M	650205M	992436M	Total Assets ($)	1672M	13700M	12615M	46033M	241379M	677037M

M = $ thousand   MM = $ million
See Pages 11 through 18 for Explanation of Ratios and Data

Current Data Sorted By Assets   **Comparative Historical Data**

						Type of Statement		
1	2	7	11	4	2	Unqualified	45	37
	2	8	4		1	Reviewed	24	22
1	9	4		1		Compiled	23	17
	4					Tax Returns	4	5
2	6	12	5	2	1	Other	28	32
	24 (4/1-9/30/02)			65 (10/1/02-3/31/03)			4/1/98-3/31/99	4/1/99-3/31/00
0-500M	500M-2MM	2-10MM	10-50MM	50-100MM	100-250MM		ALL	ALL
4	23	31	20	7	4	NUMBER OF STATEMENTS	124	113
%	%	%	%	%	%	ASSETS	%	%
	8.5	10.2	14.0			Cash & Equivalents	8.5	8.7
	37.1	28.2	22.6			Trade Receivables (net)	31.8	32.5
	25.8	25.7	30.1			Inventory	26.6	26.7
	1.7	4.6	2.1			All Other Current	1.9	2.1
	73.1	68.6	69.0			Total Current	68.8	70.0
	19.6	21.4	20.1			Fixed Assets (net)	21.3	22.9
	1.2	5.8	1.1			Intangibles (net)	3.4	2.8
	6.2	4.2	9.8			All Other Non-Current	6.4	4.3
	100.0	100.0	100.0			Total	100.0	100.0
						LIABILITIES		
	10.3	5.5	3.5			Notes Payable-Short Term	10.8	11.4
	2.6	2.5	3.6			Cur. Mat.-L/T/D	3.1	2.3
	21.1	17.1	11.3			Trade Payables	17.8	16.6
	1.4	.7	.1			Income Taxes Payable	.8	.3
	25.6	12.7	9.7			All Other Current	12.5	14.2
	60.9	38.6	28.2			Total Current	45.0	44.7
	12.4	16.7	8.9			Long Term Debt	11.1	12.6
	.2	.8	.2			Deferred Taxes	.6	.4
	3.5	8.4	7.0			All Other Non-Current	4.3	4.3
	23.0	35.4	55.6			Net Worth	39.0	38.0
	100.0	100.0	100.0			Total Liabilities & Net Worth	100.0	100.0
						INCOME DATA		
	100.0	100.0	100.0			Net Sales	100.0	100.0
	31.5	32.3	28.5			Gross Profit	28.9	29.0
	29.4	26.1	23.5			Operating Expenses	23.8	25.0
	2.1	6.3	5.0			Operating Profit	5.1	4.0
	.4	1.3	-.1			All Other Expenses (net)	.4	.7
	1.7	4.9	5.1			Profit Before Taxes	4.8	3.3
						RATIOS		
	2.1	3.9	5.1				2.2	2.6
	1.2	1.9	2.9			Current	1.5	1.6
	1.0	1.3	1.7				1.2	1.1
	1.6	1.8	3.0				1.4	1.5
	.8	1.0	1.6			Quick	.9	1.0
	.5	.7	.8				.6	.6
32	11.4	31 11.9	31 11.8				34 10.7	41 9.0
44	8.4	46 7.9	42 8.8			Sales/Receivables	47 7.8	51 7.1
58	6.3	61 5.9	56 6.5				59 6.2	64 5.7
13	27.9	43 8.4	46 8.0				31 11.6	38 9.6
46	7.9	59 6.2	68 5.4			Cost of Sales/Inventory	60 6.1	63 5.7
65	5.6	99 3.7	111 3.3				86 4.2	100 3.6
20	18.6	20 17.9	16 23.1				20 18.0	19 19.3
36	10.2	32 11.4	22 16.4			Cost of Sales/Payables	32 11.2	31 11.6
47	7.8	62 5.9	36 10.1				46 7.9	54 6.7
	6.8	3.8	3.2				5.8	5.1
	21.8	8.7	3.8			Sales/Working Capital	9.8	9.4
	-98.7	13.2	9.1				26.4	49.2
	8.5	12.0	35.7				13.3	8.2
(19)	4.0	(25) 3.4	(17) 8.8			EBIT/Interest	(112) 3.9	(100) 3.5
	1.5	1.7	2.3				1.7	1.6
		13.3				Net Profit + Depr., Dep.,	11.1	9.5
		(10) 6.4				Amort./Cur. Mat. L /T/D	(45) 2.3	(28) 3.9
		1.3					1.1	1.9
	.5	.2	.2				.2	.2
	.8	.5	.3			Fixed/Worth	.6	.6
	2.7	2.1	.6				1.2	1.4
	1.5	.7	.3				.8	.7
	2.7	2.0	.7			Debt/Worth	1.8	1.7
	21.3	4.8	2.2				3.4	4.1
	65.1	81.7	33.9				47.6	45.5
(18)	20.9	(29) 37.7	(18) 18.9			% Profit Before Taxes/Tangible Net Worth	(117) 22.4	(101) 18.2
	5.4	3.6	5.2				7.0	4.5
	17.5	27.3	16.8				18.9	14.5
	4.6	7.8	11.4			% Profit Before Taxes/Total Assets	8.6	6.6
	1.2	1.4	.4				2.4	1.9
	33.6	33.9	24.1				29.1	27.2
	20.6	14.8	9.3			Sales/Net Fixed Assets	12.7	12.8
	9.3	5.4	6.8				7.3	5.4
	4.3	2.8	2.3				2.9	2.7
	2.9	2.0	1.9			Sales/Total Assets	2.4	2.1
	2.1	1.8	1.5				1.8	1.6
	.5	.9	.9				.8	1.0
(18)	1.5	(29) 1.4	(18) 1.2			% Depr., Dep., Amort./Sales	(113) 1.4	(99) 1.6
	2.2	3.8	2.4				2.3	2.6
		1.0					1.9	1.9
		(11) 2.7				% Officers', Directors', Owners' Comp/Sales	(38) 4.3	(33) 4.0
		5.5					6.6	6.2
2196M	88693M	301804M	776315M	1015477M	1353480M	Net Sales ($)	3657620M	3233567M
814M	29322M	141336M	401994M	575140M	820017M	Total Assets ($)	1942811M	1894767M

M = $ thousand   MM = $ million
See Pages 11 through 18 for Explanation of Ratios and Data

Comparative Historical Data | **Current Data Sorted By Sales**

			Type of Statement						
20	14	27	Unqualified	1	1	2	3	4	16
14	11	15	Reviewed		1	1	6	4	3
22	17	15	Compiled			8	4		1
4	3	4	Tax Returns			1			
29	29	28	Other	2		3	3	6	8
4/1/00-3/31/01 ALL	4/1/01-3/31/02 ALL	4/1/02-3/31/03 ALL		0-1MM	1-3MM	3-5MM	5-10MM	10-25MM	25MM & OVER
				24 (4/1-9/30/02)		65 (10/1/02-3/31/03)			
89	74	89	**NUMBER OF STATEMENTS**	3	7	17	20	14	28
%	%	%	**ASSETS**	%	%	%	%	%	%
7.7	8.8	9.6	Cash & Equivalents			6.4	7.7	13.7	9.9
32.0	29.3	28.4	Trade Receivables (net)			33.4	31.0	31.5	22.3
29.7	25.2	26.7	Inventory			29.8	25.2	24.6	27.3
3.0	3.8	3.1	All Other Current			1.6	5.9	2.4	3.0
72.4	67.1	67.8	Total Current			71.2	69.9	72.2	62.4
20.0	20.9	20.7	Fixed Assets (net)			25.1	21.2	17.1	22.3
2.4	4.4	4.9	Intangibles (net)			1.6	6.1	3.2	6.9
5.2	7.6	6.6	All Other Non-Current			2.1	2.8	7.5	8.3
100.0	100.0	100.0	Total			100.0	100.0	100.0	100.0
			LIABILITIES						
10.1	8.2	8.1	Notes Payable-Short Term			7.0	6.6	5.2	6.2
2.9	2.9	2.9	Cur. Mat.-L/T/D			3.2	2.4	1.9	3.0
21.3	16.0	15.8	Trade Payables			22.4	19.0	15.3	11.7
.3	.5	.7	Income Taxes Payable			.4	1.2	.0	.2
12.4	13.6	18.1	All Other Current			18.2	15.5	13.1	10.8
47.0	41.3	45.5	Total Current			51.2	44.6	35.5	32.0
11.1	11.2	13.1	Long Term Debt			21.2	14.4	10.2	9.1
.6	.6	.5	Deferred Taxes			.1	.6	.9	.5
3.0	5.1	7.7	All Other Non-Current			3.1	12.0	2.8	11.6
38.2	41.8	33.1	Net Worth			24.5	28.4	50.5	46.8
100.0	100.0	100.0	Total Liabilities & Net Worth			100.0	100.0	100.0	100.0
			INCOME DATA						
100.0	100.0	100.0	Net Sales			100.0	100.0	100.0	100.0
28.6	30.3	30.2	Gross Profit			32.0	29.5	33.2	25.2
23.5	26.5	25.8	Operating Expenses			28.1	23.7	28.5	18.9
5.1	3.8	4.4	Operating Profit			3.8	5.8	4.7	6.3
.5	1.1	.9	All Other Expenses (net)			1.5	.8	.7	.9
4.6	2.7	3.5	Profit Before Taxes			2.4	5.0	4.0	5.4
			RATIOS						
2.3	3.2	3.2				2.9	2.1	4.8	4.5
1.6	1.7	1.8	Current			1.3	1.6	2.3	2.1
1.2	1.1	1.2				1.0	1.2	1.3	1.5
1.3	1.8	1.8				2.0	1.1	2.3	2.1
.8	.9	1.0	Quick			.8	1.0	1.7	.9
.6	.5	.6				.5	.8	.9	.7
31 11.8	36 10.2	31 11.8				31 11.9	29 12.8	35 10.4	29 12.5
48 7.6	45 8.1	44 8.4	Sales/Receivables			44 8.4	41 9.0	48 7.7	43 8.4
59 6.2	61 6.0	59 6.2				57 6.4	57 6.4	67 5.5	56 6.5
36 10.1	34 10.8	42 8.7				29 12.8	26 14.2	24 15.3	46 8.0
63 5.8	58 6.3	59 6.2	Cost of Sales/Inventory			53 6.9	57 6.4	57 6.4	62 5.9
97 3.8	100 3.7	92 3.9				89 4.1	80 4.6	118 3.1	100 3.7
21 17.1	20 18.1	18 20.0				16 22.2	20 18.0	21 17.8	17 21.5
35 10.3	26 14.0	29 12.4	Cost of Sales/Payables			39 9.4	32 11.4	27 13.3	25 14.4
60 6.1	49 7.5	43 8.5				59 6.2	51 7.2	62 5.9	36 10.1
5.3	4.2	4.4				5.5	7.0	3.1	3.4
8.9	8.8	8.1	Sales/Working Capital			15.4	9.0	6.1	6.9
22.2	35.2	20.6				NM	28.8	21.1	12.5
(78) 13.6	(65) 10.1	(73) 12.4				(14) 7.8	(18) 21.3	(10) 43.1	(25) 25.0
4.1	3.2	4.0	EBIT/Interest			4.6	5.3	3.1	5.6
1.6	.7	1.5				1.8	1.7	.4	1.3
(18) 11.0	(24) 4.8	(30) 13.6	Net Profit + Depr., Dep.,						(14) 16.3
3.9	2.1	3.5	Amort./Cur. Mat. L/T/D						4.2
1.6	1.1	2.1							2.5
.2	.2	.2				.6	.4	.1	.2
.5	.6	.5	Fixed/Worth			2.0	.7	.2	.5
1.0	1.6	2.3				2.7	1.6	.6	1.6
.9	.6	.7				1.8	1.2	.5	.4
1.7	1.5	1.8	Debt/Worth			3.7	2.1	.8	.9
4.4	5.9	5.7				14.3	4.8	3.2	4.0
(80) 55.4	(65) 41.1	(74) 52.5	% Profit Before Taxes/Tangible			(14) 65.1	(18) 91.1	65.5	(22) 33.3
26.8	12.3	20.8	Net Worth			18.9	45.9	17.3	19.7
4.5	.8	3.4				3.4	4.9	.9	6.5
17.4	16.0	17.3	% Profit Before Taxes/Total			11.3	29.1	17.2	16.8
9.5	5.0	6.6	Assets			4.4	13.6	7.2	8.2
1.7	-1.9	1.1				1.6	1.6	.2	1.4
31.1	29.9	28.5				31.4	26.4	54.8	19.9
12.9	12.8	12.3	Sales/Net Fixed Assets			17.6	14.7	17.2	8.4
7.2	5.0	6.7				7.5	7.5	7.1	5.6
3.0	3.0	2.9				4.0	3.1	3.0	2.3
2.1	2.1	2.1	Sales/Total Assets			2.9	2.6	2.0	1.8
1.9	1.5	1.6				2.3	1.8	1.6	1.5
(76) .7	(67) .7	(75) .8	% Depr., Dep., Amort./Sales			(11) .5	(19) 1.0	(13) .5	(25) .8
1.3	1.4	1.5				1.8	2.1	1.3	1.3
2.2	3.2	2.4				2.3	3.8	2.3	2.5
(25) 1.9	(22) 1.8	(22) 2.2	% Officers', Directors',						
3.9	2.9	3.5	Owners' Comp/Sales						
7.0	5.5	7.3							
2070454M	1934756M	3537965M	Net Sales ($)	1090M	15581M	61959M	151304M	220668M	3087363M
1117756M	1163835M	1968623M	Total Assets ($)	392M	8844M	25796M	65934M	109802M	1757855M

© RMA 2003

M = $ thousand   MM = $ million
See Pages 11 through 18 for Explanation of Ratios and Data

Current Data Sorted By Assets   **Comparative Historical Data**

						Type of Statement		
		1	2			Unqualified		
1	5	8	1			Reviewed		
1	7	4				Compiled		
1		2				Tax Returns		
1	2	3	4	1		Other	4/1/98-	4/1/99-
	11 (4/1-9/30/02)		33 (10/1/02-3/31/03)				3/31/99	3/31/00
0-500M	500M-2MM	2-10MM	10-50MM	50-100MM	100-250MM		ALL	ALL
4	14	18	7	1		**NUMBER OF STATEMENTS**		
%	%	%	%	%	%	**ASSETS**	%	%
	7.4	4.8			D	Cash & Equivalents	D	D
	23.1	25.7			A	Trade Receivables (net)	A	A
	15.1	8.7			T	Inventory	T	T
	1.5	3.4			A	All Other Current	A	A
	47.2	42.6				Total Current		
	44.0	50.2			N	Fixed Assets (net)	N	N
	.2	1.9			O	Intangibles (net)	O	O
	8.6	5.3			T	All Other Non-Current	T	T
	100.0	100.0				Total		
					A	**LIABILITIES**	A	A
	9.4	9.4			V	Notes Payable-Short Term	V	V
	10.3	7.9			A	Cur. Mat.-L/T/D	A	A
	7.8	6.0			I	Trade Payables	I	I
	.0	.1			L	Income Taxes Payable	L	L
	6.4	7.1			A	All Other Current	A	A
	34.0	30.5			B	Total Current	B	B
	19.8	21.9			L	Long Term Debt	L	L
	.3	1.0			E	Deferred Taxes	E	E
	11.9	4.2				All Other Non-Current		
	34.1	42.4				Net Worth		
	100.0	100.0				Total Liabilities & Net Worth		
						INCOME DATA		
	100.0	100.0				Net Sales		
	26.9	25.0				Gross Profit		
	30.0	23.9				Operating Expenses		
	-3.1	1.1				Operating Profit		
	2.4	1.7				All Other Expenses (net)		
	-5.5	-.6				Profit Before Taxes		
						RATIOS		
	1.9	1.9						
	1.3	1.3				Current		
	1.1	1.0						
	1.3	1.5						
	.9	.9				Quick		
	.6	.7						
31	11.7	37	9.7					
46	7.9	53	6.9			Sales/Receivables		
64	5.7	80	4.6					
22	16.8	9	40.4					
45	8.1	23	15.7			Cost of Sales/Inventory		
60	6.1	41	8.8					
6	64.6	8	47.2					
12	31.5	20	18.1			Cost of Sales/Payables		
27	13.4	27	13.4					
	6.5	6.6						
	16.5	18.2				Sales/Working Capital		
	218.9	NM						
	2.2	3.1						
	.5	(17)	1.5			EBIT/Interest		
	-4.1	-2.3						
						Net Profit + Depr., Dep.,		
						Amort./Cur. Mat. L./T/D		
	.8	.8						
	1.5	1.2				Fixed/Worth		
	2.3	1.6						
	.8	.7						
	2.1	1.5				Debt/Worth		
	6.0	2.3						
	5.8	20.1				% Profit Before Taxes/Tangible		
(13)	-8.5	(16)	6.5			Net Worth		
	-54.5	-18.2						
	4.4	7.1						
	-2.5	2.6				% Profit Before Taxes/Total		
	-14.7	-5.3				Assets		
	7.1	4.0						
	3.8	3.2				Sales/Net Fixed Assets		
	2.7	2.3						
	2.5	2.0						
	1.7	1.4				Sales/Total Assets		
	1.1	1.2						
	3.0	4.0						
	6.4	(17)	8.3			% Depr., Dep., Amort./Sales		
	12.1	9.2						
		1.8						
	(13)	3.9				% Officers', Directors',		
		5.0				Owners' Comp/Sales		
4918M	34004M	104217M	135097M	114307M		Net Sales ($)		
1724M	18497M	72265M	107066M	57143M		Total Assets ($)		

© RMA 2003

M = $ thousand   MM = $ million
See Pages 11 through 18 for Explanation of Ratios and Data

Comparative Historical Data | Current Data Sorted By Sales

	4/1/00-3/31/01 ALL	4/1/01-3/31/02 ALL	4/1/02-3/31/03 ALL	Type of Statement	0-1MM	1-3MM	3-5MM	5-10MM	10-25MM	25MM & OVER
			3	Unqualified					2	
			15	Reviewed		4	3	6	2	
			12	Compiled	2	6	1	3		
			3	Tax Returns		1	1	1		
			11	Other		2	2	2		1
						11 (4/1-9/30/02)		33 (10/1/02-3/31/03)		
NUMBER OF STATEMENTS			44		2	13	8	12	8	1
	%	%	%	ASSETS	%	%	%	%	%	%
			5.3	Cash & Equivalents		5.1		5.9		
	D	D	24.9	Trade Receivables (net)		22.7		28.3		
	A	A	11.6	Inventory		13.5		10.9		
	T	T	3.8	All Other Current		1.7		2.2		
	A	A	45.7	Total Current		43.0		47.3		
			47.2	Fixed Assets (net)		46.9		45.5		
	N	N	1.1	Intangibles (net)		1.2		.5		
	O	O	6.0	All Other Non-Current		9.0		6.6		
	T	T	100.0	Total		100.0		100.0		
				LIABILITIES						
	A	A	9.9	Notes Payable-Short Term		12.1		6.0		
	V	V	9.3	Cur. Mat.-L/T/D		13.2		6.4		
	A	A	7.1	Trade Payables		8.4		5.4		
	I	I	.1	Income Taxes Payable		.0		.2		
	L	L	7.8	All Other Current		6.2		8.9		
	A	A	34.3	Total Current		40.0		26.9		
	B	B	20.7	Long Term Debt		18.6		18.9		
	L	L	.7	Deferred Taxes		.5		.6		
	E	E	6.5	All Other Non-Current		11.4		6.6		
			37.9	Net Worth		29.4		46.9		
			100.0	Total Liabilities & Net Worth		100.0		100.0		
				INCOME DATA						
			100.0	Net Sales		100.0		100.0		
			26.9	Gross Profit		33.9		26.9		
			26.9	Operating Expenses		36.7		22.9		
			.0	Operating Profit		-2.8		3.9		
			1.9	All Other Expenses (net)		2.9		1.2		
			-1.9	Profit Before Taxes		-5.7		2.8		
				RATIOS						
			1.8			1.7		2.2		
			1.3	Current		1.0		1.5		
			1.0			.8		1.3		
			1.4			1.0		1.6		
			.9	Quick		.7		1.2		
			.6			.5		.9		
	34		10.8			33 11.2		39 9.4		
	53		6.8	Sales/Receivables		53 6.9		55 6.6		
	71		5.2			62 5.9		86 4.3		
	14		25.8			22 16.5		13 27.2		
	30		12.1	Cost of Sales/Inventory		48 7.7		26 14.2		
	56		6.5			92 4.0		53 6.9		
	9		40.7			6 56.6		7 50.5		
	20		18.1	Cost of Sales/Payables		24 15.2		14 26.5		
	28		13.1			50 7.3		22 16.4		
			6.5			7.5		6.5		
			18.2	Sales/Working Capital		597.5		11.8		
			471.3			-20.2		18.3		
			3.1			1.5		7.7		
	(43)		1.1	EBIT/Interest		.1		(11) 2.7		
			-.5			-2.7		.2		
			1.9	Net Profit + Depr., Dep.,						
	(16)		1.4	Amort./Cur. Mat. L/T/D						
			.8							
			.9			.9		.7		
			1.4	Fixed/Worth		1.9		1.1		
			1.9			29.8		1.4		
			.8			1.2		.6		
			1.8	Debt/Worth		2.6		1.1		
			2.9			50.1		1.7		
			9.7	% Profit Before Taxes/Tangible		(11) 4.8		29.6		
	(41)		3.7	Net Worth		-16.8		9.5		
			-19.7			-61.8		-3.4		
			4.9	% Profit Before Taxes/Total		2.2		10.9		
			1.2	Assets		-4.2		4.7		
			-4.6			-14.6		-2.0		
			5.2			6.4		5.0		
			3.5	Sales/Net Fixed Assets		4.2		3.5		
			2.6			2.1		2.4		
			2.0			2.5		2.0		
			1.6	Sales/Total Assets		1.6		1.7		
			1.2			1.0		1.2		
			4.4			3.9		3.5		
	(42)		6.7	% Depr., Dep., Amort./Sales		6.6		(11) 4.4		
			8.7			13.3		8.4		
			2.5	% Officers', Directors',						
	(25)		4.3	Owners' Comp/Sales						
			7.9							
			392543M	Net Sales ($)	1564M	21588M	34074M	75156M	145854M	114307M
			256695M	Total Assets ($)	883M	17720M	19070M	49012M	112867M	57143M

M = $ thousand   MM = $ million
See Pages 11 through 18 for Explanation of Ratios and Data

Current Data Sorted By Assets   **Comparative Historical Data**

Type of Statement

	0-500M	500M-2MM	2-10MM	10-50MM	50-100MM	100-250MM		ALL 4/1/98–3/31/99	ALL 4/1/99–3/31/00
Unqualified	1		6	11	3			32	31
Reviewed		16	43	4				56	66
Compiled	7	23	14	3				58	63
Tax Returns	7	6	3					10	16
Other	5	13	20	4		2		54	61
		46 (4/1–9/30/02)		145 (10/1/02–3/31/03)					
NUMBER OF STATEMENTS	20	58	86	22	3	2		210	237

ASSETS	0-500M %	500M-2MM %	2-10MM %	10-50MM %	50-100MM %	100-250MM %		ALL %	ALL %
Cash & Equivalents	9.0	8.9	5.7	5.7				8.8	8.0
Trade Receivables (net)	24.7	27.3	21.4	25.4				24.0	25.5
Inventory	19.8	15.7	23.9	22.3				22.8	21.2
All Other Current	1.8	2.8	2.0	7.2				2.1	2.8
Total Current	55.3	54.6	53.0	60.7				57.7	57.6
Fixed Assets (net)	35.3	38.0	39.4	30.5				34.5	33.9
Intangibles (net)	1.0	1.5	1.0	3.3				1.5	2.6
All Other Non-Current	8.4	5.9	6.6	5.5				6.3	6.0
Total	100.0	100.0	100.0	100.0				100.0	100.0
LIABILITIES									
Notes Payable-Short Term	13.5	12.9	11.5	10.1				9.0	9.1
Cur. Mat.-L/T/D	16.6	4.7	5.5	3.9				5.0	5.5
Trade Payables	9.4	15.3	10.8	9.9				9.6	11.8
Income Taxes Payable	.0	.4	.1	.2				.2	.1
All Other Current	9.7	7.7	10.1	11.5				11.8	11.0
Total Current	49.3	41.0	38.0	35.6				35.5	37.6
Long Term Debt	20.2	23.0	22.2	13.5				19.7	19.8
Deferred Taxes	.0	.5	.4	.6				.7	.6
All Other Non-Current	7.8	4.2	3.4	2.6				3.7	4.3
Net Worth	22.7	31.3	36.0	47.6				40.4	37.7
Total Liabilities & Net Worth	100.0	100.0	100.0	100.0				100.0	100.0
INCOME DATA									
Net Sales	100.0	100.0	100.0	100.0				100.0	100.0
Gross Profit	50.3	36.5	27.8	20.5				33.1	32.7
Operating Expenses	47.2	36.4	28.2	17.6				28.0	28.7
Operating Profit	3.1	.1	−.4	2.9				5.2	4.1
All Other Expenses (net)	1.7	1.4	1.6	1.9				1.5	1.1
Profit Before Taxes	1.4	−1.3	−2.0	1.0				3.6	2.9

RATIOS

	0-500M	500M-2MM	2-10MM	10-50MM	50-100MM	100-250MM		ALL	ALL
Current	1.8	2.5	2.0	3.2				3.0	2.5
	1.1	1.5	1.3	2.0				1.7	1.6
	.6	1.0	1.0	1.2				1.1	1.1
Quick	1.4	1.3	1.0	1.7				1.8	1.5
	.7	1.0	.7	1.0				(209) .9	.9
	.4	.6	.4	.6				.6	.5
Sales/Receivables	11 32.6	37 9.8	37 10.0	39 9.3				35 10.3	38 9.5
	41 8.9	48 7.6	51 7.2	66 5.6				47 7.7	52 7.1
	50 7.3	65 5.6	63 5.8	95 3.8				61 6.0	66 5.5
Cost of Sales/Inventory	0 UND	7 52.3	31 11.8	35 10.4				20 17.9	24 15.0
	10 38.0	31 11.8	56 6.5	67 5.5				58 6.2	54 6.7
	125 2.9	85 4.3	114 3.2	101 3.6				108 3.4	112 3.2
Cost of Sales/Payables	0 UND	17 22.1	21 17.7	16 23.0				13 29.0	16 23.1
	27 13.5	34 10.7	31 11.7	22 16.4				24 15.3	30 12.2
	60 6.1	60 6.1	46 7.9	50 7.3				42 8.7	48 7.6
Sales/Working Capital	9.7	4.8	6.0	3.4				4.2	4.9
	84.6	11.6	13.0	5.6				8.2	8.2
	−15.6	−371.4	−91.0	16.6				41.7	64.2
EBIT/Interest	2.4	3.3	3.2	4.5				6.7	5.1
	(16) .6	(54) .3	(78) 1.4	(17) 1.9				(192) 3.0	(218) 2.4
	−.9	−2.1	−1.7	.8				1.4	.7
Net Profit + Depr., Dep., Amort./Cur. Mat. L/T/D		3.0	2.2					5.0	3.9
		(20) .7	(22) 1.1					(86) 2.0	(93) 2.0
		.1	.2					1.2	1.0
Fixed/Worth	.5	.5	.5	.5				.4	.4
	1.7	1.2	1.2	.7				.8	.9
	NM	2.7	2.4	1.2				1.7	2.0
Debt/Worth	.8	.7	.9	.5				.6	.8
	2.9	1.8	2.3	1.0				1.6	1.8
	NM	7.7	4.9	2.6				3.6	4.2
% Profit Before Taxes/Tangible Net Worth	118.7	22.9	24.6	13.0				35.9	29.7
	(15) −.4	(50) −3.9	(80) 4.2	(21) 7.5				(194) 17.2	(216) 12.3
	−25.9	−34.0	−13.4	−4.1				6.1	1.6
% Profit Before Taxes/Total Assets	21.0	7.4	5.1	5.1				12.9	9.3
	−.6	−1.6	1.0	2.1				5.8	4.5
	−17.2	−10.2	−8.0	−.7				1.2	−.9
Sales/Net Fixed Assets	49.8	10.8	8.7	8.5				11.8	11.2
	6.7	3.9	3.9	4.7				5.6	5.8
	4.0	2.9	2.4	3.0				3.2	2.9
Sales/Total Assets	3.8	2.3	1.9	1.6				2.3	2.2
	2.7	1.8	1.4	1.3				1.7	1.7
	1.5	1.4	1.1	1.1				1.3	1.2
% Depr., Dep., Amort./Sales	1.6	2.2	2.9	2.0				1.9	2.1
	(16) 6.1	(55) 4.0	(80) 4.5	3.7				(187) 3.5	(219) 3.8
	9.1	6.9	7.9	5.2				5.9	6.7
% Officers', Directors', Owners' Comp/Sales	8.9	4.8	2.6					3.5	2.5
	(11) 12.2	(33) 8.4	(38) 3.9					(89) 5.8	(110) 5.5
	16.1	11.2	7.5					8.7	10.7
Net Sales ($)	13567M	130446M	578559M	808245M	328699M	446782M		2560123M	4239365M
Total Assets ($)	5059M	65471M	371391M	580589M	195600M	418944M		1720202M	3221663M

© RMA 2003

M = $ thousand   MM = $ million
See Pages 11 through 18 for Explanation of Ratios and Data

Comparative Historical Data | **Current Data Sorted By Sales**

	Hist 1	Hist 2	Hist 3		0-1MM	1-3MM	3-5MM	5-10MM	10-25MM	25MM & OVER
Type of Statement						46 (4/1-9/30/02)		145 (10/1/02-3/31/03)		
Unqualified	33	27	21		1	1	2	1	4	12
Reviewed	50	47	63			15	18	18	11	1
Compiled	56	53	47		10	19	4	11	2	1
Tax Returns	10	14	16		8	5	2		1	
Other	57	63	44		6	10	8	11	5	4
	4/1/00-3/31/01 ALL	4/1/01-3/31/02 ALL	4/1/02-3/31/03 ALL							
NUMBER OF STATEMENTS	206	204	191		25	50	34	41	23	18
	%	%	%	**ASSETS**	%	%	%	%	%	%
	8.3	8.3	7.1	Cash & Equivalents	8.6	7.3	7.1	5.5	8.3	6.1
	27.3	26.4	24.2	Trade Receivables (net)	22.8	23.1	21.3	26.9	23.9	28.6
	20.1	20.5	20.7	Inventory	21.9	15.5	23.6	23.8	22.5	18.4
	2.2	3.0	3.0	All Other Current	1.4	3.3	1.8	1.5	5.9	6.7
	57.9	58.2	55.0	Total Current	54.7	49.2	53.9	57.8	60.5	59.8
	33.8	34.2	37.0	Fixed Assets (net)	37.8	42.7	36.6	34.8	35.6	27.9
	2.5	2.0	1.5	Intangibles (net)	2.9	.7	.8	1.2	.7	5.0
	5.7	5.7	6.5	All Other Non-Current	4.6	7.5	8.7	6.1	3.1	7.2
	100.0	100.0	100.0	Total	100.0	100.0	100.0	100.0	100.0	100.0
				LIABILITIES						
	9.9	11.7	11.9	Notes Payable-Short Term	12.3	11.3	12.1	13.4	11.5	9.8
		5.2	6.2	Cur. Mat.-L/T/D	14.2	5.1	6.1	4.8	5.1	2.6
	11.6	13.2	11.9	Trade Payables	8.7	13.4	10.7	12.8	13.7	9.9
	.4	.1	.2	Income Taxes Payable	.3	.2	.0	.2	.2	.0
	10.2	8.6	9.6	All Other Current	8.4	4.5	7.1	14.5	12.3	16.2
	37.3	38.8	39.8	Total Current	44.0	34.5	36.0	45.7	42.9	38.5
	18.3	21.5	21.1	Long Term Debt	27.8	23.7	25.1	16.4	16.5	14.0
	.6	.5	.4	Deferred Taxes	.0	.4	.5	.6	.6	.3
	4.0	5.2	4.0	All Other Non-Current	7.7	4.4	1.8	4.7	1.8	3.5
	39.6	34.1	34.6	Net Worth	20.5	37.0	36.6	32.6	38.2	43.7
	100.0	100.0	100.0	Total Liabilities & Net Worth	100.0	100.0	100.0	100.0	100.0	100.0
				INCOME DATA						
	100.0	100.0	100.0	Net Sales	100.0	100.0	100.0	100.0	100.0	100.0
	32.8	33.0	31.9	Gross Profit	42.9	40.6	29.4	23.9	28.6	20.0
	27.9	30.8	31.4	Operating Expenses	42.5	40.8	27.8	25.8	25.1	17.7
	4.9	2.3	.6	Operating Profit	.5	-.2	1.7	-1.8	3.6	2.3
	1.4	1.4	1.6	All Other Expenses (net)	2.4	1.2	1.4	1.8	1.4	2.1
	3.5	.8	-1.1	Profit Before Taxes	-1.9	-1.4	.3	-3.7	2.2	.1
				RATIOS						
	2.5	2.5	2.3		2.2	2.4	3.0	2.0	2.4	2.4
	1.7	1.6	1.4	Current	1.4	1.5	1.4	1.2	1.3	1.7
	1.1	1.0	1.0		.8	1.0	1.0	.9	1.0	1.2
	1.7	1.6	1.2		1.3	1.2	1.1	1.3	1.7	1.5
	1.0	(203) .9	.8	Quick	.7	1.0	.7	.7	.7	.9
	.6	.6	.5		.5	.6	.5	.4	.4	.7
	40 9.1	32 11.5	36 10.0		27 13.5	36 10.1	33 10.9	40 9.0	35 10.6	43 8.5
	55 6.7	49 7.4	49 7.4	Sales/Receivables	49 7.5	47 7.8	48 7.5	53 6.9	45 8.2	66 5.6
	68 5.3	65 5.6	66 5.6		71 5.2	61 6.0	66 5.5	64 5.7	64 5.7	98 3.7
	19 19.3	17 22.0	23 15.7		0 UND	7 52.3	25 14.6	31 12.0	25 14.8	22 16.3
	57 6.4	49 7.4	48 7.5	Cost of Sales/Inventory	72 5.1	32 11.5	62 5.9	50 7.3	51 7.1	61 6.0
	104 3.5	104 3.5	107 3.4		147 2.5	84 4.3	123 3.0	106 3.4	93 3.9	101 3.6
	15 23.6	14 25.8	17 21.6		9 39.0	17 22.1	21 17.4	13 28.2	17 21.6	18 20.3
	27 13.5	26 14.2	31 12.0	Cost of Sales/Payables	31 12.0	37 9.9	29 12.8	36 10.1	30 12.3	22 16.4
	45 8.1	46 8.0	51 7.2		58 6.3	62 5.9	45 8.2	54 6.7	46 8.0	35 10.4
	4.8	4.9	5.3		6.0	4.7	5.3	7.2	5.3	4.0
	8.9	10.2	12.1	Sales/Working Capital	11.0	12.0	12.4	15.0	13.0	6.1
	37.7	207.5	-147.3		-22.9	NM	-110.1	-43.5	-104.5	19.4
	(193) 5.3	(185) 4.2	(170) 3.1		(21) 1.4	(45) 2.3	(31) 2.9	(38) 4.2	(20) 7.6	(15) 2.6
	2.4	1.5	1.3	EBIT/Interest	-.4	.6	1.2	1.3	2.9	1.3
	1.1	-.9	-1.5		-2.7	-1.8	-2.5	-2.4	1.5	-2.0
	(72) 4.3	(56) 2.9	(54) 2.6	Net Profit + Depr., Dep.,		(18) 1.8		(13) 2.6		
	2.1	1.5	1.4	Amort./Cur. Mat. L/T/D		.4		1.2		
	1.0	.4	.3			-.3		.7		
	.4	.4	.5		1.0	.5	.5	.4	.5	.4
	.9	1.1	1.1	Fixed/Worth	1.6	1.1	1.4	1.1	1.0	.6
	1.6	3.0	2.4		-16.7	2.7	2.2	2.7	1.8	1.1
	.8	.8	.7		1.5	.6	.8	.5	.9	.6
	1.5	2.0	2.1	Debt/Worth	8.2	1.2	2.3	2.6	2.1	1.4
	3.7	5.3	5.2		-29.0	3.5	5.7	4.3	4.4	2.6
	(189) 33.1	(179) 31.4	(171) 22.3	% Profit Before Taxes/Tangible	(18) 49.5	(45) 23.4	(33) 35.2	(36) 10.2	(22) 26.4	(17) 12.1
	13.9	9.5	2.5	Net Worth	-8.3	-1.4	5.1	2.5	13.0	1.4
	2.4	-12.0	-16.1		-37.6	-21.0	-15.3	-19.1	6.1	-13.8
	11.8	10.3	5.9	% Profit Before Taxes/Total	7.3	5.5	8.8	3.8	10.0	4.7
	4.6	2.2	.7	Assets	-4.4	-1.2	1.1	.7	4.3	.7
	.5	-6.3	-7.9		-16.2	-9.9	-9.3	-10.9	1.4	-4.0
	10.3	12.7	10.4		41.9	7.7	8.1	14.2	11.0	10.8
	5.6	5.5	4.7	Sales/Net Fixed Assets	3.7	3.7	3.7	5.1	6.3	6.1
	3.3	3.3	2.8		2.2	2.9	2.6	2.5	3.7	3.6
	2.2	2.3	2.1		2.4	2.4	1.9	2.0	2.9	1.8
	1.7	1.9	1.6	Sales/Total Assets	1.5	1.7	1.5	1.5	2.0	1.3
	1.3	1.3	1.2		1.2	1.1	1.1	1.1	1.4	1.1
	(189) 1.7	(191) 1.9	(178) 2.2		(22) 1.6	(47) 2.6	(33) 2.4	(36) 1.3	(22) 2.1	1.7
	3.6	3.6	4.1	% Depr., Dep., Amort./Sales	5.2	4.5	4.0	5.0	3.8	3.4
	6.4	6.0	7.4		9.3	8.3	6.8	8.0	5.4	5.1
	(89) 3.0	(98) 3.0	(85) 3.1	% Officers', Directors',	(13) 9.2	(27) 4.9	(18) 2.9	(15) 2.6	(10) 1.8	
	5.1	5.1	6.1	Owners' Comp/Sales	13.9	8.3	5.2	3.9	3.9	
	9.6	10.2	10.6		20.8	11.8	6.9	7.1	10.9	
	3625472M	2818985M	2306298M	Net Sales ($)	15246M	94843M	132991M	277036M	360378M	1425804M
	2574749M	1995136M	1637054M	Total Assets ($)	11348M	66203M	99814M	194905M	201838M	1062946M

M = $ thousand   MM = $ million
See Pages 11 through 18 for Explanation of Ratios and Data

Current Data Sorted By Assets | **Comparative Historical Data**

Type of Statement	0-500M	500M-2MM	2-10MM	10-50MM	50-100MM	100-250MM		4/1/98-3/31/99 ALL	4/1/99-3/31/00 ALL
Unqualified	2	2	4	8	1			17	20
Reviewed	2	9	14	4				23	22
Compiled	2	12	6		1			18	21
Tax Returns	4	2		1				3	4
Other	2	8	9	9		2		22	24
		28 (4/1-9/30/02)		73 (10/1/02-3/31/03)					
NUMBER OF STATEMENTS	10	33	33	22	3			83	91
ASSETS	%	%	%	%	%	%		%	%
Cash & Equivalents	4.9	4.8	11.1	8.0				10.6	9.8
Trade Receivables (net)	30.9	27.7	20.6	19.7				28.5	27.5
Inventory	16.3	24.8	23.8	22.3				17.6	22.4
All Other Current	.3	3.3	3.9	2.9				3.4	3.5
Total Current	52.4	60.5	59.4	52.9				60.2	63.2
Fixed Assets (net)	41.1	31.5	27.4	31.1				29.9	28.6
Intangibles (net)	4.7	2.3	4.7	11.6				3.2	2.7
All Other Non-Current	1.7	5.7	8.4	4.4				6.7	5.5
Total	100.0	100.0	100.0	100.0				100.0	100.0
LIABILITIES									
Notes Payable-Short Term	41.5	13.7	6.4	11.1				9.7	7.5
Cur. Mat.-L/T/D	24.3	4.5	6.6	4.7				4.6	4.2
Trade Payables	16.4	9.9	9.8	7.7				12.9	12.0
Income Taxes Payable	.0	.3	.1	.0				.4	.5
All Other Current	9.7	15.8	11.0	10.8				11.4	12.1
Total Current	91.8	44.3	33.9	34.2				39.0	36.3
Long Term Debt	31.1	16.7	24.3	21.8				15.1	16.6
Deferred Taxes	.0	.3	.5	.1				.8	.7
All Other Non-Current	4.2	6.5	4.1	8.6				8.8	7.5
Net Worth	−27.1	32.2	37.1	35.3				36.4	38.9
Total Liabilities & Net Worth	100.0	100.0	100.0	100.0				100.0	100.0
INCOME DATA									
Net Sales	100.0	100.0	100.0	100.0				100.0	100.0
Gross Profit	38.9	33.5	26.3	27.5				32.4	29.9
Operating Expenses	43.5	34.8	25.1	24.6				26.9	24.6
Operating Profit	−4.6	−1.3	1.2	2.9				5.4	5.3
All Other Expenses (net)	2.5	1.3	1.5	1.3				1.0	.7
Profit Before Taxes	−7.2	−2.6	−.4	1.5				4.4	4.5

(Columns 50-100MM and 100-250MM: DATA NOT AVAILABLE)

RATIOS

	0-500M	500M-2MM	2-10MM	10-50MM			Hist 98/99	Hist 99/00
Current	3.1	2.3	4.1	3.6			2.8	3.1
	1.0	1.4	1.9	1.4			1.7	1.9
	.4	1.1	1.1	.9			1.1	1.3
Quick	1.5	1.4	2.5	1.9			1.7	1.9
	.8	.8	.9	.7			1.0	1.0
	.4	.4	.5	.5			.6	.7
Sales/Receivables	19 19.0	38 9.7	36 10.1	42 8.7			39 9.2	41 8.9
	44 8.3	54 6.7	47 7.7	56 6.6			49 7.4	54 6.7
	56 6.5	65 5.6	61 6.0	75 4.9			68 5.3	72 5.1
Cost of Sales/Inventory	3 106.5	20 18.6	38 9.6	37 9.7			18 20.4	24 15.3
	42 8.6	53 6.9	78 4.6	77 4.7			53 6.8	56 6.6
	52 7.0	110 3.3	107 3.4	129 2.8			96 3.8	117 3.1
Cost of Sales/Payables	0 UND	9 42.8	16 23.5	19 18.9			17 21.0	13 27.5
	18 20.4	24 15.2	27 13.8	28 13.0			32 11.3	25 14.9
	26 14.2	46 7.9	38 9.5	34 10.9			51 7.2	45 8.2
Sales/Working Capital	8.7	6.7	2.6	3.1			4.2	4.4
	NM	10.2	5.0	7.2			8.1	6.4
	−4.4	68.8	25.6	−32.1			81.7	21.2
EBIT/Interest		(29) 3.9	(31) 8.6	(20) 8.6			(75) 10.8	(82) 9.4
		1.2	1.5	3.1			4.1	4.0
		−.6	−1.6	−.9			1.9	1.5
Net Profit + Depr., Dep., Amort./Cur. Mat. L/T/D			(14) 2.8				(33) 16.3	(34) 4.3
			1.3				2.5	2.5
			−.9				1.3	1.4
Fixed/Worth	.4	.4	.2	.7			.4	.4
	3.0	.9	.9	1.1			.8	.6
	−1.6	4.3	2.9	−33.5			1.8	1.6
Debt/Worth	.8	.8	.3	.8			.7	.7
	4.0	2.4	1.7	2.9			1.7	1.6
	−3.3	8.0	7.7	−754.1			4.1	3.3
% Profit Before Taxes/Tangible Net Worth		(28) 22.5	(28) 25.7	(16) 27.9			(79) 43.5	(86) 40.8
		1.1	5.2	12.5			22.0	17.4
		−14.4	−16.8	−5.0			6.1	4.0
% Profit Before Taxes/Total Assets	.4	9.1	9.8	11.2			15.9	16.2
	−11.1	−.1	.7	3.6			7.1	7.7
	−43.5	−6.7	−8.6	−5.5			2.2	1.3
Sales/Net Fixed Assets	24.7	14.2	10.7	5.7			13.3	12.5
	6.9	6.6	6.0	4.3			6.0	5.9
	2.0	3.6	3.4	3.4			4.0	4.0
Sales/Total Assets	3.9	2.5	1.7	1.6			2.4	2.3
	2.7	1.9	1.4	1.2			1.7	1.8
	1.5	1.3	1.1	1.0			1.3	1.3
% Depr., Dep., Amort./Sales	1.3	(28) 1.1	(30) 2.4	(20) 2.7			(72) 2.1	(85) 1.5
	5.6	3.7	3.5	4.6			3.3	2.9
	18.2	7.2	6.3	5.2			5.2	4.3
% Officers', Directors', Owners' Comp/Sales		(21) 3.6	(14) 2.3				(43) 3.1	(46) 3.7
		5.8	6.6				6.0	5.8
		13.0	9.0				8.8	8.8
Net Sales ($)	8394M	78216M	257318M	591023M	187976M		1159589M	1334619M
Total Assets ($)	3174M	38468M	175589M	508918M	185420M		866897M	986199M

M = $ thousand   MM = $ million
See Pages 11 through 18 for Explanation of Ratios and Data

Comparative Historical Data | Current Data Sorted By Sales

				Type of Statement						
16		11		15	Unqualified		1		3	5	6
29		23		29	Reviewed	1	8	5	7	7	1
21		28		20	Compiled	3	10	4	2	1	
3		4		7	Tax Returns	3	3				1
23		29		30	Other	2	7	3	4	8	6

4/1/00-3/31/01 ALL	4/1/01-3/31/02 ALL	4/1/02-3/31/03 ALL		28 (4/1-9/30/02)			73 (10/1/02-3/31/03)		
				0-1MM	1-3MM	3-5MM	5-10MM	10-25MM	25MM & OVER
92	95	101	NUMBER OF STATEMENTS	9	29	12	16	21	14

%	%	%	ASSETS	%	%	%	%	%	%
7.3	7.5	7.6	Cash & Equivalents		5.9	9.5	9.6	7.5	9.6
30.8	22.8	23.6	Trade Receivables (net)		27.5	22.4	22.8	21.6	20.3
23.3	22.5	22.9	Inventory		23.3	27.1	26.0	20.9	23.9
1.4	3.8	3.1	All Other Current		3.6	4.0	4.1	1.6	3.8
62.8	56.5	57.2	Total Current		60.4	63.0	62.5	51.7	57.6
28.7	31.4	31.2	Fixed Assets (net)		31.5	22.7	24.5	35.4	29.2
3.2	5.5	5.9	Intangibles (net)		2.9	6.0	4.2	9.4	8.7
5.3	6.5	5.8	All Other Non-Current		5.3	8.3	8.8	3.5	4.6
100.0	100.0	100.0	Total		100.0	100.0	100.0	100.0	100.0

			LIABILITIES						
8.6	10.4	13.2	Notes Payable-Short Term		12.6	6.1	8.1	7.0	11.5
4.2	6.4	7.2	Cur. Mat.-L/T/D		4.4	5.2	6.7	6.8	2.9
13.2	9.5	9.9	Trade Payables		11.4	6.2	13.3	9.5	8.1
.3	.3	.1	Income Taxes Payable		.2	.2	.2	.1	.1
12.0	12.1	12.3	All Other Current		14.0	15.3	11.9	10.3	9.6
38.2	38.7	42.7	Total Current		42.4	33.1	40.2	33.7	32.1
16.5	21.1	22.2	Long Term Debt		19.5	18.4	24.4	22.1	21.3
.9	.4	.3	Deferred Taxes		.3	.7	.5	.0	.4
5.7	5.4	5.9	All Other Non-Current		8.1	4.2	3.9	7.3	6.6
38.8	34.4	28.9	Net Worth		29.7	43.7	30.9	36.7	39.6
100.0	100.0	100.0	Total Liabilities & Net Worth		100.0	100.0	100.0	100.0	100.0

			INCOME DATA						
100.0	100.0	100.0	Net Sales		100.0	100.0	100.0	100.0	100.0
28.0	29.8	30.0	Gross Profit		32.8	24.0	23.3	27.7	27.1
22.9	28.4	29.6	Operating Expenses		35.0	27.1	22.3	23.5	21.9
5.1	1.5	.3	Operating Profit		-2.2	-3.1	1.0	4.2	5.2
1.7	2.1	1.6	All Other Expenses (net)		1.5	1.5	2.1	1.0	1.2
3.4	-.7	-1.3	Profit Before Taxes		-3.7	-4.6	-1.1	3.3	4.0

			RATIOS						
2.8	2.8	3.3			3.1	5.5	3.7	3.5	3.7
1.7	1.6	1.4	Current		1.5	2.2	1.6	1.3	2.2
1.1	1.0	1.0			1.1	1.3	1.0	.9	1.2
1.7	1.8	1.7			1.5	3.5	1.9	1.8	2.1
1.0	.8	.8	Quick		.9	1.0	.9	.7	1.1
.6	.4	.5			.4	.5	.4	.5	.6

44	8.4	37	9.9	38	9.6	Sales/Receivables	40	9.1	38	9.5	29	12.7	41	8.9	49	7.4
54	6.7	49	7.4	53	6.9		54	6.7	53	6.9	38	9.7	53	6.9	56	6.5
74	4.9	62	5.9	64	5.7		65	5.6	67	5.5	55	6.7	79	4.6	67	5.4
25	14.8	25	14.7	33	11.1	Cost of Sales/Inventory	19	18.8	37	10.0	34	10.7	36	10.2	73	5.0
61	5.9	64	5.7	67	5.5		53	6.9	97	3.8	73	5.0	53	6.9	88	4.2
103	3.5	108	3.4	108	3.4		108	3.4	119	3.1	96	3.8	132	2.8	117	3.1
13	28.2	10	36.6	12	29.4	Cost of Sales/Payables	9	42.8	12	30.1	13	27.5	18	19.8	17	20.9
27	13.5	21	17.3	25	14.6		24	15.2	14	26.5	24	15.2	32	11.6	28	13.1
49	7.4	42	8.6	42	8.6		46	7.9	24	15.3	50	7.2	40	9.2	32	11.2

3.9	4.0	4.1	Sales/Working Capital		4.8	4.1	3.0	3.6	3.0
7.1	9.2	9.4			9.4	5.8	9.8	16.7	4.6
28.3	-92.6	NM			68.8	12.9	NM	-35.9	20.1

	6.4		5.6		5.6	EBIT/Interest		2.5		.0		16.8		12.6		8.3
(81)	2.8	(84)	1.8	(92)	1.4		(24)	.8	(11)	-.4	(15)	1.5	(20)	3.8	(13)	4.0
	1.2		-1.0		-1.3			-4.3		-1.8		-3.0		1.4		.6

	7.2		3.1		2.5	Net Profit + Depr., Dep.,								6.2		
(36)	3.0	(30)	1.3	(32)	1.4	Amort./Cur. Mat. L/T/D							(10)	1.9		
	1.1		-.2		-.2									.0		

.3	.4	.5	Fixed/Worth		.5	.4	.1	.6	.7
.8	.9	1.1			1.2	.6	.7	1.2	.9
1.7	5.6	4.4			4.8	1.1	NM	3.4	NM

.8	1.0	.7	Debt/Worth		.8	.4	.3	.9	.6
1.7	2.1	2.5			2.4	1.3	2.0	2.8	2.5
4.4	17.8	9.7			11.3	3.9	NM	9.4	NM

	36.0		28.4		25.1	% Profit Before Taxes/Tangible Net Worth		12.5		-.4		47.0		43.6		29.0
(84)	15.0	(79)	6.9	(80)	5.3		(23)	-.2	(11)	-13.8	(12)	2.9	(17)	23.7	(11)	15.5
	2.6		-16.3		-14.6			-16.9		-32.2		-18.1		9.4		5.6

14.2	8.1	9.1	% Profit Before Taxes/Total Assets		4.1	-.9	17.1	15.9	10.8
6.0	2.6	.8			-1.0	-7.7	1.0	6.9	4.3
.9	-8.3	-8.1			-13.1	-11.3	-7.1	1.6	-.3

16.6	9.9	11.1	Sales/Net Fixed Assets		12.6	17.1	47.7	7.1	4.9
6.3	6.0	5.2			7.0	6.1	7.5	3.4	4.4
3.9	3.7	3.2			3.6	5.0	3.6	2.8	3.2

2.4	2.0	2.1	Sales/Total Assets		2.7	2.1	2.4	1.6	1.6
1.7	1.6	1.5			1.8	1.5	1.5	1.3	1.2
1.3	1.2	1.1			1.3	1.0	1.3	1.1	.9

	1.3		1.9		2.3	% Depr., Dep., Amort./Sales		2.6		.7		1.0		2.5		3.3
(79)	2.8	(91)	3.6	(91)	4.4		(25)	4.4	(10)	3.9		3.4	(18)	3.5	(13)	4.8
	4.7		5.7		6.7			6.8		8.2		7.3		5.5		6.5

	3.2		3.0		3.2	% Officers', Directors', Owners' Comp/Sales		2.9								
(43)	5.1	(36)	5.7	(46)	5.6		(20)	5.0								
	8.2		12.6		9.1			13.3								

1858510M	1153525M	1122927M	Net Sales ($)	5662M	51176M	47084M	107593M	327469M	583943M
1232670M	908915M	911569M	Total Assets ($)	4042M	30079M	32560M	67592M	266613M	510683M

M = $ thousand   MM = $ million
See Pages 11 through 18 for Explanation of Ratios and Data

Current Data Sorted By Assets							Comparative Historical Data	
							Type of Statement		
	3	2	18	15		3	Unqualified	47	55
	30	51	89	16	1		Reviewed	184	224
	16	84	51	7			Compiled	184	198
	11	16	4	1			Tax Returns	26	25
		40	64	27	3		Other	120	156
		155 (4/1-9/30/02)		397 (10/1/02-3/31/03)				4/1/98-3/31/99	4/1/99-3/31/00
	0-500M	500M-2MM	2-10MM	10-50MM	50-100MM	100-250MM		ALL	ALL
	60	193	226	66	4	3	**NUMBER OF STATEMENTS**	561	658
	%	%	%	%	%	%	**ASSETS**	%	%
	8.0	7.5	6.5	5.3			Cash & Equivalents	8.1	7.5
	29.6	26.4	28.3	25.5			Trade Receivables (net)	26.8	27.7
	9.9	15.3	17.1	16.4			Inventory	14.6	14.9
	2.3	2.8	4.1	5.3			All Other Current	2.2	2.8
	49.7	52.0	56.0	52.5			Total Current	51.7	52.9
	43.5	39.1	36.8	35.4			Fixed Assets (net)	40.4	39.4
	2.3	1.8	2.0	4.7			Intangibles (net)	2.0	2.4
	4.5	7.1	5.2	7.4			All Other Non-Current	5.9	5.3
	100.0	100.0	100.0	100.0			Total	100.0	100.0
							LIABILITIES		
	26.3	13.5	12.9	12.8			Notes Payable-Short Term	10.0	10.8
	13.1	8.0	6.5	5.3			Cur. Mat.-L/T/D	6.4	6.6
	12.7	10.4	10.4	10.9			Trade Payables	9.7	9.9
	.1	.1	.1	.3			Income Taxes Payable	.3	.3
	12.7	10.8	9.6	8.6			All Other Current	10.2	10.3
	64.9	42.8	39.6	38.0			Total Current	36.6	37.9
	30.2	22.4	17.3	17.9			Long Term Debt	21.7	21.4
	.2	.5	.9	.4			Deferred Taxes	.7	.7
	17.6	6.3	4.7	2.5			All Other Non-Current	4.8	3.7
	–13.0	28.0	37.6	41.2			Net Worth	36.2	36.3
	100.0	100.0	100.0	100.0			Total Liabilities & Net Worth	100.0	100.0
							INCOME DATA		
	100.0	100.0	100.0	100.0			Net Sales	100.0	100.0
	42.6	30.3	24.2	23.9			Gross Profit	30.7	29.6
	43.7	31.3	21.6	18.1			Operating Expenses	25.0	24.5
	–1.1	–1.0	2.6	5.8			Operating Profit	5.7	5.0
	2.0	1.9	1.8	1.9			All Other Expenses (net)	1.5	1.8
	–3.1	–2.9	.8	3.9			Profit Before Taxes	4.2	3.2
							RATIOS		
	2.2	2.4	2.3	2.3				2.2	2.3
	.8	1.2	1.4	1.4			Current	1.4	1.4
	.4	.8	1.0	1.0				1.0	1.0
	1.6	1.6	1.5	1.3				1.5	1.6
	.6	.8	.8	.8			Quick	.9	.9
	.3	.5	.6	.5				.6	.6
	23 15.6	36 10.2	43 8.4	47 7.8				36 10.2	38 9.5
	45 8.1	49 7.5	57 6.4	64 5.7			Sales/Receivables	47 7.7	50 7.2
	59 6.2	64 5.7	82 4.5	78 4.7				63 5.8	68 5.4
	6 57.8	12 30.1	21 17.6	25 14.4				16 23.4	15 24.2
	17 22.0	29 12.8	40 9.1	49 7.5			Cost of Sales/Inventory	34 10.8	35 10.5
	37 9.7	62 5.9	71 5.1	80 4.6				57 6.4	59 6.2
	12 30.8	11 32.3	14 25.6	19 19.3				12 31.7	13 28.7
	29 12.7	21 17.6	26 13.9	29 12.6			Cost of Sales/Payables	21 17.5	23 15.6
	50 7.2	45 8.1	41 8.9	49 7.5				37 9.9	38 9.6
	10.2	6.5	5.2	5.4				6.7	6.0
	–17.3	18.9	9.9	10.5			Sales/Working Capital	13.8	13.5
	–4.9	–27.7	–100.1	NM				134.5	324.7
	2.3	2.1	4.6	7.4				7.1	6.3
(56)	.3	(181) .8	(216) 2.0	(63) 2.4			EBIT/Interest	(529) 2.9	(616) 2.5
	–3.3	–2.2	–.7	1.0				1.4	.9
		2.0	2.6	2.1				3.3	3.4
		(59) 1.1	(81) 1.7	(16) 1.5			Net Profit + Depr., Dep., Amort./Cur. Mat. L /T/D	(226) 1.9	(211) 1.8
		–.3	.7	.9				1.1	.9
	.8	.5	.6	.5				.6	.6
	3.2	1.5	1.0	1.0			Fixed/Worth	1.1	1.2
	–1.4	7.5	2.3	2.6				2.4	2.4
	.8	.8	.8	.7				.9	.8
	21.5	2.3	1.9	1.9			Debt/Worth	1.8	1.8
	–3.2	14.3	4.2	5.5				3.8	4.7
	20.4	13.9	26.7	29.5				40.7	40.0
(34)	5.8	(153) –1.3	(207) 10.8	(63) 12.3			% Profit Before Taxes/Tangible Net Worth	(514) 20.6	(598) 17.6
	–30.7	–29.4	–4.3	.7				5.7	1.4
	4.9	4.5	8.2	10.1				14.4	14.4
	–1.6	–.8	3.6	5.0			% Profit Before Taxes/Total Assets	6.2	5.8
	–24.5	–11.4	–4.1	.1				1.5	.0
	11.5	10.3	7.7	7.7				7.9	7.9
	6.8	5.6	4.6	4.0			Sales/Net Fixed Assets	5.0	4.7
	3.7	2.9	2.9	2.5				3.2	3.1
	3.6	2.4	2.1	1.7				2.4	2.3
	2.5	1.8	1.6	1.2			Sales/Total Assets	1.9	1.8
	1.8	1.4	1.2	.9				1.4	1.3
	3.4	3.3	3.2	3.2				2.8	2.7
(55)	5.6	(189) 5.3	(217) 4.8	(62) 4.7			% Depr., Dep., Amort./Sales	(536) 4.5	(625) 4.6
	9.2	8.7	7.2	7.0				6.8	6.8
	6.8	3.9	2.2	1.2				3.2	3.0
(43)	12.5	(137) 6.5	(119) 3.9	(20) 1.9			% Officers', Directors', Owners' Comp/Sales	(327) 5.7	(368) 5.7
	17.7	10.4						9.3	9.3
	43657M	426763M	1642648M	1675814M	352563M	546462M	Net Sales ($)	5292837M	5733847M
	16954M	222984M	977735M	1288891M	269139M	556259M	Total Assets ($)	3202862M	3675577M

© RMA 2003

M = $ thousand   MM = $ million
See Pages 11 through 18 for Explanation of Ratios and Data

Comparative Historical Data | Current Data Sorted By Sales

Hist 1	Hist 2	Hist 3	Type of Statement	0-1MM	1-3MM	3-5MM	5-10MM	10-25MM	25MM & OVER
36	36	38	Unqualified		2	4	11	9	12
186	167	160	Reviewed	7	39	36	51	19	8
200	156	172	Compiled	32	75	27	21	14	3
35	20	37	Tax Returns	18	12	3	4		
147	176	145	Other	8	35	26	32	28	16
4/1/00-3/31/01 ALL	4/1/01-3/31/02 ALL	4/1/02-3/31/03 ALL		155 (4/1-9/30/02)			397 (10/1/02-3/31/03)		
604	555	552	**NUMBER OF STATEMENTS**	65	163	96	119	70	39
%	%	%	**ASSETS**	%	%	%	%	%	%
6.7	6.8	6.8	Cash & Equivalents	6.2	7.4	9.2	6.2	4.9	4.5
28.2	26.3	27.4	Trade Receivables (net)	22.2	27.0	28.6	29.1	29.3	26.1
14.9	14.3	15.5	Inventory	10.4	13.7	17.6	17.3	17.2	17.5
2.8	3.3	3.6	All Other Current	3.3	3.9	3.1	3.7	3.2	4.2
52.6	50.7	53.3	Total Current	42.1	52.0	58.6	56.3	54.6	52.3
39.9	41.1	38.3	Fixed Assets (net)	47.9	39.3	34.7	36.5	36.1	36.5
2.7	2.5	2.4	Intangibles (net)	1.9	2.5	1.2	2.0	2.7	6.5
4.9	5.7	6.0	All Other Non-Current	8.1	6.2	5.5	5.1	6.7	4.8
100.0	100.0	100.0	Total	100.0	100.0	100.0	100.0	100.0	100.0
			LIABILITIES						
12.3	13.4	14.5	Notes Payable-Short Term	24.4	14.6	11.2	13.5	13.9	10.4
6.6	7.5	7.6	Cur. Mat.-L/T/D	12.0	8.0	7.9	6.3	6.0	4.8
11.1	9.7	10.7	Trade Payables	10.2	10.3	9.8	11.2	11.1	13.3
.2	.1	.2	Income Taxes Payable	.1	.2	.1	.2	.1	.6
10.2	8.5	10.2	All Other Current	11.9	11.9	8.7	9.3	8.8	8.9
40.4	39.2	43.2	Total Current	58.6	45.0	37.8	40.3	39.8	38.0
22.0	24.0	20.6	Long Term Debt	28.7	21.8	19.9	19.1	15.6	16.5
.7	.6	.6	Deferred Taxes	.3	.5	.7	.8	.7	.8
4.1	4.8	6.4	All Other Non-Current	14.4	6.2	6.1	4.3	4.1	2.4
32.9	31.5	29.2	Net Worth	-2.0	25.7	35.5	35.4	39.8	42.3
100.0	100.0	100.0	Total Liabilities & Net Worth	100.0	100.0	100.0	100.0	100.0	100.0
			INCOME DATA						
100.0	100.0	100.0	Net Sales	100.0	100.0	100.0	100.0	100.0	100.0
29.8	28.0	28.3	Gross Profit	42.8	30.1	27.2	25.1	20.1	23.4
25.0	25.8	26.9	Operating Expenses	45.7	30.0	25.6	23.0	16.3	16.3
4.8	2.2	1.4	Operating Profit	-2.9	.1	1.6	2.0	3.8	7.1
2.2	2.3	1.9	All Other Expenses (net)	2.4	1.9	1.9	1.7	1.6	1.8
2.7	-.1	-.5	Profit Before Taxes	-5.3	-1.8	-.2	.3	2.2	5.3
			RATIOS						
2.0	2.2	2.3	Current	1.4	2.3	2.7	2.4	1.9	2.1
1.3	1.3	1.3		.7	1.2	1.6	1.4	1.3	1.4
1.0	.9	.9		.4	.9	1.1	.9	1.0	1.0
1.4	1.5	1.5	Quick	.9	1.6	1.9	1.4	1.4	1.3
.8	.8	.8		.4	.9	1.0	.8	.8	.8
.6	.5	.5		.2	.5	.6	.6	.5	.5
38 9.5	37 9.9	40 9.2	Sales/Receivables	23 15.6	39 9.3	37 9.8	42 8.7	46 8.0	44 8.2
51 7.2	50 7.2	54 6.8		42 8.7	54 6.8	52 7.0	54 6.7	64 5.7	55 6.7
69 5.3	69 5.3	73 5.0		60 6.1	71 5.2	79 4.6	73 5.0	81 4.5	71 5.1
13 28.5	11 32.4	15 25.0	Cost of Sales/Inventory	6 61.5	12 31.1	21 17.4	22 16.9	18 20.2	30 12.0
32 11.3	31 11.9	35 10.5		20 17.9	26 14.3	45 8.1	36 10.2	40 9.2	48 7.7
57 6.4	56 6.5	65 5.7		51 7.2	56 6.5	66 5.5	71 5.1	67 5.4	77 4.7
14 26.5	12 29.7	13 27.8	Cost of Sales/Payables	9 42.9	11 31.8	11 32.0	15 24.9	19 19.5	18 20.8
23 15.6	22 16.6	26 14.0		29 12.4	26 16.3	21 17.4	27 13.4	29 12.7	28 12.9
41 9.0	35 10.5	44 8.3		53 6.9	46 8.0	41 8.8	42 8.8	39 9.4	52 7.0
7.1	6.3	5.8	Sales/Working Capital	25.0	6.2	5.1	5.4	6.7	6.1
16.3	15.7	14.9		-13.3	16.3	7.7	13.8	12.0	9.8
-117.2	-44.3	-30.4		-4.8	-30.3	61.9	-64.6	NM	999.8
(578) 5.2	(538) 3.7	(523) 3.6	EBIT/Interest	(60) 1.6	(155) 2.6	(91) 3.5	(113) 3.9	(65) 5.9	11.1
2.3	1.4	1.4		-.2	1.0	1.5	2.0	2.4	3.5
.6	-.7	-1.1		-3.8	-1.6	-1.4	-.9	.7	1.3
(184) 3.5	(163) 2.2	(165) 2.5	Net Profit + Depr., Dep., Amort./Cur. Mat. L/T/D		(46) 2.0	(35) 2.4	(41) 3.2	(23) 2.6	(12) 2.3
1.6	1.1	1.4			1.1	1.5	1.7	1.8	1.3
.9	.2	.3			.1	-.4	.7	.6	1.0
.6	.6	.6	Fixed/Worth	.7	.6	.5	.7	.5	.6
1.3	1.3	1.2		3.1	1.4	.9	1.1	1.0	.8
3.0	3.5	3.8		-3.7	6.0	2.5	3.3	1.8	1.8
.9	.9	.8	Debt/Worth	.8	.8	.7	.8	.8	.6
2.0	2.2	2.0		7.6	2.4	1.6	2.0	1.9	1.9
5.7	6.3	8.6		-5.6	14.7	4.2	6.3	3.7	3.9
(527) 38.2	(480) 27.6	(464) 24.5	% Profit Before Taxes/Tangible Net Worth	(40) 8.6	(130) 15.3	(84) 25.3	(105) 25.8	(68) 24.7	(37) 35.5
16.0	6.8	6.7		-2.0	.7	7.2	11.4	11.1	23.7
.8	-15.3	-13.3		-40.8	-22.9	-14.0	-5.4	.1	1.9
11.8	8.4	7.2	% Profit Before Taxes/Total Assets	3.6	5.6	7.3	7.9	8.4	13.7
4.7	1.5	1.7		-4.6	.0	1.7	3.6	3.7	6.5
-1.4	-6.8	-7.0		-19.7	-9.3	-7.6	-6.2	-.1	.7
8.3	7.6	9.2	Sales/Net Fixed Assets	8.8	9.8	11.2	8.9	6.8	7.8
4.5	4.5	4.8		4.3	4.3	5.9	4.8	4.6	4.3
3.0	2.8	2.8		1.8	2.8	3.2	3.0	3.3	2.8
2.4	2.4	2.2	Sales/Total Assets	2.9	2.2	2.4	2.2	2.2	2.0
1.8	1.8	1.7		1.8	1.7	1.8	1.7	1.6	1.6
1.4	1.3	1.2		1.0	1.3	1.3	1.3	1.2	1.1
(576) 2.8	(536) 3.1	(529) 3.3	% Depr., Dep., Amort./Sales	(61) 4.5	(159) 3.4	(91) 3.3	(117) 3.0	(64) 2.8	(37) 2.9
4.6	5.1	5.0		7.7	5.8	4.4	4.8	4.5	4.4
6.8	7.6	7.6		11.8	8.8	7.1	6.5	6.6	6.0
(347) 3.2	(288) 3.1	(319) 2.9	% Officers', Directors', Owners' Comp/Sales	(45) 7.5	(114) 4.2	(60) 2.9	(64) 2.3	(30) 1.3	
5.6	5.1	5.3		11.9	6.2	5.1	3.7	2.0	
9.8	9.8	9.8		18.1	10.0	8.5	6.0	3.9	
5764631M	4896411M	4687907M	Net Sales ($)	37959M	306520M	379058M	837126M	1058014M	2069230M
3728551M	3203840M	3331962M	Total Assets ($)	26558M	196345M	239841M	530834M	763314M	1575070M

M = $ thousand   MM = $ million
See Pages 11 through 18 for Explanation of Ratios and Data

Current Data Sorted By Assets   Comparative Historical Data

0-500M	500M-2MM	2-10MM	10-50MM	50-100MM	100-250MM		4/1/98-3/31/99 ALL	4/1/99-3/31/00 ALL
						Type of Statement		
2	2	5	3	3	1	Unqualified	23	20
6	14	22	4			Reviewed	41	43
2	22	7	1			Compiled	41	41
	7	3				Tax Returns	5	8
3	14	20	9	3	2	Other	33	34
		37 (4/1-9/30/02)		118 (10/1/02-3/31/03)				
13	59	57	17	6	3	**NUMBER OF STATEMENTS**	143	146
%	%	%	%	%	%	**ASSETS**	%	%
6.4	7.3	10.5	4.7			Cash & Equivalents	8.6	8.6
29.7	32.2	21.9	17.3			Trade Receivables (net)	26.3	26.0
13.3	21.7	25.5	27.2			Inventory	22.0	23.3
.8	2.0	3.3	1.9			All Other Current	2.1	1.7
50.2	63.2	61.3	51.2			Total Current	59.0	59.7
46.7	30.4	29.9	34.1			Fixed Assets (net)	31.2	31.7
.1	1.9	2.8	10.6			Intangibles (net)	1.5	1.5
3.0	4.6	6.0	4.2			All Other Non-Current	8.3	7.0
100.0	100.0	100.0	100.0			Total	100.0	100.0
						LIABILITIES		
21.8	10.1	11.2	4.7			Notes Payable-Short Term	7.6	10.1
2.3	8.4	6.7	4.0			Cur. Mat.-L/T/D	5.6	5.2
9.4	12.7	8.8	8.0			Trade Payables	11.0	10.2
.1	.2	.1	.2			Income Taxes Payable	.3	.2
9.6	8.0	6.0	9.0			All Other Current	8.4	7.7
43.2	39.5	32.8	25.9			Total Current	32.9	33.4
14.3	19.8	13.9	12.9			Long Term Debt	18.9	19.8
.2	.3	.7	.9			Deferred Taxes	.7	.6
10.2	7.0	2.4	4.6			All Other Non-Current	4.8	4.6
32.2	33.5	50.1	55.7			Net Worth	42.7	41.6
100.0	100.0	100.0	100.0			Total Liabilities & Net Worth	100.0	100.0
						INCOME DATA		
100.0	100.0	100.0	100.0			Net Sales	100.0	100.0
53.6	34.3	31.6	31.0			Gross Profit	33.7	34.4
51.6	33.3	29.4	28.1			Operating Expenses	26.7	29.0
2.0	1.0	2.2	2.9			Operating Profit	7.0	5.4
1.6	1.3	1.0	1.5			All Other Expenses (net)	1.3	.9
.4	-.3	1.2	1.4			Profit Before Taxes	5.7	4.5
						RATIOS		
3.5	2.8	3.2	3.1				3.2	3.1
1.3	1.9	1.8	2.1			Current	1.9	1.8
.8	1.1	1.3	1.5				1.3	1.2
3.2	1.9	2.3	1.5				2.2	2.0
.9	1.0	.8	.8			Quick	1.1	1.0
.6	.6	.6	.5				.6	.7
27 13.5	43 8.5	41 8.9	39 9.3				37 9.7	39 9.3
44 8.3	56 6.5	49 7.4	45 8.1			Sales/Receivables	48 7.7	50 7.3
55 6.6	69 5.3	66 5.5	51 7.1				61 6.0	61 6.0
0 UND	10 36.1	36 10.0	51 7.2				21 17.1	31 11.9
23 15.7	42 8.6	82 4.4	114 3.2			Cost of Sales/Inventory	61 6.0	64 5.7
47 7.8	97 3.8	157 2.3	150 2.4				108 3.4	118 3.1
0 UND	16 22.5	15 23.9	17 21.0				15 24.0	16 23.1
14 25.2	31 11.8	24 14.9	19 19.6			Cost of Sales/Payables	25 14.3	25 14.8
38 9.5	42 8.7	46 8.0	33 11.0				43 8.4	40 9.1
7.2	4.7	3.0	3.2				4.4	4.0
17.3	8.3	5.8	6.7			Sales/Working Capital	7.3	7.4
NM	38.3	12.0	8.4				17.3	19.7
(10) 4.3	(56) 4.2	(51) 5.8	(14) 8.4				(127) 10.4	(130) 8.7
.1	1.5	2.0	3.9			EBIT/Interest	3.7	3.0
-4.8	-.6	.7	-1.4				1.3	1.0
	(22) 2.2	(13) 2.6					(59) 3.1	(44) 3.2
	1.5	.4				Net Profit + Depr., Dep., Amort./Cur. Mat. L/T/D	1.9	1.8
	.4	-.4					1.1	1.1
.9	.3	.3	.3				.3	.3
1.2	.9	.6	.7			Fixed/Worth	.7	.7
4.8	6.0	1.2	1.3				1.6	1.6
.8	.7	.4	.4				.5	.7
2.0	2.2	1.2	1.0			Debt/Worth	1.3	1.3
10.5	8.7	2.4	1.7				2.8	3.7
(11) 19.1	(50) 14.8	(55) 23.1	13.3				(132) 42.0	(134) 39.6
-5.5	6.6	4.6	7.6			% Profit Before Taxes/Tangible Net Worth	24.7	17.1
-26.0	-12.8	-2.9	-4.3				5.7	1.5
8.1	7.7	7.9	7.1				16.6	16.4
-4.8	1.6	2.0	3.0			% Profit Before Taxes/Total Assets	8.4	5.8
-18.6	-4.6	-3.0	-1.9				1.4	-.4
31.7	16.8	12.2	7.5				14.4	11.1
8.1	7.0	4.6	4.2			Sales/Net Fixed Assets	5.8	6.1
2.7	4.3	2.7	2.9				3.8	3.8
3.6	2.5	1.7	1.6				2.5	2.5
2.7	2.1	1.3	1.5			Sales/Total Assets	1.9	1.8
1.7	1.7	1.0	1.0				1.3	1.3
(12) 1.6	(55) 1.9	(53) 2.3	(13) 2.9				(125) 1.9	(128) 2.0
2.3	2.8	4.2	4.1			% Depr., Dep., Amort./Sales	3.3	3.5
7.6	5.5	6.1	6.8				5.3	5.5
	(34) 3.6	(25) 3.0					(72) 3.4	(66) 3.8
	7.2	6.7				% Officers', Directors', Owners' Comp/Sales	5.3	6.4
	9.9	9.6					8.4	10.1
9263M	162838M	358907M	483244M	614380M	1737523M	Net Sales ($)	1969725M	1983006M
3825M	70370M	263307M	349115M	436186M	572334M	Total Assets ($)	1330574M	1216411M

M = $ thousand   MM = $ million
See Pages 11 through 18 for Explanation of Ratios and Data

Comparative Historical Data / Current Data Sorted By Sales

				Type of Statement						
	17	10	14	Unqualified		2	2	1	3	6
	53	42	42	Reviewed	1	14	9	13	3	2
	39	39	36	Compiled	5	19	6	5	1	
	9	7	12	Tax Returns	3	5	4			
	30	46	51	Other	3	10	11	8	10	9
	4/1/00-3/31/01	4/1/01-3/31/02	4/1/02-3/31/03			37 (4/1-9/30/02)		118 (10/1/02-3/31/03)		
	ALL	ALL	ALL		0-1MM	1-3MM	3-5MM	5-10MM	10-25MM	25MM & OVER
	148	144	155	**NUMBER OF STATEMENTS**	12	50	32	27	17	17
	%	%	%	**ASSETS**	%	%	%	%	%	%
	8.2	8.7	7.8	Cash & Equivalents	5.9	8.9	11.2	5.8	6.5	3.6
	27.7	25.0	26.1	Trade Receivables (net)	23.7	30.4	26.5	24.1	22.4	21.1
	23.4	23.7	23.0	Inventory	19.6	18.5	24.5	24.9	35.1	20.6
	1.0	1.6	2.4	All Other Current	.6	1.7	3.0	3.7	3.2	1.7
	60.3	59.1	59.2	Total Current	49.7	59.5	65.2	58.5	67.2	47.0
	30.2	30.2	31.6	Fixed Assets (net)	47.8	33.7	25.9	31.8	22.4	33.3
	2.3	3.1	4.2	Intangibles (net)	.1	1.4	3.1	4.5	6.6	14.5
	7.1	7.6	5.0	All Other Non-Current	2.5	5.5	5.8	5.1	3.7	5.3
	100.0	100.0	100.0	Total	100.0	100.0	100.0	100.0	100.0	100.0
				LIABILITIES						
	11.1	8.7	10.6	Notes Payable-Short Term	23.5	10.3	9.5	12.3	7.4	4.9
	6.0	6.0	6.5	Cur. Mat.-L/T/D	1.0	9.5	6.5	6.4	4.0	4.4
	10.1	11.9	10.4	Trade Payables	8.2	10.5	10.0	10.5	13.1	9.5
	.2	.1	.1	Income Taxes Payable	.1	.1	.1	.4	.0	.2
	8.7	8.8	7.8	All Other Current	9.5	6.2	5.2	7.4	12.2	12.3
	36.1	35.5	35.4	Total Current	42.3	36.6	31.3	37.0	36.8	31.3
	19.6	18.3	16.2	Long Term Debt	20.4	17.3	16.4	14.7	11.6	16.6
	.6	.6	.5	Deferred Taxes	.0	.4	.2	1.0	1.4	.4
	5.0	3.9	6.1	All Other Non-Current	8.8	7.9	3.4	2.4	2.8	13.0
	38.6	41.6	41.7	Net Worth	28.5	37.8	48.7	44.9	47.4	38.6
	100.0	100.0	100.0	Total Liabilities & Net Worth	100.0	100.0	100.0	100.0	100.0	100.0
				INCOME DATA						
	100.0	100.0	100.0	Net Sales	100.0	100.0	100.0	100.0	100.0	100.0
	35.2	34.3	34.5	Gross Profit	52.9	36.5	33.2	28.3	30.4	31.6
	30.9	33.0	32.5	Operating Expenses	51.5	35.8	31.2	27.0	26.3	26.9
	4.4	1.3	1.9	Operating Profit	1.4	.6	2.0	1.4	4.1	4.7
	1.8	1.2	1.5	All Other Expenses (net)	1.8	1.1	.7	1.5	1.8	3.7
	2.5	.1	.4	Profit Before Taxes	−.4	−.5	1.3	−.1	2.3	1.1
				RATIOS						
	2.9	2.8	3.0		3.5	3.2	4.6	2.3	4.0	2.5
	1.7	1.8	1.7	Current	1.7	1.7	2.3	1.7	1.9	1.5
	1.2	1.1	1.2		.6	1.1	1.4	1.2	1.3	1.1
	1.8	1.6	1.8		3.3	2.0	3.2	1.3	1.5	1.3
	.9	1.0	.9	Quick	.7	1.0	1.5	.7	.7	.7
	.6	.6	.6		.3	.6	.6	.5	.5	.5
	40 9.2	37 10.0	41 8.9	Sales/Receivables	26 14.3	44 8.3	43 8.5	39 9.5	39 9.3	42 8.7
	51 7.1	48 7.6	49 7.4		40 9.2	57 6.4	53 6.9	47 7.8	46 8.0	53 6.8
	65 5.6	59 6.2	66 5.6		51 7.2	69 5.3	70 5.2	61 6.0	67 5.5	58 6.3
	30 12.1	25 14.4	24 15.2	Cost of Sales/Inventory	0 UND	9 39.7	52 7.1	20 18.1	62 5.8	37 9.9
	69 5.3	72 5.1	64 5.7		30 12.4	27 13.7	73 5.0	61 6.0	121 3.0	79 4.6
	115 3.2	108 3.4	121 3.0		108 3.4	109 3.3	150 2.4	123 3.0	177 2.1	105 3.5
	15 25.0	16 23.4	15 23.8	Cost of Sales/Payables	0 UND	15 24.9	15 24.6	17 21.2	17 21.0	18 20.2
	27 13.4	26 14.3	25 14.3		11 34.7	26 14.2	22 16.7	30 12.3	29 12.4	27 13.6
	41 8.9	41 8.9	42 8.7		42 8.8	46 7.9	39 9.4	42 8.7	49 7.4	41 9.0
	4.0	3.9	4.3	Sales/Working Capital	5.2	4.6	2.9	5.0	2.6	6.1
	7.9	7.3	7.7		10.8	8.9	4.9	8.8	5.4	23.3
	23.1	41.1	25.2		−15.6	41.8	8.0	21.8	11.0	37.9
	5.2	3.4	4.8	EBIT/Interest		3.8	6.7	5.2	6.4	7.6
(133)	1.8	(130) 1.1	(140) 1.6		(46) 1.3	(29) 1.8	(26) 1.8	(14) 2.3	(16) 1.5	
	.8	−1.3	−.6		−.9	−.6	.1	−.8	−.1	
	3.0	1.5	2.3	Net Profit + Depr., Dep., Amort./Cur. Mat. L/T/D		2.0				
(49)	1.3	(38) .4	(44) 1.1		(20) 1.1					
	.7	−.1	.1		.4					
	.3	.3	.3	Fixed/Worth	.6	.3	.3	.3	.2	.7
	.7	.7	.8		1.4	.9	.5	.8	.5	1.1
	2.2	1.7	1.7		NM	4.2	1.1	1.4	1.3	3.9
	.6	.6	.6	Debt/Worth	.3	.7	.3	.6	.4	.8
	1.3	1.3	1.4		4.0	1.8	.7	1.5	1.4	2.4
	5.6	3.8	4.8		NM	6.1	3.9	2.4	2.4	12.4
	31.4	19.3	18.2	% Profit Before Taxes/Tangible Net Worth		14.6	20.2	20.5	25.3	16.6
(132)	10.7	(130) 1.7	(140) 4.9		(45) 5.2	(30) 5.3	(26) 3.5	(15) 10.1	(15) 7.6	
	−1.2	−21.3	−12.8		−22.7	−7.7	−7.0	.1	−23.3	
	10.5	6.1	6.8	% Profit Before Taxes/Total Assets	11.3	7.7	6.3	4.1	10.0	7.1
	3.1	.1	1.7		−.7	1.1	2.8	1.8	2.1	2.1
	−2.4	−7.8	−4.8		−23.3	−5.8	−4.2	−1.7	−2.9	−6.7
	11.9	12.5	12.8	Sales/Net Fixed Assets	32.2	11.9	13.5	11.7	24.6	8.9
	6.7	6.3	5.9		6.3	5.7	5.6	5.9	8.4	3.9
	3.8	3.6	3.3		1.6	3.8	2.6	3.1	4.4	2.7
	2.3	2.6	2.3	Sales/Total Assets	3.2	2.4	2.1	2.3	1.7	2.1
	1.7	1.8	1.7		2.4	2.0	1.5	1.7	1.6	1.3
	1.3	1.3	1.1		1.2	1.5	1.0	1.1	1.3	1.0
	1.9	1.7	2.0	% Depr., Dep., Amort./Sales	1.7	2.1	1.9	1.0	2.0	3.7
(133)	3.4	(128) 3.6	(138) 3.8		(11) 2.3	(46) 4.0	(30) 3.6	(25) 3.8	(15) 3.0	(11) 6.4
	5.2	6.2	6.3		8.3	6.3	6.1	5.8	5.6	6.9
	4.4	4.2	3.6	% Officers', Directors', Owners' Comp/Sales		6.0	3.0			
(68)	7.2	(61) 6.7	(70) 7.4		(28) 7.6	(19) 5.4				
	11.1	10.9	10.5			11.5	9.0			
	1857369M	1153028M	3366155M	Net Sales ($)	7447M	102080M	127831M	192606M	256163M	2680028M
	1426715M	835585M	1695137M	Total Assets ($)	3827M	59532M	102329M	137129M	175993M	1216327M

Current Data Sorted By Assets   Comparative Historical Data

0-500M	500M-2MM	2-10MM	10-50MM	50-100MM	100-250MM	Type of Statement	4/1/98-3/31/99 ALL	4/1/99-3/31/00 ALL
		2	2	2	1	Unqualified	11	9
	3	12	1			Reviewed	20	14
3	5	5				Compiled	9	6
1	1	1				Tax Returns	3	4
1	3	5	2			Other	9	22
	12 (4/1-9/30/02)		38 (10/1/02-3/31/03)					
5	12	25	5	2	1	**NUMBER OF STATEMENTS**	52	55
%	%	%	%	%	%		%	%
						ASSETS		
	11.2	10.7				Cash & Equivalents	7.7	8.5
	32.9	25.9				Trade Receivables (net)	30.1	26.5
	11.7	25.7				Inventory	21.9	21.2
	10.6	5.0				All Other Current	7.0	5.1
	66.4	67.3				Total Current	66.8	61.3
	28.7	28.1				Fixed Assets (net)	23.4	30.0
	1.3	.5				Intangibles (net)	4.1	2.8
	3.6	4.1				All Other Non-Current	5.7	5.9
	100.0	100.0				Total	100.0	100.0
						LIABILITIES		
	24.8	14.3				Notes Payable-Short Term	14.5	18.0
	3.3	5.8				Cur. Mat.-L/T/D	2.3	3.3
	17.5	9.2				Trade Payables	17.3	14.1
	.5	.0				Income Taxes Payable	.1	.2
	12.9	15.2				All Other Current	15.2	14.9
	59.0	44.6				Total Current	49.4	50.6
	20.5	14.2				Long Term Debt	13.9	21.4
	.0	.0				Deferred Taxes	.3	.5
	7.3	5.8				All Other Non-Current	4.6	3.8
	13.2	35.3				Net Worth	31.8	23.8
	100.0	100.0				Total Liabilities & Net Worth	100.0	100.0
						INCOME DATA		
	100.0	100.0				Net Sales	100.0	100.0
	38.9	30.4				Gross Profit	26.8	31.3
	38.8	29.1				Operating Expenses	23.8	27.6
	.1	1.4				Operating Profit	3.0	3.6
	2.5	1.8				All Other Expenses (net)	1.8	2.6
	−2.4	−.5				Profit Before Taxes	1.2	1.1
						RATIOS		
	1.8	3.7				Current	1.8	1.8
	1.3	1.5					1.4	1.3
	.9	1.1					1.1	1.0
	1.4	1.5				Quick	1.2	1.3
	.8	.8					.7	.7
	.3	.5					.5	.5
	31 11.7	36 10.0				Sales/Receivables	47 7.7	33 11.0
	47 7.8	52 7.0					59 6.1	53 6.9
	81 4.5	70 5.2					82 4.5	71 5.1
	1 461.6	54 6.8				Cost of Sales/Inventory	20 18.6	19 19.6
	15 24.0	77 4.7					61 5.9	51 7.1
	61 5.9	133 2.7					115 3.2	114 3.2
	26 14.0	13 27.6				Cost of Sales/Payables	17 22.0	17 21.2
	45 8.1	21 17.4					38 9.7	32 11.3
	58 6.3	45 8.1					69 5.3	52 7.0
	8.4	3.9				Sales/Working Capital	5.0	6.5
	18.1	6.6					11.2	10.1
	−33.2	29.6					31.2	66.3
	2.6	4.3				EBIT/Interest	8.5	4.2
	(10) 1.9	(22) .7					(44) 2.4	(51) 2.0
	−.4	−3.2					.5	.8
						Net Profit + Depr., Dep., Amort./Cur. Mat. L /T/D	(16) 3.5	(20) 13.6
							.8	2.9
							−1.5	−.9
	.3	.6				Fixed/Worth	.2	.5
	2.0	.8					.6	1.0
	NM	2.7					2.6	8.3
	1.3	.8				Debt/Worth	.9	1.6
	3.6	1.9					2.8	3.7
	NM	6.0					8.0	22.0
		22.2				% Profit Before Taxes/Tangible Net Worth	44.0	39.6
		(22) −1.2					(47) 8.7	(45) 15.3
		−36.5					−8.2	2.9
	3.2	7.4				% Profit Before Taxes/Total Assets	8.5	12.8
	1.8	−.5					2.6	3.9
	−3.9	−7.2					−2.4	−.3
	99.4	16.9				Sales/Net Fixed Assets	34.7	18.1
	8.2	6.9					11.6	6.6
	3.5	3.2					4.5	3.3
	2.6	2.0				Sales/Total Assets	2.6	2.3
	1.8	1.6					1.7	1.8
	1.4	1.3					1.2	1.2
	.5	1.4				% Depr., Dep., Amort./Sales	1.1	1.3
	1.7	(23) 2.6					(46) 1.8	(51) 2.0
	7.1	5.7					3.6	5.3
		1.8				% Officers', Directors', Owners' Comp/Sales	4.1	4.1
		(11) 2.7					(13) 9.4	(24) 7.6
		4.8					10.0	11.4
5025M	31480M	159434M	77701M	257886M	280174M	Net Sales ($)	861703M	712158M
1622M	16707M	96096M	77485M	185117M	187635M	Total Assets ($)	636394M	534367M

© RMA 2003

M = $ thousand   MM = $ million
See Pages 11 through 18 for Explanation of Ratios and Data

Comparative Historical Data | Current Data Sorted By Sales

Comparative Historical Data periods: 4/1/00-3/31/01 ALL, 4/1/01-3/31/02 ALL, 4/1/02-3/31/03 ALL
Current Data grouping: **12 (4/1-9/30/02)** covers 0-1MM, 1-3MM, 3-5MM · **38 (10/1/02-3/31/03)** covers 5-10MM, 10-25MM, 25MM & OVER

4/1/00-3/31/01 ALL	4/1/01-3/31/02 ALL	4/1/02-3/31/03 ALL		0-1MM	1-3MM	3-5MM	5-10MM	10-25MM	25MM & OVER
			Type of Statement						
11	6	7	Unqualified		4	6	3	3	4
14	17	16	Reviewed	3	5	4		3	1
10	9	13	Compiled		1	2		1	
1	2	3	Tax Returns			2			
20	17	11	Other	1	4	2	3	1	
56	51	50	**NUMBER OF STATEMENTS**	4	14	14	6	8	4
%	%	%	**ASSETS**	%	%	%	%	%	%
7.9	9.5	12.5	Cash & Equivalents		13.3	6.7			
27.5	24.1	26.7	Trade Receivables (net)		27.4	26.0			
22.3	22.9	20.0	Inventory		17.1	24.2			
5.8	5.0	6.1	All Other Current		9.6	4.1			
63.6	61.6	65.3	Total Current		67.3	61.0			
27.0	30.1	29.9	Fixed Assets (net)		28.7	33.6			
4.0	3.6	.8	Intangibles (net)		1.5	.5			
5.4	4.8	4.0	All Other Non-Current		2.5	4.9			
100.0	100.0	100.0	Total		100.0	100.0			
			LIABILITIES						
15.2	14.0	16.1	Notes Payable-Short Term		22.8	9.6			
3.2	4.7	4.3	Cur. Mat.-L/T/D		5.4	6.7			
12.8	11.2	11.1	Trade Payables		14.4	8.8			
.8	.1	.2	Income Taxes Payable		.4	.0			
24.1	12.0	14.3	All Other Current		12.3	10.8			
56.0	41.9	46.0	Total Current		55.3	35.9			
16.3	24.8	18.6	Long Term Debt		23.1	21.4			
.6	.1	.1	Deferred Taxes		.1	.0			
5.8	8.2	7.1	All Other Non-Current		6.1	2.3			
21.3	25.0	28.2	Net Worth		15.3	40.3			
100.0	100.0	100.0	Total Liabilities & Net Worth		100.0	100.0			
			INCOME DATA						
100.0	100.0	100.0	Net Sales		100.0	100.0			
29.7	32.0	32.7	Gross Profit		33.6	34.6			
26.3	31.0	30.9	Operating Expenses		34.1	33.6			
3.4	1.0	1.8	Operating Profit		-.5	1.0			
1.8	1.7	2.2	All Other Expenses (net)		2.8	2.5			
1.6	-.7	-.4	Profit Before Taxes		-3.3	-1.6			
			RATIOS						
1.8	3.4	2.5	Current		2.4	3.5			
1.3	1.3	1.6			1.3	1.8			
1.0	1.0	1.1			1.0	1.2			
1.3	1.7	1.5	Quick		1.8	1.4			
.7	.7	1.0			.7	1.0			
.4	.4	.6			.3	.6			
38 9.7	29 12.5	36 10.1	Sales/Receivables	26 14.0	44 8.3				
49 7.5	44 8.3	48 7.6		46 7.9	50 7.2				
62 5.9	61 6.0	70 5.2		92 3.9	67 5.4				
16 22.2	20 18.2	9 42.2	Cost of Sales/Inventory	8 47.9	16 23.1				
64 5.7	57 6.4	56 6.6		39 9.3	84 4.3				
97 3.8	101 3.6	100 3.6		73 5.0	148 2.5				
15 24.0	14 25.6	14 26.6	Cost of Sales/Payables	16 23.0	16 22.9				
28 12.9	28 13.2	23 15.7		42 8.7	23 15.9				
48 7.7	44 8.4	47 7.8		56 6.5	42 8.7				
4.8	4.4	3.9	Sales/Working Capital		4.0	3.8			
15.0	14.4	8.4			18.1	7.3			
397.4	-318.0	41.9			-52.9	18.0			
(51) 3.6	(45) 4.4	(45) 3.5	EBIT/Interest	(11) 2.5	(13) 4.2				
1.6	1.9	1.0		1.4	1.0				
-.2	-1.2	-1.6		.1	-1.7				
5.6		7.6	Net Profit + Depr., Dep., Amort./Cur. Mat. L/T/D						
(18) 1.8		(13) 1.9							
.4		.1							
.4	.4	.6	Fixed/Worth		1.0	.4			
1.0	1.1	1.0			2.2	.8			
3.5	5.7	2.9			UND	1.7			
1.1	.6	.8	Debt/Worth		1.3	.8			
3.4	3.5	1.9			5.1	1.3			
23.2	28.1	6.5			UND	3.3			
(47) 32.5	(41) 25.8	(42) 25.3	% Profit Before Taxes/Tangible Net Worth	(11) 22.1	35.2				
7.0	9.0	3.2		4.5	.8				
-4.0	-28.6	-9.6		-8.3	-23.6				
6.1	12.3	6.2	% Profit Before Taxes/Total Assets		3.1	11.3			
2.1	3.8	.2			.3	.4			
-3.2	-9.5	-4.3			-4.2	-5.5			
37.7	27.8	20.5	Sales/Net Fixed Assets		67.1	10.4			
8.8	9.9	6.7			7.0	5.5			
3.5	3.4	2.8			2.2	3.5			
2.5	2.5	2.2	Sales/Total Assets		2.0	2.1			
1.8	1.9	1.6			1.4	1.6			
1.2	1.4	1.3			1.3	1.2			
(51) .9	(46) 1.2	(45) 1.3	% Depr., Dep., Amort./Sales	(13) .7	(11) 1.3				
2.4	2.6	3.5		5.3	2.6				
4.2	5.5	6.5		7.8	5.7				
(24) 2.2	(19) 2.0	(25) 1.9	% Officers', Directors', Owners' Comp/Sales						
4.4	3.4	4.0							
10.1	12.8	9.8							
745604M	523878M	811700M	Net Sales ($)	2605M	32107M	56933M	41829M	103506M	574720M
538965M	347051M	564662M	Total Assets ($)	1170M	21631M	43865M	32808M	65132M	400056M

Current Data Sorted By Assets

Comparative Historical Data

							Type of Statement		
		4	2	3	1	2	Unqualified	14	14
		6	3		1		Reviewed	4	8
		1	1				Compiled	11	4
		2	1				Tax Returns		2
			6	3		1	Other	5	10
	0-500M	9 (4/1-9/30/02) 500M-2MM	2-10MM	28 (10/1/02-3/31/03) 10-50MM	50-100MM	100-250MM		4/1/98-3/31/99 ALL	4/1/99-3/31/00 ALL
		13	13	6	2	3	NUMBER OF STATEMENTS	34	38
%	%	%	%	%	%	%	ASSETS	%	%
		10.0	6.3				Cash & Equivalents	7.3	8.2
D		31.8	23.7				Trade Receivables (net)	26.4	29.2
A		22.2	27.7				Inventory	21.9	22.7
T		.1	2.2				All Other Current	.8	.9
A		64.1	60.0				Total Current	56.4	60.9
		33.0	34.0				Fixed Assets (net)	38.9	34.5
N		1.6	1.1				Intangibles (net)	1.0	.9
O		1.3	4.9				All Other Non-Current	3.7	3.6
T		100.0	100.0				Total	100.0	100.0
A							LIABILITIES		
V		15.3	9.2				Notes Payable-Short Term	7.2	7.4
A		9.1	7.9				Cur. Mat.-L/T/D	5.6	6.9
I		18.7	11.7				Trade Payables	11.5	14.6
L		.1	.0				Income Taxes Payable	.1	.1
A		5.7	8.4				All Other Current	7.1	8.9
B		48.7	37.2				Total Current	31.5	37.9
L		18.8	14.9				Long Term Debt	26.6	25.7
E		.0	.8				Deferred Taxes	.8	.3
		16.7	2.1				All Other Non-Current	5.5	4.4
		15.8	45.0				Net Worth	35.6	31.7
		100.0	100.0				Total Liabilities & Net Worth	100.0	100.0
							INCOME DATA		
		100.0	100.0				Net Sales	100.0	100.0
		42.4	25.4				Gross Profit	29.5	24.9
		39.7	24.0				Operating Expenses	23.7	19.3
		2.7	1.4				Operating Profit	5.8	5.6
		2.6	1.3				All Other Expenses (net)	.9	1.1
		.1	.1				Profit Before Taxes	4.9	4.5
							RATIOS		
		2.7	3.2					2.9	2.8
		1.6	1.5				Current	1.8	1.5
		.9	1.2					1.2	1.2
		2.3	1.7					1.9	1.8
		1.1	1.1				Quick	1.1	.9
		.5	.4					.7	.6
28	13.2	36	10.2					39 9.3	43 8.5
45	8.1	52	7.0				Sales/Receivables	51 7.2	52 7.0
53	6.9	66	5.5					58 6.3	67 5.5
8	46.0	45	8.1					35 10.5	30 12.0
36	10.1	63	5.8				Cost of Sales/Inventory	56 6.6	44 8.3
69	5.3	138	2.6					89 4.1	98 3.7
14	25.8	18	20.5					15 24.4	17 22.0
41	8.9	25	14.5				Cost of Sales/Payables	26 14.1	29 12.7
80	4.6	42	8.6					38 9.5	42 8.8
	5.5		3.9					3.8	4.5
	11.0		7.9				Sales/Working Capital	7.3	10.8
	NM		NM					22.1	21.1
	1.7		11.4					7.9	8.0
(12)	1.1		1.4				EBIT/Interest	(30) 3.5	(35) 2.8
	-3.3		-1.3					1.5	1.3
							Net Profit + Depr., Dep., Amort./Cur. Mat. L /T/D	5.9	6.6
(14)								(14) 2.2	(10) 3.6
								1.0	1.4
	.7		.2					.6	.4
	1.9		.6				Fixed/Worth	1.1	.9
	-4.4		2.1					1.8	2.0
	1.3		.5					.7	.6
	4.6		1.5				Debt/Worth	1.7	1.5
	-17.0		3.1					4.1	3.0
			20.4				% Profit Before Taxes/Tangible Net Worth	35.6	32.2
			4.4					(33) 17.4	(36) 14.6
			-10.1					2.3	2.2
	3.8		6.0				% Profit Before Taxes/Total Assets	14.2	13.4
	.4		1.1					6.3	6.2
	-10.7		-5.1					1.6	1.0
	38.7		14.1					6.3	9.3
	6.2		4.5				Sales/Net Fixed Assets	4.8	4.5
	3.4		2.9					3.3	3.5
	3.1		2.0					2.1	2.3
	2.3		1.6				Sales/Total Assets	1.8	1.8
	1.7		1.4					1.4	1.5
	1.3		2.8					2.6	2.1
	3.6		5.3				% Depr., Dep., Amort./Sales	3.6	3.7
	5.8		8.3					5.8	6.2
							% Officers', Directors', Owners' Comp/Sales		2.4
								(10)	3.6
									4.6
	33196M	124222M	120310M	166987M	534292M		Net Sales ($)	821566M	959893M
	13816M	70783M	113697M	166765M	569512M		Total Assets ($)	553386M	661832M

© RMA 2003

M = $ thousand   MM = $ million
See Pages 11 through 18 for Explanation of Ratios and Data

Comparative Historical Data | Current Data Sorted By Sales

			Type of Statement	0-1MM	1-3MM	3-5MM	5-10MM	10-25MM	25MM & OVER
11	9	8	Unqualified				1	3	4
9	12	8	Reviewed		3	2	1	1	1
2	5	7	Compiled		4	3			
1	1	2	Tax Returns			1	1		
11	8	12	Other	1	1	1	3	4	2
4/1/00-3/31/01	4/1/01-3/31/02	4/1/02-3/31/03			9 (4/1-9/30/02)			28 (10/1/02-3/31/03)	
ALL	ALL	ALL							
34	35	37	**NUMBER OF STATEMENTS**	1	8	7	6	8	7
%	%	%	**ASSETS**	%	%	%	%	%	%
7.1	8.4	10.1	Cash & Equivalents						
24.0	23.6	24.7	Trade Receivables (net)						
25.6	22.3	23.0	Inventory						
.8	1.1	1.5	All Other Current						
57.5	55.3	59.3	Total Current						
35.6	37.3	33.1	Fixed Assets (net)						
1.6	3.1	2.5	Intangibles (net)						
5.4	4.3	5.1	All Other Non-Current						
100.0	100.0	100.0	Total						
			LIABILITIES						
7.9	8.4	9.7	Notes Payable-Short Term						
8.6	8.7	8.9	Cur. Mat.-L/T/D						
11.1	9.6	12.7	Trade Payables						
.1	.1	.1	Income Taxes Payable						
7.5	7.5	7.4	All Other Current						
35.2	34.3	38.8	Total Current						
15.5	15.5	14.0	Long Term Debt						
.6	.4	.5	Deferred Taxes						
3.5	3.8	7.7	All Other Non-Current						
45.1	46.0	39.0	Net Worth						
100.0	100.0	100.0	Total Liabilities & Net Worth						
			INCOME DATA						
100.0	100.0	100.0	Net Sales						
25.9	25.1	29.8	Gross Profit						
22.8	25.3	28.0	Operating Expenses						
3.1	-.1	1.8	Operating Profit						
.9	1.4	1.6	All Other Expenses (net)						
2.2	-1.6	.1	Profit Before Taxes						
			RATIOS						
2.6	3.0	3.0							
1.7	1.8	1.7	Current						
1.2	1.0	1.1							
2.1	2.1	2.3							
.9	1.1	1.1	Quick						
.5	.5	.5							
40 9.1	40 9.2	39 9.3							
53 6.9	50 7.3	51 7.2	Sales/Receivables						
59 6.2	57 6.4	63 5.8							
40 9.0	35 10.4	35 10.3							
73 5.0	65 5.6	52 7.0	Cost of Sales/Inventory						
117 3.1	92 4.0	94 3.9							
18 20.3	13 27.6	16 23.5							
28 13.1	24 15.0	25 14.3	Cost of Sales/Payables						
41 8.8	38 9.7	50 7.2							
4.1	3.6	3.5							
7.5	7.9	7.1	Sales/Working Capital						
18.1	54.1	97.3							
(31) 3.3	(31) 2.4	(34) 4.3							
2.8	1.1	1.3	EBIT/Interest						
.8	-2.3	-1.6							
			Net Profit + Depr., Dep., Amort./Cur. Mat. L/T/D						
.5	.5	.5							
.8	.7	.8	Fixed/Worth						
1.9	2.3	2.9							
.6	.4	.5							
1.2	1.1	1.7	Debt/Worth						
3.2	4.1	6.7							
21.3	16.2	12.2							
(31) 7.7	(31) 2.0	(32) 3.0	% Profit Before Taxes/Tangible Net Worth						
.3	-25.2	-7.5							
6.9	6.4	4.4							
4.2	.7	1.1	% Profit Before Taxes/Total Assets						
-1.0	-12.8	-5.1							
12.6	7.4	11.2							
4.2	4.2	5.0	Sales/Net Fixed Assets						
2.3	2.3	2.9							
2.2	2.1	2.3							
1.6	1.5	1.6	Sales/Total Assets						
1.1	1.2	1.2							
(32) 2.2	(33) 2.4	(36) 2.5							
4.4	5.9	4.7	% Depr., Dep., Amort./Sales						
6.4	7.6	7.5							
		3.5							
	(13)	6.0	% Officers', Directors', Owners' Comp/Sales						
		9.3							
1045898M	732662M	979007M	Net Sales ($)	874M	17393M	28004M	41378M	136185M	755173M
844203M	595229M	934573M	Total Assets ($)	511M	8117M	18713M	23011M	127571M	756650M

© RMA 2003

M = $ thousand   MM = $ million
See Pages 11 through 18 for Explanation of Ratios and Data

Current Data Sorted By Assets   Comparative Historical Data

0-500M	500M-2MM	2-10MM	10-50MM	50-100MM	100-250MM	Type of Statement	4/1/98-3/31/99 ALL	4/1/99-3/31/00 ALL
	2	5	2		2	Unqualified		9
	2	7	2			Reviewed		9
	2	1				Compiled		3
						Tax Returns		
1		6	2	3		Other		6
	11 (4/1-9/30/02)		24 (10/1/02-3/31/03)					4/1/99-3/31/00
1	4	19	6	3	2	NUMBER OF STATEMENTS		27
%	%	%	%	%	%		%	%
						ASSETS		
		5.5				Cash & Equivalents	D	5.8
		26.6				Trade Receivables (net)	A	24.1
		26.2				Inventory	T	31.4
		.6				All Other Current	A	1.5
		59.0				Total Current		62.8
		34.0				Fixed Assets (net)	N	30.7
		4.0				Intangibles (net)	O	2.9
		3.1				All Other Non-Current	T	3.6
		100.0				Total		100.0
						LIABILITIES	A	
		33.7				Notes Payable-Short Term	V	7.0
		5.8				Cur. Mat.-L/T/D	A	6.8
		13.1				Trade Payables	I	9.7
		.1				Income Taxes Payable	L	.1
		5.7				All Other Current	A	8.7
		58.4				Total Current	B	32.2
		18.7				Long Term Debt	L	24.7
		.4				Deferred Taxes	E	.5
		2.1				All Other Non-Current		2.8
		20.3				Net Worth		39.8
		100.0				Total Liabilities & Net Worth		100.0
						INCOME DATA		
		100.0				Net Sales		100.0
		33.6				Gross Profit		36.8
		27.2				Operating Expenses		26.2
		6.5				Operating Profit		10.7
		2.2				All Other Expenses (net)		2.0
		4.2				Profit Before Taxes		8.7
						RATIOS		
		2.9						3.3
		1.8				Current		1.9
		1.6						1.4
		1.2						1.3
		1.0				Quick		1.0
		.8						.6
	37	9.8					39	9.4
	47	7.7				Sales/Receivables	44	8.2
	67	5.5					55	6.7
	41	9.0					51	7.2
	81	4.5				Cost of Sales/Inventory	97	3.8
	163	2.2					168	2.2
	13	27.4					19	19.6
	37	10.0				Cost of Sales/Payables	26	14.2
	62	5.9					34	10.7
		3.9						3.6
		8.3				Sales/Working Capital		5.1
		13.8						12.0
		9.1						8.3
		3.6				EBIT/Interest	(26)	4.4
		1.2						2.5
						Net Profit + Depr., Dep., Amort./Cur. Mat. L /T/D		
		.4						.5
		.8				Fixed/Worth		.8
		1.2						1.7
		.7						.8
		1.3				Debt/Worth		1.7
		2.1						4.0
		31.9						51.1
	(17)	16.6				% Profit Before Taxes/Tangible Net Worth	(24)	31.2
		-.2						12.6
		13.5						22.2
		4.9				% Profit Before Taxes/Total Assets		13.4
		1.2						3.9
		8.5						18.5
		4.7				Sales/Net Fixed Assets		5.5
		3.4						3.6
		2.3						2.2
		1.8				Sales/Total Assets		1.7
		1.2						1.3
		2.3						1.2
	(17)	3.8				% Depr., Dep., Amort./Sales	(26)	2.7
		5.5						4.3
						% Officers', Directors', Owners' Comp/Sales		
1151M	19425M	120698M	198992M	239459M	438599M	Net Sales ($)		639792M
475M	4570M	72123M	126017M	231861M	390120M	Total Assets ($)		432069M

M = $ thousand   MM = $ million
See Pages 11 through 18 for Explanation of Ratios and Data

Comparative Historical Data | Current Data Sorted By Sales

				Type of Statement	0-1MM	1-3MM	3-5MM	5-10MM	10-25MM	25MM & OVER
	9	7	11	Unqualified		1	2	3	1	4
	6	5	9	Reviewed		1		5	1	2
	9	6	3	Compiled		1		1	1	
			1	Tax Returns		1				
	7	8	11	Other		2	2	2	1	4
	4/1/00-3/31/01 ALL	4/1/01-3/31/02 ALL	4/1/02-3/31/03 ALL			11 (4/1-9/30/02)		24 (10/1/02-3/31/03)		
	31	26	35	**NUMBER OF STATEMENTS**		6	4	11	4	10
	%	%	%	**ASSETS**	%	%	%	%	%	%
	4.5	5.0	5.1	Cash & Equivalents				6.8		4.2
	26.8	25.1	28.0	Trade Receivables (net)				32.5		22.7
	29.7	29.2	26.5	Inventory	D A T A			19.9		25.6
	1.9	3.2	3.0	All Other Current				.9		5.9
	63.0	62.5	62.6	Total Current	N O T			60.1		58.4
	26.4	27.8	28.1	Fixed Assets (net)				31.5		24.0
	6.4	5.1	3.9	Intangibles (net)	A V A I L A B L E			5.8		5.8
	4.2	4.7	5.4	All Other Non-Current				2.6		11.7
	100.0	100.0	100.0	Total				100.0		100.0
				LIABILITIES						
	7.6	27.5	19.7	Notes Payable-Short Term				52.0		1.8
	8.8	8.0	3.7	Cur. Mat.-L/T/D				4.7		1.3
	14.2	13.3	11.5	Trade Payables				14.8		7.8
	.4	.1	.7	Income Taxes Payable				.1		.2
	6.4	7.8	11.7	All Other Current				5.0		20.2
	37.5	56.7	47.3	Total Current				76.7		31.3
	27.1	11.5	26.0	Long Term Debt				14.1		21.0
	.9	.5	.3	Deferred Taxes				.4		.3
	4.7	6.7	5.9	All Other Non-Current				2.3		12.8
	29.8	24.7	20.4	Net Worth				6.4		34.6
	100.0	100.0	100.0	Total Liabilities & Net Worth				100.0		100.0
				INCOME DATA						
	100.0	100.0	100.0	Net Sales				100.0		100.0
	35.7	30.5	32.4	Gross Profit				35.4		24.9
	26.2	25.2	27.3	Operating Expenses				27.6		21.1
	9.4	5.2	5.2	Operating Profit				7.8		3.8
	3.0	2.7	1.6	All Other Expenses (net)				2.2		-.1
	6.5	2.5	3.6	Profit Before Taxes				5.6		3.9
				RATIOS						
	2.8	2.5	2.9	Current				3.0		4.7
	1.7	1.4	1.8					1.8		1.9
	1.2	1.0	1.5					1.6		1.2
	1.1	1.2	1.4	Quick				1.6		1.7
	.8	.6	1.0					1.2		1.0
	.6	.5	.8					1.0		.7
	42 8.7	36 10.0	39 9.5	Sales/Receivables				43 8.5		43 8.5
	52 7.1	47 7.8	51 7.1					49 7.4		62 5.9
	67 5.5	60 6.1	70 5.2					67 5.5		79 4.6
	58 6.3	50 7.3	46 8.0	Cost of Sales/Inventory				34 10.7		58 6.3
	80 4.6	76 4.8	85 4.3					63 5.8		96 3.8
	141 2.6	125 2.9	135 2.7					86 4.3		123 3.0
	27 13.5	20 17.9	12 30.4	Cost of Sales/Payables				8 44.2		0 UND
	42 8.7	31 11.6	29 12.7					24 15.2		25 14.6
	56 6.5	50 7.4	53 6.9					55 6.7		35 10.5
	4.0	3.5	3.5	Sales/Working Capital				4.3		2.5
	5.6	8.9	6.3					8.3		5.3
	20.6	245.5	13.2					12.8		16.8
	5.1	4.5	9.3	EBIT/Interest				52.5		12.0
	3.0	(24) 2.1	(34) 3.8					3.6		4.2
	2.0	.3	1.3					1.4		2.6
	(15) 4.7			Net Profit + Depr., Dep., Amort./Cur. Mat. L/T/D						
	2.8									
	.9									
	.3	.3	.4	Fixed/Worth				.3		.4
	.8	.7	.8					.8		.6
	1.7	1.8	1.2					1.1		1.2
	.8	.6	.8	Debt/Worth				.6		1.0
	1.8	2.0	1.5					.9		2.1
	3.9	4.1	2.4					2.1		2.9
	(28) 37.8	(23) 17.7	(31) 38.1	% Profit Before Taxes/Tangible Net Worth						
	21.3	10.7	14.3							
	10.2	-26.9	2.3							
	12.8	12.0	12.9	% Profit Before Taxes/Total Assets				17.9		8.8
	8.5	4.1	4.9					10.3		6.2
	3.4	-1.6	1.2					1.2		2.8
	12.5	9.6	15.3	Sales/Net Fixed Assets				14.8		9.4
	7.0	6.5	5.5					5.4		5.9
	3.7	3.9	3.6					4.7		4.7
	2.5	2.2	2.3	Sales/Total Assets				2.6		1.7
	1.8	1.8	1.7					2.3		1.4
	1.3	1.4	1.1					1.3		1.1
	(27) 1.5	(25) 1.5	(30) 1.5	% Depr., Dep., Amort./Sales						
	2.1	2.7	2.9							
	4.0	4.5	4.5							
				% Officers', Directors', Owners' Comp/Sales						
	1214520M	553947M	1018324M	Net Sales ($)		11632M	15668M	75208M	62613M	853203M
	1027894M	349349M	825166M	Total Assets ($)		9608M	10593M	43785M	34821M	726359M

Current Data Sorted By Assets   Comparative Historical Data

Type of Statement	0-500M	500M-2MM	2-10MM	10-50MM	50-100MM	100-250MM		4/1/98-3/31/99 ALL	4/1/99-3/31/00 ALL
Unqualified			12	14	3	1		47	48
Reviewed	1	4	14	2				34	30
Compiled	2	9	9					23	23
Tax Returns		2						4	6
Other	1	8	18	10	1	1		36	42
		26 (4/1-9/30/02)		86 (10/1/02-3/31/03)					
NUMBER OF STATEMENTS	4	23	53	26	4	2		144	149
ASSETS	%	%	%	%	%	%		%	%
Cash & Equivalents		7.8	8.9	8.1				7.3	8.4
Trade Receivables (net)		32.6	28.0	22.6				27.9	28.2
Inventory		32.1	31.9	26.4				29.2	31.0
All Other Current		1.0	2.7	4.1				2.3	2.3
Total Current		73.5	71.4	61.1				66.8	69.8
Fixed Assets (net)		15.9	20.9	26.4				24.6	22.6
Intangibles (net)		1.0	3.2	4.3				2.8	2.8
All Other Non-Current		9.6	4.5	8.2				5.8	4.8
Total		100.0	100.0	100.0				100.0	100.0
LIABILITIES									
Notes Payable-Short Term		14.6	10.4	5.8				8.7	11.5
Cur. Mat.-L/T/D		5.2	1.9	3.6				2.5	2.3
Trade Payables		16.0	14.1	9.0				13.4	12.4
Income Taxes Payable		.4	.1	.1				.3	.5
All Other Current		11.8	8.0	16.5				13.6	12.2
Total Current		47.9	34.6	35.0				38.4	38.8
Long Term Debt		15.0	6.3	13.0				11.7	11.9
Deferred Taxes		.3	.4	.9				.7	.5
All Other Non-Current		3.9	3.7	4.2				3.8	4.1
Net Worth		32.9	55.0	46.8				45.4	44.6
Total Liabilities & Net Worth		100.0	100.0	100.0				100.0	100.0
INCOME DATA									
Net Sales		100.0	100.0	100.0				100.0	100.0
Gross Profit		32.8	33.4	29.4				32.6	32.1
Operating Expenses		31.1	29.9	23.8				25.8	26.1
Operating Profit		1.7	3.5	5.6				6.9	6.1
All Other Expenses (net)		.9	.8	1.0				1.1	.8
Profit Before Taxes		.8	2.6	4.6				5.8	5.3
RATIOS									
Current		2.9	4.7	3.4				2.9	3.2
		1.5	2.0	2.1				1.7	1.8
		1.0	1.3	1.3				1.3	1.3
Quick		1.2	2.0	1.9				1.3	1.8
		.8	1.0	1.2				.9	.9
		.7	.7	.5				.7	.6
Sales/Receivables	32	11.3	40 9.1	44 8.3				36 10.1	37 9.9
	47	7.8	51 7.2	50 7.3				50 7.3	47 7.8
	57	6.4	70 5.2	61 6.0				63 5.8	60 6.1
Cost of Sales/Inventory	35	10.6	52 7.0	56 6.6				42 8.6	38 9.6
	65	5.6	95 3.9	87 4.2				77 4.7	78 4.7
	121	3.0	128 2.8	124 2.9				120 3.0	126 2.9
Cost of Sales/Payables	20	17.9	19 19.1	18 20.0				20 18.4	17 21.5
	25	14.9	32 11.3	24 15.3				30 12.1	30 12.2
	41	8.8	54 6.7	39 9.4				44 8.4	43 8.4
Sales/Working Capital		5.7	3.1	3.7				4.4	3.9
		11.1	4.9	4.8				7.7	6.4
		-129.3	11.9	13.1				16.8	14.7
EBIT/Interest	(20)	4.0	(48) 16.2	(24) 18.8				(129) 15.0	(130) 13.3
		2.1	3.7	4.6				4.8	4.0
		-1.4	.9	1.0				1.6	1.6
Net Profit + Depr., Dep., Amort./Cur. Mat. L/T/D			(18) 6.2					(52) 13.9	(51) 7.0
			2.1					2.7	3.0
			-.6					1.3	1.4
Fixed/Worth		.1	.2	.3				.3	.2
		.3	.3	.6				.5	.5
		1.0	.8	1.7				.9	.8
Debt/Worth		.8	.3	.5				.6	.7
		1.9	.8	.9				1.3	1.4
		6.9	2.1	4.5				3.3	2.8
% Profit Before Taxes/Tangible Net Worth	(20)	42.5	(51) 15.1	(23) 34.1				(139) 40.5	(141) 38.4
		6.2	9.5	16.9				19.4	21.6
		-3.2	1.6	1.7				5.5	5.5
% Profit Before Taxes/Total Assets		5.8	9.4	13.4				16.7	18.5
		2.9	4.0	6.1				7.8	8.0
		-2.5	.0	-1.4				2.4	1.7
Sales/Net Fixed Assets		79.8	27.3	11.0				17.7	29.9
		25.2	12.3	7.4				8.2	9.0
		5.7	5.3	4.6				4.7	4.6
Sales/Total Assets		3.7	2.4	2.1				2.5	2.5
		2.6	1.8	1.7				1.9	2.0
		1.7	1.4	1.1				1.5	1.4
% Depr., Dep., Amort./Sales	(20)	.6	(47) 1.0	(23) 1.7				(127) 1.2	(133) .8
		1.2	2.1	2.8				2.2	2.0
		2.3	3.1	4.3				3.4	3.8
% Officers', Directors', Owners' Comp/Sales			(17) 2.4					1.7	2.0
			3.3					(40) 4.7	(47) 4.1
			8.3					10.5	7.7
Net Sales ($)	3810M	75565M	476063M	831298M	338454M	344075M		4556937M	4063811M
Total Assets ($)	1255M	28256M	267081M	518108M	246427M	307846M		3063365M	2523851M

Comparative Historical Data   **Current Data Sorted By Sales**

Hist 1	Hist 2	Hist 3	Type of Statement	0-1MM	1-3MM	3-5MM	5-10MM	10-25MM	25MM & OVER
39	20	30	Unqualified			1	7	9	13
25	22	21	Reviewed	1	2	4	6	7	1
26	28	20	Compiled	1	5	5	7	2	
8	1	2	Tax Returns		1		1		
44	32	39	Other	2		4	11		7
4/1/00-3/31/01	4/1/01-3/31/02	4/1/02-3/31/03			26 (4/1-9/30/02)		86 (10/1/02-3/31/03)		
ALL	ALL	ALL							
142	103	112	**NUMBER OF STATEMENTS**	4	16	14	28	29	21

Hist 1	Hist 2	Hist 3	ASSETS	0-1MM	1-3MM	3-5MM	5-10MM	10-25MM	25MM & OVER
%	%	%		%	%	%	%	%	%
7.2	8.2	8.4	Cash & Equivalents		7.1	8.3	8.2	10.0	8.2
27.5	28.9	28.2	Trade Receivables (net)		31.2	29.1	26.3	28.9	24.5
30.0	28.4	30.0	Inventory		24.4	31.5	36.3	28.8	26.8
2.6	2.8	2.5	All Other Current		.3	1.9	2.8	3.1	4.0
67.2	68.3	69.2	Total Current		63.0	70.8	73.6	70.9	63.5
23.5	22.2	21.0	Fixed Assets (net)		23.5	19.6	18.1	20.2	26.4
3.9	3.1	3.1	Intangibles (net)		2.9	2.7	5.4	.7	4.0
5.3	6.4	6.6	All Other Non-Current		10.5	6.9	2.9	8.2	6.1
100.0	100.0	100.0	Total		100.0	100.0	100.0	100.0	100.0

Hist 1	Hist 2	Hist 3	LIABILITIES	0-1MM	1-3MM	3-5MM	5-10MM	10-25MM	25MM & OVER
11.6	9.4	11.1	Notes Payable-Short Term		15.9	7.9	9.4	9.3	6.7
3.1	2.9	4.3	Cur. Mat.-L/T/D		7.2	1.5	1.6	2.5	7.2
12.9	13.4	13.9	Trade Payables		14.0	12.4	14.3	13.9	9.4
.4	.4	.2	Income Taxes Payable		.5	.0	.2	.0	.2
11.1	10.7	10.8	All Other Current		7.0	9.8	10.2	14.8	10.7
39.1	36.8	40.2	Total Current		44.6	31.6	35.6	40.5	34.3
11.2	9.2	10.6	Long Term Debt		20.8	9.8	5.4	5.8	13.9
.6	.6	.4	Deferred Taxes		.3	.4	.5	.4	.7
3.8	3.1	4.0	All Other Non-Current		7.3	2.8	3.4	2.6	5.2
45.3	50.3	44.7	Net Worth		27.1	55.4	55.2	50.6	45.9
100.0	100.0	100.0	Total Liabilities & Net Worth		100.0	100.0	100.0	100.0	100.0

Hist 1	Hist 2	Hist 3	INCOME DATA	0-1MM	1-3MM	3-5MM	5-10MM	10-25MM	25MM & OVER
100.0	100.0	100.0	Net Sales		100.0	100.0	100.0	100.0	100.0
33.8	33.1	32.5	Gross Profit		35.2	31.2	34.2	30.9	28.7
28.7	28.8	29.2	Operating Expenses		34.2	27.0	31.1	26.5	23.4
5.1	4.2	3.4	Operating Profit		1.1	4.2	3.1	4.4	5.3
.9	.8	1.2	All Other Expenses (net)		1.5	.8	1.3	.3	1.1
4.2	3.4	2.1	Profit Before Taxes		-.4	3.3	1.8	4.1	4.2

Hist 1	Hist 2	Hist 3	RATIOS	0-1MM	1-3MM	3-5MM	5-10MM	10-25MM	25MM & OVER
2.6	3.5	3.6			2.8	4.0	5.5	2.8	4.7
1.7	1.9	1.9	Current		1.2	2.0	2.5	2.0	2.1
1.3	1.3	1.2			.9	1.6	1.3	1.2	1.4
1.4	1.8	1.8			1.6	1.8	1.9	1.8	2.5
.9	1.1	1.0	Quick		.8	1.2	.9	1.0	1.3
.6	.6	.6			.7	.7	.6	.7	.7
41 9.0	41 8.8	41 8.9			35 10.4	38 9.5	36 10.2	40 9.1	45 8.1
54 6.8	51 7.2	51 7.2	Sales/Receivables		56 6.5	48 7.7	44 8.3	50 7.3	52 7.0
68 5.4	65 5.7	67 5.5			68 5.4	55 6.6	56 6.5	70 5.2	66 5.5
46 7.9	48 7.6	52 7.0			22 16.4	48 7.6	52 7.0	51 7.2	55 6.6
86 4.3	78 4.7	85 4.3	Cost of Sales/Inventory		49 7.4	68 5.4	99 3.7	85 4.3	86 4.3
141 2.6	118 3.1	126 2.9			147 2.5	120 3.0	151 2.4	113 3.2	121 3.0
20 18.3	18 19.7	19 18.8			22 16.9	22 16.6	15 23.8	18 20.1	16 22.4
34 10.7	32 11.3	29 12.5	Cost of Sales/Payables		29 12.5	28 13.2	29 12.5	30 12.0	25 14.4
51 7.1	49 7.5	52 7.0			65 5.6	46 8.0	53 6.9	53 6.8	38 9.5
4.3	3.5	3.5			4.9	3.2	3.1	3.6	3.2
6.7	6.7	6.3	Sales/Working Capital		12.2	5.8	4.5	6.1	4.5
14.9	13.7	17.4			-50.5	8.6	14.5	15.3	12.0
12.6	17.9	9.7			3.2	16.9	15.8	12.9	22.3
(126) 3.5	(95) 3.4	(99) 3.0	EBIT/Interest		2.1	(12) 2.7	(26) 4.5	(24) 4.4	(19) 4.9
1.3	1.0	.4			-.9	1.1	.2	1.4	-.1
12.3	6.7	4.7	Net Profit + Depr., Dep.,					17.2	
(39) 3.0	(31) 1.8	(31) 2.0	Amort./Cur. Mat. L/T/D				(10) 3.8		
.6	1.2	.3					-.7		
.2	.2	.2			.1	.1	.2	.1	.4
.5	.4	.4	Fixed/Worth		1.0	.2	.2	.4	.6
1.1	.9	1.0			NM	1.1	.5	.9	1.5
.7	.4	.5			1.1	.3	.3	.4	.4
1.3	1.0	1.2	Debt/Worth		3.7	.8	.6	.9	1.4
2.9	2.7	3.5			NM	1.9	2.2	2.5	3.7
31.5	33.4	26.0	% Profit Before Taxes/Tangible		49.4	31.2	15.1	21.5	29.5
(133) 15.3	(99) 10.3	(100) 10.0	Net Worth	(12) 10.7	6.0	(26) 8.6	12.2	(18) 19.9	
3.7	.2	1.8			-4.6	-.3	2.9	2.3	1.7
13.9	13.9	9.7	% Profit Before Taxes/Total		8.6	8.3	7.6	11.8	14.4
6.3	5.8	3.9	Assets		1.8	2.7	3.9	6.0	7.1
.8	.1	-.7			-2.5	-.6	-.7	1.2	-2.4
21.2	26.6	25.0			61.2	31.7	34.0	27.3	11.0
9.9	10.7	10.8	Sales/Net Fixed Assets		17.9	14.0	13.8	10.2	7.4
4.6	5.0	5.0			4.6	5.4	6.1	5.0	4.8
2.3	2.4	2.4			3.1	2.7	2.7	2.3	2.1
1.8	2.0	1.8	Sales/Total Assets		2.2	1.9	2.0	1.8	1.8
1.4	1.4	1.3			1.4	1.6	1.2	1.5	1.3
1.0	.9	1.1			.7	1.1	.6	.8	1.8
(121) 2.1	(91) 1.9	(99) 2.1	% Depr., Dep., Amort./Sales	(12) 1.5	(12) 1.7	(27) 2.1	(24) 2.2	(20) 2.7	
3.6	3.3	3.3			3.5	2.6	4.1	3.1	4.1
2.4	1.6	2.0	% Officers', Directors',				3.2		
(48) 5.7	(31) 4.2	(29) 3.6	Owners' Comp/Sales				(12) 5.4		
9.2	9.2	9.2					10.5		
3098900M	2495037M	2069265M	Net Sales ($)	2445M	33935M	56887M	213139M	453418M	1309441M
2032966M	1744982M	1368973M	Total Assets ($)	1842M	26169M	29448M	126511M	275752M	909251M

M = $ thousand   MM = $ million
See Pages 11 through 18 for Explanation of Ratios and Data

Current Data Sorted By Assets   **Comparative Historical Data**

0-500M	500M-2MM	2-10MM	10-50MM	50-100MM	100-250MM	Type of Statement	4/1/98-3/31/99 ALL	4/1/99-3/31/00 ALL
	2	9	8		2	Unqualified	23	30
1	5	24	5			Reviewed	36	28
1	5	7	1			Compiled	13	21
	2					Tax Returns	4	2
	7	11	11	1	1	Other	35	31
	25 (4/1-9/30/02)		78 (10/1/02-3/31/03)					
2	21	51	25	1	3	**NUMBER OF STATEMENTS**	111	112
%	%	%	%	%	%	**ASSETS**	%	%
	5.6	7.5	15.4			Cash & Equivalents	11.0	10.9
	37.8	30.3	32.2			Trade Receivables (net)	31.9	31.7
	25.5	24.5	15.1			Inventory	21.5	21.3
	2.8	5.4	3.3			All Other Current	5.8	5.6
	71.8	67.8	66.0			Total Current	70.2	69.4
	20.3	20.7	23.5			Fixed Assets (net)	22.2	21.3
	2.4	4.0	6.0			Intangibles (net)	3.3	4.5
	5.6	7.5	4.6			All Other Non-Current	4.4	4.7
	100.0	100.0	100.0			Total	100.0	100.0
						LIABILITIES		
	13.4	12.4	4.3			Notes Payable-Short Term	10.2	10.1
	2.8	4.1	3.0			Cur. Mat.-L/T/D	2.9	1.9
	21.1	14.6	14.3			Trade Payables	17.5	17.7
	.2	.6	.1			Income Taxes Payable	.4	.4
	12.6	13.7	16.9			All Other Current	21.7	18.4
	50.1	45.4	38.6			Total Current	52.8	48.4
	13.3	11.1	17.4			Long Term Debt	13.8	11.0
	.5	.3	.6			Deferred Taxes	.5	.5
	22.8	3.5	5.4			All Other Non-Current	4.4	5.3
	13.3	39.7	37.9			Net Worth	28.5	34.7
	100.0	100.0	100.0			Total Liabilities & Net Worth	100.0	100.0
						INCOME DATA		
	100.0	100.0	100.0			Net Sales	100.0	100.0
	32.3	30.8	27.3			Gross Profit	28.9	29.9
	31.7	28.8	21.3			Operating Expenses	25.4	26.1
	.5	2.1	6.0			Operating Profit	3.5	3.8
	1.2	1.1	1.1			All Other Expenses (net)	.6	.8
	−.6	1.0	4.9			Profit Before Taxes	2.9	3.0
						RATIOS		
	2.5	2.1	2.8				2.3	2.6
	1.6	1.5	1.7			Current	1.5	1.6
	.9	1.2	1.2				1.1	1.1
	1.5	1.3	2.0				1.5	1.7
	.7	.8	1.2			Quick	.9	.9
	.6	.5	.7				.6	.6
	40 9.2	37 10.0	47 7.7				36 10.1	36 10.1
	51 7.1	51 7.2	56 6.5			Sales/Receivables	53 6.9	52 7.1
	71 5.2	72 5.1	88 4.1				68 5.4	70 5.2
	28 13.1	36 10.1	14 25.4				17 21.7	24 15.2
	59 6.2	63 5.8	33 11.2			Cost of Sales/Inventory	49 7.4	46 8.0
	90 4.1	95 3.8	68 5.4				77 4.8	81 4.5
	20 18.1	22 16.7	21 17.7				18 20.3	20 18.4
	33 11.1	31 11.6	42 8.6			Cost of Sales/Payables	34 10.7	33 10.9
	61 6.0	43 8.5	54 6.7				51 7.2	54 6.8
	5.9	5.2	4.1				5.4	4.9
	7.8	9.2	6.8			Sales/Working Capital	10.4	9.1
	−44.3	24.9	14.8				37.2	53.5
	4.1	7.7	14.1				13.8	16.0
	2.9	(49) 2.1	(23) 5.6			EBIT/Interest	(100) 6.0	(98) 4.5
	−1.0	.4	1.2				1.7	1.1
		3.4	7.5				4.7	7.9
	(23)	1.9	(12) 1.0			Net Profit + Depr., Dep., Amort./Cur. Mat. L /T/D	(34) 2.1	(27) 2.8
		.5	.4				1.1	.6
	.3	.3	.3				.3	.2
	1.3	.6	.7			Fixed/Worth	.7	.5
	−4.0	1.2	1.9				2.3	2.6
	.9	.8	.5				.7	.6
	4.6	1.9	2.2			Debt/Worth	1.9	1.7
	−15.6	4.2	8.9				9.2	7.9
	29.8	25.2	86.1				59.1	46.4
	(13) 12.9	(50) 8.9	(22) 13.9			% Profit Before Taxes/Tangible Net Worth	(97) 35.1	(90) 20.0
	−43.4	−3.1	6.6				10.2	5.0
	9.7	7.3	12.5				19.5	17.3
	3.1	2.5	5.9			% Profit Before Taxes/Total Assets	9.7	7.1
	−11.7	−.9	1.5				1.8	.9
	29.1	19.8	14.8				23.4	30.3
	16.8	10.9	7.1			Sales/Net Fixed Assets	11.4	10.4
	7.0	6.9	4.5				6.3	5.9
	3.0	2.4	2.0				3.1	2.7
	2.6	1.9	1.7			Sales/Total Assets	2.1	2.2
	2.2	1.6	1.1				1.7	1.5
	.9	1.2	1.4				1.0	.9
	1.2	(50) 1.8	(24) 2.2			% Depr., Dep., Amort./Sales	(98) 1.6	(96) 1.5
	2.3	2.8	3.6				2.7	2.8
		2.0					2.2	2.2
	(19)	2.8				% Officers', Directors', Owners' Comp/Sales	(40) 5.7	(27) 3.9
		5.2					8.4	9.5
1574M	70429M	481495M	868707M	108582M	610939M	Net Sales ($)	2826318M	2676561M
548M	27603M	252285M	528855M	54883M	499146M	Total Assets ($)	1564505M	1688098M

© RMA 2003

M = $ thousand   MM = $ million
See Pages 11 through 18 for Explanation of Ratios and Data

Comparative Historical Data | | | Current Data Sorted By Sales

				Type of Statement		0-1MM	1-3MM	3-5MM	5-10MM	10-25MM	25MM & OVER
	22		20		21	Unqualified		1	1	2	11	6
	32		21		35	Reviewed	1	2	7	14	9	2
	26		27		14	Compiled		5	2	3	3	1
	4		5		2	Tax Returns		1	1			
	29		29		31	Other		5	1	6	10	9
	4/1/00-		4/1/01-		4/1/02-			25 (4/1-9/30/02)		78 (10/1/02-3/31/03)		
	3/31/01		3/31/02		3/31/03							
	ALL		ALL		ALL		0-1MM	1-3MM	3-5MM	5-10MM	10-25MM	25MM & OVER
	113		102		103	NUMBER OF STATEMENTS	1	14	12	25	33	18
	%		%		%	ASSETS	%	%	%	%	%	%
	9.3		10.7		9.0	Cash & Equivalents		6.1	5.7	8.3	8.8	13.8
	34.7		33.3		31.8	Trade Receivables (net)		33.7	29.9	29.7	33.5	32.5
	19.9		21.5		22.6	Inventory		28.9	22.2	25.9	22.2	13.4
	6.0		5.2		4.4	All Other Current		3.5	3.8	6.2	3.8	4.4
	69.9		70.7		67.9	Total Current		72.2	61.6	70.0	68.3	64.1
	20.6		20.1		21.2	Fixed Assets (net)		20.0	26.1	20.2	19.5	23.8
	4.5		3.4		4.5	Intangibles (net)		1.7	3.5	3.9	4.7	8.2
	4.9		5.7		6.4	All Other Non-Current		6.1	8.9	5.9	7.5	3.9
	100.0		100.0		100.0	Total		100.0	100.0	100.0	100.0	100.0
					LIABILITIES						
	8.8		11.4		10.4	Notes Payable-Short Term		14.4	12.3	12.1	11.0	2.6
	1.7		3.2		3.9	Cur. Mat.-L/T/D		2.9	4.5	4.0	3.2	5.5
	16.6		16.3		15.6	Trade Payables		12.7	21.2	14.5	16.4	14.6
	.8		.5		.4	Income Taxes Payable		.3	1.0	.7	.2	.4
	16.8		14.4		15.5	All Other Current		11.9	7.9	15.8	14.2	18.8
	44.7		45.8		45.8	Total Current		42.1	46.9	47.0	45.0	41.9
	10.2		10.8		13.0	Long Term Debt		15.3	13.8	8.4	11.7	19.9
	.8		.5		.5	Deferred Taxes		.0	1.0	.4	.5	.8
	3.9		4.5		8.0	All Other Non-Current		32.9	1.4	5.8	1.6	8.4
	40.4		38.3		32.7	Net Worth		9.7	37.0	38.3	41.2	28.9
	100.0		100.0		100.0	Total Liabilities & Net Worth		100.0	100.0	100.0	100.0	100.0
					INCOME DATA						
	100.0		100.0		100.0	Net Sales		100.0	100.0	100.0	100.0	100.0
	28.8		28.8		30.5	Gross Profit		34.3	33.7	34.7	27.0	25.3
	25.7		26.8		27.9	Operating Expenses		35.2	31.8	31.9	24.1	19.7
	3.2		2.1		2.6	Operating Profit		−.9	1.9	2.8	2.8	5.6
	.0		.8		1.1	All Other Expenses (net)		1.6	.5	.8	1.4	1.2
	3.2		1.2		1.4	Profit Before Taxes		−2.5	1.4	2.0	1.4	4.4
					RATIOS						
	2.8		3.0		2.3			2.4	2.4	3.1	2.1	2.6
	1.7		1.6		1.5	Current		2.0	1.6	1.5	1.5	1.4
	1.2		1.1		1.1			1.2	.9	1.1	1.1	1.1
	1.6		1.9		1.4			1.4	1.4	1.3	1.5	1.9
	1.0		1.0		.8	Quick		.8	1.0	.8	.8	1.0
	.7		.6		.6			.6	.4	.4	.6	.7
42	8.6	39	9.3	41	8.9		33	10.9	36	10.2	37	9.8	45	8.1	42	8.7

Hist 00-01		Hist 01-02		Hist 02-03		Ratio	0-1MM		1-3MM		3-5MM		5-10MM		10-25MM		25MM & OVER
42	8.6	39	9.3	41	8.9				33	10.9	36	10.2	37	9.8	45	8.1	42	8.7
52	7.1	53	6.9	52	7.0	Sales/Receivables			57	6.4	44	8.2	47	7.8	56	6.5	55	6.6
71	5.2	67	5.5	75	4.9				88	4.2	59	6.1	73	5.0	80	4.6	84	4.3
18	20.0	20	18.2	27	13.4				40	9.2	36	10.1	28	13.1	28	13.3	13	28.6
45	8.1	48	7.5	58	6.3	Cost of Sales/Inventory			76	4.8	56	6.5	69	5.3	58	6.3	28	13.2
75	4.9	77	4.7	92	4.0				131	2.8	76	4.8	126	2.9	80	4.6	62	5.9
19	19.1	16	22.3	21	17.2				18	20.7	18	19.8	17	21.2	26	13.9	16	22.9
29	12.7	27	13.6	33	11.1	Cost of Sales/Payables			24	15.0	32	11.3	31	11.7	39	9.3	36	10.2
45	8.1	39	9.3	54	6.8				61	6.0	64	5.7	50	7.4	46	7.9	59	6.2

Hist 00-01	Hist 01-02	Hist 02-03	Ratio	0-1MM	1-3MM	3-5MM	5-10MM	10-25MM	25MM & OVER
5.2	5.0	5.5			5.7	6.0	5.1	5.1	4.4
8.4	8.3	8.8	Sales/Working Capital		6.9	12.2	8.8	8.8	9.6
28.0	35.1	26.9			16.6	−59.3	31.5	25.6	20.7
11.0	6.0	7.6			3.3	4.7	15.0	13.3	8.6
(101) 3.4	(93) 1.7	(98) 2.8	EBIT/Interest		.5	3.6	(24) 2.0	(32) 3.3	(15) 4.3
1.4	−.3	.9			−3.5	1.1	.4	1.2	1.2
6.5	4.3	4.2	Net Profit + Depr., Dep.,				2.1	6.0	
(33) 2.6	(27) 1.7	(42) 1.4	Amort./Cur. Mat. L/T/D			(11) 1.4	(16) 1.6		
1.3	.0	.5					−3.7	.5	
.2	.2	.3			.3	.3	.3	.3	.4
.5	.5	.6	Fixed/Worth		.6	1.3	.5	.6	.9
1.5	1.2	1.6			NM	−6.7	1.5	.8	NM
.6	.6	.8			1.2	.6	.7	.8	.7
1.4	1.6	2.2	Debt/Worth		3.2	1.4	1.8	2.1	4.5
4.0	5.4	7.5			NM	−83.0	4.8	4.4	NM
38.9	20.9	27.3	% Profit Before Taxes/Tangible		25.1		26.3	23.2	86.1
(102) 15.4	(93) 5.6	(89) 10.3	Net Worth	(11) 3.4		(23) 8.7	12.3	(14) 25.3	
3.9	−7.4	.1			−49.7		−5.5	1.1	8.9
13.9	9.7	8.8	% Profit Before Taxes/Total		5.4	12.5	10.0	7.7	11.9
5.7	1.8	3.9	Assets		−1.3	4.5	1.8	4.1	5.8
1.0	−3.2	−.1			−15.8	.5	−1.1	.3	2.0
26.0	28.7	21.8			32.9	22.6	28.1	18.0	18.2
14.8	15.6	11.3	Sales/Net Fixed Assets		15.7	10.2	13.6	10.1	8.4
6.0	6.3	5.9			6.7	5.4	5.7	6.8	5.0
2.9	2.9	2.6			2.9	2.7	2.6	2.3	2.4
2.1	2.3	2.0	Sales/Total Assets		2.3	2.3	2.0	1.9	1.8
1.7	1.6	1.5			1.3	1.6	1.4	1.7	1.3
.7	.6	1.1			1.0	1.2	1.0	1.2	1.3
(101) 1.5	(95) 1.4	(100) 1.8	% Depr., Dep., Amort./Sales		1.5	2.0	(24) 1.5	(32) 1.8	(17) 2.2
2.5	2.5	2.7			2.4	3.5	2.4	2.7	3.1
2.4	2.0	2.2						1.2	
(38) 5.0	(36) 3.7	(29) 3.3	% Officers', Directors', Owners' Comp/Sales				(11) 2.0		
8.3	7.1	7.8						2.7	
2144365M	2053986M	2141726M	Net Sales ($)	430M	31795M	50520M	177306M	515129M	1366546M
1337823M	1133427M	1363320M	Total Assets ($)	160M	16219M	24595M	103834M	323862M	894650M

M = $ thousand   MM = $ million
See Pages 11 through 18 for Explanation of Ratios and Data

Current Data Sorted By Assets   **Comparative Historical Data**

0-500M	500M-2MM	2-10MM	10-50MM	50-100MM	100-250MM		4/1/98-3/31/99 ALL	4/1/99-3/31/00 ALL
						Type of Statement		
		2		5		Unqualified	5	5
	1	1		2		Reviewed	5	6
1	3	7				Compiled	8	7
1	1					Tax Returns	1	2
	2	4				Other	11	3
						6 (4/1-9/30/02) / 24 (10/1/02-3/31/03)		
2	7	14	7			**NUMBER OF STATEMENTS**	30	23
%	%	%	%	%	%		%	%
		5.5		D	D	Cash & Equivalents	7.1	5.4
		34.1		A	A	Trade Receivables (net)	30.8	29.9
		26.6		T	T	Inventory	24.9	24.9
		6.9		A	A	All Other Current	5.4	3.9
		73.2				Total Current	68.1	64.2
		16.4		N	N	Fixed Assets (net)	22.7	25.3
		3.0		O	O	Intangibles (net)	3.6	5.0
		7.4		T	T	All Other Non-Current	5.5	5.5
		100.0				Total	100.0	100.0
				A	A	**LIABILITIES**		
		10.4		V	V	Notes Payable-Short Term	13.2	18.1
		4.7		A	A	Cur. Mat.-L/T/D	2.0	2.9
		13.6		I	I	Trade Payables	14.4	15.2
		.1		L	L	Income Taxes Payable	.4	.5
		13.3		A	A	All Other Current	14.4	11.9
		42.0		B	B	Total Current	44.3	48.6
		6.5		L	L	Long Term Debt	9.5	12.7
		.6		E	E	Deferred Taxes	.7	.4
		1.9				All Other Non-Current	2.7	1.4
		48.9				Net Worth	42.7	37.0
		100.0				Total Liabilities & Net Worth	100.0	100.0
						INCOME DATA		
		100.0				Net Sales	100.0	100.0
		26.6				Gross Profit	31.7	34.4
		23.5				Operating Expenses	26.2	29.5
		3.1				Operating Profit	5.5	4.9
		.4				All Other Expenses (net)	1.3	1.4
		2.7				Profit Before Taxes	4.1	3.5
						RATIOS		
		2.5				Current	2.9	2.2
		1.8					2.0	1.8
		1.3					1.1	1.2
		1.6				Quick	1.6	1.3
		1.0					.9	1.1
		.6					.7	.5
		46 7.9				Sales/Receivables	44 8.3	39 9.4
		53 6.9					49 7.5	50 7.3
		67 5.4					57 6.4	69 5.3
		23 15.7				Cost of Sales/Inventory	18 20.4	31 11.7
		66 5.6					55 6.7	63 5.8
		97 3.8					94 3.9	121 3.0
		14 26.7				Cost of Sales/Payables	20 17.9	27 13.4
		31 11.9					28 13.0	39 9.4
		39 9.5					43 8.6	55 6.6
		4.9				Sales/Working Capital	4.2	5.3
		8.4					7.5	8.9
		11.2					74.5	19.8
		13.1				EBIT/Interest	(27) 14.9	(22) 15.2
	(12)	4.5					5.7	6.3
		−2.0					1.8	1.0
						Net Profit + Depr., Dep., Amort./Cur. Mat. L /T/D		
		.2				Fixed/Worth	.2	.2
		.4					.4	.5
		.6					1.9	1.6
		.6				Debt/Worth	.6	.7
		1.0					1.2	1.4
		2.5					5.2	4.6
		32.7				% Profit Before Taxes/Tangible Net Worth	(28) 56.8	(19) 32.7
		13.7					26.9	20.6
		−7.7					9.8	7.5
		16.4				% Profit Before Taxes/Total Assets	15.3	14.3
		5.5					6.9	6.4
		−3.1					3.0	.4
		34.9				Sales/Net Fixed Assets	22.5	22.4
		12.6					14.9	12.7
		9.9					5.5	5.0
		2.8				Sales/Total Assets	3.2	2.9
		2.2					2.0	2.1
		1.7					1.6	1.5
		1.0				% Depr., Dep., Amort./Sales	(27) .9	(20) 1.3
	(13)	1.5					1.4	1.8
		2.3					2.7	4.1
						% Officers', Directors', Owners' Comp/Sales		(10) 3.5
								5.1
								8.1
2655M	29793M	156518M	227248M			Net Sales ($)	802012M	232111M
769M	10476M	68072M	147557M			Total Assets ($)	356212M	178044M

M = $ thousand   MM = $ million
See Pages 11 through 18 for Explanation of Ratios and Data

Comparative Historical Data   **Current Data Sorted By Sales**

			Type of Statement	0-1MM	1-3MM	3-5MM	5-10MM	10-25MM	25MM & OVER
4	5	7	Unqualified				2	1	4
3	2	4	Reviewed				2	2	
7	7	11	Compiled	2		3	4	2	
		2	Tax Returns		1				
5	8	6	Other		1	1	2	2	1
						6 (4/1-9/30/02)	24 (10/1/02-3/31/03)		
4/1/00-3/31/01 ALL	4/1/01-3/31/02 ALL	4/1/02-3/31/03 ALL	NUMBER OF STATEMENTS	0-1MM	1-3MM	3-5MM	5-10MM	10-25MM	25MM & OVER
19	25	30		2	2	4	10	7	5
%	%	%	**ASSETS**	%	%	%	%	%	%
7.0	6.9	5.7	Cash & Equivalents				4.5		
38.5	34.1	32.5	Trade Receivables (net)				34.6		
19.6	22.5	29.5	Inventory				31.0		
6.5	7.4	4.8	All Other Current				1.2		
71.6	70.9	72.5	Total Current				71.3		
23.0	19.9	18.8	Fixed Assets (net)				17.4		
1.1	2.7	2.3	Intangibles (net)				2.9		
4.4	6.5	6.4	All Other Non-Current				8.4		
100.0	100.0	100.0	Total				100.0		
			LIABILITIES						
11.1	9.7	9.7	Notes Payable-Short Term				6.0		
2.2	1.9	4.6	Cur. Mat.-L/T/D				6.1		
16.8	16.8	16.0	Trade Payables				14.0		
1.1	.9	.5	Income Taxes Payable				.8		
18.4	11.3	10.8	All Other Current				12.3		
49.7	40.6	41.5	Total Current				39.2		
10.7	11.5	10.6	Long Term Debt				6.0		
.4	.5	.3	Deferred Taxes				.8		
3.2	4.2	5.1	All Other Non-Current				2.2		
35.9	43.3	42.5	Net Worth				51.8		
100.0	100.0	100.0	Total Liabilities & Net Worth				100.0		
			INCOME DATA						
100.0	100.0	100.0	Net Sales				100.0		
30.0	29.5	30.0	Gross Profit				29.1		
26.8	28.3	26.3	Operating Expenses				26.9		
3.2	1.2	3.7	Operating Profit				2.2		
.8	.6	.3	All Other Expenses (net)				.2		
2.4	.5	3.4	Profit Before Taxes				2.0		
			RATIOS						
2.0	2.6	2.5					3.7		
1.7	1.7	1.7	Current				1.8		
1.1	1.5	1.3					1.4		
1.3	1.4	1.6					1.8		
1.0	1.2	1.0	Quick				1.1		
.6	.9	.6					.7		
43 8.6	47 7.7	40 9.2					46 7.9		
54 6.8	52 7.0	52 7.0	Sales/Receivables				56 6.5		
72 5.1	61 6.0	69 5.3					65 5.6		
21 17.1	24 15.3	39 9.4					40 9.0		
43 8.4	48 7.6	71 5.1	Cost of Sales/Inventory				77 4.7		
59 6.2	72 5.1	134 2.7					97 3.8		
23 15.7	21 17.4	20 17.9					14 25.8		
28 12.9	37 9.8	35 10.6	Cost of Sales/Payables				29 12.5		
52 7.0	56 6.5	61 6.0					39 9.5		
6.6	4.7	5.2					5.0		
7.8	8.3	7.3	Sales/Working Capital				8.4		
126.8	12.4	9.7					10.0		
11.4	9.6	14.6							
2.7 (22)	2.7 (28)	4.5	EBIT/Interest						
1.0	-5.8	-.2							
		5.6	Net Profit + Depr., Dep.,						
	(12)	1.6	Amort./Cur. Mat. L/T/D						
		.0							
.3	.3	.2					.2		
.5	.4	.4	Fixed/Worth				.3		
1.4	.8	1.0					.6		
1.1	.7	.6					.3		
1.7	1.4	1.3	Debt/Worth				1.2		
4.4	3.2	2.9					2.5		
29.3	22.1	36.7	% Profit Before Taxes/Tangible				26.7		
(18) 19.4	(24) 4.8	(28) 14.4	Net Worth				9.0		
-1.2	-27.0	.7					-7.7		
11.7	9.7	14.9	% Profit Before Taxes/Total				14.3		
5.0	2.1	5.5	Assets				2.8		
.0	-4.6	-.3					-3.1		
29.6	30.7	29.3					32.2		
11.7	12.4	12.1	Sales/Net Fixed Assets				12.6		
4.9	5.1	7.2					9.7		
3.1	3.0	2.7					2.7		
2.3	1.9	2.2	Sales/Total Assets				2.2		
1.8	1.6	1.3					1.7		
1.0	.7	1.3							
1.4 (21)	1.3 (28)	1.8	% Depr., Dep., Amort./Sales						
2.7	2.4	2.4							
	3.3	2.4	% Officers', Directors',						
(10)	5.2 (11)	4.2	Owners' Comp/Sales						
	8.4	8.4							
223311M	326064M	416214M	Net Sales ($)	1254M	4484M	15527M	74238M	123563M	197148M
170193M	186752M	226874M	Total Assets ($)	1132M	1627M	7273M	36339M	87325M	93178M

Current Data Sorted By Assets **Comparative Historical Data**

0-500M	500M-2MM	2-10MM	10-50MM	50-100MM	100-250MM	Type of Statement	4/1/98-3/31/99 ALL	4/1/99-3/31/00 ALL
2	1	6	8	3	2	Unqualified	16	14
	1	7	3			Reviewed	9	7
1	2	1				Compiled	6	4
1	2					Tax Returns		3
1	3	8	5			Other	14	9
	11 (4/1-9/30/02)		46 (10/1/02-3/31/03)					
5	9	22	16	3	2	**NUMBER OF STATEMENTS**	45	37
%	%	%	%	%	%	**ASSETS**	%	%
		8.3	7.9			Cash & Equivalents	4.7	2.7
		22.0	24.0			Trade Receivables (net)	23.0	22.9
		24.7	26.7			Inventory	32.4	31.5
		1.5	.5			All Other Current	3.3	6.1
		56.5	59.1			Total Current	63.4	63.1
		31.8	23.5			Fixed Assets (net)	26.5	23.1
		5.0	7.5			Intangibles (net)	4.7	7.4
		6.8	9.8			All Other Non-Current	5.4	6.5
		100.0	100.0			Total	100.0	100.0
						LIABILITIES		
		7.1	14.2			Notes Payable-Short Term	13.2	15.7
		3.6	2.9			Cur. Mat.-L/T/D	4.7	3.6
		12.5	10.8			Trade Payables	13.8	15.5
		.2	.7			Income Taxes Payable	.3	.3
		8.8	8.9			All Other Current	13.0	9.9
		32.2	37.6			Total Current	45.0	45.1
		15.6	15.3			Long Term Debt	17.4	23.1
		1.0	1.5			Deferred Taxes	.6	.5
		3.8	7.3			All Other Non-Current	5.2	3.6
		47.4	38.4			Net Worth	31.8	27.8
		100.0	100.0			Total Liabilities & Net Worth	100.0	100.0
						INCOME DATA		
		100.0	100.0			Net Sales	100.0	100.0
		27.7	22.3			Gross Profit	22.6	28.0
		24.6	17.9			Operating Expenses	265.1	23.7
		3.1	4.4			Operating Profit	−242.6	4.3
		1.4	1.3			All Other Expenses (net)	6.9	1.7
		1.6	3.1			Profit Before Taxes	−249.4	2.6
						RATIOS		
		3.1	2.6			Current	2.2	2.3
		1.8	1.6				1.6	1.5
		1.3	1.0				1.1	1.2
		1.8	1.4			Quick	1.2	1.1
		1.1	1.0				.7 (36)	.7
		.6	.6				.4	.3
		29 12.4	41 9.0			Sales/Receivables	28 13.0	34 10.8
		40 9.2	47 7.7				45 8.1	47 7.8
		46 7.9	66 5.6				62 5.9	61 6.0
		29 12.7	56 6.5			Cost of Sales/Inventory	54 6.8	44 8.3
		49 7.4	71 5.1				69 5.3	96 3.8
		105 3.5	104 3.5				120 3.0	137 2.7
		19 19.3	16 22.2			Cost of Sales/Payables	19 19.6	20 18.1
		27 13.4	22 16.5				28 13.1	37 9.9
		41 9.0	50 7.3				44 8.3	59 6.2
		4.2	4.1			Sales/Working Capital	5.7	5.6
		9.3	8.0				8.4	9.4
		23.9	757.1				32.9	26.1
		7.0	(15) 10.2			EBIT/Interest	(40) 6.7	(34) 4.9
		(18) 1.3	2.7				2.5	2.4
		−2.7	1.2				1.1	1.5
			(11) 5.2			Net Profit + Depr., Dep., Amort./Cur. Mat. L /T/D	(16) 7.6	(13) 4.7
			1.5				4.2	2.9
			.6				2.2	1.2
		.3	.3			Fixed/Worth	.3	.3
		.8	.8				.9	.8
		1.5	3.2				2.3	3.2
		.5	.5			Debt/Worth	.9	1.3
		1.2	3.2				2.5	3.3
		3.9	11.7				8.7	11.7
		33.1	(15) 32.0			% Profit Before Taxes/Tangible Net Worth	(38) 44.1	(29) 25.2
		(20) 9.4	17.6				17.3	19.3
		−11.1	3.0				5.9	5.6
		15.7	12.0			% Profit Before Taxes/Total Assets	12.4	8.5
		3.4	5.0				4.6	4.0
		−5.4	1.1				.3	.8
		12.5	22.7			Sales/Net Fixed Assets	15.9	18.2
		6.3	7.3				9.2	8.0
		3.4	4.7				5.5	4.6
		2.5	2.0			Sales/Total Assets	2.5	2.3
		2.0	1.6				2.1	1.8
		1.6	1.5				1.6	1.3
		1.9	(15) 1.2			% Depr., Dep., Amort./Sales	(39) 1.4	(30) 1.5
		(20) 2.9	1.9				2.1	2.7
		4.4	3.4				3.6	5.1
						% Officers', Directors', Owners' Comp/Sales		(10) 2.4
								4.4
								8.1
4703M	16755M	251114M	581909M	513612M	338144M	Net Sales ($)	1745258M	1181881M
1256M	10792M	119409M	356694M	255601M	336557M	Total Assets ($)	921284M	883861M

M = $ thousand   MM = $ million
See Pages 11 through 18 for Explanation of Ratios and Data

Comparative Historical Data / Current Data Sorted By Sales

Hist 1	Hist 2	Hist 3	Type of Statement	0-1MM	1-3MM	3-5MM	5-10MM	10-25MM	25MM & OVER
8	6	22	Unqualified	2	1		3	2	14
8	6	11	Reviewed			2	4	4	1
3	3	4	Compiled	2	1		1		
5	2	3	Tax Returns	1	2				
12	9	17	Other	1	4	1	2	6	3
4/1/00-3/31/01 ALL	4/1/01-3/31/02 ALL	4/1/02-3/31/03 ALL		11 (4/1-9/30/02)			46 (10/1/02-3/31/03)		
36	26	57	NUMBER OF STATEMENTS	6	8	3	10	12	18
%	%	%	ASSETS	%	%	%	%	%	%
7.4	4.3	6.9	Cash & Equivalents				12.1	3.2	8.1
23.5	21.1	23.1	Trade Receivables (net)				19.6	23.5	23.2
30.9	35.7	24.4	Inventory				21.7	25.9	31.9
2.2	1.5	1.6	All Other Current				1.8	1.0	1.0
64.0	62.7	56.0	Total Current				55.2	53.7	64.2
24.2	20.0	29.1	Fixed Assets (net)				30.1	34.3	22.0
5.4	5.8	6.0	Intangibles (net)				4.9	5.0	6.6
6.3	11.5	9.0	All Other Non-Current				9.8	7.0	7.1
100.0	100.0	100.0	Total				100.0	100.0	100.0
			LIABILITIES						
14.1	15.4	12.0	Notes Payable-Short Term				8.1	6.3	15.9
4.0	5.1	3.4	Cur. Mat.-L/T/D				3.0	4.4	3.0
13.8	9.2	15.1	Trade Payables				12.7	9.8	15.2
.1	.5	.3	Income Taxes Payable				.4	.2	.5
7.9	8.0	9.2	All Other Current				13.3	5.4	9.6
39.9	38.3	40.0	Total Current				37.3	26.1	44.2
24.6	15.0	28.6	Long Term Debt				15.9	16.8	13.3
.5	.9	.8	Deferred Taxes				1.5	1.0	1.0
2.4	4.9	5.4	All Other Non-Current				3.0	1.8	8.0
32.5	40.9	25.1	Net Worth				42.2	54.2	33.4
100.0	100.0	100.0	Total Liabilities & Net Worth				100.0	100.0	100.0
			INCOME DATA						
100.0	100.0	100.0	Net Sales				100.0	100.0	100.0
23.4	26.0	25.4	Gross Profit				24.8	29.1	19.3
19.3	24.0	22.7	Operating Expenses				20.8	25.3	15.8
4.1	2.1	2.7	Operating Profit				4.0	3.8	3.5
1.3	1.7	1.7	All Other Expenses (net)				1.9	1.3	1.1
2.8	.3	1.0	Profit Before Taxes				2.1	2.5	2.4
			RATIOS						
2.3	2.6	2.5	Current				2.8	3.4	2.5
1.5	1.6	1.4					1.6	2.0	1.4
1.1	1.3	1.1					1.1	1.3	1.1
1.2	1.3	1.3	Quick				1.5	1.6	1.3
.6	.7	.8					.9	1.1	.7
.4	.3	.5					.5	.8	.4
21 17.7	30 12.4	33 11.0	Sales/Receivables				23 15.9	36 10.1	36 10.1
42 8.7	44 8.3	43 8.5					38 9.7	45 8.0	44 8.4
58 6.3	53 6.8	55 6.7					43 8.5	58 6.3	54 6.8
43 8.5	59 6.2	30 12.0	Cost of Sales/Inventory				24 15.2	27 13.6	55 6.7
69 5.3	76 4.8	59 6.2					49 7.4	78 4.7	67 5.5
113 3.2	110 3.3	101 3.6					100 3.7	114 3.2	114 3.2
13 28.2	10 35.2	18 19.9	Cost of Sales/Payables				14 26.9	17 21.6	18 20.5
28 12.9	25 14.6	27 13.3					26 14.0	25 14.9	27 13.5
41 8.9	42 8.6	48 7.5					57 6.4	39 9.5	49 7.5
4.5	4.6	4.5	Sales/Working Capital				6.0	3.7	4.4
9.8	6.4	14.3					15.5	7.4	13.6
38.7	18.1	59.2					48.8	19.6	27.0
5.1	2.8	6.0	EBIT/Interest						8.9
(31) 2.1	(24) .6	(49) 1.4						(17)	1.4
.7	-.2	-1.3							-.1
4.4		3.0	Net Profit + Depr., Dep., Amort./Cur. Mat. L/T/D						4.6
(13) 1.0	(20) 1.4							(10)	1.4
.1	.1								.2
.3	.2	.4	Fixed/Worth				.5	.3	.4
.8	.5	1.0					.8	.8	.8
3.0	1.1	3.8					NM	1.3	3.2
1.0	.7	.6	Debt/Worth				.5	.4	.8
3.2	1.5	2.4					1.6	1.2	2.8
9.2	2.7	12.2					NM	2.2	11.5
48.3	16.2	31.9	% Profit Before Taxes/Tangible Net Worth					23.1	23.1
(30) 14.8	(24) -.5	(48) 9.4						9.4	(16) 12.4
4.7	-7.4	-7.2						-8.5	-4.6
12.4	5.7	10.0	% Profit Before Taxes/Total Assets				22.8	8.1	8.9
4.2	-.4	1.3					2.2	5.1	2.2
-1.0	-3.5	-5.0					-7.7	-3.7	-.2
18.9	27.8	13.3	Sales/Net Fixed Assets				11.1	9.7	27.0
10.8	11.4	6.6					7.7	6.0	9.4
5.5	4.8	4.8					5.0	3.5	5.1
2.6	2.5	2.2	Sales/Total Assets				2.6	2.4	2.1
2.1	1.8	1.8					2.1	1.7	1.8
1.7	1.4	1.3					1.6	1.3	1.5
.8	1.0	1.4	% Depr., Dep., Amort./Sales					1.5	.9
(31) 2.2	(21) 1.6	(49) 2.8					(11)	3.1	(16) 1.6
3.6	2.4	4.4						5.3	2.9
			% Officers', Directors', Owners' Comp/Sales						
1394796M	759621M	1706237M	Net Sales ($)	3667M	15032M	13074M	81139M	194546M	1398779M
808795M	432942M	1080309M	Total Assets ($)	2937M	9454M	8145M	43455M	113510M	902808M

M = $ thousand   MM = $ million
See Pages 11 through 18 for Explanation of Ratios and Data

Current Data Sorted By Assets   Comparative Historical Data

0-500M	500M-2MM	2-10MM	10-50MM	50-100MM	100-250MM	Type of Statement	4/1/98-3/31/99 ALL	4/1/99-3/31/00 ALL
		2	3			Unqualified	6	5
	3	5	2			Reviewed	9	11
1	3	1				Compiled	3	4
	1					Tax Returns	2	
1	3	3				Other	4	4
	4 (4/1-9/30/02)		24 (10/1/02-3/31/03)					
2	10	11	5			NUMBER OF STATEMENTS	24	24
%	%	%	%	%	%	ASSETS	%	%
	14.1	5.5	D	D	D	Cash & Equivalents	9.9	5.8
	35.4	21.9	A	A	A	Trade Receivables (net)	28.1	33.4
	20.2	32.1	T	T	T	Inventory	22.0	25.8
	.4	10.2	A	A	A	All Other Current	3.4	7.1
	70.1	69.7				Total Current	63.4	72.1
	27.3	25.0	N	N	N	Fixed Assets (net)	27.6	20.0
	.2	.1	O	O	O	Intangibles (net)	3.7	2.3
	2.4	5.2	T	T	T	All Other Non-Current	5.2	5.5
	100.0	100.0				Total	100.0	100.0
			A	A		LIABILITIES		
	15.9	23.6	V	V		Notes Payable-Short Term	12.6	16.4
	3.5	2.2	A	A		Cur. Mat.-L/T/D	2.8	1.5
	23.7	14.9	I	I		Trade Payables	12.6	17.5
	1.1	.0	L	L		Income Taxes Payable	.6	.2
	9.0	13.9	A	A		All Other Current	6.7	9.4
	53.3	54.5	B	B		Total Current	35.3	45.0
	21.4	13.3	L	L		Long Term Debt	20.4	13.4
	.1	.2	E	E		Deferred Taxes	.6	.2
	4.6	2.0				All Other Non-Current	5.3	4.6
	20.6	30.0				Net Worth	38.5	36.7
	100.0	100.0				Total Liabilities & Net Worth	100.0	100.0
						INCOME DATA		
	100.0	100.0				Net Sales	100.0	100.0
	38.0	32.9				Gross Profit	34.2	28.6
	34.3	29.6				Operating Expenses	26.9	22.8
	3.7	3.2				Operating Profit	7.3	5.8
	1.7	1.4				All Other Expenses (net)	1.8	3.2
	2.1	1.9				Profit Before Taxes	5.5	2.7
						RATIOS		
	3.7	2.5				Current	2.7	2.6
	1.5	1.5					1.9	1.6
	.7	.9					1.4	1.1
	3.0	1.1				Quick	1.7	1.7
	1.2	.7					(23) 1.1	1.0
	.5	.3					.7	.5
35	10.3	29 12.8				Sales/Receivables	33 11.0	44 8.3
42	8.7	47 7.8					49 7.5	68 5.4
73	5.0	54 6.8					75 4.9	84 4.4
20	18.2	80 4.6				Cost of Sales/Inventory	6 58.3	31 11.8
49	7.5	103 3.6					72 5.1	65 5.6
84	4.4	122 3.0					103 3.6	114 3.2
24	15.0	13 27.4				Cost of Sales/Payables	14 25.3	21 17.3
39	9.3	45 8.0					32 11.3	43 8.5
113	3.2	69 5.3					42 8.6	60 6.1
	4.0	5.2				Sales/Working Capital	5.6	4.6
	8.4	8.7					8.6	7.1
	-8.1	-28.9					14.5	NM
	6.9	7.2				EBIT/Interest	(21) 6.0	(23) 9.5
	1.3	2.8					3.4	4.2
	-2.4	1.2					1.8	1.6
						Net Profit + Depr., Dep., Amort./Cur. Mat. L /T/D		
	.3	.3				Fixed/Worth	.4	.3
	3.0	.8					.7	.6
	-12.8	1.5					1.6	1.4
	1.3	.6				Debt/Worth	.7	.6
	6.2	2.1					1.4	2.3
	-32.2	6.1					6.0	6.1
						% Profit Before Taxes/Tangible Net Worth	(21) 41.5	(21) 42.3
							21.0	21.3
							12.2	12.0
	21.3	11.3				% Profit Before Taxes/Total Assets	15.7	17.8
	1.9	2.5					8.8	6.7
	-3.9	.3					4.0	2.4
	30.2	25.1				Sales/Net Fixed Assets	19.9	22.3
	8.7	7.4					8.4	12.1
	5.5	4.3					6.3	5.7
	3.3	2.2				Sales/Total Assets	2.6	2.6
	2.3	1.7					1.9	1.9
	1.9	1.6					1.5	1.3
	1.4	1.3				% Depr., Dep., Amort./Sales	.9	.9
	1.9	1.6					(21) 2.2	(23) 1.8
	2.9	2.4					3.2	3.4
						% Officers', Directors', Owners' Comp/Sales		
3216M	34899M	90589M	143700M			Net Sales ($)	1181841M	530398M
723M	14128M	47069M	94609M			Total Assets ($)	434538M	327433M

Comparative Historical Data / Current Data Sorted By Sales

			Type of Statement		4 (4/1-9/30/02)			24 (10/1/02-3/31/03)		
				0-1MM	1-3MM	3-5MM	5-10MM	10-25MM	25MM & OVER
	4	5	Unqualified				2	2	1
4	4	5	Reviewed		1	2	4	3	
12	12	10	Compiled	1	1	2	1		
6	4	5	Tax Returns	1					
	3	1	Other		3	2	1	1	
5	7	7							
4/1/00-3/31/01	4/1/01-3/31/02	4/1/02-3/31/03							
ALL	ALL	ALL							
27	30	28	**NUMBER OF STATEMENTS**	2	5	6	8	6	1
%	%	%	**ASSETS**	%	%	%	%	%	%
8.9	8.8	9.0	Cash & Equivalents						
32.2	31.0	30.8	Trade Receivables (net)						
24.9	23.6	27.1	Inventory						
5.3	4.6	4.2	All Other Current						
71.2	68.0	71.1	Total Current						
19.1	25.9	23.5	Fixed Assets (net)						
2.6	1.2	.9	Intangibles (net)						
7.0	4.8	4.5	All Other Non-Current						
100.0	100.0	100.0	Total						
			LIABILITIES						
13.3	12.9	19.0	Notes Payable-Short Term						
2.1	2.8	2.2	Cur. Mat.-L/T/D						
16.6	14.0	18.9	Trade Payables						
.7	.1	.4	Income Taxes Payable						
11.6	12.2	10.9	All Other Current						
44.3	42.1	51.4	Total Current						
11.4	11.2	13.3	Long Term Debt						
.2	.2	.1	Deferred Taxes						
8.8	5.3	4.5	All Other Non-Current						
35.3	41.1	30.7	Net Worth						
100.0	100.0	100.0	Total Liabilities & Net Worth						
			INCOME DATA						
100.0	100.0	100.0	Net Sales						
33.9	30.6	32.2	Gross Profit						
26.7	27.5	28.3	Operating Expenses						
7.2	3.1	3.9	Operating Profit						
1.4	.8	1.6	All Other Expenses (net)						
5.9	2.3	2.3	Profit Before Taxes						
			RATIOS						
2.5	2.6	2.9	Current						
1.6	1.8	1.5							
1.1	1.2	1.0							
1.5	1.5	1.3	Quick						
1.0	1.0	.9							
.5	.6	.5							
39 9.3	46 7.9	38 9.6	Sales/Receivables						
54 6.7	59 6.2	49 7.4							
83 4.4	82 4.5	71 5.2							
12 30.4	23 15.6	39 9.3	Cost of Sales/Inventory						
82 4.4	71 5.1	77 4.8							
114 3.2	124 3.0	105 3.5							
21 17.6	16 23.4	15 24.3	Cost of Sales/Payables						
39 9.4	29 12.7	37 9.7							
51 7.1	51 7.1	71 5.1							
4.7	3.8	4.3	Sales/Working Capital						
8.7	6.6	8.4							
21.4	23.7	−67.8							
(25) 33.2	(27) 8.2	(27) 6.7	EBIT/Interest						
3.1	2.3	1.8							
1.5	.0	.1							
	(10) 8.3		Net Profit + Depr., Dep.,						
	3.2		Amort./Cur. Mat. L/T/D						
	1.6								
.2	.2	.3	Fixed/Worth						
.7	.6	.7							
1.8	1.3	NM							
.5	.5	.7	Debt/Worth						
2.7	1.7	1.9							
7.8	6.5	NM							
(23) 59.3	(28) 33.6	(21) 45.9	% Profit Before Taxes/Tangible						
40.8	8.0	16.1	Net Worth						
11.9	−11.4	4.9							
29.0	13.1	10.7	% Profit Before Taxes/Total						
7.5	3.8	3.7	Assets						
2.8	−2.9	−1.8							
25.5	17.6	25.3	Sales/Net Fixed Assets						
12.3	8.1	7.8							
6.3	5.3	5.2							
2.4	2.5	2.6	Sales/Total Assets						
2.0	2.0	2.1							
1.8	1.4	1.4							
(24) .8	1.3	1.3	% Depr., Dep., Amort./Sales						
1.3	2.0	1.7							
2.3	3.1	2.6							
	(11) 1.2		% Officers', Directors',						
	3.9		Owners' Comp/Sales						
	5.9								
354766M	524377M	272404M	Net Sales ($)	1764M	11879M	23776M	55646M	100614M	78725M
198793M	294807M	156529M	Total Assets ($)	859M	7229M	9867M	35618M	68835M	34121M

© RMA 2003

M = $ thousand   MM = $ million

See Pages 11 through 18 for Explanation of Ratios and Data

Current Data Sorted By Assets   Comparative Historical Data

0-500M	500M-2MM	2-10MM	10-50MM	50-100MM	100-250MM	Type of Statement	4/1/98-3/31/99 ALL	4/1/99-3/31/00 ALL
2	1	7	4	2	1	Unqualified	19	15
	3	6	3			Reviewed	13	15
1	5	8				Compiled	14	13
	4	1				Tax Returns	3	4
	3	2	6			Other	13	21
	12 (4/1-9/30/02)		47 (10/1/02-3/31/03)					
3	16	24	13	2	1	**NUMBER OF STATEMENTS**	62	68
%	%	%	%	%	%	**ASSETS**	%	%
	11.2	12.2	12.2			Cash & Equivalents	8.1	9.0
	37.0	24.6	20.8			Trade Receivables (net)	25.1	26.5
	29.3	28.6	31.5			Inventory	32.1	30.5
	1.6	3.5	5.2			All Other Current	5.7	3.5
	79.1	68.9	69.6			Total Current	70.9	69.5
	15.6	17.1	18.7			Fixed Assets (net)	16.5	20.3
	1.9	4.0	5.5			Intangibles (net)	6.8	5.8
	3.3	9.9	6.2			All Other Non-Current	5.8	4.3
	100.0	100.0	100.0			Total	100.0	100.0
						LIABILITIES		
	7.1	7.2	2.5			Notes Payable-Short Term	8.4	11.3
	5.2	1.7	3.1			Cur. Mat.-L/T/D	2.2	7.0
	27.6	15.5	9.1			Trade Payables	12.5	13.1
	.1	.7	.5			Income Taxes Payable	.4	.5
	19.0	16.1	25.4			All Other Current	24.2	21.2
	58.9	41.2	40.6			Total Current	47.5	53.2
	14.4	7.6	7.1			Long Term Debt	8.5	11.6
	.2	.6	.4			Deferred Taxes	.4	.3
	1.2	5.7	8.2			All Other Non-Current	2.0	2.9
	25.4	44.9	43.7			Net Worth	41.6	31.9
	100.0	100.0	100.0			Total Liabilities & Net Worth	100.0	100.0
						INCOME DATA		
	100.0	100.0	100.0			Net Sales	100.0	100.0
	35.2	33.3	28.3			Gross Profit	31.8	31.6
	34.0	27.0	26.2			Operating Expenses	26.4	25.8
	1.3	6.3	2.1			Operating Profit	5.4	5.8
	.4	.4	2.1			All Other Expenses (net)	1.1	1.1
	.9	5.9	-.1			Profit Before Taxes	4.3	4.6
						RATIOS		
	1.9	2.4	3.0				2.3	2.2
	1.3	1.6	2.4			Current	1.5	1.5
	1.1	1.4	1.3				1.1	1.0
	1.3	1.4	1.5				1.1	1.2
	.9	1.1	1.1			Quick	.6	.7
	.5	.4	.5				.4	.5
	(29) 12.6	(31) 11.8	(36) 10.1				(38) 9.6	(35) 10.3
	(42) 8.7	(39) 9.2	(53) 6.9			Sales/Receivables	(47) 7.7	(50) 7.3
	(55) 6.7	(58) 6.3	(65) 5.6				(61) 6.0	(65) 5.6
	(8) 45.0	(32) 11.6	(71) 5.1				(55) 6.7	(49) 7.5
	(35) 10.5	(77) 4.7	(104) 3.5			Cost of Sales/Inventory	(103) 3.5	(94) 3.9
	(106) 3.4	(157) 2.3	(189) 1.9				(135) 2.7	(132) 2.8
	(26) 13.8	(19) 19.5	(19) 18.8				(18) 20.5	(14) 26.5
	(45) 8.2	(36) 10.2	(32) 11.3			Cost of Sales/Payables	(26) 13.8	(29) 12.6
	(61) 6.0	(50) 7.2	(41) 9.0				(54) 6.8	(49) 7.4
	6.3	4.0	2.9				4.4	4.4
	18.5	6.8	3.8			Sales/Working Capital	9.0	8.9
	125.6	11.1	12.1				32.0	59.7
	14.6	66.5	10.2				15.1	7.9
	(14) 2.0	(23) 3.8	2.6			EBIT/Interest	(50) 4.2	(57) 3.5
	-1.3	2.3	-7.1				2.1	1.2
		42.1				Net Profit + Depr., Dep.,	5.2	6.7
	(13)	3.3				Amort./Cur. Mat. L /T/D	(23) 2.6	(21) 2.2
		.8					1.2	1.1
	.3	.1	.3				.2	.2
	.4	.3	.5			Fixed/Worth	.4	.5
	1.2	.6	.9				1.0	2.3
	1.4	.6	.6				.7	.8
	4.5	1.4	1.5			Debt/Worth	2.0	2.8
	14.6	2.9	4.3				9.1	6.4
	159.8	62.3	29.9			% Profit Before Taxes/Tangible	62.4	49.8
	(14) 74.3	(23) 13.0	(12) 6.1			Net Worth	(56) 21.3	(60) 27.1
	-4.2	1.4	-10.9				5.1	5.3
	21.2	23.1	8.6			% Profit Before Taxes/Total	17.9	16.2
	3.3	7.4	2.4			Assets	5.6	7.3
	-5.4	1.0	-5.5				1.6	1.6
	58.0	40.3	12.8				41.1	28.3
	31.2	22.2	7.2			Sales/Net Fixed Assets	14.8	13.4
	12.9	5.5	5.8				5.7	4.9
	5.0	2.3	1.9				2.5	2.4
	3.0	1.8	1.5			Sales/Total Assets	1.7	1.8
	2.2	1.3	1.2				1.4	1.4
	.5	.8	1.3				1.0	1.1
	(15) 1.1	(22) 1.3	(11) 2.7			% Depr., Dep., Amort./Sales	(53) 1.8	(60) 1.8
	3.9	3.1	3.0				3.0	2.7
	1.8						2.5	2.5
	(10) 3.1					% Officers', Directors',	(20) 4.1	(28) 4.1
	12.6					Owners' Comp/Sales	6.0	10.6
993M	62704M	212208M	314022M	302453M	151085M	Net Sales ($)	1803654M	2039570M
507M	19155M	122582M	227817M	146742M	169651M	Total Assets ($)	1356011M	1445349M

M = $ thousand   MM = $ million
See Pages 11 through 18 for Explanation of Ratios and Data

Comparative Historical Data | Current Data Sorted By Sales

			Type of Statement						
13	12	17	Unqualified	2			7	4	4
14	11	12	Reviewed		1	2	3	5	1
13	11	14	Compiled	1	2	3	5	3	
4	2	5	Tax Returns		3	1	1		
17	19	11	Other		1	1	4	3	2
4/1/00-3/31/01	4/1/01-3/31/02	4/1/02-3/31/03		12 (4/1-9/30/02)			47 (10/1/02-3/31/03)		
ALL	ALL	ALL		0-1MM	1-3MM	3-5MM	5-10MM	10-25MM	25MM & OVER
61	55	59	NUMBER OF STATEMENTS	3	7	7	20	15	7
%	%	%	ASSETS	%	%	%	%	%	%
6.1	6.4	11.0	Cash & Equivalents				13.4	8.9	
26.8	29.2	27.5	Trade Receivables (net)				27.1	25.5	
32.0	27.3	28.1	Inventory				23.0	32.6	
3.4	1.9	3.4	All Other Current				2.1	5.2	
68.2	64.8	70.0	Total Current				65.6	72.2	
19.4	20.5	18.0	Fixed Assets (net)				20.5	15.1	
6.3	8.0	5.5	Intangibles (net)				4.6	5.2	
6.0	6.4	6.4	All Other Non-Current				9.4	7.5	
100.0	100.0	100.0	Total				100.0	100.0	
			LIABILITIES						
14.0	12.4	6.1	Notes Payable-Short Term				5.6	5.7	
2.6	3.0	3.1	Cur. Mat.-L/T/D				2.1	3.2	
17.1	19.1	17.2	Trade Payables				14.8	17.9	
.2	1.3	.5	Income Taxes Payable				.3	1.0	
15.8	17.0	19.4	All Other Current				21.0	18.2	
49.7	52.8	46.4	Total Current				43.8	46.0	
13.9	10.9	11.9	Long Term Debt				6.6	7.6	
.2	.3	.6	Deferred Taxes				.3	.7	
3.5	3.8	4.7	All Other Non-Current				5.1	6.4	
32.9	32.0	36.4	Net Worth				44.1	39.4	
100.0	100.0	100.0	Total Liabilities & Net Worth				100.0	100.0	
			INCOME DATA						
100.0	100.0	100.0	Net Sales				100.0	100.0	
33.1	32.0	32.7	Gross Profit				35.4	28.3	
30.3	27.3	29.1	Operating Expenses				29.6	25.0	
2.8	4.7	3.6	Operating Profit				5.8	3.3	
1.5	1.5	1.1	All Other Expenses (net)				.2	2.0	
1.4	3.2	2.5	Profit Before Taxes				5.6	1.3	
			RATIOS						
1.9	1.9	2.4					2.3	2.4	
1.4	1.2	1.6	Current				1.6	1.5	
1.0	1.0	1.2					1.2	1.2	
1.0	1.0	1.3					1.5	1.1	
.6	.6	1.0	Quick				1.1	.7	
.4	.4	.5					.4	.4	
33 11.2	35 10.3	33 11.1					28 12.8	33 11.1	
48 7.5	44 8.4	47 7.8	Sales/Receivables				40 9.2	41 8.9	
63 5.8	56 6.6	59 6.2					59 6.2	63 5.8	
39 9.4	33 11.0	33 11.1					30 12.1	33 11.1	
95 3.8	78 4.7	69 5.3	Cost of Sales/Inventory				64 5.7	85 4.3	
149 2.5	113 3.2	146 2.5					146 2.5	178 2.0	
21 17.8	18 20.2	21 17.7					21 17.7	27 13.5	
36 10.2	40 9.0	36 10.0	Cost of Sales/Payables				35 10.3	37 9.7	
61 6.0	48 7.6	51 7.2					49 7.5	47 7.8	
5.1	6.4	4.4					4.8	3.2	
8.7	16.9	7.9	Sales/Working Capital				7.5	8.0	
170.7	−64.0	24.2					51.2	15.0	
9.0	11.6	13.9					30.8	10.2	
(57) 1.8	(48) 2.2	(55) 3.4	EBIT/Interest				(17) 3.7	2.7	
−.1	.1	.2					.0	.2	
7.0	7.2	14.3	Net Profit + Depr., Dep.,				33.9		
(12) 2.6	(14) 2.5	(22) 3.1	Amort./Cur. Mat. L/T/D				(10) 2.6		
−.4	1.7	.8					.5		
.2	.2	.2					.2	.2	
.6	.6	.4	Fixed/Worth				.4	.4	
2.6	2.5	1.1					.8	.8	
.9	1.2	.7					.6	1.2	
2.7	3.1	1.9	Debt/Worth				1.4	1.7	
8.3	11.9	8.9					3.5	4.3	
56.8	47.6	66.6	% Profit Before Taxes/Tangible				62.6	66.6	
(51) 18.7	(44) 22.2	(51) 12.4	Net Worth				(18) 18.1	9.1	
−1.7	−1.3	1.4					1.9	−3.3	
15.0	14.3	18.5	% Profit Before Taxes/Total				25.3	18.5	
3.1	6.1	3.6	Assets				10.8	2.2	
−1.0	−2.4	−1.3					.4	−1.3	
30.4	37.1	38.0					38.8	25.0	
9.8	9.1	12.4	Sales/Net Fixed Assets				16.3	10.4	
5.3	6.0	5.9					4.5	6.3	
2.2	2.5	2.5					2.5	2.4	
1.7	1.8	1.9	Sales/Total Assets				1.8	1.8	
1.3	1.5	1.4					1.3	1.3	
.8	.9	.8					.8	.8	
(52) 1.6	(43) 2.1	(54) 1.5	% Depr., Dep., Amort./Sales				(19) 1.3	(14) 1.4	
2.8	3.1	3.3					3.4	2.3	
2.2	2.2	2.1	% Officers', Directors',						
(21) 4.4	(15) 4.2	(20) 3.9	Owners' Comp/Sales						
8.1	10.3	10.4							
1564699M	1803848M	1043465M	Net Sales ($)	993M	15123M	30314M	147657M	242599M	606779M
1250522M	1208119M	686454M	Total Assets ($)	507M	7436M	11966M	102593M	147183M	416769M

© RMA 2003   M = $ thousand   MM = $ million
See Pages 11 through 18 for Explanation of Ratios and Data

Current Data Sorted By Assets   **Comparative Historical Data**

0-500M	500M-2MM	2-10MM	10-50MM	50-100MM	100-250MM	Type of Statement	4/1/98-3/31/99 ALL	4/1/99-3/31/00 ALL
	1	5	5	2		Unqualified	16	17
	4	7	1			Reviewed	6	7
1	5	1				Compiled	10	11
1	2					Tax Returns	2	2
1	3	6			2	Other	7	11
	13 (4/1-9/30/02)		34 (10/1/02-3/31/03)					
3	15	19	8	2		NUMBER OF STATEMENTS	41	48
%	%	%	%	%	%	ASSETS	%	%
	9.4	13.5				Cash & Equivalents	11.6	9.6
	31.1	29.4				Trade Receivables (net)	32.2	27.7
	35.6	20.6				Inventory	24.4	23.1
	2.1	4.1				All Other Current	4.2	7.7
	78.2	67.6				Total Current	72.4	68.1
	16.9	22.2				Fixed Assets (net)	19.8	19.7
	3.3	2.5				Intangibles (net)	3.9	5.7
	1.7	7.8				All Other Non-Current	3.8	6.5
	100.0	100.0				Total	100.0	100.0
						LIABILITIES		
	21.2	7.1				Notes Payable-Short Term	11.3	9.8
	6.6	4.3				Cur. Mat.-L/T/D	3.2	3.2
	16.1	15.8				Trade Payables	14.3	13.3
	.2	.3				Income Taxes Payable	.6	.6
	10.8	11.2				All Other Current	14.6	15.4
	54.9	38.8				Total Current	44.0	42.2
	15.5	15.8				Long Term Debt	13.7	14.0
	.1	.8				Deferred Taxes	.2	.3
	8.7	2.5				All Other Non-Current	4.1	5.9
	20.8	42.2				Net Worth	37.9	37.5
	100.0	100.0				Total Liabilities & Net Worth	100.0	100.0
						INCOME DATA		
	100.0	100.0				Net Sales	100.0	100.0
	31.1	28.9				Gross Profit	30.5	31.3
	30.7	25.2				Operating Expenses	25.9	26.2
	.4	3.6				Operating Profit	4.6	5.1
	2.1	.5				All Other Expenses (net)	1.6	1.2
	-1.7	3.1				Profit Before Taxes	3.0	3.9
						RATIOS		
	2.5	2.4					2.5	2.3
	1.7	1.8				Current	1.6	1.7
	1.1	1.4					1.2	1.2
	1.4	1.6					1.7	1.4
	.8	1.2				Quick	.9	.9
	.3	.8					.7	.6
	23 15.8	46 8.0					43 8.4	38 9.7
	42 8.6	57 6.4				Sales/Receivables	54 6.7	51 7.2
	63 5.8	80 4.6					68 5.4	66 5.5
	29 12.7	24 15.0					24 15.0	20 17.9
	73 5.0	64 5.7				Cost of Sales/Inventory	64 5.7	57 6.4
	176 2.1	97 3.8					90 4.1	83 4.4
	11 32.5	14 26.1					20 18.3	20 18.5
	28 12.9	31 11.7				Cost of Sales/Payables	34 10.7	35 10.6
	45 8.2	61 6.0					50 7.3	51 7.1
	5.6	4.2					4.5	4.8
	10.7	5.6				Sales/Working Capital	6.6	8.0
	51.6	12.2					15.9	22.6
	3.5	12.7					5.3	5.7
(14)	1.5	(16) 5.0				EBIT/Interest	(36) 2.4	(41) 3.0
	-2.7	1.6					1.0	.1
							3.3	9.6
	(18)					Net Profit + Depr., Dep., Amort./Cur. Mat. L /T/D	(18) 1.6	(17) 2.8
							-.7	.5
	.2	.3					.2	.2
	.7	.5				Fixed/Worth	.5	.6
	1.2	.9					.9	1.5
	1.5	.6					.8	.8
	3.9	1.8				Debt/Worth	2.1	2.5
	9.4	2.6					3.7	6.4
	67.6	41.4					33.0	38.1
(12)	1.7	(18) 14.5				% Profit Before Taxes/Tangible Net Worth	(38) 14.6	(44) 18.1
	-15.8	-1.7					.0	-6.5
	10.3	16.6					12.2	10.3
	-.7	3.8				% Profit Before Taxes/Total Assets	4.5	6.1
	-12.3	-.4					.1	-2.2
	42.3	17.5					34.1	31.6
	26.6	11.1				Sales/Net Fixed Assets	11.1	11.9
	10.3	5.8					5.2	5.7
	3.5	2.1					2.6	2.5
	2.8	1.6				Sales/Total Assets	1.9	2.0
	1.9	1.3					1.6	1.7
	1.1	1.7					.8	.7
(14)	1.6	(17) 2.2				% Depr., Dep., Amort./Sales	(34) 1.6	(40) 1.7
	3.1	4.7					2.9	3.0
							2.3	4.4
						% Officers', Directors', Owners' Comp/Sales	(13) 5.2	(13) 6.9
							10.7	8.5
3816M	39848M	184473M	199051M	132077M		Net Sales ($)	851394M	913990M
610M	16140M	103015M	140864M	125739M		Total Assets ($)	543478M	621991M

(Columns 10-50MM, 50-100MM and 100-250MM of the upper current-data sections are marked "DATA NOT AVAILABLE".)

M = $ thousand   MM = $ million
See Pages 11 through 18 for Explanation of Ratios and Data

Comparative Historical Data | Current Data Sorted By Sales

4/1/00-3/31/01 ALL	4/1/01-3/31/02 ALL	4/1/02-3/31/03 ALL	Type of Statement	0-1MM	1-3MM	3-5MM	5-10MM	10-25MM	25MM & OVER
13	9	13	Unqualified				2	8	3
11	9	12	Reviewed		4	1	3	4	
11	6	7	Compiled	1	4	1	1		
2		3	Tax Returns		2	1			
12	11	12	Other	1	4		2	3	2
					13 (4/1-9/30/02)			34 (10/1/02-3/31/03)	
49	35	47	**NUMBER OF STATEMENTS**	2	14	5	6	15	5
%	%	%	**ASSETS**	%	%	%	%	%	%
9.9	6.9	12.0	Cash & Equivalents		11.1			11.0	
28.6	29.9	27.7	Trade Receivables (net)		26.7			26.8	
24.8	20.8	24.0	Inventory		31.2			18.3	
5.2	2.5	4.0	All Other Current		2.0			6.0	
68.6	60.2	67.8	Total Current		71.1			62.1	
18.7	25.3	21.3	Fixed Assets (net)		23.8			19.1	
8.6	6.5	3.8	Intangibles (net)		3.4			2.0	
4.2	8.0	7.1	All Other Non-Current		1.7			16.7	
100.0	100.0	100.0	Total		100.0			100.0	
			LIABILITIES						
8.4	14.7	10.8	Notes Payable-Short Term		17.6			8.7	
3.1	6.2	6.2	Cur. Mat.-L/T/D		6.3			4.6	
13.9	12.3	15.6	Trade Payables		16.3			11.5	
.3	.1	.4	Income Taxes Payable		.1			.4	
19.0	13.4	14.5	All Other Current		14.4			17.0	
44.7	46.8	47.4	Total Current		54.7			42.3	
14.6	19.2	14.8	Long Term Debt		16.7			17.2	
.3	.4	.6	Deferred Taxes		.1			1.0	
3.2	7.6	6.9	All Other Non-Current		6.3			8.8	
37.2	26.1	30.3	Net Worth		22.2			30.8	
100.0	100.0	100.0	Total Liabilities & Net Worth		100.0			100.0	
			INCOME DATA						
100.0	100.0	100.0	Net Sales		100.0			100.0	
33.6	32.5	30.5	Gross Profit		31.6			34.0	
27.0	28.8	28.7	Operating Expenses		31.8			28.3	
6.6	3.7	1.9	Operating Profit		-.2			5.7	
1.9	1.5	1.6	All Other Expenses (net)		1.9			.6	
4.7	2.2	.3	Profit Before Taxes		-2.1			5.2	
			RATIOS						
2.4	2.3	2.2			1.9			2.1	
1.6	1.3	1.5	Current		1.7			1.5	
1.1	1.0	1.1			.9			1.2	
1.4	1.2	1.4			1.4			1.5	
.9	.8	.9	Quick		.8			.9	
.6	.5	.5			.3			.5	
36 10.1	36 10.1	37 9.9			22 16.5			41 8.9	
49 7.5	52 7.0	52 7.0	Sales/Receivables		52 7.0			56 6.5	
67 5.5	67 5.5	69 5.3			69 5.3			80 4.5	
40 9.2	21 17.4	25 14.5			28 13.1			25 14.5	
60 6.1	58 6.3	64 5.7	Cost of Sales/Inventory		69 5.3			41 9.0	
93 3.9	87 4.2	95 3.8			177 2.1			82 4.4	
19 19.6	13 28.8	16 23.2			16 22.7			27 13.6	
29 12.8	26 14.2	31 11.7	Cost of Sales/Payables		30 12.0			35 10.3	
45 8.0	50 7.3	61 6.0			47 7.8			61 6.0	
5.2	7.2	5.5			5.7			5.6	
8.4	12.7	9.5	Sales/Working Capital		10.5			9.2	
25.2	71.2	48.3			NM			16.0	
(37) 9.4	(30) 3.8	(41) 6.0		(13) 3.0			(13) 9.7		
2.7	1.5	1.9	EBIT/Interest	1.6			4.8		
1.1	-.8	-.8		-3.5			1.7		
(15) 13.2		(19) 2.8	Net Profit + Depr., Dep.,						
1.7		1.7	Amort./Cur. Mat. L/T/D						
.2		.5							
.3	.4	.3			.5			.4	
.5	.7	.8	Fixed/Worth		.9			.5	
1.6	-2.3	3.2			NM			5.2	
.7	.9	1.0			1.1			.8	
2.5	3.6	2.6	Debt/Worth		6.8			2.3	
7.9	-15.3	9.4			NM			30.5	
(42) 60.5	(26) 44.7	(41) 60.8	% Profit Before Taxes/Tangible	(11) 75.9			(13) 56.6		
18.8	11.1	8.4	Net Worth	6.7			9.0		
1.8	-22.8	-12.3		-17.8			.1		
17.5	16.4	11.4	% Profit Before Taxes/Total		9.8			15.0	
6.7	3.4	3.0	Assets		1.6			5.8	
.2	-7.7	-7.7			-14.0			2.5	
26.2	18.6	26.1			29.0			17.5	
13.6	11.0	12.8	Sales/Net Fixed Assets		18.3			11.5	
6.7	5.4	5.2			5.9			6.6	
2.8	2.9	3.0			3.5			2.2	
2.1	1.9	1.9	Sales/Total Assets		2.2			1.6	
1.5	1.4	1.3			1.3			1.2	
(39) .8	(26) 1.1	(41) 1.5		(13) 1.4			(13) 1.7		
1.7	1.7	2.2	% Depr., Dep., Amort./Sales	1.7			2.2		
2.3	3.7	4.5		5.0			3.8		
(12) 3.3	(10) 3.3		% Officers', Directors',						
5.8	5.0		Owners' Comp/Sales						
10.7	6.7								
668016M	489104M	559265M	Net Sales ($)	1686M	31446M	21659M	36873M	227224M	240377M
505847M	315233M	386368M	Total Assets ($)	361M	15547M	9766M	22766M	141921M	196007M

M = $ thousand   MM = $ million
See Pages 11 through 18 for Explanation of Ratios and Data

Current Data Sorted By Assets   **Comparative Historical Data**

0-500M	500M-2MM	2-10MM	10-50MM	50-100MM	100-250MM		4/1/98-3/31/99 ALL	4/1/99-3/31/00 ALL
						Type of Statement		
	1	18	16	3	4	Unqualified	32	35
1	12	29	5	2		Reviewed	46	45
2	12	8	2			Compiled	16	21
1	2	1				Tax Returns	3	4
	10	16	10	2	4	Other	30	40
	45 (4/1-9/30/02)		114 (10/1/02-3/31/03)					
4	**37**	**72**	**33**	**5**	**8**	**NUMBER OF STATEMENTS**	**127**	**145**
%	%	%	%	%	%	**ASSETS**	%	%
	4.6	10.1	7.7			Cash & Equivalents	6.6	6.3
	33.0	27.8	22.6			Trade Receivables (net)	30.1	30.4
	28.3	26.3	20.4			Inventory	25.4	25.1
	.9	3.6	6.5			All Other Current	4.2	4.6
	66.8	67.8	57.2			Total Current	66.4	66.4
	23.6	22.5	30.3			Fixed Assets (net)	23.9	24.9
	3.1	3.1	6.3			Intangibles (net)	4.2	3.4
	6.4	6.6	6.2			All Other Non-Current	5.4	5.2
	100.0	100.0	100.0			Total	100.0	100.0
						LIABILITIES		
	11.8	8.3	9.8			Notes Payable-Short Term	10.3	10.0
	4.7	3.6	4.8			Cur. Mat.-L/T/D	4.6	4.1
	15.2	10.3	8.5			Trade Payables	13.8	14.7
	.1	.2	.6			Income Taxes Payable	.3	.3
	10.3	13.3	15.6			All Other Current	13.4	11.9
	42.1	35.7	39.4			Total Current	42.4	40.9
	17.1	13.3	11.8			Long Term Debt	12.5	14.1
	.2	.4	1.2			Deferred Taxes	.8	.7
	4.6	2.6	3.5			All Other Non-Current	4.5	5.6
	35.9	47.9	44.2			Net Worth	39.8	38.7
	100.0	100.0	100.0			Total Liabilities & Net Worth	100.0	100.0
						INCOME DATA		
	100.0	100.0	100.0			Net Sales	100.0	100.0
	35.0	30.6	28.7			Gross Profit	31.7	32.4
	31.8	27.9	24.2			Operating Expenses	27.1	27.1
	3.2	2.8	4.5			Operating Profit	4.6	5.3
	1.4	.9	.7			All Other Expenses (net)	1.2	1.4
	1.8	1.9	3.8			Profit Before Taxes	3.4	3.9
						RATIOS		
	2.4	3.0	2.1				2.4	2.4
	1.5	2.0	1.3			Current	1.5	1.6
	1.1	1.3	1.1				1.2	1.2
	1.4	1.8	1.2				1.4	1.3
	.8	1.0	.7			Quick	.9	.9
	.5	.7	.5				.6	.6
	37 9.9	39 9.4	39 9.4				38 9.7	39 9.4
	50 7.2	53 6.9	50 7.3			Sales/Receivables	54 6.7	53 6.9
	57 6.4	63 5.8	71 5.2				72 5.0	71 5.2
	19 19.7	45 8.1	37 9.9				38 9.7	38 9.5
	66 5.5	76 4.8	64 5.7			Cost of Sales/Inventory	71 5.1	64 5.7
	128 2.8	112 3.3	115 3.2				104 3.5	98 3.7
	18 19.9	15 24.6	20 18.2				19 19.2	19 19.3
	34 10.9	28 13.3	25 14.8			Cost of Sales/Payables	33 11.1	34 10.7
	61 5.9	37 10.0	37 9.7				56 6.5	50 7.4
	5.9	3.7	4.4				5.3	5.2
	11.6	6.1	10.4			Sales/Working Capital	9.4	9.0
	41.8	16.4	NM				25.0	22.7
	5.9	14.1	13.4				11.0	10.7
	(35) 2.0	(66) 4.7	(31) 3.3			EBIT/Interest	(113) 4.3	(137) 4.0
	.5	.4	.5				1.4	1.4
		3.9	14.3			Net Profit + Depr., Dep.,	8.5	8.0
		(18) 2.5	(17) 3.5			Amort./Cur. Mat. L /T/D	(56) 3.1	(61) 3.0
		.2	.7				1.1	1.3
	.3	.2	.4				.3	.3
	.6	.4	1.0			Fixed/Worth	.7	.6
	1.8	1.1	1.4				1.5	1.9
	.9	.6	.7				.8	.8
	1.8	1.1	1.4			Debt/Worth	1.5	1.6
	5.8	2.3	3.2				4.3	4.6
	31.8	23.1	34.0			% Profit Before Taxes/Tangible	38.6	39.0
	(33) 8.6	(68) 12.2	(29) 19.2			Net Worth	(114) 18.6	(127) 19.6
	-4.9	.5	-2.8				6.5	9.0
	11.1	10.0	9.2			% Profit Before Taxes/Total	14.9	13.9
	3.9	4.9	6.5			Assets	7.5	6.7
	-1.0	.1	-1.2				1.8	1.8
	29.0	22.2	8.1				20.7	20.4
	13.2	9.5	4.8			Sales/Net Fixed Assets	9.9	10.7
	6.8	4.6	3.6				5.0	5.0
	3.2	2.2	1.9				2.5	2.6
	2.3	1.9	1.6			Sales/Total Assets	2.0	2.0
	1.8	1.3	1.1				1.4	1.5
	1.1	1.2	2.1				1.0	1.2
	(32) 2.6	(69) 1.9	(29) 2.8			% Depr., Dep., Amort./Sales	(117) 2.2	(127) 2.2
	3.8	4.4	5.1				3.8	3.5
	2.1	1.5				% Officers', Directors',	2.2	3.1
	(19) 5.6	(23) 2.9				Owners' Comp/Sales	(32) 3.8	(42) 4.8
	7.3	3.8					5.4	7.4
3407M	113854M	643871M	1113739M	486988M	2059525M	Net Sales ($)	2939687M	3529978M
880M	46885M	354144M	717014M	310479M	1443029M	Total Assets ($)	2032748M	2359823M

M = $ thousand   MM = $ million
See Pages 11 through 18 for Explanation of Ratios and Data

Comparative Historical Data | Current Data Sorted By Sales

					Type of Statement						
	37		39		42	Unqualified			2	11	11	18
	54		40		47	Reviewed	2	7	6	13	16	3
	40		37		24	Compiled	2	7	7	5	2	1
	7		2		4	Tax Returns		2	1	1		
	46		40		42	Other	1	6	4	11	7	13
	4/1/00-3/31/01		4/1/01-3/31/02		4/1/02-3/31/03			45 (4/1-9/30/02)		114 (10/1/02-3/31/03)		
	ALL		ALL		ALL		0-1MM	1-3MM	3-5MM	5-10MM	10-25MM	25MM & OVER
	184		158		159	NUMBER OF STATEMENTS	5	22	20	41	36	35
	%		%		%	ASSETS	%	%	%	%	%	%
	6.5		7.2		8.3	Cash & Equivalents		7.4	7.7	9.7	7.0	8.8
	30.9		28.0		26.8	Trade Receivables (net)		25.6	30.4	30.3	28.4	22.7
	26.9		23.5		24.5	Inventory		29.7	24.8	24.8	26.2	16.9
	4.1		4.9		4.1	All Other Current		1.5	2.8	3.0	5.0	7.6
	68.3		63.6		63.7	Total Current		64.3	65.6	67.8	66.5	56.0
	23.0		24.7		24.4	Fixed Assets (net)		28.2	20.5	24.6	21.9	26.2
	3.3		4.7		5.2	Intangibles (net)		2.6	4.8	1.7	4.9	10.6
	5.3		7.0		6.6	All Other Non-Current		4.9	9.1	5.9	6.6	7.2
	100.0		100.0		100.0	Total		100.0	100.0	100.0	100.0	100.0
						LIABILITIES						
	11.2		10.4		8.8	Notes Payable-Short Term		8.6	15.4	7.8	9.9	5.5
	3.0		3.7		4.3	Cur. Mat.-L/T/D		4.9	3.4	4.3	3.4	3.9
	14.3		11.7		11.4	Trade Payables		15.2	11.7	10.6	10.6	10.6
	.4		.5		.3	Income Taxes Payable		.1	.1	.2	.3	.9
	12.5		14.7		14.2	All Other Current		12.8	8.4	12.5	18.0	13.8
	41.3		41.0		39.1	Total Current		41.6	39.1	35.5	42.2	34.8
	12.5		13.0		14.2	Long Term Debt		18.6	14.2	14.8	10.1	13.3
	.6		.5		.6	Deferred Taxes		.3	.1	.6	.7	1.1
	5.3		3.5		4.6	All Other Non-Current		7.3	4.3	2.2	3.8	5.7
	40.3		42.0		41.5	Net Worth		32.2	42.3	46.9	43.3	45.1
	100.0		100.0		100.0	Total Liabilities & Net Worth		100.0	100.0	100.0	100.0	100.0
						INCOME DATA						
	100.0		100.0		100.0	Net Sales		100.0	100.0	100.0	100.0	100.0
	33.2		31.0		31.4	Gross Profit		33.0	31.7	31.5	30.7	29.1
	28.0		28.3		27.6	Operating Expenses		33.0	28.1	28.4	27.4	21.8
	5.2		2.7		3.8	Operating Profit		.1	3.6	3.1	3.3	7.3
	1.0		1.2		1.1	All Other Expenses (net)		1.1	1.3	1.0	.5	1.4
	4.3		1.5		2.7	Profit Before Taxes		−1.0	2.2	2.1	2.7	5.9
						RATIOS						
	2.4		2.5		2.6			2.1	2.9	3.7	2.3	2.6
	1.7		1.6		1.7	Current		1.4	1.4	2.0	1.9	1.4
	1.2		1.1		1.2			1.1	1.2	1.3	1.1	1.2
	1.4		1.4		1.6			1.1	1.6	1.9	1.3	1.6
	.8		.9		.8	Quick		.7	.9	1.2	.9	.8
	.6		.5		.5			.5	.5	.6	.5	.5
	38	9.5	39	9.3	38	9.5		27	13.5	41	8.8	39	9.4	39	9.4	37	9.8

	Hist 01		Hist 02		Hist 03			0-1MM		1-3MM		3-5MM		5-10MM		10-25MM		25MM & OVER
Sales/Receivables	38 / 9.5		39 / 9.3		38 / 9.5			27 / 13.5		41 / 8.8		39 / 9.4		39 / 9.4		37 / 9.8
	55 / 6.6		51 / 7.1		51 / 7.2			50 / 7.3		54 / 6.8		51 / 7.2		56 / 6.5		48 / 7.7
	70 / 5.2		67 / 5.5		64 / 5.7			66 / 5.5		72 / 5.1		60 / 6.1		66 / 5.6		66 / 5.6
Cost of Sales/Inventory	36 / 10.3		29 / 12.5		35 / 10.5			28 / 12.9		46 / 8.0		40 / 9.2		29 / 12.8		32 / 11.5
	70 / 5.2		67 / 5.5		74 / 5.0			86 / 4.2		76 / 4.8		74 / 5.0		77 / 4.7		61 / 6.0
	108 / 3.4		107 / 3.4		112 / 3.3			148 / 2.5		114 / 3.2		109 / 3.4		138 / 2.6		88 / 4.2
Cost of Sales/Payables	21 / 17.3		19 / 18.9		19 / 18.8			21 / 17.4		11 / 32.0		11 / 32.0		20 / 18.2		20 / 17.8
	34 / 10.8		29 / 12.5		28 / 13.1			31 / 11.9		29 / 12.6		28 / 13.1		28 / 12.9		26 / 14.1
	53 / 6.9		45 / 8.2		43 / 8.5			63 / 5.8		44 / 8.2		38 / 9.5		42 / 8.8		42 / 8.8

							0-1MM	1-3MM	3-5MM	5-10MM	10-25MM	25MM & OVER
	4.8		4.1		4.2	Sales/Working Capital	3.1	4.3	3.7	4.4	5.4
	8.2		9.1		8.8		11.5	9.7	6.3	6.8	10.4
	19.1		53.5		27.5		98.0	25.9	14.3	29.3	27.5
	9.8		8.5		13.6	EBIT/Interest	4.0	7.7	9.4	27.3	33.6
(167)	3.6	(145)	2.4	(149)	3.9		(21) 1.9	(19) 2.0	(36) 4.3	5.8	(32) 4.4
	1.5		.4		.5		.4	−.6	−.7	1.5	1.4
	5.7		4.3		6.3	Net Profit + Depr., Dep., Amort./Cur. Mat. L/T/D			4.9	2.6	51.9
(58)	3.3	(45)	1.9	(46)	2.4			(14) 2.8	(11) 1.4	(14) 6.4
	1.5		.3		.4			.3	−.1	1.1
	.2		.3		.3	Fixed/Worth	.3	.2	.2	.3	.4
	.6		.6		.6		.9	.5	.5	.5	1.0
	1.5		1.5		1.4		6.9	1.5	1.1	1.1	1.4
	.7		.7		.7	Debt/Worth	.9	.5	.5	.8	.7
	1.4		1.6		1.4		2.1	1.0	1.1	1.4	1.7
	4.9		4.2		3.6		10.1	5.1	2.6	3.2	3.4
	39.7		28.1		26.8	% Profit Before Taxes/Tangible Net Worth	18.9	29.6	22.7	28.7	41.1
(165)	18.3	(141)	12.5	(142)	12.2		(18) 6.0	(18) 8.5	(38) 12.3	(33) 12.1	(31) 20.3
	8.3		−2.9		.0		−9.1	−13.0	.5	3.0	6.9
	13.9		11.6		10.0	% Profit Before Taxes/Total Assets	7.6	10.5	12.3	10.0	11.0
	7.0		4.5		5.4		1.8	5.3	5.4	4.5	7.5
	1.9		−2.3		−.6		−1.9	−6.9	.2	1.4	2.5
	22.3		20.6		17.8	Sales/Net Fixed Assets	16.8	36.2	23.2	20.3	10.6
	9.5		7.9		8.2		9.7	13.1	9.4	9.7	5.7
	5.2		4.3		4.4		4.7	3.5	4.7	4.1	3.8
	2.6		2.6		2.4	Sales/Total Assets	2.6	2.5	2.6	2.3	2.1
	2.1		1.9		1.9		2.1	2.1	2.0	1.9	1.6
	1.5		1.2		1.2		1.4	1.1	1.3	1.3	1.1
	1.0		1.1		1.4	% Depr., Dep., Amort./Sales	1.4	1.2	1.5	1.0	1.7
(163)	2.0	(142)	2.3	(141)	2.4		(21) 2.6	(16) 2.3	(40) 2.4	(34) 1.7	(27) 2.6
	3.2		3.9		4.2		4.0	5.8	5.2	3.7	3.7
	3.0		2.6		1.8	% Officers', Directors', Owners' Comp/Sales	4.7		1.8		
(49)	4.6	(38)	4.2	(48)	3.6		(10) 5.8		(18) 2.4		
	8.9		6.6		6.5		7.7		4.5		
	4366063M		4257890M		4421384M	Net Sales ($)	3328M	44509M	76805M	280832M	543828M	3472082M
	2827990M		3091702M		2872431M	Total Assets ($)	3790M	28196M	48413M	164612M	359733M	2267687M

© RMA 2003   M = $ thousand   MM = $ million
See Pages 11 through 18 for Explanation of Ratios and Data

Current Data Sorted By Assets   Comparative Historical Data

0-500M	500M-2MM	2-10MM	10-50MM	50-100MM	100-250MM	Type of Statement	4/1/98-3/31/99 ALL	4/1/99-3/31/00 ALL
	1	1	4	2	3	Unqualified	31	19
	1	4	2			Reviewed	6	10
1	2	3	1			Compiled	7	10
2		1				Tax Returns	1	4
4	6	12	7		4	Other	27	14
	11 (4/1-9/30/02)		49 (10/1/02-3/31/03)					
7	10	21	13	2	7	**NUMBER OF STATEMENTS**	72	57
%	%	%	%	%	%	**ASSETS**	%	%
	2.7	14.0	14.2			Cash & Equivalents	10.9	10.2
	40.4	22.1	29.0			Trade Receivables (net)	34.1	36.1
	35.9	31.0	21.7			Inventory	24.1	25.3
	.7	8.4	3.6			All Other Current	3.0	2.3
	79.6	75.4	68.5			Total Current	72.1	73.9
	11.0	16.8	17.3			Fixed Assets (net)	15.8	15.2
	3.1	.7	10.8			Intangibles (net)	4.9	5.3
	6.3	7.1	3.4			All Other Non-Current	7.2	5.6
	100.0	100.0	100.0			Total	100.0	100.0
						LIABILITIES		
	19.7	9.3	9.8			Notes Payable-Short Term	12.5	13.9
	1.2	3.3	2.0			Cur. Mat.-L/T/D	1.5	2.8
	22.9	13.0	16.9			Trade Payables	19.2	19.4
	.4	1.1	.0			Income Taxes Payable	.5	.5
	6.4	6.9	18.0			All Other Current	16.7	8.7
	50.6	33.6	46.6			Total Current	50.4	45.3
	15.7	8.0	8.4			Long Term Debt	8.4	10.3
	.0	.2	.0			Deferred Taxes	.7	.2
	7.8	8.8	4.4			All Other Non-Current	6.3	5.4
	26.0	49.4	40.6			Net Worth	34.2	38.8
	100.0	100.0	100.0			Total Liabilities & Net Worth	100.0	100.0
						INCOME DATA		
	100.0	100.0	100.0			Net Sales	100.0	100.0
	39.8	35.4	31.2			Gross Profit	35.1	34.4
	37.0	28.2	29.8			Operating Expenses	32.3	32.2
	2.8	7.2	1.4			Operating Profit	2.8	2.2
	1.4	1.0	.9			All Other Expenses (net)	1.4	-.2
	1.4	6.2	.5			Profit Before Taxes	1.4	2.4
						RATIOS		
	2.9	6.5	2.2				2.5	2.1
	1.4	1.8	1.5			Current	1.6	1.6
	1.0	1.3	1.1				1.2	1.2
	1.8	2.9	1.3				1.5	1.5
	.8	1.0	.9			Quick	1.0	.9
	.5	.5	.6				.7	.7
	33 11.1	25 14.5	43 8.5				39 9.4	32 11.6
	47 7.8	39 9.5	53 6.9			Sales/Receivables	58 6.3	52 7.0
	78 4.7	47 7.8	79 4.6				77 4.7	68 5.3
	15 24.8	24 15.0	17 21.1				29 12.6	22 16.3
	63 5.8	90 4.1	80 4.5			Cost of Sales/Inventory	48 7.7	60 6.0
	236 1.5	148 2.5	98 3.7				111 3.3	117 3.1
	29 12.5	15 23.6	22 16.8				29 12.5	20 17.8
	52 7.1	25 14.3	31 11.8			Cost of Sales/Payables	43 8.4	37 10.0
	86 4.2	43 8.5	52 7.0				68 5.3	60 6.1
	5.9	3.4	4.7				4.7	4.6
	8.1	7.0	6.2			Sales/Working Capital	8.9	9.9
	-167.4	11.0	90.5				27.4	28.6
		84.9	26.6				17.8	13.5
	(18)	7.8	(11) 2.4			EBIT/Interest	(62) 4.3	(51) 3.7
		.2	-6.8				1.2	-.1
							43.3	6.0
						Net Profit + Depr., Dep., Amort./Cur. Mat. L /T/D	(24) 6.2	(21) 1.9
							1.4	-.3
	.0	.1	.2				.1	.1
	.6	.2	.5			Fixed/Worth	.4	.4
	1.5	.9	1.9				1.0	.9
	.7	.3	.9				.6	.7
	3.8	1.0	2.1			Debt/Worth	1.7	2.0
	19.4	3.2	4.5				4.0	4.0
		57.4	40.9				36.7	57.0
		16.1	(11) 18.6			% Profit Before Taxes/Tangible Net Worth	(64) 17.9	(52) 14.0
		-8.1	-17.4				3.9	-8.3
	31.8	30.4	14.2				14.2	18.4
	1.5	4.4	4.2			% Profit Before Taxes/Total Assets	5.7	5.0
	-6.6	-3.8	-6.6				.3	-3.0
	331.6	69.3	59.6				39.2	69.0
	64.1	22.1	13.4			Sales/Net Fixed Assets	17.3	25.7
	13.4	4.4	4.0				7.4	9.6
	4.9	2.9	2.3				3.2	4.5
	3.1	1.9	1.7			Sales/Total Assets	2.0	2.3
	1.4	1.3	1.1				1.3	1.3
		.2					.7	.3
	(16)	1.3				% Depr., Dep., Amort./Sales	(60) 1.8	(49) 1.4
		5.9					3.4	2.9
							2.0	1.9
						% Officers', Directors', Owners' Comp/Sales	(10) 3.1	(16) 5.6
							9.0	9.6
6714M	49786M	216803M	795363M	118685M	1077881M	Net Sales ($)	3954387M	2050385M
1837M	15185M	105211M	318999M	136894M	1160385M	Total Assets ($)	2131130M	1310118M

M = $ thousand   MM = $ million
See Pages 11 through 18 for Explanation of Ratios and Data

Comparative Historical Data | Current Data Sorted By Sales

			Type of Statement						
19	13	11	Unqualified				1	2	8
6	4	7	Reviewed		1		2	3	1
11	12	6	Compiled		1	1	3	1	
2	2	3	Tax Returns	2				1	
17	20	33	Other	4	3	2	8	6	10
4/1/00-3/31/01 ALL	4/1/01-3/31/02 ALL	4/1/02-3/31/03 ALL		0-1MM	1-3MM 11 (4/1-9/30/02)	3-5MM	5-10MM	10-25MM 49 (10/1/02-3/31/03)	25MM & OVER
55	51	60	**NUMBER OF STATEMENTS**	6	5	3	14	13	19
%	%	%	**ASSETS**	%	%	%	%	%	%
12.3	16.1	13.2	Cash & Equivalents				3.8	17.0	20.2
31.5	33.1	26.7	Trade Receivables (net)				31.3	25.9	25.3
23.2	23.5	26.1	Inventory				28.5	32.7	15.2
1.7	4.5	4.7	All Other Current				8.2	.8	5.3
68.6	77.2	70.7	Total Current				71.8	76.5	66.0
16.3	13.6	17.2	Fixed Assets (net)				20.6	14.5	12.8
7.0	4.1	6.9	Intangibles (net)				.0	4.8	16.5
8.0	5.1	5.3	All Other Non-Current				7.5	4.2	4.7
100.0	100.0	100.0	Total				100.0	100.0	100.0
			LIABILITIES						
10.1	11.3	12.1	Notes Payable-Short Term				12.8	12.1	5.3
2.0	1.8	2.8	Cur. Mat.-L/T/D				2.9	.9	2.1
16.4	18.6	14.7	Trade Payables				18.1	15.6	13.8
.8	.4	.6	Income Taxes Payable				1.5	.3	.6
10.1	9.7	10.2	All Other Current				5.9	6.1	18.9
39.5	41.8	40.5	Total Current				41.3	35.0	40.7
10.7	8.3	12.5	Long Term Debt				20.8	5.5	5.8
.4	.3	.1	Deferred Taxes				.2	.1	.0
4.7	4.5	6.0	All Other Non-Current				5.8	10.2	4.6
44.6	45.2	40.8	Net Worth				31.8	49.1	48.8
100.0	100.0	100.0	Total Liabilities & Net Worth				100.0	100.0	100.0
			INCOME DATA						
100.0	100.0	100.0	Net Sales				100.0	100.0	100.0
37.8	35.4	38.8	Gross Profit				29.8	32.9	39.0
31.8	32.8	35.9	Operating Expenses				25.5	27.6	40.9
6.1	2.7	2.9	Operating Profit				4.3	5.3	-1.9
.8	.4	1.0	All Other Expenses (net)				1.1	1.3	.4
5.2	2.2	1.9	Profit Before Taxes				3.2	3.9	-2.3
			RATIOS						
3.1 / 1.8 / 1.2	4.4 / 1.9 / 1.2	3.4 / 1.6 / 1.2	Current				4.2 / 1.5 / 1.2	5.9 / 1.8 / 1.4	3.5 / 1.5 / 1.2
2.3 / 1.2 / .6	3.2 / 1.0 / .7	1.4 / .9 / .5	Quick				1.4 / .7 / .5	4.1 / 1.0 / .6	2.8 / 1.0 / .6
28 13.2 / 54 6.7 / 67 5.4	33 10.9 / 45 8.1 / 68 5.4	29 12.4 / 46 8.0 / 69 5.3	Sales/Receivables				29 12.5 / 44 8.3 / 49 7.4	25 14.5 / 44 8.3 / 51 7.2	45 8.1 / 56 6.6 / 78 4.7
17 21.7 / 52 7.0 / 134 2.7	17 21.3 / 61 6.0 / 108 3.4	29 12.7 / 75 4.9 / 108 3.4	Cost of Sales/Inventory				17 22.0 / 63 5.8 / 136 2.7	41 8.9 / 83 4.4 / 177 2.1	18 20.1 / 63 5.8 / 94 3.9
27 13.8 / 39 9.3 / 68 5.3	18 20.5 / 35 10.4 / 65 5.6	20 18.3 / 37 9.8 / 59 6.2	Cost of Sales/Payables				17 21.5 / 32 11.4 / 45 8.2	19 18.8 / 26 14.2 / 54 6.8	30 12.1 / 51 7.2 / 60 6.1
3.8 / 7.4 / 23.8	3.4 / 6.2 / 16.3	4.2 / 7.6 / 25.0	Sales/Working Capital				4.2 / 8.9 / 29.0	3.9 / 6.2 / 10.9	2.0 / 5.7 / 67.2
(48) 13.9 / 3.4 / 1.4	(43) 14.5 / 2.7 / -1.3	(51) 14.2 / 2.1 / -2.5	EBIT/Interest				(12) 14.8 / 2.4 / -1.9	(12) 68.3 / 4.1 / 1.2	(16) 9.9 / 2.3 / -7.2
(16) 18.4 / 4.6 / 2.8			Net Profit + Depr., Dep., Amort./Cur. Mat. L/T/D						
.1 / .4 / 1.2	.1 / .3 / .8	.1 / .5 / 1.5	Fixed/Worth				.2 / .9 / 3.2	.1 / .2 / .7	.2 / .4 / .9
.4 / 1.6 / 4.3	.6 / 1.4 / 4.3	.6 / 1.8 / 5.6	Debt/Worth				.5 / 2.2 / 19.4	.6 / 1.2 / 2.8	.4 / 1.2 / 4.7
(50) 47.4 / 22.8 / 6.1	(47) 32.9 / 5.3 / -11.9	(54) 67.9 / 14.5 / -10.5	% Profit Before Taxes/Tangible Net Worth				(13) 70.3 / 18.0 / -25.0	26.4 / 16.1 / 1.8	(15) 40.9 / 12.4 / -11.9
18.8 / 8.2 / 1.2	12.5 / 2.7 / -6.5	12.7 / 3.7 / -7.7	% Profit Before Taxes/Total Assets				37.7 / 5.1 / -11.0	12.0 / 4.4 / 1.3	11.1 / -.4 / -7.9
52.4 / 15.7 / 5.4	57.5 / 24.7 / 7.3	60.9 / 13.9 / 4.9	Sales/Net Fixed Assets				82.3 / 19.1 / 4.0	100.1 / 41.0 / 4.3	33.2 / 8.8 / 6.4
3.6 / 1.9 / 1.1	3.6 / 2.1 / 1.4	3.3 / 1.9 / 1.2	Sales/Total Assets				4.5 / 2.1 / 1.3	3.5 / 2.2 / 1.2	1.9 / 1.2 / .9
(42) .2 / 1.2 / 5.6	(41) .6 / 1.6 / 3.2	(42) .6 / 2.4 / 4.0	% Depr., Dep., Amort./Sales				(11) .2 / 2.4 / 6.0	(11) .2 / 1.2 / 3.5	
(11) 5.3 / 6.2 / 18.0		(13) 1.8 / 11.5	% Officers', Directors', Owners' Comp/Sales						
2293675M / 1778528M	1690501M / 1221650M	2265232M / 1738511M	Net Sales ($) / Total Assets ($)	3622M / 2817M	10803M / 4824M	10876M / 7013M	102836M / 51102M	196845M / 112959M	1940250M / 1559796M

Current Data Sorted By Assets | **Comparative Historical Data**

Type of Statement	0-500M	500M-2MM	2-10MM	10-50MM	50-100MM	100-250MM	4/1/98-3/31/99 ALL	4/1/99-3/31/00 ALL
Unqualified		1	3	11	6	5	41	32
Reviewed	1	6	7				14	12
Compiled			2				6	5
Tax Returns	1	3					1	2
Other	3	2	10	8	3	1	29	31
	16 (4/1-9/30/02)			57 (10/1/02-3/31/03)				
NUMBER OF STATEMENTS	5	12	22	19	9	6	91	82
ASSETS	%	%	%	%	%	%	%	%
Cash & Equivalents		16.0	12.0	18.5			13.2	10.6
Trade Receivables (net)		36.3	30.3	24.4			33.0	32.4
Inventory		18.3	27.2	26.4			20.9	27.2
All Other Current		3.1	2.5	2.3			3.9	3.1
Total Current		73.8	72.0	71.7			71.1	73.3
Fixed Assets (net)		14.7	19.8	13.4			15.9	14.2
Intangibles (net)		8.2	3.7	8.5			5.5	6.3
All Other Non-Current		3.3	4.4	6.4			7.6	6.1
Total		100.0	100.0	100.0			100.0	100.0
LIABILITIES								
Notes Payable-Short Term		4.8	9.3	6.4			14.7	12.5
Cur. Mat.-L/T/D		3.0	2.4	4.7			2.4	3.5
Trade Payables		13.5	18.5	16.8			17.2	17.5
Income Taxes Payable		.2	.2	.3			.5	.4
All Other Current		10.9	12.2	11.8			12.7	11.6
Total Current		32.4	42.6	39.9			47.5	45.4
Long Term Debt		32.6	6.7	6.2			8.4	12.1
Deferred Taxes		1.4	.9	.1			.5	.2
All Other Non-Current		5.5	5.4	9.8			5.3	3.8
Net Worth		28.1	44.3	43.9			38.3	38.6
Total Liabilities & Net Worth		100.0	100.0	100.0			100.0	100.0
INCOME DATA								
Net Sales		100.0	100.0	100.0			100.0	100.0
Gross Profit		45.6	36.4	33.9			38.5	37.2
Operating Expenses		37.9	32.5	34.0			41.7	32.5
Operating Profit		7.6	3.9	-.1			-3.2	4.6
All Other Expenses (net)		2.3	1.1	1.0			1.1	.8
Profit Before Taxes		5.3	2.8	-1.1			-4.3	3.8
RATIOS								
Current		3.7	2.9	4.8			2.5	2.5
		2.9	1.6	1.9			1.5	1.7
		1.5	1.2	1.0			1.1	1.2
Quick		2.9	1.6	3.1			1.6	1.6
		2.0	1.0	.8			1.0	.9
		.8	.7	.5			.6	.6
Sales/Receivables		(27) 13.4	(36) 10.2	(39) 9.5			(42) 8.8	(42) 8.8
		(44) 8.2	(46) 8.0	(52) 7.1			(54) 6.8	(55) 6.6
		(69) 5.3	(52) 7.0	(64) 5.7			(68) 5.3	(66) 5.5
Cost of Sales/Inventory		(8) 44.5	(25) 14.7	(63) 5.8			(25) 14.6	(32) 11.6
		(37) 9.9	(57) 6.4	(97) 3.7			(60) 6.1	(67) 5.5
		(120) 3.0	(104) 3.5	(129) 2.8			(98) 3.7	(108) 3.4
Cost of Sales/Payables		(18) 20.6	(30) 12.2	(29) 12.7			(23) 15.8	(27) 13.3
		(30) 12.1	(46) 7.9	(47) 7.8			(43) 8.5	(44) 8.4
		(45) 8.1	(64) 5.7	(71) 5.2			(63) 5.8	(61) 6.0
Sales/Working Capital		4.3	4.0	2.4			3.6	4.6
		5.8	9.6	4.8			9.6	8.3
		14.3	25.7	59.3			45.0	18.3
EBIT/Interest		17.5	42.5	6.0			10.5	11.1
	(11)	5.8	7.3	(16) .4			(81) 2.3	(77) 3.4
		.6	1.4	-17.6			-1.7	1.1
Net Profit + Depr., Dep., Amort./Cur. Mat. L/T/D							8.3	5.6
							(26) 1.8	(18) 2.8
							-.2	.8
Fixed/Worth		.1	.3	.1			.2	.2
		.3	.6	.4			.4	.3
		97.0	.8	.7			1.0	1.3
Debt/Worth		.6	.6	.2			.6	.9
		3.9	1.8	.8			1.6	2.3
		753.4	3.6	6.5			5.1	6.5
% Profit Before Taxes/Tangible Net Worth		193.3	48.6	12.8			34.1	70.6
	(10)	30.4	25.1	(16) -1.8			(81) 14.7	(75) 24.5
		6.6	2.6	-10.6			-12.2	1.5
% Profit Before Taxes/Total Assets		24.9	17.7	10.2			9.6	15.9
		15.1	11.2	-.3			4.0	7.5
		-1.8	1.5	-4.4			-8.8	.0
Sales/Net Fixed Assets		173.6	32.0	44.6			31.0	46.4
		40.1	19.0	14.4			14.7	21.2
		9.6	5.7	7.7			7.5	9.8
Sales/Total Assets		3.4	3.0	2.4			3.0	3.1
		2.6	2.2	1.4			2.0	2.1
		1.4	1.5	1.0			1.3	1.5
% Depr., Dep., Amort./Sales			1.1	1.5			.7	1.1
		(20)	1.7	(14) 2.9			(69) 2.3	(60) 1.8
			3.9	4.3			3.9	3.4
% Officers', Directors', Owners' Comp/Sales							1.2	2.5
							(13) 3.8	(18)
							9.7	10.4
Net Sales ($)	6191M	42599M	214076M	890250M	1156615M	1194260M	4766821M	4163146M
Total Assets ($)	1026M	14329M	93707M	513929M	641338M	1045303M	2737493M	2604073M

M = $ thousand   MM = $ million
See Pages 11 through 18 for Explanation of Ratios and Data

	Comparative Historical Data				Current Data Sorted By Sales				

H1	H2	H3	Type of Statement	0-1MM	1-3MM	3-5MM	5-10MM	10-25MM	25MM & OVER
19	14	26	Unqualified		2		1	4	19
13	6	14	Reviewed		3	3	5	3	
8	8	2	Compiled				1	1	
4		4	Tax Returns		4				
21	24	27	Other	2	3	2	4	5	11
4/1/00-3/31/01 ALL	4/1/01-3/31/02 ALL	4/1/02-3/31/03 ALL			16 (4/1-9/30/02)		57 (10/1/02-3/31/03)		
65	52	73	NUMBER OF STATEMENTS	2	10	7	11	13	30
%	%	%	ASSETS	%	%	%	%	%	%
11.0	12.8	13.6	Cash & Equivalents		16.7		5.1	13.4	16.0
29.5	26.5	28.4	Trade Receivables (net)		30.5		24.8	34.1	28.1
25.6	22.3	23.2	Inventory		14.3		36.0	20.3	21.4
2.3	2.3	3.8	All Other Current		8.0		2.8	1.8	3.4
68.4	63.9	69.0	Total Current		69.5		68.7	69.5	68.9
13.1	17.5	14.7	Fixed Assets (net)		19.5		23.2	12.1	11.0
11.6	12.9	11.3	Intangibles (net)		9.6		2.6	12.5	14.6
7.0	5.7	5.0	All Other Non-Current		1.4		5.4	5.9	5.5
100.0	100.0	100.0	Total		100.0		100.0	100.0	100.0
			LIABILITIES						
13.7	8.3	6.5	Notes Payable-Short Term		7.8		9.9	7.1	3.9
3.6	4.9	3.9	Cur. Mat.-L/T/D		2.7		2.1	2.7	4.8
15.6	13.5	16.3	Trade Payables		12.4		18.1	19.8	17.6
.3	.2	.3	Income Taxes Payable		.9		.5	.3	.1
11.2	11.9	11.6	All Other Current		6.8		11.6	10.7	12.5
44.5	38.9	38.6	Total Current		30.7		42.2	40.5	38.8
13.1	11.4	15.2	Long Term Debt		38.7		5.7	6.5	10.5
.5	.7	.7	Deferred Taxes		.0		2.9	.4	.5
19.4	4.5	6.8	All Other Non-Current		7.2		6.0	6.3	8.6
22.5	44.5	38.7	Net Worth		23.4		43.1	46.3	41.7
100.0	100.0	100.0	Total Liabilities & Net Worth		100.0		100.0	100.0	100.0
			INCOME DATA						
100.0	100.0	100.0	Net Sales		100.0		100.0	100.0	100.0
39.0	38.8	36.6	Gross Profit		47.6		41.6	33.6	32.8
34.8	39.8	35.1	Operating Expenses		43.1		35.4	29.8	34.5
4.2	-1.0	1.4	Operating Profit		4.5		6.3	3.8	-1.7
.8	1.3	1.5	All Other Expenses (net)		4.7		1.0	.8	1.7
3.4	-2.3	-.1	Profit Before Taxes		-.3		5.3	3.0	-3.3
			RATIOS						
3.1	3.2	3.4			4.0		2.6	4.5	4.7
1.7	1.7	1.6	Current		3.1		1.7	1.5	1.8
1.2	1.3	1.2			1.5		1.2	1.1	1.1
1.7	2.3	2.3			3.2		1.1	2.2	3.2
.8	.9	1.0	Quick		2.0		.9	1.1	.9
.6	.6	.7			.6		.4	.7	.7
41 8.9	35 10.4	37 9.9			28 13.3		11 33.0	34 10.6	43 8.4
56 6.6	57 6.4	50 7.3	Sales/Receivables		35 9.5		38 9.5	48 7.6	62 5.9
75 4.9	70 5.2	68 5.4			72 5.0		56 6.5	52 7.0	78 4.7
41 8.9	26 14.1	20 18.0			0 UND		34 10.7	10 37.0	27 13.3
75 4.9	58 6.3	68 5.4	Cost of Sales/Inventory		34 10.8		97 3.8	54 6.8	71 5.1
113 3.2	106 3.4	112 3.3			100 3.7		136 2.7	98 3.7	112 3.3
30 12.0	21 17.0	26 13.8			16 23.1		26 14.0	14 26.4	30 12.2
41 8.9	32 11.3	41 8.9	Cost of Sales/Payables		35 10.5		59 6.2	45 8.2	41 8.8
65 5.6	64 5.7	60 6.1			50 7.4		75 4.9	56 6.5	62 5.9
4.0	4.6	3.9			3.9		4.4	3.0	2.5
7.0	7.4	7.8	Sales/Working Capital		5.8		8.0	12.2	6.5
17.4	21.0	28.4			14.7		28.9	NM	35.3
	11.4		10.3				38.0	21.1	3.0
(55) 2.9	(42) 1.0	(64) 2.4	EBIT/Interest				7.9	(12) 9.1	(25) 1.2
.1	-1.9	-.7					1.2	6.2	-3.3
37.4		11.7	Net Profit + Depr., Dep.,						
(12) 1.7		(16) 1.8	Amort./Cur. Mat. L/T/D						
.7		-2.9							
.2	.1	.1			.1		.3	.1	.1
.4	.4	.4	Fixed/Worth		.4		.7	.3	.4
4.6	2.0	1.1			NM		1.1	.8	NM
.8	.4	.5			1.0		.6	.5	.3
2.0	1.3	1.8	Debt/Worth		4.4		1.7	2.4	2.4
27.3	10.7	6.7			NM		4.7	5.1	NM
58.4	31.1	43.4					64.3	45.6	12.8
(52) 20.6	(42) 3.7	(62) 12.8	% Profit Before Taxes/Tangible Net Worth				25.5	(12) 21.9	(23) -1.1
2.0	-32.3	-4.0					1.7	13.1	-12.2
12.9	13.1	15.1			15.8		22.1	17.6	5.7
7.9	.0	4.6	% Profit Before Taxes/Total Assets		-.1		11.0	11.4	.1
-2.6	-11.7	-3.3			-10.5		.3	5.2	-4.2
37.2	30.5	42.5			110.2		42.9	35.4	34.0
17.8	14.1	15.8	Sales/Net Fixed Assets		20.9		13.9	25.5	13.8
8.1	6.9	8.5			4.3		5.5	20.5	8.8
2.7	2.4	2.8			3.9		2.7	4.5	2.4
1.7	1.9	1.8	Sales/Total Assets		1.7		2.3	2.3	1.4
1.1	1.2	1.1			1.3		1.8	1.0	.9
.9	1.1	1.1					1.3	1.1	1.0
(49) 2.0	(35) 2.3	(56) 2.1	% Depr., Dep., Amort./Sales				(10) 1.9	(10) 1.3	(21) 2.5
4.0	4.2	3.7					4.4	3.2	4.4
2.4	1.5	2.7							
(16) 6.2	(11) 3.1	(11) 6.5	% Officers', Directors', Owners' Comp/Sales						
10.1	10.5	10.4							
3108637M	2160209M	3503991M	Net Sales ($)	198M	16940M	27796M	78072M	212426M	3168559M
2223170M	1705982M	2309632M	Total Assets ($)	224M	9765M	13604M	39876M	129054M	2117109M

© RMA 2003

M = $ thousand   MM = $ million

See Pages 11 through 18 for Explanation of Ratios and Data

Current Data Sorted By Assets   **Comparative Historical Data**

0-500M	500M-2MM	2-10MM	10-50MM	50-100MM	100-250MM	Type of Statement	4/1/98-3/31/99 ALL	4/1/99-3/31/00 ALL
		3	5	1		Unqualified	29	27
	3	5	2			Reviewed	4	6
	1	2				Compiled	8	8
						Tax Returns	2	1
		6	6	1	5	Other	20	17
	3 (4/1-9/30/02)		37 (10/1/02-3/31/03)					
	4	16	13	2	5	NUMBER OF STATEMENTS	63	59
%	%	%	%	%	%	**ASSETS**	%	%
		16.0	9.0			Cash & Equivalents	13.6	10.6
		33.0	19.1			Trade Receivables (net)	27.3	30.1
		25.9	27.4			Inventory	22.6	23.8
		1.6	6.5			All Other Current	3.2	3.8
		76.6	62.0			Total Current	66.7	68.2
		15.2	14.1			Fixed Assets (net)	18.4	19.4
		2.3	13.5			Intangibles (net)	8.7	6.2
		5.8	10.4			All Other Non-Current	6.2	6.2
		100.0	100.0			Total	100.0	100.0
						LIABILITIES		
		12.4	13.5			Notes Payable-Short Term	10.8	11.2
		2.1	5.8			Cur. Mat.-L/T/D	2.3	1.7
		10.2	11.4			Trade Payables	13.2	12.8
		.0	.7			Income Taxes Payable	.4	.6
		8.9	9.9			All Other Current	14.5	12.2
		33.7	41.3			Total Current	41.2	38.5
		21.8	25.5			Long Term Debt	12.1	9.5
		.1	.0			Deferred Taxes	.4	.8
		5.7	3.1			All Other Non-Current	12.1	10.2
		38.7	30.1			Net Worth	34.2	41.0
		100.0	100.0			Total Liabilities & Net Worth	100.0	100.0
						INCOME DATA		
		100.0	100.0			Net Sales	100.0	100.0
		45.1	33.7			Gross Profit	40.6	41.4
		39.6	35.3			Operating Expenses	39.0	35.4
		5.4	-1.7			Operating Profit	1.6	6.0
		2.2	2.9			All Other Expenses (net)	1.0	1.0
		3.3	-4.6			Profit Before Taxes	.5	5.0
						RATIOS		
		3.8	3.9			Current	3.2	2.9
		2.5	2.1				2.0	2.1
		1.5	1.1				1.3	1.5
		2.8	1.9			Quick	2.3	2.0
		1.5	1.0				1.1	1.2
		.8	.5				.7	.8
		25 14.4	26 14.1			Sales/Receivables	35 10.4	39 9.5
		41 8.8	48 7.6				54 6.8	57 6.4
		75 4.9	66 5.5				69 5.3	74 4.9
		49 7.4	78 4.7			Cost of Sales/Inventory	51 7.1	40 9.1
		94 3.9	121 3.0				74 4.9	79 4.6
		154 2.4	159 2.3				112 3.2	105 3.5
		17 21.6	17 20.9			Cost of Sales/Payables	21 17.8	24 15.5
		28 12.9	28 13.2				38 9.5	41 8.9
		58 6.3	52 7.1				62 5.9	54 6.8
		3.5	2.6			Sales/Working Capital	3.0	3.8
		5.4	5.2				5.9	5.8
		7.6	22.8				19.3	13.5
		13.9	19.7			EBIT/Interest	(50) 11.1	(46) 16.1
	(15)	2.2	2.0				2.4	5.2
		1.5	-5.2				.7	1.4
						Net Profit + Depr., Dep., Amort./Cur. Mat. L /T/D	(18) 17.8	(17) 30.2
							7.9	7.1
							1.9	4.1
		.1	.2			Fixed/Worth	.2	.2
		.3	.2				.5	.4
		.8	1.3				2.1	1.0
		.6	.4			Debt/Worth	.5	.5
		1.7	.7				1.2	1.0
		6.1	4.7				9.7	4.3
		50.5	17.9			% Profit Before Taxes/Tangible Net Worth	(51) 39.4	(52) 57.6
	(13)	15.5	(11) 11.7				10.0	26.0
		4.1	-13.0				-2.0	9.7
		25.8	7.2			% Profit Before Taxes/Total Assets	12.7	19.0
		6.1	2.4				3.3	9.2
		.8	-11.5				-1.2	1.6
		58.9	23.5			Sales/Net Fixed Assets	19.4	22.3
		32.2	15.0				10.8	11.4
		9.4	8.1				6.5	7.1
		3.1	2.1			Sales/Total Assets	2.5	2.6
		2.2	1.3				1.7	1.8
		1.6	1.0				1.2	1.4
		.5	1.3			% Depr., Dep., Amort./Sales	(51) 1.2	(50) 1.5
	(13)	1.1	(10) 2.6				2.0	2.5
		2.6	6.3				4.8	4.3
						% Officers', Directors', Owners' Comp/Sales	(10)	2.6
								7.4
								16.2
	14816M	187210M	429116M	256952M	1878890M	Net Sales ($)	2457602M	3083677M
	5238M	82355M	304931M	134832M	781788M	Total Assets ($)	1918519M	2022293M

© RMA 2003

M = $ thousand   MM = $ million
See Pages 11 through 18 for Explanation of Ratios and Data

Comparative Historical Data | Current Data Sorted By Sales

					Type of Statement						
	16		12		9	Unqualified				4	5
	2		5		10	Reviewed	1	1	6	1	1
	11		8		3	Compiled	1	1	1		
	4		3			Tax Returns					
	20		10		18	Other		1	3	4	10
	4/1/00-3/31/01		4/1/01-3/31/02		4/1/02-3/31/03			3 (4/1-9/30/02)		37 (10/1/02-3/31/03)	
	ALL		ALL		ALL		0-1MM	1-3MM	3-5MM	5-10MM	10-25MM	25MM & OVER
	53		38		40	NUMBER OF STATEMENTS	2	3	10	9	16
	%		%		%	ASSETS	%	%	%	%	%	%
	11.8		15.5		14.6	Cash & Equivalents				15.0		15.1
	25.6		22.2		25.8	Trade Receivables (net)				33.6		23.3
	27.7		23.6		25.1	Inventory				19.6		26.5
	4.8		2.2		4.5	All Other Current				1.4		4.6
	69.9		63.5		70.1	Total Current				69.6		69.6
	17.3		16.9		15.1	Fixed Assets (net)				20.9		11.5
	7.4		11.6		6.8	Intangibles (net)				.7		11.6
	5.4		7.9		7.9	All Other Non-Current				8.8		7.4
	100.0		100.0		100.0	Total				100.0		100.0
						LIABILITIES						
	11.3		9.2		12.0	Notes Payable-Short Term				13.3		13.3
	4.7		3.6		7.2	Cur. Mat.-L/T/D				1.8		4.3
	11.7		12.2		13.2	Trade Payables				12.8		17.3
	.3		.3		.4	Income Taxes Payable				.0		1.0
	12.9		8.4		11.0	All Other Current				8.6		12.1
	40.9		33.7		43.8	Total Current				36.4		47.9
	10.7		17.6		18.1	Long Term Debt				9.4		20.7
	.4		.2		.2	Deferred Taxes				.0		.3
	3.9		8.4		6.0	All Other Non-Current				4.2		4.8
	44.1		40.1		32.0	Net Worth				50.0		26.4
	100.0		100.0		100.0	Total Liabilities & Net Worth				100.0		100.0
						INCOME DATA						
	100.0		100.0		100.0	Net Sales				100.0		100.0
	40.7		41.7		38.9	Gross Profit				40.5		32.7
	38.8		40.5		36.5	Operating Expenses				38.7		30.3
	1.9		1.2		2.4	Operating Profit				1.7		2.4
	−1.4		1.5		2.2	All Other Expenses (net)				.9		1.0
	3.2		−.3		.2	Profit Before Taxes				.9		1.4
						RATIOS						
	3.5		5.6		3.8					5.0		3.5
	1.6		1.8		2.3	Current				1.8		2.0
	1.2		1.2		1.2					1.2		1.0
	1.7		3.2		2.4					2.6		2.2
	.8		.9		1.2	Quick				1.4		1.1
	.5		.4		.6					.8		.6

41	8.9	35	10.5	25	14.6	Sales/Receivables			20	18.6		35	10.4
55	6.7	44	8.2	44	8.4				29	12.7		47	7.7
71	5.1	53	6.9	66	5.5				85	4.3		57	6.3
58	6.3	41	8.9	43	8.6	Cost of Sales/Inventory			22	16.6		38	9.7
93	3.9	73	5.0	85	4.3				64	5.7		68	5.4
132	2.8	145	2.5	143	2.6				145	2.5		115	3.2
20	17.8	16	22.7	18	19.9	Cost of Sales/Payables			20	17.9		21	17.2
37	9.8	29	12.7	29	12.4				28	12.9		30	12.1
69	5.3	59	6.2	56	6.5				56	6.5		60	6.1
	3.1		3.0		3.5	Sales/Working Capital				3.4			3.3
	7.5		6.9		5.4					5.7			6.4
	16.4		24.5		18.1					20.2			NM
	4.7		3.4		13.1	EBIT/Interest							19.7
(42)	2.3	(32)	1.7	(34)	2.3						(13)	3.9
	.8		−2.4		.1								1.1
	19.6		10.3		263.0	Net Profit + Depr., Dep., Amort./Cur. Mat. L/T/D							
(12)	3.0	(11)	2.1	(10)	6.3							
	.9		−.4		.4								
	.2		.2		.2	Fixed/Worth				.0			.2
	.4		.4		.3					.3			.3
	1.0		1.8		1.2					.9			NM
	.4		.3		.5	Debt/Worth				.4			.4
	1.4		2.0		1.7					.9			1.4
	3.9		9.3		4.9					2.6			NM
	28.6		28.4		39.9	% Profit Before Taxes/Tangible Net Worth							37.9
(46)	14.5	(31)	8.9	(32)	14.5						(12)	16.7
	−1.5		.5		2.4								.5
	11.2		11.6		12.7	% Profit Before Taxes/Total Assets				29.6			8.8
	5.8		2.2		6.1					4.5			6.8
	−.7		−6.8		−5.4					−6.7			−2.4
	22.9		29.4		38.2	Sales/Net Fixed Assets				74.0			38.2
	13.7		12.9		15.3					19.3			20.2
	6.1		6.3		9.0					6.2			10.5
	2.6		2.7		2.8	Sales/Total Assets				3.6			2.6
	1.7		1.8		2.0					2.5			2.0
	1.1		1.1		1.2					1.0			1.3
	.9		.9		1.0	% Depr., Dep., Amort./Sales							1.1
(40)	2.0	(36)	2.3	(29)	1.7						(10)	1.5
	3.2		4.2		3.6								3.0
	3.9		7.1		3.8	% Officers', Directors', Owners' Comp/Sales							
(10)	6.4	(12)	17.0	(10)	7.4							
	12.8		21.5		11.3								
	3184859M		1629716M		2766984M	Net Sales ($)	3201M	12981M	71652M	148078M	2531072M
	2242775M		1240245M		1309144M	Total Assets ($)	2385M	11551M	54583M	98229M	1142396M

M = $ thousand   MM = $ million
See Pages 11 through 18 for Explanation of Ratios and Data

Current Data Sorted By Assets   Comparative Historical Data

						Type of Statement		
		11	10	4	3	Unqualified	33	29
1	7	16		1		Reviewed	19	11
3	8	1				Compiled	10	11
3	5					Tax Returns	1	2
3	6	11	10	1	1	Other	27	21

0-500M	18 (4/1-9/30/02) 500M-2MM	2-10MM	87 (10/1/02-3/31/03) 10-50MM	50-100MM	100-250MM		4/1/98-3/31/99 ALL	4/1/99-3/31/00 ALL
10	26	39	20	6	4	**NUMBER OF STATEMENTS**	90	74
%	%	%	%	%	%	**ASSETS**	%	%
13.2	9.2	9.5	16.5			Cash & Equivalents	12.0	11.3
23.2	30.0	26.9	19.7			Trade Receivables (net)	26.2	25.3
23.7	28.3	32.1	19.9			Inventory	27.1	27.4
.1	1.9	4.0	6.7			All Other Current	2.7	4.5
60.2	69.3	72.5	62.7			Total Current	68.0	68.6
20.7	24.1	19.0	20.8			Fixed Assets (net)	19.7	20.5
5.4	.5	3.1	12.4			Intangibles (net)	4.8	3.9
13.7	6.1	5.3	4.0			All Other Non-Current	7.5	7.0
100.0	100.0	100.0	100.0			Total	100.0	100.0
						LIABILITIES		
14.6	28.3	13.5	7.6			Notes Payable-Short Term	10.7	10.9
3.0	4.3	3.0	2.2			Cur. Mat.-L/T/D	2.6	3.7
18.5	17.1	16.9	11.3			Trade Payables	13.3	15.1
.0	.1	.2	.0			Income Taxes Payable	.6	.3
6.9	13.8	14.9	9.5			All Other Current	9.4	10.9
43.0	63.7	48.5	30.5			Total Current	36.6	40.9
15.2	9.1	9.8	14.3			Long Term Debt	12.5	13.7
.0	.9	.5	.8			Deferred Taxes	.6	.7
5.8	4.2	1.4	2.7			All Other Non-Current	4.8	3.0
36.0	22.1	39.7	51.7			Net Worth	45.5	41.7
100.0	100.0	100.0	100.0			Total Liabilities & Net Worth	100.0	100.0
						INCOME DATA		
100.0	100.0	100.0	100.0			Net Sales	100.0	100.0
43.4	43.1	36.3	39.9			Gross Profit	38.3	38.8
31.3	38.3	32.9	42.1			Operating Expenses	32.1	34.1
12.1	4.8	3.4	-2.3			Operating Profit	6.2	4.7
.8	2.0	1.3	2.0			All Other Expenses (net)	.6	2.2
11.3	2.8	2.1	-4.3			Profit Before Taxes	5.5	2.6
						RATIOS		
7.4	3.0	2.6	4.1				3.5	3.6
1.6	1.4	1.8	2.3			Current	1.9	1.7
.8	.9	1.2	1.1				1.3	1.2
5.5	2.2	1.9	2.2				2.2	1.7
1.0	.7	.9	1.2			Quick	1.1	1.0
.5	.5	.5	.7				.6	.5

8	47.6	25	14.8	32	11.3	44	8.2					Sales/Receivables	38	9.5	37	10.0
27	13.3	50	7.2	43	8.5	52	7.0						46	7.9	49	7.4
61	6.0	69	5.3	56	6.5	69	5.3						66	5.6	61	6.0
0	UND	40	9.1	43	8.5	29	12.4					Cost of Sales/Inventory	47	7.8	47	7.8
17	21.6	74	4.9	85	4.3	82	4.5						88	4.2	88	4.1
198	1.8	140	2.6	163	2.2	121	3.0						150	2.4	135	2.7
0	UND	14	25.9	20	18.4	30	12.3					Cost of Sales/Payables	18	20.5	21	17.8
14	25.4	37	10.0	36	10.0	54	6.7						35	10.4	39	9.4
44	8.3	70	5.2	62	5.9	74	4.9						66	5.5	67	5.5

4.0	5.7	4.7	2.4				3.5	3.5
9.7	13.5	6.9	3.9			Sales/Working Capital	6.0	6.4
-40.1	-140.0	14.6	68.0				11.6	23.2

			7.0		10.1		5.0			EBIT/Interest	(72)	14.1	(61)	14.1
	(22)		2.5	(34)	3.8	(14)	.3					5.6		3.8
			-.4		-1.5		-3.6					1.6		.7

				3.3	5.7			Net Profit + Depr., Dep., Amort./Cur. Mat. L /T/D		5.3		6.8
		(14)	1.3	(11)	1.2				(38)	3.0	(28)	2.3
			-4.9		-1.2					1.3		1.2

.0	.1	.2	.2				.2	.2
.3	.6	.4	.5			Fixed/Worth	.4	.5
1.2	7.5	1.4	2.4				.7	1.3
.4	.6	.7	.3				.5	.5
1.2	1.8	1.4	.8			Debt/Worth	1.3	1.5
NM	18.6	3.7	5.3				3.1	3.8

		58.2		37.5		12.7		% Profit Before Taxes/Tangible Net Worth		56.8		38.4
	(21)	11.6	(37)	15.7	(17)	.2			(79)	22.2	(65)	20.7
		-7.7		-6.3		-57.6				10.0		1.5

42.7	18.2	13.1	6.5				21.9	17.3
24.0	6.9	6.0	-.8			% Profit Before Taxes/Total Assets	10.2	9.2
-2.9	-3.4	-7.8	-10.8				1.9	-.6
UND	30.4	25.5	12.8				27.9	26.0
43.5	15.1	13.4	8.3			Sales/Net Fixed Assets	10.4	12.1
5.9	6.3	5.7	3.7				6.0	5.4
4.8	2.7	2.5	1.8				2.5	2.5
2.5	2.2	2.0	1.3			Sales/Total Assets	2.0	1.9
1.3	1.8	1.6	1.0				1.3	1.1

		.9		1.1		2.0		% Depr., Dep., Amort./Sales		.9		.9
	(24)	2.6	(35)	2.1	(16)	3.6			(76)	2.4	(64)	2.2
		3.9		2.7		5.8				3.9		3.3

		3.4		1.4				% Officers', Directors', Owners' Comp/Sales		2.9		1.7
	(13)	7.1	(10)	2.5				(19)	4.7	(17)	4.1
		10.5		7.0					6.7		8.5

5398M	75788M	395657M	508472M	455892M	1510584M	Net Sales ($)	3240742M	2135947M
2024M	33489M	190742M	401654M	405105M	613771M	Total Assets ($)	2540313M	1479632M

© RMA 2003

M = $ thousand   MM = $ million
See Pages 11 through 18 for Explanation of Ratios and Data

Comparative Historical Data | Current Data Sorted By Sales

Hist 1	Hist 2	Hist 3	Type of Statement	0-1MM	1-3MM	3-5MM	5-10MM	10-25MM	25MM & OVER
27	20	28	Unqualified				8	8	12
9	10	25	Reviewed	1	3	5	7	8	1
13	6	12	Compiled	3	6	2	1		
2	2	8	Tax Returns	2	4	2			
21	27	32	Other	2	5	2	7	10	6
4/1/00-3/31/01 ALL	4/1/01-3/31/02 ALL	4/1/02-3/31/03 ALL		18 (4/1-9/30/02)			87 (10/1/02-3/31/03)		
72	65	105	NUMBER OF STATEMENTS	8	18	11	23	26	19
%	%	%	**ASSETS**	%	%	%	%	%	%
10.7	12.2	11.6	Cash & Equivalents		9.5	10.6	10.5	10.5	15.1
26.8	26.1	25.3	Trade Receivables (net)		25.2	34.6	24.6	26.4	20.9
25.5	26.8	26.9	Inventory		26.4	30.3	32.1	27.6	21.2
3.7	2.9	3.6	All Other Current		2.5	4.3	1.2	4.9	6.7
66.7	68.0	67.3	Total Current		63.6	79.8	68.3	69.3	63.9
23.6	20.7	21.0	Fixed Assets (net)		28.0	15.6	22.0	17.4	21.9
5.2	5.3	5.4	Intangibles (net)		.6	.2	5.3	8.2	8.9
4.5	6.0	6.3	All Other Non-Current		7.8	4.4	4.3	5.2	5.3
100.0	100.0	100.0	Total		100.0	100.0	100.0	100.0	100.0
			LIABILITIES						
7.0	10.6	14.9	Notes Payable-Short Term		30.2	19.6	15.3	8.3	5.8
4.1	2.6	3.1	Cur. Mat.-L/T/D		2.7	5.0	4.1	2.5	1.9
11.5	13.7	14.9	Trade Payables		9.9	25.6	12.9	16.6	10.2
.2	.1	.1	Income Taxes Payable		.0	.2	.2	.2	.1
11.1	11.6	12.9	All Other Current		17.5	13.2	17.0	9.3	12.3
33.9	38.6	45.9	Total Current		60.5	63.6	49.4	37.0	30.3
12.1	10.5	11.2	Long Term Debt		3.9	11.6	10.7	15.8	8.7
1.5	2.7	.7	Deferred Taxes		1.2	.0	.6	.8	.7
2.4	3.9	3.0	All Other Non-Current		.4	9.3	2.5	1.0	3.2
50.1	44.3	39.3	Net Worth		33.9	15.4	36.8	45.5	57.1
100.0	100.0	100.0	Total Liabilities & Net Worth		100.0	100.0	100.0	100.0	100.0
			INCOME DATA						
100.0	100.0	100.0	Net Sales		100.0	100.0	100.0	100.0	100.0
39.6	38.1	39.2	Gross Profit		49.1	39.0	36.9	37.5	33.3
33.0	36.0	35.3	Operating Expenses		42.2	36.6	35.6	34.3	31.4
6.6	2.1	3.8	Operating Profit		6.8	2.5	1.4	3.2	1.8
1.4	.7	1.7	All Other Expenses (net)		2.3	1.1	1.8	1.6	1.7
5.2	1.4	2.2	Profit Before Taxes		4.5	1.4	-.4	1.7	.1
			RATIOS						
3.4	3.4	3.4	Current		3.9	2.2	2.6	3.4	5.1
2.2	2.1	1.8			1.6	1.4	1.7	1.9	3.0
1.3	1.3	1.1			.6	1.0	1.0	1.2	1.7
2.2	2.1	2.1	Quick		2.3	1.1	1.1	2.0	2.5
1.0	1.1	1.0			.7	.7	.8	1.1	1.6
.6	.6	.5			.3	.6	.6	.5	.8
44 8.3	31 11.9	32 11.3	Sales/Receivables	21 17.1	39 9.4	34 10.7	39 9.3	40 9.1	
51 7.1	44 8.2	48 7.7		50 7.2	53 6.8	43 8.6	51 7.2	52 7.0	
68 5.4	60 6.1	62 5.8		64 5.7	76 4.8	53 6.9	65 5.6	67 5.5	
41 8.8	41 8.9	36 10.0	Cost of Sales/Inventory	20 18.4	40 9.1	48 7.6	41 8.9	50 7.3	
81 4.5	76 4.8	77 4.7		94 3.9	75 4.8	97 3.8	79 4.6	75 4.8	
138 2.6	138 2.7	147 2.5		168 2.2	98 3.7	169 2.2	129 2.8	137 2.7	
20 17.9	18 19.8	19 18.9	Cost of Sales/Payables	8 44.9	24 15.2	19 18.8	20 18.0	19 19.6	
31 11.8	29 12.7	36 10.0		28 13.0	68 5.4	30 12.2	41 9.0	31 11.8	
45 8.0	52 7.0	63 5.8		55 6.7	126 2.9	49 7.4	63 5.8	70 5.2	
3.0	3.8	3.4	Sales/Working Capital		4.4	5.7	4.7	3.4	2.1
5.6	6.2	6.5			12.2	12.5	7.4	6.7	3.1
11.4	22.8	31.2			-4.8	-185.0	124.0	14.5	6.3
(59) 15.7	(54) 13.0	(85) 11.6	EBIT/Interest	(15) 11.6		(21) 5.1	(22) 16.9	(14) 21.2	
4.2	2.5	3.3		3.1		2.2	6.5	3.1	
1.4	.8	-1.0		.3		-2.9	.0	-.9	
(29) 8.2	(18) 12.1	(33) 3.6	Net Profit + Depr., Dep., Amort./Cur. Mat. L/T/D			(12) 1.5			
2.8	4.1	1.5				1.1			
.8	1.8	-1.5				-8.0			
.2	.2	.2	Fixed/Worth		.1	.1	.3	.2	.1
.4	.4	.4			.5	.8	.4	.4	.4
1.0	1.1	1.4			1.7	-8.1	1.5	1.2	.9
.4	.5	.5	Debt/Worth		.3	.7	.7	.7	.3
1.0	1.1	1.4			1.5	2.3	1.5	1.1	.6
2.2	4.1	4.3			7.1	-50.4	2.8	5.0	4.2
(69) 49.0	(57) 38.2	(93) 33.5	% Profit Before Taxes/Tangible Net Worth	(16) 46.0		(21) 22.8	(23) 61.6	21.0	
16.6	16.2	11.6		17.0		9.9	20.5	5.7	
2.8	-.5	-11.9		-11.6		-19.6	-11.6	-12.8	
23.1	14.1	15.0	% Profit Before Taxes/Total Assets	24.7	17.7	7.6	21.7	12.7	
8.3	4.0	4.6		9.4	1.5	3.3	7.6	2.5	
1.0	-1.6	-5.5		-.7	-3.1	-10.8	-8.3	-10.1	
26.6	27.2	25.6	Sales/Net Fixed Assets	28.8	44.4	19.3	25.8	17.4	
9.6	14.8	12.2		14.1	15.2	11.0	12.3	9.2	
5.1	5.6	5.4		4.8	6.4	5.2	6.0	3.7	
2.6	2.8	2.5	Sales/Total Assets	2.5	3.3	2.4	2.6	1.8	
1.7	1.9	1.9		2.1	2.1	1.9	1.9	1.3	
1.1	1.5	1.3		1.6	1.6	1.4	1.3	.9	
(60) .7	(46) .9	(87) 1.1	% Depr., Dep., Amort./Sales	(16) 1.1	(10) .7	(22) 1.3	(21) 1.0	(15) 1.9	
2.1	1.9	2.2		2.6	1.9	2.2	2.1	3.5	
3.5	3.5	3.8		4.0	3.8	3.4	3.6	4.0	
(13) 1.6	(13) 3.5	(31) 2.5	% Officers', Directors', Owners' Comp/Sales	(10) 5.6					
4.1	6.4	6.4		8.7					
6.9	13.5	11.8		10.5					
2824651M	3288146M	2951791M	Net Sales ($)	3295M	36057M	44242M	162439M	426639M	2279119M
2114607M	1820477M	1646785M	Total Assets ($)	1203M	18953M	23486M	101617M	273021M	1228505M

M = $ thousand   MM = $ million
See Pages 11 through 18 for Explanation of Ratios and Data

Current Data Sorted By Assets | | | | | | | Comparative Historical Data

0-500M	500M-2MM	2-10MM	10-50MM	50-100MM	100-250MM	Type of Statement	4/1/98-3/31/99 ALL	4/1/99-3/31/00 ALL
	1	10	7	6	4	Unqualified	36	19
1	7	5				Reviewed	4	7
2	3	2				Compiled	8	5
1	3					Tax Returns	2	2
	4	10	1	3	1	Other	27	20
	14 (4/1-9/30/02)		57 (10/1/02-3/31/03)					
4	18	27	8	9	5	NUMBER OF STATEMENTS	77	53
%	%	%	%	%	%	ASSETS	%	%
	7.1	10.0				Cash & Equivalents	8.2	7.8
	40.1	31.5				Trade Receivables (net)	28.7	36.6
	25.2	25.3				Inventory	23.1	25.7
	2.0	7.1				All Other Current	3.3	5.7
	74.5	73.9				Total Current	63.3	75.9
	19.7	15.2				Fixed Assets (net)	23.6	13.2
	2.5	.6				Intangibles (net)	6.5	5.2
	3.3	10.2				All Other Non-Current	6.6	5.8
	100.0	100.0				Total	100.0	100.0
						LIABILITIES		
	16.2	13.1				Notes Payable-Short Term	9.5	11.1
	5.2	1.9				Cur. Mat.-L/T/D	4.0	3.0
	30.1	14.7				Trade Payables	16.0	17.6
	.2	.7				Income Taxes Payable	.6	.8
	9.7	10.4				All Other Current	10.2	12.4
	61.4	40.9				Total Current	40.4	44.9
	9.6	6.2				Long Term Debt	15.6	9.1
	.2	.7				Deferred Taxes	.9	.3
	.6	6.4				All Other Non-Current	13.0	11.3
	28.2	45.8				Net Worth	30.1	34.5
	100.0	100.0				Total Liabilities & Net Worth	100.0	100.0
						INCOME DATA		
	100.0	100.0				Net Sales	100.0	100.0
	41.1	39.0				Gross Profit	35.9	38.8
	42.5	38.0				Operating Expenses	43.8	31.8
	-1.4	1.0				Operating Profit	-7.8	7.0
	.7	1.2				All Other Expenses (net)	3.4	1.3
	-2.1	-.3				Profit Before Taxes	-11.3	5.7
						RATIOS		
	1.9	3.9					2.6	2.6
	1.3	2.0				Current	1.6	1.7
	1.0	1.3					1.1	1.4
	1.0	1.8					1.4	1.5
	.8	1.0				Quick	.9	.9
	.6	.6					.6	.8
	31 11.7	33 11.1					40 9.1	42 8.7
	48 7.6	45 8.1				Sales/Receivables	54 6.8	57 6.4
	53 6.9	64 5.7					75 4.9	82 4.4
	7 50.3	28 13.1					37 10.0	32 11.5
	58 6.3	75 4.9				Cost of Sales/Inventory	70 5.2	82 4.4
	98 3.7	109 3.3					118 3.1	116 3.1
	35 10.4	19 19.3					24 15.3	22 16.5
	53 6.8	30 12.1				Cost of Sales/Payables	45 8.1	35 10.6
	69 5.3	51 7.2					88 4.1	71 5.2
	8.3	3.8					4.0	3.8
	26.0	6.1				Sales/Working Capital	7.3	6.7
	NM	13.2					29.5	14.0
	5.3	13.9					13.7	10.2
	(17) 1.4	(22) 4.7				EBIT/Interest	(63) 2.9	(46) 3.3
	-9.4	-2.1					.1	1.4
						Net Profit + Depr., Dep., Amort./Cur. Mat. L /T/D	(23) 9.5 / 3.7 / .4	(15) 6.6 / 3.4 / 1.4
	.3	.1					.3	.2
	.8	.2				Fixed/Worth	.6	.4
	11.5	.5					6.2	1.5
	1.1	.5					.6	.6
	2.6	.9				Debt/Worth	2.2	1.9
	96.6	2.2					51.6	13.2
	48.8	51.7					34.1	48.2
	(15) 12.3	(26) 13.7				% Profit Before Taxes/Tangible Net Worth	(62) 17.9	(44) 30.8
	-14.9	-11.3					-2.8	5.7
	9.7	24.1					13.5	18.0
	1.7	3.2				% Profit Before Taxes/Total Assets	5.2	6.1
	-17.9	-6.4					-4.7	1.0
	48.7	45.5					18.2	40.2
	22.6	19.2				Sales/Net Fixed Assets	9.7	18.2
	11.0	9.0					4.1	10.2
	4.1	3.6					2.3	2.9
	3.3	2.3				Sales/Total Assets	1.6	2.0
	2.3	1.4					1.1	1.4
	.7	1.1					1.7	.8
	(16) 1.3	(22) 1.5				% Depr., Dep., Amort./Sales	(63) 2.7	(46) 1.5
	2.8	3.5					4.5	2.7
							2.8	2.2
						% Officers', Directors', Owners' Comp/Sales	(11) 4.6	(17) 3.9
							8.1	9.9
5648M	63151M	319555M	293878M	812336M	868383M	Net Sales ($)	2909271M	1923536M
1391M	18811M	135554M	215213M	593419M	886428M	Total Assets ($)	2034030M	1322124M

M = $ thousand   MM = $ million
See Pages 11 through 18 for Explanation of Ratios and Data

Comparative Historical Data | **Current Data Sorted By Sales**

4/1/00-3/31/01 ALL	4/1/01-3/31/02 ALL	4/1/02-3/31/03 ALL	Type of Statement	0-1MM	1-3MM	3-5MM	5-10MM	10-25MM	25MM & OVER
23	24	28	Unqualified		2	1		9	16
8	8	13	Reviewed		3	5	3		2
10	8	7	Compiled		3	3			1
4	3	4	Tax Returns	1	1	1	1		
13	24	19	Other		3	2	4	5	5
					14 (4/1-9/30/02)			57 (10/1/02-3/31/03)	
NUMBER OF STATEMENTS 58	67	71		1	10	13	9	17	21
%	%	%	**ASSETS**	%	%	%	%	%	%
11.5	9.2	10.0	Cash & Equivalents		8.4	6.3		12.1	10.2
35.4	30.1	31.2	Trade Receivables (net)		34.0	30.8		35.8	28.6
23.9	22.9	21.9	Inventory		24.3	29.9		21.9	16.9
3.1	4.2	4.8	All Other Current		3.2	3.1		7.0	4.5
73.8	66.3	67.9	Total Current		69.9	70.0		76.8	60.2
13.9	18.2	18.7	Fixed Assets (net)		22.8	19.8		13.2	18.0
4.4	7.3	6.2	Intangibles (net)		4.4	.9		4.7	14.4
7.9	8.2	7.2	All Other Non-Current		3.0	9.3		5.3	7.4
100.0	100.0	100.0	Total		100.0	100.0		100.0	100.0
			LIABILITIES						
12.7	9.5	12.2	Notes Payable-Short Term		29.4	13.1		13.1	5.2
2.2	4.3	3.5	Cur. Mat.-L/T/D		5.0	5.5		1.4	3.2
14.0	13.5	18.2	Trade Payables		21.9	15.0		16.9	16.8
1.1	.2	.5	Income Taxes Payable		.5	.1		1.1	.5
17.1	12.2	9.1	All Other Current		5.1	8.9		10.2	10.1
47.1	39.7	43.4	Total Current		61.8	42.6		42.8	35.9
6.1	9.3	9.0	Long Term Debt		11.2	9.8		6.6	9.0
.0	.4	1.0	Deferred Taxes		.0	.9		2.3	.8
6.2	6.7	4.6	All Other Non-Current		.8	3.1		3.1	6.4
40.6	43.9	42.1	Net Worth		26.2	43.6		45.4	47.8
100.0	100.0	100.0	Total Liabilities & Net Worth		100.0	100.0		100.0	100.0
			INCOME DATA						
100.0	100.0	100.0	Net Sales		100.0	100.0		100.0	100.0
40.3	38.6	38.3	Gross Profit		36.9	46.5		34.7	34.1
34.3	35.1	37.0	Operating Expenses		45.0	44.8		32.2	28.6
6.1	3.5	1.3	Operating Profit		-8.0	1.7		2.5	5.4
.5	1.5	1.4	All Other Expenses (net)		1.2	2.4		1.3	1.4
5.5	2.0	-.1	Profit Before Taxes		-9.3	-.7		1.3	4.1
			RATIOS						
3.3 / 1.9 / 1.3	3.8 / 1.9 / 1.2	2.9 / 1.8 / 1.2	Current		1.8 / 1.2 / .9	2.8 / 1.5 / 1.1		3.9 / 2.0 / 1.7	2.9 / 1.6 / 1.2
2.1 / 1.1 / .7	2.3 / 1.0 / .6	1.6 / 1.0 / .6	Quick		1.8 / .7 / .3	1.3 / .9 / .6		2.4 / 1.2 / .8	1.6 / 1.0 / .7
47 7.7 / 60 6.1 / 80 4.6	34 10.6 / 48 7.6 / 67 5.4	35 10.5 / 48 7.7 / 60 6.0	Sales/Receivables		27 13.5 / 45 8.1 / 51 7.2	28 12.9 / 49 7.5 / 57 6.4		41 9.0 / 48 7.6 / 65 5.6	40 9.1 / 54 6.7 / 76 4.8
25 14.5 / 78 4.7 / 120 3.0	26 14.0 / 61 6.0 / 101 3.6	20 17.8 / 59 6.2 / 109 3.3	Cost of Sales/Inventory		0 UND / 32 11.5 / 155 2.4	43 8.4 / 95 3.9 / 120 3.0		24 15.5 / 46 8.0 / 99 3.7	36 10.2 / 52 7.1 / 109 3.3
14 25.7 / 30 12.2 / 65 5.6	17 21.3 / 25 14.6 / 56 6.5	20 18.6 / 37 10.0 / 64 5.7	Cost of Sales/Payables		20 18.2 / 40 9.1 / 62 5.9	14 25.6 / 36 10.1 / 66 5.5		21 17.2 / 34 10.8 / 50 7.3	24 15.3 / 48 7.5 / 71 5.2
3.1 / 6.1 / 15.7	4.0 / 7.4 / 23.8	5.0 / 8.0 / 23.3	Sales/Working Capital		15.1 / 34.0 / NM	5.2 / 8.9 / 33.8		3.9 / 6.1 / 9.2	3.8 / 7.2 / 21.3
(48) 17.2 / 4.6 / 1.7	(57) 10.1 / 2.4 / .1	(60) 10.7 / 2.1 / -4.4	EBIT/Interest		(12) 8.2 / 2.6 / -2.9			(14) 36.5 / 7.3 / -5.2	(18) 19.7 / 3.8 / .8
(15) 9.7 / 4.9 / 1.3	(15) 12.3 / 4.9 / 1.5	(22) 9.9 / 2.6 / .2	Net Profit + Depr., Dep., Amort./Cur. Mat. L/T/D						
.2 / .3 / .7	.2 / .4 / 1.2	.2 / .4 / 1.3	Fixed/Worth		.6 / 1.1 / -4.5	.2 / .4 / 1.0		.1 / .2 / .5	.2 / .4 / 1.3
.5 / 1.4 / 3.7	.4 / 1.5 / 5.6	.5 / 1.5 / 3.2	Debt/Worth		1.1 / 3.0 / -83.3	.5 / 1.9 / 3.0		.4 / .9 / 1.7	.4 / 1.8 / 3.3
(52) 63.5 / 25.2 / 5.1	(56) 42.5 / 16.3 / -3.5	(62) 39.7 / 15.7 / -8.1	% Profit Before Taxes/Tangible Net Worth			30.4 / 8.8 / -17.9		(15) 68.7 / 17.4 / -4.2	(18) 29.5 / 16.1 / -.4
20.7 / 9.1 / 1.5	16.6 / 7.2 / -2.6	14.5 / 3.2 / -7.0	% Profit Before Taxes/Total Assets		7.7 / -13.1 / -57.9	19.9 / 2.2 / -10.6		25.4 / 3.2 / -6.3	12.6 / 6.2 / -2.2
38.9 / 14.9 / 7.6	26.0 / 14.7 / 6.5	32.4 / 16.9 / 7.9	Sales/Net Fixed Assets		52.1 / 18.6 / 8.6	22.1 / 11.1 / 5.9		61.1 / 28.3 / 17.1	19.4 / 9.8 / 5.6
2.9 / 1.8 / 1.1	2.8 / 2.1 / 1.2	3.5 / 2.2 / 1.2	Sales/Total Assets		3.9 / 2.7 / 2.2	3.5 / 2.3 / 1.2		3.7 / 2.5 / 1.7	2.3 / 1.2 / 1.0
(51) 1.1 / 1.8 / 3.2	(58) .9 / 2.0 / 3.2	(56) 1.0 / 1.7 / 3.6	% Depr., Dep., Amort./Sales		(11) 1.6 / 2.3 / 3.6			(13) 1.0 / 1.3 / 2.6	(15) 1.0 / 1.8 / 5.3
(18) 3.7 / 5.3 / 13.4	(18) 6.5 / 9.9 / 13.1	(20) 2.4 / 6.8 / 9.8	% Officers', Directors', Owners' Comp/Sales						
1874886M	1835773M	2362951M	Net Sales ($)	990M	17725M	49380M	58316M	253794M	1982746M
1431759M	1398853M	1850816M	Total Assets ($)	189M	6083M	26920M	33884M	140043M	1643697M

M = $ thousand   MM = $ million
See Pages 11 through 18 for Explanation of Ratios and Data

Current Data Sorted By Assets   Comparative Historical Data

0-500M	500M-2MM	2-10MM	10-50MM	50-100MM	100-250MM	Type of Statement	4/1/98-3/31/99 ALL	4/1/99-3/31/00 ALL
		1	12	1	3	Unqualified	19	16
1		9	1			Reviewed	12	9
	5					Compiled	5	3
1	1					Tax Returns	2	
1	2	6	5	5	3	Other	11	14
	15 (4/1-9/30/02)		41 (10/1/02-3/31/03)					
2	8	16	18	6	6	NUMBER OF STATEMENTS	49	42
%	%	%	%	%	%	**ASSETS**	%	%
		6.3	6.8			Cash & Equivalents	6.3	8.9
		31.8	28.0			Trade Receivables (net)	32.2	30.8
		31.8	33.7			Inventory	36.0	34.2
		3.8	2.4			All Other Current	2.8	3.3
		73.8	71.0			Total Current	77.3	77.1
		17.4	17.9			Fixed Assets (net)	14.3	14.2
		4.4	7.0			Intangibles (net)	3.8	4.3
		4.4	4.0			All Other Non-Current	4.5	4.4
		100.0	100.0			Total	100.0	100.0
						LIABILITIES		
		22.3	9.7			Notes Payable-Short Term	14.4	11.3
		1.2	1.7			Cur. Mat.-L/T/D	1.7	2.7
		15.0	12.8			Trade Payables	16.4	17.1
		.1	.5			Income Taxes Payable	.4	.3
		9.1	10.7			All Other Current	12.1	11.5
		47.7	35.5			Total Current	45.2	42.9
		10.3	7.1			Long Term Debt	11.5	11.4
		.0	.7			Deferred Taxes	.3	.2
		3.0	2.9			All Other Non-Current	4.5	2.8
		39.0	53.8			Net Worth	38.5	42.6
		100.0	100.0			Total Liabilities & Net Worth	100.0	100.0
						INCOME DATA		
		100.0	100.0			Net Sales	100.0	100.0
		33.6	33.7			Gross Profit	34.0	33.8
		29.2	26.7			Operating Expenses	27.5	27.4
		4.5	6.9			Operating Profit	6.5	6.4
		1.1	1.0			All Other Expenses (net)	.3	.6
		3.3	6.0			Profit Before Taxes	6.2	5.7
						RATIOS		
		2.7	3.5			Current	3.0	3.1
		1.4	2.4				1.8	1.7
		1.1	1.2				1.3	1.3
		1.1	1.8			Quick	1.6	1.7
		.7	1.2				.8	.9
		.5	.7				.6	.6
		31 11.7	35 10.4			Sales/Receivables	38 9.6	37 10.0
		45 8.2	51 7.2				50 7.3	52 7.0
		61 6.0	61 6.0				62 5.9	67 5.5
		38 9.5	81 4.5			Cost of Sales/Inventory	62 5.9	50 7.3
		74 4.9	94 3.9				90 4.1	88 4.1
		126 2.9	111 3.3				119 3.1	134 2.7
		16 22.5	17 21.7			Cost of Sales/Payables	21 17.1	19 19.2
		31 11.7	30 12.2				32 11.6	36 10.1
		46 7.9	42 8.8				44 8.2	62 5.9
		6.5	4.0			Sales/Working Capital	3.8	4.2
		11.3	5.5				7.3	6.8
		43.9	19.3				14.1	13.5
		28.0	45.1			EBIT/Interest	22.8	23.4
		(15) 1.9	(15) 6.1				(45) 7.0	(35) 6.8
		1.4	3.7				3.4	3.4
						Net Profit + Depr., Dep., Amort./Cur. Mat. L/T/D	15.7	8.1
							(17) 4.5	(13) 3.2
							2.0	2.0
		.1	.1			Fixed/Worth	.1	.1
		.4	.3				.3	.4
		1.3	1.1				.7	.7
		.9	.3			Debt/Worth	.6	.6
		2.0	.8				1.2	1.4
		4.3	3.3				3.8	3.5
		35.8	50.4			% Profit Before Taxes/Tangible Net Worth	59.0	48.6
		(14) 14.5	(17) 23.8				(46) 31.0	(36) 27.9
		6.5	10.7				16.2	10.3
		14.6	16.3			% Profit Before Taxes/Total Assets	20.0	21.2
		3.3	8.6				12.4	9.8
		1.6	5.5				7.6	4.3
		51.2	26.0			Sales/Net Fixed Assets	47.9	38.0
		25.3	11.3				20.9	19.5
		7.6	6.9				10.0	9.9
		2.8	2.4			Sales/Total Assets	3.2	2.9
		2.3	1.9				2.4	2.2
		1.4	1.4				1.5	1.4
		.6	1.5			% Depr., Dep., Amort./Sales	.6	.9
		(14) 1.1	(17) 2.0				(44) .9	(37) 1.2
		1.4	3.1				3.0	2.1
						% Officers', Directors', Owners' Comp/Sales		1.4
								(10) 2.5
								4.9
2543M	31871M	177860M	1104570M	631198M	1421200M	Net Sales ($)	1928949M	1765455M
350M	8323M	73548M	478355M	425334M	799136M	Total Assets ($)	999224M	851056M

M = $ thousand MM = $ million
See Pages 11 through 18 for Explanation of Ratios and Data

Comparative Historical Data / Current Data Sorted By Sales

					Type of Statement						
	8		14	17	Unqualified				1	2	14
	5		8	11	Reviewed	1		1	4	5	
	8		8	5	Compiled		2	1	2		
	3			2	Tax Returns		1	1			
	16		21	21	Other		1	1	1	3	13
	4/1/00-3/31/01		4/1/01-3/31/02	4/1/02-3/31/03			15 (4/1-9/30/02)			41 (10/1/02-3/31/03)	
	ALL		ALL	ALL		0-1MM	1-3MM	3-5MM	5-10MM	10-25MM	25MM & OVER
	40		51	56	**NUMBER OF STATEMENTS**	1	4	4	10	10	27
	%		%	%	**ASSETS**	%	%	%	%	%	%
	7.2		11.0	9.4	Cash & Equivalents				8.0	12.3	10.2
	31.3		29.5	26.8	Trade Receivables (net)				25.5	29.9	25.5
	36.3		33.2	34.0	Inventory				28.6	30.8	31.7
	2.4		3.1	3.2	All Other Current				4.2	1.8	3.7
	77.3		76.9	73.4	Total Current				66.3	74.8	71.1
	16.1		15.1	16.9	Fixed Assets (net)				21.2	19.8	16.5
	2.3		3.6	4.3	Intangibles (net)				6.2	.6	6.2
	4.3		4.4	5.3	All Other Non-Current				6.3	4.8	6.2
	100.0		100.0	100.0	Total				100.0	100.0	100.0
					LIABILITIES						
	12.8		13.9	14.4	Notes Payable-Short Term				16.7	18.2	8.7
	2.2		4.5	1.7	Cur. Mat.-L/T/D				1.5	1.6	1.6
	16.8		13.4	15.1	Trade Payables				13.8	12.9	14.0
	.4		.4	.5	Income Taxes Payable				.7	.2	.6
	9.9		11.4	10.6	All Other Current				9.6	9.0	10.6
	42.0		43.5	42.3	Total Current				42.2	41.9	35.5
	9.8		7.5	9.2	Long Term Debt				17.1	2.3	9.0
	.2		.1	.3	Deferred Taxes				.0	.3	.5
	3.9		3.3	3.6	All Other Non-Current				3.7	1.1	3.5
	44.1		45.5	44.5	Net Worth				36.9	54.4	51.5
	100.0		100.0	100.0	Total Liabilities & Net Worth				100.0	100.0	100.0
					INCOME DATA						
	100.0		100.0	100.0	Net Sales				100.0	100.0	100.0
	37.6		37.2	34.7	Gross Profit				28.9	37.2	35.4
	30.1		32.0	29.3	Operating Expenses				27.0	29.9	28.5
	7.5		5.2	5.4	Operating Profit				1.9	7.3	6.9
	1.0		.3	.7	All Other Expenses (net)				1.1	.4	.6
	6.5		4.9	4.7	Profit Before Taxes				.8	6.8	6.4
					RATIOS						
	2.9		4.3	2.9					2.7	4.5	3.3
	2.0		1.9	1.8	Current				1.4	1.5	2.4
	1.2		1.3	1.2					1.0	1.3	1.3
	1.6		1.9	1.5					1.0	1.8	1.7
	.8		1.1	.9	Quick				.8	1.1	1.0
	.6		.6	.5					.5	.6	.6
43	8.4	32	11.3	29	12.7			23	15.7	35	10.3	32	11.5
50	7.2	49	7.5	43	8.5	Sales/Receivables		40	9.1	48	7.6	46	7.9
66	5.5	60	6.1	60	6.0			51	7.2	68	5.3	61	6.0
58	6.3	53	6.9	49	7.4			26	13.9	69	5.3	62	5.9
94	3.9	87	4.2	91	4.0	Cost of Sales/Inventory		40	9.1	82	4.4	92	4.0
144	2.5	135	2.7	122	3.0			141	2.6	138	2.6	110	3.3
22	16.8	19	19.0	19	19.1			21	17.7	13	29.0	21	17.6
37	10.0	31	11.7	32	11.3	Cost of Sales/Payables		27	13.5	24	15.1	35	10.5
60	6.1	47	7.7	50	7.2			38	9.6	82	4.4	46	8.0
	4.1		2.9		4.4				3.9		2.1		4.2
	5.7		6.2		7.7	Sales/Working Capital			13.8		6.8		6.5
	20.9		15.0		19.0				NM		18.5		11.2
	13.4		19.7		20.9								38.2
(34)	4.8	(46)	4.7	(48)	6.3	EBIT/Interest					(22)	8.9
	1.6		1.2		1.7								4.6
	19.9		68.2		7.6	Net Profit + Depr., Dep.,							
(10)	5.7	(16)	9.1	(14)	5.1	Amort./Cur. Mat. L/T/D							
	2.4		2.4		2.1								
	.1		.1		.1				.2		.1		.1
	.3		.3		.4	Fixed/Worth			.4		.4		.3
	.8		.7		1.0				2.0		.5		1.0
	.6		.3		.6				.9		.5		.5
	1.2		1.3		1.4	Debt/Worth			2.5		.9		.9
	3.5		2.6		3.8				4.3		2.0		3.3
	64.7		52.0		53.1	% Profit Before Taxes/Tangible					73.9		54.3
(38)	28.9	(48)	19.2	(52)	21.3	Net Worth					12.2	(26)	25.9
	10.3		3.5		7.2						2.3		16.9
	21.3		19.4		15.5	% Profit Before Taxes/Total				10.2		38.0		18.7
	10.7		7.1		8.2	Assets				3.0		9.9		10.0
	3.2		1.1		2.1					.4		.8		6.7
	35.2		37.1		39.8					44.9		39.9		30.7
	21.2		18.4		17.3	Sales/Net Fixed Assets				17.6		18.6		9.6
	8.5		8.8		7.0					6.0		2.9		6.9
	3.3		3.0		2.9					3.2		3.0		2.8
	2.2		2.0		2.1	Sales/Total Assets				1.7		2.5		1.9
	1.4		1.5		1.4					1.3		1.2		1.5
	.4		.5		.7								1.4
(38)	1.6	(41)	1.5	(49)	1.6	% Depr., Dep., Amort./Sales					(24)	2.1
	2.4		2.5		2.9								3.1
	1.5		1.4		2.0	% Officers', Directors',							
(14)	3.4	(12)	2.8	(15)	4.2	Owners' Comp/Sales							
	7.9		5.3		7.7								
2152834M		1908999M		3369242M	Net Sales ($)	23M	8683M	14455M	64183M	167044M	3114854M
1158990M		1128390M		1785046M	Total Assets ($)	8M	2597M	5475M	35393M	177166M	1564407M

M = $ thousand   MM = $ million
See Pages 11 through 18 for Explanation of Ratios and Data

Current Data Sorted By Assets   Comparative Historical Data

Type of Statement	0-500M	500M-2MM	2-10MM	10-50MM	50-100MM	100-250MM	4/1/98-3/31/99 ALL	4/1/99-3/31/00 ALL
Unqualified			6	6	2	2	45	32
Reviewed		3	8	1			22	16
Compiled	1	6	1				18	11
Tax Returns		2	2				4	2
Other		7	11	1	1	2	52	35
		16 (4/1-9/30/02)			46 (10/1/02-3/31/03)			
NUMBER OF STATEMENTS	1	18	28	8	3	4	141	96

ASSETS	0-500M	500M-2MM	2-10MM	10-50MM	50-100MM	100-250MM	Hist 98/99	Hist 99/00
	%	%	%	%	%	%	%	%
Cash & Equivalents		6.0	8.4				9.1	9.8
Trade Receivables (net)		34.0	25.4				28.6	28.0
Inventory		30.9	33.7				26.0	27.1
All Other Current		1.1	1.8				1.6	2.0
Total Current		71.9	69.2				65.3	66.9
Fixed Assets (net)		23.4	21.8				26.6	24.1
Intangibles (net)		2.0	2.3				3.1	4.4
All Other Non-Current		2.8	6.7				5.0	4.6
Total		100.0	100.0				100.0	100.0

LIABILITIES		500M-2MM	2-10MM				Hist 98/99	Hist 99/00
Notes Payable-Short Term		19.3	11.1				9.8	11.0
Cur. Mat.-L/T/D		3.5	3.4				4.0	2.7
Trade Payables		19.9	13.1				15.3	13.6
Income Taxes Payable		.0	.4				.6	.3
All Other Current		6.8	7.1				8.8	8.3
Total Current		49.6	35.1				38.5	35.9
Long Term Debt		20.7	12.3				17.8	16.0
Deferred Taxes		.1	.7				.5	.6
All Other Non-Current		6.7	3.3				4.8	5.4
Net Worth		23.0	48.6				38.4	42.2
Total Liabilities & Net Worth		100.0	100.0				100.0	100.0

INCOME DATA		500M-2MM	2-10MM				Hist 98/99	Hist 99/00
Net Sales		100.0	100.0				100.0	100.0
Gross Profit		34.3	35.2				32.6	31.5
Operating Expenses		38.2	32.4				27.4	26.2
Operating Profit		-3.9	2.8				5.2	5.3
All Other Expenses (net)		1.5	1.8				1.3	1.0
Profit Before Taxes		-5.4	1.0				3.8	4.3

RATIOS		500M-2MM	2-10MM				Hist 98/99	Hist 99/00
Current		3.4 / 1.4 / 1.1	3.8 / 2.5 / 1.6				2.9 / 1.8 / 1.3	3.1 / 2.0 / 1.4
Quick		1.9 / .8 / .5	1.8 / 1.1 / .6				1.7 / 1.0 / .6	2.1 / 1.1 / .6
Sales/Receivables		30 12.3 / 49 7.4 / 61 6.0	39 9.4 / 45 8.1 / 63 5.8				36 10.0 / 50 7.3 / 62 5.9	43 8.6 / 51 7.1 / 66 5.5
Cost of Sales/Inventory		35 10.3 / 68 5.3 / 90 4.0	58 6.3 / 117 3.1 / 186 2.0				39 9.4 / 61 6.0 / 96 3.8	46 7.9 / 73 5.0 / 111 3.3
Cost of Sales/Payables		21 17.4 / 35 10.6 / 53 6.9	18 20.3 / 29 12.7 / 55 6.7				22 16.7 / 31 11.7 / 46 7.9	23 15.8 / 34 10.7 / 52 7.0
Sales/Working Capital		4.6 / 12.1 / 70.1	3.7 / 4.4 / 11.2				4.6 / 7.1 / 14.5	3.7 / 6.1 / 10.3
EBIT/Interest		3.5 / (17) .0 / -4.5	11.5 / (26) 2.1 / -1.7				10.0 / (128) 3.1 / .7	11.5 / (89) 3.0 / .6
Net Profit + Depr., Dep., Amort./Cur. Mat. L /T/D							(49) 9.2 / 2.5 / 1.1	(36) 6.6 / 2.3 / 1.6
Fixed/Worth		.4 / 1.0 / 5.4	.2 / .5 / 1.3				.2 / .5 / 1.5	.2 / .5 / 1.8
Debt/Worth		1.8 / 3.6 / 41.0	.5 / 1.0 / 3.0				.6 / 1.6 / 3.8	.6 / 1.4 / 4.6
% Profit Before Taxes/Tangible Net Worth		46.6 / (15) 3.5 / -167.9	38.7 / 4.2 / -24.7				45.3 / (128) 18.1 / 3.5	47.0 / (83) 19.1 / 1.6
% Profit Before Taxes/Total Assets		7.6 / -1.5 / -18.9	17.5 / 2.0 / -6.7				16.9 / 6.6 / .0	14.6 / 6.6 / -1.6
Sales/Net Fixed Assets		35.2 / 12.7 / 5.7	21.6 / 12.1 / 5.1				20.9 / 8.9 / 4.2	23.5 / 9.1 / 3.9
Sales/Total Assets		3.4 / 2.7 / 1.9	2.4 / 1.9 / 1.4				2.7 / 2.0 / 1.4	2.5 / 1.7 / 1.4
% Depr., Dep., Amort./Sales		1.0 / (15) 4.1 / 5.6	1.3 / (23) 2.4 / 3.3				1.3 / (119) 2.8 / 5.1	1.3 / (82) 2.4 / 4.5
% Officers', Directors', Owners' Comp/Sales		3.2 / (10) 4.6 / 17.0					2.2 / (43) 3.8 / 5.1	1.8 / (18) 4.5 / 7.9
Net Sales ($)	319M	61065M	265166M	224955M	367224M	712852M	4050816M	2881882M
Total Assets ($)	425M	22401M	141181M	157881M	186430M	516267M	2649925M	2090552M

Comparative Historical Data | Current Data Sorted By Sales

						Type of Statement						
	23		17		16	Unqualified				2	6	8
	14		13		12	Reviewed	1	1	3	4	3	
	16		10		8	Compiled	1	2	3	1	1	
	2		3		4	Tax Returns		2				
	24		25		22	Other	1	5	4	5	3	4

4/1/00-3/31/01 ALL	4/1/01-3/31/02 ALL	4/1/02-3/31/03 ALL		16 (4/1-9/30/02)			46 (10/1/02-3/31/03)		
			0-1MM	1-3MM	3-5MM	5-10MM	10-25MM	25MM & OVER

4/1/00-3/31/01 ALL	4/1/01-3/31/02 ALL	4/1/02-3/31/03 ALL	NUMBER OF STATEMENTS	0-1MM	1-3MM	3-5MM	5-10MM	10-25MM	25MM & OVER
79	68	62		3	10	10	14	13	12
%	%	%	ASSETS	%	%	%	%	%	%
8.7	8.0	7.2	Cash & Equivalents		9.8	6.1	7.0	8.3	6.7
30.3	27.9	27.7	Trade Receivables (net)		33.1	27.2	26.4	29.6	22.8
29.5	29.8	29.4	Inventory		17.3	36.3	38.5	29.5	21.3
2.5	3.3	3.3	All Other Current		1.8	.7	.8	5.5	6.0
71.0	69.0	67.6	Total Current		62.0	70.4	72.7	72.9	56.8
19.8	21.0	23.5	Fixed Assets (net)		28.8	26.5	16.9	20.0	27.8
3.3	3.9	3.7	Intangibles (net)		6.5	.9	.4	1.8	10.2
5.9	6.1	5.2	All Other Non-Current		2.8	2.2	10.1	5.4	5.2
100.0	100.0	100.0	Total		100.0	100.0	100.0	100.0	100.0
			LIABILITIES						
10.9	13.2	12.1	Notes Payable-Short Term		12.0	27.3	15.2	5.8	4.1
2.5	3.7	3.3	Cur. Mat.-L/T/D		2.4	2.7	3.8	3.5	3.1
15.5	14.6	14.3	Trade Payables		9.3	17.6	18.7	15.6	11.0
.4	.2	.3	Income Taxes Payable		.0	.0	.4	.3	.9
9.1	9.1	8.8	All Other Current		4.8	6.7	10.5	9.3	13.3
38.4	40.7	38.8	Total Current		28.5	54.3	48.6	34.5	32.4
12.8	13.4	14.8	Long Term Debt		24.1	10.2	14.5	10.7	13.6
.4	.3	.4	Deferred Taxes		.1	1.8	.0	.0	.3
4.7	4.9	6.4	All Other Non-Current		2.2	11.3	3.3	3.0	14.6
43.8	40.7	39.6	Net Worth		45.1	22.4	33.6	51.9	39.1
100.0	100.0	100.0	Total Liabilities & Net Worth		100.0	100.0	100.0	100.0	100.0
			INCOME DATA						
100.0	100.0	100.0	Net Sales		100.0	100.0	100.0	100.0	100.0
30.3	29.4	33.1	Gross Profit		44.4	34.7	33.6	28.6	25.4
24.9	27.6	32.6	Operating Expenses		42.6	36.4	31.9	24.4	23.1
5.4	1.8	.5	Operating Profit		1.8	-1.7	1.7	4.2	2.3
.4	1.6	1.6	All Other Expenses (net)		3.5	1.7	1.3	.7	.9
5.0	.2	-1.1	Profit Before Taxes		-1.7	-3.4	.5	3.6	1.4
			RATIOS						
2.7	2.7	3.6	Current		7.7	2.0	3.3	3.8	2.5
1.8	1.7	1.9			3.1	1.2	2.0	1.9	1.6
1.4	1.2	1.2			1.5	1.0	.9	1.6	1.2
1.6	1.3	1.6	Quick		3.6	.9	1.3	2.2	1.0
.9	.9	.9			1.9	.6	.8	1.1	.8
.6	.6	.6			1.0	.5	.4	.7	.6

43	8.4	36	10.2	42	8.8	Sales/Receivables	47	7.8	26	13.8	34	10.8	39	9.3	44	8.4
55	6.7	46	8.0	48	7.6		54	6.7	44	8.2	47	7.8	46	8.0	47	7.7
64	5.7	59	6.2	63	5.8		82	4.4	54	6.7	64	5.7	63	5.8	56	6.6
43	8.5	40	9.1	39	9.3	Cost of Sales/Inventory	38	9.7	30	12.3	69	5.3	22	16.3	25	14.3
81	4.5	79	4.6	81	4.5		77	4.8	72	5.1	100	3.7	63	5.8	72	5.1
115	3.2	126	2.9	136	2.7		105	3.5	227	1.6	196	1.9	131	2.8	118	3.1
26	14.2	19	19.0	22	16.8	Cost of Sales/Payables	13	27.2	25	14.5	13	28.4	22	16.3	25	14.6
36	10.1	34	10.9	29	12.7		22	16.5	42	8.8	36	10.2	29	12.6	27	13.3
49	7.4	49	7.4	48	7.6		41	8.9	49	7.4	70	5.2	43	8.4	39	9.3

4.2	4.5	3.7	Sales/Working Capital		2.9	7.2	3.7	3.8	4.8
6.2	6.8	5.5			4.3	31.4	4.9	5.1	8.4
12.2	19.5	19.0			11.9	NM	-20.7	10.0	23.7

	9.4		5.5		8.1	EBIT/Interest		8.2				11.1		18.4		13.2
(71)	3.6	(64)	2.7	(58)	1.6			1.4			(13)	1.6	(12)	3.6	(11)	3.6
	1.3		-3.9		-1.7			-1.5				-3.1		2.0		.2

	4.8		3.8		5.9	Net Profit + Depr., Dep., Amort./Cur. Mat. L/T/D										
(27)	1.7	(23)	2.9	(16)	2.4											
	1.0		1.0		.2											

.2	.3	.2	Fixed/Worth		.3	.5	.1	.2	.4
.5	.5	.6			.9	1.2	.4	.3	1.2
1.0	1.2	1.6			2.0	2.2	2.3	.7	NM

.7	.8	.6	Debt/Worth		.5	2.5	.8	.5	.7
1.4	1.7	1.6			2.3	3.4	1.3	1.0	1.8
2.6	3.7	6.2			4.3	16.3	11.5	1.6	NM

	49.3		28.1		36.8	% Profit Before Taxes/Tangible Net Worth		39.3				41.7		44.1		
(76)	19.0	(63)	9.4	(56)	3.8			5.3			(12)	16.2		9.0		
	3.8		-17.4		-21.5			-42.2				-20.3		-1.5		

18.3	12.1	12.3	% Profit Before Taxes/Total Assets		11.0	1.8	20.6	14.9	18.0
7.5	3.4	1.3			1.3	-7.2	3.9	3.8	5.1
1.3	-8.4	-8.1			-4.8	-14.8	-11.7	-.4	-3.5

21.9	21.7	21.3	Sales/Net Fixed Assets		33.0	35.2	31.8	26.2	15.5
13.7	10.6	10.6			6.9	9.3	13.6	12.9	6.8
6.4	5.7	4.7			3.4	4.6	7.3	7.3	3.9

2.5	2.7	2.6	Sales/Total Assets		2.9	3.2	2.9	2.6	1.9
2.0	1.9	1.9			1.9	2.4	2.1	2.1	1.6
1.6	1.4	1.2			.9	1.5	1.1	1.7	1.2

	1.1		1.1		1.3	% Depr., Dep., Amort./Sales						1.3		.9		
(67)	2.2	(55)	2.5	(51)	2.7						(12)	2.5	(12)	1.8		
	3.7		4.3		4.9							3.4		2.6		

	2.1		2.2		2.4	% Officers', Directors', Owners' Comp/Sales										
(16)	3.9	(21)	3.2	(21)	4.1											
	5.5		6.6		11.7											

3107367M	1912020M	1631581M	Net Sales ($)	1987M	21092M	40554M	96685M	219056M	1252207M
2004571M	1268340M	1024585M	Total Assets ($)	2356M	15287M	17832M	65189M	108633M	815288M

M = $ thousand   MM = $ million
See Pages 11 through 18 for Explanation of Ratios and Data

Current Data Sorted By Assets / Comparative Historical Data

0-500M	500M-2MM	2-10MM	10-50MM	50-100MM	100-250MM	Type of Statement	4/1/98-3/31/99 ALL	4/1/99-3/31/00 ALL
	1	15	7	1	2	Unqualified	38	31
	11	17	6			Reviewed	40	34
1	11	11	2			Compiled	17	25
1	3	1				Tax Returns	6	6
2	7	23	11	1		Other	45	45
	33 (4/1-9/30/02)		101 (10/1/02-3/31/03)					
4	33	67	26	2	2	NUMBER OF STATEMENTS	146	141
%	%	%	%	%	%	**ASSETS**	%	%
	4.9	7.6	14.5			Cash & Equivalents	7.6	6.9
	29.0	29.9	20.1			Trade Receivables (net)	28.6	29.6
	20.0	27.2	21.1			Inventory	21.8	19.9
	.8	1.1	1.3			All Other Current	.9	1.4
	54.6	65.9	57.0			Total Current	58.9	57.8
	39.6	26.9	33.2			Fixed Assets (net)	33.1	33.7
	.8	2.7	5.4			Intangibles (net)	4.2	3.8
	5.0	4.5	4.4			All Other Non-Current	3.8	4.7
	100.0	100.0	100.0			Total	100.0	100.0
						LIABILITIES		
	11.0	12.6	7.7			Notes Payable-Short Term	9.8	12.0
	9.0	7.0	4.1			Cur. Mat.-L/T/D	4.9	5.8
	16.2	16.8	15.8			Trade Payables	15.9	17.6
	.1	.1	.2			Income Taxes Payable	.5	.3
	9.5	7.2	9.4			All Other Current	11.1	7.3
	45.9	43.7	37.2			Total Current	42.2	42.8
	19.3	12.3	19.6			Long Term Debt	21.2	21.0
	.3	.2	.1			Deferred Taxes	.6	.4
	6.6	6.6	4.2			All Other Non-Current	3.4	4.1
	27.9	37.1	38.8			Net Worth	32.5	31.6
	100.0	100.0	100.0			Total Liabilities & Net Worth	100.0	100.0
						INCOME DATA		
	100.0	100.0	100.0			Net Sales	100.0	100.0
	34.7	23.9	20.8			Gross Profit	26.1	26.4
	35.8	22.4	18.6			Operating Expenses	24.2	22.8
	-1.1	1.5	2.2			Operating Profit	1.8	3.5
	1.3	1.1	1.0			All Other Expenses (net)	-.6	1.1
	-2.5	.4	1.1			Profit Before Taxes	2.4	2.4
						RATIOS		
	2.1	2.2	2.0			Current	2.2	2.1
	1.1	1.6	1.5				1.5	1.3
	.9	1.1	1.0				1.1	1.1
	1.3	1.7	1.5			Quick	1.5	1.2
	.7	.8	.8				.9	.9
	.6	.5	.5				.6	.6
34	10.8 / 40	9.0 / 36	10.2			Sales/Receivables	38 / 9.7 / 41	8.8
45	8.1 / 51	7.2 / 42	8.8				47 / 7.8 / 52	7.1
52	7.0 / 61	6.0 / 52	7.1				57 / 6.4 / 62	5.9
13	28.4 / 28	12.9 / 16	22.2			Cost of Sales/Inventory	25 / 14.8 / 24	15.3
36	10.0 / 47	7.7 / 52	7.0				43 / 8.5 / 45	8.2
64	5.7 / 82	4.5 / 70	5.2				74 / 4.9 / 71	5.1
17	22.1 / 21	17.4 / 22	16.9			Cost of Sales/Payables	21 / 17.2 / 25	14.5
32	11.4 / 31	11.9 / 36	10.2				33 / 11.1 / 39	9.3
52	7.0 / 51	7.2 / 49	7.4				48 / 7.6 / 54	6.7
	7.7	6.0	4.1			Sales/Working Capital	6.3	6.9
	35.9	10.7	11.1				12.6	13.7
	-82.9	27.3	203.1				61.1	60.2
	7.2	6.4	10.3			EBIT/Interest	7.9	7.5
	(30) 1.3	(63) 2.5	(23) 2.9				(130) 2.7	(133) 2.4
	-4.1	-1.1	-.6				.9	.9
		6.3	6.3			Net Profit + Depr., Dep., Amort./Cur. Mat. L/T/D	6.1	4.1
		(20) 2.0	(14) 1.9				(50) 2.3	(42) 2.2
		.2	.3				1.3	1.0
	.6	.4	.4			Fixed/Worth	.5	.5
	1.3	.7	1.0				1.0	1.1
	28.7	2.4	1.6				2.8	3.1
	.7	.7	.9			Debt/Worth	.9	1.1
	2.6	1.7	1.6				2.2	2.2
	42.0	4.8	4.1				6.4	5.8
	23.4	29.1	41.5			% Profit Before Taxes/Tangible Net Worth	50.2	47.8
	(26) 11.9	(59) 12.9	(23) 10.6				(123) 22.0	(125) 17.4
	-20.8	-4.4	-12.7				6.8	.8
	10.4	10.9	11.4			% Profit Before Taxes/Total Assets	13.9	13.9
	1.0	3.9	4.3				6.0	6.1
	-16.2	-7.3	-2.5				.6	-.4
	14.4	16.9	12.1			Sales/Net Fixed Assets	14.2	11.9
	5.5	9.6	7.3				7.3	6.5
	3.7	4.5	3.0				4.0	3.4
	3.0	2.8	2.1			Sales/Total Assets	2.6	2.7
	2.6	2.1	1.6				2.1	2.1
	1.7	1.6	1.3				1.6	1.5
	2.3	1.8	1.9			% Depr., Dep., Amort./Sales	1.8	1.9
	(31) 4.0	(62) 3.2	(24) 2.8				(128) 2.9	(127) 3.4
	8.2	4.8	4.9				4.8	5.4
	3.6	2.3					% Officers', Directors', Owners' Comp/Sales	2.4	1.9
	(18) 5.3	(18) 5.1					(47) 4.0	(46) 3.7
	10.6	7.6						9.8	
5385M	103376M	752748M	1050255M	224202M	176045M	Net Sales ($)	5437044M	3226879M
696M	43073M	324676M	573239M	110796M	303559M	Total Assets ($)	3235822M	2200921M

M = $ thousand   MM = $ million
See Pages 11 through 18 for Explanation of Ratios and Data

Comparative Historical Data — Current Data Sorted By Sales

4/1/00-3/31/01 ALL	4/1/01-3/31/02 ALL	4/1/02-3/31/03 ALL	Type of Statement	0-1MM	1-3MM	3-5MM	5-10MM	10-25MM	25MM & OVER
27	22	26	Unqualified	1	1		4	11	9
34	35	34	Reviewed		4	7	12	6	5
31	28	25	Compiled		7	8	4	3	3
8	1	5	Tax Returns	1	3		1		
53	60	44	Other	1	4	7	11	12	9
				\[33 (4/1-9/30/02)\]		\[101 (10/1/02-3/31/03)\]			
153	146	134	**NUMBER OF STATEMENTS**	3	19	22	32	32	26
%	%	%	**ASSETS**	%	%	%	%	%	%
7.1	8.2	8.5	Cash & Equivalents		8.2	6.6	9.1	6.1	13.6
30.9	26.7	27.5	Trade Receivables (net)		24.0	28.4	28.1	31.7	22.5
23.7	22.3	23.6	Inventory		12.4	20.2	27.7	25.6	25.6
.8	1.3	1.1	All Other Current		.5	1.1	.5	1.7	1.6
62.4	58.4	60.7	Total Current		45.1	56.3	65.4	65.1	63.3
29.5	32.5	31.7	Fixed Assets (net)		46.4	36.8	27.1	28.2	27.1
3.8	4.7	3.0	Intangibles (net)		2.3	1.2	1.9	3.4	6.0
4.3	4.3	4.7	All Other Non-Current		6.3	5.7	5.5	3.4	3.6
100.0	100.0	100.0	Total		100.0	100.0	100.0	100.0	100.0
			LIABILITIES						
8.1	11.0	12.1	Notes Payable-Short Term		18.0	12.3	12.2	11.2	7.6
7.0	6.2	6.6	Cur. Mat.-L/T/D		8.8	9.7	6.2	5.9	4.6
17.8	14.8	16.4	Trade Payables		14.7	14.3	14.6	18.3	19.7
.7	.3	.1	Income Taxes Payable		.0	.0	.2	.2	.3
9.7	9.2	8.1	All Other Current		4.1	9.2	6.6	6.3	10.3
43.3	41.5	43.4	Total Current		45.6	45.5	39.8	41.8	42.5
15.0	16.2	15.4	Long Term Debt		25.7	14.6	10.8	13.3	17.0
.5	.4	.2	Deferred Taxes		.2	.3	.2	.2	.2
5.0	5.1	6.0	All Other Non-Current		5.5	7.4	6.5	6.5	3.6
36.1	36.8	35.0	Net Worth		23.0	32.2	42.7	38.2	36.7
100.0	100.0	100.0	Total Liabilities & Net Worth		100.0	100.0	100.0	100.0	100.0
			INCOME DATA						
100.0	100.0	100.0	Net Sales		100.0	100.0	100.0	100.0	100.0
26.9	25.5	26.2	Gross Profit		40.4	29.2	25.5	24.0	16.8
20.6	22.8	25.4	Operating Expenses		42.8	29.0	24.7	20.9	14.3
6.3	2.7	.8	Operating Profit		-2.4	.2	.8	3.1	2.4
1.4	1.4	1.2	All Other Expenses (net)		1.5	1.4	.5	1.1	1.5
4.8	1.3	-.4	Profit Before Taxes		-3.9	-1.2	.3	2.0	.9
			RATIOS						
2.0	2.1	2.1	Current		1.7	2.3	2.6	2.1	1.9
1.3	1.4	1.5	Current		1.0	1.2	1.9	1.6	1.5
1.1	1.0	1.0	Current		.7	.8	1.1	1.2	1.2
1.3	1.5	1.5	Quick		1.2	1.5	2.0	1.2	1.4
.9	.8	.8	Quick		.7	.7	1.1	.8	.8
.6	.5	.5	Quick		.6	.5	.6	.6	.5
40 9.1	37 9.9	38 9.5	Sales/Receivables	25 14.5	41 8.9	39 9.3	41 9.0	29 12.6	
51 7.2	43 8.5	48 7.7	Sales/Receivables	46 7.9	47 7.8	50 7.3	49 7.4	41 8.8	
62 5.9	53 6.9	57 6.4	Sales/Receivables	57 6.4	54 6.7	56 6.6	62 5.9	56 6.5	
20 18.5	19 19.2	24 15.3	Cost of Sales/Inventory	5 68.5	21 17.6	32 11.5	24 14.9	27 13.5	
49 7.4	41 8.9	45 8.1	Cost of Sales/Inventory	13 27.3	37 9.9	50 7.3	44 8.4	56 6.5	
77 4.7	70 5.2	75 4.9	Cost of Sales/Inventory	45 8.1	69 5.3	97 3.8	74 4.9	70 5.2	
21 17.1	20 18.3	19 19.1	Cost of Sales/Payables	17 20.9	18 20.6	19 18.9	23 15.6	19 19.5	
38 9.7	28 13.3	34 10.9	Cost of Sales/Payables	32 11.4	28 13.1	31 11.9	35 10.4	44 8.3	
56 6.6	40 9.2	50 7.3	Cost of Sales/Payables	56 6.6	51 7.2	53 6.9	47 7.7	58 6.3	
6.9	6.2	6.2	Sales/Working Capital	7.4	7.5	4.3	6.3	5.6	
11.6	13.4	12.0	Sales/Working Capital	-198.8	19.9	7.7	11.1	11.1	
30.2	105.7	177.1	Sales/Working Capital	-34.7	-17.5	33.4	25.8	35.6	
11.8	6.6	8.0	EBIT/Interest	6.0	3.3	6.5	9.9	12.2	
(140) 4.0	(134) 2.1	(123) 2.3	EBIT/Interest	(17) 1.3	(21) .4	(29) 2.5	(31) 3.2	(24) 2.8	
1.3	.0	-1.1	EBIT/Interest	-4.7	-1.9	-1.8	.1	-.3	
5.4	3.6	4.2	Net Profit + Depr., Dep., Amort./Cur. Mat. L/T/D				4.1	11.8	
(47) 2.3	(45) 1.7	(42) 1.9	Net Profit + Depr., Dep., Amort./Cur. Mat. L/T/D				(13) 2.2	(15) 2.2	
1.1	1.1	.3	Net Profit + Depr., Dep., Amort./Cur. Mat. L/T/D				.1	.5	
.4	.5	.5	Fixed/Worth	1.0	.5	.3	.3	.5	
.8	.9	.8	Fixed/Worth	2.4	1.4	.6	.6	.8	
2.0	2.3	2.8	Fixed/Worth	-2.1	6.6	1.4	1.5	1.8	
.9	.8	.7	Debt/Worth	1.0	.7	.4	1.0	.7	
2.0	1.8	1.8	Debt/Worth	4.2	1.8	1.3	1.7	1.6	
4.0	4.2	8.4	Debt/Worth	-11.6	17.6	4.6	3.6	22.1	
52.4	38.3	29.0	% Profit Before Taxes/Tangible Net Worth	25.6	19.7	21.6	43.9	48.0	
(140) 24.6	(123) 13.8	(115) 12.0	% Profit Before Taxes/Tangible Net Worth	(14) 7.0	(19) -1.0	(28) 12.6	(30) 16.5	(23) 18.2	
7.1	-3.3	-8.9	% Profit Before Taxes/Tangible Net Worth	-72.7	-27.8	-3.6	3.7	-12.7	
19.1	13.8	10.8	% Profit Before Taxes/Total Assets	11.0	4.7	10.7	11.1	15.9	
8.7	4.0	3.0	% Profit Before Taxes/Total Assets	-5.1	-1.1	4.2	4.4	5.1	
1.6	-3.7	-7.4	% Profit Before Taxes/Total Assets	-25.4	-10.0	-4.3	-.8	-2.3	
16.3	14.9	15.9	Sales/Net Fixed Assets	11.6	12.1	16.6	19.7	20.1	
8.9	7.5	7.9	Sales/Net Fixed Assets	4.4	5.7	10.0	12.7	7.4	
4.6	4.3	4.0	Sales/Net Fixed Assets	2.1	4.0	4.8	4.6	4.4	
2.8	2.8	2.8	Sales/Total Assets	2.8	3.0	2.4	3.2	2.7	
2.2	2.3	2.1	Sales/Total Assets	2.1	2.2	2.1	2.1	1.9	
1.7	1.6	1.5	Sales/Total Assets	1.4	1.7	1.5	1.6	1.4	
1.4	1.9	2.0	% Depr., Dep., Amort./Sales	2.9	2.3	2.2	1.4	1.9	
(140) 2.6	(127) 3.4	(124) 3.3	% Depr., Dep., Amort./Sales	(18) 6.9	(20) 3.4	(29) 3.6	(31) 2.6	(24) 2.8	
4.4	5.3	6.2	% Depr., Dep., Amort./Sales	9.3	7.0	4.1	4.7	4.1	
2.3	1.6	2.6	% Officers', Directors', Owners' Comp/Sales		3.8	2.3			
(54) 3.4	(46) 4.6	(42) 4.8	% Officers', Directors', Owners' Comp/Sales		(12) 5.3	(12) 4.7			
7.3	7.3	6.8	% Officers', Directors', Owners' Comp/Sales		6.5	7.1			
4000672M	2765449M	2312011M	Net Sales ($)	1312M	40727M	90270M	226220M	499867M	1453615M
2343885M	1428441M	1356039M	Total Assets ($)	1425M	22125M	48933M	131948M	245801M	905807M

© RMA 2003

M = $ thousand   MM = $ million
See Pages 11 through 18 for Explanation of Ratios and Data

Current Data Sorted By Assets   **Comparative Historical Data**

0-500M	500M-2MM	2-10MM	10-50MM	50-100MM	100-250MM	Type of Statement	4/1/98-3/31/99 ALL	4/1/99-3/31/00 ALL
	1	3	4	5	6	Unqualified	44	28
	3	7	1			Reviewed	6	11
	2	1	2			Compiled	8	3
						Tax Returns	2	1
2	2	9	6	1	3	Other	25	24
	11 (4/1-9/30/02)		45 (10/1/02-3/31/03)					
2	6	20	13	6	9	**NUMBER OF STATEMENTS**	85	67
%	%	%	%	%	%	**ASSETS**	%	%
		7.9	12.5			Cash & Equivalents	14.1	13.9
		24.6	20.6			Trade Receivables (net)	24.5	27.1
		33.0	21.0			Inventory	22.1	22.4
		2.3	4.2			All Other Current	2.8	3.0
		67.7	58.2			Total Current	63.5	66.3
		24.9	30.4			Fixed Assets (net)	25.8	24.6
		2.6	5.1			Intangibles (net)	3.6	3.8
		4.8	6.3			All Other Non-Current	7.1	5.3
		100.0	100.0			Total	100.0	100.0
						LIABILITIES		
		13.8	4.9			Notes Payable-Short Term	6.7	5.0
		4.2	4.9			Cur. Mat.-L/T/D	3.3	3.0
		18.5	12.5			Trade Payables	11.4	12.9
		.7	.6			Income Taxes Payable	.6	.6
		10.0	16.4			All Other Current	12.0	10.9
		47.1	39.3			Total Current	34.0	32.3
		11.4	20.6			Long Term Debt	11.3	12.9
		.4	.8			Deferred Taxes	.4	.4
		10.7	1.8			All Other Non-Current	6.8	5.6
		30.4	37.5			Net Worth	47.4	48.8
		100.0	100.0			Total Liabilities & Net Worth	100.0	100.0
						INCOME DATA		
		100.0	100.0			Net Sales	100.0	100.0
		28.8	21.2			Gross Profit	28.4	36.9
		29.6	22.4			Operating Expenses	38.8	33.4
		-.8	-1.1			Operating Profit	-10.3	3.5
		3.9	2.0			All Other Expenses (net)	.8	.5
		-4.7	-3.1			Profit Before Taxes	-11.2	3.1
						RATIOS		
		2.3	2.3				3.3	3.2
		1.4	1.8			Current	2.3	2.1
		1.0	1.3				1.3	1.7
		1.0	1.1				2.2	1.8
		.7	.9			Quick	1.2	1.3
		.5	.6				.8	.8
		33 11.0	42 8.8				37 9.8	44 8.3
		43 8.5	48 7.6			Sales/Receivables	50 7.3	59 6.2
		69 5.3	64 5.7				60 6.1	79 4.6
		40 9.2	27 13.6				44 8.3	45 8.1
		60 6.1	73 5.0			Cost of Sales/Inventory	64 5.7	74 4.9
		207 1.8	109 3.3				113 3.2	118 3.1
		28 13.0	16 22.2				15 23.7	24 14.9
		45 8.1	38 9.7			Cost of Sales/Payables	33 11.1	34 10.7
		82 4.5	57 6.4				53 6.9	59 6.2
		3.8	2.6				3.0	2.8
		9.5	6.4			Sales/Working Capital	5.4	5.0
		658.0	31.2				15.8	8.8
		4.6	9.8				15.5	12.5
		(16) 1.0	(11) 1.4			EBIT/Interest	(71) 3.4	(57) 3.3
		-1.3	-3.0				.4	-.8
						Net Profit + Depr., Dep.,	15.7	7.9
						Amort./Cur. Mat. L./T/D	(31) 4.0	(20) 4.7
							2.0	3.3
		.1	.1				.3	.1
		.6	.6			Fixed/Worth	.5	.4
		11.2	NM				1.2	.9
		1.2	.4				.4	.4
		2.9	1.4			Debt/Worth	.8	.9
		17.4	NM				2.4	2.1
		22.8	13.0				34.6	39.9
		(17) 5.1	(10) -4.6			% Profit Before Taxes/Tangible Net Worth	(75) 18.0	(60) 15.2
		-18.4	-17.6				-1.4	1.1
		6.6	7.9				16.6	20.0
		.2	-.5			% Profit Before Taxes/Total Assets	7.8	6.9
		-14.4	-15.3				-1.9	-1.9
		40.4	13.8				15.2	29.0
		13.5	6.3			Sales/Net Fixed Assets	8.3	8.2
		5.9	2.8				3.3	3.1
		2.9	1.9				2.8	2.5
		1.9	1.2			Sales/Total Assets	1.6	1.5
		.7	1.0				.9	1.1
		1.3	.9				1.2	1.3
		(15) 2.9	(11) 3.6			% Depr., Dep., Amort./Sales	(70) 2.6	(54) 3.5
		10.0	6.0				5.3	5.7
							3.2	3.2
						% Officers', Directors', Owners' Comp/Sales	(18) 5.3	(13) 8.7
							14.0	20.7
1717M	20992M	166464M	343490M	1114339M	1232956M	Net Sales ($)	3242069M	3154775M
648M	8864M	92309M	240568M	387618M	1548419M	Total Assets ($)	2762805M	2350422M

M = $ thousand   MM = $ million
See Pages 11 through 18 for Explanation of Ratios and Data

Comparative Historical Data | Current Data Sorted By Sales

4/1/00-3/31/01 ALL	4/1/01-3/31/02 ALL	4/1/02-3/31/03 ALL	Type of Statement	0-1MM	1-3MM	3-5MM	5-10MM	10-25MM	25MM & OVER
23	32	19	Unqualified			1	1	5	12
7	10	11	Reviewed		3	2	3	3	
8	11	3	Compiled		1			2	
2	1	2	Tax Returns	2					
18	24	21	Other		2	3	1	8	7
					11 (4/1-9/30/02)			45 (10/1/02-3/31/03)	
58	78	56	NUMBER OF STATEMENTS	2	6	6	5	18	19
%	%	%	ASSETS	%	%	%	%	%	%
14.8	17.6	15.3	Cash & Equivalents					13.1	22.8
26.5	19.8	21.2	Trade Receivables (net)					25.3	16.3
24.6	21.7	26.6	Inventory					28.2	16.4
1.5	3.2	2.8	All Other Current					3.2	3.3
67.4	62.4	65.8	Total Current					69.7	58.9
23.1	25.0	23.8	Fixed Assets (net)					24.4	27.3
5.0	6.2	5.0	Intangibles (net)					2.9	7.9
4.6	6.4	5.3	All Other Non-Current					3.0	6.0
100.0	100.0	100.0	Total					100.0	100.0
			LIABILITIES						
5.6	9.0	9.8	Notes Payable-Short Term					9.4	1.2
2.6	3.8	3.5	Cur. Mat.-L/T/D					4.9	2.3
12.3	9.6	15.3	Trade Payables					17.1	12.1
.7	.2	.6	Income Taxes Payable					.7	.8
11.6	12.7	10.8	All Other Current					14.9	9.3
32.7	35.3	40.0	Total Current					47.0	25.7
10.8	9.8	14.3	Long Term Debt					6.1	17.9
.2	.4	.7	Deferred Taxes					1.0	1.1
6.9	4.7	5.1	All Other Non-Current					1.9	1.1
49.4	49.7	40.0	Net Worth					44.0	54.2
100.0	100.0	100.0	Total Liabilities & Net Worth					100.0	100.0
			INCOME DATA						
100.0	100.0	100.0	Net Sales					100.0	100.0
33.1	33.1	28.5	Gross Profit					23.2	22.7
27.5	31.3	30.0	Operating Expenses					21.6	28.3
5.6	1.8	-1.4	Operating Profit					1.6	-5.6
-1.0	1.0	2.0	All Other Expenses (net)					1.0	1.1
6.6	.8	-3.4	Profit Before Taxes					.6	-6.7
			RATIOS						
3.3 / 2.1 / 1.6	4.1 / 2.0 / 1.4	2.6 / 1.8 / 1.2	Current					2.5 / 1.8 / 1.2	4.0 / 2.2 / 1.6
2.0 / 1.3 / .8	2.4 / 1.2 / .6	1.8 / .9 / .6	Quick					1.6 / .8 / .6	3.0 / 1.3 / .8
46 7.9 / 57 6.3 / 77 4.7	34 10.8 / 46 7.9 / 57 6.4	37 9.7 / 48 7.6 / 64 5.7	Sales/Receivables					38 9.5 / 46 8.0 / 64 5.7	37 9.8 / 52 7.0 / 64 5.7
51 7.2 / 86 4.2 / 118 3.1	41 9.0 / 74 4.9 / 107 3.4	41 8.8 / 76 4.8 / 124 2.9	Cost of Sales/Inventory					44 8.3 / 59 6.2 / 82 4.5	37 10.0 / 71 5.2 / 109 3.4
22 16.9 / 35 10.6 / 57 6.4	14 26.2 / 25 14.5 / 42 8.7	25 14.7 / 38 9.7 / 69 5.3	Cost of Sales/Payables					19 19.4 / 38 9.7 / 53 6.8	19 19.5 / 38 9.7 / 61 6.0
2.8 / 5.1 / 10.1	2.6 / 5.4 / 16.0	2.8 / 5.4 / 27.4	Sales/Working Capital					4.2 / 6.6 / 27.6	1.5 / 2.8 / 21.3
(49) 17.2 / 6.1 / 1.9	(65) 10.6 / 1.9 / -1.3	(45) 10.2 / 1.4 / -2.1	EBIT/Interest				(14)	9.9 / 1.4 / -.1	(13) 32.5 / 1.2 / -13.1
(14) 16.9 / 9.4 / 3.3	(28) 11.3 / 5.3 / .8	(19) 5.0 / 1.7 / -1.1	Net Profit + Depr., Dep., Amort./Cur. Mat. L/T/D						
.2 / .4 / 1.0	.2 / .4 / 1.1	.2 / .4 / 1.4	Fixed/Worth					.2 / .6 / .9	.2 / .4 / 1.0
.5 / 1.0 / 2.9	.3 / 1.0 / 2.7	.5 / 1.2 / 6.8	Debt/Worth					.4 / 1.3 / 5.7	.3 / .5 / 2.1
(52) 43.6 / 19.0 / 4.0	(71) 25.0 / 6.8 / -6.4	(47) 21.6 / 2.3 / -12.9	% Profit Before Taxes/Tangible Net Worth				(16)	20.6 / 2.2 / -5.0	(16) 18.0 / -.3 / -16.6
17.6 / 9.0 / 1.7	10.7 / 1.7 / -6.1	7.7 / .6 / -11.9	% Profit Before Taxes/Total Assets					9.9 / 1.2 / -2.6	8.5 / -.5 / -22.1
22.7 / 6.2 / 3.7	24.6 / 7.7 / 3.0	25.5 / 9.6 / 3.6	Sales/Net Fixed Assets					35.1 / 7.1 / 3.8	12.3 / 5.5 / 2.5
2.2 / 1.4 / 1.0	2.4 / 1.3 / .9	2.5 / 1.3 / .8	Sales/Total Assets					2.8 / 1.9 / 1.2	1.3 / 1.0 / .7
(49) 1.3 / 2.9 / 5.3	(62) 1.3 / 2.9 / 7.1	(43) 1.3 / 2.9 / 6.0	% Depr., Dep., Amort./Sales				(15)	1.4 / 2.9 / 6.0	(15) 2.6 / 4.3 / 6.3
(10) 1.6 / 5.5 / 17.8	(14) 1.7 / 3.7 / 17.9		% Officers', Directors', Owners' Comp/Sales						
3193272M	4717305M	2879958M	Net Sales ($)	1717M	13024M	24878M	39903M	272142M	2528294M
2391966M	4149491M	2278426M	Total Assets ($)	648M	17353M	17593M	23688M	176175M	2042969M

© RMA 2003

M = $ thousand   MM = $ million
See Pages 11 through 18 for Explanation of Ratios and Data

Current Data Sorted By Assets   Comparative Historical Data

						Type of Statement		
		2	6	1		Unqualified	7	13
	1	6				Reviewed	7	6
1	2					Compiled	5	4
						Tax Returns		
		4	4			Other	7	10
	5 (4/1-9/30/02)		22 (10/1/02-3/31/03)				4/1/98-3/31/99	4/1/99-3/31/00
0-500M	500M-2MM	2-10MM	10-50MM	50-100MM	100-250MM		ALL	ALL
1	3	12	10	1		NUMBER OF STATEMENTS	26	33
%	%	%	%	%	%		%	%

0-500M	500M-2MM	2-10MM	10-50MM	50-100MM	100-250MM		4/1/98-3/31/99 ALL	4/1/99-3/31/00 ALL
						ASSETS		
		2.7	1.7			Cash & Equivalents	10.8	8.9
		27.6	23.2			Trade Receivables (net)	28.1	26.5
		25.5	32.2			Inventory	27.1	27.4
		1.7	.4			All Other Current	2.5	1.9
		57.5	57.5			Total Current	68.5	64.8
		29.4	26.4			Fixed Assets (net)	21.4	22.9
		4.4	13.7			Intangibles (net)	6.5	7.8
		8.7	2.4			All Other Non-Current	3.6	4.5
		100.0	100.0			Total	100.0	100.0
						LIABILITIES		
		8.6	12.9			Notes Payable-Short Term	10.1	11.3
		7.3	4.5			Cur. Mat.-L/T/D	3.0	4.5
		13.1	12.4			Trade Payables	12.2	12.9
		.8	.1			Income Taxes Payable	1.0	.5
		7.5	13.9			All Other Current	10.8	9.5
		37.4	43.8			Total Current	37.1	38.7
		8.2	15.0			Long Term Debt	18.5	14.3
		1.2	1.2			Deferred Taxes	.4	1.1
		12.4	13.6			All Other Non-Current	2.8	4.6
		40.8	26.4			Net Worth	41.2	41.3
		100.0	100.0			Total Liabilities & Net Worth	100.0	100.0
						INCOME DATA		
		100.0	100.0			Net Sales	100.0	100.0
		27.4	17.8			Gross Profit	29.4	28.7
		23.8	16.7			Operating Expenses	24.2	20.5
		3.6	1.1			Operating Profit	5.1	8.2
		.9	1.4			All Other Expenses (net)	1.4	1.2
		2.7	-.2			Profit Before Taxes	3.8	7.0

Note: Columns 0-500M, 500M-2MM, 50-100MM, 100-250MM marked "DATA NOT AVAILABLE" for the above sections.

RATIOS

2-10MM	10-50MM	Ratio	4/1/98-3/31/99 ALL	4/1/99-3/31/00 ALL
2.1	1.8	Current	3.6	2.7
1.6	1.4		1.9	1.6
1.3	.9		1.2	1.2
1.4	.8	Quick	1.9	1.5
.7	.6		1.1	.8
.5	.3		.6	.6
38 9.7	25 14.3	Sales/Receivables	35 10.5	38 9.7
43 8.4	38 9.6		46 7.9	51 7.2
51 7.2	50 7.3		53 6.9	67 5.5
39 9.3	49 7.5	Cost of Sales/Inventory	38 9.7	51 7.2
68 5.4	55 6.6		66 5.5	67 5.4
104 3.5	83 4.4		113 3.2	102 3.6
11 32.4	20 18.6	Cost of Sales/Payables	11 33.4	20 18.6
24 15.2	25 14.8		29 12.4	33 11.1
47 7.7	33 11.1		37 9.9	44 8.3
6.6	8.5	Sales/Working Capital	3.7	5.0
10.8	16.2		6.7	7.1
17.3	-61.0		23.9	24.1
(11) 3.9	6.5	EBIT/Interest	(21) 20.0	(31) 7.4
2.8	.8		3.2	4.4
-1.0	.4		1.7	2.3
		Net Profit + Depr., Dep., Amort./Cur. Mat. L./T/D	(11) 29.6	(10) 5.5
			8.9	2.2
			3.7	.6
.5	.6	Fixed/Worth	.3	.3
.7	1.0		.8	.9
11.9	-2.8		2.3	1.7
.5	.9	Debt/Worth	.5	.9
1.2	1.6		2.2	1.5
59.9	-16.2		6.8	8.1
(10) 21.3		% Profit Before Taxes/Tangible Net Worth	(23) 88.8	(28) 42.3
9.1			34.7	27.3
.4			11.9	12.8
10.9	8.4	% Profit Before Taxes/Total Assets	16.9	16.9
3.9	-.9		7.8	8.1
-4.0	-4.6		1.6	4.5
9.4	13.3	Sales/Net Fixed Assets	19.5	20.4
6.8	8.0		10.9	8.3
4.4	5.7		5.3	4.7
2.5	2.7	Sales/Total Assets	2.9	2.5
2.0	1.9		2.2	1.8
1.5	1.5		1.4	1.3
(11) 1.3		% Depr., Dep., Amort./Sales	(23) 1.1	(31) .8
2.1			1.6	1.7
3.9			3.9	3.3
		% Officers', Directors', Owners' Comp/Sales		

0-500M	500M-2MM	2-10MM	10-50MM	50-100MM		4/1/98-3/31/99 ALL	4/1/99-3/31/00 ALL
2189M	8204M	122679M	570966M	125601M	Net Sales ($)	569414M	1207013M
443M	3392M	57396M	273857M	86417M	Total Assets ($)	281808M	930134M

M = $ thousand MM = $ million
See Pages 11 through 18 for Explanation of Ratios and Data

Comparative Historical Data | **Current Data Sorted By Sales**

4/1/00-3/31/01 ALL	4/1/01-3/31/02 ALL	4/1/02-3/31/03 ALL		0-1MM	1-3MM	3-5MM	5-10MM	10-25MM	25MM & OVER
			Type of Statement						
7	9	9	Unqualified				1	2	6
6	5	7	Reviewed		1		2	4	
	4	3	Compiled		1	2			
			Tax Returns						
7	7	8	Other				3	1	4
				5 (4/1-9/30/02)			22 (10/1/02-3/31/03)		
20	25	27	**NUMBER OF STATEMENTS**		2	2	6	7	10
%	%	%	**ASSETS**	%	%	%	%	%	%
5.4	8.2	3.4	Cash & Equivalents	DATA NOT AVAILABLE					3.3
28.8	24.6	25.9	Trade Receivables (net)						22.2
30.4	26.0	27.6	Inventory						28.1
.8	4.4	1.2	All Other Current						.8
65.4	63.1	58.0	Total Current						54.3
26.7	25.4	26.5	Fixed Assets (net)						29.6
4.7	7.5	9.4	Intangibles (net)						13.7
3.2	4.0	6.1	All Other Non-Current						2.3
100.0	100.0	100.0	Total						100.0
			LIABILITIES						
13.2	10.9	10.4	Notes Payable-Short Term						8.2
3.3	3.1	6.0	Cur. Mat.-L/T/D						3.7
13.7	10.3	13.2	Trade Payables						11.2
.7	.9	.4	Income Taxes Payable						.1
12.4	9.5	10.1	All Other Current						13.9
43.3	34.6	40.1	Total Current						37.1
11.4	10.4	11.4	Long Term Debt						12.9
.5	.8	1.1	Deferred Taxes						1.4
1.9	6.0	12.8	All Other Non-Current						13.6
42.8	48.1	34.6	Net Worth						34.9
100.0	100.0	100.0	Total Liabilities & Net Worth						100.0
			INCOME DATA						
100.0	100.0	100.0	Net Sales						100.0
29.3	27.2	25.2	Gross Profit						24.2
22.7	23.0	22.7	Operating Expenses						19.6
6.6	4.2	2.5	Operating Profit						4.7
1.8	.9	1.3	All Other Expenses (net)						1.4
4.8	3.3	1.2	Profit Before Taxes						3.2
			RATIOS						
2.1	2.6	1.8							1.9
1.5	1.7	1.6	Current						1.7
1.2	1.2	1.1							.9
1.2	1.5	1.0							1.1
.7	.9	.6	Quick						.6
.6	.5	.5							.3
35 10.4	**34** 10.7	**30** 12.2							**25** 14.3
47 7.7	**47** 7.8	**41** 8.9	Sales/Receivables						**38** 9.6
58 6.3	**55** 6.7	**49** 7.4							**55** 6.7
49 7.5	**54** 6.7	**38** 9.6							**49** 7.5
81 4.5	**70** 5.2	**56** 6.5	Cost of Sales/Inventory						**53** 6.9
89 4.1	**83** 4.4	**85** 4.3							**82** 4.5
18 20.3	**16** 23.4	**16** 23.4							**17** 21.5
30 12.1	**26** 13.9	**24** 15.0	Cost of Sales/Payables						**25** 14.8
53 6.9	**37** 9.9	**36** 10.1							**33** 11.1
5.3	4.4	6.1							5.4
11.2	7.6	10.8	Sales/Working Capital						11.0
19.7	37.6	75.5							NM
10.4	14.0	3.4							
(18) 3.4	(21) 1.8	(25) 1.6	EBIT/Interest						
1.5	-.6	-1.4							
			Net Profit + Depr., Dep., Amort./Cur. Mat. L/T/D						
.4	.3	.5							.6
.7	.6	.7	Fixed/Worth						.8
2.2	2.0	20.8							NM
.8	.4	.7							.7
1.5	1.1	1.3	Debt/Worth						1.4
6.0	3.4	90.3							NM
48.1	24.9	21.9							
(18) 31.1	(21) 7.0	(21) 7.1	% Profit Before Taxes/Tangible Net Worth						
9.6	-14.8	-11.9							
17.7	13.1	6.6							16.3
8.1	2.7	3.2	% Profit Before Taxes/Total Assets						2.1
2.8	-6.5	-5.9							-3.2
14.2	12.7	14.1							10.6
7.5	7.3	8.3	Sales/Net Fixed Assets						6.6
5.6	5.4	6.0							4.3
2.7	2.5	2.6							2.7
1.8	1.7	2.1	Sales/Total Assets						1.7
1.6	1.4	1.6							1.5
.9	1.1	1.3							
(19) 1.9	2.8	(24) 3.0	% Depr., Dep., Amort./Sales						
3.3	4.5	4.8							
			% Officers', Directors', Owners' Comp/Sales						
1023010M	**753185M**	**829639M**	Net Sales ($)		**3657M**	**6736M**	**39823M**	**107497M**	**671926M**
573752M	**402146M**	**421505M**	Total Assets ($)		**1346M**	**2489M**	**23164M**	**44555M**	**349951M**

M = $ thousand MM = $ million

See Pages 11 through 18 for Explanation of Ratios and Data

Current Data Sorted By Assets							Comparative Historical Data	
						Type of Statement		
	2	4	4		1	Unqualified	8	18
	1	3				Reviewed	8	1
		4				Compiled	4	5
		2				Tax Returns	1	
		6	3	2		Other	12	15
8 (4/1-9/30/02)			24 (10/1/02-3/31/03)				4/1/98-3/31/99	4/1/99-3/31/00
0-500M	500M-2MM	2-10MM	10-50MM	50-100MM	100-250MM		ALL	ALL
	3	19	7	2	1	**NUMBER OF STATEMENTS**	33	39
%	%	%	%	%	%	**ASSETS**	%	%
DATA NOT AVAILABLE		14.1				Cash & Equivalents	9.5	7.7
		23.9				Trade Receivables (net)	25.6	25.6
		27.0				Inventory	26.5	27.7
		3.3				All Other Current	2.1	1.6
		68.3				Total Current	63.8	62.6
		23.9				Fixed Assets (net)	27.3	28.1
		3.2				Intangibles (net)	1.1	4.5
		4.6				All Other Non-Current	7.8	4.8
		100.0				Total	100.0	100.0
						LIABILITIES		
		7.7				Notes Payable-Short Term	12.8	13.2
		5.2				Cur. Mat.-L/T/D	4.2	3.9
		11.0				Trade Payables	10.8	12.4
		.1				Income Taxes Payable	1.0	.2
		10.5				All Other Current	10.1	13.5
		34.5				Total Current	38.8	43.3
		13.3				Long Term Debt	15.6	18.3
		.6				Deferred Taxes	.6	.4
		3.6				All Other Non-Current	7.9	15.9
		48.0				Net Worth	37.1	22.1
		100.0				Total Liabilities & Net Worth	100.0	100.0
						INCOME DATA		
		100.0				Net Sales	100.0	100.0
		36.2				Gross Profit	32.0	29.9
		31.9				Operating Expenses	25.1	21.6
		4.4				Operating Profit	6.9	8.3
		.8				All Other Expenses (net)	-21.4	2.6
		3.5				Profit Before Taxes	28.3	5.8
						RATIOS		
		4.0					2.4	2.8
		2.0				Current	1.6	1.9
		1.6					1.2	1.2
		2.8					1.6	1.5
		1.5				Quick	.8	.9
		.5					.6	.5
		34 10.6					30 12.0	40 9.0
		42 8.7				Sales/Receivables	45 8.2	49 7.5
		56 6.5					56 6.5	62 5.9
		57 6.4					49 7.5	43 8.5
		72 5.1				Cost of Sales/Inventory	76 4.8	78 4.7
		120 3.0					95 3.8	99 3.7
		15 24.2					15 23.9	22 16.9
		29 12.7				Cost of Sales/Payables	25 14.6	27 13.3
		43 8.4					38 9.6	43 8.4
		3.1					5.3	4.0
		5.5				Sales/Working Capital	8.2	6.7
		9.7					22.9	16.2
		16.1					16.9	5.6
		(17) 1.5				EBIT/Interest	(31) 6.4	(34) 2.3
		-.9					2.0	1.1
							6.1	7.7
						Net Profit + Depr., Dep., Amort./Cur. Mat. L/T/D	(12) 2.6	(15) 3.7
							1.5	1.7
		.2					.3	.4
		.5				Fixed/Worth	.6	.7
		1.1					1.3	5.5
		.4					.7	1.0
		1.3				Debt/Worth	1.4	1.9
		3.1					3.3	18.1
		47.5					78.7	46.0
		(17) 16.6				% Profit Before Taxes/Tangible Net Worth	(30) 39.1	(33) 20.0
		-.4					20.1	1.8
		22.3					29.5	13.9
		2.4				% Profit Before Taxes/Total Assets	15.1	5.8
		-1.0					6.0	.8
		20.8					12.0	14.0
		7.7				Sales/Net Fixed Assets	8.5	8.3
		4.1					5.1	3.1
		2.8					2.8	2.5
		1.8				Sales/Total Assets	2.1	1.9
		1.3					1.6	1.3
		1.5					.9	2.0
		(17) 3.4				% Depr., Dep., Amort./Sales	(29) 2.3	(33) 2.6
		5.4					3.3	4.5
								3.6
						% Officers', Directors', Owners' Comp/Sales		(10) 5.9
								9.9
	9138M	227515M	197097M	144460M	334258M	Net Sales ($)	812055M	1300972M
	3492M	112375M	143327M	127572M	216295M	Total Assets ($)	447437M	977832M

M = $ thousand MM = $ million

See Pages 11 through 18 for Explanation of Ratios and Data

Comparative Historical Data / Current Data Sorted By Sales

Type of Statement	4/1/00-3/31/01 ALL	4/1/01-3/31/02 ALL	4/1/02-3/31/03 ALL		0-1MM	1-3MM	3-5MM	5-10MM	10-25MM	25MM & OVER
Unqualified	14	9	11		1	1			5	4
Reviewed	6	3	4			2	1		1	
Compiled	6	3	4		2		1		1	
Tax Returns			2				1			1
Other	11	10	11			1			7	3
							8 (4/1-9/30/02)		24 (10/1/02-3/31/03)	
NUMBER OF STATEMENTS	37	25	32		3	4	3		14	8

(n)	%	%	%	ASSETS	%	%	%	%	%	%
	6.7	9.9	10.3	Cash & Equivalents					14.5	
	25.6	22.0	21.8	Trade Receivables (net)					26.4	
	29.2	27.8	28.9	Inventory					24.1	
	1.3	1.6	2.8	All Other Current					1.8	
	62.8	61.4	63.9	Total Current					66.8	
	28.2	30.5	28.3	Fixed Assets (net)					26.8	
	4.4	3.9	4.0	Intangibles (net)					1.8	
	4.6	4.2	3.9	All Other Non-Current					4.5	
	100.0	100.0	100.0	Total					100.0	

(DATA NOT AVAILABLE in columns 0-1MM through 5-10MM for ASSETS and LIABILITIES)

				LIABILITIES						
	14.0	8.1	6.1	Notes Payable-Short Term					5.2	
	5.8	7.3	4.7	Cur. Mat.-L/T/D					3.1	
	13.5	10.6	9.6	Trade Payables					8.8	
	.4	.1	.4	Income Taxes Payable					.1	
	10.8	8.0	14.1	All Other Current					13.0	
	44.4	34.1	34.8	Total Current					30.2	
	14.6	12.3	13.5	Long Term Debt					13.2	
	.7	.5	.5	Deferred Taxes					.6	
	9.6	4.2	5.9	All Other Non-Current					3.3	
	30.6	48.8	45.2	Net Worth					52.7	
	100.0	100.0	100.0	Total Liabilities & Net Worth					100.0	

				INCOME DATA						
	100.0	100.0	100.0	Net Sales					100.0	
	34.4	28.8	35.2	Gross Profit					37.1	
	25.8	23.8	31.5	Operating Expenses					33.5	
	8.7	5.1	3.7	Operating Profit					3.6	
	2.7	1.7	1.8	All Other Expenses (net)					1.0	
	5.9	3.3	1.9	Profit Before Taxes					2.6	

				RATIOS						
	2.3	3.5	3.4						3.5	
	1.5	2.1	2.0	Current					2.2	
	1.2	1.2	1.6						1.7	
	1.2	2.3	1.6						2.3	
	.6	1.0	1.0	Quick					1.4	
	.5	.4	.6						.8	
40 / 31 / 32	9.1	11.9	11.4						10.7 (34)	
53 / 46 / 43	6.9	8.0	8.4	Sales/Receivables					7.9 (46)	
64 / 57 / 58	5.7	6.4	6.3						6.5 (56)	
65 / 53 / 68	5.6	6.9	5.4						6.7 (55)	
97 / 72 / 95	3.8	5.1	3.8	Cost of Sales/Inventory					5.2 (70)	
131 / 108 / 119	2.8	3.4	3.1						3.9 (95)	
23 / 15 / 15	15.9	24.2	24.2						29.7 (12)	
38 / 28 / 27	9.6	13.0	13.4	Cost of Sales/Payables					15.9 (23)	
52 / 33 / 43	7.0	11.1	8.6						10.0 (37)	
	4.0	3.9	4.2						3.1	
	10.1	5.7	5.9	Sales/Working Capital					5.5	
	22.2	26.8	10.4						10.3	
(32) / (23) / (28)	3.4 / 21.3 / 23.0			EBIT/Interest					27.6 (13)	
	2.3 / 1.8 / 2.6								2.1	
	1.7 / -3.4 / -1.7								-3.8	
(12) / (10) / (12)	3.2 / 4.6 / 13.4			Net Profit + Depr., Dep.,						
	1.1 / .7 / 2.6			Amort./Cur. Mat. L/T/D						
	.6 / -.2 / .4									
	.4	.3	.3						.2	
	1.0	.6	.6	Fixed/Worth					.4	
	2.3	1.7	1.4						1.2	
	1.0	.4	.5						.4	
	2.2	1.4	1.3	Debt/Worth					1.2	
	4.8	2.5	4.5						1.8	
(32) / (24) / (28)	49.4 / 43.9 / 39.4			% Profit Before Taxes/Tangible					43.6	
	24.6 / 15.7 / 17.7			Net Worth					15.9	
	6.0 / -12.2 / 1.7								-23.2	
	17.9	25.0	15.4	% Profit Before Taxes/Total					23.2	
	6.2	4.3	2.7	Assets					7.2	
	1.6	-6.9	-3.5						-13.8	
	13.5	13.4	11.4						24.0	
	6.7	5.8	6.1	Sales/Net Fixed Assets					8.6	
	3.8	2.9	3.7						3.7	
	2.1	2.2	2.5						2.8	
	1.8	1.6	1.7	Sales/Total Assets					1.8	
	1.3	1.2	1.3						1.3	
(33) / (22) / (26)	1.4 / 1.3 / 1.7			% Depr., Dep., Amort./Sales					1.4 (11)	
	2.9 / 3.5 / 3.5								2.5	
	4.8 / 5.0 / 5.3								4.9	
(11)	1.4			% Officers', Directors',						
	4.1			Owners' Comp/Sales						
	8.3									
	1350055M	1109653M	912468M	Net Sales ($)	7414M	14788M	22054M		203410M	664802M
	954884M	942392M	603061M	Total Assets ($)	6186M	8526M	15067M		108402M	464880M

M = $ thousand   MM = $ million
See Pages 11 through 18 for Explanation of Ratios and Data

Current Data Sorted By Assets   Comparative Historical Data

						Type of Statement		
1	1	17	19	3	8	Unqualified	76	60
1	10	30	7			Reviewed	43	36
6	15	6	2		1	Compiled	23	18
3	5	2				Tax Returns	4	10
2	16	26	25	5	3	Other	64	69
	62 (4/1-9/30/02)		152 (10/1/02-3/31/03)				4/1/98-3/31/99	4/1/99-3/31/00
0-500M	500M-2MM	2-10MM	10-50MM	50-100MM	100-250MM		ALL	ALL
13	47	81	53	8	12	NUMBER OF STATEMENTS	210	193
%	%	%	%	%	%	ASSETS	%	%
16.9	8.4	8.2	11.1		18.1	Cash & Equivalents	7.8	8.1
30.3	31.9	27.6	23.9		20.0	Trade Receivables (net)	28.5	30.1
26.0	28.0	31.8	27.7		21.6	Inventory	29.3	28.7
3.7	3.1	2.9	2.5		5.8	All Other Current	1.7	2.2
77.0	71.3	70.5	65.2		65.5	Total Current	67.4	69.1
13.5	19.6	21.8	22.3		21.2	Fixed Assets (net)	23.6	22.2
2.8	2.2	2.4	7.0		8.4	Intangibles (net)	3.6	3.7
6.7	6.9	5.3	5.6		4.8	All Other Non-Current	5.4	5.0
100.0	100.0	100.0	100.0		100.0	Total	100.0	100.0
						LIABILITIES		
5.9	15.1	13.2	8.6		7.5	Notes Payable-Short Term	11.7	9.8
6.4	3.6	4.7	5.3		1.9	Cur. Mat.-L/T/D	3.5	3.7
25.7	15.9	17.7	11.8		7.0	Trade Payables	13.5	15.8
.7	.2	.3	.6		.5	Income Taxes Payable	.5	.3
15.0	12.4	12.2	10.2		17.2	All Other Current	11.3	8.9
53.7	47.3	48.1	36.6		34.1	Total Current	40.5	38.4
16.8	12.5	9.6	14.6		15.0	Long Term Debt	14.5	15.4
.0	.1	.3	.8		.3	Deferred Taxes	.5	.6
5.4	7.7	4.5	5.3		4.0	All Other Non-Current	4.3	5.3
24.0	32.5	37.5	42.8		46.6	Net Worth	40.3	40.3
100.0	100.0	100.0	100.0		100.0	Total Liabilities & Net Worth	100.0	100.0
						INCOME DATA		
100.0	100.0	100.0	100.0		100.0	Net Sales	100.0	100.0
41.1	37.1	28.3	26.6		32.2	Gross Profit	32.6	32.2
40.0	37.1	25.3	22.8		30.9	Operating Expenses	30.3	27.8
1.1	.0	3.0	3.8		1.3	Operating Profit	2.2	4.4
.8	2.0	1.4	1.5		2.9	All Other Expenses (net)	4.4	1.4
.3	-2.0	1.5	2.3		-1.6	Profit Before Taxes	-2.1	3.0
						RATIOS		
3.4	2.6	2.3	3.0		4.6		2.8	2.8
1.6	1.4	1.6	1.8		2.5	Current	1.8	1.9
1.0	1.1	1.1	1.3		1.2		1.2	1.4
2.1	1.4	1.4	1.6		1.9		1.5	1.7
.8	.9	.8	.8		1.2	Quick	.9	1.0
.3	.4	.4	.5		.7		.6	.7

27	13.3	33	11.0	34	10.6	45	8.1			40	9.1		39	9.3	44	8.3
36	10.1	49	7.4	48	7.7	52	7.1			52	7.0	Sales/Receivables	49	7.4	54	6.8
44	8.3	65	5.6	61	6.0	68	5.4			65	5.6		62	5.9	65	5.6
7	51.1	30	12.1	50	7.2	58	6.3			31	11.7		48	7.6	55	6.6
49	7.5	62	5.9	81	4.5	91	4.0			80	4.6	Cost of Sales/Inventory	81	4.5	78	4.7
115	3.2	149	2.4	115	3.2	117	3.1			128	2.9		116	3.1	110	3.3
3	123.8	14	26.2	22	16.6	21	17.7			20	18.5		23	15.9	21	17.0
29	12.5	34	10.6	32	11.5	30	12.3			28	13.2	Cost of Sales/Payables	31	11.7	37	10.0
91	4.0	57	6.4	54	6.8	46	8.0			39	9.3		46	7.9	52	7.0

	3.8		4.1		4.9		3.3		2.3		4.2	4.0
	13.5		10.1		8.3		7.0		4.0	Sales/Working Capital	7.5	6.7
	NM		42.6		23.5		13.5		40.4		20.9	12.4
	7.4		6.0		8.7		8.1		4.4		9.9	11.9
(12)	2.4	(40)	2.4	(74)	2.6	(48)	3.3	(10)	1.6	EBIT/Interest (193)	3.7 (177)	3.4
	-3.1		-5.0		.4		.9		-5.0		1.3	.8
				(24)	5.4	(23)	2.9			Net Profit + Depr., Dep.,	9.4	10.2
					1.6		1.7			Amort./Cur. Mat. L /T/D (85)	2.8 (75)	3.1
					.4		.4				1.5	1.2
	.0		.2		.3		.3		.2		.3	.2
	.5		.8		.5		.7		.4	Fixed/Worth	.6	.5
	NM		2.1		1.7		1.2		.9		1.4	1.5
	.4		.4		.8		.6		.2		.6	.7
	1.8		2.3		1.7		2.0		1.1	Debt/Worth	1.6	1.4
	NM		10.9		4.9		3.7		4.3		3.5	4.5
	63.4		25.2		25.7		34.4		47.6	% Profit Before Taxes/Tangible	39.7	41.3
(10)	18.0	(40)	5.7	(72)	12.7	(47)	16.2	(11)	.1	Net Worth (189)	21.5 (178)	20.4
	-10.6		-13.1		1.9		2.7		-10.8		7.0	3.0
	19.7		7.9		11.7		11.9		11.3		15.0	15.5
	2.0		.9		3.9		5.1		-1.1	% Profit Before Taxes/Total Assets	7.8	6.5
	-9.0		-10.6		-1.7		.3		-10.4		1.7	-.2
	186.0		34.2		25.6		14.4		9.2		20.2	23.2
	30.9		17.1		10.3		7.3		6.9	Sales/Net Fixed Assets	9.9	11.5
	14.5		6.2		5.4		3.9		5.0		4.9	5.4
	4.5		2.9		2.7		2.1		2.1		2.6	2.6
	2.4		2.2		1.9		1.5		1.2	Sales/Total Assets	2.0	2.0
	2.2		1.7		1.4		1.0		1.0		1.4	1.4
			1.3		1.2		2.0				1.2	1.4
		(35)	1.9	(75)	2.2	(48)	3.2			% Depr., Dep., Amort./Sales (180)	2.1 (167)	2.3
			3.8		4.1		5.8				3.5	3.7
			3.3		2.6						1.4	2.6
		(25)	6.1	(25)	3.8					% Officers', Directors', Owners' Comp/Sales (62)	3.6 (57)	4.9
			13.3		6.6						6.6	11.2

12925M	132166M	865634M	1837017M	661873M	3705332M	Net Sales ($)	6505761M	6108205M
3751M	57355M	399749M	1067174M	585733M	2024091M	Total Assets ($)	4235257M	4166684M

M = $ thousand   MM = $ million
See Pages 11 through 18 for Explanation of Ratios and Data

Comparative Historical Data | Current Data Sorted By Sales

						Type of Statement						
	65		49		49	Unqualified	1	1	3	9	11	24
	45		41		48	Reviewed	1	4	11	15	15	2
	43		41		30	Compiled	4	10	8	4	2	2
	8		11		10	Tax Returns	2	5	1		2	
	68		74		77	Other	5	11	3	13	18	27
	4/1/00-3/31/01 ALL		4/1/01-3/31/02 ALL		4/1/02-3/31/03 ALL		62 (4/1-9/30/02)			152 (10/1/02-3/31/03)		
							0-1MM	1-3MM	3-5MM	5-10MM	10-25MM	25MM & OVER
	229		216		214	NUMBER OF STATEMENTS	13	31	26	41	48	55
	%		%		%	**ASSETS**	%	%	%	%	%	%
	9.0		10.4		10.3	Cash & Equivalents	11.0	8.9	8.5	12.4	10.4	10.0
	29.2		26.5		26.9	Trade Receivables (net)	25.9	28.5	27.8	29.0	24.8	26.2
	29.0		29.7		28.5	Inventory	31.1	28.0	29.7	28.3	29.3	27.0
	2.6		2.3		3.2	All Other Current	5.7	2.3	3.1	1.2	3.8	4.2
	69.7		68.9		68.9	Total Current	73.7	67.7	69.2	70.9	68.2	67.4
	20.6		22.0		20.8	Fixed Assets (net)	15.7	22.0	22.1	20.2	22.3	19.9
	4.3		4.0		4.6	Intangibles (net)	.9	3.2	2.1	2.9	4.4	8.7
	5.4		5.0		5.7	All Other Non-Current	9.6	7.1	6.7	6.0	5.1	4.0
	100.0		100.0		100.0	Total	100.0	100.0	100.0	100.0	100.0	100.0
						LIABILITIES						
	11.6		13.5		11.4	Notes Payable-Short Term	11.9	13.9	12.8	13.9	8.4	10.0
	3.2		4.9		4.4	Cur. Mat.-L/T/D	5.6	3.9	3.6	3.4	5.5	4.5
	15.0		14.3		15.5	Trade Payables	15.4	17.8	16.0	14.0	16.7	13.9
	.3		.2		.4	Income Taxes Payable	.3	.3	.4	.1	.4	.6
	10.0		10.4		12.1	All Other Current	14.2	11.7	10.8	15.7	8.7	12.6
	40.1		43.3		43.7	Total Current	47.3	47.5	43.7	47.1	39.8	41.6
	12.8		14.7		12.6	Long Term Debt	22.3	12.9	10.8	8.4	13.3	13.4
	.3		.2		.4	Deferred Taxes	.0	.2	.1	.2	.4	.9
	6.7		4.6		5.4	All Other Non-Current	7.6	11.0	3.8	3.4	4.9	4.6
	40.1		37.1		37.8	Net Worth	22.7	28.4	41.6	40.8	41.6	39.5
	100.0		100.0		100.0	Total Liabilities & Net Worth	100.0	100.0	100.0	100.0	100.0	100.0
						INCOME DATA						
	100.0		100.0		100.0	Net Sales	100.0	100.0	100.0	100.0	100.0	100.0
	32.0		31.2		31.1	Gross Profit	53.4	34.7	33.3	29.2	25.8	29.0
	28.0		27.7		28.6	Operating Expenses	54.2	36.0	29.1	26.9	23.4	23.8
	4.0		3.5		2.6	Operating Profit	-.7	-1.3	4.1	2.3	2.4	5.2
	.8		1.3		1.7	All Other Expenses (net)	3.0	1.8	1.8	1.2	1.4	2.0
	3.1		2.2		.9	Profit Before Taxes	-3.7	-3.1	2.3	1.1	1.0	3.2
						RATIOS						
	3.1		2.9		3.0		3.4	2.6	2.5	3.3	3.1	3.0
	1.8		1.6		1.6	Current	1.6	1.5	1.5	1.6	1.8	1.7
	1.3		1.2		1.2		1.1	1.1	1.2	1.1	1.2	1.3
	1.7		1.5		1.5		1.7	1.4	1.2	2.2	1.8	1.3
	1.0		.8		.8	Quick	.6	.7	.9	.9	.8	.8
	.6		.5		.5		.3	.3	.4	.5	.4	.6
39	9.4	35	10.5	36	10.1		34 10.9	32 11.4	34 10.7	35 10.5	38 9.5	44 8.4
53	6.9	45	8.1	50	7.4	Sales/Receivables	42 8.7	47 7.7	47 7.7	51 7.1	48 7.7	56 6.6
65	5.6	57	6.4	61	6.0		69 5.3	57 6.4	63 5.8	62 5.9	59 6.2	65 5.6
45	8.1	46	7.9	44	8.2		36 10.1	23 16.0	41 9.0	34 10.8	54 6.8	46 8.0
74	4.9	75	4.9	81	4.5	Cost of Sales/Inventory	163 2.2	73 5.0	70 5.2	73 5.0	87 4.2	84 4.3
112	3.3	121	3.0	118	3.1		262 1.4	140 2.6	154 2.4	102 3.6	116 3.1	108 3.4
19	18.8	18	20.1	19	19.1		3 116.2	14 25.5	18 20.7	16 22.6	20 18.0	23 15.6
33	10.9	30	12.3	32	11.5	Cost of Sales/Payables	29 12.5	36 10.0	33 10.9	30 12.4	31 11.7	31 11.7
53	6.9	49	7.4	54	6.7		274 1.3	72 5.1	45 8.0	44 8.2	58 6.3	47 7.8
	3.7		4.1		3.9		2.5	4.6	4.9	4.0	3.8	3.5
	6.8		8.3		7.9	Sales/Working Capital	7.7	10.1	8.1	7.4	7.4	8.5
	15.1		24.3		21.2		24.5	147.9	23.0	60.5	14.9	16.9
	9.9		6.5		7.7		5.5	5.6	8.7	6.3	15.7	7.1
(199)	3.0	(196)	1.9	(192)	2.8	EBIT/Interest	(11) 1.2	(25) .2	(25) 2.9	(37) 1.8	(44) 3.6	(50) 3.2
	1.0		.3		-.3		-5.1	-6.3	.9	-.5	-.5	.8
	8.8		5.0		4.6	Net Profit + Depr., Dep.,					2.9	5.4
(73)	3.0	(66)	1.6	(61)	1.5	Amort./Cur. Mat. L/T/D				(19) 1.3	(22) 2.2
	1.2		.1		.4						-.5	.6
	.2		.2		.3		.1	.1	.2	.3	.3	.3
	.5		.7		.6	Fixed/Worth	.6	.9	.5	.5	.6	.6
	1.2		1.5		1.5		NM	2.9	1.2	1.8	1.5	1.0
	.5		.7		.5		.6	.3	.8	.4	.5	.6
	1.6		1.8		1.8	Debt/Worth	4.1	3.6	1.8	1.5	1.6	2.0
	3.8		5.3		5.2		NM	24.2	3.5	4.9	5.1	3.6
	43.4		36.3		28.3	% Profit Before Taxes/Tangible	16.2	42.4	30.3	18.2	26.4	42.4
(206)	18.6	(189)	12.3	(186)	12.3	Net Worth	(10) 6.0	(25) 4.3	13.6	(36) 7.8	(42) 14.9	(47) 18.7
	4.5		-2.0		-2.3		-16.4	-34.5	-3.4	-6.0	3.2	3.5
	14.6		15.6		11.5	% Profit Before Taxes/Total	6.9	10.9	11.2	12.2	11.5	12.1
	6.4		2.9		3.5	Assets	.4	-2.1	6.3	2.1	5.0	6.1
	.0		-1.9		-3.3		-11.6	-13.1	-1.2	-3.5	.3	-.7
	29.2		25.7		25.5		72.2	30.8	31.1	27.1	16.0	18.7
	11.3		10.6		10.2	Sales/Net Fixed Assets	24.6	13.2	12.7	11.8	8.5	8.2
	5.2		5.2		5.0		5.3	4.9	5.7	5.2	4.1	5.4
	2.6		2.7		2.5		2.4	2.6	2.7	2.8	2.6	2.4
	2.0		2.0		1.9	Sales/Total Assets	1.6	2.0	2.1	2.0	1.7	1.7
	1.4		1.5		1.3		.9	1.6	1.5	1.4	1.1	1.1
	.7		.8		1.4			1.7	1.3	1.0	1.6	1.8
(187)	1.9	(181)	2.2	(178)	2.5	% Depr., Dep., Amort./Sales	(22) 3.4	(24) 1.8	(39) 2.4	(43) 3.2	(42) 2.7
	3.5		3.4		4.5			7.8	2.3	3.9	5.6	5.4
	2.4		2.5		3.1	% Officers', Directors',		5.0	2.1	3.1	1.6	
(62)	4.8	(67)	4.7	(61)	4.8	Owners' Comp/Sales	(17) 9.6	(10) 3.2	(15) 4.8	(10) 2.4	
	8.6		8.4		11.3			16.0	4.2	7.3	3.6	
6596599M		5754380M		7214947M		Net Sales ($)	6891M	62487M	103605M	295336M	728104M	6018524M
5094821M		3682475M		4137853M		Total Assets ($)	6177M	35047M	55013M	174560M	497726M	3369330M

M = $ thousand   MM = $ million
See Pages 11 through 18 for Explanation of Ratios and Data

Current Data Sorted By Assets							Comparative Historical Data	
		3	10	1	1	Type of Statement Unqualified	18	13
	1		1			Reviewed	2	3
						Compiled	2	5
	3	1				Tax Returns	8	4
	2	1	7	1	2	Other	13	14
	11 (4/1-9/30/02)		23 (10/1/02-3/31/03)				4/1/98-3/31/99	4/1/99-3/31/00
0-500M	500M-2MM	2-10MM	10-50MM	50-100MM	100-250MM		ALL	ALL
	6	5	18	2	3	NUMBER OF STATEMENTS	43	39
%	%	%	%	%	%	ASSETS	%	%
D			14.5			Cash & Equivalents	11.0	15.4
A			23.1			Trade Receivables (net)	27.2	25.4
T			21.4			Inventory	26.5	21.5
A			4.0			All Other Current	3.9	3.1
			62.9			Total Current	68.6	65.5
N			21.4			Fixed Assets (net)	19.0	21.6
O			8.9			Intangibles (net)	7.5	6.0
T			6.7			All Other Non-Current	4.9	6.9
			100.0			Total	100.0	100.0
A						LIABILITIES		
V			7.4			Notes Payable-Short Term	12.8	10.4
A			1.6			Cur. Mat.-L/T/D	2.3	2.1
I			11.5			Trade Payables	12.9	12.7
L			.3			Income Taxes Payable	.8	.6
A			14.2			All Other Current	12.0	10.8
B			34.9			Total Current	40.8	36.5
L			5.0			Long Term Debt	11.0	17.4
E			.3			Deferred Taxes	.3	.2
			2.5			All Other Non-Current	14.7	12.8
			57.3			Net Worth	33.3	32.9
			100.0			Total Liabilities & Net Worth	100.0	100.0
						INCOME DATA		
			100.0			Net Sales	100.0	100.0
			47.8			Gross Profit	43.6	45.0
			45.2			Operating Expenses	43.9	39.5
			2.6			Operating Profit	−.4	5.5
			.5			All Other Expenses (net)	−.2	.7
			2.1			Profit Before Taxes	−.2	4.8
						RATIOS		
			3.7 2.7 2.1			Current	3.5 1.9 1.3	3.2 2.1 1.2
			2.3 1.8 1.0			Quick	2.1 1.0 .7	2.4 1.3 .7
			50 7.3 **60** 6.1 **71** 5.1			Sales/Receivables	**51** 7.1 **66** 5.6 **83** 4.4	**46** 8.0 **59** 6.2 **81** 4.5
			70 5.2 **111** 3.3 **161** 2.3			Cost of Sales/Inventory	**71** 5.2 **108** 3.4 **158** 2.3	**53** 6.9 **90** 4.1 **124** 2.9
			28 12.9 **43** 8.6 **70** 5.2			Cost of Sales/Payables	**26** 13.8 **39** 9.3 **62** 5.9	**29** 12.7 **44** 8.4 **66** 5.5
			2.3 3.3 6.5			Sales/Working Capital	2.6 5.6 14.4	2.7 5.2 23.7
			41.3 (16) 6.1 −5.2			EBIT/Interest	7.1 (35) 4.1 .5	32.6 (30) 5.0 .4
						Net Profit + Depr., Dep., Amort./Cur. Mat. L/T/D	4.2 (15) 2.5 −.3	
			.2 .3 .6			Fixed/Worth	.2 .5 1.5	.2 .5 1.8
			.4 .4 .8			Debt/Worth	.5 1.3 3.5	.5 1.3 7.5
			30.2 (17) 7.5 −7.0			% Profit Before Taxes/Tangible Net Worth	53.6 (35) 21.1 −12.8	60.4 (31) 21.6 4.0
			17.0 2.4 −4.2			% Profit Before Taxes/Total Assets	18.0 7.4 −5.0	19.9 10.3 −2.0
			13.4 9.9 4.4			Sales/Net Fixed Assets	22.1 9.8 4.4	17.1 9.7 4.3
			1.8 1.3 1.0			Sales/Total Assets	2.3 1.7 1.1	2.0 1.6 1.1
			2.2 (14) 3.3 4.0			% Depr., Dep., Amort./Sales	1.2 (38) 2.5 4.3	1.7 (29) 2.6 4.3
						% Officers', Directors', Owners' Comp/Sales	1.9 (11) 5.5 11.3	
	15282M	**57319M**	**636133M**	**103635M**	**363207M**	Net Sales ($)	**904707M**	**971291M**
	6669M	**27259M**	**445762M**	**128647M**	**387456M**	Total Assets ($)	**1007160M**	**801541M**

M = $ thousand MM = $ million

See Pages 11 through 18 for Explanation of Ratios and Data

Comparative Historical Data | Current Data Sorted By Sales

				Type of Statement						
13	12	15		Unqualified			2	4		9
1	2	2		Reviewed		1		1		
4	2			Compiled						
3	4	4		Tax Returns	3	1				
9	19	13		Other	2			3		8
4/1/00-3/31/01 ALL	4/1/01-3/31/02 ALL	4/1/02-3/31/03 ALL			0-1MM	11 (4/1-9/30/02) 1-3MM	3-5MM	5-10MM	23 (10/1/02-3/31/03) 10-25MM	25MM & OVER
30	39	34		NUMBER OF STATEMENTS	5	2	2	8		17
%	%	%		ASSETS	%	%	%	%	%	%
10.4	12.7	16.0		Cash & Equivalents						19.4
26.5	24.1	24.6		Trade Receivables (net)						26.0
26.4	22.3	20.0		Inventory						17.1
2.0	3.2	5.1		All Other Current						4.0
65.3	62.3	65.6		Total Current						66.4
14.6	15.9	18.0		Fixed Assets (net)						16.6
9.0	13.0	9.1		Intangibles (net)						7.9
11.1	8.8	7.2		All Other Non-Current						9.1
100.0	100.0	100.0		Total						100.0
				LIABILITIES						
8.6	7.9	8.8		Notes Payable-Short Term						4.0
1.1	2.1	2.8		Cur. Mat.-L/T/D						2.0
14.0	8.5	11.0		Trade Payables						12.0
.4	.5	.3		Income Taxes Payable						.6
7.7	10.8	13.3		All Other Current						16.3
31.9	29.7	36.2		Total Current						34.9
7.0	13.2	9.2		Long Term Debt						8.0
.3	.3	.3		Deferred Taxes						.2
18.1	13.5	5.8		All Other Non-Current						2.8
42.7	43.3	48.5		Net Worth						54.1
100.0	100.0	100.0		Total Liabilities & Net Worth						100.0
				INCOME DATA						
100.0	100.0	100.0		Net Sales						100.0
48.1	48.7	48.3		Gross Profit						51.7
43.1	41.8	44.5		Operating Expenses						46.5
5.0	6.8	3.9		Operating Profit						5.2
-1.7	1.9	.1		All Other Expenses (net)						-.4
6.7	4.9	3.8		Profit Before Taxes						5.5
				RATIOS						
4.3	3.4	4.3								3.9
2.7	2.4	2.6		Current						2.6
1.6	1.5	1.6								2.1
2.4	1.9	2.5								2.5
1.4	1.3	1.7		Quick						1.9
.6	.8	.9								1.2

51 7.2	44 8.3	43 8.4								52 7.0
67 5.4	59 6.2	56 6.5		Sales/Receivables						65 5.6
91 4.0	94 3.9	77 4.7								97 3.8
75 4.9	76 4.8	47 7.8								82 4.5
124 2.9	121 3.0	96 3.8		Cost of Sales/Inventory						113 3.2
232 1.6	167 2.2	143 2.6								147 2.5
37 10.0	28 12.9	31 11.8								36 10.2
56 6.5	40 9.2	41 8.9		Cost of Sales/Payables						53 6.9
75 4.8	60 6.1	58 6.2								66 5.5
2.4	2.6	2.2								1.9
3.2	3.8	3.6		Sales/Working Capital						3.1
8.9	7.0	11.3								5.3
26.1	13.4	45.8								67.1
(21) 3.0	(36) 4.3	(30) 8.4		EBIT/Interest					(16)	6.8
1.1	.3	-2.5								-4.9
	7.4	74.4		Net Profit + Depr., Dep.,						
	(15) 1.8	(12) 4.2		Amort./Cur. Mat. L/T/D						
	.2	1.2								
.2	.2	.1								.1
.3	.4	.3		Fixed/Worth						.3
1.0	1.9	.6								.5
.3	.4	.3								.3
1.1	1.7	.5		Debt/Worth						.4
5.1	9.3	1.4								1.0
36.1	56.5	28.9		% Profit Before Taxes/Tangible						36.2
(26) 16.0	(33) 21.9	(28) 14.8		Net Worth					(15)	13.7
.7	-.9	-5.5								-6.8
13.9	16.5	16.9		% Profit Before Taxes/Total						17.8
4.5	6.5	8.1		Assets						10.5
-.2	-1.7	-3.6								-4.9
16.5	18.4	16.1								13.6
10.4	9.0	10.9		Sales/Net Fixed Assets						11.1
4.7	5.1	6.3								6.5
2.1	1.7	2.2								1.9
1.4	1.3	1.4		Sales/Total Assets						1.2
.9	.9	.9								.9
1.7	2.0	1.6								2.2
(23) 2.7	(34) 3.1	(26) 2.7		% Depr., Dep., Amort./Sales					(16)	3.0
3.8	5.3	3.8								3.8
				% Officers', Directors', Owners' Comp/Sales						
866628M	1590376M	1175576M		Net Sales ($)	10435M	8722M	13284M	144675M		998460M
951305M	1650438M	995793M		Total Assets ($)	4835M	4050M	11065M	129710M		846133M

Note: Columns 0-1MM are marked "DATA NOT AVAILABLE".

Current Data Sorted By Assets   Comparative Historical Data

0-500M	500M-2MM	2-10MM	10-50MM	50-100MM	100-250MM	Type of Statement	4/1/98-3/31/99 ALL	4/1/99-3/31/00 ALL
		5	4	1	4	Unqualified	32	16
	1	7			1	Reviewed	11	6
	3	1			1	Compiled	2	5
	1	1				Tax Returns	2	1
2	2	5	7	1	5	Other	22	22
	12 (4/1-9/30/02)		40 (10/1/02-3/31/03)					
2	7	19	11	2	11	NUMBER OF STATEMENTS	69	50
%	%	%	%	%	%	**ASSETS**	%	%
		12.0	10.9		17.4	Cash & Equivalents	11.2	11.3
		29.4	34.2		21.7	Trade Receivables (net)	28.4	28.5
		24.6	17.5		19.0	Inventory	22.6	23.4
		5.8	12.8		10.4	All Other Current	5.7	6.5
		71.8	75.4		68.5	Total Current	67.8	69.7
		14.2	15.6		11.9	Fixed Assets (net)	21.2	18.2
		6.3	4.7		12.4	Intangibles (net)	5.7	5.1
		7.8	4.2		7.2	All Other Non-Current	5.2	7.0
		100.0	100.0		100.0	Total	100.0	100.0
						LIABILITIES		
		10.5	10.1		5.6	Notes Payable-Short Term	8.7	9.9
		2.2	1.8		1.5	Cur. Mat.-L/T/D	2.5	5.8
		9.7	11.7		9.4	Trade Payables	12.2	13.7
		.5	.2		.2	Income Taxes Payable	.5	.6
		12.3	17.6		12.6	All Other Current	12.0	12.2
		35.2	41.4		29.2	Total Current	35.9	42.2
		7.2	4.2		5.2	Long Term Debt	12.4	11.8
		.9	.1		1.1	Deferred Taxes	.8	1.4
		3.8	.8		5.8	All Other Non-Current	6.7	12.3
		52.8	53.4		58.7	Net Worth	44.2	32.3
		100.0	100.0		100.0	Total Liabilities & Net Worth	100.0	100.0
						INCOME DATA		
		100.0	100.0		100.0	Net Sales	100.0	100.0
		39.3	37.7		27.2	Gross Profit	37.3	34.7
		30.6	31.2		23.3	Operating Expenses	32.4	33.0
		8.6	6.5		4.0	Operating Profit	4.9	1.7
		1.3	.1		.6	All Other Expenses (net)	1.0	.9
		7.4	6.3		3.4	Profit Before Taxes	4.0	.8
						RATIOS		
		6.5	4.5		3.3		2.7	2.6
		2.4	2.0		3.1	Current	1.9	1.8
		1.6	1.2		1.5		1.4	1.2
		4.0	2.4		2.4		1.7	1.6
		1.3	1.1		1.8	Quick	1.1	1.1
		.6	.8		.6		.7	.6
		32 11.5	66 5.6		37 9.9		43 8.5	41 8.9
		59 6.2	74 4.9		64 5.7	Sales/Receivables	56 6.6	66 5.5
		74 4.9	105 3.5		80 4.6		81 4.5	85 4.3
		39 9.3	25 14.9		25 14.7		38 9.7	32 11.3
		93 3.9	47 7.8		85 4.3	Cost of Sales/Inventory	94 3.9	67 5.4
		174 2.1	158 2.3		172 2.1		143 2.6	134 2.7
		17 21.5	32 11.4		21 17.0		23 15.8	23 16.1
		28 12.8	43 8.5		38 9.6	Cost of Sales/Payables	40 9.2	34 10.7
		40 9.0	65 5.6		60 6.1		61 6.0	67 5.5
		2.4	2.7		2.0		3.0	3.8
		4.8	3.4		5.0	Sales/Working Capital	5.4	6.4
		7.1	15.1		6.6		9.9	11.6
		49.7					14.2	10.0
		(13) 4.3				EBIT/Interest	(63) 4.2	(47) 4.3
		1.3					1.3	1.5
						Net Profit + Depr., Dep.,	10.3	4.6
						Amort./Cur. Mat. L /T/D	(28) 4.1	(16) 2.8
							1.4	2.5
		.1	.2		.1		.2	.3
		.2	.3		.2	Fixed/Worth	.5	.5
		.6	.5		.7		1.3	1.1
		.2	.3		.4		.6	.8
		1.0	.8		.9	Debt/Worth	1.6	2.3
		2.4	3.8		2.0		3.5	4.6
		41.5	30.2		34.3	% Profit Before Taxes/Tangible	35.6	41.0
		(16) 24.7	(10) 18.7		16.6	Net Worth	(60) 19.9	(44) 22.2
		4.4	−.9		−13.0		6.0	4.6
		20.4	18.5		12.7	% Profit Before Taxes/Total	13.5	12.2
		10.8	10.2		8.2	Assets	6.3	6.2
		2.0	.2		−4.2		1.4	1.2
		28.8	12.4		18.3		14.5	23.3
		16.9	9.2		13.7	Sales/Net Fixed Assets	8.2	9.5
		5.3	6.5		5.1		5.4	5.8
		2.2	2.1		1.5		2.1	2.1
		1.9	1.3		1.1	Sales/Total Assets	1.6	1.5
		1.3	1.2		.9		1.2	1.2
		.9	1.8				1.6	1.6
		(17) 2.0	(10) 2.5			% Depr., Dep., Amort./Sales	(59) 2.3	(39) 2.3
		3.2	3.3				4.6	4.7
						% Officers', Directors',	3.4	3.9
						Owners' Comp/Sales	(11) 6.8	(11) 6.9
							13.3	9.8
1748M	20689M	168691M	483022M	93395M	2057164M	Net Sales ($)	2771771M	2611032M
461M	8901M	99075M	284189M	140743M	1580443M	Total Assets ($)	2382174M	2205282M

M = $ thousand   MM = $ million
See Pages 11 through 18 for Explanation of Ratios and Data

Comparative Historical Data | Current Data Sorted By Sales

Comparative Historical Data				Current Data Sorted By Sales					
			Type of Statement						
16	18	14	Unqualified		1		2	5	6
6	8	9	Reviewed		2		4	2	1
2	5	5	Compiled		1	2	1		1
1	2	2	Tax Returns		1	1			
14	22	22	Other	1	4	1	1	5	11
4/1/00-3/31/01 ALL	4/1/01-3/31/02 ALL	4/1/02-3/31/03 ALL		0-1MM	1-3MM (12 (4/1-9/30/02))	3-5MM	5-10MM	10-25MM (40 (10/1/02-3/31/03))	25MM & OVER
39	55	52	**NUMBER OF STATEMENTS**	1	7	5	8	12	19
%	%	%	**ASSETS**	%	%	%	%	%	%
11.5	10.8	13.2	Cash & Equivalents					17.2	15.7
26.5	27.4	30.2	Trade Receivables (net)					31.7	27.0
29.3	26.2	23.1	Inventory					15.7	18.7
4.0	6.2	7.1	All Other Current					11.6	10.2
71.3	70.6	73.6	Total Current					76.2	71.6
18.0	16.8	14.0	Fixed Assets (net)					15.2	14.2
3.1	5.6	6.4	Intangibles (net)					3.8	8.2
7.7	7.0	6.0	All Other Non-Current					4.7	5.9
100.0	100.0	100.0	Total					100.0	100.0
			LIABILITIES						
8.0	10.4	8.9	Notes Payable-Short Term					5.5	8.9
4.1	4.1	1.9	Cur. Mat.-L/T/D					1.2	1.7
12.0	12.3	11.8	Trade Payables					9.9	10.3
.9	.9	.4	Income Taxes Payable					.5	.4
12.9	11.0	13.0	All Other Current					16.2	14.2
37.9	38.8	36.0	Total Current					33.3	35.5
9.3	8.2	5.6	Long Term Debt					1.3	5.8
.4	.7	.6	Deferred Taxes					1.5	.7
5.1	5.2	2.9	All Other Non-Current					2.1	3.7
47.3	47.0	55.0	Net Worth					61.8	54.4
100.0	100.0	100.0	Total Liabilities & Net Worth					100.0	100.0
			INCOME DATA						
100.0	100.0	100.0	Net Sales					100.0	100.0
35.3	33.6	37.3	Gross Profit					36.4	31.4
29.3	28.1	29.4	Operating Expenses					29.6	26.1
6.1	5.5	7.9	Operating Profit					6.8	5.3
1.6	1.5	.6	All Other Expenses (net)					.9	.0
4.5	4.0	7.3	Profit Before Taxes					5.8	5.3
			RATIOS						
3.5 / 1.7 / 1.4	3.1 / 1.9 / 1.3	4.9 / 2.4 / 1.5	Current					4.4 / 2.6 / 1.7	3.5 / 2.0 / 1.2
2.0 / .9 / .6	1.7 / 1.0 / .7	3.1 / 1.3 / .7	Quick					3.0 / 1.6 / 1.1	2.4 / 1.1 / .6
39 9.4 / 54 6.8 / 83 4.4	43 8.5 / 60 6.1 / 92 4.0	41 8.9 / 65 5.6 / 79 4.6	Sales/Receivables					53 6.9 / 69 5.3 / 89 4.1	49 7.4 / 71 5.2 / 100 3.6
48 7.6 / 107 3.4 / 158 2.3	43 8.5 / 97 3.8 / 167 2.2	29 12.6 / 94 3.9 / 156 2.3	Cost of Sales/Inventory					25 14.6 / 42 8.7 / 121 3.0	25 14.7 / 85 4.3 / 171 2.1
22 16.7 / 32 11.3 / 50 7.3	22 16.5 / 36 10.1 / 58 6.3	19 19.1 / 33 10.9 / 56 6.5	Cost of Sales/Payables					19 19.2 / 32 11.4 / 55 6.6	26 14.0 / 38 9.6 / 58 6.2
2.8 / 6.2 / 8.6	3.1 / 4.8 / 9.7	2.4 / 4.9 / 10.0	Sales/Working Capital					2.0 / 4.3 / 6.1	2.1 / 5.0 / 10.6
(34) 19.0 / 4.4 / 1.8	(46) 10.3 / 2.9 / .8	(37) 44.8 / 6.7 / 1.3	EBIT/Interest						(16) 45.3 / 6.9 / 1.1
(16) 15.3 / 2.4 / 1.2	(19) 11.4 / 2.8 / 1.4	(18) 10.3 / 4.2 / 2.4	Net Profit + Depr., Dep., Amort./Cur. Mat. L/T/D						(11) 11.7 / 4.3 / 1.9
.2 / .4 / .8	.2 / .4 / .8	.1 / .2 / .6	Fixed/Worth					.2 / .3 / .4	.2 / .3 / .6
.4 / 1.3 / 2.8	.6 / 1.6 / 3.5	.3 / 1.0 / 2.1	Debt/Worth					.2 / .5 / 1.9	.3 / .9 / 3.8
(37) 32.6 / 17.9 / 6.5	(54) 39.1 / 19.8 / -1.1	(47) 42.2 / 21.5 / 3.9	% Profit Before Taxes/Tangible Net Worth					38.4 / 23.0 / 2.8	(18) 32.1 / 14.0 / -1.9
13.0 / 8.6 / 2.7	17.6 / 6.7 / -.5	20.0 / 9.6 / 1.2	% Profit Before Taxes/Total Assets					18.1 / 9.9 / 1.5	13.5 / 8.8 / -.5
18.9 / 10.3 / 6.3	20.9 / 10.7 / 5.0	29.3 / 13.2 / 5.4	Sales/Net Fixed Assets					19.5 / 11.9 / 6.9	18.3 / 12.4 / 4.9
2.2 / 1.7 / 1.2	1.9 / 1.5 / 1.1	2.2 / 1.5 / 1.1	Sales/Total Assets					2.2 / 1.5 / 1.2	1.6 / 1.2 / 1.0
(34) 1.7 / 2.4 / 4.0	(47) 1.2 / 2.2 / 3.4	(43) 1.1 / 2.0 / 3.3	% Depr., Dep., Amort./Sales						(16) 1.7 / 2.2 / 3.1
	(11) 4.3 / 5.5 / 9.2	(14) 2.3 / 4.3 / 6.6	% Officers', Directors', Owners' Comp/Sales						
1738280M	2263454M	2824709M	Net Sales ($)	549M	14813M	18263M	52858M	196927M	2541299M
1423000M	1756846M	2113812M	Total Assets ($)	272M	13934M	17051M	25361M	132122M	1925072M

© RMA 2003

M = $ thousand   MM = $ million
See Pages 11 through 18 for Explanation of Ratios and Data

Current Data Sorted By Assets   Comparative Historical Data

0-500M	500M-2MM	2-10MM	10-50MM	50-100MM	100-250MM	Type of Statement	4/1/98-3/31/99 ALL	4/1/99-3/31/00 ALL
	1	4	3	1	1	Unqualified	10	8
	1	4	1			Reviewed	10	13
2	3	3				Compiled	4	7
1	1					Tax Returns	1	1
		8	1			Other	14	10
3 (4/1-9/30/02)			32 (10/1/02-3/31/03)					
3	6	19	5	1	1	NUMBER OF STATEMENTS	39	39
%	%	%	%	%	%	**ASSETS**	%	%
		11.9				Cash & Equivalents	11.1	10.1
		33.5				Trade Receivables (net)	33.8	34.7
		22.4				Inventory	25.4	27.6
		4.2				All Other Current	3.3	4.7
		72.1				Total Current	73.8	77.1
		11.7				Fixed Assets (net)	19.2	17.1
		13.4				Intangibles (net)	1.6	1.4
		2.7				All Other Non-Current	5.4	4.3
		100.0				Total	100.0	100.0
						LIABILITIES		
		6.0				Notes Payable-Short Term	6.8	8.5
		4.5				Cur. Mat.-L/T/D	3.7	2.9
		16.6				Trade Payables	15.9	14.2
		.1				Income Taxes Payable	.7	.2
		12.3				All Other Current	14.4	15.6
		39.5				Total Current	41.4	41.5
		12.6				Long Term Debt	6.2	7.2
		.1				Deferred Taxes	.8	.3
		1.1				All Other Non-Current	4.8	4.5
		46.7				Net Worth	46.8	46.6
		100.0				Total Liabilities & Net Worth	100.0	100.0
						INCOME DATA		
		100.0				Net Sales	100.0	100.0
		34.8				Gross Profit	37.9	35.4
		28.7				Operating Expenses	31.3	29.7
		6.1				Operating Profit	6.5	5.7
		.1				All Other Expenses (net)	.6	.1
		6.0				Profit Before Taxes	5.9	5.6
						RATIOS		
		3.0 / 1.5 / 1.4				Current	3.0 / 1.7 / 1.4	5.1 / 2.0 / 1.2
		1.9 / 1.3 / .6				Quick	1.9 / 1.1 / .7	2.4 / 1.1 / .7
		40 9.1 / 54 6.7 / 69 5.3				Sales/Receivables	40 9.2 / 50 7.3 / 73 5.0	47 7.8 / 59 6.2 / 76 4.8
		34 10.7 / 68 5.4 / 95 3.8				Cost of Sales/Inventory	46 8.0 / 69 5.3 / 103 3.6	42 8.8 / 76 4.8 / 130 2.8
		18 20.2 / 21 17.2 / 39 9.3				Cost of Sales/Payables	20 18.1 / 35 10.4 / 49 7.4	20 18.6 / 31 11.7 / 42 8.6
		3.8 / 9.5 / 16.0				Sales/Working Capital	4.9 / 7.9 / 13.9	3.3 / 5.8 / 11.5
		(16) 12.7 / 2.6 / -2.0				EBIT/Interest	(34) 17.7 / 5.0 / 1.8	(31) 8.0 / 3.8 / 1.7
						Net Profit + Depr., Dep., Amort./Cur. Mat. L./T/D	(14) 12.0 / 2.8 / 2.0	(14) 4.5 / 2.4 / .6
		.2 / .3 / 1.3				Fixed/Worth	.2 / .4 / .9	.2 / .3 / .6
		.4 / 2.1 / 13.4				Debt/Worth	.6 / 1.0 / 2.4	.4 / 1.1 / 2.9
		(16) 55.8 / 11.8 / -6.9				% Profit Before Taxes/Tangible Net Worth	(37) 44.2 / 24.4 / 9.9	(37) 43.1 / 22.5 / 8.5
		22.9 / 9.5 / -2.5				% Profit Before Taxes/Total Assets	21.8 / 12.5 / 3.4	18.5 / 8.7 / 3.9
		43.0 / 24.3 / 8.7				Sales/Net Fixed Assets	23.9 / 13.4 / 6.0	34.6 / 16.2 / 6.2
		2.6 / 1.7 / 1.5				Sales/Total Assets	2.8 / 2.1 / 1.7	2.6 / 2.0 / 1.5
		(15) .6 / 1.4 / 2.9				% Depr., Dep., Amort./Sales	(30) 1.0 / 1.9 / 2.7	(30) .9 / 1.6 / 3.3
						% Officers', Directors', Owners' Comp/Sales	(10) 3.6 / 9.1 / 12.0	(12) 5.0 / 8.0 / 14.1
2186M	12525M	165746M	124180M	82549M	214970M	Net Sales ($)	950159M	633778M
1049M	5491M	74647M	111128M	69538M	122134M	Total Assets ($)	551554M	370206M

M = $ thousand   MM = $ million
See Pages 11 through 18 for Explanation of Ratios and Data

Comparative Historical Data | | | Current Data Sorted By Sales

			Type of Statement						
9	6	10	Unqualified		1	2	1	1	5
4	3	6	Reviewed		1		2	3	
9	10	5	Compiled	1	1	1	1	1	
1	6	4	Tax Returns	1	2	1			
13	13	10	Other		1	1	7		
4/1/00-3/31/01	4/1/01-3/31/02	4/1/02-3/31/03			3 (4/1-9/30/02)		32 (10/1/02-3/31/03)		
ALL	ALL	ALL		0-1MM	1-3MM	3-5MM	5-10MM	10-25MM	25MM & OVER
36	38	35	**NUMBER OF STATEMENTS**	2	6	5	11	6	5
%	%	%	**ASSETS**	%	%	%	%	%	%
9.7	10.8	12.2	Cash & Equivalents				8.3		
33.6	29.8	29.3	Trade Receivables (net)				31.9		
21.8	23.3	20.6	Inventory				23.1		
5.2	5.8	5.1	All Other Current				4.8		
70.3	69.6	67.2	Total Current				68.1		
15.5	18.8	16.6	Fixed Assets (net)				13.8		
7.0	6.4	9.7	Intangibles (net)				14.7		
7.2	5.2	6.5	All Other Non-Current				3.3		
100.0	100.0	100.0	Total				100.0		
			LIABILITIES						
6.3	5.5	5.4	Notes Payable-Short Term				6.8		
4.5	5.9	3.2	Cur. Mat.-L/T/D				3.0		
13.7	12.9	13.9	Trade Payables				15.2		
.4	.2	.1	Income Taxes Payable				.2		
12.8	14.9	12.4	All Other Current				10.5		
37.7	39.4	35.1	Total Current				35.8		
13.1	11.4	13.6	Long Term Debt				11.0		
.7	.6	.5	Deferred Taxes				.2		
4.2	5.0	2.0	All Other Non-Current				3.5		
44.3	43.7	48.8	Net Worth				49.5		
100.0	100.0	100.0	Total Liabilities & Net Worth				100.0		
			INCOME DATA						
100.0	100.0	100.0	Net Sales				100.0		
42.1	35.0	38.3	Gross Profit				35.4		
32.6	29.8	33.2	Operating Expenses				32.2		
9.6	5.3	5.1	Operating Profit				3.2		
.9	1.1	.3	All Other Expenses (net)				.0		
8.7	4.2	4.8	Profit Before Taxes				3.2		
			RATIOS						
3.2	3.1	3.1					5.6		
1.8	1.9	1.6	Current				1.5		
1.2	1.1	1.4					1.4		
2.4	2.5	1.9					2.0		
1.0	1.2	1.3	Quick				1.1		
.8	.5	.8					.5		
48 7.6	30 12.1	40 9.1					41 9.0		
63 5.8	50 7.3	52 7.0	Sales/Receivables				54 6.7		
76 4.8	68 5.3	67 5.4					67 5.4		
31 11.6	21 17.3	34 10.7					34 10.7		
79 4.6	64 5.7	67 5.5	Cost of Sales/Inventory				86 4.2		
131 2.8	106 3.4	106 3.4					151 2.4		
21 17.3	18 20.1	18 20.0					18 20.2		
38 9.7	29 12.6	24 15.2	Cost of Sales/Payables				20 18.1		
53 6.9	45 8.2	48 7.5					39 9.3		
3.5	4.1	3.7					2.2		
6.4	7.7	7.9	Sales/Working Capital				9.5		
14.1	33.5	17.2					13.1		
16.4	11.9	12.9					6.8		
(30) 6.0	(32) 2.1	(31) 3.5	EBIT/Interest			(10) 1.7			
1.6	.9	−.7					−1.1		
11.1	9.3		Net Profit + Depr., Dep.,						
(10) 6.2	(11) 1.2		Amort./Cur. Mat. L/T/D						
2.3	.6								
.2	.2	.2					.2		
.4	.4	.3	Fixed/Worth				.4		
1.2	1.6	.8					1.3		
.4	.4	.5					.4		
1.6	2.3	1.5	Debt/Worth				2.1		
5.6	12.5	3.8					3.9		
60.7	58.7	45.8	% Profit Before Taxes/Tangible				14.4		
(33) 32.2	(33) 15.8	(32) 9.6	Net Worth			(10) 8.2			
17.0	.5	−3.2					−5.1		
26.9	17.7	16.8	% Profit Before Taxes/Total				11.5		
10.3	5.6	5.2	Assets				1.7		
4.9	.6	−.1					−2.5		
22.9	30.0	40.6					31.8		
12.8	11.6	17.4	Sales/Net Fixed Assets				18.0		
7.0	8.1	6.8					7.8		
2.5	2.9	2.3					2.3		
1.8	1.9	1.7	Sales/Total Assets				1.9		
1.3	1.5	1.5					1.5		
.5	.5	1.4							
(30) 1.4	(32) 1.9	(29) 2.2	% Depr., Dep., Amort./Sales						
2.9	3.1	4.3							
	1.8	2.5	% Officers', Directors',						
	(15) 7.7	(19) 5.7	Owners' Comp/Sales						
	13.5	9.0							
619119M	815151M	602156M	Net Sales ($)	978M	10712M	20694M	75526M	79987M	414259M
304342M	436099M	383987M	Total Assets ($)	597M	4783M	12306M	47939M	45177M	273185M

M = $ thousand   MM = $ million
See Pages 11 through 18 for Explanation of Ratios and Data

Current Data Sorted By Assets

Comparative Historical Data

						Type of Statement		
	4	14	12	7	4	Unqualified	50	45
2	6	17	4			Reviewed	56	46
5	7	7				Compiled	16	26
	4	1				Tax Returns	6	6
3	7	11	7			Other	44	42
	29 (4/1-9/30/02)		93 (10/1/02-3/31/03)				4/1/98-3/31/99	4/1/99-3/31/00
0-500M	500M-2MM	2-10MM	10-50MM	50-100MM	100-250MM		ALL	ALL
10	28	50	23	7	4	**NUMBER OF STATEMENTS**	172	165
%	%	%	%	%	%	**ASSETS**	%	%
5.7	5.9	11.8	10.4			Cash & Equivalents	9.7	10.0
41.5	38.6	30.3	26.4			Trade Receivables (net)	30.2	30.9
34.2	24.2	26.6	25.2			Inventory	27.3	24.6
.9	5.5	3.1	2.7			All Other Current	2.4	3.7
82.3	74.2	71.7	64.7			Total Current	69.6	69.1
16.9	18.5	19.6	22.6			Fixed Assets (net)	20.0	19.8
.2	3.7	3.9	8.8			Intangibles (net)	4.2	4.5
.6	3.6	4.8	3.9			All Other Non-Current	6.2	6.6
100.0	100.0	100.0	100.0			Total	100.0	100.0
						LIABILITIES		
18.5	22.9	5.6	7.7			Notes Payable-Short Term	10.5	9.4
2.4	3.3	3.0	3.5			Cur. Mat.-L/T/D	3.3	3.1
40.4	18.7	9.3	11.4			Trade Payables	12.1	11.9
.9	.0	.6	.4			Income Taxes Payable	.3	.3
8.1	14.7	12.3	9.8			All Other Current	12.2	12.6
70.4	59.7	30.9	32.8			Total Current	38.4	37.4
52.7	18.5	10.6	11.5			Long Term Debt	12.5	14.8
.0	.0	.2	.9			Deferred Taxes	.3	.4
24.7	6.6	3.4	4.8			All Other Non-Current	4.2	5.8
−47.8	15.2	55.0	50.0			Net Worth	44.6	41.7
100.0	100.0	100.0	100.0			Total Liabilities & Net Worth	100.0	100.0
						INCOME DATA		
100.0	100.0	100.0	100.0			Net Sales	100.0	100.0
46.8	37.4	42.1	39.2			Gross Profit	40.4	42.0
43.4	37.0	37.8	34.8			Operating Expenses	37.6	37.1
3.4	.4	4.3	4.3			Operating Profit	2.8	4.9
2.0	1.9	.9	.8			All Other Expenses (net)	2.0	.7
1.5	−1.5	3.4	3.5			Profit Before Taxes	.8	4.2
						RATIOS		
2.6	1.7	4.1	4.2				3.2	3.3
1.2	1.3	2.3	1.7			Current	1.9	1.9
.8	1.0	1.7	1.1				1.3	1.3
1.4	.9	2.1	2.2				1.8	1.8
.5	.8	1.5	1.0			Quick	1.1	1.1
.4	.6	.9	.6				.6	.7
26 14.0	36 10.2	42 8.7	50 7.3				43 8.6	45 8.1
48 7.6	52 7.0	55 6.6	57 6.3			Sales/Receivables	55 6.7	59 6.1
71 5.1	64 5.7	70 5.2	65 5.6				69 5.3	73 5.0
31 11.6	22 16.3	53 6.9	64 5.7				52 7.0	49 7.4
98 3.7	54 6.7	99 3.7	110 3.3			Cost of Sales/Inventory	100 3.7	93 3.9
126 2.9	106 3.4	142 2.6	134 2.7				145 2.5	129 2.8
42 8.7	20 18.6	17 21.4	19 19.0				18 20.0	23 15.8
89 4.1	31 11.8	26 14.3	34 10.8			Cost of Sales/Payables	36 10.3	35 10.6
135 2.7	60 6.1	41 9.0	78 4.7				55 6.7	47 7.8
5.6	8.0	2.9	3.0				3.7	3.6
22.4	16.6	4.7	5.4			Sales/Working Capital	5.6	6.0
−26.3	162.1	8.5	37.5				15.3	13.3
10.1	2.8	23.0	13.3				10.2	11.6
2.2	(26) 1.0	(46) 3.7	(21) 5.1			EBIT/Interest	(147) 2.7	(141) 3.3
−2.0	−1.6	1.3	.1				1.0	1.2
		11.3	28.1				5.1	7.8
	(19) 3.3	(14) 2.4			Net Profit + Depr., Dep., Amort./Cur. Mat. L /T/D	(62) 2.1	(61) 3.0
		1.6	.2				.9	1.2
.4	.2	.1	.2				.2	.2
UND	.6	.3	.4			Fixed/Worth	.5	.4
−.1	5.5	.7	1.6				1.1	1.0
2.9	1.8	.4	.5				.5	.5
UND	3.5	.8	1.0			Debt/Worth	1.3	1.3
−1.9	20.1	1.7	3.2				3.8	3.1
	9.3	27.8	30.5				30.4	36.2
	(23) .0	(49) 10.7	(20) 13.9			% Profit Before Taxes/Tangible Net Worth	(159) 13.8	(151) 14.3
	−67.2	−.4	−3.2				−.5	2.8
22.0	5.3	12.7	18.1				13.5	13.5
9.8	.2	3.5	6.7			% Profit Before Taxes/Total Assets	5.3	6.5
−16.7	−12.3	.0	−1.3				−.5	.4
75.7	55.7	29.7	13.0				23.1	25.6
34.1	22.3	13.9	8.0			Sales/Net Fixed Assets	11.2	10.7
13.4	7.4	5.6	5.3				5.5	5.8
3.3	3.5	2.5	1.8				2.5	2.4
2.7	2.7	1.9	1.5			Sales/Total Assets	1.8	1.8
2.5	1.9	1.4	1.2				1.4	1.3
	.9	.8	1.5				1.2	1.1
	(24) 1.3	(46) 1.7	(22) 2.6			% Depr., Dep., Amort./Sales	(148) 2.1	(145) 1.9
	2.1	2.8	3.3				3.5	3.5
	3.8	2.2					3.2	2.9
	(16) 5.6	(15) 3.8				% Officers', Directors', Owners' Comp/Sales	(45) 5.3	(51) 5.0
	11.9	8.0					10.2	9.7
7475M	93229M	425677M	727531M	628922M	1047561M	Net Sales ($)	4508064M	3072687M
2623M	34716M	231233M	470871M	452878M	766664M	Total Assets ($)	2637792M	2007702M

M = $ thousand   MM = $ million
See Pages 11 through 18 for Explanation of Ratios and Data

Comparative Historical Data				Current Data Sorted By Sales					
			Type of Statement						
31	25	41	Unqualified		2	3	8	11	17
38	37	29	Reviewed	1	4	3	12	7	2
23	20	19	Compiled	3	9	4	2	1	
6	2	5	Tax Returns		1		2	2	
44	41	28	Other	2	3	5	7	6	5
4/1/00- 3/31/01 ALL	4/1/01- 3/31/02 ALL	4/1/02- 3/31/03 ALL			29 (4/1-9/30/02)		93 (10/1/02-3/31/03)		
				0-1MM	1-3MM	3-5MM	5-10MM	10-25MM	25MM & OVER
142	125	122	**NUMBER OF STATEMENTS**	6	19	17	31	25	24
%	%	%	**ASSETS**	%	%	%	%	%	%
13.6	11.4	10.4	Cash & Equivalents		9.1	7.7	11.2	8.8	15.4
29.2	28.7	31.7	Trade Receivables (net)		34.6	37.8	32.1	30.6	27.2
28.1	27.3	25.7	Inventory		27.1	24.3	27.0	25.7	22.7
3.2	3.3	3.5	All Other Current		1.3	4.9	4.3	4.1	3.2
74.1	70.7	71.2	Total Current		72.1	74.7	74.5	69.2	68.5
16.4	17.6	19.9	Fixed Assets (net)		18.6	15.4	18.7	20.4	20.2
4.8	6.3	4.9	Intangibles (net)		5.3	4.6	2.0	7.6	6.8
4.7	5.4	4.0	All Other Non-Current		4.0	5.3	4.7	2.8	4.5
100.0	100.0	100.0	Total		100.0	100.0	100.0	100.0	100.0
			LIABILITIES						
10.5	9.4	10.7	Notes Payable-Short Term		21.7	12.4	9.3	5.9	4.0
3.6	4.4	2.9	Cur. Mat.-L/T/D		3.5	3.3	2.5	3.4	2.5
12.0	12.1	14.7	Trade Payables		20.5	18.0	11.7	9.4	12.8
.6	.5	.5	Income Taxes Payable		.0	.0	.6	.7	.4
12.1	11.9	12.2	All Other Current		11.6	12.9	15.1	10.7	12.3
38.7	38.4	41.0	Total Current		57.4	46.7	39.3	30.0	32.0
9.4	12.0	15.7	Long Term Debt		19.7	14.7	12.9	9.0	8.1
.2	.2	.3	Deferred Taxes		.0	.0	.2	.8	.7
7.5	6.1	5.9	All Other Non-Current		17.7	1.0	2.8	6.0	1.9
44.3	43.4	37.1	Net Worth		5.2	37.6	44.8	54.2	57.4
100.0	100.0	100.0	Total Liabilities & Net Worth		100.0	100.0	100.0	100.0	100.0
			INCOME DATA						
100.0	100.0	100.0	Net Sales		100.0	100.0	100.0	100.0	100.0
42.2	39.7	39.8	Gross Profit		38.9	37.1	40.7	41.1	35.5
36.0	35.9	36.3	Operating Expenses		37.9	36.1	38.0	37.3	29.0
6.2	3.8	3.5	Operating Profit		.9	1.0	2.7	3.9	6.5
1.2	1.4	1.1	All Other Expenses (net)		1.4	.2	1.5	.8	.2
4.9	2.4	2.4	Profit Before Taxes		-.4	.8	1.2	3.1	6.2
			RATIOS						
3.7 2.1 1.3	3.2 2.1 1.3	3.2 2.0 1.1	Current		1.9 1.2 .9	3.5 1.4 1.1	3.2 2.1 1.3	3.5 2.2 1.6	5.0 2.6 1.2
2.2 1.2 .7	2.0 1.1 .7	1.9 1.0 .7	Quick		1.0 .8 .6	1.4 1.0 .6	2.1 1.1 .7	1.9 1.4 .8	2.8 1.4 .8
42 8.8 54 6.7 70 5.2	37 9.7 50 7.3 67 5.5	42 8.7 55 6.7 67 5.5	Sales/Receivables		30 12.0 52 7.0 64 5.7	32 11.3 54 6.7 63 5.8	40 9.2 50 7.2 66 5.5	51 7.2 60 6.1 73 5.0	49 7.5 58 6.2 75 4.8
65 5.6 106 3.4 137 2.7	51 7.2 94 3.9 147 2.5	45 8.2 94 3.9 133 2.7	Cost of Sales/Inventory		45 8.1 88 4.2 131 2.8	22 16.3 86 4.2 109 3.3	49 7.5 90 4.1 138 2.6	55 6.7 103 3.6 154 2.4	53 6.9 105 3.5 131 2.8
19 19.0 34 10.9 50 7.3	18 19.9 30 12.3 46 8.0	20 18.3 31 11.8 52 7.0	Cost of Sales/Payables		21 17.8 41 8.9 70 5.2	18 20.6 30 12.2 61 6.0	17 21.2 29 12.5 46 7.9	18 20.4 25 14.4 49 7.5	20 18.4 36 10.1 58 6.3
3.0 5.1 11.8	3.4 5.5 13.2	3.5 6.0 26.6	Sales/Working Capital		5.7 15.7 -79.9	3.8 12.6 118.2	3.4 5.4 14.0	3.3 5.3 8.2	2.3 4.0 26.9
(117) 10.7 3.1 1.4	(106) 10.0 2.6 .2	(114) 13.4 2.8 .2	EBIT/Interest		(18) 4.6 1.2 -1.3	(15) 3.2 1.5 -1.4	(30) 19.1 2.8 .2	(22) 41.3 3.9 .9	(23) 47.1 11.8 4.4
(41) 7.0 3.2 1.5	(47) 7.2 1.7 .1	(46) 12.3 2.7 .5	Net Profit + Depr., Dep., Amort./Cur. Mat. L/T/D				(11) 11.3 2.7 1.6	(11) 60.3 4.4 .7	(12) 22.6 2.5 .1
.2 .4 .9	.2 .4 1.0	.2 .4 1.2	Fixed/Worth		.4 .5 -.6	.1 .5 .7	.1 .4 .9	.2 .3 1.0	.2 .4 .9
.4 1.1 3.8	.5 1.0 3.9	.5 1.4 4.8	Debt/Worth		1.5 3.2 -3.7	.8 2.4 9.4	.6 1.2 3.4	.4 .8 2.4	.3 .7 3.4
(131) 41.3 15.8 4.3	(113) 30.4 9.1 -5.7	(108) 29.3 9.2 -2.6	% Profit Before Taxes/Tangible Net Worth		(12) 16.2 1.4 -1.8	(16) 7.9 2.6 -44.9	(30) 20.9 8.5 -15.0	(23) 29.1 18.5 .1	(23) 38.5 21.2 7.9
16.7 5.9 1.2	14.5 3.4 -3.8	13.5 3.5 -2.1	% Profit Before Taxes/Total Assets		7.4 .4 -6.9	4.5 1.0 -5.7	9.7 2.2 -5.0	17.3 6.2 -.6	18.1 9.3 4.3
31.8 13.1 7.2	29.9 13.6 7.2	30.6 12.2 5.6	Sales/Net Fixed Assets		57.5 14.1 5.4	72.3 23.1 8.0	32.5 15.5 6.7	24.9 10.2 5.4	12.9 7.8 5.0
2.5 1.8 1.3	2.5 1.9 1.3	2.7 1.9 1.4	Sales/Total Assets		2.8 2.1 1.4	3.2 2.5 1.9	3.0 1.9 1.6	2.5 1.6 1.4	2.1 1.6 1.1
(120) 1.0 1.9 2.8	(106) 1.1 2.0 3.2	(107) 1.0 1.8 3.0	% Depr., Dep., Amort./Sales		(18) .7 1.1 3.1	(14) .6 1.4 1.9	(28) .8 1.6 2.4	(23) 1.5 2.7 3.4	(20) 1.3 2.4 3.5
(39) 3.4 6.4 11.4	(29) 2.0 4.4 11.3	(36) 2.8 5.6 10.6	% Officers', Directors', Owners' Comp/Sales		(11) 3.6 7.6 13.5	(10) 3.0 5.0 10.3	(10) 2.1 3.8 10.3		
2443394M	2307172M	2930395M	Net Sales ($)	2500M	33380M	64485M	213289M	384486M	2232255M
1747989M	1535466M	1958985M	Total Assets ($)	9296M	20775M	29276M	108798M	249858M	1540982M

M = $ thousand   MM = $ million
See Pages 11 through 18 for Explanation of Ratios and Data

Current Data Sorted By Assets   **Comparative Historical Data**

0-500M	500M-2MM	2-10MM	10-50MM	50-100MM	100-250MM		4/1/98-3/31/99 ALL	4/1/99-3/31/00 ALL
						Type of Statement		
		2	3	1	1	Unqualified		4
	2	8	1			Reviewed		7
	3	1				Compiled		1
	1					Tax Returns		1
2	2	5	1			Other		7
		7 (4/1-9/30/02)	26 (10/1/02-3/31/03)					
2	8	16	5	1	1	**NUMBER OF STATEMENTS**		20
%	%	%	%	%	%	**ASSETS**	%	%
		9.7				Cash & Equivalents	D	7.3
		17.3				Trade Receivables (net)	A	25.2
		32.3				Inventory	T	33.5
		10.4				All Other Current	A	2.8
		69.7				Total Current		68.8
		17.1				Fixed Assets (net)	N	19.3
		7.4				Intangibles (net)	O	5.5
		5.7				All Other Non-Current	T	6.4
		100.0				Total		100.0
						LIABILITIES	A	
		10.2				Notes Payable-Short Term	V	9.6
		3.7				Cur. Mat.-L/T/D	A	3.5
		10.3				Trade Payables	I	10.5
		.2				Income Taxes Payable	L	.4
		9.7				All Other Current	A	15.8
		34.1				Total Current	B	39.8
		6.1				Long Term Debt	L	17.3
		.7				Deferred Taxes	E	.3
		1.4				All Other Non-Current		6.2
		57.7				Net Worth		36.4
		100.0				Total Liabilities & Net Worth		100.0
						INCOME DATA		
		100.0				Net Sales		100.0
		49.5				Gross Profit		35.2
		47.6				Operating Expenses		29.7
		1.9				Operating Profit		5.5
		.9				All Other Expenses (net)		1.8
		1.0				Profit Before Taxes		3.7
						RATIOS		
		3.7						2.4
		2.0				Current		1.9
		1.4						1.4
		2.1						1.5
		.7				Quick		.8
		.5						.5
		39 9.4						37 9.8
		44 8.2				Sales/Receivables		43 8.4
		52 7.0						52 7.1
		90 4.1						53 6.9
		125 2.9				Cost of Sales/Inventory		99 3.7
		237 1.5						143 2.5
		23 16.2						25 14.5
		37 9.8				Cost of Sales/Payables		30 12.3
		62 5.9						35 10.4
		3.1						3.9
		3.5				Sales/Working Capital		7.3
		6.4						11.1
		15.4						14.8
	(15)	1.7				EBIT/Interest	(19)	3.9
		−3.5						1.5
						Net Profit + Depr., Dep., Amort./Cur. Mat. L /T/D		
		.1						.2
		.3				Fixed/Worth		.4
		.6						.9
		.4						.9
		.9				Debt/Worth		1.5
		2.1						2.9
		25.0						32.6
	(15)	4.1				% Profit Before Taxes/Tangible Net Worth	(19)	18.9
		−12.7						6.3
		12.4						14.7
		3.2				% Profit Before Taxes/Total Assets		7.3
		−6.9						2.2
		30.0						22.2
		10.2				Sales/Net Fixed Assets		11.5
		5.9						5.9
		2.0						2.5
		1.6				Sales/Total Assets		2.0
		1.1						1.4
		.8						1.3
	(14)	1.5				% Depr., Dep., Amort./Sales	(19)	1.9
		2.5						3.7
						% Officers', Directors', Owners' Comp/Sales		
1587M	23745M	97693M	244240M	136284M	167317M	Net Sales ($)		361119M
608M	10360M	62768M	150792M	81750M	126463M	Total Assets ($)		222630M

© RMA 2003

M = $ thousand MM = $ million
See Pages 11 through 18 for Explanation of Ratios and Data

Comparative Historical Data | Current Data Sorted By Sales

					0-1MM	7 (4/1-9/30/02) 1-3MM	3-5MM	26 (10/1/02-3/31/03) 5-10MM	10-25MM	25MM & OVER
				Type of Statement						
2	2		7	Unqualified				2	1	4
10	7		10	Reviewed		2	4	3	1	
3	3		5	Compiled		2	1	2		
	1		1	Tax Returns		1				
6	5		10	Other	1	3	2	3		1
4/1/00-3/31/01	4/1/01-3/31/02		4/1/02-3/31/03							
ALL	ALL		ALL							
21	18		33	**NUMBER OF STATEMENTS**	1	8	7	10	2	5
%	%		%	**ASSETS**	%	%	%	%	%	%
9.0	7.7		11.0	Cash & Equivalents				11.6		
29.2	23.5		22.9	Trade Receivables (net)				15.8		
32.6	31.4		31.9	Inventory				32.2		
2.2	2.1		8.6	All Other Current				18.5		
73.0	64.6		74.5	Total Current				78.1		
16.1	21.4		16.2	Fixed Assets (net)				14.8		
3.8	4.4		4.3	Intangibles (net)				2.2		
7.1	9.5		5.0	All Other Non-Current				4.8		
100.0	100.0		100.0	Total				100.0		
				LIABILITIES						
9.0	13.1		12.2	Notes Payable-Short Term				10.4		
1.2	3.6		3.2	Cur. Mat.-L/T/D				2.2		
14.5	11.9		10.8	Trade Payables				12.0		
.8	.2		.3	Income Taxes Payable				.2		
12.3	12.0		11.8	All Other Current				14.2		
37.7	40.7		38.3	Total Current				38.9		
8.4	13.9		7.8	Long Term Debt				4.5		
.3	.8		.5	Deferred Taxes				.2		
3.8	10.8		5.6	All Other Non-Current				3.5		
49.7	33.7		47.7	Net Worth				52.9		
100.0	100.0		100.0	Total Liabilities & Net Worth				100.0		
				INCOME DATA						
100.0	100.0		100.0	Net Sales				100.0		
42.9	41.9		41.1	Gross Profit				42.6		
39.1	36.3		37.8	Operating Expenses				38.4		
3.8	5.5		3.3	Operating Profit				4.3		
1.0	1.6		1.0	All Other Expenses (net)				.8		
2.8	3.9		2.4	Profit Before Taxes				3.5		
				RATIOS						
4.1	2.8		2.9					3.9		
1.9	1.7		2.0	Current				2.2		
1.3	1.2		1.3					1.6		
2.4	1.2		1.6					1.7		
1.0	.7		.8	Quick				.9		
.6	.5		.5					.3		
37 9.9	31 11.9	38	9.6					17 22.1		
52 7.0	45 8.1	48	7.6	Sales/Receivables				43 8.5		
71 5.1	54 6.8	60	6.1					48 7.6		
83 4.4	78 4.7	67	5.4					68 5.3		
110 3.3	122 3.0	106	3.4	Cost of Sales/Inventory				115 3.2		
158 2.3	149 2.5	156	2.3					189 1.9		
20 18.6	14 26.3	22	16.3					12 30.5		
34 10.7	27 13.6	36	10.1	Cost of Sales/Payables				28 12.8		
94 3.9	62 5.9	54	6.8					69 5.3		
3.2	4.4		3.3					3.3		
6.6	6.2		5.1	Sales/Working Capital				4.2		
10.6	17.6		8.5					6.1		
7.8	14.0		11.7							
(18) 2.7	2.7	(31)	1.9	EBIT/Interest						
.7	1.1		-.1							
8.6			6.8	Net Profit + Depr., Dep.,						
(10) 3.1		(11)	1.9	Amort./Cur. Mat. L/T/D						
1.2			.8							
.2	.2		.2					.1		
.3	.4		.3	Fixed/Worth				.3		
.5	.9		.8					.4		
.6	.4		.5					.4		
1.1	1.1		1.1	Debt/Worth				.9		
3.2	3.4		3.0					2.4		
21.7	18.6		26.7	% Profit Before Taxes/Tangible				25.4		
(20) 14.3	(16) 9.1	(31)	8.9	Net Worth				12.5		
2.7	1.9		-12.1					-2.1		
11.7	13.0		10.8	% Profit Before Taxes/Total				14.2		
3.7	3.8		3.5	Assets				3.2		
.7	.3		-1.8					-.9		
29.3	36.2		32.7					62.9		
16.3	9.4		12.7	Sales/Net Fixed Assets				13.0		
7.6	5.6		6.7					6.6		
2.5	2.6		2.3					2.0		
1.9	1.8		1.7	Sales/Total Assets				1.8		
1.3	1.4		1.3					1.2		
.5	.3		1.0					.4		
(20) 1.3	1.8	(30)	1.6	% Depr., Dep., Amort./Sales				1.2		
2.5	3.7		2.6					2.5		
			2.7	% Officers', Directors',						
		(11)	6.3	Owners' Comp/Sales						
			9.2							
446155M	281100M		670866M	Net Sales ($)	574M	17118M	26940M	73193M	33695M	519346M
291311M	183326M		432741M	Total Assets ($)	236M	10790M	17437M	52484M	18244M	333550M

© RMA 2003   M = $ thousand   MM = $ million
See Pages 11 through 18 for Explanation of Ratios and Data

Current Data Sorted By Assets							Comparative Historical Data	
						Type of Statement		
	2	2	6		2	Unqualified	19	17
	1	5	2			Reviewed	7	10
	3	2				Compiled	6	11
						Tax Returns		
	3	3	2	1	1	Other	14	13
	8 (4/1-9/30/02)		27 (10/1/02-3/31/03)				**4/1/98-3/31/99**	**4/1/99-3/31/00**
0-500M	**500M-2MM**	**2-10MM**	**10-50MM**	**50-100MM**	**100-250MM**		**ALL**	**ALL**
	9	12	10	1	3	**NUMBER OF STATEMENTS**	46	51
%	%	%	%	%	%	**ASSETS**	%	%
DATA NOT AVAILABLE		13.8	16.5			Cash & Equivalents	7.1	7.8
		29.3	20.4			Trade Receivables (net)	27.3	30.0
		29.1	24.6			Inventory	29.5	25.2
		3.5	3.1			All Other Current	2.5	3.4
		75.7	64.6			Total Current	66.5	66.4
		17.2	24.8			Fixed Assets (net)	21.5	20.1
		1.2	3.5			Intangibles (net)	6.4	8.3
		5.9	7.1			All Other Non-Current	5.6	5.2
		100.0	100.0			Total	100.0	100.0
						LIABILITIES		
		12.2	1.0			Notes Payable-Short Term	7.3	12.4
		4.4	2.7			Cur. Mat.-L/T/D	2.5	3.0
		8.0	7.4			Trade Payables	11.4	11.1
		.5	.6			Income Taxes Payable	.3	.7
		10.3	11.2			All Other Current	10.7	11.7
		35.4	22.9			Total Current	32.3	38.8
		11.8	7.3			Long Term Debt	16.3	16.5
		.1	.0			Deferred Taxes	1.2	.8
		2.2	2.7			All Other Non-Current	4.2	7.0
		50.5	67.0			Net Worth	45.9	36.9
		100.0	100.0			Total Liabilities & Net Worth	100.0	100.0
						INCOME DATA		
		100.0	100.0			Net Sales	100.0	100.0
		42.2	42.3			Gross Profit	39.9	43.2
		36.1	43.9			Operating Expenses	33.3	37.4
		6.0	−1.6			Operating Profit	6.6	5.9
		2.0	.1			All Other Expenses (net)	1.4	1.7
		4.0	−1.7			Profit Before Taxes	5.2	4.1
						RATIOS		
		4.2	4.1				3.4	2.5
		2.3	2.8			Current	2.1	1.9
		1.6	2.0				1.4	1.3
		1.9	2.3				1.8	1.6
		1.4	1.6			Quick	1.2	1.1
		.7	1.2				.7	.6
		37 9.9	**41** 8.9				**45** 8.2	**52** 7.0
		44 8.3	**52** 7.0			Sales/Receivables	**55** 6.6	**64** 5.7
		64 5.7	**68** 5.3				**71** 5.1	**81** 4.5
		75 4.9	**70** 5.2				**75** 4.8	**56** 6.5
		95 3.9	**84** 4.4			Cost of Sales/Inventory	**103** 3.6	**107** 3.4
		116 3.1	**181** 2.0				**143** 2.6	**155** 2.4
		10 35.1	**24** 15.1				**20** 18.2	**22** 16.9
		27 13.4	**32** 11.5			Cost of Sales/Payables	**37** 10.0	**36** 10.0
		47 7.7	**39** 9.3				**44** 8.3	**63** 5.8
		4.7	2.2				3.2	3.6
		5.4	3.9			Sales/Working Capital	5.0	5.5
		7.5	5.5				9.1	11.0
		50.1					14.9	12.4
		(11) 6.4				EBIT/Interest	(43) 4.1	(46) 3.0
		1.1					1.2	1.4
							9.8	13.6
						Net Profit + Depr., Dep., Amort./Cur. Mat. L/T/D	(17) 4.1	(13) 2.4
							2.6	1.0
		.1	.1				.3	.3
		.4	.3			Fixed/Worth	.5	.6
		.6	.6				1.3	1.5
		.4	.2				.4	.7
		1.0	.6			Debt/Worth	1.3	1.2
		1.4	.9				2.9	7.5
		46.3	9.6				40.7	45.8
		(11) 22.7	−1.1			% Profit Before Taxes/Tangible Net Worth	(40) 18.6	(42) 27.8
		2.4	−11.1				4.4	8.2
		28.7	6.7				18.4	19.2
		8.5	−1.0			% Profit Before Taxes/Total Assets	6.2	6.4
		−3.0	−7.1				1.2	.7
		24.4	12.8				16.6	17.8
		17.1	9.1			Sales/Net Fixed Assets	7.8	7.5
		9.0	4.5				4.7	4.6
		2.5	1.8				2.2	2.1
		2.3	1.5			Sales/Total Assets	1.7	1.7
		1.2	1.0				1.2	1.1
		1.1					1.6	1.5
		(11) 1.8				% Depr., Dep., Amort./Sales	(39) 3.2	(36) 2.5
		2.6					5.1	5.0
							3.5	3.0
						% Officers', Directors', Owners' Comp/Sales	(11) 6.1	(14) 6.8
							9.1	10.0
	23912M	100578M	278266M	49383M	454407M	Net Sales ($)	1421462M	1922907M
	12073M	53852M	198698M	73845M	497927M	Total Assets ($)	1203075M	1754295M

M = $ thousand MM = $ million

See Pages 11 through 18 for Explanation of Ratios and Data

Comparative Historical Data

Current Data Sorted By Sales

			Type of Statement						
16	10	12	Unqualified		1	1	2	3	5
5	7	8	Reviewed		1	1	3	3	
5	13	5	Compiled		2	1		2	
4			Tax Returns						
11	9	10	Other		2	1	3		4
4/1/00-3/31/01	**4/1/01-3/31/02**	**4/1/02-3/31/03**			**8 (4/1-9/30/02)**		**27 (10/1/02-3/31/03)**		
ALL	**ALL**	**ALL**		**0-1MM**	**1-3MM**	**3-5MM**	**5-10MM**	**10-25MM**	**25MM & OVER**
41	39	35	**NUMBER OF STATEMENTS**		6	4	8	8	9
%	%	%	**ASSETS**	%	%	%	%	%	%
14.9	14.4	14.9	Cash & Equivalents	D					
25.9	24.1	25.5	Trade Receivables (net)	A					
28.4	28.5	28.0	Inventory	T					
4.3	5.0	2.7	All Other Current	A					
73.5	72.0	71.2	Total Current						
17.2	19.0	18.7	Fixed Assets (net)	N					
5.1	4.1	3.2	Intangibles (net)	O					
4.2	4.9	6.8	All Other Non-Current	T					
100.0	100.0	100.0	Total						
			LIABILITIES	A					
12.3	6.8	7.9	Notes Payable-Short Term	V					
3.7	4.3	2.8	Cur. Mat.-L/T/D	A					
11.4	8.6	10.6	Trade Payables	I					
.6	.4	.5	Income Taxes Payable	L					
12.9	14.2	10.8	All Other Current	A					
40.8	34.3	32.5	Total Current	B					
13.3	12.6	9.4	Long Term Debt	L					
.3	.2	.2	Deferred Taxes	E					
2.4	3.5	5.0	All Other Non-Current						
43.2	49.3	52.8	Net Worth						
100.0	100.0	100.0	Total Liabilities & Net Worth						
			INCOME DATA						
100.0	100.0	100.0	Net Sales						
44.4	42.3	42.6	Gross Profit						
35.3	38.9	41.0	Operating Expenses						
9.1	3.4	1.6	Operating Profit						
1.5	1.5	.8	All Other Expenses (net)						
7.6	1.9	.8	Profit Before Taxes						
			RATIOS						
3.2	3.9	3.8							
1.9	2.3	2.5	Current						
1.5	1.5	1.7							
1.8	2.3	2.1							
1.0	1.1	1.4	Quick						
.6	.7	1.0							
40 9.0	**36** 10.2	**38** 9.7							
57 6.4	**46** 7.9	**51** 7.2	Sales/Receivables						
74 5.0	**72** 5.1	**69** 5.3							
61 6.0	**72** 5.1	**74** 4.9							
117 3.1	**107** 3.4	**89** 4.1	Cost of Sales/Inventory						
163 2.2	**144** 2.5	**147** 2.5							
24 15.3	**17** 21.9	**21** 17.0							
34 10.7	**25** 14.4	**33** 11.2	Cost of Sales/Payables						
57 6.4	**46** 8.0	**54** 6.8							
3.4	2.9	2.7							
5.1	5.1	4.9	Sales/Working Capital						
8.6	7.6	7.2							
23.2	10.1	17.5							
(33) 6.4	(36) 2.7	(29) 3.5	EBIT/Interest						
3.0	-.8	-1.1							
	3.7	6.8							
	(14) 1.7	(15) 2.3	Net Profit + Depr., Dep., Amort./Cur. Mat. L/T/D						
	.2	.9							
.2	.2	.2							
.4	.4	.3	Fixed/Worth						
.9	.9	.6							
.4	.4	.3							
.9	.9	.9	Debt/Worth						
2.6	3.0	1.4							
34.1	27.4	23.5							
(37) 20.9	(37) 10.9	(32) 4.6	% Profit Before Taxes/Tangible Net Worth						
8.2	-3.9	-5.5							
17.4	10.5	12.6							
8.2	4.6	2.5	% Profit Before Taxes/Total Assets						
3.5	-3.0	-4.1							
21.0	20.3	24.1							
10.0	9.8	9.8	Sales/Net Fixed Assets						
5.6	5.4	5.7							
2.2	2.1	2.4							
1.8	1.5	1.7	Sales/Total Assets						
1.2	1.2	1.1							
1.3	1.4	1.3							
(35) 2.1	(33) 2.5	(30) 2.3	% Depr., Dep., Amort./Sales						
4.2	4.2	3.8							
6.6	3.9	3.5							
(11) 8.8	(11) 9.2	(12) 4.4	% Officers', Directors', Owners' Comp/Sales						
13.3	10.5	9.6							
1275404M	**934478M**	**906546M**	Net Sales ($)		**12831M**	**15980M**	**57407M**	**124599M**	**695729M**
1182505M	**783745M**	**836395M**	Total Assets ($)		**7462M**	**9108M**	**34388M**	**98828M**	**686609M**

M = $ thousand MM = $ million

See Pages 11 through 18 for Explanation of Ratios and Data

Current Data Sorted By Assets   Comparative Historical Data

0-500M	500M-2MM	2-10MM	10-50MM	50-100MM	100-250MM	Type of Statement	4/1/98-3/31/99 ALL	4/1/99-3/31/00 ALL
	2	5	6	1	3	Unqualified	18	18
		9				Reviewed	8	7
	2	3				Compiled		4
1	1	2				Tax Returns	4	5
	1	5	7		1	Other	17	17
		9 (4/1-9/30/02)	40 (10/1/02-3/31/03)					
1	6	24	13	1	4	**NUMBER OF STATEMENTS**	47	51
%	%	%	%	%	%	**ASSETS**	%	%
		7.4	9.5			Cash & Equivalents	8.8	9.5
		29.7	20.5			Trade Receivables (net)	24.7	27.1
		34.1	27.8			Inventory	28.3	29.1
		1.6	3.2			All Other Current	2.3	3.1
		72.8	61.1			Total Current	64.1	68.8
		14.1	18.1			Fixed Assets (net)	20.0	20.2
		6.9	12.9			Intangibles (net)	9.6	5.8
		6.2	8.0			All Other Non-Current	6.3	5.1
		100.0	100.0			Total	100.0	100.0
						LIABILITIES		
		11.4	9.7			Notes Payable-Short Term	9.5	8.3
		3.9	4.8			Cur. Mat.-L/T/D	3.3	5.0
		14.2	7.2			Trade Payables	10.6	10.6
		.3	1.1			Income Taxes Payable	.3	.5
		15.4	12.7			All Other Current	11.3	12.9
		45.4	35.6			Total Current	35.0	37.3
		13.3	13.2			Long Term Debt	15.9	14.5
		.1	.5			Deferred Taxes	.6	.6
		6.6	3.6			All Other Non-Current	6.6	7.4
		34.7	47.1			Net Worth	41.9	40.1
		100.0	100.0			Total Liabilities & Net Worth	100.0	100.0
						INCOME DATA		
		100.0	100.0			Net Sales	100.0	100.0
		42.3	53.5			Gross Profit	47.7	48.1
		40.2	50.1			Operating Expenses	41.5	44.1
		2.2	3.4			Operating Profit	6.2	4.1
		.5	1.6			All Other Expenses (net)	2.1	1.9
		1.7	1.8			Profit Before Taxes	4.1	2.2
						RATIOS		
		2.7	3.7				2.8	3.6
		1.5	1.5			Current	2.1	2.0
		1.2	1.2				1.3	1.4
		1.3	1.6				1.8	2.0
		.8	.9			Quick	1.1	1.0
		.5	.6				.6	.7
		49 7.5	50 7.4				50 7.3	47 7.8
		56 6.5	59 6.2			Sales/Receivables	60 6.1	57 6.4
		69 5.3	71 5.2				77 4.7	74 4.9
		74 4.9	122 3.0				85 4.3	89 4.1
		132 2.8	160 2.3			Cost of Sales/Inventory	125 2.9	116 3.2
		171 2.1	239 1.5				173 2.1	176 2.1
		25 14.9	23 15.8				29 12.6	22 16.7
		47 7.7	31 11.7			Cost of Sales/Payables	38 9.7	46 7.9
		57 6.4	74 4.9				61 6.0	67 5.4
		4.2	2.7				2.8	3.2
		6.7	7.0			Sales/Working Capital	4.4	5.2
		20.9	12.7				11.0	10.1
		11.4	5.7				9.6	9.1
		3.7	(11) 4.2			EBIT/Interest	(40) 2.6	(42) 2.8
		.6	1.7				1.1	-.6
						Net Profit + Depr., Dep.,	45.2	10.5
						Amort./Cur. Mat. L /T/D	(14) 5.8	(13) 2.4
							1.8	.3
		.2	.3				.2	.2
		.9	.5			Fixed/Worth	.5	.5
		-5.5	1.3				10.2	2.0
		.6	.7				.5	.4
		4.1	2.1			Debt/Worth	1.4	1.3
		-56.5	3.5				23.7	5.9
		46.5	24.4			% Profit Before Taxes/Tangible	31.9	41.0
		(17) 23.3	(11) 6.8			Net Worth	(38) 12.1	(45) 17.4
		3.8	-3.5				1.0	-7.9
		13.1	9.4			% Profit Before Taxes/Total	14.4	12.6
		5.2	3.4			Assets	4.4	5.1
		-.6	.1				.9	-4.2
		47.1	15.0				13.8	14.9
		17.7	7.8			Sales/Net Fixed Assets	8.9	8.2
		8.4	3.9				4.3	4.8
		2.2	1.7				2.0	2.0
		1.8	1.3			Sales/Total Assets	1.3	1.4
		1.4	.6				1.0	1.1
		1.5	1.6				1.3	1.4
		(21) 2.0	(11) 2.6			% Depr., Dep., Amort./Sales	(39) 2.9	(41) 2.2
		3.1	4.9				4.3	4.1
						% Officers', Directors', Owners' Comp/Sales		
562M	17559M	193888M	349854M	134922M	462344M	Net Sales ($)	1579890M	1603623M
266M	7592M	112542M	284654M	77694M	667331M	Total Assets ($)	1295079M	1343349M

Comparative Historical Data | Current Data Sorted By Sales

4/1/00-3/31/01 ALL	4/1/01-3/31/02 ALL	4/1/02-3/31/03 ALL	Type of Statement	0-1MM	1-3MM	3-5MM	5-10MM	10-25MM	25MM & OVER
16	12	17	Unqualified		1	3		8	5
8	6	9	Reviewed			2	6	1	
7	8	5	Compiled		2		2	1	
2	2	4	Tax Returns	1		1	1	1	
11	17	14	Other			3	3	2	6
44	45	49	**NUMBER OF STATEMENTS**	1	3	9	12	13	11

Date groupings: 9 (4/1-9/30/02) covers 0-1MM, 1-3MM, 3-5MM; 40 (10/1/02-3/31/03) covers 5-10MM, 10-25MM, 25MM & OVER.

%	%	%	ASSETS	%	%	%	%	%	%
8.3	10.4	9.1	Cash & Equivalents				11.4	7.4	12.9
29.3	24.8	26.8	Trade Receivables (net)				30.0	23.9	22.2
30.0	30.8	31.3	Inventory				26.9	36.4	24.3
2.3	2.4	2.0	All Other Current				1.5	2.6	1.5
69.8	68.4	69.1	Total Current				69.7	70.3	60.8
16.3	15.9	15.8	Fixed Assets (net)				15.5	13.6	20.5
7.5	9.1	8.6	Intangibles (net)				8.8	8.4	9.7
6.4	6.6	6.5	All Other Non-Current				5.9	7.7	9.0
100.0	100.0	100.0	Total				100.0	100.0	100.0
			LIABILITIES						
8.4	10.7	11.1	Notes Payable-Short Term				4.4	17.9	3.0
3.4	3.4	3.9	Cur. Mat.-L/T/D				2.4	3.6	4.1
12.5	10.6	11.7	Trade Payables				14.7	8.8	6.5
.3	.6	.6	Income Taxes Payable				.0	.9	1.4
12.6	10.9	13.8	All Other Current				17.7	10.8	14.8
37.2	36.2	41.1	Total Current				39.1	41.9	29.9
13.9	11.7	14.6	Long Term Debt				13.4	7.1	9.5
.7	.8	.3	Deferred Taxes				.1	.3	.9
5.2	4.7	4.8	All Other Non-Current				3.1	4.8	3.6
43.0	46.7	39.1	Net Worth				44.2	45.9	56.1
100.0	100.0	100.0	Total Liabilities & Net Worth				100.0	100.0	100.0
			INCOME DATA						
100.0	100.0	100.0	Net Sales				100.0	100.0	100.0
45.6	47.6	45.3	Gross Profit				41.4	48.6	50.2
39.4	42.7	43.0	Operating Expenses				37.2	44.9	44.9
6.2	4.9	2.3	Operating Profit				4.2	3.7	5.3
1.8	1.8	1.5	All Other Expenses (net)				1.2	.8	2.8
4.4	3.1	.8	Profit Before Taxes				3.0	2.9	2.6

RATIOS

4/1/00-3/31/01	4/1/01-3/31/02	4/1/02-3/31/03	Ratio	0-1MM	1-3MM	3-5MM	5-10MM	10-25MM	25MM & OVER
3.3	3.8	2.9	Current				4.6	3.7	3.7
1.9	2.0	1.6					2.4	1.4	2.2
1.4	1.3	1.2					1.2	1.2	1.5
1.7	2.2	1.4	Quick				2.3	1.2	1.9
1.1	1.0	.9					1.2	.7	1.3
.6	.6	.6					.8	.5	.9
43 8.4	47 7.8	48 7.5	Sales/Receivables			38 9.5	52 7.0	49 7.5	
60 6.1	56 6.5	59 6.2				60 6.1	55 6.6	69 5.3	
84 4.4	70 5.2	72 5.1				70 5.2	70 5.2	85 4.3	
79 4.6	82 4.5	87 4.2	Cost of Sales/Inventory			58 6.3	126 2.9	92 4.0	
122 3.0	132 2.8	130 2.8				101 3.6	160 2.3	153 2.4	
157 2.3	183 2.0	192 1.9				132 2.8	239 1.5	209 1.7	
27 13.7	21 17.7	25 14.6	Cost of Sales/Payables			25 14.4	22 16.7	28 13.1	
41 8.8	39 9.3	46 7.9				49 7.5	31 11.7	34 10.8	
64 5.7	60 6.0	62 5.9				57 6.4	72 5.1	62 5.9	
3.2	2.9	3.1	Sales/Working Capital				3.4	2.7	2.4
6.1	5.2	7.0					4.6	7.0	4.0
10.9	11.7	13.5					20.7	19.0	7.9
(41) 11.9	(44) 14.2	(46) 10.2	EBIT/Interest				11.4	(11) 15.9	(10) 39.0
4.8	2.4	3.1					5.4	3.2	9.4
1.1	.4	.7					1.6	.5	2.6
(12) 7.0	(12) 4.3	(13) 6.7	Net Profit + Depr., Dep., Amort./Cur. Mat. L/T/D						
3.0	.9	2.7							
1.7	-1.0	.7							
.2	.2	.2	Fixed/Worth				.1	.2	.2
.4	.4	.5					.5	.4	.4
.9	9.6	NM					NM	1.8	.9
.5	.4	.6	Debt/Worth				.5	.3	.5
1.3	1.0	2.1					1.0	2.2	.9
4.6	35.4	NM					NM	6.7	2.8
(36) 38.9	(35) 31.7	(37) 36.6	% Profit Before Taxes/Tangible Net Worth					46.0	27.5
22.5	9.7	17.9					(11)	20.3	(10) 13.0
4.4	-.8	1.4						-3.5	.8
14.0	13.0	9.4	% Profit Before Taxes/Total Assets				15.2	14.1	9.1
7.1	3.9	3.4					6.4	5.4	3.4
1.1	-1.1	-1.0					.5	-1.0	1.7
24.3	22.5	27.6	Sales/Net Fixed Assets				55.9	29.8	14.2
13.4	13.0	13.3					17.7	15.1	6.2
5.8	5.6	5.8					7.1	5.0	3.3
2.1	2.2	2.1	Sales/Total Assets				2.5	2.0	1.7
1.6	1.6	1.7					2.2	1.6	1.3
1.2	1.1	1.2					1.0	.9	.7
(37) 1.4	(37) .9	(41) 1.6	% Depr., Dep., Amort./Sales				(11) 1.5	(12) 1.3	
1.7	2.0	2.3					1.8	2.4	
2.6	3.6	4.1					2.4	3.9	
			% Officers', Directors', Owners' Comp/Sales						
1223398M	1209635M	1159129M	Net Sales ($)	562M	5992M	36034M	82128M	190654M	843759M
1037511M	1176401M	1150079M	Total Assets ($)	266M	2955M	20636M	65818M	157453M	902951M

M = $ thousand   MM = $ million
See Pages 11 through 18 for Explanation of Ratios and Data

Current Data Sorted By Assets   **Comparative Historical Data**

0-500M	500M-2MM	2-10MM	10-50MM	50-100MM	100-250MM	Type of Statement	4/1/98-3/31/99 ALL	4/1/99-3/31/00 ALL
	2	7	10	2	2	Unqualified	15	13
	5	8	2			Reviewed	18	22
	4	7	1			Compiled	14	15
	2					Tax Returns	1	4
1	7	12	12	2	1	Other	30	32
	15 (4/1-9/30/02)		72 (10/1/02-3/31/03)					
1	20	34	25	4	3	NUMBER OF STATEMENTS	78	86
%	%	%	%	%	%	ASSETS	%	%
	11.6	7.6	13.1			Cash & Equivalents	8.9	9.2
	29.9	32.3	28.1			Trade Receivables (net)	28.4	31.4
	29.2	29.3	24.3			Inventory	27.9	26.6
	9.2	3.2	2.6			All Other Current	4.8	2.8
	79.9	72.4	68.2			Total Current	70.0	70.0
	13.4	16.2	16.6			Fixed Assets (net)	17.9	16.2
	4.1	7.0	9.5			Intangibles (net)	5.6	8.8
	2.6	4.4	5.8			All Other Non-Current	6.5	5.0
	100.0	100.0	100.0			Total	100.0	100.0
						LIABILITIES		
	17.9	16.0	3.6			Notes Payable-Short Term	14.9	12.9
	3.8	3.7	4.9			Cur. Mat.-L/T/D	4.7	3.2
	16.0	13.3	10.0			Trade Payables	11.5	13.4
	.3	.2	.5			Income Taxes Payable	.6	.4
	19.9	12.9	14.6			All Other Current	13.0	12.4
	57.9	46.2	33.7			Total Current	44.7	42.4
	4.3	7.2	20.0			Long Term Debt	15.5	14.2
	.2	.4	.1			Deferred Taxes	.5	.3
	6.1	4.2	.9			All Other Non-Current	7.9	4.8
	31.6	42.0	45.3			Net Worth	31.4	38.3
	100.0	100.0	100.0			Total Liabilities & Net Worth	100.0	100.0
						INCOME DATA		
	100.0	100.0	100.0			Net Sales	100.0	100.0
	47.0	36.2	41.4			Gross Profit	41.5	42.6
	42.3	32.7	35.8			Operating Expenses	39.1	37.7
	4.8	3.5	5.6			Operating Profit	2.5	4.9
	1.1	1.0	.6			All Other Expenses (net)	2.1	2.0
	3.7	2.6	5.0			Profit Before Taxes	.3	2.9
						RATIOS		
	1.8	2.8	3.4				3.2	2.9
	1.5	1.8	2.2			Current	2.0	1.7
	1.2	1.1	1.4				1.4	1.3
	1.1	1.4	1.9				1.8	1.7
	.8	.8	1.4			Quick	1.0	.9
	.5	.6	.8				.7	.6
	38 9.6	46 7.9	47 7.7				42 8.6	43 8.6
	51 7.2	57 6.4	61 6.0			Sales/Receivables	53 6.8	59 6.2
	62 5.9	69 5.3	76 4.8				68 5.3	76 4.8
	31 11.6	56 6.6	62 5.9				54 6.8	48 7.5
	95 3.8	103 3.6	112 3.3			Cost of Sales/Inventory	96 3.8	88 4.2
	157 2.3	123 3.0	154 2.4				155 2.4	150 2.4
	26 14.3	14 26.7	21 17.6				21 17.5	21 17.6
	42 8.7	30 12.0	35 10.3			Cost of Sales/Payables	33 11.2	34 10.8
	70 5.2	51 7.1	54 6.8				46 7.9	49 7.4
	4.6	3.5	2.5				3.2	3.6
	6.8	6.7	3.9			Sales/Working Capital	5.7	6.8
	27.0	22.7	9.1				11.0	13.0
	9.7	5.7	13.6				8.8	7.8
	(16) 3.0	(33) 1.7	(24) 4.4			EBIT/Interest	(70) 3.5	(80) 2.5
	-3.3	.6	.3				1.5	.7
		2.7					7.2	4.7
		(16) 1.2				Net Profit + Depr., Dep., Amort./Cur. Mat. L /T/D	(31) 2.5	(23) 2.6
		.2					1.3	1.5
	.1	.2	.2				.2	.2
	.2	.5	.5			Fixed/Worth	.4	.4
	.7	1.4	1.4				1.0	1.0
	1.3	.5	.5				.5	.8
	1.7	2.3	1.7			Debt/Worth	1.6	1.8
	7.5	5.8	4.0				3.9	4.4
	70.4	27.9	31.3				39.4	35.4
	(17) 21.9	(29) 3.6	(22) 11.4			% Profit Before Taxes/Tangible Net Worth	(67) 18.1	(72) 12.2
	-12.8	-5.9	-8.0				4.9	-1.3
	16.2	6.8	12.6				15.1	15.9
	4.2	2.7	8.6			% Profit Before Taxes/Total Assets	5.6	3.4
	-9.1	-1.0	-.9				1.4	-.8
	48.6	24.7	13.7				24.8	37.1
	30.3	16.1	10.1			Sales/Net Fixed Assets	11.8	14.7
	14.2	7.7	6.1				6.3	6.6
	3.1	2.4	1.9				2.4	2.7
	2.1	1.9	1.4			Sales/Total Assets	1.7	1.7
	1.6	1.4	1.1				1.2	1.3
	1.1	.9	1.5				1.3	.8
	(15) 1.5	(33) 2.1	(18) 2.0			% Depr., Dep., Amort./Sales	(57) 2.1	(67) 1.8
	2.3	3.3	3.0				3.1	3.4
		2.1					2.3	3.3
		(12) 5.5				% Officers', Directors', Owners' Comp/Sales	(22) 6.1	(19) 5.7
		8.9					10.8	9.4
22M	54450M	278295M	887123M	321197M	343818M	Net Sales ($)	1573747M	1674016M
8M	25420M	147598M	602333M	263976M	348060M	Total Assets ($)	1297482M	1135446M

M = $ thousand   MM = $ million
See Pages 11 through 18 for Explanation of Ratios and Data

Comparative Historical Data | Current Data Sorted By Sales

	4/1/00–3/31/01 ALL	4/1/01–3/31/02 ALL	4/1/02–3/31/03 ALL	Type of Statement	0-1MM	1-3MM	3-5MM	5-10MM	10-25MM	25MM & OVER
	16	24	23	Unqualified		1	3	2	8	9
	17	20	15	Reviewed		3	4	4	4	
	15	15	12	Compiled	1	3		7		1
			2	Tax Returns		1	1			
	32	32	35	Other	2	3	4	8	6	12
						15 (4/1-9/30/02)		72 (10/1/02-3/31/03)		
	80	91	87	NUMBER OF STATEMENTS	3	11	12	21	18	22
	%	%	%	**ASSETS**	%	%	%	%	%	%
	8.1	10.8	10.3	Cash & Equivalents		16.5	7.6	7.2	12.5	11.0
	31.4	27.1	29.7	Trade Receivables (net)		25.8	31.5	33.2	26.6	28.8
	28.8	27.9	27.4	Inventory		29.5	28.7	28.1	28.7	22.9
	3.8	5.0	4.4	All Other Current		13.8	3.6	4.2	1.8	3.1
	72.1	70.8	71.8	Total Current		85.6	71.4	72.7	69.7	65.7
	16.6	15.5	16.0	Fixed Assets (net)		7.7	19.5	14.4	17.0	18.2
	5.5	8.1	7.7	Intangibles (net)		4.0	6.2	8.8	6.6	11.0
	5.9	5.5	4.5	All Other Non-Current		2.7	2.9	4.1	6.7	5.1
	100.0	100.0	100.0	Total		100.0	100.0	100.0	100.0	100.0
				LIABILITIES						
	12.7	9.7	12.0	Notes Payable-Short Term		21.9	7.2	16.8	9.9	3.7
	3.3	4.0	4.1	Cur. Mat.-L/T/D		4.4	3.5	2.0	5.5	4.8
	14.7	10.6	12.5	Trade Payables		12.8	17.3	13.9	11.6	9.8
	.4	.4	.4	Income Taxes Payable		.6	.5	.0	.1	.9
	14.2	11.7	14.9	All Other Current		9.6	25.9	15.3	10.3	16.4
	45.3	36.4	43.8	Total Current		49.3	54.4	48.1	37.4	35.7
	10.7	14.4	10.7	Long Term Debt		5.4	6.9	5.6	13.1	17.7
	.5	.2	.2	Deferred Taxes		.0	.8	.2	.2	.2
	4.0	7.8	4.4	All Other Non-Current		3.9	2.2	4.9	1.1	5.2
	39.5	41.2	40.9	Net Worth		41.4	35.7	41.2	48.3	41.2
	100.0	100.0	100.0	Total Liabilities & Net Worth		100.0	100.0	100.0	100.0	100.0
				INCOME DATA						
	100.0	100.0	100.0	Net Sales		100.0	100.0	100.0	100.0	100.0
	40.0	41.7	40.9	Gross Profit		47.3	45.2	37.0	37.9	42.4
	35.2	36.8	36.6	Operating Expenses		36.0	43.6	34.1	33.6	37.0
	4.8	4.9	4.3	Operating Profit		11.3	1.6	2.9	4.3	5.4
	1.9	1.5	1.0	All Other Expenses (net)		.5	.9	.9	.7	1.1
	3.0	3.4	3.4	Profit Before Taxes		10.8	.7	2.0	3.6	4.3
				RATIOS						
	3.0 / 1.7 / 1.2	3.2 / 2.2 / 1.4	2.9 / 1.8 / 1.2	Current		2.8 / 1.5 / 1.2	3.5 / 1.7 / 1.3	2.5 / 1.8 / 1.2	4.7 / 2.5 / 1.1	3.0 / 2.0 / 1.4
	1.5 / .8 / .6	1.9 / 1.1 / .6	1.7 / 1.0 / .6	Quick		1.1 / .9 / .5	1.7 / .9 / .5	1.3 / .8 / .6	2.3 / 1.2 / .7	1.8 / 1.2 / .7
	48 7.7 / 57 6.4 / 71 5.2	40 9.1 / 53 6.9 / 68 5.4	46 7.9 / 58 6.3 / 68 5.3	Sales/Receivables		40 9.0 / 53 6.9 / 61 6.0	42 8.8 / 51 7.1 / 64 5.7	45 8.1 / 57 6.4 / 70 5.2	43 8.5 / 58 6.2 / 65 5.6	49 7.4 / 66 5.5 / 78 4.7
	52 7.0 / 95 3.8 / 147 2.5	70 5.2 / 99 3.7 / 150 2.4	56 6.5 / 103 3.5 / 148 2.5	Cost of Sales/Inventory		21 17.1 / 133 2.7 / 169 2.2	71 5.1 / 106 3.4 / 122 3.0	38 9.6 / 106 3.4 / 137 2.7	60 6.1 / 111 3.3 / 157 2.3	55 6.6 / 101 3.6 / 161 2.3
	24 15.1 / 42 8.7 / 58 6.3	17 21.0 / 30 12.2 / 52 7.0	21 17.5 / 35 10.3 / 57 6.4	Cost of Sales/Payables		23 16.1 / 35 10.5 / 62 5.9	25 14.6 / 41 8.8 / 86 4.2	14 26.9 / 30 12.1 / 52 7.0	19 19.0 / 28 13.0 / 47 7.7	33 11.0 / 42 8.7 / 57 6.4
	4.1 / 7.1 / 20.0	3.3 / 5.3 / 9.5	3.2 / 5.4 / 16.2	Sales/Working Capital		3.2 / 6.2 / 15.2	4.5 / 7.4 / 14.0	4.0 / 6.9 / 26.5	2.4 / 4.0 / 42.1	2.8 / 4.3 / 12.3
	(72) 7.9 / 2.1 / .3	(81) 8.7 / 3.1 / 1.0	(80) 7.4 / 2.8 / -.2	EBIT/Interest		(11) 3.8 / 1.1 / -5.2	6.6 / 1.8 / .7		(17) 11.3 / 2.2 / -2.7	(21) 11.5 / 3.7 / .0
	(22) 3.5 / 1.4 / .1	(25) 9.4 / 2.6 / .8	(30) 6.9 / 1.5 / .2	Net Profit + Depr., Dep., Amort./Cur. Mat. L/T/D						
	.2 / .4 / 1.1	.2 / .4 / .9	.2 / .4 / 1.2	Fixed/Worth		.0 / .2 / .7	.2 / .4 / NM	.2 / .4 / 1.0	.2 / .5 / 1.5	.4 / .5 / 2.5
	.6 / 1.8 / 5.6	.6 / 1.4 / 5.3	.5 / 2.0 / 5.0	Debt/Worth		1.3 / 1.9 / 4.3	.5 / 1.3 / NM	.4 / 2.2 / 6.2	.3 / 1.5 / 5.3	.6 / 1.8 / 9.8
	(70) 35.6 / 15.9 / -2.0	(75) 25.9 / 14.9 / .3	(75) 39.6 / 10.8 / -6.6	% Profit Before Taxes/Tangible Net Worth		96.4 / 39.6 / 3.9	(18) 32.1 / 4.6 / -3.6		(16) 27.1 / 10.8 / -7.9	(19) 43.9 / 15.0 / -8.3
	14.4 / 5.4 / -1.7	14.0 / 6.0 / .1	10.2 / 4.2 / -1.6	% Profit Before Taxes/Total Assets		20.9 / 16.1 / 2.9	7.5 / 1.1 / -6.5	5.8 / 2.7 / -.5	9.8 / 5.0 / -3.1	14.0 / 8.8 / -1.0
	36.5 / 13.5 / 7.8	31.2 / 14.4 / 7.1	27.1 / 13.3 / 6.5	Sales/Net Fixed Assets		160.0 / 34.4 / 20.3	23.0 / 17.8 / 5.0	38.9 / 16.9 / 10.3	17.3 / 11.2 / 6.2	12.5 / 9.5 / 5.8
	2.4 / 1.9 / 1.3	2.6 / 1.6 / 1.2	2.2 / 1.8 / 1.2	Sales/Total Assets		2.2 / 2.0 / 1.6	3.1 / 1.9 / 1.4	2.5 / 2.0 / 1.3	2.2 / 1.9 / 1.1	1.8 / 1.4 / 1.0
	(67) .7 / 1.9 / 3.5	(73) .9 / 2.1 / 3.4	(72) 1.3 / 2.1 / 3.3	% Depr., Dep., Amort./Sales				1.3 / 2.3 / 4.7	(20) .9 / 2.1 / 3.4	1.0 / 1.9 / 3.3	(14) 1.7 / 2.5 / 4.1
	(18) 2.9 / 5.1 / 8.4	(23) 3.0 / 5.1 / 8.7	(18) 2.9 / 6.2 / 8.8	% Officers', Directors', Owners' Comp/Sales						
	2192208M / 1301506M	2070025M / 1567569M	1884905M / 1387395M	Net Sales ($) / Total Assets ($)	1779M / 2263M	22930M / 12860M	46546M / 24360M	152930M / 85753M	288288M / 209336M	1372432M / 1052823M

M = $ thousand   MM = $ million
See Pages 11 through 18 for Explanation of Ratios and Data

Current Data Sorted By Assets | **Comparative Historical Data**

0-500M	500M-2MM	2-10MM	10-50MM	50-100MM	100-250MM		4/1/98-3/31/99 ALL	4/1/99-3/31/00 ALL
						Type of Statement		
		5	6		2	Unqualified	9	13
		6	2			Reviewed	17	12
1	4	4				Compiled	6	12
1	1					Tax Returns	1	3
	5	9				Other	12	8
11 (4/1-9/30/02)			35 (10/1/02-3/31/03)					
2	10	24	8		2	**NUMBER OF STATEMENTS**	45	48
%	%	%	%	%	%	**ASSETS**	%	%
	5.4	7.1		DATA NOT AVAILABLE		Cash & Equivalents	8.1	7.3
	25.7	28.3				Trade Receivables (net)	30.8	29.2
	43.0	33.3				Inventory	35.4	34.0
	1.3	2.6				All Other Current	1.9	1.5
	75.3	71.3				Total Current	76.2	72.0
	19.1	19.1				Fixed Assets (net)	17.3	18.3
	.7	2.2				Intangibles (net)	2.6	3.5
	4.9	7.4				All Other Non-Current	3.9	6.2
	100.0	100.0				Total	100.0	100.0
						LIABILITIES		
	20.4	14.4				Notes Payable-Short Term	13.4	11.2
	2.5	1.5				Cur. Mat.-L/T/D	2.9	2.7
	16.3	18.3				Trade Payables	16.5	15.3
	.0	2.6				Income Taxes Payable	.2	.6
	10.6	9.1				All Other Current	11.9	12.0
	49.8	45.8				Total Current	44.9	41.8
	11.6	14.1				Long Term Debt	8.5	8.8
	.0	.2				Deferred Taxes	.2	.6
	2.5	6.9				All Other Non-Current	4.2	4.0
	36.1	33.0				Net Worth	42.2	44.8
	100.0	100.0				Total Liabilities & Net Worth	100.0	100.0
						INCOME DATA		
	100.0	100.0				Net Sales	100.0	100.0
	35.5	33.2				Gross Profit	33.5	36.1
	33.9	27.1				Operating Expenses	27.8	29.8
	1.6	6.1				Operating Profit	5.7	6.4
	.4	1.5				All Other Expenses (net)	.8	.7
	1.2	4.6				Profit Before Taxes	5.0	5.6
						RATIOS		
	2.6	2.9					3.0	3.0
	1.5	1.5				Current	1.7	1.8
	1.0	1.1					1.2	1.4
	1.3	1.6					1.4	1.4
	.6	.7				Quick	.8	.9
	.4	.5					.5	.6
	22 16.8	**30** 12.3					**31** 12.0	**34** 10.9
	40 9.2	**40** 9.1				Sales/Receivables	**46** 7.9	**44** 8.4
	52 7.1	**63** 5.8					**65** 5.6	**59** 6.2
	38 9.6	**55** 6.7					**43** 8.4	**35** 10.3
	65 5.6	**87** 4.2				Cost of Sales/Inventory	**84** 4.3	**90** 4.0
	235 1.6	**121** 3.0					**137** 2.7	**121** 3.0
	14 27.0	**17** 21.2					**21** 17.8	**16** 22.5
	25 14.6	**33** 11.0				Cost of Sales/Payables	**32** 11.5	**30** 12.1
	46 8.0	**62** 5.9					**45** 8.2	**55** 6.7
	5.2	4.9					4.0	4.5
	9.3	9.8				Sales/Working Capital	7.5	8.5
	NM	32.6					27.9	14.6
		36.7					17.1	11.0
		(23) 6.2				EBIT/Interest	(40) 4.7	(42) 5.2
		.0					2.1	3.1
							7.7	18.8
						Net Profit + Depr., Dep., Amort./Cur. Mat. L /T/D	(15) 3.3	(19) 5.8
							1.0	2.5
	.1	.2					.1	.2
	.5	.4				Fixed/Worth	.3	.4
	1.2	1.9					.7	1.0
	1.0	.6					.6	.7
	2.1	2.1				Debt/Worth	1.8	1.5
	4.5	8.0					3.1	3.4
	48.1	60.1					59.2	55.6
	12.7	(20) 38.0				% Profit Before Taxes/Tangible Net Worth	(42) 25.3	(44) 19.8
	−28.9	13.0					12.1	7.1
	12.9	21.5					19.4	17.5
	4.4	9.4				% Profit Before Taxes/Total Assets	8.4	10.6
	−6.6	−1.7					5.0	3.1
	67.5	56.8					44.0	47.4
	41.5	18.6				Sales/Net Fixed Assets	19.0	17.1
	5.8	8.1					7.6	8.5
	3.5	3.0					3.1	2.9
	2.3	2.4				Sales/Total Assets	2.4	2.3
	1.7	1.6					1.8	1.7
		1.0					.8	.8
		(21) 1.8				% Depr., Dep., Amort./Sales	(40) 1.3	(41) 1.3
		2.8					1.8	2.4
							1.9	2.3
						% Officers', Directors', Owners' Comp/Sales	(19) 4.4	(22) 4.4
							8.6	9.6
2226M	26633M	252903M	511263M		552975M	Net Sales ($)	1710386M	1205517M
379M	10514M	112654M	180994M		322689M	Total Assets ($)	846172M	653455M

© RMA 2003

M = $ thousand MM = $ million

See Pages 11 through 18 for Explanation of Ratios and Data

Comparative Historical Data | | | | | | | **Current Data Sorted By Sales**

	4/1/00-3/31/01 ALL		4/1/01-3/31/02 ALL		4/1/02-3/31/03 ALL	Type of Statement	0-1MM	1-3MM	3-5MM	5-10MM	10-25MM	25MM & OVER
	6		11		13	Unqualified				4	2	7
	13		7		8	Reviewed				1	5	2
	8		13		9	Compiled		5		3	1	
	2		2		2	Tax Returns	1		1			
	7		11		14	Other		4	1	7	2	
								11 (4/1-9/30/02)			35 (10/1/02-3/31/03)	
	36		44		46	**NUMBER OF STATEMENTS**	1	9	2	15	10	9
	%		%		%	**ASSETS**	%	%	%	%	%	%
	2.9		4.4		5.8	Cash & Equivalents				2.7	13.0	
	30.5		26.8		27.8	Trade Receivables (net)				27.3	32.0	
	37.7		36.6		35.7	Inventory				35.2	32.6	
	2.4		2.3		2.0	All Other Current				4.2	.2	
	73.5		70.1		71.3	Total Current				69.4	77.8	
	18.5		18.5		19.4	Fixed Assets (net)				16.7	17.6	
	2.9		6.8		3.1	Intangibles (net)				2.5	2.4	
	5.1		4.6		6.2	All Other Non-Current				11.4	2.3	
	100.0		100.0		100.0	Total				100.0	100.0	
						LIABILITIES						
	17.7		14.6		14.4	Notes Payable-Short Term				21.7	9.2	
	1.7		2.2		2.0	Cur. Mat.-L/T/D				.9	2.1	
	13.8		17.1		17.4	Trade Payables				17.9	19.6	
	.1		1.3		1.4	Income Taxes Payable				3.7	.6	
	12.9		14.5		11.1	All Other Current				6.5	10.7	
	46.2		49.7		46.3	Total Current				50.6	42.1	
	9.2		11.2		13.0	Long Term Debt				13.2	11.8	
	.5		.2		.2	Deferred Taxes				.2	.2	
	1.9		5.7		5.6	All Other Non-Current				6.1	9.7	
	42.2		33.2		34.9	Net Worth				29.9	36.2	
	100.0		100.0		100.0	Total Liabilities & Net Worth				100.0	100.0	
						INCOME DATA						
	100.0		100.0		100.0	Net Sales				100.0	100.0	
	37.8		33.8		33.3	Gross Profit				32.2	32.6	
	33.5		29.1		28.4	Operating Expenses				27.7	25.3	
	4.4		4.7		4.8	Operating Profit				4.4	7.3	
	1.2		1.5		1.2	All Other Expenses (net)				1.1	1.3	
	3.2		3.2		3.6	Profit Before Taxes				3.3	6.0	
						RATIOS						
	2.2		2.7		2.8					2.1	4.2	
	1.6		1.5		1.5	Current				1.4	2.1	
	1.2		1.1		1.1					1.1	1.2	
	1.0		1.1		1.3					1.1	2.0	
	.7		.6		.7	Quick				.6	1.3	
	.5		.4		.5					.4	.7	
39	9.3	33	11.0	28	13.0					35 10.5	30 12.3	
51	7.1	41	8.9	41	8.9	Sales/Receivables				53 6.9	37 9.8	
65	5.6	52	7.0	56	6.5					63 5.8	55 6.6	
74	4.9	47	7.7	43	8.5					58 6.3	22 16.8	
104	3.5	86	4.2	71	5.1	Cost of Sales/Inventory				89 4.1	67 5.4	
130	2.8	125	2.9	120	3.0					122 3.0	113 3.2	
17	22.0	15	24.5	15	24.9					23 16.0	9 38.6	
36	10.2	32	11.6	28	13.3	Cost of Sales/Payables				39 9.4	17 20.9	
48	7.5	51	7.2	60	6.0					63 5.8	52 7.0	
	5.1		4.4		5.4					5.2	4.5	
	8.1		10.8		9.8	Sales/Working Capital				15.1	7.7	
	21.6		32.1		38.8					36.3	28.9	
	5.5		8.8		16.4					6.9	69.5	
(33)	2.8	(41)	2.1	(43)	2.8	EBIT/Interest			(14)	2.5	20.6	
	1.4		1.2		1.2					-.5	1.7	
	23.3		19.9		17.0	Net Profit + Depr., Dep.,						
(13)	3.2	(15)	3.8	(13)	5.7	Amort./Cur. Mat. L/T/D						
	.4		1.1		1.8							
	.2		.2		.2					.2	.2	
	.3		.6		.5	Fixed/Worth				.5	.4	
	.9		2.1		1.8					1.3	NM	
	.7		1.1		.8					.8	.5	
	1.9		2.4		2.4	Debt/Worth				3.3	2.1	
	3.1		13.2		5.0					9.2	NM	
	40.8		64.5		51.3	% Profit Before Taxes/Tangible				55.1		
	17.9	(39)	23.5	(41)	34.6	Net Worth			(13)	22.1		
	3.0		3.6		10.6					-9.3		
	12.6		17.6		19.5	% Profit Before Taxes/Total				12.8	29.8	
	5.2		6.4		7.5	Assets				7.9	18.6	
	1.5		.5		.8					-6.0	2.7	
	35.9		48.2		53.7					52.1	216.2	
	15.6		16.3		18.6	Sales/Net Fixed Assets				18.0	20.7	
	8.0		8.0		7.0					8.9	8.3	
	2.8		3.7		3.3					3.0	3.1	
	2.2		2.1		2.4	Sales/Total Assets				2.1	2.8	
	1.6		1.6		1.7					1.6	2.4	
	.7		.3		.7					1.2		
(32)	1.1	(36)	1.2	(41)	1.5	% Depr., Dep., Amort./Sales			(13)	1.8		
	1.8		2.2		2.2					2.8		
	1.7		2.0		1.4	% Officers', Directors',						
(18)	5.1	(15)	3.0	(18)	3.0	Owners' Comp/Sales						
	9.5		5.2		5.0							
	897511M		1293425M		1346000M	Net Sales ($)	676M	16721M	7441M	112026M	166706M	1042430M
	544517M		716928M		627230M	Total Assets ($)	207M	8898M	2283M	60798M	67262M	487782M

M = $ thousand   MM = $ million
See Pages 11 through 18 for Explanation of Ratios and Data

Current Data Sorted By Assets							Comparative Historical Data	

Type of Statement

0-500M	500M-2MM	2-10MM	10-50MM	50-100MM	100-250MM	Type of Statement	4/1/98-3/31/99 ALL	4/1/99-3/31/00 ALL
1	2	3			1	Unqualified	12	8
	1	13	3			Reviewed	9	12
1	5					Compiled	7	4
1	1	1				Tax Returns	2	
1	2	6	3	1	1	Other	15	11
	5 (4/1-9/30/02)		42 (10/1/02-3/31/03)					
4	11	23	6	1	2	NUMBER OF STATEMENTS	45	35
%	%	%	%	%	%	ASSETS	%	%
	5.5	4.3				Cash & Equivalents	5.2	5.9
	35.6	31.1				Trade Receivables (net)	32.5	33.7
	44.5	34.1				Inventory	34.5	31.8
	1.2	4.5				All Other Current	1.4	1.0
	86.9	73.9				Total Current	73.6	72.4
	9.9	18.8				Fixed Assets (net)	16.8	18.2
	1.7	1.7				Intangibles (net)	5.2	4.9
	1.5	5.6				All Other Non-Current	4.4	4.5
	100.0	100.0				Total	100.0	100.0
						LIABILITIES		
	19.2	19.3				Notes Payable-Short Term	16.2	12.6
	4.1	3.3				Cur. Mat.-L/T/D	3.7	4.1
	17.2	17.4				Trade Payables	16.9	16.2
	1.2	.3				Income Taxes Payable	.3	1.2
	15.9	11.6				All Other Current	11.3	12.7
	57.6	51.8				Total Current	48.4	46.8
	4.1	5.8				Long Term Debt	11.8	9.3
	.0	.2				Deferred Taxes	.4	.2
	4.6	2.6				All Other Non-Current	5.9	4.5
	33.7	39.6				Net Worth	33.4	39.2
	100.0	100.0				Total Liabilities & Net Worth	100.0	100.0
						INCOME DATA		
	100.0	100.0				Net Sales	100.0	100.0
	31.5	35.8				Gross Profit	36.9	34.5
	34.1	32.4				Operating Expenses	31.5	29.4
	-2.6	3.4				Operating Profit	5.4	5.1
	.6	1.1				All Other Expenses (net)	1.5	1.5
	-3.2	2.3				Profit Before Taxes	3.9	3.6
						RATIOS		
	2.2	1.8					2.3	2.2
	1.4	1.4				Current	1.5	1.6
	1.1	1.2					1.1	1.2
	1.1	.9					1.4	1.2
	.7	.7				Quick	.8	.9
	.5	.5					.6	.6
	32 11.5	33 11.2					39 9.3	43 8.4
	46 8.0	43 8.6				Sales/Receivables	51 7.2	51 7.1
	54 6.7	57 6.4					57 6.4	62 5.9
	65 5.6	24 15.2					58 6.3	46 7.9
	77 4.8	91 4.0				Cost of Sales/Inventory	88 4.1	69 5.3
	105 3.5	127 2.9					138 2.6	114 3.2
	15 24.2	19 19.4					16 23.2	22 16.9
	32 11.5	38 9.6				Cost of Sales/Payables	33 11.0	30 12.1
	52 7.0	48 7.7					56 6.5	44 8.4
	5.1	6.9					5.6	5.8
	10.1	11.9				Sales/Working Capital	8.1	10.4
	17.3	32.2					36.5	25.6
	(10) 9.1	(22) 7.9					(41) 11.8	(31) 10.5
	2.8	3.1				EBIT/Interest	3.3	3.6
	-3.3	.4					1.4	.7
		(10) 4.6				Net Profit + Depr., Dep.,		10.2
		1.1				Amort./Cur. Mat. L /T/D	(18) 3.5	
		.3						1.2
	.1	.2					.3	.2
	.2	.4				Fixed/Worth	.5	.5
	5.4	.8					1.1	1.1
	.7	.8					.9	1.1
	2.4	1.6				Debt/Worth	2.5	1.8
	14.0	2.9					5.1	3.5
		(22) 33.7				% Profit Before Taxes/Tangible	(38) 59.7	(32) 36.7
		8.9				Net Worth	21.0	25.2
		-1.5					6.2	-5.0
	8.4	13.0					18.5	16.3
	2.7	3.1				% Profit Before Taxes/Total Assets	7.0	5.8
	-15.2	-.7					2.0	-1.8
	79.1	56.7					33.9	59.1
	52.5	18.0				Sales/Net Fixed Assets	17.4	16.7
	22.0	10.1					7.3	6.9
	3.9	2.9					3.1	3.1
	2.8	2.3				Sales/Total Assets	2.5	2.1
	2.4	2.1					1.9	1.9
	.4	.6					.9	.7
	.6	(22) 1.5				% Depr., Dep., Amort./Sales	(39) 1.5	(25) 1.3
	1.7	2.4					2.8	2.0
		(12) 2.1				% Officers', Directors',		2.7
		3.8				Owners' Comp/Sales	(19) 4.3	(14) 5.9
		4.7					7.2	9.2
3602M	44779M	240118M	205235M	131846M	426254M	Net Sales ($)	1013250M	1226935M
1022M	13837M	97837M	95282M	66023M	385738M	Total Assets ($)	630973M	716185M

© RMA 2003

M = $ thousand   MM = $ million
See Pages 11 through 18 for Explanation of Ratios and Data

Comparative Historical Data | Current Data Sorted By Sales

			Type of Statement	0-1MM	1-3MM	3-5MM	5-10MM	10-25MM	25MM & OVER
8	9	7	Unqualified	1		2		3	1
15	4	17	Reviewed		1		9	5	2
4	6	6	Compiled		3	3			
6	4	3	Tax Returns	1			2		
18	11	14	Other		2		3	4	5
4/1/00-3/31/01	4/1/01-3/31/02	4/1/02-3/31/03		5 (4/1-9/30/02)			42 (10/1/02-3/31/03)		
ALL	ALL	ALL							
51	34	47	**NUMBER OF STATEMENTS**	2	6	5	14	12	8
%	%	%	**ASSETS**	%	%	%	%	%	%
6.3	4.6	6.3	Cash & Equivalents				6.1	2.5	
32.9	26.0	32.3	Trade Receivables (net)				32.0	35.7	
34.1	37.0	32.6	Inventory				30.6	36.0	
1.6	1.5	3.8	All Other Current				2.7	5.6	
74.9	69.1	75.1	Total Current				71.4	79.9	
17.2	21.9	17.3	Fixed Assets (net)				21.8	11.9	
3.9	6.5	3.5	Intangibles (net)				.7	2.5	
3.9	2.4	4.1	All Other Non-Current				6.1	5.7	
100.0	100.0	100.0	Total				100.0	100.0	
			LIABILITIES						
12.4	15.3	16.4	Notes Payable-Short Term				16.6	24.1	
2.3	2.5	3.8	Cur. Mat.-L/T/D				4.1	7.6	
17.5	16.4	16.0	Trade Payables				16.4	21.8	
.2	.1	.5	Income Taxes Payable				.5	1.0	
10.6	10.0	12.0	All Other Current				12.9	12.2	
43.0	44.2	48.7	Total Current				50.5	66.8	
12.3	19.4	10.7	Long Term Debt				6.9	5.2	
.2	.2	.3	Deferred Taxes				.0	.3	
6.3	1.9	2.9	All Other Non-Current				3.4	3.9	
38.3	34.2	37.5	Net Worth				39.3	23.8	
100.0	100.0	100.0	Total Liabilities & Net Worth				100.0	100.0	
			INCOME DATA						
100.0	100.0	100.0	Net Sales				100.0	100.0	
34.2	36.1	34.0	Gross Profit				35.2	33.3	
28.5	34.1	32.2	Operating Expenses				32.0	29.9	
5.7	2.1	1.7	Operating Profit				3.1	3.4	
.9	1.0	1.2	All Other Expenses (net)				.3	1.6	
4.8	1.0	.5	Profit Before Taxes				2.8	1.8	
			RATIOS						
2.4	2.5	2.2	Current				2.0	1.4	
1.8	1.7	1.5					1.4	1.2	
1.4	1.1	1.2					1.1	1.1	
1.4	1.2	1.3	Quick				1.1	.8	
1.0	.7	.8					.8	.5	
.6	.4	.6					.6	.4	
37 9.8	27 13.3	33 11.2	Sales/Receivables				28 12.9	33 11.1	
51 7.2	36 10.1	45 8.1					48 7.6	40 9.1	
56 6.6	51 7.1	63 5.8					63 5.8	45 8.1	
45 8.1	55 6.7	32 11.3	Cost of Sales/Inventory				21 17.5	24 15.1	
73 5.0	79 4.6	77 4.8					62 5.9	73 5.0	
120 3.0	135 2.7	110 3.3					118 3.1	119 3.1	
20 17.9	18 20.0	18 19.9	Cost of Sales/Payables				17 21.8	19 19.5	
29 12.7	34 10.7	33 11.0					38 9.5	35 10.3	
52 7.1	55 6.7	45 8.1					46 7.9	54 6.7	
4.9	4.4	5.2	Sales/Working Capital				6.5	10.1	
7.6	9.1	9.1					11.4	24.9	
17.7	75.9	21.3					91.6	54.2	
(45) 13.2	(30) 10.8	(42) 8.9	EBIT/Interest				(13) 8.9	10.5	
4.6	4.1	3.0					3.9	1.2	
2.1	.2	.3					1.3	−2.0	
		(15) 5.9	Net Profit + Depr., Dep., Amort./Cur. Mat. L/T/D						
		1.2							
		.1							
.2	.3	.1	Fixed/Worth				.2	.2	
.4	.5	.5					.4	.7	
1.0	1.9	1.2					1.5	.8	
1.0	.7	.6	Debt/Worth				.6	1.5	
1.5	1.8	1.9					1.6	2.8	
3.5	7.9	5.0					4.9	10.0	
(46) 56.8	(29) 32.8	(41) 36.0	% Profit Before Taxes/Tangible Net Worth				(13) 45.0	(10) 54.3	
26.1	20.2	9.8					10.3	6.7	
13.0	−5.5	−3.4					3.3	−11.9	
19.6	13.9	12.0	% Profit Before Taxes/Total Assets				12.0	11.5	
9.0	5.9	3.1					5.5	.8	
2.4	−3.6	−1.8					1.7	−3.4	
36.6	26.5	67.2	Sales/Net Fixed Assets				59.7	79.4	
17.4	12.4	19.9					16.6	25.6	
7.8	8.1	9.8					10.5	14.8	
3.0	2.9	3.0	Sales/Total Assets				3.1	4.3	
2.3	2.2	2.5					2.3	2.5	
1.8	1.6	2.0					2.0	2.1	
(43) .8	(25) 1.0	(42) .5	% Depr., Dep., Amort./Sales				.9	(11) .3	
1.0	2.0	1.4					1.6	.7	
2.7	3.6	2.8					2.8	1.4	
(20) 2.1	(11) 3.7	(22) 2.8	% Officers', Directors', Owners' Comp/Sales				(11) 2.1		
4.9	6.1	4.6					3.9		
9.5	9.8	7.0					5.9		
1295926M	855744M	1051834M	Net Sales ($)	846M	10232M	19884M	95373M	179596M	745903M
668703M	518880M	659739M	Total Assets ($)	357M	4070M	11950M	40595M	66260M	536507M

© RMA 2003

M = $ thousand   MM = $ million
See Pages 11 through 18 for Explanation of Ratios and Data

Current Data Sorted By Assets **Comparative Historical Data**

0-500M	500M-2MM	2-10MM	10-50MM	50-100MM	100-250MM	Type of Statement	4/1/98-3/31/99 ALL	4/1/99-3/31/00 ALL
	2	1	4		2	Unqualified	8	9
	1	5	1			Reviewed	8	5
1		3				Compiled	3	3
1	1					Tax Returns	1	1
1	5	5	4	2	2	Other	13	14
	5 (4/1-9/30/02)		36 (10/1/02-3/31/03)					
3	9	14	9	2	4	**NUMBER OF STATEMENTS**	33	32
%	%	%	%	%	%	**ASSETS**	%	%
		2.2				Cash & Equivalents	7.1	9.5
		17.7				Trade Receivables (net)	26.7	29.0
		35.3				Inventory	30.3	29.6
		3.2				All Other Current	1.5	2.3
		58.4				Total Current	65.5	70.3
		23.3				Fixed Assets (net)	19.1	16.3
		5.8				Intangibles (net)	9.9	8.6
		12.4				All Other Non-Current	5.5	4.8
		100.0				Total	100.0	100.0
						LIABILITIES		
		18.1				Notes Payable-Short Term	15.1	12.5
		3.9				Cur. Mat.-L/T/D	3.3	3.9
		11.8				Trade Payables	14.9	14.0
		.6				Income Taxes Payable	.9	.1
		6.7				All Other Current	7.5	8.0
		41.2				Total Current	41.7	38.5
		8.5				Long Term Debt	14.1	12.1
		.1				Deferred Taxes	.2	.5
		1.5				All Other Non-Current	4.6	3.9
		48.8				Net Worth	39.4	45.0
		100.0				Total Liabilities & Net Worth	100.0	100.0
						INCOME DATA		
		100.0				Net Sales	100.0	100.0
		33.5				Gross Profit	34.1	37.9
		28.9				Operating Expenses	35.7	29.9
		4.6				Operating Profit	-1.6	8.0
		1.9				All Other Expenses (net)	2.0	1.0
		2.6				Profit Before Taxes	-3.5	7.0
						RATIOS		
		2.3				Current	2.6	4.3
		1.2					1.7	2.1
		1.0					1.1	1.1
		.8				Quick	1.6	3.2
		.5					.8	.8
		.3					.5	.5
	22	16.7				Sales/Receivables	34 10.8	38 9.5
	37	9.8					47 7.8	47 7.8
	43	8.5					58 6.3	57 6.4
	66	5.5				Cost of Sales/Inventory	63 5.8	49 7.5
	123	3.0					82 4.5	79 4.6
	147	2.5					126 2.9	96 3.8
	17	21.3				Cost of Sales/Payables	29 12.5	13 28.8
	28	13.2					36 10.1	26 14.3
	50	7.4					49 7.5	44 8.2
		5.3				Sales/Working Capital	5.7	4.4
		21.4					9.5	7.0
		643.9					22.2	31.1
		6.9				EBIT/Interest	(29) 10.2	14.0
		4.2					3.3	(25) 3.7
		.3					1.6	2.3
						Net Profit + Depr., Dep., Amort./Cur. Mat. L /T/D		6.6
								(10) 2.9
								1.0
		.2				Fixed/Worth	.2	.1
		.5					.5	.3
		1.0					3.1	1.1
		.6				Debt/Worth	.6	.5
		1.4					2.2	1.5
		4.5					9.8	3.7
		42.2				% Profit Before Taxes/Tangible Net Worth	(27) 67.0	(30) 48.5
		11.0					32.5	19.5
		-3.7					20.5	11.4
		14.1				% Profit Before Taxes/Total Assets	19.0	15.9
		5.7					9.8	8.8
		-1.5					3.4	3.9
		13.7				Sales/Net Fixed Assets	28.2	34.1
		9.2					10.9	19.7
		5.5					7.4	7.0
		2.3				Sales/Total Assets	2.9	2.7
		1.9					2.2	2.1
		1.3					1.6	1.6
		.8				% Depr., Dep., Amort./Sales	1.0	.6
		1.5					(25) 1.8	(28) 1.3
		3.5					2.7	2.5
						% Officers', Directors', Owners' Comp/Sales	2.4	2.2
							(10) 4.4	(14) 4.9
							6.4	8.9
2359M	21613M	134373M	327626M	249683M	813186M	Net Sales ($)	1797288M	1082244M
878M	10756M	65607M	225829M	124709M	753961M	Total Assets ($)	725966M	533078M

© RMA 2003

M = $ thousand   MM = $ million
See Pages 11 through 18 for Explanation of Ratios and Data

Comparative Historical Data | Current Data Sorted By Sales

						Type of Statement						
	6		6		9	Unqualified		1	1		2	5
	6		6		7	Reviewed		1	2	1	3	
	8		6		4	Compiled		1	2	1		
	2		1		2	Tax Returns	1	1				
	10		10		19	Other	1	3	3	1	3	8
	4/1/00-3/31/01		4/1/01-3/31/02		4/1/02-3/31/03			5 (4/1-9/30/02)			36 (10/1/02-3/31/03)	
	ALL		ALL		ALL		0-1MM	1-3MM	3-5MM	5-10MM	10-25MM	25MM & OVER
	32		29		41	NUMBER OF STATEMENTS	2	7	8	3	8	13
	%		%		%	ASSETS	%	%	%	%	%	%
	7.6		7.9		5.6	Cash & Equivalents						7.2
	28.2		24.2		20.7	Trade Receivables (net)						25.0
	29.3		32.4		31.3	Inventory						31.3
	2.0		1.9		2.2	All Other Current						2.4
	67.1		66.4		59.8	Total Current						65.8
	17.4		21.9		21.5	Fixed Assets (net)						14.8
	9.9		7.2		9.6	Intangibles (net)						15.1
	5.6		4.5		9.1	All Other Non-Current						4.3
	100.0		100.0		100.0	Total						100.0
						LIABILITIES						
	14.6		13.3		11.4	Notes Payable-Short Term						6.1
	3.4		3.6		3.2	Cur. Mat.-L/T/D						1.3
	12.6		10.9		12.4	Trade Payables						11.9
	.5		.8		.7	Income Taxes Payable						.9
	7.8		7.3		9.0	All Other Current						11.6
	38.9		35.9		36.7	Total Current						31.7
	10.5		14.2		18.0	Long Term Debt						17.4
	.9		.4		.2	Deferred Taxes						.1
	4.1		5.0		4.8	All Other Non-Current						4.7
	45.6		44.4		40.3	Net Worth						46.1
	100.0		100.0		100.0	Total Liabilities & Net Worth						100.0
						INCOME DATA						
	100.0		100.0		100.0	Net Sales						100.0
	37.7		36.6		35.1	Gross Profit						34.6
	29.7		29.7		29.1	Operating Expenses						24.6
	8.1		6.9		6.0	Operating Profit						9.9
	1.7		1.1		2.2	All Other Expenses (net)						3.8
	6.3		5.8		3.8	Profit Before Taxes						6.1
						RATIOS						
	3.3		3.1		3.1							4.2
	1.9		1.8		1.5	Current						1.9
	1.1		1.2		1.0							1.5
	2.2		1.5		1.7							1.8
	.9		.9		.7	Quick						1.1
	.5		.6		.4							.7
34	10.7	36	10.3	24	15.0						45	8.2
49	7.4	41	8.9	41	8.9	Sales/Receivables					56	6.5
58	6.3	52	7.0	57	6.4						67	5.4
55	6.7	57	6.4	48	7.6						53	6.9
80	4.6	96	3.8	97	3.8	Cost of Sales/Inventory					103	3.5
117	3.1	122	3.0	138	2.6						134	2.7
15	24.2	13	28.9	19	19.6						22	16.7
25	14.4	24	15.5	30	12.3	Cost of Sales/Payables					35	10.6
52	7.0	48	7.6	49	7.4						49	7.4
	3.8		3.8		3.8							3.3
	6.7		9.0		7.7	Sales/Working Capital						5.6
	29.3		15.5		508.6							10.5
	11.7		7.1		8.9							22.1
(24)	4.3	(24)	2.7	(39)	3.0	EBIT/Interest				(11)	1.8
	1.5		1.1		.9							.9
					3.9	Net Profit + Depr., Dep.,						
				(12)	2.5	Amort./Cur. Mat. L/T/D						
					.3							
	.2		.2		.2							.1
	.5		.5		.5	Fixed/Worth						.3
	1.7		1.0		1.7							1.3
	.6		.8		.7							.6
	1.5		1.3		1.6	Debt/Worth						1.5
	4.6		2.6		5.1							5.0
	48.7		43.2		38.5	% Profit Before Taxes/Tangible						43.7
(28)	27.5	(27)	12.0	(36)	14.5	Net Worth				(11)	21.7
	−4.8		.0		2.6							.4
	25.5		14.5		15.1	% Profit Before Taxes/Total						19.9
	13.3		6.5		5.5	Assets						8.2
	−.8		.7		−.2							−.2
	33.1		22.3		25.7							47.1
	12.6		9.8		10.2	Sales/Net Fixed Assets						12.2
	7.2		5.8		5.8							6.2
	2.4		2.5		2.3							2.3
	1.9		1.9		1.8	Sales/Total Assets						1.7
	1.5		1.5		1.3							1.3
	.9		.9		.9							.7
(26)	1.6	(25)	1.9	(35)	1.6	% Depr., Dep., Amort./Sales				(10)	1.6
	3.0		4.0		3.8							3.6
	2.9				1.2	% Officers', Directors',						
(15)	5.9			(15)	4.1	Owners' Comp/Sales						
	9.4				6.6							
	909673M		1048870M		1548840M	Net Sales ($)	1168M	11221M	27632M	17223M	134268M	1357328M
	560363M		585399M		1181740M	Total Assets ($)	809M	7187M	15745M	12605M	101777M	1043617M

© RMA 2003   M = $ thousand   MM = $ million
See Pages 11 through 18 for Explanation of Ratios and Data

Current Data Sorted By Assets   Comparative Historical Data

Type of Statement	0-500M	500M-2MM	2-10MM	10-50MM	50-100MM	100-250MM		4/1/98-3/31/99 ALL	4/1/99-3/31/00 ALL
Unqualified		3	3	11	2	3		24	16
Reviewed		8	8	1				9	9
Compiled		8	1					6	2
Tax Returns	1	1	1						1
Other	1	3	7	5	1	4		13	23
	0-500M	13 (4/1-9/30/02) 500M-2MM	2-10MM	51 (10/1/02-3/31/03) 10-50MM	50-100MM	100-250MM			
NUMBER OF STATEMENTS	2	15	20	17	3	7		52	51
ASSETS	%	%	%	%	%	%		%	%
Cash & Equivalents		13.1	8.4	9.2				5.9	6.0
Trade Receivables (net)		35.9	27.3	23.7				29.0	28.9
Inventory		25.0	37.8	30.2				29.2	32.5
All Other Current		1.6	1.6	1.8				2.0	1.0
Total Current		75.6	75.2	64.9				66.1	68.5
Fixed Assets (net)		15.7	17.1	22.7				25.1	19.5
Intangibles (net)		2.1	.7	7.4				5.6	5.8
All Other Non-Current		6.6	6.9	5.0				3.2	6.2
Total		100.0	100.0	100.0				100.0	100.0
LIABILITIES									
Notes Payable-Short Term		9.7	14.9	7.5				13.3	12.3
Cur. Mat.-L/T/D		2.2	3.3	2.0				3.8	6.0
Trade Payables		14.2	15.9	10.1				16.2	17.2
Income Taxes Payable		.1	.4	.0				.2	.4
All Other Current		6.0	11.0	14.2				10.5	10.6
Total Current		32.2	45.5	33.9				44.0	46.4
Long Term Debt		6.5	9.7	9.1				18.2	13.5
Deferred Taxes		.2	.1	.3				.5	.5
All Other Non-Current		6.6	.9	4.6				7.3	5.2
Net Worth		54.5	43.7	52.1				30.0	34.3
Total Liabilities & Net Worth		100.0	100.0	100.0				100.0	100.0
INCOME DATA									
Net Sales		100.0	100.0	100.0				100.0	100.0
Gross Profit		36.6	27.3	28.3				27.6	28.6
Operating Expenses		35.0	26.0	22.9				24.6	25.6
Operating Profit		1.7	1.2	5.4				3.0	3.0
All Other Expenses (net)		.8	.8	1.4				1.3	1.0
Profit Before Taxes		.9	.5	4.0				1.8	2.1
RATIOS									
Current		4.6 / 2.5 / 1.9	2.7 / 1.5 / 1.2	4.1 / 2.0 / 1.4				2.4 / 1.6 / 1.1	2.4 / 1.7 / 1.1
Quick		3.1 / 1.5 / .9	1.4 / .7 / .4	2.0 / .9 / .6				1.4 / .8 / .5	1.3 / .8 / .5
Sales/Receivables		30 12.1 / 40 9.2 / 63 5.8	37 9.8 / 48 7.6 / 54 6.7	45 8.1 / 58 6.3 / 65 5.6				40 9.2 / 51 7.1 / 61 6.0	40 9.2 / 51 7.2 / 61 6.0
Cost of Sales/Inventory		10 36.2 / 66 5.5 / 95 3.8	55 6.7 / 79 4.6 / 130 2.8	62 5.9 / 79 4.6 / 125 2.9				50 7.3 / 67 5.4 / 115 3.2	50 7.3 / 73 5.0 / 108 3.4
Cost of Sales/Payables		16 22.7 / 28 12.9 / 57 6.4	22 16.8 / 32 11.6 / 49 7.5	23 15.7 / 31 11.6 / 44 8.2				24 15.5 / 34 10.6 / 51 7.1	25 14.8 / 35 10.3 / 58 6.3
Sales/Working Capital		4.9 / 5.3 / 8.4	5.2 / 8.7 / 18.3	3.1 / 6.6 / 9.6				4.9 / 8.4 / 51.6	5.3 / 10.1 / 32.6
EBIT/Interest		(11) 48.7 / 6.7 / -4.5	(17) 5.9 / 2.1 / -3.8	(15) 10.1 / 2.3 / 1.1				(48) 7.8 / 3.0 / 1.6	(46) 7.2 / 2.9 / .8
Net Profit + Depr., Dep., Amort./Cur. Mat. L /T/D								(23) 3.0 / 2.1 / .9	(17) 6.7 / 2.6 / .3
Fixed/Worth		.2 / .2 / .5	.1 / .3 / .6	.3 / .4 / .9				.3 / .8 / 2.6	.2 / .4 / 1.7
Debt/Worth		.3 / .8 / 1.1	.5 / 1.3 / 3.2	.3 / .9 / 2.9				.9 / 2.8 / 6.3	.8 / 2.1 / 3.7
% Profit Before Taxes/Tangible Net Worth		(13) 35.5 / 16.0 / -4.6	(18) 29.1 / 14.4 / -8.2	(14) 23.5 / 5.5 / .7				(43) 47.8 / 24.3 / 9.9	(43) 42.1 / 21.0 / 5.0
% Profit Before Taxes/Total Assets		19.3 / 6.9 / -6.5	14.4 / 6.4 / -5.2	12.4 / 2.6 / -.7				13.8 / 5.8 / 1.4	14.3 / 5.0 / -1.4
Sales/Net Fixed Assets		31.5 / 14.9 / 11.8	24.2 / 14.9 / 10.8	15.7 / 6.9 / 4.7				18.8 / 9.2 / 4.7	27.7 / 11.7 / 5.8
Sales/Total Assets		3.4 / 2.4 / 1.6	3.0 / 2.2 / 1.8	2.0 / 1.6 / 1.1				2.8 / 1.9 / 1.5	2.6 / 2.0 / 1.4
% Depr., Dep., Amort./Sales		(11) .9 / 1.1 / 3.1	(19) .9 / 1.4 / 2.0	(15) 1.6 / 2.6 / 4.0				(43) 1.2 / 1.9 / 2.7	(41) 1.1 / 1.5 / 2.3
% Officers', Directors', Owners' Comp/Sales									(11) 2.4 / 2.8 / 5.0
Net Sales ($)	1893M	49450M	205288M	656536M	390467M	2367985M		3199493M	1397658M
Total Assets ($)	879M	18584M	92698M	401648M	242818M	1347237M		2001361M	809451M

© RMA 2003

M = $ thousand   MM = $ million

See Pages 11 through 18 for Explanation of Ratios and Data

Comparative Historical Data   Current Data Sorted By Sales

	4/1/00-3/31/01 ALL	4/1/01-3/31/02 ALL	4/1/02-3/31/03 ALL	Type of Statement	0-1MM	1-3MM	3-5MM	5-10MM	10-25MM	25MM & OVER
	12	11	19	Unqualified				4	2	13
	15	10	12	Reviewed		2		5	4	1
	14	11	9	Compiled	1	3	2	3		
	1	2	3	Tax Returns	1	1				
	12	14	21	Other	1	2	2	3	5	8
						13 (4/1-9/30/02)		51 (10/1/02-3/31/03)		
	54	48	64	**NUMBER OF STATEMENTS**	3	8	4	15	11	23
	%	%	%	**ASSETS**	%	%	%	%	%	%
	5.8	7.3	9.8	Cash & Equivalents				9.7	6.3	8.5
	30.1	27.0	27.3	Trade Receivables (net)				32.8	27.0	22.3
	30.4	31.9	29.4	Inventory				33.6	35.9	25.5
	2.2	1.7	2.0	All Other Current				2.0	.4	3.0
	68.5	67.9	68.5	Total Current				78.1	69.6	59.2
	22.4	20.9	21.7	Fixed Assets (net)				15.2	19.8	28.9
	4.4	7.8	4.1	Intangibles (net)				.7	4.7	7.4
	4.7	3.4	5.7	All Other Non-Current				6.0	5.9	4.5
	100.0	100.0	100.0	Total				100.0	100.0	100.0
				LIABILITIES						
	12.1	10.2	10.1	Notes Payable-Short Term				14.2	14.3	6.5
	4.0	3.8	2.7	Cur. Mat.-L/T/D				2.9	.9	2.4
	17.7	14.8	13.3	Trade Payables				15.4	12.4	11.5
	.4	.5	.3	Income Taxes Payable				.7	.0	.3
	11.1	11.5	11.7	All Other Current				9.7	9.6	15.3
	45.3	40.8	38.0	Total Current				42.8	37.2	36.0
	13.9	12.9	12.1	Long Term Debt				8.0	5.8	15.9
	.4	.3	.4	Deferred Taxes				.2	.3	.8
	3.3	7.6	3.6	All Other Non-Current				1.6	5.5	2.1
	37.1	38.5	45.8	Net Worth				47.4	51.3	45.2
	100.0	100.0	100.0	Total Liabilities & Net Worth				100.0	100.0	100.0
				INCOME DATA						
	100.0	100.0	100.0	Net Sales				100.0	100.0	100.0
	29.2	30.8	29.2	Gross Profit				34.2	30.3	21.6
	25.2	28.1	25.6	Operating Expenses				29.7	25.3	16.8
	3.9	2.7	3.6	Operating Profit				4.6	5.0	4.8
	1.3	1.2	1.3	All Other Expenses (net)				.1	1.9	1.8
	2.6	1.5	2.3	Profit Before Taxes				4.5	3.1	3.0
				RATIOS						
	2.5	2.6	3.0	Current				3.1	3.3	2.4
	1.7	1.5	1.8					1.7	1.5	1.8
	1.2	1.1	1.4					1.5	1.2	1.4
	1.3	1.5	1.7	Quick				1.4	1.9	1.4
	.9	.7	.9					.9	.7	.8
	.6	.5	.6					.6	.5	.6
	37 9.8	35 10.5	35 10.5	Sales/Receivables				38 9.5	44 8.3	31 11.9
	48 7.6	47 7.8	48 7.6					47 7.8	51 7.2	47 7.7
	63 5.8	58 6.3	58 6.3					58 6.3	60 6.1	58 6.3
	45 8.1	52 7.0	45 8.1	Cost of Sales/Inventory				39 9.3	60 6.0	43 8.5
	68 5.3	73 5.0	68 5.3					61 6.0	79 4.6	63 5.8
	105 3.5	116 3.2	98 3.7					120 3.1	146 2.5	79 4.6
	24 14.9	22 16.4	22 16.9	Cost of Sales/Payables				27 13.3	21 17.5	22 16.9
	32 11.5	37 10.0	31 11.8					37 10.0	28 13.0	30 12.2
	51 7.1	46 7.9	45 8.2					51 7.2	47 7.7	34 10.7
	5.4	4.5	4.6	Sales/Working Capital				5.3	3.2	4.2
	9.1	9.4	8.0					8.1	8.6	9.6
	18.8	27.1	13.4					10.3	19.9	16.2
	9.6	8.7	9.8	EBIT/Interest				17.4		9.5
(46)	3.1	(44) 2.4	(54) 2.5				(14)	4.4	(20)	4.1
	.9	1.0	.5					−1.5		1.4
	7.9	20.0	13.6	Net Profit + Depr., Dep., Amort./Cur. Mat. L/T/D						
(15)	4.3	(10) 5.3	(20) 3.8							
	.4	3.2	.5							
	.2	.2	.2	Fixed/Worth				.2	.1	.4
	.5	.6	.4					.2	.5	.7
	1.4	1.8	1.4					.4	.7	1.7
	.7	1.0	.4	Debt/Worth				.4	.4	.5
	1.9	1.8	1.1					.9	1.2	1.7
	4.0	6.4	3.4					3.2	1.8	7.8
	56.3	53.1	33.7	% Profit Before Taxes/Tangible Net Worth				28.8	21.1	53.8
(50)	18.8	(42) 11.2	(55) 13.9				(14)	12.1	(10) 7.9	(20) 20.7
	2.6	.7	−.2					−10.9	1.1	2.9
	17.0	12.8	14.6	% Profit Before Taxes/Total Assets				14.9	13.0	14.6
	5.2	4.0	5.2					6.9	2.6	5.1
	.2	.2	−1.3					−2.1	1.1	.8
	27.0	35.0	19.4	Sales/Net Fixed Assets				27.4	42.0	14.2
	13.5	16.0	11.9					18.5	10.3	6.9
	5.7	5.8	5.9					12.4	4.7	4.8
	2.9	2.5	2.4	Sales/Total Assets				3.2	2.8	2.1
	2.1	2.1	2.0					2.4	1.8	1.8
	1.6	1.6	1.5					1.7	1.2	1.6
	.9	.7	1.0	% Depr., Dep., Amort./Sales				1.0		1.4
(44)	1.7	(40) 1.5	(51) 1.7					1.5	(16)	1.8
	2.6	2.8	3.0					2.0		3.0
	1.5	3.1	3.1	% Officers', Directors', Owners' Comp/Sales						
(18)	2.7	(17) 6.6	(15) 5.6							
	9.8	10.7	11.9							
	1659378M	1500992M	3671619M	Net Sales ($)	2137M	14821M	17261M	109899M	176837M	3350664M
	1126403M	1008227M	2103864M	Total Assets ($)	1501M	9093M	6869M	67130M	111623M	1907648M

© RMA 2003

M = $ thousand   MM = $ million
See Pages 11 through 18 for Explanation of Ratios and Data

Current Data Sorted By Assets | Comparative Historical Data

0-500M	500M-2MM	2-10MM	10-50MM	50-100MM	100-250MM		4/1/98-3/31/99 ALL	4/1/99-3/31/00 ALL
						Type of Statement		
		4	5	2	1	Unqualified	14	14
		7	3			Reviewed	10	11
1	2	2				Compiled	4	7
1	1					Tax Returns		2
	2	8	8			Other	23	21
	11 (4/1-9/30/02)		36 (10/1/02-3/31/03)					
2	5	21	16	2	1	**NUMBER OF STATEMENTS**	51	55
%	%	%	%	%	%		%	%
						ASSETS		
		8.5	6.5			Cash & Equivalents	5.8	8.9
		32.4	22.1			Trade Receivables (net)	27.9	29.6
		28.8	22.6			Inventory	28.2	27.8
		2.6	2.8			All Other Current	2.7	1.7
		72.2	53.9			Total Current	64.7	67.9
		18.2	27.7			Fixed Assets (net)	24.2	21.8
		1.5	13.5			Intangibles (net)	5.4	4.7
		8.2	4.9			All Other Non-Current	5.8	5.6
		100.0	100.0			Total	100.0	100.0
						LIABILITIES		
		13.4	7.9			Notes Payable-Short Term	10.5	10.3
		3.7	4.8			Cur. Mat.-L/T/D	3.2	3.5
		15.3	8.3			Trade Payables	17.0	18.4
		.2	.1			Income Taxes Payable	.3	.5
		6.8	7.4			All Other Current	9.8	9.6
		39.4	28.5			Total Current	40.8	42.2
		12.7	15.4			Long Term Debt	17.2	14.4
		.3	1.2			Deferred Taxes	.5	.4
		5.4	4.4			All Other Non-Current	6.3	5.0
		42.1	50.4			Net Worth	35.2	37.9
		100.0	100.0			Total Liabilities & Net Worth	100.0	100.0
						INCOME DATA		
		100.0	100.0			Net Sales	100.0	100.0
		25.4	28.8			Gross Profit	25.7	31.8
		22.5	26.1			Operating Expenses	34.2	25.0
		2.9	2.7			Operating Profit	-8.5	6.8
		3.4	.3			All Other Expenses (net)	1.5	1.0
		-.4	2.4			Profit Before Taxes	-10.1	5.8
						RATIOS		
		2.5	3.7			Current	2.4	2.5
		2.0	2.1				1.7	1.6
		1.4	1.0				1.2	1.2
		1.6	2.3			Quick	1.4	1.4
		.9	1.0				.8	.9
		.6	.6				.6	.6
		44 8.2	44 8.2			Sales/Receivables	37 9.9	35 10.4
		53 6.9	53 6.9				48 7.6	45 8.1
		71 5.2	58 6.3				59 6.2	56 6.5
		41 8.9	38 9.7			Cost of Sales/Inventory	43 8.4	32 11.6
		79 4.6	74 4.9				67 5.4	62 5.9
		113 3.2	133 2.7				93 3.9	101 3.6
		15 24.5	21 17.2			Cost of Sales/Payables	23 15.9	18 19.9
		34 10.7	27 13.5				31 11.7	34 10.7
		51 7.2	37 10.0				51 7.2	50 7.3
		3.7	3.4			Sales/Working Capital	5.5	5.2
		6.4	4.7				8.2	9.1
		11.0	NM				34.6	21.1
		7.9	4.5			EBIT/Interest	(41) 6.1	(47) 8.6
		(19) 2.9	2.9				2.8	3.4
		-.3	1.0				1.6	1.4
						Net Profit + Depr., Dep., Amort./Cur. Mat. L /T/D	(12) 3.1	(16) 8.0
							2.3	1.6
							1.1	.9
		.1	.4			Fixed/Worth	.4	.2
		.5	.8				.9	.5
		.9	10.8				2.5	1.2
		.6	.5			Debt/Worth	1.4	1.0
		1.1	1.2				2.0	1.7
		4.6	20.0				7.3	4.3
		29.1	14.5			% Profit Before Taxes/Tangible Net Worth	(44) 68.9	(50) 64.6
		(20) 6.0	(13) 4.7				23.9	21.9
		-5.7	.0				4.9	7.2
		11.9	6.3			% Profit Before Taxes/Total Assets	14.8	21.5
		2.2	3.1				6.7	7.4
		-3.4	.1				.6	1.5
		25.0	8.5			Sales/Net Fixed Assets	29.2	26.2
		14.9	5.2				8.7	16.7
		6.2	3.5				4.1	5.1
		2.8	2.0			Sales/Total Assets	2.9	3.2
		2.0	1.4				1.8	2.2
		1.3	1.2				1.4	1.5
		1.1	2.4			% Depr., Dep., Amort./Sales	(39) .8	(48) .9
		(18) 2.1	(15) 3.9				1.8	1.8
		3.7	5.9				3.5	3.1
						% Officers', Directors', Owners' Comp/Sales	(10) 1.3	(13) 2.2
							3.5	4.9
							7.9	8.8
2553M	14553M	223942M	446637M	162546M	155903M	Net Sales ($)	2082763M	1826711M
845M	6636M	112705M	318122M	161408M	132669M	Total Assets ($)	1274020M	1216514M

M = $ thousand   MM = $ million
See Pages 11 through 18 for Explanation of Ratios and Data

Comparative Historical Data — Current Data Sorted By Sales

Type of Statement									
	9	10	12	Unqualified			1		5	6
	8	9	10	Reviewed		2		3	4	1
	5	5	5	Compiled		2	1		2	
	1	1	2	Tax Returns		1	1			
	17	11	18	Other	2	1		4	6	5

	4/1/00-3/31/01 ALL	4/1/01-3/31/02 ALL	4/1/02-3/31/03 ALL		0-1MM	11 (4/1-9/30/02) 1-3MM	3-5MM	36 (10/1/02-3/31/03) 5-10MM	10-25MM	25MM & OVER
NUMBER OF STATEMENTS	40	36	47		2	6	3	7	17	12
	%	%	%	**ASSETS**	%	%	%	%	%	%
	7.2	4.5	8.2	Cash & Equivalents					6.0	6.8
	30.7	26.6	26.6	Trade Receivables (net)					29.5	21.7
	25.5	29.2	27.0	Inventory					25.1	23.5
	3.1	1.2	3.9	All Other Current					3.2	1.8
	66.5	61.4	65.7	Total Current					63.8	53.8
	20.7	25.8	21.7	Fixed Assets (net)					23.0	26.1
	7.0	7.6	7.0	Intangibles (net)					7.5	15.6
	5.8	5.1	5.6	All Other Non-Current					5.7	4.6
	100.0	100.0	100.0	Total					100.0	100.0
				LIABILITIES						
	11.3	11.1	9.6	Notes Payable-Short Term					11.1	9.7
	4.9	6.6	4.2	Cur. Mat.-L/T/D					2.7	6.3
	16.5	12.6	12.8	Trade Payables					12.1	9.1
	.4	.4	.4	Income Taxes Payable					.2	1.1
	8.6	9.7	7.0	All Other Current					8.3	8.5
	41.8	40.3	34.0	Total Current					34.3	34.7
	17.3	19.9	14.7	Long Term Debt					15.2	13.9
	.6	.4	.6	Deferred Taxes					.5	1.1
	4.6	3.9	5.7	All Other Non-Current					4.9	6.6
	35.8	35.4	45.1	Net Worth					45.0	43.6
	100.0	100.0	100.0	Total Liabilities & Net Worth					100.0	100.0
				INCOME DATA						
	100.0	100.0	100.0	Net Sales					100.0	100.0
	29.1	29.1	28.0	Gross Profit					27.9	23.5
	22.8	26.0	24.9	Operating Expenses					25.1	21.1
	6.4	3.1	3.1	Operating Profit					2.8	2.4
	1.9	2.5	1.9	All Other Expenses (net)					2.7	.1
	4.5	.6	1.1	Profit Before Taxes					.1	2.3
				RATIOS						
	2.5	2.3	3.5	Current					2.9	3.7
	1.6	1.8	2.0						2.1	1.5
	1.1	1.2	1.4						1.4	.8
	1.3	1.4	1.8	Quick					1.9	2.1
	.9	.7	.9						1.0	.6
	.6	.5	.6						.6	.5
	43 8.6	40 9.1	40 9.0	Sales/Receivables					43 8.4	42 8.7
	51 7.1	48 7.6	52 7.1						51 7.1	52 7.0
	72 5.1	59 6.2	62 5.9						60 6.1	67 5.5
	36 10.2	41 8.8	38 9.5	Cost of Sales/Inventory					43 8.6	33 11.2
	58 6.3	82 4.4	79 4.6						60 6.1	85 4.3
	101 3.6	134 2.7	124 2.9						93 3.9	120 3.0
	21 17.2	23 15.8	21 17.2	Cost of Sales/Payables					21 17.3	22 16.3
	36 10.1	29 12.4	30 12.2						28 13.2	30 12.4
	58 6.3	47 7.7	42 8.6						38 9.7	37 10.0
	4.8	4.6	3.2	Sales/Working Capital					4.4	3.5
	9.1	8.1	6.2						6.5	7.6
	26.4	33.8	12.4						13.9	-23.1
	6.0	4.7	7.6	EBIT/Interest					17.4	4.1
(36)	2.0	2.0	(44) 3.5						4.3	2.6
	.4	-.8	.6						-1.1	1.0
	7.1	5.8	2.0	Net Profit + Depr., Dep., Amort./Cur. Mat. L/T/D						
(10)	3.7	(13) 1.6	(15) 1.2							
	.6	1.1	.9							
	.3	.3	.3	Fixed/Worth					.3	.4
	.8	.6	.6						.6	1.1
	1.7	1.8	1.4						4.2	NM
	1.0	1.0	.6	Debt/Worth					.6	.5
	2.2	1.8	1.3						.9	2.0
	5.8	4.5	5.7						13.1	NM
	68.8	24.4	23.4	% Profit Before Taxes/Tangible Net Worth					19.9	
(35)	31.3	(31) 5.9	(42) 5.3						(15) 5.9	
	-1.0	-2.8	-2.8						-2.5	
	14.6	7.6	8.1	% Profit Before Taxes/Total Assets					11.1	5.3
	5.1	2.7	3.3						3.9	2.6
	-2.5	-2.6	-1.6						-6.5	.3
	28.2	19.3	18.2	Sales/Net Fixed Assets					15.6	9.7
	13.8	8.5	9.5						8.6	5.2
	5.1	3.6	4.2						4.0	3.6
	2.6	2.4	2.5	Sales/Total Assets					2.8	1.9
	1.8	1.8	1.7						2.0	1.3
	1.4	1.4	1.2						1.3	1.2
	.7	.9	1.6	% Depr., Dep., Amort./Sales					1.6	2.6
(33)	2.1	(35) 2.6	(43) 2.6						(16) 2.7	(11) 3.9
	4.5	3.9	4.2						3.7	5.9
	1.6	1.3	2.2	% Officers', Directors', Owners' Comp/Sales						
(11)	4.0	(10) 4.8	(14) 5.3							
	5.2	5.8	6.9							
	1745025M	1045029M	1006134M	Net Sales ($)	1495M	12806M	12258M	53733M	286881M	638961M
	1248659M	682594M	732385M	Total Assets ($)	1422M	16655M	10231M	25797M	169215M	509065M

M = $ thousand   MM = $ million
See Pages 11 through 18 for Explanation of Ratios and Data

Current Data Sorted By Assets   **Comparative Historical Data**

Date ranges: **8 (4/1-9/30/02)** covers the 0-500M and 500M-2MM columns; **36 (10/1/02-3/31/03)** covers the 2-10MM through 100-250MM columns. Historical columns: **4/1/98-3/31/99 ALL** and **4/1/99-3/31/00 ALL**. ("DATA NOT AVAILABLE" is printed across the 50-100MM column.)

0-500M	500M-2MM	2-10MM	10-50MM	50-100MM	100-250MM		4/1/98-3/31/99 ALL	4/1/99-3/31/00 ALL
						Type of Statement		
		4	8			Unqualified	9	10
	4	6	2			Reviewed	13	11
	4	5				Compiled	8	12
1	1					Tax Returns	1	3
1		3	3		2	Other	12	19
2	9	18	13		2	**NUMBER OF STATEMENTS**	43	55
%	%	%	%	%	%	**ASSETS**	%	%
		4.8	8.0			Cash & Equivalents	7.8	10.3
		32.7	35.1			Trade Receivables (net)	35.2	35.5
		25.6	22.6			Inventory	23.1	22.2
		4.9	6.6			All Other Current	6.9	7.0
		68.1	72.4			Total Current	72.9	75.0
		23.8	20.2			Fixed Assets (net)	19.4	21.0
		3.5	1.8			Intangibles (net)	4.7	1.1
		4.6	5.6			All Other Non-Current	3.1	2.9
		100.0	100.0			Total	100.0	100.0
						LIABILITIES		
		12.5	7.5			Notes Payable-Short Term	12.9	13.7
		3.9	1.3			Cur. Mat.-L/T/D	2.4	3.8
		18.3	10.8			Trade Payables	17.4	18.5
		.1	.6			Income Taxes Payable	.3	.3
		7.9	14.1			All Other Current	12.9	12.4
		42.7	34.3			Total Current	45.9	48.6
		12.6	8.9			Long Term Debt	9.8	10.3
		.0	.2			Deferred Taxes	.3	.7
		2.8	6.8			All Other Non-Current	3.0	3.3
		41.9	49.9			Net Worth	40.9	37.1
		100.0	100.0			Total Liabilities & Net Worth	100.0	100.0
						INCOME DATA		
		100.0	100.0			Net Sales	100.0	100.0
		26.7	33.4			Gross Profit	28.7	32.1
		23.6	27.1			Operating Expenses	24.9	26.7
		3.1	6.3			Operating Profit	3.9	5.4
		.9	.8			All Other Expenses (net)	.4	.7
		2.2	5.6			Profit Before Taxes	3.4	4.6
						RATIOS		
		2.6	3.4			Current	2.3	2.7
		1.8	2.5				1.6	1.6
		1.3	1.6				1.2	1.1
		1.5	2.1			Quick	1.4	1.6
		1.0	1.2				.9	1.0
		.6	1.0				.6	.6
		43 8.4	47 7.8			Sales/Receivables	34 10.6	42 8.7
		49 7.4	58 6.3				52 7.0	51 7.1
		65 5.6	82 4.5				67 5.5	63 5.7
		26 14.0	47 7.8			Cost of Sales/Inventory	18 20.0	28 13.0
		48 7.7	62 5.9				39 9.3	42 8.7
		88 4.2	89 4.1				74 4.9	86 4.2
		25 14.9	20 18.1			Cost of Sales/Payables	22 16.9	19 18.8
		34 10.7	29 12.7				32 11.6	32 11.5
		42 8.7	34 10.8				49 7.5	57 6.4
		5.9	3.7			Sales/Working Capital	5.4	6.1
		7.6	4.3				12.5	9.8
		26.5	7.2				26.1	34.2
		15.6				EBIT/Interest	(36) 20.2	(50) 10.1
		4.6					3.7	3.7
		.0					1.4	1.4
						Net Profit + Depr., Dep., Amort./Cur. Mat. L/T/D	(15) 10.3	(17) 8.1
							1.7	3.5
							.9	1.8
		.2	.2			Fixed/Worth	.3	.2
		.5	.4				.5	.6
		1.6	.7				1.1	1.5
		.7	.6			Debt/Worth	.6	.6
		1.3	1.0				1.9	1.6
		5.2	1.5				4.6	6.4
	(16)	40.0	34.7			% Profit Before Taxes/Tangible Net Worth	(39) 41.2	(48) 52.7
		13.6	17.3				26.0	18.9
		-3.3	6.8				7.0	4.9
		13.5	18.5			% Profit Before Taxes/Total Assets	18.6	20.2
		3.4	10.9				4.8	6.3
		-1.7	1.5				.7	1.1
		35.1	18.7			Sales/Net Fixed Assets	41.8	40.1
		12.1	15.3				16.5	15.5
		5.5	4.7				7.6	6.8
		2.7	2.3			Sales/Total Assets	3.2	3.3
		2.2	1.6				2.6	2.4
		1.8	1.4				1.9	1.8
	(17)	.7	(12) 1.2			% Depr., Dep., Amort./Sales	(38) .7	(52) .5
		1.7	1.9				1.4	1.7
		2.1	4.0				2.5	2.6
	(10)	2.3				% Officers', Directors', Owners' Comp/Sales	(16) 2.2	(18) 3.8
		6.0					5.9	6.6
		10.2					13.1	9.4
635M	32684M	152461M	557510M		489773M	Net Sales ($)	970671M	910083M
107M	9719M	70500M	291702M		323680M	Total Assets ($)	633007M	535089M

M = $ thousand   MM = $ million
See Pages 11 through 18 for Explanation of Ratios and Data

Comparative Historical Data / Current Data Sorted By Sales

			Type of Statement						
9	13	12	Unqualified			1	1	3	7
25	13	12	Reviewed				4	5	3
10	7	9	Compiled		2	2	4		1
2	1	2	Tax Returns	2					
13	17	9	Other	1		5	2	1	
4/1/00-3/31/01	4/1/01-3/31/02	4/1/02-3/31/03				8 (4/1-9/30/02)	36 (10/1/02-3/31/03)		
ALL	ALL	ALL		0-1MM	1-3MM	3-5MM	5-10MM	10-25MM	25MM & OVER
59	51	44	**NUMBER OF STATEMENTS**	3	2	8	11	9	11
%	%	%	**ASSETS**	%	%	%	%	%	%
6.9	5.4	7.4	Cash & Equivalents				5.6		5.6
38.0	37.0	36.2	Trade Receivables (net)				37.5		34.6
22.3	23.4	21.7	Inventory				27.6		24.6
5.0	5.5	4.7	All Other Current				4.8		8.7
72.3	71.3	69.9	Total Current				75.5		73.5
18.7	18.6	22.7	Fixed Assets (net)				17.0		18.3
3.6	3.4	2.8	Intangibles (net)				2.4		4.5
5.4	6.1	4.7	All Other Non-Current				5.1		3.7
100.0	100.0	100.0	Total				100.0		100.0
			LIABILITIES						
16.6	14.7	11.2	Notes Payable-Short Term				11.7		8.4
2.3	3.6	2.8	Cur. Mat.-L/T/D				3.4		1.5
19.6	19.7	16.0	Trade Payables				24.4		11.5
.2	.3	.3	Income Taxes Payable				.1		.7
11.3	11.3	10.3	All Other Current				7.2		12.8
50.0	49.6	40.6	Total Current				46.7		34.8
11.3	10.1	10.4	Long Term Debt				8.8		12.0
.5	.2	.1	Deferred Taxes				.0		.3
3.9	3.9	3.3	All Other Non-Current				1.2		3.7
34.3	35.7	45.6	Net Worth				43.2		49.2
100.0	100.0	100.0	Total Liabilities & Net Worth				100.0		100.0
			INCOME DATA						
100.0	100.0	100.0	Net Sales				100.0		100.0
28.0	29.7	30.4	Gross Profit				28.8		31.6
22.9	24.3	26.7	Operating Expenses				23.6		24.9
5.0	5.5	3.7	Operating Profit				5.2		6.7
1.3	1.4	.6	All Other Expenses (net)				.8		.6
3.8	4.1	3.0	Profit Before Taxes				4.4		6.1
			RATIOS						
2.4	2.4	3.1					3.1		3.3
1.4	1.5	1.8	Current				1.9		2.5
1.0	1.1	1.3					1.3		1.8
1.3	1.5	1.6					1.5		1.6
.8	.8	1.1	Quick				.9		1.2
.6	.6	.7					.7		1.0
44 8.4	39 9.5	44 8.4					38 9.6		46 7.9
53 6.9	50 7.3	54 6.8	Sales/Receivables				53 6.9		58 6.3
75 4.9	66 5.5	71 5.2					74 4.9		78 4.7
29 12.6	27 13.6	22 16.5					34 10.6		47 7.8
55 6.6	54 6.7	47 7.7	Cost of Sales/Inventory				45 8.1		70 5.2
79 4.6	71 5.1	76 4.8					85 4.3		93 3.9
20 18.6	20 18.0	21 17.1					21 17.5		23 15.9
34 10.6	33 11.2	30 12.1	Cost of Sales/Payables				35 10.6		29 12.7
47 7.7	52 7.0	41 9.0					71 5.1		37 10.0
5.5	6.5	4.2					6.4		3.5
12.5	9.3	7.3	Sales/Working Capital				7.7		4.3
-200.8	82.8	20.0					21.5		7.7
6.3	9.6	17.5					29.1		
(56) 2.7	(49) 3.3	(38) 4.5	EBIT/Interest				12.0		
1.2	1.0	1.1					1.2		
3.9	5.9	5.7	Net Profit + Depr., Dep.,						
(12) 2.1	(19) 3.1	(17) 2.3	Amort./Cur. Mat. L/T/D						
.0	.7	-.3							
.2	.3	.2					.1		.2
.6	.5	.4	Fixed/Worth				.2		.4
2.2	.9	1.0					1.1		.7
.8	.8	.6					.6		.6
2.6	2.1	1.1	Debt/Worth				1.5		1.0
11.5	5.1	2.9					2.9		3.1
54.8	58.7	38.1	% Profit Before Taxes/Tangible				(10) 42.7		61.9
(54) 21.6	(47) 20.8	(42) 16.4	Net Worth				24.7		23.9
5.1	3.5	3.2					3.7		9.8
12.1	12.5	14.9	% Profit Before Taxes/Total				14.5		19.9
4.8	6.4	8.3	Assets				12.1		11.3
1.1	.0	.3					.8		1.3
45.1	35.2	37.3					86.8		18.7
17.7	13.9	14.1	Sales/Net Fixed Assets				34.1		15.3
5.7	7.3	5.4					9.3		6.3
3.0	3.4	3.0					3.2		2.4
2.5	2.3	2.3	Sales/Total Assets				2.5		1.6
1.8	1.7	1.6					1.8		1.4
.8	.7	1.0					(10) .3		1.2
(52) 1.5	(47) 1.6	(40) 1.7	% Depr., Dep., Amort./Sales				1.2		1.7
2.8	2.8	3.1					1.7		3.9
4.3	.8	1.3							
(22) 7.1	(19) 5.1	(18) 6.0	% Officers', Directors', Owners' Comp/Sales						
9.4	8.8	11.8							
1311627M	1322964M	1233063M	Net Sales ($)	1498M	4901M	31142M	87677M	142823M	965022M
978033M	821729M	695708M	Total Assets ($)	739M	1772M	13285M	36974M	81189M	561749M

© RMA 2003

M = $ thousand   MM = $ million
See Pages 11 through 18 for Explanation of Ratios and Data

Current Data Sorted By Assets   Comparative Historical Data

						Type of Statement		
1	1	6	5	4	2	Unqualified	27	17
1	3	10	2			Reviewed	16	17
3	6	5			1	Compiled	18	12
3	1					Tax Returns	1	2
1	2	16	3	1	3	Other	32	32
	21 (4/1-9/30/02)		59 (10/1/02-3/31/03)				4/1/98-3/31/99	4/1/99-3/31/00
0-500M	500M-2MM	2-10MM	10-50MM	50-100MM	100-250MM		ALL	ALL
9	13	37	10	5	6	NUMBER OF STATEMENTS	94	80
%	%	%	%	%	%	ASSETS	%	%
	8.8	7.5	5.0			Cash & Equivalents	6.3	6.7
	33.9	25.4	30.2			Trade Receivables (net)	32.7	30.1
	36.6	31.4	29.8			Inventory	27.4	27.8
	.5	3.4	3.4			All Other Current	3.1	3.3
	79.9	67.6	68.3			Total Current	69.5	67.8
	13.7	19.4	18.7			Fixed Assets (net)	22.4	22.5
	2.0	8.3	2.4			Intangibles (net)	3.3	4.0
	4.4	4.6	10.5			All Other Non-Current	4.9	5.7
	100.0	100.0	100.0			Total	100.0	100.0
						LIABILITIES		
	14.6	12.6	14.0			Notes Payable-Short Term	11.4	9.6
	1.9	3.1	1.7			Cur. Mat.-L/T/D	3.0	3.4
	17.6	13.0	9.6			Trade Payables	14.8	14.6
	.5	.2	.1			Income Taxes Payable	.5	.5
	7.3	11.7	16.5			All Other Current	11.5	9.4
	41.9	40.6	41.9			Total Current	41.2	37.5
	11.4	7.8	3.0			Long Term Debt	13.3	13.2
	.1	.5	.2			Deferred Taxes	.7	.7
	.2	8.5	2.1			All Other Non-Current	5.0	5.9
	46.4	42.7	52.8			Net Worth	39.9	42.6
	100.0	100.0	100.0			Total Liabilities & Net Worth	100.0	100.0
						INCOME DATA		
	100.0	100.0	100.0			Net Sales	100.0	100.0
	40.7	30.6	32.3			Gross Profit	36.9	34.5
	36.6	28.2	25.2			Operating Expenses	34.7	28.7
	4.1	2.4	7.1			Operating Profit	2.1	5.8
	.8	1.5	.7			All Other Expenses (net)	.9	1.4
	3.3	.8	6.4			Profit Before Taxes	1.2	4.3
						RATIOS		
	2.7	2.2	3.1				2.9	2.8
	2.1	1.7	1.7			Current	1.9	1.9
	1.7	1.2	1.3				1.2	1.3
	1.9	1.4	1.8				1.6	1.6
	.9	.8	.8			Quick	1.1	1.1
	.8	.5	.5				.7	.7

													Sales/Receivables				

		37	9.8	40	9.1	45	8.0	
		46	7.9	51	7.2	57	6.4	Sales/Receivables
		57	6.4	62	5.9	77	4.7	
		40	9.2	42	8.8
		49	7.5	49	7.4
		66	5.6	63	5.8

		55	6.7	46	8.0	53	6.8	
		120	3.0	85	4.3	97	3.7	Cost of Sales/Inventory
		156	2.3	147	2.5	129	2.8	
		38	9.7	39	9.4
		87	4.2	88	4.2
		124	2.9	136	2.7

		29	12.7	18	20.0	11	34.3	
		36	10.1	31	11.6	26	14.1	Cost of Sales/Payables
		52	7.1	53	6.8	39	9.5	
		19	19.2	23	16.1
		30	12.0	34	10.9
		47	7.8	48	7.6

	4.0	4.1	4.0			
	5.7	7.6	6.5			Sales/Working Capital
	9.2	20.3	14.5			

4.0	3.9
7.0	5.8
19.1	14.2

	20.7		5.4		40.5			
	1.5	(34)	2.4		17.4		EBIT/Interest	
	-1.3		-.6		4.3			
	(82)	14.3	(73)	8.5
		3.3		3.3
		.9		1.4

					Net Profit + Depr., Dep., Amort./Cur. Mat. L /T/D		
	(37)	6.7	(27)	13.4
		2.8		2.7
		1.3		1.7

.1	.3	.2			
.2	.6	.4			Fixed/Worth
1.3	1.2	.5			

.2	.3
.4	.5
1.2	1.2

.5	.9	.4			
.8	2.0	1.2			Debt/Worth
3.4	4.7	1.9			

.6	.5
1.2	1.2
4.3	5.0

	33.4		24.6		48.8		
	7.0	(34)	13.1		25.8	% Profit Before Taxes/Tangible Net Worth	
	-8.1		-8.7		6.8		
	(86)	37.2	(72)	36.4
		20.0		16.2
		1.4		4.4

16.5	9.4	21.1			
2.5	3.9	13.5			% Profit Before Taxes/Total Assets
-3.2	-3.8	4.3			

16.6	14.9
6.9	5.9
-.1	.6

50.8	19.0	21.0			
33.1	13.2	10.2			Sales/Net Fixed Assets
16.7	6.2	6.0			

25.3	20.9
12.7	10.1
7.0	5.4

3.5	2.2	2.2			
2.2	1.9	1.8			Sales/Total Assets
1.8	1.3	1.6			

2.7	2.4
2.1	2.0
1.8	1.5

	.8		1.5		1.4		
(12)	1.1	(34)	2.5		2.7	% Depr., Dep., Amort./Sales	
	2.0		3.4		3.4		
	(83)	1.2	(69)	1.4
		1.9		2.1
		3.3		3.4

			2.6				
		(12)	3.4			% Officers', Directors', Owners' Comp/Sales	
			9.1				
	(30)	4.8	(31)	2.5
		6.4		4.5
		9.1		6.2

11406M	43394M	303291M	317134M	356787M	1101999M	Net Sales ($)	1689968M	2303850M
2983M	17902M	170753M	167480M	355990M	1000587M	Total Assets ($)	1037816M	1566961M

M = $ thousand   MM = $ million
See Pages 11 through 18 for Explanation of Ratios and Data

Comparative Historical Data | Current Data Sorted By Sales

Current data periods: **21 (4/1-9/30/02)** and **59 (10/1/02-3/31/03)**. M = $ thousand   MM = $ million

4/1/00-3/31/01 ALL	4/1/01-3/31/02 ALL	4/1/02-3/31/03 ALL		0-1MM	1-3MM	3-5MM	5-10MM	10-25MM	25MM & OVER
			Type of Statement						
14	17	19	Unqualified	1			4	4	10
15	21	16	Reviewed	1	1	1	9	3	1
19	18	15	Compiled	2	6	1	5		1
3	1	4	Tax Returns	1	2	1			
23	32	26	Other	2	7	7	7	6	4
74	89	80	**NUMBER OF STATEMENTS**	5	11	10	25	13	16
%	%	%	**ASSETS**	%	%	%	%	%	%
8.3	8.0	8.6	Cash & Equivalents		9.7	12.7	5.8	3.2	11.0
32.1	28.2	27.1	Trade Receivables (net)		40.0	18.4	27.1	30.5	21.6
32.6	30.0	31.1	Inventory		28.3	38.0	31.7	36.6	20.4
2.9	3.9	2.3	All Other Current		.4	1.3	4.6	1.6	2.2
75.9	70.1	69.2	Total Current		78.4	70.4	69.1	71.9	55.2
16.6	19.4	18.5	Fixed Assets (net)		14.9	13.2	19.7	20.8	22.1
2.5	5.3	6.7	Intangibles (net)		2.3	12.5	6.4	3.5	11.2
4.9	5.2	5.6	All Other Non-Current		4.4	3.9	4.8	3.8	11.5
100.0	100.0	100.0	Total		100.0	100.0	100.0	100.0	100.0
			LIABILITIES						
10.2	9.2	11.3	Notes Payable-Short Term		14.2	6.7	12.7	19.6	4.2
2.9	3.8	2.6	Cur. Mat.-L/T/D		2.6	3.4	2.5	2.1	3.2
13.8	11.5	13.0	Trade Payables		16.1	12.4	13.4	12.5	9.8
.8	.2	.3	Income Taxes Payable		.0	.6	.2	.3	.7
11.1	10.3	11.3	All Other Current		12.1	14.5	10.7	10.9	11.7
38.8	35.0	38.5	Total Current		45.1	37.7	39.6	45.3	29.6
10.0	14.8	11.4	Long Term Debt		13.7	3.5	9.2	5.1	9.1
.4	.4	.3	Deferred Taxes		.1	.2	.4	.6	.4
5.0	4.4	8.9	All Other Non-Current		.2	10.0	6.4	4.6	13.3
45.8	45.4	40.9	Net Worth		40.9	48.6	44.4	44.4	47.6
100.0	100.0	100.0	Total Liabilities & Net Worth		100.0	100.0	100.0	100.0	100.0
			INCOME DATA						
100.0	100.0	100.0	Net Sales		100.0	100.0	100.0	100.0	100.0
36.2	35.3	32.3	Gross Profit		41.3	34.4	29.4	34.2	25.6
29.5	30.7	28.4	Operating Expenses		38.8	30.0	28.3	26.2	20.9
6.6	4.6	3.9	Operating Profit		2.5	4.4	1.1	8.1	4.8
.8	1.5	1.3	All Other Expenses (net)		1.0	1.0	1.5	1.1	1.6
5.8	3.1	2.6	Profit Before Taxes		1.5	3.4	-.4	7.0	3.1
			RATIOS						
3.1 / 2.1 / 1.5	3.6 / 2.1 / 1.4	3.1 / 1.8 / 1.3	Current		2.2 / 1.8 / 1.4	4.4 / 1.8 / 1.0	2.6 / 1.8 / 1.3	2.5 / 1.4 / 1.2	3.3 / 1.9 / 1.5
1.8 / 1.2 / .7	1.9 / 1.1 / .7	1.6 / .9 / .6	Quick		1.8 / 1.1 / .8	2.1 / .6 / .4	1.4 / .8 / .6	1.1 / .8 / .5	1.8 / .9 / .7
44 8.2 / 54 6.8 / 64 5.7	40 9.1 / 49 7.4 / 58 6.3	40 9.1 / 51 7.2 / 63 5.8	Sales/Receivables		35 10.5 / 44 8.2 / 62 5.9	0 UND / 46 7.9 / 58 6.3	44 8.3 / 51 7.2 / 63 5.8	47 7.7 / 51 7.1 / 61 6.0	42 8.6 / 60 6.1 / 76 4.8
51 7.1 / 95 3.9 / 132 2.8	58 6.3 / 87 4.2 / 137 2.7	44 8.2 / 93 3.9 / 133 2.7	Cost of Sales/Inventory		40 9.1 / 72 5.0 / 149 2.5	40 9.1 / 79 4.6 / 150 2.4	46 8.0 / 82 4.5 / 149 2.4	73 5.0 / 100 3.6 / 127 2.9	40 9.2 / 84 4.4 / 117 3.1
19 19.3 / 32 11.5 / 50 7.2	17 21.1 / 29 12.5 / 42 8.7	17 21.4 / 32 11.6 / 50 7.2	Cost of Sales/Payables		26 14.0 / 31 11.8 / 57 6.5	2 150.8 / 32 11.5 / 57 6.4	18 20.2 / 30 12.2 / 49 7.4	12 30.0 / 38 9.6 / 42 8.8	20 18.2 / 33 10.9 / 49 7.4
3.8 / 5.7 / 9.3	3.4 / 6.2 / 9.7	3.9 / 7.1 / 13.9	Sales/Working Capital		4.1 / 9.1 / 15.3	3.7 / 8.0 / -140.0	3.8 / 6.9 / 13.3	4.8 / 8.5 / 21.3	3.1 / 5.1 / 8.2
(64) 13.4 / 4.9 / 1.9	(79) 7.2 / 2.0 / .7	(72) 7.1 / 3.0 / -.1	EBIT/Interest		(10) 33.5 / 1.4 / -5.9		(24) 5.4 / 2.1 / -.3	17.4 / 5.2 / 2.2	(14) 12.2 / 3.3 / .3
(22) 9.5 / 3.4 / 1.0	(26) 4.6 / 1.8 / .7	(24) 5.3 / 1.7 / .5	Net Profit + Depr., Dep., Amort./Cur. Mat. L/T/D						(10) 7.6 / 1.8 / .8
.2 / .3 / .7	.2 / .4 / 1.1	.2 / .5 / 1.0	Fixed/Worth		.1 / .3 / .7	.2 / .3 / NM	.2 / .4 / 1.0	.4 / .5 / 1.1	.2 / .5 / 3.0
.5 / 1.2 / 2.5	.5 / 1.4 / 3.8	.6 / 1.7 / 3.3	Debt/Worth		.6 / 1.9 / 3.3	.3 / 1.2 / NM	.9 / 1.9 / 2.5	.7 / 1.7 / 4.3	.4 / 1.3 / 4.3
(71) 39.7 / 16.4 / 8.6	(84) 36.1 / 12.2 / -.6	(72) 32.7 / 13.1 / -7.2	% Profit Before Taxes/Tangible Net Worth		32.7 / 7.0 / -8.3		(24) 20.6 / 5.9 / -9.3	67.6 / 24.0 / 14.3	(13) 27.2 / 7.2 / -6.6
17.1 / 7.8 / 3.0	12.9 / 3.0 / -.7	12.6 / 4.9 / -2.2	% Profit Before Taxes/Total Assets		12.7 / 2.5 / -5.9	23.5 / 10.3 / -6.2	6.4 / 3.4 / -3.5	18.4 / 7.6 / 4.9	9.0 / 5.3 / -1.3
25.8 / 15.4 / 9.0	21.8 / 13.0 / 7.3	24.2 / 13.3 / 5.7	Sales/Net Fixed Assets		48.7 / 33.1 / 16.9	42.3 / 20.3 / 10.1	22.4 / 14.5 / 4.7	14.0 / 10.0 / 7.8	12.7 / 5.7 / 3.3
2.5 / 2.1 / 1.8	2.7 / 2.0 / 1.4	2.4 / 1.9 / 1.3	Sales/Total Assets		3.8 / 3.3 / 1.7	2.8 / 1.9 / 1.3	2.7 / 1.8 / 1.3	2.2 / 2.1 / 1.7	1.8 / 1.3 / .9
(63) 1.0 / 1.9 / 3.0	(79) 1.0 / 2.1 / 3.7	(72) 1.2 / 2.3 / 3.6	% Depr., Dep., Amort./Sales				(24) 1.3 / 2.0 / 3.7	(12) 2.4 / 2.8 / 3.3	(15) 2.3 / 3.8 / 6.7
(30) 3.1 / 4.7 / 8.2	(29) 2.6 / 4.2 / 6.9	(26) 2.6 / 4.0 / 8.3	% Officers', Directors', Owners' Comp/Sales						
1359444M	2160234M	2134011M	Net Sales ($)	2677M	25660M	42451M	170302M	226657M	1666264M
797774M	1597313M	1715695M	Total Assets ($)	1284M	10761M	26212M	99601M	116023M	1461814M

M = $ thousand   MM = $ million
See Pages 11 through 18 for Explanation of Ratios and Data

Current Data Sorted By Assets **Comparative Historical Data**

0-500M	500M-2MM	2-10MM	10-50MM	50-100MM	100-250MM	Type of Statement	ALL	ALL
	1	4	3	3	1	Unqualified	22	13
2	2	14	1			Reviewed	14	17
	6	1	1			Compiled	10	10
	2	1				Tax Returns	3	2
	5	5	8		1	Other	16	16
							4/1/98-3/31/99	4/1/99-3/31/00
	8 (4/1-9/30/02)		53 (10/1/02-3/31/03)				ALL	ALL
2	16	25	13	3	2	**NUMBER OF STATEMENTS**	65	58
%	%	%	%	%	%	**ASSETS**	%	%
	8.2	7.9	7.7			Cash & Equivalents	7.4	5.4
	34.1	23.4	22.0			Trade Receivables (net)	28.9	31.9
	26.4	35.8	21.4			Inventory	27.3	31.3
	1.1	2.1	3.3			All Other Current	.9	1.1
	69.9	69.1	54.5			Total Current	64.5	69.8
	23.3	24.6	28.8			Fixed Assets (net)	25.5	20.6
	4.5	2.0	7.9			Intangibles (net)	2.9	4.0
	2.3	4.2	8.9			All Other Non-Current	7.0	5.7
	100.0	100.0	100.0			Total	100.0	100.0
						LIABILITIES		
	16.9	14.0	9.6			Notes Payable-Short Term	7.7	13.1
	6.4	2.9	4.5			Cur. Mat.-L/T/D	4.4	3.5
	15.4	15.3	8.7			Trade Payables	15.8	17.7
	.3	.3	.0			Income Taxes Payable	.7	.3
	6.0	9.6	7.0			All Other Current	8.1	11.5
	44.9	42.1	29.8			Total Current	36.7	46.2
	21.7	14.5	8.6			Long Term Debt	20.2	12.5
	.0	.5	.7			Deferred Taxes	.4	.5
	5.4	6.0	4.3			All Other Non-Current	2.8	4.0
	28.0	37.0	56.6			Net Worth	39.9	36.8
	100.0	100.0	100.0			Total Liabilities & Net Worth	100.0	100.0
						INCOME DATA		
	100.0	100.0	100.0			Net Sales	100.0	100.0
	30.1	25.6	24.1			Gross Profit	29.9	26.6
	29.7	23.6	23.8			Operating Expenses	22.6	25.8
	.4	2.0	.3			Operating Profit	7.4	.8
	1.6	1.0	-.5			All Other Expenses (net)	.9	-3.0
	-1.2	1.0	.8			Profit Before Taxes	6.4	3.8
						RATIOS		
	2.7	2.6	3.1				2.5	2.2
	1.7	1.5	1.6			Current	2.0	1.6
	1.0	1.1	1.5				1.3	1.2
	1.8	1.3	2.1				1.7	1.2
	.9	.6	.8			Quick	1.0	.8
	.5	.4	.7				.7	.6
34 10.8	33 11.1	39 9.3					39 9.3	42 8.7
43 8.6	42 8.8	49 7.5				Sales/Receivables	47 7.8	50 7.4
56 6.5	46 7.9	59 6.2					53 6.9	58 6.3
38 9.6	62 5.9	41 8.8					38 9.6	39 9.4
52 7.0	95 3.8	56 6.5				Cost of Sales/Inventory	65 5.6	62 5.9
81 4.5	136 2.7	71 5.1					88 4.1	95 3.8
21 17.2	19 18.8	13 27.3					20 18.6	25 14.6
30 12.0	34 10.9	26 14.1				Cost of Sales/Payables	30 12.3	33 11.0
37 9.8	42 8.6	36 10.2					42 8.8	45 8.0
	5.7	3.6	5.0				4.6	6.2
	9.6	12.3	6.1			Sales/Working Capital	8.2	9.3
	NM	51.2	11.4				16.7	18.9
	2.0	10.4	28.6				18.6	8.5
	.8	(22) 1.8	(10) 4.8			EBIT/Interest	(59) 5.3	(56) 3.0
	-.8	-.8	-.9				1.8	1.4
		3.5				Net Profit + Depr., Dep.,	9.9	10.6
		(12) 1.7				Amort./Cur. Mat. L./T/D	(23) 5.6	(15) 2.7
		.6					2.4	1.3
	.2	.1	.3				.3	.3
	.7	.9	.5			Fixed/Worth	.6	.5
	2.5	2.5	1.2				1.4	1.0
	1.2	.7	.3				.6	.9
	2.5	2.6	.9			Debt/Worth	1.5	1.6
	7.7	5.3	1.5				3.5	4.5
	15.0	25.0	23.9				43.4	49.8
(14) -.1	(24) 8.7	(12) 9.9				% Profit Before Taxes/Tangible Net Worth	(59) 29.4	(51) 17.1
	-22.9	-14.1	-4.4				11.7	2.8
	1.8	14.3	12.8				22.1	17.0
	-.5	3.9	5.1			% Profit Before Taxes/Total Assets	12.5	5.8
	-8.5	-4.7	-1.9				4.3	.8
	41.6	21.2	13.6				17.3	25.9
	16.1	9.6	6.4			Sales/Net Fixed Assets	9.9	13.6
	7.5	5.6	3.1				6.0	6.1
	3.4	2.7	2.3				2.8	3.1
	2.7	1.9	1.5			Sales/Total Assets	2.3	2.1
	1.8	1.4	1.2				1.9	1.7
	1.5	1.3	1.4				1.2	1.3
(15) 2.6	(24) 2.4	(12) 2.6				% Depr., Dep., Amort./Sales	(60) 2.1	(48) 2.0
	5.1	3.6	4.6				3.4	3.0
	2.3						1.7	2.0
(11) 4.9						% Officers', Directors', Owners' Comp/Sales	(22) 3.5	(18) 4.3
	8.9						6.1	7.3
1349M	47271M	314301M	400549M	262948M	436080M	Net Sales ($)	1703101M	1005818M
691M	18723M	144265M	255695M	200372M	320519M	Total Assets ($)	915216M	556714M

M = $ thousand   MM = $ million
See Pages 11 through 18 for Explanation of Ratios and Data

Comparative Historical Data　　　　　　　　　Current Data Sorted By Sales

			Type of Statement						
9	9	12	Unqualified			1	1	3	7
14	16	19	Reviewed	2	2	2	8	4	1
8	12	8	Compiled	1	3	2	1	1	
3	4	3	Tax Returns		1	1			1
15	21	19	Other	1		4		9	4
4/1/00-	4/1/01-	4/1/02-			8 (4/1-9/30/02)		53 (10/1/02-3/31/03)		
3/31/01	3/31/02	3/31/03		0-1MM	1-3MM	3-5MM	5-10MM	10-25MM	25MM & OVER
ALL	ALL	ALL							
49	62	61	NUMBER OF STATEMENTS	4	7	10	10	17	13
%	%	%	ASSETS	%	%	%	%	%	%
6.1	8.2	7.3	Cash & Equivalents			10.6	11.4	8.1	4.9
31.0	27.3	25.9	Trade Receivables (net)			29.9	21.7	20.4	28.6
28.0	28.3	28.7	Inventory			37.8	31.9	28.8	24.0
1.2	1.9	2.0	All Other Current			1.7	1.0	3.0	2.2
66.3	65.7	63.9	Total Current			80.1	66.0	60.3	59.7
24.3	24.7	25.7	Fixed Assets (net)			17.0	25.0	26.0	26.2
3.9	4.8	5.2	Intangibles (net)			1.1	3.6	5.3	8.5
5.5	4.8	5.2	All Other Non-Current			1.8	5.3	8.4	5.6
100.0	100.0	100.0	Total			100.0	100.0	100.0	100.0
			LIABILITIES						
9.6	14.6	12.8	Notes Payable-Short Term			17.6	17.6	11.8	5.9
4.8	3.2	4.3	Cur. Mat.-L/T/D			3.5	3.0	4.3	2.4
16.9	11.9	13.3	Trade Payables			13.5	12.4	13.8	10.9
.1	.7	.3	Income Taxes Payable			.4	.6	.1	.3
7.9	7.6	8.4	All Other Current			6.4	5.9	9.9	9.5
39.2	38.1	39.0	Total Current			41.4	39.5	39.9	29.0
13.1	9.2	15.9	Long Term Debt			6.8	11.8	13.1	12.8
.3	.3	.4	Deferred Taxes			.3	.5	.7	.2
4.5	6.2	6.8	All Other Non-Current			8.7	11.7	2.5	8.0
42.9	46.1	37.9	Net Worth			42.8	36.4	43.8	50.1
100.0	100.0	100.0	Total Liabilities & Net Worth			100.0	100.0	100.0	100.0
			INCOME DATA						
100.0	100.0	100.0	Net Sales			100.0	100.0	100.0	100.0
31.2	30.8	27.0	Gross Profit			29.3	31.5	21.8	26.3
23.4	27.0	25.8	Operating Expenses			28.9	27.7	21.3	22.8
7.8	3.8	1.2	Operating Profit			.4	3.8	.5	3.4
.9	1.4	1.0	All Other Expenses (net)			1.2	.9	.2	1.0
6.9	2.4	.2	Profit Before Taxes			−.8	2.9	.2	2.4
			RATIOS						
2.7	2.8	2.6				3.2	4.6	2.7	2.9
1.8	1.9	1.6	Current			2.0	1.4	1.5	2.2
1.2	1.1	1.1				1.5	1.0	1.1	1.7
1.5	1.7	1.4				2.0	2.8	1.5	1.8
1.0	.9	.7	Quick			1.0	.6	.7	1.1
.6	.6	.5				1.5	.5	.4	.7
38　9.5	35　10.4	38　9.7		31　11.7	33　11.0	39　9.3	41　9.0		
47　7.7	42　8.6	45　8.1	Sales/Receivables	41　9.0	39　9.4	47　7.7	48　7.6		
61　6.0	54　6.8	52　7.0		45　8.1	45　8.1	63　5.8	53　6.8		
32　11.3	42　8.6	46　7.9		41　9.0	63　5.8	43　8.5	45　8.1		
55　6.7	66　5.5	66　5.5	Cost of Sales/Inventory	52　7.0	81　4.5	66　5.5	53　6.9		
99　3.7	90　4.1	98　3.7		109　3.4	145　2.5	108　3.4	76　4.8		
22　16.4	16　22.4	21　17.8		13　27.4	16　23.0	26　14.1	11　32.4		
33　11.2	25　14.6	28　13.0	Cost of Sales/Payables	25　14.5	30　12.1	40　9.2	21　17.1		
50　7.3	40　9.0	40　9.1		34　10.8	40　9.1	48　7.6	28　13.2		
5.1	4.5	4.7				5.2	2.4	4.3	4.7
9.0	6.9	8.8	Sales/Working Capital			6.7	16.8	10.1	6.2
23.6	43.0	34.6				13.7	NM	38.0	10.6
	14.5		6.1		7.3			3.9		28.5		13.2
(43)　2.8	(55)　2.7	(55)　1.6	EBIT/Interest			.4	(15)　6.4	(10)　2.9	
1.6	.2	−.7				−1.7		−.8	1.1
		4.5	Net Profit + Depr., Dep.,					10.1	
	(22)　1.7		Amort./Cur. Mat. L/T/D				(10)　2.3		
		.6						−.1	
.3	.2	.2				.2	.1	.2	.3
.6	.5	.9	Fixed/Worth			.4	1.5	.8	.5
1.6	1.4	2.5				.7	4.0	1.9	1.2
.6	.5	.8				.7	.6	.4	.6
1.2	1.1	2.0	Debt/Worth			1.6	4.2	1.8	1.1
4.5	3.4	5.9				3.0	12.0	3.5	3.7
59.0	27.8	24.1				23.8		28.9	26.6
(45)　32.1	(56)　13.9	(54)　5.6	% Profit Before Taxes/Tangible Net Worth			−5.4	(16)　15.2	(11)　9.8	
5.8	3.0	−12.5				−28.6		−43.5	2.8
26.3	11.4	11.0				12.2	9.5	16.3	11.1
7.8	5.2	1.8	% Profit Before Taxes/Total Assets			−1.9	3.9	6.1	4.6
1.8	−.2	−4.7				−9.1	−1.1	−6.1	−.1
27.8	24.4	21.2				37.5	20.4	13.9	14.9
9.8	10.6	9.5	Sales/Net Fixed Assets			19.1	10.3	6.7	8.2
6.3	5.3	5.1				11.5	4.0	4.3	4.1
3.2	3.0	2.8				3.6	2.6	2.2	2.8
2.4	2.1	1.9	Sales/Total Assets			2.8	2.0	1.5	2.0
1.7	1.6	1.3				2.2	1.4	1.4	1.4
.9	1.1	1.4					1.2	1.3	1.4
(40)　1.9	(55)　2.1	(57)　2.5	% Depr., Dep., Amort./Sales				2.3 (16)	2.7 (11)	3.0
3.2	4.0	4.3					4.0	4.5	4.0
1.9	2.5	3.0							
(18)　3.4	(24)　4.5	(19)　6.8	% Officers', Directors', Owners' Comp/Sales						
7.6	9.6	8.9							
1139771M	1576117M	1462498M	Net Sales ($)	2760M	17066M	40393M	79546M	282944M	1039789M
711333M	986444M	940265M	Total Assets ($)	2468M	10923M	16450M	45233M	211253M	653938M

© RMA 2003

M = $ thousand　　MM = $ million
See Pages 11 through 18 for Explanation of Ratios and Data

Current Data Sorted By Assets   Comparative Historical Data

0-500M	500M-2MM	2-10MM	10-50MM	50-100MM	100-250MM	Type of Statement	4/1/98-3/31/99 ALL	4/1/99-3/31/00 ALL
	3	17	11	3	4	Unqualified	47	42
	11	21	4	1	1	Reviewed	28	38
3	10	5	1			Compiled	24	24
5	6	3			1	Tax Returns	12	12
2	8	27	15	2	2	Other	44	33
	33 (4/1-9/30/02)		133 (10/1/02-3/31/03)					
10	38	73	31	6	8	NUMBER OF STATEMENTS	155	149
%	%	%	%	%	%	ASSETS	%	%
12.8	12.9	8.2	8.3			Cash & Equivalents	8.6	8.1
37.2	33.6	29.5	25.5			Trade Receivables (net)	33.1	31.0
26.1	26.5	29.7	24.8			Inventory	27.8	29.4
.8	2.7	2.2	6.3			All Other Current	3.0	3.1
76.9	75.7	69.6	64.9			Total Current	72.4	71.5
11.9	18.3	20.1	20.3			Fixed Assets (net)	17.7	17.9
.9	2.3	4.9	8.4			Intangibles (net)	4.3	4.0
10.2	3.7	5.5	6.4			All Other Non-Current	5.5	6.5
100.0	100.0	100.0	100.0			Total	100.0	100.0
						LIABILITIES		
12.3	11.0	12.4	4.4			Notes Payable-Short Term	9.5	9.4
3.9	3.1	3.9	5.8			Cur. Mat.-L/T/D	2.9	3.6
31.9	17.1	14.1	11.5			Trade Payables	16.3	17.7
.0	.2	.5	.4			Income Taxes Payable	.3	.7
21.5	7.5	10.3	14.9			All Other Current	12.6	10.3
69.6	38.9	41.1	36.9			Total Current	41.6	41.7
16.9	13.2	13.0	13.2			Long Term Debt	14.8	14.2
.2	.1	.2	.3			Deferred Taxes	.3	.4
4.7	6.0	3.5	5.4			All Other Non-Current	4.7	4.2
8.5	41.7	42.2	44.2			Net Worth	38.5	39.5
100.0	100.0	100.0	100.0			Total Liabilities & Net Worth	100.0	100.0
						INCOME DATA		
100.0	100.0	100.0	100.0			Net Sales	100.0	100.0
46.9	39.2	35.4	32.3			Gross Profit	35.7	33.7
48.7	33.4	31.2	25.6			Operating Expenses	35.6	27.0
−1.8	5.8	4.2	6.7			Operating Profit	.1	6.7
1.4	1.6	1.1	1.0			All Other Expenses (net)	1.8	1.1
−3.2	4.2	3.1	5.8			Profit Before Taxes	−1.6	5.6
						RATIOS		
2.7 / 1.3 / .7	4.6 / 1.9 / 1.3	2.9 / 1.8 / 1.3	3.1 / 2.0 / 1.4			Current	2.8 / 1.7 / 1.3	2.9 / 1.8 / 1.3
1.2 / .6 / .5	2.8 / 1.1 / .7	1.5 / .9 / .7	1.7 / 1.0 / .7	(154)		Quick	1.6 / 1.0 / .7	1.5 / .9 / .6
11 34.2 / 26 14.1 / 55 6.6	33 11.1 / 40 9.2 / 58 6.3	35 10.5 / 50 7.3 / 79 4.6	46 8.0 / 52 7.0 / 62 5.9			Sales/Receivables	40 9.2 / 51 7.1 / 75 4.9	38 9.6 / 52 7.0 / 69 5.3
3 106.0 / 29 12.6 / 300 1.2	20 18.2 / 65 5.6 / 133 2.8	49 7.5 / 82 4.5 / 149 2.5	48 7.6 / 89 4.1 / 124 2.9			Cost of Sales/Inventory	37 9.7 / 71 5.1 / 116 3.1	43 8.5 / 70 5.2 / 114 3.2
17 21.3 / 34 10.7 / 58 6.3	11 34.7 / 33 10.9 / 58 6.3	19 19.7 / 33 11.0 / 54 6.8	21 17.8 / 30 12.0 / 41 8.8			Cost of Sales/Payables	20 17.9 / 33 11.0 / 53 6.9	24 15.3 / 36 10.1 / 61 6.0
6.1 / NM / −20.7	4.0 / 6.5 / 19.5	3.9 / 6.5 / 13.8	3.9 / 6.2 / 9.3			Sales/Working Capital	4.2 / 7.1 / 13.9	4.2 / 6.9 / 16.3
	(34) 22.3 / 5.0 / 1.2	(66) 8.8 / 2.8 / .4	(30) 19.4 / 6.4 / 2.3			EBIT/Interest	(140) 13.1 / 4.2 / 1.6	(131) 14.0 / 4.6 / 1.7
	(23) 4.6 / 1.7 / .8		(14) 18.1 / 5.1 / 1.4			Net Profit + Depr., Dep., Amort./Cur. Mat. L/T/D	(47) 15.2 / 2.8 / 1.2	(45) 8.3 / 3.7 / 1.1
.0 / .3 / 16.4	.1 / .5 / 1.0	.2 / .4 / .9	.2 / .4 / 2.6			Fixed/Worth	.2 / .4 / 1.1	.2 / .4 / 1.1
1.5 / 8.4 / NM	.4 / 1.5 / 4.2	.7 / 1.5 / 2.6	.5 / 1.1 / 7.7			Debt/Worth	.8 / 1.5 / 4.3	.7 / 1.7 / 4.2
	(33) 70.5 / 29.4 / 4.9	(65) 49.4 / 14.2 / 1.1	(28) 33.7 / 17.2 / 10.1			% Profit Before Taxes/Tangible Net Worth	(138) 42.5 / 21.2 / 6.8	(136) 45.2 / 25.2 / 5.8
28.9 / −3.0 / −21.3	21.2 / 10.3 / 1.7	12.4 / 5.1 / .2	15.7 / 7.4 / 2.4			% Profit Before Taxes/Total Assets	17.2 / 7.8 / 1.2	20.2 / 8.4 / 2.0
UND / 41.0 / 13.0	38.7 / 19.0 / 7.4	23.6 / 12.9 / 5.4	18.0 / 10.8 / 6.0			Sales/Net Fixed Assets	38.4 / 16.9 / 7.6	34.0 / 15.2 / 6.8
6.4 / 3.6 / 1.8	3.3 / 2.5 / 1.7	2.8 / 1.9 / 1.4	2.0 / 1.7 / 1.2			Sales/Total Assets	2.9 / 2.1 / 1.5	2.9 / 2.1 / 1.4
	(30) .9 / 1.9 / 3.0	(69) 1.3 / 2.0 / 3.6	(25) 1.2 / 2.4 / 4.3			% Depr., Dep., Amort./Sales	(135) .8 / 1.6 / 2.9	(133) .7 / 1.6 / 2.9
	(17) 3.0 / 4.8 / 10.3	(28) 3.1 / 6.0 / 9.6				% Officers', Directors', Owners' Comp/Sales	(51) 3.6 / 5.6 / 9.7	(52) 2.2 / 4.2 / 7.5
10332M	105071M	672267M	1108339M	755984M	2511059M	Net Sales ($)	4416857M	3456335M
2753M	42487M	348302M	711554M	488569M	1446166M	Total Assets ($)	2486407M	2323945M

© RMA 2003

M = $ thousand   MM = $ million
See Pages 11 through 18 for Explanation of Ratios and Data

Comparative Historical Data / Current Data Sorted By Sales

	4/1/00-3/31/01 ALL	4/1/01-3/31/02 ALL	4/1/02-3/31/03 ALL	Type of Statement	0-1MM	1-3MM	3-5MM	5-10MM	10-25MM	25MM & OVER
	38	33	38	Unqualified		4	1	11	6	16
	30	25	38	Reviewed		9	3	10	10	6
	25	26	19	Compiled	4	5	3	5	2	
	14	12	15	Tax Returns	2	7	2	3		1
	39	52	56	Other	2	8	4	12	17	13
						33 (4/1-9/30/02)		**133 (10/1/02-3/31/03)**		
NUMBER OF STATEMENTS	146	148	166		8	33	13	41	35	36
	%	%	%	**ASSETS**	%	%	%	%	%	%
	8.5	7.2	9.4	Cash & Equivalents		11.4	11.0	7.6	8.8	7.9
	30.9	28.8	29.7	Trade Receivables (net)		28.8	30.1	33.4	30.9	25.7
	29.3	29.1	27.3	Inventory		27.7	27.6	28.8	25.9	24.9
	3.1	2.6	3.4	All Other Current		2.0	2.4	2.3	5.7	4.4
	71.7	67.7	69.7	Total Current		69.9	71.1	72.1	71.3	62.9
	17.7	20.5	19.3	Fixed Assets (net)		20.1	19.2	19.2	19.1	20.0
	5.2	5.8	5.4	Intangibles (net)		2.7	7.7	4.0	5.1	9.7
	5.5	6.0	5.6	All Other Non-Current		7.3	2.0	4.6	4.5	7.4
	100.0	100.0	100.0	Total		100.0	100.0	100.0	100.0	100.0
				LIABILITIES						
	19.1	12.3	9.7	Notes Payable-Short Term		9.7	12.5	13.6	8.1	3.5
	3.9	3.6	4.2	Cur. Mat.-L/T/D		3.1	2.8	4.2	5.9	4.0
	15.6	15.5	15.2	Trade Payables		13.8	19.6	16.2	14.7	11.7
	.4	.3	.4	Income Taxes Payable		.0	.0	.4	.8	.6
	10.5	11.8	11.4	All Other Current		7.9	8.7	8.6	14.1	13.7
	49.4	43.5	40.8	Total Current		34.5	43.6	43.0	43.5	33.5
	11.5	12.5	13.5	Long Term Debt		14.5	20.5	14.0	7.3	15.0
	.7	.3	.2	Deferred Taxes		.1	.1	.2	.2	.4
	4.9	4.8	4.9	All Other Non-Current		5.5	2.1	5.2	5.0	5.4
	33.5	38.8	40.6	Net Worth		45.4	33.6	37.6	44.0	45.7
	100.0	100.0	100.0	Total Liabilities & Net Worth		100.0	100.0	100.0	100.0	100.0
				INCOME DATA						
	100.0	100.0	100.0	Net Sales		100.0	100.0	100.0	100.0	100.0
	33.9	34.4	35.8	Gross Profit		41.7	35.8	35.2	32.6	31.5
	27.3	30.5	31.2	Operating Expenses		35.7	32.6	30.8	26.2	26.2
	6.6	3.9	4.7	Operating Profit		6.0	3.3	4.3	6.4	5.4
	1.2	1.7	1.3	All Other Expenses (net)		1.5	.8	1.3	1.0	1.3
	5.4	2.2	3.4	Profit Before Taxes		4.5	2.4	3.0	5.4	4.1
				RATIOS						
	3.2	2.4	2.9			4.5	2.1	2.9	2.9	2.7
	1.7	1.6	1.8	Current		2.2	1.7	1.7	1.8	2.2
	1.3	1.2	1.3			1.5	1.5	1.2	1.2	1.4
	1.5	1.4	1.6			2.5	1.4	1.5	1.6	1.6
	.9	.8	1.0	Quick		1.1	1.1	.9	.9	1.0
	.6	.5	.7			.6	.6	.6	.7	.7
	38 9.7	34 10.6	36 10.2		32 11.5	32 11.4	39 9.3	35 10.4	44 8.3	
	49 7.5	46 7.9	49 7.5	Sales/Receivables	44 8.2	41 8.9	51 7.1	52 7.0	50 7.3	
	68 5.4	63 5.8	64 5.7		67 5.5	56 6.5	74 5.0	63 5.8	63 5.8	
	41 8.8	37 9.9	41 8.8		20 17.9	28 13.1	46 7.8	35 10.5	50 7.3	
	70 5.2	70 5.2	81 4.5	Cost of Sales/Inventory	96 3.8	72 5.1	88 4.2	66 5.5	76 4.8	
	114 3.2	124 2.9	136 2.7		168 2.2	116 3.1	144 2.5	118 3.1	120 3.0	
	22 16.7	17 21.1	19 19.6		12 30.4	19 19.6	19 19.4	22 16.9	19 19.2	
	35 10.3	31 11.9	33 11.0	Cost of Sales/Payables	30 12.3	46 8.0	35 10.4	36 10.2	26 13.8	
	51 7.1	51 7.1	52 7.1		53 6.8	62 5.9	57 6.4	52 7.0	38 9.5	
	4.3	4.6	4.1			2.8	5.8	4.2	4.9	4.0
	7.3	8.8	6.4	Sales/Working Capital		5.4	7.6	7.6	6.5	6.3
	18.8	22.6	14.6			16.5	17.6	22.6	17.5	10.1
	14.4	7.5	11.3		13.5	20.3	7.2	21.9	14.5	
(130)	3.9	(127) 2.6	(151) 3.5	EBIT/Interest	(29) 3.2	(12) 4.0	(37) 2.5	(32) 5.7	(35) 4.9	
	1.8	.5	1.1		1.1	1.8	-.1	1.6	1.4	
	6.3	4.8	6.5				3.1	22.0	12.5	
(40)	2.5	(42) 1.5	(48) 2.2	Net Profit + Depr., Dep., Amort./Cur. Mat. L/T/D		(12) 1.5	(12) 4.3	(14) 5.1		
	1.0	.9	1.2			.7	1.5	2.2		
	.2	.2	.2			.1	.2	.2	.2	.3
	.4	.5	.4	Fixed/Worth		.4	.5	.6	.3	.5
	1.0	1.2	1.3			1.1	NM	1.6	.8	1.5
	.7	.7	.7			.5	1.0	.6	.7	.6
	1.7	1.8	1.6	Debt/Worth		1.4	1.5	2.0	1.3	1.3
	3.7	4.3	4.1			3.2	NM	5.3	2.7	5.1
	48.2	32.1	45.1		68.8	40.0	50.1	55.9	31.9	
(135)	19.6	(131) 13.7	(146) 17.2	% Profit Before Taxes/Tangible Net Worth	(31) 21.8	(10) 27.1	(34) 9.1	(33) 22.9	(32) 14.0	
	5.4	1.1	2.9		3.4	4.0	-3.3	13.4	3.3	
	19.0	12.6	15.7			25.5	14.0	9.1	19.5	9.5
	7.9	3.7	5.6	% Profit Before Taxes/Total Assets		9.0	7.0	3.9	8.1	5.5
	2.1	.1	.4			.5	1.5	-1.7	2.4	2.2
	36.3	29.4	27.1			35.3	32.1	40.9	28.0	14.2
	15.7	12.6	12.9	Sales/Net Fixed Assets		17.1	17.4	12.3	16.3	9.6
	8.1	6.3	6.2			5.0	7.9	6.7	8.1	5.6
	2.8	3.0	2.9			2.9	3.1	2.8	3.0	2.1
	2.1	2.1	1.9	Sales/Total Assets		2.0	2.5	2.1	1.8	1.7
	1.6	1.5	1.4			1.2	1.8	1.5	1.6	1.1
	.7	1.0	1.3			1.5	.7	1.3	1.1	1.5
(125)	1.5	(120) 1.9	(141) 2.1	% Depr., Dep., Amort./Sales	(28) 2.5	(10) 2.7	(36) 2.5	(31) 1.7	(31) 2.2	
	2.7	3.3	3.6		4.0	3.1	3.7	3.1	3.8	
	3.1	1.9	2.3		3.1		1.9	2.5		
(50)	6.0	(52) 5.0	(56) 4.8	% Officers', Directors', Owners' Comp/Sales	(16) 5.0		(16) 5.0	(10) 4.1		
	7.9	7.8	9.6		9.1		9.1	9.6		
	4657993M	3816132M	5163052M	Net Sales ($)	4467M	66024M	51044M	283396M	552441M	4205680M
	2953162M	2380296M	3039831M	Total Assets ($)	3718M	46485M	23037M	158917M	325931M	2481743M

© RMA 2003   **M = $ thousand   MM = $ million**
See Pages 11 through 18 for Explanation of Ratios and Data

Current Data Sorted By Assets   **Comparative Historical Data**

Item	0-500M	500M-2MM	2-10MM	10-50MM	50-100MM	100-250MM	4/1/98-3/31/99 ALL	4/1/99-3/31/00 ALL
Type of Statement								
Unqualified			6	1	5	2	12	9
Reviewed		1	5	4			10	6
Compiled	1		4				8	7
Tax Returns							3	3
Other	2	1	5	6		1	17	13
		7 (4/1-9/30/02)		37 (10/1/02-3/31/03)				
NUMBER OF STATEMENTS	3	2	20	11	5	3	50	38
	%	%	%	%	%	%	%	%
ASSETS								
Cash & Equivalents			11.2	7.8			11.9	11.7
Trade Receivables (net)			16.0	25.9			19.8	22.2
Inventory			35.9	40.8			33.6	31.5
All Other Current			3.9	2.2			4.7	5.6
Total Current			66.9	76.7			70.0	71.0
Fixed Assets (net)			19.0	18.5			19.8	18.7
Intangibles (net)			6.0	1.1			5.4	4.7
All Other Non-Current			8.0	3.6			4.7	5.6
Total			100.0	100.0			100.0	100.0
LIABILITIES								
Notes Payable-Short Term			18.2	12.4			13.2	9.2
Cur. Mat.-L/T/D			6.8	2.9			3.4	5.6
Trade Payables			13.2	14.0			18.3	16.2
Income Taxes Payable			.2	1.6			.6	.7
All Other Current			13.5	18.8			14.4	15.8
Total Current			51.9	49.7			49.8	47.6
Long Term Debt			19.8	20.1			39.0	13.1
Deferred Taxes			.8	.1			.5	.4
All Other Non-Current			8.6	4.9			6.8	4.9
Net Worth			18.9	25.3			3.9	34.0
Total Liabilities & Net Worth			100.0	100.0			100.0	100.0
INCOME DATA								
Net Sales			100.0	100.0			100.0	100.0
Gross Profit			21.3	22.7			23.6	29.7
Operating Expenses			18.1	16.8			19.9	25.1
Operating Profit			3.2	5.9			3.7	4.5
All Other Expenses (net)			.9	.9			1.2	.5
Profit Before Taxes			2.2	5.0			2.4	4.0
RATIOS								
Current			1.6	2.2			2.1	2.0
			1.2	1.4			1.5	1.5
			1.0	.9			1.2	1.1
Quick			.9	1.3			1.0	1.2
			.6	.7			.7	.7
			.2	.4			.5	.4
Sales/Receivables			7 48.7	12 30.9			10 38.2	13 28.6
			29 12.4	54 6.8			22 16.8	31 11.7
			40 9.2	78 4.7			51 7.2	50 7.3
Cost of Sales/Inventory			40 9.0	34 10.8			30 12.1	26 13.8
			60 6.1	51 7.2			58 6.3	60 6.1
			106 3.4	131 2.8			101 3.6	97 3.8
Cost of Sales/Payables			9 38.6	10 38.1			9 41.6	14 27.0
			25 14.5	22 16.4			32 11.5	23 15.8
			54 6.8	48 7.7			48 7.7	42 8.6
Sales/Working Capital			6.2	6.8			5.4	5.4
			26.6	11.4			11.9	13.2
			-308.7	-51.9			47.5	90.5
EBIT/Interest			(15) 22.9	27.2			(44) 5.7	(35) 15.9
			2.0	5.2			3.2	4.3
			-3.6	1.3			1.3	1.0
Net Profit + Depr., Dep., Amort./Cur. Mat. L/T/D							(15) 37.1	
							3.3	
							1.0	
Fixed/Worth			.4	.1			.3	.2
			6.8	.7			.6	.6
			-1.3	9.3			UND	NM
Debt/Worth			1.3	1.7			1.1	.9
			20.2	3.5			2.8	2.0
			-10.7	29.2			UND	NM
% Profit Before Taxes/Tangible Net Worth			(11) 39.3				(39) 59.1	(29) 62.4
			30.2				38.9	17.7
			19.1				15.6	3.8
% Profit Before Taxes/Total Assets			12.0	23.9			18.8	14.0
			6.4	5.0			8.0	4.3
			-2.6	.8			2.3	.1
Sales/Net Fixed Assets			28.0	53.5			43.0	49.4
			12.4	20.6			16.9	20.8
			6.5	8.0			7.0	9.2
Sales/Total Assets			2.9	3.1			3.8	3.8
			2.2	2.3			2.4	2.4
			1.4	1.4			1.6	1.7
% Depr., Dep., Amort./Sales			(17) .8				(43) .5	(32) .6
			1.8				1.0	1.0
			2.3				2.4	2.8
% Officers', Directors', Owners' Comp/Sales							(11) 2.0	(11) 1.3
							3.4	3.3
							7.6	8.3
Net Sales ($)	2631M	12027M	368923M	615622M	697095M	741637M	3830820M	1569693M
Total Assets ($)	677M	2647M	125807M	240618M	340410M	495368M	1323156M	730717M

© RMA 2003

M = $ thousand   MM = $ million
See Pages 11 through 18 for Explanation of Ratios and Data

Comparative Historical Data — Current Data Sorted By Sales

8	10	14	Type of Statement				3	3	8
6	6	9	Unqualified				3	2	4
9	7	5	Reviewed				2	4	1
1	1	1	Compiled	1					
10	18	15	Tax Returns / Other	1	2		3	2	5
4/1/00-3/31/01 ALL	4/1/01-3/31/02 ALL	4/1/02-3/31/03 ALL		0-1MM	1-3MM	3-5MM	5-10MM	10-25MM	25MM & OVER
					7 (4/1-9/30/02)		37 (10/1/02-3/31/03)		
34	42	44	**NUMBER OF STATEMENTS**	2	2		11	11	18
%	%	%	**ASSETS**	%	%	%	%	%	%
7.5	9.7	9.7	Cash & Equivalents				9.3	8.7	10.8
18.7	22.7	17.5	Trade Receivables (net)				16.6	16.5	21.2
32.2	40.5	36.4	Inventory				31.7	38.7	37.1
7.5	3.8	3.7	All Other Current				5.9	2.7	3.8
66.0	76.7	67.4	Total Current				63.4	66.5	72.9
23.4	18.1	21.9	Fixed Assets (net)				22.4	21.0	17.5
3.7	1.8	4.0	Intangibles (net)				1.4	9.6	2.8
6.9	3.4	6.8	All Other Non-Current				12.7	2.9	6.9
100.0	100.0	100.0	Total				100.0	100.0	100.0
			LIABILITIES						
12.9	16.2	13.1	Notes Payable-Short Term				10.9	14.7	16.4
6.2	4.9	4.9	Cur. Mat.-L/T/D				9.2	4.8	2.1
14.5	18.4	14.7	Trade Payables				12.1	15.0	16.8
.0	.1	.6	Income Taxes Payable				.2	.4	1.1
10.8	12.1	16.8	All Other Current				12.3	14.4	17.3
44.5	51.7	50.1	Total Current				44.7	49.2	53.7
11.4	10.6	36.1	Long Term Debt				21.8	24.2	13.8
.3	.5	.5	Deferred Taxes				.2	1.2	.4
3.9	8.0	11.2	All Other Non-Current				9.0	5.4	7.5
39.9	29.1	2.1	Net Worth				24.3	20.1	24.7
100.0	100.0	100.0	Total Liabilities & Net Worth				100.0	100.0	100.0
			INCOME DATA						
100.0	100.0	100.0	Net Sales				100.0	100.0	100.0
22.7	19.3	21.9	Gross Profit				26.8	22.7	14.8
19.7	16.5	18.9	Operating Expenses				23.0	18.8	11.3
3.0	2.8	3.0	Operating Profit				3.7	3.8	3.5
−.6	1.2	.9	All Other Expenses (net)				.4	1.9	.6
3.6	1.6	2.1	Profit Before Taxes				3.4	1.9	2.9
			RATIOS						
2.0 / 1.3 / 1.1	2.2 / 1.5 / 1.1	2.0 / 1.3 / 1.0	Current				2.2 / 1.3 / .9	1.6 / 1.1 / .9	1.7 / 1.3 / 1.0
.8 / .5 / .3	1.0 / .6 / .3	.9 / .5 / .3	Quick				1.0 / .6 / .4	.7 / .5 / .2	1.0 / .5 / .3
13 28.7 / 28 13.0 / 49 7.4	15 25.0 / 32 11.5 / 44 8.3	8 45.5 / 28 12.8 / 56 6.6	Sales/Receivables				15 25.0 / 39 9.3 / 78 4.7	7 51.1 / 31 11.9 / 56 6.5	11 33.6 / 28 12.9 / 55 6.6
24 15.4 / 63 5.8 / 95 3.9	31 11.9 / 69 5.3 / 120 3.1	40 9.1 / 59 6.2 / 105 3.5	Cost of Sales/Inventory				40 9.1 / 65 5.6 / 135 2.7	40 9.0 / 89 4.1 / 136 2.7	34 10.8 / 51 7.2 / 79 4.6
11 31.9 / 23 15.9 / 40 9.0	15 25.2 / 24 14.9 / 45 8.1	10 35.8 / 26 14.1 / 54 6.8	Cost of Sales/Payables				19 19.2 / 28 13.1 / 56 6.5	9 42.2 / 25 14.3 / 82 4.4	13 27.1 / 27 13.4 / 48 7.7
5.1 / 19.8 / 82.7	6.0 / 13.9 / 38.5	7.0 / 17.3 / −84.1	Sales/Working Capital				4.5 / 16.8 / −28.4	6.0 / 20.8 / −64.4	7.4 / 15.4 / −775.2
(29) 13.9 / 3.4 / 1.5	(41) 6.8 / 2.7 / .6	(37) 11.4 / 2.9 / .9	EBIT/Interest					(10) 23.4 / 4.1 / −4.1	(14) 16.5 / 5.0 / 1.3
(13) 3.6 / 2.0 / .5		(14) 8.2 / 2.3 / 1.3	Net Profit + Depr., Dep., Amort./Cur. Mat. L/T/D						
.3 / .6 / 1.2	.2 / .5 / 7.9	.3 / 1.2 / −3.1	Fixed/Worth				.3 / 5.5 / −2.7	.6 / −18.3 / −.8	.3 / .8 / 1.9
.7 / 1.5 / 4.3	.9 / 2.6 / 72.0	1.8 / 4.7 / −14.8	Debt/Worth				.6 / 9.6 / −14.0	.9 / −46.3 / −4.0	1.8 / 2.9 / 6.3
(30) 40.2 / 19.5 / 7.1	(33) 45.0 / 14.6 / 1.1	(31) 39.3 / 23.7 / 10.5	% Profit Before Taxes/Tangible Net Worth						(16) 45.7 / 22.5 / 6.5
15.3 / 5.2 / 2.0	16.8 / 4.7 / −.7	10.6 / 4.9 / −.4	% Profit Before Taxes/Total Assets				12.2 / 5.8 / .9	11.2 / 7.1 / −5.3	9.6 / 4.2 / .7
33.1 / 10.7 / 4.2	27.6 / 18.3 / 8.9	34.5 / 11.6 / 5.8	Sales/Net Fixed Assets				20.0 / 7.4 / 4.6	29.4 / 8.1 / 7.2	54.2 / 15.6 / 7.4
3.6 / 2.5 / 1.5	3.3 / 2.7 / 1.8	3.2 / 2.3 / 1.5	Sales/Total Assets				2.5 / 1.6 / 1.0	2.9 / 1.9 / 1.4	3.7 / 2.5 / 1.8
(29) .9 / 1.9 / 3.7	(34) .7 / 1.1 / 1.7	(38) .7 / 1.6 / 2.5	% Depr., Dep., Amort./Sales				1.0 / 2.1 / 2.8	(10) .6 / 1.0 / 2.0	(13) .5 / 1.5 / 2.3
(14) 1.9 / 3.6 / 7.6	(12) 1.4 / 3.2 / 4.9	(10) .8 / 1.4 / 2.9	% Officers', Directors', Owners' Comp/Sales						
1263475M	3770399M	2437935M	Net Sales ($)	1166M	4015M		85959M	180589M	2166206M
567760M	1054083M	1205527M	Total Assets ($)	248M	1409M		57540M	94001M	1052329M

M = $ thousand   MM = $ million
See Pages 11 through 18 for Explanation of Ratios and Data

Current Data Sorted By Assets   Comparative Historical Data

	0-500M	500M-2MM	2-10MM	10-50MM	50-100MM	100-250MM	Type of Statement	ALL 4/1/98-3/31/99	ALL 4/1/99-3/31/00
		2	8	16	8	10	Unqualified	15	23
		4	20	6	1		Reviewed	16	15
	3	6	5	1			Compiled	6	9
	1	4	4				Tax Returns	5	4
	3	4	11	15	4	4	Other	22	17
		25 (4/1-9/30/02)		115 (10/1/02-3/31/03)					
NUMBER OF STATEMENTS	7	20	48	38	13	14		64	68
	%	%	%	%	%	%	**ASSETS**	%	%
		10.8	3.5	5.1	3.8	1.5	Cash & Equivalents	4.8	5.3
		27.0	23.3	25.1	24.6	18.3	Trade Receivables (net)	22.2	23.4
		31.6	31.5	25.3	25.9	15.9	Inventory	37.5	36.0
		1.7	2.9	5.2	1.9	4.3	All Other Current	1.5	1.4
		71.1	61.3	60.6	56.2	40.0	Total Current	66.0	66.1
		22.8	30.3	27.2	33.1	31.6	Fixed Assets (net)	27.7	25.1
		1.1	3.1	6.5	2.6	18.1	Intangibles (net)	2.0	4.5
		5.0	5.3	5.6	8.1	10.3	All Other Non-Current	4.3	4.3
		100.0	100.0	100.0	100.0	100.0	Total	100.0	100.0
							LIABILITIES		
		21.0	16.4	16.9	11.7	1.0	Notes Payable-Short Term	14.0	15.5
		4.1	5.5	3.9	3.1	12.2	Cur. Mat.-L/T/D	2.6	4.2
		20.2	16.3	15.1	18.2	12.3	Trade Payables	16.2	16.8
		.0	.0	.4	.2	.0	Income Taxes Payable	.6	.4
		14.7	12.6	10.1	10.8	8.9	All Other Current	8.2	9.2
		60.0	50.9	46.4	44.0	34.4	Total Current	41.5	46.1
		13.9	19.9	12.9	9.0	19.0	Long Term Debt	21.6	20.2
		.2	.9	.4	.8	2.2	Deferred Taxes	.5	.5
		1.4	5.8	3.6	10.2	15.8	All Other Non-Current	4.7	5.3
		24.5	22.5	36.7	35.9	28.7	Net Worth	31.6	28.0
		100.0	100.0	100.0	100.0	100.0	Total Liabilities & Net Worth	100.0	100.0
							INCOME DATA		
		100.0	100.0	100.0	100.0	100.0	Net Sales	100.0	100.0
		23.0	26.6	21.9	18.5	22.4	Gross Profit	20.5	21.0
		25.1	24.4	17.3	14.4	16.4	Operating Expenses	17.4	16.3
		-2.1	2.2	4.6	4.2	6.1	Operating Profit	3.1	4.7
		-.1	1.8	.9	1.0	3.5	All Other Expenses (net)	1.3	1.3
		-2.0	.4	3.7	3.2	2.5	Profit Before Taxes	1.8	3.4
							RATIOS		
		1.7	2.1	2.4	2.2	1.7		2.2	2.3
		1.2	1.3	1.5	1.8	1.3	Current	1.6	1.5
		.9	1.0	.9	.7	.9		1.2	1.3
		1.1	1.0	1.2	1.1	.9		1.1	1.2
		.5	.7	.7	.9	.7	Quick	.6	.7
		.3	.4	.5	.4	.4		.4	.4
	19	18.9	28 13.2	31 11.7	35 10.5	38 9.7		24 15.0	27 13.6
	28	12.9	36 10.0	39 9.4	41 9.0	53 6.9	Sales/Receivables	37 9.9	37 9.8
	44	8.3	55 6.7	53 6.8	53 6.9	69 5.3		49 7.4	52 7.1
	25	14.6	40 9.1	25 14.5	20 17.9	38 9.6		48 7.6	45 8.1
	45	8.1	71 5.1	47 7.7	61 6.0	55 6.6	Cost of Sales/Inventory	63 5.8	69 5.3
	86	4.2	103 3.5	76 4.8	88 4.1	64 5.7		94 3.9	91 4.0
	14	26.7	17 21.8	16 23.1	20 18.0	33 10.9		16 22.8	18 19.8
	27	13.3	32 11.6	29 12.4	29 12.5	42 8.7	Cost of Sales/Payables	27 13.8	29 12.6
	46	7.9	55 6.6	37 9.8	39 9.3	51 7.1		42 8.8	41 8.9
		8.9	5.7	5.6	7.3	8.9		5.6	6.1
		24.0	14.1	14.5	8.9	16.0	Sales/Working Capital	10.8	9.7
		-38.5	-238.2	-36.5	-16.4	-17.5		23.3	23.1
		8.5	5.2	22.3	13.1	4.0		6.2	7.7
	(17)	3.2	(47) 1.9	(36) 4.7	5.3	1.5	EBIT/Interest	(60) 2.8	(65) 2.8
		-5.0	.2	1.5	1.0	.8		1.4	1.7
			7.6	4.6		5.2	Net Profit + Depr., Dep.,	7.7	5.6
		(14)	2.3	(15) 3.6	(10)	2.4	Amort./Cur. Mat. L./T/D	(24) 2.5	(25) 3.7
			.6	2.2		.5		1.3	2.2
		.4	.5	.4	.5	.9		.4	.5
		.7	.9	.8	.9	2.8	Fixed/Worth	.8	.9
		NM	3.1	2.9	3.3	NM		1.5	10.9
		1.3	1.0	.6	.7	3.2		1.0	1.2
		2.3	1.9	1.3	2.1	5.8	Debt/Worth	1.8	2.5
		NM	11.4	9.8	7.7	NM		5.4	69.1
		48.8	20.0	48.6	73.4	72.4	% Profit Before Taxes/Tangible	33.7	42.9
	(15)	21.8	(38) 10.1	(32) 19.8	26.6	(11) 24.0	Net Worth	(56) 21.4	(55) 25.3
		4.9	-2.9	8.5	2.8	-.9		7.7	10.0
		10.5	7.4	22.6	13.7	11.0	% Profit Before Taxes/Total	12.6	12.8
		4.6	2.2	5.9	8.9	2.0	Assets	5.5	7.2
		-17.8	-1.9	1.7	.2	-.8		1.3	2.1
		35.7	16.6	20.2	11.7	8.4		19.4	20.5
		17.4	6.5	8.2	6.2	5.3	Sales/Net Fixed Assets	9.6	10.8
		9.8	3.8	4.4	3.7	2.4		4.5	5.6
		4.3	2.7	2.5	2.7	1.5		2.9	2.8
		2.8	2.0	2.0	2.1	1.4	Sales/Total Assets	2.3	2.1
		2.1	1.5	1.5	1.4	.9		1.7	1.7
		.5	1.2	.9	.7	3.0		.7	.8
	(18)	1.1	(44) 1.9	(32) 2.5	(12) 2.2	(10) 3.5	% Depr., Dep., Amort./Sales	(54) 1.2	(63) 1.3
		2.6	4.8	4.2	4.2	6.3		2.4	2.1
		1.1	2.4					1.6	1.3
	(11)	2.2	(17) 3.5				% Officers', Directors', Owners' Comp/Sales	(20) 2.2	(27) 2.3
		5.2	5.9					3.9	3.3
	5640M	77392M	464224M	1650758M	1924155M	2658945M	Net Sales ($)	1806442M	4329808M
	1154M	26259M	220321M	780100M	904173M	2017737M	Total Assets ($)	840309M	1677167M

M = $ thousand   MM = $ million
See Pages 11 through 18 for Explanation of Ratios and Data

Comparative Historical Data | Current Data Sorted By Sales

	4/1/00-3/31/01 ALL	4/1/01-3/31/02 ALL	4/1/02-3/31/03 ALL	0-1MM	1-3MM	3-5MM	5-10MM	10-25MM	25MM & OVER
Type of Statement			25 (4/1-9/30/02)		115 (10/1/02-3/31/03)				
Unqualified	13	13	44		1	2	4	6	31
Reviewed	12	17	31		2	4	7	13	5
Compiled	15	12	15	1	7	3	1	2	1
Tax Returns	4	3	9	1	2	5	1		
Other	23	20	41	2	2	5	4	9	19
NUMBER OF STATEMENTS	67	65	140	4	14	19	17	30	56
ASSETS	%	%	%	%	%	%	%	%	%
Cash & Equivalents	3.3	5.7	5.1		4.3	11.8	2.7	2.6	4.5
Trade Receivables (net)	19.9	21.9	24.4		32.8	25.8	26.6	17.4	25.8
Inventory	41.2	34.3	27.3		26.1	26.5	32.9	32.5	23.4
All Other Current	2.4	3.8	3.3		1.6	1.4	3.8	6.8	2.5
Total Current	66.8	65.7	60.1		64.9	65.4	65.9	59.3	56.1
Fixed Assets (net)	22.0	23.4	28.3		28.2	28.6	27.5	27.2	29.1
Intangibles (net)	5.7	5.5	5.0		.0	2.0	1.0	8.4	7.1
All Other Non-Current	5.5	5.4	6.6		6.9	3.9	5.6	5.0	7.7
Total	100.0	100.0	100.0		100.0	100.0	100.0	100.0	100.0
LIABILITIES									
Notes Payable-Short Term	19.1	20.7	16.5		25.3	10.8	16.3	21.9	10.3
Cur. Mat.-L/T/D	2.7	2.7	5.5		6.7	4.4	7.9	4.4	5.6
Trade Payables	18.9	14.5	16.2		20.9	18.0	16.8	13.9	16.4
Income Taxes Payable	.1	.4	.2		.0	.0	.0	.3	.1
All Other Current	9.4	9.6	11.7		9.6	14.6	16.9	11.0	10.7
Total Current	50.3	47.9	50.0		62.4	47.9	58.0	51.5	43.1
Long Term Debt	15.9	16.3	15.1		19.6	13.9	11.2	22.4	12.6
Deferred Taxes	.6	.6	.7		.0	.4	2.3	.4	.8
All Other Non-Current	4.4	2.2	6.3		2.5	2.6	7.1	4.0	8.4
Net Worth	28.9	33.0	27.9		15.6	35.2	21.5	21.7	35.1
Total Liabilities & Net Worth	100.0	100.0	100.0		100.0	100.0	100.0	100.0	100.0
INCOME DATA									
Net Sales	100.0	100.0	100.0		100.0	100.0	100.0	100.0	100.0
Gross Profit	21.6	23.9	24.7		27.3	33.1	23.7	21.6	20.4
Operating Expenses	17.7	21.2	22.0		31.5	29.8	19.7	19.4	15.8
Operating Profit	3.9	2.7	2.8		-4.3	3.2	4.0	2.2	4.6
All Other Expenses (net)	1.6	1.5	1.3		1.4	.0	2.5	1.5	1.3
Profit Before Taxes	2.3	1.2	1.4		-5.7	3.2	1.5	.6	3.3
RATIOS									
	2.1	2.2	2.2		1.9	2.0	2.2	2.1	2.3
Current	1.5	1.5	1.3		1.1	1.3	1.3	1.2	1.4
	1.1	1.1	.9		.7	1.2	.8	.9	.9
	.9	1.3	1.1		.9	1.2	1.0	.9	1.2
Quick	.5	.6	.7		.5	.7	.6	.5	.8
	.3	.4	.4		.4	.5	.3	.3	.5
	24 15.3	22 16.5	27 13.3		27 13.4	23 15.8	32 11.6	24 15.3	37 9.9
Sales/Receivables	35 10.4	36 10.3	38 9.5		37 9.8	40 9.1	36 10.1	31 11.9	43 8.6
	47 7.7	51 7.2	54 6.8		58 6.2	61 6.0	50 7.3	39 9.4	57 6.4
	53 6.9	41 9.0	30 12.1		20 18.0	29 12.5	42 8.7	40 9.1	29 12.7
Cost of Sales/Inventory	73 5.0	65 5.6	54 6.7		56 6.6	50 7.3	70 5.2	60 6.1	48 7.6
	113 3.2	114 3.2	88 4.2		141 2.6	89 4.1	88 4.1	112 3.3	69 5.3
	17	15 25.0	19 19.0		10 36.8	20 18.3	17 21.7	12 30.6	21 17.8
Cost of Sales/Payables	34 10.6	25 14.7	32 11.6		27 13.8	37 9.9	28 12.8	23 16.1	32 11.3
	53 6.9	43 8.5	44 8.3		79 4.6	58 6.3	49 7.4	38 9.6	43 8.5
	6.8	5.2	6.3		9.1	6.3	6.0	6.5	6.6
Sales/Working Capital	10.2	12.3	16.2		24.3	13.1	19.3	16.9	12.7
	33.8	29.5	-34.3		-12.9	42.8	-20.2	-59.9	-24.1
	7.5	4.9	6.9		.8	6.5	5.0	8.7	12.7
EBIT/Interest	(66) 1.9	(60) 2.0	(131) 3.0	(12) -1.9	(17) 3.4	3.0	(27) 2.9	(55) 4.2	
	.5	.4	.5		-7.7	.3	1.0	-1.0	1.0
	9.3	6.6	5.8					12.1	6.4
Net Profit + Depr., Dep., Amort./Cur. Mat. L/T/D	(23) 4.5	(19) 1.7	(50) 2.6				(11) 3.1	(25) 2.7	
	1.2	.5	.8					1.2	1.0
	.3	.3	.5		.5	.5	.4	.5	.5
Fixed/Worth	.8	.7	.9		2.0	.7	.9	1.0	.9
	8.8	1.3	3.7		-1.2	2.0	-5.8	NM	3.6
	1.1	.8	1.0		.6	1.1	1.1	1.0	.6
Debt/Worth	2.8	2.1	2.3		13.7	1.8	2.3	2.2	2.4
	72.5	4.4	16.0		-7.7	3.8	-39.3	NM	7.3
	33.1	27.8	45.9			33.3	25.9	24.9	57.5
% Profit Before Taxes/Tangible Net Worth	(51) 15.8	(56) 10.1	(114) 15.0		(18) 21.5	(12) 11.2	(23) 13.1	(49) 24.0	
	2.4	.1	1.2			-.5	3.5	1.3	5.2
	10.7	9.1	12.2		17.5	10.4	8.7	11.6	13.4
% Profit Before Taxes/Total Assets	3.3	3.9	4.3		-5.5	7.4	3.2	4.1	5.5
	-2.2	-2.1	-1.4		-28.7	-1.5	.3	-2.1	.2
	20.3	19.8	18.6		42.9	29.5	26.6	17.0	13.1
Sales/Net Fixed Assets	11.9	11.1	8.4		12.8	10.4	8.6	8.5	7.5
	5.8	5.3	4.4		2.8	3.9	4.3	5.1	4.5
	2.9	2.8	2.9		4.8	3.2	3.5	2.7	2.5
Sales/Total Assets	2.2	2.0	2.0		1.6	2.2	2.1	1.9	2.0
	1.6	1.7	1.5		1.1	1.4	1.9	1.5	1.4
	.5	1.0	.9		.7	.7	1.2	.8	.8
% Depr., Dep., Amort./Sales	(62) 1.2	(56) 1.6	(122) 2.4		(11) 2.3	(17) 1.3	1.5	(26) 2.1	(47) 2.5
	2.3	3.4	4.4		7.4	6.2	3.9	2.9	4.6
	1.2	1.7	1.6		1.4				
% Officers', Directors', Owners' Comp/Sales	(21) 2.3	(21) 2.4	(39) 3.5		(13) 2.8				
	4.3	6.9	5.2		7.6				
Net Sales ($)	2750223M	2534872M	6781114M	2015M	29870M	75705M	141935M	458577M	6073012M
Total Assets ($)	1551030M	1338318M	3949744M	629M	20982M	37853M	65492M	262946M	3561842M

M = $ thousand   MM = $ million
See Pages 11 through 18 for Explanation of Ratios and Data

Current Data Sorted By Assets							Comparative Historical Data	
						Type of Statement		
		8	9		2	Unqualified	17	21
	2	9				Reviewed	8	13
1	8	4	2			Compiled	14	16
1	1	1				Tax Returns	1	3
1	5	11	7		1	Other	19	19
13 (4/1-9/30/02)			60 (10/1/02-3/31/03)				4/1/98-3/31/99	4/1/99-3/31/00
0-500M	500M-2MM	2-10MM	10-50MM	50-100MM	100-250MM		ALL	ALL
3	16	33	18		3	**NUMBER OF STATEMENTS**	59	72
%	%	%	%	%	%	**ASSETS**	%	%
	7.8	6.8	8.2	DATA NOT AVAILABLE		Cash & Equivalents	8.9	6.1
	17.4	19.0	13.8			Trade Receivables (net)	16.3	16.0
	42.5	41.2	30.8			Inventory	35.0	39.2
	2.1	5.2	1.5			All Other Current	1.9	2.4
	69.7	72.2	54.3			Total Current	62.2	63.7
	25.3	21.5	37.2			Fixed Assets (net)	27.0	26.4
	2.5	2.6	3.3			Intangibles (net)	4.0	5.2
	2.4	3.7	5.2			All Other Non-Current	6.8	4.7
	100.0	100.0	100.0			Total	100.0	100.0
						LIABILITIES		
	20.7	15.7	7.1			Notes Payable-Short Term	10.4	15.4
	8.9	2.9	2.9			Cur. Mat.-L/T/D	3.8	3.8
	14.0	16.1	10.6			Trade Payables	14.2	15.5
	.2	.2	.0			Income Taxes Payable	.5	.3
	3.5	7.9	10.9			All Other Current	8.4	7.2
	47.4	42.8	31.6			Total Current	37.3	42.2
	16.1	14.7	25.1			Long Term Debt	18.2	16.6
	.1	.4	1.2			Deferred Taxes	.4	.6
	5.3	4.1	4.4			All Other Non-Current	4.5	2.5
	31.1	38.0	37.8			Net Worth	39.6	38.1
	100.0	100.0	100.0			Total Liabilities & Net Worth	100.0	100.0
						INCOME DATA		
	100.0	100.0	100.0			Net Sales	100.0	100.0
	28.1	21.1	19.8			Gross Profit	21.7	20.2
	26.4	18.1	14.7			Operating Expenses	16.2	15.8
	1.7	2.9	5.1			Operating Profit	5.5	4.4
	.2	.9	3.2			All Other Expenses (net)	.9	.6
	1.4	2.0	2.0			Profit Before Taxes	4.6	3.8
						RATIOS		
	2.2	3.0	3.1				3.2	2.7
	1.5	1.6	1.8			Current	1.7	1.4
	1.2	1.2	1.1				1.0	1.1
	.9	1.1	1.5				1.2	.9
	.6	.6	.7			Quick	.6	.5
	.3	.3	.4				.3	.3
	8 43.6	**13** 28.1	**18** 20.5				**10** 36.2	**12** 29.7
	22 17.0	**26** 13.9	**27** 13.7			Sales/Receivables	**18** 20.1	**21** 17.3
	31 11.9	**42** 8.7	**43** 8.4				**33** 11.0	**40** 9.2
	38 9.5	**44** 8.4	**49** 7.4				**32** 11.4	**43** 8.5
	65 5.6	**66** 5.5	**68** 5.4			Cost of Sales/Inventory	**63** 5.8	**65** 5.6
	93 3.9	**99** 3.7	**112** 3.3				**99** 3.7	**92** 4.0
	6 58.2	**17** 22.0	**13** 27.4				**14** 26.1	**14** 26.5
	27 13.4	**26** 14.3	**21** 17.1			Cost of Sales/Payables	**23** 15.7	**24** 15.5
	37 9.9	**41** 8.9	**48** 7.6				**33** 11.1	**38** 9.6
	8.8	4.5	4.8				5.1	6.2
	16.5	12.1	8.5			Sales/Working Capital	10.8	11.1
	40.3	21.2	NM				343.4	106.1
	3.4	5.6	6.4				17.9	10.6
	(15) 1.9	(29) 2.4	2.5			EBIT/Interest	(53) 6.0	(64) 3.3
	−2.0	.7	−.8				2.6	1.8
							13.9	4.3
						Net Profit + Depr., Dep., Amort./Cur. Mat. L /T/D	(21) 5.1	(24) 2.5
							1.7	1.5
	.3	.2	.5				.3	.3
	.7	.4	.8			Fixed/Worth	.7	.7
	14.4	1.2	1.8				2.8	2.2
	.6	.6	.6				.6	.7
	2.7	1.7	1.2			Debt/Worth	1.3	1.9
	46.3	4.3	2.9				5.9	4.7
	65.0	36.1	20.5				45.5	44.5
	(13) 5.8	(31) 8.8	(15) 8.0			% Profit Before Taxes/Tangible Net Worth	(50) 22.5	(65) 23.2
	−7.4	1.7	−.9				11.9	8.9
	12.5	6.1	9.6				18.0	16.8
	1.7	3.2	4.0			% Profit Before Taxes/Total Assets	8.9	6.1
	−7.5	−.4	−2.3				4.3	2.8
	38.1	53.1	7.2				24.1	28.0
	19.4	22.6	5.8			Sales/Net Fixed Assets	10.4	13.2
	7.2	5.2	4.5				6.7	5.7
	3.9	3.9	2.3				3.4	3.2
	3.2	2.9	1.9			Sales/Total Assets	2.6	2.5
	2.5	1.6	1.4				1.8	1.9
	.7	.5	1.4				.9	.7
	(15) 1.6	(30) 1.2	2.0			% Depr., Dep., Amort./Sales	(55) 1.2	(64) 1.1
	2.1	2.6	3.8				1.8	2.3
							.6	1.3
						% Officers', Directors', Owners' Comp/Sales	(16) 1.6	(25) 2.6
							3.5	3.5
2579M	70286M	527928M	768365M		905400M	Net Sales ($)	2012519M	3481237M
635M	20859M	194772M	392939M		445293M	Total Assets ($)	1003486M	1584380M

M = $ thousand MM = $ million

See Pages 11 through 18 for Explanation of Ratios and Data

Comparative Historical Data | Current Data Sorted By Sales

					Type of Statement						
	9		8		19	Unqualified				2	6	11
	13		10		11	Reviewed		1	1	2	4	3
	17		20		15	Compiled		4	1	5	3	2
	1		4		3	Tax Returns	1	1		1		
	21		21		25	Other	1	2	1	8	8	5

	4/1/00-3/31/01 ALL	4/1/01-3/31/02 ALL	4/1/02-3/31/03 ALL		13 (4/1-9/30/02)			60 (10/1/02-3/31/03)		
				0-1MM	**1-3MM**	**3-5MM**	**5-10MM**	**10-25MM**	**25MM & OVER**
NUMBER OF STATEMENTS	61	63	73	2	8	3	18	21	21
	%	%	%	%	%	%	%	%	%
ASSETS									
Cash & Equivalents	7.1	8.5	7.6				4.6	7.5	9.2
Trade Receivables (net)	18.3	17.0	17.4				16.4	21.7	15.5
Inventory	38.6	36.1	37.6				40.5	38.1	38.8
All Other Current	4.3	3.6	3.7				5.9	3.7	3.0
Total Current	68.3	65.2	66.4				67.4	71.0	66.6
Fixed Assets (net)	22.4	25.3	27.0				27.2	23.8	24.3
Intangibles (net)	5.3	5.0	2.7				2.9	3.3	1.2
All Other Non-Current	3.9	4.5	3.9				2.5	1.9	7.9
Total	100.0	100.0	100.0				100.0	100.0	100.0
LIABILITIES									
Notes Payable-Short Term	15.4	16.8	14.0				19.4	13.9	11.4
Cur. Mat.-L/T/D	2.6	6.6	4.4				4.2	2.8	2.8
Trade Payables	14.3	11.1	14.3				13.3	16.3	13.3
Income Taxes Payable	.3	.0	.1				.0	.5	.0
All Other Current	7.5	7.1	9.0				8.4	9.0	10.0
Total Current	40.1	41.7	41.8				45.3	42.4	37.5
Long Term Debt	13.6	15.1	19.5				24.9	9.3	17.7
Deferred Taxes	.2	.4	.5				.7	1.0	.2
All Other Non-Current	1.8	4.8	6.6				5.4	4.4	3.4
Net Worth	44.2	37.9	31.6				23.7	42.9	41.3
Total Liabilities & Net Worth	100.0	100.0	100.0				100.0	100.0	100.0
INCOME DATA									
Net Sales	100.0	100.0	100.0				100.0	100.0	100.0
Gross Profit	20.1	19.3	22.4				23.9	19.2	17.2
Operating Expenses	15.4	19.3	19.1				21.1	16.2	12.7
Operating Profit	4.6	.0	3.2				2.8	3.0	4.5
All Other Expenses (net)	1.0	1.5	1.5				1.1	1.2	2.8
Profit Before Taxes	3.7	−1.5	1.8				1.7	1.8	1.7
RATIOS									
Current	3.0	3.1	2.5				2.7	2.5	3.2
	1.8	1.7	1.6				1.4	1.6	1.9
	1.2	1.0	1.1				1.1	1.3	1.2
Quick	1.0	1.4	1.1				.9	1.4	1.4
	.6	.5	.6				.5	.7	.7
	.3	.3	.4				.3	.4	.4
Sales/Receivables	13 28.1	14 26.1	14 26.2				15 24.4	16 22.8	11 34.0
	25 14.5	25 14.6	23 15.6				25 14.5	32 11.3	19 19.5
	34 10.8	38 9.5	39 9.3				36 10.2	43 8.5	31 12.0
Cost of Sales/Inventory	39 9.5	40 9.1	43 8.5				37 9.8	44 8.3	42 8.6
	64 5.7	63 5.8	65 5.6				84 4.3	64 5.7	58 6.3
	78 4.7	96 3.8	94 3.9				134 2.7	86 4.3	75 4.9
Cost of Sales/Payables	10 38.0	7 50.5	12 29.9				17 22.0	17 22.0	9 39.0
	19 19.5	18 19.8	26 13.8				28 13.3	26 13.8	15 23.8
	27 13.3	32 11.3	42 8.6				45 8.2	43 8.5	33 11.2
Sales/Working Capital	5.5	5.0	5.4				4.8	4.5	5.2
	11.3	10.3	12.1				16.3	10.4	11.7
	34.5	−236.0	30.5				99.5	19.1	24.5
EBIT/Interest	17.1	3.8	5.5				3.4	5.5	8.8
	(56) 3.9	(58) 1.5	(67) 2.3		(16)		(16) 1.7	(20) 2.9	(20) 2.9
	1.8	−1.1	−.1				−.3	.5	−.1
Net Profit + Depr., Dep., Amort./Cur. Mat. L/T/D	5.8	3.7	13.2						
	(16) 2.0	(16) 1.2	(20) 3.1						
	1.3	−.5	1.3						
Fixed/Worth	.2	.3	.3				.5	.3	.3
	.5	.8	.8				1.5	.4	.5
	1.7	1.7	1.8				2.4	1.1	.8
Debt/Worth	.6	.7	.7				1.2	.6	.5
	1.3	1.9	2.3				3.5	1.6	.9
	3.7	4.4	7.3				10.9	3.3	3.2
% Profit Before Taxes/Tangible Net Worth	44.1	23.5	37.4				46.7	36.7	36.1
	(54) 20.6	(55) 8.0	(62) 7.9		(15)		(15) 8.8	(20) 7.4	(19) 9.3
	11.0	−8.5	−1.0				−3.9	−3.5	4.1
% Profit Before Taxes/Total Assets	16.5	8.0	8.1				5.7	12.4	10.3
	7.7	1.7	2.6				1.9	3.9	4.2
	2.9	−6.2	−2.4				−6.8	−1.0	−.8
Sales/Net Fixed Assets	32.6	37.1	36.3				48.7	36.3	31.4
	14.0	13.3	10.6				12.3	12.7	9.4
	7.6	5.2	5.3				2.5	4.6	6.3
Sales/Total Assets	3.7	3.7	3.5				3.5	3.6	3.8
	2.8	2.2	2.5				2.0	2.5	2.5
	2.0	1.5	1.6				1.1	1.6	2.1
% Depr., Dep., Amort./Sales	.7	.6	.9				.9	.9	1.1
	(51) 1.1	(54) 1.6	(69) 1.6				2.0	(20) 1.2	(19) 1.4
	2.0	3.4	2.8				4.0	2.5	2.1
% Officers', Directors', Owners' Comp/Sales	1.2	1.7	.9						
	(16) 2.2	(22) 4.3	(17) 1.9						
	3.0	9.1	3.9						
Net Sales ($)	2994514M	1468186M	2274558M	941M	14663M	13038M	127303M	319208M	1799405M
Total Assets ($)	1226578M	786603M	1054498M	195M	6724M	28712M	88296M	147747M	782824M

M = $ thousand   MM = $ million
See Pages 11 through 18 for Explanation of Ratios and Data

| Current Data Sorted By Assets | | | | | | | Comparative Historical Data | |

0-500M	500M-2MM	2-10MM	10-50MM	50-100MM	100-250MM	Type of Statement	4/1/98-3/31/99 ALL	4/1/99-3/31/00 ALL
	1	2	5	1	3	Unqualified	4	9
	2	4	1		1	Reviewed	4	6
1	4	1				Compiled	2	3
2						Tax Returns	1	1
	8	7	2	1		Other	7	3
	7 (4/1-9/30/02)		39 (10/1/02-3/31/03)					
3	15	14	8	2	4	**NUMBER OF STATEMENTS**	18	22
%	%	%	%	%	%	**ASSETS**	%	%
	15.3	3.8				Cash & Equivalents	8.6	6.7
	9.1	15.6				Trade Receivables (net)	24.0	22.9
	51.1	44.3				Inventory	32.1	37.7
	1.5	.4				All Other Current	5.2	1.5
	77.0	64.0				Total Current	69.9	68.7
	16.7	24.2				Fixed Assets (net)	21.1	20.7
	.9	4.9				Intangibles (net)	4.1	4.1
	5.4	6.8				All Other Non-Current	4.9	6.5
	100.0	100.0				Total	100.0	100.0
						LIABILITIES		
	16.6	17.4				Notes Payable-Short Term	7.0	8.7
	4.2	3.5				Cur. Mat.-L/T/D	4.5	1.7
	19.8	17.3				Trade Payables	15.1	18.3
	.0	.0				Income Taxes Payable	.2	.5
	5.2	21.2				All Other Current	13.2	13.6
	45.9	59.4				Total Current	40.0	42.7
	7.0	8.6				Long Term Debt	7.3	14.9
	.0	.3				Deferred Taxes	.1	.5
	1.1	5.4				All Other Non-Current	.7	1.0
	46.0	26.2				Net Worth	51.8	40.9
	100.0	100.0				Total Liabilities & Net Worth	100.0	100.0
						INCOME DATA		
	100.0	100.0				Net Sales	100.0	100.0
	25.2	18.8				Gross Profit	27.5	20.5
	22.0	14.7				Operating Expenses	21.2	16.8
	3.2	4.1				Operating Profit	6.3	3.7
	.0	1.0				All Other Expenses (net)	1.3	.4
	3.2	3.1				Profit Before Taxes	5.0	3.3
						RATIOS		
	2.9	1.4				Current	2.6	2.3
	1.8	1.1					1.9	1.6
	1.3	.6					1.3	1.3
	1.0	.4				Quick	1.5	1.3
	.6	.3					.8	.7
	.1	.2					.5	.4
	0 999.8	2 231.0				Sales/Receivables	11 34.7	14 26.2
	8 46.2	16 23.3					20 18.0	18 20.1
	13 28.5	19 19.4					31 11.7	26 14.3
	37 9.8	24 15.5				Cost of Sales/Inventory	22 16.8	23 16.0
	69 5.3	41 9.0					42 8.8	43 8.5
	160 2.3	95 3.8					55 6.7	63 5.8
	7 50.2	1 295.3				Cost of Sales/Payables	11 34.1	12 29.7
	32 11.3	11 33.0					19 19.1	21 17.6
	75 4.9	31 11.9					35 10.3	26 13.9
	5.5	14.4				Sales/Working Capital	7.2	9.8
	11.6	36.0					12.7	12.7
	21.4	-13.3					25.1	25.9
	13.3	10.0				EBIT/Interest	19.7	28.1
	(14) 3.3	3.9					(16) 7.7	(20) 3.7
	.9	-1.6					1.1	1.8
						Net Profit + Depr., Dep., Amort./Cur. Mat. L/T/D		
	.1	.1				Fixed/Worth	.2	.4
	.4	1.0					.4	.6
	.8	70.8					.6	.9
	.7	2.0				Debt/Worth	.5	.7
	1.2	4.1					1.2	1.7
	2.5	165.3					1.9	3.8
	31.4	69.8				% Profit Before Taxes/Tangible Net Worth	63.3	33.2
	11.7	(12) 45.5					23.0	(19) 16.3
	.2	7.8					8.5	9.3
	15.4	23.0				% Profit Before Taxes/Total Assets	23.7	17.8
	7.7	7.4					11.0	9.4
	.0	-11.6					3.1	2.9
	95.2	98.4				Sales/Net Fixed Assets	49.5	28.5
	32.0	17.3					26.9	19.8
	11.7	9.4					10.7	10.0
	5.3	5.5				Sales/Total Assets	5.5	5.3
	2.5	3.6					3.8	3.5
	1.7	2.4					2.5	2.9
	.4	.3				% Depr., Dep., Amort./Sales	.6	.5
	(12) 1.0	(12) 1.0					(14) 1.1	(21) 1.0
	1.5	2.7					1.8	1.2
						% Officers', Directors', Owners' Comp/Sales		
686M	52871M	224750M	540858M	505838M	1652939M	Net Sales ($)	496664M	1344677M
551M	17135M	54256M	199966M	152871M	699066M	Total Assets ($)	188451M	401344M

M = $ thousand   MM = $ million
See Pages 11 through 18 for Explanation of Ratios and Data

Comparative Historical Data | **Current Data Sorted By Sales**

			Type of Statement						
12	10	12	Unqualified				2	1	9
5	4	8	Reviewed			1	2	2	3
14	19	6	Compiled	2	2	1			1
1		2	Tax Returns	2					
14	10	18	Other		5	2	4	4	3
4/1/00-3/31/01	4/1/01-3/31/02	4/1/02-3/31/03			7 (4/1-9/30/02)		39 (10/1/02-3/31/03)		
ALL	ALL	ALL		0-1MM	1-3MM	3-5MM	5-10MM	10-25MM	25MM & OVER
46	43	46	**NUMBER OF STATEMENTS**	4	7	4	8	7	16
%	%	%	**ASSETS**	%	%	%	%	%	%
9.8	8.6	9.9	Cash & Equivalents						10.2
20.8	17.1	14.3	Trade Receivables (net)						21.4
41.0	41.6	42.5	Inventory						31.1
.5	2.2	1.8	All Other Current						3.1
72.0	69.4	68.5	Total Current						65.9
16.5	18.0	21.1	Fixed Assets (net)						22.4
7.9	8.9	3.5	Intangibles (net)						3.5
3.6	3.7	6.9	All Other Non-Current						8.2
100.0	100.0	100.0	Total						100.0
			LIABILITIES						
12.3	10.6	14.3	Notes Payable-Short Term						10.1
4.1	2.6	3.0	Cur. Mat.-L/T/D						2.0
14.5	20.8	17.5	Trade Payables						11.9
.0	.3	.1	Income Taxes Payable						.3
19.4	19.6	14.0	All Other Current						12.0
50.3	53.9	49.0	Total Current						36.2
8.6	8.7	9.1	Long Term Debt						12.0
.1	.0	.2	Deferred Taxes						.4
5.1	1.0	4.5	All Other Non-Current						3.2
35.8	36.4	37.1	Net Worth						48.1
100.0	100.0	100.0	Total Liabilities & Net Worth						100.0
			INCOME DATA						
100.0	100.0	100.0	Net Sales						100.0
19.7	19.4	21.3	Gross Profit						15.7
17.2	17.8	17.9	Operating Expenses						11.3
2.5	1.6	3.4	Operating Profit						4.4
−1.9	.9	.6	All Other Expenses (net)						.3
4.4	.6	2.8	Profit Before Taxes						4.1
			RATIOS						
2.0	2.2	2.0							2.8
1.5	1.3	1.4	Current						1.7
1.1	1.0	1.1							1.3
1.2	1.1	1.0							1.5
.5	.5	.4	Quick						.9
.3	.2	.2							.4
10 35.7	5 69.0	7 52.7						15	25.2
17 21.5	15 24.4	15 24.8	Sales/Receivables					23	16.1
28 13.0	30 12.3	22 16.6						39	9.3
29 12.6	34 10.8	33 11.0						30	12.1
50 7.2	58 6.3	53 6.9	Cost of Sales/Inventory					46	8.0
64 5.7	99 3.7	114 3.2						55	6.6
9 40.5	11 33.3	8 46.3						12	30.3
14 26.0	21 17.7	17 20.9	Cost of Sales/Payables					16	23.0
26 14.0	48 7.6	36 10.2						24	15.1
10.0	6.6	7.2							6.2
15.6	18.9	14.2	Sales/Working Capital						11.9
56.1	−324.2	99.0							25.4
11.6	4.4	9.7							12.9
(38) 5.0	(42) 1.2	(43) 4.8	EBIT/Interest					(14)	6.6
1.3	−1.1	1.0							4.5
		2.9	Net Profit + Depr., Dep.,						
		(10) 1.8	Amort./Cur. Mat. L/T/D						
		.5							
.2	.2	.1							.1
.5	.5	.4	Fixed/Worth						.3
1.4	1.2	1.5							1.1
.9	.7	.8							.7
1.7	1.5	1.7	Debt/Worth						1.0
4.8	6.5	4.9							2.8
53.0	36.4	51.5							57.2
(38) 20.5	(37) 4.5	(41) 20.4	% Profit Before Taxes/Tangible Net Worth					(15)	23.9
8.4	−7.0	4.6							10.2
21.8	14.9	16.9							18.1
8.3	1.3	8.0	% Profit Before Taxes/Total Assets						11.4
2.0	−5.6	.8							5.0
62.3	59.1	82.7							48.0
30.1	22.3	22.5	Sales/Net Fixed Assets						15.0
11.4	11.8	9.0							6.3
5.3	3.9	4.4							4.5
4.2	2.9	2.8	Sales/Total Assets						2.8
2.9	2.2	1.9							1.9
.3	.4	.3							.3
(38) .7	(39) .8	(40) 1.1	% Depr., Dep., Amort./Sales						.7
1.1	1.8	2.2							2.2
.4	.9	1.0							
(12) 1.1	(10) 1.7	(15) 1.8	% Officers', Directors', Owners' Comp/Sales						
3.0	4.2	7.0							
1916332M	1957345M	2977942M	Net Sales ($)	1006M	11483M	17778M	50192M	114650M	2782833M
568225M	616750M	1123845M	Total Assets ($)	1150M	8279M	7049M	13556M	29809M	1064002M

M = $ thousand   MM = $ million
See Pages 11 through 18 for Explanation of Ratios and Data

Current Data Sorted By Assets | **Comparative Historical Data**

0-500M	500M-2MM	2-10MM	10-50MM	50-100MM	100-250MM	Type of Statement	44 ALL	33 ALL
	1	6	12	2	2	Unqualified	6	10
1	2	6	2			Reviewed	15	5
2	3	7	1	1		Compiled	7	7
1		1	1			Tax Returns	2	1
4	1	4	3			Other	14	10
	8 (4/1-9/30/02)		54 (10/1/02-3/31/03)				4/1/98-3/31/99	4/1/99-3/31/00
8	7	24	18	3	2	NUMBER OF STATEMENTS	44	33
%	%	%	%	%	%	**ASSETS**	%	%
		9.6	3.3			Cash & Equivalents	4.7	4.3
		34.1	25.0			Trade Receivables (net)	31.4	28.3
		23.2	34.5			Inventory	24.1	29.5
		1.5	2.0			All Other Current	.8	1.4
		68.3	64.7			Total Current	61.0	63.5
		26.3	22.3			Fixed Assets (net)	28.0	28.7
		1.6	4.5			Intangibles (net)	3.2	2.9
		3.8	8.4			All Other Non-Current	7.8	4.9
		100.0	100.0			Total	100.0	100.0
						LIABILITIES		
		13.2	25.4			Notes Payable-Short Term	20.2	14.2
		5.5	2.7			Cur. Mat.-L/T/D	4.4	3.4
		19.5	18.2			Trade Payables	20.5	22.3
		1.1	.0			Income Taxes Payable	.5	.6
		14.1	6.2			All Other Current	5.4	6.4
		53.5	52.4			Total Current	51.0	46.8
		19.6	8.0			Long Term Debt	20.6	16.6
		.1	.4			Deferred Taxes	.3	.3
		3.5	4.1			All Other Non-Current	4.4	4.7
		23.4	35.1			Net Worth	23.7	31.6
		100.0	100.0			Total Liabilities & Net Worth	100.0	100.0
						INCOME DATA		
		100.0	100.0			Net Sales	100.0	100.0
		26.1	26.5			Gross Profit	28.0	29.9
		26.6	21.7			Operating Expenses	25.9	26.9
		−.5	4.7			Operating Profit	2.1	2.9
		−.1	1.5			All Other Expenses (net)	−.2	1.7
		−.4	3.2			Profit Before Taxes	2.3	1.3
						RATIOS		
		2.2	2.5			Current	1.8	2.3
		1.3	1.2				1.2	1.4
		.9	1.0				.8	.9
		1.3	1.2			Quick	1.1	1.3
		.9	.5				.7	.8
		.6	.3				.5	.4
		28 13.1	33 11.1			Sales/Receivables	34 10.7	33 11.1
		43 8.4	42 8.6				44 8.3	45 8.1
		71 5.2	55 6.7				57 6.3	63 5.8
		18 20.4	51 7.2			Cost of Sales/Inventory	19 18.8	30 12.0
		54 6.8	99 3.7				41 8.8	53 6.8
		81 4.5	134 2.7				81 4.5	104 3.5
		19 19.5	25 14.8			Cost of Sales/Payables	26 14.3	26 13.9
		40 9.1	35 10.5				32 11.4	42 8.7
		51 7.2	53 6.9				43 8.4	65 5.6
		6.8	6.2			Sales/Working Capital	9.6	4.8
		20.9	26.5				24.1	14.0
		−32.2	NM				−36.3	−65.7
		6.9	11.4			EBIT/Interest	4.7	7.7
		(20) 2.8	2.2				(43) 2.6	(31) 2.8
		−.3	1.5				1.0	1.3
						Net Profit + Depr., Dep., Amort./Cur. Mat. L /T/D	3.6	
							(18) 2.3	
							1.1	
		.6	.4			Fixed/Worth	.5	.3
		1.1	.6				1.1	.8
		−2.7	2.2				3.7	3.8
		1.1	.7			Debt/Worth	1.4	.9
		3.5	3.0				3.3	2.7
		−22.4	6.0				7.1	6.1
		(17) 35.5	(16) 41.0			% Profit Before Taxes/Tangible Net Worth	(39) 37.0	(28) 43.7
		6.6	17.7				11.1	21.3
		1.5	4.8				.5	4.7
		11.9	12.5			% Profit Before Taxes/Total Assets	10.4	13.2
		1.8	3.2				3.3	7.1
		−5.4	1.2				.2	1.2
		43.1	22.2			Sales/Net Fixed Assets	23.8	22.2
		11.4	13.8				11.0	9.8
		5.6	6.6				7.4	4.0
		3.0	2.5			Sales/Total Assets	3.7	3.4
		2.2	2.1				2.8	2.0
		1.8	1.7				1.9	1.6
		(23) 1.0	(17) 1.0			% Depr., Dep., Amort./Sales	(39) .8	(30) .7
		2.1	2.1				1.8	1.9
		4.2	2.7				3.2	3.1
		(11) 2.6				% Officers', Directors', Owners' Comp/Sales	3.7	(10) 1.1
		3.9					(18) 5.1	2.6
		6.8					8.3	6.7
7699M	22507M	355965M	871653M	435584M	585721M	Net Sales ($)	1625969M	618158M
1964M	7238M	129869M	395006M	230023M	241921M	Total Assets ($)	631333M	301418M

© RMA 2003

M = $ thousand   MM = $ million
See Pages 11 through 18 for Explanation of Ratios and Data

Comparative Historical Data   Current Data Sorted By Sales

				Type of Statement						
14	9	23		Unqualified		1		3	4	15
10	12	11		Reviewed		1	2	2	4	2
10	9	14		Compiled	1	3	2	2	4	2
2	1	2		Tax Returns	1				1	
7	17	12		Other	3	2	1	2	2	2
4/1/00-3/31/01	4/1/01-3/31/02	4/1/02-3/31/03				8 (4/1-9/30/02)			54 (10/1/02-3/31/03)	
ALL	ALL	ALL			0-1MM	1-3MM	3-5MM	5-10MM	10-25MM	25MM & OVER
43	48	62		**NUMBER OF STATEMENTS**	5	7	5	9	15	21
%	%	%		**ASSETS**	%	%	%	%	%	%
6.7	4.7	7.0		Cash & Equivalents					8.0	4.0
33.8	31.0	29.9		Trade Receivables (net)					33.0	28.6
24.6	26.0	27.2		Inventory					25.6	30.0
1.2	.9	2.4		All Other Current					.9	4.2
66.4	62.6	66.5		Total Current					67.6	66.7
25.2	26.8	25.5		Fixed Assets (net)					25.8	24.2
4.1	3.7	3.3		Intangibles (net)					2.0	4.0
4.2	6.8	4.7		All Other Non-Current					4.7	5.1
100.0	100.0	100.0		Total					100.0	100.0
				LIABILITIES						
14.7	20.7	14.7		Notes Payable-Short Term					21.7	16.5
3.8	5.8	4.8		Cur. Mat.-L/T/D					5.4	2.2
20.7	19.1	17.9		Trade Payables					18.8	21.8
.1	.8	.5		Income Taxes Payable					1.7	.0
10.9	9.7	10.2		All Other Current					9.6	11.4
50.3	56.1	48.0		Total Current					57.3	51.9
14.2	16.8	16.5		Long Term Debt					12.3	8.7
.1	.2	.2		Deferred Taxes					.0	.4
2.7	5.0	4.6		All Other Non-Current					5.2	2.8
32.7	21.9	30.7		Net Worth					25.2	36.3
100.0	100.0	100.0		Total Liabilities & Net Worth					100.0	100.0
				INCOME DATA						
100.0	100.0	100.0		Net Sales					100.0	100.0
28.0	30.9	28.6		Gross Profit					28.2	20.6
26.4	30.9	26.2		Operating Expenses					24.6	17.1
1.6	.0	2.4		Operating Profit					3.7	3.5
1.1	1.5	.5		All Other Expenses (net)					.6	.5
.5	−1.5	1.9		Profit Before Taxes					3.0	3.0
				RATIOS						
2.3	1.6	2.4							2.0	2.3
1.4	1.2	1.3		Current					1.1	1.2
1.0	.8	1.0							.8	1.0
1.3	1.0	1.3							1.2	1.3
.8	.7	.9		Quick					.9	.7
.6	.5	.4							.5	.4
31 11.9	35 10.5	28 13.0							28 13.0	31 12.0
47 7.8	46 8.0	38 9.5		Sales/Receivables					47 7.8	34 10.6
60 6.1	57 6.4	59 6.2							78 4.7	48 7.6
20 18.7	26 13.9	20 18.3							20 18.0	16 23.5
47 7.7	59 6.1	57 6.4		Cost of Sales/Inventory					77 4.8	56 6.5
72 5.1	109 3.4	102 3.6							100 3.6	117 3.1
21 17.8	23 16.1	18 20.6							24 15.1	24 15.1
36 10.2	35 10.3	35 10.5		Cost of Sales/Payables					40 9.0	36 10.2
49 7.4	53 6.8	51 7.2							47 7.8	58 6.3
6.7	10.1	6.3							7.4	5.7
12.7	22.6	19.8		Sales/Working Capital					27.5	24.9
189.6	−26.0	215.1							−10.7	303.0
5.5	3.6	10.3							10.2	12.7
(42) 2.0	(46) 1.7	(58) 2.7		EBIT/Interest					3.3	(20) 2.7
.9	−.6	1.0							.5	1.7
2.8	3.1	7.4		Net Profit + Depr., Dep.,						
(12) 1.5	(13) 1.4	(18) 1.7		Amort./Cur. Mat. L/T/D						
1.0	.2	.6								
.4	.4	.4							.6	.4
.9	1.3	.9		Fixed/Worth					1.3	.6
1.7	8.0	3.4							−2.1	1.4
1.0	1.3	.9							1.2	1.0
1.8	2.6	1.7		Debt/Worth					4.6	1.5
6.0	28.2	21.1							−20.8	6.1
33.9	35.9	38.7							39.9	45.3
(36) 16.8	(39) 10.2	(50) 15.0		% Profit Before Taxes/Tangible Net Worth					(11) 26.0	(20) 17.7
1.4	−9.9	3.1							5.1	4.8
12.0	6.7	12.5							12.3	12.6
2.6	1.7	3.3		% Profit Before Taxes/Total Assets					4.1	3.7
−1.6	−7.8	.4							−1.5	2.2
32.3	35.8	32.4							35.8	17.9
11.9	11.8	14.0		Sales/Net Fixed Assets					8.1	13.9
4.9	4.8	6.7							5.3	6.3
3.7	3.2	3.1							2.3	2.8
2.2	2.2	2.2		Sales/Total Assets					2.1	2.1
1.7	1.6	1.8							1.8	1.8
1.0	.9	1.0							.8	1.1
(38) 2.2	(43) 2.2	(55) 2.0		% Depr., Dep., Amort./Sales					(14) 1.7	(20) 1.9
4.1	3.8	3.0							3.2	2.4
2.9	3.3	2.7		% Officers', Directors',						
(13) 4.7	(14) 6.4	(25) 4.0		Owners' Comp/Sales						
7.1	11.3	8.2								
1681638M	1181055M	2279129M		Net Sales ($)	2351M	14291M	19897M	66059M	243714M	1932817M
693692M	556228M	1006021M		Total Assets ($)	959M	4349M	15277M	33337M	121805M	830294M

© RMA 2003   **M = $ thousand   MM = $ million**
                              See Pages 11 through 18 for Explanation of Ratios and Data

Current Data Sorted By Assets   Comparative Historical Data

						Type of Statement	36	31
		2	14	5	4	Unqualified	36	31
	8	27	8			Reviewed	49	52
	8	11				Compiled	33	27
	3					Tax Returns	5	4
2	9	15	16	5	2	Other	39	46
	32 (4/1-9/30/02)		107 (10/1/02-3/31/03)				4/1/98-3/31/99	4/1/99-3/31/00
0-500M	500M-2MM	2-10MM	10-50MM	50-100MM	100-250MM		ALL	ALL
2	28	55	38	10	6	NUMBER OF STATEMENTS	162	160
%	%	%	%	%	%	**ASSETS**	%	%
	8.0	7.9	5.3	2.0		Cash & Equivalents	5.3	5.8
	29.7	27.8	25.0	22.3		Trade Receivables (net)	27.2	28.4
	15.3	17.0	14.3	9.0		Inventory	18.4	17.2
	4.5	1.2	2.7	6.5		All Other Current	2.4	1.8
	57.5	53.9	47.3	39.8		Total Current	53.2	53.2
	34.4	38.0	45.0	51.1		Fixed Assets (net)	38.1	39.5
	2.3	1.1	1.2	1.1		Intangibles (net)	2.5	2.8
	5.9	7.0	6.6	8.0		All Other Non-Current	6.1	4.5
	100.0	100.0	100.0	100.0		Total	100.0	100.0
						LIABILITIES		
	14.4	11.7	12.8	15.8		Notes Payable-Short Term	8.0	10.4
	5.6	5.3	4.6	5.0		Cur. Mat.-L/T/D	4.2	5.1
	15.9	13.4	14.3	13.4		Trade Payables	17.0	15.9
	.0	.1	.2	.0		Income Taxes Payable	.2	.1
	8.6	10.2	7.7	12.3		All Other Current	8.6	8.1
	44.5	40.8	39.6	46.6		Total Current	37.9	39.6
	21.5	19.9	30.2	27.5		Long Term Debt	19.8	20.4
	.0	.6	1.1	.8		Deferred Taxes	1.0	.7
	6.2	4.4	5.7	6.7		All Other Non-Current	6.2	4.7
	27.9	34.3	23.4	18.5		Net Worth	35.1	34.5
	100.0	100.0	100.0	100.0		Total Liabilities & Net Worth	100.0	100.0
						INCOME DATA		
	100.0	100.0	100.0	100.0		Net Sales	100.0	100.0
	28.7	22.6	19.2	20.0		Gross Profit	22.9	22.7
	26.3	20.9	14.7	14.8		Operating Expenses	17.8	17.0
	2.4	1.7	4.4	5.1		Operating Profit	5.0	5.7
	3.8	.3	2.5	2.7		All Other Expenses (net)	.9	1.4
	-1.4	1.4	1.9	2.4		Profit Before Taxes	4.1	4.3
						RATIOS		
	2.3	2.0	1.7	1.2			2.0	2.2
	1.5	1.4	1.2	.9		Current	1.4	1.3
	.7	.9	.8	.6			1.0	1.0
	1.5	1.5	1.0	.9			1.3	1.4
	.9	.9	.7	.5		Quick	.9	.9
	.5	.5	.6	.3			.6	.6
	28 13.0	38 9.6	41 8.9	30 12.0			39 9.5	38 9.6
	40 9.2	52 7.0	56 6.5	46 8.0		Sales/Receivables	47 7.7	51 7.2
	70 5.2	62 5.9	67 5.5	61 6.0			60 5.2	62 5.9
	8 48.0	26 14.3	23 15.6	16 22.9			24 15.3	25 14.3
	30 12.1	40 9.2	35 10.3	22 16.3		Cost of Sales/Inventory	35 10.4	35 10.5
	52 7.0	56 6.5	60 6.1	34 10.7			53 6.9	55 6.6
	12 29.2	17 21.3	26 13.8	29 12.5			23 16.0	19 19.2
	25 14.4	27 13.3	40 9.2	34 10.9		Cost of Sales/Payables	35 10.3	31 11.6
	49 7.5	40 9.1	52 7.0	48 7.7			47 7.7	48 7.7
	5.9	5.9	10.0	31.6			7.9	7.5
	15.5	12.5	28.2	-506.1		Sales/Working Capital	13.6	15.1
	-15.2	-75.2	-24.2	-8.3			170.6	209.1
	6.3	4.2	5.2	4.3			6.5	6.6
	(23) 1.0	(50) 1.9	(36) 2.2	2.3		EBIT/Interest	(152) 3.0	(152) 2.9
	-.5	.3	1.2	.2			1.3	1.6
		3.4	6.0				6.5	3.5
		(16) 1.5	(13) 2.4			Net Profit + Depr., Dep., Amort./Cur. Mat. L./T/D	(59) 2.4	(58) 2.1
		1.2	1.0				1.7	1.4
	.5	.6	.8	2.0			.6	.7
	1.8	1.1	1.7	3.1		Fixed/Worth	1.2	1.3
	-23.4	1.9	2.8	3.9			2.9	2.8
	.9	.7	1.5	3.3			.9	.9
	6.0	1.9	2.7	3.8		Debt/Worth	1.9	2.0
	-74.3	3.5	4.2	6.6			4.8	5.5
	31.6	22.0	45.1				41.4	46.6
	(20) .5	(47) 10.6	(36) 12.1			% Profit Before Taxes/Tangible Net Worth	(142) 19.0	(143) 23.6
	-37.3	2.4	3.7				7.3	6.8
	5.9	8.1	9.7	7.7			13.4	13.7
	-.1	3.1	3.3	4.0		% Profit Before Taxes/Total Assets	6.9	6.7
	-7.2	-2.0	.4	-3.5			1.4	2.2
	28.2	8.6	6.1	5.6			8.9	8.6
	5.9	4.9	3.3	3.2		Sales/Net Fixed Assets	5.4	5.0
	4.2	3.4	2.2	2.4			3.6	3.4
	2.6	2.2	2.1	2.2			2.5	2.6
	2.0	1.8	1.5	1.9		Sales/Total Assets	2.0	1.9
	1.8	1.5	1.2	1.2			1.6	1.5
	2.2	2.4	3.2				2.3	2.2
	(25) 3.8	3.7	(35) 4.2			% Depr., Dep., Amort./Sales	(145) 3.2	(149) 3.4
	6.3	5.4	5.5				4.6	4.9
	4.4	2.8					2.2	2.6
	(13) 6.9	(23) 6.4				% Officers', Directors', Owners' Comp/Sales	(50) 4.3	(54) 3.9
	11.9	8.6					7.0	7.6
3467M	94002M	538081M	1350498M	1302344M	988950M	Net Sales ($)	5876247M	5511477M
930M	37467M	287060M	849022M	756501M	786201M	Total Assets ($)	3552131M	3365946M

© RMA 2003

M = $ thousand   MM = $ million
See Pages 11 through 18 for Explanation of Ratios and Data

Comparative Historical Data / Current Data Sorted By Sales

							Type of Statement						
	27		24		25		Unqualified				1	3	21
	54		29		43		Reviewed	1	3	10	13	13	3
	18		23		19		Compiled		4	6	8	1	
	5		2		3		Tax Returns	1		1	1		
	39		56		49		Other		7	4	7	13	18
	4/1/00-3/31/01 ALL		4/1/01-3/31/02 ALL		4/1/02-3/31/03 ALL				32 (4/1-9/30/02)		107 (10/1/02-3/31/03)		
								0-1MM	1-3MM	3-5MM	5-10MM	10-25MM	25MM & OVER
	143		134		139		NUMBER OF STATEMENTS	2	14	21	30	30	42
	%		%		%		ASSETS	%	%	%	%	%	%
	5.5		6.7		6.5		Cash & Equivalents		6.9	6.0	9.3	10.1	2.2
	28.0		26.1		26.9		Trade Receivables (net)		28.8	27.4	27.3	24.9	26.5
	19.2		15.7		15.2		Inventory		9.3	17.4	18.8	17.1	12.8
	1.3		2.1		2.7		All Other Current		7.9	1.2	1.2	1.9	3.5
	54.1		50.5		51.4		Total Current		52.8	51.9	56.6	54.1	45.1
	37.4		38.0		40.2		Fixed Assets (net)		34.0	40.3	35.7	39.1	45.6
	2.9		3.5		1.9		Intangibles (net)		5.8	1.4	.2	.6	3.2
	5.6		8.0		6.5		All Other Non-Current		7.4	6.3	7.5	6.2	6.1
	100.0		100.0		100.0		Total		100.0	100.0	100.0	100.0	100.0
							LIABILITIES						
	12.8		11.0		12.6		Notes Payable-Short Term		15.8	13.9	13.0	11.1	12.3
	5.4		5.8		5.5		Cur. Mat.-L/T/D		5.5	6.6	3.4	6.2	6.2
	16.4		15.6		14.2		Trade Payables		11.2	17.5	11.9	14.2	15.8
	.1		.2		.1		Income Taxes Payable		.0	.1	.1	.1	.2
	9.1		8.5		9.2		All Other Current		5.6	6.7	12.2	9.3	9.8
	43.7		41.1		41.7		Total Current		38.2	44.8	40.6	40.9	44.4
	16.6		18.4		23.8		Long Term Debt		33.2	21.6	15.3	30.5	22.0
	.7		.6		.7		Deferred Taxes		.0	.2	.6	.9	1.1
	4.4		3.4		5.6		All Other Non-Current		6.9	3.8	8.0	4.6	5.3
	34.7		36.5		28.2		Net Worth		21.7	29.7	35.5	23.0	27.1
	100.0		100.0		100.0		Total Liabilities & Net Worth		100.0	100.0	100.0	100.0	100.0
							INCOME DATA						
	100.0		100.0		100.0		Net Sales		100.0	100.0	100.0	100.0	100.0
	21.6		22.9		22.8		Gross Profit		29.3	25.6	24.7	21.1	18.1
	17.9		20.4		19.7		Operating Expenses		29.9	23.4	23.7	17.6	12.8
	3.8		2.5		3.2		Operating Profit		-.5	2.2	.9	3.5	5.2
	2.0		1.7		1.9		All Other Expenses (net)		1.3	.9	.5	1.5	2.1
	1.8		.8		1.3		Profit Before Taxes		-1.9	1.3	.4	1.9	3.1
							RATIOS						
	2.0		2.1		1.9				3.6	1.9	2.3	1.7	1.3
	1.3		1.3		1.3		Current		2.1	1.5	1.4	1.4	1.1
	.9		.8		.8				.8	.7	.9	1.0	.7
	1.2		1.4		1.1				3.0	1.4	1.3	1.2	.9
	.8		.7		.8		Quick		1.4	.9	.9	.8	.6
	.5		.5		.5				.4	.4	.5	.6	.4

37	9.9	36	10.2	38	9.6	Sales/Receivables	39	9.4	35	10.4	37	9.9	38	9.7	41	8.9
49	7.4	51	7.2	51	7.2		48	7.5	43	8.4	54	6.7	47	7.7	54	6.8
59	6.2	63	5.8	62	5.8		72	5.1	67	5.4	82	4.4	59	6.2	62	5.9
22	16.8	22	16.6	23	16.2	Cost of Sales/Inventory	2	151.4	32	11.3	30	12.3	25	14.8	20	18.4
36	10.1	35	10.5	36	10.0		15	23.7	46	8.0	43	8.5	37	9.8	30	12.1
56	6.5	54	6.7	52	7.0		37	9.9	67	5.4	63	5.8	50	7.3	47	7.7
18	20.1	18	20.3	19	19.5	Cost of Sales/Payables	15	24.9	19	18.8	12	29.6	21	17.6	31	11.8
30	12.2	31	11.9	32	11.3		24	15.2	34	10.9	22	16.8	30	12.3	40	9.2
46	7.9	56	6.5	47	7.8		39	9.3	60	6.1	44	8.2	43	8.5	54	6.8
	7.5		7.8		7.5	Sales/Working Capital		5.1		6.8		4.2		6.1		13.4
	23.2		18.0		16.4			8.5		15.5		12.1		16.2		41.2
	-39.2		-21.7		-15.7			-24.4		-14.7		-64.9		-269.1		-12.2
(133)	5.7	(123)	3.5	(127)	4.6	EBIT/Interest	(11)	2.7		11.8	(28)	3.3	(26)	4.4	(41)	6.1
	2.0		2.0		2.0			1.3		1.5		1.5		2.0		2.5
	.7		-.2		.6			-3.1		.2		-.6		.9		1.6
(44)	5.7	(37)	3.3	(38)	3.9	Net Profit + Depr., Dep., Amort./Cur. Mat. L/T/D						3.9				5.3
	2.2		1.9		1.6						(11)	1.9			(14)	1.8
	1.1		.8		1.0							.9				.8
	.6		.6		.7	Fixed/Worth		.9		.5		.5		.7		1.2
	1.4		1.5		1.5			NM		1.1		1.0		1.3		2.0
	3.1		3.4		3.5			-2.1		3.9		1.7		3.1		3.3
	.9		.7		1.2	Debt/Worth		1.3		.6		1.0		1.1		2.0
	2.1		2.3		2.7			NM		1.6		1.8		2.2		3.3
	7.5		6.6		6.4			-13.9		7.6		4.3		4.7		4.7
(128)	31.5	(122)	28.4	(117)	32.9	% Profit Before Taxes/Tangible Net Worth			(17)	31.6	(27)	17.2	(26)	36.9	(38)	45.9
	10.7		10.0		10.8					12.0		5.5		12.4		21.0
	-.9		-4.3		1.1					-.5		-6.7		3.6		7.4
	10.4		8.9		8.7	% Profit Before Taxes/Total Assets		8.2		6.9		4.9		10.1		10.8
	2.9		2.7		2.7			2.6		1.3		1.2		3.3		4.7
	-1.0		-3.3		-1.4			-12.3		-3.4		-4.4		.0		1.7
	9.4		8.9		8.1	Sales/Net Fixed Assets		12.7		6.7		8.9		9.4		5.6
	5.1		4.9		4.5			6.5		5.0		4.9		4.9		3.6
	3.4		3.3		2.9			3.6		3.2		3.5		3.0		2.4
	2.6		2.3		2.2	Sales/Total Assets		2.8		2.4		2.2		2.3		2.2
	2.0		1.7		1.8			1.8		1.9		1.6		1.9		1.8
	1.6		1.4		1.4			1.4		1.6		1.2		1.4		1.3
(132)	1.9	(122)	2.9	(130)	2.7	% Depr., Dep., Amort./Sales		2.3	(18)	3.7	(29)	1.9	(29)	2.5	(38)	3.1
	3.4		3.4		3.9			3.9		4.2		3.3		4.1		3.9
	4.9		6.2		5.5			6.9		5.8		5.5		5.5		5.2
(48)	1.7	(43)	2.0	(45)	1.8	% Officers', Directors', Owners' Comp/Sales	(10)	5.7			(16)	2.9				
	5.1		4.2		5.9			7.6				6.7				
	9.7		8.7		8.7			13.2				10.4				

4586216M	4247742M	4277342M	Net Sales ($)	1143M	26147M	80339M	208916M	491417M	3469380M
2699165M	2532193M	2717181M	Total Assets ($)	2254M	18303M	45693M	142849M	289772M	2218310M

M = $ thousand   MM = $ million
See Pages 11 through 18 for Explanation of Ratios and Data

Current Data Sorted By Assets   **Comparative Historical Data**

						Type of Statement		
2		22	42	12	16	Unqualified	129	117
2	14	50	10		2	Reviewed	67	63
6	32	32	4		1	Compiled	51	37
8	8	1			1	Tax Returns	10	8
7	22	43	38	17	15	Other	140	134
	85 (4/1-9/30/02)		**322 (10/1/02-3/31/03)**				**4/1/98-**	**4/1/99-**
							3/31/99	**3/31/00**
0-500M	**500M-2MM**	**2-10MM**	**10-50MM**	**50-100MM**	**100-250MM**		**ALL**	**ALL**
25	76	148	94	29	35	NUMBER OF STATEMENTS	397	359
%	%	%	%	%	%	**ASSETS**	%	%
10.8	8.1	7.5	7.0	4.1	5.8	Cash & Equivalents	5.5	5.0
30.1	27.1	23.5	24.3	21.8	21.1	Trade Receivables (net)	23.7	24.2
14.4	26.4	27.1	25.8	19.1	17.9	Inventory	28.4	27.9
.6	1.7	2.2	3.3	2.3	2.9	All Other Current	2.1	1.9
56.0	63.3	60.3	60.4	47.3	47.6	Total Current	59.6	59.0
37.9	28.9	29.8	30.7	40.7	36.3	Fixed Assets (net)	30.6	30.7
1.5	2.0	4.4	4.1	6.7	10.4	Intangibles (net)	4.9	5.7
4.6	5.8	5.5	4.8	5.2	5.7	All Other Non-Current	4.9	4.6
100.0	100.0	100.0	100.0	100.0	100.0	Total	100.0	100.0
						LIABILITIES		
35.2	13.8	11.7	11.2	11.2	4.8	Notes Payable-Short Term	12.8	11.5
3.0	4.9	5.1	4.7	4.4	3.9	Cur. Mat.-L/T/D	3.9	3.9
22.7	14.8	14.1	16.3	16.1	16.2	Trade Payables	15.9	16.6
.0	.1	.2	.1	.2	.2	Income Taxes Payable	.2	.4
10.7	6.3	7.1	12.2	8.2	12.2	All Other Current	8.3	8.5
71.7	39.9	38.2	44.6	40.1	37.3	Total Current	41.1	40.9
26.2	18.5	16.0	15.6	17.2	15.2	Long Term Debt	18.2	19.1
.1	.2	.6	.6	1.3	1.0	Deferred Taxes	.7	.8
9.7	4.5	5.8	7.2	4.0	5.2	All Other Non-Current	5.8	6.2
-7.7	36.9	39.3	31.9	37.3	41.2	Net Worth	34.1	33.0
100.0	100.0	100.0	100.0	100.0	100.0	Total Liabilities & Net Worth	100.0	100.0
						INCOME DATA		
100.0	100.0	100.0	100.0	100.0	100.0	Net Sales	100.0	100.0
40.5	35.9	28.3	23.7	14.4	20.4	Gross Profit	25.3	26.2
42.5	31.9	24.7	17.6	10.2	14.5	Operating Expenses	21.1	20.8
-2.0	4.0	3.6	6.1	4.2	5.9	Operating Profit	4.2	5.4
1.7	2.0	1.2	1.5	1.6	1.4	All Other Expenses (net)	1.5	1.8
-3.7	2.0	2.4	4.6	2.6	4.5	Profit Before Taxes	2.7	3.6
						RATIOS		
1.9	3.9	2.5	2.3	1.8	1.7		2.3	2.3
1.1	1.8	1.4	1.4	1.3	1.2	Current	1.6	1.5
.7	.9	1.1	.9	.9	1.0		1.1	1.1
1.5	2.0	1.4	1.2	.9	1.0		1.2	1.1
.8	.9	.7	.7	.7	.8	Quick	.7	.7
.5	.5	.5	.4	.4	.5		.5	.5

31	11.9	24	15.3	29	12.6	34	10.8	35	10.5	28	12.9		
40	9.1	42	8.7	41	8.9	50	7.3	43	8.4	38	9.7	Sales/Receivables	30 12.3 33 11.1
60	6.1	65	5.6	51	7.1	65	5.6	57	6.4	49	7.5		44 8.3 46 8.0
													55 6.6 59 6.2

11	34.5	22	17.0	34	10.9	33	11.1	24	14.9	22	16.5		34 10.9 34 10.6
19	18.9	50	7.4	53	6.9	57	6.5	35	10.4	31	11.7	Cost of Sales/Inventory	59 6.2 61 6.0
58	6.3	113	3.2	99	3.7	110	3.3	74	4.9	63	5.8		103 3.6 103 3.5

16	23.4	16	22.3	18	19.8	20	18.6	28	13.1	24	15.1		22 16.4 21 17.7
36	10.1	33	11.2	28	12.9	34	10.8	33	11.0	37	9.9	Cost of Sales/Payables	35 10.4 37 10.0
78	4.7	45	8.2	50	7.3	54	6.8	42	8.6	43	8.6		48 7.5 53 6.9

10.3	4.8	5.5	4.6	7.9	8.6		5.6 5.7
33.3	9.4	10.7	11.6	27.3	24.2	Sales/Working Capital	10.1 11.9
-16.6	-51.7	50.8	-47.3	-109.4	123.9		38.1 61.0

	2.4		4.2		7.0		12.1		5.4		36.6		8.6 6.7
(21)	.8	(64)	1.9	(135)	3.2	(85)	4.0	(28)	3.3		10.4	EBIT/Interest	(366) 3.2 (333) 3.2
	-.7		-.5		1.2		1.8		1.2		3.1		1.3 1.2

		1.9		6.5		5.4		4.8		79.7		5.1 5.5
	(14)	1.3	(51)	2.1	(35)	2.7	(15)	2.4	(10)	2.2	Net Profit + Depr., Dep., Amort./Cur. Mat. L /T/D	(113) 2.4 (103) 2.7
		.2		.8		1.1		.8		.1		1.3 1.4

1.4	.2	.3	.5	.6	.8		.5 .5
4.3	.7	.8	1.1	1.4	1.0	Fixed/Worth	.9 1.1
-1.1	2.7	2.3	2.4	3.5	2.6		2.4 3.4

1.7	.4	.6	1.1	1.0	.9		.9 .9
16.9	1.7	2.0	2.2	2.5	1.8	Debt/Worth	1.9 2.4
-5.9	8.2	5.0	8.1	6.6	6.0		6.5 8.7

	37.5		24.9		41.1		43.0		25.8		40.6	% Profit Before Taxes/Tangible Net Worth	49.9 49.2
(15)	9.5	(65)	8.9	(135)	15.4	(83)	22.4	(27)	20.4	(30)	25.0		(344) 21.3 (301) 23.8
	-54.2		-2.9		2.5		9.8		3.7		8.8		7.4 7.5

5.1	10.2	11.8	12.8	8.9	13.7		14.5 15.7
-1.4	3.0	5.5	6.7	6.7	9.9	% Profit Before Taxes/Total Assets	6.8 6.9
-12.9	-3.1	.6	2.7	.8	3.7		.9 1.1

14.0	20.7	18.4	13.6	7.8	10.2		15.9 16.1
8.1	9.4	8.2	6.7	3.8	5.0	Sales/Net Fixed Assets	7.1 6.7
4.2	4.5	3.9	3.8	2.8	3.2		3.8 3.7

3.3	3.0	2.7	2.1	2.3	2.6		2.6 2.6
2.5	2.0	2.0	1.6	1.8	1.8	Sales/Total Assets	2.0 1.9
1.7	1.5	1.5	1.3	1.2	1.1		1.4 1.4

	1.9		1.8		1.5		1.8		2.1		1.3		1.3 1.4
(24)	4.0	(63)	3.1	(137)	2.7	(88)	2.9	(25)	4.5	(16)	2.7	% Depr., Dep., Amort./Sales	(325) 2.5 (299) 2.5
	5.6		5.8		4.8		5.2		5.9		4.7		4.3 4.5

	8.1		3.6		2.4		1.8					% Officers', Directors', Owners' Comp/Sales	2.3 1.4
(14)	10.1	(46)	7.0	(53)	3.9	(11)	2.4						(109) 3.6 (102) 3.6
	20.2		10.6		7.1		4.2							6.9 6.8

20188M	217042M	1561928M	4015328M	3887345M	11278940M	Net Sales ($)	21181695M	19152460M
7266M	89923M	743117M	2169542M	2104332M	5259605M	Total Assets ($)	13077731M	11702753M

M = $ thousand   MM = $ million
See Pages 11 through 18 for Explanation of Ratios and Data

Comparative Historical Data | Current Data Sorted By Sales

			Type of Statement	85 (4/1-9/30/02)		322 (10/1/02-3/31/03)			
80	81	94	Unqualified						
56	52	78	Reviewed						
40	55	75	Compiled						
11	7	18	Tax Returns						
135	120	142	Other						
4/1/00-3/31/01 ALL	4/1/01-3/31/02 ALL	4/1/02-3/31/03 ALL		0-1MM	1-3MM	3-5MM	5-10MM	10-25MM	25MM & OVER
			Type of Statement						
			Unqualified	2		4	10	14	64
			Reviewed	3	6	5	25	27	12
			Compiled	5	23	14	23	7	3
			Tax Returns	7	7	2	1		1
			Other	11	11	11	19	35	55
322	315	407	**NUMBER OF STATEMENTS**	28	47	36	78	83	135
%	%	%	**ASSETS**	%	%	%	%	%	%
5.0	5.1	7.3	Cash & Equivalents	9.3	8.7	9.2	7.5	6.8	6.0
24.5	23.9	24.4	Trade Receivables (net)	22.6	29.4	24.3	22.9	24.9	23.7
25.9	26.9	24.5	Inventory	17.7	21.9	27.0	26.4	28.4	22.7
2.0	2.2	2.3	All Other Current	.4	1.5	2.1	2.0	2.3	3.4
57.4	58.2	58.6	Total Current	50.2	61.5	62.6	58.7	62.5	55.8
31.2	30.5	31.7	Fixed Assets (net)	37.2	32.0	28.8	31.5	29.1	32.8
6.3	5.9	4.4	Intangibles (net)	2.8	1.9	4.7	3.2	4.0	6.4
5.1	5.4	5.4	All Other Non-Current	9.8	4.6	3.9	6.5	4.4	5.0
100.0	100.0	100.0	Total	100.0	100.0	100.0	100.0	100.0	100.0
			LIABILITIES						
12.0	12.4	12.8	Notes Payable-Short Term	31.1	15.3	14.3	10.6	12.4	9.3
4.0	4.3	4.7	Cur. Mat.-L/T/D	3.8	4.3	5.5	5.3	5.1	4.1
16.8	18.1	15.6	Trade Payables	14.0	15.8	14.9	13.7	13.4	18.6
.2	.2	.2	Income Taxes Payable	.1	.0	.1	.3	.2	.2
9.1	8.2	8.8	All Other Current	3.5	9.8	7.3	7.2	7.5	11.8
42.1	43.2	42.1	Total Current	52.6	45.2	42.1	37.1	38.6	43.9
19.1	18.2	17.0	Long Term Debt	31.0	15.8	21.9	15.3	15.9	15.0
.7	.6	.6	Deferred Taxes	.0	.3	.8	.5	.7	.8
5.5	9.6	6.0	All Other Non-Current	6.3	6.5	1.8	7.3	5.5	6.3
32.6	28.4	34.3	Net Worth	10.0	32.2	33.4	39.8	39.4	33.9
100.0	100.0	100.0	Total Liabilities & Net Worth	100.0	100.0	100.0	100.0	100.0	100.0
			INCOME DATA						
100.0	100.0	100.0	Net Sales	100.0	100.0	100.0	100.0	100.0	100.0
25.3	24.2	27.8	Gross Profit	49.1	31.2	31.8	30.7	26.9	19.9
21.8	20.4	23.6	Operating Expenses	44.3	30.7	30.0	26.9	22.2	14.1
3.4	3.7	4.1	Operating Profit	4.8	.5	1.8	3.8	4.7	5.8
–.1	1.9	1.5	All Other Expenses (net)	3.8	1.5	1.6	1.2	.9	1.5
3.6	1.9	2.6	Profit Before Taxes	1.0	–1.0	.3	2.5	3.8	4.2
			RATIOS						
2.2	2.3	2.3	Current	5.0	2.9	2.4	2.7	2.7	1.8
1.4	1.5	1.4		1.2	1.6	1.4	1.5	1.6	1.3
1.0	1.0	1.0		.7	.9	1.0	1.1	1.2	.9
1.1	1.2	1.3	Quick	2.4	2.0	1.3	1.4	1.5	1.0
.7	.7	.7		.8	1.0	.7	.7	.7	.7
.4	.4	.5		.5	.5	.4	.5	.5	.5
32 11.5	29 12.7	30 12.2	Sales/Receivables	28 13.1	34 10.7	23 15.6	28 12.9	30 12.2	33 11.0
43 8.5	41 9.0	43 8.6		51 7.2	43 8.6	44 8.2	40 9.2	44 8.3	43 8.5
56 6.6	53 6.9	57 6.4		69 5.3	64 5.7	57 6.4	50 7.2	57 6.4	57 6.4
29 12.7	27 13.5	26 14.3	Cost of Sales/Inventory	2 196.0	16 23.4	28 12.9	28 13.0	39 9.5	26 14.3
53 6.9	50 7.3	48 7.6		29 12.7	38 9.7	53 6.9	61 6.0	58 6.3	42 8.8
94 3.9	97 3.7	97 3.8		141 2.6	103 3.6	106 3.4	112 3.3	111 3.3	75 4.9
20 18.2	21 17.4	19 18.8	Cost of Sales/Payables	10 35.1	14 25.5	18 20.5	19 19.3	18 20.0	25 14.6
35 10.6	33 11.0	32 11.5		38 9.6	33 11.2	32 11.5	29 12.4	26 14.0	35 10.5
51 7.2	51 7.1	50 7.3		77 4.7	45 8.1	49 7.4	51 7.2	43 8.5	50 7.2
6.5	5.8	5.5	Sales/Working Capital	4.0	5.2	5.2	5.6	4.7	7.8
15.3	12.1	11.9		26.0	10.6	11.4	10.2	7.9	18.3
–142.1	–94.3	–838.7		–16.2	–21.1	–100.0	64.4	29.9	–62.8
	6.1	6.7	7.4	EBIT/Interest	3.0	2.3	4.2	6.7	8.7	15.7
(298) 2.4	(291) 2.4	(368) 3.1	EBIT/Interest	(20) .9	(40) 1.1	(33) 2.4	(72) 3.2	(76) 3.8	(127) 5.0
.7	.5	1.1		–.5	–.8	–2.0	1.2	1.8	2.1
5.3	7.1	4.7	Net Profit + Depr., Dep., Amort./Cur. Mat. L/T/D			1.6	4.1	8.8	6.1
(93) 2.3	(92) 2.4	(126) 2.1				(11) 1.4	(23) 1.9	(31) 2.2	(51) 2.9
1.3	.8	.8				1.1	1.1	.7	.9
.5	.5	.4	Fixed/Worth	.6	.3	.4	.3	.3	.5
1.3	1.2	1.0		2.0	.9	1.0	.9	.7	1.1
3.8	3.6	2.7		–4.4	9.5	2.2	2.5	2.2	2.6
1.0	1.0	.7	Debt/Worth	.8	.6	.7	.6	.6	1.0
2.2	2.4	2.1		2.6	1.4	2.2	1.8	1.9	2.3
10.0	12.0	6.8		–8.3	49.2	8.4	4.7	4.4	7.6
37.0	40.9	38.1	% Profit Before Taxes/Tangible Net Worth	26.7	20.7	38.9	33.5	40.8	45.9
(260) 17.0	(259) 18.0	(355) 17.3		(20) 4.3	(37) 7.1	(32) 13.5	(72) 15.4	(75) 20.2	(119) 24.3
3.3	1.9	2.6		–27.7	–6.1	–10.6	2.7	5.4	10.1
12.7	12.5	12.0	% Profit Before Taxes/Total Assets	8.9	5.3	11.0	11.9	13.3	13.0
5.2	4.9	5.4		.7	.5	3.1	5.3	6.3	7.4
–.6	–1.0	.3		–9.3	–5.6	–8.0	.7	1.8	3.2
14.5	16.0	16.3	Sales/Net Fixed Assets	13.0	16.7	21.9	18.8	15.8	13.9
7.1	7.4	7.2		5.2	8.3	7.7	6.4	7.9	7.0
4.1	3.7	3.8		1.8	3.8	4.7	3.6	4.0	3.8
2.6	2.7	2.7	Sales/Total Assets	2.3	2.9	2.7	2.7	2.7	2.7
2.0	2.0	1.9		1.4	2.0	2.0	2.0	1.8	1.9
1.4	1.4	1.4		.9	1.5	1.4	1.5	1.4	1.4
1.4	1.2	1.7	% Depr., Dep., Amort./Sales	2.4	2.0	1.7	1.5	1.8	1.2
(274) 2.5	(259) 2.6	(353) 2.9		(24) 4.8	(41) 3.8	(32) 2.8	(74) 2.9	(75) 2.7	(107) 2.9
4.2	4.7	5.1		7.1	5.9	7.4	5.0	4.6	4.9
2.1	2.3	2.7	% Officers', Directors', Owners' Comp/Sales	8.5	3.5	2.6	2.5	1.8	
(83) 4.0	(69) 3.7	(125) 5.0		(14) 13.9	(33) 7.4	(16) 4.9	(36) 4.0	(19) 3.3	
7.9	5.9	9.6		25.3	10.0	10.1	7.8	6.7	
19451627M	18269126M	20980771M	Net Sales ($)	14378M	91073M	141284M	603670M	1286359M	18844007M
11170889M	9938422M	10373785M	Total Assets ($)	12797M	50625M	79634M	338046M	750350M	9142333M

Current Data Sorted By Assets   Comparative Historical Data

0-500M	500M-2MM	2-10MM	10-50MM	50-100MM	100-250MM	Type of Statement	4/1/98-3/31/99 ALL	4/1/99-3/31/00 ALL
		4	7	3	1	Unqualified	18	14
	1	7	1		1	Reviewed	9	14
	3	4	1			Compiled	10	11
						Tax Returns	3	3
	2	13	9	3	1	Other	13	11
14 (4/1-9/30/02)			46 (10/1/02-3/31/03)			NUMBER OF STATEMENTS	53	53
	6	28	18	6	2			
%	%	%	%	%	%	**ASSETS**	%	%

DATA NOT AVAILABLE (columns 0-500M and 500M-2MM)

2-10MM	10-50MM	ASSETS	Hist 4/1/98-3/31/99	Hist 4/1/99-3/31/00
7.4	7.5	Cash & Equivalents	7.2	6.9
20.2	15.2	Trade Receivables (net)	19.8	19.8
35.6	34.6	Inventory	35.8	34.9
1.0	3.7	All Other Current	1.9	3.2
64.2	61.0	Total Current	64.6	64.9
25.5	27.3	Fixed Assets (net)	23.6	24.0
7.7	6.4	Intangibles (net)	6.1	6.1
2.6	5.2	All Other Non-Current	5.7	5.0
100.0	100.0	Total	100.0	100.0
		LIABILITIES		
15.4	12.0	Notes Payable-Short Term	8.1	9.8
7.0	6.6	Cur. Mat.-L/T/D	4.0	6.6
14.1	14.6	Trade Payables	12.2	9.2
.3	.1	Income Taxes Payable	.6	.1
6.6	7.1	All Other Current	10.4	14.1
43.5	40.5	Total Current	35.3	39.8
18.0	17.4	Long Term Debt	19.9	23.5
.2	.9	Deferred Taxes	.6	.4
4.6	3.1	All Other Non-Current	4.0	4.4
33.7	38.2	Net Worth	40.1	32.0
100.0	100.0	Total Liabilities & Net Worth	100.0	100.0
		INCOME DATA		
100.0	100.0	Net Sales	100.0	100.0
26.2	28.7	Gross Profit	30.9	31.8
22.3	20.7	Operating Expenses	20.5	23.2
3.9	8.0	Operating Profit	10.4	8.6
1.3	2.2	All Other Expenses (net)	−.1	.7
2.6	5.8	Profit Before Taxes	10.5	7.9

RATIOS

2-10MM	10-50MM	Ratio	Hist 4/1/98-3/31/99	Hist 4/1/99-3/31/00
2.3	2.6	Current	2.9	3.5
1.4	1.5		2.1	1.7
1.1	1.1		1.3	1.3
1.3	.6	Quick	1.1	1.1
.5	.5		.7	.7
.4	.4		.5	.4
23 15.6	33 10.9	Sales/Receivables	27 13.3	25 14.5
40 9.2	47 7.8		48 7.6	41 8.9
57 6.4	56 6.6		59 6.2	54 6.8
60 6.1	84 4.3	Cost of Sales/Inventory	70 5.2	68 5.4
97 3.8	136 2.7		99 3.7	122 3.0
129 2.8	159 2.3		161 2.3	177 2.1
18 20.5	32 11.3	Cost of Sales/Payables	22 16.7	13 27.8
34 10.8	44 8.2		33 11.1	24 15.1
46 7.9	72 5.1		51 7.1	46 8.0
3.4	4.3	Sales/Working Capital	3.0	3.3
12.3	7.5		5.5	6.2
36.0	31.1		15.7	14.0
7.7	7.9	EBIT/Interest	11.3	6.5
(26) 2.4	(17) 4.3		(45) 4.6	(48) 3.0
1.3	1.3		2.2	1.3
17.9	2.0	Net Profit + Depr., Dep., Amort./Cur. Mat. L /T/D	8.5	2.7
(10) 3.6	(11) 1.7		(26) 3.7	(12) 1.7
1.5	.8		1.4	.5
.4	.4	Fixed/Worth	.3	.2
1.0	.8		.6	.7
5.4	1.4		2.0	2.1
1.1	1.1	Debt/Worth	.6	.8
3.5	1.7		1.6	1.9
12.4	4.8		4.6	4.9
42.0	28.7	% Profit Before Taxes/Tangible Net Worth	57.4	49.8
(23) 21.1	(16) 14.3		(47) 34.1	(45) 19.1
2.6	1.2		12.4	3.4
12.7	15.2	% Profit Before Taxes/Total Assets	23.9	15.0
6.3	5.8		9.6	6.2
.7	.6		4.6	1.3
14.4	9.9	Sales/Net Fixed Assets	14.7	22.9
8.3	4.7		7.9	7.6
4.2	3.5		4.6	4.4
2.3	1.5	Sales/Total Assets	2.1	2.0
1.8	1.3		1.6	1.6
1.3	1.1		1.0	1.0
2.0	2.4	% Depr., Dep., Amort./Sales	1.0	1.9
(25) 3.4	(17) 3.3		(47) 2.3	(46) 2.7
5.7	5.1		3.9	4.4
		% Officers', Directors', Owners' Comp/Sales	1.8	2.2
			(16) 3.3	(18) 5.8
			6.1	10.8

0-500M	500M-2MM	2-10MM	10-50MM	50-100MM	100-250MM		4/1/98-3/31/99	4/1/99-3/31/00
	16900M	302640M	427002M	512941M	366911M	Net Sales ($)	1575502M	1105409M
	8727M	162064M	331605M	408967M	338389M	Total Assets ($)	1495955M	872732M

M = $ thousand   MM = $ million
See Pages 11 through 18 for Explanation of Ratios and Data

Comparative Historical Data | Current Data Sorted By Sales

						Type of Statement						
	16		13		15	Unqualified					3	5	7
	16		10		9	Reviewed			2		3	4	
	5		8		8	Compiled	1	2	2		1	2	
	2		2			Tax Returns							
	16		27		28	Other		1	1		6	12	8
	4/1/00-3/31/01 ALL		4/1/01-3/31/02 ALL		4/1/02-3/31/03 ALL		0-1MM	14 (4/1-9/30/02) 1-3MM	3-5MM		46 (10/1/02-3/31/03) 5-10MM	10-25MM	25MM & OVER
	55		60		60	NUMBER OF STATEMENTS	1	3	5		13	23	15
	%		%		%	ASSETS	%	%	%		%	%	%
	7.6		7.6		7.5	Cash & Equivalents					9.1	5.8	9.3
	19.9		23.3		18.0	Trade Receivables (net)					16.6	20.0	17.5
	28.0		32.5		35.2	Inventory					36.1	36.1	34.4
	3.2		2.3		1.7	All Other Current					.3	2.8	1.8
	58.6		65.7		62.3	Total Current					62.1	64.8	63.0
	32.6		24.4		27.8	Fixed Assets (net)					25.4	27.3	25.7
	6.2		5.6		6.5	Intangibles (net)					9.6	3.0	8.8
	2.6		4.2		3.4	All Other Non-Current					2.9	4.9	2.5
	100.0		100.0		100.0	Total					100.0	100.0	100.0
						LIABILITIES							
	10.1		12.4		13.2	Notes Payable-Short Term					8.8	17.8	9.7
	6.5		5.3		6.3	Cur. Mat.-L/T/D					8.0	6.9	3.4
	10.8		15.2		13.5	Trade Payables					14.4	15.7	10.5
	.4		.5		.2	Income Taxes Payable					.0	.4	.2
	7.8		8.8		7.4	All Other Current					6.0	6.8	10.7
	35.6		42.2		40.6	Total Current					37.3	47.6	34.4
	25.2		19.6		19.7	Long Term Debt					24.3	13.6	17.1
	.7		.4		.5	Deferred Taxes					.0	.7	.7
	4.6		4.8		4.5	All Other Non-Current					7.4	1.6	8.8
	34.0		33.1		34.8	Net Worth					31.0	36.6	39.0
	100.0		100.0		100.0	Total Liabilities & Net Worth					100.0	100.0	100.0
						INCOME DATA							
	100.0		100.0		100.0	Net Sales					100.0	100.0	100.0
	28.6		31.4		28.4	Gross Profit					24.6	25.3	26.1
	23.5		24.5		23.1	Operating Expenses					22.7	18.3	18.6
	5.1		6.9		5.3	Operating Profit					1.9	7.0	7.5
	2.0		2.9		1.7	All Other Expenses (net)					1.9	1.3	1.8
	3.1		4.1		3.6	Profit Before Taxes					.1	5.7	5.7
						RATIOS							
	2.5		2.3		2.5						3.7	1.8	3.0
	1.5		1.6		1.5	Current					1.6	1.2	1.9
	1.1		1.1		1.1						1.2	1.1	1.3
	1.1		1.0		.9						1.3	.7	1.1
	.7		.6		.6	Quick					.5	.5	.6
	.5		.4		.4						.4	.4	.5
29	12.7	32	11.5	25	14.8		20	17.8	35 10.3				29 12.6
44	8.3	47	7.7	43	8.5	Sales/Receivables	25	14.5	47 7.7				47 7.8
59	6.2	60	6.1	57	6.4		45	8.0	60 6.1				54 6.7
65	5.6	75	4.9	79	4.6		62	5.8	77 4.7				101 3.6
90	4.0	106	3.4	110	3.3	Cost of Sales/Inventory	96	3.8	104 3.5				124 3.0
133	2.7	144	2.5	151	2.4		124	3.0	142 2.6				152 2.4
18	20.3	21	17.6	22	16.6		16	22.8	32 11.3				18 20.6
31	11.9	41	8.9	40	9.2	Cost of Sales/Payables	32	11.5	41 9.0				30 12.1
53	6.9	55	6.6	51	7.2		57	6.4	50 7.3				45 8.1
	4.2		4.4		3.8						3.2	4.6	2.9
	8.3		6.7		8.4	Sales/Working Capital					10.8	12.6	4.6
	33.2		31.7		25.0						17.0	51.6	9.9
	4.6		7.1		7.3						7.5	8.8	8.9
(53)	2.4	(57)	2.8	(57)	2.7	EBIT/Interest	(11)	1.4	(22) 5.2				3.5
	.9		1.2		.9			.0	2.4					.9
	6.2		9.4		6.2	Net Profit + Depr., Dep.,					4.1		
(17)	1.9	(23)	3.1	(25)	1.7	Amort./Cur. Mat. L/T/D			(12) 1.7				
	.8		1.3		.8				1.0					
	.4		.3		.4						.4	.4	.3
	1.1		.9		.9	Fixed/Worth					1.7	.9	.8
	2.3		2.8		3.0						NM	1.4	-1.8
	.8		1.0		1.0						1.3	1.1	.7
	2.1		2.4		2.2	Debt/Worth					10.5	2.2	1.5
	5.2		10.0		10.3						NM	4.4	-12.2
	40.4		39.6		32.2	% Profit Before Taxes/Tangible					32.6	40.9	23.1
(47)	16.7	(50)	19.5	(50)	14.3	Net Worth	(10)	-7.3	(22) 25.0			(11)	17.3
	-.3		3.0		-5.9			-126.9	6.7					-1.1
	12.0		11.5		12.1	% Profit Before Taxes/Total					8.0	15.2	13.6
	6.4		5.4		5.7	Assets					3.9	6.7	6.0
	-.2		.6		-.7						-8.5	1.7	-.3
	10.3		17.1		13.3						13.9	13.9	16.0
	5.8		8.2		7.6	Sales/Net Fixed Assets					8.5	5.1	8.7
	3.8		4.4		3.6						4.9	3.5	4.7
	2.2		2.3		2.0						2.5	2.0	1.6
	1.6		1.6		1.4	Sales/Total Assets					1.6	1.4	1.4
	1.2		1.2		1.1						1.3	1.2	1.1
	2.3		1.9		2.1						2.3	1.7	3.0
(53)	3.4	(54)	3.2	(54)	3.4	% Depr., Dep., Amort./Sales	(11)		(21) 3.4			(13)	3.4
	5.8		4.5		5.3				2.7 6.0			5.3		5.1
	1.5		1.0		.9	% Officers', Directors',							
(12)	4.9	(18)	2.9	(18)	2.2	Owners' Comp/Sales							
	9.6		9.8		5.7								
1538713M		1922837M		1626394M		Net Sales ($)	542M	5313M	20199M		99662M	377729M	1122949M
1226424M		1351872M		1249752M		Total Assets ($)	621M	5612M	13914M		59320M	259630M	910655M

M = $ thousand   MM = $ million
See Pages 11 through 18 for Explanation of Ratios and Data

Current Data Sorted By Assets

Comparative Historical Data

0-500M	500M-2MM	2-10MM	10-50MM	50-100MM	100-250MM	Type of Statement	4/1/98-3/31/99 ALL	4/1/99-3/31/00 ALL
	1	9	9	2	2	Unqualified	37	37
	3	22	8		1	Reviewed	41	38
4	7	8	3			Compiled	26	31
5	7	2				Tax Returns	6	8
3	9	12	17	3	4	Other	47	41
30 (4/1-9/30/02)			111 (10/1/02-3/31/03)					
12	27	53	37	5	7	NUMBER OF STATEMENTS	157	155
%	%	%	%	%	%	ASSETS	%	%
10.9	7.8	7.4	9.3			Cash & Equivalents	6.7	8.8
25.9	24.3	19.1	18.0			Trade Receivables (net)	21.5	21.8
31.0	34.6	35.8	34.8			Inventory	31.4	32.8
4.0	3.5	3.1	4.9			All Other Current	1.9	2.4
71.8	70.1	65.5	67.0			Total Current	61.6	65.8
23.3	17.9	27.4	27.4			Fixed Assets (net)	28.0	24.8
1.1	4.9	3.1	1.2			Intangibles (net)	5.1	3.4
3.8	7.1	4.0	4.4			All Other Non-Current	5.3	6.0
100.0	100.0	100.0	100.0			Total	100.0	100.0
						LIABILITIES		
24.0	14.6	9.7	9.0			Notes Payable-Short Term	10.6	9.8
6.4	5.3	3.9	3.9			Cur. Mat.-L/T/D	4.2	4.6
16.2	14.3	10.6	11.7			Trade Payables	11.1	11.6
.0	.1	.3	.2			Income Taxes Payable	.6	.4
7.5	9.1	7.0	8.3			All Other Current	10.1	7.6
54.1	43.3	31.5	33.0			Total Current	36.6	34.0
16.3	17.8	15.5	17.1			Long Term Debt	18.6	17.4
.0	.0	.5	.7			Deferred Taxes	.6	.5
4.2	7.7	4.9	3.8			All Other Non-Current	7.5	4.6
25.4	31.2	47.5	45.4			Net Worth	36.7	43.5
100.0	100.0	100.0	100.0			Total Liabilities & Net Worth	100.0	100.0
						INCOME DATA		
100.0	100.0	100.0	100.0			Net Sales	100.0	100.0
38.1	40.0	31.7	25.3			Gross Profit	30.9	33.6
36.0	39.5	25.1	19.8			Operating Expenses	22.3	24.0
2.1	.5	6.6	5.5			Operating Profit	8.6	9.6
.8	.8	1.6	1.9			All Other Expenses (net)	2.0	1.6
1.3	-.3	5.0	3.6			Profit Before Taxes	6.6	8.0
						RATIOS		
2.6	2.8	3.5	3.8			Current	3.1	3.4
2.1	1.6	2.1	2.2				1.6	2.0
1.1	1.1	1.5	1.6				1.3	1.4
1.9	1.5	1.5	1.8			Quick	1.5	1.7
.9	.6	.8	.6				.8	.8
.2	.4	.5	.4				.4	.5
8 47.6	23 16.2	34 10.8	36 10.2			Sales/Receivables	31 11.7	30 12.1
18 20.2	31 11.8	43 8.6	46 7.9				45 8.2	42 8.6
39 9.2	50 7.3	63 5.8	59 6.1				59 6.2	56 6.5
0 UND	31 11.9	75 4.9	62 5.9			Cost of Sales/Inventory	48 7.6	51 7.2
33 11.2	79 4.6	117 3.1	115 3.2				94 3.9	87 4.2
106 3.5	169 2.2	165 2.2	204 1.8				154 2.4	146 2.5
7 50.8	14 25.7	17 22.0	19 18.7			Cost of Sales/Payables	17 21.1	15 24.0
19 19.5	32 11.3	34 10.8	32 11.2				30 12.3	30 12.3
37 10.0	55 6.7	57 6.5	49 7.4				46 7.9	51 7.1
5.4	5.6	3.4	2.4			Sales/Working Capital	3.8	3.7
9.3	10.1	4.3	4.3				6.6	5.5
71.9	25.6	8.7	8.9				15.4	11.2
	(24) 5.4	(52) 8.2	(35) 9.4			EBIT/Interest	(150) 9.5	(143) 11.5
	2.0	4.8	3.6				4.4	5.0
	-1.1	1.6	1.3				2.0	2.0
		(18) 9.3	(15) 3.6			Net Profit + Depr., Dep., Amort./Cur. Mat. L/T/D	(68) 8.3	(64) 6.1
		3.3	2.2				2.9	2.4
		1.9	1.2				1.5	1.1
.2	.2	.3	.3			Fixed/Worth	.4	.3
.4	.8	.7	.6				.7	.6
3.9	2.1	1.3	1.1				1.7	1.5
.7	1.0	.6	.6			Debt/Worth	1.0	.7
1.5	3.7	1.1	1.3				1.9	1.3
6.1	8.4	2.3	3.9				4.6	3.5
(11) 42.9	(24) 44.9	(51) 35.8	36.1			% Profit Before Taxes/Tangible Net Worth	(143) 61.3	(141) 61.0
4.0	16.9	12.3	16.0				33.5	28.3
-77.8	-15.7	5.0	4.4				13.7	10.4
25.7	11.8	13.0	12.1			% Profit Before Taxes/Total Assets	22.9	22.6
5.8	3.5	6.4	5.5				10.3	11.0
-9.8	-9.5	2.0	1.1				3.7	3.6
68.9	46.4	17.5	13.5			Sales/Net Fixed Assets	11.5	20.5
25.8	21.3	6.3	5.6				6.9	8.0
10.5	6.7	3.3	2.7				3.5	4.3
5.8	3.3	2.1	1.9			Sales/Total Assets	2.3	2.5
3.7	2.3	1.5	1.2				1.7	1.8
2.4	1.7	1.1	1.0				1.3	1.3
(10) .6	(21) .8	(50) 1.7	(33) 1.6			% Depr., Dep., Amort./Sales	(146) 1.7	(144) 1.3
1.1	2.9	3.1	2.8				2.8	2.4
5.1	5.5	5.9	4.5				4.7	3.8
	(12) 3.5	(21) 1.9				% Officers', Directors', Owners' Comp/Sales	(58) 2.1	(60) 2.4
	5.6	3.5					3.9	3.7
	7.3	5.5					8.2	8.3
17008M	78710M	433521M	1019184M	386889M	1304342M	Net Sales ($)	4214820M	2781463M
3661M	31953M	281639M	709272M	306363M	1055739M	Total Assets ($)	3265784M	2101642M

M = $ thousand   MM = $ million
See Pages 11 through 18 for Explanation of Ratios and Data

Comparative Historical Data | Current Data Sorted By Sales

			Type of Statement						
37	27	23	Unqualified			5	4	5	9
32	35	34	Reviewed	1	1	4	12	9	7
31	35	22	Compiled	1	6	4	8	2	1
9	6	14	Tax Returns	2	7	4	1		
45	55	48	Other	3	8	4	4	16	13
4/1/00-3/31/01 ALL	4/1/01-3/31/02 ALL	4/1/02-3/31/03 ALL		0-1MM	30 (4/1-9/30/02) 1-3MM	3-5MM	5-10MM	111 (10/1/02-3/31/03) 10-25MM	25MM & OVER
154	158	141	**NUMBER OF STATEMENTS**	7	22	21	29	32	30
%	%	%	**ASSETS**	%	%	%	%	%	%
6.7	7.4	8.1	Cash & Equivalents		9.5	7.1	7.9	9.9	5.8
22.2	20.4	20.3	Trade Receivables (net)		23.3	18.6	19.2	20.0	20.2
31.9	33.4	33.6	Inventory		33.0	37.6	35.7	33.0	30.6
2.2	2.6	3.9	All Other Current		2.3	4.2	2.9	3.8	6.0
63.0	63.8	65.9	Total Current		68.1	67.5	65.7	66.6	62.5
26.9	25.6	24.6	Fixed Assets (net)		17.6	22.3	29.3	29.1	21.0
5.0	6.2	4.4	Intangibles (net)		5.7	3.7	2.8	.8	9.8
5.1	4.4	5.1	All Other Non-Current		8.6	6.4	2.2	3.5	6.7
100.0	100.0	100.0	Total		100.0	100.0	100.0	100.0	100.0
			LIABILITIES						
11.7	12.2	11.3	Notes Payable-Short Term		9.2	21.5	8.9	8.5	8.1
5.0	4.4	4.3	Cur. Mat.-L/T/D		4.6	4.9	3.3	4.4	3.2
13.3	11.4	12.0	Trade Payables		16.6	9.8	10.9	12.0	11.9
.4	.2	.2	Income Taxes Payable		.0	.2	.3	.2	.3
8.3	7.3	8.1	All Other Current		8.9	8.1	6.0	8.3	10.0
38.6	35.7	35.9	Total Current		39.4	44.4	29.5	33.4	33.4
17.8	17.4	17.3	Long Term Debt		16.8	15.9	15.0	17.5	19.3
.5	.6	.5	Deferred Taxes		.0	.0	.7	.8	.6
6.0	5.4	5.2	All Other Non-Current		7.8	5.5	3.4	4.8	5.7
37.0	40.9	41.2	Net Worth		36.0	34.2	51.3	43.5	41.1
100.0	100.0	100.0	Total Liabilities & Net Worth		100.0	100.0	100.0	100.0	100.0
			INCOME DATA						
100.0	100.0	100.0	Net Sales		100.0	100.0	100.0	100.0	100.0
31.8	31.1	31.5	Gross Profit		35.4	38.0	30.7	27.5	24.9
23.8	24.2	26.7	Operating Expenses		34.3	32.8	24.9	23.4	17.2
8.0	6.9	4.8	Operating Profit		1.1	5.2	5.8	4.1	7.7
2.1	2.3	1.7	All Other Expenses (net)		1.5	1.3	1.0	2.2	2.1
5.9	4.6	3.0	Profit Before Taxes		-.4	3.9	4.8	1.9	5.6
			RATIOS						
3.2	3.4	3.4			3.5	2.9	5.9	3.3	3.5
1.7	1.9	1.9	Current		1.6	2.0	2.0	2.1	1.9
1.1	1.3	1.4			1.2	1.3	1.6	1.4	1.3
1.4	1.5	1.6			2.6	1.5	1.9	1.6	1.5
.7	.8	.7	Quick		.7	.6	.8	.8	.7
.5	.4	.5			.4	.4	.5	.5	.5
30 12.0	31 11.6	30 12.2		16 23.1	25 14.7	28 12.9	40 9.0	35 10.4	
46 7.9	47 7.8	42 8.7	Sales/Receivables	31 12.0	36 10.2	42 8.8	49 7.5	50 7.4	
62 5.9	61 6.0	59 6.2		50 7.3	60 6.1	54 6.8	61 6.0	61 5.9	
57 6.3	64 5.7	43 8.5		20 18.5	60 6.1	70 5.2	45 8.2	43 8.5	
97 3.7	108 3.4	102 3.6	Cost of Sales/Inventory	83 4.4	116 3.1	117 3.1	111 3.3	83 4.4	
154 2.4	158 2.3	168 2.2		156 2.3	183 2.0	165 2.2	164 2.2	180 2.0	
20 18.2	16 22.4	16 22.7		14 25.3	10 35.9	16 22.2	19 19.3	18 19.8	
35 10.4	30 12.1	32 11.3	Cost of Sales/Payables	28 12.8	32 11.3	25 14.8	35 10.5	29 12.4	
54 6.8	53 6.9	50 7.3		52 7.0	48 7.7	48 7.5	56 6.5	41 9.0	
3.6	3.4	3.5			5.8	2.9	3.5	2.9	3.2
6.8	5.7	5.6	Sales/Working Capital		9.3	5.1	4.3	4.8	4.5
24.0	12.5	10.2			28.7	15.1	8.7	9.1	13.5
7.3	6.8	7.8		8.4	5.9	18.8	6.2	11.1	
(141) 3.0	(148) 3.2	(131) 3.5	EBIT/Interest	(18) 2.9	(20) 2.9	4.9	(30) 3.0	(29) 6.0	
1.4	1.5	1.3		-5.2	.7	2.0	1.2	2.0	
4.5	5.6	6.2	Net Profit + Depr., Dep.,				3.9	6.8	
(51) 1.8	(45) 2.2	(48) 2.2	Amort./Cur. Mat. L/T/D			(15)	2.0	(16) 2.2	
.9	1.1	1.1				1.2	.9	
.3	.3	.3			.2	.2	.3	.4	.3
.7	.6	.7	Fixed/Worth		.6	.4	.7	.6	.8
1.9	1.7	1.5			2.1	1.1	1.2	1.3	4.7
.8	.7	.7			1.1	.6	.5	.7	.8
1.7	1.7	1.4	Debt/Worth		2.9	1.8	1.1	1.2	1.6
4.4	4.2	4.2			6.8	5.2	1.9	2.7	12.5
43.8	41.9	32.5	% Profit Before Taxes/Tangible	41.3	36.5	41.7	21.9	41.8	
(133) 20.3	(136) 18.2	(131) 13.3	Net Worth	(20) 19.4	(19) 9.3	15.6	(31) 8.4	(26) 17.2	
7.3	5.2	3.4		-44.7	-3.9	5.5	1.5	9.3	
17.5	12.4	12.2	% Profit Before Taxes/Total	13.9	9.0	14.0	10.7	9.2	
7.4	6.0	5.8	Assets	7.4	4.1	6.8	4.1	6.5	
2.5	1.5	.7		-7.3	-1.5	2.8	.7	3.4	
18.4	17.9	21.5		35.7	51.2	20.9	14.3	13.5	
7.2	6.8	8.5	Sales/Net Fixed Assets	18.3	9.9	6.6	4.8	8.1	
3.3	3.6	3.5		6.8	4.0	2.9	2.6	4.5	
2.2	2.2	2.4		3.4	2.9	2.2	1.8	2.1	
1.6	1.5	1.5	Sales/Total Assets	2.4	1.8	1.6	1.4	1.4	
1.1	1.1	1.1		1.5	1.0	1.1	1.1	1.1	
1.2	1.2	1.3		.8	1.9	1.2	1.6	1.5	
(135) 2.7	(133) 2.9	(126) 2.9	% Depr., Dep., Amort./Sales	(19) 2.1	(17) 5.6	(27) 2.8	(30) 3.3	(28) 2.4	
4.8	4.6	5.1		4.7	6.6	6.8	4.5	3.4	
2.2	2.3	2.4	% Officers', Directors',			2.3			
(56) 3.9	(51) 4.5	(45) 4.0	Owners' Comp/Sales			(13) 4.0			
6.1	7.7	6.9				5.7			
3097232M	3594038M	3239654M	Net Sales ($)	4877M	44797M	85676M	201415M	505647M	2397242M
2646328M	3251509M	2388627M	Total Assets ($)	3105M	21655M	58807M	135767M	384762M	1784531M

© RMA 2003

M = $ thousand   MM = $ million

See Pages 11 through 18 for Explanation of Ratios and Data

Current Data Sorted By Assets   Comparative Historical Data

0-500M	500M-2MM	2-10MM	10-50MM	50-100MM	100-250MM	Type of Statement	4/1/98-3/31/99 ALL	4/1/99-3/31/00 ALL
	1	3	10	1	5	Unqualified	10	17
	2	7	1			Reviewed	6	8
	3	3				Compiled	6	10
1						Tax Returns	1	
1	4	5	3		2	Other	15	9
	16 (4/1-9/30/02)		36 (10/1/02-3/31/03)					
2	10	18	14	1	7	NUMBER OF STATEMENTS	38	44
%	%	%	%	%	%	ASSETS	%	%
	7.1	6.2	9.4			Cash & Equivalents	10.7	9.0
	28.4	23.0	21.7			Trade Receivables (net)	23.2	24.3
	26.5	29.1	23.3			Inventory	27.6	28.1
	.6	8.8	1.6			All Other Current	1.0	2.7
	62.6	67.1	56.0			Total Current	62.5	64.1
	25.6	24.4	26.9			Fixed Assets (net)	24.4	26.0
	8.6	1.2	11.5			Intangibles (net)	5.5	3.6
	3.1	7.3	5.6			All Other Non-Current	7.5	6.3
	100.0	100.0	100.0			Total	100.0	100.0
						LIABILITIES		
	8.9	16.0	8.0			Notes Payable-Short Term	7.7	11.1
	2.6	4.5	6.3			Cur. Mat.-L/T/D	3.1	4.2
	17.9	12.1	10.0			Trade Payables	15.2	14.8
	.1	.1	.6			Income Taxes Payable	.3	.6
	5.7	7.2	8.4			All Other Current	11.8	13.3
	35.1	40.0	33.3			Total Current	38.1	43.9
	21.4	16.9	15.7			Long Term Debt	17.1	11.6
	.9	.2	.5			Deferred Taxes	.8	.6
	6.9	1.7	3.3			All Other Non-Current	6.1	3.7
	35.7	41.2	47.2			Net Worth	37.9	40.2
	100.0	100.0	100.0			Total Liabilities & Net Worth	100.0	100.0
						INCOME DATA		
	100.0	100.0	100.0			Net Sales	100.0	100.0
	37.7	39.7	25.4			Gross Profit	27.7	23.0
	34.0	32.6	18.3			Operating Expenses	18.2	18.7
	3.7	7.2	7.1			Operating Profit	9.6	4.2
	1.5	4.5	2.3			All Other Expenses (net)	1.4	.9
	2.2	2.7	4.8			Profit Before Taxes	8.2	3.3
						RATIOS		
	2.9	3.0	2.6			Current	2.5	2.6
	1.9	1.5	1.8				1.7	1.6
	1.3	1.2	1.0				1.4	1.0
	1.9	1.2	1.5			Quick	1.6	1.8
	.9	.7	.9				1.0	.7
	.6	.3	.5				.5	.4
	37 9.9	30 12.0	31 11.7			Sales/Receivables	33 11.2	30 12.1
	48 7.6	41 9.0	50 7.3				43 8.6	41 9.0
	59 6.2	69 5.3	68 5.4				53 6.9	61 6.0
	52 7.0	0 UND	48 7.6			Cost of Sales/Inventory	45 8.1	44 8.2
	68 5.4	87 4.2	64 5.7				71 5.1	68 5.4
	115 3.2	206 1.8	89 4.1				89 4.1	109 3.3
	16 22.4	16 22.1	16 22.6			Cost of Sales/Payables	23 16.1	18 20.1
	49 7.4	37 9.8	33 11.0				36 10.0	36 10.0
	107 3.4	86 4.3	43 8.4				47 7.7	50 7.2
	5.4	4.0	4.0			Sales/Working Capital	5.2	4.5
	7.4	7.0	7.8				8.2	9.7
	19.2	50.5	NM				15.5	-323.1
	6.8	7.4	10.7			EBIT/Interest	(33) 26.4	7.1
	1.6	5.2	2.5				8.9	(38) 3.0
	.1	.0	.8				3.2	-.7
						Net Profit + Depr., Dep., Amort./Cur. Mat. L /T/D	(12) 10.0	3.5
							2.4	(15) 1.9
							1.0	.7
	.2	.1	.4			Fixed/Worth	.4	.4
	1.1	.6	.8				.6	.8
	NM	1.2	1.7				1.5	1.5
	.8	.7	.5			Debt/Worth	.7	.6
	2.1	2.2	1.5				1.8	1.7
	NM	3.7	3.2				3.8	4.0
		22.3	34.0			% Profit Before Taxes/Tangible Net Worth	(32) 63.9	51.2
		(12) 9.4	11.2				39.4	(40) 18.4
		-10.3	-2.2				22.0	1.0
	8.7	9.0	17.0			% Profit Before Taxes/Total Assets	19.6	16.4
	1.0	4.5	5.5				14.8	6.3
	-2.5	-3.0	.0				6.6	-.7
	22.0	27.2	19.5			Sales/Net Fixed Assets	17.7	17.0
	11.5	9.6	5.9				9.1	9.3
	4.1	3.4	4.4				4.2	4.6
	2.5	2.0	1.9			Sales/Total Assets	2.9	2.8
	2.2	1.7	1.7				1.9	1.8
	1.5	1.0	1.1				1.3	1.3
		1.2	1.5			% Depr., Dep., Amort./Sales	1.1	1.6
	(17)	2.2	(13) 2.1				2.0	(38) 2.1
		7.1	3.6				2.8	3.4
						% Officers', Directors', Owners' Comp/Sales		1.4
							(11)	1.9
								3.7
1719M	24117M	156180M	492989M	497072M	1707936M	Net Sales ($)	2889007M	3023788M
559M	12450M	98940M	276346M	97501M	1074325M	Total Assets ($)	1701989M	1651957M

Comparative Historical Data

Current Data Sorted By Sales

			Type of Statement	0-1MM	1-3MM	3-5MM	5-10MM	10-25MM	25MM & OVER
11	11	20	Unqualified		2		2	3	13
6	10	10	Reviewed		1	1	4	3	1
3	8	6	Compiled		3	1	2		
1		1	Tax Returns	1					
7	11	15	Other	1	3	2	3	3	3
4/1/00-3/31/01 ALL	4/1/01-3/31/02 ALL	4/1/02-3/31/03 ALL			16 (4/1-9/30/02)		36 (10/1/02-3/31/03)		
28	40	52	NUMBER OF STATEMENTS	2	9	4	11	9	17
%	%	%	**ASSETS**	%	%	%	%	%	%
6.9	8.4	8.3	Cash & Equivalents				4.2		11.5
26.4	23.3	22.2	Trade Receivables (net)				24.1		18.1
25.0	23.6	25.2	Inventory				26.7		22.9
1.0	3.8	4.2	All Other Current				12.0		2.6
59.4	59.1	59.9	Total Current				67.0		55.1
23.4	26.9	26.6	Fixed Assets (net)				27.6		23.5
9.7	7.6	6.3	Intangibles (net)				1.1		12.8
7.4	6.4	7.2	All Other Non-Current				4.3		8.7
100.0	100.0	100.0	Total				100.0		100.0
			LIABILITIES						
13.5	11.7	9.9	Notes Payable-Short Term				15.0		5.9
4.3	4.9	4.4	Cur. Mat.-L/T/D				5.0		5.3
14.2	13.7	12.8	Trade Payables				9.9		11.5
.6	.3	.4	Income Taxes Payable				.0		.4
13.3	11.6	7.5	All Other Current				9.5		10.2
46.0	42.2	35.0	Total Current				39.5		33.4
10.4	16.9	17.1	Long Term Debt				20.9		16.3
.7	.4	.6	Deferred Taxes				.2		.7
3.1	2.0	4.9	All Other Non-Current				2.6		5.9
39.7	38.6	42.4	Net Worth				36.8		43.8
100.0	100.0	100.0	Total Liabilities & Net Worth				100.0		100.0
			INCOME DATA						
100.0	100.0	100.0	Net Sales				100.0		100.0
23.5	32.3	31.8	Gross Profit				45.4		19.9
19.8	25.7	25.8	Operating Expenses				37.7		14.4
3.7	6.6	6.0	Operating Profit				7.8		5.5
.7	2.3	2.8	All Other Expenses (net)				6.9		2.1
3.0	4.3	3.2	Profit Before Taxes				.8		3.4
			RATIOS						
2.2 / 1.3 / 1.0	2.2 / 1.3 / 1.0	2.7 / 1.7 / 1.2	Current				3.0 / 1.5 / 1.0		2.4 / 1.7 / 1.1
1.4 / .7 / .5	1.3 / .7 / .5	1.5 / .8 / .5	Quick				1.1 / .6 / .3		1.4 / .7 / .5
31 11.8 / 46 7.9 / 57 6.4	31 11.6 / 48 7.6 / 57 6.4	28 12.8 / 41 8.8 / 58 6.3	Sales/Receivables				30 12.3 / 56 6.5 / 69 5.3		20 18.5 / 34 10.7 / 52 7.0
41 8.9 / 61 5.9 / 95 3.8	36 10.0 / 68 5.4 / 107 3.4	36 10.2 / 59 6.2 / 99 3.7	Cost of Sales/Inventory				0 UND / 101 3.6 / 208 1.8		34 10.8 / 55 6.6 / 77 4.7
24 15.1 / 34 10.7 / 48 7.6	19 18.9 / 36 10.2 / 47 7.8	17 22.1 / 37 9.8 / 50 7.3	Cost of Sales/Payables				17 21.2 / 45 8.0 / 85 4.3		14 25.3 / 33 11.0 / 39 9.5
6.5 / 22.0 / -309.2	5.9 / 15.8 / 57.2	4.7 / 7.7 / 25.4	Sales/Working Capital				2.1 / 6.2 / -164.1		4.5 / 8.0 / 43.3
8.5 / (26) 2.0 / .3	11.0 / (37) 3.1 / .6	7.5 / 2.6 / .3	EBIT/Interest				7.4 / 2.3 / -.1		9.5 / 2.7 / .8
	4.8 / (12) 2.1 / .0	(24) 4.0 / 2.6 / 1.3	Net Profit + Depr., Dep., Amort./Cur. Mat. L/T/D						
.3 / .9 / NM	.4 / .8 / 1.5	.3 / .7 / 1.6	Fixed/Worth				.3 / .7 / 2.2		.5 / .7 / 1.7
.8 / 1.8 / NM	.8 / 2.0 / 4.3	.7 / 1.5 / 3.5	Debt/Worth				.9 / 2.4 / 3.5		.8 / 1.5 / 3.5
32.5 / (21) 12.7 / -3.7	61.5 / (34) 18.4 / 2.4	25.7 / (47) 9.1 / -4.1	% Profit Before Taxes/Tangible Net Worth				19.3 / 8.7 / -9.4		37.6 / (14) 8.1 / -.4
15.9 / 5.0 / -1.7	17.7 / 5.5 / -1.5	8.3 / 4.1 / -1.9	% Profit Before Taxes/Total Assets				7.4 / 5.1 / -2.9		13.2 / 3.9 / -1.3
22.3 / 7.7 / 5.0	17.8 / 8.7 / 4.1	16.3 / 6.9 / 4.5	Sales/Net Fixed Assets				12.4 / 5.8 / 3.3		15.4 / 7.1 / 5.0
3.1 / 1.9 / 1.4	2.9 / 1.8 / 1.4	2.2 / 1.8 / 1.3	Sales/Total Assets				2.0 / 1.3 / .9		1.9 / 1.8 / 1.4
(25) .9 / 2.0 / 3.1	(38) 1.1 / 2.4 / 4.1	(48) 1.5 / 2.7 / 4.0	% Depr., Dep., Amort./Sales				(10) 2.2 / 3.5 / 8.8		(16) 1.4 / 2.4 / 3.5
	(10) 1.7 / 3.1 / 4.4	(10) 1.8 / 3.6 / 6.2	% Officers', Directors', Owners' Comp/Sales						
1400853M	1420812M	2880013M	Net Sales ($)	1719M	17349M	15263M	84468M	145616M	2615598M
876343M	930812M	1560121M	Total Assets ($)	559M	13092M	7875M	66233M	81282M	1391080M

© RMA 2003

M = $ thousand   MM = $ million
See Pages 11 through 18 for Explanation of Ratios and Data

Current Data Sorted By Assets   Comparative Historical Data

0-500M	500M-2MM	2-10MM	10-50MM	50-100MM	100-250MM	Type of Statement	4/1/98-3/31/99 ALL	4/1/99-3/31/00 ALL
	5	5	5	2	5	Unqualified	30	27
	2	7	4			Reviewed	20	17
	1	6				Compiled	13	5
						Tax Returns	1	4
1	2	7	7	1		Other	16	22
	16 (4/1-9/30/02)		44 (10/1/02-3/31/03)					
1	10	25	16	3	5	**NUMBER OF STATEMENTS**	80	75
%	%	%	%	%	%		%	%
						ASSETS		
	9.2	14.3	11.8			Cash & Equivalents	8.7	11.7
	14.7	18.4	18.3			Trade Receivables (net)	21.7	22.4
	20.5	10.8	10.3			Inventory	14.2	10.6
	14.1	14.6	10.8			All Other Current	8.3	8.1
	58.5	58.2	51.2			Total Current	52.8	52.9
	26.5	31.5	43.3			Fixed Assets (net)	36.7	36.6
	3.4	2.7	.4			Intangibles (net)	3.4	2.5
	11.5	7.6	5.1			All Other Non-Current	7.1	8.0
	100.0	100.0	100.0			Total	100.0	100.0
						LIABILITIES		
	3.2	12.1	4.6			Notes Payable-Short Term	8.1	7.4
	1.8	4.1	4.1			Cur. Mat.-L/T/D	4.5	3.9
	12.6	11.9	16.1			Trade Payables	13.7	14.0
	.6	1.9	.4			Income Taxes Payable	.6	.4
	10.3	13.0	15.6			All Other Current	13.5	13.9
	28.5	43.0	40.8			Total Current	40.4	39.7
	26.7	10.8	21.7			Long Term Debt	17.7	19.3
	.0	.7	1.6			Deferred Taxes	.6	.8
	5.7	2.9	4.6			All Other Non-Current	4.4	3.9
	39.1	42.6	31.3			Net Worth	36.9	36.3
	100.0	100.0	100.0			Total Liabilities & Net Worth	100.0	100.0
						INCOME DATA		
	100.0	100.0	100.0			Net Sales	100.0	100.0
	34.5	26.9	20.2			Gross Profit	25.1	26.3
	31.9	20.0	18.1			Operating Expenses	21.5	21.5
	2.6	6.9	2.1			Operating Profit	3.5	4.8
	.6	-.2	1.5			All Other Expenses (net)	.5	.8
	2.0	7.1	.6			Profit Before Taxes	3.0	4.0
						RATIOS		
	4.1	1.9	1.8				1.8	2.1
	2.2	1.3	1.3			Current	1.4	1.4
	1.0	1.0	1.0				1.0	1.0
	1.6	1.5	1.3				1.2	1.5
	1.0	.8	.7			Quick	.8	1.0
	.2	.4	.5				.4	.5
0 UND	6 60.8	8 43.2					20 18.6	21 17.3
12 29.5	28 12.9	35 10.4				Sales/Receivables	35 10.5	39 9.3
29 12.7	45 8.0	48 7.7					55 6.6	52 7.0
0 UND	0 UND	3 140.5					0 UND	1 553.0
25 14.5	10 35.7	7 50.3				Cost of Sales/Inventory	16 22.4	11 31.8
98 3.7	20 18.2	23 16.2					52 7.0	35 10.5
7 54.1	14 25.9	17 21.6					17 21.5	15 24.1
16 23.1	19 19.1	29 12.5				Cost of Sales/Payables	27 13.5	24 15.4
43 8.6	37 9.9	49 7.4					43 8.5	48 7.6
	3.8	7.0	10.3				8.0	7.6
	10.0	21.2	19.2			Sales/Working Capital	15.1	19.0
	NM	279.8	NM				-88.8	-168.4
	(21) 15.7		(13) 5.0				(69) 7.9	(65) 7.8
	6.8		2.0			EBIT/Interest	3.3	3.4
	3.0		-2.3				1.7	1.2
						Net Profit + Depr., Dep.,	(36) 6.6	(27) 7.6
						Amort./Cur. Mat. L./T/D	3.9	2.5
							1.6	1.5
	.3	.4	.9				.5	.5
	.4	.6	1.7			Fixed/Worth	.9	.9
	NM	1.1	2.1				1.9	2.1
	.5	.6	1.2				.8	.8
	1.8	1.3	2.1			Debt/Worth	1.7	1.6
	NM	2.8	3.4				3.8	5.8
	(22) 58.2		(15) 22.8			% Profit Before Taxes/Tangible	(72) 37.3	(71) 45.7
	25.1		7.9			Net Worth	17.0	22.2
	10.6		.0				4.3	1.2
	11.3	17.2	7.7			% Profit Before Taxes/Total	12.4	15.2
	4.2	9.4	2.4			Assets	7.0	6.9
	-2.6	3.5	-2.1				1.6	.4
	32.6	26.8	9.1				13.1	13.1
	20.0	8.6	4.1			Sales/Net Fixed Assets	6.7	6.9
	3.7	4.1	3.1				3.3	2.7
	3.9	3.1	2.6				3.0	3.0
	2.2	2.4	2.1			Sales/Total Assets	2.1	2.1
	1.3	1.5	1.5				1.3	1.4
	(19) 1.5		1.0				(69) 1.2	(62) 1.2
	2.0		2.8			% Depr., Dep., Amort./Sales	1.9	1.9
	3.4		3.9				3.4	3.4
							(23) 3.2	(22) 2.3
						% Officers', Directors',	4.4	4.0
						Owners' Comp/Sales	8.5	7.8
858M	32069M	334448M	683084M	325668M	801774M	Net Sales ($)	3133892M	3025519M
248M	11054M	143364M	313203M	177498M	835857M	Total Assets ($)	2190290M	2485273M

See Pages 11 through 18 for Explanation of Ratios and Data

Comparative Historical Data				Current Data Sorted By Sales					
			Type of Statement				2	3	12
22	17	17	Unqualified				5	4	3
10	11	16	Reviewed	1	2	1	3	3	
5	10	8	Compiled	1		1			
	2	1	Tax Returns		1				
20	27	18	Other	2	2		2	5	7
4/1/00-3/31/01 ALL	4/1/01-3/31/02 ALL	4/1/02-3/31/03 ALL		0-1MM	1-3MM	3-5MM	5-10MM	10-25MM	25MM & OVER
				16 (4/1-9/30/02)			**44 (10/1/02-3/31/03)**		
57	67	60	**NUMBER OF STATEMENTS**	4	5	2	12	15	22
%	%	%	**ASSETS**	%	%	%	%	%	%
9.7	9.3	11.5	Cash & Equivalents				13.9	11.2	11.0
21.2	21.1	17.8	Trade Receivables (net)				21.2	19.0	15.7
8.7	13.2	11.7	Inventory				9.7	12.4	9.8
13.0	12.4	12.4	All Other Current				11.7	17.9	11.7
52.6	56.0	53.4	Total Current				56.6	60.4	48.2
36.2	31.4	36.9	Fixed Assets (net)				31.3	31.1	44.8
3.1	4.2	2.6	Intangibles (net)				1.5	3.3	2.3
8.2	8.3	7.2	All Other Non-Current				10.6	5.1	4.7
100.0	100.0	100.0	Total				100.0	100.0	100.0
			LIABILITIES						
6.4	9.1	7.5	Notes Payable-Short Term				9.6	14.9	2.9
5.3	4.0	3.6	Cur. Mat.-L/T/D				2.4	5.7	3.7
12.0	12.5	12.8	Trade Payables				12.0	11.9	15.7
.4	.7	1.0	Income Taxes Payable				1.2	2.1	.5
15.4	15.3	13.2	All Other Current				10.7	15.4	14.1
39.5	41.5	38.2	Total Current				35.9	49.9	36.8
18.2	18.9	17.6	Long Term Debt				8.0	15.4	19.0
1.2	.9	1.5	Deferred Taxes				.9	.1	1.9
4.5	3.4	3.7	All Other Non-Current				3.8	4.0	3.3
36.5	35.3	39.0	Net Worth				51.5	30.5	39.0
100.0	100.0	100.0	Total Liabilities & Net Worth				100.0	100.0	100.0
			INCOME DATA						
100.0	100.0	100.0	Net Sales				100.0	100.0	100.0
23.8	24.2	25.6	Gross Profit				22.8	22.3	21.0
20.7	19.8	21.1	Operating Expenses				19.6	18.3	16.8
3.1	4.4	4.5	Operating Profit				3.1	4.0	4.2
.7	1.5	.7	All Other Expenses (net)				−.5	.8	1.5
2.4	3.0	3.8	Profit Before Taxes				3.6	3.2	2.7
			RATIOS						
1.9	2.2	1.9					3.0	1.6	1.9
1.3	1.4	1.4	Current				1.5	1.2	1.4
1.0	1.0	1.0					1.1	1.0	.9
1.4	1.4	1.3					1.5	1.3	1.2
.8	.8	.8	Quick				1.0	.7	.7
.3	.5	.4					.5	.4	.5
18 19.8	20 18.2	10 37.6					17 20.9	7 51.3	9 39.9
34 10.6	34 10.7	30 12.2	Sales/Receivables				31 11.8	28 12.9	35 10.5
55 6.6	57 6.5	48 7.7					45 8.1	54 6.7	45 8.1
0 UND	1 345.1	0 UND					4 104.2	0 UND	1 281.2
6 58.7	15 23.7	8 46.0	Cost of Sales/Inventory				11 33.6	4 81.2	6 60.9
31 11.9	45 8.1	30 12.4					20 18.3	23 16.0	30 12.1
15 23.6	13 29.1	14 26.9					11 34.5	9 40.1	18 20.1
26 14.2	24 15.4	21 17.1	Cost of Sales/Payables				18 20.3	19 19.1	30 12.3
39 9.5	42 8.6	40 9.1					35 10.4	32 11.3	48 7.5
6.6	6.6	8.0					8.2	9.1	9.7
20.7	13.1	17.8	Sales/Working Capital				16.2	29.4	15.9
267.5	151.4	NM					137.0	−238.0	−36.6
9.2	4.8	7.7					25.8	8.5	5.1
(50) 2.6	(57) 3.1	(52) 3.5	EBIT/Interest				(11) 5.6	(13) 6.6	(19) 2.3
1.1	1.2	1.2					2.0	.1	1.1
5.3	3.8	4.2	Net Profit + Depr., Dep.,						2.5
(22) 1.8	(23) 2.2	(21) 1.9	Amort./Cur. Mat. L/T/D						(10) 1.5
.8	1.1	.9							.5
.4	.5	.5					.4	.5	.8
1.0	1.1	1.0	Fixed/Worth				.6	.9	1.2
1.9	2.1	1.9					1.0	2.1	1.9
.7	.9	.7					.4	1.3	.9
1.4	1.8	1.9	Debt/Worth				.7	2.8	1.7
3.9	5.0	3.2					2.4	3.7	2.7
29.4	34.4	35.5	% Profit Before Taxes/Tangible				25.0	68.0	17.9
(50) 17.1	(57) 18.8	(53) 11.4	Net Worth				(11) 11.6	(13) 49.6	(20) 7.7
2.8	3.2	3.5					6.1	17.2	.5
12.5	12.5	13.0	% Profit Before Taxes/Total				9.8	17.2	9.7
6.2	5.7	4.1	Assets				5.2	10.1	2.4
.7	.6	.3					1.7	3.8	.0
13.7	18.1	19.5					24.1	34.9	12.6
7.1	7.9	6.0	Sales/Net Fixed Assets				7.3	8.6	3.7
3.0	3.8	2.5					4.6	3.8	2.4
2.7	2.8	3.1					3.4	3.1	3.0
1.9	2.0	2.2	Sales/Total Assets				2.6	2.1	2.0
1.3	1.4	1.4					1.6	1.6	1.3
.9	.8	1.4					1.7	1.0	1.0
(47) 2.0	(58) 1.6	(50) 2.2	% Depr., Dep., Amort./Sales				(10) 2.0	(11) 2.0	(19) 1.8
4.0	4.1	3.4					3.5	3.0	3.3
3.4	1.4	1.2	% Officers', Directors',						
(10) 4.1	(18) 2.5	(18) 2.0	Owners' Comp/Sales						
8.1	4.5	5.0							
2774460M	3095069M	2177901M	Net Sales ($)	2647M	10602M	8346M	99253M	256910M	1800143M
2024303M	1737249M	1481224M	Total Assets ($)	4904M	9861M	2572M	43665M	128170M	1292052M

M = $ thousand   MM = $ million
See Pages 11 through 18 for Explanation of Ratios and Data

Current Data Sorted By Assets   **Comparative Historical Data**

Type of Statement	0-500M	500M-2MM	2-10MM	10-50MM	50-100MM	100-250MM		ALL 4/1/98-3/31/99	ALL 4/1/99-3/31/00
Unqualified		3	4	8	2	1		21	30
Reviewed	6	2	7	3				9	8
Compiled	1	2	12	2				12	9
Tax Returns		7	1					5	6
Other			8	7	3			20	23
		16 (4/1-9/30/02)		63 (10/1/02-3/31/03)					
NUMBER OF STATEMENTS	7	14	32	20	5	1		67	76

	0-500M	500M-2MM	2-10MM	10-50MM	50-100MM	100-250MM		ALL 98/99	ALL 99/00
	%	%	%	%	%	%		%	%
ASSETS									
Cash & Equivalents		7.6	9.5	14.6				10.1	8.8
Trade Receivables (net)		17.7	12.4	11.9				16.1	15.3
Inventory		34.3	37.8	33.0				33.5	33.7
All Other Current		3.3	6.7	3.5				5.0	3.9
Total Current		62.8	66.5	63.0				64.7	61.8
Fixed Assets (net)		24.1	28.5	27.0				28.7	28.2
Intangibles (net)		4.0	2.7	4.4				1.7	4.6
All Other Non-Current		9.2	2.2	5.6				4.9	5.4
Total		100.0	100.0	100.0				100.0	100.0
LIABILITIES									
Notes Payable-Short Term		17.5	11.1	5.0				7.6	8.8
Cur. Mat.-L/T/D		3.2	2.6	2.1				3.0	2.3
Trade Payables		15.0	22.4	13.7				15.4	16.2
Income Taxes Payable		.4	1.4	.0				.2	.2
All Other Current		18.5	14.9	14.3				20.7	18.2
Total Current		54.6	52.4	35.2				47.0	45.9
Long Term Debt		19.2	11.5	15.0				19.5	19.3
Deferred Taxes		.0	.6	.1				.8	.2
All Other Non-Current		2.0	6.5	1.0				2.8	5.7
Net Worth		24.3	29.1	48.6				29.8	28.9
Total Liabilities & Net Worth		100.0	100.0	100.0				100.0	100.0
INCOME DATA									
Net Sales		100.0	100.0	100.0				100.0	100.0
Gross Profit		27.0	19.6	22.3				25.9	23.8
Operating Expenses		22.1	15.1	16.2				22.2	18.5
Operating Profit		4.8	4.6	6.1				3.7	5.3
All Other Expenses (net)		.6	1.0	.3				1.3	1.9
Profit Before Taxes		4.2	3.5	5.8				2.5	3.3
RATIOS									
Current		1.9	1.7	2.8				2.0	2.0
		1.5	1.3	1.9				1.5	1.5
		.8	1.0	1.3				1.1	1.1
Quick		.9	1.2	1.4				1.1	.9
		.4	.3	.6				.6	.5
		.2	.1	.4				.4	.3
Sales/Receivables		9 40.9	2 173.6	10 37.4				7 48.7	7 49.9
		14 27.0	8 43.7	16 23.3				17 20.9	19 18.8
		23 15.8	26 14.1	24 15.4				32 11.5	27 13.3
Cost of Sales/Inventory		24 15.0	39 9.4	42 8.7				31 11.7	40 9.2
		36 10.2	63 5.8	58 6.3				52 7.0	53 6.8
		67 5.5	122 3.0	80 4.6				72 5.0	80 4.6
Cost of Sales/Payables		12 31.3	20 18.3	12 30.4				9 39.0	13 29.1
		16 22.6	33 11.2	23 15.9				20 18.0	25 14.7
		35 10.3	49 7.5	38 9.5				35 10.6	34 10.6
Sales/Working Capital		7.7	6.2	6.0				8.3	7.8
		36.8	17.7	11.4				14.5	16.0
		-43.4	93.7	16.3				92.7	119.5
EBIT/Interest		33.6	14.8	17.7				10.0	13.6
		(12) 5.6	(31) 3.2	(17) 9.8				(58) 3.8	(67) 3.8
		.8	1.8	3.2				1.5	1.6
Net Profit + Depr., Dep., Amort./Cur. Mat. L/T/D			(11) 7.2					(17) 10.0	(18) 13.4
			1.6					3.6	3.2
			.5					2.0	2.0
Fixed/Worth		.2	.5	.4				.4	.5
		1.4	1.2	.7				1.0	.9
		4.1	2.8	1.0				2.8	4.0
Debt/Worth		.9	1.2	.6				.9	.9
		3.2	2.6	1.0				2.0	3.0
		17.9	12.9	3.5				7.1	9.9
% Profit Before Taxes/Tangible Net Worth		82.7	62.0	45.0				45.9	54.4
		(12) 16.5	(29) 25.7	(19) 36.3				(56) 27.4	(61) 27.2
		-6.1	6.3	13.5				13.9	12.5
% Profit Before Taxes/Total Assets		27.7	18.5	22.3				17.0	17.0
		6.9	6.2	9.9				9.1	8.6
		-1.0	1.6	6.5				1.9	3.1
Sales/Net Fixed Assets		28.3	22.2	13.3				22.8	24.3
		19.9	9.0	8.6				11.0	12.3
		12.8	6.3	7.0				8.3	7.4
Sales/Total Assets		4.4	3.5	3.3				4.0	3.9
		3.0	2.5	2.7				3.0	3.0
		2.2	1.7	2.0				2.2	2.3
% Depr., Dep., Amort./Sales		.4	.6	.9				.8	.6
		(13) 1.2	(30) 1.5	1.3				(56) 1.3	(66) 1.3
		1.9	2.8	1.9				2.0	1.8
% Officers', Directors', Owners' Comp/Sales								(23) 1.7	(32) 1.2
								5.1	2.6
								7.4	4.8
Net Sales ($)	6906M	65712M	447564M	1167067M	564455M	150133M		2234509M	2471436M
Total Assets ($)	1817M	18899M	174767M	452271M	320731M	109918M		792898M	898180M

M = $ thousand   MM = $ million
See Pages 11 through 18 for Explanation of Ratios and Data

Comparative Historical Data | Current Data Sorted By Sales

4/1/00-3/31/01 ALL	4/1/01-3/31/02 ALL	4/1/02-3/31/03 ALL	Type of Statement	0-1MM	1-3MM	3-5MM	5-10MM	10-25MM	25MM & OVER
15	8	15	Unqualified					5	10
12	13	13	Reviewed		2	1	2	7	3
18	19	16	Compiled			1	6	6	1
4	8	9	Tax Returns	3	4	1	1		
32	20	26	Other	1	2	4	2	5	12
					16 (4/1-9/30/02)			63 (10/1/02-3/31/03)	
81	68	79	**NUMBER OF STATEMENTS**	4	8	7	11	23	26
%	%	%	**ASSETS**	%	%	%	%	%	%
11.9	15.0	11.3	Cash & Equivalents				11.5	10.7	10.9
13.4	11.9	12.3	Trade Receivables (net)				14.0	14.1	11.6
32.5	31.8	32.9	Inventory				39.3	36.1	31.0
3.0	3.7	4.8	All Other Current				9.5	4.6	4.7
60.8	62.4	61.3	Total Current				74.2	65.5	58.1
30.5	28.0	30.8	Fixed Assets (net)				22.6	28.8	32.4
2.8	5.2	3.4	Intangibles (net)				.8	3.5	4.3
5.8	4.4	4.6	All Other Non-Current				2.4	2.2	5.2
100.0	100.0	100.0	Total				100.0	100.0	100.0
			LIABILITIES						
8.2	14.2	9.7	Notes Payable-Short Term				24.4	7.1	5.9
4.4	4.2	2.6	Cur. Mat.-L/T/D				2.5	2.7	2.5
16.6	12.4	16.6	Trade Payables				16.3	23.9	13.8
.1	.1	.6	Income Taxes Payable				1.1	1.4	.0
17.4	15.1	14.9	All Other Current				15.7	9.0	17.3
46.6	46.0	44.4	Total Current				60.0	44.1	39.5
16.1	15.7	15.2	Long Term Debt				11.5	9.7	16.3
.3	.3	.3	Deferred Taxes				.2	.7	.2
4.9	4.3	3.4	All Other Non-Current				1.4	8.8	1.3
32.1	33.7	36.7	Net Worth				26.9	36.6	42.7
100.0	100.0	100.0	Total Liabilities & Net Worth				100.0	100.0	100.0
			INCOME DATA						
100.0	100.0	100.0	Net Sales				100.0	100.0	100.0
25.6	26.4	25.0	Gross Profit				18.8	21.3	20.4
20.3	21.3	20.0	Operating Expenses				15.4	15.5	14.9
5.3	5.1	5.0	Operating Profit				3.4	5.8	5.5
.9	.8	.7	All Other Expenses (net)				1.0	.6	.5
4.4	4.4	4.3	Profit Before Taxes				2.5	5.2	5.0
			RATIOS						
2.1	2.5	2.3	Current				1.7	3.0	2.8
1.5	1.5	1.6					1.4	1.3	1.8
1.0	1.0	1.0					.8	1.1	1.2
1.2	1.2	1.2	Quick				.9	1.3	1.2
.5	.7	.4					.3	.6	.5
.3	.3	.2					.2	.2	.3
6 59.7	5 79.0	5 74.6	Sales/Receivables				2 192.5	4 97.3	8 47.7
15 23.9	15 24.5	12 31.3					8 43.1	13 28.9	16 23.3
26 14.3	26 14.0	22 16.3					29 12.7	34 10.7	24 15.1
27 13.7	24 15.2	31 11.7	Cost of Sales/Inventory				32 11.5	38 9.5	38 9.6
49 7.5	57 6.4	57 6.5					56 6.5	57 6.4	58 6.3
72 5.0	85 4.3	83 4.4					124 2.9	93 3.9	76 4.8
13 27.7	8 45.0	12 30.1	Cost of Sales/Payables				14 26.4	20 18.3	11 34.5
24 15.0	18 20.5	24 14.9					32 11.4	32 11.4	16 22.5
36 10.1	35 10.3	40 9.0					49 7.4	57 6.4	34 10.8
9.4	6.2	6.1	Sales/Working Capital				6.7	6.1	5.6
17.0	12.5	16.4					15.8	23.1	12.3
−129.7	938.4	85.1					−26.1	85.1	24.3
14.0	18.7	17.0	EBIT/Interest				7.9	21.6	15.8
(71) 3.4	(62) 2.3	(70) 4.1					(10) 2.3	(22) 5.2	(21) 6.2
1.8	.9	1.6					1.1	2.5	2.7
9.8	13.5	9.1	Net Profit + Depr., Dep.,						9.9
(18) 4.4	(18) 3.0	(23) 4.2	Amort./Cur. Mat. L/T/D						(11) 5.8
.6	1.0	1.0							1.5
.5	.3	.4	Fixed/Worth				.2	.5	.4
1.0	.8	.8					.8	1.2	.7
2.5	4.0	2.5					2.7	2.0	2.2
.9	.8	.7	Debt/Worth				1.3	.8	.4
2.0	1.9	1.9					2.8	2.6	1.0
5.3	64.7	6.8					17.1	5.7	7.4
61.9	58.2	47.5	% Profit Before Taxes/Tangible				23.5	77.9	45.1
(69) 29.9	(54) 18.5	(71) 23.5	Net Worth				8.3	(21) 36.7	(23) 37.7
13.2	−.1	6.6					−.8	11.5	13.5
19.4	20.5	19.9	% Profit Before Taxes/Total				9.6	22.9	20.7
10.0	5.9	7.6	Assets				1.5	8.6	9.5
3.3	−.3	1.8					−.2	5.9	5.6
17.3	21.9	19.2	Sales/Net Fixed Assets				32.1	21.2	12.0
11.5	10.7	10.0					13.9	8.8	9.4
6.8	6.6	6.2					6.4	6.1	6.8
3.9	3.1	3.5	Sales/Total Assets				3.2	3.6	3.3
3.0	2.4	2.7					2.8	2.5	2.6
2.1	1.7	1.8					1.7	1.8	1.9
.5	.7	.8	% Depr., Dep., Amort./Sales				1.2	.6	.9
(72) 1.4	(61) 1.7	(75) 1.5					(10) 1.7	(21) 1.3	(25) 1.5
2.6	3.1	2.3					4.4	2.4	2.1
1.0	1.5	.9	% Officers', Directors',						
(32) 2.4	(24) 5.3	(25) 3.0	Owners' Comp/Sales						
4.6	8.6	7.0							
2416601M	1686349M	2401837M	Net Sales ($)	2535M	14542M	28589M	74720M	375955M	1905496M
916809M	741357M	1078403M	Total Assets ($)	826M	12931M	8878M	37141M	155715M	862912M

© RMA 2003

M = $ thousand   MM = $ million
See Pages 11 through 18 for Explanation of Ratios and Data

Current Data Sorted By Assets   **Comparative Historical Data**

Type of Statement

0-500M	500M-2MM	2-10MM	10-50MM	50-100MM	100-250MM		4/1/98-3/31/99 ALL	4/1/99-3/31/00 ALL
	2	3	6	1	1	Unqualified	12	11
2	4	5	1			Reviewed	6	6
1	4	2				Compiled	10	6
	2	10	5			Tax Returns	4	3
						Other	17	16
9 (4/1-9/30/02)		40 (10/1/02-3/31/03)						
3	12	20	12	1	1	**NUMBER OF STATEMENTS**	49	42

ASSETS

0-500M	500M-2MM	2-10MM	10-50MM	50-100MM	100-250MM		4/1/98-3/31/99 ALL	4/1/99-3/31/00 ALL
%	%	%	%	%	%		%	%
	9.9	5.2	11.5			Cash & Equivalents	7.0	9.4
	29.3	22.0	24.1			Trade Receivables (net)	20.8	23.7
	37.2	42.7	26.4			Inventory	38.2	33.7
	3.2	2.0	5.5			All Other Current	3.1	2.0
	79.6	71.9	67.5			Total Current	69.1	68.7
	11.5	19.9	15.7			Fixed Assets (net)	22.0	20.7
	.1	4.1	10.4			Intangibles (net)	2.4	5.1
	8.8	4.0	6.4			All Other Non-Current	6.5	5.5
	100.0	100.0	100.0			Total	100.0	100.0

LIABILITIES

0-500M	500M-2MM	2-10MM	10-50MM	50-100MM	100-250MM		4/1/98-3/31/99 ALL	4/1/99-3/31/00 ALL
	19.0	14.6	10.2			Notes Payable-Short Term	12.6	13.4
	2.3	4.2	7.9			Cur. Mat.-L/T/D	2.4	3.3
	17.9	17.4	12.5			Trade Payables	16.2	17.4
	.5	.2	.1			Income Taxes Payable	.4	.7
	11.8	11.8	12.8			All Other Current	19.9	12.4
	51.4	48.2	43.5			Total Current	51.6	47.2
	19.8	14.8	17.1			Long Term Debt	18.7	13.9
	.0	.2	.4			Deferred Taxes	.4	.4
	4.1	4.7	11.0			All Other Non-Current	7.6	9.6
	24.6	32.1	28.1			Net Worth	21.7	28.9
	100.0	100.0	100.0			Total Liabilities & Net Worth	100.0	100.0

INCOME DATA

0-500M	500M-2MM	2-10MM	10-50MM	50-100MM	100-250MM		4/1/98-3/31/99 ALL	4/1/99-3/31/00 ALL
	100.0	100.0	100.0			Net Sales	100.0	100.0
	28.5	26.6	23.4			Gross Profit	29.2	25.2
	25.0	23.1	15.8			Operating Expenses	22.9	19.1
	3.5	3.5	7.5			Operating Profit	6.3	6.0
	1.9	1.5	1.7			All Other Expenses (net)	1.9	1.5
	1.6	2.0	5.8			Profit Before Taxes	4.4	4.5

RATIOS

0-500M	500M-2MM	2-10MM	10-50MM	50-100MM	100-250MM		4/1/98-3/31/99 ALL	4/1/99-3/31/00 ALL
	3.6	2.8	2.2			Current	2.1	2.2
	1.8	1.6	1.5				1.4	1.5
	1.0	1.1	1.1				1.2	1.2
	2.4	.9	1.0			Quick	1.0	1.3
	.8	.6	.9				.5	.7
	.4	.3	.4				.3	.5
	11 32.9	18 20.1	16 22.2			Sales/Receivables	17 21.4	19 19.2
	31 11.6	35 10.5	30 12.2				37 9.9	41 8.8
	52 7.1	51 7.2	65 5.6				64 5.7	54 6.8
	0 UND	54 6.7	27 13.3			Cost of Sales/Inventory	38 9.5	37 9.8
	67 5.5	86 4.3	53 6.9				67 5.5	63 5.8
	123 3.0	124 2.9	93 3.9				125 2.9	108 3.4
	9 40.1	24 15.0	14 26.3			Cost of Sales/Payables	14 26.1	14 26.0
	20 18.0	36 10.0	23 15.7				27 13.5	25 14.8
	25 14.7	45 8.0	29 12.4				57 6.4	49 7.5
	5.0	4.5	6.7			Sales/Working Capital	5.8	7.5
	11.1	12.1	13.0				12.9	11.2
	NM	27.9	48.6				38.8	23.1
	10.2	11.5	10.7			EBIT/Interest	9.8	8.0
	(11) 2.0	2.3	(11) 3.6				(47) 2.9	(35) 4.3
	.9	.4	1.7				1.2	2.6
						Net Profit + Depr., Dep., Amort./Cur. Mat. L /T/D		12.6
								(11) 5.4
								3.2
	.1	.2	.2			Fixed/Worth	.3	.4
	.4	.6	2.1				.7	.7
	1.2	2.2	-1.5				NM	3.3
	.9	1.0	.8			Debt/Worth	1.2	1.0
	2.5	2.2	6.9				2.6	2.5
	9.9	4.9	-11.2				15.7	58.4
	75.7	37.3				% Profit Before Taxes/Tangible Net Worth	50.1	60.6
	(11) 30.9	(17) 27.1					(38) 28.1	(34) 34.7
	2.5	.0					10.3	16.3
	17.1	18.3	20.4			% Profit Before Taxes/Total Assets	19.7	17.0
	4.5	5.6	13.2				7.7	9.6
	-.3	-.7	5.7				1.7	4.0
	192.3	23.4	25.1			Sales/Net Fixed Assets	42.9	36.6
	49.9	16.1	16.2				14.3	11.7
	14.2	6.0	10.4				4.4	7.1
	4.9	3.1	3.2			Sales/Total Assets	3.4	3.4
	3.9	2.5	2.3				2.1	2.6
	2.0	1.8	1.4				1.5	1.7
	.4	.6	1.0			% Depr., Dep., Amort./Sales	.9	1.0
	(10) .7	(19) 1.1	(11) 1.7				(40) 1.4	(36) 1.4
	1.3	2.8	3.5				3.9	2.3
						% Officers', Directors', Owners' Comp/Sales	1.2	1.6
							(17) 2.5	(14) 4.2
							4.8	7.8
2991M	46274M	259481M	543772M	193166M	149328M	Net Sales ($)	1456412M	990025M
823M	12725M	107368M	252115M	92271M	106088M	Total Assets ($)	975644M	563119M

M = $ thousand   MM = $ million
See Pages 11 through 18 for Explanation of Ratios and Data

Comparative Historical Data / Current Data Sorted By Sales

			Type of Statement	0-1MM	1-3MM	3-5MM	5-10MM	10-25MM	25MM & OVER
13	11	12	Unqualified		1		1	5	5
7	7	7	Reviewed		2		2	3	2
10	11	8	Compiled	2	2	2	1		1
2	2	5	Tax Returns			1	2		
17	21	17	Other		1	3	4	4	5
4/1/00-3/31/01 ALL	4/1/01-3/31/02 ALL	4/1/02-3/31/03 ALL				9 (4/1-9/30/02)		40 (10/1/02-3/31/03)	
49	52	49	**NUMBER OF STATEMENTS**	2	6	6	10	12	13
%	%	%	**ASSETS**	%	%	%	%	%	%
8.3	5.5	9.1	Cash & Equivalents				8.1	6.7	10.3
20.7	21.8	22.8	Trade Receivables (net)				25.2	23.8	24.1
35.6	36.2	34.5	Inventory				37.3	34.4	30.1
4.6	4.1	3.3	All Other Current				3.0	2.0	5.9
69.2	67.6	69.7	Total Current				73.7	66.9	70.4
18.4	20.1	19.3	Fixed Assets (net)				21.8	18.6	16.8
5.3	5.4	4.4	Intangibles (net)				1.7	10.7	5.3
7.1	7.0	6.6	All Other Non-Current				2.8	3.8	7.5
100.0	100.0	100.0	Total				100.0	100.0	100.0
			LIABILITIES						
14.9	18.7	15.3	Notes Payable-Short Term				12.7	14.6	13.0
3.6	4.5	4.9	Cur. Mat.-L/T/D				2.1	4.9	9.1
16.4	15.5	15.1	Trade Payables				15.4	21.6	11.4
.3	.5	.3	Income Taxes Payable				1.0	.0	.3
9.6	11.7	11.4	All Other Current				15.6	8.2	13.1
44.8	51.0	46.9	Total Current				46.7	49.3	46.8
17.4	18.0	17.7	Long Term Debt				13.8	13.5	15.1
.4	.3	.2	Deferred Taxes				.5	.1	.3
4.4	13.6	5.7	All Other Non-Current				3.3	6.9	7.7
33.1	17.2	29.4	Net Worth				35.7	30.3	30.1
100.0	100.0	100.0	Total Liabilities & Net Worth				100.0	100.0	100.0
			INCOME DATA						
100.0	100.0	100.0	Net Sales				100.0	100.0	100.0
24.1	24.6	28.0	Gross Profit				26.4	26.4	20.7
19.9	20.1	22.3	Operating Expenses				24.9	21.5	14.7
4.2	4.6	5.6	Operating Profit				1.5	4.9	6.0
.8	2.3	2.4	All Other Expenses (net)				1.5	1.6	1.1
3.4	2.3	3.3	Profit Before Taxes				.0	3.3	4.9
			RATIOS						
2.4 / 1.5 / 1.2	2.6 / 1.5 / 1.1	2.9 / 1.6 / 1.0	Current				3.0 / 1.6 / 1.2	2.2 / 1.5 / 1.0	2.1 / 1.6 / 1.0
1.0 / .6 / .3	1.1 / .6 / .4	1.0 / .7 / .4	Quick				1.5 / .4 / .3	.9 / .6 / .4	1.0 / .8 / .4
10 35.8 / 31 11.6 / 54 6.7	16 22.9 / 31 11.9 / 47 7.7	15 24.8 / 31 11.8 / 52 7.0	Sales/Receivables				17 21.6 / 33 11.0 / 55 6.7	16 22.7 / 31 11.9 / 48 7.5	13 28.4 / 31 11.8 / 60 6.1
31 11.7 / 72 5.1 / 138 2.6	35 10.5 / 60 6.1 / 122 3.0	31 11.9 / 70 5.2 / 123 3.0	Cost of Sales/Inventory				0 UND / 92 4.0 / 132 2.8	34 10.8 / 75 4.8 / 95 3.8	4 95.9 / 51 7.2 / 75 4.8
13 27.3 / 26 14.1 / 43 8.5	14 26.4 / 24 15.4 / 36 10.1	17 21.8 / 25 14.5 / 40 9.1	Cost of Sales/Payables				22 16.5 / 25 14.6 / 36 10.1	20 17.9 / 39 9.4 / 45 8.0	12 31.7 / 22 16.8 / 29 12.8
4.2 / 9.5 / 21.5	6.0 / 11.9 / 58.6	5.5 / 14.2 / 529.2	Sales/Working Capital				5.4 / 12.2 / 31.7	7.9 / 15.4 / 756.8	7.6 / 12.0 / NM
(48) 5.3 / 1.8 / .9	(45) 6.3 / 2.3 / .8	(46) 10.1 / 2.2 / 1.0	EBIT/Interest					21.0 / 3.0 / .5	(12) 10.6 / 5.2 / 1.7
(15) 13.3 / 5.3 / 1.4	(10) 13.3 / 3.6 / .7	(11) 8.2 / 4.1 / .5	Net Profit + Depr., Dep., Amort./Cur. Mat. L/T/D						
.3 / .6 / 1.6	.3 / .6 / 8.2	.2 / .7 / 2.6	Fixed/Worth				.2 / .7 / 1.7	.3 / 1.1 / -2.5	.1 / 1.1 / NM
.9 / 2.6 / 5.9	1.0 / 2.7 / 31.9	1.0 / 2.6 / 10.0	Debt/Worth				1.0 / 2.0 / 3.5	.9 / 3.7 / -11.6	.9 / 3.9 / NM
(44) 41.6 / 16.2 / 1.5	(43) 76.9 / 16.7 / 3.0	(40) 71.9 / 30.9 / 3.9	% Profit Before Taxes/Tangible Net Worth						(10) 81.6 / 29.5 / 14.6
11.6 / 4.2 / -.1	12.5 / 4.5 / .5	19.5 / 6.8 / .5	% Profit Before Taxes/Total Assets				7.9 / 3.2 / -3.7	26.8 / 11.9 / -.5	19.7 / 12.4 / 3.8
38.0 / 12.3 / 7.6	38.7 / 12.3 / 8.1	42.5 / 16.3 / 9.9	Sales/Net Fixed Assets				34.1 / 15.9 / 4.7	19.5 / 16.1 / 9.8	43.3 / 16.7 / 12.1
3.1 / 2.1 / 1.3	3.3 / 2.3 / 1.6	3.5 / 2.6 / 1.8	Sales/Total Assets				3.9 / 2.2 / 1.6	3.3 / 2.6 / 1.9	3.3 / 2.4 / 1.9
(37) .7 / 1.9 / 3.1	(43) 1.1 / 1.7 / 3.6	(43) .6 / 1.2 / 3.0	% Depr., Dep., Amort./Sales				.6 / 1.4 / 2.9	(11) .6 / .9 / 3.6	(11) .4 / 1.2 / 2.3
(13) 2.3 / 3.5 / 4.6	(17) 1.1 / 2.1 / 4.3	(15) 1.6 / 3.7 / 4.9	% Officers', Directors', Owners' Comp/Sales						
1865605M	1862053M	1195012M	Net Sales ($)	1079M	11585M	22801M	69324M	212255M	877968M
1104755M	910409M	571390M	Total Assets ($)	564M	5013M	9958M	33301M	103457M	419097M

© RMA 2003

M = $ thousand   MM = $ million
See Pages 11 through 18 for Explanation of Ratios and Data

Current Data Sorted By Assets | Comparative Historical Data

						Type of Statement		
1		6	7	4	2	Unqualified	13	10
1	8	16	4			Reviewed	19	23
12	22	11	3		1	Compiled	43	47
20	10	8				Tax Returns	13	27
13	13	16	3		1	Other	32	39
	38 (4/1-9/30/02)		144 (10/1/02-3/31/03)				4/1/98-3/31/99	4/1/99-3/31/00
0-500M	500M-2MM	2-10MM	10-50MM	50-100MM	100-250MM		ALL	ALL
47	53	57	17	4	4	NUMBER OF STATEMENTS	120	146
%	%	%	%	%	%	ASSETS	%	%
10.5	10.2	8.6	3.9			Cash & Equivalents	6.3	8.1
20.8	28.1	26.5	21.0			Trade Receivables (net)	32.2	32.1
23.8	21.9	24.5	29.4			Inventory	17.9	18.6
2.2	1.5	3.0	2.3			All Other Current	1.4	1.4
57.3	61.7	62.6	56.6			Total Current	57.9	60.1
35.5	34.4	29.1	38.2			Fixed Assets (net)	35.8	33.5
.8	.3	2.3	2.8			Intangibles (net)	2.4	2.2
6.5	3.6	6.1	2.4			All Other Non-Current	3.9	4.1
100.0	100.0	100.0	100.0			Total	100.0	100.0
						LIABILITIES		
19.1	8.4	9.9	10.5			Notes Payable-Short Term	7.7	10.9
6.4	5.3	4.0	2.7			Cur. Mat.-L/T/D	5.1	4.9
19.2	15.3	14.0	11.2			Trade Payables	16.0	17.2
.2	.4	.5	.0			Income Taxes Payable	.6	.5
13.2	10.9	12.6	16.0			All Other Current	11.3	10.9
58.1	40.4	41.1	40.4			Total Current	40.7	44.5
23.0	19.4	15.9	14.4			Long Term Debt	21.8	22.9
.0	.2	.3	.2			Deferred Taxes	.3	.2
5.1	2.4	5.3	4.4			All Other Non-Current	3.7	3.8
13.7	37.6	37.4	40.6			Net Worth	33.4	28.6
100.0	100.0	100.0	100.0			Total Liabilities & Net Worth	100.0	100.0
						INCOME DATA		
100.0	100.0	100.0	100.0			Net Sales	100.0	100.0
41.9	34.7	30.4	33.8			Gross Profit	32.3	33.9
38.3	30.5	26.0	28.1			Operating Expenses	26.8	29.1
3.6	4.2	4.3	5.7			Operating Profit	5.5	4.8
.8	1.0	.5	.8			All Other Expenses (net)	.6	.8
2.8	3.3	3.9	4.9			Profit Before Taxes	4.9	3.9
						RATIOS		
2.1	2.5	2.2	2.2				2.4	2.2
1.3	1.5	1.5	1.5			Current	1.6	1.5
.7	1.0	1.0	1.0				1.0	1.0
1.4	1.9	1.5	1.4				1.7	1.4
.6	.9	.8	.6			Quick	1.0	.9
.3	.5	.5	.2				.6	.6

												Sales/Receivables etc.					

0	UND	15	23.9	22	16.8	17	21.7					Sales/Receivables	26	14.1	20	18.1
14	25.3	32	11.5	35	10.6	26	14.3						38	9.5	34	10.8
33	11.2	48	7.6	45	8.2	44	8.4						55	6.6	50	7.3
6	63.7	14	25.9	21	17.7	32	11.4					Cost of Sales/Inventory	18	20.1	14	26.4
25	14.9	25	14.5	31	11.6	45	8.1						31	11.8	29	12.4
50	7.3	60	6.1	62	5.9	103	3.6						47	7.7	51	7.2
6	60.3	12	29.9	14	26.6	10	38.4					Cost of Sales/Payables	13	28.4	12	30.0
23	15.9	22	16.3	24	15.1	24	15.1						24	15.0	22	16.7
39	9.3	43	8.5	37	9.8	43	8.4						37	9.9	35	10.3

11.4	8.4	7.3	6.7			Sales/Working Capital	7.6	8.3
22.4	19.5	14.1	16.2				17.9	16.2
-24.6	378.5	105.0	-204.8				UND	UND

(36)	11.5	(49)	10.7	(55)	16.5	(16)	12.8			EBIT/Interest	(114)	10.4	(137)	10.0
	2.4		3.9		3.7		6.0					5.0		4.0
	.8		1.3		1.8		2.9					1.9		1.7

		(12)	2.8	(16)	7.4					Net Profit + Depr., Dep., Amort./Cur. Mat. L./T/D	(29)	5.2	(39)	6.1
			1.7		3.3							2.5		3.8
			.8		1.0							1.5		1.6

.3	.3	.3	.6			Fixed/Worth	.5	.5
1.3	.8	.7	1.0				1.0	1.0
UND	2.8	1.9	1.6				2.7	3.4

.8	.6	.6	.9			Debt/Worth	.7	.9
3.9	2.1	2.2	1.5				1.8	2.2
UND	4.9	6.5	3.2				5.2	7.9

(36)	98.9	(46)	45.0	(53)	45.2		43.4			% Profit Before Taxes/Tangible Net Worth	(104)	65.3	(122)	80.5
	37.3		20.4		23.8		23.5					27.1		32.8
	7.1		3.8		7.7		13.4					12.2		11.2

25.9	16.1	18.3	19.5			% Profit Before Taxes/Total Assets	19.7	22.6
7.3	5.4	7.4	10.5				8.5	9.8
.8	1.0	2.0	4.2				3.4	3.3

34.4	29.1	22.6	10.0			Sales/Net Fixed Assets	16.7	22.3
16.1	11.1	11.0	5.4				8.3	11.4
7.1	5.2	5.6	4.0				5.5	6.0

6.9	3.9	3.5	2.7			Sales/Total Assets	3.8	4.2
3.9	3.1	2.7	2.2				2.9	3.2
3.0	2.4	2.1	1.7				2.1	2.4

(37)	.7	(49)	1.0	(54)	1.2	(16)	.8			% Depr., Dep., Amort./Sales	(109)	1.3	(125)	1.2
	1.4		2.1		1.8		2.0					1.8		1.8
	3.6		3.9		3.3		3.5					2.9		2.8

(34)	5.0	(27)	3.1	(22)	1.7					% Officers', Directors', Owners' Comp/Sales	(62)	2.3	(82)	2.6
	6.9		5.2		2.6							4.7		5.6
	11.1		7.4		4.6							7.8		8.6

48311M	198243M	691604M	786381M	667776M	3155934M	Net Sales ($)	2405144M	2895187M
11871M	60887M	247417M	310866M	319532M	727102M	Total Assets ($)	824578M	974370M

M = $ thousand MM = $ million
See Pages 11 through 18 for Explanation of Ratios and Data

Comparative Historical Data — Current Data Sorted By Sales

			Type of Statement						
9	12	20	Unqualified	1			1	6	12
22	17	29	Reviewed		3	4	9	12	1
46	35	49	Compiled	6	15	9	10	5	4
22	26	38	Tax Returns	15	11	4	4	4	
41	37	46	Other	9	9	5	10	8	5
4/1/00- 3/31/01 ALL	4/1/01- 3/31/02 ALL	4/1/02- 3/31/03 ALL		38 (4/1-9/30/02)			144 (10/1/02-3/31/03)		
				0-1MM	1-3MM	3-5MM	5-10MM	10-25MM	25MM & OVER
140	127	182	**NUMBER OF STATEMENTS**	31	38	22	34	35	22
%	%	%	**ASSETS**	%	%	%	%	%	%
7.6	7.4	9.3	Cash & Equivalents	10.2	11.1	11.0	7.8	7.2	9.2
29.1	27.7	24.4	Trade Receivables (net)	14.5	26.6	31.4	25.7	28.6	18.9
22.8	20.8	23.5	Inventory	21.7	22.7	20.0	27.4	26.3	20.3
1.0	1.8	2.2	All Other Current	2.5	1.2	3.1	2.4	2.4	2.5
60.5	57.7	59.5	Total Current	49.0	61.6	65.4	63.2	64.4	51.0
31.6	33.1	33.1	Fixed Assets (net)	41.5	34.6	31.1	30.2	27.0	34.3
3.0	3.8	2.0	Intangibles (net)	1.1	.5	.4	.7	3.0	8.0
4.9	5.4	5.5	All Other Non-Current	8.4	3.3	3.0	5.9	5.6	6.7
100.0	100.0	100.0	Total	100.0	100.0	100.0	100.0	100.0	100.0
			LIABILITIES						
11.0	13.8	11.7	Notes Payable-Short Term	18.8	14.2	7.6	9.9	10.5	6.1
5.9	5.8	4.9	Cur. Mat.-L/T/D	8.8	3.1	5.4	4.9	4.0	3.5
15.5	14.8	15.1	Trade Payables	17.7	16.2	15.4	15.9	13.8	9.8
.6	.3	.3	Income Taxes Payable	.3	.1	.1	1.1	.1	.0
12.7	12.3	12.4	All Other Current	11.6	10.7	15.9	11.4	13.3	12.8
45.7	46.9	44.4	Total Current	57.2	44.4	44.4	43.2	41.7	32.3
19.8	21.1	19.1	Long Term Debt	32.1	20.4	14.7	17.2	11.1	19.1
.3	.3	.2	Deferred Taxes	.0	.1	.2	.2	.5	.4
3.7	5.7	4.3	All Other Non-Current	5.6	3.1	2.0	5.3	5.3	4.0
30.5	26.0	31.9	Net Worth	5.1	32.0	38.6	34.1	41.5	44.2
100.0	100.0	100.0	Total Liabilities & Net Worth	100.0	100.0	100.0	100.0	100.0	100.0
			INCOME DATA						
100.0	100.0	100.0	Net Sales	100.0	100.0	100.0	100.0	100.0	100.0
32.6	34.6	35.1	Gross Profit	43.4	38.1	34.8	30.0	31.2	32.6
28.0	30.9	30.6	Operating Expenses	39.5	33.8	30.8	26.0	27.1	25.0
4.7	3.8	4.5	Operating Profit	3.9	4.3	4.0	4.0	4.1	7.6
1.3	1.2	.9	All Other Expenses (net)	1.4	.8	.9	.3	.5	1.6
3.4	2.6	3.6	Profit Before Taxes	2.5	3.4	3.1	3.7	3.6	6.0
			RATIOS						
2.3	1.9	2.3	Current	2.0	2.9	2.5	2.4	2.2	3.0
1.6	1.4	1.5		1.2	1.5	1.5	1.5	1.7	1.5
1.0	.9	1.0		.6	.9	1.0	1.1	1.1	1.0
1.6	1.2	1.6	Quick	1.1	1.7	2.0	1.1	1.6	1.9
.9	.8	.8		.5	.8	1.0	.8	1.0	.8
.5	.5	.4		.3	.3	.5	.6	.5	.5
21 17.3	20 18.3	12 29.4	Sales/Receivables	0 UND	11 33.5	14 25.9	20 18.6	18 20.7	15 24.1
33 10.9	32 11.4	28 13.1		13 29.0	20 17.8	37 9.8	32 11.3	31 11.9	28 13.2
49 7.5	44 8.3	44 8.2		33 11.2	48 7.6	64 5.7	45 8.2	40 9.1	42 8.7
14 25.5	16 22.6	17 20.9	Cost of Sales/Inventory	5 75.8	6 64.1	16 22.7	25 14.6	20 17.9	28 13.1
34 10.7	29 12.4	30 12.0		25 14.9	20 18.3	29 12.8	34 10.7	29 12.7	34 10.7
61 6.0	54 6.8	61 6.0		72 5.1	55 5.9	62 5.9	70 5.2	64 5.7	47 7.8
12 30.7	11 33.4	11 34.1	Cost of Sales/Payables	6 56.7	8 45.2	16 23.5	13 27.2	10 35.4	10 36.3
20 18.3	18 19.8	23 15.9		29 12.8	23 15.6	22 16.6	27 13.3	16 22.4	15 23.8
33 11.0	35 10.4	38 9.7		41 8.8	36 10.1	45 8.1	37 9.9	35 10.4	28 12.9
8.2	9.7	8.1	Sales/Working Capital	11.4	8.7	6.9	6.9	8.9	6.8
13.5	21.2	16.4		35.6	17.2	15.0	16.5	14.1	16.0
UND	-60.7	-554.4		-24.1	-92.1	183.9	64.4	52.4	-225.6
10.1	7.2	12.2	EBIT/Interest	4.7	11.9	14.6	14.0	13.2	26.7
(134) 4.0	(117) 3.4	(164) 3.9		(25) 2.3	(29) 2.0	6.2	(33) 4.1	(34) 4.6	(21) 5.8
1.4	1.6	1.5		.4	1.1	1.2	1.5	2.8	3.6
7.9	4.2	5.6	Net Profit + Depr., Dep., Amort./Cur. Mat. L/T/D				4.9	14.9	
(23) 2.1	(23) 1.8	(37) 2.5					(10) 2.4	(10) 2.5	
1.2	1.1	1.2					1.2	.7	
.4	.5	.3	Fixed/Worth	.7	.3	.2	.5	.3	.6
.8	1.2	1.0		3.0	.9	.8	.8	.6	1.0
2.3	UND	3.2		-4.3	9.0	2.2	1.7	1.5	1.9
.8	.9	.7	Debt/Worth	1.1	.6	.7	.9	.6	.7
1.6	2.9	2.2		7.3	2.4	1.9	2.3	1.3	1.4
9.4	-56.4	7.6		-7.7	15.0	8.0	4.9	4.1	7.8
62.2	58.9	51.1	% Profit Before Taxes/Tangible Net Worth	105.4	46.9	78.4	45.3	46.1	48.9
(117) 31.6	(94) 29.3	(157) 24.1		(22) 22.5	(30) 27.8	(21) 13.4	(32) 30.2	(33) 23.5	(19) 32.3
10.3	10.7	7.7		4.5	1.8	-7.1	7.2	9.4	15.8
20.7	17.4	20.8	% Profit Before Taxes/Total Assets	23.0	23.3	16.4	19.2	15.1	24.0
8.0	9.4	7.1		4.7	3.8	8.7	6.7	7.3	14.8
2.2	1.6	1.7		-2.8	1.2	.7	2.2	3.6	6.1
22.6	23.3	26.1	Sales/Net Fixed Assets	27.7	30.9	27.5	21.6	31.5	15.9
10.5	11.3	11.0		12.3	13.9	9.5	11.0	12.7	6.4
6.1	5.5	5.5		4.3	6.3	5.3	6.8	7.0	4.1
4.1	4.0	4.0	Sales/Total Assets	6.9	4.7	3.5	3.9	4.0	3.3
3.0	3.2	3.0		3.2	3.3	2.8	2.8	3.4	2.4
2.3	2.3	2.2		2.0	2.6	2.0	2.3	2.3	1.7
1.0	1.1	1.0	% Depr., Dep., Amort./Sales	.9	.6	1.4	1.3	1.0	1.3
(123) 1.7	(114) 1.9	(161) 1.8		(25) 1.5	(31) 1.7	(21) 2.3	(33) 1.8	(33) 1.6	(18) 2.2
2.9	3.1	3.5		4.7	4.0	4.0	2.7	3.0	3.3
2.5	2.4	2.6	% Officers', Directors', Owners' Comp/Sales	5.5	2.9	2.6	1.7	1.7	
(73) 4.7	(67) 4.2	(92) 5.1		(25) 7.6	(22) 5.2	(10) 4.6	(14) 2.6	(14) 3.4	
8.3	7.0	8.4		11.9	8.6	7.5	4.5	6.0	
2970085M	3060532M	5548249M	Net Sales ($)	19968M	68069M	86750M	234485M	572765M	4566212M
1147010M	1342413M	1677675M	Total Assets ($)	7787M	21554M	33764M	87663M	203440M	1323467M

M = $ thousand   MM = $ million
See Pages 11 through 18 for Explanation of Ratios and Data

Current Data Sorted By Assets   **Comparative Historical Data**

0-500M	500M-2MM	2-10MM	10-50MM	50-100MM	100-250MM	Type of Statement	4/1/98-3/31/99 ALL	4/1/99-3/31/00 ALL
		6	9	5	3	Unqualified	15	16
	1	10	3			Reviewed	11	16
1	5	6			1	Compiled	14	11
		1				Tax Returns	3	1
	1	7	5	3	1	Other	15	12
	21 (4/1-9/30/02)		47 (10/1/02-3/31/03)					
1	8	29	17	8	5	**NUMBER OF STATEMENTS**	58	56
%	%	%	%	%	%		%	%
						ASSETS		
		6.4	4.5			Cash & Equivalents	5.2	3.8
		25.8	23.7			Trade Receivables (net)	26.3	24.1
		34.5	30.5			Inventory	32.8	34.3
		3.7	6.2			All Other Current	1.5	3.0
		70.4	64.9			Total Current	65.8	65.2
		20.7	26.9			Fixed Assets (net)	24.3	26.1
		.2	1.8			Intangibles (net)	2.7	2.6
		8.7	6.3			All Other Non-Current	7.1	6.1
		100.0	100.0			Total	100.0	100.0
						LIABILITIES		
		7.5	9.2			Notes Payable-Short Term	13.3	11.3
		1.9	4.3			Cur. Mat.-L/T/D	2.7	4.0
		16.2	11.5			Trade Payables	19.1	17.8
		.1	.2			Income Taxes Payable	.4	.4
		12.1	16.0			All Other Current	9.2	11.0
		37.8	41.3			Total Current	44.7	44.4
		16.5	12.1			Long Term Debt	12.2	13.7
		.1	.3			Deferred Taxes	.2	.3
		2.8	2.3			All Other Non-Current	3.4	4.6
		42.8	44.0			Net Worth	39.6	37.0
		100.0	100.0			Total Liabilities & Net Worth	100.0	100.0
						INCOME DATA		
		100.0	100.0			Net Sales	100.0	100.0
		23.7	22.9			Gross Profit	22.8	24.8
		19.0	18.3			Operating Expenses	21.9	20.8
		4.7	4.6			Operating Profit	.9	4.0
		.5	.5			All Other Expenses (net)	1.1	.7
		4.2	4.1			Profit Before Taxes	-.2	3.3
						RATIOS		
		4.5	2.5			Current	2.8	2.2
		1.8	1.8				1.6	1.7
		1.2	1.2				1.0	1.1
		2.3	1.1			Quick	1.5	1.0
		1.1	.7				.8	.7
		.3	.5				.5	.5
		17 21.3	10 37.6			Sales/Receivables	21 17.7	20 18.6
		37 9.9	31 11.8				35 10.4	36 10.3
		47 7.8	48 7.6				48 7.6	49 7.5
		32 11.5	37 9.9			Cost of Sales/Inventory	32 11.4	37 9.8
		42 8.7	45 8.2				46 7.9	54 6.8
		82 4.5	59 6.2				84 4.3	79 4.6
		9 39.8	13 29.0			Cost of Sales/Payables	15 24.9	15 24.3
		15 23.7	19 19.3				26 14.3	24 15.0
		31 11.7	27 13.5				35 10.3	39 9.4
		4.9	6.2			Sales/Working Capital	6.5	5.4
		9.9	14.7				14.3	12.8
		35.3	28.1				88.5	54.6
		24.6	17.1			EBIT/Interest	12.3	8.5
		(27) 11.2	(15) 6.7				(48) 4.2	(48) 2.8
		1.8	3.1				1.4	1.2
						Net Profit + Depr., Dep., Amort./Cur. Mat. L./T/D	10.4	15.9
							(13) 3.8	(16) 2.0
							1.5	.5
		.2	.3			Fixed/Worth	.4	.4
		.5	.6				.7	.8
		1.6	1.1				1.3	1.5
		.3	.7			Debt/Worth	.6	.7
		1.5	1.3				1.4	2.1
		4.5	4.9				4.8	6.6
		46.4	72.5			% Profit Before Taxes/Tangible Net Worth	48.0	49.4
		(26) 22.4	32.0				(52) 26.5	(51) 25.6
		10.1	14.9				5.7	6.1
		23.9	15.9			% Profit Before Taxes/Total Assets	18.5	18.2
		9.3	9.4				9.6	9.5
		2.9	5.1				.7	.9
		53.9	19.1			Sales/Net Fixed Assets	23.5	30.7
		17.8	10.0				12.0	11.7
		9.3	6.8				8.1	7.3
		4.5	3.4			Sales/Total Assets	3.4	3.5
		3.4	2.8				2.7	2.7
		2.5	2.2				2.1	1.9
		.7	.7			% Depr., Dep., Amort./Sales	.6	.6
		(25) .9	(15) .8				(52) .9	(48) .9
		1.2	1.4				1.9	1.8
		1.6				% Officers', Directors', Owners' Comp/Sales	1.8	1.2
		(11) 2.5					(14) 3.6	(20) 1.7
		4.4					5.8	3.5
2117M	37704M	504411M	1039769M	1660186M	2444111M	Net Sales ($)	2361925M	2266646M
437M	9483M	154328M	360161M	629745M	887390M	Total Assets ($)	1008189M	952911M

M = $ thousand   MM = $ million
See Pages 11 through 18 for Explanation of Ratios and Data

Comparative Historical Data | Current Data Sorted By Sales

			Type of Statement						
15	8	23	Unqualified				1	4	18
13	9	14	Reviewed			1		10	3
16	16	13	Compiled	1	2	2	1	4	3
3	1	1	Tax Returns					1	
18	16	17	Other		2	1	1	3	10
4/1/00- 3/31/01	4/1/01- 3/31/02	4/1/02- 3/31/03		0-1MM	21 (4/1-9/30/02) 1-3MM	3-5MM	5-10MM	47 (10/1/02-3/31/03) 10-25MM	25MM & OVER
ALL	ALL	ALL							
65	50	68	NUMBER OF STATEMENTS	1	4	4	3	22	34
%	%	%	**ASSETS**	%	%	%	%	%	%
5.7	6.6	6.2	Cash & Equivalents					9.5	4.7
26.4	20.1	25.9	Trade Receivables (net)					25.2	25.6
33.8	35.4	32.2	Inventory					35.0	29.3
2.0	4.0	3.8	All Other Current					3.6	5.0
68.0	66.1	68.0	Total Current					73.3	64.6
21.9	23.2	22.5	Fixed Assets (net)					22.0	23.5
4.5	5.7	2.1	Intangibles (net)					.3	3.8
5.7	5.0	7.3	All Other Non-Current					4.5	8.0
100.0	100.0	100.0	Total					100.0	100.0
			LIABILITIES						
10.4	10.9	8.1	Notes Payable-Short Term					3.3	8.5
2.5	2.9	2.4	Cur. Mat.-L/T/D					2.0	3.0
18.1	14.9	15.1	Trade Payables					16.4	12.4
.6	.3	.1	Income Taxes Payable					.1	.2
14.5	11.4	13.9	All Other Current					12.3	17.1
46.1	40.4	39.5	Total Current					34.1	41.3
12.2	14.7	14.6	Long Term Debt					17.4	11.0
.3	.1	.2	Deferred Taxes					.1	.2
4.0	2.3	2.7	All Other Non-Current					2.7	2.7
37.4	42.5	43.0	Net Worth					45.7	44.9
100.0	100.0	100.0	Total Liabilities & Net Worth					100.0	100.0
			INCOME DATA						
100.0	100.0	100.0	Net Sales					100.0	100.0
25.3	27.6	24.3	Gross Profit					25.1	23.1
20.2	23.1	19.9	Operating Expenses					20.1	18.6
5.1	4.5	4.3	Operating Profit					4.9	4.6
.9	.9	.4	All Other Expenses (net)					.4	.4
4.3	3.6	3.9	Profit Before Taxes					4.5	4.1
			RATIOS						
2.5	2.7	3.3						5.1	2.7
1.6	1.8	1.7	Current					2.2	1.5
1.3	1.3	1.2						1.3	1.2
1.3	1.4	1.5						2.7	1.3
(64) .9	.7	.8	Quick					1.2	.8
.4	.3	.5						.4	.5
21 17.7	10 36.5	15 24.0						12 29.8	18 20.7
36 10.0	30 12.1	36 10.3	Sales/Receivables					36 10.0	36 10.3
47 7.7	43 8.5	47 7.7						45 8.1	47 7.7
35 10.4	36 10.1	33 11.2						33 11.0	32 11.4
53 6.9	51 7.2	46 7.9	Cost of Sales/Inventory					43 8.6	45 8.1
77 4.8	109 3.3	74 4.9						78 4.7	61 6.0
14 25.4	8 43.1	11 32.9						10 37.8	11 33.0
25 14.4	21 17.2	19 19.4	Cost of Sales/Payables					15 24.6	19 19.4
41 8.8	36 10.1	28 13.0						31 11.7	25 14.8
5.5	6.2	5.2						4.6	6.2
11.4	11.2	14.2	Sales/Working Capital					6.2	16.8
24.6	33.6	31.3						34.2	27.0
15.2	22.3	20.4						39.4	18.9
(58) 4.6	(45) 4.4	(62) 6.9	EBIT/Interest				(20)	9.8	(31) 11.2
1.6	1.2	2.6						2.3	3.4
13.5	7.4	11.0	Net Profit + Depr., Dep.,						
(18) 3.9	(17) 3.1	(14) 3.5	Amort./Cur. Mat. L/T/D						
1.7	.5	1.1							
.3	.3	.2						.1	.3
.5	.7	.6	Fixed/Worth					.3	.6
1.2	1.7	1.1						2.0	1.1
.6	.6	.4						.3	.6
1.8	1.6	1.4	Debt/Worth					1.2	1.3
4.5	4.4	4.0						5.3	4.0
49.7	42.4	50.9	% Profit Before Taxes/Tangible					53.1	48.1
(59) 24.8	(43) 23.1	(62) 23.1	Net Worth				(20)	24.1	(32) 28.9
12.1	8.6	10.1						9.2	10.9
18.0	20.3	18.8	% Profit Before Taxes/Total					30.5	16.7
10.7	6.7	8.9	Assets					10.2	9.1
2.7	.3	3.1						2.4	3.4
38.2	37.6	32.1						49.8	28.4
17.8	14.3	14.2	Sales/Net Fixed Assets					19.3	13.7
9.0	7.9	8.4						9.5	6.9
3.8	3.6	4.0						4.4	3.9
2.6	2.6	3.0	Sales/Total Assets					3.1	2.8
2.1	1.9	2.1						2.4	2.0
.5	.3	.5						.6	.4
(58) .9	(45) .9	(57) .9	% Depr., Dep., Amort./Sales				(19)	.9	(26) .8
1.6	1.6	1.3						1.3	1.1
1.3	1.8	1.6	% Officers', Directors',						
(18) 1.9	(15) 2.2	(13) 2.5	Owners' Comp/Sales						
1.6	4.0	4.5							
3515279M	2989636M	5688298M	Net Sales ($)	695M	10079M	16277M	21886M	337693M	5301668M
1510296M	1216159M	2041544M	Total Assets ($)	532M	6033M	9095M	6575M	113602M	1905707M

M = $ thousand   MM = $ million
See Pages 11 through 18 for Explanation of Ratios and Data

Current Data Sorted By Assets | Comparative Historical Data

0-500M	500M-2MM	2-10MM	10-50MM	50-100MM	100-250MM	Type of Statement	4/1/98-3/31/99 ALL	4/1/99-3/31/00 ALL
2	9	7	14	4	5	Unqualified	40	22
6	18	15	5			Reviewed	18	21
10	3	6	3			Compiled	39	23
7	11	2	2			Tax Returns	16	7
		15	14	1	2	Other	53	40
	39 (4/1-9/30/02)		120 (10/1/02-3/31/03)					
25	41	45	36	5	7	**NUMBER OF STATEMENTS**	166	113
%	%	%	%	%	%	**ASSETS**	%	%
8.2	8.7	6.7	5.4			Cash & Equivalents	6.2	4.7
15.7	17.7	14.5	20.7			Trade Receivables (net)	23.2	24.3
38.6	44.4	42.8	33.9			Inventory	32.1	33.0
.6	2.8	2.4	2.6			All Other Current	1.5	1.6
63.1	73.6	66.4	62.7			Total Current	63.0	63.6
31.5	20.9	26.5	27.8			Fixed Assets (net)	29.1	29.8
2.3	1.5	1.0	3.2			Intangibles (net)	3.0	2.0
3.0	4.0	6.1	6.2			All Other Non-Current	4.8	4.6
100.0	100.0	100.0	100.0			Total	100.0	100.0
						LIABILITIES		
14.9	10.1	14.3	11.7			Notes Payable-Short Term	12.1	13.7
1.8	3.7	4.3	2.7			Cur. Mat.-L/T/D	3.6	3.6
18.1	13.6	14.8	10.4			Trade Payables	11.6	12.5
.0	.2	.2	.2			Income Taxes Payable	.3	.2
11.0	12.5	14.4	10.2			All Other Current	8.2	9.7
45.8	40.0	48.1	35.3			Total Current	35.8	39.7
22.3	16.8	16.0	12.4			Long Term Debt	19.6	18.5
.0	.1	.4	.5			Deferred Taxes	.5	.6
4.6	5.2	2.9	5.7			All Other Non-Current	5.7	5.6
27.3	37.8	32.7	46.2			Net Worth	38.4	35.7
100.0	100.0	100.0	100.0			Total Liabilities & Net Worth	100.0	100.0
						INCOME DATA		
100.0	100.0	100.0	100.0			Net Sales	100.0	100.0
47.6	37.4	32.3	25.2			Gross Profit	27.7	28.9
42.6	35.6	29.4	23.2			Operating Expenses	23.1	23.1
4.9	1.8	2.9	2.1			Operating Profit	4.6	5.8
.4	1.1	1.1	.5			All Other Expenses (net)	1.4	1.7
4.5	.7	1.7	1.6			Profit Before Taxes	3.2	4.1
						RATIOS		
2.1	3.6	1.9	2.8			Current	3.4	3.2
1.7	1.9	1.5	1.7				1.9	1.6
1.0	1.3	1.1	1.3				1.2	1.1
1.1	1.7	.7	1.2			Quick	1.6	1.6
.6	.7	.4	.7				.9	.8
.1	.2	.2	.4				.4	.4
0 UND	5 66.7	4 98.1	30 12.1			Sales/Receivables	18 20.4	24 15.2
4 93.7	18 19.9	25 14.8	38 9.6				39 9.4	41 8.9
36 10.1	44 8.2	41 8.9	47 7.7				50 7.3	54 6.8
11 32.9	29 12.4	52 7.0	48 7.7			Cost of Sales/Inventory	36 10.1	40 9.2
55 6.6	105 3.5	96 3.8	79 4.6				64 5.7	73 5.0
110 3.3	206 1.8	140 2.6	122 3.0				107 3.4	109 3.3
16 22.6	14 25.9	17 21.8	12 30.9			Cost of Sales/Payables	10 35.2	13 29.0
32 11.5	28 13.0	27 13.4	22 16.5				20 18.1	24 15.5
47 7.7	42 8.6	50 7.3	32 11.3				33 11.0	39 9.3
6.9	3.7	6.7	4.6			Sales/Working Capital	4.6	4.8
10.4	6.8	13.2	8.1				7.9	8.4
NM	26.6	95.3	15.8				28.7	35.4
14.0	6.7	4.9	10.2			EBIT/Interest	7.4	8.5
(19) 1.9	(36) 2.1	(42) 2.5	(35) 4.7				(148) 3.3	(108) 2.8
1.0	-1.6	1.2	1.5				1.2	1.3
	3.2	2.7	9.0			Net Profit + Depr., Dep., Amort./Cur. Mat. L /T/D	4.9	4.4
	(12) 1.0	(15) 1.9	(18) 3.1				(48) 2.4	(30) 2.6
	.2	1.2	1.6				1.0	1.2
.2	.2	.4	.4			Fixed/Worth	.3	.3
.7	.5	.7	.5				.7	.9
66.3	1.5	1.9	.8				2.3	2.7
1.2	.5	1.1	.6			Debt/Worth	.5	.7
2.5	1.5	1.9	1.3				1.8	2.3
80.0	4.7	5.5	2.7				4.6	5.0
95.5	30.0	27.7	24.2			% Profit Before Taxes/Tangible Net Worth	33.7	37.7
(20) 18.4	(36) 7.3	(40) 11.6	(33) 12.0				(144) 18.0	(97) 21.7
-5.8	-13.5	2.3	4.0				5.5	9.5
32.3	9.4	8.8	11.0			% Profit Before Taxes/Total Assets	15.1	15.6
4.8	3.3	3.5	6.4				7.0	7.7
-1.9	-4.8	1.2	1.7				.9	1.3
72.6	36.1	31.3	12.8			Sales/Net Fixed Assets	17.6	17.3
16.8	16.1	8.1	7.6				8.7	8.0
6.3	8.5	5.2	5.2				4.9	5.3
4.7	3.5	3.1	2.6			Sales/Total Assets	3.0	2.9
3.7	2.3	2.4	2.0				2.2	2.3
2.2	1.6	1.9	1.5				1.6	1.6
.8	.7	.6	1.2			% Depr., Dep., Amort./Sales	1.1	.9
(19) 1.1	(34) 1.3	(43) 1.6	(32) 1.9				(151) 1.7	(103) 1.9
3.6	2.6	2.7	2.7				2.7	2.7
3.2	2.2	1.1				% Officers', Directors', Owners' Comp/Sales	1.4	1.5
(19) 5.5	(20) 3.7	(23) 2.5					(66) 3.2	(36) 3.4
9.4	5.0	6.7					6.2	6.8
27360M	119253M	589913M	1654448M	670078M	1739071M	Net Sales ($)	5424644M	3779213M
7262M	45006M	223846M	768550M	375829M	1047659M	Total Assets ($)	3060320M	2136237M

M = $ thousand   MM = $ million
See Pages 11 through 18 for Explanation of Ratios and Data

Comparative Historical Data | Current Data Sorted By Sales

Comp 1	Comp 2	Comp 3	Type of Statement	0-1MM	1-3MM	3-5MM	5-10MM	10-25MM	25MM & OVER
22	20	30	Unqualified				2	8	20
20	25	31	Reviewed	2	7	4	6	5	7
23	26	33	Compiled	4	13	7	2	4	3
8	15	15	Tax Returns	4	7	2	2		
34	40	50	Other	4	11	4	4	13	14
4/1/00-3/31/01 ALL	4/1/01-3/31/02 ALL	4/1/02-3/31/03 ALL		39 (4/1-9/30/02)			120 (10/1/02-3/31/03)		
107	126	159	**NUMBER OF STATEMENTS**	14	38	17	16	30	44
%	%	%	**ASSETS**	%	%	%	%	%	%
4.4	5.7	7.0	Cash & Equivalents	5.7	8.1	10.5	7.0	4.9	6.4
23.5	21.8	17.4	Trade Receivables (net)	16.7	14.5	18.3	12.3	16.6	22.2
35.2	33.3	39.6	Inventory	42.3	42.6	40.4	45.8	38.2	34.4
2.6	2.4	2.3	All Other Current	.2	1.9	1.5	3.3	3.3	2.4
65.8	63.3	66.2	Total Current	65.0	67.2	70.8	68.4	63.0	65.4
26.6	27.5	26.4	Fixed Assets (net)	32.6	26.0	23.8	25.2	28.0	25.1
2.3	2.7	2.4	Intangibles (net)	1.5	2.6	.3	.3	1.2	4.8
5.3	6.5	5.0	All Other Non-Current	.9	4.2	5.2	6.1	7.8	4.7
100.0	100.0	100.0	Total	100.0	100.0	100.0	100.0	100.0	100.0
			LIABILITIES						
14.1	12.6	12.0	Notes Payable-Short Term	13.1	12.6	11.6	13.4	14.2	9.2
4.4	2.7	3.3	Cur. Mat.-L/T/D	1.4	3.8	4.2	3.1	3.9	2.6
16.6	15.4	13.4	Trade Payables	15.0	12.2	16.3	16.7	13.6	11.4
.3	1.5	.2	Income Taxes Payable	.0	.0	.3	.2	.3	.3
12.3	12.7	11.9	All Other Current	4.5	13.7	11.6	13.9	15.1	10.1
47.6	44.9	40.8	Total Current	34.0	42.3	44.0	47.3	47.1	33.6
20.9	21.5	17.2	Long Term Debt	32.0	19.7	8.8	15.2	16.1	15.1
.3	.5	.3	Deferred Taxes	.0	.1	.2	.0	.7	.5
5.8	6.2	4.9	All Other Non-Current	6.2	3.9	5.7	4.8	6.1	4.1
25.4	26.9	36.8	Net Worth	27.9	34.0	41.3	32.8	29.9	46.6
100.0	100.0	100.0	Total Liabilities & Net Worth	100.0	100.0	100.0	100.0	100.0	100.0
			INCOME DATA						
100.0	100.0	100.0	Net Sales	100.0	100.0	100.0	100.0	100.0	100.0
27.2	30.9	33.8	Gross Profit	51.5	41.2	34.0	32.4	29.6	25.0
22.5	27.9	30.8	Operating Expenses	46.9	38.1	31.8	30.6	28.3	20.6
4.7	3.0	3.0	Operating Profit	4.7	3.0	2.2	1.8	1.2	4.5
1.4	1.6	1.0	All Other Expenses (net)	.9	1.2	.5	.8	1.0	1.0
3.3	1.4	2.0	Profit Before Taxes	3.7	1.8	1.7	1.0	.2	3.5
			RATIOS						
2.6	3.0	2.7	Current	2.2	3.4	3.1	2.0	2.0	3.0
1.5	1.6	1.7		1.8	1.6	1.7	1.4	1.5	2.2
1.1	1.1	1.2		1.6	1.1	1.1	.9	1.0	1.4
1.2	1.3	1.1	Quick	1.6	1.1	1.6	.8	.7	1.5
.7	.7	.6		.8	.5	.7	.3	.5	.9
.4	.4	.3		.1	.1	.3	.1	.3	.6
24 15.4	17 21.9	6 64.6	Sales/Receivables	0 UND	0 UND	3 112.9	4 99.9	19 19.7	25 14.7
39 9.5	35 10.3	30 12.1		5 70.3	18 20.1	13 28.4	8 47.2	33 11.1	38 9.5
50 7.4	46 7.9	45 8.2		43 8.5	51 7.2	29 12.6	31 11.9	46 8.0	47 7.7
41 9.0	39 9.5	42 8.6	Cost of Sales/Inventory	19 19.0	37 9.9	19 19.1	34 10.7	65 5.6	46 7.9
64 5.7	68 5.4	85 4.3		112 3.3	102 3.6	51 7.1	93 3.9	98 3.7	79 4.6
112 3.3	106 3.4	135 2.7		248 1.5	203 1.8	148 2.5	151 2.4	128 2.8	95 3.8
15 23.6	13 28.5	15 24.3	Cost of Sales/Payables	19 19.2	11 32.0	16 22.5	16 22.3	19 18.9	12 31.0
25 14.5	22 16.6	24 14.9		38 9.5	23 16.0	26 14.2	34 10.8	28 13.2	20 18.7
38 9.6	41 9.0	42 8.7		53 6.9	44 8.3	31 11.6	46 7.9	48 7.7	26 13.8
5.4	4.9	4.9	Sales/Working Capital	5.0	3.4	6.0	7.2	6.3	4.4
10.1	11.4	9.3		7.9	7.0	13.1	13.1	14.1	7.0
32.9	96.3	25.6		10.6	38.1	82.3	NM	NM	13.2
6.5	5.6	7.8	EBIT/Interest		7.1	10.2	2.9	4.1	11.2
(101) 2.6	(115) 2.2	(144) 2.7		(32) 1.9	2.6	1.7	(29) 1.9	(41) 5.3	
1.2	.6	1.0		-.1	-.4	.9	1.0	2.3	
6.2	4.6	3.6	Net Profit + Depr., Dep.,				3.0	9.0	
(37) 2.7	(41) 2.4	(50) 2.5	Amort./Cur. Mat. L/T/D			(15) 1.9	3.3		
.8	.8	.9				.5	2.6		
.4	.4	.3	Fixed/Worth	.3	.2	.2	.2	.5	.4
.9	.8	.6		.5	.7	.7	.6	.8	.5
2.4	2.6	1.8		NM	2.3	1.5	1.6	2.5	.8
1.3	1.0	.8	Debt/Worth	1.6	.7	.4	1.0	1.2	.6
2.4	2.1	1.7		2.3	1.6	1.4	2.3	2.4	1.4
5.2	7.3	5.2		NM	9.8	6.3	4.2	5.2	2.8
33.3	30.8	29.5	% Profit Before Taxes/Tangible	96.6	28.9	29.8	17.4	28.8	32.7
(88) 22.4	(104) 14.2	(139) 12.5	Net Worth	(11) .0	(33) 8.7	(14) 4.4	(15) 9.4	(26) 12.9	(40) 17.1
7.3	1.1	.8		-77.8	-10.9	-.7	-1.2	1.1	10.1
14.1	11.0	11.1	% Profit Before Taxes/Total	30.1	10.9	16.4	5.8	8.9	13.3
7.1	5.2	4.3	Assets	2.6	3.8	3.8	2.0	3.0	8.5
1.4	-1.3	.0		-10.5	-4.1	-.7	-.1	.1	3.7
23.4	24.2	27.9	Sales/Net Fixed Assets	36.8	27.1	59.3	41.6	31.9	15.9
10.8	10.5	11.1		11.2	13.8	21.7	21.1	7.9	8.4
5.8	5.4	5.5		3.8	5.3	7.8	5.6	5.1	5.4
3.1	3.7	3.4	Sales/Total Assets	3.9	3.7	4.4	3.4	2.7	3.3
2.4	2.3	2.3		2.2	2.0	3.2	2.7	2.0	2.2
1.7	1.7	1.7		1.6	1.6	2.4	2.3	1.6	1.7
.8	.8	.8	% Depr., Dep., Amort./Sales	.8	1.0	.6	.5	.8	.9
(94) 1.6	(107) 1.7	(137) 1.6		(10) 1.1	(30) 2.1	(16) 1.2	1.1	(28) 1.8	(37) 1.6
2.9	2.8	2.8		3.7	5.6	1.8	2.6	3.2	2.4
1.1	1.8	1.9	% Officers', Directors',		2.0			1.2	.7
(32) 2.4	(44) 3.9	(71) 3.5	Owners' Comp/Sales		(24) 3.5		(10)	2.4	(11) 1.0
4.8	7.5	6.4			7.0			10.8	2.2
3657140M	4312938M	4800123M	Net Sales ($)	8500M	67700M	68875M	107549M	498125M	4049374M
2129487M	2256741M	2468152M	Total Assets ($)	4134M	36717M	23566M	42112M	268735M	2092888M

M = $ thousand MM = $ million
See Pages 11 through 18 for Explanation of Ratios and Data

Current Data Sorted By Assets   Comparative Historical Data

	0-500M	500M-2MM	2-10MM	10-50MM	50-100MM	100-250MM		4/1/98-3/31/99 ALL	4/1/99-3/31/00 ALL
		32 (4/1-9/30/02)		114 (10/1/02-3/31/03)			Type of Statement		
Unqualified		9	11	15	2	2		30	21
Reviewed	1	9	21	5				20	18
Compiled	5	8	10	1				6	9
Tax Returns	3	10	1					6	6
Other	6		16	10		1		23	29
NUMBER OF STATEMENTS	15	36	59	31	2	3		85	83
	%	%	%	%	%	%	**ASSETS**	%	%
	9.4	8.5	6.7	5.4			Cash & Equivalents	6.7	6.4
	33.1	28.9	30.4	27.4			Trade Receivables (net)	28.5	30.5
	18.0	27.3	24.3	23.6			Inventory	24.5	27.8
	1.2	1.7	1.5	2.7			All Other Current	2.6	1.9
	61.8	66.3	63.0	59.2			Total Current	62.2	66.6
	32.1	24.2	25.7	26.0			Fixed Assets (net)	28.1	23.6
	1.1	2.4	5.4	8.0			Intangibles (net)	3.2	3.9
	4.5	7.1	5.9	6.8			All Other Non-Current	6.5	5.9
	100.0	100.0	100.0	100.0			Total	100.0	100.0
							LIABILITIES		
	13.0	12.7	11.3	7.8			Notes Payable-Short Term	9.6	15.1
	7.4	4.5	3.2	2.8			Cur. Mat.-L/T/D	2.2	2.2
	21.5	13.4	13.6	12.0			Trade Payables	14.3	13.8
	.0	.2	.7	.0			Income Taxes Payable	.6	.8
	9.6	7.9	11.5	9.6			All Other Current	11.5	11.5
	51.5	38.7	40.3	32.3			Total Current	38.2	43.4
	25.8	20.5	16.5	17.0			Long Term Debt	16.3	12.3
	.0	.6	.4	.3			Deferred Taxes	.5	.3
	1.2	3.6	6.3	3.7			All Other Non-Current	6.1	5.2
	21.0	36.5	36.5	46.7			Net Worth	38.9	38.8
	100.0	100.0	100.0	100.0			Total Liabilities & Net Worth	100.0	100.0
							INCOME DATA		
	100.0	100.0	100.0	100.0			Net Sales	100.0	100.0
	44.5	36.4	27.4	25.7			Gross Profit	28.5	28.3
	39.2	33.6	23.0	19.9			Operating Expenses	23.0	23.4
	5.3	2.8	4.4	5.8			Operating Profit	5.5	4.9
	1.0	1.2	1.2	1.2			All Other Expenses (net)	.8	.1
	4.3	1.6	3.2	4.6			Profit Before Taxes	4.7	4.8
							RATIOS		
	2.0	2.6	2.3	2.9			Current	2.8	2.3
	1.1	1.6	1.6	1.6				1.8	1.5
	.9	1.1	1.2	1.4				1.2	1.1
	1.8	1.6	1.4	1.9			Quick	1.5	1.5
	.9	.9	.9	1.0				.9	.9
	.6	.5	.6	.7				.6	.5
	20 17.9	18 19.9	28 13.1	33 11.0			Sales/Receivables	30 12.3	31 11.9
	29 12.6	38 9.6	40 9.0	40 9.0				43 8.4	41 8.8
	36 10.0	60 6.0	52 7.1	57 6.4				53 6.9	58 6.3
	21 17.6	23 15.6	29 12.8	28 13.1			Cost of Sales/Inventory	27 13.4	30 12.1
	26 13.8	52 7.0	52 7.1	47 7.8				49 7.5	53 6.8
	35 10.4	85 4.3	81 4.5	73 5.0				78 4.7	92 4.0
	17 21.0	12 29.6	16 22.7	15 24.3			Cost of Sales/Payables	15 24.0	17 22.1
	27 13.5	26 14.3	27 13.7	21 17.5				26 14.2	24 15.2
	38 9.7	38 9.6	38 9.5	38 9.5				36 10.1	37 9.8
	15.6	5.3	6.2	5.9			Sales/Working Capital	5.6	6.2
	37.1	9.8	11.2	10.4				11.1	11.6
	-52.6	27.0	31.8	16.7				25.2	34.0
	37.6	5.9	12.6	17.0			EBIT/Interest	13.5	11.6
	(12) 3.5	(33) 1.2	(54) 3.3	(28) 4.8				(78) 4.5	(76) 5.3
	-1.8	-3.0	1.3	2.6				2.1	2.3
			3.3				Net Profit + Depr., Dep., Amort./Cur. Mat. L /T/D	17.9	10.6
			(21) 1.7					(30) 5.4	(21) 3.8
			1.1					1.4	2.6
	.3	.2	.4	.4			Fixed/Worth	.3	.3
	1.2	.6	.9	.6				.6	.6
	7.7	3.4	1.9	1.1				1.5	1.8
	1.8	1.0	.8	.6			Debt/Worth	.7	.7
	2.5	1.9	2.2	1.3				1.8	2.1
	16.3	12.3	4.4	3.6				4.3	4.9
	133.5	38.4	57.6	39.5			% Profit Before Taxes/Tangible Net Worth	54.8	53.1
	(12) 94.5	(32) 14.8	(53) 18.3	(28) 17.0				(77) 25.5	(78) 35.2
	15.8	-18.7	2.2	10.2				10.1	15.2
	37.7	13.4	13.3	16.1			% Profit Before Taxes/Total Assets	17.0	22.7
	17.4	3.3	6.6	6.4				9.7	9.2
	2.8	-11.1	.9	3.9				4.6	4.4
	47.8	44.0	33.0	15.4			Sales/Net Fixed Assets	21.3	25.3
	17.1	22.4	10.6	8.6				10.0	12.2
	8.0	7.4	5.9	4.9				5.2	7.4
	5.6	3.4	3.0	2.7			Sales/Total Assets	3.3	2.9
	4.4	2.7	2.4	2.2				2.4	2.4
	2.9	2.0	1.8	1.8				1.7	1.8
		1.0	.9	1.5			% Depr., Dep., Amort./Sales	1.0	.8
		(30) 1.9	(52) 1.8	(26) 1.8				(77) 1.9	(74) 1.8
		4.0	3.1	2.7				2.7	3.0
		2.5	1.6				% Officers', Directors', Owners' Comp/Sales	2.5	2.4
		(22) 4.6	(25) 2.7					(27) 4.7	(24) 4.3
		10.2	6.5					9.2	8.8
	17356M	124928M	733840M	1428023M	291702M	698686M	Net Sales ($)	3689865M	1374456M
	4079M	44130M	290859M	602786M	182013M	498397M	Total Assets ($)	1400218M	634835M

M = $ thousand   MM = $ million
See Pages 11 through 18 for Explanation of Ratios and Data

Comparative Historical Data | Current Data Sorted By Sales

Comparative Historical Data			Type of Statement	Current Data Sorted By Sales					
			Unqualified		1	2	11	16	
19	20	30	Reviewed	1	2	5	12	9	7
19	24	36	Compiled	2	8	3	5	5	2
18	11	25	Tax Returns	1	6	4	1		
5	12	12	Other	3	10	3	9	9	9
31	24	43							
4/1/00-3/31/01	4/1/01-3/31/02	4/1/02-3/31/03		32 (4/1-9/30/02)			114 (10/1/02-3/31/03)		
ALL	ALL	ALL		0-1MM	1-3MM	3-5MM	5-10MM	10-25MM	25MM & OVER
92	91	146	**NUMBER OF STATEMENTS**	7	26	16	29	34	34
%	%	%	**ASSETS**	%	%	%	%	%	%
8.1	7.2	7.1	Cash & Equivalents		8.6	12.5	4.9	8.8	4.2
28.9	29.9	29.2	Trade Receivables (net)		29.5	25.5	28.5	28.9	31.7
23.1	24.8	24.2	Inventory		23.0	29.3	26.8	23.1	23.2
2.4	1.7	1.8	All Other Current		1.4	1.1	1.7	2.0	2.6
62.6	63.7	62.3	Total Current		62.4	68.4	62.0	62.9	61.7
26.3	25.4	26.6	Fixed Assets (net)		26.3	24.5	27.7	23.6	26.2
5.4	5.2	4.7	Intangibles (net)		1.6	2.6	5.1	7.5	5.6
5.7	5.8	6.3	All Other Non-Current		9.6	4.4	5.3	6.0	6.5
100.0	100.0	100.0	Total		100.0	100.0	100.0	100.0	100.0
			LIABILITIES						
8.4	16.3	10.7	Notes Payable-Short Term		12.5	13.1	12.2	7.6	8.7
4.4	4.3	3.8	Cur. Mat.-L/T/D		7.1	2.7	3.7	2.9	2.3
14.7	11.3	13.8	Trade Payables		17.3	13.5	15.4	12.5	11.7
.4	.1	.3	Income Taxes Payable		.1	.2	.2	1.0	.1
10.0	8.9	9.9	All Other Current		7.0	12.1	8.4	11.9	10.7
37.8	41.0	38.6	Total Current		44.0	41.6	40.0	36.0	33.5
15.4	15.3	18.5	Long Term Debt		23.7	14.8	19.4	14.3	15.9
.7	.2	.4	Deferred Taxes		.7	.2	.4	.6	.2
5.4	6.3	4.7	All Other Non-Current		3.1	5.3	7.8	3.7	4.7
40.8	37.3	37.8	Net Worth		28.4	38.1	32.4	45.5	45.7
100.0	100.0	100.0	Total Liabilities & Net Worth		100.0	100.0	100.0	100.0	100.0
			INCOME DATA						
100.0	100.0	100.0	Net Sales		100.0	100.0	100.0	100.0	100.0
29.2	29.6	31.1	Gross Profit		40.6	32.4	28.9	28.7	23.4
23.4	25.5	26.6	Operating Expenses		39.2	29.3	26.2	21.1	18.7
5.7	4.1	4.4	Operating Profit		1.4	3.1	2.7	7.6	4.7
.8	1.1	1.2	All Other Expenses (net)		1.0	1.3	1.7	.9	.8
5.0	3.0	3.3	Profit Before Taxes		.4	1.8	1.0	6.7	3.9
			RATIOS						
3.4	3.0	2.5	Current		2.2	2.7	2.3	3.1	2.6
1.6	1.6	1.6			1.3	1.5	1.6	1.8	1.8
1.2	1.2	1.2			.9	.9	1.2	1.4	1.4
1.8	1.8	1.5	Quick		1.4	1.8	1.3	1.7	1.3
1.1	.9	.9			.8	.8	.9	1.0	1.1
.7	.6	.6			.4	.5	.6	.7	.7
33 11.1	31 11.9	27 13.4	Sales/Receivables	26 13.9	13 28.9	27 13.6	28 13.1	33 11.0	
43 8.4	37 9.8	39 9.3		38 9.6	35 10.3	39 9.4	39 9.3	47 9.3	
52 7.0	59 6.2	52 7.0		52 7.0	58 6.2	51 7.1	49 7.4	58 6.3	
25 14.5	28 12.9	27 13.4	Cost of Sales/Inventory	22 16.3	28 12.8	30 12.0	31 11.9	25 14.4	
44 8.2	44 8.3	50 7.3		47 7.7	63 5.8	52 7.0	50 7.2	46 7.9	
70 5.2	70 5.2	76 4.8		88 4.1	123 3.0	83 4.4	68 5.4	74 5.4	
13 28.3	9 41.3	16 23.2	Cost of Sales/Payables	11 34.0	24 15.1	17 21.5	13 27.9	15 24.2	
25 14.6	20 18.5	25 14.8		32 11.2	29 12.4	31 11.6	21 17.4	21 17.8	
40 9.1	34 10.8	38 9.6		44 8.3	46 8.0	39 9.5	31 11.8	33 11.1	
5.8	4.9	6.3	Sales/Working Capital		5.5	6.4	7.7	4.9	6.9
11.1	11.1	11.2			21.0	9.8	14.9	10.0	10.3
24.1	29.8	29.0			-50.3	NM	27.2	20.0	16.5
(81) 9.8	(85) 7.3	(132) 10.1	EBIT/Interest	(25) 9.5	(14) 5.1	(27) 5.5	(31) 18.6	(30) 28.3	
3.8	3.0	3.3		.7	1.3	2.0	6.8	5.0	
1.6	1.3	.8		-4.3	-3.2	.8	2.9	2.8	
(24) 7.0	(21) 4.4	(30) 3.8	Net Profit + Depr., Dep., Amort./Cur. Mat. L/T/D				(13) 11.4		
2.5	1.7	2.2					3.3		
1.2	.6	1.1					1.6		
.2	.2	.3	Fixed/Worth		.2	.2	.4	.3	.3
.7	.6	.8			.9	.6	1.0	.6	.6
1.8	1.4	1.8			15.6	1.8	2.9	1.1	1.1
.7	.6	.8	Debt/Worth		1.4	1.3	1.0	.6	.7
2.0	1.9	1.9			2.2	1.8	2.5	1.7	1.3
4.2	3.7	4.1			28.9	2.9	6.3	3.3	3.5
(82) 45.4	(81) 39.3	(130) 48.9	% Profit Before Taxes/Tangible Net Worth	(22) 90.3	(14) 45.5	(26) 48.6	(30) 53.1	(32) 39.5	
26.3	18.3	18.4		17.2	17.6	7.1	21.5	16.6	
9.0	6.8	2.8		-29.8	-1.5	-1.8	9.5	10.8	
15.1	13.3	15.5	% Profit Before Taxes/Total Assets		19.9	11.4	11.8	18.8	14.5
7.8	6.0	6.5			-.5	3.0	3.1	10.1	6.6
2.4	1.4	.7			-14.1	-10.7	-.6	4.2	3.9
25.8	28.0	31.5	Sales/Net Fixed Assets		45.9	27.1	28.6	37.4	24.8
13.6	12.2	10.9			21.2	13.5	10.8	10.2	9.6
5.4	6.1	5.6			6.4	6.1	4.9	7.2	4.9
3.3	3.2	3.2	Sales/Total Assets		4.2	2.9	3.4	3.1	3.1
2.5	2.2	2.4			2.5	2.4	2.4	2.4	2.3
1.7	1.9	1.8			2.0	2.0	1.8	1.8	1.8
(83) .8	(82) .9	(120) 1.1	% Depr., Dep., Amort./Sales	(20) 1.2	(15) 1.0	(25) .9	(29) .8	(27) 1.2	
1.7	1.6	1.9		3.3	2.0	1.5	2.0	1.6	
3.1	3.0	3.5		5.1	3.6	4.0	2.8	2.6	
(27) 1.8	(31) 2.2	(56) 1.8	% Officers', Directors', Owners' Comp/Sales	(13) 2.6		(14) 1.3	(12) 1.8		
5.0	3.0	4.3		4.4		2.4	4.1		
8.6	6.5	9.8		14.1		6.4	9.6		
2057334M	2322959M	3294535M	Net Sales ($)	2579M	49846M	64319M	197731M	508356M	2471704M
1144227M	915293M	1622264M	Total Assets ($)	1066M	20226M	29197M	99970M	226450M	1245355M

M = $ thousand   MM = $ million
See Pages 11 through 18 for Explanation of Ratios and Data

Current Data Sorted By Assets   Comparative Historical Data

							Type of Statement		
	1	3	7		1		Unqualified	14	14
1	4	4	1				Reviewed	18	15
2	4	3					Compiled	10	4
2	2						Tax Returns	3	
1	4	8	3				Other	12	11
	9 (4/1-9/30/02)		42 (10/1/02-3/31/03)					4/1/98-3/31/99	4/1/99-3/31/00
0-500M	500M-2MM	2-10MM	10-50MM	50-100MM	100-250MM			ALL	ALL
6	15	18	11		1		NUMBER OF STATEMENTS	57	44
%	%	%	%	%	%		ASSETS	%	%
	4.3	4.8	4.9			D	Cash & Equivalents	5.2	5.6
	36.2	33.5	25.3			A	Trade Receivables (net)	31.9	27.1
	28.4	22.7	30.5			T	Inventory	26.8	25.0
	2.1	4.2	2.8			A	All Other Current	2.8	2.4
	71.0	65.2	63.6				Total Current	66.8	60.1
	23.0	26.7	23.9			N	Fixed Assets (net)	27.4	31.4
	2.4	1.9	2.3			O	Intangibles (net)	1.7	3.4
	3.6	6.1	10.3			T	All Other Non-Current	4.1	5.1
	100.0	100.0	100.0				Total	100.0	100.0
						A	LIABILITIES		
	18.5	12.6	7.4			V	Notes Payable-Short Term	13.1	8.6
	7.6	5.2	2.1			A	Cur. Mat.-L/T/D	5.2	4.7
	20.8	16.5	12.6			I	Trade Payables	17.0	13.1
	.0	.2	.3			L	Income Taxes Payable	.1	.3
	16.1	10.4	20.2			A	All Other Current	12.4	12.8
	63.1	44.9	42.6			B	Total Current	47.8	39.5
	26.7	9.5	7.1			L	Long Term Debt	15.3	19.4
	.7	.7	2.4			E	Deferred Taxes	.5	1.4
	.5	2.6	4.8				All Other Non-Current	3.8	3.3
	9.0	42.4	43.0				Net Worth	32.6	36.4
	100.0	100.0	100.0				Total Liabilities & Net Worth	100.0	100.0
							INCOME DATA		
	100.0	100.0	100.0				Net Sales	100.0	100.0
	27.0	26.6	24.8				Gross Profit	29.6	32.0
	29.2	26.1	21.9				Operating Expenses	25.4	26.3
	-2.2	.4	3.0				Operating Profit	4.1	5.7
	.7	.7	.4				All Other Expenses (net)	1.1	1.3
	-2.9	-.2	2.6				Profit Before Taxes	3.0	4.4
							RATIOS		
	1.7	2.1	4.3					2.1	2.4
	1.3	1.6	1.3				Current	1.4	1.6
	.9	1.1	.9					1.0	1.2
	1.1	1.1	1.1					1.3	1.4
	.6	.8	.7				Quick	.8	.8
	.4	.6	.4					.5	.5

	19	19.7	36	10.3	35	10.5			Sales/Receivables		29	12.5	30	12.0
	53	6.9	48	7.7	40	9.1					44	8.3	45	8.1
	77	4.7	54	6.7	52	7.0					58	6.3	56	6.5
	16	22.4	22	16.8	44	8.2			Cost of Sales/Inventory		26	14.0	36	10.1
	40	9.1	36	10.1	75	4.8					46	7.9	55	6.6
	97	3.8	60	6.1	101	3.6					77	4.7	85	4.3
	18	20.4	18	20.0	18	20.6			Cost of Sales/Payables		20	18.2	20	18.3
	25	14.5	27	13.7	26	14.3					33	11.2	28	13.0
	60	6.1	37	9.9	31	11.7					46	8.0	38	9.5

	8.7	7.5	3.3				Sales/Working Capital		8.7		5.9
	15.6	14.3	12.2						12.9		10.0
	-12.6	48.2	-30.1						181.9		30.9
	5.0	7.6	72.8				EBIT/Interest		7.4		8.8
	.0	2.2	2.4					(53)	2.8	(41)	5.1
	-9.6	-3.4	-2.1						1.5		2.0
							Net Profit + Depr., Dep., Amort./Cur. Mat. L /T/D		5.8		7.0
								(27)	2.5	(16)	3.5
									1.1		1.6
	.4	.3	.2				Fixed/Worth		.4		.4
	.6	.7	.6						.7		.9
	-1.6	1.2	.9						1.6		1.6
	1.0	.9	.6				Debt/Worth		1.4		1.2
	1.8	1.4	1.4						1.9		1.9
	-6.8	2.6	2.9						4.9		3.4

		20.5	40.4				% Profit Before Taxes/Tangible Net Worth		50.2		47.6
(10)		6.4	7.4					(54)	25.1	(41)	25.8
		-26.6	-30.4						7.9		12.1
	7.6	10.5	13.3				% Profit Before Taxes/Total Assets		12.5		17.6
	-3.9	2.9	3.4						6.4		8.5
	-15.3	-10.1	-5.7						2.5		3.6
	44.8	24.3	12.9				Sales/Net Fixed Assets		27.2		11.7
	14.0	10.6	9.5						11.0		7.2
	7.1	5.5	5.5						6.4		4.5
	3.1	3.4	2.6				Sales/Total Assets		3.2		3.0
	2.7	3.0	2.1						2.7		2.3
	2.0	2.0	1.7						2.1		1.5
	.9	1.6	1.2				% Depr., Dep., Amort./Sales		1.1		1.2
(14)	1.8	2.5	2.3					(54)	1.9	(41)	1.8
	3.8	3.9	2.9						2.9		2.7
							% Officers', Directors', Owners' Comp/Sales		2.0		1.7
								(31)	5.0	(15)	5.4
									8.9		11.0

4712M	53196M	230910M	351013M		349098M		Net Sales ($)	1001751M	758199M
1370M	18295M	79756M	163172M		244150M		Total Assets ($)	439365M	443393M

M = $ thousand   MM = $ million
See Pages 11 through 18 for Explanation of Ratios and Data

Comparative Historical Data | Current Data Sorted By Sales

	Hist 4/1/00-3/31/01 ALL	Hist 4/1/01-3/31/02 ALL	Hist 4/1/02-3/31/03 ALL	0-1MM	1-3MM	3-5MM	5-10MM	10-25MM	25MM & OVER
Type of Statement					9 (4/1-9/30/02)			42 (10/1/02-3/31/03)	
Unqualified	7	6	12	1	1		1	7	3
Reviewed	13	14	10		3	2	3	1	1
Compiled	8	4	9	2	2	2	1	2	
Tax Returns	1	4	4	1	2			1	
Other	16	16	16	2	1	2	4	3	3
NUMBER OF STATEMENTS	45	44	51	6	9	6	9	14	7
	%	%	%	%	%	%	%	%	%
ASSETS									
Cash & Equivalents	4.8	4.8	5.4					3.1	
Trade Receivables (net)	29.2	31.5	31.4					31.7	
Inventory	24.4	21.5	26.9					27.5	
All Other Current	3.7	2.7	3.0					2.2	
Total Current	62.1	60.5	66.7					64.5	
Fixed Assets (net)	28.8	29.0	25.3					25.7	
Intangibles (net)	4.6	4.7	2.2					1.8	
All Other Non-Current	4.4	5.8	5.8					8.0	
Total	100.0	100.0	100.0					100.0	
LIABILITIES									
Notes Payable-Short Term	12.6	12.3	12.2					7.2	
Cur. Mat.-L/T/D	5.9	8.6	5.0					4.7	
Trade Payables	15.4	14.2	17.7					14.8	
Income Taxes Payable	.3	.1	.1					.2	
All Other Current	10.0	9.0	14.3					19.6	
Total Current	44.2	44.3	49.4					46.4	
Long Term Debt	15.4	18.9	18.0					4.8	
Deferred Taxes	.6	.6	1.0					1.7	
All Other Non-Current	4.3	4.2	2.2					3.8	
Net Worth	35.4	31.9	29.5					43.3	
Total Liabilities & Net Worth	100.0	100.0	100.0					100.0	
INCOME DATA									
Net Sales	100.0	100.0	100.0					100.0	
Gross Profit	30.6	26.8	28.1					26.0	
Operating Expenses	26.7	24.3	27.3					23.1	
Operating Profit	3.9	2.5	.8					2.9	
All Other Expenses (net)	1.6	1.4	.7					.3	
Profit Before Taxes	2.3	1.1	.0					2.6	
RATIOS									
Current	2.0	2.2	2.0					2.4	
	1.5	1.4	1.5					1.4	
	1.1	1.1	1.0					1.0	
Quick	1.2	1.2	1.2					1.7	
	.8	.8	.7					.8	
	.5	.5	.5					.4	
Sales/Receivables	31 11.7	30 12.1	35 10.5					29 12.7	
	44 8.4	42 8.7	45 8.1					39 9.5	
	51 7.1	58 6.3	57 6.4					52 7.1	
Cost of Sales/Inventory	30 12.3	24 15.4	26 14.0					22 16.2	
	54 6.7	47 7.8	58 6.3					59 6.2	
	83 4.4	62 5.9	80 4.5					76 4.8	
Cost of Sales/Payables	18 20.5	15 24.4	18 20.6					15 24.5	
	27 13.5	21 17.7	26 14.3					21 17.4	
	35 10.4	34 10.6	43 8.6					28 13.1	
Sales/Working Capital	8.1	8.2	7.0					7.5	
	12.7	13.3	14.7					22.1	
	62.0	44.3	218.0					NM	
EBIT/Interest	(43) 5.6	(42) 4.5	(48) 6.9					12.4	
	2.1	1.9	1.7					6.0	
	1.1	-.1	-2.9					2.1	
Net Profit + Depr., Dep., Amort./Cur. Mat. L/T/D	(18) 4.6	(14) 4.4	(15) 8.5						
	2.2	2.2	1.1						
	1.2	1.0	-1.1						
Fixed/Worth	.5	.5	.4					.4	
	.9	.8	.6					.6	
	2.2	5.5	2.0					1.1	
Debt/Worth	.9	1.2	1.0					.6	
	2.4	1.8	1.7					1.2	
	5.3	11.2	5.0					6.5	
% Profit Before Taxes/Tangible Net Worth	(38) 40.6	(36) 37.4	(42) 34.5				(12)	42.2	
	14.4	13.2	10.5					14.9	
	1.4	-4.0	-13.1					5.5	
% Profit Before Taxes/Total Assets	13.5	8.0	10.3					12.1	
	4.4	3.7	2.4					7.1	
	-.4	-3.2	-8.3					2.0	
Sales/Net Fixed Assets	16.3	18.4	24.5					24.3	
	10.0	10.6	11.6					9.8	
	5.2	5.4	6.0					6.1	
Sales/Total Assets	3.6	3.2	3.1					3.4	
	2.7	2.6	2.6					2.9	
	1.7	1.9	2.0					2.0	
% Depr., Dep., Amort./Sales	(41) 1.2	(42) 1.3	(47) 1.2					1.6	
	2.3	2.7	2.3					2.4	
	3.1	4.0	3.5					3.1	
% Officers', Directors', Owners' Comp/Sales	(19) 2.3	(20) 2.0	(22) 1.9						
	4.6	4.9	4.8						
	6.8	6.8	7.8						
Net Sales ($)	738514M	726472M	988929M	3363M	22478M	22488M	65367M	276495M	598738M
Total Assets ($)	418557M	524694M	506743M	2499M	11023M	10116M	21849M	110066M	351190M

© RMA 2003

M = $ thousand   MM = $ million

See Pages 11 through 18 for Explanation of Ratios and Data

Current Data Sorted By Assets | **Comparative Historical Data**

	0-500M	500M-2MM	2-10MM	10-50MM	50-100MM	100-250MM	4/1/98-3/31/99 ALL	4/1/99-3/31/00 ALL
Type of Statement								
Unqualified			7	5		1	7	9
Reviewed	1	5	7	4			7	15
Compiled		6					8	7
Tax Returns		1					1	1
Other	1	5	8	3			15	11
	12 (4/1-9/30/02)		42 (10/1/02-3/31/03)					
NUMBER OF STATEMENTS	2	17	22	12		1	38	43
	%	%	%	%	%	%	%	%
ASSETS								
Cash & Equivalents		9.0	2.1	9.9	DATA NOT AVAILABLE		8.3	6.3
Trade Receivables (net)		28.1	36.5	22.7			35.9	33.6
Inventory		36.0	28.0	16.0			22.9	25.9
All Other Current		5.6	3.7	1.7			5.7	4.5
Total Current		78.6	70.2	50.2			72.7	70.3
Fixed Assets (net)		15.0	19.7	35.9			18.5	21.2
Intangibles (net)		.4	5.7	9.4			4.3	3.8
All Other Non-Current		6.0	4.4	4.5			4.5	4.7
Total		100.0	100.0	100.0			100.0	100.0
LIABILITIES								
Notes Payable-Short Term		15.3	17.8	2.6			13.9	16.6
Cur. Mat.-L/T/D		2.6	4.4	2.9			2.2	2.4
Trade Payables		16.4	13.2	11.0			17.2	18.2
Income Taxes Payable		.1	.1	.0			.4	.2
All Other Current		19.1	10.4	6.6			10.2	11.9
Total Current		53.4	45.9	23.2			43.9	49.2
Long Term Debt		6.9	5.9	14.6			11.0	11.9
Deferred Taxes		.1	.3	1.2			.2	.3
All Other Non-Current		9.0	6.2	8.1			6.6	4.1
Net Worth		30.5	41.7	53.0			38.3	34.4
Total Liabilities & Net Worth		100.0	100.0	100.0			100.0	100.0
INCOME DATA								
Net Sales		100.0	100.0	100.0			100.0	100.0
Gross Profit		31.4	27.1	29.2			32.0	29.9
Operating Expenses		31.0	25.2	24.5			27.1	25.5
Operating Profit		.4	1.9	4.8			4.9	4.3
All Other Expenses (net)		.1	.6	.7			.4	1.3
Profit Before Taxes		.4	1.3	4.1			4.5	3.1
RATIOS								
Current		2.3	2.0	2.4			2.8	2.2
		1.8	1.5	2.0			1.8	1.6
		1.2	1.0	1.4			1.3	1.1
Quick		1.3	1.2	2.0			1.6	1.2
		.8	.7	1.3			1.0	.8
		.2	.5	.8			.8	.6
Sales/Receivables		**12** 29.4	**39** 9.4	**31** 11.7			**35** 10.3	**39** 9.4
		32 11.3	**47** 7.7	**40** 9.2			**50** 7.2	**48** 7.5
		38 9.5	**54** 6.8	**45** 8.1			**69** 5.3	**64** 5.7
Cost of Sales/Inventory		**20** 18.2	**22** 16.9	**30** 12.4			**27** 13.6	**33** 11.0
		47 7.7	**51** 7.2	**39** 9.3			**45** 8.1	**45** 8.2
		91 4.0	**75** 4.9	**51** 7.1			**64** 5.7	**83** 4.4
Cost of Sales/Payables		**9** 39.9	**16** 23.4	**18** 20.3			**15** 24.1	**19** 19.1
		15 23.6	**21** 17.6	**23** 16.2			**28** 13.0	**29** 12.6
		32 11.5	**32** 11.4	**39** 9.3			**51** 7.1	**50** 7.3
Sales/Working Capital		7.5	7.7	5.9			4.9	6.5
		16.3	11.8	9.4			7.4	11.0
		41.1	127.6	16.3			16.6	50.7
EBIT/Interest		16.8	4.5	14.1			9.9	9.8
		(15) 6.4	2.4	(11) 6.1			(35) 5.6	(38) 2.7
		-1.6	.3	2.8			1.6	1.2
Net Profit + Depr., Dep., Amort./Cur. Mat. L /T/D			7.1				7.2	
			(12) 3.3				(10) 2.7	
			.6				.8	
Fixed/Worth		.2	.3	.4			.2	.2
		.3	.5	.9			.6	.5
		.8	1.2	1.7			1.6	2.0
Debt/Worth		.8	1.1	.4			.7	1.0
		2.0	1.4	1.0			1.6	1.8
		3.6	3.8	1.6			3.7	7.4
% Profit Before Taxes/Tangible Net Worth		49.2	29.6	30.2			68.4	37.2
		(16) 16.7	(20) 6.0	(11) 10.1			(32) 33.9	(37) 20.3
		-5.1	-8.0	7.1			13.5	8.7
% Profit Before Taxes/Total Assets		13.0	7.2	10.3			20.9	16.3
		4.8	2.1	6.3			11.8	6.2
		-3.3	-1.0	3.8			3.5	1.5
Sales/Net Fixed Assets		92.8	35.7	6.5			48.4	38.2
		23.9	16.9	4.5			19.4	13.1
		12.7	8.6	3.7			7.1	8.7
Sales/Total Assets		5.3	3.5	2.1			3.5	3.2
		3.8	2.9	1.9			2.6	2.3
		2.1	2.0	1.3			1.7	1.7
% Depr., Dep., Amort./Sales		.4	1.3	2.4			.6	.8
		(15) 1.1	(21) 2.2	(11) 3.4			(34) 1.1	(40) 1.3
		3.7	3.0	4.3			2.0	2.9
% Officers', Directors', Owners' Comp/Sales		1.4					3.2	2.1
		(11) 3.5					(10) 4.9	(12) 2.8
		7.5					13.3	6.7
Net Sales ($)	1230M	77478M	284329M	528543M		196101M	689509M	937558M
Total Assets ($)	597M	20158M	102954M	265577M		200092M	388450M	486485M

M = $ thousand MM = $ million

See Pages 11 through 18 for Explanation of Ratios and Data

Comparative Historical Data | Current Data Sorted By Sales

Comparative Historical Data			Type of Statement						
6	9	13	Unqualified				3	5	5
17	9	17	Reviewed	1	1	1	6	7	1
12	8	6	Compiled		2	1	3		
2	3	1	Tax Returns		1				
12	19	17	Other	1	2	2	5	5	2
4/1/00-3/31/01 ALL	4/1/01-3/31/02 ALL	4/1/02-3/31/03 ALL		0-1MM	1-3MM 12 (4/1-9/30/02)	3-5MM	5-10MM	10-25MM 42 (10/1/02-3/31/03)	25MM & OVER
49	48	54	NUMBER OF STATEMENTS	2	6	4	17	17	8
%	%	%	ASSETS	%	%	%	%	%	%
9.1	6.7	6.8	Cash & Equivalents				5.1	7.0	
33.1	28.4	30.0	Trade Receivables (net)				28.4	34.5	
23.9	24.9	27.0	Inventory				32.2	23.9	
2.4	3.3	3.6	All Other Current				1.5	3.4	
68.5	63.2	67.4	Total Current				67.3	68.8	
24.1	27.9	22.5	Fixed Assets (net)				19.3	23.3	
1.9	3.6	5.0	Intangibles (net)				7.7	4.7	
5.5	5.4	5.1	All Other Non-Current				5.7	3.2	
100.0	100.0	100.0	Total				100.0	100.0	
			LIABILITIES						
11.3	16.8	13.3	Notes Payable-Short Term				13.1	14.2	
3.3	4.7	3.3	Cur. Mat.-L/T/D				3.3	4.2	
15.9	16.6	13.8	Trade Payables				13.1	14.1	
.1	.2	.1	Income Taxes Payable				.0	.1	
15.4	10.4	14.2	All Other Current				9.6	10.6	
46.0	48.8	44.7	Total Current				39.2	43.3	
13.1	13.9	8.6	Long Term Debt				9.8	7.4	
.1	.3	.5	Deferred Taxes				.3	.1	
3.5	7.9	7.1	All Other Non-Current				6.3	7.2	
37.2	29.1	39.1	Net Worth				44.3	42.0	
100.0	100.0	100.0	Total Liabilities & Net Worth				100.0	100.0	
			INCOME DATA						
100.0	100.0	100.0	Net Sales				100.0	100.0	
30.5	31.9	29.7	Gross Profit				27.8	27.3	
25.2	27.3	27.7	Operating Expenses				25.3	24.9	
5.2	4.5	1.9	Operating Profit				2.5	2.4	
.4	1.5	.5	All Other Expenses (net)				.7	.6	
4.9	3.0	1.5	Profit Before Taxes				1.8	1.9	
			RATIOS						
2.4	2.5	2.3					2.7	2.1	
1.5	1.3	1.7	Current				1.8	1.5	
1.0	1.0	1.2					1.0	1.2	
1.5	1.3	1.4					1.2	1.4	
1.0	.7	.9	Quick				.7	.9	
.6	.5	.5					.5	.6	
29 12.6	24 15.3	31 11.9					26 14.0	32 11.5	
39 9.4	39 9.4	40 9.2	Sales/Receivables				40 9.2	40 9.0	
56 6.5	58 6.2	48 7.6					48 7.6	50 7.2	
21 17.4	26 13.8	24 15.2					25 14.7	19 18.9	
39 9.3	50 7.2	45 8.2	Cost of Sales/Inventory				59 6.2	43 8.4	
62 5.9	88 4.2	74 5.0					82 4.4	59 6.2	
14 25.8	17 20.9	15 24.2					13 27.3	17 21.6	
21 17.3	34 10.7	22 16.8	Cost of Sales/Payables				19 19.6	23 16.1	
32 11.4	49 7.4	36 10.2					39 9.4	29 12.6	
5.9	6.0	7.1					6.1	7.8	
16.8	16.6	11.8	Sales/Working Capital				11.9	11.6	
99.9	-247.5	49.8					129.0	30.9	
18.5	8.6	9.5					16.9	6.3	
(44) 5.3	(44) 2.8	(51) 3.3	EBIT/Interest				4.0	(16) 2.4	
2.1	1.1	1.1					-.6	1.1	
16.1	14.5	7.7	Net Profit + Depr., Dep.,				18.5		
(12) 5.4	(18) 2.3	(22) 3.1	Amort./Cur. Mat. L/T/D			(10)	4.2		
2.4	.7	1.7					.2		
.3	.4	.3					.3	.3	
.6	1.1	.5	Fixed/Worth				.6	.5	
1.4	3.6	1.2					1.5	1.1	
.6	.8	.7					.7	.8	
1.9	2.6	1.4	Debt/Worth				1.3	1.5	
4.4	9.7	3.5					4.3	2.8	
64.8	45.4	32.4	% Profit Before Taxes/Tangible				39.7	14.7	
(46) 33.8	(41) 20.5	(49) 10.1	Net Worth			(16)	6.1	(15) 6.8	
12.4	7.3	2.4					-11.2	1.4	
21.9	14.9	9.1	% Profit Before Taxes/Total				11.8	6.5	
11.8	6.0	4.5	Assets				4.8	2.0	
4.1	1.1	.7					-3.3	.6	
26.4	21.0	35.7					48.3	31.7	
14.8	11.0	13.1	Sales/Net Fixed Assets				17.2	13.6	
10.2	6.4	5.8					7.1	4.4	
4.1	3.3	3.8					4.0	4.0	
3.0	2.5	2.6	Sales/Total Assets				2.6	3.1	
2.3	1.9	1.8					1.9	1.7	
.6	1.0	1.1					1.3	.8	
(45) 1.2	(42) 1.8	(49) 2.4	% Depr., Dep., Amort./Sales				1.8	(16) 2.5	
2.8	3.2	3.5					3.3	3.5	
2.8	2.2	1.5	% Officers', Directors',						
(18) 6.9	(16) 4.2	(25) 3.4	Owners' Comp/Sales						
9.8	9.0	7.3							
775605M	959993M	1087681M	Net Sales ($)	1230M	10244M	16290M	127822M	282336M	649759M
334625M	459072M	589378M	Total Assets ($)	597M	4814M	4387M	52213M	127786M	399581M

© RMA 2003

M = $ thousand   MM = $ million
See Pages 11 through 18 for Explanation of Ratios and Data

Current Data Sorted By Assets   Comparative Historical Data

0-500M	500M-2MM	2-10MM	10-50MM	50-100MM	100-250MM	Type of Statement	4/1/98-3/31/99 ALL	4/1/99-3/31/00 ALL
1	6	14	2		1	Unqualified	37	18
6	30	8				Reviewed	46	41
3	19	15				Compiled	36	38
4	3	3			1	Tax Returns	11	15
2	20	19	10	3	2	Other	49	45
	31 (4/1-9/30/02)		141 (10/1/02-3/31/03)					
9	49	73	32	5	4	NUMBER OF STATEMENTS	179	157
%	%	%	%	%	%	**ASSETS**	%	%
	10.0	7.6	7.3			Cash & Equivalents	6.3	8.0
	31.5	32.7	26.0			Trade Receivables (net)	34.2	34.7
	23.9	22.5	19.6			Inventory	22.9	22.5
	1.3	3.0	2.5			All Other Current	1.8	1.9
	66.7	65.9	55.5			Total Current	65.3	67.2
	24.0	26.0	28.9			Fixed Assets (net)	26.2	24.6
	3.8	2.6	10.4			Intangibles (net)	4.2	2.1
	5.4	5.5	5.2			All Other Non-Current	4.3	6.1
	100.0	100.0	100.0			Total	100.0	100.0
						LIABILITIES		
	10.7	12.0	5.6			Notes Payable-Short Term	14.2	13.0
	4.0	3.3	3.9			Cur. Mat.-L/T/D	4.5	3.4
	15.1	18.4	12.3			Trade Payables	19.6	16.9
	.6	.2	.2			Income Taxes Payable	.4	.2
	12.4	11.7	14.4			All Other Current	12.0	13.6
	42.8	45.6	36.4			Total Current	50.6	46.9
	14.0	13.5	21.9			Long Term Debt	16.6	16.7
	.7	.3	.4			Deferred Taxes	.4	.1
	7.7	5.5	4.1			All Other Non-Current	2.4	4.3
	34.8	35.2	37.1			Net Worth	29.9	31.9
	100.0	100.0	100.0			Total Liabilities & Net Worth	100.0	100.0
						INCOME DATA		
	100.0	100.0	100.0			Net Sales	100.0	100.0
	34.3	25.7	27.5			Gross Profit	28.0	31.4
	33.7	22.8	21.2			Operating Expenses	24.0	26.3
	.5	2.9	6.3			Operating Profit	4.0	5.1
	.8	1.1	1.5			All Other Expenses (net)	1.2	.9
	-.2	1.8	4.8			Profit Before Taxes	2.7	4.2
						RATIOS		
	3.4	2.6	2.1				2.1	2.4
	1.5	1.5	1.6			Current	1.4	1.6
	1.0	1.0	1.0				1.1	1.2
	2.2	1.6	1.4				1.4	1.6
	1.1	.8	.9			Quick	(178) .9	1.0
	.6	.4	.5				.6	.6
	28 13.1	32 11.3	36 10.3				32 11.5	30 12.1
	41 9.0	46 8.0	48 7.6			Sales/Receivables	48 7.5	48 7.6
	57 6.4	64 5.7	63 5.8				64 5.7	62 5.9
	22 16.4	24 15.3	36 10.3				24 15.0	26 14.2
	43 8.4	40 9.0	49 7.4			Cost of Sales/Inventory	44 8.2	42 8.7
	86 4.2	65 5.6	69 5.3				67 5.4	63 5.8
	14 26.7	17 22.1	23 15.9				18 20.1	17 21.6
	23 15.6	29 12.5	31 11.6			Cost of Sales/Payables	28 13.1	27 13.7
	48 7.5	47 7.8	47 7.8				43 8.4	45 8.2
	5.2	6.3	6.4				6.3	6.5
	15.4	13.1	9.7			Sales/Working Capital	12.6	10.3
	NM	NM	NM				54.1	42.6
	5.4	10.5	13.7				9.5	14.8
	(42) 2.3	(67) 2.9	(30) 5.0			EBIT/Interest	(169) 3.4	(146) 4.0
	-2.7	.4	1.0				1.1	1.4
		3.9	2.0			Net Profit + Depr., Dep.,		7.2
		(18) 2.1	(10) 1.0			Amort./Cur. Mat. L./T/D	(65) 6.0 / 2.6	(41) 3.5
		.2	-.4				1.3	1.3
	.2	.3	.5				.4	.3
	1.0	.6	1.0			Fixed/Worth	.8	.7
	4.0	2.6	2.2				1.6	1.5
	.8	.6	.7				1.0	.9
	1.6	1.9	1.7			Debt/Worth	2.0	2.0
	11.3	8.4	4.9				4.1	4.7
	40.6	27.2	68.4			% Profit Before Taxes/Tangible	49.7	54.0
	(39) 9.9	(60) 11.7	(28) 21.9			Net Worth	(158) 21.6	(141) 23.0
	1.2	.8	2.2				8.3	7.6
	10.7	11.4	19.8			% Profit Before Taxes/Total	15.4	18.8
	4.3	4.3	5.4			Assets	6.6	8.0
	-7.9	-.6	-1.3				.9	1.7
	35.4	26.4	11.7				25.8	28.0
	15.3	13.3	7.9			Sales/Net Fixed Assets	11.8	13.4
	5.5	7.1	5.2				6.3	6.6
	3.3	3.1	2.2				3.4	3.6
	2.5	2.6	1.9			Sales/Total Assets	2.6	2.6
	1.8	1.9	1.6				1.8	2.0
	.7	.9	1.4				1.0	1.0
	(41) 1.5	(67) 1.8	(28) 2.3			% Depr., Dep., Amort./Sales	(164) 1.7	(145) 1.6
	3.3	2.6	3.3				2.9	2.6
	4.1	1.8					2.3	2.5
	(23) 7.7	(32) 3.5				% Officers', Directors',	(83) 4.8	(77) 5.2
	12.0	6.8				Owners' Comp/Sales	7.3	8.3
9084M	149675M	818979M	1326761M	682456M	2072950M	Net Sales ($)	2669132M	2382553M
2903M	58056M	318500M	690218M	366284M	542206M	Total Assets ($)	1493552M	1071449M

M = $ thousand   MM = $ million
See Pages 11 through 18 for Explanation of Ratios and Data

Comparative Historical Data | Current Data Sorted By Sales

				Type of Statement						
17	12	24		Unqualified		1	1	2	6	14
46	38	44		Reviewed		2	6	12	20	4
33	33	37		Compiled	3	12	6	12	4	
13	5	11		Tax Returns	2	4		1	3	1
28	42	56		Other	2	11	12	5	10	16
4/1/00-3/31/01 ALL	4/1/01-3/31/02 ALL	4/1/02-3/31/03 ALL			0-1MM	31 (4/1-9/30/02) 1-3MM	3-5MM	141 (10/1/02-3/31/03) 5-10MM	10-25MM	25MM & OVER
137	130	172		**NUMBER OF STATEMENTS**	7	30	25	32	43	35
%	%	%		**ASSETS**	%	%	%	%	%	%
7.4	8.4	7.9		Cash & Equivalents		9.7	7.5	8.5	8.7	5.3
34.4	33.6	30.6		Trade Receivables (net)		27.2	33.2	35.8	29.3	29.5
23.1	23.1	22.2		Inventory		25.3	21.4	21.2	22.0	21.7
2.5	2.7	2.2		All Other Current		.8	1.4	2.6	3.3	2.5
67.4	67.8	62.8		Total Current		63.0	63.5	68.2	63.3	59.1
25.2	23.8	26.4		Fixed Assets (net)		27.2	28.2	23.9	26.2	25.3
2.3	3.3	5.0		Intangibles (net)		4.7	1.8	1.8	5.3	10.7
5.1	5.1	5.8		All Other Non-Current		5.1	6.5	6.1	5.1	5.0
100.0	100.0	100.0		Total		100.0	100.0	100.0	100.0	100.0
				LIABILITIES						
12.8	13.5	11.3		Notes Payable-Short Term		13.3	14.3	12.1	10.2	7.3
3.5	4.2	3.4		Cur. Mat.-L/T/D		3.4	3.5	3.8	2.9	3.4
16.2	16.0	15.9		Trade Payables		11.7	13.8	22.1	15.1	16.0
.1	.3	.3		Income Taxes Payable		.2	.9	.4	.1	.2
13.5	11.7	12.1		All Other Current		10.4	10.6	6.3	15.8	15.3
46.2	45.8	43.1		Total Current		38.9	43.1	44.7	44.1	42.2
14.3	13.7	16.2		Long Term Debt		19.2	15.7	10.6	11.6	23.2
.2	.2	.4		Deferred Taxes		.0	1.2	.5	.2	.6
4.7	5.2	7.0		All Other Non-Current		5.3	8.6	4.9	4.9	7.3
34.7	35.0	33.3		Net Worth		36.5	31.4	39.2	39.2	26.7
100.0	100.0	100.0		Total Liabilities & Net Worth		100.0	100.0	100.0	100.0	100.0
				INCOME DATA						
100.0	100.0	100.0		Net Sales		100.0	100.0	100.0	100.0	100.0
29.3	28.0	29.7		Gross Profit		38.2	32.3	24.9	24.5	27.2
25.2	25.9	26.8		Operating Expenses		35.6	29.2	22.5	21.1	21.5
4.1	2.1	2.9		Operating Profit		2.6	3.2	2.4	3.4	5.7
.9	1.0	1.0		All Other Expenses (net)		1.2	1.1	1.2	.5	2.0
3.2	1.1	1.9		Profit Before Taxes		1.5	2.0	1.2	2.9	3.7
				RATIOS						
2.1	2.4	2.5				3.2	2.4	3.5	2.5	2.0
1.5	1.6	1.5		Current		1.4	1.4	1.5	1.5	1.6
1.1	1.2	1.0				1.0	1.0	1.0	.9	1.0
1.4	1.4	1.6				1.9	1.5	2.3	1.8	1.3
.9	.9	.9		Quick		1.0	.8	1.0	.9	.8
.6	.7	.5				.6	.6	.4	.4	.6
28 13.2	30 12.4	31 11.7			31 11.9	28 13.2	32 11.5	29 12.7	35 10.3	
43 8.5	46 7.9	45 8.2		Sales/Receivables	41 9.0	48 7.6	46 7.9	41 8.9	49 7.5	
59 6.2	63 5.8	60 6.1			57 6.5	66 5.5	70 5.2	56 6.5	61 6.0	
22 16.3	23 15.5	26 14.0			33 11.1	20 17.8	11 33.9	25 14.7	36 10.2	
40 9.0	40 9.1	43 8.5		Cost of Sales/Inventory	66 5.6	32 11.3	36 10.1	36 10.3	53 6.8	
61 6.0	63 5.8	72 5.0			102 3.6	58 6.3	54 6.7	54 6.7	78 4.7	
13 28.0	15 24.8	16 22.5			11 32.0	15 24.4	19 19.3	13 27.8	24 15.4	
27 13.5	26 14.1	29 12.5		Cost of Sales/Payables	17 21.3	24 15.2	33 11.2	26 13.9	35 10.5	
41 8.9	38 9.5	48 7.6			46 7.9	41 8.9	56 6.5	43 8.6	48 7.6	
7.1	5.9	6.4				4.5	7.0	5.1	6.4	7.0
14.2	13.4	12.9		Sales/Working Capital		13.1	18.1	13.5	12.0	10.2
65.5	36.5	-553.9				NM	NM	NM	-43.1	160.7
	10.4		7.2		7.7		EBIT/Interest				
(129) 3.2	(118) 2.1	(155) 2.6		EBIT/Interest	(23) 1.1	(24) 2.5	(30) 2.9	(39) 6.0	(33) 3.5	
1.3	.3	.2			-2.7	.4	.9	.8	1.2	
5.1	3.0	2.4						5.0	2.5	
(39) 2.1	(33) 1.7	(37) 1.1		Net Profit + Depr., Dep., Amort./Cur. Mat. L/T/D			(11) 1.9	(10) 1.5	
1.3	.2	-.5					-1.2	.5	
.3	.2	.3			.2	.2	.2	.3	.6	
.6	.6	.9		Fixed/Worth	.8	1.2	.6	.5	1.1	
1.5	1.9	2.6			4.8	1.7	1.8	1.9	4.7	
.9	.8	.8			.6	1.0	.5	.6	1.1	
2.0	2.0	1.9		Debt/Worth	1.7	1.7	1.8	1.3	3.6	
5.0	5.4	7.5			17.6	4.5	4.6	5.1	9.4	
49.2	35.8	39.6			39.4	37.5	24.6	35.5	68.2	
(124) 19.1	(110) 10.8	(141) 12.5		% Profit Before Taxes/Tangible Net Worth	(25) 4.8	(20) 9.3	(29) 9.9	(35) 15.0	(28) 20.4	
3.2	1.8	1.2			-3.9	-5.7	1.5	7.9	4.1	
15.7	11.5	12.9			11.1	10.5	8.5	16.4	16.2	
5.9	3.6	4.3		% Profit Before Taxes/Total Assets	1.3	4.5	3.5	8.2	4.5	
.8	-1.4	-2.0			-10.2	-2.7	.2	1.4	.3	
28.7	30.6	23.1			28.5	34.4	31.7	23.4	15.0	
13.2	12.9	11.4		Sales/Net Fixed Assets	14.8	9.9	15.1	12.7	9.2	
8.0	6.8	6.0			5.3	5.2	7.1	8.2	6.3	
3.8	3.5	3.1			3.2	3.6	3.3	3.2	2.5	
2.8	2.5	2.4		Sales/Total Assets	2.3	2.5	2.6	2.6	2.0	
2.2	1.8	1.8			1.4	1.8	2.0	2.0	1.6	
.7	.8	1.0			1.2	.5	.9	.9	1.4	
(124) 1.4	(114) 1.6	(151) 1.9		% Depr., Dep., Amort./Sales	(24) 2.0	(23) 1.6	(29) 1.6	(40) 1.7	(29) 2.0	
2.6	2.6	2.9			5.2	3.7	2.6	2.5	3.1	
2.5	2.0	2.7			4.6		2.0	1.7		
(62) 4.4	(49) 4.7	(65) 6.1		% Officers', Directors', Owners' Comp/Sales	(17) 7.2	(15) 3.3	(18) 4.5			
6.9	7.1	9.7			10.3		6.1	9.1		
2590621M	2486505M	5059905M		Net Sales ($)	4669M	58520M	99413M	236968M	681867M	3978468M
993511M	1239161M	1978167M		Total Assets ($)	2741M	30516M	42438M	97280M	311620M	1493572M

© RMA 2003

M = $ thousand   MM = $ million
See Pages 11 through 18 for Explanation of Ratios and Data

Current Data Sorted By Assets

Comparative Historical Data

0-500M	500M-2MM	2-10MM	10-50MM	50-100MM	100-250MM	Type of Statement	4/1/98-3/31/99 ALL	4/1/99-3/31/00 ALL
	1	5	2		1	Unqualified	21	16
	2	7	3			Reviewed	12	13
1	2	3				Compiled	5	11
1	3	6			1	Tax Returns	3	5
2	1		1		1	Other	9	10
	5 (4/1-9/30/02)		35 (10/1/02-3/31/03)					
4	9	21	3		3	NUMBER OF STATEMENTS	50	55
%	%	%	%	%	%		%	%

0-500M	500M-2MM	2-10MM	10-50MM	50-100MM	100-250MM		4/1/98-3/31/99 ALL	4/1/99-3/31/00 ALL
						ASSETS		
		7.9				Cash & Equivalents	11.5	10.3
		31.8		D		Trade Receivables (net)	28.9	27.8
		25.3		A		Inventory	22.9	24.3
		2.3		T		All Other Current	1.6	2.5
		67.3		A		Total Current	64.9	64.8
		26.6				Fixed Assets (net)	25.6	27.4
		.2		N		Intangibles (net)	4.8	3.4
		6.0		O		All Other Non-Current	4.7	4.4
		100.0		T		Total	100.0	100.0
						LIABILITIES		
		7.1		A		Notes Payable-Short Term	5.1	8.3
		2.9		V		Cur. Mat.-L/T/D	2.8	3.5
		21.6		A		Trade Payables	20.2	19.0
		.5		I		Income Taxes Payable	.2	.3
		10.5		L		All Other Current	9.9	7.7
		42.6		A		Total Current	38.1	38.7
		10.3		B		Long Term Debt	11.7	13.5
		1.8		L		Deferred Taxes	.2	.2
		5.4		E		All Other Non-Current	5.5	4.1
		39.8				Net Worth	44.5	43.5
		100.0				Total Liabilities & Net Worth	100.0	100.0
						INCOME DATA		
		100.0				Net Sales	100.0	100.0
		31.7				Gross Profit	33.0	32.1
		30.3				Operating Expenses	28.2	28.1
		1.5				Operating Profit	4.9	4.1
		.1				All Other Expenses (net)	.5	.8
		1.3				Profit Before Taxes	4.3	3.3
						RATIOS		
		2.3					2.5	2.6
		1.7				Current	1.8	1.8
		1.4					1.2	1.3
		1.3					1.6	1.4
		1.0				Quick	1.1	1.0
		.7					.7	.7
		29 12.6					23 15.8	25 14.9
		34 10.8				Sales/Receivables	34 10.9	31 11.7
		43 8.4					41 8.8	44 8.4
		23 16.0					24 15.4	24 15.4
		34 10.7				Cost of Sales/Inventory	32 11.3	34 10.8
		60 6.1					44 8.4	50 7.3
		20 18.0					18 20.0	19 19.5
		33 11.1				Cost of Sales/Payables	30 12.1	31 11.7
		39 9.4					50 7.3	46 7.9
		9.3					7.3	7.9
		11.3				Sales/Working Capital	13.0	11.6
		20.0					44.4	25.2
		17.3					17.5	13.0
	(19)	2.9				EBIT/Interest	(44) 6.5	(54) 5.8
		1.0					1.8	1.9
		4.4					10.4	4.3
	(10)	2.3				Net Profit + Depr., Dep., Amort./Cur. Mat. L/T/D	(18) 6.1	(15) 3.5
		.8					1.6	.3
		.3					.4	.3
		.6				Fixed/Worth	.7	.6
		1.3					1.2	1.1
		.6					.7	.7
		1.7				Debt/Worth	1.3	1.2
		2.5					3.4	2.6
		28.6					41.9	37.4
	(20)	11.6				% Profit Before Taxes/Tangible Net Worth	(47) 21.1	(51) 21.0
		.0					9.7	5.1
		16.5					18.3	16.8
		3.6				% Profit Before Taxes/Total Assets	8.0	9.3
		−1.9					2.6	2.5
		22.7					25.8	25.0
		16.4				Sales/Net Fixed Assets	15.1	14.8
		10.4					8.0	6.6
		3.9					4.3	4.2
		3.2				Sales/Total Assets	3.2	3.1
		2.6					2.4	2.2
		.9					.9	.8
	(17)	1.2				% Depr., Dep., Amort./Sales	(43) 1.2	(47) 1.2
		2.3					1.7	2.1
							1.7	1.3
						% Officers', Directors', Owners' Comp/Sales	(12) 5.7	(17) 3.7
							9.7	6.7
4314M	42281M	296827M	138682M		1866423M	Net Sales ($)	1591191M	1583280M
1447M	10550M	91095M	51587M		466519M	Total Assets ($)	691213M	695645M

M = $ thousand   MM = $ million
See Pages 11 through 18 for Explanation of Ratios and Data

Comparative Historical Data | Current Data Sorted By Sales

			Type of Statement		5 (4/1-9/30/02)		35 (10/1/02-3/31/03)		
					0-1MM	1-3MM	3-5MM	5-10MM	10-25MM	25MM & OVER
14	10	9	Unqualified						5	3
10	8	9	Reviewed				1	1	7	
12	17	6	Compiled	1	1	2	1	1		
3	5	5	Tax Returns		2		2		1	1
11	12	11	Other	1	2		2	2		2
4/1/00-3/31/01 ALL	4/1/01-3/31/02 ALL	4/1/02-3/31/03 ALL								
50	52	40	**NUMBER OF STATEMENTS**	2	5	4	6	17	6
%	%	%	**ASSETS**	%	%	%	%	%	%
6.7	9.4	7.2	Cash & Equivalents					9.0	
27.2	28.2	29.9	Trade Receivables (net)					32.9	
26.0	23.5	26.7	Inventory					22.5	
2.5	2.4	2.8	All Other Current					2.7	
62.4	63.5	66.6	Total Current					67.2	
28.3	28.7	24.6	Fixed Assets (net)					26.6	
5.3	3.2	3.7	Intangibles (net)					.2	
4.0	4.6	5.1	All Other Non-Current					6.0	
100.0	100.0	100.0	Total					100.0	
			LIABILITIES						
9.3	7.9	7.6	Notes Payable-Short Term					6.7	
2.6	3.5	3.5	Cur. Mat.-L/T/D					2.3	
18.6	19.8	20.6	Trade Payables					22.8	
.1	.1	.3	Income Taxes Payable					.7	
9.2	8.8	10.6	All Other Current					10.5	
39.9	40.2	42.6	Total Current					43.0	
16.9	15.8	11.5	Long Term Debt					10.1	
.3	.3	1.0	Deferred Taxes					1.5	
5.6	4.1	6.9	All Other Non-Current					5.3	
37.2	39.6	38.0	Net Worth					40.0	
100.0	100.0	100.0	Total Liabilities & Net Worth					100.0	
			INCOME DATA						
100.0	100.0	100.0	Net Sales					100.0	
31.5	31.3	32.9	Gross Profit					31.0	
27.8	27.3	30.6	Operating Expenses					29.7	
3.7	3.9	2.3	Operating Profit					1.3	
.6	.7	.1	All Other Expenses (net)					.0	
3.1	3.2	2.3	Profit Before Taxes					1.3	
			RATIOS						
2.0	2.4	2.4						2.4	
1.5	1.6	1.6	Current					1.7	
1.2	1.1	1.3						1.3	
1.6	1.4	1.2						1.6	
.8	.8	.9	Quick					1.0	
.5	.7	.5						.8	
26 13.9	24 14.9	26 14.3						28 13.3	
35 10.5	33 10.9	33 11.0	Sales/Receivables					34 10.8	
43 8.4	45 8.1	40 9.1						41 8.8	
27 13.6	25 14.7	25 14.7						22 16.7	
36 10.0	33 11.1	35 10.5	Cost of Sales/Inventory					30 12.3	
62 5.9	50 7.4	65 5.6						40 9.1	
18 20.6	18 20.5	21 17.5						19 18.8	
30 12.2	29 12.5	32 11.3	Cost of Sales/Payables					33 11.1	
47 7.7	45 8.1	40 9.2						43 8.5	
8.5	7.2	9.1						10.0	
18.7	16.0	14.1	Sales/Working Capital					11.3	
36.7	69.0	28.0						31.0	
10.5	9.3	12.4						20.9	
(43) 3.4	(46) 3.4	(35) 2.9	EBIT/Interest				(15) 3.4		
.9	1.1	.4						-3.2	
7.4	2.3	5.6	Net Profit + Depr., Dep.,						
(15) 3.9	(10) 1.0	(14) 2.5	Amort./Cur. Mat. L/T/D						
1.3	.3	.8							
.5	.4	.4						.3	
.9	.9	.6	Fixed/Worth					.6	
2.6	1.5	1.5						1.3	
.9	.8	.8						.6	
1.7	1.8	1.7	Debt/Worth					1.6	
6.0	3.6	3.5						2.5	
40.3	39.7	39.0	% Profit Before Taxes/Tangible					37.1	
(45) 18.3	(47) 10.9	(36) 19.0	Net Worth				(16) 20.1		
2.0	4.2	-1.3						-4.2	
17.7	16.9	18.3	% Profit Before Taxes/Total					18.4	
7.1	5.1	4.0	Assets					4.0	
-.3	.6	-1.3						-4.0	
19.3	26.6	24.5						25.7	
11.4	12.5	17.2	Sales/Net Fixed Assets					18.6	
7.0	5.6	8.8						10.4	
4.1	4.4	4.2						4.0	
2.9	3.4	3.2	Sales/Total Assets					3.5	
2.1	2.2	2.4						2.9	
.8	.4	.9						.8	
(47) 1.3	(43) 1.1	(31) 1.3	% Depr., Dep., Amort./Sales				(13) 1.0		
2.0	2.1	2.2						2.8	
1.6	1.4	.8							
(15) 3.1	(21) 2.9	(19) 5.2	% Officers', Directors', Owners' Comp/Sales						
5.6	7.2	9.8							
1281973M	1936706M	2348527M	Net Sales ($)	1308M	8362M	17917M	42259M	273576M	2005105M
603311M	967923M	621198M	Total Assets ($)	760M	3295M	5513M	11522M	82002M	518106M

© RMA 2003

M = $ thousand   MM = $ million
See Pages 11 through 18 for Explanation of Ratios and Data

Current Data Sorted By Assets | Comparative Historical Data

0-500M	500M-2MM	2-10MM	10-50MM	50-100MM	100-250MM	Type of Statement	4/1/98-3/31/99 ALL	4/1/99-3/31/00 ALL
	1		3	1		Unqualified	4	7
	2	6	1			Reviewed	7	5
1	4	1				Compiled	5	6
1						Tax Returns	3	2
	2	2	6			Other	11	10
	5 (4/1-9/30/02)		26 (10/1/02-3/31/03)					
2	9	9	10	1		NUMBER OF STATEMENTS	30	30
%	%	%	%	%	%	ASSETS	%	%
			4.5			Cash & Equivalents	10.9	10.4
			24.1			Trade Receivables (net)	31.0	31.5
			31.1			Inventory	25.1	29.0
			3.9			All Other Current	1.7	1.1
			63.7			Total Current	68.7	71.9
			27.6			Fixed Assets (net)	22.5	18.8
			2.6			Intangibles (net)	5.9	6.0
			6.1			All Other Non-Current	2.9	3.2
			100.0			Total	100.0	100.0
						LIABILITIES		
			10.6			Notes Payable-Short Term	10.3	9.7
			1.9			Cur. Mat.-L/T/D	2.5	3.3
			15.3			Trade Payables	13.6	16.0
			.2			Income Taxes Payable	.6	1.1
			13.3			All Other Current	13.5	8.8
			41.3			Total Current	40.5	39.0
			12.0			Long Term Debt	14.2	9.1
			.5			Deferred Taxes	.2	.2
			5.2			All Other Non-Current	4.1	6.5
			41.0			Net Worth	41.1	45.2
			100.0			Total Liabilities & Net Worth	100.0	100.0
						INCOME DATA		
			100.0			Net Sales	100.0	100.0
			36.9			Gross Profit	32.9	31.4
			31.6			Operating Expenses	26.9	24.3
			5.3			Operating Profit	6.0	7.0
			.8			All Other Expenses (net)	−.5	1.1
			4.5			Profit Before Taxes	6.5	5.9
						RATIOS		
			2.6				2.9	3.0
			1.5			Current	1.7	1.7
			1.2				1.3	1.3
			1.0				1.9	1.7
			.8			Quick	1.0	1.0
			.5				.7	.7
			28 13.0				30 12.3	29 12.5
			35 10.4			Sales/Receivables	40 9.1	46 8.0
			47 7.7				52 7.0	54 6.8
			46 8.0				33 11.1	32 11.4
			70 5.2			Cost of Sales/Inventory	51 7.2	58 6.3
			97 3.8				76 4.8	94 3.9
			21 17.1				10 34.8	15 24.7
			32 11.3			Cost of Sales/Payables	21 17.2	24 15.1
			43 8.6				45 8.2	42 8.6
			6.2				6.7	6.3
			15.3			Sales/Working Capital	10.6	10.7
			22.8				28.5	16.4
							13.5	21.5
						EBIT/Interest	(27) 5.7	(27) 8.0
							3.3	3.8
							7.2	
						Net Profit + Depr., Dep., Amort./Cur. Mat. L./T/D	(11) 2.9	
							1.6	
			.3				.3	.2
			.7			Fixed/Worth	.7	.4
			6.0				1.5	1.4
			.5				.7	.5
			1.6			Debt/Worth	1.8	1.2
			15.4				5.0	3.6
			53.7				83.8	75.0
			26.8			% Profit Before Taxes/Tangible Net Worth	(27) 38.6	(27) 40.3
			22.2				18.5	12.9
			19.1				23.1	25.5
			9.5			% Profit Before Taxes/Total Assets	15.1	11.9
			2.8				6.5	7.5
			19.5				31.8	51.6
			8.6			Sales/Net Fixed Assets	11.1	11.3
			5.4				7.4	7.4
			3.5				3.8	4.0
			2.4			Sales/Total Assets	2.6	2.5
			1.9				1.7	1.8
			1.0				.8	.6
			1.4			% Depr., Dep., Amort./Sales	(26) 1.6	(27) 1.3
			3.5				3.1	2.3
							1.9	2.1
						% Officers', Directors', Owners' Comp/Sales	(11) 3.0	(10) 4.1
							6.3	8.1
1908M	41646M	121885M	427251M	112904M		Net Sales ($)	730267M	922659M
418M	11579M	37967M	166722M	53530M		Total Assets ($)	368009M	496979M

(100-250MM column: DATA NOT AVAILABLE)

M = $ thousand   MM = $ million
See Pages 11 through 18 for Explanation of Ratios and Data

Comparative Historical Data | | Current Data Sorted By Sales

					Type of Statement						
	3		6		5	Unqualified			1		4
	6		4		9	Reviewed		2	4	1	2
	7		4		6	Compiled	1	2	2	1	
	7		2		1	Tax Returns			1		
	9		7		10	Other	1	1	1	1	6
	4/1/00-3/31/01 ALL		4/1/01-3/31/02 ALL		4/1/02-3/31/03 ALL		0-1MM	5 (4/1-9/30/02) 1-3MM	3-5MM	26 (10/1/02-3/31/03) 5-10MM	10-25MM	25MM & OVER
	28		23		31	**NUMBER OF STATEMENTS**	1	2	5	8	3	12
	%		%		%	**ASSETS**	%	%	%	%	%	%
	9.6		9.4		6.4	Cash & Equivalents						3.8
	34.0		26.8		31.5	Trade Receivables (net)						22.9
	31.7		32.9		32.9	Inventory						29.9
	3.7		4.4		2.0	All Other Current						4.4
	79.0		73.6		72.8	Total Current						61.1
	16.0		19.5		19.1	Fixed Assets (net)						26.6
	1.6		4.1		3.0	Intangibles (net)						6.6
	3.3		2.8		5.1	All Other Non-Current						5.8
	100.0		100.0		100.0	Total						100.0
						LIABILITIES						
	12.9		15.3		14.4	Notes Payable-Short Term						12.4
	2.0		3.2		3.5	Cur. Mat.-L/T/D						2.4
	22.3		14.9		21.2	Trade Payables						15.8
	.7		.2		.1	Income Taxes Payable						.2
	10.5		11.2		11.9	All Other Current						12.4
	48.4		44.7		51.0	Total Current						43.1
	6.0		11.7		12.1	Long Term Debt						11.4
	.1		.1		.3	Deferred Taxes						.4
	5.1		2.7		6.3	All Other Non-Current						4.4
	40.4		40.7		30.3	Net Worth						40.6
	100.0		100.0		100.0	Total Liabilities & Net Worth						100.0
						INCOME DATA						
	100.0		100.0		100.0	Net Sales						100.0
	30.2		33.2		33.8	Gross Profit						38.5
	25.8		28.6		29.9	Operating Expenses						33.6
	4.4		4.6		3.9	Operating Profit						4.9
	.1		.4		.8	All Other Expenses (net)						.8
	4.3		4.2		3.1	Profit Before Taxes						4.0
						RATIOS						
	3.2		2.5		1.9							2.4
	1.7		1.5		1.3	Current						1.4
	1.3		1.2		1.1							1.2
	1.6		1.4		1.1							.9
	.9		.7		.8	Quick						.6
	.6		.4		.5							.4
29	12.4	12	30.1	23	15.8						24	14.9
41	9.0	33	11.2	36	10.2	Sales/Receivables					35	10.4
54	6.7	49	7.5	47	7.8						45	8.1
29	12.5	31	11.9	35	10.3						40	9.2
54	6.8	53	6.9	52	7.0	Cost of Sales/Inventory					69	5.3
86	4.3	96	3.8	84	4.4						94	3.9
16	22.9	10	36.0	26	14.1						26	13.9
35	10.5	26	14.0	36	10.2	Cost of Sales/Payables					40	9.2
46	7.9	43	8.4	52	7.1						47	7.8
	5.2		5.9		7.6							6.7
	9.2		13.3		20.9	Sales/Working Capital						16.1
	28.0		26.1		56.7							26.1
	18.9		8.3		12.8							15.1
(27)	5.9	(20)	3.4	(28)	4.0	EBIT/Interest					(11)	3.8
	3.0		1.5		1.7							1.7
					2.6	Net Profit + Depr., Dep.,						
				(12)	1.7	Amort./Cur. Mat. L/T/D						
					.4							
	.2		.2		.3							.3
	.4		.3		.6	Fixed/Worth						.7
	.9		1.3		1.6							15.3
	.5		.5		1.4							.6
	1.2		1.9		2.9	Debt/Worth						2.1
	4.1		4.9		9.7							36.5
	47.6		52.1		75.6	% Profit Before Taxes/Tangible						38.4
(25)	30.0	(21)	20.5	(28)	26.5	Net Worth					(11)	26.7
	3.9		3.1		6.1							22.4
	23.0		19.6		16.8	% Profit Before Taxes/Total						16.6
	11.5		9.8		9.6	Assets						8.9
	2.0		.9		1.0							2.3
	76.4		77.1		48.7							23.5
	29.2		22.9		28.1	Sales/Net Fixed Assets						8.6
	7.9		8.6		8.5							5.8
	5.0		4.2		4.3							3.2
	2.7		2.5		3.2	Sales/Total Assets						2.4
	2.0		1.9		2.4							2.0
	.5		.7		.7							1.2
(24)	1.1	(19)	1.3	(27)	1.2	% Depr., Dep., Amort./Sales						1.4
	1.7		2.0		3.2							3.6
	1.7		1.3		2.8	% Officers', Directors',						
(13)	4.3	(11)	2.5	(18)	4.9	Owners' Comp/Sales						
	7.3		5.2		7.8							
	616957M		615910M		705594M	Net Sales ($)	638M	3888M	20984M	59034M	52010M	569040M
	270706M		263273M		270216M	Total Assets ($)	258M	1087M	6087M	18209M	14416M	230159M

M = $ thousand   MM = $ million
See Pages 11 through 18 for Explanation of Ratios and Data

MANUFACTURING—Surgical and Medical Instrument Manufacturing   NAICS 339112 (SIC 3829, 3841)

Current Data Sorted By Assets — **Comparative Historical Data**

0-500M	500M-2MM	2-10MM	10-50MM	50-100MM	100-250MM	Type of Statement	4/1/98-3/31/99 ALL	4/1/99-3/31/00 ALL
2	2	15	19	6	7	Unqualified	50	59
1	7	14	5			Reviewed	26	18
4	4	8	3	1		Compiled	18	20
1	1	1				Tax Returns	4	4
2	6	15	14	4	8	Other	41	42
	30 (4/1-9/30/02)		120 (10/1/02-3/31/03)					
10	20	53	41	11	15	NUMBER OF STATEMENTS	139	143
%	%	%	%	%	%	**ASSETS**	%	%
13.5	12.9	10.4	14.2	5.9	16.0	Cash & Equivalents	10.4	11.1
31.3	25.3	26.3	20.6	19.1	18.3	Trade Receivables (net)	25.6	25.0
22.0	23.5	25.3	17.5	20.5	14.6	Inventory	25.8	24.0
1.4	3.8	3.6	5.7	3.5	3.4	All Other Current	2.4	2.6
68.2	65.5	65.6	58.2	49.0	52.3	Total Current	64.2	62.7
23.3	26.5	20.8	25.8	25.9	20.1	Fixed Assets (net)	21.8	22.0
1.8	2.3	8.1	8.8	14.0	17.4	Intangibles (net)	8.4	9.4
5.7	5.7	5.5	7.3	11.1	10.1	All Other Non-Current	5.5	5.9
100.0	100.0	100.0	100.0	100.0	100.0	Total	100.0	100.0
						LIABILITIES		
16.5	8.1	9.9	3.8	3.2	.0	Notes Payable-Short Term	8.6	7.9
3.7	3.2	5.5	3.5	2.1	3.5	Cur. Mat.-L/T/D	2.6	3.1
12.7	16.8	11.7	11.9	7.3	5.5	Trade Payables	11.6	11.9
.0	3.1	.5	.3	1.6	.6	Income Taxes Payable	.4	.5
28.2	8.7	10.4	12.7	7.0	16.1	All Other Current	10.5	8.0
61.1	39.8	38.1	32.1	21.3	25.6	Total Current	33.8	31.4
12.3	13.4	9.4	13.5	14.3	20.3	Long Term Debt	13.2	12.3
.0	.2	.7	.5	1.0	1.4	Deferred Taxes	.6	.5
3.7	3.5	2.5	3.5	4.1	22.8	All Other Non-Current	6.8	5.5
22.9	43.2	49.4	50.5	59.2	29.9	Net Worth	45.6	50.3
100.0	100.0	100.0	100.0	100.0	100.0	Total Liabilities & Net Worth	100.0	100.0
						INCOME DATA		
100.0	100.0	100.0	100.0	100.0	100.0	Net Sales	100.0	100.0
46.0	47.5	42.7	43.6	43.8	46.1	Gross Profit	45.4	46.7
42.5	39.1	34.6	32.1	33.9	37.5	Operating Expenses	50.4	39.3
3.5	8.4	8.1	11.5	9.9	8.5	Operating Profit	-5.0	7.4
2.0	1.5	1.3	2.1	1.5	2.4	All Other Expenses (net)	.4	.1
1.5	6.9	6.8	9.5	8.4	6.1	Profit Before Taxes	-5.4	7.2
						RATIOS		
3.5	3.7	3.9	3.2	3.9	4.7	Current	4.2	3.7
2.3	1.8	1.7	2.2	2.7	2.9		2.2	2.3
.9	1.0	1.2	1.2	1.7	1.2		1.5	1.4
2.4	2.0	2.1	2.1	1.9	3.8	Quick	2.5	2.0
1.1	.8	.9	1.0	1.0	1.6		1.2	1.3
.4	.5	.6	.7	.8	.7		.7	.7
20 18.7	36 10.2	36 10.0	37 9.9	48 7.6	49 7.4	Sales/Receivables	40 9.2	41 8.8
29 12.7	41 8.9	47 7.8	47 7.8	60 6.1	68 5.4		54 6.7	53 6.9
68 5.3	50 7.3	61 6.0	60 6.1	78 4.7	75 4.9		73 5.0	65 5.6
30 12.0	43 8.5	50 7.2	38 9.6	84 4.3	68 5.4	Cost of Sales/Inventory	60 6.1	56 6.6
56 6.5	61 6.0	83 4.4	68 5.4	101 3.6	76 4.8		105 3.5	99 3.7
102 3.6	109 3.4	125 2.9	111 3.3	192 1.9	162 2.2		168 2.2	145 2.5
5 78.7	29 12.5	22 16.7	18 20.4	22 16.4	25 14.8	Cost of Sales/Payables	24 15.3	21 17.2
24 15.5	42 8.7	30 12.3	32 11.5	32 11.4	30 12.2		39 9.4	36 10.1
53 6.9	79 4.6	40 9.1	58 6.3	71 5.1	42 8.6		61 6.0	56 6.5
3.8	4.2	3.7	3.3	2.7	2.0	Sales/Working Capital	2.9	2.9
8.9	6.6	8.8	5.4	3.6	4.0		5.5	4.7
NM	NM	16.6	25.0	6.8	20.4		11.1	11.3
	(18) 12.5	(46) 11.0	(38) 62.8	(10) 13.5	(13) 77.2	EBIT/Interest	(118) 14.5	(119) 13.8
	2.8	4.5	11.0	5.1	6.8		4.2	4.4
	2.0	1.7	2.9	-1.7	1.3		1.3	1.4
		(18) 7.1	(16) 26.9			Net Profit + Depr., Dep., Amort./Cur. Mat. L /T/D	(55) 14.1	(45) 14.3
		2.1	5.2				4.2	4.7
		.5	1.8				1.4	1.9
.1	.2	.1	.2	.2	.2	Fixed/Worth	.2	.2
.6	.7	.4	.7	.8	.7		.4	.4
UND	1.5	1.1	1.4	.8	-.8		1.1	1.0
.3	.5	.5	.6	.2	.2	Debt/Worth	.4	.5
2.6	1.3	1.5	1.4	.9	.9		1.1	.9
UND	5.7	3.0	2.5	2.9	-4.8		3.0	2.8
	(17) 40.8	(52) 46.4	(38) 78.0	(10) 41.1	(10) 29.8	% Profit Before Taxes/Tangible Net Worth	(125) 39.6	(125) 48.7
	17.8	24.1	28.5	15.8	14.3		16.8	19.4
	6.6	10.6	8.4	6.0	4.9		3.4	3.8
20.2	13.4	17.6	24.2	18.1	13.5	% Profit Before Taxes/Total Assets	17.7	21.0
1.3	7.1	10.0	11.6	9.4	4.5		5.7	7.7
-2.7	1.9	2.1	4.2	2.1	.2		.6	.9
115.5	19.5	33.6	15.3	4.6	5.6	Sales/Net Fixed Assets	20.5	15.8
16.2	10.4	11.4	7.3	4.3	4.9		9.2	8.8
4.3	4.6	5.4	3.5	3.1	3.9		4.4	4.8
4.3	2.8	2.5	1.9	1.4	1.4	Sales/Total Assets	2.3	2.1
2.7	2.1	1.9	1.5	1.1	.9		1.6	1.6
1.8	1.6	1.4	1.1	.9	.7		1.0	1.1
	(18) 1.5	(44) 1.4	(36) 1.6		(12) 2.7	% Depr., Dep., Amort./Sales	(121) 1.4	(118) 1.8
	2.2	2.2	2.6		5.2		3.2	2.8
	4.5	3.9	5.0		6.0		5.0	4.7
		(22) 3.5				% Officers', Directors', Owners' Comp/Sales	(32) 3.2	(33) 3.9
		5.7					5.1	7.1
		11.1					10.4	14.8
10055M	58862M	442686M	1351163M	782516M	2442346M	Net Sales ($)	2882570M	3647763M
2706M	25203M	239675M	854171M	744353M	2374301M	Total Assets ($)	2333904M	2953974M

M = $ thousand   MM = $ million
See Pages 11 through 18 for Explanation of Ratios and Data

Comparative Historical Data | Current Data Sorted By Sales

			Type of Statement						
38	31	51	Unqualified	2	3	1	5	14	26
25	16	27	Reviewed	1	4	3	11	7	1
18	18	20	Compiled	1	7	4	4	3	1
3	1	3	Tax Returns		1		2		
26	36	49	Other	3	4	4	9	10	19
4/1/00-3/31/01 ALL	4/1/01-3/31/02 ALL	4/1/02-3/31/03 ALL		0-1MM	30 (4/1-9/30/02) 1-3MM	3-5MM	120 (10/1/02-3/31/03) 5-10MM	10-25MM	25MM & OVER
110	102	150	NUMBER OF STATEMENTS	7	19	12	31	34	47
%	%	%	ASSETS	%	%	%	%	%	%
11.5	9.0	12.2	Cash & Equivalents		13.3	13.3	10.5	11.7	13.3
25.6	25.3	23.6	Trade Receivables (net)		25.5	26.4	27.7	20.9	22.3
26.4	23.8	21.3	Inventory		20.7	22.3	26.8	19.9	19.0
4.2	3.4	4.0	All Other Current		2.9	3.3	3.8	5.0	4.1
67.7	61.5	61.2	Total Current		62.4	65.3	68.7	57.5	58.6
18.5	21.8	23.4	Fixed Assets (net)		23.1	25.6	19.8	26.9	21.6
7.3	10.0	8.4	Intangibles (net)		10.4	4.8	5.4	8.0	11.9
6.4	6.8	6.9	All Other Non-Current		4.0	4.4	6.1	7.5	7.8
100.0	100.0	100.0	Total		100.0	100.0	100.0	100.0	100.0
			LIABILITIES						
8.1	8.9	6.9	Notes Payable-Short Term		11.9	12.0	9.4	7.9	2.1
3.0	3.7	4.1	Cur. Mat.-L/T/D		7.5	5.8	3.3	4.1	3.2
11.9	14.6	11.6	Trade Payables		13.4	13.3	14.3	8.3	11.0
.8	.4	.8	Income Taxes Payable		1.1	4.1	.3	.4	.7
8.5	9.9	12.3	All Other Current		22.2	8.9	8.0	9.8	14.6
32.3	37.3	35.7	Total Current		56.1	44.0	35.3	30.5	31.7
12.5	14.0	12.7	Long Term Debt		12.9	11.6	8.9	12.2	14.5
.5	.7	.6	Deferred Taxes		.4	1.3	.1	.5	.9
3.8	5.5	5.1	All Other Non-Current		2.7	2.3	3.8	2.6	9.9
50.9	42.4	45.9	Net Worth		27.9	40.8	51.9	54.2	43.0
100.0	100.0	100.0	Total Liabilities & Net Worth		100.0	100.0	100.0	100.0	100.0
			INCOME DATA						
100.0	100.0	100.0	Net Sales		100.0	100.0	100.0	100.0	100.0
42.9	43.1	44.2	Gross Profit		48.1	41.5	41.9	42.8	45.5
37.8	36.7	35.3	Operating Expenses		41.9	37.2	33.1	34.3	34.7
5.2	6.4	8.9	Operating Profit		6.2	4.3	8.8	8.6	10.9
.5	2.5	1.7	All Other Expenses (net)		2.1	2.1	1.5	1.6	1.4
4.7	3.9	7.2	Profit Before Taxes		4.1	2.3	7.3	7.0	9.4
			RATIOS						
3.0	3.3	3.5	Current		3.9	4.1	3.5	3.8	3.1
2.4	1.7	2.0			1.8	1.3	1.7	2.1	2.5
1.5	1.1	1.2			.9	1.0	1.4	1.2	1.4
1.7	1.7	2.1	Quick		2.3	1.7	2.0	2.7	2.1
1.1	1.0	1.1			.8	.8	1.1	.9	1.2
.7	.6	.6			.4	.5	.6	.7	.7
42 8.8	40 9.0	37 9.8	Sales/Receivables	23 16.1	31 11.6	36 10.3	37 9.9	43 8.4	
53 6.8	55 6.7	48 7.6		42 8.6	47 7.8	47 7.8	47 7.8	53 6.9	
63 5.7	68 5.4	62 5.9		55 6.7	56 6.5	62 5.9	63 5.8	69 5.3	
58 6.3	52 7.0	48 7.7	Cost of Sales/Inventory	36 10.2	31 11.7	49 7.4	48 7.7	63 5.8	
108 3.4	99 3.7	80 4.6		62 5.9	63 5.8	83 4.4	69 5.3	85 4.3	
152 2.4	147 2.5	122 3.0		123 3.0	100 3.7	122 3.0	125 2.9	128 2.9	
23 15.8	25 14.4	22 16.9	Cost of Sales/Payables	20 18.1	16 22.2	22 16.7	16 22.3	25 14.8	
35 10.3	40 9.0	31 11.6		30 12.3	34 10.8	29 12.4	29 12.6	35 10.5	
58 6.3	60 6.1	57 6.4		67 5.4	55 6.7	60 6.1	38 9.5	58 6.3	
3.0	3.7	3.3	Sales/Working Capital		3.7	3.9	3.7	2.7	3.3
5.1	6.3	6.1			10.2	16.5	8.1	6.7	4.8
8.3	79.7	16.9			-31.6	NM	12.8	22.7	8.4
11.2	9.1	19.4	EBIT/Interest	12.7	4.1	17.0	39.4	51.8	
(94) 2.9	(95) 2.5	(130) 5.3		(17) 2.7	(11) 2.0	(24) 5.4	(32) 5.4	(43) 8.9	
1.3	.6	1.8		1.0	1.6	2.3	1.3	2.6	
12.9	8.7	15.3	Net Profit + Depr., Dep., Amort./Cur. Mat. L/T/D				20.4	40.4	
(36) 4.1	(38) 2.0	(56) 2.8				(13) 1.8	(24) 9.2	
1.7	1.2	1.2				.9	1.6	
.2	.2	.2	Fixed/Worth		.2	.3	.1	.2	.2
.3	.6	.5			.5	.4	.4	.6	.7
.9	2.0	1.4			6.4	1.5	.9	1.7	1.2
.5	.5	.4	Debt/Worth		.6	.9	.5	.3	.6
1.0	1.3	1.3			2.8	2.1	1.4	1.3	1.2
2.5	4.9	3.1			-60.2	2.8	2.6	2.9	3.4
36.1	31.0	44.5	% Profit Before Taxes/Tangible Net Worth	44.6	20.5	47.2	37.2	57.4	
(103) 15.8	(84) 15.6	(135) 22.7		(14) 13.2	6.9	(30) 25.1	(32) 16.7	(40) 29.6	
2.8	-.6	7.3		2.6	3.4	16.9	1.3	7.9	
13.9	14.8	17.1	% Profit Before Taxes/Total Assets		15.1	7.4	18.2	15.3	18.1
5.8	4.5	9.1			4.9	2.1	12.7	8.5	12.7
1.1	-.1	2.0			.0	1.6	5.7	.8	3.4
31.7	18.6	18.3	Sales/Net Fixed Assets		28.6	22.8	36.9	17.9	9.7
9.9	8.0	7.4			7.3	12.2	12.9	6.8	5.6
4.9	4.0	4.3			4.6	6.3	5.4	2.6	4.3
2.2	2.2	2.2	Sales/Total Assets		2.7	2.8	2.5	2.1	1.9
1.7	1.6	1.6			2.0	1.7	1.9	1.4	1.5
1.1	1.0	1.2			1.3	1.5	1.4	1.1	1.0
.8	1.4	1.6	% Depr., Dep., Amort./Sales	1.6	1.0	1.7	1.5	1.8	
(86) 2.3	(87) 3.6	(124) 2.7		(15) 2.9	1.5	(24) 2.6	(29) 2.5	(41) 3.5	
4.1	5.1	5.0		4.7	3.2	4.8	5.4	5.2	
3.2	3.0	2.6	% Officers', Directors', Owners' Comp/Sales				2.4		
(30) 4.9	(22) 5.1	(41) 4.9					(13) 4.5		
4.1	6.8	10.5					7.5		
3980666M	2976576M	5087628M	Net Sales ($)	2644M	39247M	47957M	215163M	543839M	4238778M
3214797M	2687381M	4240409M	Total Assets ($)	2528M	25653M	25495M	125662M	468658M	3592413M

M = $ thousand   MM = $ million
See Pages 11 through 18 for Explanation of Ratios and Data

Current Data Sorted By Assets   Comparative Historical Data

						Type of Statement		
1	2	15	11	6	6	Unqualified	38	31
1	5	11	1			Reviewed	17	14
4	6	4				Compiled	16	20
1	3					Tax Returns	9	7
7	8	12	6	2	2	Other	40	20
	29 (4/1-9/30/02)		85 (10/1/02-3/31/03)				4/1/98-3/31/99	4/1/99-3/31/00
0-500M	500M-2MM	2-10MM	10-50MM	50-100MM	100-250MM		ALL	ALL
14	24	42	18	8	8	**NUMBER OF STATEMENTS**	120	92
%	%	%	%	%	%	**ASSETS**	%	%
7.4	4.2	6.4	7.4			Cash & Equivalents	8.9	8.2
38.8	32.1	27.1	24.9			Trade Receivables (net)	28.0	32.0
17.3	23.5	25.4	23.3			Inventory	23.2	25.1
1.2	2.7	3.9	2.0			All Other Current	2.4	1.9
64.8	62.4	62.9	57.6			Total Current	62.4	67.1
22.9	25.5	23.5	22.8			Fixed Assets (net)	23.3	22.3
2.4	7.3	8.3	13.2			Intangibles (net)	5.9	5.1
9.9	4.8	5.3	6.4			All Other Non-Current	8.4	5.5
100.0	100.0	100.0	100.0			Total	100.0	100.0
						LIABILITIES		
20.8	8.9	8.5	7.3			Notes Payable-Short Term	10.0	10.5
4.7	3.8	3.5	4.2			Cur. Mat.-L/T/D	3.2	2.8
15.9	15.5	11.9	14.9			Trade Payables	11.9	13.4
.9	.3	1.0	.5			Income Taxes Payable	.7	.4
18.2	9.4	9.5	8.0			All Other Current	9.2	14.9
60.4	37.9	34.4	34.8			Total Current	35.0	42.0
12.1	14.4	11.7	13.6			Long Term Debt	13.4	14.2
.0	1.1	.4	.2			Deferred Taxes	.4	.5
10.9	7.5	2.2	7.8			All Other Non-Current	6.3	5.9
16.6	39.1	51.2	43.6			Net Worth	44.9	37.4
100.0	100.0	100.0	100.0			Total Liabilities & Net Worth	100.0	100.0
						INCOME DATA		
100.0	100.0	100.0	100.0			Net Sales	100.0	100.0
45.5	48.3	41.1	40.7			Gross Profit	42.6	43.8
43.5	44.0	34.2	30.1			Operating Expenses	36.0	35.6
1.9	4.3	6.9	10.6			Operating Profit	6.6	8.1
.4	1.0	.5	1.3			All Other Expenses (net)	.7	1.6
1.6	3.3	6.5	9.4			Profit Before Taxes	5.8	6.5
						RATIOS		
3.3	3.0	3.4	3.0				3.2	3.6
1.6	1.6	1.9	1.7			Current	1.9	2.1
.8	1.1	1.1	1.2				1.2	1.4
2.4	1.8	1.8	1.5				1.9	2.1
1.3	1.0	1.0	.9			Quick	1.1	1.2
.3	.5	.7	.6				.6	.8
13 28.8	34 10.6	36 10.2	40 9.1				38 9.6	42 8.7
42 8.7	46 7.9	47 7.8	48 7.6			Sales/Receivables	48 7.6	48 7.6
86 4.2	62 5.9	57 6.4	55 6.7				62 5.9	61 5.9
0 UND	17 21.7	42 8.8	62 5.9				39 9.4	46 7.9
30 12.3	47 7.7	75 4.9	79 4.6			Cost of Sales/Inventory	66 5.5	73 5.0
65 5.6	139 2.6	112 3.3	104 3.5				107 3.4	106 3.4
1 341.5	18 19.8	19 19.6	27 13.7				18 19.9	18 19.8
29 12.6	40 9.1	30 12.3	38 9.7			Cost of Sales/Payables	29 12.4	30 12.0
65 5.6	68 5.4	47 7.8	64 5.7				47 7.8	50 7.3
5.4	6.5	4.2	4.5				4.6	4.3
14.3	15.2	8.3	9.3			Sales/Working Capital	7.9	6.6
-42.1	35.6	27.8	22.6				25.2	12.6
10.5	7.9	22.6	38.3				14.8	17.7
(11) 3.0	(22) 2.8	(34) 4.6	(17) 4.9			EBIT/Interest	(103) 3.7	(78) 5.5
1.5	1.2	2.3	2.3				1.7	2.1
		4.9	7.9				16.3	13.3
		(18) 2.7	(11) 3.6			Net Profit + Depr., Dep., Amort./Cur. Mat. L /T/D	(42) 3.4	(24) 5.1
		1.6	2.2				1.2	1.5
.0	.5	.3	.4				.3	.2
.8	.9	.4	.8			Fixed/Worth	.5	.5
-.6	1.7	1.1	3.1				1.4	1.3
.5	.6	.4	.6				.5	.4
1.4	2.5	1.1	2.4			Debt/Worth	1.2	1.4
-3.8	8.3	3.2	12.0				3.9	5.0
	79.1	37.6	132.5				46.8	62.9
	(21) 20.5	(39) 23.5	(15) 64.1			% Profit Before Taxes/Tangible Net Worth	(107) 20.3	(80) 29.9
	-6.4	10.2	5.1				6.0	11.0
19.4	20.4	19.0	43.8				20.2	22.0
4.0	4.1	8.0	8.4			% Profit Before Taxes/Total Assets	8.3	10.9
-.6	1.0	4.4	1.8				2.3	3.4
UND	34.6	19.2	15.6				22.8	22.1
16.6	17.4	9.9	8.9			Sales/Net Fixed Assets	9.0	13.4
10.2	4.6	5.2	5.2				5.0	5.9
4.9	3.2	2.6	2.4				2.9	2.9
3.3	2.6	2.1	1.7			Sales/Total Assets	2.2	2.1
2.4	1.6	1.6	1.2				1.5	1.7
1.2	1.2	1.5	1.7				1.1	1.1
(10) 1.9	(20) 2.0	(37) 1.9	(17) 2.7			% Depr., Dep., Amort./Sales	(106) 2.2	(77) 2.0
2.7	3.9	3.2	3.9				4.0	3.2
	4.1	4.5					2.5	4.7
	(10) 6.1	(10) 5.7				% Officers', Directors', Owners' Comp/Sales	(42) 4.2	(26) 6.9
	13.6	9.2					7.6	11.2
17870M	69688M	388944M	801689M	704388M	1891841M	Net Sales ($)	3479897M	2957904M
4711M	28829M	198760M	479304M	553704M	1277949M	Total Assets ($)	2324787M	1802676M

© RMA 2003   M = $ thousand   MM = $ million
See Pages 11 through 18 for Explanation of Ratios and Data

Comparative Historical Data | | | **Current Data Sorted By Sales**

4/1/00-3/31/01 ALL	4/1/01-3/31/02 ALL	4/1/02-3/31/03 ALL		0-1MM	1-3MM	3-5MM	5-10MM	10-25MM	25MM & OVER
			Type of Statement		29 (4/1-9/30/02)		85 (10/1/02-3/31/03)		
19	23	41	Unqualified		2	2	6	10	21
9	8	18	Reviewed (1)		5	4	5	2	1
16	16	14	Compiled (2)		7	1	3	1	
8	7	4	Tax Returns (1)		1	2			
35	31	37	Other (3)		8	4	5	7	10
87	85	114	**NUMBER OF STATEMENTS** — 7		23	13	19	20	32
%	%	%	**ASSETS** %		%	%	%	%	%
9.4	8.2	6.5	Cash & Equivalents		4.0	4.0	8.5	6.2	7.9
30.6	27.1	28.5	Trade Receivables (net)		32.0	30.6	27.0	27.1	24.0
23.4	23.9	23.0	Inventory		20.4	32.8	22.6	24.5	21.3
1.7	3.2	3.1	All Other Current		1.7	2.7	1.8	6.2	3.2
65.0	62.3	61.1	Total Current		58.1	70.1	59.9	63.9	56.4
19.6	23.2	24.3	Fixed Assets (net)		23.9	17.4	28.4	26.2	25.5
8.2	8.9	8.4	Intangibles (net)		12.7	5.0	5.3	6.6	11.4
7.2	5.6	6.2	All Other Non-Current		5.3	7.4	6.5	3.3	6.6
100.0	100.0	100.0	Total		100.0	100.0	100.0	100.0	100.0
			LIABILITIES						
10.5	9.6	9.3	Notes Payable-Short Term		9.5	23.6	8.2	5.7	6.4
2.7	3.1	3.7	Cur. Mat.-L/T/D		4.7	5.6	3.1	3.5	3.5
13.9	13.9	13.0	Trade Payables		11.5	24.4	11.2	12.0	11.2
.5	.2	.6	Income Taxes Payable		.8	.7	1.6	.4	.2
21.5	10.3	10.5	All Other Current		9.6	13.4	8.4	10.4	9.6
49.1	37.2	37.2	Total Current		36.1	67.7	32.5	32.1	30.8
13.0	13.7	13.8	Long Term Debt		19.7	4.6	13.7	10.0	16.7
.5	.8	.5	Deferred Taxes		.5	.1	1.0	.7	.5
4.2	12.1	5.5	All Other Non-Current		7.2	3.6	4.9	3.7	5.8
33.5	36.2	42.9	Net Worth		36.4	24.0	47.9	53.6	46.2
100.0	100.0	100.0	Total Liabilities & Net Worth		100.0	100.0	100.0	100.0	100.0
			INCOME DATA						
100.0	100.0	100.0	Net Sales		100.0	100.0	100.0	100.0	100.0
45.1	42.7	43.9	Gross Profit		51.8	45.5	44.2	39.9	43.3
37.9	37.1	37.9	Operating Expenses		46.8	42.0	36.5	33.4	35.6
7.1	5.6	6.0	Operating Profit		5.0	3.6	7.6	6.5	7.7
1.0	1.7	1.0	All Other Expenses (net)		1.5	.4	1.1	-.3	1.8
6.2	3.9	5.0	Profit Before Taxes		3.5	3.2	6.6	6.9	5.9
			RATIOS						
3.6	3.6	3.3	Current		3.3	2.4	2.6	3.5	3.3
1.8	2.0	1.9			1.5	1.1	2.0	2.0	2.0
1.1	1.2	1.2			1.1	1.0	1.4	1.5	1.2
2.2	2.2	1.9	Quick		2.1	.8	1.7	1.9	2.3
1.0	.9	1.0			1.0	.6	1.2	1.1	1.0
.5	.6	.5			.6	.4	.5	.8	.5
41 8.8	38 9.7	38 9.6	Sales/Receivables	42 8.7	32 11.3	34 10.7	38 9.7	44 8.4
51 7.2	50 7.3	47 7.7		53 6.9	42 8.7	41 8.9	47 7.8	51 7.2
66 5.5	64 6.5	59 6.2		67 5.5	57 6.4	56 6.5	54 6.7	57 6.4
40 9.0	34 10.8	37 10.0	Cost of Sales/Inventory	21 17.1	16 23.1	38 9.6	37 10.0	59 6.2
75 4.9	75 4.9	67 5.5		52 7.0	93 3.9	64 5.7	68 5.3	79 4.6
112 3.3	111 3.3	108 3.4		174 2.1	151 2.4	105 3.5	90 4.0	117 3.1
17 20.9	18 19.9	20 18.2	Cost of Sales/Payables	14 26.6	32 11.5	19 19.4	17 21.2	27 13.3
33 11.0	31 11.8	33 11.1		36 10.1	64 5.7	30 12.2	25 14.4	34 10.8
55 6.6	50 7.3	52 7.0		61 6.0	76 4.8	49 7.4	46 8.0	45 8.1
4.3	4.3	4.4	Sales/Working Capital		5.2	7.3	6.0	4.3	3.4
8.0	7.1	9.0			15.2	32.3	9.4	7.4	5.5
95.4	18.8	22.9			60.9	121.3	21.1	12.5	21.4
(78) 14.6	(75) 14.1	(100) 17.7	EBIT/Interest	(21) 8.9	(11) 4.5	(16) 19.0	(17) 62.4	(31) 19.0
4.0	3.7	3.8		3.0	2.3	3.6	11.7	4.9
1.2	1.5	1.7		1.1	1.5	1.7	3.7	1.4
(25) 13.1	(26) 14.8	(42) 8.0	Net Profit + Depr., Dep., Amort./Cur. Mat. L/T/D				(11) 10.3	(16) 17.4
3.5	2.4	2.7					2.9	5.2
1.7	1.0	1.5					1.8	2.3
.2	.2	.3	Fixed/Worth		.2	.2	.3	.3	.4
.6	.6	.7			.9	.4	.5	.6	.8
1.7	1.6	1.5			-1.7	.9	1.8	1.1	1.7
.4	.5	.6	Debt/Worth		.5	1.0	.6	.3	.6
1.5	1.6	1.5			2.2	3.0	1.1	1.2	2.0
4.2	6.1	4.7			-9.5	6.1	3.3	2.7	6.2
(70) 47.3	(70) 37.0	(99) 48.2	% Profit Before Taxes/Tangible Net Worth	(16) 46.7	(12) 90.2	(18) 42.3	(18) 36.6	(29) 76.5
24.8	18.4	19.9		10.8	26.6	29.9	22.3	19.9
6.6	5.7	4.7		-10.2	7.6	7.8	11.9	3.3
19.5	15.6	20.1	% Profit Before Taxes/Total Assets		17.1	12.6	26.1	19.6	31.7
9.9	7.1	6.9			7.2	4.9	7.1	9.4	4.0
1.5	1.8	1.8			.6	2.5	1.8	5.8	1.5
28.8	28.1	20.7	Sales/Net Fixed Assets		33.8	38.8	18.8	18.6	13.0
13.4	11.4	10.4			11.9	20.2	10.4	8.2	7.5
6.5	4.6	4.9			4.6	14.4	4.3	5.2	4.0
2.7	2.9	2.8	Sales/Total Assets		2.8	3.2	2.8	3.2	2.2
2.1	1.8	2.1			2.0	2.7	2.4	2.2	1.5
1.4	1.3	1.4			1.2	1.7	1.7	1.6	1.1
(71) 1.1	(68) 1.0	(95) 1.5	% Depr., Dep., Amort./Sales	(17) 1.2	(12) 1.4	(18) 1.2	(17) 1.6	(26) 2.2
1.8	2.2	2.3		2.3	1.8	1.6	2.0	2.8
3.1	3.9	3.6		5.8	2.1	3.6	2.7	4.4
(30) 2.7	(25) 3.3	(28) 4.2	% Officers', Directors', Owners' Comp/Sales	(10) 6.2				
8.2	7.4	5.6		10.3				
13.2	12.5			15.2				
2713630M	2653408M	3874420M	Net Sales ($)	5830M	41900M	49783M	134494M	288158M	3354255M
1960648M	2028680M	2543257M	Total Assets ($)	2092M	26971M	22022M	70202M	149573M	2272397M

© RMA 2003

M = $ thousand   MM = $ million
See Pages 11 through 18 for Explanation of Ratios and Data

Current Data Sorted By Assets | Comparative Historical Data

			1	5	3		Type of Statement		
	2	2	2	2			Unqualified	10	11
	2	4	1				Reviewed	9	11
1	4						Compiled	4	4
1	1	1	5	7	2		Tax Returns	1	2
	5 (4/1-9/30/02)			34 (10/1/02-3/31/03)			Other	10	8
								4/1/98-3/31/99	4/1/99-3/31/00
0-500M	500M-2MM	2-10MM	10-50MM	50-100MM	100-250MM			ALL	ALL
2	9	9	14	5		NUMBER OF STATEMENTS		34	36
%	%	%	%	%	%	ASSETS	%	%	%
			9.4			D	Cash & Equivalents	8.7	8.8
			24.8			A	Trade Receivables (net)	24.3	25.5
			21.2			T	Inventory	25.4	28.4
			2.6			A	All Other Current	2.5	2.3
			58.0				Total Current	60.9	65.0
			27.1			N	Fixed Assets (net)	23.7	21.3
			10.6			O	Intangibles (net)	5.2	7.1
			4.3			T	All Other Non-Current	10.2	6.5
			100.0				Total	100.0	100.0
						A	LIABILITIES		
			6.8			V	Notes Payable-Short Term	7.3	7.0
			4.4			A	Cur. Mat.-L/T/D	2.1	3.9
			8.0			I	Trade Payables	9.3	10.5
			.8			L	Income Taxes Payable	.1	.3
			11.1			A	All Other Current	11.4	8.9
			31.2			B	Total Current	30.2	30.5
			14.4			L	Long Term Debt	10.4	14.1
			.9			E	Deferred Taxes	.1	.3
			8.7				All Other Non-Current	7.8	7.6
			44.9				Net Worth	51.5	47.5
			100.0				Total Liabilities & Net Worth	100.0	100.0
							INCOME DATA		
			100.0				Net Sales	100.0	100.0
			44.3				Gross Profit	45.6	43.4
			39.6				Operating Expenses	38.8	38.3
			4.7				Operating Profit	6.8	5.1
			.9				All Other Expenses (net)	.6	1.0
			3.9				Profit Before Taxes	6.2	4.2
							RATIOS		
			3.4					3.2	3.3
			2.1				Current	2.2	2.6
			1.3					1.6	1.7
			1.9					2.1	2.1
			1.2				Quick	1.2	1.3
			.8					.7	.8
		38	9.6			36	Sales/Receivables	10.2	36 10.0
		46	7.9			46		7.9	49 7.5
		56	6.5			58		6.3	57 6.4
		55	6.6			70	Cost of Sales/Inventory	5.2	70 5.2
		84	4.3			101		3.6	103 3.5
		111	3.3			139		2.6	141 2.6
		16	22.4			17	Cost of Sales/Payables	21.2	21 17.3
		23	15.6			32		11.3	30 12.3
		53	6.8			49		7.4	48 7.7
			3.6				Sales/Working Capital	3.4	3.3
			7.4					6.1	5.5
			18.6					10.3	10.9
			10.0				EBIT/Interest	10.2	13.4
			3.3			(29)		6.1	(33) 3.2
			1.4					1.3	1.5
							Net Profit + Depr., Dep., Amort./Cur. Mat. L./T/D	4.9	6.1
						(11)		3.6	(14) 2.1
								1.9	.7
			.4				Fixed/Worth	.2	.2
			.8					.4	.5
			1.6					1.0	1.2
			.5				Debt/Worth	.4	.5
			1.9					.8	1.1
			3.5					2.0	3.4
			27.1				% Profit Before Taxes/Tangible Net Worth	34.9	35.1
		(12)	10.3			(30)		15.8	(33) 17.5
			.3					3.6	4.3
			15.4				% Profit Before Taxes/Total Assets	18.5	14.8
			7.0					10.7	5.0
			.3					1.8	1.4
			13.5				Sales/Net Fixed Assets	21.6	19.1
			7.6					10.5	12.2
			3.8					5.5	5.2
			2.2				Sales/Total Assets	2.5	2.9
			1.8					1.9	1.8
			1.4					1.4	1.4
			1.6				% Depr., Dep., Amort./Sales	1.3	1.2
		(11)	2.4			(26)		2.4	(33) 1.9
			4.9					3.8	3.8
							% Officers', Directors', Owners' Comp/Sales		4.3
								(11)	7.6
									14.0
823M	37351M	87741M	568882M	498188M		Net Sales ($)		1000410M	1018360M
273M	11384M	41899M	297631M	352569M		Total Assets ($)		549280M	612731M

M = $ thousand   MM = $ million
See Pages 11 through 18 for Explanation of Ratios and Data

Comparative Historical Data | Current Data Sorted By Sales

	4/1/00-3/31/01 ALL		4/1/01-3/31/02 ALL		4/1/02-3/31/03 ALL			5 (4/1-9/30/02)		34 (10/1/02-3/31/03)		
						Type of Statement	0-1MM	1-3MM	3-5MM	5-10MM	10-25MM	25MM & OVER
	8		9		9	Unqualified				1	2	6
	7		3		6	Reviewed			1	2	2	1
	7		9		3	Compiled			2	1		
	4				5	Tax Returns	2		2	1		
	9		10		16	Other	1		1	3	3	8
	35		31		39	NUMBER OF STATEMENTS	3		6	8	7	15
	%		%		%	ASSETS	%	%	%	%	%	%
	8.2		9.8		9.8	Cash & Equivalents						11.3
	32.3		23.6		24.2	Trade Receivables (net)						24.7
	26.2		24.9		24.9	Inventory						22.5
	1.7		2.9		2.0	All Other Current						2.7
	68.3		61.3		60.9	Total Current	D A T A					61.2
	17.3		25.6		25.5	Fixed Assets (net)						22.8
	6.5		6.5		8.6	Intangibles (net)	N O T					12.7
	7.9		6.6		5.0	All Other Non-Current						3.4
	100.0		100.0		100.0	Total	A V A					100.0
						LIABILITIES	I L A B					
	9.8		10.0		7.1	Notes Payable-Short Term	L E					6.0
	4.3		2.5		2.9	Cur. Mat.-L/T/D						2.8
	12.7		8.5		11.6	Trade Payables						7.7
	.6		.8		.3	Income Taxes Payable						.8
	9.2		13.2		11.6	All Other Current						13.1
	36.6		35.0		33.6	Total Current						30.3
	14.2		11.7		13.1	Long Term Debt						12.8
	.4		.7		.5	Deferred Taxes						1.2
	6.2		2.2		6.2	All Other Non-Current						6.1
	42.7		50.4		46.5	Net Worth						49.6
	100.0		100.0		100.0	Total Liabilities & Net Worth						100.0
						INCOME DATA						
	100.0		100.0		100.0	Net Sales						100.0
	45.9		45.9		49.3	Gross Profit						48.2
	40.9		38.8		41.3	Operating Expenses						39.5
	5.0		7.1		8.0	Operating Profit						8.7
	.8		.3		.8	All Other Expenses (net)						.4
	4.2		6.7		7.1	Profit Before Taxes						8.3
						RATIOS						
	3.1 / 2.1 / 1.3		3.0 / 1.7 / 1.5		3.0 / 1.7 / 1.3	Current						3.2 / 2.4 / 1.4
	1.5 / 1.1 / .8		1.5 / 1.0 / .7		1.7 / 1.1 / .7	Quick						1.7 / 1.2 / 1.0
39 / 49 / 60	9.2 / 7.5 / 6.1	42 / 46 / 58	8.8 / 8.0 / 6.3	32 / 44 / 52	11.5 / 8.3 / 7.1	Sales/Receivables					36 / 47 / 58	10.1 / 7.8 / 6.3
27 / 93 / 165	13.4 / 3.9 / 2.2	63 / 91 / 166	5.8 / 4.0 / 2.2	44 / 83 / 132	8.2 / 4.4 / 2.8	Cost of Sales/Inventory					61 / 85 / 120	6.0 / 4.3 / 3.0
19 / 31 / 54	19.1 / 11.6 / 6.8	16 / 26 / 47	22.4 / 14.1 / 7.8	18 / 29 / 53	19.8 / 12.8 / 6.8	Cost of Sales/Payables					23 / 25 / 49	16.0 / 14.5 / 7.5
	3.3 / 5.8 / 17.6		3.4 / 5.2 / 16.2		4.3 / 8.6 / 23.4	Sales/Working Capital						2.9 / 6.3 / 11.3
(31)	10.2 / 3.5 / 2.3	(25)	9.9 / 6.4 / 1.7	(34)	16.6 / 6.0 / 1.7	EBIT/Interest					(14)	15.7 / 8.9 / 2.6
(15)	4.5 / 1.8 / .8			(12)	10.9 / 1.9 / .9	Net Profit + Depr., Dep., Amort./Cur. Mat. L/T/D						
	.2 / .5 / .9		.2 / .5 / 1.1		.3 / .6 / 1.3	Fixed/Worth						.3 / .5 / 1.5
	.7 / 1.4 / 2.5		.6 / 1.2 / 2.2		.7 / 1.6 / 3.2	Debt/Worth						.4 / 1.2 / 3.4
(32)	48.5 / 22.4 / 11.6	(29)	48.7 / 22.9 / 11.8	(37)	61.9 / 22.8 / 4.9	% Profit Before Taxes/Tangible Net Worth					(13)	50.6 / 27.7 / 10.3
	15.9 / 7.6 / 3.9		20.3 / 11.3 / 3.9		21.6 / 10.2 / 1.6	% Profit Before Taxes/Total Assets						18.3 / 13.3 / 6.2
	25.4 / 15.6 / 6.1		16.5 / 8.5 / 5.0		16.8 / 8.9 / 4.9	Sales/Net Fixed Assets						12.6 / 8.3 / 5.7
	2.8 / 2.0 / 1.2		2.5 / 1.9 / 1.3		3.0 / 2.1 / 1.3	Sales/Total Assets						2.1 / 1.7 / 1.2
(31)	.9 / 1.6 / 2.6	(28)	.6 / 2.1 / 4.2	(32)	1.3 / 2.1 / 3.5	% Depr., Dep., Amort./Sales					(12)	2.0 / 2.2 / 3.5
(12)	3.3 / 7.4 / 16.2			(13)	2.0 / 4.2 / 11.1	% Officers', Directors', Owners' Comp/Sales						
	824534M		1082709M		1192985M	Net Sales ($)	1305M		24444M	54904M	127868M	984464M
	426351M		679408M		703756M	Total Assets ($)	887M		7606M	30066M	77085M	588112M

M = $ thousand   MM = $ million
See Pages 11 through 18 for Explanation of Ratios and Data

Current Data Sorted By Assets

Comparative Historical Data

						Type of Statement		
1		1	3	1	1	Unqualified	17	9
	4	4		1		Reviewed	10	7
1	3	1				Compiled	8	6
	2	1				Tax Returns	3	3
3	2	1	5			Other	10	5
	7 (4/1-9/30/02)		28 (10/1/02-3/31/03)				4/1/98-3/31/99	4/1/99-3/31/00
0-500M	500M-2MM	2-10MM	10-50MM	50-100MM	100-250MM		ALL	ALL
5	11	8	8	2	1	NUMBER OF STATEMENTS	48	30
%	%	%	%	%	%	ASSETS	%	%
	11.1					Cash & Equivalents	8.5	9.5
	32.8					Trade Receivables (net)	24.8	26.0
	22.3					Inventory	23.6	22.5
	1.3					All Other Current	1.4	2.5
	67.5					Total Current	58.3	60.6
	15.3					Fixed Assets (net)	27.4	30.5
	14.1					Intangibles (net)	7.2	5.1
	3.1					All Other Non-Current	7.0	3.8
	100.0					Total	100.0	100.0
						LIABILITIES		
	9.1					Notes Payable-Short Term	8.1	6.8
	5.1					Cur. Mat.-L/T/D	3.4	3.8
	14.7					Trade Payables	15.0	16.3
	.4					Income Taxes Payable	.7	.3
	8.2					All Other Current	8.2	11.5
	37.5					Total Current	35.5	38.8
	21.8					Long Term Debt	19.1	15.1
	.4					Deferred Taxes	.7	.5
	12.8					All Other Non-Current	4.4	5.3
	27.5					Net Worth	40.4	40.3
	100.0					Total Liabilities & Net Worth	100.0	100.0
						INCOME DATA		
	100.0					Net Sales	100.0	100.0
	43.6					Gross Profit	42.8	40.0
	38.3					Operating Expenses	36.7	34.4
	5.3					Operating Profit	6.1	5.6
	1.5					All Other Expenses (net)	1.1	.8
	3.8					Profit Before Taxes	4.9	4.8
						RATIOS		
	2.4						2.6	2.7
	1.9					Current	1.7	1.8
	1.2						1.3	1.3
	1.9						1.7	1.8
	1.1					Quick	1.0	1.0
	.7						.6	.5

31	11.6						Sales/Receivables	33	11.2	32	11.2
36	10.3							41	8.8	38	9.6
44	8.3							54	6.8	48	7.7
19	19.5						Cost of Sales/Inventory	20	17.8	22	16.9
53	6.9							63	5.8	42	8.8
76	4.8							153	2.4	135	2.7
17	21.8						Cost of Sales/Payables	22	16.8	23	16.1
24	15.3							37	9.8	35	10.3
30	12.2							61	6.0	57	6.4

	7.5						Sales/Working Capital		5.2		5.7
	9.3								10.0		10.4
	35.2								20.7		24.4
	17.9						EBIT/Interest		9.5		11.3
(10)	2.4							(42)	3.3	(27)	6.4
	1.2								.8		2.1
							Net Profit + Depr., Dep., Amort./Cur. Mat. L /T/D		9.6		
								(17)	2.3		
									.6		
	.4						Fixed/Worth		.4		.4
	.6								.6		.6
	-5.1								2.0		2.1
	1.9						Debt/Worth		.7		.7
	3.8								1.3		1.9
	-29.6								5.0		3.8
							% Profit Before Taxes/Tangible Net Worth		52.1		57.8
								(41)	22.3	(27)	25.0
									-2.9		10.9
	31.8						% Profit Before Taxes/Total Assets		19.6		23.1
	4.8								6.9		8.4
	.3								-.3		3.5
	25.3						Sales/Net Fixed Assets		21.5		25.4
	20.5								10.5		10.1
	11.4								5.1		4.3
	4.0						Sales/Total Assets		3.6		3.8
	3.4								2.4		2.7
	1.8								1.4		1.5
							% Depr., Dep., Amort./Sales		1.0		.8
								(42)	1.8	(27)	2.3
									2.7		3.8
							% Officers', Directors', Owners' Comp/Sales		3.3		3.7
								(14)	6.4	(12)	6.0
									12.4		17.0

5007M	40583M	83115M	329890M	178965M	321690M	Net Sales ($)	1398599M	689918M
1199M	12101M	29701M	166621M	116644M	218534M	Total Assets ($)	998682M	478324M

M = $ thousand   MM = $ million
See Pages 11 through 18 for Explanation of Ratios and Data

Comparative Historical Data | Current Data Sorted By Sales

			Type of Statement						
6	7	7	Unqualified	1			1		5
7	5	9	Reviewed		1	1	4	2	1
6	6	5	Compiled	1	1	1	2		
2	2	3	Tax Returns		2			1	
9	4	11	Other	2	2	1	1	3	2
4/1/00-3/31/01 ALL	4/1/01-3/31/02 ALL	4/1/02-3/31/03 ALL		7 (4/1-9/30/02)			28 (10/1/02-3/31/03)		
				0-1MM	1-3MM	3-5MM	5-10MM	10-25MM	25MM & OVER
30	24	35	NUMBER OF STATEMENTS	4	6	3	8	6	8
%	%	%	ASSETS	%	%	%	%	%	%
10.9	10.0	9.3	Cash & Equivalents						
26.0	29.3	26.9	Trade Receivables (net)						
22.3	26.6	27.1	Inventory						
2.2	2.5	2.6	All Other Current						
61.5	68.3	65.9	Total Current						
27.8	20.7	20.2	Fixed Assets (net)						
7.6	6.9	9.1	Intangibles (net)						
3.2	4.0	4.7	All Other Non-Current						
100.0	100.0	100.0	Total						
			LIABILITIES						
9.9	9.7	9.0	Notes Payable-Short Term						
4.5	7.6	4.8	Cur. Mat.-L/T/D						
13.3	15.3	14.2	Trade Payables						
.0	.3	.4	Income Taxes Payable						
12.0	15.1	10.4	All Other Current						
39.8	48.0	38.8	Total Current						
15.7	16.1	19.1	Long Term Debt						
.6	.4	.4	Deferred Taxes						
4.4	5.7	6.7	All Other Non-Current						
39.5	29.9	35.0	Net Worth						
100.0	100.0	100.0	Total Liabilities & Net Worth						
			INCOME DATA						
100.0	100.0	100.0	Net Sales						
38.9	39.9	47.1	Gross Profit						
34.9	35.9	40.8	Operating Expenses						
4.0	4.0	6.2	Operating Profit						
1.3	1.6	1.3	All Other Expenses (net)						
2.7	2.4	4.9	Profit Before Taxes						
			RATIOS						
2.2	2.4	2.5	Current						
1.5	1.7	1.8							
1.1	1.2	1.2							
1.9	1.6	1.6	Quick						
.8	.9	1.0							
.5	.6	.5							
33 11.0	40 9.1	23 16.1	Sales/Receivables						
40 9.1	45 8.1	38 9.7							
49 7.5	65 5.6	47 7.8							
25 14.7	31 11.7	32 11.5	Cost of Sales/Inventory						
45 8.1	84 4.3	89 4.1							
122 3.0	137 2.7	132 2.8							
18 20.4	24 15.3	22 16.7	Cost of Sales/Payables						
25 14.7	34 10.7	31 11.8							
43 8.5	67 5.4	51 7.2							
6.9	4.1	7.5	Sales/Working Capital						
12.0	9.1	9.3							
67.3	17.1	19.4							
(27) 4.8	(22) 7.0	(32) 13.9	EBIT/Interest						
2.6	4.5	6.0							
1.1	.5	2.3							
		(13) 6.9	Net Profit + Depr., Dep., Amort./Cur. Mat. L/T/D						
		3.2							
		1.2							
.5	.4	.4	Fixed/Worth						
.8	.6	.6							
2.2	1.4	1.9							
.9	.7	1.0	Debt/Worth						
1.9	1.3	2.3							
5.7	13.9	13.0							
42.0	41.8	63.8	% Profit Before Taxes/Tangible Net Worth						
(27) 17.0	(19) 17.1	(29) 34.2							
2.5	8.3	16.6							
12.4	15.9	23.2	% Profit Before Taxes/Total Assets						
6.5	5.5	8.5							
-.1	-2.6	4.2							
18.1	23.6	24.3	Sales/Net Fixed Assets						
13.0	11.7	14.0							
5.6	6.8	10.1							
3.2	3.0	3.5	Sales/Total Assets						
2.2	2.2	2.4							
1.4	1.4	1.8							
1.5	.7	1.6	% Depr., Dep., Amort./Sales						
(26) 2.7	(22) 1.8	(27) 2.0							
3.7	2.9	3.1							
.6		3.9	% Officers', Directors', Owners' Comp/Sales						
(11) 3.5		(19) 8.4							
12.6		16.5							
617718M	600720M	959250M	Net Sales ($)	2262M	11403M	11565M	62496M	87121M	784403M
414992M	365308M	544800M	Total Assets ($)	1367M	3670M	2688M	22120M	51428M	463527M

M = $ thousand   MM = $ million
See Pages 11 through 18 for Explanation of Ratios and Data

Current Data Sorted By Assets / Comparative Historical Data

0-500M	500M-2MM	2-10MM	10-50MM	50-100MM	100-250MM		4/1/98-3/31/99 ALL	4/1/99-3/31/00 ALL
						Type of Statement		
1		2	1	1		Unqualified	3	4
1	1	1	1			Reviewed	9	5
5	7					Compiled	16	19
6	1					Tax Returns	2	6
5	1	1				Other	5	5
12 (4/1-9/30/02)			23 (10/1/02-3/31/03)					
18	10	4	2	1		**NUMBER OF STATEMENTS**	35	39
%	%	%	%	%	%	**ASSETS**	%	%
13.1	10.3				DATA NOT AVAILABLE	Cash & Equivalents	12.0	11.8
21.2	33.2					Trade Receivables (net)	34.4	30.8
3.5	5.8					Inventory	9.7	6.3
2.1	1.4					All Other Current	3.9	2.1
39.9	50.7					Total Current	60.0	51.0
40.3	29.4					Fixed Assets (net)	22.7	29.7
8.1	10.1					Intangibles (net)	6.6	9.7
11.6	9.7					All Other Non-Current	10.7	9.5
100.0	100.0					Total	100.0	100.0
						LIABILITIES		
15.9	9.9					Notes Payable-Short Term	5.5	8.0
14.7	5.3					Cur. Mat.-L/T/D	4.5	5.5
6.3	11.7					Trade Payables	9.3	9.2
.2	.2					Income Taxes Payable	.5	1.4
15.8	7.2					All Other Current	12.1	10.5
53.0	34.3					Total Current	32.0	34.7
25.8	22.0					Long Term Debt	19.3	27.5
.0	.9					Deferred Taxes	.4	.3
14.3	5.2					All Other Non-Current	1.9	3.2
6.9	37.6					Net Worth	46.4	34.3
100.0	100.0					Total Liabilities & Net Worth	100.0	100.0
						INCOME DATA		
100.0	100.0					Net Sales	100.0	100.0
						Gross Profit		
85.2	95.3					Operating Expenses	94.5	91.1
14.8	4.7					Operating Profit	5.5	8.9
.9	1.1					All Other Expenses (net)	.3	.7
13.9	3.6					Profit Before Taxes	5.2	8.2
						RATIOS		
2.6	3.2						3.4	2.2
.9	2.5					Current	2.1	1.6
.2	1.0						1.3	.8
2.5	2.9						2.4	1.9
.9	2.3					Quick	1.6	1.2
.1	.7						.8	.6
0 UND	**0** UND						**36** 10.2	**30** 12.3
1 453.7	**36** 10.2					Sales/Receivables	**44** 8.2	**39** 9.3
31 11.9	**41** 8.9						**51** 7.1	**48** 7.7
						Cost of Sales/Inventory		
						Cost of Sales/Payables		
10.6	8.8						6.2	9.5
−227.0	21.0					Sales/Working Capital	9.3	18.9
−15.5	NM						19.6	−34.8
20.5							10.3	10.8
(15) 13.3						EBIT/Interest	(31) 4.2	(33) 4.7
3.1							2.0	2.1
							4.9	3.6
						Net Profit + Depr., Dep., Amort./Cur. Mat. L/T/D	(16) 2.9	(17) 2.3
							1.8	.9
.4	.3						.3	.5
1.1	1.1					Fixed/Worth	.6	.9
−1.5	UND						1.0	UND
.4	.6						.6	.8
2.8	3.3					Debt/Worth	.9	2.0
−2.7	UND						1.9	UND
272.1							57.9	64.2
(11) 60.1						% Profit Before Taxes/Tangible Net Worth	(32) 17.9	(30) 20.8
10.4							4.0	8.3
71.6	16.9						17.1	18.6
30.9	−.7					% Profit Before Taxes/Total Assets	9.1	8.6
6.5	−5.4						2.8	5.5
21.7	29.9						24.2	23.5
11.7	12.3					Sales/Net Fixed Assets	15.2	12.7
7.7	7.6						9.1	7.0
6.2	4.4						4.2	4.0
4.8	3.6					Sales/Total Assets	3.1	2.9
3.4	3.1						2.5	2.1
1.0							1.7	1.4
2.0						% Depr., Dep., Amort./Sales	(32) 2.0	(35) 2.2
4.4							2.6	3.1
5.5							2.6	3.0
(14) 10.4						% Officers', Directors', Owners' Comp/Sales	(14) 11.4	(18) 11.2
24.6							16.0	19.7
17520M	**36819M**	**33944M**	**65685M**	**95185M**		Net Sales ($)	**152460M**	**322090M**
3949M	**9829M**	**12001M**	**28721M**	**65817M**		Total Assets ($)	**59822M**	**188733M**

M = $ thousand MM = $ million

See Pages 11 through 18 for Explanation of Ratios and Data

Comparative Historical Data | Current Data Sorted By Sales

4/1/00-3/31/01 ALL	4/1/01-3/31/02 ALL	4/1/02-3/31/03 ALL	Type of Statement	0-1MM	1-3MM	3-5MM	5-10MM	10-25MM	25MM & OVER
2	6	5	Unqualified	1			1	1	2
3	3	4	Reviewed		2		1	1	
12	14	12	Compiled	1	6	3	2		
5	1	7	Tax Returns	5	2		1		
6	5	7	Other	3	2	1	1		
				12 (4/1-9/30/02)		23 (10/1/02-3/31/03)			
28	29	35	**NUMBER OF STATEMENTS**	10	12	4	5	2	2
%	%	%	**ASSETS**	%	%	%	%	%	%
13.6	13.2	13.4	Cash & Equivalents	12.2	14.3				
32.2	31.3	25.1	Trade Receivables (net)	16.8	23.0				
8.6	7.5	5.4	Inventory	3.9	2.4				
1.5	.5	1.7	All Other Current	1.3	2.7				
55.9	52.5	45.6	Total Current	34.1	42.4				
27.7	32.5	34.6	Fixed Assets (net)	35.1	42.8				
6.9	8.1	8.4	Intangibles (net)	21.2	1.3				
9.6	6.9	11.4	All Other Non-Current	9.6	13.5				
100.0	100.0	100.0	Total	100.0	100.0				
			LIABILITIES						
14.4	9.5	12.2	Notes Payable-Short Term	1.6	27.7				
9.4	5.1	9.9	Cur. Mat.-L/T/D	13.1	12.5				
16.8	10.1	8.8	Trade Payables	4.3	6.9				
.3	.3	.2	Income Taxes Payable	.2	.1				
8.8	12.1	12.3	All Other Current	13.0	14.7				
49.7	37.1	43.4	Total Current	32.2	61.8				
26.9	20.5	23.6	Long Term Debt	34.9	20.5				
1.0	.5	.2	Deferred Taxes	.0	.2				
2.5	8.4	12.0	All Other Non-Current	22.4	2.8				
19.9	33.5	20.8	Net Worth	10.5	14.6				
100.0	100.0	100.0	Total Liabilities & Net Worth	100.0	100.0				
			INCOME DATA						
100.0	100.0	100.0	Net Sales	100.0	100.0				
			Gross Profit						
93.5	94.8	90.4	Operating Expenses	75.9	93.9				
6.5	5.2	9.6	Operating Profit	24.1	6.1				
1.3	.8	1.1	All Other Expenses (net)	1.1	1.1				
5.2	4.4	8.5	Profit Before Taxes	22.9	5.0				
			RATIOS						
2.3	2.4	2.9		6.7	2.4				
1.5	1.4	1.4	Current	1.7	1.1				
.9	1.0	.7		.2	.2				
2.1	2.1	2.4		6.2	2.3				
1.0	1.2	1.1	Quick	1.2	1.0				
.7	.8	.6		.1	.1				
16 23.1	33 11.1	0 UND		0 UND	0 UND				
38 9.5	39 9.4	31 11.9	Sales/Receivables	0 UND	30 12.3				
46 8.0	43 8.5	39 9.5		25 14.4	35 10.4				
			Cost of Sales/Inventory						
			Cost of Sales/Payables						
9.4	8.9	9.1		7.3	10.0				
19.5	23.0	29.2	Sales/Working Capital	NM	NM				
-241.6	403.3	-26.2		-22.3	-8.3				
6.8	9.0	14.2			16.5				
(25) 2.0	(25) 3.3	(29) 4.7	EBIT/Interest		5.8				
.9	1.7	.1			-.4				
		8.8	Net Profit + Depr., Dep.,						
		(11) 1.1	Amort./Cur. Mat. L/T/D						
		.5							
.5	.4	.3		.3	.4				
1.4	1.3	1.0	Fixed/Worth	NM	1.0				
-3.2	6.7	-6.0		-1.2	UND				
1.0	.6	.6		.2	.5				
2.6	1.9	2.5	Debt/Worth	NM	2.8				
-6.5	11.7	-17.1		-2.4	UND				
62.9	41.6	69.5	% Profit Before Taxes/Tangible						
(19) 17.8	(23) 19.3	(26) 20.9	Net Worth						
.0	11.5	-2.4							
28.3	16.9	32.7	% Profit Before Taxes/Total	117.3	32.1				
8.3	10.8	14.5	Assets	51.2	10.8				
.4	2.5	-2.7		17.2	-10.0				
35.6	21.1	19.6		22.9	25.2				
19.1	12.6	12.3	Sales/Net Fixed Assets	10.2	12.8				
8.5	7.4	7.8		7.7	7.4				
6.0	4.3	5.3		6.0	6.0				
3.4	3.4	3.9	Sales/Total Assets	4.2	4.1				
2.3	2.3	2.5		2.0	3.4				
1.8	1.3	1.5		.9	1.6				
(21) 1.9	(23) 2.1	(33) 2.0	% Depr., Dep., Amort./Sales	2.3	(11) 2.4				
3.0	2.7	3.6		5.9	3.7				
3.9	5.5	3.3	% Officers', Directors',						
(16) 8.4	(14) 8.3	(20) 7.6	Owners' Comp/Sales						
21.2	20.2	13.0							
167618M	266698M	249153M	Net Sales ($)	5228M	19856M	16896M	30825M	25957M	150391M
51104M	134024M	120317M	Total Assets ($)	1825M	4788M	4563M	10198M	14461M	84482M

© RMA 2003

M = $ thousand   MM = $ million
See Pages 11 through 18 for Explanation of Ratios and Data

Current Data Sorted By Assets   Comparative Historical Data

0-500M	500M-2MM	2-10MM	10-50MM	50-100MM	100-250MM	Type of Statement	4/1/98-3/31/99 ALL	4/1/99-3/31/00 ALL
	12	2	9	1	3	Unqualified	40	18
2	8	32	8		1	Reviewed	45	38
1	5	1	2			Compiled	20	15
1						Tax Returns	4	5
1	7	5	1	2	3	Other	23	20
	25 (4/1-9/30/02)		81 (10/1/02-3/31/03)					
4	32	40	20	3	7	**NUMBER OF STATEMENTS**	132	96
%	%	%	%	%	%	**ASSETS**	%	%
	9.4	4.9	6.5			Cash & Equivalents	5.1	7.7
	28.5	33.1	33.3			Trade Receivables (net)	28.8	27.1
	44.4	45.2	48.4			Inventory	47.1	46.5
	1.1	.9	.4			All Other Current	1.0	1.0
	83.4	84.1	88.7			Total Current	82.1	82.2
	12.2	9.7	6.4			Fixed Assets (net)	11.2	10.8
	1.2	.4	3.3			Intangibles (net)	2.4	2.8
	3.1	5.8	1.5			All Other Non-Current	4.3	4.2
	100.0	100.0	100.0			Total	100.0	100.0
						LIABILITIES		
	16.8	17.3	18.4			Notes Payable-Short Term	20.7	15.0
	1.7	1.5	1.1			Cur. Mat.-L/T/D	2.4	2.5
	19.9	18.5	22.1			Trade Payables	14.7	17.9
	.0	.2	.5			Income Taxes Payable	.5	.5
	7.2	9.7	13.8			All Other Current	8.4	6.9
	45.7	47.3	55.9			Total Current	46.6	42.9
	6.7	4.4	1.9			Long Term Debt	6.2	7.7
	.0	.0	.2			Deferred Taxes	.2	.1
	3.7	1.1	1.8			All Other Non-Current	7.6	6.6
	44.0	47.3	40.2			Net Worth	39.3	42.6
	100.0	100.0	100.0			Total Liabilities & Net Worth	100.0	100.0
						INCOME DATA		
	100.0	100.0	100.0			Net Sales	100.0	100.0
	35.6	31.5	26.8			Gross Profit	31.1	33.3
	31.2	28.3	22.9			Operating Expenses	26.6	28.4
	4.4	3.2	3.9			Operating Profit	4.4	5.0
	.7	.7	1.6			All Other Expenses (net)	1.3	1.5
	3.7	2.5	2.3			Profit Before Taxes	3.2	3.5
						RATIOS		
	3.5	2.7	2.3			Current	2.8	3.2
	1.9	1.7	1.4				1.7	1.8
	1.3	1.4	1.3				1.2	1.4
	1.5	1.1	1.0			Quick	1.1	1.4
	.9	.8	.7				.7	.7
	.5	.5	.5				.5	.5
20 18.2		37 10.0	51 7.1			Sales/Receivables	33 11.2	23 16.2
57 6.4		59 6.2	78 4.7				57 6.4	48 7.5
79 4.6		91 4.0	97 3.8				79 4.6	82 4.4
54 6.7		70 5.2	70 5.2			Cost of Sales/Inventory	80 4.5	70 5.2
129 2.8		124 2.9	121 3.0				142 2.6	141 2.6
207 1.8		225 1.6	314 1.2				217 1.7	238 1.5
10 38.1		30 12.1	32 11.6			Cost of Sales/Payables	12 29.6	12 30.6
48 7.6		49 7.5	51 7.1				32 11.4	41 8.9
115 3.2		71 5.1	105 3.5				67 5.4	91 4.0
	3.5	3.3	2.4			Sales/Working Capital	3.3	3.1
	4.2	6.0	7.7				5.5	5.6
	13.1	10.7	9.4				11.7	11.4
	19.1	4.4	17.8			EBIT/Interest	5.1	7.7
(29)	2.3	(38) 1.8	(18) 1.8				(123) 2.4	(87) 3.0
	1.5	1.2	1.0				1.3	1.7
						Net Profit + Depr., Dep., Amort./Cur. Mat. L /T/D	5.5	6.3
							(38) 2.8	(29) 2.3
							1.5	.8
	.1	.1	.0			Fixed/Worth	.1	.0
	.2	.2	.1				.2	.2
	.5	.3	.3				.6	.5
	.6	.6	1.0			Debt/Worth	.7	.6
	1.4	1.3	2.1				1.9	1.4
	3.7	2.5	3.4				4.3	3.4
	41.4	12.2	12.4			% Profit Before Taxes/Tangible Net Worth	27.7	38.2
(31)	11.8	5.5	(19) 6.2				(126) 10.0	(88) 13.2
	5.3	1.5	1.2				3.4	3.9
	11.0	5.8	7.3			% Profit Before Taxes/Total Assets	8.3	13.8
	3.4	2.3	2.3				3.0	4.5
	.5	.6	.0				1.2	1.5
	142.8	48.4	339.5			Sales/Net Fixed Assets	67.2	122.2
	35.7	25.9	58.4				23.1	28.7
	12.7	15.3	17.3				12.1	15.7
	2.7	2.5	2.3			Sales/Total Assets	2.4	2.4
	1.9	1.9	1.5				1.8	1.9
	1.4	1.1	1.0				1.3	1.4
	.4	.4	.1			% Depr., Dep., Amort./Sales	.5	.3
(24)	.7	(37) .8	(17) .3				(118) 1.1	(83) .9
	1.9	1.2	.9				1.8	1.8
	4.3	1.6				% Officers', Directors', Owners' Comp/Sales	1.6	2.4
(20)	7.1	(29) 2.7					(72) 3.3	(53) 4.0
	10.8	5.3					5.1	7.3
6162M	83163M	364624M	663188M	393622M	1917842M	Net Sales ($)	2891961M	2663856M
1524M	36563M	190698M	414795M	211498M	1089398M	Total Assets ($)	1783151M	1525558M

M = $ thousand   MM = $ million
See Pages 11 through 18 for Explanation of Ratios and Data

Comparative Historical Data | | | | | **Current Data Sorted By Sales** | | | | |

Hist 1	Hist 2	Hist 3		0-1MM	1-3MM	3-5MM	5-10MM	10-25MM	25MM & OVER
			Type of Statement						
27	30	15	Unqualified				1	4	10
44	34	53	Reviewed		9	6	18	15	5
17	11	13	Compiled	2	8	1	1	1	1
9	11	6	Tax Returns	1	3	2	2		
19	23	19	Other	3	4	2	2	2	6
4/1/00-3/31/01 ALL	4/1/01-3/31/02 ALL	4/1/02-3/31/03 ALL		25 (4/1-9/30/02)		81 (10/1/02-3/31/03)			
116	109	106	**NUMBER OF STATEMENTS**	6	24	11	21	22	22
%	%	%	**ASSETS**	%	%	%	%	%	%
5.7	6.0	7.7	Cash & Equivalents		13.8	10.9	5.2	5.0	5.3
30.6	27.5	30.7	Trade Receivables (net)		23.2	25.3	34.4	36.2	33.8
45.6	48.4	44.6	Inventory		48.3	40.8	44.6	44.2	44.9
.4	.9	1.0	All Other Current		.4	2.7	1.3	.5	1.4
82.3	82.7	84.0	Total Current		85.8	79.7	85.4	85.9	85.4
12.3	11.0	10.3	Fixed Assets (net)		11.5	9.7	10.6	7.9	9.7
1.5	1.9	1.8	Intangibles (net)		1.5	.5	.4	1.6	2.6
3.9	4.4	3.9	All Other Non-Current		1.2	10.1	3.6	4.7	2.3
100.0	100.0	100.0	Total		100.0	100.0	100.0	100.0	100.0
			LIABILITIES						
23.7	20.8	18.2	Notes Payable-Short Term		14.6	16.5	17.5	15.9	23.5
1.7	2.8	1.6	Cur. Mat.-L/T/D		.5	4.1	1.5	1.3	2.0
18.5	18.1	18.6	Trade Payables		17.5	18.9	20.4	18.9	19.3
.4	.2	.2	Income Taxes Payable		.1	.0	.1	.3	.4
7.8	8.2	9.4	All Other Current		8.8	7.5	8.2	11.2	12.4
52.2	50.1	48.0	Total Current		41.4	47.0	47.7	47.7	57.5
6.5	5.0	5.5	Long Term Debt		5.9	7.4	5.4	2.7	6.9
.1	.1	.0	Deferred Taxes		.0	.0	.0	.1	.1
4.7	5.1	2.3	All Other Non-Current		4.6	1.8	1.2	.4	3.3
36.5	39.8	44.2	Net Worth		48.1	43.8	45.7	49.1	32.2
100.0	100.0	100.0	Total Liabilities & Net Worth		100.0	100.0	100.0	100.0	100.0
			INCOME DATA						
100.0	100.0	100.0	Net Sales		100.0	100.0	100.0	100.0	100.0
29.9	28.2	32.3	Gross Profit		38.9	32.5	33.0	34.0	20.7
26.4	24.6	28.5	Operating Expenses		34.9	27.9	31.3	27.9	17.3
3.5	3.6	3.8	Operating Profit		4.0	4.6	1.7	6.1	3.4
1.1	1.9	.9	All Other Expenses (net)		1.0	.8	.9	1.0	1.3
2.4	1.7	2.9	Profit Before Taxes		3.0	3.8	.8	5.1	2.1
			RATIOS						
2.0	2.3	2.7			3.7	1.9	2.8	2.8	1.8
1.5	1.7	1.7	Current		2.4	1.6	1.7	1.8	1.4
1.2	1.3	1.3			1.6	1.4	1.3	1.3	1.2
1.0	.9	1.1			1.5	1.0	1.3	1.1	1.0
.6	.7	.8	Quick		.9	.7	.8	.8	.6
.4	.4	.5			.4	.5	.5	.6	.5
29 12.8	28 13.1	35 10.5			11 32.7	30 12.3	40 9.2	37 10.0	44 8.4
51 7.2	50 7.3	59 6.2	Sales/Receivables		54 6.8	39 9.4	58 6.3	65 5.6	66 5.6
90 4.1	82 4.5	89 4.1			76 4.8	95 3.9	74 4.9	99 3.7	89 4.1
56 6.5	70 5.2	69 5.3			47 7.7	76 4.8	72 5.1	67 5.4	63 5.8
124 2.9	123 3.0	122 3.0	Cost of Sales/Inventory		150 2.4	121 3.0	122 3.0	108 3.4	108 3.4
228 1.6	228 1.6	215 1.7			239 1.5	218 1.7	237 1.5	279 1.3	164 2.2
16 22.7	18 20.1	18 19.8			9 39.0	23 15.7	30 12.0	30 12.2	18 20.3
40 9.0	37 9.9	47 7.8	Cost of Sales/Payables		48 7.6	48 7.7	50 7.3	46 7.9	42 8.7
74 4.9	74 4.9	83 4.4			115 3.2	127 2.9	75 4.9	92 4.0	57 6.4
3.8	3.3	3.6			2.8	3.6	3.4	2.7	4.3
6.9	5.9	6.1	Sales/Working Capital		4.0	4.5	6.2	7.0	8.3
13.1	14.3	9.9			7.5	13.5	9.7	11.7	10.7
(112) 5.5	(102) 5.7	(99) 6.3		(22)	19.0	(10) 48.9	(20) 2.2	(19) 10.6	15.9
2.2	2.1	2.0	EBIT/Interest		2.5	2.5	1.5	2.4	2.4
1.2	1.1	1.1			1.1	1.0	-.6	1.5	1.0
(30) 10.4	(21) 7.1	(24) 6.9	Net Profit + Depr., Dep.,						
4.0	3.3	2.1	Amort./Cur. Mat. L/T/D						
1.8	1.6	1.3							
.1	.1	.1			.0	.1	.1	.0	.0
.2	.2	.2	Fixed/Worth		.1	.2	.3	.2	.3
.6	.5	.4			.5	.3	.4	.2	.6
1.0	.8	.7			.4	.9	.6	.5	1.7
2.1	1.6	1.6	Debt/Worth		1.2	1.3	1.6	1.2	2.5
4.2	3.7	3.2			4.0	1.9	2.6	2.2	4.9
(108) 29.9	(106) 28.8	(104) 20.2	% Profit Before Taxes/Tangible	(23)	39.3	20.4	9.7	22.3	(21) 38.4
13.0	8.5	8.7	Net Worth		9.2	10.4	2.0	11.1	10.9
3.2	.9	1.3			.3	1.8	-4.0	4.0	.4
8.2	8.5	7.8	% Profit Before Taxes/Total		10.5	8.9	3.1	10.5	12.4
4.5	2.8	2.5	Assets		3.4	4.0	.8	3.8	3.1
.8	.5	.3			-.4	1.2	-1.4	2.0	-.2
101.4	78.0	83.8			206.2	136.8	34.0	115.5	198.5
26.0	29.0	29.9	Sales/Net Fixed Assets		45.7	27.2	24.9	32.8	29.6
12.7	12.6	13.0			17.2	12.2	14.3	14.7	11.3
2.7	2.6	2.5			2.6	2.7	2.7	2.7	2.4
1.9	1.8	1.9	Sales/Total Assets		1.7	2.1	2.0	1.9	2.0
1.3	1.2	1.2			1.3	1.0	1.2	1.2	1.4
(98) .4	(94) .3	(90) .3		(19) .3	(10) .2	(20) .4	(20) .3	(18) .1	
.9	.8	.8	% Depr., Dep., Amort./Sales	.6	.7	1.0	.7	.4	
1.7	1.4	1.4		2.0	1.6	1.2	1.2	1.4	
(64) 1.4	(67) 1.5	(59) 1.9	% Officers', Directors',	(14) 3.8		(14) 1.8	(14) 1.5		
2.5	2.6	3.7	Owners' Comp/Sales	5.9		3.9	1.9		
4.4	6.7	7.6		10.3		8.2	3.1		
2886243M	3218461M	3428601M	Net Sales ($)	4873M	47844M	42013M	155785M	334926M	2843160M
1701624M	1760996M	1944476M	Total Assets ($)	4341M	27296M	27705M	93807M	229260M	1562067M

M = $ thousand   MM = $ million
See Pages 11 through 18 for Explanation of Ratios and Data

Current Data Sorted By Assets

Comparative Historical Data

Type of Statement	0-500M	500M-2MM	2-10MM	10-50MM	50-100MM	100-250MM
Unqualified			4	1		
Reviewed	2	7	9			
Compiled	1	6	1			
Tax Returns	1	1				
Other	2	3	3	1		
		9 (4/1-9/30/02)		33 (10/1/02-3/31/03)			

0-500M	500M-2MM	2-10MM	10-50MM	50-100MM	100-250MM		4/1/98-3/31/99 ALL	4/1/99-3/31/00 ALL
6	17	17	2			**NUMBER OF STATEMENTS**		
%	%	%	%	%	%	**ASSETS**	%	%
	5.5	6.0				Cash & Equivalents		
	41.5	30.9				Trade Receivables (net)		
	28.2	21.2	DATA	DATA		Inventory	DATA	DATA
	.3	1.3	NOT	NOT		All Other Current	NOT	NOT
	75.5	59.4	AVAILABLE	AVAILABLE		Total Current	AVAILABLE	AVAILABLE
	15.6	30.7				Fixed Assets (net)		
	3.6	2.7				Intangibles (net)		
	5.4	7.3				All Other Non-Current		
	100.0	100.0				Total		
						LIABILITIES		
	21.2	15.6				Notes Payable-Short Term		
	1.5	4.4				Cur. Mat.-L/T/D		
	17.1	14.4				Trade Payables		
	.2	.4				Income Taxes Payable		
	7.9	14.2				All Other Current		
	47.9	49.1				Total Current		
	11.8	20.4				Long Term Debt		
	.0	1.2				Deferred Taxes		
	4.2	11.5				All Other Non-Current		
	36.1	17.9				Net Worth		
	100.0	100.0				Total Liabilities & Net Worth		
						INCOME DATA		
	100.0	100.0				Net Sales		
	37.0	33.8				Gross Profit		
	33.5	28.1				Operating Expenses		
	3.5	5.7				Operating Profit		
	.8	2.4				All Other Expenses (net)		
	2.6	3.3				Profit Before Taxes		
						RATIOS		
	2.7	2.1						
	1.4	1.1				Current		
	1.1	.8						
	1.4	1.0						
	1.2	.8				Quick		
	.6	.5						
	33 11.0	39 9.3						
	49 7.4	44 8.4				Sales/Receivables		
	75 4.9	56 6.5						
	25 14.3	10 36.5						
	51 7.2	49 7.4				Cost of Sales/Inventory		
	96 3.8	70 5.2						
	16 22.4	22 16.9						
	30 12.3	31 11.9				Cost of Sales/Payables		
	47 7.7	39 9.4						
	6.9	7.7						
	10.2	35.8				Sales/Working Capital		
	42.5	−22.5						
	9.0	8.9						
	4.2	3.1				EBIT/Interest		
	1.3	.8						
						Net Profit + Depr., Dep., Amort./Cur. Mat. L /T/D		
	.1	.6						
	.3	1.2				Fixed/Worth		
	1.7	NM						
	1.4	1.2						
	2.2	2.0				Debt/Worth		
	4.2	NM						
	34.1	(13) 70.2						
	11.7	21.4				% Profit Before Taxes/Tangible Net Worth		
	2.0	8.9						
	14.2	29.7						
	4.1	8.1				% Profit Before Taxes/Total Assets		
	.8	−3.9						
	61.0	16.1						
	36.8	9.7				Sales/Net Fixed Assets		
	15.5	5.9						
	3.5	3.1						
	3.1	2.6				Sales/Total Assets		
	2.3	1.8						
	.4	1.1						
	.7	2.9				% Depr., Dep., Amort./Sales		
	1.6	3.6						
	(13) 4.5							
	7.8					% Officers', Directors', Owners' Comp/Sales		
	13.1							
4145M	57510M	182443M	134986M			Net Sales ($)		
1461M	19839M	71125M	62674M			Total Assets ($)		

© RMA 2003

M = $ thousand   MM = $ million
See Pages 11 through 18 for Explanation of Ratios and Data

Comparative Historical Data | Current Data Sorted By Sales

4/1/00-3/31/01 ALL	4/1/01-3/31/02 ALL	4/1/02-3/31/03 ALL	Type of Statement	0-1MM	1-3MM	3-5MM	5-10MM	10-25MM	25MM & OVER
		5	Unqualified				2	2	1
		18	Reviewed	1	5	4	3	5	
		8	Compiled		6		2		
		2	Tax Returns			1			
		9	Other	2	2		4		1
4/1/00-3/31/01 ALL	4/1/01-3/31/02 ALL	4/1/02-3/31/03 ALL		\ 9 (4/1-9/30/02)			33 (10/1/02-3/31/03)		
%	%	% 42	NUMBER OF STATEMENTS	4	13	5	11	7	2
		%	ASSETS	%	%	%	%	%	%
		8.2	Cash & Equivalents		9.7		1.7		
		36.8	Trade Receivables (net)		34.7		36.5		
D A T A	D A T A	21.7	Inventory		25.1		24.4		
		.7	All Other Current		.4		.3		
N O T	N O T	67.4	Total Current		69.9		62.9		
		23.3	Fixed Assets (net)		22.7		24.6		
A V A I L A B L E	A V A I L A B L E	2.9	Intangibles (net)		4.1		4.6		
		6.4	All Other Non-Current		3.3		7.9		
		100.0	Total		100.0		100.0		
			LIABILITIES						
		16.6	Notes Payable-Short Term		12.4		31.3		
		3.3	Cur. Mat.-L/T/D		1.8		4.9		
		15.6	Trade Payables		15.4		14.5		
		.2	Income Taxes Payable		.1		.0		
		10.3	All Other Current		5.4		6.8		
		46.0	Total Current		35.1		57.5		
		14.9	Long Term Debt		17.7		20.4		
		.5	Deferred Taxes		.0		1.8		
		13.5	All Other Non-Current		16.5		16.5		
		24.8	Net Worth		30.7		3.8		
		100.0	Total Liabilities & Net Worth		100.0		100.0		
			INCOME DATA						
		100.0	Net Sales		100.0		100.0		
		35.4	Gross Profit		37.1		31.3		
		30.6	Operating Expenses		31.4		28.2		
		4.9	Operating Profit		5.7		3.0		
		2.5	All Other Expenses (net)		1.1		2.9		
		2.4	Profit Before Taxes		4.6		.1		
			RATIOS						
		2.5 / 1.4 / 1.0	Current		4.5 / 2.6 / 1.3		1.4 / 1.1 / .8		
		1.4 / 1.0 / .6	Quick		3.2 / 1.3 / .8		.9 / .8 / .5		
		38 9.7 / 49 7.5 / 62 5.9	Sales/Receivables		31 11.9 / 48 7.5 / 71 5.1		49 7.4 / 55 6.6 / 60 6.1		
		10 35.0 / 43 8.5 / 69 5.3	Cost of Sales/Inventory		23 16.0 / 51 7.2 / 122 3.0		0 UND / 49 7.4 / 120 3.1		
		17 21.6 / 29 12.5 / 41 9.0	Cost of Sales/Payables		19 19.3 / 29 12.7 / 44 8.2		15 24.2 / 35 10.5 / 40 9.1		
		7.6 / 10.8 / NM	Sales/Working Capital		4.5 / 8.6 / 22.9		12.0 / 35.8 / -30.4		
		(39) 9.0 / 3.1 / 1.2	EBIT/Interest		(12) 10.3 / 4.7 / 1.6		3.5 / 1.7 / .3		
		(11) 4.9 / 2.5 / .8	Net Profit + Depr., Dep., Amort./Cur. Mat. L/T/D						
		.3 / .8 / 2.2	Fixed/Worth		.2 / 1.1 / 2.2		.5 / 1.2 / -.7		
		1.2 / 2.3 / 6.7	Debt/Worth		.8 / 3.2 / 7.4		2.0 / 3.2 / -3.0		
		(35) 51.1 / 17.7 / 2.6	% Profit Before Taxes/Tangible Net Worth		(12) 33.9 / 20.4 / 3.2				
		22.8 / 5.7 / .6	% Profit Before Taxes/Total Assets		23.1 / 6.1 / 1.1		8.6 / 2.4 / -8.9		
		37.7 / 14.6 / 7.5	Sales/Net Fixed Assets		33.5 / 17.2 / 4.5		22.2 / 9.7 / 7.3		
		3.3 / 2.8 / 2.2	Sales/Total Assets		3.3 / 2.4 / 2.0		3.1 / 2.6 / 1.6		
		(40) .7 / 1.5 / 3.5	% Depr., Dep., Amort./Sales		.5 / 1.2 / 4.4		.7 / 1.6 / 3.5		
		(24) 3.5 / 6.2 / 9.6	% Officers', Directors', Owners' Comp/Sales						
		379084M	Net Sales ($)	1785M	28370M	21027M	76710M	116206M	134986M
		155099M	Total Assets ($)	703M	13182M	6488M	34379M	37673M	62674M

Current Data Sorted By Assets | Comparative Historical Data

						Type of Statement		
		11	23	3	4	Unqualified	55	45
	8	17	5		1	Reviewed	31	29
3	8	13				Compiled	34	26
3	3	2				Tax Returns	12	8
7	8	23	13	4	2	Other	58	49
	43 (4/1-9/30/02)		118 (10/1/02-3/31/03)				4/1/98-3/31/99	4/1/99-3/31/00
0-500M	500M-2MM	2-10MM	10-50MM	50-100MM	100-250MM		ALL	ALL
13	27	66	41	7	7	NUMBER OF STATEMENTS	190	157
%	%	%	%	%	%	ASSETS	%	%
5.2	5.1	6.3	7.8			Cash & Equivalents	6.4	7.4
15.1	25.1	23.9	25.3			Trade Receivables (net)	23.6	25.2
45.8	42.0	40.6	32.3			Inventory	38.0	35.0
1.5	5.5	2.3	3.1			All Other Current	2.0	1.7
67.7	77.6	73.2	68.5			Total Current	70.0	69.3
19.0	13.1	19.4	18.6			Fixed Assets (net)	18.0	17.7
9.0	5.6	2.6	8.3			Intangibles (net)	6.0	6.1
4.3	3.6	4.9	4.6			All Other Non-Current	6.0	6.9
100.0	100.0	100.0	100.0			Total	100.0	100.0
						LIABILITIES		
29.6	18.4	14.1	14.0			Notes Payable-Short Term	17.8	14.2
4.9	2.8	4.7	2.3			Cur. Mat.-L/T/D	2.9	3.1
22.3	13.3	13.1	11.2			Trade Payables	11.8	12.2
1.6	.0	.5	.4			Income Taxes Payable	.3	.4
17.9	9.3	8.3	9.1			All Other Current	9.0	9.8
76.3	43.8	40.8	37.1			Total Current	41.8	39.6
24.5	13.8	13.2	9.8			Long Term Debt	14.1	13.6
.0	.1	.2	.3			Deferred Taxes	.3	.3
15.1	7.5	6.9	6.2			All Other Non-Current	7.7	5.5
-16.0	34.8	38.8	46.6			Net Worth	36.1	41.0
100.0	100.0	100.0	100.0			Total Liabilities & Net Worth	100.0	100.0
						INCOME DATA		
100.0	100.0	100.0	100.0			Net Sales	100.0	100.0
47.5	36.4	35.6	31.9			Gross Profit	34.9	36.0
43.2	36.0	29.8	27.4			Operating Expenses	35.1	31.1
4.3	.4	5.8	4.5			Operating Profit	-.2	5.0
1.6	1.0	1.1	2.4			All Other Expenses (net)	1.6	.4
2.8	-.6	4.7	2.1			Profit Before Taxes	-1.8	4.5
						RATIOS		
2.0	3.1	3.0	3.5				3.0	3.3
1.2	1.9	1.9	1.7			Current	1.7	1.8
.6	1.5	1.4	1.4				1.2	1.3
.8	1.3	1.4	1.6				1.3	1.6
.5	.7	.8	.9			Quick	.8	.8
.1	.3	.4	.6				.4	.5
0 769.0	22 17.0	28 13.0	41 9.0				28 13.1	29 12.6
6 56.7	31 11.7	41 9.0	55 6.6			Sales/Receivables	48 7.6	50 7.3
27 13.4	55 6.6	57 6.4	72 5.1				76 4.8	69 5.3
53 6.9	52 7.0	69 5.3	72 5.1				74 4.9	64 5.7
106 3.4	105 3.5	105 3.5	95 3.8			Cost of Sales/Inventory	114 3.2	106 3.4
185 2.0	184 2.0	177 2.1	129 2.8				173 2.1	137 2.7
15 24.2	14 25.7	16 22.5	20 18.3				16 22.4	17 21.5
38 9.5	30 12.1	26 14.1	27 13.4			Cost of Sales/Payables	28 12.9	30 12.1
60 6.1	47 7.7	43 8.5	40 9.1				47 7.7	49 7.5
7.0	5.2	4.1	3.7				3.7	3.7
37.4	9.0	7.2	5.2			Sales/Working Capital	5.9	6.3
-25.0	14.0	11.2	10.0				13.3	13.3
11.7	6.1	12.6	16.0				5.2	5.7
3.6	(26) 2.5	(64) 4.3	(40) 4.0			EBIT/Interest	(174) 2.0	(139) 2.4
.3	-.8	2.1	1.2				1.0	1.0
		13.5	29.9			Net Profit + Depr., Dep.,	5.6	6.3
	(24)	5.2	(17) 4.1			Amort./Cur. Mat. L /T/D	(56) 2.1	(46) 2.5
		2.4	1.3				.8	1.1
.4	.2	.2	.2				.2	.2
-13.1	.5	.5	.4			Fixed/Worth	.5	.4
-.5	1.6	1.5	1.3				1.2	1.0
3.0	.8	.6	.6				.8	.7
-25.7	2.5	2.0	1.2			Debt/Worth	1.9	1.3
-4.1	9.4	4.2	3.9				5.6	3.6
	47.5	45.6	37.0			% Profit Before Taxes/Tangible	32.3	31.4
	(22) 18.1	(60) 20.9	(38) 20.8			Net Worth	(163) 15.4	(137) 18.9
	-1.2	10.8	3.2				2.4	3.9
28.1	13.7	13.8	13.1			% Profit Before Taxes/Total	12.8	14.4
2.6	4.9	7.3	7.2			Assets	4.5	6.6
-2.1	-3.2	2.6	.7				.0	.9
50.0	66.0	39.5	27.2				32.0	34.6
23.5	24.1	14.0	9.9			Sales/Net Fixed Assets	13.9	14.3
9.0	17.1	6.7	4.2				6.0	6.7
3.6	3.3	2.7	2.3				2.2	2.6
2.8	2.3	2.0	1.7			Sales/Total Assets	1.7	1.8
2.0	1.8	1.5	1.1				1.2	1.3
.6	.8	.8	1.1				.9	.8
(10) .8	(23) 1.8	(58) 1.6	(40) 2.1			% Depr., Dep., Amort./Sales	(162) 2.0	(128) 1.7
5.7	2.8	2.5	3.7				3.2	3.1
	4.7	1.8				% Officers', Directors',	2.3	3.1
(10)	5.4	(27) 3.2				Owners' Comp/Sales	(49) 4.3	(40) 5.1
	7.6	4.3					8.7	7.8
8156M	102779M	709447M	1406714M	842694M	1574229M	Net Sales ($)	5266701M	4969859M
2998M	35977M	319585M	859363M	568438M	1260339M	Total Assets ($)	3608782M	3356886M

M = $ thousand   MM = $ million
See Pages 11 through 18 for Explanation of Ratios and Data

Comparative Historical Data / Current Data Sorted By Sales

							Type of Statement						6	8	27
	40		31		41		Unqualified						6	8	27
	27		18		31		Reviewed	1		2		8	6	11	3
	25		27		24		Compiled	3		7		5	3	6	
	8		8		8		Tax Returns	3		1		2	2		
	38		56		57		Other	7		6		5	9	14	16
	4/1/00-3/31/01 ALL		4/1/01-3/31/02 ALL		4/1/02-3/31/03 ALL				43 (4/1-9/30/02)			118 (10/1/02-3/31/03)				
								0-1MM	1-3MM		3-5MM	5-10MM	10-25MM		25MM & OVER
	138		140		161		NUMBER OF STATEMENTS	14	16		20	26	39		46
	%		%		%		ASSETS	%	%		%	%	%		%
	5.8		6.4		6.5		Cash & Equivalents	5.1	3.6		6.2	8.1	4.5		8.9
	26.2		24.6		23.9		Trade Receivables (net)	12.7	17.8		20.7	27.4	26.9		26.4
	36.2		36.5		37.9		Inventory	46.5	42.4		44.5	36.2	37.5		32.1
	2.2		2.0		3.0		All Other Current	1.2	5.1		3.7	2.8	2.0		3.5
	70.4		69.5		71.3		Total Current	65.5	68.8		75.3	74.5	71.0		70.9
	18.3		17.9		18.2		Fixed Assets (net)	16.7	24.5		17.5	17.1	17.0		18.3
	6.4		6.3		5.8		Intangibles (net)	12.4	5.2		3.6	3.8	6.2		5.9
	4.9		6.3		4.6		All Other Non-Current	5.4	1.6		3.7	4.6	5.9		4.9
	100.0		100.0		100.0		Total	100.0	100.0		100.0	100.0	100.0		100.0
							LIABILITIES								
	15.5		17.8		15.3		Notes Payable-Short Term	27.9	23.0		10.9	14.7	17.1		9.6
	3.2		3.5		3.6		Cur. Mat.-L/T/D	5.3	2.3		2.6	5.4	4.3		2.2
	14.6		14.8		12.9		Trade Payables	19.0	10.6		11.1	12.3	16.2		10.1
	.3		.2		.5		Income Taxes Payable	1.5	.0		.2	.6	.6		.4
	8.8		8.5		9.5		All Other Current	15.1	9.4		7.1	9.7	7.8		10.2
	42.4		44.8		41.8		Total Current	68.7	45.4		31.9	42.9	46.0		32.5
	12.0		11.9		13.3		Long Term Debt	22.3	26.1		10.7	10.5	11.5		10.2
	.4		.3		.2		Deferred Taxes	.0	.0		.2	.1	.3		.4
	7.5		5.9		7.2		All Other Non-Current	15.0	8.2		8.7	3.6	8.3		5.0
	37.7		37.1		37.4		Net Worth	-6.0	20.2		48.4	42.9	33.9		51.8
	100.0		100.0		100.0		Total Liabilities & Net Worth	100.0	100.0		100.0	100.0	100.0		100.0
							INCOME DATA								
	100.0		100.0		100.0		Net Sales	100.0	100.0		100.0	100.0	100.0		100.0
	36.1		36.5		35.8		Gross Profit	48.8	41.6		35.5	36.1	30.4		34.5
	30.2		31.1		31.2		Operating Expenses	48.3	41.8		30.9	29.0	26.1		28.0
	5.8		5.4		4.6		Operating Profit	.5	-.2		4.6	7.1	4.3		6.4
	1.8		1.6		1.4		All Other Expenses (net)	1.6	2.1		.2	.9	2.3		1.3
	4.0		3.8		3.2		Profit Before Taxes	-1.1	-2.3		4.4	6.2	1.9		5.2
							RATIOS								
	2.6		2.8		3.1			2.6	5.1		4.1	4.2	2.4		3.5
	1.7		1.7		1.9		Current	1.4	1.5		2.2	1.8	1.7		2.1
	1.3		1.2		1.4			.7	1.1		1.9	1.2	1.3		1.5
	1.3		1.4		1.4			1.0	.9		1.8	1.8	1.1		1.6
	.8		.7		.8		Quick	.4	.5		.7	.8	.7		1.0
	.5		.5		.5			.1	.3		.4	.5	.4		.7

							Sales/Receivables												
29	12.8	23	15.8	26	14.0			1	686.0	24	15.2	22	16.9	30	12.3	30	12.2	39	9.3
46	7.9	43	8.5	42	8.6			8	44.3	35	10.6	40	9.1	42	8.8	47	7.8	53	6.9
70	5.2	70	5.2	63	5.8			22	16.5	55	6.7	54	6.8	55	6.7	63	5.8	77	4.8
61	6.0	61	5.9	68	5.3		Cost of Sales/Inventory	82	4.4	72	5.1	90	4.0	44	8.3	50	7.4	71	5.2
103	3.5	102	3.6	103	3.5			137	2.7	189	1.9	114	3.2	100	3.7	83	4.4	94	3.9
143	2.5	157	2.3	147	2.5			254	1.4	371	1.0	179	2.0	156	2.3	124	2.9	124	2.9
17	20.9	17	21.4	18	20.8		Cost of Sales/Payables	15	23.6	12	31.3	16	23.2	18	20.7	16	22.5	20	18.5
31	11.9	26	13.9	28	13.0			38	9.7	37	9.9	30	12.0	24	15.3	26	14.2	24	15.2
46	7.9	46	7.9	42	8.8			84	4.4	62	5.9	44	8.3	39	9.2	44	8.3	36	10.1

							Sales/Working Capital							
	4.6		4.1		3.9			4.9	2.1	2.7	4.1	5.6	3.4
	7.3		7.3		6.5			14.3	9.1	5.3	9.4	9.4	4.8
	18.7		26.3		13.4			-35.2	62.1	7.4	18.8	17.6	8.3

							EBIT/Interest									
	6.8		6.9		12.0				10.5		4.4	8.7		29.0	9.6	18.6
(128)	3.0	(135)	2.9	(155)	4.2				2.6	(15)	1.0	4.3	(23)	5.1	3.9	(44)	6.2
	1.3		1.1		1.3				-.9		.0	1.1		1.9	2.1	2.5

							Net Profit + Depr.; Dep., Amort./Cur. Mat. L/T/D									
	12.2		6.0		13.5										18.0	42.0
(47)	3.4	(40)	2.4	(52)	3.6								(15)	3.8	(22)	4.5
	1.6		.9		1.4									1.1	2.4

							Fixed/Worth							
	.2		.2		.2			.4	.7	.1	.1	.2	.2
	.4		.5		.4			.7	NM	.3	.6	.6	.4
	1.1		1.1		1.5			-.6	-.9	.6	1.0	2.0	.6

							Debt/Worth							
	.8		.7		.7			1.2	2.6	.4	.3	1.0	.4
	1.7		1.7		1.7			8.0	NM	1.0	2.3	2.3	1.1
	3.7		4.7		6.8			-4.7	-10.2	2.8	3.4	7.5	1.7

							% Profit Before Taxes/Tangible Net Worth									
	39.5		46.7		45.3						36.9		43.6	47.6	39.4
(118)	19.3	(122)	18.5	(138)	21.1				(19)	20.0	(25)	20.2	(36)	20.1	(42)	23.2
	5.3		3.3		8.8					-.8		9.6	9.7	11.5

							% Profit Before Taxes/Total Assets							
	13.6		13.8		13.8			25.1	7.5	13.9	16.1	13.7	14.5
	7.0		5.1		7.2			2.1	.2	8.6	6.2	6.5	10.0
	1.9		.6		1.7			-11.4	-3.1	.7	2.5	2.7	3.9

							Sales/Net Fixed Assets							
	33.5		41.6		34.2			46.1	28.4	36.3	56.0	46.1	23.9
	13.6		16.3		14.6			19.9	13.7	18.3	20.0	13.9	11.0
	6.4		7.4		6.4			6.1	3.5	7.5	4.9	6.8	6.3

							Sales/Total Assets							
	2.8		2.8		2.7			3.0	2.3	2.4	3.0	3.2	2.5
	2.0		2.0		1.9			2.4	1.6	2.0	2.1	2.1	1.6
	1.3		1.3		1.4			1.2	.8	1.5	1.8	1.6	1.3

							% Depr., Dep., Amort./Sales												
	.9		.8		.9				.7		1.6		1.1		.6		.8		1.0
(123)	1.7	(118)	1.5	(140)	1.7			(11)	1.8	(14)	2.4	(16)	1.8	(23)	1.2	(35)	1.6	(41)	1.9
	3.0		2.8		2.8				5.6		3.6		3.4		2.4		2.2		3.4

							% Officers', Directors', Owners' Comp/Sales									
	2.4		2.2		2.4							3.0		1.8	1.2	
(44)	3.5	(57)	3.3	(50)	3.8				(10)			4.4	(10)	2.9	(11)	2.4	
	6.0		5.6		6.4							6.4		7.9	3.6	

	4012056M		3668534M		4644019M		Net Sales ($)	8273M	30083M		77465M	192101M	610145M		3725952M
	2534972M		2366382M		3046700M		Total Assets ($)	5187M	25922M		42085M	108252M	322511M		2542743M

© RMA 2003

M = $ thousand   MM = $ million
See Pages 11 through 18 for Explanation of Ratios and Data

Current Data Sorted By Assets   **Comparative Historical Data**

0-500M	500M-2MM	2-10MM	10-50MM	50-100MM	100-250MM	Type of Statement	4/1/98-3/31/99 ALL	4/1/99-3/31/00 ALL
		7	5	1	2	Unqualified	24	23
		6	3			Reviewed	16	11
1	1	1	2			Compiled	10	14
1						Tax Returns	4	6
	4	6	10	1		Other	24	10
	5 (4/1-9/30/02)		47 (10/1/02-3/31/03)					
2	6	20	20	2	2	**NUMBER OF STATEMENTS**	78	64
%	%	%	%	%	%	**ASSETS**	%	%
		6.8	7.4			Cash & Equivalents	11.3	8.1
		26.0	33.4			Trade Receivables (net)	28.2	26.8
		32.5	26.4			Inventory	29.0	35.3
		4.9	2.8			All Other Current	1.9	4.0
		70.2	70.0			Total Current	70.4	74.2
		18.7	17.8			Fixed Assets (net)	18.8	13.9
		6.5	6.8			Intangibles (net)	4.9	8.1
		4.5	5.3			All Other Non-Current	5.8	3.7
		100.0	100.0			Total	100.0	100.0
						LIABILITIES		
		20.9	18.4			Notes Payable-Short Term	12.8	20.4
		3.6	1.9			Cur. Mat.-L/T/D	3.1	1.7
		16.3	13.3			Trade Payables	11.3	13.0
		.1	.0			Income Taxes Payable	.3	.5
		12.7	10.5			All Other Current	21.3	27.1
		53.6	44.1			Total Current	48.8	62.8
		15.4	9.5			Long Term Debt	13.0	12.8
		.0	.7			Deferred Taxes	.5	.2
		5.7	5.4			All Other Non-Current	5.4	4.3
		25.4	40.3			Net Worth	32.3	19.9
		100.0	100.0			Total Liabilities & Net Worth	100.0	100.0
						INCOME DATA		
		100.0	100.0			Net Sales	100.0	100.0
		39.2	34.2			Gross Profit	36.9	36.2
		36.3	28.0			Operating Expenses	31.1	29.7
		2.9	6.2			Operating Profit	5.8	6.5
		1.9	.2			All Other Expenses (net)	1.9	.1
		1.0	6.0			Profit Before Taxes	3.9	6.4
						RATIOS		
		1.9	2.9			Current	3.2	3.0
		1.6	1.6				2.0	1.9
		1.2	1.0				1.3	1.3
		.9	1.8			Quick	2.0	1.4
		.6	.8				1.1	.8
		.4	.5				.7	.5
		30 12.1	45 8.1			Sales/Receivables	28 12.8	24 15.1
		45 8.2	64 5.7				53 6.8	46 7.9
		56 6.6	117 3.1				86 4.2	71 5.1
		32 11.5	59 6.2			Cost of Sales/Inventory	42 8.8	58 6.3
		99 3.7	90 4.0				89 4.1	99 3.7
		129 2.8	138 2.6				134 2.7	158 2.3
		17 21.0	21 17.3			Cost of Sales/Payables	14 26.4	11 32.1
		37 9.8	41 8.9				28 13.2	29 12.5
		72 5.1	62 5.9				55 6.7	46 7.9
		6.0	4.1			Sales/Working Capital	3.4	3.7
		9.5	9.1				6.0	7.0
		23.2	NM				12.6	14.0
		9.0	13.4			EBIT/Interest	9.9	6.9
		2.3	(16) 4.1				(69) 3.8	(56) 3.2
		-.3	1.5				1.5	1.4
						Net Profit + Depr., Dep., Amort./Cur. Mat. L /T/D	9.2	9.7
							(21) 5.5	(11) 4.5
							.4	2.2
		.2	.1			Fixed/Worth	.1	.2
		.6	.6				.4	.4
		2.9	NM				1.3	2.3
		.9	.5			Debt/Worth	.6	.7
		1.8	1.3				1.1	1.7
		8.0	NM				4.4	9.1
		42.9	50.8			% Profit Before Taxes/Tangible Net Worth	59.3	51.3
		(17) 7.7	(15) 32.5				(67) 26.3	(51) 25.0
		-33.7	5.4				8.3	3.1
		18.7	15.1			% Profit Before Taxes/Total Assets	23.8	20.6
		2.6	9.6				10.7	7.8
		-5.3	2.4				1.8	1.6
		27.9	32.3			Sales/Net Fixed Assets	23.6	31.8
		11.4	11.2				11.8	18.9
		8.1	5.7				6.3	10.3
		2.8	2.4			Sales/Total Assets	3.1	3.1
		2.1	1.6				1.7	2.0
		1.6	1.0				1.1	1.4
		1.2	.7			% Depr., Dep., Amort./Sales	1.0	.9
		(17) 1.6	(15) 2.0				(67) 2.3	(54) 1.8
		3.1	3.0				3.4	2.6
		2.9				% Officers', Directors', Owners' Comp/Sales	2.8	2.2
		(11) 4.7					(22) 4.5	(23) 4.5
		10.3					6.9	6.1
3041M	16146M	231851M	736294M	333446M	322458M	Net Sales ($)	2292342M	1728544M
430M	6620M	103553M	488556M	167756M	390060M	Total Assets ($)	1491303M	1071012M

M = $ thousand   MM = $ million
See Pages 11 through 18 for Explanation of Ratios and Data

Comparative Historical Data — Current Data Sorted By Sales

	4/1/00-3/31/01 ALL	4/1/01-3/31/02 ALL	4/1/02-3/31/03 ALL	0-1MM	1-3MM	3-5MM	5-10MM	10-25MM	25MM & OVER
					5 (4/1-9/30/02)			47 (10/1/02-3/31/03)	
Type of Statement									
Unqualified	9	15	15			2	2	6	5
Reviewed	5	9	9				2	3	4
Compiled	11	4	5		2		1	1	1
Tax Returns	3	1	2		2				
Other	23	16	21	2		1	5	4	9
NUMBER OF STATEMENTS	51	45	52	2	4	3	10	14	19
ASSETS	%	%	%	%	%	%	%	%	%
Cash & Equivalents	11.4	10.6	8.1				5.7	5.5	8.4
Trade Receivables (net)	27.2	27.1	26.9				24.3	24.6	34.3
Inventory	31.0	35.1	29.4				32.9	33.3	23.5
All Other Current	.9	1.2	3.3				4.3	3.5	3.3
Total Current	70.5	73.9	67.6				67.1	66.9	69.6
Fixed Assets (net)	17.0	16.6	19.1				25.4	20.5	16.1
Intangibles (net)	7.2	5.1	8.5				3.8	8.1	12.5
All Other Non-Current	5.3	4.4	4.7				3.7	4.6	1.8
Total	100.0	100.0	100.0				100.0	100.0	100.0
LIABILITIES									
Notes Payable-Short Term	15.2	12.6	20.8				27.7	24.1	13.1
Cur. Mat.-L/T/D	4.0	3.0	2.4				5.5	2.3	1.8
Trade Payables	11.6	10.9	13.6				20.6	11.0	13.6
Income Taxes Payable	.4	.2	.1				.0	.1	.1
All Other Current	9.7	12.2	11.9				16.8	8.9	10.0
Total Current	41.0	38.9	48.9				70.7	46.4	38.7
Long Term Debt	32.6	13.3	12.1				11.2	18.8	10.0
Deferred Taxes	.6	.6	.5				.1	.9	.5
All Other Non-Current	5.2	4.3	4.8				4.3	1.3	6.0
Net Worth	20.8	42.9	33.8				13.8	32.7	44.7
Total Liabilities & Net Worth	100.0	100.0	100.0				100.0	100.0	100.0
INCOME DATA									
Net Sales	100.0	100.0	100.0				100.0	100.0	100.0
Gross Profit	36.0	35.9	38.6				42.9	34.3	36.2
Operating Expenses	31.2	31.0	33.3				43.4	30.2	27.7
Operating Profit	4.9	4.9	5.3				−.5	4.0	8.5
All Other Expenses (net)	.7	1.0	1.2				2.2	1.4	1.2
Profit Before Taxes	4.1	3.9	4.1				−2.7	2.6	7.3
RATIOS									
Current	2.6	3.9	2.5				1.9	1.9	3.1
	1.8	1.9	1.6				1.3	1.5	1.7
	1.2	1.3	1.1				.8	1.1	1.3
Quick	1.7	1.8	1.5				.8	1.3	1.8
	1.0	1.0	.7				.5	.6	1.0
	.5	.5	.4				.4	.4	.7
Sales/Receivables	23 16.1	22 16.9	32 11.6				29 12.7	29 12.4	46 8.0
	57 6.4	48 7.6	49 7.5				42 8.6	45 8.1	62 5.8
	78 4.7	67 5.5	67 5.4				58 6.3	59 6.2	85 4.3
Cost of Sales/Inventory	51 7.1	50 7.3	47 7.8				70 5.2	29 12.6	55 6.6
	102 3.6	105 3.5	97 3.8				103 3.6	116 3.1	79 4.6
	143 2.5	139 2.6	136 2.7				125 2.9	191 1.9	99 3.7
Cost of Sales/Payables	15 24.5	12 29.8	20 18.7				34 10.6	19 19.7	18 19.8
	32 11.6	23 15.6	37 9.9				53 6.9	29 12.4	40 9.2
	45 8.0	41 8.9	55 6.6				81 4.5	55 6.6	50 7.3
Sales/Working Capital	4.2	3.2	5.3				6.2	5.8	4.1
	7.2	6.9	8.9				13.3	13.9	7.1
	24.1	15.5	29.1				−9.6	21.9	11.9
EBIT/Interest	(45) 12.4	(38) 6.6	(47) 9.1				2.7	10.0	(15) 23.2
	2.9	3.1	3.5				1.3	2.9	8.1
	1.7	.3	1.2				−1.4	−.7	1.9
Net Profit + Depr., Dep., Amort./Cur. Mat. L/T/D	(10) 13.5		(13) 6.1						
	4.2		1.7						
	2.0		−1.5						
Fixed/Worth	.2	.1	.2				.3	.2	.1
	.4	.4	.5				.9	.8	.3
	1.2	1.1	5.4				NM	NM	4.7
Debt/Worth	.6	.4	.8				1.2	1.0	.4
	1.6	1.7	1.7				1.8	3.3	1.4
	5.1	5.8	13.7				NM	NM	9.7
% Profit Before Taxes/Tangible Net Worth	(46) 50.6	(39) 31.8	(42) 49.1					(11) 48.6	(15) 61.0
	25.4	19.4	25.5					8.4	39.8
	9.3	−.7	3.3					−59.1	25.5
% Profit Before Taxes/Total Assets	15.1	14.2	16.8				3.2	19.2	17.2
	6.4	8.3	7.4				.8	5.3	11.0
	2.3	−1.5	.9				−11.6	−6.0	5.6
Sales/Net Fixed Assets	27.6	37.1	31.1				23.3	20.3	32.6
	14.5	14.9	11.8				10.3	10.6	12.0
	7.2	6.3	6.4				5.3	8.4	6.0
Sales/Total Assets	2.9	2.8	2.6				2.9	2.6	2.4
	1.9	2.0	1.9				2.1	1.7	1.9
	1.4	1.4	1.2				1.6	1.3	1.2
% Depr., Dep., Amort./Sales	(41) .8	(37) .8	(41) 1.3					(13) 1.3	(13) 1.1
	1.8	1.8	1.8					1.6	2.0
	2.7	3.3	3.8					2.9	4.1
% Officers', Directors', Owners' Comp/Sales	(15) 1.3	(11) 1.7	(16) 1.8						
	4.4	5.5	4.3						
	9.4	12.8	10.6						
Net Sales ($)	1705639M	1629691M	1643236M	1712M	6881M	11021M	72367M	217302M	1333953M
Total Assets ($)	897073M	1105639M	1156975M	1941M	2056M	32867M	35657M	129804M	954650M

© RMA 2003

M = $ thousand   MM = $ million
See Pages 11 through 18 for Explanation of Ratios and Data

Current Data Sorted By Assets | Comparative Historical Data

0-500M	500M-2MM	2-10MM	10-50MM	50-100MM	100-250MM	Type of Statement	ALL 4/1/98-3/31/99	ALL 4/1/99-3/31/00
	2	14	13	,3	1	Unqualified	44	35
2	20	42	10			Reviewed	55	60
6	17	11	2			Compiled	53	45
15	9	4	1		1	Tax Returns	14	14
7	21	20	9	1		Other	51	67
	37 (4/1-9/30/02)		194 (10/1/02-3/31/03)					
30	69	91	35	4	2	NUMBER OF STATEMENTS	217	221
%	%	%	%	%	%	**ASSETS**	%	%
8.1	5.6	7.1	6.4			Cash & Equivalents	8.3	8.7
27.2	36.7	39.4	30.0			Trade Receivables (net)	33.8	34.8
17.0	16.1	18.7	24.2			Inventory	19.7	19.4
1.5	2.0	3.2	5.4			All Other Current	2.3	2.6
53.8	60.4	68.5	66.0			Total Current	64.1	65.5
38.7	26.5	22.2	24.6			Fixed Assets (net)	26.9	25.8
1.4	6.1	3.4	5.7			Intangibles (net)	3.2	3.2
6.1	6.9	5.9	3.8			All Other Non-Current	5.8	5.6
100.0	100.0	100.0	100.0			Total	100.0	100.0
						LIABILITIES		
9.1	13.7	16.3	13.5			Notes Payable-Short Term	12.5	12.7
4.6	5.5	3.4	2.0			Cur. Mat.-L/T/D	3.6	3.5
18.7	16.2	17.8	14.6			Trade Payables	15.0	15.2
.0	.1	.3	.3			Income Taxes Payable	.4	.4
12.5	11.7	11.9	12.5			All Other Current	12.5	13.8
44.9	47.2	49.7	42.9			Total Current	44.0	45.7
36.5	16.3	12.4	14.5			Long Term Debt	16.1	16.5
.1	.4	.3	.5			Deferred Taxes	.4	.6
8.5	5.9	3.1	2.1			All Other Non-Current	3.2	5.3
10.0	30.2	34.5	40.0			Net Worth	36.3	31.8
100.0	100.0	100.0	100.0			Total Liabilities & Net Worth	100.0	100.0
						INCOME DATA		
100.0	100.0	100.0	100.0			Net Sales	100.0	100.0
53.8	40.5	32.7	29.6			Gross Profit	37.2	36.6
52.3	39.5	30.2	24.7			Operating Expenses	32.0	31.7
1.5	1.0	2.5	4.9			Operating Profit	5.2	4.8
.8	.9	.9	.6			All Other Expenses (net)	.9	1.1
.7	.1	1.6	4.3			Profit Before Taxes	4.3	3.7
						RATIOS		
2.3	1.8	2.1	3.0			Current	2.3	2.2
1.2	1.2	1.3	1.6				1.5	1.4
.8	1.0	1.0	1.1				1.1	1.1
1.6	1.3	1.5	1.9			Quick	1.4	1.6
(29) .7	.9	.9	.9				.9	.9
.5	.7	.6	.5				.7	.7
14 26.9	36 10.0	46 7.9	36 10.1			Sales/Receivables	35 10.4	36 10.1
25 14.6	52 7.0	58 6.3	52 7.1				49 7.5	48 7.6
37 9.9	62 5.9	73 5.0	69 5.3				66 5.5	66 5.5
0 UND	14 26.8	24 14.9	36 10.3			Cost of Sales/Inventory	18 19.8	20 17.9
41 8.8	30 12.1	41 9.0	63 5.8				40 9.0	39 9.3
76 4.8	52 7.1	57 6.4	87 4.2				74 5.0	64 5.7
7 52.7	20 18.1	21 17.6	19 18.9			Cost of Sales/Payables	18 20.8	21 21.8
41 8.9	33 11.0	35 10.3	37 9.9				31 11.9	29 12.5
74 5.0	54 6.7	53 6.9	49 7.4				46 8.0	48 7.6
11.1	11.6	6.2	4.4			Sales/Working Capital	6.4	6.6
33.4	22.9	15.6	9.5				11.7	12.9
-39.5	276.7	-417.8	38.7				59.4	62.7
5.3	(66) 6.4	(84) 6.5	(32) 13.9			EBIT/Interest	(194) 12.2	(199) 10.8
(26) 1.0	2.2	2.4	4.1				4.3	3.4
-1.3	-.7	-.4	2.1				1.6	1.3
	(17) 5.5	(35) 6.4	(17) 16.8			Net Profit + Depr., Dep., Amort./Cur. Mat. L /T/D	(76) 9.1	(67) 6.4
	1.5	3.1	3.8				3.0	3.4
	.0	1.0	2.4				1.7	1.4
.7	.5	.3	.3			Fixed/Worth	.3	.3
3.3	1.2	.9	.7				.8	.7
-7.8	4.9	1.9	1.8				1.8	1.9
1.2	1.2	.8	.9			Debt/Worth	.9	.9
5.8	3.3	2.6	2.1				1.9	2.1
-12.0	12.3	6.6	4.7				5.6	4.7
74.7	30.1	32.3	35.6			% Profit Before Taxes/Tangible Net Worth	52.8	53.0
(22) 25.7	(56) 9.2	(80) 10.3	(30) 14.4				(195) 24.7	(190) 22.4
-32.2	-14.3	-1.6	3.8				11.6	6.8
20.9	10.6	8.9	11.0			% Profit Before Taxes/Total Assets	18.6	15.1
.8	3.0	3.2	6.1				9.5	8.4
-9.0	-5.1	-2.5	2.3				2.9	1.5
30.4	22.3	25.7	20.7			Sales/Net Fixed Assets	19.2	22.0
9.8	11.9	13.7	11.3				10.8	12.4
6.2	6.6	6.7	4.3				6.2	6.5
5.3	3.4	2.9	3.0			Sales/Total Assets	3.2	3.2
3.8	2.7	2.4	1.9				2.4	2.5
2.4	2.1	1.7	1.5				1.9	1.9
1.1	1.5	1.1	1.3			% Depr., Dep., Amort./Sales	1.1	1.1
(26) 2.3	(65) 2.4	(86) 2.1	(28) 2.3				(194) 1.9	(193) 2.1
5.3	4.2	3.3	4.7				3.4	3.4
5.8	3.5	2.4				% Officers', Directors', Owners' Comp/Sales	3.4	2.8
(22) 8.8	(47) 5.2	(33) 4.3					(89) 6.4	(92) 5.3
13.3	7.6	6.4					9.4	7.9
31172M	228204M	985285M	1379140M	542748M	690997M	Net Sales ($)	3650645M	4274488M
8364M	82287M	422098M	670544M	325290M	214714M	Total Assets ($)	1875203M	1981009M

© RMA 2003

M = $ thousand   MM = $ million
See Pages 11 through 18 for Explanation of Ratios and Data

Comparative Historical Data | Current Data Sorted By Sales

Hist 1	Hist 2	Hist 3	Type of Statement	0-1MM	1-3MM	3-5MM	5-10MM	10-25MM	25MM & OVER
27	30	33	Unqualified	1			6	10	16
52	48	74	Reviewed	2	9	10	23	21	9
37	48	36	Compiled	3	10	6	12	3	2
19	11	30	Tax Returns	11	9	4	3	1	2
49	71	58	Other	4	14	10	10		8
4/1/00-3/31/01 ALL	4/1/01-3/31/02 ALL	4/1/02-3/31/03 ALL		37 (4/1-9/30/02)			194 (10/1/02-3/31/03)		
184	208	231	NUMBER OF STATEMENTS	21	42	30	54	47	37
%	%	%	ASSETS	%	%	%	%	%	%
8.1	7.6	6.6	Cash & Equivalents	9.6	5.8	3.3	9.2	5.2	6.1
36.5	34.5	35.3	Trade Receivables (net)	24.2	33.8	39.0	35.8	40.7	32.6
18.9	19.2	18.5	Inventory	16.1	17.3	14.4	17.1	19.9	24.8
2.2	2.8	3.0	All Other Current	.9	1.7	2.0	3.3	3.7	5.1
65.7	64.2	63.4	Total Current	50.9	58.6	58.7	65.4	69.6	68.7
25.8	24.8	26.4	Fixed Assets (net)	43.0	28.5	31.2	22.0	20.7	24.2
3.3	4.4	4.3	Intangibles (net)	2.0	5.2	3.8	5.3	4.7	3.1
5.1	6.6	6.0	All Other Non-Current	4.1	7.7	6.3	7.3	5.0	4.1
100.0	100.0	100.0	Total	100.0	100.0	100.0	100.0	100.0	100.0
			LIABILITIES						
13.5	14.3	13.8	Notes Payable-Short Term	6.6	14.0	15.5	12.2	19.0	12.0
3.5	4.6	4.0	Cur. Mat.-L/T/D	7.5	6.5	2.2	3.6	3.2	2.0
15.8	14.2	16.9	Trade Payables	17.2	14.8	15.4	18.1	18.7	16.1
.5	.3	.2	Income Taxes Payable	.0	.1	.0	.2	.3	.3
13.4	13.3	12.0	All Other Current	9.8	11.3	15.1	9.9	12.4	14.2
46.7	46.7	46.8	Total Current	41.1	46.7	48.2	44.1	53.6	44.7
18.5	15.3	17.4	Long Term Debt	38.7	21.1	17.9	11.7	12.5	15.4
.3	.3	.4	Deferred Taxes	.0	.4	.4	.5	.2	.1
2.8	4.4	4.7	All Other Non-Current	6.4	5.3	7.1	4.0	3.6	3.5
31.6	33.4	30.7	Net Worth	13.7	26.5	26.5	39.8	30.1	36.0
100.0	100.0	100.0	Total Liabilities & Net Worth	100.0	100.0	100.0	100.0	100.0	100.0
			INCOME DATA						
100.0	100.0	100.0	Net Sales	100.0	100.0	100.0	100.0	100.0	100.0
35.9	37.4	37.1	Gross Profit	58.1	45.0	37.9	35.7	27.7	29.6
31.9	34.5	34.8	Operating Expenses	57.2	44.4	36.2	33.2	24.8	25.1
4.0	2.9	2.3	Operating Profit	.9	.6	1.7	2.5	2.9	4.5
1.3	1.2	.9	All Other Expenses (net)	1.6	.9	.7	.9	.5	.9
2.7	1.8	1.4	Profit Before Taxes	-.7	-.3	1.0	1.6	2.4	3.6
			RATIOS						
2.0	2.2	2.0	Current	3.0	1.8	1.8	2.8	1.8	2.7
1.4	1.3	1.3		1.1	1.3	1.2	1.4	1.3	1.7
1.1	1.0	1.0		.9	.9	.9	1.1	1.0	1.2
1.3	1.3	1.4	Quick	2.4	1.2	1.4	2.1	1.3	1.6
1.0	.9	(230) .9		(20) .7	.9	.9	1.0	.9	.9
.7	.6	.6		.6	.6	.6	.6	.6	.5
39 9.4	36 10.2	36 10.0	Sales/Receivables	14 25.4	31 11.7	42 8.7	38 9.5	46 8.0	38 9.7
55 6.6	47 7.7	52 7.1		32 11.4	47 7.7	56 6.6	52 7.0	58 6.3	50 7.3
67 5.4	66 5.5	65 5.6		43 8.5	63 5.8	64 5.7	66 5.6	75 4.9	65 5.6
21 17.8	18 20.1	18 20.4	Cost of Sales/Inventory	6 59.6	17 21.3	17 21.2	14 25.7	20 18.2	35 10.5
41 8.8	42 8.7	42 8.7		47 7.8	42 8.7	31 11.6	34 10.6	44 8.2	63 5.8
63 5.8	68 5.4	68 5.4		92 4.0	74 5.0	50 7.3	52 7.1	58 6.3	83 4.4
21 17.4	19 19.6	19 18.9	Cost of Sales/Payables	6 61.5	21 17.7	15 24.0	18 20.5	21 17.5	19 18.7
34 10.6	31 11.9	35 10.5		48 7.6	35 10.4	31 11.9	33 11.0	36 10.1	32 11.5
48 7.6	47 7.8	54 6.8		82 4.5	54 6.7	56 6.5	54 6.7	48 7.7	46 7.9
7.0	7.2	7.0	Sales/Working Capital	8.5	10.2	11.3	6.3	6.5	4.7
14.4	14.6	16.6		52.4	19.6	20.6	15.5	16.6	9.2
62.6	141.6	289.0		UND	-79.7	-46.5	47.7	-150.4	22.5
6.9	6.0	6.7	EBIT/Interest	2.8	3.7	7.3	8.2	6.8	8.5
(166) 2.3	(189) 2.0	(214) 2.3		(18) .6	(40) 1.4	(29) 2.3	(50) 2.3	(42) 3.9	(35) 3.2
1.1	.6	-.3		-1.3	-2.0	.1	-.7	.7	1.2
10.0	3.3	6.4	Net Profit + Depr., Dep., Amort./Cur. Mat. L/T/D				6.2	7.1	16.8
(54) 2.6	(58) 1.3	(74) 2.9					(24) 2.7	(19) 4.0	(17) 2.9
1.0	.3	1.0					.4	1.3	2.0
.3	.3	.4	Fixed/Worth	1.0	.4	.7	.3	.3	.3
.8	.9	.9		2.4	1.7	1.2	.8	.9	.7
2.5	2.6	4.0		20.8	102.1	3.7	1.9	2.4	2.1
1.1	.9	1.0	Debt/Worth	1.1	1.0	1.4	.6	1.5	.8
2.5	2.7	3.0		5.3	3.3	4.0	2.1	3.0	2.3
5.1	7.9	10.4		69.9	188.2	8.0	6.4	11.6	4.9
38.2	38.4	36.9	% Profit Before Taxes/Tangible Net Worth	78.0	35.0	48.0	22.9	36.4	35.1
(161) 17.3	(176) 13.2	(192) 10.9		(17) 6.1	(33) 6.5	(25) 16.9	(47) 6.8	(38) 19.1	(32) 11.8
2.3	-1.9	-2.1		-33.6	-19.4	3.1	-12.3	5.7	3.2
14.3	12.4	10.5	% Profit Before Taxes/Total Assets	17.7	10.1	11.4	9.9	10.6	10.7
4.8	4.2	3.2		.0	2.3	4.6	2.9	6.1	3.8
.7	-1.4	-2.9		-13.6	-5.8	-1.8	-3.0	.9	.8
21.8	23.3	23.4	Sales/Net Fixed Assets	25.5	17.6	18.4	25.6	28.0	24.3
12.0	11.2	12.0		7.5	9.6	12.0	13.2	15.1	11.4
6.2	6.2	6.1		2.7	5.9	7.7	7.2	6.7	4.7
3.1	3.3	3.3	Sales/Total Assets	4.6	3.4	3.4	3.0	3.0	3.1
2.5	2.5	2.4		3.4	2.5	2.8	2.3	2.5	2.0
1.9	1.8	1.7		1.6	1.8	2.3	1.8	1.7	1.6
1.1	1.2	1.3	% Depr., Dep., Amort./Sales	1.1	1.8	1.5	1.3	1.0	1.1
(172) 2.0	(184) 2.2	(210) 2.2		(19) 3.0	(38) 3.4	(29) 2.0	(51) 2.1	(42) 1.7	(31) 2.0
3.5	3.3	3.5		9.3	5.2	3.0	3.3	2.6	4.1
3.3	3.3	2.8	% Officers', Directors', Owners' Comp/Sales	7.3	3.3	3.7	2.5	2.0	
(79) 6.6	(83) 6.2	(106) 5.4		(18) 9.1	(28) 5.1	(16) 6.4	(27) 3.8	(12) 5.1	
10.5	9.0	8.4		14.3	7.2	8.3	6.2	8.3	
2838591M	2908360M	3857546M	Net Sales ($)	12073M	83884M	112757M	383307M	709812M	2555713M
1504345M	1677484M	1723297M	Total Assets ($)	5772M	37434M	44320M	170956M	316391M	1148424M

© RMA 2003

M = $ thousand   MM = $ million
See Pages 11 through 18 for Explanation of Ratios and Data

MANUFACTURING—Gasket, Packing, and Sealing Device Manufacturing NAICS 339991 (SIC 3053)

Current Data Sorted By Assets | **Comparative Historical Data**

						Type of Statement		
		6	9	1	2	Unqualified	11	9
1	4	15	4			Reviewed	21	23
2	5	6				Compiled	15	14
1	1	1				Tax Returns	4	1
2	7	8	2	1	1	Other	27	24
0-500M	500M-2MM	2-10MM	10-50MM	50-100MM	100-250MM		4/1/98-3/31/99 ALL	4/1/99-3/31/00 ALL
	26 (4/1-9/30/02)		53 (10/1/02-3/31/03)					
6	17	36	15	2	3	NUMBER OF STATEMENTS	78	71
%	%	%	%	%	%	**ASSETS**	%	%
	5.7	10.6	6.1			Cash & Equivalents	6.9	5.3
	37.4	28.1	22.6			Trade Receivables (net)	27.1	30.8
	31.7	25.6	16.3			Inventory	28.4	24.4
	.8	2.6	.5			All Other Current	1.2	1.0
	75.6	66.9	45.5			Total Current	63.6	61.4
	18.2	24.8	34.7			Fixed Assets (net)	25.2	29.7
	1.2	1.6	12.1			Intangibles (net)	6.9	3.6
	4.9	6.7	7.7			All Other Non-Current	4.2	5.3
	100.0	100.0	100.0			Total	100.0	100.0
						LIABILITIES		
	12.1	9.5	10.8			Notes Payable-Short Term	9.7	11.4
	2.8	3.1	4.2			Cur. Mat.-L/T/D	3.8	4.9
	19.7	14.4	8.1			Trade Payables	14.5	15.9
	.2	.5	.9			Income Taxes Payable	.2	.2
	5.6	9.0	9.2			All Other Current	8.3	8.1
	40.5	36.5	33.1			Total Current	36.6	40.5
	10.8	11.3	18.1			Long Term Debt	15.7	15.9
	.4	.6	.9			Deferred Taxes	.5	.4
	2.4	3.2	8.7			All Other Non-Current	5.1	4.2
	45.8	48.4	39.1			Net Worth	42.1	39.0
	100.0	100.0	100.0			Total Liabilities & Net Worth	100.0	100.0
						INCOME DATA		
	100.0	100.0	100.0			Net Sales	100.0	100.0
	34.8	25.6	24.5			Gross Profit	32.6	28.2
	33.7	22.9	19.6			Operating Expenses	26.5	23.4
	1.2	2.7	4.9			Operating Profit	6.1	4.9
	.6	.8	1.5			All Other Expenses (net)	1.5	1.7
	.6	1.9	3.4			Profit Before Taxes	4.6	3.2
						RATIOS		
	3.1	4.5	2.3				2.8	2.7
	1.8	2.1	1.4			Current	1.6	1.5
	1.2	1.3	.9				1.2	1.0
	1.6	2.5	1.6				1.6	1.7
	.9	1.2	1.0			Quick	.9	.9
	.7	.7	.5				.5	.6
	38 9.5	42 8.6	38 9.7				33 10.9	39 9.4
	41 8.8	46 7.9	56 6.5			Sales/Receivables	41 9.0	47 7.8
	56 6.5	55 6.6	59 6.2				52 7.0	57 6.4
	27 13.7	32 11.3	29 12.5				34 10.7	31 11.8
	56 6.6	50 7.2	56 6.5			Cost of Sales/Inventory	54 6.8	46 7.9
	108 3.4	89 4.1	80 4.6				81 4.5	70 5.2
	17 22.0	18 20.6	14 26.7				17 21.2	15 24.3
	41 8.8	24 15.5	23 15.6			Cost of Sales/Payables	28 12.9	30 12.3
	58 6.3	38 9.5	39 9.3				46 7.9	46 7.9
	6.0	3.3	5.3				5.3	6.0
	8.3	6.9	12.6			Sales/Working Capital	9.5	10.7
	30.2	13.8	-67.2				25.1	175.0
	5.2	13.3	10.0				7.2	10.2
	(16) 2.3	(30) 2.4	2.4			EBIT/Interest	(67) 3.8	(63) 2.6
	.1	1.5	1.9				1.3	.5
		3.9	13.1			Net Profit + Depr., Dep.,	4.8	4.1
		(15) 1.9	(10) 2.4			Amort./Cur. Mat. L/T/D	(30) 2.3	(25) 1.9
		1.2	.9				1.4	.8
	.2	.3	.6				.3	.4
	.4	.4	1.3			Fixed/Worth	.7	.7
	.8	.7	4.4				1.8	1.8
	.5	.4	.9				.6	.7
	1.3	1.0	2.3			Debt/Worth	1.7	1.6
	3.5	2.4	10.2				3.7	5.1
	24.9	27.2	39.1				48.7	35.2
	7.2	(34) 7.8	(13) 19.2			% Profit Before Taxes/Tangible Net Worth	(65) 20.5	(64) 17.3
	-4.9	2.9	9.5				8.4	1.7
	6.5	9.9	12.3				14.0	15.4
	1.8	3.8	5.2			% Profit Before Taxes/Total Assets	7.6	4.6
	-1.8	1.4	4.0				2.0	-.5
	47.8	17.7	8.1				22.1	21.3
	19.5	10.1	5.8			Sales/Net Fixed Assets	10.2	8.9
	15.6	5.0	3.0				5.0	4.3
	3.8	3.0	2.0				3.3	3.0
	3.0	2.1	1.7			Sales/Total Assets	2.3	2.4
	2.3	1.6	.9				1.6	1.8
	.9	1.5	2.1				1.2	1.2
	(15) 1.3	(33) 2.5	3.3			% Depr., Dep., Amort./Sales	(68) 2.3	(63) 2.0
	1.9	4.3	4.9				3.7	3.8
		1.8					2.5	2.3
		(13) 6.3				% Officers', Directors', Owners' Comp/Sales	(25) 5.5	(19) 3.4
		10.0					8.6	6.6
4718M	54323M	329810M	524940M	150631M	499907M	Net Sales ($)	924586M	1267370M
1798M	17453M	156421M	340056M	121250M	346429M	Total Assets ($)	567748M	680190M

© RMA 2003

M = $ thousand MM = $ million
See Pages 11 through 18 for Explanation of Ratios and Data

Comparative Historical Data | Current Data Sorted By Sales

Current Data groupings: **26 (4/1-9/30/02)** covers 0-1MM and 1-3MM; **53 (10/1/02-3/31/03)** covers 5-10MM, 10-25MM, and 25MM & OVER.

7	13	18	Type of Statement						9
20	14	24	Unqualified			1	4	4	
19	15	13	Reviewed	1	4		9	10	
4	3	3	Compiled	2	4		6	1	
24	27	21	Tax Returns	2		1			
4/1/00-3/31/01 ALL	4/1/01-3/31/02 ALL	4/1/02-3/31/03 ALL	Other	1	5	4	3	4	4
				0-1MM	1-3MM	3-5MM	5-10MM	10-25MM	25MM & OVER
74	**72**	**79**	**NUMBER OF STATEMENTS**	**6**	**13**	**6**	**22**	**19**	**13**
%	%	%	**ASSETS**	%	%	%	%	%	%
6.4	5.8	8.4	Cash & Equivalents		7.6		10.3	7.5	7.5
30.9	27.9	28.0	Trade Receivables (net)		27.0		32.6	28.4	22.1
26.0	26.2	24.5	Inventory		31.0		28.0	19.8	16.5
1.3	1.0	1.5	All Other Current		.9		1.9	2.7	.3
64.6	60.9	62.4	Total Current		66.5		72.8	58.4	46.3
26.8	27.1	25.4	Fixed Assets (net)		26.4		20.8	29.9	29.0
1.8	6.2	5.5	Intangibles (net)		.4		1.6	5.1	19.2
6.8	5.8	6.7	All Other Non-Current		6.7		4.8	6.6	5.4
100.0	100.0	100.0	Total		100.0		100.0	100.0	100.0
			LIABILITIES						
14.1	10.6	10.6	Notes Payable-Short Term		10.1		11.7	9.8	3.8
4.1	4.1	3.6	Cur. Mat.-L/T/D		4.0		3.2	2.3	5.2
17.3	15.5	13.4	Trade Payables		13.0		18.8	12.3	8.0
.3	.3	.5	Income Taxes Payable		.3		.7	.3	.9
8.2	8.1	8.4	All Other Current		6.0		6.9	12.1	11.1
44.1	38.6	36.5	Total Current		33.5		41.2	36.9	29.1
13.2	17.6	14.9	Long Term Debt		16.4		9.3	13.1	21.2
.4	.3	.6	Deferred Taxes		.5		.3	1.3	.9
5.3	3.5	5.0	All Other Non-Current		2.3		2.4	3.4	14.4
37.0	40.0	43.0	Net Worth		47.3		46.8	45.3	34.4
100.0	100.0	100.0	Total Liabilities & Net Worth		100.0		100.0	100.0	100.0
			INCOME DATA						
100.0	100.0	100.0	Net Sales		100.0		100.0	100.0	100.0
31.4	32.4	29.4	Gross Profit		39.8		21.9	26.4	27.4
26.6	29.1	26.5	Operating Expenses		38.0		19.8	22.1	22.0
4.8	3.3	2.9	Operating Profit		1.8		2.0	4.2	5.4
1.3	1.6	1.4	All Other Expenses (net)		.0		.7	.8	3.8
3.5	1.7	1.5	Profit Before Taxes		1.8		1.3	3.4	1.5
			RATIOS						
2.5	2.4	3.1			4.2		3.6	2.3	2.6
1.4	1.6	1.8	Current		2.0		2.3	1.6	1.7
1.0	1.1	1.1			1.3		1.3	1.1	1.0
1.5	1.4	1.9			1.9		2.3	1.6	1.7
.7	.9	1.0	Quick		1.1		1.2	1.0	1.0
.5	.6	.7			.7		.7	.6	.6
34 10.6	33 11.2	38 9.5			35 10.4		40 9.1	42 8.6	39 9.4
46 7.9	45 8.1	47 7.8	Sales/Receivables		41 8.8		46 8.0	50 7.3	54 6.8
59 6.2	53 6.9	56 6.5			55 6.7		58 6.3	57 6.4	57 6.5
29 12.5	29 12.6	32 11.4			29 12.8		27 13.6	30 12.0	31 11.7
51 7.2	56 6.5	57 6.4	Cost of Sales/Inventory		81 4.5		50 7.2	38 9.6	57 6.4
86 4.2	97 3.8	91 4.0			128 2.9		85 4.3	63 5.8	73 5.0
21 17.4	17 21.9	17 22.0			16 23.1		17 21.2	14 26.7	15 23.9
33 11.1	30 12.1	26 14.2	Cost of Sales/Payables		27 13.7		27 13.8	22 16.2	26 14.1
46 8.0	44 8.2	46 8.0			54 6.8		46 7.9	37 9.8	38 9.7
6.4	6.4	5.1			5.2		3.5	5.9	5.1
13.1	10.1	8.3	Sales/Working Capital		7.1		7.6	13.6	8.3
606.7	38.9	33.0			17.8		18.5	31.8	NM
(67) 5.9	(68) 6.1	(71) 9.7			4.6		(17) 17.1	(18) 21.7	(12) 6.0
2.1	2.1	2.4	EBIT/Interest		2.5		3.5	2.5	2.0
.9	-.1	1.3			1.4		1.6	1.8	1.2
(26) 5.3	(24) 3.6	(31) 3.9	Net Profit + Depr., Dep.,						
1.9	1.4	1.9	Amort./Cur. Mat. L/T/D						
.3	.3	1.0							
.3	.3	.3			.2		.2	.4	.6
.9	.7	.5	Fixed/Worth		.5		.3	.6	2.7
1.6	1.6	1.3			1.2		.7	1.3	NM
.8	.7	.5			.6		.4	.5	.9
1.9	1.7	1.4	Debt/Worth		1.3		1.3	1.4	4.2
5.6	4.5	4.2			2.5		3.8	2.4	NM
(68) 39.7	(63) 40.7	(71) 36.2	% Profit Before Taxes/Tangible		12.0		(21) 32.5	(17) 36.2	(10) 63.3
16.4	7.7	10.2	Net Worth		7.6		10.9	10.2	33.8
2.3	-8.4	3.0			3.3		6.4	2.1	16.7
13.2	9.5	10.4	% Profit Before Taxes/Total		5.8		15.8	7.5	13.6
4.9	3.5	4.0	Assets		3.0		4.5	4.1	5.2
.3	-3.1	.9			1.2		2.6	1.4	1.1
23.1	20.3	18.4			22.7		39.5	11.5	9.6
10.5	9.4	9.5	Sales/Net Fixed Assets		17.7		14.8	8.1	5.8
5.6	5.1	4.7			5.5		7.6	4.2	3.4
3.1	3.3	3.0			3.1		3.0	3.1	2.2
2.5	2.2	2.1	Sales/Total Assets		2.6		2.5	2.0	1.6
1.9	1.6	1.6			1.7		1.8	1.6	1.1
(68) .9	(69) 1.1	(71) 1.5			(11) 1.5		(20) 1.1	(18) 1.7	(11) 2.1
2.0	2.1	2.4	% Depr., Dep., Amort./Sales		1.9		1.9	3.2	2.5
3.6	4.4	4.3			4.0		3.9	4.1	5.8
(23) 3.2	(23) 3.1	(26) 2.6	% Officers', Directors',						
5.5	6.0	6.6	Owners' Comp/Sales						
6.6	8.0	10.4							
1018133M	1309405M	1564329M	Net Sales ($)	3981M	27501M	22380M	153331M	291677M	1065459M
534598M	833285M	983407M	Total Assets ($)	3609M	15623M	11383M	74586M	159434M	718772M

© RMA 2003

M = $ thousand   MM = $ million
See Pages 11 through 18 for Explanation of Ratios and Data

Current Data Sorted By Assets   Comparative Historical Data

0-500M	500M-2MM	2-10MM	10-50MM	50-100MM	100-250MM	Type of Statement	4/1/98-3/31/99 ALL	4/1/99-3/31/00 ALL
		4	3	2	2	Unqualified	8	10
	1	4				Reviewed	3	6
1	1	1				Compiled	3	
2	1	1				Tax Returns	1	1
3	1	1			1	Other	10	7
	8 (4/1-9/30/02)		**20 (10/1/02-3/31/03)**					
6	3	11	3	2	3	**NUMBER OF STATEMENTS**	25	24
%	%	%	%	%	%		%	%
						ASSETS		
		9.6				Cash & Equivalents	11.3	8.0
		21.2				Trade Receivables (net)	24.9	24.5
		40.7				Inventory	38.2	36.7
		1.5				All Other Current	2.7	3.5
		72.9				Total Current	77.2	72.8
		18.2				Fixed Assets (net)	15.2	18.4
		.9				Intangibles (net)	4.2	4.3
		7.9				All Other Non-Current	3.4	4.5
		100.0				Total	100.0	100.0
						LIABILITIES		
		9.8				Notes Payable-Short Term	11.4	17.3
		1.6				Cur. Mat.-L/T/D	2.3	3.5
		10.7				Trade Payables	17.6	15.3
		.0				Income Taxes Payable	.5	1.0
		10.7				All Other Current	9.8	12.1
		32.8				Total Current	41.6	49.2
		9.8				Long Term Debt	14.7	12.8
		.7				Deferred Taxes	.4	.4
		2.2				All Other Non-Current	1.6	11.6
		54.4				Net Worth	41.6	26.0
		100.0				Total Liabilities & Net Worth	100.0	100.0
						INCOME DATA		
		100.0				Net Sales	100.0	100.0
		32.5				Gross Profit	34.4	31.7
		27.3				Operating Expenses	27.6	25.8
		5.2				Operating Profit	6.8	5.9
		.4				All Other Expenses (net)	1.5	-.1
		4.9				Profit Before Taxes	5.3	6.0
						RATIOS		
		4.6					2.8	2.7
		2.8				Current	1.9	1.9
		1.3					1.4	1.2
		1.9					1.2	1.3
		1.4				Quick	.9	.7
		.7					.7	.4
	26	13.9					32 11.4	34 10.6
	36	10.2				Sales/Receivables	50 7.4	52 7.0
	46	7.9					81 4.5	62 5.9
	67	5.4					93 3.9	73 5.0
	118	3.1				Cost of Sales/Inventory	139 2.6	126 2.9
	166	2.2					186 2.0	181 2.0
	17	21.5					19 19.4	20 18.0
	26	13.8				Cost of Sales/Payables	29 12.6	32 11.3
	30	12.2					58 6.3	56 6.5
		2.8					2.6	3.2
		4.3				Sales/Working Capital	4.6	5.6
		16.9					11.3	22.8
							5.6	6.5
						EBIT/Interest	(20) 3.1	(19) 3.0
							1.2	1.1
						Net Profit + Depr., Dep.,	21.5	27.1
						Amort./Cur. Mat. L /T/D	(10) 8.3	(10) 4.8
							1.2	1.3
		.2					.2	.3
		.3				Fixed/Worth	.4	.5
		2.0					.7	1.4
		.2					.7	.8
		.5				Debt/Worth	1.6	1.8
		5.5					4.3	7.0
		33.3					30.9	44.0
		16.5				% Profit Before Taxes/Tangible Net Worth	(23) 24.7	(20) 29.7
		6.8					10.2	7.6
		17.4					14.6	12.9
		10.6				% Profit Before Taxes/Total Assets	7.2	6.3
		2.4					1.2	.8
		28.9					54.0	22.2
		12.1				Sales/Net Fixed Assets	9.3	8.7
		6.8					5.2	4.6
		2.4					2.5	2.4
		1.9				Sales/Total Assets	1.5	1.7
		1.5					1.0	1.1
		1.1					.9	1.1
	(10)	1.6				% Depr., Dep., Amort./Sales	(21) 1.7	(21) 1.7
		2.2					3.1	3.2
						% Officers', Directors', Owners' Comp/Sales		
5548M	4852M	137611M	146521M	144287M	605896M	Net Sales ($)	766974M	1003724M
1693M	4082M	68218M	93588M	123907M	417404M	Total Assets ($)	648312M	788964M

© RMA 2003

M = $ thousand   MM = $ million
See Pages 11 through 18 for Explanation of Ratios and Data

Comparative Historical Data | Current Data Sorted By Sales

						Type of Statement						
	8		6		11	Unqualified					4	7
	7		4		5	Reviewed		1	1	1	2	
	2		6		3	Compiled	2			1		
			2		3	Tax Returns	1	1			1	
	8		11		6	Other	3	1	1	1		1
	4/1/00-3/31/01		4/1/01-3/31/02		4/1/02-3/31/03			8 (4/1-9/30/02)			20 (10/1/02-3/31/03)	
	ALL		ALL		ALL		0-1MM	1-3MM	3-5MM	5-10MM	10-25MM	25MM & OVER
	25		29		28	NUMBER OF STATEMENTS	6	3	1	3	7	8
	%		%		%	ASSETS	%	%	%	%	%	%
	6.2		6.0		7.4	Cash & Equivalents						
	23.0		20.3		22.9	Trade Receivables (net)						
	42.3		42.1		36.4	Inventory						
	1.4		1.7		2.4	All Other Current						
	72.9		70.1		69.0	Total Current						
	16.1		24.0		18.8	Fixed Assets (net)						
	6.4		3.0		1.9	Intangibles (net)						
	4.6		2.9		10.3	All Other Non-Current						
	100.0		100.0		100.0	Total						
						LIABILITIES						
	13.3		10.5		9.3	Notes Payable-Short Term						
	2.8		2.9		1.7	Cur. Mat.-L/T/D						
	14.8		20.3		12.4	Trade Payables						
	.3		.1		.2	Income Taxes Payable						
	8.3		13.6		16.1	All Other Current						
	39.5		47.5		39.8	Total Current						
	10.1		20.1		12.3	Long Term Debt						
	.8		.2		.6	Deferred Taxes						
	5.3		10.7		7.3	All Other Non-Current						
	44.4		21.5		39.9	Net Worth						
	100.0		100.0		100.0	Total Liabilities & Net Worth						
						INCOME DATA						
	100.0		100.0		100.0	Net Sales						
	32.8		37.4		35.5	Gross Profit						
	26.7		30.0		28.8	Operating Expenses						
	6.1		7.4		6.7	Operating Profit						
	2.5		1.5		1.1	All Other Expenses (net)						
	3.7		5.9		5.5	Profit Before Taxes						
						RATIOS						
	3.0		3.0		3.6							
	1.9		2.2		2.6	Current						
	1.5		1.4		1.2							
	1.1		1.3		1.8							
	.7		.8		.9	Quick						
	.5		.4		.5							
29	12.7	24	15.0	27	13.4							
47	7.8	41	9.0	40	9.2	Sales/Receivables						
55	6.6	49	7.5	54	6.7							
88	4.2	84	4.4	89	4.1							
130	2.8	122	3.0	130	2.8	Cost of Sales/Inventory						
167	2.2	189	1.9	156	2.3							
13	27.6	18	20.0	16	22.1							
31	11.6	27	13.4	24	15.0	Cost of Sales/Payables						
60	6.1	54	6.8	44	8.2							
	3.5		3.5		3.1							
	5.2		5.1		4.6	Sales/Working Capital						
	9.5		8.8		15.8							
	6.4		9.1		12.4							
(23)	3.3	(25)	2.9	(21)	4.6	EBIT/Interest						
	2.0		2.0		1.6							
						Net Profit + Depr., Dep., Amort./Cur. Mat. L/T/D						
	.3		.3		.2							
	.4		.7		.3	Fixed/Worth						
	.7		1.4		1.6							
	.8		.9		.4							
	1.2		1.4		1.0	Debt/Worth						
	3.2		4.4		5.5							
	37.9		41.6		33.7							
(23)	23.4	(26)	28.8	(26)	16.5	% Profit Before Taxes/Tangible Net Worth						
	12.7		10.0		4.8							
	12.5		18.4		16.8							
	8.7		9.8		10.5	% Profit Before Taxes/Total Assets						
	2.5		3.8		2.6							
	30.1		21.0		23.9							
	11.9		10.5		10.7	Sales/Net Fixed Assets						
	6.9		4.1		5.4							
	2.3		2.4		2.2							
	1.9		1.8		1.7	Sales/Total Assets						
	1.4		1.4		1.5							
	.6		1.1		1.1							
(22)	1.4	(25)	1.4	(25)	2.0	% Depr., Dep., Amort./Sales						
	2.3		3.5		4.2							
						% Officers', Directors', Owners' Comp/Sales						
	1285774M		1795553M		1044715M	Net Sales ($)	3946M	6454M	4186M	22086M	111339M	896704M
	852921M		858513M		708892M	Total Assets ($)	3041M	2734M	3300M	11127M	53791M	634899M

© RMA 2003   M = $ thousand   MM = $ million
See Pages 11 through 18 for Explanation of Ratios and Data

| Current Data Sorted By Assets | | | | | | | Comparative Historical Data | |

0-500M	500M-2MM	2-10MM	10-50MM	50-100MM	100-250MM	Type of Statement	4/1/98-3/31/99	4/1/99-3/31/00
		7	4		1	Unqualified	6	11
		6				Reviewed	13	6
	1					Compiled	2	5
	1					Tax Returns		1
	3	1	6			Other	17	13
	3 (4/1-9/30/02)		27 (10/1/02-3/31/03)				ALL	ALL
5	14	10			1	**NUMBER OF STATEMENTS**	38	36
%	%	%	%	%	%	**ASSETS**	%	%
		4.5	10.5			Cash & Equivalents	7.5	6.7
		23.9	22.7			Trade Receivables (net)	25.7	22.3
		42.4	30.0			Inventory	28.2	30.1
		1.1	1.2			All Other Current	.7	.8
		72.0	64.4			Total Current	62.0	60.0
D A T A N O T A V A I L A B L E		21.2	20.7	D A T A N O T A V A I L A B L E		Fixed Assets (net)	26.3	29.7
		3.1	6.0			Intangibles (net)	2.6	5.2
		3.7	8.8			All Other Non-Current	9.1	5.1
		100.0	100.0			Total	100.0	100.0
						LIABILITIES		
		11.6	4.2			Notes Payable-Short Term	9.1	6.8
		7.4	2.2			Cur. Mat.-L/T/D	8.0	6.6
		10.9	6.5			Trade Payables	10.6	8.0
		.1	.5			Income Taxes Payable	.4	.4
		6.1	10.0			All Other Current	21.2	6.4
		36.1	23.5			Total Current	49.3	28.1
		13.9	16.5			Long Term Debt	24.7	24.2
		.9	.8			Deferred Taxes	.5	.7
		4.8	5.9			All Other Non-Current	8.8	8.7
		44.3	53.2			Net Worth	16.7	38.4
		100.0	100.0			Total Liabilities & Net Worth	100.0	100.0
						INCOME DATA		
		100.0	100.0			Net Sales	100.0	100.0
		30.0	35.6			Gross Profit	32.6	34.3
		26.5	24.2			Operating Expenses	24.9	24.8
		3.5	11.3			Operating Profit	7.7	9.5
		1.1	2.8			All Other Expenses (net)	2.3	2.1
		2.4	8.6			Profit Before Taxes	5.4	7.4
						RATIOS		
		3.1	4.1			Current	3.4	4.6
		2.0	3.6				1.8	2.4
		1.5	2.2				1.4	1.8
		1.5	2.3			Quick	1.9	2.2
		.7	1.9				1.0	1.2
		.4	.9				.5	.7
		32 11.3	35 10.5			Sales/Receivables	35 10.6	33 10.9
		35 10.3	36 10.1				40 9.0	37 9.9
		45 8.0	39 9.3				47 7.8	47 7.7
		62 5.9	67 5.5			Cost of Sales/Inventory	52 7.0	66 5.5
		100 3.7	71 5.2				71 5.1	83 4.4
		154 2.4	112 3.3				104 3.5	113 3.2
		16 23.0	11 33.5			Cost of Sales/Payables	12 30.3	11 33.5
		21 17.0	11 32.3				27 13.3	19 19.6
		41 9.0	29 12.4				42 8.7	36 10.1
		4.5	3.9			Sales/Working Capital	4.7	4.3
		6.2	4.9				7.6	5.5
		11.3	7.3				14.6	9.3
		5.3				EBIT/Interest	9.5	5.2
	(13)	3.9					(32) 2.2	(29) 3.5
		1.7					.9	1.7
						Net Profit + Depr., Dep., Amort./Cur. Mat. L /T/D	4.7	5.4
							(15) 2.2	(10) 2.9
							1.1	1.6
		.3	.2			Fixed/Worth	.4	.4
		.4	.3				1.0	.9
		.9	.9				2.9	2.5
		.7	.4			Debt/Worth	.7	.9
		1.4	1.2				2.6	1.9
		2.4	2.1				6.3	3.1
		19.9	60.2			% Profit Before Taxes/Tangible Net Worth	34.2	41.5
	(13)	14.8	54.5				(31) 24.4	(31) 27.7
		8.1	21.8				4.9	11.3
		9.8	32.5			% Profit Before Taxes/Total Assets	20.0	19.3
		4.9	19.1				10.5	11.7
		1.2	10.2				.7	5.0
		34.0	21.8			Sales/Net Fixed Assets	18.9	15.7
		13.0	12.6				9.0	6.3
		5.7	6.8				5.1	4.1
		2.5	2.7			Sales/Total Assets	2.6	2.5
		2.1	2.4				2.0	1.9
		1.6	1.8				1.7	1.4
		1.0				% Depr., Dep., Amort./Sales	.9	2.1
	(13)	1.5					(29) 2.2	(27) 3.2
		3.8					3.3	4.2
						% Officers', Directors', Owners' Comp/Sales		
	11964M	136165M	384958M	253788M		Net Sales ($)	674069M	720521M
	6583M	64968M	183003M	179785M		Total Assets ($)	393762M	431788M

© RMA 2003

M = $ thousand   MM = $ million
See Pages 11 through 18 for Explanation of Ratios and Data

Comparative Historical Data				Current Data Sorted By Sales					
			Type of Statement						
5	7	12	Unqualified			1	1	5	5
4	5	6	Reviewed				4	2	
5	5	1	Compiled		1				
		1	Tax Returns		1				
13	17	10	Other		2	1		3	4
4/1/00-3/31/01	**4/1/01-3/31/02**	**4/1/02-3/31/03**			**3 (4/1-9/30/02)**			**27 (10/1/02-3/31/03)**	
ALL	**ALL**	**ALL**		**0-1MM**	**1-3MM**	**3-5MM**	**5-10MM**	**10-25MM**	**25MM & OVER**
27	34	30	**NUMBER OF STATEMENTS**		4	2	5	10	9
%	%	%	**ASSETS**	%	%	%	%	%	%
9.3	8.6	7.1	Cash & Equivalents	DATA NOT AVAILABLE				9.7	
24.2	24.3	22.9	Trade Receivables (net)					25.6	
30.4	29.7	37.2	Inventory					34.2	
1.3	.7	1.2	All Other Current					.6	
65.3	63.4	68.5	Total Current					70.2	
22.7	23.4	22.1	Fixed Assets (net)					20.0	
5.4	7.8	3.5	Intangibles (net)					5.8	
6.6	5.4	5.9	All Other Non-Current					4.0	
100.0	100.0	100.0	Total					100.0	
			LIABILITIES						
8.0	9.0	8.1	Notes Payable-Short Term					8.9	
6.0	3.9	7.1	Cur. Mat.-L/T/D					4.1	
9.3	8.9	9.0	Trade Payables					8.2	
.4	.4	.5	Income Taxes Payable					.2	
7.1	7.9	7.6	All Other Current					7.5	
30.8	30.1	32.4	Total Current					28.8	
17.0	18.9	14.8	Long Term Debt					16.8	
.9	.5	.8	Deferred Taxes					.9	
7.4	6.6	4.6	All Other Non-Current					4.0	
43.9	43.9	47.4	Net Worth					49.4	
100.0	100.0	100.0	Total Liabilities & Net Worth					100.0	
			INCOME DATA						
100.0	100.0	100.0	Net Sales					100.0	
35.8	35.9	32.5	Gross Profit					28.3	
27.0	26.8	26.9	Operating Expenses					22.2	
8.8	9.1	5.6	Operating Profit					6.1	
1.8	2.0	1.7	All Other Expenses (net)					1.7	
7.0	7.2	3.9	Profit Before Taxes					4.4	
			RATIOS						
5.0	4.1	3.7						4.3	
2.8	2.8	2.2	Current					2.5	
1.3	1.6	1.5						1.8	
2.7	2.1	2.0						2.6	
1.3	1.3	1.0	Quick					1.7	
.6	.6	.5						.6	
36 10.1	**34** 10.9	**33** 11.1						**35** 10.6	
42 8.6	**37** 9.9	**36** 10.1	Sales/Receivables					**35** 10.3	
56 6.5	**48** 7.7	**44** 8.2						**50** 7.3	
68 5.4	**56** 6.5	**70** 5.2						**42** 8.7	
92 4.0	**73** 5.0	**96** 3.8	Cost of Sales/Inventory					**69** 5.3	
112 3.3	**112** 3.3	**122** 3.0						**103** 3.5	
11 33.0	**12** 29.9	**12** 30.1						**11** 32.3	
28 13.3	**20** 18.0	**21** 17.8	Cost of Sales/Payables					**16** 22.8	
44 8.4	**29** 12.7	**32** 11.4						**22** 16.8	
3.5	4.1	4.4						3.7	
6.3	5.7	5.4	Sales/Working Capital					4.8	
16.4	8.1	10.7						11.1	
7.1	6.5	5.8							
(22) 2.7	(29) 3.6	(26) 4.2	EBIT/Interest						
1.2	2.0	1.5							
		3.1							
		(10) 2.4	Net Profit + Depr., Dep., Amort./Cur. Mat. L/T/D						
		1.2							
.3	.3	.2						.1	
.9	.6	.4	Fixed/Worth					.4	
1.5	1.1	1.0						.8	
.4	.5	.7						.4	
1.7	1.4	1.3	Debt/Worth					1.3	
5.9	3.2	2.1						2.1	
39.0	76.1	28.4							
(24) 17.8	(31) 17.9	(29) 16.0	% Profit Before Taxes/Tangible Net Worth						
2.9	8.1	7.9							
20.2	21.1	15.7						15.3	
10.9	9.1	7.1	% Profit Before Taxes/Total Assets					8.5	
1.9	3.5	1.2						2.4	
17.5	19.7	21.8						35.0	
8.1	12.7	9.6	Sales/Net Fixed Assets					15.1	
5.4	5.0	5.7						5.8	
2.5	2.7	2.5						3.0	
1.8	2.0	2.1	Sales/Total Assets					2.1	
1.4	1.5	1.6						1.6	
.7	.6	1.4							
(17) 2.4	(21) 3.1	(23) 2.0	% Depr., Dep., Amort./Sales						
3.5	3.8	4.4							
	2.9								
	(10) 4.7		% Officers', Directors', Owners' Comp/Sales						
	8.0								
706405M	**1098407M**	**786875M**	Net Sales ($)		**8655M**	**8295M**	**33876M**	**145951M**	**590098M**
504017M	**666614M**	**434339M**	Total Assets ($)		**5272M**	**3442M**	**16802M**	**68924M**	**339899M**

M = $ thousand MM = $ million

See Pages 11 through 18 for Explanation of Ratios and Data

Current Data Sorted By Assets   Comparative Historical Data

0-500M	500M-2MM	2-10MM	10-50MM	50-100MM	100-250MM	Type of Statement	4/1/98-3/31/99 ALL	4/1/99-3/31/00 ALL
2	3	27	27	13	11	Unqualified	76	81
7	30	44	8			Reviewed	55	66
12	32	20	1			Compiled	67	75
12	18	4				Tax Returns	19	28
6	35	58	27	11	5	Other	111	125
81 (4/1-9/30/02)			**332 (10/1/02-3/31/03)**					
39	118	153	63	24	16	NUMBER OF STATEMENTS	328	375
%	%	%	%	%	%	**ASSETS**	%	%
9.8	9.3	8.6	6.1	4.6	6.7	Cash & Equivalents	8.3	7.5
21.5	27.0	26.1	20.5	21.2	22.4	Trade Receivables (net)	26.5	28.1
29.7	27.3	26.2	24.2	20.3	16.7	Inventory	25.7	24.4
2.9	2.3	3.0	2.7	3.1	5.9	All Other Current	2.1	2.2
63.9	65.9	64.0	53.5	49.3	51.7	Total Current	62.5	62.2
29.6	24.2	26.4	31.6	25.7	25.9	Fixed Assets (net)	27.1	27.9
3.2	2.6	3.9	9.6	17.8	15.4	Intangibles (net)	4.5	4.7
3.2	7.3	5.7	5.3	7.2	7.0	All Other Non-Current	5.9	5.3
100.0	100.0	100.0	100.0	100.0	100.0	Total	100.0	100.0
						LIABILITIES		
18.8	12.7	12.8	7.4	5.3	3.8	Notes Payable-Short Term	11.8	10.1
5.2	4.3	3.4	3.8	3.5	5.6	Cur. Mat.-L/T/D	3.7	3.9
21.2	13.4	15.4	11.8	10.2	11.8	Trade Payables	14.5	14.7
.0	.1	.3	.2	.5	.4	Income Taxes Payable	.4	.4
18.3	10.6	8.9	8.9	14.2	10.8	All Other Current	12.1	9.9
63.5	41.2	40.8	32.1	33.7	32.5	Total Current	42.5	39.0
19.0	18.5	16.1	20.2	23.0	25.6	Long Term Debt	18.6	19.7
.0	.1	.6	.9	1.1	.9	Deferred Taxes	.6	.5
12.1	6.0	2.8	5.0	10.2	6.6	All Other Non-Current	5.1	6.1
5.4	34.2	39.6	41.7	32.0	34.4	Net Worth	33.1	34.7
100.0	100.0	100.0	100.0	100.0	100.0	Total Liabilities & Net Worth	100.0	100.0
						INCOME DATA		
100.0	100.0	100.0	100.0	100.0	100.0	Net Sales	100.0	100.0
44.9	39.7	32.2	30.1	32.5	39.3	Gross Profit	36.3	36.1
43.0	35.7	27.0	24.2	24.7	27.5	Operating Expenses	31.9	29.9
1.9	4.0	5.2	5.9	7.7	11.8	Operating Profit	4.5	6.2
1.0	1.3	1.3	1.2	3.0	3.5	All Other Expenses (net)	1.6	1.6
.9	2.7	3.9	4.7	4.7	8.3	Profit Before Taxes	2.8	4.6
						RATIOS		
2.5	2.7	2.3	2.9	2.0	2.2	Current	2.5	2.5
1.2	1.7	1.5	1.6	1.6	1.7		1.6	1.6
.6	1.1	1.1	1.2	1.2	1.3		1.1	1.1
1.2	1.4	1.3	1.4	1.1	1.1	Quick	1.4	1.5
.5	.8	.8	.8	.8	.9		(327) .8	.9
.2	.5	.6	.5	.5	.7		.5	.6
12 30.9	27 13.3	27 13.3	34 10.8	44 8.3	54 6.8	Sales/Receivables	29 12.4	34 10.9
26 13.8	40 9.0	41 8.9	41 8.9	53 6.8	66 5.6		46 8.0	47 7.7
38 9.6	49 7.4	55 6.7	59 6.2	61 6.0	79 5.8		63 5.8	63 5.8
7 52.3	26 14.3	37 9.8	43 8.6	45 8.0	50 7.3	Cost of Sales/Inventory	36 10.2	34 10.7
47 7.7	61 5.9	59 6.1	65 5.6	91 4.0	77 4.7		65 5.7	62 5.9
160 2.3	127 2.9	90 4.0	97 3.8	125 2.9	103 3.5		115 3.2	104 3.5
8 45.5	15 23.9	19 19.2	20 18.6	16 22.2	27 13.7	Cost of Sales/Payables	18 20.1	19 19.1
22 16.5	27 13.4	34 10.7	33 11.1	32 11.5	42 8.7		34 10.8	33 11.1
65 5.6	53 6.9	48 7.6	41 8.9	49 7.5	94 3.9		56 6.6	54 6.7
8.2	5.6	5.6	4.3	5.6	4.1	Sales/Working Capital	5.4	5.0
29.3	9.7	12.2	9.8	7.8	6.8		9.7	10.0
-9.8	68.8	34.9	22.3	22.5	12.1		49.5	35.2
(28) 8.1	(108) 5.5	(133) 10.8	(61) 9.1	5.5	14.1	EBIT/Interest	(287) 10.5	(332) 8.8
1.9	2.5	3.6	4.3	2.7	3.3		2.9	3.6
-.7	.2	1.5	1.9	1.1	2.2		1.2	1.3
	(28) 6.7	(38) 4.9	(17) 3.7	(12) 5.1		Net Profit + Depr., Dep.,	(104) 5.2	(103) 5.2
	2.5	2.9	2.7	1.9		Amort./Cur. Mat. L /T/D	2.2	2.5
	1.2	1.3	1.3	.7			1.1	1.5
.4	.2	.3	.4	.6	.4	Fixed/Worth	.3	.3
3.4	.6	.6	.9	1.6	1.3		.8	.8
-.6	1.7	2.1	2.1	-5.4	NM		2.8	2.5
.7	.8	.7	1.1	1.4	1.1	Debt/Worth	.8	.9
10.7	2.2	1.9	2.1	3.6	1.7		2.0	2.1
-4.0	6.3	4.6	4.1	-15.7	NM		6.6	6.0
(23) 89.8	(103) 48.0	(140) 45.9	(56) 47.0	(17) 44.5	(12) 39.9	% Profit Before Taxes/Tangible	(272) 51.6	(326) 57.2
16.1	17.5	21.9	20.7	20.7	24.5	Net Worth	23.1	25.8
-22.2	-1.5	7.4	2.9	.7	8.3		5.6	5.8
17.5	13.8	15.3	15.8	10.9	13.3	% Profit Before Taxes/Total	17.6	18.1
4.2	4.6	7.2	8.4	4.9	8.9	Assets	7.0	8.4
-9.2	-2.3	1.7	1.9	.5	1.7		.8	1.5
57.3	32.6	25.4	11.0	10.6	10.1	Sales/Net Fixed Assets	22.8	22.3
17.4	11.8	10.8	5.6	5.5	5.8		9.3	8.5
6.3	5.7	4.7	3.5	3.4	3.5		4.1	4.2
4.7	3.3	2.9	2.1	1.6	1.4	Sales/Total Assets	2.8	2.8
3.2	2.3	2.2	1.6	1.3	1.2		2.0	2.0
1.9	1.6	1.5	1.2	.9	.9		1.4	1.4
(31) .9	(105) .9	(138) 1.0	(58) 1.8	(21) 1.9	(12) 2.6	% Depr., Dep., Amort./Sales	(285) 1.0	(326) 1.2
2.2	2.1	1.9	2.6	3.1	3.9		2.1	2.1
4.6	4.9	3.7	4.7	6.9	5.1		3.9	4.3
(19) 5.8	(59) 3.3	(54) 2.2				% Officers', Directors',	(101) 3.1	(122) 2.3
9.7	4.4	3.8				Owners' Comp/Sales	5.2	4.8
16.0	8.5						11.1	8.4
40451M	341982M	1758759M	2538179M	2505092M	2752155M	Net Sales ($)	8863360M	10444578M
10586M	141071M	774371M	1455592M	1726902M	2352057M	Total Assets ($)	6189145M	6451554M

M = $ thousand   MM = $ million
See Pages 11 through 18 for Explanation of Ratios and Data

Comparative Historical Data / Current Data Sorted By Sales

Comparative Historical Data			Type of Statement	0-1MM	1-3MM	3-5MM	5-10MM	10-25MM	25MM & OVER
67	55	83	Unqualified	2	1	4	8	19	49
76	81	89	Reviewed	8	17	11	22	23	8
102	76	65	Compiled	8	25	14	13	4	1
32	22	34	Tax Returns	10	18	3	2	1	
128	113	142	Other	8	23	15	19	39	38
4/1/00-3/31/01 ALL	4/1/01-3/31/02 ALL	4/1/02-3/31/03 ALL		81 (4/1-9/30/02)			332 (10/1/02-3/31/03)		
405	347	413	NUMBER OF STATEMENTS	36	84	47	64	86	96
%	%	%	ASSETS	%	%	%	%	%	%
7.5	7.5	8.2	Cash & Equivalents	8.0	9.8	12.6	7.1	8.1	5.8
27.5	25.1	24.7	Trade Receivables (net)	15.2	25.2	25.8	26.6	27.8	23.0
26.4	27.5	25.8	Inventory	26.7	27.6	27.2	28.3	24.0	23.2
2.7	2.3	2.9	All Other Current	3.2	2.7	3.5	2.5	2.3	3.4
64.1	62.4	61.6	Total Current	53.1	65.3	69.0	64.5	62.2	55.4
25.9	26.5	26.8	Fixed Assets (net)	36.6	25.5	21.3	26.1	26.5	27.5
4.1	4.8	5.6	Intangibles (net)	3.2	3.2	3.3	3.7	5.1	11.4
5.9	6.3	6.0	All Other Non-Current	7.0	6.0	6.4	5.6	6.2	5.6
100.0	100.0	100.0	Total	100.0	100.0	100.0	100.0	100.0	100.0
			LIABILITIES						
12.5	12.8	11.8	Notes Payable-Short Term	16.7	15.1	8.6	14.1	11.4	7.4
3.7	4.2	4.0	Cur. Mat.-L/T/D	4.6	4.9	3.6	3.3	3.6	3.9
16.5	15.3	14.4	Trade Payables	16.5	14.9	13.7	13.6	15.4	13.1
.4	.4	.2	Income Taxes Payable	.0	.1	.1	.2	.3	.3
11.2	11.8	10.7	All Other Current	17.7	9.2	10.8	9.9	9.5	10.8
44.3	44.5	41.0	Total Current	55.5	44.1	36.8	41.2	40.1	35.5
16.5	18.4	18.4	Long Term Debt	19.1	20.8	18.0	15.6	15.6	20.8
.5	.3	.5	Deferred Taxes	.0	.1	.2	1.0	.3	.9
11.2	5.1	5.5	All Other Non-Current	8.6	9.2	3.1	2.6	3.2	6.5
27.5	31.7	34.5	Net Worth	16.9	25.8	41.8	39.6	40.8	36.3
100.0	100.0	100.0	Total Liabilities & Net Worth	100.0	100.0	100.0	100.0	100.0	100.0
			INCOME DATA						
100.0	100.0	100.0	Net Sales	100.0	100.0	100.0	100.0	100.0	100.0
35.7	36.0	35.5	Gross Profit	49.4	39.5	37.9	33.5	30.5	31.4
30.3	30.9	30.5	Operating Expenses	45.8	37.1	31.7	28.8	25.2	24.1
5.4	5.0	5.1	Operating Profit	3.7	2.4	6.2	4.7	5.4	7.3
1.7	1.8	1.4	All Other Expenses (net)	1.8	1.6	.9	1.5	.7	2.1
3.7	3.2	3.6	Profit Before Taxes	1.8	.8	5.3	3.2	4.7	5.2
			RATIOS						
2.3	2.2	2.4	Current	2.3	2.5	3.9	2.1	2.3	2.2
1.4	1.5	1.5		.9	1.5	2.0	1.5	1.6	1.6
1.1	1.1	1.1		.6	1.1	1.2	1.1	1.2	1.2
1.3	1.2	1.3	Quick	.9	1.3	2.3	1.3	1.3	1.2
.8	.8	.8		.4	.8	1.0	.7	.9	.8
.5	.4	.5		.2	.4	.6	.5	.6	.5
31 11.7	29 12.6	28 13.1	Sales/Receivables	3 106.4	26 13.8	28 13.2	28 13.2	30 12.2	35 10.6
44 8.3	44 8.2	41 8.9		26 14.1	38 9.5	45 8.0	39 9.5	41 9.0	49 7.4
58 6.3	57 6.4	54 6.8		43 8.5	48 7.7	57 6.4	49 7.4	53 6.8	63 5.8
33 11.0	35 10.4	35 10.5	Cost of Sales/Inventory	6 58.8	32 11.3	34 10.9	35 10.6	32 11.3	42 8.7
62 5.9	69 5.3	61 6.0		68 5.3	64 5.7	67 5.4	66 5.5	49 7.5	70 5.2
106 3.4	119 3.1	102 3.6		204 1.8	137 2.7	106 3.4	95 3.8	74 4.9	102 3.6
18 20.4	18 20.8	17 21.9	Cost of Sales/Payables	5 79.0	14 26.5	16 23.0	17 21.2	19 19.2	20 18.1
34 10.6	33 11.1	32 11.4		26 14.2	29 12.7	32 11.3	31 11.7	30 12.2	34 10.6
56 6.5	58 6.3	49 7.5		82 4.4	62 5.9	46 7.9	44 8.3	45 8.0	46 7.9
6.0	5.3	5.6	Sales/Working Capital	7.1	5.7	3.9	6.5	5.8	5.2
11.5	10.1	10.8		-61.9	9.7	6.2	12.5	11.5	9.2
53.3	47.0	43.7		-7.6	87.6	15.4	62.2	26.4	26.1
(360) 7.1	(312) 5.1	(370) 8.2	EBIT/Interest	(24) 7.0	(77) 4.4	(43) 12.1	(54) 9.0	(78) 12.3	(94) 8.1
2.7	2.2	3.2		2.4	1.6	3.5	3.3	4.5	3.5
1.2	.7	1.2		-.3	-.9	1.2	1.4	2.2	1.9
(108) 5.0	(83) 3.5	(101) 4.6	Net Profit + Depr., Dep., Amort./Cur. Mat. L/T/D		(19) 3.8	(10) 9.5	(14) 7.0	(22) 5.6	(34) 5.1
2.3	2.0	2.6			2.0	2.2	3.1	2.9	2.6
1.0	1.1	1.2			1.0	1.5	1.1	1.5	1.1
.3	.3	.3	Fixed/Worth	.3	.3	.2	.2	.3	.6
.8	.9	.8		1.9	.9	.5	.6	.6	1.0
2.2	2.5	2.8		UND	17.7	1.2	2.7	2.1	2.4
1.0	.8	.9	Debt/Worth	.5	1.1	.6	.7	.8	1.2
2.0	2.2	2.2		5.0	2.4	1.8	2.0	1.9	2.4
5.9	7.4	6.4		UND	44.0	4.3	4.4	4.7	5.8
(343) 54.2	(296) 40.0	(351) 47.3	% Profit Before Taxes/Tangible Net Worth	(27) 58.3	(65) 41.1	(44) 49.5	(56) 34.8	(80) 55.9	(79) 41.0
21.8	16.6	20.7		14.5	6.1	21.1	17.0	24.7	22.5
5.9	1.8	4.3		-15.0	-21.9	5.5	6.7	12.7	8.8
16.6	12.6	14.5	% Profit Before Taxes/Total Assets	10.3	13.8	14.3	14.4	18.7	14.1
6.4	4.7	6.1		3.5	2.4	6.7	5.1	9.6	7.6
.9	-.7	.7		-9.1	-5.5	.7	1.8	3.7	2.4
26.3	21.0	24.7	Sales/Net Fixed Assets	20.3	25.5	39.1	30.5	25.3	14.2
10.7	9.4	9.5		6.9	11.7	14.4	12.3	11.2	6.6
4.9	4.7	4.6		1.9	5.6	6.2	4.2	5.3	4.1
3.1	2.9	2.9	Sales/Total Assets	2.8	3.3	2.8	3.0	3.1	2.2
2.2	2.0	2.0		1.5	2.2	2.3	2.0	2.6	1.5
1.5	1.4	1.4		.9	1.5	1.5	1.4	1.7	1.2
(344) .9	(315) .9	(365) 1.2	% Depr., Dep., Amort./Sales	(29) 1.5	(73) 1.2	(41) 1.0	(57) 1.0	(82) 1.0	(83) 1.6
1.9	1.9	2.3		3.2	2.7	2.1	1.9	1.7	2.7
3.5	3.7	4.4		5.1	5.2	4.2	4.0	3.0	4.7
(137) 2.3	(124) 3.0	(138) 2.7	% Officers', Directors', Owners' Comp/Sales	(12) 4.1	(43) 3.8	(22) 2.9	(29) 2.6	(24) 1.8	
5.3	5.6	4.4		11.1	6.5	4.0	4.2		
9.4	9.4	9.7		23.3	9.4	7.4	9.5	11.9	
9498145M	7990472M	9936618M	Net Sales ($)	20564M	173076M	191327M	455623M	1297690M	7798338M
5274911M	4961708M	6460579M	Total Assets ($)	15966M	89563M	100928M	233003M	647025M	5374094M

WHOLESALE TRADE

Current Data Sorted By Assets   Comparative Historical Data

Type of Statement									
Unqualified	2		14	9	4	1		43	45
Reviewed	1	12	39	20	1	1		72	55
Compiled	12	24	28	5				52	55
Tax Returns	8	12	9					21	19
Other	5	21	41	23	4	1		70	66
		46 (4/1-9/30/02)		251 (10/1/02-3/31/03)				4/1/98-3/31/99	4/1/99-3/31/00
	0-500M	500M-2MM	2-10MM	10-50MM	50-100MM	100-250MM		ALL	ALL
NUMBER OF STATEMENTS	28	69	131	57	9	3		258	240
ASSETS	%	%	%	%	%	%		%	%
Cash & Equivalents	7.7	11.3	7.8	6.0				8.9	7.7
Trade Receivables (net)	22.5	15.2	15.0	18.3				17.8	18.7
Inventory	36.8	54.9	49.5	45.3				48.2	48.2
All Other Current	7.6	4.7	5.0	3.2				2.1	2.1
Total Current	74.7	86.1	77.2	72.8				76.8	76.7
Fixed Assets (net)	16.2	9.5	15.1	17.7				16.4	15.5
Intangibles (net)	.7	1.0	2.6	2.0				1.7	2.2
All Other Non-Current	8.6	3.4	5.0	7.4				5.1	5.6
Total	100.0	100.0	100.0	100.0				100.0	100.0
LIABILITIES									
Notes Payable-Short Term	25.4	33.2	35.7	37.7				31.5	29.4
Cur. Mat.-L/T/D	4.4	3.1	3.7	4.0				3.5	2.9
Trade Payables	10.9	14.2	10.2	9.5				12.7	12.5
Income Taxes Payable	.2	.0	.1	.1				.2	.3
All Other Current	31.9	9.8	9.2	9.5				11.0	9.0
Total Current	72.9	60.3	58.9	60.7				58.9	54.1
Long Term Debt	11.3	7.7	10.5	11.0				9.5	10.7
Deferred Taxes	.0	.1	.3	1.4				.3	.3
All Other Non-Current	1.1	2.8	2.6	3.3				3.7	2.9
Net Worth	14.9	29.0	27.8	23.5				27.5	31.9
Total Liabilities & Net Worth	100.0	100.0	100.0	100.0				100.0	100.0
INCOME DATA									
Net Sales	100.0	100.0	100.0	100.0				100.0	100.0
Gross Profit	25.7	18.0	18.2	18.8				18.3	19.0
Operating Expenses	24.4	17.3	16.0	17.2				15.3	15.8
Operating Profit	1.3	.7	2.2	1.6				2.9	3.2
All Other Expenses (net)	.3	.0	.2	.0				.6	.4
Profit Before Taxes	1.0	.7	2.0	1.7				2.3	2.8
RATIOS									
Current	2.0	2.1	1.6	1.4				1.8	1.9
	1.2	1.4	1.2	1.2				1.3	1.3
	.8	1.1	1.0	1.0				1.0	1.1
Quick	.8	.9	.5	.5				.7	.8
	.4	.4	(128) .3	.3			(256)	.4	(238) .4
	.2	.1	.2	.2				.2	.2
Sales/Receivables	0 UND	0 999.8	4 89.1	10 37.1				5 77.2	4 81.9
	6 56.8	4 82.5	14 26.5	19 19.6				13 28.4	14 27.0
	21 17.3	19 19.2	29 12.7	34 10.8				25 14.9	29 12.5
Cost of Sales/Inventory	4 85.0	21 17.4	30 12.1	43 8.5				24 15.3	27 13.4
	24 15.4	41 8.8	64 5.7	57 6.4				47 7.7	58 6.3
	74 4.9	90 4.1	105 3.5	90 4.1				81 4.5	92 4.0
Cost of Sales/Payables	0 UND	1 429.3	4 99.1	4 82.7				3 126.4	3 130.1
	5 69.1	6 59.1	8 43.0	10 37.5				9 42.1	9 42.7
	23 16.0	17 22.0	20 17.9	22 16.6				22 16.5	24 15.0
Sales/Working Capital	13.8	12.3	9.5	13.3				12.0	8.9
	137.6	26.2	24.2	27.2				30.9	23.6
	−54.1	70.4	103.2	99.4				155.8	77.3
EBIT/Interest	8.8	7.0	5.0	4.8				5.9	6.4
	(21) 3.2	(62) 2.3	(114) 2.0	(52) 2.1			(236)	2.8	(221) 2.6
	.8	1.0	1.1	1.4				1.4	1.4
Net Profit + Depr., Dep., Amort./Cur. Mat. L /T/D			6.9	3.6				4.1	6.7
			(22) 1.9	(18) 1.6			(65)	2.2	(57) 2.3
			.9	1.0				1.0	.7
Fixed/Worth	.0	.1	.2	.2				.1	.1
	.3	.2	.5	.6				.4	.4
	1.4	.6	1.5	2.3				1.5	1.6
Debt/Worth	1.0	1.0	1.6	2.0				1.2	1.1
	2.9	3.0	3.5	4.8				3.1	2.7
	UND	9.4	8.6	9.1				9.0	7.0
% Profit Before Taxes/Tangible Net Worth	53.4	33.4	38.8	30.4				50.1	53.7
	(22) 16.8	(60) 18.4	(119) 14.6	(53) 12.3			(234)	24.4	(219) 21.1
	7.0	5.5	1.1	5.9				8.6	7.9
% Profit Before Taxes/Total Assets	19.9	12.2	7.2	7.0				12.8	13.7
	5.9	3.9	3.1	3.5				5.1	5.0
	−.4	.2	.1	1.1				1.5	1.2
Sales/Net Fixed Assets	715.4	470.2	127.3	69.6				133.3	150.1
	75.3	84.0	39.4	37.8				51.8	40.9
	23.0	32.5	15.1	10.9				15.4	13.5
Sales/Total Assets	10.0	8.3	4.7	4.3				6.1	5.2
	5.0	5.7	3.1	2.9				4.0	3.5
	3.4	3.2	2.2	1.9				2.8	2.1
% Depr., Dep., Amort./Sales	.2	.1	.2	.3				.2	.2
	(16) .9	(49) .4	(117) .4	(53) .6			(216)	.5	(205) .5
	2.7	1.2	1.3	1.8				1.3	1.5
% Officers', Directors', Owners' Comp/Sales	1.1	.6	.6	.3				.6	.6
	(14) 4.3	(36) 1.1	(69) 1.2	(17) .5			(109)	1.4	(98) 1.6
	9.1	3.1	1.0	1.8				3.2	3.3
Net Sales ($)	101723M	550749M	2518319M	3514516M	1590339M	1192159M		10641582M	9522305M
Total Assets ($)	8096M	87328M	648788M	1180575M	669040M	528604M		2964182M	3237765M

M = $ thousand   MM = $ million
See Pages 11 through 18 for Explanation of Ratios and Data

Comparative Historical Data | Current Data Sorted By Sales

			Type of Statement						
28	27	30	Unqualified	1	2	1	1	9	16
58	55	74	Reviewed	1	2	5	16	21	29
68	77	69	Compiled	6	11	7	15	20	10
24	27	29	Tax Returns	4	1	2	10	9	3
69	72	95	Other	2	4	7	19	26	37
4/1/00-3/31/01	4/1/01-3/31/02	4/1/02-3/31/03		46 (4/1-9/30/02)			251 (10/1/02-3/31/03)		
ALL	ALL	ALL		0-1MM	1-3MM	3-5MM	5-10MM	10-25MM	25MM & OVER
247	258	297	**NUMBER OF STATEMENTS**	14	20	22	61	85	95
%	%	%	**ASSETS**	%	%	%	%	%	%
8.3	7.6	8.2	Cash & Equivalents	10.0	12.4	6.3	8.3	9.0	6.8
17.0	17.4	16.4	Trade Receivables (net)	11.8	19.0	12.0	16.6	16.8	17.1
49.2	47.0	48.1	Inventory	39.9	38.2	63.4	48.7	46.6	48.9
2.4	3.4	4.9	All Other Current	9.2	3.7	2.4	4.5	6.2	4.2
76.9	75.3	77.7	Total Current	70.9	73.4	84.2	78.1	78.6	76.9
16.7	17.2	14.7	Fixed Assets (net)	17.4	19.2	8.6	15.7	15.3	13.6
2.1	2.2	1.9	Intangibles (net)	.0	1.8	1.6	2.5	1.3	2.4
4.4	5.3	5.8	All Other Non-Current	12.0	5.6	5.6	3.7	4.9	7.1
100.0	100.0	100.0	Total	100.0	100.0	100.0	100.0	100.0	100.0
			LIABILITIES						
30.9	29.0	34.1	Notes Payable-Short Term	22.9	16.2	41.6	34.0	33.2	38.6
3.5	3.9	3.8	Cur. Mat.-L/T/D	6.1	3.8	1.6	5.4	3.9	2.7
12.3	13.0	11.2	Trade Payables	7.1	15.1	10.4	9.3	12.1	11.6
.1	.1	.1	Income Taxes Payable	.0	.2	.0	.1	.1	.1
9.0	8.8	11.4	All Other Current	34.8	18.2	6.6	8.0	12.3	8.9
55.9	54.9	60.6	Total Current	70.9	53.5	60.2	56.9	61.7	61.9
10.6	11.6	10.4	Long Term Debt	12.0	12.6	14.7	11.6	8.8	9.4
.4	.3	.5	Deferred Taxes	.0	.1	.2	.3	.4	.8
4.3	4.2	2.6	All Other Non-Current	1.0	1.0	1.6	3.6	2.6	2.6
28.8	28.9	26.0	Net Worth	16.5	32.8	23.3	27.6	26.4	25.3
100.0	100.0	100.0	Total Liabilities & Net Worth	100.0	100.0	100.0	100.0	100.0	100.0
			INCOME DATA						
100.0	100.0	100.0	Net Sales	100.0	100.0	100.0	100.0	100.0	100.0
18.9	20.7	19.1	Gross Profit	33.1	35.1	20.8	20.6	16.4	14.9
16.9	18.5	17.5	Operating Expenses	30.8	33.7	18.5	19.2	14.4	13.4
2.0	2.1	1.7	Operating Profit	2.3	1.5	2.3	1.4	2.0	1.5
.5	.7	.2	All Other Expenses (net)	.9	.7	.7	.1	.2	.0
1.5	1.4	1.5	Profit Before Taxes	1.4	.8	1.5	1.3	1.8	1.5
			RATIOS						
1.9	2.0	1.7		4.9	3.2	2.0	1.9	1.5	1.5
1.3	1.3	1.2	Current	1.2	1.7	1.4	1.3	1.2	1.2
1.1	1.0	1.1		.8	1.2	1.1	1.1	1.0	1.0
(246) .7	(254) .7	(294) .6		.5	1.2	.7	.7	.6	(92) .5
.4	.4	.3	Quick	.2	.8	.2	.3	.3	.3
.2	.2	.2		.2	.3	.1	.2	.1	.2
5 71.8	5 71.4	4 94.1		0 UND	1 274.1	0 UND	4 89.0	4 91.1	5 75.4
13 27.7	14 26.6	12 29.4	Sales/Receivables	5 72.0	16 22.1	5 70.5	13 28.4	12 30.0	12 30.3
25 14.4	30 12.3	27 13.5		21 17.3	43 8.6	40 9.1	26 14.2	28 13.2	26 13.8
28 13.0	27 13.6	28 13.1		24 15.2	19 19.4	47 7.7	20 17.8	22 16.4	34 10.8
61 5.9	53 6.9	54 6.8	Cost of Sales/Inventory	73 5.0	62 5.9	133 2.7	46 8.0	57 6.3	51 7.2
100 3.7	98 3.7	96 3.8		109 3.3	137 2.7	177 2.1	95 3.8	99 3.7	66 5.5
3 119.9	3 119.6	3 122.3		0 UND	1 353.6	1 510.6	2 158.2	5 81.1	3 110.6
9 41.0	10 37.6	8 44.9	Cost of Sales/Payables	4 83.7	14 26.8	4 87.2	7 53.0	10 37.7	8 44.6
25 14.7	28 12.9	20 18.1		13 28.2	38 9.6	31 11.6	18 20.6	20 17.9	16 22.2
10.7	8.9	11.1		3.3	4.5	3.8	8.8	13.9	16.8
26.5	24.8	26.1	Sales/Working Capital	UND	11.0	17.1	21.4	28.4	33.8
89.2	227.0	112.8		−21.1	22.9	47.7	53.9	253.4	136.1
3.7	4.0	5.5			9.8	6.3	5.4	5.3	5.3
(228) 1.8	(234) 1.8	(261) 2.2	EBIT/Interest		2.3	(18) 2.2	(53) 1.8	(78) 1.9	(85) 2.7
1.0	1.0	1.2			.2	.9	.5	1.2	1.5
2.2	2.3	4.7	Net Profit + Depr., Dep.,					4.9	5.3
(40) 1.4	(44) 1.1	(49) 1.8	Amort./Cur. Mat. L/T/D				(15) 1.8	1.8	(22) 1.9
.6	.1	.9						.8	1.1
.1	.1	.1		.0	.1	.1	.2	.1	.1
.6	.5	.4	Fixed/Worth	.2	.4	.2	.4	.5	.4
1.6	1.8	1.5		UND	1.4	1.7	1.5	1.7	1.5
1.2	1.4	1.6		.7	.5	1.8	1.4	1.8	2.1
3.3	3.2	3.7	Debt/Worth	1.6	1.3	5.2	3.1	4.0	3.8
8.4	8.7	8.8		UND	3.4	18.7	10.7	8.9	6.3
38.7	37.7	33.6	% Profit Before Taxes/Tangible	27.6	20.9	53.2	37.9	34.8	33.5
(226) 16.7	(237) 13.4	(265) 15.6	Net Worth	(11) 12.3	(16) 13.7	(19) 22.8	(53) 15.6	(78) 14.0	(88) 17.9
3.0	1.5	4.1		.0	3.7	2.3	−.1	3.3	8.8
9.2	8.3	8.3	% Profit Before Taxes/Total	24.0	11.2	11.9	7.5	8.0	7.7
3.5	3.0	3.7	Assets	3.0	4.1	3.9	2.6	2.5	4.3
.2	.0	.5		−3.1	−5.2	.3	−1.7	.5	1.7
142.3	129.7	146.1		UND	59.5	555.6	123.4	176.9	134.8
38.4	35.3	46.9	Sales/Net Fixed Assets	46.2	23.5	45.5	41.0	60.4	49.2
12.6	10.5	15.9		6.7	9.1	22.8	16.6	13.7	17.4
5.9	5.2	5.7		3.7	5.9	5.2	5.7	6.1	5.9
3.6	3.3	3.5	Sales/Total Assets	3.1	2.5	2.5	3.8	3.2	4.2
2.4	2.0	2.3		1.5	1.3	1.5	2.6	2.3	2.5
(192) .2	(211) .2	(243) .2			(13) .6	(13) .2	(49) .3	(76) .2	(84) .1
.6	.6	.5	% Depr., Dep., Amort./Sales		1.9	.6	.7	.4	.4
1.5	1.9	1.6			3.5	1.1	1.9	1.6	1.3
(122) .4	(111) .6	(137) .5	% Officers', Directors',				(32) .8	(46) .6	(35) .4
1.5	1.5	1.1	Owners' Comp/Sales				1.7	.9	.7
3.4	3.9	2.7					3.6	1.7	1.3
12100085M	8221409M	9467805M	Net Sales ($)	6532M	37573M	86574M	448370M	1342262M	7546494M
3188924M	2512613M	3122431M	Total Assets ($)	3458M	23439M	42555M	179259M	443822M	2429898M

M = $ thousand   MM = $ million
See Pages 11 through 18 for Explanation of Ratios and Data

Current Data Sorted By Assets   Comparative Historical Data

Type of Statement	0-500M	500M-2MM	2-10MM	10-50MM	50-100MM	100-250MM		4/1/98-3/31/99 ALL	4/1/99-3/31/00 ALL
Unqualified	1	2	19	19	8	10		70	86
Reviewed	3	30	76	15	1			190	177
Compiled	23	49	49	8				182	146
Tax Returns	32	23	12	1				49	51
Other	14	35	49	29	5	4		163	176
	136 (4/1-9/30/02)			381 (10/1/02-3/31/03)					
NUMBER OF STATEMENTS	73	139	205	72	14	14		654	636
ASSETS	%	%	%	%	%	%		%	%
Cash & Equivalents	9.3	6.8	4.6	3.5	1.9	4.1		5.2	5.1
Trade Receivables (net)	24.1	23.5	24.2	22.1	18.0	19.1		25.4	25.0
Inventory	44.4	49.0	50.6	50.3	53.4	41.9		49.1	48.9
All Other Current	1.2	1.8	2.1	2.4	3.6	2.4		1.7	1.5
Total Current	79.0	81.1	81.6	78.3	77.0	67.5		81.4	80.5
Fixed Assets (net)	15.2	12.2	11.4	11.4	13.0	9.6		11.8	12.4
Intangibles (net)	3.5	2.0	2.3	3.4	6.0	18.8		1.8	2.4
All Other Non-Current	2.3	4.8	4.7	6.9	4.0	4.1		5.0	4.7
Total	100.0	100.0	100.0	100.0	100.0	100.0		100.0	100.0
LIABILITIES									
Notes Payable-Short Term	16.4	13.3	19.7	14.7	12.2	8.0		14.1	15.6
Cur. Mat.-L/T/D	4.2	3.6	1.9	2.3	1.5	2.2		2.9	2.7
Trade Payables	32.5	19.5	21.7	20.5	17.3	15.3		22.5	22.3
Income Taxes Payable	.1	.1	.2	.4	.1	.1		.2	.2
All Other Current	18.3	8.2	7.5	8.1	5.8	10.6		7.0	7.3
Total Current	71.5	44.7	50.9	46.0	37.0	36.2		46.6	48.2
Long Term Debt	19.4	15.5	7.6	11.5	21.3	15.6		10.9	11.8
Deferred Taxes	.0	.2	.1	.1	.0	.2		.1	.2
All Other Non-Current	7.5	5.5	3.6	4.2	8.7	4.8		4.1	4.7
Net Worth	1.6	34.2	37.7	38.3	32.9	43.2		38.3	35.1
Total Liabilities & Net Worth	100.0	100.0	100.0	100.0	100.0	100.0		100.0	100.0
INCOME DATA									
Net Sales	100.0	100.0	100.0	100.0	100.0	100.0		100.0	100.0
Gross Profit	37.7	32.9	31.1	30.6	33.7	30.4		30.9	31.0
Operating Expenses	36.3	30.1	28.8	26.4	28.9	27.9		27.8	27.6
Operating Profit	1.4	2.9	2.3	4.3	4.8	2.5		3.1	3.5
All Other Expenses (net)	.7	.6	.4	.8	.8	1.4		.6	.7
Profit Before Taxes	.7	2.2	1.9	3.5	4.0	1.0		2.5	2.7
RATIOS									
Current	2.4	2.9	2.3	2.3	3.5	3.1		2.7	2.6
	1.4	1.9	1.6	1.7	2.2	2.0		1.8	1.7
	.8	1.4	1.2	1.3	1.5	1.3		1.3	1.3
Quick	.9	1.0	.8	.8	.9	1.2		1.0	1.0
	.5	.7	.5	.5	.7	.8		(653) .6	.6
	.3	.5	.3	.4	.4	.2		.4	.4
Sales/Receivables	8 44.6	22 16.5	25 14.8	29 12.6	26 14.1	32 11.3		26 14.3	24 15.2
	22 16.3	32 11.4	35 10.5	34 10.9	38 9.6	34 10.7		35 10.4	34 10.8
	36 10.1	40 9.1	45 8.1	48 7.7	42 8.7	49 7.4		45 8.2	45 8.0
Cost of Sales/Inventory	34 10.8	65 5.6	70 5.2	80 4.6	106 3.5	89 4.1		70 5.2	70 5.2
	68 5.4	100 3.7	115 3.2	128 2.9	142 2.6	121 3.0		105 3.5	110 3.3
	133 2.7	155 2.4	170 2.1	181 2.0	175 2.1	175 2.1		148 2.5	158 2.3
Cost of Sales/Payables	19 19.1	22 16.8	23 15.7	29 12.8	20 18.3	26 13.8		27 13.7	27 13.5
	38 9.6	35 10.4	37 9.8	45 8.2	38 9.6	45 8.1		42 8.8	41 8.9
	69 5.3	55 6.7	69 5.3	65 5.6	81 4.5	54 6.7		59 6.2	61 6.0
Sales/Working Capital	7.9	4.5	4.9	4.0	3.5	3.6		4.8	4.6
	15.6	7.1	8.0	7.6	5.1	6.1		7.6	8.0
	-29.6	13.3	16.0	12.5	9.8	9.6		13.6	15.1
EBIT/Interest	5.2	5.6	7.2	9.4	10.0	11.2		7.0	7.3
	(63) 1.4	(127) 2.4	(190) 3.3	(70) 4.2	3.9	3.9		(603) 2.9	(582) 2.6
	-1.4	1.2	1.5	1.2	2.3	2.9		1.4	1.3
Net Profit + Depr., Dep., Amort./Cur. Mat. L./T/D		2.8	7.4	6.4				4.7	5.5
		(40) 1.7	(63) 1.9	(24) 2.6				(204) 2.0	(156) 1.8
		1.0	.8	1.0				1.0	.9
Fixed/Worth	.1	.1	.1	.1	.3	.2		.1	.1
	.7	.2	.3	.2	.4	.3		.3	.3
	-.6	.7	.6	.6	.5	NM		.6	.6
Debt/Worth	1.1	.8	.9	1.0	1.5	.9		.8	.8
	4.3	1.8	1.9	1.9	2.4	3.4		1.8	1.9
	-3.6	4.8	4.0	4.0	4.1	NM		3.7	4.4
% Profit Before Taxes/Tangible Net Worth	35.1	23.2	31.8	25.8	45.2	31.9		32.5	32.0
	(45) 14.4	(124) 9.2	(197) 13.9	(67) 15.3	(13) 26.3	(11) 17.5		(619) 13.9	(578) 14.5
	-.7	2.4	3.2	4.0	14.0	9.0		4.0	4.8
% Profit Before Taxes/Total Assets	9.9	8.5	9.9	9.5	16.1	12.6		11.3	11.1
	1.1	3.6	3.6	5.1	5.5	10.3		4.6	4.1
	-8.0	.5	.9	1.0	3.9	2.6		1.2	.9
Sales/Net Fixed Assets	103.2	81.9	61.7	51.8	33.6	43.9		58.3	58.0
	34.6	35.9	35.1	31.2	17.7	28.1		30.3	29.4
	19.9	19.6	16.6	13.5	10.3	11.7		15.7	15.2
Sales/Total Assets	5.4	3.3	3.1	2.7	2.5	2.1		3.2	3.1
	3.6	2.5	2.4	2.1	1.9	1.7		2.5	2.4
	2.6	2.0	1.8	1.6	1.6	1.2		1.9	1.8
% Depr., Dep., Amort./Sales	.5	.5	.5	.5	.9	.8		.5	.5
	(56) 1.1	(118) 1.0	(188) .9	(67) .9	(13) 1.2	(12) 1.5		(579) .9	(553) .9
	2.3	1.6	1.4	1.3	1.4	1.7		1.5	1.4
% Officers', Directors', Owners' Comp/Sales	2.5	2.3	1.5	1.4				2.0	2.0
	(44) 5.4	(70) 3.9	(82) 3.1	(21) 3.5				(305) 3.3	(281) 3.0
	8.5	5.6	5.7	5.7				5.4	5.1
Net Sales ($)	80798M	459864M	2349199M	2897055M	2127354M	4192106M		10290254M	11983936M
Total Assets ($)	20797M	165879M	953741M	1360235M	973225M	2497736M		4942436M	5746287M

© RMA 2003   M = $ thousand   MM = $ million
See Pages 11 through 18 for Explanation of Ratios and Data

Comparative Historical Data / Current Data Sorted By Sales

			Type of Statement						
69	58	59	Unqualified	1	3	2	3	16	34
162	117	125	Reviewed	3	9	19	32	43	19
162	154	129	Compiled	9	41	27	28	18	6
45	36	68	Tax Returns	18	25	10	9	5	1
159	177	136	Other	10	26	16	21	32	31
4/1/00-3/31/01 ALL	4/1/01-3/31/02 ALL	4/1/02-3/31/03 ALL		136 (4/1-9/30/02) 0-1MM	1-3MM	3-5MM	381 (10/1/02-3/31/03) 5-10MM	10-25MM	25MM & OVER
597	542	517	**NUMBER OF STATEMENTS**	41	104	74	93	114	91
%	%	%	**ASSETS**	%	%	%	%	%	%
5.3	5.2	5.6	Cash & Equivalents	8.9	7.7	5.4	5.9	3.8	3.8
24.5	24.1	23.4	Trade Receivables (net)	22.0	22.1	23.1	25.3	23.5	23.7
48.4	48.0	49.1	Inventory	40.9	48.9	49.8	49.7	50.4	50.2
1.7	1.7	2.0	All Other Current	.6	2.2	1.4	1.8	2.6	2.3
79.9	79.0	80.1	Total Current	72.4	80.9	79.6	82.7	80.4	80.0
12.2	12.5	12.1	Fixed Assets (net)	19.4	12.1	12.7	11.5	11.5	9.9
2.6	3.3	3.1	Intangibles (net)	4.4	1.9	3.3	1.4	2.3	6.4
5.2	5.1	4.7	All Other Non-Current	3.8	5.1	4.4	4.3	5.8	3.7
100.0	100.0	100.0	Total	100.0	100.0	100.0	100.0	100.0	100.0
			LIABILITIES						
16.1	16.8	16.3	Notes Payable-Short Term	12.3	15.9	15.9	16.9	19.1	14.9
3.2	3.0	2.7	Cur. Mat.-L/T/D	5.4	3.2	3.0	2.7	1.8	1.9
22.8	22.1	22.2	Trade Payables	33.3	21.2	18.5	21.6	23.0	20.7
.2	.1	.2	Income Taxes Payable	.1	.1	.1	.2	.3	.3
7.7	8.5	9.3	All Other Current	20.9	9.9	9.4	7.0	8.0	7.5
50.1	50.6	50.7	Total Current	72.0	50.2	46.9	48.3	52.1	45.3
11.5	13.1	12.5	Long Term Debt	29.1	15.5	11.9	7.9	9.0	11.4
.2	.1	.1	Deferred Taxes	.0	.1	.2	.1	.1	.1
4.1	4.0	4.9	All Other Non-Current	6.9	8.9	2.8	2.8	3.7	4.8
34.2	32.2	31.8	Net Worth	−8.0	25.2	38.3	40.8	35.1	38.4
100.0	100.0	100.0	Total Liabilities & Net Worth	100.0	100.0	100.0	100.0	100.0	100.0
			INCOME DATA						
100.0	100.0	100.0	Net Sales	100.0	100.0	100.0	100.0	100.0	100.0
31.4	31.6	32.5	Gross Profit	43.3	33.6	32.9	32.7	29.4	29.9
28.6	28.8	29.8	Operating Expenses	41.0	31.4	30.9	30.2	26.6	25.9
2.8	2.8	2.7	Operating Profit	2.3	2.2	2.0	2.5	2.8	4.0
1.0	.9	.6	All Other Expenses (net)	1.0	.8	.6	.2	.5	.8
1.8	1.9	2.1	Profit Before Taxes	1.3	1.4	1.4	2.3	2.4	3.2
			RATIOS						
2.6	2.4	2.5		2.9	2.9	2.5	2.6	2.2	2.8
1.6	1.6	1.7	Current	1.4	1.8	1.9	1.7	1.6	1.7
1.2	1.2	1.3		.7	1.2	1.3	1.3	1.2	1.3
1.0	.9	.9		1.0	1.0	.9	.9	.8	.9
.6	.6	.6	Quick	.5	.6	.6	.6	.5	.6
.4	.3	.4		.3	.4	.4	.5	.3	.4

Sales/Receivables

25	14.9	24	15.1	23	15.9		10	36.8	21	17.5	23	15.8	23	15.6	25	14.9	28	13.1
33	10.9	33	11.1	33	11.1	Sales/Receivables	25	14.4	28	13.0	33	10.9	34	10.6	34	10.7	34	10.6
45	8.0	44	8.3	42	8.6		41	8.9	38	9.5	44	8.5	44	8.2	43	8.5	45	8.2
68	5.4	68	5.4	65	5.6		38	9.6	62	5.8	57	6.4	64	5.7	65	5.6	80	4.5
110	3.3	105	3.5	106	3.4	Cost of Sales/Inventory	105	3.5	111	3.3	109	3.4	101	3.6	103	3.6	115	3.2
160	2.3	149	2.5	165	2.2		177	2.1	166	2.2	169	2.2	159	2.3	166	2.2	160	2.3
27	13.3	24	15.1	24	15.2		27	13.4	22	16.3	18	20.3	23	13.5	27	13.5	26	13.9
44	8.4	41	8.8	38	9.6	Cost of Sales/Payables	54	6.8	37	10.0	30	12.3	35	10.4	43	8.4	44	8.2
64	5.7	64	5.7	65	5.6		84	4.3	61	6.0	55	6.7	66	5.5	66	5.5	65	5.6

			Ratio						
4.6	5.1	4.7		4.5	4.4	4.8	5.2	5.6	4.0
8.5	9.1	8.2	Sales/Working Capital	10.0	7.7	7.2	8.0	8.9	7.6
18.3	18.6	16.2		−16.8	17.5	12.8	14.0	17.3	12.2
5.1	5.8	6.7		7.2	4.1	5.4	7.0	7.9	9.5
(546) 2.2	(498) 2.4	(478) 2.8	EBIT/Interest	(34) 1.2	(91) 1.7	(69) 2.1	(87) 3.4	(108) 3.2	(89) 4.3
1.1	1.1	1.2		−1.5	.7	1.1	1.8	1.2	2.3
4.0	4.1	4.6	Net Profit + Depr., Dep.,	4.5	3.0	3.1	2.9	9.4	7.4
(142) 1.9	(138) 1.8	(146) 2.0	Amort./Cur. Mat. L/T/D		(20) 1.5	(23) 1.6	(30) 1.7	(36) 2.3	(37) 2.9
.6	.9	1.0			.6	1.0	.6	.9	1.8
.1	.1	.1		.1	.1	.1	.1	.1	.1
.3	.3	.3	Fixed/Worth	.5	.4	.3	.2	.3	.3
.8	.9	.7		−.8	6.9	1.0	.5	.6	.6
.9	1.0	.9		1.0	1.0	.7	.9	.9	1.0
2.2	2.3	2.0	Debt/Worth	4.7	2.3	1.6	1.6	2.3	2.2
4.6	5.6	4.9		−2.9	29.2	4.6	3.1	4.1	4.5
28.3	30.2	29.9	% Profit Before Taxes/Tangible	18.4	23.3	19.6	37.0	35.5	31.9
(533) 10.6	(485) 14.2	(457) 13.2	Net Worth	(23) 3.6	(83) 9.6	(66) 8.5	(91) 16.7	(111) 13.2	(83) 18.0
2.5	3.2	2.8		−.9	−.2	1.8	3.3	2.5	9.0
10.1	9.6	9.6	% Profit Before Taxes/Total	13.6	7.6	6.8	11.0	10.1	10.6
3.4	3.6	3.9	Assets	.6	2.4	3.2	4.0	4.4	6.3
.5	.4	.5		−10.4	−1.8	.3	1.7	.6	2.3
54.3	58.6	64.7		85.8	90.1	85.4	54.3	61.1	54.6
29.1	29.8	34.2	Sales/Net Fixed Assets	26.0	38.0	32.3	34.2	31.8	34.3
15.2	15.7	17.0		8.5	20.0	11.8	18.3	15.1	18.1
3.1	3.2	3.2		4.5	3.4	3.2	3.3	3.2	2.9
2.4	2.5	2.4	Sales/Total Assets	2.7	2.4	2.4	2.6	2.3	2.3
1.9	1.9	1.9		1.9	1.9	1.8	1.9	1.9	1.7
.6	.5	.5		.7	.5	.7	.5	.5	.5
(503) 1.0	(463) .9	(454) 1.0	% Depr., Dep., Amort./Sales	(31) 1.9	(87) 1.0	(63) 1.2	(85) .9	(106) .9	(82) .8
1.5	1.5	1.5		2.8	1.8	1.8	1.4	1.3	1.3
1.8	1.6	2.0	% Officers', Directors',	2.9	2.4	2.2	2.0	1.5	.9
(265) 3.1	(238) 3.4	(217) 3.4	Owners' Comp/Sales	(22) 6.5	(60) 3.9	(38) 4.5	(38) 3.2	(35) 2.9	(24) 1.9
5.7	5.8	6.1		10.0	5.6	5.6	4.6	4.6	3.4
12480272M	13619002M	12106376M	Net Sales ($)	27512M	195810M	286568M	676638M	1747664M	9172184M
6324437M	5987632M	5971613M	Total Assets ($)	11355M	90746M	146942M	282774M	775788M	4664008M

M = $ thousand   MM = $ million
See Pages 11 through 18 for Explanation of Ratios and Data

Current Data Sorted By Assets | Comparative Historical Data

0-500M	500M-2MM	2-10MM	10-50MM	50-100MM	100-250MM	Type of Statement	4/1/98-3/31/99 ALL	4/1/99-3/31/00 ALL
	1	4	10	2	3	Unqualified	21	23
2	6	11	13	2		Reviewed	32	34
5	13	19	6			Compiled	64	54
9	8	4			1	Tax Returns	9	9
6	6	14	8	3	1	Other	45	36
	25 (4/1-9/30/02)		132 (10/1/02-3/31/03)					
22	34	52	37	7	5	NUMBER OF STATEMENTS	171	156
%	%	%	%	%	%	**ASSETS**	%	%
10.5	9.4	5.5	4.6			Cash & Equivalents	6.7	5.4
21.9	28.2	28.2	27.6			Trade Receivables (net)	28.9	28.9
35.6	35.3	41.8	42.0			Inventory	38.7	39.1
3.0	1.5	2.1	3.3			All Other Current	1.7	2.4
71.0	74.4	77.6	77.5			Total Current	76.0	75.9
21.9	20.6	17.1	16.5			Fixed Assets (net)	16.6	17.7
2.0	.5	1.7	2.6			Intangibles (net)	2.5	1.2
5.1	4.5	3.5	3.3			All Other Non-Current	4.9	5.2
100.0	100.0	100.0	100.0			Total	100.0	100.0
						LIABILITIES		
6.7	11.3	9.6	13.7			Notes Payable-Short Term	11.9	11.6
2.2	3.5	4.7	2.3			Cur. Mat.-L/T/D	3.0	2.2
31.3	29.1	36.4	27.1			Trade Payables	33.8	34.5
.0	.1	.0	.4			Income Taxes Payable	.3	.2
11.1	7.8	6.8	6.7			All Other Current	6.1	5.1
51.2	51.7	57.5	50.1			Total Current	55.0	53.6
20.4	11.1	9.8	6.6			Long Term Debt	10.4	13.9
.0	.0	.2	.3			Deferred Taxes	.2	.2
5.4	1.5	2.6	3.0			All Other Non-Current	2.7	4.5
23.1	35.7	29.9	40.0			Net Worth	31.8	27.8
100.0	100.0	100.0	100.0			Total Liabilities & Net Worth	100.0	100.0
						INCOME DATA		
100.0	100.0	100.0	100.0			Net Sales	100.0	100.0
37.8	31.3	23.5	26.5			Gross Profit	25.7	27.3
36.6	29.5	21.9	23.6			Operating Expenses	23.3	25.7
1.3	1.8	1.6	2.9			Operating Profit	2.4	1.6
.7	.2	−.1	.0			All Other Expenses (net)	.1	.2
.6	1.6	1.7	3.0			Profit Before Taxes	2.4	1.4
						RATIOS		
2.6	1.9	2.0	2.2			Current	1.7	1.9
1.3	1.5	1.3	1.5				1.3	1.4
.9	1.1	1.1	1.2				1.1	1.2
1.4	1.2	.9	1.0			Quick	1.0	.9
.5	.7	.5	.6				.6 (155)	.6
.2	.4	.4	.4				.5	.5
5 76.2	18 20.7	22 16.3	31 11.6			Sales/Receivables	25 14.5	24 15.0
16 22.9	25 14.3	32 11.6	39 9.3				36 10.1	37 10.0
35 10.5	36 10.1	39 9.4	50 7.2				46 8.0	48 7.6
41 8.9	33 11.2	53 6.9	67 5.4			Cost of Sales/Inventory	44 8.3	50 7.3
48 7.5	58 6.3	67 5.4	87 4.2				67 5.4	68 5.3
75 4.8	76 4.8	88 4.1	114 3.2				91 4.0	92 4.0
18 20.5	29 12.5	42 8.8	26 13.8			Cost of Sales/Payables	36 10.3	38 9.6
34 10.9	49 7.5	56 6.5	49 7.5				58 6.3	60 6.1
78 4.7	70 5.2	82 4.5	82 4.5				81 4.5	81 4.5
9.2	7.9	8.7	5.8			Sales/Working Capital	8.0	7.1
22.1	16.4	18.7	9.0				14.3	12.9
−92.9	67.9	60.1	17.2				41.0	36.2
9.0	5.0	7.3	14.5			EBIT/Interest	7.7	7.5
(18) 2.8	(31) 3.1	(48) 3.5	(35) 7.6				(159) 3.7	(144) 3.1
.4	1.1	1.6	2.9				1.9	1.4
		6.1	7.2			Net Profit + Depr., Dep., Amort./Cur. Mat. L./T/D	5.4	5.3
	(22)	2.7	(12) 2.2				(58) 2.8	(54) 2.6
		1.2	.9				1.7	1.6
.2	.2	.2	.2			Fixed/Worth	.2	.2
.8	.7	.6	.4				.5	.5
−1.3	1.3	1.2	.7				1.1	1.1
.7	1.0	1.3	.9			Debt/Worth	1.4	1.4
4.2	2.1	2.8	1.6				2.5	2.5
−6.7	4.3	5.8	3.1				5.3	5.6
34.8	33.1	31.6	25.0			% Profit Before Taxes/Tangible Net Worth	37.0	32.4
(15) 13.2	15.4	(48) 13.7	(35) 18.8				(159) 20.6	(145) 15.0
1.1	4.7	6.1	8.0				8.6	5.8
11.8	9.0	6.7	10.3			% Profit Before Taxes/Total Assets	10.5	8.3
1.1	5.1	3.7	6.6				5.4	3.5
−4.1	1.4	1.5	3.1				1.9	1.0
68.6	43.7	57.4	35.7			Sales/Net Fixed Assets	41.7	42.7
26.0	22.1	24.5	22.3				22.2	20.8
11.1	13.1	12.1	10.9				11.5	11.2
4.6	4.1	3.7	3.3			Sales/Total Assets	3.5	3.5
4.1	3.5	3.0	2.6				2.8	2.9
3.3	2.6	2.5	2.0				2.3	2.2
.7	.9	.7	.4			% Depr., Dep., Amort./Sales	.6	.6
(17) 1.4	(31) 1.2	(47) 1.1	(35) 1.1				(157) 1.1	(145) 1.2
2.8	1.6	1.6	1.7				1.5	1.8
	2.9	1.1	.7			% Officers', Directors', Owners' Comp/Sales	1.2	1.5
	(18) 4.8	(20) 1.7	(13) 1.8				(69) 1.9	(55) 2.3
	6.1	3.9	8.1					5.1
25672M	153779M	756115M	1686209M	931643M	1577765M	Net Sales ($)	4521999M	4659816M
6960M	40772M	232095M	674459M	438336M	584817M	Total Assets ($)	1660540M	1727073M

© RMA 2003

M = $ thousand   MM = $ million
See Pages 11 through 18 for Explanation of Ratios and Data

Comparative Historical Data | Current Data Sorted By Sales

					25 (4/1-9/30/02)		132 (10/1/02-3/31/03)		
Type of Statement	4/1/00-3/31/01 ALL	4/1/01-3/31/02 ALL	4/1/02-3/31/03 ALL	0-1MM	1-3MM	3-5MM	5-10MM	10-25MM	25MM & OVER
Unqualified	16	19	20				1	3	16
Reviewed	44	33	34	1	4	2	4	4	19
Compiled	61	62	43	2	6	7	13	10	5
Tax Returns	15	20	22	1	11	3	5	1	1
Other	46	38	38	3	5	3	8	7	12
NUMBER OF STATEMENTS	182	172	157	7	26	15	31	25	53
ASSETS	%	%	%	%	%	%	%	%	%
Cash & Equivalents	6.1	5.9	7.1		10.5	7.3	8.1	4.5	5.5
Trade Receivables (net)	28.3	26.2	27.1		22.4	31.0	27.2	25.4	29.5
Inventory	38.9	40.5	39.0		38.2	35.2	38.1	42.3	41.1
All Other Current	1.8	2.0	2.4		2.3	2.0	1.5	5.1	2.0
Total Current	75.1	74.6	75.7		73.4	75.5	74.9	77.3	78.1
Fixed Assets (net)	18.1	18.5	18.6		21.0	19.6	19.7	17.4	16.1
Intangibles (net)	2.0	1.7	1.8		.6	.0	1.3	2.7	2.6
All Other Non-Current	4.8	5.2	3.9		4.9	4.9	4.1	2.7	3.2
Total	100.0	100.0	100.0		100.0	100.0	100.0	100.0	100.0
LIABILITIES									
Notes Payable-Short Term	10.9	11.4	10.9		9.2	10.7	8.4	11.6	13.6
Cur. Mat.-L/T/D	3.1	3.4	3.3		4.4	2.9	4.4	4.0	2.0
Trade Payables	33.7	34.4	31.0		30.1	31.4	38.8	32.0	26.7
Income Taxes Payable	.2	.2	.2		.1	.0	.1	.2	.4
All Other Current	7.6	8.7	7.8		10.6	5.8	5.1	10.5	7.4
Total Current	55.5	58.1	53.1		54.3	50.8	56.8	58.4	50.0
Long Term Debt	11.3	11.8	10.8		19.8	9.7	11.8	7.5	7.4
Deferred Taxes	.2	.2	.2		.0	.0	.2	.1	.3
All Other Non-Current	2.8	4.5	3.3		3.4	1.7	3.2	1.6	4.0
Net Worth	30.1	25.4	32.6		22.4	37.8	28.1	32.4	38.3
Total Liabilities & Net Worth	100.0	100.0	100.0		100.0	100.0	100.0	100.0	100.0
INCOME DATA									
Net Sales	100.0	100.0	100.0		100.0	100.0	100.0	100.0	100.0
Gross Profit	28.1	27.5	28.1		37.7	28.9	26.7	26.0	24.2
Operating Expenses	26.7	26.2	26.0		36.4	26.8	24.9	23.1	21.9
Operating Profit	1.4	1.3	2.1		1.3	2.1	1.8	2.8	2.3
All Other Expenses (net)	−.6	.1	.1		.5	.4	.0	.0	.0
Profit Before Taxes	2.0	1.2	1.9		.8	1.7	1.8	2.9	2.4
RATIOS									
Current	1.8	1.8	2.1		2.1	2.7	1.9	2.0	2.1
	1.4	1.4	1.4		1.4	1.5	1.2	1.3	1.5
	1.1	1.1	1.1		1.0	1.2	1.1	1.1	1.2
Quick	.9	.8	1.0		1.1	1.5	.9	.7	1.0
	.6	.5	.6		.6	.7	.6	.5	.6
	.4	.4	.4		.3	.5	.4	.3	.4
Sales/Receivables	23 16.0	19 18.9	20 18.1		10 38.2	17 21.2	23 15.8	20 18.6	31 12.0
	34 10.8	30 12.2	33 11.1		19 19.2	34 10.8	30 12.1	27 13.6	40 9.2
	47 7.8	42 8.8	44 8.3		38 9.6	46 7.9	38 9.7	37 9.7	50 7.3
Cost of Sales/Inventory	46 8.0	49 7.4	46 7.9		45 8.2	30 12.3	53 6.9	42 8.7	58 6.3
	70 5.2	67 5.4	67 5.4		60 6.0	63 5.8	65 5.6	73 5.0	71 5.1
	91 4.0	87 4.2	89 4.1		83 4.4	119 3.1	82 4.4	106 3.4	91 4.0
Cost of Sales/Payables	31 11.9	31 11.9	27 13.5		28 13.0	32 11.4	41 8.9	20 18.2	22 16.4
	55 6.6	55 6.7	52 7.0		52 7.0	47 7.7	61 6.0	51 7.2	47 7.7
	84 4.3	76 4.8	76 4.8		64 5.7	76 4.8	86 4.2	68 5.3	78 4.7
Sales/Working Capital	8.5	8.3	7.5		8.8	7.0	7.7	8.9	6.5
	14.9	15.6	14.3		13.8	16.4	18.9	22.2	11.3
	86.8	78.2	49.6		UND	27.4	74.8	72.0	19.6
EBIT/Interest	7.1	6.7	10.0		5.0	5.3	9.3	14.3	14.7
	(171) 2.7	(161) 2.6	(144) 3.8		(23) 2.9	(13) 3.4	(29) 3.1	4.1	(49) 5.5
	1.3	1.1	1.7		.2	1.4	1.6	2.3	2.5
Net Profit + Depr., Dep., Amort./Cur. Mat. L/T/D	4.8	3.1	5.4				6.9		4.7
	(60) 2.4	(53) 2.0	(46) 2.2				(11) 2.3		(16) 2.2
	1.0	1.2	1.0				.5		.9
Fixed/Worth	.3	.3	.2		.2	.2	.2	.3	.2
	.6	.6	.6		.9	.4	.6	.6	.4
	1.4	1.6	1.2		NM	1.1	1.3	1.3	.7
Debt/Worth	1.3	1.1	1.0		1.0	.9	1.3	1.2	.9
	2.2	2.6	2.3		3.4	1.9	3.1	2.6	1.8
	6.2	6.3	5.3		NM	3.7	5.5	5.7	3.1
% Profit Before Taxes/Tangible Net Worth	26.3	25.0	28.7		33.9	22.4	31.1	35.5	25.8
	(166) 13.2	(155) 14.0	(142) 16.8		(20) 17.7	11.9	(29) 13.4	(23) 20.0	(49) 18.3
	5.5	4.8	6.2		−6.0	6.1	5.9	9.3	7.5
% Profit Before Taxes/Total Assets	8.8	7.9	9.2		10.2	7.0	6.6	12.3	10.0
	3.8	3.7	4.5		4.0	4.5	4.0	4.3	5.6
	1.0	.5	1.3		−3.2	1.9	1.4	2.6	2.9
Sales/Net Fixed Assets	41.4	46.0	44.2		62.8	49.1	34.6	52.3	42.7
	22.1	20.5	23.2		23.3	20.9	24.9	23.9	22.3
	12.1	11.0	11.3		10.3	16.0	11.6	11.9	10.9
Sales/Total Assets	3.7	3.9	3.7		4.4	4.0	3.5	3.8	3.5
	3.0	3.1	3.1		3.5	3.3	3.0	3.2	2.7
	2.4	2.4	2.4		2.5	2.5	2.6	2.4	2.2
% Depr., Dep., Amort./Sales	.6	.6	.6		.8	.5	.7	.8	.4
	(170) 1.1	(151) 1.2	(140) 1.1		(22) 1.6	(13) .9	(30) 1.1	(22) 1.2	(48) 1.0
	1.9	2.0	1.7		2.7	1.4	1.7	1.7	1.4
% Officers', Directors', Owners' Comp/Sales	1.1	1.2	1.2		3.4		1.2		.6
	(79) 2.1	(76) 2.5	(63) 2.9		(13) 6.1		(15) 2.5		(18) 1.1
	5.4	5.0	5.4		7.7		4.3		4.2
Net Sales ($)	4965611M	4923476M	5131183M	4309M	46375M	61445M	221719M	388269M	4409066M
Total Assets ($)	1852848M	1882247M	1977439M	1724M	16401M	28341M	76766M	153924M	1700283M

M = $ thousand   MM = $ million
See Pages 11 through 18 for Explanation of Ratios and Data

Current Data Sorted By Assets   Comparative Historical Data

0-500M	500M-2MM	2-10MM	10-50MM	50-100MM	100-250MM	Type of Statement	4/1/98-3/31/99 ALL	4/1/99-3/31/00 ALL
				1		Unqualified	4	3
2	3	7	4			Reviewed	8	4
4	6	1				Compiled	16	14
6	11	1				Tax Returns	7	7
	8	3	3		2	Other	6	13
17 (4/1-9/30/02)			45 (10/1/02-3/31/03)					
12	28	12	7	1	2	NUMBER OF STATEMENTS	41	41
%	%	%	%	%	%	**ASSETS**	%	%
11.3	3.6	3.1				Cash & Equivalents	3.8	6.9
16.1	14.8	20.1				Trade Receivables (net)	13.1	15.9
34.8	44.1	41.8				Inventory	46.0	43.8
.2	2.1	1.1				All Other Current	.9	1.1
62.4	64.6	66.1				Total Current	63.7	67.7
31.8	22.7	23.1				Fixed Assets (net)	31.9	24.8
3.1	4.3	4.5				Intangibles (net)	.8	2.2
2.7	8.3	6.3				All Other Non-Current	3.6	5.3
100.0	100.0	100.0				Total	100.0	100.0
						LIABILITIES		
11.9	14.1	28.8				Notes Payable-Short Term	21.8	15.1
7.3	6.4	.9				Cur. Mat.-L/T/D	5.2	4.5
9.9	11.0	10.8				Trade Payables	9.7	10.4
.1	.0	.0				Income Taxes Payable	.1	.2
25.9	8.6	9.2				All Other Current	9.9	4.2
55.0	40.1	49.6				Total Current	46.7	34.4
20.8	11.4	13.6				Long Term Debt	17.8	15.5
.0	.0	.2				Deferred Taxes	.2	.3
12.8	3.4	1.9				All Other Non-Current	3.1	5.8
11.4	45.0	34.6				Net Worth	32.1	44.0
100.0	100.0	100.0				Total Liabilities & Net Worth	100.0	100.0
						INCOME DATA		
100.0	100.0	100.0				Net Sales	100.0	100.0
53.9	45.5	26.5				Gross Profit	43.9	35.9
55.5	43.4	26.9				Operating Expenses	41.5	31.9
-1.6	2.2	-.5				Operating Profit	2.4	3.9
1.2	.7	.4				All Other Expenses (net)	1.9	.7
-2.8	1.4	-.8				Profit Before Taxes	.5	3.2
						RATIOS		
2.7	2.9	2.1				Current	2.1	4.1
1.2	1.8	1.5					1.5	2.2
.8	1.0	.7					1.0	1.2
1.0	1.2	1.0				Quick	.6	1.8
.5	(27) .5	.4					.3	.6
.2	.2	.1					.2	.2
0 UND	6 57.4	10 37.3				Sales/Receivables	1 288.2	4 94.9
16 22.9	21 17.2	22 16.5					18 19.7	17 21.9
29 12.5	34 10.7	41 8.9					32 11.2	29 12.8
47 7.8	45 8.1	49 7.4				Cost of Sales/Inventory	48 7.6	48 7.5
73 5.0	112 3.2	82 4.4					118 3.1	91 4.0
144 2.5	239 1.5	108 3.4					220 1.7	161 2.3
0 UND	6 60.1	4 92.7				Cost of Sales/Payables	1 460.9	2 201.4
14 25.9	19 19.5	13 28.1					11 31.8	15 24.3
28 13.1	42 8.7	29 12.5					56 6.5	38 9.5
8.1	5.0	5.8				Sales/Working Capital	7.7	4.3
19.0	11.8	10.6					13.4	9.1
-37.5	NM	-182.1					NM	23.3
3.6	8.3	6.0				EBIT/Interest	4.3	9.6
(11) 1.2	(25) 3.9	2.6					(40) 1.4	(35) 3.4
-1.0	1.1	-.2					-.5	1.1
						Net Profit + Depr., Dep., Amort./Cur. Mat. L /T/D		
.5	.3	.1				Fixed/Worth	.3	.2
1.9	.5	.3					.6	.5
-1.0	.9	2.7					2.9	.9
1.1	.5	1.2				Debt/Worth	1.0	.5
6.3	1.0	2.2					2.2	1.5
-5.0	5.0	7.3					4.4	4.1
	17.8	20.9				% Profit Before Taxes/Tangible Net Worth	27.5	29.7
	(24) 10.2	(11) 14.7					(36) 10.5	(39) 15.9
	2.2	-17.4					-10.3	6.0
9.3	9.3	7.3				% Profit Before Taxes/Total Assets	12.3	12.8
.4	4.5	2.0					1.7	5.9
-25.8	.2	-2.9					-6.3	.9
37.2	30.3	103.3				Sales/Net Fixed Assets	23.4	32.9
13.0	13.5	16.4					10.9	15.5
4.3	6.7	5.7					3.2	5.6
4.8	3.7	2.9				Sales/Total Assets	3.3	3.7
3.2	2.2	2.2					2.1	2.3
2.1	1.7	1.8					1.6	1.7
1.2	.8	.7				% Depr., Dep., Amort./Sales	.6	.8
2.1	(23) 2.4	(11) 1.4					(38) 2.4	(35) 1.5
8.8	3.2	3.2					4.4	2.7
	3.4					% Officers', Directors', Owners' Comp/Sales	2.7	1.5
	(18) 5.7						(17) 4.1	(25) 4.8
	7.9						6.7	6.6
12579M	71639M	106958M	233474M	43932M	845179M	Net Sales ($)	311336M	234055M
3703M	27226M	49476M	120079M	68722M	391049M	Total Assets ($)	144518M	153785M

M = $ thousand   MM = $ million
See Pages 11 through 18 for Explanation of Ratios and Data

Comparative Historical Data   Current Data Sorted By Sales

							Type of Statement						
	3		1		1		Unqualified						1
	8		6		16		Reviewed	1	2	3	4	2	4
	21		21		11		Compiled	6	4			1	
	9		9		18		Tax Returns	4	8	5	1		
	10		11		16		Other	1	5	2	4		4
	4/1/00- 3/31/01 ALL		4/1/01- 3/31/02 ALL		4/1/02- 3/31/03 ALL			17 (4/1-9/30/02)			45 (10/1/02-3/31/03)		
								0-1MM	1-3MM	3-5MM	5-10MM	10-25MM	25MM & OVER
	51		48		62		NUMBER OF STATEMENTS	12	19	10	9	3	9
	%		%		%		ASSETS	%	%	%	%	%	%
	7.5		5.9		4.9		Cash & Equivalents	9.3	6.3	2.1			
	18.8		19.7		17.1		Trade Receivables (net)	16.5	12.4	21.6			
	40.8		46.4		41.4		Inventory	40.1	40.1	36.6			
	2.1		.6		1.7		All Other Current	.1	2.3	2.3			
	69.1		72.6		65.0		Total Current	66.0	61.0	62.7			
	24.2		20.0		24.9		Fixed Assets (net)	29.5	25.6	25.7			
	2.6		1.1		4.1		Intangibles (net)	2.2	6.4	1.2			
	5.1		7.3		6.0		All Other Non-Current	2.4	7.0	10.4			
	100.0		100.0		100.0		Total	100.0	100.0	100.0			
							LIABILITIES						
	16.1		24.4		17.4		Notes Payable-Short Term	10.5	13.2	15.3			
	7.6		3.4		4.9		Cur. Mat.-L/T/D	10.6	5.3	3.8			
	12.1		14.3		10.4		Trade Payables	12.1	7.2	13.6			
	.4		.1		.1		Income Taxes Payable	.1	.0	.0			
	6.9		6.3		12.4		All Other Current	14.6	16.4	8.0			
	43.3		48.5		45.1		Total Current	47.9	42.1	40.6			
	19.3		15.2		14.6		Long Term Debt	14.3	20.3	8.9			
	.2		.1		.2		Deferred Taxes	.0	.0	.0			
	5.3		6.6		4.7		All Other Non-Current	12.6	4.0	1.9			
	32.0		29.7		35.4		Net Worth	25.2	33.6	48.6			
	100.0		100.0		100.0		Total Liabilities & Net Worth	100.0	100.0	100.0			
							INCOME DATA						
	100.0		100.0		100.0		Net Sales	100.0	100.0	100.0			
	38.9		41.5		42.1		Gross Profit	56.1	43.2	42.4			
	34.8		39.9		40.8		Operating Expenses	58.8	42.8	39.6			
	4.2		1.6		1.3		Operating Profit	-2.6	.4	2.8			
	.7		1.6		.8		All Other Expenses (net)	1.4	.9	.1			
	3.5		.0		.5		Profit Before Taxes	-4.0	-.4	2.7			
							RATIOS						
	3.6		2.6		2.6			4.7	2.8	3.2			
	1.9		1.6		1.5		Current	1.5	1.5	1.9			
	1.3		1.2		1.0			.9	.9	.8			
	1.0		.9		1.0			1.4	1.1				
	.7		.5	(61)	.5		Quick	.6	.4				
	.3		.2		.2			.2	.3				
9	39.2	10	36.1	7	53.5			1	487.9	5	73.2	1	456.9
21	17.7	24	15.4	25	14.8		Sales/Receivables	29	12.7	16	22.4	27	13.5
39	9.5	40	9.2	34	10.8			43	8.4	26	14.1	39	9.4
49	7.5	64	5.7	51	7.2			55	6.7	32	11.2	44	8.4
90	4.0	99	3.7	108	3.4		Cost of Sales/Inventory	151	2.4	115	3.2	54	6.8
143	2.5	197	1.9	148	2.5			384	1.0	206	1.8	100	3.6
6	66.1	5	67.1	6	59.9			0	UND	5	67.6	0	UND
15	23.9	18	20.3	20	18.5		Cost of Sales/Payables	17	21.5	16	22.7	23	16.0
44	8.2	54	6.8	33	11.2			81	4.5	30	12.3	35	10.3
	4.8		5.2		5.7			3.2	5.3	7.3			
	8.5		10.3		12.7		Sales/Working Capital	16.2	9.2	18.4			
	22.1		35.0		-618.5			NM	-67.7	-37.8			
	4.4		4.0		6.3				6.2	14.6			
(44)	2.5	(45)	2.0	(58)	3.4		EBIT/Interest	(18)	1.4	5.4			
	.7		1.2		1.0				.2	4.3			
	2.1		4.4		3.0		Net Profit + Depr., Dep.,						
(13)	1.4	(10)	1.6	(13)	1.7		Amort./Cur. Mat. L/T/D						
	.4		.9		.9								
	.2		.3		.2			.2	.3	.3			
	.5		.6		.6		Fixed/Worth	1.7	.7	.6			
	1.3		2.8		1.9			-1.0	1.8	.8			
	.7		1.0		.8			.6	.6	.3			
	1.5		1.9		1.6		Debt/Worth	2.5	1.4	.9			
	6.1		12.5		7.3			-7.6	19.2	3.5			
	23.9		40.4		25.3		% Profit Before Taxes/Tangible		28.6				
(43)	10.3	(39)	16.0	(52)	12.2		Net Worth	(15)	8.6				
	.6		3.1		1.1				.6				
	13.9		8.1		9.8		% Profit Before Taxes/Total	5.0	6.7	13.5			
	4.5		4.3		3.7		Assets	-.4	.6	8.9			
	-.1		.7		-1.3			-27.0	-2.6	4.2			
	27.5		41.7		36.0			37.8	28.1	30.5			
	11.9		13.3		14.8		Sales/Net Fixed Assets	5.9	13.3	18.5			
	6.4		9.7		5.8			4.1	5.8	12.4			
	3.6		3.2		3.5			3.0	3.6	5.0			
	2.3		2.4		2.5		Sales/Total Assets	1.8	2.1	3.6			
	1.9		1.8		1.7			1.2	1.8	2.5			
	.6		.8		.8		% Depr., Dep., Amort./Sales		.6	1.2			
(48)	1.6	(41)	1.3	(56)	1.5			(10)	2.3	(17)	2.6		
	2.4		2.3		3.2				9.9	3.9			
	2.5		2.8		2.8		% Officers', Directors',			3.2			
(29)	4.7	(28)	6.0	(30)	5.7		Owners' Comp/Sales	(13)	7.1				
	7.7		10.7		10.2				10.5				
	504683M		225853M		1313761M		Net Sales ($)	7887M	37253M	38414M	66376M	49065M	1114766M
	359838M		95152M		660255M		Total Assets ($)	5214M	17312M	11560M	38879M	18686M	568604M

© RMA 2003   M = $ thousand   MM = $ million
See Pages 11 through 18 for Explanation of Ratios and Data

Current Data Sorted By Assets   **Comparative Historical Data**

Type of Statement	0-500M	500M-2MM	2-10MM	10-50MM	50-100MM	100-250MM		4/1/98-3/31/99 ALL	4/1/99-3/31/00 ALL
Unqualified		1	17	14	3			50	38
Reviewed	1	20	40	10				89	103
Compiled	9	26	16	1				59	58
Tax Returns	3	12	3					15	16
Other	5	15	26	12	2	1		46	75
	41 (4/1-9/30/02)		196 (10/1/02-3/31/03)						
NUMBER OF STATEMENTS	18	74	102	37	5	1		259	290
	%	%	%	%	%	%		%	%
ASSETS									
Cash & Equivalents	16.1	9.5	9.4	9.2				8.0	8.2
Trade Receivables (net)	22.4	34.3	41.6	42.9				40.6	43.8
Inventory	40.1	36.7	25.4	23.4				28.4	27.3
All Other Current	3.0	2.9	3.2	2.9				1.8	2.4
Total Current	81.7	83.3	79.6	78.4				78.8	81.7
Fixed Assets (net)	10.7	10.8	13.2	10.6				14.0	12.2
Intangibles (net)	.2	1.2	1.6	1.6				1.8	1.6
All Other Non-Current	7.4	4.7	5.6	9.4				5.4	4.4
Total	100.0	100.0	100.0	100.0				100.0	100.0
LIABILITIES									
Notes Payable-Short Term	16.9	15.2	17.7	14.8				17.6	16.8
Cur. Mat.-L/T/D	6.3	2.3	2.2	1.0				2.2	2.1
Trade Payables	27.6	22.4	18.6	17.6				22.8	22.0
Income Taxes Payable	.0	.1	.2	.3				.4	.4
All Other Current	17.3	15.3	15.0	15.2				12.1	14.1
Total Current	68.2	55.3	53.7	48.9				55.1	55.3
Long Term Debt	15.5	8.1	6.0	5.6				7.8	8.0
Deferred Taxes	.0	.0	.0	.7				.3	.2
All Other Non-Current	7.2	5.4	4.3	5.8				4.9	5.3
Net Worth	9.2	31.1	36.0	38.9				31.9	31.2
Total Liabilities & Net Worth	100.0	100.0	100.0	100.0				100.0	100.0
INCOME DATA									
Net Sales	100.0	100.0	100.0	100.0				100.0	100.0
Gross Profit	38.2	29.8	27.9	25.8				29.8	28.7
Operating Expenses	38.0	29.1	26.3	22.9				27.1	25.4
Operating Profit	.2	.7	1.6	2.8				2.7	3.3
All Other Expenses (net)	.4	.6	.2	.0				-.1	.2
Profit Before Taxes	-.2	.1	1.4	2.9				2.8	3.0
RATIOS									
Current	3.0	2.1	1.9	2.4				2.2	2.1
	1.1	1.6	1.5	1.5				1.4	1.4
	.7	1.1	1.2	1.3				1.1	1.2
Quick	1.1	1.3	1.2	1.6				1.3	1.3
	.5	.9	.9	1.1				.9	1.0
	.1	.4	.7	.8				.5	.7
Sales/Receivables	0 UND	18 20.1	27 13.7	32 11.4				28 12.8	29 12.6
	12 29.4	34 10.6	38 9.6	49 7.4				40 9.1	44 8.2
	20 18.0	53 6.9	55 6.6	61 6.0				58 6.3	60 6.1
Cost of Sales/Inventory	0 UND	23 15.8	11 32.9	12 31.3				16 23.3	13 27.2
	23 16.2	60 6.1	27 13.7	24 15.3				41 9.0	31 11.9
	104 3.5	117 3.1	75 4.9	56 6.5				82 4.4	75 4.9
Cost of Sales/Payables	4 92.0	15 24.7	12 30.0	18 19.9				18 19.7	14 25.7
	28 13.0	26 13.8	21 17.3	23 16.1				30 12.1	28 13.0
	62 5.9	46 7.9	43 8.6	29 12.7				46 7.9	44 8.2
Sales/Working Capital	16.1	5.5	8.5	7.3				7.3	8.2
	211.7	13.3	15.8	12.0				14.5	15.4
	-23.8	50.1	43.9	22.9				47.7	35.5
EBIT/Interest	4.3	5.9	9.5	14.9				8.3	9.7
	(14) .3	(64) 2.0	(94) 2.8	(30) 2.8				(235) 3.6	(261) 4.0
	-.6	-.9	1.2	1.4				1.5	1.6
Net Profit + Depr., Dep., Amort./Cur. Mat. L/T/D		5.8	10.4	28.2				8.6	10.9
		(17) 2.2	(31) 3.4	(12) 4.6				(84) 3.5	(84) 3.9
		1.0	.8	1.9				1.1	1.1
Fixed/Worth	.3	.1	.1	.1				.1	.1
	10.7	.2	.3	.2				.3	.3
	-.4	1.1	1.0	.5				.9	.8
Debt/Worth	1.5	1.0	1.0	.8				1.0	1.1
	71.1	1.8	2.0	1.9				2.4	2.5
	-4.4	6.3	4.9	3.7				4.7	5.2
% Profit Before Taxes/Tangible Net Worth	100.0	23.5	32.0	40.9				49.2	56.2
	(11) 13.0	(62) 9.6	(96) 13.9	(35) 17.3				(240) 25.5	(265) 27.3
	-7.8	-6.9	2.8	5.0				9.5	8.6
% Profit Before Taxes/Total Assets	22.9	9.7	10.9	18.7				14.8	14.4
	.3	2.5	4.2	4.4				7.2	7.2
	-6.7	-3.2	.4	1.4				2.3	2.1
Sales/Net Fixed Assets	230.6	127.1	92.7	71.7				82.5	91.6
	65.1	51.6	43.8	34.7				36.5	43.2
	30.0	26.8	19.5	23.0				18.6	23.1
Sales/Total Assets	9.7	4.2	4.5	4.2				4.3	4.6
	5.6	3.2	3.4	3.4				3.3	3.5
	3.4	2.4	2.6	2.5				2.4	2.6
% Depr., Dep., Amort./Sales	.4	.3	.4	.4				.4	.4
	(13) .8	(61) .6	(93) .7	(36) .7				(225) .6	(250) .7
	1.4	.9	1.2	1.1				1.2	1.1
% Officers', Directors', Owners' Comp/Sales	3.0	2.2	1.7	1.0				1.9	1.8
	(15) 7.4	(37) 3.2	(43) 2.7	(14) 1.6				(108) 3.1	(112) 3.6
	10.0	5.8	5.4					6.0	6.0
Net Sales ($)	44848M	330760M	1691323M	2478638M	1146143M	323225M		4874098M	6975652M
Total Assets ($)	5902M	91521M	470122M	745864M	353228M	108851M		1622045M	2016988M

M = $ thousand   MM = $ million
See Pages 11 through 18 for Explanation of Ratios and Data

Comparative Historical Data			Type of Statement	Current Data Sorted By Sales					
27	25	35	Unqualified		1			13	21
101	66	71	Reviewed	1	4	8	17	24	17
69	66	52	Compiled	5	15	12	10	9	1
22	25	18	Tax Returns	2	5	3	6	2	
75	96	61	Other	2	4	6	11	22	16
4/1/00-3/31/01 ALL	4/1/01-3/31/02 ALL	4/1/02-3/31/03 ALL		41 (4/1-9/30/02)			196 (10/1/02-3/31/03)		
				0-1MM	1-3MM	3-5MM	5-10MM	10-25MM	25MM & OVER
294	278	237	**NUMBER OF STATEMENTS**	10	29	29	44	70	55
%	%	%	**ASSETS**	%	%	%	%	%	%
9.3	8.7	9.7	Cash & Equivalents	3.3	7.3	14.0	12.3	10.2	7.2
41.5	37.3	38.2	Trade Receivables (net)	23.2	23.0	29.3	37.9	43.2	47.6
27.0	29.3	29.9	Inventory	53.1	47.2	35.9	27.5	23.8	23.0
2.8	2.9	3.1	All Other Current	5.2	1.7	1.8	3.8	3.1	3.4
80.7	78.1	80.9	Total Current	84.9	79.2	80.9	81.4	80.3	81.3
12.4	13.2	11.8	Fixed Assets (net)	5.7	15.9	11.4	10.8	12.8	10.7
2.2	2.1	1.4	Intangibles (net)	.6	1.0	1.6	.6	1.2	2.3
4.7	6.5	6.0	All Other Non-Current	8.8	4.0	6.1	7.2	5.7	5.7
100.0	100.0	100.0	Total	100.0	100.0	100.0	100.0	100.0	100.0
			LIABILITIES						
15.4	15.4	16.2	Notes Payable-Short Term	25.9	14.2	17.1	14.3	17.0	15.6
2.1	3.0	2.3	Cur. Mat.-L/T/D	5.7	4.1	2.0	2.0	2.3	1.1
23.4	21.5	20.6	Trade Payables	22.8	17.1	22.0	25.4	19.6	18.7
.3	.2	.2	Income Taxes Payable	.0	.0	.0	.2	.3	.2
16.9	15.7	15.4	All Other Current	14.1	12.5	13.3	17.0	14.4	18.3
58.1	55.8	54.7	Total Current	68.6	47.9	54.4	58.9	53.6	53.9
7.3	8.5	7.4	Long Term Debt	18.0	16.3	7.6	4.2	5.1	6.0
.1	.2	.1	Deferred Taxes	.0	.0	.0	.2	.0	.5
3.8	5.3	5.0	All Other Non-Current	10.6	7.4	2.0	7.7	2.6	5.3
30.6	30.2	32.8	Net Worth	2.7	28.4	36.0	29.1	38.6	34.4
100.0	100.0	100.0	Total Liabilities & Net Worth	100.0	100.0	100.0	100.0	100.0	100.0
			INCOME DATA						
100.0	100.0	100.0	Net Sales	100.0	100.0	100.0	100.0	100.0	100.0
28.9	29.0	28.9	Gross Profit	42.6	34.2	30.5	29.1	27.4	24.6
25.9	27.3	27.6	Operating Expenses	44.2	32.9	29.8	27.9	25.7	22.8
3.0	1.6	1.3	Operating Profit	-1.6	1.2	.7	1.2	1.7	1.8
.3	.5	.3	All Other Expenses (net)	1.7	.6	.3	.0	.3	.0
2.7	1.1	1.0	Profit Before Taxes	-3.3	.7	.4	1.2	1.4	1.8
			RATIOS						
1.9	2.0	2.0	Current	3.6	3.0	1.9	2.2	1.9	2.0
1.3	1.4	1.5		1.1	1.7	1.7	1.5	1.5	1.4
1.1	1.1	1.1		.8	1.0	1.2	1.0	1.2	1.2
1.2	1.2	1.3	Quick	1.0	1.3	1.3	1.3	1.3	1.4
.9	(277) .8	.9		.2	.5	.9	.8	1.0	1.0
.6	.5	.6		.0	.2	.5	.5	.7	.8
25 14.6	19 19.4	23 15.6	Sales/Receivables	0 UND	2 161.3	21 17.1	20 18.4	28 12.8	31 11.7
41 8.9	35 10.4	38 9.7		30 12.2	19 19.1	30 12.0	33 11.2	39 9.4	49 7.5
61 6.0	53 6.9	56 6.5		57 6.4	50 7.4	46 7.9	54 6.8	54 6.8	59 6.2
12 31.3	11 32.2	11 31.9	Cost of Sales/Inventory	0 UND	50 7.3	28 13.2	8 45.9	11 33.2	10 35.9
30 12.2	32 11.6	36 10.1		211 1.7	94 3.9	62 5.9	32 11.3	22 16.8	22 16.5
75 4.9	85 4.3	86 4.2		396 .9	189 1.9	90 4.0	76 4.8	52 7.0	52 7.1
16 23.3	13 27.5	13 27.9	Cost of Sales/Payables	2 170.1	9 40.5	13 28.6	13 29.1	13 29.0	16 22.5
29 12.6	26 14.1	25 14.7		65 5.6	26 14.0	26 14.1	29 12.5	23 16.0	22 16.6
46 7.9	43 8.4	43 8.5		165 2.2	49 7.5	49 7.5	49 7.4	36 10.1	27 13.6
8.6	9.1	7.3	Sales/Working Capital	2.5	3.9	6.4	8.5	8.5	9.6
17.9	18.6	15.0		21.5	8.5	12.2	15.0	16.5	15.0
59.0	67.0	42.3		-16.1	NM	26.9	999.8	44.7	27.9
8.2	6.3	8.0	EBIT/Interest		6.7	6.3	7.6	10.3	13.9
(269) 3.0	(253) 2.5	(207) 2.3		(27) 1.9	(22) 2.3	(39) 2.0	(65) 2.6	(46) 3.2	
1.5	.6	.4		-1.0	1.2	.8	.7	1.6	
9.6	4.4	9.8	Net Profit + Depr., Dep., Amort./Cur. Mat. L/T/D				7.4	10.2	20.6
(83) 3.2	(63) 1.9	(62) 2.8				(14) 2.3	(21) 5.5	(18) 2.8	
1.2	.6	.9				.7	.8	1.7	
.2	.1	.1	Fixed/Worth	.2	.1	.0	.1	.1	.1
.4	.4	.3		1.5	.4	.2	.3	.2	.3
1.0	1.1	1.2		-.3	3.4	1.0	1.6	.8	.7
1.3	1.2	1.0	Debt/Worth	3.7	1.2	1.0	1.1	.9	1.0
2.8	2.6	2.0		60.0	1.8	1.6	2.2	1.9	2.0
6.6	7.0	5.7		-6.9	16.6	5.4	9.9	3.6	5.0
52.5	41.4	32.0	% Profit Before Taxes/Tangible Net Worth		26.8	16.9	23.4	32.5	40.9
(268) 21.8	(246) 14.9	(210) 12.8		(23) 7.4	(26) 9.4	(35) 11.9	(68) 11.9	(51) 18.4	
8.3	1.3	.8		-7.8	2.3	2.2	.5	5.0	
14.7	11.5	10.7	% Profit Before Taxes/Total Assets	8.3	9.8	9.4	10.6	10.9	12.6
5.7	4.0	3.2		-6.7	1.8	2.3	3.1	3.4	5.1
2.2	-.8	-1.3		-17.5	-4.3	-.1	-.5	.1	.8
84.0	85.8	106.8	Sales/Net Fixed Assets	UND	139.6	137.7	106.5	119.3	76.7
43.4	45.0	45.6		52.6	30.6	60.7	48.0	50.5	41.5
20.0	22.1	23.9		31.9	14.7	24.6	22.9	20.2	28.7
4.6	5.0	4.5	Sales/Total Assets	3.3	4.4	4.0	5.0	4.8	4.6
3.5	3.7	3.4		2.0	2.4	3.1	3.7	3.8	3.6
2.5	2.6	2.6		1.0	1.8	2.5	2.7	2.8	3.0
.4	.4	.3	% Depr., Dep., Amort./Sales		.4	.1	.5	.4	.3
(248) .6	(235) .6	(209) .7			(24) .6	(22) .6	(42) .7	(62) .7	(53) .6
1.1	1.0	1.1			1.3	1.1	.9	1.2	1.0
1.7	1.7	1.8	% Officers', Directors', Owners' Comp/Sales		4.0	2.1	1.8	1.7	1.1
(126) 3.9	(135) 2.7	(110) 2.9			(15) 5.6	(18) 2.7	(26) 2.8	(24) 2.6	(21) 1.8
6.2	5.5	5.6			9.1	4.6	4.8	4.6	5.5
7568717M	6617749M	6014937M	Net Sales ($)	6291M	60490M	113517M	309997M	1128561M	4396081M
2630439M	1949524M	1775488M	Total Assets ($)	4296M	25679M	38412M	91721M	349109M	1266271M

M = $ thousand   MM = $ million
See Pages 11 through 18 for Explanation of Ratios and Data

Current Data Sorted By Assets

Comparative Historical Data

						Type of Statement		
	2	15	21	1	2	Unqualified	49	48
	11	42	14			Reviewed	99	74
6	16	20	6			Compiled	65	49
8	10	6				Tax Returns	12	21
5	19	24	22	4	3	Other	69	47

	37 (4/1-9/30/02)		217 (10/1/02-3/31/03)				4/1/98-3/31/99	4/1/99-3/31/00
0-500M	500M-2MM	2-10MM	10-50MM	50-100MM	100-250MM		ALL	ALL
19	58	107	60	5	5	NUMBER OF STATEMENTS	294	239
%	%	%	%	%	%	ASSETS	%	%
18.3	5.5	5.8	4.4			Cash & Equivalents	5.6	6.1
30.1	29.8	35.7	32.3			Trade Receivables (net)	33.6	34.1
31.4	42.3	39.3	42.4			Inventory	41.4	39.0
4.4	2.5	2.0	3.3			All Other Current	1.9	2.1
84.2	80.1	82.9	82.3			Total Current	82.5	81.2
12.3	10.9	12.1	10.1			Fixed Assets (net)	10.6	12.2
.7	3.0	1.0	2.7			Intangibles (net)	2.0	1.7
2.8	6.0	4.0	4.9			All Other Non-Current	4.9	4.8
100.0	100.0	100.0	100.0			Total	100.0	100.0
						LIABILITIES		
19.1	13.1	16.7	17.5			Notes Payable-Short Term	18.1	18.7
25.2	2.7	1.7	1.2			Cur. Mat.-L/T/D	2.4	2.4
26.5	20.8	23.1	19.5			Trade Payables	20.5	20.9
.3	.1	.3	.3			Income Taxes Payable	.3	.4
17.4	10.7	9.6	9.7			All Other Current	9.7	9.1
88.5	47.5	51.4	48.1			Total Current	51.1	51.5
8.9	10.0	7.8	7.5			Long Term Debt	8.4	7.4
.0	.1	.1	.1			Deferred Taxes	.2	.1
3.2	5.6	4.6	4.1			All Other Non-Current	5.0	4.2
−.5	36.9	36.1	40.2			Net Worth	35.3	36.7
100.0	100.0	100.0	100.0			Total Liabilities & Net Worth	100.0	100.0
						INCOME DATA		
100.0	100.0	100.0	100.0			Net Sales	100.0	100.0
37.4	33.7	30.0	28.7			Gross Profit	28.5	29.4
35.1	32.3	27.1	24.7			Operating Expenses	25.5	25.7
2.3	1.4	3.0	4.0			Operating Profit	3.0	3.7
.7	.6	.3	.4			All Other Expenses (net)	.2	.5
1.6	.8	2.6	3.6			Profit Before Taxes	2.8	3.2
						RATIOS		
2.1	2.4	2.3	2.6			Current	2.3	2.1
1.2	1.6	1.6	1.8				1.6	1.5
.8	1.3	1.3	1.3				1.3	1.2
1.3	1.3	1.3	1.3			Quick	1.1	1.1
.7	.7	.7	.7				.8	.7
.2	.4	.5	.5				.5	.5
7 52.0	22 16.4	32 11.6	32 11.3			Sales/Receivables	30 12.2	30 12.2
27 13.3	36 10.2	40 9.1	40 9.2				41 9.0	39 9.3
41 8.9	54 6.8	60 6.1	54 6.8				55 6.6	55 6.6
1 334.0	27 13.5	32 11.3	49 7.4			Cost of Sales/Inventory	45 8.1	37 9.7
10 36.8	84 4.4	68 5.3	77 4.8				68 5.4	69 5.3
171 2.1	173 2.1	113 3.2	108 3.4				109 3.3	107 3.4
10 38.1	14 25.4	19 18.8	15 24.1			Cost of Sales/Payables	16 22.5	19 19.6
28 13.2	34 10.7	34 10.7	26 14.0				28 13.2	30 12.0
50 7.2	63 5.8	54 6.7	51 7.2				49 7.5	48 7.6
7.7	4.6	6.1	4.5			Sales/Working Capital	5.8	6.6
30.4	10.0	10.0	9.7				9.8	10.4
−41.9	22.2	20.6	16.9				19.6	24.0
14.0	12.3	7.4	16.8			EBIT/Interest	8.5	7.9
(15) 1.7	(54) 2.2	(96) 3.8	(55) 4.4				(270) 2.9	(221) 3.0
−.9	.6	2.0	2.2				1.5	1.6
		20.6	15.0			Net Profit + Depr., Dep., Amort./Cur. Mat. L./T/D	12.9	12.5
	(25) 5.1	(19) 4.1					(88) 3.5	(60) 3.3
	1.4	1.3					1.3	1.3
.0	.1	.1	.1			Fixed/Worth	.1	.1
.3	.3	.2	.2				.2	.2
2.7	.8	.6	.5				.6	.5
1.0	.8	1.0	.7			Debt/Worth	1.0	1.0
3.3	1.5	2.2	1.8				2.0	1.9
77.3	5.9	3.8	3.5				4.3	4.0
86.8	31.3	41.3	40.7			% Profit Before Taxes/Tangible Net Worth	44.6	44.6
(15) 22.4	(48) 8.2	(102) 16.9	(59) 22.2				(274) 20.3	(223) 19.8
.6	.2	6.2	10.3				6.3	6.4
11.6	14.1	11.3	13.8			% Profit Before Taxes/Total Assets	13.2	15.1
1.7	3.3	5.3	6.3				5.1	6.0
−4.7	−1.0	1.7	3.0				1.8	2.1
UND	110.9	98.9	80.9			Sales/Net Fixed Assets	99.7	92.5
59.4	39.5	51.7	44.7				46.7	46.4
29.7	23.5	18.9	18.4				20.1	21.8
6.3	3.9	3.9	3.8			Sales/Total Assets	3.8	4.0
4.3	2.8	3.1	2.7				3.0	3.0
2.4	2.0	2.2	2.0				2.2	2.1
.7	.4	.3	.4			% Depr., Dep., Amort./Sales	.3	.3
(11) .8	(46) .8	(94) .7	(53) .6				(246) .6	(211) .6
2.3	1.2	1.1	.9				1.0	1.1
	2.4	1.4	.9			% Officers', Directors', Owners' Comp/Sales	1.7	1.5
	(36) 5.9	(51) 2.3	(20) 1.7				(133) 3.6	(111) 2.5
	10.8	6.5	8.9				5.9	4.8
24077M	198921M	1657411M	3456806M	773351M	1399585M	Net Sales ($)	5657962M	5354294M
5117M	69964M	535898M	1215026M	368140M	786825M	Total Assets ($)	2350472M	2004403M

© RMA 2003

M = $ thousand   MM = $ million

See Pages 11 through 18 for Explanation of Ratios and Data

Comparative Historical Data | **Current Data Sorted By Sales**

4/1/00-3/31/01 ALL	4/1/01-3/31/02 ALL	4/1/02-3/31/03 ALL		0-1MM	1-3MM	3-5MM	5-10MM	10-25MM	25MM & OVER
			Type of Statement						
38	34	41	Unqualified	1			4	12	24
75	60	67	Reviewed	1	5	4	15	25	17
56	69	45	Compiled	3	10	8	10	9	5
12	18	24	Tax Returns	6	10	3	3	2	
66	69	77	Other	3	11	9	10	12	32
				37 (4/1-9/30/02)		217 (10/1/02-3/31/03)			
247	250	254	**NUMBER OF STATEMENTS**	14	36	24	42	60	78
%	%	%	**ASSETS**	%	%	%	%	%	%
7.0	8.0	6.4	Cash & Equivalents	14.4	8.2	4.4	6.7	6.1	4.7
31.8	31.3	32.8	Trade Receivables (net)	25.7	26.1	33.8	33.7	35.7	34.0
38.7	39.6	39.8	Inventory	45.8	45.3	34.2	39.1	39.2	38.7
2.4	2.3	2.6	All Other Current	.0	3.4	4.5	2.3	1.8	2.9
80.0	81.1	81.5	Total Current	85.9	83.0	76.9	81.8	82.7	80.3
11.8	12.0	11.5	Fixed Assets (net)	13.4	11.1	11.6	12.6	11.6	10.6
2.0	1.9	2.5	Intangibles (net)	.0	1.2	4.9	1.1	1.6	4.2
6.3	5.0	4.5	All Other Non-Current	.7	4.7	6.7	4.4	4.1	4.8
100.0	100.0	100.0	Total	100.0	100.0	100.0	100.0	100.0	100.0
			LIABILITIES						
16.5	19.2	16.0	Notes Payable-Short Term	26.9	14.5	13.4	12.3	15.7	17.8
2.9	2.1	3.6	Cur. Mat.-L/T/D	.4	16.6	1.1	1.4	1.7	1.6
21.1	20.0	21.8	Trade Payables	17.4	22.5	22.6	22.9	23.4	20.1
.3	.3	.3	Income Taxes Payable	.1	.1	.3	.7	.1	.3
10.3	9.5	10.4	All Other Current	16.9	9.6	15.6	8.6	9.9	9.4
51.1	51.0	52.0	Total Current	61.6	63.2	53.1	45.8	50.8	49.0
8.4	7.7	9.1	Long Term Debt	13.9	11.4	6.6	10.1	6.0	9.7
.2	.3	.1	Deferred Taxes	.0	.0	.1	.1	.1	.1
5.4	5.1	4.6	All Other Non-Current	5.3	5.7	5.3	5.8	3.0	4.3
35.0	35.9	34.2	Net Worth	19.2	19.7	34.9	38.2	40.1	36.9
100.0	100.0	100.0	Total Liabilities & Net Worth	100.0	100.0	100.0	100.0	100.0	100.0
			INCOME DATA						
100.0	100.0	100.0	Net Sales	100.0	100.0	100.0	100.0	100.0	100.0
30.6	32.5	31.4	Gross Profit	44.9	35.8	30.2	32.7	28.7	28.6
27.3	29.8	28.3	Operating Expenses	42.1	34.4	29.0	29.9	25.8	24.0
3.3	2.7	3.0	Operating Profit	2.8	1.4	1.2	2.8	2.9	4.6
.1	.8	.5	All Other Expenses (net)	2.2	.7	.2	.1	.3	.6
3.2	1.9	2.5	Profit Before Taxes	.6	.8	1.1	2.7	2.6	4.0
			RATIOS						
2.3	2.3	2.4		3.9	2.3	1.8	2.8	2.4	2.4
1.6	1.6	1.6	Current	1.9	1.6	1.4	1.6	1.6	1.6
1.2	1.2	1.3		1.0	1.2	1.2	1.4	1.3	1.3
1.2	1.3	1.3		1.5	1.2	1.1	1.5	1.2	1.3
.7	.7	.7	Quick	.8	.6	.6	.7	.8	.7
.5	.5	.5		.2	.2	.4	.5	.6	.5
23 15.5	**24** 15.0	**29** 12.5		**14** 25.4	**13** 27.6	**30** 12.3	**30** 12.1	**30** 12.1	**30** 12.1
35 10.3	**37** 9.8	**38** 9.6	Sales/Receivables	**33** 11.1	**38** 9.5	**37** 9.9	**37** 9.7	**39** 9.3	**40** 9.2
48 7.6	**51** 7.2	**55** 6.7		**52** 7.1	**60** 6.1	**53** 6.9	**64** 5.7	**55** 6.7	**53** 6.9
35 10.3	**34** 10.6	**38** 9.6		**1** 361.7	**52** 7.0	**15** 23.9	**52** 7.0	**31** 11.9	**45** 8.1
71 5.2	**66** 5.5	**72** 5.1	Cost of Sales/Inventory	**162** 2.3	**153** 2.4	**55** 6.7	**81** 4.5	**58** 6.3	**62** 5.9
115 3.2	**131** 2.8	**123** 3.0		**333** 1.1	**267** 1.4	**105** 3.5	**136** 2.7	**94** 3.9	**93** 3.9
17 21.6	**14** 25.4	**18** 20.5		**11** 32.7	**12** 29.3	**17** 21.9	**19** 19.4	**22** 16.3	**16** 22.9
30 12.2	**28** 13.1	**32** 11.3	Cost of Sales/Payables	**29** 12.4	**39** 9.4	**36** 10.2	**40** 9.1	**33** 11.0	**26** 14.0
51 7.2	**47** 7.8	**55** 6.7		**54** 6.7	**94** 3.9	**61** 5.9	**63** 5.8	**48** 7.5	**47** 7.8
6.1	5.7	5.2		3.6	4.1	6.6	4.8	6.7	5.7
10.4	10.8	10.0	Sales/Working Capital	11.5	8.9	13.1	7.3	11.0	10.1
23.6	24.7	23.9		-88.5	28.8	44.9	13.4	21.6	20.3
10.3	6.3	11.9		18.0	9.4	8.9	6.5	11.1	14.8
(227) 2.9	(225) 2.6	(230) 3.6	EBIT/Interest	(10) 1.6	(35) 1.5	(22) 2.1	(38) 3.8	(52) 3.8	(73) 4.4
1.5	1.2	1.5		.0	-.9	.6	2.0	1.8	2.6
8.4	14.4	12.0					11.7	20.0	15.0
(54) 3.1	(57) 3.9	(58) 4.5	Net Profit + Depr., Dep., Amort./Cur. Mat. L/T/D				(10) 4.5	(18) 5.1	(19) 8.0
1.2	1.0	1.3					1.7	1.1	2.0
.1	.1	.1		.0	.1	.1	.1	.1	.1
.2	.2	.2	Fixed/Worth	.1	.3	.3	.2	.2	.3
.6	.6	.7		1.5	-5.5	.8	.6	.6	.6
.9	.8	.9		.7	.9	1.1	.9	.9	1.2
2.0	1.9	2.1	Debt/Worth	1.8	2.0	2.0	2.1	2.0	2.1
4.2	3.8	4.0		9.2	-24.0	5.2	3.6	3.4	4.0
49.7	38.8	41.6		96.7	24.8	23.0	38.3	35.7	47.4
(232) 20.7	(230) 13.2	(233) 19.2	% Profit Before Taxes/Tangible Net Worth	(13) 25.5	(26) 6.4	(20) 7.9	(41) 17.7	(59) 14.7	(74) 24.2
6.3	3.2	5.3		-11.2	.5	-.9	5.6	6.1	15.9
15.1	11.9	12.8		16.9	10.8	11.9	11.3	11.2	15.9
5.7	4.0	5.4	% Profit Before Taxes/Total Assets	2.3	1.0	2.0	5.7	5.6	8.1
1.3	.7	1.4		-4.5	-3.7	-.8	2.1	1.6	3.6
89.1	86.2	94.4		UND	79.5	67.2	194.5	94.3	79.6
43.4	43.9	48.0	Sales/Net Fixed Assets	327.1	45.9	36.1	39.3	52.4	44.9
20.5	21.9	20.0		12.8	18.4	24.1	16.4	20.1	18.9
4.0	4.0	3.9		3.9	3.7	4.0	3.6	4.1	4.1
3.0	3.0	3.0	Sales/Total Assets	2.2	2.2	3.0	2.9	3.2	3.1
2.2	2.2	2.1		1.5	1.1	2.3	2.0	2.2	2.2
.3	.3	.4			.4	.4	.3	.3	.4
(210) .6	(218) .6	(210) .7	% Depr., Dep., Amort./Sales		(29) .8	(22) .7	(34) .8	(55) .7	(65) .6
.9	.9	1.1			1.3	1.2	1.2	1.0	.9
1.9	2.0	1.5			2.7	2.2	1.5	1.1	.9
(118) 3.3	(119) 3.5	(117) 3.3	% Officers', Directors', Owners' Comp/Sales		(22) 5.5	(15) 6.1	(26) 2.4	(26) 2.4	(25) 1.7
6.3	6.5	7.5			10.0	11.1	6.3	5.4	7.1
5319108M	**5771850M**	**7510151M**	Net Sales ($)	**8244M**	**76398M**	**95782M**	**308925M**	**1023771M**	**5997031M**
1835590M	**2151623M**	**2980970M**	Total Assets ($)	**4428M**	**51199M**	**33186M**	**134010M**	**360261M**	**2397886M**

M = $ thousand MM = $ million

See Pages 11 through 18 for Explanation of Ratios and Data

Current Data Sorted By Assets   **Comparative Historical Data**

						Type of Statement		
1	9	66	76	15	6	Unqualified	165	190
9	51	151	36	3		Reviewed	262	254
11	77	55	7			Compiled	210	196
11	23	14	1			Tax Returns	38	32
12	49	83	50	12	6	Other	173	193

		152 (4/1-9/30/02)		682 (10/1/02-3/31/03)			4/1/98-3/31/99	4/1/99-3/31/00
0-500M	500M-2MM	2-10MM	10-50MM	50-100MM	100-250MM		ALL	ALL
44	209	369	170	30	12	NUMBER OF STATEMENTS	848	865
%	%	%	%	%	%	ASSETS	%	%
8.7	6.6	5.0	5.4	4.5	3.2	Cash & Equivalents	5.3	5.0
40.5	39.1	33.6	30.1	27.5	27.2	Trade Receivables (net)	36.0	35.7
29.5	33.3	37.0	34.1	30.4	31.0	Inventory	34.7	34.6
.5	2.1	2.3	2.6	6.6	3.3	All Other Current	2.2	2.2
79.1	81.0	77.9	72.3	69.0	64.6	Total Current	78.2	77.6
14.5	13.2	15.5	18.7	21.7	16.9	Fixed Assets (net)	15.0	15.3
1.2	1.1	1.2	1.8	2.7	7.5	Intangibles (net)	1.6	1.7
5.1	4.7	5.4	7.3	6.5	10.9	All Other Non-Current	5.2	5.4
100.0	100.0	100.0	100.0	100.0	100.0	Total	100.0	100.0
						LIABILITIES		
26.3	23.4	21.4	19.3	15.5	7.4	Notes Payable-Short Term	21.3	21.1
3.8	2.4	2.8	2.7	3.6	3.4	Cur. Mat.-L/T/D	2.3	2.5
23.2	17.6	13.2	10.7	10.0	19.3	Trade Payables	15.7	15.7
.0	.2	.2	.1	.2	.5	Income Taxes Payable	.2	.3
10.3	9.1	7.5	9.0	7.0	6.3	All Other Current	7.2	7.8
63.7	52.6	45.2	41.8	36.3	37.0	Total Current	46.7	47.4
4.3	8.4	8.9	12.2	18.6	19.9	Long Term Debt	9.9	10.3
.0	.1	.2	.3	1.2	.3	Deferred Taxes	.3	.3
8.7	3.0	3.8	2.3	1.8	7.9	All Other Non-Current	4.4	4.0
23.2	35.9	41.8	43.4	42.1	35.0	Net Worth	38.7	38.0
100.0	100.0	100.0	100.0	100.0	100.0	Total Liabilities & Net Worth	100.0	100.0
						INCOME DATA		
100.0	100.0	100.0	100.0	100.0	100.0	Net Sales	100.0	100.0
25.8	21.7	20.4	20.3	22.0	18.5	Gross Profit	18.9	19.6
25.0	19.9	18.3	16.8	18.0	15.1	Operating Expenses	16.0	16.3
.8	1.8	2.2	3.5	4.0	3.4	Operating Profit	2.9	3.3
.6	.4	.4	.5	.4	1.0	All Other Expenses (net)	.5	.6
.2	1.4	1.7	3.0	3.6	2.4	Profit Before Taxes	2.3	2.7
						RATIOS		
2.6	2.3	2.6	3.1	3.8	3.0		2.7	2.4
1.5	1.5	1.6	1.6	1.8	1.7	Current	1.6	1.6
1.1	1.2	1.3	1.3	1.3	1.2		1.3	1.3
1.9	1.3	1.3	1.6	1.7	1.6		1.5	1.3
.9	.9	.8	.8	.9	.8	Quick	(847) .9	(864) .9
.4	.5	.5	.5	.6	.5		.6	.6
12 30.5	19 19.2	24 15.3	25 14.4	26 13.8	16 22.2		24 15.2	23 15.7
22 16.5	31 12.0	33 11.0	36 10.0	33 11.1	30 12.3	Sales/Receivables	33 11.1	33 11.2
41 8.9	43 8.5	43 8.5	45 8.0	46 7.9	37 9.7		44 8.2	43 8.4
2 188.7	15 24.7	30 12.3	37 10.0	43 8.4	36 10.1		26 13.9	26 14.1
22 16.6	36 10.2	47 7.8	51 7.2	57 6.4	42 8.6	Cost of Sales/Inventory	44 8.4	44 8.3
76 4.8	72 5.1	71 5.2	69 5.3	75 4.9	55 6.6		68 5.4	68 5.3
4 84.6	7 53.3	8 45.1	9 42.1	12 31.6	15 24.7		9 42.5	9 41.5
13 28.6	14 25.8	14 25.5	13 28.2	19 19.5	17 21.4	Cost of Sales/Payables	16 22.6	16 23.1
26 13.8	31 11.9	25 14.7	21 17.6	24 15.5	19 19.4		27 13.5	26 13.8
6.9	8.2	7.0	5.8	5.3	7.5		6.8	7.2
25.8	15.4	11.6	10.1	8.9	12.2	Sales/Working Capital	12.6	12.9
107.4	42.9	23.6	21.7	14.8	31.7		25.1	26.9
9.0	6.3	8.8	10.5	6.9	5.7		5.9	8.0
(33) 2.0	(196) 2.7	(353) 3.1	(160) 4.1	(29) 3.8	2.1	EBIT/Interest	(788) 2.8	(823) 3.1
−6.7	1.1	1.4	2.2	1.5	1.4		1.5	1.8
	6.8	7.6	16.3	7.9		Net Profit + Depr., Dep.,	8.2	6.8
	(30) 2.5	(129) 2.7	(48) 4.9	(15) 2.6		Amort./Cur. Mat. L /T/D	(244) 2.8	(268) 2.9
	1.2	1.3	1.3	1.7			1.4	1.5
.0	.1	.1	.2	.3	.4		.1	.1
.2	.2	.3	.4	.5	.7	Fixed/Worth	.3	.3
.8	.7	.6	.7	.8	1.0		.7	.7
.5	.8	.7	.6	.8	1.2		.8	.8
2.2	1.9	1.6	1.5	2.1	3.1	Debt/Worth	1.8	1.9
9.2	3.7	2.9	3.2	3.2	4.4		3.9	3.6
66.7	36.5	27.3	30.4	28.1	47.3	% Profit Before Taxes/Tangible	34.3	39.4
(35) 25.3	(189) 12.6	(354) 12.7	(163) 16.6	17.7	8.6	Net Worth	(798) 18.1	(820) 21.0
−6.6	1.1	4.1	7.1	4.0	7.1		6.9	9.6
21.8	11.1	10.6	12.9	10.7	11.0	% Profit Before Taxes/Total	12.5	13.6
3.9	3.6	4.7	6.8	7.0	3.4	Assets	6.4	7.2
−10.2	.2	1.3	2.9	1.1	.9		2.1	2.9
UND	189.6	62.7	48.6	21.9	37.3		83.6	75.2
117.3	49.5	27.2	19.0	12.7	19.7	Sales/Net Fixed Assets	31.7	31.7
30.8	20.8	14.4	9.7	9.7	10.8		14.1	13.6
9.3	6.2	4.6	3.8	3.3	4.6		4.8	4.8
5.4	4.0	3.4	2.9	2.6	3.4	Sales/Total Assets	3.5	3.5
3.0	2.7	2.5	2.2	1.8	1.7		2.5	2.6
.2	.3	.4	.4	.7	.2		.3	.3
(25) 1.0	(179) .7	(350) .8	(158) 1.0	(26) .9	(10) .8	% Depr., Dep., Amort./Sales	(761) .7	(789) .7
2.3	1.5	1.3	1.6	2.0	1.5		1.2	1.2
1.1	1.7	1.1	1.2				1.3	1.3
(24) 4.8	(113) 2.8	(150) 2.0	(31) 1.8			% Officers', Directors',	(363) 2.4	(356) 2.3
14.0	4.2	3.7	3.0			Owners' Comp/Sales	4.2	4.2
88373M	1264975M	6829362M	11707830M	5153437M	8474851M	Net Sales ($)	28278536M	34702436M
12567M	262360M	1829977M	3815558M	2057040M	1948409M	Total Assets ($)	7591214M	9348473M

M = $ thousand   MM = $ million
See Pages 11 through 18 for Explanation of Ratios and Data

Comparative Historical Data / Current Data Sorted By Sales

			Type of Statement	1	2	2	10	42	116
138	137	173	Unqualified	1	2	2	10	42	116
230	175	250	Reviewed	3	9	20	55	96	67
194	179	150	Compiled	7	22	38	31	43	9
39	52	49	Tax Returns	7	13	6	12	10	1
194	218	212	Other	3	24	16	32	60	77
4/1/00-3/31/01 ALL	4/1/01-3/31/02 ALL	4/1/02-3/31/03 ALL		152 (4/1-9/30/02)			682 (10/1/02-3/31/03)		
				0-1MM	1-3MM	3-5MM	5-10MM	10-25MM	25MM & OVER
795	761	834	NUMBER OF STATEMENTS	21	70	82	140	251	270
%	%	%	**ASSETS**	%	%	%	%	%	%
5.2	5.4	5.6	Cash & Equivalents	8.5	8.4	5.5	6.4	5.7	4.3
35.3	35.0	34.3	Trade Receivables (net)	25.9	30.6	33.9	36.9	34.6	34.4
34.7	34.0	34.7	Inventory	34.6	36.0	37.3	33.4	34.7	34.4
2.3	2.4	2.4	All Other Current	.7	2.2	2.1	1.7	2.4	3.0
77.5	76.8	77.1	Total Current	69.8	77.1	78.9	78.3	77.4	76.1
15.6	15.7	15.8	Fixed Assets (net)	27.4	14.8	14.4	15.5	15.8	15.6
1.3	1.5	1.4	Intangibles (net)	.3	1.0	1.3	1.9	1.1	1.8
5.6	6.0	5.7	All Other Non-Current	2.5	7.1	5.5	4.3	5.7	6.4
100.0	100.0	100.0	Total	100.0	100.0	100.0	100.0	100.0	100.0
			LIABILITIES						
20.9	21.5	21.3	Notes Payable-Short Term	27.7	26.4	20.5	20.1	20.6	21.1
2.9	3.0	2.8	Cur. Mat.-L/T/D	.9	4.6	2.4	3.4	2.4	2.6
14.8	14.8	14.3	Trade Payables	21.5	14.8	16.7	15.7	14.1	12.4
.3	.2	.2	Income Taxes Payable	.1	.3	.1	.1	.2	.2
7.8	7.8	8.3	All Other Current	11.4	8.0	7.5	8.4	7.9	8.8
46.7	47.2	46.9	Total Current	61.6	54.0	47.2	47.8	45.1	45.0
9.4	9.9	9.7	Long Term Debt	8.9	9.9	10.5	9.3	8.2	11.2
.3	.2	.2	Deferred Taxes	.0	.0	.2	.2	.3	.3
3.4	3.4	3.6	All Other Non-Current	15.2	4.7	2.7	4.8	3.0	2.4
40.3	39.2	39.6	Net Worth	14.3	31.3	39.4	38.0	43.4	41.1
100.0	100.0	100.0	Total Liabilities & Net Worth	100.0	100.0	100.0	100.0	100.0	100.0
			INCOME DATA						
100.0	100.0	100.0	Net Sales	100.0	100.0	100.0	100.0	100.0	100.0
19.3	20.2	21.0	Gross Profit	37.9	26.5	22.1	23.1	19.2	18.6
16.5	17.7	18.7	Operating Expenses	36.0	25.8	20.4	20.9	16.7	15.7
2.8	2.6	2.4	Operating Profit	1.9	.7	1.7	2.2	2.5	3.0
.4	.5	.5	All Other Expenses (net)	1.0	.8	.4	.6	.3	.4
2.3	2.0	1.9	Profit Before Taxes	.9	-.1	1.3	1.6	2.2	2.6
			RATIOS						
2.5	2.7	2.6	Current	3.4	2.6	2.6	2.4	2.5	2.8
1.6	1.6	1.6		2.1	1.6	1.7	1.6	1.6	1.6
1.3	1.2	1.3		.8	1.0	1.3	1.3	1.3	1.2
1.4	1.4	1.4	Quick	1.4	1.4	1.2	1.4	1.3	1.5
(793) .8	(760) .8	.8		.8	.7	.8	.9	.8	.8
.5	.5	.5		.2	.3	.5	.5	.6	.6
23 15.8	23 15.6	23 16.1	Sales/Receivables	4 92.7	14 25.2	23 16.0	27 13.8	23 16.0	23 15.7
32 11.4	33 11.0	33 11.2		21 17.5	38 9.7	31 11.7	35 10.4	31 11.7	33 11.0
43 8.5	45 8.2	43 8.4		44 8.3	57 6.4	47 7.7	46 8.0	43 8.6	42 8.7
24 15.1	27 13.7	27 13.5	Cost of Sales/Inventory	8 46.1	24 15.4	28 12.8	24 15.2	26 14.2	30 12.0
45 8.2	44 8.3	46 7.9		77 4.7	73 5.0	50 7.3	47 7.7	47 7.8	43 8.5
65 5.6	70 5.2	71 5.2		146 2.5	117 3.1	89 4.1	66 5.5	58 6.3	
8 46.5	8 44.7	8 44.8	Cost of Sales/Payables	2 197.2	6 60.1	8 45.5	8 44.3	8 44.7	9 42.9
14 25.3	15 24.1	14 25.9		23 15.9	20 18.3	19 19.2	15 23.8	13 27.9	13 28.2
25 14.8	25 14.5	25 14.4		50 7.3	35 10.6	36 10.1	29 12.6	25 14.4	20 18.4
7.3	6.9	6.7	Sales/Working Capital	5.0	5.0	5.7	6.7	7.1	7.2
13.0	12.7	12.6		16.4	9.3	11.7	11.9	12.8	13.0
30.4	27.2	28.1		-14.3	184.0	25.5	29.0	24.9	27.8
6.3	6.6	8.3	EBIT/Interest	7.1	5.3	5.9	8.4	8.7	10.0
(746) 2.5	(717) 2.7	(783) 3.1		(13) 2.0	(62) 1.1	(77) 2.3	(135) 2.6	(236) 3.2	(260) 4.1
1.4	1.4	1.4		-5.2	-2.2	.5	1.1	1.6	2.1
5.5	7.8	8.2	Net Profit + Depr., Dep., Amort./Cur. Mat. L/T/D		2.3	12.4	6.5	7.3	11.9
(231) 2.2	(193) 2.6	(231) 2.7		(11) .3	(15) 2.1	(32) 2.7	(88) 2.6	(85) 4.0	
1.1	1.1	1.3		-.7	-.6	.7	1.3	1.6	
.1	.1	.1	Fixed/Worth	.0	.1	.1	.2	.1	.1
.3	.3	.3		.3	.3	.3	.3	.3	.4
.7	.7	.7		3.2	1.4	.8	.6	.7	.7
.7	.8	.7	Debt/Worth	.3	.9	.7	.8	.7	.7
1.7	1.7	1.7		2.3	2.1	1.5	1.6	1.5	1.8
3.4	3.5	3.3		NM	7.0	3.3	3.4	2.5	3.4
33.0	30.5	30.4	% Profit Before Taxes/Tangible Net Worth	51.5	29.8	33.2	31.4	27.7	31.4
(757) 16.6	(722) 14.6	(783) 14.0		(16) 19.1	(60) 6.6	(74) 7.8	(126) 12.1	(243) 12.5	(264) 18.9
5.3	4.3	3.8		.0	-13.3	-.4	1.7	5.2	8.1
12.6	12.0	11.5	% Profit Before Taxes/Total Assets	15.5	9.8	11.9	10.9	11.2	12.6
5.8	5.4	4.9		4.0	.4	2.6	3.6	4.6	6.8
1.6	1.2	1.0		-6.2	-8.2	-.9	.3	1.8	2.9
75.2	74.1	71.8	Sales/Net Fixed Assets	UND	81.9	81.9	66.7	83.4	60.7
31.5	29.1	28.8		24.6	37.2	31.3	30.7	27.2	25.7
14.6	13.4	13.3		2.9	8.7	11.9	15.2	13.3	13.4
4.9	4.5	4.7	Sales/Total Assets	3.7	4.3	4.7	4.6	4.6	4.8
3.6	3.4	3.4		2.1	2.5	3.3	3.4	3.5	3.5
2.6	2.5	2.4		1.6	1.8	2.4	2.4	2.5	2.6
.3	.3	.4	% Depr., Dep., Amort./Sales	1.0	.4	.4	.4	.4	.3
(727) .7	(670) .7	(748) .8		(11) 2.9	(57) 1.3	(71) .8	(132) .9	(233) .7	(244) .7
1.2	1.3	1.5		6.8	2.5	1.5	1.8	1.3	1.2
1.4	1.3	1.3	% Officers', Directors', Owners' Comp/Sales	1.0	2.0	1.9	1.4	1.2	.7
(343) 2.3	(300) 2.2	(321) 2.3		(10) 11.4	(39) 3.4	(46) 3.0	(73) 2.3	(99) 2.1	(54) 1.4
4.6	3.9	4.0		18.5	6.8	4.1	4.2	3.3	3.1
32327033M	30549731M	33518828M	Net Sales ($)	11627M	141282M	331412M	1047697M	4047040M	27939770M
8731406M	8448941M	9925911M	Total Assets ($)	6233M	64535M	117072M	351017M	1358055M	8028999M

M = $ thousand   MM = $ million
See Pages 11 through 18 for Explanation of Ratios and Data

Current Data Sorted By Assets   **Comparative Historical Data**

	0-500M	500M-2MM	2-10MM	10-50MM	50-100MM	100-250MM	Type of Statement	4/1/98-3/31/99 ALL	4/1/99-3/31/00 ALL
	3	1	17	10	7	1	Unqualified	49	57
	4	8	51	10			Reviewed	95	81
	7	23	28	1			Compiled	74	63
	6	14	5				Tax Returns	16	20
	4	19	28	12	1	1	Other	68	62
		47 (4/1-9/30/02)		214 (10/1/02-3/31/03)					
	24	65	129	33	8	2	**NUMBER OF STATEMENTS**	302	283
	%	%	%	%	%	%	**ASSETS**	%	%
	15.5	7.4	6.0	3.6			Cash & Equivalents	6.3	6.9
	31.3	32.3	28.9	27.8			Trade Receivables (net)	34.8	33.0
	18.5	27.5	28.2	31.0			Inventory	27.0	27.0
	1.3	2.0	3.2	2.7			All Other Current	1.8	1.4
	66.6	69.2	66.3	65.1			Total Current	70.0	68.2
	27.1	25.4	24.4	26.4			Fixed Assets (net)	21.6	24.1
	4.2	1.6	2.1	.9			Intangibles (net)	1.8	2.4
	2.1	3.9	7.2	7.6			All Other Non-Current	6.6	5.2
	100.0	100.0	100.0	100.0			Total	100.0	100.0
							LIABILITIES		
	30.7	11.2	13.8	11.2			Notes Payable-Short Term	13.1	13.5
	7.8	3.7	4.0	5.9			Cur. Mat.-L/T/D	3.5	3.3
	20.6	17.0	18.4	18.6			Trade Payables	21.8	20.4
	.3	.2	.3	.3			Income Taxes Payable	.4	.4
	5.4	16.2	5.9	8.9			All Other Current	7.8	7.4
	64.8	48.4	42.3	44.9			Total Current	46.6	44.9
	18.3	16.3	10.5	12.6			Long Term Debt	11.9	12.5
	.0	.8	.5	.4			Deferred Taxes	.3	.4
	.8	5.0	4.6	4.8			All Other Non-Current	3.4	2.6
	16.1	29.5	42.1	37.3			Net Worth	37.8	39.7
	100.0	100.0	100.0	100.0			Total Liabilities & Net Worth	100.0	100.0
							INCOME DATA		
	100.0	100.0	100.0	100.0			Net Sales	100.0	100.0
	36.4	35.5	26.9	27.4			Gross Profit	26.5	28.8
	33.2	31.8	23.6	22.0			Operating Expenses	22.8	24.0
	3.2	3.7	3.3	5.4			Operating Profit	3.7	4.8
	.2	.6	.4	.9			All Other Expenses (net)	.1	.8
	3.1	3.1	2.9	4.5			Profit Before Taxes	3.5	4.1
							RATIOS		
	3.1	2.7	2.5	2.1				2.2	2.2
	1.5	1.6	1.5	1.6			Current	1.5	1.5
	.8	1.0	1.2	1.1				1.2	1.2
	2.2	1.6	1.4	1.1				1.3	1.4
	1.1	.9	.8	.6			Quick	(282) .9	.9
	.5	.5	.5	.5				.6	.6
	8 44.7	24 15.0	31 11.9	35 10.4				33 11.0	29 12.6
	34 10.8	33 11.1	38 9.5	43 8.6			Sales/Receivables	44 8.3	40 9.1
	50 7.3	54 6.8	50 7.3	54 6.8				55 6.6	55 6.7
	0 UND	8 44.3	30 12.2	32 11.5				21 17.4	17 21.5
	22 16.5	44 8.3	50 7.3	56 6.5			Cost of Sales/Inventory	44 8.2	46 8.0
	38 9.6	79 4.6	74 4.9	132 2.8				75 4.9	82 4.4
	2 169.6	14 26.5	17 21.0	20 17.9				20 17.9	20 18.5
	20 18.2	26 14.0	31 11.9	40 9.1			Cost of Sales/Payables	33 11.0	30 12.0
	42 8.7	51 7.2	47 7.8	58 6.3				52 7.1	51 7.2
	7.8	6.4	6.3	6.2				6.6	7.1
	18.2	12.4	11.3	8.4			Sales/Working Capital	11.2	12.4
	−68.4	−170.2	24.5	28.2				26.2	32.6
	11.4	9.9	10.1	13.7				8.6	11.7
	(22) 3.3	(62) 4.1	(117) 4.3	(31) 5.1			EBIT/Interest	(274) 3.6	(267) 4.2
	−1.4	1.1	1.6	1.9				2.0	2.0
		5.0	4.6	17.5			Net Profit + Depr., Dep.,	5.4	6.2
		(11) 1.8	(42) 2.5	(14) 5.3			Amort./Cur. Mat. L./T/D	(89) 2.3	(86) 3.1
		.9	1.0	1.7				1.3	1.6
	.3	.2	.2	.3				.2	.3
	.5	.5	.5	.7			Fixed/Worth	.5	.5
	2.3	2.0	1.2	1.5				1.0	1.2
	1.1	.9	.6	.7				.8	.8
	2.3	2.5	1.6	1.9			Debt/Worth	1.8	1.7
	51.5	6.3	4.4	4.0				3.9	3.8
	53.8	53.3	25.0	45.2			% Profit Before Taxes/Tangible	41.5	46.2
	(19) 28.6	(59) 20.8	(123) 14.6	(32) 22.9			Net Worth	(287) 22.6	(270) 21.0
	12.6	3.7	4.0	9.8				10.1	10.3
	19.5	12.8	11.5	14.2				13.7	14.8
	9.3	5.6	6.3	8.8			% Profit Before Taxes/Total Assets	8.2	7.8
	−1.4	.3	1.0	3.1				3.3	3.4
	49.1	42.8	38.9	18.5				39.7	42.5
	22.0	18.3	16.1	12.0			Sales/Net Fixed Assets	18.2	14.9
	10.9	6.5	5.4	4.1				6.8	6.6
	5.0	3.7	3.2	2.9				3.6	3.5
	4.1	2.9	2.5	2.2			Sales/Total Assets	2.7	2.8
	2.7	1.9	1.8	1.5				1.8	2.0
	.8	.9	.8	.8				.7	.6
	(20) 2.4	(57) 1.5	(120) 1.5	(30) 1.7			% Depr., Dep., Amort./Sales	(273) 1.3	(253) 1.3
	4.0	3.4	3.1	2.3				2.5	2.5
	2.7	1.9	1.4				% Officers', Directors',	2.0	1.9
	(13) 5.4	(31) 3.7	(50) 2.5				Owners' Comp/Sales	(121) 3.2	(113) 3.0
	7.1	4.9	5.8					5.8	5.8
	40264M	219869M	1539582M	1389103M	950598M	374674M	Net Sales ($)	5323834M	6823677M
	7925M	77623M	600992M	652451M	610758M	296394M	Total Assets ($)	2223440M	2997258M

M = $ thousand   MM = $ million
See Pages 11 through 18 for Explanation of Ratios and Data

Comparative Historical Data | Current Data Sorted By Sales

	4/1/00-3/31/01 ALL	4/1/01-3/31/02 ALL	4/1/02-3/31/03 ALL	Type of Statement	0-1MM	1-3MM	3-5MM	5-10MM	10-25MM	25MM & OVER
	41	28	39	Unqualified	1	2		10	8	18
	99	76	73	Reviewed	1	6	6	18	31	11
	84	84	59	Compiled	4	14	15	14	11	1
	19	20	25	Tax Returns	5	7	5	4	3	1
	75	81	65	Other	5	13	6	13	15	13
					47 (4/1-9/30/02)		214 (10/1/02-3/31/03)			
NUMBER OF STATEMENTS	318	289	261		16	42	32	59	68	44
	%	%	%	ASSETS	%	%	%	%	%	%
	6.4	7.3	6.9	Cash & Equivalents	11.0	10.9	8.9	5.4	5.8	3.5
	31.9	31.7	29.4	Trade Receivables (net)	20.0	26.8	26.5	34.1	30.2	30.2
	28.5	27.7	27.2	Inventory	22.8	21.6	30.4	25.2	28.8	31.7
	2.1	2.3	2.6	All Other Current	.5	2.4	.9	3.0	3.7	2.6
	68.9	69.1	66.1	Total Current	54.3	61.7	66.8	67.7	68.6	68.0
	22.5	22.2	25.7	Fixed Assets (net)	35.1	30.8	23.6	24.8	23.1	23.9
	2.0	2.4	2.2	Intangibles (net)	8.8	1.7	2.4	1.1	2.0	2.1
	6.6	6.4	6.1	All Other Non-Current	1.8	5.8	7.2	6.5	6.3	6.0
	100.0	100.0	100.0	Total	100.0	100.0	100.0	100.0	100.0	100.0
				LIABILITIES						
	13.5	13.2	13.9	Notes Payable-Short Term	43.3	11.2	9.9	10.8	14.2	12.7
	3.7	3.8	4.4	Cur. Mat.-L/T/D	6.8	4.3	2.9	4.2	4.6	4.9
	18.6	19.9	17.9	Trade Payables	13.0	20.1	14.6	17.7	19.0	18.4
	.2	.2	.3	Income Taxes Payable	.1	.1	.5	.2	.3	.3
	7.4	9.5	8.8	All Other Current	20.9	11.6	9.6	4.9	7.1	9.0
	43.3	46.7	45.3	Total Current	84.2	47.3	37.4	37.8	45.2	45.4
	12.6	14.2	13.4	Long Term Debt	28.4	17.9	9.8	13.5	10.0	11.2
	.3	.3	.6	Deferred Taxes	.1	1.2	.0	.5	.5	.8
	4.7	3.6	4.2	All Other Non-Current	.8	4.3	4.4	6.0	4.0	3.4
	39.0	35.3	36.5	Net Worth	−13.6	29.4	48.4	42.2	40.4	39.2
	100.0	100.0	100.0	Total Liabilities & Net Worth	100.0	100.0	100.0	100.0	100.0	100.0
				INCOME DATA						
	100.0	100.0	100.0	Net Sales	100.0	100.0	100.0	100.0	100.0	100.0
	28.6	29.1	30.0	Gross Profit	47.6	36.0	33.0	26.1	26.3	26.9
	24.9	25.4	26.3	Operating Expenses	45.6	31.6	27.3	23.3	23.0	22.6
	3.7	3.7	3.7	Operating Profit	2.0	4.3	5.7	2.8	3.3	4.3
	.5	.8	.5	All Other Expenses (net)	2.6	.2	.0	.4	.7	.4
	3.1	2.9	3.2	Profit Before Taxes	−.6	4.2	5.8	2.4	2.6	3.9
				RATIOS						
	2.5 / 1.6 / 1.2	2.5 / 1.6 / 1.1	2.6 / 1.6 / 1.1	Current	2.5 / .8 / .6	2.8 / 1.5 / .9	3.3 / 1.8 / 1.2	2.9 / 1.5 / 1.3	2.2 / 1.4 / 1.1	2.2 / 1.6 / 1.3
	1.4 / .9 / .6	1.5 / .9 / .6	1.4 / .8 / .5	Quick	2.2 / .7 / .3	1.9 / .9 / .4	1.8 / .9 / .6	1.4 / .9 / .7	1.4 / .8 / .5	1.1 / .8 / .5
	31 12.0 / 39 9.4 / 50 7.2	30 12.3 / 39 9.4 / 54 6.7	28 12.9 / 38 9.6 / 51 7.2	Sales/Receivables	11 32.8 / 35 10.4 / 50 7.4	21 17.5 / 31 11.9 / 55 6.6	20 18.5 / 30 12.1 / 42 8.7	35 10.5 / 41 8.8 / 57 6.4	30 12.3 / 37 9.9 / 48 7.6	34 10.7 / 41 8.9 / 53 6.9
	24 15.3 / 48 7.6 / 79 4.6	26 14.2 / 50 7.4 / 84 4.3	21 17.4 / 47 7.8 / 76 4.8	Cost of Sales/Inventory	6 59.1 / 28 13.1 / 49 7.4	2 200.6 / 20 18.0 / 70 5.2	35 10.3 / 49 7.4 / 73 5.0	23 15.6 / 50 7.3 / 77 4.7	27 13.7 / 50 7.4 / 66 5.5	34 10.7 / 67 5.4 / 103 3.6
	17 21.7 / 30 12.1 / 45 8.0	18 20.3 / 34 10.8 / 53 6.8	17 21.7 / 28 12.9 / 49 7.4	Cost of Sales/Payables	0 UND / 16 23.5 / 87 4.2	13 28.2 / 31 11.9 / 70 5.2	13 27.6 / 22 16.4 / 49 7.4	17 21.0 / 32 11.2 / 46 8.0	17 21.0 / 28 12.9 / 52 7.1	21 17.3 / 29 12.4 / 49 7.4
	6.2 / 10.8 / 29.7	6.2 / 10.7 / 32.9	6.1 / 11.1 / 32.6	Sales/Working Capital	13.2 / −34.1 / −7.7	5.9 / 13.9 / −45.3	5.1 / 9.2 / 24.9	5.6 / 9.1 / 16.6	6.8 / 12.6 / 45.5	6.2 / 9.7 / 17.2
	(298) 9.0 / 3.2 / 1.3	(270) 9.6 / 3.4 / 1.3	(242) 11.2 / 4.4 / 1.6	EBIT/Interest	(15) 5.1 / 1.0 / −1.6	(40) 10.8 / 3.9 / .6	(28) 14.9 / 5.7 / 2.3	(55) 9.4 / 2.9 / 1.5	(62) 10.8 / 4.1 / 1.7	(42) 15.3 / 5.2 / 2.5
	(81) 5.5 / 2.6 / 1.3	(86) 4.8 / 2.0 / 1.3	(76) 5.5 / 2.9 / 1.2	Net Profit + Depr., Dep., Amort./Cur. Mat. L/T/D				(19) 3.2 / 2.1 / 1.0	(25) 4.9 / 2.3 / .7	(18) 16.6 / 5.3 / 3.1
	.2 / .5 / 1.2	.2 / .5 / 1.4	.2 / .5 / 1.4	Fixed/Worth	.3 / 2.1 / −10.4	.3 / .7 / 2.5	.2 / .4 / 1.3	.2 / .4 / 1.2	.2 / .5 / 1.3	.3 / .6 / 1.1
	.7 / 1.7 / 3.9	.7 / 1.8 / 5.4	.7 / 1.8 / 5.2	Debt/Worth	2.2 / NM / −4.8	1.0 / 2.2 / 7.0	.5 / 1.0 / 4.6	.6 / 1.6 / 4.4	.7 / 1.8 / 4.0	.7 / 1.4 / 5.2
	(295) 40.3 / 14.9 / 3.7	(250) 32.5 / 15.4 / 4.9	(243) 36.7 / 16.8 / 5.2	% Profit Before Taxes/Tangible Net Worth		(37) 59.5 / 23.0 / 2.3	(31) 51.8 / 21.3 / 9.4	(58) 26.6 / 9.1 / 2.9	(66) 28.2 / 16.7 / 3.8	(43) 45.2 / 18.7 / 9.3
	14.5 / 5.1 / 1.2	13.6 / 6.6 / 1.2	12.4 / 6.3 / 1.0	% Profit Before Taxes/Total Assets	13.6 / 1.0 / −17.5	15.9 / 5.8 / −.1	16.8 / 8.9 / 3.3	9.6 / 4.4 / .8	11.1 / 6.6 / 1.0	15.6 / 8.0 / 3.2
	43.9 / 18.5 / 7.7	48.6 / 17.0 / 7.1	36.2 / 15.2 / 5.4	Sales/Net Fixed Assets	44.6 / 9.6 / 2.0	26.9 / 10.2 / 3.7	32.2 / 15.6 / 7.3	43.5 / 16.3 / 5.4	39.6 / 18.0 / 7.4	27.3 / 12.6 / 5.1
	3.6 / 2.9 / 2.0	3.6 / 2.7 / 1.9	3.5 / 2.6 / 1.8	Sales/Total Assets	4.3 / 1.9 / .7	3.4 / 2.4 / 1.3	3.6 / 2.9 / 1.9	3.1 / 2.6 / 1.8	3.6 / 2.8 / 2.1	3.1 / 2.5 / 1.7
	(288) .6 / 1.3 / 2.3	(259) .6 / 1.4 / 2.6	(237) .9 / 1.6 / 3.1	% Depr., Dep., Amort./Sales	(13) 1.1 / 3.7 / 8.2	(36) .9 / 2.8 / 6.9	(30) 1.1 / 1.6 / 3.8	(56) .9 / 1.5 / 3.1	(64) .7 / 1.5 / 2.0	(38) .7 / 1.5 / 2.7
	(146) 1.8 / 3.0 / 5.7	(137) 1.8 / 3.0 / 5.6	(101) 1.8 / 3.3 / 5.6	% Officers', Directors', Owners' Comp/Sales		(16) 3.4 / 4.9 / 7.6	(19) 1.9 / 3.6 / 4.7	(29) 3.1 / 3.1 / 5.8	(22) 1.2 / 2.3 / 5.1	(10) .3 / 1.3 / 5.9
	4953773M	4301438M	4514090M	Net Sales ($)	10473M	80582M	130757M	417790M	1031071M	2843417M
	2134382M	2150228M	2246143M	Total Assets ($)	7992M	45555M	61714M	193309M	441492M	1496081M

© RMA 2003

M = $ thousand   MM = $ million

See Pages 11 through 18 for Explanation of Ratios and Data

WHOLESALE—Roofing, Siding, and Insulation Material Merchant Wholesalers NAICS 423330 (SIC 5033)

Current Data Sorted By Assets

Comparative Historical Data

						Type of Statement		
		7	9	3	1	Unqualified	26	24
1	3	18	3			Reviewed	64	44
5	12	11	3		1	Compiled	27	38
1	7	1				Tax Returns	8	6
	8	17	9	1		Other	45	52
	22 (4/1-9/30/02)		99 (10/1/02-3/31/03)				4/1/98-3/31/99	4/1/99-3/31/00
0-500M	500M-2MM	2-10MM	10-50MM	50-100MM	100-250MM		ALL	ALL
7	30	54	24	4	2	**NUMBER OF STATEMENTS**	170	164
%	%	%	%	%	%	**ASSETS**	%	%
	5.1	6.1	3.6			Cash & Equivalents	6.3	6.0
	39.0	37.2	38.4			Trade Receivables (net)	39.3	37.7
	27.9	32.2	30.4			Inventory	30.3	31.4
	2.7	2.5	3.8			All Other Current	1.6	2.3
	74.6	78.0	76.2			Total Current	77.6	77.4
	18.0	14.1	16.0			Fixed Assets (net)	15.1	15.3
	1.9	3.1	2.7			Intangibles (net)	2.3	2.2
	5.5	4.8	5.1			All Other Non-Current	5.1	5.1
	100.0	100.0	100.0			Total	100.0	100.0
						LIABILITIES		
	16.9	15.5	17.4			Notes Payable-Short Term	14.9	14.2
	6.6	2.4	1.9			Cur. Mat.-L/T/D	2.4	2.2
	27.6	25.1	26.6			Trade Payables	27.8	26.3
	.1	.2	.4			Income Taxes Payable	.2	.3
	6.3	8.2	6.2			All Other Current	6.9	7.3
	57.5	51.3	52.4			Total Current	52.1	50.5
	14.9	4.3	8.1			Long Term Debt	11.3	9.9
	.1	.1	.4			Deferred Taxes	.2	.3
	2.1	3.3	1.5			All Other Non-Current	4.9	4.0
	25.3	41.0	37.5			Net Worth	31.4	35.3
	100.0	100.0	100.0			Total Liabilities & Net Worth	100.0	100.0
						INCOME DATA		
	100.0	100.0	100.0			Net Sales	100.0	100.0
	25.6	22.2	25.1			Gross Profit	24.7	23.5
	23.3	19.6	23.8			Operating Expenses	21.4	20.8
	2.2	2.6	1.3			Operating Profit	3.3	2.8
	.4	.5	.2			All Other Expenses (net)	.8	.4
	1.8	2.2	1.0			Profit Before Taxes	2.5	2.4
						RATIOS		
	1.8	2.2	2.0				2.1	2.0
	1.3	1.5	1.4			Current	1.4	1.5
	1.1	1.2	1.1				1.2	1.2
	1.2	1.3	1.1				1.3	1.2
	.8	.8	.7			Quick	.8	.8
	.5	.6	.6				.6	.6
	33 11.0	32 11.5	36 10.2				34 10.8	31 11.9
	43 8.5	47 7.8	49 7.5			Sales/Receivables	46 8.0	44 8.3
	61 6.0	57 6.4	59 6.1				56 6.5	58 6.3
	23 15.8	33 11.0	33 11.1				29 12.4	28 13.0
	47 7.8	45 8.2	54 6.8			Cost of Sales/Inventory	44 8.2	46 8.0
	70 5.2	76 4.8	68 5.4				64 5.7	70 5.2
	25 14.4	25 14.9	30 12.3				29 12.7	25 14.5
	39 9.4	35 10.3	47 7.8			Cost of Sales/Payables	40 9.2	38 9.6
	59 6.2	50 7.4	58 6.3				58 6.2	55 6.7
	7.1	8.8	9.0				7.2	7.6
	17.1	13.2	12.7			Sales/Working Capital	12.7	13.4
	69.6	28.7	29.2				26.5	26.0
	6.3	14.0	11.4				8.1	7.6
	(28) 3.4	(51) 5.3	(23) 5.7			EBIT/Interest	(154) 3.2	(146) 2.9
	.5	2.4	2.3				1.8	1.7
		8.8	13.8				6.4	8.3
		(18) 4.0	(13) 5.7			Net Profit + Depr., Dep., Amort./Cur. Mat. L/T/D	(52) 2.7	(57) 2.4
		2.7	1.4				1.4	1.3
	.3	.2	.2				.2	.2
	.9	.4	.4			Fixed/Worth	.5	.4
	7.0	.7	1.0				1.0	1.0
	.9	.7	.9				.9	.9
	4.6	1.6	1.9			Debt/Worth	2.4	2.1
	83.8	2.9	3.5				6.2	4.7
	57.7	38.0	25.8				36.4	37.3
	(24) 22.4	(51) 14.7	(23) 17.9			% Profit Before Taxes/Tangible Net Worth	(149) 18.5	(150) 19.0
	−3.1	6.0	11.0				9.1	6.5
	10.6	12.2	9.1				12.5	11.2
	5.4	6.4	8.2			% Profit Before Taxes/Total Assets	6.0	5.6
	−2.1	2.9	3.9				2.1	1.8
	85.7	47.6	30.3				46.3	55.5
	24.3	24.9	19.5			Sales/Net Fixed Assets	25.9	28.1
	10.5	15.1	9.7				15.5	14.0
	3.8	3.8	3.5				3.8	3.6
	2.7	3.2	2.8			Sales/Total Assets	3.1	3.1
	2.4	2.3	2.3				2.6	2.6
	.6	.6	.7				.6	.6
	(26) .8	(53) 1.0	(23) .9			% Depr., Dep., Amort./Sales	(144) 1.0	(149) .9
	2.1	1.6	1.4				1.5	1.5
	1.4	1.6					1.6	1.1
	(19) 3.6	(24) 2.9				% Officers', Directors', Owners' Comp/Sales	(63) 2.7	(47) 3.1
	4.8	5.6					4.2	5.2
17617M	110837M	809721M	1243823M	792255M	613901M	Net Sales ($)	3693341M	4837464M
2181M	38026M	263976M	437462M	327359M	258071M	Total Assets ($)	1279116M	1711860M

M = $ thousand   MM = $ million
See Pages 11 through 18 for Explanation of Ratios and Data

Comparative Historical Data — Current Data Sorted By Sales

Type of Statement	4/1/00-3/31/01 ALL	4/1/01-3/31/02 ALL	4/1/02-3/31/03 ALL	0-1MM	1-3MM	3-5MM	5-10MM	10-25MM	25MM & OVER
Unqualified	13	15	20			1	1	5	13
Reviewed	30	36	25			3	6	9	7
Compiled	30	27	32	3	5	8	6	5	5
Tax Returns	7	18	9	1	4	3			1
Other	47	48	35		3	3	7	13	9
(period)					22 (4/1-9/30/02)		99 (10/1/02-3/31/03)		
NUMBER OF STATEMENTS	127	144	121	4	12	18	20	32	35

ASSETS (%)

Cash & Equivalents	5.6	6.5	6.6		12.6	5.8	3.0	7.4	6.3
Trade Receivables (net)	37.1	38.1	36.8		36.1	39.0	32.5	40.0	37.7
Inventory	30.1	28.1	29.6		19.2	28.0	37.2	28.3	29.5
All Other Current	3.0	3.1	3.3		5.2	1.6	4.4	2.5	3.3
Total Current	75.8	75.7	76.3		73.2	74.4	77.1	78.1	76.8
Fixed Assets (net)	16.0	16.2	15.6		17.0	17.7	13.7	13.4	15.8
Intangibles (net)	2.3	2.3	3.1		.0	6.2	2.3	3.6	3.0
All Other Non-Current	5.9	5.8	5.0		9.8	1.6	7.0	4.9	4.4
Total	100.0	100.0	100.0		100.0	100.0	100.0	100.0	100.0

LIABILITIES

Notes Payable-Short Term	16.0	13.9	15.4		4.8	17.0	22.6	14.7	13.6
Cur. Mat.-L/T/D	3.1	2.7	3.4		8.3	6.5	3.7	1.4	2.1
Trade Payables	23.5	26.3	25.4		24.4	33.0	25.5	23.8	25.6
Income Taxes Payable	.3	.3	.2		.1	.2	.0	.3	.3
All Other Current	7.1	7.6	7.1		4.2	4.7	8.9	9.5	6.1
Total Current	49.9	50.7	51.6		41.7	61.4	60.8	49.7	47.7
Long Term Debt	11.7	9.1	8.7		13.1	9.7	8.3	5.5	8.8
Deferred Taxes	.1	.6	.2		.0	.1	.3	.1	.4
All Other Non-Current	3.2	2.2	2.3		.0	2.2	2.5	2.6	2.3
Net Worth	35.1	37.4	37.2		45.1	26.6	28.2	42.2	40.8
Total Liabilities & Net Worth	100.0	100.0	100.0		100.0	100.0	100.0	100.0	100.0

INCOME DATA

Net Sales	100.0	100.0	100.0		100.0	100.0	100.0	100.0	100.0
Gross Profit	24.1	23.8	25.1		26.7	25.2	23.8	21.8	26.1
Operating Expenses	21.1	21.4	21.9		24.4	21.7	21.2	19.6	22.2
Operating Profit	3.0	2.5	3.2		2.3	3.5	2.6	2.2	3.8
All Other Expenses (net)	.7	.6	.7		-.2	.4	1.6	.8	.1
Profit Before Taxes	2.3	1.9	2.5		2.5	3.0	1.0	1.4	3.7

RATIOS

Current	2.2 / 1.5 / 1.2	2.2 / 1.5 / 1.1	2.2 / 1.4 / 1.1		3.5 / 2.0 / 1.1	1.8 / 1.2 / .9	1.6 / 1.2 / 1.1	2.2 / 1.4 / 1.2	2.2 / 1.5 / 1.2
Quick	1.1 / .8 / .6	1.3 / .8 / .6	1.2 / .8 / .6		2.9 / 1.2 / .7	1.2 / .7 / .5	.9 / .6 / .4	1.4 / .9 / .6	1.2 / .9 / .6
Sales/Receivables	28 13.1 / 43 8.5 / 57 6.4	33 11.1 / 43 8.5 / 54 6.7	33 11.2 / 45 8.0 / 57 6.4		18 19.8 / 41 8.8 / 58 6.3	38 9.7 / 50 7.3 / 65 5.6	23 15.8 / 41 8.9 / 53 6.9	35 10.3 / 47 7.8 / 64 5.7	33 11.0 / 45 8.0 / 56 6.5
Cost of Sales/Inventory	29 12.7 / 47 7.8 / 65 5.6	25 14.5 / 43 8.6 / 64 5.7	28 13.0 / 46 7.9 / 70 5.2		0 788.9 / 28 12.8 / 73 5.0	23 15.7 / 56 6.6 / 73 5.0	29 12.8 / 62 5.9 / 95 3.9	28 13.2 / 41 8.8 / 61 6.0	38 9.5 / 46 7.9 / 66 5.5
Cost of Sales/Payables	19 19.0 / 32 11.4 / 48 7.6	24 15.2 / 33 11.0 / 52 7.1	25 14.8 / 36 10.2 / 53 6.8		17 20.9 / 28 13.0 / 48 7.6	35 10.4 / 47 7.7 / 87 4.2	22 16.3 / 38 9.6 / 49 7.4	24 15.5 / 35 10.3 / 49 7.5	26 13.9 / 32 11.6 / 54 6.7
Sales/Working Capital	7.4 / 14.6 / 28.6	7.7 / 12.9 / 34.4	7.8 / 13.1 / 35.9		3.9 / 11.7 / 63.2	6.1 / 16.1 / -30.9	9.8 / 34.0 / 77.0	8.8 / 13.0 / 23.9	7.3 / 12.3 / 27.1
EBIT/Interest	(116) 5.7 / 2.8 / 1.4	(132) 6.6 / 3.2 / 1.4	(112) 11.4 / 4.7 / 2.0		20.3 / 4.5 / -2.0	(17) 7.8 / 4.2 / 3.3	(17) 5.8 / 2.2 / -.2	(30) 14.8 / 5.4 / 3.1	(33) 13.9 / 6.5 / 2.6
Net Profit + Depr., Dep., Amort./Cur. Mat. L/T/D	(39) 6.2 / 2.0 / 1.1	(32) 6.9 / 3.3 / 1.5	(39) 11.2 / 4.2 / 2.1					(13) 14.3 / 5.6 / 2.7	(18) 12.5 / 3.5 / 1.0
Fixed/Worth	.2 / .4 / 1.0	.2 / .4 / .9	.2 / .4 / 1.2		.1 / .3 / 1.1	.3 / .9 / 6.9	.3 / .5 / 2.5	.1 / .3 / .6	.2 / .4 / .8
Debt/Worth	1.2 / 2.0 / 4.2	.8 / 1.8 / 4.0	.7 / 2.0 / 5.0		.5 / .9 / 5.5	1.9 / 4.6 / 29.7	.9 / 2.3 / 68.4	.7 / 1.6 / 3.9	.8 / 1.8 / 2.9
% Profit Before Taxes/Tangible Net Worth	(121) 39.0 / 18.1 / 4.2	(135) 33.6 / 17.6 / 5.0	(110) 40.1 / 19.8 / 7.0		42.0 / 9.3 / -7.7	(15) 55.4 / 28.6 / 19.1	(16) 28.5 / 10.6 / 2.4	(30) 61.6 / 18.5 / 5.4	(34) 29.7 / 21.6 / 14.0
% Profit Before Taxes/Total Assets	10.1 / 5.6 / 1.4	10.9 / 6.0 / 1.0	12.1 / 6.7 / 2.3		23.9 / 4.3 / -3.4	12.6 / 7.1 / 3.4	7.4 / 3.1 / -2.6	13.0 / 7.9 / 3.0	11.9 / 8.5 / 5.1
Sales/Net Fixed Assets	51.9 / 28.1 / 16.2	49.4 / 27.0 / 14.8	54.0 / 24.7 / 13.0		62.1 / 30.6 / 12.9	43.1 / 14.7 / 10.1	65.7 / 27.4 / 14.3	62.8 / 26.8 / 15.8	50.8 / 24.2 / 15.1
Sales/Total Assets	3.7 / 3.2 / 2.6	3.9 / 3.3 / 2.6	3.8 / 2.9 / 2.4		5.1 / 2.5 / 2.0	3.6 / 2.6 / 2.0	3.9 / 3.0 / 2.4	3.7 / 3.3 / 2.3	3.9 / 2.9 / 2.5
% Depr., Dep., Amort./Sales	(114) .6 / 1.0 / 1.5	(126) .6 / 1.0 / 1.6	(110) .6 / .9 / 1.6		(11) .6 / .8 / 1.9	(17) .3 / .7 / 2.3	(16) .6 / 1.0 / 1.9	.6 / 1.0 / 1.6	(32) .7 / .9 / 1.4
% Officers', Directors', Owners' Comp/Sales	(49) 1.7 / 3.1 / 5.4	(58) 1.3 / 2.9 / 5.3	(51) 1.5 / 3.3 / 5.2		(10) 1.3 / 4.4 / 11.1	(11) 1.9 / 3.5 / 4.2		(13) 1.3 / 1.9 / 6.5	
Net Sales ($)	3643300M	4047037M	3588154M	3119M	25656M	71571M	150942M	508023M	2828843M
Total Assets ($)	1248705M	1406217M	1327075M	1763M	10088M	29949M	53908M	178710M	1052657M

M = $ thousand   MM = $ million
See Pages 11 through 18 for Explanation of Ratios and Data

Current Data Sorted By Assets

Comparative Historical Data

Type of Statement								
	1	2	12	13	6	2	Unqualified	32	33
	2	20	49	12			Reviewed	66	66
	4	23	17				Compiled	48	47
	4	11	4	1			Tax Returns	12	13
	3	16	22	11	5	1	Other	39	57

	0-500M	37 (4/1-9/30/02) 500M-2MM	2-10MM	204 (10/1/02-3/31/03) 10-50MM	50-100MM	100-250MM		4/1/98-3/31/99 ALL	4/1/99-3/31/00 ALL
	14	72	104	37	11	3	NUMBER OF STATEMENTS	197	216
	%	%	%	%	%	%	ASSETS	%	%
	15.7	6.4	5.7	8.3	3.0		Cash & Equivalents	7.2	6.9
	30.2	39.8	37.3	34.5	31.0		Trade Receivables (net)	40.7	40.7
	30.6	29.9	33.1	24.9	27.7		Inventory	26.6	28.2
	1.2	1.8	2.2	2.6	2.9		All Other Current	2.3	2.1
	77.6	77.9	78.3	70.4	64.7		Total Current	76.8	77.9
	15.7	17.4	15.8	19.4	20.1		Fixed Assets (net)	17.6	16.5
	1.8	.1	1.1	3.3	11.2		Intangibles (net)	1.4	1.2
	4.8	4.5	4.8	7.0	4.0		All Other Non-Current	4.2	4.4
	100.0	100.0	100.0	100.0	100.0		Total	100.0	100.0
							LIABILITIES		
	22.7	13.3	14.7	13.4	11.9		Notes Payable-Short Term	11.9	13.1
	1.5	2.2	3.4	1.9	1.8		Cur. Mat.-L/T/D	3.6	2.3
	19.7	22.2	18.7	15.8	12.9		Trade Payables	24.9	23.4
	.4	.2	.4	.2	.1		Income Taxes Payable	.3	.4
	7.3	12.7	8.2	8.5	13.3		All Other Current	8.4	9.1
	51.6	50.6	45.3	39.7	39.9		Total Current	49.1	48.3
	5.5	9.8	7.9	12.3	15.7		Long Term Debt	12.1	8.6
	.4	.1	.4	.3	1.7		Deferred Taxes	.3	.4
	2.8	2.2	3.1	1.3	.9		All Other Non-Current	4.5	5.6
	39.7	37.3	43.3	46.4	41.8		Net Worth	34.0	37.1
	100.0	100.0	100.0	100.0	100.0		Total Liabilities & Net Worth	100.0	100.0
							INCOME DATA		
	100.0	100.0	100.0	100.0	100.0		Net Sales	100.0	100.0
	27.2	27.6	27.3	22.7	24.6		Gross Profit	25.4	27.1
	21.3	25.5	23.8	18.9	19.6		Operating Expenses	21.9	23.2
	5.8	2.0	3.5	3.8	5.0		Operating Profit	3.5	4.0
	.2	.6	.4	.3	.9		All Other Expenses (net)	.1	.3
	5.6	1.4	3.0	3.5	4.1		Profit Before Taxes	3.4	3.7
							RATIOS		
	3.1	2.9	2.5	2.9	2.6			2.2	2.4
	1.6	1.5	1.7	1.8	1.6	Current	1.5	1.6
	.9	1.1	1.4	1.2	1.3		1.2	1.3
	2.1	1.7	1.4	1.9	1.2			1.4	1.5
	.7	1.0	.9	1.1	1.0	Quick	1.0	1.0
	.3	.6	.7	.6	.6		.7	.7

Sales/Receivables:

9	41.5	27	13.5	33	11.1	30	12.2	36	10.2	35	10.4	37	9.9
30	12.1	40	9.2	44	8.2	39	9.3	41	8.8	46	7.9	47	7.8
46	7.9	57	6.4	61	6.0	54	6.8	45	8.1	59	6.2	56	6.5

Cost of Sales/Inventory:

3	115.4	17	21.4	32	11.5	19	19.1	40	9.1	20	18.6	27	13.6
59	6.2	43	8.4	54	6.8	39	9.3	57	6.4	40	9.2	46	8.0
98	3.7	77	4.7	80	4.6	62	5.9	65	5.6	63	5.8	67	5.4

Cost of Sales/Payables:

11	33.7	17	20.9	16	23.4	11	32.2	16	22.3	21	17.6	20	18.4
28	13.2	31	11.8	25	14.4	25	14.7	22	16.9	35	10.4	34	10.8
41	9.0	52	7.1	40	9.2	35	10.6	30	12.1	54	6.8	50	7.3

Sales/Working Capital:

	9.3		6.7		6.5		5.7		8.3		7.1		6.8
	16.0		10.7		8.7		11.0		10.2		11.6		12.0
	−124.4		41.5		16.2		23.2		19.3		29.9		21.6

EBIT/Interest:

	41.0		8.6		10.8		9.6		9.2		8.4		14.3
(11)	4.4	(67)	3.3	(99)	4.3	(35)	5.0	(10)	4.0	(176)	3.8	(198)	4.6
	−3.5		.9		2.1		2.1		3.2		1.6		2.4

Net Profit + Depr., Dep., Amort./Cur. Mat. L /T/D:

			3.5		10.9		14.6				5.2		7.8
		(12)	1.3	(36)	5.4	(11)	4.6			(64)	2.4	(62)	3.3
			.7		2.9		1.3				1.1		1.9

Fixed/Worth:

	.1		.1		.1		.2		.3		.2		.2
	.5		.3		.3		.3		.7		.4		.4
	−1.7		.8		.7		.8		1.2		1.1		.7

Debt/Worth:

	.4		.6		.6		.7		.9		.9		.8
	.8		1.5		1.3		1.2		1.4		2.0		1.6
	−37.7		4.0		2.9		2.7		4.5		4.5		3.3

% Profit Before Taxes/Tangible Net Worth:

	64.5		34.7		34.0		31.1				51.9		49.4
(10)	48.8	(66)	14.9	(101)	19.5	(35)	19.3			(180)	22.5	(205)	22.9
	18.2		2.0		5.4		6.4				7.4		11.7

% Profit Before Taxes/Total Assets:

	39.2		15.2		13.1		12.3		12.1		14.9		17.2
	23.5		4.8		6.2		7.9		7.8		6.8		7.9
	−7.6		.2		1.7		3.0		4.8		1.8		3.8

Sales/Net Fixed Assets:

	308.4		59.5		56.1		36.3		48.2		54.3		53.2
	48.0		32.3		27.4		18.5		15.6		25.6		27.5
	13.2		15.7		13.8		9.1		7.3		12.2		14.5

Sales/Total Assets:

	5.6		4.0		3.8		3.6		3.5		3.9		3.8
	3.5		3.4		2.9		2.8		2.7		3.1		3.2
	1.8		2.7		2.3		1.9		1.6		2.4		2.6

% Depr., Dep., Amort./Sales:

	.4		.6		.5		.5				.6		.6
(10)	1.4	(64)	.8	(96)	.8	(34)	1.0			(175)	1.1	(199)	.9
	4.6		1.7		1.5		2.0				1.7		1.7

% Officers', Directors', Owners' Comp/Sales:

			3.4		1.1						1.5		1.7
		(40)	4.6	(37)	2.2					(77)	3.4	(90)	3.3
			7.2		4.4						6.1		6.1

	18081M	289082M	1538173M	2116049M	1874288M	805074M	Net Sales ($)	5674955M	7279216M
	4445M	82932M	512791M	718492M	773090M	385425M	Total Assets ($)	1927114M	2637528M

M = $ thousand   MM = $ million
See Pages 11 through 18 for Explanation of Ratios and Data

Comparative Historical Data | Current Data Sorted By Sales

			Type of Statement						
22	24	36	Unqualified		2		1	11	22
46	42	83	Reviewed	1	7	11	20	26	18
72	68	44	Compiled	3	9	8	13	11	11
18	16	20	Tax Returns	4	6	2	4	3	1
63	64	58	Other	2	5	11	11	12	17
4/1/00-3/31/01	4/1/01-3/31/02	4/1/02-3/31/03			37 (4/1-9/30/02)		204 (10/1/02-3/31/03)		
ALL	ALL	ALL		0-1MM	1-3MM	3-5MM	5-10MM	10-25MM	25MM & OVER
221	214	241	**NUMBER OF STATEMENTS**	10	29	32	49	63	58
%	%	%	**ASSETS**	%	%	%	%	%	%
7.4	7.3	6.7	Cash & Equivalents	11.5	7.6	5.9	6.4	7.6	5.2
38.4	37.1	36.7	Trade Receivables (net)	22.4	35.4	43.1	37.8	35.5	36.4
30.5	29.8	30.3	Inventory	38.3	28.1	27.8	32.6	31.9	27.7
1.8	2.9	2.1	All Other Current	.1	1.3	1.6	2.3	2.8	2.3
78.0	77.2	75.8	Total Current	72.4	72.5	78.4	79.0	77.8	71.6
16.3	16.9	17.2	Fixed Assets (net)	22.5	21.8	15.6	14.3	14.5	20.1
2.0	1.4	1.8	Intangibles (net)	.0	.0	1.1	1.3	2.2	3.6
3.7	4.6	5.2	All Other Non-Current	5.1	5.8	4.9	5.4	5.5	4.7
100.0	100.0	100.0	Total	100.0	100.0	100.0	100.0	100.0	100.0
			LIABILITIES						
16.1	14.2	14.3	Notes Payable-Short Term	21.9	16.3	16.1	11.9	13.8	13.6
3.1	3.8	2.6	Cur. Mat.-L/T/D	.0	1.9	3.7	2.7	2.0	2.0
20.8	20.2	19.0	Trade Payables	24.2	22.9	16.8	23.0	15.9	17.6
.2	.3	.3	Income Taxes Payable	.1	.4	.1	.2	.5	.2
9.1	9.9	9.8	All Other Current	5.6	12.6	9.0	10.9	9.3	9.0
49.2	48.4	46.0	Total Current	51.9	54.2	45.7	48.7	42.8	42.3
9.8	10.1	9.4	Long Term Debt	9.5	13.0	10.0	7.0	7.5	11.5
.1	.1	.3	Deferred Taxes	.2	.1	.2	.4	.3	.5
4.3	3.7	2.4	All Other Non-Current	2.2	3.1	1.8	3.4	2.3	1.8
36.6	37.6	41.8	Net Worth	36.3	29.5	42.3	40.5	47.1	43.9
100.0	100.0	100.0	Total Liabilities & Net Worth	100.0	100.0	100.0	100.0	100.0	100.0
			INCOME DATA						
100.0	100.0	100.0	Net Sales	100.0	100.0	100.0	100.0	100.0	100.0
26.3	26.8	26.5	Gross Profit	25.7	31.9	25.5	26.1	27.6	23.5
22.7	23.2	23.1	Operating Expenses	22.9	29.4	21.9	24.0	23.3	19.8
3.6	3.6	3.3	Operating Profit	2.8	2.5	3.6	2.1	4.3	3.7
.1	.6	.5	All Other Expenses (net)	1.5	1.0	.6	.2	.2	.4
3.5	2.9	2.9	Profit Before Taxes	1.3	1.5	3.0	1.9	4.1	3.3
			RATIOS						
2.5	2.5	2.7		4.5	2.4	4.0	2.7	2.8	2.6
1.6	1.6	1.7	Current	1.6	1.5	1.5	1.8	1.7	1.7
1.2	1.2	1.2		.7	1.1	1.1	1.3	1.4	1.2
1.4	1.5	1.5		1.9	1.2	2.4	1.6	1.3	1.4
.9	.9	.9	Quick	.4	.9	.9	1.0	.9	1.0
.6	.6	.6		.2	.5	.7	.7	.7	.6
33 11.1	32 11.5	29 12.5		7 49.3	25 14.9	30 12.3	28 13.1	29 12.4	32 11.5
41 8.8	40 9.2	41 8.9	Sales/Receivables	37 9.8	40 9.2	46 8.0	42 8.7	38 9.5	38 9.5
58 6.3	55 6.6	56 6.6		60 6.1	65 5.7	64 5.7	62 5.8	52 7.1	52 7.0
26 14.1	27 13.4	25 14.9		57 6.4	15 25.0	12 31.6	24 15.1	26 14.1	25 14.5
45 8.0	44 8.4	47 7.8	Cost of Sales/Inventory	86 4.2	54 6.8	45 8.1	49 7.4	49 7.5	40 9.1
69 5.3	65 5.6	76 4.8		134 2.7	86 4.2	73 5.0	80 4.6	79 4.6	62 5.9
15 23.8	16 23.3	16 22.8		26 13.8	23 16.1	9 38.5	21 17.1	15 25.1	16 22.4
28 13.2	28 13.1	26 13.8	Cost of Sales/Payables	34 10.7	41 8.9	25 14.8	31 11.7	23 15.8	24 15.3
46 7.9	42 8.6	40 9.1		105 3.5	73 5.0	38 9.7	43 8.5	35 10.5	36 10.1
6.9	6.8	6.7		3.9	7.4	5.3	6.3	6.1	7.6
11.6	11.0	10.2	Sales/Working Capital	16.0	12.7	11.7	9.6	7.9	11.1
26.6	27.6	24.6		-4.5	29.4	44.4	20.7	15.6	24.6
	10.6		9.4		10.7		8.4	12.0	8.5	16.2	10.8
(201) 4.1	(196) 3.4	(225) 4.2	EBIT/Interest	(27) 3.2	(30) 3.1	(47) 3.3	(59) 4.3	(55) 5.5	
1.8	1.4	1.9			-.1	1.7	1.3	2.4	3.2
5.9	5.8	9.3	Net Profit + Depr., Dep.,				10.9	10.0	14.1
(50) 3.0	(49) 2.4	(68) 4.1	Amort./Cur. Mat. L/T/D			(15) 4.1	(25) 5.2	(19) 5.1	
1.8	1.2	2.0					.9	2.9	2.6
.2	.2	.1		.0	.2	.1	.1	.1	.2
.4	.4	.4	Fixed/Worth	.4	.4	.3	.2	.3	.4
.8	.9	.8		-2.0	2.0	1.2	.5	.6	.9
.9	.8	.6		.3	.7	.3	.6	.6	.8
2.0	1.9	1.3	Debt/Worth	.8	2.0	1.9	1.4	1.2	1.3
3.9	3.8	3.0		-5.1	7.9	4.2	3.0	2.5	2.9
47.7	40.6	34.7	% Profit Before Taxes/Tangible		40.9	50.6	34.7	30.5	33.2
(209) 23.6	(199) 17.0	(223) 19.3	Net Worth	(25) 16.2	(31) 11.7	(45) 8.2	(61) 21.1	(54) 20.5	
8.2	5.6	5.1			.4	2.0	3.1	9.1	8.8
16.9	15.1	14.0	% Profit Before Taxes/Total	39.2	11.6	18.6	14.9	14.1	12.6
7.1	6.0	6.5	Assets	23.5	6.3	3.3	4.0	8.2	7.7
2.5	1.7	1.6		-9.4	-1.6	1.1	1.0	3.2	3.3
56.6	51.2	51.3		UND	42.8	75.3	69.4	53.1	42.9
28.8	27.5	27.3	Sales/Net Fixed Assets	16.5	22.2	31.4	38.3	26.6	20.4
14.3	13.0	12.4		4.3	10.9	16.5	17.4	15.2	9.4
4.1	3.8	3.9		3.7	3.4	3.9	4.2	3.9	3.7
3.2	3.2	3.0	Sales/Total Assets	1.9	2.8	3.0	3.4	3.0	3.0
2.5	2.6	2.4		1.4	2.2	2.4	2.5	2.4	2.5
.4	.4	.5			.6	.4	.5	.5	.6
(194) .9	(187) .9	(215) .9	% Depr., Dep., Amort./Sales	(26) 1.4	(28) .8	(44) .8	(60) .9	(50) 1.0	
1.5	1.5	1.8			3.3	1.7	1.3	1.6	1.8
1.3	1.5	1.5			4.2	2.5	1.7	1.2	.7
(100) 2.7	(77) 3.3	(91) 3.6	% Officers', Directors', Owners' Comp/Sales	(17) 5.3	(12) 4.4	(22) 3.6	(24) 2.5	(11) 1.1	
6.4	6.6	6.1			10.1	7.6	5.6	4.4	2.1
5536528M	6138628M	6640747M	Net Sales ($)	5331M	61444M	130736M	361625M	987563M	5094048M
1952682M	2096909M	2477175M	Total Assets ($)	3241M	24471M	52987M	127993M	369855M	1898628M

M = $ thousand   MM = $ million
See Pages 11 through 18 for Explanation of Ratios and Data

Current Data Sorted By Assets							Comparative Historical Data	
						Type of Statement		
	1	3	4			Unqualified	8	9
	5	13	3			Reviewed	12	16
1		5	1			Compiled	10	8
	1					Tax Returns	2	1
	3	1	1	1		Other	9	10
	5 (4/1-9/30/02)		38 (10/1/02-3/31/03)				**4/1/98-3/31/99**	**4/1/99-3/31/00**
0-500M	**500M-2MM**	**2-10MM**	**10-50MM**	**50-100MM**	**100-250MM**		**ALL**	**ALL**
1	10	22	9	1		**NUMBER OF STATEMENTS**	41	44
%	%	%	%	%	%	**ASSETS**	%	%
	8.3	9.7			DATA NOT AVAILABLE	Cash & Equivalents	7.4	6.8
	36.5	28.4				Trade Receivables (net)	37.6	34.3
	38.0	41.3				Inventory	36.6	37.3
	1.4	2.1				All Other Current	1.8	3.0
	84.3	81.4				Total Current	83.4	81.4
	6.8	12.3				Fixed Assets (net)	9.1	10.8
	2.2	.9				Intangibles (net)	2.6	2.6
	6.8	5.4				All Other Non-Current	4.8	5.3
	100.0	100.0				Total	100.0	100.0
						LIABILITIES		
	20.4	20.0				Notes Payable-Short Term	22.1	18.7
	1.2	2.0				Cur. Mat.-L/T/D	1.6	1.5
	21.9	20.6				Trade Payables	21.8	21.1
	.7	.2				Income Taxes Payable	.2	.3
	7.7	9.4				All Other Current	7.6	7.9
	52.0	52.2				Total Current	53.4	49.6
	3.3	7.8				Long Term Debt	6.5	7.3
	.0	.1				Deferred Taxes	.1	.3
	12.1	2.5				All Other Non-Current	4.0	3.0
	32.6	37.4				Net Worth	36.0	39.9
	100.0	100.0				Total Liabilities & Net Worth	100.0	100.0
						INCOME DATA		
	100.0	100.0				Net Sales	100.0	100.0
	36.1	29.3				Gross Profit	26.4	29.5
	34.2	27.4				Operating Expenses	22.2	25.7
	1.9	2.0				Operating Profit	4.2	3.8
	.5	.1				All Other Expenses (net)	.3	.5
	1.4	1.9				Profit Before Taxes	3.9	3.3
						RATIOS		
	2.3	2.5					1.9	2.2
	1.5	1.5				Current	1.5	1.6
	1.2	1.2					1.2	1.3
	1.9	1.0					1.3	1.3
	.8	.6				Quick	.8	.8
	.5	.5					.5	.5
	32 11.4	**25** 14.7					**29** 12.4	**36** 10.2
	38 9.5	**32** 11.4				Sales/Receivables	**43** 8.5	**47** 7.8
	74 4.9	**48** 7.6					**55** 6.7	**62** 5.9
	36 10.1	**41** 8.9					**35** 10.5	**41** 9.0
	60 6.1	**78** 4.7				Cost of Sales/Inventory	**56** 6.5	**57** 6.5
	107 3.4	**105** 3.5					**114** 3.2	**137** 2.7
	30 12.4	**13** 29.1					**13** 28.4	**25** 14.4
	37 9.8	**33** 11.1				Cost of Sales/Payables	**30** 12.2	**39** 9.4
	74 4.9	**49** 7.4					**54** 6.7	**59** 6.2
	5.0	4.9					5.9	5.5
	11.5	9.3				Sales/Working Capital	10.5	8.3
	25.3	34.3					22.9	16.4
		4.1					12.5	12.3
		(20) 2.2				EBIT/Interest	(37) 3.5	(40) 3.7
		.5					1.6	1.7
								9.4
						Net Profit + Depr., Dep., Amort./Cur. Mat. L /T/D		(16) 3.5
								1.8
	.1	.1					.1	.1
	.2	.3				Fixed/Worth	.3	.2
	NM	.8					.5	.5
	.9	.8					1.4	1.1
	2.9	2.0				Debt/Worth	2.1	1.8
	NM	5.1					3.7	3.1
		32.3					63.0	34.9
		(21) 11.0				% Profit Before Taxes/Tangible Net Worth	(38) 20.4	(43) 15.1
		.0					8.7	8.7
	10.3	9.5					17.8	9.1
	1.6	3.1				% Profit Before Taxes/Total Assets	7.1	5.4
	−4.1	−.9					1.4	2.2
	125.6	92.2					119.8	86.0
	53.1	34.0				Sales/Net Fixed Assets	49.8	52.2
	25.7	12.6					19.2	16.6
	4.0	3.6					4.0	3.6
	3.0	3.0				Sales/Total Assets	3.0	2.6
	1.9	2.1					2.0	1.8
		.5					.4	.3
		(19) 1.0				% Depr., Dep., Amort./Sales	(34) .7	(36) .8
		2.0					1.0	2.0
		1.3					.7	1.5
		(10) 1.8				% Officers', Directors', Owners' Comp/Sales	(18) 1.8	(17) 3.2
		4.8					3.0	5.1
747M	40069M	325181M	343965M	199732M		Net Sales ($)	504271M	1022398M
264M	13063M	113915M	137063M	68547M		Total Assets ($)	174433M	420129M

M = $ thousand MM = $ million

See Pages 11 through 18 for Explanation of Ratios and Data

Comparative Historical Data — Current Data Sorted By Sales

	4/1/00-3/31/01 ALL	4/1/01-3/31/02 ALL	4/1/02-3/31/03 ALL	0-1MM	1-3MM	3-5MM	5-10MM	10-25MM	25MM & OVER
Type of Statement									
Unqualified	6	4	8		1		1	4	2
Reviewed	13	16	21			4	4	8	5
Compiled	19	14	7	1		1	3	2	1
Tax Returns	4	2	1						
Other	13	11	6		2		1	1	2
				5 (4/1-9/30/02)			38 (10/1/02-3/31/03)		
NUMBER OF STATEMENTS	55	47	43	1	3	5	9	15	10
	%	%	%	%	%	%	%	%	%
ASSETS									
Cash & Equivalents	6.6	7.9	7.5					8.1	2.9
Trade Receivables (net)	33.4	29.2	32.9					29.0	47.4
Inventory	36.7	40.5	39.4					39.6	36.3
All Other Current	.8	2.1	1.7					2.1	2.1
Total Current	77.5	79.8	81.6					78.8	88.7
Fixed Assets (net)	12.5	12.0	10.9					14.7	7.4
Intangibles (net)	4.2	2.2	1.2					.9	1.6
All Other Non-Current	5.8	6.0	6.4					5.5	2.3
Total	100.0	100.0	100.0					100.0	100.0
LIABILITIES									
Notes Payable-Short Term	15.1	14.0	18.9					23.5	18.7
Cur. Mat.-L/T/D	4.6	6.1	1.4					1.0	1.3
Trade Payables	23.7	20.2	21.4					18.9	27.2
Income Taxes Payable	.1	.1	.8					.3	2.2
All Other Current	6.9	7.7	10.8					9.5	17.6
Total Current	50.4	48.0	53.3					53.3	67.0
Long Term Debt	11.1	8.4	6.7					5.1	9.9
Deferred Taxes	.2	.2	.1					.2	.0
All Other Non-Current	2.6	11.6	6.0					5.7	3.3
Net Worth	35.7	31.8	33.8					35.7	19.8
Total Liabilities & Net Worth	100.0	100.0	100.0					100.0	100.0
INCOME DATA									
Net Sales	100.0	100.0	100.0					100.0	100.0
Gross Profit	29.3	28.6	30.2					30.8	22.4
Operating Expenses	25.8	27.0	28.2					29.0	20.1
Operating Profit	3.5	1.6	2.0					1.8	2.3
All Other Expenses (net)	.8	.5	.4					.4	.4
Profit Before Taxes	2.7	1.1	1.7					1.4	2.0
RATIOS									
Current	2.1	2.9	2.0					2.0	1.7
	1.6	1.8	1.5					1.5	1.4
	1.2	1.3	1.2					1.2	1.0
Quick	1.3	1.3	1.1					.9	1.1
	.8	.8	.6					.6	.7
	.5	.5	.5					.4	.5
Sales/Receivables	28 13.0	25 14.7	27 13.4					26 14.1	28 12.8
	39 9.3	35 10.4	36 10.1					34 10.7	51 7.1
	54 6.8	49 7.5	63 5.8					46 7.9	77 4.7
Cost of Sales/Inventory	38 9.7	39 9.3	39 9.2					39 9.2	33 11.1
	53 6.9	73 5.0	69 5.3					78 4.7	48 7.5
	104 3.5	100 3.6	104 3.5					96 3.8	76 4.8
Cost of Sales/Payables	22 16.8	15 24.4	15 25.0					27 13.7	10 35.4
	36 10.1	30 12.0	37 9.9					37 9.9	43 8.4
	56 6.5	49 7.4	52 7.0					52 7.1	53 6.9
Sales/Working Capital	5.6	6.0	5.1					5.2	8.4
	12.4	9.1	9.8					9.8	12.6
	30.1	17.8	29.3					32.4	−189.1
EBIT/Interest	4.5	4.4	5.8					5.8	
	(50) 2.5	(40) 2.2	(39) 1.9					3.1	
	1.1	.7	.3					1.1	
Net Profit + Depr., Dep., Amort./Cur. Mat. L/T/D	5.4	2.9							
	(17) 1.4	(10) .5							
	.4	−2.4							
Fixed/Worth	.1	.0	.1					.1	.0
	.3	.2	.2					.2	.2
	.7	.7	.8					1.4	−.8
Debt/Worth	.9	.7	.9					.8	1.3
	2.4	1.7	2.2					2.2	2.0
	4.9	4.3	4.7					5.2	−44.2
% Profit Before Taxes/Tangible Net Worth	24.9	22.8	32.7					39.7	
	(51) 13.4	(45) 9.6	(38) 10.9					11.0	
	3.8	.8	.4					1.5	
% Profit Before Taxes/Total Assets	9.8	9.6	8.2					9.7	7.8
	4.7	4.2	2.5					3.5	4.1
	.4	.1	−1.5					.4	−1.6
Sales/Net Fixed Assets	102.3	130.4	162.6					98.2	519.9
	53.3	49.3	42.7					35.8	143.2
	11.9	22.2	18.2					11.1	34.5
Sales/Total Assets	3.7	3.6	3.4					3.4	4.1
	2.9	2.9	2.8					2.8	2.9
	2.0	2.0	2.1					2.0	2.5
% Depr., Dep., Amort./Sales	.4	.3	.5					.4	
	(45) .8	(39) .8	(31) .9				(14)	1.0	
	1.9	1.3	2.1					1.3	
% Officers', Directors', Owners' Comp/Sales	1.4	1.8	1.4						
	(29) 3.7	(21) 2.8	(18) 4.1						
	5.5	5.2	7.5						
Net Sales ($)	1636524M	745579M	909694M	747M	5188M	18704M	65916M	246662M	572477M
Total Assets ($)	617435M	278045M	332852M	264M	3017M	7626M	29887M	100330M	191728M

© RMA 2003

M = $ thousand   MM = $ million

See Pages 11 through 18 for Explanation of Ratios and Data

Current Data Sorted By Assets | Comparative Historical Data

0-500M	500M-2MM	2-10MM	10-50MM	50-100MM	100-250MM	Type of Statement	4/1/98-3/31/99 ALL	4/1/99-3/31/00 ALL
1		11	9		1	Unqualified	38	32
1	17	32	5			Reviewed	62	56
8	22	9	1			Compiled	59	53
5	12	1				Tax Returns	15	15
7	12	16	5	1	2	Other	49	44
	48 (4/1-9/30/02)		129 (10/1/02-3/31/03)					
22	63	69	19	1	3	NUMBER OF STATEMENTS	223	200
%	%	%	%	%	%	**ASSETS**	%	%
12.4	8.9	7.3	6.7			Cash & Equivalents	6.3	7.1
24.1	32.2	34.1	31.5			Trade Receivables (net)	32.0	32.6
34.6	33.8	30.5	21.4			Inventory	33.9	35.5
.7	2.0	3.1	6.3			All Other Current	2.4	2.7
71.9	76.9	74.9	65.9			Total Current	74.6	77.9
17.6	16.7	15.8	18.3			Fixed Assets (net)	16.1	13.8
.9	2.5	2.3	5.8			Intangibles (net)	3.0	2.2
9.6	4.0	6.9	10.0			All Other Non-Current	6.3	6.1
100.0	100.0	100.0	100.0			Total	100.0	100.0
						LIABILITIES		
24.5	13.5	14.3	10.4			Notes Payable-Short Term	12.0	15.1
5.5	4.6	3.5	4.0			Cur. Mat.-L/T/D	3.9	3.5
18.3	20.9	20.3	12.9			Trade Payables	18.2	18.4
.2	.2	.4	.2			Income Taxes Payable	.4	.3
14.9	12.8	11.9	17.0			All Other Current	14.2	16.8
63.5	52.0	50.5	44.4			Total Current	48.7	54.0
20.0	15.0	6.0	11.3			Long Term Debt	12.8	11.7
.0	.1	.3	.5			Deferred Taxes	.4	.2
7.5	3.9	5.4	5.8			All Other Non-Current	5.3	5.9
9.1	29.0	37.9	38.0			Net Worth	32.8	28.3
100.0	100.0	100.0	100.0			Total Liabilities & Net Worth	100.0	100.0
						INCOME DATA		
100.0	100.0	100.0	100.0			Net Sales	100.0	100.0
45.5	41.3	36.7	39.0			Gross Profit	38.8	39.2
47.0	38.7	33.2	35.6			Operating Expenses	35.0	36.7
-1.5	2.6	3.6	3.4			Operating Profit	3.8	2.5
.4	.9	.3	.0			All Other Expenses (net)	.4	.4
-1.9	1.7	3.3	3.4			Profit Before Taxes	3.4	2.0
						RATIOS		
2.5	2.2	2.1	2.3			Current	2.1	2.0
1.1	1.6	1.5	1.4				1.5	1.4
.9	1.1	1.1	1.2				1.2	1.1
1.4	1.3	1.2	1.2			Quick	1.1	1.1
.6	.8	.8	.9				.8	.7
.3	.5	.5	.4				.5	.5
8 45.3	24 15.3	30 12.2	35 10.5			Sales/Receivables	27 13.4	29 12.5
21 17.1	31 11.9	36 10.2	42 8.6				37 9.9	40 9.0
34 10.7	41 9.0	50 7.3	66 5.6				51 7.1	50 7.3
11 33.8	27 13.6	30 12.2	21 17.3			Cost of Sales/Inventory	41 8.9	47 7.8
44 8.3	65 5.6	63 5.8	79 4.6				72 5.1	84 4.4
87 4.2	106 3.4	100 3.6	103 3.3				110 3.3	117 3.1
4 82.9	22 16.7	20 18.4	18 20.5			Cost of Sales/Payables	19 18.8	18 20.6
27 13.3	32 11.5	36 10.2	23 15.8				31 11.7	34 10.7
48 7.6	52 7.0	55 6.7	38 9.6				55 6.7	54 6.8
8.1	7.1	7.0	7.3			Sales/Working Capital	6.7	6.7
201.4	13.5	13.6	8.2				12.3	12.3
-46.0	62.4	41.8	33.1				32.9	44.6
10.9	10.5	8.8	12.5			EBIT/Interest	7.9	9.2
(21) 1.9	(53) 3.1	(63) 3.6	(16) 3.0				(211) 3.0	(183) 2.9
-.8	.1	1.7	1.5				1.6	1.4
	8.0	5.2				Net Profit + Depr., Dep., Amort./Cur. Mat. L /T/D	4.5	6.0
	(10) 1.7	(26) 1.8					(75) 1.9	(52) 1.7
	.8	1.1					1.3	.8
.1	.2	.1	.1			Fixed/Worth	.2	.2
.8	.3	.3	.6				.4	.4
-.7	1.7	.8	1.4				.9	1.2
.7	.8	.9	.7			Debt/Worth	1.2	1.3
6.6	2.0	1.8	2.1				2.3	2.5
-4.4	6.9	4.3	3.6				4.1	5.8
52.1	28.6	45.5	27.2			% Profit Before Taxes/Tangible Net Worth	42.2	36.4
(13) 7.8	(52) 14.8	(66) 18.9	(17) 16.8				(203) 19.8	(174) 13.5
-14.3	3.3	5.2	8.2				8.0	4.5
17.6	11.6	14.4	11.0			% Profit Before Taxes/Total Assets	12.9	10.0
1.0	5.3	5.5	5.6				5.8	4.3
-10.3	-1.2	1.7	2.0				2.2	.9
139.9	81.0	56.8	50.9			Sales/Net Fixed Assets	55.3	58.6
44.7	31.1	30.3	15.8				26.0	29.0
14.6	17.4	10.2	5.7				11.0	14.5
7.1	4.8	4.1	2.9			Sales/Total Assets	4.0	3.8
4.1	3.5	3.0	1.9				2.9	2.7
2.8	2.3	2.2	1.4				2.1	2.1
.2	.5	.5	.8			% Depr., Dep., Amort./Sales	.7	.7
(11) .9	(55) 1.2	(62) .8	(16) 1.7				(192) 1.2	(162) 1.2
2.5	2.5	1.9	3.2				2.3	2.4
3.4	2.9	1.9				% Officers', Directors', Owners' Comp/Sales	2.3	2.3
(12) 6.2	(35) 4.1	(24) 2.5					(94) 3.9	(85) 3.7
8.4	5.7	5.2					6.7	6.7
31425M	272016M	967434M	747609M	107436M	2267210M	Net Sales ($)	2827521M	3018115M
6655M	75025M	312648M	333784M	94716M	518103M	Total Assets ($)	1096480M	1377630M

Comparative Historical Data

Current Data Sorted By Sales

Type of Statement

Type of Statement	4/1/00-3/31/01 ALL	4/1/01-3/31/02 ALL	4/1/02-3/31/03 ALL	0-1MM	1-3MM	3-5MM	5-10MM	10-25MM	25MM & OVER
Unqualified	24	14	22	2	1	5	4	6	11
Reviewed	40	39	55		5	5	22	17	4
Compiled	50	51	39	5	8	11	9	4	2
Tax Returns	11	18	18	1	11	2	3	1	
Other	49	46	43	3	11	5	4	10	10

Right-side date spans: **48 (4/1-9/30/02)** covers 0-1MM, 1-3MM, 3-5MM; **129 (10/1/02-3/31/03)** covers 5-10MM, 10-25MM, 25MM & OVER.

NUMBER OF STATEMENTS	174	168	177	11	36	23	42	38	27

ASSETS (%)

	Hist 174	Hist 168	Hist 177	0-1MM	1-3MM	3-5MM	5-10MM	10-25MM	25MM & OVER
Cash & Equivalents	9.1	8.0	8.4	5.2	14.5	6.3	4.0	10.8	6.8
Trade Receivables (net)	33.4	32.3	31.8	21.3	22.5	31.6	37.1	36.1	34.4
Inventory	31.3	33.7	30.9	33.8	34.7	35.0	31.0	28.4	24.7
All Other Current	1.9	2.5	2.8	.4	1.3	3.7	3.0	2.1	6.0
Total Current	75.7	76.6	74.0	60.7	73.0	76.6	75.1	77.4	71.8
Fixed Assets (net)	14.7	13.4	16.4	30.3	17.0	17.5	16.2	14.6	12.1
Intangibles (net)	3.1	3.3	2.9	1.7	3.3	1.1	1.5	2.9	6.7
All Other Non-Current	6.4	6.8	6.7	7.3	6.7	4.8	7.2	5.1	9.3
Total	100.0	100.0	100.0	100.0	100.0	100.0	100.0	100.0	100.0

LIABILITIES

	Hist 174	Hist 168	Hist 177	0-1MM	1-3MM	3-5MM	5-10MM	10-25MM	25MM & OVER
Notes Payable-Short Term	12.7	14.1	14.7	38.3	15.5	12.4	15.9	10.5	10.0
Cur. Mat.-L/T/D	3.7	3.8	4.2	7.9	4.5	3.4	5.3	3.2	2.5
Trade Payables	19.0	19.4	19.1	15.4	18.3	19.6	19.4	22.0	16.7
Income Taxes Payable	.3	.3	.3	.0	.5	.3	.2	.5	.2
All Other Current	16.8	14.3	13.1	8.2	11.2	17.2	13.8	11.5	15.0
Total Current	52.5	51.9	51.3	69.8	49.9	53.0	54.6	47.6	44.4
Long Term Debt	10.5	11.5	11.8	29.2	19.6	5.8	10.9	4.2	11.3
Deferred Taxes	.1	.1	.2	.0	.0	.1	.4	.1	.4
All Other Non-Current	6.7	5.4	5.1	2.6	5.9	5.0	4.1	5.2	6.4
Net Worth	30.2	31.2	31.6	-1.6	24.5	36.1	30.0	42.8	37.4
Total Liabilities & Net Worth	100.0	100.0	100.0	100.0	100.0	100.0	100.0	100.0	100.0

INCOME DATA

	Hist 174	Hist 168	Hist 177	0-1MM	1-3MM	3-5MM	5-10MM	10-25MM	25MM & OVER
Net Sales	100.0	100.0	100.0	100.0	100.0	100.0	100.0	100.0	100.0
Gross Profit	37.6	37.2	39.9	56.3	41.2	43.3	38.7	36.7	34.9
Operating Expenses	35.2	35.4	37.2	59.6	37.7	40.6	37.0	32.3	31.4
Operating Profit	2.4	1.8	2.7	-3.3	3.4	2.7	1.7	4.4	3.4
All Other Expenses (net)	.2	.7	.5	3.2	.6	-.1	.6	.3	.2
Profit Before Taxes	2.2	1.1	2.2	-6.5	2.8	2.8	1.1	4.0	3.2

RATIOS (values given as upper / median / lower)

Ratio	Hist 174	Hist 168	Hist 177	0-1MM	1-3MM	3-5MM	5-10MM	10-25MM	25MM & OVER
Current	2.2 / 1.5 / 1.1	2.2 / 1.5 / 1.1	2.2 / 1.5 / 1.1	1.6 / 1.0 / .5	3.1 / 1.6 / 1.2	2.0 / 1.5 / 1.1	2.0 / 1.3 / 1.1	2.4 / 1.7 / 1.2	2.2 / 1.5 / 1.3
Quick	1.3 / .8 / .5	(167) 1.2 / .7 / .5	1.2 / .8 / .5	.6 / .4 / .3	1.6 / .9 / .4	1.0 / .7 / .5	1.0 / .7 / .5	1.5 / 1.0 / .6	1.5 / .9 / .5
Sales/Receivables	28 12.9 / 37 9.9 / 52 7.1	26 13.8 / 35 10.5 / 48 7.6	25 14.4 / 33 11.0 / 46 7.9	24 15.4 / 34 10.9 / 49 7.5	15 24.7 / 24 15.2 / 33 11.2	25 14.4 / 31 11.9 / 42 8.7	31 11.7 / 36 10.1 / 50 7.4	29 12.5 / 36 10.2 / 52 7.0	30 12.2 / 37 9.8 / 48 7.6
Cost of Sales/Inventory	29 12.5 / 62 5.9 / 98 3.7	28 13.2 / 71 5.2 / 111 3.3	25 14.6 / 64 5.7 / 101 3.6	30 12.0 / 82 4.4 / 201 1.8	13 29.1 / 66 5.5 / 106 3.4	37 9.8 / 58 6.3 / 107 3.4	25 14.5 / 64 5.7 / 103 3.5	22 16.7 / 61 6.0 / 99 3.7	14 25.7 / 56 6.5 / 82 4.4
Cost of Sales/Payables	19 19.4 / 32 11.5 / 48 7.5	16 22.5 / 31 12.0 / 49 7.4	19 19.4 / 30 12.1 / 50 7.3	32 11.5 / 49 7.5 / 71 5.2	13 27.6 / 28 12.9 / 52 7.0	19 19.5 / 33 11.1 / 49 7.4	19 19.6 / 28 13.0 / 56 6.5	19 19.0 / 36 10.2 / 55 6.7	18 20.5 / 23 15.8 / 38 9.7
Sales/Working Capital	7.3 / 12.5 / 37.9	6.5 / 11.2 / 37.8	7.2 / 14.7 / 65.7	5.2 / -200.5 / -5.8	4.8 / 10.8 / 53.3	9.3 / 12.6 / 155.6	8.1 / 20.5 / 80.1	6.2 / 11.8 / 33.0	7.7 / 12.4 / 21.4
EBIT/Interest	(158) 6.7 / 2.8 / 1.3	(157) 5.0 / 2.3 / .9	(156) 9.6 / 3.2 / 1.1	(10) .8 / -.1 / -5.6	(31) 12.2 / 4.4 / 1.0	(20) 10.6 / 5.0 / 1.3	(41) 6.8 / 3.1 / .7	(31) 12.3 / 4.9 / 1.6	(23) 13.5 / 4.8 / 1.6
Net Profit + Depr., Dep., Amort./Cur. Mat. L/T/D	(47) 8.5 / 2.3 / 1.0	(39) 6.5 / 2.2 / .8	(47) 4.9 / 1.6 / 1.0				(14) 5.0 / 1.8 / 1.3	(14) 6.0 / 1.5 / 1.1	
Fixed/Worth	.1 / .4 / 1.2	.1 / .3 / 1.3	.1 / .3 / 1.5	.4 / 20.6 / -1.2	.1 / .4 / -3.0	.2 / .4 / 1.1	.2 / .5 / 1.0	.1 / .3 / .9	.1 / .2 / 1.0
Debt/Worth	1.1 / 2.5 / 5.8	.9 / 2.3 / 7.6	.9 / 2.0 / 6.4	5.8 / 27.6 / -4.0	.8 / 2.0 / -24.5	.8 / 1.6 / 4.4	.9 / 2.2 / 4.2	.7 / 1.6 / 3.2	1.0 / 2.1 / 4.8
% Profit Before Taxes/Tangible Net Worth	(151) 39.5 / 15.3 / 4.8	(142) 32.8 / 11.8 / 1.1	(151) 37.4 / 16.8 / 4.0		(26) 28.1 / 12.9 / 4.1	(21) 45.9 / 21.6 / 4.3	(38) 25.3 / 10.5 / 1.1	(36) 48.4 / 21.7 / 10.2	(24) 44.8 / 23.8 / 9.8
% Profit Before Taxes/Total Assets	11.3 / 4.6 / 1.0	8.9 / 3.3 / -.5	12.7 / 5.5 / .7	-2.5 / -5.5 / -12.8	14.7 / 6.4 / .1	16.3 / 8.6 / .8	6.9 / 3.4 / -.8	16.9 / 8.6 / 1.5	13.5 / 7.1 / 2.4
Sales/Net Fixed Assets	71.5 / 33.9 / 14.3	66.6 / 34.2 / 15.3	71.3 / 30.6 / 13.5	120.0 / 8.4 / 3.9	75.0 / 41.0 / 17.4	40.6 / 31.1 / 13.7	52.3 / 23.9 / 17.3	62.4 / 41.3 / 10.1	76.6 / 43.5 / 13.0
Sales/Total Assets	4.0 / 3.1 / 2.1	4.1 / 2.9 / 2.2	4.3 / 3.1 / 2.2	3.5 / 2.0 / 1.4	4.6 / 3.2 / 2.0	5.0 / 3.5 / 2.4	4.2 / 3.0 / 2.5	4.4 / 3.0 / 2.1	4.2 / 3.1 / 1.7
% Depr., Dep., Amort./Sales	(143) .5 / 1.2 / 2.1	(131) .6 / 1.2 / 2.3	(147) .6 / 1.1 / 2.3		(23) .5 / 1.2 / 1.8	(19) .5 / 1.2 / 3.3	(41) .6 / 1.2 / 2.5	(33) .3 / .7 / 1.6	(23) .7 / 1.1 / 1.9
% Officers', Directors', Owners' Comp/Sales	(77) 2.0 / 4.4 / 7.3	(76) 2.7 / 4.1 / 7.0	(74) 2.3 / 3.7 / 5.9		(20) 3.4 / 4.3 / 6.6	(16) 2.7 / 4.5 / 5.8	(15) 2.1 / 2.9 / 4.7	(13) 2.3 / 3.0 / 7.2	
Net Sales ($)	4751168M	2382591M	4393130M	7870M	73140M	90612M	316070M	599363M	3306075M
Total Assets ($)	1698219M	1160945M	1340931M	5108M	29231M	27907M	105613M	222166M	950906M

M = $ thousand   MM = $ million
See Pages 11 through 18 for Explanation of Ratios and Data

Current Data Sorted By Assets   **Comparative Historical Data**

0-500M	500M-2MM	2-10MM	10-50MM	50-100MM	100-250MM	Type of Statement	4/1/98-3/31/99 ALL	4/1/99-3/31/00 ALL
1	5	19	21	5	7	Unqualified	67	62
1	13	32	7			Reviewed	72	59
6	24	12				Compiled	62	59
12	15	2				Tax Returns	27	26
12	31	32	19	3	3	Other	113	112
	45 (4/1-9/30/02)		237 (10/1/02-3/31/03)					
32	88	97	47	8	10	**NUMBER OF STATEMENTS**	341	318
%	%	%	%	%	%	**ASSETS**	%	%
17.5	10.5	13.4	15.3		18.4	Cash & Equivalents	10.7	9.5
35.9	46.0	43.6	36.4		33.7	Trade Receivables (net)	47.2	46.2
13.2	21.9	18.5	18.7		21.5	Inventory	20.0	20.4
1.0	2.3	2.0	4.2		8.4	All Other Current	2.5	2.4
67.7	80.7	77.5	74.7		82.1	Total Current	80.4	78.5
20.3	11.1	12.7	9.2		8.2	Fixed Assets (net)	11.1	12.0
1.3	3.2	4.7	9.3		4.6	Intangibles (net)	3.3	4.3
10.7	5.0	5.2	6.8		5.1	All Other Non-Current	5.2	5.2
100.0	100.0	100.0	100.0		100.0	Total	100.0	100.0
						LIABILITIES		
26.6	14.8	14.1	12.7		7.3	Notes Payable-Short Term	14.4	13.5
7.9	2.6	1.8	1.7		.9	Cur. Mat.-L/T/D	2.2	2.3
23.0	25.4	27.3	20.0		21.8	Trade Payables	27.4	26.6
.0	.6	.2	.3		.5	Income Taxes Payable	.4	.3
17.0	13.7	10.9	18.1		11.1	All Other Current	13.0	13.1
74.5	57.0	54.3	52.9		41.6	Total Current	57.4	55.9
15.4	5.5	4.0	6.2		6.4	Long Term Debt	8.3	8.3
.0	.2	.3	.1		.2	Deferred Taxes	.1	.2
3.5	8.6	4.7	4.3		5.9	All Other Non-Current	4.8	4.3
6.6	28.7	36.7	36.5		46.0	Net Worth	29.3	31.4
100.0	100.0	100.0	100.0		100.0	Total Liabilities & Net Worth	100.0	100.0
						INCOME DATA		
100.0	100.0	100.0	100.0		100.0	Net Sales	100.0	100.0
44.9	34.4	30.2	32.8		30.2	Gross Profit	31.2	30.3
44.4	31.8	27.0	29.7		26.0	Operating Expenses	30.1	26.2
.5	2.6	3.2	3.1		4.3	Operating Profit	1.1	4.0
.7	.4	.4	.2		-.2	All Other Expenses (net)	-.1	.2
-.1	2.2	2.8	3.0		4.5	Profit Before Taxes	1.2	3.8
						RATIOS		
1.8	2.3	2.2	1.9		3.7		1.9	2.0
1.2	1.3	1.3	1.4		2.0	Current	1.4	1.4
.9	1.0	1.0	1.1		1.4		1.1	1.1
1.5	1.7	1.6	1.5		3.2		1.4	1.4
1.0	.9	1.0	.9		1.1	Quick	1.0	1.0
.5	.6	.7	.7		.8		.7	.7
9 42.7	24 15.0	34 10.9	27 13.7		27 13.5		29 12.4	29 12.6
30 12.3	37 9.9	40 9.1	45 8.0		56 6.5	Sales/Receivables	43 8.4	42 8.7
52 7.0	57 6.4	55 6.6	70 5.2		90 4.0		62 5.9	59 6.2
0 UND	10 37.9	3 105.5	6 61.0		0 UND		7 49.2	6 64.1
4 102.2	25 14.7	19 18.8	21 17.6		28 13.1	Cost of Sales/Inventory	22 16.5	21 17.6
29 12.6	47 7.8	44 8.3	40 9.2		60 6.1		42 8.7	42 8.7
7 50.3	16 22.1	19 19.4	21 17.2		23 15.8		18 19.9	17 21.6
31 11.8	30 12.2	30 12.3	32 11.3		43 8.5	Cost of Sales/Payables	36 10.2	33 11.0
70 5.2	49 7.4	50 7.3	53 6.9		57 6.4		6.5	56 6.5
15.7	8.6	8.3	6.9		2.2		9.4	9.5
45.8	21.5	21.0	17.7		5.8	Sales/Working Capital	17.6	19.1
-88.8	131.3	228.7	79.6		14.2		47.3	60.8
(26) 23.1	(76) 12.0	(81) 12.4	(38) 13.2		14.4		(292) 14.4	(273) 17.6
7.0	3.2	3.4	3.1			EBIT/Interest	4.1	4.4
-1.3	.7	1.2	.7				1.4	1.7
	(16) 8.2	(19) 6.5	(14) 21.5			Net Profit + Depr., Dep.,	(66) 16.0	(58) 8.6
	4.7	2.9	2.6			Amort./Cur. Mat. L./T/D	4.6	4.0
	1.0	1.2	.7				2.1	1.6
.1	.1	.1	.1		.1		.1	.1
.8	.3	.3	.2		.2	Fixed/Worth	.3	.3
2.3	1.0	1.3	1.0		.3		.8	1.1
.6	1.0	.9	1.3		.6		1.1	1.0
2.5	2.5	2.2	2.6		1.4	Debt/Worth	2.7	2.6
21.2	8.0	9.4	11.4		4.2		5.9	7.4
(25) 142.2	(77) 70.4	(85) 52.8	(40) 57.2		51.4	% Profit Before Taxes/Tangible	(307) 60.1	(277) 71.6
34.3	24.0	18.1	18.9		22.2	Net Worth	30.2	30.6
-.5	.0	2.8	.1		11.0		7.3	10.5
38.2	15.9	13.1	12.9		19.9	% Profit Before Taxes/Total	18.2	21.1
7.2	5.2	5.0	3.3		8.5	Assets	7.0	7.2
-5.4	-.5	.6	-.7		4.1		1.5	2.1
184.5	143.0	164.5	124.7		149.3		150.1	126.1
37.8	56.9	60.5	36.7		48.3	Sales/Net Fixed Assets	57.5	50.9
17.6	22.9	27.5	18.4		10.2		20.0	21.1
8.6	5.6	5.1	4.9		3.7		5.2	5.4
4.9	4.1	3.8	2.6		2.4	Sales/Total Assets	3.9	3.9
2.8	2.9	2.5	1.7		1.3		2.5	2.6
(18) .5	(67) .3	(78) .2	(36) .2			% Depr., Dep., Amort./Sales	(270) .2	(242) .3
1.4	.7	.6	.7				.6	.6
2.2	1.4	1.4	1.8				1.4	1.4
(14) 4.5	(44) 2.2	(29) 1.2				% Officers', Directors',	(128) 1.4	(113) 1.6
7.3	4.5	2.6				Owners' Comp/Sales	3.5	4.1
9.1	7.3	4.2					7.2	8.4
44420M	454007M	1752098M	3121802M	1567803M	4409536M	Net Sales ($)	13123571M	15619929M
8331M	101963M	436145M	935729M	562277M	1724037M	Total Assets ($)	4697514M	4835888M

M = $ thousand   MM = $ million
See Pages 11 through 18 for Explanation of Ratios and Data

Comparative Historical Data | Current Data Sorted By Sales

	4/1/00-3/31/01	4/1/01-3/31/02	4/1/02-3/31/03	Type of Statement	0-1MM	1-3MM	3-5MM	5-10MM	10-25MM	25MM & OVER
	45	46	58	Unqualified	1	1	1	7	14	34
	51	39	53	Reviewed	2	2	4	14	21	10
	67	52	42	Compiled	2	18	8	7	6	1
	24	16	29	Tax Returns	4	8	8	7	2	
	95	117	100	Other	7	15	11	17	22	28
	ALL	ALL	ALL		45 (4/1-9/30/02)			237 (10/1/02-3/31/03)		
NUMBER OF STATEMENTS	282	270	282		16	44	32	52	65	73

ASSETS (%)

	Hist1	Hist2	Hist3		0-1MM	1-3MM	3-5MM	5-10MM	10-25MM	25MM & OVER
Cash & Equivalents	9.6	11.8	13.7		19.8	10.9	15.3	10.2	16.2	13.5
Trade Receivables (net)	48.0	44.3	41.7		25.5	39.5	42.6	41.2	44.8	43.9
Inventory	22.3	19.6	19.1		19.2	14.2	16.0	24.0	18.1	20.8
All Other Current	2.5	3.2	2.7		1.0	2.7	1.8	2.0	2.5	4.0
Total Current	82.5	78.9	77.2		65.5	67.3	75.8	77.4	81.6	82.2
Fixed Assets (net)	10.5	11.0	12.0		19.6	18.4	10.5	12.4	9.5	9.2
Intangibles (net)	2.9	4.8	4.8		5.6	.9	9.2	6.9	3.7	4.5
All Other Non-Current	4.2	5.2	6.0		9.3	13.5	4.5	3.3	5.2	4.1
Total	100.0	100.0	100.0		100.0	100.0	100.0	100.0	100.0	100.0

LIABILITIES

	Hist1	Hist2	Hist3		0-1MM	1-3MM	3-5MM	5-10MM	10-25MM	25MM & OVER
Notes Payable-Short Term	17.4	16.5	15.3		14.2	19.6	21.8	12.6	13.0	14.2
Cur. Mat.-L/T/D	2.5	2.6	2.7		1.5	2.2	8.7	3.3	1.3	1.3
Trade Payables	29.6	26.8	24.8		14.6	20.0	19.8	24.4	28.0	29.5
Income Taxes Payable	.3	.4	.3		.4	.4	.5	.4	.2	.4
All Other Current	12.5	11.9	13.7		10.9	13.9	15.5	15.3	10.3	15.0
Total Current	62.3	58.1	56.8		41.6	56.2	66.1	55.9	52.9	60.4
Long Term Debt	6.8	5.8	6.2		6.6	8.3	12.5	4.5	4.2	5.2
Deferred Taxes	.2	.2	.2		.3	.4	.0	.0	.4	.1
All Other Non-Current	3.8	5.9	5.9		5.2	7.7	5.2	7.5	5.6	4.2
Net Worth	26.9	30.0	30.9		46.3	27.5	16.1	32.1	37.0	30.0
Total Liabilities & Net Worth	100.0	100.0	100.0		100.0	100.0	100.0	100.0	100.0	100.0

INCOME DATA

	Hist1	Hist2	Hist3		0-1MM	1-3MM	3-5MM	5-10MM	10-25MM	25MM & OVER
Net Sales	100.0	100.0	100.0		100.0	100.0	100.0	100.0	100.0	100.0
Gross Profit	29.2	31.3	33.4		51.6	45.4	36.2	34.9	29.6	23.3
Operating Expenses	27.2	28.9	30.9		52.4	42.9	32.6	31.6	26.4	21.7
Operating Profit	2.0	2.4	2.5		-.9	2.4	3.6	3.3	3.2	1.7
All Other Expenses (net)	.7	.6	.3		1.2	.7	.4	.4	.2	.1
Profit Before Taxes	1.3	1.8	2.2		-2.0	1.8	3.3	3.0	3.0	1.5

RATIOS

	Hist1	Hist2	Hist3		0-1MM	1-3MM	3-5MM	5-10MM	10-25MM	25MM & OVER
Current	1.9	2.2	2.1		2.7	2.0	3.0	2.1	2.5	1.7
	1.3	1.4	1.4		2.0	1.1	1.5	1.3	1.7	1.3
	1.1	1.0	1.1		1.2	.9	1.1	1.1	1.0	1.1
Quick	1.3	1.5	1.5		2.6	1.4	2.5	1.3	1.9	1.3
	.9	1.0	1.0		1.5	.9	1.1	.9	1.2	.9
	.7	.7	.7		.8	.5	.8	.6	.8	.7
Sales/Receivables	30 / 12.2	27 / 13.5	27 / 13.7		13 / 28.8	27 / 13.6	24 / 15.2	25 / 14.9	34 / 10.7	27 / 13.7
	42 / 8.8	40 / 9.2	39 / 9.4		37 / 9.9	39 / 9.4	42 / 8.6	35 / 10.3	40 / 9.1	42 / 8.7
	60 / 6.1	58 / 6.3	60 / 6.1		119 / 3.1	60 / 6.0	72 / 5.1	44 / 8.2	53 / 6.9	65 / 5.6
Cost of Sales/Inventory	8 / 46.7	6 / 58.2	5 / 74.9		0 / UND	0 / UND	3 / 113.2	6 / 60.8	7 / 51.2	5 / 76.9
	24 / 15.0	20 / 17.9	21 / 17.7		28 / 12.9	20 / 18.1	18 / 20.6	27 / 13.3	19 / 18.8	20 / 18.0
	44 / 8.3	42 / 8.7	43 / 8.5		106 / 3.4	52 / 7.0	47 / 7.7	48 / 7.7	41 / 8.9	34 / 10.6
Cost of Sales/Payables	18 / 20.1	16 / 23.1	18 / 20.1		10 / 34.8	14 / 25.4	12 / 30.0	14 / 27.0	20 / 18.5	22 / 17.0
	35 / 10.5	33 / 11.2	31 / 11.7		67 / 5.4	32 / 11.4	29 / 12.6	28 / 13.3	32 / 11.3	30 / 12.1
	59 / 6.2	51 / 7.1	53 / 6.9		189 / 1.9	61 / 6.0	44 / 8.3	49 / 7.4	51 / 7.2	53 / 6.9
Sales/Working Capital	10.6	9.4	8.1		2.7	9.1	5.6		6.9	8.7
	22.4	20.5	19.5		11.8	45.7	14.4	23.4	13.2	22.6
	119.5	142.8	118.0		34.9	-49.6	97.3	107.2	172.6	73.4
EBIT/Interest	9.7	10.7	13.6		17.0	21.7	18.2	12.8	10.3	13.6
	(242) 2.3	(232) 2.5	(235) 3.5		(10) 5.1	(37) 3.9	(26) 3.1	(46) 3.4	(53) 2.9	(63) 4.6
	.9	.1	1.0		-1.1	.0	.9	-.3	1.0	1.4
Net Profit + Depr., Dep., Amort./Cur. Mat. L/T/D	10.5	11.5	10.4					8.6	4.0	27.7
	(53) 2.6	(40) 3.1	(54) 3.9					(10) 3.0	(12) 2.2	(24) 5.3
	.2	.8	1.0					1.0	1.1	.9
Fixed/Worth	.1	.1	.1		.2	.1	.0	.2	.1	.1
	.4	.4	.3		.4	.6	.3	.4	.2	.2
	1.2	1.4	1.3		1.3	1.7	1.0	1.2	1.2	.9
Debt/Worth	1.2	1.0	.9		.4	.9	.6	1.5	.8	1.5
	3.0	2.8	2.4		.8	3.6	1.9	2.6	2.2	2.8
	8.6	12.0	8.4		3.3	6.5	29.9	10.5	10.3	8.3
% Profit Before Taxes/Tangible Net Worth	61.1	66.0	59.8		49.8	79.8	70.8	75.4	55.5	51.1
	(246) 20.2	(219) 24.5	(244) 21.0		(14) 15.2	(37) 26.7	(26) 21.8	(43) 20.0	(59) 18.5	(65) 22.7
	2.6	2.4	1.5		-1.3	-9.1	4.5	2.4	1.2	4.8
% Profit Before Taxes/Total Assets	15.7	16.9	14.8		24.1	15.9	20.6	17.3	13.1	12.5
	4.6	4.8	5.6		6.9	6.4	5.0	3.3	5.2	6.0
	-.1	-1.3	-.2		-4.6	-3.5	-.2	-.6	.1	.8
Sales/Net Fixed Assets	181.1	151.5	150.2		38.2	83.2	228.0	92.0	164.6	213.0
	61.9	61.3	51.6		18.2	33.7	62.5	54.9	53.2	68.5
	25.5	25.5	20.4		8.8	15.8	18.4	26.3	34.1	24.2
Sales/Total Assets	5.8	5.6	5.3		2.9	5.1	5.1	6.0	5.2	5.9
	4.0	4.1	3.8		2.3	3.4	2.9	4.1	4.2	4.1
	2.9	2.6	2.4		1.1	2.2	2.2	2.8	2.5	2.5
% Depr., Dep., Amort./Sales	.2	.2	.3			.6	.2	.3	.2	.2
	(212) .5	(213) .5	(209) .7			(32) 1.1	(19) .6	(41) .7	(53) .6	(57) .5
	1.2	1.3	1.6			2.4	1.4	1.6	1.3	1.0
% Officers', Directors', Owners' Comp/Sales	1.2	1.6	2.0			4.6	2.2	2.2	1.9	.4
	(107) 3.2	(84) 2.9	(92) 4.0			(19) 6.4	(17) 4.3	(23) 3.8	(19) 2.8	(11) 1.1
	6.2	6.4	7.4			10.3	7.4	7.5	4.7	1.9
Net Sales ($)	12454389M	13556740M	11349666M		8434M	84949M	126763M	375969M	1048369M	9705182M
Total Assets ($)	3332339M	3877026M	3768482M		6349M	40944M	46428M	121579M	416532M	3136650M

© RMA 2003

M = $ thousand   MM = $ million
See Pages 11 through 18 for Explanation of Ratios and Data

Current Data Sorted By Assets | Comparative Historical Data

Type of Statement	0-500M	500M-2MM	2-10MM	10-50MM	50-100MM	100-250MM	4/1/98-3/31/99 ALL	4/1/99-3/31/00 ALL
Unqualified		1	12	6	2	5	19	13
Reviewed		18	37	8			55	59
Compiled	8	21	13	1			50	39
Tax Returns	3	11	3				10	12
Other	7	17	24	10			33	40
		36 (4/1-9/30/02)		171 (10/1/02-3/31/03)				
NUMBER OF STATEMENTS	18	68	89	25	2	5	167	163
	%	%	%	%	%	%	%	%
ASSETS								
Cash & Equivalents	13.6	6.5	5.9	9.5			6.8	7.7
Trade Receivables (net)	29.5	38.4	32.0	29.3			33.9	35.3
Inventory	32.4	38.9	37.4	28.7			32.8	30.8
All Other Current	.5	1.7	3.0	5.4			3.3	2.1
Total Current	76.0	85.5	78.3	72.8			76.7	75.9
Fixed Assets (net)	16.6	7.6	12.8	16.6			14.5	15.5
Intangibles (net)	1.1	1.0	2.7	6.1			3.2	2.5
All Other Non-Current	6.3	5.9	6.2	4.5			5.6	6.1
Total	100.0	100.0	100.0	100.0			100.0	100.0
LIABILITIES								
Notes Payable-Short Term	6.9	17.3	16.5	11.0			15.3	13.3
Cur. Mat.-L/T/D	3.3	1.7	3.6	3.4			2.6	3.0
Trade Payables	23.3	25.9	21.4	14.7			21.8	22.0
Income Taxes Payable	.2	.1	.1	.3			.4	.5
All Other Current	13.6	9.8	11.7	12.8			10.8	11.6
Total Current	47.3	54.9	53.4	42.3			51.0	50.4
Long Term Debt	13.8	5.2	9.1	8.8			8.6	11.2
Deferred Taxes	.3	.1	.0	.3			.1	.1
All Other Non-Current	5.2	2.2	3.3	7.2			2.4	3.2
Net Worth	33.5	37.5	34.3	41.4			37.9	35.0
Total Liabilities & Net Worth	100.0	100.0	100.0	100.0			100.0	100.0
INCOME DATA								
Net Sales	100.0	100.0	100.0	100.0			100.0	100.0
Gross Profit	35.1	28.5	29.6	32.5			30.2	31.1
Operating Expenses	33.1	26.9	27.5	25.8			28.6	28.2
Operating Profit	2.0	1.7	2.1	6.7			1.5	2.9
All Other Expenses (net)	.8	−.5	.4	2.7			−3.1	−1.0
Profit Before Taxes	1.2	2.1	1.7	4.0			4.7	3.9
RATIOS								
Current	2.6	2.4	2.0	3.2			2.1	2.1
	1.5	1.6	1.5	2.0			1.5	1.5
	1.1	1.2	1.1	1.2			1.2	1.2
Quick	1.5	1.3	1.0	1.8			1.1	1.2
	.9	.9	.7	.9			.8	.8
	.5	.5	.5	.6			.5	.5
Sales/Receivables	16 / 22.4	28 / 13.0	27 / 13.3	30 / 12.0			27 / 13.7	28 / 13.1
	29 / 12.4	39 / 9.3	42 / 8.7	48 / 7.7			41 / 9.0	41 / 8.9
	43 / 8.5	51 / 7.2	56 / 6.5	62 / 5.9			54 / 6.7	55 / 6.7
Cost of Sales/Inventory	18 / 20.7	26 / 13.8	40 / 9.1	38 / 9.5			37 / 10.0	23 / 15.6
	29 / 12.7	62 / 5.9	71 / 5.2	63 / 5.8			54 / 6.7	51 / 7.1
	82 / 4.5	113 / 3.2	111 / 3.3	105 / 3.5			86 / 4.3	81 / 4.5
Cost of Sales/Payables	18 / 20.7	17 / 21.8	17 / 21.7	18 / 20.8			18 / 20.4	18 / 19.8
	31 / 11.7	34 / 10.7	32 / 11.6	25 / 14.4			35 / 10.6	34 / 10.6
	41 / 8.9	56 / 6.5	59 / 6.2	39 / 9.3			52 / 7.0	49 / 7.4
Sales/Working Capital	5.8	5.3	6.4	4.9			7.6	7.3
	15.2	10.7	11.9	6.8			11.2	12.1
	76.1	31.6	54.5	24.6			32.5	42.4
EBIT/Interest	9.5	8.0	9.6	16.5			7.8	9.6
	(15) 2.5	(62) 3.4	(83) 3.3	7.1			(149) 2.7	(143) 3.7
	−1.3	.2	1.1	1.7			1.6	1.7
Net Profit + Depr., Dep., Amort./Cur. Mat. L/T/D		5.7	9.1				10.0	7.2
	(15) 1.6	(31) 2.3					(59) 3.0	(58) 2.6
	−.4	.6					1.3	1.0
Fixed/Worth	.1	.1	.1	.1			.2	.1
	.6	.2	.3	.4			.4	.3
	1.5	.4	1.2	1.4			.8	.9
Debt/Worth	.6	.8	1.0	.8			.8	1.0
	3.5	1.9	2.2	1.9			1.9	2.2
	7.5	5.0	6.1	4.8			4.5	4.4
% Profit Before Taxes/Tangible Net Worth	108.8	40.1	33.1	36.3			37.0	44.9
	(16) 20.9	(65) 10.9	(82) 13.7	(22) 19.3			(159) 18.0	(148) 23.7
	−19.6	3.2	3.1	1.1			6.6	10.3
% Profit Before Taxes/Total Assets	31.5	14.6	10.2	15.6			11.9	15.2
	3.3	3.9	3.3	7.5			5.5	7.2
	−8.1	.4	.3	1.2			1.5	2.4
Sales/Net Fixed Assets	172.7	162.6	78.9	58.9			61.0	82.5
	33.4	57.3	36.8	26.3			31.4	35.4
	19.3	28.7	13.4	7.7			15.5	16.8
Sales/Total Assets	6.3	3.9	3.5	3.2			3.8	4.0
	3.7	3.2	2.8	2.3			3.0	3.1
	2.1	2.4	2.1	1.6			2.4	2.3
% Depr., Dep., Amort./Sales	.6	.3	.5	.5			.5	.4
	(15) .9	(54) 1.0	(81) .7	(22) 1.0			(148) .7	(148) .7
	3.7	1.5	1.2	3.2			1.4	1.5
% Officers', Directors', Owners' Comp/Sales	2.5	2.5	1.8				2.1	1.8
	(10) 4.2	(32) 4.1	(37) 2.8				(95) 3.8	(86) 3.4
	8.1	6.7	4.1				6.2	6.5
Net Sales ($)	19912M	253589M	1324390M	900576M	335993M	1237551M	2734411M	3104781M
Total Assets ($)	4810M	76283M	450036M	401120M	171705M	615317M	1159691M	1369946M

M = $ thousand   MM = $ million
See Pages 11 through 18 for Explanation of Ratios and Data

Comparative Historical Data				Current Data Sorted By Sales					
			Type of Statement						
8	14	26	Unqualified		1		3	7	15
58	49	63	Reviewed		8	6	22	15	12
53	46	43	Compiled	5	13	11	9	4	1
16	13	17	Tax Returns	2	7	4	1	2	1
36	53	58	Other	2	11	7	13	15	10
4/1/00-3/31/01 ALL	4/1/01-3/31/02 ALL	4/1/02-3/31/03 ALL			36 (4/1-9/30/02)		171 (10/1/02-3/31/03)		
				0-1MM	1-3MM	3-5MM	5-10MM	10-25MM	25MM & OVER
171	175	207	**NUMBER OF STATEMENTS**	9	40	28	48	43	39
%	%	%	**ASSETS**	%	%	%	%	%	%
6.8	6.1	7.1	Cash & Equivalents		10.1	4.6	4.6	6.6	8.5
35.9	34.7	33.4	Trade Receivables (net)		30.8	36.2	31.0	36.7	32.9
33.9	36.5	35.7	Inventory		40.4	44.0	38.2	32.5	28.2
2.0	2.0	2.7	All Other Current		.8	1.5	3.3	3.4	4.6
78.5	79.4	78.9	Total Current		82.1	86.2	77.1	79.2	74.2
12.7	12.7	11.8	Fixed Assets (net)		8.0	8.6	15.8	12.6	11.0
2.8	2.9	3.4	Intangibles (net)		2.4	.1	3.1	2.1	9.1
6.0	5.0	5.9	All Other Non-Current		7.5	5.0	4.1	6.2	5.7
100.0	100.0	100.0	Total		100.0	100.0	100.0	100.0	100.0
			LIABILITIES						
13.9	15.9	14.8	Notes Payable-Short Term		16.8	19.6	16.2	14.2	11.0
3.5	3.6	2.9	Cur. Mat.-L/T/D		1.9	2.5	3.9	3.3	2.3
21.5	21.6	22.0	Trade Payables		27.9	21.2	21.4	22.6	17.2
.2	.2	.1	Income Taxes Payable		.1	.3	.1	.2	.2
11.1	9.6	11.3	All Other Current		8.5	7.1	11.2	11.9	15.3
50.2	50.9	51.2	Total Current		55.1	50.7	52.8	52.2	45.9
8.4	9.8	8.7	Long Term Debt		4.0	8.2	12.0	5.6	10.8
.1	.2	.1	Deferred Taxes		.1	.1	.1	.2	.2
4.1	4.2	3.7	All Other Non-Current		3.0	2.0	4.9	2.1	5.2
37.1	35.0	36.3	Net Worth		37.8	38.9	30.3	40.0	37.8
100.0	100.0	100.0	Total Liabilities & Net Worth		100.0	100.0	100.0	100.0	100.0
			INCOME DATA						
100.0	100.0	100.0	Net Sales		100.0	100.0	100.0	100.0	100.0
29.6	30.1	29.9	Gross Profit		32.9	27.0	30.1	27.9	28.6
27.2	27.6	27.3	Operating Expenses		31.4	23.6	28.9	25.2	23.5
2.3	2.5	2.5	Operating Profit		1.5	3.4	1.2	2.7	5.1
.2	.3	.5	All Other Expenses (net)		–.3	.5	.1	.2	1.9
2.1	2.2	2.1	Profit Before Taxes		1.8	3.0	1.1	2.5	3.2
			RATIOS						
2.3	2.2	2.3	Current		2.5	2.5	1.9	2.6	2.2
1.6	1.6	1.5			1.5	1.7	1.5	1.5	1.5
1.2	1.2	1.2			1.1	1.3	1.0	1.1	1.3
1.3	1.2	1.2	Quick		1.1	1.6	1.0	1.5	1.3
.8	.8	.8			.7	1.0	.8	.8	.8
.6	.6	.5			.5	.4	.4	.6	.6
28 13.2	28 13.0	28 13.0	Sales/Receivables		19 19.5	28 13.2	26 14.1	35 10.5	25 14.7
43 8.5	40 9.0	41 8.9			36 10.2	41 9.0	39 9.5	42 8.7	41 9.0
59 6.1	56 6.5	54 6.7			48 7.5	53 6.9	54 6.7	63 5.8	54 6.7
29 12.8	35 10.3	32 11.6	Cost of Sales/Inventory		26 14.0	28 12.9	33 11.0	38 9.7	24 14.9
54 6.8	61 6.0	63 5.8			64 5.7	73 5.0	79 4.6	53 6.9	49 7.4
98 3.7	97 3.8	106 3.5			139 2.6	113 3.2	118 3.1	83 4.4	73 5.0
17 21.9	18 20.3	18 20.8	Cost of Sales/Payables		26 14.2	8 43.7	14 25.3	19 19.1	16 22.5
29 12.4	29 12.5	32 11.5			40 9.1	26 13.8	34 10.7	31 11.7	25 14.4
49 7.5	53 6.9	54 6.8			66 5.6	46 7.9	61 6.0	58 6.3	38 9.7
6.0	6.3	5.8	Sales/Working Capital		5.0	5.3	6.0	6.0	6.5
11.2	11.6	10.9			8.8	8.4	11.0	10.7	12.4
27.7	27.5	42.1			57.5	15.8	66.0	43.7	24.2
(157) 8.1	(163) 7.8	(192) 9.5	EBIT/Interest		(37) 12.7	(26) 9.1	(45) 4.5	(39) 13.7	(38) 14.8
3.4	2.9	3.4			3.6	4.0	2.1	4.2	4.6
1.3	1.2	1.0			–2.2	1.4	.1	2.1	1.3
(49) 7.1	(48) 4.1	(59) 7.0	Net Profit + Depr., Dep., Amort./Cur. Mat. L/T/D				(10) 4.9	(19) 8.9	(14) 26.1
3.5	2.5	1.9					1.7	2.4	3.7
1.2	1.1	.4					1.0	.9	.3
.1	.1	.1	Fixed/Worth		.0	.0	.1	.1	.2
.3	.3	.3			.1	.2	.4	.2	.4
.8	.9	.9			.6	.4	2.5	.8	2.5
.9	1.0	.9	Debt/Worth		.8	.6	1.1	.8	.9
1.8	1.9	2.0			2.0	1.9	2.7	1.9	2.9
5.1	5.0	6.4			4.7	4.8	12.1	4.5	8.1
(156) 36.0	(158) 33.1	(188) 39.2	% Profit Before Taxes/Tangible Net Worth		(38) 57.0	38.5	(41) 35.5	(42) 33.1	(32) 44.1
14.0	15.0	13.9			12.8	12.5	9.9	16.3	19.5
1.1	3.0	1.9			–8.1	3.3	3.9	5.8	3.1
10.8	12.2	11.8	% Profit Before Taxes/Total Assets		10.3	20.0	5.1	14.5	18.1
5.0	4.1	3.7			3.7	4.0	3.0	5.9	6.0
.2	.8	.3			–4.3	1.1	–.4	.9	.9
97.0	81.8	95.3	Sales/Net Fixed Assets		189.6	128.7	79.4	79.6	75.4
37.3	43.6	40.5			47.6	57.3	28.4	40.3	46.6
17.1	15.4	19.9			27.5	27.3	10.7	17.7	23.0
3.8	3.9	3.7	Sales/Total Assets		3.9	3.8	3.4	3.5	3.8
3.0	3.0	2.9			2.9	3.1	2.7	2.9	3.2
2.2	2.2	2.2			2.0	2.3	2.1	2.2	2.3
(149) .3	(147) .3	(177) .5	% Depr., Dep., Amort./Sales		(33) .4	(22) .3	(43) .6	(37) .5	(35) .4
.8	.7	.8			1.0	.8	.9	.7	.7
1.4	1.5	1.5			1.7	1.4	2.1	1.0	1.5
(99) 2.5	(86) 2.2	(84) 2.0	% Officers', Directors', Owners' Comp/Sales		(21) 3.1	(13) 2.0	(18) 2.3	(18) 2.2	(10) 1.1
4.5	3.5	3.3			6.2	3.3	2.9	2.9	1.6
7.0	6.4	5.3			9.3	4.4	5.3	3.6	3.6
2585062M	3186365M	4072011M	Net Sales ($)	4978M	80612M	111114M	343204M	695315M	2836788M
1002487M	1222633M	1719271M	Total Assets ($)	2105M	33544M	43942M	154563M	295063M	1190054M

M = $ thousand   MM = $ million
See Pages 11 through 18 for Explanation of Ratios and Data

Current Data Sorted By Assets   **Comparative Historical Data**

	0-500M	500M-2MM	2-10MM	10-50MM	50-100MM	100-250MM	Type of Statement	4/1/98-3/31/99 ALL	4/1/99-3/31/00 ALL
Unqualified		2	23	27	7	2		58	46
Reviewed	2	13	26	5				54	56
Compiled	6	24	21					66	67
Tax Returns	11	17	8	1				22	21
Other	10	27	33	11	2	4		92	87
	68 (4/1-9/30/02)		214 (10/1/02-3/31/03)						
NUMBER OF STATEMENTS	29	83	111	44	9	6		292	277
	%	%	%	%	%	%	**ASSETS**	%	%
	14.9	9.1	8.3	5.6			Cash & Equivalents	7.2	7.1
	27.4	39.3	37.9	32.0			Trade Receivables (net)	36.2	38.6
	27.3	26.3	27.5	29.7			Inventory	29.5	28.0
	2.7	2.9	1.7	3.4			All Other Current	1.5	1.3
	72.4	77.5	75.4	70.6			Total Current	74.4	75.0
	16.4	15.9	14.1	16.4			Fixed Assets (net)	14.2	13.2
	2.4	1.8	4.2	8.5			Intangibles (net)	3.9	5.6
	9.0	4.7	6.3	4.5			All Other Non-Current	7.4	6.2
	100.0	100.0	100.0	100.0			Total	100.0	100.0
							LIABILITIES		
	23.2	14.6	10.9	16.6			Notes Payable-Short Term	14.8	15.6
	9.9	3.4	3.7	3.0			Cur. Mat.-L/T/D	3.2	3.0
	29.5	24.9	22.3	19.5			Trade Payables	23.3	24.4
	.2	.2	.4	.4			Income Taxes Payable	.5	.3
	8.7	10.5	9.6	12.8			All Other Current	9.0	9.9
	71.5	53.7	46.9	52.4			Total Current	50.9	53.2
	25.2	9.5	8.8	10.4			Long Term Debt	11.5	12.4
	.0	.2	.1	.4			Deferred Taxes	.2	.2
	3.6	7.9	5.0	4.2			All Other Non-Current	2.8	4.5
	-.3	28.8	39.1	32.6			Net Worth	34.6	29.7
	100.0	100.0	100.0	100.0			Total Liabilities & Net Worth	100.0	100.0
							INCOME DATA		
	100.0	100.0	100.0	100.0			Net Sales	100.0	100.0
	45.5	39.7	36.6	35.0			Gross Profit	35.3	36.7
	37.0	36.4	31.7	31.4			Operating Expenses	32.1	32.8
	8.6	3.3	4.9	3.6			Operating Profit	3.2	3.9
	.3	.4	.5	1.2			All Other Expenses (net)	.5	.4
	8.3	2.9	4.4	2.4			Profit Before Taxes	2.7	3.5
							RATIOS		
	2.8	2.1	2.8	1.8				2.1	2.2
	1.3	1.4	1.6	1.3			Current	1.5	1.5
	.9	1.0	1.1	1.1				1.2	1.1
	1.3	1.4	1.7	1.1				1.3	1.3
	.6	.8	1.0	.7			Quick	.9	.8
	.4	.6	.6	.5				.6	.6
	0 UND	31 11.8	35 10.4	41 8.9				34 10.8	39 9.3
	24 15.5	42 8.7	43 8.6	50 7.4			Sales/Receivables	45 8.1	51 7.2
	50 7.3	59 6.2	58 6.3	66 5.5				58 6.3	68 5.3
	1 315.5	21 17.5	25 14.7	48 7.6				34 10.7	37 9.9
	40 9.1	50 7.3	51 7.2	79 4.6			Cost of Sales/Inventory	57 6.4	57 6.4
	66 5.5	71 5.1	79 4.6	125 2.9				92 4.0	87 4.2
	0 UND	26 14.3	24 15.5	21 17.4				24 15.1	24 15.5
	33 10.9	44 8.2	34 10.9	43 8.5			Cost of Sales/Payables	39 9.4	46 7.9
	64 5.7	72 5.1	62 5.8	67 5.5				64 5.7	75 4.8
	8.7	8.0	6.0	6.3				6.7	6.2
	26.9	16.0	11.0	12.2			Sales/Working Capital	12.2	11.4
	-35.6	115.9	33.5	34.5				30.9	38.7
	11.0	13.1	19.3	7.1				8.1	7.3
(19)	4.2	(75) 3.6	(99) 5.7	(43) 2.8			EBIT/Interest	(262) 3.3	(254) 2.7
	.2	1.7	2.0	1.1				1.4	1.3
		3.9	6.6	17.3				7.4	5.9
		(15) 3.2	(29) 2.4	(17) 2.8			Net Profit + Depr., Dep., Amort./Cur. Mat. L /T/D	(89) 3.2	(78) 2.0
		1.3	1.0	.7				1.3	1.0
	.1	.1	.1	.3				.1	.1
	.8	.4	.3	.5			Fixed/Worth	.3	.3
	-2.7	1.3	.8	2.8				.9	1.2
	1.0	1.3	.7	1.3				1.0	1.0
	11.9	2.5	2.0	3.2			Debt/Worth	2.0	2.7
	-4.0	5.4	5.9	8.8				4.8	7.2
	361.1	52.8	56.3	35.0				48.4	46.1
(19)	72.6	(75) 30.0	(103) 28.3	(37) 22.3			% Profit Before Taxes/Tangible Net Worth	(270) 20.5	(236) 21.2
	16.0	10.6	7.2	.0				6.1	5.6
	48.8	16.8	22.0	9.6				14.1	14.8
	16.0	6.7	7.0	5.4			% Profit Before Taxes/Total Assets	5.5	5.0
	-5.1	1.9	2.2	.1				1.0	.8
	722.2	112.4	97.9	37.8				85.0	99.4
	56.0	33.7	42.7	22.8			Sales/Net Fixed Assets	32.4	38.9
	23.7	13.2	11.5	7.3				12.1	12.0
	8.4	4.1	3.9	3.3				3.7	3.5
	4.2	3.4	2.9	1.9			Sales/Total Assets	2.8	2.8
	2.4	2.4	2.1	1.3				1.9	1.7
	.4	.4	.4	.9				.4	.5
(17)	1.0	(65) .9	(91) .8	(43) 1.4			% Depr., Dep., Amort./Sales	(235) .8	(215) .9
	1.8	2.1	2.7	2.5				2.2	2.6
	3.3	3.5	1.5					2.4	2.7
(14)	5.8	(45) 5.3	(47) 3.2				% Officers', Directors', Owners' Comp/Sales	(105) 4.0	(101) 5.0
	13.1	6.9	6.1					7.0	8.7
	32012M	330476M	1693758M	2298714M	1385080M	1558694M	Net Sales ($)	5411163M	4965419M
	6495M	97705M	525681M	1095283M	576561M	987388M	Total Assets ($)	2313414M	2308246M

M = $ thousand   MM = $ million
See Pages 11 through 18 for Explanation of Ratios and Data

Comparative Historical Data — **Current Data Sorted By Sales**

4/1/00-3/31/01 ALL	4/1/01-3/31/02 ALL	4/1/02-3/31/03 ALL	Type of Statement	0-1MM	1-3MM	3-5MM	5-10MM	10-25MM	25MM & OVER
46	43	61	Unqualified			1	9	16	35
46	39	46	Reviewed		6	6	13	14	7
68	59	51	Compiled	3	7	12	17	10	2
22	25	37	Tax Returns	5	13	7	8	2	2
72	69	87	Other	6	7	12	12	20	20
				68 (4/1-9/30/02)		214 (10/1/02-3/31/03)			
254	235	282	NUMBER OF STATEMENTS	14	43	38	59	62	66
%	%	%	**ASSETS**	%	%	%	%	%	%
8.4	8.8	8.9	Cash & Equivalents	17.5	12.1	6.2	11.5	7.3	5.5
38.4	36.1	35.5	Trade Receivables (net)	30.2	30.6	40.1	34.2	40.5	33.7
27.9	29.4	27.7	Inventory	19.8	22.5	26.5	27.2	30.6	31.2
1.8	2.5	2.5	All Other Current	.4	4.3	1.4	2.8	1.5	3.2
76.4	76.8	74.6	Total Current	68.0	69.5	74.2	75.7	79.8	73.7
13.3	13.6	15.2	Fixed Assets (net)	12.0	23.0	17.2	16.3	10.7	13.1
4.8	4.8	4.5	Intangibles (net)	4.2	2.2	1.4	4.2	3.9	8.6
5.5	4.8	5.7	All Other Non-Current	16.1	5.4	7.2	3.8	5.6	4.6
100.0	100.0	100.0	Total	100.0	100.0	100.0	100.0	100.0	100.0
			LIABILITIES						
14.7	13.8	14.3	Notes Payable-Short Term	38.3	10.9	15.1	10.3	13.1	15.6
2.7	3.5	4.0	Cur. Mat.-L/T/D	6.1	8.2	3.9	3.7	3.1	2.2
25.8	22.6	23.0	Trade Payables	34.0	20.1	24.4	21.9	26.0	19.8
.4	.4	.4	Income Taxes Payable	.0	.1	.3	.7	.2	.4
9.1	9.7	10.6	All Other Current	7.7	11.2	11.4	8.4	9.2	13.6
52.7	49.9	52.3	Total Current	86.0	50.7	55.2	45.0	51.6	51.6
11.1	12.8	10.8	Long Term Debt	21.7	15.7	14.6	10.4	5.9	8.2
.2	.3	.1	Deferred Taxes	.0	.2	.1	.1	.1	.2
4.8	4.0	5.4	All Other Non-Current	6.7	7.3	7.3	4.3	5.9	3.5
31.2	33.0	31.3	Net Worth	−14.5	26.2	22.8	40.2	36.4	36.5
100.0	100.0	100.0	Total Liabilities & Net Worth	100.0	100.0	100.0	100.0	100.0	100.0
			INCOME DATA						
100.0	100.0	100.0	Net Sales	100.0	100.0	100.0	100.0	100.0	100.0
38.2	36.1	38.2	Gross Profit	47.9	46.9	39.4	41.7	32.8	31.8
33.5	32.3	33.4	Operating Expenses	39.7	42.6	35.8	36.7	27.5	27.4
4.7	3.9	4.8	Operating Profit	8.3	4.3	3.6	4.9	5.3	4.5
.5	.7	.6	All Other Expenses (net)	.3	.7	.5	.7	.1	1.1
4.2	3.2	4.2	Profit Before Taxes	8.0	3.6	3.1	4.2	5.2	3.4
			RATIOS						
2.4	2.4	2.4	Current	2.1	2.7	2.3	2.6	2.5	2.1
1.5	1.5	1.5		1.2	1.7	1.4	1.7	1.4	1.5
1.1	1.2	1.1		.7	.9	1.0	1.2	1.1	1.1
1.5	1.4	1.4	Quick	1.8	1.5	1.4	1.7	1.7	1.3
.9	.8	.9		.6	.8	.9	1.0	.9	.7
.6	.6	.5		.4	.5	.5	.7	.6	.5
36 10.1	33 11.1	33 11.1	Sales/Receivables	6 62.5	17 21.0	33 10.9	31 11.9	36 10.2	35 10.3
48 7.6	44 8.2	43 8.6		43 8.5	42 8.7	47 7.7	41 8.8	45 8.1	42 8.7
62 5.9	62 5.9	59 6.2		60 6.1	70 5.2	63 5.8	53 6.9	62 5.9	55 6.6
31 11.6	32 11.3	26 14.2	Cost of Sales/Inventory	0 UND	16 23.5	24 15.2	25 14.6	28 13.3	44 8.2
57 6.4	58 6.3	55 6.6		43 8.4	45 8.1	45 8.1	57 6.4	56 6.5	66 5.5
88 4.3	86 4.3	85 4.3		73 5.0	95 3.9	77 4.8	85 4.3	81 4.5	91 4.0
26 13.9	23 15.9	22 16.6	Cost of Sales/Payables	0 UND	14 26.7	25 14.7	22 16.4	26 14.2	19 19.1
48 7.6	40 9.0	38 9.5		48 7.6	42 8.7	38 9.5	39 9.4	46 7.9	32 11.5
76 4.8	64 5.7	65 5.6		89 4.1	77 4.7	71 5.2	61 6.0	68 5.4	51 7.1
5.7	6.4	6.2	Sales/Working Capital	8.4	5.7	6.5	6.1	6.4	6.1
10.5	12.0	12.8		37.2	15.4	15.8	9.9	11.7	12.2
36.9	35.5	53.0		−11.3	−44.4	319.8	25.7	48.5	42.4
10.5	9.0	13.4	EBIT/Interest		11.5	12.0	15.8	20.7	12.1
(222) 3.3	(207) 2.7	(249) 4.0			(34) 3.7	(34) 1.9	(53) 6.0	(56) 6.0	(63) 3.6
1.4	1.4	1.5			1.3	−1.2	2.2	2.2	1.5
4.4	5.1	6.2	Net Profit + Depr., Dep., Amort./Cur. Mat. L/T/D				3.5	12.5	6.7
(53) 2.3	(60) 2.5	(70) 2.7				(12) 1.6	(19) 6.1	(23) 2.8	
1.4	1.2	1.0				1.0	1.6	.8	
.1	.1	.1	Fixed/Worth	.0	.1	.1	.1	.1	.2
.3	.3	.4		UND	.6	.5	.4	.2	.4
.9	1.2	1.2		−.2	3.3	2.7	.9	.7	1.1
1.0	1.0	1.0	Debt/Worth	2.7	.8	1.1	1.0	.8	1.0
2.4	2.5	2.4		UND	2.3	2.6	1.8	2.3	2.8
6.1	7.0	7.1		−3.4	12.4	6.3	3.4	7.3	8.4
50.8	49.2	53.4	% Profit Before Taxes/Tangible Net Worth		74.0	65.1	54.0	55.9	40.3
(226) 23.0	(207) 19.6	(247) 28.3		(36) 37.7	(33) 15.6	(57) 28.3	(57) 27.3	(57) 24.0	
7.3	6.5	7.8		9.3	−6.8	13.0	7.1	7.7	
18.1	14.5	20.0	% Profit Before Taxes/Total Assets	47.3	23.5	22.5	18.2	20.5	13.6
5.8	5.4	6.8		6.1	7.5	3.5	7.3	7.2	6.8
1.7	.7	1.4		−5.7	−4.0	−2.5	3.4	2.1	1.3
94.7	97.4	94.6	Sales/Net Fixed Assets	UND	165.0	122.0	62.0	131.1	87.1
36.9	33.1	33.4		84.0	24.6	29.3	28.2	61.3	31.2
15.0	13.9	11.0		22.8	6.5	10.0	10.9	17.8	9.5
3.7	3.9	3.9	Sales/Total Assets	4.6	3.5	4.1	4.0	3.9	3.9
2.9	3.1	3.0		2.4	2.5	3.4	3.1	3.2	2.8
2.0	2.0	2.0		2.0	2.0	2.3	2.2	2.3	1.6
.4	.4	.4	% Depr., Dep., Amort./Sales		.6	.3	.5	.3	.4
(204) .8	(197) .9	(229) 1.1		(32) 1.8	(29) 1.4	(49) 1.2	(52) .7	(59) 1.1	
1.8	2.0	2.2		5.1	2.2	3.0	1.4	2.1	
3.0	2.3	2.4	% Officers', Directors', Owners' Comp/Sales		3.4	4.1	2.4	1.6	.8
(96) 4.9	(107) 4.3	(113) 4.3		(22) 5.0	(20) 5.9	(26) 3.7	(28) 2.9	(11) 2.4	
7.6	7.9	6.9		10.0	8.1	6.5	6.0	4.0	
5790492M	6149914M	7298734M	Net Sales ($)	6325M	77202M	146247M	417030M	1006025M	5645905M
2460510M	2942797M	3289113M	Total Assets ($)	2091M	33003M	54246M	166658M	412074M	2621041M

© RMA 2003   M = $ thousand   MM = $ million
See Pages 11 through 18 for Explanation of Ratios and Data

Current Data Sorted By Assets   **Comparative Historical Data**

0-500M	500M-2MM	2-10MM	10-50MM	50-100MM	100-250MM		4/1/98-3/31/99 ALL	4/1/99-3/31/00 ALL
						Type of Statement		
	1	2	1		1	Unqualified	4	9
1	2	3				Reviewed	13	6
2	3	2				Compiled	6	7
						Tax Returns	2	
2	3	1	6		1	Other	6	8
	5 (4/1-9/30/02)		23 (10/1/02-3/31/03)					
3	8	8	7		2	**NUMBER OF STATEMENTS**	31	30
%	%	%	%	%	%		%	%
						ASSETS		
			DATA			Cash & Equivalents	8.2	5.1
			NOT			Trade Receivables (net)	33.8	29.9
			AVAILABLE			Inventory	34.3	36.8
						All Other Current	2.5	1.5
						Total Current	78.9	73.3
						Fixed Assets (net)	14.0	12.4
						Intangibles (net)	2.6	6.7
						All Other Non-Current	4.5	7.5
						Total	100.0	100.0
						LIABILITIES		
						Notes Payable-Short Term	10.9	12.3
						Cur. Mat.-L/T/D	2.4	2.2
						Trade Payables	25.1	23.5
						Income Taxes Payable	.3	.1
						All Other Current	10.3	8.0
						Total Current	49.0	46.2
						Long Term Debt	10.0	13.2
						Deferred Taxes	.3	.3
						All Other Non-Current	6.8	13.0
						Net Worth	33.9	27.3
						Total Liabilities & Net Worth	100.0	100.0
						INCOME DATA		
						Net Sales	100.0	100.0
						Gross Profit	35.6	35.5
						Operating Expenses	31.7	33.7
						Operating Profit	3.9	1.8
						All Other Expenses (net)	.2	.6
						Profit Before Taxes	3.8	1.2
						RATIOS		
						Current	2.2 / 1.8 / 1.3	2.0 / 1.7 / 1.2
						Quick	1.5 / .8 / .5	1.0 / .8 / .5
						Sales/Receivables	34 10.9 / 39 9.4 / 55 6.6	35 10.5 / 41 9.0 / 54 6.7
						Cost of Sales/Inventory	25 14.5 / 61 5.9 / 159 2.3	45 8.1 / 82 4.4 / 125 2.9
						Cost of Sales/Payables	23 15.8 / 34 10.7 / 95 3.9	30 12.1 / 51 7.1 / 76 4.8
						Sales/Working Capital	4.8 / 8.9 / 26.1	6.2 / 9.4 / 14.2
						EBIT/Interest	(26) 6.1 / 3.5 / 2.1	(26) 5.9 / 2.6 / .5
						Net Profit + Depr., Dep., Amort./Cur. Mat. L /T/D	(12) 17.7 / 4.7 / 1.1	
						Fixed/Worth	.1 / .3 / 1.4	.1 / .5 / 2.3
						Debt/Worth	.8 / 2.1 / 7.5	1.1 / 1.7 / 17.4
						% Profit Before Taxes/Tangible Net Worth	(27) 48.0 / 30.6 / 13.9	(24) 38.1 / 14.7 / 5.7
						% Profit Before Taxes/Total Assets	22.2 / 7.4 / 4.1	10.6 / 4.8 / −.3
						Sales/Net Fixed Assets	67.8 / 24.1 / 10.6	62.5 / 20.6 / 13.4
						Sales/Total Assets	3.5 / 2.3 / 2.0	3.4 / 2.7 / 1.7
						% Depr., Dep., Amort./Sales	(28) .6 / .9 / 2.1	(26) .5 / 1.0 / 2.0
						% Officers', Directors', Owners' Comp/Sales	(20) 2.7 / 4.1 / 7.6	(16) 3.3 / 3.7 / 6.4
3572M	26606M	156212M	335087M		420986M	Net Sales ($)	389551M	1348481M
997M	8262M	42727M	134049M		458755M	Total Assets ($)	184867M	761491M

M = $ thousand   MM = $ million
See Pages 11 through 18 for Explanation of Ratios and Data

Comparative Historical Data | Current Data Sorted By Sales

						Type of Statement						
	3		3		4	Unqualified					1	3
	9		7		6	Reviewed	1	1		2	2	
	8		6		5	Compiled		2	2		1	
	1		1		2	Tax Returns		2				
	11		10		11	Other		2		1	1	7
	4/1/00-3/31/01 ALL		4/1/01-3/31/02 ALL		4/1/02-3/31/03 ALL		0-1MM	5 (4/1-9/30/02) 1-3MM	3-5MM	23 (10/1/02-3/31/03) 5-10MM	10-25MM	25MM & OVER
	32		27		28	NUMBER OF STATEMENTS	1	7	2	3	5	10
	%		%		%	ASSETS	%	%	%	%	%	%
	5.7		4.2		5.6	Cash & Equivalents						6.0
	31.4		30.7		30.0	Trade Receivables (net)						27.8
	38.5		40.2		37.7	Inventory						36.3
	2.6		3.1		2.9	All Other Current						3.6
	78.3		78.3		76.2	Total Current						73.7
	10.5		9.9		13.8	Fixed Assets (net)						14.3
	4.4		4.6		7.4	Intangibles (net)						9.3
	6.8		6.9		2.6	All Other Non-Current						2.6
	100.0		100.0		100.0	Total						100.0
						LIABILITIES						
	15.5		19.1		17.1	Notes Payable-Short Term						20.4
	2.6		2.6		3.9	Cur. Mat.-L/T/D						5.4
	24.4		22.3		30.0	Trade Payables						41.6
	.3		.3		.2	Income Taxes Payable						.3
	8.2		8.9		9.5	All Other Current						10.8
	51.0		53.1		60.7	Total Current						78.4
	11.9		5.9		17.2	Long Term Debt						24.4
	.2		.5		.1	Deferred Taxes						.0
	3.1		2.5		4.0	All Other Non-Current						1.7
	33.8		38.0		18.1	Net Worth						-4.6
	100.0		100.0		100.0	Total Liabilities & Net Worth						100.0
						INCOME DATA						
	100.0		100.0		100.0	Net Sales						100.0
	36.2		41.2		42.5	Gross Profit						42.3
	32.0		33.6		39.3	Operating Expenses						39.7
	4.2		7.6		3.2	Operating Profit						2.6
	1.3		1.3		1.5	All Other Expenses (net)						2.1
	2.9		6.2		1.7	Profit Before Taxes						.5
						RATIOS						
	1.9		2.0		2.3							2.0
	1.7		1.6		1.6	Current						1.7
	1.2		1.1		1.1							.9
	1.1		1.1		1.2							1.1
	.9		.6		.8	Quick						.8
	.5		.5		.5							.4
33	11.2	36	10.3	26	13.9						13	27.5
44	8.3	44	8.2	38	9.6	Sales/Receivables					30	12.3
64	5.7	61	6.0	49	7.5						44	8.2
40	9.2	40	9.2	37	10.0						23	16.0
95	3.8	121	3.0	103	3.5	Cost of Sales/Inventory					108	3.4
198	1.8	184	2.0	193	1.9						232	1.6
21	17.7	19	18.9	27	13.3						33	11.1
43	8.5	38	9.7	54	6.8	Cost of Sales/Payables					75	4.9
75	4.8	109	3.4	97	3.8						201	1.8
	4.9		4.8		5.5							5.4
	8.4		10.6		13.1	Sales/Working Capital						11.6
	25.6		46.2		35.9							NM
	7.1		9.4		10.6							14.2
(28)	2.5	(23)	3.8	(26)	3.2	EBIT/Interest						2.2
	1.5		2.0		1.6							.4
					3.7	Net Profit + Depr., Dep.,						
				(10)	1.5	Amort./Cur. Mat. L/T/D						
					.5							
	.1		.1		.2							.3
	.3		.3		.5	Fixed/Worth						.6
	.9		.7		-.5							-.2
	1.1		.9		.9							1.2
	1.8		1.4		2.8	Debt/Worth						4.0
	4.5		5.4		-6.2							-3.4
	40.6		55.5		54.4							
(29)	20.4	(26)	29.9	(20)	24.1	% Profit Before Taxes/Tangible Net Worth						
	10.4		13.1		3.8							
	11.7		17.3		17.7							11.1
	5.4		7.6		4.2	% Profit Before Taxes/Total Assets						2.1
	2.0		3.0		1.2							-4.0
	99.5		92.7		89.1							86.5
	23.8		23.6		27.3	Sales/Net Fixed Assets						20.0
	15.1		15.9		10.7							7.7
	3.6		3.3		3.9							4.7
	2.6		2.1		3.1	Sales/Total Assets						3.1
	1.6		1.7		1.8							1.6
	.3		.3		.4							
(22)	.8	(19)	.8	(24)	.9	% Depr., Dep., Amort./Sales						
	1.9		1.7		2.3							
	1.7		2.2		1.8							
(15)	4.0	(11)	3.8	(13)	4.1	% Officers', Directors', Owners' Comp/Sales						
	7.2		5.9		6.9							
	1126344M		829448M		942463M	Net Sales ($)	765M	12793M	7325M	18782M	79913M	822885M
	685586M		467092M		644790M	Total Assets ($)	376M	5814M	2055M	7796M	43685M	585064M

© RMA 2003   M = $ thousand   MM = $ million
See Pages 11 through 18 for Explanation of Ratios and Data

WHOLESALE—Other Professional Equipment and Supplies Merchant Wholesalers NAICS 423490 (SIC 5049)

Current Data Sorted By Assets

Comparative Historical Data

							Type of Statement			
	1	2	6	5		1	Unqualified		17	13
	2	11	19	4			Reviewed		15	23
	3	8	3				Compiled		18	14
	7	4	2				Tax Returns		8	5
		11	8	4			Other		14	11
		17 (4/1-9/30/02)			84 (10/1/02-3/31/03)				4/1/98-3/31/99 ALL	4/1/99-3/31/00 ALL
	0-500M	500M-2MM	2-10MM	10-50MM	50-100MM	100-250MM				
	13	36	38	13		1	NUMBER OF STATEMENTS		72	66
	%	%	%	%	%	%	ASSETS		%	%
	13.9	9.6	6.5	5.5			Cash & Equivalents		8.5	9.1
	39.1	34.5	37.7	20.0			Trade Receivables (net)		35.4	33.3
	30.2	32.7	29.9	31.2			Inventory		30.4	30.9
	3.1	2.8	2.0	4.6			All Other Current		2.1	3.5
	86.3	79.5	76.1	61.2			Total Current		76.3	76.8
	5.7	9.0	11.4	25.2			Fixed Assets (net)		15.3	13.3
	4.0	4.2	7.2	8.0			Intangibles (net)		4.0	4.1
	3.4	7.3	5.3	5.6			All Other Non-Current		4.4	5.9
	100.0	100.0	100.0	100.0			Total		100.0	100.0
							LIABILITIES			
	18.4	9.4	16.1	13.5			Notes Payable-Short Term		11.3	15.6
	1.6	4.7	3.1	4.7			Cur. Mat.-L/T/D		2.9	3.1
	18.2	27.1	22.8	11.7			Trade Payables		22.3	22.6
	.0	.4	.2	.1			Income Taxes Payable		.2	.1
	15.6	8.5	12.1	8.8			All Other Current		11.8	9.8
	53.9	50.2	54.2	38.7			Total Current		48.4	51.2
	6.3	5.9	7.1	20.0			Long Term Debt		10.9	10.5
	.5	.3	.1	.9			Deferred Taxes		.1	.1
	5.6	6.5	2.3	.3			All Other Non-Current		5.7	1.1
	34.2	37.1	36.3	40.0			Net Worth		34.8	37.1
	100.0	100.0	100.0	100.0			Total Liabilities & Net Worth		100.0	100.0
							INCOME DATA			
	100.0	100.0	100.0	100.0			Net Sales		100.0	100.0
	41.0	35.6	32.7	39.2			Gross Profit		32.0	34.1
	38.6	31.7	28.9	34.8			Operating Expenses		27.8	28.2
	2.5	3.8	3.8	4.4			Operating Profit		4.2	5.8
	−.1	.4	−.2	1.7			All Other Expenses (net)		1.0	.3
	2.5	3.5	4.0	2.7			Profit Before Taxes		3.3	5.6
							RATIOS			
	2.6	2.9	2.3	2.7					2.7	2.3
	2.1	1.6	1.4	1.6			Current		1.6	1.4
	1.2	1.1	1.2	1.0					1.2	1.1
	1.9	1.4	1.4	1.0					1.4	1.3
	1.2	.9	.9	.7			Quick		.8	.8
	.5	.6	.6	.4					.6	.5
	16 23.2	25 14.5	35 10.3	19 19.5					31 11.8	35 10.4
	33 11.0	37 9.8	44 8.3	36 10.1			Sales/Receivables		44 8.3	46 8.0
	56 6.5	54 6.8	56 6.5	55 6.6					58 6.3	59 6.2
	3 115.6	34 10.9	26 13.8	72 5.1					24 15.1	34 10.6
	73 5.0	59 6.1	52 7.0	81 4.5			Cost of Sales/Inventory		62 5.9	70 5.2
	238 1.5	94 3.9	92 4.0	176 2.1					96 3.8	99 3.7
	0 UND	26 13.8	23 15.9	19 18.8					18 20.4	20 18.7
	12 30.6	47 7.7	39 9.3	26 13.9			Cost of Sales/Payables		35 10.4	43 8.4
	57 6.4	59 6.2	68 5.4	53 6.9					58 6.2	62 5.9
	4.7	6.2	6.6	5.3					6.3	6.4
	12.8	13.9	10.9	9.8			Sales/Working Capital		9.4	13.2
	27.1	33.8	32.0	−111.2					33.9	31.1
		(34) 24.5	(33) 16.1	16.4					(63) 13.3	(58) 10.9
		3.1	5.8	5.8			EBIT/Interest		3.0	4.9
		1.4	1.4	1.5					1.5	2.2
			(10) 113.1				Net Profit + Depr., Dep.,		(21) 8.0	(17) 5.0
			4.2				Amort./Cur. Mat. L/T/D		2.7	2.7
			1.8						.6	1.3
	.0	.1	.1	.2					.1	.1
	.2	.2	.3	.6			Fixed/Worth		.3	.3
	−3.9	.6	.7	NM					1.2	.8
	.8	.7	.9	.5					.8	.8
	2.1	1.9	2.0	1.6			Debt/Worth		2.3	1.9
	−53.1	4.9	4.4	NM					5.1	4.6
		(30) 50.5	(34) 48.3	(10) 33.9			% Profit Before Taxes/Tangible		(64) 50.9	(58) 46.1
		20.1	23.1	17.5			Net Worth		26.1	22.5
		4.3	3.2	10.4					8.3	12.5
	17.2	15.2	16.9	13.9					17.8	14.8
	8.5	7.0	6.3	6.7			% Profit Before Taxes/Total		6.0	7.5
	1.1	.5	1.2	1.4			Assets		2.2	3.6
	UND	125.2	67.8	33.9					64.2	70.4
	81.8	46.6	31.5	11.8			Sales/Net Fixed Assets		31.3	31.2
	30.7	21.9	14.6	3.8					14.1	15.8
	6.5	3.8	3.5	2.5					3.7	3.3
	3.6	3.0	2.7	2.2			Sales/Total Assets		2.9	2.6
	1.8	2.5	2.2	1.5					2.1	2.0
		(25) .5	(34) .6	(12) .4					(58) .5	(55) .5
		1.1	.9	2.5			% Depr., Dep., Amort./Sales		.9	.9
		2.1	2.2	4.9					2.1	1.8
	(10) 5.0	(14) 3.1	(16) 1.3						(40) 2.1	(30) 1.7
	6.1	5.5	1.9				% Officers', Directors',		3.0	3.8
	8.5	8.2	3.8				Owners' Comp/Sales		4.7	8.3
	19800M	142613M	487624M	669881M		441840M	Net Sales ($)		2139050M	1545210M
	4303M	44932M	168726M	337223M		110528M	Total Assets ($)		1071191M	656302M

Left vertical text in columns 5 and 6: **D A T A   N O T   A V A I L A B L E**

© RMA 2003

M = $ thousand   MM = $ million
See Pages 11 through 18 for Explanation of Ratios and Data

Comparative Historical Data | Current Data Sorted By Sales

			Type of Statement						
11	10	15	Unqualified	1		2	1	3	8
13	23	36	Reviewed	2	4	2	13	11	4
11	23	14	Compiled	2	5	4	2	1	
4	11	13	Tax Returns		6	4	2	1	
20	17	23	Other		5	8	3	3	4
4/1/00- 3/31/01 ALL	4/1/01- 3/31/02 ALL	4/1/02- 3/31/03 ALL		17 (4/1-9/30/02)			84 (10/1/02-3/31/03)		
				0-1MM	1-3MM	3-5MM	5-10MM	10-25MM	25MM & OVER
59	84	101	**NUMBER OF STATEMENTS**	5	20	20	21	19	16
%	%	%	**ASSETS**	%	%	%	%	%	%
6.6	8.6	8.3	Cash & Equivalents		11.3	12.0	8.0	5.4	4.3
32.7	38.1	34.6	Trade Receivables (net)		36.1	32.2	36.0	40.5	30.0
34.4	30.4	31.0	Inventory		29.0	29.2	32.6	30.9	30.0
2.2	2.8	3.0	All Other Current		2.6	3.0	2.6	1.2	5.9
75.9	79.9	76.9	Total Current		79.0	76.4	79.2	78.0	70.2
12.8	13.3	11.5	Fixed Assets (net)		8.2	9.7	10.7	14.1	17.8
4.9	2.5	5.7	Intangibles (net)		6.4	9.9	2.0	2.6	6.8
6.4	4.3	5.8	All Other Non-Current		6.3	3.9	8.1	5.3	5.2
100.0	100.0	100.0	Total		100.0	100.0	100.0	100.0	100.0
			LIABILITIES						
13.3	17.0	14.0	Notes Payable-Short Term		17.2	13.7	8.4	13.3	19.8
6.4	3.1	3.7	Cur. Mat.-L/T/D		4.9	3.2	4.3	2.7	3.5
24.1	22.1	22.5	Trade Payables		25.4	20.3	27.2	24.1	16.7
.4	.3	.2	Income Taxes Payable		.2	.4	.4	.0	.1
11.7	11.2	10.7	All Other Current		11.7	11.2	13.0	9.2	8.0
55.9	53.6	51.1	Total Current		59.4	48.8	53.4	49.4	48.1
9.4	10.5	8.2	Long Term Debt		5.2	10.6	4.9	8.6	12.9
.2	.1	.3	Deferred Taxes		.2	.3	.0	.0	.7
2.4	3.0	4.0	All Other Non-Current		6.3	6.7	2.3	2.0	.2
32.2	32.7	36.5	Net Worth		28.9	33.6	39.4	40.1	38.0
100.0	100.0	100.0	Total Liabilities & Net Worth		100.0	100.0	100.0	100.0	100.0
			INCOME DATA						
100.0	100.0	100.0	Net Sales		100.0	100.0	100.0	100.0	100.0
33.7	32.4	35.4	Gross Profit		43.1	35.1	32.2	27.5	34.3
30.3	28.9	31.6	Operating Expenses		39.5	31.9	27.8	24.6	29.6
3.4	3.5	3.7	Operating Profit		3.6	3.1	4.4	2.9	4.8
.2	.6	.3	All Other Expenses (net)		.7	.0	−.3	.2	1.2
3.3	2.9	3.4	Profit Before Taxes		2.9	3.2	4.7	2.7	3.6
			RATIOS						
2.3	2.2	2.5			2.2	3.3	2.3	2.5	2.3
1.4	1.5	1.6	Current		1.2	1.9	1.5	1.6	1.3
1.1	1.1	1.1			1.1	1.2	1.1	1.2	1.0
1.1	1.3	1.4			1.1	1.5	1.3	1.4	1.0
.7	.8	.8	Quick		.6	1.1	.8	.9	.7
.5	.6	.6			.5	.6	.6	.6	.6
32 11.5	32 11.4	31 11.9			31 11.7	23 16.2	26 13.9	36 10.3	22 16.9
43 8.5	45 8.1	42 8.8	Sales/Receivables		37 9.7	38 9.7	41 8.9	45 8.1	39 9.3
63 5.8	63 5.8	54 6.7			56 6.5	47 7.8	54 6.8	60 6.1	58 6.3
43 8.5	27 13.4	28 13.0			16 22.5	22 16.7	22 16.7	27 13.7	33 10.9
75 4.9	57 6.4	60 6.1	Cost of Sales/Inventory		77 4.7	47 7.7	45 8.0	56 6.5	75 4.9
125 2.9	102 3.6	101 3.6			132 2.8	91 4.0	97 4.2	86 4.2	108 3.4
26 14.3	20 18.6	19 19.1			13 28.2	20 18.5	18 20.7	25 14.8	20 18.6
42 8.6	35 10.4	36 10.0	Cost of Sales/Payables		49 7.4	36 10.2	47 7.7	35 10.3	29 12.5
64 5.7	54 6.8	65 5.7			88 4.1	54 6.8	70 5.2	68 5.4	42 8.7
6.0	6.4	6.1			6.7	6.0	7.8	6.4	5.8
12.1	13.6	11.9	Sales/Working Capital		20.5	14.5	15.0	10.7	14.4
67.0	37.0	36.2			76.7	25.0	181.3	21.8	73.9
(57) 11.6	(78) 8.8	(87) 16.8		(18) 13.5	(17) 23.0	(19) 28.6	(16) 11.9	16.9	
4.2	3.4	5.0	EBIT/Interest	2.8	3.2	5.8	6.3	6.1	
1.1	1.4	1.4		1.4	.8	1.4	3.5	1.7	
(12) 9.6	(22) 7.6	(18) 7.6	Net Profit + Depr., Dep.,						
4.2	3.5	3.4	Amort./Cur. Mat. L/T/D						
.7	1.1	1.3							
.1	.1	.1			.1	.1	.1	.2	.1
.4	.3	.2	Fixed/Worth		.2	.2	.3	.2	.4
.7	1.0	.8			1.0	.7	.6	.6	3.6
.7	.9	.8			1.5	.8	.8	.6	.6
2.1	2.5	1.9	Debt/Worth		3.0	1.4	1.9	1.4	2.3
7.5	5.3	6.6			NM	8.8	4.3	3.3	7.0
45.1	42.8	48.5	% Profit Before Taxes/Tangible	72.0	49.1	66.8	41.4	44.1	
(48) 22.2	(73) 19.6	(84) 22.4	Net Worth	(15) 20.2	(16) 12.1	(19) 30.1	(17) 23.2	(14) 17.5	
6.8	8.8	5.4		8.4	−1.8	3.7	10.7	8.8	
14.1	13.3	15.8	% Profit Before Taxes/Total		14.3	18.0	21.6	14.1	17.9
5.4	6.1	7.1	Assets		5.0	7.6	6.4	7.6	7.2
1.3	1.8	1.2			1.2	.4	.6	1.3	1.6
65.1	84.2	119.2			253.9	122.9	110.3	59.4	144.3
30.7	32.6	35.9	Sales/Net Fixed Assets		45.2	38.9	44.9	29.7	27.3
13.5	14.0	15.6			16.6	22.7	18.6	14.7	6.8
3.5	3.6	3.6			3.6	4.8	3.8	3.5	3.1
2.6	2.8	2.8	Sales/Total Assets		2.7	3.1	2.9	2.9	2.4
2.1	2.2	2.2			2.1	2.2	2.4	2.5	1.9
.5	.3	.5		.2	.8	.5	.6	.3	
(48) 1.0	(69) 1.0	(80) 1.0	% Depr., Dep., Amort./Sales	(13) 1.6	(14) 1.1	(18) .9	(18) .8	(15) 1.3	
1.8	2.0	2.2		2.2	2.2	2.1	2.2	2.9	
2.9	2.2	1.8	% Officers', Directors',				1.2		
(29) 4.1	(43) 4.1	(44) 4.5	Owners' Comp/Sales			(10) 2.8			
6.5	7.7	7.5					6.5		
1043551M	1377547M	1761758M	Net Sales ($)	2145M	44605M	79289M	142932M	293671M	1199116M
496450M	717330M	665712M	Total Assets ($)	1289M	18712M	28134M	48403M	109552M	459622M

Current Data Sorted By Assets   Comparative Historical Data

0-500M	500M-2MM	2-10MM	10-50MM	50-100MM	100-250MM	Type of Statement	4/1/98-3/31/99 ALL	4/1/99-3/31/00 ALL
3	4	28	54	21	9	Unqualified	118	140
3	28	108	26			Reviewed	154	142
6	42	37	3			Compiled	114	114
7	13	4	1			Tax Returns	14	23
4	35	66	44	8	4	Other	134	147
110 (4/1-9/30/02)			448 (10/1/02-3/31/03)					
23	122	243	128	29	13	NUMBER OF STATEMENTS	534	566
%	%	%	%	%	%	ASSETS	%	%
7.5	8.2	5.3	3.7	3.1	3.1	Cash & Equivalents	4.9	5.1
33.0	37.7	32.1	26.3	28.9	23.5	Trade Receivables (net)	34.0	34.2
27.4	37.2	41.6	44.6	41.1	37.9	Inventory	38.1	38.4
2.7	1.4	1.7	1.6	2.2	.9	All Other Current	1.4	1.4
70.7	84.5	80.8	76.1	75.3	65.4	Total Current	78.4	79.2
21.5	11.7	14.0	18.2	17.5	25.0	Fixed Assets (net)	15.1	14.4
2.1	1.3	1.4	1.9	5.1	2.0	Intangibles (net)	1.7	2.3
5.7	2.5	3.8	3.8	2.0	7.6	All Other Non-Current	4.9	4.2
100.0	100.0	100.0	100.0	100.0	100.0	Total	100.0	100.0
						LIABILITIES		
20.7	19.2	21.1	23.5	29.4	6.2	Notes Payable-Short Term	19.9	20.5
6.5	3.0	2.9	2.3	2.3	.8	Cur. Mat.-L/T/D	2.4	2.5
27.2	24.0	22.7	15.9	15.4	14.4	Trade Payables	23.6	23.7
.4	.1	.1	.3	.3	.6	Income Taxes Payable	.2	.2
5.4	6.5	6.2	5.3	9.2	10.2	All Other Current	7.3	6.7
60.2	52.7	53.0	47.3	56.6	32.3	Total Current	53.4	53.6
5.3	10.0	7.7	10.3	8.7	23.3	Long Term Debt	8.8	9.0
.0	.2	.1	.4	.3	1.3	Deferred Taxes	.3	.4
1.7	3.6	5.2	3.0	2.3	4.1	All Other Non-Current	4.1	4.8
32.8	33.4	34.0	39.0	32.0	38.9	Net Worth	33.4	32.2
100.0	100.0	100.0	100.0	100.0	100.0	Total Liabilities & Net Worth	100.0	100.0
						INCOME DATA		
100.0	100.0	100.0	100.0	100.0	100.0	Net Sales	100.0	100.0
34.5	25.6	21.7	20.0	16.2	15.0	Gross Profit	21.1	21.4
32.0	23.3	19.1	16.6	12.5	11.5	Operating Expenses	17.8	17.8
2.5	2.2	2.5	3.4	3.7	3.5	Operating Profit	3.3	3.5
.3	.8	1.1	.5	1.2	.7	All Other Expenses (net)	1.0	.8
2.1	1.4	1.4	2.9	2.5	2.7	Profit Before Taxes	2.3	2.7
						RATIOS		
2.4	2.7	2.3	2.5	1.9	3.7		2.2	2.2
1.3	1.6	1.4	1.6	1.3	2.3	Current	1.4	1.4
.8	1.2	1.1	1.1	1.1	1.3		1.1	1.1
1.8	1.5	1.0	.9	.8	1.3		1.1	1.1
.7	.9	.6	.6	.6	.9	Quick	.7	.7
.4	.5	.4	.4	.4	.5		.5	.5
10 37.5	30 12.0	33 11.1	35 10.4	41 8.8	31 11.9		33 11.0	35 10.3
30 12.0	43 8.5	43 8.5	43 8.4	46 7.9	39 9.4	Sales/Receivables	41 8.9	44 8.2
46 7.9	57 6.4	53 6.9	49 7.4	58 6.3	52 7.0		51 7.2	53 6.9
13 28.8	25 14.7	45 8.1	57 6.4	62 5.9	63 5.8		37 9.8	40 9.2
23 16.0	67 5.4	73 5.0	97 3.8	82 4.4	97 3.8	Cost of Sales/Inventory	63 5.8	70 5.2
55 6.7	97 3.8	119 3.1	130 2.8	122 3.0	105 3.5		98 3.7	106 3.4
14 25.4	18 20.0	21 17.6	20 18.0	17 20.9	20 18.3		20 18.2	22 16.5
25 14.4	34 10.8	34 10.7	30 12.1	32 11.3	31 11.8	Cost of Sales/Payables	34 10.8	36 10.0
58 6.3	52 7.0	54 6.7	43 8.4	46 8.0	40 9.1		51 7.2	55 6.7
7.5	5.6	5.4	4.8	6.9	4.4		6.6	6.0
17.5	10.5	11.3	8.8	12.3	5.5	Sales/Working Capital	13.0	11.6
-57.7	27.0	29.5	23.6	32.7	12.7		32.9	37.7
45.1	7.1	5.6	7.5	5.6	6.1		6.0	6.5
(18) 8.1	(114) 2.1	(229) 2.1	(124) 2.9	2.6	3.7	EBIT/Interest	(480) 2.5	(519) 2.6
.7	.6	1.0	1.5	1.1	2.7		1.3	1.2
	5.5	4.1	11.6	3.3			8.2	5.9
	(24) 1.8	(59) 2.1	(34) 3.5	(11) 1.3		Net Profit + Depr., Dep., Amort./Cur. Mat. L /T/D	(139) 2.8	(121) 2.6
	.5	1.0	1.2	-.3			1.4	1.1
.1	.1	.1	.2	.2	.3		.1	.1
.4	.3	.3	.4	.5	.6	Fixed/Worth	.3	.4
2.3	1.2	1.0	1.2	1.9	2.1		1.0	1.0
.6	.8	1.1	.8	1.4	1.0		1.0	1.1
1.1	1.9	2.4	2.0	3.3	1.9	Debt/Worth	2.5	2.4
6.4	8.3	5.3	4.2	6.5	5.5		5.8	5.9
86.4	26.1	26.4	28.0	30.6	19.6		36.0	42.8
(19) 27.1	(105) 11.8	(226) 10.6	(125) 12.8	(27) 15.3	15.2	% Profit Before Taxes/Tangible Net Worth	(493) 19.3	(528) 20.0
14.0	-1.9	1.0	5.1	3.8	5.8		6.5	4.0
31.5	10.5	8.0	8.3	8.8	6.9		11.7	11.7
13.7	3.1	2.6	4.0	2.9	5.5	% Profit Before Taxes/Total Assets	5.2	5.0
1.5	-1.1	-.1	1.2	.5	2.2		1.1	.8
130.8	174.5	105.4	38.3	90.5	19.6		75.1	86.9
25.6	33.8	28.8	16.8	11.6	6.0	Sales/Net Fixed Assets	28.3	27.4
10.8	19.0	11.7	7.6	6.7	4.2		13.0	10.3
6.2	4.2	3.2	2.8	2.3	2.8		3.7	3.5
4.1	3.1	2.4	2.2	1.9	1.8	Sales/Total Assets	2.8	2.6
2.8	2.2	1.8	1.6	1.5	1.6		2.1	1.9
.5	.3	.3	.7	.8	.9		.4	.4
(13) 1.4	(101) 1.1	(220) .8	(116) 1.0	(27) 1.2	1.3	% Depr., Dep., Amort./Sales	(482) .8	(494) .8
2.1	1.7	1.8	1.9	1.6	2.2		1.4	1.6
4.5	1.9	1.5	.9				1.5	1.5
(13) 6.1	(83) 3.4	(101) 1.9	(32) 1.9			% Officers', Directors', Owners' Comp/Sales	(220) 2.7	(222) 2.7
11.3	6.4	3.0					5.4	5.4
31588M	576138M	3244302M	6576004M	4297713M	4434583M	Net Sales ($)	18890226M	18992796M
5750M	166734M	1215261M	2906717M	2048429M	2133366M	Total Assets ($)	6904198M	8373785M

M = $ thousand   MM = $ million
See Pages 11 through 18 for Explanation of Ratios and Data

Comparative Historical Data				Current Data Sorted By Sales					
104	104	119	**Type of Statement** Unqualified	1	2	3	8	26	79
148	134	165	Reviewed	1	7	16	49	65	27
113	116	88	Compiled	4	24	15	25	12	8
22	20	25	Tax Returns	2	9	7	6		1
147	168	161	Other	3	13	18	29	43	55
4/1/00-3/31/01 ALL	4/1/01-3/31/02 ALL	4/1/02-3/31/03 ALL		110 (4/1-9/30/02) 0-1MM	1-3MM	448 (10/1/02-3/31/03) 3-5MM	5-10MM	10-25MM	25MM & OVER
534	542	558	**NUMBER OF STATEMENTS**	11	55	59	117	146	170
%	%	%	**ASSETS**	%	%	%	%	%	%
4.5	4.4	5.5	Cash & Equivalents	8.4	8.7	5.6	7.2	5.8	2.7
34.4	31.6	31.7	Trade Receivables (net)	24.4	27.3	33.6	34.5	32.3	30.5
40.5	39.4	40.6	Inventory	25.2	38.6	41.3	39.9	39.4	43.7
1.2	1.4	1.7	All Other Current	5.4	.8	1.2	1.9	2.0	1.4
80.6	76.9	79.5	Total Current	63.5	75.4	81.6	83.4	79.5	78.3
14.3	16.3	15.2	Fixed Assets (net)	24.4	19.1	13.7	12.1	15.6	15.6
1.9	1.5	1.7	Intangibles (net)	2.5	2.6	1.4	1.6	1.0	2.3
3.2	5.3	3.6	All Other Non-Current	9.6	3.0	3.3	2.9	3.9	3.8
100.0	100.0	100.0	Total	100.0	100.0	100.0	100.0	100.0	100.0
			LIABILITIES						
22.6	22.0	21.3	Notes Payable-Short Term	9.9	22.3	22.6	19.8	19.6	23.7
2.2	2.7	2.9	Cur. Mat.-L/T/D	7.1	4.7	4.4	2.0	3.0	1.9
22.8	20.7	21.0	Trade Payables	15.9	21.5	17.9	25.1	22.3	18.4
.2	.2	.2	Income Taxes Payable	.0	.2	.1	.2	.3	.2
6.9	7.5	6.3	All Other Current	6.6	5.0	4.1	6.5	6.9	6.7
54.7	53.1	51.6	Total Current	39.6	53.6	49.0	53.7	52.0	50.9
8.5	9.5	9.1	Long Term Debt	14.6	12.7	9.9	6.4	8.1	10.1
.2	.2	.3	Deferred Taxes	.0	.1	.4	.2	.1	.4
3.4	4.3	4.0	All Other Non-Current	2.2	6.3	5.1	4.1	4.1	2.9
33.2	32.8	35.0	Net Worth	43.6	27.3	35.6	35.6	35.7	35.7
100.0	100.0	100.0	Total Liabilities & Net Worth	100.0	100.0	100.0	100.0	100.0	100.0
			INCOME DATA						
100.0	100.0	100.0	Net Sales	100.0	100.0	100.0	100.0	100.0	100.0
21.8	22.2	22.2	Gross Profit	41.9	33.3	24.5	23.9	20.4	17.0
18.1	19.5	19.5	Operating Expenses	38.6	30.4	22.7	21.5	17.3	14.1
3.6	2.6	2.7	Operating Profit	3.3	2.9	1.8	2.4	3.1	2.9
1.2	1.2	.9	All Other Expenses (net)	.3	1.8	.6	.9	.9	.7
2.4	1.4	1.9	Profit Before Taxes	3.0	1.1	1.1	1.5	2.2	2.3
			RATIOS						
2.2	2.4	2.4		2.4	2.7	2.9	2.2	2.4	2.4
1.4	1.4	1.5	Current	2.0	1.7	1.7	1.5	1.4	1.5
1.1	1.1	1.1		.8	.9	1.3	1.2	1.1	1.1
1.0	1.1	1.1		1.5	1.6	1.3	1.2	1.1	.9
(533) .6	.7	.7	Quick	.8	.6	.7	.7	.6	.7
.5	.4	.4		.4	.3	.5	.4	.4	.4
34 10.7	32 11.3	33 11.1		5 79.5	30 12.0	35 10.4	31 11.9	33 11.0	35 10.4
45 8.2	41 8.9	43 8.5	Sales/Receivables	34 10.6	44 8.4	45 8.2	44 8.2	42 8.7	43 8.4
53 6.9	52 7.0	53 6.9		65 5.6	51 7.1	61 6.0	57 6.5	51 7.2	51 7.1
43 8.4	43 8.5	45 8.2		1 567.0	33 11.1	57 6.4	28 13.1	41 8.9	51 7.2
73 5.0	74 4.9	76 4.8	Cost of Sales/Inventory	46 8.0	87 4.2	87 4.2	68 5.4	67 5.4	80 4.5
109 3.3	112 3.3	115 3.2		187 2.0	129 2.8	120 3.0	132 2.8	103 3.6	116 3.2
21 17.7	21 17.3	19 19.0		14 26.9	22 16.8	15 25.2	21 17.2	19 19.0	19 19.3
35 10.4	32 11.4	32 11.3	Cost of Sales/Payables	36 10.3	36 10.1	29 12.6	36 10.2	33 11.2	29 12.6
52 7.0	49 7.5	51 7.2		73 5.0	70 5.2	48 7.7	58 6.2	50 7.3	41 9.0
6.1	6.0	5.3		3.3	4.2	4.2	5.8	5.5	5.4
13.0	11.4	10.4	Sales/Working Capital	9.5	9.4	9.3	10.0	13.9	10.1
36.5	34.8	29.2		-57.7	-68.7	16.3	24.7	40.3	26.3
5.3	4.5	6.4			7.4	4.5	6.5	6.5	6.6
(492) 2.4	(511) 1.9	(527) 2.5	EBIT/Interest	(53) 2.2	(56) 1.6	(111) 2.1	(134) 2.7	(167) 2.9	2.9
1.2	.7	1.1		.6	.7	.9	1.0	1.4	
7.6	3.8	6.0				2.8	3.5	6.6	10.4
(119) 2.6	(113) 1.8	(134) 2.2	Net Profit + Depr., Dep., Amort./Cur. Mat. L/T/D		(13) 1.9	(26) 1.6	(38) 2.6	(50) 3.1	3.1
1.0	.4	.9			.6	.3	1.3	1.0	
.1	.1	.1		.0	.1	.1	.1	.1	.1
.4	.4	.3	Fixed/Worth	.3	.5	.3	.3	.3	.4
1.0	1.1	1.1		1.1	8.3	1.2	.8	1.1	1.0
1.0	1.0	1.0		.6	.9	.8	.9	1.0	1.1
2.7	2.3	2.1	Debt/Worth	1.1	2.0	1.9	1.9	2.4	2.1
6.2	5.5	5.5		2.6	71.0	5.9	6.4	4.2	5.5
36.3	28.1	27.4		51.7	37.4	18.2	25.3	32.5	26.7
(499) 17.8	(505) 9.9	(515) 12.3	% Profit Before Taxes/Tangible Net Worth	25.0	(43) 10.3	(53) 10.2	(109) 10.9	(134) 12.0	(165) 14.4
4.2	-.9	2.0		3.4	.0	-4.7	1.0	1.7	5.5
11.6	7.7	8.7		18.0	10.3	7.9	8.5	10.0	8.1
4.4	3.0	3.4	% Profit Before Taxes/Total Assets	6.2	3.4	2.5	2.6	3.5	3.9
.8	-.9	.2		.8	-1.3	-1.0	-.4	.1	.9
90.9	67.0	85.6		UND	68.0	88.7	130.3	86.3	61.9
27.8	23.3	23.7	Sales/Net Fixed Assets	10.8	18.4	26.0	31.5	24.1	18.2
12.4	10.6	10.2		7.9	7.2	15.0	15.1	9.7	8.0
3.5	3.3	3.4		3.6	3.7	3.3	3.7	3.5	3.2
2.6	2.5	2.4	Sales/Total Assets	2.2	2.2	2.3	2.6	2.6	2.3
2.0	1.9	1.8		1.3	1.4	1.8	1.9	2.0	1.8
.4	.4	.4			.9	.4	.4	.4	.4
(459) .8	(464) 1.0	(490) .9	% Depr., Dep., Amort./Sales		(45) 1.5	(51) 1.1	(100) .9	(134) .8	(154) .9
1.5	1.9	1.8			2.6	2.2	1.8	1.5	1.6
1.6	1.5	1.6			3.1	1.8	1.8	1.4	.6
(228) 2.7	(226) 2.8	(233) 3.0	% Officers', Directors', Owners' Comp/Sales		(36) 6.0	(33) 2.6	(67) 3.8	(53) 2.6	(38) 1.3
4.7	5.2	5.8			8.4	5.2	5.4	4.0	2.4
17540303M	18199922M	19160328M	Net Sales ($)	4368M	115523M	234773M	813985M	2375118M	15616561M
7562167M	8315400M	8476257M	Total Assets ($)	3220M	67840M	106239M	354888M	1010891M	6933179M

M = $ thousand   MM = $ million
See Pages 11 through 18 for Explanation of Ratios and Data

WHOLESALE—Coal and Other Mineral and Ore Merchant Wholesalers NAICS 423520 (SIC 5052)

Current Data Sorted By Assets   **Comparative Historical Data**

0-500M	500M-2MM	2-10MM	10-50MM	50-100MM	100-250MM	Type of Statement	4/1/98-3/31/99 ALL	4/1/99-3/31/00 ALL
	1	2	3	1		Unqualified	10	14
		3	2			Reviewed	6	10
	2	3				Compiled	9	5
1	2	2				Tax Returns		2
1		6	4			Other	10	12
		3 (4/1-9/30/02)	30 (10/1/02-3/31/03)					
2	5	16	9	1		**NUMBER OF STATEMENTS**	35	43
%	%	%	%	%	%	**ASSETS**	%	%
		18.1				Cash & Equivalents	8.3	10.2
		41.1				Trade Receivables (net)	36.7	38.9
		17.7				Inventory	16.4	18.7
		2.4			D	All Other Current	7.5	4.7
		79.4			A	Total Current	68.9	72.5
		15.6			T	Fixed Assets (net)	18.5	17.2
		.5			A	Intangibles (net)	2.5	3.1
		4.5			N	All Other Non-Current	10.0	7.1
		100.0			O	Total	100.0	100.0
					T	**LIABILITIES**		
		12.3			A	Notes Payable-Short Term	18.0	13.4
		.5			V	Cur. Mat.-L/T/D	1.5	4.1
		31.9			A	Trade Payables	25.9	24.4
		.6			I	Income Taxes Payable	.3	.3
		4.2			L	All Other Current	5.9	9.5
		49.5			A	Total Current	51.6	51.8
		7.6			B	Long Term Debt	9.0	10.0
		.3			L	Deferred Taxes	.3	.4
		6.5			E	All Other Non-Current	6.4	7.6
		36.1				Net Worth	32.6	30.1
		100.0				Total Liabilities & Net Worth	100.0	100.0
						INCOME DATA		
		100.0				Net Sales	100.0	100.0
		12.1				Gross Profit	15.1	12.8
		10.3				Operating Expenses	12.8	11.0
		1.8				Operating Profit	2.3	1.7
		−.1				All Other Expenses (net)	−1.7	−.2
		1.9				Profit Before Taxes	4.0	1.9
						RATIOS		
		2.3					1.9	2.3
		2.0				Current	1.2	1.3
		1.2					.9	1.0
		2.0					1.4	1.3
		1.4				Quick	.6	.8
		.9					.4	.7
	25	14.6					20 18.3	28 13.1
	40	9.0				Sales/Receivables	32 11.6	40 9.1
	47	7.8					45 8.1	56 6.5
	0	UND					0 UND	0 999.8
	2	153.7				Cost of Sales/Inventory	11 31.9	32 11.5
	62	5.9					44 8.2	49 7.5
	16	23.1					10 37.2	8 43.5
	24	15.0				Cost of Sales/Payables	26 13.9	27 13.4
	51	7.2					49 7.5	38 9.5
		4.9					10.8	8.5
		11.5				Sales/Working Capital	29.3	17.6
		50.3					−88.0	101.6
		55.3					7.3	12.2
	(15)	3.9				EBIT/Interest	(30) 1.6	(41) 4.1
		1.3					.6	1.1
								10.0
						Net Profit + Depr., Dep., Amort./Cur. Mat. L /T/D		(13) 2.1
								1.3
		.0					.1	.1
		.3				Fixed/Worth	.4	.6
		1.4					1.6	1.4
		.8					.9	.9
		1.0				Debt/Worth	2.5	2.0
		11.1					7.7	11.3
		26.0					34.1	35.3
	(13)	11.9				% Profit Before Taxes/Tangible Net Worth	(29) 15.0	(36) 18.0
		3.1					.8	9.3
		9.6					15.0	13.4
		4.0				% Profit Before Taxes/Total Assets	4.0	5.2
		.5					−.1	.9
		774.8					356.1	458.2
		57.9				Sales/Net Fixed Assets	50.3	65.0
		13.7					6.7	6.6
		5.7					6.2	5.8
		3.7				Sales/Total Assets	3.7	3.5
		1.8					2.0	1.8
		.0					.1	.2
	(14)	.2				% Depr., Dep., Amort./Sales	(28) .3	(34) .8
		3.0					2.9	2.3
								.9
						% Officers', Directors', Owners' Comp/Sales		(12) 1.2
								5.4
2621M	27208M	340844M	480985M	177333M		Net Sales ($)	1206924M	2083695M
750M	5300M	81322M	224392M	65542M		Total Assets ($)	304646M	868109M

M = $ thousand   MM = $ million
See Pages 11 through 18 for Explanation of Ratios and Data

	Comparative Historical Data						Current Data Sorted By Sales					

Type of Statement

	8		3		7	Unqualified					1		2	4
	7		4		5	Reviewed					1		1	3
	7		8		5	Compiled		1			1		2	1
	3		2		5	Tax Returns		1	3					1
	14		13		11	Other		1	1				5	4
	4/1/00-		4/1/01-		4/1/02-			3 (4/1-9/30/02)			30 (10/1/02-3/31/03)			
	3/31/01		3/31/02		3/31/03									
	ALL		ALL		ALL		0-1MM	1-3MM	3-5MM	5-10MM			10-25MM	25MM & OVER
	39		30		33	**NUMBER OF STATEMENTS**	3		4	3			10	13

						ASSETS								
	%		%		%		%	%	%	%			%	%
	12.5		12.0		15.2	Cash & Equivalents	D						21.2	9.4
	36.2		44.6		40.0	Trade Receivables (net)	A						34.4	42.3
	17.7		13.8		16.8	Inventory	T						20.5	19.9
	3.9		3.3		3.0	All Other Current	A						2.5	3.6
	70.3		73.7		75.0	Total Current							78.6	75.2
	16.6		16.1		16.3	Fixed Assets (net)	N						16.6	14.7
	3.0		2.4		1.8	Intangibles (net)	O						.5	3.3
	10.2		7.8		6.9	All Other Non-Current	T						4.3	6.8
	100.0		100.0		100.0	Total							100.0	100.0

						LIABILITIES								
	12.7		14.3		15.6	Notes Payable-Short Term	A						10.6	21.3
	4.6		2.8		2.4	Cur. Mat.-L/T/D	V						1.3	2.0
	25.6		29.5		30.5	Trade Payables	A						23.5	30.6
	.2		.4		.4	Income Taxes Payable	I						.0	.4
	5.0		7.7		4.3	All Other Current	L						4.5	5.4
	48.1		54.7		53.2	Total Current	A						39.9	59.8
	7.5		5.4		9.9	Long Term Debt	B						8.1	4.8
	2.4		.1		.3	Deferred Taxes	L						.4	.3
	6.0		6.3		4.6	All Other Non-Current	E						2.5	8.1
	36.1		33.5		32.1	Net Worth							49.0	26.9
	100.0		100.0		100.0	Total Liabilities & Net Worth							100.0	100.0

						INCOME DATA								
	100.0		100.0		100.0	Net Sales							100.0	100.0
	11.3		13.2		12.0	Gross Profit							9.5	8.6
	12.6		11.4		10.2	Operating Expenses							9.8	6.4
	−1.2		1.8		1.8	Operating Profit							−.3	2.2
	−1.4		.1		.1	All Other Expenses (net)							.0	.1
	.2		1.6		1.7	Profit Before Taxes							−.3	2.1

						RATIOS								
	2.2		2.1		2.2								3.5	1.8
	1.5		1.4		1.5	Current							2.1	1.3
	1.1		1.0		1.0								1.4	.8

	1.8		1.5		1.7								2.4	1.1
	1.0		1.0		1.0	Quick							1.7	.8
	.7		.6		.8								.9	.6

28	12.9	29	12.6	28	13.0						30	12.3	24	15.1
41	9.0	41	8.9	42	8.6	Sales/Receivables					38	9.5	45	8.0
52	7.0	48	7.7	48	7.5						54	6.8	47	7.7

1	414.3	0	UND	0	UND						0	UND	2	167.7
25	14.7	7	55.9	23	15.9	Cost of Sales/Inventory					20	18.0	34	10.6
74	4.9	46	7.9	45	8.1						62	5.9	42	8.7

18	20.6	17	21.3	16	22.4						16	23.4	17	21.6
32	11.5	27	13.8	26	14.0	Cost of Sales/Payables					23	15.7	22	16.3
49	7.5	41	8.9	54	6.7						81	4.5	35	10.6

	5.6		7.0		6.2								3.5	10.1
	13.6		15.0		16.5	Sales/Working Capital							5.9	22.6
	43.9		NM		121.5								45.0	−38.6

	5.5		12.5		12.7								56.6	16.1
(37)	1.8	(29)	4.0	(31)	4.4	EBIT/Interest						6.2	(12)	4.0
	.7		.9		2.0								.9	2.0

					5.0	Net Profit + Depr., Dep.,								
			(11)		2.3	Amort./Cur. Mat. L/T/D								
					1.4									

	.0		.1		.0								.0	.1
	.5		.5		.4	Fixed/Worth							.2	.6
	.8		1.2		1.2								.6	1.8

	.7		.6		.9								.3	1.4
	2.2		2.7		1.9	Debt/Worth							.9	3.2
	5.7		11.8		16.3								4.6	5.8

	22.2		34.9		34.7	% Profit Before Taxes/Tangible							12.9	72.9
(35)	9.8	(26)	11.0	(28)	14.9	Net Worth						5.5	(11)	21.1
	−.1		1.4		5.4								−.5	10.6

	5.7		9.7		9.6								6.6	12.6
	1.9		3.6		3.5	% Profit Before Taxes/Total							3.6	4.5
	−.9		.0		1.6	Assets							−.4	2.0

	395.1		585.0		726.5								386.4	393.6
	35.3		57.9		60.1	Sales/Net Fixed Assets							57.9	27.2
	6.6		8.9		13.1								9.4	15.5

	4.6		6.6		4.6								4.0	6.3
	2.7		3.6		3.1	Sales/Total Assets							2.4	3.7
	1.4		2.0		2.0								1.5	2.6

	.2		.0		.1									.1
(30)	1.1	(22)	.8	(26)	.6	% Depr., Dep., Amort./Sales								.4
	3.8		2.3		3.0									1.0

	1.1		.6		1.5	% Officers', Directors',								
(17)	1.7	(12)	1.4	(12)	2.1	Owners' Comp/Sales								
	4.2		4.8		3.8									

	1895273M		1310440M		1028991M	Net Sales ($)		3905M	17723M	25537M			149642M	832184M
	686262M		314316M		377306M	Total Assets ($)		1435M	8166M	7889M			90549M	269267M

M = $ thousand   MM = $ million
See Pages 11 through 18 for Explanation of Ratios and Data

Current Data Sorted By Assets   Comparative Historical Data

Type of Statement	0-500M	500M-2MM	2-10MM	10-50MM	50-100MM	100-250MM	4/1/98-3/31/99 ALL	4/1/99-3/31/00 ALL
Unqualified		4	26	36	6	5	118	118
Reviewed	5	24	104	21	1		191	160
Compiled	8	45	39	7			137	120
Tax Returns	9	21	6	2			22	31
Other	8	24	45	31	4	1	123	132
	90 (4/1-9/30/02)			392 (10/1/02-3/31/03)				
NUMBER OF STATEMENTS	30	118	220	97	11	6	591	561

ASSETS	0-500M %	500M-2MM %	2-10MM %	10-50MM %	50-100MM %	100-250MM %	Hist %	Hist %
Cash & Equivalents	10.9	8.1	5.2	6.7	4.0		5.7	5.5
Trade Receivables (net)	34.5	35.9	39.6	39.1	38.9		39.8	40.9
Inventory	27.7	36.2	34.9	33.7	32.3		35.2	34.9
All Other Current	3.6	1.6	2.5	2.5	5.4		2.0	1.4
Total Current	76.7	81.7	82.1	82.0	80.5		82.6	82.7
Fixed Assets (net)	13.9	10.4	11.8	11.6	12.7		11.2	10.8
Intangibles (net)	2.2	1.7	1.3	2.4	1.5		1.6	2.3
All Other Non-Current	7.2	6.1	4.8	4.0	5.2		4.6	4.3
Total	100.0	100.0	100.0	100.0	100.0		100.0	100.0
LIABILITIES								
Notes Payable-Short Term	32.1	13.9	17.5	14.3	7.5		17.5	17.2
Cur. Mat.-L/T/D	3.8	3.1	1.8	2.6	6.1		2.5	2.0
Trade Payables	33.3	26.5	22.3	22.8	22.1		25.0	26.5
Income Taxes Payable	.6	.1	.2	.2	.1		.3	.3
All Other Current	13.4	9.3	7.9	7.5	6.2		8.6	8.8
Total Current	83.2	53.0	49.7	47.4	42.2		53.8	54.7
Long Term Debt	9.9	9.7	7.1	7.1	7.2		8.9	9.2
Deferred Taxes	.3	.1	.2	.2	.4		.2	.2
All Other Non-Current	9.4	3.9	4.5	2.2	6.0		4.3	4.0
Net Worth	-2.8	33.3	38.6	43.1	44.3		32.7	31.9
Total Liabilities & Net Worth	100.0	100.0	100.0	100.0	100.0		100.0	100.0
INCOME DATA								
Net Sales	100.0	100.0	100.0	100.0	100.0		100.0	100.0
Gross Profit	50.9	30.6	27.6	22.3	24.6		26.2	26.3
Operating Expenses	54.7	29.2	25.2	19.5	22.9		23.1	23.1
Operating Profit	-3.7	1.4	2.4	2.8	1.7		3.1	3.1
All Other Expenses (net)	.0	.6	.4	.1	.9		.6	.4
Profit Before Taxes	-3.7	.8	2.0	2.7	.8		2.4	2.7

RATIOS	0-500M	500M-2MM	2-10MM	10-50MM	50-100MM	100-250MM	Hist	Hist
Current	2.2	2.3	2.4	2.4	3.4		2.2	2.2
	1.2	1.6	1.6	1.7	2.0		1.6	1.5
	.8	1.2	1.3	1.3	1.6		1.2	1.2
Quick	1.2	1.3	1.2	1.4	1.5		1.2	1.2
	.8	.9	.9	1.0	1.2		.9 (560)	.9
	.4	.6	.7	.7	.9		.6	.6
Sales/Receivables	10 37.8	33 11.1	40 9.1	42 8.6	41 8.9		38 9.6	41 9.0
	32 11.5	43 8.6	49 7.5	49 7.4	45 8.0		46 7.9	49 7.4
	56 6.5	55 6.6	59 6.2	59 6.2	54 6.8		58 6.2	61 6.8
Cost of Sales/Inventory	3 116.6	35 10.3	39 9.4	41 8.9	43 8.5		37 9.8	39 9.3
	45 8.1	61 6.0	57 6.4	54 6.7	53 6.8		55 6.6	58 6.2
	89 4.1	99 3.7	84 4.3	77 4.7	66 5.5		81 4.5	84 4.4
Cost of Sales/Payables	20 18.7	23 16.2	24 15.4	28 13.1	28 13.1		26 13.9	28 13.2
	36 10.1	43 8.4	34 10.8	37 9.9	33 11.0		36 10.0	39 9.3
	70 5.2	65 5.7	49 7.5	45 8.1	40 9.2		51 7.1	56 6.6
Sales/Working Capital	9.0	5.9	5.4	6.0	4.7		6.3	6.1
	65.7	10.1	9.6	8.7	7.4		10.2	10.6
	-26.9	34.4	18.1	12.9	10.6		20.7	23.7
EBIT/Interest	(21) 6.6	(110) 6.4	(203) 7.9	(86) 14.0	(10) 32.0		(548) 6.6	(513) 7.2
	-.9	2.2	2.8	5.5	4.6		3.3	3.3
	-8.3	.1	1.3	1.5	2.4		1.6	1.6
Net Profit + Depr., Dep., Amort./Cur. Mat. L /T/D		(20) 4.5	(66) 6.0	(27) 8.2			(194) 7.3	(187) 7.3
		1.6	2.7	2.3			2.5	2.8
		-.2	1.0	.9			1.2	1.3
Fixed/Worth	.0	.1	.1	.1	.1		.1	.1
	.6	.2	.2	.2	.2		.3	.3
	-1.0	.7	.6	.5	.4		.6	.6
Debt/Worth	.9	.8	.9	.7	.3		1.0	1.0
	9.5	1.9	1.7	1.3	1.5		2.1	2.3
	-5.0	4.2	3.4	2.7	2.3		4.1	4.8
% Profit Before Taxes/Tangible Net Worth	(18) 59.0	(104) 29.0	(208) 26.0	(93) 26.5	(10) 14.5		(547) 35.3	(512) 36.0
	12.0	8.7	11.9	13.9	8.1		19.3	18.0
	-19.1	-2.7	2.4	5.1	3.9		8.0	6.7
% Profit Before Taxes/Total Assets	19.4	8.1	9.8	13.5	4.9		11.1	11.6
	-6.7	2.8	3.2	4.8	4.1		5.8	5.7
	-26.2	-1.7	.7	1.4	.3		1.9	1.5
Sales/Net Fixed Assets	332.5	103.8	69.6	83.7	61.9		86.5	85.0
	54.4	49.5	39.9	35.8	23.3		43.3	45.1
	18.0	21.1	18.0	14.2	16.9		19.7	20.8
Sales/Total Assets	5.7	3.7	3.6	3.5	3.5		3.7	3.6
	4.1	3.0	2.9	2.8	2.9		3.0	2.9
	2.7	2.3	2.2	2.1	2.0		2.4	2.3
% Depr., Dep., Amort./Sales	(20) .6	(102) .3	(202) .5	(92) .4	.5		(512) .4	(496) .4
	1.3	.7	.7	.6	.8		.6	.6
	1.7	1.1	1.2	1.0	1.1		1.0	1.0
% Officers', Directors', Owners' Comp/Sales	(20) 4.1	(61) 3.0	(93) 1.5	(26) .9			(242) 1.8	(224) 1.6
	9.0	4.5	2.6	1.2			3.2	3.1
	17.9	7.9	3.0					5.7
Net Sales ($)	40497M	459500M	3100949M	5864397M	2152674M	1700012M	16238127M	15340986M
Total Assets ($)	8789M	144722M	1043667M	2184294M	741903M	783288M	5832205M	5752214M

Comparative Historical Data   Current Data Sorted By Sales

			Type of Statement						
75	64	77	Unqualified		2	2	6	17	50
144	121	155	Reviewed	1	9	16	43	55	31
156	129	99	Compiled	5	23	16	26	18	11
28	13	38	Tax Returns	5	14	9	4	4	2
113	123	113	Other	2	18	10	19	31	33
4/1/00-3/31/01	4/1/01-3/31/02	4/1/02-3/31/03		90 (4/1-9/30/02)		392 (10/1/02-3/31/03)			
ALL	ALL	ALL		0-1MM	1-3MM	3-5MM	5-10MM	10-25MM	25MM & OVER
516	450	482	**NUMBER OF STATEMENTS**	13	66	53	98	125	127
%	%	%	**ASSETS**	%	%	%	%	%	%
5.9	5.7	6.5	Cash & Equivalents	12.7	9.3	6.4	6.7	5.0	5.6
39.1	37.7	38.2	Trade Receivables (net)	27.2	33.6	36.3	36.0	40.6	41.8
34.5	36.0	34.4	Inventory	38.6	33.8	35.9	33.9	35.8	32.6
2.2	2.4	2.4	All Other Current	.3	3.2	1.1	2.5	2.3	2.9
81.7	81.7	81.4	Total Current	78.9	80.0	79.6	79.0	83.6	82.8
11.4	11.1	11.6	Fixed Assets (net)	10.2	12.9	12.7	13.4	10.4	10.3
2.3	2.2	1.9	Intangibles (net)	4.3	1.3	1.4	.9	1.8	3.1
4.5	5.0	5.1	All Other Non-Current	6.7	5.8	6.2	6.7	4.2	3.8
100.0	100.0	100.0	Total	100.0	100.0	100.0	100.0	100.0	100.0
			LIABILITIES						
16.3	18.1	16.9	Notes Payable-Short Term	37.6	14.9	16.9	15.5	18.9	14.8
2.6	2.8	2.5	Cur. Mat.-L/T/D	2.1	3.9	3.0	2.2	1.6	2.7
25.1	22.6	24.1	Trade Payables	45.8	23.5	25.3	22.8	22.3	24.3
.3	.2	.2	Income Taxes Payable	.1	.4	.1	.2	.2	.3
9.1	7.9	8.5	All Other Current	11.2	10.2	10.8	7.5	8.0	7.6
53.5	51.6	52.1	Total Current	96.8	53.0	56.1	48.1	51.0	49.6
7.9	8.6	7.9	Long Term Debt	8.4	9.8	12.1	8.9	5.5	6.6
.2	.2	.2	Deferred Taxes	.0	.2	.1	.2	.1	.2
3.5	3.2	4.2	All Other Non-Current	17.7	4.8	3.9	5.1	3.2	2.9
34.9	36.4	35.6	Net Worth	−23.0	32.2	27.8	37.7	40.1	40.6
100.0	100.0	100.0	Total Liabilities & Net Worth	100.0	100.0	100.0	100.0	100.0	100.0
			INCOME DATA						
100.0	100.0	100.0	Net Sales	100.0	100.0	100.0	100.0	100.0	100.0
27.9	27.5	28.6	Gross Profit	38.6	38.8	33.2	30.6	25.2	22.3
24.9	24.9	26.8	Operating Expenses	48.0	37.7	32.0	28.3	22.8	19.5
2.9	2.6	1.8	Operating Profit	−9.4	1.1	1.2	2.3	2.4	2.8
.5	.6	.4	All Other Expenses (net)	.7	.4	.7	.3	.3	.2
2.4	2.0	1.5	Profit Before Taxes	−10.1	.7	.5	2.0	2.1	2.5
			RATIOS						
2.2	2.4	2.4		3.8	2.9	2.0	2.6	2.2	2.3
1.5	1.6	1.6	Current	1.2	1.7	1.3	1.5	1.6	1.7
1.2	1.2	1.2		.7	1.1	1.1	1.2	1.3	1.3
1.3	1.3	1.3		2.4	1.5	1.1	1.3	1.2	1.4
(515) .9	.8	.9	Quick	.7	.9	.8	.9	.9	1.0
.6	.6	.6		.2	.5	.5	.6	.7	.7
38 9.7	38 9.6	38 9.5		23 16.1	27 13.4	36 10.1	38 9.5	39 9.3	42 8.8
47 7.7	47 7.8	47 7.8	Sales/Receivables	39 9.3	43 8.5	46 7.9	45 8.1	48 7.5	48 7.5
58 6.3	58 6.3	58 6.3		59 6.2	60 6.0	64 5.7	56 6.5	57 6.4	58 6.3
38 9.5	38 9.5	38 9.7		59 6.2	32 11.4	31 12.0	40 9.1	38 9.6	37 10.0
56 6.6	60 6.1	57 6.4	Cost of Sales/Inventory	105 3.5	58 6.3	76 4.8	62 5.9	56 6.5	50 7.3
86 4.2	96 3.8	87 4.2		232 1.6	115 3.2	124 3.0	84 4.3	83 4.6	69 5.3
25 14.3	25 14.9	24 15.0		26 13.9	23 15.6	23 16.0	24 15.0	23 15.6	27 13.4
38 9.6	35 10.4	36 10.2	Cost of Sales/Payables	51 7.2	45 8.1	54 6.8	38 9.7	32 11.5	34 10.8
55 6.6	49 7.4	52 7.0		90 4.0	70 5.2	80 4.6	52 7.1	45 8.1	43 8.5
6.4	6.1	5.8		3.5	5.2	6.0	5.1	6.1	6.4
10.9	9.9	9.8	Sales/Working Capital	20.3	9.3	10.4	9.8	10.4	9.7
22.1	19.3	20.3		−8.2	59.4	67.5	20.7	17.9	17.1
7.5	6.1	8.4			6.4	5.3	7.1	8.1	13.8
(473) 3.0	(412) 2.3	(436) 2.9	EBIT/Interest	(60) 2.3	(50) 1.5	(91) 2.7	(113) 3.1	(115) 4.6	
1.4	1.1	1.1			−1.5	−.9	1.1	1.3	1.9
7.3	5.5	6.6	Net Profit + Depr., Dep.,			2.0	5.8	8.6	9.2
(148) 3.1	(125) 1.9	(126) 2.5	Amort./Cur. Mat. L/T/D		(11) 1.2	(29) 2.3	(33) 4.9	(43) 2.8	
1.1	.4	.9				.7	.7	1.2	1.0
.1	.1	.1		.0	.1	.1	.1	.1	.1
.3	.3	.2	Fixed/Worth	.5	.3	.4	.2	.2	.2
.6	.6	.6		.0	.8	.9	.9	.5	.5
1.0	.9	.9		.4	.8	1.2	.8	.9	.8
2.0	1.9	1.7	Debt/Worth	4.3	1.9	2.6	1.7	1.7	1.5
4.2	4.0	3.9		−1.9	8.0	4.5	3.9	3.1	3.0
34.4	28.1	27.0			36.1	18.2	29.3	27.6	26.1
(469) 17.0	(419) 11.4	(437) 11.0	% Profit Before Taxes/Tangible Net Worth	(56) 8.5	(45) 4.9	(91) 12.0	(119) 11.2	(119) 14.2	
5.1	1.5	2.1			.5	−14.5	1.7	2.0	6.0
11.1	9.7	10.0		−1.3	8.3	8.1	8.5	11.5	11.4
4.9	3.1	3.4	% Profit Before Taxes/Total Assets	−12.1	3.1	1.4	3.1	3.7	4.3
1.3	.3	.3		−42.6	−3.2	−2.9	.4	.7	2.2
86.6	72.2	77.7		473.7	91.0	72.0	68.7	77.8	85.9
41.9	38.7	41.0	Sales/Net Fixed Assets	50.8	45.0	31.3	34.1	43.6	41.5
20.6	19.0	17.8		12.0	18.9	14.5	15.9	22.2	18.2
3.6	3.6	3.6		3.7	3.6	3.3	3.6	3.7	3.6
3.0	2.8	2.9	Sales/Total Assets	2.4	2.7	2.7	2.9	3.0	3.1
2.4	2.3	2.2		1.3	2.0	2.0	2.1	2.5	2.4
.3	.4	.4			.4	.6	.5	.4	.4
(433) .6	(388) .7	(433) .7	% Depr., Dep., Amort./Sales	(54) .8	(46) .8	(92) .8	(113) .6	(121) .6	
1.0	1.2	1.1			1.3	1.5	1.5	1.0	.9
1.7	1.4	1.6			3.7	2.9	2.2	1.3	.9
(207) 3.5	(183) 2.9	(200) 3.5	% Officers', Directors', Owners' Comp/Sales	(35) 6.0	(27) 5.3	(50) 3.4	(47) 2.3	(33) 1.5	
7.0	5.2	6.5			10.7	11.3	5.1	4.1	3.1
15243008M	14324383M	13318029M	Net Sales ($)	7627M	131441M	209553M	717769M	2004539M	10247100M
5383763M	5209199M	4906663M	Total Assets ($)	4261M	54033M	83174M	298007M	710221M	3756967M

M = $ thousand   MM = $ million
See Pages 11 through 18 for Explanation of Ratios and Data

Current Data Sorted By Assets   **Comparative Historical Data**

0-500M	500M-2MM	2-10MM	10-50MM	50-100MM	100-250MM	Type of Statement	4/1/98-3/31/99 ALL	4/1/99-3/31/00 ALL
	2	10	15	5	1	Unqualified	38	42
	6	15	9			Reviewed	44	34
1	9	12	3			Compiled	27	24
1	3	4				Tax Returns	7	4
3	9	14	13		2	Other	51	35
	28 (4/1-9/30/02)		109 (10/1/02-3/31/03)					
5	29	55	40	5	3	NUMBER OF STATEMENTS	167	139
%	%	%	%	%	%	**ASSETS**	%	%
	9.5	7.8	7.5			Cash & Equivalents	6.1	7.3
	31.3	32.3	35.9			Trade Receivables (net)	32.9	33.3
	41.6	42.2	41.7			Inventory	41.2	39.9
	1.7	2.2	1.2			All Other Current	2.2	1.8
	84.1	84.5	86.2			Total Current	82.4	82.3
	9.1	8.8	9.5			Fixed Assets (net)	9.7	10.0
	.3	4.0	1.8			Intangibles (net)	3.0	3.0
	6.5	2.6	2.5			All Other Non-Current	4.9	4.7
	100.0	100.0	100.0			Total	100.0	100.0
						LIABILITIES		
	25.6	15.6	16.0			Notes Payable-Short Term	17.0	14.0
	1.2	2.6	4.1			Cur. Mat.-L/T/D	1.5	2.2
	25.6	22.2	22.5			Trade Payables	26.9	27.4
	.2	.1	.0			Income Taxes Payable	.2	.3
	13.6	8.9	11.9			All Other Current	6.8	8.1
	66.2	49.4	54.6			Total Current	52.4	52.0
	6.7	3.3	1.8			Long Term Debt	8.5	6.8
	.1	.0	.0			Deferred Taxes	.2	.2
	6.1	2.3	3.3			All Other Non-Current	5.1	4.4
	20.9	44.9	40.3			Net Worth	33.9	36.5
	100.0	100.0	100.0			Total Liabilities & Net Worth	100.0	100.0
						INCOME DATA		
	100.0	100.0	100.0			Net Sales	100.0	100.0
	29.2	21.3	21.6			Gross Profit	23.6	23.2
	25.4	18.2	17.8			Operating Expenses	22.6	20.5
	3.8	3.1	3.8			Operating Profit	.9	2.7
	1.1	.1	.5			All Other Expenses (net)	−.3	.4
	2.7	3.0	3.2			Profit Before Taxes	1.3	2.3
						RATIOS		
	2.1	2.7	2.2			Current	2.2	2.3
	1.6	1.8	1.6				1.5	1.6
	1.2	1.4	1.2				1.3	1.2
	1.3	1.2	1.3			Quick	1.0	1.2
	.7	.8	.8				.7	.7
	.5	.5	.5				.5	.5
	21 17.1	24 15.4	25 14.7			Sales/Receivables	30 12.4	27 13.4
	30 12.0	35 10.3	41 8.9				37 9.9	39 9.4
	45 8.2	49 7.5	61 6.0				49 7.5	49 7.5
	35 10.4	33 11.2	44 8.3			Cost of Sales/Inventory	39 9.4	39 9.4
	66 5.5	56 6.5	68 5.4				64 5.7	59 6.2
	106 3.4	93 3.9	89 4.1				96 3.8	84 4.3
	12 29.3	15 24.9	15 25.2			Cost of Sales/Payables	24 15.4	21 17.6
	32 11.3	25 14.7	29 12.5				37 9.8	37 10.0
	65 5.6	47 7.8	42 8.7				56 6.5	58 6.3
	7.6	5.7	5.9			Sales/Working Capital	6.2	6.4
	12.0	9.2	10.4				10.2	11.8
	29.5	17.8	25.9				21.5	23.9
	9.6	17.9	17.2			EBIT/Interest	(150) 6.5	(125) 6.4
	(27) 4.3	(47) 3.9	(35) 4.8				3.0	3.3
	1.6	1.9	2.5				1.6	1.6
						Net Profit + Depr., Dep., Amort./Cur. Mat. L /T/D	(38) 6.2 / 2.3 / 1.3	(36) 14.8 / 4.7 / 1.9
	.0	.0	.1			Fixed/Worth	.1	.1
	.1	.1	.2				.2	.2
	.5	.3	.4				.7	.5
	.8	.6	.8			Debt/Worth	1.1	.9
	1.6	1.1	1.7				2.7	2.3
	6.9	3.2	3.5				4.9	4.2
	38.6	63.5	51.8			% Profit Before Taxes/Tangible Net Worth	(154) 39.2	(130) 37.1
	(26) 16.0	(52) 17.4	31.7				16.9	19.4
	4.2	6.0	5.4				6.3	4.3
	15.9	12.9	19.9			% Profit Before Taxes/Total Assets	12.3	12.0
	6.7	6.1	9.5				5.1	5.4
	1.4	1.5	2.5				1.5	1.7
	351.5	179.4	180.0			Sales/Net Fixed Assets	149.7	145.5
	83.0	93.0	63.8				59.5	46.6
	28.0	28.5	23.6				19.8	20.3
	4.5	4.6	3.8			Sales/Total Assets	4.0	4.1
	3.3	3.4	3.0				3.1	3.0
	2.7	2.2	2.5				2.1	2.3
	.2	.2	.2			% Depr., Dep., Amort./Sales	(146) .3	(120) .2
	(25) .5	(46) .4	(34) .6				.5	.6
	1.1	.5	1.0				1.2	1.0
	1.3	1.0				% Officers', Directors', Owners' Comp/Sales	(70) 1.2	(54) 1.2
	(20) 2.3	(27) 1.4					2.2	2.1
	5.1	2.4					4.5	4.7
3746M	146558M	853341M	2436538M	1181097M	947395M	Net Sales ($)	5279282M	5473349M
789M	36672M	256732M	757462M	354907M	401990M	Total Assets ($)	2184506M	1804600M

M = $ thousand   MM = $ million
See Pages 11 through 18 for Explanation of Ratios and Data

Comparative Historical Data   **Current Data Sorted By Sales**

					28 (4/1-9/30/02)	109 (10/1/02-3/31/03)			
			Type of Statement	0-1MM	1-3MM	3-5MM	5-10MM	10-25MM	25MM & OVER
23	27	33	Unqualified		1	1	2	8	21
24	21	30	Reviewed		1	4	7	7	11
28	27	25	Compiled	1	5	3	6	7	3
8	3	8	Tax Returns	1		1	5	1	
43	34	41	Other	3	3	4	4	8	19
4/1/00-3/31/01 ALL	4/1/01-3/31/02 ALL	4/1/02-3/31/03 ALL							
126	112	137	**NUMBER OF STATEMENTS**	5	10	13	24	31	54
%	%	%	**ASSETS**	%	%	%	%	%	%
6.7	7.5	8.6	Cash & Equivalents		4.7	11.8	6.3	10.7	7.1
33.2	34.5	32.4	Trade Receivables (net)		20.9	31.5	29.4	34.1	36.4
40.7	39.2	40.5	Inventory		44.0	38.6	42.3	40.2	42.7
1.4	.9	1.8	All Other Current		2.1	.6	3.7	1.2	1.6
82.1	82.2	83.3	Total Current		71.7	82.5	81.7	86.1	87.8
9.0	9.2	10.2	Fixed Assets (net)		15.9	13.0	8.8	9.4	6.4
2.8	3.1	2.6	Intangibles (net)		.8	2.0	6.0	1.8	2.3
6.2	5.5	3.9	All Other Non-Current		11.6	2.5	3.5	2.6	3.4
100.0	100.0	100.0	Total		100.0	100.0	100.0	100.0	100.0
			LIABILITIES						
17.3	19.8	18.4	Notes Payable-Short Term		46.5	13.7	10.6	18.4	16.2
1.8	1.9	2.9	Cur. Mat.-L/T/D		2.0	8.6	1.1	3.2	2.1
24.8	23.2	22.9	Trade Payables		28.6	26.0	17.6	20.5	25.0
.2	.1	.1	Income Taxes Payable		.0	.2	.3	.0	.0
7.7	8.1	11.6	All Other Current		25.3	11.7	9.5	6.0	11.2
51.8	53.1	55.8	Total Current		102.3	60.2	39.1	48.1	54.5
6.4	6.1	4.0	Long Term Debt		5.4	2.3	7.8	2.5	2.8
.1	.0	.0	Deferred Taxes		.1	.0	.1	.0	.0
5.6	9.0	6.1	All Other Non-Current		4.7	9.9	1.8	2.5	2.7
36.1	31.8	34.0	Net Worth		−12.5	27.6	51.2	46.9	40.0
100.0	100.0	100.0	Total Liabilities & Net Worth		100.0	100.0	100.0	100.0	100.0
			INCOME DATA						
100.0	100.0	100.0	Net Sales		100.0	100.0	100.0	100.0	100.0
23.2	24.5	24.4	Gross Profit		37.8	26.4	24.5	22.9	19.4
21.2	21.7	21.0	Operating Expenses		34.0	25.5	20.2	19.0	15.6
2.0	2.8	3.4	Operating Profit		3.8	.9	4.3	4.0	3.7
−.5	.4	.4	All Other Expenses (net)		1.7	.3	.7	.5	.2
2.5	2.4	3.0	Profit Before Taxes		2.1	.6	3.6	3.5	3.6
			RATIOS						
2.4	2.6	2.4	Current		1.4	2.3	3.6	2.7	2.3
1.6	1.5	1.6			1.2	1.6	2.1	1.6	1.6
1.2	1.1	1.2			1.1	1.1	1.6	1.4	1.2
1.2	1.2	1.2	Quick		.7	1.3	1.9	1.2	1.1
.8	.7	.8			.5	.7	.8	.9	.8
.5	.5	.5			.2	.5	.6	.5	.6
28 13.1	28 13.0	23 15.8	Sales/Receivables	12 29.2	29 12.8	21 17.3	26 13.9		24 15.3
38 9.5	36 10.2	36 10.2		31 11.9	44 8.2	31 11.8	36 10.2		39 9.4
53 6.9	51 7.1	50 7.3		48 7.7	62 5.9	48 7.6	49 7.5		53 6.9
40 9.1	34 10.8	36 10.3	Cost of Sales/Inventory	58 6.3	40 9.2	34 10.6	33 11.2		42 8.8
59 6.1	58 6.3	62 5.9		114 3.2	72 5.1	68 5.4	53 6.9		61 6.0
87 4.2	82 4.4	93 3.9		155 2.4	126 2.9	94 3.9	84 4.3		88 4.2
22 16.8	17 21.9	15 24.8	Cost of Sales/Payables	22 16.7	19 19.7	8 43.7	14 25.8		16 23.5
37 9.9	32 11.6	28 13.0		61 5.9	34 10.8	25 14.8	26 13.9		29 12.7
54 6.8	50 7.3	47 7.8		89 4.1	68 5.3	43 8.6	48 7.6		40 9.0
6.2	6.1	5.9	Sales/Working Capital		9.4	4.3	5.0	6.3	6.7
10.8	11.0	10.8			25.3	12.0	7.1	10.8	10.8
22.6	32.6	25.2			137.8	87.3	14.7	16.0	25.6
(113) 10.8	(101) 8.0	(119) 13.3	EBIT/Interest	4.8	(11) 11.6	(18) 17.5	(30) 18.3		(47) 19.0
3.5	2.7	4.3		1.9	3.2	4.4	4.7		6.1
1.4	1.1	2.1		1.3	1.2	1.9	2.6		2.5
(22) 9.2	(15) 7.0	(20) 7.9	Net Profit + Depr., Dep., Amort./Cur. Mat. L/T/D						(10) 21.7
2.8	2.3	5.3							7.1
1.7	1.1	1.5							2.4
.1	.1	.1	Fixed/Worth		.1	.0	.0	.0	.1
.2	.2	.2			.3	.1	.1	.1	.2
.5	.5	.4			.7	NM	.3	.3	.2
.9	.7	.6	Debt/Worth		.9	.7	.4	.6	.8
2.1	1.7	1.5			2.4	4.4	1.1	.9	1.7
5.6	6.5	4.4			7.8	NM	2.2	3.2	4.3
(117) 41.7	(102) 34.0	(128) 46.9	% Profit Before Taxes/Tangible Net Worth		(10) 63.5	(22) 44.4	64.5	53.6	
16.6	13.6	21.9			29.6	16.0	16.9	30.2	
5.1	1.4	6.2			3.1	4.0	8.0	9.1	
14.3	16.3	16.6	% Profit Before Taxes/Total Assets		11.9	11.2	17.0	19.6	19.1
5.3	4.9	6.6			3.9	6.0	7.3	5.8	8.9
1.4	.5	1.7			1.2	.8	2.9	1.6	3.1
159.9	123.0	204.5	Sales/Net Fixed Assets		193.0	379.5	194.1	174.8	308.9
49.4	52.6	71.0			24.2	54.0	77.0	92.9	87.0
22.9	25.3	24.1			8.1	26.1	21.3	37.8	30.4
3.8	4.1	4.5	Sales/Total Assets		3.1	3.8	5.0	4.8	4.5
3.1	3.3	3.2			2.6	2.8	3.0	3.4	3.4
2.3	2.6	2.4			2.0	1.5	2.4	2.2	2.6
(103) .3	(96) .2	(114) .2	% Depr., Dep., Amort./Sales		.1	(19) .2	(26) .2	(45) .1	
.5	.4	.4			.8	.4	.4	.4	
1.0	.9	1.0			1.4	.7	.8	.8	
(46) 1.2	(36) 1.3	(62) 1.0	% Officers', Directors', Owners' Comp/Sales				(15) 1.0	(16) 1.1	(12) .3
2.2	2.4	1.9					2.0	1.7	.8
4.2	5.9	3.4					2.6	2.4	1.0
3829733M	3644936M	5568675M	Net Sales ($)	3746M	21894M	53215M	183618M	501885M	4804317M
1408712M	1321958M	1808552M	Total Assets ($)	789M	9330M	27521M	74302M	161888M	1534722M

Current Data Sorted By Assets   Comparative Historical Data

Type of Statement								
4	5	26	24	8	6	Unqualified	67	70
3	29	63	8			Reviewed	115	98
5	39	33	2			Compiled	97	94
6	11	3				Tax Returns	22	28
6	31	41	26	7	3	Other	111	92
92 (4/1-9/30/02)			297 (10/1/02-3/31/03)				4/1/98-3/31/99	4/1/99-3/31/00
0-500M	500M-2MM	2-10MM	10-50MM	50-100MM	100-250MM		ALL	ALL
24	115	166	60	15	9	NUMBER OF STATEMENTS	412	382
%	%	%	%	%	%	ASSETS	%	%
12.8	9.3	8.3	8.6	7.8		Cash & Equivalents	8.6	7.9
36.4	37.3	37.3	33.3	34.2		Trade Receivables (net)	37.4	41.5
26.7	32.0	35.2	37.6	31.9		Inventory	32.8	30.6
4.8	2.3	2.4	2.7	1.8		All Other Current	2.0	2.1
80.6	80.9	83.1	82.2	75.6		Total Current	80.8	82.1
12.5	11.2	8.8	9.5	10.2		Fixed Assets (net)	11.5	10.6
2.3	2.7	2.4	3.8	9.1		Intangibles (net)	2.0	2.5
4.5	5.2	5.7	4.5	5.0		All Other Non-Current	5.7	4.8
100.0	100.0	100.0	100.0	100.0		Total	100.0	100.0
						LIABILITIES		
18.4	15.0	16.8	13.1	10.4		Notes Payable-Short Term	15.0	15.5
8.1	2.4	2.1	2.0	1.3		Cur. Mat.-L/T/D	2.6	2.3
23.8	24.5	23.2	20.4	24.0		Trade Payables	23.4	25.7
.3	.2	.5	.2	.1		Income Taxes Payable	.6	.3
13.5	10.5	10.1	9.0	8.2		All Other Current	9.5	9.1
64.0	52.6	52.7	44.6	43.9		Total Current	51.1	52.9
6.8	8.8	5.0	6.3	17.5		Long Term Debt	9.6	8.0
.1	.0	.1	.1	.7		Deferred Taxes	.2	.2
21.3	3.9	5.0	4.5	2.0		All Other Non-Current	5.2	3.3
7.8	34.7	37.2	44.5	35.9		Net Worth	33.9	35.6
100.0	100.0	100.0	100.0	100.0		Total Liabilities & Net Worth	100.0	100.0
						INCOME DATA		
100.0	100.0	100.0	100.0	100.0		Net Sales	100.0	100.0
35.7	33.2	28.6	26.0	20.8		Gross Profit	30.9	30.2
33.5	31.7	25.9	24.9	18.8		Operating Expenses	32.2	26.6
2.2	1.5	2.7	1.1	2.0		Operating Profit	−1.2	3.7
.1	.4	.6	.3	.3		All Other Expenses (net)	.3	.3
2.1	1.1	2.1	.8	1.7		Profit Before Taxes	−1.6	3.3
						RATIOS		
2.4	2.3	2.5	3.1	2.7		Current	2.3	2.3
1.4	1.7	1.6	2.0	1.8			1.7	1.5
1.0	1.2	1.2	1.3	1.4			1.3	1.2
1.7	1.4	1.2	1.3	1.3		Quick	1.4	1.3
.9	.9	.9	.9	1.1			.9	.9
.5	.6	.6	.6	.7			.6	.6
17 21.5	31 12.0	33 11.1	35 10.4	44 8.2		Sales/Receivables	32 11.3	34 10.6
33 11.0	40 9.1	42 8.7	46 7.9	53 6.9			43 8.5	48 7.6
45 8.1	54 6.7	57 6.4	57 6.4	60 6.1			54 6.7	61 6.0
16 22.4	25 14.4	30 12.1	42 8.7	36 10.1		Cost of Sales/Inventory	29 12.6	28 13.3
39 9.5	54 6.8	60 6.1	72 5.1	64 5.7			55 6.6	48 7.6
54 6.7	93 3.9	95 3.8	115 3.2	79 4.6			88 4.1	81 4.5
17 20.9	23 15.6	20 18.1	18 20.4	26 14.1		Cost of Sales/Payables	21 17.5	23 15.8
36 10.2	37 9.8	33 11.0	36 10.2	33 10.9			35 10.4	39 9.4
49 7.4	55 6.7	50 7.4	49 7.4	57 6.4			52 7.0	59 6.2
7.1	6.5	5.3	4.0	5.3		Sales/Working Capital	6.0	6.4
19.2	11.5	9.2	6.1	10.3			10.9	11.1
808.6	28.1	26.6	16.7	11.7			21.8	26.4
(21) 20.3	(99) 4.8	(149) 10.9	(54) 9.8	(13) 19.0		EBIT/Interest	(371) 7.8	(338) 12.4
2.6	2.0	2.5	3.5	2.6			3.4	3.1
−.8	−.7	1.0	−.6	.9			1.4	1.4
	(15) 5.1	(40) 7.9	(20) 24.3			Net Profit + Depr., Dep., Amort./Cur. Mat. L /T/D	(107) 7.2	(102) 5.8
	1.0	2.7	2.4				2.6	2.2
	.3	.7	.5				1.2	.9
.1	.1	.1	.1	.1		Fixed/Worth	.1	.1
.3	.2	.2	.2	.2			.3	.2
.9	.8	.5	.6	.8			.7	.6
.8	.8	.9	.6	.7		Debt/Worth	1.0	1.0
2.4	2.1	1.7	1.5	1.6			2.0	2.1
14.0	9.3	4.5	2.9	4.6			4.6	4.9
(19) 60.0	(100) 45.6	(159) 33.4	(57) 30.1	(13) 18.2		% Profit Before Taxes/Tangible Net Worth	(377) 43.7	(352) 50.6
26.4	8.7	11.0	9.3	9.0			18.6	19.7
.0	−4.0	.4	−7.5	1.3			4.8	5.8
21.4	8.1	11.7	9.0	9.6		% Profit Before Taxes/Total Assets	14.3	14.5
8.6	2.2	3.1	4.1	2.4			5.8	5.9
−2.2	−2.7	.4	−3.5	.2			1.2	1.3
214.9	160.6	121.3	86.2	69.8		Sales/Net Fixed Assets	100.1	123.3
57.5	60.8	52.3	39.7	26.3			39.7	46.1
36.7	15.2	28.5	15.3	10.2			19.8	22.3
5.4	4.1	3.9	3.5	3.4		Sales/Total Assets	4.2	4.0
4.0	3.2	2.8	2.7	2.3			3.1	3.2
3.3	2.4	2.2	1.8	1.8			2.2	2.3
(15) .4	(90) .3	(140) .4	(50) .4	(13) .6		% Depr., Dep., Amort./Sales	(350) .3	(328) .3
.7	.7	.7	.6	1.0			.7	.7
2.3	1.5	1.1	1.2	1.6			1.2	1.3
(13) 4.5	(61) 3.3	(71) 1.8	(13) .8			% Officers', Directors', Owners' Comp/Sales	(171) 2.2	(154) 1.7
5.8	5.6	2.8	2.0				3.8	3.6
7.8	9.7	4.3	3.8				6.8	6.3
31208M	468324M	2303734M	3669116M	2909730M	2405944M	Net Sales ($)	9168570M	9844469M
7062M	137599M	760332M	1306111M	1092738M	1213587M	Total Assets ($)	3567535M	3924516M

M = $ thousand   MM = $ million
See Pages 11 through 18 for Explanation of Ratios and Data

Comparative Historical Data | Current Data Sorted By Sales

Type of Statement									
53 / 55 / 73			Unqualified	2	2	4	6	18	41
90 / 84 / 103			Reviewed		12	9	31	39	12
103 / 91 / 79			Compiled	1	22	14	20	20	2
20 / 18 / 20			Tax Returns	4	3	5	5	3	
98 / 109 / 114			Other	4	23	8	19	28	32
4/1/00-3/31/01 ALL	4/1/01-3/31/02 ALL	4/1/02-3/31/03 ALL		0-1MM	1-3MM	3-5MM	5-10MM	10-25MM	25MM & OVER
				92 (4/1-9/30/02)		297 (10/1/02-3/31/03)			
364	357	389	NUMBER OF STATEMENTS	11	62	40	81	108	87

ASSETS

%	%	%		%	%	%	%	%	%
7.8	8.5	8.9	Cash & Equivalents	12.8	7.3	11.8	12.1	7.2	7.3
38.5	33.1	36.2	Trade Receivables (net)	28.6	33.0	37.8	35.4	38.1	37.3
33.1	36.8	33.9	Inventory	31.9	33.0	31.3	32.9	35.4	35.0
2.4	2.9	2.6	All Other Current	7.6	1.8	1.8	2.9	2.3	2.8
81.8	81.4	81.6	Total Current	81.0	75.1	82.7	83.4	83.0	82.4
10.8	10.3	10.0	Fixed Assets (net)	13.1	13.9	10.1	10.0	7.7	9.6
2.2	2.6	3.1	Intangibles (net)	2.4	3.0	3.5	1.9	3.5	3.9
5.2	5.7	5.3	All Other Non-Current	3.5	8.1	3.7	4.8	5.8	4.2
100.0	100.0	100.0	Total	100.0	100.0	100.0	100.0	100.0	100.0

LIABILITIES

17.4	17.0	15.2	Notes Payable-Short Term	24.6	15.9	14.4	11.9	18.6	12.9
2.2	2.6	2.5	Cur. Mat.-L/T/D	13.9	2.6	3.0	1.9	2.0	1.8
24.6	20.8	23.1	Trade Payables	21.2	20.0	25.4	23.6	20.7	27.0
.4	.2	.3	Income Taxes Payable	.5	.1	.2	.6	.2	.2
8.7	9.7	10.2	All Other Current	16.7	8.9	8.0	11.9	9.2	11.2
53.3	50.3	51.3	Total Current	76.9	47.5	51.1	49.9	50.7	53.1
8.9	9.0	7.0	Long Term Debt	14.3	9.5	10.3	4.6	4.4	8.4
.2	.2	.1	Deferred Taxes	.0	.0	.0	.1	.1	.2
3.6	3.2	5.4	All Other Non-Current	3.8	11.1	2.3	2.9	5.8	4.7
34.0	37.4	36.1	Net Worth	4.9	32.0	36.3	42.5	38.9	33.6
100.0	100.0	100.0	Total Liabilities & Net Worth	100.0	100.0	100.0	100.0	100.0	100.0

INCOME DATA

100.0	100.0	100.0	Net Sales	100.0	100.0	100.0	100.0	100.0	100.0
29.9	30.5	29.5	Gross Profit	34.8	36.6	32.1	34.5	26.3	21.9
26.1	28.4	27.5	Operating Expenses	31.8	34.9	31.4	32.0	24.3	19.6
3.8	2.1	2.0	Operating Profit	3.0	1.7	.7	2.5	2.0	2.3
.5	.6	.4	All Other Expenses (net)	1.6	.8	.0	.3	.4	.5
3.3	1.5	1.6	Profit Before Taxes	1.4	.9	.7	2.2	1.6	1.8

RATIOS

2.1 1.5 1.2	2.6 1.7 1.2	2.5 1.7 1.2	Current	2.8 1.6 .5	2.5 1.9 1.1	3.0 1.6 1.2	2.8 1.7 1.2	2.3 1.7 1.2	2.4 1.6 1.3
1.2 .8 .6	1.3 .8 .6	1.3 .9 .6	Quick	1.3 .5 .1	1.4 .9 .5	1.6 .9 .6	1.8 1.0 .7	1.2 .9 .6	1.2 .9 .6
35 10.5 47 7.8 57 6.4	29 12.5 41 8.9 53 6.8	32 11.4 42 8.6 56 6.5	Sales/Receivables	0 UND 52 7.0 73 5.0	32 11.3 42 8.7 62 5.9	28 13.1 43 8.5 54 6.7	30 12.2 38 9.5 52 7.0	34 10.6 42 8.8 55 6.6	37 10.0 46 7.9 57 6.4
32 11.4 57 6.4 84 4.3	35 10.3 64 5.7 103 3.6	31 11.7 58 6.2 95 3.8	Cost of Sales/Inventory	7 52.0 45 8.1 201 1.8	31 11.9 70 5.2 116 3.1	16 23.0 49 7.4 83 4.4	34 10.6 60 6.0 102 3.6	34 10.7 59 6.2 87 4.2	34 10.8 55 6.6 90 4.1
21 17.6 35 10.6 60 6.1	17 21.7 31 11.7 51 7.2	22 16.6 36 10.2 50 7.3	Cost of Sales/Payables	21 17.0 49 7.4 64 5.7	22 16.6 39 9.5 50 7.3	29 12.7 40 9.2 59 6.1	20 17.9 36 10.2 58 6.3	18 20.0 29 12.4 46 8.0	24 15.4 36 10.1 49 7.4
6.9 11.7 26.3	5.1 9.4 26.0	5.4 9.4 25.7	Sales/Working Capital	2.7 14.0 -6.1	5.1 8.5 49.2	6.2 9.6 23.0	4.9 9.2 26.9	5.6 9.4 23.9	5.5 9.6 23.0
(326) 8.9 3.4 1.6	(312) 7.7 2.3 -.3	(344) 8.0 2.5 .4	EBIT/Interest	(10) 12.5 2.8 -1.4	(54) 4.9 2.3 -.6	(35) 3.7 1.6 -.2	(68) 14.6 1.7 -.2	(96) 7.0 2.4 1.0	(81) 14.5 4.2 1.1
(77) 11.5 3.2 1.4	(74) 10.8 1.5 -.1	(88) 8.2 2.6 .7	Net Profit + Depr., Dep., Amort./Cur. Mat. L/T/D		(12) 4.7 2.2 .1	(13) 6.1 .9 .3	(26) 7.5 2.4 .9	(34) 15.4 3.1 1.0	
.1 .2 .6	.1 .2 .7	.1 .2 .6	Fixed/Worth	.0 .2 -.5	.1 .2 1.0	.1 .2 .9	.1 .2 .5	.1 .2 .5	.1 .2 .5
1.1 2.3 5.4	.7 1.8 4.6	.8 1.8 4.9	Debt/Worth	1.2 7.0 -3.0	.6 1.6 9.6	.8 2.0 10.2	.6 1.6 3.9	.9 2.1 4.8	.8 1.7 4.6
(333) 63.5 23.2 5.9	(325) 36.5 12.2 -4.7	(357) 33.2 10.0 -1.7	% Profit Before Taxes/Tangible Net Worth		(52) 26.6 3.6 -8.5	(36) 33.9 3.3 -2.7	(78) 42.0 4.3 -2.8	(103) 32.8 11.7 .0	(81) 40.2 12.7 1.3
16.5 6.6 1.6	11.7 3.9 -3.2	10.1 3.0 -1.2	% Profit Before Taxes/Total Assets	21.9 5.2 -2.7	8.6 1.8 -4.4	7.0 1.5 -1.8	13.7 2.6 -1.4	9.7 3.3 .0	11.2 4.9 .2
127.3 50.3 21.9	109.9 45.4 19.8	118.9 52.2 22.0	Sales/Net Fixed Assets	UND 99.7 7.7	76.9 47.3 14.0	119.6 56.9 15.3	129.8 54.5 22.6	138.7 54.6 30.1	103.2 44.1 22.1
4.0 3.0 2.4	3.9 2.9 2.1	3.9 3.0 2.1	Sales/Total Assets	4.7 2.6 1.7	3.5 2.7 2.0	3.5 2.9 2.1	4.1 3.0 2.2	4.1 2.9 2.3	4.1 3.1 2.0
(304) .3 .6 1.2	(286) .3 .7 1.2	(317) .4 .7 1.3	% Depr., Dep., Amort./Sales		(45) .5 .9 2.3	(32) .3 .7 1.3	(66) .4 .7 1.4	(92) .3 .6 1.1	(76) .4 .6 1.2
(165) 1.7 4.0 7.3	(151) 2.1 3.8 7.3	(159) 2.3 3.7 6.7	% Officers', Directors', Owners' Comp/Sales		(29) 4.6 6.6 9.8	(23) 3.0 4.8 8.2	(41) 2.9 3.8 8.1	(47) 1.4 2.7 3.7	(14) .6 1.8 2.5
10906307M	10238234M	11788056M	Net Sales ($)	5864M	119337M	156205M	567791M	1640212M	9298647M
3822813M	4019967M	4517429M	Total Assets ($)	5559M	51083M	60474M	230489M	623700M	3546124M

M = $ thousand   MM = $ million
See Pages 11 through 18 for Explanation of Ratios and Data

Current Data Sorted By Assets

Comparative Historical Data

Type of Statement	0-500M	500M-2MM	2-10MM	10-50MM	50-100MM	100-250MM		4/1/98-3/31/99 ALL	4/1/99-3/31/00 ALL
Unqualified		2	20	18	4	1		43	41
Reviewed	1	16	48	8	1			92	77
Compiled	3	22	19	1				78	80
Tax Returns	9	9	4					17	17
Other	1	14	26	15	3			71	50
		48 (4/1-9/30/02)		197 (10/1/02-3/31/03)					
NUMBER OF STATEMENTS	14	63	117	42	8	1		301	265

ASSETS	%	%	%	%	%	%		%	%
Cash & Equivalents	7.6	8.4	5.7	4.2				6.2	5.6
Trade Receivables (net)	28.6	29.7	29.7	26.9				34.0	31.8
Inventory	47.1	41.9	42.5	44.6				39.8	42.7
All Other Current	.2	1.8	3.2	2.1				1.4	1.6
Total Current	83.5	81.7	81.1	77.7				81.4	81.7
Fixed Assets (net)	9.2	12.1	12.6	13.7				11.6	10.8
Intangibles (net)	1.2	1.8	2.4	2.3				2.7	2.6
All Other Non-Current	6.0	4.4	3.9	6.3				4.3	4.8
Total	100.0	100.0	100.0	100.0				100.0	100.0

LIABILITIES									
Notes Payable-Short Term	9.1	13.8	17.9	17.1				14.8	16.0
Cur. Mat.-L/T/D	6.0	3.3	2.7	4.0				2.6	2.7
Trade Payables	26.5	19.1	16.3	13.6				21.6	19.4
Income Taxes Payable	.0	.3	.2	.3				.4	.3
All Other Current	10.5	5.4	6.9	5.8				7.1	9.6
Total Current	52.1	41.9	44.0	40.7				46.5	47.9
Long Term Debt	17.0	8.8	10.9	9.4				8.6	7.5
Deferred Taxes	.0	.3	.1	.6				.2	.1
All Other Non-Current	7.2	7.0	3.0	3.3				4.8	3.5
Net Worth	23.7	42.0	41.9	45.9				39.9	40.9
Total Liabilities & Net Worth	100.0	100.0	100.0	100.0				100.0	100.0

INCOME DATA									
Net Sales	100.0	100.0	100.0	100.0				100.0	100.0
Gross Profit	36.6	35.7	32.1	30.7				30.8	31.5
Operating Expenses	35.6	32.7	28.5	27.1				27.6	28.1
Operating Profit	.9	3.0	3.6	3.6				3.2	3.4
All Other Expenses (net)	−.2	.4	.6	1.0				−.3	.3
Profit Before Taxes	1.2	2.6	3.0	2.6				3.4	3.1

RATIOS

Ratio	0-500M	500M-2MM	2-10MM	10-50MM	50-100MM	100-250MM		98-99 ALL	99-00 ALL
Current	3.3	3.8	3.0	2.8				2.7	2.6
	2.0	2.1	1.8	1.9				1.8	1.7
	1.3	1.4	1.4	1.4				1.3	1.4
Quick	1.2	1.7	1.4	1.3				1.4	1.3
	1.0	1.0	.8	.8				.9	.7
	.5	.6	.5	.4				.5	.5
Sales/Receivables	16 23.5	27 13.4	32 11.6	39 9.3				32 11.4	31 11.8
	29 12.7	36 10.2	41 8.9	45 8.1				42 8.7	41 8.9
	42 8.7	45 8.0	50 7.3	55 6.6				55 6.7	52 7.1
Cost of Sales/Inventory	45 8.1	57 6.4	60 6.0	74 4.9				44 8.4	50 7.2
	76 4.8	84 4.3	88 4.2	111 3.3				75 4.9	85 4.3
	115 3.2	112 3.2	160 2.3	177 2.1				119 3.1	137 2.7
Cost of Sales/Payables	19 19.2	15 25.0	17 22.0	17 21.2				22 16.2	20 18.3
	28 13.0	28 12.9	29 12.6	31 11.7				34 10.8	35 10.6
	51 7.1	49 7.4	44 8.3	46 7.9				50 7.3	50 7.3
Sales/Working Capital	6.1	4.5	4.4	4.1				5.0	5.1
	10.3	7.6	7.0	6.0				7.7	7.8
	28.8	19.9	12.0	9.1				15.8	15.8
EBIT/Interest	16.5	(58) 7.9	(106) 9.8	(38) 6.2				(281) 9.8	(246) 9.2
	1.9	3.4	3.7	2.6				3.5	3.2
	−.2	1.4	1.4	1.8				1.4	1.5
Net Profit + Depr., Dep., Amort./Cur. Mat. L/T/D		(17) 4.1	(45) 5.5	(13) 5.9				(103) 5.0	(72) 7.5
		1.2	2.3	.6				1.7	2.5
		.1	.9	.4				.9	1.1
Fixed/Worth	.1	.1	.1	.1				.1	.1
	.2	.2	.3	.2				.3	.2
	NM	.6	.6	.6				.6	.5
Debt/Worth	.7	.6	.7	.7				.7	.7
	2.2	1.1	1.5	1.3				1.6	1.5
	NM	4.3	3.0	2.7				3.7	3.5
% Profit Before Taxes/Tangible Net Worth	(11) 23.9	(57) 31.7	(108) 27.9	16.7				(278) 33.7	(252) 34.2
	12.3	8.4	13.4	8.9				15.7	16.0
	.0	2.6	3.0	5.0				5.1	6.6
% Profit Before Taxes/Total Assets	11.2	10.3	12.1	8.1				13.8	12.0
	3.3	3.4	5.0	3.2				6.0	5.6
	−3.0	.8	.9	1.9				1.7	1.8
Sales/Net Fixed Assets	186.0	84.3	64.4	47.5				75.5	66.6
	83.6	32.1	32.7	23.0				31.9	32.5
	21.9	16.7	14.5	8.3				17.9	17.1
Sales/Total Assets	5.2	3.6	3.1	2.6				3.5	3.3
	3.7	3.0	2.4	2.1				2.7	2.6
	2.8	2.5	1.9	1.4				2.1	2.0
% Depr., Dep., Amort./Sales	(12) .4	(50) .4	(107) .5	(39) .5				(265) .4	(229) .4
	.5	.8	.9	1.1				.8	.8
	.9	1.3	1.5	1.7				1.2	1.2
% Officers', Directors', Owners' Comp/Sales		(31) 3.1	(52) 1.7	(11) 1.5				(134) 2.4	(115) 2.0
		5.4	2.9	1.9				4.2	3.7
		13.7	5.7	5.1				7.2	7.6
Net Sales ($)	16637M	251864M	1468104M	1783904M	960536M	668019M		5267342M	5182655M
Total Assets ($)	4412M	83157M	555272M	873097M	553753M	172472M		2189964M	2145307M

M = $ thousand   MM = $ million
See Pages 11 through 18 for Explanation of Ratios and Data

Comparative Historical Data | Current Data Sorted By Sales

Hist 4/1/00-3/31/01 ALL	Hist 4/1/01-3/31/02 ALL	Hist 4/1/02-3/31/03 ALL	Type of Statement	0-1MM	1-3MM	3-5MM	5-10MM	10-25MM	25MM & OVER
35	31	45	Unqualified		1		6	12	26
71	65	74	Reviewed		3	10	24	26	11
91	92	45	Compiled	3	11	10	13	8	
19	24	22	Tax Returns	3	8	8	3		
76	72	59	Other	1	4	14	10	11	19
					48 (4/1-9/30/02)		197 (10/1/02-3/31/03)		
292	284	245	NUMBER OF STATEMENTS	7	27	42	56	57	56
%	%	%	**ASSETS**	%	%	%	%	%	%
5.2	6.1	6.1	Cash & Equivalents		11.5	5.3	7.4	3.7	4.6
29.1	28.5	29.0	Trade Receivables (net)		28.7	25.2	29.7	30.6	30.3
44.4	44.6	43.2	Inventory		38.7	45.9	43.2	43.2	42.2
1.8	1.5	2.4	All Other Current		1.1	3.1	2.4	3.3	1.9
80.5	80.6	80.7	Total Current		80.0	79.5	82.7	80.8	79.0
11.5	12.6	12.4	Fixed Assets (net)		10.8	12.0	12.8	13.8	12.2
2.2	1.7	2.3	Intangibles (net)		3.1	4.4	1.5	.9	2.5
5.8	5.0	4.6	All Other Non-Current		6.1	4.1	2.9	4.4	6.3
100.0	100.0	100.0	Total		100.0	100.0	100.0	100.0	100.0
			LIABILITIES						
17.8	15.5	16.2	Notes Payable-Short Term		11.8	14.2	18.7	19.4	14.7
2.7	2.8	3.2	Cur. Mat.-L/T/D		4.3	2.8	2.0	3.5	3.3
19.4	18.4	17.3	Trade Payables		20.3	17.1	13.6	17.5	18.0
.3	.2	.2	Income Taxes Payable		.0	.3	.3	.3	.0
7.8	8.2	6.6	All Other Current		8.2	4.3	7.4	7.0	6.9
47.9	45.1	43.4	Total Current		44.7	38.6	41.9	47.7	43.0
9.4	11.2	10.3	Long Term Debt		15.4	11.2	12.6	5.9	8.2
.1	.1	.2	Deferred Taxes		.2	.2	.1	.2	.4
3.3	3.6	4.4	All Other Non-Current		5.9	3.5	4.5	4.2	3.0
39.3	39.9	41.6	Net Worth		33.8	46.4	40.9	41.9	45.4
100.0	100.0	100.0	Total Liabilities & Net Worth		100.0	100.0	100.0	100.0	100.0
			INCOME DATA						
100.0	100.0	100.0	Net Sales		100.0	100.0	100.0	100.0	100.0
32.3	32.0	32.9	Gross Profit		38.0	34.9	35.8	29.2	29.6
28.9	28.8	29.6	Operating Expenses		35.6	31.1	32.4	25.9	25.7
3.4	3.2	3.3	Operating Profit		2.4	3.8	3.4	3.2	3.8
.9	.8	.6	All Other Expenses (net)		.5	.8	.5	.4	.8
2.5	2.4	2.7	Profit Before Taxes		1.9	3.0	2.9	2.9	3.0
			RATIOS						
2.5	2.6	3.0	Current		3.2	3.8	3.1	2.6	2.7
1.7	1.9	1.9			2.1	2.3	1.9	1.6	1.9
1.3	1.4	1.4			1.3	1.6	1.4	1.4	1.4
1.2	1.2	1.4	Quick		1.8	1.6	1.5	1.0	1.3
(291) .7	.7	.8			1.0	1.0	.8	.7	.8
.4	.5	.5			.6	.5	.6	.4	.4
28 12.9	27 13.6	31 11.7	Sales/Receivables		24 14.9	32 11.3	31 11.8	32 11.6	34 10.7
40 9.1	37 10.0	40 9.1			35 10.4	37 10.0	39 9.5	43 8.4	44 8.3
51 7.1	48 7.6	50 7.4			48 7.6	47 7.8	46 7.9	50 7.2	50 7.4
57 6.4	55 6.7	58 6.3	Cost of Sales/Inventory		48 7.6	69 5.3	63 5.8	53 6.9	53 6.9
91 4.0	94 3.9	93 3.9			87 4.2	108 3.4	86 4.2	73 5.0	92 4.0
148 2.5	147 2.5	142 2.6			126 2.9	154 2.4	132 2.8	139 2.6	143 2.5
20 18.0	20 18.7	17 20.9	Cost of Sales/Payables		18 20.2	15 24.5	14 26.4	18 20.4	19 19.2
34 10.7	30 12.0	30 12.0			38 9.6	28 12.8	24 14.9	31 11.7	33 11.1
51 7.1	48 7.6	46 7.9			61 6.0	58 6.2	38 9.5	48 7.6	48 7.7
5.2	5.0	4.4	Sales/Working Capital		3.4	4.0	4.7	5.6	4.3
8.2	7.3	7.1			7.4	5.6	7.3	8.7	7.0
14.1	13.3	12.0			19.9	8.4	12.2	12.5	12.1
6.7	5.8	8.0	EBIT/Interest		7.2	7.0	9.5	12.0	9.2
(268) 2.8	(262) 2.4	(225) 3.3			(25) 1.7	(40) 3.0	(51) 3.4	(51) 3.3	(51) 4.0
1.1	1.2	1.5			−.5	1.2	1.4	1.6	2.1
7.3	8.4	4.7	Net Profit + Depr., Dep., Amort./Cur. Mat. L/T/D				4.9	8.2	8.4
(84) 3.1	(75) 1.9	(80) 1.3					(24) 1.3	(24) 1.7	(18) 2.7
.8	.7	.6					.9	.4	.6
.1	.1	.1	Fixed/Worth		.1	.1	.1	.1	.1
.2	.3	.2			.2	.2	.3	.3	.2
.6	.6	.6			22.6	.4	.7	.5	.7
.7	.7	.7	Debt/Worth		.8	.5	.7	.8	.7
1.6	1.6	1.4			2.9	1.0	1.6	1.4	1.3
3.6	3.4	3.2			88.2	3.1	3.1	2.7	3.1
27.7	28.4	25.7	% Profit Before Taxes/Tangible Net Worth		27.3	32.6	24.8	25.5	28.7
(272) 13.3	(269) 10.9	(227) 10.6			(21) 12.3	(39) 5.9	(52) 11.4	(54) 12.9	12.9
2.0	2.4	3.6			−2.0	1.5	3.0	5.1	6.8
11.8	9.8	10.2	% Profit Before Taxes/Total Assets		10.1	8.1	10.6	12.4	11.0
4.2	4.1	4.5			2.3	2.8	4.7	4.5	5.7
.5	.7	1.0			−1.9	.7	1.2	1.8	2.8
64.9	62.5	69.2	Sales/Net Fixed Assets		98.2	79.4	68.8	47.9	51.6
30.1	30.5	30.6			31.4	23.4	32.1	25.7	33.6
17.0	14.9	16.0			21.1	11.4	15.9	11.8	19.5
3.2	3.3	3.2	Sales/Total Assets		3.6	2.9	3.3	3.2	3.2
2.6	2.6	2.6			2.9	2.5	2.7	2.6	2.4
2.0	2.0	1.9			1.8	1.8	2.0	1.9	1.7
.4	.5	.5	% Depr., Dep., Amort./Sales		.5	.4	.4	.6	.5
(261) .8	(242) .8	(216) .9			(21) .8	(34) 1.0	(50) .8	(54) .9	(52) .8
1.4	1.5	1.5			1.4	1.8	1.3	1.5	1.4
2.5	2.4	1.7	% Officers', Directors', Owners' Comp/Sales		8.1	1.8	2.6	1.2	1.6
(129) 4.5	(135) 4.0	(102) 3.9			(12) 13.7	(22) 3.9	(29) 4.2	(22) 1.6	(13) 2.0
8.9	7.0	8.1			16.8	7.7	9.1	3.3	4.9
6071706M	6055185M	5149064M	Net Sales ($)	4643M	53637M	165073M	392444M	892765M	3640502M
2509039M	2506478M	2242163M	Total Assets ($)	3213M	21903M	80961M	163738M	373188M	1599160M

© RMA 2003   M = $ thousand   MM = $ million
See Pages 11 through 18 for Explanation of Ratios and Data

Current Data Sorted By Assets — Comparative Historical Data

						Type of Statement		
	12	17	29	3	1	Unqualified	77	73
1	28	89	17	2		Reviewed	132	138
6	26	25	3			Compiled	86	89
7	8	7				Tax Returns	17	15
7	16	24	14	4	1	Other	82	73
	60 (4/1-9/30/02)			287 (10/1/02-3/31/03)			4/1/98-3/31/99	4/1/99-3/31/00
0-500M	500M-2MM	2-10MM	10-50MM	50-100MM	100-250MM		ALL	ALL
21	90	162	63	9	2	NUMBER OF STATEMENTS	394	388
%	%	%	%	%	%	**ASSETS**	%	%
17.3	7.1	4.8	4.6			Cash & Equivalents	6.4	5.4
25.5	32.9	34.2	32.1			Trade Receivables (net)	33.4	33.6
29.0	41.3	41.4	39.0			Inventory	39.6	38.9
.3	2.3	3.2	3.4			All Other Current	1.7	2.2
72.1	83.6	83.6	79.2			Total Current	81.1	80.1
20.3	11.1	10.4	12.6			Fixed Assets (net)	12.6	11.8
.5	.9	1.4	3.0			Intangibles (net)	1.2	2.3
7.1	4.4	4.5	5.2			All Other Non-Current	5.1	5.8
100.0	100.0	100.0	100.0			Total	100.0	100.0
						LIABILITIES		
13.3	13.5	17.6	23.2			Notes Payable-Short Term	15.9	14.8
3.5	3.4	2.6	1.7			Cur. Mat.-L/T/D	2.1	2.0
14.0	23.7	20.5	17.9			Trade Payables	23.5	23.2
.1	.4	.3	.2			Income Taxes Payable	.4	.3
12.0	12.9	11.2	8.8			All Other Current	7.3	8.9
43.0	53.9	52.2	51.9			Total Current	49.1	49.2
14.9	8.6	6.6	6.2			Long Term Debt	8.3	8.3
.0	.2	.2	.1			Deferred Taxes	.3	.3
4.2	2.6	2.5	3.5			All Other Non-Current	4.2	3.9
37.8	34.7	38.5	38.2			Net Worth	38.1	38.3
100.0	100.0	100.0	100.0			Total Liabilities & Net Worth	100.0	100.0
						INCOME DATA		
100.0	100.0	100.0	100.0			Net Sales	100.0	100.0
40.2	28.9	27.9	26.2			Gross Profit	27.2	26.8
37.9	27.5	25.9	23.2			Operating Expenses	24.5	24.5
2.3	1.4	1.9	2.9			Operating Profit	2.7	2.3
.2	-.4	.2	.3			All Other Expenses (net)	.2	-.3
2.1	1.8	1.7	2.7			Profit Before Taxes	2.5	2.5
						RATIOS		
4.9	2.4	2.1	2.2				2.4	2.5
1.8	1.6	1.5	1.4			Current	1.6	1.7
1.0	1.2	1.3	1.2				1.3	1.2
3.1	1.1	1.0	1.1				1.2	1.2
1.3	.8	.7	.6			Quick	.8	.8
.5	.5	.5	.5				.6	.5
8 43.1	28 13.0	37 9.8	38 9.7				34 10.7	34 10.7
19 18.9	37 9.8	44 8.4	44 8.3			Sales/Receivables	42 8.8	44 8.4
33 11.2	48 7.6	54 6.7	52 7.0				51 7.2	51 7.1
10 38.0	43 8.6	49 7.5	57 6.4				46 7.9	48 7.7
33 10.9	70 5.2	80 4.6	77 4.7			Cost of Sales/Inventory	72 5.1	73 5.0
70 5.2	110 3.3	111 3.3	105 3.5				99 3.7	103 3.6
0 UND	27 13.7	24 15.4	25 14.8				26 14.0	26 14.1
17 21.3	36 10.1	34 10.9	32 11.4			Cost of Sales/Payables	37 10.0	39 9.4
29 12.7	56 6.5	47 7.7	44 8.4				51 7.1	55 6.6
6.2	6.2	5.9	6.2				5.7	5.3
15.5	9.8	9.6	10.7			Sales/Working Capital	9.3	8.8
NM	21.0	15.6	22.3				17.3	18.6
14.3	10.0	8.4	7.7				8.0	7.1
(20) 5.0	(79) 3.6	(153) 3.0	(60) 3.4			EBIT/Interest	(369) 3.3	(361) 3.3
1.1	1.5	1.6	1.4				1.7	1.6
	7.0	8.1	9.5				8.3	7.2
	(18) 1.6	(66) 2.9	(34) 4.3			Net Profit + Depr., Dep., Amort./Cur. Mat. L /T/D	(144) 3.0	(138) 3.2
	.4	.9	1.5				1.4	1.6
.1	.1	.1	.2				.1	.1
.4	.2	.2	.3			Fixed/Worth	.3	.2
NM	.5	.5	.6				.6	.6
.3	.9	.9	1.0				.8	.8
1.8	1.6	2.0	1.9			Debt/Worth	1.7	1.8
NM	4.3	3.4	3.9				3.7	3.6
88.9	25.9	23.1	29.2				31.9	32.1
(16) 32.4	(83) 10.2	(155) 10.2	(58) 14.3			% Profit Before Taxes/Tangible Net Worth	(368) 15.1	(358) 14.6
9.4	4.3	3.1	7.1				5.8	5.6
31.7	10.7	7.2	10.5				10.4	11.1
8.1	4.0	4.0	4.3			% Profit Before Taxes/Total Assets	5.2	5.0
1.6	1.1	.9	1.4				2.1	1.7
213.2	95.1	79.6	42.4				56.7	62.0
37.7	37.5	38.5	25.3			Sales/Net Fixed Assets	29.4	35.2
16.6	19.4	19.7	12.8				16.7	17.7
6.0	3.6	3.2	3.1				3.5	3.3
4.4	3.1	2.6	2.6			Sales/Total Assets	2.8	2.8
2.8	2.4	2.1	2.0				2.3	2.1
.3	.4	.4	.5				.5	.4
(14) 1.2	(74) .7	(145) .7	(62) .8			% Depr., Dep., Amort./Sales	(356) .8	(363) .7
2.5	1.3	1.1	1.1				1.2	1.1
3.2	2.5	1.6	.9				1.5	1.5
(13) 8.6	(39) 5.0	(85) 2.7	(17) 1.3			% Officers', Directors', Owners' Comp/Sales	(175) 3.0	(174) 3.4
15.3	7.4	5.1					5.6	6.1
26415M	332169M	1990610M	3376045M	1666149M	853473M	Net Sales ($)	8913278M	8807761M
6009M	111755M	734617M	1311360M	607117M	376814M	Total Assets ($)	3428328M	3401052M

M = $ thousand   MM = $ million
See Pages 11 through 18 for Explanation of Ratios and Data

Comparative Historical Data | Current Data Sorted By Sales

			Type of Statement						
53	54	62	Unqualified		7	4	8	15	28
110	85	137	Reviewed	2	6	17	40	51	21
110	95	60	Compiled	2	15	14	13	14	2
17	14	22	Tax Returns	3	8	5	2	4	
78	93	66	Other	3	11	6	16	11	19

					60 (4/1-9/30/02)		287 (10/1/02-3/31/03)		
4/1/00-3/31/01 ALL	4/1/01-3/31/02 ALL	4/1/02-3/31/03 ALL		0-1MM	1-3MM	3-5MM	5-10MM	10-25MM	25MM & OVER
368	341	347	**NUMBER OF STATEMENTS**	10	47	46	79	95	70
%	%	%	**ASSETS**	%	%	%	%	%	%
5.5	6.3	6.0	Cash & Equivalents	18.2	8.7	8.8	5.7	4.7	2.9
35.2	33.9	32.9	Trade Receivables (net)	12.8	31.0	28.7	32.0	37.1	34.9
38.9	38.3	40.1	Inventory	25.7	38.3	47.2	40.7	39.3	39.2
1.5	1.8	2.9	All Other Current	.6	3.1	1.0	2.8	3.5	3.5
81.1	80.2	81.9	Total Current	57.3	81.0	85.7	81.3	84.6	80.6
11.9	12.9	11.8	Fixed Assets (net)	32.0	13.5	8.7	11.8	9.8	12.7
2.0	2.1	1.5	Intangibles (net)	.8	.3	2.0	1.4	1.4	2.5
4.9	4.8	4.8	All Other Non-Current	9.9	5.3	3.6	5.5	4.3	4.3
100.0	100.0	100.0	Total	100.0	100.0	100.0	100.0	100.0	100.0
			LIABILITIES						
15.9	16.2	17.2	Notes Payable-Short Term	17.8	10.4	15.9	15.5	18.9	22.2
3.0	2.6	2.9	Cur. Mat.-L/T/D	4.5	4.2	2.8	2.7	2.1	3.1
23.6	21.3	20.6	Trade Payables	7.5	21.3	21.2	19.4	22.2	20.8
.4	.5	.3	Income Taxes Payable	.2	.3	.1	.4	.2	.3
8.3	9.1	11.1	All Other Current	13.6	10.2	13.5	12.7	10.9	8.4
51.2	49.7	52.2	Total Current	43.6	46.5	53.6	50.7	54.4	54.9
8.3	8.2	7.8	Long Term Debt	26.8	9.5	8.2	7.8	5.6	6.7
.3	.3	.2	Deferred Taxes	.0	.3	.2	.2	.2	.3
3.9	3.6	2.9	All Other Non-Current	7.4	2.7	1.7	3.4	2.7	2.9
36.3	38.2	36.9	Net Worth	22.2	41.0	36.3	37.8	37.2	35.3
100.0	100.0	100.0	Total Liabilities & Net Worth	100.0	100.0	100.0	100.0	100.0	100.0
			INCOME DATA						
100.0	100.0	100.0	Net Sales	100.0	100.0	100.0	100.0	100.0	100.0
27.3	28.1	28.5	Gross Profit	48.8	31.8	28.5	29.0	26.9	24.6
25.0	25.7	26.5	Operating Expenses	48.5	29.4	28.2	26.9	24.8	22.2
2.2	2.4	1.9	Operating Profit	.3	2.4	.3	2.1	2.1	2.4
.5	.3	.1	All Other Expenses (net)	.1	-.5	.7	-.2	-.1	.6
1.7	2.1	1.9	Profit Before Taxes	.2	2.9	-.4	2.3	2.2	1.8
			RATIOS						
2.2	2.4	2.2		3.4	3.2	2.5	2.3	2.0	2.1
1.6	1.6	1.5	Current	1.6	1.8	1.6	1.5	1.5	1.4
1.3	1.2	1.2		.6	1.3	1.2	1.3	1.3	1.2
1.1	1.2	1.1		3.0	1.5	1.1	1.0	1.1	1.0
.8	.8	.7	Quick	.5	.8	.8	.8	.7	.7
.6	.5	.5		.2	.4	.4	.5	.5	.5
35	10.5	33	10.9	34	10.8		Sales/Receivables	0 UND	27 13.6	26 14.3	35 10.4	38 9.5	37 9.7

35	10.5	33	10.9	34	10.8	Sales/Receivables	0	UND	27	13.6	26	14.3	35	10.4	38	9.5	37	9.7
42	8.6	42	8.7	41	8.8		8	43.1	34	10.7	37	9.9	42	8.7	44	8.3	44	8.3
54	6.8	52	7.0	51	7.2		20	18.5	47	7.7	49	7.5	50	7.3	53	6.8	52	7.0
44	8.3	41	8.9	48	7.7	Cost of Sales/Inventory	0	UND	34	10.8	50	7.4	49	7.5	43	8.4	53	6.8
72	5.1	73	5.0	73	5.0		31	11.7	74	4.9	86	4.3	72	5.1	74	4.9	67	5.4
100	3.7	106	3.4	108	3.4		115	3.2	139	2.6	137	2.7	111	3.3	105	3.5	86	4.3
25	14.7	24	15.1	24	15.5	Cost of Sales/Payables	0	UND	22	16.9	22	16.5	25	14.3	24	15.4	25	14.7
38	9.7	35	10.4	33	11.1		11	31.8	33	11.1	35	10.4	32	11.4	34	10.8	36	10.3
50	7.3	49	7.4	48	7.6		41	8.9	59	6.2	51	7.1	47	7.7	46	8.0	46	8.0

5.7	5.7	6.0	Sales/Working Capital	10.8	4.2	4.8	5.8	6.5	6.9
10.2	9.5	10.0		32.6	8.7	9.1	9.9	10.1	12.2
19.8	18.7	19.6		-12.0	16.6	20.7	17.6	17.8	24.1
(339) 5.6	(309) 6.3	(321) 9.3	EBIT/Interest		15.4	4.1	8.5	9.0	8.6
2.3	2.6	3.3		(44)	7.1	(40) 1.8	(72) 2.9	(90) 3.4	(66) 3.6
1.3	1.3	1.5			2.0	.9	1.6	1.7	1.5
(109) 5.9	(98) 8.8	(125) 8.6	Net Profit + Depr., Dep., Amort./Cur. Mat. L/T/D				8.3	8.7	9.6
2.1	2.5	3.0				(25) 3.2	(41) 2.6	(40) 4.3	
1.2	1.1	1.1				.9	1.0	1.6	
.1	.1	.1	Fixed/Worth	.2	.1	.0	.1	.1	.2
.3	.3	.3		2.9	.2	.2	.2	.2	.3
.6	.6	.6		-2.7	.5	.6	.5	.4	.6
.8	.7	.9	Debt/Worth	1.0	.4	.7	.8	1.0	1.1
1.9	1.7	1.9		3.8	1.2	1.6	1.7	2.1	2.1
4.0	4.2	3.8		-12.5	3.2	8.1	3.4	3.6	3.9
(340) 30.3	(314) 25.9	(321) 26.1	% Profit Before Taxes/Tangible Net Worth		37.7	11.6	21.5	26.4	27.7
12.6	13.0	11.6		(42)	15.5	(43) 7.3	(74) 9.9	(91) 11.0	(65) 14.5
3.3	3.7	4.1			5.9	.1	4.0	3.2	7.6
9.5	10.1	9.5	% Profit Before Taxes/Total Assets	25.2	14.8	4.5	10.0	7.0	10.5
4.1	4.8	4.1		5.8	7.2	2.3	4.1	4.0	4.3
.7	.8	1.0		-1.6	2.9	.0	1.3	1.0	1.5
63.8	68.4	67.5	Sales/Net Fixed Assets	170.2	72.3	124.0	86.4	62.3	50.3
33.0	30.5	33.9		22.3	30.8	49.4	34.6	38.2	28.7
17.2	16.3	18.3		5.4	15.1	21.0	17.3	19.5	17.6
3.5	3.4	3.4	Sales/Total Assets	6.2	4.0	3.4	3.5	3.3	3.4
2.9	2.8	2.8		3.1	2.8	2.9	2.8	2.7	2.8
2.3	2.3	2.2		2.4	2.0	2.0	2.1	2.3	2.3
(313) .4	(281) .5	(305) .4	% Depr., Dep., Amort./Sales		.4	.4	.4	.4	.5
.7	.8	.7		(36)	.9	(38) .7	(68) .7	(88) .7	(69) .7
1.1	1.3	1.2			2.0	1.2	1.3	1.0	.9
(170) 1.6	(154) 1.6	(158) 1.7	% Officers', Directors', Owners' Comp/Sales		3.1	1.7	2.0	1.6	.9
3.2	3.2	3.3		(20)	8.0	(29) 4.5	(39) 3.6	(44) 2.4	(22) 1.7
5.8	6.3	6.5			12.8	6.7	6.4	3.7	3.4
7623907M	8816414M	8244861M	Net Sales ($)	6661M	96202M	177996M	564421M	1501224M	5898357M
3141044M	3166708M	3147672M	Total Assets ($)	2919M	41635M	73033M	220354M	609540M	2200191M

M = $ thousand   MM = $ million
See Pages 11 through 18 for Explanation of Ratios and Data

Current Data Sorted By Assets   Comparative Historical Data

	0-500M	500M-2MM	2-10MM	10-50MM	50-100MM	100-250MM	Type of Statement	4/1/98-3/31/99 ALL	4/1/99-3/31/00 ALL
	1	7	16	21	4	2	Unqualified	54	59
	1	17	43	6	1		Reviewed	77	77
	4	24	10	2			Compiled	68	62
	6	8	5			2	Tax Returns	11	9
	5	15	21	11	2		Other	40	59
		50 (4/1-9/30/02)		184 (10/1/02-3/31/03)					
NUMBER OF STATEMENTS	17	71	95	40	7	4		250	266
ASSETS %	%	%	%	%	%	%		%	%
Cash & Equivalents	12.3	6.3	6.4	3.4				7.4	6.0
Trade Receivables (net)	34.0	42.6	41.2	37.5				39.7	39.5
Inventory	27.0	31.8	35.4	34.9				34.3	34.4
All Other Current	4.9	2.3	3.0	3.4				2.1	2.0
Total Current	78.2	83.0	85.9	79.2				83.5	82.0
Fixed Assets (net)	14.0	10.0	9.7	11.9				10.6	11.0
Intangibles (net)	5.3	1.7	.4	2.4				1.9	2.0
All Other Non-Current	2.5	5.3	4.0	6.5				4.1	5.0
Total	100.0	100.0	100.0	100.0				100.0	100.0
LIABILITIES									
Notes Payable-Short Term	28.8	17.6	16.8	22.3				17.3	17.0
Cur. Mat.-L/T/D	1.9	3.0	2.6	2.6				2.5	2.2
Trade Payables	22.5	26.5	22.1	15.9				22.7	22.8
Income Taxes Payable	.0	.2	.2	.2				.2	.4
All Other Current	12.8	8.9	10.8	10.6				10.9	9.2
Total Current	66.1	56.1	52.5	51.6				53.6	51.5
Long Term Debt	20.0	8.6	6.9	8.5				6.5	7.7
Deferred Taxes	.0	.3	.4	.0				.2	.2
All Other Non-Current	9.5	3.1	4.7	3.7				2.5	3.7
Net Worth	4.4	32.0	35.4	36.3				37.3	36.9
Total Liabilities & Net Worth	100.0	100.0	100.0	100.0				100.0	100.0
INCOME DATA									
Net Sales	100.0	100.0	100.0	100.0				100.0	100.0
Gross Profit	37.0	28.5	25.9	23.8				25.8	28.3
Operating Expenses	36.0	26.2	23.7	21.0				23.4	25.0
Operating Profit	1.0	2.3	2.2	2.8				2.4	3.3
All Other Expenses (net)	.4	.2	.1	.6				−.1	.4
Profit Before Taxes	.6	2.2	2.1	2.3				2.5	2.9
RATIOS									
Current	2.4	2.1	2.0	2.0				2.2	2.2
	1.3	1.5	1.5	1.5				1.6	1.6
	.9	1.1	1.3	1.2				1.2	1.3
Quick	1.6	1.3	1.2	1.1				1.3	1.3
	.7	.9	.8	.8				.9	.9
	.4	.6	.6	.5				.6	.6
Sales/Receivables	4 103.0	32 11.4	38 9.5	40 9.2				36 10.2	34 10.7
	33 11.2	43 8.4	48 7.6	50 7.4				46 7.9	46 8.0
	46 7.9	63 5.8	60 6.1	56 6.5				58 6.3	60 6.0
Cost of Sales/Inventory	6 57.1	14 26.0	30 12.3	44 8.4				28 13.0	28 13.3
	19 18.9	51 7.2	68 5.4	66 5.5				61 5.9	60 6.0
	54 6.8	97 3.8	86 4.2	91 4.0				93 3.9	97 3.8
Cost of Sales/Payables	0 UND	24 15.1	21 17.2	14 27.0				20 18.4	21 17.7
	30 12.1	40 9.1	34 10.6	26 14.2				33 11.0	34 10.7
	57 6.4	57 6.4	51 7.2	36 10.1				53 6.9	52 7.0
Sales/Working Capital	10.4	6.7	6.3	6.3				6.3	6.0
	25.1	11.5	9.0	10.7				10.1	10.6
	UND	30.5	16.4	20.4				20.1	19.3
EBIT/Interest	(12) 1.2	(69) 11.6	(90) 9.8	(39) 6.1				(227) 9.1	(243) 9.1
	−2.2	2.1	3.5	3.6				3.2	3.2
	−4.4	1.3	1.4	1.4				1.6	1.6
Net Profit + Depr., Dep., Amort./Cur. Mat. L/T/D		(15) 5.8	(33) 9.2	(17) 5.6				(95) 8.9	(83) 8.6
		1.6	2.2	2.6				4.0	3.1
		.4	1.3	.0				1.6	1.2
Fixed/Worth	.0	.1	.1	.1				.1	.1
	.4	.3	.2	.3				.2	.2
	−.3	.7	.5	.6				.5	.6
Debt/Worth	1.5	1.0	1.0	1.1				.9	.9
	5.9	2.1	1.9	2.0				1.9	1.8
	−2.8	5.8	3.9	3.1				3.8	3.6
% Profit Before Taxes/Tangible Net Worth	(11) 33.3	(67) 40.3	(89) 27.6	(38) 28.5				(239) 37.2	(250) 37.6
	4.2	11.1	11.7	16.0				19.2	17.8
	.0	2.1	3.4	3.1				5.9	6.2
% Profit Before Taxes/Total Assets	10.2	9.5	9.9	9.5				12.1	12.7
	.0	2.2	4.3	6.6				5.6	5.7
	−16.1	.5	1.2	1.0				1.8	1.1
Sales/Net Fixed Assets	UND	95.9	109.4	61.8				91.4	88.7
	74.1	40.7	52.7	33.0				43.9	45.4
	18.7	24.0	23.9	15.4				20.5	19.8
Sales/Total Assets	6.9	3.8	3.4	3.1				3.6	3.7
	5.1	3.2	3.0	2.8				2.9	3.0
	3.6	2.6	2.5	2.3				2.3	2.3
% Depr., Dep., Amort./Sales		(59) .4	(89) .4	(38) .4				(221) .4	(233) .4
		.7	.7	.8				.6	.7
		1.2	1.0	1.5				1.0	1.1
% Officers', Directors', Owners' Comp/Sales	(11) 2.9	(40) 2.7	(36) 1.7					(101) 1.8	(98) 2.6
	6.4	4.7	2.9					3.2	4.1
	10.1	6.9	6.1					7.0	7.4
Net Sales ($)	22849M	282133M	1336447M	2171741M	1434433M	2260702M		5355673M	4874451M
Total Assets ($)	4476M	85672M	447381M	816496M	495406M	712997M		2157494M	1819841M

© RMA 2003

M = $ thousand   MM = $ million
See Pages 11 through 18 for Explanation of Ratios and Data

Comparative Historical Data   Current Data Sorted By Sales

			Type of Statement						
41	41	51	Unqualified	1	4	1	7	7	31
60	49	68	Reviewed	1	6	6	25	20	10
67	61	40	Compiled	1	11	13	8	5	2
8	12	21	Tax Returns	1	8	3	4	3	2
59	74	54	Other	2	9	2	14	14	13
4/1/00-3/31/01	4/1/01-3/31/02	4/1/02-3/31/03			50 (4/1-9/30/02)			184 (10/1/02-3/31/03)	
ALL	ALL	ALL		0-1MM	1-3MM	3-5MM	5-10MM	10-25MM	25MM & OVER
235	237	234	**NUMBER OF STATEMENTS**	6	38	25	58	49	58
%	%	%	**ASSETS**	%	%	%	%	%	%
4.7	5.5	6.1	Cash & Equivalents		6.9	10.7	5.9	6.3	3.2
40.4	39.5	39.9	Trade Receivables (net)		33.0	39.9	43.4	44.0	38.4
35.4	35.4	33.7	Inventory		35.4	28.9	31.7	33.8	36.2
2.2	2.5	2.9	All Other Current		3.8	2.5	2.6	2.8	3.2
82.8	82.9	82.6	Total Current		79.2	82.0	83.5	86.9	81.0
10.6	10.4	10.8	Fixed Assets (net)		12.7	12.9	10.7	8.3	11.5
1.7	2.1	1.7	Intangibles (net)		4.7	.3	.6	.2	2.8
4.8	4.6	4.8	All Other Non-Current		3.3	4.8	5.1	4.6	4.6
100.0	100.0	100.0	Total		100.0	100.0	100.0	100.0	100.0
			LIABILITIES						
18.2	18.4	18.6	Notes Payable-Short Term		23.3	11.6	16.5	16.5	21.3
2.6	2.7	2.7	Cur. Mat.-L/T/D		3.2	3.7	2.2	2.1	3.0
23.7	23.1	22.2	Trade Payables		23.2	23.2	26.3	22.6	16.6
.3	.2	.2	Income Taxes Payable		.1	.1	.2	.2	.2
9.9	9.1	10.5	All Other Current		10.9	6.4	10.1	11.3	12.2
54.7	53.6	54.2	Total Current		60.7	45.1	55.2	52.8	53.5
6.9	8.8	9.3	Long Term Debt		13.1	8.4	7.5	6.8	10.3
.3	.2	.3	Deferred Taxes		.2	.6	.4	.2	.1
3.8	2.4	4.2	All Other Non-Current		4.0	5.0	3.6	4.4	3.2
34.4	35.0	32.1	Net Worth		22.0	41.0	33.3	35.9	32.9
100.0	100.0	100.0	Total Liabilities & Net Worth		100.0	100.0	100.0	100.0	100.0
			INCOME DATA						
100.0	100.0	100.0	Net Sales		100.0	100.0	100.0	100.0	100.0
26.9	27.6	27.2	Gross Profit		32.7	26.4	26.7	25.6	24.4
23.6	24.8	24.8	Operating Expenses		30.3	24.5	25.3	23.1	21.5
3.3	2.8	2.3	Operating Profit		2.5	1.8	1.4	2.5	2.9
.5	.4	.3	All Other Expenses (net)		.6	.3	-.1	.1	.6
2.8	2.4	2.0	Profit Before Taxes		1.8	1.6	1.5	2.3	2.3
			RATIOS						
2.0	2.2	2.1	Current		2.3	2.7	2.0	2.0	2.1
1.5	1.5	1.5			1.6	1.9	1.5	1.7	1.5
1.2	1.2	1.2			1.0	1.3	1.2	1.3	1.2
1.2	1.2	1.2	Quick		1.1	1.5	1.3	1.3	1.1
.8	.9	.8			.7	1.1	.8	.9	.7
.6	.5	.6			.5	.8	.6	.7	.6
36 10.0	36 10.2	35 10.3	Sales/Receivables	26 14.2	26 14.1	38 9.6	40 9.1	39 9.4	
45 8.1	44 8.3	44 8.2		37 9.8	39 9.3	50 7.3	49 7.4	44 8.2	
60 6.1	57 6.4	59 6.2		56 6.6	60 6.1	60 6.1	63 5.8	55 6.6	
30 12.1	27 13.6	28 13.2	Cost of Sales/Inventory	18 20.0	15 23.9	21 17.0	29 12.5	42 8.8	
58 6.3	62 5.9	60 6.1		57 6.4	42 8.7	48 7.5	66 5.5	65 5.6	
94 3.9	95 3.9	88 4.2		101 3.6	83 4.4	86 4.2	82 4.4	84 4.3	
23 15.9	21 17.5	19 18.8	Cost of Sales/Payables	20 17.9	20 18.7	24 15.2	22 16.8	13 27.7	
34 10.6	35 10.4	34 10.8		39 9.3	30 12.0	39 9.3	33 11.1	23 15.9	
51 7.1	54 6.7	51 7.2		62 5.9	52 7.0	56 6.5	46 8.0	37 9.9	
6.5	6.0	6.7	Sales/Working Capital		6.8	5.4	7.1	6.1	7.3
10.3	10.4	10.7			13.2	7.4	12.1	9.1	10.7
18.2	18.8	21.7			999.8	15.5	22.1	14.9	21.8
(219) 8.4	(216) 10.1	(221) 7.6	EBIT/Interest	(35) 7.3	(24) 8.2	(56) 6.5	(46) 13.7	(57) 7.6	
2.9	3.0	3.0		1.7	2.0	2.8	3.7	4.1	
1.4	1.4	1.3		-1.2	1.1	1.3	1.3	1.4	
(82) 11.1	(66) 10.0	(72) 8.9	Net Profit + Depr., Dep., Amort./Cur. Mat. L/T/D			(22) 5.4	(16) 9.8	(24) 19.9	
2.9	2.7	2.2				2.0	2.4	3.9	
1.1	1.2	.7				1.1	.3	.6	
.1	.1	.1	Fixed/Worth		.1	.1	.1	.1	.1
.2	.2	.3			.4	.2	.3	.1	.3
.6	.5	.6			3.7	.5	.5	.4	.7
1.1	1.0	1.0	Debt/Worth		1.0	.8	1.2	.8	1.2
2.2	1.9	2.0			4.2	1.3	2.0	2.0	2.1
4.0	4.0	5.5			48.7	2.5	4.7	3.9	5.7
(224) 38.8	(220) 33.3	(213) 30.3	% Profit Before Taxes/Tangible Net Worth	(31) 55.6	23.8	(55) 24.2	(46) 23.7	(52) 31.8	
17.0	14.3	11.7		18.1	8.7	8.1	13.8	20.7	
4.7	5.1	2.8		1.1	.4	2.7	3.1	5.0	
14.0	12.9	9.8	% Profit Before Taxes/Total Assets		12.1	10.9	6.6	10.8	10.8
5.3	4.9	3.7			3.1	1.9	2.6	4.3	6.6
1.4	1.3	.6			-2.6	.1	.8	.9	1.1
103.9	93.9	99.6	Sales/Net Fixed Assets		123.4	113.6	91.1	110.2	70.0
41.2	41.2	41.0			42.4	37.5	37.1	64.8	36.2
21.8	21.6	20.5			17.1	17.5	25.5	23.4	17.1
3.6	3.7	3.6	Sales/Total Assets		4.2	3.6	3.8	3.5	3.4
3.0	2.9	3.0			3.2	3.1	3.1	3.0	2.9
2.4	2.3	2.5			2.1	2.5	2.6	2.5	2.4
(205) .3	(200) .3	(205) .4	% Depr., Dep., Amort./Sales	(25) .4	(22) .5	(55) .4	(47) .4	(54) .4	
.6	.6	.7		.9	.9	.7	.6	.7	
1.1	1.0	1.1		1.2	1.4	1.2	.9	.9	
(92) 2.4	(89) 2.1	(95) 2.0	% Officers', Directors', Owners' Comp/Sales	(23) 2.5	(17) 2.2	(23) 2.6	(20) 1.7	(10) 1.0	
4.2	4.2	4.1		4.6	4.7	4.1	3.6	1.6	
7.7	7.9	7.4		8.1	8.1	5.7	9.8	4.8	
6244865M	5180293M	7508305M	Net Sales ($)	2756M	73784M	98142M	427675M	789647M	6116301M
1897579M	1906642M	2562428M	Total Assets ($)	1631M	25899M	33608M	145151M	283885M	2072254M

M = $ thousand   MM = $ million
See Pages 11 through 18 for Explanation of Ratios and Data

Current Data Sorted By Assets   **Comparative Historical Data**

						Type of Statement		
	1	4		5	1	Unqualified	9	8
1	4	6				Reviewed	14	17
2	7	6				Compiled	12	17
3	2	1				Tax Returns	2	3
2	3	6		3		Other	18	13
	4 (4/1-9/30/02)			53 (10/1/02-3/31/03)			4/1/98-3/31/99	4/1/99-3/31/00
0-500M	500M-2MM	2-10MM	10-50MM	50-100MM	100-250MM		ALL	ALL
8	17	23	8	1		NUMBER OF STATEMENTS	55	58

0-500M	500M-2MM	2-10MM	10-50MM	50-100MM	100-250MM		98-99 ALL	99-00 ALL
%	%	%	%	%	%	**ASSETS**	%	%
	13.4	7.7			D	Cash & Equivalents	5.9	6.5
	34.7	27.6			A	Trade Receivables (net)	33.3	36.2
	29.6	40.9			T	Inventory	37.9	37.1
	1.8	1.1			A	All Other Current	1.7	3.0
	79.5	77.3				Total Current	78.8	82.9
	13.2	14.3			N	Fixed Assets (net)	14.0	11.0
	.7	2.8			O	Intangibles (net)	2.4	3.0
	6.5	5.6			T	All Other Non-Current	4.7	3.1
	100.0	100.0				Total	100.0	100.0
					A	**LIABILITIES**		
	13.7	20.7			V	Notes Payable-Short Term	21.1	16.1
	1.7	1.4			A	Cur. Mat.-L/T/D	1.9	3.4
	24.5	17.0			I	Trade Payables	20.1	36.2
	.5	.4			L	Income Taxes Payable	.1	.6
	12.5	6.2			A	All Other Current	9.4	11.6
	52.9	45.7			B	Total Current	52.5	67.9
	8.5	5.4			L	Long Term Debt	14.4	8.2
	.3	.2			E	Deferred Taxes	.2	.2
	2.4	4.5				All Other Non-Current	4.6	4.8
	35.9	44.3				Net Worth	28.3	18.9
	100.0	100.0				Total Liabilities & Net Worth	100.0	100.0
						INCOME DATA		
	100.0	100.0				Net Sales	100.0	100.0
	27.1	27.0				Gross Profit	26.1	25.1
	26.9	24.6				Operating Expenses	24.0	23.2
	.2	2.4				Operating Profit	2.2	2.0
	−.5	−.1				All Other Expenses (net)	.1	−.2
	.7	2.5				Profit Before Taxes	2.1	2.2
						RATIOS		
	2.1	2.4					2.1	2.2
	1.6	1.7				Current	1.5	1.5
	1.1	1.3					1.2	1.2
	1.6	1.3					1.0	1.1
	.7	.7				Quick	.8	.7
	.6	.5					.6	.5
	28 13.2	27 13.6					29 12.4	31 11.9
	38 9.7	33 11.1				Sales/Receivables	38 9.6	38 9.5
	58 6.3	46 7.9					57 6.4	50 7.4
	11 33.3	54 6.8					36 10.3	27 13.6
	38 9.5	67 5.5				Cost of Sales/Inventory	70 5.2	66 5.5
	93 3.9	118 3.1					109 3.3	104 3.5
	15 24.8	16 22.6					17 21.5	23 16.1
	29 12.4	26 14.0				Cost of Sales/Payables	32 11.2	34 10.7
	66 5.5	44 8.2					44 8.3	54 6.8
	7.1	5.6					5.9	6.6
	9.6	8.8				Sales/Working Capital	10.7	10.4
	38.3	35.2					20.6	29.4
	6.1	13.7					5.5	7.2
	(15) 2.4	(20) 3.9				EBIT/Interest	(52) 3.0	(54) 2.9
	2.0	1.5					1.3	1.2
						Net Profit + Depr., Dep.,	3.2	2.9
						Amort./Cur. Mat. L /T/D	(13) 2.2	(19) 2.2
							.8	1.3
	.2	.1					.1	.2
	.3	.2				Fixed/Worth	.3	.3
	.8	.4					.9	.8
	.9	.8					1.2	1.1
	1.5	1.5				Debt/Worth	2.3	2.1
	4.8	2.2					4.2	4.5
	27.8	33.1				% Profit Before Taxes/Tangible	38.9	36.7
	(16) 7.3	12.7				Net Worth	(50) 16.4	(50) 16.4
	2.6	5.9					4.9	3.1
	5.9	12.9				% Profit Before Taxes/Total	9.7	12.3
	3.4	4.7				Assets	5.1	4.0
	.9	2.2					1.1	.6
	97.0	91.2					72.2	62.8
	36.8	29.2				Sales/Net Fixed Assets	28.3	34.7
	14.9	16.3					15.8	19.8
	4.1	3.3					3.6	3.9
	3.1	2.9				Sales/Total Assets	2.9	3.0
	2.3	2.2					2.1	2.6
	.3	.4					.4	.4
	(15) .7	1.1				% Depr., Dep., Amort./Sales	(49) .8	(52) .8
	1.9	2.1					1.3	1.4
	3.0					% Officers', Directors',	2.4	2.5
	(11) 4.7					Owners' Comp/Sales	(22) 4.3	(28) 4.0
	9.4						7.8	6.5
10570M	85566M	282719M	485732M	161822M		Net Sales ($)	1630364M	1671298M
2596M	23187M	104342M	211243M	52728M		Total Assets ($)	719249M	709462M

(The far-right current-data column is marked: **DATA NOT AVAILABLE**)

M = $ thousand   MM = $ million
See Pages 11 through 18 for Explanation of Ratios and Data

Comparative Historical Data | | **Current Data Sorted By Sales**

Hist 4/1/00-3/31/01 ALL	Hist 4/1/01-3/31/02 ALL	Hist 4/1/02-3/31/03 ALL	Type of Statement	0-1MM	1-3MM	3-5MM	5-10MM	10-25MM	25MM & OVER
12	9	11	Unqualified			1	1	2	7
9	9	11	Reviewed		1	2	3	5	
13	12	15	Compiled	1	2	6	4	2	
3	4	6	Tax Returns		3	1	1	1	
19	18	14	Other	2	1	3	1	4	3
				4 (4/1-9/30/02)		53 (10/1/02-3/31/03)			
56	52	57	**NUMBER OF STATEMENTS**	3	7	13	10	14	10
%	%	%	**ASSETS**	%	%	%	%	%	%
4.8	8.7	9.1	Cash & Equivalents			11.3	13.7	6.3	2.8
35.4	34.3	28.7	Trade Receivables (net)			33.6	30.6	28.4	27.8
37.4	36.8	37.1	Inventory			25.5	39.8	41.5	42.6
3.4	1.3	1.5	All Other Current			2.2	1.0	.9	2.7
81.0	81.1	76.5	Total Current			72.5	85.0	77.1	75.9
12.3	11.7	13.7	Fixed Assets (net)			20.7	7.2	12.3	9.9
1.6	1.4	3.2	Intangibles (net)			.2	4.0	2.4	10.1
5.1	5.9	6.7	All Other Non-Current			6.5	3.8	8.2	4.2
100.0	100.0	100.0	Total			100.0	100.0	100.0	100.0
			LIABILITIES						
19.9	17.6	14.4	Notes Payable-Short Term			17.0	16.1	20.4	9.1
2.7	2.8	2.0	Cur. Mat.-L/T/D			2.3	1.4	.7	3.6
21.6	22.4	20.0	Trade Payables			25.2	14.7	21.3	16.8
.4	.2	.3	Income Taxes Payable			.7	.0	.7	.0
8.7	9.3	8.0	All Other Current			9.3	6.2	7.4	4.9
53.4	52.3	44.8	Total Current			54.5	38.5	50.6	34.4
9.2	7.8	10.0	Long Term Debt			15.6	1.7	2.8	11.8
.1	.1	.2	Deferred Taxes			.1	.2	.1	.2
4.6	4.1	5.9	All Other Non-Current			1.5	4.5	5.7	.3
32.7	35.7	39.2	Net Worth			28.3	55.1	40.8	53.3
100.0	100.0	100.0	Total Liabilities & Net Worth			100.0	100.0	100.0	100.0
			INCOME DATA						
100.0	100.0	100.0	Net Sales			100.0	100.0	100.0	100.0
27.1	27.7	28.6	Gross Profit			24.7	27.8	25.1	24.3
25.0	25.8	26.2	Operating Expenses			24.8	25.7	22.7	20.8
2.1	2.0	2.4	Operating Profit			−.1	2.1	2.4	3.5
.0	.3	.1	All Other Expenses (net)			−1.2	.2	−.1	.5
2.1	1.7	2.2	Profit Before Taxes			1.1	1.9	2.5	3.0
			RATIOS						
2.2	2.2	2.4				1.8	3.7	2.1	3.3
1.5	1.6	1.7	Current			1.4	2.7	1.4	2.2
1.2	1.2	1.3				1.0	1.6	1.3	1.5
1.2	1.3	1.4				1.2	2.4	.8	1.2
.7	.8	(56) .7	Quick			.6	1.4	.6	.8
.5	.5	.6				.6	.7	.6	.6
31 11.8	32 11.4	27 13.7				29 12.5	26 14.0	21 17.4	32 11.6
40 9.2	41 8.9	34 10.8	Sales/Receivables			36 10.0	33 10.9	32 11.4	37 9.8
51 7.2	56 6.5	46 7.9				58 6.3	40 9.2	46 7.9	41 8.8
29 12.5	35 10.5	28 13.3				5 68.6	36 10.1	39 9.4	61 5.9
73 5.0	75 4.8	66 5.5	Cost of Sales/Inventory			38 9.5	57 6.4	72 5.1	90 4.0
112 3.2	111 3.3	104 3.5				85 4.3	121 3.0	108 3.4	106 3.4
19 19.3	24 15.3	18 20.0				23 16.0	12 29.8	16 22.7	20 18.6
32 11.5	32 11.5	29 12.6	Cost of Sales/Payables			29 12.4	18 20.0	29 12.6	32 11.3
48 7.7	55 6.7	44 8.2				79 4.6	29 12.7	45 8.1	43 8.5
5.6	5.6	6.1				8.8	5.3	7.0	4.0
11.3	11.0	9.2	Sales/Working Capital			15.4	7.1	10.7	7.1
27.2	20.7	29.5				NM	8.9	42.2	11.4
4.4	5.5	6.1				4.9		20.9	
(49) 2.5	(47) 3.4	(49) 2.9	EBIT/Interest			2.4	(12)	5.8	
1.3	1.3	1.9				1.7		2.4	
5.6	5.8	6.2	Net Profit + Depr., Dep.,						
(19) 3.2	(17) 2.5	(13) 2.8	Amort./Cur. Mat. L/T/D						
2.0	1.1	.6							
.1	.1	.1				.3	.0	.1	.1
.3	.2	.3	Fixed/Worth			.4	.1	.3	.2
.7	.5	.9				1.4	.2	.5	.9
.8	.8	.6				1.5	.5	.8	.5
2.0	1.8	1.5	Debt/Worth			1.9	.8	2.0	.8
3.8	4.1	4.3				6.3	1.6	2.6	4.7
28.9	22.3	33.8				28.6	19.4	35.9	
(51) 13.4	(49) 9.9	(53) 12.7	% Profit Before Taxes/Tangible Net Worth	(12)	11.3	5.5	14.1	
2.7	2.8	4.9				4.0	2.4	6.4	
10.2	7.5	11.0				7.7	11.0	14.8	11.2
4.9	3.7	4.3	% Profit Before Taxes/Total Assets			3.8	2.5	6.5	5.6
1.0	.8	2.1				1.3	1.4	2.2	2.9
79.9	97.5	92.1				59.5	127.9	84.0	50.5
44.5	36.2	32.7	Sales/Net Fixed Assets			21.9	92.1	26.5	32.7
19.2	15.3	14.7				13.8	26.9	14.8	14.0
3.6	3.7	3.6				3.6	3.8	3.4	3.1
2.9	2.7	2.8	Sales/Total Assets			2.8	3.5	2.8	2.6
2.4	2.1	2.2				2.3	2.5	2.2	2.2
.4	.3	.3				.3		.3	.5
(48) 1.0	(47) .8	(53) 1.0	% Depr., Dep., Amort./Sales	(12)	.6		1.1	1.0
1.4	1.3	2.0				1.8		2.2	1.5
2.0	1.6	1.7	% Officers', Directors',						
(27) 4.5	(23) 3.8	(25) 3.5	Owners' Comp/Sales						
7.8	5.7	5.9							
1345271M	866947M	1026409M	Net Sales ($)	1488M	13001M	49536M	79185M	209576M	673623M
543656M	325725M	394096M	Total Assets ($)	1093M	3932M	21218M	26302M	69042M	272509M

© RMA 2003   M = $ thousand   MM = $ million
See Pages 11 through 18 for Explanation of Ratios and Data

Current Data Sorted By Assets   Comparative Historical Data

						Type of Statement		
	1	19	36	14	24	Unqualified	127	134
	16	37	11	1	1	Reviewed	84	86
6	19	25	5			Compiled	62	58
6	9	6				Tax Returns	20	20
2	12	25	13	8	6	Other	74	72
	41 (4/1-9/30/02)		261 (10/1/02-3/31/03)				4/1/98- 3/31/99	4/1/99- 3/31/00
0-500M	500M-2MM	2-10MM	10-50MM	50-100MM	100-250MM		ALL	ALL
14	57	112	65	23	31	NUMBER OF STATEMENTS	367	370
%	%	%	%	%	%	ASSETS	%	%
18.2	7.3	5.1	3.3	3.1	2.5	Cash & Equivalents	6.2	5.3
13.9	27.5	17.5	14.1	15.5	18.1	Trade Receivables (net)	18.4	18.8
36.7	41.7	48.7	56.1	56.8	45.4	Inventory	49.8	49.9
1.1	1.0	1.8	2.0	1.3	3.1	All Other Current	1.9	2.4
69.8	77.4	73.1	75.4	76.7	69.1	Total Current	76.3	76.4
21.6	15.7	22.1	19.6	18.1	22.2	Fixed Assets (net)	19.0	18.8
2.1	1.7	1.1	.6	.3	.7	Intangibles (net)	.9	1.3
6.5	5.2	3.7	4.4	4.9	8.0	All Other Non-Current	3.7	3.5
100.0	100.0	100.0	100.0	100.0	100.0	Total	100.0	100.0
						LIABILITIES		
29.5	24.8	26.8	36.9	41.2	25.5	Notes Payable-Short Term	27.8	27.1
2.6	4.5	5.9	5.0	4.3	2.8	Cur. Mat.-L/T/D	3.7	4.3
9.5	19.0	13.0	8.0	7.5	14.3	Trade Payables	14.7	15.2
.2	.2	.2	.2	1.1	.3	Income Taxes Payable	.3	.2
6.5	6.7	6.0	5.5	8.2	7.7	All Other Current	10.1	7.5
48.2	55.1	51.9	55.7	62.2	50.6	Total Current	56.6	54.5
18.5	9.4	11.5	11.7	10.5	10.7	Long Term Debt	11.3	12.3
.0	.1	.8	1.3	.9	.7	Deferred Taxes	.5	.4
1.3	3.3	3.7	2.1	1.4	3.0	All Other Non-Current	2.8	2.7
32.0	32.1	32.2	29.2	25.0	35.0	Net Worth	28.9	30.0
100.0	100.0	100.0	100.0	100.0	100.0	Total Liabilities & Net Worth	100.0	100.0
						INCOME DATA		
100.0	100.0	100.0	100.0	100.0	100.0	Net Sales	100.0	100.0
29.4	27.4	27.8	23.0	20.4	22.4	Gross Profit	25.9	24.7
27.8	25.1	25.2	20.2	18.1	19.3	Operating Expenses	21.6	20.5
1.6	2.3	2.6	2.8	2.3	3.1	Operating Profit	4.3	4.1
.7	1.0	.7	1.2	1.7	.9	All Other Expenses (net)	.9	1.2
.9	1.3	1.9	1.6	.6	2.2	Profit Before Taxes	3.4	2.9
						RATIOS		
3.3	2.0	2.0	1.8	1.6	1.7		1.9	1.9
2.0	1.4	1.4	1.3	1.3	1.3	Current	1.4	1.4
1.3	1.0	1.1	1.1	1.0	1.1		1.1	1.1
2.0	1.1	.7	.4	.4	.6		.7	.7
.9	.6	.4	.3	.3	.4	Quick	.4	.4
.3	.3	.2	.2	.2	.3	(366)	.2	.2

												Sales/Receivables				
0	UND	23	16.0	21	17.1	23	15.6	33	10.9	38	9.6		22	16.9	22	16.7
16	23.3	37	9.7	33	11.2	31	11.8	38	9.6	47	7.8		33	11.2	33	11.2
38	9.7	54	6.8	44	8.3	43	8.4	48	7.6	55	6.6		45	8.1	45	8.1

												Cost of Sales/Inventory				
11	32.6	42	8.7	65	5.7	109	3.3	100	3.6	108	3.4		59	6.1	64	5.7
55	6.6	76	4.8	126	2.9	181	2.0	171	2.1	155	2.4		121	3.0	125	2.9
103	3.5	162	2.3	229	1.6	232	1.6	265	1.4	197	1.9		198	1.8	191	1.9

												Cost of Sales/Payables				
0	UND	12	31.1	13	28.3	10	37.3	11	33.9	39	9.3		11	32.3	11	31.9
5	68.0	34	10.6	24	14.9	16	22.3	20	18.5	51	7.2		24	15.0	29	12.7
31	11.9	55	6.6	44	8.3	32	11.3	37	9.9	59	6.1		52	7.0	51	7.1

						Sales/Working Capital		
3.9	5.9	4.2	4.9	4.0	4.9		5.6	5.3
13.7	9.9	8.9	9.2	7.5	8.2		9.8	10.6
84.6	72.4	24.0	15.3	101.4	34.9		22.1	29.8

									EBIT/Interest				
	4.8		4.7		4.1		3.1		4.5		4.1		4.6		4.4
(13)	-.8	(55)	1.9	(109)	1.9		1.8	(22)	2.0	(29)	2.0	(341)	2.4	(352)	2.4
	-2.6		1.0		1.0		1.1		.7		1.4		1.5		1.4

								Net Profit + Depr., Dep., Amort./Cur. Mat. L /T/D				
			3.1		4.5		6.9						6.7		7.8
		(15)	1.0	(46)	2.1	(20)	1.3					(124)	3.4	(109)	2.6
			.1		1.1		.1						1.1		.8

						Fixed/Worth		
.1	.1	.2	.2	.2	.3		.2	.2
.8	.4	.4	.4	.3	.5		.4	.4
1.3	1.3	1.4	1.1	.9	.9		1.0	1.1

						Debt/Worth		
.6	1.2	1.4	1.6	2.2	1.3		1.3	1.4
1.8	2.1	2.6	2.8	2.6	2.0		2.9	2.9
NM	6.7	4.9	5.5	4.3	3.2		4.9	5.5

									% Profit Before Taxes/Tangible Net Worth				
	47.2		25.2		28.8		14.8		15.1		15.6		30.0		29.2
(11)	9.7	(52)	9.0	(111)	8.8	(63)	9.0	(21)	9.2		7.8	(353)	18.1	(351)	17.7
	-12.5		-1.0		.2		3.4		4.1		4.8		8.0		6.1

						% Profit Before Taxes/Total Assets		
16.0	8.1	6.5	4.9	4.7	5.9		8.7	8.4
-1.6	2.5	2.4	2.2	2.6	2.4		4.5	4.4
-5.9	-.3	.0	.1	.0	1.2		1.9	1.3

						Sales/Net Fixed Assets		
91.6	83.3	48.3	35.5	30.2	13.4		49.8	50.3
36.2	21.2	17.8	16.6	15.1	7.9		20.4	20.4
5.4	12.7	5.5	6.6	5.8	4.7		7.4	7.5

						Sales/Total Assets		
6.1	3.2	2.3	1.8	1.8	1.6		2.7	2.6
3.3	2.4	1.6	1.5	1.4	1.4		1.8	1.9
1.7	1.7	1.3	1.2	1.1	1.3		1.4	1.4

									% Depr., Dep., Amort./Sales				
	.6		.6		.7		.6				1.0		.6		.6
(10)	1.1	(45)	1.5	(100)	1.7	(53)	1.4			(17)	1.3	(306)	1.0	(298)	1.1
	2.6		2.5		7.9		4.7				2.6		2.7		2.4

								% Officers', Directors', Owners' Comp/Sales				
			1.8		1.1		.7						1.3		1.3
		(34)	2.9	(44)	2.1	(17)	1.2					(134)	2.7	(131)	2.7
			5.1		5.3								5.8		5.8

13782M	184587M	1064119M	2372715M	2388320M	6786153M	Net Sales ($)	13951938M	14917092M
3441M	72084M	578157M	1527332M	1581967M	4780776M	Total Assets ($)	9391123M	9734278M

© RMA 2003   M = $ thousand   MM = $ million
See Pages 11 through 18 for Explanation of Ratios and Data

Comparative Historical Data | Current Data Sorted By Sales

Type of Statement	4/1/00-3/31/01	4/1/01-3/31/02	4/1/02-3/31/03		0-1MM	1-3MM	3-5MM	5-10MM	10-25MM	25MM & OVER
Unqualified	78	91	94				2	6	16	70
Reviewed	54	68	66			10	9	19	21	7
Compiled	63	73	55		8	15	9	13	9	1
Tax Returns	20	17	21		4	8	3	3	3	
Other	93	98	66		3	5	9	13	14	22
	4/1/00-3/31/01 ALL	4/1/01-3/31/02 ALL	4/1/02-3/31/03 ALL		41 (4/1-9/30/02)		261 (10/1/02-3/31/03)			
NUMBER OF STATEMENTS	308	347	302		15	38	32	54	63	100
ASSETS	%	%	%		%	%	%	%	%	%
Cash & Equivalents	5.0	5.1	5.3		19.3	6.2	5.2	5.8	4.9	2.9
Trade Receivables (net)	19.2	18.6	18.4		13.2	19.9	21.9	19.8	19.1	16.2
Inventory	49.7	49.9	48.7		37.3	41.8	48.4	46.3	50.5	53.3
All Other Current	1.7	2.0	1.7		1.8	1.3	.9	1.2	2.5	2.0
Total Current	75.6	75.7	74.1		71.6	69.3	76.3	73.1	77.0	74.4
Fixed Assets (net)	18.4	17.8	20.0		15.1	25.1	19.5	21.0	19.2	19.0
Intangibles (net)	1.5	2.0	1.0		1.3	1.6	1.5	.4	1.3	.8
All Other Non-Current	4.5	4.5	4.8		12.0	3.9	2.6	5.5	2.5	5.8
Total	100.0	100.0	100.0		100.0	100.0	100.0	100.0	100.0	100.0
LIABILITIES										
Notes Payable-Short Term	28.3	29.0	29.7		34.9	26.1	20.8	29.4	29.3	33.5
Cur. Mat.-L/T/D	4.6	4.6	4.9		1.7	5.6	5.1	4.0	5.8	4.9
Trade Payables	14.2	12.3	12.6		5.0	14.5	19.1	12.0	14.1	10.4
Income Taxes Payable	.3	.2	.3		.2	.2	.1	.1	.3	.4
All Other Current	10.4	7.1	6.4		5.5	5.0	6.2	6.3	6.6	6.9
Total Current	57.8	53.3	53.8		47.4	51.4	51.4	51.7	56.0	56.1
Long Term Debt	11.8	12.4	11.3		20.9	14.5	9.4	10.3	9.6	11.0
Deferred Taxes	.6	.6	.7		.1	.5	.5	.7	.5	1.1
All Other Non-Current	2.2	2.3	2.9		.9	4.4	2.3	5.8	2.0	1.8
Net Worth	27.5	31.4	31.2		30.7	29.1	36.5	31.4	31.8	30.0
Total Liabilities & Net Worth	100.0	100.0	100.0		100.0	100.0	100.0	100.0	100.0	100.0
INCOME DATA										
Net Sales	100.0	100.0	100.0		100.0	100.0	100.0	100.0	100.0	100.0
Gross Profit	25.3	25.0	25.7		37.5	28.2	32.5	28.1	23.5	20.8
Operating Expenses	21.4	22.0	23.1		30.9	27.2	29.1	24.9	21.6	18.4
Operating Profit	3.8	3.0	2.6		6.6	1.0	3.4	3.2	1.9	2.4
All Other Expenses (net)	1.2	1.5	1.0		2.4	.7	.9	1.2	.5	1.2
Profit Before Taxes	2.6	1.5	1.6		4.2	.2	2.6	2.0	1.5	1.2
RATIOS										
Current	1.8	1.9	1.9		3.8	1.9	2.0	2.0	1.6	1.8
Current	1.4	1.4	1.4		2.2	1.3	1.6	1.4	1.3	1.3
Current	1.1	1.2	1.1		1.0	1.0	1.1	1.1	1.1	1.1
Quick	.7	.8	.7		2.7	.9	1.0	.9	.6	.5
Quick	.4	.4	.4		.9	.5	.5	.4	.4	.3
Quick	.2	.2	.2		.2	.2	.3	.3	.2	.2
Sales/Receivables	21 · 17.4	20 · 18.2	25 · 14.7		0 · UND	21 · 17.3	21 · 17.7	25 · 14.8	23 · 16.0	29 · 12.6
Sales/Receivables	34 · 10.9	35 · 10.3	35 · 10.6		31 · 11.7	33 · 10.9	37 · 9.7	33 · 11.2	32 · 11.4	37 · 9.8
Sales/Receivables	48 · 7.6	50 · 7.3	47 · 7.7		53 · 6.8	52 · 7.0	50 · 7.4	44 · 8.3	44 · 8.2	48 · 7.6
Cost of Sales/Inventory	63 · 5.8	65 · 5.6	66 · 5.5		23 · 16.2	42 · 8.7	52 · 7.0	63 · 5.8	62 · 5.8	104 · 3.5
Cost of Sales/Inventory	132 · 2.8	139 · 2.6	131 · 2.8		106 · 3.5	76 · 4.8	104 · 3.5	132 · 2.8	112 · 3.3	164 · 2.2
Cost of Sales/Inventory	202 · 1.8	211 · 1.7	218 · 1.7		166 · 2.2	229 · 1.6	235 · 1.6	201 · 1.8	222 · 1.6	209 · 1.7
Cost of Sales/Payables	11 · 34.4	10 · 37.3	11 · 32.3		0 · UND	6 · 60.5	11 · 34.2	13 · 28.1	13 · 29.0	13 · 28.7
Cost of Sales/Payables	22 · 16.4	22 · 16.8	24 · 15.5		15 · 25.1	35 · 10.6	37 · 9.9	20 · 18.2	20 · 17.9	24 · 15.2
Cost of Sales/Payables	50 · 7.3	46 · 8.0	45 · 8.1		34 · 10.9	65 · 5.6	64 · 5.7	40 · 9.1	44 · 8.4	45 · 8.1
Sales/Working Capital	5.4	4.7	4.7		3.3	5.8	4.5	4.5	4.9	4.9
Sales/Working Capital	9.6	9.4	8.9		4.0	9.3	7.5	9.3	9.4	8.8
Sales/Working Capital	23.6	20.9	22.4		463.5	NM	28.1	20.8	26.5	18.6
EBIT/Interest	4.1	2.7	4.0		4.7	3.0	9.0	4.1	3.2	3.8
EBIT/Interest	(294) 1.9	(327) 1.6	(293) 1.9		(14) 1.7	(37) 1.5	(52) 3.5	(61) 1.8	(97) 2.1	1.9
EBIT/Interest	1.2	1.1	1.0		−1.8	−.7	1.3	.8	1.2	1.2
Net Profit + Depr., Dep., Amort./Cur. Mat. L/T/D	6.0	6.8	4.7				4.7	3.5	7.6	8.0
Net Profit + Depr., Dep., Amort./Cur. Mat. L/T/D	(86) 1.7	(96) 2.2	(91) 1.9			(11) 1.9	(21) 1.8	(28) 2.2	(21) 1.9	1.9
Net Profit + Depr., Dep., Amort./Cur. Mat. L/T/D	.9	1.0	.7				1.0	.8	1.0	.0
Fixed/Worth	.2	.2	.2		.0	.2	.2	.1	.2	.2
Fixed/Worth	.4	.3	.4		.1	.9	.4	.4	.3	.5
Fixed/Worth	1.2	1.1	1.2		1.1	2.8	1.1	1.5	1.1	.9
Debt/Worth	1.4	1.4	1.4		.6	1.4	1.0	1.4	1.4	1.8
Debt/Worth	2.7	2.5	2.5		1.6	2.4	1.9	2.6	2.9	2.5
Debt/Worth	5.2	4.8	4.8		25.4	7.3	4.5	5.6	4.8	4.2
% Profit Before Taxes/Tangible Net Worth	24.6	19.4	20.5		65.7	16.7	42.4	22.8	22.5	15.1
% Profit Before Taxes/Tangible Net Worth	(290) 13.6	(324) 9.9	(289) 8.9		(12) 16.0	(35) 6.2	(30) 15.5	(53) 9.3	(62) 9.1	(97) 8.4
% Profit Before Taxes/Tangible Net Worth	5.2	1.6	1.3		−9.5	−14.2	3.2	−1.3	2.5	3.9
% Profit Before Taxes/Total Assets	7.4	5.6	5.9		12.1	5.7	10.7	6.3	6.4	5.0
% Profit Before Taxes/Total Assets	3.5	2.4	2.3		1.0	1.4	5.0	2.5	2.3	2.3
% Profit Before Taxes/Total Assets	1.0	.4	.1		−7.1	−4.4	.9	−.4	.5	.7
Sales/Net Fixed Assets	45.8	48.5	44.2		UND	41.8	74.3	48.3	51.3	28.9
Sales/Net Fixed Assets	19.7	20.2	16.5		49.8	16.4	18.8	18.4	20.9	13.6
Sales/Net Fixed Assets	7.0	6.9	5.8		4.2	4.4	9.7	5.4	8.3	5.7
Sales/Total Assets	2.5	2.4	2.3		2.0	2.5	2.8	2.9	2.4	1.8
Sales/Total Assets	1.8	1.7	1.6		1.6	1.8	2.2	1.7	1.7	1.5
Sales/Total Assets	1.3	1.3	1.3		.9	1.2	1.1	1.3	1.4	1.3
% Depr., Dep., Amort./Sales	.6	.5	.7			.6	.8	.7	.6	.7
% Depr., Dep., Amort./Sales	(250) 1.1	(275) 1.1	(233) 1.4		(32) 1.9	(26) 1.6	(51) 1.3	(54) 1.1	(61) 1.3	
% Depr., Dep., Amort./Sales	2.4	2.7	3.8			4.3	4.0	6.7	4.1	3.3
% Officers', Directors', Owners' Comp/Sales	1.3	1.2	1.2			2.2	1.3	1.8	.7	.7
% Officers', Directors', Owners' Comp/Sales	(116) 2.7	(116) 2.3	(108) 2.4		(26) 4.4	(15) 2.4	(24) 3.9	(27) 1.2	(11) 1.2	
% Officers', Directors', Owners' Comp/Sales	5.2	4.8	5.1			5.7	4.3	7.0	2.1	2.1
Net Sales ($)	11979638M	15253088M	12809676M		8678M	81439M	126754M	377464M	960968M	11254373M
Total Assets ($)	8238796M	10382354M	8543757M		9136M	51832M	81754M	241491M	567806M	7591738M

© RMA 2003

M = $ thousand   MM = $ million
See Pages 11 through 18 for Explanation of Ratios and Data

Current Data Sorted By Assets   Comparative Historical Data

0-500M	500M-2MM	2-10MM	10-50MM	50-100MM	100-250MM	Type of Statement	4/1/98-3/31/99 ALL	4/1/99-3/31/00 ALL
	5	12	21	1	1	Unqualified	56	59
1	8	50	16			Reviewed	105	104
6	28	53	8			Compiled	132	118
8	12	14	2			Tax Returns	31	41
2	22	53	27	2		Other	125	107
	73 (4/1-9/30/02)		279 (10/1/02-3/31/03)					
17	75	182	74	3	1	**NUMBER OF STATEMENTS**	449	429
%	%	%	%	%	%	**ASSETS**	%	%
14.1	6.4	5.5	4.4			Cash & Equivalents	4.8	5.2
12.2	13.7	14.5	14.7			Trade Receivables (net)	14.7	15.4
50.4	60.4	64.7	58.6			Inventory	61.8	60.2
1.4	1.4	1.8	2.8			All Other Current	2.0	2.0
78.1	82.0	86.5	80.5			Total Current	83.4	82.8
16.9	12.1	9.0	12.0			Fixed Assets (net)	11.1	12.1
.9	.7	.7	1.7			Intangibles (net)	.8	.8
4.1	5.3	3.8	5.8			All Other Non-Current	4.8	4.4
100.0	100.0	100.0	100.0			Total	100.0	100.0
						LIABILITIES		
12.3	25.4	27.9	27.0			Notes Payable-Short Term	27.2	25.8
3.8	3.0	2.0	2.2			Cur. Mat.-L/T/D	3.0	2.9
21.6	15.3	21.5	21.5			Trade Payables	21.2	20.3
.4	.3	.3	.2			Income Taxes Payable	.3	.2
8.3	11.7	8.6	7.2			All Other Current	7.2	8.2
46.4	55.8	60.2	58.1			Total Current	58.9	57.4
14.0	14.8	5.4	8.7			Long Term Debt	8.6	8.4
.0	.1	.1	.4			Deferred Taxes	.2	.1
11.9	4.3	2.4	2.5			All Other Non-Current	2.5	3.2
27.4	25.0	31.9	30.4			Net Worth	29.9	30.8
100.0	100.0	100.0	100.0			Total Liabilities & Net Worth	100.0	100.0
						INCOME DATA		
100.0	100.0	100.0	100.0			Net Sales	100.0	100.0
36.3	26.7	19.8	20.2			Gross Profit	21.3	22.5
35.5	24.0	18.3	17.8			Operating Expenses	19.3	20.9
.8	2.8	1.5	2.5			Operating Profit	2.0	1.6
-.4	1.2	-.1	.4			All Other Expenses (net)	.0	.3
1.2	1.6	1.6	2.0			Profit Before Taxes	2.0	1.3
						RATIOS		
4.4	2.0	1.8	1.7				1.8	1.8
2.4	1.6	1.4	1.3			Current	1.4	1.4
1.2	1.1	1.2	1.2				1.1	1.2
1.4	.6	.6	.6				.6	.6
.4	(74) .3	.3	.3			Quick	(448) .3	(428) .3
.2	.1	.1	.1				.1	.1
0 UND	7 52.9	8 46.6	8 47.0				7 52.9	8 45.1
11 31.9	15 24.3	15 24.9	23 15.7			Sales/Receivables	18 20.2	18 20.3
30 12.2	28 13.0	34 10.9	37 9.8				34 10.7	36 10.0
46 7.9	88 4.2	93 3.9	92 4.0				90 4.1	89 4.1
120 3.0	135 2.7	129 2.8	132 2.8			Cost of Sales/Inventory	139 2.6	127 2.9
172 2.1	217 1.7	188 1.9	167 2.2				188 1.9	183 2.0
9 41.6	7 55.9	8 43.7	13 27.2				8 44.6	9 39.8
26 14.1	17 21.4	25 14.4	35 10.4			Cost of Sales/Payables	24 15.2	26 14.0
113 3.2	58 6.3	63 5.8	72 5.1				74 4.9	71 5.1
2.5	5.2	5.6	6.4				6.2	5.9
9.2	9.5	9.1	10.2			Sales/Working Capital	10.1	9.9
28.0	26.2	18.1	19.3				19.7	18.5
28.0	5.9	4.9	7.3				4.5	4.6
(15) 2.0	(69) 1.8	(175) 2.4	(72) 2.3			EBIT/Interest	(427) 2.2	(413) 1.9
-.7	1.0	1.2	1.4				1.4	1.0
		3.4	10.2				5.4	3.9
		(67) 1.7	(28) 3.5			Net Profit + Depr., Dep., Amort./Cur. Mat. L/T/D	(144) 2.2	(135) 1.9
		.8	1.8				.8	.8
.0	.1	.1	.1				.1	.1
.4	.3	.2	.4			Fixed/Worth	.3	.3
1.7	1.2	.5	.8				.7	.7
.5	1.4	1.3	1.6				1.4	1.3
2.2	3.4	2.5	2.9			Debt/Worth	3.0	2.7
5.2	9.5	5.0	5.2				5.8	5.7
32.0	37.4	22.6	29.1				26.3	22.1
(15) 17.2	(66) 13.1	(178) 9.1	(72) 15.3			% Profit Before Taxes/Tangible Net Worth	(433) 12.5	(410) 9.2
-.3	.4	2.4	4.7				4.8	1.1
13.8	9.0	6.0	7.1				7.4	6.7
2.4	2.4	2.7	3.7			% Profit Before Taxes/Total Assets	3.3	2.8
-3.7	-.8	.5	1.0				1.2	.1
82.9	74.1	61.7	50.5				66.2	59.9
41.3	38.1	32.6	22.6			Sales/Net Fixed Assets	34.6	33.1
13.7	16.1	18.0	11.8				15.2	14.5
4.5	3.0	2.9	2.5				2.8	2.9
2.5	2.3	2.4	2.1			Sales/Total Assets	2.2	2.2
1.7	1.6	1.7	1.7				1.6	1.6
1.1	.4	.5	.5				.5	.5
(12) 1.4	(65) .9	(165) .7	(64) .8			% Depr., Dep., Amort./Sales	(400) .8	(400) .8
4.2	1.7	1.1	1.3				1.3	1.2
2.9	1.6	.7	.6				.9	1.0
(10) 5.4	(39) 3.6	(100) 1.4	(23) 1.4			% Officers', Directors', Owners' Comp/Sales	(204) 1.9	(199) 1.9
13.0	6.2	2.5	2.5				4.2	3.9
15590M	242151M	1971308M	3169205M	397134M	549920M	Net Sales ($)	6058615M	5996760M
5419M	91965M	851884M	1514597M	192495M	216594M	Total Assets ($)	3259103M	2846995M

Comparative Historical Data | Current Data Sorted By Sales

				Type of Statement						
	36	47	40	Unqualified	1	1	2	6	9	21
	76	87	75	Reviewed	1	4	10	19	24	17
	114	124	95	Compiled	7	18	13	28	22	7
	35	38	36	Tax Returns	3	11	10	2	8	2
	102	117	106	Other	4	13	8	23	37	21
	4/1/00- 3/31/01 ALL	4/1/01- 3/31/02 ALL	4/1/02- 3/31/03 ALL		73 (4/1-9/30/02)			279 (10/1/02-3/31/03)		
					0-1MM	1-3MM	3-5MM	5-10MM	10-25MM	25MM & OVER
	363	413	352	**NUMBER OF STATEMENTS**	16	47	43	78	100	68
	%	%	%	**ASSETS**	%	%	%	%	%	%
	4.3	5.5	5.8	Cash & Equivalents	9.9	7.4	7.8	6.5	4.3	4.1
	15.1	14.6	14.3	Trade Receivables (net)	6.7	13.0	12.8	15.5	14.6	16.2
	60.8	60.8	61.7	Inventory	56.6	59.4	64.3	64.0	61.4	60.6
	2.2	1.7	1.9	All Other Current	2.4	1.1	1.1	1.7	2.8	1.9
	82.4	82.5	83.8	Total Current	75.6	80.9	86.0	87.7	83.1	82.9
	11.7	11.5	10.7	Fixed Assets (net)	18.5	12.4	10.2	8.9	10.0	10.9
	.9	1.0	1.0	Intangibles (net)	.7	1.1	.0	.7	.8	2.2
	5.0	5.1	4.6	All Other Non-Current	5.2	5.6	3.8	2.8	6.1	4.0
	100.0	100.0	100.0	Total	100.0	100.0	100.0	100.0	100.0	100.0
				LIABILITIES						
	25.7	25.5	26.7	Notes Payable-Short Term	15.1	27.7	28.7	24.9	27.6	28.2
	3.0	2.0	2.3	Cur. Mat.-L/T/D	2.4	3.6	2.8	2.3	1.8	2.0
	20.6	20.6	20.1	Trade Payables	9.8	18.4	15.8	20.4	21.8	23.4
	.2	.3	.3	Income Taxes Payable	.8	.3	.0	.4	.3	.2
	7.5	10.6	9.1	All Other Current	10.7	6.8	10.7	9.5	9.4	8.2
	57.0	59.0	58.4	Total Current	38.8	56.9	58.1	57.4	60.8	62.0
	9.5	8.3	8.4	Long Term Debt	17.8	15.1	9.7	5.1	7.3	6.4
	.2	.2	.2	Deferred Taxes	.0	.2	.0	.2	.2	.3
	3.4	3.1	3.3	All Other Non-Current	4.4	7.6	2.3	2.9	2.4	2.7
	30.0	29.4	29.6	Net Worth	38.7	20.3	29.9	34.4	29.3	28.6
	100.0	100.0	100.0	Total Liabilities & Net Worth	100.0	100.0	100.0	100.0	100.0	100.0
				INCOME DATA						
	100.0	100.0	100.0	Net Sales	100.0	100.0	100.0	100.0	100.0	100.0
	22.1	21.8	22.1	Gross Profit	35.5	30.1	23.2	20.3	18.6	20.0
	20.0	19.8	20.2	Operating Expenses	29.2	28.5	21.8	18.6	17.4	17.4
	2.1	2.0	1.9	Operating Profit	6.3	1.6	1.4	1.7	1.2	2.7
	.6	.6	.3	All Other Expenses (net)	2.9	.6	.0	-.2	-.1	.6
	1.5	1.4	1.6	Profit Before Taxes	3.4	1.0	1.4	1.9	1.3	2.1
				RATIOS						
	1.9	1.8	1.8		4.2	1.9	1.8	2.1	1.6	1.6
	1.4	1.4	1.4	Current	2.2	1.4	1.4	1.6	1.3	1.3
	1.2	1.2	1.2		.9	1.1	1.2	1.3	1.1	1.2
	.6	.6	.6		.9	.4	.6	.7	.6	.6
(362) .3		(351) .3		Quick	(15) .3	.2	.3	.4	.3	.3
	.1	.1	.1		.1	.1	.1	.1	.1	.1
8 47.3	7 55.8	7 49.7		Sales/Receivables	3 130.9	7 52.9	9 42.0	7 53.0	7 49.4	8 45.9
17 21.0	15 24.5	15 24.2			9 40.1	21 17.0	15 24.6	13 27.2	15 24.5	23 15.6
36 10.1	36 10.1	33 10.9			15 24.6	32 11.4	33 11.1	36 10.1	34 10.8	36 10.0
86 4.2	84 4.4	91 4.0		Cost of Sales/Inventory	86 4.2	94 3.9	95 3.8	93 3.9	88 4.2	86 4.3
135 2.7	124 2.9	130 2.8			186 2.0	154 2.4	170 2.1	130 2.8	113 3.2	117 3.1
185 2.0	177 2.1	184 2.0			268 1.4	251 1.5	211 1.7	188 1.9	168 2.2	156 2.3
9 39.9	9 39.7	9 40.9		Cost of Sales/Payables	7 52.6	9 40.4	8 45.9	7 51.9	9 39.2	11 33.1
30 12.3	28 13.1	24 14.9			13 27.4	28 13.2	18 20.0	21 17.6	24 15.0	34 10.6
74 4.9	64 5.7	63 5.8			65 5.6	71 5.1	63 5.8	57 6.4	63 5.8	73 5.0
	5.6	6.2	5.7	Sales/Working Capital	2.1	4.5	4.8	5.0	6.6	6.8
	9.8	10.3	9.6		7.7	9.4	7.0	7.8	12.5	11.4
	21.1	20.6	19.2		NM	26.1	15.0	13.0	21.8	20.2
	4.0	4.8	5.7		9.7	4.2	2.8	9.5	4.1	7.6
(345) 1.9	(400) 2.2	(335) 2.2		EBIT/Interest	(13) 2.0	1.8	(37) 1.5	(74) 3.1	(97) 2.0	(67) 3.5
	1.1	1.2	1.1		.5	.4	1.0	1.1	1.2	1.6
	4.3	4.6	4.6	Net Profit + Depr., Dep.,				2.8	3.9	12.4
(106) 2.0	(110) 2.1	(105) 2.1	Amort./Cur. Mat. L/T/D			(26) 1.6	(39) 2.0	(25) 2.9
	.8	1.0	1.3					.5	.8	1.9
	.1	.1	.1	Fixed/Worth	.0	.1	.1	.1	.2	.1
	.3	.3	.3		.2	.4	.3	.2	.3	.3
	.8	.7	.7		NM	1.6	.7	.4	.6	.8
	1.4	1.3	1.3	Debt/Worth	.3	1.5	1.3	1.0	1.4	1.6
	2.6	2.7	2.6		2.4	3.4	2.4	1.8	3.1	2.8
	6.3	5.4	5.4		NM	7.2	6.4	3.7	5.4	5.0
	22.1	22.7	27.2	% Profit Before Taxes/Tangible	31.6	51.0	17.5	20.9	25.3	35.0
(340) 9.8	(391) 11.0	(334) 11.0	Net Worth	(12) 7.8	(42) 15.8	(42) 5.8	(75) 9.0	(98) 9.4	(65) 16.0
	2.4	2.8	2.6		-.1	2.3	-.2	1.1	2.4	10.1
	6.3	6.8	6.6	% Profit Before Taxes/Total	11.7	7.3	4.9	6.4	5.2	8.4
	2.5	3.2	2.7	Assets	3.3	2.5	.9	3.4	2.5	4.6
	.4	.6	.3		-2.3	-2.3	-.1	.2	.4	1.3
	61.5	61.8	66.2	Sales/Net Fixed Assets	83.2	73.1	45.9	96.4	58.9	67.5
	33.7	33.2	32.6		27.3	38.2	32.2	34.2	31.9	33.1
	14.5	14.9	15.6		5.1	17.1	18.0	16.6	16.2	13.9
	2.9	3.0	2.9	Sales/Total Assets	2.4	2.9	2.5	3.1	3.0	2.8
	2.2	2.3	2.2		1.5	2.1	1.9	2.4	2.5	2.3
	1.7	1.8	1.7		.9	1.6	1.5	1.7	1.7	1.9
	.5	.5	.5	% Depr., Dep., Amort./Sales	.9	.6	.5	.4	.5	.4
(333) .8	(381) .7	(309) .8		(13) 2.5	(36) .9	(40) .9	(69) .7	(91) .8	(60) .7
	1.3	1.2	1.3		7.6	1.5	1.6	1.0	1.2	1.0
	1.1	1.0	.9	% Officers', Directors',		2.7	1.3	1.0	.7	.4
(176) 2.1	(198) 1.9	(172) 1.7	Owners' Comp/Sales		(23) 5.4	(23) 5.4	(46) 1.5	(54) 1.5	(19) 1.0
	3.9	3.4	3.6			8.5	4.3	3.6	2.3	2.5
	5450021M	7273178M	6345308M	Net Sales ($)	10774M	96244M	173845M	552766M	1508325M	4003354M
	2580664M	3302610M	2872954M	Total Assets ($)	7649M	47601M	99206M	248729M	705844M	1763925M

M = $ thousand   MM = $ million
See Pages 11 through 18 for Explanation of Ratios and Data

WHOLESALE—Industrial Machinery and Equipment Merchant Wholesalers NAICS 423830 (SIC 5084, 5085)

Current Data Sorted By Assets | **Comparative Historical Data**

	0-500M	500M-2MM	2-10MM	10-50MM	50-100MM	100-250MM	Type of Statement	4/1/98-3/31/99 ALL	4/1/99-3/31/00 ALL
	2	12	91	74	22	13	Unqualified	223	224
	12	99	219	47	1		Reviewed	395	358
	29	151	106	8			Compiled	332	311
	23	42	14	2			Tax Returns	68	77
	26	93	131	46	7	4	Other	278	281
	\>\>\> 297 (4/1-9/30/02)			977 (10/1/02-3/31/03) \>\>\>					
NUMBER OF STATEMENTS	92	397	561	177	30	17	NUMBER OF STATEMENTS	1296	1251
	%	%	%	%	%	%	**ASSETS**	%	%
	12.3	7.3	5.9	5.5	3.0	5.8	Cash & Equivalents	6.7	6.7
	34.4	35.4	33.6	28.1	21.5	19.4	Trade Receivables (net)	33.7	34.1
	30.2	36.1	37.6	34.5	31.6	35.8	Inventory	35.2	34.8
	1.6	1.8	2.2	3.2	3.6	6.7	All Other Current	2.1	2.4
	78.5	80.6	79.2	71.4	59.7	67.7	Total Current	77.6	77.9
	15.3	13.6	13.8	19.8	24.5	15.0	Fixed Assets (net)	15.5	15.0
	.8	1.2	1.6	3.4	7.0	9.9	Intangibles (net)	1.6	1.8
	5.4	4.7	5.4	5.4	8.8	7.4	All Other Non-Current	5.3	5.3
	100.0	100.0	100.0	100.0	100.0	100.0	Total	100.0	100.0
							LIABILITIES		
	21.4	16.3	18.5	18.6	14.6	11.0	Notes Payable-Short Term	14.8	15.7
	3.9	3.3	3.4	4.3	6.6	3.5	Cur. Mat.-L/T/D	3.7	3.7
	25.3	23.7	20.4	16.2	11.3	14.3	Trade Payables	21.4	20.9
	.5	.2	.2	.3	.2	.1	Income Taxes Payable	.3	.3
	16.5	9.9	9.7	9.1	11.4	8.2	All Other Current	10.4	10.8
	67.6	53.4	52.3	48.6	44.0	37.0	Total Current	50.6	51.4
	12.7	8.4	8.2	11.1	18.4	17.5	Long Term Debt	10.5	10.4
	.1	.1	.2	.5	1.2	.3	Deferred Taxes	.4	.3
	4.9	3.7	3.3	3.6	2.1	4.1	All Other Non-Current	3.2	3.4
	14.7	34.3	35.9	36.2	34.4	41.1	Net Worth	35.3	34.5
	100.0	100.0	100.0	100.0	100.0	100.0	Total Liabilities & Net Worth	100.0	100.0
							INCOME DATA		
	100.0	100.0	100.0	100.0	100.0	100.0	Net Sales	100.0	100.0
	35.1	32.4	29.3	27.5	26.6	25.5	Gross Profit	28.6	28.9
	34.2	31.2	27.5	24.4	23.2	23.0	Operating Expenses	25.4	26.1
	.9	1.2	1.8	3.1	3.3	2.5	Operating Profit	3.2	2.8
	1.1	.6	.6	.9	1.2	1.3	All Other Expenses (net)	.5	.5
	-.1	.7	1.2	2.2	2.2	1.2	Profit Before Taxes	2.7	2.2
							RATIOS		
	2.1	2.4	2.1	1.9	2.0	2.6	Current	2.2	2.2
	1.3	1.6	1.5	1.4	1.3	1.8		1.5	1.5
	.9	1.2	1.2	1.1	1.1	1.6		1.2	1.2
	1.4	1.2	1.1	1.0	.8	1.1	Quick	1.2	1.2
	.7	.8	.7	.7	.6	.6		(1294) .8	.8
	.4	.5	.5	.4	.4	.4		.5	.5
	18 20.8	31 11.7	36 10.2	38 9.7	33 10.9	39 9.3	Sales/Receivables	31 11.6	33 11.0
	30 12.1	42 8.6	45 8.1	46 8.0	46 7.9	43 8.5		42 8.7	44 8.3
	46 7.9	55 6.7	56 6.5	53 6.8	61 6.0	54 6.7		54 6.8	56 6.5
	8 44.7	31 11.8	39 9.4	46 7.9	65 5.6	59 6.2	Cost of Sales/Inventory	35 10.5	35 10.5
	35 10.4	63 5.8	70 5.2	70 5.2	85 4.3	93 3.9		59 6.2	59 6.2
	81 4.5	112 3.3	112 3.3	112 3.3	130 2.8	211 1.7		101 3.6	103 3.5
	7 55.2	22 16.8	21 17.2	21 17.2	16 22.3	23 16.2	Cost of Sales/Payables	19 19.4	19 19.0
	35 10.5	35 10.5	34 10.8	31 11.8	29 12.7	33 11.1		33 11.0	33 11.1
	61 6.0	56 6.5	52 7.1	46 7.9	45 8.2	65 5.6		51 7.2	51 7.1
	8.5	5.7	5.6	5.2	5.4	2.9	Sales/Working Capital	6.3	5.9
	25.2	10.3	10.2	11.1	9.5	4.2		11.4	10.8
	-72.8	30.2	24.3	26.7	NM	8.4		24.5	27.3
	(77) 8.2	(356) 4.9	(519) 5.5	(166) 7.2	(29) 5.7	(16) 3.4	EBIT/Interest	(1185) 6.7	(1129) 6.4
	1.3	1.9	2.4	2.6	2.3	2.0		2.9	2.7
	-5.0	.1	1.0	1.1	1.3	.1		1.5	1.3
		(94) 4.2	(194) 3.5	(75) 7.5	(13) 2.8		Net Profit + Depr., Dep., Amort./Cur. Mat. L./T/D	(463) 5.0	(372) 3.9
		2.1	1.5	2.5	1.2			2.2	1.7
		.8	.7	.7	.2			1.1	.9
	.1	.1	.1	.2	.2	.2	Fixed/Worth	.1	.1
	.5	.3	.3	.5	1.0	.4		.4	.3
	12.1	.9	.8	1.4	1.9	1.0		.9	.9
	1.0	.8	1.0	1.0	1.6	.8	Debt/Worth	1.0	1.0
	3.0	1.9	2.1	2.2	2.4	1.6		2.0	2.1
	UND	4.6	4.4	4.3	4.3	9.4		4.4	4.9
	(70) 57.0	(355) 19.0	(532) 23.9	(165) 23.6	(29) 31.5	(15) 14.4	% Profit Before Taxes/Tangible Net Worth	(1206) 35.4	(1168) 32.2
	12.6	6.4	8.5	12.2	10.5	7.5		17.2	15.8
	-20.3	-2.8	.6	1.9	3.0	-3.5		6.3	4.3
	16.8	6.4	7.2	7.8	7.3	5.0	% Profit Before Taxes/Total Assets	11.5	10.5
	1.4	2.2	2.6	3.2	2.7	2.4		5.3	4.5
	-8.9	-1.9	.0	.3	.8	-2.2		1.8	1.0
	168.6	76.3	65.7	38.4	35.9	44.2	Sales/Net Fixed Assets	66.0	64.0
	40.2	36.5	29.4	15.6	9.3	8.9		28.8	30.2
	19.5	16.4	12.4	6.8	3.2	5.4		11.6	12.7
	5.6	3.8	3.3	2.9	2.0	1.7	Sales/Total Assets	3.7	3.6
	3.8	3.0	2.6	2.0	1.7	1.4		2.8	2.7
	2.8	2.1	1.9	1.5	1.1	1.0		2.0	1.9
	(59) .6	(349) .5	(515) .5	(167) .6	(26) .6	(10) .9	% Depr., Dep., Amort./Sales	(1146) .5	(1084) .5
	1.1	1.0	1.0	1.2	1.4	1.2		.9	.9
	2.2	1.7	1.8	2.8	5.1	2.8		1.7	1.7
	(47) 4.2	(229) 2.4	(215) 2.0	(29) .9			% Officers', Directors', Owners' Comp/Sales	(533) 2.0	(503) 2.1
	6.3	4.4	3.2	1.9				3.7	3.9
	10.4	7.5	5.1					6.9	
	127655M	1397987M	6897045M	7988221M	3406707M	3916953M	Net Sales ($)	24076055M	23676242M
	25812M	470382M	2635894M	3649812M	2161902M	2711513M	Total Assets ($)	11056754M	11612074M

© RMA 2003

M = $ thousand   MM = $ million
See Pages 11 through 18 for Explanation of Ratios and Data

Comparative Historical Data | Current Data Sorted By Sales

				Type of Statement						
160	163	214		Unqualified	1	8	7	25	72	101
308	255	378		Reviewed	10	48	56	82	140	42
356	328	294		Compiled	18	86	74	73	36	7
62	58	81		Tax Returns	15	31	15	11	7	2
283	334	307		Other	16	57	45	63	63	63
4/1/00-3/31/01 ALL	4/1/01-3/31/02 ALL	4/1/02-3/31/03 ALL			297 (4/1-9/30/02)			977 (10/1/02-3/31/03)		
					0-1MM	1-3MM	3-5MM	5-10MM	10-25MM	25MM & OVER
1169	1138	1274		NUMBER OF STATEMENTS	60	230	197	254	318	215
%	%	%		ASSETS	%	%	%	%	%	%
6.2	6.1	6.7		Cash & Equivalents	10.9	7.4	8.1	6.6	5.6	4.9
34.8	31.9	33.0		Trade Receivables (net)	21.9	30.8	34.2	36.4	34.8	30.4
34.8	36.2	36.0		Inventory	41.3	37.1	37.1	36.0	36.0	32.2
2.5	2.3	2.3		All Other Current	3.3	1.2	2.3	1.8	2.1	3.9
78.3	76.5	77.9		Total Current	77.4	76.6	81.7	80.9	78.5	71.4
14.6	15.9	14.9		Fixed Assets (net)	16.5	16.0	12.3	13.3	14.8	18.0
1.7	2.1	1.9		Intangibles (net)	.3	1.4	1.4	1.3	1.6	4.6
5.5	5.4	5.3		All Other Non-Current	5.8	6.0	4.6	4.6	5.2	6.0
100.0	100.0	100.0		Total	100.0	100.0	100.0	100.0	100.0	100.0
				LIABILITIES						
17.0	17.5	17.9		Notes Payable-Short Term	23.1	17.7	16.1	18.9	17.6	17.2
3.5	3.6	3.6		Cur. Mat.-L/T/D	3.3	3.7	3.1	3.4	3.6	4.4
21.9	20.2	20.9		Trade Payables	17.7	21.5	22.1	23.6	20.4	17.4
.2	.2	.2		Income Taxes Payable	.2	.3	.3	.2	.2	.2
9.9	9.6	10.2		All Other Current	11.1	12.9	8.1	9.0	9.8	10.9
52.6	51.2	52.8		Total Current	55.4	56.1	49.9	55.2	51.7	50.1
9.3	10.0	9.4		Long Term Debt	14.0	10.6	8.7	7.3	8.4	11.4
.3	.3	.2		Deferred Taxes	.0	.1	.1	.2	.3	.5
2.9	3.5	3.6		All Other Non-Current	7.9	3.2	3.9	3.2	3.0	3.8
35.0	34.9	34.0		Net Worth	22.6	29.9	37.3	34.1	36.7	34.2
100.0	100.0	100.0		Total Liabilities & Net Worth	100.0	100.0	100.0	100.0	100.0	100.0
				INCOME DATA						
100.0	100.0	100.0		Net Sales	100.0	100.0	100.0	100.0	100.0	100.0
29.1	30.2	30.4		Gross Profit	41.2	35.4	31.8	29.3	27.6	25.9
26.4	28.2	28.6		Operating Expenses	40.3	34.2	30.2	27.9	25.3	23.4
2.7	2.1	1.8		Operating Profit	.9	1.2	1.7	1.3	2.3	2.5
.5	.7	.7		All Other Expenses (net)	1.9	.9	.4	.6	.5	.7
2.2	1.3	1.1		Profit Before Taxes	−1.0	.3	1.3	.7	1.8	1.8
				RATIOS						
2.0	2.2	2.1			3.0	2.5	2.2	2.0	2.1	1.9
1.4	1.5	1.5		Current	1.8	1.5	1.6	1.5	1.5	1.4
1.2	1.2	1.2			1.0	1.0	1.3	1.1	1.2	1.2
	1.1	1.1	1.2		1.3	1.2	1.3	1.2	1.1	1.0
(1168)	.8	.7	.7	Quick	.6	.6	.8	.8	.8	.7
	.5	.5	.5		.2	.4	.5	.5	.5	.5
34 10.7	31 11.7	33 11.0			16 22.4	29 12.5	32 11.3	36 10.1	35 10.4	35 10.4
44 8.3	42 8.8	44 8.3		Sales/Receivables	27 13.4	42 8.7	45 8.1	46 8.0	43 8.4	45 8.1
57 6.5	54 6.7	55 6.7			52 7.0	57 6.4	56 6.5	56 6.5	54 6.8	53 6.9
33 11.1	39 9.3	36 10.1			35 10.4	34 10.8	28 12.9	37 10.0	37 9.8	39 9.2
61 6.0	65 5.6	67 5.4		Cost of Sales/Inventory	98 3.7	78 4.7	72 5.1	62 5.9	65 5.6	65 5.6
105 3.5	113 3.2	110 3.3			312 1.2	142 2.6	127 2.9	102 3.6	93 3.9	93 3.9
20 17.9	19 18.9	21 17.7			1 278.6	18 20.4	21 17.6	24 15.5	21 17.1	19 19.1
34 10.7	33 11.0	34 10.8		Cost of Sales/Payables	33 11.2	39 9.4	35 10.5	38 9.6	32 11.3	29 12.6
56 6.5	55 6.6	54 6.8			61 6.0	69 5.3	56 6.5	54 6.8	47 7.8	43 8.5
6.5	5.8	5.7			2.8	4.5	5.0	6.2	6.7	6.8
11.6	10.8	10.6		Sales/Working Capital	7.9	10.5	8.8	11.7	11.4	12.8
27.8	26.8	28.4			UND	292.2	21.1	27.5	26.0	27.6
	5.6	4.7	5.6		4.6	5.6	4.7	4.8	6.7	6.5
(1069)	2.4	(1040) 1.8	(1163) 2.2	EBIT/Interest	(51) 1.2	(210) 1.9	(171) 1.9	(237) 2.1	(291) 2.8	(203) 2.6
	1.2	.6	.7		−6.7	.0	.2	.3	1.3	1.1
	4.6	4.0	4.5	Net Profit + Depr., Dep.,		4.6	3.9	3.2	4.9	6.6
(333)	1.6	(327) 1.6	(386) 1.7	Amort./Cur. Mat. L/T/D		(40) 2.0	(56) 1.7	(79) 1.6	(122) 1.8	(85) 1.7
	.7	.5	.6			.6	.8	.3	.9	.5
	.1	.1	.1		.1	.1	.1	.1	.1	.2
	.3	.3	.4	Fixed/Worth	.5	.4	.2	.3	.3	.5
	.9	.9	1.0		10.0	1.6	.8	.8	.8	1.4
	1.0	1.0	.9		.6	.7	.8	1.0	1.0	1.2
	2.1	2.1	2.0	Debt/Worth	2.3	2.0	1.7	2.0	2.0	2.4
	4.5	4.6	4.7		UND	6.4	3.9	4.8	4.1	4.6
	30.7	26.3	23.6	% Profit Before Taxes/Tangible	28.2	20.5	20.2	21.6	26.6	25.2
(1103)	13.2	(1055) 9.0	(1166) 8.3	Net Worth	(47) 1.3	(193) 6.5	(185) 7.0	(235) 7.0	(307) 10.8	(199) 11.4
	3.2	−1.2	.0		−35.6	−5.3	−2.1	.0	2.1	1.4
	9.3	7.9	7.3	% Profit Before Taxes/Total	12.5	6.6	6.4	6.5	8.1	7.7
	3.8	2.5	2.6	Assets	.3	2.1	2.2	1.9	3.3	3.2
	.7	−1.2	−.6		−11.4	−3.0	−1.4	−1.2	.5	.2
	65.3	62.9	64.9		137.3	64.9	67.0	77.2	67.7	44.1
	29.1	27.9	29.3	Sales/Net Fixed Assets	20.0	27.2	35.7	37.0	29.3	18.9
	12.2	10.8	11.7		9.8	10.2	16.2	16.1	12.6	8.4
	3.6	3.5	3.5		3.8	3.5	3.5	3.6	3.5	3.2
	2.7	2.6	2.6	Sales/Total Assets	2.1	2.5	2.7	2.8	2.7	2.4
	1.9	1.9	1.8		.9	1.7	1.9	2.1	2.0	1.6
	.4	.5	.6		.4	.4	.5	.5	.5	.6
(1016)	.9	(982) .9	(1126) 1.0	% Depr., Dep., Amort./Sales	(39) 1.7	(185) 1.2	(178) 1.0	(230) .9	(302) .9	(192) 1.0
	1.7	2.0	1.9		3.2	2.3	1.8	1.6	1.6	2.3
	2.2	2.1	2.2	% Officers', Directors',	5.2	3.5	2.5	1.9	1.9	1.0
(488)	3.9	(425) 3.7	(522) 4.0	Owners' Comp/Sales	(25) 7.9	(132) 5.1	(107) 4.2	(115) 3.3	(111) 2.9	(32) 1.5
	6.4	6.6	6.4		12.9	8.4	6.5	5.1	4.8	3.6
22384003M	22282756M	23734568M		Net Sales ($)	35253M	463441M	773782M	1800361M	5079663M	15582068M
10677430M	11082306M	11655315M		Total Assets ($)	25103M	245052M	329097M	755335M	2112527M	8188201M

© RMA 2003   M = $ thousand   MM = $ million
See Pages 11 through 18 for Explanation of Ratios and Data

Current Data Sorted By Assets   Comparative Historical Data

						Type of Statement		
1	8	34	37	3	2	Unqualified	113	112
5	39	108	30			Reviewed	232	214
11	64	52	3			Compiled	185	171
12	26	4				Tax Returns	25	35
11	47	59	35	10	5	Other	178	172
	128 (4/1-9/30/02)		478 (10/1/02-3/31/03)				4/1/98-3/31/99 ALL	4/1/99-3/31/00 ALL
0-500M	500M-2MM	2-10MM	10-50MM	50-100MM	100-250MM	NUMBER OF STATEMENTS		
40	184	257	105	13	7		733	704
%	%	%	%	%	%	ASSETS	%	%
14.7	7.3	5.9	6.5	6.5		Cash & Equivalents	5.3	5.6
30.7	33.6	32.3	29.9	21.5		Trade Receivables (net)	34.6	35.6
30.8	38.2	38.3	33.7	37.0		Inventory	37.8	37.4
2.8	1.3	2.0	3.0	2.0		All Other Current	1.7	1.5
78.9	80.5	78.5	73.1	67.0		Total Current	79.4	80.2
15.7	12.4	13.5	14.9	7.9		Fixed Assets (net)	13.0	12.9
3.2	2.3	3.5	6.0	19.6		Intangibles (net)	2.2	2.2
2.2	4.8	4.5	6.1	5.6		All Other Non-Current	5.4	4.7
100.0	100.0	100.0	100.0	100.0		Total	100.0	100.0
						LIABILITIES		
28.8	13.7	17.1	18.3	14.4		Notes Payable-Short Term	15.8	15.8
8.3	4.2	2.5	2.8	5.8		Cur. Mat.-L/T/D	2.5	2.4
24.7	23.3	18.2	15.5	16.0		Trade Payables	22.0	21.4
.1	.1	.3	.3	1.2		Income Taxes Payable	.3	.3
8.2	8.4	8.0	7.8	4.6		All Other Current	7.5	7.4
70.0	49.7	46.1	44.7	42.1		Total Current	48.1	47.2
22.5	10.4	9.3	8.4	9.7		Long Term Debt	8.9	9.6
.0	.1	.1	.5	.5		Deferred Taxes	.2	1.1
4.9	5.2	3.4	2.2	1.2		All Other Non-Current	4.3	3.3
2.6	34.6	41.1	44.2	46.5		Net Worth	38.5	38.8
100.0	100.0	100.0	100.0	100.0		Total Liabilities & Net Worth	100.0	100.0
						INCOME DATA		
100.0	100.0	100.0	100.0	100.0		Net Sales	100.0	100.0
35.7	31.6	29.6	28.7	33.3		Gross Profit	29.3	29.6
35.6	30.2	27.4	25.2	23.9		Operating Expenses	25.7	26.0
.1	1.3	2.2	3.5	9.3		Operating Profit	3.6	3.5
.8	.5	.5	.3	1.7		All Other Expenses (net)	.5	.5
-.7	.8	1.7	3.2	7.7		Profit Before Taxes	3.1	3.1
						RATIOS		
2.1	2.8	2.7	2.8	2.8			2.5	2.6
1.3	1.6	1.8	1.7	1.4		Current	1.7	1.7
.9	1.2	1.3	1.2	1.0			1.2	1.3
1.6	1.3	1.2	1.5	1.3			1.2	1.3
.7	.8	.8	.8	.6		Quick	.8	.9
.4	.6	.5	.5	.3			.6	.6
15 24.6	31 11.8	34 10.8	36 10.3	35 10.4			34 10.7	36 10.1
28 13.2	39 9.4	41 8.9	43 8.4	52 7.1		Sales/Receivables	41 8.8	43 8.4
40 9.0	50 7.3	50 7.3	52 7.0	56 6.5			49 7.4	53 6.9
8 45.1	39 9.5	45 8.0	47 7.7	71 5.1			40 9.0	40 9.1
39 9.4	69 5.3	68 5.3	72 5.1	96 3.8		Cost of Sales/Inventory	62 5.9	63 5.8
114 3.2	107 3.4	113 3.2	106 3.4	224 1.6			97 3.8	100 3.6
0 UND	22 16.3	18 20.1	22 16.5	20 18.1			22 16.6	22 16.9
36 10.3	35 10.3	31 11.7	30 12.3	37 9.9		Cost of Sales/Payables	34 10.7	34 10.8
62 5.8	55 6.7	46 7.9	40 9.0	68 5.4			49 7.4	50 7.3
6.6	5.4	5.5	4.8	3.5			5.7	5.5
21.7	10.4	8.6	8.1	6.6		Sales/Working Capital	9.7	9.3
-56.8	31.9	17.4	25.1	513.9			23.8	19.9
5.8	6.2	7.0	7.3	9.9			7.7	7.0
(33) .9	(165) 2.1	(239) 2.8	(95) 4.0	(11) 3.1		EBIT/Interest	(663) 3.0	(638) 3.1
-2.7	-.1	1.3	1.5	.5			1.5	1.5
	2.2	5.0	8.4				6.0	6.4
	(47) 1.1	(79) 1.9	(44) 3.5			Net Profit + Depr., Dep., Amort./Cur. Mat. L /T/D	(241) 2.8	(231) 2.9
	.2	.9	1.1				1.1	1.4
.1	.1	.1	.2	.1			.1	.1
1.7	.3	.2	.3	.2		Fixed/Worth	.3	.3
-1.6	1.0	.7	.8	NM			.7	.7
1.4	.8	.8	.6	.7			.8	.7
15.1	1.8	1.6	1.5	2.2		Debt/Worth	1.7	1.7
-6.0	5.2	3.6	3.5	NM			3.8	3.8
34.5	22.9	26.5	25.9	21.6			33.4	33.6
(24) 7.7	(159) 8.2	(239) 10.7	(97) 13.0	(10) 15.0		% Profit Before Taxes/Tangible Net Worth	(682) 17.5	(657) 16.3
-72.1	.6	2.5	3.6	4.7			6.5	5.8
10.6	8.7	9.6	10.7	12.2			12.1	13.0
3.6	2.4	3.7	4.8	4.9		% Profit Before Taxes/Total Assets	5.9	5.5
-11.4	-2.9	.8	1.3	.8			1.6	1.7
227.4	90.1	73.5	49.1	60.0			64.1	64.6
39.9	34.4	34.6	22.5	30.6		Sales/Net Fixed Assets	33.0	34.5
15.6	17.0	15.4	10.6	24.7			16.8	17.2
6.0	3.9	3.5	3.1	2.5			3.7	3.6
3.8	3.0	2.8	2.5	1.5		Sales/Total Assets	3.0	3.0
2.3	2.2	2.0	1.8	.9			2.2	2.2
.8	.5	.5	.7				.5	.5
(32) 1.2	(156) 1.1	(240) .8	(93) 1.0			% Depr., Dep., Amort./Sales	(645) .8	(620) .8
2.2	1.7	1.6	1.7				1.4	1.4
5.5	2.9	1.8	1.6				2.2	2.2
(18) 7.5	(93) 4.8	(114) 3.1	(23) 2.6			% Officers', Directors', Owners' Comp/Sales	(336) 4.3	(328) 3.9
7.4	5.5	5.5	4.3				7.0	7.0
46412M	702403M	3205928M	4865060M	1408587M	1862682M	Net Sales ($)	12324379M	13230593M
11669M	222083M	1178423M	2084461M	860467M	1131125M	Total Assets ($)	4824091M	5252841M

M = $ thousand   MM = $ million
See Pages 11 through 18 for Explanation of Ratios and Data

Comparative Historical Data | | | | **Current Data Sorted By Sales**

			Type of Statement	1	2	6	9	20	47
88	85	85	Unqualified	1	2	6	9	20	47
164	136	182	Reviewed	2	10	29	51	61	29
191	198	130	Compiled	11	29	29	31	24	6
42	33	42	Tax Returns	6	22	7	6	1	
191	171	167	Other	10	25	24	33	32	43

4/1/00-3/31/01 ALL	4/1/01-3/31/02 ALL	4/1/02-3/31/03 ALL		128 (4/1-9/30/02)			478 (10/1/02-3/31/03)		
				0-1MM	1-3MM	3-5MM	5-10MM	10-25MM	25MM & OVER
676	623	606	**NUMBER OF STATEMENTS**	30	88	95	130	138	125
%	%	%	**ASSETS**	%	%	%	%	%	%
5.1	6.0	7.0	Cash & Equivalents	16.0	9.3	5.4	6.1	6.8	5.5
35.5	32.7	31.9	Trade Receivables (net)	18.1	30.3	31.5	32.4	34.3	33.2
36.8	37.6	36.8	Inventory	41.0	33.8	38.4	41.0	35.0	34.1
1.9	2.1	2.0	All Other Current	1.3	2.2	1.6	1.6	2.4	2.4
79.4	78.3	77.6	Total Current	76.4	75.7	76.9	81.2	78.5	75.2
12.3	13.2	13.5	Fixed Assets (net)	13.8	16.3	16.1	11.3	12.7	12.5
3.2	3.1	4.2	Intangibles (net)	2.0	4.6	2.5	2.7	3.9	7.6
5.2	5.3	4.7	All Other Non-Current	7.8	3.4	4.5	4.9	4.9	4.7
100.0	100.0	100.0	Total	100.0	100.0	100.0	100.0	100.0	100.0
			LIABILITIES						
17.0	17.4	16.8	Notes Payable-Short Term	30.4	13.5	17.0	15.3	16.5	17.7
2.5	2.8	3.6	Cur. Mat.-L/T/D	5.7	5.0	4.6	2.4	2.8	3.6
21.7	19.7	19.6	Trade Payables	16.9	22.4	20.1	19.3	19.0	18.8
.3	.3	.2	Income Taxes Payable	.1	.1	.1	.3	.2	.4
7.3	7.8	8.0	All Other Current	6.5	9.9	7.8	8.2	8.0	7.1
48.8	48.0	48.2	Total Current	59.5	50.9	49.6	45.5	46.4	47.6
9.7	9.0	10.5	Long Term Debt	14.3	17.5	10.6	9.2	7.5	9.3
.1	.2	.2	Deferred Taxes	.0	.1	.1	.3	.1	.4
4.0	3.3	4.0	All Other Non-Current	8.2	7.5	4.2	3.4	2.1	2.9
37.2	39.4	37.1	Net Worth	18.0	24.0	35.6	41.6	43.9	39.7
100.0	100.0	100.0	Total Liabilities & Net Worth	100.0	100.0	100.0	100.0	100.0	100.0
			INCOME DATA						
100.0	100.0	100.0	Net Sales	100.0	100.0	100.0	100.0	100.0	100.0
29.5	29.5	30.5	Gross Profit	40.0	34.5	30.5	31.0	28.2	27.3
26.2	26.7	28.3	Operating Expenses	40.7	33.3	29.6	28.2	25.8	23.4
3.3	2.8	2.2	Operating Profit	-.8	1.2	.9	2.8	2.4	4.0
.7	.8	.6	All Other Expenses (net)	.6	1.0	.5	.7	.1	.8
2.6	2.0	1.7	Profit Before Taxes	-1.4	.2	.4	2.1	2.3	3.1
			RATIOS						
2.6	2.8	2.7	Current	5.8	2.8	2.6	3.0	2.6	2.4
1.6	1.7	1.7		1.8	1.6	1.5	1.8	1.8	1.6
1.2	1.2	1.2		.9	1.1	1.1	1.2	1.3	1.2
1.3	1.3	1.3	Quick	2.0	1.4	1.1	1.3	1.3	1.2
.8	.8	.8		.7	.8	.8	.8	.9	.8
.6	.5	.5		.3	.5	.5	.5	.6	.5
36 10.3	33 11.1	33 11.0	Sales/Receivables	15 23.9	28 13.2	32 11.3	32 11.3	34 10.6	35 10.5
44 8.3	41 8.9	41 9.0		29 12.8	38 9.6	40 9.2	39 9.3	43 8.4	43 8.6
53 6.8	50 7.3	51 7.2		47 7.8	51 7.1	51 7.2	48 7.6	51 7.1	52 7.0
41 8.8	42 8.7	42 8.7	Cost of Sales/Inventory	32 11.4	36 10.0	45 8.2	42 8.7	41 8.8	41 8.9
62 5.9	67 5.5	69 5.3		119 3.1	72 5.1	76 4.8	73 5.0	62 5.9	66 5.5
99 3.7	106 3.5	110 3.3		216 1.7	119 3.1	118 3.1	116 3.2	90 4.1	93 3.9
22 16.4	18 19.8	20 18.2	Cost of Sales/Payables	7 54.1	22 16.8	23 15.9	16 22.8	19 19.3	22 16.3
34 10.8	30 12.2	33 11.2		36 10.2	37 9.9	36 10.2	32 11.3	28 13.2	32 11.6
50 7.3	49 7.4	48 7.6		85 4.3	62 5.9	52 7.0	50 7.3	41 8.9	42 8.7
5.7	5.2	5.2	Sales/Working Capital	2.5	4.8	4.8	5.0	5.8	5.7
9.6	9.4	9.2		7.5	11.0	9.9	8.6	8.6	10.4
22.9	24.2	24.7		-25.0	50.9	32.0	19.3	15.8	27.6
(599) 7.4	(560) 6.6	(550) 6.7	EBIT/Interest	(21) 7.2	(80) 5.6	(86) 4.9	(120) 7.4	(126) 6.8	(117) 9.0
2.7	2.2	2.6		1.5	1.8	2.0	2.3	3.4	3.3
1.3	.9	1.0		-3.3	-1.1	.0	1.0	1.6	1.5
(215) 6.6	(166) 4.7	(181) 5.0	Net Profit + Depr., Dep., Amort./Cur. Mat. L/T/D		(15) 2.2	(26) 2.4	(44) 3.9	(43) 5.0	(49) 8.1
3.0	1.9	1.7			1.0	.9	1.7	1.9	3.2
1.3	.7	.6			-.4	.0	.8	.8	1.1
.1	.1	.1	Fixed/Worth	.0	.2	.1	.1	.1	.1
.3	.3	.3		.1	.7	.4	.2	.2	.3
.8	.7	1.0		5.8	NM	1.5	.6	.5	.8
.8	.7	.8	Debt/Worth	.5	.8	.9	.8	.7	.8
1.9	1.6	1.7		1.7	3.3	1.9	1.5	1.4	2.0
4.5	4.0	5.1		-23.7	-44.8	5.2	3.7	2.6	5.0
(624) 34.9	(572) 30.5	(534) 25.3	% Profit Before Taxes/Tangible Net Worth	(22) 23.5	(65) 27.7	(84) 20.2	(122) 27.1	(129) 26.6	(112) 29.8
15.1	11.4	10.3		6.4	8.8	6.1	9.2	12.1	14.1
3.7	.7	1.9		-30.3	-.2	-.7	1.0	3.7	3.6
12.1	10.9	9.6	% Profit Before Taxes/Total Assets	9.4	8.4	7.8	10.2	9.7	10.9
4.9	4.1	3.5		4.0	3.0	2.1	3.0	4.4	4.8
.8	-.1	.1		-19.5	-5.5	-3.1	.1	1.6	1.3
70.0	71.1	71.0	Sales/Net Fixed Assets	184.2	55.6	68.9	85.2	78.8	59.1
35.0	34.0	31.7		34.3	23.8	30.1	39.3	32.5	30.0
16.7	16.2	14.4		9.7	11.4	14.9	20.4	14.9	14.1
3.7	3.6	3.5	Sales/Total Assets	3.0	3.7	3.5	3.7	3.6	3.5
2.9	2.8	2.8		1.8	2.6	2.7	3.0	2.9	2.7
2.1	2.0	2.0		1.2	1.7	1.9	2.1	2.1	2.1
(579) .4	(542) .4	(535) .5	% Depr., Dep., Amort./Sales	(24) .7	(78) .8	(79) .6	(118) .4	(130) .5	(106) .6
.8	.8	.9		1.3	1.4	1.1	.8	.8	.9
1.4	1.4	1.6		3.4	2.4	1.6	1.5	1.5	1.4
(301) 2.2	(284) 2.1	(250) 2.3	% Officers', Directors', Owners' Comp/Sales	(12) 6.6	(50) 3.5	(45) 2.8	(64) 1.8	(51) 1.8	(28) 1.6
3.8	3.9	3.8		10.4	5.4	4.4	3.0	3.2	2.6
6.6	6.1	6.4		14.9	10.4	7.1	5.2	4.6	4.0
12758597M	10931687M	12091072M	Net Sales ($)	20845M	170876M	376199M	945823M	2180430M	8396899M
5395088M	4580510M	5488228M	Total Assets ($)	14638M	86386M	162112M	388908M	922002M	3914182M

M = $ thousand   MM = $ million
See Pages 11 through 18 for Explanation of Ratios and Data

Current Data Sorted By Assets　　　　　　　　**Comparative Historical Data**

						Type of Statement		
	1	7	5		2	Unqualified	15	20
4	14	31	8			Reviewed	47	47
6	18	10				Compiled	42	49
7	6	4				Tax Returns	9	11
6	14	12		6		Other	34	42
	30 (4/1-9/30/02)			131 (10/1/02-3/31/03)			4/1/98-3/31/99	4/1/99-3/31/00
0-500M	500M-2MM	2-10MM	10-50MM	50-100MM	100-250MM		ALL	ALL
23	53	64	19		2	NUMBER OF STATEMENTS	147	169
%	%	%	%	%	%	**ASSETS**	%	%
6.8	4.9	7.1	2.3			Cash & Equivalents	5.2	6.8
35.8	30.4	32.7	28.3			Trade Receivables (net)	34.0	35.1
32.9	37.4	36.0	36.7			Inventory	34.7	31.5
.7	3.2	4.4	3.3			All Other Current	1.3	1.5
76.2	75.9	80.1	70.6			Total Current	75.2	74.8
16.3	14.1	11.4	16.5			Fixed Assets (net)	15.1	15.1
4.5	6.2	2.6	5.1			Intangibles (net)	4.1	3.9
2.9	3.8	5.9	7.9			All Other Non-Current	5.6	6.2
100.0	100.0	100.0	100.0			Total	100.0	100.0
						LIABILITIES		
7.2	16.6	16.6	23.9			Notes Payable-Short Term	15.1	15.8
8.1	4.1	3.8	2.5			Cur. Mat.-L/T/D	4.7	3.0
26.2	22.9	24.7	18.7			Trade Payables	23.3	21.0
.3	.0	.1	.2			Income Taxes Payable	.3	.2
11.2	7.6	9.8	11.8			All Other Current	7.7	10.0
52.9	51.2	54.9	57.1			Total Current	51.0	50.0
28.8	11.2	8.4	9.8			Long Term Debt	13.9	13.9
.0	.1	.1	.3			Deferred Taxes	.1	.2
5.9	6.9	3.0	1.9			All Other Non-Current	4.3	5.1
12.3	30.7	33.6	30.9			Net Worth	30.7	30.9
100.0	100.0	100.0	100.0			Total Liabilities & Net Worth	100.0	100.0
						INCOME DATA		
100.0	100.0	100.0	100.0			Net Sales	100.0	100.0
36.9	35.2	29.2	30.0			Gross Profit	33.6	33.4
36.2	32.6	27.1	26.6			Operating Expenses	30.9	30.0
.8	2.6	2.0	3.4			Operating Profit	2.7	3.4
1.5	.5	.2	.6			All Other Expenses (net)	.6	.7
−.8	2.0	1.8	2.8			Profit Before Taxes	2.2	2.7
						RATIOS		
3.4	2.2	1.9	1.5				2.2	2.3
1.5	1.4	1.5	1.2			Current	1.6	1.5
1.2	1.1	1.1	1.0				1.1	1.2
1.8	1.0	1.1	.8				1.1	1.4
.9	.7	.8	.4			Quick	.8	.8
.7	.4	.5	.3				.5	.6
24 15.2	20 18.2	28 13.1	22 16.9				29 12.7	31 11.8
31 11.7	35 10.4	37 9.8	31 11.9			Sales/Receivables	36 10.1	39 9.4
44 8.2	48 7.5	48 7.6	45 8.1				48 7.6	52 7.0
29 12.4	49 7.4	35 10.4	38 9.7				37 10.0	35 10.4
52 7.0	60 6.1	55 6.6	55 6.7			Cost of Sales/Inventory	54 6.7	54 6.8
84 4.4	91 4.0	85 4.3	94 3.9				82 4.5	84 4.3
19 19.6	17 20.9	24 14.9	17 21.2				20 18.2	16 22.6
32 11.3	34 10.8	39 9.3	28 13.2			Cost of Sales/Payables	35 10.3	30 12.1
63 5.8	62 5.8	49 7.4	45 8.0				53 6.9	49 7.4
6.5	7.0	8.2	14.6				8.2	7.8
11.9	13.2	12.9	23.5			Sales/Working Capital	12.0	12.3
27.9	44.4	40.1	154.7				39.2	23.9
4.3	7.7	9.0	9.2				(139) 4.7	(160) 6.7
(20) 1.1	(50) 3.0	(59) 3.1	4.4			EBIT/Interest	2.3	3.0
−1.0	1.0	1.3	2.8				1.3	1.6
	2.9	6.6	5.4			Net Profit + Depr., Dep.,	5.1	4.1
	(14) 1.7	(23) 1.9	(10) 3.2			Amort./Cur. Mat. L./T/D	(54) 2.0	(59) 1.9
	.5	.5	1.4				.8	1.1
.1	.2	.1	.3				.2	.2
.4	.6	.3	.8			Fixed/Worth	.5	.4
14.0	1.3	.8	1.5				1.4	.9
1.0	1.0	1.1	1.7				1.2	1.2
4.2	2.8	2.6	2.4			Debt/Worth	2.7	2.5
−37.5	13.8	6.3	5.2				7.2	5.6
61.4	58.4	38.1	79.3			% Profit Before Taxes/Tangible	39.6	47.7
(17) 7.3	(44) 20.3	(61) 17.1	(17) 21.3			Net Worth	(130) 15.9	(148) 22.0
−10.3	.7	1.9	13.7				4.8	8.5
14.6	15.2	11.2	11.3			% Profit Before Taxes/Total	8.8	12.9
2.3	3.7	4.7	6.7			Assets	4.1	6.4
−4.7	.0	.7	4.1				1.1	1.8
69.0	77.4	76.6	39.2				58.5	63.0
23.0	30.4	36.3	24.3			Sales/Net Fixed Assets	26.4	30.7
10.9	13.1	17.8	15.3				15.6	15.8
4.7	3.9	3.9	4.0				4.0	3.9
3.8	3.0	3.0	3.2			Sales/Total Assets	3.4	3.2
2.7	2.4	2.4	2.5				2.5	2.2
.7	.6	.5	.6				.6	.5
(18) 1.4	(49) 1.1	(60) .8	(18) .8			% Depr., Dep., Amort./Sales	(127) .9	(154) 1.0
3.2	1.8	1.2	1.5				1.3	1.6
2.8	2.1	1.3				% Officers', Directors',	2.5	2.4
(15) 5.5	(26) 4.1	(30) 2.3				Owners' Comp/Sales	(81) 4.0	(79) 4.5
7.1	7.7	3.3					6.9	7.3
23652M	209437M	936154M	1031268M		402459M	Net Sales ($)	1527497M	2120038M
6480M	64553M	290889M	325120M		316681M	Total Assets ($)	675373M	923764M

(Columns 50-100MM and 100-250MM: **DATA NOT AVAILABLE**)

M = $ thousand　　MM = $ million
See Pages 11 through 18 for Explanation of Ratios and Data

Comparative Historical Data | Current Data Sorted By Sales

			Type of Statement	0-1MM	1-3MM	3-5MM	5-10MM	10-25MM	25MM & OVER
14	13	15	Unqualified				1	6	8
42	37	57	Reviewed	2	6	8	14	13	14
41	38	34	Compiled	4	11	5	7	6	1
12	12	17	Tax Returns	4	6	2	3	1	1
46	48	38	Other	2	9	8	8	5	6
4/1/00-3/31/01 ALL	4/1/01-3/31/02 ALL	4/1/02-3/31/03 ALL		30 (4/1-9/30/02)			131 (10/1/02-3/31/03)		
155	148	161	**NUMBER OF STATEMENTS**	12	32	23	33	31	30
%	%	%	**ASSETS**	%	%	%	%	%	%
6.2	7.6	5.7	Cash & Equivalents	4.1	6.5	7.6	4.3	5.5	5.8
33.4	29.1	31.5	Trade Receivables (net)	23.3	32.4	32.7	33.3	35.7	26.8
32.9	34.8	35.8	Inventory	36.0	35.3	32.6	36.6	34.3	39.5
2.0	3.2	3.3	All Other Current	6.1	1.8	2.9	3.6	4.4	2.8
74.4	74.6	76.4	Total Current	69.5	76.1	75.9	77.7	79.8	74.8
16.0	16.4	13.8	Fixed Assets (net)	20.6	12.6	17.2	14.6	8.2	14.5
3.6	3.6	4.8	Intangibles (net)	7.2	7.3	2.3	2.2	4.3	6.4
6.0	5.3	5.0	All Other Non-Current	2.7	3.9	4.5	5.5	7.6	4.3
100.0	100.0	100.0	Total	100.0	100.0	100.0	100.0	100.0	100.0
			LIABILITIES						
17.4	14.9	15.9	Notes Payable-Short Term	5.5	15.5	12.7	17.0	19.8	17.7
3.4	3.1	4.4	Cur. Mat.-L/T/D	10.9	4.4	4.5	4.4	3.1	2.9
20.5	20.3	23.4	Trade Payables	19.1	25.0	21.8	22.7	26.3	22.4
.2	.1	.1	Income Taxes Payable	.0	.0	.4	.0	.1	.1
10.4	8.6	9.5	All Other Current	13.2	7.8	7.7	9.5	10.6	9.8
51.9	47.0	53.2	Total Current	48.6	52.8	47.1	53.6	59.8	52.9
11.8	12.8	12.7	Long Term Debt	37.1	13.3	10.8	11.8	7.6	10.2
.1	.1	.2	Deferred Taxes	.1	.0	.0	.2	.1	.6
4.3	5.0	4.6	All Other Non-Current	10.6	1.7	10.7	4.0	2.8	3.1
31.9	35.0	29.3	Net Worth	3.6	32.2	31.4	30.4	29.6	33.3
100.0	100.0	100.0	Total Liabilities & Net Worth	100.0	100.0	100.0	100.0	100.0	100.0
			INCOME DATA						
100.0	100.0	100.0	Net Sales	100.0	100.0	100.0	100.0	100.0	100.0
33.1	35.4	32.4	Gross Profit	42.5	34.0	32.9	32.1	28.3	30.6
30.9	32.6	30.1	Operating Expenses	42.3	32.4	29.7	29.4	26.8	27.1
2.3	2.8	2.3	Operating Profit	.1	1.6	3.3	2.7	1.5	3.5
.5	.8	.6	All Other Expenses (net)	2.0	.8	.6	.0	.4	.4
1.8	2.1	1.7	Profit Before Taxes	-1.9	.8	2.7	2.7	1.1	3.1
			RATIOS						
2.4	2.4	2.0	Current	4.9	2.5	3.0	2.0	1.7	1.8
1.5	1.5	1.4		1.8	1.5	1.4	1.3	1.4	1.4
1.1	1.2	1.1		.9	1.2	1.2	1.0	1.0	1.2
1.2	1.2	1.0	Quick	1.7	1.0	1.1	1.0	1.0	.9
.8	.8	.7		.8	.7	.8	.7	.8	.5
.5	.5	.5		.4	.4	.5	.4	.5	.3
28 13.2	20 18.4	26 14.1	Sales/Receivables	24 15.3	22 16.5	31 11.7	27 13.6	30 12.1	19 18.9
38 9.7	34 10.8	35 10.4		28 13.1	41 8.9	39 9.4	41 8.8	37 9.9	26 13.9
51 7.1	45 8.1	47 7.8		36 10.1	51 7.1	57 6.4	51 7.2	44 8.3	38 9.6
37 10.0	38 9.7	37 9.8	Cost of Sales/Inventory	53 6.9	31 11.8	40 9.2	47 7.7	34 10.8	37 9.8
55 6.6	57 6.4	58 6.3		73 5.0	56 6.5	59 6.1	59 6.2	54 6.7	52 7.1
87 3.9	93 3.9	86 4.2		119 3.1	96 3.8	87 4.2	81 4.5	79 4.6	90 4.1
17 21.0	17 21.8	21 17.3	Cost of Sales/Payables	26 14.2	18 20.0	17 22.0	20 18.0	22 16.6	21 17.6
31 11.9	31 11.8	34 10.8		41 8.9	33 10.9	37 9.8	34 10.8	38 9.7	31 11.9
51 7.2	55 6.7	54 6.7		73 5.0	69 5.3	63 5.8	53 6.9	66 5.6	45 8.1
7.0	6.4	7.8	Sales/Working Capital	4.4	6.6	4.9	7.8	11.0	10.9
12.9	11.2	13.9		10.3	11.7	14.5	12.2	16.4	17.5
32.5	25.9	40.5		NM	26.3	40.9	98.7	118.9	27.5
(145) 6.4	(133) 5.5	(150) 8.0	EBIT/Interest	(10) 1.1	(30) 7.0	(22) 11.1	(31) 9.5	(29) 8.6	(28) 9.0
2.7	2.1	3.0		.0	3.0	3.2	2.0	2.7	5.4
1.4	1.0	1.0		-6.5	.3	1.2	1.3	.2	3.0
(42) 5.0	(35) 4.1	(52) 4.5	Net Profit + Depr., Dep., Amort./Cur. Mat. L/T/D				7.9	3.2	6.5
1.9	1.6	1.7					(13) 2.0	(11) .9	(14) 3.2
.9	.7	.6					1.0	.3	1.4
.2	.2	.2	Fixed/Worth	.1	.2	.2	.1	.2	.2
.4	.4	.4		1.0	.5	.7	.6	.3	.5
.9	1.1	1.4		-1.5	2.1	1.2	1.3	.6	1.4
.9	.9	1.1	Debt/Worth	1.1	.7	.6	1.0	1.7	1.5
2.1	2.5	2.7		4.3	1.8	3.2	2.6	3.3	2.4
4.4	5.1	7.9		-6.6	67.6	6.9	9.3	7.2	5.3
(137) 33.4	(130) 32.9	(140) 48.5	% Profit Before Taxes/Tangible Net Worth		(26) 55.5	(21) 63.9	(29) 50.4	(29) 25.8	(27) 65.3
16.5	11.0	17.9			16.8	19.7	13.3	14.7	29.6
4.6	.4	1.6			-3.1	-.7	1.9	-14.2	17.1
11.4	10.7	13.3	% Profit Before Taxes/Total Assets	1.7	15.7	9.0	16.1	7.6	17.5
5.9	3.2	4.5		-2.1	5.2	3.5	2.5	4.5	7.6
1.1	-.3	.3		-22.0	-1.3	.3	.8	-2.1	4.8
55.9	56.5	69.6	Sales/Net Fixed Assets	190.4	67.2	44.0	72.4	69.1	91.8
30.3	26.0	30.4		13.9	30.0	25.9	29.9	52.1	33.6
15.3	12.3	16.0		6.9	21.2	11.1	14.4	25.4	16.7
4.1	3.9	4.0	Sales/Total Assets	4.4	3.5	3.5	4.0	4.0	4.3
3.1	3.1	3.1		2.7	3.1	2.7	3.2	3.0	3.6
2.2	2.3	2.4		1.3	2.3	2.2	2.5	2.5	2.9
(134) .5	(127) .5	(146) .6	% Depr., Dep., Amort./Sales		(27) .8	.5	(30) .5	.6	(26) .4
1.0	.8	1.0			1.1	1.2	1.0	.8	.8
1.6	1.8	1.6			2.0	1.7	1.6	1.2	1.4
(75) 2.6	(71) 2.5	(77) 1.8	% Officers', Directors', Owners' Comp/Sales		(18) 4.2	(12) 1.6	(18) 2.1	(12) 1.0	(11) 1.2
4.9	3.9	3.0			5.9	2.9	2.6	1.8	1.8
7.9	7.0	5.6			8.6	4.7	4.3	3.1	3.2
2310040M	1840596M	2602970M	Net Sales ($)	6594M	56688M	90872M	250565M	475171M	1723080M
910571M	707049M	1003723M	Total Assets ($)	3159M	21090M	37220M	81228M	159701M	701325M

M = $ thousand   MM = $ million
See Pages 11 through 18 for Explanation of Ratios and Data

Current Data Sorted By Assets   Comparative Historical Data

Type of Statement

	0-500M	500M-2MM	2-10MM	10-50MM	50-100MM	100-250MM		4/1/98-3/31/99 ALL	4/1/99-3/31/00 ALL
Unqualified	1	2	10	9				26	31
Reviewed		13	29	9	1			40	35
Compiled	3	21	13	3				41	36
Tax Returns	7	5	3					11	20
Other	2	14	19	8	1	3		53	32
	47 (4/1-9/30/02)			126 (10/1/02-3/31/03)					
NUMBER OF STATEMENTS	13	55	74	26	2	3		171	154

ASSETS

	%	%	%	%	%	%		%	%
Cash & Equivalents	16.8	10.7	6.0	4.5				7.6	6.0
Trade Receivables (net)	27.8	27.4	26.8	21.3				26.6	26.0
Inventory	34.1	43.6	43.8	48.3				43.1	42.5
All Other Current	2.4	1.5	2.5	3.2				1.6	2.5
Total Current	81.1	83.3	79.1	77.3				78.9	77.0
Fixed Assets (net)	9.6	11.9	13.2	13.3				14.4	15.4
Intangibles (net)	7.0	.4	1.9	1.7				.9	1.8
All Other Non-Current	2.4	4.4	5.8	7.7				5.8	5.8
Total	100.0	100.0	100.0	100.0				100.0	100.0

LIABILITIES

Notes Payable-Short Term	14.1	19.3	19.2	22.7				18.3	19.8
Cur. Mat.-L/T/D	3.6	2.9	2.4	4.7				2.6	2.3
Trade Payables	34.0	23.4	19.1	15.5				20.5	21.0
Income Taxes Payable	.0	.1	.1	.2				.3	.4
All Other Current	13.9	9.4	9.3	5.5				8.2	9.9
Total Current	65.7	55.2	50.2	48.5				49.9	53.4
Long Term Debt	13.3	8.1	6.6	12.5				11.6	12.2
Deferred Taxes	.0	.1	.5	1.8				.4	.3
All Other Non-Current	13.0	3.8	3.1	3.5				5.6	3.6
Net Worth	8.1	32.8	39.7	33.7				32.5	30.5
Total Liabilities & Net Worth	100.0	100.0	100.0	100.0				100.0	100.0

INCOME DATA

Net Sales	100.0	100.0	100.0	100.0				100.0	100.0
Gross Profit	35.3	29.3	28.8	25.5				28.4	27.3
Operating Expenses	33.5	28.3	26.1	20.1				23.0	23.9
Operating Profit	1.8	1.0	2.7	5.5				5.4	3.4
All Other Expenses (net)	.9	.0	.2	1.5				1.0	-.1
Profit Before Taxes	.9	1.0	2.5	4.0				4.4	3.5

RATIOS

	0-500M	500M-2MM	2-10MM	10-50MM	50-100MM	100-250MM		Hist 1	Hist 2
Current	1.9	2.3	2.3	2.4				2.2	2.6
	1.2	1.6	1.5	1.5				1.6	1.6
	.9	1.2	1.2	1.2				1.2	1.2
Quick	1.3	1.1	1.0	.8				1.0	1.2
	.5	.7	.7	.5			(170)	.7	.7
	.4	.4	.4	.3				.4	.4
Sales/Receivables	18 19.9	20 17.9	21 17.1	20 17.8			23	16.1	23 15.7
	30 12.3	32 11.3	39 9.4	41 8.9			36	10.1	39 9.4
	46 8.0	48 7.6	51 7.2	50 7.4			53	6.9	53 6.9
Cost of Sales/Inventory	27 13.4	46 8.0	51 7.2	54 6.7			47	7.7	47 7.8
	51 7.2	77 4.8	88 4.2	106 3.4			78	4.7	81 4.5
	86 4.2	126 2.9	130 2.8	188 1.9			159	2.3	152 2.4
Cost of Sales/Payables	20 18.6	20 18.2	17 20.9	13 27.5			17	22.1	16 22.4
	55 6.6	35 10.5	37 9.9	37 9.8			35	10.5	34 10.7
	68 5.4	52 7.0	56 6.5	50 7.2			58	6.2	52 7.0
Sales/Working Capital	10.6	5.4	5.4	4.7				4.8	4.5
	17.7	11.4	10.2	8.3				9.3	8.9
	-45.7	22.7	14.9	26.1				22.6	27.9
EBIT/Interest	2.6	14.0	8.0	9.3				10.4	8.7
	(10) .7	(52) 2.3	(66) 2.6	2.5			(158)	3.8	(137) 3.1
	-1.1	.8	1.0	1.3				1.7	1.3
Net Profit + Depr., Dep., Amort./Cur. Mat. L/T/D		5.7	6.7	2.7				9.6	4.7
		(19) 2.1	(22) 4.9	(11) .8			(49)	4.3	(45) 1.7
		.8	1.0	.1				2.0	.5
Fixed/Worth	.1	.1	.1	.1				.1	.1
	2.2	.2	.2	.3				.2	.2
	-.6	1.0	.4	.7				.7	.9
Debt/Worth	2.3	.9	.8	.9				1.0	.9
	21.8	2.3	1.8	2.2				1.9	2.0
	-7.4	8.2	3.2	5.2				4.0	5.0
% Profit Before Taxes/Tangible Net Worth		31.4	29.1	28.0				41.9	40.2
	(49)	9.7	(72) 8.2	14.4			(163)	25.1	(145) 16.7
		-1.1	.8	3.9				8.6	4.4
% Profit Before Taxes/Total Assets	8.7	10.8	8.8	8.9				13.8	11.1
	.4	2.9	4.0	4.5				7.0	5.0
	-7.2	-.8	.2	.7				2.5	1.3
Sales/Net Fixed Assets	214.5	100.6	72.9	45.7				76.7	91.6
	55.5	49.1	34.3	24.9				32.0	32.1
	21.7	19.4	18.7	12.4				11.6	9.1
Sales/Total Assets	5.4	4.0	3.2	2.8				3.6	3.3
	3.1	2.9	2.2	2.0				2.5	2.3
	2.0	2.1	1.6	1.1				1.6	1.7
% Depr., Dep., Amort./Sales	.2	.4	.4	.7				.4	.4
	(10) .4	(49) .9	(65) .9	(24) 1.0			(146)	.9	(129) .7
	.8	1.2	2.0	1.4				1.8	1.8
% Officers', Directors', Owners' Comp/Sales		2.4	1.9					2.1	2.0
	(35)	3.6	(31) 3.5				(69)	3.9	(65) 3.5
		5.9						6.4	5.8
Net Sales ($)	16542M	209806M	889170M	1051464M	377353M	746549M		3040277M	3197878M
Total Assets ($)	4263M	68996M	358839M	506138M	145954M	537121M		1554276M	2022201M

© RMA 2003

M = $ thousand   MM = $ million
See Pages 11 through 18 for Explanation of Ratios and Data

Comparative Historical Data | Current Data Sorted By Sales

	Type of Statement		47 (4/1-9/30/02)		126 (10/1/02-3/31/03)		

4/1/00-3/31/01 ALL	4/1/01-3/31/02 ALL	4/1/02-3/31/03 ALL		0-1MM	1-3MM	3-5MM	5-10MM	10-25MM	25MM & OVER
18	22	22	Unqualified		2		3	8	9
30	28	52	Reviewed		4	10	17	12	9
38	42	37	Compiled		14	7	12	4	
22	13	15	Tax Returns	5	6		3	1	
42	48	47	Other	3	7	10	5	12	10
150	153	173	NUMBER OF STATEMENTS	8	33	27	40	37	28
%	%	%	ASSETS	%	%	%	%	%	%
6.5	6.1	8.0	Cash & Equivalents		11.2	9.6	6.8	4.2	5.2
27.0	25.0	26.1	Trade Receivables (net)		24.7	24.5	27.8	28.8	24.2
42.2	43.6	43.8	Inventory		43.7	50.0	41.7	43.1	46.3
2.2	2.4	2.6	All Other Current		1.0	3.1	2.6	1.9	4.6
77.9	77.1	80.5	Total Current		80.5	87.2	79.0	78.0	80.3
14.9	14.9	12.2	Fixed Assets (net)		13.5	8.6	13.9	12.4	11.1
1.4	2.3	1.9	Intangibles (net)		1.2	.5	.9	2.9	2.6
5.8	5.7	5.5	All Other Non-Current		4.8	3.6	6.1	6.7	6.0
100.0	100.0	100.0	Total		100.0	100.0	100.0	100.0	100.0
			LIABILITIES						
17.5	21.1	19.4	Notes Payable-Short Term		20.1	17.7	18.3	19.6	21.1
3.9	3.3	2.9	Cur. Mat.-L/T/D		3.9	2.3	2.3	3.0	2.7
19.5	16.9	21.2	Trade Payables		22.9	20.8	20.9	18.9	21.4
.2	.3	.1	Income Taxes Payable		.2	.0	.2	.2	.1
9.5	6.9	9.1	All Other Current		9.2	9.7	11.0	8.5	6.8
50.5	48.6	52.7	Total Current		56.2	50.5	52.6	50.2	52.1
11.6	11.2	8.4	Long Term Debt		11.4	4.3	6.2	8.1	8.4
.4	.5	.5	Deferred Taxes		.1	1.5	.6	.1	.8
3.7	3.7	4.1	All Other Non-Current		5.0	2.7	4.5	3.7	2.0
33.8	36.0	34.3	Net Worth		27.3	41.0	36.1	37.8	36.7
100.0	100.0	100.0	Total Liabilities & Net Worth		100.0	100.0	100.0	100.0	100.0
			INCOME DATA						
100.0	100.0	100.0	Net Sales		100.0	100.0	100.0	100.0	100.0
25.9	29.9	28.8	Gross Profit		32.1	31.9	30.1	25.1	20.7
22.5	26.2	26.1	Operating Expenses		31.9	27.5	28.5	21.5	16.5
3.5	3.7	2.7	Operating Profit		.2	4.4	1.6	3.6	4.3
1.0	1.3	.4	All Other Expenses (net)		.1	.4	−.1	.7	.8
2.5	2.4	2.3	Profit Before Taxes		.0	4.0	1.8	2.9	3.5
			RATIOS						
2.5	2.4	2.3			2.7	2.7	2.0	2.2	2.1
1.6	1.5	1.5	Current		1.4	1.8	1.5	1.4	1.4
1.2	1.2	1.2			1.1	1.3	1.1	1.2	1.3
1.1	1.0	1.0			.9	1.2	1.1	.9	.9
.6	.6	.6	Quick		.6	.7	.7	.6	.6
.4	.4	.4			.4	.5	.4	.4	.4

24	15.5	21	17.2	21	17.5	Sales/Receivables	20	18.4	21	17.6	21	17.6	24	15.0	15	24.1
42	8.7	36	10.2	37	9.9		32	11.3	35	10.3	37	9.8	37	9.9	40	9.2
55	6.6	55	6.7	49	7.5		53	6.9	46	8.0	48	7.5	52	7.0	58	6.3
51	7.2	48	7.5	49	7.5	Cost of Sales/Inventory	42	8.7	64	5.7	47	7.8	43	8.6	48	7.6
84	4.3	88	4.1	78	4.7		80	4.5	110	3.3	77	4.7	69	5.3	63	5.8
141	2.6	175	2.1	136	2.7		168	2.2	208	1.8	101	3.6	141	2.6	145	2.5
19	19.5	18	20.0	19	19.3	Cost of Sales/Payables	18	19.8	18	19.7	25	14.8	15	24.6	14	25.8
35	10.3	33	11.2	37	9.8		40	9.1	35	10.5	41	8.8	32	11.4	31	11.7
60	6.1	54	6.8	56	6.5		68	5.4	49	7.4	57	6.4	46	7.9	54	6.8

4.3	4.6	5.5	Sales/Working Capital	3.8	4.2	6.8	6.0	6.1
8.4	9.2	9.9		14.8	6.5	10.7	10.9	9.2
23.2	19.3	21.6		31.8	13.0	23.2	17.1	21.2

(137)	4.9	(143)	6.4	(159)	10.3	EBIT/Interest	(29)	6.3	(26)	15.4	(36)	12.0	(33)	6.8	13.1
	2.2		2.4		2.4			1.1		4.3		2.0		3.4	4.1
	1.1		1.0		.9			−1.7		1.2		.7		1.9	1.3

(34)	4.6	(38)	4.3	(52)	5.8	Net Profit + Depr., Dep., Amort./Cur. Mat. L/T/D					(13)	5.7	(14)	5.7	
	1.9		2.0		1.9							2.1		2.1	
	.4		.5		.6							.9		1.1	

.1	.1	.1	Fixed/Worth	.1	.0	.1	.1	.1
.3	.3	.2		.4	.2	.2	.2	.2
.8	.8	.9		NM	.3	.8	.4	.6
1.0	.9	.9	Debt/Worth	1.1	.7	1.1	.8	.9
2.1	1.9	2.1		2.3	1.3	1.9	2.1	2.1
4.6	3.9	5.1		NM	3.2	3.7	4.5	3.9

(138)	34.4	(141)	32.0	(158)	31.1	% Profit Before Taxes/Tangible Net Worth	(25)	21.3	(25)	45.2	(39)	25.5	46.0	(27)	30.5
	12.8		11.7		9.6			2.4		11.1		7.6	13.0		18.0
	3.1		1.5		1.4			−18.7		1.7		−2.1	6.9		1.6

9.4	9.0	9.0	% Profit Before Taxes/Total Assets	5.6	12.3	10.1	9.0	15.2
3.8	4.4	3.7		.2	4.7	2.3	4.9	4.8
.4	.2	−.1		−8.0	.6	−.8	1.8	.6
91.5	59.9	82.6	Sales/Net Fixed Assets	126.9	387.2	70.3	77.9	134.3
34.7	28.4	38.0		49.8	39.2	41.8	38.2	35.3
11.7	10.6	18.5		15.7	18.1	19.4	21.9	19.3
3.2	3.2	3.5	Sales/Total Assets	3.9	3.4	3.6	3.6	3.7
2.2	2.2	2.4		2.2	2.3	2.8	2.6	2.2
1.5	1.4	1.7		1.5	1.6	1.9	1.6	1.7

(123)	.4	(131)	.4	(152)	.4	% Depr., Dep., Amort./Sales	(29)	.3	(20)	.4	(38)	.4	(33)	.4	(25)	.3
	.7		.9		.8			.8		.8		.8		.6		1.0
	1.9		1.9		1.4			2.0		1.5		1.8		1.3		1.2

(68)	2.3	(61)	2.5	(81)	2.2	% Officers', Directors', Owners' Comp/Sales	(19)	2.5	(15)	2.4	(20)	2.2	(17)	1.7	
	3.2		4.0		3.6			4.3		4.3		3.6		2.7	
	5.5		8.8		6.5			9.9		8.7		4.4		5.7	

3167475M	3578296M	3290884M	Net Sales ($)	4919M	70233M	108440M	279571M	610554M	2217167M
1926911M	1817840M	1621311M	Total Assets ($)	2821M	45521M	63690M	117434M	279335M	1112510M

© RMA 2003 M = $ thousand MM = $ million
See Pages 11 through 18 for Explanation of Ratios and Data

Current Data Sorted By Assets

Comparative Historical Data

0-500M	500M-2MM	2-10MM	10-50MM	50-100MM	100-250MM	Type of Statement	4/1/98-3/31/99 ALL	4/1/99-3/31/00 ALL
1		16	22	7	3	Unqualified	45	33
1	10	41	7	1		Reviewed	54	64
12	19	13	1			Compiled	63	60
10	13	6				Tax Returns	24	19
6	17	21	10	2	1	Other	64	61
50 (4/1-9/30/02)		189 (10/1/02-3/31/03)						
30	59	97	40	9	4	**NUMBER OF STATEMENTS**	250	237
%	%	%	%	%	%	**ASSETS**	%	%
7.5	7.6	5.5	5.2			Cash & Equivalents	6.7	6.7
25.1	29.3	29.7	29.6			Trade Receivables (net)	25.7	25.8
47.2	43.6	44.6	41.9			Inventory	46.4	46.2
.4	4.2	2.1	2.6			All Other Current	2.4	1.7
80.2	84.8	81.9	79.3			Total Current	81.3	80.4
12.0	9.6	10.4	10.7			Fixed Assets (net)	10.8	10.8
3.6	2.6	2.3	4.3			Intangibles (net)	2.9	3.4
4.2	3.1	5.3	5.7			All Other Non-Current	5.0	5.4
100.0	100.0	100.0	100.0			Total	100.0	100.0
						LIABILITIES		
18.8	22.0	18.4	18.5			Notes Payable-Short Term	16.5	18.1
6.4	4.4	2.2	2.7			Cur. Mat.-L/T/D	2.5	2.0
25.0	20.4	20.8	21.1			Trade Payables	20.4	20.3
.2	.3	.2	.1			Income Taxes Payable	.2	.2
7.5	6.7	9.0	8.0			All Other Current	10.0	11.4
57.9	54.0	50.6	50.5			Total Current	49.7	52.1
16.4	11.2	6.2	5.7			Long Term Debt	9.9	8.4
.0	.0	.1	.0			Deferred Taxes	.1	.2
9.3	4.2	3.5	8.4			All Other Non-Current	7.4	7.6
16.4	30.7	39.6	35.4			Net Worth	32.9	31.7
100.0	100.0	100.0	100.0			Total Liabilities & Net Worth	100.0	100.0
						INCOME DATA		
100.0	100.0	100.0	100.0			Net Sales	100.0	100.0
34.9	31.1	31.8	26.6			Gross Profit	29.7	30.4
31.6	28.5	27.4	22.8			Operating Expenses	26.3	26.6
3.4	2.6	4.5	3.8			Operating Profit	3.4	3.7
.6	.6	.7	.7			All Other Expenses (net)	1.0	1.1
2.8	2.0	3.8	3.2			Profit Before Taxes	2.4	2.6
						RATIOS		
3.1	2.5	2.6	2.1				2.6	2.7
1.5	1.6	1.6	1.4			Current	1.6	1.7
.9	1.1	1.2	1.2				1.2	1.2
1.1	1.2	1.2	1.2				1.0	1.0
.6	.7	.7	.7			Quick	(249) .6	.6
.3	.3	.4	.4				.3	.4
3 110.6	14 25.7	27 13.6	25 14.8				17 20.9	16 23.1
20 17.9	32 11.5	38 9.5	35 10.4			Sales/Receivables	34 10.7	32 11.5
45 8.2	50 7.3	57 6.4	81 4.5				56 6.6	52 7.0
30 12.0	38 9.5	55 6.6	77 4.7				56 6.6	53 6.8
59 6.2	70 5.2	87 4.2	92 4.0			Cost of Sales/Inventory	91 4.0	86 4.2
184 2.0	117 3.1	145 2.5	155 2.3				144 2.5	136 2.7
10 35.8	7 52.2	12 29.4	14 27.0				14 26.5	15 25.0
23 15.6	27 13.7	30 12.0	28 13.2			Cost of Sales/Payables	29 12.4	30 12.1
63 5.8	50 7.3	58 6.2	62 5.9				53 6.8	51 7.2
4.7	5.1	4.6	4.3				5.1	5.3
15.2	9.5	9.8	7.5			Sales/Working Capital	8.5	9.3
-151.3	25.1	24.0	16.7				21.1	19.3
(27) 4.3	(49) 5.6	(93) 10.3	(38) 11.2				(230) 5.7	(225) 6.4
3.1	1.7	5.2	4.1			EBIT/Interest	2.5	2.8
1.2	.9	2.0	2.0				1.3	1.5
		(20) 4.7	(14) 42.3			Net Profit + Depr., Dep.,	(61) 6.9	(45) 10.2
		1.6	6.1			Amort./Cur. Mat. L /T/D	2.8	2.2
		1.0	2.8				.7	1.2
.1	.1	.1	.1				.1	.1
.4	.2	.2	.3			Fixed/Worth	.2	.2
-14.2	.8	.7	.6				.5	.8
1.5	.8	.8	.7				.9	.8
4.3	2.2	1.7	2.3			Debt/Worth	2.0	2.3
-13.9	11.0	3.8	4.4				4.7	5.3
(20) 80.6	(52) 56.7	(91) 46.8	(38) 36.2			% Profit Before Taxes/Tangible	(232) 37.9	(213) 42.8
14.6	10.1	20.5	19.5			Net Worth	16.6	19.4
1.7	3.1	6.3	6.9				4.2	6.5
22.1	15.7	14.9	11.4			% Profit Before Taxes/Total	11.6	13.1
9.0	2.6	6.6	5.2			Assets	5.3	5.9
1.4	.0	2.5	.7				.9	2.1
113.1	102.7	108.5	88.3				88.9	96.3
46.1	46.4	41.9	31.3			Sales/Net Fixed Assets	41.4	41.5
17.9	23.5	20.7	11.0				21.4	19.1
4.9	4.3	3.5	2.8				3.6	3.6
3.7	3.3	2.6	1.7			Sales/Total Assets	2.5	2.7
2.5	2.3	1.9	1.2				1.8	1.9
(23) .6	(47) .4	(87) .4	(36) .3				(217) .4	(204) .4
.8	.7	.6	.9			% Depr., Dep., Amort./Sales	.7	.7
1.3	1.2	1.3	1.6				1.2	1.4
(14) 2.7	(38) 2.7	(45) 1.5				% Officers', Directors',	(102) 2.4	(114) 2.0
4.4	4.9	2.6				Owners' Comp/Sales	3.5	3.3
5.7	8.0	4.0					7.1	6.6
31243M	238598M	1103301M	1928266M	1569023M	1138876M	Net Sales ($)	5819074M	5717534M
8766M	67432M	424636M	919051M	642431M	601842M	Total Assets ($)	2499005M	2362229M

M = $ thousand   MM = $ million
See Pages 11 through 18 for Explanation of Ratios and Data

Comparative Historical Data — Current Data Sorted By Sales

Hist 1	Hist 2	Hist 3	Type of Statement	0-1MM	1-3MM	3-5MM	5-10MM	10-25MM	25MM & OVER
21	18	49	Unqualified		2		5	12	30
59	45	59	Reviewed		1	8	18	26	6
67	47	45	Compiled	10	10	6	13	5	1
18	20	29	Tax Returns	6	10	7	5	1	
63	61	57	Other	6	11	7	10	15	8
4/1/00-3/31/01 ALL	4/1/01-3/31/02 ALL	4/1/02-3/31/03 ALL		50 (4/1-9/30/02) 0-1MM	1-3MM	3-5MM	189 (10/1/02-3/31/03) 5-10MM	10-25MM	25MM & OVER
228	191	239	NUMBER OF STATEMENTS	22	34	28	51	59	45
%	%	%	**ASSETS**	%	%	%	%	%	%
5.7	5.5	6.2	Cash & Equivalents	10.4	4.8	6.2	5.8	5.9	6.1
26.3	29.6	29.2	Trade Receivables (net)	15.6	28.3	31.8	29.6	32.7	29.8
48.7	46.1	44.1	Inventory	54.4	48.2	40.2	41.1	42.9	43.6
2.1	2.7	2.5	All Other Current	.4	1.3	4.1	4.0	2.0	2.4
82.8	84.0	82.0	Total Current	80.9	82.6	82.4	80.4	83.4	81.9
9.6	9.2	10.2	Fixed Assets (net)	12.3	10.6	10.9	12.4	7.8	9.2
3.0	2.6	3.1	Intangibles (net)	3.2	2.8	3.9	2.0	3.7	3.0
4.6	4.3	4.7	All Other Non-Current	3.6	4.0	2.9	5.2	5.1	5.9
100.0	100.0	100.0	Total	100.0	100.0	100.0	100.0	100.0	100.0
			LIABILITIES						
21.6	18.8	19.3	Notes Payable-Short Term	20.3	24.6	17.2	17.7	19.3	17.7
2.4	3.6	3.3	Cur. Mat.-L/T/D	7.2	5.1	4.2	1.8	2.4	2.5
20.2	22.3	21.2	Trade Payables	17.3	19.9	19.7	22.0	22.3	22.7
.2	.3	.2	Income Taxes Payable	.0	.3	.6	.2	.1	.3
8.5	8.4	8.2	All Other Current	6.0	6.9	9.2	7.2	9.5	8.9
52.9	53.5	52.2	Total Current	50.9	56.8	50.8	48.9	53.6	52.1
7.7	7.3	8.7	Long Term Debt	21.4	11.3	10.8	6.8	4.4	7.2
.1	.1	.0	Deferred Taxes	.0	.0	.0	.1	.0	.1
6.1	8.0	5.5	All Other Non-Current	10.2	7.0	4.3	3.9	5.4	4.7
33.2	31.1	33.5	Net Worth	17.4	24.9	34.0	40.3	36.5	35.9
100.0	100.0	100.0	Total Liabilities & Net Worth	100.0	100.0	100.0	100.0	100.0	100.0
			INCOME DATA						
100.0	100.0	100.0	Net Sales	100.0	100.0	100.0	100.0	100.0	100.0
29.6	29.9	30.7	Gross Profit	38.9	34.2	29.2	32.8	29.8	23.5
26.1	26.3	26.9	Operating Expenses	36.0	31.4	25.9	28.3	25.7	19.5
3.5	3.6	3.8	Operating Profit	2.9	2.8	3.3	4.5	4.0	4.1
1.2	1.4	.7	All Other Expenses (net)	1.0	.7	.2	.8	.6	.7
2.3	2.2	3.1	Profit Before Taxes	1.9	2.1	3.1	3.7	3.4	3.3
			RATIOS						
2.2 / 1.5 / 1.2	2.2 / 1.6 / 1.2	2.6 / 1.6 / 1.2	Current	3.3 / 1.6 / 1.2	2.6 / 1.6 / .9	2.6 / 1.7 / 1.4	3.3 / 1.6 / 1.2	2.1 / 1.4 / 1.2	2.5 / 1.6 / 1.2
1.0 / .6 / .3	1.0 / .6 / .4	1.2 / .7 / .4	Quick	1.0 / .5 / .3	1.1 / .6 / .2	1.3 / .8 / .4	1.2 / .7 / .5	1.2 / .6 / .4	1.2 / .7 / .4
15 24.3 / 36 10.1 / 59 6.2	20 18.0 / 37 10.0 / 64 5.7	20 18.7 / 35 10.5 / 58 6.3	Sales/Receivables	0 UND / 27 13.6 / 47 7.7	6 58.1 / 38 9.7 / 57 6.4	21 17.7 / 34 10.6 / 59 6.2	19 19.1 / 37 9.9 / 58 6.3	23 16.1 / 37 9.9 / 54 6.7	25 14.7 / 33 11.0 / 68 5.3
64 5.7 / 103 3.5 / 146 2.5	59 6.1 / 92 3.9 / 142 2.6	49 7.4 / 83 4.4 / 142 2.6	Cost of Sales/Inventory	50 7.3 / 218 1.7 / 421 .9	48 7.7 / 90 4.0 / 167 2.2	39 9.4 / 69 5.3 / 95 3.8	49 7.4 / 88 4.1 / 134 2.7	54 6.7 / 78 4.7 / 120 3.0	60 6.1 / 89 4.1 / 137 2.7
16 23.1 / 33 11.0 / 57 6.4	17 21.0 / 37 9.9 / 55 6.6	12 29.6 / 29 12.5 / 55 6.7	Cost of Sales/Payables	0 UND / 20 18.1 / 41 9.0	10 38.3 / 28 12.8 / 69 5.3	11 32.8 / 25 14.4 / 45 8.1	14 25.4 / 33 11.2 / 57 6.4	10 36.9 / 26 14.0 / 60 6.1	18 19.9 / 35 10.3 / 57 6.4
5.3 / 9.7 / 21.9	5.2 / 9.6 / 20.3	4.6 / 9.8 / 25.2	Sales/Working Capital	2.1 / 4.6 / 21.4	3.8 / 10.9 / -42.2	5.5 / 7.7 / 13.9	4.4 / 9.8 / 21.0	5.6 / 10.5 / 32.7	4.8 / 9.9 / 21.9
(211) 5.9 / 2.5 / 1.2	(179) 7.4 / 2.6 / 1.2	(220) 9.3 / 3.4 / 1.5	EBIT/Interest	(17) 3.6 / 1.6 / -.6	(32) 3.8 / 2.7 / 1.3	(23) 6.4 / 2.3 / .7	(47) 13.2 / 3.3 / 1.5	9.9 / 5.5 / 2.2	(42) 13.9 / 4.3 / 2.0
(40) 4.6 / 1.8 / .9	(36) 6.6 / 2.1 / .7	(48) 11.7 / 2.7 / 1.0	Net Profit + Depr., Dep., Amort./Cur. Mat. L/T/D				(12) 2.4 / 1.1 / -.1	(10) 11.4 / 3.0 / 1.2	(18) 46.3 / 11.4 / 5.2
.1 / .2 / .7	.1 / .2 / .8	.1 / .3 / .7	Fixed/Worth	.1 / .4 / -2.6	.1 / .3 / 2.4	.1 / .3 / .5	.1 / .3 / 1.0	.1 / .2 / .5	.1 / .2 / .6
1.1 / 2.3 / 6.0	1.0 / 2.2 / 7.4	.9 / 2.2 / 6.0	Debt/Worth	1.6 / 4.5 / -13.2	1.1 / 3.8 / 20.3	.7 / 1.6 / 3.8	.4 / 1.7 / 8.4	1.1 / 2.1 / 4.0	1.0 / 2.3 / 5.1
(203) 35.7 / 19.0 / 5.4	(171) 35.0 / 17.7 / 2.4	(213) 46.5 / 18.2 / 5.0	% Profit Before Taxes/Tangible Net Worth	(15) 22.8 / 5.9 / .0	(28) 66.3 / 12.0 / 3.6	(24) 36.6 / 14.6 / -.4	(47) 46.2 / 14.6 / 5.2	(56) 49.4 / 25.7 / 11.2	(43) 38.4 / 20.2 / 12.0
11.4 / 5.1 / .9	12.4 / 4.8 / .6	14.8 / 6.1 / 1.3	% Profit Before Taxes/Total Assets	22.1 / 2.8 / -.1	10.0 / 4.2 / .9	17.4 / 8.3 / -.1	17.1 / 4.3 / 1.0	15.1 / 6.6 / 2.7	12.0 / 6.1 / 2.6
108.3 / 47.2 / 20.9	137.2 / 46.7 / 20.8	101.6 / 41.9 / 20.2	Sales/Net Fixed Assets	74.5 / 28.1 / 13.7	107.9 / 37.6 / 19.0	102.1 / 46.5 / 17.1	107.1 / 39.9 / 15.4	109.6 / 55.5 / 25.0	106.0 / 44.7 / 20.9
3.5 / 2.6 / 1.8	3.5 / 2.6 / 1.8	3.7 / 2.7 / 1.8	Sales/Total Assets	4.3 / 2.0 / .9	3.6 / 2.6 / 1.8	4.2 / 3.0 / 2.4	3.7 / 2.7 / 1.7	3.9 / 2.8 / 1.9	2.9 / 2.4 / 1.6
(188) .3 / .6 / 1.2	(155) .2 / .6 / 1.2	(204) .4 / .7 / 1.2	% Depr., Dep., Amort./Sales	(16) .7 / 1.0 / 2.2	(26) .4 / .8 / 1.5	(22) .5 / .7 / 1.2	(48) .4 / .7 / 1.3	(52) .4 / .6 / 1.0	(40) .2 / .5 / 1.2
(109) 1.9 / 3.5 / 5.8	(82) 2.1 / 3.5 / 5.8	(105) 2.2 / 3.4 / 6.4	% Officers', Directors', Owners' Comp/Sales		(19) 3.5 / 5.0 / 8.1	(17) 2.2 / 4.1 / 5.5	(25) 2.2 / 2.9 / 6.3	(29) 1.3 / 2.0 / 3.6	
4261310M	4683020M	6009307M	Net Sales ($)	12197M	63961M	111525M	377928M	931669M	4512027M
1910389M	2237151M	2664158M	Total Assets ($)	8232M	29186M	37983M	172622M	410609M	2005526M

M = $ thousand   MM = $ million
See Pages 11 through 18 for Explanation of Ratios and Data

WHOLESALE—Toy and Hobby Goods and Supplies Merchant Wholesalers   NAICS 423920 (SIC 5092)

Current Data Sorted By Assets | **Comparative Historical Data**

0-500M	500M-2MM	2-10MM	10-50MM	50-100MM	100-250MM	Type of Statement	4/1/98-3/31/99 ALL	4/1/99-3/31/00 ALL
	1	8	14	4	1	Unqualified	27	29
	6	22	3			Reviewed	27	25
1	18	6				Compiled	32	30
4	11	2				Tax Returns	5	5
3	8	13	10	1	2	Other	37	24
	26 (4/1-9/30/02)		112 (10/1/02-3/31/03)					
8	44	51	27	5	3	**NUMBER OF STATEMENTS**	128	113
%	%	%	%	%	%	**ASSETS**	%	%
	12.3	6.5	12.0			Cash & Equivalents	8.4	6.9
	27.0	28.2	28.0			Trade Receivables (net)	26.9	27.2
	41.9	39.1	34.6			Inventory	40.0	43.9
	2.1	3.7	3.3			All Other Current	2.7	2.5
	83.3	77.4	77.9			Total Current	78.0	80.5
	10.5	12.8	13.7			Fixed Assets (net)	13.2	11.2
	2.8	3.1	5.0			Intangibles (net)	3.1	2.6
	3.4	6.7	3.4			All Other Non-Current	5.7	5.7
	100.0	100.0	100.0			Total	100.0	100.0
						LIABILITIES		
	11.2	19.9	12.4			Notes Payable-Short Term	20.1	19.2
	1.6	2.2	1.8			Cur. Mat.-L/T/D	2.3	1.2
	17.2	19.8	19.5			Trade Payables	18.4	15.7
	.3	.2	.3			Income Taxes Payable	.3	.5
	10.6	10.0	11.0			All Other Current	9.1	9.6
	40.8	52.0	45.0			Total Current	50.1	46.1
	6.7	6.6	7.9			Long Term Debt	9.1	7.2
	.0	.2	.0			Deferred Taxes	.1	.1
	6.5	4.5	2.9			All Other Non-Current	4.5	6.6
	45.9	36.8	44.2			Net Worth	36.1	39.9
	100.0	100.0	100.0			Total Liabilities & Net Worth	100.0	100.0
						INCOME DATA		
	100.0	100.0	100.0			Net Sales	100.0	100.0
	38.6	33.5	34.9			Gross Profit	34.2	36.2
	35.1	29.4	27.1			Operating Expenses	29.9	31.1
	3.5	4.2	7.8			Operating Profit	4.3	5.2
	.4	.9	.5			All Other Expenses (net)	1.1	.9
	3.2	3.3	7.2			Profit Before Taxes	3.2	4.3
						RATIOS		
	4.0 / 2.0 / 1.5	2.0 / 1.4 / 1.1	2.8 / 1.6 / 1.2			Current	2.4 / 1.6 / 1.2	2.8 / 1.7 / 1.3
	2.1 / 1.0 / .5	1.0 / .6 / .3	1.5 / .8 / .6			Quick	1.0 / .7 / .4	1.4 / .7 / .5
	20 18.4 / 34 10.9 / 49 7.4	29 12.8 / 43 8.4 / 57 6.4	28 13.0 / 49 7.5 / 69 5.3			Sales/Receivables	24 14.9 / 37 9.8 / 54 6.8	27 13.3 / 41 9.0 / 69 5.3
	31 11.6 / 117 3.1 / 189 1.9	47 7.8 / 84 4.3 / 204 1.8	69 5.3 / 84 4.4 / 109 3.3			Cost of Sales/Inventory	55 6.6 / 94 3.9 / 149 2.4	68 5.4 / 120 3.0 / 193 1.9
	8 48.6 / 19 18.8 / 54 6.8	18 20.8 / 38 9.5 / 64 5.7	20 17.9 / 40 9.0 / 66 5.5			Cost of Sales/Payables	16 / 32 11.5 / 59 6.2	17 21.7 / 32 11.5 / 59 6.1
	3.1 / 5.9 / 16.2	6.0 / 8.4 / 44.8	4.3 / 8.6 / 19.4			Sales/Working Capital	5.2 / 10.4 / 20.5	3.0 / 8.0 / 15.4
	(40) 19.0 / 3.7 / 1.0	(49) 10.6 / 4.5 / 1.4	(26) 17.8 / 8.5 / 3.5			EBIT/Interest	(118) 6.4 / 2.4 / 1.3	(104) 8.5 / 2.7 / 1.2
		(15) 11.5 / 3.1 / 1.3				Net Profit + Depr., Dep., Amort./Cur. Mat. L /T/D	(32) 15.2 / 3.6 / 1.5	(31) 7.1 / 4.2 / 1.4
	.0 / .1 / .5	.1 / .3 / .8	.1 / .2 / .6			Fixed/Worth	.1 / .3 / .7	.1 / .2 / .5
	.4 / .9 / 2.7	.9 / 1.6 / 5.9	.7 / 1.5 / 3.4			Debt/Worth	.9 / 2.0 / 4.3	.7 / 1.7 / 3.8
	(41) 46.7 / 22.3 / 1.2	(47) 59.1 / 19.4 / 1.4	(25) 67.4 / 33.6 / 19.4			% Profit Before Taxes/Tangible Net Worth	(120) 40.5 / 15.3 / 3.7	(101) 43.8 / 16.3 / 4.0
	17.7 / 4.6 / −.5	14.3 / 6.0 / .9	25.5 / 13.5 / 3.4			% Profit Before Taxes/Total Assets	12.9 / 4.7 / 1.0	14.5 / 5.2 / 1.3
	176.5 / 77.4 / 13.2	137.3 / 41.3 / 10.6	68.2 / 38.1 / 10.3			Sales/Net Fixed Assets	84.2 / 32.8 / 13.9	67.1 / 30.6 / 14.3
	3.9 / 2.6 / 1.6	3.0 / 2.2 / 1.5	2.6 / 2.3 / 1.6			Sales/Total Assets	3.3 / 2.3 / 1.6	2.9 / 2.0 / 1.4
	(35) .1 / .6 / 1.3	(46) .4 / .7 / 1.8	(21) .7 / 1.2 / 1.7			% Depr., Dep., Amort./Sales	(114) .4 / .8 / 1.4	(97) .5 / .8 / 1.4
	(23) 2.5 / 5.1 / 12.4	(29) 2.1 / 3.8 / 8.5				% Officers', Directors', Owners' Comp/Sales	(61) 1.6 / 3.4 / 6.1	(53) 1.8 / 3.7 / 7.3
8386M	171956M	652945M	1270260M	797283M	683065M	Net Sales ($)	2800553M	2464251M
2153M	53244M	273543M	610995M	352173M	391217M	Total Assets ($)	1653281M	1311773M

M = $ thousand   MM = $ million
See Pages 11 through 18 for Explanation of Ratios and Data

Comparative Historical Data | Current Data Sorted By Sales

						Type of Statement						
	20		13		28	Unqualified		1		1	8	18
	26		22		31	Reviewed		1	6	9	11	4
	32		36		25	Compiled	4	7	4	8	2	
	10		6		17	Tax Returns	4	7	3	3		
	24		41		37	Other	2	3	5	8	7	12
	4/1/00-3/31/01 ALL		4/1/01-3/31/02 ALL		4/1/02-3/31/03 ALL		26 (4/1-9/30/02) 0-1MM	1-3MM	3-5MM	112 (10/1/02-3/31/03) 5-10MM	10-25MM	25MM & OVER
	112		118		138	NUMBER OF STATEMENTS	10	19	18	29	28	34
	%		%		%	ASSETS	%	%	%	%	%	%
	6.5		7.9		10.2	Cash & Equivalents	7.0	12.1	13.5	9.5	8.2	10.7
	26.7		25.9		26.7	Trade Receivables (net)	13.5	24.8	24.2	24.1	32.6	30.4
	44.0		39.8		39.5	Inventory	63.2	36.1	41.8	39.5	35.4	36.7
	3.2		3.1		2.9	All Other Current	.7	1.6	1.4	3.4	4.4	3.3
	80.4		76.8		79.4	Total Current	84.4	74.5	80.8	76.6	80.6	81.1
	10.7		13.9		12.0	Fixed Assets (net)	6.5	13.8	13.7	12.4	11.2	11.9
	3.0		3.9		3.4	Intangibles (net)	4.0	4.5	.0	3.0	4.0	4.2
	5.9		5.3		5.3	All Other Non-Current	5.2	7.2	5.4	8.0	4.2	2.8
	100.0		100.0		100.0	Total	100.0	100.0	100.0	100.0	100.0	100.0
						LIABILITIES						
	20.1		18.1		14.8	Notes Payable-Short Term	18.3	10.1	15.1	16.4	16.2	13.7
	2.6		2.8		2.7	Cur. Mat.-L/T/D	14.2	2.6	2.6	1.3	1.8	1.5
	15.3		15.7		18.8	Trade Payables	21.0	7.6	15.8	23.0	23.1	19.0
	.4		.1		.2	Income Taxes Payable	.0	.0	.0	.4	.1	.5
	9.8		10.1		10.5	All Other Current	14.9	9.9	9.6	9.8	8.9	11.9
	48.2		46.8		47.1	Total Current	68.4	30.3	43.2	50.9	50.1	46.6
	5.2		7.2		7.0	Long Term Debt	2.6	3.7	8.7	10.2	5.8	7.3
	.1		.2		.1	Deferred Taxes	.0	.0	.2	.1	.0	.1
	5.3		5.9		5.1	All Other Non-Current	17.1	6.4	5.6	5.0	3.3	2.0
	41.2		39.9		40.8	Net Worth	11.9	59.6	42.2	33.8	40.8	44.0
	100.0		100.0		100.0	Total Liabilities & Net Worth	100.0	100.0	100.0	100.0	100.0	100.0
						INCOME DATA						
	100.0		100.0		100.0	Net Sales	100.0	100.0	100.0	100.0	100.0	100.0
	36.2		37.9		36.4	Gross Profit	41.8	42.8	40.4	35.6	31.9	33.4
	33.0		33.2		31.3	Operating Expenses	43.3	39.2	34.6	31.7	27.0	25.0
	3.2		4.6		5.0	Operating Profit	-1.4	3.5	5.8	3.9	4.9	8.4
	.8		1.1		.6	All Other Expenses (net)	1.4	.3	.8	.9	.3	.5
	2.4		3.5		4.4	Profit Before Taxes	-2.8	3.2	4.9	3.1	4.6	7.9
						RATIOS						
	2.6		2.6		3.1		3.5	6.8	3.3	2.0	2.9	2.9
	1.6		1.6		1.7	Current	1.8	2.9	1.9	1.6	1.5	1.7
	1.2		1.2		1.2		.8	1.5	1.3	1.1	1.1	1.3
	1.1		1.3		1.6		1.8	3.5	2.0	1.0	1.3	1.5
	.7	(117)	.7		.8	Quick	.2	1.6	.7	.6	.8	.9
	.4		.4		.5		.1	.5	.3	.3	.6	.6

26	13.8	24	15.2	23	15.9		0	UND	21	17.4	20	18.1	18	20.8	26	14.3	32	11.4
37	9.9	40	9.1	39	9.2	Sales/Receivables	23	16.0	39	9.4	35	10.6	38	9.6	42	8.8	48	7.6
60	6.1	56	6.5	56	6.5		55	6.6	50	7.3	47	7.8	54	6.8	59	6.2	61	5.9
64	5.7	58	6.3	53	6.9		97	3.8	79	4.6	51	7.1	27	13.3	40	9.2	59	6.2
113	3.2	101	3.6	95	3.8	Cost of Sales/Inventory	170	2.1	125	2.9	96	3.8	89	4.1	65	5.6	86	4.2
211	1.7	225	1.6	145	2.5		569	.6	174	2.1	196	1.9	216	1.7	110	3.3	106	3.4
16	23.4	15	24.1	13	28.0		0	UND	5	70.6	9	39.4	16	22.2	16	22.7	19	18.9
32	11.5	31	11.9	30	12.0	Cost of Sales/Payables	20	18.3	13	27.9	29	12.6	35	10.3	27	13.5	39	9.4
54	6.8	55	6.7	60	6.1		128	2.9	54	6.7	62	5.8	65	5.6	63	5.8	57	6.4
	4.0		4.0		4.0			1.3		2.9		3.3		5.3		6.6		4.3
	8.8		8.8		7.3	Sales/Working Capital		3.1		4.3		6.5		8.6		13.1		7.6
	20.5		19.0		20.5			-198.5		8.1		11.4		108.9		31.3		15.4
	6.1		7.0		17.1					16.1		21.0		22.5		17.0		20.7
(105)	2.1	(106)	2.8	(126)	6.6	EBIT/Interest			(15)	2.9	(17)	3.8	(27)	5.9	(27)	5.0	(32)	11.3
	1.0		1.2		1.5					-1.3		1.2		1.8		1.9		4.9
	5.0		5.4		11.6	Net Profit + Depr., Dep.,												19.7
(26)	2.9	(19)	2.2	(30)	4.1	Amort./Cur. Mat. L/T/D											(10)	10.4
	.6		1.0		2.6													7.9
	.1		.1		.1			.1		.0		.0		.1		.0		.1
	.2		.3		.2	Fixed/Worth		.3		.2		.1		.2		.2		.2
	.6		.7		.6			UND		.5		.8		.9		.8		.5
	.7		.8		.6			.7		.2		.6		.8		.8		.8
	1.9		1.5		1.5	Debt/Worth		9.1		.5		1.1		1.6		1.8		1.6
	3.5		3.1		4.2			-10.5		1.7		3.4		5.8		4.9		2.4
	35.9		45.2		56.0	% Profit Before Taxes/Tangible				31.7		46.7		26.3		104.5		71.8
(107)	16.8	(107)	14.6	(126)	25.1	Net Worth			(18)	12.6	(16)	24.7	(26)	15.0	(27)	29.8	(32)	38.3
	.7		1.7		3.4					-.4		2.2		2.7		4.4		26.4
	14.1		17.0		18.2	% Profit Before Taxes/Total		-.1		17.1		22.1		10.1		19.3		25.9
	3.8		6.5		7.4	Assets		-2.4		4.8		7.3		5.9		7.8		16.3
	.0		.5		.7			-21.8		-1.5		.6		1.1		2.1		9.1
	77.7		70.4		132.4			136.7		165.8		176.9		134.5		146.4		74.0
	33.8		31.0		45.3	Sales/Net Fixed Assets		32.3		41.0		97.6		35.2		54.9		29.2
	17.1		8.7		11.9			10.7		7.3		11.5		11.5		20.3		11.1
	3.0		3.1		3.2			3.5		2.7		3.4		3.8		4.2		2.8
	2.2		2.2		2.4	Sales/Total Assets		1.3		2.0		2.7		2.2		2.7		2.4
	1.5		1.4		1.7			.7		1.6		1.5		1.7		1.9		1.9
	.4		.4		.4					.3		.1		.5		.4		.5
(92)	.6	(97)	.8	(116)	.8	% Depr., Dep., Amort./Sales			(16)	.8	(14)	.4	(25)	.8	(24)	.7	(29)	1.0
	1.6		2.0		1.8					2.4		2.5		2.3		1.5		1.6
	2.3		2.0		2.2					3.2		2.9		2.9		1.6		
(57)	3.7	(57)	3.4	(64)	4.7	% Officers', Directors',			(12)	10.4	(10)	4.9	(15)	5.6	(13)	2.4		
	6.3		5.8		9.6	Owners' Comp/Sales				12.6		12.6		12.6		8.7		4.4

2555777M		2799544M		3583895M	Net Sales ($)	6975M	38180M	68357M	202691M	484382M	2783310M
1279213M		1484520M		1683325M	Total Assets ($)	5996M	20025M	34027M	101044M	211510M	1310723M

Current Data Sorted By Assets   Comparative Historical Data

0-500M	500M-2MM	2-10MM	10-50MM	50-100MM	100-250MM	Type of Statement	4/1/98-3/31/99 ALL	4/1/99-3/31/00 ALL
		4	12	5	5	Unqualified	28	31
3	13	47	16		.	Reviewed	78	94
11	23	34	3			Compiled	89	83
4	10	1				Tax Returns	14	23
4	12	34	15	2	3	Other	72	62
	52 (4/1-9/30/02)		209 (10/1/02-3/31/03)					
22	58	120	46	7	8	**NUMBER OF STATEMENTS**	281	293
%	%	%	%	%	%	**ASSETS**	%	%
22.7	6.7	7.1	6.2			Cash & Equivalents	7.1	8.0
23.4	22.4	27.9	23.6			Trade Receivables (net)	24.2	28.6
18.6	19.3	20.8	22.5			Inventory	22.0	21.1
1.7	3.3	2.7	2.5			All Other Current	2.8	2.3
66.5	51.7	58.5	54.8			Total Current	56.0	60.0
27.8	37.3	32.8	33.7			Fixed Assets (net)	34.2	30.8
1.4	.6	2.7	3.3			Intangibles (net)	2.3	2.7
4.3	10.4	6.0	8.3			All Other Non-Current	7.5	6.4
100.0	100.0	100.0	100.0			Total	100.0	100.0
						LIABILITIES		
17.7	9.8	16.4	13.2			Notes Payable-Short Term	15.0	15.1
2.8	6.1	4.5	6.4			Cur. Mat.-L/T/D	4.8	4.3
15.2	14.0	16.3	14.1			Trade Payables	13.4	16.9
.0	.5	.1	.1			Income Taxes Payable	.2	.2
13.1	7.4	8.0	6.0			All Other Current	6.2	7.3
48.8	37.7	45.2	39.8			Total Current	39.5	43.9
5.0	23.5	14.6	13.5			Long Term Debt	16.2	15.3
.0	.3	.4	.9			Deferred Taxes	.4	.3
22.0	5.0	7.1	7.1			All Other Non-Current	5.4	6.3
24.2	33.5	32.7	38.7			Net Worth	38.5	34.2
100.0	100.0	100.0	100.0			Total Liabilities & Net Worth	100.0	100.0
						INCOME DATA		
100.0	100.0	100.0	100.0			Net Sales	100.0	100.0
32.4	32.7	26.0	23.8			Gross Profit	24.8	26.9
27.2	29.4	23.3	18.0			Operating Expenses	24.0	24.5
5.2	3.3	2.7	5.8			Operating Profit	.7	2.4
1.7	.7	.6	1.1			All Other Expenses (net)	.9	.0
3.5	2.6	2.2	4.6			Profit Before Taxes	–.2	2.4
						RATIOS		
3.7	2.6	2.1	2.0			Current	2.6	2.3
1.7	1.3	1.4	1.3				1.5	1.4
1.1	.9	1.0	1.0				1.0	1.0
3.1	1.2	1.5	1.1			Quick	1.4	1.5
1.2	.7	.8	.8				.8	.8
.5	.4	.4	.5				.4	.5
0 UND	11 33.1	21 17.6	30 12.2			Sales/Receivables	15 24.4	23 15.8
11 32.2	19 19.3	32 11.5	35 10.3				26 13.9	40 9.2
39 9.3	43 8.4	42 8.7	42 8.6				36 10.0	51 7.2
0 UND	7 48.8	10 36.8	18 20.8			Cost of Sales/Inventory	11 31.8	14 25.9
15 23.6	18 19.8	26 14.1	41 8.8				25 14.5	32 11.3
39 9.4	59 6.2	60 6.1	72 5.1				60 6.1	65 5.6
0 UND	6 62.0	11 33.8	15 23.7			Cost of Sales/Payables	6 56.7	12 31.0
13 28.5	19 19.7	21 17.6	24 15.4				16 22.5	26 13.8
38 9.7	34 10.8	35 10.4	44 8.3				28 12.8	43 8.4
8.4	8.6	9.8	7.7			Sales/Working Capital	8.4	7.1
21.7	44.7	18.7	15.4				19.4	17.9
234.6	–70.5	–306.6	–315.4				407.0	438.9
33.1	6.6	5.7	10.7			EBIT/Interest	3.5	4.5
(14) 6.4	(55) 2.2	(112) 2.4	(45) 4.6				(257) 1.4	(265) 2.1
1.3	1.1	1.2	1.7				–.2	1.1
	3.4	6.8	2.9			Net Profit + Depr., Dep., Amort./Cur. Mat. L /T/D	2.5	6.0
	(10) 2.5	(29) 3.3	(11) 1.8				(67) 1.3	(67) 2.6
	1.8	1.4	.9				.3	1.4
.2	.5	.4	.5			Fixed/Worth	.4	.3
.6	1.1	.9	.9				.8	.9
NM	2.6	3.2	2.5				2.3	2.4
.4	1.0	.8	.8			Debt/Worth	.6	.8
1.7	2.0	1.8	1.9				1.9	2.0
NM	5.1	8.8	5.3				4.0	6.5
50.0	48.0	25.4	41.6			% Profit Before Taxes/Tangible Net Worth	17.1	32.1
(17) 38.8	(51) 19.1	(101) 9.6	(43) 19.2				(246) 4.5	(262) 13.8
.0	5.2	2.6	6.4				–8.5	2.6
34.8	12.9	7.9	13.7			% Profit Before Taxes/Total Assets	7.2	9.1
14.1	4.3	3.1	8.5				1.1	3.2
.0	1.1	.9	2.2				–4.7	.3
70.1	20.3	21.2	10.9			Sales/Net Fixed Assets	22.7	21.5
24.5	9.2	10.2	7.0				10.2	8.9
13.3	5.3	4.8	4.3				5.0	5.2
9.9	4.7	4.1	2.8			Sales/Total Assets	4.5	3.7
4.8	3.4	3.0	2.4				3.0	2.6
2.7	2.0	1.9	1.6				2.0	1.8
.6	1.5	.9	1.3			% Depr., Dep., Amort./Sales	1.1	1.1
(16) 1.5	(53) 2.9	(115) 2.3	(43) 2.8				(261) 2.1	(267) 2.4
3.6	5.2	4.4	4.1				3.9	4.2
3.7	3.2	1.2				% Officers', Directors', Owners' Comp/Sales	1.3	1.6
(10) 6.2	(36) 4.6	(61) 1.9					(140) 3.0	(139) 3.0
13.6	7.1	4.2					5.2	5.1
32114M	227849M	1796171M	2376755M	1108599M	3172667M	Net Sales ($)	7187568M	6019716M
5341M	65775M	534638M	1103387M	444601M	1412608M	Total Assets ($)	2603860M	2612416M

Comparative Historical Data / Current Data Sorted By Sales

Type of Statement	33	20	26			1		4	21
Unqualified	33	20	26			1		4	21
Reviewed	71	74	79	2	6	7	14	26	24
Compiled	91	72	71	7	15	14	20	10	5
Tax Returns	24	14	15	2	1	6	5	1	
Other	60	70	70		16	4	9	21	20
	4/1/00-3/31/01	4/1/01-3/31/02	4/1/02-3/31/03	52 (4/1-9/30/02)			209 (10/1/02-3/31/03)		
	ALL	ALL	ALL	0-1MM	1-3MM	3-5MM	5-10MM	10-25MM	25MM & OVER
NUMBER OF STATEMENTS	279	250	261	11	38	32	48	62	70
ASSETS	%	%	%	%	%	%	%	%	%
Cash & Equivalents	7.4	6.5	8.0	17.2	8.6	11.5	8.3	7.0	5.2
Trade Receivables (net)	28.2	26.5	25.5	17.5	18.8	21.2	23.0	27.5	32.2
Inventory	20.8	21.9	20.4	21.2	17.2	18.7	21.9	23.2	19.1
All Other Current	3.3	3.2	2.8	.8	2.2	4.5	1.7	3.5	2.7
Total Current	59.6	58.1	56.6	56.7	46.8	55.9	55.0	61.2	59.2
Fixed Assets (net)	31.4	32.9	33.6	37.9	37.6	36.2	37.2	29.2	31.0
Intangibles (net)	2.5	2.6	2.7	2.8	1.6	3.4	1.4	2.2	4.2
All Other Non-Current	6.4	6.3	7.1	2.6	14.1	4.5	6.3	7.5	5.5
Total	100.0	100.0	100.0	100.0	100.0	100.0	100.0	100.0	100.0
LIABILITIES									
Notes Payable-Short Term	14.9	15.7	13.9	28.1	11.7	8.4	12.8	16.3	13.9
Cur. Mat.-L/T/D	4.0	4.4	5.0	2.0	5.4	6.7	5.3	5.0	4.2
Trade Payables	15.6	15.6	15.2	13.0	10.3	11.7	15.5	17.0	17.8
Income Taxes Payable	.3	.1	.2	.0	.5	.3	.1	.1	.1
All Other Current	7.4	8.2	8.0	15.2	6.4	7.5	10.0	7.7	6.8
Total Current	42.2	44.0	42.2	58.3	34.3	34.6	43.8	46.2	42.8
Long Term Debt	14.0	16.0	16.0	5.5	23.5	18.6	17.5	14.5	12.7
Deferred Taxes	.3	.6	.4	.0	.0	.7	.2	.6	.6
All Other Non-Current	4.1	5.2	7.9	23.2	12.2	6.4	4.9	6.2	7.3
Net Worth	39.4	34.3	33.5	12.9	30.0	39.8	33.7	32.5	36.6
Total Liabilities & Net Worth	100.0	100.0	100.0	100.0	100.0	100.0	100.0	100.0	100.0
INCOME DATA									
Net Sales	100.0	100.0	100.0	100.0	100.0	100.0	100.0	100.0	100.0
Gross Profit	25.3	25.4	26.9	34.1	38.6	32.7	29.7	23.6	17.9
Operating Expenses	22.2	24.1	23.3	31.5	33.0	28.6	27.2	20.8	13.9
Operating Profit	3.1	1.3	3.6	2.6	5.6	4.1	2.5	2.8	4.0
All Other Expenses (net)	.8	1.0	.8	1.0	2.3	.3	.7	.4	.5
Profit Before Taxes	2.3	.3	2.9	1.5	3.2	3.8	1.9	2.4	3.5
RATIOS									
Current	2.5	2.0	2.1	3.0	3.0	2.8	2.4	2.1	2.0
	1.5	1.4	1.4	1.5	1.4	1.6	1.3	1.4	1.4
	1.0	1.0	1.0	.4	.8	1.0	1.0	1.0	1.1
Quick	1.4	1.2	1.4	3.0	1.8	2.2	1.4	1.3	1.2
	.8	.8	.8	.8	.8	.9	.7	.8	.9
	.5	.4	.5	.2	.4	.5	.5	.5	.6
Sales/Receivables	18 20.4	20 17.9	19 19.4	0 UND	10 37.7	9 41.8	16 22.2	21 17.0	28 13.2
	30 12.3	32 11.5	32 11.5	11 33.0	25 14.6	21 17.5	30 12.3	31 11.9	35 10.3
	40 9.1	44 8.3	43 8.5	43 8.5	44 8.2	47 7.8	40 9.1	41 8.8	44 8.3
Cost of Sales/Inventory	10 35.4	12 31.5	10 34.9	8 46.3	2 152.7	6 63.6	12 29.8	15 24.3	9 39.0
	26 14.3	28 13.2	24 15.0	33 11.2	25 14.7	15 24.0	26 14.1	29 12.4	23 16.1
	54 6.8	57 6.5	59 6.2	66 5.5	106 3.4	55 6.9	62 5.9	52 7.0	52 7.1
Cost of Sales/Payables	7 53.8	10 35.3	9 41.6	0 UND	0 UND	6 60.2	14 26.2	9 41.8	13 29.1
	18 20.1	22 16.5	22 16.5	33 11.0	18 20.1	15 24.0	20 18.1	24 14.9	22 16.5
	32 11.3	38 9.6	35 10.3	55 6.6	33 11.0	29 12.6	35 10.4	37 9.7	35 10.4
Sales/Working Capital	7.9	8.5	8.7	6.5	7.0	8.5	9.6	10.6	9.4
	19.0	18.3	19.5	10.9	25.5	14.5	26.8	17.2	22.1
	252.5	-839.8	-514.0	-16.1	-15.1	-243.5	182.4	-316.9	121.6
EBIT/Interest	(255) 5.2	(228) 3.4	(239) 6.5		(35) 6.6	(27) 6.8	6.1	(58) 6.2	(65) 8.1
	2.3	1.1	2.9		2.8	2.2	2.2	2.5	4.2
	1.1	-.2	1.3		1.0	1.5	1.2	1.2	1.8
Net Profit + Depr., Dep., Amort./Cur. Mat. L/T/D	(67) 6.8	(56) 3.7	(55) 3.9					(20) 4.1	(15) 3.3
	2.2	1.7	2.3					2.1	2.0
	1.2	.7	1.3					1.3	1.2
Fixed/Worth	.3	.4	.4	.3	.5	.3	.4	.4	.5
	.7	.8	.9	.9	1.4	1.0	1.0	.7	1.0
	1.8	2.6	2.9	-17.1	45.6	2.4	1.9	2.8	2.5
Debt/Worth	.7	.8	.8	.3	.9	.5	.8	.8	1.0
	1.7	2.2	1.9	2.8	2.6	1.5	1.8	1.7	2.1
	4.8	5.9	7.2	-20.6	114.6	3.4	5.0	7.8	6.5
% Profit Before Taxes/Tangible Net Worth	(255) 31.4	(216) 19.9	(224) 42.1		(30) 44.3	(27) 47.3	(41) 53.3	(55) 28.5	(63) 41.2
	11.7	2.7	14.6		22.4	11.5	8.4	12.6	18.6
	1.8	-8.8	4.2		2.9	4.2	1.3	2.6	8.5
% Profit Before Taxes/Total Assets	11.3	6.8	12.1	29.2	13.8	14.2	11.7	10.2	12.8
	4.0	.6	4.5	3.9	5.5	4.9	3.1	2.9	6.2
	.3	-4.1	1.0	.0	-.3	1.7	.5	.6	2.2
Sales/Net Fixed Assets	28.7	20.7	21.2	29.3	17.1	26.4	16.7	25.6	25.3
	10.4	9.2	9.5	13.0	6.3	9.2	10.4	11.6	9.3
	5.7	4.5	4.9	3.7	2.4	4.5	4.9	6.0	5.3
Sales/Total Assets	4.5	4.0	4.1	6.6	3.7	5.0	4.1	4.2	4.2
	3.1	2.7	2.8	2.6	2.0	2.9	3.0	3.2	2.7
	2.1	1.9	2.0	2.0	1.2	1.8	2.0	2.2	2.1
% Depr., Dep., Amort./Sales	(247) .7	(230) .7	(236) 1.1		(33) 2.0	(29) 1.5	1.5	(59) .9	(60) .7
	1.9	2.2	2.5		3.4	3.3	3.1	1.7	1.9
	3.6	4.2	4.3		5.5	5.6	5.0	3.5	3.3
% Officers', Directors', Owners' Comp/Sales	(136) 1.3	(118) 1.6	(116) 1.6		(17) 3.8	(20) 3.2	(24) 2.0	(30) 1.0	(17) .6
	2.8	2.9	3.3		5.8	6.0	3.8	1.7	1.1
	5.1	5.9	5.6		12.0	7.1	4.7	3.7	2.3
Net Sales ($)	7738759M	6627604M	8714155M	6432M	73895M	126016M	350600M	991483M	7165729M
Total Assets ($)	3121685M	2739115M	3566350M	2789M	45365M	55797M	131070M	370402M	2960927M

M = $ thousand   MM = $ million
See Pages 11 through 18 for Explanation of Ratios and Data

Current Data Sorted By Assets | **Comparative Historical Data**

Type of Statement	0-500M	500M-2MM	2-10MM	10-50MM	50-100MM	100-250MM	4/1/98-3/31/99 ALL	4/1/99-3/31/00 ALL
Unqualified	1	10	4	11	2		30	23
Reviewed	3	12	42	7			58	51
Compiled	5	10	13	1			44	45
Tax Returns	2	11	5	4			18	10
Other			10		2	1	28	22
	45 (4/1-9/30/02)		111 (10/1/02-3/31/03)					
NUMBER OF STATEMENTS	11	43	74	23	4	1	178	151

ASSETS	%	%	%	%	%	%	%	%
Cash & Equivalents	6.9	5.2	9.7	8.5			5.9	6.7
Trade Receivables (net)	24.8	27.9	37.6	27.4			28.0	31.3
Inventory	60.3	56.9	42.3	47.7			54.6	49.0
All Other Current	2.9	1.0	1.6	6.7			1.2	1.4
Total Current	94.9	91.0	91.1	90.2			89.7	88.5
Fixed Assets (net)	1.4	3.9	3.6	3.9			5.6	5.8
Intangibles (net)	.2	.2	.4	2.1			.9	1.4
All Other Non-Current	3.5	4.9	4.8	3.8			3.7	4.3
Total	100.0	100.0	100.0	100.0			100.0	100.0

LIABILITIES								
Notes Payable-Short Term	6.3	17.0	12.3	15.4			22.1	19.2
Cur. Mat.-L/T/D	.3	1.9	.6	2.0			1.5	2.0
Trade Payables	37.5	24.0	30.8	27.2			21.7	23.3
Income Taxes Payable	.0	.0	.5	.3			.2	.2
All Other Current	5.4	9.6	10.3	14.3			6.9	8.4
Total Current	49.6	52.6	54.6	59.2			52.4	53.1
Long Term Debt	15.6	4.0	4.1	.8			4.6	4.3
Deferred Taxes	.0	.0	.0	.0			.0	.1
All Other Non-Current	3.8	5.2	5.2	2.6			7.3	4.7
Net Worth	31.1	38.1	36.1	37.3			35.7	37.7
Total Liabilities & Net Worth	100.0	100.0	100.0	100.0			100.0	100.0

INCOME DATA								
Net Sales	100.0	100.0	100.0	100.0			100.0	100.0
Gross Profit	33.9	30.9	24.1	25.9			27.6	27.0
Operating Expenses	31.3	30.0	20.2	20.6			23.0	24.4
Operating Profit	2.6	.9	3.9	5.3			4.6	2.6
All Other Expenses (net)	–.2	.7	.9	1.4			1.3	.3
Profit Before Taxes	2.7	.2	3.0	3.9			3.3	2.3

RATIOS								
Current	2.9	2.6	2.2	2.0			2.4	2.4
	2.3	2.1	1.7	1.5			1.7	1.7
	1.5	1.2	1.3	1.2			1.3	1.3
Quick	1.2	1.1	1.2	.8			.9	1.0
	.8	.6	.9	.5			.7	.7
	.2	.3	.6	.3			.4	.4
Sales/Receivables	1 399.8	22 16.4	36 10.2	41 9.0			16 22.5	23 16.2
	21 17.3	44 8.3	66 5.5	72 5.1			50 7.3	46 8.0
	66 5.5	71 5.2	105 3.5	97 3.8			89 4.1	87 4.2
Cost of Sales/Inventory	49 7.5	76 4.8	43 8.5	97 3.8			83 4.4	60 6.1
	103 3.5	151 2.4	97 3.8	161 2.3			140 2.6	111 3.3
	206 1.8	281 1.3	173 2.1	193 1.9			215 1.7	178 2.1
Cost of Sales/Payables	24 15.5	26 14.2	42 8.7	36 10.2			19 19.6	26 14.1
	73 5.0	50 7.3	63 5.8	79 4.6			42 8.6	46 8.0
	112 3.3	89 4.1	100 3.7	107 3.4			84 4.3	84 4.4
Sales/Working Capital	5.2	3.2	3.4	3.5			3.4	3.7
	7.4	5.5	5.8	6.1			5.5	6.3
	13.2	12.8	9.6	9.3			11.2	13.3
EBIT/Interest		(38) 6.8	(71) 10.6	(21) 5.2			(164) 4.7	(139) 6.3
		1.5	4.1	2.0			2.2	2.4
		1.0	1.6	1.2			1.4	1.2
Net Profit + Depr., Dep., Amort./Cur. Mat. L /T/D							(35) 5.3	(25) 6.7
							2.1	1.9
							.6	.6
Fixed/Worth	.0	.0	.0	.0			.0	.0
	.0	.0	.0	.1			.1	.0
	.0	.1	.1	.1			.3	.2
Debt/Worth	.6	.6	1.0	.9			1.1	.8
	2.7	1.2	2.0	2.3			2.6	1.8
	52.2	5.2	3.8	3.8			5.5	4.2
% Profit Before Taxes/Tangible Net Worth	(10) 98.0	(41) 15.3	(71) 32.0	(22) 31.0			(173) 32.6	(145) 27.4
	25.8	5.8	10.3	9.5			14.6	9.8
	–.6	.3	3.2	1.5			4.7	2.9
% Profit Before Taxes/Total Assets	20.8	6.2	9.9	8.2			9.1	9.9
	4.8	1.5	2.9	3.4			4.0	3.2
	.0	.1	1.1	.3			1.3	.7
Sales/Net Fixed Assets	UND	656.0	340.2	158.3			217.6	280.8
	UND	144.1	165.8	64.6			88.8	110.5
	246.2	38.2	60.9	26.8			31.8	36.3
Sales/Total Assets	5.1	2.9	2.9	1.9			2.6	3.0
	3.4	1.9	2.0	1.6			2.0	2.1
	2.1	1.4	1.4	1.2			1.4	1.4
% Depr., Dep., Amort./Sales		(31) .1	(60) .1	.2			(152) .1	(116) .1
		.3	.2	.5			.3	.3
		.8	.5	.8			.7	.8
% Officers', Directors', Owners' Comp/Sales		(30) 2.7	(48) 1.3				(108) 1.4	(95) 1.5
		4.7	2.9				3.1	3.0
		8.8	4.2					5.3
Net Sales ($)	15896M	128132M	778933M	619691M	568289M	224294M	2898169M	2618086M
Total Assets ($)	3624M	50982M	359874M	419172M	322530M	129775M	1651832M	1476475M

Comparative Historical Data | Current Data Sorted By Sales

			Type of Statement						
26	32	17	Unqualified			1	1	7	8
49	44	60	Reviewed	2	8	8	17	21	4
45	35	29	Compiled	1	10	5	7	5	1
14	9	20	Tax Returns	6	4	1	6	3	
25	26	30	Other	2	6	4	4	8	6
4/1/00-3/31/01 ALL	4/1/01-3/31/02 ALL	4/1/02-3/31/03 ALL		45 (4/1-9/30/02)			111 (10/1/02-3/31/03)		
				0-1MM	1-3MM	3-5MM	5-10MM	10-25MM	25MM & OVER
159	146	156	NUMBER OF STATEMENTS	11	28	19	35	44	19
%	%	%	ASSETS	%	%	%	%	%	%
5.6	6.3	8.1	Cash & Equivalents	6.1	4.6	4.8	6.8	14.2	5.8
30.6	30.5	32.0	Trade Receivables (net)	20.4	24.1	41.9	30.1	38.7	28.6
50.4	49.5	48.0	Inventory	55.2	64.6	43.4	51.5	37.1	42.6
1.1	1.5	2.2	All Other Current	3.9	.6	.8	1.5	2.3	6.3
87.7	87.8	90.3	Total Current	85.7	93.9	90.9	89.9	92.4	83.3
5.5	5.5	3.8	Fixed Assets (net)	3.6	2.6	4.4	4.2	3.2	5.5
2.2	2.1	.8	Intangibles (net)	.2	.4	.2	.5	1.2	1.9
4.6	4.6	5.1	All Other Non-Current	10.5	3.1	4.6	5.3	3.1	9.4
100.0	100.0	100.0	Total	100.0	100.0	100.0	100.0	100.0	100.0
			LIABILITIES						
21.5	21.4	13.7	Notes Payable-Short Term	10.6	17.9	16.7	11.3	11.7	15.0
1.0	1.4	1.2	Cur. Mat.-L/T/D	4.1	.9	.7	.8	1.5	.4
21.3	20.6	28.5	Trade Payables	22.8	26.3	30.0	31.2	29.0	27.2
.4	.2	.3	Income Taxes Payable	.0	.0	.1	.5	.5	.3
8.9	7.1	10.4	All Other Current	2.1	12.3	6.7	6.1	14.1	15.7
53.1	50.7	54.1	Total Current	39.5	57.4	54.2	49.9	56.8	58.7
4.1	4.9	4.6	Long Term Debt	20.8	2.3	4.2	6.2	1.6	2.7
.1	.1	.1	Deferred Taxes	.0	.0	.0	.0	.0	.6
7.0	5.4	5.1	All Other Non-Current	5.1	2.5	10.6	4.8	4.0	6.6
35.7	38.9	36.2	Net Worth	34.6	37.9	31.1	39.1	37.4	31.5
100.0	100.0	100.0	Total Liabilities & Net Worth	100.0	100.0	100.0	100.0	100.0	100.0
			INCOME DATA						
100.0	100.0	100.0	Net Sales	100.0	100.0	100.0	100.0	100.0	100.0
27.0	30.3	27.1	Gross Profit	38.0	35.4	27.6	20.1	25.3	25.5
22.9	26.4	24.0	Operating Expenses	38.0	32.9	26.6	17.7	19.8	21.4
4.2	3.9	3.1	Operating Profit	.0	2.5	1.0	2.4	5.4	4.1
.9	1.5	.9	All Other Expenses (net)	.9	.7	.7	.5	1.2	1.1
3.3	2.4	2.3	Profit Before Taxes	−.9	1.8	.3	1.8	4.2	2.9
			RATIOS						
2.6	2.8	2.4	Current	2.7	2.6	2.6	2.8	2.2	1.7
1.6	1.7	1.7		2.6	2.0	1.8	1.9	1.6	1.3
1.3	1.3	1.3		1.5	1.2	1.3	1.3	1.3	1.2
1.0	1.1	1.1	Quick	1.2	.9	1.6	1.1	1.4	.9
.6	.7	.8		.3	.5	1.0	.7	1.0	.6
.4	.4	.4		.2	.2	.6	.5	.6	.4
24 15.2	30 12.0	28 13.3	Sales/Receivables	1 358.5	19 18.8	46 7.9	29 12.6	35 10.6	27 13.4
52 7.1	60 6.1	60 6.1		29 12.8	44 8.3	73 5.0	55 6.7	65 5.6	62 5.9
78 4.7	85 4.3	91 4.0		72 5.1	84 4.3	108 3.4	79 4.6	97 4.6	93 3.9
64 5.7	73 5.0	66 5.5	Cost of Sales/Inventory	206 1.8	117 3.1	60 6.1	66 5.5	34 10.8	75 4.8
125 2.9	144 2.5	121 3.0		281 1.3	179 2.0	96 3.8	120 3.0	79 4.6	123 3.0
183 2.0	208 1.8	193 1.9		357 1.0	297 1.2	186 2.0	193 1.9	135 2.7	173 2.1
20 18.0	24 15.4	35 10.4	Cost of Sales/Payables	66 5.6	34 10.6	33 11.2	47 7.8	16 22.3	28 13.2
44 8.3	50 7.2	62 5.9		89 4.1	49 7.4	68 5.3	64 5.7	50 7.3	73 5.0
77 4.7	84 4.4	104 3.5		112 3.3	110 3.3	115 3.2	92 4.0	98 3.7	121 3.0
3.8	3.6	3.5	Sales/Working Capital	1.6	3.3	2.9	3.1	4.4	5.3
6.3	5.7	5.9		3.3	5.3	5.1	4.6	7.0	8.4
13.9	11.5	10.1		7.1	9.9	12.8	13.0	10.1	12.9
(150) 6.3	(138) 5.1	(143) 7.6	EBIT/Interest		(23) 3.0	6.9	(34) 7.1	(41) 13.9	(17) 5.2
2.3	1.6	2.6			1.5	2.3	3.6	4.9	2.2
1.4	1.0	1.2			1.1	1.1	1.2	1.9	1.2
(25) 18.7	(20) 9.8	(17) 11.6	Net Profit + Depr., Dep., Amort./Cur. Mat. L/T/D						
2.8	4.4	3.0							
1.3	.0	.3							
.0	.0	.0	Fixed/Worth	.0	.0	.0	.0	.0	.0
.1	.1	.1		.0	.0	.1	.1	.0	.1
.3	.3	.1		.5	.1	.2	.1	.1	.2
.8	.7	.8	Debt/Worth	.6	.6	.7	.9	.9	1.7
2.3	1.9	2.0		2.0	1.9	2.1	1.5	2.0	2.7
6.2	5.3	3.9		10.5	3.9	4.8	3.9	3.6	6.1
(148) 31.7	(139) 24.3	(148) 28.2	% Profit Before Taxes/Tangible Net Worth	(10) 12.3	(27) 34.9	(18) 14.6	(34) 14.8	(41) 38.9	(18) 38.6
14.6	7.8	9.5		1.8	5.8	6.8	7.1	19.6	12.2
4.7	.5	1.7		−11.3	.4	1.7	.9	7.5	2.2
9.7	8.4	8.2	% Profit Before Taxes/Total Assets	2.3	11.3	7.3	6.9	15.0	7.6
3.7	2.3	2.6		.2	1.2	2.3	2.5	5.4	4.1
1.3	.1	.3		−1.6	.1	.3	.3	2.3	.5
340.6	221.6	384.4	Sales/Net Fixed Assets	UND	999.8	388.2	266.5	884.3	195.2
107.1	81.5	147.0		246.2	213.1	203.4	149.8	165.7	64.6
37.5	28.1	43.4		22.4	45.6	41.5	59.8	46.6	29.1
3.0	2.7	2.8	Sales/Total Assets	2.1	2.6	2.9	2.8	3.1	2.4
2.0	1.9	1.9		1.3	1.7	2.1	2.0	2.2	1.8
1.5	1.4	1.4		1.0	1.4	1.4	1.4	1.6	1.3
(120) .1	(124) .1	(121) .1	% Depr., Dep., Amort./Sales		(19) .1	(17) .1	(28) .1	(35) .1	(18) .1
.2	.4	.3			.3	.4	.2	.3	.5
.7	.9	.8			.8	.9	.5	.6	1.0
(98) 1.3	(90) 1.6	(98) 1.5	% Officers', Directors', Owners' Comp/Sales		(19) 3.3	(14) 2.1	(27) 1.5	(24) 1.0	
2.9	3.9	3.4			5.5	3.7	2.8	2.8	
5.8	6.2	6.1			8.6	7.5	3.7	6.9	
3690061M	5830063M	2335235M	Net Sales ($)	6309M	53313M	70045M	234351M	692045M	1279172M
2045063M	2244197M	1285957M	Total Assets ($)	5188M	32380M	36874M	129630M	347949M	733936M

Current Data Sorted By Assets   Comparative Historical Data

						Type of Statement		
		4	24	24	3	4	Unqualified	50	29
2	25	56	6		1	Reviewed	59	59
15	41	33	4			Compiled	81	69
12	15	11	4			Tax Returns	26	25
11	26	42	8	2	3	Other	68	81

0-500M	72 (4/1-9/30/02) 500M-2MM	2-10MM	304 (10/1/02-3/31/03) 10-50MM	50-100MM	100-250MM		4/1/98-3/31/99 ALL	4/1/99-3/31/00 ALL
40	111	166	46	6	7	NUMBER OF STATEMENTS	284	263
%	%	%	%	%	%	**ASSETS**	%	%
14.1	11.7	7.8	6.4			Cash & Equivalents	8.8	10.6
25.4	31.3	34.6	34.4			Trade Receivables (net)	32.4	32.6
28.0	35.5	36.3	37.6			Inventory	35.2	33.1
3.8	2.4	2.2	1.4			All Other Current	2.2	2.1
71.2	81.0	80.8	79.8			Total Current	78.5	78.3
19.2	13.5	11.6	10.3			Fixed Assets (net)	12.8	12.9
1.6	2.3	2.9	6.1			Intangibles (net)	2.1	3.0
8.0	3.2	4.7	3.8			All Other Non-Current	6.6	5.8
100.0	100.0	100.0	100.0			Total	100.0	100.0
						LIABILITIES		
33.3	14.7	17.6	18.3			Notes Payable-Short Term	16.7	18.3
2.6	3.0	2.3	3.2			Cur. Mat.-L/T/D	2.3	2.3
20.3	19.3	25.6	19.6			Trade Payables	22.2	20.6
.0	.1	.5	.2			Income Taxes Payable	.2	.3
15.3	11.9	7.9	8.5			All Other Current	10.0	7.8
71.5	49.1	53.9	49.7			Total Current	51.5	49.4
13.6	6.9	7.3	4.8			Long Term Debt	9.6	8.6
.0	.0	.1	.4			Deferred Taxes	.1	.2
7.1	5.4	4.3	3.8			All Other Non-Current	3.7	5.1
7.7	38.6	34.4	42.1			Net Worth	35.0	36.8
100.0	100.0	100.0	100.0			Total Liabilities & Net Worth	100.0	100.0
						INCOME DATA		
100.0	100.0	100.0	100.0			Net Sales	100.0	100.0
44.1	32.3	28.6	29.3			Gross Profit	29.8	31.0
40.7	30.5	25.6	22.6			Operating Expenses	26.3	26.5
3.4	1.7	3.0	6.7			Operating Profit	3.5	4.6
1.1	.4	.7	.5			All Other Expenses (net)	.7	.2
2.2	1.4	2.3	6.2			Profit Before Taxes	2.8	4.4
						RATIOS		
1.7	3.0	2.3	2.5				2.4	2.5
1.0	1.6	1.4	1.7			Current	1.5	1.5
.8	1.2	1.1	1.2				1.2	1.1
.9	1.8	1.2	1.2				1.3	1.3
.6	.8	.8	.8			Quick	.9 (262)	.9
.3	.5	.5	.5				.5	.6

											Sales/Receivables				
4	85.6	22	16.9	33	11.2	37	9.8					26	13.9	29	12.7
23	15.9	35	10.5	45	8.0	47	7.8					40	9.1	41	8.9
42	8.6	47	7.7	58	6.3	71	5.1					57	6.4	57	6.4
10	36.5	27	13.5	39	9.3	67	5.4				Cost of Sales/Inventory	31	11.8	27	13.7
33	11.2	57	6.4	73	5.0	95	3.8					62	5.9	62	5.9
100	3.7	103	3.5	108	3.4	123	3.0					103	3.6	104	3.5
13	28.3	14	25.9	22	16.4	12	31.0				Cost of Sales/Payables	14	25.3	15	24.3
29	12.7	28	13.2	37	9.8	31	11.9					34	10.7	31	11.6
55	6.7	49	7.5	58	6.3	59	6.2					58	6.2	59	6.2

					Sales/Working Capital		
12.4	5.5	6.0	4.5			5.4	5.2
198.8	11.1	11.3	7.1			11.2	10.2
-28.2	34.6	27.9	27.6			27.4	32.4

								EBIT/Interest				
	7.5		7.7		7.6		25.9			7.8		10.7
(31)	2.1	(96)	3.4	(155)	2.9	(41)	5.1		(251)	2.9	(237)	3.1
	.3		.1		1.4		1.9			1.2		1.6

							Net Profit + Depr., Dep., Amort./Cur. Mat. L /T/D				
			6.2		12.5		14.2		9.7		7.6
	(15)		1.2	(44)	2.5	(17)	3.7	(70)	4.0	(56)	2.1
			-.7		1.0		1.3		1.2		.8

					Fixed/Worth		
.1	.1	.1	.1			.1	.1
.6	.3	.3	.2			.2	.3
8.1	1.0	.7	.8			.8	.7
1.1	.6	1.0	.9		Debt/Worth	.9	.9
2.6	2.0	2.4	2.0			2.0	2.0
NM	5.5	5.4	3.6			5.1	5.4

							% Profit Before Taxes/Tangible Net Worth				
	80.1		47.7		34.7		50.0		40.1		48.7
(30)	16.3	(100)	10.5	(152)	13.8	(43)	24.1	(252)	20.0	(239)	21.7
	-1.9		1.4		3.7		9.5		5.0		5.9

					% Profit Before Taxes/Total Assets		
18.0	11.8	11.4	20.7			15.9	15.8
3.4	3.3	3.7	10.5			5.8	5.9
-2.9	-.3	1.2	2.0			1.1	1.9
78.3	126.1	107.1	67.1		Sales/Net Fixed Assets	107.5	97.2
31.0	38.1	43.8	28.8			41.7	39.6
11.2	14.4	17.9	17.7			17.7	16.3
5.2	4.2	3.6	2.6		Sales/Total Assets	3.8	3.6
3.7	3.0	2.7	2.3			2.8	2.7
2.3	2.4	2.0	1.6			2.2	2.0

							% Depr., Dep., Amort./Sales				
	.6		.3		.3		.3		.4		.3
(27)	1.0	(90)	.9	(152)	.7	(41)	.7	(243)	.7	(223)	.8
	2.1		1.8		1.4		1.3		1.3		1.5

							% Officers', Directors', Owners' Comp/Sales				
	2.1		2.7		1.9		1.4		2.2		2.2
(24)	5.1	(71)	4.0	(80)	3.7	(14)	2.2	(121)	3.7	(135)	3.8
	9.0		6.8		5.3		4.4		7.9		7.4

45242M	463835M	2252895M	2148437M	1161267M	1959526M	Net Sales ($)	5549689M	4198615M
11219M	136753M	755872M	933549M	415328M	1080865M	Total Assets ($)	2110985M	2016816M

Comparative Historical Data — Current Data Sorted By Sales

			Type of Statement						
42	38	59	Unqualified			1	10	16	32
67	56	90	Reviewed		7	14	31	29	9
101	84	93	Compiled	10	21	13	29	12	8
46	31	42	Tax Returns	6	14	4	11	3	4
82	98	92	Other	5	18	19	13	25	12
4/1/00-3/31/01 ALL	4/1/01-3/31/02 ALL	4/1/02-3/31/03 ALL		72 (4/1-9/30/02)			304 (10/1/02-3/31/03)		
				0-1MM	1-3MM	3-5MM	5-10MM	10-25MM	25MM & OVER
338	307	376	NUMBER OF STATEMENTS	21	60	51	94	85	65
%	%	%	ASSETS	%	%	%	%	%	%
9.3	9.1	9.3	Cash & Equivalents	17.2	10.9	9.6	9.2	7.1	8.3
33.6	33.4	32.5	Trade Receivables (net)	18.3	28.0	33.1	32.3	36.9	35.6
34.2	34.0	34.9	Inventory	28.8	31.1	33.2	38.1	37.5	33.9
2.6	2.8	2.4	All Other Current	5.3	3.8	1.7	2.1	1.7	2.1
79.6	79.3	79.2	Total Current	69.6	73.8	77.6	81.7	83.1	79.9
12.5	13.0	13.0	Fixed Assets (net)	19.1	17.5	14.7	11.9	9.9	11.0
2.9	3.4	3.2	Intangibles (net)	3.1	3.1	3.5	2.4	2.6	5.0
5.0	4.2	4.6	All Other Non-Current	8.1	5.6	4.1	4.1	4.4	4.0
100.0	100.0	100.0	Total	100.0	100.0	100.0	100.0	100.0	100.0
			LIABILITIES						
16.8	17.2	18.0	Notes Payable-Short Term	35.0	20.3	15.7	17.2	16.5	15.6
2.2	2.8	2.7	Cur. Mat.-L/T/D	1.9	4.0	3.0	1.5	3.6	2.2
22.5	22.9	22.6	Trade Payables	14.1	19.9	19.7	22.6	24.8	27.0
.3	.2	.3	Income Taxes Payable	.0	.0	.1	.5	.5	.2
9.1	9.8	10.1	All Other Current	15.2	10.4	10.0	11.7	6.6	10.6
51.0	52.7	53.7	Total Current	66.2	54.6	48.4	53.5	52.0	55.5
10.8	9.4	7.8	Long Term Debt	19.1	10.2	9.1	6.9	4.6	6.3
.1	.1	.1	Deferred Taxes	.0	.0	.1	.1	.1	.4
4.0	3.9	4.8	All Other Non-Current	13.6	4.4	7.2	3.1	4.2	3.4
34.2	33.9	33.6	Net Worth	1.1	30.7	35.2	36.4	39.1	34.3
100.0	100.0	100.0	Total Liabilities & Net Worth	100.0	100.0	100.0	100.0	100.0	100.0
			INCOME DATA						
100.0	100.0	100.0	Net Sales	100.0	100.0	100.0	100.0	100.0	100.0
30.7	30.2	31.2	Gross Profit	48.8	38.9	30.7	30.0	27.4	25.4
25.7	27.2	28.0	Operating Expenses	44.9	38.2	27.3	27.2	23.8	20.4
5.0	3.0	3.2	Operating Profit	3.8	.8	3.4	2.8	3.5	4.9
.9	.7	.6	All Other Expenses (net)	1.8	.9	.6	.5	.4	.7
4.1	2.3	2.5	Profit Before Taxes	2.1	−.1	2.8	2.4	3.2	4.3
			RATIOS						
2.5 1.6 1.2	2.3 1.5 1.1	2.3 1.5 1.1	Current	4.3 1.1 .8	2.1 1.6 .9	3.4 1.5 1.1	2.3 1.4 1.2	2.5 1.5 1.2	2.3 1.3 1.0
1.4 .9 .5	1.3 .8 .5	1.2 .8 .5	Quick	.9 .6 .4	1.3 .7 .5	1.8 .8 .5	1.3 .7 .5	1.4 .9 .6	1.1 .8 .5
28 13.2 41 9.0 56 6.6	29 12.6 40 9.0 56 6.5	27 13.4 41 8.9 56 6.5	Sales/Receivables	0 UND 25 14.8 61 6.0	21 17.4 35 10.4 46 7.9	24 15.5 41 8.9 63 5.8	25 14.8 40 9.2 56 6.5	34 10.6 44 8.2 57 6.4	31 11.9 44 8.3 59 6.2
28 13.3 61 6.0 108 3.4	31 11.6 64 5.7 108 3.4	34 10.9 67 5.4 109 3.4	Cost of Sales/Inventory	10 37.7 75 4.9 181 2.0	25 14.9 63 5.8 109 3.3	30 12.1 69 5.3 110 3.3	39 9.4 66 5.5 109 3.3	39 9.4 68 5.4 106 3.4	34 10.8 68 5.3 96 3.8
15 23.9 32 11.5 58 6.3	14 25.7 31 11.7 53 6.9	18 20.8 33 10.9 57 6.4	Cost of Sales/Payables	2 175.1 48 7.7 71 5.1	16 23.2 38 9.6 63 5.8	22 16.6 33 11.0 59 6.1	15 24.0 31 11.9 57 6.5	20 18.5 34 10.7 56 6.5	21 17.4 32 11.3 52 7.1
5.6 10.0 26.2	5.5 10.9 36.9	5.7 11.7 41.9	Sales/Working Capital	3.6 44.7 −16.7	5.6 18.6 −107.6	4.8 8.5 42.6	6.3 11.3 21.7	6.0 11.1 26.7	5.9 13.1 124.7
(298) 8.8 2.9 1.4	(260) 6.6 2.5 1.0	(336) 8.9 3.0 1.2	EBIT/Interest	(15) 2.5 1.0 −.5	(51) 6.4 1.7 −.2	(45) 7.8 2.2 1.0	(85) 11.3 3.1 1.3	(81) 9.2 3.5 1.4	(59) 19.9 5.6 1.9
(56) 19.6 2.5 1.0	(53) 6.9 2.5 1.4	(80) 10.9 2.4 .8	Net Profit + Depr., Dep., Amort./Cur. Mat. L/T/D				(19) 5.3 1.5 .6	(28) 9.6 2.4 .8	(21) 37.1 7.5 1.4
.1 .2 .8	.1 .3 1.0	.1 .3 1.0	Fixed/Worth	.1 .6 −6.2	.1 .4 2.0	.0 .3 3.3	.1 .2 .7	.1 .2 .6	.1 .4 1.0
.8 1.9 4.5	.8 2.3 5.9	.9 2.3 5.7	Debt/Worth	.7 5.3 −12.7	.8 2.5 7.9	.8 2.6 10.6	.9 1.7 3.9	.8 2.1 4.7	1.0 2.6 6.0
(307) 47.7 21.3 5.5	(272) 40.9 14.7 3.3	(335) 43.0 14.0 3.4	% Profit Before Taxes/Tangible Net Worth	(14) 52.4 −.7 −21.9	(52) 57.4 8.3 −1.9	(44) 53.3 16.8 3.4	(87) 30.7 12.0 3.4	(82) 43.3 14.8 4.0	(56) 52.7 24.5 7.7
16.7 6.3 1.7	11.1 4.3 .1	12.4 3.9 .7	% Profit Before Taxes/Total Assets	13.4 3.1 −2.3	10.4 1.8 −5.9	11.8 3.6 .5	11.7 3.7 1.2	12.4 4.2 1.2	15.9 7.6 2.4
125.7 40.4 17.8	94.2 36.1 16.5	100.8 36.7 15.4	Sales/Net Fixed Assets	262.0 14.2 5.4	61.7 23.9 11.4	113.4 36.9 11.8	155.7 53.6 17.9	83.2 40.0 18.7	100.7 34.7 17.9
4.0 2.9 2.1	3.6 2.7 2.1	3.8 2.7 2.1	Sales/Total Assets	2.7 2.0 1.0	4.6 2.9 1.9	3.1 2.6 1.8	3.8 2.9 2.1	3.9 2.8 2.3	3.8 2.6 2.3
(265) .3 .7 1.6	(242) .4 .8 1.5	(320) .3 .8 1.6	% Depr., Dep., Amort./Sales	(11) .6 1.3 6.3	(50) .6 1.2 2.3	(39) .4 1.0 2.3	(85) .2 .7 1.4	(78) .3 .6 1.1	(57) .3 .6 1.2
(165) 2.4 4.4 8.0	(134) 2.1 3.8 7.8	(191) 2.1 3.8 6.9	% Officers', Directors', Owners' Comp/Sales	(12) 2.0 5.1 10.0	(40) 2.7 3.1 13.5	(26) 2.6 3.1 5.4	(52) 2.6 3.8 8.3	(39) 2.1 4.0 6.3	(22) 1.0 1.6 3.8
7684634M	5995687M	8031202M	Net Sales ($)	8986M	119637M	193083M	678820M	1331335M	5699341M
3315155M	2617032M	3333586M	Total Assets ($)	6184M	49864M	84836M	267987M	527646M	2397069M

M = $ thousand   MM = $ million
See Pages 11 through 18 for Explanation of Ratios and Data

Current Data Sorted By Assets   Comparative Historical Data

0-500M	500M-2MM	2-10MM	10-50MM	50-100MM	100-250MM	Type of Statement	4/1/98-3/31/99 ALL	4/1/99-3/31/00 ALL
		5	9	6	2	Unqualified	20	23
	3	15	1	1		Reviewed	20	30
3	6	7				Compiled	13	23
4	3					Tax Returns	4	3
2	7	10	7		3	Other	20	20
	16 (4/1-9/30/02)		78 (10/1/02-3/31/03)					
9	19	37	17	7	5	**NUMBER OF STATEMENTS**	77	99
%	%	%	%	%	%	**ASSETS**	%	%
	6.8	5.4	2.0			Cash & Equivalents	4.5	6.0
	40.9	49.3	38.1			Trade Receivables (net)	43.8	48.0
	27.3	21.3	35.3			Inventory	24.7	22.4
	2.4	3.6	1.0			All Other Current	2.3	1.2
	77.4	79.6	76.4			Total Current	75.3	77.7
	12.9	14.2	12.0			Fixed Assets (net)	16.0	14.7
	4.4	2.9	5.8			Intangibles (net)	2.6	1.8
	5.2	3.3	5.8			All Other Non-Current	6.1	5.8
	100.0	100.0	100.0			Total	100.0	100.0
						LIABILITIES		
	16.6	22.2	15.1			Notes Payable-Short Term	16.6	18.3
	2.3	4.3	5.9			Cur. Mat.-L/T/D	3.2	2.7
	24.2	26.1	20.8			Trade Payables	24.5	26.5
	.0	.1	.2			Income Taxes Payable	.1	.3
	6.5	5.6	8.3			All Other Current	9.0	7.4
	49.6	58.3	50.2			Total Current	53.5	55.1
	17.3	7.8	18.8			Long Term Debt	14.1	11.4
	.0	.1	.1			Deferred Taxes	.1	.1
	2.4	8.5	6.8			All Other Non-Current	5.6	4.8
	30.6	25.4	24.0			Net Worth	26.7	28.6
	100.0	100.0	100.0			Total Liabilities & Net Worth	100.0	100.0
						INCOME DATA		
	100.0	100.0	100.0			Net Sales	100.0	100.0
	27.8	21.6	23.3			Gross Profit	20.4	23.1
	23.9	20.6	19.2			Operating Expenses	18.3	20.2
	3.9	1.0	4.0			Operating Profit	2.1	2.9
	.2	.4	1.8			All Other Expenses (net)	.8	.4
	3.7	.6	2.2			Profit Before Taxes	1.3	2.6
						RATIOS		
	2.3	1.8	2.5				2.3	2.1
	1.9	1.4	1.4			Current	1.5	1.4
	1.2	1.1	1.0				1.1	1.1
	1.6	1.4	1.4				1.6	1.5
	.9	.9	.7			Quick	.9	1.0
	.7	.7	.5				.6	.7
	35 10.5	34 10.9	37 9.8				32 11.5	37 9.8
	44 8.3	40 9.0	44 8.2			Sales/Receivables	41 9.0	44 8.2
	54 6.8	53 6.9	56 6.5				51 7.2	57 6.4
	17 22.1	6 58.4	28 13.1				13 28.5	12 30.9
	40 9.1	23 15.8	62 5.9			Cost of Sales/Inventory	27 13.4	25 14.7
	65 5.6	40 9.2	98 3.7				45 8.1	46 8.0
	27 13.7	17 21.9	24 15.1				16 22.7	20 18.7
	42 8.8	30 12.3	32 11.4			Cost of Sales/Payables	25 14.8	28 12.8
	46 7.9	40 9.2	51 7.2				39 9.3	44 8.3
	4.6	11.0	7.3				8.8	8.3
	7.7	21.5	10.2			Sales/Working Capital	16.2	14.9
	30.7	56.1	157.6				79.5	46.7
	11.4	5.4	2.9				4.7	5.1
	(16) 2.5	(36) 2.6	(16) 1.8			EBIT/Interest	(69) 2.1	(91) 2.9
	.5	1.6	1.5				.8	1.4
		3.6	6.3				6.9	8.1
		(10) 1.6	(10) 2.7			Net Profit + Depr., Dep., Amort./Cur. Mat. L./T/D	(22) 3.5	(18) 1.9
		.4	.9				1.1	.2
	.1	.1	.1				.1	.1
	.2	.3	.3			Fixed/Worth	.5	.3
	1.5	2.9	1.3				2.0	1.0
	1.0	1.4	2.3				1.2	1.3
	2.5	3.5	3.7			Debt/Worth	2.9	2.4
	27.5	7.7	12.7				16.0	8.3
	77.6	60.9	32.4				30.9	44.4
	(16) 25.5	(32) 8.5	(16) 16.6			% Profit Before Taxes/Tangible Net Worth	(66) 18.0	(89) 19.7
	1.5	1.4	6.5				2.8	3.8
	16.7	11.0	5.2				9.1	10.8
	3.5	2.1	3.1			% Profit Before Taxes/Total Assets	3.9	4.6
	.0	.7	1.4				−.6	.7
	141.3	212.3	161.8				145.2	145.0
	47.4	73.5	37.3			Sales/Net Fixed Assets	33.7	54.1
	20.1	17.8	13.5				11.0	16.5
	4.8	5.4	4.0				5.1	4.9
	3.4	4.4	2.7			Sales/Total Assets	3.9	3.9
	1.6	2.6	2.1				2.6	2.6
	.1	.1	.2				.2	.2
	(14) .5	(35) .4	(15) .8			% Depr., Dep., Amort./Sales	(68) .5	(88) .6
	1.9	1.1	1.2				1.0	1.3
		1.4					1.4	1.3
		(17) 2.6				% Officers', Directors', Owners' Comp/Sales	(31) 2.8	(42) 2.6
		3.7					6.3	6.1
14743M	93078M	724378M	1194526M	1468635M	2350529M	Net Sales ($)	4688010M	6828883M
1935M	24697M	177687M	391115M	443428M	695049M	Total Assets ($)	1433311M	1896715M

M = $ thousand   MM = $ million
See Pages 11 through 18 for Explanation of Ratios and Data

Comparative Historical Data / Current Data Sorted By Sales

	4/1/00-3/31/01 ALL	4/1/01-3/31/02 ALL	4/1/02-3/31/03 ALL		0-1MM	1-3MM	3-5MM	5-10MM	10-25MM	25MM & OVER
Type of Statement						16 (4/1-9/30/02)		78 (10/1/02-3/31/03)		
Unqualified	20	18	22			1		1	3	18
Reviewed	18	20	20			1		1	9	6
Compiled	23	22	16		2	3	2	4	5	
Tax Returns	3	7	7		3	2		2		
Other	34	27	29		1	4	3	2	8	11
NUMBER OF STATEMENTS	98	94	94		6	10	8	10	25	35
	%	%	%		%	%	%	%	%	%
ASSETS										
Cash & Equivalents	3.2	7.5	7.4			16.1		12.7	5.2	3.5
Trade Receivables (net)	52.2	49.6	43.1			27.5		40.3	52.3	47.8
Inventory	23.6	21.9	25.1			14.8		14.6	25.1	26.1
All Other Current	1.3	2.0	3.1			3.0		2.6	3.8	1.6
Total Current	80.3	81.1	78.7			61.4		70.2	86.3	79.0
Fixed Assets (net)	13.3	12.7	13.0			31.4		12.0	10.4	10.6
Intangibles (net)	2.1	2.6	4.2			.9		13.5	.5	5.7
All Other Non-Current	4.2	3.6	4.1			6.3		4.3	2.7	4.7
Total	100.0	100.0	100.0			100.0		100.0	100.0	100.0
LIABILITIES										
Notes Payable-Short Term	22.5	21.3	18.9			10.3		16.9	25.3	19.5
Cur. Mat.-L/T/D	2.0	3.3	3.9			2.8		7.4	2.8	4.4
Trade Payables	27.7	29.7	25.2			29.9		27.8	28.5	22.2
Income Taxes Payable	.0	.1	.1			.0		.1	.1	.2
All Other Current	7.9	6.3	6.6			8.3		4.9	6.6	8.0
Total Current	60.1	60.7	54.7			51.3		57.0	63.2	54.3
Long Term Debt	9.0	25.4	12.3			19.0		4.5	6.4	15.2
Deferred Taxes	.2	.1	.1			.0		.0	.0	.3
All Other Non-Current	4.3	3.5	8.6			26.9		27.6	4.6	2.9
Net Worth	26.3	10.2	24.3			2.8		10.9	25.7	27.4
Total Liabilities & Net Worth	100.0	100.0	100.0			100.0		100.0	100.0	100.0
INCOME DATA										
Net Sales	100.0	100.0	100.0			100.0		100.0	100.0	100.0
Gross Profit	20.8	21.9	24.5			38.5		25.8	22.4	17.9
Operating Expenses	18.3	19.4	21.7			36.6		23.3	20.2	16.2
Operating Profit	2.5	2.5	2.8			1.9		2.5	2.3	1.8
All Other Expenses (net)	.7	1.2	.7			.3		1.4	.5	.6
Profit Before Taxes	1.8	1.3	2.1			1.6		1.0	1.8	1.1
RATIOS										
Current	1.9 1.4 1.1	1.9 1.4 1.1	2.0 1.4 1.1			2.6 2.0 .7		1.9 1.2 .8	1.7 1.3 1.1	1.9 1.4 1.2
Quick	1.3 1.0 .7	1.4 1.0 .7	1.4 .9 .6			2.0 1.1 .5		1.6 .8 .6	1.2 .9 .6	1.3 1.0 .6
Sales/Receivables	37 9.9 43 8.4 54 6.8	34 10.8 42 8.6 52 7.0	34 10.8 42 8.7 53 6.9			5 67.7 35 10.4 51 7.1		30 12.2 40 9.0 45 8.1	35 10.4 47 7.7 56 6.5	36 10.0 45 8.2 59 6.2
Cost of Sales/Inventory	11 32.6 27 13.5 49 7.4	6 56.5 23 15.5 47 7.7	9 39.6 29 12.7 58 6.3			2 208.1 36 10.2 55 6.6		0 UND 13 27.7 35 10.3	8 43.7 29 12.5 52 7.0	17 20.9 27 13.7 46 7.9
Cost of Sales/Payables	18 20.1 27 13.4 45 8.1	16 22.9 25 14.4 43 8.5	20 18.6 32 11.5 44 8.2			23 16.0 36 10.2 51 7.2		31 11.8 40 9.1 46 7.9	23 15.8 33 11.1 48 7.6	17 21.5 24 15.0 38 9.6
Sales/Working Capital	10.3 21.2 67.7	9.6 17.2 62.5	8.2 18.0 63.8			3.4 7.3 −63.8		24.2 51.9 −45.5	10.1 28.0 59.2	9.6 14.7 49.6
EBIT/Interest	(95) 5.3 1.9 1.1	(88) 5.5 1.6 .8	(85) 5.0 2.4 1.4						(24) 5.4 1.9 1.7	3.5 2.3 1.3
Net Profit + Depr., Dep., Amort./Cur. Mat. L/T/D	(11) 18.2 3.5 .9	(19) 6.7 3.4 1.0	(27) 6.0 1.8 .5							(18) 7.6 3.2 1.3
Fixed/Worth	.1 .3 1.1	.1 .3 1.4	.1 .4 1.6			.3 .9 NM		.1 .9 −.6	.1 .2 .8	.1 .5 3.4
Debt/Worth	1.5 3.4 8.3	1.6 3.5 8.2	1.4 3.5 16.9			.7 14.7 −4.1		3.3 52.7 −3.0	1.4 3.7 7.0	1.9 3.4 16.3
% Profit Before Taxes/Tangible Net Worth	(87) 52.1 17.4 4.0	(82) 30.5 10.4 .0	(80) 60.7 12.7 2.9						(24) 57.0 10.2 4.7	(31) 33.5 11.0 2.6
% Profit Before Taxes/Total Assets	11.6 3.1 .2	7.4 2.5 −.8	11.5 3.0 .7			28.4 5.5 −3.7		12.9 3.3 1.3	11.0 2.3 1.1	5.9 2.8 .6
Sales/Net Fixed Assets	297.9 59.5 15.7	288.3 71.1 21.2	208.4 48.9 16.9			41.0 10.1 2.5		UND 70.6 7.3	301.1 108.7 21.7	188.6 41.7 20.6
Sales/Total Assets	5.0 4.1 3.0	5.4 4.2 2.8	4.9 3.7 2.3			4.7 2.4 1.3		5.6 4.2 2.4	5.4 4.3 2.5	4.9 4.0 2.6
% Depr., Dep., Amort./Sales	(78) .1 .4 1.0	(73) .1 .3 .8	(79) .2 .5 1.1						(24) .1 .3 1.3	(30) .2 .4 .9
% Officers', Directors', Owners' Comp/Sales	(38) 1.3 2.7 7.4	(46) 1.1 2.2 4.6	(33) 1.2 2.9 4.3						(13) 1.4 2.5 3.2	
Net Sales ($)	7002943M	5800813M	5845889M		3822M	18550M	32302M	75829M	426130M	5289256M
Total Assets ($)	1740162M	1339112M	1733911M		1524M	9906M	13911M	28994M	123594M	1555982M

© RMA 2003

M = $ thousand   MM = $ million
See Pages 11 through 18 for Explanation of Ratios and Data

Current Data Sorted By Assets   **Comparative Historical Data**

						Type of Statement		
		1	6	7	1	Unqualified	29	27
2	9	28	7			Reviewed	30	39
2	17	6	1			Compiled	68	58
7	7	2				Tax Returns	23	16
6	8	15	6		1	Other	51	41
	25 (4/1-9/30/02)		114 (10/1/02-3/31/03)				4/1/98-3/31/99	4/1/99-3/31/00
0-500M	500M-2MM	2-10MM	10-50MM	50-100MM	100-250MM		ALL	ALL
17	42	57	21		2	NUMBER OF STATEMENTS	201	181
%	%	%	%	%	%	ASSETS	%	%
9.9	9.7	7.0	2.9			Cash & Equivalents	7.5	7.3
54.1	38.6	41.9	32.1			Trade Receivables (net)	44.0	42.0
25.2	26.3	26.5	35.5			Inventory	24.3	24.8
.0	.9	1.9	3.9			All Other Current	2.1	2.0
89.2	75.5	77.3	74.4			Total Current	77.8	76.1
8.6	14.9	14.8	15.7			Fixed Assets (net)	12.7	14.4
1.7	3.2	1.9	6.3			Intangibles (net)	4.1	4.1
.5	6.4	5.9	3.7			All Other Non-Current	5.4	5.5
100.0	100.0	100.0	100.0			Total	100.0	100.0
						LIABILITIES		
4.8	16.0	16.4	14.4			Notes Payable-Short Term	14.3	15.2
8.3	2.3	2.8	1.5			Cur. Mat.-L/T/D	2.6	2.2
40.3	23.1	27.3	15.6			Trade Payables	24.5	22.9
.0	.2	.2	1.4			Income Taxes Payable	.4	.4
5.8	10.2	10.5	12.8			All Other Current	10.1	10.9
59.2	51.8	57.2	45.8			Total Current	51.9	51.5
16.4	10.5	9.5	8.2			Long Term Debt	11.7	12.0
.0	.1	.1	.6			Deferred Taxes	.1	.1
8.2	7.6	4.8	6.4			All Other Non-Current	3.2	4.3
16.1	30.0	28.4	39.1			Net Worth	33.1	32.2
100.0	100.0	100.0	100.0			Total Liabilities & Net Worth	100.0	100.0
						INCOME DATA		
100.0	100.0	100.0	100.0			Net Sales	100.0	100.0
33.9	33.9	28.8	27.3			Gross Profit	31.8	32.5
31.3	32.3	27.5	22.6			Operating Expenses	29.9	30.0
2.6	1.7	1.2	4.8			Operating Profit	1.8	2.6
.6	.1	.5	.6			All Other Expenses (net)	.4	.4
2.0	1.5	.8	4.1			Profit Before Taxes	1.4	2.2
						RATIOS		
2.9	2.1	2.1	2.7				2.2	2.1
1.6	1.7	1.4	1.6			Current	1.5	1.5
1.2	1.0	1.0	1.2				1.2	1.2
1.5	1.3	1.2	1.1				1.4	1.3
1.2	1.0	.9	.8			Quick	1.0	1.0
.7	.6	.6	.5				.7	.7

28	13.2	23	15.8	34	10.8	33	11.2			Sales/Receivables	30	12.0	30	12.0
39	9.5	35	10.3	40	9.1	40	9.1				38	9.5	40	9.1
68	5.3	47	7.8	50	7.3	64	5.7				52	7.0	56	6.6
3	116.2	12	29.6	16	23.3	29	12.5			Cost of Sales/Inventory	12	30.3	16	23.4
29	12.6	28	13.0	32	11.5	70	5.2				27	13.6	34	10.8
61	6.0	70	5.2	58	6.3	108	3.4				60	6.1	65	5.6
25	14.4	17	22.0	22	16.7	20	18.5			Cost of Sales/Payables	22	16.9	21	17.2
39	9.4	29	12.5	34	10.8	26	14.3				31	11.7	32	11.3
112	3.3	49	7.5	47	7.7	38	9.5				46	8.0	46	7.9

7.8	8.6	8.6	5.7			Sales/Working Capital	9.1	7.9
14.3	14.2	17.3	8.2				16.2	14.8
31.4	UND	224.0	32.6				39.7	36.4

	9.5		7.7		8.3		12.9	EBIT/Interest		6.9		6.5
(11)	2.2	(40)	2.5	(54)	2.7	(19)	3.4		(179)	2.6	(160)	2.3
	.7		1.0		1.1		1.4			1.1		1.0
					4.9			Net Profit + Depr., Dep., Amort./Cur. Mat. L./T/D		7.1		7.7
		(13)			1.8				(47)	3.2	(39)	3.4
					1.0					1.4		1.0
	.0		.2		.1		.2	Fixed/Worth		.1		.2
	.4		.5		.3		.5			.3		.4
	UND		2.2		2.5		1.4			.9		1.3
	.9		.9		1.1		.8	Debt/Worth		1.1		1.1
	3.8		1.9		2.5		1.8			2.1		2.4
	-8.7		18.0		9.6		5.0			4.5		5.9
	59.7		29.5		40.6		49.5	% Profit Before Taxes/Tangible Net Worth		46.4		38.7
(12)	20.0	(36)	9.5	(47)	14.3	(20)	27.6		(183)	18.1	(161)	13.7
	.0		.1		4.5		5.7			4.1		1.8
	12.6		9.8		9.7		17.5	% Profit Before Taxes/Total Assets		14.4		12.2
	3.5		3.5		3.2		7.2			4.9		3.7
	.0		.0		.4		1.2			.5		.3
	UND		71.4		96.6		55.6	Sales/Net Fixed Assets		108.8		83.3
	159.7		41.0		46.5		20.1			42.2		32.5
	30.3		16.8		14.2		10.6			19.5		14.9
	5.8		4.9		4.8		3.6	Sales/Total Assets		5.3		4.5
	4.4		3.8		3.7		2.5			4.1		3.5
	3.3		2.8		2.5		1.5			2.7		2.5
	.3		.5		.4		.6	% Depr., Dep., Amort./Sales		.4		.5
(10)	.9	(39)	.8	(52)	.7	(17)	1.2		(171)	.8	(156)	.8
	1.6		1.4		1.2		2.9			1.4		1.5
	2.5		2.3		1.5			% Officers', Directors', Owners' Comp/Sales		2.7		2.5
(11)	3.8	(18)	3.2	(25)	1.9				(112)	4.6	(87)	4.5
	15.3		5.2		4.0					7.5		7.5

16433M	179218M	897346M	1130102M		515494M	Net Sales ($)	3319888M	3598005M
3387M	47748M	242420M	404384M		282570M	Total Assets ($)	1395601M	1312565M

M = $ thousand   MM = $ million
See Pages 11 through 18 for Explanation of Ratios and Data

Comparative Historical Data | | | | Current Data Sorted By Sales

4/1/00-3/31/01 ALL	4/1/01-3/31/02 ALL	4/1/02-3/31/03 ALL	Type of Statement	0-1MM	1-3MM	3-5MM	5-10MM	10-25MM	25MM & OVER
9	13	15	Unqualified			1		6	8
29	29	46	Reviewed	1	5	4	7	21	8
44	44	26	Compiled		8	7	6	3	2
10	13	16	Tax Returns	4	4	3	4	1	
40	45	36	Other	4	5	3	8	8	8
					25 (4/1-9/30/02)		114 (10/1/02-3/31/03)		
132	144	139	NUMBER OF STATEMENTS	9	22	18	25	39	26
%	%	%	**ASSETS**	%	%	%	%	%	%
6.4	8.0	7.6	Cash & Equivalents		10.4	8.8	8.4	5.6	5.2
41.9	39.9	40.5	Trade Receivables (net)		40.2	39.8	38.7	42.6	37.6
24.8	24.7	27.8	Inventory		25.5	23.3	25.8	28.0	32.2
2.9	2.8	1.7	All Other Current		.1	1.8	.8	3.0	2.4
76.0	75.3	77.6	Total Current		76.2	73.7	73.7	79.2	77.3
13.8	14.8	14.4	Fixed Assets (net)		12.5	20.3	16.0	14.2	14.0
5.7	4.5	2.9	Intangibles (net)		4.1	2.6	1.7	2.4	4.4
4.5	5.4	5.1	All Other Non-Current		7.1	3.5	8.6	4.2	4.3
100.0	100.0	100.0	Total		100.0	100.0	100.0	100.0	100.0
			LIABILITIES						
14.4	15.7	14.5	Notes Payable-Short Term		13.2	10.9	15.8	18.5	15.4
2.9	4.4	3.1	Cur. Mat.-L/T/D		3.2	2.6	3.6	2.6	1.4
24.5	22.7	25.6	Trade Payables		25.4	23.7	22.4	27.1	21.1
.1	.2	.4	Income Taxes Payable		.0	.6	.1	.2	1.1
9.9	10.7	10.3	All Other Current		12.3	7.0	9.0	10.4	13.7
51.9	53.7	53.8	Total Current		54.2	44.6	50.9	58.9	52.8
11.9	9.2	10.4	Long Term Debt		10.7	15.4	11.1	7.9	5.9
.2	.3	.1	Deferred Taxes		.1	.0	.1	.2	.3
5.7	4.3	6.3	All Other Non-Current		9.6	6.1	1.1	6.2	6.3
30.4	32.4	29.4	Net Worth		25.4	33.8	36.8	26.8	34.8
100.0	100.0	100.0	Total Liabilities & Net Worth		100.0	100.0	100.0	100.0	100.0
			INCOME DATA						
100.0	100.0	100.0	Net Sales		100.0	100.0	100.0	100.0	100.0
32.0	32.4	31.0	Gross Profit		38.7	35.3	29.2	26.4	28.0
30.4	31.1	28.7	Operating Expenses		36.2	33.0	28.5	24.9	23.5
1.7	1.3	2.2	Operating Profit		2.5	2.3	.6	1.6	4.5
.7	.9	.4	All Other Expenses (net)		.4	.4	.1	.6	.5
.9	.4	1.8	Profit Before Taxes		2.1	1.8	.5	1.0	4.1
			RATIOS						
2.1	2.3	2.1	Current		2.0	2.3	2.2	2.1	2.1
1.4	1.5	1.5			1.6	1.9	1.7	1.4	1.6
1.1	1.1	1.1			1.0	1.3	1.0	1.0	1.1
1.4	1.5	1.3	Quick		1.3	1.4	1.5	1.1	1.1
.9	.9	.9			.9	1.1	.8	.9	.8
.7	.6	.6			.6	.9	.6	.6	.6
33 11.0	29 12.5	30 12.0	Sales/Receivables		28 13.0	22 16.6	29 12.7	33 11.0	30 12.4
42 8.6	36 10.0	39 9.3			47 7.8	39 9.5	37 9.9	42 8.6	39 9.4
54 6.8	47 7.8	50 7.3			74 4.9	48 7.6	45 8.1	54 6.8	45 8.1
15 23.6	14 25.8	17 22.0	Cost of Sales/Inventory		0 UND	13 27.8	8 45.4	16 23.3	22 16.5
31 11.8	28 12.8	35 10.4			34 10.7	26 14.0	28 12.8	37 9.9	37 9.8
65 5.6	68 5.4	75 4.9			124 2.9	70 5.2	75 4.9	60 6.1	80 4.6
20 17.9	16 22.8	20 18.0	Cost of Sales/Payables		27 13.3	14 26.8	21 17.4	13 27.4	22 16.3
36 10.1	28 12.9	32 11.5			34 10.6	31 11.9	29 12.7	31 11.7	28 12.8
54 6.7	44 8.2	48 7.6			70 5.2	59 6.2	43 8.6	49 7.5	37 9.8
8.3	8.5	7.4	Sales/Working Capital		5.3	8.5	8.7	8.2	6.5
14.8	16.2	13.4			12.2	12.6	18.8	14.8	12.4
44.0	68.1	65.0			UND	26.4	326.9	326.4	54.2
(118) 5.5	(128) 5.2	(126) 8.1	EBIT/Interest	(20) 6.4	(17) 6.9	(24) 10.2	(37) 8.5	(24) 22.2	
2.0	1.7	2.6		1.6	3.7	2.5	2.1	4.2	
1.0	.5	1.1		1.0	2.1	.0	-.2	2.1	
(25) 4.5	(27) 4.1	(29) 4.5	Net Profit + Depr., Dep., Amort./Cur. Mat. L/T/D					(10) 3.7	
1.8	2.0	1.9						1.8	
.8	.3	1.0						.8	
.2	.1	.1	Fixed/Worth		.2	.2	.1	.2	.2
.4	.4	.4			.5	.5	.4	.5	.4
2.2	1.1	1.8			NM	1.7	1.3	2.8	1.1
1.1	1.0	1.0	Debt/Worth		1.0	.9	.7	1.1	.9
3.0	2.0	2.4			1.7	2.1	2.0	2.7	2.3
10.3	7.2	10.9			NM	8.0	4.5	15.7	5.2
(117) 32.4	(127) 33.3	(117) 41.0	% Profit Before Taxes/Tangible Net Worth	(17) 18.7	(17) 47.0	(23) 39.3	(31) 47.2	(24) 49.8	
9.4	7.5	13.9		3.5	18.0	9.4	10.2	34.5	
1.2	-3.2	1.1		-1.0	10.1	-.5	-.2	10.0	
9.6	10.7	11.4	% Profit Before Taxes/Total Assets		9.4	8.7	12.3	9.0	17.4
2.4	2.1	3.6			1.9	4.5	2.7	2.8	8.1
.0	-1.6	.2			.0	3.4	-2.2	-2.1	2.2
76.4	90.4	95.8	Sales/Net Fixed Assets		117.9	61.7	77.2	113.4	78.6
29.7	35.7	40.9			51.8	27.4	34.0	40.9	32.0
16.8	15.9	14.0			15.0	12.7	16.0	13.5	10.9
4.6	5.1	4.7	Sales/Total Assets		4.4	5.0	5.1	4.7	4.8
3.6	3.7	3.6			2.8	3.8	3.8	3.5	3.6
2.3	2.6	2.5			1.8	3.0	3.0	2.5	2.5
(109) .5	(119) .3	(119) .4	% Depr., Dep., Amort./Sales		(17) .7	(16) .4	.4	(34) .4	(22) .3
.9	.7	.7			1.2	.7	.8	.6	.9
1.5	1.4	1.5			2.1	1.2	1.5	1.0	1.5
(68) 3.3	(78) 2.3	(57) 1.7	% Officers', Directors', Owners' Comp/Sales		(11) 2.0	(11) 2.5	(10) 1.4	(19) 1.3	
5.2	4.3	2.7			3.8	3.5	2.0	2.0	
8.7	7.1	4.7			9.7	4.6	3.9	3.9	
3025040M	2744718M	2738593M	Net Sales ($)	3957M	41329M	72725M	172722M	636079M	1811781M
1426719M	1107299M	980509M	Total Assets ($)	1007M	20390M	22067M	52921M	227458M	656666M

M = $ thousand   MM = $ million
See Pages 11 through 18 for Explanation of Ratios and Data

Current Data Sorted By Assets   Comparative Historical Data

			6	10	2		Type of Statement		
	13		50	16	1		Unqualified	34	28
7	30		17				Reviewed	79	73
4	9		3			1	Compiled	44	58
2	16		21	9	2		Tax Returns	11	6
							Other	53	53
	55 (4/1-9/30/02)			164 (10/1/02-3/31/03)				4/1/98- 3/31/99	4/1/99- 3/31/00
0-500M	500M-2MM		2-10MM	10-50MM	50-100MM	100-250MM		ALL	ALL
13	68		97	35	5	1	NUMBER OF STATEMENTS	221	218
%	%		%	%	%	%	ASSETS	%	%
11.4	7.5		5.2	4.8			Cash & Equivalents	5.5	5.9
50.0	39.3		39.7	42.2			Trade Receivables (net)	39.8	41.7
22.8	31.5		28.8	27.0			Inventory	28.6	29.4
.3	2.2		2.4	5.3			All Other Current	1.7	1.5
84.5	80.5		76.1	79.2			Total Current	75.5	78.5
11.8	13.0		15.4	12.4			Fixed Assets (net)	16.0	13.8
.0	2.1		3.5	1.9			Intangibles (net)	2.4	2.0
3.7	4.4		5.0	6.5			All Other Non-Current	6.1	5.8
100.0	100.0		100.0	100.0			Total	100.0	100.0
							LIABILITIES		
19.3	9.1		15.7	19.7			Notes Payable-Short Term	15.7	15.8
.2	4.0		2.8	2.3			Cur. Mat.-L/T/D	2.9	2.2
41.7	25.9		26.4	24.5			Trade Payables	25.3	28.6
.0	.2		.2	.3			Income Taxes Payable	.2	.3
2.1	6.4		6.6	9.7			All Other Current	7.0	7.2
63.3	45.6		51.7	56.6			Total Current	51.0	54.1
14.7	10.6		11.1	9.9			Long Term Debt	12.6	11.3
.0	.1		.3	.1			Deferred Taxes	.3	.2
6.6	3.0		3.0	1.4			All Other Non-Current	3.9	2.9
15.4	40.8		33.9	32.1			Net Worth	32.2	31.4
100.0	100.0		100.0	100.0			Total Liabilities & Net Worth	100.0	100.0
							INCOME DATA		
100.0	100.0		100.0	100.0			Net Sales	100.0	100.0
26.1	25.8		22.6	20.3			Gross Profit	25.5	24.4
26.4	24.1		20.9	18.3			Operating Expenses	23.3	22.4
−.2	1.6		1.7	1.9			Operating Profit	2.2	2.0
.7	.2		.4	.3			All Other Expenses (net)	.6	.3
−1.0	1.4		1.3	1.7			Profit Before Taxes	1.7	1.7
							RATIOS		
1.9	3.4		2.1	1.9				2.2	2.1
1.2	1.9		1.4	1.4			Current	1.5	1.5
.9	1.2		1.2	1.1				1.2	1.2
1.5	1.8		1.2	1.2				1.3	1.3
1.0	1.1		.9	.8			Quick	1.0	.9
.6	.7		.6	.6				.6	.7

									Sales/ Receivables				
31	11.9	28	13.3	30	12.2	32	11.4			30	12.0	32	11.2
42	8.7	33	10.9	35	10.4	40	9.1			37	9.8	40	9.2
65	5.7	42	8.6	43	8.6	47	7.8			45	8.1	48	7.5
0	UND	24	15.2	24	15.2	22	16.4		Cost of Sales/Inventory	24	15.3	25	14.4
32	11.4	36	10.1	35	10.6	32	11.3			36	10.1	38	9.5
68	5.4	58	6.3	47	7.8	50	7.3			51	7.1	52	7.0
23	16.2	19	19.6	18	20.1	20	18.3		Cost of Sales/Payables	18	19.9	20	17.9
43	8.5	26	14.1	27	13.5	26	13.9			29	12.5	31	11.7
79	4.6	42	8.7	42	8.7	36	10.1			44	8.4	47	7.8

						Sales/Working Capital		
8.2		6.9		10.0	9.9		9.1	8.8
24.1		10.9		18.1	15.8		15.1	15.6
UND		35.5		35.6	59.8		35.6	37.5

								EBIT/Interest				
	12.6		13.6		6.1		9.4			6.3		7.2
(10)	2.7	(61)	2.9	(86)	2.8		3.9		(206)	2.6	(207)	3.1
	−.5		1.0		1.3		2.1			1.3		1.4

								Net Profit + Depr., Dep., Amort./Cur. Mat. L./T/D				
			2.8		10.7		7.2			5.9		6.2
		(10)	1.8	(29)	2.1	(15)	3.6		(74)	1.8	(72)	3.2
			.1		1.0		1.0			.6		1.7

						Fixed/Worth		
.0		.1		.1	.1		.2	.1
.1		.2		.3	.3		.4	.4
NM		1.2		1.5	1.0		1.1	.8

						Debt/Worth		
1.0		.5		1.0	1.4		1.1	1.1
3.2		1.5		2.3	2.7		2.2	2.2
−40.5		6.1		6.1	5.7		5.2	4.5

								% Profit Before Taxes/Tangible Net Worth				
			27.7		30.4		36.2			33.8		35.5
		(63)	5.7	(85)	9.9		20.3		(200)	15.1	(201)	16.3
			.5		2.3		9.2			4.6		5.7

						% Profit Before Taxes/Total Assets		
17.4		8.2		7.4	8.0		10.1	9.9
2.2		2.7		3.4	5.8		4.2	4.6
−4.4		−.1		.6	1.6		1.3	1.6

						Sales/Net Fixed Assets		
UND		115.2		114.3	90.0		88.0	100.4
469.0		58.1		49.2	41.9		36.8	43.3
34.5		20.2		17.0	19.2		13.1	16.5

						Sales/Total Assets		
5.4		5.1		5.0	4.8		4.8	4.7
4.1		4.0		4.0	3.8		3.7	3.8
2.8		3.1		3.0	2.8		2.9	2.9

								% Depr., Dep., Amort./Sales				
			.4		.3		.4			.4		.3
		(51)	.7	(86)	.6	(33)	.6		(199)	.7	(196)	.6
			1.3		1.3		1.2			1.3		1.1

							% Officers', Directors', Owners' Comp/Sales				
		1.8		1.1			1.7		1.7	
	(40)	3.1	(45)	1.8			3.0	(116)	2.9	
		6.7		3.4			5.6		5.2	

14303M	370972M	1812819M	2408466M	1362032M	876334M	Net Sales ($)	5920911M	5750341M
3386M	84244M	456719M	655489M	348294M	238385M	Total Assets ($)	1943259M	1721763M

M = $ thousand   MM = $ million
See Pages 11 through 18 for Explanation of Ratios and Data

Comparative Historical Data | Current Data Sorted By Sales

4/1/00-3/31/01 ALL	4/1/01-3/31/02 ALL	4/1/02-3/31/03 ALL	Type of Statement	0-1MM	1-3MM	3-5MM	5-10MM	10-25MM	25MM & OVER
26	28	18	Unqualified				1	5	12
65	56	80	Reviewed		2	1	15	32	30
56	62	54	Compiled	4	12	8	16	11	3
12	10	17	Tax Returns	3	4	4	4	1	1
51	62	50	Other	1	6	3	11	14	15
					55 (4/1-9/30/02)		164 (10/1/02-3/31/03)		
210	218	219	**NUMBER OF STATEMENTS**	8	24	16	47	63	61
%	%	%	**ASSETS**	%	%	%	%	%	%
5.4	5.3	6.2	Cash & Equivalents		5.6	12.8	4.4	5.1	5.6
41.9	41.6	40.8	Trade Receivables (net)		37.9	36.2	40.1	40.0	45.4
27.9	26.8	29.0	Inventory		29.4	27.6	30.5	31.6	26.3
3.0	2.1	2.7	All Other Current		1.8	2.4	1.3	1.7	4.7
78.3	75.9	78.6	Total Current		74.7	78.9	76.4	78.4	82.1
13.5	14.9	13.8	Fixed Assets (net)		17.6	14.4	16.1	13.4	10.2
2.8	3.2	2.6	Intangibles (net)		2.5	1.4	2.9	4.0	1.5
5.4	6.1	5.0	All Other Non-Current		5.2	5.2	4.5	4.3	6.2
100.0	100.0	100.0	Total		100.0	100.0	100.0	100.0	100.0
			LIABILITIES						
16.4	16.3	14.1	Notes Payable-Short Term		10.4	5.5	14.8	14.0	16.7
2.5	2.6	2.9	Cur. Mat.-L/T/D		6.6	3.0	3.1	2.7	1.7
27.7	23.9	27.0	Trade Payables		27.1	19.1	28.1	26.5	27.9
.3	.3	.2	Income Taxes Payable		.1	.2	.3	.3	.2
7.2	7.4	6.9	All Other Current		3.3	8.8	5.9	7.1	9.0
54.1	50.4	51.0	Total Current		47.4	36.5	52.3	50.6	55.4
10.3	13.1	11.3	Long Term Debt		13.2	13.6	10.7	11.0	9.3
.2	.1	.2	Deferred Taxes		.1	.0	.4	.2	.1
2.7	3.0	2.9	All Other Non-Current		4.2	6.5	1.6	3.0	1.7
32.7	33.5	34.6	Net Worth		35.0	43.4	35.1	35.3	33.4
100.0	100.0	100.0	Total Liabilities & Net Worth		100.0	100.0	100.0	100.0	100.0
			INCOME DATA						
100.0	100.0	100.0	Net Sales		100.0	100.0	100.0	100.0	100.0
25.2	24.7	23.3	Gross Profit		29.1	25.7	25.6	22.4	19.3
22.7	22.0	21.7	Operating Expenses		26.5	25.0	24.0	20.5	17.7
2.5	2.6	1.6	Operating Profit		2.6	.7	1.5	1.9	1.7
.6	.7	.3	All Other Expenses (net)		.5	.1	.4	.3	.2
1.9	2.0	1.3	Profit Before Taxes		2.1	.6	1.1	1.5	1.5
			RATIOS						
2.1	2.2	2.3	Current		3.0	4.4	2.1	2.3	2.0
1.4	1.4	1.6			1.6	3.0	1.5	1.8	1.5
1.1	1.1	1.1			1.1	1.3	1.1	1.1	1.2
1.2	1.4	1.4	Quick		1.3	3.2	1.2	1.4	1.3
.8	.9	.9			1.1	1.9	.8	1.0	.9
.6	.6	.6			.6	.7	.6	.6	.7
31 11.6	31 11.9	30 12.3	Sales/Receivables		24 15.3	30 12.3	32 11.5	28 13.1	31 11.7
38 9.5	37 9.8	36 10.1			38 9.5	35 10.3	36 10.1	34 10.7	39 9.4
47 7.7	46 7.9	45 8.1			53 6.8	38 9.7	47 7.8	39 9.3	46 8.0
24 15.5	22 16.5	22 16.4	Cost of Sales/Inventory		18 19.9	26 14.1	26 14.0	27 13.7	19 19.1
36 10.0	35 10.4	34 10.7			34 10.8	36 10.1	38 9.6	35 10.6	31 11.7
53 6.9	50 7.4	52 7.0			74 4.9	48 7.6	58 6.3	50 7.3	45 8.2
20 18.6	17 21.4	19 19.0	Cost of Sales/Payables		21 17.1	18 20.8	24 15.5	17 21.4	20 18.2
30 12.0	25 14.3	27 13.4			35 10.3	23 16.0	34 10.8	24 15.2	26 13.8
45 8.1	41 8.9	42 8.7			53 6.9	29 12.5	49 7.4	36 10.3	35 10.4
9.5	8.9	8.5	Sales/Working Capital		6.7	5.5	9.1	8.9	10.4
17.5	15.9	14.1			13.1	8.4	15.5	13.7	18.2
50.8	46.0	36.2			39.4	27.6	42.4	36.9	35.6
(196) 6.6	(201) 6.0	(198) 10.4	EBIT/Interest	(21) 7.6	(14) 25.1	(43) 11.5	(57) 9.6	(58) 14.8	
2.5	2.5	3.0			2.4	1.6	3.0	2.7	4.1
1.2	1.2	1.4			.1	-.2	1.4	1.4	1.7
(53) 4.4	(49) 12.5	(54) 6.8	Net Profit + Depr., Dep., Amort./Cur. Mat. L/T/D				(19) 12.3	(20) 10.4	
2.8	3.5	2.2						2.2	3.9
1.5	1.1	1.0						1.4	.8
.1	.1	.1	Fixed/Worth		.1	.1	.1	.1	.1
.3	.3	.3			.3	.3	.4	.2	.3
.9	.9	1.1			2.1	4.5	2.3	1.1	.5
1.0	1.1	.9	Debt/Worth		.7	.3	.9	.9	1.3
2.4	2.4	2.2			3.3	1.3	1.9	2.2	2.3
6.7	6.0	6.1			8.7	8.9	7.5	6.5	4.6
(194) 44.1	(200) 37.8	(198) 32.2	% Profit Before Taxes/Tangible Net Worth	(22) 55.2	(13) 23.9	(43) 26.4	(55) 32.4	(60) 34.9	
16.0	16.0	11.3			7.1	11.5	5.9	8.8	18.5
4.0	3.1	2.2			-4.4	-.1	2.0	2.7	7.6
11.0	10.8	8.3	% Profit Before Taxes/Total Assets		18.1	8.6	6.7	6.8	9.8
4.4	3.9	3.5			1.9	3.0	3.5	2.7	5.4
1.1	.4	.6			-1.9	-.2	.4	.8	1.6
107.1	106.9	140.4	Sales/Net Fixed Assets		252.6	66.1	110.2	152.0	140.6
41.3	44.9	54.6			42.3	36.2	48.5	66.4	57.6
16.9	16.4	17.9			10.5	17.8	15.4	21.5	28.2
4.8	4.8	4.9	Sales/Total Assets		4.4	4.3	4.6	5.4	5.1
3.9	3.9	3.9			3.4	3.7	3.6	4.4	4.1
2.9	2.9	3.0			2.5	2.8	3.0	2.9	3.5
(175) .3	(185) .3	(180) .3	% Depr., Dep., Amort./Sales	(18) .4	(13) .8	(37) .4	(54) .3	(54) .2	
.7	.6	.7			.7	1.0	1.1	.5	.5
1.1	1.2	1.3			1.6	2.9	1.9	1.2	.8
(101) 1.6	(94) 1.7	(100) 1.3	% Officers', Directors', Owners' Comp/Sales	(12) 1.3	(10) 2.8	(30) 1.8	(32) 1.1	(12) .6	
2.8	3.1	2.3			5.4	4.5	2.5	1.7	1.7
5.4	5.6	5.2			6.1	8.4	5.4	2.6	2.5
7452738M	7009773M	6844926M	Net Sales ($)	4364M	54806M	64538M	332987M	1033372M	5354859M
2294125M	2172496M	1786517M	Total Assets ($)	1989M	17303M	19009M	101369M	289176M	1357671M

© RMA 2003

M = $ thousand   MM = $ million
See Pages 11 through 18 for Explanation of Ratios and Data

Current Data Sorted By Assets | | | | | | **Comparative Historical Data**

0-500M	500M-2MM	2-10MM	10-50MM	50-100MM	100-250MM	Type of Statement	4/1/98-3/31/99 ALL	4/1/99-3/31/00 ALL
	5	13	26	6	10	Unqualified	49	43
	8	27	16	1		Reviewed	32	31
3	19	12	2	1		Compiled	27	34
1	12	5				Tax Returns	16	9
4	16	24	16	2	4	Other	61	43
	39 (4/1-9/30/02)		194 (10/1/02-3/31/03)					
8	60	81	60	10	14	**NUMBER OF STATEMENTS**	185	160
%	%	%	%	%	%	**ASSETS**	%	%
	13.5	10.1	5.4	4.1	3.6	Cash & Equivalents	7.8	9.8
	37.1	36.7	31.3	31.6	31.9	Trade Receivables (net)	34.9	34.1
	26.7	30.9	35.7	25.0	36.4	Inventory	34.3	33.0
	5.2	2.6	4.0	2.6	2.5	All Other Current	2.1	3.2
	82.5	80.4	76.4	63.3	74.3	Total Current	79.1	80.2
	9.2	9.4	11.4	21.8	12.2	Fixed Assets (net)	10.5	10.9
	4.1	2.6	7.0	12.5	10.0	Intangibles (net)	5.3	4.2
	4.2	7.7	5.3	2.4	3.5	All Other Non-Current	5.0	4.7
	100.0	100.0	100.0	100.0	100.0	Total	100.0	100.0
						LIABILITIES		
	10.1	17.0	14.2	7.0	11.2	Notes Payable-Short Term	16.0	13.3
	2.5	1.5	1.3	1.0	.5	Cur. Mat.-L/T/D	1.9	3.5
	27.7	25.4	27.1	27.6	35.0	Trade Payables	28.0	27.1
	.1	.1	.3	.1	.9	Income Taxes Payable	.3	.5
	14.6	14.0	10.1	8.7	7.7	All Other Current	9.8	10.4
	55.0	58.1	53.0	44.4	55.2	Total Current	56.1	54.7
	13.1	5.3	9.0	10.9	19.4	Long Term Debt	10.4	8.6
	.0	.5	.6	1.0	.2	Deferred Taxes	.3	.2
	3.8	4.1	1.6	6.3	2.2	All Other Non-Current	4.8	2.1
	28.0	32.0	35.8	37.3	22.9	Net Worth	28.4	34.4
	100.0	100.0	100.0	100.0	100.0	Total Liabilities & Net Worth	100.0	100.0
						INCOME DATA		
	100.0	100.0	100.0	100.0	100.0	Net Sales	100.0	100.0
	32.0	31.2	26.5	25.0	17.4	Gross Profit	28.0	31.3
	28.1	26.9	20.0	22.4	11.5	Operating Expenses	24.0	27.2
	3.9	4.3	6.5	2.5	5.9	Operating Profit	4.0	4.2
	.2	.4	1.1	2.4	.9	All Other Expenses (net)	.8	.1
	3.7	3.9	5.4	.1	5.0	Profit Before Taxes	3.1	4.1
						RATIOS		
	2.3	2.0	1.9	1.7	2.0	Current	1.9	2.2
	1.5	1.4	1.4	1.4	1.5		1.5	1.4
	1.1	1.1	1.2	1.2	1.0		1.1	1.2
	1.5	1.1	1.1	1.3	1.0	Quick	1.1	1.3
	.9	.8	.7	.8	.6		.8	.7
	.6	.5	.5	.4	.5		.5	.5
	21 17.0	25 14.7	23 16.2	27 13.3	19 18.8	Sales/Receivables	24 15.2	25 14.9
	30 12.3	37 9.9	34 10.8	43 8.5	36 10.3		38 9.7	39 9.4
	41 9.0	47 7.8	55 6.6	58 6.3	50 7.3		52 7.0	53 6.8
	13 28.3	23 16.0	35 10.4	18 19.9	29 12.4	Cost of Sales/Inventory	28 13.1	31 11.8
	31 11.6	45 8.1	54 6.7	36 10.2	39 9.3		53 6.9	56 6.5
	62 5.9	84 4.3	98 3.7	58 6.2	82 4.5		82 4.4	105 3.5
	15 23.7	20 18.3	26 14.2	27 13.3	28 13.2	Cost of Sales/Payables	23 16.1	23 16.0
	27 13.7	38 9.7	43 8.4	31 11.6	37 9.8		39 9.4	38 9.5
	49 7.5	56 6.6	64 5.7	36 10.2	48 7.6		54 6.8	60 6.1
	7.9	8.9	7.7	7.4	7.6	Sales/Working Capital	8.6	6.9
	16.5	18.7	13.8	23.0	18.4		14.8	13.8
	71.8	70.6	26.3	NM	NM		40.6	35.7
	22.0	20.6	16.6	9.5	12.0	EBIT/Interest	10.2	11.8
(47)	5.7	(72) 7.4	(59) 5.5	2.9	3.5		(164) 3.5	(136) 4.4
	1.2	2.4	3.5	-1.4	1.9		1.5	2.0
		9.9	61.0			Net Profit + Depr., Dep., Amort./Cur. Mat. L./T/D	18.4	14.2
	(21) 3.1	(20) 5.8					(50) 4.1	(29) 3.1
	1.6	1.8					1.2	1.3
	.0	.0	.1	.1	.3	Fixed/Worth	.1	.1
	.2	.2	.3	.2	1.2		.3	.3
	1.1	.7	.9	1.5	-.9		1.1	.8
	.9	1.2	1.3	1.3	3.3	Debt/Worth	1.3	1.0
	2.4	2.6	2.5	2.6	14.4		2.9	2.3
	10.8	7.7	5.7	3.5	-38.5		7.0	6.3
	83.6	91.4	65.5		46.5	% Profit Before Taxes/Tangible Net Worth	62.0	64.0
(47)	38.2	(72) 38.0	(56) 28.4		(10) 32.9		(162) 24.4	(144) 30.0
	13.4	16.1	11.9		12.8		6.6	9.9
	27.6	26.8	12.6	9.6	13.4	% Profit Before Taxes/Total Assets	18.2	21.6
	9.5	9.9	6.7	.9	4.5		6.6	7.0
	2.2	3.0	3.5	-2.6	1.8		1.3	2.3
	284.4	299.9	125.0	159.7	140.8	Sales/Net Fixed Assets	162.8	137.1
	81.4	71.4	63.5	78.6	47.3		56.6	57.8
	30.5	32.6	16.8	1.1	29.9		23.0	23.0
	7.0	4.5	4.0	5.6	5.6	Sales/Total Assets	4.7	4.3
	4.9	3.7	3.1	3.9	3.3		3.4	3.1
	2.9	2.2	2.2	.5	2.0		2.4	2.2
	.2	.2	.2		.2	% Depr., Dep., Amort./Sales	.2	.2
(43)	.5	(68) .6	(52) .5		(13) .7		(148) .5	(124) .5
	1.5	1.0	1.0		1.4		1.2	1.2
	2.1	1.4	.5			% Officers', Directors', Owners' Comp/Sales	1.4	1.6
(30)	4.8	(41) 2.6	(10) 2.2				(67) 3.1	(61) 4.3
	9.6	5.7	5.0				6.8	7.9
11790M	389724M	1541506M	3885661M	2336378M	7846008M	Net Sales ($)	12199170M	10791712M
2457M	72441M	393994M	1203664M	636124M	2094261M	Total Assets ($)	3206075M	3022176M

M = $ thousand   MM = $ million
See Pages 11 through 18 for Explanation of Ratios and Data

Comparative Historical Data / Current Data Sorted By Sales

	4/1/00-3/31/01 ALL	4/1/01-3/31/02 ALL	4/1/02-3/31/03 ALL	0-1MM	1-3MM	3-5MM	5-10MM	10-25MM	25MM & OVER
Type of Statement									
Unqualified	42	36	60	1		3	6	12	38
Reviewed	35	31	52		1	3	7	14	27
Compiled	36	36	37	2	7	5	11	7	5
Tax Returns	8	8	18	1		6	7	3	1
Other	43	61	66	3	4	6	12	17	24
				39 (4/1-9/30/02)		194 (10/1/02-3/31/03)			
NUMBER OF STATEMENTS	164	172	233	7	12	23	43	53	95
ASSETS	%	%	%	%	%	%	%	%	%
Cash & Equivalents	8.6	7.6	9.4		12.4	9.3	11.3	12.0	6.0
Trade Receivables (net)	34.1	35.2	34.2		15.0	35.3	35.2	37.0	35.3
Inventory	32.6	35.0	31.4		33.2	28.1	26.0	30.3	35.2
All Other Current	3.6	2.4	3.9		7.6	4.6	3.2	3.2	3.4
Total Current	78.9	80.2	78.9		68.3	77.3	75.6	82.5	79.9
Fixed Assets (net)	9.5	9.3	10.3		5.5	12.1	10.1	8.6	11.1
Intangibles (net)	6.2	5.3	4.9		11.0	1.6	7.6	3.9	4.6
All Other Non-Current	5.4	5.3	5.9		15.3	9.0	6.7	5.0	4.4
Total	100.0	100.0	100.0		100.0	100.0	100.0	100.0	100.0
LIABILITIES									
Notes Payable-Short Term	15.5	17.3	13.9		19.1	10.5	8.0	13.4	16.7
Cur. Mat.-L/T/D	2.7	2.1	1.6		1.8	2.2	2.9	1.7	.8
Trade Payables	28.0	27.6	27.3		13.6	25.7	24.8	26.6	30.5
Income Taxes Payable	.3	.3	.2		.0	.1	.1	.2	.2
All Other Current	8.3	10.2	12.5		25.2	9.3	16.2	14.4	9.5
Total Current	54.8	57.5	55.6		59.7	47.8	52.1	56.4	57.8
Long Term Debt	9.5	9.0	9.3		21.0	9.5	13.8	4.6	8.5
Deferred Taxes	.3	.2	.4		.0	.0	.6	.6	.4
All Other Non-Current	3.2	4.3	3.2		3.6	5.1	2.5	4.4	2.4
Net Worth	32.1	28.9	31.5		15.7	37.5	31.1	34.0	30.9
Total Liabilities & Net Worth	100.0	100.0	100.0		100.0	100.0	100.0	100.0	100.0
INCOME DATA									
Net Sales	100.0	100.0	100.0		100.0	100.0	100.0	100.0	100.0
Gross Profit	29.3	25.2	29.0		40.3	35.8	34.8	32.5	20.5
Operating Expenses	25.3	21.5	24.4		37.3	32.9	29.5	27.0	15.5
Operating Profit	3.9	3.8	4.6		2.9	2.9	5.3	5.5	5.0
All Other Expenses (net)	.7	.6	.6		.8	.3	.3	.8	.7
Profit Before Taxes	3.3	3.1	4.0		2.2	2.6	4.9	4.7	4.3
RATIOS									
Current	2.0 / 1.5 / 1.1	1.9 / 1.4 / 1.1	2.0 / 1.4 / 1.1		4.0 / 1.6 / .4	2.8 / 1.9 / 1.3	2.3 / 1.5 / 1.1	1.9 / 1.4 / 1.1	1.7 / 1.4 / 1.1
Quick	1.1 / .7 / .5	1.0 / .7 / .5	1.2 / .8 / .5		2.5 / .4 / .1	1.8 / .9 / .5	1.4 / .9 / .6	1.2 / .9 / .6	1.1 / .7 / .5
Sales/Receivables	26 13.8 / 38 9.5 / 53 6.9	23 15.5 / 36 10.1 / 48 7.5	23 16.2 / 34 10.7 / 47 7.8		2 206.5 / 22 16.3 / 45 8.0	25 14.5 / 35 10.4 / 49 7.4	23 15.6 / 34 10.7 / 46 7.9	23 15.8 / 39 9.3 / 49 7.4	21 17.4 / 33 11.1 / 45 8.0
Cost of Sales/Inventory	28 13.0 / 57 6.4 / 96 3.8	26 14.1 / 45 8.2 / 91 4.0	22 16.6 / 44 8.3 / 80 4.5		35 10.4 / 56 6.5 / 108 3.4	17 21.0 / 35 10.4 / 87 4.2	20 18.4 / 35 10.3 / 59 6.2	23 16.0 / 46 8.0 / 112 3.3	24 15.0 / 45 8.2 / 79 4.6
Cost of Sales/Payables	25 14.6 / 39 9.3 / 60 6.1	19 19.1 / 33 11.1 / 52 7.1	21 17.5 / 34 10.7 / 54 6.8		13 27.8 / 25 14.8 / 43 8.5	23 15.6 / 33 11.0 / 56 6.5	18 20.2 / 32 11.4 / 54 6.7	19 19.6 / 38 9.5 / 55 6.7	23 15.7 / 34 10.7 / 50 7.3
Sales/Working Capital	6.7 / 15.2 / 33.0	8.3 / 17.3 / 66.5	8.3 / 16.8 / 58.8		5.3 / 40.4 / -3.9	5.8 / 12.3 / 17.8	8.7 / 16.8 / 78.8	7.7 / 15.2 / 49.5	9.9 / 18.7 / 49.3
EBIT/Interest	(142) 8.9 / 2.6 / 1.2	(149) 9.4 / 2.9 / 1.3	(207) 17.5 / 5.9 / 2.0			(17) 12.8 / 2.7 / .1	(34) 18.2 / 7.8 / 1.5	(48) 21.3 / 8.7 / 2.6	(94) 16.5 / 6.0 / 2.7
Net Profit + Depr., Dep., Amort./Cur. Mat. L/T/D	(30) 12.8 / 2.9 / .8	(43) 9.9 / 2.9 / 1.4	(51) 10.9 / 3.7 / 1.6					(11) 5.8 / 1.7 / 1.4	(28) 24.6 / 6.5 / 2.6
Fixed/Worth	.1 / .3 / 1.0	.1 / .4 / 1.3	.1 / .2 / .9		.0 / .1 / NM	.1 / .2 / 1.1	.0 / .2 / 3.3	.1 / .2 / .6	.1 / .3 / .9
Debt/Worth	1.2 / 2.9 / 12.0	1.3 / 3.1 / 15.0	1.2 / 2.7 / 8.0		1.0 / 6.8 / -3.2	.6 / 1.3 / 7.3	1.1 / 2.7 / 22.7	.9 / 3.4 / 7.3	1.4 / 3.0 / 7.2
% Profit Before Taxes/Tangible Net Worth	(143) 60.8 / 21.4 / 6.2	(150) 59.7 / 24.9 / 8.2	(202) 83.3 / 33.4 / 11.7			(18) 48.7 / 17.2 / 3.8	(33) 108.3 / 36.4 / 12.4	(48) 83.5 / 36.5 / 18.7	(88) 78.1 / 33.0 / 11.9
% Profit Before Taxes/Total Assets	15.0 / 5.3 / .8	13.8 / 5.3 / 1.0	21.6 / 7.3 / 2.2		32.7 / 6.2 / -4.0	15.3 / 6.9 / 1.4	29.0 / 11.4 / .9	24.9 / 8.0 / 4.0	16.9 / 6.4 / 3.1
Sales/Net Fixed Assets	169.2 / 63.4 / 24.9	186.2 / 69.5 / 28.3	239.2 / 71.7 / 28.4		UND / 178.4 / 35.0	211.8 / 61.1 / 14.3	509.9 / 71.8 / 29.8	215.7 / 70.7 / 24.2	167.2 / 76.0 / 33.2
Sales/Total Assets	4.6 / 3.0 / 2.0	5.4 / 3.5 / 2.4	5.2 / 3.7 / 2.3		4.1 / 2.6 / 1.6	5.5 / 3.0 / 2.1	5.6 / 3.9 / 2.4	5.2 / 3.3 / 2.2	5.3 / 3.8 / 2.8
% Depr., Dep., Amort./Sales	(125) .1 / .4 / 1.1	(135) .2 / .4 / 1.0	(189) .2 / .5 / 1.1			(19) .3 / .6 / 1.5	(30) .2 / .9 / 1.6	(42) .3 / .7 / 1.4	(88) .1 / .3 / .8
% Officers', Directors', Owners' Comp/Sales	(61) 1.6 / 3.7 / 6.8	(63) .9 / 2.5 / 5.9	(88) 1.4 / 3.1 / 6.8			(10) .9 / 6.1 / 10.9	(17) 2.5 / 3.0 / 5.6	(25) 1.6 / 3.1 / 6.7	(23) .6 / 1.3 / 3.0
Net Sales ($)	13489394M	13926323M	16011067M	4841M	23164M	86224M	323631M	891326M	14681881M
Total Assets ($)	3674212M	3705696M	4402941M	4243M	10998M	31831M	178492M	327380M	3849997M

© RMA 2003

M = $ thousand   MM = $ million
See Pages 11 through 18 for Explanation of Ratios and Data

Current Data Sorted By Assets   **Comparative Historical Data**

0-500M	500M-2MM	2-10MM	10-50MM	50-100MM	100-250MM	Type of Statement	4/1/98-3/31/99 ALL	4/1/99-3/31/00 ALL
	1	9	6	1	3	Unqualified	44	41
2	11	39	10			Reviewed	66	52
2	10	8				Compiled	54	25
1	3	3			1	Tax Returns	9	9
	10	12	8	2		Other	48	28
	30 (4/1-9/30/02)		112 (10/1/02-3/31/03)					
5	35	71	24	3	4	NUMBER OF STATEMENTS	221	155
%	%	%	%	%	%	**ASSETS**	%	%
	8.5	12.0	5.7			Cash & Equivalents	8.1	7.9
	37.1	32.7	29.1			Trade Receivables (net)	32.8	33.5
	35.4	39.0	38.7			Inventory	40.0	38.9
	2.5	2.7	1.4			All Other Current	2.7	3.3
	83.5	86.3	74.9			Total Current	83.6	83.6
	7.4	6.5	9.8			Fixed Assets (net)	9.0	9.9
	2.2	3.3	5.6			Intangibles (net)	2.1	1.6
	7.0	3.9	9.6			All Other Non-Current	5.3	5.0
	100.0	100.0	100.0			Total	100.0	100.0
						LIABILITIES		
	13.9	14.1	10.4			Notes Payable-Short Term	16.5	19.2
	1.1	2.0	2.2			Cur. Mat.-L/T/D	2.0	1.2
	23.2	23.2	23.4			Trade Payables	21.8	21.4
	.1	.3	.7			Income Taxes Payable	.2	.3
	10.4	9.0	8.9			All Other Current	8.3	8.9
	48.8	48.7	45.6			Total Current	48.8	51.1
	6.9	4.7	9.7			Long Term Debt	8.0	6.4
	.1	.0	.0			Deferred Taxes	.1	.1
	3.1	3.8	7.2			All Other Non-Current	3.9	4.7
	41.1	42.8	37.5			Net Worth	39.1	37.8
	100.0	100.0	100.0			Total Liabilities & Net Worth	100.0	100.0
						INCOME DATA		
	100.0	100.0	100.0			Net Sales	100.0	100.0
	31.4	27.6	29.0			Gross Profit	27.1	26.9
	29.7	24.7	24.1			Operating Expenses	23.9	23.3
	1.7	2.9	4.9			Operating Profit	3.2	3.6
	.7	1.2	1.4			All Other Expenses (net)	.8	.8
	1.0	1.7	3.5			Profit Before Taxes	2.4	2.8
						RATIOS		
	2.4	2.3	2.3				2.6	2.2
	1.8	1.6	1.5			Current	1.6	1.6
	1.5	1.3	1.3				1.3	1.3
	1.6	1.3	1.2				1.3	1.3
	1.2	.8	.9			Quick	.8	.8
	.5	.6	.4				.5	.4
	32 11.3	27 13.4	31 11.9				31 11.8	28 13.0
	45 8.0	48 7.6	43 8.6			Sales/Receivables	44 8.4	47 7.7
	64 5.7	64 5.7	51 7.1				61 6.0	61 6.0
	20 18.6	47 7.7	39 9.4				44 8.4	43 8.4
	66 5.5	80 4.6	81 4.5			Cost of Sales/Inventory	73 5.0	67 5.5
	117 3.1	120 3.0	120 3.0				126 2.9	116 3.1
	13 27.2	27 13.8	27 13.3				19 19.2	17 22.0
	35 10.3	43 8.5	46 8.0			Cost of Sales/Payables	37 9.9	33 10.9
	59 6.1	59 6.2	60 6.0				60 6.1	58 6.3
	4.8	4.3	5.8				5.0	5.0
	8.5	8.0	11.1			Sales/Working Capital	7.9	8.1
	15.7	13.1	15.6				14.6	15.4
	9.1	11.8	23.3				6.6	6.4
	(31) 2.3	(61) 3.0	(20) 4.4			EBIT/Interest	(193) 3.0	(141) 2.4
	-.6	1.6	2.2				1.3	1.4
		17.6					12.4	22.9
		(15) 3.1				Net Profit + Depr., Dep., Amort./Cur. Mat. L /T/D	(39) 3.7	(32) 5.7
		1.8					1.6	2.2
	.0	.0	.1				.0	.0
	.1	.1	.1			Fixed/Worth	.1	.2
	.6	.2	.5				.4	.4
	.6	.8	.7				.8	.9
	1.0	1.6	1.8			Debt/Worth	1.7	1.9
	4.1	2.9	3.4				3.7	4.4
	20.9	34.7	42.7				30.5	41.1
	(31) 8.3	(69) 12.8	(22) 24.2			% Profit Before Taxes/Tangible Net Worth	(210) 16.0	(148) 16.1
	.4	2.8	5.7				4.9	5.6
	9.0	11.0	14.2				12.3	12.4
	2.6	5.1	6.1			% Profit Before Taxes/Total Assets	5.4	5.0
	-2.1	.7	2.8				1.5	1.8
	177.3	212.9	162.5				244.4	168.0
	57.4	75.6	52.1			Sales/Net Fixed Assets	60.7	54.5
	24.5	32.5	22.0				22.9	20.1
	3.8	3.0	3.2				3.7	3.2
	2.6	2.5	2.5			Sales/Total Assets	2.7	2.7
	2.0	1.9	1.8				1.9	1.9
	.2	.3	.2				.2	.2
	(27) .6	(53) .4	(21) .5			% Depr., Dep., Amort./Sales	(183) .5	(139) .5
	.9	.8	1.2				.9	1.0
	2.6	2.0					1.6	1.8
	(22) 4.4	(38) 3.8				% Officers', Directors', Owners' Comp/Sales	(116) 3.4	(82) 3.0
	7.1	7.4					5.9	5.5
14380M	137212M	923961M	1057502M	1466738M	1376014M	Net Sales ($)	4048275M	2750939M
1284M	40925M	338829M	438090M	234484M	749405M	Total Assets ($)	1672584M	1128951M

M = $ thousand   MM = $ million
See Pages 11 through 18 for Explanation of Ratios and Data

Comparative Historical Data | Current Data Sorted By Sales

Type of Statement	4/1/00-3/31/01 ALL	4/1/01-3/31/02 ALL	4/1/02-3/31/03 ALL	0-1MM	1-3MM	3-5MM	5-10MM	10-25MM	25MM & OVER
Unqualified	25	18	20				2	8	10
Reviewed	57	36	62	2	6	5	18	20	11
Compiled	36	35	20		4	7	5	4	
Tax Returns	5	12	8		2	1	1	3	1
Other	33	26	32	1	1	7	5	10	8
				30 (4/1-9/30/02)		112 (10/1/02-3/31/03)			
NUMBER OF STATEMENTS	156	127	142	3	13	20	31	45	30

	%	%	%	%	%	%	%	%	%
ASSETS									
Cash & Equivalents	7.8	8.2	9.6		4.1	6.6	13.7	13.0	5.6
Trade Receivables (net)	36.2	32.9	31.9		31.7	39.4	30.5	31.8	30.3
Inventory	41.2	40.2	37.8		39.7	32.5	37.7	37.2	38.9
All Other Current	2.2	2.0	2.3		3.2	2.1	2.2	3.1	1.1
Total Current	87.4	83.2	81.7		78.8	80.5	84.1	85.1	76.0
Fixed Assets (net)	6.2	8.6	8.3		10.5	8.2	7.3	6.0	12.4
Intangibles (net)	1.7	2.8	3.7		4.6	6.4	1.6	3.4	4.6
All Other Non-Current	4.7	5.3	6.2		6.1	4.9	7.0	5.4	7.0
Total	100.0	100.0	100.0		100.0	100.0	100.0	100.0	100.0
LIABILITIES									
Notes Payable-Short Term	21.8	19.9	13.0		25.1	11.3	8.8	14.9	10.5
Cur. Mat.-L/T/D	1.5	1.5	1.8		3.2	1.4	2.4	1.7	1.3
Trade Payables	22.7	22.3	22.5		13.8	24.8	23.4	24.3	21.9
Income Taxes Payable	.2	.1	.3		.1	.2	.3	.2	.7
All Other Current	8.5	8.6	11.4		6.7	8.1	14.7	9.0	12.1
Total Current	54.7	52.4	49.1		49.0	45.9	49.7	50.2	46.5
Long Term Debt	6.0	7.3	6.5		13.2	7.9	2.8	5.0	8.3
Deferred Taxes	.1	.0	.0		.2	.0	.1	.0	.0
All Other Non-Current	5.0	4.2	5.0		9.2	3.7	2.6	4.9	6.9
Net Worth	34.3	35.9	39.4		28.4	42.4	44.9	39.9	38.1
Total Liabilities & Net Worth	100.0	100.0	100.0		100.0	100.0	100.0	100.0	100.0
INCOME DATA									
Net Sales	100.0	100.0	100.0		100.0	100.0	100.0	100.0	100.0
Gross Profit	27.4	28.6	29.4		34.8	32.2	28.8	26.5	28.2
Operating Expenses	23.9	25.8	26.6		35.9	30.6	25.9	22.0	25.6
Operating Profit	3.5	2.8	2.9		-1.1	1.5	2.8	4.6	2.6
All Other Expenses (net)	1.3	.9	1.1		1.4	1.9	.5	1.2	.6
Profit Before Taxes	2.2	1.9	1.8		-2.5	-.3	2.3	3.3	2.0

RATIOS

Ratio	4/1/00-3/31/01	4/1/01-3/31/02	4/1/02-3/31/03	0-1MM	1-3MM	3-5MM	5-10MM	10-25MM	25MM & OVER
Current	2.0	2.3	2.3		2.3	2.9	2.6	2.2	2.4
	1.6	1.6	1.7		1.7	1.7	1.7	1.6	1.7
	1.3	1.3	1.3		1.1	1.4	1.5	1.3	1.3
Quick	1.1	1.1	1.4		1.4	1.6	1.9	1.4	1.2
	.7	.7	.8		.5	1.1	.8	.8	.9
	.5	.5	.5		.3	.7	.6	.6	.4
Sales/Receivables	33 11.0	29 12.7	29 12.6		38 9.7	35 10.5	22 16.6	26 13.9	30 12.0
	49 7.4	42 8.7	44 8.2		49 7.5	49 7.4	55 6.7	39 9.4	40 9.2
	64 5.7	60 6.0	59 6.1		64 5.7	80 4.6	66 5.5	58 6.3	52 7.0
Cost of Sales/Inventory	45 8.1	43 8.5	39 9.4		58 6.3	24 14.9	37 9.9	41 8.9	33 11.1
	76 4.8	76 4.8	79 4.6		102 3.6	77 4.7	83 4.4	64 5.7	72 5.1
	123 3.0	122 3.0	120 3.0		194 1.9	101 3.6	142 2.6	115 3.2	120 3.0
Cost of Sales/Payables	22 16.5	19 19.0	22 16.5		14 25.3	16 22.6	27 13.8	19 19.7	19 19.7
	35 10.3	37 9.9	43 8.6		32 11.5	52 7.0	43 8.4	39 9.4	43 8.6
	55 6.7	53 6.9	60 6.1		60 6.1	73 5.0	65 5.6	55 6.7	58 6.3
Sales/Working Capital	5.4	5.2	4.7		4.0	4.7	3.8	5.4	5.2
	9.3	9.1	8.5		5.1	7.4	6.9	9.8	9.8
	15.0	16.7	14.8		NM	15.1	10.5	17.2	15.6
EBIT/Interest	(145) 4.5	(117) 5.3	(121) 11.1		5.3	(17) 12.5	(25) 8.7	(37) 12.4	(27) 22.1
	1.8	1.9	3.0		1.0	2.7	2.7	3.9	4.9
	1.2	.7	1.3		-2.0	.1	.9	1.9	2.7
Net Profit + Depr., Dep., Amort./Cur. Mat. L/T/D	(33) 15.9	(21) 7.8	(24) 13.0						
	3.9	2.3	3.3						
	1.1	.1	1.9						
Fixed/Worth	.0	.1	.0		.0	.1	.0	.0	.1
	.1	.1	.1		.2	.1	.1	.1	.2
	.3	.5	.4		NM	1.2	.2	.2	.4
Debt/Worth	1.1	1.0	.8		.7	.5	.6	.8	.9
	2.2	2.0	1.6		1.3	1.4	1.5	1.5	1.9
	4.4	3.2	3.2		NM	4.6	2.1	3.1	4.5
% Profit Before Taxes/Tangible Net Worth	(145) 31.2	(117) 30.8	(130) 34.6		(10) 11.1	(17) 33.8	(30) 27.8	(44) 39.9	(27) 35.0
	14.1	12.0	13.1		6.7	10.7	11.1	17.2	24.1
	3.9	.2	2.4		-7.5	1.7	.5	5.4	9.6
% Profit Before Taxes/Total Assets	10.8	10.0	12.2		5.9	11.0	10.0	16.5	12.3
	3.9	3.6	4.9		.0	2.3	4.9	5.5	6.1
	.8	-.5	.7		-9.6	-2.1	.2	1.2	3.2
Sales/Net Fixed Assets	221.5	128.3	192.9		171.6	127.8	259.0	207.4	153.1
	87.7	56.8	63.4		35.6	48.0	65.8	97.5	53.5
	33.7	23.8	25.5		12.7	21.0	31.8	33.6	17.1
Sales/Total Assets	3.4	3.6	3.4		2.6	3.5	3.7	3.4	3.9
	2.5	2.6	2.5		2.0	2.5	2.4	2.8	2.7
	2.0	2.0	1.9		1.5	2.0	1.9	2.2	1.9
% Depr., Dep., Amort./Sales	(118) .2	(102) .2	(108) .2		(11) .2	(14) .4	(23) .2	(33) .2	(25) .2
	.4	.4	.5		.8	.8	.5	.4	.5
	.8	.9	.9		1.4	1.0	1.3	.7	1.2
% Officers', Directors', Owners' Comp/Sales	(88) 1.7	(63) 1.8	(70) 2.1		(10) 2.3	(11) 3.4	(17) 2.0	(24) 2.1	
	3.6	4.1	3.9		5.0	6.0	3.9	3.8	
	6.5	6.6	8.3		9.1	10.9	6.5	9.3	
Net Sales ($)	2531112M	2603218M	4975807M	1245M	24057M	74329M	218451M	710113M	3947612M
Total Assets ($)	985999M	994942M	1803017M	1400M	12870M	32978M	94721M	281453M	1379595M

M = $ thousand   MM = $ million
See Pages 11 through 18 for Explanation of Ratios and Data

Current Data Sorted By Assets   **Comparative Historical Data**

Type of Statement	0-500M	500M-2MM	2-10MM	10-50MM	50-100MM	100-250MM	4/1/98-3/31/99 ALL	4/1/99-3/31/00 ALL
Unqualified	2	1	11	20	6	6	41	39
Reviewed	1	12	37	9	1		38	35
Compiled	3	12	6	3			27	32
Tax Returns	1	8	1				6	8
Other	3	7	12	3		2	38	30
		22 (4/1-9/30/02)		145 (10/1/02-3/31/03)				
NUMBER OF STATEMENTS	10	40	67	35	7	8	150	144
ASSETS	%	%	%	%	%	%	%	%
Cash & Equivalents	15.4	11.5	8.0	8.6			10.3	7.5
Trade Receivables (net)	30.8	35.3	34.8	30.5			31.2	31.7
Inventory	47.2	34.7	41.4	45.1			39.0	41.1
All Other Current	.0	.9	1.8	2.4			3.0	1.9
Total Current	93.4	82.4	86.0	86.6			83.5	82.2
Fixed Assets (net)	2.3	11.1	8.1	6.1			9.9	10.2
Intangibles (net)	1.2	.8	1.8	2.2			1.4	1.5
All Other Non-Current	3.1	5.7	4.2	5.1			5.1	6.0
Total	100.0	100.0	100.0	100.0			100.0	100.0
LIABILITIES								
Notes Payable-Short Term	16.8	13.4	22.2	17.4			20.7	21.1
Cur. Mat.-L/T/D	3.2	1.4	1.4	3.6			2.4	1.6
Trade Payables	12.4	25.0	19.1	18.0			19.1	19.4
Income Taxes Payable	.0	.1	.5	.1			.3	.3
All Other Current	32.2	5.7	10.0	8.5			7.1	6.9
Total Current	64.7	45.5	53.2	47.7			49.5	49.4
Long Term Debt	5.9	12.6	5.5	7.2			7.9	8.2
Deferred Taxes	.0	.1	.0	.1			.1	.1
All Other Non-Current	5.5	5.2	3.0	2.8			5.5	4.3
Net Worth	23.9	36.6	38.3	42.3			36.9	38.0
Total Liabilities & Net Worth	100.0	100.0	100.0	100.0			100.0	100.0
INCOME DATA								
Net Sales	100.0	100.0	100.0	100.0			100.0	100.0
Gross Profit	29.4	29.7	29.8	25.5			27.3	27.6
Operating Expenses	24.8	26.9	25.1	20.7			24.5	24.5
Operating Profit	4.6	2.7	4.6	4.8			2.7	3.1
All Other Expenses (net)	2.7	1.0	1.0	.6			1.0	.8
Profit Before Taxes	1.9	1.7	3.7	4.2			1.8	2.3
RATIOS								
Current	1.9	3.5	3.0	3.0			2.8	2.6
	1.6	2.0	1.5	2.0			1.7	1.6
	1.2	1.3	1.3	1.3			1.3	1.2
Quick	1.1	2.0	1.3	1.3			1.6	1.2
	.9	.8	.7	.7			.8	.8
	.3	.6	.5	.4			.4	.5
Sales/Receivables	7 52.6	23 15.7	25 14.8	29 12.8			28 13.2	28 12.9
	43 8.5	36 10.1	42 8.6	43 8.5			41 8.8	42 8.8
	65 5.6	76 4.8	72 5.0	80 4.5			59 6.2	60 6.0
Cost of Sales/Inventory	7 52.2	26 13.9	45 8.1	61 6.0			39 9.3	46 7.9
	113 3.2	65 5.6	75 4.9	92 4.0			74 4.9	92 4.0
	219 1.7	121 3.0	132 2.8	153 2.4			127 2.9	141 2.6
Cost of Sales/Payables	0 UND	19 19.0	17 22.0	17 21.3			16 22.3	16 22.5
	16 22.5	31 12.0	27 13.4	27 13.6			30 12.3	33 11.1
	94 3.9	62 5.9	47 7.8	51 7.2			54 6.8	50 7.3
Sales/Working Capital	3.8	5.4	5.5	3.6			4.5	4.9
	7.9	7.1	7.9	7.4			7.9	8.4
	162.8	20.9	15.4	11.4			16.3	15.8
EBIT/Interest		12.0	7.3	8.0			6.7	7.1
		(35) 4.5	(61) 4.1	(33) 6.2			(127) 2.4	(127) 2.6
		1.1	2.3	2.5			1.2	1.4
Net Profit + Depr., Dep., Amort./Cur. Mat. L /T/D			17.6				7.0	19.3
			(18) 7.6				(29) 2.0	(31) 3.2
			1.0				.2	1.3
Fixed/Worth	.0	.0	.0	.0			.1	.0
	.0	.2	.1	.1			.2	.1
	.3	1.1	.4	.2			.6	.4
Debt/Worth	1.2	.6	.8	.6			.8	.9
	2.3	2.0	2.0	1.6			2.0	1.7
	NM	7.3	3.4	3.8			4.5	4.9
% Profit Before Taxes/Tangible Net Worth		35.7	38.5	45.2			42.9	39.4
		(35) 9.7	(64) 27.2	(33) 30.2			(142) 16.4	(137) 15.3
		.8	11.8	9.0			2.6	4.8
% Profit Before Taxes/Total Assets	13.4	14.6	13.0	15.1			13.0	11.7
	3.5	5.1	7.8	9.8			5.0	4.9
	−1.4	.1	4.2	4.0			.5	1.4
Sales/Net Fixed Assets	UND	362.9	183.9	183.5			137.4	227.3
	UND	55.1	59.2	88.1			49.5	60.0
	507.2	13.0	28.6	28.0			17.5	21.9
Sales/Total Assets	3.7	3.7	3.4	3.3			3.4	3.2
	2.5	2.8	2.6	2.4			2.5	2.5
	1.4	2.2	1.9	1.5			1.8	1.9
% Depr., Dep., Amort./Sales		.2	.3	.2			.3	.2
		(29) .6	(57) .5	(32) .3			(117) .6	(115) .5
		1.6	.7	1.0			1.4	1.2
% Officers', Directors', Owners' Comp/Sales		2.4	1.0	1.4			1.5	1.9
		(26) 4.0	(36) 2.7	(14) 2.0			(58) 3.2	(71) 4.0
		6.1	5.5	4.9			6.1	7.0
Net Sales ($)	10372M	132980M	940621M	1922663M	984532M	2405143M	4516540M	4522637M
Total Assets ($)	2358M	46040M	346839M	740885M	498439M	1171922M	2053488M	1885068M

M = $ thousand   MM = $ million
See Pages 11 through 18 for Explanation of Ratios and Data

Comparative Historical Data   **Current Data Sorted By Sales**

			Type of Statement						
34	22	46	Unqualified	2	1		4	9	30
32	31	60	Reviewed	1	5	3	21	22	8
30	29	24	Compiled	4	4	5	3	8	1
9	4	10	Tax Returns	2	3	3	1	1	
32	34	27	Other	3	3	5	2	7	7
4/1/00-3/31/01	4/1/01-3/31/02	4/1/02-3/31/03		22 (4/1-9/30/02)			145 (10/1/02-3/31/03)		
ALL	ALL	ALL		0-1MM	1-3MM	3-5MM	5-10MM	10-25MM	25MM & OVER
137	120	167	**NUMBER OF STATEMENTS**	12	16	16	31	47	45
%	%	%	**ASSETS**	%	%	%	%	%	%
8.3	10.6	8.9	Cash & Equivalents	19.2	10.0	10.6	8.6	7.8	6.3
31.8	29.7	33.3	Trade Receivables (net)	29.1	33.3	34.5	30.5	35.6	33.4
41.0	41.1	40.9	Inventory	45.8	37.6	30.6	44.7	41.8	41.0
2.5	2.2	1.9	All Other Current	.3	.1	1.9	.7	2.0	3.8
83.6	83.6	85.0	Total Current	94.5	81.1	77.6	84.5	87.2	84.5
8.7	7.7	8.2	Fixed Assets (net)	4.0	11.1	14.0	9.5	6.5	7.2
2.6	2.1	1.8	Intangibles (net)	1.1	.5	1.5	1.2	2.1	2.8
5.1	6.6	4.9	All Other Non-Current	.4	7.3	6.8	4.8	4.2	5.6
100.0	100.0	100.0	Total	100.0	100.0	100.0	100.0	100.0	100.0
			LIABILITIES						
26.5	21.3	18.2	Notes Payable-Short Term	18.0	9.4	21.0	17.6	21.2	17.6
1.6	1.9	3.0	Cur. Mat.-L/T/D	.0	1.9	1.9	1.7	1.4	7.2
16.3	18.6	19.6	Trade Payables	10.6	30.2	23.4	15.5	22.1	17.0
.2	.3	.3	Income Taxes Payable	.0	.0	.2	.0	.8	.2
6.9	7.5	10.6	All Other Current	26.9	3.8	6.4	7.8	11.7	11.0
51.5	49.7	51.6	Total Current	55.4	45.2	52.9	42.6	57.2	52.9
4.8	4.8	7.7	Long Term Debt	22.8	15.0	3.5	7.1	5.0	5.9
.1	.2	.1	Deferred Taxes	.0	.0	.3	.0	.1	.1
4.3	5.0	3.6	All Other Non-Current	4.5	5.5	7.7	1.3	3.6	2.9
39.2	40.4	37.0	Net Worth	17.3	34.4	35.6	49.0	34.2	38.2
100.0	100.0	100.0	Total Liabilities & Net Worth	100.0	100.0	100.0	100.0	100.0	100.0
			INCOME DATA						
100.0	100.0	100.0	Net Sales	100.0	100.0	100.0	100.0	100.0	100.0
29.1	29.1	28.6	Gross Profit	31.0	32.4	31.5	30.2	27.4	25.6
25.9	25.7	24.3	Operating Expenses	30.0	30.3	25.6	24.8	23.4	20.9
3.3	3.4	4.3	Operating Profit	1.0	2.1	5.9	5.5	4.0	4.7
1.0	1.2	1.0	All Other Expenses (net)	3.5	.7	.9	.9	.9	.8
2.2	2.2	3.2	Profit Before Taxes	-2.5	1.4	5.0	4.6	3.1	3.9
			RATIOS						
2.7	2.6	2.9		3.4	2.9	2.0	4.7	2.2	2.6
1.7	1.7	1.6	Current	1.6	2.2	1.3	1.7	1.5	1.6
1.2	1.3	1.3		1.3	1.3	1.0	1.3	1.3	1.3
1.2	1.5	1.3		2.9	1.4	1.3	2.6	1.2	1.2
.8	.8	.8	Quick	1.0	.8	.7	.8	.7	.8
.4	.5	.5		.4	.5	.5	.4	.5	.4
27 13.3	25 14.7	25 14.4		23 15.5	18 20.1	22 16.5	25 14.8	30 12.2	28 13.2
38 9.5	41 9.0	42 8.6	Sales/Receivables	56 6.5	38 9.6	36 10.1	40 9.1	45 8.0	43 8.5
63 5.8	59 6.2	73 5.0		110 3.3	83 4.4	62 5.9	73 5.0	73 5.0	72 5.1
42 8.7	42 8.6	40 9.1		67 5.5	21 17.5	25 14.6	64 5.7	46 8.0	44 8.3
87 4.2	90 4.1	80 4.6	Cost of Sales/Inventory	147 2.5	118 3.1	36 10.2	119 3.1	75 4.9	78 4.7
143 2.6	142 2.6	133 2.8		378 1.0	171 2.1	90 4.1	179 2.0	122 3.0	112 3.3
14 26.2	19 18.9	17 21.5		4 102.7	20 17.9	20 17.9	12 30.3	17 21.5	19 19.5
28 13.1	31 11.9	30 12.1	Cost of Sales/Payables	34 10.7	36 10.0	33 10.9	30 12.3	27 13.4	32 11.5
55 6.7	55 6.7	51 7.2		95 3.8	101 3.6	61 6.0	46 8.0	53 6.9	43 8.6
5.1	4.8	5.1		1.3	3.9	7.4	4.2	5.5	4.9
8.5	7.5	7.4	Sales/Working Capital	4.1	6.3	12.9	6.6	8.5	7.5
20.7	16.0	16.2		18.6	13.2	320.5	13.9	16.2	16.4
5.4	5.5	8.0			11.1	10.3	15.5	5.6	7.9
(126) 2.6	(104) 2.5	(149) 4.4	EBIT/Interest		(12) 4.5	4.3	(29) 4.8	(42) 3.9	(43) 4.8
1.1	1.3	1.9			1.8	.2	2.1		2.5
10.1	5.4	17.3	Net Profit + Depr., Dep.,					19.3	15.3
(32) 2.5	(16) 1.8	(36) 4.8	Amort./Cur. Mat. L/T/D					(14) 5.4	(12) 3.9
1.1	.4	1.3						.7	2.2
.0	.0	.0		.0	.0	.1	.0	.0	.0
.1	.1	.1	Fixed/Worth	.0	.2	.3	.1	.1	.1
.5	.4	.4		1.1	1.4	1.0	.4	.2	.3
.8	.6	.8		1.5	.6	.8	.3	.9	.8
1.7	1.9	1.9	Debt/Worth	11.5	1.6	3.3	1.3	1.9	1.6
4.1	4.9	4.0		NM	19.5	5.2	2.4	3.4	3.6
32.8	38.2	39.7	% Profit Before Taxes/Tangible		19.9	42.5	41.1	37.1	45.4
(125) 15.3	(112) 18.3	(153) 25.4	Net Worth		(13) 6.3	(15) 31.7	(30) 24.7	(44) 22.4	(42) 31.7
2.7	3.1	6.3			.5	-1.0	9.1	6.5	18.5
12.7	13.5	13.9	% Profit Before Taxes/Total	4.5	9.7	22.1	16.1	11.7	15.7
4.5	5.3	7.7	Assets	.0	5.0	8.3	8.9	7.5	10.4
.5	1.1	2.4		-11.3	.6	.0	3.8	3.1	5.6
214.3	218.7	225.2		UND	UND	185.5	138.6	237.5	175.1
58.6	61.7	61.8	Sales/Net Fixed Assets	UND	34.4	49.5	49.0	88.1	56.9
18.8	24.9	24.6		29.7	13.0	13.4	22.2	34.0	22.2
3.4	3.4	3.3		2.6	3.0	3.8	3.4	4.0	3.4
2.5	2.6	2.6	Sales/Total Assets	1.3	2.6	3.0	2.2	2.7	2.7
1.8	1.8	1.9		.8	1.8	2.6	1.6	1.9	1.9
.2	.2	.2			.3	.3	.3	.2	.2
(108) .5	(92) .5	(133) .5	% Depr., Dep., Amort./Sales		(11) 1.1	(13) .5	(27) .6	(38) .4	(42) .5
1.3	1.3	1.1			3.0	1.6	.9	.7	1.3
1.7	1.7	1.4				2.4	.8	1.1	1.3
(64) 3.2	(62) 3.0	(83) 2.8	% Officers', Directors', Owners' Comp/Sales		(11) 3.9	(16) 3.4	(29) 2.1	(15) 1.9	
7.3	5.5	5.2			8.8	4.4	6.4	3.3	
4316287M	3579198M	6396311M	Net Sales ($)	6503M	32357M	58677M	233633M	770233M	5294908M
1882129M	1611309M	2806483M	Total Assets ($)	5622M	15592M	19933M	122251M	323636M	2319449M

M = $ thousand   MM = $ million
See Pages 11 through 18 for Explanation of Ratios and Data

Current Data Sorted By Assets | Comparative Historical Data

						Type of Statement		
	1	19	17	4	2	Unqualified	24	31
2	14	22	7	1	1	Reviewed	45	45
1	9	3				Compiled	20	24
4	4	2				Tax Returns	7	6
	10	9	8			Other	25	27

0-500M	30 (4/1-9/30/02) 500M-2MM	2-10MM	110 (10/1/02-3/31/03) 10-50MM	50-100MM	100-250MM		4/1/98-3/31/99 ALL	4/1/99-3/31/00 ALL
7	38	55	32	5	3	NUMBER OF STATEMENTS	121	133

%	%	%	%	%	%	ASSETS	%	%
	10.8	14.6	6.2			Cash & Equivalents	10.7	8.1
	31.4	30.8	35.7			Trade Receivables (net)	30.3	34.3
	38.8	37.6	36.8			Inventory	42.0	38.9
	3.2	3.5	2.3			All Other Current	1.4	1.9
	84.1	86.5	80.9			Total Current	84.4	83.2
	6.5	6.7	8.4			Fixed Assets (net)	8.4	9.8
	.3	.5	3.4			Intangibles (net)	2.0	1.4
	9.1	6.3	7.2			All Other Non-Current	5.3	5.6
	100.0	100.0	100.0			Total	100.0	100.0

						LIABILITIES		
	21.0	14.4	14.8			Notes Payable-Short Term	21.8	20.8
	.6	3.0	2.1			Cur. Mat.-L/T/D	1.1	1.1
	23.2	20.2	16.5			Trade Payables	17.3	18.0
	.1	.1	.1			Income Taxes Payable	.4	.3
	9.8	10.2	13.4			All Other Current	10.9	9.5
	54.7	47.8	46.9			Total Current	51.5	49.7
	5.4	3.5	3.0			Long Term Debt	6.6	6.3
	.0	.0	.1			Deferred Taxes	.1	.1
	8.2	4.9	4.4			All Other Non-Current	3.2	8.1
	31.6	43.7	45.5			Net Worth	38.6	35.8
	100.0	100.0	100.0			Total Liabilities & Net Worth	100.0	100.0

						INCOME DATA		
	100.0	100.0	100.0			Net Sales	100.0	100.0
	32.9	29.8	28.9			Gross Profit	27.2	31.7
	30.3	26.4	23.7			Operating Expenses	24.6	27.8
	2.5	3.4	5.1			Operating Profit	2.5	3.9
	.5	.5	.6			All Other Expenses (net)	.3	.6
	2.0	2.9	4.6			Profit Before Taxes	2.3	3.3

						RATIOS		
	3.0	3.0	2.5			Current	2.6	2.6
	1.5	1.7	1.7				1.7	1.7
	1.2	1.3	1.3				1.3	1.3
	1.4	1.9	1.2			Quick	1.3	1.5
	.9	.8	.8			(120)	.9	.8
	.4	.4	.6				.5	.6
17	21.0	20 18.5	30 12.3			Sales/Receivables	29 12.7	29 12.5
34	10.9	43 8.5	48 7.6				42 8.7	45 8.0
57	6.4	61 5.9	64 5.7				62 5.9	66 5.5
35	10.3	33 11.2	48 7.6			Cost of Sales/Inventory	52 7.0	44 8.3
79	4.6	66 5.5	64 5.7				86 4.3	74 4.9
142	2.6	135 2.7	105 3.5				137 2.7	128 2.9
11	32.4	16 22.8	15 24.6			Cost of Sales/Payables	11 33.5	13 28.7
28	13.2	31 11.9	30 12.3				27 13.5	24 15.1
67	5.5	59 6.2	49 7.4				49 7.5	47 7.8
	4.5	4.6	4.8			Sales/Working Capital	4.3	4.5
	9.4	8.1	7.6				7.1	7.4
	21.9	13.8	20.1				14.5	16.7
	14.2	8.1	14.5			EBIT/Interest	5.7	7.2
(35)	4.6	(50) 3.0	(28) 5.5			(106)	2.4	(124) 2.9
	.9	1.5	2.6				1.2	1.4
						Net Profit + Depr., Dep.,	10.8	18.9
						Amort./Cur. Mat. L/T/D	(24) 6.0	(25) 3.4
							.8	.3
	.0	.0	.0			Fixed/Worth	.0	.1
	.1	.1	.1				.2	.1
	.3	.2	.5				.4	.4
	.5	.5	.6			Debt/Worth	.7	.8
	1.5	1.4	1.4				1.7	1.5
	3.4	3.1	2.6				3.2	3.6
	42.7	29.0	50.8			% Profit Before Taxes/Tangible	37.5	39.9
(32)	12.4	(53) 12.5	(30) 33.0			Net Worth (112)	17.7	(124) 17.7
	1.0	3.1	8.3				3.5	4.4
	16.5	15.0	20.9			% Profit Before Taxes/Total	12.7	15.2
	4.7	4.8	8.5			Assets	5.5	7.3
	.1	1.2	2.9				1.0	1.5
	251.3	243.2	208.5			Sales/Net Fixed Assets	167.9	146.1
	65.2	123.6	64.5				47.0	49.4
	31.7	35.4	30.6				20.1	22.2
	4.6	3.4	3.4			Sales/Total Assets	3.4	3.6
	3.1	2.5	2.6				2.4	2.7
	2.0	1.9	1.9				1.9	1.8
	.2	.2	.2			% Depr., Dep., Amort./Sales	.2	.3
(29)	.4	(45) .3	(26) .4			(102)	.5	(108) .5
	.6	.7	1.2				1.1	1.0
	1.9	2.2	1.7			% Officers', Directors',	1.5	1.7
(16)	2.7	(28) 3.4	(14) 2.4			Owners' Comp/Sales (57)	2.7	(77) 2.8
	4.8	5.7	3.9				5.1	6.3
5943M	150197M	824845M	1824534M	828353M	1009717M	Net Sales ($)	2761915M	3578749M
2028M	44663M	282321M	656543M	362119M	403543M	Total Assets ($)	1155493M	1506279M

M = $ thousand   MM = $ million
See Pages 11 through 18 for Explanation of Ratios and Data

Comparative Historical Data · Current Data Sorted By Sales

			Type of Statement	0-1MM	1-3MM	3-5MM	5-10MM	10-25MM	25MM & OVER
22	18	43	Unqualified				4	10	27
29	28	47	Reviewed	2	2	7	11	16	9
16	16	13	Compiled	1	5	3	3	1	
8	4	10	Tax Returns	3	3	3	1		
27	21	27	Other	1	5	5	6	5	7
4/1/00-3/31/01	4/1/01-3/31/02	4/1/02-3/31/03			30 (4/1-9/30/02)		110 (10/1/02-3/31/03)		
ALL	ALL	ALL							
102	87	140	**NUMBER OF STATEMENTS**	7	15	18	25	32	43
%	%	%	**ASSETS**	%	%	%	%	%	%
9.6	8.9	10.9	Cash & Equivalents		11.2	13.1	13.0	11.3	6.8
32.0	29.7	31.7	Trade Receivables (net)		27.3	25.0	30.6	36.7	37.0
39.9	45.9	38.2	Inventory		47.7	35.4	36.1	37.5	37.0
3.8	3.4	3.0	All Other Current		.8	7.2	2.1	2.4	2.9
85.3	87.9	83.7	Total Current		87.0	80.7	81.7	87.9	83.8
8.0	5.7	6.8	Fixed Assets (net)		5.1	7.8	8.5	7.3	5.0
1.4	.9	1.7	Intangibles (net)		.8	1.0	.4	.4	4.2
5.3	5.5	7.8	All Other Non-Current		7.2	10.5	9.5	4.4	7.0
100.0	100.0	100.0	Total		100.0	100.0	100.0	100.0	100.0
			LIABILITIES						
21.4	21.6	16.6	Notes Payable-Short Term		16.9	19.9	18.8	11.8	15.6
2.3	3.0	2.9	Cur. Mat.-L/T/D		1.8	1.2	3.4	2.0	2.2
19.5	14.7	19.1	Trade Payables		12.3	20.8	24.0	22.9	16.5
.4	.3	.1	Income Taxes Payable		.2	.1	.1	.1	.1
7.1	7.9	10.9	All Other Current		12.9	7.6	7.3	11.1	14.3
50.7	47.5	49.6	Total Current		44.1	49.7	53.5	47.9	48.7
5.2	3.6	4.7	Long Term Debt		5.8	2.3	7.4	3.2	5.4
.1	.2	.1	Deferred Taxes		.0	.0	.1	.1	.2
7.4	6.4	5.5	All Other Non-Current		3.6	4.0	10.7	4.6	4.7
36.6	42.4	40.1	Net Worth		46.5	44.1	28.4	44.2	41.0
100.0	100.0	100.0	Total Liabilities & Net Worth		100.0	100.0	100.0	100.0	100.0
			INCOME DATA						
100.0	100.0	100.0	Net Sales		100.0	100.0	100.0	100.0	100.0
33.1	32.5	30.6	Gross Profit		37.0	29.5	33.8	26.8	29.1
27.7	27.4	27.1	Operating Expenses		32.5	28.2	32.9	23.3	23.1
5.4	5.1	3.5	Operating Profit		4.5	1.2	.9	3.4	6.0
1.3	1.4	.6	All Other Expenses (net)		1.4	-.2	.8	.1	.9
4.1	3.7	2.9	Profit Before Taxes		3.2	1.4	.1	3.3	5.1
			RATIOS						
2.5	2.8	2.7	Current		3.0	4.2	2.8	3.0	2.1
1.7	1.8	1.7			2.3	1.6	1.7	1.7	1.8
1.2	1.4	1.3			1.2	1.3	1.2	1.3	1.3
1.3	1.6	1.4	Quick		1.3	1.9	1.5	1.9	1.2
.8	(86) .7	.8			.9	.8	1.1	1.0	.8
.4	.4	.4			.4	.2	.4	.6	.6
26 14.1	24 15.3	20 18.4	Sales/Receivables		19 18.8	6 61.1	25 14.6	27 13.7	24 15.1
41 8.9	39 9.5	40 9.0			32 11.4	28 12.9	41 9.0	49 7.4	49 7.5
60 6.1	54 6.8	62 5.9			87 4.2	54 6.7	54 6.8	70 5.2	62 5.9
41 9.0	55 6.6	42 8.6	Cost of Sales/Inventory		91 4.0	30 12.3	29 12.4	45 8.0	45 8.1
76 4.8	83 4.4	75 4.9			115 3.2	76 4.8	83 4.4	55 6.6	61 6.0
124 2.9	130 2.8	125 2.9			211 1.7	104 3.5	135 2.7	129 2.8	99 3.7
11 33.9	11 32.7	12 29.8	Cost of Sales/Payables		5 68.6	15 25.0	17 20.9	11 33.4	16 22.8
28 13.0	20 18.3	29 12.8			21 17.2	31 11.8	44 8.3	28 13.1	29 12.7
47 7.8	40 9.0	54 6.8			66 5.6	64 5.7	60 6.1	67 5.4	35 10.3
5.3	4.6	4.7	Sales/Working Capital		3.2	4.8	4.1	5.1	5.0
7.8	8.0	8.4			4.6	8.7	8.5	7.8	9.8
17.7	13.5	16.8			8.8	17.8	21.5	15.4	15.7
7.2	6.7	10.8	EBIT/Interest		30.8	6.2	10.9	7.8	15.2
(95) 2.4	(82) 2.4	(127) 3.4			(14) 2.8	(20) 2.8	(31) 2.3	(41) 3.2	5.2
1.5	1.3	1.5			.8	-.8	-.6	2.0	2.6
44.9	15.8	26.0	Net Profit + Depr., Dep., Amort./Cur. Mat. L/T/D						48.8
(15) 9.1	(12) 7.3	(21) 2.4						(10)	3.8
1.2	.9	.2							.5
.0	.0	.0	Fixed/Worth		.0	.0	.1	.0	.0
.1	.1	.1			.1	.1	.2	.1	.1
.3	.2	.3			.3	.2	.7	.1	.3
.8	.6	.5	Debt/Worth		.4	.4	.5	.5	.9
1.8	1.4	1.4			1.4	1.3	1.8	1.5	1.5
3.5	2.9	3.7			2.1	2.6	4.2	3.0	4.0
56.0	57.2	45.9	% Profit Before Taxes/Tangible Net Worth		41.9	18.1	32.5	28.3	68.6
(95) 20.9	(83) 15.9	(127) 17.7			(13) 12.5	(16) 6.5	(22) 11.5	(31) 10.5	(40) 42.3
4.3	3.5	3.4			-1.0	-5.3	-7.0	3.5	17.1
20.9	16.1	16.4	% Profit Before Taxes/Total Assets		18.0	8.3	14.8	11.2	22.8
7.3	6.2	6.8			4.8	1.9	4.8	4.9	9.0
2.1	1.2	1.2			-1.0	-3.1	-3.7	1.5	4.2
248.3	145.2	237.0	Sales/Net Fixed Assets		108.8	289.2	175.3	333.7	225.2
83.5	61.6	81.9			58.2	66.9	71.5	136.4	84.8
24.8	33.9	33.1			26.9	31.7	23.4	63.6	35.5
3.5	3.7	3.5	Sales/Total Assets		2.7	3.7	4.4	3.6	3.6
2.8	2.7	2.8			2.0	3.0	2.4	2.9	3.0
2.1	2.2	1.9			1.5	1.8	1.8	2.1	2.5
(76) .2	(74) .2	(113) .2	% Depr., Dep., Amort./Sales		(12) .3	(14) .2	(20) .3	(28) .1	(35) .2
.4	.3	.4			.4	.3	.4	.3	.4
.8	.7	.8			.5	.9	.8	.7	.9
(56) 1.6	(53) 1.5	(67) 1.8	% Officers', Directors', Owners' Comp/Sales				(12) 1.4	(19) 2.3	(20) 1.4
3.4	2.8	2.7					2.6	3.5	2.5
7.5	7.2	5.7					4.4	6.2	4.2
2494434M	2642957M	4643589M	Net Sales ($)	4972M	26369M	69840M	178560M	518510M	3845338M
1060506M	1003499M	1751217M	Total Assets ($)	2914M	14181M	29803M	78686M	197443M	1428190M

Current Data Sorted By Assets — **Comparative Historical Data**

0-500M	500M-2MM	2-10MM	10-50MM	50-100MM	100-250MM	Type of Statement	4/1/98-3/31/99 ALL	4/1/99-3/31/00 ALL
		4	10	3	4	Unqualified	20	23
	6	17	3			Reviewed	24	21
	2	5		1		Compiled	7	10
2	3					Tax Returns	3	4
2	3	9	9	4		Other	20	17
	15 (4/1-9/30/02)		71 (10/1/02-3/31/03)					
4	13	35	22	8	4	**NUMBER OF STATEMENTS**	74	75
%	%	%	%	%	%	**ASSETS**	%	%
	8.1	7.0	9.1			Cash & Equivalents	8.9	8.6
	41.9	39.7	35.6			Trade Receivables (net)	29.8	30.9
	38.0	41.3	35.7			Inventory	42.7	39.1
	.2	3.1	3.9			All Other Current	3.2	4.3
	88.2	91.1	84.2			Total Current	84.6	82.9
	8.8	5.0	7.6			Fixed Assets (net)	7.1	7.7
	.8	1.2	1.4			Intangibles (net)	3.5	2.5
	2.2	2.7	6.8			All Other Non-Current	4.7	7.0
	100.0	100.0	100.0			Total	100.0	100.0
						LIABILITIES		
	19.6	23.4	12.0			Notes Payable-Short Term	21.7	20.8
	2.1	.3	1.8			Cur. Mat.-L/T/D	3.1	.6
	26.6	23.3	14.7			Trade Payables	15.8	20.7
	.0	.1	.2			Income Taxes Payable	.2	.2
	7.1	8.7	10.3			All Other Current	7.9	27.4
	55.3	55.8	39.0			Total Current	48.8	69.8
	7.9	1.1	7.6			Long Term Debt	6.3	4.4
	.2	.0	.5			Deferred Taxes	.3	.4
	8.7	3.2	3.4			All Other Non-Current	5.4	3.7
	27.9	39.9	49.5			Net Worth	39.1	21.7
	100.0	100.0	100.0			Total Liabilities & Net Worth	100.0	100.0
						INCOME DATA		
	100.0	100.0	100.0			Net Sales	100.0	100.0
	30.5	28.9	33.7			Gross Profit	31.4	29.3
	26.0	25.7	26.7			Operating Expenses	28.3	26.7
	4.5	3.2	7.0			Operating Profit	3.1	2.7
	1.5	1.6	.6			All Other Expenses (net)	1.1	.4
	3.0	1.6	6.4			Profit Before Taxes	2.0	2.3
						RATIOS		
	2.4	2.5	4.4			Current	2.6	2.4
	1.7	1.6	2.2				1.6	1.6
	1.1	1.3	1.5				1.3	1.2
	1.4	1.3	2.2			Quick	1.2	1.3
	1.1	.9	1.0				.7	.7
	.5	.6	.8				.3	.3
	46 7.9	40 9.0	41 8.9			Sales/Receivables	33 11.1	32 11.4
	54 6.7	55 6.7	56 6.5				52 7.1	49 7.5
	70 5.2	84 4.4	69 5.3				74 4.9	70 5.2
	30 12.2	44 8.3	48 7.5			Cost of Sales/Inventory	74 5.0	53 6.9
	62 5.9	88 4.1	79 4.6				110 3.3	91 4.0
	148 2.5	143 2.6	108 3.4				159 2.3	145 2.5
	23 15.6	18 20.2	13 27.8			Cost of Sales/Payables	19 19.3	20 18.3
	37 9.7	43 8.4	25 14.3				34 10.7	37 9.9
	69 5.3	88 4.2	42 8.7				58 6.3	62 5.9
	4.2	4.0	3.2			Sales/Working Capital	3.6	4.1
	8.7	4.8	5.1				6.3	7.4
	16.5	11.2	10.2				14.4	24.9
	8.7	6.7	23.1			EBIT/Interest	7.4	9.2
	(12) 4.6	(32) 3.1	(20) 5.0				(64) 2.5	(66) 3.2
	1.3	1.5	3.3				.9	1.0
						Net Profit + Depr., Dep., Amort./Cur. Mat. L/T/D	22.7	24.5
							(16) 7.4	(17) 2.6
							-.3	-1.9
	.0	.0	.0			Fixed/Worth	.1	.1
	.1	.0	.1				.1	.1
	.5	.1	.3				.4	.3
	1.3	.5	.5			Debt/Worth	.9	.8
	2.1	1.7	1.0				1.7	1.8
	6.5	3.2	1.7				3.8	3.8
	43.9	29.1	35.6			% Profit Before Taxes/Tangible Net Worth	31.8	31.4
	(12) 25.1	(34) 7.3	(21) 14.8				(67) 14.0	(66) 17.4
	10.9	3.1	7.6				.8	5.1
	18.0	11.0	26.9			% Profit Before Taxes/Total Assets	14.9	13.7
	8.9	3.6	5.6				4.9	5.2
	1.3	.7	3.8				-.1	.5
	716.5	630.7	106.5			Sales/Net Fixed Assets	124.9	116.2
	85.8	105.2	47.3				49.1	50.5
	12.6	50.7	27.0				22.5	28.1
	3.9	3.2	2.6			Sales/Total Assets	2.6	2.8
	2.5	2.4	2.6				1.9	2.2
	1.8	1.5	1.9				1.5	1.7
	.1	.2	.4			% Depr., Dep., Amort./Sales	.3	.3
	(10) .3	(25) .4	(20) .5				(59) .5	(64) .6
	1.3	1.0	.9				1.0	.9
		2.4				% Officers', Directors', Owners' Comp/Sales	2.0	1.7
		(16) 3.4					(35) 4.2	(29) 4.3
		4.4					8.6	8.2
2677M	43102M	439994M	1214300M	799443M	751738M	Net Sales ($)	2403680M	2787680M
1093M	16425M	179260M	475011M	499820M	566334M	Total Assets ($)	1341796M	1419980M

M = $ thousand   MM = $ million
See Pages 11 through 18 for Explanation of Ratios and Data

Comparative Historical Data   Current Data Sorted By Sales

12 21 8 2 22	7 14 15 4 27	21 26 8 5 26	Type of Statement				2 5 5 · 4	1 9 1 · 5	18 4 1 · 13
			Unqualified / Reviewed / Compiled / Tax Returns / Other		5 · · 1 ·	3 1 2 2 ·			
				2 2	1				
4/1/00-3/31/01 ALL	4/1/01-3/31/02 ALL	4/1/02-3/31/03 ALL		**15 (4/1-9/30/02)**			**71 (10/1/02-3/31/03)**		
				0-1MM	1-3MM	3-5MM	5-10MM	10-25MM	25MM & OVER
65	67	86	**NUMBER OF STATEMENTS**	4	6	8	16	16	36
%	%	%	**ASSETS**	%	%	%	%	%	%
9.5	8.4	9.4	Cash & Equivalents				10.7	3.3	12.5
35.5	31.8	35.8	Trade Receivables (net)				35.6	43.2	33.3
39.7	41.3	37.8	Inventory				42.4	41.3	31.9
2.5	3.9	2.6	All Other Current				.5	4.1	4.1
87.2	85.3	85.6	Total Current				89.2	91.8	81.9
5.4	6.9	7.2	Fixed Assets (net)				6.3	4.1	7.7
2.3	3.0	2.2	Intangibles (net)				.1	2.3	3.5
5.2	4.8	5.0	All Other Non-Current				4.3	1.8	6.9
100.0	100.0	100.0	Total				100.0	100.0	100.0
			LIABILITIES						
24.4	19.8	18.1	Notes Payable-Short Term				12.9	38.8	11.0
.8	3.7	1.3	Cur. Mat.-L/T/D				.1	.6	1.3
16.4	16.8	18.8	Trade Payables				20.1	21.8	16.4
.2	.1	.2	Income Taxes Payable				.0	.2	.3
7.3	10.9	8.6	All Other Current				8.7	9.2	8.7
49.0	51.3	47.1	Total Current				41.9	70.7	37.7
22.6	5.8	8.2	Long Term Debt				1.4	1.4	7.2
.3	.3	.2	Deferred Taxes				.0	.0	.4
7.9	6.2	5.0	All Other Non-Current				3.6	3.3	2.6
20.1	36.4	39.5	Net Worth				53.1	24.7	52.1
100.0	100.0	100.0	Total Liabilities & Net Worth				100.0	100.0	100.0
			INCOME DATA						
100.0	100.0	100.0	Net Sales				100.0	100.0	100.0
31.7	33.2	32.6	Gross Profit				28.7	29.1	35.3
27.9	29.4	27.9	Operating Expenses				24.0	26.6	28.7
3.8	3.8	4.7	Operating Profit				4.7	2.5	6.6
1.2	2.1	1.3	All Other Expenses (net)				.6	2.8	.7
2.7	1.7	3.4	Profit Before Taxes				4.1	−.3	5.9
			RATIOS						
3.0	3.0	2.7					3.2	1.8	4.0
1.8	1.7	2.0	Current				2.2	1.4	2.3
1.5	1.4	1.4					1.7	1.2	1.6
1.3	1.3	1.8					1.8	1.1	2.2
.9	(65) .8	1.0	Quick				1.2	.8	1.0
.6	.5	.7					.7	.4	.8
39 9.4	39 9.3	41 8.9					41 8.9	48 7.6	38 9.5
52 7.0	52 7.0	56 6.5	Sales/Receivables				49 7.4	59 6.2	59 6.2
67 5.4	75 4.9	70 5.2					90 4.0	73 5.0	68 5.4
58 6.3	64 5.7	47 7.7					49 7.4	33 10.9	48 7.6
92 4.0	107 3.4	84 4.4	Cost of Sales/Inventory				107 3.4	86 4.2	68 5.4
139 2.6	146 2.5	138 2.6					176 2.1	126 2.9	113 3.2
13 27.4	18 20.5	18 20.3					18 19.8	13 27.3	19 19.4
27 13.4	35 10.3	29 12.5	Cost of Sales/Payables				41 8.9	21 17.0	30 12.3
53 6.9	61 6.0	56 6.5					113 3.2	61 6.0	44 8.3
3.9	3.9	3.8					3.2	6.4	2.9
6.6	5.6	5.1	Sales/Working Capital				4.2	8.8	4.7
10.3	12.6	11.2					4.8	13.4	10.4
5.5	6.3	9.1					7.0	4.2	24.1
(60) 3.1	(62) 2.1	(77) 3.5	EBIT/Interest				(15) 3.4	(15) 3.0	(31) 5.4
1.7	.7	1.5					2.3	1.0	3.3
45.2	4.9	15.8	Net Profit + Depr., Dep.,						
(11) 9.0	(12) 1.3	(12) 4.4	Amort./Cur. Mat. L/T/D						
1.3	.1	.3							
.0	.1	.0					.0	.0	.0
.1	.1	.1	Fixed/Worth				.0	.1	.1
.3	.4	.3					.1	.3	.3
.7	.8	.6					.4	1.4	.5
1.8	1.5	1.5	Debt/Worth				1.1	2.7	1.0
3.3	4.0	2.9					1.9	5.0	1.8
30.7	41.8	38.1	% Profit Before Taxes/Tangible				36.2	28.9	48.7
(59) 17.8	(59) 16.4	(80) 14.8	Net Worth				8.2	(15) 14.8	(35) 14.4
5.7	1.8	5.4					4.6	6.2	5.8
13.8	11.7	13.2	% Profit Before Taxes/Total				16.1	9.3	22.6
6.4	3.1	5.2	Assets				4.9	3.9	8.0
2.4	−.8	1.3					2.1	.5	2.6
124.5	118.1	175.9					712.0	591.9	91.0
57.5	54.7	62.5	Sales/Net Fixed Assets				98.3	97.5	30.3
32.9	27.0	23.9					43.8	42.2	20.7
2.9	2.6	2.9					2.5	3.1	2.7
2.2	2.2	2.3	Sales/Total Assets				2.0	2.4	2.5
1.6	1.6	1.6					1.4	2.1	1.7
.3	.4	.2					.2	.1	.4
(54) .6	(48) .6	(67) .5	% Depr., Dep., Amort./Sales				(10) .6	(13) .3	(31) .6
.9	1.1	1.1					1.0	.7	1.2
1.6	3.4	2.5					2.5		
(26) 3.7	(29) 5.9	(34) 3.6	% Officers', Directors', Owners' Comp/Sales				(12) 3.6		
8.7	9.2	6.2					4.4		
2458430M	2223563M	3251254M	Net Sales ($)	2433M	12004M	29938M	122493M	239115M	2845271M
1358014M	1313875M	1737943M	Total Assets ($)	1321M	9263M	10705M	65737M	99158M	1551759M

© RMA 2003

M = $ thousand   MM = $ million
See Pages 11 through 18 for Explanation of Ratios and Data

Current Data Sorted By Assets   **Comparative Historical Data**

0-500M	500M-2MM	2-10MM	10-50MM	50-100MM	100-250MM	Type of Statement	4/1/98-3/31/99	4/1/99-3/31/00
1	2	27	35	11	16	Unqualified	89	92
4	8	53	19	1		Reviewed	99	88
6	28	25	3		1	Compiled	81	70
8	18	4				Tax Returns	30	27
	19	47	25	7	9	Other	105	88
	119 (4/1-9/30/02)			257 (10/1/02-3/31/03)				
19	75	156	82	19	25	NUMBER OF STATEMENTS	404 ALL	365 ALL
%	%	%	%	%	%	**ASSETS**	%	%
9.6	14.3	5.9	6.0	3.8	4.3	Cash & Equivalents	6.3	7.1
26.2	30.9	36.2	31.7	25.3	23.6	Trade Receivables (net)	32.6	33.3
34.3	30.1	31.7	28.1	28.0	30.6	Inventory	30.4	30.3
.2	1.7	3.2	2.1	2.6	4.1	All Other Current	2.0	2.2
70.3	76.9	77.1	67.9	59.6	62.6	Total Current	71.3	73.0
19.8	15.2	15.6	22.2	29.0	21.7	Fixed Assets (net)	19.3	18.8
3.3	1.1	2.1	1.9	2.7	7.0	Intangibles (net)	3.1	2.0
6.7	6.8	5.3	7.9	8.7	8.7	All Other Non-Current	6.4	6.2
100.0	100.0	100.0	100.0	100.0	100.0	Total	100.0	100.0
						LIABILITIES		
22.9	10.9	18.3	13.7	18.7	9.8	Notes Payable-Short Term	16.4	14.8
11.8	2.5	2.2	2.9	2.2	3.0	Cur. Mat.-L/T/D	3.0	2.4
21.0	28.2	25.4	20.7	20.7	22.8	Trade Payables	24.7	25.1
.1	.4	.2	.2	.2	.1	Income Taxes Payable	.3	.2
34.4	7.8	7.2	8.3	6.7	14.5	All Other Current	10.4	8.0
90.2	49.8	53.4	45.8	48.5	50.3	Total Current	54.9	50.5
9.5	9.6	9.5	13.3	14.4	17.9	Long Term Debt	13.6	12.6
.0	.2	.1	.6	1.2	.6	Deferred Taxes	.3	.3
3.6	7.2	4.2	2.7	2.6	4.8	All Other Non-Current	4.6	3.8
-3.4	33.2	32.7	37.7	33.3	26.4	Net Worth	26.8	32.8
100.0	100.0	100.0	100.0	100.0	100.0	Total Liabilities & Net Worth	100.0	100.0
						INCOME DATA		
100.0	100.0	100.0	100.0	100.0	100.0	Net Sales	100.0	100.0
33.0	23.5	16.7	16.3	14.5	14.2	Gross Profit	17.7	18.3
30.3	20.5	14.9	14.5	12.9	12.0	Operating Expenses	15.6	16.3
2.7	2.9	1.9	1.8	1.6	2.2	Operating Profit	2.1	2.0
.4	-.1	.1	-.2	.5	1.0	All Other Expenses (net)	.4	.4
2.4	3.0	1.8	1.9	1.2	1.3	Profit Before Taxes	1.7	1.6
						RATIOS		
3.3	2.6	2.0	2.1	1.6	1.5	Current	2.0	2.1
1.3	1.5	1.4	1.5	1.2	1.3		1.4	1.4
1.0	1.1	1.1	1.1	1.0	1.0		1.1	1.1
(18) 1.4	1.5	1.1	1.3	.8	.7	Quick	1.1	1.2
.7	.8	.8	.8	.6	.6		.8	.8
.2	.6	.5	.6		.3		.5	.6
6 / 64.6	11 / 34.4	18 / 20.8	15 / 24.6	7 / 50.0	9 / 39.0	Sales/Receivables	16 / 22.3	14 / 26.4
19 / 18.7	20 / 17.8	26 / 13.8	25 / 14.5	25 / 14.4	11 / 32.6		23 / 15.7	24 / 15.3
37 / 9.7	30 / 12.0	34 / 10.7	32 / 11.3	31 / 11.7	23 / 16.0		32 / 11.5	34 / 10.8
18 / 19.7	10 / 36.1	16 / 22.2	18 / 20.8	16 / 22.5	17 / 21.8	Cost of Sales/Inventory	16 / 22.8	16 / 22.5
30 / 12.0	25 / 14.8	27 / 13.5	23 / 15.9	25 / 14.3	23 / 16.2		26 / 14.2	27 / 13.3
57 / 6.4	44 / 8.3	40 / 9.1	33 / 11.1	37 / 9.8	35 / 10.5		40 / 9.0	42 / 8.7
12 / 29.8	11 / 33.3	10 / 37.5	10 / 35.4	14 / 26.4	11 / 33.6	Cost of Sales/Payables	11 / 32.0	12 / 30.8
19 / 18.8	22 / 16.9	21 / 17.2	18 / 20.5	17 / 21.1	16 / 23.3		19 / 19.4	19 / 19.2
33 / 11.1	35 / 10.3	33 / 11.1	27 / 13.7	26 / 14.3	26 / 14.2		31 / 11.8	31 / 11.6
8.8	13.7	13.3	12.8	21.2	24.9	Sales/Working Capital	12.5	12.9
34.2	24.8	21.6	24.6	44.9	36.1		25.5	22.8
-613.0	89.7	72.7	62.6	-683.7	408.2		140.5	71.2
(15) 15.9	(63) 12.4	(147) 13.3	(77) 9.3	(24) 10.9	7.2	EBIT/Interest	(358) 5.7	(338) 6.8
5.5	4.3	2.7	4.6	3.3	2.7		2.6	3.2
.7	1.3	1.5	2.2	.7	1.5		1.4	1.5
	(15) 3.0	(40) 8.9	(40) 12.6	(13) 6.3	(13) 3.6	Net Profit + Depr., Dep., Amort./Cur. Mat. L/T/D	(127) 6.1	(126) 6.4
	1.8	3.1	4.2	2.7	1.0		2.7	3.0
	.8	1.2	2.1	1.3	.7		1.6	1.6
.1	.1	.1	.3	.6	.5	Fixed/Worth	.2	.2
.6	.4	.4	.6	1.0	1.0		.6	.5
-6.8	.8	1.1	1.2	1.5	1.8		1.6	1.1
.6	.7	1.2	.9	1.0	2.3	Debt/Worth	1.1	1.1
5.1	1.9	2.5	2.3	2.7	3.9		2.4	2.4
-9.3	4.9	5.8	3.4	4.1	10.1		6.2	5.0
(13) 76.4	(68) 54.4	(144) 29.9	(80) 47.0	(18) 30.1	(23) 56.3	% Profit Before Taxes/Tangible Net Worth	(367) 36.0	(342) 40.8
15.3	21.2	14.8	19.3	15.0	15.0		17.1	19.2
3.3	3.3	5.2	10.3	-4.1	6.1		6.0	7.9
30.1	23.4	9.0	10.8	9.1	6.6	% Profit Before Taxes/Total Assets	10.9	11.7
1.7	5.6	4.6	6.4	4.1	3.9		5.1	5.2
-.9	.8	1.6	3.4	-.6	1.4		1.5	1.9
748.0	188.5	141.9	53.3	27.8	77.7	Sales/Net Fixed Assets	91.4	101.0
41.9	63.5	48.6	27.4	16.9	22.5		36.2	39.6
16.5	24.1	21.7	14.1	8.4	12.9		16.2	15.7
7.2	7.2	6.9	6.5	6.1	7.0	Sales/Total Assets	6.6	7.2
5.0	5.2	4.8	5.1	4.4	5.7		4.9	4.9
3.1	3.7	3.5	3.6	3.6	3.9		3.3	3.4
(12) .6	(66) .2	(145) .2	(77) .4	(18) .5	(16) .4	% Depr., Dep., Amort./Sales	(349) .3	(323) .3
2.0	.6	.4	.6	.8	.7		.6	.6
2.5	1.1	.8	1.0	1.7	.9		1.1	1.0
	(45) .9	(73) .8	(21) .3			% Officers', Directors', Owners' Comp/Sales	(137) .8	(133) .7
	1.9	1.4	.9				1.6	1.7
	3.6	4.2	1.8				3.2	3.2
22926M	523712M	4238745M	10049596M	6634707M	24935885M	Net Sales ($)	36456752M	34714161M
4343M	85357M	782258M	1866218M	1441211M	3931607M	Total Assets ($)	7503570M	6369702M

Comparative Historical Data | Current Data Sorted By Sales

73	62	91	Type of Statement	1		2	3	7	80
79	72	82	Unqualified	1	1		6	34	38
69	77	60	Reviewed	2	6	8	20	10	14
31	21	28	Compiled	3	6	6	7	4	4
79	97	115	Tax Returns	4	8	9	11	25	58
4/1/00-3/31/01	4/1/01-3/31/02	4/1/02-3/31/03	Other						
ALL	ALL	ALL		119 (4/1-9/30/02)			257 (10/1/02-3/31/03)		
				0-1MM	1-3MM	3-5MM	5-10MM	10-25MM	25MM & OVER
331	329	376	NUMBER OF STATEMENTS	11	21	23	47	80	194
%	%	%	**ASSETS**	%	%	%	%	%	%
6.5	6.9	7.6	Cash & Equivalents	9.2	11.7	10.8	10.5	10.6	4.7
34.4	32.5	32.3	Trade Receivables (net)	32.5	21.5	26.4	35.2	33.0	33.1
29.7	30.4	30.5	Inventory	31.4	31.1	30.0	29.7	30.9	30.4
1.7	1.9	2.5	All Other Current	.0	.2	3.0	2.6	1.9	3.1
72.2	71.8	72.8	Total Current	73.2	64.5	70.3	78.1	76.3	71.3
18.3	19.5	18.2	Fixed Assets (net)	13.1	25.2	19.5	14.2	15.4	19.8
2.3	2.8	2.3	Intangibles (net)	1.2	4.0	3.8	.4	1.5	2.7
7.2	6.0	6.7	All Other Non-Current	12.5	6.4	6.4	7.3	6.8	6.2
100.0	100.0	100.0	Total	100.0	100.0	100.0	100.0	100.0	100.0
			LIABILITIES						
16.3	18.1	15.5	Notes Payable-Short Term	19.0	14.9	15.9	12.1	14.1	16.8
2.1	2.7	3.0	Cur. Mat.-L/T/D	13.8	5.3	1.6	4.1	1.7	2.5
23.9	23.2	24.3	Trade Payables	18.4	26.6	21.9	30.2	24.5	23.2
.2	.2	.2	Income Taxes Payable	.1	.2	.6	.3	.2	.2
8.5	8.3	9.4	All Other Current	6.8	30.5	7.1	8.4	6.9	8.8
51.0	52.5	52.4	Total Current	58.1	77.6	47.1	55.1	47.4	51.5
12.2	12.6	11.1	Long Term Debt	10.7	8.5	10.4	11.1	10.5	11.8
.3	.3	.3	Deferred Taxes	.0	.0	.3	.1	.2	.5
3.2	3.7	4.4	All Other Non-Current	2.5	1.9	5.1	7.0	6.1	3.4
33.2	30.9	31.7	Net Worth	28.7	12.0	37.1	26.6	35.8	32.9
100.0	100.0	100.0	Total Liabilities & Net Worth	100.0	100.0	100.0	100.0	100.0	100.0
			INCOME DATA						
100.0	100.0	100.0	Net Sales	100.0	100.0	100.0	100.0	100.0	100.0
18.0	18.6	18.5	Gross Profit	35.9	37.1	27.1	19.8	17.5	14.6
16.0	16.6	16.4	Operating Expenses	29.8	33.0	24.0	17.1	15.6	13.1
2.0	2.0	2.1	Operating Profit	6.1	4.2	3.1	2.7	2.0	1.5
.4	.3	.1	All Other Expenses (net)	.4	.5	−.1	.2	.0	.1
1.6	1.7	2.0	Profit Before Taxes	5.7	3.7	3.2	2.5	2.0	1.4
			RATIOS						
2.1	2.1	2.0		3.6	2.2	3.5	2.4	2.2	1.9
1.4	1.4	1.4	Current	1.2	1.4	1.3	1.5	1.5	1.4
1.1	1.1	1.1		1.0	1.0	1.0	1.1	1.2	1.1
1.1	1.1	1.2		1.8	.9	1.7	1.3	1.3	1.1
.8 (328)	.8 (375)	.8	Quick	1.0 (20)	.7	.7	.9	.9	.7
.6	.5	.5		.6	.3	.5	.6	.6	.5
16 23.1	12 29.3	13 27.7		23 15.6	9 42.6	18 20.8	13 27.8	20 18.1	11 32.6
26 14.3	24 15.3	24 15.3	Sales/Receivables	37 9.7	19 18.9	21 17.0	27 13.6	27 13.6	22 16.5
36 10.2	35 10.5	32 11.4		50 7.3	29 12.4	32 11.3	41 8.9	33 10.9	30 12.3
16 23.0	17 21.4	16 22.3		12 29.3	19 19.5	23 15.9	10 36.1	20 17.9	16 22.5
25 14.4	26 13.9	25 14.6	Cost of Sales/Inventory	28 13.0	37 9.7	37 9.9	25 14.5	30 12.3	23 16.1
42 8.8	41 8.8	39 9.3		73 5.0	55 6.6	76 4.8	60 6.0	41 9.0	32 11.5
11 32.8	10 36.2	11 34.1		9 39.2	18 19.8	11 32.0	12 30.5	10 37.5	10 36.8
18 20.6	19 19.7	19 19.1	Cost of Sales/Payables	28 13.0	29 12.4	22 16.9	24 15.3	22 16.7	17 21.7
31 11.6	30 12.2	31 11.8		41 8.9	47 7.7	37 9.8	34 10.7	36 10.1	26 14.3
12.6	13.8	13.6		5.0	7.9	8.0	9.3	11.3	15.5
25.6	26.3	25.5	Sales/Working Capital	21.9	23.3	27.3	17.6	19.0	31.9
121.8	71.0	89.3		−613.0	NM	999.8	64.0	33.1	127.3
5.5	7.0	11.0			16.0	10.7	7.4	15.1	10.3
(302) 2.8	(301) 2.7	(345) 3.5	EBIT/Interest	(18) 2.7	(20) 2.2	(40) 3.9	(74) 3.6	(186) 3.5	
1.6	1.4	1.7		.8	−.1	1.8	1.4	1.8	
6.6	5.9	7.6	Net Profit + Depr., Dep.,			4.1	9.7	8.2	
(107) 2.8	(89) 2.1	(123) 2.8	Amort./Cur. Mat. L/T/D	(10) 1.0	(21) 2.7	(83) 3.3			
1.7	1.1	1.1		.4	1.7	1.5			
.2	.2	.2		.0	.2	.1	.1	.1	.3
.5	.5	.5	Fixed/Worth	.1	.6	.6	.4	.3	.7
1.1	1.1	1.2		UND	2.3	1.5	.8	.9	1.3
1.0	.9	1.0		.4	.7	.6	1.0	1.0	1.1
2.5	2.3	2.5	Debt/Worth	2.3	1.7	2.2	2.4	1.9	2.8
5.2	5.3	5.3		−108.0	8.2	7.0	6.8	3.9	5.0
35.9	34.0	42.6	% Profit Before Taxes/Tangible		54.5	52.1	48.7	31.0	41.1
(313) 16.0	(293) 16.1	(346) 16.9	Net Worth	(18) 16.1	(20) 25.1	(43) 17.3	(74) 15.4	(183) 17.6	
6.1	6.4	6.6		−.2	−2.1	8.5	8.5	8.7	
10.0	10.5	11.0	% Profit Before Taxes/Total	7.5	29.6	23.4	9.2	14.4	9.6
4.9	4.5	4.9	Assets	1.7	2.4	5.8	4.7	4.8	5.2
1.5	1.1	1.7		.0	−.3	−1.5	2.2	1.5	2.3
106.9	86.0	109.5		UND	73.4	110.0	190.5	139.9	88.0
38.6	37.4	38.6	Sales/Net Fixed Assets	295.5	33.2	28.2	84.4	41.8	33.5
15.2	17.5	17.0		16.5	6.8	10.3	24.1	20.8	16.7
6.8	6.9	7.0		5.7	5.9	5.4	6.7	5.7	7.5
5.0	5.0	5.0	Sales/Total Assets	3.3	3.9	4.4	5.0	4.7	5.5
3.4	3.5	3.6		2.7	2.5	2.8	3.3	3.4	4.1
.3	.3	.3			.7	.3	.2	.2	.3
(285) .6	(279) .6	(334) .6	% Depr., Dep., Amort./Sales	(18) 1.7	(19) .8	(43) .6	(76) .5	(173) .5	
1.0	1.1	1.0		2.8	2.0	1.0	1.0	.8	
.9	.8	.8			1.7	.9	.9	.9	.4
(128) 1.7	(120) 1.8	(147) 1.6	% Officers', Directors', Owners' Comp/Sales	(14) 4.1	(11) 3.7	(28) 1.8	(34) 1.8	(58) .9	
2.9	2.8	3.5		7.1	4.5	3.3	4.4	1.6	
36848127M	38266351M	46405571M	Net Sales ($)	5210M	46223M	99353M	346587M	1330888M	44577310M
6785522M	7102157M	8110994M	Total Assets ($)	2246M	13904M	29928M	93761M	334212M	7636943M

© RMA 2003

M = $ thousand   MM = $ million
See Pages 11 through 18 for Explanation of Ratios and Data

Current Data Sorted By Assets · Comparative Historical Data

0-500M	500M-2MM	2-10MM	10-50MM	50-100MM	100-250MM	Type of Statement	4/1/98-3/31/99 ALL	4/1/99-3/31/00 ALL
		6	17	2	2	Unqualified	36	31
1	7	16	7			Reviewed	33	24
1	3	9				Compiled	20	24
		2				Tax Returns	4	4
2	5	16	10		4	Other	25	26
	34 (4/1-9/30/02)		78 (10/1/02-3/31/03)					
4	16	49	34	3	6	NUMBER OF STATEMENTS	118	109
%	%	%	%	%	%	**ASSETS**	%	%
	7.5	6.5	7.9			Cash & Equivalents	6.4	6.5
	27.7	31.3	26.4			Trade Receivables (net)	30.1	32.5
	30.7	32.6	27.2			Inventory	28.0	25.3
	4.5	4.4	4.2			All Other Current	3.1	2.2
	70.4	74.7	65.7			Total Current	67.6	66.4
	19.0	16.6	23.8			Fixed Assets (net)	22.8	24.3
	1.2	1.5	1.9			Intangibles (net)	4.4	2.1
	9.4	7.2	8.7			All Other Non-Current	5.2	7.1
	100.0	100.0	100.0			Total	100.0	100.0
						LIABILITIES		
	13.5	18.3	15.4			Notes Payable-Short Term	16.9	15.3
	6.8	1.6	2.6			Cur. Mat.-L/T/D	2.4	3.4
	24.3	24.2	16.6			Trade Payables	21.4	21.1
	.0	.1	.3			Income Taxes Payable	.2	.2
	7.1	8.9	9.1			All Other Current	9.8	9.2
	51.6	53.1	44.1			Total Current	50.6	49.2
	10.2	10.1	12.6			Long Term Debt	15.4	14.4
	.0	.1	.5			Deferred Taxes	.4	.4
	5.1	3.3	1.6			All Other Non-Current	6.0	4.0
	33.1	33.3	41.3			Net Worth	27.6	31.9
	100.0	100.0	100.0			Total Liabilities & Net Worth	100.0	100.0
						INCOME DATA		
	100.0	100.0	100.0			Net Sales	100.0	100.0
	23.3	19.0	18.8			Gross Profit	18.4	20.7
	19.7	16.6	15.3			Operating Expenses	17.8	18.1
	3.6	2.4	3.5			Operating Profit	.5	2.7
	.1	.5	-.1			All Other Expenses (net)	.5	-.5
	3.5	1.9	3.6			Profit Before Taxes	.0	3.2
						RATIOS		
	2.1	1.9	2.1			Current	2.1	1.9
	1.3	1.4	1.4				1.3	1.4
	1.2	1.1	1.1				1.0	1.0
	1.2	1.1	1.3			Quick	1.2	1.2
	.8	.7	.8			(117)	.7	.8
	.4	.5	.5				.5	.6
	10 36.4	18 20.3	20 17.9			Sales/Receivables	15 23.9	20 18.6
	14 26.9	25 14.8	27 13.3				25 14.7	28 13.1
	21 17.5	30 12.0	38 9.6				35 10.5	35 10.5
	10 36.4	21 17.7	22 16.7			Cost of Sales/Inventory	18 20.4	14 25.2
	20 18.7	26 13.8	36 10.0				26 13.8	24 15.3
	39 9.2	43 8.5	61 6.0				39 9.5	41 8.9
	12 29.4	14 27.0	13 27.4			Cost of Sales/Payables	11 32.2	12 29.3
	17 21.5	19 19.1	20 18.1				18 20.1	20 18.1
	31 12.0	26 14.2	29 12.7				25 14.5	30 12.1
	14.5	11.5	8.8			Sales/Working Capital	12.5	11.2
	45.1	26.9	20.0				27.9	28.3
	57.5	63.7	39.0				372.7	261.1
	14.9	6.3	9.1			EBIT/Interest	6.7	6.9
(15)	6.7	(43) 2.7	(28) 3.8				(111) 2.2	(96) 3.2
	1.3	1.3	2.1				1.3	1.4
		(11) 8.0				Net Profit + Depr., Dep., Amort./Cur. Mat. L /T/D	8.3	5.5
		3.1					(33) 2.8	(30) 2.5
		1.0					1.7	1.0
	.0	.1	.2			Fixed/Worth	.3	.2
	.2	.4	.8				.8	.7
	1.0	1.1	1.2				3.4	1.8
	1.0	1.0	.9			Debt/Worth	1.4	1.3
	1.7	2.7	1.5				3.2	2.5
	5.8	6.4	5.1				16.1	5.9
	63.9	53.2	36.1			% Profit Before Taxes/Tangible Net Worth	44.9	40.4
(15)	17.0	(45) 21.6	(33) 14.6				(99) 19.7	(99) 20.2
	3.5	3.4	9.9				7.8	5.4
	27.6	12.8	9.5			% Profit Before Taxes/Total Assets	11.0	11.5
	5.6	4.6	7.0				4.1	5.0
	1.9	1.3	3.3				1.3	1.7
	288.7	145.9	40.2			Sales/Net Fixed Assets	98.1	82.9
	85.2	48.7	18.1				26.7	27.7
	16.8	20.4	8.1				11.0	8.2
	8.1	5.9	4.9			Sales/Total Assets	6.5	6.2
	6.3	5.0	3.1				4.4	4.0
	3.6	3.6	2.2				3.1	2.6
	.3	.2	.3			% Depr., Dep., Amort./Sales	.4	.3
(10)	.4	(43) .5	(30) .9				(100) .6	(94) .8
	1.9	1.0	1.6				1.4	1.9
		(19) .9				% Officers', Directors', Owners' Comp/Sales	.7	.7
		1.1					(32) 1.6	(32) 1.3
		1.4					3.1	2.5
6237M	132341M	1214258M	2882535M	905088M	2377648M	Net Sales ($)	7291436M	5253849M
1419M	20781M	246283M	765438M	169513M	894858M	Total Assets ($)	1699634M	1251368M

© RMA 2003

M = $ thousand   MM = $ million
See Pages 11 through 18 for Explanation of Ratios and Data

Comparative Historical Data				Current Data Sorted By Sales					
			Type of Statement						
25	21	27	Unqualified				3	11	24
24	20	24	Reviewed		1		7	4	9
29	26	17	Compiled		1	2	1	1	3
3	1	6	Tax Returns		1	1	1	2	
21	27	38	Other	1		2	3	9	22
4/1/00-3/31/01 ALL	4/1/01-3/31/02 ALL	4/1/02-3/31/03 ALL		0-1MM	34 (4/1-9/30/02) 1-3MM	3-5MM	5-10MM	78 (10/1/02-3/31/03) 10-25MM	25MM & OVER
102	95	112	**NUMBER OF STATEMENTS**	1	3	6	14	28	60
%	%	%	**ASSETS**	%	%	%	%	%	%
5.5	6.2	7.0	Cash & Equivalents				3.7	8.6	7.3
33.8	30.0	28.2	Trade Receivables (net)				22.8	30.1	29.6
26.2	29.3	31.1	Inventory				36.1	33.7	29.7
3.2	1.8	4.0	All Other Current				7.8	2.1	3.6
68.8	67.3	70.3	Total Current				70.5	74.5	70.3
22.5	22.5	20.1	Fixed Assets (net)				22.7	16.1	20.4
1.4	2.5	1.5	Intangibles (net)				1.2	1.3	1.8
7.3	7.7	8.2	All Other Non-Current				5.6	8.2	7.5
100.0	100.0	100.0	Total				100.0	100.0	100.0
			LIABILITIES						
18.8	17.4	17.2	Notes Payable-Short Term				24.7	12.9	16.8
2.6	2.3	2.7	Cur. Mat.-L/T/D				4.1	1.7	2.2
20.0	22.4	23.4	Trade Payables				16.9	27.2	22.6
.1	.1	.2	Income Taxes Payable				.0	.0	.3
9.6	6.9	8.5	All Other Current				8.8	9.6	7.6
51.1	49.1	52.0	Total Current				54.5	51.5	49.5
14.3	13.1	11.8	Long Term Debt				14.2	6.9	11.2
.5	.4	.3	Deferred Taxes				.0	.0	.5
8.2	6.0	4.1	All Other Non-Current				3.3	2.1	3.3
25.8	31.4	31.8	Net Worth				28.0	39.6	35.5
100.0	100.0	100.0	Total Liabilities & Net Worth				100.0	100.0	100.0
			INCOME DATA						
100.0	100.0	100.0	Net Sales				100.0	100.0	100.0
20.8	19.1	19.4	Gross Profit				20.9	19.0	17.6
18.4	17.5	16.4	Operating Expenses				18.8	16.1	14.9
2.4	1.6	3.0	Operating Profit				2.1	2.9	2.7
.8	.6	.2	All Other Expenses (net)				.4	.2	.0
1.6	1.0	2.8	Profit Before Taxes				1.8	2.7	2.7
			RATIOS						
1.8	2.0	2.0	Current				2.2	1.9	1.9
1.4	1.4	1.4					1.3	1.5	1.4
1.1	1.1	1.1					1.1	1.1	1.1
1.2	1.2	1.1	Quick				1.1	1.1	1.2
.8	.7	.7					.6	.8	.7
.6	.5	.5					.3	.5	.5
16 23.0	15 24.0	15 23.6	Sales/Receivables				9 38.9	18 20.8	17 21.9
26 13.9	23 16.0	23 15.7					19 19.0	24 15.1	24 15.3
35 10.4	31 11.9	34 10.6					34 10.7	29 12.4	36 10.2
13 28.4	15 23.6	18 20.0	Cost of Sales/Inventory				17 21.3	21 17.1	18 20.7
23 15.8	26 14.0	28 13.1					29 12.5	33 10.9	25 14.6
39 9.4	44 8.3	55 6.7					51 7.2	62 5.9	53 6.9
12 30.6	13 28.6	14 26.0	Cost of Sales/Payables				6 56.6	16 23.5	14 26.8
19 19.3	20 18.4	20 18.1					16 23.1	21 17.1	20 18.1
27 13.7	29 12.8	31 11.9					26 14.2	36 10.2	28 12.9
12.9	11.5	11.4	Sales/Working Capital				9.7	10.2	11.4
32.5	27.8	25.8					37.6	28.5	24.0
107.3	75.4	60.7					76.7	57.3	64.2
4.4	6.0	8.3	EBIT/Interest				(13) 6.4	(23) 18.4	(52) 6.7
(95) 2.3	(89) 2.1	(95) 3.4					2.8	4.9	3.4
1.3	.9	1.5					1.2	1.5	1.8
6.0	4.9	7.6	Net Profit + Depr., Dep., Amort./Cur. Mat. L/T/D						5.0
(32) 3.4	(30) 2.2	(24) 2.0						(12)	2.5
1.3	1.2	1.2							1.2
.2	.2	.1	Fixed/Worth				.0	.1	.1
.6	.7	.5					.6	.4	.7
1.6	1.4	1.2					1.8	.8	1.2
1.2	1.1	.9	Debt/Worth				1.0	.8	.9
2.6	2.2	2.4					3.2	1.4	2.5
6.4	4.5	5.7					15.5	3.1	5.2
31.8	28.1	48.9	% Profit Before Taxes/Tangible Net Worth				(13) 69.2	(27) 38.9	(58) 46.4
(91) 13.6	(86) 12.2	(104) 16.1					17.9	14.7	16.1
4.9	4.5	6.8					2.5	3.4	10.0
9.6	7.4	10.5	% Profit Before Taxes/Total Assets				11.3	14.9	9.6
4.7	3.6	5.2					3.6	5.5	5.9
1.3	.0	1.8					1.0	1.6	2.5
124.1	140.6	160.6	Sales/Net Fixed Assets				988.2	160.6	102.6
32.7	29.5	31.5					47.1	48.4	26.1
11.8	11.5	13.4					14.7	15.0	13.1
6.4	6.2	6.1	Sales/Total Assets				6.8	5.9	6.2
4.7	4.7	4.4					3.9	4.7	4.6
3.1	3.3	2.7					2.9	3.4	2.6
.2	.3	.3	% Depr., Dep., Amort./Sales				(11) .3	(23) .3	(53) .3
(79) .6	(76) .8	(93) .6					.6	.4	.6
1.5	1.4	1.4					1.8	1.4	1.3
.7	.6	.7	% Officers', Directors', Owners' Comp/Sales						.6
(38) 1.5	(31) 1.0	(35) 1.1						(18)	1.0
3.5	3.3	1.6							1.3
6186473M	7289274M	7518107M	Net Sales ($)	839M	5398M	23591M	109955M	475675M	6902649M
1301164M	1872773M	2098292M	Total Assets ($)	304M	1115M	13520M	28467M	143879M	1911007M

© RMA 2003 M = $ thousand MM = $ million
See Pages 11 through 18 for Explanation of Ratios and Data

Current Data Sorted By Assets   Comparative Historical Data

						Type of Statement		
	1	3	9	3	3	Unqualified	19	21
	2	13	3	1		Reviewed	18	16
1	4	5	3			Compiled	23	23
3	2	4	1			Tax Returns	2	3
3	5	11	2			Other	18	18
	21 (4/1-9/30/02)		61 (10/1/02-3/31/03)				4/1/98-3/31/99	4/1/99-3/31/00
0-500M	500M-2MM	2-10MM	10-50MM	50-100MM	100-250MM		ALL	ALL
7	14	36	18	4	3	NUMBER OF STATEMENTS	80	81
%	%	%	%	%	%	**ASSETS**	%	%
	7.1	6.7	9.5			Cash & Equivalents	6.4	9.2
	43.5	43.5	35.8			Trade Receivables (net)	44.9	37.8
	23.2	24.2	21.1			Inventory	20.7	23.0
	1.3	1.3	.7			All Other Current	1.0	1.8
	75.1	75.8	67.0			Total Current	73.0	71.9
	18.2	18.3	22.4			Fixed Assets (net)	17.9	19.9
	.3	1.9	1.3			Intangibles (net)	1.6	2.0
	6.3	4.0	9.2			All Other Non-Current	7.4	6.3
	100.0	100.0	100.0			Total	100.0	100.0
						LIABILITIES		
	9.5	7.7	6.7			Notes Payable-Short Term	19.8	11.1
	4.1	2.3	3.6			Cur. Mat.-L/T/D	2.5	2.4
	24.4	37.6	33.0			Trade Payables	37.9	33.7
	.1	.2	.1			Income Taxes Payable	.1	.3
	17.7	11.4	9.7			All Other Current	7.0	8.3
	55.7	59.3	53.1			Total Current	67.4	55.8
	10.7	9.8	7.7			Long Term Debt	8.3	11.4
	.0	.0	.5			Deferred Taxes	.5	.4
	9.7	1.7	3.1			All Other Non-Current	8.8	2.7
	23.9	29.3	35.5			Net Worth	14.9	29.7
	100.0	100.0	100.0			Total Liabilities & Net Worth	100.0	100.0
						INCOME DATA		
	100.0	100.0	100.0			Net Sales	100.0	100.0
	18.3	17.7	17.3			Gross Profit	16.4	16.6
	19.2	16.9	12.8			Operating Expenses	14.7	14.6
	−1.0	.8	4.5			Operating Profit	1.8	2.0
	−.5	−.1	.5			All Other Expenses (net)	.0	.1
	−.5	.9	4.1			Profit Before Taxes	1.8	1.9
						RATIOS		
	2.4	1.4	1.7				1.5	1.7
	1.6	1.2	1.3			Current	1.2	1.3
	.9	1.1	1.0				1.0	1.1
	1.7	1.1	1.3				1.1	1.2
	1.2	.7	1.0			Quick	.8	.9
	.4	.6	.5				.6	.6
13 28.1	20 18.5	21 17.8					24 15.4	18 20.2
20 18.3	24 14.9	25 14.5				Sales/Receivables	32 11.4	25 14.4
31 11.9	38 9.7	35 10.4					39 9.3	33 11.0
0 UND	7 52.3	11 33.1					8 44.6	8 44.6
18 19.9	25 14.8	14 25.4				Cost of Sales/Inventory	16 23.2	16 22.9
34 10.9	39 9.3	36 10.1					28 13.1	29 12.6
4 91.3	17 21.4	21 17.2					21 17.6	17 21.5
19 18.9	28 12.9	26 14.3				Cost of Sales/Payables	29 12.8	24 15.3
43 8.6	42 8.8	41 8.9					42 8.7	34 10.9
	15.3	20.1	13.8				20.4	17.7
	23.1	43.0	32.8			Sales/Working Capital	45.6	36.4
	−74.7	163.9	NM				UND	259.3
		10.9	28.5				9.9	15.0
	(29) 3.4	(17) 7.1				EBIT/Interest	(71) 4.1	(71) 4.3
	1.7	3.6					2.2	2.4
						Net Profit + Depr., Dep.,	7.6	11.3
						Amort./Cur. Mat. L./T/D	(26) 2.5	(28) 4.6
							1.9	2.5
	.0	.1	.1				.1	.2
	.6	.5	.4			Fixed/Worth	.6	.6
	NM	1.0	1.2				1.2	1.2
	.8	1.4	1.0				1.5	1.2
	1.5	3.5	2.3			Debt/Worth	2.9	2.4
	NM	5.9	4.2				8.6	5.5
	53.4	32.5	48.7				45.6	40.7
	(11) 15.6	(35) 20.9	(17) 30.0			% Profit Before Taxes/Tangible	(73) 21.5	(76) 20.5
	−15.1	7.3	16.8			Net Worth	9.6	11.9
	22.1	8.7	16.1				9.9	12.6
	2.8	4.3	8.6			% Profit Before Taxes/Total	6.3	6.2
	−8.4	1.0	5.9			Assets	2.4	2.8
	489.4	421.7	380.7				205.8	111.2
	59.9	35.1	26.4			Sales/Net Fixed Assets	42.0	34.6
	12.6	19.8	5.8				14.7	18.2
	8.6	6.6	7.4				6.8	6.9
	5.4	5.4	3.8			Sales/Total Assets	5.0	5.3
	2.9	3.5	2.4				3.4	3.8
		.2	.2				.2	.2
	(32) .8	(15) .8				% Depr., Dep., Amort./Sales	(73) .7	(73) .6
	1.8	2.8					1.4	1.1
		.5					.8	.6
	(17) 1.7					% Officers', Directors',	(35) 1.3	(25) 1.5
	3.1					Owners' Comp/Sales	2.1	2.4
10861M	96043M	1078038M	1531949M	3085360M	1424876M	Net Sales ($)	4969753M	6234663M
1376M	16203M	173693M	339827M	317323M	424653M	Total Assets ($)	1019816M	1260519M

M = $ thousand   MM = $ million
See Pages 11 through 18 for Explanation of Ratios and Data

Comparative Historical Data | Current Data Sorted By Sales

			Type of Statement	0-1MM	1-3MM	3-5MM	5-10MM	10-25MM	25MM & OVER
19	14	19	Unqualified			1	1	2	15
16	12	19	Reviewed				2	4	13
18	18	13	Compiled			2	2	5	3
4	3	10	Tax Returns			1	1	3	1
18	19	21	Other		3	1	1	6	6
4/1/00- 3/31/01 ALL	4/1/01- 3/31/02 ALL	4/1/02- 3/31/03 ALL		21 (4/1-9/30/02)			61 (10/1/02-3/31/03)		
75	66	82	NUMBER OF STATEMENTS	4	4	7	10	19	38

%	%	%	ASSETS	%	%	%	%	%	%
6.9	8.9	8.0	Cash & Equivalents				9.1	5.3	8.7
41.7	42.0	39.3	Trade Receivables (net)				46.3	36.6	43.3
22.8	20.1	21.8	Inventory				17.7	31.5	18.2
2.1	1.5	1.2	All Other Current				1.1	.9	1.6
73.5	72.4	70.3	Total Current				74.2	74.3	71.8
18.7	20.7	21.3	Fixed Assets (net)				16.9	18.5	18.9
2.3	2.0	2.2	Intangibles (net)				1.9	1.5	1.4
5.4	4.9	6.2	All Other Non-Current				7.0	5.7	7.8
100.0	100.0	100.0	Total				100.0	100.0	100.0

			LIABILITIES						
16.1	8.8	6.7	Notes Payable-Short Term				9.0	7.6	6.3
2.5	2.6	4.4	Cur. Mat.-L/T/D				2.9	2.4	2.3
34.4	31.3	31.8	Trade Payables				28.0	30.7	34.8
.2	.1	.2	Income Taxes Payable				.0	.2	.2
8.7	11.1	13.3	All Other Current				26.1	12.1	13.4
61.9	53.9	56.4	Total Current				66.0	53.1	57.0
10.4	10.6	13.2	Long Term Debt				9.6	9.0	8.0
.3	.2	.1	Deferred Taxes				.0	.0	.3
1.9	1.4	4.1	All Other Non-Current				1.6	5.1	2.6
25.4	33.9	26.2	Net Worth				22.8	32.7	32.2
100.0	100.0	100.0	Total Liabilities & Net Worth				100.0	100.0	100.0

			INCOME DATA						
100.0	100.0	100.0	Net Sales				100.0	100.0	100.0
17.6	17.2	18.6	Gross Profit				16.2	23.4	12.3
16.4	15.5	17.2	Operating Expenses				16.4	21.5	10.2
1.2	1.7	1.5	Operating Profit				−.2	1.9	2.1
.5	−.1	.0	All Other Expenses (net)				−.9	.3	−.1
.7	1.8	1.4	Profit Before Taxes				.6	1.6	2.2

			RATIOS						
1.7	1.6	1.6	Current				2.3	2.2	1.6
1.3	1.4	1.2					1.3	1.3	1.3
1.0	1.1	1.0					1.0	1.0	1.1
1.1	1.3	1.3	Quick				1.7	1.3	1.3
.9	.9	.8					1.0	.7	.8
.6	.6	.5					.4	.5	.6
23 16.2	20 18.4	16 22.6	Sales/Receivables				12 30.5	20 18.4	18 20.6
29 12.7	24 15.0	22 16.3					25 14.8	25 14.7	23 16.2
39 9.5	35 10.4	34 10.7					59 6.1	37 9.8	31 11.8
9 41.7	6 58.4	6 59.1	Cost of Sales/Inventory				0 UND	12 30.8	4 101.7
15 23.7	13 27.9	17 21.5					6 60.3	30 12.2	14 26.7
32 11.4	25 14.5	35 10.3					31 11.6	61 6.0	24 15.2
20 18.6	15 23.9	14 25.9	Cost of Sales/Payables				2 183.7	18 20.0	16 23.0
30 12.2	25 14.7	24 15.3					6 65.8	23 15.6	23 15.8
41 8.9	31 11.7	39 9.5					60 6.1	42 8.6	32 11.6
16.9	17.6	17.4	Sales/Working Capital				17.0	12.3	22.1
34.1	32.3	42.9					30.4	21.7	43.8
−999.8	95.1	−877.5					NM	−366.3	150.5
9.8	12.4	12.2	EBIT/Interest					6.3	22.9
(65) 3.0	(54) 3.7	(67) 4.1						(15) 2.0	(32) 7.5
1.5	1.8	1.8						1.7	3.4
9.4	12.0	14.4	Net Profit + Depr., Dep., Amort./Cur. Mat. L/T/D						
(16) 3.1	(14) 5.8	(11) 1.8							
1.1	1.8	1.3							
.1	.1	.1	Fixed/Worth				.0	.1	.1
.6	.4	.7					.3	.7	.4
1.5	1.1	1.5					1.0	3.5	1.1
1.4	1.4	1.3	Debt/Worth				1.1	.8	1.2
2.9	2.2	2.9					1.4	3.1	2.8
6.5	5.0	6.1					5.9	10.4	4.6
41.5	38.4	39.8	% Profit Before Taxes/Tangible Net Worth					25.8	44.6
(68) 18.3	(62) 19.6	(74) 21.0						(17) 16.6	(37) 24.4
9.6	10.9	7.5						7.1	11.1
10.0	13.0	12.3	% Profit Before Taxes/Total Assets				14.6	9.3	12.9
5.2	6.2	4.9					3.7	4.0	7.3
1.0	2.1	1.0					−8.4	1.0	3.2
288.6	310.1	327.9	Sales/Net Fixed Assets				999.8	232.8	462.5
32.6	32.5	32.3					44.5	36.2	38.9
15.7	13.9	12.9					16.9	14.6	14.6
6.4	7.9	8.2	Sales/Total Assets				9.2	6.6	9.6
5.2	5.9	5.2					4.6	5.1	6.0
3.3	3.3	3.1					3.2	2.7	3.7
.2	.1	.2	% Depr., Dep., Amort./Sales					.1	.2
(61) .6	(56) .7	(68) .9						(18) 1.1	(30) .5
1.3	1.2	2.0						2.9	1.3
.8	.9	.6	% Officers', Directors', Owners' Comp/Sales						.4
(31) 1.8	(33) 1.7	(35) 1.9							(12) .7
3.3	3.4	4.4							3.5
4999538M	4944394M	7227127M	Net Sales ($)	2414M	7601M	29549M	74641M	296770M	6816152M
1145947M	980688M	1273075M	Total Assets ($)	1140M	1519M	10886M	18963M	91696M	1148871M

M = $ thousand   MM = $ million
See Pages 11 through 18 for Explanation of Ratios and Data

Current Data Sorted By Assets | Comparative Historical Data

	1	2	2	1	3	Type of Statement			
	1	10	5		1	Unqualified		11	16
	5	8	1			Reviewed		23	16
						Compiled		16	16
						Tax Returns		3	2
	2	6	3			Other		19	20
	16 (4/1-9/30/02)		35 (10/1/02-3/31/03)					4/1/98-3/31/99	4/1/99-3/31/00
0-500M	500M-2MM	2-10MM	10-50MM	50-100MM	100-250MM			ALL	ALL
9		26	11	1	4	NUMBER OF STATEMENTS		72	70
%	%	%	%	%	%	ASSETS		%	%
		5.9	7.6			Cash & Equivalents		6.4	5.0
		46.5	48.2			Trade Receivables (net)		41.1	35.7
		16.1	20.8			Inventory		18.1	19.3
		1.1	2.4			All Other Current		1.9	3.1
		69.6	79.0			Total Current		67.4	63.2
		20.0	16.0			Fixed Assets (net)		22.7	27.2
		1.6	1.5			Intangibles (net)		2.2	2.8
		8.8	3.5			All Other Non-Current		7.7	6.7
		100.0	100.0			Total		100.0	100.0
						LIABILITIES			
		13.8	22.0			Notes Payable-Short Term		13.5	14.5
		5.8	2.0			Cur. Mat.-L/T/D		2.7	2.6
		34.3	31.8			Trade Payables		27.1	22.7
		.0	.0			Income Taxes Payable		.5	.4
		8.3	8.7			All Other Current		8.8	5.6
		62.2	64.5			Total Current		52.6	45.7
		7.5	11.0			Long Term Debt		9.9	13.9
		.0	1.6			Deferred Taxes		1.3	1.4
		7.3	2.0			All Other Non-Current		1.7	5.0
		22.9	20.9			Net Worth		34.6	34.0
		100.0	100.0			Total Liabilities & Net Worth		100.0	100.0
						INCOME DATA			
		100.0	100.0			Net Sales		100.0	100.0
		10.6	11.5			Gross Profit		14.4	14.2
		10.6	10.0			Operating Expenses		12.3	12.0
		.0	1.5			Operating Profit		2.1	2.1
		.2	.2			All Other Expenses (net)		.4	.4
		−.3	1.2			Profit Before Taxes		1.7	1.8
						RATIOS			
		1.6	1.7					1.8	2.1
		1.2	1.2			Current		1.3	1.4
		1.0	.9					1.0	1.1
		1.2	1.3					1.2	1.4
		.9	.8			Quick		.9	.8
		.6	.6					.6	.5
	14	26.8	20	17.8				15	24.6	16	23.5
	19	19.7	27	13.6		Sales/Receivables		22	16.9	21	17.1
	24	15.4	33	11.1				27	13.6	29	12.8
	3	135.7	7	51.3				4	102.8	6	61.9
	7	50.6	12	30.6		Cost of Sales/Inventory		9	39.5	14	25.3
	10	35.0	21	17.6				30	12.1	52	7.0
	9	40.5	11	32.9				9	39.7	10	35.9
	18	19.8	19	19.1		Cost of Sales/Payables		15	24.6	14	25.2
	23	16.1	33	11.0				22	16.9	23	15.6
		26.0	18.6					18.4	13.6
		91.5	37.3			Sales/Working Capital		42.4	26.0
		NM	−69.8					NM	UND
		10.1	12.2					9.0	8.5
	(23)	3.2	4.0			EBIT/Interest	(68)	3.1	(61)	4.2
		1.1	2.1					1.5	2.0
						Net Profit + Depr., Dep., Amort./Cur. Mat. L /T/D		9.2	17.6
							(22)	2.7	(11)	2.1
								.7	1.6
		.1	.0					.1	.2
		.6	.8			Fixed/Worth		.6	.9
		1.8	5.9					1.4	1.9
		1.6	2.0					.8	.9
		4.1	4.7			Debt/Worth		1.9	2.2
		7.0	22.6					7.5	4.5
		69.3				% Profit Before Taxes/Tangible Net Worth		40.4	46.1
	(25)	22.5					(64)	16.5	(62)	19.9
		3.7						8.4	10.4
		9.0	15.1			% Profit Before Taxes/Total Assets		12.8	13.3
		5.9	4.9					5.3	8.4
		.3	2.6					1.4	3.2
		779.1	999.8					453.5	90.0
		57.4	34.1			Sales/Net Fixed Assets		41.2	23.2
		25.9	25.5					9.9	6.3
		11.5	7.7					9.6	7.9
		9.3	6.0			Sales/Total Assets		6.5	5.3
		5.5	5.5					2.9	2.6
		.1	.1					.1	.4
	(24)	.3	(10)	.4		% Depr., Dep., Amort./Sales	(59)	.6	(54)	.8
		.8	.7					1.7	1.6
						% Officers', Directors', Owners' Comp/Sales		.4	1.0
							(30)	1.0	(18)	1.4
								1.9	2.2
	96841M	1025077M	1257361M	43253M	1807032M	Net Sales ($)		4050331M	6600490M
	9734M	122929M	192413M	56667M	726364M	Total Assets ($)		1241433M	2551098M

M = $ thousand MM = $ million
See Pages 11 through 18 for Explanation of Ratios and Data

(D A T A N O T A V A I L A B L E — column 0-500M)

Comparative Historical Data — Current Data Sorted By Sales

4/1/00-3/31/01 ALL	4/1/01-3/31/02 ALL	4/1/02-3/31/03 ALL	Type of Statement	0-1MM	1-3MM	3-5MM	5-10MM	10-25MM	25MM & OVER
8	6	9	Unqualified					2	7
19	17	17	Reviewed	1				2	14
10	22	14	Compiled	1	3			2	8
1	2		Tax Returns						
16	12	11	Other			1		4	6
				16 (4/1-9/30/02)		**35 (10/1/02-3/31/03)**			
54	59	51	NUMBER OF STATEMENTS	2		2	4	10	35
%	%	%	**ASSETS**	%	%	%	%	%	%
3.1	6.2	5.4	Cash & Equivalents	D	D			6.2	5.9
39.1	37.3	43.8	Trade Receivables (net)	A	A			43.2	44.9
17.7	15.7	19.0	Inventory	T	T			16.7	18.2
1.9	3.5	1.4	All Other Current	A	A			1.1	1.6
61.8	62.8	69.5	Total Current					67.2	70.6
27.3	27.1	21.6	Fixed Assets (net)	N	N			17.8	22.0
3.1	2.0	1.6	Intangibles (net)	O	O			2.7	1.4
7.7	8.1	7.3	All Other Non-Current	T	T			12.3	5.9
100.0	100.0	100.0	Total					100.0	100.0
			LIABILITIES	A	A				
18.0	14.2	14.8	Notes Payable-Short Term	V	V			19.4	15.1
2.9	3.3	4.1	Cur. Mat.-L/T/D	A	A			10.5	2.6
25.1	24.2	30.0	Trade Payables	I	I			29.8	31.8
.3	.3	.1	Income Taxes Payable	L	L			.0	.1
6.6	8.4	8.6	All Other Current	A	A			17.6	6.2
52.9	50.3	57.6	Total Current	B	B			77.5	55.8
14.1	11.5	11.5	Long Term Debt	L	L			3.8	12.5
.8	1.1	.5	Deferred Taxes	E	E			.0	.8
4.1	3.9	4.7	All Other Non-Current					2.3	5.2
28.1	33.2	25.6	Net Worth					16.4	25.8
100.0	100.0	100.0	Total Liabilities & Net Worth					100.0	100.0
			INCOME DATA						
100.0	100.0	100.0	Net Sales					100.0	100.0
11.5	15.0	11.8	Gross Profit					16.1	10.8
10.5	13.4	11.0	Operating Expenses					16.1	9.2
1.0	1.6	.8	Operating Profit					.0	1.5
1.1	.7	.4	All Other Expenses (net)					.2	.5
-.1	1.0	.4	Profit Before Taxes					-.3	1.0
			RATIOS						
1.8 / 1.2 / 1.0	1.6 / 1.2 / 1.0	1.7 / 1.3 / 1.0	Current					1.5 / 1.1 / .9	1.7 / 1.2 / .9
1.3 / .8 / .5	1.2 / .8 / .6	1.2 / .8 / .6	Quick					1.2 / .8 / .6	1.2 / .8 / .6
18 20.3 / 22 16.7 / 30 12.2	16 23.3 / 22 16.6 / 28 12.9	16 22.6 / 20 18.5 / 25 14.7	Sales/Receivables					13 27.8 / 18 19.9 / 28 13.1	16 22.6 / 20 18.5 / 25 14.7
6 63.4 / 10 35.4 / 23 16.2	4 96.9 / 8 44.0 / 24 15.0	4 82.9 / 9 42.8 / 20 17.9	Cost of Sales/Inventory					0 UND / 5 78.1 / 15 23.7	5 68.9 / 9 40.8 / 20 17.9
10 35.5 / 17 21.0 / 23 15.8	11 34.7 / 16 23.0 / 22 16.4	9 38.5 / 18 20.2 / 23 16.1	Cost of Sales/Payables					6 57.1 / 20 17.8 / 35 10.4	9 38.5 / 17 21.4 / 21 17.7
19.6 / 50.1 / -498.6	20.9 / 50.1 / -335.0	23.4 / 45.2 / -304.0	Sales/Working Capital					26.3 / 522.5 / NM	23.4 / 50.8 / -289.3
(49) 7.3 / 2.2 / 1.0	(54) 6.8 / 2.6 / 1.4	(46) 9.0 / 3.0 / 1.2	EBIT/Interest						(33) 9.4 / 3.1 / 1.7
(13) 6.6 / 2.3 / 1.2	(15) 5.2 / 1.9 / .5	(10) 6.3 / 1.5 / -1.0	Net Profit + Depr., Dep., Amort./Cur. Mat. L/T/D						
.2 / 1.0 / 2.1	.3 / .8 / 1.6	.1 / .6 / 2.2	Fixed/Worth					.1 / .5 / 1.1	.1 / .9 / 2.7
1.1 / 2.6 / 7.0	.9 / 2.2 / 5.8	1.6 / 2.8 / 7.4	Debt/Worth					1.3 / 1.9 / 11.9	2.0 / 3.8 / 8.2
(49) 35.9 / 11.6 / 1.6	(54) 30.8 / 12.2 / 3.9	(48) 52.6 / 20.5 / 2.1	% Profit Before Taxes/Tangible Net Worth						(33) 61.0 / 20.7 / 4.3
9.5 / 3.5 / .0	7.8 / 3.8 / .7	9.2 / 4.3 / .4	% Profit Before Taxes/Total Assets					7.9 / 5.4 / 1.8	9.6 / 4.9 / 1.4
138.4 / 31.1 / 7.1	81.0 / 29.5 / 7.7	351.3 / 48.7 / 19.2	Sales/Net Fixed Assets					453.9 / 91.2 / 17.6	705.5 / 37.4 / 25.5
7.6 / 5.6 / 2.9	9.0 / 5.8 / 2.9	11.1 / 8.1 / 5.4	Sales/Total Assets					11.7 / 7.5 / 4.5	10.9 / 9.1 / 5.5
(45) .3 / .6 / 1.8	(51) .2 / .6 / 1.7	(42) .1 / .3 / .7	% Depr., Dep., Amort./Sales					.1 / .4 / 1.4	(27) .1 / .3 / .6
(23) .5 / 1.2 / 2.3	(19) .4 / 1.6 / 1.8	(15) .3 / 1.5 / 2.1	% Officers', Directors', Owners' Comp/Sales						
3567733M	3082997M	4229564M	Net Sales ($)			8513M	30454M	167965M	4022632M
1174366M	843677M	1108107M	Total Assets ($)			1763M	10189M	26426M	1069729M

M = $ thousand   MM = $ million
See Pages 11 through 18 for Explanation of Ratios and Data

Current Data Sorted By Assets   Comparative Historical Data

	0-500M	500M-2MM	2-10MM	10-50MM	50-100MM	100-250MM	Type of Statement	4/1/98-3/31/99 ALL	4/1/99-3/31/00 ALL
			7	5	1	2	Unqualified	17	16
	1	6	9	4	1		Reviewed	28	27
	3	8	10				Compiled	22	26
		4	1				Tax Returns	7	4
	2	2	9	8			Other	28	24
		26 (4/1-9/30/02)		57 (10/1/02-3/31/03)					
NUMBER OF STATEMENTS	6	20	36	17	2	2		102	97
	%	%	%	%	%	%	**ASSETS**	%	%
		7.2	8.8	3.0			Cash & Equivalents	8.3	6.6
		19.2	28.1	25.0			Trade Receivables (net)	27.8	29.2
		36.2	32.8	39.4			Inventory	36.9	34.1
		2.0	2.2	1.9			All Other Current	.8	1.1
		64.6	71.9	69.2			Total Current	73.8	70.9
		20.2	21.3	19.3			Fixed Assets (net)	17.6	20.5
		2.9	2.7	3.5			Intangibles (net)	2.6	3.6
		12.4	4.1	8.0			All Other Non-Current	6.1	4.9
		100.0	100.0	100.0			Total	100.0	100.0
							LIABILITIES		
		10.9	20.7	30.4			Notes Payable-Short Term	17.7	18.7
		2.4	2.6	3.2			Cur. Mat.-L/T/D	2.2	2.0
		18.7	12.9	16.3			Trade Payables	22.7	17.9
		.3	.2	.1			Income Taxes Payable	.5	.3
		5.0	4.9	5.7			All Other Current	6.8	6.4
		37.3	41.3	55.7			Total Current	49.9	45.3
		18.4	15.9	8.9			Long Term Debt	10.7	13.4
		.4	.6	.2			Deferred Taxes	.2	.3
		1.6	5.5	3.0			All Other Non-Current	3.6	4.9
		42.4	36.7	32.2			Net Worth	35.6	36.0
		100.0	100.0	100.0			Total Liabilities & Net Worth	100.0	100.0
							INCOME DATA		
		100.0	100.0	100.0			Net Sales	100.0	100.0
		31.6	25.0	22.3			Gross Profit	24.2	24.1
		28.6	21.1	19.3			Operating Expenses	21.6	21.2
		2.9	3.9	3.0			Operating Profit	2.6	2.9
		.2	.7	1.0			All Other Expenses (net)	.7	.7
		2.8	3.2	2.0			Profit Before Taxes	1.9	2.2
							RATIOS		
		3.5	3.0	1.6			Current	2.4	2.4
		1.6	1.5	1.1				1.5	1.5
		1.2	1.2	1.1				1.1	1.1
		1.8	1.5	.7			Quick	1.2	1.2
		.5	.9	.5				.7	.7
		.3	.5	.3				.4	.5
		7 49.4	20 18.5	27 13.7			Sales/Receivables	19 19.2	18 20.1
		18 20.5	26 13.9	32 11.4				28 13.0	28 12.9
		26 14.2	38 9.7	39 9.3				40 9.1	40 9.1
		25 14.5	24 15.3	40 9.2			Cost of Sales/Inventory	25 14.4	20 18.5
		39 9.4	38 9.6	64 5.7				46 8.0	43 8.5
		81 4.5	57 6.4	132 2.8				88 4.1	77 4.7
		10 37.6	7 50.6	15 24.7			Cost of Sales/Payables	12 29.7	10 37.0
		18 20.6	13 28.1	28 13.2				24 15.0	23 16.1
		39 9.4	27 13.3	39 9.3				44 8.4	38 9.6
		8.2	7.3	9.2			Sales/Working Capital	9.0	8.4
		13.1	16.1	35.7				16.0	18.2
		42.8	32.8	62.5				45.3	47.1
		31.5	7.9	5.4			EBIT/Interest	6.8	6.3
		(19) 2.9	(33) 2.9	3.1				(95) 3.2	(95) 2.9
		1.6	1.7	1.9				1.7	1.6
			10.0				Net Profit + Depr., Dep., Amort./Cur. Mat. L./T/D	7.8	9.4
			(14) 4.6					(27) 2.4	(33) 2.7
			3.0					1.8	1.6
		.1	.2	.3			Fixed/Worth	.1	.2
		.6	.5	.8				.5	.6
		1.2	1.6	1.2				1.2	1.3
		.7	.7	1.4			Debt/Worth	1.0	.9
		1.6	2.6	3.3				1.8	2.5
		3.5	5.3	7.4				4.8	5.5
		34.7	40.2	45.0			% Profit Before Taxes/Tangible Net Worth	42.7	50.5
		(18) 16.9	(34) 23.3	(16) 24.5				(93) 22.6	(89) 20.8
		7.8	5.8	6.6				12.0	6.1
		12.9	15.1	10.6			% Profit Before Taxes/Total Assets	13.5	12.5
		5.5	6.4	4.9				7.1	6.6
		1.8	3.3	3.9				2.9	1.9
		81.2	62.2	49.7			Sales/Net Fixed Assets	99.8	76.1
		28.4	28.6	19.3				30.0	26.2
		9.0	6.0	5.2				10.9	8.9
		5.1	5.0	3.8			Sales/Total Assets	5.5	5.2
		3.7	3.4	2.8				3.5	3.4
		2.7	2.1	1.6				2.1	2.4
		.4	.3	.4			% Depr., Dep., Amort./Sales	.4	.5
		(18) 1.2	(32) 1.2	(16) 1.0				(91) .9	(87) .9
		2.6	2.2	2.0				1.9	1.7
		1.7	1.0				% Officers', Directors', Owners' Comp/Sales	1.2	1.0
		(10) 2.1	(12) 1.9					(44) 2.1	(46) 2.3
		5.8	2.9					4.8	4.9
Net Sales ($)	6386M	96511M	618282M	895129M	696742M	522439M		3095604M	2800133M
Total Assets ($)	1878M	25058M	155724M	329620M	180793M	376224M		1262906M	982788M

© RMA 2003

M = $ thousand   MM = $ million
See Pages 11 through 18 for Explanation of Ratios and Data

Comparative Historical Data | Current Data Sorted By Sales

H1	H2	H3	Type of Statement	0-1MM	1-3MM	3-5MM	5-10MM	10-25MM	25MM & OVER
12	15	15	Unqualified					5	10
23	22	21	Reviewed	1		2	4	9	5
26	19	21	Compiled	1	5	3	5	5	2
6	10	5	Tax Returns		3	1	1		
15	24	21	Other	1	1	3	5	3	8
4/1/00-3/31/01 ALL	4/1/01-3/31/02 ALL	4/1/02-3/31/03 ALL			26 (4/1-9/30/02)			57 (10/1/02-3/31/03)	
82	90	83	NUMBER OF STATEMENTS	3	9	9	15	22	25
%	%	%	ASSETS	%	%	%	%	%	%
7.6	7.9	6.9	Cash & Equivalents				12.9	6.8	3.0
27.7	26.6	24.3	Trade Receivables (net)				22.6	29.0	28.1
35.8	33.9	33.9	Inventory				30.5	34.0	39.7
2.8	1.8	3.4	All Other Current				2.3	2.5	2.4
73.8	70.3	68.5	Total Current				68.4	72.3	73.2
18.5	20.4	21.8	Fixed Assets (net)				26.3	18.7	18.7
3.0	2.6	2.7	Intangibles (net)				.9	4.7	1.3
4.6	6.6	7.1	All Other Non-Current				4.3	4.3	6.8
100.0	100.0	100.0	Total				100.0	100.0	100.0
			LIABILITIES						
26.4	21.3	19.4	Notes Payable-Short Term				9.3	23.2	27.6
2.3	3.1	2.6	Cur. Mat.-L/T/D				2.9	2.5	2.1
18.3	21.1	15.6	Trade Payables				17.2	14.0	16.1
.3	.2	.2	Income Taxes Payable				.5	.1	.2
6.6	8.1	5.2	All Other Current				6.5	5.0	7.0
53.8	53.7	43.1	Total Current				36.4	44.8	53.0
13.2	13.1	15.1	Long Term Debt				19.4	12.5	10.2
.3	.2	.4	Deferred Taxes				.2	.9	.2
2.7	5.6	3.6	All Other Non-Current				5.6	2.7	1.7
30.0	27.2	37.9	Net Worth				38.4	39.1	34.9
100.0	100.0	100.0	Total Liabilities & Net Worth				100.0	100.0	100.0
			INCOME DATA						
100.0	100.0	100.0	Net Sales				100.0	100.0	100.0
24.2	25.3	26.1	Gross Profit				25.8	24.9	17.5
20.3	23.1	23.5	Operating Expenses				21.8	21.3	14.8
3.9	2.2	2.6	Operating Profit				3.9	3.6	2.7
.8	.8	.4	All Other Expenses (net)				.9	.6	.7
3.1	1.3	2.2	Profit Before Taxes				3.0	3.0	2.0
			RATIOS						
2.2	2.1	2.6					3.6	2.5	2.2
1.4	1.4	1.5	Current				1.7	1.5	1.3
1.1	1.0	1.1					1.2	1.2	1.1
1.0	1.0	1.3					2.1	1.3	.9
.7	.7	.7	Quick				.8	.7	.6
.5	.4	.4					.6	.5	.4
16 22.6	14 25.4	18 20.7	Sales/Receivables				17 21.4	21 17.2	20 18.1
27 13.7	25 14.8	25 14.4					25 14.6	28 13.1	30 12.2
39 9.4	37 9.7	35 10.4					41 8.8	35 10.4	39 9.3
22 16.6	21 17.7	27 13.6	Cost of Sales/Inventory				36 10.1	23 16.2	23 15.7
43 8.4	42 8.7	45 8.1					41 8.8	34 10.6	57 6.4
74 4.9	83 4.4	82 4.4					57 6.4	77 4.7	99 3.7
9 42.9	10 36.4	10 37.4	Cost of Sales/Payables				12 30.3	8 47.1	12 29.9
20 18.1	21 17.4	19 19.6					19 19.6	17 21.7	24 15.1
42 8.7	38 9.6	34 10.7					34 10.7	31 11.8	34 10.7
9.8	9.4	8.1	Sales/Working Capital				6.5	9.6	9.2
16.1	23.2	15.8					13.5	15.5	21.0
49.1	NM	59.0					19.3	41.8	58.2
(72) 7.4	(80) 4.3	(78) 6.8	EBIT/Interest				(14) 11.3	(21) 9.1	8.4
2.5	2.0	3.0					2.5	3.3	3.1
1.5	1.1	1.6					1.5	2.5	1.8
(17) 6.8	(28) 9.0	(31) 8.2	Net Profit + Depr., Dep., Amort./Cur. Mat. L/T/D					(10) 8.3	
3.0	3.1	3.1						3.5	
1.5	1.3	1.9						2.4	
.2	.2	.2	Fixed/Worth				.1	.2	.3
.4	.6	.6					.4	.5	.5
1.0	1.4	1.2					3.2	1.4	.9
1.0	1.0	.8	Debt/Worth				.7	.6	1.1
2.4	3.0	2.1					2.1	2.3	2.5
5.2	9.7	5.2					5.0	5.6	4.4
36.3	34.3	39.3	% Profit Before Taxes/Tangible Net Worth				(14) 35.0	(20) 35.3	44.4
(75) 20.7	(77) 12.9	(78) 20.3					19.3	14.3	26.1
9.9	3.1	5.2					6.5	5.4	9.8
12.6	10.6	11.3	% Profit Before Taxes/Total Assets				13.7	11.9	11.3
5.8	4.0	5.2					6.8	5.2	5.9
1.5	.4	2.6					1.6	3.2	3.6
76.4	92.2	60.7	Sales/Net Fixed Assets				48.9	68.3	64.9
26.0	23.4	25.8					13.8	28.6	20.8
11.7	8.7	6.3					4.8	6.7	7.8
5.2	5.8	4.9	Sales/Total Assets				4.5	5.4	5.3
3.6	3.6	3.3					2.9	3.8	3.7
2.8	2.3	2.0					2.1	2.1	1.8
.4	.3	.4	% Depr., Dep., Amort./Sales				(12) .4	(20) .4	(23) .2
(68) .7	(80) .9	(73) 1.2					1.4	1.0	1.1
1.5	1.9	2.4					2.4	2.3	2.0
.9	1.1	.7	% Officers', Directors', Owners' Comp/Sales						.4
(39) 1.8	(39) 2.2	(34) 3.0						(10)	.7
3.1	3.6	3.1							1.4
2350082M	6495206M	2835489M	Net Sales ($)	2233M	15345M	36037M	107895M	332202M	2341777M
917634M	950996M	1069297M	Total Assets ($)	1032M	8896M	14836M	37643M	106321M	900569M

© RMA 2003

M = $ thousand   MM = $ million
See Pages 11 through 18 for Explanation of Ratios and Data

Current Data Sorted By Assets / Comparative Historical Data

0-500M	500M-2MM	2-10MM	10-50MM	50-100MM	100-250MM	Type of Statement	4/1/98-3/31/99 ALL	4/1/99-3/31/00 ALL
	3	16	18	3	2	Unqualified	50	45
2	17	40	5			Reviewed	73	54
5	26	12	3			Compiled	59	39
2	9	5				Tax Returns	23	20
3	15	34	8		1	Other	62	61
	63 (4/1-9/30/02)		166 (10/1/02-3/31/03)					
12	70	107	34	3	3	**NUMBER OF STATEMENTS**	267	219
%	%	%	%	%	%	**ASSETS**	%	%
13.3	14.2	7.5	4.7			Cash & Equivalents	8.2	8.7
29.1	38.2	38.6	28.1			Trade Receivables (net)	37.4	38.2
21.5	21.4	31.2	40.8			Inventory	26.9	27.9
5.8	2.2	2.3	3.1			All Other Current	2.3	3.7
69.7	76.0	79.6	76.7			Total Current	74.9	78.4
17.7	17.4	13.8	17.2			Fixed Assets (net)	16.9	14.9
9.0	2.3	1.2	1.4			Intangibles (net)	1.6	1.6
3.6	4.3	5.4	4.8			All Other Non-Current	6.6	5.1
100.0	100.0	100.0	100.0			Total	100.0	100.0
						LIABILITIES		
16.4	15.0	22.0	28.0			Notes Payable-Short Term	22.9	23.8
5.2	2.8	2.0	1.7			Cur. Mat.-L/T/D	2.4	1.8
29.4	24.9	28.0	15.5			Trade Payables	25.4	23.5
.0	.3	.3	.8			Income Taxes Payable	.1	.2
4.4	7.1	7.2	5.5			All Other Current	7.1	8.0
55.4	50.2	59.6	51.5			Total Current	58.0	57.3
27.5	8.9	6.3	10.2			Long Term Debt	9.2	7.5
.0	.0	.3	.6			Deferred Taxes	.2	.2
25.7	6.1	3.5	2.6			All Other Non-Current	5.9	4.7
-8.6	34.8	30.3	35.0			Net Worth	26.7	30.3
100.0	100.0	100.0	100.0			Total Liabilities & Net Worth	100.0	100.0
						INCOME DATA		
100.0	100.0	100.0	100.0			Net Sales	100.0	100.0
19.4	15.2	14.4	14.0			Gross Profit	14.7	14.3
17.3	13.3	12.3	11.3			Operating Expenses	13.2	12.4
2.0	1.9	2.1	2.7			Operating Profit	1.5	1.9
.6	.4	.4	.4			All Other Expenses (net)	.3	.1
1.4	1.5	1.7	2.3			Profit Before Taxes	1.2	1.9
						RATIOS		
2.8 1.5 .7	2.9 1.4 1.1	1.8 1.3 1.1	2.0 1.5 1.2			Current	1.7 1.3 1.1	1.8 1.3 1.1
1.4 1.0 .5	1.9 1.1 .6	1.2 .7 .5	.9 .6 .4		(266)	Quick	1.1 .7 .5	1.2 .8 .6
7 55.7 11 32.6 32 11.3	10 35.5 24 15.3 33 11.2	25 14.8 30 12.1 43 8.6	25 14.6 34 10.8 38 9.7			Sales/Receivables	21 17.5 30 12.3 40 9.2	20 17.9 30 12.1 41 9.0
0 UND 6 61.1 57 6.4	2 159.0 8 44.8 28 12.8	13 27.1 31 11.9 50 7.4	38 9.7 52 7.0 83 4.4			Cost of Sales/Inventory	8 44.6 25 14.7 43 8.5	8 45.2 23 15.7 47 7.8
2 157.9 16 22.6 37 9.9	5 73.7 14 27.0 27 13.4	14 26.3 27 13.3 36 10.2	9 40.8 18 19.9 32 11.5			Cost of Sales/Payables	9 42.1 20 18.0 33 10.9	7 50.9 19 19.6 29 12.5
12.4 66.7 -42.4	13.1 29.7 83.4	12.8 25.1 130.8	6.9 12.1 27.6			Sales/Working Capital	13.4 32.8 147.1	11.7 26.3 97.1
(10) 16.6 2.4 1.1	(60) 9.0 3.4 1.0	(96) 9.1 2.8 1.3	(33) 5.4 3.0 1.6			EBIT/Interest	(245) 4.9 2.4 1.2	(198) 6.0 2.5 1.3
	(11) 4.9 3.0 .2	(32) 9.9 2.2 1.1	(13) 3.2 1.9 1.4			Net Profit + Depr., Dep., Amort./Cur. Mat. L /T/D	(55) 9.9 2.9 1.1	(41) 6.7 3.3 1.3
.0 NM -.3	.1 .4 1.3	.1 .3 .9	.0 .3 1.0			Fixed/Worth	.1 .5 1.3	.1 .4 .9
1.1 -3.8 -2.4	1.1 2.5 7.1	1.4 2.7 6.1	1.0 2.7 4.7			Debt/Worth	1.2 3.4 8.0	1.2 3.2 6.2
	(60) 41.5 13.7 3.3	(101) 40.9 17.6 5.0	(33) 23.6 16.7 7.0			% Profit Before Taxes/Tangible Net Worth	(242) 42.8 18.7 5.1	(197) 47.4 22.0 8.0
35.9 10.5 1.4	10.7 4.2 .2	11.2 3.4 .9	7.3 5.1 1.8			% Profit Before Taxes/Total Assets	10.1 4.2 .8	12.4 5.4 1.6
UND 100.6 17.5	138.0 50.1 26.1	216.3 69.9 20.0	467.5 60.2 6.7			Sales/Net Fixed Assets	174.7 53.4 16.9	294.1 59.4 23.2
8.3 6.6 4.0	7.9 6.3 3.6	5.8 4.5 3.1	4.3 3.2 2.0			Sales/Total Assets	6.3 4.7 3.3	6.7 4.7 3.0
	(62) .2 .4 1.0	(94) .2 .4 1.0	(33) .0 .3			% Depr., Dep., Amort./Sales	(230) .2 .5 1.2	(180) .1 .4 .9
	(37) 1.1 2.0 3.4	(52) .7 1.4				% Officers', Directors', Owners' Comp/Sales	(113) .8 1.6	(99) .8 1.7 3.1
32156M 3596M	567009M 87693M	2309562M 513346M	2603327M 780297M	661145M 191345M	748830M 358202M	Net Sales ($) Total Assets ($)	7457347M 2257048M	6624802M 2017938M

© RMA 2003
M = $ thousand   MM = $ million
See Pages 11 through 18 for Explanation of Ratios and Data

Comparative Historical Data | Current Data Sorted By Sales

			Type of Statement		0-1MM	1-3MM	3-5MM	5-10MM	10-25MM	25MM & OVER
33	34	42	Unqualified			1	2	3	7	29
54	54	64	Reviewed			1	4	13	25	21
60	42	46	Compiled		2	7	6	13	12	6
22	18	16	Tax Returns			6	2	2	6	
52	63	61	Other		2	3	5	11	23	17
4/1/00-3/31/01 ALL	4/1/01-3/31/02 ALL	4/1/02-3/31/03 ALL			\<-- 63 (4/1-9/30/02) -->		\<------ 166 (10/1/02-3/31/03) ------>			
221	211	229	**NUMBER OF STATEMENTS**		4	18	19	42	73	73
%	%	%	**ASSETS**		%	%	%	%	%	%
9.1	8.5	9.3	Cash & Equivalents			16.2	12.5	11.5	8.0	7.2
39.8	36.7	36.1	Trade Receivables (net)			22.2	30.6	32.0	41.0	38.1
27.5	30.0	30.0	Inventory			28.7	19.3	29.3	27.5	36.0
1.9	2.6	2.5	All Other Current			3.4	1.9	3.7	1.5	2.9
78.3	77.7	77.9	Total Current			70.6	64.3	76.5	78.0	84.2
14.6	14.7	15.4	Fixed Assets (net)			20.7	20.9	19.4	14.9	10.3
1.6	2.1	1.9	Intangibles (net)			3.1	10.6	.4	1.4	.9
5.5	5.5	4.8	All Other Non-Current			5.7	4.2	3.7	5.8	4.5
100.0	100.0	100.0	Total			100.0	100.0	100.0	100.0	100.0
			LIABILITIES							
20.8	21.1	21.3	Notes Payable-Short Term			12.3	15.0	21.7	18.1	27.4
2.3	2.2	2.3	Cur. Mat.-L/T/D			4.9	1.9	3.6	2.3	1.2
25.4	24.5	25.1	Trade Payables			22.9	26.7	18.6	29.0	24.2
.2	.3	.4	Income Taxes Payable			.1	.7	.2	.2	.6
8.7	6.6	6.7	All Other Current			3.2	3.0	8.8	7.2	6.7
57.5	54.7	55.7	Total Current			43.6	47.3	52.8	56.8	60.1
8.2	8.4	8.7	Long Term Debt			15.9	9.6	10.9	6.6	5.8
.2	.2	.2	Deferred Taxes			.0	.5	.0	.3	.3
3.9	4.7	5.3	All Other Non-Current			6.1	10.2	6.9	4.7	2.7
30.3	31.9	30.1	Net Worth			34.5	32.5	29.3	31.6	31.0
100.0	100.0	100.0	Total Liabilities & Net Worth			100.0	100.0	100.0	100.0	100.0
			INCOME DATA							
100.0	100.0	100.0	Net Sales			100.0	100.0	100.0	100.0	100.0
15.2	14.4	14.8	Gross Profit			24.2	22.6	12.5	13.9	12.0
13.2	12.3	12.6	Operating Expenses			21.3	17.6	10.4	12.4	9.9
2.0	2.1	2.2	Operating Profit			2.9	5.0	2.1	1.4	2.1
–.1	.6	.4	All Other Expenses (net)			.6	.1	.8	.3	.4
2.1	1.5	1.7	Profit Before Taxes			2.3	4.9	1.3	1.2	1.7
			RATIOS							
1.9	2.0	2.0				5.6	2.7	3.0	1.8	1.8
1.3	1.4	1.4	Current			1.5	1.2	1.4	1.4	1.4
1.1	1.1	1.1				1.0	1.1	1.1	1.1	1.1
1.2	1.3	1.3				3.8	1.3	1.5	1.3	1.1
.8	.8	.8	Quick			.9	.9	.7	1.0	.7
.6	.5	.5				.3	.7	.5	.6	.5
21 / 17.2	19 / 19.1	21 / 17.3				7 / 53.5	9 / 41.4	16 / 22.8	22 / 16.2	25 / 14.8
29 / 12.5	28 / 13.2	28 / 13.0	Sales/Receivables			11 / 32.6	25 / 14.7	30 / 12.3	29 / 12.5	28 / 13.1
39 / 9.3	39 / 9.5	39 / 9.4				34 / 10.6	46 / 8.0	40 / 9.0	38 / 9.5	36 / 10.2
8 / 47.0	10 / 37.8	7 / 52.8				7 / 55.1	1 / 681.0	6 / 63.6	7 / 56.1	16 / 23.2
24 / 15.3	26 / 14.0	27 / 13.6	Cost of Sales/Inventory			36 / 10.3	11 / 31.9	29 / 12.5	22 / 16.9	35 / 10.5
47 / 7.8	50 / 7.4	54 / 6.8				71 / 5.2	57 / 6.4	49 / 7.5	44 / 8.2	55 / 6.6
8 / 45.6	8 / 43.7	10 / 37.9				4 / 94.4	12 / 31.0	3 / 145.4	12 / 29.2	11 / 33.2
21 / 17.7	20 / 18.2	21 / 17.4	Cost of Sales/Payables			17 / 21.0	27 / 13.6	11 / 34.3	22 / 16.7	22 / 16.7
33 / 11.1	33 / 11.2	33 / 11.1				34 / 10.6	62 / 5.8	29 / 12.6	33 / 11.0	33 / 11.1
11.3	11.6	11.5				6.3	7.5	12.0	14.2	11.7
26.3	22.1	25.4	Sales/Working Capital			15.5	19.5	22.8	27.2	25.1
96.6	73.1	73.9				-202.9	114.9	212.4	95.5	41.7
(197) 5.5	(194) 5.5	(205) 8.0			(14) 6.6	13.0	(36) 7.2	(66) 9.1	(67) 7.5	
2.4	2.3	2.9	EBIT/Interest		2.5	4.0	1.8	3.3	2.9	
1.3	1.3	1.3			1.0	1.2	1.0	1.2	1.8	
(50) 9.0	(42) 8.4	(57) 5.9	Net Profit + Depr., Dep.,					(23) 5.3	(23) 10.4	
2.8	4.3	2.1	Amort./Cur. Mat. L/T/D					1.4	2.1	
1.4	1.7	1.1						.3	1.8	
.1	.1	.1				.0	.3	.1	.2	.1
.4	.4	.3	Fixed/Worth			.2	.5	.5	.4	.2
.9	.9	1.2				NM	3.1	1.5	1.1	.5
1.1	1.1	1.2				.2	1.1	1.2	1.3	1.5
2.8	2.8	2.8	Debt/Worth			1.3	3.1	2.5	2.7	2.9
6.7	6.1	6.9				-18.5	10.6	7.1	6.3	5.6
(202) 36.7	(198) 40.2	(205) 37.4	% Profit Before Taxes/Tangible		(13) 38.1	(16) 37.1	(36) 32.3	(68) 39.8	(71) 37.3	
18.0	15.3	17.3	Net Worth		15.9	26.4	10.9	17.2	19.9	
7.3	5.1	5.1			4.9	4.7	2.6	3.7	8.0	
10.5	9.3	10.2	% Profit Before Taxes/Total			15.9	12.9	10.1	10.3	9.5
4.7	4.7	4.1	Assets			5.0	6.1	2.4	3.4	4.7
1.3	1.2	.9				.6	.5	.0	.5	2.1
203.8	213.5	198.2				UND	70.1	161.5	133.3	460.5
56.9	69.7	68.9	Sales/Net Fixed Assets			52.3	30.0	54.4	64.8	105.7
24.3	22.4	20.3				11.5	15.7	25.2	31.8	
7.3	6.3	6.5				4.7	4.7	6.6	7.1	6.1
4.9	4.5	4.5	Sales/Total Assets			3.4	3.3	3.9	5.6	4.6
3.2	3.1	3.1				2.2	1.8	3.0	3.6	3.2
(181) .2	(171) .2	(202) .1	% Depr., Dep., Amort./Sales		(12) .2	(18) .2	(36) .3	(71) .2	(63) .1	
.5	.4	.4			1.1	1.1	.5	.4	.2	
1.0	1.0	1.0			2.6	3.3	1.0	1.0	.7	
(102) 1.1	(101) .8	(102) .8	% Officers', Directors',			(11) 1.3	(19) .8	(42) .8	(21) .5	
1.9	1.6	1.7	Owners' Comp/Sales			4.3	1.6	2.1	1.0	
3.4	2.9	3.3				5.8	2.4	3.2	2.1	
8525579M	7580109M	6922029M	Net Sales ($)		2673M	39442M	78182M	310190M	1143057M	5348485M
2312729M	2353453M	1934479M	Total Assets ($)		1006M	15912M	36600M	80669M	307324M	1492968M

Current Data Sorted By Assets　　　　　　　　　　　Comparative Historical Data

							Type of Statement		
	1	14	13	3	2		Unqualified	29	36
	10	37	8	1			Reviewed	63	67
1	22	17	5				Compiled	44	52
3	9	5					Tax Returns	7	9
3	9	23	8	1	1		Other	36	35
	43 (4/1-9/30/02)		153 (10/1/02-3/31/03)					4/1/98-3/31/99	4/1/99-3/31/00
0-500M	500M-2MM	2-10MM	10-50MM	50-100MM	100-250MM			ALL	ALL
7	51	96	34	5	3		NUMBER OF STATEMENTS	179	199
%	%	%	%	%	%		ASSETS	%	%
	8.9	7.5	3.4				Cash & Equivalents	7.4	6.4
	43.2	40.4	35.7				Trade Receivables (net)	39.0	39.2
	24.7	24.0	30.6				Inventory	23.4	24.8
	1.3	2.4	1.8				All Other Current	2.2	1.7
	78.1	74.3	71.5				Total Current	72.0	72.1
	16.0	17.7	18.4				Fixed Assets (net)	20.2	20.0
	.4	1.4	6.0				Intangibles (net)	2.1	2.6
	5.5	6.7	4.1				All Other Non-Current	5.7	5.4
	100.0	100.0	100.0				Total	100.0	100.0
							LIABILITIES		
	15.7	14.2	17.8				Notes Payable-Short Term	16.4	17.8
	2.3	4.3	1.2				Cur. Mat.-L/T/D	2.0	2.6
	25.4	25.1	20.4				Trade Payables	23.4	23.0
	.7	.4	.2				Income Taxes Payable	.2	.2
	11.2	8.1	15.5				All Other Current	6.0	7.9
	55.3	52.0	55.1				Total Current	48.0	51.6
	7.0	8.2	12.3				Long Term Debt	12.6	11.3
	.0	.1	.0				Deferred Taxes	.1	.1
	5.3	4.6	3.3				All Other Non-Current	8.9	3.8
	32.4	35.1	29.3				Net Worth	30.3	33.1
	100.0	100.0	100.0				Total Liabilities & Net Worth	100.0	100.0
							INCOME DATA		
	100.0	100.0	100.0				Net Sales	100.0	100.0
	16.7	15.5	13.2				Gross Profit	17.5	17.4
	16.0	13.8	10.9				Operating Expenses	15.7	15.4
	.7	1.7	2.3				Operating Profit	1.8	2.1
	.0	.2	.5				All Other Expenses (net)	.2	.2
	.7	1.5	1.7				Profit Before Taxes	1.6	1.9
							RATIOS		
	2.3	1.9	1.5					2.1	2.0
	1.7	1.5	1.3				Current	1.5	1.4
	1.0	1.1	1.1					1.1	1.1
	1.6	1.3	1.0					1.4	1.3
	1.1	.9	.7				Quick	1.0	.9
	.6	.6	.5					.7	.7

	16	23.4	16	23.4	17	21.9				Sales/Receivables	15	24.3	16	23.4
	19	19.0	20	18.0	21	17.5					20	18.1	22	16.6
	27	13.7	28	13.2	29	12.4					29	12.8	28	13.2
	7	55.9	8	43.8	14	26.3				Cost of Sales/Inventory	9	42.8	9	41.3
	13	27.4	16	23.4	22	16.7					14	25.6	16	22.9
	23	15.9	28	13.1	37	9.8					25	14.3	26	13.9
	7	50.7	10	36.7	9	38.9				Cost of Sales/Payables	9	39.5	7	54.0
	14	26.4	15	24.3	13	27.3					14	26.0	13	27.7
	21	17.5	22	16.8	18	19.8					22	16.3	21	17.1
		17.1		16.9		19.6				Sales/Working Capital		16.0		15.9
		27.8		27.9		35.2						31.2		29.9
		183.2		71.4		86.6						78.0		86.3
		12.7		11.5		12.1				EBIT/Interest		6.7		8.6
	(46)	3.4	(86)	4.3	(30)	3.8					(156)	2.7	(174)	3.4
		1.1		1.6		2.1						1.3		1.4
				15.3						Net Profit + Depr., Dep.,		6.7		8.5
			(24)	3.5						Amort./Cur. Mat. L /T/D	(49)	2.9	(52)	3.5
				1.1								1.8		1.6
		.1		.1		.2				Fixed/Worth		.2		.2
		.3		.3		.9						.5		.5
		1.1		1.1		1.9						1.1		1.2
		.6		1.1		1.4				Debt/Worth		.9		1.0
		1.6		1.9		3.5						2.1		2.1
		4.6		5.1		11.3						5.3		5.9
		36.5		36.5		53.0				% Profit Before Taxes/Tangible		33.3		45.3
	(43)	11.7	(90)	17.1	(31)	23.5				Net Worth	(167)	13.1	(181)	18.9
		2.2		6.3		11.5						5.1		6.2
		12.6		12.4		14.8				% Profit Before Taxes/Total		10.8		14.6
		5.2		5.5		6.3				Assets		4.7		6.0
		.5		1.5		2.5						1.3		1.4
		246.6		169.8		175.4				Sales/Net Fixed Assets		133.6		139.8
		67.5		61.7		40.1						44.8		41.1
		26.2		19.3		16.5						17.6		18.1
		10.0		9.4		7.5				Sales/Total Assets		9.3		8.4
		7.3		6.0		5.1						6.1		6.1
		4.4		4.5		3.8						4.1		4.2
		.2		.2		.3				% Depr., Dep., Amort./Sales		.3		.2
	(43)	.6	(86)	.5	(28)	.7					(157)	.6	(171)	.5
		1.1		1.0		1.1						1.1		1.1
		1.5		.9						% Officers', Directors',		.8		.8
	(27)	2.4	(57)	1.2						Owners' Comp/Sales	(84)	1.5	(92)	1.5
		4.3		2.5										

17687M	471957M	3261906M	4387914M	2514376M	2553250M	Net Sales ($)	6854886M　9418156M
1912M	58769M	480821M	736109M	358216M	502913M	Total Assets ($)	1498484M　1592283M

M = $ thousand　　MM = $ million
See Pages 11 through 18 for Explanation of Ratios and Data

Comparative Historical Data | Current Data Sorted By Sales

			Type of Statement	0-1MM	1-3MM	3-5MM	5-10MM	10-25MM	25MM & OVER
29	21	33	Unqualified			1		2	30
49	35	56	Reviewed			3	2	22	29
49	44	45	Compiled	1	4	6	4	13	17
10	7	17	Tax Returns			3	7	3	4
43	52	45	Other	2	3	3	9	10	18
4/1/00-3/31/01 ALL	**4/1/01-3/31/02 ALL**	**4/1/02-3/31/03 ALL**				43 (4/1-9/30/02)		153 (10/1/02-3/31/03)	
180	159	196	**NUMBER OF STATEMENTS**	3	7	16	22	50	98
%	%	%	**ASSETS**	%	%	%	%	%	%
7.3	6.1	7.3	Cash & Equivalents			6.8	6.1	9.1	6.0
39.2	39.3	39.3	Trade Receivables (net)			30.1	34.8	44.6	40.3
24.3	25.4	25.6	Inventory			27.8	24.0	20.6	28.6
1.5	1.9	1.9	All Other Current			1.3	2.3	1.3	2.3
72.3	72.8	74.2	Total Current			66.0	67.2	75.6	77.2
19.0	19.9	17.6	Fixed Assets (net)			21.1	23.7	17.2	15.2
2.5	2.0	2.3	Intangibles (net)			.6	.9	1.0	3.1
6.3	5.4	5.9	All Other Non-Current			12.4	8.2	6.2	4.4
100.0	100.0	100.0	Total			100.0	100.0	100.0	100.0
			LIABILITIES						
16.2	14.2	15.2	Notes Payable-Short Term			9.1	17.6	12.9	16.4
2.8	2.9	3.6	Cur. Mat.-L/T/D			2.4	4.3	4.3	2.3
23.3	22.3	24.4	Trade Payables			16.0	27.2	25.9	25.3
.1	.3	.4	Income Taxes Payable			2.1	.1	.2	.3
7.1	7.7	10.8	All Other Current			16.0	6.9	8.4	10.7
49.4	47.4	54.4	Total Current			45.6	56.0	51.7	55.1
10.1	10.2	9.4	Long Term Debt			9.9	20.5	6.3	8.2
.1	.1	.1	Deferred Taxes			.0	.1	.1	.0
2.7	3.5	4.5	All Other Non-Current			4.0	3.8	8.0	3.3
37.6	38.8	31.6	Net Worth			40.5	19.5	33.9	33.3
100.0	100.0	100.0	Total Liabilities & Net Worth			100.0	100.0	100.0	100.0
			INCOME DATA						
100.0	100.0	100.0	Net Sales			100.0	100.0	100.0	100.0
14.7	14.8	15.9	Gross Profit			20.3	18.2	16.2	12.5
13.1	13.1	14.5	Operating Expenses			18.2	16.4	14.7	10.7
1.6	1.7	1.4	Operating Profit			2.0	1.8	1.5	1.8
.0	.3	.2	All Other Expenses (net)			−.5	.3	.1	.2
1.6	1.3	1.2	Profit Before Taxes			2.6	1.5	1.4	1.5
			RATIOS						
2.0 / 1.4 / 1.1	2.4 / 1.5 / 1.1	1.9 / 1.4 / 1.1	Current			2.8 / 1.6 / 1.1	1.9 / 1.1 / .9	2.3 / 1.6 / 1.2	1.7 / 1.4 / 1.2
1.3 / .9 / .6	1.4 / 1.0 / .6	1.3 / .9 / .6	Quick			1.8 / 1.1 / .5	1.2 / .7 / .4	1.6 / 1.1 / .7	1.2 / .9 / .6
15 23.6 / 20 17.9 / 28 12.9	14 25.4 / 20 18.3 / 29 12.7	15 23.8 / 20 18.7 / 27 13.6	Sales/Receivables			17 21.2 / 21 17.2 / 33 11.1	12 29.2 / 19 19.6 / 27 13.8	16 22.2 / 21 17.1 / 28 12.9	15 24.2 / 19 18.8 / 26 14.0
9 41.3 / 16 23.5 / 25 14.6	9 42.3 / 16 23.4 / 25 14.7	9 40.5 / 16 23.1 / 28 13.1	Cost of Sales/Inventory			11 34.0 / 24 15.3 / 46 7.9	11 32.6 / 18 20.8 / 33 11.2	8 46.6 / 12 30.8 / 20 18.0	8 43.6 / 16 22.7 / 27 13.6
8 43.8 / 14 25.9 / 20 18.3	7 49.3 / 12 29.4 / 17 21.1	9 41.1 / 15 25.0 / 21 17.5	Cost of Sales/Payables			6 61.8 / 18 20.8 / 24 15.1	12 31.7 / 16 23.2 / 26 14.1	9 38.5 / 14 25.3 / 21 17.6	9 42.4 / 13 27.3 / 19 19.3
17.4 / 35.6 / 75.0	15.7 / 28.5 / 76.6	18.0 / 30.2 / 88.5	Sales/Working Capital			9.1 / 23.5 / 76.5	18.5 / 44.9 / −53.9	17.7 / 23.5 / 77.4	20.5 / 34.7 / 74.1
(163) 6.0 / 2.8 / 1.3	(142) 7.7 / 3.5 / 1.4	(174) 11.5 / 4.2 / 1.7	EBIT/Interest			(14) 8.8 / 2.4 / −.5	8.9 / 4.2 / 1.8	(45) 13.7 / 4.2 / 1.6	(87) 12.3 / 4.8 / 2.1
(40) 8.3 / 2.3 / 1.2	(27) 7.1 / 2.5 / 1.3	(41) 10.3 / 4.4 / 2.2	Net Profit + Depr., Dep., Amort./Cur. Mat. L/T/D					(11) 25.6 / 4.4 / 2.9	(24) 10.7 / 4.2 / 1.8
.1 / .4 / 1.0	.1 / .4 / 1.1	.1 / .4 / 1.3	Fixed/Worth			.1 / .4 / 1.2	.1 / .7 / NM	.1 / .3 / 1.6	.1 / .3 / 1.2
.9 / 2.1 / 3.8	.7 / 1.9 / 3.8	1.0 / 2.3 / 5.8	Debt/Worth			.3 / 1.4 / 4.5	1.3 / 1.9 / NM	.6 / 2.2 / 5.9	1.3 / 2.5 / 5.2
(173) 37.2 / 13.9 / 4.0	(153) 39.2 / 16.0 / 3.6	(174) 41.8 / 17.6 / 6.8	% Profit Before Taxes/Tangible Net Worth			(13) 20.5 / 6.9 / 1.1	(17) 53.2 / 26.9 / 8.9	(45) 43.6 / 17.8 / 6.9	(93) 43.7 / 20.0 / 10.2
12.4 / 4.7 / .9	12.7 / 5.5 / .6	12.6 / 5.5 / 1.6	% Profit Before Taxes/Total Assets			9.3 / 4.9 / −.9	16.0 / 8.4 / 2.7	12.8 / 5.4 / 1.5	12.9 / 5.4 / 2.1
144.6 / 54.0 / 19.3	170.0 / 45.6 / 18.1	194.4 / 59.9 / 19.6	Sales/Net Fixed Assets			96.4 / 26.3 / 15.1	179.0 / 42.8 / 9.1	171.7 / 60.9 / 22.3	302.6 / 75.6 / 22.9
9.1 / 6.4 / 4.6	9.3 / 6.6 / 4.7	9.4 / 6.2 / 4.3	Sales/Total Assets			6.4 / 4.6 / 3.4	8.8 / 6.6 / 3.3	9.2 / 7.1 / 4.9	10.0 / 7.0 / 4.6
(159) .2 / .5 / 1.1	(137) .1 / .5 / 1.1	(166) .2 / .5 / 1.1	% Depr., Dep., Amort./Sales			(13) .7 / 1.1 / 1.4	(19) .4 / .6 / 1.2	(47) .2 / .6 / 1.0	(80) .1 / .3 / .8
(94) .7 / 1.3 / 3.1	(76) .9 / 1.6 / 2.8	(98) .9 / 1.5 / 3.0	% Officers', Directors', Owners' Comp/Sales					(33) 1.2 / 1.6 / 3.1	(44) .6 / 1.0 / 1.6
9145826M	9204596M	13207090M	Net Sales ($)	1744M	15077M	61303M	158952M	809073M	12160941M
1598945M	1455704M	2138740M	Total Assets ($)	387M	10789M	19436M	40776M	136224M	1931128M

M = $ thousand   MM = $ million
See Pages 11 through 18 for Explanation of Ratios and Data

Current Data Sorted By Assets   **Comparative Historical Data**

Type of Statement	0-500M	500M-2MM	2-10MM	10-50MM	50-100MM	100-250MM	4/1/98-3/31/99 ALL	4/1/99-3/31/00 ALL
Unqualified		2	15	17	5	1	30	29
Reviewed	2	9	42	11			66	70
Compiled	5	17	35	8			79	78
Tax Returns	8	15	4	1			24	20
Other	1	8	31	17	1	1	63	59
	95 (4/1-9/30/02)			161 (10/1/02-3/31/03)				
NUMBER OF STATEMENTS	16	51	127	54	6	2	262	256
ASSETS	%	%	%	%	%	%	%	%
Cash & Equivalents	11.3	12.2	10.4	7.7			8.5	9.2
Trade Receivables (net)	28.6	44.9	40.8	38.8			41.9	41.2
Inventory	14.0	8.5	10.4	8.1			10.2	10.3
All Other Current	3.6	6.3	4.1	7.3			4.1	4.8
Total Current	57.5	71.8	65.6	61.9			64.6	65.5
Fixed Assets (net)	32.1	20.1	22.2	26.1			24.2	23.3
Intangibles (net)	4.4	1.9	2.2	4.8			2.8	3.0
All Other Non-Current	6.0	6.1	9.9	7.2			8.5	8.3
Total	100.0	100.0	100.0	100.0			100.0	100.0
LIABILITIES								
Notes Payable-Short Term	5.8	8.4	9.1	8.9			9.8	12.7
Cur. Mat.-L/T/D	4.5	3.1	2.4	1.8			2.5	2.8
Trade Payables	31.0	31.2	33.5	22.8			31.8	32.7
Income Taxes Payable	.8	.2	.3	.2			.5	.3
All Other Current	11.7	9.2	8.9	9.5			8.8	11.7
Total Current	53.8	52.1	54.2	43.3			53.5	60.2
Long Term Debt	22.9	8.8	10.7	11.5			11.2	12.4
Deferred Taxes	.2	.2	.3	.7			.6	.5
All Other Non-Current	2.8	4.0	2.2	2.6			2.9	1.6
Net Worth	20.4	34.8	32.6	42.0			31.8	25.3
Total Liabilities & Net Worth	100.0	100.0	100.0	100.0			100.0	100.0
INCOME DATA								
Net Sales	100.0	100.0	100.0	100.0			100.0	100.0
Gross Profit	25.2	21.4	19.8	19.8			19.0	19.6
Operating Expenses	24.1	20.2	17.2	15.6			17.2	17.7
Operating Profit	1.1	1.3	2.6	4.3			1.8	1.9
All Other Expenses (net)	.0	−.1	.3	.4			.4	.2
Profit Before Taxes	1.2	1.4	2.3	3.8			1.5	1.7
RATIOS								
Current	2.0	1.9	1.6	1.9			1.7	1.6
	1.1	1.3	1.2	1.4			1.3	1.2
	.8	1.1	1.0	1.1			1.0	.9
Quick	1.5	1.5	1.2	1.4			1.4	1.2
	.8	1.1	.9	1.0			1.0	1.0
	.3	.8	.6	.8			.7	.6
Sales/Receivables	0 799.9	13 27.6	21 17.8	25 14.8			19 19.7	21 17.7
	11 34.5	24 15.1	28 13.2	32 11.6			28 13.3	30 12.2
	31 11.7	33 11.1	36 10.2	46 7.9			36 10.1	41 9.0
Cost of Sales/Inventory	2 228.5	0 UND	3 138.0	3 116.2			2 171.7	1 537.9
	4 88.0	3 125.0	5 67.3	7 49.1			6 60.2	5 67.3
	12 30.9	9 38.8	12 31.6	15 24.7			12 31.6	12 29.9
Cost of Sales/Payables	1 247.2	9 42.0	15 24.4	15 25.0			14 25.3	15 24.7
	19 19.7	20 17.8	26 14.1	22 16.8			23 15.7	25 14.9
	32 11.5	32 11.5	40 9.2	34 10.7			35 10.5	38 9.7
Sales/Working Capital	66.6	18.1	22.7	11.2			19.0	20.0
	155.8	35.0	50.9	26.0			48.3	55.2
	−43.3	141.8	−880.4	85.7			−682.5	−166.5
EBIT/Interest	7.7	10.2	16.1	16.0			10.2	8.5
	3.9	(45) 3.0	(118) 4.8	(47) 5.2			(228) 2.9	(223) 2.5
	−2.0	.4	1.8	2.1			1.2	1.1
Net Profit + Depr., Dep., Amort./Cur. Mat. L /T/D		(10) 12.2	(32) 11.0	(16) 10.3			(79) 6.9	(66) 5.2
		4.0	3.7	6.9			3.2	2.3
		.4	1.4	3.3			1.3	1.4
Fixed/Worth	.5	.2	.2	.2			.3	.3
	1.3	.5	.6	.6			.7	.7
	−3.0	1.2	1.3	1.4			1.8	2.0
Debt/Worth	1.0	.8	1.1	1.0			1.1	1.2
	3.1	2.2	2.5	1.6			2.1	2.7
	−6.5	7.4	5.0	3.0			5.3	8.8
% Profit Before Taxes/Tangible Net Worth	(10) 59.5	(46) 42.5	(118) 38.5	(51) 36.0			(231) 40.2	(222) 39.3
	18.1	11.6	18.1	22.1			15.9	17.1
	−1.0	.3	6.5	8.7			3.6	2.5
% Profit Before Taxes/Total Assets	17.7	9.2	11.7	14.2			12.9	9.0
	11.6	4.0	4.5	6.4			4.3	4.4
	−4.8	.0	1.3	2.4			.6	.3
Sales/Net Fixed Assets	109.6	230.4	104.9	77.2			84.8	95.0
	37.4	44.8	40.2	18.4			31.7	29.9
	16.7	17.4	14.1	7.7			11.6	11.8
Sales/Total Assets	16.4	9.8	7.5	5.5			8.1	7.1
	9.1	7.1	5.6	3.8			5.5	5.3
	4.2	4.0	3.4	2.3			3.4	3.3
% Depr., Dep., Amort./Sales	(13) .3	(43) .1	(112) .3	(47) .4			(231) .3	(228) .3
	.9	.7	.7	1.0			.7	.7
	2.2	1.7	1.4	2.5			1.6	1.5
% Officers', Directors', Owners' Comp/Sales	(15) 2.4	(26) 1.4	(61) .9	(10) .6			(117) .9	(116) .9
	4.5	2.6	1.4	1.3			2.0	1.7
	5.8	5.2	2.7	1.3			3.5	3.1
Net Sales ($)	58697M	408287M	3546551M	4246604M	7168819M	1035421M	9167926M	9743348M
Total Assets ($)	5162M	55775M	618746M	1073354M	377913M	295730M	2612249M	2541168M

© RMA 2003

M = $ thousand   MM = $ million
See Pages 11 through 18 for Explanation of Ratios and Data

Comparative Historical Data				Type of Statement		Current Data Sorted By Sales				
31	41	40		Unqualified		1	1	2	7	29
49	38	64		Reviewed		2		8	23	31
87	91	65		Compiled		7	8	11	20	19
16	19	28		Tax Returns	1	8	6	9	4	
68	71	59		Other	1		3	9	18	28
4/1/00-3/31/01 ALL	4/1/01-3/31/02 ALL	4/1/02-3/31/03 ALL					95 (4/1-9/30/02)		161 (10/1/02-3/31/03)	
					0-1MM	1-3MM	3-5MM	5-10MM	10-25MM	25MM & OVER
251	260	256		NUMBER OF STATEMENTS	2	18	18	39	72	107
%	%	%		ASSETS	%	%	%	%	%	%
8.3	9.8	10.2		Cash & Equivalents		9.7	9.3	11.0	9.8	10.4
40.8	40.2	39.9		Trade Receivables (net)		26.5	30.6	37.3	41.4	43.8
10.4	10.3	9.9		Inventory		13.8	13.4	6.8	11.7	8.6
5.6	5.7	5.2		All Other Current		2.4	5.3	5.8	5.8	5.2
65.1	66.0	65.2		Total Current		52.5	58.6	60.9	68.6	68.1
23.5	23.6	23.7		Fixed Assets (net)		37.3	37.7	26.1	20.7	20.6
3.5	2.9	2.8		Intangibles (net)		4.3	.9	2.1	1.3	3.6
7.9	7.5	8.2		All Other Non-Current		6.0	2.9	10.9	9.4	7.7
100.0	100.0	100.0		Total		100.0	100.0	100.0	100.0	100.0
				LIABILITIES						
9.8	10.2	8.6		Notes Payable-Short Term		8.7	6.7	7.7	10.9	7.8
2.7	2.2	2.6		Cur. Mat.-L/T/D		5.4	3.7	2.4	3.3	1.5
31.7	29.4	30.1		Trade Payables		15.8	23.1	28.7	35.7	30.8
.4	.2	.3		Income Taxes Payable		.4	.3	.1	.2	.4
8.9	10.1	9.5		All Other Current		9.3	10.7	8.0	9.1	10.0
53.5	52.1	51.1		Total Current		39.5	44.6	46.9	59.1	50.6
12.7	12.0	11.4		Long Term Debt		22.3	21.1	13.5	10.7	7.6
.6	.5	.3		Deferred Taxes		.1	.4	.2	.3	.4
2.5	3.0	2.7		All Other Non-Current		2.6	4.0	5.0	1.9	2.3
30.7	32.4	34.4		Net Worth		35.5	29.9	34.4	27.9	39.2
100.0	100.0	100.0		Total Liabilities & Net Worth		100.0	100.0	100.0	100.0	100.0
				INCOME DATA						
100.0	100.0	100.0		Net Sales		100.0	100.0	100.0	100.0	100.0
19.5	20.7	20.3		Gross Profit		36.4	30.3	24.1	18.5	15.4
17.8	18.3	17.6		Operating Expenses		32.4	23.9	21.2	16.2	13.1
1.6	2.5	2.7		Operating Profit		4.1	6.4	2.9	2.3	2.2
.3	.6	.2		All Other Expenses (net)		.4	.2	.2	.4	.2
1.3	1.9	2.4		Profit Before Taxes		3.7	6.3	2.7	1.9	2.1
				RATIOS						
1.8	1.8	1.8				2.0	2.4	1.9	1.5	1.8
1.3	1.3	1.2		Current		1.4	1.3	1.3	1.2	1.3
1.0	1.0	1.0				.8	1.1	1.0	1.0	1.0
1.5	1.3	1.4				1.5	1.7	1.7	1.1	1.4
1.0	1.0	1.0		Quick		.9	1.0	1.1	.9	1.0
.7	.7	.7				.6	.5	.7	.6	.8
22 16.7	21 17.0	20 17.8			0 UND	1 301.4	9 41.8	21 17.0	22 16.3	
30 12.2	29 12.7	27 13.4		Sales/Receivables	31 11.8	20 17.8	25 14.5	29 12.5	27 13.4	
39 9.4	40 9.1	36 10.1			64 5.7	36 10.0	33 11.0	40 9.2	33 11.2	
2 179.3	2 162.1	2 170.2			1 398.8	0 UND	0 817.7	2 157.7	3 138.0	
5 69.6	6 59.4	6 66.2		Cost of Sales/Inventory	13 27.3	4 92.3	6 62.0	6 59.0	5 73.5	
13 27.6	17 21.7	13 27.1			33 11.2	16 22.3	15 25.0	14 27.0	9 42.2	
13 28.7	15 23.9	13 27.1			3 130.2	1 270.0	13 27.7	21 17.6	13 27.9	
23 15.6	25 14.5	23 15.6		Cost of Sales/Payables	13 28.5	20 18.2	22 16.6	30 12.0	20 18.1	
37 9.9	39 9.3	35 10.3			35 10.4	41 9.0	40 9.1	46 7.9	30 12.1	
16.8	15.9	18.1			5.3	7.9	20.8	18.3	21.5	
36.8	36.2	46.1		Sales/Working Capital	28.7	25.9	56.3	55.5	44.7	
-999.8	316.9	422.9			-62.2	132.1	-164.7	-338.6	229.7	
	7.8		11.1		14.1		EBIT/Interest		12.3		5.9		15.1		7.6		16.8
(226) 3.1	(231) 3.2	(233) 4.4		EBIT/Interest		1.9	(16) 2.5	(38) 3.6	(64) 3.5	(95) 7.1
1.1	1.5	1.5				-.8	.3	1.0	1.3	2.7
6.6	9.5	10.7		Net Profit + Depr., Dep.,					7.6	16.5
(70) 2.9	(69) 3.2	(63) 4.4		Amort./Cur. Mat. L/T/D				(17) 3.0	(31) 7.0	
1.4	1.5	1.5						1.1	3.2	
.2	.2	.2				.5	.4	.3	.2	.2
.6	.6	.6		Fixed/Worth		.9	.8	.8	.5	.5
1.6	1.6	1.4				2.0	3.6	1.5	1.6	.9
1.1	1.1	1.0				.8	.8	.8	1.5	1.0
2.1	2.4	2.3		Debt/Worth		2.5	2.0	2.2	2.7	1.8
6.9	5.9	4.7				5.5	4.7	7.8	7.7	3.2
43.1	44.1	38.9		% Profit Before Taxes/Tangible		40.8	38.2	31.1	39.4	41.5
(228) 15.9	(235) 18.8	(233) 17.2		Net Worth	(15) 12.9	(15) 12.9	(33) 13.2	(66) 18.3	(103) 20.3
3.9	5.6	5.6				-11.6	1.1	.2	4.8	9.4
12.9	13.3	12.7		% Profit Before Taxes/Total		18.5	14.7	12.1	9.1	16.0
4.6	4.8	4.9		Assets		2.2	4.3	4.1	4.3	6.6
.5	1.2	1.2				-5.0	-1.4	.0	.6	2.2
101.3	145.5	107.4				30.5	34.5	69.5	129.3	141.8
32.2	31.3	33.7		Sales/Net Fixed Assets		12.3	17.0	31.1	42.9	41.8
13.2	9.9	12.9				5.2	2.7	7.4	14.0	19.2
7.1	7.5	7.6				3.9	8.5	9.7	7.4	7.6
5.4	5.2	5.4		Sales/Total Assets		3.0	3.5	5.7	4.9	6.2
2.9	2.5	3.1				2.0	1.8	2.3	3.3	4.3
.3	.2	.3				.5	1.4	.3	.2	.3
(216) .7	(220) .6	(220) .7		% Depr., Dep., Amort./Sales		1.8	(16) 1.9	(28) .9	(66) .2	(91) .6
1.4	1.6	1.6				4.0	2.7	2.7	1.4	1.1
.9	1.1	1.2		% Officers', Directors',		2.8	2.2	1.3	1.1	.7
(112) 1.9	(97) 2.1	(112) 1.8		Owners' Comp/Sales	(12) 5.1	(10) 3.6	(18) 2.3	(32) 1.6	(38) 1.3
3.8	3.8	3.8				13.4	7.4	4.5	3.7	2.0
8111533M	8760071M	16464379M		Net Sales ($)	1919M	35730M	70390M	276023M	1255168M	14825149M
2406271M	2460326M	2426680M		Total Assets ($)	3318M	18120M	37155M	84781M	336949M	1946357M

M = $ thousand   MM = $ million
See Pages 11 through 18 for Explanation of Ratios and Data

Current Data Sorted By Assets | **Comparative Historical Data**

0-500M	500M-2MM	2-10MM	10-50MM	50-100MM	100-250MM	Type of Statement	4/1/98-3/31/99 ALL	4/1/99-3/31/00 ALL
	2	14	33	6	1	Unqualified	57	50
	13	51	15			Reviewed	61	53
6	19	26	1			Compiled	66	53
10	14	5		1		Tax Returns	18	13
6	14	32	22	4	2	Other	76	63
	56 (4/1-9/30/02)			241 (10/1/02-3/31/03)				
22	62	128	71	11	3	NUMBER OF STATEMENTS	278	232
%	%	%	%	%	%	**ASSETS**	%	%
13.3	8.2	7.0	7.7	5.6		Cash & Equivalents	7.8	6.9
24.3	31.2	30.7	27.1	15.2		Trade Receivables (net)	27.4	30.8
26.8	28.5	28.0	29.8	23.3		Inventory	27.7	28.9
.4	1.1	2.9	2.8	2.5		All Other Current	2.5	2.5
64.8	69.0	68.6	67.4	46.6		Total Current	65.5	68.9
24.8	19.0	21.2	23.5	32.5		Fixed Assets (net)	23.1	21.9
4.3	6.9	4.0	3.1	16.1		Intangibles (net)	5.0	3.2
6.2	5.1	6.1	5.9	4.8		All Other Non-Current	6.4	5.9
100.0	100.0	100.0	100.0	100.0		Total	100.0	100.0
						LIABILITIES		
9.7	9.0	15.4	16.1	7.9		Notes Payable-Short Term	13.6	15.7
8.3	5.9	4.3	3.5	4.1		Cur. Mat.-L/T/D	3.5	3.2
30.6	22.3	23.7	20.8	10.4		Trade Payables	22.7	23.6
.0	.1	.3	.1	.3		Income Taxes Payable	.4	.3
10.5	13.5	8.8	9.3	9.1		All Other Current	6.9	7.2
59.2	50.7	52.5	49.8	31.8		Total Current	47.2	49.9
12.9	25.1	13.5	8.8	20.0		Long Term Debt	15.0	13.0
.0	.1	.3	.3	.7		Deferred Taxes	.2	.3
4.5	2.7	5.4	5.4	4.8		All Other Non-Current	3.5	5.7
23.4	21.4	28.3	37.9	42.6		Net Worth	34.0	31.1
100.0	100.0	100.0	100.0	100.0		Total Liabilities & Net Worth	100.0	100.0
						INCOME DATA		
100.0	100.0	100.0	100.0	100.0		Net Sales	100.0	100.0
32.6	31.3	26.9	25.1	37.5		Gross Profit	27.9	27.6
26.7	28.7	24.0	20.2	31.2		Operating Expenses	24.3	23.9
5.9	2.5	2.9	4.9	6.3		Operating Profit	3.5	3.8
1.3	.6	.7	.4	1.1		All Other Expenses (net)	.2	.7
4.6	1.9	2.2	4.5	5.2		Profit Before Taxes	3.3	3.1
						RATIOS		
1.9	2.0	1.8	2.1	1.7		Current	2.0	2.1
1.1	1.5	1.3	1.3	1.4			1.4	1.4
.6	1.0	1.0	1.0	1.1			1.0	1.0
1.5	1.5	1.0	1.1	.9		Quick	1.1	1.2
.6	.7	.7	.6	.8			.7 (231)	.7
.3	.5	.5	.4	.4			.5	.5
7 51.9	19 19.1	23 16.2	23 15.9	17 21.0		Sales/Receivables	20 18.3	22 16.5
21 17.1	30 12.3	31 12.0	30 12.1	29 12.8			27 13.4	29 12.4
32 11.4	39 9.3	44 8.3	40 9.2	34 10.9			37 9.8	43 8.6
2 161.5	14 26.7	19 19.0	27 13.6	25 14.6		Cost of Sales/Inventory	18 20.2	19 19.3
31 11.7	35 10.4	35 10.5	42 8.7	42 8.6			38 9.6	36 10.3
58 6.3	62 5.8	71 5.1	74 4.9	71 5.1			70 5.2	65 5.7
9 40.4	11 33.9	16 23.0	18 20.8	16 23.1		Cost of Sales/Payables	15 23.6	14 26.4
25 14.7	25 14.7	25 14.4	26 13.9	21 17.7			27 13.4	27 13.3
74 5.0	43 8.5	54 6.7	47 7.8	37 10.0			45 8.1	45 8.0
11.7	10.9	9.6	9.2	14.7		Sales/Working Capital	10.5	10.4
69.1	24.3	26.2	14.7	24.4			19.6	19.8
-18.0	-344.8	NM	89.7	90.5			139.1	133.7
22.2	8.0	8.7	28.7	9.4		EBIT/Interest	7.1	8.0
(18) 4.4	(51) 3.5	(118) 3.0	(67) 7.5	(10) 4.0			(255) 3.2	(209) 3.1
1.7	1.7	1.4	2.7	2.1			1.4	1.5
	3.0	5.2	20.7			Net Profit + Depr., Dep., Amort./Cur. Mat. L /T/D	6.5	9.3
	(10) 1.9	(41) 2.7	(25) 6.3				(84) 3.2	(56) 3.9
	1.1	1.0	2.3				1.5	1.9
.4	.2	.1	.2	.7		Fixed/Worth	.2	.2
1.1	.8	.6	.7	.9			.6	.6
-1.6	6.8	2.3	1.4	4.1			1.8	1.9
1.1	1.0	1.2	.7	.8		Debt/Worth	1.0	.9
3.8	2.6	2.9	2.1	1.5			2.4	2.8
-16.4	NM	8.8	5.5	10.8			7.7	7.9
78.6	60.7	50.3	42.0			% Profit Before Taxes/Tangible Net Worth	47.0	45.2
(15) 44.6	(47) 27.1	(110) 19.0	(66) 22.9				(245) 22.0	(201) 20.5
18.6	8.4	5.5	11.8				8.4	9.1
28.5	12.2	10.7	14.7	18.5		% Profit Before Taxes/Total Assets	14.0	14.1
13.7	5.4	4.8	7.4	8.1			6.3	7.3
4.1	.4	1.2	2.8	2.5			1.7	1.9
94.8	86.5	105.0	44.1	18.5		Sales/Net Fixed Assets	68.0	73.3
21.7	34.1	26.0	19.1	10.4			18.4	22.9
9.4	12.7	9.2	7.7	4.1			7.6	8.5
8.0	5.3	4.6	4.3	3.5		Sales/Total Assets	4.7	4.9
4.8	3.8	3.1	2.9	2.3			3.2	3.4
3.0	2.0	2.1	2.0	1.8			2.1	2.2
.9	.4	.3	.4			% Depr., Dep., Amort./Sales	.5	.4
(18) 1.8	(51) 1.3	(120) .9	(68) .8				(240) 1.2	(199) 1.0
3.0	4.1	2.1	1.5				2.9	2.4
3.1	1.6	.9	1.2			% Officers', Directors', Owners' Comp/Sales	1.4	1.2
(13) 5.9	(30) 2.8	(59) 1.9	(18) 1.8				(115) 2.7	(93) 2.6
10.8	4.3	3.3	3.3				5.3	6.0
31119M	319074M	2217336M	5074729M	1804638M	2526607M	Net Sales ($)	8084577M	8537319M
5646M	76118M	603097M	1471800M	706178M	452083M	Total Assets ($)	2844551M	2447976M

M = $ thousand   MM = $ million
See Pages 11 through 18 for Explanation of Ratios and Data

Comparative Historical Data / Current Data Sorted By Sales

Hist 1	Hist 2	Hist 3	Type of Statement	0-1MM	1-3MM	3-5MM	5-10MM	10-25MM	25MM & OVER
51	44	56	Unqualified	1		3		13	39
53	45	79	Reviewed		6	3	17	28	25
75	57	52	Compiled	3	8	5	17	13	6
29	21	30	Tax Returns	5	10	6	4	4	1
72	85	80	Other	4	8	5	13	18	32
4/1/00-3/31/01 ALL	4/1/01-3/31/02 ALL	4/1/02-3/31/03 ALL		56 (4/1-9/30/02)			241 (10/1/02-3/31/03)		
280	252	297	NUMBER OF STATEMENTS	13	32	22	51	76	103
%	%	%	**ASSETS**	%	%	%	%	%	%
7.7	7.1	7.8	Cash & Equivalents	6.3	9.4	12.5	5.4	8.6	7.1
30.8	28.7	29.0	Trade Receivables (net)	22.4	22.4	31.2	30.2	29.7	30.3
28.7	28.3	28.4	Inventory	30.8	26.5	25.1	23.7	30.3	30.4
1.8	2.0	2.3	All Other Current	1.1	1.1	.9	4.3	1.9	2.4
69.0	66.2	67.5	Total Current	60.7	59.4	69.7	63.6	70.5	70.2
22.2	23.3	21.8	Fixed Assets (net)	23.1	25.8	20.5	23.5	20.2	21.1
3.3	4.7	4.9	Intangibles (net)	8.2	8.1	4.3	6.6	3.5	3.7
5.6	5.8	5.8	All Other Non-Current	8.0	6.7	5.5	6.3	5.8	5.0
100.0	100.0	100.0	Total	100.0	100.0	100.0	100.0	100.0	100.0
			LIABILITIES						
17.6	17.7	13.5	Notes Payable-Short Term	8.0	12.5	12.3	14.8	13.8	14.0
3.0	5.1	4.9	Cur. Mat.-L/T/D	8.3	8.0	5.5	4.8	5.1	3.2
22.6	21.3	22.8	Trade Payables	25.6	15.9	25.1	20.9	25.2	23.1
.2	.2	.2	Income Taxes Payable	.0	.0	.3	.4	.2	.2
7.0	7.4	10.0	All Other Current	21.4	7.5	12.6	10.7	8.8	9.3
50.4	51.8	51.3	Total Current	63.3	44.0	55.8	51.6	53.0	49.8
13.5	12.9	15.0	Long Term Debt	19.6	25.7	27.5	17.5	10.9	10.1
.2	.3	.2	Deferred Taxes	.0	.0	.0	.4	.4	.2
4.0	5.9	4.3	All Other Non-Current	.7	6.5	2.4	5.0	5.6	3.1
31.8	29.1	29.2	Net Worth	16.3	23.8	14.3	25.5	30.1	36.8
100.0	100.0	100.0	Total Liabilities & Net Worth	100.0	100.0	100.0	100.0	100.0	100.0
			INCOME DATA						
100.0	100.0	100.0	Net Sales	100.0	100.0	100.0	100.0	100.0	100.0
27.7	29.0	28.0	Gross Profit	30.1	40.1	38.1	27.2	28.0	22.2
24.8	25.5	24.4	Operating Expenses	28.3	34.9	34.9	24.6	24.6	18.1
2.9	3.5	3.6	Operating Profit	1.8	5.2	3.1	2.7	3.5	4.1
.7	1.1	.7	All Other Expenses (net)	1.3	1.7	.6	.8	.4	.4
2.2	2.4	3.0	Profit Before Taxes	.5	3.5	2.5	1.9	3.0	3.7
			RATIOS						
1.9	1.9	1.9	Current	1.3	2.1	2.5	1.9	1.8	2.1
1.4	1.2	1.3		1.0	1.4	1.5	1.3	1.3	1.4
1.0	1.0	1.0		.6	.8	.9	1.0	1.0	1.1
1.1	1.1	1.2	Quick	.6	1.3	1.6	1.1	1.1	1.1
.8	.6	.7		.4	.7	.8	.7	.7	.7
.5	.4	.4		.2	.4	.5	.5	.5	.5
21 17.0	20 17.8	21 17.5	Sales/Receivables	18 19.8	18 20.7	17 21.8	23 15.6	22 16.9	21 17.6
30 12.4	31 11.9	30 12.3		22 16.4	34 10.8	26 14.2	37 9.8	30 12.2	27 13.4
42 8.8	40 9.0	40 9.2		34 10.8	50 7.3	38 9.6	51 7.2	41 9.0	35 10.5
17 21.0	20 18.5	21 17.1	Cost of Sales/Inventory	14 26.5	26 14.1	8 47.8	17 21.3	22 16.6	23 16.1
34 10.8	36 10.3	36 10.1		54 6.8	46 8.0	41 8.8	35 10.5	34 10.6	34 10.9
70 5.2	70 5.2	70 5.2		90 4.0	129 2.8	77 4.7	66 5.5	84 4.4	52 7.0
14 25.7	14 26.7	16 23.2	Cost of Sales/Payables	9 40.3	7 48.9	17 21.0	13 27.5	17 21.9	16 22.6
27 13.7	29 12.7	25 14.5		38 9.6	19 19.2	30 12.2	31 11.6	27 13.3	22 16.4
47 7.8	42 8.7	48 7.6		77 4.7	47 7.8	41 8.8	55 6.7	56 6.5	37 9.9
9.5	10.0	10.1	Sales/Working Capital	17.9	7.3	10.4	9.5	10.0	11.7
23.0	30.8	24.7		90.4	45.8	23.3	23.2	24.7	21.7
145.5	-205.4	NM		-14.8	-79.5	-77.9	-240.8	95.0	69.2
(263) 7.1	(225) 6.5	(267) 11.1	EBIT/Interest	(10) 23.7	(28) 12.0	(17) 7.8	(47) 5.6	(67) 10.0	(98) 20.6
2.8	2.7	3.8		3.6	2.4	3.5	2.9	4.5	5.1
1.3	1.1	1.7		.6	1.1	1.0	1.0	1.7	2.7
(74) 8.8	(66) 6.8	(81) 7.2	Net Profit + Depr., Dep., Amort./Cur. Mat. L/T/D				(18) 3.8	(22) 4.7	(34) 20.2
3.8	3.0	2.8					2.7	2.6	5.9
1.9	1.5	1.6					1.4	1.0	2.4
.2	.2	.2	Fixed/Worth	.5	.2	.2	.2	.1	.2
.6	.7	.7		1.5	1.1	1.4	.8	.5	.6
1.8	3.4	2.3		-1.5	-2.9	-2.4	3.7	2.0	1.2
1.0	1.1	1.0	Debt/Worth	1.2	1.2	1.3	1.1	1.0	.8
2.4	3.1	2.8		8.1	3.9	5.5	2.7	2.6	2.4
6.6	10.4	8.5		-6.7	-22.4	-7.9	15.2	8.6	5.5
(245) 39.7	(213) 52.8	(250) 51.8	% Profit Before Taxes/Tangible Net Worth	(23) 60.7	(16) 79.7	(41) 38.4	(66) 40.8	(96) 50.0	
17.5	18.8	25.2		27.1	30.9	13.1	25.3	26.2	
6.3	5.7	8.4		4.5	6.4	3.9	6.9	13.0	
12.3	12.8	13.8	% Profit Before Taxes/Total Assets	16.8	18.4	14.0	8.5	13.5	15.8
5.5	5.0	5.8		5.8	5.6	3.2	5.3	5.3	7.4
1.3	.2	1.6		-2.0	.0	1.7	.0	1.9	3.7
66.5	92.3	81.5	Sales/Net Fixed Assets	58.0	49.8	58.1	66.4	111.9	85.7
26.3	20.8	23.8		13.3	20.6	24.0	21.4	31.4	23.9
8.6	7.0	8.4		6.8	5.4	11.5	6.7	9.2	9.6
5.1	4.8	4.8	Sales/Total Assets	3.8	5.0	5.3	3.8	4.7	5.8
3.5	3.1	3.2		2.3	2.1	4.0	2.7	3.2	4.0
2.2	2.1	2.1		1.8	1.5	2.5	1.9	2.3	2.4
(242) .4	(204) .3	(267) .4	% Depr., Dep., Amort./Sales	(12) .9	(25) .7	(18) .7	(45) .5	(74) .2	(93) .3
.9	1.2	1.0		1.6	3.1	1.3	1.4	.8	.7
2.6	2.9	2.2		3.0	7.8	3.5	2.4	2.0	1.5
(116) 1.2	(106) 1.3	(121) 1.3	% Officers', Directors', Owners' Comp/Sales		(17) 1.8	(13) 2.4	(22) 1.2	(36) 1.1	(28) .7
2.6	2.8	2.1			3.9	6.3	2.0	2.0	1.3
4.8	5.3	4.9			6.8	10.4	4.1	4.4	2.0
11568284M	9770632M	11973503M	Net Sales ($)	8709M	64684M	90061M	369598M	1199469M	10240982M
3381548M	2947910M	3314922M	Total Assets ($)	3898M	35652M	27035M	156418M	427848M	2664071M

Current Data Sorted By Assets | **Comparative Historical Data**

Date ranges: 183 (4/1-9/30/02) covers columns 0-500M, 500M-2MM, 2-10MM; 128 (10/1/02-3/31/03) covers 10-50MM, 50-100MM, 100-250MM. Historical columns: 4/1/98-3/31/99 ALL and 4/1/99-3/31/00 ALL.

0-500M	500M-2MM	2-10MM	10-50MM	50-100MM	100-250MM	Type of Statement	4/1/98-3/31/99 ALL	4/1/99-3/31/00 ALL
3	18	92	52	6	4	Unqualified	110	109
4	17	42	8			Reviewed	73	80
1	9	8	1			Compiled	31	29
	5	3				Tax Returns	3	10
	5	18	11	4		Other	31	35
8	54	163	72	10	4	**NUMBER OF STATEMENTS**	248	263
%	%	%	%	%	%	**ASSETS**	%	%
	16.3	7.6	4.0	6.9		Cash & Equivalents	12.1	10.4
	16.0	19.5	17.7	21.3		Trade Receivables (net)	22.0	19.5
	24.3	32.2	35.9	32.2		Inventory	24.0	27.7
	4.1	3.4	4.9	8.2		All Other Current	3.3	3.5
	60.8	62.8	62.5	68.6		Total Current	61.4	61.1
	29.6	29.6	29.2	18.6		Fixed Assets (net)	28.3	27.9
	.3	.4	1.1	.8		Intangibles (net)	3.1	3.0
	9.3	7.2	7.2	12.0		All Other Non-Current	7.3	8.0
	100.0	100.0	100.0	100.0		Total	100.0	100.0
						LIABILITIES		
	10.2	16.9	20.8	23.1		Notes Payable-Short Term	11.7	15.6
	3.8	2.2	1.5	1.4		Cur. Mat.-L/T/D	2.1	2.4
	10.9	15.8	16.6	13.6		Trade Payables	18.7	16.6
	.3	.6	.5	.0		Income Taxes Payable	.4	.3
	6.5	8.8	6.8	21.2		All Other Current	11.2	10.3
	31.7	44.2	46.2	59.3		Total Current	44.1	45.1
	8.0	8.1	13.7	16.9		Long Term Debt	10.2	10.4
	.5	1.1	1.2	.3		Deferred Taxes	1.0	.9
	2.1	2.1	1.2	1.9		All Other Non-Current	1.8	2.0
	57.7	44.5	37.7	21.7		Net Worth	42.8	41.5
	100.0	100.0	100.0	100.0		Total Liabilities & Net Worth	100.0	100.0
						INCOME DATA		
	100.0	100.0	100.0	100.0		Net Sales	100.0	100.0
	15.1	13.4	11.9	7.9		Gross Profit	12.4	15.4
	14.1	11.8	9.9	5.7		Operating Expenses	11.7	13.6
	1.0	1.7	2.0	2.2		Operating Profit	.8	1.7
	−.1	.1	.4	.5		All Other Expenses (net)	−.4	−.1
	1.1	1.6	1.6	1.7		Profit Before Taxes	1.1	1.9
						RATIOS		
	4.0 2.0 1.3	1.9 1.4 1.2	1.5 1.3 1.1	1.4 1.1 1.0		Current	1.9 1.3 1.1	1.8 1.3 1.1
	2.3 1.0 .5	.9 .5 .3	.8 .4 .2	.9 .6 .2		Quick	1.2 .7 .4	1.1 .6 .3
	3 110.8 9 41.9 22 17.0	9 40.1 16 23.2 34 10.9	8 46.1 16 22.5 34 10.8	8 48.0 24 15.0 40 9.1		Sales/Receivables	8 46.1 17 21.9 29 12.4	8 48.2 19 18.8 34 10.7
	5 72.0 27 13.7 52 7.0	23 15.9 44 8.4 75 4.9	29 12.5 52 7.0 76 4.8	0 UND 32 11.3 124 2.9		Cost of Sales/Inventory	10 36.5 26 13.9 47 7.8	16 22.1 37 10.0 69 5.3
	1 309.0 6 60.8 22 16.4	6 56.6 16 22.7 28 12.9	11 33.3 17 21.3 34 10.7	3 106.0 11 34.4 39 9.3		Cost of Sales/Payables	5 71.5 14 26.1 32 11.3	6 62.8 17 22.1 38 9.6
	7.0 15.2 28.8	8.8 16.7 45.8	13.0 24.3 43.6	7.8 37.0 NM		Sales/Working Capital	12.0 27.8 90.8	11.2 21.6 78.3
	(47) 6.5 3.0 1.0	(156) 7.1 3.4 1.5	(70) 5.2 3.4 2.0			EBIT/Interest	(229) 5.4 2.2 1.1	(246) 5.0 2.4 1.1
	(14) 6.7 4.1 1.5	(57) 6.2 3.4 1.7	(26) 11.9 4.3 1.9			Net Profit + Depr., Dep., Amort./Cur. Mat. L /T/D	(92) 6.7 3.1 1.4	(94) 7.2 3.4 1.7
	.2 .5 .9	.4 .7 .9	.5 .8 1.2	.2 .6 1.6		Fixed/Worth	.4 .7 1.2	.4 .7 1.2
	.3 .6 1.9	.7 1.4 2.4	1.0 1.7 3.1	2.3 4.7 10.4		Debt/Worth	.8 1.6 3.0	.8 1.6 3.1
	(53) 15.3 6.7 .1	(162) 15.4 8.7 2.8	(71) 21.3 10.4 4.8	25.6 22.1 9.7		% Profit Before Taxes/Tangible Net Worth	(242) 19.5 8.8 1.4	(254) 20.3 8.7 1.5
	7.7 3.9 .0	8.0 3.5 .8	7.4 3.3 2.1	6.3 2.9 2.4		% Profit Before Taxes/Total Assets	6.9 3.2 .3	8.1 3.3 .4
	27.8 13.6 7.6	17.1 9.8 6.2	18.3 8.5 5.9	296.3 14.4 7.7		Sales/Net Fixed Assets	29.0 12.8 7.9	22.1 10.3 6.0
	5.1 3.6 2.4	4.0 2.9 2.0	3.6 2.7 2.0	4.8 2.3 1.5		Sales/Total Assets	5.4 3.5 2.3	4.1 2.8 1.9
	(53) .7 1.1 2.0	(157) 1.0 1.5 2.0	(68) 1.0 1.4 1.9			% Depr., Dep., Amort./Sales	(239) .6 1.1 1.8	(245) .8 1.5 2.2
	(19) .9 1.7 2.4	(29) .4 1.3 2.4				% Officers', Directors', Owners' Comp/Sales	(77) .5 1.3	(72) .7 1.8 3.4
9742M 2500M	306620M 72481M	2366643M 738584M	5124494M 1527825M	2778610M 766218M	867286M 608668M	Net Sales ($) Total Assets ($)	10220043M 2526262M	9078780M 3207101M

© RMA 2003

M = $ thousand   MM = $ million
See Pages 11 through 18 for Explanation of Ratios and Data

Comparative Historical Data — Current Data Sorted By Sales

			Type of Statement	0-1MM	1-3MM	3-5MM	5-10MM	10-25MM	25MM & OVER
72	163	175	Unqualified	1	5	8	42	50	69
69	60	71	Reviewed	4	5	10	23	15	14
22	21	19	Compiled	1	5	3	3	6	1
4	3	8	Tax Returns	1	4			3	
39	44	38	Other	2		4	8	8	16
4/1/00-3/31/01 ALL	4/1/01-3/31/02 ALL	4/1/02-3/31/03 ALL		183 (4/1-9/30/02)			128 (10/1/02-3/31/03)		
206	291	311	NUMBER OF STATEMENTS	7	21	25	76	82	100
%	%	%	ASSETS	%	%	%	%	%	%
9.5	9.2	8.2	Cash & Equivalents		16.3	8.5	10.8	7.6	5.2
19.8	16.4	18.8	Trade Receivables (net)		21.7	18.3	15.1	16.4	23.4
29.3	30.1	31.7	Inventory		29.4	34.1	32.1	31.9	30.5
3.1	3.4	4.1	All Other Current		4.5	3.0	2.7	4.5	5.0
61.7	59.2	62.8	Total Current		72.0	63.8	60.8	60.5	64.2
28.2	32.0	29.0	Fixed Assets (net)		22.7	26.1	31.6	30.9	27.0
2.6	1.3	.5	Intangibles (net)		.0	.5	.5	.2	1.1
7.5	7.5	7.7	All Other Non-Current		5.3	9.6	7.2	8.4	7.7
100.0	100.0	100.0	Total		100.0	100.0	100.0	100.0	100.0
			LIABILITIES						
16.1	14.8	17.0	Notes Payable-Short Term		16.2	16.0	15.3	15.9	19.7
2.4	2.4	2.4	Cur. Mat.-L/T/D		2.6	4.5	2.6	2.5	1.3
18.0	15.5	15.0	Trade Payables		12.6	11.6	13.4	13.2	18.9
.2	.5	.5	Income Taxes Payable		.1	.1	.5	.7	.5
9.8	8.1	8.1	All Other Current		7.4	5.7	6.5	10.9	8.4
46.5	41.3	43.0	Total Current		38.8	37.8	38.3	43.2	48.7
11.0	10.0	9.6	Long Term Debt		11.2	5.2	9.2	8.1	12.2
.8	1.1	1.0	Deferred Taxes		.2	.7	1.2	1.0	1.0
1.9	1.6	2.0	All Other Non-Current		2.8	2.2	1.3	2.6	1.4
39.9	46.1	44.4	Net Worth		47.0	54.2	49.9	45.1	36.6
100.0	100.0	100.0	Total Liabilities & Net Worth		100.0	100.0	100.0	100.0	100.0
			INCOME DATA						
100.0	100.0	100.0	Net Sales		100.0	100.0	100.0	100.0	100.0
16.1	14.2	13.7	Gross Profit		20.9	18.4	13.6	11.4	11.5
14.3	12.3	12.1	Operating Expenses		20.2	14.6	12.2	10.1	9.7
1.8	1.8	1.6	Operating Profit		.7	3.8	1.4	1.3	1.8
-.2	.3	.1	All Other Expenses (net)		.1	.7	-.3	.2	.2
2.0	1.5	1.5	Profit Before Taxes		.6	3.0	1.7	1.1	1.5
			RATIOS						
1.7	2.0	2.0	Current		4.2	2.5	2.2	1.7	1.5
1.3	1.4	1.4			2.0	1.8	1.6	1.3	1.3
1.1	1.1	1.2			1.2	1.3	1.2	1.1	1.1
.9	1.0	1.0	Quick		2.2	1.6	1.2	.9	.9
.5	.5	.5			.8	.7	.6	.4	.5
.3	.3	.3			.3	.4	.3	.3	.3
10 36.9	6 57.9	7 49.5	Sales/Receivables		4 99.2	6 57.6	7 54.9	8 47.8	9 41.2
19 19.0	14 25.4	15 23.7			12 29.3	19 19.6	16 23.4	12 30.0	18 20.5
36 10.2	30 12.0	33 11.1			58 6.3	40 9.0	32 11.2	24 15.3	34 10.7
19 18.7	18 19.8	21 17.4	Cost of Sales/Inventory		17 21.1	27 13.5	21 17.0	25 14.5	20 18.6
43 8.4	39 9.4	42 8.7			51 7.1	58 6.3	54 6.8	41 9.0	39 9.4
84 4.4	72 5.1	75 4.9			124 2.9	124 2.9	80 4.6	62 5.8	60 6.0
9 40.2	6 56.5	6 64.2	Cost of Sales/Payables		1 277.6	2 149.4	5 66.5	4 93.7	9 40.4
21 17.5	17 21.6	14 25.4			8 48.1	22 16.4	14 26.1	11 33.9	17 21.5
39 9.4	30 12.3	29 12.7			16 22.3	37 9.8	34 10.7	25 14.4	31 11.6
9.7	10.0	9.1	Sales/Working Capital		4.2	5.5	7.5	14.5	15.0
22.1	21.9	18.1			7.3	7.0	14.1	20.6	27.5
96.6	48.2	41.2			16.4	14.8	25.4	44.9	48.7
(192) 3.8	(278) 4.5	(291) 6.7	EBIT/Interest	(19) 5.3	(24) 7.1	(70) 6.1	(80) 7.5	(94) 5.2	
2.1	2.5	3.2		2.8	4.1	2.8	3.9	3.2	
1.1	1.4	1.5		.1	1.3	1.3	1.4	1.9	
(56) 4.8	(110) 7.3	(107) 6.5	Net Profit + Depr., Dep., Amort./Cur. Mat. L/T/D			(28) 6.9	(29) 6.2	(37) 10.6	
2.5	4.2	3.5				3.6	3.5	4.8	
1.2	2.0	1.8				1.8	1.1	2.1	
.4	.5	.4	Fixed/Worth		.2	.3	.3	.5	.4
.7	.7	.7			.3	.4	.7	.7	.7
1.3	1.1	1.0			1.0	.6	1.0	1.0	1.0
.8	.6	.7	Debt/Worth		.4	.4	.5	.6	1.1
1.8	1.2	1.4			1.2	.6	1.1	1.3	1.8
3.8	2.7	2.6			2.7	2.1	2.1	2.6	3.7
(202) 19.0	(289) 16.2	(308) 16.4	% Profit Before Taxes/Tangible Net Worth		18.8	20.4	(75) 12.4	(81) 15.1	(99) 21.6
8.4	8.4	8.8			7.1	8.3	6.4	9.9	11.2
1.5	3.4	3.0			-2.3	1.1	1.7	3.5	5.6
6.5	6.9	7.1	% Profit Before Taxes/Total Assets		7.5	10.0	6.1	8.7	7.1
2.7	3.6	3.4			4.0	5.4	3.2	3.7	3.3
.4	1.3	1.0			-1.3	.6	.6	1.3	2.1
20.4	18.4	20.5	Sales/Net Fixed Assets		40.0	20.7	13.8	17.7	21.8
9.5	9.0	10.2			19.1	11.3	7.9	9.7	11.0
5.6	6.0	6.3			6.1	6.6	5.8	7.3	6.9
3.8	4.3	4.0	Sales/Total Assets		4.2	3.2	3.5	4.4	4.8
2.5	2.9	2.9			2.4	2.2	2.5	3.2	3.1
1.8	2.0	2.0			1.4	1.5	1.4	2.3	2.2
(198) .8	(276) .9	(295) .9	% Depr., Dep., Amort./Sales	(19) .8	.8	(74) 1.0	(80) 1.0	(91) .7	
1.4	1.5	1.5		1.8	1.5	1.6	1.5	1.2	
2.3	2.2	2.0		2.2	2.7	2.3	1.9	1.7	
(65) .6	(47) .5	(53) .4	% Officers', Directors', Owners' Comp/Sales			(15) .4	(14) .2		
1.5	1.0	1.0				1.7	1.1		
2.4	1.9	2.3				5.5	1.6		
7795755M	13281679M	11453395M	Net Sales ($)	3304M	46068M	101333M	570053M	1317247M	9415390M
2675684M	3718139M	3716276M	Total Assets ($)	3901M	23939M	54295M	247346M	450668M	2936127M

M = $ thousand   MM = $ million
See Pages 11 through 18 for Explanation of Ratios and Data

Current Data Sorted By Assets **Comparative Historical Data**

	0-500M	500M-2MM	2-10MM	10-50MM	50-100MM	100-250MM	Type of Statement	4/1/98-3/31/99 ALL	4/1/99-3/31/00 ALL
Unqualified	1	5	3			1	Unqualified	5	6
Reviewed	1	2		1			Reviewed	5	6
Compiled	6	3					Compiled	14	12
Tax Returns		2	1	2			Tax Returns	2	5
Other							Other	8	14
		3 (4/1-9/30/02)		25 (10/1/02-3/31/03)					
	8	12	4	3		1	NUMBER OF STATEMENTS	34	43
	%	%	%	%	%	%	**ASSETS**	%	%
		18.0					Cash & Equivalents	5.8	5.8
		24.2					Trade Receivables (net)	25.1	29.4
		27.0					Inventory	23.7	24.9
		3.9					All Other Current	−.5	3.5
		73.1					Total Current	54.1	63.5
		20.3					Fixed Assets (net)	33.4	27.3
		.0					Intangibles (net)	1.6	1.8
		6.6					All Other Non-Current	10.9	7.4
		100.0					Total	100.0	100.0
							LIABILITIES		
		42.2					Notes Payable-Short Term	19.2	24.1
		6.8					Cur. Mat.-L/T/D	5.8	1.4
		13.5					Trade Payables	10.2	11.8
		.0					Income Taxes Payable	.1	.1
		4.3					All Other Current	8.1	10.8
		66.9					Total Current	43.4	48.2
		4.2					Long Term Debt	13.3	12.0
		.1					Deferred Taxes	.2	.3
		2.7					All Other Non-Current	4.3	1.4
		26.0					Net Worth	38.9	38.1
		100.0					Total Liabilities & Net Worth	100.0	100.0
							INCOME DATA		
		100.0					Net Sales	100.0	100.0
		15.6					Gross Profit	19.5	28.4
		14.4					Operating Expenses	19.9	21.8
		1.2					Operating Profit	−.3	6.5
		.7					All Other Expenses (net)	−.2	1.0
		.5					Profit Before Taxes	−.1	5.5
							RATIOS		
		1.8 / 1.0 / .8					Current	2.2 / 1.4 / .9	2.5 / 1.3 / .9
		1.1 / .7 / .2					Quick	(32) 1.6 / 1.0 / .3	(42) 2.0 / .6 / .3
		5 76.8 / 9 38.4 / 18 19.9					Sales/Receivables	0 UND / 5 70.5 / 26 14.3	2 192.4 / 12 31.1 / 24 15.0
		1 550.5 / 15 25.0 / 34 10.6					Cost of Sales/Inventory	0 999.8 / 17 21.1 / 54 6.8	3 115.6 / 20 18.4 / 39 9.3
		2 218.0 / 4 81.1 / 12 31.7					Cost of Sales/Payables	0 UND / 2 148.1 / 13 29.0	1 587.5 / 6 57.8 / 17 21.4
		21.9 / NM / −50.5					Sales/Working Capital	15.9 / 173.7 / −64.2	14.8 / 41.8 / −187.0
							EBIT/Interest	(33) 7.0 / 2.5 / 1.4	(39) 6.0 / 2.8 / 1.5
							Net Profit + Depr., Dep., Amort./Cur. Mat. L /T/D		
		.2 / .8 / 33.6					Fixed/Worth	.2 / .6 / 3.0	.2 / .4 / 1.6
		.8 / 7.4 / 461.6					Debt/Worth	.3 / 2.3 / 7.7	.7 / 1.9 / 4.2
		(10) 68.1 / 14.1 / −17.2					% Profit Before Taxes/Tangible Net Worth	(31) 45.9 / 20.1 / 3.3	(40) 50.5 / 20.0 / 3.6
		9.2 / 2.6 / −3.3					% Profit Before Taxes/Total Assets	17.1 / 7.4 / .3	17.3 / 8.0 / 1.7
		390.5 / 72.3 / 13.4					Sales/Net Fixed Assets	135.8 / 28.3 / 5.9	200.1 / 60.8 / 9.4
		28.0 / 6.7 / 4.5					Sales/Total Assets	16.1 / 7.3 / 2.0	11.8 / 6.3 / 2.2
		(11) .2 / .4 / 1.0					% Depr., Dep., Amort./Sales	(31) .1 / .5 / 2.3	(37) .1 / .2 / 2.3
							% Officers', Directors', Owners' Comp/Sales		(15) .5 / 1.8 / 7.7
Net Sales ($)	57715M	236280M	88489M	171702M		65715M	Net Sales ($)	1495822M	2717101M
Total Assets ($)	2294M	14053M	20548M	56343M		183168M	Total Assets ($)	383057M	794226M

(50-100MM column: DATA NOT AVAILABLE)

© RMA 2003

M = $ thousand   MM = $ million
See Pages 11 through 18 for Explanation of Ratios and Data

Comparative Historical Data | Current Data Sorted By Sales

			Type of Statement						
1	3	1	Unqualified						1
4	6	9	Reviewed	1		1	5		2
10	11	4	Compiled	1	1	1	1		1
5	2	9	Tax Returns	2	2	2	2		1
6	4	5	Other				3		2
4/1/00-3/31/01	4/1/01-3/31/02	4/1/02-3/31/03			3 (4/1-9/30/02)		25 (10/1/02-3/31/03)		
ALL	ALL	ALL		0-1MM	1-3MM	3-5MM	5-10MM	10-25MM	25MM & OVER
26	26	28	**NUMBER OF STATEMENTS**	4	3	3	11		7
%	%	%	**ASSETS**	%	%	%	%	%	%
12.1	19.7	18.3	Cash & Equivalents					10.5	
22.6	18.3	22.5	Trade Receivables (net)	D				26.0	
25.8	17.6	24.8	Inventory	A				26.4	
2.1	4.1	3.2	All Other Current	T				4.3	
62.6	59.7	68.8	Total Current	A				67.1	
29.0	23.0	20.5	Fixed Assets (net)					16.6	
3.3	6.8	1.7	Intangibles (net)	N				2.5	
5.2	10.4	9.0	All Other Non-Current	O				13.8	
100.0	100.0	100.0	Total	T				100.0	
			LIABILITIES	A					
18.4	15.7	29.6	Notes Payable-Short Term	V				36.4	
1.6	3.7	3.9	Cur. Mat.-L/T/D	A				8.0	
11.0	9.5	8.5	Trade Payables	I				11.6	
.4	.0	.0	Income Taxes Payable	L				.0	
15.7	16.9	8.1	All Other Current	A				15.1	
47.1	45.9	50.0	Total Current	B				71.0	
11.2	14.8	12.5	Long Term Debt	L				5.5	
.2	.0	.1	Deferred Taxes	E				.0	
1.7	1.2	2.8	All Other Non-Current					3.0	
39.7	38.1	34.5	Net Worth					20.5	
100.0	100.0	100.0	Total Liabilities & Net Worth					100.0	
			INCOME DATA						
100.0	100.0	100.0	Net Sales					100.0	
19.7	29.4	16.3	Gross Profit					8.8	
15.7	22.9	13.3	Operating Expenses					7.8	
3.9	6.6	2.9	Operating Profit					1.0	
−.1	−.1	.1	All Other Expenses (net)					.0	
4.0	6.7	2.9	Profit Before Taxes					1.0	
			RATIOS						
2.6	1.9	2.8						1.3	
1.2	1.2	1.2	Current					1.0	
1.0	.9	.9						.7	
2.1	1.3	1.8						.9	
(25) .9	.8	.8	Quick					.5	
.4	.4	.4						.2	
2 240.9	2 154.7	3 132.1						1 280.3	
8 43.1	13 27.6	8 44.2	Sales/Receivables					6 59.3	
23 15.7	37 9.8	21 17.6						21 17.4	
1 427.8	1 435.8	1 494.7						0 999.8	
14 26.0	13 27.4	11 33.4	Cost of Sales/Inventory					6 63.7	
30 12.0	39 9.2	24 15.3						23 15.7	
1 691.6	1 523.7	1 590.1						1 579.5	
3 123.3	6 62.0	2 154.2	Cost of Sales/Payables					3 121.8	
10 35.2	30 12.3	12 31.7						13 28.3	
18.1	7.3	15.2						47.1	
76.7	86.6	102.9	Sales/Working Capital					−999.8	
UND	−61.2	−385.6						−172.9	
14.5	21.4	6.1							
(22) 3.9	(22) 3.5	(22) 2.1	EBIT/Interest						
1.2	1.0	.9							
			Net Profit + Depr., Dep., Amort./Cur. Mat. L/T/D						
.2	.2	.2						.2	
.6	.5	.7	Fixed/Worth					.9	
1.5	2.0	1.4						1.8	
.4	.9	.8						2.7	
2.5	2.7	2.7	Debt/Worth					4.1	
4.4	6.2	7.9						8.3	
34.5	35.3	53.1						60.6	
(24) 14.3	(23) 12.8	(25) 17.0	% Profit Before Taxes/Tangible Net Worth					12.5	
3.6	6.2	2.4						−13.7	
16.0	12.1	12.4						11.0	
6.1	6.0	5.0	% Profit Before Taxes/Total Assets					1.7	
1.3	.0	1.0						−4.1	
227.3	120.7	167.0						292.3	
34.4	39.9	68.0	Sales/Net Fixed Assets					75.7	
9.4	5.3	20.5						62.4	
11.5	10.2	28.5						39.9	
7.7	3.2	7.7	Sales/Total Assets					8.6	
3.2	1.2	4.0						4.1	
.1	.1	.2						.1	
(24) .3	(24) .5	(25) .4	% Depr., Dep., Amort./Sales					.3	
2.4	2.6	.8						.6	
.2		.1							
(10) 1.1		(11) .9	% Officers', Directors', Owners' Comp/Sales						
2.1		2.2							
532591M	1007041M	619901M	Net Sales ($)	7289M	10255M	18637M	166626M		417094M
244064M	420733M	276406M	Total Assets ($)	1750M	1316M	3173M	25711M		244456M

© RMA 2003

M = $ thousand   MM = $ million
See Pages 11 through 18 for Explanation of Ratios and Data

Current Data Sorted By Assets / Comparative Historical Data

						Type of Statement		
	2	7	18	2	4	Unqualified	26	28
	3	12	7			Reviewed	13	15
2	6	11				Compiled	10	18
3	4	4	1			Tax Returns	5	4
1	1	6	9		1	Other	14	17
	44 (4/1-9/30/02)		61 (10/1/02-3/31/03)				4/1/98-3/31/99	4/1/99-3/31/00
0-500M	500M-2MM	2-10MM	10-50MM	50-100MM	100-250MM		ALL	ALL
6	16	40	35	3	5	NUMBER OF STATEMENTS	68	82
%	%	%	%	%	%	ASSETS	%	%
	10.3	7.4	9.1			Cash & Equivalents	11.0	12.7
	39.2	32.5	28.7			Trade Receivables (net)	33.5	26.9
	28.2	33.7	35.6			Inventory	29.7	31.4
	3.9	5.6	4.1			All Other Current	6.1	2.5
	81.5	79.2	77.5			Total Current	80.3	73.5
	9.3	13.2	13.3			Fixed Assets (net)	14.5	16.6
	.3	3.0	.6			Intangibles (net)	.4	1.9
	8.8	4.5	8.6			All Other Non-Current	4.8	8.0
	100.0	100.0	100.0			Total	100.0	100.0
						LIABILITIES		
	2.8	20.1	25.8			Notes Payable-Short Term	24.7	19.3
	2.4	2.3	.9			Cur. Mat.-L/T/D	1.7	2.7
	37.1	24.0	15.3			Trade Payables	16.6	16.4
	.3	.4	.3			Income Taxes Payable	.8	.5
	10.0	10.6	8.2			All Other Current	8.0	11.0
	52.6	57.4	50.6			Total Current	51.8	49.9
	3.1	5.1	9.2			Long Term Debt	5.8	11.0
	.0	.1	.2			Deferred Taxes	.3	.3
	1.9	3.7	3.5			All Other Non-Current	3.1	3.8
	42.4	33.8	36.4			Net Worth	39.1	35.0
	100.0	100.0	100.0			Total Liabilities & Net Worth	100.0	100.0
						INCOME DATA		
	100.0	100.0	100.0			Net Sales	100.0	100.0
	18.0	14.8	17.6			Gross Profit	15.3	19.2
	15.9	12.6	13.7			Operating Expenses	12.2	16.1
	2.1	2.2	3.9			Operating Profit	3.0	3.1
	−.5	.1	.4			All Other Expenses (net)	.6	.5
	2.5	2.0	3.5			Profit Before Taxes	2.4	2.6
						RATIOS		
	2.5	2.0	2.5				1.9	2.2
	1.7	1.4	1.3			Current	1.4	1.3
	1.1	1.1	1.1				1.2	1.1
	1.7	1.2	1.6				1.3	1.2
	1.0	.7	.7			Quick	.8	.7
	.6	.3	.3				.4	.5

15	23.6	19	19.4	25	14.5			Sales/Receivables	18	20.6	19	19.7
35	10.5	30	12.1	36	10.3				28	13.3	28	13.2
68	5.3	41	8.9	55	6.6				45	8.1	51	7.1
0	UND	14	26.7	17	22.0			Cost of Sales/Inventory	5	80.8	15	24.1
35	10.5	28	12.9	44	8.3				23	15.6	46	7.9
61	6.0	72	5.1	162	2.2				82	4.4	96	3.8
9	41.8	12	29.4	6	58.6			Cost of Sales/Payables	4	89.1	5	77.0
33	10.9	25	14.7	16	23.5				15	23.8	17	22.1
62	5.9	44	8.4	48	7.6				37	9.8	38	9.6
	7.2		9.0		5.9			Sales/Working Capital		7.8		7.4
	16.3		19.5		13.8					15.6		17.4
	54.6		91.9		25.0					41.8		51.5
	20.7		12.3		5.8			EBIT/Interest		5.3		8.4
(13)	9.5	(38)	4.1	(27)	2.8				(63)	2.3	(76)	3.7
	1.1		1.4		1.5					1.4		1.4
			8.8					Net Profit + Depr., Dep., Amort./Cur. Mat. L /T/D		8.1		28.0
		(12)	2.2						(15)	2.9	(10)	5.7
			.6							1.8		1.9
	.0		.1		.1			Fixed/Worth		.1		.1
	.1		.4		.2					.3		.3
	.4		1.3		.5					.6		.9
	.6		1.1		.7			Debt/Worth		.8		.9
	1.2		2.5		2.5					1.9		2.0
	6.4		5.9		5.7					3.9		4.9
	27.7		33.9		41.0			% Profit Before Taxes/Tangible Net Worth		41.9		39.7
(15)	18.5	(38)	17.4		20.5					15.7	(73)	20.0
	3.5		6.9		7.4					3.9		3.8
	13.0		11.1		11.5			% Profit Before Taxes/Total Assets		10.6		13.7
	3.9		5.5		6.1					4.4		7.3
	.5		1.2		1.1					1.6		.7
	999.8		112.3		233.9			Sales/Net Fixed Assets		202.4		159.5
	223.3		35.3		35.6					47.0		35.3
	36.0		15.9		11.5					11.5		8.0
	6.2		5.3		3.9			Sales/Total Assets		5.5		4.7
	4.3		3.7		2.1					3.1		2.5
	2.5		2.5		1.4					1.7		1.6
	.1		.1		.1			% Depr., Dep., Amort./Sales		.1		.1
(12)	.3	(39)	.6	(30)	.5			(61)	.5	(65)	.6
	1.0		.9		1.9					1.3		2.1
			.9					% Officers', Directors', Owners' Comp/Sales		1.1		1.2
		(16)	1.5						(17)	2.0	(28)	2.5
			3.6							4.6		6.6

8761M	90294M	863204M	2020556M	372765M	1361480M	Net Sales ($)	3751193M	2967188M
1659M	19668M	208462M	676630M	215295M	796688M	Total Assets ($)	1363038M	1231740M

© RMA 2003

M = $ thousand   MM = $ million
See Pages 11 through 18 for Explanation of Ratios and Data

Comparative Historical Data　　　　　　　Current Data Sorted By Sales

			Type of Statement						
26	28	33	Unqualified		1		3	8	21
16	16	22	Reviewed			1	2	9	10
22	21	19	Compiled	1	3	3	4	5	3
4	7	12	Tax Returns	2	3		3	4	
19	20	19	Other		2		2		12
4/1/00- 3/31/01 ALL	4/1/01- 3/31/02 ALL	4/1/02- 3/31/03 ALL			44 (4/1-9/30/02)		61 (10/1/02-3/31/03)		
				0-1MM	1-3MM	3-5MM	5-10MM	10-25MM	25MM & OVER
87	92	105	**NUMBER OF STATEMENTS**	3	9	4	14	29	46
%	%	%	**ASSETS**	%	%	%	%	%	%
10.8	9.3	9.0	Cash & Equivalents				7.8	10.8	7.0
30.7	30.9	29.9	Trade Receivables (net)				20.3	33.3	31.4
31.2	27.4	32.3	Inventory				40.5	26.1	36.3
3.7	5.7	4.5	All Other Current				5.3	3.7	5.6
76.5	73.3	75.7	Total Current				73.9	73.9	80.3
15.5	17.3	15.5	Fixed Assets (net)				12.7	16.1	12.8
1.4	2.0	1.5	Intangibles (net)				.8	3.5	.7
6.6	7.8	7.4	All Other Non-Current				12.6	6.5	6.2
100.0	100.0	100.0	Total				100.0	100.0	100.0
			LIABILITIES						
24.2	25.4	19.1	Notes Payable-Short Term				14.9	15.1	25.6
1.9	1.5	1.9	Cur. Mat.-L/T/D				2.1	1.8	1.3
16.5	18.9	21.3	Trade Payables				26.1	20.0	19.2
.4	.3	.3	Income Taxes Payable				.3	.5	.2
10.4	10.2	10.4	All Other Current				6.9	13.2	9.7
53.4	56.3	53.0	Total Current				50.3	50.7	56.1
7.8	7.6	8.3	Long Term Debt				6.9	5.2	8.1
.2	.2	.1	Deferred Taxes				.4	.1	.2
2.1	3.7	3.4	All Other Non-Current				2.6	5.3	2.3
36.6	32.1	35.2	Net Worth				39.8	38.8	33.4
100.0	100.0	100.0	Total Liabilities & Net Worth				100.0	100.0	100.0
			INCOME DATA						
100.0	100.0	100.0	Net Sales				100.0	100.0	100.0
16.4	19.6	17.5	Gross Profit				22.3	20.3	10.6
13.4	17.3	14.6	Operating Expenses				18.9	17.3	7.4
3.0	2.4	2.9	Operating Profit				3.5	3.0	3.2
.1	.6	.2	All Other Expenses (net)				.1	.0	.4
3.0	1.7	2.7	Profit Before Taxes				3.3	3.0	2.8
			RATIOS						
1.8	1.7	2.0					2.1	2.1	1.9
1.3	1.3	1.4	Current				1.5	1.5	1.3
1.1	1.1	1.1					1.1	1.1	1.1
1.1	1.0	1.3					1.1	1.5	1.1
.7	.7	.7	Quick				.5	.9	.7
.4	.4	.3					.3	.4	.3
21　17.4	17　21.3	19　19.5					16　22.7	26　13.8	19　19.4
33　11.1	30　12.0	32　11.2	Sales/Receivables				25　14.9	35　10.3	30　12.1
53　6.8	46　7.9	47　7.7					39　9.3	45　8.1	45　8.0
12　30.4	12　30.7	15　23.8					0　UND	11　33.3	16　22.5
46　7.9	33　11.0	43　8.5	Cost of Sales/Inventory				64　5.7	41　9.0	42　8.7
99　3.7	72　5.1	87　4.2					228　1.6	74　4.9	90　4.0
5　74.3	5　66.7	8　47.5					12　31.0	5　68.7	8　47.3
15　24.7	20　18.7	21　17.2	Cost of Sales/Payables				29　12.5	24　15.4	17　22.1
35　10.3	40　9.1	45　8.1					74　5.0	48　7.5	32　11.4
8.1	9.9	8.3					8.0	8.3	10.9
17.8	22.3	15.7	Sales/Working Capital				15.5	13.5	17.8
74.9	90.8	42.5					77.9	40.2	39.3
5.2	5.2	9.5					18.1	12.0	7.1
(79)　2.3	(81)　2.6	(92)　3.9	EBIT/Interest			(13)　2.7	(24)　7.2	(41)　4.0
1.4	.9	1.5					1.3	1.3	2.2
16.4	7.0	6.1							
(16)　3.5	(17)　2.8	(20)　2.6	Net Profit + Depr., Dep., Amort./Cur. Mat. L/T/D						
1.0	1.0	1.0							
.1	.1	.1					.1	.1	.0
.3	.5	.3	Fixed/Worth				.3	.4	.2
.8	1.0	.9					.9	1.0	.6
.9	1.2	.9					.8	.6	1.2
1.9	2.3	2.3	Debt/Worth				1.4	2.3	2.6
4.7	7.0	5.8					6.4	6.6	5.3
41.2	33.8	37.7					22.2	42.1	41.2
(83)　20.9	(85)　14.2	(99)　18.5	% Profit Before Taxes/Tangible Net Worth				16.6	(28)　20.4	(45)　21.9
7.0	−.4	7.4					1.0	8.2	9.3
11.9	9.8	10.9					14.0	13.2	9.2
5.2	3.8	5.9	% Profit Before Taxes/Total Assets				5.1	7.6	6.3
1.3	.0	1.1					.5	1.4	2.9
105.2	140.3	230.9					270.8	79.8	489.0
30.4	26.8	35.7	Sales/Net Fixed Assets				31.6	26.2	63.6
10.1	7.7	12.2					10.7	11.8	19.8
4.3	4.2	5.2					5.1	4.4	5.7
2.9	3.1	3.0	Sales/Total Assets				2.8	3.2	2.7
1.7	2.0	1.8					1.5	2.0	1.9
.2	.1	.1					.2	.2	.1
(77)　.6	(80)　.6	(92)　.6	% Depr., Dep., Amort./Sales			(13)　.9	(28)　.9	(38)　.2
1.4	1.9	1.4					2.5	1.8	.6
.7	.8	.8						.9	.5
(21)　1.7	(31)　1.6	(35)　1.0	% Officers', Directors', Owners' Comp/Sales				(14)　1.5	(12)　1.5
3.4	4.2	2.0						2.7	1.1
2481803M	3762915M	4717060M	Net Sales ($)	2247M	19376M	15553M	104251M	469158M	4106475M
984881M	1604253M	1918402M	Total Assets ($)	426M	9497M	6583M	59305M	177219M	1665372M

M = $ thousand　　MM = $ million
See Pages 11 through 18 for Explanation of Ratios and Data

Current Data Sorted By Assets   **Comparative Historical Data**

0-500M	500M-2MM	2-10MM	10-50MM	50-100MM	100-250MM	Type of Statement	4/1/98-3/31/99 ALL	4/1/99-3/31/00 ALL
1		6	7	4		Unqualified	26	15
	7	18	5			Reviewed	22	26
4	13	6		1		Compiled	34	35
2	1	3				Tax Returns	7	9
1	10	15	13	1	2	Other	21	33
	16 (4/1-9/30/02)		104 (10/1/02-3/31/03)					
8	31	48	25	6	2	**NUMBER OF STATEMENTS**	110	118
%	%	%	%	%	%	**ASSETS**	%	%
	6.0	6.1	2.4			Cash & Equivalents	6.2	5.8
	41.7	39.6	43.0			Trade Receivables (net)	39.0	40.8
	31.4	30.1	30.6			Inventory	25.3	27.3
	.7	2.6	2.4			All Other Current	1.6	1.8
	79.8	78.5	78.5			Total Current	72.2	75.7
	14.8	16.4	13.9			Fixed Assets (net)	18.5	15.9
	2.6	.9	2.5			Intangibles (net)	3.6	3.4
	2.9	4.2	5.2			All Other Non-Current	5.6	5.0
	100.0	100.0	100.0			Total	100.0	100.0
						LIABILITIES		
	14.8	13.0	17.1			Notes Payable-Short Term	13.7	16.1
	4.9	1.4	1.3			Cur. Mat.-L/T/D	26.9	2.2
	30.9	26.9	26.9			Trade Payables	25.6	28.8
	.6	.5	.1			Income Taxes Payable	.4	.2
	6.9	9.5	13.6			All Other Current	18.1	7.0
	58.1	51.3	59.0			Total Current	84.8	54.3
	10.0	7.3	14.5			Long Term Debt	106.9	9.0
	.1	.4	.1			Deferred Taxes	.3	.2
	5.4	2.1	5.7			All Other Non-Current	3.2	4.5
	26.4	39.0	20.7			Net Worth	−95.2	32.0
	100.0	100.0	100.0			Total Liabilities & Net Worth	100.0	100.0
						INCOME DATA		
	100.0	100.0	100.0			Net Sales	100.0	100.0
	30.6	25.0	17.2			Gross Profit	26.4	26.1
	28.5	21.8	15.0			Operating Expenses	22.2	22.2
	2.1	3.2	2.1			Operating Profit	4.2	4.0
	.3	.4	.5			All Other Expenses (net)	.8	1.1
	1.8	2.8	1.6			Profit Before Taxes	3.4	2.9
						RATIOS		
	1.8	2.5	1.7			Current	2.0	1.9
	1.4	1.4	1.4				1.4	1.3
	1.1	1.2	1.1				1.1	1.1
	1.1	1.3	1.1			Quick	1.2	1.1
	.9	.9	.7				.9	.9
	.5	.6	.6				.6	.6
	31 11.8	34 10.7	42 8.8			Sales/Receivables	35 10.5	36 10.2
	43 8.6	42 8.8	54 6.7				43 8.4	47 7.8
	52 7.0	57 6.4	71 5.1				56 6.5	58 6.3
	33 11.0	36 10.1	27 13.3			Cost of Sales/Inventory	25 14.7	31 11.8
	43 8.4	49 7.5	56 6.5				42 8.8	46 7.9
	73 5.0	75 4.9	84 4.4				66 5.5	72 5.1
	27 13.7	21 17.1	27 13.4			Cost of Sales/Payables	26 13.9	28 12.9
	43 8.5	36 10.2	38 9.7				37 10.0	45 8.2
	69 5.3	53 6.9	63 5.8				55 6.6	61 5.9
	9.9	6.5	7.5			Sales/Working Capital	8.4	7.9
	17.2	13.0	13.4				15.5	14.9
	49.0	31.3	40.4				38.4	52.7
	8.4	8.1	10.7			EBIT/Interest	9.2	9.5
	(29) 4.4	(42) 4.6	(22) 2.5				(100) 3.7	(107) 3.6
	−.1	1.3	1.4				1.9	1.6
		6.7				Net Profit + Depr., Dep.,		8.1 7.2
		(14) 3.1				Amort./Cur. Mat. L./T/D	(22) 3.2 (20) 2.8	
		.6					1.7 1.5	
	.2	.1	.0			Fixed/Worth	.2	.1
	.7	.3	.4				.4	.4
	4.9	.7	1.0				1.7	1.3
	1.3	.7	1.6			Debt/Worth	1.1	1.2
	2.9	1.6	3.2				2.4	2.4
	26.7	3.4	11.9				6.2	6.7
	50.4	36.9	73.3			% Profit Before Taxes/Tangible	48.6	52.0
	(25) 17.0	(45) 25.2	(23) 22.0			Net Worth	(95) 25.9	(110) 27.4
	1.4	3.1	4.0				11.2	10.5
	12.7	13.8	10.7			% Profit Before Taxes/Total	15.6	15.0
	4.8	5.8	3.3			Assets	7.3	6.8
	−2.6	.4	1.3				3.1	2.0
	66.1	144.6	400.1			Sales/Net Fixed Assets	77.1	124.8
	21.0	36.7	46.8				29.7	36.5
	14.5	9.1	11.0				9.7	11.1
	3.9	4.2	3.3			Sales/Total Assets	4.0	3.8
	3.1	2.9	2.9				3.0	3.1
	2.7	2.2	2.1				2.2	2.4
	.5	.2	.3			% Depr., Dep., Amort./Sales	.5	.3
	(27) 1.3	(42) 1.2	(19) .6				(94) .9	(102) .7
	2.2	2.3	1.5				2.4	2.2
	2.4	1.4				% Officers', Directors',	1.9	1.8
	(18) 4.3	(30) 3.0				Owners' Comp/Sales	(44) 4.0	(61) 3.6
	4.8	6.5					8.0	5.8
11725M	121019M	638791M	1473247M	1330621M	957753M	Net Sales ($)	2867491M	2007609M
2347M	36577M	211459M	516458M	439426M	292763M	Total Assets ($)	1022168M	995981M

© RMA 2003

M = $ thousand   MM = $ million
See Pages 11 through 18 for Explanation of Ratios and Data

Comparative Historical Data | Current Data Sorted By Sales

4/1/00-3/31/01 ALL	4/1/01-3/31/02 ALL	4/1/02-3/31/03 ALL	Type of Statement	0-1MM	1-3MM	3-5MM	5-10MM	10-25MM	25MM & OVER
15	15	18	Unqualified	1			1	5	11
25	22	30	Reviewed		5	4	6	9	6
39	32	24	Compiled	1	4	6	7	5	1
6	4	6	Tax Returns	1	2		1	2	
39	34	42	Other		6	5	6	11	14
					16 (4/1-9/30/02)		104 (10/1/02-3/31/03)		
124	107	120	NUMBER OF STATEMENTS	3	17	15	21	32	32
%	%	%	**ASSETS**	%	%	%	%	%	%
6.3	6.1	5.4	Cash & Equivalents		6.4	3.4	8.3	5.1	4.8
41.4	39.1	40.1	Trade Receivables (net)		40.2	42.6	36.4	41.9	40.3
27.3	26.7	29.9	Inventory		31.9	25.4	30.5	32.4	27.8
2.7	3.1	1.9	All Other Current		.7	1.3	2.2	2.0	2.7
77.8	75.0	77.4	Total Current		79.2	72.6	77.4	81.5	75.6
14.1	17.3	17.2	Fixed Assets (net)		17.0	19.6	18.3	14.0	17.0
3.1	3.5	1.7	Intangibles (net)		1.8	5.4	.3	.5	2.0
5.0	4.2	3.8	All Other Non-Current		2.0	2.4	4.0	4.1	5.4
100.0	100.0	100.0	Total		100.0	100.0	100.0	100.0	100.0
			LIABILITIES						
15.5	16.8	14.5	Notes Payable-Short Term		14.5	19.6	10.7	13.9	15.0
2.1	3.5	2.6	Cur. Mat.-L/T/D		3.3	7.7	1.4	1.2	2.1
31.3	26.4	27.5	Trade Payables		31.5	26.9	25.1	27.6	27.8
.3	.0	.4	Income Taxes Payable		.4	1.1	.7	.1	.1
7.7	7.5	10.9	All Other Current		9.8	3.6	5.8	12.6	13.8
57.0	54.3	55.9	Total Current		59.4	58.9	43.7	55.4	58.9
9.3	11.0	9.8	Long Term Debt		12.2	12.9	5.4	8.7	10.4
.3	.3	.2	Deferred Taxes		.1	.1	.4	.2	.1
3.3	3.4	3.7	All Other Non-Current		1.3	7.1	4.1	1.7	4.5
30.2	30.9	30.3	Net Worth		27.0	21.0	46.4	34.0	26.2
100.0	100.0	100.0	Total Liabilities & Net Worth		100.0	100.0	100.0	100.0	100.0
			INCOME DATA						
100.0	100.0	100.0	Net Sales		100.0	100.0	100.0	100.0	100.0
21.3	23.3	25.5	Gross Profit		30.8	31.6	30.6	21.1	19.6
18.4	20.1	22.4	Operating Expenses		27.8	29.0	27.2	18.7	16.2
2.8	3.2	3.0	Operating Profit		3.0	2.6	3.3	2.4	3.3
.9	1.1	.6	All Other Expenses (net)		1.0	.8	.0	.1	.5
1.9	2.1	2.5	Profit Before Taxes		2.0	1.8	3.4	2.3	2.9
			RATIOS						
1.8	2.0	2.0	Current		2.0	1.4	3.3	2.2	1.7
1.4	1.3	1.4			1.3	1.3	1.8	1.4	1.2
1.1	1.1	1.1			1.1	1.1	1.3	1.2	1.0
1.2	1.1	1.1	Quick		1.2	1.1	1.8	1.2	1.1
.8	.8	.8			.9	.8	1.1	.9	.8
.6	.6	.6			.5	.5	.7	.7	.5
35 10.4	33 11.2	34 10.8	Sales/Receivables		33 11.1	38 9.6	30 12.3	36 10.1	33 10.9
46 8.0	41 8.9	43 8.5			41 8.9	43 8.5	41 8.9	44 8.4	47 7.8
57 6.4	55 6.6	59 6.2			79 4.6	52 7.0	52 7.0	64 5.7	58 6.3
18 20.4	24 15.3	28 13.1	Cost of Sales/Inventory		36 10.1	24 15.0	38 9.6	36 10.1	20 17.9
38 9.5	41 8.9	46 7.9			67 5.5	42 8.7	43 8.4	48 7.6	46 8.0
74 4.9	59 6.2	75 4.8			109 3.3	63 5.8	73 5.0	70 5.2	77 4.8
26 13.8	24 15.4	25 14.5	Cost of Sales/Payables		28 13.0	22 16.4	19 19.5	25 14.5	28 12.9
41 8.9	35 10.5	39 9.4			54 6.7	42 8.7	35 10.3	36 10.2	37 9.8
59 6.2	49 7.4	58 6.3			93 3.9	67 5.4	60 6.1	50 7.3	56 6.5
8.0	9.1	7.4	Sales/Working Capital		5.7	9.9	4.6	6.8	7.7
18.1	15.1	15.3			27.2	18.2	14.1	11.5	26.5
55.6	73.3	47.2			53.4	50.2	19.0	31.2	123.9
6.4	4.7	9.0	EBIT/Interest		3.4	6.5	15.4	7.3	18.7
(107) 2.9	(94) 2.5	(105) 4.2			(14) 1.2	4.1	(19) 6.8	(27) 4.2	(28) 4.9
1.7	1.1	1.2			-4.5	-.7	2.4	1.2	1.6
4.8	4.1	7.1	Net Profit + Depr., Dep., Amort./Cur. Mat. L/T/D						
(24) 2.2	(25) 2.3	(27) 3.2							
.9	.4	1.4							
.1	.1	.1	Fixed/Worth		.1	.6	.1	.1	.0
.3	.5	.4			.7	1.0	.3	.3	.3
1.1	2.1	1.1			NM	7.3	.7	.8	1.1
1.4	1.1	1.2	Debt/Worth		1.3	1.7	.6	.9	1.5
2.7	2.9	2.3			2.4	4.8	1.1	2.0	2.7
6.8	7.7	5.0			NM	44.1	2.8	4.7	7.0
56.8	54.7	46.9	% Profit Before Taxes/Tangible Net Worth		38.1	61.5	34.5	48.7	74.4
(117) 27.1	(95) 22.2	(108) 19.5			(13) 3.5	(12) 20.6	17.0	(30) 26.2	(30) 29.1
10.4	6.0	3.6			-20.4	-20.8	4.8	4.4	5.6
12.0	11.8	12.7	% Profit Before Taxes/Total Assets		5.7	13.1	15.2	11.8	17.5
5.7	5.2	5.0			.7	4.8	6.7	4.4	6.5
2.1	.8	.4			-4.8	-3.9	1.9	.4	1.4
251.1	131.0	130.4	Sales/Net Fixed Assets		203.6	54.7	63.9	165.6	634.2
48.2	33.8	32.4			20.9	18.7	32.0	58.6	42.0
14.2	9.8	9.7			11.8	9.6	9.8	9.7	9.0
4.2	4.2	3.9	Sales/Total Assets		4.2	3.8	4.1	4.3	4.2
3.1	3.0	3.0			2.7	3.1	3.0	2.9	3.0
2.3	2.2	2.3			2.0	2.7	2.3	2.2	2.3
.2	.3	.3	% Depr., Dep., Amort./Sales		.3	.9	.6	.2	.2
(93) .8	(88) .8	(101) 1.0			(13) .5	(14) 2.2	(20) 1.1	(26) .8	(26) .5
1.6	2.3	2.2			2.5	2.9	2.0	1.7	1.9
1.3	1.2	1.6	% Officers', Directors', Owners' Comp/Sales		3.4		1.7	1.4	
(62) 3.2	(45) 2.2	(59) 3.2			(10) 4.6		(13) 3.2	(18) 2.8	
5.7	5.3	5.7			7.1		5.1	4.8	
3539057M	4350616M	4533156M	Net Sales ($)	1072M	36252M	61271M	142594M	528255M	3763712M
1414313M	1742837M	1499030M	Total Assets ($)	370M	16611M	21161M	48890M	196336M	1215662M

M = $ thousand   MM = $ million
See Pages 11 through 18 for Explanation of Ratios and Data

WHOLESALE—Other Chemical and Allied Products Merchant Wholesalers NAICS 424690 (SIC 5169)

Current Data Sorted By Assets | **Comparative Historical Data**

Type of Statement	0-500M	500M-2MM	2-10MM	10-50MM	50-100MM	100-250MM	4/1/98-3/31/99 ALL	4/1/99-3/31/00 ALL
Unqualified		2	22	28	5	2	63	60
Reviewed	2	11	64	10	2		82	87
Compiled	6	21	15	1			70	60
Tax Returns	7	7					18	19
Other	7	16	37	20	2	5	61	66
		56 (4/1-9/30/02)		236 (10/1/02-3/31/03)				
NUMBER OF STATEMENTS	22	57	138	59	9	7	294	292

ASSETS	0-500M %	500M-2MM %	2-10MM %	10-50MM %	50-100MM %	100-250MM %	4/1/98-3/31/99 ALL %	4/1/99-3/31/00 ALL %
Cash & Equivalents	11.1	9.0	6.3	5.2			7.7	6.9
Trade Receivables (net)	40.3	38.4	38.4	34.4			39.0	37.8
Inventory	18.6	23.7	28.6	24.4			24.3	26.5
All Other Current	.9	1.7	2.8	2.3			1.9	2.0
Total Current	70.9	72.8	76.1	66.3			72.9	73.3
Fixed Assets (net)	19.3	18.1	16.9	24.7			18.9	18.5
Intangibles (net)	3.1	3.4	1.3	3.2			2.5	2.6
All Other Non-Current	6.7	5.7	5.7	5.8			5.6	5.6
Total	100.0	100.0	100.0	100.0			100.0	100.0

LIABILITIES	0-500M	500M-2MM	2-10MM	10-50MM	50-100MM	100-250MM	ALL	ALL
Notes Payable-Short Term	7.8	11.3	16.8	14.7			15.5	14.4
Cur. Mat.-L/T/D	4.5	6.4	2.4	2.0			2.4	2.4
Trade Payables	29.0	28.0	28.7	22.3			26.7	28.2
Income Taxes Payable	.0	.0	.3	.3			.3	.3
All Other Current	9.5	11.9	9.8	8.1			7.5	8.1
Total Current	50.7	57.7	58.0	47.5			52.4	53.4
Long Term Debt	12.1	12.1	5.9	9.6			11.8	9.6
Deferred Taxes	.0	.3	.1	.3			.2	.4
All Other Non-Current	.9	4.6	4.2	2.5			4.0	4.4
Net Worth	36.3	25.3	31.8	40.1			31.5	32.2
Total Liabilities & Net Worth	100.0	100.0	100.0	100.0			100.0	100.0

INCOME DATA	0-500M	500M-2MM	2-10MM	10-50MM	50-100MM	100-250MM	ALL	ALL
Net Sales	100.0	100.0	100.0	100.0			100.0	100.0
Gross Profit	37.3	32.0	24.2	26.3			26.9	28.8
Operating Expenses	34.4	29.7	21.0	22.2			23.9	25.1
Operating Profit	2.9	2.3	3.2	4.1			3.0	3.6
All Other Expenses (net)	1.0	.5	.4	.7			.6	.8
Profit Before Taxes	1.8	1.8	2.8	3.4			2.3	2.8

RATIOS	0-500M	500M-2MM	2-10MM	10-50MM	50-100MM	100-250MM	ALL	ALL
Current	2.8 / 1.3 / 1.0	2.0 / 1.3 / 1.0	1.7 / 1.3 / 1.1	2.2 / 1.3 / 1.1			2.0 / 1.4 / 1.1	2.0 / 1.4 / 1.1
Quick	2.0 / .8 / .6	1.3 / .9 / .6	1.1 / .8 / .5	1.3 / .9 / .6			1.3 / .9 / .6	1.2 / .9 / .6
Sales/Receivables	10 36.2 / 38 9.6 / 50 7.3	33 10.9 / 41 9.0 / 54 6.7	37 10.0 / 44 8.4 / 56 6.5	39 9.4 / 43 8.5 / 49 7.5			36 10.3 / 44 8.4 / 56 6.5	38 9.7 / 46 7.9 / 55 6.6
Cost of Sales/Inventory	0 UND / 22 16.6 / 60 6.1	14 25.5 / 37 9.8 / 64 5.7	25 14.7 / 42 8.6 / 72 5.0	31 11.9 / 43 8.5 / 73 5.0			19 18.9 / 39 9.5 / 68 5.4	26 14.2 / 45 8.1 / 66 5.5
Cost of Sales/Payables	12 31.6 / 40 9.2 / 57 6.4	20 18.4 / 44 8.4 / 64 5.7	30 12.0 / 44 8.3 / 60 6.0	25 14.8 / 42 8.7 / 57 6.4			25 14.8 / 38 9.6 / 56 6.5	31 11.7 / 44 8.2 / 59 6.2
Sales/Working Capital	7.8 / 19.5 / NM	8.8 / 20.6 / NM	8.6 / 17.7 / 77.0	6.6 / 15.7 / 53.8			8.8 / 15.7 / 66.4	7.7 / 14.5 / 51.5
EBIT/Interest	(15) 20.4 / 3.4 / -2.4	(49) 7.1 / 2.0 / 1.1	(120) 10.3 / 3.7 / 1.1	(54) 15.4 / 3.5 / 2.2			(266) 6.9 / 3.0 / 1.4	(255) 8.0 / 3.1 / 1.5
Net Profit + Depr., Dep., Amort./Cur. Mat. L/T/D		(11) 2.5 / 1.3 / 1.0	(37) 11.3 / 5.0 / 1.5	(20) 10.0 / 5.3 / 1.5			(79) 7.5 / 3.5 / 1.7	(91) 9.3 / 3.4 / 1.3
Fixed/Worth	.0 / .4 / 1.7	.1 / .3 / 3.9	.1 / .3 / 1.1	.2 / .6 / 1.0			.1 / .4 / 1.3	.1 / .4 / 1.2
Debt/Worth	.6 / 2.4 / 6.3	1.0 / 2.9 / 22.3	1.2 / 2.3 / 5.0	.8 / 2.0 / 3.7			1.0 / 2.4 / 5.1	1.0 / 2.2 / 6.2
% Profit Before Taxes/Tangible Net Worth	(19) 78.9 / 11.9 / -5.4	(48) 32.5 / 11.5 / 1.8	(128) 41.8 / 16.3 / 5.1	(57) 28.9 / 18.5 / 6.9			(264) 40.6 / 18.4 / 6.4	(261) 40.0 / 19.0 / 6.8
% Profit Before Taxes/Total Assets	36.6 / 2.6 / -4.0	8.0 / 3.0 / .2	11.9 / 4.6 / 1.4	10.9 / 6.0 / 1.5			12.1 / 5.4 / 1.1	12.3 / 5.2 / 1.7
Sales/Net Fixed Assets	999.8 / 26.3 / 15.6	118.7 / 26.3 / 11.8	150.7 / 31.1 / 9.9	45.7 / 12.7 / 5.3			120.2 / 27.8 / 9.2	84.2 / 27.3 / 8.4
Sales/Total Assets	4.8 / 3.7 / 2.9	4.5 / 3.2 / 2.4	3.8 / 3.1 / 2.2	3.4 / 2.5 / 1.8			4.1 / 3.2 / 2.1	3.9 / 3.0 / 2.0
% Depr., Dep., Amort./Sales	(16) .3 / 1.1 / 3.3	(45) .5 / 1.2 / 2.6	(125) .2 / .7 / 1.9	(55) .7 / 1.5 / 3.1			(253) .3 / 1.0 / 2.1	(255) .4 / 1.0 / 2.3
% Officers', Directors', Owners' Comp/Sales		(28) 3.2 / 5.6 / 8.8	(61) 1.2 / 2.4 / 4.5	(11) 1.2 / 2.1 / 2.7			(127) 2.1 / 3.4 / 6.2	(116) 1.4 / 3.8 / 6.9
Net Sales ($)	28746M	235447M	2066842M	2966514M	1027438M	2705323M	5318614M	6297743M
Total Assets ($)	6124M	69773M	679777M	1216012M	600642M	1056938M	2342539M	2639541M

© RMA 2003

M = $ thousand   MM = $ million
See Pages 11 through 18 for Explanation of Ratios and Data

Comparative Historical Data / Current Data Sorted By Sales

			Type of Statement						
47	49	59	Unqualified		1	6	11	41	
72	70	89	Reviewed	1	3	6	17	43	19
82	62	43	Compiled	4	11	7	11	9	1
17	13	14	Tax Returns	2	7	4	1		
73	75	87	Other	4	13	10	19	14	27
4/1/00- 3/31/01	4/1/01- 3/31/02	4/1/02- 3/31/03			56 (4/1-9/30/02)		236 (10/1/02-3/31/03)		
ALL	ALL	ALL		0-1MM	1-3MM	3-5MM	5-10MM	10-25MM	25MM & OVER
291	269	292	**NUMBER OF STATEMENTS**	11	34	28	54	77	88
%	%	%	**ASSETS**	%	%	%	%	%	%
7.8	7.3	7.0	Cash & Equivalents	6.1	10.5	7.6	8.7	6.6	5.0
39.1	38.2	37.3	Trade Receivables (net)	27.8	32.3	37.1	38.2	40.1	37.7
26.4	26.5	25.7	Inventory	25.1	22.9	24.1	24.1	27.4	26.9
1.8	2.1	2.3	All Other Current	.8	3.8	1.9	1.4	2.5	2.5
75.2	74.0	72.4	Total Current	59.9	69.5	70.6	72.4	76.5	72.0
16.8	17.7	19.3	Fixed Assets (net)	25.2	18.8	25.8	18.0	17.0	19.6
2.5	2.7	2.6	Intangibles (net)	4.2	5.0	1.0	1.9	1.1	3.6
5.5	5.5	5.7	All Other Non-Current	10.8	6.7	2.6	7.7	5.4	4.8
100.0	100.0	100.0	Total	100.0	100.0	100.0	100.0	100.0	100.0
			LIABILITIES						
15.2	15.8	14.2	Notes Payable-Short Term	12.0	8.4	12.5	15.2	16.5	14.5
2.7	2.8	3.4	Cur. Mat.-L/T/D	3.2	6.2	6.3	3.5	2.0	2.5
27.8	28.3	26.7	Trade Payables	21.2	27.1	26.2	27.4	29.0	25.0
.2	.3	.3	Income Taxes Payable	.1	.1	.1	.3	.2	.4
8.7	7.8	10.1	All Other Current	12.5	8.8	11.2	12.5	8.5	9.9
54.6	55.0	54.6	Total Current	49.0	50.6	56.4	58.9	56.3	52.2
9.0	8.8	8.8	Long Term Debt	20.0	13.2	14.1	5.9	5.6	8.5
.3	.3	.2	Deferred Taxes	.0	.2	.4	.1	.1	.4
3.4	3.3	3.7	All Other Non-Current	.2	6.0	2.1	3.6	5.5	2.2
32.7	32.7	32.8	Net Worth	30.8	30.1	27.1	31.5	32.6	36.8
100.0	100.0	100.0	Total Liabilities & Net Worth	100.0	100.0	100.0	100.0	100.0	100.0
			INCOME DATA						
100.0	100.0	100.0	Net Sales	100.0	100.0	100.0	100.0	100.0	100.0
27.7	27.3	27.2	Gross Profit	37.1	38.5	29.6	29.0	24.8	22.0
24.2	23.8	23.9	Operating Expenses	32.9	36.0	27.6	25.8	21.0	18.2
3.5	3.5	3.4	Operating Profit	4.2	2.5	1.9	3.3	3.8	3.7
.5	.6	.6	All Other Expenses (net)	2.0	.6	1.1	.3	.4	.5
3.0	3.0	2.8	Profit Before Taxes	2.1	1.9	.9	2.9	3.3	3.2
			RATIOS						
1.9	1.9	1.9		1.9	2.6	2.4	1.7	1.9	1.9
1.3	1.3	1.3	Current	1.3	1.3	1.4	1.3	1.4	1.3
1.1	1.1	1.1		.8	1.0	1.1	.9	1.1	1.1
1.2	1.2	1.2		1.1	1.4	1.5	1.1	1.3	1.1
.8	.8	.8	Quick	.7	.9	1.0	.8	.8	.8
.6	.6	.6		.3	.6	.6	.5	.6	.6
39 9.4	34 10.8	36 10.1		12 29.2	26 14.0	37 10.0	36 10.1	37 9.8	38 9.5
47 7.7	43 8.5	43 8.5	Sales/Receivables	49 7.5	36 10.1	45 8.1	45 8.2	43 8.5	43 8.4
57 6.4	52 7.0	55 6.7		50 7.2	56 6.6	61 6.0	60 6.1	49 7.5	53 6.9
23 15.7	20 18.4	23 15.7		15 25.0	11 32.0	19 19.4	16 23.4	26 13.9	26 13.9
46 8.0	44 8.3	42 8.8	Cost of Sales/Inventory	49 7.4	50 7.3	47 7.7	36 10.1	38 9.7	42 8.7
72 5.1	74 5.0	71 5.2		61 6.0	75 4.9	80 4.6	82 4.4	61 6.0	69 5.3
28 13.0	26 13.8	26 13.9		22 16.4	18 20.0	24 15.4	29 12.5	29 12.6	26 14.0
44 8.3	39 9.4	43 8.5	Cost of Sales/Payables	45 8.1	42 8.6	52 7.1	45 8.1	39 9.4	41 8.9
62 5.9	62 5.9	57 6.4		68 5.3	69 5.3	65 5.6	78 4.7	51 7.1	51 7.1
8.0	9.2	8.4		7.3	6.2	6.3	10.3	8.6	9.1
15.5	18.6	16.5	Sales/Working Capital	22.2	18.4	12.4	18.1	18.0	16.4
66.5	68.3	70.5		−15.4	NM	41.7	−57.6	54.9	45.2
	8.0	10.3			4.3	6.7	13.5	11.1	12.6
(268) 3.0	(249) 2.7	(252) 3.4	EBIT/Interest	(28) 1.4	2.0	(45) 5.1	(63) 3.6	(81) 4.0
1.3	1.5	1.6			.3	1.0	2.0	1.4	2.0
	5.9	9.7	6.9	Net Profit + Depr., Dep.,			9.4	12.2	7.2
(74) 2.6	(69) 2.8	(74) 3.2	Amort./Cur. Mat. L/T/D	(11) 2.5	(21) 5.0	(32) 4.3
.8	1.6	1.4				1.1	1.2	1.6
.1	.1	.1		.1	.0	.1	.1	.1	.1
.3	.5	.4	Fixed/Worth	1.0	.4	.7	.4	.3	.5
1.3	1.2	1.2		−2.2	3.3	1.4	1.3	1.0	1.0
1.0	1.1	1.0		.2	.8	.9	1.1	1.1	.9
2.6	2.4	2.3	Debt/Worth	3.0	3.3	2.3	2.1	2.3	2.3
6.5	6.1	5.5		−13.4	23.4	6.2	4.8	5.3	4.4
45.7	43.7	34.4			38.4	20.2	51.1	35.8	30.7
(265) 18.5	(243) 19.3	(267) 16.9	% Profit Before Taxes/Tangible Net Worth	(27) 9.5	(26) 11.1	(50) 15.1	(71) 21.4	(85) 20.4
4.5	6.2	5.3		.2	.0	5.6	7.2	9.8
11.7	13.5	11.0		26.4	9.4	6.1	10.1	14.4	10.7
5.7	5.2	4.7	% Profit Before Taxes/Total Assets	1.5	1.4	2.5	4.6	4.8	6.6
1.1	1.0	1.0		−.8	−2.4	.0	1.9	1.3	1.6
133.7	115.2	121.5		50.4	651.4	80.5	78.8	193.3	158.4
32.5	26.3	22.8	Sales/Net Fixed Assets	19.3	23.7	14.8	18.6	40.9	23.7
8.8	9.7	8.5		9.7	9.4	7.2	11.3	7.7	7.5
3.8	4.1	3.8		3.7	4.4	3.8	3.5	4.0	3.6
3.0	3.1	3.0	Sales/Total Assets	2.9	3.3	2.9	2.8	3.3	3.0
1.9	2.0	2.1		1.4	2.1	1.7	2.0	2.4	1.9
.3	.3	.3			.3	.8	.5	.2	.3
(248) .9	(224) .9	(254) 1.1	% Depr., Dep., Amort./Sales	(26) 1.6	(24) 2.4	(45) 1.0	(72) .7	(79) 1.1
2.1	2.3	2.4		2.9	3.5	2.3	1.8	2.0
2.2	2.1	1.6			3.2	2.0	2.3	1.1	.6
(117) 3.8	(97) 3.6	(108) 3.0	% Officers', Directors', Owners' Comp/Sales	(14) 5.0	(13) 4.4	(22) 5.1	(41) 2.4	(15) 2.1
6.7	5.7	5.8		7.6	6.2	6.8	3.9	3.0
5966497M	7543428M	9030310M	Net Sales ($)	5786M	70073M	118047M	393419M	1266395M	7176590M
2529317M	3596464M	3629266M	Total Assets ($)	3619M	26450M	50997M	159978M	452956M	2935266M

M = $ thousand   MM = $ million
See Pages 11 through 18 for Explanation of Ratios and Data

Current Data Sorted By Assets　　　　　　　Comparative Historical Data

Type of Statement	0-500M	500M-2MM	2-10MM	10-50MM	50-100MM	100-250MM		4/1/98-3/31/99 ALL	4/1/99-3/31/00 ALL
Unqualified			10	23	4	4		60	53
Reviewed		8	61	24	1			105	119
Compiled	4	25	46	13				120	96
Tax Returns	1	5	6		1			14	17
Other	2	6	27	29	1	1		80	68
	108 (4/1-9/30/02)			194 (10/1/02-3/31/03)					
NUMBER OF STATEMENTS	7	44	150	89	7	5		379	353

	0-500M %	500M-2MM %	2-10MM %	10-50MM %	50-100MM %	100-250MM %		ALL %	ALL %
ASSETS									
Cash & Equivalents		7.0	9.5	7.0				9.4	9.1
Trade Receivables (net)		35.0	27.9	23.2				23.2	25.6
Inventory		15.2	13.0	10.1				12.8	12.9
All Other Current		3.3	3.8	4.3				2.4	3.6
Total Current		60.5	54.2	44.6				47.8	51.1
Fixed Assets (net)		30.7	36.6	43.8				41.7	39.9
Intangibles (net)		.9	1.9	3.5				2.6	2.7
All Other Non-Current		7.8	7.2	8.1				7.9	6.2
Total		100.0	100.0	100.0				100.0	100.0
LIABILITIES									
Notes Payable-Short Term		13.5	8.5	6.8				7.4	7.8
Cur. Mat.-L/T/D		3.5	4.9	4.4				4.2	3.8
Trade Payables		24.6	24.3	19.9				18.8	21.0
Income Taxes Payable		.2	.2	.1				.3	.2
All Other Current		9.6	6.6	7.2				7.7	9.0
Total Current		51.4	44.4	38.4				38.4	42.0
Long Term Debt		17.3	19.6	24.6				22.1	20.3
Deferred Taxes		.1	.4	1.1				.8	1.0
All Other Non-Current		4.9	2.1	1.8				3.4	2.8
Net Worth		26.4	33.5	34.0				35.3	33.9
Total Liabilities & Net Worth		100.0	100.0	100.0				100.0	100.0
INCOME DATA									
Net Sales		100.0	100.0	100.0				100.0	100.0
Gross Profit		14.3	12.4	13.0				17.2	18.6
Operating Expenses		13.8	12.1	12.9				15.8	17.6
Operating Profit		.5	.3	.1				1.4	1.0
All Other Expenses (net)		.1	-.2	-.3				-.2	-.4
Profit Before Taxes		.4	.5	.4				1.6	1.4
RATIOS									
Current		1.8 / 1.2 / .9	1.5 / 1.2 / 1.0	1.5 / 1.1 / .8				1.6 / 1.2 / .9	1.7 / 1.2 / .9
Quick		1.3 / .9 / .5	1.1 / .8 / .6	1.1 / .7 / .5				1.2 / .8 / .5	1.2 / .8 / .6
Sales/Receivables		14 25.4 / 23 15.7 / 32 11.3	12 30.8 / 18 20.2 / 26 14.2	10 34.9 / 16 22.5 / 22 16.3				9 38.5 / 16 22.5 / 28 13.1	12 29.4 / 22 16.8 / 32 11.5
Cost of Sales/Inventory		6 63.1 / 9 41.4 / 15 23.6	5 67.0 / 10 38.0 / 16 23.0	5 72.2 / 9 40.7 / 14 25.5				6 59.2 / 11 33.5 / 18 20.3	7 55.8 / 12 30.4 / 23 16.2
Cost of Sales/Payables		10 36.8 / 16 23.0 / 24 15.5	14 25.9 / 18 20.5 / 23 15.6	13 28.4 / 17 21.3 / 23 15.7				12 29.6 / 17 21.1 / 23 15.5	15 25.0 / 20 17.8 / 29 12.6
Sales/Working Capital		20.0 / 58.5 / -370.5	25.5 / 60.0 / 999.8	23.4 / 148.3 / -66.0				20.9 / 81.8 / -178.3	18.1 / 54.6 / -121.6
EBIT/Interest		(40) 3.1 / .1 / -3.3	(141) 4.0 / 2.0 / .9	(87) 5.7 / 2.3 / .9				(362) 5.1 / 2.3 / 1.4	(323) 4.8 / 2.4 / 1.2
Net Profit + Depr., Dep., Amort./Cur. Mat. L /T/D			(53) 3.2 / 2.3 / 1.0	(39) 5.7 / 1.9 / 1.2				(160) 3.7 / 2.1 / 1.3	(131) 4.4 / 2.6 / 1.2
Fixed/Worth		.5 / 1.0 / 3.8	.7 / 1.0 / 1.8	.8 / 1.5 / 2.5				.7 / 1.3 / 2.5	.7 / 1.2 / 2.6
Debt/Worth		.9 / 2.9 / 14.0	1.1 / 2.4 / 4.1	1.4 / 2.7 / 4.5				1.1 / 2.0 / 4.0	1.1 / 2.1 / 4.7
% Profit Before Taxes/Tangible Net Worth		(37) 16.0 / .8 / -23.6	(144) 16.9 / 6.2 / .1	(88) 20.9 / 8.8 / -.9				(353) 23.8 / 12.3 / 4.9	(323) 22.8 / 10.1 / 2.8
% Profit Before Taxes/Total Assets		3.2 / -2.9 / -8.2	5.0 / 2.1 / -.3	6.3 / 2.5 / -.3				8.0 / 3.8 / 1.5	7.4 / 3.4 / .5
Sales/Net Fixed Assets		48.5 / 26.6 / 8.8	29.0 / 14.5 / 8.2	17.1 / 9.6 / 6.2				22.2 / 10.8 / 6.0	21.9 / 10.3 / 5.2
Sales/Total Assets		7.7 / 5.6 / 3.6	6.7 / 5.1 / 3.6	5.4 / 4.6 / 3.3				5.8 / 4.2 / 3.0	5.4 / 3.9 / 2.6
% Depr., Dep., Amort./Sales		(41) .7 / 1.1 / 1.6	(144) .8 / 1.2 / 1.9	(86) .9 / 1.5 / 2.3				(366) .9 / 1.5 / 2.2	(338) .9 / 1.6 / 2.5
% Officers', Directors', Owners' Comp/Sales		(22) .9 / 1.8 / 2.3	(64) .5 / .7 / 1.2	(24) .2 / .4 / .6				(170) .7 / 1.1 / 2.0	(145) .6 / 1.0 / 1.9
Net Sales ($)	9072M	371148M	4028814M	8895421M	1734235M	1961610M		13341760M	14503134M
Total Assets ($)	1890M	55792M	732652M	1837204M	439027M	787906M		3576319M	3867142M

M = $ thousand   MM = $ million
See Pages 11 through 18 for Explanation of Ratios and Data

Comparative Historical Data | Current Data Sorted By Sales

			Type of Statement						
51	44	41	Unqualified				1	7	33
92	83	94	Reviewed		2		13	33	46
87	104	88	Compiled	1	7	7	13	28	32
17	18	13	Tax Returns		2		3	6	2
82	77	66	Other	1	5	1	5	15	43
4/1/00- 3/31/01 ALL	4/1/01- 3/31/02 ALL	4/1/02- 3/31/03 ALL		0-1MM	108 (4/1-9/30/02) 1-3MM	3-5MM	5-10MM	194 (10/1/02-3/31/03) 10-25MM	25MM & OVER
329	326	302	**NUMBER OF STATEMENTS**	2	12	8	35	89	156
%	%	%	**ASSETS**	%	%	%	%	%	%
8.5	9.3	8.4	Cash & Equivalents		5.0		5.7	9.5	8.3
28.2	24.8	27.2	Trade Receivables (net)		20.1		27.7	28.0	26.8
12.7	12.3	12.7	Inventory		18.1		12.7	13.7	11.0
2.9	4.2	3.9	All Other Current		2.6		4.6	3.1	4.2
52.4	50.6	52.2	Total Current		45.9		50.7	54.4	50.4
37.5	38.6	37.8	Fixed Assets (net)		40.7		35.9	37.6	39.2
3.0	3.1	2.4	Intangibles (net)		3.5		2.6	1.2	3.0
7.1	7.7	7.6	All Other Non-Current		10.0		10.8	6.8	7.4
100.0	100.0	100.0	Total		100.0		100.0	100.0	100.0
			LIABILITIES						
8.8	9.2	9.0	Notes Payable-Short Term		20.5		10.6	8.0	7.9
4.2	4.5	4.5	Cur. Mat.-L/T/D		6.7		5.1	4.6	4.4
22.9	19.4	22.6	Trade Payables		15.7		17.2	23.4	23.9
.2	.2	.2	Income Taxes Payable		.4		.1	.2	.1
7.3	8.6	7.3	All Other Current		4.4		8.1	7.0	7.2
43.4	41.9	43.5	Total Current		47.7		41.1	43.2	43.6
20.0	22.3	21.2	Long Term Debt		38.1		16.5	20.7	21.8
.6	.7	.6	Deferred Taxes		.0		.4	.5	.8
2.5	2.4	2.5	All Other Non-Current		9.3		2.9	2.9	1.8
33.4	32.7	32.2	Net Worth		4.9		39.2	32.7	32.1
100.0	100.0	100.0	Total Liabilities & Net Worth		100.0		100.0	100.0	100.0
			INCOME DATA						
100.0	100.0	100.0	Net Sales		100.0		100.0	100.0	100.0
13.6	15.3	13.1	Gross Profit		19.3		20.6	12.3	11.3
13.3	14.1	12.9	Operating Expenses		22.8		19.9	11.9	10.9
.4	1.1	.2	Operating Profit		−3.5		.8	.3	.4
−.2	.0	−.2	All Other Expenses (net)		−1.8		−.2	−.1	−.3
.6	1.1	.5	Profit Before Taxes		−1.7		1.0	.4	.7
			RATIOS						
1.5	1.8	1.6			1.5		1.8	1.7	1.5
1.2	1.3	1.2	Current		1.2		1.4	1.3	1.1
.9	1.0	1.0			.8		1.0	1.0	.9
1.1	1.3	1.1			.8		1.2	1.2	1.1
.8	.8	.8	Quick		.5		.9	.9	.7
.6	.5	.6			.4		.6	.6	.5
11 33.8	10 35.8	12 31.5		10 36.0		13 27.3	12 30.7	11 33.8	
19 18.9	16 23.0	18 20.0	Sales/Receivables	19 19.6		24 15.3	19 19.6	17 21.5	
30 12.0	25 14.4	27 13.4		31 11.9		39 9.3	29 12.5	23 15.7	
5 70.3	5 68.1	6 65.7		9 38.7		8 48.1	6 57.7	4 91.8	
10 37.9	9 41.3	9 38.8	Cost of Sales/Inventory	17 22.1		15 24.2	10 37.5	8 46.4	
16 22.3	15 24.3	16 23.1		32 11.3		27 13.3	16 23.5	14 26.2	
13 27.1	10 36.5	13 28.0		7 53.9		14 25.2	14 25.4	13 28.6	
18 20.7	14 25.5	18 20.7	Cost of Sales/Payables	11 32.4		21 17.5	18 20.4	17 22.0	
24 15.5	20 17.8	24 15.3		42 8.7		27 13.3	24 15.3	23 16.0	
25.4	19.1	22.5		20.2		12.9	21.3	31.5	
64.6	48.7	73.3	Sales/Working Capital	65.8		27.3	46.5	137.9	
−175.5	−310.4	−251.1		−49.6		−999.8	NM	−169.3	
4.4	5.1	4.2		1.7		3.3	3.7	5.0	
(312) 2.0	(314) 2.0	(285) 1.9	EBIT/Interest	(10) −.3		(32) 1.3	(84) 1.7	(152) 2.4	
1.1	1.0	.5		−1.3		−1.1	.1	1.1	
5.0	3.2	3.5	Net Profit + Depr., Dep.,			4.3	2.9	4.5	
(129) 2.2	(105) 1.8	(107) 2.1	Amort./Cur. Mat. L/T/D			(15) .6	(29) 2.1	(61) 1.9	
1.1	.9	1.0				.2	1.0	1.2	
.7	.6	.7		.6		.4	.6	.7	
1.3	1.2	1.2	Fixed/Worth	NM		1.0	1.0	1.3	
2.5	2.8	2.4		−1.1		2.2	2.5	2.1	
1.3	1.0	1.1		1.6		.9	1.1	1.4	
2.4	2.3	2.4	Debt/Worth	NM		1.5	2.4	2.6	
4.6	5.3	4.5		−3.4		4.1	4.5	4.4	
20.3	21.0	18.6	% Profit Before Taxes/Tangible			18.3	14.5	20.2	
(304) 9.3	(292) 10.1	(285) 6.2	Net Worth			(33) 4.0	(84) 4.6	(153) 9.5	
1.6	1.8	−2.8				−11.1	−5.0	1.8	
7.1	7.2	5.2	% Profit Before Taxes/Total		2.3		5.0	4.2	5.8	
2.6	2.8	1.9	Assets		−5.1		.7	1.5	2.5	
.1	.1	−1.6			−15.3		−4.9	−2.1	.4	
28.3	30.0	29.0			33.2		24.5	27.4	29.8	
12.8	12.6	12.8	Sales/Net Fixed Assets		10.2		9.1	13.3	13.5	
7.2	7.1	7.3			5.3		5.1	7.4	7.9	
6.7	7.1	6.5			5.4		5.0	6.5	7.0	
4.7	4.9	4.8	Sales/Total Assets		3.9		3.5	4.9	5.1	
3.2	3.4	3.5			2.6		2.4	3.5	3.8	
.7	.7	.8		1.5		1.2	.9	.7	
(312) 1.3	(312) 1.2	(288) 1.3	% Depr., Dep., Amort./Sales	(11) 1.9		(33) 1.6	(87) 1.2	(149) 1.2	
2.0	1.9	1.9		2.8		2.5	1.9	1.8	
.4	.5	.4	% Officers', Directors',			.9	.5	.3	
(134) .9	(124) .8	(114) .7	Owners' Comp/Sales	(14) 1.6		(44) .7	(47) .5	
1.8	1.8	1.7			3.4		1.4	.8	
18895336M	16865574M	17000300M	Net Sales ($)	1105M	24019M	32691M	259732M	1490543M	15192210M
4097681M	3945537M	3854471M	Total Assets ($)	169M	6840M	8869M	144259M	347112M	3347222M

© RMA 2003

M = $ thousand   MM = $ million
See Pages 11 through 18 for Explanation of Ratios and Data

Current Data Sorted By Assets **Comparative Historical Data**

						Type of Statement		
1	5	22	42	12	9	Unqualified	89	94
2	18	103	45			Reviewed	161	163
6	36	71	13	2		Compiled	149	134
8	9	11	1			Tax Returns	20	21
8	30	59	54	6	8	Other	121	102
	177 (4/1-9/30/02)		404 (10/1/02-3/31/03)				4/1/98-3/31/99	4/1/99-3/31/00
0-500M	500M-2MM	2-10MM	10-50MM	50-100MM	100-250MM		ALL	ALL
25	98	266	155	20	17	NUMBER OF STATEMENTS	540	514
%	%	%	%	%	%	ASSETS	%	%
13.2	12.1	9.2	7.5	4.8	4.8	Cash & Equivalents	10.2	8.5
30.4	37.1	30.7	26.6	30.0	30.3	Trade Receivables (net)	24.4	28.7
16.9	14.5	13.4	10.9	11.1	15.7	Inventory	12.9	12.7
3.1	2.2	3.1	4.6	4.8	1.8	All Other Current	2.8	2.6
63.5	66.0	56.4	49.6	50.7	52.6	Total Current	50.3	52.6
28.0	23.9	32.7	38.1	33.4	29.3	Fixed Assets (net)	38.2	37.0
5.6	2.7	2.4	3.4	7.8	11.2	Intangibles (net)	2.9	2.8
2.9	7.4	8.4	8.9	8.1	6.8	All Other Non-Current	8.6	7.6
100.0	100.0	100.0	100.0	100.0	100.0	Total	100.0	100.0
						LIABILITIES		
7.2	10.9	10.3	9.8	9.2	9.6	Notes Payable-Short Term	7.6	8.8
4.0	3.8	4.3	4.2	2.6	1.9	Cur. Mat.-L/T/D	4.2	4.0
20.6	26.7	24.0	23.6	29.4	18.7	Trade Payables	20.2	23.2
.1	.1	.3	.3	.3	.3	Income Taxes Payable	.3	.2
4.6	10.7	7.3	8.0	12.0	11.5	All Other Current	8.7	7.9
36.5	52.2	46.2	45.9	53.5	42.0	Total Current	41.0	44.2
25.1	11.7	18.0	22.5	18.5	23.6	Long Term Debt	20.1	19.8
.0	.2	.5	1.1	1.5	1.7	Deferred Taxes	.7	.8
9.8	3.8	2.8	3.0	3.1	6.7	All Other Non-Current	2.7	3.2
28.6	31.9	32.6	27.6	23.4	26.0	Net Worth	35.5	31.9
100.0	100.0	100.0	100.0	100.0	100.0	Total Liabilities & Net Worth	100.0	100.0
						INCOME DATA		
100.0	100.0	100.0	100.0	100.0	100.0	Net Sales	100.0	100.0
24.9	17.1	14.6	14.2	13.9	12.1	Gross Profit	17.6	17.4
23.9	16.1	13.8	12.8	11.5	9.8	Operating Expenses	16.2	16.2
1.0	1.1	.8	1.4	2.4	2.3	Operating Profit	1.4	1.2
.4	.2	-.2	.1	1.4	1.4	All Other Expenses (net)	-.1	-.1
.6	.8	.9	1.4	1.0	.9	Profit Before Taxes	1.5	1.3
						RATIOS		
3.0	1.9	1.6	1.4	1.4	1.3	Current	1.6	1.6
2.0	1.3	1.2	1.1	1.1	1.1		1.2	1.1
1.1	1.0	.9	.8	.8	.9		.9	.9
2.2	1.5	1.1	1.0	.8	1.0	Quick	1.2	1.1
1.1	1.0	.8	.7	.7	.7		.8	.8
.7	.6	.6	.5	.5	.6		.5	.5
4 92.2	13 29.1	12 30.2	11 31.9	17 21.8	16 22.8	Sales/Receivables	10 37.3	12 29.4
21 17.4	25 14.4	23 15.9	19 18.7	24 15.3	30 12.2		18 20.3	24 15.3
41 9.0	41 8.9	34 10.8	32 11.3	27 13.4	45 8.0		30 12.2	37 9.9
3 145.2	2 241.9	3 107.6	4 87.5	5 71.4	7 51.3	Cost of Sales/Inventory	5 66.6	5 70.8
9 40.2	9 41.1	9 42.4	9 42.5	10 37.5	12 30.2		11 34.2	11 33.4
32 11.6	26 14.2	21 17.0	15 23.8	17 21.8	19 19.4		19 19.6	20 18.0
3 110.3	11 34.4	13 28.7	14 25.7	17 21.2	17 21.8	Cost of Sales/Payables	12 30.6	16 23.4
17 21.0	17 21.9	19 18.8	20 18.5	26 14.1	19 19.0		18 20.2	22 16.6
25 14.7	31 11.8	28 13.1	29 12.8	32 11.4	34 10.8		26 14.2	32 11.3
14.1	14.7	19.5	29.9	30.8	33.9	Sales/Working Capital	21.3	19.3
23.4	38.6	64.2	165.2	168.6	83.2		70.6	85.5
72.4	-178.8	-183.5	-66.1	-54.7	NM		-111.4	-77.8
(20) 6.0	(81) 5.4	(251) 4.7	(149) 4.8	(19) 10.0	(16) 2.5	EBIT/Interest	(495) 5.1	(477) 4.7
2.7	2.0	2.1	2.1	3.6	2.0		2.3	2.2
-.4	-.3	1.1	1.3	1.4	1.1		1.4	1.1
	(27) 1.8	(87) 4.4	(70) 4.1			Net Profit + Depr., Dep., Amort./Cur. Mat. L /T/D	(226) 3.8	(195) 3.5
	1.1	1.8	2.3				2.1	2.0
	.2	1.1	1.3				1.3	1.1
.3	.3	.5	.8	1.0	.1	Fixed/Worth	.6	.5
.8	.8	1.1	1.8	1.8	2.0		1.2	1.4
4.6	2.4	2.1	3.0	11.2	3.1		2.5	2.8
.8	.8	1.3	1.8	1.9	3.1	Debt/Worth	1.1	1.2
1.8	1.8	2.5	3.4	3.9	3.8		2.2	2.7
18.1	10.2	4.6	8.0	22.2	9.2		4.3	5.4
(21) 62.2	(79) 28.4	(254) 20.9	(147) 33.2	(17) 49.6	(15) 21.3	% Profit Before Taxes/Tangible Net Worth	(508) 26.6	(474) 28.0
20.5	7.3	10.0	13.2	14.9	16.8		13.6	12.7
-5.2	.5	1.4	3.5	5.8	2.2		4.2	2.4
17.8	8.0	5.5	5.8	10.1	4.5	% Profit Before Taxes/Total Assets	8.6	7.6
5.6	2.5	2.8	2.9	4.7	3.1		4.0	3.5
-5.0	-2.1	.3	.8	1.6	.7		1.3	.5
60.9	68.2	39.0	26.2	40.7	548.2	Sales/Net Fixed Assets	27.4	30.6
19.9	29.8	14.4	12.3	12.5	10.9		11.7	11.5
13.0	14.1	8.0	6.7	3.9	5.8		6.2	5.5
7.8	8.2	6.7	6.1	7.3	5.6	Sales/Total Assets	6.1	5.5
4.6	4.9	4.5	4.2	4.3	2.8		4.2	3.8
3.8	3.3	3.1	2.9	2.0	2.1		3.0	2.6
(19) .8	(86) .6	(256) .6	(147) .8	(17) .7	(12) .7	% Depr., Dep., Amort./Sales	(510) .9	(474) .8
2.0	1.2	1.2	1.3	1.4	1.9		1.5	1.5
3.0	1.7	1.9	1.8	3.3	3.1		2.2	2.4
	(47) .7	(121) .5	(37) .2			% Officers', Directors', Owners' Comp/Sales	(232) .7	(201) .7
	1.4	1.0	.4				1.4	1.4
	2.6	2.1	.9				3.2	3.9
43473M	838721M	6828721M	15532883M	6180619M	9492438M	Net Sales ($)	22783211M	24498625M
7884M	124438M	1296855M	3301782M	1300562M	2470570M	Total Assets ($)	5405377M	6854350M

© RMA 2003

M = $ thousand   MM = $ million
See Pages 11 through 18 for Explanation of Ratios and Data

Comparative Historical Data | Current Data Sorted By Sales

Current data columns: **177 (4/1-9/30/02)** covers 0-1MM / 1-3MM / 3-5MM; **404 (10/1/02-3/31/03)** covers 5-10MM / 10-25MM / 25MM & OVER.

4/1/00-3/31/01 ALL	4/1/01-3/31/02 ALL	4/1/02-3/31/03 ALL	Type of Statement	0-1MM	1-3MM	3-5MM	5-10MM	10-25MM	25MM & OVER
81	83	91	Unqualified	1	1	1	3	16	69
137	139	168	Reviewed	2	1	11	21	51	82
141	143	128	Compiled		17	10	24	38	39
33	21	29	Tax Returns	3	6	1	5	8	6
128	103	165	Other	2	12	7	20	27	97
520	489	581	**NUMBER OF STATEMENTS**	8	37	30	73	140	293
%	%	%	**ASSETS**	%	%	%	%	%	%
8.2	8.7	9.1	Cash & Equivalents		10.9	12.9	7.2	10.0	8.6
32.0	28.7	30.6	Trade Receivables (net)		24.2	27.9	34.0	30.7	31.0
13.3	13.1	13.1	Inventory		12.5	19.2	15.3	15.2	10.6
2.6	3.6	3.4	All Other Current		2.8	4.3	3.0	3.3	3.6
56.0	54.1	56.2	Total Current		50.4	64.2	59.5	59.2	53.8
33.1	34.2	32.4	Fixed Assets (net)		36.7	27.9	28.7	31.0	34.0
3.4	2.6	3.3	Intangibles (net)		5.1	1.3	4.0	1.8	3.8
7.5	9.2	8.1	All Other Non-Current		7.7	6.6	7.8	8.0	8.5
100.0	100.0	100.0	Total		100.0	100.0	100.0	100.0	100.0
			LIABILITIES						
10.8	9.4	10.0	Notes Payable-Short Term		9.4	12.6	10.2	10.9	9.5
4.5	4.2	4.0	Cur. Mat.-L/T/D		4.1	4.2	4.7	3.9	3.9
25.5	22.2	24.3	Trade Payables		17.0	15.0	24.5	23.4	26.5
.3	.3	.2	Income Taxes Payable		.2	.1	.2	.2	.3
7.5	8.1	8.2	All Other Current		6.9	9.2	8.5	6.9	8.9
48.6	44.2	46.8	Total Current		37.5	41.0	48.1	45.3	49.2
18.4	20.4	18.6	Long Term Debt		27.5	17.7	15.7	15.7	19.6
.6	.7	.7	Deferred Taxes		.3	.5	.3	.5	.9
3.8	4.1	3.4	All Other Non-Current		8.9	2.5	4.0	3.5	2.6
28.5	30.6	30.5	Net Worth		25.8	38.2	31.9	35.0	27.7
100.0	100.0	100.0	Total Liabilities & Net Worth		100.0	100.0	100.0	100.0	100.0
			INCOME DATA						
100.0	100.0	100.0	Net Sales		100.0	100.0	100.0	100.0	100.0
14.0	14.5	15.3	Gross Profit		28.1	27.9	18.0	15.1	11.4
13.3	13.6	14.2	Operating Expenses		26.7	24.7	17.1	14.0	10.4
.7	.9	1.1	Operating Profit		1.4	3.1	.8	1.1	1.0
-.2	.1	.1	All Other Expenses (net)		.4	.9	-.1	-.2	.1
.9	.8	1.0	Profit Before Taxes		1.0	2.2	.9	1.3	.9
			RATIOS						
1.5 / 1.1 / .9	1.6 / 1.2 / .9	1.6 / 1.2 / .9	Current		2.9 / 1.4 / .9	2.4 / 1.4 / 1.0	1.8 / 1.3 / 1.0	1.8 / 1.3 / 1.0	1.4 / 1.1 / .8
1.1 / .8 / .6	1.1 / .8 / .5	1.1 / .8 / .6	Quick		1.9 / 1.0 / .6	1.6 / .9 / .7	1.4 / .9 / .6	1.2 / .9 / .6	1.0 / .8 / .5
13 27.5 / 23 15.8 / 36 10.1	11 33.7 / 19 19.7 / 31 11.7	12 29.8 / 22 16.5 / 35 10.4	Sales/Receivables		7 52.8 / 30 12.4 / 45 8.2	23 16.2 / 35 10.4 / 47 7.8	17 22.0 / 26 13.9 / 41 8.9	14 25.6 / 26 14.2 / 34 10.7	11 33.2 / 18 20.0 / 30 12.3
4 93.7 / 9 40.8 / 19 19.7	4 92.4 / 8 43.7 / 17 22.0	4 104.1 / 9 41.5 / 19 19.5	Cost of Sales/Inventory		4 97.1 / 15 24.0 / 28 13.2	13 28.5 / 25 14.5 / 55 6.7	4 89.8 / 11 34.2 / 33 11.1	4 91.9 / 10 36.0 / 25 14.8	3 115.4 / 7 48.8 / 13 27.6
14 26.1 / 20 18.6 / 28 13.1	11 33.6 / 16 22.6 / 23 15.7	13 27.8 / 19 18.8 / 29 12.7	Cost of Sales/Payables		13 29.0 / 22 16.9 / 45 8.2	10 34.9 / 25 14.4 / 45 8.1	13 27.3 / 22 16.9 / 33 11.0	13 27.9 / 21 17.3 / 31 11.8	13 27.6 / 17 21.2 / 25 14.6
23.0 / 76.3 / -108.4	22.2 / 66.6 / -164.9	20.2 / 69.3 / -114.2	Sales/Working Capital		17.0 / 30.1 / -65.1	5.1 / 13.1 / NM	13.7 / 33.2 / -262.0	16.4 / 39.4 / 825.7	37.6 / 155.8 / -73.1
(489) 4.3 / 1.9 / 1.1	(467) 4.3 / 2.1 / 1.2	(536) 4.9 / 2.1 / 1.1	EBIT/Interest	(30) 4.5 / 2.0 / -1.2	(29) 5.2 / 2.6 / .5	(65) 4.2 / 2.0 / .1	(130) 5.0 / 2.2 / 1.2	(274) 4.9 / 2.1 / 1.3	
(171) 3.6 / 1.9 / 1.1	(184) 3.6 / 2.1 / 1.1	(197) 3.7 / 1.8 / 1.0	Net Profit + Depr., Dep., Amort./Cur. Mat. L/T/D				(19) 1.6 / 1.2 / .6	(49) 3.9 / 1.7 / .8	(114) 5.0 / 2.4 / 1.3
.5 / 1.4 / 3.0	.6 / 1.2 / 2.5	.5 / 1.2 / 2.5	Fixed/Worth		.6 / 1.5 / -2.1	.3 / .5 / 1.9	.3 / .9 / 1.9	.5 / .9 / 1.9	.7 / 1.5 / 2.8
1.5 / 3.0 / 6.6	1.3 / 2.5 / 5.4	1.3 / 2.7 / 6.3	Debt/Worth		.8 / 2.7 / -7.5	.8 / 1.4 / 3.2	1.3 / 2.1 / 7.0	.9 / 2.3 / 4.0	1.8 / 3.3 / 7.3
(471) 26.6 / 11.9 / 3.5	(458) 25.6 / 12.4 / 3.6	(533) 25.9 / 11.6 / 2.1	% Profit Before Taxes/Tangible Net Worth	(27) 47.6 / 13.5 / 2.1	(26) 27.8 / 4.2 / .6	(65) 19.7 / 7.5 / -1.6	(132) 23.6 / 8.6 / 2.6	(275) 27.5 / 13.8 / 3.9	
6.8 / 2.6 / .6	6.6 / 3.2 / .8	6.3 / 2.9 / .6	% Profit Before Taxes/Total Assets		8.4 / 3.5 / -5.4	7.7 / 1.4 / -1.1	6.3 / 1.9 / -2.3	6.3 / 3.2 / .6	6.1 / 3.0 / .7
37.2 / 15.9 / 8.4	34.1 / 15.7 / 8.4	39.0 / 15.3 / 8.3	Sales/Net Fixed Assets		25.7 / 13.1 / 5.7	46.1 / 16.0 / 4.6	42.3 / 14.4 / 7.3	36.2 / 15.4 / 8.4	40.4 / 15.5 / 9.5
6.7 / 4.4 / 3.2	6.8 / 4.8 / 3.4	6.7 / 4.5 / 3.1	Sales/Total Assets		5.0 / 3.3 / 2.4	3.7 / 2.7 / 1.5	5.6 / 3.5 / 2.7	5.9 / 4.1 / 3.0	7.6 / 5.4 / 3.6
(479) .7 / 1.1 / 1.9	(455) .5 / 1.0 / 1.7	(537) .7 / 1.2 / 1.9	% Depr., Dep., Amort./Sales	(34) 1.3 / 2.1 / 4.9	(25) 1.1 / 1.7 / 3.9	(66) .8 / 1.5 / 2.3	(133) .7 / 1.2 / 1.9	(273) .6 / 1.1 / 1.7	
(217) .5 / 1.0 / 2.4	(204) .5 / 1.0 / 2.5	(215) .4 / 1.0 / 2.2	% Officers', Directors', Owners' Comp/Sales	(14) 1.5 / 3.0 / 5.8	(14) .7 / 2.6 / 4.7	(36) 1.1 / 1.6 / 2.5	(69) .5 / .9 / 1.6	(80) .2 / .6 / 1.0	
33720477M	37729184M	38916855M	Net Sales ($)	5353M	77160M	115166M	553644M	2386214M	35779318M
7138620M	6740149M	8502091M	Total Assets ($)	2045M	30172M	72360M	162174M	686619M	7548721M

M = $ thousand   MM = $ million
See Pages 11 through 18 for Explanation of Ratios and Data

Current Data Sorted By Assets   Comparative Historical Data

0-500M	500M-2MM	2-10MM	10-50MM	50-100MM	100-250MM		4/1/98-3/31/99 ALL	4/1/99-3/31/00 ALL
						Type of Statement		
1	3	38	48	10	4	Unqualified	121	131
	12	70	31	2		Reviewed	147	131
2	23	38	5			Compiled	111	110
6	2	9	2			Tax Returns	17	14
3	6	41	55	11	4	Other	114	123
	62 (4/1-9/30/02)		364 (10/1/02-3/31/03)					
12	46	196	141	23	8	**NUMBER OF STATEMENTS**	510	509
%	%	%	%	%	%	**ASSETS**	%	%
13.1	11.5	11.5	10.4	8.0		Cash & Equivalents	12.2	13.2
8.0	5.8	11.4	10.3	5.1		Trade Receivables (net)	11.3	11.9
37.8	33.7	22.6	15.8	15.1		Inventory	24.2	23.2
.3	3.6	3.0	2.3	3.0		All Other Current	2.2	2.1
59.2	54.6	48.5	38.7	31.3		Total Current	50.0	50.5
18.9	25.5	24.8	23.1	27.1		Fixed Assets (net)	24.3	22.9
14.6	11.9	16.1	28.8	33.2		Intangibles (net)	15.7	16.1
7.3	8.0	10.6	9.4	8.5		All Other Non-Current	10.1	10.5
100.0	100.0	100.0	100.0	100.0		Total	100.0	100.0
						LIABILITIES		
14.7	12.6	8.0	6.6	1.8		Notes Payable-Short Term	8.2	7.8
2.0	6.0	3.7	5.8	3.1		Cur. Mat.-L/T/D	4.5	3.9
19.0	10.4	11.1	9.8	11.0		Trade Payables	11.3	12.1
.0	.5	.2	.1	.1		Income Taxes Payable	.2	.2
31.5	11.3	9.1	6.6	5.8		All Other Current	8.3	8.1
67.1	40.7	32.0	28.8	21.8		Total Current	32.4	32.2
17.3	24.7	22.3	27.4	45.1		Long Term Debt	22.0	21.9
.2	.2	.3	.3	.0		Deferred Taxes	.3	.3
8.2	2.9	3.7	3.1	5.4		All Other Non-Current	3.4	3.5
7.2	31.5	41.7	40.3	27.8		Net Worth	41.9	42.1
100.0	100.0	100.0	100.0	100.0		Total Liabilities & Net Worth	100.0	100.0
						INCOME DATA		
100.0	100.0	100.0	100.0	100.0		Net Sales	100.0	100.0
18.3	24.3	25.6	24.7	25.1		Gross Profit	24.3	24.4
16.8	22.4	22.3	20.3	19.4		Operating Expenses	21.3	21.2
1.5	1.9	3.3	4.4	5.6		Operating Profit	3.0	3.1
.4	.1	.5	.7	1.4		All Other Expenses (net)	.3	.0
1.2	1.8	2.7	3.7	4.2		Profit Before Taxes	2.7	3.1
						RATIOS		
1.6	2.1	2.4	2.2	1.9			2.5	2.6
.9	1.4	1.5	1.3	1.4		Current	1.6	1.5
.8	1.0	1.1	.8	.9			1.1	1.1
.5	.7	1.3	1.1	1.0			1.3	1.4
(11) .3	.4	.6	.7	.5		Quick	(509) .7	(507) .7
.0	.2	.3	.3	.2			.4	.4
0 UND	0 999.8	1 269.4	2 169.9	1 250.8			2 197.9	2 210.5
0 UND	2 191.5	5 78.4	4 92.8	2 161.3		Sales/Receivables	5 72.4	5 71.5
7 56.0	6 61.0	19 19.1	22 16.5	10 35.5			19 18.7	20 18.3
12 31.6	16 22.6	14 25.6	14 26.6	10 35.9			16 23.0	15 24.3
24 15.5	27 13.6	24 14.9	19 19.7	20 18.5		Cost of Sales/Inventory	23 15.7	23 15.7
42 8.7	36 10.0	32 11.2	30 12.4	31 11.8			35 10.5	33 11.1
0 UND	3 130.2	6 62.2	7 50.5	9 41.3			5 68.9	7 55.8
5 79.3	9 40.9	11 33.2	12 29.3	14 26.4		Cost of Sales/Payables	11 34.1	12 31.0
16 22.6	13 28.5	17 21.7	17 21.5	23 15.8			17 21.2	18 20.3
26.3	19.3	13.8	12.2	14.6			12.0	12.4
-79.2	47.4	27.4	50.1	42.5		Sales/Working Capital	24.4	27.1
-21.7	-458.7	150.4	-78.3	-111.0			113.2	145.2
5.7	6.4	12.0	11.2	14.0			8.4	9.3
(10) 1.2	(41) 3.3	(171) 4.9	(129) 4.5	4.7		EBIT/Interest	(455) 3.3	(443) 3.6
-9.3	1.7	2.0	2.8	1.8			1.6	1.6
	3.5	8.4	3.2				5.5	6.5
	(12) 2.2	(49) 2.5	(24) 2.3			Net Profit + Depr., Dep., Amort./Cur. Mat. L /T/D	(145) 2.5	(123) 2.4
	1.0	1.1	1.3				1.3	1.3
.3	.4	.3	.5	.8			.3	.3
NM	.9	.9	2.0	2.8		Fixed/Worth	.8	.8
-.4	-3.0	4.9	-1.2	-.5			18.6	8.7
2.0	.9	.7	1.1	.9			.6	.7
NM	2.7	2.2	4.9	6.6		Debt/Worth	1.7	1.9
-2.3	-8.4	15.5	-4.1	-2.0			52.2	32.5
	50.3	57.8	57.1	105.0			50.3	58.2
	(33) 11.0	(152) 30.1	(77) 29.9	(13) 45.9		% Profit Before Taxes/Tangible Net Worth	(389) 24.0	(392) 24.7
	-.6	12.4	17.0	19.5			7.5	8.2
11.9	18.6	19.3	15.8	17.8			17.0	18.1
4.2	7.2	9.2	10.0	13.4		% Profit Before Taxes/Total Assets	7.9	8.3
-4.5	1.3	3.1	5.4	5.2			2.5	2.6
66.5	46.3	36.3	36.0	31.0			37.6	40.5
44.1	27.9	23.3	15.6	9.5		Sales/Net Fixed Assets	19.6	22.7
24.8	15.1	11.7	9.1	6.9			10.8	11.1
11.3	7.8	5.6	4.1	3.9			5.3	5.6
7.1	6.2	4.4	3.2	2.8		Sales/Total Assets	3.9	4.2
4.2	4.0	3.1	2.5	2.2			2.8	2.9
	.7	.8	.7	.9			.8	.8
	(44) 1.1	(183) 1.2	(127) 1.3	(19) 1.3		% Depr., Dep., Amort./Sales	(462) 1.3	(449) 1.2
	1.8	1.7	1.7	1.9			1.7	1.7
	1.9	1.1	.4				1.3	1.2
	(27) 2.9	(81) 1.6	(34) .9			% Officers', Directors', Owners' Comp/Sales	(202) 2.5	(197) 2.2
	9.3	2.5	2.6				3.9	3.4
25896M	389193M	4354475M	9759518M	5120513M	3604748M	Net Sales ($)	16722554M	18810068M
3392M	60812M	1000863M	3005240M	1643036M	1192302M	Total Assets ($)	5157571M	5836739M

© RMA 2003

M = $ thousand   MM = $ million
See Pages 11 through 18 for Explanation of Ratios and Data

Comparative Historical Data | Current Data Sorted By Sales

90 / 91 / 104 etc. (4/1/00)	(4/1/01)	(4/1/02)	Type of Statement	0-1MM	1-3MM	3-5MM	5-10MM	10-25MM	25MM & OVER
90	91	104	Unqualified	1	1		1	28	73
123	82	115	Reviewed		1	2	17	42	53
111	112	68	Compiled		2	11	10	29	16
15	16	19	Tax Returns	1	3	3	1	7	4
125	124	120	Other		3	1	7	27	82
4/1/00-3/31/01 ALL	4/1/01-3/31/02 ALL	4/1/02-3/31/03 ALL		62 (4/1-9/30/02)		364 (10/1/02-3/31/03)			
464	425	426	**NUMBER OF STATEMENTS**	2	10	17	36	133	228
%	%	%	**ASSETS**	%	%	%	%	%	%
10.8	12.0	10.9	Cash & Equivalents		19.9	5.7	8.6	11.7	10.9
10.7	10.9	10.1	Trade Receivables (net)		2.3	10.8	7.5	10.0	10.9
22.7	21.4	21.6	Inventory		26.9	35.0	27.2	23.5	18.4
2.6	2.6	2.7	All Other Current		1.1	1.6	3.6	2.8	2.8
46.9	46.9	45.4	Total Current		50.2	53.2	46.9	48.0	42.9
23.9	23.3	24.0	Fixed Assets (net)		23.6	24.8	29.4	23.4	23.5
18.0	19.5	20.9	Intangibles (net)		25.3	11.5	16.8	17.3	24.3
11.3	10.3	9.7	All Other Non-Current		.9	10.5	7.0	11.3	9.2
100.0	100.0	100.0	Total		100.0	100.0	100.0	100.0	100.0
			LIABILITIES						
8.3	8.4	7.9	Notes Payable-Short Term		11.0	14.6	13.3	7.9	6.3
4.8	4.6	4.5	Cur. Mat.-L/T/D		2.4	4.8	3.6	4.5	4.7
10.9	11.3	10.8	Trade Payables		13.0	13.0	7.5	10.6	11.3
.2	.2	.2	Income Taxes Payable		.0	.2	.0	.3	.1
8.2	7.8	9.0	All Other Current		18.7	20.3	8.7	8.8	7.9
32.4	32.2	32.4	Total Current		45.1	53.0	33.1	32.1	30.3
22.6	23.0	25.2	Long Term Debt		17.6	22.6	25.2	22.9	27.1
.3	.3	.3	Deferred Taxes		.0	.3	.4	.2	.3
4.1	3.1	3.6	All Other Non-Current		1.3	2.9	2.5	3.5	3.8
40.5	41.4	38.5	Net Worth		35.9	21.2	38.7	41.3	38.5
100.0	100.0	100.0	Total Liabilities & Net Worth		100.0	100.0	100.0	100.0	100.0
			INCOME DATA						
100.0	100.0	100.0	Net Sales		100.0	100.0	100.0	100.0	100.0
24.7	25.1	25.0	Gross Profit		28.1	23.4	24.6	25.6	24.6
21.6	22.0	21.3	Operating Expenses		22.2	22.8	21.7	22.6	20.3
3.1	3.1	3.7	Operating Profit		5.9	.6	3.0	3.1	4.3
.3	.5	.6	All Other Expenses (net)		3.2	-.1	.7	.4	.6
2.8	2.6	3.1	Profit Before Taxes		2.7	.7	2.3	2.7	3.8
			RATIOS						
2.3	2.4	2.2			9.2	1.6	2.3	2.3	2.3
1.4	1.4	1.4	Current		.8	1.4	1.3	1.5	1.4
1.0	1.0	1.0			.7	.8	.9	1.1	.9
1.1	1.3	1.1			4.0	.6	.9	1.3	1.2
(461) .6	.6	(425) .6	Quick		.4	(16) .4	.4	.6	.6
.3	.3	.3			.1	.2	.1	.3	.3
2 242.5	1 245.5	1 263.5			0 UND	1 349.7	0 790.9	1 252.8	2 204.4
4 81.6	5 78.0	4 96.1	Sales/Receivables		0 UND	9 40.3	3 123.1	4 82.2	4 94.7
19 19.4	19 19.3	18 19.8			1 279.7	18 20.6	17 21.3	19 19.3	19 18.7
16 23.3	14 25.7	14 25.9			15 23.8	25 14.5	19 19.3	15 24.7	13 29.1
24 15.5	22 16.3	24 15.5	Cost of Sales/Inventory		29 12.7	33 11.2	27 13.7	25 14.4	19 19.6
34 10.8	32 11.4	32 11.4			50 7.4	42 8.7	40 9.1	34 10.7	30 12.2
6 57.3	6 59.8	6 61.7			0 UND	8 46.4	3 106.1	6 63.7	7 53.2
12 31.4	12 31.5	11 32.2	Cost of Sales/Payables		2 182.0	11 33.1	9 39.2	12 31.1	12 31.0
18 20.1	18 20.6	17 21.7			12 31.4	16 23.5	14 27.0	16 22.3	18 20.0
14.4	13.0	14.1			20.6	24.4	14.3	13.4	13.8
33.3	32.3	33.6	Sales/Working Capital		-31.1	42.7	33.5	26.8	36.6
978.1	-491.4	-288.5			-20.2	-64.2	-98.8	119.7	-230.4
8.1	9.4	10.9				3.4	7.2	7.7	14.0
(415) 3.0	(385) 3.5	(382) 4.3	EBIT/Interest			(15) 1.1	(33) 2.0	(114) 3.8	(211) 5.3
1.4	1.8	2.1				.6	1.3	2.0	3.1
5.1	4.0	5.3					4.0	11.7	4.5
(107) 2.3	(95) 1.9	(92) 2.4	Net Profit + Depr., Dep., Amort./Cur. Mat. L/T/D				(10) 1.5	(30) 3.8	(43) 2.4
1.0	1.2	1.3					.6	1.3	1.4
.3	.3	.4			.9	.5	.3	.3	.5
.9	.9	1.1	Fixed/Worth		NM	1.0	1.3	.8	1.3
-62.8	-5.4	-2.0			-.4	-2.1	NM	NM	-1.5
.7	.7	.8			1.3	1.1	.8	.7	.9
2.1	2.1	2.7	Debt/Worth		NM	2.6	3.0	2.2	3.6
-75.8	-12.2	-7.5			-6.3	-8.3	NM	-40.8	-4.7
59.4	60.3	57.6				32.7	39.4	52.9	74.3
(344) 28.1	(303) 29.8	(286) 30.5	% Profit Before Taxes/Tangible Net Worth			(11) .0	(27) 11.0	(99) 26.0	(143) 38.6
10.0	12.0	13.2				-1.9	3.2	11.4	19.6
17.1	16.5	17.6			27.6	5.9	12.6	15.8	19.1
8.0	7.4	9.3	% Profit Before Taxes/Total Assets		8.6	1.2	3.4	8.4	10.7
2.3	3.2	3.5			-.7	-.7	1.5	2.8	6.2
39.2	39.5	37.8			60.4	41.1	32.9	41.3	37.7
20.0	21.7	20.5	Sales/Net Fixed Assets		34.0	18.1	18.3	24.7	19.9
10.5	10.6	10.3			20.9	9.2	8.4	11.3	10.1
5.3	5.3	5.4			7.3	6.8	6.6	5.6	5.0
4.0	3.9	3.7	Sales/Total Assets		4.8	4.1	3.7	4.1	3.6
2.9	2.8	2.8			3.3	2.3	2.3	3.0	2.7
.7	.7	.7				.9	.9	.7	.7
(418) 1.2	(391) 1.3	(389) 1.2	% Depr., Dep., Amort./Sales			(16) 1.4	(35) 1.6	(121) 1.2	(208) 1.1
1.8	1.9	1.7				2.5	2.4	1.7	1.6
1.0	1.0	.9				1.9	1.6	1.1	.6
(191) 1.9	(152) 1.9	(147) 1.8	% Officers', Directors', Owners' Comp/Sales			(10) 3.6	(24) 2.2	(53) 1.9	(56) 1.2
3.3	3.3	3.4				7.2	3.5	3.5	2.5
17313697M	20861310M	23254343M	Net Sales ($)	699M	18747M	67309M	282904M	2199450M	20685234M
5233445M	6552343M	6905645M	Total Assets ($)	300M	12544M	19314M	94313M	603750M	6175424M

M = $ thousand   MM = $ million

See Pages 11 through 18 for Explanation of Ratios and Data

Current Data Sorted By Assets   Comparative Historical Data

						Type of Statement		
	3	7	16	8	13	Unqualified	39	28
	4	17	7	1	1	Reviewed	21	17
3	4	12	1	1		Compiled	29	18
2	4	3	1			Tax Returns	7	2
	6	17	12	6	4	Other	25	34
	38 (4/1-9/30/02)		115 (10/1/02-3/31/03)				4/1/98-3/31/99	4/1/99-3/31/00
0-500M	500M-2MM	2-10MM	10-50MM	50-100MM	100-250MM		ALL	ALL
5	21	56	37	16	18	**NUMBER OF STATEMENTS**	121	99
%	%	%	%	%	%	**ASSETS**	%	%
	5.5	8.5	7.2	5.3	2.6	Cash & Equivalents	8.7	7.3
	20.4	25.8	22.1	24.1	25.3	Trade Receivables (net)	21.4	24.7
	54.9	41.6	41.5	36.7	39.7	Inventory	41.3	40.9
	1.2	3.8	2.2	2.9	3.0	All Other Current	3.4	3.4
	81.9	79.8	73.0	69.0	70.6	Total Current	74.7	76.4
	9.3	9.4	11.8	10.3	11.0	Fixed Assets (net)	12.1	13.2
	2.1	4.9	7.2	12.2	10.2	Intangibles (net)	5.3	5.4
	6.7	5.9	8.0	8.6	8.2	All Other Non-Current	7.9	5.0
	100.0	100.0	100.0	100.0	100.0	Total	100.0	100.0
						LIABILITIES		
	18.3	11.3	11.4	8.1	12.2	Notes Payable-Short Term	14.4	13.6
	3.2	1.2	1.1	8.1	1.1	Cur. Mat.-L/T/D	2.3	2.3
	29.4	25.2	25.2	19.7	21.0	Trade Payables	24.9	27.0
	.1	.1	.1	.3	.4	Income Taxes Payable	.1	.3
	8.5	10.6	11.5	12.5	10.8	All Other Current	8.0	10.1
	59.5	48.4	49.4	48.7	45.5	Total Current	49.8	53.3
	9.8	4.8	9.7	24.9	18.9	Long Term Debt	13.7	17.3
	.1	.1	.0	.1	.9	Deferred Taxes	.1	.1
	4.6	1.8	5.3	3.9	5.0	All Other Non-Current	4.1	5.9
	25.9	44.9	35.6	22.4	29.7	Net Worth	32.3	23.3
	100.0	100.0	100.0	100.0	100.0	Total Liabilities & Net Worth	100.0	100.0
						INCOME DATA		
	100.0	100.0	100.0	100.0	100.0	Net Sales	100.0	100.0
	28.1	26.6	23.8	24.8	24.7	Gross Profit	25.2	26.6
	24.7	22.1	21.3	20.2	19.7	Operating Expenses	22.4	21.3
	3.4	4.4	2.6	4.6	4.9	Operating Profit	2.8	5.2
	.3	.2	.2	.5	.0	All Other Expenses (net)	.3	.6
	3.1	4.2	2.4	4.1	4.9	Profit Before Taxes	2.5	4.7
						RATIOS		
	2.2	2.9	2.2	2.0	2.4		2.1	2.1
	1.3	1.6	1.7	1.4	1.8	Current	1.5	1.5
	1.1	1.3	1.1	1.1	1.2		1.2	1.2
	.6	1.2	1.0	.8	.9		.9	.9
	.5	.7	.6	.6	.6	Quick	(120) .6	.6
	.2	.4	.4	.3	.4		.3	.4

												Ratio				
2	195.2	16	22.2	11	31.9	23	16.1	26	14.0	Sales/Receivables	5	72.2	7	54.7
23	16.0	28	13.2	32	11.4	36	10.2	37	9.9		25	14.5	34	10.6
58	6.3	50	7.3	47	7.7	49	7.4	52	7.1		44	8.3	53	6.9
35	10.3	34	10.7	45	8.2	48	7.6	54	6.8	Cost of Sales/Inventory	33	11.1	41	8.9
87	4.2	56	6.5	65	5.6	61	6.0	77	4.7		56	6.6	56	6.5
177	2.1	100	3.6	94	3.9	82	4.4	91	4.0		81	4.5	78	4.7
21	17.7	16	23.1	23	15.7	17	21.6	25	14.7	Cost of Sales/Payables	17	21.0	17	21.0
51	7.2	35	10.4	41	8.8	31	11.8	40	9.1		30	12.4	36	10.2
96	3.8	56	6.5	55	6.7	53	6.9	50	7.3		51	7.2	61	6.0

	4.5	6.9	6.5	8.2	5.9	Sales/Working Capital	8.0	7.8
	18.2	11.8	13.5	13.9	10.9		14.4	14.8
	118.7	29.3	76.3	56.4	30.1		35.7	27.4
	6.7	28.9	13.3	19.8	13.6	EBIT/Interest	9.2	15.0
	3.4 (46)	9.2 (33)	4.2 (15)	7.1	4.2		(105) 3.2 (90)	5.3
	1.6	2.2	2.4	2.2	2.2		1.7	2.1
						Net Profit + Depr., Dep., Amort./Cur. Mat. L/T/D	5.7	10.6
							(29) 2.4 (23)	6.2
							1.2	1.4
	.1	.0	.1	.1	.4	Fixed/Worth	.1	.1
	.4	.2	.5	.5	.6		.3	.3
	.8	.4	1.9	4.4	NM		1.1	.9
	1.5	.6	.8	1.8	1.8	Debt/Worth	1.2	1.2
	3.0	1.4	2.1	3.6	3.7		3.0	2.8
	8.2	2.8	25.5	8.7	NM		7.9	6.8
	47.9	61.7	46.7	57.2	83.4	% Profit Before Taxes/Tangible Net Worth	51.5	54.0
	27.9 (19)	22.9 (52)	29.6 (30)	38.7 (13)	43.2 (14)		(108) 26.1 (85)	37.4
	14.2	9.5	11.9	16.9	17.6		10.9	21.9
	13.2	22.4	15.1	20.3	15.7	% Profit Before Taxes/Total Assets	14.4	17.5
	5.4	9.3	5.9	9.5	8.1		5.9	9.7
	.8	2.9	2.8	3.4	3.6		2.3	4.5
	166.2	181.3	85.7	116.2	44.0	Sales/Net Fixed Assets	86.5	114.9
	48.9	80.8	40.6	38.1	27.6		49.3	48.8
	21.5	29.8	19.6	14.7	17.8		22.5	19.2
	5.3	4.7	3.4	3.7	3.0	Sales/Total Assets	4.4	4.3
	2.8	3.5	2.8	2.3	2.5		3.4	3.1
	1.8	2.4	2.3	1.8	2.3		2.3	2.3
	.1	.3	.3	.4	.4	% Depr., Dep., Amort./Sales	.4	.4
	.5 (18)	.4 (48)	.6 (35)	1.2 (11)	.7 (16)		(100) .6 (78)	.6
	1.1	.8	1.2	2.5	1.3		1.0	1.0
	2.2	1.7				% Officers', Directors', Owners' Comp/Sales	2.2	2.7
	3.1 (14)	3.1 (26)					(39) 4.3 (27)	3.9
	4.2	6.5					7.8	6.3

9445M	109363M	949408M	2511461M	2938847M	7341625M	Net Sales ($)	7173865M	8786759M
1496M	27148M	261885M	827248M	1131056M	2804283M	Total Assets ($)	2258069M	2838989M

© RMA 2003

M = $ thousand   MM = $ million
See Pages 11 through 18 for Explanation of Ratios and Data

Comparative Historical Data   Current Data Sorted By Sales

			Type of Statement						
27	35	47	Unqualified			3		5	39
27	26	30	Reviewed	1	2	3		11	13
23	18	21	Compiled	4	5	4		6	2
4	8	10	Tax Returns	3	2	2		3	
37	26	45	Other	4	3	3		13	22
4/1/00- 3/31/01 ALL	4/1/01- 3/31/02 ALL	4/1/02- 3/31/03 ALL		0-1MM	**38 (4/1-9/30/02)** 1-3MM	3-5MM	**115 (10/1/02-3/31/03)** 5-10MM	10-25MM	25MM & OVER
118	113	153	**NUMBER OF STATEMENTS**	12	12	15		38	76
%	%	%	**ASSETS**	%	%	%		%	%
6.1	6.8	7.5	Cash & Equivalents	14.6	6.1	5.2		9.4	6.1
24.8	26.6	23.1	Trade Receivables (net)	12.7	19.1	23.5		24.8	24.4
39.8	39.3	42.5	Inventory	58.6	50.7	43.0		40.8	39.5
4.2	4.1	2.8	All Other Current	.8	.5	9.2		2.2	2.4
75.0	76.8	75.9	Total Current	86.7	76.4	80.8		77.3	72.4
12.7	9.8	10.1	Fixed Assets (net)	3.8	11.6	7.4		10.7	11.0
6.1	5.1	6.8	Intangibles (net)	3.1	7.2	2.7		5.0	9.1
6.2	8.2	7.2	All Other Non-Current	6.4	4.8	9.0		7.0	7.5
100.0	100.0	100.0	Total	100.0	100.0	100.0		100.0	100.0
			LIABILITIES						
10.7	11.5	12.2	Notes Payable-Short Term	22.9	8.1	15.2		13.2	10.1
2.8	1.4	2.3	Cur. Mat.-L/T/D	2.2	2.6	2.3		1.3	2.7
25.5	24.9	24.6	Trade Payables	24.6	28.6	22.0		26.3	23.6
.4	.2	.2	Income Taxes Payable	.1	.1	.1		.2	.2
14.7	10.0	11.6	All Other Current	16.7	6.4	22.8		10.9	9.7
54.0	48.0	50.8	Total Current	66.6	45.8	62.4		51.9	46.3
12.7	12.1	10.8	Long Term Debt	12.0	7.3	5.3		4.2	15.6
.1	.1	.2	Deferred Taxes	.0	.3	.0		.1	.3
2.9	4.5	3.9	All Other Non-Current	8.1	1.3	4.8		2.0	4.3
30.3	35.2	34.3	Net Worth	13.3	45.3	27.5		41.7	33.5
100.0	100.0	100.0	Total Liabilities & Net Worth	100.0	100.0	100.0		100.0	100.0
			INCOME DATA						
100.0	100.0	100.0	Net Sales	100.0	100.0	100.0		100.0	100.0
26.4	27.1	25.6	Gross Profit	27.9	27.5	28.3		26.5	23.9
21.8	22.8	21.8	Operating Expenses	24.4	21.9	26.0		22.8	19.9
4.6	4.2	3.8	Operating Profit	3.6	5.7	2.3		3.7	3.9
1.0	.5	.2	All Other Expenses (net)	1.2	.1	.5		.1	.1
3.6	3.7	3.6	Profit Before Taxes	2.4	5.6	1.8		3.5	3.9
			RATIOS						
2.0	2.5	2.3		2.6	2.9	1.4		2.9	2.1
1.4	1.6	1.5	Current	1.7	1.7	1.2		1.4	1.7
1.1	1.1	1.1		1.0	1.4	1.1		1.0	1.2
.9	1.2	1.0		.7	1.1	.7		1.3	1.0
(117) .6	(112) .7	.6	Quick	.4	.6	.4		.6	.7
.3	.4	.4		.3	.3	.2		.4	.4
9 40.0	14 25.9	13 27.9		0 UND	2 229.8	5 67.6	11 34.0	15 23.8
32 11.4	33 11.1	31 11.9	Sales/Receivables	0 UND	39 9.3	32 11.2	21 17.3	32 11.6
50 7.3	48 7.6	48 7.5		65 5.6	66 5.5	50 7.3	40 9.2	44 8.4
38 9.5	36 10.2	41 8.8		52 7.1	86 4.2	30 12.1	32 11.5	42 8.6
54 6.8	54 6.7	62 5.9	Cost of Sales/Inventory	146 2.5	148 2.5	68 5.4	55 6.6	60 6.0
95 3.9	79 4.6	94 3.9		213 1.7	181 2.0	129 2.8	76 4.8	78 4.7
20 18.5	22 16.8	18 19.8		27 13.7	35 10.4	12 29.7	15 23.9	21 17.6
34 10.6	35 10.5	37 9.9	Cost of Sales/Payables	62 5.9	70 5.2	27 13.3	28 13.1	36 10.2
54 6.8	51 7.1	55 6.6		97 3.8	112 3.2	55 6.6	55 6.7	50 7.3
7.3	6.6	6.7		2.9	2.9	10.2		7.5	6.8
14.3	12.2	13.5	Sales/Working Capital	6.2	4.4	18.2		16.1	13.3
51.8	32.9	53.5		NM	25.4	105.1		166.1	31.7
14.2	11.3	14.4		3.9	72.2	8.4		17.7	17.5
(102) 4.4	(100) 4.1	(136) 4.8	EBIT/Interest	(10) 1.6	(10) 5.9	(14) 3.5	(32) 7.1	(70) 5.9
2.0	1.8	2.2		−1.7	3.1	1.9		1.7	3.0
9.6	15.3	11.1	Net Profit + Depr., Dep.,					14.4
(23) 1.7	(24) 4.6	(31) 3.2	Amort./Cur. Mat. L/T/D					(19) 9.0
.7	2.0	1.7						2.5
.1	.1	.1		.0	.0	.1		.1	.1
.3	.2	.3	Fixed/Worth	.2	.2	.3		.2	.4
2.1	.9	.9		.4	1.0	.6		.7	1.4
1.2	1.1	1.0		2.3	.5	1.6		.5	1.1
2.6	2.5	2.3	Debt/Worth	3.7	1.4	3.3		1.7	2.5
12.3	4.9	8.3		NM	4.5	10.5		10.4	8.4
62.9	63.0	59.1	% Profit Before Taxes/Tangible		54.0	47.3		68.3	60.4
(95) 26.6	(100) 27.9	(129) 28.9	Net Worth	(10)	19.3	(13) 21.3	(33) 28.4	(64) 33.9
11.7	9.6	14.5			7.8	9.5		8.5	16.7
16.6	17.1	16.6	% Profit Before Taxes/Total	11.0	14.2	12.8		22.8	17.5
8.9	7.5	6.7	Assets	3.9	7.8	5.9		6.4	8.4
3.0	2.1	2.9		−4.8	2.6	1.2		1.5	4.4
128.9	136.2	145.1		UND	921.3	156.6		173.0	86.6
54.4	57.8	48.2	Sales/Net Fixed Assets	178.3	90.0	84.4		65.4	40.4
18.4	25.4	22.5		17.2	19.0	41.1		22.6	19.7
4.2	4.3	4.3		4.9	4.1	5.1		4.7	3.8
3.2	3.4	2.9	Sales/Total Assets	2.0	1.9	3.2		3.7	2.9
2.1	2.4	2.2		1.5	1.3	2.3		2.4	2.4
.2	.3	.3				.2		.3	.4
(99) .6	(94) .6	(130) .5	% Depr., Dep., Amort./Sales			(14) .4	(33) .4	(67) .6
1.2	1.2	1.2				.6		.9	1.2
1.3	1.2	2.1				2.2		1.8	1.2
(41) 2.6	(43) 2.3	(52) 3.1	% Officers', Directors',			(13) 3.0	(15) 3.7	(13) 2.9
5.4	4.5	4.5	Owners' Comp/Sales			5.0		10.2	4.4
6825800M	8735615M	13860149M	Net Sales ($)	19528M	43729M	115105M		606615M	13075172M
2396430M	2994651M	5053116M	Total Assets ($)	9590M	27361M	42247M		234127M	4739791M

M = $ thousand   MM = $ million
See Pages 11 through 18 for Explanation of Ratios and Data

Current Data Sorted By Assets   Comparative Historical Data

0-500M	500M-2MM	2-10MM	10-50MM	50-100MM	100-250MM		4/1/98-3/31/99 ALL	4/1/99-3/31/00 ALL
						Type of Statement		
5	64	299	208	21	12	Unqualified	71	75
1	25	53	13	1		Reviewed	74	70
9	27	23	3			Compiled	84	76
5	13	2				Tax Returns	14	16
2	38	59	27	3	2	Other	78	64
402 (4/1-9/30/02)			513 (10/1/02-3/31/03)					
22	167	436	251	25	14	**NUMBER OF STATEMENTS**	321	301
%	%	%	%	%	%	**ASSETS**	%	%
7.9	9.5	5.3	4.3	3.4	2.7	Cash & Equivalents	6.8	7.4
25.8	19.6	21.1	20.2	21.9	28.7	Trade Receivables (net)	28.5	27.9
25.5	29.2	27.8	28.5	35.5	25.6	Inventory	29.2	29.2
1.8	2.6	3.4	3.6	7.0	4.6	All Other Current	2.8	2.5
60.9	61.0	57.6	56.7	67.8	61.7	Total Current	67.2	67.1
29.3	24.1	26.1	25.7	21.6	20.3	Fixed Assets (net)	23.4	23.2
2.3	.5	.4	.8	1.8	4.3	Intangibles (net)	1.5	1.4
7.4	14.5	15.9	16.8	8.8	13.7	All Other Non-Current	7.9	8.4
100.0	100.0	100.0	100.0	100.0	100.0	Total	100.0	100.0
						LIABILITIES		
10.2	10.4	14.4	19.5	25.6	15.6	Notes Payable-Short Term	14.1	15.2
3.7	1.9	2.0	1.9	1.4	1.5	Cur. Mat.-L/T/D	2.5	2.8
17.5	14.8	17.0	16.7	17.4	16.9	Trade Payables	20.3	19.3
.1	.2	.3	.4	.4	.4	Income Taxes Payable	.3	.3
12.7	6.0	5.4	5.6	10.4	9.1	All Other Current	10.0	9.7
44.2	33.3	39.1	44.1	55.3	43.6	Total Current	47.3	47.2
26.3	7.4	7.1	9.9	11.7	15.9	Long Term Debt	11.3	11.6
.0	.2	.2	.4	.7	.1	Deferred Taxes	.5	.4
1.9	2.2	1.1	1.6	2.6	4.5	All Other Non-Current	3.7	3.1
27.7	56.9	52.5	44.1	29.7	35.8	Net Worth	37.2	37.8
100.0	100.0	100.0	100.0	100.0	100.0	Total Liabilities & Net Worth	100.0	100.0
						INCOME DATA		
100.0	100.0	100.0	100.0	100.0	100.0	Net Sales	100.0	100.0
28.8	22.4	19.1	17.3	20.2	19.1	Gross Profit	21.1	21.4
30.5	21.6	18.1	16.3	17.7	16.5	Operating Expenses	19.2	19.7
-1.7	.9	1.0	1.1	2.4	2.6	Operating Profit	1.9	1.8
.2	-.8	-.8	-.5	.1	.0	All Other Expenses (net)	-.2	-.2
-2.0	1.6	1.8	1.6	2.3	2.6	Profit Before Taxes	2.1	2.0
						RATIOS		
3.3	3.2	1.9	1.4	1.3	1.6		2.0	2.0
1.3	2.0	1.4	1.2	1.2	1.3	Current	1.4	1.4
.8	1.4	1.2	1.1	1.1	1.2		1.1	1.1
1.6	1.8	.9	.7	.6	1.0		1.1	1.1
.7	.9	.7	.5	.4	.7	Quick	.7	.7
.4	.5	.4	.4	.3	.6		.4	.5
7 50.6	17 21.1	20 18.1	19 18.7	30 12.2	35 10.4		20 18.4	22 16.7
21 17.0	25 14.9	30 12.2	28 13.0	38 9.7	47 7.8	Sales/Receivables	33 10.9	34 10.6
29 12.5	39 9.3	43 8.5	45 8.1	51 7.2	93 3.9		54 6.8	54 6.8
14 26.1	29 12.6	38 9.7	38 9.6	58 6.3	36 10.3		22 16.5	27 13.7
43 8.5	57 6.4	56 6.5	53 6.9	79 4.6	57 6.4	Cost of Sales/Inventory	42 8.6	48 7.6
64 5.7	82 4.5	78 4.7	75 4.9	144 2.5	70 5.2		78 4.7	80 4.6
8 46.2	12 31.0	19 18.9	18 19.8	20 18.0	24 15.1		13 28.3	15 25.0
14 26.5	23 16.1	30 12.2	27 13.4	38 9.7	36 10.2	Cost of Sales/Payables	26 13.8	29 12.8
47 7.8	38 9.5	45 8.0	45 8.1	67 5.4	45 8.1		48 7.6	50 7.4
11.2	5.4	8.1	12.6	11.1	7.0		7.4	7.8
28.6	8.4	13.1	22.0	18.9	11.3	Sales/Working Capital	15.2	15.5
-22.7	19.4	25.2	31.4	35.4	26.7		57.3	50.9
6.6	10.1	8.1	5.3	6.0	4.7		4.6	4.7
(18) 1.7	(137) 3.6	(410) 3.7	(245) 3.1	(24) 3.0	3.5	EBIT/Interest	(300) 2.3	(283) 2.5
-2.0	.9	1.8	1.7	1.8	1.6		1.4	1.4
	9.0	6.5	6.9	24.7	5.0		7.1	6.4
	(36) 4.1	(203) 3.8	(175) 3.9	(17) 7.7	(10) 3.6	Net Profit + Depr., Dep., Amort./Cur. Mat. L/T/D	(111) 2.8	(117) 3.1
	1.8	2.2	2.5	1.9	2.6		1.6	1.6
.1	.2	.3	.4	.6	.4		.3	.3
.6	.4	.5	.6	.7	.6	Fixed/Worth	.6	.6
NM	.7	.7	.8	.9	.8		1.1	1.1
.5	.3	.5	.9	1.6	1.3		.9	.9
1.5	.6	.8	1.2	2.4	2.2	Debt/Worth	1.9	1.9
NM	1.7	1.6	2.0	3.5	3.0		4.7	3.9
46.0	16.9	13.2	12.8	18.6	25.2		27.7	25.2
(17) 9.7	(163) 7.2	(428) 7.2	(247) 6.8	(24) 13.0	(13) 11.5	% Profit Before Taxes/Tangible Net Worth	(302) 13.6	(292) 12.0
-1.3	.8	2.6	3.2	5.1	5.7		4.2	3.5
11.9	8.4	6.7	5.4	5.8	7.6		9.1	7.7
2.3	3.9	3.6	3.2	3.9	4.7	% Profit Before Taxes/Total Assets	4.3	4.3
-4.7	.1	1.3	1.3	2.5	2.1		1.4	1.3
67.5	21.0	12.7	11.9	11.8	14.5		33.1	29.2
19.5	12.4	8.3	8.2	8.2	10.3	Sales/Net Fixed Assets	14.0	12.3
5.4	6.9	5.9	6.2	5.9	6.0		6.6	6.4
5.5	3.2	2.8	2.7	2.4	2.4		3.9	3.5
3.5	2.4	2.1	2.1	1.7	2.0	Sales/Total Assets	2.7	2.5
1.9	1.7	1.6	1.7	1.3	1.7		1.9	1.8
.7	1.0	1.4	1.4	1.3	1.3		.7	.8
(18) 1.8	(160) 1.5	(433) 1.9	(246) 1.9	1.6	(13) 1.6	% Depr., Dep., Amort./Sales	(295) 1.5	(280) 1.4
3.4	2.4	2.6	2.6	2.9	2.4		2.6	2.7
	1.7	.5					1.0	1.1
	(38) 2.7	(31) 1.3				% Officers', Directors', Owners' Comp/Sales	(113) 1.8	(114) 2.1
	5.2	2.8					4.4	3.4
30922M	551914M	5101409M	12613110M	3214017M	4036919M	Net Sales ($)	10780169M	9806241M
7973M	219807M	2246444M	5536694M	1687884M	2021118M	Total Assets ($)	4333311M	4358199M

Comparative Historical Data | Current Data Sorted By Sales

Note: Historical periods — 4/1/00-3/31/01 ALL (310); 4/1/01-3/31/02 ALL (1024); 4/1/02-3/31/03 ALL (915). Current periods — 402 (4/1-9/30/02) and 513 (10/1/02-3/31/03). M = $ thousand, MM = $ million.

	4/1/00-3/31/01 ALL	4/1/01-3/31/02 ALL	4/1/02-3/31/03 ALL	0-1MM	1-3MM	3-5MM	5-10MM	10-25MM	25MM & OVER
Type of Statement									
Unqualified	73	672	609	4	37	49	115	189	215
Reviewed	68	79	93		14	14	26	24	15
Compiled	79	87	62	3	22	13	12	7	5
Tax Returns	26	27	20		13	3	4		
Other	64	159	131	1	18	30	31	21	30
NUMBER OF STATEMENTS	310	1024	915	8	104	109	188	241	265
ASSETS	%	%	%	%	%	%	%	%	%
Cash & Equivalents	6.5	6.4	5.8		9.8	7.2	6.1	4.8	4.2
Trade Receivables (net)	28.5	20.3	20.8		18.0	21.2	19.6	22.0	22.0
Inventory	28.4	26.0	28.4		26.7	27.3	28.4	28.4	29.4
All Other Current	2.6	3.0	3.4		2.7	4.0	2.6	3.5	4.0
Total Current	66.1	55.7	58.4		57.1	59.7	56.7	58.7	59.6
Fixed Assets (net)	24.7	26.1	25.5		25.5	22.9	26.9	25.6	24.9
Intangibles (net)	1.4	.7	.7		1.0	.6	.3	.2	1.2
All Other Non-Current	7.8	17.6	15.5		16.4	16.7	16.1	15.5	14.3
Total	100.0	100.0	100.0		100.0	100.0	100.0	100.0	100.0
LIABILITIES									
Notes Payable-Short Term	16.6	12.9	15.3		10.8	10.7	12.4	17.1	19.6
Cur. Mat.-L/T/D	3.1	2.2	2.0		1.9	2.4	1.7	2.1	1.8
Trade Payables	18.8	17.5	16.6		13.9	15.4	15.3	17.6	18.2
Income Taxes Payable	.2	.4	.3		.1	.3	.3	.3	.4
All Other Current	8.8	5.6	5.9		5.7	5.9	5.7	5.3	6.5
Total Current	47.6	38.5	40.0		32.5	34.7	35.4	42.4	46.5
Long Term Debt	11.9	8.8	8.6		9.4	7.4	6.5	7.0	10.7
Deferred Taxes	.4	.3	.3		.1	.3	.2	.3	.4
All Other Non-Current	3.5	1.3	1.6		1.1	2.5	1.0	1.4	1.9
Net Worth	36.6	51.1	49.5		57.0	55.2	56.8	48.9	40.5
Total Liabilities & Net Worth	100.0	100.0	100.0		100.0	100.0	100.0	100.0	100.0
INCOME DATA									
Net Sales	100.0	100.0	100.0		100.0	100.0	100.0	100.0	100.0
Gross Profit	23.2	19.5	19.5		25.2	22.6	20.1	18.3	16.4
Operating Expenses	22.0	18.1	18.5		24.4	22.0	19.1	17.1	15.1
Operating Profit	1.2	1.4	1.0		.8	.6	1.1	1.2	1.3
All Other Expenses (net)	-.3	-.3	-.7		-.8	-1.0	-.9	-.7	-.3
Profit Before Taxes	1.5	1.7	1.7		1.6	1.6	2.0	1.9	1.6
RATIOS									
Current	2.0	1.9	1.9		3.8	2.6	2.3	1.6	1.4
	1.4	1.4	1.4		2.0	1.8	1.6	1.3	1.2
	1.1	1.2	1.2		1.3	1.3	1.3	1.2	1.1
Quick	1.1	1.0	1.0		2.0	1.4	1.1	.9	.8
	(309) .7	(1023) .7	.7		.9	.8	.7	.6	.5
	.5	.4	.4		.4	.5	.4	.4	.4
Sales/Receivables	22 16.8	18 20.5	19 18.8		17 21.9	19 18.9	19 19.1	21 17.7	20 18.5
	33 10.9	28 13.0	29 12.5		24 15.0	30 12.3	28 12.9	31 11.7	28 13.0
	55 6.6	41 8.9	43 8.5		43 8.5	49 7.5	41 8.9	44 8.3	44 8.3
Cost of Sales/Inventory	27 13.4	32 11.3	37 9.9		31 11.8	41 8.9	38 9.7	37 9.8	36 10.0
	50 7.2	50 7.3	56 6.5		62 5.9	65 5.6	60 6.1	53 6.9	52 7.0
	85 4.3	74 4.9	78 4.7		85 4.3	83 4.4	83 4.4	76 4.8	70 5.2
Cost of Sales/Payables	13 27.7	18 19.9	17 21.0		11 31.8	16 22.8	18 20.5	19 19.5	18 20.1
	28 13.2	29 12.5	28 13.0		23 15.8	32 11.5	27 13.6	30 12.3	28 13.2
	47 7.8	46 7.8	44 8.3		45 8.2	49 7.5	41 8.8	46 7.9	45 8.2
Sales/Working Capital	7.5	8.6	8.3		4.6	5.5	7.3	10.8	12.8
	19.2	17.1	14.5		7.5	8.5	10.8	17.0	23.5
	68.3	30.4	28.0		19.5	20.4	19.4	26.3	33.6
EBIT/Interest	4.5	5.2	7.0		6.6	9.3	9.9	7.6	5.2
	(291) 1.9	(954) 2.7	(848) 3.3		(84) 2.3	(88) 3.4	(174) 4.1	(236) 3.3	(259) 3.1
	1.2	1.4	1.6		-.3	1.2	2.0	1.9	1.7
Net Profit + Depr., Dep., Amort./Cur. Mat. L/T/D	6.0	7.0	7.1		19.6	6.4	6.2	6.6	7.5
	(98) 3.0	(558) 3.9	(441) 3.9		(15) 4.4	(32) 3.1	(66) 4.0	(144) 3.8	(184) 4.0
	1.5	2.4	2.3		2.8	1.3	2.4	2.3	2.5
Fixed/Worth	.3	.3	.3		.2	.2	.3	.4	.5
	.6	.5	.5		.3	.4	.5	.5	.6
	1.2	.7	.8		.9	.6	.7	.7	.8
Debt/Worth	.8	.5	.5		.2	.3	.4	.6	.9
	1.8	.9	1.0		.6	.5	.6	1.0	1.4
	4.4	1.7	1.9		2.0	1.7	1.3	1.6	2.4
% Profit Before Taxes/Tangible Net Worth	23.1	12.5	13.7		15.0	12.6	12.9	13.4	15.4
	(294) 9.2	(1004) 7.2	(892) 7.2		(101) 5.3	(104) 6.9	(187) 6.7	(237) 7.4	(258) 8.0
	2.7	2.6	2.6		-1.6	1.5	2.2	3.4	3.7
% Profit Before Taxes/Total Assets	7.3	6.3	6.5		7.0	6.8	7.2	6.8	5.7
	2.9	3.6	3.5		2.5	3.3	3.8	3.6	3.6
	.6	1.2	1.1		-1.6	.6	1.3	1.6	1.4
Sales/Net Fixed Assets	30.2	13.4	14.1		17.9	16.2	12.9	12.9	13.2
	12.1	8.7	8.7		10.2	9.0	8.2	8.3	9.3
	6.0	6.2	6.1		5.5	5.7	5.7	6.3	6.7
Sales/Total Assets	3.4	2.8	2.8		2.7	2.5	2.8	2.8	2.9
	2.5	2.1	2.1		1.8	1.9	2.0	2.2	2.3
	1.9	1.7	1.7		1.5	1.5	1.6	1.8	1.8
% Depr., Dep., Amort./Sales	.8	1.3	1.3		1.2	1.2	1.4	1.4	1.3
	(293) 1.5	(1003) 1.9	(895) 1.8		(97) 1.8	(106) 2.1	(186) 2.0	(240) 1.8	(258) 1.8
	2.7	2.6	2.6		3.0	3.2	2.6	2.6	2.3
% Officers', Directors', Owners' Comp/Sales	1.0	1.2	1.0		2.0	1.8	1.0	.5	.5
	(117) 2.1	(122) 2.7	(90) 2.0		(28) 4.7	(14) 2.5	(21) 1.8	(11) 1.3	(16) .7
	3.9	4.6	4.7		5.8	5.9	5.9	2.6	2.3
Net Sales ($)	9869077M	26944641M	25548291M	4860M	211666M	432104M	1399862M	3907730M	19592069M
Total Assets ($)	4547045M	11979821M	11719920M	2918M	115213M	242287M	702339M	1843001M	8814162M

M = $ thousand   MM = $ million
See Pages 11 through 18 for Explanation of Ratios and Data

Current Data Sorted By Assets   Comparative Historical Data

0-500M	500M-2MM	2-10MM	10-50MM	50-100MM	100-250MM		4/1/98-3/31/99 ALL	4/1/99-3/31/00 ALL
						Type of Statement		
	2	6	5	3	2	Unqualified	11	14
	3	1	2			Reviewed	8	10
3	2					Compiled	6	8
2	5	3	2	1	2	Tax Returns	2	4
						Other	21	14
	13 (4/1-9/30/02)		31 (10/1/02-3/31/03)					
5	12	10	9	4	4	**NUMBER OF STATEMENTS**	48	50
%	%	%	%	%	%	**ASSETS**	%	%
	5.6	6.3				Cash & Equivalents	11.0	5.9
	31.3	25.9				Trade Receivables (net)	29.1	32.0
	33.4	27.2				Inventory	32.1	30.2
	6.8	5.8				All Other Current	2.0	3.9
	77.1	65.2				Total Current	74.2	72.1
	12.5	19.2				Fixed Assets (net)	12.0	13.3
	1.8	6.1				Intangibles (net)	8.9	6.6
	8.6	9.5				All Other Non-Current	4.9	7.9
	100.0	100.0				Total	100.0	100.0
						LIABILITIES		
	8.0	15.1				Notes Payable-Short Term	10.5	12.5
	1.4	1.9				Cur. Mat.-L/T/D	3.9	2.5
	38.9	29.4				Trade Payables	31.9	28.8
	2.9	.0				Income Taxes Payable	.5	.1
	9.9	7.4				All Other Current	9.9	15.4
	61.2	53.9				Total Current	56.8	59.2
	15.5	5.8				Long Term Debt	12.8	8.3
	.2	.2				Deferred Taxes	.2	.2
	11.9	4.5				All Other Non-Current	3.3	6.3
	11.2	35.6				Net Worth	26.9	25.9
	100.0	100.0				Total Liabilities & Net Worth	100.0	100.0
						INCOME DATA		
	100.0	100.0				Net Sales	100.0	100.0
	30.5	42.9				Gross Profit	33.3	35.6
	28.1	38.7				Operating Expenses	28.9	33.1
	2.4	4.2				Operating Profit	4.4	2.5
	1.6	-.6				All Other Expenses (net)	.8	.5
	.8	4.8				Profit Before Taxes	3.6	2.0
						RATIOS		
	5.4	3.1				Current	2.0	1.8
	1.3	1.2					1.3	1.2
	1.0	.9					1.1	1.0
	1.1	1.1				Quick	1.0	.9
	.8	.8					.8	.6
	.3	.4					.5	.4
	19 19.6	19 19.4				Sales/Receivables	29 12.7	24 15.3
	42 8.7	37 9.8					39 9.5	46 7.9
	64 5.7	45 8.0					62 5.9	75 4.9
	5 76.6	28 13.0				Cost of Sales/Inventory	38 9.6	23 16.1
	68 5.3	57 6.4					76 4.8	66 5.5
	209 1.7	150 2.4					132 2.8	137 2.7
	32 11.4	25 14.4				Cost of Sales/Payables	35 10.4	31 12.0
	53 6.8	60 6.1					70 5.2	63 5.8
	74 4.9	107 3.4					104 3.5	83 4.4
	2.6	7.3				Sales/Working Capital	5.0	6.7
	13.5	19.1					17.4	14.5
	NM	NM					62.8	-178.9
	9.9	29.6				EBIT/Interest	7.6	6.4
	1.6	5.7					(44) 4.1	(48) 2.3
	.2	-.1					1.9	1.1
						Net Profit + Depr., Dep., Amort./Cur. Mat. L /T/D	13.9	4.2
							(13) 1.5	(15) 2.3
							.6	1.4
	.2	.2				Fixed/Worth	.2	.2
	.3	.7					.6	.6
	NM	-13.1					3.2	2.0
	1.4	.8				Debt/Worth	1.5	1.8
	7.2	1.8					2.7	3.2
	NM	-66.8					37.8	22.0
						% Profit Before Taxes/Tangible Net Worth	47.8	34.4
							(38) 17.9	(42) 13.5
							7.4	2.2
	4.2	13.9				% Profit Before Taxes/Total Assets	16.9	7.8
	1.5	6.1					4.7	3.6
	-5.2	-.9					2.9	.3
	57.9	29.8				Sales/Net Fixed Assets	52.1	60.7
	40.9	18.9					31.7	27.9
	20.0	9.7					14.1	15.3
	4.1	4.0				Sales/Total Assets	3.1	3.5
	2.0	2.7					2.2	2.3
	1.1	2.1					1.8	1.7
	.3	1.0				% Depr., Dep., Amort./Sales	.7	.6
	.6	1.4					(39) .9	(43) 1.0
	2.7	1.9					2.0	1.8
						% Officers', Directors', Owners' Comp/Sales	1.4	2.7
							(18) 3.5	(17) 3.8
							4.9	5.0
5706M	32866M	153322M	528481M	501591M	1096873M	Net Sales ($)	2006656M	1269357M
1298M	13697M	48151M	220660M	272572M	792918M	Total Assets ($)	919950M	582413M

M = $ thousand   MM = $ million
See Pages 11 through 18 for Explanation of Ratios and Data

Comparative Historical Data | | | | **Current Data Sorted By Sales** | | | | | |

			Type of Statement						
11	7	10	Unqualified					1	9
12	12	10	Reviewed		1	1		5	3
8	10	4	Compiled	1		2	1		
1	1	5	Tax Returns	4	1				
17	10	15	Other	1	3	4	2		5
4/1/00-3/31/01	4/1/01-3/31/02	4/1/02-3/31/03			13 (4/1-9/30/02)			31 (10/1/02-3/31/03)	
ALL	ALL	ALL		0-1MM	1-3MM	3-5MM	5-10MM	10-25MM	25MM & OVER
49	40	44	NUMBER OF STATEMENTS	6	5	7	3	6	17
%	%	%	ASSETS	%	%	%	%	%	%
9.2	5.6	7.2	Cash & Equivalents						9.5
33.4	34.0	24.8	Trade Receivables (net)						22.0
26.4	30.0	29.5	Inventory						30.9
2.9	5.1	5.3	All Other Current						5.9
71.9	74.6	66.8	Total Current						68.3
10.7	16.1	14.8	Fixed Assets (net)						14.0
10.0	3.0	6.2	Intangibles (net)						8.2
7.3	6.3	12.1	All Other Non-Current						9.5
100.0	100.0	100.0	Total						100.0
			LIABILITIES						
10.1	11.3	8.4	Notes Payable-Short Term						6.9
2.3	1.9	1.5	Cur. Mat.-L/T/D						1.4
37.9	31.4	31.1	Trade Payables						37.4
.1	.3	.8	Income Taxes Payable						.1
9.1	12.7	16.4	All Other Current						13.7
59.5	57.5	58.3	Total Current						59.5
9.6	10.6	17.2	Long Term Debt						12.1
.1	.5	.3	Deferred Taxes						.6
3.0	4.1	6.0	All Other Non-Current						4.1
27.8	27.4	18.1	Net Worth						23.8
100.0	100.0	100.0	Total Liabilities & Net Worth						100.0
			INCOME DATA						
100.0	100.0	100.0	Net Sales						100.0
32.7	37.5	38.0	Gross Profit						36.1
28.7	33.7	33.8	Operating Expenses						30.6
3.9	3.8	4.2	Operating Profit						5.5
.6	1.3	1.3	All Other Expenses (net)						1.8
3.3	2.5	2.9	Profit Before Taxes						3.7
			RATIOS						
1.7	2.3	2.3							1.4
1.3	1.5	1.2	Current						1.1
1.0	1.0	.9							.9
1.0	1.0	.9							.8
.7	.7	.6	Quick						.5
.5	.5	.4							.4
27 13.3	28 13.1	18 20.8							19 19.0
42 8.8	40 9.1	40 9.0	Sales/Receivables						43 8.5
68 5.4	75 4.9	49 7.4							47 7.8
13 28.1	25 14.8	22 16.9							20 18.3
55 6.6	71 5.1	72 5.1	Cost of Sales/Inventory						82 4.4
116 3.2	164 2.2	130 2.8							122 3.0
45 8.1	29 12.7	28 12.9							61 6.0
75 4.8	63 5.8	65 5.6	Cost of Sales/Payables						85 4.3
102 3.6	98 3.7	91 4.0							103 3.5
6.7	4.6	6.1							7.7
19.3	7.8	19.1	Sales/Working Capital						57.8
NM	-336.6	-34.4							-34.7
23.0	7.4	6.9							6.0
(48) 4.3	(37) 2.3	(42) 2.8	EBIT/Interest					(15)	3.7
1.0	.4	1.0							1.4
3.4	4.5	4.7	Net Profit + Depr., Dep.,						
(14) 1.2	(14) 2.2	(13) 1.9	Amort./Cur. Mat. L/T/D						
.5	1.1	.7							
.2	.1	.2							.2
.4	.4	.8	Fixed/Worth						1.2
-1.0	3.4	-9.6							NM
1.8	.8	1.4							2.3
3.1	2.3	5.8	Debt/Worth						5.5
-25.1	23.4	-22.2							NM
72.1	26.6	34.3	% Profit Before Taxes/Tangible						64.3
(36) 27.1	(33) 8.4	(30) 11.8	Net Worth					(13)	17.9
4.5	-5.9	7.2							9.9
13.5	11.4	8.8	% Profit Before Taxes/Total						7.7
5.5	3.3	3.9	Assets						4.8
.2	-1.6	.1							1.4
62.3	71.6	46.3							46.6
32.1	32.1	25.2	Sales/Net Fixed Assets						24.5
20.2	9.6	11.2							10.0
3.2	3.2	3.1							2.8
2.3	2.1	2.2	Sales/Total Assets						2.2
1.6	1.6	1.3							2.0
.5	.5	.6							.7
(37) .8	(34) 1.0	(40) 1.1	% Depr., Dep., Amort./Sales					(15)	1.1
1.7	1.5	1.9							1.4
1.9	1.6	1.8	% Officers', Directors',						
(16) 3.5	(16) 4.2	(19) 4.9	Owners' Comp/Sales						
5.1	5.2	10.5							
2120225M	1372156M	2318839M	Net Sales ($)	2075M	9246M	28893M	23366M	98465M	2156794M
1116616M	650863M	1349296M	Total Assets ($)	2367M	5589M	11056M	7343M	47547M	1275394M

© RMA 2003
M = $ thousand   MM = $ million
See Pages 11 through 18 for Explanation of Ratios and Data

Current Data Sorted By Assets   **Comparative Historical Data**

						Type of Statement		
	2	4	11	2	3	Unqualified	30	22
4	9	21	2			Reviewed	48	43
9	19	10				Compiled	62	33
	1	4				Tax Returns	16	17
4	13	12	7	1	3	Other	42	40
0-500M	**500M-2MM**	**2-10MM**	**10-50MM**	**50-100MM**	**100-250MM**		**4/1/98-3/31/99 ALL**	**4/1/99-3/31/00 ALL**
50 (4/1-9/30/02)			91 (10/1/02-3/31/03)					
17	44	51	20	3	6	NUMBER OF STATEMENTS	198	155
%	%	%	%	%	%	**ASSETS**	%	%
9.4	8.3	7.7	5.9			Cash & Equivalents	9.1	6.3
29.2	24.2	25.4	30.1			Trade Receivables (net)	21.7	26.4
28.3	28.2	26.4	25.2			Inventory	27.6	28.5
.1	3.7	4.5	5.1			All Other Current	2.6	2.6
67.0	64.4	64.0	66.3			Total Current	61.1	63.8
27.2	25.2	27.5	24.7			Fixed Assets (net)	29.4	26.2
1.3	1.5	1.2	3.7			Intangibles (net)	2.7	3.4
4.5	8.9	7.4	5.3			All Other Non-Current	6.8	6.6
100.0	100.0	100.0	100.0			Total	100.0	100.0
						LIABILITIES		
13.0	10.9	10.3	12.5			Notes Payable-Short Term	13.8	12.8
1.7	5.1	5.2	3.0			Cur. Mat.-L/T/D	4.8	3.7
18.6	15.8	14.7	15.7			Trade Payables	16.1	17.8
.1	.6	.3	1.2			Income Taxes Payable	.5	.4
15.6	9.3	6.3	12.3			All Other Current	9.3	7.5
49.1	41.7	36.8	44.7			Total Current	44.6	42.2
25.5	18.7	12.4	11.5			Long Term Debt	16.1	15.9
.0	.3	.1	.6			Deferred Taxes	.9	.9
3.9	9.1	2.0	2.4			All Other Non-Current	4.6	5.2
21.5	30.2	48.8	40.8			Net Worth	33.8	35.8
100.0	100.0	100.0	100.0			Total Liabilities & Net Worth	100.0	100.0
						INCOME DATA		
100.0	100.0	100.0	100.0			Net Sales	100.0	100.0
43.4	38.4	31.7	30.3			Gross Profit	37.8	35.4
39.7	35.9	29.3	26.9			Operating Expenses	32.5	31.1
3.7	2.5	2.5	3.3			Operating Profit	5.3	4.3
.6	1.3	.7	.5			All Other Expenses (net)	1.1	1.0
3.1	1.1	1.8	2.8			Profit Before Taxes	4.1	3.3
						RATIOS		
3.2 1.4 .7	2.5 1.5 1.0	3.2 1.6 1.2	2.7 1.7 1.0			Current	2.5 1.4 1.0	2.6 1.5 1.1
1.7 .8 .4	1.2 .7 .4	1.8 .9 .6	1.5 .9 .5			Quick	1.1 .7 .4	1.3 .8 .4
10 36.4 20 18.2 29 12.7	14 26.8 23 15.6 39 9.4	19 19.3 32 11.5 42 8.7	28 13.2 50 7.3 69 5.3			Sales/Receivables	14 25.6 29 12.5 43 8.6	18 20.5 33 11.2 44 8.4
8 43.4 15 25.1 112 3.3	6 64.7 40 9.2 108 3.4	14 25.5 50 7.2 112 3.3	20 18.0 44 8.3 198 1.8			Cost of Sales/Inventory	15 23.9 48 7.6 125 2.9	20 17.9 51 7.1 113 3.2
7 50.1 35 10.4 45 8.2	8 45.3 24 15.4 35 10.5	10 36.7 23 15.6 33 11.0	15 24.8 25 14.7 48 7.6			Cost of Sales/Payables	13 27.9 30 12.2 46 8.0	13 27.0 29 12.7 45 8.1
7.5 32.9 -30.2	5.8 14.5 -241.6	4.6 15.8 65.8	4.8 10.2 NM			Sales/Working Capital	6.1 16.0 UND	6.1 14.0 65.0
(14) 5.8 1.9 -.9	(38) 5.7 2.4 1.0	(45) 9.6 3.5 1.1	7.3 3.0 1.8			EBIT/Interest	(190) 6.3 2.7 1.1	(147) 7.0 2.9 1.2
	(16) 8.6 2.2 .6	(15) 5.4 3.5 .9	(10) 5.8 3.3 1.7			Net Profit + Depr., Dep., Amort./Cur. Mat. L/T/D	(56) 4.7 1.8 .7	(49) 5.9 2.5 1.4
.3 1.3 NM	.2 .5 3.1	.2 .5 1.3	.4 .7 1.9			Fixed/Worth	.3 .8 2.1	.3 .7 1.4
1.4 2.9 NM	1.0 1.9 9.8	.4 1.0 3.9	.7 1.5 2.1			Debt/Worth	.8 1.9 6.4	.9 1.6 4.8
(13) 98.1 8.6 -9.9	(38) 31.3 10.5 .6	(48) 25.1 9.7 1.7	(18) 29.1 9.7 2.7			% Profit Before Taxes/Tangible Net Worth	(170) 37.8 16.9 7.0	(132) 35.6 17.7 6.6
19.9 6.3 -6.1	9.9 4.5 -.3	11.4 4.0 .5	7.9 2.9 1.1			% Profit Before Taxes/Total Assets	14.0 5.1 .9	13.9 6.0 .6
63.4 36.9 8.0	59.1 19.8 5.3	26.2 13.7 5.0	39.8 13.6 2.8			Sales/Net Fixed Assets	28.8 11.4 4.6	33.0 13.8 5.1
6.1 3.8 2.8	3.9 3.0 1.7	4.2 2.4 1.6	3.1 2.3 1.0			Sales/Total Assets	3.9 2.6 1.4	4.2 2.9 1.6
(12) .5 1.8 3.2	(38) .6 1.1 3.5	(48) .7 1.6 3.2	.6 1.0 2.2			% Depr., Dep., Amort./Sales	(179) .9 1.6 3.1	(134) .9 1.6 2.7
(10) 2.1 5.2 8.4	(28) 2.8 4.9 8.5	(26) 1.5 2.5 5.3				% Officers', Directors', Owners' Comp/Sales	(96) 2.8 4.7 7.3	(70) 2.0 3.9 6.8
25673M 5391M	171740M 53220M	611032M 224058M	891785M 408677M	379299M 216379M	1455847M 1073392M	Net Sales ($) Total Assets ($)	3149574M 1398373M	2936405M 1504329M

© RMA 2003

M = $ thousand   MM = $ million
See Pages 11 through 18 for Explanation of Ratios and Data

Comparative Historical Data | Current Data Sorted By Sales

			Type of Statement						
13	18	22	Unqualified		1	2	1	5	13
28	21	32	Reviewed		4	3	10	11	4
39	39	33	Compiled	5	8	7	8	5	
11	13	14	Tax Returns	2	5	4	1	2	
42	52	40	Other	3	8	4	9	7	9
4/1/00-3/31/01 ALL	4/1/01-3/31/02 ALL	4/1/02-3/31/03 ALL		0-1MM	1-3MM	3-5MM	5-10MM	10-25MM	25MM & OVER
					50 (4/1-9/30/02)		91 (10/1/02-3/31/03)		
133	143	141	**NUMBER OF STATEMENTS**	10	26	20	29	30	26
%	%	%	**ASSETS**	%	%	%	%	%	%
6.8	8.0	7.9	Cash & Equivalents	2.8	9.1	8.7	7.5	9.7	6.6
26.1	24.4	25.4	Trade Receivables (net)	13.8	21.5	22.7	23.5	32.5	30.1
27.0	27.9	27.4	Inventory	38.1	33.4	23.9	30.0	21.5	23.7
2.8	2.8	3.6	All Other Current	.1	4.3	1.3	4.9	4.3	3.8
62.7	63.1	64.3	Total Current	54.8	68.2	56.6	65.9	67.9	64.2
25.9	27.1	25.8	Fixed Assets (net)	38.1	22.8	33.2	26.6	22.9	21.1
2.9	3.5	2.7	Intangibles (net)	.2	2.8	.8	1.4	1.9	7.3
8.5	6.2	7.1	All Other Non-Current	7.0	6.2	9.3	6.1	7.2	7.4
100.0	100.0	100.0	Total	100.0	100.0	100.0	100.0	100.0	100.0
			LIABILITIES						
11.3	12.1	11.3	Notes Payable-Short Term	11.2	13.3	9.2	11.1	11.5	10.9
4.1	4.1	4.4	Cur. Mat.-L/T/D	1.5	6.2	5.2	5.2	2.9	3.9
19.2	16.3	15.5	Trade Payables	10.4	12.9	10.3	12.0	21.9	20.9
.7	.8	.8	Income Taxes Payable	.0	.9	.1	.1	.6	2.5
8.6	11.3	9.3	All Other Current	2.9	13.9	9.7	7.5	7.6	10.9
43.9	44.6	41.3	Total Current	26.0	47.2	34.5	35.9	44.5	49.1
13.8	13.1	15.9	Long Term Debt	38.7	22.9	15.4	14.8	8.7	10.0
.8	.5	.4	Deferred Taxes	.0	.1	.4	.1	.2	1.1
4.9	4.7	5.2	All Other Non-Current	3.9	11.2	5.1	2.3	2.4	6.2
36.6	37.1	37.2	Net Worth	31.4	18.6	44.6	46.8	44.3	33.6
100.0	100.0	100.0	Total Liabilities & Net Worth	100.0	100.0	100.0	100.0	100.0	100.0
			INCOME DATA						
100.0	100.0	100.0	Net Sales	100.0	100.0	100.0	100.0	100.0	100.0
36.7	35.1	35.4	Gross Profit	53.8	38.9	37.4	33.8	29.2	32.2
33.2	30.8	32.6	Operating Expenses	46.0	38.3	35.0	30.6	26.6	29.1
3.5	4.3	2.8	Operating Profit	7.8	.6	2.4	3.2	2.5	3.1
1.1	1.1	1.1	All Other Expenses (net)	2.5	1.6	.4	.8	.3	1.6
2.4	3.2	1.7	Profit Before Taxes	5.3	-1.0	2.0	2.4	2.3	1.5
			RATIOS						
2.3	2.5	2.7	Current	8.4	4.0	3.5	3.7	2.7	1.9
1.4	1.4	1.5		1.5	1.6	1.6	1.9	1.5	1.3
1.0	1.0	1.0		.7	.9	.7	1.2	1.2	1.0
1.2	1.1	1.5	Quick	1.5	1.5	2.1	2.2	1.6	1.1
.7	(142) .7	.8		.7	.5	.7	.7	1.0	.8
.4	.4	.4		.2	.2	.5	.5	.7	.5
16 22.3	16 23.3	18 19.9	Sales/Receivables	0 UND	11 32.9	15 24.6	11 32.2	26 14.1	27 13.5
31 11.9	29 12.4	30 12.1		19 19.0	29 12.4	20 18.1	33 11.1	32 11.3	35 10.4
44 8.3	42 8.6	46 8.0		26 14.0	45 8.2	34 10.8	49 7.4	44 8.3	52 7.0
17 22.1	13 27.3	14 27.0	Cost of Sales/Inventory	12 29.4	11 32.1	0 UND	24 15.3	5 77.0	20 18.3
39 9.3	42 8.6	44 8.3		146 2.5	70 5.2	33 11.2	56 6.6	39 9.3	28 13.1
130 2.8	122 3.0	119 3.1		411 .9	241 1.5	68 5.3	105 3.5	97 3.8	146 2.5
12 31.4	12 31.4	12 31.1	Cost of Sales/Payables	0 UND	7 51.1	8 45.7	6 63.4	14 26.0	25 14.6
28 13.2	25 14.7	24 15.1		35 10.4	23 15.6	23 15.6	16 22.9	25 14.8	37 9.9
43 8.4	47 7.8	40 9.2		54 6.8	46 7.9	33 11.2	27 13.5	44 8.3	62 5.9
6.4	5.9	5.1	Sales/Working Capital	3.2	3.6	5.8	4.8	6.1	7.6
17.9	18.1	14.9		21.7	10.4	15.8	10.7	19.2	22.1
492.1	-367.2	NM		-44.6	-35.6	-15.7	61.9	45.9	-289.2
4.9	6.6	6.6	EBIT/Interest		4.2	6.4	6.9	17.0	8.1
(127) 2.3	(125) 2.7	(126) 2.6			(23) 1.3	(15) 2.0	(27) 2.9	(26) 4.9	3.0
1.0	1.1	1.1			-1.1	1.0	1.4	.2	1.7
5.6	5.8	5.4	Net Profit + Depr., Dep., Amort./Cur. Mat. L/T/D					7.9	9.4
(40) 2.5	(36) 1.8	(46) 2.9						(10) 3.8	(15) 3.4
.4	.4	.8						-1.1	1.8
.3	.3	.2	Fixed/Worth	.1	.3	.1	.2	.2	.4
.6	.7	.6		1.1	2.3	.7	.4	.5	.8
2.2	1.7	2.2		4.9	-1.4	1.5	2.8	1.0	5.6
.8	.8	.8	Debt/Worth	1.4	.9	.7	.4	.7	1.3
1.7	1.6	1.6		1.8	5.4	1.6	1.0	1.1	2.3
6.3	5.1	5.1		5.4	-7.5	2.9	5.1	3.9	32.3
24.8	38.2	31.3	% Profit Before Taxes/Tangible Net Worth		31.3	24.5	32.9	27.4	65.2
(117) 12.5	(126) 15.1	(122) 9.0			(18) 3.5	8.0	(25) 6.7	(29) 16.4	(21) 11.7
1.1	1.6	1.6			-48.6	.5	2.9	.3	5.6
9.7	14.2	10.8	% Profit Before Taxes/Total Assets	9.6	9.9	11.1	10.1	12.5	10.1
4.2	4.9	3.8		4.5	1.7	5.7	4.1	6.1	2.8
-.1	.4	.4		-8.5	-8.9	.2	1.3	-.2	1.9
36.5	30.4	37.7	Sales/Net Fixed Assets	44.9	35.9	60.3	37.1	44.0	34.3
12.7	12.8	18.0		9.7	14.7	12.1	18.5	21.0	14.8
6.3	5.9	4.9		2.8	4.9	3.9	4.1	7.1	5.0
4.4	4.3	3.9	Sales/Total Assets	3.2	4.0	3.6	3.8	5.3	3.8
2.9	2.9	2.7		2.1	2.2	2.6	2.7	2.9	2.8
1.7	1.8	1.6		1.3	1.3	2.2	1.6	1.8	1.2
.6	.7	.7	% Depr., Dep., Amort./Sales		.6	.9	.6	.6	.6
(120) 1.3	(131) 1.3	(126) 1.3			(22) 2.0	(16) 1.8	1.3	(27) 1.0	(25) 1.0
2.9	2.6	3.3			3.9	4.6	3.3	1.9	3.1
2.1	1.9	2.0	% Officers', Directors', Owners' Comp/Sales		2.2	2.3	2.7	1.4	
(64) 3.6	(71) 3.4	(70) 4.4			(16) 5.3	(12) 4.8	(15) 4.8	(15) 2.1	
6.2	5.8	6.8			11.3	6.9	6.2	2.9	
2433654M	2659100M	3535376M	Net Sales ($)	7038M	48093M	77727M	201227M	464891M	2736400M
1530192M	1577073M	1981117M	Total Assets ($)	4009M	30573M	30851M	104220M	226571M	1584893M

© RMA 2003

M = $ thousand   MM = $ million
See Pages 11 through 18 for Explanation of Ratios and Data

Current Data Sorted By Assets   **Comparative Historical Data**

0-500M	500M-2MM	2-10MM	10-50MM	50-100MM	100-250MM	Type of Statement	4/1/98-3/31/99 ALL	4/1/99-3/31/00 ALL
		7	7	2	4	Unqualified	21	23
	5	26	6			Reviewed	36	27
	8	23	4			Compiled	38	22
1	2	2				Tax Returns	4	9
	3	5	6	1	3	Other	24	15
	32 (4/1-9/30/02)		83 (10/1/02-3/31/03)					
1	18	63	23	3	7	**NUMBER OF STATEMENTS**	123	96
%	%	%	%	%	%	**ASSETS**	%	%
	11.2	8.0	8.1			Cash & Equivalents	8.3	9.8
	29.8	33.2	36.7			Trade Receivables (net)	32.5	33.2
	38.4	37.6	30.9			Inventory	38.2	37.1
	1.8	2.0	2.2			All Other Current	1.3	1.5
	81.2	80.7	78.0			Total Current	80.3	81.6
	10.1	11.4	13.0			Fixed Assets (net)	11.1	10.7
	1.1	2.2	.4			Intangibles (net)	3.2	2.9
	7.7	5.6	8.6			All Other Non-Current	5.4	4.8
	100.0	100.0	100.0			Total	100.0	100.0
						LIABILITIES		
	23.2	20.9	34.3			Notes Payable-Short Term	20.6	17.1
	.8	2.7	1.2			Cur. Mat.-L/T/D	2.0	3.0
	16.1	16.6	13.2			Trade Payables	17.1	17.5
	.1	.5	2.0			Income Taxes Payable	.4	.6
	8.5	7.6	10.0			All Other Current	7.5	6.7
	48.7	48.2	60.8			Total Current	47.6	45.0
	4.7	8.5	4.4			Long Term Debt	8.6	9.1
	.1	.2	.0			Deferred Taxes	.3	.2
	4.2	2.5	1.6			All Other Non-Current	3.2	2.8
	42.4	40.6	33.2			Net Worth	40.4	43.0
	100.0	100.0	100.0			Total Liabilities & Net Worth	100.0	100.0
						INCOME DATA		
	100.0	100.0	100.0			Net Sales	100.0	100.0
	14.8	8.7	9.2			Gross Profit	11.9	11.5
	13.2	7.9	8.3			Operating Expenses	9.8	9.0
	1.6	.8	1.0			Operating Profit	2.1	2.5
	.1	.0	.4			All Other Expenses (net)	.1	.3
	1.5	.8	.6			Profit Before Taxes	2.0	2.2
						RATIOS		
	2.2	2.5	1.5			Current	2.5	3.2
	1.9	1.6	1.2				1.7	1.8
	1.2	1.2	1.0				1.2	1.3
	1.2	1.6	.9			Quick	1.3	1.5
	.8	.8	.6				.8	.9
	.6	.5	.5				.6	.7
	9 42.1	10 35.8	13 29.1			Sales/Receivables	13 28.4	10 35.0
	17 21.5	14 25.8	18 20.2				17 21.3	15 24.1
	29 12.6	19 19.2	23 15.6				22 16.3	21 17.2
	16 23.0	10 37.2	10 37.7			Cost of Sales/Inventory	14 25.6	11 34.2
	23 16.2	17 21.6	18 20.0				22 16.7	15 23.7
	27 13.5	26 14.0	22 16.8				32 11.4	28 13.1
	1 269.9	3 115.2	4 88.6			Cost of Sales/Payables	4 81.4	3 104.3
	4 91.5	6 58.7	7 61.4				9 42.1	8 47.3
	15 24.5	12 30.0	10 36.1				13 27.8	14 25.4
	11.3	16.9	34.4			Sales/Working Capital	13.5	12.2
	20.2	27.5	72.1				23.2	25.5
	48.9	57.3	−359.7				52.1	51.1
	7.6	9.2	10.0			EBIT/Interest	7.1	9.2
	(15) 2.0	(57) 3.6	(22) 2.8				(112) 2.9	(90) 4.5
	1.5	1.8	1.1				1.4	2.0
		3.9				Net Profit + Depr., Dep.,	8.7	12.5
		(18) 2.3				Amort./Cur. Mat. L /T/D	(41) 2.9	(28) 7.2
		.7					1.4	2.6
	.1	.1	.2			Fixed/Worth	.1	.1
	.2	.2	.3				.3	.2
	.7	.7	.9				.7	.5
	.7	.7	1.0			Debt/Worth	.7	.5
	1.3	1.9	3.3				2.2	1.7
	3.3	3.7	6.1				5.0	3.7
	48.6	27.0	32.9			% Profit Before Taxes/Tangible	34.2	40.6
	(17) 10.0	(60) 15.2	11.4			Net Worth	(118) 21.6	(92) 20.7
	2.6	6.1	5.5				8.7	10.2
	11.9	10.6	6.9			% Profit Before Taxes/Total	14.1	18.5
	3.8	4.7	3.7			Assets	6.2	8.1
	.6	2.5	.7				2.3	2.8
	191.3	290.1	210.3			Sales/Net Fixed Assets	186.0	349.2
	92.2	106.5	74.6				85.6	97.5
	53.8	39.5	42.8				39.5	38.7
	9.7	11.7	10.3			Sales/Total Assets	9.2	11.9
	7.7	8.4	8.8				7.0	8.6
	5.1	6.3	5.2				4.7	5.5
	.2	.1	.2			% Depr., Dep., Amort./Sales	.2	.1
	(15) .3	(55) .3	(22) .2				(108) .3	(80) .3
	.7	.5	.5				.5	.5
	1.2	.3				% Officers', Directors',	.4	.4
	(12) 1.9	(34) .6				Owners' Comp/Sales	(52) .7	(46) .7
	4.3	1.3					1.3	1.3
1728M	161082M	2735663M	3884394M	641597M	7102866M	Net Sales ($)	9136075M	8687475M
168M	21300M	299120M	520667M	175604M	1007540M	Total Assets ($)	1350330M	1402422M

M = $ thousand   MM = $ million
See Pages 11 through 18 for Explanation of Ratios and Data

Comparative Historical Data | Current Data Sorted By Sales

13	14	20	Type of Statement		1	1	18
26	31	37	Unqualified	3	1	6	27
31	40	35	Reviewed	1	3	10	20
4	7	5	Compiled	1	1	1	1
12	23	18	Tax Returns / Other	2 / 1	1 / 2	1 / 2	1 / 12

Type of Statement distribution (Unqualified / Reviewed / Compiled / Tax Returns / Other):
- 1-3MM: Compiled 1, Tax Returns 2, Other 1
- 3-5MM: Reviewed 3, Compiled 1, Tax Returns 1, Other 1
- 5-10MM: Unqualified 1, Reviewed 1, Compiled 3, Other 2
- 10-25MM: Unqualified 1, Reviewed 6, Compiled 10, Tax Returns 1, Other 2
- 25MM & OVER: Unqualified 18, Reviewed 27, Compiled 20, Tax Returns 1, Other 12

Time periods (left): 4/1/00–3/31/01 ALL (86); 4/1/01–3/31/02 ALL (115); 4/1/02–3/31/03 ALL (115)
Right periods: 32 (4/1–9/30/02); 83 (10/1/02–3/31/03)

4/1/00–3/31/01 ALL	4/1/01–3/31/02 ALL	4/1/02–3/31/03 ALL		0-1MM	1-3MM	3-5MM	5-10MM	10-25MM	25MM & OVER
86	115	115	**NUMBER OF STATEMENTS**		4	6	7	20	78
%	%	%	**ASSETS**	%	%	%	%	%	%
7.0	9.1	8.4	Cash & Equivalents					6.8	8.1
35.0	33.7	32.9	Trade Receivables (net)					25.0	35.8
38.6	37.0	35.7	Inventory					40.2	34.6
2.2	1.8	2.1	All Other Current					1.2	2.3
82.7	81.6	79.1	Total Current					73.1	80.8
10.7	10.4	11.8	Fixed Assets (net)					15.5	10.9
1.9	2.3	2.4	Intangibles (net)					2.5	2.7
4.7	5.8	6.7	All Other Non-Current					8.9	5.6
100.0	100.0	100.0	Total					100.0	100.0
			LIABILITIES						
21.5	20.8	23.8	Notes Payable-Short Term					24.4	24.6
2.7	2.7	2.0	Cur. Mat.-L/T/D					1.7	2.2
16.5	16.1	16.2	Trade Payables					13.3	16.5
.4	1.0	.7	Income Taxes Payable					.4	.9
6.8	10.6	8.1	All Other Current					10.5	8.6
47.9	51.2	50.9	Total Current					50.4	52.7
5.3	6.8	8.1	Long Term Debt					8.1	7.7
.1	.1	.1	Deferred Taxes					.2	.1
1.8	3.1	2.6	All Other Non-Current					3.2	2.7
44.9	38.8	38.2	Net Worth					38.1	36.8
100.0	100.0	100.0	Total Liabilities & Net Worth					100.0	100.0
			INCOME DATA						
100.0	100.0	100.0	Net Sales					100.0	100.0
11.5	11.2	10.1	Gross Profit					12.5	7.5
10.0	9.9	8.8	Operating Expenses					11.2	6.1
1.5	1.2	1.3	Operating Profit					1.3	1.4
.1	.2	.3	All Other Expenses (net)					.6	.3
1.3	1.0	1.0	Profit Before Taxes					.7	1.1

(For columns 0-1MM through 5-10MM the ASSETS / LIABILITIES / INCOME DATA percentages are marked "DATA NOT AVAILABLE.")

RATIOS

4/1/00–3/31/01 ALL	4/1/01–3/31/02 ALL	4/1/02–3/31/03 ALL		10-25MM	25MM & OVER
2.8 / 1.8 / 1.2	2.3 / 1.7 / 1.2	2.3 / 1.5 / 1.2	Current	2.0 / 1.6 / .9	2.2 / 1.4 / 1.2
1.5 / .8 / .5	1.2 / .8 / .6	1.2 / .7 / .5	Quick	.8 / .6 / .4	1.1 / .7 / .5
11 33.3 / 17 22.1 / 22 16.5	9 38.8 / 14 26.3 / 21 17.4	10 35.0 / 16 23.5 / 22 16.4	Sales/Receivables	9 39.3 / 16 22.2 / 25 14.5	11 34.1 / 15 24.7 / 19 18.8
12 29.6 / 18 19.9 / 29 12.4	10 37.7 / 16 22.4 / 26 14.1	10 35.6 / 18 19.8 / 26 14.0	Cost of Sales/Inventory	21 17.2 / 24 15.2 / 43 8.6	9 40.0 / 15 25.1 / 21 17.3
4 99.7 / 7 53.1 / 15 23.7	3 108.0 / 6 57.8 / 11 32.7	3 114.8 / 7 55.8 / 13 28.3	Cost of Sales/Payables	4 90.9 / 10 37.3 / 13 27.5	3 114.3 / 6 63.4 / 11 34.4
13.0 / 26.5 / 57.0	15.6 / 30.3 / 61.3	16.9 / 29.4 / 89.9	Sales/Working Capital	15.3 / 25.9 / -203.3	21.2 / 34.7 / 90.7
(75) 8.6 / 2.7 / 1.4	(100) 8.0 / 3.1 / 1.8	(104) 8.2 / 3.0 / 1.6	EBIT/Interest	(18) 4.8 / 1.9 / .9	(72) 9.9 / 3.4 / 1.8
(26) 9.4 / 2.9 / 1.5	(30) 7.0 / 3.5 / 1.6	(32) 4.0 / 2.1 / .9	Net Profit + Depr., Dep., Amort./Cur. Mat. L/T/D		(23) 10.0 / 3.0 / 1.8
.1 / .2 / .6	.1 / .3 / .5	.1 / .3 / .8	Fixed/Worth	.2 / .3 / 1.1	.1 / .3 / .8
.6 / 1.2 / 2.7	.8 / 1.9 / 3.7	.8 / 1.9 / 4.2	Debt/Worth	.8 / 1.6 / 3.5	1.0 / 2.2 / 4.3
(79) 25.4 / 14.2 / 6.7	(106) 36.8 / 17.2 / 7.8	(108) 27.1 / 14.5 / 4.6	% Profit Before Taxes/Tangible Net Worth	(18) 15.8 / 5.7 / -.8	(74) 27.9 / 18.0 / 8.8
11.5 / 6.1 / 1.7	11.6 / 5.4 / 1.9	9.6 / 4.3 / 1.6	% Profit Before Taxes/Total Assets	6.2 / 3.3 / .3	10.7 / 5.6 / 2.5
167.8 / 83.1 / 53.4	203.7 / 93.2 / 48.6	221.2 / 91.8 / 39.1	Sales/Net Fixed Assets	122.4 / 75.3 / 23.1	277.4 / 97.8 / 52.5
10.5 / 8.0 / 5.8	11.1 / 8.7 / 5.9	10.5 / 8.1 / 5.9	Sales/Total Assets	9.3 / 6.3 / 4.5	11.5 / 8.9 / 7.2
(78) .1 / .2 / .5	(90) .1 / .2 / .5	(101) .2 / .3 / .6	% Depr., Dep., Amort./Sales	(18) .3 / .6 / .8	(71) .1 / .2 / .4
(48) .4 / 1.0 / 3.2	(53) .3 / .8 / 1.7	(55) .3 / .6 / 1.5	% Officers', Directors', Owners' Comp/Sales	(12) .4 / 1.3 / 2.3	(33) .3 / .5 / .7

4/1/00–3/31/01	4/1/01–3/31/02	4/1/02–3/31/03		1-3MM	3-5MM	5-10MM	10-25MM	25MM & OVER
8456705M	10666140M	14527330M	Net Sales ($)	8109M	23431M	52071M	336073M	14107646M
1089099M	1542566M	2024399M	Total Assets ($)	4342M	6243M	19410M	89662M	1904742M

M = $ thousand   MM = $ million
See Pages 11 through 18 for Explanation of Ratios and Data

WHOLESALE—Paint, Varnish, and Supplies Merchant Wholesalers   NAICS 424950   (SIC 5198)

Current Data Sorted By Assets   **Comparative Historical Data**

0-500M	500M-2MM	2-10MM	10-50MM	50-100MM	100-250MM	Type of Statement	4/1/98-3/31/99 ALL	4/1/99-3/31/00 ALL
	1	2	4	1	2	Unqualified	7	11
	5	9	5		1	Reviewed	16	14
1	10	3	2			Compiled	14	14
2	4	3				Tax Returns	6	7
	3	7	4		1	Other	12	12
	9 (4/1-9/30/02)		61 (10/1/02-3/31/03)					
3	23	24	15	1	4	**NUMBER OF STATEMENTS**	55	58
%	%	%	%	%	%	**ASSETS**	%	%
	8.1	7.8	9.3			Cash & Equivalents	7.0	7.2
	33.6	29.3	28.1			Trade Receivables (net)	32.4	32.4
	43.5	41.1	38.3			Inventory	35.1	33.4
	1.1	1.1	2.6			All Other Current	1.9	1.4
	86.4	79.3	78.3			Total Current	76.4	74.3
	9.2	14.1	9.8			Fixed Assets (net)	14.7	16.7
	.7	1.4	6.6			Intangibles (net)	4.3	2.7
	3.8	5.2	5.3			All Other Non-Current	4.6	6.3
	100.0	100.0	100.0			Total	100.0	100.0
						LIABILITIES		
	12.5	15.5	6.9			Notes Payable-Short Term	17.4	10.7
	1.3	1.7	1.2			Cur. Mat.-L/T/D	2.8	2.4
	30.4	25.9	18.9			Trade Payables	26.4	24.7
	.4	.4	.1			Income Taxes Payable	.2	.5
	7.9	8.1	9.6			All Other Current	6.3	6.3
	52.6	51.6	36.7			Total Current	53.2	44.5
	5.4	8.1	14.4			Long Term Debt	9.1	10.7
	.0	.4	.2			Deferred Taxes	.1	.1
	2.2	6.5	5.2			All Other Non-Current	10.6	9.5
	39.9	33.4	43.5			Net Worth	27.1	35.2
	100.0	100.0	100.0			Total Liabilities & Net Worth	100.0	100.0
						INCOME DATA		
	100.0	100.0	100.0			Net Sales	100.0	100.0
	34.2	34.1	30.4			Gross Profit	31.3	36.2
	31.1	32.0	26.6			Operating Expenses	28.4	32.8
	3.1	2.0	3.7			Operating Profit	2.9	3.4
	.0	.3	.5			All Other Expenses (net)	.5	.1
	3.1	1.8	3.2			Profit Before Taxes	2.4	3.3
						RATIOS		
	2.7	2.7	4.0			Current	2.1	3.1
	1.8	1.5	2.2				1.4	1.9
	1.3	1.1	1.5				1.2	1.0
	1.4	1.4	1.9			Quick	1.1	1.6
	.8	.7	1.1				.7	.8
	.6	.5	.6				.5	.5
	26 14.0	33 11.2	27 13.3			Sales/Receivables	29 12.6	34 10.8
	40 9.1	40 9.2	42 8.7				37 9.9	41 8.8
	49 7.4	49 7.4	50 7.4				53 6.9	53 6.9
	45 8.1	47 7.8	45 8.1			Cost of Sales/Inventory	45 8.1	40 9.0
	77 4.8	81 4.5	72 5.1				65 5.6	75 4.8
	110 3.3	131 2.8	86 4.2				105 3.5	115 3.2
	31 11.8	26 14.1	13 28.3			Cost of Sales/Payables	28 13.2	35 10.3
	51 7.2	44 8.3	32 11.3				42 8.7	46 8.0
	80 4.5	67 5.4	44 8.2				63 5.8	65 5.6
	6.5	4.7	4.7			Sales/Working Capital	5.8	5.1
	9.5	10.6	7.4				11.6	9.9
	16.3	28.5	11.2				26.4	130.3
	33.1	9.4	10.1			EBIT/Interest	(50) 7.4	(50) 9.7
	(20) 6.7	(19) 2.5	(14) 5.2				2.4	3.9
	2.3	1.5	2.7				1.3	1.7
						Net Profit + Depr., Dep., Amort./Cur. Mat. L /T/D	(19) 5.0	(18) 14.4
							2.8	3.2
							1.3	1.0
	.1	.1	.1			Fixed/Worth	.2	.2
	.2	.3	.2				.4	.5
	.8	.5	.7				1.4	1.3
	.6	.6	.4			Debt/Worth	1.0	.8
	1.2	2.4	1.5				2.1	1.5
	7.7	5.5	5.0				11.6	6.3
	42.2	23.2	32.7			% Profit Before Taxes/Tangible Net Worth	(43) 33.3	(51) 40.2
	(21) 21.6	(22) 16.3	(13) 15.2				18.5	18.4
	6.5	6.3	4.2				6.4	4.3
	22.0	10.1	12.7			% Profit Before Taxes/Total Assets	10.0	14.7
	6.4	4.7	5.1				5.1	6.4
	2.5	.8	2.1				1.3	2.0
	71.2	91.1	65.1			Sales/Net Fixed Assets	76.8	30.6
	43.8	26.5	37.4				23.8	18.7
	27.4	11.1	15.4				12.1	12.4
	4.0	3.3	3.6			Sales/Total Assets	3.5	3.9
	3.3	2.5	2.9				2.9	2.5
	2.6	1.9	1.9				2.1	1.9
	.4	.5	.6			% Depr., Dep., Amort./Sales	(41) .6	(52) 1.0
	.7	(22) 1.0	(13) .7				1.1	1.4
	1.2	1.7	1.2				1.8	2.2
	2.4					% Officers', Directors', Owners' Comp/Sales	(21) 2.3	(16) 1.7
	(11) 4.4						3.3	3.7
	8.2						5.7	6.4
2316M	88900M	249199M	954803M	114289M	1121028M	Net Sales ($)	1658609M	1714372M
676M	27361M	100031M	350525M	66639M	796038M	Total Assets ($)	910336M	889575M

© RMA 2003

M = $ thousand   MM = $ million
See Pages 11 through 18 for Explanation of Ratios and Data

Comparative Historical Data | **Current Data Sorted By Sales**

4/1/00-3/31/01 ALL	4/1/01-3/31/02 ALL	4/1/02-3/31/03 ALL		0-1MM	1-3MM	3-5MM	5-10MM	10-25MM	25MM & OVER
			Type of Statement		9 (4/1-9/30/02)		61 (10/1/02-3/31/03)		
5	5	10	Unqualified		1	1	3	1	7
7	11	20	Reviewed		2	4		5	6
17	16	16	Compiled		5	3	4	3	1
2	5	9	Tax Returns	2	1	4	1	1	
17	10	15	Other		1	1	4	4	5
48	47	70	**NUMBER OF STATEMENTS**	2	10	13	12	14	19
%	%	%	**ASSETS**	%	%	%	%	%	%
5.4	5.7	8.4	Cash & Equivalents		4.1	13.0	6.4	10.8	6.9
35.2	31.0	30.2	Trade Receivables (net)		29.5	29.8	33.9	31.7	26.9
36.4	36.3	39.8	Inventory		48.0	41.7	44.3	34.8	35.7
2.3	2.8	1.5	All Other Current		1.2	1.1	1.0	1.1	2.5
79.4	75.8	79.9	Total Current		82.7	85.7	85.7	78.4	72.0
11.2	14.2	11.9	Fixed Assets (net)		10.8	9.3	9.4	16.0	12.1
2.9	3.6	3.5	Intangibles (net)		1.4	.2	.3	2.1	10.3
6.5	6.4	4.7	All Other Non-Current		5.1	4.8	4.6	3.5	5.7
100.0	100.0	100.0	Total		100.0	100.0	100.0	100.0	100.0
			LIABILITIES						
15.0	16.2	11.9	Notes Payable-Short Term		13.2	9.5	17.3	16.6	7.3
2.3	4.7	2.1	Cur. Mat.-L/T/D		1.2	1.2	1.1	2.2	1.2
28.9	21.7	24.9	Trade Payables		20.6	34.2	35.1	20.1	17.3
.5	.1	.4	Income Taxes Payable		.5	.4	.5	.3	.3
7.3	9.2	7.7	All Other Current		12.4	4.2	7.6	8.4	8.0
54.0	52.0	47.0	Total Current		47.8	49.5	61.6	47.5	34.0
6.0	7.8	9.5	Long Term Debt		7.1	4.7	3.3	10.4	15.2
.1	.1	.2	Deferred Taxes		.0	.2	.4	.2	.3
3.6	7.3	6.6	All Other Non-Current		12.2	6.4	6.7	2.7	5.6
36.3	32.7	36.6	Net Worth		32.9	39.1	28.0	39.2	45.0
100.0	100.0	100.0	Total Liabilities & Net Worth		100.0	100.0	100.0	100.0	100.0
			INCOME DATA						
100.0	100.0	100.0	Net Sales		100.0	100.0	100.0	100.0	100.0
34.0	35.4	33.3	Gross Profit		40.6	37.5	26.7	33.2	31.2
31.7	33.9	30.0	Operating Expenses		39.7	34.6	23.6	29.6	26.2
2.3	1.5	3.4	Operating Profit		1.0	2.9	3.1	3.7	5.0
–.3	.5	.4	All Other Expenses (net)		–.2	.4	.2	.2	1.0
2.7	1.1	2.9	Profit Before Taxes		1.2	2.5	2.9	3.5	4.0
			RATIOS						
2.2 / 1.5 / 1.1	2.3 / 1.4 / 1.1	3.1 / 1.7 / 1.3	Current		3.7 / 1.7 / 1.3	2.6 / 1.8 / 1.3	3.2 / 1.6 / 1.0	1.9 / 1.5 / 1.4	3.7 / 2.2 / 1.4
1.0 / .8 / .5	1.0 / .7 / .5	1.5 / .8 / .5	Quick		1.4 / .8 / .6	1.4 / .8 / .5	1.8 / .6 / .5	1.4 / .8 / .5	1.7 / 1.1 / .6
33 11.0 / 40 9.0 / 52 7.0	30 12.0 / 44 8.3 / 56 6.5	31 11.9 / 40 9.1 / 50 7.4	Sales/Receivables		32 11.5 / 41 9.0 / 50 7.3	29 12.5 / 40 9.1 / 52 7.0	26 13.9 / 40 9.0 / 55 6.6	30 12.2 / 39 9.5 / 47 7.8	32 11.4 / 42 8.6 / 56 6.5
48 7.6 / 72 5.0 / 107 3.4	41 8.8 / 77 4.8 / 124 2.9	50 7.3 / 75 4.9 / 123 3.0	Cost of Sales/Inventory		63 5.8 / 81 4.5 / 214 1.7	42 8.6 / 110 3.3 / 145 2.5	45 8.2 / 68 5.3 / 94 3.9	36 10.1 / 73 5.0 / 93 3.9	52 7.1 / 73 5.0 / 88 4.2
25 14.5 / 49 7.5 / 62 5.9	27 13.5 / 42 8.7 / 65 5.6	26 13.9 / 42 8.7 / 64 5.7	Cost of Sales/Payables		19 19.1 / 49 7.4 / 74 4.9	40 9.0 / 67 5.5 / 109 3.4	27 13.3 / 43 8.5 / 64 5.7	14 25.9 / 33 11.1 / 56 6.5	25 14.7 / 33 10.9 / 50 7.3
5.4 / 11.0 / 31.4	4.9 / 12.4 / 41.0	5.5 / 9.8 / 15.9	Sales/Working Capital		5.6 / 8.4 / NM	4.2 / 10.2 / 16.0	6.4 / 16.9 / NM	7.8 / 10.6 / 14.4	4.7 / 7.4 / 12.5
(43) 7.5 / 3.5 / 1.5	(44) 7.1 / 2.8 / 1.1	(61) 11.1 / 3.6 / 1.6	EBIT/Interest			(10) 43.7 / 5.6 / –.2	(10) 37.7 / 6.2 / 1.4		(11) 9.4 / 2.9 / 1.8	10.4 / 4.1 / 2.7
(12) 10.5 / 2.7 / .8	(14) 4.6 / 1.0 / .0	(20) 15.2 / 6.2 / 3.5	Net Profit + Depr., Dep., Amort./Cur. Mat. L/T/D						
.1 / .3 / .8	.2 / .5 / 1.5	.1 / .3 / .9	Fixed/Worth			.1 / .4 / NM	.1 / .2 / .7	.1 / .2 / .4	.2 / .3 / .6	.1 / .2 / 1.0
.7 / 1.7 / 5.0	.8 / 2.5 / 10.2	.6 / 1.7 / 5.9	Debt/Worth			.3 / 1.6 / NM	.5 / 1.2 / 6.3	.4 / 1.7 / 29.3	1.0 / 2.2 / 3.3	.5 / 1.5 / 5.0
(44) 37.0 / 16.5 / 5.2	(41) 54.3 / 14.5 / 1.2	(61) 36.6 / 18.5 / 6.4	% Profit Before Taxes/Tangible Net Worth				(12) 48.4 / 19.3 / 8.1	(10) 28.0 / 20.1 / 7.4	31.4 / 16.3 / 8.9	(16) 38.2 / 17.4 / 4.1
9.8 / 5.5 / 1.2	10.7 / 4.2 / .0	13.4 / 5.8 / 1.9	% Profit Before Taxes/Total Assets			17.9 / 3.1 / –1.5	18.2 / 7.1 / .4	17.3 / 3.6 / .8	11.5 / 6.9 / 2.5	12.7 / 7.4 / 2.1
96.5 / 27.3 / 16.4	52.9 / 24.2 / 11.7	67.2 / 32.7 / 16.3	Sales/Net Fixed Assets			125.2 / 36.5 / 13.8	84.8 / 49.8 / 22.6	115.6 / 40.9 / 24.2	39.9 / 26.5 / 13.4	62.0 / 35.0 / 15.4
3.9 / 2.8 / 2.1	3.4 / 2.7 / 1.9	3.6 / 2.9 / 2.0	Sales/Total Assets			3.4 / 2.7 / 2.0	3.4 / 2.9 / 1.9	4.0 / 3.4 / 2.3	3.4 / 3.0 / 2.2	3.5 / 2.2 / 1.7
(39) .5 / 1.0 / 1.8	(41) .6 / 1.2 / 1.9	(62) .5 / .9 / 1.5	% Depr., Dep., Amort./Sales				(11) .4 / .6 / 1.4	(13) .3 / .7 / 1.9	(14) .7 / 1.0 / 1.1	.6 / .7 / 1.4
(20) 1.8 / 3.2 / 5.7	(17) 1.6 / 3.0 / 4.5	(26) 1.5 / 3.6 / 5.7	% Officers', Directors', Owners' Comp/Sales						
1422184M / 786782M	728449M / 313524M	2530535M / 1341270M	Net Sales ($) / Total Assets ($)	879M / 245M	22152M / 13597M	50014M / 20917M	82221M / 27732M	206037M / 87163M	2169232M / 1191616M

M = $ thousand   MM = $ million
See Pages 11 through 18 for Explanation of Ratios and Data

Current Data Sorted By Assets   Comparative Historical Data

						Type of Statement		
2	5	26	31	5	7	Unqualified	78	72
1	31	83	15	2		Reviewed	144	113
18	43	30	2		1	Compiled	123	113
15	28	9			1	Tax Returns	35	31
11	36	45	27	4	5	Other	123	127
98 (4/1-9/30/02)			385 (10/1/02-3/31/03)				4/1/98-3/31/99	4/1/99-3/31/00
0-500M	500M-2MM	2-10MM	10-50MM	50-100MM	100-250MM		ALL	ALL
47	143	193	75	11	14	NUMBER OF STATEMENTS	503	456
%	%	%	%	%	%	ASSETS	%	%
9.7	12.6	8.0	6.8	3.8	5.1	Cash & Equivalents	8.9	8.9
28.6	35.0	31.4	29.5	26.9	21.6	Trade Receivables (net)	32.2	32.9
34.9	34.4	35.8	35.6	34.5	35.3	Inventory	35.3	34.6
4.2	2.5	2.3	2.2	2.8	2.1	All Other Current	1.9	1.5
77.4	84.4	77.5	74.1	68.0	64.2	Total Current	78.3	77.9
12.3	9.3	13.2	16.0	21.9	12.3	Fixed Assets (net)	13.7	13.5
3.7	2.2	2.6	4.4	4.9	14.9	Intangibles (net)	2.7	2.8
6.6	4.2	6.7	5.5	5.2	8.6	All Other Non-Current	5.4	5.8
100.0	100.0	100.0	100.0	100.0	100.0	Total	100.0	100.0
						LIABILITIES		
19.9	14.8	17.4	16.5	15.4	7.8	Notes Payable-Short Term	17.1	17.7
5.5	3.4	3.1	3.0	2.8	1.9	Cur. Mat.-L/T/D	2.3	2.8
25.0	22.4	21.6	19.0	15.2	15.5	Trade Payables	20.8	20.9
1.0	.3	.2	.2	.2	1.0	Income Taxes Payable	.3	.3
14.9	12.2	8.4	7.4	15.2	5.4	All Other Current	9.7	10.8
66.3	53.1	50.7	46.1	48.8	31.5	Total Current	50.2	52.4
13.3	9.3	7.2	11.9	13.0	28.4	Long Term Debt	8.4	9.9
.0	.1	.2	.3	.2	.7	Deferred Taxes	.2	.2
4.7	5.8	6.6	4.3	3.4	10.1	All Other Non-Current	5.8	5.4
15.7	31.8	35.2	37.5	34.7	29.2	Net Worth	35.4	32.1
100.0	100.0	100.0	100.0	100.0	100.0	Total Liabilities & Net Worth	100.0	100.0
						INCOME DATA		
100.0	100.0	100.0	100.0	100.0	100.0	Net Sales	100.0	100.0
38.4	33.6	31.4	31.9	36.7	36.7	Gross Profit	31.8	32.4
35.1	30.9	27.7	26.2	32.6	26.3	Operating Expenses	29.5	28.3
3.2	2.8	3.7	5.7	4.1	10.3	Operating Profit	2.3	4.1
.7	.9	.6	.8	1.5	2.2	All Other Expenses (net)	.7	.6
2.5	1.9	3.1	4.8	2.6	8.2	Profit Before Taxes	1.6	3.6
						RATIOS		
2.2	2.6	2.4	2.8	2.3	3.3		2.4	2.2
1.3	1.6	1.5	1.5	1.3	2.4	Current	1.6	1.4
.9	1.2	1.2	1.2	1.1	1.5		1.2	1.2
1.5	1.5	1.3	1.3	.9	1.2		1.3	1.3
(46) .7	.9	.8	.7	.6	.8	Quick	.8	.8
.3	.5	.5	.5	.4	.6		.5	.5
10 36.3	23 15.7	23 15.8	33 11.1	25 14.6	27 13.7		23 15.7	26 14.3
26 14.3	39 9.3	37 9.7	43 8.5	48 7.6	34 10.8	Sales/Receivables	38 9.6	39 9.4
38 9.5	54 6.8	55 6.6	57 6.3	74 5.0	58 6.3		56 6.5	57 6.4
12 31.5	20 17.8	37 9.8	37 9.8	69 5.3	71 5.1		28 12.9	28 13.0
40 9.2	53 6.9	66 5.6	72 5.1	105 3.5	95 3.8	Cost of Sales/Inventory	67 5.5	63 5.8
110 3.3	121 3.0	108 3.4	146 2.5	175 2.1	133 2.7		121 3.0	116 3.1
6 62.3	14 25.5	18 20.1	18 20.0	34 10.7	26 14.0		14 25.7	15 24.1
32 11.4	34 10.6	33 11.0	32 11.6	38 9.7	42 8.8	Cost of Sales/Payables	32 11.4	35 10.6
63 5.8	55 6.6	53 6.9	58 6.2	54 6.7	51 7.1		56 6.6	57 6.4
7.4	4.7	5.3	4.9	4.8	3.7		5.6	6.1
23.5	9.8	9.9	10.2	10.0	6.5	Sales/Working Capital	10.7	12.4
-52.3	30.2	31.3	27.9	34.1	10.2		29.9	34.5
16.7	8.5	9.5	9.0	6.6	9.8		7.2	7.2
(37) 3.4	(125) 3.0	(176) 4.3	(70) 4.5	3.8	3.0	EBIT/Interest	(445) 2.8	(408) 3.2
-.5	1.0	1.8	2.5	1.5	1.8		1.3	1.5
	6.1	5.0	10.5			Net Profit + Depr., Dep.,	7.6	7.1
	(18) 2.2	(50) 2.4	(24) 2.7			Amort./Cur. Mat. L /T/D	(107) 2.9	(104) 3.0
	.2	1.0	.9				1.3	1.2
.1	.0	.1	.2	.4	.2		.1	.1
.4	.2	.3	.4	.6	.5	Fixed/Worth	.3	.3
4.3	.5	1.0	1.0	1.0	-.6		.8	.9
1.0	.9	.8	.7	1.1	1.3		1.0	.9
3.2	2.5	2.0	1.9	2.3	7.4	Debt/Worth	2.0	2.1
UND	9.2	4.4	7.8	2.4	-10.7		5.1	5.8
70.3	47.6	39.5	50.6	41.3	104.5	% Profit Before Taxes/Tangible	43.8	52.4
(36) 24.7	(123) 12.3	(176) 19.0	(68) 22.3	(10) 15.6	(10) 57.9	Net Worth	(455) 17.3	(402) 21.4
-2.9	1.3	6.4	12.0	2.6	18.7		5.9	8.1
17.1	14.0	13.1	13.3	7.2	21.2	% Profit Before Taxes/Total	12.9	14.7
1.4	4.4	7.5	6.9	4.2	7.9	Assets	5.0	6.5
-3.9	-.3	2.1	3.2	.6	1.3		1.0	2.2
178.3	240.4	100.8	60.4	33.7	37.8		109.5	91.6
49.1	75.2	45.8	23.4	9.1	18.4	Sales/Net Fixed Assets	39.3	40.8
21.4	30.2	15.8	9.0	4.0	9.0		17.2	16.6
5.5	4.2	3.7	3.0	2.5	3.2		4.0	3.8
3.9	2.9	2.7	2.4	2.1	1.8	Sales/Total Assets	2.7	2.8
2.2	2.1	2.1	1.9	1.3	1.1		1.9	2.0
.5	.2	.4	.4		.3		.3	.4
(26) 1.0	(109) .6	(170) .6	(67) .9		(10) 1.0	% Depr., Dep., Amort./Sales	(413) .7	(386) .7
1.8	1.3	1.5	1.8		2.5		1.4	1.5
2.6	2.3	1.8	1.6				2.1	1.9
(24) 4.4	(87) 3.8	(91) 3.2	(24) 2.3			% Officers', Directors', Owners' Comp/Sales	(240) 4.3	(232) 3.9
9.2	6.2	6.2	5.8				7.7	6.4
56812M	563887M	2708853M	4435890M	1517220M	6147621M	Net Sales ($)	9746577M	10450469M
13397M	166380M	854502M	1639735M	786580M	2671731M	Total Assets ($)	3908424M	4191130M

M = $ thousand   MM = $ million
See Pages 11 through 18 for Explanation of Ratios and Data

Comparative Historical Data | Current Data Sorted By Sales

						Type of Statement						
	65		57		76	Unqualified	2	2	1	5	19	47
	118		107		132	Reviewed	1	11	18	43	39	20
	135		140		94	Compiled	8	30	18	16	16	6
	36		29		53	Tax Returns	14	17	12	6	3	1
	119		132		128	Other	7	16	20	28	24	33
	4/1/00- 3/31/01 ALL		4/1/01- 3/31/02 ALL		4/1/02- 3/31/03 ALL		98 (4/1-9/30/02)			385 (10/1/02-3/31/03)		
							0-1MM	1-3MM	3-5MM	5-10MM	10-25MM	25MM & OVER
	473		465		483	NUMBER OF STATEMENTS	32	76	69	98	101	107
	%		%		%	ASSETS	%	%	%	%	%	%
	8.8		8.8		9.2	Cash & Equivalents	12.0	10.4	11.2	11.5	6.9	6.2
	32.2		30.8		31.5	Trade Receivables (net)	19.2	31.0	31.2	35.3	34.7	29.1
	34.4		35.6		35.2	Inventory	36.1	38.2	36.1	33.0	33.6	35.8
	2.2		2.4		2.5	All Other Current	5.9	1.8	1.5	3.2	2.5	2.1
	77.6		77.7		78.4	Total Current	73.2	81.4	80.0	83.0	77.7	73.2
	13.7		13.2		12.6	Fixed Assets (net)	13.7	10.6	12.6	10.4	13.3	14.8
	2.9		3.4		3.3	Intangibles (net)	4.9	3.4	1.9	1.9	2.5	5.5
	5.7		5.7		5.8	All Other Non-Current	8.1	4.6	5.5	4.6	6.5	6.5
	100.0		100.0		100.0	Total	100.0	100.0	100.0	100.0	100.0	100.0
						LIABILITIES						
	17.0		18.6		16.4	Notes Payable-Short Term	22.1	14.7	14.7	17.4	17.0	15.7
	3.0		3.4		3.4	Cur. Mat.-L/T/D	4.2	3.7	3.6	3.8	2.5	3.1
	20.5		19.8		21.4	Trade Payables	19.4	21.0	21.3	22.2	22.0	21.2
	.3		.3		.3	Income Taxes Payable	1.4	.2	.2	.3	.3	.2
	10.6		9.4		10.1	All Other Current	14.6	8.9	15.1	11.2	7.0	8.1
	51.4		51.6		51.6	Total Current	61.7	48.5	54.8	54.9	48.8	48.4
	9.0		9.3		9.9	Long Term Debt	12.2	13.7	9.2	6.0	6.6	13.5
	.2		.2		.2	Deferred Taxes	.0	.1	.1	.1	.3	.3
	7.5		5.9		5.8	All Other Non-Current	5.4	7.2	9.2	4.7	4.3	5.4
	32.1		33.1		32.5	Net Worth	20.7	30.6	26.7	34.3	39.9	32.5
	100.0		100.0		100.0	Total Liabilities & Net Worth	100.0	100.0	100.0	100.0	100.0	100.0
						INCOME DATA						
	100.0		100.0		100.0	Net Sales	100.0	100.0	100.0	100.0	100.0	100.0
	34.2		32.9		33.1	Gross Profit	36.1	38.6	33.4	33.2	30.6	30.4
	30.6		29.2		29.2	Operating Expenses	32.8	36.3	30.6	29.5	26.0	25.0
	3.5		3.8		3.9	Operating Profit	3.3	2.3	2.8	3.7	4.6	5.4
	.5		.9		.8	All Other Expenses (net)	1.6	.8	.6	.8	.4	1.0
	3.1		2.9		3.1	Profit Before Taxes	1.7	1.5	2.2	2.9	4.2	4.4
						RATIOS						
	2.3		2.5		2.6		2.4	3.4	2.8	2.3	2.0	2.7
	1.5		1.5		1.6	Current	1.3	1.9	1.6	1.5	1.5	1.4
	1.1		1.1		1.2		.8	1.2	1.2	1.1	1.3	1.1
	1.2		1.2		1.3		1.0	2.4	1.4	1.3	1.3	1.1
	.8		.8	(482)	.8	Quick	.4	(75) .8	.8	.8	.9	.7
	.5		.5		.5		.2	.5	.5	.6	.6	.6
26	13.9	23	15.8	23	15.7		1	672.2	25	14.8	22	16.9	27	13.3	26	14.3	21	17.5
41	8.9	36	10.0	38	9.6	Sales/Receivables	27	13.6	38	9.6	34	10.8	40	9.0	39	9.4	38	9.6
56	6.5	51	7.1	55	6.7		71	5.1	58	6.3	51	7.1	56	6.5	54	6.8	53	6.9
29	12.5	32	11.6	33	10.9		27	13.4	29	12.5	29	12.7	35	10.3	34	10.8	35	10.4
67	5.4	67	5.5	65	5.6	Cost of Sales/Inventory	100	3.7	78	4.7	57	6.4	65	5.6	59	6.2	69	5.3
122	3.0	125	2.9	118	3.1		175	2.1	169	2.2	125	2.9	100	3.6	104	3.5	120	3.0
16	22.2	14	25.5	18	20.5		1	254.5	18	19.7	14	25.7	19	19.0	18	20.3	18	20.0
32	11.4	30	12.2	34	10.7	Cost of Sales/Payables	35	10.5	40	9.2	31	11.8	36	10.2	32	11.5	33	11.0
57	6.4	47	7.7	54	6.7		104	3.5	64	5.7	49	7.4	53	6.8	51	7.2	51	7.2
	5.6		5.6		5.1		2.7	3.7	5.1	5.7	6.2	5.1
	10.8		11.3		10.0	Sales/Working Capital	9.3	8.2	9.5	9.8	11.9	11.9
	39.2		35.7		32.6		−64.8	23.0	34.1	38.2	24.8	32.9
	7.6		7.2		9.1			7.1		6.6		10.9		9.8		10.1		8.5
(417)	2.9	(417)	2.6	(433)	3.6	EBIT/Interest	(23)	1.8	(67)	2.7	(62)	3.2	(87)	3.2	(91)	5.0	(103)	4.4
	1.4		1.0		1.5			.4		.4		1.2		1.3		2.4		2.2
	9.6		6.5		5.8	Net Profit + Depr., Dep.,				6.8		4.2		3.2		6.9		8.3
(108)	2.8	(92)	2.5	(105)	2.4	Amort./Cur. Mat. L/T/D			(10)	3.7	(12)	2.1	(17)	1.0	(32)	2.7	(33)	3.0
	1.0		.8		1.0					.8		.5		.2		1.4		1.2
	.1		.1		.1		.0	.0	.1	.1	.1	.2
	.3		.3		.3	Fixed/Worth	.3	.2	.3	.2	.2	.4
	.9		1.1		1.0		2.8	1.3	1.2	.6	.7	1.1
	1.0		.9		.8		.8	.7	.8	.9	.8	.9
	2.2		2.3		2.2	Debt/Worth	3.3	2.7	2.3	2.1	1.8	2.2
	5.4		7.2		7.4		UND	13.7	13.7	6.0	4.0	9.7
	53.1		45.3		46.1	% Profit Before Taxes/Tangible		48.1		44.9		40.0		38.3		55.7		55.3
(431)	21.0	(409)	16.6	(423)	19.7	Net Worth	(24)	9.8	(63)	9.1	(55)	18.1	(92)	17.4	(97)	25.0	(92)	23.1
	5.9		2.5		4.9			−4.4		−3.2		4.1		3.4		11.9		11.9
	14.5		13.0		13.3	% Profit Before Taxes/Total	11.3	12.1	11.5	13.2	14.7	13.5
	5.9		5.3		6.1	Assets	.4	3.0	4.5	6.4	8.6	6.9
	1.7		.2		.9		−3.3	−2.6	.6	.7	3.7	3.0
	91.1		97.4		116.6		306.7	197.4	155.3	148.9	97.5	72.5
	34.7		39.9		44.2	Sales/Net Fixed Assets	43.6	44.4	63.8	60.3	43.9	26.4
	14.4		14.8		16.7		8.9	19.9	22.2	24.7	18.7	9.8
	3.9		3.8		3.8		2.4	3.9	4.2	4.0	3.9	3.7
	2.7		2.8		2.8	Sales/Total Assets	1.5	2.7	2.8	3.0	2.9	2.6
	1.9		2.0		2.0		1.1	1.8	2.0	2.1	2.2	1.9
	.3		.3		.4		.8	.3	.3	.3	.3	.5
(390)	.7	(371)	.7	(391)	.7	% Depr., Dep., Amort./Sales	(17)	1.8	(55)	.9	(53)	.6	(81)	.6	(93)	.7	(92)	.8
	1.6		1.6		1.6		3.5	1.7	1.2	1.2	1.4	1.8
	2.2		2.2		2.0	% Officers', Directors',	2.3	3.1	2.3	2.2	1.4	.9
(234)	3.9	(207)	4.0	(229)	3.3	Owners' Comp/Sales	(13)	3.8	(50)	5.2	(34)	3.8	(55)	3.9	(48)	2.5	(29)	2.2
	6.2		7.0		6.4		12.4	7.4	5.9	6.6	5.2	4.5
	11594361M		12510145M		15430283M	Net Sales ($)	16896M	148092M	281255M	704461M	1671479M	12608100M
	5276685M		4922863M		6132325M	Total Assets ($)	11438M	71748M	113527M	261832M	607881M	5065899M

© RMA 2003

M = $ thousand   MM = $ million
See Pages 11 through 18 for Explanation of Ratios and Data

RETAIL TRADE

Current Data Sorted By Assets   Comparative Historical Data

0-500M	500M-2MM	2-10MM	10-50MM	50-100MM	100-250MM	Type of Statement	4/1/98-3/31/99 ALL	4/1/99-3/31/00 ALL
2	7	63	76	14	10	Unqualified	256	184
3	14	262	155	6	4	Reviewed	513	426
10	35	128	41	4		Compiled	255	241
21	35	149	46		1	Tax Returns	159	164
13	73	789	440	14	11	Other	2501	2173
	176 (4/1-9/30/02)		2250 (10/1/02-3/31/03)					
49	164	1391	758	38	26	**NUMBER OF STATEMENTS**	3684	3188
%	%	%	%	%	%	**ASSETS**	%	%
10.9	7.9	8.7	10.8	7.3	8.7	Cash & Equivalents	7.9	8.2
7.5	9.8	7.4	8.9	10.0	10.9	Trade Receivables (net)	7.9	7.1
62.8	65.4	67.3	56.4	48.3	45.5	Inventory	64.3	65.7
2.0	2.2	2.6	2.9	4.4	2.5	All Other Current	3.6	3.2
83.3	85.3	86.0	79.1	70.0	67.6	Total Current	83.6	84.3
7.9	10.4	8.5	12.6	16.3	20.9	Fixed Assets (net)	9.4	8.9
1.6	.9	1.3	1.8	2.6	1.5	Intangibles (net)	2.0	2.1
7.0	3.5	4.1	6.4	11.1	10.0	All Other Non-Current	5.0	4.6
100.0	100.0	100.0	100.0	100.0	100.0	Total	100.0	100.0
						LIABILITIES		
45.1	43.4	54.7	50.9	42.2	42.5	Notes Payable-Short Term	53.1	55.4
3.0	3.4	2.1	2.4	3.5	2.4	Cur. Mat.-L/T/D	1.5	1.5
5.2	5.9	4.3	4.2	3.5	4.2	Trade Payables	4.5	4.0
.1	.2	.1	.1	.1	.2	Income Taxes Payable	.2	.1
12.6	10.2	10.4	10.8	9.7	12.8	All Other Current	8.9	8.4
66.0	63.1	71.6	68.5	59.0	62.2	Total Current	68.1	69.4
9.2	9.0	6.3	8.8	14.6	16.0	Long Term Debt	6.9	6.4
.0	.1	.1	.3	.6	.3	Deferred Taxes	.5	.5
9.9	5.1	2.4	2.4	3.4	2.3	All Other Non-Current	2.3	2.6
14.6	22.6	19.6	20.0	22.5	19.2	Net Worth	22.2	21.0
100.0	100.0	100.0	100.0	100.0	100.0	Total Liabilities & Net Worth	100.0	100.0
						INCOME DATA		
100.0	100.0	100.0	100.0	100.0	100.0	Net Sales	100.0	100.0
17.3	15.9	12.4	12.7	15.6	15.6	Gross Profit	12.6	13.3
16.6	15.4	11.9	11.7	13.2	14.0	Operating Expenses	11.1	11.6
.8	.5	.5	1.0	2.4	1.6	Operating Profit	1.4	1.6
.1	-.1	-.5	-.6	-.3	.3	All Other Expenses (net)	.1	.0
.7	.6	1.0	1.6	2.6	1.3	Profit Before Taxes	1.4	1.7
						RATIOS		
2.3	1.7	1.4	1.3	1.3	1.2		1.4	1.4
1.2	1.3	1.2	1.1	1.2	1.1	Current	1.2	1.2
1.0	1.1	1.1	1.0	1.1	.9		1.1	1.1
(48) .7	(160) .4	(1387) .3	(757) .4	.4	.4		(3667) .3	(3180) .3
.2	.2	.2	.3	.3	.3	Quick	.2	.2
.1	.1	.1	.2	.2	.2		.1	.1
0 UND	1 267.2	3 134.9	4 83.6	5 67.2	6 61.0		2 193.7	2 214.1
0 999.8	4 87.3	5 71.6	7 52.3	10 36.1	11 33.1	Sales/Receivables	5 77.8	4 84.8
8 47.3	9 41.5	9 42.6	11 32.0	17 21.6	17 21.9		9 40.6	8 45.1
29 12.7	47 7.8	53 6.9	48 7.7	52 7.1	53 6.9		46 8.0	50 7.3
51 7.2	72 5.1	70 5.2	63 5.8	67 5.4	62 5.9	Cost of Sales/Inventory	60 6.0	64 5.7
104 3.5	94 3.9	89 4.1	78 4.7	80 4.7	74 5.0		77 4.7	82 4.5
0 UND	1 377.1	1 248.8	2 186.3	3 142.6	3 111.0		1 247.4	2 241.2
0 999.8	3 144.6	3 141.2	3 115.4	4 84.3	4 81.3	Cost of Sales/Payables	3 142.3	3 140.6
7 50.9	8 48.1	5 78.2	5 68.3	5 43.8	5 43.5		5 80.3	5 80.1
11.2	11.4	18.0	21.6	16.7	30.5		18.1	18.8
41.2	23.5	31.1	38.5	29.7	95.3	Sales/Working Capital	31.5	31.9
UND	71.4	85.7	166.8	53.0	-98.0		82.1	78.9
(29) 3.0	(127) 3.6	(1038) 7.4	(555) 11.4	(32) 8.4	(20) 12.7		(3301) 6.0	(2759) 7.5
2.2	1.6	2.8	4.3	4.0	4.1	EBIT/Interest	2.8	3.3
.4	.7	1.1	1.9	1.5	2.5		1.4	1.6
	(14) 3.2	(137) 6.6	(98) 4.5	(10) 8.4		Net Profit + Depr., Dep.,	(390) 9.6	(313) 8.1
	1.3	2.6	1.6	1.5		Amort./Cur. Mat. L./T/D	3.0	2.4
	.0	.8	.8	1.0			1.0	.9
.0	.1	.2	.2	.2	.4		.1	.2
.2	.3	.4	.6	.8	1.3	Fixed/Worth	.4	.3
3.3	1.3	1.1	1.5	1.3	4.9		.9	.9
1.5	1.6	2.7	2.8	2.4	3.2		2.4	2.5
5.0	4.0	5.2	5.0	3.7	5.3	Debt/Worth	4.2	4.5
UND	17.8	11.4	10.6	6.6	17.0		8.9	9.4
(39) 70.2	(136) 27.6	(1265) 40.1	(712) 50.4	(36) 39.3	(25) 77.4	% Profit Before Taxes/Tangible	(3392) 54.1	(2946) 60.3
43.7	10.2	18.9	28.7	23.3	22.2	Net Worth	27.0	32.8
5.5	.4	4.2	12.4	10.5	13.3		10.1	12.8
9.7	6.5	7.1	8.7	8.6	7.7	% Profit Before Taxes/Total	10.5	11.2
4.9	2.1	2.9	4.7	4.4	5.0	Assets	5.3	5.7
.0	-.8	.4	1.7	1.5	2.9		1.5	1.8
UND	223.8	155.7	103.2	84.2	74.0		168.9	161.7
171.1	79.0	82.2	50.4	22.9	17.7	Sales/Net Fixed Assets	78.7	81.4
32.2	37.4	40.8	19.8	9.6	8.2		38.3	38.6
7.2	5.2	5.0	4.6	4.0	3.9		5.5	5.3
4.9	4.1	4.0	3.8	3.3	3.1	Sales/Total Assets	4.5	4.3
3.2	2.9	3.3	3.1	1.9	2.5		3.6	3.4
(24) .2	(130) .1	(1245) .1	(708) .2	(37) .3	(21) .2		(3203) .1	(2820) .1
.3	.2	.3	.3	.4	.5	% Depr., Dep., Amort./Sales	.2	.2
.8	.6	.4	.4	1.0	.8		.4	.4
(18) 1.0	(90) .6	(890) .3	(424) .2	(17) .1			(2406) .3	(2093) .3
2.9	1.1	.6	.4	.3		% Officers', Directors',	.5	.5
4.7	2.2	1.1	1.0	1.1		Owners' Comp/Sales	.9	.9
117042M	946871M	32502823M	55710232M	7968935M	13431196M	Net Sales ($)	125516943M	120246543M
11394M	214599M	7641529M	14584711M	2604956M	3948948M	Total Assets ($)	29211485M	29304058M

M = $ thousand   MM = $ million
See Pages 11 through 18 for Explanation of Ratios and Data

Comparative Historical Data | | | Type of Statement | Current Data Sorted By Sales

Hist 1	Hist 2	Hist 3	Type of Statement	0-1MM	1-3MM	3-5MM	5-10MM	10-25MM	25MM & OVER
147	143	172	Unqualified	2		3	6	32	129
385	366	444	Reviewed	2	2	1	32	134	273
201	247	218	Compiled	3	11	15	34	75	80
161	182	252	Tax Returns	14	16	12	30	82	98
1209	1135	1340	Other	10	21	32	105	449	723
4/1/00-3/31/01 ALL	4/1/01-3/31/02 ALL	4/1/02-3/31/03 ALL		176 (4/1-9/30/02)			2250 (10/1/02-3/31/03)		
2103	2073	2426	NUMBER OF STATEMENTS	31	50	63	207	772	1303
%	%	%	ASSETS	%	%	%	%	%	%
7.2	9.0	9.3	Cash & Equivalents	6.8	13.5	8.0	7.6	8.1	10.3
8.2	8.7	8.1	Trade Receivables (net)	5.8	10.4	8.0	7.7	7.3	8.7
66.7	62.1	63.2	Inventory	58.1	54.8	66.5	67.1	67.9	60.0
2.9	3.1	2.7	All Other Current	1.4	2.0	1.3	1.8	2.7	2.9
84.9	82.8	83.3	Total Current	72.0	80.7	83.8	84.3	85.9	81.9
8.9	10.4	10.2	Fixed Assets (net)	14.3	13.7	12.0	10.7	8.3	10.9
1.4	1.8	1.5	Intangibles (net)	1.1	1.3	1.2	1.2	1.4	1.6
4.7	5.0	5.0	All Other Non-Current	12.3	4.3	2.9	3.8	4.3	5.6
100.0	100.0	100.0	Total	100.0	100.0	100.0	100.0	100.0	100.0
			LIABILITIES						
56.2	51.3	52.3	Notes Payable-Short Term	48.2	36.6	41.2	47.0	56.5	51.8
2.2	1.8	2.3	Cur. Mat.-L/T/D	3.0	4.2	4.1	1.9	2.0	2.4
4.5	4.8	4.4	Trade Payables	4.2	4.5	4.0	5.1	4.3	4.4
.1	.2	.1	Income Taxes Payable	.2	.1	.2	.1	.1	.2
9.1	10.3	10.5	All Other Current	11.0	10.5	8.2	11.1	9.5	11.2
72.2	68.4	69.6	Total Current	66.7	55.9	57.8	65.2	72.3	70.0
7.0	7.7	7.6	Long Term Debt	16.3	9.9	13.4	8.7	6.5	7.5
.1	.1	.2	Deferred Taxes	.1	.1	.2	.1	.1	.2
2.1	2.7	2.7	All Other Non-Current	6.2	10.2	5.4	3.2	2.7	2.2
18.5	21.1	19.9	Net Worth	10.4	23.9	23.1	22.8	18.5	20.1
100.0	100.0	100.0	Total Liabilities & Net Worth	100.0	100.0	100.0	100.0	100.0	100.0
			INCOME DATA						
100.0	100.0	100.0	Net Sales	100.0	100.0	100.0	100.0	100.0	100.0
12.5	12.9	12.9	Gross Profit	22.0	25.7	16.3	14.7	12.3	12.1
11.5	11.8	12.2	Operating Expenses	20.9	24.5	15.7	14.3	11.9	11.2
1.0	1.1	.7	Operating Profit	1.1	1.3	.6	.4	.3	.9
.1	-.1	-.5	All Other Expenses (net)	.4	.0	.3	-.3	-.6	-.5
.9	1.2	1.2	Profit Before Taxes	.6	1.3	.3	.8	.9	1.4
			RATIOS						
1.3 / 1.1 / 1.0	1.4 / 1.2 / 1.1	1.3 / 1.2 / 1.1	Current	2.4 / 1.1 / 1.0	2.1 / 1.4 / 1.1	1.8 / 1.3 / 1.2	1.6 / 1.2 / 1.1	1.3 / 1.2 / 1.1	1.3 / 1.1 / 1.0
(2092) .3 / .2 / .1	(2066) .4 / .2 / .1	(2416) .3 / .2 / .1	Quick	(30) .8 / .2 / .1	1.0 / .3 / .1	(62) .6 / .2 / .1	(204) .3 / .2 / .1	(768) .3 / .2 / .1	(1302) .4 / .2 / .2
3 137.2 / 5 68.3 / 9 38.9	3 135.7 / 5 69.0 / 10 38.0	3 121.4 / 6 64.4 / 10 36.9	Sales/Receivables	0 UND / 0 769.0 / 18 20.0	0 999.8 / 5 80.7 / 16 22.3	1 373.5 / 5 71.1 / 11 32.7	2 155.8 / 5 74.0 / 11 32.4	3 127.5 / 5 70.6 / 9 38.6	4 102.8 / 6 60.7 / 10 37.5
52 7.1 / 66 5.5 / 82 4.4	43 8.4 / 58 6.3 / 75 4.9	51 7.2 / 67 5.5 / 86 4.3	Cost of Sales/Inventory	38 9.5 / 94 3.9 / 155 2.3	42 8.8 / 96 3.8 / 158 2.3	56 6.5 / 84 4.3 / 130 2.8	66 5.5 / 87 4.2 / 113 3.2	60 6.1 / 76 4.8 / 93 3.9	46 8.0 / 59 6.2 / 73 5.0
2 232.3 / 3 138.9 / 5 77.2	2 242.9 / 3 138.5 / 5 75.6	2 232.9 / 3 128.8 / 5 71.9	Cost of Sales/Payables	0 UND / 0 UND / 13 28.6	0 999.8 / 5 68.9 / 17 21.7	1 385.2 / 3 132.8 / 9 41.6	1 263.0 / 3 135.7 / 8 48.4	1 257.4 / 3 140.6 / 5 71.2	2 209.2 / 3 123.4 / 5 77.8
20.0 / 37.4 / 136.3	18.9 / 33.5 / 101.5	18.4 / 32.9 / 97.6	Sales/Working Capital	10.2 / 72.0 / -44.2	4.1 / 14.0 / 71.2	5.5 / 15.0 / 36.6	11.1 / 20.1 / 47.8	17.5 / 30.6 / 88.5	21.9 / 39.4 / 134.2
(1915) 3.6 / 1.8 / 1.0	(1813) 5.2 / 2.4 / 1.3	(1801) 8.3 / 3.0 / 1.3	EBIT/Interest	(15) 2.5 / 1.2 / -1.1	(38) 3.8 / 2.4 / 1.0	(51) 3.2 / 1.5 / .1	(162) 3.5 / 1.5 / .6	(597) 6.8 / 2.4 / 1.0	(938) 11.3 / 4.5 / 1.9
(207) 5.5 / 2.3 / .9	(196) 5.3 / 2.0 / .9	(267) 5.6 / 2.0 / .8	Net Profit + Depr., Dep., Amort./Cur. Mat. L/T/D				(23) 3.0 / 1.9 / .7	(64) 4.6 / 1.8 / .6	(174) 6.7 / 2.2 / .9
.2 / .4 / 1.2	.2 / .4 / 1.1	.2 / .4 / 1.3	Fixed/Worth	.2 / .8 / -2.0	.0 / .2 / 2.2	.1 / .3 / 1.1	.1 / .3 / 1.3	.2 / .4 / 1.2	.2 / .5 / 1.2
2.9 / 5.4 / 12.1	2.4 / 4.5 / 10.1	2.6 / 5.0 / 11.5	Debt/Worth	2.0 / 12.0 / -17.4	1.3 / 2.8 / 18.1	1.8 / 3.4 / 11.1	1.8 / 4.5 / 13.2	3.0 / 5.8 / 14.0	2.6 / 4.8 / 9.8
(1900) 40.6 / 17.6 / 3.2	(1884) 48.0 / 24.0 / 8.3	(2213) 43.7 / 22.0 / 6.1	% Profit Before Taxes/Tangible Net Worth	(21) 187.1 / 12.5 / 1.6	(44) 50.9 / 16.3 / .6	(53) 20.5 / 8.1 / -4.2	(180) 23.1 / 7.5 / .0	(692) 36.4 / 17.4 / 3.0	(1223) 50.4 / 28.0 / 12.2
6.7 / 2.6 / .2	9.4 / 4.2 / 1.1	7.7 / 3.7 / .7	% Profit Before Taxes/Total Assets	8.8 / .8 / -.8	7.8 / 2.4 / -1.4	4.9 / 1.3 / -1.5	4.8 / 1.8 / -.3	6.1 / 2.3 / .1	9.2 / 4.8 / 1.6
162.4 / 77.7 / 36.6	150.6 / 75.6 / 34.4	139.2 / 69.2 / 29.8	Sales/Net Fixed Assets	UND / 22.1 / 8.8	332.9 / 51.1 / 13.7	219.5 / 69.6 / 24.2	160.3 / 64.9 / 26.2	163.6 / 77.4 / 37.0	126.3 / 67.2 / 27.0
5.1 / 4.2 / 3.4	5.6 / 4.4 / 3.5	4.8 / 4.0 / 3.2	Sales/Total Assets	6.3 / 3.1 / 1.3	4.2 / 2.7 / 1.6	4.5 / 3.2 / 2.2	4.3 / 3.3 / 2.6	4.5 / 3.8 / 3.0	5.2 / 4.2 / 3.4
(1828) .1 / .2 / .4	(1849) .1 / .2 / .4	(2165) .1 / .3 / .4	% Depr., Dep., Amort./Sales	(12) .4 / 1.2 / 4.5	(36) .2 / .5 / 1.1	(49) .1 / .3 / .8	(175) .1 / .3 / .6	(679) .1 / .3 / .4	(1214) .1 / .3 / .4
(1281) .3 / .6 / 1.0	(1267) .3 / .6 / 1.1	(1447) .3 / .6 / 1.2	% Officers', Directors', Owners' Comp/Sales		(20) .2 / 3.0 / 4.1	(34) .7 / 1.3 / 2.3	(125) .5 / .9 / 1.7	(501) .4 / .6 / 1.1	(760) .2 / .4 / 1.0
82391859M	84318247M	110677099M	Net Sales ($)	13716M	96479M	245665M	1575680M	13318098M	95427461M
20994435M	20152169M	29006137M	Total Assets ($)	10734M	58109M	119060M	635366M	3876849M	24306019M

M = $ thousand   MM = $ million
See Pages 11 through 18 for Explanation of Ratios and Data

Current Data Sorted By Assets　　　　　　　　　　　　　Comparative Historical Data

0-500M	500M-2MM	2-10MM	10-50MM	50-100MM	100-250MM	Type of Statement		4/1/98-3/31/99 ALL	4/1/99-3/31/00 ALL
3	4	6	4	1		Unqualified		16	12
2	19	19	5			Reviewed		36	37
52	76	23			1	Compiled		162	139
89	72	14	1		1	Tax Returns		97	117
20	53	36	1	1		Other		123	146
	70 (4/1-9/30/02)		433 (10/1/02-3/31/03)						
166	224	98	11	2	2	NUMBER OF STATEMENTS		434	451
%	%	%	%	%	%			%	%
						ASSETS			
9.5	7.2	6.1	3.7			Cash & Equivalents		7.7	7.7
5.3	11.1	16.9	40.8			Trade Receivables (net)		12.0	10.3
69.0	64.4	55.3	30.5			Inventory		60.3	63.4
1.5	2.1	4.7	.8			All Other Current		3.4	2.4
85.4	84.8	83.1	75.8			Total Current		83.3	83.8
11.4	10.7	9.7	6.4			Fixed Assets (net)		11.6	11.3
.6	.6	1.4	.6			Intangibles (net)		1.1	.8
2.7	3.8	5.8	17.2			All Other Non-Current		4.0	4.0
100.0	100.0	100.0	100.0			Total		100.0	100.0
						LIABILITIES			
42.1	39.6	40.7	46.8			Notes Payable-Short Term		39.2	43.6
4.1	2.9	2.1	8.1			Cur. Mat.-L/T/D		2.6	3.0
4.5	5.3	5.9	4.3			Trade Payables		6.8	6.0
.1	.1	.1	.5			Income Taxes Payable		.3	.4
8.8	10.5	9.5	3.5			All Other Current		9.2	8.1
59.6	58.5	58.2	63.3			Total Current		58.1	61.1
16.5	8.9	7.5	4.9			Long Term Debt		11.3	12.6
.0	.0	.1	.4			Deferred Taxes		.1	.2
9.7	7.4	6.2	3.6			All Other Non-Current		5.7	6.7
14.3	25.2	28.0	27.8			Net Worth		24.8	19.4
100.0	100.0	100.0	100.0			Total Liabilities & Net Worth		100.0	100.0
						INCOME DATA			
100.0	100.0	100.0	100.0			Net Sales		100.0	100.0
19.2	17.9	19.8	29.1			Gross Profit		19.0	18.2
16.7	15.7	16.6	23.7			Operating Expenses		16.1	15.4
2.5	2.2	3.2	5.4			Operating Profit		2.9	2.8
.9	.7	.9	1.5			All Other Expenses (net)		.6	.6
1.5	1.5	2.3	3.9			Profit Before Taxes		2.3	2.2
						RATIOS			
2.9	2.2	1.8	1.4					2.4	2.3
1.4	1.3	1.4	1.3			Current		1.4	1.3
1.0	1.1	1.1	1.1					1.1	1.1
.6	.5	.7	1.2					.7	.6
(162) .2	(221) .2	(96) .3	.6			Quick		(424) .2	(445) .2
.1	.1	.1	.2					.1	.1
0 UND	0 UND	1 391.6	18 20.5					0 UND	0 UND
0 UND	2 165.6	4 90.2	92 3.9			Sales/Receivables		2 189.8	1 264.1
2 151.5	9 40.8	29 12.8	339 1.1					10 35.2	6 59.4
37 9.7	39 9.4	35 10.5	32 11.3					37 10.0	38 9.7
65 5.6	61 6.0	59 6.2	39 9.3			Cost of Sales/Inventory		57 6.3	56 6.5
96 3.8	86 4.3	93 3.9	79 4.6					85 4.3	82 4.5
0 UND	0 UND	1 421.8	10 36.0					0 UND	0 UND
0 UND	2 226.8	3 133.0	12 29.5			Cost of Sales/Payables		2 167.3	2 223.5
4 96.6	6 62.4	7 50.6	19 19.3					7 51.0	6 60.8
8.2	9.2	7.6	5.4					8.0	9.3
26.9	21.4	21.5	9.3			Sales/Working Capital		21.8	24.0
176.2	64.9	46.0	27.4					80.3	133.1
5.3	4.8	4.9	8.6					4.9	4.1
(142) 1.9	(205) 2.1	(86) 1.9	2.1			EBIT/Interest		(409) 2.3	(427) 2.3
.9	.9	.9	1.4					1.1	1.2
	3.9	5.2				Net Profit + Depr., Dep.,		8.4	8.5
(11) 2.2	(10) 2.1				Amort./Cur. Mat. L /T/D		(27) 3.9	(33) 3.0
.8	.0						1.8	1.0
.0	.0	.1	.1					.0	.1
.3	.3	.2	.2			Fixed/Worth		.3	.2
2.5	1.0	.6	.5					1.2	1.2
1.5	1.3	1.8	1.3					1.2	1.5
5.5	3.9	3.2	3.6			Debt/Worth		3.4	3.9
−61.7	12.0	8.2	7.7					10.3	13.0
65.3	50.3	48.0	38.7			% Profit Before Taxes/Tangible		63.0	71.4
(121) 28.9	(193) 16.3	(93) 17.9	21.2			Net Worth		(377) 25.5	(389) 28.2
.4	3.3	7.1	11.5					6.3	10.0
17.5	10.1	10.3	11.0			% Profit Before Taxes/Total		14.5	13.9
5.4	4.0	3.5	4.6			Assets		6.5	6.4
.0	−.4	1.4	2.5					.9	1.0
UND	448.2	262.9	49.0					375.2	451.6
190.4	95.5	88.1	31.3			Sales/Net Fixed Assets		87.9	105.8
34.6	31.7	31.5	21.0					25.0	29.1
8.2	6.6	5.9	1.8					7.0	7.2
5.1	4.6	3.7	1.2			Sales/Total Assets		4.5	4.7
3.4	2.5	2.1	.9					2.7	3.0
.1	.1	.1	.1					.1	.1
(91) .4	(164) .2	(74) .2	(10) .3			% Depr., Dep., Amort./Sales		(297) .3	(321) .2
.8	.6	.5	1.2					.7	.5
1.4	.9	.6						.9	1.1
(81) 2.5	(135) 1.6	(65) 1.2				% Officers', Directors',		(208) 1.8	(252) 1.9
4.5	3.6	2.7				Owners' Comp/Sales		3.6	3.3
290152M	1157842M	1633930M	354544M	160812M	378426M	Net Sales ($)		2391778M	5574078M
47203M	231813M	372996M	167628M	154862M	316215M	Total Assets ($)		629909M	1291351M

© RMA 2003

M = $ thousand　　MM = $ million
See Pages 11 through 18 for Explanation of Ratios and Data

Comparative Historical Data — Current Data Sorted By Sales

			Type of Statement						
9	16	18	Unqualified	•	5	1	4	6	2
31	32	45	Reviewed	1	4	7	15	12	6
152	129	152	Compiled	25	49	24	34	12	8
109	145	177	Tax Returns	23	81	34	25	9	5
100	115	111	Other	16	23	19	21	22	10
4/1/00-3/31/01 ALL	4/1/01-3/31/02 ALL	4/1/02-3/31/03 ALL		0-1MM	1-3MM	3-5MM	5-10MM	10-25MM	25MM & OVER
					70 (4/1-9/30/02)		433 (10/1/02-3/31/03)		
401	437	503	NUMBER OF STATEMENTS	65	162	85	99	61	31
%	%	%	**ASSETS**	%	%	%	%	%	%
7.4	6.5	7.7	Cash & Equivalents	6.8	7.0	9.7	7.2	8.0	7.8
11.6	12.0	11.2	Trade Receivables (net)	14.3	8.8	12.2	11.9	9.5	14.9
61.7	63.3	63.2	Inventory	54.0	64.8	62.3	64.2	67.9	63.9
3.1	2.3	2.5	All Other Current	3.2	3.0	2.6	1.2	2.0	2.8
83.8	84.1	84.5	Total Current	78.3	83.7	86.9	84.5	87.5	89.4
11.6	10.8	10.6	Fixed Assets (net)	18.3	11.3	8.6	9.6	6.6	7.4
1.0	.7	.8	Intangibles (net)	.6	.7	1.1	.7	.6	1.0
3.6	4.4	4.1	All Other Non-Current	2.9	4.3	3.4	5.2	5.4	2.2
100.0	100.0	100.0	Total	100.0	100.0	100.0	100.0	100.0	100.0
			LIABILITIES						
39.7	41.1	40.7	Notes Payable-Short Term	34.6	41.5	37.0	45.2	41.0	44.2
3.3	3.8	3.2	Cur. Mat.-L/T/D	5.8	3.3	2.9	1.1	5.7	.4
6.1	5.8	5.1	Trade Payables	3.3	3.0	6.4	7.2	6.9	6.2
.1	.2	.1	Income Taxes Payable	.1	.1	.1	.2	.2	.1
10.0	9.7	9.5	All Other Current	7.1	9.5	9.8	9.2	9.9	14.3
59.3	60.6	58.7	Total Current	51.0	57.4	56.2	62.8	63.8	65.2
11.8	11.8	11.0	Long Term Debt	20.8	13.6	8.4	9.5	3.9	3.3
.0	.0	.0	Deferred Taxes	.0	.0	.0	.0	.1	.1
5.7	7.6	8.1	All Other Non-Current	18.3	5.6	9.0	4.6	7.2	10.0
23.1	20.0	22.2	Net Worth	9.9	23.4	26.4	23.1	25.1	21.5
100.0	100.0	100.0	Total Liabilities & Net Worth	100.0	100.0	100.0	100.0	100.0	100.0
			INCOME DATA						
100.0	100.0	100.0	Net Sales	100.0	100.0	100.0	100.0	100.0	100.0
18.7	17.9	19.0	Gross Profit	30.4	21.3	15.1	15.6	14.3	14.2
16.2	15.5	16.5	Operating Expenses	26.0	18.5	13.3	13.6	11.4	14.5
2.5	2.4	2.5	Operating Profit	4.3	2.8	1.8	1.9	2.9	-.3
.6	.9	.8	All Other Expenses (net)	2.0	.8	.4	.4	1.4	-.8
1.9	1.5	1.7	Profit Before Taxes	2.3	2.0	1.4	1.5	1.5	.5
			RATIOS						
2.0	2.1	2.3		4.0	2.7	2.7	1.7	1.7	1.6
1.3	1.3	1.3	Current	2.0	1.4	1.4	1.3	1.3	1.3
1.1	1.1	1.1		1.1	1.1	1.1	1.1	1.1	1.2
.6	.6	.6		1.5	.6	.8	.5	.5	.5
(396) .2	(432) .2	(494) .2	Quick	.3	(157) .2	(83) .3	(59) .2	.2	.2
.1	.1	.1		.0	.1	.1	.1	.1	.1
0 UND	0 UND	0 UND		0 UND	0 UND	0 UND	0 999.8	1 541.5	1 634.0
2 194.8	2 213.5	2 210.0	Sales/Receivables	0 UND	1 379.9	1 289.7	2 165.9	2 170.1	4 88.2
9 40.1	10 37.1	10 38.3		21 17.4	8 43.3	9 41.8	11 31.9	6 58.6	12 31.5
36 10.1	36 10.2	38 9.7		58 6.3	51 7.2	35 10.5	35 10.5	32 11.3	25 14.7
56 6.5	56 6.6	62 5.9	Cost of Sales/Inventory	107 3.4	72 5.1	48 7.6	50 7.4	47 7.8	39 9.3
83 4.4	83 4.4	91 4.0		159 2.3	106 3.4	71 5.1	71 5.1	69 5.3	56 6.5
0 UND	0 UND	0 UND		0 UND	0 UND	0 UND	0 999.8	0 802.5	0 970.3
2 193.7	2 163.4	2 229.3	Cost of Sales/Payables	0 UND	1 583.7	2 181.9	2 174.0	2 177.9	2 178.5
7 50.5	7 55.3	6 62.3		9 38.8	4 81.5	6 56.2	6 56.7	8 47.7	6 57.5
9.7	10.0	8.2		2.8	7.0	10.2	11.1	16.8	19.0
25.0	24.3	22.0	Sales/Working Capital	7.7	16.4	23.3	29.0	29.1	36.2
107.2	115.2	77.8		43.3	86.9	65.4	111.4	102.5	53.8
3.8	4.0	4.9		3.5	4.2	5.6	4.3	7.5	11.5
(376) 1.9	(412) 2.1	(448) 2.0	EBIT/Interest	(56) 1.6	(145) 1.8	(79) 2.7	(86) 1.9	(55) 2.3	(27) 1.9
1.1	1.2	1.0		.2	.9	.9	1.0	1.5	1.4
7.2	8.0	3.7	Net Profit + Depr., Dep.,				4.1		
(24) 2.3	(24) 1.8	(23) 2.1	Amort./Cur. Mat. L/T/D				(10) 3.1		
.5	1.0	.3					1.7		
.1	.0	.0		.0	.0	.0	.0	.1	.1
.3	.3	.2	Fixed/Worth	.5	.3	.1	.2	.2	.2
1.2	1.2	1.2		-6.9	1.5	.8	1.0	.9	.4
1.6	1.6	1.4		1.2	1.1	1.0	1.9	2.4	2.2
3.8	4.3	3.9	Debt/Worth	6.0	3.7	3.1	3.9	4.2	3.2
12.8	14.7	15.7		-6.0	14.2	19.2	11.4	11.2	5.8
66.3	64.6	51.1		42.6	51.5	40.4	50.4	78.0	47.9
(345) 26.9	(371) 27.9	(421) 19.3	% Profit Before Taxes/Tangible Net Worth	(40) 7.7	(135) 16.3	(71) 22.2	(88) 20.8	(58) 23.4	(29) 27.0
6.9	7.4	3.9		-1.0	3.6	3.5	4.4	8.1	6.4
13.1	12.9	12.8		13.5	12.6	13.3	10.3	12.9	14.4
5.5	5.4	4.0	% Profit Before Taxes/Total Assets	3.2	3.7	5.7	4.2	3.5	3.4
.4	.9	.1		-.6	.0	-.5	-.3	1.7	1.7
479.2	560.6	664.1		421.5	791.0	948.5	689.9	395.5	761.1
99.1	96.8	109.1	Sales/Net Fixed Assets	37.3	76.3	126.5	113.4	155.0	148.9
30.9	31.9	31.4		8.1	25.7	39.9	38.6	59.3	37.1
6.9	6.8	6.7		3.5	5.6	7.3	7.6	8.4	8.7
4.6	4.8	4.4	Sales/Total Assets	2.0	3.9	5.5	5.0	5.7	6.5
2.9	3.0	2.5		1.3	2.3	3.6	3.1	3.8	5.1
.1	.1	.1		.2	.2	.1	.1	.1	.1
(272) .2	(299) .3	(341) .2	% Depr., Dep., Amort./Sales	(42) .7	(105) .4	(54) .2	(70) .2	(47) .1	(23) .2
.6	.6	.7		2.0	1.0	.4	.5	.2	.4
.9	1.0	.9		3.4	1.4	1.0	.7	.6	.5
(222) 1.9	(246) 1.8	(286) 1.8	% Officers', Directors', Owners' Comp/Sales	(24) 5.7	(101) 2.6	(48) 1.7	(54) 1.3	(39) .9	(20) 1.0
3.8	3.6	3.7		7.3	4.3	4.1	1.9	1.4	2.6
3285217M	3618290M	3975706M	Net Sales ($)	36989M	301504M	334715M	692919M	928346M	1681233M
1018780M	1004302M	1290717M	Total Assets ($)	24438M	106322M	83315M	203564M	228923M	644155M

M = $ thousand   MM = $ million
See Pages 11 through 18 for Explanation of Ratios and Data

Current Data Sorted By Assets   Comparative Historical Data

						Type of Statement		
1	8	2 19	2 10			Unqualified	4	5
2	46	31	1			Reviewed	28	22
6	20	16	1			Compiled	81	97
12	74	77	20			Tax Returns	28	25
	37 (4/1-9/30/02)		311 (10/1/02-3/31/03)			Other	59	53
							4/1/98-3/31/99	4/1/99-3/31/00
0-500M	500M-2MM	2-10MM	10-50MM	50-100MM	100-250MM		ALL	ALL
21	148	145	34			NUMBER OF STATEMENTS	200	202
%	%	%	%	%	%	ASSETS	%	%
11.5	7.0	7.0	7.2			Cash & Equivalents	6.0	7.6
2.4	2.5	2.4	3.7			Trade Receivables (net)	2.8	2.8
65.6	76.0	80.8	76.6			Inventory	75.9	75.8
.2	.7	.6	.6			All Other Current	1.0	.9
79.7	86.3	90.8	88.0			Total Current	85.7	87.1
18.7	10.4	6.9	7.7			Fixed Assets (net)	11.6	9.5
.5	2.3	1.4	2.4			Intangibles (net)	.8	.7
1.1	1.0	1.0	1.9			All Other Non-Current	2.0	2.6
100.0	100.0	100.0	100.0			Total	100.0	100.0
						LIABILITIES		
21.2	26.4	29.0	21.4			Notes Payable-Short Term	49.3	52.5
1.7	1.9	2.0	.1			Cur. Mat.-L/T/D	1.7	1.5
26.1	29.2	34.4	41.0			Trade Payables	5.0	5.1
.0	.1	.2	.2			Income Taxes Payable	.2	.2
8.2	7.7	8.6	11.1			All Other Current	7.9	7.9
57.3	65.3	74.2	73.9			Total Current	63.9	67.3
18.5	6.7	3.5	3.6			Long Term Debt	9.0	5.8
.0	.0	.0	.1			Deferred Taxes	.1	.1
4.1	2.7	1.9	1.6			All Other Non-Current	2.8	2.6
20.1	25.4	20.3	20.9			Net Worth	24.2	24.2
100.0	100.0	100.0	100.0			Total Liabilities & Net Worth	100.0	100.0
						INCOME DATA		
100.0	100.0	100.0	100.0			Net Sales	100.0	100.0
28.8	22.1	17.4	16.0			Gross Profit	20.3	19.6
26.0	19.4	14.9	13.2			Operating Expenses	17.2	16.2
2.8	2.7	2.6	2.8			Operating Profit	3.1	3.3
2.0	1.0	.7	.7			All Other Expenses (net)	1.1	1.0
.8	1.6	1.8	2.0			Profit Before Taxes	2.1	2.4
						RATIOS		
2.1	1.6	1.4	1.3				1.6	1.5
1.3	1.2	1.2	1.1			Current	1.2	1.2
1.0	1.1	1.1	1.1				1.1	1.1
.4	.2	.2	.2				.2	.2
.2	.1	.1	.1			Quick (199) (201)	.1	.1
.1	.1	.1	.0				.0	.1
0 UND	0 UND	0 986.8	1 259.0				0 999.8	0 999.8
1 344.0	1 445.1	2 215.2	4 98.1			Sales/Receivables	1 309.7	2 198.6
6 64.5	4 98.2	4 91.5	6 58.4				5 81.0	4 81.8
70 5.2	105 3.5	111 3.3	111 3.3				93 3.9	93 3.9
122 3.0	139 2.6	139 2.6	132 2.8			Cost of Sales/Inventory	122 3.0	126 2.9
222 1.6	194 1.9	168 2.2	145 2.5				160 2.3	157 2.3
1 615.7	1 248.0	3 141.3	3 111.0				0 988.9	1 559.3
16 22.8	23 15.7	19 19.1	79 4.6			Cost of Sales/Payables	2 151.6	2 154.5
103 3.5	101 3.6	120 3.1	125 2.9				7 49.2	6 60.4
6.1	7.7	10.6	12.7				9.8	8.5
24.1	15.4	17.7	30.5			Sales/Working Capital	19.0	21.0
-313.2	34.8	37.0	44.8				51.4	44.2
2.8	3.2	3.5	3.9				3.0	3.0
(19) 1.7	(140) 1.8	(137) 1.9	(32) 2.6			EBIT/Interest (188) (191)	1.8	1.7
.6	1.1	1.4	1.7				1.2	1.3
	6.2	4.5					8.0	13.2
(13) 3.2	(11) 1.4				Net Profit + Depr., Dep., Amort./Cur. Mat. L./T/D (31) (30)	2.6	4.1
	1.8	1.2					.9	2.2
.2	.1	.1	.1				.1	.1
.7	.3	.3	.2			Fixed/Worth	.4	.3
5.3	.9	.8	.6				1.2	1.0
1.8	1.8	2.8	2.5				2.1	2.0
6.0	3.8	5.4	5.0			Debt/Worth	4.2	3.9
18.4	8.3	9.2	11.2				9.9	10.8
74.9	32.5	49.7	44.7				42.4	44.2
(17) 42.9	(139) 16.4	(138) 22.0	(32) 30.3			% Profit Before Taxes/Tangible Net Worth (184) (187)	20.3	25.1
11.6	3.8	9.9	16.3				5.5	9.3
9.5	6.3	6.9	7.0				9.1	9.7
4.7	3.5	3.3	4.1			% Profit Before Taxes/Total Assets	4.3	4.4
-2.6	.7	1.2	2.1				1.2	1.7
100.5	168.2	181.1	148.8				133.7	148.0
33.9	51.0	66.5	94.5			Sales/Net Fixed Assets	51.2	57.1
13.5	19.7	29.0	30.4				19.3	23.6
3.7	3.4	3.2	2.8				3.5	3.5
3.0	2.4	2.6	2.6			Sales/Total Assets	2.9	2.7
1.9	1.9	2.1	2.4				2.2	2.2
.5	.3	.2	.2				.2	.2
(13) .9	(108) .6	(115) .4	(25) .2			% Depr., Dep., Amort./Sales (169) (173)	.5	.3
1.9	1.2	.6	.4				.9	.7
1.3	1.0	1.0	.4				.8	.9
(11) 5.7	(82) 2.0	(99) 1.8	(22) .6			% Officers', Directors', Owners' Comp/Sales (105) (121)	1.7	1.7
10.8	3.3	2.6	1.3				4.4	3.5
19624M	487304M	1625692M	1775487M			Net Sales ($)	2398673M	2564552M
6700M	181565M	609566M	679092M			Total Assets ($)	938671M	846179M

DATA NOT AVAILABLE (columns 50-100MM and 100-250MM)

M = $ thousand   MM = $ million
See Pages 11 through 18 for Explanation of Ratios and Data

Comparative Historical Data | Current Data Sorted By Sales

			Type of Statement						
5	4	4	Unqualified					2	2
37	35	38	Reviewed	1	4	3	8	13	9
168	174	80	Compiled	2	24	17	20	15	2
63	45	43	Tax Returns	5	18	3	8	8	1
231	95	183	Other	8	34	35	49	35	22
4/1/00-	4/1/01-	4/1/02-			37 (4/1-9/30/02)		311 (10/1/02-3/31/02)		
3/31/01	3/31/02	3/31/03							
ALL	ALL	ALL		0-1MM	1-3MM	3-5MM	5-10MM	10-25MM	25MM & OVER
504	353	348	**NUMBER OF STATEMENTS**	16	80	58	85	73	36
%	%	%	**ASSETS**	%	%	%	%	%	%
5.6	7.2	7.3	Cash & Equivalents	12.2	8.2	5.5	6.1	8.2	7.2
2.7	2.8	2.5	Trade Receivables (net)	2.2	2.2	2.4	3.0	2.1	3.6
76.5	75.8	77.4	Inventory	56.7	71.9	81.6	82.0	79.5	77.3
.5	.8	.6	All Other Current	.2	.8	.7	.5	.6	.6
85.3	86.5	87.9	Total Current	71.2	83.1	90.2	91.7	90.3	88.7
10.8	9.9	9.2	Fixed Assets (net)	24.7	13.1	7.8	6.4	6.5	7.8
2.8	2.3	1.8	Intangibles (net)	2.6	2.3	1.7	1.3	1.9	1.6
1.1	1.3	1.1	All Other Non-Current	1.6	1.5	.3	.7	1.2	2.0
100.0	100.0	100.0	Total	100.0	100.0	100.0	100.0	100.0	100.0
			LIABILITIES						
19.8	23.6	26.7	Notes Payable-Short Term	12.8	28.6	26.5	29.6	25.7	23.9
1.9	1.8	1.8	Cur. Mat.-L/T/D	1.9	2.9	.9	1.2	2.7	.2
38.0	33.4	32.4	Trade Payables	16.5	24.2	33.4	36.2	35.9	39.7
.1	.1	.1	Income Taxes Payable	.0	.1	.0	.1	.2	.2
11.3	9.2	8.4	All Other Current	10.6	6.7	9.7	7.4	9.0	10.9
71.1	68.1	69.4	Total Current	41.8	62.4	70.5	74.5	73.4	75.0
5.7	5.6	5.8	Long Term Debt	24.1	7.7	6.2	3.7	3.1	3.3
.0	.0	.0	Deferred Taxes	.0	.0	.1	.0	.0	.1
1.8	2.2	2.3	All Other Non-Current	4.8	2.6	2.7	2.3	1.7	1.5
21.3	24.0	22.5	Net Worth	29.3	27.3	20.6	19.6	21.8	20.1
100.0	100.0	100.0	Total Liabilities & Net Worth	100.0	100.0	100.0	100.0	100.0	100.0
			INCOME DATA						
100.0	100.0	100.0	Net Sales	100.0	100.0	100.0	100.0	100.0	100.0
19.3	19.3	20.0	Gross Profit	41.3	22.5	19.7	18.0	17.3	15.4
15.8	16.2	17.3	Operating Expenses	37.3	19.8	17.2	15.5	14.5	13.0
3.5	3.0	2.7	Operating Profit	4.0	2.7	2.5	2.5	2.8	2.4
2.1	1.5	.9	All Other Expenses (net)	2.6	1.1	1.0	.7	.8	.7
1.4	1.5	1.7	Profit Before Taxes	1.4	1.6	1.5	1.8	2.0	1.7
			RATIOS						
1.3	1.4	1.4		4.0	1.6	1.4	1.3	1.4	1.3
1.1	1.2	1.2	Current	1.5	1.3	1.2	1.2	1.2	1.1
1.1	1.1	1.1		.9	1.1	1.1	1.1	1.1	1.1
.2	.2	.2		.4	.3	.2	.1	.2	.2
(501) .1	(352) .1	.1	Quick	.3	.1	.1	.1	.1	.1
.0	.0	.0		.0	.0	.0	.0	.1	.0
0 999.8	0 999.8	0 999.8		0 UND	0 UND	0 UND	0 999.8	0 999.8	1 271.7
1 271.0	2 230.6	1 247.7	Sales/Receivables	1 589.5	1 275.7	1 656.4	1 333.4	2 181.6	3 108.8
4 84.3	4 85.7	4 85.7		8 47.6	5 80.0	4 101.5	3 106.4	4 92.5	6 60.9
99 3.7	95 3.9	105 3.5		101 3.6	105 3.5	109 3.4	108 3.4	98 3.7	105 3.5
130 2.8	123 3.0	137 2.7	Cost of Sales/Inventory	222 1.6	161 2.3	137 2.7	131 2.8	124 3.0	132 2.8
165 2.2	162 2.3	178 2.0		339 1.1	215 1.7	185 2.0	158 2.3	159 2.3	143 2.6
4 90.3	3 131.2	2 157.3		0 UND	0 903.7	3 120.0	2 180.5	3 117.6	3 115.4
69 5.3	35 10.3	23 15.7	Cost of Sales/Payables	15 25.1	13 29.0	23 16.0	46 7.9	25 14.7	64 5.7
122 3.0	104 3.5	109 3.3		117 3.1	96 3.8	113 3.2	113 3.2	101 3.6	124 3.0
12.1	10.5	9.7		3.8	6.2	9.3	10.4	12.1	13.7
24.1	20.7	17.7	Sales/Working Capital	8.4	13.7	15.4	18.7	23.2	30.5
67.0	40.6	38.2		−32.9	28.4	28.2	33.5	48.3	39.8
2.1	2.4	3.2		2.1	3.2	3.1	3.0	4.5	3.6
(480) 1.3	(342) 1.5	(328) 1.9	EBIT/Interest	(13) 1.1	(75) 1.7	1.8	(81) 2.0	(67) 1.9	(34) 2.5
1.0	1.0	1.3		.5	1.1	1.1	1.4	1.4	1.5
5.7	6.8	5.7	Net Profit + Depr., Dep.,						
(68) 2.0	(43) 3.8	(30) 3.2	Amort./Cur. Mat. L/T/D						
.9	1.5	1.2							
.1	.1	.1		.0	.1	.1	.1	.1	.1
.4	.3	.3	Fixed/Worth	.9	.3	.3	.2	.3	.2
1.4	1.1	.9		NM	1.2	.9	.5	1.0	.6
2.5	2.2	2.4		.7	1.5	2.5	2.9	2.3	2.6
5.3	4.5	4.7	Debt/Worth	5.3	3.5	4.5	4.9	5.8	5.0
13.6	8.9	9.1		NM	8.3	7.0	8.2	13.1	10.6
38.0	42.3	44.1	% Profit Before Taxes/Tangible	56.4	36.1	32.0	54.8	72.6	44.3
(457) 17.7	(325) 16.6	(326) 21.1	Net Worth	(12) 12.4	(75) 15.0	(54) 22.0	(82) 21.1	(69) 27.6	(34) 29.2
4.2	4.8	7.4		1.0	1.7	3.9	10.3	10.4	13.1
6.2	6.8	6.8	% Profit Before Taxes/Total	5.0	7.2	6.1	9.0	9.0	6.8
2.3	3.0	3.6	Assets	.7	3.4	3.5	4.1	3.3	3.9
.4	.7	1.0		−2.2	.4	.7	1.6	1.6	2.0
174.4	167.7	168.5		109.0	98.0	170.4	216.8	174.9	227.3
58.1	59.1	61.4	Sales/Net Fixed Assets	21.7	34.4	51.6	79.7	71.9	94.5
17.9	19.0	22.6		2.9	10.9	27.0	33.4	31.3	27.3
3.3	3.5	3.2		2.4	2.8	3.5	3.4	3.5	2.9
2.7	2.8	2.6	Sales/Total Assets	1.8	2.2	2.5	2.8	2.9	2.7
2.1	2.1	2.0		.7	1.7	2.0	2.3	2.3	2.4
.2	.2	.2		1.5	.3	.2	.2	.2	.1
(378) .4	(283) .4	(261) .4	% Depr., Dep., Amort./Sales	(10) 1.9	(61) .6	(44) .6	(59) .4	(60) .3	(27) .2
.7	.8	.9		4.8	1.1	1.4	.7	.7	.4
.9	1.0	.9			1.3	1.2	1.1	.6	.4
(283) 1.6	(219) 1.8	(214) 1.7	% Officers', Directors',	(47)	(441) 2.3	(33) 2.2	(57) 2.0	(45) 1.3	(25) .6
2.7	3.1	3.1	Owners' Comp/Sales		3.4	3.7	2.8	2.1	1.3
6264069M	3978578M	3908107M	Net Sales ($)	9063M	155409M	222668M	620105M	1067980M	1832882M
2185681M	1426885M	1476923M	Total Assets ($)	7066M	76732M	90057M	232810M	377914M	692344M

© RMA 2003

M = $ thousand   MM = $ million
See Pages 11 through 18 for Explanation of Ratios and Data

Current Data Sorted By Assets   Comparative Historical Data

0-500M	500M-2MM	2-10MM	10-50MM	50-100MM	100-250MM	Type of Statement	4/1/98-3/31/99 ALL	4/1/99-3/31/00 ALL
		3	1		1	Unqualified	4	2
	5	19				Reviewed	21	24
	18	38	2			Compiled	76	81
5	15	27				Tax Returns	13	22
4	17	47	8	2		Other	52	48
	35 (4/1-9/30/02)		177 (10/1/02-3/31/03)					
9	55	134	11	2	1	**NUMBER OF STATEMENTS**	166	177
%	%	%	%	%	%	**ASSETS**	%	%
	7.9	9.2	6.0			Cash & Equivalents	10.4	11.0
	2.9	4.0	3.6			Trade Receivables (net)	4.8	4.7
	73.6	66.6	43.3			Inventory	64.6	64.7
	.8	2.3	1.9			All Other Current	1.5	1.7
	85.2	82.1	54.9			Total Current	81.4	82.1
	11.7	11.6	25.5			Fixed Assets (net)	13.3	12.2
	.9	3.5	7.2			Intangibles (net)	2.2	2.1
	2.2	2.8	12.4			All Other Non-Current	3.2	3.6
	100.0	100.0	100.0			Total	100.0	100.0
						LIABILITIES		
	36.1	33.6	18.5			Notes Payable-Short Term	30.5	28.8
	2.4	3.6	2.5			Cur. Mat.-L/T/D	1.6	1.8
	11.6	12.3	9.9			Trade Payables	10.6	11.3
	.1	.3	.7			Income Taxes Payable	.3	.3
	9.0	10.3	9.2			All Other Current	10.4	9.7
	59.3	60.1	40.7			Total Current	53.4	51.9
	10.1	7.5	19.0			Long Term Debt	9.0	9.1
	.0	.0	.0			Deferred Taxes	.0	.1
	1.8	2.4	2.5			All Other Non-Current	2.2	4.5
	28.8	29.9	37.9			Net Worth	35.3	34.4
	100.0	100.0	100.0			Total Liabilities & Net Worth	100.0	100.0
						INCOME DATA		
	100.0	100.0	100.0			Net Sales	100.0	100.0
	20.9	21.7	26.8			Gross Profit	22.1	22.3
	18.5	18.2	22.1			Operating Expenses	18.0	17.8
	2.3	3.6	4.7			Operating Profit	4.2	4.5
	.2	-.2	-.2			All Other Expenses (net)	.6	.2
	2.1	3.8	5.0			Profit Before Taxes	3.6	4.3
						RATIOS		
	1.8	1.8	1.8				2.0	2.5
	1.3	1.3	1.5			Current	1.4	1.5
	1.1	1.1	1.1				1.2	1.2
	.2	.4	.4				.5	.6
	.1	.2	.1			Quick	(165) .2	(174) .3
	.1	.1	.1				.1	.1
	0 999.8	2 219.3	2 200.0				1 275.7	1 260.7
	2 154.7	4 93.4	3 105.0			Sales/Receivables	4 85.3	4 100.7
	7 55.6	7 54.9	7 54.3				8 46.1	7 54.2
93 3.9	77 4.7	57 6.4				Cost of Sales/Inventory	73 5.0	73 5.0
123 3.0	107 3.4	78 4.7					97 3.8	99 3.7
193 1.9	151 2.4	131 2.8					142 2.6	129 2.8
3 129.5	5 70.3	10 36.2				Cost of Sales/Payables	5 78.9	5 66.9
8 43.8	11 31.9	13 27.5					10 36.4	11 32.4
20 18.2	24 15.2	48 7.6					21 17.7	23 16.1
	7.7	8.5	9.1				7.4	6.7
	13.4	14.2	20.4			Sales/Working Capital	12.5	11.6
	29.3	33.1	51.8				22.2	22.5
	7.5	13.1	89.5				7.5	9.8
	(49) 2.4	(124) 5.1	(10) 6.0			EBIT/Interest	(153) 2.9	(163) 4.4
	.9	2.4	2.9				1.4	1.9
		20.4				Net Profit + Depr., Dep., Amort./Cur. Mat. L /T/D	13.5	11.2
		(17) 5.7					(27) 3.0	(23) 4.4
		3.0					1.3	2.0
	.1	.1	.2				.1	.1
	.4	.3	.5			Fixed/Worth	.3	.3
	1.2	1.0	4.4				.8	.8
	1.3	1.4	.6				1.0	.9
	3.3	2.9	1.8			Debt/Worth	2.1	2.4
	7.9	7.3	8.2				5.0	5.0
	39.1	60.1				% Profit Before Taxes/Tangible Net Worth	43.3	60.3
	(51) 16.6	(119) 35.1					(155) 25.0	(164) 34.8
	-4.1	16.4					11.7	13.5
	10.8	19.3	20.3			% Profit Before Taxes/Total Assets	18.2	19.9
	3.8	8.1	7.5				6.8	9.5
	-.6	3.2	6.1				2.7	3.9
	88.6	74.3	48.1			Sales/Net Fixed Assets	82.5	87.8
	45.5	38.8	13.4				38.8	41.9
	15.1	18.6	4.1				16.2	18.4
	3.6	3.6	2.9			Sales/Total Assets	3.7	3.9
	2.6	2.7	2.0				2.9	3.1
	1.8	2.2	1.9				2.3	2.3
	.4	.3	.4			% Depr., Dep., Amort./Sales	.4	.3
	(48) .6	(115) .6	.9				(144) .6	(143) .5
	1.0	.9	3.4				.9	.8
	1.7	1.0				% Officers', Directors', Owners' Comp/Sales	1.6	1.4
	(40) 2.8	(77) 1.8					(99) 2.5	(109) 2.3
	4.1	3.0					4.5	3.7
13325M	197282M	1468466M	394517M	304827M	254232M	Net Sales ($)	1018036M	1225684M
2606M	68446M	516072M	165803M	117426M	115229M	Total Assets ($)	337689M	413975M

M = $ thousand   MM = $ million
See Pages 11 through 18 for Explanation of Ratios and Data

Comparative Historical Data　　　　Current Data Sorted By Sales

Hist 1	Hist 2	Hist 3	Type of Statement	0-1MM	1-3MM	3-5MM	5-10MM	10-25MM	25MM & OVER
1	4	5	Unqualified					4	1
25	20	24	Reviewed	1	2	2	6	12	1
78	62	58	Compiled	1	8	7	17	25	
16	27	47	Tax Returns	3	8	7	21	8	
47	65	78	Other	4	9	9	24	23	10
4/1/00-3/31/01	4/1/01-3/31/02	4/1/02-3/31/03		35 (4/1-9/30/02)		177 (10/1/02-3/31/02)			
ALL	ALL	ALL							
167	178	212	**NUMBER OF STATEMENTS**	9	27	24	68	72	12
%	%	%	**ASSETS**	%	%	%	%	%	%
8.2	9.6	8.7	Cash & Equivalents		6.8	7.1	9.7	9.8	5.1
4.1	4.7	4.3	Trade Receivables (net)		2.8	2.6	4.9	4.2	9.4
68.1	66.4	66.4	Inventory		73.0	72.8	66.7	63.9	45.3
1.5	1.0	1.8	All Other Current		.8	.4	2.0	2.5	2.8
81.9	81.8	81.2	Total Current		83.4	82.9	83.2	80.5	62.6
11.1	13.5	12.6	Fixed Assets (net)		12.5	13.7	10.6	12.1	26.4
3.2	2.3	2.9	Intangibles (net)		.7	.7	4.5	3.1	4.2
3.8	2.4	3.3	All Other Non-Current		3.3	2.7	1.8	4.3	6.8
100.0	100.0	100.0	Total		100.0	100.0	100.0	100.0	100.0
			LIABILITIES						
31.4	32.4	32.9	Notes Payable-Short Term		41.6	43.7	33.0	28.7	19.5
2.4	1.9	3.6	Cur. Mat.-L/T/D		7.8	3.2	4.0	2.4	2.3
13.1	11.9	12.2	Trade Payables		13.2	11.5	11.7	12.2	10.6
.2	.3	.3	Income Taxes Payable		.1	.1	.3	.5	.2
10.1	9.8	9.5	All Other Current		7.6	6.6	8.3	12.2	12.3
57.2	56.3	58.5	Total Current		70.2	65.0	57.3	56.0	44.9
6.9	10.1	9.6	Long Term Debt		7.6	13.6	8.9	7.1	21.5
.0	.0	.0	Deferred Taxes		.0	.0	.0	.0	.0
3.1	2.5	3.3	All Other Non-Current		3.0	2.9	2.5	2.3	9.6
32.8	31.1	28.6	Net Worth		19.1	18.6	31.3	34.6	23.9
100.0	100.0	100.0	Total Liabilities & Net Worth		100.0	100.0	100.0	100.0	100.0
			INCOME DATA						
100.0	100.0	100.0	Net Sales		100.0	100.0	100.0	100.0	100.0
21.8	21.6	22.1	Gross Profit		20.1	19.4	20.5	23.0	29.3
18.0	18.0	18.7	Operating Expenses		19.0	18.8	16.8	18.5	26.0
3.8	3.7	3.3	Operating Profit		1.2	.6	3.7	4.4	3.3
.0	.3	.0	All Other Expenses (net)		.8	−.5	.1	−.5	.2
3.8	3.3	3.4	Profit Before Taxes		.4	1.1	3.6	4.9	3.2
			RATIOS						
1.8	1.8	1.8	Current		1.4	1.6	1.8	2.1	2.2
1.4	1.3	1.3			1.2	1.2	1.3	1.4	1.3
1.1	1.2	1.1			1.0	1.1	1.1	1.1	.9
.4	.4	.4	Quick		.2	.2	.4	.4	.5
(163) .2	(177) .2	.2			.1	.1	.2	.2	.2
.1	.1	.1			.0	.0	.1	.1	.1
1 300.2	1 295.5	1 316.6	Sales/Receivables		0 UND	1 403.1	2 221.8	2 201.1	3 126.6
4 100.7	3 108.7	4 103.9			2 157.8	2 165.2	4 93.3	4 97.0	6 63.5
7 53.2	7 51.2	7 54.3			7 52.4	5 77.4	7 50.7	7 56.0	10 35.2
78 4.7	76 4.8	77 4.7	Cost of Sales/Inventory		117 3.1	112 3.3	76 4.8	69 5.3	39 9.4
99 3.7	102 3.6	112 3.2			170 2.1	137 2.7	113 3.2	94 3.9	69 5.3
135 2.7	142 2.6	156 2.3			234 1.6	156 2.3	153 2.4	117 3.1	127 2.9
5 67.5	5 80.1	5 80.5	Cost of Sales/Payables		3 129.5	3 145.1	5 76.9	5 73.9	12 31.2
11 33.0	11 34.1	11 34.1			9 41.7	9 41.9	9 39.7	12 30.8	14 25.4
24 15.0	22 16.3	23 15.9			21 17.5	20 18.1	20 17.9	25 14.9	35 10.5
8.3	8.3	8.4	Sales/Working Capital		9.2	8.3	8.5	8.4	20.5
13.8	12.6	14.3			13.4	20.8	13.5	13.9	20.9
27.4	22.8	35.5			70.0	39.0	28.1	33.7	NM
11.4	7.8	11.4	EBIT/Interest		(23) 2.9	5.1	(61) 11.9	(66) 23.9	66.7
(152) 3.8	(165) 3.3	(193) 4.3			1.5	2.5	4.7	7.4	3.9
1.6	1.7	1.6			.3	.3	1.8	3.3	2.5
14.8	24.5	13.8	Net Profit + Depr., Dep., Amort./Cur. Mat. L/T/D					(10) 26.8	
(27) 5.1	(21) 12.3	(25) 5.6						13.8	
2.5	4.6	2.0						5.0	
.1	.1	.1	Fixed/Worth		.1	.2	.1	.2	.4
.3	.3	.4			.4	.5	.4	.3	.6
.8	1.0	1.2			1.3	3.9	1.2	.8	NM
1.1	1.3	1.4	Debt/Worth		2.3	2.6	1.4	.9	1.2
2.7	2.8	3.0			5.2	6.0	2.7	2.0	2.9
6.5	5.9	7.8			10.3	13.0	7.1	6.1	NM
65.0	53.3	49.3	% Profit Before Taxes/Tangible Net Worth		(25) 27.3	(21) 39.3	(61) 59.5	(63) 60.8	
(157) 30.5	(163) 30.0	(185) 26.9			9.7	16.6	35.5	33.8	
12.6	14.7	12.0			−47.4	−9.4	16.3	19.5	
18.8	16.6	18.4	% Profit Before Taxes/Total Assets		5.7	7.7	20.1	22.0	19.4
7.9	7.7	6.8			1.7	4.2	6.8	14.4	7.6
2.6	2.8	2.0			−3.0	−2.2	3.0	5.1	6.3
93.3	94.4	75.3	Sales/Net Fixed Assets		71.7	76.5	121.2	67.0	38.4
40.6	37.4	37.3			21.0	45.6	47.0	40.7	13.1
22.4	14.8	15.6			12.0	10.7	15.6	21.6	5.5
3.9	3.7	3.6	Sales/Total Assets		2.6	3.0	3.6	4.1	3.6
3.0	3.0	2.6			1.9	2.5	2.6	3.2	2.6
2.4	2.2	2.0			1.6	2.0	2.1	2.5	2.0
.3	.3	.4	% Depr., Dep., Amort./Sales		(20) .4	(22) .3	(57) .3	(64) .3	(11) .5
(140) .5	(145) .6	(179) .6			.8	.5	.5	.6	.9
.8	1.0	1.0			1.3	1.0	.9	.9	2.0
1.4	1.2	1.2	% Officers', Directors', Owners' Comp/Sales		(21) 1.8	(16) 1.2	(40) 1.3	(41) .6	
(97) 2.1	(116) 2.4	(128) 2.0			2.5	2.4	2.1	1.6	
3.5	3.7	4.0			3.8	3.5	4.8	2.5	
1383616M	1807216M	2632649M	Net Sales ($)	5243M	56342M	95054M	502014M	1054916M	919080M
457584M	619117M	985582M	Total Assets ($)	3602M	29328M	43213M	190015M	355778M	363646M

M = $ thousand　　MM = $ million
See Pages 11 through 18 for Explanation of Ratios and Data

RETAIL—Boat Dealers   NAICS 441222 (SIC 5551)

Current Data Sorted By Assets   —   Comparative Historical Data

0-500M	500M-2MM	2-10MM	10-50MM	50-100MM	100-250MM	Type of Statement	4/1/98-3/31/99 ALL	4/1/99-3/31/00 ALL
		1	4			Unqualified	12	4
2	8	15	2			Reviewed	47	49
7	40	34	3		1	Compiled	94	96
10	26	9	1			Tax Returns	32	26
9	32	30	7	2		Other	61	55
39 (4/1-9/30/02)			204 (10/1/02-3/31/03)					
28	106	89	17	2	1	**NUMBER OF STATEMENTS**	246	230
%	%	%	%	%	%	**ASSETS**	%	%
7.7	7.9	7.1	6.9			Cash & Equivalents	7.3	7.7
7.5	3.3	3.9	2.4			Trade Receivables (net)	4.8	4.4
59.8	74.7	71.3	74.8			Inventory	67.5	68.8
3.2	.5	.9	1.6			All Other Current	.8	1.4
78.3	86.4	83.1	85.8			Total Current	80.4	82.3
18.3	10.6	13.4	9.5			Fixed Assets (net)	14.8	13.4
1.1	1.2	1.5	3.3			Intangibles (net)	1.8	1.2
2.4	1.9	2.0	1.4			All Other Non-Current	3.0	3.0
100.0	100.0	100.0	100.0			Total	100.0	100.0
						LIABILITIES		
30.2	37.5	42.7	27.5			Notes Payable-Short Term	39.5	39.3
1.0	1.9	1.9	3.5			Cur. Mat.-L/T/D	2.3	3.0
10.0	12.6	12.8	28.8			Trade Payables	8.7	7.9
.0	.1	.2	.2			Income Taxes Payable	.4	.2
19.3	11.2	8.9	12.0			All Other Current	7.4	12.1
60.5	63.4	66.5	72.0			Total Current	58.3	62.5
18.8	9.1	11.2	10.3			Long Term Debt	8.9	9.3
.0	.0	.0	.3			Deferred Taxes	.1	.1
23.2	4.3	1.7	2.4			All Other Non-Current	5.6	3.3
-2.5	23.2	20.6	15.0			Net Worth	27.0	24.8
100.0	100.0	100.0	100.0			Total Liabilities & Net Worth	100.0	100.0
						INCOME DATA		
100.0	100.0	100.0	100.0			Net Sales	100.0	100.0
32.7	24.9	20.6	18.8			Gross Profit	23.2	23.6
31.9	22.0	18.0	17.2			Operating Expenses	23.4	19.6
.8	2.9	2.5	1.5			Operating Profit	-.2	3.9
.3	1.4	.8	.2			All Other Expenses (net)	-2.0	1.0
.5	1.5	1.8	1.3			Profit Before Taxes	1.8	2.9
						RATIOS		
2.4	1.6	1.4	1.2			Current	1.8	1.7
1.5	1.4	1.2	1.1				1.3	1.3
1.0	1.1	1.0	1.1				1.1	1.1
.7	.2	.3	.2			Quick	.3	.3
.2	.1	.1	.1				(242) .1	(229) .1
.0	.1	.1	.1				.1	.1
0 UND	0 UND	1 411.3	2 178.6			Sales/Receivables	1 294.9	1 293.0
3 116.8	2 146.1	3 121.2	3 110.4				4 83.7	4 92.1
7 50.3	8 46.6	10 38.2	7 50.1				10 37.7	9 40.1
36 10.0	124 2.9	129 2.8	121 3.0			Cost of Sales/Inventory	98 3.7	95 3.8
136 2.7	180 2.0	169 2.2	168 2.2				149 2.5	147 2.5
221 1.6	239 1.5	234 1.6	230 1.6				203 1.8	203 1.8
0 UND	2 241.2	1 248.0	2 166.5			Cost of Sales/Payables	2 193.9	2 181.7
1 314.0	6 57.3	6 62.6	15 24.2				5 67.1	5 70.1
18 19.9	19 19.0	24 15.5	157 2.3				19 18.7	15 24.6
6.4	5.0	8.5	12.8			Sales/Working Capital	7.1	7.4
20.0	9.7	16.0	21.8				13.8	13.0
NM	31.6	61.9	43.3				32.9	37.2
(24) 9.1	(102) 2.7	(85) 4.2	3.1			EBIT/Interest	(235) 3.5	(226) 4.5
1.6	1.6	1.8	2.0				2.0	2.2
-.3	1.1	1.1	1.2				1.2	1.4
	(15) 4.1	(19) 4.8				Net Profit + Depr., Dep., Amort./Cur. Mat. L/T/D	(48) 8.6	(42) 7.8
	3.1	3.1					3.7	3.0
	.8	.8					1.7	1.7
.2	.1	.2	.2			Fixed/Worth	.2	.2
.8	.4	.5	.6				.4	.4
-1.7	1.1	1.3	2.1				1.1	1.1
.9	2.0	2.7	5.2			Debt/Worth	1.6	1.7
9.7	4.0	5.2	6.9				4.1	3.9
-4.6	10.4	11.9	39.6				8.9	9.8
(16) 72.7	(93) 29.0	(79) 41.1	(14) 56.2			% Profit Before Taxes/Tangible Net Worth	(226) 42.9	(207) 48.5
33.6	10.8	17.7	34.1				19.8	23.9
1.5	4.0	5.5	6.2				6.7	11.1
19.8	5.9	6.3	5.1			% Profit Before Taxes/Total Assets	10.4	10.7
1.7	2.7	2.6	2.7				4.4	4.9
-6.9	.7	.4	.7				1.1	1.9
66.7	86.7	71.7	91.5			Sales/Net Fixed Assets	80.5	92.7
30.8	41.4	27.5	70.3				27.3	36.0
16.3	15.8	11.8	16.0				10.0	10.2
5.8	2.8	2.4	2.6			Sales/Total Assets	3.0	3.1
2.6	2.0	1.8	2.1				2.2	2.2
1.7	1.6	1.5	1.6				1.7	1.6
(19) .5	(87) .4	(77) .3	(14) .2			% Depr., Dep., Amort./Sales	(208) .4	(185) .4
.9	.7	.6	.6				.7	.6
1.7	1.5	1.3	1.0				1.3	1.2
(15) 2.4	(65) 1.3	(40) 1.0				% Officers', Directors', Owners' Comp/Sales	(126) 1.3	(119) 1.4
5.6	2.6	1.9					2.4	2.6
9.8	4.1	3.7					4.4	4.8
28858M	304936M	769023M	821499M	275796M	408149M	Net Sales ($)	1760737M	2263268M
8285M	129153M	380848M	352861M	170179M	128412M	Total Assets ($)	1097247M	1119369M

M = $ thousand   MM = $ million
See Pages 11 through 18 for Explanation of Ratios and Data

Comparative Historical Data | Current Data Sorted By Sales

Hist 1	Hist 2	Hist 3	Type of Statement	0-1MM	1-3MM	3-5MM	5-10MM	10-25MM	25MM & OVER
2	5	5	Unqualified					1	4
33	37	27	Reviewed	1	6	4	5	10	1
118	122	85	Compiled	7	30	21	19	4	4
43	32	46	Tax Returns	10	16	12	3	4	1
109	62	80	Other	7	24	12	16	12	9
4/1/00- 3/31/01 ALL	4/1/01- 3/31/02 ALL	4/1/02- 3/31/03 ALL		39 (4/1-9/30/02)			204 (10/1/02-3/31/02)		
305	258	243	**NUMBER OF STATEMENTS**	25	76	49	43	31	19
%	%	%	**ASSETS**	%	%	%	%	%	%
7.1	8.3	7.5	Cash & Equivalents	6.2	6.8	6.7	7.4	12.3	7.0
3.6	4.2	3.9	Trade Receivables (net)	6.9	3.6	3.1	3.8	3.5	4.6
72.7	69.3	71.4	Inventory	59.9	73.5	75.6	74.3	68.7	64.9
.7	1.2	1.0	All Other Current	3.6	.5	.4	.9	1.0	1.5
84.1	83.0	83.9	Total Current	76.5	84.3	85.9	86.4	85.5	78.0
11.5	13.0	12.8	Fixed Assets (net)	17.9	13.2	11.0	11.7	10.3	15.2
2.3	1.8	1.4	Intangibles (net)	2.2	1.2	1.2	.7	2.0	2.9
2.1	2.3	1.9	All Other Non-Current	3.4	1.3	1.9	1.1	2.2	4.0
100.0	100.0	100.0	Total	100.0	100.0	100.0	100.0	100.0	100.0
			LIABILITIES						
30.7	31.6	37.6	Notes Payable-Short Term	29.9	36.7	42.9	42.0	40.3	23.9
1.8	3.3	2.2	Cur. Mat.-L/T/D	3.0	1.1	4.0	.7	.5	6.5
20.5	16.4	13.4	Trade Payables	5.6	13.5	11.2	15.0	15.6	21.4
.1	.2	.1	Income Taxes Payable	.0	.0	.1	.1	.3	.2
13.8	12.2	11.3	All Other Current	20.9	10.1	7.7	9.9	12.3	14.0
67.0	63.6	64.6	Total Current	59.4	61.5	65.9	67.8	69.0	65.9
8.0	10.7	11.3	Long Term Debt	22.4	11.5	9.3	7.4	7.8	16.5
.0	.0	.0	Deferred Taxes	.0	.0	.0	.0	.0	.2
3.5	3.3	5.3	All Other Non-Current	27.6	4.3	2.3	1.9	1.3	2.2
21.5	22.7	18.7	Net Worth	−9.4	22.8	22.4	22.9	21.9	15.1
100.0	100.0	100.0	Total Liabilities & Net Worth	100.0	100.0	100.0	100.0	100.0	100.0
			INCOME DATA						
100.0	100.0	100.0	Net Sales	100.0	100.0	100.0	100.0	100.0	100.0
22.9	23.6	23.7	Gross Profit	36.4	26.2	21.6	20.1	19.5	17.8
19.4	20.8	21.3	Operating Expenses	35.2	23.2	18.7	17.6	17.6	16.4
3.4	2.8	2.4	Operating Profit	1.2	2.9	2.9	2.4	1.9	1.4
1.5	1.5	1.0	All Other Expenses (net)	1.7	1.4	1.2	.7	−.2	.3
1.9	1.4	1.4	Profit Before Taxes	−.6	1.6	1.6	1.7	2.2	1.1
			RATIOS						
1.5	1.6	1.6	Current	2.4	1.6	1.6	1.6	1.4	1.2
1.2	1.2	1.2		1.7	1.3	1.2	1.2	1.2	1.1
1.1	1.1	1.1		1.1	1.1	1.0	1.1	1.0	1.1
.2	.3	.3	Quick	.6	.2	.2	.3	.4	.3
(304) .1	.1	.1		.1	.1	.1	.1	.1	.2
.0	.1	.1		.1	.1	.0	.1	.1	.1
1 517.3	1 649.9	0 939.0	Sales/Receivables	0 UND	0 UND	0 999.8	1 411.3	1 367.2	2 195.2
3 124.8	4 84.9	3 121.2		3 110.2	3 119.1	2 165.3	3 133.6	3 134.6	4 88.4
8 48.4	8 43.8	8 44.9		15 24.8	8 43.3	8 43.0	6 56.4	8 46.6	8 44.0
113 3.2	110 3.3	120 3.0	Cost of Sales/Inventory	97 3.8	133 2.7	121 3.0	111 3.3	108 3.4	109 3.3
169 2.2	162 2.3	169 2.2		219 1.7	193 1.9	165 2.2	155 2.3	160 2.3	147 2.5
235 1.6	229 1.6	230 1.6		334 1.1	278 1.3	224 1.6	222 1.6	209 1.7	191 1.9
2 198.4	2 222.7	1 285.1	Cost of Sales/Payables	0 UND	1 269.4	1 729.6	2 212.0	2 159.7	2 208.1
10 35.4	8 47.8	6 60.6		1 437.0	7 49.0	3 112.6	7 55.0	7 52.3	5 80.9
66 5.5	33 10.9	23 15.9		17 21.1	32 11.6	18 20.7	29 12.6	22 16.4	118 3.1
8.6	7.3	6.9	Sales/Working Capital	2.3	5.0	6.1	8.6	11.8	15.4
15.3	13.8	13.8		8.3	11.2	12.6	16.5	17.4	28.2
38.2	33.4	45.3		NM	26.5	95.0	49.1	61.7	43.7
3.3	2.9	3.9	EBIT/Interest	2.1	2.6	3.6	4.3	7.2	3.5
(290) 1.7	(243) 1.6	(231) 1.7		(22) 1.2	(75) 1.5	(46) 2.2	(41) 1.9	(28) 2.8	2.1
1.2	1.6	1.1		−1.3	1.0	1.2	1.1	1.2	1.1
5.6	7.7	4.4	Net Profit + Depr., Dep., Amort./Cur. Mat. L/T/D		4.8		17.9		
(42) 2.9	(29) 3.1	(39) 2.7			(10) 3.7		(10) 4.5		
1.1	1.3	.1			.7		2.2		
.1	.2	.2	Fixed/Worth	.1	.2	.1	.1	.2	.4
.4	.5	.5		3.1	.5	.4	.4	.4	.8
1.6	2.1	1.8		−.6	1.9	1.6	.9	1.1	3.0
2.4	2.1	2.3	Debt/Worth	1.2	1.8	2.1	2.3	2.6	4.2
5.7	4.8	4.8		20.5	4.4	4.9	4.3	5.2	5.9
17.4	14.5	15.1		−3.6	14.5	26.6	8.3	9.6	11.4
47.1	32.0	41.3	% Profit Before Taxes/Tangible Net Worth	39.0	26.1	47.8	37.3	48.0	55.0
(264) 23.7	(224) 12.7	(205) 14.9		(13) 3.5	(65) 8.9	(41) 19.4	(40) 12.9	(30) 27.2	(16) 44.3
9.0	2.1	4.8		−1.4	2.3	7.0	5.8	7.3	4.3
8.0	7.1	6.1	% Profit Before Taxes/Total Assets	2.5	5.3	6.8	6.8	10.7	5.6
3.2	2.7	2.6		.6	2.5	3.3	3.2	3.6	3.5
.8	.1	.4		−8.6	.1	.9	.7	.9	.6
102.3	85.4	77.1	Sales/Net Fixed Assets	62.1	66.2	129.7	73.7	70.3	86.5
40.8	33.8	33.9		25.6	24.8	61.6	32.0	39.3	25.7
15.2	12.3	13.5		4.8	11.9	17.6	18.2	13.8	8.3
2.8	2.7	2.8	Sales/Total Assets	2.5	2.5	2.8	3.2	2.7	3.2
2.0	2.1	2.0		1.6	1.8	2.1	2.2	2.1	2.2
1.5	1.6	1.6		1.1	1.4	1.6	1.6	1.8	1.6
.3	.4	.4	% Depr., Dep., Amort./Sales	.5	.4	.3	.2	.3	.3
(242) .6	(213) .7	(199) .7		(16) 1.1	(64) .9	(38) .7	(38) .5	(28) .6	(15) .6
1.1	1.4	1.4		2.5	1.9	1.3	.9	1.0	1.1
1.3	1.4	1.2	% Officers', Directors', Owners' Comp/Sales	1.5	1.4	1.0	1.1	.6	
(164) 2.1	(134) 2.3	(127) 2.2		(18) 5.1	(40) 3.0	(27) 1.7	(19) 2.1	(17) 1.3	
3.5	4.3	4.3		10.2	4.9	3.7	3.1	3.2	
3386210M	2159781M	2608261M	Net Sales ($)	14592M	151067M	189398M	304284M	441746M	1507174M
1795588M	1123775M	1169738M	Total Assets ($)	9972M	82730M	95833M	148767M	196930M	635506M

M = $ thousand   MM = $ million
See Pages 11 through 18 for Explanation of Ratios and Data

Current Data Sorted By Assets   Comparative Historical Data

Type of Statement	0-500M	500M-2MM	2-10MM	10-50MM	50-100MM	100-250MM		4/1/98-3/31/99 ALL	4/1/99-3/31/00 ALL
Unqualified		1	7	6	1	2		16	14
Reviewed	1	5	21	3	1			19	15
Compiled	11	17	11					20	25
Tax Returns	11	19	9					11	17
Other	7	18	28	17	3	1		25	36
		42 (4/1-9/30/02)		158 (10/1/02-3/31/03)					
NUMBER OF STATEMENTS	30	60	76	26	5	3		91	107
	%	%	%	%	%	%		%	%
ASSETS									
Cash & Equivalents	12.3	7.1	8.0	6.9				7.0	7.3
Trade Receivables (net)	13.0	11.0	13.0	11.3				13.2	14.2
Inventory	49.8	58.5	56.5	46.4				46.6	51.0
All Other Current	.3	.5	3.5	2.7				3.7	3.4
Total Current	75.4	77.1	81.0	67.3				70.5	75.8
Fixed Assets (net)	16.8	18.9	13.2	19.4				21.8	19.0
Intangibles (net)	2.1	1.1	1.1	1.8				2.1	1.1
All Other Non-Current	5.7	2.9	4.7	11.5				5.6	4.1
Total	100.0	100.0	100.0	100.0				100.0	100.0
LIABILITIES									
Notes Payable-Short Term	19.2	33.2	40.0	43.6				27.3	33.6
Cur. Mat.-L/T/D	2.3	3.0	3.6	5.0				5.4	5.3
Trade Payables	7.7	13.2	11.0	5.4				10.6	10.6
Income Taxes Payable	.3	.0	.1	.7				.1	.1
All Other Current	11.7	6.8	9.3	7.2				10.1	8.7
Total Current	41.3	56.3	64.0	61.9				53.5	58.3
Long Term Debt	18.2	16.8	8.0	15.3				17.1	11.8
Deferred Taxes	.0	.0	.3	.9				.3	.3
All Other Non-Current	10.5	4.6	2.9	1.4				2.4	4.5
Net Worth	29.9	22.4	24.7	20.5				26.7	25.1
Total Liabilities & Net Worth	100.0	100.0	100.0	100.0				100.0	100.0
INCOME DATA									
Net Sales	100.0	100.0	100.0	100.0				100.0	100.0
Gross Profit	28.9	23.9	20.8	18.1				24.8	20.3
Operating Expenses	27.7	22.4	19.1	14.4				23.0	17.2
Operating Profit	1.2	1.5	1.7	3.8				1.8	3.2
All Other Expenses (net)	.3	1.6	.0	1.4				.0	1.4
Profit Before Taxes	.9	-.1	1.6	2.4				1.9	1.7
RATIOS									
Current	3.3	2.3	1.5	1.3				1.9	1.7
	1.9	1.1	1.2	1.1				1.2	1.3
	1.2	1.0	1.1	.9				1.0	1.1
Quick	1.9	.8	.5	.4				.6	.7
	.5 (59)	.4 (74)	.3	.3				.3 (105)	.4
	.1	.1	.1	.2				.2	.1
Sales/Receivables	0 UND	2 155.6	3 105.1	8 47.6				2 149.0	2 209.2
	4 87.7	8 46.2	8 45.0	14 26.8				18 20.1	11 32.4
	17 21.0	20 18.7	21 17.3	27 13.3				38 9.5	27 13.6
Cost of Sales/Inventory	26 13.8	50 7.3	47 7.8	51 7.1				40 9.1	43 8.5
	55 6.6	86 4.2	76 4.8	66 5.5				80 4.6	77 4.7
	81 4.5	143 2.5	102 3.6	85 4.3				154 2.4	150 2.4
Cost of Sales/Payables	0 UND	1 324.4	3 121.7	2 190.4				2 163.0	3 131.2
	2 241.4	11 33.5	8 45.4	3 105.2				11 32.2	8 45.4
	16 22.5	31 11.7	21 17.7	17 21.3				31 11.7	28 13.0
Sales/Working Capital	5.6	8.6	10.6	18.3				7.0	7.5
	15.1	22.3	26.5	38.7				19.7	20.4
	63.2	999.8	77.7	-62.0				782.0	92.0
EBIT/Interest	6.6	2.8	5.6	5.5				3.7	4.7
	(20) 2.3	(46) 1.5	(66) 2.1	(23) 3.2				(85) 2.1	(96) 2.0
	.4	-.3	1.4	1.7				1.3	1.2
Net Profit + Depr., Dep., Amort./Cur. Mat. L /T/D			2.4					4.0	4.3
		(14)	1.3					(24) 1.3	(17) 3.4
			.9					.4	1.9
Fixed/Worth	.0	.1	.1	.3				.2	.2
	.5	1.0	.3	.9				.6	.4
	2.6	3.1	.9	3.1				1.7	1.7
Debt/Worth	1.0	1.9	1.9	3.1				1.6	1.5
	2.2	4.9	3.6	4.9				3.8	3.6
	7.0	23.3	7.2	9.9				7.0	8.8
% Profit Before Taxes/Tangible Net Worth	51.3	29.9	37.8	72.8				36.6	45.4
	(25) 26.1	(51) 12.7	(72) 12.3	(25) 15.8				(82) 17.9	(93) 22.4
	1.1	-3.7	6.9	2.5				5.0	8.4
% Profit Before Taxes/Total Assets	17.6	4.7	8.0	11.7				6.2	10.6
	6.0	1.3	2.5	4.2				3.2	4.4
	-.6	-4.3	1.2	.5				.9	1.1
Sales/Net Fixed Assets	362.8	144.9	113.7	83.3				64.4	95.7
	46.5	34.5	60.8	17.9				20.7	32.7
	18.3	7.2	19.7	7.9				5.9	7.8
Sales/Total Assets	5.9	4.9	4.2	3.6				3.7	4.1
	4.0	2.9	3.3	2.8				2.2	2.5
	2.9	1.9	2.3	2.0				1.4	1.7
% Depr., Dep., Amort./Sales	.3	.3	.2	.3				.4	.3
	(21) 1.3	(46) .9	(69) .4	(21) .4				(80) 1.2	(87) .6
	2.3	1.8	1.3	1.3				3.0	1.8
% Officers', Directors', Owners' Comp/Sales	1.4	1.2	.4	.3				1.2	.7
	(21) 3.7	(40) 2.5	(41) 1.1	(15) .4				(36) 3.5	(48) 1.7
	6.6	4.7	2.0	.5				5.2	4.1
Net Sales ($)	39134M	243742M	1365288M	1509200M	832162M	560268M		2464168M	1725278M
Total Assets ($)	8492M	70611M	389095M	509237M	320551M	478518M		1225960M	669515M

RETAIL—All Other Motor Vehicle Dealers NAICS 441229 (SIC 5599)

Comparative Historical Data			Type of Statement	Current Data Sorted By Sales					
6	13	17	Unqualified		1		3	3	10
17	20	31	Reviewed	1	1	4	4	12	9
28	29	39	Compiled	8	12	4	11	4	
17	16	39	Tax Returns	6	15	7	5	6	
34	28	74	Other	8	8	7	6	18	27
4/1/00-3/31/01 ALL	4/1/01-3/31/02 ALL	4/1/02-3/31/03 ALL		42 (4/1-9/30/02)			158 (10/1/02-3/31/02)		
				0-1MM	1-3MM	3-5MM	5-10MM	10-25MM	25MM & OVER
102	106	200	**NUMBER OF STATEMENTS**	23	37	22	29	43	46
%	%	%	**ASSETS**	%	%	%	%	%	%
5.8	8.9	8.2	Cash & Equivalents	12.1	8.8	4.1	7.7	6.7	9.4
13.0	13.6	12.0	Trade Receivables (net)	16.1	8.9	7.6	18.3	12.1	10.5
53.4	49.9	54.4	Inventory	40.6	54.3	63.2	49.6	60.8	54.0
2.6	2.1	2.4	All Other Current	.8	.9	.6	2.3	3.8	4.0
74.8	74.4	77.0	Total Current	69.6	72.8	75.5	78.0	83.5	78.0
20.2	17.4	16.4	Fixed Assets (net)	20.7	20.6	21.0	17.2	10.6	13.8
1.4	3.0	1.3	Intangibles (net)	4.3	1.3	.4	.3	1.1	1.1
3.5	5.2	5.3	All Other Non-Current	5.4	5.2	3.1	4.4	4.9	7.2
100.0	100.0	100.0	Total	100.0	100.0	100.0	100.0	100.0	100.0
			LIABILITIES						
29.9	32.0	35.5	Notes Payable-Short Term	22.1	25.3	32.4	29.7	44.6	47.0
6.2	4.9	3.5	Cur. Mat.-L/T/D	2.2	4.9	2.4	2.8	5.0	2.4
11.6	8.8	10.5	Trade Payables	4.3	11.6	20.3	14.9	9.3	6.6
.3	.2	.2	Income Taxes Payable	.1	.2	.0	.2	.3	.1
10.8	11.7	8.5	All Other Current	14.7	4.3	5.4	9.0	6.9	11.3
58.8	57.5	58.2	Total Current	43.4	46.2	60.5	56.6	66.1	67.5
13.8	10.6	13.4	Long Term Debt	23.6	18.3	16.0	11.1	7.6	9.8
.3	.2	.3	Deferred Taxes	.0	.0	.0	.1	.7	.6
3.2	3.1	4.2	All Other Non-Current	5.6	9.1	6.0	2.2	2.7	1.6
23.9	28.6	23.9	Net Worth	27.4	26.4	17.4	29.9	22.8	20.5
100.0	100.0	100.0	Total Liabilities & Net Worth	100.0	100.0	100.0	100.0	100.0	100.0
			INCOME DATA						
100.0	100.0	100.0	Net Sales	100.0	100.0	100.0	100.0	100.0	100.0
21.6	22.7	22.2	Gross Profit	36.1	30.4	21.9	23.7	16.8	13.0
19.8	19.8	20.4	Operating Expenses	33.2	28.2	21.4	21.4	14.9	11.8
1.8	2.9	1.8	Operating Profit	2.9	2.2	.5	2.3	1.9	1.3
1.7	2.0	1.0	All Other Expenses (net)	2.6	1.4	1.1	.6	.0	.9
.1	.9	.9	Profit Before Taxes	.3	.8	-.6	1.7	1.9	.4
			RATIOS						
1.8	1.9	1.7		4.3	3.1	1.5	1.9	1.4	1.3
1.2	1.2	1.2	Current	1.7	1.5	1.1	1.3	1.2	1.1
1.0	1.0	1.0		1.0	.9	.9	1.0	1.1	1.0
.6	.7	.6		2.7	.9	.5	.7	.5	.4
.2	.4 (197)	.3	Quick	.5	.4 (20)	.2	.5 (42)	.2	.3
.1	.2	.1		.0	.1	.1	.2	.2	.2
1 289.0	2 189.8	3 131.2		0 UND	1 254.0	0 UND	4 98.0	3 142.4	5 72.8
12 30.5	13 27.6	9 42.5	Sales/Receivables	6 59.3	8 45.5	9 42.4	12 31.6	10 35.9	9 42.5
22 16.5	31 11.8	20 18.0		25 14.9	22 16.5	17 20.9	33 11.1	26 13.9	16 23.3
48 7.6	40 9.2	46 7.9		12 29.4	65 5.6	55 6.7	21 17.7	47 7.8	47 7.8
78 4.7	73 5.0	71 5.1	Cost of Sales/Inventory	46 8.0	87 4.2	114 3.2	59 6.2	78 4.7	63 5.8
154 2.4	158 2.3	113 3.2		243 1.5	141 2.6	150 2.4	92 4.0	98 3.7	81 4.5
1 313.3	3 120.3	2 189.5		0 UND	0 UND	11 34.5	4 86.9	3 144.9	2 190.4
6 59.1	10 35.5	8 47.7	Cost of Sales/Payables	3 137.3	13 28.6	21 17.2	12 29.8	5 67.5	4 103.7
20 18.1	22 16.7	21 17.2		23 15.7	32 11.5	83 4.4	37 9.8	17 20.9	8 44.2
9.7	7.8	10.6		3.3	5.5	9.9	9.1	13.7	18.3
20.8	17.1	24.0	Sales/Working Capital	15.6	14.7	48.5	25.5	26.7	34.4
473.8	163.2	181.0		59.3	-37.6	-48.0	314.4	97.7	198.1
	2.9	2.7	4.5		2.5	4.7	1.9	4.7	8.5	5.8
(95) 1.4	(88) 1.6	(161) 2.0	EBIT/Interest	(12) 1.6	(32) 1.9	(17) .7	(25) 2.5	(37) 2.8	(38) 2.8
.9	1.1	1.2		.0	.2	-.8	1.5	1.4	1.4
3.4	4.7	2.6	Net Profit + Depr., Dep.,						7.8
(21) 1.1	(13) 1.7	(28) 1.6	Amort./Cur. Mat. L/T/D					(10)	2.3
.8	.7	.9							1.3
.2	.1	.1		.1	.1	.1	.1	.1	.1
.6	.5	.5	Fixed/Worth	1.0	1.1	1.0	.4	.3	.5
1.7	1.6	2.1		3.3	3.6	4.7	1.0	.6	1.2
1.9	1.6	1.9		1.2	1.4	3.3	1.1	2.1	2.8
3.8	3.3	4.2	Debt/Worth	4.0	2.7	7.9	2.2	4.2	4.9
8.4	13.3	9.2		19.7	13.7	76.8	7.2	7.7	7.9
33.5	29.1	39.9	% Profit Before Taxes/Tangible	40.6	43.1	37.6	24.8	37.0	55.0
(92) 13.3	(96) 14.3	(181) 13.9	Net Worth	(18) 3.0	(31) 15.6	(18) -.5	(40) 15.2	(45) 17.8	14.5
2.0	2.2	3.2		-3.3	2.7	-23.8	6.8	9.0	4.6
6.7	5.8	8.2	% Profit Before Taxes/Total	9.3	11.5	3.3	7.8	8.3	10.7
2.0	2.5	2.3	Assets	2.1	2.4	-1.4	3.1	2.6	2.4
-.7	.1	.3		-1.5	-3.9	-4.8	1.4	1.1	1.1
76.3	126.6	132.7		145.8	133.5	64.5	88.1	139.9	166.6
24.4	37.4	40.5	Sales/Net Fixed Assets	35.6	40.3	27.5	34.8	84.1	56.9
7.5	10.9	10.8		4.1	4.8	7.4	15.2	22.8	10.3
3.9	4.3	4.5		4.1	4.0	3.4	5.6	4.5	4.6
2.7	2.9	3.2	Sales/Total Assets	2.7	2.9	2.5	3.2	3.5	3.4
2.0	1.8	2.2		.9	1.5	2.0	2.5	2.6	2.5
.3	.3	.3		1.3	.3	.4	.4	.2	.2
(87) .9	(81) .8	(164) .6	% Depr., Dep., Amort./Sales	(15) 1.4	(30) .5	(18) 1.1	(25) .9	(36) .4	(40) .3
1.7	2.3	1.8		6.0	1.9	3.1	1.8	1.2	1.0
.9	.7	.6		3.5	1.3	1.5	.7	.6	.3
(45) 1.9	(48) 2.2	(121) 1.4	% Officers', Directors', Owners' Comp/Sales	(11) 4.3	(27) 2.8	(15) 1.9	(17) 2.0	(24) 1.2	(27) .4
3.0	5.2	3.6		6.7	6.7	3.5	4.6	2.3	.6
2685646M	1998818M	4549794M	Net Sales ($)	14183M	70290M	87785M	217744M	663495M	3496297M
1022045M	877604M	1776504M	Total Assets ($)	15105M	48055M	39677M	81580M	215361M	1376726M

M = $ thousand   MM = $ million
See Pages 11 through 18 for Explanation of Ratios and Data

Current Data Sorted By Assets   Comparative Historical Data

Type of Statement	0-500M	500M-2MM	2-10MM	10-50MM	50-100MM	100-250MM		4/1/98-3/31/99 ALL	4/1/99-3/31/00 ALL
Unqualified	1	2	8	13	3	2		30	27
Reviewed	1	20	39	7	1	1		59	51
Compiled	24	46	28	1	1	1		162	128
Tax Returns	22	26	2	1	1	1		58	47
Other	22	22	28	10	1	3		102	93
		75 (4/1-9/30/02)		259 (10/1/02-3/31/03)					
NUMBER OF STATEMENTS	70	116	105	31	7	5		411	346
	%	%	%	%	%	%		%	%
ASSETS									
Cash & Equivalents	7.3	6.4	5.3	5.9				7.9	6.8
Trade Receivables (net)	14.9	21.1	19.7	18.6				17.6	17.6
Inventory	50.4	43.2	49.0	36.3				45.8	46.1
All Other Current	2.3	2.1	2.5	1.7				1.4	1.4
Total Current	74.9	72.7	76.6	62.5				72.8	71.9
Fixed Assets (net)	16.7	18.0	16.7	28.9				20.2	20.0
Intangibles (net)	3.3	2.3	2.2	1.5				2.4	2.7
All Other Non-Current	5.1	7.0	4.5	7.0				4.6	5.4
Total	100.0	100.0	100.0	100.0				100.0	100.0
LIABILITIES									
Notes Payable-Short Term	9.7	10.4	13.0	11.1				8.0	8.3
Cur. Mat.-L/T/D	4.3	3.4	3.0	3.6				4.5	4.0
Trade Payables	26.5	24.0	25.0	20.8				24.3	22.7
Income Taxes Payable	.4	.1	.1	.1				.2	.2
All Other Current	7.2	5.0	9.6	7.2				8.2	7.4
Total Current	48.1	42.8	50.7	42.9				45.2	42.7
Long Term Debt	33.5	16.9	11.3	14.3				17.1	17.8
Deferred Taxes	.0	.0	.2	.5				.1	.1
All Other Non-Current	10.8	5.1	3.1	4.5				4.4	3.6
Net Worth	7.5	35.1	34.7	37.9				33.2	35.8
Total Liabilities & Net Worth	100.0	100.0	100.0	100.0				100.0	100.0
INCOME DATA									
Net Sales	100.0	100.0	100.0	100.0				100.0	100.0
Gross Profit	39.6	35.5	34.5	32.9				36.5	37.0
Operating Expenses	37.1	32.6	32.6	29.6				34.0	34.0
Operating Profit	2.5	2.9	1.9	3.3				2.5	3.0
All Other Expenses (net)	.5	.6	.1	1.5				.3	.3
Profit Before Taxes	2.0	2.3	1.8	1.8				2.2	2.7
RATIOS									
Current	4.4	2.5	2.0	2.0				2.7	2.8
	1.9	1.7	1.4	1.4				1.7	1.7
	1.0	1.2	1.1	1.1				1.2	1.2
Quick	1.0	1.0	.8	.9				1.0	1.0
	.4	.6	.5	.5			(410)	.6 (345)	.6
	.3	.4	.3	.2				.3	.3
Sales/Receivables	5 70.6	16 23.4	16 23.2	13 27.2			10	36.4 10	37.4
	16 22.8	27 13.5	28 13.1	30 12.0			22	17.0 23	16.2
	30 12.3	37 9.9	33 10.9	39 9.4			32	11.4 33	11.1
Cost of Sales/Inventory	55 6.6	48 7.6	59 6.2	58 6.3			53	6.9 57	6.4
	102 3.6	91 4.0	91 4.0	81 4.5			84	4.3 91	4.0
	158 2.3	147 2.5	136 2.7	124 2.9			130	2.8 146	2.5
Cost of Sales/Payables	21 17.6	25 14.4	30 12.3	28 13.2			26	13.8 27	13.3
	33 10.9	44 8.3	48 7.6	47 7.8			42	8.6 43	8.5
	54 6.8	66 5.5	63 5.8	74 4.9			62	5.9 62	5.8
Sales/Working Capital	4.1	4.9	6.3	6.8				5.6	4.9
	9.1	10.0	12.2	11.7				10.2	10.0
	309.3	24.0	35.2	36.7				37.1	29.3
EBIT/Interest	5.8	6.2	7.1	6.8				6.4	6.8
	(56) 2.2	(110) 3.1	(99) 3.0	(26) 4.2			(363)	2.7 (310)	2.9
	.5	1.0	1.3	2.6				1.3	1.4
Net Profit + Depr., Dep., Amort./Cur. Mat. L/T/D		2.2	4.1	6.6				5.1	4.8
	(22) 1.5	(37) 1.9	(11) 4.3				(107)	2.2 (104)	2.4
	.3	.7	1.5					1.0	1.1
Fixed/Worth	.2	.2	.2	.3				.2	.2
	.8	.4	.4	.8				.5	.5
	-3.0	1.2	.9	1.6				1.3	1.3
Debt/Worth	1.6	.9	1.1	.7				.8	.9
	3.4	1.9	2.0	2.1				1.9	1.8
	-7.3	5.8	4.0	4.5				4.9	4.8
% Profit Before Taxes/Tangible Net Worth	57.1	27.5	31.9	28.1				37.4	36.5
	(48) 12.7	(104) 10.8	(99) 15.2	(30) 20.1			(366)	17.9 (316)	16.8
	.6	.7	3.1	6.0				4.6	5.6
% Profit Before Taxes/Total Assets	16.4	8.8	9.0	9.4				12.5	10.9
	2.6	3.9	4.1	5.6				5.5	5.2
	-.5	.1	.5	1.8				1.0	1.6
Sales/Net Fixed Assets	109.8	47.7	52.1	22.1				41.4	38.5
	24.9	22.1	23.9	11.1				20.2	20.1
	13.4	12.3	14.2	4.5				10.7	10.2
Sales/Total Assets	4.2	3.7	3.6	3.1				3.8	3.6
	2.8	2.6	2.9	2.4				2.8	2.8
	2.2	2.1	2.2	1.7				2.1	2.0
% Depr., Dep., Amort./Sales	.5	.8	.7	1.0				.8	.8
	(55) 1.1	(107) 1.3	(100) 1.2	(27) 1.7			(361)	1.4 (304)	1.3
	2.4	1.8	1.8	2.2				2.0	2.1
% Officers', Directors', Owners' Comp/Sales	3.1	2.0	1.5					2.2	2.0
	(43) 5.2	(71) 3.3	(45) 2.4				(209)	4.1 (171)	3.6
	8.3	6.1	5.1					6.7	5.9
Net Sales ($)	66409M	363759M	1363562M	1545632M	864286M	1699004M		4745085M	5416225M
Total Assets ($)	20969M	128229M	463094M	667290M	509989M	762352M		1573624M	2103760M

M = $ thousand   MM = $ million
See Pages 11 through 18 for Explanation of Ratios and Data

Comparative Historical Data — Current Data Sorted By Sales

Hist 1	Hist 2	Hist 3	Type of Statement	0-1MM	1-3MM	3-5MM	5-10MM	10-25MM	25MM & OVER
16	19	29	Unqualified	1	1	1	2	6	18
45	32	68	Reviewed	2	10	9	13	25	9
100	82	100	Compiled	13	38	21	15	10	3
43	40	51	Tax Returns	17	18	10	4	1	1
67	77	86	Other	22	13	10	16	10	15
4/1/00-3/31/01 ALL	4/1/01-3/31/02 ALL	4/1/02-3/31/03 ALL		75 (4/1-9/30/02)			259 (10/1/02-3/31/02)		
271	250	334	**NUMBER OF STATEMENTS**	55	80	51	50	52	46
%	%	%	**ASSETS**	%	%	%	%	%	%
7.3	6.5	6.1	Cash & Equivalents	6.4	6.3	6.5	5.5	4.8	6.9
18.0	18.5	18.9	Trade Receivables (net)	14.6	18.2	21.8	21.2	20.0	18.2
46.1	45.7	45.8	Inventory	49.8	46.8	44.8	47.5	45.5	38.6
2.1	1.5	2.2	All Other Current	3.2	1.8	3.0	1.2	2.5	1.5
73.4	72.1	72.9	Total Current	74.0	73.1	76.1	75.4	72.8	65.2
18.4	18.9	18.4	Fixed Assets (net)	15.8	18.5	15.8	19.5	18.4	22.7
2.5	2.9	2.8	Intangibles (net)	3.5	2.1	2.3	1.6	2.1	5.6
5.7	6.1	5.9	All Other Non-Current	6.7	6.3	5.9	3.5	6.7	6.5
100.0	100.0	100.0	Total	100.0	100.0	100.0	100.0	100.0	100.0
			LIABILITIES						
8.7	9.0	11.1	Notes Payable-Short Term	9.2	10.2	12.2	12.2	13.7	9.7
3.7	3.3	3.4	Cur. Mat.-L/T/D	3.9	4.3	3.3	3.1	2.4	3.0
24.5	22.5	24.3	Trade Payables	21.2	23.6	26.0	26.0	25.0	24.8
.2	.2	.2	Income Taxes Payable	.4	.1	.1	.2	.1	.3
7.2	8.1	7.2	All Other Current	5.6	6.5	5.8	7.5	10.1	8.2
44.3	43.0	46.2	Total Current	40.3	44.7	47.4	49.0	51.3	46.1
16.0	17.5	18.7	Long Term Debt	37.4	22.4	13.2	10.2	9.7	15.6
.2	.2	.1	Deferred Taxes	.0	.0	.0	.1	.3	.4
5.3	5.0	5.7	All Other Non-Current	13.3	2.8	8.0	2.9	4.1	3.4
34.3	34.3	29.2	Net Worth	9.0	30.1	31.3	37.7	34.6	34.4
100.0	100.0	100.0	Total Liabilities & Net Worth	100.0	100.0	100.0	100.0	100.0	100.0
			INCOME DATA						
100.0	100.0	100.0	Net Sales	100.0	100.0	100.0	100.0	100.0	100.0
36.8	38.0	35.9	Gross Profit	40.5	37.0	33.7	35.2	32.7	34.9
34.3	35.4	33.2	Operating Expenses	37.1	34.6	31.9	33.1	30.5	31.0
2.5	2.6	2.6	Operating Profit	3.4	2.4	1.8	2.1	2.2	3.9
.2	.2	.5	All Other Expenses (net)	.3	.8	.8	.1	.4	.8
2.3	2.4	2.1	Profit Before Taxes	3.2	1.7	1.0	2.0	1.8	3.2
			RATIOS						
2.8	2.8	2.5		4.4	2.6	2.5	1.9	1.9	1.8
1.7	1.8	1.6	Current	2.5	1.6	1.6	1.4	1.3	1.4
1.2	1.2	1.1		1.2	1.1	1.1	1.2	1.1	1.1
.9	1.0	.9		1.1	1.0	1.0	.9	.7	.9
.6	.6	.5	Quick	.6	.6	.6	.5	.4	.5
.3	.4	.3		.3	.3	.3	.3	.3	.3
11 34.0	13 27.3	12 31.1		8 45.8	9 40.0	15 24.8	14 26.2	16 22.6	8 44.0
23 15.7	23 15.8	25 14.4	Sales/Receivables	21 17.1	23 15.9	29 12.6	25 14.6	28 12.9	28 13.0
33 10.9	33 11.1	35 10.3		36 10.2	35 10.3	35 10.4	39 9.4	32 11.5	36 10.2
55 6.6	62 5.9	55 6.6		77 4.7	54 6.8	45 8.2	57 6.4	57 6.4	48 7.6
92 4.0	102 3.6	94 3.9	Cost of Sales/Inventory	133 2.8	95 3.8	92 3.9	92 4.0	85 4.3	80 4.6
137 2.7	150 2.4	146 2.5		192 1.9	145 2.5	147 2.5	126 2.9	127 2.9	118 3.1
27 13.7	24 15.1	27 13.7		16 22.9	28 12.9	26 13.9	27 13.4	28 13.1	33 10.9
44 8.3	44 8.4	43 8.5	Cost of Sales/Payables	29 12.4	41 8.8	44 8.3	48 7.6	46 7.9	54 6.8
67 5.4	67 5.5	63 5.8		54 6.8	61 6.0	77 4.7	63 5.8	63 5.8	67 5.4
4.9	4.9	5.4		3.6	4.7	5.5	6.6	7.3	7.1
10.0	9.0	10.8	Sales/Working Capital	6.1	9.3	9.8	11.9	20.0	15.4
27.8	28.9	35.7		15.0	55.4	35.4	24.7	55.3	38.7
(239) 5.7	(225) 6.5	(303) 6.1		(43) 5.4	(76) 5.6	(47) 5.8	(48) 8.3	(48) 9.2	(41) 8.9
2.7	2.5	3.2	EBIT/Interest	2.8	2.0	2.4	4.3	3.7	5.0
1.2	1.2	1.2		1.3	.5	.8	1.5	1.4	2.1
(74) 3.8	(50) 4.2	(84) 3.9			(17) 1.9	(10) 2.1	(14) 2.8	(21) 5.6	(18) 6.5
1.7	2.5	2.0	Net Profit + Depr., Dep., Amort./Cur. Mat. L/T/D		.6	1.0	2.2	2.3	2.6
.9	.7	.8			.2	-2.5	1.0	1.0	2.1
.2	.2	.2		.2	.1	.2	.2	.2	.3
.4	.4	.5	Fixed/Worth	.4	.5	.4	.4	.4	.7
1.3	1.5	1.4		5.0	1.5	1.2	.9	1.2	2.0
.9	.8	1.1		1.2	1.1	1.0	1.0	1.1	1.0
1.8	1.9	2.1	Debt/Worth	3.7	1.9	2.2	1.9	1.9	2.1
4.8	5.3	6.0		-40.2	8.2	6.9	3.8	3.4	6.0
(243) 31.5	(224) 34.4	(289) 34.5		(40) 71.7	(67) 21.2	(43) 26.3	(49) 36.0	(49) 37.6	(41) 34.6
14.8	14.1	14.6	% Profit Before Taxes/Tangible Net Worth	17.4	7.6	11.6	15.2	18.4	20.8
4.0	3.0	2.8		.5	-.7	2.1	5.7	3.1	14.1
10.0	10.7	10.4		16.0	7.5	8.5	9.1	10.4	9.8
4.4	4.5	4.5	% Profit Before Taxes/Total Assets	5.3	2.6	2.7	5.4	3.3	6.7
1.0	.5	.4		.3	-1.4	-.3	2.0	.9	3.0
44.7	38.0	51.0		106.7	59.1	47.3	53.4	46.7	27.0
20.1	19.5	21.3	Sales/Net Fixed Assets	19.6	22.3	25.6	27.7	20.5	14.8
12.1	10.9	11.5		13.5	11.0	16.0	11.7	11.8	8.4
3.8	3.4	3.7		3.3	3.5	3.9	3.8	3.7	3.5
2.7	2.6	2.7	Sales/Total Assets	2.2	2.5	2.7	3.0	2.9	2.7
2.0	2.0	2.1		1.5	2.1	2.0	2.3	2.2	1.8
(245) .8	(230) .8	(300) .7		(40) .9	(75) .7	(47) .8	(49) .8	(48) .8	(41) .7
1.3	1.4	1.3	% Depr., Dep., Amort./Sales	1.4	1.1	1.3	1.2	1.2	1.6
2.0	2.3	1.9		3.1	1.7	1.8	1.9	1.7	2.0
(142) 1.9	(135) 1.9	(171) 2.0		(27) 3.6	(56) 2.4	(29) 1.7	(27) .7	(20) 2.1	(12) .3
3.6	3.3	3.3	% Officers', Directors', Owners' Comp/Sales	6.6	4.3	2.7	2.9	2.5	1.6
6.2	6.3	6.3		8.4	6.7	4.7	5.1	4.6	13.2
3246513M	2542901M	5902652M	Net Sales ($)	37571M	155768M	203129M	380035M	819679M	4306470M
1261522M	1099956M	2551923M	Total Assets ($)	19165M	65771M	79381M	139911M	339849M	1907846M

© RMA 2003

M = $ thousand   MM = $ million
See Pages 11 through 18 for Explanation of Ratios and Data

Current Data Sorted By Assets | Comparative Historical Data

						Type of Statement		
1		1	1	3		Unqualified		
8	1	2	2			Reviewed		
12	9	8	1			Compiled		
3	3	1				Tax Returns		
	5	5	1	1		Other		
	10 (4/1-9/30/02)			**58 (10/1/02-3/31/03)**			4/1/98-3/31/99	4/1/99-3/31/00
0-500M	500M-2MM	2-10MM	10-50MM	50-100MM	100-250MM		ALL	ALL
24	18	17	5	4		**NUMBER OF STATEMENTS**		
%	%	%	%	%	%	**ASSETS**	%	%
9.8	11.1	4.2			D	Cash & Equivalents	D	D
17.4	19.8	26.1			A	Trade Receivables (net)	A	A
40.0	38.5	47.0			T	Inventory	T	T
.8	1.2	3.0			A	All Other Current	A	A
68.1	70.6	80.3				Total Current		
25.1	18.8	16.8			N	Fixed Assets (net)	N	N
1.8	.1	.5			O	Intangibles (net)	O	O
4.9	10.4	2.4			T	All Other Non-Current	T	T
100.0	100.0	100.0				Total		
					A	**LIABILITIES**	A	A
12.6	3.6	13.6			V	Notes Payable-Short Term	V	V
7.7	2.2	1.5			A	Cur. Mat.-L/T/D	A	A
32.6	29.0	30.2			I	Trade Payables	I	I
.3	.3	.1			L	Income Taxes Payable	L	L
13.3	6.3	6.9			A	All Other Current	A	A
66.6	41.4	52.4			B	Total Current	B	B
30.5	11.8	8.4			L	Long Term Debt	L	L
.0	.0	.0			E	Deferred Taxes	E	E
21.0	4.6	5.5				All Other Non-Current		
-18.1	42.1	33.7				Net Worth		
100.0	100.0	100.0				Total Liabilities & Net Worth		
						INCOME DATA		
100.0	100.0	100.0				Net Sales		
43.7	33.5	34.4				Gross Profit		
43.3	32.1	33.2				Operating Expenses		
.3	1.4	1.3				Operating Profit		
.9	-.7	.5				All Other Expenses (net)		
-.5	2.0	.7				Profit Before Taxes		
						RATIOS		
2.6	2.8	2.9						
1.5	1.6	1.4				Current		
.7	1.1	1.2						
1.1	1.1	.9						
.6	.8	.6				Quick		
.2	.4	.3						
(1) 338.3	(7) 52.6	(16) 22.6						
(12) 31.0	(19) 19.0	(30) 12.0				Sales/Receivables		
(24) 15.5	(29) 12.5	(50) 7.2						
(17) 21.2	(24) 15.1	(54) 6.7						
(33) 11.2	(65) 5.6	(87) 4.2				Cost of Sales/Inventory		
(115) 3.2	(108) 3.4	(129) 2.8						
(11) 34.3	(27) 13.8	(30) 12.1						
(30) 12.2	(46) 7.9	(42) 8.8				Cost of Sales/Payables		
(73) 5.0	(69) 5.3	(75) 4.9						
7.7	5.6	6.5						
30.1	12.2	10.7				Sales/Working Capital		
-20.1	124.2	22.1						
2.8	17.0	5.9						
(20) .9	(17) 6.1	2.0				EBIT/Interest		
-2.0	2.0	.4						
						Net Profit + Depr., Dep., Amort./Cur. Mat. L./T/D		
.2	.2	.2						
1.4	.4	.4				Fixed/Worth		
-1.1	.8	1.0						
1.1	.8	1.0						
6.5	1.3	2.1				Debt/Worth		
-5.2	2.8	6.3						
38.2	38.4	19.3						
(15) 9.8	(16) 10.9	7.7				% Profit Before Taxes/Tangible Net Worth		
-1.2	2.7	-.8						
7.1	13.2	4.8						
-.4	4.5	1.2				% Profit Before Taxes/Total Assets		
-7.5	1.3	-2.1						
69.6	49.0	44.0						
33.4	25.7	28.6				Sales/Net Fixed Assets		
12.3	14.5	16.2						
8.1	5.4	3.8						
5.2	3.0	3.0				Sales/Total Assets		
3.2	2.2	2.0						
.7	.6	.7						
(21) 1.9	(15) 1.3	1.3				% Depr., Dep., Amort./Sales		
3.0	1.8	1.5						
2.6	.3							
(15) 4.0	(12) 1.6					% Officers', Directors', Owners' Comp/Sales		
7.5	3.7							
29163M	94459M	227030M	280399M	713765M		Net Sales ($)		
5339M	24350M	79141M	99468M	290486M		Total Assets ($)		

M = $ thousand　　MM = $ million
See Pages 11 through 18 for Explanation of Ratios and Data

Comparative Historical Data / Current Data Sorted By Sales

	4/1/00-3/31/01 ALL	4/1/01-3/31/02 ALL	4/1/02-3/31/03 ALL	Type of Statement	0-1MM	1-3MM	3-5MM	5-10MM	10-25MM	25MM & OVER
			6	Unqualified	1				1	4
			5	Reviewed			1		2	2
			26	Compiled	6	6	7	1	5	1
			16	Tax Returns	3	9	1	3	2	
			15	Other	3		1	6		3
						10 (4/1-9/30/02)		58 (10/1/02-3/31/03)		
			68	NUMBER OF STATEMENTS	13	15	10	10	10	10
	%	%	%	**ASSETS**	%	%	%	%	%	%
	D A T A N O T A V A I L A B L E	D A T A N O T A V A I L A B L E	7.9	Cash & Equivalents	8.0	11.1	9.3	7.0	4.6	6.0
			20.8	Trade Receivables (net)	9.4	20.9	16.5	26.8	30.4	24.3
			41.2	Inventory	46.1	35.2	47.4	32.9	44.4	42.8
			1.5	All Other Current	1.9	.2	2.3	3.9	.2	1.0
			71.5	Total Current	65.4	67.5	75.5	70.6	79.7	74.1
			21.3	Fixed Assets (net)	31.9	21.4	13.7	23.8	17.0	16.9
			1.3	Intangibles (net)	1.5	1.6	.2	.0	.9	3.4
			5.9	All Other Non-Current	1.2	9.5	10.7	5.7	2.4	5.7
			100.0	Total	100.0	100.0	100.0	100.0	100.0	100.0
				LIABILITIES						
			10.0	Notes Payable-Short Term	12.4	9.9	7.1	5.1	14.9	9.5
			3.9	Cur. Mat.-L/T/D	12.2	2.7	2.0	1.9	1.7	1.2
			30.6	Trade Payables	35.0	30.0	27.0	28.3	28.9	33.2
			.3	Income Taxes Payable	.6	.0	.4	.0	.1	.4
			8.7	All Other Current	13.6	10.4	5.5	8.9	6.6	5.0
			53.4	Total Current	73.9	53.0	42.0	44.2	52.2	49.4
			17.9	Long Term Debt	44.6	16.3	7.7	14.0	8.6	9.0
			.0	Deferred Taxes	.0	.0	.0	.0	.0	.3
			10.5	All Other Non-Current	32.3	6.1	7.2	3.1	8.3	1.9
			18.1	Net Worth	−50.7	24.5	43.1	38.7	30.9	39.5
			100.0	Total Liabilities & Net Worth	100.0	100.0	100.0	100.0	100.0	100.0
				INCOME DATA						
			100.0	Net Sales	100.0	100.0	100.0	100.0	100.0	100.0
			36.5	Gross Profit	47.8	42.1	31.2	36.9	29.1	25.6
			35.2	Operating Expenses	46.9	41.8	29.5	36.7	27.5	22.2
			1.3	Operating Profit	1.0	.3	1.7	.2	1.6	3.3
			.3	All Other Expenses (net)	1.3	.2	−.4	−.2	.6	.0
			1.0	Profit Before Taxes	−.3	.1	2.1	.4	1.0	3.4
				RATIOS						
			2.6 / 1.5 / 1.1	Current	2.5 / 1.8 / .6	2.9 / 1.3 / .8	3.3 / 1.8 / 1.1	2.8 / 1.5 / 1.3	2.2 / 1.6 / 1.2	2.1 / 1.5 / 1.1
			1.0 / .6 / .3	Quick	.8 / .4 / .1	1.2 / .6 / .3	1.0 / .6 / .3	1.0 / .8 / .5	1.1 / .6 / .4	1.2 / .5 / .4
		9 / 20 / 32	40.6 / 18.1 / 11.3	Sales/Receivables	1 585.5 / 4 88.6 / 25 14.4	5 72.8 / 15 23.7 / 25 14.9	7 52.6 / 20 17.9 / 30 12.2	10 34.8 / 19 19.2 / 40 9.0	17 22.1 / 26 13.9 / 49 7.4	19 19.2 / 27 13.6 / 35 10.6
		30 / 65 / 110	12.0 / 5.7 / 3.3	Cost of Sales/Inventory	29 12.4 / 115 3.2 / 135 2.7	19 18.9 / 36 10.2 / 61 6.0	24 15.1 / 64 5.7 / 215 1.7	37 10.0 / 69 5.3 / 95 3.8	39 9.4 / 77 4.7 / 104 3.5	48 7.6 / 67 5.5 / 108 3.4
		23 / 44 / 67	15.5 / 8.4 / 5.5	Cost of Sales/Payables	13 28.0 / 57 6.5 / 114 3.2	13 28.6 / 45 8.1 / 72 5.1	14 26.6 / 49 7.5 / 72 5.1	26 13.9 / 32 11.5 / 50 7.3	24 15.1 / 39 9.5 / 61 6.0	42 8.8 / 50 7.3 / 56 6.5
			6.3 / 14.1 / 93.5	Sales/Working Capital	5.6 / 13.3 / −14.0	11.1 / 21.7 / −34.0	3.7 / 21.7 / 111.5	6.3 / 14.2 / 25.0	7.2 / 9.9 / 39.5	7.9 / 10.6 / 49.5
			11.8 / (62) 2.9 / .7	EBIT/Interest	(10) 4.1 / 1.2 / −4.6	(14) 3.5 / 1.5 / −.3	16.7 / 8.5 / 1.2		9.7 / 2.1 / 1.1	
			7.2 / (17) 2.3 / 1.7	Net Profit + Depr., Dep., Amort./Cur. Mat. L/T/D						
			.2 / .5 / 1.7	Fixed/Worth	.3 / 6.4 / −.4	.3 / .7 / 3.5	.1 / .2 / .8	.3 / .6 / 1.4	.2 / .4 / .9	.2 / .4 / 1.1
			1.0 / 2.6 / 6.9	Debt/Worth	1.5 / 8.2 / −3.3	1.0 / 3.0 / 19.2	.7 / 1.2 / 2.8	.7 / 1.6 / 6.0	1.6 / 2.9 / 3.9	.9 / 2.1 / 4.1
			26.6 / (58) 11.5 / 1.2	% Profit Before Taxes/Tangible Net Worth		(12) 14.9 / 4.9 / −4.0		27.8 / 10.2 / −4.3	22.1 / 11.4 / .2	40.0 / 19.8 / 13.7
			9.1 / 2.4 / −1.1	% Profit Before Taxes/Total Assets	8.4 / 1.2 / −40.7	2.8 / .0 / −2.6	20.7 / 7.2 / .5	6.0 / 2.9 / −2.4	7.4 / 2.9 / .1	11.1 / 8.2 / 4.5
			54.6 / 25.8 / 12.5	Sales/Net Fixed Assets	60.8 / 12.8 / 5.2	57.9 / 25.3 / 15.5	262.4 / 33.8 / 19.0	37.5 / 23.7 / 13.4	69.4 / 31.4 / 22.0	64.9 / 26.4 / 12.2
			5.2 / 3.4 / 2.6	Sales/Total Assets	6.9 / 3.1 / 2.8	6.2 / 5.0 / 4.2	6.1 / 2.5 / 1.8	4.3 / 3.1 / 3.0	4.9 / 3.2 / 2.2	3.6 / 2.9 / 2.5
			.7 / (61) 1.3 / 2.2	% Depr., Dep., Amort./Sales	(10) 1.7 / 2.5 / 3.8	.5 / 1.5 / 2.4		.9 / 1.5 / 1.6		
			1.1 / (39) 2.7 / 4.9	% Officers', Directors', Owners' Comp/Sales		(11) 2.0 / 4.0 / 4.7				
			1344816M	Net Sales ($)	7784M	29040M	37398M	70448M	154690M	1045456M
			498784M	Total Assets ($)	7796M	6813M	12910M	21799M	51306M	398160M

© RMA 2003

M = $ thousand   MM = $ million
See Pages 11 through 18 for Explanation of Ratios and Data

Current Data Sorted By Assets   Comparative Historical Data

						Type of Statement		
	4	23	22	9	6	Unqualified	50	58
2	29	58	11		1	Reviewed	147	131
17	73	39	5			Compiled	205	177
31	40	15	1		1	Tax Returns	72	82
11	50	39	23	5	4	Other	153	134
	123 (4/1-9/30/02)		396 (10/1/02-3/31/03)				4/1/98-3/31/99	4/1/99-3/31/00
0-500M	500M-2MM	2-10MM	10-50MM	50-100MM	100-250MM		ALL	ALL
61	196	174	62	14	12	NUMBER OF STATEMENTS	627	582
%	%	%	%	%	%	ASSETS	%	%
13.0	9.5	9.9	7.4	6.1	7.7	Cash & Equivalents	8.2	8.4
12.5	12.0	15.0	18.2	24.9	11.0	Trade Receivables (net)	16.6	15.8
47.5	54.7	46.4	39.1	30.3	32.3	Inventory	48.4	49.0
1.1	1.7	2.3	3.1	3.9	2.2	All Other Current	1.7	1.6
74.1	77.8	73.6	67.8	65.2	53.1	Total Current	74.9	74.7
14.6	15.4	19.6	24.4	24.3	35.6	Fixed Assets (net)	16.6	17.8
3.9	1.3	1.5	2.7	.4	10.0	Intangibles (net)	2.3	2.1
7.4	5.5	5.3	5.2	10.1	1.2	All Other Non-Current	6.1	5.4
100.0	100.0	100.0	100.0	100.0	100.0	Total	100.0	100.0
						LIABILITIES		
10.0	9.5	9.3	10.4	16.7	8.2	Notes Payable-Short Term	10.5	9.0
4.5	2.3	2.7	2.1	1.2	5.4	Cur. Mat.-L/T/D	2.8	2.2
18.8	18.2	18.3	18.9	12.6	10.1	Trade Payables	18.3	18.9
.1	.4	.3	.3	.0	.8	Income Taxes Payable	.4	.4
17.6	16.0	18.0	16.6	11.3	14.5	All Other Current	17.2	18.0
51.1	46.4	48.6	48.4	41.8	39.1	Total Current	49.2	48.5
22.3	13.5	11.0	13.5	16.1	13.9	Long Term Debt	12.5	12.5
.0	.1	.1	.1	.1	.3	Deferred Taxes	.2	.1
11.0	4.8	5.0	3.5	2.1	11.8	All Other Non-Current	5.5	5.4
15.6	35.3	35.4	34.6	40.0	34.9	Net Worth	32.6	33.5
100.0	100.0	100.0	100.0	100.0	100.0	Total Liabilities & Net Worth	100.0	100.0
						INCOME DATA		
100.0	100.0	100.0	100.0	100.0	100.0	Net Sales	100.0	100.0
42.1	41.0	40.6	41.5	42.7	40.7	Gross Profit	38.7	40.0
38.2	38.6	38.0	38.5	38.1	35.6	Operating Expenses	36.1	37.5
3.9	2.3	2.5	3.0	4.6	5.1	Operating Profit	2.5	2.5
.8	.3	.3	-.1	1.1	1.0	All Other Expenses (net)	.0	-.3
3.1	2.1	2.2	3.1	3.5	4.2	Profit Before Taxes	2.5	2.8
						RATIOS		
2.7	2.7	2.4	2.1	2.0	2.9		2.4	2.4
1.8	1.7	1.4	1.4	1.6	1.4	Current	1.6	1.5
1.0	1.2	1.1	1.0	1.2	1.2		1.2	1.1
1.2	.8	.9	.8	1.0	1.0		.9	.9
.5	.3	.4	.4	.8	.5	Quick (622) / (579)	.4	.4
.1	.1	.1	.1	.3	.1		.1	.2

												Sales/Receivables				
0	UND	0	UND	1	293.2	2	171.5	4	87.6	0	999.8		2	217.3	1	296.1
3	111.8	5	77.2	6	63.6	5	66.8	11	34.5	0	775.5		10	35.9	9	42.2
20	18.4	20	17.9	34	10.6	58	6.3	133	2.7	3	120.8		32	11.5	29	12.6
33	11.2	68	5.4	70	5.2	71	5.1	87	4.2	63	5.8	Cost of Sales/Inventory	64	5.7	70	5.2
91	4.0	117	3.1	118	3.1	102	3.6	127	2.9	84	4.4		110	3.3	108	3.4
145	2.5	181	2.0	162	2.3	122	3.0	155	2.4	122	3.0		156	2.3	158	2.3
10	36.9	17	21.0	21	17.7	25	14.6	27	13.3	12	31.1	Cost of Sales/Payables	19	19.3	17	21.8
26	13.8	28	12.9	35	10.3	37	10.0	35	10.5	32	11.6		31	11.7	33	11.2
47	7.8	53	6.9	56	6.6	57	6.4	48	7.6	43	8.6		48	7.6	58	6.3

7.9	5.0	5.9	8.2	3.9	8.0	Sales/Working Capital	5.4	5.5
13.0	9.7	13.1	15.7	7.9	14.3		11.4	11.9
UND	30.7	42.8	999.8	29.9	35.2		31.7	42.3
18.0	8.6	10.5	19.0	10.9		EBIT/Interest (560) / (507)	9.4	9.8
(52) 3.3	(164) 2.7	(160) 3.3	(56) 4.0	(13) 4.6			3.0	3.6
1.0	1.1	1.3	1.9	2.6			1.4	1.4
	5.6	7.1	16.4			Net Profit + Depr., Dep., Amort./Cur. Mat. L/T/D (147) / (128)	5.9	6.8
	(28) 2.5	(40) 2.3	(26) 4.4				2.7	2.6
	.6	.9	1.3				1.0	1.1
.1	.1	.2	.3	.3	.5	Fixed/Worth	.2	.2
.7	.3	.4	.8	.6	1.0		.4	.5
-3.7	.8	1.3	2.6	1.0	NM		1.3	1.4
1.7	.7	1.0	1.2	1.0	.7	Debt/Worth	.9	.9
5.4	1.7	2.0	2.7	1.3	1.2		2.2	2.0
-28.4	4.5	4.1	6.1	4.6	NM		5.6	5.1
103.0	33.3	31.6	52.7	36.5		% Profit Before Taxes/Tangible Net Worth (559) / (511)	39.7	40.9
(42) 26.5	(177) 12.7	(163) 13.4	(57) 21.6	23.6			16.9	18.5
1.7	3.0	4.0	8.1	12.0			4.7	6.5
29.6	11.2	9.6	15.8	12.9	12.4	% Profit Before Taxes/Total Assets	12.5	13.2
6.8	4.1	4.4	6.9	7.2	6.3		5.2	6.0
.0	.7	1.0	2.0	3.4	1.4		1.3	1.7
240.7	70.8	47.6	33.0	11.8	11.0	Sales/Net Fixed Assets	57.6	52.8
40.5	30.9	23.1	10.9	6.9	7.3		25.3	24.5
21.1	13.3	8.8	5.9	5.0	3.6		11.9	10.5
6.0	4.0	3.6	3.5	2.4	2.8	Sales/Total Assets	3.9	4.0
3.7	2.9	2.7	2.7	1.4	2.2		2.8	2.8
2.3	2.0	1.8	1.9	1.1	1.2		2.0	1.9
.5	.5	.6	.7	1.2		% Depr., Dep., Amort./Sales (557) / (511)	.5	.5
(39) .9	(163) .8	(152) .9	(56) 1.1	(12) 1.5			.8	.8
1.7	1.4	1.3	1.7	2.5			1.3	1.2
2.4	2.1	1.4	.6			% Officers', Directors', Owners' Comp/Sales (288) / (297)	2.0	2.0
(40) 5.1	(118) 3.9	(91) 2.9	(15) 1.5				3.7	3.8
7.7	6.3	4.8	6.0				6.3	6.9
62386M	689387M	2372105M	3972046M	1990966M	4600092M	Net Sales ($)	13781185M	14827349M
16330M	210662M	822636M	1468849M	1055945M	2048722M	Total Assets ($)	5596486M	6398099M

M = $ thousand   MM = $ million
See Pages 11 through 18 for Explanation of Ratios and Data

Comparative Historical Data | Current Data Sorted By Sales

Hist 1	Hist 2	Hist 3	Type of Statement	0-1MM	1-3MM	3-5MM	5-10MM	10-25MM	25MM & OVER
37	40	64	Unqualified		1	4	1	11	47
104	88	101	Reviewed	1	12	12	21	40	15
164	160	134	Compiled	18	41	28	25	15	7
76	63	88	Tax Returns	19	35	11	16	6	1
134	119	132	Other	12	34	19	15	23	29
4/1/00-3/31/01	4/1/01-3/31/02	4/1/02-3/31/03		123 (4/1-9/30/02)		396 (10/1/02-3/31/03)			
ALL	ALL	ALL							
515	470	519	**NUMBER OF STATEMENTS**	50	123	74	78	95	99
%	%	%	**ASSETS**	%	%	%	%	%	%
8.3	8.4	9.7	Cash & Equivalents	10.3	10.4	11.0	10.2	8.8	7.8
16.1	13.7	14.1	Trade Receivables (net)	10.0	12.5	11.9	13.5	17.6	17.0
48.9	49.8	48.0	Inventory	45.1	51.6	53.0	52.1	45.9	40.1
1.8	1.8	2.1	All Other Current	1.6	1.7	1.7	1.0	2.9	3.1
75.1	73.7	73.9	Total Current	67.1	76.1	77.7	76.8	75.3	68.0
17.5	18.4	18.5	Fixed Assets (net)	19.1	17.4	15.0	17.1	17.4	24.3
2.2	2.6	2.0	Intangibles (net)	3.7	2.1	.9	.5	1.8	3.4
5.2	5.3	5.6	All Other Non-Current	10.1	4.5	6.4	5.7	5.6	4.3
100.0	100.0	100.0	Total	100.0	100.0	100.0	100.0	100.0	100.0
			LIABILITIES						
11.9	11.7	9.8	Notes Payable-Short Term	8.7	10.7	7.7	9.6	10.5	10.2
2.6	2.7	2.7	Cur. Mat.-L/T/D	5.3	2.2	1.9	2.7	2.7	2.7
19.3	17.8	18.0	Trade Payables	12.0	16.1	19.6	17.8	20.3	20.3
.1	.3	.3	Income Taxes Payable	.1	.2	.4	.6	.3	.3
17.2	21.6	16.8	All Other Current	13.9	15.0	18.9	17.6	18.0	17.0
51.1	54.2	47.6	Total Current	39.9	44.2	48.5	48.3	51.8	50.6
11.9	11.3	13.8	Long Term Debt	22.6	18.2	10.1	12.1	9.9	11.5
.1	.1	.1	Deferred Taxes	.0	.0	.1	.1	.1	.2
4.7	13.5	5.5	All Other Non-Current	15.1	4.4	4.9	2.4	5.0	5.5
32.2	20.9	33.0	Net Worth	22.3	33.2	36.3	37.2	33.3	32.2
100.0	100.0	100.0	Total Liabilities & Net Worth	100.0	100.0	100.0	100.0	100.0	100.0
			INCOME DATA						
100.0	100.0	100.0	Net Sales	100.0	100.0	100.0	100.0	100.0	100.0
39.9	41.2	41.1	Gross Profit	45.4	42.5	39.4	42.0	38.4	40.2
37.3	38.8	38.3	Operating Expenses	39.5	40.6	37.3	39.4	36.4	36.5
2.6	2.4	2.8	Operating Profit	5.9	1.9	2.1	2.6	2.0	3.7
.1	.4	.4	All Other Expenses (net)	.8	.6	.3	.1	-.1	.6
2.5	1.9	2.4	Profit Before Taxes	5.1	1.3	1.8	2.6	2.1	3.1
			RATIOS						
2.1	2.3	2.5	Current	4.6	3.0	2.5	2.2	2.2	1.8
1.5	1.5	1.6		2.2	1.8	1.7	1.5	1.4	1.3
1.1	1.1	1.1		1.0	1.3	1.3	1.2	1.1	1.0
.9	.8	.9	Quick	1.3	1.1	.8	.7	1.0	.8
(513) .4	(464) .4	.4		.5	.4	.4	.4	.3	.4
.1	.1	.1		.2	.1	.1	.1	.1	.1
1 294.8	1 650.8	0 826.4	Sales/Receivables	0 UND	0 UND	0 999.8	0 963.3	1 341.4	2 213.9
7 51.0	5 69.2	5 73.4		7 51.6	7 55.7	4 85.4	5 71.8	5 78.4	4 82.0
28 12.9	23 16.1	25 14.5		39 9.5	24 15.4	20 18.7	23 16.1	37 9.7	32 11.3
66 5.5	71 5.1	65 5.6	Cost of Sales/Inventory	44 8.3	75 4.9	55 6.7	82 4.5	44 8.2	64 5.7
107 3.4	109 3.4	111 3.3		120 3.0	126 2.9	108 3.4	124 2.9	98 3.7	94 3.9
155 2.4	163 2.2	158 2.3		219 1.7	205 1.8	158 2.3	167 2.2	142 2.6	117 3.1
19 18.8	19 19.5	19 18.8	Cost of Sales/Payables	6 64.2	19 19.3	18 19.8	20 18.1	20 18.6	23 15.7
34 10.7	31 11.7	32 11.3		27 13.3	30 12.4	28 13.2	36 10.2	34 10.7	34 10.6
53 6.9	50 7.3	53 6.9		50 7.2	57 6.4	42 8.6	57 6.4	52 7.0	51 7.1
6.2	5.9	5.7	Sales/Working Capital	3.2	4.2	5.7	5.8	7.1	9.2
13.3	12.3	11.5		8.2	8.3	10.5	10.6	15.8	19.6
46.3	58.9	40.7		UND	22.3	30.7	40.2	72.7	196.6
8.2	7.0	10.4	EBIT/Interest	13.8	5.6	8.1	9.8	14.1	14.0
(464) 2.8	(403) 2.5	(454) 3.3		(41) 2.5	(107) 2.0	(61) 3.2	(70) 3.7	(85) 3.9	(90) 5.8
1.3	1.0	1.3		.9	.3	1.3	1.8	1.3	2.3
6.1	4.7	9.0	Net Profit + Depr., Dep., Amort./Cur. Mat. L/T/D		6.6	6.7	3.1	9.4	12.6
(104) 2.4	(86) 1.6	(108) 3.1			(13) 1.7	(14) 1.5	(15) 2.0	(27) 3.4	(34) 6.1
1.0	.8	1.1			.5	.1	1.2	1.1	3.1
.2	.2	.1	Fixed/Worth	.1	.1	.1	.1	.2	.3
.5	.5	.4		.8	.4	.4	.4	.4	.7
1.4	1.6	1.5		UND	2.6	.9	.8	1.6	1.9
.9	.9	.9	Debt/Worth	.9	.7	.9	.9	1.0	1.2
2.3	2.1	2.1		3.7	1.9	1.8	1.6	2.6	2.3
5.9	6.0	5.4		-31.4	11.0	4.3	3.2	5.4	5.7
39.0	38.8	36.9	% Profit Before Taxes/Tangible Net Worth	73.5	23.2	33.1	32.7	40.3	46.7
(454) 15.7	(409) 14.2	(462) 15.1		(37) 15.8	(103) 9.6	(69) 13.9	(77) 15.1	(87) 15.1	(89) 23.5
4.8	2.8	4.5		3.1	.6	4.4	5.1	3.7	10.8
12.2	12.4	12.1	% Profit Before Taxes/Total Assets	20.3	8.2	9.5	9.9	11.3	15.8
5.1	4.2	4.9		4.8	3.3	5.3	5.1	5.1	7.1
1.1	.3	1.0		.0	-1.4	1.3	1.5	.8	2.5
49.9	53.6	53.7	Sales/Net Fixed Assets	120.2	65.8	78.9	53.6	50.3	35.7
25.1	26.0	25.3		15.5	30.9	34.6	26.5	23.6	14.1
10.7	10.6	9.5		5.5	10.8	14.4	10.4	11.2	5.9
4.0	4.0	3.9	Sales/Total Assets	3.1	3.6	4.3	3.7	4.3	4.2
2.9	2.8	2.8		1.9	2.6	3.2	2.8	3.0	2.9
2.1	1.8	1.9		1.1	1.8	2.4	1.9	2.3	2.0
.5	.5	.6	% Depr., Dep., Amort./Sales	.9	.4	.5	.6	.5	.7
(452) .8	(405) .9	(430) .9		(32) 1.5	(101) .8	(60) .8	(65) .8	(86) .9	(86) 1.1
1.3	1.3	1.5		2.8	1.6	1.3	1.2	1.3	1.7
1.8	1.7	1.7	% Officers', Directors', Owners' Comp/Sales	2.3	3.0	1.8	1.8	1.3	.7
(268) 3.4	(257) 3.3	(267) 3.6		(27) 5.4	(79) 4.9	(43) 3.3	(46) 2.8	(47) 2.6	(25) 1.5
6.0	6.5	6.2		10.9	7.3	6.2	5.3	4.8	5.0
13128939M	9613059M	13686982M	Net Sales ($)	30639M	238467M	301634M	546987M	1461959M	11107296M
5379060M	3975344M	5623144M	Total Assets ($)	21066M	114505M	113151M	241654M	543873M	4588895M

Current Data Sorted By Assets   Comparative Historical Data

						Type of Statement	4/1/98-3/31/99 ALL	4/1/99-3/31/00 ALL
2	2	5	2			Unqualified	5	10
2	17	24	3			Reviewed	45	40
18	40	20	4		1	Compiled	111	90
34	36	7	18			Tax Returns	48	50
17	27	18	4			Other	59	59
0-500M	500M-2MM	2-10MM	10-50MM	50-100MM	100-250MM			
	66 (4/1-9/30/02)			217 (10/1/02-3/31/03)				
73	122	74	13		1	**NUMBER OF STATEMENTS**	268	249
%	%	%	%	%	%	**ASSETS**	%	%
14.1	8.1	9.1	8.6			Cash & Equivalents	8.4	9.2
19.6	28.6	30.1	19.7			Trade Receivables (net)	27.2	27.6
34.5	33.9	35.2	33.9			Inventory	35.3	36.1
2.2	2.3	3.7	1.6			All Other Current	2.3	2.0
70.3	72.9	78.1	63.8			Total Current	73.1	74.8
18.4	17.2	15.1	14.2			Fixed Assets (net)	17.9	16.4
2.4	3.6	1.6	16.5			Intangibles (net)	2.8	3.1
8.8	6.4	5.1	5.4			All Other Non-Current	6.2	5.8
100.0	100.0	100.0	100.0			Total	100.0	100.0
						LIABILITIES		
9.7	11.9	13.7	11.6			Notes Payable-Short Term	11.1	11.0
6.0	3.4	2.6	3.0			Cur. Mat.-L/T/D	4.5	3.9
27.7	17.5	19.5	22.6			Trade Payables	22.0	20.3
.4	.5	.3	.1			Income Taxes Payable	.4	.5
12.7	13.6	12.2	11.3			All Other Current	13.7	13.2
56.4	46.9	48.3	48.6			Total Current	51.6	48.9
16.2	13.8	7.9	13.0			Long Term Debt	16.3	13.8
.0	.2	.1	.0			Deferred Taxes	.1	.1
7.9	4.4	2.7	3.3			All Other Non-Current	5.3	4.8
19.5	34.6	41.0	35.0			Net Worth	26.7	32.4
100.0	100.0	100.0	100.0			Total Liabilities & Net Worth	100.0	100.0
						INCOME DATA		
100.0	100.0	100.0	100.0			Net Sales	100.0	100.0
37.5	34.8	34.1	38.9			Gross Profit	35.1	34.7
34.8	33.5	31.4	34.2			Operating Expenses	32.3	31.3
2.7	1.3	2.7	4.7			Operating Profit	2.9	3.4
.4	.3	.2	.5			All Other Expenses (net)	.1	.3
2.3	1.0	2.5	4.2			Profit Before Taxes	2.8	3.1
						RATIOS		
3.0	2.2	2.5	1.7				2.5	2.6
1.6	1.5	1.6	1.3			Current	1.5	1.5
.8	1.2	1.2	1.0				1.1	1.1
1.3	1.3	1.7	1.1				1.3	1.4
(72) .7	.8	.8	.6			Quick	.7 (248)	.8
.3	.4	.5	.1				.3	.3
3 112.8	11 32.5	17 21.3	4 103.1				11 33.3	11 33.4
13 27.1	25 14.5	36 10.2	33 11.0			Sales/Receivables	23 15.5	25 14.7
22 17.0	40 9.2	46 7.9	38 9.7				39 9.3	40 9.2
18 20.1	24 15.2	27 13.7	30 12.0				21 17.3	22 16.4
35 10.5	42 8.6	62 5.9	66 5.5			Cost of Sales/Inventory	45 8.1	47 7.8
65 5.6	71 5.2	121 3.0	91 4.0				85 4.3	86 4.2
13 27.5	13 28.1	15 23.6	22 16.7				15 25.1	15 24.7
25 14.7	22 16.9	27 13.7	31 11.9			Cost of Sales/Payables	26 14.0	24 15.0
40 9.2	37 9.8	42 8.6	70 5.2				46 7.9	43 8.5
9.8	7.8	6.7	7.5				7.5	7.4
23.7	14.4	11.2	26.7			Sales/Working Capital	16.3	13.7
-53.2	46.8	25.5	698.8				101.1	42.2
10.5	10.7	12.4	24.4				10.3	10.9
(55) 3.8	(115) 3.0	(64) 3.9	4.8			EBIT/Interest	(239) 3.7	(212) 4.0
1.2	1.1	1.7	3.1				1.4	1.9
	(33) 4.4	(17) 6.4				Net Profit + Depr., Dep.,	8.5	5.8
	1.6	2.6				Amort./Cur. Mat. L /T/D	(59) 3.1	(52) 2.2
	.7	.9					1.7	.9
.3	.2	.1	.2				.1	.1
.6	.4	.3	.6			Fixed/Worth	.4	.4
19.4	1.3	.7	-1.2				2.2	1.3
.8	.9	.7	1.1				1.0	.9
2.5	2.1	1.7	3.2			Debt/Worth	2.3	1.9
UND	5.0	3.1	-5.9				11.4	6.8
84.6	39.9	40.4					60.2	53.2
(55) 32.3	(108) 16.0	(72) 16.5				% Profit Before Taxes/Tangible Net Worth	(220) 27.1	(218) 25.8
8.1	2.8	6.6					8.6	9.5
31.2	12.1	12.1	22.1				17.1	17.6
10.8	5.2	5.6	6.4			% Profit Before Taxes/Total Assets	7.5	7.2
.6	.4	1.7	3.6				1.3	2.6
106.9	56.1	65.0	56.4				74.4	69.8
34.9	29.0	29.1	52.1			Sales/Net Fixed Assets	33.2	37.6
19.3	15.4	14.0	17.7				15.6	18.0
6.9	4.8	4.2	3.4				5.0	4.8
5.3	3.7	2.9	3.1			Sales/Total Assets	3.7	3.7
4.1	2.6	2.3	2.2				2.7	2.6
.5	.5	.4	.4				.4	.4
(54) .8	(107) .9	(71) .7	.8			% Depr., Dep., Amort./Sales	(234) .8	(210) .8
1.5	1.4	1.2	1.3				1.3	1.3
3.9	2.3	1.9					2.6	2.9
(49) 5.8	(82) 3.9	(43) 3.4				% Officers', Directors', Owners' Comp/Sales	(148) 4.5	(136) 4.6
8.9	6.1	8.9					7.3	8.5
92572M	465760M	1025824M	859599M		679934M	Net Sales ($)	1430626M	1912461M
16968M	128728M	313925M	290277M		216923M	Total Assets ($)	426622M	591932M

Data not available for 50-100MM column (shown as "DATA NOT AVAILABLE").

M = $ thousand   MM = $ million
See Pages 11 through 18 for Explanation of Ratios and Data

Comparative Historical Data | | | | Current Data Sorted By Sales

			Type of Statement						
6	7	11	Unqualified	3	1	1	1	1	4
42	26	46	Reviewed	1	7	6	12	12	8
93	70	83	Compiled	11	26	16	17	8	5
42	24	77	Tax Returns	13	38	8	14	4	
50	49	66	Other	10	16	14	10	10	6
4/1/00- 3/31/01 ALL	4/1/01- 3/31/02 ALL	4/1/02- 3/31/03 ALL		0-1MM	1-3MM	3-5MM	5-10MM	10-25MM	25MM & OVER
				66 (4/1-9/30/02)			217 (10/1/02-3/31/03)		
233	176	283	NUMBER OF STATEMENTS	38	88	45	54	35	23
%	%	%	ASSETS	%	%	%	%	%	%
8.4	8.7	9.9	Cash & Equivalents	14.9	10.8	7.7	8.9	9.6	5.4
28.5	27.3	26.2	Trade Receivables (net)	16.0	24.9	27.8	30.7	30.9	26.6
35.5	36.3	34.5	Inventory	39.8	34.4	31.2	32.2	36.4	34.7
2.2	2.9	2.6	All Other Current	.4	2.8	2.2	2.9	4.2	3.3
74.6	75.2	73.1	Total Current	71.1	73.0	68.9	74.7	81.0	70.0
15.9	15.5	16.9	Fixed Assets (net)	17.4	17.4	18.9	16.6	14.1	15.3
3.1	3.1	3.3	Intangibles (net)	2.7	3.4	3.6	1.6	1.1	11.2
6.5	6.1	6.6	All Other Non-Current	8.7	6.2	8.7	7.2	3.8	3.5
100.0	100.0	100.0	Total	100.0	100.0	100.0	100.0	100.0	100.0
			LIABILITIES						
11.5	11.1	11.9	Notes Payable-Short Term	14.3	9.9	12.7	9.8	13.6	16.6
3.3	2.8	3.8	Cur. Mat.-L/T/D	5.9	4.2	3.1	3.8	2.1	3.3
21.3	19.2	21.4	Trade Payables	23.9	21.2	19.5	19.3	19.5	30.5
.3	.2	.4	Income Taxes Payable	.5	.3	.8	.3	.2	.1
13.4	16.0	12.9	All Other Current	12.9	10.5	12.8	16.8	11.7	14.1
49.7	49.3	50.5	Total Current	57.6	46.1	48.9	50.0	47.1	64.6
13.5	10.4	12.8	Long Term Debt	21.0	13.8	14.6	8.5	7.8	10.1
.2	.0	.1	Deferred Taxes	.0	.0	.1	.4	.1	.1
3.2	2.8	4.8	All Other Non-Current	9.4	4.1	7.0	3.6	1.9	2.6
33.4	37.3	31.9	Net Worth	12.0	36.0	29.5	37.6	43.2	22.6
100.0	100.0	100.0	Total Liabilities & Net Worth	100.0	100.0	100.0	100.0	100.0	100.0
			INCOME DATA						
100.0	100.0	100.0	Net Sales	100.0	100.0	100.0	100.0	100.0	100.0
36.0	35.8	35.5	Gross Profit	40.4	35.9	35.5	33.7	32.1	34.7
32.6	33.5	33.3	Operating Expenses	40.1	32.5	35.5	31.1	29.4	32.0
3.3	2.3	2.1	Operating Profit	.4	3.4	.0	2.5	2.6	2.7
.5	.1	.3	All Other Expenses (net)	.3	.6	.1	.3	-.2	.3
2.9	2.2	1.9	Profit Before Taxes	.1	2.9	-.1	2.3	2.8	2.3
			RATIOS						
2.4	2.3	2.4	Current	3.0	3.2	2.3	2.0	3.1	1.5
1.5	1.6	1.5		1.7	1.6	1.4	1.5	1.6	1.2
1.1	1.2	1.1		.8	1.1	1.1	1.2	1.3	1.0
1.4	1.2	1.4	Quick	1.2	1.4	1.5	1.3	2.1	.9
(232) .8	.7	(282) .7		.6	.8	(44) .8	.8	.8	.6
.4	.4	.4		.3	.4	.4	.4	.5	.3
12 31.5	11 32.1	10 35.5	Sales/Receivables	9 42.9	8 45.2	11 33.3	14 27.0	17 21.5	4 89.0
26 14.2	26 14.1	22 16.3		16 22.2	19 18.8	29 12.8	29 12.8	34 10.8	26 14.3
40 9.1	40 9.1	39 9.4		23 16.0	36 10.1	43 8.5	39 9.4	45 8.1	44 8.4
24 15.2	31 12.0	23 16.1	Cost of Sales/Inventory	28 13.2	21 17.3	21 17.4	20 18.6	21 17.8	27 13.7
48 7.6	50 7.3	45 8.1		63 5.8	43 8.5	40 9.1	43 8.5	61 5.9	47 7.8
82 4.4	87 4.2	83 4.4		108 3.4	76 4.8	61 6.0	69 5.3	104 3.5	82 4.4
14 25.8	14 25.4	14 25.9	Cost of Sales/Payables	16 22.7	13 28.4	12 30.8	14 26.6	14 25.6	19 18.9
25 14.6	25 14.8	24 15.2		25 14.5	25 14.8	24 15.5	21 17.8	26 13.8	27 13.6
39 9.4	36 10.1	40 9.1		51 7.1	43 8.6	39 9.4	37 9.7	40 9.1	56 6.5
7.6	7.4	8.0	Sales/Working Capital	7.3	6.8	8.3	9.5	6.6	12.1
14.9	14.4	14.7		13.4	14.6	16.0	16.2	10.3	41.1
45.6	36.3	66.7		-46.6	68.2	118.4	46.8	22.8	819.8
10.2	17.2	11.1	EBIT/Interest	3.8	11.5	9.6	11.9	17.2	12.2
(197) 3.6	(154) 3.5	(248) 3.7		(29) 1.2	(76) 4.4	(40) 2.3	(49) 4.5	(31) 5.4	4.1
1.5	1.1	1.4		-5.6	1.5	.5	1.6	2.0	1.6
8.2	3.5	5.9	Net Profit + Depr., Dep., Amort./Cur. Mat. L/T/D		9.2	3.5	7.5		
(47) 3.5	(27) 1.6	(58) 2.0			(13) 2.2	(10) 1.3	(20) 2.2		
1.6	.6	1.1			1.3	.8	.7		
.2	.1	.2	Fixed/Worth	.1	.2	.2	.2	.1	.3
.4	.4	.4		.4	.4	.5	.4	.3	.6
1.1	.9	1.5		-1.0	1.7	1.7	.9	.7	-8.5
.9	.7	.9	Debt/Worth	.8	.7	.7	1.0	.6	2.1
1.8	1.7	2.2		2.2	2.2	2.9	1.9	1.3	5.2
5.7	4.4	6.8		-4.7	9.0	13.9	4.0	2.8	-19.5
49.6	41.0	48.0	% Profit Before Taxes/Tangible Net Worth	41.3	65.0	45.3	37.5	39.8	71.4
(211) 20.6	(159) 14.8	(244) 18.7		(25) 2.4	(77) 25.2	(38) 17.4	(53) 16.4	(34) 19.2	(17) 22.9
6.7	2.4	5.8		-2.2	6.3	6.0	6.6	10.8	7.3
15.1	11.8	16.3	% Profit Before Taxes/Total Assets	17.3	22.6	13.8	13.3	14.5	19.1
7.2	6.3	6.0		1.6	7.3	4.0	6.7	8.6	5.7
1.8	.4	1.1		-5.3	2.2	-.6	1.7	3.0	1.2
67.6	76.1	62.0	Sales/Net Fixed Assets	92.6	69.9	48.4	58.7	70.4	58.4
37.5	34.3	32.2		29.0	33.9	26.2	36.9	32.4	43.8
19.8	17.6	17.0		12.7	16.9	14.1	22.0	18.1	19.2
5.0	5.0	5.1	Sales/Total Assets	5.2	5.5	5.1	4.8	4.3	4.9
4.0	3.8	3.8		3.6	4.2	3.5	3.9	3.1	3.4
2.8	2.5	2.6		2.3	2.4	2.6	3.2	2.6	2.9
.5	.5	.5	% Depr., Dep., Amort./Sales	.6	.5	.5	.5	.3	.4
(201) .9	(148) .8	(246) .8		(26) 1.1	(74) .8	(37) 1.0	(53) .9	(34) .6	(22) .8
1.3	1.3	1.4		2.3	1.5	1.6	1.3	.9	1.3
2.5	2.3	2.4	% Officers', Directors', Owners' Comp/Sales	4.5	3.6	2.9	1.8	1.6	
(133) 4.6	(102) 3.7	(177) 4.1		(24) 7.5	(61) 4.7	(27) 4.6	(38) 2.5	(23) 3.4	
8.1	6.4	7.1		11.4	7.0	7.1	4.8	8.9	
2130384M	1434764M	3123689M	Net Sales ($)	25900M	170823M	172021M	369599M	536851M	1848495M
579375M	437711M	966821M	Total Assets ($)	12184M	59344M	56447M	108968M	164517M	565361M

M = $ thousand   MM = $ million
See Pages 11 through 18 for Explanation of Ratios and Data

Current Data Sorted By Assets   Comparative Historical Data

	0-500M	500M-2MM	2-10MM	10-50MM	50-100MM	100-250MM	Type of Statement		4/1/98-3/31/99 ALL	4/1/99-3/31/00 ALL
		2	7	5	1	5	Unqualified		19	17
	1	3	4	1			Reviewed		21	20
	9	14	11				Compiled		47	57
	15	12					Tax Returns		30	25
	10	6	7	7		1	Other		45	42
	| 21 (4/1-9/30/02) |		| 100 (10/1/02-3/31/03) |							
NUMBER OF STATEMENTS	35	37	29	13	1	6			162	161

	%	%	%	%	%	%	ASSETS		%	%
	15.2	10.8	8.2	6.8			Cash & Equivalents		10.0	9.6
	14.0	9.5	10.6	12.1			Trade Receivables (net)		15.6	14.9
	48.7	60.7	46.0	40.7			Inventory		41.5	48.4
	.4	1.7	2.5	7.5			All Other Current		1.2	1.8
	78.3	82.7	67.4	67.1			Total Current		68.3	74.7
	14.3	13.2	25.1	20.8			Fixed Assets (net)		23.2	17.5
	3.4	1.0	4.7	4.6			Intangibles (net)		2.8	2.6
	4.1	3.2	2.8	7.5			All Other Non-Current		5.6	5.2
	100.0	100.0	100.0	100.0			Total		100.0	100.0
							LIABILITIES			
	9.5	9.1	12.1	16.9			Notes Payable-Short Term		10.6	10.5
	2.8	5.2	4.5	1.3			Cur. Mat.-L/T/D		3.2	3.2
	16.6	24.1	16.2	18.7			Trade Payables		17.6	19.3
	.1	.2	.2	.3			Income Taxes Payable		.6	.3
	16.5	13.8	14.1	8.2			All Other Current		15.2	10.7
	45.6	52.3	47.0	45.5			Total Current		47.2	44.1
	23.2	8.4	12.5	7.1			Long Term Debt		19.2	15.2
	.0	.0	.1	2.2			Deferred Taxes		.3	.1
	10.7	8.2	2.1	4.2			All Other Non-Current		4.9	5.4
	20.5	31.1	38.3	41.1			Net Worth		28.4	35.2
	100.0	100.0	100.0	100.0			Total Liabilities & Net Worth		100.0	100.0
							INCOME DATA			
	100.0	100.0	100.0	100.0			Net Sales		100.0	100.0
	45.0	44.8	44.3	47.2			Gross Profit		42.6	40.8
	40.2	42.0	39.1	43.8			Operating Expenses		38.1	36.8
	4.9	2.8	5.2	3.4			Operating Profit		4.5	4.0
	.6	.7	1.5	.0			All Other Expenses (net)		.9	.9
	4.3	2.0	3.8	3.3			Profit Before Taxes		3.7	3.0
							RATIOS			
	3.5	2.8	2.3	2.2					2.5	2.9
	2.0	1.8	1.4	1.3			Current		1.6	1.7
	1.2	1.2	1.1	1.1					1.1	1.2
	1.4	.9	.6	.8					1.0	1.0
	(34) .7	(34) .4	.4	.5			Quick		(161) .5	(159) .5
	.2	.2	.1	.1					.3	.2
	0 UND	0 UND	0 923.7	1 537.6					0 964.2	0 911.1
	2 187.4	6 58.0	2 155.4	7 54.1			Sales/Receivables		13 28.6	11 34.0
	19 18.9	27 13.3	24 14.9	35 10.5					36 10.1	30 12.0
	41 8.8	73 5.0	79 4.6	72 5.1					57 6.4	56 6.6
	84 4.3	120 3.0	118 3.1	130 2.8			Cost of Sales/Inventory		98 3.7	107 3.4
	136 2.7	204 1.8	170 2.1	185 2.0					147 2.5	151 2.4
	8 46.9	24 15.2	19 19.4	37 10.0					16 22.2	19 19.6
	19 19.2	40 9.1	35 10.3	56 6.5			Cost of Sales/Payables		36 10.3	39 9.5
	44 8.3	71 5.1	64 5.7	69 5.3					53 6.9	62 5.9
	6.5	4.9	4.9	6.6					5.5	5.5
	10.6	10.1	19.5	11.2			Sales/Working Capital		11.2	10.0
	29.9	35.8	133.7	60.8					45.8	24.9
	11.1	14.9	8.0	24.0					10.5	11.8
	(21) 4.7	(32) 2.7	(26) 3.5	(12) 8.0			EBIT/Interest		(148) 3.8	(144) 4.6
	.2	.8	2.0	2.0					1.6	1.3
			10.5						8.2	7.8
			(12) 3.1				Net Profit + Depr., Dep., Amort./Cur. Mat. L /T/D		(40) 3.5	(30) 2.4
			1.6						1.7	1.5
	.1	.1	.2	.4					.3	.1
	.4	.3	.7	.6			Fixed/Worth		.5	.4
	-5.0	1.1	1.3	1.1					2.1	1.5
	.8	.6	1.0	.7					.9	.7
	1.7	1.6	2.0	1.7			Debt/Worth		2.2	2.0
	-32.4	7.9	3.5	4.5					8.0	5.9
	80.8	31.6	29.5	31.2			% Profit Before Taxes/Tangible		54.3	62.6
	(25) 45.4	(30) 16.4	(26) 17.8	(12) 22.1			Net Worth		(132) 24.7	(142) 25.7
	14.5	-1.1	4.9	13.3					10.0	7.6
	35.1	12.3	10.3	14.4			% Profit Before Taxes/Total		20.6	21.3
	14.9	4.4	6.1	9.0			Assets		6.7	8.0
	2.0	-.1	2.2	1.6					2.4	1.3
	153.0	72.4	34.5	18.3					41.8	62.8
	41.0	38.9	17.5	11.5			Sales/Net Fixed Assets		18.7	25.0
	14.9	17.6	8.2	8.3					8.8	10.8
	5.6	4.2	3.8	2.9					3.7	4.0
	4.2	3.0	2.7	2.1			Sales/Total Assets		2.7	2.9
	2.8	2.5	1.2	1.6					1.8	2.2
	.5	.4	.6	.9					.6	.6
	(22) .9	(34) .6	(28) .8	(11) 1.1			% Depr., Dep., Amort./Sales		(140) 1.1	(131) 1.0
	1.9	1.2	1.6	1.5					1.6	1.8
	3.2	2.0	1.5						2.9	2.7
	(20) 5.0	(24) 4.7	(15) 3.7				% Officers', Directors', Owners' Comp/Sales		(74) 3.6	(75) 4.6
	9.5	9.6	4.3						8.0	8.4
	37510M	119133M	340544M	800976M	216892M	2258618M	Net Sales ($)		3732113M	4508806M
	9299M	38944M	127980M	356669M	80314M	1141322M	Total Assets ($)		1687167M	1924109M

© RMA 2003

M = $ thousand   MM = $ million
See Pages 11 through 18 for Explanation of Ratios and Data

Comparative Historical Data | Current Data Sorted By Sales

			Type of Statement	0-1MM	1-3MM	3-5MM	5-10MM	10-25MM	25MM & OVER
11	17	20	Unqualified		1	1	1	4	13
14	12	9	Reviewed	1	2		1	4	1
37	38	34	Compiled	3	17	4	8	1	1
38	23	27	Tax Returns	8	13	3	3		
39	44	31	Other	4	11	2	2	7	5
4/1/00-3/31/01 ALL	4/1/01-3/31/02 ALL	4/1/02-3/31/03 ALL		21 (4/1-9/30/02)			100 (10/1/02-3/31/03)		
139	134	121	NUMBER OF STATEMENTS	16	44	10	15	16	20
%	%	%	ASSETS	%	%	%	%	%	%
8.0	9.0	10.9	Cash & Equivalents	18.9	12.3	7.0	5.1	7.8	10.3
16.3	11.1	11.1	Trade Receivables (net)	9.3	13.2	4.0	17.4	11.1	6.7
48.8	50.7	51.1	Inventory	49.4	53.0	58.8	55.5	47.2	44.2
1.6	2.2	2.3	All Other Current	.2	1.0	3.7	.6	2.4	7.5
74.8	73.0	75.4	Total Current	77.7	79.4	73.6	78.7	68.4	68.8
17.6	19.8	17.6	Fixed Assets (net)	10.6	16.7	24.2	11.9	23.3	21.4
2.6	2.9	3.2	Intangibles (net)	6.4	.8	.0	6.5	3.1	4.8
5.1	4.3	3.9	All Other Non-Current	5.3	3.1	2.2	2.9	5.2	5.1
100.0	100.0	100.0	Total	100.0	100.0	100.0	100.0	100.0	100.0
			LIABILITIES						
12.0	11.5	10.3	Notes Payable-Short Term	8.0	9.9	4.9	10.2	17.9	9.7
3.1	3.3	3.7	Cur. Mat.-L/T/D	1.1	3.7	8.5	3.5	6.6	1.5
19.1	21.3	20.3	Trade Payables	10.0	21.6	16.5	25.2	16.0	27.5
.3	.2	.2	Income Taxes Payable	.2	.1	.6	.1	.1	.7
12.7	13.6	13.9	All Other Current	21.9	10.4	23.6	10.0	16.1	11.5
47.3	50.0	48.5	Total Current	41.2	45.7	54.1	48.9	56.7	50.7
13.7	13.2	13.4	Long Term Debt	26.7	15.5	15.4	5.0	10.5	5.9
.2	.1	.3	Deferred Taxes	.0	.0	.3	.0	.1	1.5
7.3	5.9	6.7	All Other Non-Current	18.3	7.2	3.6	4.6	1.9	3.1
31.6	30.7	31.1	Net Worth	13.7	31.5	26.7	41.5	30.9	38.7
100.0	100.0	100.0	Total Liabilities & Net Worth	100.0	100.0	100.0	100.0	100.0	100.0
			INCOME DATA						
100.0	100.0	100.0	Net Sales	100.0	100.0	100.0	100.0	100.0	100.0
40.0	43.9	44.5	Gross Profit	45.2	44.7	44.3	44.5	45.4	43.1
36.8	40.9	40.4	Operating Expenses	40.8	40.5	39.1	40.7	41.1	39.7
3.2	3.0	4.1	Operating Profit	4.4	4.2	5.3	3.8	4.3	3.4
1.0	1.1	.9	All Other Expenses (net)	.7	1.0	.6	.8	.7	1.0
2.2	1.9	3.3	Profit Before Taxes	3.7	3.2	4.6	3.0	3.7	2.4
			RATIOS						
2.5	2.4	2.6		5.5	3.4	2.9	2.3	1.5	2.5
1.6	1.6	1.7	Current	2.3	2.0	2.3	1.7	1.3	1.3
1.2	1.1	1.1		1.2	1.4	.8	1.2	1.0	1.0
.9	.7	.9		2.0	1.0		.9	.5	.6
(137) .5	(132) .4	(117) .4	Quick	.6	(42) .5		.3	.3	.4
.2	.1	.2		.2	.2		.2	.1	.1
0 UND	0 UND	0 UND		0 UND	0 UND	0 UND	0 826.4	1 419.0	0 UND
15 24.4	5 75.1	3 116.9	Sales/Receivables	0 UND	11 34.1	0 999.8	12 29.7	4 95.5	1 286.4
32 11.3	19 19.0	25 14.9		12 30.8	27 13.5	11 33.7	37 9.8	21 17.6	15 24.7
55 6.6	70 5.2	65 5.6		32 11.4	57 6.4	80 4.6	83 4.4	80 4.5	57 6.4
102 3.6	111 3.3	117 3.1	Cost of Sales/Inventory	115 3.2	117 3.1	125 2.9	116 3.1	119 3.1	108 3.4
172 2.1	165 2.2	169 2.2		178 2.0	208 1.8	178 2.0	155 2.2	175 2.1	134 2.7
17 21.8	22 16.4	16 22.8		0 UND	14 25.3	7 55.6	33 11.2	21 17.1	35 10.3
35 10.5	41 8.8	38 9.7	Cost of Sales/Payables	12 29.5	38 9.6	26 14.1	59 6.2	42 8.8	50 7.3
58 6.3	65 5.7	62 5.8		23 16.2	67 5.4	65 5.6	72 5.1	58 6.3	75 4.9
5.5	6.6	6.0		4.9	4.8	4.5	5.2	9.0	6.3
9.8	11.9	11.6	Sales/Working Capital	10.0	10.0	9.1	11.2	17.3	22.3
35.8	118.6	33.4		26.8	17.8	−42.6	38.2	NM	178.5
8.1	10.1	15.9		11.6	10.5		19.0	11.7	33.8
(121) 2.8	(128) 2.7	(98) 3.8	EBIT/Interest	(11) .8	(30) 2.2		4.7	(15) 3.9	(18) 13.1
1.1	1.0	1.3		−.2	.8		2.0	2.4	3.4
8.3	6.9	12.6	Net Profit + Depr., Dep.,						
(23) 1.8	(19) 2.4	(26) 5.0	Amort./Cur. Mat. L/T/D						
.9	.6	1.7							
.2	.2	.1		.1	.1	.1	.1	.3	.3
.5	.5	.5	Fixed/Worth	.4	.3	.8	.5	.6	.7
2.3	1.7	1.4		−.4	1.5	−.6	.7	1.1	1.8
.8	1.1	.7		.4	.6	.5	.7	1.5	.6
2.1	2.1	1.8	Debt/Worth	4.1	1.5	1.1	1.6	2.4	1.7
10.1	6.5	6.0		−7.7	3.9	−5.7	•4.8	4.1	5.1
35.3	37.0	38.3	% Profit Before Taxes/Tangible	51.7	55.0		30.0	35.4	30.5
(115) 15.8	(116) 17.3	(99) 20.9	Net Worth	(10) 14.5	(37) 26.1		(13) 15.9	(14) 23.2	(18) 21.1
2.1	2.2	5.6		2.0	2.6		−.8	16.1	8.9
12.7	13.8	15.6	% Profit Before Taxes/Total	31.0	19.7	14.9	13.9	12.5	13.7
4.5	4.9	6.7	Assets	2.3	8.1	8.3	5.5	7.2	8.2
.2	−.3	1.4		−2.9	.7	2.2	1.1	4.1	2.3
52.4	45.8	63.2		138.5	111.3	65.8	57.4	26.1	27.6
22.4	20.2	24.0	Sales/Net Fixed Assets	30.6	40.8	22.4	32.1	16.7	11.0
11.0	10.4	11.0		18.2	11.0	7.0	18.5	8.7	9.5
3.6	3.9	4.2		5.6	4.4	4.7	4.1	3.8	3.3
2.7	3.0	3.0	Sales/Total Assets	3.4	3.1	3.2	3.2	2.6	2.3
2.1	2.1	2.1		1.8	2.4	1.5	2.7	2.1	2.0
.6	.5	.5		.5	.4	.4	.7	.6	.8
(112) 1.0	(109) .9	(99) .9	% Depr., Dep., Amort./Sales	(12) .7	(31) .5	.7	.9	.8	(15) 1.2
1.7	1.7	1.5		2.1	1.9	2.4	1.4	1.4	1.8
3.2	2.5	2.3	% Officers', Directors',		2.9		1.7		
(74) 4.6	(71) 4.9	(64) 4.1	Owners' Comp/Sales		(27) 5.3		(11) 2.4		
8.2	8.0	9.1			9.8		5.6		
4367134M	4128381M	3773673M	Net Sales ($)	8766M	78479M	37278M	104892M	242899M	3301359M
1661508M	1700341M	1754528M	Total Assets ($)	2915M	32186M	15680M	42258M	105911M	1555578M

M = $ thousand   MM = $ million
See Pages 11 through 18 for Explanation of Ratios and Data

Current Data Sorted By Assets   Comparative Historical Data

	0-500M	500M-2MM	2-10MM	10-50MM	50-100MM	100-250MM		4/1/98-3/31/99 ALL	4/1/99-3/31/00 ALL
Unqualified			3	1	1	4		11	16
Reviewed		7	7	1	1			19	22
Compiled	6	19	7	2				41	45
Tax Returns	10	10	2					18	13
Other	7	13	10	2		2		41	33
		32 (4/1-9/30/02)		81 (10/1/02-3/31/03)					
NUMBER OF STATEMENTS	23	49	29	4	2	6		130	129
	%	%	%	%	%	%		%	%
ASSETS									
Cash & Equivalents	10.9	10.5	11.8					9.9	10.0
Trade Receivables (net)	15.0	14.5	17.2					17.9	18.3
Inventory	49.7	44.6	47.1					41.8	43.6
All Other Current	1.2	2.7	3.6					2.9	1.7
Total Current	76.8	72.3	79.6					72.5	73.6
Fixed Assets (net)	17.3	16.8	14.4					19.2	18.3
Intangibles (net)	.9	4.0	1.5					3.8	3.2
All Other Non-Current	5.0	6.9	4.5					4.5	4.9
Total	100.0	100.0	100.0					100.0	100.0
LIABILITIES									
Notes Payable-Short Term	16.7	16.3	10.4					16.8	15.9
Cur. Mat.-L/T/D	6.4	3.9	2.2					2.7	2.7
Trade Payables	24.4	26.1	24.2					17.7	20.6
Income Taxes Payable	.2	.6	.4					.3	.3
All Other Current	12.1	10.2	14.2					11.4	9.8
Total Current	59.8	57.1	51.4					48.9	49.2
Long Term Debt	15.8	13.6	6.6					13.6	12.5
Deferred Taxes	.1	.1	.2					.1	.2
All Other Non-Current	3.7	4.8	3.4					3.4	4.3
Net Worth	20.7	24.4	38.3					34.0	33.9
Total Liabilities & Net Worth	100.0	100.0	100.0					100.0	100.0
INCOME DATA									
Net Sales	100.0	100.0	100.0					100.0	100.0
Gross Profit	37.7	31.8	33.4					31.8	32.1
Operating Expenses	36.2	29.4	30.9					28.2	29.4
Operating Profit	1.5	2.4	2.5					3.6	2.7
All Other Expenses (net)	.0	.3	.2					.1	.1
Profit Before Taxes	1.6	2.1	2.4					3.5	2.6
RATIOS									
Current	1.9 / 1.4 / 1.1	1.8 / 1.3 / 1.0	2.1 / 1.4 / 1.2					2.3 / 1.4 / 1.1	2.3 / 1.5 / 1.1
Quick	.8 / .5 / .2	.6 / .3 / .2	1.0 / .4 / .3					1.0 / .5 / .2	1.0 / .6 / .3
Sales/Receivables	3 139.3 / 7 54.9 / 36 10.0	4 82.5 / 10 34.9 / 19 19.6	5 67.6 / 13 28.6 / 27 13.7					6 60.5 / 16 22.8 / 35 10.4	7 55.5 / 14 26.9 / 34 10.7
Cost of Sales/Inventory	40 9.1 / 61 5.9 / 104 3.5	39 9.4 / 58 6.2 / 124 3.0	43 8.5 / 66 5.5 / 105 3.5					42 8.6 / 73 5.0 / 103 3.6	44 8.4 / 75 4.8 / 104 3.5
Cost of Sales/Payables	20 18.4 / 35 10.6 / 58 6.3	12 30.1 / 30 12.3 / 53 6.9	15 24.8 / 34 10.8 / 57 6.4					11 34.0 / 23 16.2 / 51 7.2	12 29.2 / 24 15.4 / 55 6.6
Sales/Working Capital	9.0 / 19.3 / 89.5	8.0 / 27.8 / 208.5	6.3 / 16.1 / 36.4					7.0 / 14.5 / 41.1	6.9 / 16.1 / 41.8
EBIT/Interest	(16) 11.0 / 2.0 / 1.5	(46) 14.0 / 4.1 / 1.1	(26) 15.9 / 8.9 / 3.2					(110) 6.4 / 2.3 / 1.3	(115) 7.3 / 2.8 / 1.4
Net Profit + Depr., Dep., Amort./Cur. Mat. L /T/D		(11) 2.5 / 1.8 / 1.1						(29) 8.0 / 4.0 / 1.3	(27) 7.2 / 2.5 / 1.6
Fixed/Worth	.2 / .7 / -8.0	.2 / .5 / 1.5	.2 / .3 / .6					.2 / .5 / 2.0	.2 / .5 / 1.4
Debt/Worth	1.3 / 4.9 / -15.1	1.2 / 2.3 / 8.9	1.0 / 2.1 / 3.6					.9 / 2.4 / 7.5	.9 / 2.2 / 5.8
% Profit Before Taxes/Tangible Net Worth	(15) 89.1 / 15.2 / .4	(43) 43.7 / 20.2 / 6.1	34.7 / 24.1 / 8.2					(113) 39.4 / 17.6 / 6.5	(112) 39.5 / 16.4 / 3.5
% Profit Before Taxes/Total Assets	12.4 / 4.9 / .3	10.9 / 4.7 / 1.5	10.7 / 5.5 / 2.5					12.8 / 5.2 / 1.2	13.1 / 5.1 / 1.2
Sales/Net Fixed Assets	72.9 / 36.2 / 13.1	69.4 / 26.7 / 12.7	57.3 / 35.8 / 20.5					52.6 / 25.6 / 8.9	55.9 / 30.7 / 12.0
Sales/Total Assets	5.6 / 3.8 / 2.7	4.8 / 3.5 / 2.3	4.2 / 3.6 / 2.6					4.0 / 3.0 / 2.1	4.3 / 3.1 / 2.1
% Depr., Dep., Amort./Sales	(19) .5 / 1.0 / 1.7	(42) .5 / .9 / 1.6	(25) .4 / .8 / 1.2					(113) .5 / .9 / 1.8	(108) .6 / .9 / 1.7
% Officers', Directors', Owners' Comp/Sales	(17) 3.9 / 6.4 / 10.8	(30) 2.0 / 2.8 / 4.8	(13) 1.4 / 2.6 / 3.9					(69) 1.9 / 2.9 / 5.9	(72) 1.8 / 3.8 / 6.1
Net Sales ($)	26409M	227908M	462101M	170683M	669113M	2321260M		3414203M	2097044M
Total Assets ($)	6504M	51333M	131487M	46620M	149612M	908076M		1209424M	797018M

M = $ thousand   MM = $ million
See Pages 11 through 18 for Explanation of Ratios and Data

Comparative Historical Data | Current Data Sorted By Sales

			Type of Statement						
9	8	8	Unqualified				1	1	6
11	18	15	Reviewed		1	3	3	5	3
36	25	34	Compiled	2	11	8	7	3	3
18	12	22	Tax Returns	7	7	4	4		
19	22	34	Other	5	10	2	6	6	5
4/1/00-3/31/01 ALL	4/1/01-3/31/02 ALL	4/1/02-3/31/03 ALL		32 (4/1-9/30/02)			81 (10/1/02-3/31/03)		
				0-1MM	1-3MM	3-5MM	5-10MM	10-25MM	25MM & OVER
93	85	113	NUMBER OF STATEMENTS	14	29	18	20	15	17
%	%	%	**ASSETS**	%	%	%	%	%	%
9.3	9.6	11.0	Cash & Equivalents	11.1	7.5	13.7	11.8	12.3	11.9
17.5	14.9	15.4	Trade Receivables (net)	11.9	13.6	16.6	16.4	16.7	17.7
46.2	47.5	46.5	Inventory	41.8	49.9	43.0	48.9	44.8	47.1
2.5	2.0	2.6	All Other Current	2.0	3.2	1.3	4.3	.6	3.4
75.5	74.1	75.5	Total Current	66.8	74.2	74.5	81.4	74.4	80.0
17.6	17.2	16.4	Fixed Assets (net)	24.8	15.7	15.2	12.0	19.5	14.4
1.9	4.5	2.4	Intangibles (net)	1.5	4.4	3.0	1.2	1.2	1.6
5.0	4.2	5.7	All Other Non-Current	6.9	5.6	7.2	5.4	5.0	4.0
100.0	100.0	100.0	Total	100.0	100.0	100.0	100.0	100.0	100.0
			LIABILITIES						
19.7	13.2	14.1	Notes Payable-Short Term	17.3	17.4	16.9	10.6	8.9	11.3
3.1	1.9	3.7	Cur. Mat.-L/T/D	9.0	3.6	3.3	3.8	1.9	1.2
21.3	23.4	25.6	Trade Payables	16.6	21.7	22.8	31.4	30.6	31.2
.3	.2	.5	Income Taxes Payable	.3	.1	.2	1.6	.2	.4
11.2	12.1	12.1	All Other Current	13.0	6.6	10.3	15.0	17.0	14.9
55.5	50.8	55.9	Total Current	56.1	49.4	53.4	62.5	58.6	59.0
12.7	10.9	11.8	Long Term Debt	24.6	10.5	9.0	14.6	7.1	7.6
.2	.0	.1	Deferred Taxes	.1	.0	.2	.3	.0	.0
6.1	4.9	4.4	All Other Non-Current	2.2	4.3	4.8	7.2	2.0	4.9
25.5	33.4	27.8	Net Worth	17.0	35.8	32.6	15.4	32.3	28.4
100.0	100.0	100.0	Total Liabilities & Net Worth	100.0	100.0	100.0	100.0	100.0	100.0
			INCOME DATA						
100.0	100.0	100.0	Net Sales	100.0	100.0	100.0	100.0	100.0	100.0
31.8	29.7	33.0	Gross Profit	42.6	36.6	29.8	32.2	29.3	26.4
29.9	26.9	30.6	Operating Expenses	40.7	34.4	27.2	30.2	26.8	23.4
1.9	2.8	2.4	Operating Profit	1.9	2.2	2.6	2.1	2.4	3.0
.0	.5	.1	All Other Expenses (net)	.5	−.1	.6	.1	.2	−.1
1.9	2.4	2.2	Profit Before Taxes	1.4	2.3	2.0	2.0	2.3	3.2
			RATIOS						
1.9	2.3	1.9		2.1	1.8	1.9	2.2	1.4	1.5
1.3	1.5	1.4	Current	1.4	1.5	1.4	1.4	1.3	1.3
1.1	1.1	1.1		.9	1.2	1.0	1.1	1.0	1.1
.8	.8	.8		1.0	.7	1.0	1.0	.8	.9
.4	.5	.4	Quick	.5	.3	.5	.4	.4	.4
.2	.2	.2		.2	.1	.3	.2	.3	.2
6 58.0	4 85.9	4 87.0		3 143.9	3 130.3	4 99.4	7 54.7	5 80.5	3 105.0
13 28.5	11 32.9	11 33.4	Sales/Receivables	9 41.8	10 34.9	15 25.1	12 30.0	9 40.2	8 48.5
27 13.7	21 17.1	23 16.0		37 9.9	22 16.4	20 18.2	24 15.4	13 28.6	32 11.3
50 7.2	45 8.1	41 8.9		40 9.1	49 7.4	31 11.7	49 7.4	38 9.7	47 7.8
74 4.9	66 5.5	66 5.5	Cost of Sales/Inventory	69 5.3	104 3.5	49 7.4	66 5.5	43 8.5	72 5.0
98 3.7	102 3.6	108 3.4		114 3.2	146 2.5	95 3.9	107 3.4	66 5.5	92 3.9
12 29.4	17 21.4	14 25.6		12 31.0	26 14.0	8 47.9	13 27.8	18 19.8	9 40.6
30 12.1	30 12.1	32 11.5	Cost of Sales/Payables	30 12.3	35 10.6	17 21.9	35 10.5	27 13.4	32 11.4
53 6.9	50 7.3	55 6.6		44 8.4	61 5.9	56 6.5	60 6.1	45 8.1	59 6.2
8.0	8.5	8.2		7.6	6.2	8.9	5.7	16.6	12.6
16.6	14.5	20.2	Sales/Working Capital	20.1	13.2	23.6	18.6	26.6	20.2
53.8	47.2	61.6		−201.1	46.7	NM	66.0	100.8	28.9
	5.6		8.3		15.0		5.2		23.4		8.7		17.8		15.9		27.8
(83) 2.4	(77) 3.5	(99) 5.1	EBIT/Interest	(12) 1.8	(25) 3.3	(15) 4.1	(18) 8.6	(14) 9.2	(15) 6.0
1.2	1.1	1.8		.6	1.2	1.2	2.3	4.5	3.1
12.9	11.3	4.1	Net Profit + Depr., Dep.,						
(20) 4.6	(20) 4.0	(24) 2.0	Amort./Cur. Mat. L/T/D						
1.3	1.9	1.1							
.2	.2	.2		.4	.1	.2	.2	.3	.2
.6	.5	.5	Fixed/Worth	2.0	.4	.4	.3	.6	.4
1.5	1.2	1.0		−1.7	1.7	1.2	.6	.9	.7
1.4	1.0	1.3		1.3	.9	1.0	1.4	1.1	1.7
2.9	2.4	2.6	Debt/Worth	5.2	2.2	1.6	2.6	2.5	2.7
5.1	6.0	6.0		−10.0	11.2	6.4	4.0	4.6	6.0
33.7	39.8	45.8	% Profit Before Taxes/Tangible		56.4	30.9	35.9	58.6	64.0
(85) 16.9	(77) 22.4	(99) 23.9	Net Worth	(26) 24.4	(16) 13.0	(18) 19.9	(14) 30.5	26.6	
5.2	3.0	8.9			−1.5	6.6	8.6	20.7	15.8
9.4	13.6	12.0	% Profit Before Taxes/Total	8.8	13.8	8.0	8.5	13.2	17.7
4.5	5.5	5.5	Assets	4.2	5.5	5.0	5.4	8.5	6.7
1.2	.6	2.3		−.6	−1.4	2.3	2.9	5.4	4.0
62.3	59.5	66.3		61.0	58.7	73.8	66.1	76.5	174.9
32.7	33.9	33.2	Sales/Net Fixed Assets	15.5	25.8	28.3	38.4	35.8	47.5
12.4	15.1	13.2		7.4	10.8	16.3	25.5	13.8	11.3
4.4	4.4	4.7		4.9	4.4	4.8	4.7	6.0	4.2
3.4	3.5	3.6	Sales/Total Assets	2.9	2.8	3.8	3.6	4.4	3.8
2.4	2.6	2.6		1.9	2.1	3.0	2.7	3.2	2.8
.5	.6	.5		.4	.7	.4	.5	.3	.4
(81) .8	(72) .8	(98) .8	% Depr., Dep., Amort./Sales	(12) 1.1	(22) 1.3	(16) .8	(18) .9	(14) .6	(16) .5
1.4	1.3	1.3		1.7	2.4	1.1	1.5	1.0	1.0
2.2	1.8	2.1	% Officers', Directors',		2.2	2.7	1.4		
(56) 3.4	(49) 3.4	(60) 3.3	Owners' Comp/Sales	(19) 3.6	(12) 3.5	(12) 2.1			
7.5	5.5	6.0		6.0	5.7	3.5			
4103666M	2299005M	3877474M	Net Sales ($)	9398M	53175M	72123M	149199M	261635M	3331944M
1224477M	725432M	1293632M	Total Assets ($)	3382M	18764M	19920M	48332M	61623M	1141611M

© RMA 2003
M = $ thousand   MM = $ million
See Pages 11 through 18 for Explanation of Ratios and Data

Current Data Sorted By Assets								Comparative Historical Data	
	1	1 3	2 14	6 3	2 1	1	**Type of Statement** Unqualified	21	14
	9	13	6				Reviewed Compiled	25 36	22 25
	13	10	3				Tax Returns	21	19
	6	7	8			1	Other	24	34
	0-500M	28 (4/1-9/30/02) 500M-2MM	2-10MM	10-50MM	82 (10/1/02-3/31/03) 50-100MM	100-250MM		4/1/98-3/31/99 ALL	4/1/99-3/31/00 ALL
	29	34	33	9	3	2	**NUMBER OF STATEMENTS**	127	114
	%	%	%	%	%	%	**ASSETS**	%	%
	14.0	9.5	8.7				Cash & Equivalents	7.6	8.8
	7.0	19.9	22.5				Trade Receivables (net)	20.9	21.5
	40.0	36.9	39.3				Inventory	42.1	39.6
	3.0	2.4	3.9				All Other Current	1.5	1.2
	64.1	68.6	74.4				Total Current	72.1	71.0
	23.9	22.0	19.7				Fixed Assets (net)	19.0	18.4
	2.4	4.4	2.3				Intangibles (net)	3.6	5.8
	9.7	5.0	3.6				All Other Non-Current	5.3	4.8
	100.0	100.0	100.0				Total	100.0	100.0
							LIABILITIES		
	12.7	16.4	10.3				Notes Payable-Short Term	13.6	12.5
	8.1	3.2	5.0				Cur. Mat.-L/T/D	3.8	3.7
	16.7	20.1	25.7				Trade Payables	24.3	21.6
	.1	.1	.4				Income Taxes Payable	.3	.3
	10.7	9.4	11.0				All Other Current	10.5	11.4
	48.3	49.2	52.4				Total Current	52.4	49.5
	29.1	13.5	8.3				Long Term Debt	14.3	13.5
	.0	.4	.2				Deferred Taxes	.1	.1
	7.8	2.9	2.8				All Other Non-Current	4.9	2.5
	14.8	34.0	36.3				Net Worth	28.4	34.4
	100.0	100.0	100.0				Total Liabilities & Net Worth	100.0	100.0
							INCOME DATA		
	100.0	100.0	100.0				Net Sales	100.0	100.0
	45.2	35.5	32.1				Gross Profit	36.9	38.7
	43.3	34.3	28.8				Operating Expenses	33.7	35.9
	1.9	1.1	3.4				Operating Profit	3.2	2.8
	1.0	.2	.2				All Other Expenses (net)	1.0	.9
	.8	.9	3.2				Profit Before Taxes	2.2	1.9
							RATIOS		
	4.0	1.9	1.9					1.9	2.1
	1.3	1.5	1.4				Current	1.4	1.4
	.9	1.0	1.1					1.1	1.2
	1.6	1.0	1.0					.9	.9
(28)	.4	.6	.6				Quick	.5	.6
	.1	.3	.3					.2	.3
0	UND	**10** 37.2	**7** 52.1					**7** 53.7	**7** 53.6
3	127.9	**24** 15.2	**24** 15.3				Sales/Receivables	**18** 20.0	**23** 16.0
12	31.4	**39** 9.2	**39** 9.3					**41** 9.0	**42** 8.7
16	22.4	**30** 12.0	**36** 10.1					**45** 8.1	**47** 7.7
64	5.7	**61** 6.0	**59** 6.2				Cost of Sales/Inventory	**80** 4.5	**75** 4.9
140	2.6	**130** 2.8	**104** 3.5					**120** 3.0	**119** 3.1
0	UND	**15** 24.7	**23** 15.6					**21** 17.0	**22** 16.7
23	16.2	**39** 9.3	**34** 10.6				Cost of Sales/Payables	**37** 9.9	**40** 9.2
50	7.3	**50** 7.3	**52** 7.1					**61** 6.0	**64** 5.7
	10.6	6.1	10.6					7.5	8.2
	31.5	15.2	18.8				Sales/Working Capital	15.1	12.4
	-46.1	NM	37.4					49.7	34.2
	11.3	3.7	19.5					6.4	6.8
(23)	3.1	(29) 1.7	(28) 2.6				EBIT/Interest	(117) 2.2	(101) 2.7
	-.1	-1.0	1.0					1.0	1.1
			3.9				Net Profit + Depr., Dep.,		8.7	9.8
		(12) 2.0					Amort./Cur. Mat. L /T/D	(36) 1.7	(26) 2.7
			.2					1.0	1.2
	.3	.1	.2					.2	.2
	.7	.7	.5				Fixed/Worth	.4	.5
	-3.3	4.8	1.2					1.4	1.7
	.8	1.0	1.2					1.1	1.2
	4.7	1.9	2.1				Debt/Worth	2.1	2.1
	-11.0	10.6	3.3					5.8	6.9
	136.6	31.7	43.0				% Profit Before Taxes/Tangible	34.2	35.7
(21)	36.8	(29) 6.4	(32) 20.7				Net Worth	(114) 14.0	(100) 14.2
	-4.8	-4.4	1.7					1.6	3.4
	19.8	9.8	21.8				% Profit Before Taxes/Total	10.1	11.6
	6.9	2.5	4.7				Assets	3.6	4.1
	-8.0	-2.5	.8					.1	.2
	63.1	69.8	61.9					44.3	45.8
	20.8	18.7	22.2				Sales/Net Fixed Assets	21.5	21.7
	10.8	8.8	10.8					11.9	9.4
	4.9	4.0	4.9					4.3	3.8
	3.8	2.8	3.1				Sales/Total Assets	3.1	2.7
	2.4	2.2	2.4					2.2	2.0
	.7	.7	.3				% Depr., Dep., Amort./Sales	.5	.7
(21)	1.6	(29) 1.1	(31) .9					(113) 1.0	(100) 1.1
	2.6	2.1	1.7					2.0	2.3
	3.3	1.9	1.8				% Officers', Directors',	1.9	1.9
(20)	7.0	(20) 3.9	(16) 4.3				Owners' Comp/Sales	(66) 3.2	(49) 4.9
	14.5	7.0	8.2					7.5	7.6
	26722M	106056M	503535M	655679M	923203M	1088224M	Net Sales ($)	4323630M	4348411M
	6817M	35304M	145336M	165002M	209231M	354303M	Total Assets ($)	1544684M	1370235M

Comparative Historical Data   Current Data Sorted By Sales

				Type of Statement						
17		15		12	Unqualified		1			2	9
16		15		22	Reviewed		1	5	1	11	4
33		13		28	Compiled	6	9	5	5	2	1
12		15		26	Tax Returns	6	13	4	1	2	
30		31		22	Other	6	3	3	2	4	4
4/1/00-		4/1/01-		4/1/02-			28 (4/1-9/30/02)			82 (10/1/02-3/31/03)	
3/31/01		3/31/02		3/31/03		0-1MM	1-3MM	3-5MM	5-10MM	10-25MM	25MM & OVER
ALL		ALL		ALL							
108		89		110	NUMBER OF STATEMENTS	18	27	17	9	21	18
%		%		%	ASSETS	%	%	%	%	%	%
9.6		9.4		10.1	Cash & Equivalents	14.8	12.2	7.4		10.3	7.1
19.3		20.8		17.3	Trade Receivables (net)	4.3	14.9	21.3		27.4	18.1
41.6		39.8		40.2	Inventory	42.5	36.3	34.2		38.2	52.6
2.3		2.9		2.9	All Other Current	2.8	2.0	3.5		5.3	1.8
72.8		72.9		70.4	Total Current	64.5	65.4	66.4		81.3	79.6
19.1		17.8		21.3	Fixed Assets (net)	23.9	23.2	25.6		11.6	16.8
2.5		2.4		2.8	Intangibles (net)	2.5	5.1	2.2		2.8	1.4
5.6		6.9		5.4	All Other Non-Current	9.1	6.3	5.8		4.4	2.3
100.0		100.0		100.0	Total	100.0	100.0	100.0		100.0	100.0
				LIABILITIES						
10.5		15.2		14.1	Notes Payable-Short Term	15.1	14.0	15.4		12.6	16.9
3.4		5.7		4.7	Cur. Mat.-L/T/D	9.6	4.0	4.7		2.4	3.2
24.6		25.9		21.4	Trade Payables	13.6	17.4	21.2		31.8	23.8
.6		.3		.4	Income Taxes Payable	.1	.0	.1		.2	1.4
9.1		9.8		10.2	All Other Current	11.8	8.8	7.0		10.5	9.4
48.2		56.9		50.9	Total Current	50.3	44.2	48.3		57.4	54.7
10.6		14.4		15.2	Long Term Debt	38.3	16.2	13.2		4.6	6.7
.1		.1		.2	Deferred Taxes	.0	.1	.6		.1	.1
4.1		3.1		4.0	All Other Non-Current	9.4	3.9	1.3		3.4	2.5
37.0		25.5		29.8	Net Worth	2.0	35.6	36.6		34.6	35.9
100.0		100.0		100.0	Total Liabilities & Net Worth	100.0	100.0	100.0		100.0	100.0
				INCOME DATA						
100.0		100.0		100.0	Net Sales	100.0	100.0	100.0		100.0	100.0
35.6		36.3		36.2	Gross Profit	49.5	37.1	33.1		27.3	32.0
32.8		34.7		34.0	Operating Expenses	49.1	34.2	32.4		24.6	29.0
2.8		1.6		2.2	Operating Profit	.5	2.9	.7		2.7	2.9
−.6		.2		.4	All Other Expenses (net)	1.2	.8	−.4		.4	.1
3.4		1.4		1.8	Profit Before Taxes	−.7	2.0	1.1		2.3	2.9
				RATIOS						
2.2		2.0		2.1		4.5	2.2	2.7		1.8	2.2
1.5		1.4		1.4	Current	1.1	1.5	1.4		1.3	1.5
1.2		1.1		1.1		.7	1.0	.9		1.2	1.3
1.0		.9		1.0		1.3	1.4	1.0		1.0	1.0
.6	(88)	.6	(109)	.5	Quick	(17) .3	.6	.5		.6	.5
.3		.2		.2		.1	.2	.3		.3	.1
5 75.6	6	64.3	4	97.6		0 UND	3 117.8	12 29.3		9 40.1	4 88.6
14 25.3	17	21.6	15	25.0	Sales/Receivables	2 152.7	18 20.7	27 13.5		26 14.2	8 48.2
40 9.1	41	8.9	35	10.4		7 53.8	37 10.0	39 9.4		40 9.0	19 18.8
38 9.6	41	8.9	34	10.6		30 12.3	18 20.8	21 17.0		32 11.6	45 8.0
72 5.1	69	5.3	63	5.8	Cost of Sales/Inventory	111 3.3	61 6.0	72 5.1		51 7.2	64 5.7
102 3.6	103	3.6	113	3.2		217 1.7	127 2.9	123 3.6		81 4.5	88 4.1
21 17.6	20	17.9	17	20.9		0 UND	11 31.9	15 23.8		26 13.9	19 19.5
32 11.6	38	9.6	32	11.5	Cost of Sales/Payables	14 26.9	29 12.5	40 9.0		38 9.5	23 15.6
57 6.4	61	5.9	50	7.4		56 6.6	46 7.9	54 6.8		54 6.8	46 8.0
7.3		8.7		9.6		6.4	7.2	5.6		11.2	10.7
13.2		16.9		17.4	Sales/Working Capital	84.9	17.1	14.7		19.5	14.8
37.3		59.2		113.7		−13.6	177.4	−34.0		26.7	22.9
11.4		7.0		11.7		11.2	8.2	4.0		21.3	30.3
(96) 3.3	(80)	1.5	(94)	2.8	EBIT/Interest	(13) 1.0	(22) 3.0	(16) 1.5	(17)	2.2	(17) 7.8
1.5		.5		.8		−1.2	−.3	.9		−.4	2.1
10.9		11.6		8.4	Net Profit + Depr., Dep.,						
(32) 2.7	(20)	3.1	(26)	2.9	Amort./Cur. Mat. L/T/D						
.8		1.3		1.2							
.2		.2		.2		.3	.1	.2		.2	.3
.4		.5		.6	Fixed/Worth	4.2	.6	.6		.4	.4
1.1		1.8		2.0		−.6	2.4	2.2		.9	.6
.8		1.0		1.1		.6	.8	.9		1.2	1.3
2.0		2.5		2.1	Debt/Worth	15.9	2.7	1.4		2.2	1.7
4.3		10.8		5.9		−3.3	8.9	4.3		3.7	2.3
53.2		31.9		51.1		104.8	65.9	19.4		43.0	57.4
(101) 19.8	(72)	14.0	(95)	20.4	% Profit Before Taxes/Tangible Net Worth	(10) 18.0	(25) 24.2	(14) 5.2	(20)	26.6	(17) 25.7
5.3		.3		1.0		−11.3	−6.9	−.1		2.4	9.8
16.2		13.4		15.7		11.3	27.3	5.6		21.8	21.5
6.5		2.3		4.7	% Profit Before Taxes/Total Assets	−2.6	7.1	1.8		5.2	9.7
1.5		−1.9		−.7		−13.7	−4.1	−.2		.7	2.2
64.4		54.9		51.0		45.1	84.2	26.2		133.7	51.7
29.8		23.4		21.4	Sales/Net Fixed Assets	18.8	30.3	15.2		33.2	27.6
9.9		14.2		10.4		8.7	8.8	6.6		16.8	13.5
4.5		4.5		4.8		4.6	4.6	4.0		4.9	6.3
3.1		3.2		3.3	Sales/Total Assets	2.8	3.2	2.7		3.6	4.1
2.2		2.3		2.4		2.2	2.1	2.3		2.8	2.8
.5		.6		.6		.8	.6	.8		.3	.5
(92) .9	(72)	.9	(92)	1.0	% Depr., Dep., Amort./Sales	(12) 1.4	(21) 1.8	(16) 1.5		.7	(13) .8
1.7		1.6		2.0		2.0	2.8	2.2		1.0	1.1
2.2		2.3		2.2		3.6	1.0			1.7	
(43) 6.0	(48)	4.8	(58)	4.4	% Officers', Directors', Owners' Comp/Sales	(11) 13.3	(17) 4.1		(11)	4.1	
9.9		7.9		10.4		15.4	9.0			6.9	
5914361M		5368160M		3303419M	Net Sales ($)	9778M	46129M	63716M	61627M	321780M	2800389M
2068152M		1514114M		915993M	Total Assets ($)	3452M	17264M	24187M	23069M	91024M	756997M

M = $ thousand   MM = $ million
See Pages 11 through 18 for Explanation of Ratios and Data

Current Data Sorted By Assets							Comparative Historical Data	
						Type of Statement		
	2	8	5	1		Unqualified	30	28
2	6	11				Reviewed	21	28
9	10	6				Compiled	46	54
18	4					Tax Returns	31	28
7	12	7	5			Other	76	62
	24 (4/1-9/30/02)		89 (10/1/02-3/31/03)				**4/1/98-3/31/99**	**4/1/99-3/31/00**
0-500M	**500M-2MM**	**2-10MM**	**10-50MM**	**50-100MM**	**100-250MM**		**ALL**	**ALL**
36	34	32	10	1		**NUMBER OF STATEMENTS**	204	200
%	%	%	%	%	%	**ASSETS**	%	%
11.6	11.8	16.2	17.3		DATA NOT AVAILABLE	Cash & Equivalents	11.1	10.3
36.9	37.8	42.1	30.4			Trade Receivables (net)	40.4	43.6
26.4	22.0	16.3	8.5			Inventory	20.5	21.7
1.5	2.9	2.5	4.7			All Other Current	2.0	2.9
76.4	74.5	77.2	60.9			Total Current	74.0	78.5
15.2	15.8	15.5	14.2			Fixed Assets (net)	17.7	13.6
.3	2.6	3.0	18.4			Intangibles (net)	3.2	3.5
8.2	7.1	4.3	6.5			All Other Non-Current	5.1	4.3
100.0	100.0	100.0	100.0			Total	100.0	100.0
						LIABILITIES		
14.5	15.9	10.0	6.7			Notes Payable-Short Term	14.7	15.9
4.2	5.2	1.5	1.6			Cur. Mat.-L/T/D	2.7	2.4
33.4	24.6	28.3	9.0			Trade Payables	22.1	25.7
.2	.1	.0	.3			Income Taxes Payable	.5	.4
17.9	10.8	11.9	23.0			All Other Current	13.3	13.2
70.2	56.5	51.7	40.7			Total Current	53.3	57.6
22.8	11.4	6.2	10.0			Long Term Debt	11.9	10.2
.1	.0	.1	.4			Deferred Taxes	.3	.5
10.9	1.6	5.4	11.4			All Other Non-Current	7.8	3.9
-4.1	30.4	36.6	37.5			Net Worth	26.7	27.8
100.0	100.0	100.0	100.0			Total Liabilities & Net Worth	100.0	100.0
						INCOME DATA		
100.0	100.0	100.0	100.0			Net Sales	100.0	100.0
39.2	32.4	29.0	47.3			Gross Profit	35.6	33.6
40.4	32.4	26.2	47.9			Operating Expenses	32.9	31.3
-1.2	.0	2.8	-.6			Operating Profit	2.7	2.4
.1	.3	.5	.6			All Other Expenses (net)	.4	.1
-1.3	-.3	2.3	-1.3			Profit Before Taxes	2.3	2.2
						RATIOS		
2.7	2.2	1.9	2.4				2.1	1.9
1.2	1.3	1.5	1.2			Current	1.5	1.4
.8	.9	1.0	1.1				1.2	1.1
1.4	1.4	1.7	1.6				1.5	1.3
.7	.9	1.0	1.0			Quick	1.0	.9
.5	.6	.7	.8				.7	.6
16 23.4	**20** 18.4	**12** 30.3	**34** 10.8				**20** 18.0	**22** 16.7
22 16.5	**34** 10.8	**40** 9.2	**51** 7.1			Sales/Receivables	**35** 10.5	**35** 10.5
31 11.8	**41** 8.9	**61** 6.0	**83** 4.4				**54** 6.7	**54** 6.8
7 54.4	**7** 55.7	**1** 275.3	**0** UND				**4** 83.6	**6** 59.0
21 17.4	**23** 16.1	**13** 27.2	**13** 29.2			Cost of Sales/Inventory	**19** 19.5	**21** 17.4
49 7.5	**44** 8.3	**27** 13.5	**55** 6.6				**41** 8.8	**44** 8.2
10 36.3	**14** 25.5	**18** 20.0	**18** 19.9				**15** 24.0	**15** 24.8
26 13.9	**29** 12.6	**29** 12.8	**24** 15.3			Cost of Sales/Payables	**28** 12.9	**29** 12.7
45 8.1	**47** 7.7	**52** 7.0	**60** 6.1				**46** 7.9	**46** 7.9
12.7	9.8	9.7	6.4				8.5	9.8
51.9	35.7	22.1	17.6			Sales/Working Capital	18.7	20.2
-33.7	-113.1	98.3	33.8				55.3	83.5
6.0	9.4	9.4					10.7	9.4
(32) 1.7	(32) 1.6	(28) 4.0				EBIT/Interest	(177) 4.0	(178) 3.6
-1.5	-1.4	1.5					1.4	1.1
							7.2	7.3
						Net Profit + Depr., Dep., Amort./Cur. Mat. L /T/D	(39) 4.2	(41) 3.8
							1.7	1.0
.2	.1	.1	.2				.1	.1
1.0	.3	.3	.6			Fixed/Worth	.4	.4
-.5	UND	1.0	NM				1.3	1.3
1.0	.6	1.0	1.5				1.0	1.1
8.4	1.8	2.2	3.5			Debt/Worth	2.2	2.7
-4.3	UND	4.6	NM				6.8	11.0
73.4	24.8	38.2					66.8	60.8
(22) 16.0	(27) 6.2	(30) 13.2				% Profit Before Taxes/Tangible Net Worth	(184) 29.3	(169) 23.1
-1.9	-16.3	2.0					5.8	7.5
15.8	5.4	9.8	6.9				19.2	14.7
3.5	1.7	4.7	1.4			% Profit Before Taxes/Total Assets	7.5	6.5
-7.0	-7.7	.6	-2.3				1.2	.5
111.4	70.7	122.5	78.7				88.0	115.4
44.3	34.8	37.0	26.5			Sales/Net Fixed Assets	34.0	43.7
28.4	18.9	19.1	19.5				16.9	22.2
7.7	5.8	5.9	2.7				5.5	5.5
5.9	4.3	4.0	1.8			Sales/Total Assets	4.2	4.3
4.6	2.7	2.9	1.4				2.8	3.0
.4	.5	.5					.4	.4
(26) 1.0	(30) 1.1	(30) .9				% Depr., Dep., Amort./Sales	(159) .8	(158) .8
1.5	2.1	1.8					1.5	1.7
3.7	2.5						2.2	2.2
(27) 6.2	(13) 3.3					% Officers', Directors', Owners' Comp/Sales	(87) 3.6	(95) 3.7
12.2	8.3						10.1	8.4
51349M	**174879M**	**599136M**	**418887M**	**280998M**		Net Sales ($)	**4030071M**	**4993985M**
9089M	**37658M**	**130430M**	**216103M**	**73369M**		Total Assets ($)	**1270037M**	**1735495M**

M = $ thousand MM = $ million

See Pages 11 through 18 for Explanation of Ratios and Data

Comparative Historical Data   Current Data Sorted By Sales

			Type of Statement						
10	7	16	Unqualified				4	4	8
23	19	19	Reviewed	1	3	2	5	6	2
37	26	25	Compiled	4	8	4	4	5	
21	19	22	Tax Returns	6	13	1	1	1	
43	34	31	Other	3	7	6	5	6	4
4/1/00-3/31/01 ALL	4/1/01-3/31/02 ALL	4/1/02-3/31/03 ALL		24 (4/1-9/30/02) 0-1MM	1-3MM	3-5MM	89 (10/1/02-3/31/03) 5-10MM	10-25MM	25MM & OVER
134	105	113	**NUMBER OF STATEMENTS**	14	31	13	19	22	14
%	%	%	**ASSETS**	%	%	%	%	%	%
11.3	11.8	13.4	Cash & Equivalents	17.2	7.9	13.4	10.7	17.9	18.0
44.6	36.2	37.8	Trade Receivables (net)	34.3	35.8	34.2	39.2	46.4	33.7
16.9	22.9	20.8	Inventory	25.1	21.4	25.0	27.1	13.9	13.4
2.8	2.6	2.5	All Other Current	1.5	2.9	1.7	1.3	3.1	4.3
75.6	73.6	74.5	Total Current	78.0	68.0	74.4	78.3	81.3	69.4
13.7	15.5	15.5	Fixed Assets (net)	11.3	18.6	19.1	15.5	16.3	8.4
4.4	5.2	3.4	Intangibles (net)	.0	3.8	1.8	.9	1.2	13.8
6.3	5.7	6.6	All Other Non-Current	10.5	9.5	4.7	5.4	1.2	8.4
100.0	100.0	100.0	Total	100.0	100.0	100.0	100.0	100.0	100.0
			LIABILITIES						
17.3	15.3	12.9	Notes Payable-Short Term	7.2	18.9	12.6	18.0	7.9	6.9
4.5	3.9	3.5	Cur. Mat.-L/T/D	8.6	2.9	8.8	1.1	1.2	1.5
27.9	23.9	27.1	Trade Payables	31.6	26.8	24.3	25.3	32.6	19.9
.5	.9	.1	Income Taxes Payable	.0	.2	.2	.0	.0	.2
13.5	13.9	14.4	All Other Current	9.7	18.2	12.4	12.4	12.6	17.9
63.7	57.9	58.0	Total Current	57.1	67.0	58.3	56.8	54.4	46.4
9.2	17.2	13.4	Long Term Debt	17.7	22.0	22.5	4.8	5.4	5.5
.2	.2	.1	Deferred Taxes	.2	.0	.1	.1	.0	.4
5.9	6.0	6.5	All Other Non-Current	22.0	3.3	3.0	4.3	3.3	9.2
21.0	18.7	22.0	Net Worth	2.9	7.6	16.2	34.1	36.8	38.4
100.0	100.0	100.0	Total Liabilities & Net Worth	100.0	100.0	100.0	100.0	100.0	100.0
			INCOME DATA						
100.0	100.0	100.0	Net Sales	100.0	100.0	100.0	100.0	100.0	100.0
36.4	37.8	34.8	Gross Profit	46.6	38.3	36.2	29.5	24.6	37.3
35.7	36.6	34.5	Operating Expenses	48.4	38.8	34.2	28.6	23.0	37.4
.6	1.2	.3	Operating Profit	-1.8	-.5	2.0	.9	1.6	-.1
-.7	.6	.3	All Other Expenses (net)	.8	-.1	.6	.3	.4	.2
1.4	.7	.0	Profit Before Taxes	-2.6	-.4	1.4	.6	1.2	-.3
			RATIOS						
2.0	2.0	2.1		5.1	2.5	2.3	2.0	1.9	1.9
1.2	1.3	1.3	Current	1.1	1.1	1.1	1.6	1.4	1.4
.9	1.0	.9		.8	.8	.9	1.0	1.0	1.1
1.4	1.5	1.5		2.9	1.3	1.4	1.6	1.7	1.3
.9	.8	.9	Quick	1.0	.8	.8	.9	1.1	1.0
.6	.6	.6		.6	.6	.4	.5	.7	.9

24	15.0	20	18.1	17	21.0	Sales/Receivables	14	25.4	17	21.2	16	22.2	22	16.2	13	28.0	24	15.3
43	8.5	32	11.4	30	12.1		27	13.4	26	13.8	22	16.4	35	10.3	28	12.8	42	8.8
59	6.2	51	7.1	46	7.9		35	10.3	43	8.4	43	8.5	43	8.4	65	5.6	72	5.0
4	97.9	7	55.2	5	74.0	Cost of Sales/Inventory	9	39.8	4	97.3	8	44.8	14	26.1	2	172.0	1	477.6
15	23.8	19	19.0	17	21.1		22	16.3	14	26.3	25	14.8	22	16.6	12	31.4	11	34.1
33	11.0	41	8.9	43	8.5		55	6.7	43	8.5	31	11.7	56	6.6	25	14.8	45	8.2
17	20.9	14	25.3	16	22.5	Cost of Sales/Payables	7	55.9	12	31.4	18	20.7	21	17.4	16	23.4	17	21.3
30	12.0	24	15.3	28	13.0		39	9.3	23	15.7	24	15.2	30	12.0	28	13.1	27	13.4
55	6.6	47	7.7	47	7.7		84	4.3	43	8.4	53	6.9	46	7.9	51	7.1	44	8.3
	10.8		9.8		10.0	Sales/Working Capital		7.6		11.5		14.4		9.4		10.5		8.7
	24.5		20.2		25.5			NM		66.0		35.3		14.7		22.1		18.1
	-111.6		-463.5		-135.0			-32.2		-25.2		-37.6		999.8		85.5		26.3
	7.9		5.1		6.6	EBIT/Interest		6.0		9.5		5.8		9.2		12.5		6.7
(125)	2.5	(95)	1.8	(101)	2.0		(11)	2.0	(30)	1.5	(12)	2.2	(17)	2.9	(19)	3.0	(12)	2.4
	.8		-1.2		-.5			-1.5		-4.1		.1		-.4		-4.5		1.3
	4.7		3.5		2.9	Net Profit + Depr., Dep., Amort./Cur. Mat. L/T/D												
(23)	1.8	(14)	.2	(16)	.4												
	-1.4		-2.2		-.6												
	.1		.2		.1	Fixed/Worth		.1		.2		.1		.1		.1		.1
	.5		.6		.5			.5		.6		6.6		.2		.4		.3
	3.9		UND		8.2			-.3		-.7		-.7		2.5		1.0		1.8
	1.2		1.0		1.1	Debt/Worth		.5		.8		1.4		1.1		.9		1.4
	4.0		2.5		2.6			7.7		2.6		11.3		1.4		2.4		2.7
	36.8		UND		48.1			-3.2		-5.7		-6.7		5.2		4.3		11.7
	63.5		42.1		37.7	% Profit Before Taxes/Tangible Net Worth				28.0				18.7		46.2		41.6
(106)	16.5	(79)	10.6	(88)	7.7				(20)	10.2			(18)	7.2	(21)	12.9	(12)	10.0
	1.5		-3.3		-.6					-11.3				-3.7		-17.9		2.1
	12.0		9.7		9.5	% Profit Before Taxes/Total Assets		15.7		14.6		8.4		6.1		14.0		7.2
	3.5		3.1		2.4			5.1		1.5		1.9		3.1		5.3		2.2
	-1.0		-2.8		-3.4			-3.0		-8.5		-5.6		-2.1		-4.5		.5
	104.0		102.8		85.2	Sales/Net Fixed Assets		178.9		48.9		70.2		70.5		149.7		230.7
	37.4		37.0		36.3			45.6		30.8		52.0		35.7		47.7		33.2
	18.4		20.3		21.0			25.8		19.3		18.7		21.7		18.8		20.6
	5.3		5.8		6.0	Sales/Total Assets		7.7		6.3		7.0		5.4		6.7		4.9
	3.8		3.8		4.5			5.5		5.0		4.4		4.5		5.5		2.8
	2.6		2.8		2.8			3.5		3.3		2.5		2.9		3.6		1.7
	.3		.3		.5	% Depr., Dep., Amort./Sales				.6		.5		.6		.3		.3
(103)	.9	(77)	.9	(94)	1.0				(28)	1.4	(10)	.9	(15)	1.1	(21)	.8	(11)	.8
	1.6		1.9		1.7					1.6		2.4		1.8		1.1		2.1
	2.1		2.2		2.5	% Officers', Directors', Owners' Comp/Sales		5.5		3.1								
(59)	3.7	(47)	4.0	(50)	4.9		(11)	9.6	(19)	5.1								
	7.9		7.8		8.9			22.9		7.9								
2895438M		1903357M		1525249M		Net Sales ($)	8390M		59556M		49874M		137033M		372400M		897996M
892218M		553124M		466649M		Total Assets ($)	2043M		17152M		14081M		35357M		90187M		307829M

© RMA 2003

M = $ thousand   MM = $ million
See Pages 11 through 18 for Explanation of Ratios and Data

Current Data Sorted By Assets   Comparative Historical Data

0-500M	500M-2MM	2-10MM	10-50MM	50-100MM	100-250MM	Type of Statement	4/1/98-3/31/99 ALL	4/1/99-3/31/00 ALL
1	3	8				Unqualified	3	3
1		4				Reviewed	5	6
2	2	1				Compiled	11	12
3		2				Tax Returns	2	4
						Other	11	7
	10 (4/1-9/30/02)		17 (10/1/02-3/31/03)					
7	5	15				**NUMBER OF STATEMENTS**	32	32
%	%	%	%	%	%	**ASSETS**	%	%
		10.7	D	D	D	Cash & Equivalents	7.4	11.0
		16.8	A	A	A	Trade Receivables (net)	16.0	13.4
		42.0	T	T	T	Inventory	47.2	44.8
		2.6	A	A	A	All Other Current	1.5	1.0
		72.0				Total Current	72.1	70.0
		21.4	N	N	N	Fixed Assets (net)	19.2	24.7
		2.3	O	O	O	Intangibles (net)	3.7	2.5
		4.3	T	T	T	All Other Non-Current	5.1	2.8
		100.0				Total	100.0	100.0
			A	A	A	**LIABILITIES**		
		4.6	V	V	V	Notes Payable-Short Term	10.4	4.4
		5.5	A	A	A	Cur. Mat.-L/T/D	3.8	3.7
		15.9	I	I	I	Trade Payables	26.0	26.9
		.7	L	L	L	Income Taxes Payable	.2	.4
		8.4	A	A	A	All Other Current	7.2	7.4
		35.1	B	B	B	Total Current	47.6	42.8
		12.3	L	L	L	Long Term Debt	12.8	19.6
		.0	E	E	E	Deferred Taxes	.3	.3
		6.5				All Other Non-Current	1.4	2.3
		46.0				Net Worth	37.9	35.0
		100.0				Total Liabilities & Net Worth	100.0	100.0
						INCOME DATA		
		100.0				Net Sales	100.0	100.0
		37.7				Gross Profit	33.9	35.3
		31.4				Operating Expenses	30.6	31.3
		6.3				Operating Profit	3.3	4.0
		.9				All Other Expenses (net)	−.3	.5
		5.4				Profit Before Taxes	3.5	3.6
						RATIOS		
		2.8					2.0	2.5
		2.0				Current	1.4	1.8
		1.8					1.1	1.3
		1.6					.8	1.0
		.6				Quick	.4	.5
		.4					.2	.3
		4 82.2					9 42.8	6 61.7
		13 28.8				Sales/Receivables	17 21.4	14 26.6
		51 7.1					35 10.6	28 13.1
		54 6.7					56 6.5	53 6.9
		85 4.3				Cost of Sales/Inventory	96 3.8	88 4.1
		110 3.3					148 2.5	123 3.0
		13 29.1					32 11.5	18 19.7
		33 11.1				Cost of Sales/Payables	42 8.7	42 8.6
		52 7.0					70 5.2	69 5.3
		4.1					5.9	5.5
		7.6				Sales/Working Capital	14.9	9.5
		12.3					41.7	35.2
		20.1					8.3	18.4
		(13) 8.4				EBIT/Interest	(30) 2.7	(30) 4.4
		2.4					1.2	2.3
						Net Profit + Depr., Dep., Amort./Cur. Mat. L /T/D	(10) 7.1 / 2.5 / 1.4	
		.1					.2	.2
		.4				Fixed/Worth	.6	.7
		.9					1.6	1.2
		.4					.9	.6
		1.4				Debt/Worth	1.7	1.7
		3.4					5.0	5.4
		75.6					38.8	44.0
		(14) 25.4				% Profit Before Taxes/Tangible Net Worth	(28) 16.9	(28) 22.3
		6.9					5.5	10.3
		21.2					9.5	13.5
		13.0				% Profit Before Taxes/Total Assets	4.3	7.5
		3.0					.8	3.3
		56.9					35.2	37.4
		20.5				Sales/Net Fixed Assets	17.7	17.0
		4.2					11.3	6.6
		3.3					3.7	3.7
		2.6				Sales/Total Assets	2.9	2.9
		1.6					2.1	2.0
		.6					.7	.8
		1.1				% Depr., Dep., Amort./Sales	(28) 1.4	(28) 1.6
		4.0					2.7	3.2
							1.7	3.2
						% Officers', Directors', Owners' Comp/Sales	(13) 6.6	(13) 6.2
							10.2	10.7
2831M	19513M	179678M				Net Sales ($)	681993M	794687M
856M	7071M	58852M				Total Assets ($)	334418M	300639M

M = $ thousand   MM = $ million
See Pages 11 through 18 for Explanation of Ratios and Data

Comparative Historical Data | Current Data Sorted By Sales

Type of Statement									
2	1		Unqualified	1	1	1	5	3	1
10	8	12	Reviewed	1		2	1		1
12	19	5	Compiled	1	3		1		
10	3	5	Tax Returns	1			1		
6	10	5	Other	3	1		1		
4/1/00-3/31/01 ALL	4/1/01-3/31/02 ALL	4/1/02-3/31/03 ALL		10 (4/1-9/30/02)			17 (10/1/02-3/31/03)		
				0-1MM	1-3MM	3-5MM	5-10MM	10-25MM	25MM & OVER
40	41	27	NUMBER OF STATEMENTS	6	5	3	8	3	2
%	%	%	ASSETS	%	%	%	%	%	%
6.0	11.3	11.2	Cash & Equivalents						
13.8	11.1	17.0	Trade Receivables (net)						
47.2	41.7	31.6	Inventory						
.6	2.6	1.7	All Other Current						
67.5	66.7	61.4	Total Current						
23.2	26.0	29.7	Fixed Assets (net)						
5.5	2.6	2.8	Intangibles (net)						
3.7	4.8	6.2	All Other Non-Current						
100.0	100.0	100.0	Total						
			LIABILITIES						
8.7	4.6	4.2	Notes Payable-Short Term						
4.3	4.7	4.8	Cur. Mat.-L/T/D						
24.2	22.8	15.7	Trade Payables						
.4	.2	.4	Income Taxes Payable						
9.8	8.5	9.6	All Other Current						
47.4	40.8	34.8	Total Current						
22.4	21.5	12.5	Long Term Debt						
.3	.0	.1	Deferred Taxes						
2.5	3.9	6.1	All Other Non-Current						
27.4	33.8	46.6	Net Worth						
100.0	100.0	100.0	Total Liabilities & Net Worth						
			INCOME DATA						
100.0	100.0	100.0	Net Sales						
37.4	40.6	46.0	Gross Profit						
35.2	37.8	41.2	Operating Expenses						
2.2	2.8	4.8	Operating Profit						
1.1	.6	.7	All Other Expenses (net)						
1.2	2.2	4.1	Profit Before Taxes						
			RATIOS						
2.1	2.8	3.0	Current						
1.6	1.5	1.8							
1.1	1.3	1.2							
.7	.9	1.8	Quick						
.4	.6	.9							
.2	.3	.3							
7 52.4	4 92.9	6 56.2	Sales/Receivables						
10 35.9	8 43.8	15 23.9							
25 14.6	25 14.8	37 9.8							
67 5.5	56 6.6	46 8.0	Cost of Sales/Inventory						
103 3.5	90 4.1	85 4.3							
153 2.4	128 2.9	106 3.5							
24 15.0	27 13.3	13 29.1	Cost of Sales/Payables						
48 7.6	48 7.6	33 11.1							
75 4.9	69 5.3	72 5.1							
7.3	5.7	6.8	Sales/Working Capital						
11.2	10.5	8.6							
112.7	21.2	41.2							
(36) 4.6	(36) 8.5	(21) 19.3	EBIT/Interest						
2.0	2.7	5.5							
1.1	1.1	1.5							
			Net Profit + Depr., Dep., Amort./Cur. Mat. L/T/D						
.3	.2	.2	Fixed/Worth						
.8	.7	.6							
NM	1.6	1.2							
1.2	.8	.4	Debt/Worth						
3.4	2.1	1.1							
−44.9	5.9	3.0							
(29) 21.3	(35) 47.1	(24) 46.9	% Profit Before Taxes/Tangible Net Worth						
8.8	8.8	17.8							
1.6	−1.2	1.3							
8.6	15.6	21.2	% Profit Before Taxes/Total Assets						
3.1	3.2	8.5							
.6	−.1	.0							
39.0	39.6	45.1	Sales/Net Fixed Assets						
17.2	14.3	15.3							
6.9	6.7	3.3							
3.7	3.2	4.3	Sales/Total Assets						
2.9	2.7	2.3							
1.7	2.1	1.6							
(35) .7	(36) 1.2	(25) .7	% Depr., Dep., Amort./Sales						
2.0	2.4	2.3							
4.1	4.9	6.3							
(21) 1.6	(23) 1.6	(17) 3.1	% Officers', Directors', Owners' Comp/Sales						
4.9	4.6	4.5							
8.5	9.1	9.9							
812005M	1436310M	202022M	Net Sales ($)	1522M	8423M	13526M	58308M	43432M	76811M
217566M	400728M	66779M	Total Assets ($)	563M	6461M	9378M	23892M	13071M	13414M

© RMA 2003

M = $ thousand   MM = $ million

See Pages 11 through 18 for Explanation of Ratios and Data

Current Data Sorted By Assets   Comparative Historical Data

						Type of Statement		
1	4	28	38	11	3	Unqualified	116	109
2	52	119	36	2		Reviewed	242	223
16	76	86	5			Compiled	248	247
21	34	20	1		1	Tax Returns	71	67
12	47	55	37	5	3	Other	166	151
	103 (4/1-9/30/02)		612 (10/1/02-3/31/03)				4/1/98-3/31/99	4/1/99-3/31/00
0-500M	500M-2MM	2-10MM	10-50MM	50-100MM	100-250MM		ALL	ALL
52	213	308	117	18	7	NUMBER OF STATEMENTS	843	797
%	%	%	%	%	%	ASSETS	%	%
8.1	5.7	6.0	5.0	7.7		Cash & Equivalents	6.0	6.9
28.2	30.5	31.1	29.0	24.6		Trade Receivables (net)	30.5	30.5
33.7	37.6	34.6	29.6	25.9		Inventory	33.7	32.7
2.5	1.2	2.0	3.3	6.9		All Other Current	2.2	2.0
72.5	75.0	73.8	66.9	65.1		Total Current	72.4	72.2
21.3	17.4	18.3	23.4	27.0		Fixed Assets (net)	19.0	19.3
.7	1.7	1.4	2.2	3.4		Intangibles (net)	1.6	1.5
5.5	6.0	6.5	7.6	4.5		All Other Non-Current	7.0	7.1
100.0	100.0	100.0	100.0	100.0		Total	100.0	100.0
						LIABILITIES		
19.5	15.5	15.5	16.5	9.6		Notes Payable-Short Term	13.4	13.3
9.6	4.1	2.9	2.9	1.8		Cur. Mat.-L/T/D	3.1	3.0
20.1	17.9	15.2	12.6	10.3		Trade Payables	16.6	16.1
.1	.2	.2	.1	.1		Income Taxes Payable	.3	.3
8.3	7.5	8.3	7.3	9.5		All Other Current	7.8	7.9
57.6	45.2	42.1	39.4	31.3		Total Current	41.2	40.5
13.4	13.2	11.0	12.6	18.3		Long Term Debt	13.4	13.2
.0	.1	.2	.4	.5		Deferred Taxes	.3	.2
6.4	3.4	3.7	4.4	1.9		All Other Non-Current	3.4	3.8
22.6	38.1	42.9	43.2	48.0		Net Worth	41.7	42.2
100.0	100.0	100.0	100.0	100.0		Total Liabilities & Net Worth	100.0	100.0
						INCOME DATA		
100.0	100.0	100.0	100.0	100.0		Net Sales	100.0	100.0
30.9	27.3	25.9	26.6	26.0		Gross Profit	25.7	26.1
29.1	25.7	24.4	23.9	21.2		Operating Expenses	22.7	23.0
1.8	1.6	1.6	2.7	4.9		Operating Profit	3.0	3.0
1.0	.3	.1	.0	.7		All Other Expenses (net)	.3	-.1
.7	1.4	1.5	2.7	4.2		Profit Before Taxes	2.7	3.1
						RATIOS		
2.6	2.7	2.9	2.6	3.6		Current	2.7	2.9
1.2	1.7	1.8	1.6	1.8			1.9	1.8
.9	1.2	1.3	1.3	1.3			1.3	1.4
1.2	1.2	1.5	1.3	1.5		Quick	1.4	1.5
.7	.8	.9	.9	1.0	(841)		.9	1.0
.3	.5	.6	.6	.7			.6	.7
7 49.9	23 16.2	29 12.5	27 13.3	26 13.9		Sales/Receivables	27 13.5	27 13.6
22 16.6	31 11.6	38 9.6	39 9.4	33 11.2			37 9.8	37 9.9
43 8.5	44 8.3	48 7.5	47 7.7	44 8.2			50 7.2	48 7.6
10 36.9	38 9.6	41 9.0	41 8.9	33 11.2		Cost of Sales/Inventory	39 9.3	37 9.8
42 8.8	57 6.4	59 6.2	52 7.0	44 8.3			55 6.7	54 6.8
112 3.3	88 4.1	79 4.6	71 5.2	70 5.2			79 4.6	78 4.7
6 66.1	15 23.6	15 23.8	15 23.6	14 26.7		Cost of Sales/Payables	17 22.0	16 23.1
24 15.1	22 16.6	22 16.3	20 18.2	19 19.5			25 14.9	24 15.4
52 7.0	38 9.7	35 10.5	28 13.1	23 15.7			36 10.2	34 10.9
10.4	6.4	5.8	6.2	4.9		Sales/Working Capital	5.9	5.7
37.6	10.2	9.2	10.6	7.3			9.0	9.1
-186.0	23.4	17.7	17.1	13.5			18.0	17.7
(44) 8.0	(202) 6.8	(286) 7.0	(115) 9.0	(17) 10.3		EBIT/Interest	(789) 6.7	7.5
2.0	2.1	2.9	3.5	8.7			3.0	(729) 3.1
.2	.5	1.4	2.2	3.8			1.5	1.7
	(48) 3.0	(98) 5.4	(52) 7.1			Net Profit + Depr., Dep.,	(282) 6.2	5.3
	1.4	2.5	3.8			Amort./Cur. Mat. L /T/D	2.5	(266) 2.5
	.5	1.2	2.0				1.3	1.5
.1	.2	.2	.3	.3		Fixed/Worth	.2	.2
.7	.4	.4	.5	.6			.4	.4
UND	1.1	.8	1.0	1.0			.8	.8
.6	.8	.6	.7	.4		Debt/Worth	.7	.7
3.0	1.6	1.4	1.5	1.3			1.5	1.5
UND	4.2	3.0	2.8	2.9			3.0	2.9
(39) 48.5	(192) 29.2	(289) 23.8	(113) 25.4	30.8		% Profit Before Taxes/Tangible	(799) 29.3	32.0
10.1	9.6	10.7	14.8	22.4		Net Worth	15.2	(753) 16.3
-6.5	-.4	3.2	7.1	10.6			5.5	6.1
18.5	9.1	8.9	10.2	12.3		% Profit Before Taxes/Total	11.7	12.8
3.6	3.2	4.2	5.8	9.5		Assets	5.8	6.2
-3.0	-1.0	1.1	2.5	6.4			1.9	2.1
75.4	45.5	34.2	21.0	20.6		Sales/Net Fixed Assets	36.7	36.9
23.1	21.6	18.3	12.7	12.1			20.0	18.9
11.4	13.1	10.8	7.5	7.0			9.9	10.1
4.9	3.9	3.4	3.3	3.7		Sales/Total Assets	3.6	3.6
3.6	3.1	2.8	2.5	2.5			2.8	2.9
2.8	2.3	2.2	2.1	1.5			2.2	2.2
(35) .8	(183) .7	(295) .7	(115) .9	(16) .9		% Depr., Dep., Amort./Sales	(780) .7	(745) .6
1.4	1.2	1.1	1.2	1.2			1.0	1.0
2.6	2.0	1.5	1.7	2.1			1.6	1.5
(36) 2.8	(125) 2.0	(159) 1.3	(42) 1.0			% Officers', Directors',	(399) 1.4	(377) 1.5
5.8	3.0	2.2	1.4			Owners' Comp/Sales	2.6	2.7
9.6	5.8	3.8	3.1				4.4	5.1
53290M	851180M	4061298M	6478429M	3105668M	3678515M	Net Sales ($)	14334122M	15227120M
14355M	247421M	1400755M	2441185M	1162352M	1082529M	Total Assets ($)	5522978M	5755276M

M = $ thousand   MM = $ million
See Pages 11 through 18 for Explanation of Ratios and Data

Comparative Historical Data / Current Data Sorted By Sales

Type of Statement	70	78	85		1	2	1	7	24	50
Unqualified	70	78	85		1	2	1	7	24	50
Reviewed	186	203	211			16	27	48	79	41
Compiled	206	221	183		11	38	37	52	38	7
Tax Returns	67	59	77		14	22	15	18	6	2
Other	150	161	159		5	29	26	21	29	49
	4/1/00-3/31/01 ALL	4/1/01-3/31/02 ALL	4/1/02-3/31/03 ALL		103 (4/1-9/30/02) 0-1MM	1-3MM	3-5MM	612 (10/1/02-3/31/03) 5-10MM	10-25MM	25MM & OVER
NUMBER OF STATEMENTS	679	722	715		31	107	106	146	176	149
	%	%	%	**ASSETS**	%	%	%	%	%	%
Cash & Equivalents	7.2	6.8	5.9		8.3	5.7	5.6	7.2	6.2	4.1
Trade Receivables (net)	29.0	29.7	30.1		23.3	25.1	30.8	30.5	32.7	31.0
Inventory	33.5	33.1	34.4		39.7	37.8	37.4	33.5	33.2	31.0
All Other Current	2.7	2.6	2.2		2.2	1.9	.8	2.2	2.1	3.2
Total Current	72.3	72.2	72.5		73.4	70.5	74.6	73.4	74.3	69.4
Fixed Assets (net)	18.7	19.3	19.4		18.5	20.1	18.3	18.2	18.6	22.2
Intangibles (net)	1.8	1.6	1.6		.6	1.8	1.5	2.1	.7	2.4
All Other Non-Current	7.1	6.9	6.4		7.5	7.6	5.6	6.3	6.4	6.0
Total	100.0	100.0	100.0		100.0	100.0	100.0	100.0	100.0	100.0
				LIABILITIES						
Notes Payable-Short Term	14.5	14.8	16.1		25.1	13.2	15.3	15.7	16.0	17.5
Cur. Mat.-L/T/D	3.3	3.4	3.7		10.5	5.8	3.3	3.2	2.6	2.9
Trade Payables	15.4	15.2	15.8		13.5	17.4	17.4	16.2	15.2	14.3
Income Taxes Payable	.2	.2	.2		.2	.2	.2	.2	.2	.1
All Other Current	8.4	7.8	7.9		6.4	6.8	10.8	7.1	7.6	8.2
Total Current	41.7	41.4	43.8		55.6	43.5	46.9	42.5	41.7	43.0
Long Term Debt	12.0	13.4	12.4		13.4	16.9	12.5	12.3	9.5	12.3
Deferred Taxes	.2	.2	.2		.1	.0	.1	.3	.2	.3
All Other Non-Current	3.5	3.6	3.9		4.9	4.5	3.6	3.9	3.2	4.5
Net Worth	42.6	41.4	39.7		26.3	35.1	36.9	41.1	45.4	39.8
Total Liabilities & Net Worth	100.0	100.0	100.0		100.0	100.0	100.0	100.0	100.0	100.0
				INCOME DATA						
Net Sales	100.0	100.0	100.0		100.0	100.0	100.0	100.0	100.0	100.0
Gross Profit	26.3	26.9	26.9		31.7	30.4	27.5	25.3	25.6	26.0
Operating Expenses	23.9	24.3	25.0		29.6	29.0	26.9	23.6	23.4	23.1
Operating Profit	2.4	2.6	1.9		2.1	1.3	.6	1.7	2.2	2.9
All Other Expenses (net)	.2	.5	.2		.9	.5	.5	.1	-.1	.2
Profit Before Taxes	2.2	2.1	1.7		1.2	.8	.1	1.7	2.3	2.7
				RATIOS						
Current	2.7	2.9	2.8		3.9	2.9	2.6	2.9	2.9	2.5
	1.8	1.8	1.7		1.2	1.7	1.7	1.8	1.8	1.7
	1.3	1.3	1.3		.9	1.2	1.2	1.3	1.3	1.3
Quick	1.4	1.5	1.4		1.3	1.2	1.3	1.5	1.5	1.2
	.9 (721)	.9	.8		.7	.7	.8	.9	.9	.8
	.5	.6	.6		.2	.4	.5	.6	.6	.6
Sales/Receivables	24 15.2	26 14.0	25 14.5		4 90.6	16 22.7	26 14.1	26 13.8	29 12.5	27 13.3
	34 10.7	37 10.0	35 10.3		21 17.1	28 13.2	34 10.7	37 9.9	38 9.6	36 10.0
	45 8.1	48 7.6	46 7.9		44 8.3	45 8.1	48 7.6	47 7.7	48 7.5	44 8.3
Cost of Sales/Inventory	38 9.7	38 9.7	37 9.8		14 25.9	41 8.8	44 8.4	35 10.4	38 9.6	35 10.4
	53 6.9	54 6.7	55 6.6		114 3.2	72 5.1	57 6.4	57 6.4	56 6.6	49 7.5
	77 4.7	80 4.6	80 4.6		158 2.3	117 3.1	87 4.2	78 4.7	70 5.2	65 5.6
Cost of Sales/Payables	13 27.4	15 23.8	15 24.5		5 76.0	15 24.9	16 22.6	15 24.4	15 23.6	14 25.2
	21 17.5	23 16.0	22 16.7		23 15.6	23 15.9	25 14.9	23 15.7	21 17.3	19 19.1
	33 11.2	34 10.8	34 10.6		43 8.5	44 8.3	43 8.5	37 9.9	32 11.3	27 13.6
Sales/Working Capital	6.0	5.5	6.1		4.8	5.2	5.7	6.0	6.7	6.7
	9.8	9.9	10.2		36.4	9.8	10.3	9.0	9.6	11.0
	18.9	19.0	21.1		-101.6	28.3	32.2	20.4	15.8	19.7
EBIT/Interest	6.5	5.9	7.5		7.6	5.1	6.5	7.0	8.4	8.8
	(634) 2.5	(675) 2.5	(671) 3.0		(24) 2.1	(102) 1.5	(100) 2.0	(136) 2.4	(162) 3.2	(147) 4.4
	1.3	1.2	1.2		.7	.1	.2	1.2	1.7	2.3
Net Profit + Depr., Dep., Amort./Cur. Mat. L/T/D	4.6	5.8	6.2			1.2	4.1	4.0	7.7	10.2
	(190) 1.9	(198) 2.4	(211) 2.5			(14) .5	(26) 1.6	(47) 1.8	(63) 2.7	(59) 4.2
	.9	.9	1.1			-1.5	.8	.7	1.2	2.4
Fixed/Worth	.2	.2	.2		.1	.2	.2	.2	.2	.3
	.4	.4	.4		.3	.5	.4	.4	.4	.5
	.9	.9	1.0		5.0	1.4	1.2	.9	.8	.9
Debt/Worth	.7	.6	.7		.4	.8	.7	.7	.5	.9
	1.4	1.5	1.6		3.7	1.7	1.6	1.5	1.4	1.7
	3.0	3.3	3.2		UND	5.1	4.4	3.3	2.7	2.9
% Profit Before Taxes/Tangible Net Worth	30.2	26.1	26.2		83.5	23.3	22.1	24.6	25.2	29.6
	(639) 12.7	(677) 10.9	(657) 11.7		(24) 12.8	(91) 5.7	(93) 8.0	(134) 10.3	(171) 13.5	(144) 16.8
	3.7	2.8	2.8		-3.8	-6.3	-.9	2.9	4.2	8.2
% Profit Before Taxes/Total Assets	10.6	9.7	9.7		16.4	8.7	7.3	9.1	10.6	10.5
	5.2	4.3	4.2		5.2	1.7	3.0	3.4	4.9	6.8
	1.1	.7	.7		-.9	-2.7	-1.8	.7	1.7	2.4
Sales/Net Fixed Assets	38.7	38.0	35.7		205.7	36.3	42.5	40.7	35.7	30.4
	20.2	18.6	18.5		32.8	19.0	19.0	18.6	19.2	15.1
	10.8	9.7	10.6		7.1	9.1	10.9	11.4	11.3	9.1
Sales/Total Assets	3.8	3.7	3.6		3.6	3.7	3.5	3.6	3.6	3.7
	3.0	2.8	2.9		3.0	2.6	3.0	2.9	2.9	3.0
	2.3	2.2	2.2		1.6	1.9	2.1	2.2	2.5	2.3
% Depr., Dep., Amort./Sales	.6	.7	.8		.7	.8	.8	.8	.7	.8
	(620) 1.0	(673) 1.0	(649) 1.1		(20) 1.6	(86) 1.5	(94) 1.2	(136) 1.1	(170) 1.0	(143) 1.2
	1.5	1.6	1.7		5.7	2.5	1.9	1.7	1.5	1.6
% Officers', Directors', Owners' Comp/Sales	1.4	1.4	1.4		1.8	2.3	1.8	1.8	1.1	1.0
	(337) 2.5	(372) 2.7	(363) 2.6		(16) 6.6	(71) 4.1	(62) 3.0	(86) 2.7	(82) 2.1	(46) 1.5
	4.4	4.8	5.2		9.6	8.0	6.1	4.6	3.4	3.1
Net Sales ($)	13104662M	13646997M	18228380M		17915M	213847M	419548M	1064391M	2786183M	13726496M
Total Assets ($)	4920189M	5227226M	6348597M		7657M	87605M	160133M	409112M	1048141M	4635949M

M = $ thousand   MM = $ million

See Pages 11 through 18 for Explanation of Ratios and Data

Current Data Sorted By Assets   Comparative Historical Data

						Type of Statement		
1	13	5	1		1	Unqualified	9	8
8	15	4	2			Reviewed	20	16
6	5					Compiled	38	28
4	11	4				Tax Returns	10	17
						Other	17	23
	29 (4/1-9/30/02)			51 (10/1/02-3/31/03)			4/1/98-3/31/99	4/1/99-3/31/00
0-500M	500M-2MM	2-10MM	10-50MM	50-100MM	100-250MM		ALL	ALL
19	44	13	3		1	**NUMBER OF STATEMENTS**	94	92
%	%	%	%	%	%	**ASSETS**	%	%
10.9	10.5	6.6				Cash & Equivalents	8.7	9.5
23.3	23.4	15.7				Trade Receivables (net)	28.9	27.1
45.5	38.1	30.8				Inventory	36.6	31.7
.7	1.3	3.0				All Other Current	1.6	1.7
80.3	73.4	56.0				Total Current	75.8	70.0
7.8	11.8	19.1				Fixed Assets (net)	15.9	21.1
2.0	2.0	.8				Intangibles (net)	1.2	3.0
9.9	12.9	24.0				All Other Non-Current	7.1	5.9
100.0	100.0	100.0				Total	100.0	100.0
						LIABILITIES		
12.0	8.6	9.0				Notes Payable-Short Term	8.6	12.7
2.5	2.4	2.5				Cur. Mat.-L/T/D	3.0	3.4
26.7	25.0	21.1				Trade Payables	22.9	21.6
.3	.9	.2				Income Taxes Payable	.5	.4
11.4	7.6	10.7				All Other Current	11.6	8.2
52.9	44.5	43.6				Total Current	46.6	46.4
10.5	5.8	9.2				Long Term Debt	12.0	14.0
.0	.0	.0				Deferred Taxes	.1	.1
8.5	18.9	19.3				All Other Non-Current	5.1	6.4
28.0	30.8	27.9				Net Worth	36.2	33.1
100.0	100.0	100.0				Total Liabilities & Net Worth	100.0	100.0
						INCOME DATA		
100.0	100.0	100.0				Net Sales	100.0	100.0
34.8	34.3	36.1				Gross Profit	35.2	38.9
31.2	33.9	36.9				Operating Expenses	31.9	36.0
3.5	.5	−.9				Operating Profit	3.3	2.9
.1	.3	−.2				All Other Expenses (net)	.5	.6
3.4	.2	−.7				Profit Before Taxes	2.8	2.3

Data not available (10-50MM, 50-100MM, 100-250MM columns)

						RATIOS		
3.3	3.0	2.1					2.7	2.4
1.5	1.7	1.4				Current	1.8	1.6
1.3	1.2	.8					1.3	1.2
1.2	1.6	.7					1.4	1.4
.7	.6	.5				Quick	.9	.8
.3	.2	.2					.5	.4
16 23.5	15 23.6	14 26.3					21 17.4	19 18.7
22 16.7	25 14.6	32 11.3				Sales/Receivables	30 12.1	31 11.8
44 8.4	38 9.6	44 8.2					46 8.0	47 7.8
52 7.0	42 8.6	57 6.4					29 12.5	21 17.6
81 4.5	76 4.8	118 3.1				Cost of Sales/Inventory	68 5.4	61 6.0
114 3.2	134 2.7	170 2.1					107 3.4	112 3.3
20 18.3	13 28.1	26 14.0					20 18.7	19 19.6
38 9.5	45 8.1	68 5.4				Cost of Sales/Payables	35 10.4	35 10.5
51 7.2	85 4.3	157 2.3					52 7.0	62 5.9
5.9	5.5	6.8					6.1	6.3
9.7	7.2	20.6				Sales/Working Capital	9.5	12.4
21.8	24.6	−19.7					23.5	40.3
8.9	12.8	4.1					8.5	6.9
(15) 4.0	(38) 1.6	(12) 1.0				EBIT/Interest	(85) 2.8	(83) 3.4
2.0	−3.0	−2.2					1.3	1.0
	2.7					Net Profit + Depr., Dep.,		6.0
	(18) .2					Amort./Cur. Mat. L /T/D	5.9	3.0
	−2.5						(30) 2.6 (31)	1.6
							1.3	
.0	.1	.2					.1	.2
.2	.3	.5				Fixed/Worth	.4	.5
.8	1.3	2.7					1.0	1.7
1.3	.5	1.4					.6	.7
2.7	2.2	2.3				Debt/Worth	1.7	1.5
23.9	12.1	11.1					5.3	7.5
98.1	13.6	9.2					32.4	30.7
(16) 44.5	(37) 6.1	(11) 7.8				% Profit Before Taxes/Tangible Net Worth	(84) 18.2	(75) 15.4
−4.2	−15.6	−9.8					7.0	2.9
20.8	8.5	3.2					15.5	13.9
9.1	1.9	.3				% Profit Before Taxes/Total Assets	6.4	6.7
−.7	−4.4	−4.8					1.3	.8
UND	73.4	37.8					59.2	37.6
177.0	27.6	24.5				Sales/Net Fixed Assets	26.1	18.3
25.0	15.5	8.3					13.6	10.3
4.6	3.5	3.1					4.0	3.9
3.4	2.7	1.6				Sales/Total Assets	3.1	2.9
2.6	1.7	1.1					2.3	2.1
.3	.6	.7					.7	.9
(11) .6	(36) .9	1.4				% Depr., Dep., Amort./Sales	(82) 1.2	(83) 1.2
1.0	1.4	1.8					1.8	1.8
3.2	4.3						2.0	3.0
(11) 6.4	(26) 5.2					% Officers', Directors', Owners' Comp/Sales	(42) 5.0 (41)	5.2
7.2	6.8						7.5	7.5
20808M	131870M	101187M	100396M		177257M	Net Sales ($)	627534M	570928M
6147M	48684M	53248M	49822M		170362M	Total Assets ($)	242923M	235012M

M = $ thousand   MM = $ million
See Pages 11 through 18 for Explanation of Ratios and Data

Comparative Historical Data | Current Data Sorted By Sales

				Type of Statement						
6	4		2	Unqualified		13		4	1	2
15	15		21	Reviewed	1	14	5	2		2
30	23		27	Compiled	6	7	2	1		
8	11		11	Tax Returns	1	7	2	5	2	
19	22		19	Other	1	7	4			
4/1/00-3/31/01 ALL	4/1/01-3/31/02 ALL		4/1/02-3/31/03 ALL		0-1MM	29 (4/1-9/30/02) 1-3MM	3-5MM	51 (10/1/02-3/31/03) 5-10MM	10-25MM	25MM & OVER
78	75		80	**NUMBER OF STATEMENTS**	9	41	11	12	3	4
%	%		%	**ASSETS**	%	%	%	%	%	%
7.4	8.3		9.6	Cash & Equivalents		8.5	10.3	14.1		
27.5	27.5		22.0	Trade Receivables (net)		21.6	29.4	18.3		
32.7	32.3		38.0	Inventory		39.9	31.5	42.2		
1.8	3.4		2.2	All Other Current		1.6	.4	3.1		
69.4	71.5		71.8	Total Current		71.6	71.6	77.7		
21.4	17.6		12.5	Fixed Assets (net)		10.9	16.3	13.9		
2.1	1.8		1.8	Intangibles (net)		2.0	3.2	.7		
7.1	9.1		13.9	All Other Non-Current		15.6	8.9	7.7		
100.0	100.0		100.0	Total		100.0	100.0	100.0		
				LIABILITIES						
10.8	9.8		9.7	Notes Payable-Short Term		10.2	10.0	2.2		
3.1	4.3		2.5	Cur. Mat.-L/T/D		1.9	5.1	2.3		
20.2	20.7		24.0	Trade Payables		25.2	22.5	25.8		
.3	.2		.6	Income Taxes Payable		1.0	.0	.2		
8.0	8.8		8.9	All Other Current		8.2	11.1	13.2		
42.4	43.9		45.7	Total Current		46.6	48.6	43.7		
17.9	14.5		7.8	Long Term Debt		7.3	7.3	8.1		
.4	.2		.0	Deferred Taxes		.0	.0	.0		
3.4	6.1		15.8	All Other Non-Current		19.0	7.9	14.6		
36.0	35.3		30.6	Net Worth		27.2	36.2	33.6		
100.0	100.0		100.0	Total Liabilities & Net Worth		100.0	100.0	100.0		
				INCOME DATA						
100.0	100.0		100.0	Net Sales		100.0	100.0	100.0		
38.0	36.6		34.8	Gross Profit		33.5	35.1	39.0		
35.6	34.5		33.7	Operating Expenses		31.7	33.5	40.7		
2.5	2.1		1.1	Operating Profit		1.8	1.7	-1.7		
.6	.6		.2	All Other Expenses (net)		.5	.0	-.7		
1.8	1.5		.9	Profit Before Taxes		1.4	1.7	-1.0		
				RATIOS						
2.7	2.5		2.7			2.7	4.4	2.6		
1.9	1.6		1.6	Current		1.5	1.2	2.0		
1.2	1.1		1.2			1.2	.9	1.5		
1.5	1.4		1.2			1.2	2.3	1.2		
.8	.7		.6	Quick		.5	.6	.7		
.4	.5		.3			.2	.5	.3		

19	18.7	21	17.3	16	23.1		15	24.2	26	13.9	5	73.7					
31	11.8	33	11.1	25	14.4	Sales/Receivables	24	15.1	32	11.5	18	20.6					
50	7.2	49	7.5	40	9.1		38	9.5	43	8.4	36	10.0					
34	10.6	28	12.9	49	7.4		53	6.9	41	9.0	41	9.0					
74	4.9	69	5.3	81	4.5	Cost of Sales/Inventory	104	3.5	59	6.2	86	4.2					
107	3.4	111	3.3	134	2.7		151	2.4	71	5.1	124	2.9					
22	16.7	24	15.0	19	19.7		12	29.4	13	28.3	31	11.8					
38	9.6	37	9.8	43	8.5	Cost of Sales/Payables	52	7.1	19	19.3	42	8.6					
62	5.9	57	6.4	83	4.4		95	3.9	82	4.5	74	4.9					
	5.7		6.4		5.8			5.3		6.8		6.4					
	8.8		9.2		8.4	Sales/Working Capital		7.9		26.4		7.4					
	31.8		33.3		26.5			20.3		-35.8		10.4					
	8.6		2.7		7.2			8.5		31.3							
(69)	2.9	(61)	1.5	(68)	2.6	EBIT/Interest	(36)	3.4	(10)	11.1							
	1.0		.4		-1.7			-1.0		-1.4							
	9.7		2.2		2.6	Net Profit + Depr., Dep.,		2.4									
(22)	3.7	(20)	1.3	(26)	.9	Amort./Cur. Mat. L/T/D	(16)	.2									
	2.0		.2		-2.1			-2.4									
	.2		.2		.1			.1		.1		.1					
	.4		.3		.3	Fixed/Worth		.3		.9		.3					
	1.2		1.3		.9			.8		3.8		NM					
	.8		.7		.7			.9		.4		.6					
	1.5		1.9		2.3	Debt/Worth		3.1		2.1		2.0					
	4.2		4.7		11.7			12.0		12.7		NM					
	37.5		19.5		29.9	% Profit Before Taxes/Tangible		26.5									
(69)	13.6	(66)	8.0	(68)	8.3	Net Worth	(36)	7.6									
	1.3		-1.2		-9.7			-21.5									
	10.6		7.6		9.2	% Profit Before Taxes/Total		10.9		26.3		4.2					
	4.7		2.1		3.0	Assets		2.8		4.3		-2.4					
	.1		-.6		-4.2			-4.2		-.6		-9.3					
	37.6		51.0		88.4			87.0		57.0		84.7					
	19.6		28.0		31.4	Sales/Net Fixed Assets		37.5		27.6		30.3					
	9.1		12.3		14.7			16.9		12.7		13.9					
	3.5		3.9		3.6			3.3		4.8		3.8					
	2.7		2.6		2.7	Sales/Total Assets		2.5		3.0		3.0					
	1.9		1.8		1.7			1.7		2.6		2.6					
	.8		.4		.6			.6				.8					
(71)	1.5	(67)	.9	(64)	1.0	% Depr., Dep., Amort./Sales	(31)	.8			(11)	1.2					
	2.0		1.7		1.6			1.2				1.6					
	2.9		3.2		4.1	% Officers', Directors',		5.1									
(33)	5.5	(41)	5.6	(44)	5.4	Owners' Comp/Sales	(25)	5.9									
	7.7		10.6		7.2			8.5									

611988M	442215M		531518M	Net Sales ($)	6786M	75333M	42398M	82258M	47090M	277653M
269624M	185875M		328263M	Total Assets ($)	2675M	42019M	15686M	28681M	19018M	220184M

© RMA 2003

M = $ thousand   MM = $ million
See Pages 11 through 18 for Explanation of Ratios and Data

RETAIL—Hardware Stores NAICS 444130 (SIC 5072, 5251)

| Current Data Sorted By Assets | | | | | | | Comparative Historical Data | |

						Type of Statement		
1	2	6	5	1	2	Unqualified	24	14
	20	28	6			Reviewed	70	52
23	57	27	3			Compiled	121	105
14	29	7	2			Tax Returns	44	46
17	33	16	8	1	1	Other	102	99
	58 (4/1-9/30/02)		251 (10/1/02-3/31/03)				4/1/98-3/31/99	4/1/99-3/31/00
0-500M	500M-2MM	2-10MM	10-50MM	50-100MM	100-250MM		ALL	ALL
55	141	84	24	2	3	NUMBER OF STATEMENTS	361	316
%	%	%	%	%	%	ASSETS	%	%
7.4	6.8	4.3	5.0			Cash & Equivalents	6.5	6.0
10.0	13.2	17.7	14.5			Trade Receivables (net)	13.7	12.4
60.0	49.8	46.4	47.7			Inventory	49.6	49.6
.9	2.1	1.5	2.6			All Other Current	1.6	1.1
78.3	71.9	70.0	69.8			Total Current	71.5	69.2
13.6	15.9	20.3	18.5			Fixed Assets (net)	17.0	17.3
1.5	1.5	1.4	1.7			Intangibles (net)	1.8	3.3
6.6	10.7	8.3	10.1			All Other Non-Current	9.7	10.3
100.0	100.0	100.0	100.0			Total	100.0	100.0
						LIABILITIES		
17.0	7.6	11.3	20.4			Notes Payable-Short Term	10.5	8.9
3.4	3.1	4.6	2.1			Cur. Mat.-L/T/D	3.2	3.5
16.5	14.8	16.3	13.4			Trade Payables	15.6	15.5
.1	.4	.2	.1			Income Taxes Payable	.2	.3
6.6	7.2	6.9	5.9			All Other Current	7.3	9.8
43.7	33.1	39.3	41.9			Total Current	36.9	37.9
22.3	20.3	16.5	12.8			Long Term Debt	19.1	18.3
.1	.0	.1	.3			Deferred Taxes	.1	.1
8.3	4.7	2.8	6.8			All Other Non-Current	4.2	4.5
25.6	41.8	41.3	38.2			Net Worth	39.7	39.2
100.0	100.0	100.0	100.0			Total Liabilities & Net Worth	100.0	100.0
						INCOME DATA		
100.0	100.0	100.0	100.0			Net Sales	100.0	100.0
38.0	36.6	33.8	31.8			Gross Profit	34.1	34.5
35.0	33.8	32.3	28.9			Operating Expenses	31.3	31.5
3.0	2.8	1.5	2.8			Operating Profit	2.8	3.0
.6	.1	.2	.3			All Other Expenses (net)	.1	.2
2.4	2.7	1.2	2.5			Profit Before Taxes	2.7	2.9
						RATIOS		
3.9	4.0	2.8	3.1				3.4	3.2
2.2	2.5	1.8	1.7			Current	2.1	2.1
1.5	1.6	1.4	1.3				1.4	1.4
.8	1.3	1.0	.7				1.0	.9
.5	(140) .5	.5	.5			Quick	(360) .5	(315) .5
.2	.3	.2	.2				.3	.2

											Sales/Receivables				
6	65.4	8	47.1	10	37.4	7	54.6					9	41.3	7	49.0
11	34.5	13	27.5	21	17.6	18	20.3			Sales/Receivables		16	22.8	13	27.9
16	23.5	28	13.2	37	9.8	39	9.4					30	12.2	26	14.2
81	4.5	93	3.9	75	4.9	75	4.8					80	4.6	84	4.3
130	2.8	121	3.0	114	3.2	107	3.4			Cost of Sales/Inventory		120	3.0	123	3.0
195	1.9	176	2.1	170	2.1	160	2.3					161	2.3	163	2.2
7	54.6	16	22.1	20	18.1	18	19.8					18	20.1	17	21.4
24	15.1	29	12.8	35	10.5	28	13.1			Cost of Sales/Payables		32	11.3	30	12.2
49	7.5	45	8.1	53	6.9	45	8.1					51	7.2	50	7.2

3.8	3.9	4.9	5.2			Sales/Working Capital	4.4	4.5
7.4	6.2	7.5	9.2				7.0	7.3
16.8	10.0	12.3	16.4				13.7	15.7
8.9	8.0	6.2	9.7				5.3	5.7
(46) 2.6	(120) 2.8	(74) 2.1	3.6			EBIT/Interest	(326) 2.5	(298) 2.9
.2	1.3	1.0	1.3				1.2	1.4
	5.4	3.1	13.4			Net Profit + Depr., Dep.,	3.4	4.2
	(28) 2.3	(27) 1.2	(11) 5.3			Amort./Cur. Mat. L /T/D	(92) 1.8	(78) 2.2
	.5	.3	.5				1.0	1.2
.1	.1	.2	.3				.2	.1
.4	.3	.4	.5			Fixed/Worth	.4	.4
9.2	.9	.9	1.2				1.2	1.1
.8	.6	.7	.6				.6	.7
1.7	1.6	1.4	2.2			Debt/Worth	1.6	1.6
UND	3.5	3.2	3.6				4.2	4.5
45.0	30.3	21.3	31.0			% Profit Before Taxes/Tangible	34.6	36.9
(42) 14.0	(127) 12.4	(81) 8.8	(22) 11.7			Net Worth	(333) 14.3	(286) 14.1
6.0	2.8	.2	6.4				3.4	3.8
14.3	12.9	8.2	10.3			% Profit Before Taxes/Total	11.7	11.3
6.5	4.9	3.0	5.3			Assets	5.0	5.3
-2.4	.7	.0	.4				.9	1.5
95.0	46.8	32.2	30.1				41.0	45.2
26.1	23.0	16.1	13.1			Sales/Net Fixed Assets	20.9	21.3
14.0	10.1	7.3	9.5				9.4	9.1
3.8	3.0	2.8	2.8				3.1	2.9
2.9	2.5	2.2	2.2			Sales/Total Assets	2.3	2.4
2.1	1.9	1.7	1.8				1.8	1.8
.6	.6	.9	.8				.8	.7
(43) 1.0	(123) 1.3	(74) 1.2	(23) 1.2			% Depr., Dep., Amort./Sales	(317) 1.2	(279) 1.2
2.4	2.3	1.8	1.6				2.0	2.1
4.2	2.4	1.6				% Officers', Directors',	2.2	2.2
(28) 5.6	(96) 4.4	(40) 3.0				Owners' Comp/Sales	(192) 3.8	(165) 3.7
10.9	7.8	3.9					6.6	6.3
48534M	375234M	811708M	1098778M	356176M	1072241M	Net Sales ($)	3057121M	2695162M
16485M	149651M	361878M	464938M	148498M	465860M	Total Assets ($)	1265222M	1080082M

© RMA 2003

M = $ thousand   MM = $ million
See Pages 11 through 18 for Explanation of Ratios and Data

Comparative Historical Data | Current Data Sorted By Sales

			Type of Statement						
9	11	17	Unqualified	1	1	2	1	4	8
38	42	54	Reviewed		8	10	16	14	6
88	85	110	Compiled	19	48	18	17	5	3
44	34	52	Tax Returns	10	30	5	1	5	1
67	57	76	Other	14	25	13	11	3	10
4/1/00-3/31/01 ALL	4/1/01-3/31/02 ALL	4/1/02-3/31/03 ALL		58 (4/1-9/30/02) 0-1MM	1-3MM	3-5MM	251 (10/1/02-3/31/03) 5-10MM	10-25MM	25MM & OVER
246	229	309	**NUMBER OF STATEMENTS**	44	112	48	46	31	28
%	%	%	**ASSETS**	%	%	%	%	%	%
5.9	6.1	6.0	Cash & Equivalents	5.3	7.1	7.4	5.0	5.0	3.5
12.2	13.3	13.8	Trade Receivables (net)	7.4	11.6	15.3	19.9	20.4	13.5
52.0	48.9	50.5	Inventory	62.4	50.1	47.8	47.3	44.5	50.4
1.3	1.3	1.8	All Other Current	1.8	1.7	1.7	2.1	.7	2.7
71.4	69.6	72.2	Total Current	76.8	70.4	72.2	74.2	70.5	70.1
17.3	17.8	17.0	Fixed Assets (net)	14.7	17.4	16.4	16.0	18.3	20.2
1.9	3.1	1.7	Intangibles (net)	1.1	1.6	1.5	2.0	.5	3.5
9.4	9.5	9.2	All Other Non-Current	7.3	10.5	9.9	7.8	10.7	6.2
100.0	100.0	100.0	Total	100.0	100.0	100.0	100.0	100.0	100.0
			LIABILITIES						
8.7	8.0	11.3	Notes Payable-Short Term	11.1	10.1	8.0	13.3	11.1	18.5
3.7	3.8	3.5	Cur. Mat.-L/T/D	2.9	3.6	3.5	5.2	2.6	2.0
15.7	15.6	15.5	Trade Payables	13.2	14.6	15.8	19.4	15.4	15.3
.2	.2	.2	Income Taxes Payable	.0	.5	.1	.2	.3	.1
7.1	8.1	7.0	All Other Current	7.8	7.3	5.8	6.0	7.1	8.2
35.3	35.6	37.4	Total Current	35.0	36.0	33.3	44.1	36.5	44.1
19.1	20.6	19.0	Long Term Debt	29.0	20.6	17.9	13.6	13.7	13.9
.1	.1	.1	Deferred Taxes	.1	.0	.0	.1	.3	.2
4.8	6.3	5.0	All Other Non-Current	8.9	4.8	5.4	1.3	3.5	6.4
40.6	37.4	38.5	Net Worth	27.0	38.6	43.3	40.9	46.0	35.5
100.0	100.0	100.0	Total Liabilities & Net Worth	100.0	100.0	100.0	100.0	100.0	100.0
			INCOME DATA						
100.0	100.0	100.0	Net Sales	100.0	100.0	100.0	100.0	100.0	100.0
35.0	35.3	35.7	Gross Profit	39.8	37.3	36.4	32.9	29.9	32.3
33.1	33.1	33.1	Operating Expenses	38.3	34.7	33.6	30.1	27.9	29.0
1.9	2.2	2.5	Operating Profit	1.5	2.7	2.8	2.8	2.0	3.4
.1	.4	.2	All Other Expenses (net)	.6	.2	.1	.2	-.3	.7
1.8	1.8	2.3	Profit Before Taxes	.9	2.5	2.7	2.6	2.3	2.7
			RATIOS						
3.8	3.7	3.7		6.6	4.0	3.4	2.6	2.8	2.4
2.1	2.2	2.2	Current	2.5	2.5	2.6	1.8	1.7	1.8
1.5	1.4	1.5		1.4	1.5	1.5	1.3	1.5	1.3
1.0	1.0	1.1		.9	1.1	1.2	1.0	1.1	.7
.5	.5	(308) .5	Quick	.4	.5	(47) .6	.5	.7	.5
.3	.2	.2		.2	.2	.3	.2	.4	.2
8 43.2	7 49.8	7 49.8		4 91.2	8 48.6	6 65.0	11 33.2	11 34.6	5 68.4
14 26.7	15 24.5	14 26.5	Sales/Receivables	11 32.1	12 29.3	15 25.0	20 18.4	26 14.0	15 24.5
25 14.6	27 13.4	29 12.4		20 18.4	25 14.6	34 10.8	43 8.4	39 9.4	38 9.7
88 4.2	81 4.5	85 4.3		137 2.7	93 3.9	78 4.7	70 5.2	57 6.4	81 4.5
120 3.0	121 3.0	120 3.0	Cost of Sales/Inventory	179 2.0	121 3.0	114 3.2	108 3.4	83 4.4	104 3.5
178 2.0	163 2.2	171 2.1		262 1.4	172 2.1	167 2.2	161 2.3	120 3.0	149 2.5
17 21.3	18 20.0	17 21.3		0 UND	17 22.0	17 22.0	22 16.3	15 23.8	18 19.8
29 12.8	29 12.7	30 12.3	Cost of Sales/Payables	25 14.3	30 12.3	29 12.7	34 10.6	22 16.4	30 12.1
48 7.7	46 7.9	50 7.4		68 5.4	43 8.5	53 6.9	59 6.2	41 8.8	44 8.3
4.2	4.4	4.2		2.6	4.1	4.4	5.4	5.7	5.7
6.4	6.7	7.0	Sales/Working Capital	4.0	6.5	6.8	9.1	7.0	10.2
11.8	12.9	12.3		10.5	11.2	10.2	14.9	12.4	16.4
5.0	4.8	8.1		7.7	7.8	8.4	15.1	9.5	8.3
(225) 2.1	(213) 2.1	(269) 2.8	EBIT/Interest	(36) 2.4	(93) 2.5	(43) 4.0	(43) 3.2	(27) 4.1	(27) 3.2
.7	1.1	1.1		-.7	1.2	1.4	1.0	1.6	1.1
3.8	4.5	5.5			5.2	12.4	2.6	6.1	13.4
(58) 1.7	(53) 2.0	(73) 2.4	Net Profit + Depr., Dep., Amort./Cur. Mat. L/T/D		(21) 1.9	(10) 2.0	(15) .6	(14) 2.8	(11) 5.3
.7	1.1	.5			.7	.1	.0	1.3	.5
.1	.2	.2		.0	.2	.1	.1	.1	.3
.4	.4	.4	Fixed/Worth	.4	.4	.4	.3	.3	.6
1.1	1.1	1.0		8.1	1.1	.9	.7	.8	1.2
.7	.6	.7		.8	.6	.7	.6	.6	1.2
1.6	1.7	1.5	Debt/Worth	2.8	1.6	1.4	1.7	1.0	2.2
3.8	4.8	3.7		NM	4.2	2.9	2.9	1.9	3.6
27.7	27.6	29.2		46.5	25.3	28.4	31.0	17.6	40.4
(224) 9.9	(203) 10.4	(277) 11.9	% Profit Before Taxes/Tangible Net Worth	(33) 12.3	(98) 11.5	(45) 15.0	(45) 10.9	(30) 9.6	(26) 23.7
.1	1.6	2.2		.4	.9	3.3	1.8	.3	2.5
9.4	9.1	11.5		10.6	10.5	12.4	12.7	9.2	11.3
3.6	3.2	4.7	% Profit Before Taxes/Total Assets	4.9	4.6	4.7	5.4	5.2	4.9
-1.2	.2	.2		-6.0	.2	1.5	.5	.2	.4
49.2	40.5	41.1		97.7	42.1	42.7	40.3	55.4	29.1
21.0	20.4	19.6	Sales/Net Fixed Assets	21.2	23.1	18.6	20.1	17.6	14.3
9.4	8.7	9.2		7.1	9.4	9.6	12.2	7.6	9.1
3.1	3.0	3.1		2.8	3.0	3.2	3.2	3.0	3.3
2.3	2.4	2.4	Sales/Total Assets	2.0	2.5	2.4	2.5	2.4	2.3
1.8	1.8	1.8		1.1	1.9	1.8	1.7	2.2	1.9
.7	.7	.7		.8	.7	.7	.7	.8	.8
(222) 1.1	(200) 1.2	(266) 1.2	% Depr., Dep., Amort./Sales	(31) 1.2	(102) 1.5	(41) 1.2	(40) 1.0	(29) 1.1	(23) 1.2
2.0	2.2	2.0		2.4	2.5	1.6	1.3	1.8	1.7
2.9	2.0	2.3		3.7	2.7	2.0	2.1	1.3	
(132) 4.6	(136) 4.0	(168) 4.0	% Officers', Directors', Owners' Comp/Sales	(21) 5.3	(75) 4.5	(32) 3.8	(22) 3.0	(14) 2.0	
7.0	6.1	4.0		11.6	7.1	6.7	6.2	3.3	
2771100M	2517327M	3762671M	Net Sales ($)	27586M	204026M	188955M	328481M	469173M	2544450M
990644M	1153657M	1607310M	Total Assets ($)	18552M	93100M	86254M	158179M	191739M	1059486M

© RMA 2003

M = $ thousand   MM = $ million
See Pages 11 through 18 for Explanation of Ratios and Data

Current Data Sorted By Assets   Comparative Historical Data

						Type of Statement		
1	5	12	6	2	4	Unqualified		
7	22	37	15	1		Reviewed		
13	25	26	3			Compiled		
7	9	4	4			Tax Returns		
	16	9	4		1	Other		
							4/1/98- 3/31/99 ALL	4/1/99- 3/31/00 ALL

0-500M	500M-2MM	2-10MM	10-50MM	50-100MM	100-250MM			
	40 (4/1-9/30/02)			189 (10/1/02-3/31/03)				
28	77	88	28	4	4	**NUMBER OF STATEMENTS**		
%	%	%	%	%	%	**ASSETS**	%	%
13.8	6.3	5.3	6.2			Cash & Equivalents	D	D
27.2	34.1	33.0	30.7			Trade Receivables (net)	A	A
28.1	32.9	35.7	22.6			Inventory	T	T
2.8	1.9	2.1	7.1			All Other Current	A	A
72.0	75.2	76.1	66.6			Total Current		
19.4	17.1	15.6	20.0			Fixed Assets (net)	N	N
3.1	1.5	.6	1.4			Intangibles (net)	O	O
5.6	6.2	7.7	12.0			All Other Non-Current	T	T
100.0	100.0	100.0	100.0			Total		
						LIABILITIES	A	A
8.0	16.3	18.9	21.9			Notes Payable-Short Term	V	V
3.7	4.7	2.9	2.8			Cur. Mat.-L/T/D	A	A
24.6	21.9	18.5	15.1			Trade Payables	I	I
.5	.1	.1	.1			Income Taxes Payable	L	L
12.4	8.0	6.0	5.7			All Other Current	A	A
49.1	51.0	46.5	45.5			Total Current	B	B
24.2	12.5	9.6	13.0			Long Term Debt	L	L
.1	.1	.4	.3			Deferred Taxes	E	E
25.7	2.2	4.0	1.8			All Other Non-Current		
.8	34.1	39.6	39.3			Net Worth		
100.0	100.0	100.0	100.0			Total Liabilities & Net Worth		
						INCOME DATA		
100.0	100.0	100.0	100.0			Net Sales		
38.0	30.1	27.7	24.0			Gross Profit		
35.9	29.1	25.6	22.4			Operating Expenses		
2.1	1.0	2.2	1.7			Operating Profit		
.6	.5	.4	−.5			All Other Expenses (net)		
1.5	.5	1.7	2.2			Profit Before Taxes		
						RATIOS		
2.4	2.1	2.5	1.8					
1.6	1.7	1.7	1.4			Current		
1.2	1.1	1.3	1.1					
1.6	1.3	1.2	1.2					
1.0	(76) .9	.8	.8			Quick		
.4	.5	.5	.4					

12	30.7	25	14.3	30	12.4	32	11.4				Sales/Receivables
27	13.7	36	10.1	43	8.4	51	7.1				
39	9.4	57	6.3	52	7.0	69	5.3				
0	UND	35	10.3	38	9.5	30	12.3				Cost of Sales/Inventory
32	11.4	48	7.6	57	6.4	50	7.2				
94	3.9	89	4.1	98	3.7	60	6.0				
9	40.2	20	18.3	20	18.3	13	27.3				Cost of Sales/Payables
35	10.6	33	11.0	33	10.9	33	11.2				
55	6.6	48	7.6	43	8.6	45	8.1				

0-500M	500M-2MM	2-10MM	10-50MM				
6.9	6.7	5.2	7.0			Sales/Working Capital	
12.9	12.0	8.8	12.0				
103.1	42.6	19.2	28.8				
(24) 13.0	(74) 5.3	(81) 6.0	(25) 5.7			EBIT/Interest	
2.0	1.5	2.8	2.6				
−1.5	−1.3	1.4	1.1				
	(18) 3.3	(27) 3.4	(13) 5.8			Net Profit + Depr., Dep., Amort./Cur. Mat. L /T/D	
	.8	2.0	1.4				
	−.8	1.3	.1				
.3	.2	.2	.1			Fixed/Worth	
.7	.4	.4	.4				
3.9	.9	.8	.9				
.8	.9	.7	1.0			Debt/Worth	
6.2	1.9	1.7	1.9				
−8.4	5.1	3.3	3.0				
(20) 117.6	(68) 24.2	(84) 28.0	18.8			% Profit Before Taxes/Tangible Net Worth	
51.5	7.4	13.3	9.2				
−35.7	−7.4	3.8	1.6				
18.8	7.6	8.4	6.8			% Profit Before Taxes/Total Assets	
2.0	1.3	3.9	3.1				
−15.1	−5.0	.9	.5				
60.2	48.6	49.1	49.4			Sales/Net Fixed Assets	
35.7	27.1	24.9	17.1				
13.0	13.6	11.3	3.6				
5.1	4.2	3.5	3.2			Sales/Total Assets	
3.6	3.1	2.6	1.9				
2.8	2.2	2.1	.8				
(17) 1.0	(69) .6	(82) .5	(27) .6			% Depr., Dep., Amort./Sales	
1.6	1.2	.9	1.1				
2.2	2.0	1.6	3.3				
(17) 4.2	(41) 2.2	(49) 1.6	(13) .5			% Officers', Directors', Owners' Comp/Sales	
8.5	4.4	3.5	1.5				
13.0	6.7	5.9	2.8				

0-500M	500M-2MM	2-10MM	10-50MM	50-100MM	100-250MM			
31719M	308819M	1107505M	1293199M	431774M	1239409M	Net Sales ($)		
7480M	92986M	409741M	615326M	227097M	639749M	Total Assets ($)		

M = $ thousand   MM = $ million
See Pages 11 through 18 for Explanation of Ratios and Data

Comparative Historical Data | Current Data Sorted By Sales

Type of Statement	4/1/00-3/31/01 ALL	4/1/01-3/31/02 ALL	4/1/02-3/31/03 ALL	0-1MM	1-3MM	3-5MM	5-10MM	10-25MM	25MM & OVER
				40 (4/1-9/30/02)			189 (10/1/02-3/31/03)		
Unqualified			29		1	1	5	7	15
Reviewed			76	1	8	7	29	17	14
Compiled			61	5	13	6	22	13	2
Tax Returns			26	9	8	5	2	2	
Other			37	3	11	6	7	7	3
NUMBER OF STATEMENTS	DATA NOT AVAILABLE	DATA NOT AVAILABLE	229	18	41	25	65	46	34

ASSETS
	%	%	%	%	%	%	%	%	%
Cash & Equivalents			6.7	9.6	10.8	7.5	4.9	6.8	3.1
Trade Receivables (net)			32.1	22.5	31.0	31.7	29.7	37.8	35.4
Inventory			31.8	36.2	26.5	32.1	36.3	30.6	28.6
All Other Current			3.1	3.4	1.6	1.0	3.1	3.3	5.8
Total Current			73.6	71.7	69.8	72.3	74.0	78.6	72.8
Fixed Assets (net)			17.3	19.3	22.0	14.8	16.3	14.9	17.7
Intangibles (net)			1.7	4.4	1.5	1.2	1.2	.4	3.7
All Other Non-Current			7.3	4.6	6.7	11.8	8.4	6.1	5.8
Total			100.0	100.0	100.0	100.0	100.0	100.0	100.0

LIABILITIES
Notes Payable-Short Term			16.7	8.1	10.9	17.3	16.8	22.5	19.8
Cur. Mat.-L/T/D			3.7	3.9	6.1	2.8	3.5	2.3	3.5
Trade Payables			19.7	22.2	20.0	23.3	16.8	21.4	19.0
Income Taxes Payable			.2	.0	.4	.1	.1	.1	.1
All Other Current			7.5	9.0	7.2	11.2	6.6	7.1	6.2
Total Current			47.7	43.3	44.7	54.7	43.8	53.4	48.6
Long Term Debt			13.4	26.3	20.5	7.4	11.6	8.6	12.5
Deferred Taxes			.3	.0	.2	.0	.5	.2	.3
All Other Non-Current			5.8	11.5	4.2	18.7	3.3	4.0	2.3
Net Worth			32.8	18.9	30.4	19.2	40.8	33.7	36.4
Total Liabilities & Net Worth			100.0	100.0	100.0	100.0	100.0	100.0	100.0

INCOME DATA
Net Sales			100.0	100.0	100.0	100.0	100.0	100.0	100.0
Gross Profit			29.3	41.6	31.8	33.4	27.0	27.0	23.9
Operating Expenses			27.5	40.0	30.2	33.1	25.7	24.2	21.3
Operating Profit			1.8	1.5	1.6	.3	1.3	2.9	2.6
All Other Expenses (net)			.4	–.3	.8	.4	.1	.3	.7
Profit Before Taxes			1.4	1.9	.8	–.1	1.2	2.5	1.9

RATIOS
Current			2.3 / 1.6 / 1.2	2.7 / 1.6 / 1.3	2.7 / 1.8 / 1.1	2.2 / 1.6 / 1.0	2.4 / 1.8 / 1.3	2.0 / 1.5 / 1.2	2.1 / 1.4 / 1.2
Quick			(228) 1.3 / .8 / .5	1.4 / .6 / .3	1.6 / .9 / .6	(24) 1.3 / .9 / .5	1.3 / .8 / .5	1.3 / .8 / .5	1.2 / .8 / .5
Sales/Receivables	28 13.1 / 39 9.3 / 54 6.8			14 26.0 / 31 11.9 / 50 7.3	26 14.2 / 34 10.7 / 58 6.3	26 13.8 / 40 9.2 / 62 5.9	28 13.3 / 36 10.0 / 50 7.3	31 11.6 / 44 8.3 / 53 6.9	31 11.9 / 51 7.1 / 61 6.0
Cost of Sales/Inventory	33 11.2 / 51 7.1 / 88 4.1			21 17.4 / 82 4.4 / 140 2.6	19 18.7 / 50 7.3 / 117 3.1	36 10.0 / 51 7.1 / 96 3.8	38 9.7 / 58 6.3 / 100 3.7	31 11.8 / 48 7.6 / 78 4.7	34 10.7 / 49 7.4 / 58 6.3
Cost of Sales/Payables	19 19.6 / 33 11.0 / 46 8.0			11 32.3 / 40 9.1 / 68 5.4	14 25.2 / 36 10.2 / 57 6.4	24 14.9 / 41 9.0 / 66 5.5	18 20.5 / 29 12.6 / 38 9.6	20 18.3 / 34 10.7 / 49 7.5	19 19.7 / 34 10.6 / 41 9.0
Sales/Working Capital	6.1 / 11.2 / 28.5			4.7 / 11.4 / 65.9	4.8 / 10.7 / 56.0	7.2 / 13.0 / NM	5.0 / 9.2 / 17.7	7.3 / 11.0 / 29.2	7.6 / 11.9 / 18.7
EBIT/Interest	(212) 5.7 / 2.3 / .9			(15) 4.4 / .0 / –1.9	(39) 8.8 / 1.8 / .2	(24) 4.0 / .6 / –2.9	(57) 4.3 / 2.6 / 1.2	(44) 8.7 / 3.2 / 1.8	(33) 5.7 / 2.6 / 1.1
Net Profit + Depr., Dep., Amort./Cur. Mat. L/T/D	(65) 3.5 / 1.8 / .6						(23) 3.4 / 1.4 / .7	(13) 5.8 / 2.4 / 1.9	(18) 3.6 / 1.6 / .5
Fixed/Worth	.2 / .4 / 1.0			.2 / 1.3 / NM	.3 / .7 / 2.5	.2 / .4 / .6	.2 / .4 / .7	.1 / .4 / 1.0	.2 / .4 / .9
Debt/Worth	.9 / 1.9 / 4.9			1.2 / 6.2 / –10.7	.5 / 2.2 / 33.6	.7 / 1.5 / 6.4	.9 / 1.4 / 3.0	1.0 / 2.4 / 4.2	1.1 / 2.1 / 3.5
% Profit Before Taxes/Tangible Net Worth	(207) 29.5 / 11.2 / 1.5			(13) 81.4 / –6.0 / –51.9	(34) 49.8 / 8.4 / –3.9	(22) 23.0 / 2.4 / –13.4	(62) 18.3 / 7.5 / 2.0	(43) 45.3 / 17.4 / 5.4	(33) 28.8 / 11.2 / 2.3
% Profit Before Taxes/Total Assets	8.4 / 2.8 / –.2			13.8 / –2.8 / –10.0	13.0 / 1.3 / –2.8	4.8 / –.9 / –8.7	7.0 / 2.8 / .5	9.2 / 5.0 / 1.8	6.2 / 4.2 / .3
Sales/Net Fixed Assets	49.1 / 25.2 / 11.1			57.3 / 40.3 / 9.4	35.7 / 17.5 / 9.6	47.6 / 21.8 / 16.2	50.3 / 25.2 / 12.5	49.0 / 29.5 / 12.0	58.7 / 27.1 / 10.6
Sales/Total Assets	3.8 / 2.8 / 2.0			3.6 / 3.0 / 1.3	3.9 / 2.4 / 1.9	4.3 / 3.3 / 2.2	3.8 / 2.9 / 2.0	4.1 / 2.7 / 2.2	3.4 / 3.0 / 1.9
% Depr., Dep., Amort./Sales	(203) .6 / 1.1 / 1.9			(12) .9 / 1.5 / 2.2	(33) 1.0 / 1.7 / 2.9	(23) .5 / 1.3 / 1.6	(63) .6 / 1.0 / 1.7	(38) .5 / .9 / 1.6	.6 / .9 / 1.8
% Officers', Directors', Owners' Comp/Sales	(122) 1.8 / 3.7 / 7.3			(10) 6.5 / 10.3 / 15.3	(24) 2.7 / 5.2 / 9.7	(13) 2.4 / 5.8 / 9.7	(36) 1.6 / 2.9 / 5.8	(24) .8 / 3.3 / 9.4	(15) .8 / 1.5 / 3.0
Net Sales ($)	4412425M			9923M	85182M	94262M	458371M	696998M	3067689M
Total Assets ($)	1992379M			4909M	35948M	41567M	244213M	262751M	1402991M

M = $ thousand   MM = $ million
See Pages 11 through 18 for Explanation of Ratios and Data

Current Data Sorted By Assets　　　　　　　　　　　　　　　　**Comparative Historical Data**

0-500M	500M-2MM	2-10MM	10-50MM	50-100MM	100-250MM	Type of Statement	4/1/98-3/31/99 ALL	4/1/99-3/31/00 ALL
	6	5	11		1	Unqualified	13	13
3	15	19	5			Reviewed	51	46
22	49	12	2		1	Compiled	91	84
30	20	3		1		Tax Returns	46	40
10	23	13	6			Other	74	55
	50 (4/1-9/30/02)		207 (10/1/02-3/31/03)					
65	113	52	24	1	2	**NUMBER OF STATEMENTS**	275	238
%	%	%	%	%	%	**ASSETS**	%	%
9.9	8.6	8.0	7.2			Cash & Equivalents	9.6	9.6
10.9	13.7	15.1	17.9			Trade Receivables (net)	12.6	12.2
34.2	35.5	33.7	27.3			Inventory	34.7	32.3
1.2	3.1	3.2	5.0			All Other Current	1.1	1.4
56.1	60.9	60.0	57.3			Total Current	58.0	55.6
36.7	32.0	32.2	34.1			Fixed Assets (net)	32.6	35.9
1.9	2.7	.9	2.2			Intangibles (net)	2.4	2.5
5.2	4.4	6.9	6.3			All Other Non-Current	7.0	6.0
100.0	100.0	100.0	100.0			Total	100.0	100.0
						LIABILITIES		
17.7	13.4	11.3	12.7			Notes Payable-Short Term	12.4	13.3
8.7	4.7	2.8	4.6			Cur. Mat.-L/T/D	5.2	4.4
12.7	15.5	13.5	13.8			Trade Payables	13.0	14.2
.1	.1	.9	1.3			Income Taxes Payable	.4	.4
7.9	6.9	7.5	6.9			All Other Current	8.3	8.4
47.0	40.6	36.0	39.3			Total Current	39.2	40.8
25.6	20.0	15.1	17.2			Long Term Debt	19.4	23.1
.0	.5	.4	.7			Deferred Taxes	.5	.7
12.9	5.6	3.4	4.7			All Other Non-Current	7.5	5.8
14.4	33.3	45.2	38.1			Net Worth	33.4	29.6
100.0	100.0	100.0	100.0			Total Liabilities & Net Worth	100.0	100.0
						INCOME DATA		
100.0	100.0	100.0	100.0			Net Sales	100.0	100.0
47.2	36.5	38.0	35.6			Gross Profit	40.9	42.0
45.5	34.2	34.7	31.3			Operating Expenses	36.1	37.4
1.8	2.3	3.3	4.3			Operating Profit	4.8	4.6
1.0	1.0	.6	-.3			All Other Expenses (net)	1.4	1.2
.7	1.3	2.7	4.7			Profit Before Taxes	3.4	3.4
						RATIOS		
3.2	2.7	2.8	2.2				2.6	2.5
1.6	1.5	1.8	1.5			Current	1.5	1.5
.8	1.1	1.2	1.2				1.1	1.0
1.4	1.4	1.2	1.0				1.3	1.2
(63) .5	(112) .5	.8	.7			Quick	(273) .5	(237) .5
.1	.1	.2	.3				.2	.2
0 UND	4 94.1	5 67.0	7 51.0				3 123.0	2 161.5
3 105.3	11 32.6	13 28.3	24 15.2			Sales/Receivables	11 32.9	9 38.7
13 27.7	29 12.6	37 9.9	71 5.1				28 13.0	24 15.1
14 26.1	40 9.1	26 14.0	40 9.1				34 10.7	27 13.5
43 8.6	69 5.3	74 4.9	79 4.6			Cost of Sales/Inventory	67 5.5	57 6.4
102 3.6	120 3.0	153 2.4	153 2.4				128 2.9	126 2.9
0 UND	13 27.7	13 27.2	19 19.0				8 48.5	6 56.2
9 40.0	27 13.5	26 14.2	34 10.7			Cost of Sales/Payables	20 18.6	25 14.9
31 11.6	47 7.7	41 8.9	51 7.2				43 8.5	47 7.8
8.0	7.1	5.2	6.1				6.9	8.5
23.7	13.5	11.8	9.7			Sales/Working Capital	14.6	17.0
-45.1	117.7	32.3	23.2				97.1	-340.4
6.9	5.3	12.2	7.4				6.3	5.7
(60) 2.3	(104) 2.2	(51) 4.8	(23) 2.1			EBIT/Interest	(254) 3.1	(218) 2.6
-.5	.4	1.5	1.2				1.4	1.1
	2.9	6.0					4.8	5.0
	(23) 1.9	(19) 2.7				Net Profit + Depr., Dep., Amort./Cur. Mat. L /T/D	(65) 2.5	(56) 2.0
	.5	1.1					1.2	1.4
.4	.4	.3	.3				.4	.4
1.7	1.0	.6	1.0			Fixed/Worth	.9	1.1
33.3	4.5	1.3	2.3				2.2	3.1
.8	.8	.6	.9				.7	.8
3.9	1.9	1.3	1.7			Debt/Worth	1.7	2.0
-63.9	9.9	2.7	4.6				5.7	6.3
75.0	28.3	31.9	29.0				45.8	40.4
(48) 22.9	(93) 10.8	(50) 10.3	16.7			% Profit Before Taxes/Tangible Net Worth	(237) 19.2	(203) 17.9
.6	1.0	3.9	2.0				7.0	5.0
13.7	9.5	9.2	9.4				15.8	15.0
5.1	3.5	5.1	4.4			% Profit Before Taxes/Total Assets	6.3	5.9
-8.9	-1.5	1.1	1.0				1.7	.6
29.5	23.5	18.3	13.1				24.0	21.8
13.6	10.1	10.0	5.3			Sales/Net Fixed Assets	10.0	9.9
6.1	4.9	4.0	3.6				5.2	4.2
6.0	3.7	3.7	2.4				4.0	4.1
4.3	2.6	2.3	1.8			Sales/Total Assets	2.6	2.8
2.8	1.7	1.5	1.2				1.7	1.8
1.4	1.0	1.2	1.5				1.0	1.2
(55) 2.2	(105) 2.0	(48) 1.7	(23) 2.0			% Depr., Dep., Amort./Sales	(254) 1.9	(208) 2.2
4.2	3.3	2.9	3.3				3.4	3.9
4.0	2.4	1.6					2.5	2.7
(39) 5.9	(64) 3.5	(25) 2.9				% Officers', Directors', Owners' Comp/Sales	(148) 4.2	(125) 4.7
8.4	5.7	5.5					7.3	7.6
72393M	358982M	597047M	995888M	480850M	3486560M	Net Sales ($)	2331482M	1592131M
17274M	124983M	226208M	526165M	61914M	341646M	Total Assets ($)	970423M	581561M

© RMA 2003

M = $ thousand　　MM = $ million
See Pages 11 through 18 for Explanation of Ratios and Data

Comparative Historical Data				Current Data Sorted By Sales					
			Type of Statement						
5	9	23	Unqualified		3	2	2	4	12
45	38	42	Reviewed	3	8	8	10	9	4
81	61	86	Compiled	16	33	17	10	8	2
42	31	54	Tax Returns	17	23	7	6		1
51	59	52	Other	9	19	7	3	10	4
4/1/00-3/31/01 ALL	4/1/01-3/31/02 ALL	4/1/02-3/31/03 ALL		50 (4/1-9/30/02) 0-1MM	207 (10/1/02-3/31/03) 1-3MM	3-5MM	5-10MM	10-25MM	25MM & OVER
224	198	257	**NUMBER OF STATEMENTS**	45	86	41	31	31	23
%	%	%	**ASSETS**	%	%	%	%	%	%
9.0	8.1	8.7	Cash & Equivalents	9.0	7.8	9.7	9.7	9.0	8.2
12.3	13.1	13.9	Trade Receivables (net)	8.1	12.3	13.0	18.0	19.8	19.6
38.5	36.2	33.8	Inventory	34.0	35.3	36.3	33.5	32.0	26.1
2.0	2.2	2.8	All Other Current	.2	3.5	2.5	3.6	2.6	4.8
61.7	59.7	59.2	Total Current	51.3	58.9	61.5	64.8	63.4	58.7
29.8	32.6	33.4	Fixed Assets (net)	40.9	34.5	30.1	25.9	30.0	35.4
2.5	2.1	2.1	Intangibles (net)	2.6	1.7	3.7	.5	1.5	2.3
6.0	5.6	5.3	All Other Non-Current	5.2	4.9	4.7	8.8	5.0	3.6
100.0	100.0	100.0	Total	100.0	100.0	100.0	100.0	100.0	100.0
			LIABILITIES						
13.0	14.1	14.0	Notes Payable-Short Term	18.5	16.3	7.9	13.5	12.4	10.3
4.2	4.6	5.3	Cur. Mat.-L/T/D	9.5	5.8	3.3	2.5	3.7	4.2
16.6	13.8	14.1	Trade Payables	10.7	13.0	17.6	13.5	17.3	14.9
.2	.5	.4	Income Taxes Payable	.1	.1	.2	1.9	.5	.4
9.5	9.2	7.2	All Other Current	8.7	4.8	10.0	8.4	6.3	8.2
43.6	42.2	41.0	Total Current	47.5	39.9	39.1	39.7	40.2	38.1
20.3	23.0	21.5	Long Term Debt	24.1	24.7	19.7	12.6	13.2	31.2
.5	.7	.4	Deferred Taxes	.0	.5	.2	.4	.4	.9
4.6	5.3	6.8	All Other Non-Current	14.7	7.8	5.3	1.2	2.7	3.7
31.0	28.7	30.3	Net Worth	13.6	27.1	35.7	46.0	43.5	26.2
100.0	100.0	100.0	Total Liabilities & Net Worth	100.0	100.0	100.0	100.0	100.0	100.0
			INCOME DATA						
100.0	100.0	100.0	Net Sales	100.0	100.0	100.0	100.0	100.0	100.0
39.1	41.7	39.3	Gross Profit	48.6	40.9	37.0	34.1	32.0	36.9
35.4	38.0	36.7	Operating Expenses	44.9	39.4	34.6	31.0	28.8	32.7
3.7	3.8	2.6	Operating Profit	3.7	1.4	2.4	3.1	3.2	4.1
.7	1.3	.8	All Other Expenses (net)	1.7	1.0	.6	.1	.6	−.1
3.0	2.4	1.8	Profit Before Taxes	2.0	.4	1.8	3.0	2.6	4.3
			RATIOS						
2.3	2.8	2.8	Current	2.4	4.0	2.7	3.1	2.7	2.7
1.6	1.5	1.6		1.5	1.8	1.6	1.8	1.7	1.6
1.0	1.0	1.1		.7	1.0	1.3	1.2	1.1	1.2
1.0	1.2	1.4	Quick	.9	1.5	1.1	1.7	1.4	1.1
(222) .4	(197) .4	(254) .6		(44) .3	(84) .5	.6	.7	.8	.7
.2	.2	.2		.1	.1	.2	.3	.3	.4
3 131.3	4 102.9	3 138.8	Sales/Receivables	0 UND	3 111.2	4 96.3	3 112.2	5 67.1	4 90.5
10 35.1	11 34.6	9 39.5		4 103.2	9 40.0	9 39.9	18 20.5	27 13.7	12 29.9
25 14.5	31 11.8	29 12.7		17 21.2	24 15.1	20 18.0	42 8.6	37 9.9	29 12.7
38 9.6	36 10.2	28 13.1	Cost of Sales/Inventory	22 16.5	33 10.9	41 9.0	26 14.3	20 18.4	11 34.2
79 4.6	76 4.8	68 5.4		65 5.6	76 4.8	65 5.6	53 6.9	68 5.4	55 6.6
133 2.7	136 2.7	125 2.9		194 1.9	135 2.7	115 3.2	102 3.6	107 3.4	81 4.5
11 32.9	10 36.5	9 40.4	Cost of Sales/Payables	0 UND	8 44.0	16 22.2	7 54.1	18 20.6	11 33.7
26 14.1	24 15.0	23 15.9		17 21.7	20 17.9	27 13.4	18 20.1	28 13.1	32 11.4
51 7.1	47 7.8	42 8.6		37 9.9	48 7.6	44 8.3	35 10.3	45 8.1	41 9.0
7.4	6.8	7.0	Sales/Working Capital	6.0	6.9	7.7	5.4	9.1	6.9
14.1	13.8	13.9		28.4	12.3	11.7	13.9	15.4	12.5
NM	NM	96.2		−27.1	−157.8	38.5	47.0	29.7	48.8
6.0	5.8	6.7	EBIT/Interest	6.3	4.5	6.1	14.0	10.8	11.3
(211) 2.5	(191) 2.1	(241) 2.6		(42) 1.8	(80) 2.1	(37) 2.0	(30) 6.3	(29) 4.1	4.2
1.3	1.1	.8		−.9	.4	.0	1.2	1.9	1.5
4.1	4.6	5.0	Net Profit + Depr., Dep., Amort./Cur. Mat. L/T/D		5.4	4.2		5.2	
(51) 2.2	(44) 2.1	(54) 2.1			(10) 2.1	(12) 2.6		(15) 1.5	
.9	.9	1.0			.4	.7		.9	
.3	.4	.4	Fixed/Worth	.4	.5	.3	.1	.4	.5
.8	1.0	.9		1.4	1.3	.9	.5	.6	1.0
2.7	3.3	4.3		−35.2	12.9	2.7	1.3	1.2	3.0
.7	.9	.8	Debt/Worth	.9	.8	.7	.6	.6	.9
2.0	2.1	1.8		3.9	2.8	2.4	1.2	1.3	1.6
9.7	10.3	8.7		−22.9	39.2	6.7	2.6	4.0	3.9
36.6	32.6	35.5	% Profit Before Taxes/Tangible Net Worth	75.0	33.0	19.1	33.8	41.4	45.7
(189) 16.7	(165) 16.9	(217) 12.6		(31) 19.8	(69) 13.8	(35) 7.2	(30) 11.2	(30) 11.8	(22) 18.9
5.1	2.6	2.2		.0	.4	.3	2.6	7.3	5.8
12.8	11.0	10.8	% Profit Before Taxes/Total Assets	18.1	9.9	7.1	16.3	8.7	12.9
5.0	4.2	4.3		3.3	4.1	3.2	4.8	4.4	8.7
1.1	.4	−.7		−11.2	−2.8	−.8	.9	2.5	1.7
31.9	22.1	22.3	Sales/Net Fixed Assets	22.4	25.2	23.3	24.8	21.1	18.7
12.0	10.2	10.6		6.8	9.8	12.5	13.5	10.6	11.1
5.7	4.8	4.7		2.9	5.0	5.9	5.1	5.9	3.7
3.8	3.7	4.4	Sales/Total Assets	4.9	4.3	4.0	4.0	4.8	6.0
2.7	2.5	2.7		2.6	2.7	2.5	2.9	2.7	2.6
1.9	1.7	1.7		1.2	1.7	1.9	1.9	1.7	1.9
.9	1.1	1.2	% Depr., Dep., Amort./Sales	1.5	1.2	1.2	1.2	.8	1.0
(201) 1.8	(178) 1.9	(233) 2.0		(38) 2.5	(79) 2.0	(40) 2.0	(27) 1.9	(29) 1.3	(20) 1.7
3.0	3.5	3.3		5.7	3.9	3.0	2.7	3.0	2.9
2.9	2.4	2.5	% Officers', Directors', Owners' Comp/Sales	4.7	2.9	2.0	2.2	1.1	
(131) 4.3	(109) 3.9	(133) 4.3		(23) 5.9	(50) 4.4	(24) 3.4	(20) 3.0	(13) 1.7	
6.6	6.6	6.4		8.4	6.4	6.1	5.9	3.9	
1244198M	3090997M	5991720M	Net Sales ($)	26593M	164423M	155994M	211174M	467602M	4965934M
558422M	988547M	1298190M	Total Assets ($)	14207M	71670M	69579M	114850M	202133M	825751M

© RMA 2003

M = $ thousand   MM = $ million

See Pages 11 through 18 for Explanation of Ratios and Data

Current Data Sorted By Assets   Comparative Historical Data

Type of Statement	0-500M	500M-2MM	2-10MM	10-50MM	50-100MM	100-250MM	4/1/98-3/31/99 ALL	4/1/99-3/31/00 ALL
Unqualified	2	3	18	42	19	19	137	131
Reviewed	2	13	65	21	5	2	155	140
Compiled	37	63	64	17	1		339	255
Tax Returns	74	65	15	3		1	126	110
Other	20	54	71	37	10	15	292	300
		164 (4/1-9/30/02)			594 (10/1/02-3/31/03)			
NUMBER OF STATEMENTS	135	198	233	120	35	37	1049	936
ASSETS	%	%	%	%	%	%	%	%
Cash & Equivalents	12.7	11.7	14.2	12.5	7.1	9.6	11.5	11.0
Trade Receivables (net)	4.3	4.9	5.0	4.5	5.3	6.9	4.9	4.7
Inventory	44.4	31.8	22.6	22.5	18.6	19.6	26.9	27.9
All Other Current	2.6	3.4	2.9	3.5	1.9	2.6	2.1	2.6
Total Current	64.0	51.8	44.8	43.1	32.9	38.7	45.4	46.2
Fixed Assets (net)	25.5	36.8	41.0	44.1	54.8	48.5	41.5	40.9
Intangibles (net)	4.8	2.5	4.2	3.9	4.4	4.4	4.1	5.3
All Other Non-Current	5.8	8.9	10.0	8.9	7.8	8.4	9.0	7.6
Total	100.0	100.0	100.0	100.0	100.0	100.0	100.0	100.0
LIABILITIES								
Notes Payable-Short Term	4.9	4.4	4.6	3.4	1.1	1.1	4.4	4.5
Cur. Mat.-L/T/D	3.5	4.6	5.1	5.4	4.7	4.8	4.4	4.6
Trade Payables	23.4	21.6	16.9	17.4	16.4	15.1	17.3	17.6
Income Taxes Payable	.3	.2	.3	.2	.4	.2	.2	.2
All Other Current	15.2	11.0	9.3	9.7	9.9	17.0	9.5	10.1
Total Current	47.3	41.9	36.2	36.1	32.4	38.3	35.9	37.1
Long Term Debt	30.3	31.7	28.0	25.4	28.5	27.7	28.5	29.5
Deferred Taxes	.0	.1	.1	.7	1.5	.8	.4	.4
All Other Non-Current	14.6	7.4	3.8	4.1	5.0	4.3	4.7	3.9
Net Worth	7.8	19.0	31.9	33.8	32.6	29.0	30.5	29.2
Total Liabilities & Net Worth	100.0	100.0	100.0	100.0	100.0	100.0	100.0	100.0
INCOME DATA								
Net Sales	100.0	100.0	100.0	100.0	100.0	100.0	100.0	100.0
Gross Profit	24.1	23.3	26.0	25.8	26.8	26.1	23.7	24.7
Operating Expenses	23.1	22.1	24.8	23.8	24.8	24.2	22.5	23.2
Operating Profit	1.0	1.1	1.1	2.0	2.0	1.9	1.3	1.4
All Other Expenses (net)	−.2	−.1	−.1	−.1	.2	.1	−.3	−.2
Profit Before Taxes	1.1	1.2	1.3	2.1	1.8	1.8	1.5	1.7
RATIOS								
Current	3.5	2.4	2.0	1.7	1.3	1.4	2.1	1.9
	1.8	1.4	1.3	1.2	1.0	1.1	1.3	1.2
	.9	.8	.9	.9	.7	.9	.9	.9
Quick	1.0	.9	.9	.8	.5	.6	.9	.8
	(129) .4	(196) .4	(229) .5	.4	.3	.3	(1036) .4	(921) .4
	.1	.1	.2	.2	.2	.3	.2	.2
Sales/Receivables	0 UND	0 999.8	0 895.1	1 257.0	2 176.1	3 113.7	0 755.8	0 827.2
	0 999.8	1 383.0	1 245.8	3 139.8	4 97.6	4 82.7	2 205.7	2 208.5
	1 262.4	3 113.9	4 93.6	5 77.1	6 60.0	6 62.2	4 85.3	4 89.4
Cost of Sales/Inventory	15 23.7	15 23.8	15 23.8	17 22.0	15 23.6	19 18.9	15 24.7	16 23.4
	24 14.9	25 14.9	21 17.3	22 16.6	23 15.6	23 15.6	21 17.6	22 16.4
	40 9.2	32 11.3	29 12.8	30 12.3	30 12.3	33 11.1	29 12.5	31 11.7
Cost of Sales/Payables	3 122.6	6 59.6	9 38.6	11 32.1	14 25.2	16 23.5	7 50.6	8 45.1
	10 37.1	12 30.0	15 24.5	17 21.8	20 18.5	19 18.7	13 27.2	15 25.1
	19 19.1	20 18.6	21 17.3	24 15.1	26 14.3	24 15.0	20 18.0	22 16.3
Sales/Working Capital	16.0	16.8	19.7	23.0	42.6	33.2	21.0	21.3
	32.3	46.6	56.9	75.3	−384.4	86.4	62.5	69.6
	−197.7	−99.8	−98.0	−96.1	−27.5	−216.8	−100.3	−96.8
EBIT/Interest	7.7	5.4	6.4	7.6	8.2	6.2	6.4	6.0
	(96) 3.2	(169) 2.6	(214) 2.9	(113) 4.1	2.5	(35) 2.5	(940) 2.8	(851) 2.7
	.3	1.1	1.1	1.6	1.6	1.3	1.2	1.2
Net Profit + Depr., Dep., Amort./Cur. Mat. L./T/D		2.2	5.7	5.5	6.1	31.4	4.6	4.4
	(22) 1.4	(54) 1.9	(51) 2.3	(20) 3.0	(10) 2.0		(276) 2.4	(231) 2.3
	.9	1.3	1.6	2.2	1.0		1.3	1.4
Fixed/Worth	.2	.6	.7	.9	1.4	1.1	.6	.7
	1.3	2.2	1.4	1.6	2.2	1.5	1.6	1.8
	−1.5	−18.8	4.5	4.3	4.0	3.9	5.1	6.7
Debt/Worth	.9	1.1	1.0	1.2	1.3	1.1	.9	1.1
	5.2	4.2	2.3	2.4	2.6	2.5	2.6	3.0
	−5.5	−46.9	8.3	7.1	6.5	5.3	9.6	13.2
% Profit Before Taxes/Tangible Net Worth	76.7	69.7	45.0	47.4	24.3	24.2	47.6	49.4
	(90) 43.6	(145) 22.0	(196) 18.3	(110) 23.9	(32) 15.2	(33) 16.4	(876) 20.6	(768) 23.0
	11.8	7.2	3.5	11.3	8.2	6.7	6.3	7.6
% Profit Before Taxes/Total Assets	19.5	12.7	12.8	11.9	8.5	9.5	14.0	13.1
	5.8	5.8	5.2	7.7	4.0	5.3	5.9	6.0
	−3.5	1.0	.5	2.2	1.2	1.3	1.0	1.2
Sales/Net Fixed Assets	162.9	41.7	24.2	19.5	8.7	8.9	32.9	30.1
	42.1	19.2	12.9	10.6	7.1	7.8	13.7	13.4
	17.2	9.0	7.3	6.3	5.7	5.1	6.5	6.4
Sales/Total Assets	11.9	8.5	6.3	5.8	4.9	4.5	7.3	7.2
	7.6	6.2	4.8	4.6	3.9	3.4	5.1	5.0
	5.0	3.7	3.3	3.4	3.1	2.8	3.4	3.3
% Depr., Dep., Amort./Sales	.4	.6	.8	1.0	1.5	1.2	.7	.8
	(103) .8	(185) 1.0	(221) 1.4	(117) 1.4	(32) 1.8	(20) 1.6	(966) 1.2	(851) 1.2
	1.6	1.6	1.9	1.8	2.2	2.0	1.9	2.0
% Officers', Directors', Owners' Comp/Sales	1.3	.5	.5	.3			.6	.8
	(73) 2.2	(98) 1.5	(85) .8	(26) .8			(392) 1.5	(341) 1.5
	3.8	2.5	1.9	1.9			3.2	3.2
Net Sales ($)	325743M	1392728M	5610768M	12454366M	9559666M	22484935M	51738156M	57798848M
Total Assets ($)	37410M	214375M	1116253M	2668087M	2448698M	5986933M	12307524M	13173452M

© RMA 2003

M = $ thousand   MM = $ million

See Pages 11 through 18 for Explanation of Ratios and Data

Comparative Historical Data   Current Data Sorted By Sales

			Type of Statement						
101	91	103	Unqualified		2	3	1	4	93
130	122	108	Reviewed	1	3	4	13	38	49
256	251	182	Compiled	10	25	25	40	44	38
141	138	158	Tax Returns	19	47	39	25	19	9
253	274	207	Other	8	23	13	31	44	88
4/1/00-3/31/01 ALL	4/1/01-3/31/02 ALL	4/1/02-3/31/03 ALL		0-1MM	164 (4/1-9/30/02) 1-3MM	3-5MM	5-10MM	594 (10/1/02-3/31/03) 10-25MM	25MM & OVER
881	876	758	NUMBER OF STATEMENTS	38	100	84	110	149	277
%	%	%	ASSETS	%	%	%	%	%	%
11.9	11.6	12.4	Cash & Equivalents	9.6	10.4	12.5	12.1	15.2	12.2
4.8	4.8	4.9	Trade Receivables (net)	2.2	4.4	3.8	7.2	4.4	5.1
26.6	25.5	28.6	Inventory	35.1	35.0	33.2	30.4	27.7	23.7
2.5	2.4	3.0	All Other Current	3.3	2.2	2.2	3.2	4.1	2.9
45.9	44.3	48.9	Total Current	50.2	52.0	51.7	52.9	51.4	43.8
41.1	42.1	38.6	Fixed Assets (net)	34.4	37.2	34.4	36.4	35.7	43.5
4.8	5.1	3.8	Intangibles (net)	4.3	4.7	3.0	3.7	3.7	3.9
8.2	8.4	8.6	All Other Non-Current	11.1	6.1	10.8	7.0	9.2	8.8
100.0	100.0	100.0	Total	100.0	100.0	100.0	100.0	100.0	100.0
			LIABILITIES						
5.1	4.1	4.1	Notes Payable-Short Term	9.5	3.9	4.1	5.7	4.6	2.4
4.2	4.5	4.7	Cur. Mat.-L/T/D	2.6	2.9	4.4	5.1	5.1	5.4
18.2	17.3	19.2	Trade Payables	9.6	17.5	22.4	21.9	19.7	18.9
.2	.1	.3	Income Taxes Payable	.6	.1	.3	.2	.2	.3
10.6	9.8	11.3	All Other Current	20.8	10.5	13.8	9.1	10.9	10.5
38.3	35.8	39.6	Total Current	43.0	35.0	45.0	42.0	40.5	37.6
31.5	32.2	29.0	Long Term Debt	51.8	36.5	24.4	27.2	28.9	25.2
.3	.3	.3	Deferred Taxes	.0	.0	.2	.1	.1	.6
4.7	6.3	6.8	All Other Non-Current	11.3	11.9	11.5	6.2	5.2	4.0
25.1	25.4	24.4	Net Worth	−6.1	16.6	18.9	24.5	25.2	32.6
100.0	100.0	100.0	Total Liabilities & Net Worth	100.0	100.0	100.0	100.0	100.0	100.0
			INCOME DATA						
100.0	100.0	100.0	Net Sales	100.0	100.0	100.0	100.0	100.0	100.0
23.4	23.5	24.9	Gross Profit	31.0	23.1	25.8	22.7	25.1	25.4
22.9	22.1	23.6	Operating Expenses	28.5	22.2	23.8	22.1	24.2	23.7
.4	1.3	1.3	Operating Profit	2.5	.9	2.0	.6	.9	1.6
−.9	−.1	−.1	All Other Expenses (net)	2.3	−.2	−.2	−.1	−.5	−.1
1.3	1.4	1.4	Profit Before Taxes	.3	1.1	2.2	.7	1.3	1.8
			RATIOS						
2.0	2.0	2.2		6.0	3.6	2.7	2.2	2.1	1.6
1.3	1.3	1.3	Current	1.8	1.9	1.5	1.4	1.3	1.2
.9	.9	.9		1.0	.9	.7	.8	.9	.9
.9	.9	.8		1.1	1.1	1.0	.9	1.0	.7
(874) .4	(866) .4	(746) .4	Quick	(36) .4	(97) .4	(82) .4	(109) .4	(147) .5	(275) .4
.2	.2	.2		.0	.1	.1	.1	.2	.2
0 781.9	0 999.8	0 999.8		0 UND	0 UND	0 999.8	0 999.8	0 999.8	1 329.9
2 211.7	2 205.1	2 237.9	Sales/Receivables	0 UND	1 699.9	1 479.4	1 307.9	1 259.8	3 141.7
4 90.2	4 81.6	4 90.8		2 177.7	3 108.5	2 188.2	4 102.1	3 105.7	5 74.3
14 26.6	13 27.7	16 23.2		30 12.2	15 24.4	14 25.7	14 25.6	15 23.9	16 22.5
21 17.4	20 18.1	23 16.0	Cost of Sales/Inventory	44 8.3	27 13.7	24 15.1	22 16.8	22 16.7	22 16.6
30 12.4	29 12.5	32 11.3		84 4.3	41 9.0	33 11.0	28 13.0	30 12.3	28 12.9
8 45.0	8 47.8	8 45.4		0 UND	2 178.2	7 53.2	7 52.2	9 41.8	12 29.6
14 25.4	14 26.0	14 25.7	Cost of Sales/Payables	6 59.6	9 38.7	13 28.5	13 29.0	14 26.9	17 21.2
21 17.1	21 17.7	21 17.0		15 24.2	19 19.6	24 15.4	20 18.6	21 17.5	23 15.7
22.0	21.7	19.7		10.1	12.8	16.8	20.2	20.1	27.7
63.6	61.5	55.5	Sales/Working Capital	22.0	31.6	38.3	53.8	51.3	97.4
−103.4	−112.1	−98.7		UND	−231.5	−53.4	−83.6	−113.8	−102.2
5.6	6.0	6.6		6.1	5.0	5.0	7.0	7.2	7.5
(777) 2.3	(788) 2.4	(662) 2.9	EBIT/Interest	(28) 2.6	(81) 2.0	(63) 2.4	(95) 2.6	(134) 3.1	(261) 3.6
.9	1.1	1.2		.4	.0	1.1	.9	1.0	1.6
5.2	4.5	4.6	Net Profit + Depr., Dep.,		2.1	2.9	4.5	5.4	
(174) 2.4	(164) 2.4	(164) 2.1	Amort./Cur. Mat. L/T/D		(13) .9	(14) 1.7	(30) 2.3	(104) 2.4	
1.2	1.2	1.3			.7	1.1	1.5	1.3	
.7	.7	.6		.5	.4	.4	.4	.7	.9
2.0	1.9	1.6	Fixed/Worth	3.6	2.4	2.1	1.3	1.5	1.6
10.3	16.4	7.2		−15.8	−2.6	−14.5	−32.0	5.5	4.0
1.1	1.2	1.1		1.5	.8	.8	.9	1.1	1.2
3.2	3.2	2.8	Debt/Worth	6.5	5.0	3.3	2.3	2.9	2.5
20.0	33.3	16.9		−20.0	−6.4	−33.9	−46.5	21.3	6.6
46.2	46.9	50.2	% Profit Before Taxes/Tangible	62.9	67.5	46.0	50.2	60.3	44.8
(702) 20.8	(687) 21.3	(606) 21.5	Net Worth	(27) 40.0	(68) 26.3	(59) 18.3	(81) 20.0	(120) 23.5	(251) 21.1
4.3	6.4	6.7		5.3	7.7	5.3	4.5	4.2	8.2
12.3	13.3	12.9	% Profit Before Taxes/Total	10.5	13.8	14.3	12.9	14.4	12.0
5.0	5.1	5.7	Assets	3.0	4.0	5.8	4.8	6.3	6.8
−.2	.7	.7		−3.4	−4.7	1.6	−.5	.5	1.9
32.2	28.1	34.5		36.7	99.1	68.2	54.1	33.6	20.8
14.2	13.5	14.7	Sales/Net Fixed Assets	12.9	17.9	25.5	22.2	16.4	10.6
6.7	6.4	7.6		4.1	5.4	7.8	9.2	9.5	7.2
7.3	7.3	7.3		5.7	8.8	8.6	9.3	7.2	6.3
5.1	4.9	5.2	Sales/Total Assets	3.4	5.0	5.9	6.6	5.6	4.7
3.5	3.4	3.5		1.7	2.7	3.4	3.7	3.9	3.5
.7	.7	.8		.5	.5	.6	.6	.8	.9
(812) 1.2	(811) 1.3	(678) 1.2	% Depr., Dep., Amort./Sales	(28) 1.8	(84) 1.0	(72) 1.1	(99) 1.0	(142) 1.4	(253) 1.3
1.8	2.0	1.8		4.2	2.0	2.1	1.7	1.8	1.8
.8	.7	.6	% Officers', Directors',	2.3	1.3	1.2	.7	.5	.3
(325) 1.5	(332) 1.5	(283) 1.4	Owners' Comp/Sales	(15) 3.8	(48) 2.4	(46) 1.9	(54) 1.3	(60) .8	(60) .8
2.5	2.9	2.6		10.0	3.7	3.1	2.1	1.9	1.5
49658617M	53849076M	51828206M	Net Sales ($)	22967M	199246M	335441M	783668M	2377890M	48108994M
12009782M	12261760M	12471756M	Total Assets ($)	16544M	63285M	119393M	163855M	498977M	11609702M

M = $ thousand   MM = $ million
See Pages 11 through 18 for Explanation of Ratios and Data

Current Data Sorted By Assets   Comparative Historical Data

	0-500M	500M-2MM	2-10MM	10-50MM	50-100MM	100-250MM	Type of Statement	4/1/98-3/31/99 ALL	4/1/99-3/31/00 ALL
			1	2			Unqualified		
	3	3	3	2			Reviewed		
	7	6	3				Compiled		
	1	1	3	1			Tax Returns		
			3				Other		
	3 (4/1-9/30/02)			33 (10/1/02-3/31/03)					
NUMBER OF STATEMENTS	11	10	10	5					
	%	%	%	%	%	%	**ASSETS**	%	%
	18.5	13.9	5.6		D	D	Cash & Equivalents	D	D
	2.1	2.6	8.4		A	A	Trade Receivables (net)	A	A
	35.7	22.4	17.0		T	T	Inventory	T	T
	.2	3.3	5.1		A	A	All Other Current	A	A
	56.5	42.1	36.0				Total Current		
	33.3	51.8	55.7		N	N	Fixed Assets (net)	N	N
	6.6	4.5	.5		O	O	Intangibles (net)	O	O
	3.6	1.6	7.8		T	T	All Other Non-Current	T	T
	100.0	100.0	100.0				Total		
					A	A	**LIABILITIES**	A	A
	24.0	2.2	10.6		V	V	Notes Payable-Short Term	V	V
	.8	8.9	3.8		A	A	Cur. Mat.-L/T/D	A	A
	7.5	13.0	9.8		I	I	Trade Payables	I	I
	.0	.0	.0		L	L	Income Taxes Payable	L	L
	16.3	2.4	6.4		A	A	All Other Current	A	A
	48.5	26.5	30.7		B	B	Total Current	B	B
	21.8	50.2	33.4		L	L	Long Term Debt	L	L
	.0	.0	.4		E	E	Deferred Taxes	E	E
	14.9	2.6	2.6				All Other Non-Current		
	14.7	20.7	32.9				Net Worth		
	100.0	100.0	100.0				Total Liabilities & Net Worth		
							INCOME DATA		
	100.0	100.0	100.0				Net Sales		
	30.6	21.7	20.8				Gross Profit		
	27.5	22.5	16.0				Operating Expenses		
	3.1	−.9	4.9				Operating Profit		
	.4	.1	3.6				All Other Expenses (net)		
	2.7	−1.0	1.3				Profit Before Taxes		
							RATIOS		
	1.8	3.6	2.1						
	1.4	1.5	1.1				Current		
	1.1	.6	.7						
	1.7	1.2	.8						
(10)	.5	.6	.5				Quick		
	.3	.1	.2						
	0 UND	0 UND	0 UND						
	0 UND	1 437.8	2 164.4				Sales/Receivables		
	0 999.8	1 301.1	8 47.1						
	13 27.9	10 37.0	9 38.5						
	25 14.6	13 27.1	13 27.8				Cost of Sales/Inventory		
	68 5.4	26 13.9	24 15.2						
	0 UND	5 80.3	2 186.1						
	0 UND	9 39.3	12 31.4				Cost of Sales/Payables		
	8 47.4	16 22.8	20 18.2						
	14.0	25.5	29.0						
	22.3	43.3	66.6				Sales/Working Capital		
	196.8	−35.8	−89.6						
							EBIT/Interest		
							Net Profit + Depr., Dep., Amort./Cur. Mat. L /T/D		
	.2	1.0	.8						
	4.2	4.6	1.9				Fixed/Worth		
	−.8	−10.2	9.8						
	2.9	1.3	.9						
	4.8	4.5	3.1				Debt/Worth		
	−8.9	−12.6	11.8						
							% Profit Before Taxes/Tangible Net Worth		
	15.7	7.7	10.5						
	2.1	1.0	.5				% Profit Before Taxes/Total Assets		
	−12.9	−7.2	−.8						
	83.7	53.7	17.1						
	27.7	12.1	7.3				Sales/Net Fixed Assets		
	9.1	3.5	3.1						
	6.9	6.6	6.0						
	4.0	5.7	3.8				Sales/Total Assets		
	2.5	2.7	1.8						
	.5	.5	1.2						
(10)	1.0	1.5	1.3				% Depr., Dep., Amort./Sales		
	1.8	2.9	2.5						
							% Officers', Directors', Owners' Comp/Sales		
	12076M	67000M	186386M	356277M			Net Sales ($)		
	2351M	11386M	44952M	91976M			Total Assets ($)		

Comparative Historical Data   Current Data Sorted By Sales

			Type of Statement						
		2	Unqualified						2
		3	Reviewed						3
		9	Compiled	2	3		2	2	
		16	Tax Returns	6	3	2	3	2	
		6	Other	1			1	2	2
4/1/00-3/31/01 ALL	4/1/01-3/31/02 ALL	4/1/02-3/31/03 ALL		0-1MM	3 (4/1-9/30/02) 1-3MM	3-5MM	33 (10/1/02-3/31/03) 5-10MM	10-25MM	25MM & OVER
		36	NUMBER OF STATEMENTS	9	6	2	6	6	7
%	%	%	ASSETS	%	%	%	%	%	%
D	D	13.3	Cash & Equivalents						
A	A	4.4	Trade Receivables (net)						
T	T	24.3	Inventory						
A	A	2.5	All Other Current						
		44.6	Total Current						
N	N	46.5	Fixed Assets (net)						
O	O	3.4	Intangibles (net)						
T	T	5.5	All Other Non-Current						
		100.0	Total						
A	A		LIABILITIES						
V	V	10.9	Notes Payable-Short Term						
A	A	4.3	Cur. Mat.-L/T/D						
I	I	10.4	Trade Payables						
L	L	.2	Income Taxes Payable						
A	A	8.4	All Other Current						
B	B	34.2	Total Current						
L	L	33.8	Long Term Debt						
E	E	.2	Deferred Taxes						
		6.0	All Other Non-Current						
		25.7	Net Worth						
		100.0	Total Liabilities & Net Worth						
			INCOME DATA						
		100.0	Net Sales						
		23.0	Gross Profit						
		21.0	Operating Expenses						
		2.0	Operating Profit						
		1.0	All Other Expenses (net)						
		1.0	Profit Before Taxes						
			RATIOS						
		1.8							
		1.4	Current						
		.8							
		1.1							
	(35)	.6	Quick						
		.2							
	0	UND							
	1	442.0	Sales/Receivables						
	5	66.9							
	11	33.6							
	16	23.3	Cost of Sales/Inventory						
	36	10.1							
	0	UND							
	8	45.5	Cost of Sales/Payables						
	16	22.2							
		20.2							
		45.3	Sales/Working Capital						
		NM							
		4.8							
	(29)	2.5	EBIT/Interest						
		.4							
			Net Profit + Depr., Dep., Amort./Cur. Mat. L/T/D						
		.7							
		2.3	Fixed/Worth						
		UND							
		1.2							
		3.5	Debt/Worth						
		UND							
		32.3							
	(28)	8.9	% Profit Before Taxes/Tangible Net Worth						
		−2.0							
		9.5							
		2.1	% Profit Before Taxes/Total Assets						
		−2.1							
		35.3							
		12.2	Sales/Net Fixed Assets						
		4.7							
		5.8							
		4.0	Sales/Total Assets						
		2.8							
		.7							
	(35)	1.3	% Depr., Dep., Amort./Sales						
		2.4							
		.6							
	(19)	2.0	% Officers', Directors', Owners' Comp/Sales						
		4.6							
		621739M	Net Sales ($)	4953M	12024M	8981M	43843M	115136M	436802M
		150665M	Total Assets ($)	4864M	2557M	3823M	9112M	24108M	106201M

© RMA 2003   M = $ thousand   MM = $ million
See Pages 11 through 18 for Explanation of Ratios and Data

Current Data Sorted By Assets / Comparative Historical Data

0-500M	500M-2MM	2-10MM	10-50MM	50-100MM	100-250MM		4/1/98-3/31/99 ALL	4/1/99-3/31/00 ALL
						Type of Statement		
	4		1			Unqualified	2	2
1	5		1			Reviewed	4	4
3	7	2	1			Compiled	13	7
5	2					Tax Returns	8	9
4	5	2	1			Other	8	12
9 (4/1-9/30/02)		35 (10/1/02-3/31/03)						
13	23	4	4			**NUMBER OF STATEMENTS**	35	34
%	%	%	%	%	%	**ASSETS**	%	%
7.3	9.7			DATA NOT AVAILABLE	DATA NOT AVAILABLE	Cash & Equivalents	10.1	18.8
4.8	11.7					Trade Receivables (net)	16.2	12.2
26.9	22.1					Inventory	23.3	16.5
.5	4.2					All Other Current	4.3	1.4
39.6	47.6					Total Current	53.9	48.9
35.0	35.1					Fixed Assets (net)	31.0	37.0
10.6	1.4					Intangibles (net)	5.2	4.8
14.6	15.9					All Other Non-Current	9.9	9.3
100.0	100.0					Total	100.0	100.0
						LIABILITIES		
2.1	12.2					Notes Payable-Short Term	8.1	7.4
12.9	4.3					Cur. Mat.-L/T/D	5.8	1.8
17.0	17.5					Trade Payables	19.0	18.3
.7	.6					Income Taxes Payable	.0	.2
4.5	11.9					All Other Current	12.9	10.1
37.2	46.5					Total Current	45.9	37.8
64.9	17.7					Long Term Debt	18.8	11.7
.0	.3					Deferred Taxes	.1	.3
17.5	3.4					All Other Non-Current	3.0	5.3
-19.8	32.2					Net Worth	32.2	44.9
100.0	100.0					Total Liabilities & Net Worth	100.0	100.0
						INCOME DATA		
100.0	100.0					Net Sales	100.0	100.0
32.1	34.6					Gross Profit	30.8	37.5
30.4	33.7					Operating Expenses	28.9	36.7
1.7	.8					Operating Profit	1.8	.8
.6	-.3					All Other Expenses (net)	.2	-.4
1.1	1.2					Profit Before Taxes	1.6	1.3
						RATIOS		
5.0	1.9						2.0	2.3
1.4	1.0					Current	1.2	1.6
.5	.6						.8	.9
2.5	1.0						1.1	1.7
(11) .6	.5					Quick	.5	.8
.2	.2						.2	.4
0 UND	0 UND						1 471.7	1 447.8
0 UND	4 101.3					Sales/Receivables	6 65.5	7 53.1
1 522.3	21 17.1						20 18.3	14 25.3
11 34.1	10 36.6						9 41.0	9 41.8
14 26.5	25 14.7					Cost of Sales/Inventory	13 27.4	23 16.2
36 10.2	41 8.8						24 15.2	35 10.5
0 UND	8 47.7						6 64.7	10 38.1
10 38.1	17 21.0					Cost of Sales/Payables	13 28.7	22 16.6
23 16.2	31 12.0						27 13.3	53 6.9
18.8	19.6						18.7	16.0
121.0	-388.6					Sales/Working Capital	59.4	35.9
-29.3	-21.2						-46.6	-68.5
5.0	15.9						6.5	10.9
(10) 1.3	(21) 5.9					EBIT/Interest	(30) 2.6	(24) 2.9
-1.3	1.8						.9	.6
						Net Profit + Depr., Dep., Amort./Cur. Mat. L /T/D		
2.3	.3						.3	.5
-5.4	1.1					Fixed/Worth	1.2	.7
-.6	9.5						5.3	2.3
2.9	.6						1.0	.4
-14.4	1.7					Debt/Worth	2.2	1.1
-2.7	11.7						12.3	4.5
	58.0						47.3	31.9
	(19) 15.1					% Profit Before Taxes/Tangible Net Worth	(29) 20.8	(29) 15.1
	4.3						-2.0	.6
19.4	11.8						17.1	12.8
3.3	7.6					% Profit Before Taxes/Total Assets	7.3	5.4
-2.9	1.6						-.2	-1.8
40.7	44.0						58.9	23.0
24.1	17.7					Sales/Net Fixed Assets	25.3	11.1
7.9	8.5						10.9	5.3
8.3	5.3						8.2	6.9
5.0	4.0					Sales/Total Assets	6.1	4.4
3.4	3.1						4.8	1.9
.9	.7						.5	.9
(10) 1.8	(19) 2.1					% Depr., Dep., Amort./Sales	(30) .9	(33) 1.8
4.4	3.5						1.7	3.7
	1.4						1.7	1.8
	(12) 2.9					% Officers', Directors', Owners' Comp/Sales	(19) 2.6	(17) 3.7
	5.9						5.6	5.9
15821M	104873M	154968M	392903M			Net Sales ($)	571387M	612069M
3141M	24581M	19418M	98777M			Total Assets ($)	190593M	258923M

M = $ thousand MM = $ million

See Pages 11 through 18 for Explanation of Ratios and Data

Comparative Historical Data | | | | Current Data Sorted By Sales

Hist 1	Hist 2	Hist 3	Type of Statement	0-1MM	1-3MM	3-5MM	5-10MM	10-25MM	25MM & OVER
2	2	5	Unqualified		1	1	2		1
4	8	7	Reviewed		2	1	3		1
9	14	13	Compiled	1	8	1	1	1	2
11	7	7	Tax Returns	5		1	1		
15	20	12	Other	2	3	1	2	1	3
4/1/00- 3/31/01	4/1/01- 3/31/02	4/1/02- 3/31/03			9 (4/1-9/30/02)		35 (10/1/02-3/31/03)		
ALL	ALL	ALL							
41	51	44	**NUMBER OF STATEMENTS**	8	14	4	9	2	7
%	%	%	**ASSETS**	%	%	%	%	%	%
15.9	19.1	10.8	Cash & Equivalents		11.8				
13.0	14.5	11.7	Trade Receivables (net)		4.2				
15.4	18.4	22.8	Inventory		23.7				
2.7	5.3	3.1	All Other Current		1.0				
47.1	57.3	48.4	Total Current		40.7				
38.3	29.8	33.6	Fixed Assets (net)		40.2				
4.9	4.8	4.3	Intangibles (net)		.4				
9.7	8.0	13.6	All Other Non-Current		18.5				
100.0	100.0	100.0	Total		100.0				
			LIABILITIES						
9.2	12.9	8.7	Notes Payable-Short Term		8.0				
3.4	3.3	6.4	Cur. Mat.-L/T/D		2.6				
16.8	20.4	17.6	Trade Payables		9.8				
.2	.1	.5	Income Taxes Payable		.4				
8.4	14.5	8.9	All Other Current		8.4				
38.0	51.2	42.1	Total Current		29.1				
26.0	18.6	30.3	Long Term Debt		19.1				
.3	.1	.1	Deferred Taxes		.3				
1.0	3.2	8.4	All Other Non-Current		10.4				
34.7	26.9	19.0	Net Worth		40.9				
100.0	100.0	100.0	Total Liabilities & Net Worth		100.0				
			INCOME DATA						
100.0	100.0	100.0	Net Sales		100.0				
33.4	35.1	32.3	Gross Profit		37.7				
31.9	32.9	31.0	Operating Expenses		35.6				
1.6	2.2	1.2	Operating Profit		2.1				
-.3	.7	-.1	All Other Expenses (net)		-.3				
1.9	1.5	1.4	Profit Before Taxes		2.4				
			RATIOS						
2.1	1.7	2.9			12.2				
1.4	1.1	1.2	Current		1.2				
.8	.8	.7			.5				
1.4	1.0	1.5			3.0				
(40) .7	(50) .6	(42) .6	Quick		.5				
.5	.3	.3			.0				
0 UND	1 390.5	0 UND			0 UND				
4 87.5	5 75.5	1 253.7	Sales/Receivables		0 UND				
21 17.5	17 21.7	18 20.6			4 81.3				
9 42.1	9 41.1	10 35.1			12 30.2				
19 18.8	21 17.8	22 16.3	Cost of Sales/Inventory		22 16.3				
33 11.1	38 9.6	39 9.4			41 9.0				
6 59.2	6 57.4	7 56.1			0 UND				
20 18.7	22 16.6	15 23.6	Cost of Sales/Payables		9 39.8				
31 11.6	34 10.6	24 15.4			21 17.5				
14.4	17.8	18.2			7.4				
39.0	145.0	124.9	Sales/Working Capital		NM				
-65.6	-44.3	-34.1			-17.3				
6.4	5.6	14.5			8.1				
(34) 2.4	(42) 2.5	(39) 4.1	EBIT/Interest	(11)	3.4				
.9	.9	1.3			1.7				
			Net Profit + Depr., Dep., Amort./Cur. Mat. L/T/D						
.3	.4	.2			.1				
1.1	1.1	1.6	Fixed/Worth		.9				
NM	3.2	-10.0			5.9				
.7	1.1	.7			.3				
2.3	2.5	2.8	Debt/Worth		1.3				
NM	31.8	-21.0			6.8				
44.3	41.8	48.1			28.1				
(31) 20.8	(40) 22.6	(32) 24.4	% Profit Before Taxes/Tangible Net Worth	(12)	17.8				
1.2	.1	9.4			10.0				
19.9	15.7	13.1			10.9				
5.8	7.9	7.4	% Profit Before Taxes/Total Assets		7.4				
-.1	.0	.8			2.2				
29.1	33.8	43.4			64.3				
10.6	17.0	18.1	Sales/Net Fixed Assets		9.6				
6.3	8.8	8.5			4.0				
6.7	4.8	6.6			4.7				
3.9	3.7	4.4	Sales/Total Assets		3.6				
2.5	3.0	3.2			1.9				
1.0	.5	.7			1.2				
(39) 1.5	(43) 1.5	(36) 1.8	% Depr., Dep., Amort./Sales	(10)	3.3				
3.7	2.7	3.5			4.0				
1.7	1.8	1.2							
(24) 3.5	(23) 3.4	(22) 2.8	% Officers', Directors', Owners' Comp/Sales						
4.0	6.1	5.5							
1014155M	1132588M	668565M	Net Sales ($)	5219M	28121M	16240M	59878M	22891M	536216M
358046M	309376M	145917M	Total Assets ($)	1450M	9666M	3391M	12596M	3531M	115283M

M = $ thousand   MM = $ million
See Pages 11 through 18 for Explanation of Ratios and Data

RETAIL—Fruit and Vegetable Markets NAICS 445230 (SIC 5148, 5431)

Current Data Sorted By Assets | **Comparative Historical Data**

						Type of Statement	4/1/98-3/31/99 ALL	4/1/99-3/31/00 ALL
1	2	3				Unqualified		3
	7	3				Reviewed		6
5	3					Compiled		9
	1		1			Tax Returns		3
						Other		4
0-500M	500M-2MM	2-10MM	10-50MM	50-100MM	100-250MM			
	3 (4/1-9/30/02)		23 (10/1/02-3/31/03)					
6	13	6	1			NUMBER OF STATEMENTS		25
%	%	%	%	%	%	ASSETS	%	%
	16.5			D	D	Cash & Equivalents	D	10.6
	9.8			A	A	Trade Receivables (net)	A	9.3
	16.0			T	T	Inventory	T	20.0
	.6			A	A	All Other Current	A	2.4
	43.0					Total Current		42.3
	44.7			N	N	Fixed Assets (net)	N	50.2
	4.2			O	O	Intangibles (net)	O	2.0
	8.2			T	T	All Other Non-Current	T	5.5
	100.0					Total		100.0
				A	A	**LIABILITIES**	A	
	9.9			V	V	Notes Payable-Short Term	V	6.2
	4.1			A	A	Cur. Mat.-L/T/D	A	6.0
	24.6			I	I	Trade Payables	I	18.6
	.0			L	L	Income Taxes Payable	L	.4
	6.8			A	A	All Other Current	A	12.2
	45.4			B	B	Total Current	B	43.4
	29.8			L	L	Long Term Debt	L	29.8
	.0			E	E	Deferred Taxes	E	.3
	1.2					All Other Non-Current		1.8
	23.7					Net Worth		24.8
	100.0					Total Liabilities & Net Worth		100.0
						INCOME DATA		
	100.0					Net Sales		100.0
	34.1					Gross Profit		32.2
	29.0					Operating Expenses		27.5
	5.1					Operating Profit		4.7
	.7					All Other Expenses (net)		1.4
	4.4					Profit Before Taxes		3.3
						RATIOS		
	3.0							1.5
	.7					Current		1.0
	.6							.7
	1.4							1.0
	.7					Quick		.7
	.1							.1
0	UND						0	UND
3	144.9					Sales/Receivables	1	391.9
14	26.7						10	37.1
2	172.9						7	55.4
7	52.6					Cost of Sales/Inventory	14	26.7
16	22.3						29	12.7
4	81.4						7	53.8
11	33.5					Cost of Sales/Payables	14	26.3
30	12.2						26	13.9
	20.5							57.7
	−58.1					Sales/Working Capital		323.7
	−24.3							−20.8
	14.1							5.6
(11)	7.2					EBIT/Interest	(20)	2.8
	.1							1.3
						Net Profit + Depr., Dep., Amort./Cur. Mat. L/T/D		
	.6							.7
	3.6					Fixed/Worth		2.5
	−4.3							522.3
	.5							1.0
	4.3					Debt/Worth		2.7
	−14.1							544.8
								59.7
						% Profit Before Taxes/Tangible Net Worth	(20)	17.7
								4.8
	28.8							15.5
	16.0					% Profit Before Taxes/Total Assets		4.3
	−4.1							.6
	29.9							24.8
	17.7					Sales/Net Fixed Assets		10.3
	9.1							3.9
	10.1							8.4
	8.1					Sales/Total Assets		5.2
	3.0							2.0
	.8							.6
(12)	1.0					% Depr., Dep., Amort./Sales	(24)	1.2
	1.6							1.8
								.9
						% Officers', Directors', Owners' Comp/Sales	(12)	4.6
								7.3
13429M	92442M	201202M	189279M			Net Sales ($)		412209M
1430M	12445M	19463M	34802M			Total Assets ($)		81369M

M = $ thousand   MM = $ million
See Pages 11 through 18 for Explanation of Ratios and Data

Comparative Historical Data | Current Data Sorted By Sales

						Type of Statement						
	2		2			Unqualified						
	4		3		6	Reviewed	1		2		1	2
	12		5		10	Compiled		2	1	2	5	
	5		2		8	Tax Returns	2	3	1	2		
	5		6		2	Other			1			1
	4/1/00-3/31/01 ALL		4/1/01-3/31/02 ALL		4/1/02-3/31/03 ALL		0-1MM	3 (4/1-9/30/02) 1-3MM	3-5MM	23 (10/1/02-3/31/03) 5-10MM	10-25MM	25MM & OVER
	28		18		26	NUMBER OF STATEMENTS	3	5	5	4	6	3
	%		%		%	ASSETS	%	%	%	%	%	%
	18.0		14.9		17.0	Cash & Equivalents						
	13.7		8.4		11.0	Trade Receivables (net)						
	15.4		18.4		19.7	Inventory						
	1.0		5.6		1.9	All Other Current						
	48.0		47.2		49.6	Total Current						
	39.3		44.8		41.6	Fixed Assets (net)						
	3.3		3.4		3.3	Intangibles (net)						
	9.3		1.9		5.6	All Other Non-Current						
	100.0		100.0		100.0	Total						
						LIABILITIES						
	7.0		11.2		6.4	Notes Payable-Short Term						
	5.1		4.9		3.4	Cur. Mat.-L/T/D						
	23.9		28.2		21.6	Trade Payables						
	.1		.1		.1	Income Taxes Payable						
	15.6		10.5		10.8	All Other Current						
	51.8		54.9		42.3	Total Current						
	15.4		31.1		24.2	Long Term Debt						
	.3		.6		.3	Deferred Taxes						
	2.6		6.0		5.8	All Other Non-Current						
	29.9		7.4		27.4	Net Worth						
	100.0		100.0		100.0	Total Liabilities & Net Worth						
						INCOME DATA						
	100.0		100.0		100.0	Net Sales						
	31.6		32.1		33.9	Gross Profit						
	27.7		28.2		29.6	Operating Expenses						
	3.9		3.9		4.3	Operating Profit						
	.7		.6		.5	All Other Expenses (net)						
	3.2		3.3		3.8	Profit Before Taxes						
						RATIOS						
	1.4		1.2		2.3							
	1.0		.8		1.2	Current						
	.6		.5		.7							
	1.0		.9		1.3							
	.6		.3		.6	Quick						
	.3		.1		.2							
0	UND	0	UND	0	UND							
1	401.6	1	482.7	1	546.5	Sales/Receivables						
14	25.2	6	63.1	15	24.8							
4	86.6	6	63.2	3	113.9							
10	35.3	16	23.5	11	32.1	Cost of Sales/Inventory						
15	23.8	38	9.6	21	17.2							
8	43.3	12	29.3	4	93.6							
14	25.7	28	13.0	9	41.1	Cost of Sales/Payables						
33	11.2	33	10.9	27	13.4							
	62.0		82.5		34.3							
	392.3		−58.5		126.4	Sales/Working Capital						
	−28.6		−20.2		−37.2							
	7.4		4.4		12.5							
(22)	3.0	(15)	2.2	(18)	4.1	EBIT/Interest						
	1.1		.3		.6							
						Net Profit + Depr., Dep., Amort./Cur. Mat. L/T/D						
	.4		.6		.5							
	1.2		5.0		1.9	Fixed/Worth						
	7.5		−3.1		NM							
	.9		2.7		.6							
	2.0		6.5		2.7	Debt/Worth						
	13.3		−9.1		NM							
	91.3		112.1		123.5							
(22)	29.3	(12)	38.8	(20)	34.9	% Profit Before Taxes/Tangible Net Worth						
	2.7		−2.1		5.0							
	21.8		17.6		37.2							
	7.6		5.7		12.6	% Profit Before Taxes/Total Assets						
	1.1		−1.2		−.4							
	48.2		34.3		36.4							
	21.7		12.6		21.6	Sales/Net Fixed Assets						
	10.8		3.2		10.5							
	9.9		8.4		10.9							
	7.6		4.1		7.4	Sales/Total Assets						
	4.3		2.2		4.2							
	.5		.7		.8							
(24)	1.0	(17)	1.4	(22)	1.0	% Depr., Dep., Amort./Sales						
	1.9		2.0		1.6							
	.8				1.4							
(16)	2.2			(16)	3.2	% Officers', Directors', Owners' Comp/Sales						
	7.2				7.8							
	364631M		460484M		496352M	Net Sales ($)	1998M	10143M	20065M	23943M	118462M	321741M
	59929M		117165M		68140M	Total Assets ($)	801M	2870M	5695M	2060M	14415M	42299M

M = $ thousand   MM = $ million
See Pages 11 through 18 for Explanation of Ratios and Data

Current Data Sorted By Assets   Comparative Historical Data

						Type of Statement		
	1		1	2		Unqualified	4	7
			2	1		Reviewed	3	3
		3	1			Compiled	9	10
	13	3				Tax Returns	4	5
	1	1	6	1		Other	7	7
		10 (4/1-9/30/02)		26 (10/1/02-3/31/03)			4/1/98-3/31/99	4/1/99-3/31/00
	0-500M	500M-2MM	2-10MM	10-50MM	50-100MM	100-250MM	ALL	ALL
	15	7	10	4		NUMBER OF STATEMENTS	27	32
	%	%	%	%	%	%	ASSETS	%	%
	12.6		5.7				Cash & Equivalents	13.6	19.7
	3.1		14.7		D	D	Trade Receivables (net)	8.9	13.6
	20.8		28.4		A	A	Inventory	26.3	22.9
	1.7		.6		T	T	All Other Current	2.5	1.3
	38.2		49.4		A	A	Total Current	51.3	57.5
	38.7		40.5				Fixed Assets (net)	39.6	31.9
	13.0		4.2		N	N	Intangibles (net)	4.2	5.8
	10.1		6.0		O	O	All Other Non-Current	4.9	4.8
	100.0		100.0		T	T	Total	100.0	100.0
							LIABILITIES		
	10.3		9.3		A	A	Notes Payable-Short Term	10.0	8.2
	3.7		3.4		V	V	Cur. Mat.-L/T/D	3.6	2.6
	12.2		17.9		A	A	Trade Payables	19.0	19.2
	.0		.4		I	I	Income Taxes Payable	.5	.4
	3.0		8.5		L	L	All Other Current	8.3	9.0
	29.2		39.4		A	A	Total Current	41.4	39.4
	36.5		23.8		B	B	Long Term Debt	23.1	16.2
	.0		.9		L	L	Deferred Taxes	.5	.4
	18.0		8.0		E	E	All Other Non-Current	.6	11.0
	16.4		27.9				Net Worth	34.4	33.1
	100.0		100.0				Total Liabilities & Net Worth	100.0	100.0
							INCOME DATA		
	100.0		100.0				Net Sales	100.0	100.0
	66.7		41.0				Gross Profit	45.1	46.1
	65.0		35.9				Operating Expenses	39.4	40.8
	1.7		5.1				Operating Profit	5.7	5.3
	1.4		1.3				All Other Expenses (net)	.7	.0
	.3		3.8				Profit Before Taxes	5.0	5.3
							RATIOS		
	3.3		2.2					2.5	3.5
	.9		1.2				Current	1.5	1.5
	.5		.7					.8	.7
	1.4		1.1					1.0	2.3
	.5		.5				Quick	.6	.8
	.2		.1					.2	.2

					Sales/Receivables		
0	UND	3	134.5			0	UND	0	UND
0	UND	16	22.8			4	101.0	5	73.5
0	UND	35	10.3			15	24.0	23	15.8

					Cost of Sales/Inventory		
10	36.6	30	12.2			28	12.9	27	13.5
20	18.2	56	6.5			51	7.2	52	7.0
65	5.6	145	2.5			92	4.0	85	4.3

					Cost of Sales/Payables		
0	UND	13	27.6			6	62.3	4	99.2
32	11.5	27	13.5			27	13.4	33	11.0
52	7.0	68	5.4			49	7.4	68	5.4

			Sales/Working Capital		
12.0	7.5			8.6	6.8
−453.0	27.1			23.7	21.9
−32.5	−62.8			−37.6	−30.7

				EBIT/Interest		
	8.2	10.8			11.9	13.7
(13)	.5	2.1		(25)	2.9	(26)	3.6
	−1.7	1.4			1.3	.8

			Net Profit + Depr., Dep., Amort./Cur. Mat. L/T/D

			Fixed/Worth		
.2	.8			.4	.3
1.2	1.8			1.4	1.2
−21.2	2.9			5.4	6.9

			Debt/Worth		
1.0	1.5			.5	1.1
UND	3.0			1.7	1.9
−8.6	5.8			10.7	7.8

			% Profit Before Taxes/Tangible Net Worth		
				39.5	83.6
			(22)	20.5	(26)	29.1
				8.6	5.6

			% Profit Before Taxes/Total Assets		
6.6	13.1			20.7	42.0
−2.3	3.8			7.7	9.8
−12.7	1.8			1.2	.2

			Sales/Net Fixed Assets		
58.1	20.0			21.5	46.3
14.2	6.2			13.5	12.7
3.6	3.4			4.3	3.8

			Sales/Total Assets		
5.2	2.9			6.6	4.6
4.4	2.3			3.5	3.1
2.3	1.9			1.9	1.6

				% Depr., Dep., Amort./Sales		
	.9	1.2			1.2	1.2
(13)	2.3	2.6		(22)	1.9	(29)	2.5
	5.5	3.9			2.7	3.2

			% Officers', Directors', Owners' Comp/Sales		
				2.7	2.0
		(13)	11.5	(12)	9.0
			14.3	13.4

				Net Sales ($)		
11153M	13272M	186679M	247699M	Net Sales ($)	450930M	331837M
2869M	5741M	54603M	113282M	Total Assets ($)	271056M	141664M

M = $ thousand   MM = $ million
See Pages 11 through 18 for Explanation of Ratios and Data

Comparative Historical Data | Current Data Sorted By Sales

			Type of Statement						
2	2	3	Unqualified					1	2
2	2	4	Reviewed	1	1			2	
7	6	4	Compiled	2	1	1			
5	7	16	Tax Returns	12	4				
6	3	9	Other	1	1		3	2	2
4/1/00-3/31/01	4/1/01-3/31/02	4/1/02-3/31/03			10 (4/1-9/30/02)			26 (10/1/02-3/31/03)	
ALL	ALL	ALL		0-1MM	1-3MM	3-5MM	5-10MM	10-25MM	25MM & OVER
22	20	36	NUMBER OF STATEMENTS	13	8	2	4	5	4
%	%	%	**ASSETS**	%	%	%	%	%	%
19.9	26.0	11.1	Cash & Equivalents	11.5					
9.1	11.7	9.0	Trade Receivables (net)	3.5					
20.3	19.6	26.6	Inventory	21.3					
1.4	3.9	1.5	All Other Current	1.8					
50.6	61.3	48.3	Total Current	38.1					
37.5	27.6	34.9	Fixed Assets (net)	36.3					
4.8	1.3	9.3	Intangibles (net)	16.9					
6.8	9.8	7.5	All Other Non-Current	8.8					
100.0	100.0	100.0	Total	100.0					
			LIABILITIES						
8.2	7.4	9.0	Notes Payable-Short Term	11.3					
2.6	2.3	3.8	Cur. Mat.-L/T/D	4.4					
14.7	14.1	13.9	Trade Payables	11.4					
.3	.1	.1	Income Taxes Payable	.0					
13.6	15.9	6.1	All Other Current	3.4					
39.3	39.7	32.8	Total Current	30.5					
29.0	12.8	29.6	Long Term Debt	40.2					
.2	.0	.3	Deferred Taxes	.0					
5.5	5.8	10.5	All Other Non-Current	18.8					
25.9	41.7	26.8	Net Worth	10.5					
100.0	100.0	100.0	Total Liabilities & Net Worth	100.0					
			INCOME DATA						
100.0	100.0	100.0	Net Sales	100.0					
50.4	49.1	53.2	Gross Profit	68.5					
47.4	44.1	49.9	Operating Expenses	67.0					
3.1	4.9	3.4	Operating Profit	1.5					
2.2	2.4	1.2	All Other Expenses (net)	1.8					
.8	2.5	2.2	Profit Before Taxes	−.3					
			RATIOS						
2.1	2.7	2.7		4.4					
1.2	1.5	1.6	Current	.9					
.6	1.0	.8		.6					
1.3	1.6	1.2		1.1					
.6	.9	.5	Quick	.5					
.1	.3	.3		.2					
0 UND	0 UND	0 UND		0 UND					
1 295.3	0 UND	2 195.2	Sales/Receivables	0 UND					
22 16.5	20 17.9	20 18.6		0 UND					
13 28.5	8 45.0	18 20.3		11 34.5					
46 7.9	41 8.9	43 8.4	Cost of Sales/Inventory	20 18.2					
78 4.7	78 4.7	121 3.0		73 5.0					
15 24.2	2 153.3	11 32.5		0 UND					
29 12.5	10 36.6	23 15.9	Cost of Sales/Payables	23 15.6					
53 6.9	35 10.5	54 6.8		55 6.6					
6.1	5.9	8.5		11.2					
43.9	26.2	22.4	Sales/Working Capital	−453.0					
−24.7	UND	−58.7		−29.4					
(19) 4.3	(15) 8.5	(32) 10.8		(10) 6.5					
2.0	3.6	2.5	EBIT/Interest	−.2					
.1	2.0	.6		−1.9					
			Net Profit + Depr., Dep., Amort./Cur. Mat. L/T/D						
.3	.2	.4		.2					
2.7	.6	1.3	Fixed/Worth	4.2					
UND	2.3	4.0		−13.2					
1.0	.7	1.0		2.4					
3.0	1.4	3.6	Debt/Worth	−171.0					
UND	9.9	UND		−3.5					
87.3	39.6	40.6							
(17) 31.4	(19) 24.4	(27) 20.1	% Profit Before Taxes/Tangible Net Worth						
−.7	.0	9.6							
16.4	17.2	11.6		1.4					
7.4	9.6	2.9	% Profit Before Taxes/Total Assets	−6.9					
−3.3	.8	−2.3		−16.3					
35.8	88.8	32.7		73.6					
7.9	28.8	6.8	Sales/Net Fixed Assets	14.2					
3.3	6.5	4.2		4.0					
4.1	7.0	4.5		4.8					
2.7	3.5	2.5	Sales/Total Assets	3.1					
1.7	2.6	2.0		1.8					
1.3	.2	.9		.8					
(19) 2.0	(19) .9	(34) 2.4	% Depr., Dep., Amort./Sales	(11) 3.8					
4.6	2.2	4.4		8.3					
	3.4	2.7							
	(12) 7.1	(14) 3.7	% Officers', Directors', Owners' Comp/Sales						
	15.8	11.0							
181389M	149106M	458803M	Net Sales ($)	7381M	13763M	7821M	31431M	87930M	310477M
63586M	41218M	176495M	Total Assets ($)	2449M	5626M	2779M	19171M	34580M	111890M

M = $ thousand   MM = $ million
See Pages 11 through 18 for Explanation of Ratios and Data

Current Data Sorted By Assets   Comparative Historical Data

						Type of Statement		
	1	1	2	4	1	2	Unqualified	19	15
		3	7	1			Reviewed	10	8
	5	8	1				Compiled	32	23
	22	12	3	1		1	Tax Returns	15	19
	5	13	13	4	2	1	Other	30	30
		19 (4/1-9/30/02)		94 (10/1/02-3/31/03)				4/1/98-3/31/99	4/1/99-3/31/00
	0-500M	500M-2MM	2-10MM	10-50MM	50-100MM	100-250MM		ALL	ALL
	33	37	26	10	3	4	NUMBER OF STATEMENTS	106	95
	%	%	%	%	%	%	ASSETS	%	%
	13.2	12.1	11.8	9.6			Cash & Equivalents	8.7	9.8
	1.1	10.5	14.7	4.5			Trade Receivables (net)	9.5	11.0
	24.2	20.0	22.3	23.7			Inventory	24.7	22.4
	.4	.5	3.3	1.7			All Other Current	2.3	1.9
	39.0	43.3	52.0	39.5			Total Current	45.2	45.0
	42.0	41.8	38.2	39.7			Fixed Assets (net)	41.3	41.9
	11.9	8.4	3.8	8.2			Intangibles (net)	6.4	6.4
	7.2	6.5	6.0	12.6			All Other Non-Current	7.1	6.6
	100.0	100.0	100.0	100.0			Total	100.0	100.0
							LIABILITIES		
	2.3	6.6	6.7	2.3			Notes Payable-Short Term	8.5	9.3
	3.9	2.6	3.3	4.2			Cur. Mat.-L/T/D	4.1	4.6
	8.9	14.2	19.8	19.3			Trade Payables	15.3	14.1
	.1	.1	.1	.0			Income Taxes Payable	.2	.2
	15.5	9.7	15.6	8.0			All Other Current	11.8	7.7
	30.7	33.3	45.4	33.7			Total Current	39.9	35.9
	45.2	26.3	22.7	14.9			Long Term Debt	24.5	32.0
	.0	.0	.1	.2			Deferred Taxes	.4	.3
	12.8	4.0	6.1	3.2			All Other Non-Current	11.5	5.4
	11.3	36.4	25.7	48.0			Net Worth	23.7	26.3
	100.0	100.0	100.0	100.0			Total Liabilities & Net Worth	100.0	100.0
							INCOME DATA		
	100.0	100.0	100.0	100.0			Net Sales	100.0	100.0
	51.9	43.1	41.9	28.9			Gross Profit	40.5	42.0
	48.4	38.0	37.8	25.3			Operating Expenses	41.2	38.2
	3.5	5.1	4.0	3.6			Operating Profit	−.7	3.8
	2.8	1.7	1.1	.1			All Other Expenses (net)	.2	1.0
	.7	3.3	2.9	3.5			Profit Before Taxes	−.9	2.8
							RATIOS		
	5.2	2.0	1.9	1.9				1.7	2.4
	2.0	1.4	1.2	1.1			Current	1.1	1.2
	.8	.8	.8	.8				.8	.8
	2.0	1.2	1.0	.8				.8	1.3
	.3	.6	(25) .7	.4			Quick	.4	(93) .5
	.2	.2	.3	.3				.2	.2
	0 UND	0 UND	3 126.7	2 156.0				0 UND	0 UND
	0 UND	2 200.1	15 24.6	4 96.7			Sales/Receivables	3 143.0	2 154.8
	1 479.2	21 17.1	29 12.7	6 62.5				20 18.0	20 18.1
	6 59.9	8 44.9	12 30.5	11 33.8				14 25.3	17 22.1
	20 18.0	20 18.6	29 12.7	24 15.3			Cost of Sales/Inventory	32 11.4	34 10.7
	53 6.9	59 6.2	74 4.9	58 6.3				56 6.6	64 5.7
	0 UND	5 79.1	13 29.2	16 23.5				12 31.7	9 42.5
	4 86.0	21 17.7	30 12.3	21 17.3			Cost of Sales/Payables	22 16.7	20 18.6
	20 18.2	35 10.4	52 7.0	42 8.6				39 9.4	38 9.5
	16.2	9.9	13.8	9.2				15.5	13.8
	69.6	38.7	32.8	NM			Sales/Working Capital	102.6	39.2
	−85.3	−39.6	−43.6	−76.0				−37.6	−52.7
	2.8	9.4	5.5					6.2	6.7
(22)	1.3	(32) 5.4	(19) 1.8				EBIT/Interest	(97) 2.7	(86) 2.8
	−.7	1.0	−.1					1.0	1.0
							Net Profit + Depr., Dep.,	4.4	5.1
							Amort./Cur. Mat. L./T/D	(32) 2.0	(23) 1.7
								.8	.9
	.6	.5	.3	.4				.5	.6
	2.1	1.5	.9	.9			Fixed/Worth	1.8	2.1
	−2.3	2.9	3.3	2.4				10.0	13.5
	1.4	1.0	.9	.7				1.0	1.2
	3.9	2.2	2.1	1.4			Debt/Worth	3.3	3.0
	−3.1	8.5	4.2	2.5				20.2	24.7
	80.2	74.7	51.4				% Profit Before Taxes/Tangible	62.8	65.9
(20)	17.4	(30) 30.4	(22) 29.2				Net Worth	(84) 25.2	(75) 27.4
	1.9	2.3	−3.4					5.4	3.3
	16.3	22.8	18.5	21.0			% Profit Before Taxes/Total	15.9	20.3
	4.6	5.2	4.1	12.5			Assets	7.5	7.8
	−4.8	.1	−2.4	4.0				−.1	.4
	25.8	31.1	35.4	14.3				24.1	20.7
	11.6	7.8	7.9	8.4			Sales/Net Fixed Assets	11.3	10.5
	4.2	3.0	3.4	6.2				4.4	4.0
	6.7	3.4	5.1	6.0				5.6	5.0
	3.4	2.7	3.2	3.7			Sales/Total Assets	3.4	3.2
	2.2	1.6	1.8	1.9				2.0	2.1
	1.4	1.0	.6					1.0	1.1
(27)	3.8	(31) 2.0	(23) 1.9				% Depr., Dep., Amort./Sales	(92) 1.7	(85) 2.1
	5.2	4.4	3.9					3.2	4.2
	1.4	1.8	2.0				% Officers', Directors',	1.8	2.4
(18)	4.1	(19) 2.8	(10) 3.2				Owners' Comp/Sales	(45) 3.5	(41) 3.7
	7.3	10.0	4.9					7.1	7.2
	31044M	142767M	348931M	1002149M	313619M	2146076M	Net Sales ($)	4317022M	3018823M
	6793M	37939M	100066M	266271M	234619M	660197M	Total Assets ($)	1556094M	867491M

M = $ thousand   MM = $ million
See Pages 11 through 18 for Explanation of Ratios and Data

Comparative Historical Data   Current Data Sorted By Sales

			Type of Statement						
6	7	11	Unqualified	1	1				9
14	13	11	Reviewed	1	1		5	2	2
19	26	14	Compiled	4	6		2	2	
29	29	39	Tax Returns	17	14	5	1		2
31	36	38	Other	4	10	4	4	7	9
4/1/00-	4/1/01-	4/1/02-			19 (4/1-9/30/02)			94 (10/1/02-3/31/03)	
3/31/01	3/31/02	3/31/03							
ALL	ALL	ALL		0-1MM	1-3MM	3-5MM	5-10MM	10-25MM	25MM & OVER
99	111	113	**NUMBER OF STATEMENTS**	27	32	9	12	11	22
%	%	%	**ASSETS**	%	%	%	%	%	%
10.7	10.9	12.0	Cash & Equivalents	10.3	14.4		14.2	13.2	10.7
9.7	8.5	8.1	Trade Receivables (net)	1.0	8.1		11.1	17.6	11.1
21.9	20.3	21.6	Inventory	16.9	17.5		24.7	27.2	22.3
3.0	3.6	1.4	All Other Current	.4	.9		1.5	3.7	2.1
45.2	43.3	43.1	Total Current	28.7	40.9		51.5	61.7	46.2
43.2	39.3	40.4	Fixed Assets (net)	50.6	44.3		38.9	28.1	32.7
5.3	7.8	9.4	Intangibles (net)	14.2	7.5		5.8	3.1	12.3
6.2	9.6	7.1	All Other Non-Current	6.5	7.3		3.7	7.1	8.9
100.0	100.0	100.0	Total	100.0	100.0		100.0	100.0	100.0
			LIABILITIES						
5.0	8.8	4.8	Notes Payable-Short Term	2.0	6.5		6.4	6.5	3.5
5.1	3.7	3.4	Cur. Mat.-L/T/D	4.3	3.3		5.9	1.4	3.4
17.6	14.3	14.1	Trade Payables	4.3	9.9		15.4	24.2	24.5
.3	.1	.1	Income Taxes Payable	.1	.2		.2	.0	.2
9.1	12.5	12.4	All Other Current	10.7	14.5		14.3	11.7	13.1
37.0	39.4	34.9	Total Current	21.4	34.3		42.3	43.8	44.6
27.8	29.9	29.8	Long Term Debt	44.8	36.7		16.4	19.1	16.4
.2	.1	.2	Deferred Taxes	.0	.0		.1	.0	.8
4.6	4.9	7.4	All Other Non-Current	10.8	5.2		4.0	1.4	10.5
30.7	25.7	27.7	Net Worth	23.0	23.8		37.2	35.6	27.7
100.0	100.0	100.0	Total Liabilities & Net Worth	100.0	100.0		100.0	100.0	100.0
			INCOME DATA						
100.0	100.0	100.0	Net Sales	100.0	100.0		100.0	100.0	100.0
39.4	41.8	43.7	Gross Profit	56.5	48.4		44.1	38.7	29.8
35.6	37.8	39.4	Operating Expenses	53.3	42.9		39.3	35.6	26.0
3.8	4.0	4.2	Operating Profit	3.2	5.5		4.8	3.1	3.8
1.0	.7	1.9	All Other Expenses (net)	3.0	2.6		.9	.0	1.6
2.8	3.3	2.3	Profit Before Taxes	.2	2.9		3.9	3.1	2.2
			RATIOS						
2.9	2.3	2.1		5.0	2.1		2.0	1.7	2.2
1.5	1.2	1.4	Current	1.5	1.2		1.2	1.4	1.3
.8	.7	.8		.5	.9		.7	1.1	.8
1.3	1.0	1.1		2.0	1.4		.9	1.0	1.3
(97) .5	.5	(112) .6	Quick	.3	.7		.7	.8	.4
.2	.2	.3		.2	.3		.3	.3	.3
0 UND	0 UND	0 UND		0 UND	0 UND		1 562.7	4 101.1	3 137.1
2 187.8	2 201.2	2 166.5	Sales/Receivables	0 UND	1 309.0		12 31.7	11 33.0	6 60.2
23 15.7	15 23.7	13 28.2		1 434.0	27 13.7		28 12.8	22 16.7	12 30.0
12 30.3	10 36.0	10 36.3		4 87.2	10 37.9		11 32.3	16 23.4	11 33.8
24 15.0	20 18.2	21 17.0	Cost of Sales/Inventory	20 18.0	19 19.2		40 9.2	27 13.4	23 15.7
61 5.9	56 6.6	55 6.7		41 8.9	54 6.7		77 4.7	50 7.3	53 6.9
6 65.4	5 68.7	7 51.6		0 UND	3 124.2		13 27.9	16 23.3	16 22.8
19 19.2	17 21.2	19 18.8	Cost of Sales/Payables	0 UND	16 22.5		31 11.9	23 16.0	22 16.5
33 11.1	34 10.9	36 10.3		19 18.8	31 11.8		54 6.8	42 8.7	38 9.6
10.7	11.8	12.8		13.7	10.7		11.5	15.5	10.5
34.0	85.5	43.5	Sales/Working Capital	113.0	60.7		26.5	33.0	78.1
-55.6	-40.7	-59.3		-17.5	-113.3		-24.5	43.5	-59.8
6.5	7.8	7.4		2.2	8.0		13.9		7.5
(86) 3.0	(89) 2.9	(87) 1.8	EBIT/Interest	(16) 1.0	(28) 2.3		4.1		(17) 3.4
1.1	1.1	.6		-.2	.6		.3		.2
2.6	2.4	36.4	Net Profit + Depr., Dep.,						
(16) 1.6	(13) 1.3	(10) 3.1	Amort./Cur. Mat. L/T/D						
1.2	.4	1.7							
.7	.5	.5		.8	.6		.4	.2	.4
1.8	1.7	1.6	Fixed/Worth	2.7	1.5		1.3	.7	1.6
4.6	5.6	11.0		-2.7	4.1		3.0	2.3	NM
.9	1.0	1.0		1.0	1.0		1.5	1.4	.7
2.6	2.8	2.4	Debt/Worth	5.5	2.3		2.4	1.9	2.0
7.8	10.5	104.3		-4.0	7.5		3.9	6.3	NM
48.6	58.4	60.5	% Profit Before Taxes/Tangible	62.2	96.2		75.0	48.3	48.4
(78) 19.6	(91) 38.5	(86) 27.5	Net Worth	(16) 16.0	(25) 21.0	(11) 28.7	(10) 14.3	(17) 31.7
3.9	6.8	1.0		.0	1.7		-19.8	-3.4	-.4
18.4	20.4	19.5	% Profit Before Taxes/Total	13.9	25.0		22.5	13.6	19.9
6.8	10.0	5.2	Assets	2.0	4.9		12.7	3.4	7.2
1.0	.8	-1.1		-8.5	-.9		-3.5	-.9	-1.5
26.1	36.4	26.0		18.6	22.0		30.3	62.2	41.7
8.8	10.7	8.9	Sales/Net Fixed Assets	4.8	7.0		7.3	15.0	11.8
4.4	4.1	4.1		1.9	4.3		4.0	6.4	6.2
5.5	6.0	5.2		4.1	4.5		3.4	6.0	6.6
3.4	3.6	2.9	Sales/Total Assets	2.2	2.8		3.1	5.1	3.5
2.2	2.0	1.9		1.2	2.0		2.4	3.5	1.9
.8	.7	1.1		3.8	1.1		.7		.6
(90) 1.7	(85) 1.8	(91) 2.3	% Depr., Dep., Amort./Sales	(23) 4.8	(28) 1.9		1.6	(14) 1.5
3.1	3.5	4.6		9.4	4.2		3.4		2.4
2.1	2.4	1.7	% Officers', Directors',	2.5	2.7				
(42) 3.3	(46) 4.9	(49) 3.2	Owners' Comp/Sales	(13) 6.8	(17) 5.0				
6.9	5.9	7.1		9.5	9.4				
2835967M	3062246M	3984586M	Net Sales ($)	13201M	60161M	39482M	93076M	182137M	3596529M
951943M	1085150M	1305885M	Total Assets ($)	7488M	24553M	18381M	32996M	45374M	1177093M

M = $ thousand   MM = $ million
                            See Pages 11 through 18 for Explanation of Ratios and Data

Current Data Sorted By Assets | Comparative Historical Data

	0-500M	500M-2MM	2-10MM	10-50MM	50-100MM	100-250MM	Type of Statement	4/1/98-3/31/99 ALL	4/1/99-3/31/00 ALL
	2	1	3	5		1	Unqualified		
		13	7	3			Reviewed	4	6
	28	32	6	1			Compiled	21	20
	68	33	5	1			Tax Returns	56	58
	13	16	12	7	1		Other	55	43
		56 (4/1-9/30/02)		202 (10/1/02-3/31/03)				33	33
	111	95	33	17	1	1	**NUMBER OF STATEMENTS**	169	160
	%	%	%	%	%	%	**ASSETS**	%	%
	10.2	14.1	13.4	9.0			Cash & Equivalents	11.6	10.1
	1.1	1.7	5.7	2.3			Trade Receivables (net)	3.8	2.2
	53.8	44.1	44.1	50.3			Inventory	51.6	49.2
	.8	1.0	1.6	1.3			All Other Current	.7	1.4
	65.9	60.9	64.7	62.9			Total Current	67.7	62.9
	13.5	21.3	21.9	21.5			Fixed Assets (net)	18.6	19.1
	14.6	11.5	8.8	7.8			Intangibles (net)	7.9	11.8
	6.0	6.2	4.6	7.8			All Other Non-Current	5.8	6.2
	100.0	100.0	100.0	100.0			Total	100.0	100.0
							LIABILITIES		
	7.4	9.5	5.6	10.0			Notes Payable-Short Term	7.7	6.8
	4.3	2.8	3.5	3.0			Cur. Mat.-L/T/D	4.7	5.2
	16.7	23.8	24.9	20.7			Trade Payables	20.1	18.9
	.1	.3	.0	.3			Income Taxes Payable	.2	.2
	8.3	12.8	13.0	7.0			All Other Current	11.0	12.3
	36.8	49.2	47.0	40.9			Total Current	43.7	43.5
	22.8	22.3	13.2	11.4			Long Term Debt	21.7	22.1
	.0	.0	.0	.1			Deferred Taxes	.2	.0
	14.5	4.3	8.6	5.2			All Other Non-Current	9.6	13.6
	25.9	24.1	31.2	42.3			Net Worth	24.8	20.7
	100.0	100.0	100.0	100.0			Total Liabilities & Net Worth	100.0	100.0
							INCOME DATA		
	100.0	100.0	100.0	100.0			Net Sales	100.0	100.0
	22.0	23.1	25.1	24.7			Gross Profit	21.6	21.8
	20.7	20.4	22.9	20.8			Operating Expenses	20.1	19.7
	1.3	2.7	2.2	3.9			Operating Profit	1.5	2.1
	−.1	.4	.3	−.3			All Other Expenses (net)	.2	−.3
	1.4	2.3	1.9	4.1			Profit Before Taxes	1.3	2.5
							RATIOS		
	9.9	2.1	2.1	2.0				3.3	3.1
	2.2	1.4	1.5	1.7			Current	1.8	1.5
	1.1	.9	1.0	1.2				1.1	1.0
	1.2	.6	.8	.6				.9	.6
	(107) .4	.3	.4	.3			Quick	(164) .3	(157) .2
	.1	.1	.1	.1				.1	.1
	0 UND	0 UND	0 999.8	0 UND				0 UND	0 UND
	0 UND	0 999.8	2 177.7	1 290.1			Sales/Receivables	0 999.8	0 UND
	0 999.8	1 284.3	8 43.7	4 88.8				2 154.0	2 171.4
	33 11.2	40 9.1	38 9.5	53 6.9				39 9.4	36 10.1
	46 7.9	58 6.3	53 6.9	63 5.8			Cost of Sales/Inventory	52 7.0	55 6.6
	62 5.8	78 4.7	84 4.4	81 4.5				77 4.7	75 4.8
	0 UND	7 52.6	15 25.1	20 18.7				2 212.1	2 171.5
	3 126.6	28 13.2	27 13.7	29 12.7			Cost of Sales/Payables	17 22.0	16 23.4
	27 13.4	50 7.2	56 6.5	38 9.6				33 10.9	32 11.4
	9.1	9.6	9.8	10.0				9.0	10.2
	15.6	21.8	17.9	12.0			Sales/Working Capital	16.0	21.5
	103.1	−102.1	191.1	31.7				79.4	−230.9
	10.0	9.2	11.2	16.8				7.2	5.7
	(75) 3.7	(87) 2.9	(29) 3.7	(16) 4.8			EBIT/Interest	(142) 2.9	(130) 3.0
	1.0	1.3	1.2	2.1				1.0	1.5
		1.7		8.0			Net Profit + Depr., Dep.,		12.6	4.6
		(11) 1.2	(11)	3.5			Amort./Cur. Mat. L /T/D	(25) 3.4	(23) 1.4
		.5		.9				1.8	.6
	.1	.2	.3	.3				.1	.2
	.6	.9	.8	.6			Fixed/Worth	.7	1.0
	−2.7	−3.4	NM	1.3				−2.6	−3.3
	.7	1.5	1.1	.7				.8	1.1
	4.8	4.3	3.0	1.9			Debt/Worth	2.9	3.4
	−7.1	−8.1	NM	3.0				−10.2	−8.9
	84.2	64.2	44.5	79.5			% Profit Before Taxes/Tangible	48.6	57.0
	(73) 38.3	(65) 24.2	(25) 14.8	(15) 20.7			Net Worth	(113) 18.6	(109) 24.2
	13.1	7.2	6.0	5.3				7.0	10.4
	19.6	14.0	14.4	18.8			% Profit Before Taxes/Total	14.7	14.7
	9.0	5.1	3.2	7.6			Assets	5.2	7.3
	.0	.9	1.0	1.9				.3	3.1
	260.2	75.1	48.5	41.1				102.0	103.9
	86.1	26.9	23.3	19.4			Sales/Net Fixed Assets	40.7	38.2
	25.6	9.5	7.8	9.9				15.0	12.5
	7.2	4.9	5.9	4.3				6.0	5.7
	5.1	3.5	3.2	3.3			Sales/Total Assets	4.4	4.2
	3.2	2.4	2.3	2.6				2.9	2.9
	.3	.3	.4	.6				.3	.4
	(64) .8	(85) .8	(32) .8	(13) 1.0			% Depr., Dep., Amort./Sales	(148) .7	(134) .7
	1.8	1.6	1.3	1.3				1.4	1.4
	2.2	1.3	1.0				% Officers', Directors',	1.6	1.4
	(67) 2.9	(56) 2.4	(13) 2.7				Owners' Comp/Sales	(79) 2.5	(89) 2.2
	4.1	4.1	4.1					5.0	4.1
	143744M	389091M	526128M	1203427M	107157M	347409M	Net Sales ($)	2314215M	1062419M
	29241M	95849M	140503M	347995M	72136M	140115M	Total Assets ($)	673168M	333407M

Comparative Historical Data

Current Data Sorted By Sales

			Type of Statement						
8	8	12	Unqualified		2	1	1	2	6
18	25	23	Reviewed		3	2	8	7	3
59	63	67	Compiled	13	32	10	6	5	1
52	39	107	Tax Returns	35	53	11	5	2	1
29	43	49	Other	5	11	6	8	9	10
4/1/00-3/31/01 ALL	4/1/01-3/31/02 ALL	4/1/02-3/31/03 ALL		56 (4/1-9/30/02)	202 (10/1/02-3/31/03)				
				0-1MM	1-3MM	3-5MM	5-10MM	10-25MM	25MM & OVER
166	178	258	**NUMBER OF STATEMENTS**	53	101	30	28	25	21
%	%	%	**ASSETS**	%	%	%	%	%	%
11.6	12.9	11.9	Cash & Equivalents	8.9	11.8	15.8	13.3	15.2	8.5
1.9	2.3	2.0	Trade Receivables (net)	.3	2.1	1.4	3.1	3.9	2.8
50.2	45.8	48.5	Inventory	48.8	48.3	46.7	53.4	47.9	45.3
1.0	1.9	1.0	All Other Current	.2	.9	1.9	1.7	.8	2.0
64.8	62.8	63.4	Total Current	58.3	63.2	65.6	71.5	67.9	58.6
19.2	18.2	18.2	Fixed Assets (net)	20.6	16.0	20.9	15.4	16.2	25.3
8.5	11.3	12.2	Intangibles (net)	13.4	15.4	6.4	9.6	11.1	6.9
7.5	7.7	6.1	All Other Non-Current	7.7	5.4	7.1	3.6	4.9	9.2
100.0	100.0	100.0	Total	100.0	100.0	100.0	100.0	100.0	100.0
			LIABILITIES						
7.5	6.7	8.1	Notes Payable-Short Term	7.7	7.7	7.7	7.3	10.8	9.4
3.8	3.8	3.5	Cur. Mat.-L/T/D	5.6	2.9	1.9	3.9	3.3	3.2
20.8	21.4	20.6	Trade Payables	10.2	19.7	28.9	28.3	28.6	19.0
.4	.3	.2	Income Taxes Payable	.1	.2	.4	.4	.2	.3
12.7	8.7	10.4	All Other Current	6.6	13.5	9.4	9.6	11.2	6.8
45.2	40.8	42.8	Total Current	30.3	44.0	48.4	49.5	54.1	38.6
20.0	19.7	20.6	Long Term Debt	31.5	21.9	17.4	15.1	9.1	12.7
.1	.1	.0	Deferred Taxes	.0	.0	.0	.0	.1	.3
8.5	8.8	9.3	All Other Non-Current	20.0	8.7	4.9	2.3	4.2	7.3
26.2	30.6	27.2	Net Worth	18.3	25.3	29.4	33.1	32.5	41.2
100.0	100.0	100.0	Total Liabilities & Net Worth	100.0	100.0	100.0	100.0	100.0	100.0
			INCOME DATA						
100.0	100.0	100.0	Net Sales	100.0	100.0	100.0	100.0	100.0	100.0
22.2	23.3	23.0	Gross Profit	25.8	21.7	23.6	21.9	22.1	24.0
20.0	21.2	20.9	Operating Expenses	24.4	19.6	21.2	19.2	20.4	20.3
2.2	2.0	2.1	Operating Profit	1.4	2.1	2.4	2.7	1.7	3.7
.0	.0	.1	All Other Expenses (net)	.5	.0	.3	.1	.2	-.1
2.2	2.0	2.0	Profit Before Taxes	.9	2.1	2.1	2.6	1.5	3.8
			RATIOS						
2.8	3.3	3.2		9.8	4.0	2.1	2.0	2.1	2.0
1.5	1.7	1.6	Current	2.5	1.9	1.3	1.5	1.4	1.7
1.0	1.0	1.0		1.0	1.1	1.0	1.0	.9	1.2
.7	.9	.8		3.0	.9	.5	.6	.8	.4
(163) .3	(177) .4	(254) .3	Quick	(51) .3	(99) .4	.3	.3	.4	.3
.1	.1	.1		.0	.1	.1	.1	.1	.2
0 UND	0 UND	0 UND		0 UND	0 UND	0 UND	0 UND	0 UND	0 989.7
0 UND	0 UND	0 UND	Sales/Receivables	0 UND	0 UND	0 999.8	1 587.9	1 503.6	2 177.7
1 331.8	2 153.2	1 288.4		0 UND	1 398.6	2 204.0	3 118.5	6 56.5	5 73.9
35 10.5	33 11.0	38 9.7		38 9.7	38 9.6	34 10.9	42 8.7	31 11.8	44 8.3
48 7.6	54 6.8	53 6.9	Cost of Sales/Inventory	55 6.6	50 7.3	53 6.9	60 6.1	44 8.4	59 6.2
66 5.6	73 5.0	72 5.1		83 4.4	69 5.3	68 5.4	81 4.5	68 5.3	69 5.3
3 126.5	2 150.0	0 852.7		0 UND	0 UND	12 30.5	11 33.7	12 29.3	14 25.9
18 20.3	22 16.6	19 19.1	Cost of Sales/Payables	0 UND	21 17.4	27 13.7	38 9.6	21 17.5	24 14.9
36 10.1	39 9.4	37 9.8		18 20.5	34 10.8	55 6.6	57 6.3	45 8.2	30 12.1
10.2	8.7	9.6		7.4	9.5	12.4	9.5	12.3	11.1
23.4	18.5	17.8	Sales/Working Capital	12.7	14.9	27.3	18.6	23.6	14.5
-269.2	136.8	486.0		UND	136.3	-335.6	NM	-127.3	34.7
7.0	5.8	9.0		3.8	9.6	11.3	16.3	8.9	14.7
(142) 3.1	(156) 3.0	(209) 3.7	EBIT/Interest	(35) 1.7	(79) 4.3	(26) 3.0	(26) 5.7	(23) 2.9	(20) 4.6
1.7	1.8	1.3		.3	1.1	1.4	2.4	1.5	2.1
5.5	6.3	5.5						8.4	
(21) 2.1	(22) 2.7	(31) 3.5	Net Profit + Depr., Dep., Amort./Cur. Mat. L/T/D					(10) 3.2	
1.7	1.2	1.1						1.4	
.2	.2	.2		.1	.1	.3	.1	.2	.4
.9	.6	.8	Fixed/Worth	.8	1.2	.6	.8	.5	.7
-3.7	6.7	-3.9		-3.6	-.7	7.4	1.8	NM	1.3
1.1	1.2	1.2		1.3	.9	1.1	1.3	1.3	.7
3.6	2.9	3.3	Debt/Worth	13.8	4.0	4.0	3.0	2.6	2.0
-9.2	UND	-15.1		-9.4	-5.5	27.7	5.9	-41.3	3.3
59.4	49.6	66.0		87.5	72.5	41.6	69.6	50.5	79.5
(116) 23.3	(134) 19.5	(180) 23.6	% Profit Before Taxes/Tangible Net Worth	(31) 20.0	(65) 28.6	(24) 23.5	(23) 37.7	(18) 13.6	(19) 22.9
8.9	6.0	7.4		7.1	9.7	6.3	10.2	5.7	7.4
12.6	13.3	15.6		14.1	16.5	14.0	22.2	11.0	18.8
6.2	5.2	6.3	% Profit Before Taxes/Total Assets	5.8	8.9	5.1	10.7	3.2	7.6
1.8	1.8	.9		-1.9	1.1	1.1	1.9	2.1	2.3
93.3	96.4	130.6		162.6	156.1	99.0	77.1	165.9	39.1
35.1	31.7	37.8	Sales/Net Fixed Assets	43.0	49.0	36.1	32.2	40.3	18.6
13.1	13.2	14.3		11.7	16.5	13.2	22.5	14.5	6.6
6.1	5.4	5.7		5.5	5.8	5.3	5.4	6.9	4.4
4.1	4.1	4.0	Sales/Total Assets	3.1	4.1	4.2	4.2	5.9	3.3
3.0	2.8	2.7		2.0	2.7	3.1	3.3	3.1	2.6
.3	.4	.4		.5	.4	.3	.2	.4	.7
(132) .7	(151) .8	(196) .8	% Depr., Dep., Amort./Sales	(30) 1.5	(74) .8	(27) .8	(25) .5	(23) .6	(17) 1.2
1.4	1.3	1.6		2.6	1.8	1.8	1.1	1.2	1.5
1.3	1.7	1.6		2.5	1.8	1.7	1.0	1.2	
(101) 2.6	(98) 2.6	(141) 2.7	% Officers', Directors', Owners' Comp/Sales	(29) 2.8	(62) 3.0	(18) 2.4	(15) 1.9	(12) 2.4	
4.4	4.4	3.9		6.4	4.5	2.8	2.7	6.5	
3887787M	2379452M	2716956M	Net Sales ($)	33812M	181290M	116501M	197642M	386345M	1801366M
922775M	728649M	825839M	Total Assets ($)	12488M	52154M	32844M	67755M	86119M	574479M

M = $ thousand   MM = $ million
See Pages 11 through 18 for Explanation of Ratios and Data

Current Data Sorted By Assets   Comparative Historical Data

0-500M	500M-2MM	2-10MM	10-50MM	50-100MM	100-250MM	Type of Statement	4/1/98-3/31/99 ALL	4/1/99-3/31/00 ALL
		2	7	2	1	Unqualified	17	22
1	7	14	2	1		Reviewed	32	24
21	42	14	2			Compiled	89	74
32	29	5			2	Tax Returns	37	41
11	28	16	2	4		Other	48	51
	59 (4/1-9/30/02)		184 (10/1/02-3/31/03)					
65	106	51	11	7	3	**NUMBER OF STATEMENTS**	223	212
%	%	%	%	%	%	**ASSETS**	%	%
11.8	12.4	12.0	7.3			Cash & Equivalents	7.3	8.5
21.2	22.9	28.6	25.0			Trade Receivables (net)	22.4	22.1
48.5	38.9	31.5	31.9			Inventory	44.2	42.8
2.7	2.4	3.7	8.1			All Other Current	2.0	2.1
84.1	76.7	75.8	72.3			Total Current	75.9	75.5
11.1	12.3	14.4	13.8			Fixed Assets (net)	14.1	12.8
1.3	4.7	4.7	1.0			Intangibles (net)	3.9	5.0
3.4	6.3	5.1	12.9			All Other Non-Current	6.1	6.7
100.0	100.0	100.0	100.0			Total	100.0	100.0
						LIABILITIES		
12.2	5.6	10.4	10.4			Notes Payable-Short Term	7.9	8.1
2.2	2.8	2.9	5.9			Cur. Mat.-L/T/D	4.0	3.8
26.5	22.8	25.6	21.4			Trade Payables	23.1	25.8
.3	.2	.3	.0			Income Taxes Payable	.3	.3
8.3	7.7	5.3	10.8			All Other Current	7.8	6.5
49.5	39.1	44.5	48.6			Total Current	43.1	44.4
14.7	13.4	12.2	13.4			Long Term Debt	16.0	18.6
.0	.0	.1	.2			Deferred Taxes	.2	.1
4.1	2.8	4.5	6.4			All Other Non-Current	4.3	5.2
31.7	44.7	38.7	31.3			Net Worth	36.4	31.7
100.0	100.0	100.0	100.0			Total Liabilities & Net Worth	100.0	100.0
						INCOME DATA		
100.0	100.0	100.0	100.0			Net Sales	100.0	100.0
25.6	24.3	27.1	27.1			Gross Profit	26.8	25.2
22.6	20.6	22.4	22.5			Operating Expenses	24.6	22.7
3.0	3.7	4.7	4.6			Operating Profit	2.2	2.4
−.1	.1	−.1	−.4			All Other Expenses (net)	−.2	.2
3.1	3.6	4.8	5.0			Profit Before Taxes	2.4	2.3
						RATIOS		
3.4	3.3	2.3	1.9			Current	2.8	2.7
2.0	2.0	1.7	1.5				2.0	1.9
1.3	1.3	1.3	1.2				1.3	1.2
1.8	1.6	1.3	.9			Quick	1.2	1.2
.8	.9	.8	.6			(222)	.7	.7
.4	.5	.6	.4				.4	.3
1 401.7	9 39.4	15 24.6	11 33.6			Sales/Receivables	9 42.9	10 36.6
12 29.8	15 23.6	25 14.8	31 11.7				16 23.3	16 23.5
20 18.3	22 16.8	33 11.0	46 7.9				25 14.8	25 14.7
25 14.8	24 15.4	24 15.1	26 14.1			Cost of Sales/Inventory	34 10.6	31 11.7
35 10.3	33 11.2	35 10.6	42 8.7				49 7.5	46 8.0
55 6.7	47 7.8	44 8.4	74 4.9				65 5.6	63 5.8
9 40.9	12 31.7	18 20.4	25 14.6			Cost of Sales/Payables	16 22.5	16 23.3
20 18.2	19 19.4	26 14.2	38 9.6				22 16.4	24 15.5
29 12.6	27 13.3	43 8.4	39 9.3				38 9.7	38 9.7
11.1	8.9	8.3	8.7			Sales/Working Capital	8.1	8.8
15.5	13.3	14.5	10.6				12.6	13.7
42.9	28.6	29.5	36.6				25.1	29.9
26.7	(86) 23.5	(49) 29.3	17.6			EBIT/Interest	11.9	10.4
(46) 7.2	7.1	7.0	9.8				(202) 3.9	(181) 3.4
2.9	3.9	3.0	3.3				1.5	1.6
	2.9	9.3				Net Profit + Depr., Dep.,	3.2	4.3
	(14) 1.5	(16) 2.7				Amort./Cur. Mat. L /T/D	(57) 1.4	(49) 1.8
	.7	1.1					.8	1.0
.0	.1	.2	.1			Fixed/Worth	.1	.1
.2	.3	.5	.4				.4	.4
.7	.6	.9	1.0				1.3	3.0
.6	.6	1.1	1.0			Debt/Worth	.8	.9
1.7	1.5	2.0	1.6				1.9	2.0
12.8	3.7	4.7	4.9				7.8	22.4
129.6	65.1	76.7	66.2			% Profit Before Taxes/Tangible	52.8	48.4
(55) 52.7	(100) 36.7	(49) 40.2	(10) 23.5			Net Worth	(189) 23.9	(168) 23.1
12.6	13.5	16.1	13.1				6.7	7.0
35.1	26.0	22.9	14.8			% Profit Before Taxes/Total	17.9	15.9
15.1	13.7	12.0	11.1			Assets	6.9	6.6
4.3	6.3	4.0	5.5				1.4	2.2
552.7	142.3	56.8	69.2			Sales/Net Fixed Assets	94.1	101.2
90.5	60.8	36.2	23.8				40.6	49.8
37.7	27.0	21.9	17.3				22.1	24.7
8.3	6.6	5.4	4.5			Sales/Total Assets	5.7	5.8
6.6	5.3	4.4	3.0				4.5	4.4
4.8	4.3	3.2	1.5				3.2	3.3
.2	.3	.3	.6			% Depr., Dep., Amort./Sales	.3	.3
(44) .5	(92) .5	(47) .6	1.0				(190) .6	(183) .6
.9	.8	1.0	2.2				1.0	1.1
1.4	2.2	.4				% Officers', Directors',	2.1	2.2
(41) 3.2	(64) 4.1	(24) 2.2				Owners' Comp/Sales	(109) 3.4	(111) 3.3
5.6	6.4	3.5					5.7	5.5
130324M	580363M	867086M	753727M	1986922M	4593014M	Net Sales ($)	4335891M	3928549M
18987M	107384M	210425M	225265M	542022M	554742M	Total Assets ($)	1317053M	1362198M

M = $ thousand   MM = $ million
See Pages 11 through 18 for Explanation of Ratios and Data

Comparative Historical Data | Current Data Sorted By Sales

				Type of Statement						
	13	14	12	Unqualified					2	10
	24	19	23	Reviewed			3	7	8	5
	73	63	79	Compiled	4	18	19	23	15	
	42	50	68	Tax Returns	7	25	21	9	4	2
	51	52	61	Other	5	7	16	11	12	10
	4/1/00-3/31/01 ALL	4/1/01-3/31/02 ALL	4/1/02-3/31/03 ALL		\<-- 59 (4/1-9/30/02) -->			\<-- 184 (10/1/02-3/31/03) -->		
					0-1MM	1-3MM	3-5MM	5-10MM	10-25MM	25MM & OVER
	203	198	243	NUMBER OF STATEMENTS	16	50	59	50	41	27
	%	%	%	ASSETS	%	%	%	%	%	%
	9.3	10.8	11.6	Cash & Equivalents	8.3	11.6	14.0	10.1	14.4	6.6
	23.3	22.4	23.6	Trade Receivables (net)	18.5	19.9	23.4	27.0	24.1	26.4
	41.0	42.4	39.8	Inventory	38.4	49.0	38.5	38.5	33.8	38.2
	2.4	2.9	3.0	All Other Current	6.8	1.5	3.8	1.9	3.8	2.7
	76.0	78.5	78.0	Total Current	72.0	82.0	79.7	77.5	76.1	74.0
	13.0	12.5	12.6	Fixed Assets (net)	15.7	11.0	10.3	13.8	15.1	12.5
	5.6	4.2	3.9	Intangibles (net)	5.5	3.1	3.6	3.7	3.1	6.7
	5.3	4.8	5.6	All Other Non-Current	6.9	4.0	6.4	5.0	5.6	6.8
	100.0	100.0	100.0	Total	100.0	100.0	100.0	100.0	100.0	100.0
				LIABILITIES						
	7.9	7.3	8.5	Notes Payable-Short Term	26.3	8.5	5.3	6.4	7.6	10.0
	3.2	3.3	2.9	Cur. Mat.-L/T/D	2.9	2.7	2.6	2.5	2.5	5.1
	23.4	24.6	24.3	Trade Payables	15.7	21.7	26.0	24.5	28.1	24.7
	.2	.2	.2	Income Taxes Payable	.0	.3	.2	.2	.3	.3
	8.7	7.7	7.4	All Other Current	5.9	7.9	8.8	6.7	7.2	6.3
	43.4	43.2	43.4	Total Current	50.8	41.1	42.9	40.3	45.7	46.4
	17.6	16.2	14.1	Long Term Debt	21.1	13.7	13.8	13.1	8.9	21.4
	.2	.1	.1	Deferred Taxes	.0	.0	.0	.0	.1	.2
	5.3	6.1	3.7	All Other Non-Current	.9	4.8	1.9	4.1	4.9	4.5
	33.5	34.4	38.8	Net Worth	27.4	40.3	41.4	42.5	40.4	27.6
	100.0	100.0	100.0	Total Liabilities & Net Worth	100.0	100.0	100.0	100.0	100.0	100.0
				INCOME DATA						
	100.0	100.0	100.0	Net Sales	100.0	100.0	100.0	100.0	100.0	100.0
	25.4	26.2	25.4	Gross Profit	37.6	24.0	25.2	24.3	23.8	26.1
	23.0	23.1	21.7	Operating Expenses	32.1	20.3	21.4	21.0	19.7	22.8
	2.4	3.1	3.8	Operating Profit	5.5	3.6	3.8	3.2	4.0	3.4
	.1	.4	.1	All Other Expenses (net)	-.2	.2	.2	-.2	-.4	.8
	2.3	2.7	3.7	Profit Before Taxes	5.8	3.5	3.6	3.5	4.4	2.6
				RATIOS						
	2.8	3.1	3.0	Current	7.4	3.1	3.6	3.1	2.2	2.5
	1.9	2.0	1.9		1.8	2.3	1.7	2.0	1.6	1.7
	1.3	1.4	1.3		1.0	1.5	1.3	1.3	1.3	1.4
(202)	1.3	1.2	1.5	Quick	2.5	1.6	2.0	1.3	1.3	.9
	.8	.8	.8		.6	.8	.9	.9	.8	.6
	.5	.5	.5		.3	.4	.5	.5	.5	.4
	10 35.8	9 40.7	8 44.1	Sales/Receivables	0 UND	7 52.6	7 49.3	10 37.0	6 57.0	11 33.5
	17 21.7	16 23.3	16 23.1		19 19.0	14 26.0	14 25.8	17 21.3	19 19.1	22 16.7
	26 14.2	24 15.1	26 14.2		56 6.5	21 17.6	21 17.6	25 14.8	31 11.7	33 11.0
	28 13.1	28 13.1	25 14.8	Cost of Sales/Inventory	31 11.7	29 12.8	21 17.5	24 15.3	22 16.8	26 13.9
	41 9.0	38 9.7	35 10.6		55 6.6	40 9.2	31 11.8	33 11.2	31 11.6	41 9.0
	55 6.6	56 6.5	50 7.2		100 3.6	56 6.6	40 9.0	44 8.3	42 8.7	57 6.4
	15 25.0	13 29.2	14 26.1	Cost of Sales/Payables	1 288.7	9 40.2	10 35.0	13 27.1	17 21.1	20 18.7
	20 18.1	21 17.2	21 17.2		28 13.2	19 19.7	19 20.0	19 17.5	22 16.9	24 15.0
	31 11.6	36 10.2	31 11.9		30 12.0	29 12.7	28 13.1	28 13.2	37 10.0	39 9.3
	8.9	8.1	9.3	Sales/Working Capital	4.8	9.1	8.9	10.2	9.7	9.1
	13.6	12.3	14.4		13.3	12.4	17.6	12.9	18.5	14.5
	29.2	25.7	29.9		376.7	19.4	36.7	33.0	30.9	26.0
(178) (171) (201)	10.1	11.1	21.0	EBIT/Interest	(11) 9.2	(36) 13.9	(47) 31.3	(41) 35.1	(40) 41.1	(26) 10.4
	4.4	4.4	6.8		3.1	5.4	14.0	6.0	13.3	4.4
	1.5	1.7	3.1		.8	2.7	3.9	3.0	4.0	2.4
(45) (33) (43)	4.2	7.4	10.1	Net Profit + Depr., Dep., Amort./Cur. Mat. L/T/D					(11) 30.7	(13) 9.9
	2.4	1.8	1.9						3.1	2.4
	1.4	1.1	1.0						1.2	1.0
	.1	.1	.1	Fixed/Worth	.0	.0	.1	.1	.2	.3
	.4	.4	.3		.5	.2	.2	.3	.4	.5
	1.7	1.0	.7		NM	.9	.5	.6	.8	5.0
	.8	.8	.7	Debt/Worth	.4	.6	.4	.6	.9	1.5
	1.8	1.9	1.7		2.7	1.3	1.6	1.7	1.5	3.2
	20.3	6.5	4.9		-10.8	9.2	3.3	4.6	2.8	18.5
(161) (167) (221)	50.0	53.6	77.8	% Profit Before Taxes/Tangible Net Worth	(11) 135.5	(44) 114.0	(55) 85.6	(49) 64.7	(40) 79.5	(22) 76.8
	23.4	24.2	37.0		59.4	25.0	43.4	46.9	39.4	25.1
	7.8	8.0	13.8		9.1	6.2	13.5	20.3	18.7	11.8
	17.0	18.3	25.7	% Profit Before Taxes/Total Assets	23.1	28.4	35.6	21.9	24.1	14.9
	8.4	9.1	13.1		10.9	12.4	16.2	13.6	12.5	10.2
	1.8	2.1	5.4		-.7	2.7	7.3	6.0	5.5	3.7
	125.8	132.4	127.2	Sales/Net Fixed Assets	245.9	311.6	275.7	120.6	65.7	69.2
	52.0	53.6	54.5		34.7	77.7	86.2	54.9	36.2	31.8
	25.0	26.7	25.7		12.4	35.2	36.6	26.2	20.1	23.8
	6.1	6.4	6.6	Sales/Total Assets	4.8	6.9	7.7	6.6	6.1	4.8
	4.8	4.7	5.0		3.7	5.6	5.7	5.4	5.0	4.0
	3.6	3.6	3.9		1.7	4.4	4.3	4.4	3.6	3.4
(165) (164) (202)	.3	.3	.3	% Depr., Dep., Amort./Sales		(39) .3	(47) .2	(43) .3	(40) .3	(24) .4
	.5	.5	.6			.5	.5	.5	.5	.6
	.9	.9	.9			.9	.9	.8	1.0	1.1
(110) (113) (133)	2.2	1.9	1.7	% Officers', Directors', Owners' Comp/Sales		(31) 1.2	(40) 2.0	(29) 2.7	(22) .4	
	3.4	3.2	3.2			3.0	3.9	4.3	1.8	
	5.0	5.9	6.1			5.2	7.0	6.4	3.2	
	4140120M	3554242M	8911436M	Net Sales ($)	9944M	100593M	231925M	342349M	684654M	7541971M
	1465235M	937743M	1658825M	Total Assets ($)	9050M	20704M	45179M	69214M	179580M	1335098M

Current Data Sorted By Assets

Comparative Historical Data

							Type of Statement			
			1	1		2	Unqualified		6	5
		4	2	1			Reviewed		7	7
6		5	1				Compiled		7	6
7							Tax Returns		3	2
5			2	2	1		Other		3	8
	15 (4/1-9/30/02)			25 (10/1/02-3/31/03)					4/1/98-3/31/99	4/1/99-3/31/00
0-500M	500M-2MM	2-10MM	10-50MM	50-100MM	100-250MM				ALL	ALL
18	9	6	4	1	2		NUMBER OF STATEMENTS		26	28
%	%	%	%	%	%		ASSETS		%	%
16.1							Cash & Equivalents		4.9	5.1
9.0							Trade Receivables (net)		23.0	24.7
42.4							Inventory		37.5	43.0
.2							All Other Current		3.5	1.3
67.6							Total Current		69.0	74.1
28.3							Fixed Assets (net)		16.3	15.3
2.4							Intangibles (net)		8.6	4.6
1.6							All Other Non-Current		6.2	6.0
100.0							Total		100.0	100.0
							LIABILITIES			
10.9							Notes Payable-Short Term		11.3	15.5
3.4							Cur. Mat.-L/T/D		4.8	5.5
11.8							Trade Payables		23.0	22.9
.0							Income Taxes Payable		.5	.2
15.8							All Other Current		10.6	5.7
41.9							Total Current		50.1	49.8
26.6							Long Term Debt		12.2	16.0
.1							Deferred Taxes		.1	.2
14.1							All Other Non-Current		5.9	8.2
17.4							Net Worth		31.6	25.7
100.0							Total Liabilities & Net Worth		100.0	100.0
							INCOME DATA			
100.0							Net Sales		100.0	100.0
44.6							Gross Profit		38.2	41.6
35.5							Operating Expenses		34.1	39.5
9.1							Operating Profit		4.2	2.1
1.2							All Other Expenses (net)		.6	1.2
7.9							Profit Before Taxes		3.5	.9
							RATIOS			
5.8									2.0	1.8
1.7							Current		1.5	1.4
1.0									1.1	1.2
2.5									.9	.8
.4							Quick		.5	.6
.1									.3	.4
0	UND							14	26.7	15	24.5
0	UND						Sales/Receivables	28	13.2	37	9.9
11	32.2							40	9.2	54	6.7
45	8.1							33	10.9	85	4.3
77	4.7						Cost of Sales/Inventory	80	4.6	98	3.7
161	2.3							103	3.5	110	3.3
0	UND							26	13.9	23	15.6
18	20.5						Cost of Sales/Payables	40	9.0	35	10.5
47	7.8							66	5.5	78	4.7
	4.6								9.5	7.2
	15.8						Sales/Working Capital		14.9	10.7
	288.3								NM	23.3
	9.4								5.0	4.4
(14)	2.7						EBIT/Interest	(22)	3.0	(27)	1.9
	.5								1.5	1.1
							Net Profit + Depr., Dep.,		4.0	2.9
							Amort./Cur. Mat. L./T/D	(13)	2.1	(17)	1.4
									.3	.4
	.1								.1	.3
	3.8						Fixed/Worth		.5	.7
	−3.3								1.6	NM
	1.1								1.4	1.3
	10.1						Debt/Worth		2.9	2.4
	−14.8								12.5	NM
	83.0						% Profit Before Taxes/Tangible		41.1	31.8
(10)	47.2						Net Worth	(21)	24.1	(21)	16.7
	11.3								10.0	2.3
	43.3						% Profit Before Taxes/Total		14.3	10.9
	7.0						Assets		7.1	3.6
	−3.0								2.2	.3
	159.2								117.7	47.6
	17.9						Sales/Net Fixed Assets		25.0	24.9
	3.8								13.8	16.8
	4.6								4.2	3.9
	2.7						Sales/Total Assets		2.9	2.7
	1.8								2.1	2.4
	.6								.5	.6
(16)	1.6						% Depr., Dep., Amort./Sales	(23)	.9	(26)	1.2
	2.6								1.6	1.8
							% Officers', Directors',		1.6	1.6
							Owners' Comp/Sales	(11)	2.1	(12)	1.9
									11.4	5.6
13487M	38897M	67579M	236454M	176188M	690049M		Net Sales ($)		545347M	652961M
4004M	12469M	26143M	119846M	66582M	345358M		Total Assets ($)		200211M	234210M

M = $ thousand   MM = $ million
See Pages 11 through 18 for Explanation of Ratios and Data

Comparative Historical Data / Current Data Sorted By Sales

4/1/00-3/31/01 ALL	4/1/01-3/31/02 ALL	4/1/02-3/31/03 ALL	Type of Statement	0-1MM	1-3MM	3-5MM	5-10MM	10-25MM	25MM & OVER
					15 (4/1-9/30/02)			25 (10/1/02-3/31/03)	
6	4	4	Unqualified						4
6	3	7	Reviewed		1	1	3	1	1
6	5	12	Compiled	4	4	2	2		
	1	7	Tax Returns	5	2				
5	5	10	Other	4	1	1		1	3
23	18	40	**NUMBER OF STATEMENTS**	13	8	4	5	2	8
%	%	%	**ASSETS**	%	%	%	%	%	%
3.4	4.5	13.8	Cash & Equivalents	16.2					
16.0	20.5	15.1	Trade Receivables (net)	3.4					
41.6	38.2	36.4	Inventory	40.2					
1.8	1.7	1.7	All Other Current	.1					
62.9	64.9	67.0	Total Current	60.0					
12.0	14.4	23.7	Fixed Assets (net)	36.7					
8.3	12.1	5.3	Intangibles (net)	3.0					
16.8	8.6	4.0	All Other Non-Current	.3					
100.0	100.0	100.0	Total	100.0					
			LIABILITIES						
13.7	11.8	7.8	Notes Payable-Short Term	8.4					
5.1	4.2	3.3	Cur. Mat.-L/T/D	2.7					
19.7	20.9	18.4	Trade Payables	8.9					
.1	.0	.1	Income Taxes Payable	.0					
17.7	7.5	14.1	All Other Current	6.2					
56.3	44.4	43.6	Total Current	26.2					
10.7	13.2	16.7	Long Term Debt	33.2					
.2	.2	.4	Deferred Taxes	.1					
5.4	8.6	9.3	All Other Non-Current	16.6					
27.5	33.6	29.9	Net Worth	23.8					
100.0	100.0	100.0	Total Liabilities & Net Worth	100.0					
			INCOME DATA						
100.0	100.0	100.0	Net Sales	100.0					
39.0	39.3	46.3	Gross Profit	47.3					
35.2	37.4	39.4	Operating Expenses	36.3					
3.8	1.9	6.9	Operating Profit	11.0					
1.1	.6	1.2	All Other Expenses (net)	2.1					
2.7	1.3	5.6	Profit Before Taxes	8.9					
			RATIOS						
1.6	2.3	2.4	Current	6.1					
1.2	1.4	1.6		1.9					
.8	1.2	1.1		1.1					
.5	1.0	1.4	Quick	3.3					
.3	.5	.5		.5					
.2	.4	.2		.1					
13 27.6	17 22.0	0 UND	Sales/Receivables	0 UND					
17 21.0	26 14.2	16 22.2		0 UND					
33 10.9	30 12.0	35 10.5		2 220.7					
53 6.9	50 7.3	53 6.9	Cost of Sales/Inventory	60 6.1					
88 4.2	83 4.4	70 5.2		135 2.7					
117 3.1	96 3.8	126 2.9		173 2.1					
17 21.9	29 12.7	17 21.1	Cost of Sales/Payables	0 UND					
40 9.1	41 9.0	45 8.0		19 19.3					
67 5.5	60 6.1	58 6.2		48 7.5					
9.2	10.0	5.1	Sales/Working Capital	4.1					
22.6	17.3	14.2		11.6					
−15.4	32.7	102.7		82.2					
(20) 5.4	(17) 2.9	(33) 8.5	EBIT/Interest	(11) 5.7					
2.1	1.5	3.4		1.9					
.3	.8	1.1		.3					
		(10) 6.2	Net Profit + Depr., Dep., Amort./Cur. Mat. L/T/D						
		3.0							
		1.5							
.1	.3	.2	Fixed/Worth	.4					
.6	.6	.7		6.5					
2.4	NM	5.4		−5.4					
1.5	1.5	1.5	Debt/Worth	.9					
3.1	2.9	2.4		6.1					
46.2	NM	12.7		−15.2					
(19) 35.0	(14) 14.8	(32) 57.8	% Profit Before Taxes/Tangible Net Worth						
11.6	7.4	31.4							
−11.5	−2.2	10.9							
11.0	8.7	31.0	% Profit Before Taxes/Total Assets	43.2					
4.0	2.4	6.2		6.2					
−2.6	−.4	.8		−3.7					
73.7	58.1	47.8	Sales/Net Fixed Assets	26.1					
42.8	28.2	19.1		9.0					
21.4	15.9	7.5		2.9					
3.9	3.6	3.8	Sales/Total Assets	2.9					
2.7	2.8	2.7		2.2					
1.5	2.3	1.9		1.4					
(13) .5	(14) .6	(37) .6	% Depr., Dep., Amort./Sales	(12) 1.5					
.8	1.1	1.6		2.2					
2.0	1.7	2.8		2.8					
		(22) 1.9	% Officers', Directors', Owners' Comp/Sales						
		2.8							
		8.5							
813510M	734070M	1222654M	Net Sales ($)	5985M	12890M	17147M	34370M	24337M	1127925M
411685M	335168M	574402M	Total Assets ($)	2706M	3741M	7595M	11692M	8120M	540548M

M = $ thousand   MM = $ million
See Pages 11 through 18 for Explanation of Ratios and Data

RETAIL—Optical Goods Stores NAICS 446130 (SIC 5995)

Current Data Sorted By Assets | **Comparative Historical Data**

						Type of Statement		
	1	1	1	2		Unqualified	4	1
1	3	2				Reviewed	13	13
5	5	3				Compiled	22	21
26	2		5		1	Tax Returns	38	26
3	3			1	1	Other	40	36
	11 (4/1-9/30/02)			54 (10/1/02-3/31/03)			4/1/98-3/31/99 ALL	4/1/99-3/31/00 ALL
0-500M	500M-2MM	2-10MM	10-50MM	50-100MM	100-250MM			
35	14	11	3		2	NUMBER OF STATEMENTS	117	97
%	%	%	%	%	%	ASSETS	%	%
14.1	6.4	8.4				Cash & Equivalents	9.5	9.7
8.6	10.0	22.0		D		Trade Receivables (net)	14.9	13.3
41.0	30.9	19.5		A		Inventory	33.7	36.8
2.7	1.0	1.1		T		All Other Current	2.0	1.4
66.5	48.3	51.0		A		Total Current	60.1	61.2
17.9	30.4	36.4				Fixed Assets (net)	24.2	23.8
3.2	12.1	2.7		N		Intangibles (net)	8.2	6.8
12.4	9.2	9.9		O		All Other Non-Current	7.5	8.3
100.0	100.0	100.0		T		Total	100.0	100.0
				A		LIABILITIES		
6.6	2.5	9.1		V		Notes Payable-Short Term	9.5	12.1
6.7	5.4	4.4		A		Cur. Mat.-L/T/D	5.5	7.1
23.9	14.3	17.0		I		Trade Payables	18.2	19.0
.1	.3	.0		L		Income Taxes Payable	.3	.2
12.4	8.7	9.3		A		All Other Current	10.3	10.6
49.7	31.1	39.9		B		Total Current	43.9	49.0
25.2	24.1	24.1		L		Long Term Debt	22.4	21.5
.1	.0	.1		E		Deferred Taxes	.2	.1
9.1	6.5	7.4				All Other Non-Current	5.1	2.9
15.8	38.3	28.5				Net Worth	28.5	26.4
100.0	100.0	100.0				Total Liabilities & Net Worth	100.0	100.0
						INCOME DATA		
100.0	100.0	100.0				Net Sales	100.0	100.0
48.6	47.5	61.9				Gross Profit	51.3	47.3
41.6	44.5	52.5				Operating Expenses	46.4	43.0
7.0	3.0	9.5				Operating Profit	5.0	4.3
1.0	.7	2.8				All Other Expenses (net)	.7	.6
6.0	2.3	6.6				Profit Before Taxes	4.3	3.7
						RATIOS		
2.6	3.7	2.5					2.4	2.1
1.5	1.8	1.2				Current	1.4	1.4
.9	.9	.7					.9	.9
.8	.8	1.2					1.0	1.1
.6	.4	.9				Quick	.5 (95)	.6
.2	.2	.3					.2	.2

						Sales/Receivables		
0	UND	0 UND	10	37.7			4	81.6	1	360.0
2	189.0	5 68.7	20	18.2			12	31.4	9	39.0
8	45.0	15 23.7	58	6.3			26	14.0	23	15.7

						Cost of Sales/Inventory				
50	7.3	40 9.1	48	7.6			41	9.0	47	7.8
92	4.0	74 4.9	73	5.0			78	4.7	88	4.2
136	2.7	102 3.6	90	4.0			151	2.4	140	2.6

						Cost of Sales/Payables				
5	72.9	9 41.8	20	18.0			19	19.2	20	18.0
38	9.6	24 15.4	34	10.7			44	8.2	39	9.4
66	5.6	35 10.5	133	2.7			69	5.3	69	5.3

						Sales/Working Capital		
7.6	7.2	9.8					6.7	8.0
23.6	16.7	48.4					18.9	20.1
−99.0	−64.4	−18.2					−62.6	−70.1

						EBIT/Interest		
	8.8	6.5						7.6	8.2
(27)	3.9	(13) 2.1					(102) 2.6	(85) 2.5
	−.4	−1.3						1.1	1.0

						Net Profit + Depr., Dep., Amort./Cur. Mat. L/T/D		
							6.2	7.0
						(17)	2.7 (18)	2.4
							.5	1.1

						Fixed/Worth		
.1	.4	.1					.2	.2
1.1	1.2	1.1					.9	1.0
−1.0	−2.1	−6.1					15.2	−10.9

						Debt/Worth		
.9	.5	1.2					.9	1.0
11.6	1.7	2.0					3.3	3.0
−8.0	−6.0	−9.1					UND	−26.8

						% Profit Before Taxes/Tangible Net Worth		
	90.8	56.3					84.0	84.3
(19)	14.9	(10) 17.7					(89) 22.6	(68) 29.3
	−27.3	−9.7					3.8	5.0

						% Profit Before Taxes/Total Assets		
39.3	12.5	21.0					20.5	18.8
7.9	3.7	12.5					6.2	6.9
−12.4	−8.8	3.6					.3	.3

						Sales/Net Fixed Assets		
113.4	26.5	14.6					38.8	42.4
31.4	16.0	7.1					15.4	20.2
12.0	6.5	3.1					7.6	6.8

						Sales/Total Assets		
5.6	4.6	3.4					4.1	3.9
3.5	2.7	2.4					2.8	2.8
2.3	1.9	1.7					1.7	2.0

						% Depr., Dep., Amort./Sales		
	.4	.8	.7				.7	.7
(26)	.9	(13) 1.0	2.0			(91)	1.7 (83)	1.6
	2.2	1.9	2.4				2.9	2.8

						% Officers', Directors', Owners' Comp/Sales		
	3.4	3.4					3.2	2.6
(21)	7.0	(10) 7.6				(55)	6.9 (48)	6.1
	15.5	13.0					12.5	11.5

24600M	40102M	173679M	134865M		1588602M	Net Sales ($)	2178239M	753133M
6644M	13112M	59187M	48459M		447804M	Total Assets ($)	956252M	317879M

© RMA 2003

M = $ thousand   MM = $ million
See Pages 11 through 18 for Explanation of Ratios and Data

Comparative Historical Data / Current Data Sorted By Sales

			Type of Statement						
3	1	4	Unqualified	1					3
6	3	6	Reviewed		2		2	2	
21	18	13	Compiled	3	6	2	1	1	
15	19	29	Tax Returns	22	4	2			1
23	15	13	Other	3	3		2	2	3
4/1/00-3/31/01 ALL	4/1/01-3/31/02 ALL	4/1/02-3/31/03 ALL		11 (4/1-9/30/02) 0-1MM	1-3MM	54 (10/1/02-3/31/03) 3-5MM	5-10MM	10-25MM	25MM & OVER
68	56	65	NUMBER OF STATEMENTS	28	16	4	5	5	7
%	%	%	**ASSETS**	%	%	%	%	%	%
8.5	8.2	10.6	Cash & Equivalents	15.8	6.2				
14.8	11.6	11.1	Trade Receivables (net)	7.7	9.2				
35.9	38.0	33.5	Inventory	39.8	36.8				
2.6	2.2	1.9	All Other Current	1.6	4.2				
61.8	60.0	57.1	Total Current	64.9	56.4				
24.4	22.2	25.5	Fixed Assets (net)	18.3	22.9				
8.2	9.6	6.7	Intangibles (net)	3.7	11.0				
5.6	8.3	10.6	All Other Non-Current	13.1	9.6				
100.0	100.0	100.0	Total	100.0	100.0				
			LIABILITIES						
12.7	9.1	5.7	Notes Payable-Short Term	6.5	5.7				
4.5	4.1	6.5	Cur. Mat.-L/T/D	5.5	8.9				
21.5	17.8	19.4	Trade Payables	20.9	14.9				
.2	.1	.1	Income Taxes Payable	.1	.2				
15.8	9.8	10.8	All Other Current	11.9	9.5				
54.6	40.8	42.6	Total Current	44.8	39.0				
19.5	19.0	25.4	Long Term Debt	26.5	27.6				
.3	.0	.1	Deferred Taxes	.2	.0				
5.2	10.9	8.6	All Other Non-Current	6.7	5.5				
20.4	29.2	23.2	Net Worth	21.8	27.8				
100.0	100.0	100.0	Total Liabilities & Net Worth	100.0	100.0				
			INCOME DATA						
100.0	100.0	100.0	Net Sales	100.0	100.0				
48.0	53.0	52.0	Gross Profit	52.3	51.1				
45.3	47.1	45.6	Operating Expenses	44.5	46.7				
2.7	5.9	6.4	Operating Profit	7.9	4.4				
1.0	1.3	1.3	All Other Expenses (net)	1.4	.7				
1.7	4.6	5.1	Profit Before Taxes	6.4	3.7				
			RATIOS						
2.1	2.6	2.5	Current	2.6	4.9				
1.3	1.5	1.5		2.0	1.5				
.8	1.0	.8		1.0	.7				
1.0	.8	.8	Quick	.8	.7				
.4	.4	.4		.6	.4				
.2	.2	.2		.2	.2				
1 433.1	1 543.7	0 UND	Sales/Receivables	0 UND	1 383.4				
9 41.6	5 75.4	5 66.7		0 UND	5 72.2				
27 13.6	16 23.5	16 23.1		7 49.9	23 16.0				
37 9.9	53 6.9	48 7.6	Cost of Sales/Inventory	76 4.8	53 6.8				
80 4.6	92 4.0	85 4.3		95 3.8	88 4.1				
125 2.9	165 2.2	112 3.3		138 2.6	124 2.9				
19 19.7	14 26.7	10 35.6	Cost of Sales/Payables	0 UND	8 44.7				
39 9.3	38 9.7	33 10.9		26 14.1	31 11.8				
66 5.5	76 4.8	61 6.0		56 6.6	60 6.0				
7.7	7.6	7.9	Sales/Working Capital	7.2	6.4				
29.2	16.2	22.0		14.9	17.8				
-39.3	NM	-63.9		NM	-22.0				
9.7	8.4	8.7	EBIT/Interest	11.6	5.6				
(63) 2.0	(47) 2.4	(54) 3.8		(20) 4.1	(15) 1.1				
-.5	1.0	.4		.3	-1.4				
5.9			Net Profit + Depr., Dep., Amort./Cur. Mat. L/T/D						
(12) 1.7									
.6									
.3	.1	.2	Fixed/Worth	.0	.2				
.9	.9	1.2		.8	.9				
-14.8	-25.8	-3.3		-4.7	-1.3				
1.0	.8	1.1	Debt/Worth	.7	1.1				
3.0	2.8	2.7		7.3	3.6				
-33.6	-115.3	-8.0		-11.1	-5.3				
66.5	63.2	45.9	% Profit Before Taxes/Tangible Net Worth	119.9	46.6				
(49) 14.7	(41) 28.2	(40) 22.5		(16) 27.4	(10) -.5				
-1.8	7.0	-4.2		-6.1	-35.6				
22.9	20.3	16.3	% Profit Before Taxes/Total Assets	33.0	33.3				
3.7	7.1	7.9		10.2	4.1				
-2.8	.6	-2.5		-8.2	-14.5				
49.8	84.2	63.1	Sales/Net Fixed Assets	167.8	24.7				
19.2	21.1	17.4		39.6	16.5				
7.3	7.5	6.7		9.7	9.6				
4.6	4.4	4.7	Sales/Total Assets	6.2	4.0				
2.9	2.6	2.9		3.3	2.7				
2.1	1.7	1.9		1.8	2.1				
.8	.6	.7	% Depr., Dep., Amort./Sales	.4	.9				
(59) 1.6	(42) 1.1	(53) 1.2		(20) .9	(15) 1.4				
3.2	2.6	2.3		2.3	2.2				
2.3	3.3	2.8	% Officers', Directors', Owners' Comp/Sales	3.6	5.1				
(36) 4.6	(33) 7.4	(34) 7.1		(18) 7.2	(10) 7.6				
8.3	13.1	14.3		16.5	13.6				
3779428M	3870264M	1961848M	Net Sales ($)	10612M	26473M	14871M	32112M	76567M	1801213M
698573M	811087M	575206M	Total Assets ($)	4549M	11811M	3999M	13704M	28513M	512630M

M = $ thousand   MM = $ million
See Pages 11 through 18 for Explanation of Ratios and Data

Current Data Sorted By Assets   Comparative Historical Data

0-500M	500M-2MM	2-10MM	10-50MM	50-100MM	100-250MM	Type of Statement	4/1/98-3/31/99 ALL	4/1/99-3/31/00 ALL
	1	6	17	4	3	Unqualified		
2	6	21	17		1	Reviewed		
28	37	30	5		1	Compiled		
73	49	11		1		Tax Returns		
29	35	27	16	5	1	Other		
	70 (4/1-9/30/02)		356 (10/1/02-3/31/03)					
132	128	95	55	10	6	**NUMBER OF STATEMENTS**		
%	%	%	%	%	%	**ASSETS**	%	%
14.6	7.3	8.1	8.8	7.0		Cash & Equivalents	D	D
5.6	6.0	8.7	8.4	6.2		Trade Receivables (net)	A	A
31.8	14.8	13.3	12.4	15.5		Inventory	T	T
1.7	3.0	3.2	2.8	2.0		All Other Current	A	A
53.6	31.1	33.3	32.4	30.6		Total Current		
27.1	57.7	56.2	56.7	60.1		Fixed Assets (net)	N	N
11.4	4.7	2.9	2.4	5.1		Intangibles (net)	O	O
7.9	6.6	7.5	8.4	4.2		All Other Non-Current	T	T
100.0	100.0	100.0	100.0	100.0		Total		
						LIABILITIES	A	A
3.0	3.5	5.6	3.3	.1		Notes Payable-Short Term	V	V
2.1	4.2	4.9	4.7	3.1		Cur. Mat.-L/T/D	A	A
18.5	12.1	15.1	15.6	16.2		Trade Payables	I	I
.4	.3	.1	.0	.0		Income Taxes Payable	L	L
11.5	6.4	7.0	6.7	5.0		All Other Current	A	A
35.4	26.4	32.7	30.3	24.5		Total Current	B	B
24.3	47.8	40.0	38.7	47.8		Long Term Debt	L	L
.1	.0	.1	1.0	1.2		Deferred Taxes	E	E
18.6	8.3	5.3	2.9	4.4		All Other Non-Current		
21.6	17.4	22.0	27.1	22.1		Net Worth		
100.0	100.0	100.0	100.0	100.0		Total Liabilities & Net Worth		
						INCOME DATA		
100.0	100.0	100.0	100.0	100.0		Net Sales		
17.3	16.9	15.5	20.1	19.2		Gross Profit		
16.5	15.9	14.6	18.2	17.5		Operating Expenses		
.7	1.0	.9	1.9	1.7		Operating Profit		
−.4	.0	−.1	.1	.1		All Other Expenses (net)		
1.1	1.0	1.0	1.8	1.5		Profit Before Taxes		
						RATIOS		
4.4	3.0	1.5	1.5	1.5				
1.7	1.5	1.0	1.0	1.0		Current		
1.0	.7	.7	.8	.8				
1.8	1.2	.9	.8	.8				
(130) .6	(127) .5	.5	.6	.5		Quick		
.2	.2	.2	.4	.3				
0 UND	0 UND	1 249.7	2 162.7	2 192.8				
1 392.4	1 370.6	4 85.8	5 79.1	3 107.6		Sales/Receivables		
3 136.7	4 103.7	8 43.3	7 51.8	15 23.9				
8 47.0	7 52.1	7 52.6	8 45.1	11 33.2				
11 32.1	12 30.6	11 31.9	13 28.5	14 25.5		Cost of Sales/Inventory		
17 21.9	18 19.8	17 22.0	18 20.3	16 22.8				
1 259.5	1 329.3	8 48.6	11 32.6	14 25.2				
6 60.0	7 51.3	13 28.3	17 22.1	20 18.4		Cost of Sales/Payables		
11 33.8	14 25.5	18 20.3	23 15.5	25 14.3				
27.2	28.2	37.7	32.2	18.8				
56.5	76.9	804.6	316.9	NM		Sales/Working Capital		
986.3	−49.5	−39.1	−86.7	−80.1				
5.8	2.9	3.2	3.7					
(72) 2.4	(112) 1.6	(92) 1.6	(52) 2.0			EBIT/Interest		
−.1	.0	.9	1.3					
	1.6	5.3	3.3			Net Profit + Depr., Dep.,		
	(12) 1.1	(27) 1.8	(26) 2.1			Amort./Cur. Mat. L /T/D		
	.1	.7	.8					
.2	1.2	1.0	1.2	1.3				
.8	5.5	3.4	2.5	2.9		Fixed/Worth		
−3.4	−30.5	10.0	4.9	NM				
.7	2.1	2.2	1.7	1.5				
3.1	8.8	4.2	3.1	3.3		Debt/Worth		
−5.7	−34.7	14.4	8.0	NM				
71.9	71.3	27.9	23.5			% Profit Before Taxes/Tangible		
(89) 29.3	(90) 32.7	(82) 9.8	(49) 8.5			Net Worth		
9.9	1.4	1.1	4.1					
23.3	8.8	7.0	5.9	11.9		% Profit Before Taxes/Total		
8.6	3.2	2.1	2.9	3.7		Assets		
−1.7	−2.3	−.2	.8	.6				
416.0	21.4	15.3	10.0	11.8				
65.3	5.8	8.3	5.5	5.8		Sales/Net Fixed Assets		
14.6	3.2	3.5	3.4	3.5				
17.3	6.6	6.3	5.2	5.2				
10.0	3.5	4.2	3.5	3.8		Sales/Total Assets		
5.9	2.2	2.4	2.6	2.2				
.3	1.0	1.0	1.2	1.2				
(97) .8	(114) 1.4	(90) 1.6	(54) 1.8	2.2		% Depr., Dep., Amort./Sales		
1.4	2.5	2.4	2.3	3.2				
.7	.8	.5	.5			% Officers', Directors',		
(78) 1.3	(53) 1.5	(41) .7	(12) .9			Owners' Comp/Sales		
2.2	3.3	1.5	1.7					
308438M	670089M	2299574M	4403219M	2457438M	4284085M	Net Sales ($)		
32160M	135997M	438893M	1187944M	646303M	949932M	Total Assets ($)		

M = $ thousand   MM = $ million
See Pages 11 through 18 for Explanation of Ratios and Data

Comparative Historical Data | Current Data Sorted By Sales

			Type of Statement						
		31	Unqualified				2	3	26
		47	Reviewed	1	1	2	3	13	27
		101	Compiled	5	32	16	14	16	18
		134	Tax Returns	9	73	33	12	5	2
		113	Other	6	29	22	13	15	28
4/1/00- 3/31/01 ALL	4/1/01- 3/31/02 ALL	4/1/02- 3/31/03 ALL		70 (4/1-9/30/02)			356 (10/1/02-3/31/03)		
				0-1MM	1-3MM	3-5MM	5-10MM	10-25MM	25MM & OVER
		426	NUMBER OF STATEMENTS	21	135	73	44	52	101
%	%	%	ASSETS	%	%	%	%	%	%
D A T A N O T	D A T A N O T	9.9	Cash & Equivalents	8.1	10.6	10.7	9.5	10.0	8.9
		6.8	Trade Receivables (net)	3.9	3.4	6.7	6.2	9.2	11.0
		19.4	Inventory	25.1	22.9	18.6	14.9	21.2	15.2
		2.5	All Other Current	.3	1.1	4.2	4.3	2.2	3.1
		38.7	Total Current	37.4	38.0	40.2	34.9	42.6	38.2
		47.8	Fixed Assets (net)	48.3	45.6	46.0	51.2	46.2	51.4
		6.1	Intangibles (net)	10.6	8.4	8.5	3.3	4.5	2.6
		7.4	All Other Non-Current	3.8	8.0	5.2	10.6	6.7	7.8
		100.0	Total	100.0	100.0	100.0	100.0	100.0	100.0
A V A I L A B L E	A V A I L A B L E		LIABILITIES						
		3.6	Notes Payable-Short Term	2.5	2.9	1.8	3.5	8.8	3.7
		3.8	Cur. Mat.-L/T/D	3.6	2.9	2.3	4.9	5.5	4.6
		15.4	Trade Payables	10.2	13.4	13.2	11.3	20.8	19.6
		.2	Income Taxes Payable	.0	.1	.8	.2	.2	.1
		8.1	All Other Current	4.4	6.2	12.9	8.6	8.0	7.7
		31.1	Total Current	20.6	25.5	30.9	28.5	43.3	35.8
		37.5	Long Term Debt	46.8	41.6	35.9	41.3	31.2	32.6
		.2	Deferred Taxes	.0	.0	.2	.1	.1	.7
		10.0	All Other Non-Current	10.3	17.1	12.7	5.3	3.3	4.1
		21.2	Net Worth	22.3	15.9	20.3	24.8	22.1	26.7
		100.0	Total Liabilities & Net Worth	100.0	100.0	100.0	100.0	100.0	100.0
			INCOME DATA						
		100.0	Net Sales	100.0	100.0	100.0	100.0	100.0	100.0
		17.1	Gross Profit	26.4	15.8	17.9	16.3	18.3	16.1
		16.1	Operating Expenses	24.1	15.0	16.0	15.1	17.7	15.6
		1.0	Operating Profit	2.3	.8	1.9	1.2	.6	.6
		−.1	All Other Expenses (net)	.2	−.2	−.1	.3	−.1	−.3
		1.2	Profit Before Taxes	2.0	1.0	2.0	.9	.7	.9
			RATIOS						
		2.4		6.0	4.2	4.9	2.4	1.5	1.4
		1.3	Current	2.1	1.6	1.5	1.4	1.0	1.0
		.8		1.1	.8	.8	.8	.7	.8
		1.0		2.1	1.6	1.7	1.1	.9	.8
	(423)	.5	Quick	.8	(132) .6	.5	.4	.4	.5
		.2		.2	.2	.2	.2	.2	.3
0	UND			0 UND	0 UND	0 UND	0 957.9	1 298.9	3 128.4
2	176.0		Sales/Receivables	0 UND	0 999.8	1 346.4	2 203.8	3 105.6	5 71.9
5	70.7			4 86.0	3 129.8	3 125.9	6 56.8	8 47.5	10 36.9
8	48.4			22 16.9	9 41.8	6 63.0	5 79.3	7 51.2	8 45.6
12	30.7		Cost of Sales/Inventory	32 11.5	13 28.6	9 38.7	11 31.8	12 30.2	12 30.9
17	21.2			45 8.2	18 20.5	14 26.0	15 23.7	17 21.2	17 21.5
3	126.2			0 UND	1 373.0	1 251.9	1 249.6	10 38.2	11 32.2
10	37.1		Cost of Sales/Payables	4 85.8	7 52.6	6 65.9	7 49.8	14 25.6	17 22.1
17	21.7			25 14.6	11 32.0	10 37.5	16 22.3	19 19.6	21 17.4
		29.8		9.4	24.9	29.3	32.7	44.2	42.7
		86.2	Sales/Working Capital	20.7	60.5	65.7	81.6	979.9	748.4
		−78.2		UND	−163.9	−81.5	−56.9	−40.2	−75.0
		3.7		5.5	4.1	3.1	4.0	3.3	3.6
	(343)	1.7	EBIT/Interest	(15) 1.6	(96) 1.5	(51) 2.0	(39) 1.7	(46) 1.3	(96) 2.0
		.6		−.7	−.1	1.1	.7	.3	1.3
		3.1	Net Profit + Depr., Dep.,					2.6	3.5
	(70)	1.8	Amort./Cur. Mat. L/T/D				(13) .9	(44) 2.1	
		.8						.2	1.2
		.8		.9	.4	.5	.7	.8	1.0
		2.9	Fixed/Worth	3.2	4.7	2.8	3.6	3.6	2.3
		32.0		−6.2	−7.2	−25.6	9.2	14.4	4.9
		1.6		2.5	1.2	1.2	1.4	2.2	1.7
		4.1	Debt/Worth	3.5	7.3	4.4	3.9	5.6	3.1
		206.4		−10.9	−8.6	−15.8	13.3	29.8	7.2
		55.7		106.2	66.1	80.2	41.7	36.7	25.4
	(323)	17.8	% Profit Before Taxes/Tangible Net Worth	(15) 55.6	(85) 29.6	(50) 30.3	(37) 22.8	(45) 3.5	(91) 12.0
		3.2		.0	7.7	6.9	3.3	−21.9	4.8
		10.1		13.8	13.6	14.9	10.3	6.3	6.6
		3.5	% Profit Before Taxes/Total Assets	3.3	5.6	6.1	3.7	.9	3.3
		−.5		−3.9	−2.4	.7	−.4	−3.9	.8
		46.7		57.2	101.0	131.0	23.3	48.2	16.6
		9.7	Sales/Net Fixed Assets	4.9	11.8	12.5	10.7	9.9	8.7
		4.0		2.2	3.8	3.2	4.5	5.6	5.0
		8.8		5.5	11.6	11.9	8.6	10.0	6.6
		5.0	Sales/Total Assets	2.4	5.6	5.2	5.3	5.2	4.6
		2.8		1.3	2.9	2.4	2.8	3.4	3.1
		.8		1.3	.6	.4	.8	.6	1.0
	(367)	1.3	% Depr., Dep., Amort./Sales	(14) 1.5	(112) 1.3	(61) 1.2	(39) 1.4	(47) 1.3	(94) 1.4
		2.2		3.9	2.2	2.1	2.5	2.2	2.1
		.6			.8	.8	.5	.6	.4
	(186)	1.2	% Officers', Directors', Owners' Comp/Sales	(72) 1.4	(36) 1.3	(18) 1.2	(25) .7	(26) .7	2.2
		2.3			2.3	3.2	1.6	1.6	1.6
14422843M			Net Sales ($)	13392M	270678M	281607M	304809M	852155M	12700202M
3391229M			Total Assets ($)	9035M	73110M	101715M	79197M	198966M	2929206M

© RMA 2003

M = $ thousand   MM = $ million
See Pages 11 through 18 for Explanation of Ratios and Data

Current Data Sorted By Assets   Comparative Historical Data

0-500M	500M-2MM	2-10MM	10-50MM	50-100MM	100-250MM	Type of Statement	4/1/98-3/31/99 ALL	4/1/99-3/31/00 ALL
	3	10	44	12	9	Unqualified	96	88
6	20	34	31	1		Reviewed	108	101
39	64	46	6		1	Compiled	245	186
85	63	17	2		1	Tax Returns	145	128
28	51	47	39	8	10	Other	249	212
134 (4/1-9/30/02)			**543 (10/1/02-3/31/03)**					
158	201	154	122	21	21	**NUMBER OF STATEMENTS**	843	715
%	%	%	%	%	%	**ASSETS**	%	%
11.9	9.8	8.9	8.7	9.0	3.6	Cash & Equivalents	10.9	9.8
5.8	7.2	8.0	8.9	8.7	9.6	Trade Receivables (net)	8.6	8.6
25.5	12.6	12.1	10.9	7.1	14.2	Inventory	14.6	15.6
2.9	2.5	2.0	2.2	1.6	1.6	All Other Current	2.3	2.4
46.1	32.2	31.0	30.7	26.6	28.9	Total Current	36.3	36.4
40.7	56.7	58.9	58.9	58.2	52.1	Fixed Assets (net)	51.7	52.6
6.2	4.9	2.8	2.7	3.7	8.8	Intangibles (net)	5.0	4.9
7.1	6.3	7.4	7.7	11.5	10.1	All Other Non-Current	7.0	6.2
100.0	100.0	100.0	100.0	100.0	100.0	Total	100.0	100.0
						LIABILITIES		
3.9	6.1	4.6	3.8	3.3	1.0	Notes Payable-Short Term	4.2	5.0
3.4	3.5	4.8	4.2	3.7	2.8	Cur. Mat.-L/T/D	4.0	4.3
15.5	13.6	14.9	16.0	13.6	14.9	Trade Payables	14.4	16.4
.1	.1	.1	.4	.1	.2	Income Taxes Payable	.3	.2
14.6	9.5	9.4	6.9	5.8	10.1	All Other Current	8.5	9.5
37.5	32.9	33.7	31.3	26.5	28.9	Total Current	31.5	35.3
34.1	47.1	37.9	34.2	37.1	30.8	Long Term Debt	35.8	35.9
.0	.3	.3	.8	.6	1.1	Deferred Taxes	.4	.4
11.7	6.4	5.6	3.0	1.4	2.5	All Other Non-Current	7.2	6.4
16.7	13.3	22.5	30.7	34.3	36.6	Net Worth	25.2	22.0
100.0	100.0	100.0	100.0	100.0	100.0	Total Liabilities & Net Worth	100.0	100.0
						INCOME DATA		
100.0	100.0	100.0	100.0	100.0	100.0	Net Sales	100.0	100.0
18.4	18.1	18.3	16.5	16.9	16.1	Gross Profit	20.8	19.9
17.3	17.5	17.4	15.6	15.1	14.9	Operating Expenses	19.1	19.4
1.1	.6	.9	.9	1.9	1.1	Operating Profit	1.7	.5
.3	.5	.3	-.4	.0	.2	All Other Expenses (net)	.3	-.8
.8	.1	.6	1.3	1.9	1.0	Profit Before Taxes	1.4	1.3
						RATIOS		
3.5	2.0	1.6	1.2	1.3	1.5		2.0	1.7
1.5	1.2	.9	1.0	.9	1.0	Current	1.1	1.1
.9	.7	.6	.7	.8	.8		.7	.7
1.4	.9	.9	.8	.9	.8		1.1	1.0
(157) .5	(200) .5	(153) .5	.5	(20) .5	.5	Quick	(837) .6	(713) .5
.2	.2	.2	.3	.4	.3		.3	.3
0 UND	0 999.8	2 198.7	3 133.3	3 107.1	2 156.0		1 351.4	1 391.0
1 346.9	2 180.5	4 97.1	5 75.3	6 58.4	6 74.9	Sales/Receivables	3 111.0	4 101.5
3 130.8	6 61.4	8 43.3	10 38.0	16 22.5	16 22.3		9 42.9	9 39.6
6 61.8	7 52.6	7 52.2	7 54.2	8 48.4	6 58.7		7 53.7	8 47.4
10 36.3	10 36.0	10 36.1	11 34.7	10 35.4	11 34.5	Cost of Sales/Inventory	10 35.0	11 32.6
16 22.9	14 25.8	14 26.4	16 23.5	14 25.9	19 19.6		15 23.6	17 21.8
0 UND	3 118.3	8 45.9	11 32.5	15 24.1	10 35.0		5 73.9	6 62.1
5 79.5	8 46.4	14 25.7	15 23.8	19 19.4	16 22.5	Cost of Sales/Payables	12 31.6	14 26.9
11 34.4	14 25.5	20 18.6	22 16.9	28 13.0	28 13.1		19 19.7	21 17.1
29.8	32.9	39.4	83.0	45.6	60.5		29.8	35.5
65.7	166.5	-479.2	-356.8	-145.8	229.0	Sales/Working Capital	186.3	225.6
-303.7	-40.9	-31.9	-48.6	-35.3	-55.9		-56.6	-46.4
5.2	3.0	3.1	3.8	3.0	2.8		4.8	4.0
(109) 2.1	(177) 1.2	(147) 1.5	(117) 1.9	2.2	1.9	EBIT/Interest	(737) 2.1	(626) 1.9
.5	.1	.4	1.2	.8	.5		1.0	.9
	2.4	4.8	3.6				4.5	4.5
	(17) 1.4	(34) 2.0	(35) 1.7			Net Profit + Depr., Dep., Amort./Cur. Mat. L /T/D	(173) 2.2	(141) 2.4
	.7	.9	1.2				1.3	1.2
.5	1.3	1.3	1.4	1.3	1.0		.9	1.1
2.2	5.9	3.1	2.4	2.2	2.2	Fixed/Worth	2.4	2.5
-4.1	-5.8	10.5	4.2	4.6	5.5		12.4	18.5
1.0	1.7	2.0	1.6	1.1	.9		1.1	1.3
4.5	8.4	4.5	2.7	2.7	2.4	Debt/Worth	3.3	3.6
-8.5	-9.5	19.1	5.2	5.6	13.7		20.2	34.2
83.7	43.4	28.7	23.7	19.1	19.0		42.9	37.9
(109) 24.7	(127) 12.6	(126) 7.0	(115) 11.6	(19) 13.8	(18) 8.3	% Profit Before Taxes/Tangible Net Worth	(674) 19.6	(555) 16.5
4.6	-4.5	-3.8	1.2	4.1	-1.0		5.4	2.2
16.2	7.7	5.3	6.3	5.9	3.6		11.4	9.7
5.9	1.5	1.5	3.3	2.9	2.0	% Profit Before Taxes/Total Assets	4.9	4.0
-4.7	-4.0	-2.1	.6	-.9	-.8		.2	-.5
127.6	20.4	15.3	10.4	7.3	10.7		23.8	19.0
23.8	6.8	6.7	6.5	5.2	5.1	Sales/Net Fixed Assets	8.5	8.2
8.3	3.1	3.4	4.0	2.6	4.3		3.9	4.0
14.9	7.0	6.4	5.4	3.6	3.6		7.3	7.1
9.0	3.9	3.8	4.0	2.5	2.6	Sales/Total Assets	4.4	4.1
4.7	2.5	2.2	2.8	1.4	2.3		2.7	2.6
.6	1.1	1.1	1.2	1.3	1.1		1.0	1.1
(116) 1.0	(187) 1.7	(147) 1.6	(120) 1.8	(20) 1.7	(12) 2.0	% Depr., Dep., Amort./Sales	(749) 1.6	(642) 1.8
1.9	2.7	2.4	2.2	2.5	2.4		2.5	2.6
1.2	.9	.3	.2				.8	.8
(86) 2.0	(76) 1.6	(61) .5	(34) .5			% Officers', Directors', Owners' Comp/Sales	(363) 1.6	(271) 1.5
3.2	2.5	1.1	1.2				3.2	3.1
364171M	1210879M	3414712M	11740615M	4112774M	14820584M	Net Sales ($)	27124271M	21175985M
39553M	224870M	732328M	2749747M	1472373M	3369375M	Total Assets ($)	7978306M	6357405M

© RMA 2003

M = $ thousand   MM = $ million

See Pages 11 through 18 for Explanation of Ratios and Data

Comparative Historical Data | Current Data Sorted By Sales

61/83/189/196/204	70/88/175/146/210	78/92/156/168/183	Type of Statement	0-1MM	1-3MM	3-5MM	5-10MM	10-25MM	25MM & OVER
61	70	78	Unqualified		2	3	1	7	65
83	88	92	Reviewed	3	5	7	10	23	44
189	175	156	Compiled	9	46	29	24	29	19
196	146	168	Tax Returns	19	80	33	20	9	7
204	210	183	Other	6	33	21	25	28	70
4/1/00-3/31/01 ALL	4/1/01-3/31/02 ALL	4/1/02-3/31/03 ALL		134 (4/1-9/30/02)		543 (10/1/02-3/31/03)			
733	689	677	NUMBER OF STATEMENTS	37	166	93	80	96	205
%	%	%	ASSETS	%	%	%	%	%	%
10.3	10.7	9.6	Cash & Equivalents	7.8	9.0	11.1	9.6	11.3	9.1
8.6	8.0	7.5	Trade Receivables (net)	2.9	4.7	5.4	8.1	11.1	9.7
17.0	15.6	15.1	Inventory	14.1	17.8	13.5	16.1	16.6	12.6
1.9	2.4	2.4	All Other Current	6.0	1.7	2.0	1.4	3.3	2.4
37.8	36.7	34.6	Total Current	30.8	33.2	32.0	35.2	42.4	33.8
50.5	51.6	53.7	Fixed Assets (net)	57.0	56.6	52.0	52.3	47.4	55.1
5.7	4.2	4.4	Intangibles (net)	5.0	5.4	7.2	2.5	3.0	3.7
6.0	7.5	7.2	All Other Non-Current	7.4	4.8	8.7	9.9	7.3	7.4
100.0	100.0	100.0	Total	100.0	100.0	100.0	100.0	100.0	100.0
			LIABILITIES						
5.0	4.0	4.6	Notes Payable-Short Term	8.4	5.1	4.2	4.1	5.4	3.4
3.6	3.4	3.9	Cur. Mat.-L/T/D	4.7	3.5	4.1	4.3	3.4	4.0
15.0	15.3	14.8	Trade Payables	9.3	10.4	10.7	14.2	21.9	18.3
.2	.2	.1	Income Taxes Payable	.3	.1	.1	.1	.1	.3
10.0	8.6	10.1	All Other Current	16.7	8.5	15.0	8.9	8.2	9.3
33.8	31.3	33.6	Total Current	39.4	27.7	34.0	31.7	39.0	35.3
35.4	37.2	38.8	Long Term Debt	35.4	50.6	45.0	35.8	32.3	31.3
.5	.4	.4	Deferred Taxes	.6	.0	.1	.2	.4	.7
7.7	7.9	6.5	All Other Non-Current	5.8	11.1	9.6	7.9	3.2	2.6
22.7	23.2	20.7	Net Worth	18.8	10.5	11.3	24.4	25.1	30.0
100.0	100.0	100.0	Total Liabilities & Net Worth	100.0	100.0	100.0	100.0	100.0	100.0
			INCOME DATA						
100.0	100.0	100.0	Net Sales	100.0	100.0	100.0	100.0	100.0	100.0
17.0	17.8	17.8	Gross Profit	26.8	19.2	17.7	19.9	15.7	15.3
16.5	16.5	16.9	Operating Expenses	25.2	18.3	16.3	18.6	15.6	14.6
.4	1.3	.9	Operating Profit	1.6	.9	1.4	1.2	.1	.7
−.5	.4	.2	All Other Expenses (net)	1.3	.8	.6	−.1	−.3	−.2
1.0	1.0	.7	Profit Before Taxes	.3	.2	.8	1.3	.4	.9
			RATIOS						
1.9	2.0	1.8	Current	2.7	3.1	2.2	2.3	1.7	1.2
1.2	1.2	1.1		1.0	1.5	1.2	1.1	1.1	.9
.8	.7	.7		.2	.7	.7	.7	.7	.7
(728) 1.0	(680) 1.1	(673) .9	Quick	1.1	(165) 1.4	1.2	(78) 1.1	1.0	(204) .8
.5	.5	.5		.3	.5	.4	.6	.5	.5
.3	.3	.2		.0	.2	.2	.3	.3	.3
1 590.2	1 544.3	1 535.9	Sales/Receivables	0 UND	0 UND	0 UND	1 657.8	2 181.2	3 144.8
3 120.7	3 119.7	3 126.6		1 648.0	1 257.0	1 285.1	2 150.2	4 86.8	5 76.7
8 46.8	7 52.3	7 52.1		4 100.2	4 96.1	5 74.0	12 30.6	10 38.4	9 38.8
7 53.1	6 59.5	7 54.2	Cost of Sales/Inventory	6 60.7	8 47.7	6 61.0	6 60.7	7 53.9	7 54.4
10 36.4	9 38.6	10 35.7		15 24.5	12 31.1	8 45.1	10 36.4	11 34.1	10 36.8
15 24.0	14 25.9	15 24.8		28 13.1	16 23.3	12 30.3	13 27.1	15 23.7	14 25.8
5 73.5	5 74.4	4 84.2	Cost of Sales/Payables	0 UND	1 523.8	2 153.4	3 128.8	8 44.8	11 33.3
11 33.5	10 36.0	11 32.8		3 123.7	5 69.8	7 55.6	12 31.6	14 26.8	15 23.7
17 20.9	16 22.5	17 21.3		13 27.8	11 31.8	12 29.6	19 18.8	19 19.6	21 17.1
33.9	31.7	36.4	Sales/Working Capital	22.6	29.1	41.4	24.7	33.6	78.4
115.7	138.7	281.9		465.0	69.1	166.4	209.6	162.4	−253.8
−59.2	−66.0	−47.0		−6.6	−63.1	−26.6	−67.0	−47.9	−45.2
(617) 3.9	(593) 4.3	(592) 3.6	EBIT/Interest	(26) 3.3	(138) 3.2	(77) 4.3	(70) 5.6	(84) 3.1	(197) 3.7
1.7	1.8	1.7		2.1	1.4	1.3	1.6	1.5	1.9
.8	.9	.4		.5	.1	.3	.5	.1	.9
(125) 3.4	(107) 3.5	(100) 3.9	Net Profit + Depr., Dep., Amort./Cur. Mat. L/T/D				(11) 4.7	(18) 2.9	(58) 4.1
1.9	1.8	1.7					2.3	1.3	2.0
1.0	1.1	1.1					1.8	.7	1.3
1.0	.9	1.1	Fixed/Worth	.7	1.0	1.0	.8	.9	1.3
2.7	2.4	2.8		5.4	10.2	3.6	2.6	2.2	2.3
39.9	12.7	57.7		−3.7	−4.5	−5.6	−10.0	6.4	4.7
1.3	1.2	1.6	Debt/Worth	.9	1.8	1.6	.8	1.4	1.6
3.8	3.2	4.0		6.0	12.7	6.6	3.6	3.6	2.9
74.3	21.5	90.4		−6.9	−6.7	−9.4	−64.6	9.3	6.4
(563) 38.5	(552) 40.6	(514) 34.1	% Profit Before Taxes/Tangible Net Worth	(25) 46.7	(101) 87.9	(61) 40.1	(57) 44.9	(82) 26.8	(188) 23.6
15.6	16.1	12.8		18.7	23.3	18.7	10.1	5.1	11.6
2.6	3.1	−.5		−2.1	2.3	−.8	−1.4	−9.6	1.2
9.4	9.5	7.6	% Profit Before Taxes/Total Assets	8.8	11.9	7.9	8.7	6.9	5.7
3.5	3.8	2.4		4.3	3.5	1.1	1.8	1.8	2.9
−.5	.0	−2.2		−5.4	−4.8	−3.7	−2.5	−2.7	−.2
29.1	29.1	21.4	Sales/Net Fixed Assets	34.0	27.0	34.5	19.3	28.2	15.3
9.4	9.3	8.0		6.1	7.1	9.6	8.7	12.4	7.9
4.3	4.2	4.0		1.8	3.0	3.7	4.4	4.7	4.6
8.4	8.5	7.6	Sales/Total Assets	5.4	9.3	8.5	7.2	8.5	6.4
4.5	4.9	4.2		3.0	4.2	4.2	4.6	5.3	4.2
2.9	2.9	2.6		1.5	2.4	2.5	2.6	3.0	3.0
(647) .7	(610) .7	(602) 1.0	% Depr., Dep., Amort./Sales	(30) 1.1	(140) 1.0	(73) 1.0	(77) .8	(91) .8	(191) 1.0
1.4	1.3	1.6		2.1	1.9	1.7	1.6	1.4	1.5
2.1	2.0	2.4		4.8	3.1	2.7	2.3	2.2	2.1
(310) .6	(287) .5	(265) .5	% Officers', Directors', Owners' Comp/Sales	(19) 1.7	(79) 1.5	(29) 1.0	(33) .5	(41) .3	(64) .2
1.2	1.1	1.3		3.9	1.9	2.0	1.0	.7	.5
2.5	2.6	2.5		9.0	3.1	3.4	1.4	2.0	1.0
31251754M	31464232M	35663735M	Net Sales ($)	21561M	345678M	357503M	588775M	1579024M	32771194M
7149574M	7024439M	8588246M	Total Assets ($)	10517M	114611M	111546M	174060M	452843M	7724669M

M = $ thousand   MM = $ million
See Pages 11 through 18 for Explanation of Ratios and Data

Current Data Sorted By Assets   **Comparative Historical Data**

0-500M	500M-2MM	2-10MM	10-50MM	50-100MM	100-250MM		4/1/98-3/31/99 ALL	4/1/99-3/31/00 ALL
						Type of Statement		
		2	3	1	3	Unqualified	14	13
3	7	6	3			Reviewed	24	30
5	9	9				Compiled	48	53
6	7	1			1	Tax Returns	6	12
2	4	10	2	1	1	Other	36	28
16	27	28	8	2	5	**NUMBER OF STATEMENTS**	128	136
%	%	%	%	%	%	**ASSETS**	%	%
9.0	12.4	8.9				Cash & Equivalents	7.8	9.4
8.2	9.4	8.7				Trade Receivables (net)	7.5	9.4
62.9	52.6	39.4				Inventory	58.2	54.8
1.0	.9	1.8				All Other Current	1.1	1.3
81.0	75.3	58.8				Total Current	74.7	75.0
12.0	16.5	26.1				Fixed Assets (net)	17.1	15.8
2.0	3.3	2.2				Intangibles (net)	2.7	3.0
4.8	5.0	12.9				All Other Non-Current	5.5	6.2
100.0	100.0	100.0				Total	100.0	100.0
						LIABILITIES		
11.9	4.8	11.4				Notes Payable-Short Term	11.4	9.8
1.6	3.5	2.6				Cur. Mat.-L/T/D	3.1	3.6
15.2	20.6	15.5				Trade Payables	19.4	17.1
.1	.1	.0				Income Taxes Payable	.4	.3
11.4	7.6	13.7				All Other Current	9.2	9.6
40.2	36.7	43.2				Total Current	43.6	40.5
15.0	15.4	19.8				Long Term Debt	12.7	14.6
.0	.0	.0				Deferred Taxes	.1	.2
8.1	5.9	3.7				All Other Non-Current	4.6	5.3
36.8	42.1	33.2				Net Worth	39.0	39.4
100.0	100.0	100.0				Total Liabilities & Net Worth	100.0	100.0
						INCOME DATA		
100.0	100.0	100.0				Net Sales	100.0	100.0
45.2	50.2	45.0				Gross Profit	44.2	43.3
42.9	47.2	45.7				Operating Expenses	41.0	39.8
2.3	3.0	-.7				Operating Profit	3.1	3.5
.2	-.1	.9				All Other Expenses (net)	.3	.9
2.2	3.1	-1.6				Profit Before Taxes	2.8	2.6
						RATIOS		
4.6	3.7	2.4				Current	3.4	3.4
2.8	2.2	1.8					1.9	1.9
1.4	1.2	.9					1.2	1.3
1.1	1.1	.7				Quick	.7	.9
.4	.6	.3					.3	.3
.1	.1	.2					.1	.1
0 999.8	0 UND	0 901.2				Sales/Receivables	0 999.8	1 516.5
3 109.5	4 98.1	3 104.3					5 73.9	7 55.5
20 18.4	19 19.5	23 16.2					17 21.3	21 17.3
105 3.5	93 3.9	84 4.4				Cost of Sales/Inventory	102 3.6	92 3.9
149 2.4	140 2.6	129 2.8					157 2.3	147 2.5
264 1.4	236 1.5	177 2.1					219 1.7	223 1.6
14 25.8	19 19.1	23 15.8				Cost of Sales/Payables	22 16.6	21 17.3
32 11.3	41 8.8	39 9.3					41 8.8	36 10.1
45 8.1	102 3.6	61 6.0					76 4.8	78 4.7
3.3	3.8	5.2				Sales/Working Capital	4.0	3.9
5.3	7.3	8.7					6.8	6.5
14.9	12.1	-28.0					21.9	14.8
14.9	7.2	3.4				EBIT/Interest	6.5	5.6
(12) 1.9	(24) 1.9	(25) 1.2					(109) 3.4	(116) 2.8
1.0	-1.0	-5.0					1.4	1.4
						Net Profit + Depr., Dep., Amort./Cur. Mat. L /T/D	5.3	3.2
							(31) 2.2	(29) 1.8
							.9	.8
.1	.1	.2				Fixed/Worth	.1	.1
.4	.4	.5					.3	.3
NM	.8	2.4					.7	1.0
.7	.6	.7				Debt/Worth	.7	.7
1.4	1.4	1.5					1.4	1.7
NM	4.3	8.2					3.6	4.5
24.4	20.4	21.5				% Profit Before Taxes/Tangible Net Worth	33.9	35.8
(12) 4.8	(26) 8.3	(24) 4.6					(117) 15.1	(125) 12.4
.0	-3.1	-13.0					3.0	2.9
9.0	7.1	8.1				% Profit Before Taxes/Total Assets	12.5	10.0
2.9	1.4	.9					5.2	4.9
-2.0	-1.7	-11.1					1.0	1.2
397.8	58.8	26.6				Sales/Net Fixed Assets	56.2	57.2
40.6	24.2	10.5					18.6	25.5
9.9	12.3	6.8					9.8	10.0
3.8	2.9	3.1				Sales/Total Assets	3.0	3.1
2.5	2.5	2.3					2.4	2.3
1.6	2.0	1.6					1.7	1.7
.4	.5	1.0				% Depr., Dep., Amort./Sales	.5	.4
(13) .8	(21) .9	(27) 1.8					(109) 1.2	(115) 1.0
2.0	1.9	2.8					1.9	1.7
3.9	3.9	2.5				% Officers', Directors', Owners' Comp/Sales	4.0	3.3
(11) 7.8	(20) 6.1	(13) 4.9					(48) 5.6	(70) 5.6
11.5	9.7	7.7					8.5	8.2
13965M	66527M	260848M	273157M	476237M	2078454M	Net Sales ($)	3929213M	2860443M
5153M	27652M	124264M	135953M	127709M	810933M	Total Assets ($)	1669281M	1272257M

© RMA 2003

M = $ thousand   MM = $ million
See Pages 11 through 18 for Explanation of Ratios and Data

Comparative Historical Data			Type of Statement	Current Data Sorted By Sales					
14	9	9	Unqualified				1	2	6
19	20	19	Reviewed	2	5	4	3	3	2
35	31	23	Compiled	5	10	4	2	2	
12	12	15	Tax Returns	3	8	1	1	1	1
22	26	20	Other	2	4	3	3	6	2
4/1/00-3/31/01 ALL	4/1/01-3/31/02 ALL	4/1/02-3/31/03 ALL		30 (4/1-9/30/02)			56 (10/1/02-3/31/03)		
				0-1MM	1-3MM	3-5MM	5-10MM	10-25MM	25MM & OVER
102	98	86	**NUMBER OF STATEMENTS**	12	27	12	10	14	11
%	%	%	**ASSETS**	%	%	%	%	%	%
11.0	11.3	10.9	Cash & Equivalents	5.3	12.9	7.8	11.2	8.6	18.1
8.0	8.0	8.6	Trade Receivables (net)	11.8	6.7	7.2	12.7	10.7	4.5
53.7	52.1	48.8	Inventory	54.1	51.6	49.4	43.5	42.9	47.5
1.1	1.6	1.4	All Other Current	.8	1.3	.2	2.3	2.3	2.0
73.8	73.0	69.7	Total Current	72.0	72.5	64.6	69.7	64.5	72.1
17.2	19.1	20.7	Fixed Assets (net)	18.2	19.9	13.4	22.9	27.2	22.7
2.2	2.5	2.3	Intangibles (net)	2.0	1.9	8.2	.0	.9	1.0
6.7	5.4	7.4	All Other Non-Current	7.8	5.7	13.8	7.4	7.4	4.1
100.0	100.0	100.0	Total	100.0	100.0	100.0	100.0	100.0	100.0
			LIABILITIES						
9.7	13.0	7.8	Notes Payable-Short Term	15.2	5.8	8.2	5.2	12.9	.2
3.1	4.0	2.7	Cur. Mat.-L/T/D	2.6	1.8	4.3	3.4	2.6	2.6
17.6	18.6	16.5	Trade Payables	9.7	18.2	18.7	19.0	18.1	12.7
.5	.1	.2	Income Taxes Payable	.2	.1	.0	.1	.0	1.4
11.7	10.0	10.8	All Other Current	9.3	10.8	9.0	15.9	8.1	13.5
42.8	45.8	38.0	Total Current	37.1	36.6	40.3	43.6	41.8	30.4
11.3	13.4	17.4	Long Term Debt	16.5	20.5	15.4	10.3	20.7	15.5
.0	.1	.1	Deferred Taxes	.0	.0	.0	.1	.5	.0
3.9	5.6	5.2	All Other Non-Current	10.8	4.5	7.7	.8	3.8	3.6
42.0	35.1	39.3	Net Worth	35.8	38.3	36.6	45.2	33.2	50.5
100.0	100.0	100.0	Total Liabilities & Net Worth	100.0	100.0	100.0	100.0	100.0	100.0
			INCOME DATA						
100.0	100.0	100.0	Net Sales	100.0	100.0	100.0	100.0	100.0	100.0
43.5	43.1	45.8	Gross Profit	49.4	50.5	42.7	46.1	39.5	41.2
40.9	41.4	43.9	Operating Expenses	42.0	50.2	41.9	47.8	38.9	35.4
2.7	1.8	1.9	Operating Profit	7.4	.3	.8	-1.7	.6	5.8
.8	1.0	.6	All Other Expenses (net)	.9	1.0	-.6	-.5	.7	1.2
1.9	.8	1.3	Profit Before Taxes	6.5	-.7	1.4	-1.2	.0	4.5
			RATIOS						
3.4 1.9 1.2	2.7 1.7 1.2	3.3 2.1 1.3	Current	4.9 2.6 1.3	4.1 2.3 1.2	3.1 1.9 .9	2.2 1.8 1.2	2.6 1.8 1.5	3.4 2.3 1.8
(101) 1.0 .3 .1	.9 .4 .1	1.1 .4 .2	Quick	1.1 .5 .1	1.1 .5 .1	.6 .2 .1	.8 .5 .3	.8 .4 .2	1.5 .8 .2
0 999.8 3 116.7 17 21.6	0 UND 3 123.9 21 17.6	0 UND 4 98.9 20 18.2	Sales/Receivables	0 UND 8 45.3 36 10.1	0 UND 4 99.7 10 37.5	0 UND 3 130.7 8 44.0	0 UND 6 58.5 42 8.7	1 516.1 3 116.1 24 15.3	0 UND 3 104.5 12 31.5
84 4.4 125 2.9 187 2.0	89 4.1 143 2.6 210 1.7	90 4.0 134 2.7 194 1.9	Cost of Sales/Inventory	134 2.7 222 1.6 327 1.1	90 4.0 135 2.7 249 1.5	110 3.3 137 2.7 169 2.2	83 4.4 108 3.4 143 2.6	68 5.4 119 3.1 154 2.4	49 7.5 84 4.4 226 1.6
15 24.3 31 11.7 67 5.4	20 17.9 40 9.0 68 5.3	16 22.8 40 9.2 61 6.0	Cost of Sales/Payables	0 UND 38 9.6 45 8.1	16 23.1 36 10.1 67 5.4	23 15.8 49 7.4 74 4.9	15 24.1 48 7.6 65 5.6	28 13.1 41 9.0 60 6.1	11 32.8 26 13.9 53 6.9
4.7 6.7 25.5	4.9 7.3 45.9	3.9 6.6 19.7	Sales/Working Capital	3.3 4.4 16.2	3.9 6.6 22.6	3.6 10.0 NM	6.0 9.2 NM	5.1 8.1 24.0	5.0 5.9 7.4
(93) 9.0 2.7 .8	(81) 3.8 1.6 -.1	(75) 6.5 1.6 -.8	EBIT/Interest		(24) 8.5 1.3 -.3	(11) 7.4 1.4 -1.9		(12) 4.5 1.5 -3.6	(10) 51.7 8.5 2.1
(23) 4.4 1.8 .7	(18) 2.9 1.5 .4	(19) 4.5 .5 -1.1	Net Profit + Depr., Dep., Amort./Cur. Mat. L/T/D						
.1 .3 .8	.2 .4 1.2	.2 .4 .9	Fixed/Worth	.0 .3 NM	.2 .5 1.1	.2 .4 NM	.2 .5 .8	.2 .4 1.5	.3 .5 .6
.5 1.4 3.2	.7 1.9 4.6	.7 1.3 4.3	Debt/Worth	.8 1.7 NM	.6 1.5 4.6	.5 1.8 NM	.7 1.0 2.2	.9 1.5 6.1	.6 1.0 1.7
(94) 26.1 9.3 -1.5	(87) 20.8 5.6 -6.9	(77) 25.5 8.0 -3.1	% Profit Before Taxes/Tangible Net Worth		(25) 9.4 3.2 -3.1		23.3 1.2 -24.7	(13) 28.1 15.2 -9.2	34.6 25.5 -.5
10.1 4.4 -.7	7.0 1.6 -2.4	8.7 1.4 -4.6	% Profit Before Taxes/Total Assets	9.0 4.0 .0	5.7 .7 -6.3	10.0 1.5 -6.0	6.0 .7 -12.0	8.4 5.0 -11.6	18.5 12.8 -.1
73.0 23.1 11.1	60.8 20.0 7.7	48.4 16.3 7.8	Sales/Net Fixed Assets	88.0 24.2 6.9	53.8 24.2 8.7	213.3 19.6 10.8	29.2 11.5 7.9	42.9 11.1 3.9	22.4 10.2 7.9
3.3 2.7 2.0	3.1 2.3 1.7	3.1 2.4 1.8	Sales/Total Assets	2.3 1.7 .9	3.5 2.5 1.5	2.6 2.4 1.6	3.3 2.7 2.2	3.1 2.6 1.6	3.6 2.5 2.0
(85) .4 .8 1.7	(78) .5 1.1 2.3	(75) .6 1.4 2.3	% Depr., Dep., Amort./Sales		(24) .3 .9 2.7		1.1 1.6 2.8	.8 1.4 2.5	(10) .8 1.7 2.3
(48) 3.4 6.2 11.2	(51) 2.1 4.2 8.6	(48) 3.5 6.0 9.8	% Officers', Directors', Owners' Comp/Sales		(21) 4.0 6.2 11.0				
2460728M 1024157M	1355894M 689294M	3169188M 1231664M	Net Sales ($) Total Assets ($)	7189M 6169M	48150M 38911M	46378M 26064M	70275M 26895M	240614M 113106M	2756582M 1020519M

M = $ thousand   MM = $ million
See Pages 11 through 18 for Explanation of Ratios and Data

Current Data Sorted By Assets　　　　**Comparative Historical Data**

Type of Statement	0-500M	500M-2MM	2-10MM	10-50MM	50-100MM	100-250MM		4/1/98-3/31/99 ALL	4/1/99-3/31/00 ALL
Unqualified			2	11	4	7		19	18
Reviewed	2	7	8					24	20
Compiled	9	9	3					31	30
Tax Returns	7	5						13	13
Other	8	6	8	4	1	2		26	22
	26 (4/1-9/30/02)			77 (10/1/02-3/31/03)					
NUMBER OF STATEMENTS	26	27	21	15	5	9		113	103
	%	%	%	%	%	%	**ASSETS**	%	%
	10.1	9.6	12.5	12.9			Cash & Equivalents	13.7	12.7
	5.3	9.6	5.8	10.1			Trade Receivables (net)	8.2	8.2
	60.4	50.0	49.3	39.0			Inventory	50.5	51.8
	.9	1.7	3.7	5.0			All Other Current	1.2	3.0
	76.6	70.8	71.3	66.9			Total Current	73.6	75.6
	14.6	21.7	15.1	26.6			Fixed Assets (net)	17.8	16.9
	1.5	1.6	5.3	.1			Intangibles (net)	2.8	3.2
	7.3	5.8	8.3	6.4			All Other Non-Current	5.8	4.3
	100.0	100.0	100.0	100.0			Total	100.0	100.0
							LIABILITIES		
	19.5	8.6	8.9	6.7			Notes Payable-Short Term	13.1	10.7
	2.7	4.7	1.9	1.9			Cur. Mat.-L/T/D	1.9	2.1
	9.4	24.7	26.0	22.0			Trade Payables	16.7	19.8
	.1	.3	.5	1.8			Income Taxes Payable	.6	.4
	7.8	7.8	11.6	12.1			All Other Current	10.4	10.6
	39.5	46.1	48.9	44.5			Total Current	42.7	43.5
	18.5	6.6	4.9	10.5			Long Term Debt	12.4	11.7
	.0	.1	.1	.3			Deferred Taxes	.2	.1
	4.0	1.4	6.2	6.2			All Other Non-Current	5.1	4.5
	37.9	45.8	39.8	38.5			Net Worth	39.5	40.2
	100.0	100.0	100.0	100.0			Total Liabilities & Net Worth	100.0	100.0
							INCOME DATA		
	100.0	100.0	100.0	100.0			Net Sales	100.0	100.0
	41.3	41.6	45.4	42.6			Gross Profit	42.4	43.5
	36.7	39.2	43.9	39.2			Operating Expenses	39.6	41.2
	4.7	2.5	1.5	3.4			Operating Profit	2.7	2.4
	.8	.6	.5	.5			All Other Expenses (net)	.4	.2
	3.9	1.9	1.0	3.0			Profit Before Taxes	2.3	2.2
							RATIOS		
	3.0	2.8	2.3	2.3				2.8	3.0
	2.4	1.6	1.7	1.5			Current	1.8	1.7
	1.4	1.0	1.0	1.1				1.3	1.3
	.6	.7	1.1	.9				1.0	1.0
	.2	.4	.3	.6			Quick	(112) .3	(102) .3
	.1	.1	.1	.1				.1	.1
	0 UND	0 UND	0 UND	0 UND				0 999.8	0 999.8
	1 394.2	3 118.4	2 225.3	3 115.6			Sales/Receivables	3 115.0	2 164.4
	4 85.6	13 27.9	8 46.9	7 51.8				20 17.8	18 20.2
	90 4.0	89 4.1	66 5.5	66 5.5				75 4.9	71 5.1
	127 2.9	121 3.0	135 2.7	75 4.9			Cost of Sales/Inventory	102 3.6	104 3.5
	196 1.9	148 2.5	193 1.9	110 3.3				160 2.3	150 2.4
	7 55.9	32 11.3	32 11.5	28 13.2				20 18.1	21 17.2
	20 18.2	49 7.5	55 6.6	47 7.8			Cost of Sales/Payables	33 11.2	38 9.6
	28 12.9	59 6.2	102 3.6	58 6.3				57 6.4	54 6.7
	4.3	5.1	4.7	6.9				4.4	4.6
	7.7	12.3	9.9	21.3			Sales/Working Capital	10.6	9.4
	30.3	999.8	-543.7	68.5				26.9	22.0
	6.4	11.7	26.2	80.0				7.0	12.7
	(22) 2.1	(25) 2.0	(17) 6.4	(14) 11.9			EBIT/Interest	(95) 2.8	(84) 2.9
	-.2	.8	1.8	2.1				1.0	.3
								25.0	13.3
				(24)			Net Profit + Depr., Dep., Amort./Cur. Mat. L /T/D	(24) 5.4	(20) 3.4
								1.7	1.5
	.1	.2	.2	.4				.2	.2
	.4	.4	.5	.6			Fixed/Worth	.4	.4
	.7	1.1	.9	1.0				1.1	.9
	.4	.5	.7	.9				.6	.5
	1.2	1.1	1.2	1.3			Debt/Worth	1.4	1.4
	3.1	1.8	4.2	3.6				4.1	4.5
	55.3	29.6	21.2	40.4				30.8	31.1
	(21) 10.4	(25) 11.2	(19) 8.6	19.0			% Profit Before Taxes/Tangible Net Worth	(99) 12.2	(90) 12.2
	-3.7	-.8	3.4	7.0				3.2	.1
	18.6	11.1	9.2	17.8				13.8	14.8
	4.9	4.6	2.7	7.1			% Profit Before Taxes/Total Assets	5.1	4.3
	-5.9	-.4	1.3	1.2				.4	-1.4
	77.3	41.1	42.7	38.5				42.3	45.5
	31.4	16.3	18.7	13.7			Sales/Net Fixed Assets	18.6	20.9
	13.3	9.7	11.1	5.9				11.7	11.9
	4.1	4.0	3.5	4.1				3.7	3.9
	3.0	2.6	2.7	2.5			Sales/Total Assets	2.7	3.0
	2.0	1.9	1.8	2.3				1.9	2.0
	.4	.4	.7	.9				.6	.5
	(16) .8	(26) .8	(18) 1.2	(13) 1.9			% Depr., Dep., Amort./Sales	(100) 1.2	(87) 1.0
	1.6	1.6	1.9	2.4				2.0	1.9
	3.6	3.5						2.5	3.4
	(17) 6.5	(20) 4.6					% Officers', Directors', Owners' Comp/Sales	(51) 4.0	(51) 5.9
	8.5	6.7						9.8	9.5
	19571M	97681M	270178M	1147885M	909925M	3443125M	Net Sales ($)	4888806M	2966043M
	6924M	34383M	101105M	351013M	408678M	1696968M	Total Assets ($)	1888323M	1030829M

© RMA 2003　　　　M = $ thousand　　MM = $ million
See Pages 11 through 18 for Explanation of Ratios and Data

Comparative Historical Data | | | | **Current Data Sorted By Sales** | | | | | |

			Type of Statement						
12	16	24	Unqualified				1	1	22
15	16	17	Reviewed	2	3	2	6	4	
25	30	21	Compiled	6	7	2	4	2	
12	11	12	Tax Returns	7	2	3			
29	24	29	Other	8	5		4	5	7
4/1/00-3/31/01 ALL	4/1/01-3/31/02 ALL	4/1/02-3/31/03 ALL		0-1MM	26 (4/1-9/30/02) 1-3MM	3-5MM	77 (10/1/02-3/31/03) 5-10MM	10-25MM	25MM & OVER
93	97	103	**NUMBER OF STATEMENTS**	23	17	7	15	12	29
%	%	%	**ASSETS**	%	%	%	%	%	%
11.6	13.8	12.2	Cash & Equivalents	10.5	7.0		11.4	14.9	16.3
5.8	7.0	6.9	Trade Receivables (net)	.6	7.6		3.1	9.2	6.4
54.7	47.8	47.1	Inventory	59.0	55.7		55.6	45.5	30.1
2.3	1.7	2.4	All Other Current	.9	.5		4.5	.9	4.1
74.5	70.4	68.6	Total Current	76.7	70.9		74.6	70.5	56.9
17.8	22.0	21.1	Fixed Assets (net)	16.8	14.8		18.3	13.7	31.3
2.7	3.0	3.3	Intangibles (net)	.1	4.7		3.1	5.3	5.1
5.0	4.7	6.9	All Other Non-Current	6.4	9.7		3.9	10.5	6.7
100.0	100.0	100.0	Total	100.0	100.0		100.0	100.0	100.0
			LIABILITIES						
11.4	12.2	10.0	Notes Payable-Short Term	19.8	10.1		4.4	11.0	4.1
2.7	3.2	2.8	Cur. Mat.-L/T/D	2.7	5.5		1.8	1.6	1.5
16.8	16.2	19.1	Trade Payables	8.0	22.2		21.1	33.4	17.9
.6	.4	.5	Income Taxes Payable	.1	.2		.7	.2	1.1
13.0	10.4	9.7	All Other Current	8.2	5.7		14.8	8.2	11.6
44.5	42.5	42.0	Total Current	38.8	43.7		42.8	54.4	36.2
10.0	13.6	10.9	Long Term Debt	19.4	11.0		5.2	4.3	12.1
.1	.0	.1	Deferred Taxes	.0	.0		.2	.0	.3
5.4	4.1	3.9	All Other Non-Current	3.0	4.3		4.0	5.9	4.3
40.1	39.8	43.2	Net Worth	38.8	41.1		47.8	35.4	47.0
100.0	100.0	100.0	Total Liabilities & Net Worth	100.0	100.0		100.0	100.0	100.0
			INCOME DATA						
100.0	100.0	100.0	Net Sales	100.0	100.0		100.0	100.0	100.0
41.0	42.9	42.0	Gross Profit	42.3	40.8		48.4	41.3	40.1
37.7	40.2	38.3	Operating Expenses	37.5	37.8		45.6	40.6	34.8
3.3	2.7	3.7	Operating Profit	4.9	3.0		2.8	.7	5.3
.9	1.1	.6	All Other Expenses (net)	1.1	.8		.0	.6	.5
2.4	1.5	3.1	Profit Before Taxes	3.7	2.2		2.7	.1	4.8
			RATIOS						
2.7	2.6	2.6		3.2	3.2		2.4	1.8	2.2
1.9	1.7	1.7	Current	2.4	1.5		1.8	1.5	1.5
1.3	1.2	1.2		1.6	1.1		1.4	.9	1.1
.7	1.0	.9		.7	.8		1.0	1.0	1.1
(92) .4	.4	.3	Quick	.2	.3		.2	.3	.6
.1	.2	.1		.1	.1		.1	.1	.3
0 UND	0 UND	0 UND		0 UND	0 UND		0 UND	0 806.2	0 UND
2 235.8	2 168.0	3 142.0	Sales/Receivables	1 451.5	1 253.2		0 827.0	7 52.0	3 121.0
10 37.3	10 36.5	11 34.4		11 34.4	15 25.1		7 55.9	26 13.8	7 51.8
66 5.5	62 5.9	66 5.5		100 3.6	95 3.9		104 3.5	40 9.2	45 8.1
114 3.2	92 4.0	106 3.5	Cost of Sales/Inventory	141 2.6	129 2.8		133 2.8	79 4.6	70 5.2
167 2.2	150 2.4	151 2.4		201 1.8	165 2.2		213 1.7	154 2.4	95 3.8
23 15.9	20 18.0	24 15.5		5 75.4	29 12.6		31 11.7	38 9.7	28 13.0
34 10.7	34 10.7	37 10.0	Cost of Sales/Payables	19 18.8	38 9.7		46 7.9	55 6.7	37 9.7
46 7.9	50 7.3	56 6.5		24 15.1	67 5.5		100 3.6	82 4.4	53 6.9
4.8	5.8	5.2		2.7	5.1		4.6	6.3	7.1
10.1	11.1	9.9	Sales/Working Capital	7.4	12.3		8.4	30.8	16.0
19.7	42.1	48.5		26.8	520.3		17.0	-273.9	57.1
10.0	9.9	21.7		6.0	11.7		27.4	28.9	129.4
(78) 2.5	(80) 2.3	(88) 3.8	EBIT/Interest	(19) 2.2	2.0		(12) 2.8	(10) 5.4	(23) 9.2
.9	.9	1.1		-.2	.3		1.8	-1.3	2.2
9.3	19.7	16.4							
(17) 2.5	(13) 2.2	(21) 2.5	Net Profit + Depr., Dep., Amort./Cur. Mat. L/T/D						
.7	1.2	-.4							
.2	.2	.3		.1	.2		.2	.2	.4
.4	.5	.5	Fixed/Worth	.4	.4		.4	.3	.6
1.0	1.3	1.0		.8	1.0		1.0	1.6	1.6
.6	.6	.6		.4	.4		.7	.7	.6
1.3	1.0	1.1	Debt/Worth	1.1	1.6		.8	1.2	1.1
3.0	5.7	2.5		2.2	3.4		2.2	6.4	3.7
35.8	37.4	34.4		57.2	25.4		21.2	32.4	36.8
(83) 13.5	(81) 14.4	(92) 11.3	% Profit Before Taxes/Tangible Net Worth	(19) 10.8	(14) 9.3		8.6	(10) 8.1	(27) 26.0
3.5	.4	3.3		-1.0	-2.1		3.4	3.9	8.5
12.3	13.0	13.8		24.9	9.4		11.2	12.2	20.2
4.5	5.2	5.5	% Profit Before Taxes/Total Assets	5.3	3.8		2.7	3.3	8.5
.7	-.3	.4		-5.9	-2.1		1.8	-6.3	1.5
54.7	43.2	41.1		107.1	56.1		41.7	57.2	17.1
20.0	19.8	16.3	Sales/Net Fixed Assets	31.2	19.1		16.3	27.3	8.2
9.9	9.0	8.4		10.9	11.4		8.7	17.0	4.9
3.8	3.9	3.7		4.3	3.4		3.7	5.1	3.0
2.6	2.8	2.6	Sales/Total Assets	3.0	2.5		2.7	3.2	2.4
2.0	2.1	1.9		1.8	1.9		1.8	2.2	2.1
.6	.5	.6		.4	.4		1.0	.3	1.3
(75) .9	(80) .9	(81) 1.1	% Depr., Dep., Amort./Sales	(14) .9	(15) .7		(14) 1.4	(11) .7	(20) 2.1
1.5	1.9	2.0		1.7	1.2		2.0	1.4	2.7
3.1	2.9	2.3		4.4	3.0				
(41) 5.7	(47) 5.0	(47) 4.6	% Officers', Directors', Owners' Comp/Sales	(13) 6.5	(13) 4.6				
8.7	8.1	6.8		8.5	6.6				
3945383M	5014957M	5888365M	Net Sales ($)	14428M	32674M	27428M	104759M	201206M	5507870M
1384310M	1984938M	2599071M	Total Assets ($)	7091M	14110M	9660M	45862M	68170M	2454178M

M = $ thousand   MM = $ million
See Pages 11 through 18 for Explanation of Ratios and Data

Current Data Sorted By Assets   **Comparative Historical Data**

0-500M	500M-2MM	2-10MM	10-50MM	50-100MM	100-250MM	Type of Statement	4/1/98-3/31/99 ALL	4/1/99-3/31/00 ALL
		1	3	1	1	Unqualified	25	19
	3	5	6			Reviewed	20	17
6	9	3			1	Compiled	30	25
9	2	1				Tax Returns	21	21
6	2	4	8	1	2	Other	28	18
16 (4/1-9/30/02)			58 (10/1/02-3/31/03)					
21	16	14	17	2	4	NUMBER OF STATEMENTS	124	100
%	%	%	%	%	%	**ASSETS**	%	%
13.2	10.2	5.4	12.3			Cash & Equivalents	8.1	11.3
2.8	8.2	8.9	3.8			Trade Receivables (net)	5.9	6.1
57.1	43.4	50.8	44.4			Inventory	55.4	49.1
1.2	4.4	7.2	6.0			All Other Current	1.1	1.2
74.3	66.1	72.3	66.5			Total Current	70.6	67.7
12.7	20.2	17.1	26.4			Fixed Assets (net)	20.3	23.6
5.4	2.1	.6	.7			Intangibles (net)	2.8	2.3
7.6	11.6	10.0	6.4			All Other Non-Current	6.3	6.3
100.0	100.0	100.0	100.0			Total	100.0	100.0
						LIABILITIES		
17.1	20.9	12.8	3.3			Notes Payable-Short Term	9.2	9.0
2.5	3.9	2.1	3.5			Cur. Mat.-L/T/D	3.1	2.8
18.0	11.8	23.1	19.0			Trade Payables	15.4	13.6
.0	.1	.3	.1			Income Taxes Payable	.3	.3
15.0	7.2	7.1	9.0			All Other Current	8.8	10.1
52.7	43.9	45.5	34.9			Total Current	36.9	36.0
12.7	12.9	3.6	10.9			Long Term Debt	15.4	15.0
.0	.0	.0	.1			Deferred Taxes	.0	.2
7.3	4.7	6.1	3.3			All Other Non-Current	6.1	2.7
27.3	38.5	44.8	50.8			Net Worth	41.6	46.2
100.0	100.0	100.0	100.0			Total Liabilities & Net Worth	100.0	100.0
						INCOME DATA		
100.0	100.0	100.0	100.0			Net Sales	100.0	100.0
43.8	44.7	38.5	47.7			Gross Profit	40.1	41.0
39.3	41.9	37.8	44.8			Operating Expenses	36.6	37.2
4.5	2.7	.7	2.8			Operating Profit	3.6	3.8
.6	-.7	-.3	-.7			All Other Expenses (net)	.9	.0
3.9	3.5	1.0	3.6			Profit Before Taxes	2.7	3.8
						RATIOS		
3.2	2.0	2.6	2.5			Current	3.1	3.2
2.5	1.8	1.4	2.1				1.9	1.9
1.0	1.1	1.2	1.4				1.5	1.4
.5	.7	.6	.7			Quick	.8	.9
.2	.3	.2	.3				.3	.4
.1	.1	.0	.2				.1	.1
0 UND	0 UND	1 424.6	0 UND			Sales/Receivables	0 999.8	0 UND
0 UND	0 UND	2 165.0	3 142.0				3 132.4	2 227.3
3 112.0	13 27.1	18 20.2	9 40.2				13 28.9	12 30.7
50 7.3	51 7.2	53 6.8	94 3.9			Cost of Sales/Inventory	86 4.2	76 4.8
127 2.9	109 3.3	113 3.2	134 2.7				143 2.6	122 3.0
190 1.9	239 1.5	153 2.4	175 2.1				200 1.8	187 1.9
13 27.3	6 57.6	21 17.1	28 12.9			Cost of Sales/Payables	15 24.4	15 24.2
36 10.0	29 12.4	30 12.1	40 9.1				27 13.3	30 12.2
61 6.0	71 5.1	57 6.4	58 6.3				53 6.9	48 7.6
4.1	5.8	7.2	4.8			Sales/Working Capital	4.4	4.7
9.1	11.9	11.6	7.9				7.7	7.8
NM	50.3	57.9	23.4				15.7	18.9
10.0	27.6	29.8	29.4			EBIT/Interest	7.8	10.7
(15) 5.7	3.1	4.6	(16) 8.6				(101) 3.1	(92) 4.9
1.1	.1	.6	2.1				1.3	1.3
						Net Profit + Depr., Dep., Amort./Cur. Mat. L./T/D	12.8	6.2
							(31) 2.6	(24) 3.2
							1.1	2.0
.1	.3	.1	.2			Fixed/Worth	.2	.2
.3	.6	.3	.5				.5	.4
NM	1.1	.6	.7				.9	1.0
.6	.8	.6	.6			Debt/Worth	.6	.6
1.2	1.4	1.2	.8				1.3	1.2
NM	4.1	2.1	1.9				3.7	2.7
48.9	39.8	30.4	35.4			% Profit Before Taxes/Tangible Net Worth	31.7	39.0
(16) 12.8	(15) 18.1	(13) 10.0	9.1				(113) 17.4	(96) 15.0
3.8	-10.9	1.3	5.0				4.4	5.4
18.0	19.5	13.1	19.2			% Profit Before Taxes/Total Assets	13.5	14.9
5.4	7.0	3.7	4.4				5.9	7.0
1.2	-3.0	-.7	2.0				1.3	1.5
187.7	24.2	51.4	33.3			Sales/Net Fixed Assets	35.0	31.9
31.1	13.5	26.1	9.8				17.6	11.5
18.0	7.0	9.0	5.9				9.2	6.8
5.0	3.2	5.1	3.4			Sales/Total Assets	3.5	3.1
2.8	2.2	2.7	2.3				2.4	2.3
2.2	1.4	2.1	1.9				1.8	1.7
.4	1.1	.5	.7			% Depr., Dep., Amort./Sales	.6	.6
(13) .6	(14) 1.6	(13) 1.0	(16) 1.6				(103) 1.2	(89) 1.3
1.7	2.0	1.6	2.6				1.9	2.2
2.6	2.7					% Officers', Directors', Owners' Comp/Sales	2.4	1.9
(15) 4.9	(11) 4.5						(53) 5.1	(44) 4.2
11.0	7.9						7.3	9.9
24989M	39120M	194502M	999165M	661237M	2906853M	Net Sales ($)	3443374M	4407887M
5719M	17347M	68691M	391313M	186335M	507213M	Total Assets ($)	1475810M	2078182M

© RMA 2003

M = $ thousand   MM = $ million

See Pages 11 through 18 for Explanation of Ratios and Data

Comparative Historical Data   Current Data Sorted By Sales

4/1/00-3/31/01	4/1/01-3/31/02	4/1/02-3/31/03	Type of Statement	0-1MM	1-3MM	3-5MM	5-10MM	10-25MM	25MM & OVER
15	8	6	Unqualified					2	4
14	15	14	Reviewed		2	1	1	4	6
19	17	19	Compiled	3	9	2	1	3	1
18	25	12	Tax Returns	6	3	2	1		
34	29	23	Other	5	2	1		5	10
ALL	ALL	ALL		16 (4/1-9/30/02)			58 (10/1/02-3/31/03)		
100	94	74	**NUMBER OF STATEMENTS**	14	16	6	3	14	21
%	%	%	**ASSETS**	%	%	%	%	%	%
11.5	13.8	10.0	Cash & Equivalents	7.2	11.3			6.8	9.8
5.6	6.0	5.4	Trade Receivables (net)	1.2	6.5			10.1	3.5
48.1	47.0	49.5	Inventory	60.9	49.2			47.6	45.7
1.7	2.5	4.4	All Other Current	1.7	1.6			6.2	6.0
66.8	69.3	69.4	Total Current	71.1	68.7			70.6	65.0
23.8	18.6	19.2	Fixed Assets (net)	14.4	18.5			20.0	25.6
4.1	4.2	3.1	Intangibles (net)	6.0	1.9			.8	3.3
5.2	7.9	8.4	All Other Non-Current	8.5	10.9			8.5	6.0
100.0	100.0	100.0	Total	100.0	100.0			100.0	100.0
			LIABILITIES						
9.0	8.3	14.2	Notes Payable-Short Term	29.5	15.6			10.0	8.4
3.0	1.6	3.3	Cur. Mat.-L/T/D	2.5	2.9			4.2	2.9
15.4	17.5	18.3	Trade Payables	16.2	15.3			23.3	21.3
.2	.1	.2	Income Taxes Payable	.0	.1			.3	.5
9.7	13.4	10.2	All Other Current	11.0	12.2			7.5	9.8
37.4	40.9	46.2	Total Current	59.3	46.2			45.3	42.9
17.8	11.6	14.4	Long Term Debt	17.1	11.1			5.2	24.7
.0	.5	.1	Deferred Taxes	.0	.0			.0	.2
4.7	4.2	5.3	All Other Non-Current	4.4	10.5			5.4	3.7
40.0	42.8	34.0	Net Worth	19.3	32.2			44.0	28.4
100.0	100.0	100.0	Total Liabilities & Net Worth	100.0	100.0			100.0	100.0
			INCOME DATA						
100.0	100.0	100.0	Net Sales	100.0	100.0			100.0	100.0
41.0	41.2	42.9	Gross Profit	42.1	48.3			39.8	42.7
37.3	38.8	40.4	Operating Expenses	43.0	41.1			37.6	41.5
3.7	2.4	2.5	Operating Profit	−.9	7.2			2.2	1.2
1.2	.1	−.2	All Other Expenses (net)	.9	−.9			−.1	−.5
2.5	2.3	2.7	Profit Before Taxes	−1.8	8.2			2.2	1.7
			RATIOS						
3.8	3.7	2.6		4.1	2.8			2.6	2.4
2.0	2.0	1.8	Current	2.1	1.8			1.4	1.6
1.2	1.3	1.1		.9	1.0			1.2	1.0
.9	.9	.6		.5	.5			.7	.6
(99) .4	.4	.3	Quick	.1	.2			.3	.3
.1	.1	.1		.0	.2			.1	.1
0 UND	0 UND	0 UND		0 UND	0 UND			1 334.4	0 UND
2 165.3	1 329.7	2 192.5	Sales/Receivables	0 UND	0 UND			3 118.2	3 142.0
9 38.7	12 31.5	8 47.4		4 98.5	14 27.0			24 15.4	6 62.6
64 5.7	60 6.1	55 6.6		110 3.3	53 6.9			53 6.8	76 4.8
125 2.9	107 3.4	112 3.2	Cost of Sales/Inventory	182 2.0	128 2.8			113 3.2	96 3.8
181 2.0	181 2.0	190 1.9		223 1.6	200 1.8			139 2.6	143 2.6
13 28.2	10 34.8	18 20.0		7 55.6	16 23.0			21 17.1	26 14.3
32 11.6	33 11.2	35 10.4	Cost of Sales/Payables	40 9.2	36 10.0			33 11.1	39 9.4
56 6.5	60 6.1	60 6.1		71 5.2	71 5.1			57 6.4	56 6.5
4.7	4.6	5.7		3.6	6.0			5.8	6.2
8.5	8.7	11.4	Sales/Working Capital	5.5	10.1			11.6	12.8
28.9	24.9	74.8		−65.0	NM			57.9	−320.5
11.1	13.2	16.2		6.5	27.2			29.8	22.6
(89) 3.8	(79) 2.6	(65) 4.5	EBIT/Interest	(11) 1.3	(13) 2.5			8.2	(18) 4.9
1.2	.0	1.1		−10.7	.2			2.5	1.2
5.0	5.5	12.2	Net Profit + Depr., Dep.,						
(19) 2.6	(15) 1.4	(18) 2.5	Amort./Cur. Mat. L/T/D						
1.6	.2	.9							
.2	.1	.1		.1	.2			.1	.3
.5	.4	.5	Fixed/Worth	.3	.6			.4	.6
1.2	.9	1.2		NM	2.8			.8	1.6
.7	.6	.6		.9	.6			.7	.6
1.3	1.1	1.2	Debt/Worth	1.6	1.6			1.3	.9
3.7	3.4	3.1		NM	19.8			2.1	5.1
51.6	45.2	39.9	% Profit Before Taxes/Tangible	41.8	51.9			31.0	27.8
(87) 18.7	(84) 11.0	(66) 10.4	Net Worth	(11) 9.2	(13) 10.3		(13) 13.8		(20) 7.9
4.2	.7	1.8		1.4	−17.4			7.9	2.0
18.4	20.9	15.4	% Profit Before Taxes/Total	8.8	26.1			16.5	12.4
6.6	5.0	4.6	Assets	2.5	6.2			4.4	4.0
1.0	−2.0	.3		−7.0	−2.4			2.7	.5
36.0	58.7	51.4		33.5	107.0			51.4	23.7
13.0	20.2	16.3	Sales/Net Fixed Assets	22.4	14.9			14.7	12.5
7.9	8.5	9.6		14.0	7.0			8.0	7.8
3.7	3.7	3.8		2.8	4.8			5.1	3.8
2.4	2.6	2.6	Sales/Total Assets	2.3	2.3			2.6	3.1
1.6	1.7	2.1		2.1	1.6			2.0	2.1
.6	.6	.6		.3	.7			.5	.8
(79) 1.1	(77) .9	(59) 1.4	% Depr., Dep., Amort./Sales	(10) .9	(12) 1.5		(13) 1.0		(17) 1.7
2.3	1.7	2.0		2.0	1.9			1.7	2.5
2.8	1.3	2.4	% Officers', Directors',		2.8				
(40) 4.4	(44) 6.0	(33) 4.2	Owners' Comp/Sales		(12) 4.2				
8.2	10.0	10.4			11.9				
4621503M	2271378M	4825866M	Net Sales ($)	7936M	25566M	22554M	20277M	223788M	4525745M
1857394M	830749M	1176618M	Total Assets ($)	3648M	12547M	7067M	5081M	89401M	1058874M

M = $ thousand   MM = $ million
See Pages 11 through 18 for Explanation of Ratios and Data

Current Data Sorted By Assets **Comparative Historical Data**

0-500M	500M-2MM	2-10MM	10-50MM	50-100MM	100-250MM	Type of Statement	4/1/98-3/31/99 ALL	4/1/99-3/31/00 ALL
	1	1				Unqualified	1	1
1	1	3				Reviewed	3	5
2	7	1	1			Compiled	9	13
7		1				Tax Returns	1	2
1	5	2	1			Other	5	7
	4 (4/1-9/30/02)		31 (10/1/02-3/31/03)					
11	14	8	2			NUMBER OF STATEMENTS	19	28
%	%	%	%	%	%	**ASSETS**	%	%
14.5	7.9			DATA	DATA	Cash & Equivalents	9.1	10.6
7.9	20.1			NOT	NOT	Trade Receivables (net)	16.6	20.3
61.5	51.7			AVAILABLE	AVAILABLE	Inventory	48.2	48.5
1.2	3.6					All Other Current	.8	1.7
85.2	83.3					Total Current	74.7	81.2
11.1	11.9					Fixed Assets (net)	12.7	12.0
2.2	.1					Intangibles (net)	2.4	3.2
1.5	4.7					All Other Non-Current	10.2	3.6
100.0	100.0					Total	100.0	100.0
						LIABILITIES		
9.9	14.5					Notes Payable-Short Term	15.8	14.1
.2	2.8					Cur. Mat.-L/T/D	2.5	2.6
17.5	26.2					Trade Payables	21.5	21.2
.0	.1					Income Taxes Payable	.1	.3
9.0	13.2					All Other Current	5.5	8.4
36.6	56.8					Total Current	45.5	46.6
32.7	5.8					Long Term Debt	12.2	17.7
.0	.1					Deferred Taxes	.0	.0
3.8	7.2					All Other Non-Current	6.4	2.2
26.9	30.0					Net Worth	35.9	33.4
100.0	100.0					Total Liabilities & Net Worth	100.0	100.0
						INCOME DATA		
100.0	100.0					Net Sales	100.0	100.0
47.5	44.6					Gross Profit	49.4	48.8
41.7	42.6					Operating Expenses	49.8	46.6
5.7	2.0					Operating Profit	-.4	2.2
2.5	.3					All Other Expenses (net)	-7.4	-.2
3.2	1.7					Profit Before Taxes	7.0	2.4
						RATIOS		
6.6	2.3					Current	2.5	3.8
3.7	1.6						1.6	1.5
1.2	1.1						1.2	1.3
1.3	.9					Quick	.9	1.2
.6	.5						.6	.7
.2	.2						.2	.4
0 UND	4 86.4					Sales/Receivables	5 71.2	13 28.6
0 UND	22 16.9						29 12.8	32 11.4
25 14.3	51 7.1						52 7.0	50 7.2
155 2.4	62 5.9					Cost of Sales/Inventory	120 3.0	117 3.1
209 1.7	119 3.1						236 1.5	188 1.9
245 1.5	266 1.4						331 1.1	320 1.1
6 59.0	24 15.2					Cost of Sales/Payables	33 11.1	21 17.5
11 33.7	57 6.4						57 6.5	52 7.1
99 3.7	146 2.5						181 2.0	121 3.0
3.7	4.2					Sales/Working Capital	3.6	3.5
5.5	9.7						5.4	7.9
22.1	36.8						12.0	12.7
	11.2					EBIT/Interest	4.0	3.7
	(13) 2.0						(17) .4	(24) 1.5
	-.6						-2.0	.9
						Net Profit + Depr., Dep., Amort./Cur. Mat. L /T/D		
.0	.1					Fixed/Worth	.2	.1
.3	.4						.4	.3
.8	.7						.5	.7
.2	.8					Debt/Worth	.9	1.0
.7	2.5						1.8	2.1
1.8	3.6						4.5	4.5
	27.7					% Profit Before Taxes/Tangible Net Worth	33.1	32.8
	(12) .7						(18) -1.1	(25) 7.1
	-8.8						-14.3	.9
27.8	18.8					% Profit Before Taxes/Total Assets	9.5	10.3
4.2	2.4						-.7	3.4
-2.1	-1.9						-8.6	.4
498.0	80.7					Sales/Net Fixed Assets	41.4	41.8
35.5	25.2						16.8	19.4
12.9	12.6						9.6	8.8
3.5	4.7					Sales/Total Assets	2.5	2.6
2.6	2.7						1.5	2.1
1.5	1.6						1.2	1.3
						% Depr., Dep., Amort./Sales	.6	.4
							(17) 1.3	(22) .9
							2.3	1.7
						% Officers', Directors', Owners' Comp/Sales	8.0	5.6
							(12) 12.0	(16) 8.2
							15.0	14.8
7794M	52785M	81883M	85879M			Net Sales ($)	59102M	286014M
2853M	17522M	34631M	29292M			Total Assets ($)	25983M	126423M

© RMA 2003

M = $ thousand   MM = $ million
See Pages 11 through 18 for Explanation of Ratios and Data

Comparative Historical Data / Current Data Sorted By Sales

	4/1/00-3/31/01 ALL	4/1/01-3/31/02 ALL	4/1/02-3/31/03 ALL	Type of Statement	0-1MM	1-3MM	3-5MM	5-10MM	10-25MM	25MM & OVER
	2	1	2	Unqualified				2		
	8	5	6	Reviewed	1	1		2	1	1
	16	11	10	Compiled	2	2	4	1	1	
	4	3	8	Tax Returns	6	1		1	1	
	7	12	9	Other	1		1	1		1
						4 (4/1-9/30/02)		31 (10/1/02-3/31/03)		
	37	32	35	**NUMBER OF STATEMENTS**	10	8	5	6	4	2
	%	%	%	**ASSETS**	%	%	%	%	%	%
	11.8	12.9	15.6	Cash & Equivalents	12.0					
	17.5	13.1	14.9	Trade Receivables (net)	5.9					
	50.5	46.4	49.7	Inventory	66.9					
	2.5	4.2	3.1	All Other Current	1.8					
	82.4	76.6	83.3	Total Current	86.6					
	10.8	15.6	11.8	Fixed Assets (net)	9.2					
	2.3	1.2	.8	Intangibles (net)	2.4					
	4.6	6.6	4.0	All Other Non-Current	1.8					
	100.0	100.0	100.0	Total	100.0					
				LIABILITIES						
	14.8	10.0	10.7	Notes Payable-Short Term	13.4					
	1.3	5.7	2.3	Cur. Mat.-L/T/D	.2					
	20.2	18.1	23.5	Trade Payables	21.5					
	.3	.2	.1	Income Taxes Payable	.0					
	16.7	12.3	11.0	All Other Current	8.7					
	53.2	46.3	47.6	Total Current	43.8					
	9.8	9.9	13.2	Long Term Debt	32.6					
	.2	.0	.1	Deferred Taxes	.0					
	4.1	12.1	4.6	All Other Non-Current	4.2					
	32.6	31.8	34.5	Net Worth	19.4					
	100.0	100.0	100.0	Total Liabilities & Net Worth	100.0					
				INCOME DATA						
	100.0	100.0	100.0	Net Sales	100.0					
	45.1	48.6	46.6	Gross Profit	47.7					
	42.0	44.8	43.7	Operating Expenses	43.5					
	3.1	3.8	3.0	Operating Profit	4.2					
	.7	.6	.4	All Other Expenses (net)	1.6					
	2.4	3.2	2.5	Profit Before Taxes	2.6					
				RATIOS						
	3.2 / 1.5 / 1.3	2.4 / 1.6 / 1.2	3.7 / 1.7 / 1.2	Current	4.9 / 2.3 / 1.2					
	1.3 / .7 / .2	1.0 / .5 / .2	1.1 / .6 / .3	Quick	.9 / .5 / .2					
	2 240.3 / 24 15.4 / 41 8.9	0 UND / 15 24.0 / 37 9.8	0 999.8 / 14 26.7 / 45 8.1	Sales/Receivables	0 UND / 0 UND / 34 10.9					
	95 3.9 / 163 2.2 / 241 1.5	99 3.7 / 160 2.3 / 272 1.3	70 5.2 / 163 2.2 / 245 1.5	Cost of Sales/Inventory	167 2.2 / 219 1.7 / 279 1.3					
	12 29.7 / 55 6.6 / 94 3.9	14 25.7 / 39 9.3 / 86 4.2	22 16.5 / 53 6.9 / 117 3.1	Cost of Sales/Payables	9 40.8 / 59 6.2 / 123 3.0					
	3.8 / 6.0 / 15.7	4.3 / 7.5 / 15.8	3.9 / 7.7 / 22.1	Sales/Working Capital	3.2 / 4.3 / 23.1					
	7.6 / (29) 2.1 / .9	5.2 / (30) 2.1 / 1.2	18.9 / (29) 2.8 / -.3	EBIT/Interest						
				Net Profit + Depr., Dep., Amort./Cur. Mat. L/T/D						
	.1 / .2 / .6	.1 / .3 / .6	.1 / .4 / .6	Fixed/Worth	.0 / .2 / NM					
	.8 / 2.0 / 5.3	.8 / 1.6 / 4.6	.6 / 1.2 / 3.0	Debt/Worth	.5 / .9 / NM					
	27.7 / (34) 8.3 / 1.0	28.8 / (29) 7.6 / .8	30.7 / (31) 6.7 / -3.7	% Profit Before Taxes/Tangible Net Worth						
	8.8 / 3.9 / -.3	10.4 / 2.9 / .4	15.0 / 3.6 / -1.9	% Profit Before Taxes/Total Assets	12.5 / 3.1 / -3.1					
	124.9 / 28.1 / 12.7	87.3 / 19.2 / 10.0	76.8 / 25.5 / 12.6	Sales/Net Fixed Assets	UND / 35.5 / 11.6					
	3.0 / 2.3 / 1.5	3.0 / 2.0 / 1.3	4.2 / 2.6 / 1.5	Sales/Total Assets	3.3 / 2.2 / 1.3					
	.4 / (30) .9 / 1.4	.3 / (24) .9 / 1.7	.3 / (26) 1.0 / 2.2	% Depr., Dep., Amort./Sales						
	5.9 / (21) 8.1 / 13.6	4.3 / (14) 7.8 / 15.1	3.3 / (19) 5.9 / 9.2	% Officers', Directors', Owners' Comp/Sales						
	247516M	226186M	228341M	Net Sales ($)	5869M	16874M	17539M	39501M	62679M	85879M
	97396M	95629M	84298M	Total Assets ($)	2960M	10318M	5792M	13072M	22864M	29292M

M = $ thousand   MM = $ million
See Pages 11 through 18 for Explanation of Ratios and Data

Current Data Sorted By Assets   Comparative Historical Data

Type of Statement	0-500M	500M-2MM	2-10MM	10-50MM	50-100MM	100-250MM		4/1/98-3/31/99	4/1/99-3/31/00
Unqualified			4	7	1	2		9	11
Reviewed	1	8	10	2		1		18	14
Compiled	5	9	11	1	1			26	29
Tax Returns	18	14	3	5				20	18
Other	13	10	12		1	2		31	34
			16 (4/1-9/30/02)		124 (10/1/02-3/31/03)			ALL	ALL
NUMBER OF STATEMENTS	37	41	40	15	2	5		104	106

ASSETS	%	%	%	%	%	%		%	%
Cash & Equivalents	17.5	12.6	6.6	7.8				9.6	9.9
Trade Receivables (net)	8.9	10.8	11.8	11.5				11.4	14.5
Inventory	46.2	44.0	38.1	45.2				50.5	45.9
All Other Current	.8	3.4	3.3	2.6				1.7	1.5
Total Current	73.5	70.8	59.8	67.1				73.2	71.8
Fixed Assets (net)	14.9	22.9	32.5	21.5				18.6	20.3
Intangibles (net)	3.5	2.0	2.1	7.3				2.7	2.7
All Other Non-Current	8.1	4.3	5.7	4.1				5.5	5.3
Total	100.0	100.0	100.0	100.0				100.0	100.0

LIABILITIES									
Notes Payable-Short Term	8.0	11.5	7.4	11.0				11.6	15.1
Cur. Mat.-L/T/D	10.3	2.5	3.2	1.4				3.1	2.5
Trade Payables	18.9	17.0	17.6	15.0				20.9	17.7
Income Taxes Payable	.8	.2	.4	.6				.5	.3
All Other Current	13.2	8.1	9.6	11.1				10.0	10.3
Total Current	51.2	39.4	38.3	39.2				46.1	45.9
Long Term Debt	40.2	14.2	20.6	11.7				12.9	14.9
Deferred Taxes	.0	.0	.0	.3				.0	.1
All Other Non-Current	30.5	5.8	5.6	4.8				12.5	8.8
Net Worth	-21.8	40.6	35.5	44.1				28.5	30.2
Total Liabilities & Net Worth	100.0	100.0	100.0	100.0				100.0	100.0

INCOME DATA									
Net Sales	100.0	100.0	100.0	100.0				100.0	100.0
Gross Profit	44.9	43.6	45.2	43.1				42.7	41.4
Operating Expenses	40.8	38.0	40.0	36.4				39.3	37.3
Operating Profit	4.1	5.6	5.3	6.6				3.4	4.1
All Other Expenses (net)	.7	1.4	1.4	1.3				1.4	1.9
Profit Before Taxes	3.3	4.2	3.8	5.4				2.0	2.2

RATIOS

Ratio	0-500M	500M-2MM	2-10MM	10-50MM	50-100MM	100-250MM		4/1/98-3/31/99	4/1/99-3/31/00
Current	3.4	3.0	2.5	2.0				2.5	3.2
	1.9	1.9	1.8	1.6				1.6	1.7
	1.2	1.2	1.1	1.3				1.2	1.1
Quick	1.6	1.0	1.0	.9				(103) .8	1.0
	.4	.5	.3	.3				.4	(103) .6
	.2	.1	.1	.1				.2	.1
Sales/Receivables	0 UND	0 UND	0 UND	1 541.0				0 999.8	0 UND
	0 UND	1 265.9	4 87.9	2 194.9				5 73.6	4 93.5
	17 21.6	31 11.9	38 9.7	48 7.6				26 13.9	40 9.2
Cost of Sales/Inventory	39 9.3	62 5.9	70 5.2	82 4.5				73 5.0	61 6.0
	90 4.0	136 2.7	92 4.0	151 2.4				102 3.6	113 3.2
	179 2.0	239 1.5	171 2.1	199 1.8				165 2.2	169 2.2
Cost of Sales/Payables	3 116.6	14 25.6	23 16.0	28 12.8				21 17.6	13 28.4
	12 30.5	35 10.4	45 8.2	42 8.8				50 7.3	38 9.7
	47 7.8	63 5.8	68 5.4	58 6.3				66 5.5	67 5.5
Sales/Working Capital	5.7	4.4	6.3	4.4				6.0	5.4
	10.8	8.2	9.2	8.9				11.2	10.3
	217.2	32.2	59.0	24.4				24.3	60.2
EBIT/Interest	(29) 7.9	(39) 12.2	8.7	(14) 13.1				(93) 5.9	(93) 7.9
	3.4	3.9	2.8	5.7				3.0	2.2
	1.2	1.7	1.4	3.5				.9	1.1
Net Profit + Depr., Dep., Amort./Cur. Mat. L /T/D			(11) 3.8					(16) 4.2	(18) 4.7
			2.7					2.2	1.5
			1.1					1.0	.8
Fixed/Worth	.1	.2	.3	.2				.1	.2
	.3	.6	.9	.3				.5	.5
	3.0	1.2	2.5	1.9				1.6	1.7
Debt/Worth	.8	.4	.7	.8				.9	.8
	3.0	1.9	2.0	1.3				2.2	2.0
	NM	4.6	4.5	4.1				6.6	5.6
% Profit Before Taxes/Tangible Net Worth	(28) 79.8	(38) 44.0	(37) 48.2	(14) 62.0				(87) 51.8	(96) 46.1
	31.9	23.1	16.3	33.0				22.9	14.6
	5.0	5.4	5.0	14.0				2.6	1.6
% Profit Before Taxes/Total Assets	30.3	17.0	12.0	17.7				13.8	15.2
	14.3	7.6	4.5	12.9				6.6	3.9
	.9	1.2	1.1	8.4				-.7	.5
Sales/Net Fixed Assets	100.0	43.8	28.9	38.7				54.0	61.1
	43.2	13.7	14.2	13.8				20.0	20.1
	16.4	7.1	3.8	7.2				11.1	9.3
Sales/Total Assets	5.0	3.3	3.2	2.9				3.6	3.5
	3.8	2.3	2.4	1.7				2.9	2.4
	2.3	1.3	1.5	1.5				2.1	1.8
% Depr., Dep., Amort./Sales	(23) .6	(35) .7	(36) .8	(12) .8				(90) .5	(89) .6
	.9	1.0	1.4	1.2				1.0	1.3
	1.6	1.6	2.3	2.5				1.8	2.1
% Officers', Directors', Owners' Comp/Sales	(19) 2.4	(27) 3.5	(20) 3.0					(42) 2.8	(51) 2.9
	5.0	5.8	5.3					4.6	4.7
	5.9	10.6	11.7					8.0	7.0
Net Sales ($)	35348M	117700M	396978M	713750M	231561M	1777254M		1675239M	967573M
Total Assets ($)	9178M	50689M	167399M	343314M	110420M	808348M		930117M	521274M

© RMA 2003

M = $ thousand   MM = $ million
See Pages 11 through 18 for Explanation of Ratios and Data

Comparative Historical Data | **Current Data Sorted By Sales**

			Type of Statement						
9	10	14	Unqualified			1	2	2	9
13	16	21	Reviewed	2	2	4	7	4	2
35	30	27	Compiled	2	12	5	5	1	2
22	10	35	Tax Returns	16	11	5	1	1	1
29	30	43	Other	7	13	4	5	4	10
4/1/00-3/31/01 ALL	4/1/01-3/31/02 ALL	4/1/02-3/31/03 ALL		0-1MM	16 (4/1-9/30/02) 1-3MM	3-5MM	124 (10/1/02-3/31/03) 5-10MM	10-25MM	25MM & OVER
108	96	140	**NUMBER OF STATEMENTS**	27	38	19	20	12	24
%	%	%	**ASSETS**	%	%	%	%	%	%
9.3	8.9	11.8	Cash & Equivalents	11.6	14.4	13.3	8.5	7.1	11.8
11.4	13.8	10.3	Trade Receivables (net)	5.6	11.1	9.0	14.0	7.8	13.5
46.6	46.2	43.0	Inventory	55.5	35.5	43.3	41.7	46.5	39.7
1.8	2.3	2.5	All Other Current	2.7	1.8	3.0	1.6	4.5	2.7
69.1	71.2	67.6	Total Current	75.4	62.8	68.6	65.9	65.9	67.8
20.5	22.5	23.2	Fixed Assets (net)	16.8	25.7	24.6	27.2	27.1	20.2
4.1	2.3	3.5	Intangibles (net)	2.9	3.4	2.6	.9	1.6	7.9
6.3	4.0	5.7	All Other Non-Current	4.9	8.0	4.1	6.0	5.5	4.1
100.0	100.0	100.0	Total	100.0	100.0	100.0	100.0	100.0	100.0
			LIABILITIES						
17.0	10.1	9.1	Notes Payable-Short Term	13.4	6.6	8.0	8.5	15.3	6.6
4.0	4.6	4.8	Cur. Mat.-L/T/D	3.6	8.6	4.3	3.3	3.1	2.5
24.7	21.9	17.5	Trade Payables	20.0	13.5	16.4	22.5	20.3	16.3
.1	.3	.5	Income Taxes Payable	.1	.7	.5	.1	1.2	.9
10.8	11.4	10.1	All Other Current	14.0	9.0	9.3	9.3	5.9	10.9
56.6	48.3	42.1	Total Current	51.0	38.6	38.4	43.8	45.7	37.2
14.8	17.6	22.3	Long Term Debt	51.6	19.5	13.9	14.3	8.6	13.8
.1	.1	.1	Deferred Taxes	.0	.0	.1	.0	.1	.2
6.0	7.8	12.6	All Other Non-Current	37.9	7.8	4.5	5.6	5.7	7.4
22.3	26.1	23.0	Net Worth	−40.5	34.1	43.1	36.3	39.9	41.5
100.0	100.0	100.0	Total Liabilities & Net Worth	100.0	100.0	100.0	100.0	100.0	100.0
			INCOME DATA						
100.0	100.0	100.0	Net Sales	100.0	100.0	100.0	100.0	100.0	100.0
42.2	43.3	44.3	Gross Profit	45.7	43.3	49.3	40.9	49.7	40.3
39.1	39.6	39.1	Operating Expenses	43.4	36.1	43.4	36.9	45.7	34.0
3.1	3.7	5.2	Operating Profit	2.3	7.3	5.9	4.0	4.0	6.3
1.2	1.0	1.3	All Other Expenses (net)	1.5	1.2	1.3	1.0	.3	1.7
2.0	2.8	3.9	Profit Before Taxes	.8	6.0	4.6	3.0	3.7	4.6
			RATIOS						
2.1	2.4	2.8	Current	2.9	3.0	3.4	2.4	2.2	2.4
1.4	1.5	1.8		2.0	1.9	1.9	1.6	1.5	1.9
1.0	1.1	1.2		1.0	1.3	1.1	1.3	1.1	1.3
(107) .7	.9	1.0	Quick	.8	1.3	1.0	1.0	.8	1.2
.3	.4	.4		.3	.6	.3	.4	.2	.4
.1	.1	.1		.0	.2	.1	.2	.1	.2
0 UND	0 999.8	0 UND	Sales/Receivables	0 UND	0 UND	0 UND	0 UND	0 UND	1 488.2
3 129.0	4 103.9	2 207.1		0 UND	0 UND	3 108.2	6 59.2	2 153.7	2 197.5
27 13.6	35 10.5	27 13.3		9 39.4	19 18.8	31 11.7	37 9.8	21 17.5	36 10.2
57 6.4	61 6.0	58 6.3	Cost of Sales/Inventory	82 4.4	38 9.6	79 4.6	53 6.9	66 5.5	48 7.6
102 3.6	120 3.0	112 3.3		182 2.0	86 4.2	139 2.6	93 3.9	104 3.5	103 3.5
158 2.0	192 1.9	184 2.0		250 1.5	139 2.6	176 2.1	155 2.4	225 1.6	153 2.4
23 15.6	20 18.0	14 25.3	Cost of Sales/Payables	6 65.7	4 92.1	18 19.8	17 21.1	26 14.1	18 20.6
49 7.5	47 7.7	37 9.8		29 12.8	25 14.7	46 8.0	40 9.1	58 6.3	40 9.2
70 5.2	78 4.7	59 6.1		54 6.7	59 6.2	95 3.8	73 5.0	81 4.5	55 6.6
7.8	5.6	5.1	Sales/Working Capital	2.8	5.7	4.3	6.4	6.2	5.2
15.4	10.9	9.2		8.1	10.0	7.7	9.3	9.8	7.9
163.1	52.0	35.0		566.0	34.3	92.3	31.2	76.8	23.4
(99) 6.0	(80) 6.9	(129) 8.9	EBIT/Interest	(22) 4.5	(34) 14.2	(18) 8.6	9.6	8.6	(23) 16.5
2.1	3.2	3.8		1.7	4.9	3.3	2.6	4.9	6.9
.5	1.6	1.4		.4	2.5	1.7	1.4	2.1	2.4
(23) 7.2	(15) 5.8	(23) 3.8	Net Profit + Depr., Dep., Amort./Cur. Mat. L/T/D						
2.3	1.6	2.6							
.5	.9	.6							
.2	.2	.2	Fixed/Worth	.0	.2	.1	.1	.3	.2
.7	.6	.5		.3	.5	.6	.7	.5	.5
2.7	1.9	1.8		−33.7	3.0	1.2	1.6	1.2	1.6
1.1	.9	.7	Debt/Worth	.9	.5	.3	.6	.9	.7
2.8	3.0	1.8		3.2	2.4	1.9	1.8	1.3	1.3
13.8	5.6	6.6		−12.8	6.8	3.9	4.8	2.6	6.0
(90) 50.3	(86) 71.6	(123) 51.5	% Profit Before Taxes/Tangible Net Worth	(18) 33.6	(35) 93.4	(18) 36.3	(19) 41.1	(11) 57.0	(22) 66.1
23.0	29.5	24.3		7.2	35.3	18.0	16.3	15.1	36.1
3.0	7.0	5.7		.0	12.6	7.6	1.7	3.5	6.3
15.9	17.9	19.1	% Profit Before Taxes/Total Assets	21.2	29.3	18.5	11.8	21.8	19.5
5.2	6.6	8.4		1.7	12.8	5.8	2.7	6.9	13.2
−.8	1.2	1.4		−2.5	4.5	1.9	1.0	2.7	3.2
52.3	40.1	53.3	Sales/Net Fixed Assets	88.2	58.0	46.2	43.5	20.1	59.4
23.8	19.1	16.6		35.0	15.0	14.6	15.0	15.2	16.7
10.6	8.0	7.5		10.2	6.8	5.9	7.1	6.7	7.9
4.2	4.0	3.6	Sales/Total Assets	3.7	4.6	3.0	3.6	3.5	3.1
2.9	2.6	2.5		2.0	2.8	2.4	3.0	2.8	2.3
2.0	1.8	1.6		1.4	1.5	1.5	1.8	1.8	1.7
(86) .4	(78) .5	(111) .7	% Depr., Dep., Amort./Sales	(16) 1.0	(31) .6	(14) .7	(19) .8	1.2	(19) .6
1.0	1.2	1.1		1.2	.9	1.2	1.1	1.5	1.0
1.9	2.2	1.8		3.1	1.6	1.8	1.6	2.2	1.5
(59) 2.2	(46) 2.7	(70) 2.9	% Officers', Directors', Owners' Comp/Sales	(14) 4.2	(20) 2.1	(13) 3.5	(12) 2.7		
4.2	4.3	5.0		5.1	4.2	6.5	5.7		
8.0	7.3	9.1		6.1	8.1	13.2	12.6		
2197795M	1276487M	3272591M	Net Sales ($)	16078M	68758M	75654M	144674M	184873M	2782554M
674623M	552182M	1489348M	Total Assets ($)	10664M	33559M	45630M	60933M	80660M	1257902M

M = $ thousand   MM = $ million
See Pages 11 through 18 for Explanation of Ratios and Data

Current Data Sorted By Assets   Comparative Historical Data

0-500M	500M-2MM	2-10MM	10-50MM	50-100MM	100-250MM	Type of Statement	4/1/98-3/31/99 ALL	4/1/99-3/31/00 ALL
		1	5		1	Unqualified	16	13
1	1	12	1			Reviewed	13	19
6	12	3	4			Compiled	29	23
7	5		4			Tax Returns	14	7
3	6	4	4		1	Other	28	28
\<14 (4/1-9/30/02)\>			\<63 (10/1/02-3/31/03)\>					
17	24	20	14		2	NUMBER OF STATEMENTS	100	90
%	%	%	%	%	%	ASSETS	%	%
3.5	10.7	7.5	6.3			Cash & Equivalents	7.4	7.9
3.0	5.6	5.1	2.6			Trade Receivables (net)	4.2	5.1
72.8	62.2	66.6	59.2			Inventory	66.1	66.9
1.8	4.8	1.3	6.8			All Other Current	.6	.8
81.0	83.3	80.5	74.8			Total Current	78.4	80.7
8.4	7.9	14.2	15.6			Fixed Assets (net)	12.5	12.4
.8	2.8	.3	1.4			Intangibles (net)	4.2	2.5
9.8	6.0	4.9	8.2			All Other Non-Current	5.0	4.4
100.0	100.0	100.0	100.0			Total	100.0	100.0
						LIABILITIES		
7.5	8.2	12.4	6.3			Notes Payable-Short Term	12.2	14.3
4.6	1.8	4.2	4.8			Cur. Mat.-L/T/D	3.4	2.5
20.9	25.8	20.3	14.7			Trade Payables	19.4	19.8
.0	.1	.1	.0			Income Taxes Payable	.2	.3
7.5	4.2	8.9	12.8			All Other Current	6.2	7.0
40.5	40.2	45.9	38.6			Total Current	41.4	43.8
27.9	9.8	6.0	15.2			Long Term Debt	11.2	12.8
.0	.0	.0	.0			Deferred Taxes	.1	.1
11.8	6.8	6.2	4.2			All Other Non-Current	5.3	3.8
19.8	43.2	41.8	41.9			Net Worth	42.0	39.5
100.0	100.0	100.0	100.0			Total Liabilities & Net Worth	100.0	100.0
						INCOME DATA		
100.0	100.0	100.0	100.0			Net Sales	100.0	100.0
40.3	44.6	39.6	37.9			Gross Profit	40.8	40.5
37.7	41.9	38.1	34.6			Operating Expenses	37.8	37.2
2.6	2.7	1.5	3.3			Operating Profit	3.0	3.3
2.4	−.2	.5	−.5			All Other Expenses (net)	.2	.9
.2	2.9	.9	3.8			Profit Before Taxes	2.8	2.4

(Columns for 50-100MM and 100-250MM marked "DATA NOT AVAILABLE".)

RATIOS

0-500M	500M-2MM	2-10MM	10-50MM	Ratio	4/1/98-3/31/99 ALL	4/1/99-3/31/00 ALL
3.8	3.5	2.7	4.9	Current	3.0	3.0
2.2	2.1	1.6	3.1		2.0	2.0
1.5	1.5	1.4	1.1		1.4	1.4
.4	.8	.6	.9	Quick	(99) .5	.7
.1	.2	.1	.2		.2	.2
.0	.0	.1	.1		.1	.0
0 UND	0 UND	0 UND	0 UND	Sales/Receivables	0 UND	0 UND
0 UND	1 510.0	1 589.8	3 136.4		1 340.7	1 387.5
4 81.9	6 56.6	4 102.8	5 77.6		6 60.2	5 71.7
139 2.6	102 3.6	108 3.4	102 3.6	Cost of Sales/Inventory	121 3.0	111 3.3
207 1.8	155 2.3	165 2.2	178 2.1		162 2.2	177 2.1
373 1.0	372 1.4	269 1.4	219 1.7		220 1.7	240 1.5
36 10.2	38 9.6	30 12.1	17 21.5	Cost of Sales/Payables	22 16.5	25 14.9
48 7.6	67 5.5	51 7.1	29 12.5		42 8.6	42 8.8
104 3.5	89 4.1	81 4.5	44 8.4		63 5.8	63 5.8
2.6	2.1	4.5	3.0	Sales/Working Capital	4.2	3.9
4.0	5.2	7.6	4.4		6.5	6.4
28.1	16.7	14.3	NM		13.6	14.4
(16) 7.0	(16) 37.8	(16) 8.2	(10) 3.9	EBIT/Interest	(85) 8.2	(75) 6.9
1.4	2.1	3.2	2.1		3.4	2.4
−.5	.6	1.3	.9		.9	1.1
		(11) 2.6		Net Profit + Depr., Dep., Amort./Cur. Mat. L/T/D	(27) 12.6	(15) 15.5
		1.5			2.1	1.3
		.6			.6	.9
.1	.1	.2	.1	Fixed/Worth	.1	.1
.4	.2	.2	.3		.3	.3
−2.0	.4	.6	2.0		.9	.6
.9	.6	.5	.3	Debt/Worth	.7	.7
3.1	1.6	1.6	1.0		1.5	1.4
−18.7	6.6	3.1	4.6		4.0	4.1
(12) 83.2	58.7	(19) 22.2	(12) 19.3	% Profit Before Taxes/Tangible Net Worth	(91) 36.5	(82) 27.9
28.7	3.8	12.5	9.6		14.7	12.1
−7.8	−3.3	2.9	.2		2.6	2.6
14.7	20.2	9.4	16.1	% Profit Before Taxes/Total Assets	14.0	12.4
.9	2.0	4.3	3.7		5.4	4.3
−7.9	−1.5	.7	.4		.4	.3
108.9	45.3	38.7	25.5	Sales/Net Fixed Assets	48.8	60.9
36.7	32.9	22.6	17.4		23.9	29.9
17.0	19.4	8.9	9.9		14.2	14.5
2.9	3.3	3.0	2.9	Sales/Total Assets	3.1	3.3
1.9	2.2	2.3	2.3		2.4	2.4
1.5	1.3	1.8	1.9		2.0	1.8
(13) .5	(21) .5	(19) .6	.8	% Depr., Dep., Amort./Sales	(88) .5	(75) .4
1.0	.8	.9	1.2		1.0	.8
1.2	1.3	1.6	1.8		1.6	1.4
	(13) 3.0	(11) 2.0		% Officers', Directors', Owners' Comp/Sales	(49) 3.0	(44) 2.8
	5.9	2.4			4.7	4.0
	9.4	3.8			8.1	8.2

0-500M	500M-2MM	2-10MM	10-50MM	100-250MM		4/1/98-3/31/99 ALL	4/1/99-3/31/00 ALL
10693M	69284M	235836M	778081M	700899M	Net Sales ($)	1990109M	2929455M
4399M	26191M	93193M	308093M	365510M	Total Assets ($)	938707M	1297355M

M = $ thousand   MM = $ million
See Pages 11 through 18 for Explanation of Ratios and Data

Comparative Historical Data / Current Data Sorted By Sales

			Type of Statement	0-1MM	1-3MM	3-5MM	5-10MM	10-25MM	25MM & OVER
11	5	7	Unqualified					1	6
12	13	15	Reviewed	2		2	4	5	2
22	28	25	Compiled	8	7	1	4	1	4
9	8	12	Tax Returns	5	3	1	3		
16	22	18	Other	5	2	4	1	1	5
4/1/00-3/31/01 ALL	4/1/01-3/31/02 ALL	4/1/02-3/31/03 ALL		14 (4/1-9/30/02)			63 (10/1/02-3/31/03)		
70	76	77	NUMBER OF STATEMENTS	20	12	8	12	8	17
%	%	%	**ASSETS**	%	%	%	%	%	%
11.5	7.4	7.3	Cash & Equivalents	5.7	9.6		9.2		6.9
4.2	6.9	4.5	Trade Receivables (net)	2.2	8.3		5.1		3.2
60.6	66.0	64.8	Inventory	75.6	58.0		61.2		59.9
1.1	.8	3.5	All Other Current	2.3	1.1		3.9		5.6
77.4	81.2	80.1	Total Current	85.8	77.1		79.4		75.6
14.0	13.2	11.4	Fixed Assets (net)	5.5	9.8		8.5		18.3
3.4	1.1	1.5	Intangibles (net)	1.5	3.7		.7		1.5
5.2	3.9	7.0	All Other Non-Current	7.2	9.5		11.3		4.6
100.0	100.0	100.0	Total	100.0	100.0		100.0		100.0
			LIABILITIES						
10.7	14.2	8.6	Notes Payable-Short Term	7.6	8.9		8.6		6.4
4.3	2.8	3.5	Cur. Mat.-L/T/D	3.4	3.8		1.3		4.1
19.8	19.5	21.0	Trade Payables	16.7	24.8		26.4		16.9
.1	.1	.1	Income Taxes Payable	.0	.3		.0		.0
6.9	6.3	7.7	All Other Current	6.4	4.3		11.2		10.6
41.9	42.9	41.0	Total Current	34.2	42.1		47.6		38.0
15.1	12.7	14.0	Long Term Debt	21.8	16.4		9.4		13.6
.2	.1	.1	Deferred Taxes	.0	.0		.1		.3
3.8	6.7	7.1	All Other Non-Current	14.8	4.9		1.3		3.7
38.3	36.9	37.9	Net Worth	29.2	36.5		41.7		44.3
100.0	100.0	100.0	Total Liabilities & Net Worth	100.0	100.0		100.0		100.0
			INCOME DATA						
100.0	100.0	100.0	Net Sales	100.0	100.0		100.0		100.0
40.6	41.0	40.8	Gross Profit	44.1	40.5		38.6		37.2
37.2	37.3	38.2	Operating Expenses	41.4	39.8		34.1		33.2
3.3	3.7	2.6	Operating Profit	2.7	.7		4.4		4.0
.5	1.5	.5	All Other Expenses (net)	2.5	-1.2		-.9		.4
2.8	2.2	2.1	Profit Before Taxes	.2	1.9		5.3		3.5
			RATIOS						
3.4	3.5	3.5	Current	4.3	3.5		2.2		4.3
2.2	2.0	2.1		3.1	1.8		1.8		2.6
1.3	1.3	1.4		1.9	1.4		1.2		1.5
.8	.5	.6	Quick	.4	1.0		.6		.9
.3	.2	.2		.1	.3		.3		.2
.1	.1	.0		.0	.1		.1		.1
0 UND	0 UND	0 UND	Sales/Receivables	0 UND	0 UND		0 UND		0 UND
1 653.0	2 203.4	1 453.6		1 605.5	0 UND		0 928.1		2 179.1
4 90.4	7 50.5	4 89.2		4 103.5	9 42.0		10 37.4		4 90.6
92 4.0	113 3.2	109 3.3	Cost of Sales/Inventory	219 1.7	80 4.6		87 4.2		96 3.8
138 2.6	170 2.1	178 2.1		373 1.0	155 2.3		116 3.1		149 2.5
211 1.7	267 1.4	282 1.3		483 .8	199 1.8		174 2.1		205 1.8
21 17.6	23 15.8	30 12.2	Cost of Sales/Payables	38 9.6	28 12.9		18 20.4		21 17.1
36 10.1	42 8.6	49 7.5		59 6.2	53 6.9		45 8.2		34 10.8
69 5.3	78 4.7	83 4.4		124 3.0	85 4.3		77 4.7		50 7.3
3.8	3.4	3.0	Sales/Working Capital	1.5	3.8		5.8		3.2
6.1	5.9	5.2		2.6	8.2		9.0		5.2
18.0	17.7	15.8		3.9	23.1		23.6		21.8
7.3	9.1	8.2	EBIT/Interest	3.7			63.9		4.6
(57) 2.6	(68) 2.6	(60) 2.1		(18) 1.4			(10) 13.9		(12) 2.1
.9	.4	.6		.0			3.1		1.1
3.4	7.0	6.0	Net Profit + Depr., Dep., Amort./Cur. Mat. L/T/D						
(14) 1.1	(19) 2.2	(19) 1.6							
.3	.5	.6							
.1	.1	.1	Fixed/Worth	.0	.1		.1		.2
.3	.3	.2		.2	.3		.2		.3
1.1	.7	.6		2.8	.7		.4		.7
.6	.8	.6	Debt/Worth	.7	.8		.6		.4
1.9	1.7	1.5		3.1	3.1		1.6		.9
7.6	5.1	6.0		53.1	7.3		5.9		1.9
54.9	37.8	40.4	% Profit Before Taxes/Tangible Net Worth	68.5	76.0		64.0		20.0
(62) 23.0	(69) 14.7	(69) 8.9		(16) 2.4	(11) .4		35.1		(15) 10.2
2.8	.9	.2		-12.8	-2.7		4.0		.9
18.5	13.4	13.0	% Profit Before Taxes/Total Assets	6.6	12.2		33.8		16.1
4.0	5.2	2.9		.6	.1		10.6		4.0
.0	-.1	-.7		-2.9	-6.9		.9		.6
66.3	46.5	44.0	Sales/Net Fixed Assets	117.4	43.6		79.5		26.0
28.2	24.8	28.7		34.0	32.9		34.5		15.7
11.6	13.4	14.4		17.4	18.5		27.2		8.2
3.4	3.1	3.1	Sales/Total Assets	1.9	3.2		4.8		3.3
2.4	2.4	2.2		1.4	2.4		3.1		2.4
1.7	1.8	1.6		1.2	2.0		2.2		2.0
.4	.5	.6	% Depr., Dep., Amort./Sales	.6	.7		.2		.7
(55) .7	(62) .9	(68) 1.0		(14) 1.0	(11) 1.0		.8		(15) 1.1
1.4	1.3	1.4		1.4	1.2		1.4		1.7
2.7	2.8	2.2	% Officers', Directors', Owners' Comp/Sales	4.3					
(32) 3.7	(42) 4.7	(40) 3.9		(10) 6.1					
6.0	7.1	8.5		11.0					
2465173M	1987311M	1794793M	Net Sales ($)	10846M	20743M	33048M	85817M	112719M	1531620M
1220177M	1062293M	797386M	Total Assets ($)	8479M	9565M	16703M	39566M	45799M	677274M

M = $ thousand   MM = $ million
See Pages 11 through 18 for Explanation of Ratios and Data

Current Data Sorted By Assets   Comparative Historical Data

						Type of Statement		
1	1	2	12	3	2	Unqualified	18	23
1	11	27	8			Reviewed	44	41
13	41	25	2		1	Compiled	99	97
23	31	17	1	1		Tax Returns	47	50
3	25	12	6			Other	82	67
	101 (4/1-9/30/02)		167 (10/1/02-3/31/03)				4/1/98-3/31/99	4/1/99-3/31/00
0-500M	500M-2MM	2-10MM	10-50MM	50-100MM	100-250MM		ALL	ALL
40	109	83	29	4	3	NUMBER OF STATEMENTS	290	278

0-500M	500M-2MM	2-10MM	10-50MM	50-100MM	100-250MM		4/1/98-3/31/99 ALL	4/1/99-3/31/00 ALL
%	%	%	%	%	%	**ASSETS**	%	%
12.8	8.0	6.0	5.2			Cash & Equivalents	5.3	7.5
5.3	7.0	10.3	13.2			Trade Receivables (net)	10.8	9.9
59.1	70.0	66.8	60.1			Inventory	67.4	65.3
3.6	1.4	1.6	2.6			All Other Current	.9	1.3
80.9	86.4	84.8	81.2			Total Current	84.4	84.1
14.5	8.3	9.7	12.4			Fixed Assets (net)	11.1	10.4
1.3	1.2	1.2	.7			Intangibles (net)	1.3	1.8
3.3	4.0	4.4	5.7			All Other Non-Current	3.1	3.7
100.0	100.0	100.0	100.0			Total	100.0	100.0
						LIABILITIES		
14.9	9.9	12.1	9.2			Notes Payable-Short Term	12.5	12.5
1.5	3.0	3.2	3.5			Cur. Mat.-L/T/D	3.1	2.9
11.3	21.7	18.9	20.2			Trade Payables	21.2	21.4
.0	.1	.2	.0			Income Taxes Payable	.4	.2
12.2	6.6	9.9	11.8			All Other Current	8.8	11.3
40.0	41.3	44.3	44.6			Total Current	46.0	48.3
15.2	14.7	8.0	7.9			Long Term Debt	12.1	12.6
.0	.0	.1	.4			Deferred Taxes	.1	.1
7.9	5.0	3.4	1.9			All Other Non-Current	4.8	4.3
36.9	38.9	44.1	45.1			Net Worth	36.9	34.7
100.0	100.0	100.0	100.0			Total Liabilities & Net Worth	100.0	100.0
						INCOME DATA		
100.0	100.0	100.0	100.0			Net Sales	100.0	100.0
46.1	45.0	42.8	48.7			Gross Profit	43.6	43.4
39.5	40.8	39.1	43.5			Operating Expenses	37.7	38.8
6.6	4.2	3.7	5.1			Operating Profit	5.9	4.7
1.6	1.3	.9	.3			All Other Expenses (net)	1.1	.6
5.0	3.0	2.8	4.9			Profit Before Taxes	4.8	4.0
						RATIOS		
4.6	3.2	2.9	3.0				3.0	3.2
2.2	2.2	1.9	1.7			Current	1.8	1.9
1.5	1.6	1.5	1.4				1.3	1.4
(39) .8	.6	.7	.9				.7	.7
.5	.3	.2	.3			Quick	.3 (277)	.3
.2	.1	.1	.1				.1	.1
0 UND	2 214.6	3 106.1	8 48.2				1 294.0	0 999.8
0 UND	9 41.4	13 28.6	16 22.7			Sales/Receivables	9 39.4	11 33.6
11 34.1	25 14.5	31 12.0	37 10.0				34 10.9	29 12.4
87 4.2	205 1.8	222 1.6	250 1.5				186 2.0	167 2.2
192 1.9	331 1.1	299 1.2	291 1.3			Cost of Sales/Inventory	268 1.4	254 1.4
356 1.0	469 .8	375 1.0	387 .9				380 1.0	358 1.0
0 UND	46 7.9	38 9.5	37 9.8				34 10.7	28 12.8
18 20.3	84 4.3	68 5.4	103 3.5			Cost of Sales/Payables	68 5.3	61 6.0
69 5.3	130 2.8	116 3.2	178 2.0				112 3.3	111 3.3
2.3	2.2	2.5	2.7				2.6	2.7
4.8	3.3	4.0	4.6			Sales/Working Capital	4.5	4.5
10.0	5.4	7.0	6.6				9.2	9.5
(31) 8.8	(101) 5.3	(80) 6.9	(26) 9.7				(266) 8.0	(260) 6.6
3.6	2.4	3.0	3.6			EBIT/Interest	3.1	3.0
1.6	1.2	1.1	1.9				1.6	1.5
	(15) 2.3	(32) 3.0	(11) 4.3			Net Profit + Depr., Dep.,	(68) 4.7	(56) 3.5
	.9	.9	2.1			Amort./Cur. Mat. L./T/D	2.0	2.0
	.4	.2	.8				.6	.9
.0	.1	.1	.1				.1	.1
.1	.2	.1	.3			Fixed/Worth	.2	.2
1.7	.5	.4	.5				.6	.5
.6	.8	.9	.7				.9	1.0
1.4	1.7	1.3	1.1			Debt/Worth	1.9	1.9
32.4	3.6	2.5	2.4				3.8	3.9
50.0	22.1	20.2	21.5			% Profit Before Taxes/Tangible	39.8	36.5
(31) 16.9	(101) 10.1	(81) 6.4	13.0			Net Worth	(263) 16.5	(262) 16.1
2.1	1.7	.3	2.8				5.2	6.5
21.4	7.4	8.7	11.4				12.8	12.1
6.1	3.5	3.0	4.9			% Profit Before Taxes/Total Assets	5.4	5.1
1.2	.6	.2	1.2				1.7	1.6
384.7	73.4	51.6	20.2				55.6	57.6
38.3	28.6	25.4	11.4			Sales/Net Fixed Assets	24.1	25.2
11.9	11.9	9.5	9.0				12.0	11.9
3.5	1.9	1.9	1.8				2.3	2.3
2.6	1.5	1.5	1.4			Sales/Total Assets	1.7	1.7
1.3	1.2	1.1	1.2				1.3	1.3
.4	.4	.5	.8				.4	.4
(28) .8	(90) .9	(78) .8	(28) 1.2			% Depr., Dep., Amort./Sales	(250) .8	(245) .8
1.3	1.5	1.3	2.1				1.5	1.5
5.6	4.4	2.2	2.7				3.2	3.5
(27) 9.7	(77) 6.0	(50) 3.9	(10) 5.1			% Officers', Directors', Owners' Comp/Sales	(151) 5.7	(150) 6.0
12.1	8.9	7.9	6.1				8.0	9.3
31692M	199723M	552306M	833160M	548383M	503966M	Net Sales ($)	3696409M	4469224M
11805M	129551M	359517M	556547M	276555M	354640M	Total Assets ($)	2317927M	2793937M

M = $ thousand   MM = $ million
See Pages 11 through 18 for Explanation of Ratios and Data

Comparative Historical Data　　　　　　　Current Data Sorted By Sales

	4/1/00-3/31/01 ALL	4/1/01-3/31/02 ALL	4/1/02-3/31/03 ALL	0-1MM	1-3MM	3-5MM	5-10MM	10-25MM	25MM & OVER
Type of Statement				101 (4/1-9/30/02)			167 (10/1/02-3/31/03)		
Unqualified	13	15	20		2		1	5	12
Reviewed	41	24	47	2	9	8	13	13	2
Compiled	98	88	81	18	31	17	11	3	1
Tax Returns	45	50	72	21	34	7	8	2	
Other	54	53	48	12	21	2	1	8	4
NUMBER OF STATEMENTS	251	230	268	53	97	34	34	31	19
ASSETS	%	%	%	%	%	%	%	%	%
Cash & Equivalents	6.0	7.1	7.7	7.5	9.7	5.3	8.6	4.7	5.1
Trade Receivables (net)	9.0	9.8	8.7	5.1	6.6	16.2	6.6	11.3	15.4
Inventory	67.6	66.7	65.9	68.2	65.8	67.0	68.3	62.7	58.6
All Other Current	1.2	1.5	2.0	2.4	2.3	1.6	.6	2.0	3.4
Total Current	83.8	85.1	84.3	83.3	84.4	90.2	84.1	80.8	82.5
Fixed Assets (net)	10.3	9.7	10.3	10.2	10.5	6.6	9.0	13.0	14.0
Intangibles (net)	1.8	1.3	1.1	1.3	1.6	.8	.6	.5	1.0
All Other Non-Current	4.1	3.9	4.2	5.3	3.4	2.5	6.3	5.7	2.5
Total	100.0	100.0	100.0	100.0	100.0	100.0	100.0	100.0	100.0
LIABILITIES									
Notes Payable-Short Term	12.4	11.0	11.1	17.0	8.7	13.8	7.7	10.7	8.8
Cur. Mat.-L/T/D	3.3	4.0	2.8	1.2	3.5	3.2	3.2	3.1	2.2
Trade Payables	21.1	20.3	19.0	11.8	22.0	20.3	17.8	21.5	19.6
Income Taxes Payable	.2	.3	.1	.1	.1	.2	.4	.0	.2
All Other Current	8.2	8.2	9.3	9.1	7.4	9.6	10.1	12.8	12.3
Total Current	45.3	43.8	42.4	39.1	41.8	46.9	39.2	48.1	43.1
Long Term Debt	12.8	11.5	12.2	15.9	14.3	8.2	6.4	9.4	13.3
Deferred Taxes	.1	.1	.1	.0	.0	.0	.2	.5	.4
All Other Non-Current	3.5	4.3	4.5	8.1	4.7	4.2	2.5	1.9	1.7
Net Worth	38.4	40.3	40.8	36.9	39.2	40.6	51.6	40.2	41.5
Total Liabilities & Net Worth	100.0	100.0	100.0	100.0	100.0	100.0	100.0	100.0	100.0
INCOME DATA									
Net Sales	100.0	100.0	100.0	100.0	100.0	100.0	100.0	100.0	100.0
Gross Profit	44.0	45.4	44.8	48.1	44.4	42.6	42.1	44.2	46.8
Operating Expenses	39.0	41.7	40.2	41.6	40.1	39.6	39.2	39.0	42.1
Operating Profit	5.1	3.7	4.5	6.5	4.3	3.0	2.9	5.1	4.7
All Other Expenses (net)	.8	1.2	1.1	1.9	1.1	1.3	.2	.6	1.1
Profit Before Taxes	4.3	2.5	3.4	4.6	3.2	1.7	2.6	4.5	3.6
RATIOS									
Current	3.1	3.4	3.3	5.8	3.2	2.5	3.5	2.2	3.3
	2.0	2.0	2.0	2.6	2.1	1.9	2.0	1.6	1.9
	1.4	1.4	1.5	1.5	1.6	1.6	1.5	1.3	1.4
Quick	.6	.7	.7	.8	.6	.7	1.0	.7	.9
	.3	(229) .3	(267) .3	(52) .3	.3	.3	.3	.2	.4
	.1	.1	.1	.1	.1	.1	.1	.1	.1
Sales/Receivables	1　447.6	1　340.3	2　202.6	0　UND	1　464.6	5　68.6	3　120.9	4　100.6	4　87.3
	10　38.2	11　32.0	9　41.3	7　48.7	8　43.3	16　22.3	8　44.6	10　36.8	13　27.3
	25　14.5	27　13.6	27　13.6	18　20.8	26　14.3	45　8.2	22　16.7	37　10.0	46　7.9
Cost of Sales/Inventory	189　1.9	210　1.7	190　1.9	209　1.7	191　1.9	159　2.3	190　1.9	244　1.5	164　2.2
	271　1.3	280　1.3	296　1.2	380　1.0	308　1.2	274　1.3	267　1.4	285　1.3	212　1.7
	363　1.0	381　1.0	401　.9	617　.6	432　.8	367　1.0	317　1.2	371　1.0	297　1.2
Cost of Sales/Payables	34　10.8	33　11.2	36　10.2	0　UND	40　9.2	44　8.3	34　10.9	48　7.6	30　12.0
	70　5.2	76　4.8	71　5.1	46　8.0	77　4.7	71　5.2	51　7.1	87　4.2	53　6.9
	118　3.1	129　2.8	120　3.1	115　3.2	133　2.7	113　3.2	84　4.3	139　2.6	98　3.7
Sales/Working Capital	2.6	2.4	2.3	1.6	2.3	3.0	2.5	2.9	3.0
	4.1	4.0	3.7	2.6	3.6	3.6	4.2	4.1	5.6
	8.1	7.7	6.8	5.5	6.6	6.0	8.2	8.5	7.7
EBIT/Interest	7.4	5.8	6.8	7.8	4.9	6.9	7.6	7.5	11.0
	(236) 3.1	(218) 2.7	(245) 2.7	(47) 2.7	(84) 2.4	3.0	(33) 3.2	(28) 2.4	6.6
	1.7	1.1	1.2	.9	1.3	.3	.9	1.7	1.9
Net Profit + Depr., Dep., Amort./Cur. Mat. L/T/D	3.3	2.6	3.4		2.3	2.5	5.3	3.1	28.7
	(61) 1.7	(47) 1.4	(63) 1.4		(15) 1.4	(12) .4	(13) 1.1	(10) .7	(10) 3.2
	.7	.5	.4		.5	-.5	.6	-1.6	1.4
Fixed/Worth	.1	.1	.1	.0	.1	.0	.1	.2	.1
	.2	.2	.2	.1	.2	.1	.1	.4	.4
	.5	.5	.5	1.6	.6	.2	.3	.7	.5
Debt/Worth	.8	.7	.7	.5	.9	1.0	.5	.9	.6
	1.8	1.7	1.4	1.5	1.7	1.4	1.0	1.5	1.4
	3.3	3.6	3.2	24.3	3.9	2.4	1.7	2.9	3.1
% Profit Before Taxes/Tangible Net Worth	31.4	23.7	22.8	24.6	23.3	23.5	14.9	19.6	29.8
	(235) 14.6	(215) 11.3	(248) 10.2	(42) 6.9	(89) 11.1	8.5	6.3	(18) 11.8	18.3
	5.7	3.0	1.4	1.1	2.4	-7.3	-.1	1.4	7.6
% Profit Before Taxes/Total Assets	10.4	9.3	9.7	10.3	7.6	9.3	11.3	10.4	13.2
	5.5	4.0	3.7	3.9	3.3	3.6	3.1	4.0	5.3
	2.1	.5	.7	.2	1.0	-1.8	.0	.8	1.0
Sales/Net Fixed Assets	57.0	68.5	68.0	112.1	62.4	102.2	44.5	16.1	27.9
	26.0	23.8	25.1	26.7	26.7	53.8	27.4	10.1	11.4
	13.2	10.7	9.9	7.4	11.1	21.1	14.1	8.3	9.3
Sales/Total Assets	2.2	2.1	2.0	2.0	2.1	2.3	2.1	1.8	2.3
	1.7	1.6	1.5	1.2	1.5	1.7	1.8	1.4	1.8
	1.3	1.2	1.2	.8	1.2	1.2	1.4	1.3	1.5
% Depr., Dep., Amort./Sales	.3	.3	.5	.6	.4	.3	.5	.7	.9
	(212) .7	(190) .7	(230) .9	(39) 1.1	(78) 1.0	(33) .5	(33) .9	(29) .9	(18) 2.0
	1.4	1.6	1.5	2.1	1.5	1.1	1.2	1.5	2.3
% Officers', Directors', Owners' Comp/Sales	3.7	3.4	3.2	5.7	4.2	2.8	2.0	1.5	
	(143) 6.4	(122) 5.7	(165) 5.7	(33) 8.2	(72) 5.7	(22) 5.5	(19) 6.9	(14) 2.9	
	9.7	8.8	9.3	10.9	9.2	7.1	9.5	5.4	
Net Sales ($)	2957681M	2436196M	2669230M	30896M	183090M	139397M	235785M	482918M	1597144M
Total Assets ($)	1709668M	1570333M	1688615M	29103M	134625M	91592M	149451M	366798M	917046M

© RMA 2003

M = $ thousand　　MM = $ million
See Pages 11 through 18 for Explanation of Ratios and Data

Current Data Sorted By Assets   **Comparative Historical Data**

0-500M	500M-2MM	2-10MM	10-50MM	50-100MM	100-250MM	Type of Statement	4/1/98-3/31/99 ALL	4/1/99-3/31/00 ALL
3	2	7	10	4	3	Unqualified	21	22
19	18	19	5			Reviewed	46	47
31	43	20	6			Compiled	140	126
14	19	6	2			Tax Returns	67	49
	29	21		2	2	Other	76	89
60 (4/1-9/30/02)		225 (10/1/02-3/31/03)						
67	111	73	23	6	5	NUMBER OF STATEMENTS	350	333
%	%	%	%	%	%	ASSETS	%	%
7.5	8.2	5.8	4.1			Cash & Equivalents	6.9	7.9
7.6	8.5	10.6	8.4			Trade Receivables (net)	6.4	8.8
64.8	62.0	57.1	50.6			Inventory	64.2	60.1
.5	.6	2.2	.7			All Other Current	1.2	1.4
80.5	79.3	75.6	63.8			Total Current	78.8	78.2
14.1	13.5	16.8	16.8			Fixed Assets (net)	14.4	14.8
1.3	3.0	3.2	12.2			Intangibles (net)	2.5	2.9
4.1	4.3	4.4	7.2			All Other Non-Current	4.3	4.2
100.0	100.0	100.0	100.0			Total	100.0	100.0
						LIABILITIES		
15.1	11.7	13.1	14.5			Notes Payable-Short Term	13.1	12.4
5.3	2.7	3.2	3.6			Cur. Mat.-L/T/D	2.9	3.5
29.3	22.2	25.9	24.4			Trade Payables	25.6	22.3
.0	.2	.1	.0			Income Taxes Payable	.2	.3
13.7	7.6	7.4	9.2			All Other Current	9.4	10.7
63.4	44.5	49.7	51.7			Total Current	51.1	49.2
20.9	9.4	10.2	17.4			Long Term Debt	14.2	12.0
.0	.1	.1	.0			Deferred Taxes	.2	.1
7.5	8.2	4.6	3.3			All Other Non-Current	5.0	6.8
8.1	37.8	35.4	27.6			Net Worth	29.5	31.9
100.0	100.0	100.0	100.0			Total Liabilities & Net Worth	100.0	100.0
						INCOME DATA		
100.0	100.0	100.0	100.0			Net Sales	100.0	100.0
36.2	35.5	35.9	40.8			Gross Profit	35.7	35.6
35.9	34.1	33.1	35.3			Operating Expenses	33.1	33.2
.3	1.5	2.9	5.5			Operating Profit	2.5	2.4
1.0	.6	.7	2.4			All Other Expenses (net)	.5	.7
−.7	.8	2.2	3.2			Profit Before Taxes	2.0	1.7
						RATIOS		
2.2	3.1	2.2	1.6				2.3	2.3
1.5	1.8	1.6	1.4			Current	1.6	1.7
1.0	1.2	1.1	1.0				1.2	1.2
.5	1.0	.6	.4				.5	.6
.2	(109) .3	.2	.1			Quick (345) ... (332)	.2	.2
.1	.1	.1	.1				.1	.1
0 UND	0 999.8	0 749.5	2 194.9				0 UND	0 999.8
1 266.5	4 102.2	3 105.2	4 89.8			Sales/Receivables	3 144.1	3 112.1
9 40.9	17 21.7	14 25.5	18 20.4				10 38.1	16 22.6
85 4.3	82 4.4	96 3.8	88 4.1				96 3.8	91 4.0
140 2.6	133 2.7	129 2.8	137 2.7			Cost of Sales/Inventory	135 2.7	125 2.9
208 1.8	209 1.7	171 2.1	171 2.1				195 1.9	177 2.1
20 17.9	19 19.3	35 10.5	51 7.2				25 14.4	24 15.1
56 6.5	42 8.8	51 7.1	64 5.7			Cost of Sales/Payables	45 8.0	44 8.3
87 4.2	77 4.8	78 4.7	81 4.5				75 4.9	67 5.4
5.7	5.0	5.6	7.7				5.2	5.5
13.9	8.1	10.3	18.7			Sales/Working Capital	9.1	9.1
UND	20.9	38.2	127.7				23.4	20.1
3.1	6.3	10.7	7.9				6.4	5.9
(59) 1.0	(102) 2.0	(67) 2.4	(21) 3.8			EBIT/Interest (312) ... (295)	2.6	2.4
−2.0	1.0	1.1	2.4				1.2	1.1
	7.2	3.4				Net Profit + Depr., Dep.,	5.9	7.2
	(16) 1.7	(16) 1.7				Amort./Cur. Mat. L /T/D (77) ... (65)	3.5	2.7
	.9	.7					1.6	1.3
.1	.1	.2	.2				.1	.1
.6	.3	.4	.7			Fixed/Worth	.4	.4
−1.9	.8	1.2	1.9				1.5	1.2
1.8	.8	1.0	1.7				1.1	.9
6.7	1.6	2.3	3.9			Debt/Worth	2.2	2.2
−7.6	4.1	4.8	7.2				7.8	6.9
25.7	21.2	32.0	55.7			% Profit Before Taxes/Tangible	32.8	38.3
(47) 7.1	(96) 8.2	(68) 14.0	(20) 34.1			Net Worth (296) ... (287)	15.2	15.5
−9.8	1.8	3.0	5.2				3.7	4.7
8.7	7.2	8.7	11.0			% Profit Before Taxes/Total	10.6	11.6
1.1	2.7	3.7	8.1			Assets	4.8	5.0
−8.2	.1	.5	1.1				.5	.5
116.0	67.6	48.6	60.3				65.9	60.6
37.0	33.2	22.6	21.2			Sales/Net Fixed Assets	28.8	28.0
14.4	14.3	10.6	11.7				13.3	12.2
4.0	3.4	3.3	2.8				3.3	3.4
2.8	2.7	2.3	2.5			Sales/Total Assets	2.5	2.6
2.1	1.7	1.8	1.9				2.0	2.1
.6	.5	.5	.6				.5	.5
(51) 1.1	(95) .8	(69) 1.0	(21) .8			% Depr., Dep., Amort./Sales (304) ... (282)	.9	.9
2.0	1.6	1.6	1.9				1.5	1.6
4.4	2.2	1.5					2.0	2.2
(45) 6.4	(68) 4.0	(30) 3.3				% Officers', Directors', Owners' Comp/Sales (190) ... (178)	3.6	4.1
12.3	6.7	5.3					6.0	7.0
58720M	369664M	771797M	1025127M	1029722M	1610416M	Net Sales ($)	5609766M	7461960M
19278M	130894M	297175M	432084M	509369M	742279M	Total Assets ($)	2472229M	2972860M

© RMA 2003   M = $ thousand   MM = $ million
See Pages 11 through 18 for Explanation of Ratios and Data

Comparative Historical Data | Current Data Sorted By Sales

4/1/00-3/31/01 ALL	4/1/01-3/31/02 ALL	4/1/02-3/31/03 ALL	Type of Statement	0-1MM	1-3MM	3-5MM	5-10MM	10-25MM	25MM & OVER
13	16	26	Unqualified			2		5	19
36	35	45	Reviewed	2	7	7	17	7	5
107	92	84	Compiled	11	35	10	19	5	4
41	52	56	Tax Returns	26	14	12	4		
70	58	74	Other	14	18	11	16	7	8
				60 (4/1-9/30/02)			225 (10/1/02-3/31/03)		
267	253	285	**NUMBER OF STATEMENTS**	53	74	42	56	24	36
%	%	%	**ASSETS**	%	%	%	%	%	%
6.3	8.3	7.1	Cash & Equivalents	6.8	8.9	5.3	8.2	4.7	5.9
7.5	6.3	8.8	Trade Receivables (net)	6.9	6.5	9.5	11.0	15.6	7.2
60.3	60.5	60.1	Inventory	65.3	61.2	61.3	58.7	51.7	56.5
1.7	1.8	1.1	All Other Current	.4	.5	1.0	1.9	2.4	1.1
75.9	76.9	77.0	Total Current	79.4	77.1	77.1	79.9	74.3	70.7
16.8	15.4	15.1	Fixed Assets (net)	14.9	13.6	14.7	15.1	15.4	18.5
3.2	3.2	3.5	Intangibles (net)	2.3	4.2	2.8	1.2	6.6	5.9
4.1	4.5	4.4	All Other Non-Current	3.4	5.1	5.3	3.7	3.7	4.9
100.0	100.0	100.0	Total	100.0	100.0	100.0	100.0	100.0	100.0
			LIABILITIES						
13.1	13.1	13.0	Notes Payable-Short Term	14.6	12.0	13.9	12.5	10.7	14.0
3.5	3.0	3.4	Cur. Mat.-L/T/D	5.3	3.9	1.9	3.3	2.6	2.4
24.2	23.1	24.8	Trade Payables	24.0	25.2	27.7	22.4	27.1	24.2
.3	.3	.2	Income Taxes Payable	.1	.1	.1	.2	.2	.9
8.9	8.9	9.2	All Other Current	10.7	9.3	6.2	10.0	8.1	9.9
50.0	48.4	50.7	Total Current	54.6	50.5	49.9	48.4	48.8	51.4
15.7	12.1	12.9	Long Term Debt	21.4	14.0	7.4	8.9	9.7	12.4
.1	.1	.1	Deferred Taxes	.0	.0	.2	.1	.1	.1
5.2	5.2	6.4	All Other Non-Current	8.2	10.3	5.5	5.2	1.6	2.1
28.9	34.3	29.9	Net Worth	15.7	25.1	37.0	37.3	39.8	34.1
100.0	100.0	100.0	Total Liabilities & Net Worth	100.0	100.0	100.0	100.0	100.0	100.0
			INCOME DATA						
100.0	100.0	100.0	Net Sales	100.0	100.0	100.0	100.0	100.0	100.0
36.1	37.7	36.2	Gross Profit	37.5	38.0	32.6	35.1	35.6	37.0
33.9	34.8	34.2	Operating Expenses	37.9	36.1	31.1	32.2	32.6	32.8
2.2	2.9	2.0	Operating Profit	-.4	2.0	1.5	2.9	3.0	4.2
1.2	.9	.9	All Other Expenses (net)	1.2	1.3	.8	.3	.7	.7
1.0	1.9	1.1	Profit Before Taxes	-1.6	.6	.7	2.6	2.3	3.6
			RATIOS						
2.3	2.7	2.5		2.3	3.1	2.7	2.7	1.9	1.7
1.6	1.7	1.6	Current	1.5	1.7	1.6	1.8	1.6	1.4
1.1	1.2	1.1		1.0	1.2	1.1	1.2	1.1	1.1
.5	.5	.7		.5	.9	.5	1.0	.7	.4
(265) .2	(251) .2	(283) .2	Quick	.1	(73) .3	(41) .3	.3	.3	.1
.0	.1	.1		.0	.1	.1	.1	.1	.1
0 951.0	0 UND	0 999.8		0 UND	0 UND	0 845.8	1 724.7	1 485.0	2 212.4
3 111.8	2 196.0	3 115.8	Sales/Receivables	2 211.0	3 145.9	4 100.2	5 72.3	4 93.5	4 98.2
15 25.1	10 36.0	14 25.8		6 57.3	13 27.1	18 20.8	17 21.7	38 9.6	6 63.4
96 3.8	92 4.0	88 4.2		92 4.0	94 3.9	92 4.0	71 5.2	61 6.0	85 4.3
138 2.6	135 2.7	133 2.7	Cost of Sales/Inventory	178 2.1	130 2.8	137 2.7	118 3.1	114 3.2	130 2.8
192 1.9	183 2.0	189 1.9		281 1.3	213 1.7	179 2.0	162 2.3	158 2.3	164 2.2
27 13.3	25 14.7	27 13.7		20 18.6	20 17.9	30 12.0	19 19.2	32 11.4	38 9.5
45 8.1	46 7.9	49 7.4	Cost of Sales/Payables	57 6.4	45 8.0	44 8.2	46 7.9	45 8.1	59 6.1
77 4.8	69 5.3	81 4.5		94 3.9	84 4.4	88 4.2	62 5.9	62 5.9	77 4.7
5.1	5.2	5.5		5.1	4.9	5.6	4.8	8.2	6.9
9.5	8.8	10.3	Sales/Working Capital	12.3	8.5	9.2	9.9	10.0	15.8
29.4	23.4	34.1		57.5	24.3	56.1	19.6	34.7	56.0
3.9	6.9	6.6		3.1	5.7	5.9	8.5	10.9	20.7
(250) 1.9	(227) 2.3	(259) 2.1	EBIT/Interest	(46) 1.2	(65) 1.5	(41) 2.6	(50) 2.0	2.4	(33) 6.5
.8	1.0	.9		-2.7	-.2	1.1	1.1	1.4	2.4
8.7	7.4	10.6	Net Profit + Depr., Dep.,		11.0			2.1	33.1
(49) 2.0	(42) 2.4	(48) 2.1	Amort./Cur. Mat. L/T/D		(11) 1.7			(10) 1.1	(10) 15.9
.9	1.2	.9			.4			.3	3.5
.2	.1	.1		.2	.1	.2	.1	.2	.3
.5	.4	.4	Fixed/Worth	.7	.3	.4	.4	.4	.6
1.9	1.2	1.3		-2.4	-19.5	1.0	.8	1.1	1.1
1.0	.8	1.0		1.8	.9	1.0	.8	1.1	1.3
2.3	2.0	2.3	Debt/Worth	4.2	2.2	1.7	1.8	2.2	2.2
9.6	6.3	8.0		-20.3	-43.5	3.1	4.8	3.9	6.0
26.1	35.5	29.6	% Profit Before Taxes/Tangible	26.0	18.3	25.2	30.9	25.2	65.7
(224) 10.3	(220) 14.2	(242) 11.9	Net Worth	(39) 7.4	(55) 7.2	(38) 8.0	(53) 12.6	(23) 13.9	(34) 30.2
1.6	1.3	.9		-9.1	.3	1.1	1.9	7.9	11.9
8.3	10.7	8.8	% Profit Before Taxes/Total	8.1	7.4	8.9	7.7	7.5	16.9
2.9	4.2	3.2	Assets	1.2	2.5	2.7	3.4	4.6	9.7
-.7	.0	-.2		-6.4	-1.3	.1	.5	1.6	4.4
62.0	63.0	60.9		76.6	103.4	49.2	68.8	46.5	49.4
23.9	24.8	27.3	Sales/Net Fixed Assets	22.3	37.2	24.1	28.4	19.6	19.4
9.9	11.8	12.9		10.6	14.4	13.9	12.0	14.8	7.6
3.2	3.4	3.4		3.0	3.2	3.4	3.9	3.8	3.2
2.5	2.5	2.5	Sales/Total Assets	2.1	2.6	2.6	2.8	3.0	2.5
1.9	1.9	1.9		1.5	1.7	2.2	2.1	1.8	2.1
.5	.5	.5		.7	.3	.5	.5	.7	.7
(235) 1.0	(214) 1.0	(246) .9	% Depr., Dep., Amort./Sales	(39) 1.4	(59) .7	(41) .9	(54) .7	(21) 1.0	(32) 1.0
2.1	1.8	1.8		3.3	1.8	1.9	1.4	1.5	1.9
2.1	2.3	2.2		4.4	2.7	2.0	1.5	1.4	
(147) 3.8	(141) 4.3	(147) 4.3	% Officers', Directors',	(34) 6.4	(47) 4.7	(27) 3.7	(23) 3.2	(11) 2.4	
6.3	7.0	7.6	Owners' Comp/Sales	12.1	6.8	8.2	5.8	7.1	
3994007M	3380517M	4865446M	Net Sales ($)	30987M	136633M	165143M	413348M	348855M	3770480M
1704586M	1413097M	2131079M	Total Assets ($)	16605M	75098M	66168M	161660M	132668M	1678880M

© RMA 2003

M = $ thousand   MM = $ million
See Pages 11 through 18 for Explanation of Ratios and Data

Current Data Sorted By Assets   Comparative Historical Data

							Type of Statement		
	3	3			2		Unqualified	13	5
	10	1					Reviewed	7	8
9	4	1					Compiled	31	18
8	7	2	1				Tax Returns	12	5
	5 (4/1-9/30/02)		46 (10/1/02-3/31/03)				Other	27	23
								4/1/98-	4/1/99-
								3/31/99	3/31/00
0-500M	500M-2MM	2-10MM	10-50MM	50-100MM	100-250MM			ALL	ALL
17	24	7	1		2	NUMBER OF STATEMENTS		90	59
%	%	%	%	%	%	%	ASSETS	%	%
16.4	9.1						Cash & Equivalents	9.8	10.3
.7	8.0						Trade Receivables (net)	6.0	3.7
62.1	59.7						Inventory	57.8	58.6
3.3	1.8						All Other Current	1.7	.9
82.6	78.7						Total Current	75.3	73.5
8.4	12.5						Fixed Assets (net)	16.4	16.0
8.0	1.5						Intangibles (net)	3.9	4.8
1.0	7.3						All Other Non-Current	4.4	5.6
100.0	100.0						Total	100.0	100.0
							LIABILITIES		
15.7	10.4						Notes Payable-Short Term	13.3	13.5
3.7	3.4						Cur. Mat.-L/T/D	3.7	3.3
15.1	21.0						Trade Payables	17.8	17.8
.0	.3						Income Taxes Payable	.1	.2
37.5	13.8						All Other Current	10.8	8.9
72.0	48.9						Total Current	45.7	43.7
20.2	14.4						Long Term Debt	16.8	11.3
.0	.0						Deferred Taxes	.1	.1
1.0	7.1						All Other Non-Current	5.4	7.7
6.8	29.6						Net Worth	32.0	37.3
100.0	100.0						Total Liabilities & Net Worth	100.0	100.0
							INCOME DATA		
100.0	100.0						Net Sales	100.0	100.0
41.7	42.6						Gross Profit	40.8	42.5
39.7	40.2						Operating Expenses	39.8	40.4
2.1	2.5						Operating Profit	1.1	2.1
1.7	.9						All Other Expenses (net)	1.7	.4
.3	1.6						Profit Before Taxes	−.7	1.7
							RATIOS		
3.5	2.8							2.9	3.2
1.6	1.9						Current	1.7	2.0
.8	1.1							1.2	1.2
1.2	.6							.8	.6
.3	.3						Quick	(88) .3	(58) .3
.0	.1							.1	.1
0 UND	0 999.8							0 UND	0 UND
0 UND	2 203.3						Sales/Receivables	1 413.9	0 999.8
1 709.9	10 35.1							10 36.2	4 97.7
63 5.8	84 4.3							84 4.3	88 4.1
128 2.9	169 2.2						Cost of Sales/Inventory	133 2.7	156 2.3
145 2.5	259 1.4							197 1.9	208 1.8
0 UND	15 24.2							10 38.4	19 19.4
16 22.2	42 8.8						Cost of Sales/Payables	36 10.1	39 9.3
30 12.3	58 6.3							63 5.8	60 6.1
5.9	4.2							5.0	4.5
13.9	7.4						Sales/Working Capital	9.1	8.8
−44.8	52.4							48.3	28.1
6.5	5.9							6.3	7.7
(15) 2.3	(21) 2.7						EBIT/Interest	(78) 2.8	(52) 1.9
−2.3	1.0							1.1	.4
							Net Profit + Depr., Dep.,	2.1	5.2
							Amort./Cur. Mat. L /T/D	(18) .9	(17) 2.1
								.4	.0
.1	.1							.2	.1
.6	.3						Fixed/Worth	.4	.4
−.2	2.5							1.9	.7
1.0	1.1							.9	.7
8.5	2.6						Debt/Worth	2.5	2.4
−2.9	9.5							6.1	4.3
76.4	52.0						% Profit Before Taxes/Tangible	43.6	32.0
(10) 26.2	(20) 18.3						Net Worth	(79) 13.5	(54) 13.4
10.8	−.7							3.4	−1.7
18.7	11.6							15.4	10.5
6.6	4.0						% Profit Before Taxes/Total	5.2	4.1
−21.8	−1.0						Assets	−.4	−3.2
300.7	55.1							59.0	44.1
33.1	32.8						Sales/Net Fixed Assets	21.2	25.2
20.3	16.4							13.8	13.3
5.4	3.6							3.5	3.5
3.4	2.6						Sales/Total Assets	2.8	2.7
2.1	1.5							1.9	1.8
	.5							.6	.6
(20)	.8						% Depr., Dep., Amort./Sales	(67) 1.2	(49) 1.0
	1.5							2.0	2.3
	1.3						% Officers', Directors',	2.3	1.8
(12)	3.2						Owners' Comp/Sales	(34) 3.2	(25) 3.4
	5.0							6.9	6.0
16631M	71442M	58960M	39684M		875048M	Net Sales ($)		2895546M	1720651M
4759M	26307M	21728M	33923M		413802M	Total Assets ($)		1131858M	742851M

DATA NOT AVAILABLE

M = $ thousand   MM = $ million
See Pages 11 through 18 for Explanation of Ratios and Data

Comparative Historical Data				Current Data Sorted By Sales					
			Type of Statement						
5	7	2	Unqualified						2
6	8	6	Reviewed		1	1	2	2	
20	15	11	Compiled	1	6	2	2		
4	6	14	Tax Returns	5	6	1	2		
17	22	18	Other	6	7	1	3		1
4/1/00-3/31/01	4/1/01-3/31/02	4/1/02-3/31/03		5 (4/1-9/30/02)		46 (10/1/02-3/31/03)			
ALL	ALL	ALL		0-1MM	1-3MM	3-5MM	5-10MM	10-25MM	25MM & OVER
52	58	51	**NUMBER OF STATEMENTS**	12	20	5	9	2	3
%	%	%	**ASSETS**	%	%	%	%	%	%
9.2	11.5	11.5	Cash & Equivalents	19.1	8.9				
9.6	9.5	5.8	Trade Receivables (net)	.4	1.7				
56.9	52.8	58.9	Inventory	58.5	66.3				
3.3	2.8	2.8	All Other Current	.8	3.7				
79.0	76.5	79.0	Total Current	78.8	80.6				
13.7	16.1	11.3	Fixed Assets (net)	8.6	11.0				
2.6	2.3	4.3	Intangibles (net)	9.2	2.4				
4.6	5.0	5.4	All Other Non-Current	3.4	6.0				
100.0	100.0	100.0	Total	100.0	100.0				
			LIABILITIES						
10.0	12.1	12.7	Notes Payable-Short Term	12.0	14.0				
2.8	4.6	3.8	Cur. Mat.-L/T/D	1.4	4.5				
21.5	16.7	19.7	Trade Payables	10.6	18.3				
.3	.4	.2	Income Taxes Payable	.1	.3				
12.1	9.7	21.1	All Other Current	52.4	14.9				
46.6	43.6	57.5	Total Current	76.5	52.1				
17.5	21.2	16.5	Long Term Debt	24.9	11.5				
.1	.2	.1	Deferred Taxes	.1	.0				
5.9	9.0	5.0	All Other Non-Current	.1	4.8				
29.9	26.1	20.9	Net Worth	−1.6	31.6				
100.0	100.0	100.0	Total Liabilities & Net Worth	100.0	100.0				
			INCOME DATA						
100.0	100.0	100.0	Net Sales	100.0	100.0				
39.0	41.8	43.1	Gross Profit	45.2	42.3				
38.1	37.6	40.6	Operating Expenses	43.1	40.1				
.9	4.1	2.6	Operating Profit	2.1	2.2				
.0	1.4	1.2	All Other Expenses (net)	2.0	1.2				
.8	2.7	1.4	Profit Before Taxes	.1	1.0				
			RATIOS						
3.0	3.5	2.8		3.1	3.6				
1.9	2.0	1.5	Current	1.6	1.9				
1.2	1.2	1.1		.8	.8				
.7	1.0	.6		1.4	.4				
(51) .4	.4	.3	Quick	.3	.1				
.1	.1	.0		.0	.0				
0 UND	0 UND	0 UND		0 UND	0 UND				
2 214.3	3 129.4	1 420.0	Sales/Receivables	0 UND	1 339.4				
14 25.2	14 26.1	7 54.8		0 UND	3 111.6				
83 4.4	89 4.1	87 4.2		90 4.1	82 4.4				
129 2.8	122 3.0	129 2.8	Cost of Sales/Inventory	143 2.6	156 2.3				
183 2.0	170 2.1	216 1.7		258 1.4	241 1.5				
21 17.0	14 26.6	13 27.1		0 UND	6 59.4				
38 9.5	28 13.0	30 12.2	Cost of Sales/Payables	21 17.1	22 16.7				
54 6.8	49 7.5	53 6.9		45 8.2	52 7.0				
5.1	4.3	5.3		4.4	4.2				
9.3	9.1	13.6	Sales/Working Capital	9.2	8.1				
25.7	33.7	57.1		−131.1	−44.6				
6.3	11.4	6.3			6.5				
(47) 1.6	(55) 2.4	(46) 2.5	EBIT/Interest		(19) 1.4				
−.3	.9	.7			−.8				
	8.4		Net Profit + Depr., Dep.,						
	(12) 1.8		Amort./Cur. Mat. L/T/D						
	.9								
.1	.1	.1		.1	.1				
.4	.4	.5	Fixed/Worth	.6	.4				
.9	2.2	7.8		−.2	−.9				
.8	.9	1.4		1.4	.6				
1.9	2.6	3.6	Debt/Worth	8.8	2.0				
4.7	6.7	−28.3		−1.9	−9.9				
32.4	52.9	51.3			30.6				
(44) 11.2	(49) 21.0	(38) 18.3	% Profit Before Taxes/Tangible Net Worth		(13) 12.0				
−15.3	3.3	1.1			2.7				
14.5	16.0	12.2		17.8	10.2				
1.9	4.9	5.9	% Profit Before Taxes/Total Assets	2.4	1.1				
−5.0	−.2	−1.8		−18.1	−2.1				
84.3	67.0	59.0		103.9	57.6				
38.1	29.5	32.8	Sales/Net Fixed Assets	29.4	40.4				
14.6	11.4	15.7		14.0	18.7				
4.2	3.8	3.7		3.5	3.2				
3.0	2.9	2.7	Sales/Total Assets	2.1	2.6				
2.1	1.8	1.9		1.4	1.8				
.3	.6	.7			.5				
(38) .8	(42) .8	(35) 1.1	% Depr., Dep., Amort./Sales		(15) .9				
1.8	1.7	1.8			2.4				
2.4	2.2	1.8			2.4				
(19) 4.4	(29) 4.0	(27) 3.5	% Officers', Directors', Owners' Comp/Sales		(12) 4.0				
7.1	5.3	5.1			5.0				
1782188M	2127473M	1061765M	Net Sales ($)	6584M	36292M	17626M	63990M	22541M	914732M
913638M	871882M	500519M	Total Assets ($)	3738M	15690M	6849M	19736M	6781M	447725M

© RMA 2003

M = $ thousand   MM = $ million

See Pages 11 through 18 for Explanation of Ratios and Data

Current Data Sorted By Assets   Comparative Historical Data

						Type of Statement		
		1	7	1		Unqualified	14	9
1	5	14	1			Reviewed	23	29
6	15	10	2			Compiled	45	37
2	5					Tax Returns	10	16
5	11	5	1		2	Other	33	23
	41 (4/1-9/30/02)		53 (10/1/02-3/31/03)				4/1/98-3/31/99	4/1/99-3/31/00
0-500M	500M-2MM	2-10MM	10-50MM	50-100MM	100-250MM		ALL	ALL
14	36	30	11	1	2	NUMBER OF STATEMENTS	125	114
%	%	%	%	%	%	ASSETS	%	%
10.5	7.5	6.6	7.0			Cash & Equivalents	6.4	6.0
8.1	13.1	10.4	23.5			Trade Receivables (net)	16.9	13.0
60.8	61.1	61.7	44.4			Inventory	55.0	56.3
.9	4.9	1.1	1.6			All Other Current	1.6	1.9
80.3	86.6	79.7	76.4			Total Current	80.0	77.1
14.0	10.7	12.7	12.8			Fixed Assets (net)	12.6	16.8
.9	.6	1.0	1.8			Intangibles (net)	2.4	2.1
4.8	2.1	6.6	9.0			All Other Non-Current	5.0	4.0
100.0	100.0	100.0	100.0			Total	100.0	100.0
						LIABILITIES		
23.2	14.1	19.9	9.0			Notes Payable-Short Term	17.8	15.0
1.8	2.8	5.9	1.1			Cur. Mat.-L/T/D	4.3	3.5
45.8	17.1	13.0	19.8			Trade Payables	17.5	20.1
.0	.1	.8	1.0			Income Taxes Payable	.4	.2
7.0	11.6	13.0	12.5			All Other Current	8.3	9.8
77.9	45.8	52.5	43.4			Total Current	48.2	48.7
6.4	7.7	6.2	13.9			Long Term Debt	13.7	15.2
.0	.0	.0	1.7			Deferred Taxes	.3	.3
2.8	2.1	4.1	2.7			All Other Non-Current	3.1	4.7
13.0	44.4	37.1	38.3			Net Worth	34.6	31.1
100.0	100.0	100.0	100.0			Total Liabilities & Net Worth	100.0	100.0
						INCOME DATA		
100.0	100.0	100.0	100.0			Net Sales	100.0	100.0
43.0	41.6	45.1	38.2			Gross Profit	41.1	42.1
40.3	39.3	42.1	33.6			Operating Expenses	38.0	38.6
2.7	2.3	3.0	4.6			Operating Profit	3.1	3.4
.3	.7	.6	.4			All Other Expenses (net)	.4	1.0
2.3	1.6	2.4	4.2			Profit Before Taxes	2.7	2.4
						RATIOS		
2.1	3.6	2.1	2.2				2.5	2.0
1.6	2.0	1.6	1.8			Current	1.7	1.7
.6	1.6	1.2	1.7				1.2	1.2
.4	1.0	.7	1.3				.8	.6
.2	.3	.3	.7			Quick	.4	.3
.1		.1	.3				.2	.1

											Sales/Receivables				
0	UND	3	104.4	5	80.0	16	23.0					7	53.8	5	73.2
6	59.0	12	29.8	10	36.6	32	11.3					18	20.7	12	30.6
14	26.3	29	12.7	18	20.8	82	4.5					40	9.2	28	13.2
47	7.7	113	3.2	179	2.0	71	5.1			Cost of Sales/Inventory		111	3.3	105	3.5
138	2.7	202	1.8	220	1.7	138	2.6					168	2.2	167	2.2
228	1.6	280	1.3	252	1.4	208	1.8					243	1.5	242	1.5
30	12.0	18	19.9	14	25.8	31	11.6			Cost of Sales/Payables		18	20.4	19	18.7
40	9.2	39	9.4	47	7.7	55	6.6					38	9.6	43	8.5
64	5.7	85	4.3	73	5.0	67	5.5					87	4.2	88	4.1

								Sales/Working Capital		
6.5		3.3		4.3		6.0			4.1	4.6
9.7		5.4		6.9		6.4			7.2	7.9
−12.1		8.5		12.2		11.2			13.8	16.7

								EBIT/Interest		
	7.8		10.7		5.2		26.6		4.4	3.8
(10)	5.3	(32)	3.6	(28)	2.3	5.3		(118)	2.2	(110) 2.0
	1.5		1.2		1.5		1.7		1.4	1.2

							Net Profit + Depr., Dep., Amort./Cur. Mat. L /T/D		
				5.3				2.6	3.5
		(16)		3.3			(39)	1.5	(34) 1.5
				.9				.6	.9

							Fixed/Worth		
.0		.1		.2		.1		.1	.2
.1		.2		.3		.2		.3	.4
1.0		.5		.5		.5		.6	.8

							Debt/Worth		
1.1		.6		1.3		.7		1.1	1.3
1.8		1.2		1.9		2.3		2.3	2.6
3.4		2.5		2.6		3.5		4.7	5.2

								% Profit Before Taxes/Tangible Net Worth		
	37.0		17.7		19.5		35.2		34.9	35.0
(12)	16.1	(33)	5.6	(29)	11.5	16.7		(118)	13.3	(109) 13.5
	2.4		3.5		4.1		9.0		3.4	2.7

							% Profit Before Taxes/Total Assets		
11.4		7.8		7.0		16.8		9.0	9.2
2.5		4.0		4.0		3.4		4.4	3.6
−3.5		.8		1.3		2.3		1.5	.8

							Sales/Net Fixed Assets		
393.7		123.1		27.8		51.3		58.4	48.2
95.7		36.9		19.4		23.2		32.6	23.9
22.6		13.5		12.1		18.0		12.1	9.1

							Sales/Total Assets		
5.1		3.1		2.3		2.8		2.7	2.7
2.5		2.1		1.9		2.0		1.9	2.0
1.8		1.5		1.5		1.7		1.4	1.4

								% Depr., Dep., Amort./Sales		
			.4		.7		.4		.5	.5
(25)		(28)	.7		1.1		1.0		(108) .9	(96) .9
			1.5		1.8		1.7		1.4	2.0

								% Officers', Directors', Owners' Comp/Sales		
			2.0		3.5				2.5	3.1
(21)		(15)	3.6		6.0			(45)	4.8	(49) 5.7
			6.4		10.6				7.8	7.6

13709M	98904M	220366M	486654M	40510M	496265M	Net Sales ($)	1587574M	1753472M
4332M	42075M	114452M	237846M	84308M	214816M	Total Assets ($)	761650M	773950M

M = $ thousand   MM = $ million
See Pages 11 through 18 for Explanation of Ratios and Data

Comparative Historical Data | Current Data Sorted By Sales

Type of Statement	4/1/00-3/31/01 ALL	4/1/01-3/31/02 ALL	4/1/02-3/31/03 ALL	0-1MM	1-3MM	3-5MM	5-10MM	10-25MM	25MM & OVER
Unqualified	5	3	9				1	1	7
Reviewed	20	14	21		4	6	7	2	2
Compiled	33	25	33	6	12	6	6	1	2
Tax Returns	10	15	7	2	3	2			2
Other	26	17	24	4	7		6		3
	4/1/00-3/31/01 ALL	4/1/01-3/31/02 ALL	4/1/02-3/31/03 ALL	41 (4/1-9/30/02)			53 (10/1/02-3/31/03)		
NUMBER OF STATEMENTS	94	74	94	12	26	18	20	4	14
ASSETS	%	%	%	%	%	%	%	%	%
Cash & Equivalents	5.7	7.4	7.5	9.4	8.9	6.3	5.7		7.1
Trade Receivables (net)	13.5	9.4	13.5	15.1	9.7	8.9	11.1		25.1
Inventory	54.6	55.6	58.4	59.6	58.8	70.5	58.5		43.9
All Other Current	2.9	2.9	2.6	2.2	3.9	1.3	3.5		1.4
Total Current	76.7	75.3	82.0	86.4	81.3	86.9	78.8		77.5
Fixed Assets (net)	17.8	16.9	12.2	11.8	13.3	8.6	14.4		13.8
Intangibles (net)	1.2	2.4	1.0	.5	1.5	.6	.3		
All Other Non-Current	4.3	5.5	4.8	1.3	3.9	3.9	6.5		6.4
Total	100.0	100.0	100.0	100.0	100.0	100.0	100.0		100.0
LIABILITIES									
Notes Payable-Short Term	13.9	22.1	16.3	19.8	15.0	18.8	19.8		8.2
Cur. Mat.-L/T/D	3.6	3.8	3.5	.9	3.9	6.1	4.0		1.6
Trade Payables	20.6	15.8	20.3	42.1	20.4	18.3	12.9		18.0
Income Taxes Payable	.3	.1	.4	.0	.1	.1	.9		.8
All Other Current	10.2	7.3	11.3	6.5	5.8	14.0	17.2		11.6
Total Current	48.5	49.1	51.7	69.2	45.2	57.3	54.9		40.2
Long Term Debt	17.7	12.8	8.7	5.3	11.3	5.6	4.1		15.5
Deferred Taxes	.4	.2	.2	.0	.0	.0	.0		.9
All Other Non-Current	3.9	4.1	2.9	3.2	1.9	2.3	5.3		2.3
Net Worth	29.5	33.8	36.5	22.2	41.7	34.8	35.7		41.1
Total Liabilities & Net Worth	100.0	100.0	100.0	100.0	100.0	100.0	100.0		100.0
INCOME DATA									
Net Sales	100.0	100.0	100.0	100.0	100.0	100.0	100.0		100.0
Gross Profit	42.9	45.2	42.6	38.3	46.9	42.6	41.2		39.9
Operating Expenses	39.6	42.4	39.6	37.7	43.2	40.4	38.5		34.7
Operating Profit	3.3	2.8	3.0	.6	3.7	2.1	2.6		5.2
All Other Expenses (net)	.5	1.0	.6	.7	.6	.6	.5		.6
Profit Before Taxes	2.8	1.8	2.4	-.1	3.1	1.5	2.1		4.6
RATIOS									
Current	2.2	2.3	2.5	3.9	3.7	1.9	2.0		2.4
	1.6	1.6	1.7	1.8	2.0	1.7	1.6		1.9
	1.1	1.3	1.4	1.3	1.6	1.2	1.2		1.7
Quick	.7	.7	.8	1.7	1.1	.4	.4		1.2
	.3	.3	.3	.3	.3	.2	.3		.7
	.1	.1	.2	.1	.1	.1	.1		.4
Sales/Receivables	5 79.1	3 139.3	4 83.0	2 159.5	1 253.8	3 133.3	4 83.4		13 28.0
	16 22.8	11 33.1	12 29.8	11 32.2	12 31.1	8 43.5	11 34.5		26 13.9
	33 11.1	22 16.3	30 12.2	50 7.2	20 18.0	17 21.5	16 22.4		66 5.5
Cost of Sales/Inventory	119 3.1	134 2.7	112 3.2	96 3.8	112 3.2	181 2.0	126 2.9		73 5.0
	181 2.0	185 2.0	197 1.9	221 1.7	212 1.7	209 1.7	182 2.0		96 3.8
	236 1.5	270 1.3	248 1.5	260 1.4	295 1.2	250 1.5	223 1.6		167 2.2
Cost of Sales/Payables	24 15.1	15 24.5	21 17.4	34 10.6	21 17.4	26 14.0	12 29.8		24 14.9
	54 6.7	39 9.3	45 8.1	45 8.1	40 9.0	52 7.0	21 17.6		42 8.7
	94 3.9	70 5.2	72 5.1	75 4.8	91 4.0	90 4.1	63 5.8		65 5.6
Sales/Working Capital	4.4	4.4	4.3	2.1	3.2	5.1	5.4		5.1
	8.1	6.5	6.4	5.8	5.1	6.6	9.3		6.4
	20.1	14.9	11.4	10.0	9.3	16.6	23.7		10.7
EBIT/Interest	5.0	4.6	7.7		10.4	5.5	5.2		28.4
	(86) 2.3	(72) 2.1	(84) 3.1		(23) 6.0	(16) 1.9	2.8		6.6
	1.2	1.2	1.5		1.2	.5	1.7		1.7
Net Profit + Depr., Dep., Amort./Cur. Mat. L/T/D	10.9	3.7	5.0				6.3		
	(28) 4.3	(27) 1.0	(30) 2.6				(12) 3.6		
	1.4	.6	.9				1.5		
Fixed/Worth	.1	.1	.1	.0	.1	.1	.2		.1
	.3	.3	.3	.0	.3	.3	.3		.2
	1.5	.9	.5	.3	.6	.4	.5		.6
Debt/Worth	1.1	1.1	.8	.4	.5	1.1	1.3		.6
	2.1	1.9	1.7	1.8	1.3	2.0	1.8		2.2
	5.1	4.0	2.7	2.8	2.3	4.3	2.5		4.0
% Profit Before Taxes/Tangible Net Worth	33.4	26.2	23.1	9.4	22.7	32.4	20.1		36.3
	(87) 14.9	(69) 9.6	(88) 10.2	(11) 5.6	(23) 11.2	(17) 5.5	(19) 11.5		21.8
	3.9	2.8	3.9	-1.6	3.2	-3.6	6.8		9.6
% Profit Before Taxes/Total Assets	9.0	8.4	8.0	5.1	9.8	4.5	7.7		19.3
	4.7	2.7	3.9	1.8	4.6	2.7	4.5		5.8
	.8	.5	1.2	-8.4	.8	-.9	2.0		2.3
Sales/Net Fixed Assets	41.6	43.8	62.7	806.5	81.9	103.8	33.7		45.9
	22.9	21.2	25.5	95.7	21.7	32.8	16.9		23.1
	8.4	8.5	13.6	24.8	9.0	19.4	12.5		16.8
Sales/Total Assets	2.6	2.9	2.6	2.2	2.9	2.6	2.6		2.9
	1.9	1.9	2.1	1.8	2.0	2.1	2.3		2.2
	1.5	1.4	1.5	1.5	1.4	1.4	1.8		1.7
% Depr., Dep., Amort./Sales	.6	.6	.5		.5	.4	.6		.7
	(84) .9	(63) .9	(73) .9	(16)	(16) 1.0	(16) .9	(18) .8		1.1
	2.5	1.8	1.8		2.2	1.3	1.5		1.8
% Officers', Directors', Owners' Comp/Sales	2.7	2.9	3.3		3.2	2.3			
	(39) 5.0	(38) 5.5	(44) 5.3	(14)	4.4	(12) 4.5			
	8.0	8.5	8.3		5.9	10.2			
Net Sales ($)	1193524M	537954M	1356408M	8266M	45854M	69610M	140659M	60168M	1031851M
Total Assets ($)	618313M	259317M	697829M	4766M	27103M	34957M	65009M	44919M	521075M

© RMA 2003

M = $ thousand   MM = $ million

See Pages 11 through 18 for Explanation of Ratios and Data

Current Data Sorted By Assets   Comparative Historical Data

0-500M	500M-2MM	2-10MM	10-50MM	50-100MM	100-250MM	Type of Statement	4/1/98-3/31/99 ALL	4/1/99-3/31/00 ALL
	1	5	3	3	3	Unqualified	11	10
	4	6	1			Reviewed	8	10
3	9	2				Compiled	18	19
8	4					Tax Returns	12	5
4	8	8	3			Other	36	31
	19 (4/1-9/30/02)		56 (10/1/02-3/31/03)					
15	26	21	7	3	3	NUMBER OF STATEMENTS	85	75
%	%	%	%	%	%	ASSETS	%	%
8.3	12.3	15.1				Cash & Equivalents	10.7	13.5
2.1	12.8	3.5				Trade Receivables (net)	6.7	6.8
60.9	46.6	46.2				Inventory	53.4	51.4
.7	1.8	2.8				All Other Current	1.6	1.6
72.0	73.6	67.7				Total Current	72.4	73.4
19.1	17.9	28.2				Fixed Assets (net)	20.8	21.6
3.7	.0	1.4				Intangibles (net)	3.0	2.0
5.2	8.5	2.7				All Other Non-Current	3.9	3.0
100.0	100.0	100.0				Total	100.0	100.0
						LIABILITIES		
8.0	9.1	4.1				Notes Payable-Short Term	9.4	9.7
3.9	2.3	2.6				Cur. Mat.-L/T/D	2.3	2.1
32.0	29.4	25.7				Trade Payables	22.9	26.5
.0	.0	.5				Income Taxes Payable	.5	.4
9.8	11.7	7.7				All Other Current	8.1	10.1
53.7	52.5	40.6				Total Current	43.3	48.8
30.1	12.8	9.7				Long Term Debt	15.1	13.5
.0	.1	.4				Deferred Taxes	.2	.1
11.8	2.3	4.0				All Other Non-Current	8.1	3.1
4.4	32.3	45.4				Net Worth	33.3	34.5
100.0	100.0	100.0				Total Liabilities & Net Worth	100.0	100.0
						INCOME DATA		
100.0	100.0	100.0				Net Sales	100.0	100.0
42.3	35.6	38.9				Gross Profit	41.1	39.0
40.1	31.8	35.1				Operating Expenses	37.9	35.1
2.3	3.8	3.8				Operating Profit	3.2	3.8
.7	1.1	.6				All Other Expenses (net)	1.0	.6
1.5	2.7	3.1				Profit Before Taxes	2.3	3.3
						RATIOS		
3.4	2.3	3.0					3.1	2.7
1.6	1.7	1.8				Current	1.7	1.8
.9	.8	1.2					1.3	1.0
.4	.7	1.0					1.0	.7
.2	.4	.4				Quick (83)	.3	.3
.0	.1	.2					.1	.1
0 UND	1 724.8	0 999.8					0 984.4	0 754.3
0 UND	4 90.1	3 137.9				Sales/Receivables	3 143.6	3 130.1
0 999.8	23 16.1	6 58.6					10 38.4	13 27.9
91 4.0	50 7.3	70 5.2					79 4.6	76 4.8
121 3.0	72 5.1	91 4.0				Cost of Sales/Inventory	120 3.0	111 3.3
127 2.9	152 2.4	109 3.3					178 2.0	182 2.0
7 55.0	24 15.1	29 12.5					19 18.9	22 16.7
62 5.9	42 8.8	46 7.9				Cost of Sales/Payables	41 8.9	51 7.2
91 4.0	79 4.6	64 5.7					73 5.0	84 4.3
6.9	6.1	6.5					5.0	5.5
12.6	13.9	10.1				Sales/Working Capital	9.4	9.8
−80.1	−37.0	31.4					21.3	243.4
3.6	23.7	33.4					9.5	11.7
(11) 1.8	(24) 4.5	(20) 6.2				EBIT/Interest	(73) 3.1	(66) 2.8
.1	-.6	.1					1.0	1.0
						Net Profit + Depr., Dep.,	10.0	34.2
						Amort./Cur. Mat. L /T/D	(13) 2.0	(12) 4.9
							.9	1.4
.4	.1	.3					.2	.2
UND	.5	.7				Fixed/Worth	.5	.7
−5.2	3.7	1.3					1.7	3.9
5.0	.8	.4					.9	.7
UND	2.2	1.7				Debt/Worth	1.9	2.0
−15.0	15.2	2.8					7.4	10.1
	89.8	48.2				% Profit Before Taxes/Tangible	41.0	61.8
	(23) 16.9	(20) 12.1				Net Worth	(72) 18.1	(61) 25.4
	14.1	-4.2					2.0	2.3
12.4	23.6	20.0					15.8	17.7
5.7	7.8	7.6				% Profit Before Taxes/Total Assets	4.8	4.9
-1.7	-2.3	-2.2					.0	.2
52.8	74.8	19.6					36.7	45.3
32.6	30.4	11.2				Sales/Net Fixed Assets	15.4	13.5
9.2	11.1	6.9					9.2	6.6
3.5	4.5	3.4					3.5	3.4
3.2	3.2	3.1				Sales/Total Assets	2.5	2.6
2.6	2.0	2.4					1.7	2.0
1.0	.4	1.1					.9	.7
(10) 1.9	(22) .8	1.6				% Depr., Dep., Amort./Sales	(77) 1.4	(66) 1.3
3.8	1.7	2.6					2.2	2.1
4.8	1.3						1.7	1.3
(10) 5.7	(10) 5.8					% Officers', Directors', Owners' Comp/Sales	(29) 4.3	(26) 2.4
10.5	10.9						10.1	5.5
13691M	96591M	316654M	310963M	160744M	1229423M	Net Sales ($)	859250M	935992M
4127M	29544M	110349M	145542M	204287M	544446M	Total Assets ($)	387951M	412962M

© RMA 2003

M = $ thousand   MM = $ million
See Pages 11 through 18 for Explanation of Ratios and Data

Comparative Historical Data　　　　　　　　　　　　　　　Current Data Sorted By Sales

4/1/00-3/31/01 ALL	4/1/01-3/31/02 ALL	4/1/02-3/31/03 ALL	Type of Statement	0-1MM	1-3MM	3-5MM	5-10MM	10-25MM	25MM & OVER
10	9	15	Unqualified	1				5	9
12	8	11	Reviewed		1	1	3	5	1
15	14	14	Compiled	1	4	5	4		
14	7	12	Tax Returns	6	6				
22	20	23	Other	3	4	3	3	8	2
				19 (4/1-9/30/02)			56 (10/1/02-3/31/03)		
73	58	75	**NUMBER OF STATEMENTS**	11	15	9	10	18	12
%	%	%	**ASSETS**	%	%	%	%	%	%
10.8	13.0	12.0	Cash & Equivalents	4.7	11.7		17.0	13.9	9.7
6.0	6.3	7.6	Trade Receivables (net)	.9	7.1		14.8	5.7	8.0
54.8	52.0	46.7	Inventory	60.0	51.3		38.3	46.3	33.6
2.0	1.2	2.7	All Other Current	1.0	.3		2.9	4.8	3.7
73.5	72.5	68.9	Total Current	66.5	70.4		73.1	70.6	55.0
18.7	19.6	22.3	Fixed Assets (net)	27.3	16.9		20.2	26.2	25.9
2.5	1.6	1.9	Intangibles (net)	.8	2.8		.0	1.5	4.9
5.3	6.3	7.0	All Other Non-Current	5.3	10.0		6.7	1.7	14.2
100.0	100.0	100.0	Total	100.0	100.0		100.0	100.0	100.0
			LIABILITIES						
8.0	10.1	6.2	Notes Payable-Short Term	8.9	7.4		.0	3.4	4.2
2.5	2.8	2.4	Cur. Mat.-L/T/D	2.1	4.0		1.3	2.8	1.1
24.6	25.3	26.5	Trade Payables	38.4	27.6		25.8	25.9	17.0
.1	.2	.2	Income Taxes Payable	.0	.0		.7	.2	.3
11.1	10.0	11.4	All Other Current	10.2	11.0		10.2	8.4	20.0
46.3	48.5	46.8	Total Current	59.7	50.1		38.0	40.6	42.6
14.0	15.8	16.1	Long Term Debt	25.5	27.7		6.1	10.9	15.4
.1	.2	.2	Deferred Taxes	.0	.0		.0	.5	.2
5.4	3.7	4.9	All Other Non-Current	7.5	8.2		5.8	1.4	4.1
34.2	31.9	32.0	Net Worth	7.3	13.9		50.1	46.6	37.7
100.0	100.0	100.0	Total Liabilities & Net Worth	100.0	100.0		100.0	100.0	100.0
			INCOME DATA						
100.0	100.0	100.0	Net Sales	100.0	100.0		100.0	100.0	100.0
40.1	38.7	39.2	Gross Profit	42.6	33.7		40.8	37.7	44.4
38.4	36.7	35.6	Operating Expenses	40.1	31.9		32.4	33.8	41.7
1.7	2.0	3.6	Operating Profit	2.5	1.8		8.4	3.9	2.7
−.4	.7	.9	All Other Expenses (net)	1.9	1.2		.8	.9	.8
2.2	1.3	2.7	Profit Before Taxes	.6	.6		7.5	3.1	1.9
			RATIOS						
2.7	3.0	2.7	Current	2.3	3.0		2.9	3.1	2.7
1.7	1.5	1.6		1.0	1.6		2.2	1.8	1.5
1.1	1.1	1.0		.8	.7		1.5	1.1	.9
.8	1.0	.9	Quick	.3	.6		1.6	1.1	.9
(72) .4	(56) .3	.4		.1	.4		.8	.4	.4
.1	.2	.1		.0	.1		.4	.2	.1
1　608.0	0　UND	0　UND	Sales/Receivables	0　UND	0　UND		0　UND	1　400.3	3　133.7
3　120.8	3　131.2	3　128.3		0　UND	2　179.6		1　399.2	4　91.0	10　38.0
10　35.7	11　34.5	11　33.1		0　UND	14　26.8		24　15.0	8　47.0	28　12.9
86　4.2	80　4.5	65　5.7	Cost of Sales/Inventory	102　3.6	58　6.3		36　10.0	65　5.6	73　5.0
123　3.0	104　3.5	92　4.0		121　3.0	107　3.4		72　5.1	90　4.0	108　3.4
187　1.9	145　2.5	125　2.9		180　2.0	165　2.2		86　4.3	106　3.5	172　2.1
25　14.6	25　14.8	26　14.2	Cost of Sales/Payables	32　11.4	13　28.2		28　13.2	29　12.4	25　14.4
53　6.9	44　8.4	44　8.4		70　5.2	43　8.4		38　9.5	45　8.1	44　8.3
83　4.4	87　4.2	74　4.9		115　3.2	98　3.7		64　5.7	63　5.8	83　4.4
5.0	5.0	6.1	Sales/Working Capital	6.9	3.8		5.9	5.1	6.2
10.6	10.5	11.2		112.1	8.9		10.6	10.0	8.4
31.6	33.7	112.1		−15.9	−28.8		18.7	49.7	NM
13.4	8.3	20.4	EBIT/Interest		3.8		224.4	37.6	10.3
(66) 3.7	(51) 2.5	(67) 3.9		(12) .6			20.3	(17) 9.3	(11) 2.3
.9	.5	.3			−3.5		6.5	.2	.5
12.3	92.2	14.4	Net Profit + Depr., Dep.,						
(15) 4.5	(10) 7.1	(12) 2.9	Amort./Cur. Mat. L/T/D						
1.7	1.6	.5							
.2	.2	.3	Fixed/Worth	2.1	.1		.1	.2	.3
.4	.4	.7		UND	8.6		.4	.5	.7
1.5	1.9	3.1		−7.8	−9.8		1.3	1.2	1.8
.6	.7	.7	Debt/Worth	4.5	1.0		.4	.4	.7
2.4	2.2	2.4		UND	34.7		.9	1.4	2.0
4.7	5.0	11.2		−30.7	−38.3		2.6	2.9	3.5
34.4	39.5	67.1	% Profit Before Taxes/Tangible		250.3		107.4	42.3	28.8
(64) 17.3	(48) 15.0	(64) 16.9	Net Worth	(10) 35.2			57.8	(17) 12.3	(11) 4.5
5.2	1.3	2.9			9.9		16.1	−.7	−4.6
11.2	12.1	13.9	% Profit Before Taxes/Total	8.2	12.5		43.2	13.7	4.5
5.5	4.4	5.5	Assets	.0	4.4		28.6	7.9	2.8
.3	−2.1	−1.3		−1.7	−5.9		6.7	−2.1	−.8
51.8	54.9	46.7	Sales/Net Fixed Assets	49.0	98.0		118.6	25.2	12.6
19.1	15.1	13.4		18.3	24.6		24.8	12.6	7.9
8.7	8.6	6.7		6.6	9.2		8.2	6.5	4.9
3.5	3.4	3.7	Sales/Total Assets	3.5	3.4		6.4	3.5	2.6
2.6	2.6	2.8		2.8	2.9		3.8	3.2	2.0
1.7	1.9	2.1		2.5	1.8		2.7	2.1	1.1
.6	.7	.8	% Depr., Dep., Amort./Sales		.8			1.0	1.3
(63) 1.3	(51) 1.1	(64) 1.4		(12) 1.3				1.6	(10) 1.7
2.1	1.9	2.1			3.1			2.5	2.3
2.2	2.6	1.6	% Officers', Directors',						
(27) 4.4	(22) 5.6	(28) 4.8	Owners' Comp/Sales						
7.7	9.2	8.4							
923112M	973047M	2128066M	Net Sales ($)	6027M	28960M	34439M	70944M	301133M	1686563M
435597M	425445M	1038295M	Total Assets ($)	3310M	11988M	10152M	19852M	110074M	882919M

M = $ thousand   MM = $ million
See Pages 11 through 18 for Explanation of Ratios and Data

Current Data Sorted By Assets   Comparative Historical Data

Periods: 7 (4/1–9/30/02) covering 500M-2MM; 56 (10/1/02–3/31/03) covering 2-10MM through 100-250MM

0-500M	500M-2MM	2-10MM	10-50MM	50-100MM	100-250MM	Type of Statement	4/1/98-3/31/99 ALL	4/1/99-3/31/00 ALL
		4		9	4	Unqualified	28	20
1	3	3				Reviewed	14	6
1	4	3	4			Compiled	5	6
4	2	2	1			Tax Returns	2	
	2	9	1		3	Other	16	10
6	**11**	**17**	**13**	**9**	**7**	**NUMBER OF STATEMENTS**	**65**	**42**
%	%	%	%	%	%	**ASSETS**	%	%
	12.0	8.3	13.9			Cash & Equivalents	7.3	8.5
	13.9	7.3	7.2			Trade Receivables (net)	13.2	15.8
	38.0	40.4	38.1			Inventory	39.8	41.2
	1.8	5.0	1.0			All Other Current	1.4	1.4
	65.7	61.1	60.2			Total Current	61.7	67.0
	27.8	27.3	22.1			Fixed Assets (net)	27.7	23.6
	1.0	1.9	5.1			Intangibles (net)	2.1	1.8
	5.5	9.8	12.6			All Other Non-Current	8.5	7.7
	100.0	100.0	100.0			Total	100.0	100.0
						LIABILITIES		
	8.6	10.5	3.4			Notes Payable-Short Term	6.4	8.5
	3.0	1.7	1.6			Cur. Mat.-L/T/D	2.3	1.7
	15.8	17.9	10.1			Trade Payables	12.4	11.8
	.0	.2	.4			Income Taxes Payable	.3	.2
	17.2	11.6	7.4			All Other Current	9.0	9.0
	44.6	41.9	22.9			Total Current	30.5	31.2
	16.4	17.4	14.3			Long Term Debt	22.3	16.7
	.4	.0	1.2			Deferred Taxes	.7	.2
	3.0	.8	4.3			All Other Non-Current	6.4	3.4
	35.6	39.9	57.3			Net Worth	40.0	48.4
	100.0	100.0	100.0			Total Liabilities & Net Worth	100.0	100.0
						INCOME DATA		
	100.0	100.0	100.0			Net Sales	100.0	100.0
	35.9	35.8	34.0			Gross Profit	33.4	35.4
	24.3	30.4	33.3			Operating Expenses	38.7	33.4
	11.5	5.4	.7			Operating Profit	−5.3	2.1
	2.4	−.3	−.3			All Other Expenses (net)	−7.2	−2.9
	9.1	5.7	1.0			Profit Before Taxes	1.9	5.0
						RATIOS		
	4.4	2.4	4.6			Current	3.6	3.8
	1.5	1.8	2.4				2.2	2.4
	.9	1.2	1.7				1.4	1.6
	1.8	.8	2.4			Quick	1.5	1.9
	.8	(16) .3	1.0				.8	.7
	.3	.2	.5				.2	.3
0 UND	7 49.9	1 514.6	2 227.4			Sales/Receivables	0 999.8	2 227.3
17 21.8		3 116.9	9 42.8				8 43.5	9 42.5
		9 40.6	27 13.3				56 6.6	56 6.5
4 82.8	76 4.8	18 20.2	81 4.5			Cost of Sales/Inventory	71 5.1	63 5.8
268 1.4		58 6.3	109 3.3				100 3.7	106 3.5
		170 2.1	150 2.4				141 2.6	141 2.6
0 UND	9 41.3	10 37.0	10 35.0			Cost of Sales/Payables	14 25.9	14 26.6
42 8.7		30 12.3	35 10.4				28 12.9	32 11.2
		55 6.6	50 7.3				51 7.2	50 7.4
	9.5	6.1	4.2			Sales/Working Capital	3.6	3.8
	15.3	11.1	5.3				6.3	6.4
	−7.6	110.3	7.8				12.7	10.5
		(16) 18.8	(12) 7.2			EBIT/Interest	(56) 8.0	(35) 8.9
		5.8	3.8				3.3	3.0
		1.4	−2.7				1.9	1.6
						Net Profit + Depr., Dep., Amort./Cur. Mat. L /T/D	(26) 7.4	(17) 5.0
							2.6	2.1
							1.2	1.0
	.0	.1	.2			Fixed/Worth	.3	.2
	.6	.2	.5				.8	.4
	8.5	2.2	1.1				1.4	1.5
	1.0	.6	.2			Debt/Worth	.8	.3
	1.4	1.4	1.1				1.8	1.2
	13.4	2.7	3.2				2.8	2.5
		(14) 64.5	(12) 21.4			% Profit Before Taxes/Tangible Net Worth	(61) 26.1	(39) 29.5
		18.2	14.0				18.5	15.4
		6.4	−2.4				4.5	7.7
	14.4	23.2	10.6			% Profit Before Taxes/Total Assets	10.9	11.3
	4.5	7.0	5.8				6.2	6.6
	−2.6	2.2	−.7				1.7	3.1
	133.7	74.3	15.2			Sales/Net Fixed Assets	15.4	31.1
	15.6	30.4	9.4				7.6	9.0
	1.1	3.4	6.5				5.3	5.5
	4.5	4.4	2.7			Sales/Total Assets	2.6	2.6
	1.8	2.5	1.9				1.9	2.1
	.6	1.4	1.1				1.3	1.6
		(14) .4	(11) .8			% Depr., Dep., Amort./Sales	(55) .9	(35) .9
		.9	1.2				1.5	1.4
		2.5	2.5				2.3	2.3
		(10) .9				% Officers', Directors', Owners' Comp/Sales	(17) .7	
		3.0					1.9	
		6.3					5.5	
9183M	43536M	211272M	724139M	1550433M	1813304M	Net Sales ($)	7044843M	4647506M
1464M	13776M	68663M	337413M	693390M	1085471M	Total Assets ($)	3709040M	2472921M

M = $ thousand   MM = $ million
See Pages 11 through 18 for Explanation of Ratios and Data

Comparative Historical Data | Current Data Sorted By Sales

4/1/00-3/31/01 ALL	4/1/01-3/31/02 ALL	4/1/02-3/31/03 ALL	Type of Statement	0-1MM	1-3MM	3-5MM	5-10MM	10-25MM	25MM & OVER
6	13	17	Unqualified					3	14
9	3	11	Reviewed	1		1	2	1	6
6	11	9	Compiled	1	3	1	3	1	
6	3	9	Tax Returns	3	4	1			1
15	12	17	Other	1		2	4	3	7
				7 (4/1-9/30/02)			56 (10/1/02-3/31/03)		
42	42	63	NUMBER OF STATEMENTS	6	7	5	9	8	28
%	%	%	ASSETS	%	%	%	%	%	%
10.6	11.2	10.0	Cash & Equivalents						12.1
13.1	10.5	8.4	Trade Receivables (net)						9.0
43.7	38.0	36.4	Inventory						36.9
2.0	6.3	3.0	All Other Current						2.4
69.4	66.0	57.8	Total Current						60.5
20.9	22.4	29.3	Fixed Assets (net)						25.1
2.5	5.5	3.4	Intangibles (net)						5.9
7.2	6.1	9.5	All Other Non-Current						8.5
100.0	100.0	100.0	Total						100.0
			LIABILITIES						
7.8	3.0	7.8	Notes Payable-Short Term						4.4
1.6	2.2	1.7	Cur. Mat.-L/T/D						1.5
13.0	12.1	14.5	Trade Payables						13.7
.3	.2	.2	Income Taxes Payable						.3
7.1	7.5	10.0	All Other Current						9.2
29.8	25.1	34.2	Total Current						29.0
16.4	16.7	18.1	Long Term Debt						15.2
.2	.7	1.0	Deferred Taxes						.8
6.4	2.0	4.2	All Other Non-Current						3.8
47.2	55.4	42.4	Net Worth						51.1
100.0	100.0	100.0	Total Liabilities & Net Worth						100.0
			INCOME DATA						
100.0	100.0	100.0	Net Sales						100.0
35.4	33.9	36.4	Gross Profit						33.0
35.0	30.4	32.1	Operating Expenses						30.0
.4	3.5	4.3	Operating Profit						3.0
−1.2	.7	.6	All Other Expenses (net)						.3
1.6	2.8	3.7	Profit Before Taxes						2.7
			RATIOS						
4.5	5.8	3.5	Current						3.4
2.3	2.6	1.9	Current						2.0
1.8	1.8	1.3	Current						1.5
2.2	1.8	1.2	Quick						1.4
.8	.8	(62) .5	Quick						.7
.1	.4	.2	Quick						.2
1 644.7	1 299.4	1 487.8	Sales/Receivables						1 357.7
4 91.6	6 57.9	4 82.4	Sales/Receivables						5 73.9
37 9.8	21 17.0	18 20.3	Sales/Receivables						21 17.4
59 6.2	50 7.3	34 10.7	Cost of Sales/Inventory						48 7.6
83 4.4	80 4.6	81 4.5	Cost of Sales/Inventory						81 4.5
146 2.5	113 3.2	161 2.3	Cost of Sales/Inventory						131 2.8
15 23.8	12 30.2	9 41.3	Cost of Sales/Payables						13 27.8
30 12.1	31 11.9	30 12.3	Cost of Sales/Payables						34 10.8
51 7.1	48 7.5	45 8.1	Cost of Sales/Payables						41 9.0
4.0	3.9	5.0	Sales/Working Capital						4.6
6.3	6.3	8.6	Sales/Working Capital						7.8
14.1	9.7	69.8	Sales/Working Capital						13.1
6.5	15.4	11.9	EBIT/Interest						14.5
(31) 2.3	(32) 3.4	(53) 4.4	EBIT/Interest						(25) 4.5
1.0	1.4	1.5	EBIT/Interest						1.7
5.2		15.0	Net Profit + Depr., Dep., Amort./Cur. Mat. L/T/D						
(13) 1.6		(13) 4.5	Net Profit + Depr., Dep., Amort./Cur. Mat. L/T/D						
.3		2.7	Net Profit + Depr., Dep., Amort./Cur. Mat. L/T/D						
.1	.2	.2	Fixed/Worth						.3
.5	.4	.6	Fixed/Worth						.6
1.4	1.2	1.7	Fixed/Worth						1.0
.5	.2	.5	Debt/Worth						.4
1.2	.9	1.3	Debt/Worth						1.3
3.0	2.4	3.3	Debt/Worth						2.3
27.8	23.6	30.8	% Profit Before Taxes/Tangible Net Worth						26.1
(38) 12.3	(38) 10.7	(54) 14.0	% Profit Before Taxes/Tangible Net Worth						(26) 15.9
1.8	1.5	3.1	% Profit Before Taxes/Tangible Net Worth						5.9
10.9	10.7	12.8	% Profit Before Taxes/Total Assets						12.9
4.3	4.2	5.2	% Profit Before Taxes/Total Assets						6.3
−1.1	1.0	1.5	% Profit Before Taxes/Total Assets						2.4
39.1	48.3	34.2	Sales/Net Fixed Assets						18.6
12.6	11.2	10.0	Sales/Net Fixed Assets						9.2
5.5	6.2	4.5	Sales/Net Fixed Assets						6.0
3.6	3.5	3.8	Sales/Total Assets						3.2
2.3	2.3	2.1	Sales/Total Assets						2.2
1.5	1.3	1.3	Sales/Total Assets						1.6
.4	.4	.6	% Depr., Dep., Amort./Sales						.7
(32) 1.3	(36) .9	(53) 1.2	% Depr., Dep., Amort./Sales						(23) 1.2
2.2	2.0	2.6	% Depr., Dep., Amort./Sales						2.2
1.0	1.4	1.9	% Officers', Directors', Owners' Comp/Sales						
(13) 3.3	(11) 3.3	(21) 4.4	% Officers', Directors', Owners' Comp/Sales						
12.0	12.0	10.3	% Officers', Directors', Owners' Comp/Sales						
2497356M	3584411M	4351867M	Net Sales ($)	2861M	13919M	20122M	68150M	104553M	4142262M
1453887M	1702723M	2200177M	Total Assets ($)	5139M	11720M	17308M	23807M	190476M	1951727M

M = $ thousand   MM = $ million
See Pages 11 through 18 for Explanation of Ratios and Data

Current Data Sorted By Assets   Comparative Historical Data

							Type of Statement		
1	2	2	6	1	5		Unqualified	26	20
2	3	10	9				Reviewed	23	24
17	14	7	1				Compiled	44	67
21	14	4					Tax Returns	29	38
11	11	6	7	3	1		Other	81	53

	41 (4/1-9/30/02)			117 (10/1/02-3/31/03)				4/1/98-3/31/99	4/1/99-3/31/00
0-500M	500M-2MM	2-10MM	10-50MM	50-100MM	100-250MM			ALL	ALL
52	44	29	23	4	6	NUMBER OF STATEMENTS	203	202
%	%	%	%	%	%	**ASSETS**	%	%
12.7	7.7	10.1	8.3			Cash & Equivalents	9.9	8.0
7.9	8.7	6.7	6.9			Trade Receivables (net)	4.9	6.7
49.9	44.8	51.9	50.1			Inventory	51.3	52.3
3.3	1.4	4.1	2.3			All Other Current	1.6	1.7
73.7	62.7	72.8	67.5			Total Current	67.6	68.8
19.1	27.9	18.6	22.6			Fixed Assets (net)	21.3	20.8
2.8	1.0	1.9	3.5			Intangibles (net)	4.4	3.8
4.4	8.5	6.6	6.3			All Other Non-Current	6.7	6.6
100.0	100.0	100.0	100.0			Total	100.0	100.0
						LIABILITIES		
10.0	8.7	12.1	9.3			Notes Payable-Short Term	7.4	10.3
3.2	2.1	1.2	2.1			Cur. Mat.-L/T/D	3.3	3.1
20.9	12.4	19.8	12.4			Trade Payables	15.6	18.7
.3	.2	.2	.2			Income Taxes Payable	.4	.3
7.5	7.6	9.9	9.9			All Other Current	11.1	11.2
41.8	31.1	43.2	33.9			Total Current	37.8	43.7
26.3	24.9	12.5	15.2			Long Term Debt	19.1	17.9
.0	.0	.2	.1			Deferred Taxes	.2	.1
7.5	5.3	9.4	8.1			All Other Non-Current	4.9	7.2
24.3	38.6	34.8	42.7			Net Worth	38.0	31.1
100.0	100.0	100.0	100.0			Total Liabilities & Net Worth	100.0	100.0
						INCOME DATA		
100.0	100.0	100.0	100.0			Net Sales	100.0	100.0
40.6	35.6	37.6	39.2			Gross Profit	36.8	38.0
38.2	32.1	34.5	37.3			Operating Expenses	33.5	34.5
2.5	3.5	3.2	1.9			Operating Profit	3.3	3.4
.4	.7	.5	.0			All Other Expenses (net)	.3	.8
2.1	2.7	2.6	1.9			Profit Before Taxes	2.9	2.6
						RATIOS		
4.4	5.0	3.5	2.7				3.3	3.0
2.1	2.4	1.9	2.0			Current	1.9	1.7
1.2	1.4	1.2	1.4				1.3	1.1
1.4	1.1	1.0	.9				.9	.6
.3	.4	.4	.3			Quick	(199) .3	(198) .2
.1	.1	.1	.1				.1	.1
0 UND	0 UND	0 UND	0 872.7				0 UND	0 UND
1 273.8	1 463.0	2 146.6	2 229.5			Sales/Receivables	1 309.0	1 464.4
6 57.1	17 21.9	11 32.5	4 83.4				5 68.2	7 54.6
30 12.0	26 13.8	74 4.9	65 5.6				64 5.7	47 7.8
88 4.2	80 4.6	129 2.8	113 3.2			Cost of Sales/Inventory	106 3.4	105 3.5
155 2.4	162 2.3	190 1.9	193 1.9				171 2.1	175 2.1
5 76.7	5 77.1	16 22.7	18 20.6				11 34.5	11 33.0
23 16.2	14 26.0	38 9.5	32 11.4			Cost of Sales/Payables	25 14.7	27 13.6
44 8.2	38 9.7	57 6.4	47 7.8				48 7.5	49 7.5
5.0	4.5	4.4	4.3				5.1	5.9
11.0	9.8	9.0	8.1			Sales/Working Capital	10.1	12.0
44.3	41.2	28.5	14.3				29.1	96.0
6.0	8.4	18.2	12.0				8.6	6.3
(39) 1.5	(39) 2.8	(21) 3.2	(21) 3.1			EBIT/Interest	(184) 3.7	(174) 3.7
.0	.1	1.9	2.2				1.4	1.4
			9.2			Net Profit + Depr., Dep.,	10.0	6.9
			(10) 3.2			Amort./Cur. Mat. L /T/D	(46) 3.1	(34) 3.4
			1.6				.9	1.0
.1	.2	.1	.3				.1	.2
.8	.5	.3	.4			Fixed/Worth	.5	.6
23.9	1.8	1.7	1.6				1.8	1.9
.4	.7	.8	.7				.6	.9
2.9	1.4	2.3	1.5			Debt/Worth	1.5	2.6
109.2	4.3	3.8	2.6				5.6	8.8
82.6	22.1	70.2	45.7			% Profit Before Taxes/Tangible	48.9	50.0
(40) 12.4	(39) 7.8	(27) 24.3	(21) 13.9			Net Worth	(170) 23.4	(167) 21.3
-.9	-5.4	9.2	5.6				5.7	6.6
18.5	10.4	20.4	12.1			% Profit Before Taxes/Total	15.2	16.4
4.1	3.9	5.8	4.8			Assets	8.0	7.5
-3.1	-2.1	3.1	1.9				1.5	1.9
127.8	58.6	65.7	23.7				65.0	61.0
34.7	15.9	19.6	15.7			Sales/Net Fixed Assets	18.9	21.3
12.3	6.5	10.3	8.5				8.5	9.7
5.7	4.2	3.4	3.1				4.1	4.8
3.4	3.0	2.2	2.3			Sales/Total Assets	2.7	2.9
2.6	2.0	1.5	1.7				1.8	2.1
.8	.4	.4	1.0				.6	.7
(36) 1.3	(39) 1.0	(26) 1.1	1.2			% Depr., Dep., Amort./Sales	(162) 1.2	(165) 1.1
2.0	1.8	1.9	1.8				2.1	1.8
1.9	1.9	1.2				% Officers', Directors',	2.0	1.9
(29) 4.8	(30) 5.0	(14) 3.5				Owners' Comp/Sales	(76) 3.6	(90) 3.2
8.1	7.8	6.0					5.9	5.8
55516M	172381M	377947M	1260267M	789267M	2611870M	Net Sales ($)	8864169M	7115854M
13246M	43904M	139394M	499365M	279285M	1039315M	Total Assets ($)	3621470M	2634661M

© RMA 2003

M = $ thousand   MM = $ million
See Pages 11 through 18 for Explanation of Ratios and Data

Comparative Historical Data | Current Data Sorted By Sales

			Type of Statement	0-1MM	1-3MM	3-5MM	5-10MM	10-25MM	25MM & OVER
15	21	17	Unqualified		2		2		13
22	18	24	Reviewed	2		3	2	8	9
65	64	39	Compiled	8	19	7	1	4	
35	44	39	Tax Returns	12	17	5	3	1	1
51	42	39	Other	8	10	4	3	3	11
4/1/00-3/31/01	4/1/01-3/31/02	4/1/02-3/31/03			41 (4/1-9/30/02)		117 (10/1/02-3/31/03)		
ALL	ALL	ALL							
188	189	158	**NUMBER OF STATEMENTS**	30	48	19	11	16	34
%	%	%	**ASSETS**	%	%	%	%	%	%
9.3	10.5	10.2	Cash & Equivalents	10.5	10.7	7.6	13.6	7.6	10.7
7.5	7.9	7.8	Trade Receivables (net)	5.6	7.7	14.5	10.5	6.4	6.0
50.9	49.1	48.2	Inventory	54.7	46.0	38.3	55.8	50.3	47.7
2.6	2.4	2.7	All Other Current	2.6	2.4	2.2	4.0	3.9	2.4
70.2	69.9	68.9	Total Current	73.5	66.8	62.6	83.9	68.3	66.8
20.2	21.7	22.1	Fixed Assets (net)	21.2	25.3	26.2	12.2	16.9	21.7
3.2	2.5	2.2	Intangibles (net)	3.2	1.5	.7	1.4	2.7	3.3
6.3	5.9	6.8	All Other Non-Current	2.2	6.4	10.5	2.5	12.1	8.1
100.0	100.0	100.0	Total	100.0	100.0	100.0	100.0	100.0	100.0
			LIABILITIES						
11.4	10.4	9.4	Notes Payable-Short Term	10.2	7.5	16.6	9.0	11.8	6.5
2.3	2.8	2.3	Cur. Mat.-L/T/D	4.5	1.8	1.7	1.3	1.5	2.0
16.3	16.5	17.0	Trade Payables	19.4	15.8	9.6	21.7	18.8	18.2
.2	.2	.3	Income Taxes Payable	.3	.2	.4	.1	.2	.4
13.7	10.6	8.3	All Other Current	5.3	7.0	8.7	9.5	10.2	11.4
43.9	40.6	37.3	Total Current	39.7	32.3	37.0	41.6	42.6	38.6
18.2	16.9	21.0	Long Term Debt	29.6	28.4	18.5	9.3	7.8	14.6
.1	.1	.1	Deferred Taxes	.1	.0	.0	.1	.2	.2
8.8	5.7	7.7	All Other Non-Current	4.8	8.4	11.0	3.1	6.9	9.5
29.1	36.8	33.8	Net Worth	26.0	30.9	33.5	45.8	42.6	37.1
100.0	100.0	100.0	Total Liabilities & Net Worth	100.0	100.0	100.0	100.0	100.0	100.0
			INCOME DATA						
100.0	100.0	100.0	Net Sales	100.0	100.0	100.0	100.0	100.0	100.0
36.2	37.3	38.2	Gross Profit	46.2	36.1	35.5	34.9	35.4	37.9
34.1	34.6	35.3	Operating Expenses	42.8	33.9	33.2	33.0	31.0	34.5
2.2	2.8	2.9	Operating Profit	3.4	2.2	2.3	2.0	4.5	3.4
.6	.7	.5	All Other Expenses (net)	.5	.9	.1	-.5	.2	.8
1.6	2.1	2.4	Profit Before Taxes	3.0	1.3	2.2	2.5	4.3	2.6
			RATIOS						
3.1	3.6	3.9		4.7	6.5	3.2	3.9	4.7	2.7
1.9	1.8	2.1	Current	2.4	2.9	1.9	2.0	1.8	1.9
1.1	1.2	1.3		1.3	1.4	1.3	1.4	1.1	1.3
.7	.9	1.0		1.0	1.8	1.0	1.4	1.2	.9
(184) .3	(186) .3	.3	Quick	.3	.4	.3	.5	.4	.3
.1	.1	.1		.1	.1	.1	.1	.0	.1
0 UND	0 UND	0 UND		0 UND	0 UND	0 999.8	0 UND	0 UND	0 UND
1 246.9	1 321.6	2 218.6	Sales/Receivables	0 UND	2 195.4	3 141.7	2 185.4	1 248.8	2 158.3
13 27.2	10 37.1	8 47.1		7 49.7	10 35.9	28 13.2	21 17.7	6 56.5	7 53.1
41 8.9	46 8.0	41 8.9		89 4.1	33 11.2	13 28.9	26 14.1	49 7.5	63 5.8
100 3.6	100 3.7	104 3.5	Cost of Sales/Inventory	144 2.5	71 5.2	68 5.4	123 3.0	112 3.3	109 3.3
165 2.2	160 2.3	168 2.2		205 1.8	133 2.7	189 1.9	194 1.9	160 2.6	163 2.2
9 42.4	9 40.8	10 36.6		12 29.3	2 205.2	5 70.2	15 23.9	15 24.5	21 17.0
23 15.8	25 14.8	28 12.9	Cost of Sales/Payables	38 9.6	14 26.6	13 27.1	28 13.1	29 12.4	36 10.0
44 8.4	45 8.2	48 7.5		68 5.4	37 9.8	36 10.1	58 6.3	53 6.9	49 7.5
5.3	4.9	4.5		3.5	4.6	4.6	5.3	4.7	4.5
10.7	9.8	9.7	Sales/Working Capital	5.7	10.0	17.1	9.7	12.9	9.5
54.7	37.9	29.8		14.1	31.3	46.5	16.1	53.5	25.0
8.3	7.3	7.1		3.2	6.6	10.9		20.1	13.9
(165) 2.9	(167) 2.2	(130) 2.9	EBIT/Interest	(22) 1.0	(40) 2.0	(17) 4.7		(12) 4.9	(32) 3.6
1.0	.6	.8		.0	-.8	1.7		2.5	2.1
8.6	5.5	10.3	Net Profit + Depr., Dep.,						10.4
(31) 3.0	(35) 2.5	(23) 4.2	Amort./Cur. Mat. L/T/D					(12)	4.3
1.5	.5	1.0							1.6
.2	.2	.2		.1	.2	.1	.0	.2	.3
.6	.4	.5	Fixed/Worth	.8	.6	.9	.4	.4	.5
1.8	1.3	1.9		10.1	2.6	2.8	.5	.9	2.0
.8	.6	.7		.5	.6	.5	.8	.6	.8
2.3	1.6	2.0	Debt/Worth	4.0	2.0	2.0	1.0	1.8	1.8
9.2	4.7	6.3		90.4	8.1	4.6	2.5	2.6	4.3
38.6	39.1	48.8	% Profit Before Taxes/Tangible	39.5	76.7	24.5	70.2	104.5	48.1
(155) 18.8	(170) 15.1	(137) 15.4	Net Worth	(24) 5.9	(39) 11.5	(16) 15.2	14.2	(15) 23.9	(32) 27.9
4.7	.3	2.3		-13.1	-3.0	7.8	-4.4	8.2	6.6
15.8	12.4	17.3	% Profit Before Taxes/Total	14.9	17.9	11.5	20.0	22.3	17.9
5.2	4.3	4.8	Assets	2.8	2.4	6.9	6.3	7.8	5.2
.0	-.2	-.4		-3.5	-3.3	2.8	-2.3	3.1	2.4
52.5	55.0	57.2		154.3	55.9	59.3	109.0	66.2	23.8
22.9	22.8	21.5	Sales/Net Fixed Assets	27.0	19.7	16.7	42.3	29.8	15.5
10.8	10.7	9.7		7.3	7.1	10.7	17.8	14.5	9.7
4.4	4.3	4.2		3.3	5.7	4.3	4.2	5.6	3.6
2.9	3.0	2.9	Sales/Total Assets	2.5	3.4	2.9	3.3	2.4	2.7
2.0	2.3	2.0		1.5	2.0	1.4	2.3	2.0	2.0
.4	.5	.7		1.1	.7	.4	.4	.4	1.0
(162) .7	(163) 1.0	(131) 1.2	% Depr., Dep., Amort./Sales	(19) 1.9	(40) 1.3	(17) .9	(10) .7	(14) .8	(31) 1.5
1.6	1.7	1.9		3.4	1.9	1.4	1.8	1.5	1.8
1.6	1.9	1.6		3.6	1.6				
(84) 4.3	(93) 4.0	(78) 4.1	% Officers', Directors',	(19) 6.8	(30) 4.0				
7.9	7.5	7.7	Owners' Comp/Sales	10.3	6.2				
5588957M	5638378M	5267248M	Net Sales ($)	16503M	83563M	71851M	88706M	259252M	4747373M
2140993M	2068787M	2014509M	Total Assets ($)	7956M	33127M	37827M	28029M	96987M	1810583M

M = $ thousand   MM = $ million
See Pages 11 through 18 for Explanation of Ratios and Data

Current Data Sorted By Assets							Comparative Historical Data	
						Type of Statement		
		1				Unqualified	4	
1	1					Reviewed	12	7
19	5	2				Compiled	33	28
26	6	1		1		Tax Returns	21	16
7	1	1			3	Other	16	23
28 (4/1-9/30/02)		47 (10/1/02-3/31/03)					**4/1/98-3/31/99**	**4/1/99-3/31/00**
0-500M	**500M-2MM**	**2-10MM**	**10-50MM**	**50-100MM**	**100-250MM**		**ALL**	**ALL**
53	13	5		1	3	**NUMBER OF STATEMENTS**	86	74
%	%	%	%	%	%	**ASSETS**	%	%
12.6	13.3		D A T A			Cash & Equivalents	12.0	9.6
12.3	17.3					Trade Receivables (net)	16.3	19.1
23.1	22.8					Inventory	24.3	24.4
2.2	1.0					All Other Current	2.0	1.8
50.0	54.5					Total Current	54.6	54.9
37.6	35.3		N O T			Fixed Assets (net)	35.7	33.9
9.0	.1					Intangibles (net)	3.8	4.9
3.4	10.2					All Other Non-Current	5.9	6.4
100.0	100.0					Total	100.0	100.0
			A V A I L A B L E			**LIABILITIES**		
10.5	5.8					Notes Payable-Short Term	6.7	8.0
8.1	3.7					Cur. Mat.-L/T/D	4.9	4.5
18.5	17.5					Trade Payables	17.7	16.7
.0	.3					Income Taxes Payable	.3	.5
15.4	5.8					All Other Current	14.0	13.4
52.5	33.1					Total Current	43.5	43.1
44.9	21.0					Long Term Debt	29.7	35.0
.1	.2					Deferred Taxes	.2	.2
7.4	2.2					All Other Non-Current	3.9	5.1
-4.9	43.5					Net Worth	22.7	16.5
100.0	100.0					Total Liabilities & Net Worth	100.0	100.0
						INCOME DATA		
100.0	100.0					Net Sales	100.0	100.0
53.6	48.1					Gross Profit	52.6	53.5
52.6	48.1					Operating Expenses	49.8	50.3
1.0	-.1					Operating Profit	2.8	3.1
1.0	-.5					All Other Expenses (net)	.0	.1
.0	.5					Profit Before Taxes	2.7	3.0
						RATIOS		
2.4	2.8						2.5	2.2
1.1	1.6					Current	1.5	1.4
.6	.9						1.0	1.0
1.0	1.8						1.6	1.3
.6	1.0					Quick	.7	.7
.2	.3						.3	.4
2 206.9	**12** 31.4						**8** 48.3	**7** 55.9
14 26.0	**16** 22.4					Sales/Receivables	**15** 25.0	**18** 20.4
22 16.5	**31** 11.9						**22** 16.3	**29** 12.8
24 15.5	**35** 10.5						**22** 16.9	**26** 14.0
39 9.4	**61** 5.9					Cost of Sales/Inventory	**47** 7.8	**52** 7.1
90 4.1	**74** 4.9						**81** 4.5	**85** 4.3
10 36.4	**26** 14.1						**22** 16.9	**18** 20.0
35 10.4	**40** 9.1					Cost of Sales/Payables	**34** 10.8	**32** 11.3
63 5.8	**60** 6.1						**51** 7.1	**52** 7.0
11.4	7.5						8.4	9.4
84.6	11.2					Sales/Working Capital	17.3	20.8
-12.3	-78.7						-133.8	240.1
4.9	10.2						6.7	6.1
(49) 2.3	(11) 5.5					EBIT/Interest	(79) 2.8	(65) 2.4
.2	.7						1.3	.8
							5.3	8.0
						Net Profit + Depr., Dep., Amort./Cur. Mat. L /T/D	(20) 2.1	(12) 3.2
							1.4	1.9
.8	.3						.4	.4
13.4	.5					Fixed/Worth	1.0	1.2
-.9	2.4						19.7	-2.7
2.6	.6						.8	.8
UND	1.2					Debt/Worth	1.9	1.9
-2.8	3.1						30.2	-7.1
155.6	20.3						50.3	48.0
(27) 39.4	(12) 9.6					% Profit Before Taxes/Tangible Net Worth	(66) 21.1	(51) 19.3
2.3	-4.5						4.6	4.2
19.7	7.3						15.6	20.1
4.7	5.5					% Profit Before Taxes/Total Assets	7.1	6.4
-5.3	-2.2						1.0	-.6
29.8	21.4						24.1	25.2
10.7	9.5					Sales/Net Fixed Assets	10.6	12.0
3.6	4.0						5.3	6.0
5.3	3.8						4.5	5.0
3.6	2.4					Sales/Total Assets	3.3	3.5
2.1	2.0						2.2	2.1
1.3	1.3						1.2	1.1
(42) 2.9	2.6					% Depr., Dep., Amort./Sales	(77) 1.8	(65) 1.8
5.0	4.0						3.1	3.1
4.7	4.1						3.9	4.3
(30) 7.3	(11) 5.6					% Officers', Directors', Owners' Comp/Sales	(50) 6.6	(40) 5.7
11.3	7.5						9.9	9.4
32967M	**33920M**	**74046M**		**320739M**	**2165628M**	Net Sales ($)	**744653M**	**217449M**
10152M	**12035M**	**27505M**		**61965M**	**536493M**	Total Assets ($)	**400950M**	**64909M**

M = $ thousand MM = $ million

See Pages 11 through 18 for Explanation of Ratios and Data

Comparative Historical Data | | | Current Data Sorted By Sales

					Type of Statement						
	1		2		1	Unqualified					1
	4		4		2	Reviewed	1		1		1	
	27		24		26	Compiled	15	8	1	1	1	1
	20		20		34	Tax Returns	23	7	2		1	1
	17		10		12	Other	6	2			1	3
	4/1/00-3/31/01 ALL		4/1/01-3/31/02 ALL		4/1/02-3/31/03 ALL		0-1MM	28 (4/1-9/30/02) 1-3MM	3-5MM	5-10MM	47 (10/1/02-3/31/03) 10-25MM	25MM & OVER
	69		60		75	**NUMBER OF STATEMENTS**	45	17	4	1	4	4
	%		%		%	**ASSETS**	%	%	%	%	%	%
	14.0		10.9		13.6	Cash & Equivalents	11.5	15.0				
	17.0		18.8		12.9	Trade Receivables (net)	11.2	16.4				
	23.4		22.3		22.6	Inventory	22.4	24.1				
	2.1		3.1		2.3	All Other Current	1.5	3.0				
	56.5		55.1		51.4	Total Current	46.5	58.4				
	32.7		33.2		36.7	Fixed Assets (net)	39.7	35.4				
	4.6		5.2		6.7	Intangibles (net)	10.3	.7				
	6.2		6.4		5.2	All Other Non-Current	3.5	5.5				
	100.0		100.0		100.0	Total	100.0	100.0				
						LIABILITIES						
	6.0		8.6		8.7	Notes Payable-Short Term	10.7	7.6				
	5.2		6.5		7.1	Cur. Mat.-L/T/D	7.0	9.1				
	21.2		20.8		19.6	Trade Payables	17.1	19.8				
	.2		.2		.2	Income Taxes Payable	.0	.3				
	19.5		16.8		12.8	All Other Current	14.4	11.7				
	52.2		52.9		48.3	Total Current	49.3	48.5				
	28.9		34.4		37.8	Long Term Debt	49.0	25.3				
	.3		.3		.1	Deferred Taxes	.0	.3				
	6.4		2.9		5.8	All Other Non-Current	8.1	2.6				
	12.2		9.5		7.9	Net Worth	−6.4	23.3				
	100.0		100.0		100.0	Total Liabilities & Net Worth	100.0	100.0				
						INCOME DATA						
	100.0		100.0		100.0	Net Sales	100.0	100.0				
	52.8		52.5		51.8	Gross Profit	54.4	49.6				
	51.9		50.9		50.9	Operating Expenses	53.7	48.1				
	.8		1.6		.9	Operating Profit	.7	1.5				
	.1		.9		.7	All Other Expenses (net)	.8	.4				
	.7		.7		.3	Profit Before Taxes	−.1	1.1				
						RATIOS						
	2.2		2.5		2.2		2.4	2.5				
	1.3		1.4		1.2	Current	1.2	1.2				
	1.0		.8		.7		.6	.9				
	1.3		1.5		1.2		1.0	1.5				
	.7	(59)	.8		.6	Quick	.6	.6				
	.4		.4		.3		.2	.2				
7	54.4	11	33.1	4	102.2		0 UND	7 52.3				
17	21.0	18	20.3	14	25.7	Sales/Receivables	14 25.5	15 23.9				
27	13.4	28	13.3	23	16.2		23 15.9	22 16.6				
23	15.9	27	13.7	23	15.7		24 15.5	31 11.8				
45	8.1	42	8.7	44	8.3	Cost of Sales/Inventory	44 8.2	59 6.2				
82	4.5	75	4.9	83	4.4		103 3.5	70 5.2				
21	17.7	16	23.3	19	18.8		3 112.2	21 17.0				
28	13.0	31	11.7	40	9.1	Cost of Sales/Payables	35 10.4	41 9.0				
48	7.6	66	5.6	61	6.0		74 5.0	62 5.9				
	11.4		8.6		10.7		10.7	10.5				
	24.3		34.2		45.4	Sales/Working Capital	84.6	46.5				
	−397.7		−66.3		−17.8		−12.3	−62.2				
	4.0		4.8		5.9		4.0	7.8				
(60)	1.8	(51)	2.5	(69)	2.4	EBIT/Interest	(41) 1.5	(15) 3.0				
	.0		.9		.4		.1	.7				
	3.5		3.8		3.0	Net Profit + Depr., Dep.,						
(14)	1.6	(12)	1.9	(11)	2.3	Amort./Cur. Mat. L/T/D						
	.4		1.1		2.0							
	.4		.5		.6		1.3	.5				
	1.3		1.4		3.3	Fixed/Worth	13.4	.7				
	−11.4		−2.2		−1.4		−.9	−4.7				
	.9		1.1		1.2		3.1	.7				
	2.7		2.3		5.5	Debt/Worth	UND	2.4				
	−25.7		−6.0		−3.4		−2.7	−8.0				
	31.7		49.0		55.6	% Profit Before Taxes/Tangible	155.6	37.3				
(48)	9.8	(40)	10.5	(47)	12.9	Net Worth	(23) 24.3	(12) 10.1				
	−2.8		−.2		1.4		1.5	−1.2				
	13.4		14.4		14.2	% Profit Before Taxes/Total	20.0	13.8				
	2.7		2.5		4.7	Assets	4.1	4.7				
	−3.2		−1.1		−3.1		−5.3	−2.2				
	23.5		31.2		30.3		21.8	24.3				
	12.7		13.3		10.5	Sales/Net Fixed Assets	9.6	11.0				
	7.4		7.1		4.4		3.3	5.9				
	4.8		5.3		4.8		4.8	5.2				
	3.6		3.5		3.1	Sales/Total Assets	2.6	3.4				
	2.5		2.2		2.1		1.6	2.3				
	1.1		1.0		1.2		1.6	1.2				
(61)	2.0	(56)	1.7	(62)	2.4	% Depr., Dep., Amort./Sales	(34) 3.5	2.5				
	3.1		2.8		4.2		5.3	3.1				
	3.6		3.1		3.8	% Officers', Directors',	4.2	4.7				
(37)	6.7	(38)	5.6	(47)	5.6	Owners' Comp/Sales	(23) 8.4	(14) 5.6				
	9.6		7.7		9.5		14.5	8.4				
	1895855M		467708M		2627300M	Net Sales ($)	20144M	30521M	16222M	5725M	68321M	2486367M
	500708M		235386M		648150M	Total Assets ($)	7901M	10266M	4020M	5428M	22077M	598458M

© RMA 2003

M = $ thousand   MM = $ million
See Pages 11 through 18 for Explanation of Ratios and Data

Current Data Sorted By Assets — Comparative Historical Data

Type of Statement	0-500M	500M-2MM	2-10MM	10-50MM	50-100MM	100-250MM		4/1/98-3/31/99 ALL	4/1/99-3/31/00 ALL
Unqualified			1	2		1		9	8
Reviewed	1	6	8					19	16
Compiled	10	24	5					47	41
Tax Returns	15	14	1			1		15	8
Other	10	9	6	1	1			32	17
	30 (4/1-9/30/02)			86 (10/1/02-3/31/03)					
NUMBER OF STATEMENTS	36	53	21	3	1	2		122	90
ASSETS	%	%	%	%	%	%		%	%
Cash & Equivalents	11.4	7.8	5.6					7.9	6.9
Trade Receivables (net)	24.3	28.0	39.7					27.1	31.2
Inventory	37.2	36.5	32.6					36.9	35.8
All Other Current	1.0	2.6	1.6					2.1	1.9
Total Current	73.8	75.0	79.5					74.0	75.8
Fixed Assets (net)	15.5	15.5	12.1					18.1	16.5
Intangibles (net)	7.2	3.4	2.5					2.6	2.2
All Other Non-Current	3.5	6.1	5.9					5.2	5.5
Total	100.0	100.0	100.0					100.0	100.0
LIABILITIES									
Notes Payable-Short Term	12.6	13.2	16.3					8.9	13.6
Cur. Mat.-L/T/D	5.9	4.0	2.4					3.9	3.4
Trade Payables	29.9	23.2	22.5					23.9	28.0
Income Taxes Payable	.0	.1	.7					.2	.2
All Other Current	8.4	11.5	9.4					11.4	9.0
Total Current	56.8	52.0	51.4					48.4	54.2
Long Term Debt	25.7	14.1	6.8					16.1	15.9
Deferred Taxes	.1	.0	.1					.1	.1
All Other Non-Current	7.9	2.0	5.9					3.2	2.8
Net Worth	9.5	31.9	35.8					32.3	27.0
Total Liabilities & Net Worth	100.0	100.0	100.0					100.0	100.0
INCOME DATA									
Net Sales	100.0	100.0	100.0					100.0	100.0
Gross Profit	40.2	39.4	29.3					35.5	35.3
Operating Expenses	39.8	37.6	27.1					33.7	33.2
Operating Profit	.3	1.7	2.1					1.7	2.1
All Other Expenses (net)	.5	.3	.0					.0	.2
Profit Before Taxes	–.1	1.4	2.1					1.7	1.9
RATIOS									
Current	1.8	2.1	2.0					2.3	2.0
	1.3	1.5	1.6					1.6	1.5
	1.0	1.1	1.3					1.1	1.1
Quick	1.2	1.0	1.2					1.3	1.1
	.6	.7	.9				(119)	.7	.7
	.3	.4	.6					.4	.5
Sales/Receivables	0 UND	10 35.7	19 19.3				17 21.9	18 19.8
	25 14.7	28 13.0	31 11.8				29 12.4	29 12.6
	34 10.8	39 9.3	40 9.0				38 9.7	40 9.1
Cost of Sales/Inventory	15 24.7	28 12.9	21 17.1				28 12.9	27 13.4
	61 6.0	66 5.5	37 9.9				58 6.3	58 6.3
	106 3.4	118 3.1	56 6.5				107 3.4	115 3.2
Cost of Sales/Payables	26 14.0	22 17.0	16 22.5				21 17.8	24 15.0
	33 11.0	34 10.6	20 17.8				32 11.3	41 9.0
	79 4.6	54 6.8	35 10.5				58 6.3	65 5.6
Sales/Working Capital	11.2	9.3	10.5					7.2	7.6
	21.2	13.4	13.9					12.9	15.1
	NM	59.6	22.7					42.8	43.3
EBIT/Interest	(32) 6.5	(50) 5.0	13.0				(113) 7.4	(84) 7.4
	1.6	2.0	4.4				2.7	2.2
	–4.1	–1.3	2.9				1.2	1.0
Net Profit + Depr., Dep., Amort./Cur. Mat. L /T/D		(15) 1.7					(41) 6.4	(25) 7.8
		.8					2.6	2.4
		.3					.8	1.4
Fixed/Worth	.3	.2	.2					.3	.2
	1.4	.5	.3					.5	.5
	–.8	1.9	.8					1.2	1.6
Debt/Worth	1.7	1.1	1.0					1.1	1.3
	12.5	2.1	1.6					2.2	2.9
	–3.6	9.1	6.4					7.8	7.9
% Profit Before Taxes/Tangible Net Worth	(24) 68.0	(45) 33.0	(19) 45.5				(108) 49.3	(75) 43.8
	9.7	11.5	29.5				15.3	19.0
	–13.0	–3.9	17.6				5.5	2.8
% Profit Before Taxes/Total Assets	9.3	7.2	12.7					11.3	11.5
	.1	2.6	6.9					4.3	3.3
	–8.5	–3.3	4.2					.7	–.3
Sales/Net Fixed Assets	101.7	61.7	102.0					46.0	62.2
	39.0	34.8	58.5					21.1	28.4
	18.9	15.4	28.9					11.8	13.2
Sales/Total Assets	5.4	4.5	5.7					4.4	4.7
	3.7	3.2	4.7					3.1	3.4
	2.6	2.5	3.6					2.3	2.5
% Depr., Dep., Amort./Sales	(29) .4	(45) .6	(20) .4				(111) .5	(77) .6
	1.0	1.2	.8				1.1	1.0
	1.8	1.9	1.1				1.7	1.5
% Officers', Directors', Owners' Comp/Sales	(21) 2.8	(31) 1.4	(12) .9				(63) 2.3	(44) 2.5
	6.3	3.4	2.1				4.2	4.4
	10.2	6.4	3.0				8.2	6.1
Net Sales ($)	45393M	210122M	377720M	76910M	185699M	1504792M		1994709M	838795M
Total Assets ($)	10729M	57173M	85037M	36021M	60040M	346314M		582220M	422534M

M = $ thousand   MM = $ million
See Pages 11 through 18 for Explanation of Ratios and Data

Comparative Historical Data / Current Data Sorted By Sales

						Type of Statement							
	10		2 10		4 15	Unqualified		9	2 6	2 14	2 5	1 7 5	3 2
	23		22		39	Reviewed		8	15	4	5	5	1
	11		7		31	Compiled		8	15	4	2	1	2
	15		20		27	Tax Returns		4	9	4	3	5	
	4/1/00- 3/31/01		4/1/01- 3/31/02		4/1/02- 3/31/03	Other							
	ALL		ALL		ALL			30 (4/1-9/30/02)		86 (10/1/02-3/31/03)			
								0-1MM	1-3MM	3-5MM	5-10MM	10-25MM	25MM & OVER
	59		61		116	NUMBER OF STATEMENTS		21	32	24	12	19	8
	%		%		%	ASSETS		%	%	%	%	%	%
	10.1		9.2		8.3	Cash & Equivalents		12.8	7.8	8.8	8.4	5.5	
	28.7		27.3		28.8	Trade Receivables (net)		12.9	24.8	33.4	39.8	38.1	
	35.3		35.2		36.0	Inventory		40.7	37.4	32.8	34.7	32.4	
	1.0		2.8		2.0	All Other Current		2.1	2.0	2.5	1.0	1.8	
	75.0		74.6		75.0	Total Current		68.4	72.0	77.4	83.9	77.8	
	14.3		14.6		14.7	Fixed Assets (net)		17.0	20.9	12.0	8.8	10.6	
	1.9		5.3		4.8	Intangibles (net)		8.4	5.4	1.6	2.2	5.4	
	8.7		5.6		5.4	All Other Non-Current		6.2	1.7	9.0	5.1	6.2	
	100.0		100.0		100.0	Total		100.0	100.0	100.0	100.0	100.0	
						LIABILITIES							
	8.8		9.2		13.8	Notes Payable-Short Term		10.2	9.8	16.1	16.7	18.5	
	4.6		4.2		4.2	Cur. Mat.-L/T/D		5.8	5.5	3.6	4.3	2.0	
	28.4		24.1		24.9	Trade Payables		26.5	24.8	26.8	24.8	20.5	
	.3		.4		.2	Income Taxes Payable		.0	.0	.3	.1	.7	
	10.2		9.1		10.4	All Other Current		8.0	11.1	7.1	17.3	10.6	
	52.3		47.0		53.6	Total Current		50.5	51.2	54.0	63.3	52.3	
	15.8		15.3		16.3	Long Term Debt		34.3	18.3	11.3	10.8	6.0	
	.1		.0		.1	Deferred Taxes		.1	.0	.2	.0	.1	
	4.6		4.7		5.0	All Other Non-Current		10.2	2.3	3.2	1.9	6.5	
	27.2		32.9		25.1	Net Worth		4.8	28.2	31.4	23.9	35.1	
	100.0		100.0		100.0	Total Liabilities & Net Worth		100.0	100.0	100.0	100.0	100.0	
						INCOME DATA							
	100.0		100.0		100.0	Net Sales		100.0	100.0	100.0	100.0	100.0	
	35.1		35.6		37.7	Gross Profit		47.4	39.2	36.1	35.8	31.8	
	33.8		34.0		36.1	Operating Expenses		46.1	37.3	35.6	35.3	29.0	
	1.3		1.6		1.6	Operating Profit		1.3	1.9	.6	.6	2.8	
	.3		.4		.4	All Other Expenses (net)		1.6	.5	-.5	-.3	.1	
	1.0		1.2		1.2	Profit Before Taxes		-.3	1.4	1.1	.8	2.7	
						RATIOS							
	2.0		2.2		1.9			2.3	2.0	1.9	1.8	1.9	
	1.5		1.6		1.5	Current		1.3	1.4	1.5	1.3	1.6	
	1.3		1.3		1.1			1.0	1.0	1.2	1.1	1.3	
	1.0		1.2		1.1			1.2	1.3	1.0	1.0	1.2	
	.8		.8		.7	Quick		.6	.5	.8	.8	.9	
	.5		.4		.4			.3	.2	.6	.6	.6	
12	30.6	6	63.4	10	36.8		0	UND	0 UND	21 17.1	16 23.0	19 18.9	
28	13.0	27	13.4	28	13.0	Sales/Receivables	24	15.0	21 17.7	30 12.3	34 10.9	31 12.0	
38	9.5	35	10.3	39	9.4		34	10.8	34 10.8	40 9.2	44 8.2	41 9.0	
23	16.0	23	15.6	22	16.8		37	9.9	23 15.8	19 19.4	18 19.9	14 26.0	
50	7.3	49	7.5	57	6.4	Cost of Sales/Inventory	91	4.0	67 5.4	32 11.3	46 7.9	37 9.9	
112	3.2	114	3.2	114	3.2		147	2.5	119 3.1	122 3.0	86 6.2	73 5.0	
24	15.0	21	17.2	20	18.7		23	16.1	26 14.0	19 19.3	19 18.7	16 23.1	
35	10.4	30	12.3	33	11.2	Cost of Sales/Payables	56	6.5	35 10.5	34 10.8	33 11.1	19 18.8	
54	6.8	45	8.1	52	7.0		119	3.1	41 9.0	55 6.6	39 9.2	34 10.7	
	8.6		7.8		9.5			8.0	9.5	9.2	11.5	10.5	
	14.9		13.9		14.8	Sales/Working Capital		16.3	17.5	11.4	22.5	13.9	
	30.2		23.7		62.6			NM	NM	44.5	138.3	25.6	
	4.8		6.0		6.4			6.6	4.1	5.6	5.1	14.5	
(56)	2.4	(57)	2.3	(109)	2.5	EBIT/Interest	(18)	2.2	(29) 2.2	2.0	(11) 1.2	4.4	
	.9		.9		-.8			-3.4	-3.7	-1.1	-1.6	2.9	
	4.3		1.6		2.5	Net Profit + Depr., Dep.,							
(14)	.9	(15)	.6	(22)	1.4	Amort./Cur. Mat. L/T/D							
	-.3		-.9		.3								
	.2		.2		.2			.3	.3	.1	.2	.2	
	.6		.4		.5	Fixed/Worth		4.2	1.1	.3	.4	.3	
	.9		1.3		4.4			-.6	18.3	1.3	1.0	.7	
	1.1		1.0		1.2			1.5	1.5	1.0	1.7	1.0	
	2.5		2.0		3.0	Debt/Worth		16.6	3.1	1.8	3.1	1.6	
	6.5		7.1		33.7			-2.8	61.3	9.3	-11.4	7.0	
	35.7		32.2		45.2	% Profit Before Taxes/Tangible		369.7	51.0	21.3	20.4	61.2	
(50)	8.6	(55)	11.8	(92)	19.3	Net Worth	(14)	24.9	(25) 24.0	(19) 10.0	(11) 12.0	(18) 32.5	
	-.1		.9		-1.9			-14.9	-7.9	-5.6	-13.7	11.4	
	10.0		10.4		9.9	% Profit Before Taxes/Total		9.0	15.9	6.6	6.4	14.2	
	3.9		3.1		4.2	Assets		2.5	3.5	1.4	.7	7.4	
	-.9		.0		-3.5			-15.5	-6.3	-2.7	-3.3	4.0	
	59.4		74.6		76.8			78.3	43.6	80.8	84.8	90.0	
	30.1		34.9		37.8	Sales/Net Fixed Assets		25.0	22.6	39.5	60.4	56.6	
	16.6		16.4		18.9			9.9	9.9	25.1	39.5	33.2	
	4.9		5.2		5.0			3.5	5.2	4.8	5.2	5.8	
	3.9		3.5		3.6	Sales/Total Assets		2.6	3.6	3.6	4.4	4.8	
	2.8		2.7		2.6			2.4	2.5	2.7	3.3	3.5	
	.4		.4		.5			.8	.6	.6	.3	.5	
(53)	1.0	(56)	.8	(98)	1.0	% Depr., Dep., Amort./Sales	(18)	1.5	(24) 1.5	(21) 1.1	(11) .5	(17) .8	
	1.4		1.2		1.8			3.8	2.7	1.4	1.7	1.1	
	1.6		1.5		1.4			5.1	.8	1.7		1.1	
(30)	3.9	(32)	3.6	(67)	4.1	% Officers', Directors', Owners' Comp/Sales	(13)	6.9	(18) 2.1	(14) 4.5		(10) 2.1	
	6.8		5.9		7.2			11.5	6.5	7.6		3.0	
	525409M		1167853M		2400636M	Net Sales ($)		15374M	58551M	92561M	78018M	297148M	1858984M
	132180M		315885M		595314M	Total Assets ($)		6050M	17840M	26457M	18425M	77605M	448937M

M = $ thousand   MM = $ million
See Pages 11 through 18 for Explanation of Ratios and Data

RETAIL—Gift, Novelty, and Souvenir Stores   NAICS 453220 (SIC 5199, 5947)

Current Data Sorted By Assets   **Comparative Historical Data**

Type of Statement	0-500M	500M-2MM	2-10MM	10-50MM	50-100MM	100-250MM		4/1/98-3/31/99 ALL	4/1/99-3/31/00 ALL
Unqualified		4	3					14	14
Reviewed	3	9	8	3	2	4		27	35
Compiled	26	30	11					68	52
Tax Returns	26	14	4			1		41	39
Other	13	20	10	4		3		47	36
	45 (4/1-9/30/02)			153 (10/1/02-3/31/03)					
NUMBER OF STATEMENTS	68	77	36	7	2	8		197	176
	%	%	%	%	%	%		%	%
ASSETS									
Cash & Equivalents	13.8	12.8	13.8					12.9	13.0
Trade Receivables (net)	3.3	9.5	6.9					5.4	6.7
Inventory	56.9	45.0	36.3					50.8	50.5
All Other Current	1.2	1.8	1.2					1.6	1.3
Total Current	75.2	69.1	58.1					70.8	71.4
Fixed Assets (net)	17.1	19.6	31.0					22.1	19.1
Intangibles (net)	3.3	4.4	4.5					2.4	3.5
All Other Non-Current	4.5	6.8	6.4					4.8	6.0
Total	100.0	100.0	100.0					100.0	100.0
LIABILITIES									
Notes Payable-Short Term	11.3	10.8	7.7					8.4	9.3
Cur. Mat.-L/T/D	7.5	3.6	3.9					2.6	3.3
Trade Payables	15.2	19.2	17.4					13.6	16.8
Income Taxes Payable	.2	.2	.3					.3	.2
All Other Current	16.8	10.8	6.0					12.1	11.3
Total Current	51.0	44.5	35.3					36.9	40.9
Long Term Debt	20.4	16.6	23.1					19.6	18.5
Deferred Taxes	.1	.0	.0					.1	.2
All Other Non-Current	10.0	8.3	3.4					5.9	8.0
Net Worth	18.6	30.5	38.1					37.5	32.4
Total Liabilities & Net Worth	100.0	100.0	100.0					100.0	100.0
INCOME DATA									
Net Sales	100.0	100.0	100.0					100.0	100.0
Gross Profit	47.2	46.4	45.7					47.3	44.9
Operating Expenses	45.5	44.2	40.7					43.0	39.5
Operating Profit	1.7	2.2	5.0					4.3	5.4
All Other Expenses (net)	1.0	.9	1.4					.7	.8
Profit Before Taxes	.7	1.4	3.6					3.6	4.5
RATIOS									
Current	3.6	3.1	3.0					4.2	3.1
	1.7	1.6	1.8					2.2	2.0
	1.0	1.1	1.2					1.3	1.3
Quick	.7	.9	1.0					1.3	.9
	(66) .4	(76) .3	.6					.5	(173) .4
	.1	.1	.2					.1	.1
Sales/Receivables	0 UND	0 UND	0 UND					0 UND	0 UND
	0 UND	1 703.3	0 758.2					0 999.8	0 999.8
	2 208.1	7 50.0	7 54.3					5 75.8	9 41.2
Cost of Sales/Inventory	91 4.0	73 5.0	68 5.3					84 4.3	86 4.3
	175 2.1	124 2.9	103 3.6					129 2.8	127 2.9
	241 1.5	201 1.8	190 1.9					197 1.9	193 1.9
Cost of Sales/Payables	2 186.7	15 25.0	25 14.7					8 45.2	16 23.5
	19 19.5	40 9.1	34 10.6					30 12.1	34 10.9
	67 5.4	67 5.5	79 4.6					55 6.7	60 6.1
Sales/Working Capital	3.7	4.7	5.3					4.5	4.5
	9.1	9.2	9.6					7.5	8.2
	NM	32.2	18.9					16.8	20.2
EBIT/Interest	5.2	10.4	6.0					8.7	8.1
	(57) 1.7	(69) 2.0	(33) 2.9					(177) 2.8	(155) 2.8
	-1.4	-.5	.6					1.3	1.0
Net Profit + Depr., Dep., Amort./Cur. Mat. L /T/D								3.9	4.6
								(27) 2.2	(36) 1.9
								.7	1.0
Fixed/Worth	.1	.2	.3					.2	.2
	.6	.8	.8					.5	.5
	UND	1.8	2.9					1.4	1.6
Debt/Worth	.9	.8	.7					.6	.7
	3.1	2.0	1.6					1.6	2.0
	-8.8	8.3	6.9					4.7	8.6
% Profit Before Taxes/Tangible Net Worth	67.9	41.8	40.7					42.2	46.2
	(49) 23.3	(67) 6.2	(33) 14.4					(175) 16.7	(151) 20.6
	1.8	-7.7	.0					5.2	3.3
% Profit Before Taxes/Total Assets	18.5	10.5	9.9					17.1	17.7
	4.9	2.0	4.1					6.4	7.2
	-3.7	-3.3	-.4					1.2	.0
Sales/Net Fixed Assets	86.2	33.9	17.2					39.9	40.9
	22.2	22.6	9.2					16.6	19.3
	9.4	8.3	4.3					7.3	8.4
Sales/Total Assets	3.1	3.3	2.9					3.3	3.5
	2.5	2.4	2.2					2.4	2.5
	1.9	1.7	1.6					1.9	1.9
% Depr., Dep., Amort./Sales	.7	.7	.9					.8	.7
	(51) 1.3	(63) 1.2	(34) 1.9					(168) 1.4	(154) 1.4
	2.2	2.1	2.8					2.1	2.3
% Officers', Directors', Owners' Comp/Sales	3.1	2.7	.7					3.0	2.9
	(27) 5.6	(44) 4.5	(18) 2.2					(104) 5.4	(88) 4.9
	9.1	7.4	6.4					8.1	8.1
Net Sales ($)	45991M	194590M	333968M	141669M	529566M	3187368M		2962955M	4139316M
Total Assets ($)	17774M	74992M	159962M	98863M	155218M	1403761M		1305614M	1893058M

M = $ thousand   MM = $ million
See Pages 11 through 18 for Explanation of Ratios and Data

Comparative Historical Data | Current Data Sorted By Sales

10	4	16	Type of Statement		1	3	1	5	6
10	4	16	Unqualified		1	3	1	5	6
17	21	20	Reviewed	1	8	5	3	3	
54	38	67	Compiled	20	29	7	8	3	
35	48	45	Tax Returns	23	14	2	5		1
44	53	50	Other	15	13	6	5	7	4
4/1/00-3/31/01 ALL	4/1/01-3/31/02 ALL	4/1/02-3/31/03 ALL		0-1MM	1-3MM	3-5MM	5-10MM	10-25MM	25MM & OVER
				45 (4/1-9/30/02)			**153 (10/1/02-3/31/03)**		
160	164	198	**NUMBER OF STATEMENTS**	59	65	23	22	18	11
%	%	%	**ASSETS**	%	%	%	%	%	%
9.8	10.7	13.5	Cash & Equivalents	13.1	13.3	13.5	11.5	14.1	19.4
8.9	7.1	6.4	Trade Receivables (net)	2.0	9.1	9.3	4.0	11.5	4.1
50.6	52.1	46.8	Inventory	58.3	43.9	42.7	38.6	38.2	40.7
2.1	1.0	1.5	All Other Current	1.5	1.6	1.4	.9	1.5	2.1
71.3	70.8	68.1	Total Current	75.0	67.9	67.0	54.9	65.3	66.2
19.1	20.4	21.8	Fixed Assets (net)	17.3	22.8	21.2	30.3	23.7	21.6
4.7	3.2	4.2	Intangibles (net)	3.3	2.7	6.2	6.2	6.4	6.1
4.9	5.5	5.8	All Other Non-Current	4.4	6.5	5.5	8.5	4.6	6.1
100.0	100.0	100.0	Total	100.0	100.0	100.0	100.0	100.0	100.0
			LIABILITIES						
11.1	13.6	10.4	Notes Payable-Short Term	13.2	10.6	7.3	5.0	12.8	6.8
3.8	2.6	4.8	Cur. Mat.-L/T/D	6.1	5.6	3.3	3.0	3.9	.6
14.9	13.9	17.1	Trade Payables	13.6	19.9	19.1	12.0	22.6	17.2
.3	.3	.2	Income Taxes Payable	.1	.2	.3	.1	.4	1.4
11.3	10.2	12.1	All Other Current	15.1	10.7	12.5	10.7	7.1	15.4
41.3	40.6	44.6	Total Current	48.0	47.0	42.5	30.7	46.8	41.4
22.3	20.5	19.8	Long Term Debt	22.9	19.9	11.3	24.4	14.3	19.7
.1	.1	.1	Deferred Taxes	.1	.0	.1	.0	.1	.5
7.8	6.8	7.4	All Other Non-Current	10.8	6.3	11.5	3.4	3.2	2.3
28.5	32.1	28.1	Net Worth	18.2	26.7	34.6	41.5	35.6	36.1
100.0	100.0	100.0	Total Liabilities & Net Worth	100.0	100.0	100.0	100.0	100.0	100.0
			INCOME DATA						
100.0	100.0	100.0	Net Sales	100.0	100.0	100.0	100.0	100.0	100.0
46.2	45.1	46.7	Gross Profit	48.0	45.0	47.8	47.9	45.7	46.2
42.1	41.8	43.7	Operating Expenses	46.1	42.9	44.1	43.8	41.0	38.3
4.1	3.3	3.0	Operating Profit	1.9	2.2	3.7	4.1	4.6	7.9
1.7	1.3	1.0	All Other Expenses (net)	1.5	.7	.6	1.1	1.2	.7
2.4	2.0	2.0	Profit Before Taxes	.4	1.4	3.1	3.0	3.4	7.2
			RATIOS						
3.1 / 1.9 / 1.3	3.3 / 1.9 / 1.3	3.1 / 1.6 / 1.1	Current	4.3 / 1.7 / 1.0	3.0 / 1.6 / 1.1	3.4 / 2.0 / 1.3	4.1 / 2.0 / 1.2	2.0 / 1.3 / .9	2.2 / 1.8 / 1.0
(158) .9 / .4 / .1	(163) .9 / .4 / .1	(195) .9 / .4 / .1	Quick	(56) .7 / .3 / .0	.9 / .5 / .2	1.7 / .4 / .1	1.1 / .4 / .0	.7 / .5 / .3	1.0 / .8 / .1
0 UND / 0 752.2 / 12 29.5	0 UND / 1 472.6 / 9 40.1	0 UND / 0 UND / 5 77.5	Sales/Receivables	0 UND / 0 UND / 1 282.3	0 UND / 0 999.8 / 5 74.4	0 UND / 1 258.2 / 23 16.2	0 UND / 0 UND / 3 131.2	0 UND / 3 105.7 / 26 14.0	0 UND / 2 238.3 / 9 38.8
82 4.5 / 136 2.7 / 208 1.8	82 4.5 / 128 2.8 / 198 1.8	75 4.9 / 128 2.8 / 212 1.7	Cost of Sales/Inventory	137 2.7 / 192 1.9 / 336 1.1	79 4.6 / 126 2.9 / 204 1.8	62 5.9 / 112 3.3 / 171 2.1	58 6.2 / 90 4.1 / 166 2.2	62 5.9 / 113 3.2 / 149 2.4	65 5.6 / 92 4.0 / 111 3.3
13 27.8 / 29 12.6 / 60 6.1	8 47.2 / 27 13.7 / 54 6.7	11 31.8 / 34 10.6 / 66 5.5	Cost of Sales/Payables	2 218.0 / 22 16.5 / 74 5.0	12 30.1 / 38 9.5 / 77 4.7	30 12.1 / 40 9.1 / 64 5.7	8 47.2 / 24 15.1 / 45 8.2	30 12.3 / 36 10.1 / 90 4.1	17 21.1 / 47 7.8 / 59 6.2
5.1 / 7.5 / 19.0	5.1 / 8.1 / 14.1	4.6 / 9.6 / 37.6	Sales/Working Capital	3.1 / 7.7 / 194.2	5.1 / 9.9 / 42.2	4.3 / 9.6 / 20.1	6.6 / 13.4 / 46.9	7.7 / 12.7 / -140.5	5.8 / 9.7 / 98.2
(146) 5.8 / 2.3 / .6	(141) 5.6 / 2.3 / .2	(176) 7.3 / 2.3 / .2	EBIT/Interest	(51) 5.0 / 1.5 / -1.7	(55) 9.0 / 2.0 / .1	(21) 13.4 / 3.4 / .7	(20) 5.5 / 2.4 / -.7	9.6 / 3.0 / 1.3	191.9 / 15.3 / 6.1
(27) 4.1 / 1.4 / .6	(18) 6.8 / 2.9 / 1.2	(29) 5.8 / 2.0 / .2	Net Profit + Depr., Dep., Amort./Cur. Mat. L/T/D						
.2 / .6 / 3.2	.2 / .6 / 2.5	.2 / .7 / 4.0	Fixed/Worth	.1 / .6 / -2.1	.2 / .9 / 1.8	.2 / .6 / 1.6	.3 / .8 / 2.3	.3 / .6 / 3.0	.3 / .6 / 1.0
.9 / 2.2 / 11.5	.7 / 2.0 / 7.1	.8 / 2.1 / 17.8	Debt/Worth	.8 / 3.2 / -8.3	1.0 / 2.4 / 10.6	.5 / 1.4 / 10.9	.6 / 2.0 / 5.8	1.1 / 1.9 / 7.9	.8 / 1.2 / 2.5
(131) 44.8 / 18.2 / 2.3	(146) 45.8 / 17.0 / -1.0	(165) 48.4 / 16.1 / -1.5	% Profit Before Taxes/Tangible Net Worth	(41) 46.6 / 24.8 / 1.2	(57) 48.4 / 7.6 / -4.3	(19) 41.0 / 8.0 / .0	(20) 41.1 / 10.7 / -10.5	60.6 / 24.0 / -1.4	(10) 76.1 / 47.9 / 27.4
13.7 / 6.1 / -1.1	14.3 / 5.1 / -1.5	15.2 / 3.8 / -2.0	% Profit Before Taxes/Total Assets	17.6 / 2.9 / -11.0	9.8 / 2.1 / -2.3	17.4 / 3.2 / .0	14.1 / 3.4 / -2.3	10.7 / 5.0 / .1	26.9 / 19.3 / 10.9
51.0 / 20.2 / 8.1	44.5 / 17.7 / 7.3	36.4 / 14.9 / 7.6	Sales/Net Fixed Assets	83.8 / 21.6 / 8.2	27.1 / 15.8 / 7.5	59.1 / 14.7 / 7.8	20.6 / 11.4 / 5.5	38.9 / 12.6 / 6.9	25.1 / 10.8 / 8.6
3.4 / 2.5 / 1.7	3.6 / 2.5 / 1.7	3.1 / 2.4 / 1.7	Sales/Total Assets	2.7 / 2.0 / 1.4	3.2 / 2.5 / 1.7	3.7 / 2.7 / 1.9	3.6 / 2.4 / 1.9	3.1 / 2.3 / 1.7	3.0 / 2.5 / 2.0
(137) .6 / 1.4 / 2.3	(135) .6 / 1.3 / 2.2	(162) .8 / 1.4 / 2.4	% Depr., Dep., Amort./Sales	(42) .6 / 1.3 / 2.5	(55) .8 / 1.2 / 2.2	(19) .9 / 1.5 / 2.1	(20) .7 / 1.7 / 2.4	.5 / 1.4 / 2.8	
(79) 3.2 / 4.8 / 8.1	(80) 2.0 / 4.4 / 8.7	(90) 2.5 / 4.5 / 7.6	% Officers', Directors', Owners' Comp/Sales	(24) 3.3 / 5.9 / 8.2	(33) 2.7 / 4.2 / 6.4	(15) 2.5 / 5.6 / 6.5	(11) .8 / 2.0 / 6.5		
2382520M / 1324290M	3586902M / 1929581M	4433152M / 1910570M	Net Sales ($) / Total Assets ($)	29596M / 16881M	107190M / 51247M	87600M / 44049M	169985M / 82896M	285855M / 144137M	3752926M / 1571360M

M = $ thousand   MM = $ million
See Pages 11 through 18 for Explanation of Ratios and Data

Current Data Sorted By Assets / Comparative Historical Data

	0-500M	500M-2MM	2-10MM	10-50MM	50-100MM	100-250MM		4/1/98-3/31/99 ALL	4/1/99-3/31/00 ALL
		8 (4/1-9/30/02)		59 (10/1/02-3/31/03)			Type of Statement		
Unqualified			2	1		1		9	4
Reviewed		1	4	1				15	13
Compiled	6	8	8	1				38	29
Tax Returns	7	6	2					17	12
Other	9	6	2	1		2		26	27
NUMBER OF STATEMENTS	22	21	18	3		3		105	85
	%	%	%	%	%	%	**ASSETS**	%	%
Cash & Equivalents	10.4	12.0	7.6					10.2	7.2
Trade Receivables (net)	13.3	19.8	7.3					17.3	15.6
Inventory	53.1	27.6	50.5		D			41.6	45.4
All Other Current	2.6	11.5	4.9		A			2.4	4.7
Total Current	79.4	71.0	70.3		T			71.5	72.9
Fixed Assets (net)	17.3	24.0	20.3		A			21.9	19.2
Intangibles (net)	1.2	.9	.7		N			2.2	3.8
All Other Non-Current	2.2	4.1	8.7		O			4.4	4.1
Total	100.0	100.0	100.0		T			100.0	100.0
					A		**LIABILITIES**		
Notes Payable-Short Term	13.7	22.1	20.3		V			16.7	17.1
Cur. Mat.-L/T/D	1.5	.5	1.4		A			2.5	3.3
Trade Payables	8.0	5.4	4.8		I			10.3	9.6
Income Taxes Payable	.3	.0	.0		L			.2	.1
All Other Current	10.1	12.9	8.5		A			12.5	12.8
Total Current	33.7	41.0	35.2		B			42.2	42.9
Long Term Debt	8.2	12.5	24.8		L			15.9	15.4
Deferred Taxes	.0	.0	.0		E			.0	.1
All Other Non-Current	14.6	7.7	3.1					7.7	3.8
Net Worth	43.6	38.9	36.9					34.1	37.9
Total Liabilities & Net Worth	100.0	100.0	100.0					100.0	100.0
							INCOME DATA		
Net Sales	100.0	100.0	100.0					100.0	100.0
Gross Profit	49.6	60.4	57.5					46.7	50.0
Operating Expenses	43.4	49.0	52.8					40.7	43.7
Operating Profit	6.3	11.4	4.7					6.0	6.3
All Other Expenses (net)	1.7	1.9	3.5					1.1	-1.5
Profit Before Taxes	4.5	9.5	1.2					4.8	7.8
							RATIOS		
Current	20.5	10.7	6.8					4.2	3.2
	5.0	6.0	2.3					1.9	1.8
	1.3	1.5	1.3					1.3	1.2
Quick	9.4	9.9	1.8					1.7	1.2
	(21) .8	(20) 3.2	(16) .4					(84) .7	.6
	.2	.8	.1					.2	.2
Sales/Receivables	0 UND	0 UND	0 UND					0 UND	0 UND
	0 UND	16 22.3	9 40.5					13 29.1	18 20.0
	53 6.9	83 4.4	32 11.3					65 5.6	55 6.6
Cost of Sales/Inventory	87 4.2	35 10.5	145 2.5					53 6.9	104 3.5
	164 2.2	131 2.8	318 1.1					161 2.3	197 1.9
	305 1.2	265 1.4	1203 .3					258 1.4	308 1.2
Cost of Sales/Payables	0 UND	0 UND	4 97.6					0 UND	3 124.8
	0 UND	6 58.1	16 23.5					13 28.9	19 19.6
	45 8.2	45 8.1	49 7.5					39 9.4	41 8.9
Sales/Working Capital	1.9	1.7	1.5					2.8	2.7
	3.3	4.3	2.2					8.3	6.2
	13.6	13.2	7.1					33.2	19.4
EBIT/Interest	16.2	10.2	5.9					10.6	10.2
	(19) 3.7	(18) 4.2	(17) 2.4					(94) 3.4	(80) 3.7
	.6	2.6	.9					1.3	1.7
Net Profit + Depr., Dep., Amort./Cur. Mat. L /T/D								76.7	3.4
								(16) 4.1	(13) 1.9
								.9	.4
Fixed/Worth	.0	.0	.1					.1	.1
	.2	.1	.3					.5	.4
	1.1	1.1	.8					1.8	1.0
Debt/Worth	.3	.2	.4					.7	.6
	1.0	1.0	1.2					1.7	1.7
	10.7	3.1	4.8					14.0	6.0
% Profit Before Taxes/Tangible Net Worth	38.4	34.3	27.5					58.9	60.2
	(18) 22.5	(20) 18.9	(16) 9.3					(85) 22.8	(77) 27.6
	9.8	11.1	-.1					11.1	7.2
% Profit Before Taxes/Total Assets	20.3	15.0	6.5					21.0	15.9
	11.8	8.8	2.9					7.6	8.0
	.0	6.8	-.3					1.9	2.7
Sales/Net Fixed Assets	93.7	62.1	32.0					51.6	36.4
	21.5	26.5	10.7					17.0	15.3
	9.9	8.9	4.6					7.2	5.6
Sales/Total Assets	3.8	3.3	1.4					3.7	2.4
	1.9	1.5	.9					1.9	1.6
	1.5	1.0	.6					1.2	1.0
% Depr., Dep., Amort./Sales	(14) .5	(15) .2	(17) .5					(76) .7	(62) .5
	1.5	.5	1.3					1.4	1.4
	2.6	1.6	1.8					2.6	2.3
% Officers', Directors', Owners' Comp/Sales		(11) 5.4	(10) 2.8					(44) 3.0	(39) 3.0
		10.4	9.4					5.5	7.0
		13.9	11.9					8.8	10.2
Net Sales ($)	11325M	52633M	89906M	56714M		854165M		2031423M	647080M
Total Assets ($)	5669M	20651M	73487M	35333M		537556M		814574M	577114M

© RMA 2003

M = $ thousand   MM = $ million
See Pages 11 through 18 for Explanation of Ratios and Data

Comparative Historical Data | | | Current Data Sorted By Sales

			Type of Statement						
6	7	4	Unqualified			1	1	1	1
6	7	5	Reviewed		2	1	1	1	
32	31	23	Compiled	7	9	1	4	2	
16	20	15	Tax Returns	9	2	3	1		
23	30	20	Other	12	4	1		1	2
4/1/00-3/31/01	4/1/01-3/31/02	4/1/02-3/31/03		8 (4/1-9/30/02)			59 (10/1/02-3/31/03)		
ALL	ALL	ALL		0-1MM	1-3MM	3-5MM	5-10MM	10-25MM	25MM & OVER
83	95	67	NUMBER OF STATEMENTS	28	17	7	7	5	3
%	%	%	ASSETS	%	%	%	%	%	%
6.9	7.8	9.8	Cash & Equivalents	8.5	15.1				
13.9	13.4	14.1	Trade Receivables (net)	16.1	11.8				
46.5	42.7	41.5	Inventory	43.3	53.5				
5.2	5.0	7.2	All Other Current	8.3	4.2				
72.5	68.9	72.6	Total Current	76.2	84.6				
17.3	20.7	20.4	Fixed Assets (net)	20.5	8.2				
3.2	5.2	1.9	Intangibles (net)	.9	1.6				
7.0	5.2	5.0	All Other Non-Current	2.4	5.6				
100.0	100.0	100.0	Total	100.0	100.0				
			LIABILITIES						
20.2	17.7	17.6	Notes Payable-Short Term	11.9	15.8				
2.5	2.1	1.2	Cur. Mat.-L/T/D	.6	1.8				
8.0	4.5	6.2	Trade Payables	4.8	8.9				
.1	.1	.1	Income Taxes Payable	.3	.0				
9.4	11.1	10.2	All Other Current	8.5	12.2				
40.3	35.5	35.4	Total Current	25.9	38.7				
11.4	16.8	14.4	Long Term Debt	12.5	4.7				
.1	.1	.0	Deferred Taxes	.0	.0				
5.9	7.9	8.5	All Other Non-Current	11.6	8.4				
42.3	39.7	41.7	Net Worth	49.9	48.2				
100.0	100.0	100.0	Total Liabilities & Net Worth	100.0	100.0				
			INCOME DATA						
100.0	100.0	100.0	Net Sales	100.0	100.0				
48.7	51.4	55.7	Gross Profit	56.0	53.3				
43.2	43.2	48.0	Operating Expenses	45.6	50.4				
5.5	8.1	7.7	Operating Profit	10.4	3.0				
.0	3.1	2.1	All Other Expenses (net)	2.3	1.5				
5.5	5.0	5.5	Profit Before Taxes	8.1	1.4				
			RATIOS						
4.2	5.2	8.3		16.4	6.5				
1.9	2.5	3.7	Current	6.2	2.6				
1.3	1.3	1.4		2.2	1.4				
1.4	1.5	3.8		11.1	3.0				
(93) .5	(93) .7	(63) 1.1	Quick	(27) 1.4	(16) .9				
.2	.1	.2		.2	.2				
0 UND	0 UND	0 UND		0 UND	0 UND				
7 53.3	8 46.4	11 34.5	Sales/Receivables	0 UND	16 22.3				
63 5.8	65 5.6	59 6.1		75 4.9	77 4.7				
82 4.4	102 3.6	70 5.2		109 3.4	186 2.0				
185 2.0	184 2.0	165 2.2	Cost of Sales/Inventory	162 2.3	294 1.2				
371 1.0	299 1.2	332 1.1		321 1.1	638 .6				
0 UND	0 UND	0 UND		0 UND	2 171.0				
15 23.9	6 56.3	11 34.1	Cost of Sales/Payables	0 UND	13 28.1				
43 8.4	34 10.6	47 7.8		42 8.7	60 6.0				
2.5	2.0	1.8		1.8	1.6				
5.3	5.2	2.9	Sales/Working Capital	2.7	2.1				
23.2	27.0	10.1		9.3	5.1				
7.7	6.7	10.6		10.9	5.4				
(75) 3.5	(85) 2.2	(59) 3.8	EBIT/Interest	(25) 3.8	(16) 3.5				
1.5	.9	1.6		1.7	1.2				
	3.3		Net Profit + Depr., Dep.,						
	(10) 1.1		Amort./Cur. Mat. L/T/D						
	.4								
.1	.1	.1		.1	.0				
.3	.5	.2	Fixed/Worth	.2	.1				
.8	1.2	1.1		1.3	.3				
.6	.5	.3		.3	.5				
1.5	1.5	1.0	Debt/Worth	.8	1.0				
3.5	5.3	4.2		2.7	3.4				
34.3	41.3	33.6	% Profit Before Taxes/Tangible	33.6	34.1				
(78) 17.6	(82) 20.0	(59) 16.8	Net Worth	(24) 18.9	15.0				
4.0	4.3	8.5		8.4	.9				
13.4	15.0	16.7	% Profit Before Taxes/Total	19.3	13.3				
5.8	6.6	8.0	Assets	9.5	7.1				
1.6	.0	2.2		3.6	.8				
74.8	42.4	51.2		57.6	335.2				
19.5	14.6	15.9	Sales/Net Fixed Assets	18.5	28.3				
8.6	6.7	6.9		9.6	6.7				
2.7	2.4	2.2		2.0	2.0				
1.7	1.5	1.5	Sales/Total Assets	1.6	1.1				
1.0	1.1	1.0		1.1	.8				
.5	.5	.4		.4	.4				
(55) .9	(73) 1.0	(51) 1.2	% Depr., Dep., Amort./Sales	(16) 1.5	(14) .5				
1.9	2.2	2.5		2.8	1.4				
3.7	3.4	3.3	% Officers', Directors',	2.3	9.1				
(37) 7.6	(43) 6.0	(32) 9.1	Owners' Comp/Sales	(11) 7.9	(11) 10.8				
10.6	10.6	11.5		10.9	16.3				
2215733M	1218085M	1064743M	Net Sales ($)	14444M	31591M	25541M	47416M	91586M	854165M
1149832M	912133M	672696M	Total Assets ($)	10983M	34910M	23666M	21726M	43855M	537556M

© RMA 2003   M = $ thousand   MM = $ million
See Pages 11 through 18 for Explanation of Ratios and Data

Current Data Sorted By Assets   Comparative Historical Data

Type of Statement

	0-500M	500M-2MM	2-10MM	10-50MM	50-100MM	100-250MM	Type of Statement	ALL 4/1/98-3/31/99	ALL 4/1/99-3/31/00
		1	1	4	1		Unqualified	4	7
	10	6	6				Reviewed	16	30
	4	43	16	1		1	Compiled	71	78
	2	12	2	1			Tax Returns	16	18
		16	5	1			Other	36	25
		20 (4/1-9/30/02)		112 (10/1/02-3/31/03)					
NUMBER OF STATEMENTS	16	78	30	6	1	1		143	158

ASSETS

	0-500M %	500M-2MM %	2-10MM %	10-50MM %	50-100MM %	100-250MM %		ALL %	ALL %
Cash & Equivalents	9.9	9.6	8.5					10.0	8.1
Trade Receivables (net)	4.2	6.1	9.1					7.1	4.9
Inventory	53.5	58.9	49.5					55.8	61.5
All Other Current	5.4	3.8	2.0					2.2	2.9
Total Current	72.9	78.4	69.1					75.2	77.4
Fixed Assets (net)	15.6	13.0	23.0					16.7	15.6
Intangibles (net)	.0	1.1	.4					1.1	1.8
All Other Non-Current	11.5	7.5	7.5					7.0	5.3
Total	100.0	100.0	100.0					100.0	100.0

LIABILITIES

	0-500M	500M-2MM	2-10MM	10-50MM	50-100MM	100-250MM		ALL	ALL
Notes Payable-Short Term	31.6	38.9	32.1					40.2	44.8
Cur. Mat.-L/T/D	.2	1.7	4.2					2.4	2.3
Trade Payables	2.5	4.6	4.6					5.1	5.1
Income Taxes Payable	.0	.1	.1					.2	.1
All Other Current	12.7	11.5	8.7					10.1	10.1
Total Current	47.0	56.7	49.7					57.9	62.3
Long Term Debt	15.9	8.3	14.7					11.7	8.3
Deferred Taxes	.0	.0	.1					.0	.0
All Other Non-Current	8.2	5.5	5.8					4.3	2.9
Net Worth	28.9	29.4	29.7					26.1	26.5
Total Liabilities & Net Worth	100.0	100.0	100.0					100.0	100.0

INCOME DATA

	0-500M	500M-2MM	2-10MM	10-50MM	50-100MM	100-250MM		ALL	ALL
Net Sales	100.0	100.0	100.0					100.0	100.0
Gross Profit	26.7	23.7	23.8					25.0	22.7
Operating Expenses	21.6	22.6	22.3					22.1	20.3
Operating Profit	5.2	1.1	1.5					2.9	2.4
All Other Expenses (net)	1.0	.3	.4					-.5	-.2
Profit Before Taxes	4.1	.8	1.1					3.4	2.6

RATIOS

	0-500M	500M-2MM	2-10MM	10-50MM	50-100MM	100-250MM		ALL	ALL
Current	2.6	1.9	2.0					1.8	1.6
	1.6	1.3	1.2					1.2	1.2
	1.1	1.0	1.1					1.0	1.0
Quick	.9	.5	.6					.6	.4
	.3	.2	.3				(157)	.2	.2
	.1	.1	.2					.1	.1
Sales/Receivables	0 UND	0 UND	5 78.7					1 601.2	0 UND
	1 645.9	3 111.5	11 34.4					3 107.9	3 130.5
	10 35.9	16 22.8	20 17.9					11 32.3	10 36.1
Cost of Sales/Inventory	52 7.0	85 4.3	92 4.0					72 5.0	80 4.5
	137 2.7	137 2.7	130 2.8					112 3.3	118 3.1
	206 1.8	181 2.0	162 2.3					170 2.2	165 2.2
Cost of Sales/Payables	0 UND	0 UND	1 471.1					0 819.5	1 521.2
	0 UND	2 159.1	9 42.8					3 106.7	4 88.0
	4 93.9	8 44.6	18 20.4					11 34.2	9 38.4
Sales/Working Capital	4.4	5.6	5.1					7.0	8.7
	9.0	12.3	13.4					19.9	19.8
	195.1	88.4	70.8					142.7	147.7
EBIT/Interest	17.2	2.8	5.0					3.6	3.5
	(14) 2.6	(72) 1.5	(27) 1.3				(134)	2.1	(151) 1.8
	-.5	-.1	.7					1.2	1.1
Net Profit + Depr., Dep., Amort./Cur. Mat. L/T/D								6.3	3.3
							(17)	2.4	(19) 1.2
								1.6	.7
Fixed/Worth	.0	.2	.2					.2	.2
	.3	.4	.6					.6	.7
	NM	1.2	2.1					1.5	1.4
Debt/Worth	1.2	1.1	1.0					1.1	1.7
	1.5	3.5	2.7					3.8	4.1
	NM	8.0	8.2					10.7	12.5
% Profit Before Taxes/Tangible Net Worth	93.3	37.4	26.6					49.1	48.0
	(12) 27.2	(68) 8.1	(28) 8.3				(128)	23.2	(141) 19.5
	1.0	-5.1	-3.2					5.8	5.0
% Profit Before Taxes/Total Assets	32.5	6.4	8.5					12.0	10.3
	8.2	2.0	1.4					4.6	4.3
	-2.6	-2.6	-1.5					1.0	.8
Sales/Net Fixed Assets	396.9	75.6	28.6					52.4	60.4
	45.9	24.9	14.9					26.2	23.3
	13.4	11.2	4.8					9.4	10.7
Sales/Total Assets	3.5	3.1	2.6					3.3	3.4
	2.4	1.9	2.1					2.4	2.4
	1.4	1.6	1.3					1.6	1.7
% Depr., Dep., Amort./Sales	.2	.4	.4					.4	.4
	(12) .4	(66) .8	1.0				(124)	.7	(138) .7
	1.5	1.3	2.2					1.2	1.2
% Officers', Directors', Owners' Comp/Sales		1.8	1.0					1.4	1.6
	(44)	2.4	(18) 1.4				(73)	2.9	(75) 2.4
		4.4	5.5					4.8	4.8
Net Sales ($)	16041M	190465M	217836M	153270M	22516M	17324M		768667M	1029571M
Total Assets ($)	5437M	86327M	104772M	100037M	74780M	141477M		333233M	443840M

Comparative Historical Data | Current Data Sorted By Sales

4/1/00-3/31/01 ALL	4/1/01-3/31/02 ALL	4/1/02-3/31/03 ALL	Type of Statement	0-1MM	1-3MM	3-5MM	5-10MM	10-25MM	25MM & OVER
7	4	7	Unqualified		1		2	2	2
30	25	12	Reviewed		9		2		1
56	68	71	Compiled	7	35	13	10	5	1
17	20	18	Tax Returns	4	10	2	2		
33	30	24	Other	3	11	4	3	2	1
				20 (4/1-9/30/02)			112 (10/1/02-3/31/03)		
143	147	132	NUMBER OF STATEMENTS	14	66	19	19	9	5
%	%	%	ASSETS	%	%	%	%	%	%
6.1	8.7	9.1	Cash & Equivalents	8.0	8.7	11.3	12.5		
6.4	5.7	7.0	Trade Receivables (net)	8.8	5.7	4.6	5.6		
58.1	57.8	54.7	Inventory	50.0	56.3	64.9	50.5		
2.5	3.1	3.5	All Other Current	3.2	3.5	3.6	4.5		
73.1	75.3	74.2	Total Current	70.0	74.2	84.4	73.1		
19.2	15.6	16.9	Fixed Assets (net)	17.6	15.9	12.2	19.1		
2.0	2.1	1.1	Intangibles (net)	.0	1.2	.8	.0		
5.6	7.1	7.7	All Other Non-Current	12.4	8.7	2.6	7.8		
100.0	100.0	100.0	Total	100.0	100.0	100.0	100.0		
			LIABILITIES						
37.9	42.0	36.0	Notes Payable-Short Term	33.9	36.5	42.5	34.4		
3.6	3.2	2.1	Cur. Mat.-L/T/D	.4	2.9	.7	.4		
6.0	5.4	4.3	Trade Payables	.5	5.0	4.3	3.8		
.1	.1	.1	Income Taxes Payable	.0	.0	.0	.2		
8.1	9.7	11.5	All Other Current	7.9	11.6	9.9	10.5		
55.8	60.5	54.0	Total Current	42.7	56.0	57.4	49.3		
9.7	9.4	11.0	Long Term Debt	21.5	11.7	4.9	5.6		
.1	.1	.0	Deferred Taxes	.0	.0	.0	.0		
5.1	6.0	5.9	All Other Non-Current	3.5	9.2	2.8	1.7		
29.2	24.1	29.0	Net Worth	32.3	23.1	34.9	43.3		
100.0	100.0	100.0	Total Liabilities & Net Worth	100.0	100.0	100.0	100.0		
			INCOME DATA						
100.0	100.0	100.0	Net Sales	100.0	100.0	100.0	100.0		
24.7	22.0	24.6	Gross Profit	27.7	25.1	21.8	24.4		
22.8	20.6	22.7	Operating Expenses	23.6	23.5	21.2	22.3		
1.9	1.4	1.9	Operating Profit	4.1	1.6	.5	2.1		
.0	.7	.7	All Other Expenses (net)	3.1	.6	-1.1	-.5		
1.9	.8	1.3	Profit Before Taxes	1.0	1.0	1.6	2.7		
			RATIOS						
1.9	1.6	2.1		2.7	1.9	2.0	2.5		
1.2	1.2	1.3	Current	1.5	1.3	1.2	1.2		
1.0	1.0	1.0		.9	1.0	1.1	1.0		
.4	.5	.6		.9	.6	.3	.9		
(141) .2	(146) .2	.2	Quick	.2	.2	.2	.3		
.1	.1	.1		.0	.1	.1	.2		
1 703.9	0 999.8	0 999.8		0 UND	0 UND	0 914.4	2 230.3		
3 110.8	4 84.2	5 68.6	Sales/Receivables	2 180.0	4 99.1	2 173.5	6 57.5		
16 23.3	13 27.9	17 21.1		11 32.4	17 21.0	12 29.5	17 21.6		
85 4.3	84 4.4	84 4.3		113 3.2	96 3.8	85 4.3	50 7.3		
131 2.8	120 3.1	135 2.7	Cost of Sales/Inventory	250 1.5	151 2.4	126 2.9	97 3.8		
191 1.9	179 2.0	179 2.0		458 .8	188 1.9	177 2.1	139 2.6		
1 410.5	0 999.8	0 UND		0 UND	0 UND	0 999.8	1 537.1		
4 95.2	3 127.8	3 104.3	Cost of Sales/Payables	0 UND	2 173.1	4 88.5	6 60.0		
12 30.7	10 35.5	11 32.3		3 124.8	11 32.4	15 24.6	12 30.3		
6.6	7.7	5.4		2.3	6.0	5.2	6.9		
16.0	22.0	12.3	Sales/Working Capital	4.8	10.7	17.7	14.9		
131.5	-999.8	105.0		-33.7	160.3	34.0	-999.8		
3.4	3.1	4.1		4.3	2.5	7.4	11.5		
(134) 1.6	(137) 1.4	(120) 1.6	EBIT/Interest	(12) 2.0	(63) 1.4	(16) 1.7	(16) 3.6		
.8	.7	.5		-.5	-.4	.6	1.3		
5.8	7.7	5.1	Net Profit + Depr., Dep.,						
(19) 1.7	(18) 1.9	(11) 1.1	Amort./Cur. Mat. L/T/D						
1.0	.4	-.6							
.2	.2	.2		.0	.2	.1	.1		
.6	.6	.4	Fixed/Worth	.4	.5	.4	.3		
1.5	1.7	1.6		1.3	10.0	.8	1.0		
1.3	1.6	1.1		1.0	1.4	.8	.4		
3.3	3.8	2.9	Debt/Worth	1.4	4.1	2.5	2.0		
8.7	16.5	7.9		8.5	180.7	7.2	3.5		
38.7	37.9	37.3	% Profit Before Taxes/Tangible	59.7	41.9	33.3	32.8		
(125) 9.4	(126) 10.2	(115) 9.0	Net Worth	(13) 1.2	(51) 6.4	11.6	19.7		
.5	-5.1	-1.7		-18.6	-13.4	-3.0	2.3		
8.0	8.1	7.5	% Profit Before Taxes/Total	10.8	5.8	9.4	14.2		
2.6	1.8	2.1	Assets	.7	1.7	5.1	4.8		
-.8	-1.8	-1.2		-4.4	-4.2	-.9	.6		
46.0	54.0	68.0		UND	67.2	106.0	64.3		
19.4	20.4	21.6	Sales/Net Fixed Assets	10.7	24.2	32.0	22.1		
7.4	9.5	8.8		2.5	10.6	9.0	10.6		
3.0	3.1	2.8		1.9	2.6	3.3	3.7		
2.1	2.3	2.0	Sales/Total Assets	.8	1.8	2.3	2.4		
1.5	1.6	1.4		.6	1.4	1.8	1.9		
.4	.4	.4			.4	.4	.5		
(130) .8	(134) .7	(116) .8	% Depr., Dep., Amort./Sales	(58) .8	(18) .7	(17) .8			
2.0	1.6	1.5			1.4	1.4	1.2		
1.4	1.6	1.4	% Officers', Directors',		1.9	1.8	.9		
(57) 2.3	(70) 2.8	(67) 2.3	Owners' Comp/Sales	(35) 3.4	(12) 2.1	(10) 1.3			
4.2	4.4	4.9			5.8	3.1	3.4		
1045708M	884236M	617452M	Net Sales ($)	7173M	122486M	72692M	129820M	135087M	150194M
651580M	434120M	512830M	Total Assets ($)	8443M	70339M	32037M	69201M	257796M	75014M

M = $ thousand   MM = $ million
See Pages 11 through 18 for Explanation of Ratios and Data

RETAIL—Tobacco Stores NAICS 453991 (SIC 5194, 5199, 5993)

Current Data Sorted By Assets | **Comparative Historical Data**

Type of Statement

0-500M	500M-2MM	2-10MM	10-50MM	50-100MM	100-250MM	Type of Statement	4/1/98-3/31/99 ALL	4/1/99-3/31/00 ALL
					1	Unqualified	1	2
	1	1	1			Reviewed	7	2
3	1	2				Compiled	11	7
6	1	1				Tax Returns	3	5
2		2				Other	9	9
	3 (4/1-9/30/02)		19 (10/1/02-3/31/03)					
11	3	6	1		1	NUMBER OF STATEMENTS	31	25

ASSETS

0-500M %	500M-2MM %	2-10MM %	10-50MM %	50-100MM %	100-250MM %		%	%
15.8						Cash & Equivalents	10.6	13.7
10.0				D		Trade Receivables (net)	8.9	9.6
44.0				A		Inventory	42.4	43.6
2.1				T		All Other Current	2.2	1.7
71.9				A		Total Current	64.1	68.6
18.3						Fixed Assets (net)	26.3	23.3
3.5				N		Intangibles (net)	4.7	4.5
6.3				O		All Other Non-Current	4.9	3.5
100.0				T		Total	100.0	100.0

LIABILITIES

0-500M	500M-2MM	2-10MM	10-50MM	50-100MM	100-250MM			
6.8				A		Notes Payable-Short Term	10.4	6.7
12.0				V		Cur. Mat.-L/T/D	2.7	2.1
31.6				A		Trade Payables	22.2	16.5
.0				I		Income Taxes Payable	.5	.1
14.8				L		All Other Current	7.4	18.4
65.2				A		Total Current	43.2	43.8
26.0				B		Long Term Debt	17.5	21.6
.0				L		Deferred Taxes	.0	.0
10.5				E		All Other Non-Current	7.3	4.2
−1.7						Net Worth	32.0	30.4
100.0						Total Liabilities & Net Worth	100.0	100.0

INCOME DATA

0-500M	500M-2MM	2-10MM	10-50MM	50-100MM	100-250MM			
100.0						Net Sales	100.0	100.0
30.9						Gross Profit	28.5	22.6
32.1						Operating Expenses	23.6	20.1
−1.1						Operating Profit	4.9	2.5
.6						All Other Expenses (net)	.6	.1
−1.7						Profit Before Taxes	4.3	2.4

RATIOS

0-500M	500M-2MM	2-10MM	10-50MM	50-100MM	100-250MM		4/1/98-3/31/99	4/1/99-3/31/00
1.4						Current	2.3	3.4
1.3							1.6	1.6
.5							1.2	1.2
1.2						Quick	.9	1.3
.3							.4	.7
.0							.2	.2
0 UND						Sales/Receivables	1 442.3	1 247.3
1 289.1							5 73.1	5 71.0
13 28.7							12 31.0	7 49.4
14 26.6						Cost of Sales/Inventory	26 14.1	18 20.8
33 11.1							55 6.6	33 11.1
77 4.7							129 2.8	67 5.4
13 28.4						Cost of Sales/Payables	14 25.2	1 280.3
22 16.7							27 13.4	13 27.0
79 4.6							37 9.9	22 16.9
15.0						Sales/Working Capital	6.2	8.0
51.3							15.2	27.4
−13.3							50.8	63.2
						EBIT/Interest	(29) 8.4	(21) 8.4
							4.0	4.8
							1.6	1.5
						Net Profit + Depr., Dep., Amort./Cur. Mat. L /T/D		
.1						Fixed/Worth	.2	.3
−4.5							.9	.7
−.5							2.0	2.3
3.8						Debt/Worth	1.1	1.0
−11.0							2.3	2.4
−4.8							5.9	7.9
						% Profit Before Taxes/Tangible Net Worth	(27) 55.4	(20) 69.0
							27.2	41.0
							11.6	25.5
14.9						% Profit Before Taxes/Total Assets	16.8	21.4
−7.1							6.9	14.2
−18.5							3.8	3.2
222.3						Sales/Net Fixed Assets	45.9	88.8
133.9							18.5	27.4
12.7							7.9	9.6
9.2						Sales/Total Assets	5.8	8.1
4.6							3.2	5.0
3.1							1.7	2.9
						% Depr., Dep., Amort./Sales	(28) .4	(22) .3
							.7	.5
							1.5	.8
						% Officers', Directors', Owners' Comp/Sales	(13) 1.3	
							3.9	
							7.7	
16759M	19546M	114608M	86666M		342712M	Net Sales ($)	315190M	1123375M
3123M	4517M	20905M	10506M		102713M	Total Assets ($)	117846M	250572M

M = $ thousand   MM = $ million
See Pages 11 through 18 for Explanation of Ratios and Data

Comparative Historical Data

Current Data Sorted By Sales

				Type of Statement						
	2	2		Unqualified			1		1	
	1	2		Reviewed				1	1	
6	8	6		Compiled	2	1		2	1	
3	4	8		Tax Returns	1	6		1		
4	3	4		Other		1	1	2		
4/1/00-3/31/01	4/1/01-3/31/02	4/1/02-3/31/03				3 (4/1-9/30/02)		19 (10/1/02-3/31/03)		
ALL	ALL	ALL			0-1MM	1-3MM	3-5MM	5-10MM	10-25MM	25MM & OVER
13	18	22		NUMBER OF STATEMENTS	3	8	1	1	6	3
%	%	%		ASSETS	%	%	%	%	%	%
8.6	7.4	12.0		Cash & Equivalents						
9.2	10.7	10.2		Trade Receivables (net)						
57.8	51.6	47.9		Inventory						
1.4	1.5	3.4		All Other Current						
77.0	71.2	73.5		Total Current						
18.5	22.4	19.2		Fixed Assets (net)						
.7	1.1	3.2		Intangibles (net)						
3.8	5.3	4.0		All Other Non-Current						
100.0	100.0	100.0		Total						
				LIABILITIES						
26.2	12.6	12.0		Notes Payable-Short Term						
5.5	7.0	7.9		Cur. Mat.-L/T/D						
28.5	21.4	27.3		Trade Payables						
.1	.0	.0		Income Taxes Payable						
11.0	6.6	10.0		All Other Current						
71.3	47.6	57.3		Total Current						
12.5	16.9	20.6		Long Term Debt						
.0	.3	.0		Deferred Taxes						
6.7	6.2	6.5		All Other Non-Current						
9.5	26.3	15.7		Net Worth						
100.0	100.0	100.0		Total Liabilities & Net Worth						
				INCOME DATA						
100.0	100.0	100.0		Net Sales						
22.4	22.7	25.8		Gross Profit						
23.9	20.8	24.5		Operating Expenses						
−1.5	1.9	1.2		Operating Profit						
.7	−.1	.4		All Other Expenses (net)						
−2.1	2.0	.9		Profit Before Taxes						
				RATIOS						
1.8	3.4	1.9								
.9	1.4	1.3		Current						
.9	1.0	.9								
.6	1.0	.9								
.2	.5	.3		Quick						
.0	.1	.1								
0 UND	0 UND	1 383.0								
1 422.0	3 115.4	3 120.4		Sales/Receivables						
15 24.5	11 32.5	12 29.9								
24 15.4	28 13.0	25 14.7								
56 6.5	33 11.1	41 9.0		Cost of Sales/Inventory						
148 2.5	92 4.0	71 5.2								
11 34.3	3 130.8	12 31.6								
18 20.5	23 15.8	21 17.6		Cost of Sales/Payables						
37 10.0	28 13.1	40 9.2								
17.1	9.4	12.2								
−97.3	31.9	49.8		Sales/Working Capital						
−57.6	UND	−67.4								
3.5	17.0	11.6								
(12) 1.3	(16) 3.9	(18) 4.7		EBIT/Interest						
−.5	.9	1.2								
				Net Profit + Depr., Dep., Amort./Cur. Mat. L/T/D						
.8	.1	.3								
1.2	.9	1.0		Fixed/Worth						
−2.9	UND	−1.8								
2.1	.9	1.4								
9.5	2.5	6.3		Debt/Worth						
−36.2	UND	−10.1								
	175.0	97.8		% Profit Before Taxes/Tangible Net Worth						
(15)	44.4	(14) 35.3								
	12.4	15.1								
5.6	15.8	14.0		% Profit Before Taxes/Total Assets						
1.2	10.3	8.5								
−11.9	−.2	−8.6								
116.5	93.9	171.3								
47.1	31.9	50.1		Sales/Net Fixed Assets						
10.5	10.6	14.6								
7.5	8.3	7.7								
4.5	5.4	4.8		Sales/Total Assets						
2.5	3.2	3.4								
.4	.2	.3								
(11) .7	(14) .7	(20) .6		% Depr., Dep., Amort./Sales						
2.5	1.3	1.6								
		1.9		% Officers', Directors', Owners' Comp/Sales						
		(13) 2.9								
		7.0								
111021M	651177M	580291M		Net Sales ($)	2309M	12955M	3244M	6299M	88890M	466594M
33977M	204244M	141764M		Total Assets ($)	790M	2760M	352M	1836M	16976M	119050M

© RMA 2003   M = $ thousand   MM = $ million
See Pages 11 through 18 for Explanation of Ratios and Data

Current Data Sorted By Assets   Comparative Historical Data

0-500M	500M-2MM	2-10MM	10-50MM	50-100MM	100-250MM	Type of Statement	4/1/98-3/31/99 ALL	4/1/99-3/31/00 ALL
	2	15	13	3	3	Unqualified	37	33
1	18	32	2			Reviewed	64	54
22	46	24				Compiled	114	109
54	34	11	1		2	Tax Returns	78	74
30	32	28	3	2	7	Other	101	105
61 (4/1-9/30/02)			324 (10/1/02-3/31/03)					
107	132	110	19	5	12	NUMBER OF STATEMENTS	394	375
%	%	%	%	%	%	ASSETS	%	%
10.6	10.0	8.1	11.5		7.0	Cash & Equivalents	9.3	9.2
10.8	15.5	17.9	17.6		12.4	Trade Receivables (net)	17.9	18.2
42.5	43.5	36.9	31.2		37.5	Inventory	39.3	42.5
1.7	2.4	2.8	2.4		4.7	All Other Current	2.1	1.3
65.6	71.4	65.7	62.6		61.6	Total Current	68.7	71.2
24.3	21.8	24.5	30.3		25.9	Fixed Assets (net)	21.8	20.4
3.7	1.2	4.2	1.6		9.3	Intangibles (net)	3.3	3.1
6.4	5.6	5.6	5.5		3.2	All Other Non-Current	6.2	5.3
100.0	100.0	100.0	100.0		100.0	Total	100.0	100.0
						LIABILITIES		
11.6	11.8	13.2	14.1		8.5	Notes Payable-Short Term	10.7	13.2
4.6	3.6	3.3	2.1		.7	Cur. Mat.-L/T/D	3.4	4.3
18.4	22.5	19.4	15.1		18.5	Trade Payables	20.3	17.9
.2	.2	.2	.3		.9	Income Taxes Payable	.3	.2
12.4	11.0	9.8	10.9		10.2	All Other Current	13.1	18.9
47.3	49.0	45.9	42.5		38.9	Total Current	47.8	54.5
26.8	15.6	15.2	16.8		22.7	Long Term Debt	17.3	16.0
.0	.0	.3	.3		.3	Deferred Taxes	.2	.3
12.1	5.1	4.1	.9		14.3	All Other Non-Current	6.9	4.9
13.7	30.3	34.5	39.4		23.9	Net Worth	27.8	24.4
100.0	100.0	100.0	100.0		100.0	Total Liabilities & Net Worth	100.0	100.0
						INCOME DATA		
100.0	100.0	100.0	100.0		100.0	Net Sales	100.0	100.0
44.5	39.5	38.5	37.0		42.9	Gross Profit	40.7	40.3
40.8	36.8	35.0	30.5		35.5	Operating Expenses	38.8	37.1
3.6	2.6	3.5	6.4		7.4	Operating Profit	1.8	3.2
1.4	1.1	.3	1.7		1.3	All Other Expenses (net)	1.4	-.4
2.2	1.5	3.2	4.7		6.1	Profit Before Taxes	.5	3.6
						RATIOS		
2.8	2.3	2.0	2.8		2.0		2.9	2.5
1.5	1.5	1.5	1.4		1.5	Current	1.6	1.6
1.0	1.1	1.0	1.1		1.4		1.1	1.1
1.2	.9	.9	1.3		.9		1.2	1.0
(105) .5	.5	.5	.7		.4	Quick	(390) .6	(374) .6
.1	.2	.2	.2		.2		.2	.2
0 UND	0 920.8	3 123.6	5 76.2		0 UND		1 307.8	2 217.3
2 166.7	11 33.9	16 22.7	11 34.2		15 24.0	Sales/Receivables	13 27.7	16 23.4
16 23.3	26 13.8	40 9.0	64 5.7		51 7.2		43 8.4	42 8.7
19 19.3	32 11.4	36 10.2	49 7.5		79 4.6		40 9.2	47 7.8
63 5.8	80 4.6	74 5.0	95 3.8		104 3.5	Cost of Sales/Inventory	76 4.8	88 4.2
147 2.5	155 2.4	123 3.0	137 2.7		159 2.3		133 2.7	154 2.4
1 258.5	13 28.1	21 17.5	14 25.7		33 11.0		12 30.5	12 31.0
28 13.2	34 10.6	33 10.9	32 11.5		47 7.7	Cost of Sales/Payables	30 12.1	32 11.3
55 6.6	67 5.4	64 5.7	53 6.9		72 5.1		56 6.5	63 5.7
7.0	7.4	7.1	6.0		4.2		6.3	6.0
24.0	13.6	14.1	10.2		10.6	Sales/Working Capital	11.2	11.9
-206.5	70.9	118.8	86.4		13.1		42.4	50.8
6.8	7.4	7.7	19.3		6.8		9.2	7.7
(84) 2.5	(120) 2.3	(101) 3.1	6.4		(11) 3.1	EBIT/Interest	(354) 3.4	(340) 2.9
-.9	.8	1.3	1.0		1.8		1.5	1.3
	3.2	9.9				Net Profit + Depr., Dep.,	4.8	4.3
	(21) 1.1	(26) 2.0				Amort./Cur. Mat. L/T/D	(73) 2.0	(60) 1.8
	.7	.8					1.0	1.0
.2	.2	.2	.2		.8		.2	.2
1.0	.6	.6	.5		1.1	Fixed/Worth	.5	.6
-1.4	2.3	1.5	1.7		-3.6		2.0	1.8
1.0	.9	1.0	.8		1.7		.8	.9
5.0	2.4	2.0	1.8		2.8	Debt/Worth	1.9	2.5
-6.1	7.9	5.8	4.2		-12.3		7.4	8.1
84.7	39.2	38.5	53.7			% Profit Before Taxes/Tangible	49.1	57.6
(68) 26.7	(113) 14.4	(96) 14.6	(18) 15.9			Net Worth	(331) 21.5	(322) 20.0
1.0	.8	3.4	1.2				8.8	7.0
16.4	12.5	11.9	13.8		16.0	% Profit Before Taxes/Total	16.2	14.5
7.2	4.1	4.1	8.4		9.0	Assets	6.7	5.9
-7.1	-.2	.8	.1		5.0		2.0	1.4
109.6	55.6	37.8	41.3		30.4		54.2	53.7
25.4	23.5	18.4	16.2		9.0	Sales/Net Fixed Assets	21.0	21.1
11.1	8.9	8.0	2.5		4.8		9.4	9.7
6.1	4.4	3.6	3.0		2.9		4.0	3.9
3.5	3.0	2.6	2.2		2.0	Sales/Total Assets	2.8	2.7
2.2	1.9	1.8	1.1		1.6		2.0	1.9
.8	.6	.7	1.1				.6	.6
(73) 1.6	(118) 1.2	(97) 1.3	(17) 1.3			% Depr., Dep., Amort./Sales	(340) 1.1	(306) 1.2
3.2	2.5	2.4	2.5				2.4	2.4
3.2	2.6	1.8				% Officers', Directors',	2.2	2.2
(56) 6.0	(74) 4.9	(55) 2.9				Owners' Comp/Sales	(190) 4.0	(176) 4.4
8.0	8.0	6.8					6.6	7.4
103204M	443606M	1346182M	900720M	629578M	4413094M	Net Sales ($)	5175746M	5242326M
25805M	132997M	481185M	403185M	355410M	1964934M	Total Assets ($)	2484113M	2478255M

© RMA 2003

M = $ thousand   MM = $ million
See Pages 11 through 18 for Explanation of Ratios and Data

Comparative Historical Data | Current Data Sorted By Sales

30	28	36	Type of Statement						
43	55	53	Unqualified			3	5	11	17
125	107	92	Reviewed	1	7	13	13	15	4
109	88	102	Compiled	18	36	7	16	14	1
127	122	102	Tax Returns	34	40	10	11	5	2
4/1/00-	4/1/01-	4/1/02-	Other	19	26	15	16	13	13
3/31/01	3/31/02	3/31/03			61 (4/1-9/30/02)			324 (10/1/02-3/31/03)	
ALL	ALL	ALL		0-1MM	1-3MM	3-5MM	5-10MM	10-25MM	25MM & OVER
434	400	385	NUMBER OF STATEMENTS	72	109	48	61	58	37
%	%	%	ASSETS	%	%	%	%	%	%
9.2	9.6	9.7	Cash & Equivalents	10.5	10.6	8.2	8.7	8.2	11.1
16.3	15.6	15.0	Trade Receivables (net)	9.5	12.9	14.7	18.3	21.2	16.7
41.5	41.3	40.3	Inventory	42.1	41.1	42.1	39.7	40.4	33.2
1.7	1.7	2.4	All Other Current	1.5	2.6	3.1	2.0	2.3	3.1
68.7	68.2	67.3	Total Current	63.6	67.2	68.1	68.6	72.1	64.1
21.2	22.5	23.8	Fixed Assets (net)	26.6	24.8	21.3	23.1	19.8	26.2
4.1	3.4	3.0	Intangibles (net)	3.8	2.0	3.9	2.5	3.3	4.3
6.0	5.9	5.8	All Other Non-Current	6.0	6.0	6.7	5.8	4.8	5.4
100.0	100.0	100.0	Total	100.0	100.0	100.0	100.0	100.0	100.0
			LIABILITIES						
10.9	11.2	12.1	Notes Payable-Short Term	10.8	11.2	12.3	16.4	12.0	10.4
3.4	3.6	3.7	Cur. Mat.-L/T/D	4.1	4.8	3.5	3.5	2.7	1.6
19.2	18.6	19.9	Trade Payables	16.6	19.8	21.4	19.0	25.1	17.6
.3	.2	.2	Income Taxes Payable	.1	.2	.2	.2	.2	.5
12.1	10.8	11.0	All Other Current	11.5	11.5	9.7	10.3	11.0	11.3
46.0	44.5	46.9	Total Current	43.0	47.5	47.1	49.4	51.0	41.5
17.2	20.0	18.7	Long Term Debt	29.5	22.3	15.6	12.5	11.3	12.6
.2	.1	.2	Deferred Taxes	.0	.0	.2	.2	.3	.4
6.9	7.0	6.8	All Other Non-Current	13.2	6.0	6.2	4.8	2.8	6.9
29.8	28.4	27.5	Net Worth	14.2	24.1	30.9	33.1	34.6	38.6
100.0	100.0	100.0	Total Liabilities & Net Worth	100.0	100.0	100.0	100.0	100.0	100.0
			INCOME DATA						
100.0	100.0	100.0	Net Sales	100.0	100.0	100.0	100.0	100.0	100.0
41.1	42.4	40.6	Gross Profit	49.3	41.0	38.0	35.4	39.0	36.6
38.1	39.3	36.9	Operating Expenses	45.3	38.5	33.8	33.1	34.8	29.8
3.0	3.2	3.6	Operating Profit	4.0	2.5	4.3	2.3	4.2	6.8
.4	1.0	1.0	All Other Expenses (net)	2.0	1.0	1.4	.3	.5	.2
2.6	2.2	2.7	Profit Before Taxes	2.0	1.5	2.9	1.9	3.6	6.6
			RATIOS						
2.7	2.7	2.2		3.4	2.6	2.1	1.8	2.1	2.4
1.6	1.5	1.5	Current	1.5	1.5	1.5	1.4	1.5	1.5
1.1	1.1	1.1		1.0	1.0	1.0	1.0	1.0	1.2
1.1	1.1	1.0		1.2	1.0	.8	.9	.9	1.3
(432) .5	(396) .6	(383) .5	Quick	.5	(107) .5	.3	.5	.6	.6
.2	.2	.2		.1	.2	.1	.2	.3	.3
0 777.6	0 999.8	0 886.2		0 UND	0 UND	0 999.8	3 116.2	3 140.0	4 84.7
11 33.5	10 35.6	8 45.5	Sales/Receivables	4 103.9	5 70.1	4 83.7	18 20.2	17 21.4	14 26.2
35 10.3	35 10.5	30 12.0		21 17.2	24 15.4	24 10.8	41 8.8	59 6.2	
38 9.6	38 9.5	31 11.6		23 15.9	25 14.8	24 15.0	36 10.3	35 10.3	49 7.5
84 4.3	80 4.6	76 4.8	Cost of Sales/Inventory	115 3.2	67 5.4	80 4.5	61 6.0	76 4.8	85 4.3
139 2.6	157 2.3	144 2.5		216 1.7	150 2.4	134 2.7	112 3.3	115 3.2	119 3.1
13 29.1	13 28.8	13 27.9		2 206.5	6 59.5	16 22.6	18 19.8	23 16.0	17 21.5
32 11.4	30 12.0	34 10.9	Cost of Sales/Payables	36 10.2	32 11.5	34 10.8	33 11.1	37 9.9	34 10.8
64 5.7	64 5.7	62 5.9		75 4.9	69 5.3	58 6.3	54 6.7	60 6.1	57 6.4
6.3	6.1	7.0		6.0	6.3	9.5	9.9	6.9	5.8
12.5	12.7	14.5	Sales/Working Capital	15.8	16.9	14.5	18.7	10.7	12.1
75.0	43.7	122.7		373.6	-207.6	NM	98.8	149.9	39.1
6.8	6.0	7.7		4.2	6.0	18.4	10.6	7.7	19.3
(385) 2.8	(345) 2.3	(340) 3.0	EBIT/Interest	(56) 1.5	(95) 2.2	(43) 3.3	(58) 2.9	(53) 4.0	(35) 6.1
1.1	.7	.9		-1.2	-.2	1.6	1.0	1.6	1.8
4.0	4.4	7.7	Net Profit + Depr., Dep.,				5.9	12.0	
(56) 1.8	(73) 1.8	(61) 1.8	Amort./Cur. Mat. L/T/D				(16) 1.2	(15) 5.4	
.9	.9	.8					.4	1.9	
.2	.2	.2		.2	.2	.2	.3	.2	.3
.6	.6	.7	Fixed/Worth	1.0	1.1	.7	.6	.5	.8
2.4	3.5	4.1		-2.8	-27.2	1.9	1.2	1.3	1.6
.9	.9	1.0		1.1	.9	1.0	1.0	1.1	.6
2.3	2.5	2.4	Debt/Worth	4.1	3.3	2.3	2.0	2.2	1.8
10.8	13.8	13.1		-5.9	-118.7	9.1	5.0	5.8	6.2
50.6	44.1	45.0	% Profit Before Taxes/Tangible	57.4	43.3	46.8	34.2	51.7	74.9
(357) 17.6	(323) 16.2	(308) 16.3	Net Worth	(48) 25.0	(81) 11.8	(40) 19.9	(54) 13.2	(53) 20.7	(32) 20.8
3.9	1.6	1.7		-.6	1.1	3.7	.7	5.1	10.2
14.9	12.8	13.8	% Profit Before Taxes/Total	15.0	10.6	14.6	11.9	13.5	18.6
5.3	4.6	5.0	Assets	7.8	3.3	6.3	3.1	4.8	8.8
.4	-.9	.0		-6.7	-5.0	.9	-.1	1.4	4.2
53.5	47.8	44.9		47.7	48.7	76.3	41.8	43.0	33.7
20.5	20.5	21.9	Sales/Net Fixed Assets	17.9	18.4	30.2	20.1	30.3	16.2
9.1	8.0	8.6		6.0	8.3	12.5	10.5	10.4	6.3
4.1	4.0	4.4		4.1	4.4	5.2	4.4	4.5	3.2
2.8	2.8	2.9	Sales/Total Assets	2.4	3.0	3.2	2.6	3.1	2.4
1.9	1.8	1.9		1.5	1.9	2.4	2.0	2.4	1.7
.6	.6	.7		.9	.7	.5	.8	.6	1.0
(350) 1.2	(326) 1.3	(318) 1.3	% Depr., Dep., Amort./Sales	(48) 1.9	(94) 1.6	(41) 1.0	(49) 1.2	(55) 1.1	(31) 1.5
2.3	2.7	2.7		4.8	3.1	2.2	2.2	1.9	3.2
2.6	2.3	2.3	% Officers', Directors',	4.2	2.7	2.6	2.2	1.8	.8
(223) 4.4	(201) 4.7	(194) 4.4	Owners' Comp/Sales	(34) 7.5	(60) 5.4	(29) 3.8	(31) 3.5	(30) 2.6	(10) 3.6
7.5	7.4	8.0		12.8	8.1	8.8	6.1	4.0	7.4
7133819M	5451211M	7836384M	Net Sales ($)	39378M	197820M	188069M	429374M	862183M	6119560M
3315772M	2541233M	3363516M	Total Assets ($)	18597M	81285M	74827M	192304M	300057M	2696446M

Current Data Sorted By Assets   Comparative Historical Data

0-500M	500M-2MM	2-10MM	10-50MM	50-100MM	100-250MM		4/1/98-3/31/99 ALL	4/1/99-3/31/00 ALL
	1	10	18	3	12	Unqualified	48	39
	4	14	9	1		Reviewed	25	29
2	10	11	1			Compiled	19	25
5	3	1				Tax Returns	9	7
2	6	22	13	2	6	Other	54	48
	38 (4/1-9/30/02)		118 (10/1/02-3/31/03)					
9	24	58	41	6	18	**NUMBER OF STATEMENTS**	155	148
%	%	%	%	%	%	**ASSETS**	%	%
	13.4	11.2	11.3		8.7	Cash & Equivalents	8.4	9.7
	20.8	12.9	10.4		14.4	Trade Receivables (net)	15.0	13.5
	39.1	46.9	39.5		33.0	Inventory	41.6	40.6
	3.4	3.8	8.2		4.6	All Other Current	3.1	3.6
	76.7	74.8	69.4		60.7	Total Current	68.1	67.4
	11.6	13.8	15.4		21.5	Fixed Assets (net)	14.8	16.5
	2.4	3.6	8.3		6.7	Intangibles (net)	7.6	8.0
	9.3	7.9	6.9		11.1	All Other Non-Current	9.6	8.1
	100.0	100.0	100.0		100.0	Total	100.0	100.0
						LIABILITIES		
	12.7	9.7	6.4		2.6	Notes Payable-Short Term	12.1	11.6
	11.0	4.1	4.2		2.3	Cur. Mat.-L/T/D	2.6	2.3
	27.3	26.5	21.7		16.2	Trade Payables	25.4	22.6
	.8	.1	.1		.5	Income Taxes Payable	.3	.3
	15.3	13.4	13.1		12.4	All Other Current	13.0	14.6
	67.2	53.8	45.6		34.0	Total Current	53.4	51.4
	9.7	7.1	8.6		21.3	Long Term Debt	8.5	13.7
	.2	.1	.1		.6	Deferred Taxes	.3	.2
	4.4	2.2	4.2		5.2	All Other Non-Current	5.4	4.3
	18.6	36.8	41.5		38.9	Net Worth	32.4	30.3
	100.0	100.0	100.0		100.0	Total Liabilities & Net Worth	100.0	100.0
						INCOME DATA		
	100.0	100.0	100.0		100.0	Net Sales	100.0	100.0
	38.7	45.1	46.9		46.2	Gross Profit	43.2	42.0
	37.4	41.2	43.0		39.7	Operating Expenses	40.7	38.7
	1.3	3.9	3.9		6.5	Operating Profit	2.5	3.4
	1.0	.2	.5		.8	All Other Expenses (net)	2.0	.5
	.3	3.7	3.4		5.7	Profit Before Taxes	.5	2.8
						RATIOS		
	2.3	2.0	3.0		3.1		1.9	2.4
	1.5	1.5	1.5		2.1	Current	1.3	1.5
	1.0	1.1	1.1		1.2		1.0	1.0
	1.2	.9	1.3		1.6		.8	.9
	.7	.3	.4		1.1	Quick	(154) .4	(147) .4
	.3	.1	.1		.3		.1	.1
	3 106.2	3 134.8	2 240.1		8 47.6		3 121.2	2 153.5
	15 23.7	10 36.8	8 47.5		22 16.4	Sales/Receivables	9 40.0	7 55.0
	25 14.7	26 14.1	16 22.8		36 10.1		24 15.3	26 14.3
	25 14.7	56 6.5	64 5.7		51 7.1		50 7.4	52 7.0
	54 6.7	91 4.0	90 4.0		91 4.0	Cost of Sales/Inventory	81 4.5	82 4.5
	107 3.4	144 2.5	118 3.1		130 2.8		123 3.0	114 3.2
	22 17.0	27 13.7	26 14.0		27 13.7		25 14.6	23 15.9
	34 10.7	39 9.3	40 9.0		41 8.8	Cost of Sales/Payables	42 8.6	37 9.9
	54 6.8	65 5.7	65 5.7		61 6.0		66 5.5	60 6.1
	8.1	7.9	7.5		5.7		8.8	8.4
	19.4	17.1	14.9		8.4	Sales/Working Capital	20.1	15.2
	NM	77.1	140.1		20.9		UND	NM
	9.3	22.1	14.0		13.2		20.1	12.9
	(22) 2.1	(49) 6.4	(36) 6.2		(17) 7.6	EBIT/Interest	(141) 4.1	(133) 4.7
	-2.8	2.6	2.5		2.2		1.6	1.4
						Net Profit + Depr., Dep., Amort./Cur. Mat. L /T/D	14.7	5.5
							(38) 5.6	(33) 2.4
							1.7	.8
	.1	.1	.1		.4		.2	.2
	.4	.3	.4		.7	Fixed/Worth	.5	.5
	NM	.9	1.6		1.1		1.6	1.5
	.7	.8	.7		.8		1.2	.9
	2.2	1.8	2.6		2.1	Debt/Worth	2.1	2.0
	NM	4.9	5.8		5.2		7.3	6.7
	76.9	60.7	97.4		71.6		50.2	48.0
	(18) 17.9	(52) 28.1	(36) 36.2		(16) 45.5	% Profit Before Taxes/Tangible Net Worth	(129) 24.5	(120) 24.8
	3.7	10.3	14.7		21.0		8.6	5.7
	15.8	25.6	18.3		19.8		18.7	20.2
	4.4	8.9	10.5		11.5	% Profit Before Taxes/Total Assets	7.5	7.2
	-14.2	2.9	3.5		4.1		1.7	1.2
	217.8	60.0	51.9		19.6		77.0	55.9
	62.2	35.5	25.8		12.0	Sales/Net Fixed Assets	29.4	26.0
	16.8	18.2	13.5		8.1		13.3	12.7
	5.4	4.7	4.2		2.8		4.4	4.5
	3.7	3.3	3.0		2.3	Sales/Total Assets	3.2	3.2
	2.7	2.4	2.0		2.0		2.2	2.2
	.2	.5	.6				.5	.6
	(17) .6	(51) .9	(35) .9			% Depr., Dep., Amort./Sales	(124) .9	(127) 1.1
	2.4	1.5	1.6				1.6	1.8
		1.4					1.8	1.9
		(17) 3.5				% Officers', Directors', Owners' Comp/Sales	(46) 3.2	(47) 3.8
		7.4					7.1	6.6
8087M	114661M	1159204M	3278819M	1450952M	6548536M	Net Sales ($)	9643659M	9028869M
2212M	28483M	295370M	1032262M	418400M	2917453M	Total Assets ($)	3479763M	3374760M

M = $ thousand   MM = $ million
See Pages 11 through 18 for Explanation of Ratios and Data

Comparative Historical Data | Current Data Sorted By Sales

			Type of Statement						
25	24	44	Unqualified		1		3	2	38
18	10	28	Reviewed			3	5	5	15
31	34	24	Compiled	1	6	3	6	4	4
8	12	9	Tax Returns	4	1	1	3		
49	56	51	Other	2	2	2	10	10	25
4/1/00-3/31/01 ALL	4/1/01-3/31/02 ALL	4/1/02-3/31/03 ALL		0-1MM	38 (4/1-9/30/02) 1-3MM	3-5MM	118 (10/1/02-3/31/03) 5-10MM	10-25MM	25MM & OVER
131	136	156	NUMBER OF STATEMENTS	7	10	9	27	21	82
%	%	%	**ASSETS**	%	%	%	%	%	%
9.8	11.5	11.9	Cash & Equivalents		10.8		9.6	11.3	11.9
16.7	16.0	13.7	Trade Receivables (net)		24.4		15.9	11.3	13.0
40.9	40.0	41.2	Inventory		31.0		46.2	51.0	38.4
2.9	3.7	4.8	All Other Current		.9		2.9	1.7	6.9
70.3	71.2	71.6	Total Current		67.1		74.6	75.3	70.3
14.6	15.1	14.3	Fixed Assets (net)		17.1		12.2	13.5	16.2
6.3	6.1	5.5	Intangibles (net)		2.7		1.0	3.8	6.4
8.7	8.3	8.6	All Other Non-Current		13.0		12.2	7.4	7.2
100.0	100.0	100.0	Total		100.0		100.0	100.0	100.0
			LIABILITIES						
12.0	8.4	9.0	Notes Payable-Short Term		15.1		10.2	12.4	4.7
2.4	3.3	5.6	Cur. Mat.-L/T/D		1.4		5.6	3.4	3.1
24.6	23.2	23.5	Trade Payables		22.2		23.5	25.1	24.6
.3	.4	.3	Income Taxes Payable		.1		.0	.2	.2
10.2	9.6	12.7	All Other Current		7.3		16.3	11.9	13.8
49.5	44.9	51.1	Total Current		46.1		55.6	52.9	46.4
9.7	9.9	9.8	Long Term Debt		10.3		9.4	5.2	10.6
.1	.2	.2	Deferred Taxes		.7		.0	.1	.2
6.4	4.5	4.0	All Other Non-Current		2.8		4.0	2.5	3.7
34.2	40.6	34.9	Net Worth		40.2		31.0	39.3	39.1
100.0	100.0	100.0	Total Liabilities & Net Worth		100.0		100.0	100.0	100.0
			INCOME DATA						
100.0	100.0	100.0	Net Sales		100.0		100.0	100.0	100.0
43.2	45.9	44.2	Gross Profit		35.9		45.4	45.3	44.5
39.7	41.6	40.3	Operating Expenses		37.0		43.8	40.6	40.1
3.5	4.3	4.0	Operating Profit		-1.0		1.6	4.6	4.4
.6	.7	.6	All Other Expenses (net)		1.9		.4	.3	.4
2.9	3.6	3.4	Profit Before Taxes		-2.9		1.2	4.3	4.0
			RATIOS						
2.5	3.2	2.6	Current		2.7		2.3	1.9	2.9
1.5	1.7	1.6			1.5		1.6	1.5	1.7
1.0	1.1	1.1			1.1		1.0	1.1	1.1
(130) .9	1.2	1.2	Quick		1.1		1.0	1.1	1.3
.5	.6	.4			.6		.4	.2	.5
.2	.2	.1			.4		.1	.1	.1
3 130.3	3 111.3	3 120.2	Sales/Receivables	4 97.2	19 19.3		6 62.6	3 144.6	3 124.0
10 38.1	11 33.0	10 36.3					15 25.2	7 55.2	10 37.7
29 12.4	29 12.7	25 14.6		30 12.2			26 14.2	27 13.7	23 16.2
49 7.5	48 7.6	50 7.4	Cost of Sales/Inventory	21 17.1	42 8.7		61 6.0	63 5.8	48 7.6
84 4.3	80 4.6	88 4.2					102 3.6	102 3.6	77 4.7
118 3.1	123 3.0	126 2.9		116 3.2			149 2.4	157 2.3	114 3.2
24 15.0	20 18.0	26 14.3	Cost of Sales/Payables	14 25.2	36 10.1		27 13.7	29 12.4	26 13.9
37 9.8	35 10.3	39 9.4					37 9.9	40 9.2	39 9.3
63 5.8	63 5.8	62 5.9		59 6.2			61 5.9	72 5.1	61 6.0
7.7	5.9	7.4	Sales/Working Capital		6.7		6.6	7.9	7.2
14.5	12.5	13.2			15.2		12.2	12.6	14.3
999.8	108.4	57.3			NM		132.6	49.7	39.7
(117) 11.1	(114) 14.7	(135) 19.6	EBIT/Interest				5.9	27.9	21.3
4.2	3.9	6.2					(26) 1.9	(20) 7.0	(67) 7.6
1.5	.9	1.9					-.8	2.7	3.2
(21) 10.0	(22) 13.0	(27) 8.2	Net Profit + Depr., Dep., Amort./Cur. Mat. L/T/D						22.0
3.7	4.3	3.2						(16)	5.1
.7	1.5	1.2							3.1
.2	.2	.1	Fixed/Worth		.1		.1	.1	.2
.4	.4	.4			.4		.2	.3	.5
1.1	1.2	1.2			1.0		1.3	.8	1.2
.9	.7	.8	Debt/Worth		.6		.8	.9	.8
2.0	1.7	2.1			1.4		1.6	1.5	2.2
5.2	6.4	5.7			4.5		5.8	3.9	5.3
(108) 58.5	(116) 56.1	(133) 67.9	% Profit Before Taxes/Tangible Net Worth				39.9	70.3	73.3
29.5	28.9	31.5					(23) 11.7	(20) 31.1	(71) 41.9
8.2	3.2	11.9					1.3	11.0	15.6
17.8	19.1	20.0	% Profit Before Taxes/Total Assets		9.8		8.8	26.5	21.8
8.5	7.4	9.0			4.3		1.4	9.3	11.5
.8	.1	2.0			-20.1		-2.8	4.0	4.0
54.1	56.1	67.1	Sales/Net Fixed Assets		210.6		66.7	73.6	40.4
31.5	30.3	30.6			19.5		35.6	37.9	25.6
14.5	14.7	15.1			9.8		24.6	18.3	13.8
4.3	4.9	4.4	Sales/Total Assets		3.7		4.7	4.2	4.5
3.2	3.3	3.0			2.9		2.9	3.0	3.2
2.2	2.2	2.2			1.8		2.2	2.6	2.3
(105) .5	(104) .6	(121) .5	% Depr., Dep., Amort./Sales				(24) .5	(17) .5	(63) .7
.8	1.0	.9					1.0	.9	.9
1.4	1.5	1.7					1.3	1.3	1.7
(43) 1.8	(44) 1.8	(41) 1.6	% Officers', Directors', Owners' Comp/Sales				(14) 1.6		(13) 1.4
3.8	4.0	3.5					3.6		2.5
7.4	8.0	6.9					7.1		5.2
7017402M	7851916M	12560259M	Net Sales ($)	3706M	20862M	36278M	209819M	322130M	11967464M
2451291M	2784377M	4694180M	Total Assets ($)	1582M	8765M	15226M	74204M	106771M	4487632M

© RMA 2003

M = $ thousand   MM = $ million
See Pages 11 through 18 for Explanation of Ratios and Data

Current Data Sorted By Assets   **Comparative Historical Data**

Type of Statement	0-500M	500M-2MM	2-10MM	10-50MM	50-100MM	100-250MM		4/1/98-3/31/99 ALL	4/1/99-3/31/00 ALL
Unqualified			6	2		2		12	13
Reviewed	1	6	12	4				31	20
Compiled	4	20	5					50	41
Tax Returns	10	5						14	12
Other	5	8	13	6	1			31	28
	32 (4/1-9/30/02)			78 (10/1/02-3/31/03)					
NUMBER OF STATEMENTS	20	39	36	12	1	2		138	114

	0-500M %	500M-2MM %	2-10MM %	10-50MM %	50-100MM %	100-250MM %		138 ALL %	114 ALL %
ASSETS									
Cash & Equivalents	8.0	9.2	8.0	6.2				8.6	8.5
Trade Receivables (net)	3.4	8.8	7.2	9.0				7.3	6.8
Inventory	13.8	17.0	15.9	11.5				15.2	16.2
All Other Current	.2	3.2	4.5	3.4				1.1	1.7
Total Current	25.5	38.2	35.6	30.0				32.2	33.2
Fixed Assets (net)	54.4	50.3	52.1	59.5				58.2	55.1
Intangibles (net)	6.4	7.1	4.8	5.2				4.8	5.6
All Other Non-Current	13.7	4.4	7.5	5.3				4.7	6.1
Total	100.0	100.0	100.0	100.0				100.0	100.0
LIABILITIES									
Notes Payable-Short Term	12.4	7.8	4.5	4.6				7.1	6.3
Cur. Mat.-L/T/D	10.7	7.0	9.3	6.1				9.8	8.9
Trade Payables	7.9	13.0	15.4	12.5				12.6	13.5
Income Taxes Payable	.0	.4	.4	.2				.2	.3
All Other Current	13.6	10.4	8.1	7.2				8.3	7.9
Total Current	44.6	38.5	37.7	30.6				37.9	36.9
Long Term Debt	45.8	29.9	24.5	39.9				30.2	29.4
Deferred Taxes	.0	.2	1.0	3.2				.8	.9
All Other Non-Current	16.3	5.1	10.3	.6				4.6	5.1
Net Worth	-6.8	26.3	26.4	25.7				26.5	27.7
Total Liabilities & Net Worth	100.0	100.0	100.0	100.0				100.0	100.0
INCOME DATA									
Net Sales	100.0	100.0	100.0	100.0				100.0	100.0
Gross Profit	42.6	45.9	51.4	45.4				47.0	46.1
Operating Expenses	41.0	45.1	48.8	44.1				43.3	44.0
Operating Profit	1.6	.8	2.6	1.3				3.7	2.1
All Other Expenses (net)	.5	.2	.6	.5				1.3	.6
Profit Before Taxes	1.1	.6	1.9	.8				2.4	1.5
RATIOS									
Current	.9 / .6 / .3	2.1 / 1.0 / .6	1.1 / .9 / .7	1.6 / .9 / .7				1.5 / .8 / .5	1.4 / .9 / .5
Quick	(19) .4 / .1 / .0	.9 / .4 / .2	.5 / .3 / .2	.8 / .5 / .3				.7 / .4 / .1	.7 / .3 / .2
Sales/Receivables	0 UND / 0 UND / 2 222.1	1 422.6 / 4 86.5 / 14 25.3	3 112.0 / 6 62.2 / 13 28.4	3 121.0 / 5 68.8 / 33 11.2				1 588.7 / 3 117.4 / 9 42.4	1 308.5 / 3 104.3 / 11 33.8
Cost of Sales/Inventory	6 58.8 / 21 17.3 / 46 7.9	25 14.6 / 34 10.6 / 45 8.1	25 14.5 / 42 8.7 / 60 6.1	27 13.4 / 29 12.4 / 38 9.7				22 16.6 / 33 11.0 / 48 7.6	25 14.7 / 34 10.7 / 48 7.5
Cost of Sales/Payables	0 UND / 2 154.0 / 23 15.9	11 32.7 / 27 13.7 / 37 9.8	18 19.8 / 39 9.4 / 59 6.2	26 14.0 / 38 9.7 / 45 8.1				15 24.2 / 27 13.4 / 41 9.0	18 20.3 / 28 12.9 / 43 8.5
Sales/Working Capital	-161.9 / -43.0 / -11.9	17.6 / -382.3 / -16.8	90.5 / -66.4 / -26.1	13.6 / -72.4 / -19.3				26.1 / -42.0 / -11.9	23.5 / -75.5 / -15.1
EBIT/Interest	3.7 / .9 / -2.4	(37) 2.9 / 1.8 / .4	(35) 4.3 / 1.7 / .8	4.1 / 1.4 / .0				(131) 3.2 / 1.8 / 1.1	(110) 4.3 / 2.1 / .9
Net Profit + Depr., Dep., Amort./Cur. Mat. L /T/D			(14) 3.4 / 2.5 / 1.4					(43) 2.8 / 1.8 / 1.3	(37) 3.4 / 1.8 / 1.4
Fixed/Worth	1.4 / -2.7 / -1.2	.8 / 2.6 / 361.5	1.2 / 2.1 / NM	1.6 / 2.9 / 12.4				1.5 / 2.8 / 8.0	1.1 / 2.3 / 34.0
Debt/Worth	1.6 / -23.5 / -2.4	1.2 / 3.8 / 482.5	1.3 / 3.6 / NM	1.9 / 2.5 / 18.5				1.3 / 3.4 / 10.2	1.2 / 3.0 / 48.8
% Profit Before Taxes/Tangible Net Worth		(30) 38.9 / 14.6 / -2.5	(27) 26.1 / 8.9 / -6.2	(11) 24.6 / 6.8 / -8.4				(115) 35.7 / 16.7 / 4.8	(90) 39.4 / 19.0 / 6.0
% Profit Before Taxes/Total Assets	21.1 / -.7 / -13.4	8.4 / 3.1 / -2.8	7.3 / 2.2 / -.7	6.1 / 1.4 / -2.6				8.4 / 4.3 / .1	10.5 / 4.4 / -.1
Sales/Net Fixed Assets	18.2 / 7.3 / 3.7	9.7 / 6.8 / 4.1	7.8 / 5.3 / 3.6	4.9 / 3.4 / 2.9				7.1 / 4.6 / 3.2	7.8 / 4.4 / 3.1
Sales/Total Assets	6.4 / 4.2 / 2.4	4.4 / 3.1 / 2.4	3.4 / 2.8 / 1.9	2.8 / 2.0 / 1.8				3.7 / 2.8 / 1.9	3.7 / 2.7 / 2.0
% Depr., Dep., Amort./Sales	(19) 1.5 / 6.0 / 10.3	(37) 3.8 / 5.4 / 7.3	3.7 / 5.3 / 7.7	3.5 / 6.0 / 7.8				(134) 4.2 / 5.7 / 7.5	(109) 4.4 / 5.8 / 7.4
% Officers', Directors', Owners' Comp/Sales	(13) 4.4 / 5.3 / 10.0	(23) 1.8 / 3.8 / 6.6	(13) .9 / 1.6 / 4.3					(72) 2.6 / 4.0 / 6.5	(57) 2.1 / 4.0 / 5.4
Net Sales ($)	22372M	158611M	443419M	424714M	57323M	360340M		1349199M	1420874M
Total Assets ($)	4985M	43976M	157876M	197956M	53310M	334079M		709358M	744456M

© RMA 2003

M = $ thousand   MM = $ million
See Pages 11 through 18 for Explanation of Ratios and Data

Comparative Historical Data — Current Data Sorted By Sales

			Type of Statement						
5	8	10	Unqualified				3	1	6
18	13	23	Reviewed		2	4	5	10	2
38	29	29	Compiled	5	10	4	7	3	
20	10	15	Tax Returns	9	4	2			
27	27	33	Other	3	4	3	10	7	6
4/1/00-3/31/01 ALL	4/1/01-3/31/02 ALL	4/1/02-3/31/03 ALL		0-1MM	1-3MM	3-5MM	5-10MM	10-25MM	25MM & OVER
				32 (4/1-9/30/02)			78 (10/1/02-3/31/03)		
108	87	110	**NUMBER OF STATEMENTS**	17	20	13	25	21	14
%	%	%	**ASSETS**	%	%	%	%	%	%
8.7	9.8	8.1	Cash & Equivalents	4.3	14.2	7.4	8.3	5.5	8.7
8.1	7.8	7.2	Trade Receivables (net)	3.0	7.6	5.3	9.4	9.7	5.7
16.9	16.8	15.4	Inventory	12.2	12.6	16.3	21.0	15.6	11.6
1.7	1.9	3.1	All Other Current	4.9	2.3	.8	4.4	2.3	2.9
35.5	36.3	33.8	Total Current	24.4	36.8	29.8	43.1	33.1	28.8
52.2	50.7	52.4	Fixed Assets (net)	60.7	51.7	49.8	44.9	54.6	55.9
5.0	4.7	6.6	Intangibles (net)	7.3	8.2	5.7	3.7	6.2	10.4
7.3	8.3	7.2	All Other Non-Current	7.6	3.3	14.7	8.4	6.1	4.9
100.0	100.0	100.0	Total	100.0	100.0	100.0	100.0	100.0	100.0
			LIABILITIES						
7.8	8.7	7.0	Notes Payable-Short Term	12.7	5.3	10.2	6.5	4.8	3.4
8.1	9.1	8.2	Cur. Mat.-L/T/D	8.9	9.1	4.7	7.0	9.5	9.5
13.0	12.8	12.6	Trade Payables	7.6	8.7	14.2	13.5	18.6	11.9
.2	.2	.3	Income Taxes Payable	.0	.0	1.1	.2	.5	.0
8.9	9.3	9.7	All Other Current	10.5	10.9	12.0	10.7	6.3	8.4
38.0	40.2	37.8	Total Current	39.8	34.0	42.3	38.0	39.7	33.2
31.6	28.6	31.7	Long Term Debt	55.9	28.3	31.2	22.8	28.3	28.9
.5	.5	.8	Deferred Taxes	.0	.0	.6	.5	1.3	2.6
7.0	6.9	9.3	All Other Non-Current	13.5	9.4	10.0	10.2	4.6	8.6
22.9	23.8	20.4	Net Worth	−9.2	28.3	15.8	28.5	26.0	26.7
100.0	100.0	100.0	Total Liabilities & Net Worth	100.0	100.0	100.0	100.0	100.0	100.0
			INCOME DATA						
100.0	100.0	100.0	Net Sales	100.0	100.0	100.0	100.0	100.0	100.0
46.5	44.4	46.7	Gross Profit	45.2	49.1	48.8	46.0	46.1	45.4
44.7	42.8	44.8	Operating Expenses	41.9	47.6	49.0	44.1	44.9	41.8
1.8	1.6	1.9	Operating Profit	3.2	1.5	−.1	1.9	1.2	3.6
.6	.9	.5	All Other Expenses (net)	.5	.5	−.1	.3	.7	1.6
1.2	.7	1.3	Profit Before Taxes	2.8	1.0	.0	1.6	.6	2.0
			RATIOS						
1.5	1.5	1.5	Current	1.2	2.1	1.5	1.4	1.0	1.4
1.0	1.0	.9		.8	.8	.9	1.0	.8	.9
.6	.5	.6		.2	.6	.4	.7	.6	.7
.8	(86) .9	(109) .7	Quick	(16) .6	1.2	.5	.9	.6	.7
.4	.4	.3		.2	.4	.3	.4	.3	.4
.2	.2	.2		.0	.1	.1	.2	.2	.3
2 180.0	2 189.2	1 342.1	Sales/Receivables	0 UND	0 879.3	2 197.9	1 256.5	4 88.3	3 123.9
6 61.1	4 81.7	4 94.0		0 UND	3 109.6	4 86.5	6 60.5	6 59.3	3 108.4
13 28.1	12 31.7	12 29.4		1 262.4	25 14.8	7 53.5	15 21.6	19 19.4	10 37.1
23 15.8	23 15.6	24 15.2	Cost of Sales/Inventory	10 38.1	11 32.6	18 20.8	32 11.2	24 15.1	25 14.5
36 10.2	34 10.8	35 10.6		25 14.5	33 10.9	39 9.3	42 8.7	33 11.0	29 12.4
50 7.3	49 7.4	47 7.7		45 8.1	45 7.3	45 8.1	59 6.1	57 6.4	37 9.8
17 21.2	16 22.2	12 30.0	Cost of Sales/Payables	0 UND	9 40.8	14 26.3	15 23.6	17 20.9	22 16.4
28 13.0	25 14.4	27 13.6		1 255.5	23 15.7	23 16.2	29 12.5	46 8.0	32 11.2
50 7.3	41 8.8	46 8.0		30 12.3	42 8.8	34 10.7	56 6.5	59 6.2	39 9.4
21.4	16.6	29.8	Sales/Working Capital	112.7	9.4	40.4	20.5	NM	28.9
−761.7	−415.0	−93.3		−54.8	−71.8	−119.3	255.2	−57.5	−110.8
−17.2	−15.2	−17.7		−10.5	−16.7	−12.2	−27.6	−19.0	−23.9
(103) 3.5	(82) 2.9	(106) 3.6	EBIT/Interest	(16) 3.7	3.1	5.2	(23) 7.6	3.3	(13) 5.0
1.6	1.4	1.6		1.1	1.3	1.8	2.2	1.4	1.3
.8	−.7	.2		−2.0	.4	−2.0	.9	−.1	.4
(20) 6.4	(20) 2.6	(24) 3.3	Net Profit + Depr., Dep., Amort./Cur. Mat. L/T/D				(10) 4.6		
2.2	1.5	1.8					2.9		
1.0	.9	1.2					1.7		
1.1	1.1	1.2	Fixed/Worth	1.4	.5	1.5	.7	1.2	1.5
2.6	2.1	2.7		−8.7	2.5	3.5	1.7	3.0	6.0
16.0	9.7	−16.7		−1.3	−19.0	−2.7	7.4	−35.7	NM
1.3	1.3	1.4	Debt/Worth	2.3	.8	1.1	1.4	1.4	1.8
3.6	2.6	4.4		−20.7	2.2	6.0	3.0	4.0	7.7
31.2	21.1	−27.6		−2.5	−24.4	−15.7	10.7	−68.0	NM
(85) 29.9	(69) 26.3	(77) 26.2	% Profit Before Taxes/Tangible Net Worth		(14) 23.0		(22) 35.2	(15) 24.9	(11) 21.0
15.3	10.5	7.6			6.0		9.9	2.9	7.3
3.6	−2.3	−4.7			−5.7		.2	−8.4	−31.3
7.5	8.3	8.2	% Profit Before Taxes/Total Assets	9.1	5.9	8.7	8.8	4.2	8.8
2.5	1.9	2.0		.5	1.1	3.7	3.8	1.4	1.1
−1.2	−7.2	−2.9		−13.4	−3.0	−12.6	.1	−3.1	−2.2
8.4	10.4	9.5	Sales/Net Fixed Assets	9.9	7.4	14.8	17.1	8.0	5.7
5.4	5.7	5.0		3.7	4.4	8.7	6.8	5.0	3.6
3.5	3.5	3.5		2.5	3.1	4.3	4.2	3.8	3.2
3.6	4.3	4.2	Sales/Total Assets	4.4	3.2	5.4	4.6	3.6	3.7
2.8	2.7	2.9		2.6	2.6	3.5	3.3	2.8	2.4
2.0	1.9	1.9		1.7	1.7	3.1	1.9	2.1	1.7
(102) 4.1	(81) 3.5	(104) 3.6	% Depr., Dep., Amort./Sales	3.8	(19) 4.2	3.1	(23) 2.8	3.8	(11) 3.9
5.9	5.2	5.4		6.4	6.3	4.7	4.7	6.0	4.7
8.2	7.3	7.6		14.6	8.0	7.1	8.3	7.6	7.0
(53) 1.7	(37) 1.4	(50) 1.5	% Officers', Directors', Owners' Comp/Sales	(11) 3.9	(13) 3.1		(14) 1.4		
3.6	4.1	4.0		5.3	4.6		3.2		
5.1	8.1	5.4		9.7	7.5		4.8		
1161028M	2126596M	1466779M	Net Sales ($)	11930M	37197M	48645M	193898M	319841M	855268M
566898M	1022916M	792182M	Total Assets ($)	6344M	17721M	12588M	68467M	132559M	554503M

M = $ thousand   MM = $ million
See Pages 11 through 18 for Explanation of Ratios and Data

Current Data Sorted By Assets   Comparative Historical Data

							Type of Statement		
		1	15	22	1	5	Unqualified	40	43
6	28	56	8	1			Reviewed	109	113
15	28	20	1	1			Compiled	66	70
12	19	3					Tax Returns	23	25
6	7	11	5	2	1		Other	44	29
	134 (4/1-9/30/02)			140 (10/1/02-3/31/03)				4/1/98-3/31/99	4/1/99-3/31/00
0-500M	500M-2MM	2-10MM	10-50MM	50-100MM	100-250MM		**NUMBER OF STATEMENTS**	ALL	ALL
39	83	105	36	5	6			282	280
%	%	%	%	%	%		**ASSETS**	%	%
21.2	12.5	11.7	8.1				Cash & Equivalents	10.8	10.4
19.1	27.1	27.0	20.3				Trade Receivables (net)	20.0	23.9
12.4	10.0	10.6	9.5				Inventory	10.8	9.7
1.4	2.6	3.7	4.2				All Other Current	3.2	3.0
54.1	52.3	53.0	42.2				Total Current	44.8	47.1
33.4	29.5	29.8	44.2				Fixed Assets (net)	35.7	35.6
5.1	7.6	6.6	7.4				Intangibles (net)	7.8	6.8
7.4	10.6	10.6	6.2				All Other Non-Current	11.8	10.5
100.0	100.0	100.0	100.0				Total	100.0	100.0
							LIABILITIES		
12.4	6.6	10.1	6.4				Notes Payable-Short Term	8.6	7.5
5.9	6.0	4.6	4.4				Cur. Mat.-L/T/D	5.7	5.2
14.6	15.1	16.4	18.0				Trade Payables	14.0	15.5
.1	.2	.1	.1				Income Taxes Payable	.2	.2
21.7	20.9	18.0	12.7				All Other Current	13.0	13.7
54.7	48.8	49.2	41.6				Total Current	41.4	42.1
25.2	19.3	14.0	25.3				Long Term Debt	24.3	21.1
.5	.3	.5	1.3				Deferred Taxes	.6	.7
4.7	3.3	5.0	3.6				All Other Non-Current	6.3	5.1
14.9	28.3	31.2	28.3				Net Worth	27.4	31.0
100.0	100.0	100.0	100.0				Total Liabilities & Net Worth	100.0	100.0
							INCOME DATA		
100.0	100.0	100.0	100.0				Net Sales	100.0	100.0
29.2	25.7	21.3	16.5				Gross Profit	25.9	26.7
29.0	24.5	20.7	15.8				Operating Expenses	24.5	25.5
.2	1.2	.6	.7				Operating Profit	1.4	1.2
.3	.3	–.1	–.1				All Other Expenses (net)	.5	–.3
–.1	.9	.7	.9				Profit Before Taxes	.9	1.4
							RATIOS		
1.9	1.7	1.4	1.2					1.7	1.7
1.0	1.1	1.1	1.0				Current	1.1	1.1
.8	.7	.7	.8					.8	.8
1.4	1.2	1.1	.9					1.2	1.2
.8	.8	.8	.6				Quick	(281) .8	.8
.5	.5	.5	.4					.5	.5
5 74.2	14 25.4	14 26.5	10 38.1					11 33.3	13 29.0
16 23.5	25 14.5	22 16.8	15 24.3				Sales/Receivables	19 19.4	25 14.8
25 14.6	39 9.3	34 10.6	31 11.9					29 12.4	36 10.3
2 211.7	4 85.0	5 68.8	6 64.5					6 59.8	5 67.8
9 40.5	12 31.2	11 33.8	10 37.3				Cost of Sales/Inventory	13 29.1	11 34.5
21 17.3	21 17.2	19 19.6	23 28.4					22 16.9	23 16.0
5 78.8	10 36.1	11 34.3	14 25.3					11 33.2	12 29.2
17 21.8	17 21.5	15 24.3	19 19.4				Cost of Sales/Payables	16 22.5	21 17.6
26 14.1	28 13.1	22 16.3	25 14.8					24 15.4	30 12.2
19.4	16.7	20.7	32.5					17.1	17.0
UND	110.0	99.4	–946.2				Sales/Working Capital	101.7	90.9
–25.0	–23.5	–29.6	–33.2					–36.0	–40.5
3.0	5.5	4.4	4.2					3.8	4.7
(34) 1.0	(77) 1.4	(96) 1.9	(35) 1.7				EBIT/Interest	(267) 1.9	(256) 1.8
–1.0	–1.3	.7	.9					.6	1.0
	2.9	2.7	2.9					3.4	3.8
	(19) 1.7	(43) 1.8	(19) 2.0				Net Profit + Depr., Dep., Amort./Cur. Mat. L /T/D	(94) 1.7	(95) 1.6
	.7	.8	1.0					1.1	.9
.5	.4	.5	1.2					.7	.6
1.2	1.4	1.2	2.4				Fixed/Worth	1.6	1.5
–2.2	38.6	3.6	7.7					28.0	5.9
1.0	1.1	1.2	2.0					1.1	1.0
2.5	3.1	3.1	2.7				Debt/Worth	2.9	2.4
–5.1	125.3	10.3	14.7					77.5	14.3
22.4	24.0	20.9	23.1					26.9	23.8
(26) 9.7	(63) 6.7	(90) 8.6	(30) 8.2				% Profit Before Taxes/Tangible Net Worth	(213) 12.4	(226) 9.4
–4.2	–7.5	–1.8	1.7					2.0	1.1
7.4	7.8	4.7	5.7					7.6	8.1
.0	1.8	1.9	2.0				% Profit Before Taxes/Total Assets	3.0	3.2
–11.4	–4.6	–1.5	–.2					–1.1	.1
29.7	21.3	25.8	16.1					18.5	20.5
17.3	13.8	16.1	8.9				Sales/Net Fixed Assets	11.5	11.0
8.0	7.9	8.3	4.9					6.1	6.0
6.7	4.4	5.3	5.1					4.6	4.7
5.2	3.3	3.8	3.3				Sales/Total Assets	3.3	3.3
3.3	2.4	2.7	2.4					2.4	2.3
1.0	1.2	.9	1.2					1.3	1.3
(35) 2.2	(77) 2.2	(103) 1.6	1.6				% Depr., Dep., Amort./Sales	(264) 1.9	(261) 2.1
3.0	4.2	2.4	2.5					2.8	3.2
3.4	1.8	1.0						1.3	1.5
(28) 5.0	(50) 2.8	(57) 2.1					% Officers', Directors', Owners' Comp/Sales	(152) 2.7	(149) 3.4
10.1	5.1	3.5						5.6	6.8
64750M	327573M	2258010M	2951956M	1796834M	1742838M		Net Sales ($)	5848453M	6123800M
12264M	92513M	506240M	792415M	331461M	942008M		Total Assets ($)	2018260M	1995962M

M = $ thousand   MM = $ million
See Pages 11 through 18 for Explanation of Ratios and Data

Comparative Historical Data   Current Data Sorted By Sales

4/1/00-3/31/01 ALL	4/1/01-3/31/02 ALL	4/1/02-3/31/03 ALL	Type of Statement	0-1MM	1-3MM	3-5MM	5-10MM	10-25MM	25MM & OVER
33	20	44	Unqualified				6	5	33
90	70	99	Reviewed		13	9	24	24	29
77	61	65	Compiled	6	24	9	11	6	9
21	26	34	Tax Returns	6	15	6	6	1	
36	37	32	Other	3	6	4	4	6	9
				134 (4/1-9/30/02)			140 (10/1/02-3/31/03)		
257	214	274	NUMBER OF STATEMENTS	15	58	28	51	42	80
%	%	%	**ASSETS**	%	%	%	%	%	%
11.2	16.5	12.7	Cash & Equivalents	26.1	15.3	12.8	12.4	12.3	8.5
29.0	23.2	25.0	Trade Receivables (net)	9.4	23.7	27.4	25.0	26.8	27.3
10.6	10.9	10.5	Inventory	10.1	11.0	10.0	11.6	10.1	9.8
2.9	2.5	3.1	All Other Current	2.3	1.5	1.1	3.9	4.5	3.9
53.7	53.1	51.3	Total Current	47.9	51.5	51.4	52.8	53.7	49.5
30.8	30.2	32.0	Fixed Assets (net)	41.6	31.1	26.6	30.4	27.1	36.3
6.9	7.7	7.3	Intangibles (net)	1.9	6.7	10.2	7.0	7.9	7.6
8.6	9.1	9.5	All Other Non-Current	8.5	10.7	11.8	9.9	11.3	6.6
100.0	100.0	100.0	Total	100.0	100.0	100.0	100.0	100.0	100.0
			LIABILITIES						
9.1	6.1	8.6	Notes Payable-Short Term	4.9	10.0	6.0	6.8	9.5	9.8
4.5	4.7	5.1	Cur. Mat.-L/T/D	6.8	5.7	5.5	5.3	4.8	4.3
18.9	14.6	16.1	Trade Payables	9.9	13.8	13.6	15.7	16.2	20.1
.3	.4	.1	Income Taxes Payable	.0	.3	.0	.0	.0	.1
14.3	19.8	18.6	All Other Current	21.7	18.5	29.2	22.5	15.2	13.9
47.2	45.6	48.6	Total Current	43.3	48.2	54.4	50.4	45.7	48.1
20.2	19.8	18.9	Long Term Debt	30.4	22.9	16.7	16.0	12.1	20.1
.5	.5	.6	Deferred Taxes	.0	.5	.4	.6	.4	1.0
6.6	7.6	4.3	All Other Non-Current	4.2	4.6	2.6	2.9	7.7	3.8
25.5	26.5	27.6	Net Worth	22.1	23.7	26.0	30.2	34.1	26.9
100.0	100.0	100.0	Total Liabilities & Net Worth	100.0	100.0	100.0	100.0	100.0	100.0
			INCOME DATA						
100.0	100.0	100.0	Net Sales	100.0	100.0	100.0	100.0	100.0	100.0
20.8	22.2	23.1	Gross Profit	31.9	29.4	24.1	24.4	23.2	15.5
19.3	20.5	22.2	Operating Expenses	28.2	28.6	23.9	23.7	22.7	14.7
1.4	1.6	.8	Operating Profit	3.7	.7	.3	.7	.5	.8
.3	.1	.1	All Other Expenses (net)	1.4	.4	.3	–.4	.0	.1
1.2	1.5	.7	Profit Before Taxes	2.3	.4	–.1	1.1	.6	.7
			RATIOS						
1.7 1.1 .8	1.7 1.1 .8	1.5 1.1 .8	Current	1.9 1.3 .5	1.9 1.1 .8	1.6 1.0 .7	1.5 1.1 .7	1.8 1.2 .7	1.3 1.0 .8
1.3 .8 .6	1.3 .9 .6	1.1 .8 .5	Quick	1.5 .8 .4	1.4 .8 .5	1.0 .8 .5	1.1 .7 .5	1.3 .8 .5	1.0 .7 .4
13 27.7 25 14.4 35 10.5	12 31.6 19 19.4 27 13.7	12 30.3 22 16.8 33 10.9	Sales/Receivables	5 74.2 10 37.9 18 20.0	12 29.9 24 15.2 33 11.0	19 19.4 31 11.9 41 8.9	14 25.4 23 15.6 33 11.0	17 22.0 25 14.7 44 8.3	10 34.9 19 18.8 31 11.6
5 72.5 10 37.4 16 22.9	4 82.0 9 38.5 16 22.6	5 76.9 11 34.2 20 18.6	Cost of Sales/Inventory	1 588.0 15 24.4 23 16.0	6 61.9 14 26.3 26 14.0	3 122.6 8 45.0 24 15.4	7 51.8 13 28.3 21 17.5	6 63.5 11 34.5 18 20.5	4 89.7 10 37.5 14 25.4
12 30.8 17 20.9 27 13.7	8 47.5 13 27.9 19 18.7	11 34.8 17 21.5 26 14.2	Cost of Sales/Payables	2 158.5 17 21.4 26 14.1	7 48.7 15 23.7 29 12.6	9 39.1 19 19.0 28 13.2	10 36.0 15 24.3 26 14.2	12 30.7 18 20.7 26 14.1	13 28.2 17 21.5 25 14.6
17.4 71.7 –51.5	19.5 87.8 –50.3	18.9 137.2 –29.9	Sales/Working Capital	13.2 50.6 –8.8	17.4 115.3 –36.5	22.9 NM –16.4	18.7 78.8 –17.5	11.8 70.0 –30.3	32.5 395.8 –52.7
5.7 (237) 2.3 1.0	6.0 (198) 2.6 1.3	4.5 (253) 1.7 .0	EBIT/Interest	5.6 (13) 2.2 .1	3.8 (51) .8 –1.1	6.2 (27) 1.4 –2.2	5.8 (48) 2.0 .3	4.1 (36) 1.7 –.9	4.1 (78) 1.9 1.1
4.4 (91) 2.1 1.0	3.9 (72) 2.1 1.6	2.8 (93) 1.9 .8	Net Profit + Depr., Dep., Amort./Cur. Mat. L/T/D		2.9 (14) 2.3 .5		2.2 (17) 1.2 .7	2.8 (18) 2.1 .8	3.4 (35) 2.0 1.2
.6 1.6 134.2	.5 1.5 12.5	.5 1.4 9.2	Fixed/Worth	.3 1.4 12.6	.4 1.3 –2.5	.5 1.3 –6.8	.4 1.4 5.2	.5 1.0 2.6	.9 2.0 7.7
1.2 3.1 447.1	1.4 3.2 29.3	1.3 3.1 29.6	Debt/Worth	1.6 2.5 13.7	.9 2.4 –6.6	1.2 3.4 –15.5	1.2 3.3 13.5	.9 1.9 8.2	2.0 3.4 23.7
36.0 (196) 15.7 3.1	42.2 (167) 19.3 5.2	22.3 (216) 8.6 –1.9	% Profit Before Taxes/Tangible Net Worth	80.4 (13) 18.2 .0	17.2 (39) 4.6 –11.1	32.3 (20) 8.8 –10.3	27.5 (43) 7.5 –3.3	21.2 (35) 8.5 –2.1	23.1 (66) 9.4 2.4
9.2 3.9 .1	11.3 4.6 1.1	5.8 1.9 –2.5	% Profit Before Taxes/Total Assets	8.0 4.3 –2.7	8.9 .5 –9.2	6.8 1.3 –5.5	6.7 3.1 –1.6	5.1 1.2 –5.5	5.0 2.0 .4
28.4 15.3 8.8	27.4 16.6 9.3	25.1 14.0 7.4	Sales/Net Fixed Assets	29.7 10.0 3.1	24.9 13.6 7.5	25.3 15.3 8.7	22.7 12.5 6.2	22.3 15.6 10.7	26.4 13.4 6.7
5.6 4.0 3.0	6.1 4.2 3.1	5.1 3.6 2.7	Sales/Total Assets	5.0 3.0 1.7	5.3 3.3 2.4	4.0 3.3 2.7	4.6 3.5 2.7	4.8 3.9 2.7	6.2 4.5 2.9
.8 (243) 1.5 2.3	1.0 (201) 1.6 2.5	1.1 (260) 1.8 2.8	% Depr., Dep., Amort./Sales	1.7 (13) 2.5 4.7	1.4 (54) 2.4 4.4	1.2 (27) 2.0 3.8	1.1 (48) 2.2 2.9	1.2 (41) 1.6 2.5	.7 (77) 1.3 2.0
1.5 (127) 2.6 5.1	1.2 (127) 2.6 5.3	1.3 (144) 2.7 4.8	% Officers', Directors', Owners' Comp/Sales		2.1 (36) 3.0 6.4	2.5 (21) 3.0 4.8	1.4 (31) 2.8 4.8	1.3 (22) 2.2 4.0	.5 (26) .8 1.8
10346540M 2315204M	7796994M 2003462M	9141961M 2676901M	Net Sales ($) Total Assets ($)	9772M 5598M	119029M 36969M	103966M 35401M	382695M 123134M	608613M 184979M	7917886M 2290820M

M = $ thousand   MM = $ million
See Pages 11 through 18 for Explanation of Ratios and Data

Current Data Sorted By Assets

Comparative Historical Data

0-500M	500M-2MM	2-10MM	10-50MM	50-100MM	100-250MM	Type of Statement	ALL 4/1/98-3/31/99	ALL 4/1/99-3/31/00
1	1	1	3	1	2	Unqualified	22	13
1	2	13	5			Reviewed	32	19
1	10	6				Compiled	29	26
3	3					Tax Returns	5	2
	6	5	5			Other	21	19
	31 (4/1-9/30/02)		38 (10/1/02-3/31/03)					
6	22	25	13	1	2	**NUMBER OF STATEMENTS**	109	79
%	%	%	%	%	%	**ASSETS**	%	%
	8.3	9.3	8.5			Cash & Equivalents	8.3	10.2
	18.1	22.2	9.3			Trade Receivables (net)	15.6	20.1
	10.5	9.6	7.9			Inventory	11.6	9.7
	.9	1.6	5.2			All Other Current	3.3	2.5
	37.8	42.8	30.9			Total Current	38.8	42.5
	48.7	41.6	57.9			Fixed Assets (net)	45.6	45.1
	9.7	4.9	6.5			Intangibles (net)	3.9	4.1
	3.7	10.7	4.7			All Other Non-Current	11.6	8.3
	100.0	100.0	100.0			Total	100.0	100.0
						LIABILITIES		
	9.8	6.6	1.4			Notes Payable-Short Term	7.0	5.9
	5.5	3.9	6.8			Cur. Mat.-L/T/D	7.3	5.4
	14.4	16.5	6.2			Trade Payables	11.0	14.1
	.0	.0	.4			Income Taxes Payable	.3	.4
	6.1	9.5	4.7			All Other Current	7.5	7.5
	35.9	36.4	19.5			Total Current	33.1	33.2
	23.2	17.6	27.1			Long Term Debt	23.9	19.6
	1.2	.8	2.7			Deferred Taxes	1.2	1.2
	2.5	5.7	7.0			All Other Non-Current	3.6	4.5
	37.2	39.5	43.7			Net Worth	38.2	41.5
	100.0	100.0	100.0			Total Liabilities & Net Worth	100.0	100.0
						INCOME DATA		
	100.0	100.0	100.0			Net Sales	100.0	100.0
	45.3	35.7	44.2			Gross Profit	40.6	43.0
	42.6	33.3	38.6			Operating Expenses	37.0	36.8
	2.7	2.5	5.6			Operating Profit	3.5	6.2
	.7	−.1	.4			All Other Expenses (net)	.5	1.1
	2.0	2.6	5.2			Profit Before Taxes	3.0	5.1
						RATIOS		
	2.5	1.9	2.2				2.1	2.2
	.9	1.2	1.8			Current	1.2	1.3
	.6	.9	.9				.8	.9
	1.7	1.5	1.5				1.2	1.5
	.6	.9	.7			Quick	.7	.8
	.4	.4	.5				.4	.5
	15 24.4	15 24.3	11 32.2				14 25.2	21 17.6
	29 12.7	26 13.9	21 17.5			Sales/Receivables	23 15.7	30 12.0
	46 8.0	44 8.3	31 11.7				37 9.9	50 7.4
	15 24.5	11 33.9	16 22.5				15 24.8	12 30.1
	21 17.0	23 16.1	27 13.7			Cost of Sales/Inventory	31 11.9	26 14.0
	47 7.7	47 7.8	45 8.1				51 7.1	53 6.9
	16 22.7	13 28.0	17 21.6				17 21.7	20 18.1
	31 11.6	27 13.5	23 15.7			Cost of Sales/Payables	27 13.6	33 11.2
	75 4.9	37 9.9	40 9.1				43 8.6	56 6.5
	8.4	12.3	5.5				9.5	7.5
	−71.2	39.2	11.0			Sales/Working Capital	62.7	35.5
	−14.0	−59.6	−163.0				−25.8	−54.4
	(16) 5.1	(24) 9.8	10.5				(101) 5.5	(67) 7.8
	2.2	3.5	2.7			EBIT/Interest	2.2	3.4
	.2	.0	1.6				1.1	1.7
		(12) 5.8				Net Profit + Depr., Dep.,	(47) 8.3	(31) 5.0
		2.3				Amort./Cur. Mat. L /T/D	2.8	2.4
		1.5					1.5	1.4
	.7	.6	.9				.6	.6
	2.7	1.2	2.0			Fixed/Worth	1.2	1.3
	UND	1.9	2.7				3.0	4.1
	.7	.8	.7				.8	.5
	3.0	2.0	1.9			Debt/Worth	1.8	1.9
	UND	4.9	3.3				4.3	5.5
	(18) 66.2	(23) 38.1	27.9			% Profit Before Taxes/Tangible	(97) 26.0	(69) 32.0
	13.0	14.7	18.9			Net Worth	13.2	17.8
	5.4	−5.7	6.7				3.6	5.3
	9.5	10.6	10.3			% Profit Before Taxes/Total	10.0	12.1
	4.2	3.7	4.6			Assets	3.8	7.1
	−1.3	−1.8	2.1				.4	2.0
	7.8	9.6	3.6				9.1	10.9
	4.4	5.9	3.2			Sales/Net Fixed Assets	4.2	4.2
	2.5	4.1	2.0				2.4	2.3
	2.9	3.1	2.1				2.9	2.9
	2.1	2.3	1.7			Sales/Total Assets	1.9	1.8
	1.6	1.8	1.1				1.3	1.3
	(20) 4.4	(23) 2.4	4.0			% Depr., Dep., Amort./Sales	(99) 2.3	(72) 2.2
	6.1	4.0	5.1				4.8	4.8
	7.0	6.5	5.8				7.0	7.2
	(10) 2.6	(13) 1.4				% Officers', Directors',	(32) 1.0	(28) 1.6
	3.9	3.0				Owners' Comp/Sales	2.6	3.9
	6.5	10.5					6.1	6.6
7300M	66071M	266308M	410974M	81589M	355491M	Net Sales ($)	2222051M	1016285M
2038M	29347M	110581M	259982M	67071M	243828M	Total Assets ($)	1807106M	609482M

M = $ thousand   MM = $ million
See Pages 11 through 18 for Explanation of Ratios and Data

Comparative Historical Data / Current Data Sorted By Sales

Hist 1	Hist 2	Hist 3	Type of Statement	0-1MM	1-3MM	3-5MM	5-10MM	10-25MM	25MM & OVER
5	11	9	Unqualified	1		1		2	5
16	9	21	Reviewed		2	2	6	8	3
26	26	17	Compiled		4	7	3	3	
2	5	6	Tax Returns	1	5				
13	14	16	Other	1	4	3	1	4	3
4/1/00-3/31/01 ALL	4/1/01-3/31/02 ALL	4/1/02-3/31/03 ALL			31 (4/1-9/30/02)			38 (10/1/02-3/31/02)	
62	65	69	NUMBER OF STATEMENTS	3	15	13	10	17	11
%	%	%	ASSETS	%	%	%	%	%	%
6.7	9.3	8.3	Cash & Equivalents		8.3	8.7	6.9	8.6	8.7
20.1	18.8	19.0	Trade Receivables (net)		21.2	16.6	22.6	21.7	13.4
11.6	13.0	9.8	Inventory		12.2	11.6	9.7	8.5	9.4
2.3	3.4	2.4	All Other Current		.3	1.6	1.7	4.0	2.6
40.6	44.5	39.5	Total Current		42.0	38.5	40.9	42.7	34.2
45.2	42.5	46.5	Fixed Assets (net)		46.4	46.9	41.0	47.2	53.0
5.1	3.7	7.4	Intangibles (net)		8.4	6.6	5.7	4.5	5.1
9.0	9.3	6.6	All Other Non-Current		3.2	8.1	12.3	5.6	7.7
100.0	100.0	100.0	Total		100.0	100.0	100.0	100.0	100.0
			LIABILITIES						
6.6	5.4	5.9	Notes Payable-Short Term		8.7	9.7	3.9	5.4	1.8
5.2	3.9	5.0	Cur. Mat.-L/T/D		3.7	4.4	5.8	4.3	5.9
15.2	15.0	13.9	Trade Payables		16.4	7.8	20.8	17.1	9.3
.2	.1	.1	Income Taxes Payable		.0	.0	.0	.0	.4
9.8	12.1	8.3	All Other Current		10.9	6.7	9.0	8.6	5.6
37.1	36.5	33.2	Total Current		39.7	28.7	39.4	35.5	23.0
25.5	26.8	21.3	Long Term Debt		19.6	21.0	20.2	18.4	25.0
1.3	.9	1.4	Deferred Taxes		1.5	.9	.2	.6	4.2
4.0	4.5	5.0	All Other Non-Current		6.3	6.5	2.1	6.1	3.8
32.2	31.3	39.1	Net Worth		32.7	42.9	38.1	39.4	44.0
100.0	100.0	100.0	Total Liabilities & Net Worth		100.0	100.0	100.0	100.0	100.0
			INCOME DATA						
100.0	100.0	100.0	Net Sales		100.0	100.0	100.0	100.0	100.0
35.6	33.7	39.9	Gross Profit		42.6	41.4	35.4	39.2	35.6
33.1	30.2	36.6	Operating Expenses		39.2	38.9	33.4	34.9	32.2
2.5	3.6	3.2	Operating Profit		3.4	2.4	2.0	4.3	3.4
−.2	1.1	.2	All Other Expenses (net)		.5	.7	.0	.1	−.6
2.7	2.5	3.0	Profit Before Taxes		2.8	1.7	2.1	4.2	4.0
			RATIOS						
1.5	2.1	2.1			2.9	3.2	1.6	2.0	2.1
1.1	1.4	1.4	Current		1.1	1.4	1.4	1.2	1.6
.7	.8	.8			.5	.8	.6	.9	.9
1.0	1.5	1.5			2.0	1.9	1.2	1.2	1.5
.7	.8	.8	Quick		.5	.7	.8	.8	1.0
.5	.4	.4			.4	.5	.3	.5	.5
13 27.9	12 30.3	15 24.3		2 235.3	17 21.1	23 16.1	9 38.9	12 30.9	
25 14.6	19 19.0	27 13.5	Sales/Receivables	30 12.3	29 12.7	28 12.8	21 17.5	26 14.2	
49 7.5	32 11.6	43 8.5		52 7.1	45 8.1	55 6.7	40 9.2	40 9.1	
12 31.1	8 43.2	15 24.8		16 22.7	16 22.8	6 62.4	6 60.6	14 25.7	
22 16.6	20 18.4	24 15.3	Cost of Sales/Inventory	30 12.1	31 11.7	21 17.4	23 16.1	24 15.2	
40 9.2	38 9.6	43 8.4		47 7.8	63 5.8	44 8.3	40 9.1	44 8.3	
14 26.0	8 43.4	15 23.9		15 25.1	7 49.8	26 14.0	15 25.2	18 20.6	
33 11.1	17 21.4	27 13.3	Cost of Sales/Payables	30 12.0	25 14.9	30 12.3	27 13.3	24 15.0	
51 7.1	30 12.2	47 7.8		67 5.4	32 11.3	66 5.5	44 8.3	44 8.4	
14.7	11.3	9.1			8.7	5.3	13.3	11.6	7.3
99.2	27.0	26.2	Sales/Working Capital		186.5	18.4	17.4	39.3	13.5
−46.1	−32.5	−37.8			−13.6	−27.7	−22.2	−151.4	−59.6
(58) 4.8	(61) 6.9	(60) 7.4		(11) 6.2	4.5		(16) 27.3	5.2	
2.0	2.4	2.8	EBIT/Interest	3.7	1.5		5.4	2.7	
.8	1.1	.8		−1.3	−.4		2.3	2.3	
(17) 4.6	(20) 4.2	(27) 3.3	Net Profit + Depr., Dep., Amort./Cur. Mat. L/T/D						
2.3	2.5	2.4							
1.3	1.9	1.6							
.8	.6	.7			.6	.4	1.1	.6	.8
1.9	1.7	1.5	Fixed/Worth		2.3	1.6	1.5	1.2	1.3
6.5	6.0	3.1			UND	3.1	1.9	4.3	2.7
1.3	.8	.8			.5	.6	1.3	.7	.7
2.7	2.1	1.9	Debt/Worth		4.1	2.0	2.2	1.9	1.4
9.6	12.9	5.1			UND	4.5	3.3	5.6	2.9
42.0	43.8	38.1	% Profit Before Taxes/Tangible Net Worth	149.5	23.1	21.6	39.9	21.7	
(54) 12.0	(55) 21.2	(62) 15.0		(12) 22.3	(12) 8.5	10.6	(16) 20.1	19.4	
−4.4	4.8	5.4		4.9	−5.9	−5.7	7.7	6.2	
10.0	14.9	10.2	% Profit Before Taxes/Total Assets		18.7	5.8	6.9	11.6	11.4
3.7	6.6	4.6			7.4	1.9	3.8	7.5	6.9
−.6	.5	−.3			−1.7	−3.3	−1.0	2.2	3.3
12.3	12.8	7.8			11.5	8.3	8.3	9.0	4.8
6.4	7.2	4.7	Sales/Net Fixed Assets		4.6	5.8	6.4	4.2	3.4
2.6	3.6	2.6			2.6	2.1	4.1	2.7	2.7
3.6	4.2	3.0			3.0	2.8	2.9	3.8	2.2
2.5	2.6	2.1	Sales/Total Assets		2.0	2.2	2.3	2.8	1.8
1.7	1.9	1.6			1.6	1.1	1.9	1.7	1.4
(58) 1.5	(54) 1.0	(63) 3.3	% Depr., Dep., Amort./Sales	(14) 4.4	(12) 3.5	3.6	(16) 2.3	3.0	
3.8	2.9	5.1		6.0	5.7	4.9	4.7	3.9	
6.4	4.6	6.5		8.6	7.2	6.1	6.4	5.1	
(27) 1.3	(21) 1.3	(29) 1.7	% Officers', Directors', Owners' Comp/Sales						
3.6	4.6	3.5							
11.4	6.8	5.9							
870475M	1243826M	1187733M	Net Sales ($)	833M	26101M	50015M	69841M	276569M	764374M
383589M	495602M	712847M	Total Assets ($)	3467M	12540M	35651M	37836M	156426M	466927M

© RMA 2003

M = $ thousand   MM = $ million
See Pages 11 through 18 for Explanation of Ratios and Data

	Current Data Sorted By Assets							Comparative Historical Data	
							Type of Statement		
	1	2	1	4		2	Unqualified	5	7
	1	2	5	4			Reviewed	3	4
	4	3	1				Compiled	10	5
	9	8					Tax Returns	3	3
	3	6	2	4	1	2	Other	4	3
		9 (4/1-9/30/02)		49 (10/1/02-3/31/03)				4/1/98-3/31/99	4/1/99-3/31/00
	0-500M	500M-2MM	2-10MM	10-50MM	50-100MM	100-250MM		ALL	ALL
	17	19	9	8	1	4	NUMBER OF STATEMENTS	25	22
	%	%	%	%	%	%	ASSETS	%	%
	9.4	11.2					Cash & Equivalents	14.5	14.3
	18.0	25.0					Trade Receivables (net)	20.4	18.2
	16.4	26.9					Inventory	18.9	21.8
	7.1	2.1					All Other Current	2.2	2.7
	51.0	65.2					Total Current	55.9	57.0
	24.8	18.9					Fixed Assets (net)	26.4	32.1
	10.7	7.3					Intangibles (net)	4.7	2.2
	13.4	8.6					All Other Non-Current	12.9	8.7
	100.0	100.0					Total	100.0	100.0
							LIABILITIES		
	21.2	14.3					Notes Payable-Short Term	5.3	14.4
	8.1	4.5					Cur. Mat.-L/T/D	4.8	4.5
	29.1	21.0					Trade Payables	23.3	14.3
	.1	.0					Income Taxes Payable	.8	1.2
	13.1	11.1					All Other Current	8.7	14.1
	71.5	50.9					Total Current	43.0	48.5
	12.9	12.2					Long Term Debt	25.0	19.4
	.0	.0					Deferred Taxes	.2	.0
	8.1	18.3					All Other Non-Current	9.0	8.5
	7.5	18.6					Net Worth	22.8	23.7
	100.0	100.0					Total Liabilities & Net Worth	100.0	100.0
							INCOME DATA		
	100.0	100.0					Net Sales	100.0	100.0
	45.6	36.1					Gross Profit	45.3	58.8
	44.2	34.8					Operating Expenses	42.4	52.9
	1.3	1.3					Operating Profit	3.0	5.9
	.4	1.1					All Other Expenses (net)	−.1	1.8
	.9	.2					Profit Before Taxes	3.0	4.1
							RATIOS		
	2.1	3.3						2.2	2.0
	.9	1.3					Current	1.3	1.3
	.3	.8						.9	1.0
	.9	1.6						1.4	1.4
	.5	.7					Quick	.9	.8
	.2	.4						.5	.3
0	UND	12 29.5						5 72.9	0 UND
8	47.1	26 14.1					Sales/Receivables	18 20.6	18 20.8
32	11.6	40 9.1						32 11.3	40 9.2
0	UND	14 25.7						0 UND	0 UND
18	20.0	47 7.7					Cost of Sales/Inventory	36 10.2	55 6.6
48	7.5	92 4.0						69 5.3	138 2.6
12	31.0	13 28.1						19 19.1	12 31.2
50	7.3	33 11.0					Cost of Sales/Payables	38 9.6	35 10.3
76	4.8	47 7.8						62 5.9	68 5.3
	38.9	7.0						11.1	9.7
	−54.5	23.2					Sales/Working Capital	22.7	35.6
	−8.6	−15.4						−52.5	NM
		7.8						8.3	9.3
	(16)	3.8					EBIT/Interest	(20) 3.8	(18) 4.5
		1.2						.8	1.1
							Net Profit + Depr., Dep., Amort./Cur. Mat. L /T/D		
	.5	.1						.3	.4
	10.5	1.9					Fixed/Worth	.6	.9
	−.5	−1.9						1.7	2.0
	1.2	1.4						.5	.8
	55.0	8.1					Debt/Worth	2.4	2.2
	−2.7	−16.5						−30.6	5.4
	781.8	78.1						48.4	34.7
(11)	77.6	(13) 10.8					% Profit Before Taxes/Tangible Net Worth	(18) 11.3	(19) 21.0
	.0	3.9						−2.6	7.6
	27.7	9.0						19.5	12.1
	3.3	5.7					% Profit Before Taxes/Total Assets	3.7	5.0
	−5.4	.7						−.9	.5
	86.9	102.2						45.9	32.9
	26.2	30.6					Sales/Net Fixed Assets	18.7	14.6
	11.1	12.6						4.3	4.8
	7.3	5.8						5.2	4.1
	4.2	3.1					Sales/Total Assets	3.1	2.9
	2.9	2.2						2.0	2.0
	.2	.9						.7	.6
(11)	1.1	(13) 1.8					% Depr., Dep., Amort./Sales	(17) 2.1	(19) 1.9
	1.7	4.4						6.0	3.2
							% Officers', Directors', Owners' Comp/Sales		
	17782M	71667M	205843M	397331M	338079M	1138458M	Net Sales ($)	2188118M	1545459M
	3252M	17829M	53589M	148890M	72267M	685778M	Total Assets ($)	445604M	575097M

© RMA 2003

M = $ thousand   MM = $ million
See Pages 11 through 18 for Explanation of Ratios and Data

Comparative Historical Data | Current Data Sorted By Sales

4/1/00-3/31/01 ALL	4/1/01-3/31/02 ALL	4/1/02-3/31/03 ALL	Type of Statement	0-1MM	1-3MM	3-5MM	5-10MM	10-25MM	25MM & OVER
4	7	7	Unqualified		2		1	4	3
5	2	8	Reviewed					2	3
10	17	8	Compiled	3	4			1	
2	5	17	Tax Returns	7	5	4	1		
6	9	18	Other	2	3	2	4		7
				9 (4/1-9/30/02)			49 (10/1/02-3/31/02)		
27	40	58	**NUMBER OF STATEMENTS**	12	14	6	6	7	13
%	%	%	**ASSETS**	%	%	%	%	%	%
11.3	15.9	10.9	Cash & Equivalents	8.3	9.0				13.8
21.4	17.8	19.4	Trade Receivables (net)	18.4	20.0				16.2
21.2	20.9	21.5	Inventory	25.4	23.1				24.9
9.8	4.8	5.2	All Other Current	.3	8.5				8.1
63.7	59.4	57.1	Total Current	52.4	60.6				63.0
23.6	26.6	22.6	Fixed Assets (net)	25.2	19.5				18.7
4.6	4.4	10.9	Intangibles (net)	6.5	10.9				13.1
8.0	9.7	9.3	All Other Non-Current	15.9	8.9				5.2
100.0	100.0	100.0	Total	100.0	100.0				100.0
			LIABILITIES						
12.8	10.8	14.8	Notes Payable-Short Term	9.2	24.7				6.8
4.9	7.0	7.2	Cur. Mat.-L/T/D	10.0	2.9				11.9
21.1	19.8	20.2	Trade Payables	31.3	20.2				14.0
.9	.5	.2	Income Taxes Payable	.0	.2				.5
14.9	13.0	14.4	All Other Current	11.3	13.2				25.6
54.6	51.0	56.8	Total Current	61.8	61.2				58.8
14.9	17.5	14.4	Long Term Debt	17.5	10.5				24.2
.0	.2	.4	Deferred Taxes	.0	.0				1.0
4.9	3.5	9.2	All Other Non-Current	22.9	11.4				2.8
25.6	27.9	19.2	Net Worth	-2.2	16.8				13.2
100.0	100.0	100.0	Total Liabilities & Net Worth	100.0	100.0				100.0
			INCOME DATA						
100.0	100.0	100.0	Net Sales	100.0	100.0				100.0
50.1	47.1	45.3	Gross Profit	51.5	38.6				52.5
45.6	43.6	42.1	Operating Expenses	53.0	36.0				44.6
4.5	3.5	3.2	Operating Profit	-1.6	2.6				7.9
1.5	.8	.8	All Other Expenses (net)	1.1	.4				.8
3.0	2.6	2.4	Profit Before Taxes	-2.7	2.1				7.0
			RATIOS						
1.9	3.1	2.3	Current	2.7	3.1				1.9
1.1	1.4	1.0		.9	1.3				1.1
.7	.7	.6		.4	.8				.9
1.2	2.0	.9	Quick	.9	1.1				.9
.6	.7	.6		.4	.7				.5
.3	.2	.3		.2	.3				.3
3 111.1	1 251.3	4 86.2	Sales/Receivables	0 UND	2 214.2				4 86.9
18 19.8	13 29.0	23 16.1		12 29.4	26 13.8				13 29.1
39 9.4	38 9.5	36 10.2		33 11.2	36 10.0				43 8.5
9 40.5	7 54.3	14 26.1	Cost of Sales/Inventory	0 UND	9 40.9				32 11.3
34 10.8	32 11.4	43 8.4		26 14.3	48 7.5				89 4.1
104 3.5	63 5.8	86 4.2		80 4.6	87 4.2				107 3.4
18 20.3	11 31.9	17 21.8	Cost of Sales/Payables	25 14.8	6 62.5				18 20.6
46 8.0	29 12.4	36 10.1		64 5.7	31 11.6				36 10.1
74 4.9	53 6.9	58 6.3		146 2.5	51 7.1				54 6.8
12.0	7.3	11.0	Sales/Working Capital	NM	10.2				11.1
120.1	18.3	NM		-33.8	38.9				41.7
-22.0	-49.4	-15.3		-8.2	-35.9				-91.4
9.3	4.8	13.9	EBIT/Interest		10.6				35.5
(22) 2.6	(32) 3.4	(44) 6.4			(10) 3.6			(12)	10.5
-.5	.8	1.2			.7				3.2
			Net Profit + Depr., Dep., Amort./Cur. Mat. L/T/D						
.2	.2	.5	Fixed/Worth	.4	.5				.9
.5	1.0	2.0		12.0	2.5				2.7
5.2	16.3	-2.2		-.3	UND				-.4
.9	1.0	1.1	Debt/Worth	.9	2.3				1.2
4.6	2.0	9.7		72.5	9.9				52.3
26.2	217.2	-10.1		-2.2	UND				-2.5
91.4	76.9	145.7	% Profit Before Taxes/Tangible Net Worth		781.8				
(23) 23.7	(31) 24.6	(40) 40.9			(11) 77.6				
5.9	6.0	9.5			4.4				
30.6	18.8	21.8	% Profit Before Taxes/Total Assets	10.7	25.7				27.4
4.2	6.9	8.3		.0	4.4				18.6
-10.6	.4	.5		-12.6	-.9				9.0
72.3	40.8	60.5	Sales/Net Fixed Assets	84.3	180.8				53.6
16.5	18.7	25.6		30.2	27.9				19.1
5.9	6.3	8.9		8.7	11.1				7.6
5.2	4.1	4.9	Sales/Total Assets	5.3	7.1				4.1
3.1	2.9	3.1		3.1	3.5				3.4
2.0	2.4	2.2		2.1	2.2				1.8
.7	.4	.8	% Depr., Dep., Amort./Sales		.6				.7
(20) 2.3	(34) 1.5	(43) 1.3			(10) 1.5			(10)	1.3
5.1	4.9	3.1			6.4				3.0
1.5	2.1	2.3	% Officers', Directors', Owners' Comp/Sales						
(11) 8.4	(16) 5.0	(21) 3.5							
9.5	10.9	12.2							
1344809M	2104725M	2169160M	Net Sales ($)	7318M	26546M	22969M	46876M	128688M	1936763M
469241M	737075M	981605M	Total Assets ($)	2662M	7473M	9756M	10042M	64320M	887352M

M = $ thousand   MM = $ million
See Pages 11 through 18 for Explanation of Ratios and Data

TRANSPORTATION
AND WAREHOUSING

Current Data Sorted By Assets   Comparative Historical Data

0-500M	500M-2MM	2-10MM	10-50MM	50-100MM	100-250MM	Type of Statement	4/1/98-3/31/99 ALL	4/1/99-3/31/00 ALL
1		2	4	4	1	Unqualified	27	15
		2	1			Reviewed	3	7
	1	4	3			Compiled	9	8
2	3					Tax Returns	5	4
	2	6	3		7	Other	12	11
4 (4/1-9/30/02)		42 (10/1/02-3/31/03)						
3	6	14	11	4	8	**NUMBER OF STATEMENTS**	56	45
%	%	%	%	%	%	**ASSETS**	%	%
		6.2	7.2			Cash & Equivalents	10.1	12.0
		14.0	6.1			Trade Receivables (net)	16.6	15.2
		11.4	7.3			Inventory	6.3	7.7
		2.2	2.7			All Other Current	3.9	3.9
		33.9	23.2			Total Current	36.9	38.8
		53.9	65.2			Fixed Assets (net)	52.5	47.0
		3.1	3.5			Intangibles (net)	2.3	4.4
		9.1	8.0			All Other Non-Current	8.3	9.8
		100.0	100.0			Total	100.0	100.0
						LIABILITIES		
		5.1	2.3			Notes Payable-Short Term	3.3	5.7
		10.3	6.3			Cur. Mat.-L/T/D	5.0	5.0
		8.1	5.3			Trade Payables	13.1	11.0
		.2	1.7			Income Taxes Payable	.1	.3
		6.0	12.9			All Other Current	12.0	12.4
		29.7	28.5			Total Current	33.5	34.4
		34.2	25.1			Long Term Debt	36.1	32.0
		.5	.4			Deferred Taxes	1.2	.8
		2.7	13.5			All Other Non-Current	4.1	4.2
		33.0	32.5			Net Worth	25.0	28.6
		100.0	100.0			Total Liabilities & Net Worth	100.0	100.0
						INCOME DATA		
		100.0	100.0			Net Sales	100.0	100.0
						Gross Profit		
		101.7	107.6			Operating Expenses	117.3	92.3
		-1.7	-7.6			Operating Profit	-17.3	7.7
		1.2	.8			All Other Expenses (net)	3.0	2.3
		-2.8	-8.4			Profit Before Taxes	-20.3	5.4
						RATIOS		
		2.2	1.5				1.9	1.9
		1.1	.7			Current	1.0	1.1
		.7	.4				.6	.9
		1.1	1.0				1.4	1.4
		.9	.3			Quick	(55) .7	.7
		.3	.3				.4	.5
		9 40.1	12 31.4				13 29.2	7 53.6
		27 13.6	15 24.3			Sales/Receivables	32 11.4	24 15.3
		37 9.9	43 8.6				45 8.1	36 10.1
						Cost of Sales/Inventory		
						Cost of Sales/Payables		
		6.0	14.2				8.5	6.0
		113.7	-17.2			Sales/Working Capital	268.0	76.7
		-19.4	-3.9				-14.0	-37.1
		2.4	10.3				7.6	5.3
		1.2	1.9			EBIT/Interest	(45) 1.9	(40) 2.1
		-1.8	-3.7				.8	1.0
						Net Profit + Depr., Dep., Amort./Cur. Mat. L /T/D	(23) 5.8 / 2.6 / 1.1	(11) 3.6 / 1.5 / .8
		.7	.9				.9	.9
		1.2	2.3			Fixed/Worth	2.3	1.8
		15.2	-15.9				7.8	7.2
		.7	.8				1.3	1.2
		2.0	1.6			Debt/Worth	3.8	2.7
		20.1	-22.7				11.6	12.6
	(12)	34.6					48.7	83.5
		1.7				% Profit Before Taxes/Tangible Net Worth	(46) 21.0	(37) 16.4
		-20.9					.2	3.4
		4.7	10.7				9.2	19.1
		.4	2.0			% Profit Before Taxes/Total Assets	2.5	4.4
		-7.0	-8.1				-1.6	.3
		6.5	2.3				7.7	11.3
		3.2	1.5			Sales/Net Fixed Assets	2.6	3.3
		1.7	.8				1.2	1.1
		4.2	1.5				2.4	2.8
		1.5	.9			Sales/Total Assets	1.3	1.8
		1.1	.5				.8	.7
		3.1	4.1				2.2	2.6
		6.4	8.6			% Depr., Dep., Amort./Sales	(48) 4.9	(39) 4.3
		12.8	11.8				12.7	8.4
						% Officers', Directors', Owners' Comp/Sales	(11) 1.3 / 3.3 / 7.9	
3723M	23721M	229915M	184216M	314611M	2374326M	Net Sales ($)	4167394M	2778454M
1027M	7396M	86089M	198857M	282149M	1314228M	Total Assets ($)	2112355M	1426509M

M = $ thousand   MM = $ million
See Pages 11 through 18 for Explanation of Ratios and Data

Comparative Historical Data				Current Data Sorted By Sales					
			Type of Statement						
5	1	12	Unqualified	1			1	3	7
9	2	3	Reviewed		1			2	
8	10	8	Compiled		3	1	1	3	
4	1	5	Tax Returns		3		2		
21	20	18	Other	1		1	3	4	9
4/1/00-3/31/01 ALL	4/1/01-3/31/02 ALL	4/1/02-3/31/03 ALL		0-1MM	4 (4/1-9/30/02) 1-3MM	3-5MM	5-10MM	42 (10/1/02-3/31/03) 10-25MM	25MM & OVER
47	34	46	**NUMBER OF STATEMENTS**	2	7	2	7	12	16
%	%	%	**ASSETS**	%	%	%	%	%	%
9.3	12.6	13.7	Cash & Equivalents					3.8	18.4
16.4	19.7	12.4	Trade Receivables (net)					13.2	9.6
7.9	8.1	6.7	Inventory					10.0	8.4
4.0	3.0	2.2	All Other Current					3.1	2.8
37.6	43.4	35.0	Total Current					30.1	39.2
51.1	44.0	51.9	Fixed Assets (net)					57.1	48.7
3.0	5.1	2.6	Intangibles (net)					4.6	2.3
8.3	7.5	10.5	All Other Non-Current					8.3	9.8
100.0	100.0	100.0	Total					100.0	100.0
			LIABILITIES						
9.9	7.4	4.4	Notes Payable-Short Term					4.9	6.8
5.4	5.4	6.1	Cur. Mat.-L/T/D					6.7	5.6
13.9	15.5	8.8	Trade Payables					8.1	10.0
.3	.4	.8	Income Taxes Payable					.6	1.5
14.7	10.2	13.2	All Other Current					7.0	15.1
44.1	38.9	33.3	Total Current					27.3	39.1
29.6	35.3	25.2	Long Term Debt					23.0	23.6
1.0	1.1	1.3	Deferred Taxes					.5	2.5
4.3	6.6	12.3	All Other Non-Current					12.8	8.8
21.0	18.1	27.9	Net Worth					36.4	26.0
100.0	100.0	100.0	Total Liabilities & Net Worth					100.0	100.0
			INCOME DATA						
100.0	100.0	100.0	Net Sales					100.0	100.0
			Gross Profit						
93.0	99.4	100.7	Operating Expenses					100.4	96.3
7.0	.6	-.7	Operating Profit					-.4	3.7
2.6	1.9	1.8	All Other Expenses (net)					1.1	2.0
4.4	-1.3	-2.5	Profit Before Taxes					-1.5	1.7
			RATIOS						
1.4	1.6	1.7						1.7	1.5
.9	1.0	1.0	Current					1.0	1.1
.4	.8	.6						.6	.7
1.0	1.2	1.2						1.0	1.2
.5	.8	.7	Quick					.6	.9
.3	.4	.3						.3	.5
10 35.0	16 23.0	9 40.1						10 37.3	7 53.8
30 12.2	29 12.7	25 14.8	Sales/Receivables					17 21.2	27 13.7
46 8.0	36 10.0	38 9.6						36 10.1	40 9.2
			Cost of Sales/Inventory						
			Cost of Sales/Payables						
18.2	11.8	13.4						8.0	14.3
-113.6	-98.3	NM	Sales/Working Capital					NM	200.9
-7.8	-22.1	-8.0						-8.0	-9.2
(37) 4.2	(30) 4.2	(42) 3.0						2.9	(15) 5.6
1.7	1.2	1.1	EBIT/Interest					1.7	2.8
-.5	-1.0	-3.4						-2.9	-3.3
		(16) 2.4	Net Profit + Depr., Dep.,						
		1.3	Amort./Cur. Mat. L/T/D						
		.3							
1.0	.7	.8						.9	.8
2.0	4.6	1.2	Fixed/Worth					1.1	1.3
9.9	-6.5	21.4						16.2	6.5
1.7	1.7	.8						.6	.8
5.3	7.9	1.6	Debt/Worth					2.3	1.6
29.0	-12.7	27.4						21.2	12.5
(38) 86.1	(24) 61.7	(36) 34.6	% Profit Before Taxes/Tangible				(10) 49.8		(13) 34.2
23.6	11.9	5.5	Net Worth					10.7	17.8
-7.0	-60.0	-14.7						-1.7	-5.7
16.2	11.5	8.6	% Profit Before Taxes/Total					5.7	10.7
3.9	1.6	.8	Assets					1.6	5.6
-4.1	-8.3	-7.6						-7.7	-13.9
16.6	14.9	6.8						5.1	6.8
2.8	5.0	2.5	Sales/Net Fixed Assets					2.2	5.1
1.3	1.9	1.3						1.0	1.5
3.8	4.3	2.9						2.4	2.7
1.7	1.9	1.5	Sales/Total Assets					1.3	2.1
.8	1.1	.8						.7	1.0
(40) 1.5	(24) .6	(42) 2.3						3.5	(13) .7
4.1	2.8	5.5	% Depr., Dep., Amort./Sales					6.5	2.5
12.9	15.1	11.8						9.0	9.0
(13) 1.2		(13) 1.3	% Officers', Directors',						
2.1		4.7	Owners' Comp/Sales						
2.9		18.3							
1537747M	3052315M	3130512M	Net Sales ($)	717M	14207M	7144M	51285M	191296M	2865863M
723702M	1620630M	1889746M	Total Assets ($)	2082M	38232M	10220M	27567M	163589M	1648056M

M = $ thousand   MM = $ million
See Pages 11 through 18 for Explanation of Ratios and Data

Current Data Sorted By Assets   Comparative Historical Data

0-500M	500M-2MM	2-10MM	10-50MM	50-100MM	100-250MM	Type of Statement	4/1/98-3/31/99 ALL	4/1/99-3/31/00 ALL
	1	7	6		3	Unqualified	15	18
1	1	8	3			Reviewed	9	11
3	3	8	2			Compiled	28	15
1	10	1	1			Tax Returns	14	3
3	8	14	10	1		Other	33	29
	22 (4/1-9/30/02)			72 (10/1/02-3/31/03)				
8	22	38	22	1	3	NUMBER OF STATEMENTS	99	76
%	%	%	%	%	%	ASSETS	%	%
	6.3	7.1	6.6			Cash & Equivalents	10.9	11.5
	22.0	13.1	18.0			Trade Receivables (net)	16.5	13.7
	2.6	11.2	6.8			Inventory	7.5	9.1
	7.6	3.0	2.1			All Other Current	2.6	4.6
	38.5	34.4	33.5			Total Current	37.5	38.9
	48.9	52.9	57.3			Fixed Assets (net)	52.3	53.9
	1.3	2.4	.4			Intangibles (net)	2.4	1.3
	11.3	10.2	8.8			All Other Non-Current	7.7	5.9
	100.0	100.0	100.0			Total	100.0	100.0
						LIABILITIES		
	12.5	9.5	6.2			Notes Payable-Short Term	8.1	7.0
	10.9	5.8	4.8			Cur. Mat.-L/T/D	16.8	4.6
	11.1	9.2	8.5			Trade Payables	10.4	8.1
	.3	.1	.6			Income Taxes Payable	.3	.1
	5.7	7.7	8.5			All Other Current	20.6	7.3
	40.5	32.4	28.7			Total Current	56.2	27.1
	37.9	47.0	42.9			Long Term Debt	56.1	42.1
	.0	.8	2.5			Deferred Taxes	1.0	1.4
	5.8	1.4	1.6			All Other Non-Current	5.0	2.4
	15.8	18.5	24.2			Net Worth	−18.3	26.9
	100.0	100.0	100.0			Total Liabilities & Net Worth	100.0	100.0
						INCOME DATA		
	100.0	100.0	100.0			Net Sales	100.0	100.0
						Gross Profit		
	95.7	93.2	94.7			Operating Expenses	120.7	92.8
	4.3	6.8	5.3			Operating Profit	−20.7	7.2
	2.1	2.3	2.1			All Other Expenses (net)	4.9	1.7
	2.3	4.5	3.2			Profit Before Taxes	−25.6	5.5
						RATIOS		
	2.0	2.1	1.5				2.0	2.4
	1.0	1.2	1.0			Current	1.2	1.4
	.5	.8	.7				.6	.9
	1.3	1.2	1.3				1.4	1.7
(21)	.9	.7	.6			Quick	.8	.8
	.4	.4	.4				.4	.5
	0 UND	16 22.4	21 17.0				7 56.1	5 73.4
	26 13.8	27 13.6	35 10.3			Sales/Receivables	28 13.0	25 14.7
	34 10.7	36 10.0	78 4.7				51 7.1	47 7.7
						Cost of Sales/Inventory		
						Cost of Sales/Payables		
	16.4	9.4	10.3				7.7	7.2
	NM	23.9	154.0			Sales/Working Capital	36.2	25.4
	−16.9	−27.9	−15.1				−11.8	−71.8
	8.9	4.0	5.3				5.7	5.3
(18)	1.0	(36) 2.5	(21) 2.6			EBIT/Interest	(76) 2.9	(70) 2.2
	−2.4	1.1	1.4				1.1	.9
							4.3	3.6
						Net Profit + Depr., Dep., Amort./Cur. Mat. L/T/D	(22) 2.1	(26) 2.4
							1.1	1.2
	.7	1.2	1.3				.8	.9
	3.9	3.8	2.3			Fixed/Worth	1.9	2.0
	−5.6	−40.2	4.5				−29.9	6.0
	.7	1.4	1.7				1.1	1.3
	11.1	5.9	3.4			Debt/Worth	2.8	2.7
	−7.9	−58.9	8.7				−26.0	10.1
	45.3	58.3	36.4				38.8	48.9
(14)	9.7	(27) 27.0	(20) 27.8			% Profit Before Taxes/Tangible Net Worth	(73) 23.5	(67) 14.7
	−28.5	4.5	13.7				9.3	4.6
	13.3	10.9	10.8				14.0	10.9
	2.3	6.2	5.6			% Profit Before Taxes/Total Assets	4.7	4.3
	−17.5	.3	1.9				−3.6	−.1
	14.1	6.1	3.1				9.5	5.8
	5.4	2.8	2.2			Sales/Net Fixed Assets	2.2	2.2
	1.8	1.2	1.0				1.0	1.2
	4.5	2.2	1.7				2.5	2.1
	2.8	1.3	1.3			Sales/Total Assets	1.4	1.3
	1.0	.9	.8				.6	.8
	1.5	2.7	3.8				2.1	2.9
(17)	4.3	(34) 5.0	(21) 8.0			% Depr., Dep., Amort./Sales	(86) 7.1	(68) 6.8
	18.6	9.2	11.8				17.0	13.5
	2.6	1.9					1.7	1.8
(10)	4.8	(14) 2.5				% Officers', Directors', Owners' Comp/Sales	(27) 5.0	(24) 3.4
	8.0	6.3					8.3	7.2
12014M	68662M	329487M	626795M	36327M	496568M	Net Sales ($)	1410022M	1402103M
2564M	24542M	203931M	436860M	58590M	470617M	Total Assets ($)	1171037M	1195412M

M = $ thousand   MM = $ million
See Pages 11 through 18 for Explanation of Ratios and Data

Comparative Historical Data | Current Data Sorted By Sales

Type of Statement	4/1/00-3/31/01 ALL	4/1/01-3/31/02 ALL	4/1/02-3/31/03 ALL	0-1MM	1-3MM	3-5MM	5-10MM	10-25MM	25MM & OVER
					22 (4/1-9/30/02)		72 (10/1/02-3/31/03)		
Unqualified	11	16	16	1		1	4	5	5
Reviewed	8	14	13		1	2	4	6	
Compiled	17	20	16	1	6	4	2	2	1
Tax Returns	15	8	13	4	3	3	2	1	
Other	25	33	36	1	8	5	8	8	6
NUMBER OF STATEMENTS	76	91	94	7	18	15	20	22	12
ASSETS	%	%	%	%	%	%	%	%	%
Cash & Equivalents	8.6	7.2	7.4		11.5	9.3	5.2	5.6	6.9
Trade Receivables (net)	16.2	16.1	17.5		18.9	16.5	22.7	12.6	25.2
Inventory	8.2	10.1	8.1		10.2	5.2	8.8	7.6	12.0
All Other Current	5.6	3.6	4.0		6.8	.9	4.7	2.6	2.3
Total Current	38.6	37.1	37.1		47.3	31.9	41.4	28.4	46.4
Fixed Assets (net)	52.4	50.5	51.4		46.6	54.5	44.1	62.9	36.5
Intangibles (net)	3.0	2.6	1.4		1.2	.5	3.4	1.3	.9
All Other Non-Current	6.0	9.9	10.0		4.9	13.1	11.1	7.4	16.2
Total	100.0	100.0	100.0		100.0	100.0	100.0	100.0	100.0
LIABILITIES									
Notes Payable-Short Term	8.9	11.6	9.2		8.4	11.0	7.9	6.9	2.4
Cur. Mat.-L/T/D	5.5	5.6	6.3		8.3	6.8	7.1	6.3	1.9
Trade Payables	10.4	7.9	9.8		6.7	9.5	14.1	8.3	14.5
Income Taxes Payable	.7	.4	.5		.1	.0	.8	.2	2.1
All Other Current	16.1	9.7	8.1		10.2	10.5	6.0	5.0	15.9
Total Current	41.6	35.3	33.8		33.7	37.8	35.8	26.7	36.9
Long Term Debt	37.1	44.8	40.9		35.9	55.4	32.3	52.6	24.8
Deferred Taxes	.8	1.1	1.1		.1	.9	1.6	1.5	2.3
All Other Non-Current	14.6	2.9	3.0		7.3	.1	1.8	1.5	6.6
Net Worth	5.9	15.9	21.2		22.9	5.8	28.6	17.7	29.5
Total Liabilities & Net Worth	100.0	100.0	100.0		100.0	100.0	100.0	100.0	100.0
INCOME DATA									
Net Sales	100.0	100.0	100.0		100.0	100.0	100.0	100.0	100.0
Gross Profit									
Operating Expenses	97.0	93.9	94.1		96.0	94.4	93.6	96.5	92.5
Operating Profit	3.0	6.1	5.9		4.0	5.6	6.4	3.5	7.5
All Other Expenses (net)	−.2	3.5	2.1		2.1	2.3	.7	2.4	.4
Profit Before Taxes	3.2	2.6	3.7		1.8	3.3	5.6	1.1	7.1
RATIOS									
Current	2.0	2.0	1.9		3.5	1.8	2.2	1.4	1.6
	1.2	1.2	1.1		1.5	1.1	1.3	1.0	1.4
	.6	.7	.8		.8	.7	.8	.7	1.1
Quick	1.3	1.2	(93) 1.3		1.7	1.5	1.6	.8	1.3
	.6	.7	.7		1.0	.9	.7	.5	.8
	.2	.4	.4		.5	.4	.4	.4	.6
Sales/Receivables	1 380.3	13 28.4	17 21.9		1 274.6	6 57.9	23 16.2	20 18.5	24 15.5
	23 15.8	29 12.8	27 13.3		26 13.9	26 14.2	32 11.2	26 14.2	33 11.0
	46 7.9	51 7.2	37 9.8		35 10.5	37 9.8	43 8.4	39 9.4	67 5.4
Cost of Sales/Inventory									
Cost of Sales/Payables									
Sales/Working Capital	8.5	8.1	10.1		6.6	12.9	8.3	17.4	12.5
	43.2	33.0	40.3		16.2	55.1	19.0	532.6	19.3
	−15.5	−17.8	−23.2		−33.2	−17.1	−29.4	−15.1	42.4
EBIT/Interest	(65) 4.4	(77) 3.2	(85) 5.3		(13) 5.2	(14) 3.8	7.4	4.1	(11) 22.3
	1.8	1.7	2.2		.5	2.5	3.3	1.6	5.5
	.4	.6	.9		−2.4	−.2	1.3	1.0	3.3
Net Profit + Depr., Dep., Amort./Cur. Mat. L/T/D		(22) 3.6	(23) 4.1						
		2.1	2.7						
		.7	1.1						
Fixed/Worth	.9	.9	1.0		.5	.8	.7	2.0	.7
	2.3	2.2	2.9		1.6	6.3	1.4	4.3	1.8
	−34.1	22.5	NM		−4.4	−7.6	NM	NM	2.9
Debt/Worth	1.2	1.7	1.3		.4	1.5	.8	1.7	1.4
	3.7	3.8	4.2		2.5	10.1	2.0	5.6	2.3
	−36.2	59.1	NM		−7.4	−24.4	NM	NM	5.2
% Profit Before Taxes/Tangible Net Worth	(54) 54.5	(72) 51.2	(71) 50.3		(13) 51.2	(10) 226.6	(15) 40.0	(17) 38.9	(11) 50.3
	21.2	14.1	25.8		10.4	65.9	24.7	28.8	26.6
	4.5	−3.8	5.3		−40.8	1.1	8.6	8.4	19.9
% Profit Before Taxes/Total Assets	14.4	8.0	11.9		11.3	14.7	12.5	10.7	11.1
	3.6	2.5	5.2		3.9	5.9	6.8	3.2	8.1
	−3.9	−2.7	−.2		−12.8	−9.5	1.3	.2	4.7
Sales/Net Fixed Assets	8.6	8.1	8.4		12.3	15.9	23.4	3.5	41.6
	2.8	2.8	2.7		3.6	2.7	4.8	2.4	4.7
	1.5	1.5	1.2		2.0	1.1	1.8	1.3	1.6
Sales/Total Assets	2.8	2.6	2.7		3.2	4.3	3.8	2.0	2.7
	1.6	1.6	1.5		1.8	1.9	1.5	1.5	1.8
	.8	.9	.9		.9	.8	1.1	.9	1.0
% Depr., Dep., Amort./Sales	(63) 1.6	(78) 2.0	(82) 2.2		(17) 1.8	(13) 3.6	(17) 1.1	5.0	(10) .6
	6.2	5.1	5.0		5.0	5.0	3.8	7.4	1.4
	14.6	10.2	9.6		18.6	7.7	8.1	10.5	4.1
% Officers', Directors', Owners' Comp/Sales	(27) 2.7	(28) 2.1	(32) 1.9						
	6.4	3.8	3.4						
	11.7	6.3	6.3						
Net Sales ($)	1083773M	1847007M	1569853M	2817M	34138M	60385M	132954M	384708M	954851M
Total Assets ($)	834097M	1475534M	1197104M	8884M	29646M	46433M	99331M	308962M	703848M

M = $ thousand   MM = $ million
See Pages 11 through 18 for Explanation of Ratios and Data

Current Data Sorted By Assets   Comparative Historical Data

0-500M	500M-2MM	2-10MM	10-50MM	50-100MM	100-250MM		4/1/98-3/31/99 ALL	4/1/99-3/31/00 ALL
						Type of Statement		
		1	6	3	6	Unqualified	36	21
		4	2			Reviewed	5	4
1		2				Compiled	4	3
1		1				Tax Returns	3	1
2	1	5	6	1	2	Other	23	19
							4 (4/1-9/30/02)	41 (10/1/02-3/31/03)
4	2	13	14	4	8	**NUMBER OF STATEMENTS**	71	48
%	%	%	%	%	%	**ASSETS**	%	%
		12.1	8.5			Cash & Equivalents	8.1	10.8
		7.4	11.0			Trade Receivables (net)	12.7	16.8
		1.6	2.0			Inventory	2.2	2.0
		3.4	1.9			All Other Current	1.6	5.9
		24.5	23.4			Total Current	24.7	35.5
		58.1	66.3			Fixed Assets (net)	66.0	56.8
		3.4	2.9			Intangibles (net)	4.7	3.7
		14.0	7.4			All Other Non-Current	4.7	4.1
		100.0	100.0			Total	100.0	100.0
						LIABILITIES		
		9.2	3.3			Notes Payable-Short Term	2.0	3.1
		5.6	3.8			Cur. Mat.-L/T/D	4.5	4.5
		7.2	7.6			Trade Payables	9.9	6.7
		1.4	.2			Income Taxes Payable	.4	.3
		7.2	5.4			All Other Current	9.1	25.4
		30.6	20.3			Total Current	26.0	40.0
		24.7	26.9			Long Term Debt	29.3	23.4
		2.7	11.7			Deferred Taxes	4.3	3.6
		5.1	8.4			All Other Non-Current	6.4	6.6
		36.9	32.8			Net Worth	34.0	26.4
		100.0	100.0			Total Liabilities & Net Worth	100.0	100.0
						INCOME DATA		
		100.0	100.0			Net Sales	100.0	100.0
						Gross Profit		
		77.9	88.1			Operating Expenses	82.8	86.0
		22.1	11.9			Operating Profit	17.2	14.0
		2.2	3.2			All Other Expenses (net)	4.1	3.6
		19.9	8.7			Profit Before Taxes	13.1	10.5
						RATIOS		
		1.6	2.3			Current	1.3	1.5
		.7	.8				.9	1.0
		.5	.5				.6	.6
		1.4	1.7			Quick	1.1	1.3
		.7	.6				.7	.7
		.3	.4				.5	.4
		(11) 34.4	(20) 18.3			Sales/Receivables	(30) 12.2	(17) 21.5
		(37) 9.8	(43) 8.4				(50) 7.3	(38) 9.6
		(50) 7.3	(63) 5.8				(71) 5.1	(58) 6.3
						Cost of Sales/Inventory		
						Cost of Sales/Payables		
		8.9	5.5			Sales/Working Capital	12.0	10.2
		−14.2	−17.3				−56.6	−519.0
		−4.4	−8.8				−7.6	−8.5
		7.8	8.1			EBIT/Interest	7.8	5.4
		(13) 4.1	4.2				(66) 3.7	(37) 3.1
		1.5	1.9				1.7	1.7
						Net Profit + Depr., Dep., Amort./Cur. Mat. L /T/D	(34) 4.5 / 2.4 / 1.5	(15) 3.3 / 2.3 / 1.4
		1.2	1.6			Fixed/Worth	1.4	.9
		2.1	2.5				2.5	2.1
		3.0	9.2				4.4	3.7
		1.2	1.4			Debt/Worth	1.3	1.1
		2.3	2.4				2.5	2.3
		5.6	10.5				4.6	4.3
		45.2	35.3			% Profit Before Taxes/Tangible Net Worth	(64) 38.4	(43) 39.4
		(13) 31.4	18.9				22.0	18.5
		7.8	3.2				10.0	4.6
		21.7	6.3			% Profit Before Taxes/Total Assets	13.5	13.3
		10.4	4.1				7.4	6.3
		2.1	.4				2.8	1.2
		3.3	3.0			Sales/Net Fixed Assets	1.8	3.0
		1.9	.6				.9	1.1
		.7	.4				.5	.7
		1.3	1.2			Sales/Total Assets	.9	1.9
		.7	.5				.6	.7
		.4	.3				.4	.5
		(12) 3.9	3.3			% Depr., Dep., Amort./Sales	(66) 5.5	(39) 5.9
		6.3	8.9				7.6	8.3
		12.6	10.8				10.0	12.8
						% Officers', Directors', Owners' Comp/Sales		
3588M	884M	77942M	221415M	123115M	876892M	Net Sales ($)	1837027M	870961M
1184M	2272M	84834M	307322M	247577M	1044646M	Total Assets ($)	2939812M	1591561M

M = $ thousand   MM = $ million
See Pages 11 through 18 for Explanation of Ratios and Data

Comparative Historical Data | Current Data Sorted By Sales

Type of Statement	4/1/00-3/31/01 ALL	4/1/01-3/31/02 ALL	4/1/02-3/31/03 ALL	0-1MM	1-3MM	3-5MM	5-10MM	10-25MM	25MM & OVER
Unqualified	16	17	17	1	1		1	6	8
Reviewed	4	3	6			1	3	2	
Compiled	6	9	3		2		1		
Tax Returns		1	2	1				1	
Other	23	17	17	3	1	2	5	3	3

Periods: 4 (4/1-9/30/02); 41 (10/1/02-3/31/03)

	Hist 4/1/00-3/31/01 ALL	Hist 4/1/01-3/31/02 ALL	Hist 4/1/02-3/31/03 ALL		0-1MM	1-3MM	3-5MM	5-10MM	10-25MM	25MM & OVER
NUMBER OF STATEMENTS	49	47	45		5	4	3	10	12	11
	%	%	%	**ASSETS**	%	%	%	%	%	%
	5.2	5.5	7.0	Cash & Equivalents				7.4	11.7	1.3
	12.6	10.4	8.7	Trade Receivables (net)				5.3	10.8	11.9
	4.0	2.8	2.5	Inventory				1.9	1.9	4.8
	1.6	3.5	3.1	All Other Current				4.0	2.2	2.0
	23.4	22.3	21.4	Total Current				18.6	26.5	20.0
	69.3	67.0	66.0	Fixed Assets (net)				63.6	61.4	67.5
	3.0	5.6	4.1	Intangibles (net)				4.5	3.2	8.5
	4.3	5.1	8.6	All Other Non-Current				13.3	8.9	3.9
	100.0	100.0	100.0	Total				100.0	100.0	100.0
				LIABILITIES						
	3.1	2.0	5.4	Notes Payable-Short Term				1.8	10.0	5.3
	3.8	4.0	5.1	Cur. Mat.-L/T/D				2.8	3.1	4.1
	10.7	6.3	7.6	Trade Payables				5.4	8.2	8.6
	.2	.5	.5	Income Taxes Payable				.0	.1	.2
	7.3	9.3	8.8	All Other Current				6.1	6.2	4.8
	25.2	22.2	27.4	Total Current				16.2	27.7	22.9
	27.8	24.2	32.8	Long Term Debt				27.3	28.6	21.6
	5.7	4.8	6.1	Deferred Taxes				10.0	7.7	5.8
	6.0	5.5	10.4	All Other Non-Current				8.9	11.9	12.4
	35.3	43.5	23.3	Net Worth				37.7	24.2	37.4
	100.0	100.0	100.0	Total Liabilities & Net Worth				100.0	100.0	100.0
				INCOME DATA						
	100.0	100.0	100.0	Net Sales				100.0	100.0	100.0
				Gross Profit						
	85.0	84.8	84.5	Operating Expenses				85.9	88.6	85.7
	15.0	15.2	15.5	Operating Profit				14.1	11.4	14.3
	4.7	3.2	4.0	All Other Expenses (net)				4.3	2.3	4.3
	10.3	11.9	11.6	Profit Before Taxes				9.8	9.2	10.1
				RATIOS						
	1.3	1.9	1.7	Current				1.9	2.2	1.9
	.8	.7	.8					.8	1.0	1.0
	.5	.5	.5					.6	.4	.7
	1.0	.9	1.1	Quick				1.6	1.7	.7
	.6	.6	.6					.4	.9	.6
	.3	.3	.3					.3	.3	.4
	32 11.5	20 18.5	18 20.3	Sales/Receivables				19 19.2	18 20.6	28 12.9
	52 7.0	44 8.3	39 9.5					35 10.3	36 10.1	57 6.4
	68 5.4	62 5.9	60 6.1					42 8.7	69 5.3	68 5.4
				Cost of Sales/Inventory						
				Cost of Sales/Payables						
	12.7	8.9	8.5	Sales/Working Capital				6.5	5.1	10.0
	−24.7	−13.8	−19.3					−20.2	NM	53.8
	−5.9	−6.3	−6.1					−6.1	−8.4	−7.5
	4.8	5.7	8.8	EBIT/Interest					4.8	10.5
	(45) 2.9	(44) 2.6	(44) 3.9						2.5	4.9
	1.6	1.3	1.4						1.2	1.4
	5.5	2.8	3.0	Net Profit + Depr., Dep., Amort./Cur. Mat. L/T/D						
	(19) 1.7	(19) 1.6	(17) 2.1							
	.6	1.2	1.3							
	1.1	1.1	1.4	Fixed/Worth				1.5	1.1	1.3
	2.4	1.8	2.8					2.3	2.9	3.3
	4.6	3.7	9.7					7.9	8.3	8.8
	.9	.7	1.4	Debt/Worth				1.3	1.2	.7
	2.0	1.6	3.2					2.6	2.5	3.5
	4.5	3.5	10.7					8.2	9.8	9.9
	40.2	28.8	46.1	% Profit Before Taxes/Tangible Net Worth				33.5	40.4	193.7
	(44) 15.1	(42) 13.8	(39) 25.7					14.3	(10) 20.1	(10) 18.7
	3.3	3.9	9.6					−2.8	2.0	15.1
	11.2	10.7	13.4	% Profit Before Taxes/Total Assets				11.7	6.6	11.1
	4.9	4.5	5.4					3.6	3.6	6.4
	1.7	1.3	.7					1.8	.4	2.2
	1.4	2.1	2.5	Sales/Net Fixed Assets				2.6	3.3	1.5
	.7	.8	.9					.7	1.6	1.1
	.5	.5	.5					.4	.5	.6
	1.0	1.1	1.2	Sales/Total Assets				1.0	1.4	1.1
	.6	.7	.7					.6	1.1	.8
	.4	.4	.4					.3	.4	.4
	5.6	4.6	4.8	% Depr., Dep., Amort./Sales					2.9	6.2
	(45) 9.0	(44) 8.4	(43) 7.1						(10) 6.3	7.0
	11.5	11.9	11.5						10.1	9.8
				% Officers', Directors', Owners' Comp/Sales						
	784972M	1035489M	1303836M	Net Sales ($)	2272M	6361M	11308M	68538M	208453M	1006904M
	1403382M	1754544M	1687835M	Total Assets ($)	5712M	10820M	20411M	153472M	347829M	1149591M

M = $ thousand   MM = $ million
See Pages 11 through 18 for Explanation of Ratios and Data

Current Data Sorted By Assets   Comparative Historical Data

0-500M	500M-2MM	2-10MM	10-50MM	50-100MM	100-250MM	Type of Statement	4/1/98-3/31/99 ALL	4/1/99-3/31/00 ALL
		1	12	7	9	Unqualified	14	18
	1	1	2			Reviewed	5	2
4	5	6				Compiled	8	14
	2	2				Tax Returns	1	1
	3	6	10	2	1	Other	17	18
	11 (4/1-9/30/02)		63 (10/1/02-3/31/03)					
4	11	16	24	9	10	**NUMBER OF STATEMENTS**	45	53
%	%	%	%	%	%	**ASSETS**	%	%
	5.5	8.3	8.1		7.2	Cash & Equivalents	15.6	9.2
	18.7	13.3	23.7		7.9	Trade Receivables (net)	18.1	19.8
	5.9	2.1	1.5		1.8	Inventory	1.6	3.2
	.3	1.5	3.2		1.1	All Other Current	3.0	2.0
	30.5	25.2	36.5		18.1	Total Current	38.3	34.2
	42.9	64.1	48.9		70.9	Fixed Assets (net)	52.4	53.7
	3.1	.5	2.8		5.7	Intangibles (net)	2.2	1.7
	23.6	10.3	11.8		5.3	All Other Non-Current	7.1	10.4
	100.0	100.0	100.0		100.0	Total	100.0	100.0
						LIABILITIES		
	10.3	5.2	1.8		1.5	Notes Payable-Short Term	6.2	2.6
	5.6	7.4	6.4		6.1	Cur. Mat.-L/T/D	4.8	4.4
	14.4	5.7	18.2		3.5	Trade Payables	11.6	11.1
	.0	2.2	.2		.1	Income Taxes Payable	.7	.2
	10.9	5.4	7.8		4.3	All Other Current	9.4	8.8
	41.2	25.8	34.4		15.5	Total Current	32.7	27.1
	43.5	30.5	29.7		35.5	Long Term Debt	51.5	30.5
	.0	2.6	2.7		5.9	Deferred Taxes	1.9	1.7
	11.6	.2	1.8		5.7	All Other Non-Current	1.5	6.6
	3.7	40.9	31.4		37.4	Net Worth	12.4	34.0
	100.0	100.0	100.0		100.0	Total Liabilities & Net Worth	100.0	100.0
						INCOME DATA		
	100.0	100.0	100.0		100.0	Net Sales	100.0	100.0
						Gross Profit		
	92.0	94.2	91.9		87.2	Operating Expenses	96.8	89.8
	8.0	5.8	8.1		12.8	Operating Profit	3.2	10.2
	6.9	3.3	2.3		4.1	All Other Expenses (net)	-5.5	2.8
	1.1	2.5	5.8		8.6	Profit Before Taxes	8.7	7.3
						RATIOS		
	2.3	2.6	1.7		2.1		2.6	1.9
	.8	.7	1.1		1.0	Current	1.2	1.1
	.3	.3	.6		.7		.8	.7
	2.3	1.8	1.6		1.9		2.3	1.6
	.5	.7	.9		.8	Quick	1.1	1.0
	.2	.2	.4		.5		.7	.5
	9 42.5	2 202.0	31 11.6		33 11.2		26 13.9	21 17.2
	26 13.8	36 10.1	42 8.7		44 8.3	Sales/Receivables	40 9.1	45 8.0
	44 8.2	63 5.8	58 6.3		63 5.8		55 6.7	58 6.3
						Cost of Sales/Inventory		
						Cost of Sales/Payables		
	8.1	7.5	10.7		6.2		6.5	7.6
	-22.8	-13.8	59.4		NM	Sales/Working Capital	41.7	39.3
	-5.9	-4.2	-11.2		-21.5		-20.7	-23.7
		6.9	(23) 6.1		4.8		(36) 6.5	(49) 6.2
		1.9	2.2		2.6	EBIT/Interest	2.6	2.5
		.0	.7		1.8		1.0	1.6
						Net Profit + Depr., Dep., Amort./Cur. Mat. L/T/D	(11) 4.4	(13) 5.4
							2.3	1.9
							1.2	1.3
	1.1	1.0	.5		1.5		.6	.8
	2.1	1.3	2.3		2.7	Fixed/Worth	1.8	1.6
	-4.0	3.2	4.2		5.5		7.9	3.6
	3.2	.5	.8		1.1		.7	1.0
	14.2	1.3	3.0		2.2	Debt/Worth	2.0	1.9
	-5.0	2.8	11.1		7.6		8.3	4.6
	(15)	30.0	(21) 28.1		35.1	% Profit Before Taxes/Tangible Net Worth	(38) 47.8	(49) 43.0
		7.6	11.1		19.9		19.5	20.8
		-2.0	-5.3		9.7		9.4	7.4
	8.9	10.7	8.9		7.3	% Profit Before Taxes/Total Assets	16.4	13.5
	4.9	3.3	3.6		4.6		7.7	5.9
	-1.9	-2.1	-1.5		2.7		-1.6	2.6
	111.3	3.6	29.9		1.1	Sales/Net Fixed Assets	18.4	5.4
	4.3	1.3	2.6		.7		1.5	2.1
	1.4	.7	1.0		.6		.9	.9
	3.2	1.4	2.9		.8	Sales/Total Assets	2.7	2.3
	1.4	.9	1.5		.5		.9	1.0
	.8	.5	.7		.4		.6	.6
	(10) 1.5	4.0	(23) 1.6			% Depr., Dep., Amort./Sales	(35) 1.8	(45) 2.9
	6.1	7.7	5.4				6.6	5.6
	13.4	20.6	10.0				11.6	10.7
						% Officers', Directors', Owners' Comp/Sales		(12) 2.7
								4.3
								8.9
3138M	23886M	81170M	740994M	394431M	985061M	Net Sales ($)	3234006M	1161099M
848M	12784M	68154M	489182M	686422M	1561176M	Total Assets ($)	1250085M	1672382M

M = $ thousand   MM = $ million
See Pages 11 through 18 for Explanation of Ratios and Data

Comparative Historical Data | Current Data Sorted By Sales

Hist 1	Hist 2	Hist 3	Type of Statement	0-1MM	1-3MM	3-5MM	5-10MM	10-25MM	25MM & OVER
12	14	29	Unqualified		1		1	8	20
5	4	2	Reviewed		1		1		
14	12	17	Compiled	5	6	1	3	2	
3	4	4	Tax Returns	1	2		1		
10	20	22	Other		5	3	2	3	9
4/1/00-3/31/01 ALL	4/1/01-3/31/02 ALL	4/1/02-3/31/03 ALL		11 (4/1-9/30/02)			63 (10/1/02-3/31/03)		
44	54	74	**NUMBER OF STATEMENTS**	6	14	4	8	13	29
%	%	%	**ASSETS**	%	%	%	%	%	%
11.1	10.6	7.8	Cash & Equivalents		7.1			11.1	6.6
15.5	18.7	15.8	Trade Receivables (net)		9.8			13.9	18.3
1.7	2.3	2.2	Inventory		.3			2.0	1.2
3.8	2.0	1.9	All Other Current		1.2			2.9	2.3
32.1	33.5	27.6	Total Current		18.5			30.0	28.3
61.1	57.3	59.4	Fixed Assets (net)		58.5			60.7	58.3
1.5	2.4	2.2	Intangibles (net)		.9			1.1	4.0
5.3	6.7	10.8	All Other Non-Current		22.1			8.3	9.4
100.0	100.0	100.0	Total		100.0			100.0	100.0
			LIABILITIES						
3.8	4.4	3.5	Notes Payable-Short Term		3.1			.2	2.2
5.1	4.5	6.6	Cur. Mat.-L/T/D		7.7			8.6	5.3
9.5	9.0	10.1	Trade Payables		10.6			10.2	13.1
.2	.5	.6	Income Taxes Payable		.0			.2	.2
7.8	5.5	6.6	All Other Current		7.1			5.2	6.7
26.4	24.0	27.5	Total Current		28.5			24.4	27.5
34.6	34.4	43.6	Long Term Debt		72.9			24.2	39.4
1.4	2.1	2.7	Deferred Taxes		1.1			3.7	4.0
2.6	4.4	3.6	All Other Non-Current		9.3			1.9	2.9
34.9	35.1	22.6	Net Worth		−11.6			45.9	26.3
100.0	100.0	100.0	Total Liabilities & Net Worth		100.0			100.0	100.0
			INCOME DATA						
100.0	100.0	100.0	Net Sales		100.0			100.0	100.0
			Gross Profit						
91.0	86.8	90.7	Operating Expenses		97.8			90.9	90.8
9.0	13.2	9.3	Operating Profit		2.2			9.1	9.2
3.3	4.1	3.9	All Other Expenses (net)		4.4			1.8	3.5
5.7	9.1	5.5	Profit Before Taxes		−2.3			7.3	5.7
			RATIOS						
1.6 / 1.1 / .6	2.0 / 1.2 / .8	1.8 / 1.0 / .5	Current		2.9 / .4 / .2			2.8 / 1.1 / .6	1.6 / 1.1 / .7
1.3 / 1.0 / .5	1.8 / 1.0 / .6	1.8 / .8 / .4	Quick		2.9 / .3 / .1			2.5 / .9 / .4	1.4 / 1.0 / .5
21 17.4 / 39 9.2 / 67 5.4	24 15.0 / 43 8.4 / 60 6.1	14 25.8 / 38 9.5 / 57 6.4	Sales/Receivables		0 UND / 26 13.9 / 37 9.8			18 20.4 / 38 9.6 / 55 6.7	33 11.2 / 41 8.8 / 57 6.4
			Cost of Sales/Inventory						
			Cost of Sales/Payables						
9.4 / 49.5 / −12.2	6.0 / 23.7 / −23.1	9.8 / −123.6 / −8.8	Sales/Working Capital		7.8 / −6.8 / −3.8			2.9 / 57.0 / −8.3	11.2 / 51.0 / −31.7
(40) 4.1 / 2.0 / .1	(46) 6.2 / 2.5 / 1.7	(71) 5.3 / 2.2 / 1.1	EBIT/Interest		(13) 3.6 / 1.6 / −.5			(12) 6.3 / 3.0 / 1.9	3.9 / 2.0 / 1.2
(12) 3.9 / 1.2 / .5	(13) 3.3 / 2.0 / 1.4	(21) 2.1 / 1.5 / 1.0	Net Profit + Depr., Dep., Amort./Cur. Mat. L/T/D						(12) 2.0 / 1.2 / .9
1.0 / 1.8 / 6.7	.9 / 2.0 / 4.9	1.1 / 2.4 / 4.2	Fixed/Worth		.3 / 1.8 / NM			.9 / 1.3 / 3.5	1.3 / 2.8 / 6.7
1.0 / 2.3 / 7.5	.9 / 2.2 / 6.7	1.2 / 2.9 / 9.0	Debt/Worth		.7 / 2.8 / −13.3			.6 / 1.1 / 3.7	1.6 / 3.4 / 11.9
(40) 35.6 / 15.3 / −4.4	(50) 58.7 / 23.2 / 12.9	(65) 32.6 / 17.1 / 2.6	% Profit Before Taxes/Tangible Net Worth		(10) 36.0 / 7.1 / −3.7			29.5 / 15.4 / 3.3	(26) 26.2 / 17.2 / 3.4
12.2 / 4.6 / −2.3	13.3 / 7.6 / 2.6	9.0 / 4.4 / .0	% Profit Before Taxes/Total Assets		9.3 / 2.6 / −5.0			7.3 / 4.0 / 2.0	7.4 / 4.2 / .6
4.7 / 1.4 / .8	5.9 / 1.3 / .7	5.0 / 1.5 / .7	Sales/Net Fixed Assets		11.1 / 1.9 / .6			4.2 / 2.0 / .8	9.1 / 1.1 / .7
2.0 / .9 / .5	2.5 / .8 / .5	1.9 / .9 / .5	Sales/Total Assets		1.5 / .9 / .5			1.7 / .9 / .6	2.7 / .8 / .5
(42) 2.9 / 8.6 / 10.6	(45) 3.2 / 7.1 / 11.1	(69) 3.1 / 7.2 / 11.0	% Depr., Dep., Amort./Sales		(13) 2.3 / 8.3 / 38.6			3.9 / 5.9 / 10.1	(25) 1.8 / 8.0 / 10.5
(10) .8 / 5.1 / 7.2		(14) 3.3 / 6.3 / 9.3	% Officers', Directors', Owners' Comp/Sales						
1199363M	1952884M	2228680M	Net Sales ($)	3412M	27298M	15689M	56585M	222732M	1902964M
1331803M	1892663M	2818566M	Total Assets ($)	3385M	36727M	8533M	84584M	284879M	2400458M

M = $ thousand   MM = $ million
See Pages 11 through 18 for Explanation of Ratios and Data

Current Data Sorted By Assets   Comparative Historical Data

	149 (4/1-9/30/02)		767 (10/1/02-3/31/03)				Type of Statement	4/1/98-3/31/99	4/1/99-3/31/00
2	5	21	19	7	8	Unqualified	71	64
13	55	115	25	3		Reviewed	255	217
57	121	60	5			Compiled	321	278
82	61	15	4		1	Tax Returns	136	142
33	83	89	27	4	1	Other	241	246
0-500M	**500M-2MM**	**2-10MM**	**10-50MM**	**50-100MM**	**100-250MM**		**ALL**	**ALL**
187	325	300	80	14	10	**NUMBER OF STATEMENTS**	1024	947
%	%	%	%	%	%	**ASSETS**	%	%
16.4	9.8	8.1	6.0	9.5	7.5	Cash & Equivalents	10.2	9.7
21.2	31.1	30.7	24.6	21.2	15.7	Trade Receivables (net)	26.8	26.6
2.2	1.7	1.8	1.9	1.3	9.6	Inventory	1.6	1.5
6.2	4.9	4.1	4.3	2.4	9.4	All Other Current	3.2	3.3
46.0	47.4	44.7	36.8	34.4	42.2	Total Current	41.7	41.1
42.1	41.3	43.0	52.0	55.3	46.1	Fixed Assets (net)	47.1	46.9
2.7	2.6	2.4	3.2	5.6	7.4	Intangibles (net)	2.3	2.6
9.1	8.6	9.9	8.0	4.7	4.4	All Other Non-Current	8.9	9.4
100.0	100.0	100.0	100.0	100.0	100.0	Total	100.0	100.0
						LIABILITIES		
13.5	8.6	9.3	6.8	2.7	2.2	Notes Payable-Short Term	8.2	7.4
11.9	7.8	8.2	9.0	5.9	4.8	Cur. Mat.-L/T/D	8.6	8.2
9.3	11.7	11.4	10.4	7.6	8.0	Trade Payables	9.8	10.1
.1	.3	.5	.2	.0	.4	Income Taxes Payable	.3	.3
12.8	9.4	8.3	8.5	8.2	17.3	All Other Current	9.4	9.0
47.6	37.8	37.8	34.9	24.3	32.7	Total Current	36.3	35.0
30.7	25.1	23.3	25.8	25.1	30.5	Long Term Debt	27.5	26.6
.1	.4	1.3	2.3	1.8	4.1	Deferred Taxes	1.0	1.0
6.2	3.5	2.5	3.7	.5	5.5	All Other Non-Current	4.0	3.6
15.4	33.2	35.2	33.4	48.3	27.1	Net Worth	31.2	33.8
100.0	100.0	100.0	100.0	100.0	100.0	Total Liabilities & Net Worth	100.0	100.0
						INCOME DATA		
100.0	100.0	100.0	100.0	100.0	100.0	Net Sales	100.0	100.0
						Gross Profit		
95.9	96.8	96.3	94.8	93.8	94.7	Operating Expenses	95.0	95.1
4.1	3.2	3.7	5.2	6.2	5.3	Operating Profit	5.0	4.9
1.2	.9	1.6	1.8	1.5	2.3	All Other Expenses (net)	.8	.9
2.9	2.3	2.1	3.3	4.7	3.0	Profit Before Taxes	4.2	4.0
						RATIOS		
3.0	2.4	1.7	1.5	1.9	1.8		2.1	2.0
1.1	1.3	1.1	1.1	1.4	1.1	Current	1.2	1.2
.4	.7	.8	.8	.8	.8		.7	.7
2.8	1.9	1.5	1.4	1.7	1.0		1.9	1.8
.9	1.1	1.0	.9	1.2	.8	Quick	(1019) 1.1	(945) 1.1
.3	.6	.7	.6	.7	.6		.6	.6
0 UND	19 18.7	28 13.1	30 12.3	34 10.7	0 UND		17 21.7	17 21.0
11 34.1	34 10.8	39 9.4	40 9.2	37 9.9	34 10.7	Sales/Receivables	34 10.8	34 10.7
33 11.2	50 7.3	49 7.4	49 7.4	46 7.9	53 6.9		47 7.8	48 7.5
						Cost of Sales/Inventory		
						Cost of Sales/Payables		
13.2	9.6	14.0	16.8	8.3	13.7		11.7	11.9
128.3	34.9	58.7	87.9	23.2	141.1	Sales/Working Capital	48.6	47.8
-14.8	-26.0	-42.0	-18.0	-42.8	-32.7		-24.5	-22.9
(147) 7.5	(293) 5.6	(285) 5.0	(74) 4.8	5.8			(908) 5.9	(818) 6.5
1.9	2.0	2.1	2.3	3.2		EBIT/Interest	2.9	2.6
-.4	.2	.8	1.2	2.6			1.4	1.1
(11) 5.3	(65) 3.2	(119) 2.9	(42) 2.5			Net Profit + Depr., Dep.,	(305) 3.0	(243) 2.9
3.3	1.7	1.5	1.3			Amort./Cur. Mat. L/T/D	1.7	1.7
.7	.9	.9	1.0				1.1	1.1
.3	.5	.6	1.0	.8	.9		.7	.6
1.7	1.3	1.4	1.4	1.4	1.7	Fixed/Worth	1.4	1.4
-8.5	4.0	2.7	3.5	1.8	NM		3.9	3.9
.5	.7	1.1	1.1	.8	1.3		.9	.8
4.0	2.1	2.2	2.1	1.1	2.5	Debt/Worth	2.0	2.0
-9.4	7.8	4.0	4.7	1.9	NM		6.7	6.1
(127) 95.2	(272) 39.5	(283) 29.3	(74) 25.7	32.9		% Profit Before Taxes/Tangible	(896) 51.3	(823) 42.5
32.1	11.5	12.0	11.1	12.3		Net Worth	21.8	18.2
1.2	-6.0	-.2	1.6	7.3			7.9	3.8
26.3	10.2	10.2	7.9	7.9	9.4	% Profit Before Taxes/Total	15.3	14.6
5.9	3.2	3.6	3.7	5.6	6.0	Assets	7.1	6.2
-3.9	-3.0	-.5	.7	3.5	3.4		2.0	.7
45.5	20.1	15.7	7.1	4.8	27.8		13.4	13.6
11.8	8.6	6.1	3.6	2.5	3.7	Sales/Net Fixed Assets	5.9	5.7
4.8	3.6	3.1	1.8	1.6	1.9		3.1	2.8
7.7	4.1	3.6	2.8	2.3	5.3		4.0	3.7
4.6	3.0	2.5	1.9	1.6	1.7	Sales/Total Assets	2.6	2.5
2.7	2.0	1.8	1.2	1.2	1.1		1.8	1.6
(142) 2.6	(284) 2.0	(286) 2.0	(77) 2.9	(13) 2.4			(920) 2.4	(829) 2.4
5.1	4.7	4.3	4.5	4.7		% Depr., Dep., Amort./Sales	4.9	4.9
11.5	9.4	6.9	10.4	7.4			8.8	8.6
(98) 2.7	(151) 2.2	(113) 1.5	(13) .9			% Officers', Directors',	(416) 2.2	(391) 2.0
4.7	4.1	2.8	1.6			Owners' Comp/Sales	4.4	4.2
9.8	6.1	5.1	2.4				8.0	7.2
216547M	1228527M	3520682M	3183871M	1817705M	7246559M	Net Sales ($)	10640508M	9997169M
44086M	366671M	1277510M	1464341M	1012168M	1729425M	Total Assets ($)	5145563M	5326897M

© RMA 2003

M = $ thousand   MM = $ million
See Pages 11 through 18 for Explanation of Ratios and Data

Comparative Historical Data | Current Data Sorted By Sales

Current Data periods: 149 (4/1-9/30/02); 767 (10/1/02-3/31/03)

4/1/00-3/31/01 ALL	4/1/01-3/31/02 ALL	4/1/02-3/31/03 ALL		0-1MM	1-3MM	3-5MM	5-10MM	10-25MM	25MM & OVER
			Type of Statement						
53	52	62	Unqualified	8	4	3	9	12	34
193	184	211	Reviewed		27	32	60	66	18
297	270	243	Compiled	36	82	43	53	25	4
144	132	163	Tax Returns	65	57	15	14	8	4
244	257	237	Other	30	49	33	41	52	32
931	895	916	**NUMBER OF STATEMENTS**	139	219	126	177	163	92
%	%	%	**ASSETS**	%	%	%	%	%	%
9.2	9.2	10.2	Cash & Equivalents	14.7	12.0	9.3	8.9	8.1	7.0
27.1	26.1	28.1	Trade Receivables (net)	11.9	25.8	29.3	32.5	37.7	30.4
1.6	1.7	1.9	Inventory	1.0	2.6	1.8	1.1	1.7	3.9
3.9	4.0	4.8	All Other Current	4.9	4.3	5.9	5.0	4.5	4.9
41.8	41.0	45.1	Total Current	32.5	44.8	46.3	47.4	52.0	46.2
46.9	46.5	43.2	Fixed Assets (net)	56.4	42.4	41.3	40.2	38.1	42.7
2.8	3.0	2.7	Intangibles (net)	3.3	2.7	1.4	2.0	2.9	4.7
8.5	9.5	9.0	All Other Non-Current	7.8	10.0	11.1	10.3	6.9	6.5
100.0	100.0	100.0	Total	100.0	100.0	100.0	100.0	100.0	100.0
			LIABILITIES						
8.8	9.2	9.5	Notes Payable-Short Term	10.0	9.8	9.7	9.4	9.6	8.0
9.0	9.3	8.8	Cur. Mat.-L/T/D	12.7	7.9	8.2	8.4	8.4	7.5
10.0	10.3	10.9	Trade Payables	5.3	10.2	10.9	11.1	15.5	12.6
.2	.4	.3	Income Taxes Payable	.1	.2	.3	.5	.3	.4
9.1	9.9	9.7	All Other Current	9.0	10.6	9.3	8.9	9.3	11.5
37.3	39.1	39.3	Total Current	37.1	38.8	38.6	38.1	43.1	40.0
28.0	29.8	25.8	Long Term Debt	39.3	26.8	25.1	21.0	20.7	22.0
1.0	.9	.9	Deferred Taxes	.1	.4	.5	1.3	1.2	2.0
3.7	4.7	3.7	All Other Non-Current	8.8	2.7	3.7	2.8	2.0	3.4
30.1	25.6	30.4	Net Worth	14.7	31.3	32.0	36.8	33.0	32.5
100.0	100.0	100.0	Total Liabilities & Net Worth	100.0	100.0	100.0	100.0	100.0	100.0
			INCOME DATA						
100.0	100.0	100.0	Net Sales	100.0	100.0	100.0	100.0	100.0	100.0
			Gross Profit						
95.8	96.0	96.2	Operating Expenses	90.3	97.3	97.0	97.7	97.4	96.2
4.2	4.0	3.8	Operating Profit	9.7	2.7	3.0	2.3	2.6	3.8
1.0	1.6	1.3	All Other Expenses (net)	4.7	.6	1.0	.6	.7	.9
3.2	2.4	2.5	Profit Before Taxes	5.0	2.1	2.0	1.7	2.0	2.8
			RATIOS						
1.9	1.9	2.0	Current	2.7	2.7	2.4	2.0	1.6	1.6
1.1	1.1	1.2		.9	1.3	1.1	1.2	1.2	1.1
.7	.6	.7		.3	.6	.8	.8	.9	.9
1.7	1.7	1.7	Quick	2.1	2.4	2.1	1.8	1.4	1.5
(929) 1.0	1.0	1.0		.6	1.1	1.0	1.1	1.0	.9
.6	.5	.6		.2	.5	.6	.7	.8	.7
18 20.8	17 21.2	18 20.5	Sales/Receivables	0 UND	8 43.0	20 17.9	28 12.9	28 13.0	31 11.8
34 10.6	31 11.6	34 10.8		6 58.0	27 13.4	34 10.6	39 9.2	37 9.8	38 9.6
49 7.4	46 8.0	46 7.9		30 12.0	47 7.7	47 7.7	53 6.9	46 7.9	48 7.7
			Cost of Sales/Inventory						
			Cost of Sales/Payables						
13.2	13.6	12.2	Sales/Working Capital	11.3	9.6	11.0	11.4	18.4	15.0
63.2	74.7	53.4		-56.3	36.3	82.5	40.9	47.1	60.4
-19.5	-18.6	-26.5		-6.1	-20.4	-36.7	-35.5	-64.9	-52.2
4.8	4.5	5.5	EBIT/Interest	6.3	5.5	4.4	5.1	6.6	5.6
(841) 2.2	(809) 1.8	(822) 2.1		(110) 1.4	(190) 1.9	(116) 2.1	(164) 2.0	(155) 2.5	(87) 2.5
1.0	.5	.6		-.1	-.3	.4	.9	1.1	1.3
2.9	2.6	3.1	Net Profit + Depr., Dep., Amort./Cur. Mat. L/T/D		3.6	4.6	2.8	2.6	2.9
(234) 1.5	(204) 1.3	(245) 1.5		(30) 1.7	(33) 1.5	(64) 1.6	(71) 1.5	(39) 1.4
.9	.8	1.0			.7	.8	1.0	1.0	1.0
.6	.7	.6	Fixed/Worth	1.1	.5	.4	.5	.6	.8
1.6	1.7	1.4		3.4	1.4	1.4	1.2	1.1	1.4
4.8	6.2	4.0		-9.7	5.6	3.3	2.8	2.4	3.4
.9	1.0	.9	Debt/Worth	1.0	.6	.8	.8	1.3	1.1
2.4	2.6	2.2		5.3	2.4	2.0	1.9	2.1	2.3
8.5	12.2	7.7		-11.4	11.3	6.2	3.8	4.0	5.0
40.9	36.2	38.5	% Profit Before Taxes/Tangible Net Worth	83.5	43.6	38.7	24.7	36.4	42.2
(784) 16.0	(729) 12.8	(778) 13.5		(93) 20.2	(176) 11.0	(113) 16.8	(161) 10.0	(152) 15.7	(83) 14.8
2.3	.4	-.8		-.9	-7.7	-5.0	-.1	.9	4.4
11.8	10.6	11.6	% Profit Before Taxes/Total Assets	17.6	14.2	10.3	9.5	11.8	9.4
4.7	3.4	3.9		2.1	3.6	4.2	3.6	5.0	5.5
.2	-2.2	-1.2		-3.1	-3.8	-2.4	-.5	.3	1.0
14.3	16.2	18.9	Sales/Net Fixed Assets	11.4	20.8	19.0	15.9	26.1	22.9
6.2	6.4	7.3		3.5	8.6	8.7	7.5	10.8	5.9
2.8	3.0	3.3		1.2	3.7	4.1	3.6	4.3	3.2
4.1	4.1	4.3	Sales/Total Assets	4.1	5.0	4.3	3.8	5.0	4.2
2.6	2.7	2.8		1.8	3.0	2.9	2.8	3.3	2.5
1.7	1.7	1.8		.8	1.9	2.1	1.8	2.4	1.8
2.2	2.2	2.2	% Depr., Dep., Amort./Sales	6.4	2.6	1.9	2.2	1.4	1.3
(833) 4.7	(780) 5.3	(805) 4.5		(117) 10.8	(181) 5.4	(109) 4.4	(166) 4.4	(153) 3.2	(79) 3.4
8.7	9.4	8.6		19.6	10.2	6.8	6.9	5.8	5.2
2.3	2.1	2.0	% Officers', Directors', Owners' Comp/Sales	3.0	2.5	2.5	1.6	1.5	.9
(393) 4.0	(392) 4.0	(379) 3.5		(59) 6.9	(111) 4.3	(60) 4.0	(74) 2.5	(60) 2.7	(15) 1.6
7.5	7.2	6.8		12.3	7.4	5.9	5.0	4.5	2.9
9682450M	10987562M	17213891M	Net Sales ($)	71471M	427478M	490491M	1268508M	2542372M	12413571M
4889124M	4906013M	5894201M	Total Assets ($)	74357M	193085M	263155M	577130M	920378M	3866096M

Current Data Sorted By Assets | **Comparative Historical Data**

Type of Statement	0-500M	500M-2MM	2-10MM	10-50MM	50-100MM	100-250MM	4/1/98-3/31/99 ALL	4/1/99-3/31/00 ALL
Unqualified	1	6	24	88	41	29	204	192
Reviewed	9	48	125	45	2		297	283
Compiled	38	123	88	12	1	1	361	326
Tax Returns	32	38	17			2	69	84
Other	32	53	101	85	12	12	364	303
	141 (4/1-9/30/02)			924 (10/1/02-3/31/03)				
NUMBER OF STATEMENTS	112	268	355	230	56	44	1295	1188
ASSETS	%	%	%	%	%	%	%	%
Cash & Equivalents	11.2	8.1	6.8	6.2	3.9	7.2	7.5	7.1
Trade Receivables (net)	30.3	31.2	29.7	26.3	17.9	19.0	25.3	26.5
Inventory	2.0	1.6	1.4	1.7	2.5	2.1	1.7	1.4
All Other Current	4.2	4.4	4.5	4.0	3.5	3.3	3.4	3.3
Total Current	47.7	45.3	42.4	38.2	27.7	31.6	37.9	38.2
Fixed Assets (net)	39.1	44.2	47.0	51.5	61.5	56.6	51.7	51.1
Intangibles (net)	1.3	2.5	1.5	2.5	4.1	6.6	2.3	2.7
All Other Non-Current	11.8	8.0	9.0	7.9	6.6	5.2	8.1	8.0
Total	100.0	100.0	100.0	100.0	100.0	100.0	100.0	100.0
LIABILITIES								
Notes Payable-Short Term	13.6	9.7	8.4	7.5	5.8	2.9	6.9	6.9
Cur. Mat.-L/T/D	10.2	10.9	12.0	10.5	13.1	6.9	10.6	10.4
Trade Payables	17.4	11.2	9.6	9.7	6.7	7.2	8.8	9.4
Income Taxes Payable	.1	.2	.3	.2	.2	.2	.3	.3
All Other Current	18.5	10.0	10.1	9.5	10.4	11.3	9.4	8.7
Total Current	59.9	41.9	40.3	37.3	36.2	28.5	36.1	35.7
Long Term Debt	38.6	27.6	23.8	23.4	30.2	27.6	29.9	28.4
Deferred Taxes	.1	.5	1.8	3.3	5.4	3.6	2.0	1.8
All Other Non-Current	10.0	3.6	2.5	1.9	6.5	3.7	3.3	3.5
Net Worth	-8.7	26.4	31.6	34.1	21.6	36.6	28.7	30.7
Total Liabilities & Net Worth	100.0	100.0	100.0	100.0	100.0	100.0	100.0	100.0
INCOME DATA								
Net Sales	100.0	100.0	100.0	100.0	100.0	100.0	100.0	100.0
Gross Profit								
Operating Expenses	96.9	97.0	96.6	96.1	96.1	95.1	95.4	96.1
Operating Profit	3.1	3.0	3.4	3.8	3.9	4.9	4.6	3.9
All Other Expenses (net)	1.7	1.3	1.4	1.4	2.4	1.5	.7	.7
Profit Before Taxes	1.4	1.7	2.0	2.4	1.5	3.4	3.9	3.1
RATIOS								
Current	1.9	1.7	1.5	1.4	1.1	1.6	1.7	1.7
	.9	1.0	1.0	1.0	.8	1.1	1.0	1.0
	.3	.6	.7	.7	.6	.7	.7	.7
Quick	1.6	1.4	1.3	1.2	.9	1.4	1.5	1.5
	(110) .7	.9	.9	.8	.6	.9	(1292) .9	(1186) .9
	.3	.5	.6	.6	.4	.6	.6	.6
Sales/Receivables	0 UND	18 20.0	27 13.4	31 11.7	28 13.0	33 11.0	23 16.2	25 14.6
	19 18.7	30 12.1	36 10.1	38 9.6	35 10.5	39 9.4	33 11.0	35 10.4
	33 10.9	42 8.6	45 8.1	46 7.9	40 9.1	44 8.2	42 8.7	45 8.2
Cost of Sales/Inventory								
Cost of Sales/Payables								
Sales/Working Capital	20.2	19.1	21.7	17.6	39.3	18.4	17.6	17.7
	-142.3	241.7	764.7	NM	-25.6	90.6	288.5	194.8
	-12.1	-22.9	-21.2	-19.2	-10.3	-27.4	-19.2	-18.0
EBIT/Interest	4.4	5.0	3.9	4.6	4.9	7.1	5.3	5.0
	(96) 1.5	(245) 2.0	(337) 2.0	(221) 2.2	(54) 1.6	(43) 2.8	(1208) 2.8	(1101) 2.5
	-.8	.3	.8	1.0	1.1	1.1	1.5	1.2
Net Profit + Depr., Dep., Amort./Cur. Mat. L /T/D		2.7	1.9	2.0	4.9		2.6	2.3
		(60) 1.4	(125) 1.2	(109) 1.2	(25) 1.2		(469) 1.5	(407) 1.4
		.7	.8	.8	.8		1.0	1.0
Fixed/Worth	.4	.6	.8	1.0	1.9	1.1	.9	.9
	7.5	1.9	1.7	1.7	3.4	1.7	2.0	2.0
	-1.3	9.9	3.5	3.5	7.0	4.4	4.5	4.7
Debt/Worth	1.9	1.3	1.2	1.1	2.1	.9	1.2	1.1
	38.9	2.9	2.4	2.2	3.5	2.0	2.6	2.5
	-3.3	19.6	5.5	5.4	9.5	5.5	6.6	7.3
% Profit Before Taxes/Tangible Net Worth	100.0	43.5	35.1	22.4	20.7	24.4	44.6	39.9
	(60) 21.1	(218) 17.7	(330) 12.7	(215) 10.9	(48) 11.5	(41) 16.4	(1132) 24.6	(1055) 19.5
	2.8	-3.9	.0	.4	4.1	7.0	10.1	5.1
% Profit Before Taxes/Total Assets	14.1	10.9	8.5	6.9	5.7	10.9	13.0	11.9
	2.2	3.7	3.5	3.3	1.9	4.4	6.6	5.3
	-10.6	-2.7	-.8	.1	.3	.7	2.4	.9
Sales/Net Fixed Assets	131.1	22.7	12.2	7.8	4.8	6.1	10.5	10.7
	15.5	8.1	5.4	4.0	2.5	3.5	4.4	4.4
	5.7	4.0	3.1	2.4	1.9	2.0	2.5	2.5
Sales/Total Assets	8.2	5.0	3.9	2.9	2.3	2.5	3.7	3.7
	5.2	3.3	2.6	2.2	1.7	1.8	2.4	2.4
	2.7	2.1	1.9	1.5	1.4	1.4	1.6	1.6
% Depr., Dep., Amort./Sales	.9	2.2	2.3	2.9	3.9	1.8	2.5	2.6
	(84) 5.0	(229) 5.3	(340) 5.1	(225) 5.3	(40) 7.2	(10) 2.6	(1168) 5.8	(1060) 5.8
	12.1	9.2	8.9	8.8	9.1	3.8	9.3	9.6
% Officers', Directors', Owners' Comp/Sales	1.5	1.7	1.2	.7	2.2		1.5	1.5
	(43) 3.5	(138) 3.1	(140) 2.0	(45) 1.7	(11) 3.0		(466) 3.0	(464) 3.2
	8.8	6.1	4.3	8.4	7.9		5.7	6.2
Net Sales ($)	170061M	1169679M	4873376M	11729257M	8293126M	16845908M	36135270M	32712996M
Total Assets ($)	28685M	314812M	1695457M	5122150M	4011556M	7112957M	19158935M	17294219M

M = $ thousand   MM = $ million
See Pages 11 through 18 for Explanation of Ratios and Data

Comparative Historical Data | Current Data Sorted By Sales

Hist 1	Hist 2	Hist 3	Type of Statement	0-1MM	1-3MM	3-5MM	5-10MM	10-25MM	25MM & OVER
137	145	189	Unqualified	1	2	4	6	31	145
205	219	229	Reviewed	6	15	21	51	84	52
268	309	263	Compiled	21	65	53	61	50	13
74	79	89	Tax Returns	23	30	14	8	12	2
279	368	295	Other	19	35	29	43	64	105
4/1/00-3/31/01 ALL	4/1/01-3/31/02 ALL	4/1/02-3/31/03 ALL		141 (4/1-9/30/02)		924 (10/1/02-3/31/03)			
963	1120	1065	NUMBER OF STATEMENTS	70	147	121	169	241	317
%	%	%	**ASSETS**	%	%	%	%	%	%
6.8	7.4	7.3	Cash & Equivalents	12.0	8.4	8.9	6.8	6.9	5.9
28.0	27.7	28.3	Trade Receivables (net)	10.7	25.9	30.2	32.2	31.4	28.2
1.4	1.5	1.7	Inventory	3.0	1.9	1.2	1.3	1.2	1.9
3.1	3.8	4.3	All Other Current	6.0	3.3	5.0	3.7	4.0	4.5
39.3	40.4	41.6	Total Current	31.7	39.5	45.2	44.0	43.6	40.5
49.5	48.1	47.6	Fixed Assets (net)	57.3	48.6	42.2	45.3	46.8	48.9
2.9	2.8	2.3	Intangibles (net)	.5	2.9	1.6	2.2	1.6	3.3
8.3	8.7	8.5	All Other Non-Current	10.5	9.0	11.0	8.5	8.0	7.3
100.0	100.0	100.0	Total	100.0	100.0	100.0	100.0	100.0	100.0
			LIABILITIES						
8.2	8.7	8.7	Notes Payable-Short Term	6.2	13.1	7.8	8.9	8.0	7.9
10.1	10.8	11.0	Cur. Mat.-L/T/D	11.3	11.7	10.7	11.8	12.1	9.7
9.8	10.7	10.6	Trade Payables	4.6	12.6	13.6	9.8	10.7	10.2
.2	.3	.2	Income Taxes Payable	.1	.1	.1	.4	.2	.2
10.1	10.3	10.9	All Other Current	15.1	10.6	8.9	10.3	10.7	11.3
38.4	40.8	41.4	Total Current	37.3	48.2	41.1	41.2	41.6	39.3
27.1	26.2	26.7	Long Term Debt	49.3	35.6	26.7	24.3	21.8	22.6
1.8	1.8	1.9	Deferred Taxes	.3	.3	.8	1.3	2.2	3.4
3.3	3.3	3.7	All Other Non-Current	10.7	4.7	4.3	2.3	2.8	2.8
29.4	27.9	26.3	Net Worth	2.4	11.1	27.1	30.8	31.5	31.9
100.0	100.0	100.0	Total Liabilities & Net Worth	100.0	100.0	100.0	100.0	100.0	100.0
			INCOME DATA						
100.0	100.0	100.0	Net Sales	100.0	100.0	100.0	100.0	100.0	100.0
			Gross Profit						
96.2	96.5	96.5	Operating Expenses	87.4	97.7	97.0	97.0	97.3	96.9
3.8	3.5	3.5	Operating Profit	12.6	2.3	3.0	3.0	2.7	3.1
1.1	1.4	1.5	All Other Expenses (net)	8.6	.9	.9	1.0	.9	1.1
2.7	2.1	2.0	Profit Before Taxes	4.0	1.4	2.0	1.9	1.8	1.9
			RATIOS						
1.6	1.6	1.5		2.1	1.3	1.7	1.5	1.5	1.5
1.0	1.0	1.0	Current	.7	.8	1.1	1.0	1.0	1.0
.7	.6	.6		.2	.5	.7	.7	.7	.7
1.4	1.4	1.3		2.0	1.1	1.4	1.4	1.3	1.2
(961) .9	(1118) .9	(1063) .8	Quick	(68) .6	.7	.9	.9	.9	.8
.6	.5	.5		.2	.5	.5	.6	.6	.6
25 14.6	**23** 15.6	**24** 15.0		**0** UND	**14** 26.1	**17** 21.2	**25** 14.3	**28** 13.1	**31** 11.8
35 10.3	**33** 11.0	**35** 10.6	Sales/Receivables	**0** UND	**28** 12.9	**31** 11.8	**35** 10.5	**36** 10.1	**38** 9.7
45 8.1	**43** 8.6	**43** 8.4		**31** 12.0	**39** 9.5	**45** 8.1	**45** 8.2	**44** 8.3	**45** 8.1
			Cost of Sales/Inventory						
			Cost of Sales/Payables						
17.5	18.0	20.3		8.9	38.2	14.8	19.1	23.5	22.5
999.8	793.2	UND	Sales/Working Capital	-37.1	-55.0	202.6	270.3	216.3	999.8
-18.4	-17.6	-18.6		-3.8	-9.7	-28.4	-24.1	-21.8	-21.1
4.6	4.0	4.5		5.4	3.1	4.2	5.1	4.4	4.9
(886) 2.1	(1038) 1.7	(996) 2.0	EBIT/Interest	(51) 1.8	(137) 1.3	(112) 2.3	(159) 2.3	(231) 2.0	(306) 2.2
.8	.6	.7		.4	-.4	.7	.8	.7	1.1
2.1	2.0	2.1			3.7	2.5	1.9	2.0	2.3
(285) 1.3	(331) 1.2	(330) 1.3	Net Profit + Depr., Dep., Amort./Cur. Mat. L/T/D		(21) 1.6	(36) 1.4	(49) 1.2	(99) 1.2	(121) 1.3
.9	.8	.8			1.0	.6	.9	.8	.8
.9	.8	.8		1.1	.7	.6	.7	.9	1.0
1.9	1.9	1.9	Fixed/Worth	4.7	3.2	1.9	1.6	1.7	1.8
4.7	4.7	5.2		-4.1	-10.2	5.2	3.3	3.9	3.8
1.1	1.1	1.2		1.2	1.5	1.2	1.3	1.1	1.2
2.6	2.7	2.7	Debt/Worth	9.8	5.2	2.8	2.5	2.4	2.3
7.1	7.6	9.0		-8.8	-13.4	12.5	5.9	5.5	5.7
35.9	30.7	33.6		40.0	46.7	38.6	38.1	34.5	23.5
(829) 15.2	(971) 11.3	(912) 12.7	% Profit Before Taxes/Tangible Net Worth	(45) 13.4	(99) 12.7	(103) 17.6	(151) 14.7	(223) 12.7	(291) 12.0
1.1	-.9	.4		.0	-6.9	3.5	-1.0	-.4	2.8
10.1	10.0	8.6		7.8	10.6	9.8	10.0	8.5	7.4
4.0	3.2	3.4	% Profit Before Taxes/Total Assets	2.5	1.4	3.8	3.7	3.5	3.4
-.8	-1.6	-.9		-3.7	-8.2	-1.1	-.9	-.9	.3
11.7	13.4	14.2		11.5	18.0	21.7	16.4	13.6	10.6
4.9	5.7	5.6	Sales/Net Fixed Assets	3.1	5.7	7.5	6.8	5.7	4.4
2.6	2.9	2.9		.5	3.1	4.0	3.4	3.2	2.5
3.9	4.1	4.2		3.0	5.3	5.2	4.6	4.1	3.3
2.5	2.7	2.6	Sales/Total Assets	1.8	2.9	3.2	2.9	2.8	2.3
1.6	1.7	1.8		.4	1.9	1.9	2.0	1.9	1.6
2.0	2.1	2.3		4.8	4.2	1.8	2.6	2.3	2.1
(850) 4.9	(970) 4.9	(928) 5.3	% Depr., Dep., Amort./Sales	(61) 16.4	(121) 8.0	(105) 4.8	(151) 5.4	(231) 4.8	(259) 4.2
8.9	9.0	9.0		33.9	12.1	7.9	9.2	8.1	7.6
1.4	1.3	1.4		5.6	1.7	2.0	1.3	1.0	.9
(374) 2.8	(391) 2.7	(382) 2.5	% Officers', Directors', Owners' Comp/Sales	(17) 8.5	(71) 3.9	(63) 3.1	(79) 2.1	(88) 1.7	(64) 2.2
5.8	5.1	5.8		20.4	6.8	5.1	4.2	3.8	8.8
28189156M	35053547M	43081407M	Net Sales ($)	30041M	296059M	472651M	1232590M	3824300M	37225766M
14058029M	16321409M	18285617M	Total Assets ($)	47202M	134287M	284521M	568787M	1596473M	15654347M

© RMA 2003

M = $ thousand   MM = $ million
See Pages 11 through 18 for Explanation of Ratios and Data

Current Data Sorted By Assets

Comparative Historical Data

						Type of Statement		
			4		6	Unqualified		
	1	3	2			Reviewed		
1	2	4		1		Compiled		
2	1	4	10	1	6	Tax Returns		
						Other		
3 (4/1-9/30/02)			47 (10/1/02-3/31/03)				4/1/98-3/31/99	4/1/99-3/31/00
0-500M	500M-2MM	2-10MM	10-50MM	50-100MM	100-250MM		ALL	ALL
3	6	11	16	2	12	NUMBER OF STATEMENTS		
%	%	%	%	%	%	ASSETS	%	%
		7.6	5.5		6.3	Cash & Equivalents	D	D
		40.1	27.8		17.3	Trade Receivables (net)	A	A
		.6	.6		1.1	Inventory	T	T
		3.4	6.7		3.9	All Other Current	A	A
		51.7	40.7		28.6	Total Current		
		38.0	53.5		65.8	Fixed Assets (net)	N	N
		2.9	.1		1.1	Intangibles (net)	O	O
		7.4	5.8		4.6	All Other Non-Current	T	T
		100.0	100.0		100.0	Total		
						LIABILITIES	A	A
		10.7	9.5		3.5	Notes Payable-Short Term	V	V
		9.0	10.4		8.9	Cur. Mat.-L/T/D	A	A
		14.4	11.2		5.2	Trade Payables	I	I
		.1	.1		.1	Income Taxes Payable	L	L
		10.8	7.3		10.6	All Other Current	A	A
		45.0	38.6		28.2	Total Current	B	B
		17.1	24.2		28.5	Long Term Debt	L	L
		1.3	3.8		4.1	Deferred Taxes	E	E
		.9	1.7		2.0	All Other Non-Current		
		35.7	31.7		37.2	Net Worth		
		100.0	100.0		100.0	Total Liabilities & Net Worth		
						INCOME DATA		
		100.0	100.0		100.0	Net Sales		
						Gross Profit		
		98.1	91.8		94.2	Operating Expenses		
		1.9	8.2		5.8	Operating Profit		
		.2	2.0		1.9	All Other Expenses (net)		
		1.7	6.2		3.9	Profit Before Taxes		
						RATIOS		
		1.6	1.5		1.7	Current		
		1.2	.9		1.0			
		1.0	.5		.9			
		1.5	1.5		1.0	Quick		
		1.2	.8		.9			
		1.0	.5		.7			
		30 12.3	31 11.8		34 10.9	Sales/Receivables		
		35 10.3	38 9.6		39 9.5			
		51 7.2	48 7.6		40 9.0			
						Cost of Sales/Inventory		
						Cost of Sales/Payables		
		25.7	16.9		18.4	Sales/Working Capital		
		50.7	-51.0		NM			
		-225.8	-9.2		-39.7			
		9.8	4.4		4.1	EBIT/Interest		
		(10) 3.3	2.0		3.3			
		.6	1.1		2.1			
						Net Profit + Depr., Dep., Amort./Cur. Mat. L /T/D		
		.7	.6		1.1	Fixed/Worth		
		1.0	2.6		1.7			
		2.0	3.8		3.7			
		.8	1.0		1.3	Debt/Worth		
		1.9	3.2		1.6			
		7.9	5.2		3.9			
		41.0	42.0		21.7	% Profit Before Taxes/Tangible Net Worth		
		24.6	14.2		14.7			
		-4.4	1.2		10.0			
		13.5	6.6		8.0	% Profit Before Taxes/Total Assets		
		4.2	3.2		5.9			
		-1.5	.5		3.7			
		35.0	7.6		3.9	Sales/Net Fixed Assets		
		10.9	4.7		2.5			
		4.9	2.6		1.9			
		4.5	3.2		2.0	Sales/Total Assets		
		3.5	2.3		1.7			
		2.3	1.8		1.4			
		1.0	3.6			% Depr., Dep., Amort./Sales		
		(10) 2.6	5.9					
		7.2	10.2					
						% Officers', Directors', Owners' Comp/Sales		
2425M	28999M	165413M	873347M	225987M	3333383M	Net Sales ($)		
738M	7618M	46848M	357855M	159613M	1982686M	Total Assets ($)		

M = $ thousand   MM = $ million
See Pages 11 through 18 for Explanation of Ratios and Data

Comparative Historical Data | Current Data Sorted By Sales

4/1/00-3/31/01 ALL	4/1/01-3/31/02 ALL	4/1/02-3/31/03 ALL	Type of Statement	0-1MM	1-3MM	3-5MM	5-10MM	10-25MM	25MM & OVER
		10	Unqualified				1		9
		6	Reviewed					2	2
		8	Compiled	1	1			2	2
		2	Tax Returns				2		2
		24	Other	2		2	1	3	16
				3 (4/1-9/30/02)			47 (10/1/02-3/31/03)		
		50	**NUMBER OF STATEMENTS**	3	1	3	7	7	29
%	%	%	**ASSETS**	%	%	%	%	%	%
D	D	5.8	Cash & Equivalents						6.1
A	A	29.2	Trade Receivables (net)						26.2
T	T	.7	Inventory						.8
A	A	4.5	All Other Current						5.5
		40.2	Total Current						38.6
N	N	51.3	Fixed Assets (net)						56.5
O	O	.9	Intangibles (net)						.5
T	T	7.6	All Other Non-Current						4.4
		100.0	Total						100.0
A	A		**LIABILITIES**						
V	V	7.5	Notes Payable-Short Term						8.7
A	A	10.1	Cur. Mat.-L/T/D						9.2
I	I	9.8	Trade Payables						9.1
L	L	.1	Income Taxes Payable						.1
A	A	10.3	All Other Current						9.3
B	B	37.8	Total Current						36.4
L	L	22.4	Long Term Debt						23.5
E	E	2.6	Deferred Taxes						3.6
		1.9	All Other Non-Current						1.8
		35.3	Net Worth						34.7
		100.0	Total Liabilities & Net Worth						100.0
			INCOME DATA						
		100.0	Net Sales						100.0
			Gross Profit						
		95.2	Operating Expenses						95.9
		4.8	Operating Profit						4.1
		1.2	All Other Expenses (net)						1.6
		3.6	Profit Before Taxes						2.5
			RATIOS						
		1.7							1.6
		1.1	Current						1.0
		.7							.7
		1.5							1.5
		1.0	Quick						.9
		.6							.6
	31	11.8						33	11.2
	37	10.0	Sales/Receivables					39	9.4
	45	8.1						47	7.8
			Cost of Sales/Inventory						
			Cost of Sales/Payables						
		19.2							16.4
		86.3	Sales/Working Capital						−225.8
		−20.4							−17.4
		5.8							3.9
	(47)	2.9	EBIT/Interest					(28)	2.7
		1.0							1.6
		2.3	Net Profit + Depr., Dep.,						
	(12)	1.2	Amort./Cur. Mat. L/T/D						
		.9							
		.8							.9
		1.7	Fixed/Worth						1.8
		3.4							3.7
		1.1							1.2
		1.7	Debt/Worth						2.0
		4.4							5.0
		24.6	% Profit Before Taxes/Tangible						21.9
	(49)	14.6	Net Worth						14.6
		.2							6.0
		7.6	% Profit Before Taxes/Total						6.5
		4.1	Assets						4.1
		.0							1.9
		11.8							5.2
		4.4	Sales/Net Fixed Assets						3.6
		2.5							2.3
		3.5							2.7
		2.1	Sales/Total Assets						2.0
		1.6							1.5
		2.1							2.7
	(36)	5.2	% Depr., Dep., Amort./Sales					(18)	5.3
		9.0							8.0
		.5	% Officers', Directors',						
	(12)	1.3	Owners' Comp/Sales						
		4.8							
		4629554M	Net Sales ($)	1646M	1764M	10874M	47896M	116359M	4451015M
		2555358M	Total Assets ($)	1035M	330M	34093M	13274M	32377M	2474249M

(Columns 4/1/00-3/31/01 ALL and 4/1/01-3/31/02 ALL: DATA NOT AVAILABLE)

M = $ thousand   MM = $ million
See Pages 11 through 18 for Explanation of Ratios and Data

Current Data Sorted By Assets   Comparative Historical Data

						Type of Statement		
	1	1	1			Unqualified		
2	1	3				Reviewed		
1	3	4				Compiled		
3	1	1	1			Tax Returns		
2	3	4				Other		

0-500M	500M-2MM	2-10MM	10-50MM	50-100MM	100-250MM		4/1/98-3/31/99 ALL	4/1/99-3/31/00 ALL
	3 (4/1-9/30/02)		29 (10/1/02-3/31/03)					
8	9	13	2			NUMBER OF STATEMENTS		
%	%	%	%	%	%	**ASSETS**	%	%
		6.3		DATA	DATA	Cash & Equivalents	DATA	DATA
		26.5		NOT	NOT	Trade Receivables (net)	NOT	NOT
		.9		AVAILABLE	AVAILABLE	Inventory	AVAILABLE	AVAILABLE
		10.9				All Other Current		
		44.6				Total Current		
		47.7				Fixed Assets (net)		
		1.2				Intangibles (net)		
		6.5				All Other Non-Current		
		100.0				Total		
						LIABILITIES		
		2.6				Notes Payable-Short Term		
		6.1				Cur. Mat.-L/T/D		
		11.6				Trade Payables		
		.3				Income Taxes Payable		
		7.0				All Other Current		
		27.6				Total Current		
		16.2				Long Term Debt		
		1.4				Deferred Taxes		
		2.9				All Other Non-Current		
		51.8				Net Worth		
		100.0				Total Liabilities & Net Worth		
						INCOME DATA		
		100.0				Net Sales		
						Gross Profit		
		95.6				Operating Expenses		
		4.4				Operating Profit		
		.8				All Other Expenses (net)		
		3.6				Profit Before Taxes		
						RATIOS		
		8.0				Current		
		1.4						
		1.2						
		6.5				Quick		
		1.2						
		.7						
		28 13.0				Sales/Receivables		
		39 9.4						
		47 7.7						
						Cost of Sales/Inventory		
						Cost of Sales/Payables		
		4.8				Sales/Working Capital		
		21.6						
		35.7						
		4.9				EBIT/Interest		
		(12) 1.7						
		1.2						
						Net Profit + Depr., Dep., Amort./Cur. Mat. L /T/D		
		.6				Fixed/Worth		
		.9						
		1.2						
		.3				Debt/Worth		
		.9						
		2.3						
		40.0				% Profit Before Taxes/Tangible Net Worth		
		7.1						
		.5						
		7.1				% Profit Before Taxes/Total Assets		
		2.6						
		.2						
		12.0				Sales/Net Fixed Assets		
		5.2						
		2.1						
		3.6				Sales/Total Assets		
		2.5						
		1.1						
		1.7				% Depr., Dep., Amort./Sales		
		5.2						
		10.1						
						% Officers', Directors', Owners' Comp/Sales		
14055M	26727M	170210M	62323M			Net Sales ($)		
1654M	7021M	65533M	52624M			Total Assets ($)		

© RMA 2003

M = $ thousand   MM = $ million
See Pages 11 through 18 for Explanation of Ratios and Data

Comparative Historical Data   Current Data Sorted By Sales

			Type of Statement						
		3	Unqualified		1			1	1
		6	Reviewed	1			2	3	
		8	Compiled	1	3	1	2	1	
		5	Tax Returns	2	1	1	1		1
		10	Other	2	1	3	1	2	
4/1/00-3/31/01 ALL	4/1/01-3/31/02 ALL	4/1/02-3/31/03 ALL		0-1MM	3 (4/1-9/30/02) 1-3MM	3-5MM	29 (10/1/02-3/31/03) 5-10MM	10-25MM	25MM & OVER
		32	NUMBER OF STATEMENTS	6	6	5	6	7	2
%	%	%	ASSETS	%	%	%	%	%	%
D	D	8.4	Cash & Equivalents						
A	A	21.9	Trade Receivables (net)						
T	T	1.8	Inventory						
A	A	5.4	All Other Current						
		37.4	Total Current						
N	N	54.1	Fixed Assets (net)						
O	O	1.4	Intangibles (net)						
T	T	7.1	All Other Non-Current						
		100.0	Total						
A	A		LIABILITIES						
V	V	18.1	Notes Payable-Short Term						
A	A	6.1	Cur. Mat.-L/T/D						
I	I	11.8	Trade Payables						
L	L	.3	Income Taxes Payable						
A	A	4.9	All Other Current						
B	B	41.2	Total Current						
L	L	26.2	Long Term Debt						
E	E	1.1	Deferred Taxes						
		4.7	All Other Non-Current						
		26.8	Net Worth						
		100.0	Total Liabilities & Net Worth						
			INCOME DATA						
		100.0	Net Sales						
			Gross Profit						
		97.9	Operating Expenses						
		2.1	Operating Profit						
		1.2	All Other Expenses (net)						
		.9	Profit Before Taxes						
			RATIOS						
		1.9							
		1.2	Current						
		.6							
		1.6							
		1.0	Quick						
		.3							
	10	37.3							
	30	12.3	Sales/Receivables						
	46	7.9							
			Cost of Sales/Inventory						
			Cost of Sales/Payables						
		12.1							
		36.6	Sales/Working Capital						
		−16.3							
		7.0							
	(30)	1.7	EBIT/Interest						
		.2							
			Net Profit + Depr., Dep., Amort./Cur. Mat. L/T/D						
		.8							
		1.7	Fixed/Worth						
		17.3							
		.6							
		2.1	Debt/Worth						
		20.1							
		42.4							
	(25)	9.1	% Profit Before Taxes/Tangible Net Worth						
		.1							
		9.8							
		2.4	% Profit Before Taxes/Total Assets						
		−2.8							
		15.9							
		3.6	Sales/Net Fixed Assets						
		2.1							
		3.7							
		2.2	Sales/Total Assets						
		1.1							
		2.3							
	(30)	6.9	% Depr., Dep., Amort./Sales						
		14.7							
		2.2							
	(11)	5.1	% Officers', Directors', Owners' Comp/Sales						
		6.4							
		273315M	Net Sales ($)	1219M	11226M	16971M	45467M	117715M	80717M
		126832M	Total Assets ($)	1147M	4726M	11715M	18356M	70282M	20606M

Current Data Sorted By Assets   **Comparative Historical Data**

0-500M	500M-2MM	2-10MM	10-50MM	50-100MM	100-250MM	Type of Statement	4/1/98-3/31/99 ALL	4/1/99-3/31/00 ALL
			1	2	2	1	Unqualified		
	2					Reviewed		
	6					Compiled		
2	1	1	2			Tax Returns		
1	5	2	4			Other		
			2 (4/1-9/30/02)		30 (10/1/02-3/31/03)			
3	14	4	8	2	1	**NUMBER OF STATEMENTS**		
%	%	%	%	%	%	**ASSETS**	%	%
	3.8					Cash & Equivalents	D	D
	47.6					Trade Receivables (net)	A	A
	1.6					Inventory	T	T
	5.5					All Other Current	A	A
	58.4					Total Current		
	38.6					Fixed Assets (net)	N	N
	.1					Intangibles (net)	O	O
	2.9					All Other Non-Current	T	T
	100.0					Total		
						LIABILITIES	A	A
	4.1					Notes Payable-Short Term	V	V
	8.6					Cur. Mat.-L/T/D	A	A
	20.6					Trade Payables	I	I
	.0					Income Taxes Payable	L	L
	16.6					All Other Current	A	A
	49.9					Total Current	B	B
	23.0					Long Term Debt	L	L
	.1					Deferred Taxes	E	E
	7.7					All Other Non-Current		
	19.4					Net Worth		
	100.0					Total Liabilities & Net Worth		
						INCOME DATA		
	100.0					Net Sales		
						Gross Profit		
	98.0					Operating Expenses		
	2.0					Operating Profit		
	−.2					All Other Expenses (net)		
	2.1					Profit Before Taxes		
						RATIOS		
	1.8					Current		
	1.2							
	.9							
	1.4					Quick		
	1.1							
	.8							
21	17.7					Sales/Receivables		
28	13.1							
77	4.7							
						Cost of Sales/Inventory		
						Cost of Sales/Payables		
	13.2					Sales/Working Capital		
	61.4							
	−80.7							
	9.2					EBIT/Interest		
	4.0							
	1.1							
						Net Profit + Depr., Dep., Amort./Cur. Mat. L /T/D		
	.1					Fixed/Worth		
	2.4							
	NM							
	1.4					Debt/Worth		
	6.0							
	NM							
	100.0					% Profit Before Taxes/Tangible Net Worth		
	(11) 20.7							
	6.0							
	13.5					% Profit Before Taxes/Total Assets		
	5.4							
	.2							
	UND					Sales/Net Fixed Assets		
	17.5							
	2.4							
	7.4					Sales/Total Assets		
	4.2							
	1.8							
	1.3					% Depr., Dep., Amort./Sales		
	(11) 8.0							
	13.1							
						% Officers', Directors', Owners' Comp/Sales		
1303M	89684M	73551M	499466M	509986M	350934M	Net Sales ($)		
457M	18914M	19574M	202464M	158381M	137586M	Total Assets ($)		

M = $ thousand   MM = $ million
See Pages 11 through 18 for Explanation of Ratios and Data

Comparative Historical Data — Current Data Sorted By Sales

4/1/00-3/31/01 ALL	4/1/01-3/31/02 ALL	4/1/02-3/31/03 ALL		0-1MM	1-3MM	3-5MM	5-10MM	10-25MM	25MM & OVER
			Type of Statement		2 (4/1-9/30/02)		30 (10/1/02-3/31/03)		
		6	Unqualified					1	5
		5	Reviewed				1	3	1
		8	Compiled	2	3		2	1	
		2	Tax Returns	1		1			
		11	Other		2		2	2	5
		32	**NUMBER OF STATEMENTS**	3	5	1	5	7	11
%	%	%	**ASSETS**	%	%	%	%	%	%
D	D	4.2	Cash & Equivalents						4.7
A	A	36.4	Trade Receivables (net)						27.3
T	T	2.0	Inventory						3.3
A	A	5.4	All Other Current						6.4
		47.9	Total Current						41.8
N	N	42.9	Fixed Assets (net)						44.7
O	O	2.1	Intangibles (net)						6.0
T	T	7.0	All Other Non-Current						7.6
		100.0	Total						100.0
A	A		**LIABILITIES**						
V	V	4.3	Notes Payable-Short Term						4.9
A	A	8.3	Cur. Mat.-L/T/D						6.3
I	I	16.5	Trade Payables						10.8
L	L	.6	Income Taxes Payable						.4
A	A	16.4	All Other Current						18.4
B	B	46.2	Total Current						40.7
L	L	18.3	Long Term Debt						11.8
E	E	2.1	Deferred Taxes						4.3
		8.8	All Other Non-Current						8.3
		24.7	Net Worth						34.9
		100.0	Total Liabilities & Net Worth						100.0
			INCOME DATA						
		100.0	Net Sales						100.0
			Gross Profit						
		96.8	Operating Expenses						97.5
		3.1	Operating Profit						2.5
		.3	All Other Expenses (net)						.6
		2.8	Profit Before Taxes						1.9
			RATIOS						
		1.6	Current						1.7
		1.2							1.3
		.7							.8
		1.2	Quick						1.6
		1.0							.9
		.6							.7
	22	16.3	Sales/Receivables					29	12.7
	34	10.8						35	10.4
	56	6.5						47	7.7
			Cost of Sales/Inventory						
			Cost of Sales/Payables						
		16.9	Sales/Working Capital						16.3
		74.1							28.1
		−40.9							−34.0
		5.9	EBIT/Interest						7.8
	(30)	2.8							2.2
		.4							−.2
			Net Profit + Depr., Dep., Amort./Cur. Mat. L/T/D						
		.7	Fixed/Worth						.8
		2.0							1.9
		4.6							4.3
		1.1	Debt/Worth						.8
		3.0							2.1
		20.3							6.7
		67.7	% Profit Before Taxes/Tangible Net Worth						21.7
	(27)	17.8						(10)	14.3
		6.0							−2.8
		12.5	% Profit Before Taxes/Total Assets						8.3
		4.7							4.5
		−1.3							−1.8
		25.8	Sales/Net Fixed Assets						8.7
		6.4							6.0
		3.2							5.0
		4.8	Sales/Total Assets						3.1
		3.1							2.8
		2.0							2.3
		1.7	% Depr., Dep., Amort./Sales						
	(25)	4.6							
		11.6							
			% Officers', Directors', Owners' Comp/Sales						
		1524924M	Net Sales ($)	1303M	9848M	3236M	37470M	111536M	1361531M
		537376M	Total Assets ($)	457M	7340M	969M	7949M	31888M	488773M

M = $ thousand   MM = $ million
See Pages 11 through 18 for Explanation of Ratios and Data

TRANSPORTATION—Taxi Service NAICS 485310 (SIC 4121, 4899)

Current Data Sorted By Assets   **Comparative Historical Data**

Type of Statement								
		2	1			Unqualified		1
	2	5				Reviewed		2
2	3	3				Compiled		7
5	3	1				Tax Returns		2
2		3	3		1	Other		9

	7 (4/1-9/30/02)			26 (10/1/02-3/31/03)			4/1/98-3/31/99	4/1/99-3/31/00
0-500M	500M-2MM	2-10MM	10-50MM	50-100MM	100-250MM		ALL	ALL
9	8	11	4	1		NUMBER OF STATEMENTS		21
%	%	%	%	%	%	ASSETS	%	%
		10.2				Cash & Equivalents		10.8
		13.8				Trade Receivables (net)		10.4
		2.4				Inventory		.8
		11.9				All Other Current		6.4
		38.3				Total Current		28.3
		31.5				Fixed Assets (net)		49.9
		19.5				Intangibles (net)		2.4
		10.8				All Other Non-Current		19.4
		100.0				Total		100.0
						LIABILITIES		
		14.4				Notes Payable-Short Term		7.8
		7.2				Cur. Mat.-L/T/D		5.2
		7.7				Trade Payables		7.3
		1.3				Income Taxes Payable		.5
		10.9				All Other Current		24.0
		41.5				Total Current		44.7
		23.0				Long Term Debt		26.6
		.1				Deferred Taxes		.3
		7.6				All Other Non-Current		6.3
		27.8				Net Worth		22.0
		100.0				Total Liabilities & Net Worth		100.0
						INCOME DATA		
		100.0				Net Sales		100.0
						Gross Profit		
		93.6				Operating Expenses		92.7
		6.4				Operating Profit		7.3
		2.6				All Other Expenses (net)		1.0
		3.7				Profit Before Taxes		6.3
						RATIOS		
		1.1						1.8
		1.0				Current		.8
		.7						.3
		1.0						1.4
		.6				Quick		.6
		.4					(20)	.3
	3	137.0					0	UND
	20	18.2				Sales/Receivables	11	34.7
	46	8.0					26	14.0
						Cost of Sales/Inventory		
						Cost of Sales/Payables		
		14.2						27.1
		−122.6				Sales/Working Capital		−28.0
		−14.0						−7.4
		11.7						7.2
		5.2				EBIT/Interest	(19)	4.1
		−.3						1.5
						Net Profit + Depr., Dep., Amort./Cur. Mat. L /T/D		
		.8						.8
		2.4				Fixed/Worth		2.4
		−1.4						6.1
		.7						1.3
		8.1				Debt/Worth		2.3
		−5.0						11.5
						% Profit Before Taxes/Tangible Net Worth		88.6
							(18)	21.0
								8.8
		18.2				% Profit Before Taxes/Total Assets		17.4
		6.9						8.6
		−4.4						2.6
		9.8				Sales/Net Fixed Assets		9.5
		5.6						5.1
		4.1						2.7
		2.3				Sales/Total Assets		3.1
		1.3						2.1
		1.2						1.4
		2.5				% Depr., Dep., Amort./Sales		4.3
	(10)	10.8					(18)	8.0
		13.7						16.2
						% Officers', Directors', Owners' Comp/Sales		3.4
							(10)	6.0
								11.7
10001M	28362M	77997M	165764M	62825M		Net Sales ($)		264150M
2954M	7739M	47025M	116065M	59636M		Total Assets ($)		163338M

(Columns 0-500M, 500M-2MM, 10-50MM, 50-100MM, 100-250MM marked "DATA NOT AVAILABLE"; column 4/1/98-3/31/99 ALL marked "DATA NOT AVAILABLE")

M = $ thousand   MM = $ million
See Pages 11 through 18 for Explanation of Ratios and Data

Comparative Historical Data | | | | Current Data Sorted By Sales

			Type of Statement	0-1MM	1-3MM	3-5MM	5-10MM	10-25MM	25MM & OVER
1	1	3	Unqualified				1	1	1
	3	2	Reviewed				2		
5	4	10	Compiled	1	3	2	3	1	
3	5	9	Tax Returns	2	5	2	1		
11	7	9	Other	1	1	2		1	3
4/1/00-3/31/01	4/1/01-3/31/02	4/1/02-3/31/03			7 (4/1-9/30/02)			26 (10/1/02-3/31/03)	
ALL	ALL	ALL							
20	20	33	**NUMBER OF STATEMENTS**	4	9	6	7	3	4
%	%	%	**ASSETS**	%	%	%	%	%	%
8.3	8.8	14.3	Cash & Equivalents						
15.4	10.7	19.7	Trade Receivables (net)						
1.3	.4	1.0	Inventory						
9.7	2.2	6.0	All Other Current						
34.7	22.2	41.0	Total Current						
36.1	41.8	35.0	Fixed Assets (net)						
14.3	22.2	13.6	Intangibles (net)						
14.9	13.9	10.4	All Other Non-Current						
100.0	100.0	100.0	Total						
			LIABILITIES						
4.1	6.5	10.0	Notes Payable-Short Term						
9.4	11.1	4.7	Cur. Mat.-L/T/D						
5.7	8.0	9.1	Trade Payables						
.2	.8	2.2	Income Taxes Payable						
10.1	26.1	11.7	All Other Current						
29.4	52.4	37.6	Total Current						
21.3	23.1	21.8	Long Term Debt						
.4	.3	.2	Deferred Taxes						
3.5	6.6	5.8	All Other Non-Current						
45.4	17.6	34.5	Net Worth						
100.0	100.0	100.0	Total Liabilities & Net Worth						
			INCOME DATA						
100.0	100.0	100.0	Net Sales						
			Gross Profit						
88.4	91.6	88.8	Operating Expenses						
11.6	8.3	11.2	Operating Profit						
.9	1.2	2.7	All Other Expenses (net)						
10.7	7.2	8.5	Profit Before Taxes						
			RATIOS						
2.3	1.0	2.0	Current						
1.0	.7	1.0							
.3	.3	.7							
1.3	.9	1.7	Quick						
.7	.6	1.0							
.2	.2	.4							
1 265.3	2 158.4	3 105.9	Sales/Receivables						
19 19.4	8 43.9	18 20.0							
45 8.2	25 14.6	44 8.3							
			Cost of Sales/Inventory						
			Cost of Sales/Payables						
11.1	-206.3	8.8	Sales/Working Capital						
NM	-35.9	235.5							
-10.1	-10.1	-16.6							
8.1	8.9	21.8	EBIT/Interest						
(16) 1.8	(19) 5.9	(29) 7.5							
1.2	1.5	2.3							
			Net Profit + Depr., Dep., Amort./Cur. Mat. L/T/D						
.4	.9	.4	Fixed/Worth						
1.0	1.8	1.7							
11.0	-1.0	NM							
.5	1.2	1.8	Debt/Worth						
1.7	3.4	3.1							
16.6	-2.9	NM							
28.0	94.6	116.4	% Profit Before Taxes/Tangible Net Worth						
(16) 14.1	(12) 27.8	(25) 40.4							
.8	7.0	23.4							
18.4	19.5	27.6	% Profit Before Taxes/Total Assets						
4.8	12.3	11.2							
.9	2.6	3.9							
15.5	7.2	17.6	Sales/Net Fixed Assets						
6.7	4.9	8.5							
3.9	3.1	4.4							
3.1	4.0	3.9	Sales/Total Assets						
2.1	2.6	2.2							
1.3	1.1	1.3							
2.1	3.6	1.9	% Depr., Dep., Amort./Sales						
(17) 5.3	(18) 6.4	(28) 4.7							
9.2	11.3	12.9							
		3.1	% Officers', Directors', Owners' Comp/Sales						
	(19)	4.7							
		12.1							
361800M	402812M	344949M	Net Sales ($)	2446M	14416M	20428M	50201M	42180M	215278M
230618M	269923M	233419M	Total Assets ($)	1209M	5190M	12493M	24346M	63590M	126591M

© RMA 2003

M = $ thousand   MM = $ million
See Pages 11 through 18 for Explanation of Ratios and Data

	Current Data Sorted By Assets						Comparative Historical Data	
Type of Statement								
Unqualified		1	4	5			32	23
Reviewed		9	27	7			39	42
Compiled	4	10	17	1			38	35
Tax Returns	3	5	3	1	1		11	9
Other	6	1	7	1	1		16	26
	44 (4/1-9/30/02)		70 (10/1/02-3/31/03)				4/1/98-3/31/99	4/1/99-3/31/00
	0-500M	500M-2MM	2-10MM	10-50MM	50-100MM	100-250MM	ALL	ALL
NUMBER OF STATEMENTS	13	26	58	15	2		136	135
	%	%	%	%	%	%	%	%
ASSETS								
Cash & Equivalents	15.3	12.0	10.3	5.3		D	10.3	11.3
Trade Receivables (net)	11.3	8.9	8.9	9.2		A	10.7	9.4
Inventory	4.2	1.3	2.1	4.6		T	2.7	2.5
All Other Current	.4	1.9	1.4	4.7		A	1.9	2.6
Total Current	31.3	24.1	22.6	23.9			25.6	25.8
Fixed Assets (net)	53.4	64.0	66.9	64.4		N	64.3	64.1
Intangibles (net)	2.4	4.0	1.7	1.3		O	3.2	3.3
All Other Non-Current	12.9	7.8	8.8	10.4		T	6.9	6.8
Total	100.0	100.0	100.0	100.0			100.0	100.0
LIABILITIES						A		
Notes Payable-Short Term	4.5	1.3	6.9	9.7		V	5.6	7.6
Cur. Mat.-L/T/D	7.5	19.5	11.3	10.3		A	12.5	13.0
Trade Payables	3.9	3.0	3.7	3.1		I	9.3	3.8
Income Taxes Payable	.0	.5	.3	.2		L	.1	.2
All Other Current	23.8	7.8	10.3	12.3		A	6.3	6.6
Total Current	39.7	32.1	32.5	35.6		B	33.8	31.2
Long Term Debt	26.3	41.4	29.3	27.5		L	32.3	31.7
Deferred Taxes	.5	.5	2.5	2.3		E	1.6	1.7
All Other Non-Current	4.9	1.4	1.8	4.1			3.4	2.3
Net Worth	28.7	24.6	33.8	30.5			28.8	33.2
Total Liabilities & Net Worth	100.0	100.0	100.0	100.0			100.0	100.0
INCOME DATA								
Net Sales	100.0	100.0	100.0	100.0			100.0	100.0
Gross Profit								
Operating Expenses	94.2	92.6	94.7	89.0			92.7	93.7
Operating Profit	5.8	7.4	5.3	11.0			7.2	6.3
All Other Expenses (net)	.5	3.7	2.1	4.2			1.9	2.4
Profit Before Taxes	5.3	3.7	3.2	6.8			5.4	3.9
RATIOS								
Current	1.9	1.4	1.1	1.0			1.7	1.6
	.8	.7	.8	.8			.9	.9
	.4	.3	.3	.4			.4	.5
Quick	1.9	1.0	1.1	.9			1.5	1.3
	.8	.6	.6	.5			.7	.7
	.4	.3	.2	.1			.3	.3
Sales/Receivables	0 UND	0 UND	6 56.4	9 39.7			3 120.6	3 108.5
	1 288.0	13 28.7	13 27.2	24 14.9			12 30.2	15 24.2
	25 14.5	30 12.0	25 14.6	44 8.4			35 10.5	32 11.3
Cost of Sales/Inventory								
Cost of Sales/Payables								
Sales/Working Capital	15.7	37.4	39.1	375.3			14.5	19.9
	-57.5	-20.8	-23.0	-16.5			-76.6	-35.2
	-25.4	-7.8	-6.3	-4.3			-7.2	-8.4
EBIT/Interest		5.1	4.3	3.5			5.7	3.8
		(25) 2.1	(56) 2.1	(14) 2.5			(124) 2.3	(124) 2.1
		1.0	1.2	1.2			1.5	1.1
Net Profit + Depr., Dep., Amort./Cur. Mat. L /T/D		3.3	2.3				1.8	2.2
		(10) 2.7	(22) 1.0				(55) 1.2	(50) 1.5
		1.7	.9				.9	1.0
Fixed/Worth	1.0	1.1	1.3	1.3			1.2	1.2
	1.4	3.4	2.4	2.3			2.1	2.5
	3.2	UND	5.4	3.4			4.2	5.3
Debt/Worth	.9	1.2	1.2	1.6			1.0	1.1
	2.1	3.0	2.2	2.4			2.3	2.7
	30.7	UND	6.1	5.0			4.5	5.7
% Profit Before Taxes/Tangible Net Worth	107.5	48.7	22.3	25.5			41.1	32.2
	(11) 63.7	(20) 24.9	(52) 13.6	(14) 19.4			(120) 22.6	(120) 15.1
	17.4	6.6	6.8	3.5			9.4	2.9
% Profit Before Taxes/Total Assets	33.8	12.6	9.4	8.8			14.0	9.7
	22.6	4.3	4.1	6.1			6.2	4.8
	4.2	-.4	1.3	1.7			2.6	.6
Sales/Net Fixed Assets	10.5	4.5	2.9	3.1			4.2	3.5
	5.6	2.6	1.9	1.6			2.2	2.3
	3.3	1.6	1.5	1.0			1.5	1.5
Sales/Total Assets	4.9	2.4	1.9	1.9			2.1	2.2
	3.5	1.8	1.4	1.2			1.4	1.5
	2.1	1.1	1.1	.8			1.0	1.0
% Depr., Dep., Amort./Sales	2.2	8.5	8.1	5.7			6.9	7.5
	(12) 10.8	(25) 12.4	11.9	12.9			(135) 10.6	(127) 12.0
	13.8	16.0	14.9	18.1			14.7	15.3
% Officers', Directors', Owners' Comp/Sales		4.3	2.3				2.7	2.7
		(18) 7.6	(39) 4.3				(75) 4.5	(73) 6.7
		10.4	7.6				10.1	11.5
Net Sales ($)	11430M	53277M	397948M	381242M	153863M		1234774M	2706839M
Total Assets ($)	3453M	29792M	252419M	281612M	143801M		823795M	1231748M

M = $ thousand MM = $ million

See Pages 11 through 18 for Explanation of Ratios and Data

Comparative Historical Data				**Current Data Sorted By Sales**					
			Type of Statement						
16	10	10	Unqualified	1	1	1	1	4	3
26	24	43	Reviewed	1	10	8	14	8	2
30	27	32	Compiled	3	11	10	7		1
11	12	13	Tax Returns	4	5	1	1	1	1
12	14	16	Other	5	2	2	4	1	1
4/1/00-3/31/01 ALL	4/1/01-3/31/02 ALL	4/1/02-3/31/03 ALL		0-1MM	44 (4/1-9/30/02) 1-3MM	3-5MM	70 (10/1/02-3/31/03) 5-10MM	10-25MM	25MM & OVER
95	87	114	**NUMBER OF STATEMENTS**	13	29	22	27	15	8
%	%	%	**ASSETS**	%	%	%	%	%	%
12.6	9.2	10.8	Cash & Equivalents	14.3	10.2	11.8	12.4	5.7	
10.8	10.1	9.1	Trade Receivables (net)	8.7	9.2	5.5	9.5	10.7	
3.3	2.6	2.5	Inventory	.0	2.1	1.4	1.0	2.1	
2.6	2.1	1.9	All Other Current	.3	1.0	1.9	2.2	1.5	
29.2	23.9	24.3	Total Current	23.2	22.5	20.6	25.1	20.0	
60.5	66.0	64.2	Fixed Assets (net)	65.6	63.4	70.5	65.7	63.7	
3.0	2.1	2.3	Intangibles (net)	3.4	3.0	.9	2.3	2.4	
7.3	7.9	9.2	All Other Non-Current	7.8	11.1	8.0	6.9	13.9	
100.0	100.0	100.0	Total	100.0	100.0	100.0	100.0	100.0	
			LIABILITIES						
6.1	8.7	5.6	Notes Payable-Short Term	2.2	5.0	2.8	5.8	5.5	
11.1	11.9	12.7	Cur. Mat.-L/T/D	12.7	14.9	14.7	10.2	12.5	
3.8	3.4	3.5	Trade Payables	1.6	3.8	3.0	4.0	3.5	
.3	.1	.3	Income Taxes Payable	.0	.4	.1	.4	.3	
6.8	6.9	11.4	All Other Current	7.7	16.7	3.8	16.3	8.8	
28.2	31.1	33.5	Total Current	24.2	40.9	24.4	36.6	30.6	
31.5	37.9	31.7	Long Term Debt	42.9	29.4	38.8	26.6	31.3	
1.7	2.4	1.7	Deferred Taxes	.5	1.3	2.6	1.2	3.6	
2.6	2.9	2.4	All Other Non-Current	4.7	2.3	1.3	.9	5.2	
35.9	25.8	30.6	Net Worth	27.7	26.1	32.9	34.7	29.3	
100.0	100.0	100.0	Total Liabilities & Net Worth	100.0	100.0	100.0	100.0	100.0	
			INCOME DATA						
100.0	100.0	100.0	Net Sales	100.0	100.0	100.0	100.0	100.0	
			Gross Profit						
94.3	94.0	93.3	Operating Expenses	90.9	92.5	94.7	94.6	91.6	
5.7	5.9	6.7	Operating Profit	9.1	7.5	5.3	5.4	8.4	
2.0	3.0	2.5	All Other Expenses (net)	2.2	2.9	1.8	2.5	4.0	
3.7	2.9	4.2	Profit Before Taxes	6.9	4.6	3.5	2.9	4.4	
			RATIOS						
1.9	1.2	1.2		1.9	1.0	1.3	1.4	1.0	
1.0	.8	.7	Current	.7	.7	.7	.8	.8	
.5	.4	.4		.4	.3	.4	.2	.4	
1.7	1.0	1.0		1.9	.9	1.1	1.1	.9	
.8	.7	.6	Quick	.7	.5	.6	.6	.5	
.4	.3	.3		.4	.3	.3	.1	.3	
3 108.5	4 95.1	5 77.5		0 UND	0 999.8	4 90.7	7 49.8	9 42.9	
20 18.5	18 20.5	13 27.4	Sales/Receivables	0 UND	11 33.2	13 27.5	13 27.1	15 24.4	
37 9.8	31 11.8	27 13.5		25 14.5	31 11.6	21 17.5	24 15.4	29 12.5	
			Cost of Sales/Inventory						
			Cost of Sales/Payables						
13.1	29.1	39.1		15.7	NM	35.0	24.5	−97.2	
194.3	−37.2	−26.3	Sales/Working Capital	−50.5	−16.3	−25.5	−18.9	−16.5	
−11.4	−7.7	−7.8		−7.6	−7.8	−10.1	−4.3	−7.8	
3.4	2.5	4.3		6.9	4.4	3.5	7.5	3.4	
(87) 2.1	(80) 1.4	(106) 2.5	EBIT/Interest	(10) 4.0	(27) 2.6	2.3	(26) 2.4	(13) 2.1	
1.0	.7	1.2		1.0	.7	1.5	1.1	1.1	
2.2	2.1	2.8			3.2		5.7		
(42) 1.3	(27) 1.2	(37) 1.3	Net Profit + Depr., Dep., Amort./Cur. Mat. L/T/D		(10) 2.2		(10) 1.5		
.9	.9	1.0			1.2		.9		
1.1	1.3	1.2		1.3	1.1	1.3	.9	1.9	
2.0	3.1	2.3	Fixed/Worth	2.1	3.3	2.2	2.3	2.6	
5.0	12.7	6.5		6.5	UND	4.3	6.6	5.6	
.9	1.2	1.2		1.2	1.0	1.1	.7	2.0	
2.4	3.2	2.3	Debt/Worth	2.6	2.8	1.7	2.0	2.4	
5.6	16.2	7.6		6.8	UND	4.5	7.5	7.6	
28.2	35.4	41.4		71.2	50.8	20.1	35.9	23.8	
(87) 13.6	(73) 8.7	(99) 17.4	% Profit Before Taxes/Tangible Net Worth	(11) 42.5	(23) 26.2	(20) 13.1	(24) 13.4	(13) 18.3	
2.1	2.3	6.7		.0	12.4	6.4	5.1	6.0	
8.0	8.4	10.6		28.6	11.8	8.2	10.5	8.8	
4.0	2.1	5.4	% Profit Before Taxes/Total Assets	13.3	8.2	4.1	3.9	5.5	
.0	−.4	1.0		.2	−1.7	3.2	.3	1.8	
4.2	3.8	3.7		6.3	3.9	2.6	3.7	3.2	
2.3	2.1	2.2	Sales/Net Fixed Assets	3.1	2.4	1.8	2.0	1.7	
1.5	1.4	1.6		1.2	1.7	1.5	1.6	1.3	
2.3	2.0	2.2		3.5	2.3	1.8	2.2	1.9	
1.4	1.5	1.5	Sales/Total Assets	2.1	1.6	1.4	1.4	1.3	
1.0	1.0	1.1		1.0	1.1	1.1	1.1	1.0	
5.6	6.8	7.9		10.5	9.0	7.5	8.2	8.5	
(91) 10.6	(82) 12.1	(111) 11.9	% Depr., Dep., Amort./Sales	(11) 13.0	13.5	11.9	11.3	12.8	
15.4	16.2	15.0		14.3	16.4	15.8	14.3	14.1	
2.8	2.9	2.8			4.7	2.9	1.2		
(61) 5.1	(51) 5.3	(74) 5.1	% Officers', Directors', Owners' Comp/Sales	(19) 7.2	(17) 4.3	(16) 3.5			
10.3	10.8	9.2			10.3	8.8	8.7		
2771183M	648580M	997760M	Net Sales ($)	8630M	56071M	85444M	200403M	219445M	427767M
987457M	452459M	711077M	Total Assets ($)	6126M	47045M	59797M	148409M	184410M	265290M

M = $ thousand   MM = $ million
See Pages 11 through 18 for Explanation of Ratios and Data

Current Data Sorted By Assets

Comparative Historical Data

			2	3			Type of Statement		9	4
		2	14	1			Unqualified		21	16
4		10	11	2			Reviewed		21	16
4		8					Compiled		14	18
2		10	9	2	1		Tax Returns		5	4
							Other		16	10
	12 (4/1-9/30/02)			73 (10/1/02-3/31/03)					4/1/98-3/31/99	4/1/99-3/31/00
0-500M	500M-2MM	2-10MM	10-50MM	50-100MM	100-250MM				ALL	ALL
10	30	36	8	1			NUMBER OF STATEMENTS		65	52
%	%	%	%	%	%		ASSETS		%	%
12.5	8.3	6.9					Cash & Equivalents		8.2	12.6
12.3	8.9	7.7				D	Trade Receivables (net)		11.7	5.3
.0	1.2	1.7				A	Inventory		2.1	3.4
5.1	1.9	4.4				T	All Other Current		2.2	3.2
29.9	20.2	20.6				A	Total Current		24.1	24.5
62.2	68.2	73.0				N	Fixed Assets (net)		66.5	68.8
2.2	1.3	1.9				O	Intangibles (net)		2.4	.5
5.7	10.2	4.5				T	All Other Non-Current		7.0	6.2
100.0	100.0	100.0					Total		100.0	100.0
						A	LIABILITIES			
8.1	6.3	2.4				V	Notes Payable-Short Term		3.4	5.4
16.8	14.7	13.4				A	Cur. Mat.-L/T/D		9.9	12.1
10.2	5.8	5.5				I	Trade Payables		3.1	3.3
.0	.7	.0				L	Income Taxes Payable		.2	.2
16.8	6.2	8.5				A	All Other Current		9.4	13.6
51.9	33.7	29.9				B	Total Current		26.0	34.5
92.0	58.6	42.6				L	Long Term Debt		38.8	36.2
.6	.0	2.4				E	Deferred Taxes		1.3	1.5
42.8	6.1	2.8					All Other Non-Current		8.1	3.1
−87.3	1.6	22.3					Net Worth		25.8	24.7
100.0	100.0	100.0					Total Liabilities & Net Worth		100.0	100.0
							INCOME DATA			
100.0	100.0	100.0					Net Sales		100.0	100.0
							Gross Profit			
102.8	93.8	93.3					Operating Expenses		90.7	95.5
−2.8	6.2	6.7					Operating Profit		9.3	4.5
1.9	4.3	3.2					All Other Expenses (net)		2.2	1.7
−4.7	1.9	3.4					Profit Before Taxes		7.1	2.8
							RATIOS			
1.6	1.3	1.4							1.5	1.5
.7	.5	.7					Current		1.0	.9
.4	.2	.3							.4	.4
1.6	1.1	1.0							1.3	1.1
.6	.4	.5					Quick		.7	.5
.3	.2	.3							.3	.3
0 UND	0 UND	8 48.4						6	65.4	3 135.7
0 UND	7 52.6	13 28.5					Sales/Receivables	20	18.5	17 21.6
24 14.9	22 16.8	25 14.4						37	9.9	24 15.4
							Cost of Sales/Inventory			
							Cost of Sales/Payables			
57.8	29.7	32.1							16.4	17.5
−29.0	−14.1	−20.9					Sales/Working Capital		−189.5	−91.6
−12.4	−6.1	−6.3							−8.5	−6.7
1.9	2.0	2.9							4.9	2.9
−.6	(28) 1.0	(35) 1.9					EBIT/Interest	(62)	2.0	(48) 1.4
−2.3	−.5	1.1							1.0	.9
		2.1					Net Profit + Depr., Dep.,		2.0	1.7
	(20)	1.2					Amort./Cur. Mat. L /T/D	(25)	1.6	(19) 1.1
		.9							1.1	.5
25.3	2.0	1.9							1.2	1.2
−10.5	17.3	2.9					Fixed/Worth		2.1	2.1
−.4	−2.4	6.9							4.1	−151.8
32.5	1.8	1.8							.9	1.0
−15.2	20.1	2.9					Debt/Worth		2.1	3.0
−1.6	−4.5	7.6							4.7	−188.7
	42.5	33.8							42.4	18.9
(16)	15.1	(30) 13.6					% Profit Before Taxes/Tangible Net Worth	(56)	17.3	(38) 8.0
	−5.4	4.5							3.3	.7
16.1	8.7	7.9							14.2	8.2
−7.9	.6	3.5					% Profit Before Taxes/Total Assets		3.8	3.2
−50.9	−4.7	.2							.0	−.8
13.7	4.5	2.5							2.9	3.4
7.7	2.7	1.6					Sales/Net Fixed Assets		1.9	1.9
2.5	1.6	1.1							1.3	1.3
7.4	2.7	1.8							1.8	1.8
3.9	1.9	1.2					Sales/Total Assets		1.3	1.3
1.8	1.1	.9							.9	.9
	6.8	6.3							6.4	7.8
(29)	12.1	(33) 10.0					% Depr., Dep., Amort./Sales	(61)	9.6	10.3
	17.1	15.0							16.4	16.5
	1.3	1.3							1.8	2.3
(11)	3.4	(10) 2.7					% Officers', Directors', Owners' Comp/Sales	(26)	3.2	(28) 3.7
	8.9	9.0							5.1	6.3
15176M	66604M	236053M	188902M	95423M			Net Sales ($)		360916M	262721M
2487M	33468M	180060M	155100M	66919M			Total Assets ($)		352391M	198045M

© RMA 2003

Comparative Historical Data   Current Data Sorted By Sales

	4/1/00-3/31/01 ALL	4/1/01-3/31/02 ALL	4/1/02-3/31/03 ALL		12 (4/1-9/30/02) 0-1MM	1-3MM	73 (10/1/02-3/31/03) 3-5MM	5-10MM	10-25MM	25MM & OVER
Type of Statement										
Unqualified	7	8	5			1	1	1		2
Reviewed	4	12	17		1	2	1	8	5	
Compiled	20	29	27		4	10	4	6	3	
Tax Returns	1	7	12		3	6	3			
Other	10	31	24		4	7	6	3	3	1
NUMBER OF STATEMENTS	42	87	85		12	26	15	18	11	3
	%	%	%		%	%	%	%	%	%
ASSETS										
Cash & Equivalents	7.9	8.3	8.1		7.8	9.3	6.4	9.5	5.0	
Trade Receivables (net)	6.9	8.2	8.4		8.8	7.3	10.8	5.9	10.5	
Inventory	1.5	1.9	1.3		.0	1.0	1.2	2.1	1.9	
All Other Current	2.8	3.6	3.5		2.1	2.1	2.4	5.5	6.1	
Total Current	19.0	22.1	21.2		18.7	19.8	20.8	23.0	23.5	
Fixed Assets (net)	72.7	63.0	69.5		74.1	69.5	73.4	64.9	68.3	
Intangibles (net)	1.8	3.4	1.8		2.1	2.1	.9	1.8	.9	
All Other Non-Current	6.5	11.4	7.5		5.0	8.7	4.9	10.3	7.3	
Total	100.0	100.0	100.0		100.0	100.0	100.0	100.0	100.0	
LIABILITIES										
Notes Payable-Short Term	4.1	3.3	4.4		5.4	5.7	2.7	4.8	2.2	
Cur. Mat.-L/T/D	11.2	14.7	14.0		17.9	12.8	13.1	10.8	18.2	
Trade Payables	3.8	6.1	5.9		7.4	5.2	6.4	2.3	10.9	
Income Taxes Payable	.2	.1	.3		.0	.0	1.4	.0	.0	
All Other Current	9.7	10.6	8.4		7.1	9.5	2.4	13.7	6.7	
Total Current	29.0	34.7	33.0		37.8	33.3	26.1	31.6	38.1	
Long Term Debt	46.0	42.2	52.9		97.3	60.1	52.7	32.7	28.0	
Deferred Taxes	.8	1.5	1.3		.5	.0	.4	3.4	3.0	
All Other Non-Current	2.4	6.9	8.6		7.6	5.6	1.3	22.9	4.0	
Net Worth	21.7	14.8	4.3		−43.2	1.0	19.5	9.4	26.8	
Total Liabilities & Net Worth	100.0	100.0	100.0		100.0	100.0	100.0	100.0	100.0	
INCOME DATA										
Net Sales	100.0	100.0	100.0		100.0	100.0	100.0	100.0	100.0	
Gross Profit										
Operating Expenses	93.4	95.7	94.7		85.9	98.5	93.0	96.9	94.6	
Operating Profit	6.6	4.3	5.3		14.1	1.5	7.0	3.1	5.4	
All Other Expenses (net)	2.7	2.9	3.3		9.0	2.6	3.6	1.0	2.9	
Profit Before Taxes	3.9	1.4	2.0		5.1	−1.1	3.4	2.1	2.5	
RATIOS										
Current	1.3	1.2	1.3		.8	1.1	1.8	1.2	1.4	
	.7	.7	.7		.5	.6	1.6	.7	.5	
	.2	.3	.3		.2	.3	.4	.6	.2	
Quick	1.1	.9	1.0		.8	.9	1.8	.8	.8	
	.5	.4	.4		.4	.4	1.0	.5	.3	
	.2	.2	.2		.1	.2	.2	.2	.1	
Sales/Receivables	2 152.2	1 374.0	3 126.2		0 UND	0 UND	7 50.9	5 70.6	6 63.0	
	13 28.8	13 29.0	12 30.2		4 97.7	11 34.0	13 28.1	12 29.4	9 40.7	
	24 15.4	25 14.8	24 15.3		17 21.1	24 15.3	30 12.1	25 14.7	18 20.5	
Cost of Sales/Inventory										
Cost of Sales/Payables										
Sales/Working Capital	36.9	32.4	61.0		−29.9	767.7	14.0	49.8	18.7	
	−25.8	−16.9	−19.7		−15.2	−15.3	69.5	−122.5	−12.6	
	−6.8	−6.1	−6.8		−5.8	−6.1	−7.3	−9.5	−4.5	
EBIT/Interest	3.6	2.4	2.8		3.4	1.8	2.8	4.1	3.7	
	(79) 1.7	(82) 1.2	1.4		(10) .8	.9	(14) 1.3	2.0	1.9	
	.9	.1	−.1		−1.3	−.7	.6	−3.1	1.1	
Net Profit + Depr., Dep., Amort./Cur. Mat. L/T/D	(14) 1.8	(20) 1.8	(30) 1.9					2.0		
	1.1	1.0	1.3					(11) 1.2		
	.7	.7	1.0					1.0		
Fixed/Worth	1.4	1.4	2.0		3.4	2.3	1.9	1.3	1.8	
	3.4	4.6	3.5		−12.3	NM	2.8	2.4	2.4	
	−26.5	−5.3	−6.7		−.6	−2.4	12.3	NM	4.0	
Debt/Worth	1.0	1.4	1.8		2.6	3.4	1.5	1.2	1.5	
	3.4	7.0	3.7		−16.0	NM	2.8	2.3	2.3	
	−31.5	−8.1	−11.9		−2.1	−4.5	12.7	NM	6.0	
% Profit Before Taxes/Tangible Net Worth	27.6	23.5	38.0			35.8	38.4	35.3	24.2	
	(31) 10.2	(58) 6.9	(58) 13.6		(13) 9.3	(13) 9.9	(14) 13.7	(10) 9.0		
	2.7	−8.7	.9			−9.0	−5.2	4.9	.6	
% Profit Before Taxes/Total Assets	7.9	7.4	8.2		11.4	3.4	5.9	8.8	9.3	
	3.2	1.2	2.0		1.2	−.2	2.0	4.3	3.7	
	−.5	−4.1	−3.1		−26.9	−6.9	−1.5	−5.9	.2	
Sales/Net Fixed Assets	2.8	4.3	3.9		10.8	4.5	3.7	2.8	4.3	
	1.9	2.5	2.2		1.6	2.5	2.2	2.0	1.8	
	1.5	1.5	1.3		.8	1.5	.9	1.4	1.5	
Sales/Total Assets	2.1	2.7	2.4		4.3	2.7	2.6	1.9	2.3	
	1.4	1.6	1.5		1.3	1.6	1.9	1.5	1.5	
	1.1	1.0	1.0		.7	1.0	.7	1.1	1.1	
% Depr., Dep., Amort./Sales	2.5	3.4	5.9		6.1	5.6	9.8	5.0	6.6	
	(80) 7.6	(80) 8.2	9.8		(11) 11.2	(25) 12.5	(13) 11.9	(17) 9.0	7.6	
	13.2	14.1	14.2		19.0	18.7	14.9	13.4	10.0	
% Officers', Directors', Owners' Comp/Sales	1.4	1.4	1.5			1.2				
	(20) 3.0	(36) 3.1	(29) 2.8		(13) 3.4					
	8.1	7.2	8.6			9.7				
Net Sales ($)	303361M	707783M	602158M		6572M	52547M	56081M	130331M	143269M	213358M
Total Assets ($)	239163M	499154M	438034M		9213M	38055M	48297M	111346M	94273M	136850M

© RMA 2003   M = $ thousand   MM = $ million
See Pages 11 through 18 for Explanation of Ratios and Data

Current Data Sorted By Assets   **Comparative Historical Data**

0-500M	500M-2MM	2-10MM	10-50MM	50-100MM	100-250MM	Type of Statement	4/1/98-3/31/99	4/1/99-3/31/00
	1	17	8	1		Unqualified	21	21
	4	6	1			Reviewed	13	13
3	12	3				Compiled	31	22
12	3					Tax Returns	10	14
1	6	11	4		1	Other	28	26
	36 (4/1-9/30/02)		58 (10/1/02-3/31/03)					
16	26	37	13		1	**NUMBER OF STATEMENTS**	**103** ALL	**96** ALL
%	%	%	%	%	%		%	%
						ASSETS		
26.4	15.5	11.6	7.5			Cash & Equivalents	13.2	11.3
8.9	22.3	28.4	32.0			Trade Receivables (net)	25.1	24.7
.1	.1	.5	2.2			Inventory	.6	.6
3.9	1.3	4.4	4.6			All Other Current	2.5	2.1
39.4	39.1	44.9	46.2			Total Current	41.4	38.7
43.0	43.7	45.4	34.4			Fixed Assets (net)	44.4	46.6
12.2	7.1	2.7	8.4			Intangibles (net)	5.5	4.6
5.4	10.1	7.0	10.9			All Other Non-Current	8.7	10.0
100.0	100.0	100.0	100.0			Total	100.0	100.0
						LIABILITIES		
13.9	7.4	7.3	8.4			Notes Payable-Short Term	9.4	7.1
4.9	11.6	7.1	8.1			Cur. Mat.-L/T/D	7.6	9.9
3.6	3.0	6.9	10.8			Trade Payables	6.6	7.0
.1	2.5	.8	.1			Income Taxes Payable	.2	.8
20.5	8.6	12.6	9.0			All Other Current	8.1	11.8
43.0	33.1	34.8	36.4			Total Current	31.9	36.5
54.1	21.5	16.9	15.3			Long Term Debt	23.9	27.1
.0	.3	.8	.0			Deferred Taxes	.9	.7
17.3	1.8	2.0	4.6			All Other Non-Current	4.1	4.0
−14.3	43.2	45.5	43.7			Net Worth	39.2	31.7
100.0	100.0	100.0	100.0			Total Liabilities & Net Worth	100.0	100.0
						INCOME DATA		
100.0	100.0	100.0	100.0			Net Sales	100.0	100.0
						Gross Profit		
95.3	94.7	93.6	95.8			Operating Expenses	95.5	93.4
4.7	5.3	6.4	4.2			Operating Profit	4.5	6.6
4.0	1.6	1.9	2.3			All Other Expenses (net)	.4	.9
.7	3.7	4.5	1.9			Profit Before Taxes	4.1	5.7
						RATIOS		
3.8	2.7	2.8	2.4				3.0	2.7
1.2	1.1	1.5	1.3			Current	1.3	1.2
.8	.7	.9	.9				.7	.6
1.7	2.7	2.7	2.0				2.9	2.4
1.2	1.1	1.4	1.2			Quick	1.2	1.1
.6	.6	.7	.7				.7	.6
0 UND	0 UND	29 12.4	36 10.3				9 39.0	12 30.7
7 51.8	23 15.5	52 7.0	57 6.4			Sales/Receivables	35 10.4	39 9.4
19 19.5	66 5.5	76 4.8	70 5.2				65 5.6	71 5.2
						Cost of Sales/Inventory		
						Cost of Sales/Payables		
23.1	9.0	5.3	5.9				6.5	7.9
44.0	52.5	13.2	25.3			Sales/Working Capital	22.7	35.5
−18.7	−13.3	NM	NM				−28.5	−20.8
5.3	13.6	6.0	18.3				8.8	5.9
(13) .8	3.5	(31) 3.6	4.4			EBIT/Interest	(87) 3.1	(85) 3.1
−2.5	1.8	1.0	1.7				1.3	1.4
		2.4				Net Profit + Depr., Dep.,	3.7	3.0
	(10)	.9				Amort./Cur. Mat. L./T/D	(26) 2.0	(26) 1.4
		.5					1.1	1.1
1.0	.6	.5	.4				.6	.8
2.2	1.1	.9	.9			Fixed/Worth	1.3	1.2
−3.3	5.4	1.7	3.2				3.2	3.8
1.4	.8	.5	.4				.6	.9
4.1	1.8	1.0	2.8			Debt/Worth	1.8	2.0
−5.5	5.9	2.9	7.6				5.6	6.1
161.0	71.8	21.0	52.8			% Profit Before Taxes/Tangible	51.7	57.0
(11) 28.0	(21) 12.3	(34) 9.1	19.2			Net Worth	(88) 22.3	(85) 21.1
−96.0	4.6	1.0	5.5				5.0	8.0
31.4	20.0	11.9	7.3			% Profit Before Taxes/Total	18.8	16.4
8.1	7.3	4.6	3.5			Assets	6.8	8.1
−17.0	2.3	−.1	2.2				.0	1.6
18.2	11.8	9.3	21.2				10.9	8.1
8.4	6.7	3.9	7.4			Sales/Net Fixed Assets	4.8	4.9
2.7	3.9	2.3	3.1				2.9	3.1
5.8	3.6	2.6	2.8				3.6	3.2
2.9	2.6	1.8	1.9			Sales/Total Assets	2.2	2.0
1.5	1.9	1.2	1.4				1.5	1.3
6.7	3.9	3.3	1.0				2.8	3.7
(12) 9.9	(24) 6.1	(36) 7.0	(12) 3.0			% Depr., Dep., Amort./Sales	(95) 6.3	(91) 6.3
19.1	7.4	12.4	7.0				9.1	9.6
	2.7	3.2				% Officers', Directors',	3.0	2.7
	(17) 4.0	(14) 5.2				Owners' Comp/Sales	(34) 5.5	(35) 4.3
	6.2	9.1					10.4	6.4
14442M	79541M	302699M	499395M	125518M	497038M	Net Sales ($)	845871M	884814M
3981M	30857M	155360M	230651M	69155M	237438M	Total Assets ($)	429285M	566950M

M = $ thousand   MM = $ million
See Pages 11 through 18 for Explanation of Ratios and Data

Comparative Historical Data | | | **Current Data Sorted By Sales**

			Type of Statement	0-1MM	1-3MM	3-5MM	5-10MM	10-25MM	25MM & OVER
15	16	27	Unqualified	2	1	3	9	5	7
14	11	11	Reviewed		2	3	3	2	1
28	29	18	Compiled	3	9	3	3		
17	15	15	Tax Returns	10	2	3	3		
22	27	23	Other	1	6	4	3	4	5
4/1/00-3/31/01	4/1/01-3/31/02	4/1/02-3/31/03		**36 (4/1-9/30/02)**			**58 (10/1/02-3/31/03)**		
ALL	ALL	ALL		0-1MM	1-3MM	3-5MM	5-10MM	10-25MM	25MM & OVER
96	98	94	NUMBER OF STATEMENTS	16	20	16	18	11	13
%	%	%	**ASSETS**	%	%	%	%	%	%
10.2	11.5	14.5	Cash & Equivalents	20.7	17.1	13.7	10.3	19.4	5.4
21.2	24.9	24.2	Trade Receivables (net)	9.2	15.2	23.9	31.9	36.5	35.7
.7	1.2	.6	Inventory	.1	.1	.2	.8	.2	3.0
2.3	4.1	3.4	All Other Current	4.0	1.5	.9	3.4	8.0	5.0
34.3	41.7	42.7	Total Current	34.0	33.9	38.7	46.3	64.0	49.1
54.3	47.1	42.6	Fixed Assets (net)	47.8	51.7	43.4	45.1	26.3	31.3
3.8	4.0	6.6	Intangibles (net)	10.6	4.2	10.6	2.8	1.0	10.6
7.6	7.2	8.1	All Other Non-Current	7.7	10.2	7.3	5.8	8.6	9.1
100.0	100.0	100.0	Total	100.0	100.0	100.0	100.0	100.0	100.0
			LIABILITIES						
15.2	9.2	8.5	Notes Payable-Short Term	10.7	10.7	5.6	6.5	8.6	8.5
9.5	8.0	8.1	Cur. Mat.-L/T/D	5.9	11.6	9.6	6.6	7.5	6.1
5.4	6.5	5.7	Trade Payables	3.1	2.9	3.9	4.8	11.6	11.9
.2	.9	1.0	Income Taxes Payable	.2	1.0	1.2	2.4	.9	.1
7.2	8.8	12.6	All Other Current	20.3	5.3	15.4	9.3	16.9	11.9
37.6	33.5	36.0	Total Current	40.2	31.5	35.8	29.6	45.4	38.5
27.0	25.7	25.6	Long Term Debt	53.8	25.7	16.8	19.5	5.8	26.7
1.0	.7	.4	Deferred Taxes	.0	.2	.5	1.4	.0	.0
4.8	9.0	5.0	All Other Non-Current	17.3	1.8	2.1	1.8	5.1	2.6
29.7	31.2	33.1	Net Worth	−11.3	40.8	44.8	47.7	43.7	32.2
100.0	100.0	100.0	Total Liabilities & Net Worth	100.0	100.0	100.0	100.0	100.0	100.0
			INCOME DATA						
100.0	100.0	100.0	Net Sales	100.0	100.0	100.0	100.0	100.0	100.0
			Gross Profit						
92.5	94.9	94.5	Operating Expenses	92.5	92.0	97.5	95.4	94.8	95.5
7.5	5.1	5.5	Operating Profit	7.5	8.0	2.5	4.6	5.2	4.5
2.2	1.5	2.3	All Other Expenses (net)	4.5	2.5	3.4	.8	.5	1.3
5.3	3.5	3.2	Profit Before Taxes	3.0	5.4	−.9	3.7	4.7	3.1
			RATIOS						
2.5	2.7	2.5	Current	4.1	2.6	3.1	3.8	2.4	1.9
1.1	1.4	1.4		1.2	1.3	1.3	1.6	1.4	1.3
.6	.8	.8		.8	.2	.7	1.1	1.2	.9
2.3	2.4	2.5	Quick	2.4	2.5	2.9	3.7	2.3	1.5
1.0	1.1	1.2		1.2	1.3	1.3	1.3	1.3	1.2
.4	.6	.7		.6	.6	.8	.9	.9	.7
0 738.5	7 54.4	11 32.1	Sales/Receivables	0 UND	0 UND	14 26.2	34 10.9	32 11.3	41 8.8
30 12.3	33 11.0	39 9.3		11 32.8	18 20.8	34 10.7	55 6.7	59 6.1	57 6.4
68 5.4	72 5.0	64 5.7		24 15.5	70 5.2	73 5.0	77 4.8	86 4.3	65 5.6
			Cost of Sales/Inventory						
			Cost of Sales/Payables						
7.8	5.9	7.5	Sales/Working Capital	9.5	6.8	7.0	6.8	5.9	8.9
95.6	23.2	26.6		44.0	31.1	52.5	14.5	9.7	25.3
−11.1	−29.0	−27.1		−18.7	−8.7	−32.8	NM	28.0	NM
(85) 7.0	(90) 6.9	(85) 8.6	EBIT/Interest	(14) 5.3	(19) 13.3	(15) 6.2	(16) 5.7		36.0
3.0	2.4	2.9		1.1	4.2	2.8	3.1		5.9
1.1	.8	.9		−2.0	1.0	−.3	1.1		1.8
(26) 3.4	(30) 4.1	(24) 5.5	Net Profit + Depr., Dep., Amort./Cur. Mat. L/T/D						
1.3	1.5	1.6							
.7	1.0	.9							
.8	.6	.5	Fixed/Worth	1.0	.6	.6	.7	.3	.4
1.6	1.3	1.0		1.5	1.1	1.3	.9	.5	1.1
6.4	4.1	3.5		−3.3	22.7	6.2	1.9	.5	3.7
.6	.6	.7	Debt/Worth	.9	.7	.4	.5	.5	.9
1.8	2.2	1.6		3.1	1.4	1.6	1.0	1.5	4.5
7.9	8.8	7.3		−5.5	30.4	8.2	3.3	4.0	7.6
(80) 59.5	(84) 40.8	(80) 44.4	% Profit Before Taxes/Tangible Net Worth	(11) 106.2	(17) 76.6	(13) 43.9	(17) 17.0	(10) 49.9	(12) 68.2
16.8	14.7	12.8		4.6	7.8	11.9	8.4	33.2	23.9
3.8	.4	1.6		−22.4	.5	−7.4	.7	11.1	15.8
19.5	14.3	15.0	% Profit Before Taxes/Total Assets	27.7	21.7	14.5	7.6	20.6	11.0
5.6	5.3	5.1		2.5	5.0	6.2	4.3	12.0	6.2
.8	−.4	−.1		−9.0	.1	−4.9	.5	3.4	2.2
7.9	10.3	10.7	Sales/Net Fixed Assets	14.1	9.1	12.5	9.3	27.6	21.2
3.7	5.1	5.7		5.1	4.1	5.8	4.5	9.4	9.4
1.9	2.4	2.7		1.7	2.0	3.0	2.7	3.9	5.1
2.8	3.4	3.1	Sales/Total Assets	3.3	3.3	3.6	2.8	3.2	3.0
1.9	2.0	2.1		2.0	1.9	2.4	1.9	2.5	2.1
1.3	1.4	1.5		.9	1.1	1.5	1.5	1.8	1.8
(90) 3.5	(90) 3.4	(85) 3.2	% Depr., Dep., Amort./Sales	(13) 3.3	(19) 6.5	(14) 3.6	(17) 3.2	(10) 1.0	(12) 1.5
6.0	6.4	6.5		9.7	8.4	6.6	5.7	3.9	3.4
10.2	9.6	10.9		19.2	12.7	11.5	10.5	6.5	7.3
(44) 2.5	(41) 2.9	(40) 3.0	% Officers', Directors', Owners' Comp/Sales		(11) 2.6	(11) 3.5			
5.5	5.8	5.5			7.3	4.3			
8.6	9.2	10.5			17.9	6.0			
872376M	1147253M	1518633M	Net Sales ($)	8940M	42952M	59833M	122728M	177757M	1106423M
418295M	589032M	727442M	Total Assets ($)	9521M	28344M	33740M	66742M	78243M	510852M

M = $ thousand   MM = $ million
See Pages 11 through 18 for Explanation of Ratios and Data

Current Data Sorted By Assets　　　　　　　　　　　Comparative Historical Data

3 2 1	1 3 2 6	2 3 1 3	4 2	1	1 1	Type of Statement		
						Unqualified	4	5
						Reviewed	9	11
						Compiled	6	5
						Tax Returns	7	3
						Other	11	7
	5 (4/1-9/30/02)		31 (10/1/02-3/31/03)				4/1/98-3/31/99	4/1/99-3/31/00
0-500M	500M-2MM	2-10MM	10-50MM	50-100MM	100-250MM		ALL	ALL
6	12	9	6	1	2	NUMBER OF STATEMENTS	37	31
%	%	%	%	%	%		%	%
						ASSETS		
	17.9					Cash & Equivalents	16.4	12.4
	3.4					Trade Receivables (net)	7.0	9.7
	2.8					Inventory	2.2	4.7
	.8					All Other Current	4.1	1.3
	25.0					Total Current	29.8	28.1
	60.7					Fixed Assets (net)	53.7	53.9
	.4					Intangibles (net)	1.0	1.8
	13.8					All Other Non-Current	15.6	16.2
	100.0					Total	100.0	100.0
						LIABILITIES		
	7.5					Notes Payable-Short Term	14.1	25.0
	11.2					Cur. Mat.-L/T/D	6.2	5.2
	7.0					Trade Payables	4.9	8.8
	.1					Income Taxes Payable	.2	.5
	5.2					All Other Current	16.2	36.4
	31.0					Total Current	41.6	75.8
	49.3					Long Term Debt	30.4	29.0
	.0					Deferred Taxes	.6	.8
	2.9					All Other Non-Current	4.9	5.1
	16.8					Net Worth	22.6	-10.6
	100.0					Total Liabilities & Net Worth	100.0	100.0
						INCOME DATA		
	100.0					Net Sales	100.0	100.0
						Gross Profit		
	89.5					Operating Expenses	97.5	94.8
	10.5					Operating Profit	2.5	5.2
	2.3					All Other Expenses (net)	3.8	-1.3
	8.1					Profit Before Taxes	-1.3	6.5
						RATIOS		
	2.6						2.2	2.0
	.8					Current	1.0	.8
	.2						.5	.3
	2.3						2.1	1.6
	.7					Quick	.7	.7
	.2						.3	.2
	0 UND						0 UND	1 578.6
	1 431.2					Sales/Receivables	3 114.8	7 52.0
	7 54.4						24 15.5	27 13.4
						Cost of Sales/Inventory		
						Cost of Sales/Payables		
	42.0						7.1	7.0
	-41.8					Sales/Working Capital	-118.9	-54.0
	-7.8						-7.7	-10.1
	5.4						(32) 7.0	(25) 5.2
(10)	2.1					EBIT/Interest	3.3	2.1
	.2						1.5	1.1
							3.5	
						Net Profit + Depr., Dep., Amort./Cur. Mat. L /T/D	(15) 3.0	
							1.7	
	.5						.8	.7
	4.4					Fixed/Worth	2.1	1.9
	-9.7						5.9	-56.5
	.7						.8	.6
	9.7					Debt/Worth	2.5	1.9
	-7.5						8.2	-68.6
						% Profit Before Taxes/Tangible	(30) 34.8	(23) 21.6
						Net Worth	21.1	12.1
							7.2	3.6
	41.4					% Profit Before Taxes/Total	19.4	7.1
	11.4					Assets	6.4	3.6
	-1.4						2.1	-.5
	12.5						8.9	13.3
	2.9					Sales/Net Fixed Assets	2.6	2.3
	1.7						1.2	1.5
	3.2						2.2	2.8
	2.2					Sales/Total Assets	1.4	1.5
	1.4						.8	1.0
	3.4						(34) 2.8	(27) 2.9
(10)	7.1					% Depr., Dep., Amort./Sales	6.4	5.6
	19.6						8.8	8.6
						% Officers', Directors',		4.3
						Owners' Comp/Sales	(12)	9.0
								13.7
10179M	31351M	44442M	157584M	85552M	1051676M	Net Sales ($)	490727M	415493M
1855M	12714M	43284M	101171M	98557M	367112M	Total Assets ($)	468411M	363328M

M = $ thousand　　MM = $ million
See Pages 11 through 18 for Explanation of Ratios and Data

Comparative Historical Data | Current Data Sorted By Sales

Type of Statement					5 (4/1-9/30/02)		31 (10/1/02-3/31/03)			
					0-1MM	1-3MM	3-5MM	5-10MM	10-25MM	25MM & OVER
Unqualified	8	4	5			1			1	4
Reviewed	5	2	5				1	1	2	
Compiled	2	4	9		3	3	1	2		
Tax Returns	4	3	6		1	3	1			1
Other	17	22	11		2	3	3	2		1
	4/1/00-3/31/01 ALL	4/1/01-3/31/02 ALL	4/1/02-3/31/03 ALL							
NUMBER OF STATEMENTS	36	35	36		6	10	6	5	3	6

	%	%	%	ASSETS	%	%	%	%	%	%
	12.6	13.4	15.6	Cash & Equivalents		12.5				
	8.3	3.5	4.1	Trade Receivables (net)		3.0				
	2.6	4.6	3.1	Inventory		2.7				
	1.4	1.5	2.9	All Other Current		3.1				
	25.0	23.0	25.7	Total Current		21.3				
	57.0	63.6	57.9	Fixed Assets (net)		61.0				
	1.5	1.8	3.8	Intangibles (net)		9.1				
	16.5	11.7	12.6	All Other Non-Current		8.5				
	100.0	100.0	100.0	Total		100.0				

				LIABILITIES						
	8.1	18.0	4.6	Notes Payable-Short Term		.0				
	7.5	4.6	6.6	Cur. Mat.-L/T/D		8.1				
	4.6	3.9	8.6	Trade Payables		12.6				
	.0	.0	.1	Income Taxes Payable		.0				
	10.2	14.8	17.6	All Other Current		31.7				
	30.4	41.3	37.5	Total Current		52.4				
	40.6	45.4	47.4	Long Term Debt		57.7				
	.4	.2	.7	Deferred Taxes		.0				
	19.3	3.1	5.3	All Other Non-Current		2.6				
	9.3	10.0	9.3	Net Worth		−12.7				
	100.0	100.0	100.0	Total Liabilities & Net Worth		100.0				

				INCOME DATA						
	100.0	100.0	100.0	Net Sales		100.0				
				Gross Profit						
	85.8	87.1	90.3	Operating Expenses		93.6				
	14.2	12.9	9.6	Operating Profit		6.4				
	11.3	7.7	5.2	All Other Expenses (net)		1.4				
	2.8	5.2	4.5	Profit Before Taxes		5.0				

				RATIOS						
	1.4	2.0	1.5	Current		2.7				
	1.0	.8	.8			.9				
	.2	.2	.2			.2				
	1.2	1.3	1.3	Quick		1.8				
	.6	.5	.6			.7				
	.2	.1	.2			.2				
	2 229.3	0 UND	0 UND	Sales/Receivables		0 UND				
	6 58.3	1 264.9	2 230.6			0 797.3				
	25 14.6	8 47.3	9 38.7			10 38.1				
				Cost of Sales/Inventory						
				Cost of Sales/Payables						
	8.2	12.4	27.1	Sales/Working Capital		17.0				
	NM	−41.5	−24.6			NM				
	−6.0	−5.2	−8.1			−10.3				
	4.8	3.4	4.8	EBIT/Interest						
(28)	1.7	(27) 1.8	(29) 2.1							
	.8	.1	.5							
				Net Profit + Depr., Dep., Amort./Cur. Mat. L/T/D						
	1.4	1.6	1.2	Fixed/Worth		2.4				
	2.2	3.6	2.9			NM				
	13.7	−30.8	−7.5			−4.0				
	1.8	1.3	1.2	Debt/Worth		3.2				
	4.1	4.7	4.0			NM				
	15.4	−34.5	−7.5			−5.5				
	56.7	68.9	47.5	% Profit Before Taxes/Tangible Net Worth						
(28)	22.1	(25) 10.3	(24) 20.7							
	.8	−4.9	−.2							
	11.1	12.8	14.8	% Profit Before Taxes/Total Assets		40.4				
	2.4	5.7	5.8			11.4				
	−1.1	−1.8	−2.9			−4.8				
	4.1	5.0	4.7	Sales/Net Fixed Assets		7.2				
	1.9	2.1	2.9			2.8				
	.9	.9	1.6			1.5				
	1.6	2.2	2.5	Sales/Total Assets		2.6				
	1.2	1.6	1.7			1.6				
	.6	.7	1.1			1.1				
	2.9	2.3	4.3	% Depr., Dep., Amort./Sales		3.4				
(35)	6.1	(33) 6.2	(32) 6.7			8.4				
	11.6	10.3	10.7			18.7				
			3.8	% Officers', Directors', Owners' Comp/Sales						
		(15)	7.2							
			15.0							
	609221M	367464M	1380784M	Net Sales ($)	3590M	19448M	24768M	38166M	60938M	1233874M
	753365M	342815M	624693M	Total Assets ($)	10913M	12450M	8575M	25915M	42074M	524766M

M = $ thousand   MM = $ million
See Pages 11 through 18 for Explanation of Ratios and Data

Current Data Sorted By Assets   Comparative Historical Data

Type of Statement	0-500M	500M-2MM	2-10MM	10-50MM	50-100MM	100-250MM		4/1/98-3/31/99 ALL	4/1/99-3/31/00 ALL
Unqualified		1	7	7		4		38	33
Reviewed		2	9					14	12
Compiled	3	10	7	2				22	20
Tax Returns	6	4	3					12	13
Other	2	10	22	8	2	5		43	56
	15 (4/1-9/30/02)			99 (10/1/02-3/31/03)					
NUMBER OF STATEMENTS	11	27	48	17	2	9		129	134
ASSETS	%	%	%	%	%	%		%	%
Cash & Equivalents	9.5	10.0	5.8	3.3				6.5	8.7
Trade Receivables (net)	21.9	21.1	16.5	13.3				18.0	15.2
Inventory	19.2	19.3	8.6	10.7				11.7	13.6
All Other Current	1.1	3.5	4.3	2.6				4.6	3.2
Total Current	51.6	53.9	35.3	29.8				40.8	40.6
Fixed Assets (net)	42.9	36.9	45.4	48.8				49.4	48.7
Intangibles (net)	2.1	2.0	9.7	9.8				3.7	4.2
All Other Non-Current	3.5	7.2	9.6	11.6				6.1	6.4
Total	100.0	100.0	100.0	100.0				100.0	100.0
LIABILITIES									
Notes Payable-Short Term	5.4	20.7	8.7	7.9				11.2	10.7
Cur. Mat.-L/T/D	8.6	3.6	6.2	3.3				4.5	4.9
Trade Payables	18.0	12.9	9.7	5.1				10.6	10.7
Income Taxes Payable	.0	.0	.1	.3				.5	.3
All Other Current	9.4	14.1	8.6	6.0				7.9	15.2
Total Current	41.4	51.3	33.2	22.7				34.7	41.9
Long Term Debt	62.3	18.4	32.2	38.2				26.9	30.7
Deferred Taxes	.0	.3	.1	1.9				.5	.3
All Other Non-Current	7.7	10.7	6.0	5.2				5.9	4.0
Net Worth	−11.4	19.3	28.4	32.0				32.1	23.1
Total Liabilities & Net Worth	100.0	100.0	100.0	100.0				100.0	100.0
INCOME DATA									
Net Sales	100.0	100.0	100.0	100.0				100.0	100.0
Gross Profit									
Operating Expenses	98.5	92.9	91.2	94.7				100.7	92.7
Operating Profit	1.5	7.1	8.8	5.3				−.7	7.3
All Other Expenses (net)	1.2	3.6	5.0	3.1				−.8	1.6
Profit Before Taxes	.3	3.4	3.8	2.2				.0	5.7
RATIOS									
Current	2.1	2.3	1.6	2.1				2.1	2.0
	1.4	1.2	1.1	1.2				1.3	1.2
	.9	.5	.4	.6				.9	.8
Quick	2.1	1.7	1.2	1.5				1.3	1.4
	1.1	.5	.6	.4				.8	.7
	.2	.1	.2	.4				.5	.3
Sales/Receivables	9 41.7	9 41.8	11 34.0	25 14.5				18 20.7	11 31.9
	18 20.4	24 15.0	21 17.2	34 10.7				30 12.0	25 14.9
	26 14.0	44 8.4	37 9.9	52 7.0				45 8.0	48 7.7
Cost of Sales/Inventory									
Cost of Sales/Payables									
Sales/Working Capital	8.4	9.8	11.6	6.7				6.8	8.0
	46.3	49.3	522.9	13.6				17.0	27.4
	−67.2	−5.8	−9.7	−12.4				−76.8	−21.6
EBIT/Interest	4.2	10.6	7.5	2.8				5.5	6.2
	1.6 (23)	1.8 (40)	2.5	2.2				2.7 (113)	2.9 (121)
	−.4	−.1	1.5	1.3				1.4	1.2
Net Profit + Depr., Dep., Amort./Cur. Mat. L /T/D								3.9	6.9
								2.5 (31)	2.2 (25)
								1.1	.8
Fixed/Worth	.6	.3	.9	.7				.8	.9
	−10.3	1.9	2.1	4.2				1.5	1.6
	−2.6	6.1	6.7	−32.6				5.9	7.3
Debt/Worth	1.7	.8	1.2	1.9				1.0	.9
	−14.2	2.5	3.5	5.3				2.5	2.9
	−8.4	18.3	34.9	−59.1				9.6	18.7
% Profit Before Taxes/Tangible Net Worth		87.9	50.5	52.2				49.5 (107)	54.9
	(21)	37.3	17.9 (37)	27.1 (12)				20.6 (107)	20.9
		1.4	5.5	10.4				4.3	3.3
% Profit Before Taxes/Total Assets	13.3	18.2	12.8	6.4				13.2	13.4
	3.7	1.8	5.4	4.2				4.8	5.4
	−11.2	−3.0	.4	.8				.6	.5
Sales/Net Fixed Assets	23.7	51.4	15.9	11.4				10.5	10.6
	9.6	8.2	3.5	2.3				3.7	4.0
	3.5	3.5	1.6	.9				1.3	1.1
Sales/Total Assets	5.5	3.7	2.0	1.3				2.7	2.6
	3.9	2.7	1.4	1.0				1.8	1.6
	2.9	1.4	1.0	.6				.7	.6
% Depr., Dep., Amort./Sales	2.7	.9	1.6	2.6				1.6	1.6
	4.3 (10)	2.7 (26)	3.5 (42)	4.4 (15)				3.9 (119)	3.9 (116)
	13.1	4.9	5.9	10.8				9.6	10.0
% Officers', Directors', Owners' Comp/Sales			1.0					1.4	2.6
			2.1 (16)					3.0 (37)	3.8 (41)
			3.3					6.5	8.2
Net Sales ($)	12354M	101075M	383579M	409178M	145852M	1053525M		2424199M	4803785M
Total Assets ($)	3102M	35049M	252645M	377723M	164817M	1255699M		2430078M	3772405M

M = $ thousand   MM = $ million
See Pages 11 through 18 for Explanation of Ratios and Data

Comparative Historical Data				Current Data Sorted By Sales					
			Type of Statement						
23	17	19	Unqualified		1		4	9	5
19	18	11	Reviewed			2	4	5	
24	31	22	Compiled	2	5	7	5	2	1
9	9	13	Tax Returns	4	6	1	1	1	
44	43	49	Other	6	7	8	8	13	7
4/1/00-3/31/01 ALL	4/1/01-3/31/02 ALL	4/1/02-3/31/03 ALL		0-1MM	15 (4/1-9/30/02) 1-3MM	3-5MM	5-10MM	99 (10/1/02-3/31/03) 10-25MM	25MM & OVER
119	118	114	**NUMBER OF STATEMENTS**	12	19	18	22	30	13
%	%	%	**ASSETS**	%	%	%	%	%	%
6.6	8.8	6.7	Cash & Equivalents	9.7	6.7	8.2	7.2	5.6	3.2
20.7	22.8	17.1	Trade Receivables (net)	5.6	16.3	21.8	16.0	16.1	26.1
11.9	14.1	12.7	Inventory	12.5	16.8	11.0	11.3	10.7	16.1
3.1	3.1	3.4	All Other Current	1.5	1.8	3.9	3.4	4.8	3.7
42.3	48.8	39.8	Total Current	29.3	41.6	44.9	37.9	37.1	49.2
46.5	39.5	44.0	Fixed Assets (net)	53.5	45.7	44.5	46.1	46.0	23.5
4.3	2.7	7.4	Intangibles (net)	10.6	3.0	1.8	10.0	6.7	15.6
7.0	9.0	8.9	All Other Non-Current	6.6	9.7	8.8	6.0	10.1	11.8
100.0	100.0	100.0	Total	100.0	100.0	100.0	100.0	100.0	100.0
			LIABILITIES						
7.6	11.4	10.5	Notes Payable-Short Term	15.3	7.4	21.4	7.7	8.2	5.6
4.4	5.5	5.1	Cur. Mat.-L/T/D	2.7	5.4	6.2	5.7	5.4	3.3
11.2	16.7	10.2	Trade Payables	6.6	10.7	14.0	13.0	6.6	10.7
.4	1.2	.3	Income Taxes Payable	.0	.0	.3	.0	.0	1.8
9.3	16.6	10.4	All Other Current	4.0	10.0	19.4	8.0	6.7	16.9
32.7	51.4	36.4	Total Current	28.6	33.5	61.3	34.3	27.0	38.4
29.5	26.5	31.8	Long Term Debt	52.7	37.8	20.8	32.4	32.4	16.6
.7	.3	.5	Deferred Taxes	.0	.0	.5	.2	.9	1.2
3.2	24.9	6.9	All Other Non-Current	8.5	20.8	1.4	2.3	5.2	4.2
33.8	-3.1	24.4	Net Worth	10.2	7.9	15.9	30.8	34.5	39.6
100.0	100.0	100.0	Total Liabilities & Net Worth	100.0	100.0	100.0	100.0	100.0	100.0
			INCOME DATA						
100.0	100.0	100.0	Net Sales	100.0	100.0	100.0	100.0	100.0	100.0
			Gross Profit						
95.1	95.0	92.1	Operating Expenses	85.5	93.3	95.4	93.1	90.8	93.0
4.9	5.0	7.9	Operating Profit	14.5	6.6	4.6	6.9	9.2	7.0
2.4	3.2	4.0	All Other Expenses (net)	12.4	4.5	3.9	2.2	2.3	2.6
2.5	1.9	3.9	Profit Before Taxes	2.1	2.2	.7	4.6	6.9	4.4
			RATIOS						
2.1	2.1	1.9		2.0	2.3	1.4	1.4	2.0	3.6
1.3	1.3	1.2	Current	.6	1.2	.9	1.0	1.3	1.4
.8	.9	.5		.3	.6	.5	.4	.8	1.0
1.4	1.6	1.4		1.9	1.7	1.2	1.1	1.6	1.7
.9	.8	.6	Quick	.4	.9	.4	.6	.7	.7
.4	.4	.2		.1	.2	.2	.2	.4	.4
18 20.8	16 22.8	12 30.5		0 UND	6 57.2	10 36.8	11 32.7	20 18.6	28 13.1
29 12.6	29 12.6	26 13.8	Sales/Receivables	12 30.5	23 15.6	22 16.3	14 25.6	34 10.8	48 7.5
43 8.5	46 8.0	42 8.7		33 11.0	32 11.3	32 11.2	35 10.3	54 6.7	61 6.0
			Cost of Sales/Inventory						
			Cost of Sales/Payables						
7.9	8.3	10.6		17.9	8.2	11.2	25.0	6.5	6.5
23.3	21.8	38.4	Sales/Working Capital	-4.2	27.5	NM	NM	18.9	14.3
-28.5	-37.2	-10.0		-1.7	-15.7	-5.7	-8.2	-12.4	-630.9
(110) 6.4	(102) 5.1	(101) 6.5			(14) 4.1	(17) 5.4	(20) 9.0	(29) 5.2	30.9
2.3	2.2	2.2	EBIT/Interest		1.6	1.5	2.9	2.6	5.3
.4	1.0	.9			-1.3	-1.0	1.5	1.5	2.2
(13) 6.7	(20) 2.7	(17) 4.0	Net Profit + Depr., Dep.,						
1.8	1.7	2.3	Amort./Cur. Mat. L/T/D						
1.0	.6	1.3							
.5	.5	.6		1.4	.1	.4	1.2	.6	.1
1.4	1.1	2.1	Fixed/Worth	12.3	1.9	1.5	2.4	1.8	1.0
6.3	4.9	-42.9		-8.3	-2.6	-3.6	6.8	5.7	-7.3
.7	.8	1.0		4.5	.7	1.1	1.7	.8	.6
1.8	2.4	3.7	Debt/Worth	NM	2.3	4.2	3.5	3.5	1.8
9.2	6.9	-19.8		-8.5	-8.7	-8.4	17.1	33.5	-13.3
(99) 40.6	(103) 39.2	(84) 52.7	% Profit Before Taxes/Tangible		(13) 20.4	(13) 73.1	(18) 70.4	(25) 52.0	
17.0	17.5	21.9	Net Worth		4.9	10.3	38.7	27.8	
.3	.9	3.8			-14.3	-7.3	7.5	3.8	
12.4	12.7	13.1	% Profit Before Taxes/Total	8.9	9.8	13.5	21.8	9.6	14.4
5.2	4.3	4.1	Assets	2.7	.4	.9	9.0	4.3	9.2
-1.6	-1.1	-.9		-5.2	-3.0	-10.7	1.7	1.4	3.1
21.3	22.8	16.3		17.4	23.7	25.7	20.0	13.8	28.6
3.9	6.1	4.1	Sales/Net Fixed Assets	2.3	7.9	4.2	4.2	3.0	6.6
1.3	2.5	1.5		.3	1.2	2.3	2.0	.9	3.1
3.1	3.5	2.8		2.6	3.9	3.5	3.4	2.0	2.5
1.8	2.0	1.4	Sales/Total Assets	.4	2.2	1.7	1.8	1.3	1.5
.8	1.2	.8		.2	.5	1.3	1.1	.6	1.2
(108) 1.1	(110) 1.2	(102) 1.5		(10) 3.6	(18) 1.4	(16) 1.5	(19) 1.1	(29) 1.7	(10) .5
3.4	2.1	3.5	% Depr., Dep., Amort./Sales	17.3	5.2	3.1	3.1	3.5	2.0
8.9	4.4	6.7		37.0	8.8	4.2	5.1	10.1	3.0
(34) 1.6	(42) 1.5	(38) 1.4	% Officers', Directors',					(11) .4	
2.9	3.7	3.0	Owners' Comp/Sales					1.6	
4.4	7.0	7.7						3.8	
3668045M	2695594M	2105563M	Net Sales ($)	5832M	35507M	69130M	157619M	438477M	1398998M
3253882M	1633782M	2089035M	Total Assets ($)	14011M	63748M	44867M	103712M	934182M	928515M

M = $ thousand   MM = $ million
See Pages 11 through 18 for Explanation of Ratios and Data

Current Data Sorted By Assets / Comparative Historical Data

0-500M	500M-2MM	2-10MM	10-50MM	50-100MM	100-250MM	Type of Statement	4/1/98-3/31/99 ALL	4/1/99-3/31/00 ALL
	1	4	5	2	4	Unqualified	18	23
	4	2	3			Reviewed	7	9
	3	4		1		Compiled	11	9
	2	1				Tax Returns	1	
	1	7	3	3	2	Other	17	22
			49 (10/1/02-3/31/03)					
3 (4/1-9/30/02)	11	18	11	6	6	**NUMBER OF STATEMENTS**	54	63
%	%	%	%	%	%	**ASSETS**	%	%
	10.7	13.7	4.0			Cash & Equivalents	9.5	10.9
	36.0	22.3	27.4			Trade Receivables (net)	19.7	22.0
D	6.4	3.9	4.2			Inventory	5.1	3.4
A	3.1	5.2	4.0			All Other Current	3.2	2.9
T	56.2	45.0	39.6			Total Current	37.4	39.2
A	31.2	45.0	44.5			Fixed Assets (net)	49.5	51.7
	.0	.2	6.1			Intangibles (net)	2.5	1.3
N	12.6	9.8	9.7			All Other Non-Current	10.6	7.8
O	100.0	100.0	100.0			Total	100.0	100.0
T						**LIABILITIES**		
	7.5	5.8	5.1			Notes Payable-Short Term	6.4	6.1
A	1.0	4.6	7.7			Cur. Mat.-L/T/D	5.3	5.1
V	18.2	6.4	13.2			Trade Payables	10.1	9.4
A	.0	.6	.1			Income Taxes Payable	.1	.1
I	6.8	15.5	11.9			All Other Current	9.9	11.2
L	33.6	33.0	38.1			Total Current	31.9	31.9
A	1.2	19.3	30.6			Long Term Debt	22.3	23.4
B	.0	.6	1.3			Deferred Taxes	1.7	1.1
L	8.2	5.9	2.9			All Other Non-Current	5.6	4.0
E	57.0	41.2	27.1			Net Worth	38.6	39.7
	100.0	100.0	100.0			Total Liabilities & Net Worth	100.0	100.0
						INCOME DATA		
	100.0	100.0	100.0			Net Sales	100.0	100.0
						Gross Profit		
	94.7	90.9	92.1			Operating Expenses	92.6	91.5
	5.3	9.1	7.9			Operating Profit	7.4	8.5
	–1.1	.4	8.1			All Other Expenses (net)	3.3	.8
	6.5	8.7	–.2			Profit Before Taxes	4.1	7.6
						RATIOS		
	3.7	2.4	1.7				2.0	2.1
	2.3	1.4	.9			Current	1.1	1.4
	1.3	1.2	.6				.7	.8
	3.6	2.0	1.1				1.6	1.9
	2.3	1.3	.7			Quick	1.0	1.3
	.6	.8	.5				.4	.7
	28 13.2	22 16.8	39 9.5				26 14.1	30 12.3
	47 7.8	35 10.4	54 6.7			Sales/Receivables	43 8.5	46 7.9
	117 3.1	58 6.3	71 5.2				63 5.7	61 6.0
						Cost of Sales/Inventory		
						Cost of Sales/Payables		
	3.8	6.4	5.8				5.4	7.3
	6.4	10.0	–23.7			Sales/Working Capital	25.8	17.5
	41.3	28.7	–9.3				–22.7	–20.5
		(17) 17.6	(10) 1.8				(46) 5.7	(57) 8.0
		4.7	.9			EBIT/Interest	2.1	2.4
		2.0	–5.5				.9	1.4
							(21) 3.3	(21) 4.3
						Net Profit + Depr., Dep., Amort./Cur. Mat. L /T/D	2.3	2.6
							1.1	1.3
	.3	.6	.7				.7	.8
	.5	.8	2.1			Fixed/Worth	1.4	1.2
	1.0	1.9	18.6				3.5	2.5
	.2	.9	1.4				.9	.7
	.5	1.6	2.6			Debt/Worth	2.1	1.5
	2.6	4.1	42.0				4.4	4.3
	43.9	38.3				% Profit Before Taxes/Tangible Net Worth	(49) 37.5	(58) 47.2
	22.3	15.9					18.5	23.0
	.0	6.3					3.7	4.7
	23.3	18.1	3.7			% Profit Before Taxes/Total Assets	12.0	19.5
	3.7	7.3	.3				4.0	6.6
	.0	2.0	–6.4				.2	.9
	25.4	10.4	9.9			Sales/Net Fixed Assets	11.1	7.7
	8.2	4.0	4.5				2.8	3.2
	3.0	1.5	1.5				.9	1.1
	2.9	2.6	3.2			Sales/Total Assets	2.6	2.4
	2.3	1.4	1.3				1.3	1.5
	1.2	1.0	1.0				.6	.7
	(10) 2.0	(16) 2.6	1.8			% Depr., Dep., Amort./Sales	(51) 1.6	(55) 2.1
	3.7	4.4	4.4				5.9	5.5
	6.1	9.4	12.0				12.4	9.9
						% Officers', Directors', Owners' Comp/Sales		
	33762M	214984M	328571M	252588M	1384969M	Net Sales ($)	3620894M	3772788M
	14924M	101574M	215717M	454156M	1045904M	Total Assets ($)	1696170M	2000833M

M = $ thousand   MM = $ million
See Pages 11 through 18 for Explanation of Ratios and Data

Comparative Historical Data — Current Data Sorted By Sales

			Type of Statement						
26	19	16	Unqualified		3		1	5	7
5	3	9	Reviewed	1	1	1	3		3
14	15	8	Compiled		4		2		2
1	3	3	Tax Returns		2				
22	23	16	Other	1	1	3		2	9
4/1/00-3/31/01	4/1/01-3/31/02	4/1/02-3/31/03			3 (4/1-9/30/02)		49 (10/1/02-3/31/03)		
ALL	ALL	ALL		0-1MM	1-3MM	3-5MM	5-10MM	10-25MM	25MM & OVER
68	63	52	**NUMBER OF STATEMENTS**	2	11	4	7	7	21
%	%	%	**ASSETS**	%	%	%	%	%	%
9.6	9.2	9.3	Cash & Equivalents		11.5				7.3
23.8	22.2	24.0	Trade Receivables (net)		19.6				26.1
2.7	3.6	3.8	Inventory		2.7				1.9
5.3	3.4	3.9	All Other Current		1.5				4.3
41.3	38.5	40.9	Total Current		35.4				39.5
46.3	46.5	47.3	Fixed Assets (net)		55.5				47.9
2.8	2.5	2.0	Intangibles (net)		.4				2.0
9.5	12.5	9.7	All Other Non-Current		8.8				10.6
100.0	100.0	100.0	Total		100.0				100.0
			LIABILITIES						
7.0	4.9	4.8	Notes Payable-Short Term		1.3				2.7
5.1	4.4	4.5	Cur. Mat.-L/T/D		3.9				4.3
9.0	7.6	10.2	Trade Payables		10.4				10.9
.2	.2	.3	Income Taxes Payable		.0				.1
10.7	11.5	10.8	All Other Current		6.7				15.7
32.0	28.7	30.6	Total Current		22.4				33.8
19.6	20.2	21.5	Long Term Debt		27.3				22.2
.8	.5	1.5	Deferred Taxes		.9				3.2
5.8	8.2	7.2	All Other Non-Current		1.4				7.9
41.7	42.5	39.2	Net Worth		48.0				32.8
100.0	100.0	100.0	Total Liabilities & Net Worth		100.0				100.0
			INCOME DATA						
100.0	100.0	100.0	Net Sales		100.0				100.0
			Gross Profit						
92.1	91.1	90.2	Operating Expenses		83.6				91.4
7.9	8.9	9.8	Operating Profit		16.4				8.6
.6	5.0	3.1	All Other Expenses (net)		6.3				3.6
7.3	3.9	6.7	Profit Before Taxes		10.0				5.0
			RATIOS						
1.9	2.2	2.3			3.8				1.7
1.5	1.4	1.3	Current		3.2				1.3
.8	1.0	.9			.7				.7
1.6	1.8	2.0			3.8				1.4
1.2	1.2	1.2	Quick		1.6				1.1
.6	.8	.6			.6				.6
26 13.8	26 14.0	28 13.1		1 314.0				39 9.3	
46 7.9	50 7.4	48 7.6	Sales/Receivables	23 15.9				49 7.5	
65 5.6	62 5.9	63 5.8		62 5.9				55 6.6	
			Cost of Sales/Inventory						
			Cost of Sales/Payables						
7.3	5.9	5.9			3.2				7.8
16.1	15.2	17.2	Sales/Working Capital		5.7				24.6
-28.9	-129.8	-27.8			-15.3				-20.4
8.7	5.5	11.5							6.6
(60) 2.9	(52) 2.8	(45) 3.4	EBIT/Interest						3.2
1.3	1.4	1.1							1.2
5.5	1.6	7.0	Net Profit + Depr., Dep.,						
(18) 2.1	(15) 1.2	(14) 1.5	Amort./Cur. Mat. L/T/D						
1.0	.8	.4							
.7	.7	.5			.5				.7
1.1	1.0	1.4	Fixed/Worth		1.0				1.5
2.5	2.2	2.6			2.2				3.5
.6	.7	.9			.2				1.4
1.6	1.4	2.1	Debt/Worth		1.6				2.4
3.4	3.3	4.8			6.9				6.0
47.0	24.6	30.7	% Profit Before Taxes/Tangible		65.4				38.2
(60) 17.5	(58) 11.5	(49) 18.2	Net Worth	(10) 13.0				(20) 21.7	
3.4	.0	1.7			2.2				-1.8
15.2	8.9	11.3	% Profit Before Taxes/Total		20.2				8.1
5.8	4.1	4.1	Assets		4.7				5.2
.4	.0	.4			.4				.8
9.8	8.2	9.9			5.4				10.0
4.6	3.4	3.2	Sales/Net Fixed Assets		2.2				6.2
1.3	1.2	1.2			.8				1.0
3.1	2.5	2.7			1.9				3.4
1.5	1.3	1.3	Sales/Total Assets		1.2				1.7
.9	.8	.8			.8				.6
2.1	2.0	2.7			3.9				1.5
(57) 4.5	(54) 3.9	(45) 4.4	% Depr., Dep., Amort./Sales	(10) 6.5				(17) 3.3	
8.5	9.2	9.7			9.9				7.0
	.1		% Officers', Directors',						
	(13) 1.9		Owners' Comp/Sales						
	5.6								
3474138M	3780617M	2214874M	Net Sales ($)	881M	25507M	16272M	51190M	105606M	2015418M
2259898M	2802968M	1832275M	Total Assets ($)	2627M	38537M	11679M	31095M	161492M	1586845M

M = $ thousand   MM = $ million

See Pages 11 through 18 for Explanation of Ratios and Data

Current Data Sorted By Assets   **Comparative Historical Data**

Date ranges: 13 (4/1-9/30/02)   72 (10/1/02-3/31/03)

0-500M	500M-2MM	2-10MM	10-50MM	50-100MM	100-250MM	Type of Statement	4/1/98-3/31/99 ALL	4/1/99-3/31/00 ALL
		5	6	2	3	Unqualified	12	11
		5	1			Reviewed	11	9
4	9	11		1		Compiled	11	25
4	4	1				Tax Returns	4	
	5	14	5	3	2	Other	14	19
8	18	36	12	6	5	**NUMBER OF STATEMENTS**	52	64
%	%	%	%	%	%	**ASSETS**	%	%
	10.5	4.6	7.2			Cash & Equivalents	8.7	9.1
	15.9	17.0	16.3			Trade Receivables (net)	16.1	17.9
	.0	.4	1.5			Inventory	1.1	.8
	1.6	5.2	4.2			All Other Current	1.6	2.9
	28.0	27.2	29.2			Total Current	27.6	30.7
	65.2	61.7	64.2			Fixed Assets (net)	63.0	56.1
	.0	.8	.0			Intangibles (net)	1.2	.8
	6.8	10.3	6.6			All Other Non-Current	8.3	12.3
	100.0	100.0	100.0			Total	100.0	100.0
						LIABILITIES		
	7.5	3.5	2.0			Notes Payable-Short Term	1.9	4.8
	10.6	10.0	13.3			Cur. Mat.-L/T/D	5.5	4.6
	2.9	9.3	8.4			Trade Payables	5.8	9.2
	.2	.1	.1			Income Taxes Payable	.2	.3
	2.1	5.7	8.2			All Other Current	8.3	7.9
	23.3	28.7	32.0			Total Current	21.6	26.8
	48.0	41.0	30.0			Long Term Debt	37.6	30.8
	.4	1.1	3.2			Deferred Taxes	2.1	1.7
	5.8	5.0	1.9			All Other Non-Current	3.5	3.6
	22.5	24.2	32.9			Net Worth	35.1	37.1
	100.0	100.0	100.0			Total Liabilities & Net Worth	100.0	100.0
						INCOME DATA		
	100.0	100.0	100.0			Net Sales	100.0	100.0
						Gross Profit		
	85.7	92.5	92.3			Operating Expenses	86.7	90.1
	14.3	7.5	7.7			Operating Profit	13.3	9.9
	4.5	4.8	2.8			All Other Expenses (net)	3.0	3.3
	9.8	2.6	4.9			Profit Before Taxes	10.3	6.5
						RATIOS		
	4.5	1.6	2.2				2.3	2.0
	1.2	.9	1.1			Current	1.5	1.3
	.4	.5	.4				.6	.8
	4.5	1.0	1.9				2.0	1.7
	.9	.8	.8			Quick	1.3	1.2
	.3	.4	.4				.5	.5
0 UND		15 23.6	36 10.1				8 45.5	25 14.4
28 13.2		43 8.6	46 7.9			Sales/Receivables	41 8.9	43 8.4
72 5.1		75 4.9	73 5.0				56 6.6	57 6.4
						Cost of Sales/Inventory		
						Cost of Sales/Payables		
	5.9	11.7	4.6				9.2	8.8
	29.3	−65.1	66.5			Sales/Working Capital	14.4	34.2
	−9.4	−6.0	−7.7				−16.6	−18.4
	3.9	3.1	5.7				7.5	6.3
	(17) 2.4	(35) 1.7	2.8			EBIT/Interest	(43) 3.6	(57) 2.9
	.8	.4	1.6				1.7	1.3
		3.0					2.9	5.4
		(12) 1.3				Net Profit + Depr., Dep., Amort./Cur. Mat. L /T/D	(17) 2.4	(18) 3.3
		.5					1.3	1.8
	1.1	1.5	1.1				1.0	.9
	3.3	2.2	2.1			Fixed/Worth	2.1	1.6
	−30.4	10.1	5.2				4.2	3.2
	.8	1.4	1.3				.7	.7
	5.5	2.7	1.9			Debt/Worth	1.9	1.8
	−31.8	11.6	6.0				5.0	4.9
	69.7	28.8	31.2				64.7	33.4
	(12) 20.0	(32) 12.5	(11) 16.2			% Profit Before Taxes/Tangible Net Worth	(50) 29.9	(59) 12.1
	−1.2	−5.0	6.7				12.9	4.5
	12.0	6.6	7.2				20.1	11.0
	4.0	2.1	4.4			% Profit Before Taxes/Total Assets	7.5	4.1
	−.8	−1.9	1.8				2.8	1.0
	3.2	4.3	2.9				3.7	4.7
	2.4	1.6	1.9			Sales/Net Fixed Assets	2.0	2.1
	1.4	.6	1.4				.9	.8
	2.2	2.0	1.6				2.0	2.0
	1.5	.9	1.2			Sales/Total Assets	1.2	1.0
	.8	.5	.8				.7	.6
	5.5	2.3	4.2				3.1	4.1
	11.5	(34) 7.9	(11) 5.1			% Depr., Dep., Amort./Sales	(44) 5.9	(57) 6.9
	18.0	16.1	9.0				9.4	10.3
		2.1					1.3	2.4
		(13) 5.1				% Officers', Directors', Owners' Comp/Sales	(14) 4.7	(24) 3.8
		9.7					13.6	8.1
6928M	30304M	246298M	421373M	245526M	471825M	Net Sales ($)	917176M	941775M
2185M	18549M	184179M	325384M	439179M	749351M	Total Assets ($)	930455M	1248182M

M = $ thousand   MM = $ million
See Pages 11 through 18 for Explanation of Ratios and Data

Comparative Historical Data | Current Data Sorted By Sales

				Type of Statement						
11	15	16		Unqualified		1	2	2	2	9
14	10	6		Reviewed	1		1	2	2	
20	24	25		Compiled	7	9	4	3	1	1
3	7	9		Tax Returns	4	4			1	
22	20	29		Other	4	4	4	4	6	7
4/1/00- 3/31/01 ALL	4/1/01- 3/31/02 ALL	4/1/02- 3/31/03 ALL			13 (4/1-9/30/02)			72 (10/1/02-3/31/03)		
					0-1MM	1-3MM	3-5MM	5-10MM	10-25MM	25MM & OVER
70	76	85		**NUMBER OF STATEMENTS**	16	18	11	11	12	17
%	%	%		**ASSETS**	%	%	%	%	%	%
6.9	9.6	7.9		Cash & Equivalents	13.1	6.7	8.5	4.7	6.5	7.1
17.5	17.5	16.1		Trade Receivables (net)	14.2	14.2	12.8	21.1	18.8	16.9
.9	1.6	.5		Inventory	.2	.0	.0	.6	1.3	1.1
2.3	2.4	3.5		All Other Current	.5	2.1	9.8	1.7	3.7	4.7
27.6	31.0	28.1		Total Current	28.0	23.1	31.1	28.1	30.3	29.7
62.2	58.8	63.3		Fixed Assets (net)	64.1	69.7	56.6	61.0	63.2	61.8
.8	.4	.6		Intangibles (net)	.1	.6	.2	.9	.5	1.1
9.3	9.7	8.1		All Other Non-Current	7.8	6.6	12.1	10.0	6.1	7.4
100.0	100.0	100.0		Total	100.0	100.0	100.0	100.0	100.0	100.0
				LIABILITIES						
4.9	2.8	4.1		Notes Payable-Short Term	4.5	4.1	8.8	5.1	1.6	1.6
5.6	6.8	9.1		Cur. Mat.-L/T/D	6.5	10.8	7.5	7.8	12.5	9.3
8.5	7.6	7.4		Trade Payables	2.5	5.1	5.5	13.3	9.4	10.4
.3	.3	.1		Income Taxes Payable	.0	.5	.2	.0	.1	.0
8.8	7.8	5.9		All Other Current	7.5	3.6	4.5	4.4	7.6	7.7
28.2	25.3	26.6		Total Current	21.0	24.1	26.4	30.6	31.1	29.0
36.4	38.5	42.8		Long Term Debt	53.6	51.2	36.4	33.4	31.1	42.3
1.8	1.5	1.6		Deferred Taxes	1.5	.2	.7	1.3	2.7	3.4
4.3	7.0	5.6		All Other Non-Current	14.9	6.4	3.9	2.9	1.9	1.3
29.3	27.6	23.3		Net Worth	9.0	18.1	32.5	31.8	33.2	24.0
100.0	100.0	100.0		Total Liabilities & Net Worth	100.0	100.0	100.0	100.0	100.0	100.0
				INCOME DATA						
100.0	100.0	100.0		Net Sales	100.0	100.0	100.0	100.0	100.0	100.0
				Gross Profit						
90.7	88.0	91.1		Operating Expenses	81.2	95.9	89.1	96.4	92.4	92.2
9.3	12.0	8.9		Operating Profit	18.8	4.1	10.9	3.6	7.6	7.7
3.9	4.1	3.9		All Other Expenses (net)	7.3	4.4	3.6	2.9	2.3	2.1
5.4	7.9	5.0		Profit Before Taxes	11.4	−.3	7.3	.7	5.3	5.6
				RATIOS						
2.0	2.1	1.8			5.9	1.9	3.1	1.3	2.1	1.7
1.0	1.2	1.0		Current	1.0	.7	1.4	.9	1.1	1.4
.6	.8	.5			.3	.3	.9	.8	1.0	.6
2.0	2.0	1.5			5.7	1.0	1.4	1.2	1.6	1.5
.9	1.1	.9		Quick	1.0	.6	.9	.8	1.0	1.1
.5	.6	.4			.3	.1	.0	.6	.6	.4
27 13.6	28 13.2	16 23.0			6 62.2	0 UND	0 UND	24 15.1	38 9.5	32 11.6
45 8.2	46 7.9	41 9.0		Sales/Receivables	28 13.1	35 10.3	21 17.8	45 8.1	49 7.4	43 8.5
63 5.8	63 5.8	68 5.4			84 4.3	87 4.2	67 5.5	73 5.0	63 5.8	57 6.4
				Cost of Sales/Inventory						
				Cost of Sales/Payables						
9.3	6.7	8.1			6.6	20.0	5.3	20.8	7.6	6.2
−549.1	20.2	157.7		Sales/Working Capital	NM	−22.0	15.0	−51.3	66.5	12.0
−8.4	−32.1	−11.0			−4.0	−4.1	−30.3	−19.8	NM	−17.4
6.6	6.0	3.7			7.4	2.7	5.8	2.3	5.9	4.6
(64) 2.8	(74) 3.0	(81) 2.0		EBIT/Interest	(12) 2.2	1.5	3.3	1.2	2.8	2.1
.9	1.2	1.0			−.1	.7	2.5	−.3	1.6	1.3
2.3	5.1	3.5		Net Profit + Depr., Dep.,						
(18) 1.6	(21) 2.3	(25) 1.4		Amort./Cur. Mat. L/T/D						
1.4	1.6	.8								
.9	1.2	1.4			1.4	1.8	.7	1.1	1.2	1.7
1.9	1.7	2.4		Fixed/Worth	3.6	5.8	2.0	1.8	1.8	2.4
6.4	5.9	11.2			−17.5	−27.7	3.8	6.4	3.1	NM
.8	1.2	1.3			1.5	1.5	.9	.9	1.4	1.4
1.9	2.0	2.7		Debt/Worth	12.4	5.2	1.7	2.1	1.8	2.2
5.8	6.5	19.4			−19.6	−33.1	6.1	10.2	4.0	NM
28.5	37.9	31.2		% Profit Before Taxes/Tangible	71.3	29.7	57.0	15.5	49.8	21.9
(61) 13.8	(64) 20.6	(69) 14.4		Net Worth	(11) 35.4	(12) 13.1	(10) 14.3	5.3	17.7	(13) 13.6
5.3	7.5	3.1			6.6	.5	−3.1	−13.8	5.9	6.0
11.7	12.2	8.2		% Profit Before Taxes/Total	15.3	9.6	14.9	4.2	14.5	6.2
5.4	5.1	3.6		Assets	6.4	1.3	6.8	1.5	4.4	3.6
−.2	.6	.2			−1.0	−.8	1.8	−3.5	1.8	1.4
3.7	3.9	3.5			4.0	2.9	6.2	4.9	2.9	3.0
1.8	1.8	1.9		Sales/Net Fixed Assets	1.9	1.7	3.0	2.5	1.9	1.1
.8	1.0	.8			.5	.5	1.5	1.0	1.3	.7
2.0	1.8	2.1			2.7	2.0	2.2	2.2	2.0	1.5
1.0	1.0	1.0		Sales/Total Assets	.9	1.2	1.3	1.5	1.2	.7
.6	.7	.5			.3	.4	.5	.7	.9	.5
3.4	4.3	4.0			6.2	4.2	5.0	1.9	3.4	4.7
(63) 8.6	(73) 6.8	(81) 8.5		% Depr., Dep., Amort./Sales	14.4	9.4	(10) 8.5	2.4	(11) 6.5	(15) 8.8
12.3	11.5	12.3			23.3	16.1	13.6	8.1	9.0	9.9
2.3	2.3	2.8		% Officers', Directors',						
(18) 4.7	(19) 5.1	(21) 6.1		Owners' Comp/Sales						
11.8	8.6	10.4								
1107754M	1448519M	1422254M		Net Sales ($)	10662M	30462M	44731M	82796M	203221M	1050382M
1258486M	1646472M	1718827M		Total Assets ($)	20747M	44912M	44428M	60043M	194832M	1353865M

M = $ thousand   MM = $ million
See Pages 11 through 18 for Explanation of Ratios and Data

Current Data Sorted By Assets   Comparative Historical Data

0-500M	500M-2MM	2-10MM	10-50MM	50-100MM	100-250MM	Type of Statement	4/1/98-3/31/99 ALL	4/1/99-3/31/00 ALL
1	1	5	7	1	2	Unqualified	18	13
1	1	6	2			Reviewed	6	2
1	4	3	3			Compiled	7	8
1			1			Tax Returns	2	3
3	1	7	7	3	3	Other	6	8
	8 (4/1-9/30/02)		55 (10/1/02-3/31/03)					
6	**7**	**21**	**20**	**4**	**5**	**NUMBER OF STATEMENTS**	**39**	**34**
%	%	%	%	%	%	**ASSETS**	%	%
		8.8	10.6			Cash & Equivalents	12.1	10.7
		17.5	14.9			Trade Receivables (net)	22.5	12.9
		1.8	1.9			Inventory	1.2	.9
		6.2	4.9			All Other Current	3.3	2.3
		34.4	32.3			Total Current	39.1	26.8
		49.7	60.6			Fixed Assets (net)	52.1	61.4
		2.4	.9			Intangibles (net)	1.4	.4
		13.5	6.2			All Other Non-Current	7.4	11.3
		100.0	100.0			Total	100.0	100.0
						LIABILITIES		
		4.7	5.7			Notes Payable-Short Term	5.5	5.8
		5.2	8.1			Cur. Mat.-L/T/D	4.4	5.8
		6.8	9.1			Trade Payables	10.8	5.7
		.2	.2			Income Taxes Payable	.2	.4
		10.8	3.1			All Other Current	6.9	8.2
		27.7	26.3			Total Current	27.8	26.0
		25.7	27.5			Long Term Debt	24.8	28.1
		1.1	1.5			Deferred Taxes	.5	.9
		9.9	.8			All Other Non-Current	2.6	5.1
		35.6	43.9			Net Worth	44.4	40.0
		100.0	100.0			Total Liabilities & Net Worth	100.0	100.0
						INCOME DATA		
		100.0	100.0			Net Sales	100.0	100.0
						Gross Profit		
		87.8	84.8			Operating Expenses	79.8	94.2
		12.2	15.2			Operating Profit	20.2	5.8
		6.7	2.9			All Other Expenses (net)	3.3	3.5
		5.6	12.3			Profit Before Taxes	16.9	2.3
						RATIOS		
		1.9	2.6				2.4	1.3
		1.4	1.2			Current	1.3	1.0
		.6	.7				.6	.6
		1.6	2.1				2.1	1.2
		.8	.9			Quick	1.1	.7
		.3	.5				.5	.4
		4 102.5	35 10.4				22 16.7	28 13.1
		36 10.1	60 6.1			Sales/Receivables	43 8.5	40 9.1
		63 5.8	85 4.3				66 5.5	61 6.0
						Cost of Sales/Inventory		
						Cost of Sales/Payables		
		6.4	4.3				8.9	18.6
		17.5	16.4			Sales/Working Capital	20.0	-136.1
		-6.8	-13.5				-9.2	-7.9
		16.8	5.8				(30) 30.1	7.4
		(17) 4.4	(19) 3.4			EBIT/Interest	6.2	(29) 2.1
		1.1	1.5				1.8	.0
						Net Profit + Depr., Dep., Amort./Cur. Mat. L /T/D		
		1.0	.9				.5	.9
		1.9	1.2			Fixed/Worth	1.6	2.2
		3.1	3.2				3.1	4.2
		1.0	.4				.5	.5
		2.3	1.8			Debt/Worth	1.4	1.6
		7.4	3.9				4.8	5.3
		50.9	31.9				(37) 132.1	32.1
		(19) 16.0	(19) 11.7			% Profit Before Taxes/Tangible Net Worth	49.1	(32) 7.5
		-5.3	6.9				14.6	-11.1
		13.8	9.7				45.2	10.2
		5.1	4.8			% Profit Before Taxes/Total Assets	15.5	1.9
		-.9	2.0				1.5	-5.8
		9.4	3.2				18.9	4.2
		2.6	1.3			Sales/Net Fixed Assets	1.8	1.7
		.8	.6				.8	.5
		3.0	1.4				4.0	2.2
		1.2	.7			Sales/Total Assets	1.1	1.0
		.3	.4				.6	.4
		1.8	5.4				(31) 1.3	4.1
		(20) 5.5	(19) 9.1			% Depr., Dep., Amort./Sales	4.4	(32) 10.3
		17.1	11.9				9.8	13.5
						% Officers', Directors', Owners' Comp/Sales		
6077M	13752M	205066M	451978M	283556M	1324305M	Net Sales ($)	770042M	392603M
1960M	7073M	121045M	434164M	214229M	840576M	Total Assets ($)	1235142M	684618M

M = $ thousand   MM = $ million
See Pages 11 through 18 for Explanation of Ratios and Data

Comparative Historical Data			Type of Statement	Current Data Sorted By Sales					
8	8	16	Unqualified		1		5	3	6
4	2	10	Reviewed	2	2	1	1	3	1
10	15	11	Compiled	1	5	3	1	1	
5	2	2	Tax Returns		1			1	
11	9	24	Other	3	6	2	1	5	7
4/1/00-3/31/01	4/1/01-3/31/02	4/1/02-3/31/03			8 (4/1-9/30/02)		55 (10/1/02-3/31/03)		
ALL	ALL	ALL		0-1MM	1-3MM	3-5MM	5-10MM	10-25MM	25MM & OVER
38	36	63	**NUMBER OF STATEMENTS**	6	15	7	8	13	14
%	%	%	**ASSETS**	%	%	%	%	%	%
10.3	10.8	9.2	Cash & Equivalents		5.7			7.0	8.2
11.1	19.2	19.7	Trade Receivables (net)		14.6			21.0	22.2
1.4	2.8	3.2	Inventory		4.0			2.5	6.1
5.7	4.0	5.2	All Other Current		6.5			6.3	7.1
28.6	36.9	37.4	Total Current		30.9			36.8	43.6
58.9	54.7	50.6	Fixed Assets (net)		56.9			56.9	43.9
1.2	2.3	3.6	Intangibles (net)		3.0			1.0	5.2
11.4	6.2	8.3	All Other Non-Current		9.2			5.3	7.4
100.0	100.0	100.0	Total		100.0			100.0	100.0
			LIABILITIES						
7.7	5.1	6.1	Notes Payable-Short Term		8.6			6.0	1.9
7.3	6.5	7.1	Cur. Mat.-L/T/D		6.6			7.3	7.4
4.6	12.4	7.4	Trade Payables		3.6			8.8	9.4
.2	.4	.2	Income Taxes Payable		.1			.0	.5
5.4	5.7	7.2	All Other Current		4.9			4.6	9.7
25.3	30.1	27.9	Total Current		23.8			26.7	28.7
31.2	32.5	24.6	Long Term Debt		31.3			20.6	21.5
.8	1.6	1.1	Deferred Taxes		.4			2.5	2.4
7.8	3.8	4.7	All Other Non-Current		2.2			2.6	5.7
34.8	32.1	41.6	Net Worth		42.3			47.6	41.7
100.0	100.0	100.0	Total Liabilities & Net Worth		100.0			100.0	100.0
			INCOME DATA						
100.0	100.0	100.0	Net Sales		100.0			100.0	100.0
			Gross Profit						
79.7	83.0	86.3	Operating Expenses		86.9			95.1	87.7
20.3	17.0	13.7	Operating Profit		13.1			4.9	12.3
5.7	4.7	3.8	All Other Expenses (net)		7.9			2.4	1.2
14.6	12.3	10.0	Profit Before Taxes		5.2			2.5	11.1
			RATIOS						
1.5	2.1	2.2			2.2			3.5	2.1
1.1	1.3	1.3	Current		1.2			1.5	1.8
.6	.7	.6			.1			.7	1.2
1.4	1.9	1.7			1.4			3.4	1.6
.8	1.0	1.0	Quick		.9			.9	1.1
.4	.4	.4			.1			.5	.8
0 UND	23 15.6	18 20.8		0 UND			34 10.8	25 14.6	
36 10.1	43 8.4	50 7.2	Sales/Receivables	42 8.7			55 6.6	41 9.0	
62 5.9	67 5.5	72 5.1		65 5.6			74 4.9	66 5.5	
			Cost of Sales/Inventory						
			Cost of Sales/Payables						
10.8	7.3	5.0			4.5			4.6	5.5
68.7	16.0	15.7	Sales/Working Capital		46.6			15.3	10.4
-7.5	-12.0	-16.9			-1.7			-13.6	47.6
(32) 5.2	(29) 15.4	(53) 7.2		(13) 7.0			13.4	(12) 10.2	
2.5	4.5	3.7	EBIT/Interest	3.7			2.9	6.1	
.4	1.5	1.3		1.3			1.5	1.3	
	(10) 5.5	(13) 3.5							
	1.5	2.2	Net Profit + Depr., Dep., Amort./Cur. Mat. L/T/D						
	.3	1.1							
1.0	.7	.8			.8			.8	.8
2.0	1.9	1.2	Fixed/Worth		1.3			1.9	1.2
3.8	3.8	2.8			2.7			2.6	1.5
1.1	.7	.6			.9			.3	.6
2.0	2.3	1.5	Debt/Worth		1.3			2.0	1.4
4.1	6.6	4.5			4.6			3.5	2.9
(32) 44.8	(31) 45.5	(57) 35.7		(14) 24.7			17.8	(12) 46.4	
26.9	18.3	14.3	% Profit Before Taxes/Tangible Net Worth	15.1			8.7	18.0	
6.2	4.0	4.6		2.4			2.4	7.1	
19.0	16.6	11.5			9.8			7.0	16.2
6.3	4.6	6.7	% Profit Before Taxes/Total Assets		5.1			2.6	8.6
-.5	1.2	.2			.1			1.5	1.4
8.8	6.5	8.6			3.6			6.8	12.2
1.5	1.6	2.6	Sales/Net Fixed Assets		1.3			2.2	5.0
.4	.9	1.0			.3			.9	2.4
2.4	1.8	2.6			2.8			3.0	3.6
.8	1.2	1.2	Sales/Total Assets		.8			1.3	1.7
.4	.5	.5			.3			.7	1.0
(31) 5.0	(29) 2.0	(52) 2.5		(12) 7.0			3.0		
12.0	8.4	6.7	% Depr., Dep., Amort./Sales	11.2			5.4		
17.8	14.5	11.8		19.8			10.7		
(13) 2.3	(10) 1.7	(14) 2.3							
4.6	3.0	3.9	% Officers', Directors', Owners' Comp/Sales						
	7.4	5.8							
390675M	908241M	2284734M	Net Sales ($)	3571M	27899M	28835M	64170M	231484M	1928775M
725018M	916445M	1619047M	Total Assets ($)	10474M	63509M	38794M	124299M	238908M	1143063M

M = $ thousand   MM = $ million
See Pages 11 through 18 for Explanation of Ratios and Data

Current Data Sorted By Assets   Comparative Historical Data

Type of Statement	0-500M	500M-2MM	2-10MM	10-50MM	50-100MM	100-250MM		4/1/98-3/31/99 ALL	4/1/99-3/31/00 ALL
Unqualified		3	2	2	1			14	7
Reviewed	5	4	4	2				14	10
Compiled	15	14	8					45	38
Tax Returns	26	10	2					32	32
Other	12	9	13	3		1		46	36
	17 (4/1-9/30/02)			119 (10/1/02-3/31/03)					
NUMBER OF STATEMENTS	58	40	29	7	1	1		151	123

	0-500M %	500M-2MM %	2-10MM %	10-50MM %	50-100MM %	100-250MM %		%	%
ASSETS									
Cash & Equivalents	12.1	10.8	6.6					13.6	11.9
Trade Receivables (net)	14.7	13.3	10.2					10.1	12.7
Inventory	15.6	12.7	9.0					15.9	15.5
All Other Current	3.9	2.5	1.4					1.2	1.9
Total Current	46.4	39.4	27.2					40.7	42.0
Fixed Assets (net)	39.2	47.8	57.0					45.4	42.1
Intangibles (net)	5.4	8.6	4.3					7.3	7.1
All Other Non-Current	9.0	4.2	11.4					6.7	8.8
Total	100.0	100.0	100.0					100.0	100.0
LIABILITIES									
Notes Payable-Short Term	12.6	2.2	4.9					8.4	7.4
Cur. Mat.-L/T/D	5.7	8.3	5.6					6.1	7.8
Trade Payables	13.4	11.0	7.4					11.2	13.1
Income Taxes Payable	.1	.3	.2					.2	.5
All Other Current	30.6	8.8	9.2					23.3	12.9
Total Current	62.4	30.6	27.4					49.4	41.7
Long Term Debt	33.9	34.8	42.4					37.6	30.5
Deferred Taxes	.0	.0	.1					.3	.1
All Other Non-Current	8.0	6.1	6.3					4.1	4.7
Net Worth	-4.3	28.5	23.8					8.6	23.0
Total Liabilities & Net Worth	100.0	100.0	100.0					100.0	100.0
INCOME DATA									
Net Sales	100.0	100.0	100.0					100.0	100.0
Gross Profit									
Operating Expenses	98.4	95.9	89.8					95.0	94.4
Operating Profit	1.6	4.1	10.2					5.0	5.6
All Other Expenses (net)	.6	2.0	6.2					2.0	1.6
Profit Before Taxes	1.0	2.0	4.0					3.0	3.9
RATIOS									
Current	2.9	2.9	1.6					2.0	1.9
	1.2	1.4	1.1					1.1	1.1
	.5	.5	.5					.6	.6
Quick	1.9	1.6	1.3					1.3	1.2
	.4	.8	.7					(121) .6	.6
	.1	.2	.3					.2	.3
Sales/Receivables	0 UND	2 242.5	2 205.1					1 483.7	2 227.5
	8 44.9	9 42.4	6 60.4					4 83.9	8 47.2
	25 14.4	25 14.6	25 14.9					19 19.2	25 14.5
Cost of Sales/Inventory									
Cost of Sales/Payables									
Sales/Working Capital	10.6	10.4	16.5					14.5	14.5
	171.8	36.0	117.9					108.0	103.9
	-16.2	-21.1	-17.0					-14.1	-16.0
EBIT/Interest	(47) 8.5	(38) 6.7	(24) 12.4					(125) 6.0	(106) 7.2
	2.5	1.9	2.3					2.1	2.6
	-.5	.2	1.2					.8	.9
Net Profit + Depr., Dep., Amort./Cur. Mat. L/T/D								3.4	6.3
								(23) 2.3	(17) 2.5
								1.3	1.6
Fixed/Worth	.6	.6	1.0					.5	.7
	2.4	1.6	3.2					2.2	2.1
	-.8	96.0	NM					-6.3	-12.0
Debt/Worth	1.2	.8	1.9					1.1	1.2
	5.0	3.3	3.9					3.9	3.9
	-4.5	NM	NM					-7.8	-29.7
% Profit Before Taxes/Tangible Net Worth	(36) 60.6	(30) 74.6	(22) 70.9					(109) 73.7	(90) 68.9
	26.3	12.4	19.2					22.4	30.6
	.5	-4.5	10.3					6.3	10.8
% Profit Before Taxes/Total Assets	17.6	17.7	15.1					20.5	17.6
	4.3	3.9	4.6					5.6	9.0
	-5.3	-1.9	.7					-.1	.9
Sales/Net Fixed Assets	37.4	22.5	10.4					22.6	24.3
	11.9	6.6	2.6					7.5	7.6
	6.5	1.7	1.5					2.2	3.2
Sales/Total Assets	6.5	4.1	2.8					4.5	4.4
	4.3	2.6	1.9					2.3	2.5
	2.4	1.3	.9					1.2	1.6
% Depr., Dep., Amort./Sales	(53) 1.3	(35) .9	(26) 2.4					(136) 1.6	(106) 1.1
	2.6	2.8	3.0					3.4	2.2
	6.6	8.1	6.8					7.6	5.1
% Officers', Directors', Owners' Comp/Sales	(29) 3.9	(22) 2.0	(13) 1.5					(56) 3.5	(64) 3.0
	7.5	4.1	3.2					5.4	5.4
	12.5	7.2	4.3					8.8	9.0
Net Sales ($)	52747M	139762M	269002M	462813M	67710M	38223M		1486438M	887134M
Total Assets ($)	12607M	44989M	131011M	104350M	54947M	183197M		829113M	541954M

© RMA 2003

M = $ thousand   MM = $ million
See Pages 11 through 18 for Explanation of Ratios and Data

Comparative Historical Data | Current Data Sorted By Sales

			Type of Statement	0-1MM	1-3MM	3-5MM	5-10MM	10-25MM	25MM & OVER
6	12	8	Unqualified		1		2	2	3
8	12	15	Reviewed	2	7	2	1	2	1
59	50	37	Compiled	11	12	5	5	4	
44	32	38	Tax Returns	21	11	5	1		
32	50	38	Other	12	7	5	5	6	3
4/1/00-3/31/01 ALL	4/1/01-3/31/02 ALL	4/1/02-3/31/03 ALL		17 (4/1-9/30/02)		119 (10/1/02-3/31/03)			
149	156	136	**NUMBER OF STATEMENTS**	46	38	17	14	14	7
%	%	%	**ASSETS**	%	%	%	%	%	%
10.4	10.9	10.7	Cash & Equivalents	11.5	8.5	13.1	10.6	8.6	
14.9	13.2	12.9	Trade Receivables (net)	10.6	13.7	11.2	18.9	17.4	
16.3	15.5	13.6	Inventory	11.5	13.1	19.2	9.5	17.2	
2.3	2.2	3.3	All Other Current	4.0	3.0	1.4	.6	3.3	
43.8	41.9	40.5	Total Current	37.7	38.3	44.9	39.6	46.5	
43.8	42.9	45.5	Fixed Assets (net)	49.7	46.2	39.1	47.5	41.0	
5.9	8.3	6.2	Intangibles (net)	3.7	9.6	6.4	7.0	5.7	
6.4	6.9	7.8	All Other Non-Current	8.9	5.9	9.6	5.9	6.7	
100.0	100.0	100.0	Total	100.0	100.0	100.0	100.0	100.0	
			LIABILITIES						
8.1	12.9	7.8	Notes Payable-Short Term	11.2	5.9	2.7	7.5	6.0	
6.6	4.8	6.6	Cur. Mat.-L/T/D	6.3	7.9	5.9	2.6	7.9	
13.0	14.3	11.3	Trade Payables	7.3	13.7	14.8	10.9	14.4	
.2	.2	.2	Income Taxes Payable	.1	.3	.0	.1	.2	
13.3	23.4	19.0	All Other Current	30.2	13.7	8.3	7.2	15.8	
41.3	55.5	44.8	Total Current	55.0	41.5	31.7	28.3	44.4	
32.3	32.6	36.6	Long Term Debt	41.3	39.5	30.9	29.4	28.3	
.1	.3	.2	Deferred Taxes	.0	.1	.0	.1	.8	
4.5	5.8	6.8	All Other Non-Current	9.4	5.1	7.1	3.5	8.0	
21.8	5.8	11.6	Net Worth	-5.8	13.8	30.2	38.7	18.5	
100.0	100.0	100.0	Total Liabilities & Net Worth	100.0	100.0	100.0	100.0	100.0	
			INCOME DATA						
100.0	100.0	100.0	Net Sales	100.0	100.0	100.0	100.0	100.0	
			Gross Profit						
93.3	96.1	95.4	Operating Expenses	96.1	95.9	94.5	95.1	95.6	
6.7	3.9	4.6	Operating Profit	3.9	4.1	5.5	4.9	4.4	
3.5	2.8	2.5	All Other Expenses (net)	2.8	2.6	2.3	1.4	1.8	
3.3	1.0	2.1	Profit Before Taxes	1.1	1.5	3.2	3.6	2.6	
			RATIOS						
2.3	1.9	2.6		3.7	2.7	2.3	2.3	1.6	
1.1	1.1	1.2	Current	1.2	1.3	1.2	1.3	1.1	
.6	.5	.5		.5	.4	.9	.6	.7	
1.4	1.3	1.5		2.5	1.6	1.0	2.0	1.3	
.6	.5	.6	Quick	.6	.4	.8	1.0	.6	
.3	.2	.2		.1	.1	.4	.4	.3	
1 304.9	2 187.4	1 374.7		0 UND	0 UND	2 166.9	3 144.6	3 105.3	
13 27.6	8 47.7	8 44.2	Sales/Receivables	4 81.5	9 39.1	9 39.5	6 60.2	14 25.9	
30 12.1	28 13.0	26 14.2		21 17.6	26 13.9	24 15.1	26 13.8	43 8.5	
			Cost of Sales/Inventory						
			Cost of Sales/Payables						
12.0	12.5	10.9		10.7	8.9	12.0	20.3	17.1	
90.5	83.6	69.9	Sales/Working Capital	171.8	55.3	81.2	45.6	46.6	
-20.2	-11.1	-17.4		-15.4	-11.9	NM	-28.3	-35.2	
(125) 5.6	(132) 3.4	(116) 7.7		(35) 7.5	(34) 6.3	(15) 4.7	23.9	(13) 16.9	
1.8	1.2	2.2	EBIT/Interest	1.3	2.2	1.4	7.8	2.5	
.8	-.3	.6		-1.2	.5	.1	1.5	1.1	
(12) 2.9	(18) 1.8	(14) 3.1	Net Profit + Depr., Dep.,						
1.7	1.1	1.9	Amort./Cur. Mat. L/T/D						
.7	.2	.9							
.6	.7	.7		.9	.6	.4	.6	.9	
2.5	2.7	2.3	Fixed/Worth	3.4	3.7	1.5	1.3	2.4	
UND	-4.1	-4.5		-3.1	-.9	-6.3	3.9	NM	
1.2	1.4	1.2		1.3	.7	.6	.8	2.2	
3.8	5.5	4.3	Debt/Worth	5.8	5.4	2.2	2.4	5.7	
UND	-7.9	-10.5		-6.8	-4.7	-37.8	12.8	NM	
(113) 72.3	(105) 73.0	(94) 63.2	% Profit Before Taxes/Tangible	(30) 61.8	(23) 54.1	(12) 65.8	(13) 99.8	(11) 86.5	
23.7	15.5	19.8	Net Worth	23.9	17.9	16.1	40.3	15.3	
3.8	-1.0	4.3		-.5	6.4	-6.2	8.5	-2.5	
17.8	10.7	16.8	% Profit Before Taxes/Total	12.7	14.7	28.2	23.8	20.2	
4.3	1.6	4.2	Assets	1.8	4.2	2.5	6.7	9.2	
-1.0	-5.4	-1.2		-6.2	-2.2	-2.1	2.3	1.1	
23.2	27.7	21.2		18.7	31.8	44.2	42.2	21.7	
7.7	7.8	9.1	Sales/Net Fixed Assets	8.9	8.9	10.2	9.6	8.2	
2.7	2.6	2.4		2.4	1.7	3.4	2.0	2.9	
4.9	4.2	4.8		5.3	4.5	4.5	5.6	4.5	
2.6	2.4	2.8	Sales/Total Assets	2.8	2.6	3.4	2.4	2.8	
1.5	1.2	1.4		1.4	1.2	2.1	1.6	1.7	
(133) 1.2	(129) 1.3	(121) 1.4	% Depr., Dep., Amort./Sales	(41) 1.7	(34) 1.2	(15) .9	(13) .8	1.5	
3.4	2.9	2.7		4.6	3.2	2.8	2.8	2.4	
7.2	6.4	6.9		13.3	7.3	10.7	4.7	2.7	
(77) 2.6	(73) 2.9	(65) 2.6	% Officers', Directors',	(23) 4.4	(18) 2.5		2.0		
5.5	5.5	4.4	Owners' Comp/Sales	9.3	4.6		(11) 2.7		
9.1	9.6	9.2		12.8	8.1		4.0		
1410357M	1256007M	1030257M	Net Sales ($)	23618M	64149M	64193M	108561M	235733M	534003M
644535M	841481M	531101M	Total Assets ($)	15583M	37066M	24510M	47936M	102728M	303278M

M = $ thousand   MM = $ million
See Pages 11 through 18 for Explanation of Ratios and Data

Current Data Sorted By Assets   Comparative Historical Data

0-500M	500M-2MM	2-10MM	10-50MM	50-100MM	100-250MM	Type of Statement	4/1/98-3/31/99 ALL	4/1/99-3/31/00 ALL
	1					Unqualified		5
	4	5	3			Reviewed		8
1	1	1				Compiled		4
5	1	1		1		Tax Returns		
3	3	3	3			Other		5
	5 (4/1-9/30/02)		31 (10/1/02-3/31/03)					
9	10	10	6	1		NUMBER OF STATEMENTS		22
%	%	%	%	%	%	**ASSETS**	%	%
	6.1	8.7				Cash & Equivalents		5.4
	36.3	25.8				Trade Receivables (net)		30.5
	.3	6.4				Inventory		7.2
	.3	1.2				All Other Current		3.6
	43.0	42.1				Total Current		46.6
	42.0	34.7				Fixed Assets (net)		30.1
	6.0	.2				Intangibles (net)		3.7
	8.9	23.0				All Other Non-Current		19.5
	100.0	100.0				Total		100.0
						LIABILITIES		
	10.7	7.9				Notes Payable-Short Term		12.6
	2.5	3.4				Cur. Mat.-L/T/D		7.9
	10.4	7.8				Trade Payables		10.7
	.0	.1				Income Taxes Payable		.1
	5.2	7.5				All Other Current		12.3
	28.9	26.7				Total Current		43.7
	34.2	30.3				Long Term Debt		13.8
	.8	1.5				Deferred Taxes		1.1
	11.7	7.3				All Other Non-Current		9.6
	24.5	34.2				Net Worth		31.8
	100.0	100.0				Total Liabilities & Net Worth		100.0
						INCOME DATA		
	100.0	100.0				Net Sales		100.0
						Gross Profit		31.6
	82.3	82.6				Operating Expenses		23.1
	17.7	17.4				Operating Profit		8.5
	15.7	5.4				All Other Expenses (net)		3.1
	2.0	12.0				Profit Before Taxes		5.4

(Columns 10-50MM, 50-100MM, 100-250MM and 4/1/98-3/31/99 ALL for ASSETS / LIABILITIES: DATA NOT AVAILABLE)

0-500M	500M-2MM	2-10MM	10-50MM	50-100MM	100-250MM	RATIOS	4/1/98-3/31/99 ALL	4/1/99-3/31/00 ALL
	5.5	2.6				Current		1.6
	1.2	1.0						1.1
	.9	.3						.8
	5.5	2.6				Quick		1.5
	1.1	.6						1.0
	.8	.1						.5
	0 UND	0 UND				Sales/Receivables	30	12.1
	40 9.2	36 10.2					43	8.5
	56 6.5	45 8.2					64	5.7
						Cost of Sales/Inventory	0	UND
							0	UND
							14	25.8
						Cost of Sales/Payables	6	58.1
							18	20.7
							41	9.0
	8.1	10.2				Sales/Working Capital		20.3
	60.2	NM						54.3
	NM	-12.4						-36.8
						EBIT/Interest		7.8
							(17)	3.6
								2.5
						Net Profit + Depr., Dep., Amort./Cur. Mat. L /T/D		
	.3	.1				Fixed/Worth		.6
	1.2	.2						1.2
	NM	12.3						NM
	.8	.5				Debt/Worth		.8
	9.7	1.9						2.6
	NM	12.3						NM
						% Profit Before Taxes/Tangible Net Worth		51.6
							(17)	31.4
								11.3
	25.5	14.4				% Profit Before Taxes/Total Assets		14.2
	4.9	8.2						8.1
	.2	3.7						3.5
	395.5	210.2				Sales/Net Fixed Assets		69.1
	5.5	23.6						12.6
	1.0	2.6						2.4
	5.6	3.8				Sales/Total Assets		3.8
	1.7	3.1						1.6
	1.0	.3						1.0
						% Depr., Dep., Amort./Sales		.5
							(15)	2.1
								5.9
						% Officers', Directors', Owners' Comp/Sales		
7265M	29888M	91257M	264602M	141835M		Net Sales ($)		390622M
1229M	9791M	37841M	123420M	54861M		Total Assets ($)		219307M

M = $ thousand   MM = $ million
See Pages 11 through 18 for Explanation of Ratios and Data

Comparative Historical Data / Current Data Sorted By Sales

4/1/00-3/31/01 ALL	4/1/01-3/31/02 ALL	4/1/02-3/31/03 ALL	Type of Statement	0-1MM	1-3MM	3-5MM	5-10MM	10-25MM	25MM & OVER
2		1	Unqualified	1					
1		12	Reviewed	2	2		3	3	2
2	1	3	Compiled	2				1	
	1	8	Tax Returns	4				1	1
3	2	12	Other	3	3	1	3		2
						5 (4/1-9/30/02)		31 (10/1/02-3/31/03)	
8	4	36	**NUMBER OF STATEMENTS**	12	7	1	6	5	5
%	%	%	**ASSETS**	%	%	%	%	%	%
		9.1	Cash & Equivalents	6.7					
		28.4	Trade Receivables (net)	13.2					
		5.7	Inventory	.2					
		.9	All Other Current	1.2					
		44.1	Total Current	21.2					
		36.4	Fixed Assets (net)	62.8					
		3.3	Intangibles (net)	3.7					
		16.1	All Other Non-Current	12.2					
		100.0	Total	100.0					
			LIABILITIES						
		13.0	Notes Payable-Short Term	12.4					
		4.9	Cur. Mat.-L/T/D	11.2					
		14.3	Trade Payables	18.4					
		.0	Income Taxes Payable	.0					
		23.8	All Other Current	2.1					
		56.1	Total Current	44.1					
		39.4	Long Term Debt	58.9					
		.6	Deferred Taxes	.1					
		6.5	All Other Non-Current	4.0					
		-2.6	Net Worth	-7.2					
		100.0	Total Liabilities & Net Worth	100.0					
			INCOME DATA						
		100.0	Net Sales	100.0					
			Gross Profit						
		88.4	Operating Expenses	72.8					
		11.6	Operating Profit	27.2					
		7.2	All Other Expenses (net)	20.4					
		4.4	Profit Before Taxes	6.8					
			RATIOS						
		2.0 1.0 .5	Current	.9 .4 .2					
		2.0 .8 .4	Quick	.8 .4 .1					
	0 33 46	UND. 11.0 8.0	Sales/Receivables	0 UND 29 12.6					
			Cost of Sales/Inventory						
			Cost of Sales/Payables						
		9.0 151.2 -14.7	Sales/Working Capital	NM -12.6 -3.5					
	(22)	8.1 3.2 1.7	EBIT/Interest						
			Net Profit + Depr., Dep., Amort./Cur. Mat. L/T/D						
		.2 1.2 28.6	Fixed/Worth	1.6 5.3 -1.8					
		1.0 4.0 -20.2	Debt/Worth	2.2 21.2 -3.1					
	(26)	69.2 16.9 6.3	% Profit Before Taxes/Tangible Net Worth						
		13.8 5.6 1.1	% Profit Before Taxes/Total Assets	9.9 1.4 -11.9					
		139.2 11.3 2.7	Sales/Net Fixed Assets	8.5 2.4 .2					
		4.3 2.7 1.4	Sales/Total Assets	2.7 1.5 .2					
	(28)	.6 3.1 13.1	% Depr., Dep., Amort./Sales						
	(10)	1.4 8.0 23.2	% Officers', Directors', Owners' Comp/Sales						
209601M	63993M	534847M	Net Sales ($)	5304M	12989M	3893M	41117M	87116M	384428M
119638M	41262M	227142M	Total Assets ($)	11807M	20202M	944M	9878M	28446M	155865M

M = $ thousand   MM = $ million
See Pages 11 through 18 for Explanation of Ratios and Data

Current Data Sorted By Assets · Comparative Historical Data

	0-500M	500M-2MM	2-10MM	10-50MM	50-100MM	100-250MM	Type of Statement		4/1/98-3/31/99 ALL	4/1/99-3/31/00 ALL
	1	2	13	14	4	1	Unqualified		46	44
	1	11	34	12	1		Reviewed		63	62
	10	21	23	2			Compiled		67	74
	15	13	3				Tax Returns		12	27
	8	22	31	16	1	1	Other		63	59
		38 (4/1-9/30/02)		222 (10/1/02-3/31/03)						
	35	69	104	44	6	2	NUMBER OF STATEMENTS		251	266
	%	%	%	%	%	%	ASSETS		%	%
	15.9	6.4	7.5	7.6			Cash & Equivalents		11.4	11.1
	35.7	55.0	52.3	45.3			Trade Receivables (net)		49.4	50.6
	3.9	.8	1.3	.8			Inventory		.8	.7
	3.4	5.3	5.8	6.7			All Other Current		4.5	4.1
	59.0	67.4	66.8	60.3			Total Current		66.1	66.6
	22.6	22.2	20.7	29.0			Fixed Assets (net)		21.5	23.3
	4.1	2.0	4.9	2.0			Intangibles (net)		3.3	3.3
	14.3	8.4	7.7	8.6			All Other Non-Current		9.0	6.8
	100.0	100.0	100.0	100.0			Total		100.0	100.0
							LIABILITIES			
	12.7	10.7	12.7	7.4			Notes Payable-Short Term		14.1	14.3
	15.7	6.5	3.3	6.2			Cur. Mat.-L/T/D		3.6	4.2
	16.9	25.8	27.5	22.0			Trade Payables		27.8	37.9
	.1	.5	.2	.1			Income Taxes Payable		.4	.5
	27.5	9.9	13.8	9.4			All Other Current		10.7	12.2
	73.0	53.4	57.5	45.2			Total Current		56.5	69.2
	17.0	15.7	8.5	18.0			Long Term Debt		11.7	11.5
	.1	.7	.6	1.2			Deferred Taxes		.6	.6
	11.2	4.5	3.4	2.2			All Other Non-Current		3.2	9.8
	−1.3	25.6	29.9	33.4			Net Worth		27.9	8.9
	100.0	100.0	100.0	100.0			Total Liabilities & Net Worth		100.0	100.0
							INCOME DATA			
	100.0	100.0	100.0	100.0			Net Sales		100.0	100.0
							Gross Profit			
	96.6	98.6	96.5	94.2			Operating Expenses		94.5	96.0
	3.4	1.4	3.5	5.8			Operating Profit		5.5	4.0
	.9	.8	.3	1.2			All Other Expenses (net)		.9	1.0
	2.5	.6	3.2	4.5			Profit Before Taxes		4.6	3.0
							RATIOS			
	2.9	1.8	1.5	1.6					1.7	1.6
	1.2	1.2	1.1	1.3			Current		1.2	1.2
	.5	.9	.9	1.0					1.0	1.0
	2.1	1.6	1.3	1.5					1.5	1.6
	.7	1.2	1.0	1.1			Quick	(250)	1.1	1.1
	.4	.9	.8	.7					.9	.9
0 UND		24 15.1	33 11.1	32 11.5				26 13.9	26 14.0	
24 15.4		34 10.9	41 8.9	47 7.8			Sales/Receivables	45 8.1	42 8.6	
36 10.1		50 7.2	62 5.9	63 5.8				64 5.7	56 6.5	
							Cost of Sales/Inventory			
							Cost of Sales/Payables			
	13.5	20.4	14.1	8.1					12.4	13.6
	52.2	40.8	67.5	31.9			Sales/Working Capital		36.1	43.4
	−15.7	−134.7	−65.8	821.4					−245.8	−118.9
	10.2	20.4	15.2	10.6					13.3	13.7
(24)	2.6	(62) 3.1	(92) 3.7	(41) 3.8			EBIT/Interest	(207)	3.8	(226) 3.8
	−.1	−1.1	1.7	1.6					1.7	1.6
		4.8	4.8	7.5					7.1	8.8
		(11) 1.3	(31) 1.9	(15) 4.8			Net Profit + Depr., Dep., Amort./Cur. Mat. L /T/D	(67)	2.2	(65) 3.1
		−.5	.8	1.3					1.3	1.2
	.1	.1	.2	.3					.2	.2
	1.2	.4	.6	.7			Fixed/Worth		.6	.6
	−1.4	2.7	2.5	1.9					1.8	1.9
	1.5	.9	1.3	1.6					1.2	1.3
	4.0	2.9	3.0	2.1			Debt/Worth		2.8	2.8
	−4.0	15.8	7.0	4.6					7.5	7.6
	119.2	57.1	52.5	32.4			% Profit Before Taxes/Tangible Net Worth		62.1	64.1
(22)	29.5	(58) 13.3	(87) 22.1	(43) 14.6				(217)	28.7	(235) 29.2
	−3.5	−1.0	9.0	6.8					10.6	12.4
	21.7	15.5	13.7	9.3			% Profit Before Taxes/Total Assets		17.7	15.6
	5.1	4.9	5.5	3.5					7.3	7.0
	−3.2	−2.6	1.3	1.7					2.1	1.5
	307.6	155.1	95.4	43.2					130.0	174.7
	64.0	58.2	31.8	13.9			Sales/Net Fixed Assets		30.6	30.0
	10.9	11.0	9.5	6.4					8.6	8.4
	8.6	8.5	5.3	4.6					6.3	6.5
	5.7	5.4	3.9	3.0			Sales/Total Assets		4.2	4.3
	2.8	2.8	2.5	1.7					2.0	2.0
	.3	.2	.3	.5					.4	.3
(24)	.8	(60) .5	(94) .9	(40) 1.8			% Depr., Dep., Amort./Sales	(195)	1.2	(224) 1.0
	3.5	2.1	3.0	5.4					3.3	3.0
	3.0	1.2	.6				% Officers', Directors', Owners' Comp/Sales		1.6	1.4
(20)	7.2	(37) 2.6	(19) 2.0					(94)	4.0	(89) 2.9
	18.9	4.5	5.1						6.4	6.6
	56324M	500043M	2049167M	2796972M	917506M	130065M	Net Sales ($)		5650823M	6178361M
	8728M	85738M	506815M	843070M	387242M	255138M	Total Assets ($)		2209528M	2259138M

M = $ thousand MM = $ million
See Pages 11 through 18 for Explanation of Ratios and Data

Comparative Historical Data | **Current Data Sorted By Sales**

	H: 4/1/00-3/31/01 ALL	H: 4/1/01-3/31/02 ALL	H: 4/1/02-3/31/03 ALL	Type of Statement	0-1MM	1-3MM	3-5MM	5-10MM	10-25MM	25MM & OVER
	36	32	35	Unqualified			3	2	10	20
	44	50	59	Reviewed	3	5	3	9	17	22
	77	58	56	Compiled	2	11	8	11	18	6
	21	27	31	Tax Returns	12	4	5	5	4	1
	64	98	79	Other	4	11	8	16	16	24
						38 (4/1-9/30/02)			222 (10/1/02-3/31/03)	
NUMBER OF STATEMENTS	242	265	260		21	31	27	43	65	73
	%	%	%	**ASSETS**	%	%	%	%	%	%
Cash & Equivalents	9.6	9.0	8.3		18.0	8.9	5.4	9.1	6.4	7.5
Trade Receivables (net)	50.1	47.5	48.5		20.3	41.4	49.0	50.7	57.3	50.4
Inventory	.9	1.6	1.6		6.3	.7	1.2	1.1	.9	1.5
All Other Current	3.5	4.6	5.3		6.8	6.1	4.2	4.3	6.1	4.8
Total Current	64.1	62.6	63.7		51.4	57.2	59.8	65.3	70.6	64.3
Fixed Assets (net)	23.3	25.8	23.8		31.0	23.5	27.9	23.6	19.2	24.6
Intangibles (net)	4.2	3.3	3.5		2.0	4.0	2.5	4.4	4.0	3.1
All Other Non-Current	8.4	8.3	9.0		15.5	15.2	9.9	6.6	6.1	8.0
Total	100.0	100.0	100.0		100.0	100.0	100.0	100.0	100.0	100.0
				LIABILITIES						
Notes Payable-Short Term	10.2	12.8	10.9		11.1	10.2	8.5	11.6	14.9	8.2
Cur. Mat.-L/T/D	4.4	5.2	6.5		25.1	5.0	5.9	3.8	4.2	5.7
Trade Payables	26.4	24.4	24.2		6.8	18.6	20.2	27.2	26.6	29.3
Income Taxes Payable	.3	.2	.3		.1	1.0	.1	.1	.2	.2
All Other Current	12.9	11.5	13.6		32.1	17.5	8.3	12.0	13.1	9.8
Total Current	54.3	54.1	55.5		75.2	52.3	43.0	54.7	59.1	53.2
Long Term Debt	12.5	15.0	14.0		31.5	15.1	20.8	10.7	7.7	13.6
Deferred Taxes	.5	.7	.7		.2	.2	.8	.2	1.0	1.1
All Other Non-Current	4.5	4.4	4.5		9.0	12.4	.7	2.9	4.5	2.3
Net Worth	28.2	25.8	25.2		-16.0	20.0	34.6	31.6	27.7	29.7
Total Liabilities & Net Worth	100.0	100.0	100.0		100.0	100.0	100.0	100.0	100.0	100.0
				INCOME DATA						
Net Sales	100.0	100.0	100.0		100.0	100.0	100.0	100.0	100.0	100.0
Gross Profit										
Operating Expenses	95.6	95.9	96.6		92.0	96.7	93.7	97.1	98.2	97.3
Operating Profit	4.4	4.1	3.4		8.0	3.3	6.3	2.9	1.8	2.7
All Other Expenses (net)	.1	1.3	.7		2.4	.8	2.1	.1	.5	.3
Profit Before Taxes	4.3	2.9	2.6		5.6	2.4	4.2	2.8	1.4	2.4
				RATIOS						
Current	1.8	1.6	1.6		3.3	1.5	2.1	1.7	1.7	1.4
	1.2	1.1	1.2		1.5	1.0	1.3	1.2	1.2	1.1
	.9	.9	.9		.5	.6	.9	.9	.9	1.0
Quick	1.6	1.5	1.5		2.6	1.2	2.1	1.4	1.5	1.4
	1.1	1.0	1.1		.7	1.0	1.3	1.2	1.1	1.1
	.8	.8	.7		.3	.5	.7	.9	.8	.8
Sales/Receivables	26 13.9	27 13.5	26 13.8		0 UND	14 26.0	29 12.6	30 12.3	29 12.4	30 12.3
	41 9.0	38 9.6	38 9.6		7 55.2	35 10.4	47 7.8	37 9.8	38 9.7	41 8.9
	62 5.9	56 6.5	55 6.6		57 6.4	105 3.5	87 4.2	60 6.0	50 7.3	52 7.0
Cost of Sales/Inventory										
Cost of Sales/Payables										
Sales/Working Capital	13.0	16.3	17.0		2.5	17.4	7.1	12.6	17.7	19.4
	44.5	70.3	52.6		18.4	-76.5	25.9	27.5	63.1	65.8
	-79.7	-44.3	-71.7		-20.4	-13.0	-88.0	-189.8	-48.1	-454.3
EBIT/Interest	(209) 15.1	(232) 10.1	(226) 13.6		(14) 5.2	(25) 11.9	(20) 24.9	(39) 20.0	(60) 12.1	(68) 12.0
	4.2	2.7	3.4		1.6	3.6	2.4	5.0	3.2	3.7
	1.4	1.0	1.2		-.5	-.3	1.1	1.8	.0	1.8
Net Profit + Depr., Dep., Amort./Cur. Mat. L/T/D	(48) 10.3	(59) 5.9	(63) 4.9						(20) 4.8	(29) 6.1
	2.7	1.8	1.7						1.4	2.4
	1.4	.9	.8						.4	1.2
Fixed/Worth	.2	.2	.2		.1	.2	.1	.1	.2	.3
	.5	.8	.6		.8	.5	.4	.5	.9	.6
	2.2	2.9	2.7		-1.9	-10.0	3.1	1.5	3.0	2.2
Debt/Worth	1.2	1.5	1.4		.8	1.5	1.2	.9	1.1	1.7
	3.0	3.2	2.9		3.3	5.2	2.7	2.7	2.7	2.9
	8.3	8.0	7.3		-3.9	-23.7	5.0	6.6	18.5	5.4
% Profit Before Taxes/Tangible Net Worth	(208) 57.9	(226) 52.5	(218) 52.9		(14) 60.0	(22) 103.8	(24) 80.2	(38) 61.6	(53) 40.0	(67) 38.6
	29.5	20.1	18.5		3.9	23.2	20.5	33.5	19.9	14.9
	9.9	2.9	4.9		-7.6	-6.1	5.2	9.5	3.7	6.7
% Profit Before Taxes/Total Assets	17.8	12.1	13.1		11.4	20.8	16.6	13.9	11.4	10.9
	6.7	4.5	5.0		1.8	5.1	7.3	6.1	5.1	3.8
	1.7	.0	.6		-3.2	-2.8	.3	2.9	-.7	1.7
Sales/Net Fixed Assets	148.1	113.5	110.9		56.2	86.4	80.6	162.6	122.6	66.3
	28.9	28.9	32.4		9.2	29.4	34.7	30.3	59.9	29.2
	9.0	6.9	8.2		3.9	9.8	3.7	6.9	13.7	9.3
Sales/Total Assets	6.5	6.2	6.0		3.7	6.1	5.4	6.2	6.9	5.7
	4.0	3.9	4.1		2.2	3.7	2.5	4.2	4.7	4.5
	2.1	2.1	2.3		.6	1.8	.8	2.7	3.3	2.7
% Depr., Dep., Amort./Sales	(204) .3	(210) .3	(223) .3		(15) .8	(22) .4	(25) .2	(35) .3	(61) .2	(65) .3
	1.0	1.1	.8		6.0	1.4	1.0	1.0	.7	.8
	3.0	3.4	3.3		8.5	5.8	5.3	2.8	2.6	2.6
% Officers', Directors', Owners' Comp/Sales	(81) 2.0	(92) 1.4	(85) 1.2		(12) 3.5	(17) 3.1		(18) 1.2	(19) .7	(10) .7
	3.8	3.1	3.2		11.0	4.0		3.3	1.3	1.6
	8.6	9.3	5.7		22.9	7.6		4.9	2.6	2.4
Net Sales ($)	10580716M	8154428M	6450077M		10224M	64108M	109673M	311933M	1037612M	4916527M
Total Assets ($)	2591831M	3191010M	2086731M		10337M	31250M	122025M	104597M	285807M	1532715M

M = $ thousand   MM = $ million
See Pages 11 through 18 for Explanation of Ratios and Data

Current Data Sorted By Assets							Comparative Historical Data	
						Type of Statement		
2	1	2				Unqualified	2	4
1	1	8	1			Reviewed	12	8
1	3	1	2			Compiled	9	16
5	2					Tax Returns	2	2
3	7	5	6			Other	11	9
	8 (4/1-9/30/02)		43 (10/1/02-3/31/03)				**4/1/98-3/31/99 ALL**	**4/1/99-3/31/00 ALL**
0-500M	**500M-2MM**	**2-10MM**	**10-50MM**	**50-100MM**	**100-250MM**			
12	14	16	9			**NUMBER OF STATEMENTS**	36	39
%	%	%	%	%	%	**ASSETS**	%	%
20.1	6.5	11.1		DATA NOT AVAILABLE	DATA NOT AVAILABLE	Cash & Equivalents	8.0	10.7
36.2	34.9	25.8				Trade Receivables (net)	34.7	30.1
7.6	9.9	13.1				Inventory	12.7	12.2
1.2	2.0	1.4				All Other Current	2.6	7.1
65.0	53.2	51.5				Total Current	58.1	60.1
21.6	39.7	40.2				Fixed Assets (net)	32.3	27.5
8.0	2.1	3.2				Intangibles (net)	4.3	3.3
5.4	5.1	5.1				All Other Non-Current	5.2	9.1
100.0	100.0	100.0				Total	100.0	100.0
						LIABILITIES		
14.0	8.7	7.2				Notes Payable-Short Term	10.0	8.2
11.3	3.7	6.4				Cur. Mat.-L/T/D	3.3	5.0
17.9	27.0	11.1				Trade Payables	15.8	13.2
.0	.2	.0				Income Taxes Payable	.3	.1
17.5	4.1	5.3				All Other Current	11.2	11.5
60.8	43.7	30.0				Total Current	40.7	38.1
15.1	26.7	22.2				Long Term Debt	19.5	15.1
.0	.0	.0				Deferred Taxes	.1	.3
5.8	2.5	.4				All Other Non-Current	1.7	29.1
18.3	27.1	47.3				Net Worth	37.9	17.5
100.0	100.0	100.0				Total Liabilities & Net Worth	100.0	100.0
						INCOME DATA		
100.0	100.0	100.0				Net Sales	100.0	100.0
						Gross Profit		
95.3	95.9	93.0				Operating Expenses	92.1	95.0
4.7	4.1	7.0				Operating Profit	7.9	5.0
1.1	1.2	1.4				All Other Expenses (net)	1.7	.9
3.6	2.9	5.6				Profit Before Taxes	6.1	4.2
						RATIOS		
1.7	2.0	2.3					2.5	2.7
1.1	1.2	1.5				Current	1.5	1.9
.7	.8	1.2					.9	1.0
1.5	1.4	1.5					1.8	1.9
.8	.9	1.1				Quick	.9	1.0
.6	.6	.8					.7	.7
12 29.3	**25** 14.7	**19** 19.0					**28** 12.8	**17** 20.9
28 13.0	**47** 7.8	**37** 9.9				Sales/Receivables	**43** 8.5	**38** 9.5
42 8.7	**61** 6.0	**53** 6.8					**65** 5.7	**59** 6.2
						Cost of Sales/Inventory		
						Cost of Sales/Payables		
21.6	11.2	7.3					6.4	5.6
117.4	50.7	16.4				Sales/Working Capital	16.0	19.3
−24.1	−29.7	37.3					−68.2	UND
	8.4	13.5					11.8	15.6
	(12) 2.6	(13) 5.0				EBIT/Interest	(29) 6.0	(29) 4.6
	.7	3.5					1.8	1.6
								3.2
						Net Profit + Depr., Dep., Amort./Cur. Mat. L /T/D		(11) 1.9
								−.3
.3	.2	.3					.3	.3
1.7	1.6	.8				Fixed/Worth	.8	.9
NM	4.9	2.8					2.9	2.2
1.3	.8	.5					.8	.8
5.7	2.6	1.1				Debt/Worth	1.7	2.1
NM	22.8	2.8					4.3	4.4
	47.5	36.0					58.6	65.5
	(12) 18.5	(15) 25.2				% Profit Before Taxes/Tangible Net Worth	(30) 38.4	(31) 16.7
	−7.3	8.2					12.5	2.4
25.6	20.7	19.5					28.5	25.1
12.3	3.7	14.1				% Profit Before Taxes/Total Assets	14.7	7.5
3.6	−1.2	2.9					3.8	.0
127.1	29.4	22.1					22.6	36.6
32.4	11.1	6.3				Sales/Net Fixed Assets	11.7	15.6
12.1	3.1	2.9					4.2	6.2
8.5	3.8	3.1					3.8	4.0
4.5	3.0	2.3				Sales/Total Assets	2.7	2.8
3.3	2.0	1.7					2.0	2.1
	.7	1.1					.9	1.1
	(10) 1.7	2.0				% Depr., Dep., Amort./Sales	(32) 2.1	(33) 2.2
	7.1	4.3					4.5	4.4
							3.5	2.7
						% Officers', Directors', Owners' Comp/Sales	(17) 6.0	(15) 5.3
							10.2	11.1
18352M	**43893M**	**221854M**	**482560M**			Net Sales ($)	**407493M**	**399244M**
2769M	**14993M**	**78958M**	**192838M**			Total Assets ($)	**185734M**	**148346M**

M = $ thousand MM = $ million

See Pages 11 through 18 for Explanation of Ratios and Data

Comparative Historical Data | Current Data Sorted By Sales

			Type of Statement						
4	4	5	Unqualified	1	1	1		1	1
9	12	11	Reviewed		2	1	1	4	3
8	5	7	Compiled		3	2		1	1
1	3	7	Tax Returns	3	2	2			
12	16	21	Other	2	6	3	3	1	6
4/1/00-3/31/01 ALL	4/1/01-3/31/02 ALL	4/1/02-3/31/03 ALL		8 (4/1-9/30/02)			43 (10/1/02-3/31/03)		
				0-1MM	1-3MM	3-5MM	5-10MM	10-25MM	25MM & OVER
34	40	51	**NUMBER OF STATEMENTS**	6	14	9	4	7	11
%	%	%	**ASSETS**	%	%	%	%	%	%
6.0	8.7	10.4	Cash & Equivalents		7.4				6.0
35.5	31.9	31.3	Trade Receivables (net)		38.8				33.4
16.0	14.4	13.0	Inventory		9.1				26.4
2.4	4.6	1.9	All Other Current		1.3				3.3
59.9	59.6	56.7	Total Current		56.6				69.0
28.6	30.9	33.6	Fixed Assets (net)		36.1				21.9
2.0	4.5	4.8	Intangibles (net)		2.3				6.5
9.5	5.0	4.9	All Other Non-Current		5.0				2.6
100.0	100.0	100.0	Total		100.0				100.0
			LIABILITIES						
11.1	11.4	9.3	Notes Payable-Short Term		8.7				7.7
6.3	6.8	6.2	Cur. Mat.-L/T/D		10.6				2.1
14.4	13.8	18.8	Trade Payables		17.3				21.1
.3	.1	.3	Income Taxes Payable		.2				1.1
7.3	12.9	9.0	All Other Current		8.0				11.1
39.5	45.1	43.7	Total Current		44.7				43.1
11.8	17.9	20.4	Long Term Debt		25.9				10.1
.2	.2	.0	Deferred Taxes		.0				.1
10.1	8.9	3.2	All Other Non-Current		1.3				4.7
38.4	27.9	32.7	Net Worth		28.1				42.1
100.0	100.0	100.0	Total Liabilities & Net Worth		100.0				100.0
			INCOME DATA						
100.0	100.0	100.0	Net Sales		100.0				100.0
			Gross Profit						
94.7	94.4	94.7	Operating Expenses		96.6				94.3
5.3	5.6	5.3	Operating Profit		3.4				5.7
1.1	2.3	1.2	All Other Expenses (net)		.9				.7
4.2	3.3	4.1	Profit Before Taxes		2.5				5.0
			RATIOS						
2.6	2.1	2.0			2.0				3.1
1.5	1.3	1.4	Current		1.1				1.4
1.0	.9	.9			.9				1.4
1.7	1.3	1.3			1.7				1.7
1.0	.9	.9	Quick		.9				.8
.7	.6	.6			.7				.6
33 10.9	29 12.5	20 18.5		31 11.7				26 14.1	
53 6.9	43 8.4	39 9.4	Sales/Receivables	47 7.8				46 7.9	
71 5.1	57 6.4	56 6.5		62 5.9				58 6.3	
			Cost of Sales/Inventory						
			Cost of Sales/Payables						
5.8	7.5	11.6			15.3				10.7
16.9	20.1	22.7	Sales/Working Capital		54.6				12.8
-282.1	-55.6	-55.4			-30.2				17.0
14.1	9.5	11.1			6.4				104.5
(25) 3.9	(35) 3.2	(43) 3.7	EBIT/Interest	(13) 2.2				(10) 4.5	
.9	1.1	1.8			1.0				2.2
		21.6	Net Profit + Depr., Dep.,						
	(11) 3.2		Amort./Cur. Mat. L/T/D						
	1.3								
.3	.4	.3			.5				.2
.6	1.2	1.2	Fixed/Worth		2.1				.5
1.3	NM	3.3			4.3				1.4
.9	1.1	.7			1.2				.3
1.6	2.2	2.3	Debt/Worth		3.4				2.0
3.2	NM	6.3			22.8				3.4
40.3	40.5	48.6			82.3				60.0
(30) 17.8	(30) 24.1	(44) 30.7	% Profit Before Taxes/Tangible Net Worth	(12) 23.1				(10) 31.2	
7.1	9.4	7.2			5.9				12.3
14.8	14.2	19.8			5.7				20.8
7.1	7.3	8.3	% Profit Before Taxes/Total Assets		3.5				8.3
.1	1.6	2.1			.4				2.2
23.6	27.2	35.8			31.2				49.2
15.7	12.4	10.0	Sales/Net Fixed Assets		11.0				25.0
5.2	4.1	4.2			3.1				8.4
3.4	3.6	4.0			4.0				4.0
2.7	2.8	2.9	Sales/Total Assets		2.9				3.1
1.8	1.3	2.1			2.0				2.7
.9	1.2	.9			1.4				.5
(33) 1.8	(36) 2.3	(43) 1.8	% Depr., Dep., Amort./Sales	(11) 2.1				(10) 1.3	
2.7	4.1	4.3			6.6				1.6
3.8	1.5	1.9							
(16) 5.0	(19) 3.4	(24) 4.7	% Officers', Directors', Owners' Comp/Sales						
11.0	5.2	7.7							
374749M	554153M	766659M	Net Sales ($)	2716M	30724M	36344M	25976M	98937M	571962M
140862M	225038M	289558M	Total Assets ($)	1934M	11961M	12975M	10103M	46715M	205870M

M = $ thousand   MM = $ million
See Pages 11 through 18 for Explanation of Ratios and Data

Current Data Sorted By Assets　　　　　　　　Comparative Historical Data

0-500M	500M-2MM	2-10MM	10-50MM	50-100MM	100-250MM	Type of Statement	13	10
2	2	5	9	2	2	Unqualified	13	10
	8	8	3	1		Reviewed	17	13
9	11	4	1			Compiled	23	22
5	5	7			1	Tax Returns	16	7
3	13	10	6	1	1	Other	19	27
13 (4/1-9/30/02)			**106 (10/1/02-3/31/03)**				**4/1/98- 3/31/99 ALL**	**4/1/99- 3/31/00 ALL**
19	39	34	19	4	4	**NUMBER OF STATEMENTS**	88	79
%	%	%	%	%	%	**ASSETS**	%	%
5.5	14.2	8.2	6.9			Cash & Equivalents	6.4	13.1
26.3	34.8	33.4	21.2			Trade Receivables (net)	30.9	28.4
8.7	6.7	4.9	3.0			Inventory	4.0	6.1
6.3	4.6	2.2	7.4			All Other Current	3.5	2.2
46.8	60.3	48.7	38.5			Total Current	44.7	49.8
39.7	28.8	43.8	42.0			Fixed Assets (net)	46.5	40.3
3.3	2.1	2.6	7.1			Intangibles (net)	2.2	3.1
10.1	8.8	4.9	12.5			All Other Non-Current	6.6	6.9
100.0	100.0	100.0	100.0			Total	100.0	100.0
						LIABILITIES		
30.5	11.7	7.0	8.4			Notes Payable-Short Term	9.2	9.0
17.1	6.7	7.1	4.7			Cur. Mat.-L/T/D	8.0	9.3
14.5	24.7	13.5	7.8			Trade Payables	14.0	14.1
.7	.2	.0	.7			Income Taxes Payable	.3	.3
10.3	15.4	11.1	14.1			All Other Current	7.2	16.6
73.1	58.7	38.7	35.7			Total Current	38.6	49.3
47.0	13.5	32.2	15.0			Long Term Debt	29.3	20.3
.0	.5	.1	1.4			Deferred Taxes	1.1	1.0
8.1	5.4	3.9	2.6			All Other Non-Current	2.8	5.2
−28.2	21.9	25.0	45.2			Net Worth	28.1	24.2
100.0	100.0	100.0	100.0			Total Liabilities & Net Worth	100.0	100.0
						INCOME DATA		
100.0	100.0	100.0	100.0			Net Sales	100.0	100.0
						Gross Profit		
94.5	97.4	86.9	89.8			Operating Expenses	91.7	92.4
5.5	2.6	13.1	10.2			Operating Profit	8.3	7.6
3.8	.6	4.1	.5			All Other Expenses (net)	3.7	1.1
1.7	2.0	9.0	9.7			Profit Before Taxes	4.6	6.5
						RATIOS		
1.0	1.7	1.7	1.5			Current	1.9	1.7
.6	1.3	1.2	1.2				1.3	1.1
.2	.7	.7	.6				.6	.7
.9	1.5	1.5	1.4			Quick	1.6	1.6
.5	1.0	1.0	.7				1.0	.9
.1	.2	.5	.5				.5	.4
0 UND	0 UND	17 21.9	26 14.0			Sales/Receivables	27 13.4	16 23.5
14 26.6	33 10.9	39 9.5	37 9.8				41 8.8	35 10.5
31 11.8	58 6.3	62 5.9	49 7.4				60 6.1	51 7.2
						Cost of Sales/Inventory		
						Cost of Sales/Payables		
−856.0	7.6	9.4	10.9			Sales/Working Capital	10.5	11.4
−20.2	29.9	48.6	26.6				41.5	39.2
−14.6	−16.7	−17.8	−10.4				−17.9	−25.2
(17) 3.6	(32) 15.2	(30) 17.8	(15) 17.4			EBIT/Interest	(74) 7.0	(69) 7.4
1.2	2.5	4.4	2.7				3.2	2.3
−2.1	.5	1.6	1.3				1.7	.7
						Net Profit + Depr., Dep., Amort./Cur. Mat. L /T/D	(35) 6.8	(19) 2.6
							2.2	1.5
							1.0	.7
.9	.2	.7	.6			Fixed/Worth	.4	.5
UND	.7	1.6	1.0				1.3	1.3
−.4	−19.2	11.5	2.3				7.8	4.0
2.7	1.1	1.3	.6			Debt/Worth	1.2	1.0
−10.0	2.9	2.8	1.5				2.6	2.9
−2.8	−24.9	14.8	3.9				10.7	10.3
	43.1	60.4	40.8			% Profit Before Taxes/Tangible Net Worth	48.6	50.3
	(29) 28.9	(29) 22.0	(18) 11.1				(74) 23.0	(65) 18.9
	.4	7.9	5.5				7.6	7.4
21.3	13.7	16.3	7.9			% Profit Before Taxes/Total Assets	18.2	15.3
3.0	5.0	5.6	5.6				7.4	4.5
−14.9	−.7	2.0	1.3				1.4	−1.3
71.7	73.5	34.9	16.4			Sales/Net Fixed Assets	19.0	21.7
13.1	18.9	4.6	5.7				5.3	9.8
3.8	6.2	2.2	1.4				1.9	2.3
6.2	5.6	4.2	3.1			Sales/Total Assets	3.8	3.9
4.0	3.7	2.0	1.5				2.2	2.3
2.3	1.6	1.1	.9				1.2	1.2
(12) .6	1.1	.9	1.6			% Depr., Dep., Amort./Sales	2.0	1.3
6.0	(30) 3.6	(32) 2.6	(18) 3.6				(79) 4.2	(66) 3.6
11.4	9.6	15.1	6.4				8.1	7.6
	1.6	1.5				% Officers', Directors', Owners' Comp/Sales	2.0	2.0
	(15) 3.2	(11) 2.3					(30) 3.4	(30) 3.7
	4.7						7.0	8.6
19540M	182889M	404659M	763420M	371402M	1069870M	Net Sales ($)	1395993M	1027514M
4498M	44968M	148706M	429712M	284045M	669223M	Total Assets ($)	904940M	729719M

© RMA 2003

M = $ thousand　　MM = $ million
See Pages 11 through 18 for Explanation of Ratios and Data

Comparative Historical Data   Current Data Sorted By Sales

				Type of Statement						
11	10		20	Unqualified	1	2	2	2	6	7
17	17		22	Reviewed	1	5	2	4	6	4
27	26		25	Compiled	8	3	3	6	3	2
11	16		18	Tax Returns	3	5	3	4	2	1
25	25		34	Other	6	6	4	5	4	9
4/1/00- 3/31/01 ALL	4/1/01- 3/31/02 ALL		4/1/02- 3/31/03 ALL		0-1MM	1-3MM	3-5MM	5-10MM	10-25MM	25MM & OVER
					13 (4/1-9/30/02)			106 (10/1/02-3/31/03)		
91	94		119	NUMBER OF STATEMENTS	19	21	14	21	21	23
%	%		%	ASSETS	%	%	%	%	%	%
7.4	7.2		9.5	Cash & Equivalents	6.1	8.4	12.5	13.1	10.6	7.2
30.5	27.9		29.5	Trade Receivables (net)	21.6	18.2	38.0	35.3	31.0	34.4
6.3	4.9		6.1	Inventory	5.2	5.9	13.1	7.2	2.3	5.2
4.7	6.6		4.7	All Other Current	1.8	6.8	5.6	2.5	5.6	6.0
48.9	46.6		49.8	Total Current	34.8	39.3	69.2	58.1	49.5	52.8
39.9	39.8		38.6	Fixed Assets (net)	53.4	47.0	15.0	36.1	42.3	32.0
3.3	4.8		3.3	Intangibles (net)	3.8	3.3	1.8	1.4	1.4	7.3
7.8	8.9		8.3	All Other Non-Current	8.0	10.4	14.0	4.5	6.8	7.9
100.0	100.0		100.0	Total	100.0	100.0	100.0	100.0	100.0	100.0
				LIABILITIES						
14.0	9.5		12.3	Notes Payable-Short Term	21.1	8.2	27.0	9.7	4.9	9.0
8.6	7.9		8.3	Cur. Mat.-L/T/D	16.8	6.0	9.2	6.5	6.1	6.1
15.8	12.2		15.9	Trade Payables	8.5	13.7	21.9	20.0	19.4	13.6
.2	.2		.3	Income Taxes Payable	.4	.4	.1	.1	.1	.6
11.0	12.6		12.7	All Other Current	12.6	16.8	6.8	14.0	12.0	12.0
49.6	42.4		49.6	Total Current	59.5	45.3	64.9	50.2	42.4	41.9
24.5	25.5		27.3	Long Term Debt	45.6	36.2	15.7	17.3	17.1	29.8
.5	1.0		.6	Deferred Taxes	.1	.8	.0	.2	1.2	1.2
3.7	3.7		5.6	All Other Non-Current	8.9	5.3	6.1	2.4	3.7	7.7
21.6	27.4		16.8	Net Worth	−13.9	12.5	13.3	29.8	35.5	19.5
100.0	100.0		100.0	Total Liabilities & Net Worth	100.0	100.0	100.0	100.0	100.0	100.0
				INCOME DATA						
100.0	100.0		100.0	Net Sales	100.0	100.0	100.0	100.0	100.0	100.0
				Gross Profit						
93.2	91.8		92.4	Operating Expenses	89.2	91.9	85.7	94.8	95.2	94.7
6.8	8.2		7.6	Operating Profit	10.8	8.1	14.3	5.2	4.8	5.3
1.6	2.7		2.6	All Other Expenses (net)	6.2	3.5	1.1	1.0	1.1	2.4
5.2	5.4		5.1	Profit Before Taxes	4.5	4.6	13.2	4.2	3.8	2.9
				RATIOS						
1.4	1.7		1.7		1.0	1.5	1.8	1.7	2.1	1.8
1.0	1.1		1.2	Current	.6	.9	1.4	1.3	1.2	1.3
.5	.7		.6		.2	.5	.5	.8	.7	1.1
1.2	1.4		1.4		1.0	1.3	1.4	1.4	1.8	1.5
.7	(93) .9		.9	Quick	.3	.6	.8	.9	1.0	1.0
.3	.3		.4		.1	.1	.1	.5	.5	.6

22	16.4	4	92.6	9	42.6		0	UND	0	UND	0	UND	14	25.7	12	30.8	27	13.7

Sales/Receivables:

	0-1MM	1-3MM	3-5MM	5-10MM	10-25MM	25MM & OVER
22 / 38 / 51	16.4 / 9.5 / 7.2					
4 / 30 / 55	92.6 / 12.2 / 6.6					
9 / 31 / 52	42.6 / 11.8 / 7.0					
0 15 29	UND 23.7 12.4	0 14 62 — UND 26.6 5.9	0 36 58 — UND 10.3 6.3	14 47 79 — 25.7 7.8 4.6	12 38 52 — 30.8 9.7 7.0	27 37 49 — 13.7 9.8 7.4

Cost of Sales/Inventory (no data)

Cost of Sales/Payables (no data)

Sales/Working Capital:

14.7 / −162.8 / −8.8	19.0 / 78.7 / −19.5		10.9 / 48.0 / −16.6		−856.0 / −16.0 / −1.3	6.7 / −62.7 / −15.7	7.5 / 21.5 / −9.1	9.0 / 36.0 / −38.7	8.1 / 39.8 / −27.5	10.9 / 22.0 / 78.0

EBIT/Interest:

(77) 4.5 / 1.8 / .7	(77) 5.6 / 2.2 / 1.1	(98) 8.8 / 2.7 / 1.0	(17) 8.7 / 1.2 / −1.1	(17) 2.2 / 1.0 / −1.3	(11) 10.3 / 1.9 / 1.1	(18) 18.0 / 3.8 / 2.0	(17) 28.0 / 5.0 / 2.8	(18) 16.9 / 2.8 / 1.4

Net Profit + Depr., Dep., Amort./Cur. Mat. L/T/D:

(18) 2.8 / 1.2 / .4	(23) 3.7 / 2.2 / 1.0	(19) 3.8 / 1.5 / .6

Fixed/Worth:

.6 / 2.4 / 9.2	.5 / 1.4 / 5.3	.6 / 1.3 / 21.3	.9 / 3.8 / −1.0	.7 / 1.6 / −3.9	.1 / .4 / −.6	.4 / 1.0 / 6.0	.4 / 1.0 / 4.7	.4 / 1.4 / 2.2

Debt/Worth:

1.9 / 4.4 / 18.8	.9 / 3.0 / 25.7	1.2 / 3.0 / 166.3	1.7 / 22.0 / −3.5	1.7 / 8.7 / −10.5	1.3 / 2.7 / −2.8	1.1 / 2.6 / 7.5	1.0 / 2.9 / 6.0	1.0 / 2.1 / 3.7

% Profit Before Taxes/Tangible Net Worth:

(74) 57.7 / 22.9 / 3.6	(76) 49.2 / 16.8 / 4.9	(91) 56.2 / 20.7 / 5.4	(11) 78.4 / 32.1 / .0	(14) 48.7 / 9.8 / −10.8	(10) 44.4 / 22.9 / 6.0	(17) 65.6 / 30.8 / 6.1	(20) 52.3 / 21.3 / 8.7	(19) 43.1 / 19.8 / 5.4

% Profit Before Taxes/Total Assets:

14.9 / 4.1 / −1.1	16.4 / 5.5 / .6	13.8 / 5.3 / .4	21.3 / 2.9 / −13.0	7.8 / 3.0 / −5.4	24.3 / 6.5 / .4	16.3 / 8.4 / 2.5	13.0 / 5.8 / 3.9	7.9 / 5.6 / 1.3

Sales/Net Fixed Assets:

26.5 / 6.9 / 2.7	31.0 / 10.1 / 2.9	39.8 / 8.6 / 2.5	28.4 / 2.9 / .9	18.4 / 7.2 / 2.5	381.7 / 42.6 / 27.5	38.9 / 6.2 / 3.1	38.6 / 7.8 / 1.4	31.3 / 10.3 / 3.0

Sales/Total Assets:

3.7 / 2.3 / 1.3	4.7 / 2.6 / 1.5	4.9 / 2.5 / 1.3	3.7 / 1.9 / .8	4.8 / 2.0 / .9	7.2 / 3.7 / 2.1	4.7 / 3.3 / 1.5	5.8 / 3.1 / 1.0	4.1 / 2.9 / 1.4

% Depr., Dep., Amort./Sales:

(79) 1.1 / 4.3 / 8.8	(81) 1.0 / 3.1 / 8.3	(94) 1.1 / 3.4 / 9.6	(13) 4.4 / 11.0 / 29.4	(17) 4.2 / 7.6 / 19.7	(10) .8 / 1.2 / 4.3	(19) .9 / 2.5 / 8.6	(18) 1.1 / 1.9 / 9.0	(17) .6 / 1.5 / 3.6

% Officers', Directors', Owners' Comp/Sales:

(35) 2.5 / 4.8 / 6.2	(34) 1.7 / 3.7 / 5.4	(35) 1.6 / 3.3 / 5.6

1922871M	1222934M	2811780M	Net Sales ($)	11950M	36018M	55183M	144955M	331587M	2232087M
1221369M	744731M	1581152M	Total Assets ($)	14066M	31914M	62144M	65607M	255342M	1152079M

M = $ thousand   MM = $ million
See Pages 11 through 18 for Explanation of Ratios and Data

Current Data Sorted By Assets   Comparative Historical Data

0-500M	500M-2MM	2-10MM	10-50MM	50-100MM	100-250MM	Type of Statement	4/1/98-3/31/99 ALL	4/1/99-3/31/00 ALL
1	1	1	4	1	1	Unqualified	9	16
3	5	7				Reviewed	14	16
9	3	4				Compiled	21	21
4	5				1	Tax Returns	6	5
	5	6	3		1	Other	27	21
10 (4/1-9/30/02)			55 (10/1/02-3/31/03)					
17	19	18	7	1	3	**NUMBER OF STATEMENTS**	77	79
%	%	%	%	%	%	**ASSETS**	%	%
9.3	4.9	5.8				Cash & Equivalents	9.2	9.2
25.3	44.0	50.6				Trade Receivables (net)	36.0	33.0
1.3	3.4	1.4				Inventory	.9	2.1
2.9	7.7	3.0				All Other Current	3.0	2.0
38.9	60.1	60.9				Total Current	49.1	46.3
40.6	24.4	22.0				Fixed Assets (net)	34.3	39.6
4.4	5.0	8.9				Intangibles (net)	8.5	6.9
16.0	10.5	8.1				All Other Non-Current	8.1	7.3
100.0	100.0	100.0				Total	100.0	100.0
						LIABILITIES		
12.5	15.1	18.1				Notes Payable-Short Term	7.6	12.4
8.7	4.6	7.4				Cur. Mat.-L/T/D	8.4	6.7
13.4	16.1	21.2				Trade Payables	13.8	14.3
2.1	.0	.1				Income Taxes Payable	.8	.9
11.7	14.9	9.1				All Other Current	10.6	9.0
48.4	50.7	56.0				Total Current	41.2	43.3
40.8	12.9	12.0				Long Term Debt	22.1	24.1
.4	.1	.3				Deferred Taxes	.4	.8
7.1	4.8	7.7				All Other Non-Current	3.3	5.2
3.4	31.5	24.0				Net Worth	33.0	26.6
100.0	100.0	100.0				Total Liabilities & Net Worth	100.0	100.0
						INCOME DATA		
100.0	100.0	100.0				Net Sales	100.0	100.0
						Gross Profit		
95.7	98.0	97.0				Operating Expenses	93.4	94.7
4.3	2.0	3.0				Operating Profit	6.6	5.3
3.4	.9	.2				All Other Expenses (net)	1.4	1.9
.9	1.1	2.8				Profit Before Taxes	5.1	3.4
						RATIOS		
1.5	2.0	1.8					1.7	1.7
.7	1.3	1.1				Current	1.2	1.1
.2	.7	.8					.8	.7
1.3	1.6	1.6					1.6	1.5
.7	.8	1.1				Quick	1.0	1.0
.2	.5	.8					.7	.6
0 UND	25 14.4	34 10.9					22 16.4	25 14.7
16 22.4	30 12.3	40 9.1				Sales/Receivables	33 11.2	34 10.7
33 10.9	42 8.8	50 7.3					49 7.4	48 7.6
						Cost of Sales/Inventory		
						Cost of Sales/Payables		
58.5	12.8	14.4					14.7	17.6
-53.9	53.6	53.6				Sales/Working Capital	62.0	88.0
-16.9	-21.2	-25.2					-35.2	-20.8
12.4	6.8	10.9					8.6	6.8
(16) 1.2	2.1	(16) 3.1				EBIT/Interest	(66) 3.6	(73) 2.7
-1.8	.1	1.9					1.9	1.2
						Net Profit + Depr., Dep., Amort./Cur. Mat. L /T/D	4.4 / (25) 2.1 / 1.5	4.8 / (25) 1.8 / .7
1.4	.2	.4					.6	.6
-4.3	.8	1.5				Fixed/Worth	1.6	1.5
-1.2	3.5	-66.6					5.1	5.4
3.6	1.0	2.2					1.3	1.2
-13.4	2.1	3.6				Debt/Worth	3.3	3.3
-5.5	31.6	-160.5					9.0	12.4
	61.3	77.0					87.8	59.2
	(17) 12.8	(13) 34.6				% Profit Before Taxes/Tangible Net Worth	(63) 47.2	(64) 22.7
	-12.4	10.8					17.8	6.7
27.9	18.9	17.0					23.0	14.7
2.0	5.2	6.5				% Profit Before Taxes/Total Assets	9.0	5.8
-12.0	-2.4	2.1					3.3	.4
66.1	71.1	75.0					30.5	25.7
11.4	33.4	22.9				Sales/Net Fixed Assets	12.4	9.2
8.7	7.9	11.6					5.8	4.1
7.7	5.6	5.3					5.1	4.8
5.5	4.6	4.3				Sales/Total Assets	3.6	3.2
3.3	3.1	3.3					2.3	1.8
1.3	.7	.5					1.8	1.1
(15) 2.4	(16) 1.1	1.6				% Depr., Dep., Amort./Sales	(64) 3.4	(66) 3.1
9.1	2.0	3.3					6.9	6.8
1.5	3.5						2.5	2.4
(13) 3.9	(11) 4.5					% Officers', Directors', Owners' Comp/Sales	(31) 4.6	(35) 4.4
5.4	6.5						8.7	9.3
28920M	102140M	351301M	341902M	81357M	830512M	Net Sales ($)	1960472M	2805861M
4381M	21025M	80971M	154689M	75647M	549630M	Total Assets ($)	917470M	1457875M

M = $ thousand   MM = $ million
See Pages 11 through 18 for Explanation of Ratios and Data

Comparative Historical Data			Type of Statement	Current Data Sorted By Sales					
10	7	8	Unqualified		1		4	1	6
14	15	13	Reviewed		1		4	4	4
17	17	10	Compiled	2	1	1	1	4	1
8	7	15	Tax Returns	6	4	2	2		1
27	33	19	Other	1	2	6	5	2	3
4/1/00-3/31/01 ALL	4/1/01-3/31/02 ALL	4/1/02-3/31/03 ALL		0-1MM	10 (4/1-9/30/02) 1-3MM	3-5MM	5-10MM	55 (10/1/02-3/31/03) 10-25MM	25MM & OVER
76	79	65	NUMBER OF STATEMENTS	9	9	9	12	11	15
%	%	%	ASSETS	%	%	%	%	%	%
8.2	7.8	6.6	Cash & Equivalents				9.5	5.2	6.9
37.3	35.0	37.3	Trade Receivables (net)				41.8	48.2	36.0
4.0	2.4	1.9	Inventory				4.5	2.5	.7
2.5	4.0	5.0	All Other Current				8.6	5.3	5.5
52.1	49.1	50.8	Total Current				64.4	61.3	49.1
32.3	33.5	31.4	Fixed Assets (net)				20.7	26.8	34.5
8.3	7.6	6.7	Intangibles (net)				5.0	5.1	6.8
7.4	9.8	11.1	All Other Non-Current				9.9	6.8	9.6
100.0	100.0	100.0	Total				100.0	100.0	100.0
			LIABILITIES						
9.3	9.9	13.2	Notes Payable-Short Term				25.3	6.9	8.7
7.1	6.8	6.3	Cur. Mat.-L/T/D				7.7	8.9	3.3
12.7	13.2	15.4	Trade Payables				17.0	11.3	18.9
.3	.2	1.0	Income Taxes Payable				.0	.2	1.7
10.9	9.4	11.5	All Other Current				10.5	13.3	7.9
40.4	39.4	47.3	Total Current				60.5	40.6	40.4
24.2	22.2	20.8	Long Term Debt				16.0	9.9	13.6
.5	.5	.8	Deferred Taxes				.2	.7	2.4
4.8	5.6	6.1	All Other Non-Current				2.7	7.9	4.9
30.0	32.3	24.9	Net Worth				20.7	40.9	38.7
100.0	100.0	100.0	Total Liabilities & Net Worth				100.0	100.0	100.0
			INCOME DATA						
100.0	100.0	100.0	Net Sales				100.0	100.0	100.0
			Gross Profit						
95.2	97.8	96.2	Operating Expenses				97.4	96.5	94.8
4.7	2.2	3.8	Operating Profit				2.6	3.5	5.2
1.1	1.3	1.4	All Other Expenses (net)				.1	.0	.6
3.7	.9	2.4	Profit Before Taxes				2.5	3.5	4.6
			RATIOS						
2.0	2.0	1.6					2.4	2.2	1.6
1.3	1.2	1.2	Current				1.0	1.4	1.2
.9	.9	.7					.7	1.1	.9
1.9	1.7	1.5					1.4	1.7	1.2
1.1	1.0	1.0	Quick				.8	1.3	1.1
.8	.7	.6					.5	1.0	.9
25 14.6	23 16.1	25 14.5					24 15.0	31 11.9	36 10.2
37 10.0	34 10.7	34 10.6	Sales/Receivables				30 12.1	39 9.3	41 8.9
45 8.1	43 8.5	45 8.1					46 8.0	49 7.4	47 7.8
			Cost of Sales/Inventory						
			Cost of Sales/Payables						
13.1	14.8	17.5					26.6	12.8	13.3
41.3	47.1	62.3	Sales/Working Capital				NM	28.5	46.8
-130.3	-45.5	-21.6					-22.9	56.8	-172.7
6.3	6.5	9.4					7.3	15.1	9.9
(71) 1.6	(72) 1.8	(60) 2.6	EBIT/Interest				3.5	(10) 6.9	(12) 3.5
.0	.1	.6					1.0	2.4	.0
2.1	4.2	4.4							
(18) 1.6	(16) 2.3	(15) 2.5	Net Profit + Depr., Dep., Amort./Cur. Mat. L/T/D						
.9	1.1	.5							
.7	.5	.6					.7	.2	.4
1.4	1.3	1.5	Fixed/Worth				1.6	1.4	1.2
11.9	10.5	-10.8					NM	1.5	1.5
1.2	.9	1.0					1.5	.7	.7
3.2	2.0	3.8	Debt/Worth				5.3	1.3	2.4
76.0	26.0	-13.6					NM	3.8	6.5
60.8	43.5	69.9							60.1
(58) 18.3	(64) 11.9	(46) 21.0	% Profit Before Taxes/Tangible Net Worth					(13) 15.4	
-9.9	-3.7	-1.4							1.3
16.2	14.5	17.3					18.6	21.4	12.0
2.9	3.7	6.0	% Profit Before Taxes/Total Assets				8.4	8.4	7.0
-5.1	-2.5	-1.1					.2	4.6	-.2
51.0	46.0	55.1					49.2	97.3	36.0
14.0	16.5	14.6	Sales/Net Fixed Assets				34.7	16.8	9.8
5.8	6.5	8.0					15.3	11.5	2.3
5.7	5.5	5.5					6.5	5.4	5.3
3.9	3.7	4.1	Sales/Total Assets				4.6	4.4	2.4
2.0	2.1	2.6					3.8	2.9	1.3
1.2	.6	1.0					.6	.5	1.5
(61) 3.0	(65) 2.2	(57) 2.0	% Depr., Dep., Amort./Sales		(11) 1.3		(10) 2.5	(12) 2.5	
4.8	5.0	4.9					2.2	4.8	5.3
3.1	2.7	2.9							
(36) 4.5	(33) 5.3	(36) 4.5	% Officers', Directors', Owners' Comp/Sales						
7.0	9.4	6.7							
2265852M	1971786M	1736132M	Net Sales ($)	4957M	19170M	35447M	87540M	172834M	1416184M
1172695M	881604M	886343M	Total Assets ($)	1609M	5265M	9093M	18612M	51806M	799958M

M = $ thousand   MM = $ million
See Pages 11 through 18 for Explanation of Ratios and Data

Current Data Sorted By Assets   Comparative Historical Data

0-500M	500M-2MM	2-10MM	10-50MM	50-100MM	100-250MM	Type of Statement	4/1/98-3/31/99 ALL	4/1/99-3/31/00 ALL
7	1	7	10	5	3	Unqualified	42	50
	14	28	11	1		Reviewed	66	60
15	25	27	1			Compiled	98	99
20	27	11			2	Tax Returns	50	31
9	48	43	13	4	1	Other	98	85
	37 (4/1-9/30/02)			296 (10/1/02-3/31/03)				
51	115	116	35	10	6	NUMBER OF STATEMENTS	354	325
%	%	%	%	%	%	ASSETS	%	%
15.4	8.4	6.8	4.9	5.2		Cash & Equivalents	8.9	7.7
19.2	15.4	16.1	14.2	25.4		Trade Receivables (net)	15.6	20.9
3.1	1.3	2.2	.9	5.0		Inventory	1.9	1.9
3.6	1.7	2.1	3.6	1.0		All Other Current	2.2	2.4
41.3	26.8	27.2	23.6	36.6		Total Current	28.5	32.9
48.3	66.2	61.5	59.4	39.3		Fixed Assets (net)	61.7	54.6
1.7	1.9	2.3	2.8	14.8		Intangibles (net)	2.0	2.5
8.7	5.1	9.0	14.1	9.3		All Other Non-Current	7.8	10.0
100.0	100.0	100.0	100.0	100.0		Total	100.0	100.0
						LIABILITIES		
8.5	3.3	4.3	6.3	8.0		Notes Payable-Short Term	6.0	6.4
9.9	3.5	4.7	4.6	2.5		Cur. Mat.-L/T/D	4.8	4.6
7.1	6.2	6.7	6.8	10.7		Trade Payables	5.8	9.0
.1	.2	.3	.1	.1		Income Taxes Payable	.3	.3
20.5	7.7	7.2	11.4	12.5		All Other Current	8.3	9.1
46.0	20.8	23.3	29.1	33.8		Total Current	25.1	29.4
30.0	48.7	46.6	32.6	20.9		Long Term Debt	42.8	42.5
.0	.0	.4	1.0	.5		Deferred Taxes	.3	.6
11.2	5.1	3.7	3.2	1.8		All Other Non-Current	6.1	4.2
12.8	25.4	26.1	34.0	42.9		Net Worth	25.7	23.4
100.0	100.0	100.0	100.0	100.0		Total Liabilities & Net Worth	100.0	100.0
						INCOME DATA		
100.0	100.0	100.0	100.0	100.0		Net Sales	100.0	100.0
						Gross Profit		
87.8	74.0	81.9	88.6	95.7		Operating Expenses	82.4	82.4
12.2	26.0	18.1	11.4	4.3		Operating Profit	17.6	17.6
5.0	13.0	10.9	5.9	2.9		All Other Expenses (net)	8.5	7.5
7.1	13.0	7.3	5.5	1.5		Profit Before Taxes	9.1	10.1
						RATIOS		
5.7	2.9	1.9	1.5	1.5		Current	2.3	1.9
1.3	1.1	1.2	1.0	1.0			1.2	1.1
.3	.3	.5	.4	.8			.5	.5
4.7	2.6	1.7	1.3	1.3		Quick	2.0	1.7
1.1	1.0	1.0	.7	1.0		(352)	1.0	1.0
.3	.2	.4	.4	.6			.4	.4
0 UND	0 UND	3 115.2	28 13.0	35 10.4		Sales/Receivables	0 UND	3 108.3
14 25.4	9 39.1	32 11.5	37 9.7	48 7.7			24 14.9	32 11.4
34 10.7	38 9.7	47 7.8	50 7.2	62 5.9			42 8.8	50 7.3
						Cost of Sales/Inventory		
						Cost of Sales/Payables		
9.0	8.4	8.5	14.8	10.5		Sales/Working Capital	9.4	11.0
32.4	50.9	39.3	999.8	477.1			41.2	68.3
−9.0	−9.4	−8.3	−6.3	−79.0			−8.9	−11.6
(32) 12.5	(63) 7.2	(84) 5.9	(31) 4.2	7.7		EBIT/Interest	(245) 6.6	(233) 7.6
3.7	3.5	2.8	1.6	4.1			3.3	3.2
.9	1.7	1.0	1.1	2.2			1.7	1.7
	(11) 29.5	(27) 2.8	(14) 5.8			Net Profit + Depr., Dep., Amort./Cur. Mat. L /T/D	(74) 4.3	(79) 3.9
	6.7	1.5	2.2				2.2	2.1
	2.5	.9	1.1				1.1	1.0
.6	.9	.9	.9	.9		Fixed/Worth	.9	.8
1.3	2.6	2.7	2.4	1.4			2.2	2.2
9.6	44.5	15.8	4.1	2.2			8.1	11.9
.4	.9	1.2	1.2	1.8		Debt/Worth	.9	1.2
2.0	3.6	3.0	2.2	2.0			2.3	2.9
−9.9	101.6	22.2	7.3	2.9			10.6	22.3
(36) 83.4	(89) 63.2	(92) 34.9	(34) 28.4	39.5		% Profit Before Taxes/Tangible Net Worth	(293) 45.4	(266) 50.1
24.7	26.5	13.8	10.2	23.2			24.1	22.5
−16.0	11.9	3.0	1.3	9.5			10.0	9.0
33.8	13.9	9.3	7.3	9.9		% Profit Before Taxes/Total Assets	15.1	13.0
10.6	6.4	4.1	3.3	5.9			6.9	5.9
−3.9	1.0	−.4	.3	2.2			2.0	1.6
25.6	9.9	9.4	3.9	10.3		Sales/Net Fixed Assets	8.1	11.2
9.1	.6	1.2	1.7	5.1			1.5	2.0
1.3	.2	.3	.6	2.3			.4	.5
5.0	2.8	2.5	1.6	3.1		Sales/Total Assets	2.6	2.8
2.9	.5	.8	1.0	1.7			1.0	1.0
1.2	.2	.3	.4	.8			.3	.3
(43) 2.0	(97) 2.9	(107) 2.8	3.3			% Depr., Dep., Amort./Sales	(318) 2.8	(292) 2.3
4.4	8.2	5.5	4.7				6.3	5.6
8.2	16.2	12.7	10.1				13.3	11.8
(20) 3.7	(33) 2.9	(34) 2.3	(10) 1.1			% Officers', Directors', Owners' Comp/Sales	(97) 2.8	(89) 2.1
10.5	10.5	5.1	2.6				6.8	5.9
18.9	11.3	11.3	4.9				11.1	11.4
35033M	221574M	869184M	808063M	1955287M	621342M	Net Sales ($)	3103819M	5393419M
12633M	130868M	557021M	792303M	864188M	823923M	Total Assets ($)	2254866M	2959685M

© RMA 2003

M = $ thousand   MM = $ million
See Pages 11 through 18 for Explanation of Ratios and Data

Comparative Historical Data | | Current Data Sorted By Sales

			Type of Statement						
28	27	26	Unqualified		3	1	3	8	11
44	44	61	Reviewed	6	13	11	10	11	10
89	93	68	Compiled	35	14	7	5	7	
36	42	60	Tax Returns	47	8		1	3	1
86	127	118	Other	52	17	10	14	15	10
4/1/00- 3/31/01	4/1/01- 3/31/02	4/1/02- 3/31/03			37 (4/1-9/30/02)		296 (10/1/02-3/31/03)		
ALL	ALL	ALL		0-1MM	1-3MM	3-5MM	5-10MM	10-25MM	25MM & OVER
283	333	333	NUMBER OF STATEMENTS	140	55	29	33	44	32
%	%	%	ASSETS	%	%	%	%	%	%
8.2	9.0	8.4	Cash & Equivalents	6.7	13.1	8.8	10.7	7.9	5.4
18.3	17.5	16.3	Trade Receivables (net)	4.3	19.4	20.6	27.1	31.5	27.2
1.6	2.3	2.0	Inventory	.2	3.9	4.9	2.8	2.2	3.1
2.9	4.1	2.3	All Other Current	1.0	4.1	2.5	1.8	3.2	3.6
31.0	32.9	29.0	Total Current	12.3	40.7	36.7	42.3	44.8	39.3
56.9	54.8	60.5	Fixed Assets (net)	80.0	49.9	55.2	45.3	38.5	44.4
3.2	3.1	2.5	Intangibles (net)	1.5	3.8	1.0	3.6	.8	7.0
8.8	9.2	8.0	All Other Non-Current	6.2	5.6	7.0	8.8	15.8	9.3
100.0	100.0	100.0	Total	100.0	100.0	100.0	100.0	100.0	100.0
			LIABILITIES						
5.9	7.3	5.0	Notes Payable-Short Term	3.5	6.6	4.3	5.4	4.5	9.4
5.9	4.1	5.0	Cur. Mat.-L/T/D	5.6	3.9	5.9	3.2	4.5	5.7
6.4	7.5	6.6	Trade Payables	1.7	6.7	11.7	8.2	12.4	13.5
.2	.2	.2	Income Taxes Payable	.0	.4	.1	.2	.6	.2
12.1	11.0	9.9	All Other Current	8.7	8.3	6.5	10.2	15.8	12.3
30.6	30.1	26.6	Total Current	19.6	26.0	28.5	27.2	37.8	41.1
39.9	45.1	42.5	Long Term Debt	63.1	32.5	38.9	25.7	19.0	23.0
.4	.2	.3	Deferred Taxes	.0	.1	.2	.2	.9	1.5
5.4	5.4	5.2	All Other Non-Current	4.3	11.8	4.1	3.1	3.2	3.5
23.8	19.2	25.3	Net Worth	13.1	29.5	28.2	43.7	39.2	30.9
100.0	100.0	100.0	Total Liabilities & Net Worth	100.0	100.0	100.0	100.0	100.0	100.0
			INCOME DATA						
100.0	100.0	100.0	Net Sales	100.0	100.0	100.0	100.0	100.0	100.0
			Gross Profit						
83.0	82.6	81.2	Operating Expenses	67.4	87.3	88.8	90.3	96.0	94.5
17.0	17.4	18.8	Operating Profit	32.6	12.7	11.2	9.7	4.0	5.5
8.8	9.8	10.0	All Other Expenses (net)	18.6	6.4	4.9	2.6	1.4	2.6
8.2	7.6	8.8	Profit Before Taxes	14.0	6.3	6.3	7.1	2.6	2.9
			RATIOS						
2.0	2.0	2.4		3.0	4.7	2.5	2.1	1.9	1.5
1.1	1.1	1.1	Current	.7	1.5	1.3	1.4	1.2	1.0
.6	.6	.5		.2	.7	.8	1.2	.8	.6
1.8	1.7	1.8		2.5	3.1	1.9	1.9	1.7	1.3
(282) 1.0	(332) .8	1.0	Quick	.6	1.1	1.3	1.3	1.0	.9
.4	.4	.3		.2	.5	.7	.9	.7	.5
5 75.4	0 UND	0 UND		0 UND	7 50.0	21 17.7	34 10.7	31 11.8	34 10.6
32 11.6	27 13.5	26 14.0	Sales/Receivables	0 UND	26 14.0	34 10.7	44 8.3	37 9.9	42 8.6
47 7.7	46 7.9	43 8.4		15 24.4	41 9.0	51 7.2	55 6.7	49 7.4	51 7.1
			Cost of Sales/Inventory						
			Cost of Sales/Payables						
11.8	10.3	9.1		9.8	7.5	7.4	8.1	12.1	15.4
103.7	89.5	48.3	Sales/Working Capital	-15.5	26.0	20.9	16.7	44.7	65.6
-10.9	-11.2	-9.3		-4.4	-15.7	-48.4	45.2	-31.9	-11.2
7.0	5.3	6.2		4.8	7.6	4.2	7.6	8.8	6.1
(192) 2.9	(228) 2.5	(223) 3.1	EBIT/Interest	(58) 3.0	(43) 4.0	(26) 2.4	(29) 4.1	(37) 2.9	(30) 3.2
1.4	1.2	1.2		1.3	1.5	1.0	1.1	.8	1.3
3.5	5.5	5.4	Net Profit + Depr., Dep.,					9.4	5.3
(57) 1.8	(46) 1.9	(59) 2.4	Amort./Cur. Mat. L/T/D				(12) 1.7	(16) 1.4	
1.1	1.0	1.3						1.0	.9
.7	.8	.8		1.8	.6	1.1	.4	.4	.8
2.5	2.4	2.3	Fixed/Worth	5.6	1.4	2.2	1.1	.9	1.6
11.9	11.5	11.8		-21.5	6.8	8.2	3.0	2.4	4.3
1.0	1.3	1.1		1.6	.4	1.2	.7	.8	1.3
2.9	3.4	2.6	Debt/Worth	7.0	1.9	2.2	1.6	1.8	2.6
17.9	20.9	28.8		-21.8	38.0	8.2	4.0	3.1	7.4
49.2	54.2	45.8	% Profit Before Taxes/Tangible	48.2	66.2	31.5	63.2	39.6	38.7
(227) 20.7	(265) 20.9	(267) 19.1	Net Worth	(96) 21.8	(43) 18.1	(24) 18.5	(32) 16.3	(43) 11.9	(29) 21.9
7.3	4.3	3.1		7.0	2.3	1.1	1.9	-2.5	6.7
12.0	12.4	12.5	% Profit Before Taxes/Total	11.2	14.5	10.7	21.3	13.3	9.6
5.2	4.3	5.0	Assets	5.0	4.3	4.7	6.6	4.7	4.7
1.0	.3	.3		.2	.3	-.2	.4	-.6	1.0
9.9	12.7	9.8		.8	16.7	12.6	14.6	14.8	8.5
2.3	2.5	1.7	Sales/Net Fixed Assets	.3	6.3	1.8	3.2	9.7	5.5
.4	.4	.3		.2	.5	.6	1.4	2.7	2.5
2.7	2.8	2.9		.7	3.8	3.3	3.0	4.5	3.1
1.2	1.2	1.0	Sales/Total Assets	.3	1.6	1.1	1.6	2.7	1.8
.4	.3	.3		.2	.5	.6	.9	1.2	1.4
2.0	1.9	2.8		6.3	2.1	1.9	1.9	1.7	2.4
(261) 5.4	(299) 4.9	(294) 5.4	% Depr., Dep., Amort./Sales	(119) 13.5	(50) 5.0	(26) 6.5	(29) 3.6	(42) 3.1	(28) 3.0
11.6	11.6	13.5		19.6	9.9	9.3	5.5	4.3	4.4
3.0	2.8	2.5	% Officers', Directors',	3.3	3.8	4.0	1.8	1.6	
(85) 6.0	(96) 7.2	(98) 6.1	Owners' Comp/Sales	(32) 9.3	(21) 9.3	(11) 6.7	(11) 3.1	(17) 3.0	
10.1	13.3	11.9		17.5	11.5	9.6	6.3	7.8	
3933204M	4127997M	4510483M	Net Sales ($)	58147M	105139M	112465M	244304M	734461M	3255967M
2662078M	3123130M	3180936M	Total Assets ($)	193951M	186810M	159298M	202514M	776980M	1661383M

M = $ thousand   MM = $ million
See Pages 11 through 18 for Explanation of Ratios and Data

TRANSPORTATION—Refrigerated Warehousing and Storage NAICS 493120 (SIC 4222, 4226)

Current Data Sorted By Assets						Type of Statement	Comparative Historical Data	
		6	6	5	1	Unqualified	22	19
	4	10	10			Reviewed	24	27
4	10	8	2			Compiled	15	13
1	4	1				Tax Returns	4	4
2	7	8	4	2	4	Other	27	24
	13 (4/1-9/30/02)		86 (10/1/02-3/31/03)				4/1/98-3/31/99	4/1/99-3/31/00
0-500M	500M-2MM	2-10MM	10-50MM	50-100MM	100-250MM		ALL	ALL
7	25	33	22	7	5	NUMBER OF STATEMENTS	92	87
%	%	%	%	%	%	ASSETS	%	%
	6.9	8.6	5.9			Cash & Equivalents	6.9	6.3
	20.7	14.6	8.4			Trade Receivables (net)	11.5	10.4
	3.4	4.1	.6			Inventory	2.0	2.6
	5.5	3.3	1.9			All Other Current	−1.0	1.3
	36.5	30.6	16.9			Total Current	19.4	20.6
	55.8	59.2	69.7			Fixed Assets (net)	68.9	71.1
	3.3	5.0	.5			Intangibles (net)	2.8	1.8
	4.3	5.2	12.9			All Other Non-Current	8.9	6.5
	100.0	100.0	100.0			Total	100.0	100.0
						LIABILITIES		
	6.7	6.0	3.1			Notes Payable-Short Term	7.4	4.3
	7.2	5.9	4.5			Cur. Mat.-L/T/D	5.9	7.3
	10.9	4.6	2.3			Trade Payables	4.4	4.2
	.0	.1	.4			Income Taxes Payable	.2	.4
	14.4	5.2	5.7			All Other Current	9.7	6.7
	39.1	21.8	16.0			Total Current	27.6	22.8
	33.5	33.5	51.6			Long Term Debt	39.0	46.8
	.3	.4	.9			Deferred Taxes	.8	1.0
	6.4	2.0	4.7			All Other Non-Current	3.2	3.0
	20.6	42.2	26.8			Net Worth	29.4	26.5
	100.0	100.0	100.0			Total Liabilities & Net Worth	100.0	100.0
						INCOME DATA		
	100.0	100.0	100.0			Net Sales	100.0	100.0
						Gross Profit		
	87.2	86.3	76.7			Operating Expenses	86.0	84.7
	12.8	13.7	23.3			Operating Profit	14.0	15.3
	6.6	4.9	15.0			All Other Expenses (net)	7.9	7.8
	6.2	8.8	8.3			Profit Before Taxes	6.1	7.5
						RATIOS		
	2.6	3.3	1.9				2.1	1.8
	.8	1.2	1.3			Current	1.1	1.1
	.4	.8	.8				.6	.5
	2.2	2.4	1.6				2.0	1.8
	.7	1.1	1.0			Quick	.9	.8
	.4	.6	.7				.4	.4
10	37.2	23	16.0	27	13.3		26	14.0	22	16.7
26	14.0	41	9.0	40	9.0	Sales/Receivables	36	10.2	35	10.5
47	7.8	51	7.2	58	6.3		48	7.6	54	6.7
						Cost of Sales/Inventory		
						Cost of Sales/Payables		
	8.1	5.9	6.3				7.9	7.9
	−37.0	23.1	22.8			Sales/Working Capital	UND	66.5
	−10.9	−17.5	−17.0				−7.9	−9.6
	11.0	10.9	3.6				3.5	3.1
(19)	2.3	(27)	2.4	(19)	2.5	EBIT/Interest	(75)	2.3	(75)	1.9
	−1.9	1.0	1.3				1.2	1.2
			3.2			Net Profit + Depr., Dep.,	4.2	2.9
		(12)	2.5			Amort./Cur. Mat. L /T/D	(27)	2.1	(21)	2.1
			2.1				1.0	1.4
	.7	.7	2.0				1.3	1.6
	7.7	1.4	2.8			Fixed/Worth	2.7	3.7
	−12.3	3.4	5.2				8.9	9.3
	.7	.5	1.7				1.2	1.1
	7.5	1.9	2.6			Debt/Worth	2.6	3.3
	−20.8	3.4	6.2				8.9	11.7
	56.8	29.2	28.7				38.6	34.5
(17)	24.6	(29)	17.8	(20)	15.7	% Profit Before Taxes/Tangible Net Worth	(83)	14.4	(75)	17.2
	8.8	2.5	5.5				3.4	5.7
	14.7	15.1	9.5				10.5	7.8
	6.6	7.2	4.6			% Profit Before Taxes/Total Assets	4.1	5.2
	−3.8	.7	.8				−.3	.9
	18.4	3.3	1.4				1.9	1.6
	4.3	1.3	.8			Sales/Net Fixed Assets	1.0	.9
	.8	.7	.5				.6	.5
	3.3	1.8	.9				1.2	.9
	2.1	.8	.5			Sales/Total Assets	.6	.7
	.6	.5	.3				.4	.5
	2.5	3.8	7.6				5.6	6.1
(23)	5.3	(32)	7.3	9.8		% Depr., Dep., Amort./Sales	(84)	9.8	(85)	9.1
	15.9	9.4	14.6				13.2	13.3
		2.2					3.0	2.8
		(13)	3.8			% Officers', Directors', Owners' Comp/Sales	(28)	5.7	(24)	4.9
		10.3					9.0	7.7
8441M	59697M	335774M	331238M	566082M	787275M	Net Sales ($)	1409854M	1385470M
2051M	29334M	186059M	440460M	503038M	771758M	Total Assets ($)	2041725M	1246853M

© RMA 2003

M = $ thousand   MM = $ million
See Pages 11 through 18 for Explanation of Ratios and Data

Comparative Historical Data				Current Data Sorted By Sales					
			Type of Statement		1	3	5	3	6
19	14	18	Unqualified		1	3	5	3	6
12	16	24	Reviewed	1	6	4	5	6	2
18	22	24	Compiled	4	8	8	2		2
3	3	6	Tax Returns	4	1	1			
24	24	27	Other	3	6	6	5	1	6
4/1/00-3/31/01	4/1/01-3/31/02	4/1/02-3/31/03		13 (4/1-9/30/02)			86 (10/1/02-3/31/03)		
ALL	ALL	ALL		0-1MM	1-3MM	3-5MM	5-10MM	10-25MM	25MM & OVER
76	79	99	**NUMBER OF STATEMENTS**	12	22	22	17	10	16
%	%	%	**ASSETS**	%	%	%	%	%	%
8.3	7.0	7.1	Cash & Equivalents	11.2	6.1	4.7	8.0	5.0	9.1
12.4	13.3	14.9	Trade Receivables (net)	6.0	14.5	15.8	17.7	16.7	16.4
2.1	1.7	2.6	Inventory	.4	4.0	2.4	1.8	1.3	4.5
1.9	2.8	3.4	All Other Current	3.0	6.4	1.8	4.1	3.5	1.1
24.7	25.0	28.0	Total Current	20.6	31.1	24.7	31.6	26.5	31.1
64.2	64.7	61.3	Fixed Assets (net)	73.2	54.6	63.3	57.9	61.9	61.9
3.2	2.0	3.4	Intangibles (net)	.9	7.7	3.5	.8	5.6	.8
7.9	8.3	7.3	All Other Non-Current	5.3	6.7	8.5	9.7	6.0	6.2
100.0	100.0	100.0	Total	100.0	100.0	100.0	100.0	100.0	100.0
			LIABILITIES						
3.7	4.6	5.1	Notes Payable-Short Term	3.9	6.6	4.5	5.3	5.4	4.5
5.3	5.8	5.4	Cur. Mat.-L/T/D	9.5	7.4	3.6	4.6	5.1	5.4
6.2	5.3	6.9	Trade Payables	4.3	6.3	9.2	7.9	5.0	6.8
.3	.1	.1	Income Taxes Payable	.0	.0	.1	.5	.0	.1
5.8	6.6	9.6	All Other Current	5.4	14.4	9.0	14.4	4.7	5.1
21.3	22.4	27.2	Total Current	23.2	34.7	26.5	32.8	20.2	19.3
41.9	39.6	38.5	Long Term Debt	52.6	32.1	39.5	36.0	42.2	35.7
.6	.9	.7	Deferred Taxes	.0	.0	1.0	.4	1.8	1.2
4.8	2.2	3.9	All Other Non-Current	6.2	3.3	8.0	.9	1.9	1.5
31.5	34.9	29.7	Net Worth	18.0	29.8	25.0	29.9	33.8	42.2
100.0	100.0	100.0	Total Liabilities & Net Worth	100.0	100.0	100.0	100.0	100.0	100.0
			INCOME DATA						
100.0	100.0	100.0	Net Sales	100.0	100.0	100.0	100.0	100.0	100.0
			Gross Profit						
85.2	86.0	84.4	Operating Expenses	74.2	85.6	82.3	86.4	86.2	90.1
14.8	14.0	15.6	Operating Profit	25.8	14.4	17.7	13.6	13.8	9.9
6.0	6.7	7.9	All Other Expenses (net)	17.1	7.1	10.1	4.1	6.7	3.9
8.7	7.3	7.7	Profit Before Taxes	8.7	7.3	7.7	9.5	7.0	5.9
			RATIOS						
2.0	1.9	2.5	Current	3.1	2.3	2.7	2.4	1.5	2.5
1.1	1.3	1.2		.9	.8	1.2	1.2	1.2	1.3
.6	.7	.7		.3	.5	.6	.7	.9	1.0
1.7	1.6	1.8	Quick	2.6	1.2	2.1	2.1	1.3	2.2
1.0	.9	.9		.9	.6	1.1	1.1	1.0	1.1
.5	.5	.6		.3	.4	.5	.5	.7	.9
22 16.4	23 15.5	21 17.1	Sales/Receivables	0 UND	7 52.7	12 31.4	25 14.5	36 10.2	27 13.6
36 10.2	37 9.8	35 10.3		21 17.5	30 12.0	33 11.0	45 8.2	45 8.0	36 10.1
48 7.6	48 7.6	48 7.7		40 9.2	44 8.3	44 8.2	60 6.1	54 6.8	50 7.3
			Cost of Sales/Inventory						
			Cost of Sales/Payables						
8.6	9.1	9.5	Sales/Working Capital	6.2	7.4	6.8	11.8	14.0	11.1
44.3	34.0	45.9		-70.7	-21.2	31.4	23.1	36.1	28.6
-12.1	-15.5	-13.6		-6.8	-10.9	-10.3	-11.9	-43.0	NM
(61) 3.5	(65) 3.9	(81) 5.9	EBIT/Interest		(18) 9.5	(18) 7.3	(14) 8.3	4.6	(15) 5.6
2.4	1.9	2.3			2.5	2.3	3.3	2.1	2.1
1.3	1.0	1.1			-.9	.4	1.3	.9	1.2
(17) 4.7	(23) 2.8	(25) 3.2	Net Profit + Depr., Dep., Amort./Cur. Mat. L/T/D						
2.2	1.7	2.5							
1.1	.9	1.7							
1.2	.9	1.1	Fixed/Worth	2.8	1.1	1.1	1.0	1.0	.9
2.4	2.4	2.6		8.6	2.3	2.7	2.1	2.5	2.1
8.0	4.4	6.5		189.9	NM	NM	5.5	3.8	2.8
1.2	.9	.9	Debt/Worth	2.6	1.3	.9	.5	1.0	.5
2.5	2.2	2.7		8.3	3.0	2.5	2.0	2.9	1.9
7.6	4.9	7.3		189.6	NM	NM	5.1	4.7	3.5
(65) 39.2	(72) 28.3	(83) 29.4	% Profit Before Taxes/Tangible Net Worth	(10) 52.6	(17) 36.4	(17) 27.2	(14) 51.3		22.3
22.3	11.8	17.4		15.2	10.0	19.1	27.0		17.1
4.6	1.4	4.3		-10.7	-10.3	13.1	7.5		2.5
10.9	8.8	11.5	% Profit Before Taxes/Total Assets	4.7	10.2	12.0	16.2	6.4	11.2
5.1	3.9	4.7		2.1	4.9	6.1	11.7	4.5	5.2
1.2	.0	.2		-1.4	-4.9	-.2	1.7	-.2	1.0
2.7	3.9	4.3	Sales/Net Fixed Assets	2.9	7.5	4.6	3.3	10.3	4.2
1.1	1.1	1.3		.4	1.9	1.5	1.3	1.0	2.0
.5	.5	.6		.3	.6	.5	.9	.5	.6
1.5	1.6	2.2	Sales/Total Assets	.7	2.5	2.5	2.1	2.9	2.7
.7	.7	.8		.4	.9	.8	1.0	.8	1.1
.4	.4	.4		.2	.3	.5	.5	.5	.5
(67) 2.6	(75) 3.5	(94) 4.1	% Depr., Dep., Amort./Sales	(10) 8.6	(21) 5.5	3.0	(16) 4.5	3.2	(15) 1.7
6.6	7.2	8.1		12.6	9.4	6.7	7.3	7.8	7.6
11.2	14.1	13.4		17.8	22.7	10.7	10.3	14.9	10.5
(18) 2.7	(20) 2.0	(26) 3.1	% Officers', Directors', Owners' Comp/Sales			(11) 2.4			
5.7	6.3	4.1				3.8			
9.6	18.9	10.5				5.7			
2356701M	988570M	2088507M	Net Sales ($)	5708M	43303M	84994M	116832M	151413M	1686257M
1307986M	1108549M	1932700M	Total Assets ($)	15191M	88071M	240211M	141858M	233686M	1213683M

M = $ thousand   MM = $ million
See Pages 11 through 18 for Explanation of Ratios and Data

Current Data Sorted By Assets | Comparative Historical Data

						Type of Statement		
	6	9	10	1	3	Unqualified	35	21
2	7	10	3			Reviewed	11	16
2	5	2	2			Compiled	11	10
	4	1				Tax Returns	2	3
	5	8	4		1	Other	4	4
	39 (4/1-9/30/02)			46 (10/1/02-3/31/03)			4/1/98-3/31/99	4/1/99-3/31/00
0-500M	500M-2MM	2-10MM	10-50MM	50-100MM	100-250MM		ALL	ALL
4	27	30	19	2	3	NUMBER OF STATEMENTS	63	54
%	%	%	%	%	%	**ASSETS**	%	%
	9.4	7.3	5.5			Cash & Equivalents	13.9	9.1
	19.3	15.7	15.8			Trade Receivables (net)	16.6	20.4
	18.8	20.7	19.6			Inventory	8.8	12.8
	4.7	7.1	7.0			All Other Current	5.1	3.1
	52.2	50.7	48.0			Total Current	44.4	45.4
	39.7	42.1	43.8			Fixed Assets (net)	46.6	41.0
	2.4	.7	.3			Intangibles (net)	.4	2.2
	5.7	6.5	7.9			All Other Non-Current	8.6	11.4
	100.0	100.0	100.0			Total	100.0	100.0
						LIABILITIES		
	13.9	12.1	15.6			Notes Payable-Short Term	7.1	12.9
	3.7	4.0	4.2			Cur. Mat.-L/T/D	3.9	2.2
	12.9	10.9	4.5			Trade Payables	10.9	9.0
	.0	.3	.2			Income Taxes Payable	.0	.2
	7.0	10.6	11.4			All Other Current	9.4	8.4
	37.6	37.9	35.8			Total Current	31.4	32.7
	15.9	18.1	16.5			Long Term Debt	14.0	16.4
	.5	1.1	1.1			Deferred Taxes	.5	.8
	1.1	1.1	3.6			All Other Non-Current	4.3	2.4
	44.9	41.8	43.0			Net Worth	49.7	47.8
	100.0	100.0	100.0			Total Liabilities & Net Worth	100.0	100.0
						INCOME DATA		
	100.0	100.0	100.0			Net Sales	100.0	100.0
						Gross Profit		
	93.4	85.2	88.5			Operating Expenses	91.3	92.0
	6.6	14.8	11.5			Operating Profit	8.7	8.0
	1.7	1.4	1.6			All Other Expenses (net)	1.4	-.8
	4.9	13.4	9.9			Profit Before Taxes	7.3	8.8
						RATIOS		
	1.6	2.9	2.0			Current	2.7	2.7
	1.3	1.1	1.1				1.5	1.3
	.8	.9	1.0				.9	1.0
	1.2	1.6	1.2			Quick	2.0	1.7
	.6	.6	.4				1.0	.9
	.3	.1	.2				.5	.4
	5 73.8	8 48.3	11 34.1			Sales/Receivables	8 45.0	10 35.4
	16 22.6	17 21.3	23 15.6				18 19.9	27 13.4
	45 8.1	30 12.1	100 3.6				35 10.4	48 7.7
						Cost of Sales/Inventory		
						Cost of Sales/Payables		
	12.3	8.9	4.1			Sales/Working Capital	6.5	6.1
	28.7	37.1	31.2				19.9	24.9
	-51.0	-72.4	126.0				-92.4	-165.4
	(25) 4.1	(29) 10.8	12.3			EBIT/Interest	(59) 14.0	(49) 8.5
	2.7	3.3	4.7				3.0	3.6
	.8	2.0	1.5				1.3	1.8
		(10) 4.4	9.0			Net Profit + Depr., Dep.,	(19) 4.7	(17) 6.2
		1.6	(12) 5.0			Amort./Cur. Mat. L /T/D	1.2	3.5
		1.1	1.4				.2	1.1
	.4	.6	.6			Fixed/Worth	.5	.4
	.9	1.0	1.0				.8	.9
	1.9	1.8	1.6				1.6	1.5
	.6	.5	.6			Debt/Worth	.4	.4
	1.1	1.9	1.8				1.1	1.2
	2.7	3.0	3.1				2.4	2.5
	(24) 18.3	(29) 37.0	28.8			% Profit Before Taxes/Tangible	(62) 22.4	(52) 21.6
	6.2	11.9	13.5			Net Worth	9.6	14.9
	.4	8.5	9.9				2.4	8.3
	8.3	13.3	12.5			% Profit Before Taxes/Total	12.0	10.6
	3.1	4.4	5.0			Assets	4.8	6.9
	.2	2.8	2.4				.7	2.4
	17.4	11.3	6.5			Sales/Net Fixed Assets	14.5	14.7
	9.2	6.0	2.9				5.5	5.6
	4.1	2.6	.9				1.3	1.0
	4.5	3.7	1.9			Sales/Total Assets	4.0	3.8
	2.9	2.9	1.1				2.1	1.8
	1.4	1.1	.6				.7	.6
	1.2	1.1	1.8			% Depr., Dep., Amort./Sales	1.0	.9
	1.9	1.6	3.1				(61) 1.9	(51) 2.1
	4.1	3.0	9.0				7.5	7.0
		(10) 2.1				% Officers', Directors',	1.9	.5
		3.2				Owners' Comp/Sales	(17) 3.4	(14) 1.8
		4.7					13.2	4.3
2758M	121983M	327028M	578099M	199160M	1789548M	Net Sales ($)	1695691M	1416405M
1203M	34207M	135968M	365884M	131230M	480770M	Total Assets ($)	538673M	541367M

M = $ thousand   MM = $ million
See Pages 11 through 18 for Explanation of Ratios and Data

Comparative Historical Data | **Current Data Sorted By Sales**

Hist 1	Hist 2	Hist 3	Type of Statement	0-1MM	1-3MM	3-5MM	5-10MM	10-25MM	25MM & OVER
19	19	29	Unqualified	2	1		8	6	12
17	13	22	Reviewed	2	5	4	6	4	1
13	9	11	Compiled	3	2	1	1	3	1
2	1	5	Tax Returns	1	1	1		2	
12	11	18	Other	3	2	1	5	4	3
4/1/00-3/31/01 ALL	4/1/01-3/31/02 ALL	4/1/02-3/31/03 ALL		39 (4/1-9/30/02)			46 (10/1/02-3/31/03)		
63	53	85	NUMBER OF STATEMENTS	11	11	7	20	19	17
%	%	%	**ASSETS**	%	%	%	%	%	%
8.7	8.7	7.3	Cash & Equivalents	7.9	11.7		10.0	6.1	3.9
17.1	16.7	17.3	Trade Receivables (net)	12.8	16.8		15.3	25.1	16.9
18.6	21.4	20.0	Inventory	3.1	24.9		9.7	24.7	33.0
4.1	5.9	6.5	All Other Current	5.9	3.5		7.1	3.8	10.0
48.6	52.6	51.1	Total Current	29.7	57.0		42.1	59.8	63.7
43.1	37.7	40.9	Fixed Assets (net)	64.7	33.6		49.2	32.4	28.7
.9	1.8	1.3	Intangibles (net)	1.3	1.3		2.3	1.1	.7
7.5	7.9	6.7	All Other Non-Current	4.4	8.1		6.3	6.6	6.8
100.0	100.0	100.0	Total	100.0	100.0		100.0	100.0	100.0
			LIABILITIES						
16.5	15.6	13.9	Notes Payable-Short Term	5.8	16.8		11.3	11.2	17.5
3.4	2.7	4.1	Cur. Mat.-L/T/D	7.1	5.5		4.0	2.3	4.1
11.0	11.7	10.1	Trade Payables	3.9	11.4		6.3	13.9	12.6
.1	.1	.2	Income Taxes Payable	.3	.0		.3	.0	.2
7.9	9.5	9.4	All Other Current	2.2	10.2		9.1	10.4	15.6
38.9	39.6	37.7	Total Current	19.3	44.0		30.9	37.8	50.1
20.6	16.8	17.4	Long Term Debt	35.4	13.2		10.2	15.9	11.7
.5	.7	.8	Deferred Taxes	.4	1.1		1.0	.7	1.2
1.2	2.3	1.6	All Other Non-Current	.5	1.9		3.3	1.1	.8
38.8	40.5	42.4	Net Worth	44.3	39.8		54.6	44.5	36.2
100.0	100.0	100.0	Total Liabilities & Net Worth	100.0	100.0		100.0	100.0	100.0
			INCOME DATA						
100.0	100.0	100.0	Net Sales	100.0	100.0		100.0	100.0	100.0
			Gross Profit						
92.1	88.3	89.3	Operating Expenses	74.6	87.3		88.0	95.0	91.4
7.9	11.7	10.7	Operating Profit	25.4	12.7		12.0	5.0	8.6
3.2	2.2	1.5	All Other Expenses (net)	9.0	1.5		-.5	.6	.8
4.7	9.5	9.2	Profit Before Taxes	16.3	11.2		12.5	4.4	7.8
			RATIOS						
2.0	2.1	2.0	Current	3.3	1.4		2.8	3.7	1.6
1.2	1.3	1.2		1.0	1.2		1.3	1.5	1.1
.9	1.0	.9		.3	.8		.9	1.1	1.1
1.3	1.7	1.4	Quick	1.6	1.0		2.4	2.9	.6
.6	.5	.6		.8	.6		.7	1.1	.3
.2	.2	.2		.3	.4		.3	.3	.2
7 54.8	9 42.6	8 46.3	Sales/Receivables	0 UND	4 97.1		9 40.8	8 44.6	10 35.1
18 19.8	25 14.8	19 19.4		69 5.3	15 23.8		16 23.3	26 14.0	19 19.4
46 8.0	48 7.6	40 9.0		93 3.9	45 8.1		29 12.6	38 9.6	30 12.1
			Cost of Sales/Inventory						
			Cost of Sales/Payables						
11.0	8.9	8.5	Sales/Working Capital	2.5	5.7		8.7	7.6	10.8
21.5	18.3	31.9		95.2	26.5		36.0	28.7	26.5
-52.3	-153.8	-102.0		-4.4	-23.5		-67.5	64.5	72.9
(54) 3.7	(49) 4.9	(82) 7.4	EBIT/Interest		7.1		25.5	(18) 6.5	9.1
1.6	2.2	3.1			3.7		4.1	3.1	4.7
.9	1.2	1.7			2.7		1.9	1.5	2.1
(16) 6.7	(17) 11.6	(28) 7.2	Net Profit + Depr., Dep., Amort./Cur. Mat. L/T/D						
3.0	5.4	1.6							
1.2	2.7	.8							
.4	.5	.5	Fixed/Worth	.7	.3		.7	.5	.5
1.1	.8	1.0		1.9	1.2		.9	.8	.6
2.2	1.7	1.8		2.6	2.2		1.4	1.0	1.2
.6	.6	.6	Debt/Worth	.6	.6		.3	.4	1.1
2.0	1.6	1.5		1.1	1.5		.9	2.1	1.8
5.0	5.0	3.0		2.9	2.9		2.7	4.4	3.8
(60) 26.0	(49) 22.2	(81) 30.0	% Profit Before Taxes/Tangible Net Worth	(10) 25.0	(10) 73.2		(19) 30.9	24.3	31.4
16.1	11.1	11.1		10.3	11.3		10.6	10.5	20.7
.2	1.7	4.9		1.2	3.1		4.6	4.9	10.6
10.5	9.8	11.0	% Profit Before Taxes/Total Assets	7.4	26.6		21.7	8.8	13.2
3.4	4.1	4.3		4.2	3.3		6.3	3.2	7.0
.0	1.1	1.8		.2	1.6		2.5	1.9	2.1
12.7	16.0	15.2	Sales/Net Fixed Assets	2.0	18.4		9.0	24.6	22.4
5.5	5.7	6.0		.7	8.6		4.4	10.0	11.0
1.6	2.0	2.0		.2	5.9		1.4	5.8	3.7
3.0	3.3	3.7	Sales/Total Assets	1.0	2.9		4.3	5.1	4.4
2.0	2.0	2.0		.5	2.1		2.4	3.6	2.2
.9	.9	.9		.2	1.4		.7	1.7	1.3
(61) 1.1	(51) 1.0	(84) 1.1	% Depr., Dep., Amort./Sales	(10) 7.5	1.8		1.4	.6	.6
2.4	1.9	2.0		14.1	2.1		2.3	1.1	1.6
6.0	4.0	5.0		18.8	4.1		7.0	1.8	3.1
(15) 2.1	(14) .6	(23) 1.4	% Officers', Directors', Owners' Comp/Sales						
4.1	2.4	3.2							
6.8	6.5	4.9							
2289660M	660159M	3018576M	Net Sales ($)	5616M	23339M	29111M	144503M	271483M	2544524M
684424M	447097M	1149262M	Total Assets ($)	17895M	14619M	17722M	127992M	130235M	840799M

Current Data Sorted By Assets   Comparative Historical Data

0-500M	500M-2MM	2-10MM	10-50MM	50-100MM	100-250MM	Type of Statement	4/1/98-3/31/99 ALL	4/1/99-3/31/00 ALL
		2	6	2		Unqualified	8	9
2	2	11				Reviewed	11	17
1	2	3				Compiled	17	11
3	3	1				Tax Returns	9	7
2	3	5	2			Other	14	12
		8 (4/1-9/30/02)		**42 (10/1/02-3/31/03)**				
8	10	22	8	2		**NUMBER OF STATEMENTS**	59	56
%	%	%	%	%	%	**ASSETS**	%	%
	10.4	8.6				Cash & Equivalents	10.3	9.8
	24.5	34.5				Trade Receivables (net)	13.2	17.4
	12.4	6.1				Inventory	3.0	2.9
	.2	2.6				All Other Current	2.7	2.1
	47.5	51.8				Total Current	29.2	32.2
	41.4	37.8				Fixed Assets (net)	60.6	49.5
	8.6	1.3				Intangibles (net)	3.8	5.9
	2.4	9.2				All Other Non-Current	6.4	12.5
	100.0	100.0				Total	100.0	100.0
						LIABILITIES		
	12.0	15.9				Notes Payable-Short Term	8.6	6.7
	5.8	2.7				Cur. Mat.-L/T/D	4.8	4.0
	11.1	17.6				Trade Payables	5.2	9.5
	.0	.0				Income Taxes Payable	.1	.3
	24.0	9.5				All Other Current	8.8	7.0
	52.9	45.6				Total Current	27.5	27.4
	26.1	17.5				Long Term Debt	34.2	33.7
	.0	.3				Deferred Taxes	.6	.7
	2.6	1.2				All Other Non-Current	3.8	4.7
	18.4	35.3				Net Worth	33.8	33.5
	100.0	100.0				Total Liabilities & Net Worth	100.0	100.0
						INCOME DATA		
	100.0	100.0				Net Sales	100.0	100.0
						Gross Profit		
	96.2	86.2				Operating Expenses	77.9	80.7
	3.8	13.8				Operating Profit	22.1	19.3
	4.6	4.5				All Other Expenses (net)	9.9	5.7
	–.8	9.4				Profit Before Taxes	12.3	13.6
						RATIOS		
	2.0	2.7					2.8	2.5
	1.4	1.2				Current	1.5	1.2
	.6	.6					.6	.7
	1.5	2.5					2.7	2.3
	.9	1.0				Quick	1.1	1.1
	.5	.5					.4	.5
	15 25.0	31 11.7					0 UND	20 18.4
	37 9.8	46 7.9				Sales/Receivables	23 15.5	37 9.8
	53 6.9	52 7.0					44 8.3	56 6.5
						Cost of Sales/Inventory		
						Cost of Sales/Payables		
	7.2	7.6					7.1	6.4
	18.0	27.7				Sales/Working Capital	18.1	22.5
	–15.0	–9.5					–12.7	–26.5
		44.7					8.0	9.1
	(18)	4.3				EBIT/Interest	(41) 3.2	(36) 3.8
		1.5					1.9	1.6
							7.0	4.1
						Net Profit + Depr., Dep., Amort./Cur. Mat. L /T/D	(12) 2.9	(12) 1.9
							1.8	.5
	.9	.2					1.0	.7
	2.7	.9				Fixed/Worth	2.6	1.4
	–1.1	6.4					30.1	8.6
	1.6	.6					.7	.7
	3.0	2.6				Debt/Worth	2.8	1.6
	–5.4	16.1					30.0	12.7
		58.7					56.3	78.3
	(18)	29.8				% Profit Before Taxes/Tangible Net Worth	(46) 27.7	(46) 38.9
		11.0					10.8	11.1
	5.1	19.2					20.2	25.3
	–2.6	7.5				% Profit Before Taxes/Total Assets	7.7	8.7
	–6.7	2.0					2.9	2.4
	41.7	43.9					9.5	15.9
	4.3	21.0				Sales/Net Fixed Assets	1.2	1.6
	1.1	.7					.5	.8
	3.8	3.8					2.4	2.4
	2.0	2.7				Sales/Total Assets	.9	.9
	.8	.6					.4	.5
		.7					3.8	2.4
	(20)	2.0				% Depr., Dep., Amort./Sales	(54) 7.5	(52) 6.3
		10.2					12.5	12.2
							4.8	2.3
						% Officers', Directors', Owners' Comp/Sales	(11) 8.7	(10) 4.9
							11.5	13.1
7563M	25340M	293957M	227567M	616259M		Net Sales ($)	422799M	621729M
2194M	10800M	109565M	183567M	175992M		Total Assets ($)	419416M	407214M

(Columns 0-500M, 10-50MM, 50-100MM, and 100-250MM: DATA NOT AVAILABLE)

M = $ thousand   MM = $ million
See Pages 11 through 18 for Explanation of Ratios and Data

Comparative Historical Data   Current Data Sorted By Sales

Type of Statement									
							1	5	4
Unqualified	3	4	10				1	5	4
Reviewed	11	14	15	1	4	1	4	2	3
Compiled	16	24	6	2	2	1			
Tax Returns	8	6	7	1	5		1		1
Other	12	22	12	3	4	1	2	2	
	4/1/00-3/31/01 ALL	4/1/01-3/31/02 ALL	4/1/02-3/31/03 ALL	_	8 (4/1-9/30/02)	_	_	42 (10/1/02-3/31/03)	_
				0-1MM	1-3MM	3-5MM	5-10MM	10-25MM	25MM & OVER
NUMBER OF STATEMENTS	50	70	50	7	15	3	8	9	8
	%	%	%	%	%	%	%	%	%
ASSETS									
Cash & Equivalents	9.5	10.3	8.5		9.3				
Trade Receivables (net)	18.3	21.9	29.0		23.2				
Inventory	4.7	4.1	5.4		5.6				
All Other Current	4.1	5.2	2.3		2.0				
Total Current	36.6	41.5	45.2		40.1				
Fixed Assets (net)	51.2	45.4	43.3		51.2				
Intangibles (net)	2.7	3.9	5.3		7.4				
All Other Non-Current	9.6	9.3	6.2		1.4				
Total	100.0	100.0	100.0		100.0				
LIABILITIES									
Notes Payable-Short Term	3.8	5.6	12.5		18.8				
Cur. Mat.-L/T/D	3.9	6.8	5.4		4.0				
Trade Payables	10.5	13.1	12.3		5.5				
Income Taxes Payable	.1	.3	.1		.0				
All Other Current	8.1	10.7	12.2		24.0				
Total Current	26.3	36.5	42.5		52.3				
Long Term Debt	33.5	28.7	24.3		24.2				
Deferred Taxes	.7	.7	.7		.0				
All Other Non-Current	6.3	3.3	3.8		8.8				
Net Worth	33.2	30.9	28.7		14.6				
Total Liabilities & Net Worth	100.0	100.0	100.0		100.0				
INCOME DATA									
Net Sales	100.0	100.0	100.0		100.0				
Gross Profit									
Operating Expenses	85.5	87.5	87.6		89.2				
Operating Profit	14.5	12.5	12.4		10.8				
All Other Expenses (net)	4.1	4.4	6.1		8.8				
Profit Before Taxes	10.4	8.1	6.3		2.0				
RATIOS									
Current	2.2 1.5 .7	1.9 1.3 .9	2.6 1.3 .6		1.5 .7 .3				
Quick	1.8 .9 .5	1.5 1.0 .5	1.5 .9 .5		1.3 .6 .2				
Sales/Receivables	10 37.4 / 32 11.3 / 48 7.7	15 24.2 / 34 10.7 / 49 7.4	25 14.4 / 44 8.2 / 50 7.4		3 119.0 / 39 9.4 / 49 7.5				
Cost of Sales/Inventory									
Cost of Sales/Payables									
Sales/Working Capital	6.7 20.1 -31.9	10.1 23.1 -103.3	8.2 31.1 -10.8		10.2 -19.5 -1.7				
EBIT/Interest	(38) 11.7 3.5 2.0	(50) 8.2 2.6 1.4	(42) 10.7 2.3 .3		(12) 5.4 .4 -.9				
Net Profit + Depr., Dep., Amort./Cur. Mat. L/T/D		(10) 5.0 2.1 .3	(11) 2.9 2.1 .7						
Fixed/Worth	.7 1.8 5.8	.5 2.0 4.9	.5 2.4 10.2		1.1 8.6 -1.1				
Debt/Worth	.6 2.8 7.7	.9 3.1 7.3	.9 3.0 24.4		.8 12.7 -4.8				
% Profit Before Taxes/Tangible Net Worth	(45) 60.9 35.6 8.8	(62) 71.1 34.8 4.8	(39) 54.1 27.7 4.6						
% Profit Before Taxes/Total Assets	21.9 7.5 2.4	20.3 6.6 1.9	16.3 4.4 -1.9		14.4 -.7 -9.2				
Sales/Net Fixed Assets	17.3 2.9 .7	30.2 4.4 .8	36.0 7.0 .7		28.8 4.7 .7				
Sales/Total Assets	3.5 1.5 .5	3.8 2.0 .6	3.9 2.2 .6		5.1 2.0 .6				
% Depr., Dep., Amort./Sales	(48) 1.0 2.6 10.0	(59) .7 3.0 9.1	(44) 1.3 3.0 10.9		(13) 2.2 4.8 11.1				
% Officers', Directors', Owners' Comp/Sales	(11) 3.6 5.6 15.0	(20) 2.1 6.0 12.0	(18) 3.6 6.1 12.4		(10) 3.6 5.7 14.4				
Net Sales ($)	584627M	1508166M	1170686M	2730M	25844M	13078M	58330M	156826M	913878M
Total Assets ($)	427598M	806522M	482118M	11243M	40808M	13123M	39139M	94005M	283800M

M = $ thousand   MM = $ million
See Pages 11 through 18 for Explanation of Ratios and Data

INFORMATION

	Current Data Sorted By Assets							Comparative Historical Data	
	1	1	3	12	8	2	**Type of Statement**		
		4	7	1	1		Unqualified	32	39
	4	3	4	1			Reviewed	15	14
	2	5	2				Compiled	23	17
	6	6	6	10			Tax Returns	10	11
							Other	24	24
		16 (4/1-9/30/02)		73 (10/1/02-3/31/03)				4/1/98-3/31/99	4/1/99-3/31/00
	0-500M	500M-2MM	2-10MM	10-50MM	50-100MM	100-250MM		ALL	ALL
	13	19	22	24	9	2	**NUMBER OF STATEMENTS**	104	105
	%	%	%	%	%	%	**ASSETS**	%	%
	21.6	14.1	15.1	12.8			Cash & Equivalents	9.4	10.3
	24.9	26.6	22.8	16.7			Trade Receivables (net)	24.9	22.5
	1.3	4.7	3.5	3.5			Inventory	4.5	3.9
	7.3	2.5	1.8	1.5			All Other Current	2.6	2.5
	55.1	47.8	43.2	34.5			Total Current	41.4	39.2
	34.2	26.3	35.0	40.0			Fixed Assets (net)	33.0	34.5
	5.8	10.5	13.7	15.7			Intangibles (net)	15.6	16.8
	4.8	15.3	8.0	9.8			All Other Non-Current	9.9	9.6
	100.0	100.0	100.0	100.0			Total	100.0	100.0
							LIABILITIES		
	11.5	1.2	3.1	.9			Notes Payable-Short Term	6.1	6.0
	1.0	4.2	7.0	3.6			Cur. Mat.-L/T/D	6.1	5.3
	15.2	9.1	9.2	4.9			Trade Payables	11.0	8.7
	.0	.1	1.4	.0			Income Taxes Payable	.2	.3
	11.1	7.0	12.9	18.0			All Other Current	15.0	12.4
	38.8	21.5	33.6	27.5			Total Current	38.4	32.7
	12.8	37.4	20.8	25.1			Long Term Debt	27.1	31.3
	.0	.2	.1	1.4			Deferred Taxes	.7	.8
	2.6	9.5	11.3	6.5			All Other Non-Current	6.9	6.9
	45.9	31.4	34.3	39.5			Net Worth	26.8	28.3
	100.0	100.0	100.0	100.0			Total Liabilities & Net Worth	100.0	100.0
							INCOME DATA		
	100.0	100.0	100.0	100.0			Net Sales	100.0	100.0
	54.8	65.0	46.0	48.4			Gross Profit	46.9	48.4
	52.1	59.7	37.0	41.8			Operating Expenses	42.2	41.6
	2.7	5.3	9.0	6.6			Operating Profit	4.7	6.8
	1.1	.7	1.6	1.8			All Other Expenses (net)	2.4	1.7
	1.6	4.6	7.4	4.7			Profit Before Taxes	2.3	5.1
							RATIOS		
	8.6	6.3	2.6	2.3				1.9	1.8
	1.4	2.1	1.2	1.4			Current	1.1	1.2
	.7	1.0	1.0	1.0				.8	.8
	5.7	6.3	2.4	2.0				1.6	1.5
	1.2	2.0	1.1	1.3			Quick	.9	1.1
	.7	.9	.7	.8				.6	.6
	0　UND	23　15.6	35　10.4	32　11.4				32　11.3	32　11.3
	28　13.0	34　10.7	40　9.1	37　9.8			Sales/Receivables	39　9.3	42　8.8
	40　9.0	67　5.5	60　6.1	48　7.6				50　7.2	49　7.4
	0　UND	0　UND	4　82.4	6　61.9				0　UND	0　UND
	0　UND	8　44.3	9　41.2	13　27.4			Cost of Sales/Inventory	9　39.1	10　35.0
	1　434.8	30　12.3	31　11.8	20　18.7				22　16.6	27　13.5
	14　25.2	15　24.5	18　20.7	13　28.1				11　32.0	14　25.9
	32　11.4	22　16.7	27　13.4	18　20.3			Cost of Sales/Payables	23　15.6	25　14.9
	66　5.5	48　7.5	54　6.7	35　10.4				45　8.1	41　8.8
	5.4	5.8	7.7	5.4				11.8	10.8
	24.7	9.4	25.0	19.2			Sales/Working Capital	52.5	41.8
	−21.2	154.6	NM	NM				−31.7	−20.1
		5.5	15.1	5.1				7.2	6.5
	(16)	1.8	(19) 3.9	(19) 3.7			EBIT/Interest	(94) 2.2	(98) 2.9
		−1.1	1.2	2.2				.9	1.4
								6.3	6.2
							Net Profit + Depr., Dep., Amort./Cur. Mat. L /T/D	(36) 2.9	(33) 2.2
								.9	1.9
	.4	.1	.6	.8				.6	.8
	.6	3.6	1.7	1.2			Fixed/Worth	1.8	1.8
	NM	−1.8	−6.3	NM				−1.5	−2.5
	.1	.1	.8	.7				1.0	1.3
	.7	5.3	2.4	1.5			Debt/Worth	4.4	3.6
	NM	−8.0	−13.9	NM				−5.2	−6.1
	20.2	74.4	37.7	40.5				39.1	40.4
	(10) 4.1	(13) 29.8	(15) 15.1	(18) 21.3			% Profit Before Taxes/Tangible Net Worth	(71) 21.5	(71) 23.3
	−28.4	1.3	2.9	2.2				.6	5.6
	22.7	25.0	17.5	15.3				13.5	13.2
	5.2	8.1	7.8	7.4			% Profit Before Taxes/Total Assets	4.5	6.5
	−.9	.1	.8	2.5				−1.1	1.7
	19.2	19.2	14.5	5.7				15.2	11.6
	12.3	9.4	6.6	4.0			Sales/Net Fixed Assets	6.3	5.5
	8.3	4.4	2.4	2.6				3.2	2.8
	5.3	2.9	2.3	1.8				2.9	2.5
	3.5	2.3	1.8	1.5			Sales/Total Assets	1.9	1.6
	2.2	1.1	1.2	1.1				1.2	1.1
	1.2	1.7	3.2	3.5				1.7	2.4
	1.9	(15) 3.0	(20) 4.2	(22) 4.6			% Depr., Dep., Amort./Sales	(93) 3.5	(88) 4.0
	3.0	6.7	6.1	6.1				5.1	6.2
		3.8						3.1	3.2
	(10)	7.2					% Officers', Directors', Owners' Comp/Sales	(25) 6.0	(26) 6.1
		16.5						10.2	12.4
	12337M	41288M	182272M	765895M	759965M	190443M	Net Sales ($)	4571804M	2712235M
	3601M	19959M	97650M	559281M	667131M	297907M	Total Assets ($)	2465772M	2295268M

M = $ thousand　　MM = $ million
See Pages 11 through 18 for Explanation of Ratios and Data

Comparative Historical Data   Current Data Sorted By Sales

			Type of Statement	0-1MM	1-3MM	3-5MM	5-10MM	10-25MM	25MM & OVER
22	19	27	Unqualified		2		1	6	18
12	11	13	Reviewed	1	3	2	3	4	
14	18	12	Compiled	3	3	4	1	1	
6	8	9	Tax Returns	4	2	2	1		
23	32	28	Other	4	1	1	3	5	6
4/1/00-3/31/01 ALL	4/1/01-3/31/02 ALL	4/1/02-3/31/03 ALL		16 (4/1-9/30/02)		73 (10/1/02-3/31/03)			
77	88	89	NUMBER OF STATEMENTS	12	19	9	9	16	24
%	%	%	**ASSETS**	%	%	%	%	%	%
9.1	10.6	14.6	Cash & Equivalents	22.9	16.6			16.8	9.9
24.4	24.2	20.7	Trade Receivables (net)	18.9	25.0			22.8	14.3
4.2	3.1	3.3	Inventory	1.2	4.1			5.3	2.4
1.9	2.9	2.7	All Other Current	6.9	2.2			.9	2.0
39.6	40.9	41.3	Total Current	50.0	48.0			45.8	28.7
34.6	32.0	33.6	Fixed Assets (net)	26.4	31.5			28.2	38.5
17.0	17.1	15.6	Intangibles (net)	9.9	12.7			14.9	25.3
8.8	10.1	9.5	All Other Non-Current	13.7	7.8			11.0	7.5
100.0	100.0	100.0	Total	100.0	100.0			100.0	100.0
			LIABILITIES						
8.0	3.1	3.1	Notes Payable-Short Term	6.4	5.2			1.0	.7
5.1	5.4	4.7	Cur. Mat.-L/T/D	2.3	1.9			4.3	5.5
10.1	8.6	8.1	Trade Payables	10.3	8.8			8.3	4.2
.3	.4	.4	Income Taxes Payable	.0	.6			.1	.0
13.6	10.0	12.6	All Other Current	8.0	9.1			19.3	15.4
37.1	27.5	28.9	Total Current	26.9	25.5			33.0	25.9
28.4	31.2	26.3	Long Term Debt	13.5	35.4			15.1	34.5
.6	.4	.6	Deferred Taxes	.0	.2			.7	1.5
10.4	14.3	7.8	All Other Non-Current	5.7	4.4			10.4	7.7
23.4	26.6	36.4	Net Worth	53.9	34.5			40.8	30.4
100.0	100.0	100.0	Total Liabilities & Net Worth	100.0	100.0			100.0	100.0
			INCOME DATA						
100.0	100.0	100.0	Net Sales	100.0	100.0			100.0	100.0
49.7	49.0	52.8	Gross Profit	56.9	64.1			43.2	51.9
44.6	44.2	46.2	Operating Expenses	56.9	53.1			40.4	41.5
5.1	4.8	6.6	Operating Profit	.0	11.0			2.9	10.4
1.5	2.3	1.8	All Other Expenses (net)	.6	1.6			1.3	3.3
3.6	2.5	4.8	Profit Before Taxes	-.6	9.4			1.6	7.2
			RATIOS						
1.8	2.3	2.7		8.9	6.8			3.2	1.7
1.3	1.5	1.4	Current	1.8	2.1			2.0	1.1
.9	1.0	.9		.6	.7			1.2	.9
1.4	2.0	2.3		8.0	6.8			2.8	1.3
1.1	1.2	1.2	Quick	1.6	2.0			1.7	.9
.7	.8	.8		.6	.7			1.0	.8
34 10.7	33 11.2	30 12.0		0 UND	24 15.0			31 11.8	32 11.5
42 8.8	40 9.1	36 10.1	Sales/Receivables	28 13.2	34 10.7			39 9.3	35 10.3
51 7.2	50 7.3	48 7.6		41 8.9	51 7.2			52 7.1	45 8.1
2 217.8	0 UND	0 UND		0 UND	0 UND			7 51.5	5 75.2
11 31.8	8 48.5	8 44.3	Cost of Sales/Inventory	0 UND	2 168.7			13 29.0	11 34.5
21 17.0	18 20.3	20 18.7		0 UND	30 12.3			29 12.6	19 18.8
14 26.7	12 30.6	14 26.1		11 34.4	17 21.9			15 25.1	11 33.2
26 13.9	23 16.1	22 16.9	Cost of Sales/Payables	15 24.1	27 13.3			26 14.0	17 22.1
53 6.9	44 8.3	51 7.2		70 5.2	65 5.6			48 7.7	40 9.1
12.0	8.0	6.8		2.7	7.1			4.3	14.1
23.1	18.1	23.4	Sales/Working Capital	20.6	12.1			9.2	113.9
-109.0	-123.1	-51.1		-21.8	-23.3			31.7	-42.9
4.2	6.7	9.6			15.8			8.6	6.0
(70) 2.3	(78) 1.9	(74) 3.7	EBIT/Interest		(16) 3.8			(12) 3.7	(22) 3.6
1.0	.1	1.1			1.5			1.2	2.1
3.3	4.7	8.5	Net Profit + Depr., Dep.,						
(22) 1.5	(17) 1.6	(20) 2.0	Amort./Cur. Mat. L/T/D						
.8	.8	1.3							
.9	.5	.6		.1	.4			.5	1.0
1.8	2.2	2.1	Fixed/Worth	.5	3.6			.8	7.8
-3.0	-1.6	-4.0		4.7	-1.5			NM	-1.1
1.5	.8	.5		.1	.1			.6	1.1
3.2	3.7	2.4	Debt/Worth	.5	3.4			1.0	11.0
-6.3	-4.9	-9.2		9.1	-3.5			NM	-3.0
33.2	44.4	43.0		5.4	80.3			35.1	73.5
(53) 17.9	(58) 11.7	(61) 15.9	% Profit Before Taxes/Tangible Net Worth	(10) 2.4	(14) 42.0			(12) 11.9	(14) 29.7
1.8	-.4	1.3		-40.4	12.7			-9.1	4.2
13.6	13.5	16.1		6.0	31.9			17.1	15.4
5.8	4.4	7.7	% Profit Before Taxes/Total Assets	1.3	11.0			7.4	9.5
.1	-2.7	.8		-8.6	5.2			.7	3.8
9.6	15.5	13.1		14.1	23.6			11.6	5.8
5.6	5.7	5.8	Sales/Net Fixed Assets	11.5	11.4			6.2	4.1
3.0	3.1	3.1		5.8	4.2			3.2	2.6
2.5	2.7	2.4		3.8	3.5			2.5	1.7
1.8	1.9	1.7	Sales/Total Assets	1.8	2.7			1.6	1.4
1.2	1.1	1.1		1.0	1.3			1.2	.9
1.9	1.7	2.1		1.2	1.8			3.0	2.9
(61) 3.2	(77) 3.6	(79) 3.8	% Depr., Dep., Amort./Sales	(11) 1.9	(16) 3.2			(14) 4.3	(22) 4.5
6.0	6.4	6.2		3.0	6.6			6.1	6.7
2.7	2.4	3.8	% Officers', Directors',						
(18) 6.0	(22) 5.0	(22) 7.3	Owners' Comp/Sales						
9.5	8.4	16.5							
2398116M	2790753M	1952200M	Net Sales ($)	7960M	35945M	35898M	69367M	296100M	1506930M
1894535M	1735629M	1645529M	Total Assets ($)	5496M	20139M	21171M	42444M	272989M	1283290M

M = $ thousand   MM = $ million
See Pages 11 through 18 for Explanation of Ratios and Data

Current Data Sorted By Assets | Comparative Historical Data

	0-500M	500M-2MM	2-10MM	10-50MM	50-100MM	100-250MM		4/1/98-3/31/99 ALL	4/1/99-3/31/00 ALL
Type of Statement									
Unqualified	1	2	5	9	4	2		27	21
Reviewed		4	7	4				19	19
Compiled	4	9	5	2				10	16
Tax Returns	1	1	2	1				13	5
Other	4	4	15	2	1	2		23	19
		21 (4/1-9/30/02)		70 (10/1/02-3/31/03)					
NUMBER OF STATEMENTS	10	20	34	18	5	4		92	80
	%	%	%	%	%	%		%	%
ASSETS									
Cash & Equivalents	11.3	16.2	11.5	17.9				12.4	13.2
Trade Receivables (net)	29.2	34.1	30.0	18.6				31.5	30.2
Inventory	1.0	4.8	8.9	6.1				7.3	8.1
All Other Current	9.3	6.2	6.1	5.8				2.6	4.5
Total Current	50.8	61.3	56.6	48.3				53.7	56.0
Fixed Assets (net)	24.7	21.4	17.3	22.1				19.7	20.5
Intangibles (net)	8.6	5.9	17.5	17.7				16.2	13.9
All Other Non-Current	16.1	11.4	8.7	11.9				10.4	9.6
Total	100.0	100.0	100.0	100.0				100.0	100.0
LIABILITIES									
Notes Payable-Short Term	14.7	3.8	4.6	.8				5.1	8.6
Cur. Mat.-L/T/D	8.4	2.9	6.1	7.6				5.8	5.7
Trade Payables	17.6	14.0	16.3	10.3				19.8	16.4
Income Taxes Payable	.5	.3	.4	1.3				.4	.3
All Other Current	25.0	12.7	29.2	21.2				24.0	20.8
Total Current	66.3	33.8	56.6	41.2				55.0	51.8
Long Term Debt	29.4	11.9	26.2	14.3				24.5	20.1
Deferred Taxes	.0	.7	.3	.1				.6	.4
All Other Non-Current	19.3	14.4	8.2	16.0				23.1	10.1
Net Worth	−15.1	39.2	8.8	28.4				−3.2	17.5
Total Liabilities & Net Worth	100.0	100.0	100.0	100.0				100.0	100.0
INCOME DATA									
Net Sales	100.0	100.0	100.0	100.0				100.0	100.0
Gross Profit	56.4	42.3	48.5	46.9				44.0	45.5
Operating Expenses	56.4	39.3	41.6	40.1				39.1	40.8
Operating Profit	.0	2.9	6.8	6.8				4.9	4.7
All Other Expenses (net)	1.2	−.4	2.8	1.1				1.1	1.0
Profit Before Taxes	−1.3	3.3	4.0	5.7				3.8	3.7
RATIOS									
Current	1.6	3.1	1.5	2.4				1.8	2.0
	.8	1.8	1.2	1.1				1.0	1.2
	.4	1.3	.7	.7				.7	.7
Quick	1.3	2.6	1.1	1.4				1.4	1.5
	.5	1.5	1.0	1.0				.9	.9
	.3	1.2	.5	.5				.5	.5
Sales/Receivables	0 UND	34 10.9	34 10.8	25 14.8				26 14.3	29 12.8
	34 10.8	41 9.0	45 8.2	37 9.9				42 8.8	42 8.7
	56 6.6	51 7.2	58 6.3	63 5.8				64 5.7	61 6.0
Cost of Sales/Inventory	0 UND	0 UND	0 UND	0 UND				0 UND	0 UND
	0 UND	1 419.2	7 50.1	16 22.3				13 29.0	10 34.9
	7 55.4	12 30.4	30 12.2	53 6.8				37 9.9	38 9.7
Cost of Sales/Payables	4 95.9	11 32.7	22 16.5	21 17.5				18 20.1	12 31.1
	39 9.4	21 17.2	44 8.4	31 11.7				41 8.9	27 13.8
	81 4.5	39 9.3	78 4.6	63 5.8				68 5.3	51 7.1
Sales/Working Capital	19.2	5.6	11.9	5.4				10.5	7.3
	−61.2	14.6	37.3	37.1				130.7	48.7
	−9.0	30.3	−13.2	−9.1				−13.8	−16.5
EBIT/Interest		(16) 46.5	(28) 9.5	(14) 42.0				13.0	10.6
		8.0	2.3	5.7				(80) 4.7	(64) 3.6
		2.4	−1.0	2.2				1.3	.8
Net Profit + Depr., Dep., Amort./Cur. Mat. L /T/D								5.1	4.1
								(23) 3.1	(17) 1.5
								1.2	.1
Fixed/Worth	.4	.2	.4	.5				.5	.5
	1.3	.4	2.6	1.1				26.6	3.9
	−1.0	1.4	−.2	−1.4				−.4	−.3
Debt/Worth	2.3	.6	1.7	1.4				1.9	1.2
	NM	1.2	9.2	8.1				NM	14.0
	−4.0	2.5	−2.6	−9.9				−3.1	−3.6
% Profit Before Taxes/Tangible Net Worth		83.5	126.9	70.4				74.5	69.8
		(18) 16.6	(20) 23.8	(12) 36.8				(46) 41.9	(47) 36.9
		2.4	−20.4	12.1				16.9	.0
% Profit Before Taxes/Total Assets	34.6	21.1	24.0	13.3				19.2	18.2
	2.6	7.9	9.6	7.5				7.7	9.3
	−17.7	1.7	−6.1	1.8				1.2	−.8
Sales/Net Fixed Assets	42.2	62.7	60.6	27.4				35.9	34.3
	15.1	18.1	37.6	10.8				17.2	19.7
	10.2	9.6	6.5	4.5				8.7	8.8
Sales/Total Assets	5.1	4.0	3.1	2.0				3.9	3.4
	4.4	3.1	2.2	1.4				2.2	2.4
	2.5	2.4	1.5	1.1				1.5	1.6
% Depr., Dep., Amort./Sales		.7	.9	1.3				1.1	1.0
		(18) 1.6	(25) 1.6	(16) 3.1				(67) 1.7	(58) 1.7
		4.2	3.0	4.2				3.4	3.5
% Officers', Directors', Owners' Comp/Sales								1.8	2.4
								(29) 4.7	(25) 5.1
								9.0	6.9
Net Sales ($)	9637M	78413M	368028M	602806M	307314M	657490M		2337839M	1660120M
Total Assets ($)	2219M	24527M	164652M	437066M	374927M	590890M		1429782M	1145755M

© RMA 2003

M = $ thousand   MM = $ million
See Pages 11 through 18 for Explanation of Ratios and Data

Comparative Historical Data | Current Data Sorted By Sales

Hist 4/1/00-3/31/01 ALL	Hist 4/1/01-3/31/02 ALL	Hist 4/1/02-3/31/03 ALL		0-1MM	1-3MM	3-5MM	5-10MM	10-25MM	25MM & OVER
			Type of Statement		21 (4/1-9/30/02)		70 (10/1/02-3/31/03)		
19	23	23	Unqualified	1	2	1	2	5	12
21	18	15	Reviewed			2	5	4	4
13	13	20	Compiled	2	5	6	4	2	1
6	4	5	Tax Returns	1	1			3	
19	28	28	Other	2	6	2	5	7	6
78	86	91	**NUMBER OF STATEMENTS**	6	14	11	16	21	23
%	%	%	**ASSETS**	%	%	%	%	%	%
12.7	11.1	13.7	Cash & Equivalents		14.4	13.5	14.3	11.5	16.2
31.9	27.6	26.6	Trade Receivables (net)		27.6	29.0	34.8	29.1	17.1
6.1	5.5	6.2	Inventory		3.6	7.0	5.8	10.1	5.2
2.6	3.8	6.4	All Other Current		6.2	3.8	4.8	7.7	5.5
53.3	48.0	52.9	Total Current		51.7	53.2	59.7	58.5	43.9
19.9	20.4	19.5	Fixed Assets (net)		20.9	24.3	12.2	21.9	16.6
15.8	19.3	16.5	Intangibles (net)		7.8	11.0	20.0	12.4	27.8
11.0	12.4	11.2	All Other Non-Current		19.6	11.5	8.1	7.2	11.6
100.0	100.0	100.0	Total		100.0	100.0	100.0	100.0	100.0
			LIABILITIES						
9.5	12.6	4.5	Notes Payable-Short Term		10.1	.6	6.9	3.4	.5
3.9	5.9	5.7	Cur. Mat.-L/T/D		5.8	3.8	3.3	7.3	7.2
15.5	14.0	13.9	Trade Payables		15.9	10.6	21.5	11.5	10.9
.3	.3	.5	Income Taxes Payable		.0	.3	.4	1.4	.0
20.8	18.4	22.5	All Other Current		15.3	19.4	33.9	22.2	21.0
50.0	51.3	47.2	Total Current		47.1	34.6	66.0	45.8	39.6
18.9	20.7	21.6	Long Term Debt		14.9	10.9	17.1	31.2	18.8
.7	.5	.6	Deferred Taxes		.4	.8	.2	.4	1.4
14.4	14.9	13.1	All Other Non-Current		19.1	2.1	11.0	7.3	16.8
15.9	12.6	17.5	Net Worth		18.5	51.5	5.7	15.3	23.4
100.0	100.0	100.0	Total Liabilities & Net Worth		100.0	100.0	100.0	100.0	100.0
			INCOME DATA						
100.0	100.0	100.0	Net Sales		100.0	100.0	100.0	100.0	100.0
49.3	47.5	46.9	Gross Profit		49.9	42.1	44.0	51.3	43.6
45.0	44.2	41.7	Operating Expenses		48.3	38.5	35.5	44.9	37.2
4.3	3.4	5.2	Operating Profit		1.7	3.6	8.4	6.5	6.4
1.8	1.4	1.8	All Other Expenses (net)		.3	.5	3.9	1.0	2.7
2.5	2.0	3.4	Profit Before Taxes		1.3	3.1	4.5	5.5	3.7
			RATIOS						
1.8	1.6	1.9			2.3	2.5	2.3	1.8	1.4
1.2	1.1	1.2	Current		1.5	1.5	1.2	1.3	1.1
.9	.8	.7			.5	.9	.8	1.0	.7
1.5	1.3	1.3			1.8	2.5	1.7	1.2	1.1
1.1	.9	1.1	Quick		1.4	1.0	1.1	1.1	.9
.7	.6	.6			.5	.8	.6	.6	.6
28 12.9	30 12.1	26 14.2		14 25.6	29 12.6	26 14.1		35 10.4	24 15.0
48 7.7	40 9.1	41 9.0	Sales/Receivables	50 7.3	40 9.1	39 9.4		45 8.1	35 10.5
65 5.6	56 6.5	55 6.7		60 6.1	44 8.2	63 5.8		51 7.1	60 6.1
0 UND	0 UND	0 UND		0 UND	1 721.0	0 UND		0 UND	0 UND
7 50.0	6 57.0	6 57.6	Cost of Sales/Inventory	0 UND	13 28.3	0 UND		13 27.2	8 47.6
26 14.2	19 19.1	22 16.5		11 33.1	31 11.8	10 35.1		82 4.4	29 12.4
12 30.0	15 24.9	19 19.5		9 38.8	1 447.5	17 21.2		20 17.9	22 16.5
30 12.0	35 10.3	31 11.9	Cost of Sales/Payables	30 12.1	22 16.5	48 7.5		26 13.8	31 11.9
80 4.6	71 5.2	66 5.6		69 5.3	33 11.0	88 4.2		55 6.7	62 5.8
11.1	13.3	7.8		5.8	7.0	16.9		9.1	7.3
32.0	42.5	27.2	Sales/Working Capital	15.6	13.2	29.2		26.6	47.6
-37.1	-17.6	-18.0		-11.9	-56.7	-18.5		-277.7	-10.8
8.8	7.2	15.1		21.2		20.5	13.5		16.2
(67) 3.1	(77) 2.5	(75) 3.5	EBIT/Interest	(12) 2.1		(14) 7.6	(16) 2.3		(20) 4.7
.7	-.2	.2		-.9		1.5	-1.0		.4
11.5	5.7	4.3	Net Profit + Depr., Dep., Amort./Cur. Mat. L/T/D						
(17) 2.0	(15) 3.1	(15) 1.6							
.9	1.6	.3							
.5	.4	.3			.1	.1	.3	.3	.7
2.3	4.9	1.2	Fixed/Worth		.7	.7	1.9	1.2	2.4
-.5	-.3	-.3			-1.6	1.9	-.2	-1.4	-.1
1.5	1.7	1.4			.7	.6	1.9	1.4	3.2
8.0	11.4	4.5	Debt/Worth		1.9	1.0	4.4	5.2	16.0
-3.5	-2.5	-4.3			-4.2	3.2	-2.5	-10.8	-2.1
62.0	69.3	82.5	% Profit Before Taxes/Tangible Net Worth		34.4			134.4	76.7
(48) 26.0	(48) 24.7	(58) 23.1			(10) 14.3			(14) 26.5	(13) 43.7
-8.3	3.7	.9			4.8			-20.1	13.9
14.9	12.5	18.2	% Profit Before Taxes/Total Assets		12.1	10.8	30.5	19.1	13.8
7.1	6.9	7.4			3.7	6.4	14.8	10.6	7.2
-1.3	-3.6	-2.0			-2.8	1.4	-2.6	-5.9	-1.4
40.7	35.0	47.6	Sales/Net Fixed Assets		81.2	73.3	58.2	40.6	43.3
21.6	18.0	18.6			17.2	17.3	43.3	17.8	17.9
7.6	6.6	8.8			8.6	7.1	25.4	5.9	4.8
3.4	3.1	3.3	Sales/Total Assets		3.8	3.3	4.2	3.0	2.0
2.4	2.1	2.2			2.5	2.4	2.8	2.2	1.3
1.6	1.3	1.4			1.2	1.6	1.6	1.6	.9
1.1	1.1	1.2	% Depr., Dep., Amort./Sales		1.2	.8	.6	1.3	1.3
(57) 2.3	(67) 2.5	(72) 1.8		(11) 2.5	(10) 1.7	(12) 1.2		(17) 1.7	(17) 2.5
3.8	4.9	3.4		4.0	5.4	1.8		3.2	4.0
3.7	3.0	3.5	% Officers', Directors', Owners' Comp/Sales						
(18) 6.2	(20) 5.9	(25) 5.5							
9.4	8.9	7.1							
1377357M	1834711M	2023688M	Net Sales ($)	3915M	26421M	44133M	116060M	330706M	1502453M
969048M	1400420M	1594281M	Total Assets ($)	1043M	15511M	19808M	54531M	184944M	1318444M

© RMA 2003

M = $ thousand   MM = $ million
See Pages 11 through 18 for Explanation of Ratios and Data

Current Data Sorted By Assets   Comparative Historical Data

0-500M	500M-2MM	2-10MM	10-50MM	50-100MM	100-250MM	Type of Statement	4/1/98-3/31/99 ALL	4/1/99-3/31/00 ALL
	1	11	14	6	7	Unqualified	35	40
	3	14	3	1		Reviewed	35	27
5	4	3				Compiled	13	13
3	2	3				Tax Returns	6	5
1	1	14	11	1	1	Other	36	31
	30 (4/1-9/30/02)		79 (10/1/02-3/31/03)					
9	11	45	28	8	8	**NUMBER OF STATEMENTS**	125	116
%	%	%	%	%	%	**ASSETS**	%	%
	12.8	8.4	9.3			Cash & Equivalents	8.6	8.6
	25.4	33.3	22.9			Trade Receivables (net)	27.5	30.6
	26.7	26.2	24.8			Inventory	30.1	30.7
	2.6	4.4	4.2			All Other Current	3.7	3.0
	67.5	72.4	61.2			Total Current	70.0	72.9
	17.3	14.0	13.3			Fixed Assets (net)	14.4	12.7
	9.8	6.0	12.9			Intangibles (net)	5.1	5.4
	5.4	7.5	12.6			All Other Non-Current	10.6	8.9
	100.0	100.0	100.0			Total	100.0	100.0
						LIABILITIES		
	10.0	8.6	11.2			Notes Payable-Short Term	10.3	10.7
	8.2	4.5	2.1			Cur. Mat.-L/T/D	2.7	2.5
	15.2	19.6	13.5			Trade Payables	14.4	17.9
	.0	.4	.6			Income Taxes Payable	.3	.3
	10.9	14.2	14.1			All Other Current	14.9	15.2
	44.3	47.3	41.5			Total Current	42.7	46.6
	13.4	9.4	7.2			Long Term Debt	9.7	10.8
	.2	.1	.3			Deferred Taxes	.4	.4
	4.6	9.7	12.2			All Other Non-Current	8.2	8.0
	37.6	33.5	38.9			Net Worth	39.0	34.3
	100.0	100.0	100.0			Total Liabilities & Net Worth	100.0	100.0
						INCOME DATA		
	100.0	100.0	100.0			Net Sales	100.0	100.0
	49.7	49.9	51.8			Gross Profit	51.5	50.1
	44.7	45.9	48.1			Operating Expenses	48.8	45.7
	5.1	4.0	3.7			Operating Profit	2.7	4.4
	1.4	.8	.8			All Other Expenses (net)	1.3	.6
	3.6	3.2	2.8			Profit Before Taxes	1.4	3.8
						RATIOS		
	2.6	2.3	2.4			Current	2.4	2.3
	1.5	1.5	1.6				1.6	1.7
	.9	1.1	1.1				1.3	1.3
	1.3	1.2	1.6			Quick	1.4	1.3
	.9	.9	.8				.9	.9
	.6	.5	.5				.6	.6
	35 10.5	46 7.9	34 10.7			Sales/Receivables	39 9.3	40 9.1
	54 6.7	61 6.0	56 6.6				62 5.9	63 5.8
	61 6.0	84 4.3	84 4.3				81 4.5	93 3.9
	24 15.4	29 12.5	85 4.3			Cost of Sales/Inventory	57 6.4	44 8.3
	117 3.1	117 3.1	128 2.8				140 2.6	139 2.6
	187 1.9	185 2.0	229 1.6				250 1.5	250 1.5
	5 78.2	30 12.3	26 14.1			Cost of Sales/Payables	30 12.0	31 11.6
	35 10.3	61 6.0	50 7.3				54 6.8	56 6.5
	118 3.1	111 3.3	106 3.4				94 3.9	115 3.2
	3.3	3.6	3.8			Sales/Working Capital	3.3	3.4
	6.5	6.7	6.9				6.1	5.5
	-46.6	26.3	73.9				12.2	12.4
	5.3	10.6	7.4			EBIT/Interest	9.1	11.6
	(10) 1.3	(39) 2.7	(21) 2.1				(113) 3.2	(102) 3.5
	-4.0	1.1	.2				1.3	1.3
		3.5	10.7			Net Profit + Depr., Dep., Amort./Cur. Mat. L /T/D	9.6	5.0
		(11) 1.4	(10) 2.2				(35) 2.8	(29) 2.1
		.7	-1.0				1.2	1.1
	.1	.1	.1			Fixed/Worth	.1	.1
	.2	.4	.4				.3	.3
	24.7	2.5	1.2				.8	1.2
	.9	.8	1.0			Debt/Worth	.7	.8
	1.7	2.0	1.6				1.7	1.7
	98.7	8.4	4.0				5.0	5.2
		39.8	41.7			% Profit Before Taxes/Tangible Net Worth	39.0	43.7
		(37) 12.2	(23) 9.1				(116) 16.9	(100) 18.6
		2.5	-3.9				4.9	3.9
	13.6	11.8	13.1			% Profit Before Taxes/Total Assets	11.7	14.5
	1.5	3.0	5.7				5.3	7.2
	-2.8	.3	-2.1				1.3	.8
	53.1	42.5	34.9			Sales/Net Fixed Assets	55.0	61.8
	18.8	19.8	23.6				24.7	23.0
	11.4	9.5	6.7				7.2	9.6
	3.0	2.3	1.8			Sales/Total Assets	2.0	2.1
	2.0	1.8	1.4				1.6	1.5
	1.3	1.4	1.0				1.2	1.2
		.7	1.7			% Depr., Dep., Amort./Sales	.8	.7
		(39) 1.3	(21) 2.6				(108) 1.4	(88) 1.5
		2.6	3.9				3.2	2.4
		1.6				% Officers', Directors', Owners' Comp/Sales	6.1	2.2
		(12) 4.7					(30) 8.3	(27) 7.5
		7.9					11.8	13.7
8295M	23115M	421924M	1081559M	704630M	1324980M	Net Sales ($)	3233940M	2214002M
2693M	11715M	227702M	699591M	547568M	1213683M	Total Assets ($)	2365701M	1721306M

Comparative Historical Data | Current Data Sorted By Sales

	4/1/00-3/31/01 ALL	4/1/01-3/31/02 ALL	4/1/02-3/31/03 ALL	Type of Statement	0-1MM	1-3MM	3-5MM	5-10MM	10-25MM	25MM & OVER
	32	33	39	Unqualified		1	1	4	14	19
	26	22	21	Reviewed	1	2	1	8	6	3
	13	15	12	Compiled	4	4	3		1	
	10	5	8	Tax Returns	1	4	1	1	1	
	24	38	29	Other	1	3	4	6	4	11
						30 (4/1-9/30/02)			79 (10/1/02-3/31/03)	
NUMBER OF STATEMENTS	105	113	109		7	14	10	19	26	33
	%	%	%	**ASSETS**	%	%	%	%	%	%
Cash & Equivalents	8.8	9.1	9.0			11.2	3.8	7.5	12.9	8.9
Trade Receivables (net)	29.4	28.4	27.8			27.1	28.0	33.2	27.5	25.1
Inventory	28.3	28.8	24.5			24.4	29.2	26.7	24.2	20.2
All Other Current	3.0	3.3	4.0			4.8	2.2	1.8	6.3	3.6
Total Current	69.6	69.5	65.4			67.5	63.1	69.2	71.0	57.8
Fixed Assets (net)	14.3	13.8	14.9			17.7	13.7	20.3	8.8	15.0
Intangibles (net)	6.6	7.1	9.8			7.7	10.8	3.3	8.4	16.6
All Other Non-Current	9.5	9.5	9.9			7.0	12.3	7.1	11.8	10.6
Total	100.0	100.0	100.0			100.0	100.0	100.0	100.0	100.0
				LIABILITIES						
Notes Payable-Short Term	10.8	20.3	14.6			9.1	9.0	7.5	10.9	5.5
Cur. Mat.-L/T/D	2.2	2.6	3.8			6.8	9.2	3.2	2.1	3.0
Trade Payables	17.3	12.9	16.7			12.1	14.9	20.4	18.6	11.6
Income Taxes Payable	.3	.3	.4			.0	.0	.5	.7	.4
All Other Current	14.3	17.2	13.7			9.7	16.0	12.0	13.8	16.2
Total Current	44.9	53.3	49.2			37.7	49.3	43.7	46.1	36.7
Long Term Debt	13.2	12.3	15.7			12.8	17.0	11.3	2.3	17.4
Deferred Taxes	.3	.2	.3			.3	.0	.1	.1	.6
All Other Non-Current	6.8	7.0	10.0			17.1	6.2	4.9	11.9	10.4
Net Worth	34.8	27.3	24.9			32.1	27.6	40.0	39.6	34.9
Total Liabilities & Net Worth	100.0	100.0	100.0			100.0	100.0	100.0	100.0	100.0
				INCOME DATA						
Net Sales	100.0	100.0	100.0			100.0	100.0	100.0	100.0	100.0
Gross Profit	51.3	54.2	51.3			47.7	68.2	51.4	48.3	46.5
Operating Expenses	44.6	48.8	46.6			43.5	67.0	44.8	44.0	39.2
Operating Profit	6.7	5.3	4.7			4.2	1.2	6.6	4.3	7.3
All Other Expenses (net)	1.0	1.4	1.5			.5	1.8	1.0	.4	2.8
Profit Before Taxes	5.7	4.0	3.2			3.7	−.6	5.6	3.9	4.4
				RATIOS						
Current	2.4	2.5	2.3			2.5	2.2	2.3	2.3	2.5
	1.6	1.8	1.5			2.1	1.3	1.5	1.5	1.8
	1.3	1.2	1.1			1.1	1.0	1.1	1.2	1.2
Quick	1.5	1.5	1.4			1.7	1.2	1.5	1.3	1.6
	.9	.8	.9			1.0	.5	.9	.9	1.1
	.5	.5	.5			.7	.4	.6	.5	.7
Sales/Receivables	36 10.1	37 9.7	39 9.4		28 12.8	42 8.6	43 8.5	38 9.7	40 9.0	
	62 5.9	60 6.0	56 6.5		52 7.0	60 6.1	54 6.8	55 6.6	63 5.8	
	97 3.8	99 3.7	84 4.3		101 3.6	129 2.8	98 3.7	70 5.2	95 3.9	
Cost of Sales/Inventory	50 7.2	78 4.6	28 13.2		11 32.4	78 4.7	44 8.4	25 14.5	38 9.5	
	132 2.8	155 2.3	117 3.1		93 3.9	175 2.1	117 3.1	124 2.9	108 3.4	
	248 1.5	285 1.3	182 2.0		197 1.9	762 .5	175 2.1	231 1.6	131 2.8	
Cost of Sales/Payables	32 11.4	23 15.7	22 16.3		0 UND	36 10.2	23 15.6	38 9.6	20 18.2	
	60 6.1	50 7.3	55 6.6		28 13.2	56 6.5	66 5.6	66 5.6	37 9.8	
	113 3.2	89 4.1	96 3.8		60 6.1	251 1.5	120 3.0	88 4.2	85 4.3	
Sales/Working Capital	3.4	3.1	3.6			2.9	2.7	3.9	3.5	3.9
	6.3	5.3	7.1			6.5	6.7	5.4	7.3	6.7
	17.8	20.1	52.5			NM	−272.7	89.3	21.9	15.2
EBIT/Interest	11.3	6.0	8.5			6.0	6.1	10.2	10.6	12.5
	(89) 3.3	(97) 2.4	(94) 3.4		(13) 2.7	1.4	(16) 4.1	(19) 2.4	(29) 5.6	
	.7	.8	.7			.3	.0	1.8	−.1	1.4
Net Profit + Depr., Dep., Amort./Cur. Mat. L/T/D	5.1	4.2	4.1							4.3
	(23) 1.8	(26) 1.9	(25) 2.0						(11) 2.7	
	1.3	1.0	.6							.1
Fixed/Worth	.1	.1	.1			.1	.1	.1	.1	.2
	.3	.3	.5			.5	.5	.6	.2	.6
	2.4	1.7	2.5			6.8	−3.1	2.5	.7	−4.0
Debt/Worth	.8	.8	.8			.9	.8	.5	.9	.7
	2.0	1.6	1.8			1.6	1.8	2.7	1.5	2.5
	25.5	7.4	26.2			29.6	−13.4	4.2	5.7	−9.3
% Profit Before Taxes/Tangible Net Worth	38.7	34.7	38.2			70.7		56.1	39.3	40.4
	(84) 22.6	(95) 14.5	(85) 13.4			(12) 15.9		(17) 16.5	(22) 9.4	(24) 20.0
	3.0	1.6	.1			−3.1		7.3	−3.7	5.9
% Profit Before Taxes/Total Assets	17.2	10.7	12.6			15.9	3.5	14.6	15.0	17.0
	6.9	4.2	5.3			3.7	.8	7.0	2.7	8.8
	.2	−.7	−.1			−.8	−5.7	3.2	−.6	1.3
Sales/Net Fixed Assets	55.6	55.1	37.2			49.9	25.3	36.8	48.5	32.6
	24.0	21.6	18.3			18.0	15.5	10.8	30.9	15.3
	8.1	8.3	7.8			12.2	10.0	5.0	15.7	5.8
Sales/Total Assets	2.0	1.9	2.2			3.5	1.8	2.3	2.4	1.9
	1.6	1.5	1.6			2.0	1.4	1.8	1.8	1.4
	1.2	1.2	1.2			1.1	.7	1.4	1.4	1.1
% Depr., Dep., Amort./Sales	.7	.6	.9			.8		1.0	.6	1.7
	(77) 1.3	(87) 1.4	(85) 1.8			(10) 2.0		(18) 1.6	(20) 1.4	(25) 2.6
	3.0	2.6	3.0			3.4		3.2	2.6	4.5
% Officers', Directors', Owners' Comp/Sales	1.5	3.8	3.7							
	(38) 6.3	(30) 6.5	(27) 6.5							
	10.3	14.6	11.9							
Net Sales ($)	2479414M	2636435M	3564503M		3681M	27173M	41975M	135042M	434744M	2921888M
Total Assets ($)	1842226M	1975888M	2702952M		1865M	15411M	34837M	83741M	274296M	2292802M

M = $ thousand   MM = $ million
See Pages 11 through 18 for Explanation of Ratios and Data

Current Data Sorted By Assets

Comparative Historical Data

	0-500M	500M-2MM	2-10MM	10-50MM	50-100MM	100-250MM	Type of Statement	4/1/98-3/31/99 ALL	4/1/99-3/31/00 ALL
		1	2	2	2		Unqualified		
		1	4	1			Reviewed		
	1	8	1				Compiled		
	4	1					Tax Returns		
	1	5	2	1			Other		
		5 (4/1-9/30/02)		32 (10/1/02-3/31/03)					
	6	16	9	4	2		NUMBER OF STATEMENTS		
	%	%	%	%	%	%	ASSETS	%	%
		8.0				D	Cash & Equivalents	D	D
		38.3				A	Trade Receivables (net)	A	A
		3.7				T	Inventory	T	T
		.7				A	All Other Current	A	A
		50.7					Total Current		
		35.5				N	Fixed Assets (net)	N	N
		3.4				O	Intangibles (net)	O	O
		10.4				T	All Other Non-Current	T	T
		100.0					Total		
						A	LIABILITIES	A	A
		9.5				V	Notes Payable-Short Term	V	V
		4.5				A	Cur. Mat.-L/T/D	A	A
		11.9				I	Trade Payables	I	I
		.1				L	Income Taxes Payable	L	L
		10.2				A	All Other Current	A	A
		36.1				B	Total Current	B	B
		15.4				L	Long Term Debt	L	L
		.3				E	Deferred Taxes	E	E
		13.0					All Other Non-Current		
		35.2					Net Worth		
		100.0					Total Liabilities & Net Worth		
							INCOME DATA		
		100.0					Net Sales		
							Gross Profit		
		93.8					Operating Expenses		
		6.2					Operating Profit		
		3.0					All Other Expenses (net)		
		3.2					Profit Before Taxes		
							RATIOS		
		2.5							
		1.6					Current		
		1.1							
		2.1							
		1.5					Quick		
		.9							
	31	11.7							
	40	9.1					Sales/Receivables		
	59	6.2							
							Cost of Sales/Inventory		
							Cost of Sales/Payables		
		8.2							
		13.0					Sales/Working Capital		
		67.2							
		17.8							
	(15)	2.2					EBIT/Interest		
		-.2							
							Net Profit + Depr., Dep., Amort./Cur. Mat. L /T/D		
		.5							
		1.2					Fixed/Worth		
		6.9							
		.8							
		1.7					Debt/Worth		
		31.3							
		38.6					% Profit Before Taxes/Tangible		
	(15)	22.3					Net Worth		
		-37.0							
		21.4					% Profit Before Taxes/Total		
		1.3					Assets		
		-4.3							
		23.3							
		7.7					Sales/Net Fixed Assets		
		4.9							
		4.8							
		2.5					Sales/Total Assets		
		2.1							
		1.3							
	(13)	3.1					% Depr., Dep., Amort./Sales		
		4.7							
							% Officers', Directors', Owners' Comp/Sales		
	6573M	58956M	74480M	128086M	101065M		Net Sales ($)		
	1341M	18590M	32500M	58634M	132541M		Total Assets ($)		

© RMA 2003

M = $ thousand   MM = $ million
See Pages 11 through 18 for Explanation of Ratios and Data

Comparative Historical Data

Current Data Sorted By Sales

			Type of Statement						
		7	Unqualified		1	1	1		4
		6	Reviewed		2	2	2	2	
		10	Compiled		3	5	1	1	
		5	Tax Returns	2	2	1			
		9	Other	2	3	1	1	1	1
					5 (4/1-9/30/02)		32 (10/1/02-3/31/03)		
4/1/00-3/31/01 ALL	4/1/01-3/31/02 ALL	4/1/02-3/31/03 ALL		0-1MM	1-3MM	3-5MM	5-10MM	10-25MM	25MM & OVER
		37	NUMBER OF STATEMENTS	4	9	10	5	4	5
%	%	%	ASSETS	%	%	%	%	%	%
D	D	13.0	Cash & Equivalents			5.9			
A	A	31.3	Trade Receivables (net)			44.1			
T	T	5.9	Inventory			3.8			
A	A	1.6	All Other Current			.9			
		51.7	Total Current			54.8			
N	N	33.2	Fixed Assets (net)			30.9			
O	O	6.5	Intangibles (net)			9.9			
T	T	8.5	All Other Non-Current			4.4			
		100.0	Total			100.0			
A	A		LIABILITIES						
V	V	10.1	Notes Payable-Short Term			12.5			
A	A	4.8	Cur. Mat.-L/T/D			5.0			
I	I	11.5	Trade Payables			10.0			
L	L	.1	Income Taxes Payable			.1			
A	A	17.0	All Other Current			11.5			
B	B	43.4	Total Current			39.1			
L	L	18.7	Long Term Debt			18.4			
E	E	.2	Deferred Taxes			.1			
		10.9	All Other Non-Current			17.9			
		26.8	Net Worth			24.5			
		100.0	Total Liabilities & Net Worth			100.0			
			INCOME DATA						
		100.0	Net Sales			100.0			
			Gross Profit						
		94.4	Operating Expenses			95.0			
		5.6	Operating Profit			5.0			
		2.7	All Other Expenses (net)			4.7			
		2.9	Profit Before Taxes			.3			
			RATIOS						
		2.5				2.6			
		1.5	Current			1.5			
		.9				.8			
		2.0				2.2			
		1.3	Quick			1.3			
		.6				.8			
	32	11.5			33	11.2			
	43	8.5	Sales/Receivables		41	9.0			
	56	6.5			86	4.2			
			Cost of Sales/Inventory						
			Cost of Sales/Payables						
		6.6				6.9			
		14.9	Sales/Working Capital			22.0			
		−82.0				−68.7			
		12.3				20.8			
	(33)	2.5	EBIT/Interest			.7			
		.0				−2.9			
			Net Profit + Depr., Dep., Amort./Cur. Mat. L/T/D						
		.4				.4			
		1.4	Fixed/Worth			4.3			
		6.9				NM			
		1.0				1.0			
		2.6	Debt/Worth			8.5			
		25.4				NM			
		51.8	% Profit Before Taxes/Tangible Net Worth						
	(31)	31.8							
		−1.6							
		21.2	% Profit Before Taxes/Total Assets			23.2			
		6.9				−.3			
		−1.3				−8.2			
		23.3	Sales/Net Fixed Assets			23.6			
		7.9				8.5			
		4.4				6.3			
		3.8	Sales/Total Assets			5.2			
		2.3				2.8			
		1.6				2.2			
		1.3	% Depr., Dep., Amort./Sales			1.5			
	(29)	3.1				2.7			
		5.7				4.6			
		3.9	% Officers', Directors', Owners' Comp/Sales						
	(19)	5.8							
		11.3							
		369160M	Net Sales ($)	2121M	18536M	37148M	32458M	62409M	216488M
		243606M	Total Assets ($)	1194M	8349M	13266M	16254M	27072M	177471M

© RMA 2003

M = $ thousand   MM = $ million
See Pages 11 through 18 for Explanation of Ratios and Data

Current Data Sorted By Assets　　　　　　　　　　　Comparative Historical Data

0-500M	500M-2MM	2-10MM	10-50MM	50-100MM	100-250MM		4/1/98-3/31/99 ALL	4/1/99-3/31/00 ALL
						Type of Statement		
		5	7	3	1	Unqualified	21	27
	3	6	5			Reviewed	19	19
1	3	1	1			Compiled	18	16
1	3					Tax Returns	13	7
4	7	8	9	1	1	Other	47	28
		11 (4/1-9/30/02)		59 (10/1/02-3/31/03)				
6	16	20	22	4	2	**NUMBER OF STATEMENTS**	118	97
%	%	%	%	%	%	**ASSETS**	%	%
	12.4	11.6	10.8			Cash & Equivalents	11.3	11.6
	32.2	33.7	23.7			Trade Receivables (net)	32.4	30.1
	14.7	23.3	11.4			Inventory	13.9	13.9
	1.7	5.4	5.3			All Other Current	3.7	3.5
	61.0	73.9	51.1			Total Current	61.3	59.1
	21.6	14.3	31.6			Fixed Assets (net)	22.8	20.9
	4.6	7.3	11.7			Intangibles (net)	7.1	11.3
	12.8	4.5	5.5			All Other Non-Current	8.8	8.7
	100.0	100.0	100.0			Total	100.0	100.0
						LIABILITIES		
	7.9	8.9	6.8			Notes Payable-Short Term	10.7	8.5
	4.8	1.6	5.7			Cur. Mat.-L/T/D	2.8	3.4
	22.7	20.4	11.9			Trade Payables	15.1	16.2
	.9	.3	.1			Income Taxes Payable	.2	.4
	17.6	14.5	20.6			All Other Current	22.3	22.3
	53.8	45.6	45.2			Total Current	51.2	50.8
	19.7	3.2	14.7			Long Term Debt	22.2	18.8
	.0	.6	.6			Deferred Taxes	1.0	.4
	6.4	16.4	5.3			All Other Non-Current	6.7	10.0
	20.1	34.2	34.2			Net Worth	18.9	20.0
	100.0	100.0	100.0			Total Liabilities & Net Worth	100.0	100.0
						INCOME DATA		
	100.0	100.0	100.0			Net Sales	100.0	100.0
	46.3	49.9	43.0			Gross Profit	47.0	49.5
	43.6	45.6	36.4			Operating Expenses	40.2	42.8
	2.7	4.3	6.6			Operating Profit	6.7	6.7
	.1	.1	1.8			All Other Expenses (net)	1.1	.6
	2.6	4.2	4.8			Profit Before Taxes	5.7	6.0
						RATIOS		
	1.7	2.4	1.7				2.2	2.0
	1.3	1.9	1.1			Current	1.3	1.3
	.9	1.1	.9				1.0	.9
	1.4	1.7	1.2				1.5	1.5
	1.1	1.2	.7			Quick　(117)	1.0	1.0
	.4	.4	.5				.6	.6
	20　17.9	24　14.9	30　12.1				31　11.8	31　11.6
	38　9.7	47　7.8	46　7.9			Sales/Receivables	46　8.0	48　7.5
	62　5.9	67　5.4	64　5.7				69　5.3	68　5.4
	0　UND	0　UND	15　25.1				0　UND	1　298.3
	18　20.8	40　9.1	29　12.4			Cost of Sales/Inventory	22　16.5	35　10.3
	102　3.6	176　2.1	74　5.0				80　4.6	103　3.6
	12　29.3	19　19.7	24　15.4				17　22.1	23　16.1
	48　7.7	35　10.6	37　9.9			Cost of Sales/Payables	35　10.4	44　8.4
	90　4.1	102　3.6	62　5.9				62　5.9	70　5.2
	10.9	5.2	6.7				7.3	6.6
	20.1	7.2	48.7			Sales/Working Capital	23.3	16.5
	−47.2	36.5	−33.5				−184.0	−42.2
	20.5	46.5	8.9				15.3	13.3
	(12) 1.8	(18) 7.2	(19) 3.3			EBIT/Interest	(100) 4.0	(88) 3.8
	.3	1.4	.9				1.5	1.6
						Net Profit + Depr., Dep.,	3.9	4.2
						Amort./Cur. Mat. L /T/D　(32)	2.2 (22)	2.1
							1.2	1.5
	.1	.1	.4				.3	.2
	1.2	.4	1.5			Fixed/Worth	.9	1.2
	NM	.9	5.0				10.1	14.5
	1.8	.7	1.2				.8	1.1
	3.4	1.8	3.7			Debt/Worth	2.7	3.5
	NM	9.1	12.0				93.5	63.8
	215.1	58.8	72.0			% Profit Before Taxes/Tangible	73.2	75.9
	(12) 68.3	(17) 22.3	(20) 32.0			Net Worth	(91) 29.4	(75) 38.0
	15.3	10.0	.1				8.8	12.8
	31.4	17.6	15.4			% Profit Before Taxes/Total	21.8	21.7
	10.5	8.9	6.1			Assets	9.8	6.8
	−5.1	2.7	.1				3.2	1.6
	75.3	43.1	16.3				26.5	33.2
	17.4	17.0	7.5			Sales/Net Fixed Assets	14.7	15.0
	8.0	10.5	2.6				6.6	7.0
	3.5	2.8	2.0				3.3	2.9
	2.6	2.1	1.7			Sales/Total Assets	2.1	2.1
	1.9	1.4	.9				1.6	1.5
	1.8	.9	2.0				1.2	1.0
	(11) 2.1	(17) 2.0	(20) 5.1			% Depr., Dep., Amort./Sales　(99)	2.3 (75)	2.1
	5.3	3.4	6.4				3.8	4.0
						% Officers', Directors',	2.4	4.1
						Owners' Comp/Sales　(43)	7.0 (36)	8.2
							13.9	13.3
7640M	49507M	204726M	816422M	427382M	478237M	Net Sales ($)	2983596M	3629037M
1606M	19007M	92498M	499891M	214672M	369266M	Total Assets ($)	1505359M	1909299M

M = $ thousand　　MM = $ million
See Pages 11 through 18 for Explanation of Ratios and Data

Comparative Historical Data | Current Data Sorted By Sales

						Type of Statement						
	22		21		16	Unqualified		1	1	5	9	
	15		11		14	Reviewed	3	1	4	3	3	
	13		12		6	Compiled	2	2	1		1	
	5		11		4	Tax Returns	2	1	1			
	38		38		30	Other	3	4	5	5	4	9
	4/1/00-3/31/01 ALL		4/1/01-3/31/02 ALL		4/1/02-3/31/03 ALL			11 (4/1-9/30/02)			59 (10/1/02-3/31/03)	
							0-1MM	1-3MM	3-5MM	5-10MM	10-25MM	25MM & OVER
	93		93		70	NUMBER OF STATEMENTS	3	11	10	12	12	22
	%		%		%	ASSETS	%	%	%	%	%	%
	8.3		10.4		11.6	Cash & Equivalents		14.2	8.3	6.6	14.3	12.0
	30.6		26.7		29.4	Trade Receivables (net)		21.9	26.8	43.5	19.4	30.4
	12.8		14.3		15.0	Inventory		11.1	31.6	16.0	11.8	11.3
	3.5		4.7		4.9	All Other Current		3.9	1.4	4.5	7.6	5.9
	55.2		56.1		60.9	Total Current		51.1	68.1	70.6	53.1	59.7
	26.1		26.1		22.7	Fixed Assets (net)		32.3	14.8	13.3	29.9	23.7
	10.1		9.4		9.6	Intangibles (net)		10.2	3.3	11.4	13.1	9.5
	8.6		8.4		6.7	All Other Non-Current		6.5	13.8	4.7	3.9	7.1
	100.0		100.0		100.0	Total		100.0	100.0	100.0	100.0	100.0
						LIABILITIES						
	8.3		15.8		9.6	Notes Payable-Short Term		25.7	8.2	9.4	4.3	6.5
	5.8		5.2		5.7	Cur. Mat.-L/T/D		5.5	1.6	2.1	1.4	6.0
	12.0		12.8		18.0	Trade Payables		19.3	10.9	19.9	14.8	15.7
	.6		.1		.3	Income Taxes Payable		.5	.8	.5	.1	.2
	15.2		15.8		23.4	All Other Current		46.1	15.1	21.9	10.7	22.3
	41.9		49.7		57.1	Total Current		97.0	36.6	53.8	31.3	50.6
	21.9		19.0		12.6	Long Term Debt		17.7	12.2	4.3	12.3	16.2
	.4		.3		.4	Deferred Taxes		.0	.0	1.1	.3	.4
	11.9		7.6		18.9	All Other Non-Current		25.4	16.9	7.2	17.3	8.8
	23.9		23.4		11.1	Net Worth		−40.1	34.3	33.7	38.7	24.0
	100.0		100.0		100.0	Total Liabilities & Net Worth		100.0	100.0	100.0	100.0	100.0
						INCOME DATA						
	100.0		100.0		100.0	Net Sales		100.0	100.0	100.0	100.0	100.0
	47.6		47.5		47.4	Gross Profit		49.5	39.3	56.4	44.0	46.0
	42.1		43.4		42.4	Operating Expenses		46.9	34.9	50.1	39.6	35.0
	5.4		4.1		5.0	Operating Profit		2.6	4.4	6.3	4.5	11.0
	1.9		1.4		.7	All Other Expenses (net)		1.0	1.2	.3	1.3	1.4
	3.5		2.7		4.3	Profit Before Taxes		1.7	3.2	6.0	3.1	9.6
						RATIOS						
	2.2		2.2		2.0			1.6	2.7	2.2	3.0	1.5
	1.4		1.4		1.2	Current		1.0	1.9	1.4	2.0	1.1
	1.0		.9		.9			.4	1.3	.9	1.1	.9
	1.8		1.5		1.5			1.1	1.7	1.5	1.7	1.1
	1.0		.8		.8	Quick		1.0	1.1	.8	1.5	.7
	.6		.5		.5			.2	.4	.3	.6	.5

36	10.3	29	12.6	24	15.1	Sales/Receivables	0 UND	23 15.7	36 10.2	20 18.5	39 9.3	
49	7.5	46	7.9	46	8.0		18 20.7	43 8.5	47 7.7	34 10.8	52 7.1	
72	5.1	63	5.8	63	5.8		52 7.0	57 6.4	91 4.0	59 6.2	63 5.8	
2	196.7	1	313.9	0	UND	Cost of Sales/Inventory	0 UND	0 UND	0 UND	12 31.5	0 UND	
33	10.9	24	15.1	20	18.3		2 170.6	93 3.9	8 45.5	20 18.6	29 12.4	
98	3.7	114	3.2	106	3.4		20 18.7	205 1.8	196 1.9	88 4.1	74 5.0	
18	20.2	17	21.5	19	19.3	Cost of Sales/Payables	10 35.5	7 50.9	22 16.9	9 39.8	26 14.3	
33	10.9	32	11.5	38	9.6		38 9.6	18 19.7	62 5.9	26 14.2	38 9.6	
59	6.2	67	5.5	88	4.2		141 2.6	76 4.8	100 3.6	58 6.3	78 4.7	
	6.5		6.4		6.7	Sales/Working Capital	21.7	2.7	5.5	4.3	11.7	
	13.9		12.8		21.5		225.7	10.4	9.9	7.2	42.3	
	−336.3		−44.9		−49.2		−3.3	14.1	−54.8	NM	−34.6	
	9.2		9.5		13.7	EBIT/Interest			23.1	41.8	22.4	
(86)	3.3	(81)	2.3	(59)	3.9			(11) 4.7	(11) 4.5	(18) 4.4	
	.8		.1		1.0				2.1	−.5	3.3	
	4.6		2.8		3.3	Net Profit + Depr., Dep., Amort./Cur. Mat. L/T/D						
(26)	2.1	(19)	.9	(20)	2.0							
	.8		.5		.9							
	.4		.3		.2	Fixed/Worth	.9	.1	.1	.4	.3	
	1.1		.9		.9		3.7	.3	.3	.9	.9	
	5.5		8.6		NM		−.6	NM	1.7	35.1	5.0	
	.8		.7		1.0	Debt/Worth	2.3	.6	1.3	.7	1.3	
	2.8		2.3		3.1		18.2	2.1	2.4	1.0	4.2	
	9.7		UND		NM		−1.9	NM	11.2	56.1	12.4	
	55.7		43.7		80.9	% Profit Before Taxes/Tangible Net Worth			128.8	40.3	85.4	
(72)	24.1	(70)	15.2	(53)	33.5			(11) 50.8	(10) 20.1	(18) 53.8	
	2.1		−4.4		10.0				10.5	−15.0	29.5	
	21.1		18.3		26.2	% Profit Before Taxes/Total Assets	32.7	28.5	23.5	28.2	33.3	
	6.4		5.0		8.2		7.4	1.9	5.5	7.8	14.8	
	−1.0		−2.1		1.5		1.9	−4.7	3.0	−2.6	3.9	
	19.4		28.7		31.2	Sales/Net Fixed Assets	26.2	104.6	60.7	26.3	29.2	
	12.5		11.8		14.2		11.5	16.1	20.9	5.6	13.2	
	5.2		4.8		6.8		7.5	9.2	13.7	2.6	6.1	
	2.6		2.7		2.8	Sales/Total Assets	5.0	2.8	2.8	3.0	2.3	
	2.0		1.9		2.0		3.5	2.2	2.2	1.5	1.9	
	1.4		1.3		1.4		1.9	1.3	1.3	.9	1.7	
	.9		.8		1.1	% Depr., Dep., Amort./Sales			.8		1.0	
(80)	2.4	(74)	2.3	(57)	2.4				(10) 1.7		2.1	
	4.8		5.3		5.3				3.2		6.0	
	3.2		3.5		2.2	% Officers', Directors', Owners' Comp/Sales						
(32)	4.8	(33)	7.3	(15)	6.1							
	9.7		13.1		8.5							

2743577M		1813885M		1983914M		Net Sales ($)	2549M	19848M	38700M	83381M	199005M	1640431M
1650871M		973410M		1196940M		Total Assets ($)	1538M	7678M	20828M	48495M	151238M	967163M

© RMA 2003   M = $ thousand   MM = $ million
See Pages 11 through 18 for Explanation of Ratios and Data

Current Data Sorted By Assets   **Comparative Historical Data**

	0-500M	500M-2MM	2-10MM	10-50MM	50-100MM	100-250MM	Type of Statement	4/1/98-3/31/99 ALL	4/1/99-3/31/00 ALL
		4	10	15	11	10	Unqualified	81	65
		7	10	2		1	Reviewed	17	21
		12	5				Compiled	19	24
	5	6	2				Tax Returns	11	12
	10	10	14	14	6	6	Other	90	70
		24 (4/1-9/30/02)		136 (10/1/02-3/31/03)					
NUMBER OF STATEMENTS	15	39	41	31	17	17		218	192
	%	%	%	%	%	%	**ASSETS**	%	%
	7.0	18.7	21.6	28.8	35.7	23.5	Cash & Equivalents	22.3	19.4
	30.2	43.1	35.7	28.8	26.7	19.7	Trade Receivables (net)	37.6	38.4
	6.5	4.2	3.3	1.1	3.3	1.2	Inventory	3.2	3.6
	10.4	3.8	5.7	4.4	5.3	6.4	All Other Current	4.6	4.6
	54.1	69.8	66.3	63.1	71.0	50.8	Total Current	67.7	66.1
	25.1	17.0	9.6	18.8	11.8	10.7	Fixed Assets (net)	16.5	15.8
	8.2	5.0	13.1	11.6	13.0	25.7	Intangibles (net)	7.4	7.9
	12.6	8.2	11.0	6.5	4.2	12.7	All Other Non-Current	8.4	10.2
	100.0	100.0	100.0	100.0	100.0	100.0	Total	100.0	100.0
							LIABILITIES		
	41.6	13.7	4.8	.7	3.9	3.0	Notes Payable-Short Term	8.8	8.0
	8.7	3.4	2.0	3.4	1.8	2.3	Cur. Mat.-L/T/D	3.5	3.4
	18.6	12.1	10.6	7.1	7.7	4.2	Trade Payables	12.9	10.3
	.2	1.0	.3	3.1	1.1	3.9	Income Taxes Payable	.3	.7
	26.1	19.3	36.8	27.9	28.5	25.2	All Other Current	26.3	25.8
	95.2	49.5	54.6	42.1	43.1	38.6	Total Current	51.8	48.3
	20.3	12.6	7.1	16.1	3.2	14.9	Long Term Debt	9.7	11.0
	.2	.2	.7	.2	.4	.2	Deferred Taxes	.8	.9
	2.5	15.4	17.4	12.9	5.4	5.6	All Other Non-Current	9.9	9.7
	-18.1	22.3	20.2	28.7	47.9	40.7	Net Worth	27.9	30.1
	100.0	100.0	100.0	100.0	100.0	100.0	Total Liabilities & Net Worth	100.0	100.0
							INCOME DATA		
	100.0	100.0	100.0	100.0	100.0	100.0	Net Sales	100.0	100.0
							Gross Profit		
	100.3	98.2	96.5	97.7	99.7	95.3	Operating Expenses	154.8	94.0
	-.3	1.8	3.5	2.3	.3	4.7	Operating Profit	-54.8	6.0
	.7	.7	.9	2.8	.0	2.1	All Other Expenses (net)	6.3	.5
	-.9	1.1	2.7	-.5	.3	2.6	Profit Before Taxes	-61.0	5.5
							RATIOS		
	1.2	4.0	1.8	2.2	3.4	2.6		3.2	3.1
	.9	1.7	1.3	1.7	1.5	1.3	Current	1.8	1.7
	.1	1.0	1.0	1.1	1.1	.8		1.0	1.0
	.8	3.6	1.7	2.2	3.3	2.3		2.9	2.9
	.4	1.5	1.2	1.6	1.3	1.2	Quick	1.5 (191)	1.4
	.1	.8	.8	1.1	.9	.6		.9	.8
	0 UND	33 10.9	28 13.2	46 7.9	59 6.1	56 6.6		44 8.4	36 10.1
	26 14.1	49 7.5	55 6.6	62 5.8	76 4.8	75 4.9	Sales/Receivables	73 5.0	59 6.2
	54 6.7	76 4.8	81 4.5	88 4.2	88 4.1	97 3.8		95 3.8	88 4.1
							Cost of Sales/Inventory		
							Cost of Sales/Payables		
	25.0	5.7	7.7	3.1	1.9	2.9		3.6	4.2
	-43.7	11.4	21.8	6.8	6.3	7.0	Sales/Working Capital	8.1	10.1
	-7.7	999.8	UND	17.8	86.1	-8.6		169.2	NM
	(14) 6.6	(34) 16.4	(30) 19.0	(26) 33.9		(13) 10.5		(161) 31.6	(134) 24.4
	2.2	3.8	6.2	10.3		.8	EBIT/Interest	6.6	6.2
	-7.4	-2.4	1.7	-12.3		-2.6		-2.3	.2
				(10) 12.2			Net Profit + Depr., Dep.,	(51) 20.7	(29) 42.6
				5.2			Amort./Cur. Mat. L/T/D	5.2	4.0
				1.5				1.5	1.2
	.4	.1	.1	.2	.1	.1		.2	.2
	-25.0	.6	.6	.5	.3	.4	Fixed/Worth	.5	.4
	-.5	1.8	-1.4	9.8	1.0	NM		1.7	2.6
	2.8	.7	1.4	.8	.5	.6		.6	.6
	-213.0	1.4	4.6	1.8	1.3	2.0	Debt/Worth	1.5	1.8
	-4.2	13.6	-6.1	22.2	4.8	NM		7.1	10.7
		(31) 30.6	(29) 105.5	(24) 49.6	(14) 39.9	(13) 37.3	% Profit Before Taxes/Tangible	(175) 69.3	(152) 86.7
		16.8	51.0	29.4	3.3	3.2	Net Worth	30.6	34.9
		7.1	5.9	-107.2	-18.4	-32.0		3.3	9.6
	40.9	14.1	24.4	15.2	15.9	15.3	% Profit Before Taxes/Total	22.6	27.8
	4.2	5.9	6.3	6.3	.0	-.4	Assets	10.5	11.7
	-35.1	-1.7	-.8	-20.0	-6.6	-3.8		-4.8	-.2
	79.0	95.0	68.8	31.2	18.9	18.3		29.0	34.9
	24.1	25.2	32.1	12.2	10.6	9.9	Sales/Net Fixed Assets	15.4	18.7
	10.8	13.3	18.5	5.5	6.6	6.5		8.6	11.7
	6.9	4.5	3.4	1.8	1.4	1.4		3.1	3.7
	4.2	3.3	2.0	1.4	1.2	1.0	Sales/Total Assets	2.0	2.2
	3.1	2.0	1.5	1.1	.8	.6		1.3	1.4
	(11) .4	(28) 1.0	(23) .6	(16) 2.4	(11) 1.6		% Depr., Dep., Amort./Sales	(159) 1.6	(130) 1.1
	1.3	1.9	1.9	5.8	5.3			2.9	2.4
	2.3	3.0	2.5	9.0	7.2			5.2	4.2
	(10) 4.4	(20) 2.7	(12) 3.1				% Officers', Directors',	(38) 5.6	(47) 3.5
	11.3	7.2	8.9				Owners' Comp/Sales	9.2	8.1
	25.1	13.1	15.5					15.2	13.1
	19369M	150807M	451716M	1192537M	1517270M	2606830M	Net Sales ($)	7485360M	7622240M
	3386M	44742M	193421M	853170M	1229181M	2674508M	Total Assets ($)	5307661M	5383849M

M = $ thousand   MM = $ million
See Pages 11 through 18 for Explanation of Ratios and Data

Comparative Historical Data | | | | Current Data Sorted By Sales

				Type of Statement	0-1MM	24 (4/1-9/30/02) 1-3MM	3-5MM	136 (10/1/02-3/31/03) 5-10MM	10-25MM	25MM & OVER
	40	36	50	Unqualified			3	5	11	31
	18	14	20	Reviewed		2	3	9	3	3
	27	28	17	Compiled	1	7	3	3	3	
	11	9	13	Tax Returns	1	7	4	1		
	65	59	60	Other	5	9	8	5	11	22
	4/1/00- 3/31/01 ALL	4/1/01- 3/31/02 ALL	4/1/02- 3/31/03 ALL							
	161	146	160	NUMBER OF STATEMENTS	7	25	21	23	28	56
	%	%	%	ASSETS	%	%	%	%	%	%
	21.0	21.2	22.6	Cash & Equivalents		12.0	17.7	27.1	26.3	27.2
	37.4	34.7	33.0	Trade Receivables (net)		31.7	45.9	39.3	36.1	26.1
	3.4	3.2	3.2	Inventory		7.2	2.6	2.1	3.0	2.0
	3.5	4.1	5.5	All Other Current		2.5	6.4	2.6	5.2	6.0
	65.4	63.3	64.3	Total Current		53.4	72.6	71.1	70.6	61.2
	15.5	16.8	15.0	Fixed Assets (net)		26.4	12.3	11.2	7.6	16.5
	8.4	10.9	11.7	Intangibles (net)		4.2	8.1	10.5	9.2	15.9
	10.7	9.0	9.0	All Other Non-Current		16.0	7.0	7.2	12.6	6.3
	100.0	100.0	100.0	Total		100.0	100.0	100.0	100.0	100.0
				LIABILITIES						
	9.4	10.7	9.4	Notes Payable-Short Term		23.1	9.0	3.7	4.8	1.9
	2.2	2.4	3.2	Cur. Mat.-L/T/D		5.5	5.6	.9	2.4	2.8
	12.7	10.1	10.0	Trade Payables		10.7	10.2	15.5	8.1	7.2
	.7	1.7	1.5	Income Taxes Payable		.4	.8	.1	1.0	3.2
	20.4	24.0	27.7	All Other Current		14.9	22.8	27.1	42.5	25.8
	45.4	48.9	51.8	Total Current		54.5	48.4	47.3	58.9	40.9
	8.7	11.3	11.8	Long Term Debt		16.3	15.5	5.6	5.8	13.5
	.4	.7	.4	Deferred Taxes		.3	.4	.9	.1	.2
	8.2	19.6	12.1	All Other Non-Current		6.0	17.5	26.8	10.7	8.9
	37.3	19.6	23.9	Net Worth		22.8	18.2	19.4	24.6	36.5
	100.0	100.0	100.0	Total Liabilities & Net Worth		100.0	100.0	100.0	100.0	100.0
				INCOME DATA						
	100.0	100.0	100.0	Net Sales		100.0	100.0	100.0	100.0	100.0
				Gross Profit						
	97.0	95.6	97.7	Operating Expenses		98.5	94.7	97.0	98.1	97.8
	3.0	4.4	2.3	Operating Profit		1.5	5.3	3.0	1.9	2.2
	-.7	1.0	1.2	All Other Expenses (net)		.8	.4	.4	2.0	1.3
	3.7	3.4	1.1	Profit Before Taxes		.6	5.0	2.6	-.2	1.0
				RATIOS						
	3.1	2.5	2.2			2.3	2.3	3.0	2.1	2.5
	1.7	1.5	1.4	Current		1.2	1.3	1.8	1.3	1.5
	1.0	1.0	1.0			.4	1.1	1.0	1.0	1.1
	2.7	2.2	2.1			2.1	2.2	3.0	1.8	2.2
	1.5	1.3	1.2	Quick		.8	1.2	1.7	1.3	1.4
	.9	.8	.8			.4	.9	.9	.9	.9
37	9.9	31 11.8	35 10.3		22 16.8	34 10.8	38 9.6	27 13.7	49 7.5	
59	6.2	54 6.7	58 6.3	Sales/Receivables	40 9.1	78 4.7	54 6.7	57 6.4	67 5.5	
91	4.0	81 4.5	81 4.5		74 4.9	99 3.7	62 5.9	81 4.5	87 4.2	
				Cost of Sales/Inventory						
				Cost of Sales/Payables						
	3.6	5.2	4.8			6.2	6.2	6.4	5.6	3.1
	11.4	14.2	11.6	Sales/Working Capital		25.0	13.1	10.2	20.0	7.3
	-182.0	-414.8	UND			-9.9	112.3	999.8	NM	28.3
	27.9	22.6	16.1			8.4	12.7	20.0	34.3	17.6
(119)	3.8	(109) 3.5	(126) 3.8	EBIT/Interest	(23) 3.7	(16) 3.3	(19) 5.5	(21) 4.2	(41) 2.7	
	.2	-1.3	-1.7			-4.3	-1.5	.7	-15.5	-1.9
	14.3	21.9	7.5							8.3
(26)	6.7	(19) 3.6	(26) 3.7	Net Profit + Depr., Dep., Amort./Cur. Mat. L/T/D					(13) 3.7	
	1.1	-.4	1.0							1.3
	.1	.2	.1			.2	.2	.2	.1	.2
	.3	.5	.6	Fixed/Worth		.7	.8	.6	.2	.5
	1.8	1.9	-10.0			NM	19.0	-1.1	NM	6.9
	.5	.9	.8			.7	1.3	.8	1.3	.7
	1.4	1.9	2.5	Debt/Worth		1.8	4.6	4.7	2.3	1.6
	16.0	17.0	-28.5			NM	42.8	-6.4	NM	18.8
	65.4	81.7	57.7			24.3	125.5	84.3	74.0	40.6
(133)	19.6	(115) 29.8	(118) 20.2	% Profit Before Taxes/Tangible Net Worth	(19) 14.4	(17) 51.0	(15) 19.7	(21) 38.5	(44) 8.8	
	1.8	-8.9	-4.8			6.0	9.0	2.1	-6.9	-24.2
	24.2	24.1	16.9			13.8	29.9	13.9	25.0	15.4
	5.7	5.0	4.6	% Profit Before Taxes/Total Assets		5.9	5.5	1.3	6.8	1.2
	-1.5	-7.4	-4.8			-4.6	-.7	-2.3	-16.0	-5.3
	37.2	43.4	40.2			62.1	59.4	56.4	71.2	20.6
	18.9	19.6	20.0	Sales/Net Fixed Assets		18.8	29.1	25.2	35.6	10.6
	11.1	9.4	9.8			9.2	17.3	16.5	18.4	5.7
	3.6	3.8	3.3			4.6	3.3	4.5	3.8	1.7
	2.1	2.2	1.8	Sales/Total Assets		3.1	2.8	3.2	1.9	1.2
	1.2	1.3	1.2			1.8	1.6	1.6	1.3	1.0
	.9	.6	1.2			.8	.4	1.4	.4	2.5
(116)	1.9	(98) 2.1	(96) 2.2	% Depr., Dep., Amort./Sales	(20) 2.0	(14) 1.7	(13) 1.9	(15) 1.4	(30) 6.4	
	3.6	3.3	4.6			2.7	2.9	3.0	2.2	8.1
	4.2	4.4	2.4				6.0			
(43)	6.7	(40) 6.5	(49) 7.2	% Officers', Directors', Owners' Comp/Sales		(15) 7.3				
	13.3	15.9	14.3			14.1				
	8665951M	5035150M	5938529M	Net Sales ($)	3041M	46305M	81463M	175541M	455431M	5176748M
	5031275M	3608058M	4998408M	Total Assets ($)	3926M	17563M	36431M	81174M	430238M	4429076M

M = $ thousand   MM = $ million
See Pages 11 through 18 for Explanation of Ratios and Data

Current Data Sorted By Assets

Comparative Historical Data

0-500M	500M-2MM	2-10MM	10-50MM	50-100MM	100-250MM	Type of Statement	4/1/98-3/31/99 ALL	4/1/99-3/31/00 ALL
		5	6	2	1	Unqualified	18	18
1	6	17	3			Reviewed	37	26
4	9	9	2		1	Compiled	28	37
9	11	2	2			Tax Returns	10	9
6	11	9	2	1	1	Other	45	36
	28 (4/1-9/30/02)		90 (10/1/02-3/31/03)					
20	37	42	13	3	3	NUMBER OF STATEMENTS	138	126
%	%	%	%	%	%	**ASSETS**	%	%
21.9	10.6	11.6	7.4			Cash & Equivalents	10.9	10.4
27.5	24.3	29.7	17.7			Trade Receivables (net)	27.7	30.3
1.3	4.7	5.1	9.7			Inventory	3.5	4.1
.7	3.7	5.9	2.1			All Other Current	2.9	3.7
51.4	43.2	52.4	37.0			Total Current	45.0	48.5
27.3	32.1	32.6	36.5			Fixed Assets (net)	40.2	38.9
5.4	10.8	6.1	5.6			Intangibles (net)	5.4	5.5
15.9	13.9	8.9	20.9			All Other Non-Current	9.4	7.1
100.0	100.0	100.0	100.0			Total	100.0	100.0
						LIABILITIES		
46.9	11.6	8.4	13.2			Notes Payable-Short Term	8.0	10.2
23.4	5.6	6.4	3.4			Cur. Mat.-L/T/D	6.2	7.4
29.5	12.2	14.1	7.6			Trade Payables	13.7	13.9
.5	.6	1.5	.8			Income Taxes Payable	.7	.5
20.3	15.8	16.2	20.9			All Other Current	16.5	13.6
120.7	45.9	46.5	45.9			Total Current	45.0	45.5
24.1	23.7	20.6	17.7			Long Term Debt	23.6	20.3
.0	1.3	.4	1.0			Deferred Taxes	1.1	1.2
13.8	6.9	7.2	13.9			All Other Non-Current	7.1	6.9
-58.6	22.3	25.3	21.5			Net Worth	23.1	26.1
100.0	100.0	100.0	100.0			Total Liabilities & Net Worth	100.0	100.0
						INCOME DATA		
100.0	100.0	100.0	100.0			Net Sales	100.0	100.0
						Gross Profit		
95.0	94.0	96.9	94.1			Operating Expenses	94.4	93.8
5.0	6.0	3.1	5.9			Operating Profit	5.6	6.2
.9	2.5	1.6	3.3			All Other Expenses (net)	2.4	2.0
4.1	3.5	1.6	2.6			Profit Before Taxes	3.1	4.2
						RATIOS		
1.3	2.2	1.7	1.1				2.0	1.7
.7	1.1	1.1	.9			Current	1.1	1.0
.2	.4	.7	.5				.6	.7
1.3	1.7	1.4	.8				1.8	1.6
.7	1.1	.9	.5			Quick	.9	.8
.1	.3	.6	.4				.5	.5
0 UND	0 UND	34 10.6	22 16.2				28 13.0	30 12.3
21 17.0	42 8.6	46 7.9	47 7.8			Sales/Receivables	50 7.2	51 7.2
44 8.3	63 5.8	61 6.0	63 5.8				67 5.5	70 5.2
						Cost of Sales/Inventory		
						Cost of Sales/Payables		
47.3	8.0	9.4	251.2				9.2	8.2
-32.1	122.9	66.0	-24.4			Sales/Working Capital	117.3	UND
-2.5	-6.8	-18.3	-7.1				-12.4	-15.6
4.6	6.2	3.6	13.6				9.5	8.4
(11) 1.0	(31) 1.4	(35) 1.6	(11) 4.0			EBIT/Interest	(124) 2.4	(109) 2.6
-2.3	-.9	-.2	1.3				1.0	.5
	10.7	4.5				Net Profit + Depr., Dep.,	4.0	4.3
	(11) 1.9	(20) 1.8				Amort./Cur. Mat. L /T/D	(43) 2.5	(33) 2.5
	.2	1.0					1.3	1.3
.1	.4	.6	.5				.6	.6
1.3	1.6	1.5	1.7			Fixed/Worth	1.5	1.7
-12.7	NM	8.6	25.5				6.9	11.5
1.8	.9	1.3	1.0				.9	1.1
9.1	3.9	4.1	3.0			Debt/Worth	2.3	3.0
-4.3	-10.8	36.0	47.5				21.3	43.4
213.0	94.8	45.8	68.1			% Profit Before Taxes/Tangible	57.1	63.0
(12) 7.1	(27) 11.3	(34) 11.1	(11) 21.7			Net Worth	(109) 22.9	(99) 23.1
-8.2	-16.3	-2.2	8.8				5.6	.9
41.3	17.4	9.6	11.0			% Profit Before Taxes/Total	19.4	18.5
3.4	5.5	2.2	5.3			Assets	5.8	6.8
-14.3	-7.5	-2.1	1.2				-1.4	-.6
73.2	25.7	34.1	28.3				16.0	20.3
17.5	10.4	6.3	5.5			Sales/Net Fixed Assets	5.6	6.6
8.2	4.6	3.4	1.5				2.6	2.6
4.7	3.4	3.1	2.3				3.4	3.1
4.0	2.4	2.1	1.6			Sales/Total Assets	2.0	2.0
2.9	1.5	1.5	.8				1.4	1.3
2.0	2.1	1.8	1.4				2.5	2.4
(14) 4.2	(29) 3.9	(36) 5.0	(11) 5.6			% Depr., Dep., Amort./Sales	(115) 5.5	(101) 6.2
6.1	9.3	9.3	13.3				9.7	10.8
7.3	6.5	2.2				% Officers', Directors',	4.8	5.2
(12) 10.2	(18) 8.9	(19) 5.7				Owners' Comp/Sales	(56) 8.3	(45) 7.6
15.2	12.5	8.6					13.0	13.3
20452M	94057M	476239M	467541M	188086M	332665M	Net Sales ($)	1277033M	1179220M
5357M	38177M	199081M	271743M	217287M	580860M	Total Assets ($)	856211M	713442M

M = $ thousand   MM = $ million
See Pages 11 through 18 for Explanation of Ratios and Data

Comparative Historical Data | Current Data Sorted By Sales

			Type of Statement						
18	13	14	Unqualified			1	3	3	7
24	17	27	Reviewed		3	9	8	6	1
24	19	25	Compiled	3	6	3	4	4	5
16	14	22	Tax Returns	10	6	4	1	1	
52	48	30	Other	6	10	2	4	5	3
4/1/00-3/31/01	4/1/01-3/31/02	4/1/02-3/31/03		28 (4/1-9/30/02)			90 (10/1/02-3/31/03)		
ALL	ALL	ALL		0-1MM	1-3MM	3-5MM	5-10MM	10-25MM	25MM & OVER
134	111	118	**NUMBER OF STATEMENTS**	19	25	19	20	19	16
%	%	%	**ASSETS**	%	%	%	%	%	%
11.8	10.4	13.3	Cash & Equivalents	14.7	14.0	12.9	9.9	14.2	14.2
29.2	25.3	25.9	Trade Receivables (net)	20.3	29.9	22.0	32.0	20.0	30.6
4.4	6.0	5.6	Inventory	.4	3.6	7.7	6.5	2.8	14.7
3.4	3.1	3.7	All Other Current	.9	4.7	1.5	1.4	10.6	2.5
48.8	44.9	48.5	Total Current	36.3	52.2	44.2	49.8	47.6	62.0
34.9	36.2	31.4	Fixed Assets (net)	36.3	33.1	28.2	36.0	33.8	18.1
6.7	7.1	7.1	Intangibles (net)	4.5	3.9	16.9	7.4	5.5	5.1
9.5	11.8	13.0	All Other Non-Current	22.9	10.7	10.7	6.8	13.1	14.9
100.0	100.0	100.0	Total	100.0	100.0	100.0	100.0	100.0	100.0
			LIABILITIES						
12.0	9.3	16.3	Notes Payable-Short Term	18.4	30.8	9.6	13.9	5.5	15.1
8.1	5.7	8.5	Cur. Mat.-L/T/D	24.0	6.9	4.9	7.8	5.2	1.6
11.6	10.5	15.2	Trade Payables	20.0	17.6	16.3	12.3	7.3	17.8
.4	.4	.9	Income Taxes Payable	.6	.2	.2	1.5	.1	3.4
17.0	17.4	17.4	All Other Current	12.0	17.2	17.1	14.9	19.9	24.6
49.1	43.3	58.3	Total Current	74.9	72.7	48.2	50.4	37.9	62.5
20.1	21.9	21.9	Long Term Debt	36.2	23.6	21.1	15.7	21.6	11.5
.7	.4	.7	Deferred Taxes	.0	.6	2.5	.2	.7	.3
9.8	7.6	8.9	All Other Non-Current	6.2	13.8	5.1	6.6	5.5	16.1
20.3	26.8	10.1	Net Worth	−17.2	−10.7	23.1	27.1	34.3	9.5
100.0	100.0	100.0	Total Liabilities & Net Worth	100.0	100.0	100.0	100.0	100.0	100.0
			INCOME DATA						
100.0	100.0	100.0	Net Sales	100.0	100.0	100.0	100.0	100.0	100.0
			Gross Profit						
94.2	94.1	95.1	Operating Expenses	88.8	96.6	99.5	97.1	93.6	94.6
5.8	5.9	4.9	Operating Profit	11.2	3.4	.5	2.9	6.4	5.4
1.5	3.0	2.0	All Other Expenses (net)	4.5	1.1	1.3	1.2	2.4	2.1
4.2	2.9	2.8	Profit Before Taxes	6.7	2.4	−.8	1.7	4.0	3.3
			RATIOS						
1.7	2.3	1.7		1.1	3.9	1.5	1.6	2.1	1.5
1.0	1.0	1.0	Current	.5	1.1	1.2	1.1	1.1	.9
.6	.7	.5		.2	.6	.4	.8	.7	.5
1.5	1.9	1.4		1.1	3.3	1.3	1.4	1.7	1.2
.9	.9	.8	Quick	.4	1.1	.9	.9	1.0	.6
.5	.5	.4		.1	.4	.4	.6	.5	.4
19 18.9	12 29.5	19 19.2		0 UND	23 15.9	11 34.5	42 8.6	19 18.8	34 10.7
43 8.4	43 8.4	43 8.4	Sales/Receivables	6 59.2	46 7.9	41 8.9	53 6.8	44 8.4	41 8.9
65 5.6	73 5.0	62 5.9		45 8.2	64 5.7	47 7.8	62 5.9	62 5.9	98 3.7
			Cost of Sales/Inventory						
			Cost of Sales/Payables						
10.3	7.7	8.6		80.5	6.3	10.9	10.9	6.1	3.9
234.5	130.3	NM	Sales/Working Capital	−10.6	36.5	80.0	161.4	45.7	−42.3
−16.4	−16.0	−10.6		−5.1	−9.3	−9.2	−34.2	−15.9	−10.7
	8.9	7.3	5.1		3.8	7.7	3.6	5.8	12.0	8.2
(119) 2.6	(95) 1.9	(93) 1.7	EBIT/Interest	(11) 1.0	(21) .9	(17) 2.5	(17) 1.6	(15) 3.6	(12) 2.9
.7	−.3	−.7		−.9	−3.8	−.7	.4	1.9	1.1
4.9	5.5	5.1	Net Profit + Depr., Dep.,			11.2	13.7		
(33) 2.4	(27) 2.9	(36) 1.9	Amort./Cur. Mat. L/T/D		(10) 2.0	(12) 3.4			
1.4	.6	1.0				−.3	1.5		
.3	.3	.4		.2	.3	.5	.5	.2	.1
1.7	1.2	1.5	Fixed/Worth	2.1	1.6	2.4	1.5	.9	1.4
36.8	6.7	15.6		18.8	−2.2	−.8	2.7	7.6	36.8
1.2	.8	1.2		1.8	.4	1.3	1.5	.8	2.5
3.6	2.7	3.8	Debt/Worth	9.5	3.8	5.7	2.6	1.7	7.0
168.8	22.5	NM		−97.0	−6.0	−4.8	4.9	19.7	NM
79.6	74.1	62.8	% Profit Before Taxes/Tangible	295.8	89.9	36.6	39.1	76.8	66.7
(103) 28.9	(91) 21.9	(89) 11.3	Net Worth	(14) 28.9	(17) 11.3	(13) 5.7	(17) 8.4	(16) 22.3	(12) 38.6
6.5	2.3	1.3		−18.2	−12.4	−31.0	−6.5	8.8	7.1
18.2	13.9	13.2	% Profit Before Taxes/Total	44.3	24.0	10.9	8.9	20.3	8.2
6.8	4.2	3.3	Assets	3.2	1.0	2.9	3.3	5.3	2.9
.1	−3.5	−4.6		−7.9	−31.5	−4.7	.1	.3	.6
29.3	28.3	31.5		27.5	22.2	29.7	29.8	48.6	135.6
9.5	7.5	10.0	Sales/Net Fixed Assets	7.1	9.0	11.5	7.6	6.1	28.3
3.5	3.1	4.2		2.1	4.8	5.1	3.4	2.4	6.6
3.2	3.2	3.5		4.5	4.0	4.6	3.3	2.2	3.6
2.2	2.1	2.1	Sales/Total Assets	1.5	2.4	2.5	2.3	1.6	1.7
1.4	1.4	1.4		1.0	1.7	1.6	1.7	1.2	.7
1.1	1.6	2.0		4.9	2.3	1.7	2.4	1.9	.1
(105) 3.7	(85) 4.2	(92) 4.8	% Depr., Dep., Amort./Sales	(14) 9.1	(18) 4.4	(18) 2.7	(17) 6.3	(14) 5.8	(11) .8
8.8	8.8	9.3		10.9	7.3	7.0	9.5	12.0	5.1
3.1	4.7	4.8	% Officers', Directors',	10.0	7.1	6.0	2.5		
(54) 7.6	(41) 9.8	(52) 8.5	Owners' Comp/Sales	(10) 12.3	(11) 8.7	(13) 8.7	(10) 5.2		
13.9	16.3	11.6		16.9	11.5	10.2	7.9		
2964270M	2170607M	1579040M	Net Sales ($)	10430M	45405M	75083M	148887M	284465M	1014770M
2255285M	2035911M	1312505M	Total Assets ($)	8299M	21756M	37585M	68205M	202627M	974033M

Current Data Sorted By Assets   **Comparative Historical Data**

Type of Statement

	0-500M	500M-2MM	2-10MM	10-50MM	50-100MM	100-250MM		4/1/98-3/31/99 ALL	4/1/99-3/31/00 ALL
Unqualified			6					10	17
Reviewed		4	1	7				8	9
Compiled	4	3	10	5	8	6		19	18
Tax Returns	2	6	3	4				5	6
Other	3	7	11	8	1	2		23	27
		14 (4/1-9/30/02)		87 (10/1/02-3/31/03)					
NUMBER OF STATEMENTS	9	20	31	24	9	8		65	77
	%	%	%	%	%	%		%	%
ASSETS									
Cash & Equivalents		18.2	7.6	12.5				11.5	10.2
Trade Receivables (net)		1.2	2.6	.3				.4	1.7
Inventory		.5	.7	1.0				1.2	1.2
All Other Current		1.1	2.1	1.3				2.9	3.0
Total Current		21.1	13.0	15.2				16.1	16.1
Fixed Assets (net)		69.9	78.4	72.0				68.4	71.7
Intangibles (net)		1.6	2.2	1.7				6.5	4.7
All Other Non-Current		7.3	6.4	11.1				9.0	7.6
Total		100.0	100.0	100.0				100.0	100.0
LIABILITIES									
Notes Payable-Short Term		6.2	4.1	1.5				2.7	3.5
Cur. Mat.-L/T/D		5.8	5.2	6.1				6.5	6.0
Trade Payables		9.0	6.7	3.5				8.1	6.7
Income Taxes Payable		.1	.0	.1				.4	.1
All Other Current		19.3	5.5	5.1				8.2	8.9
Total Current		40.4	21.5	16.4				26.0	25.1
Long Term Debt		42.4	51.6	42.9				45.0	41.9
Deferred Taxes		.0	.0	.4				.4	.2
All Other Non-Current		3.9	8.8	6.2				2.7	6.8
Net Worth		13.2	18.1	34.1				26.0	26.0
Total Liabilities & Net Worth		100.0	100.0	100.0				100.0	100.0
INCOME DATA									
Net Sales		100.0	100.0	100.0				100.0	100.0
Gross Profit									
Operating Expenses		89.3	82.9	84.0				91.5	90.2
Operating Profit		10.7	17.1	16.0				8.5	9.8
All Other Expenses (net)		3.8	8.7	5.9				4.0	4.5
Profit Before Taxes		6.9	8.4	10.1				4.5	5.3
RATIOS									
Current		3.3	1.2	3.2				.8	1.2
		.7	.5	1.3				.6	.5
		.4	.1	.3				.2	.2
Quick		3.1	1.1	2.8				.8	.9
		.7	.3	.6				(64) .4	(76) .4
		.3	.1	.3				.2	.1
Sales/Receivables		0 UND	0 UND	0 UND				0 UND	0 UND
		0 UND	0 UND	1 686.2				0 UND	0 UND
		1 475.8	0 UND	3 140.9				2 169.2	2 234.1
Cost of Sales/Inventory									
Cost of Sales/Payables									
Sales/Working Capital		13.2	32.6	8.2				−247.1	56.4
		−43.8	−16.0	27.1				−14.3	−13.9
		−6.1	−6.3	−7.8				−7.0	−5.2
EBIT/Interest		6.4	3.8	7.3				4.5	5.1
	(13)	2.0	(25) 2.5	(19) 2.7				(58) 2.1	(59) 1.7
		.9	1.4	1.8				1.2	1.0
Net Profit + Depr., Dep., Amort./Cur. Mat. L/T/D								4.7	5.6
								(11) 2.0	(10) 2.8
								1.1	1.5
Fixed/Worth		1.7	1.9	.7				1.8	1.5
		6.7	4.8	3.8				3.6	3.3
		−3.4	19.4	10.1				13.2	16.9
Debt/Worth		1.3	1.8	.6				1.6	1.0
		6.5	5.1	3.7				3.6	3.5
		−5.1	18.8	11.0				23.1	31.2
% Profit Before Taxes/Tangible Net Worth		200.9	63.5	54.5				38.5	41.9
	(14)	50.0	(25) 22.1	(22) 32.9				(53) 19.3	(59) 11.4
		12.0	8.3	16.6				5.2	2.1
% Profit Before Taxes/Total Assets		20.2	12.1	12.7				8.5	9.7
		9.7	4.8	6.1				5.4	3.4
		−1.5	2.0	3.6				−1.5	.0
Sales/Net Fixed Assets		5.8	3.4	2.3				3.1	3.4
		2.7	.9	1.2				1.5	1.1
		1.3	.4	.8				.8	.7
Sales/Total Assets		2.6	1.5	1.4				2.0	1.4
		1.6	.9	.8				.9	.9
		1.1	.4	.6				.6	.6
% Depr., Dep., Amort./Sales		2.6	4.8	4.8				4.0	4.9
	(19)	5.7	(30) 7.4	6.0				(59) 6.2	(66) 7.1
		12.4	10.7	11.1				8.2	10.2
% Officers', Directors', Owners' Comp/Sales								1.6	3.1
								(17) 4.1	(18) 4.7
								7.6	10.2
Net Sales ($)	13348M	44320M	146439M	514836M	542322M	1128995M		1225365M	1326344M
Total Assets ($)	2432M	22346M	141404M	511562M	640797M	1222575M		1317228M	1494449M

Comparative Historical Data				Current Data Sorted By Sales					
			Type of Statement						
15	20	27	Unqualified	1	1	1	2	5	17
7	6	10	Reviewed		3		5	2	
15	15	21	Compiled	5	8	3	4		1
10	4	11	Tax Returns	3	5	1	2		
29	31	32	Other	3	10	5	3	4	7
4/1/00-3/31/01 ALL	4/1/01-3/31/02 ALL	4/1/02-3/31/03 ALL		0-1MM	14 (4/1-9/30/02) 1-3MM	3-5MM	87 (10/1/02-3/31/03) 5-10MM	10-25MM	25MM & OVER
76	76	101	**NUMBER OF STATEMENTS**	12	27	10	16	11	25
%	%	%	**ASSETS**	%	%	%	%	%	%
9.5	10.9	14.0	Cash & Equivalents	13.9	17.5	12.6	11.4	15.4	11.9
1.0	1.3	1.8	Trade Receivables (net)	.2	1.1	7.8	.3	.3	2.8
1.0	1.3	1.1	Inventory	.7	.5	.6	.7	2.0	2.1
3.6	1.5	1.4	All Other Current	.4	1.9	2.0	1.2	1.3	1.1
15.2	15.0	18.3	Total Current	15.3	21.0	23.0	13.4	19.0	17.9
73.8	73.7	71.7	Fixed Assets (net)	72.0	72.3	63.6	72.0	66.8	76.0
5.0	3.3	2.1	Intangibles (net)	1.2	.9	4.4	3.1	.8	2.9
6.0	8.0	7.9	All Other Non-Current	11.6	5.9	9.0	11.5	13.4	3.1
100.0	100.0	100.0	Total	100.0	100.0	100.0	100.0	100.0	100.0
			LIABILITIES						
3.4	3.9	3.0	Notes Payable-Short Term	17.4	1.1	.1	.3	.8	1.8
4.8	6.0	5.6	Cur. Mat.-L/T/D	2.7	5.9	5.5	11.7	4.1	3.6
5.7	7.4	6.9	Trade Payables	5.9	8.0	11.2	5.5	6.1	5.6
.1	.0	.1	Income Taxes Payable	.0	.1	.0	.0	.2	.1
12.4	5.8	10.8	All Other Current	4.6	14.5	32.4	4.6	5.6	7.6
26.3	23.3	26.4	Total Current	30.6	29.5	49.3	22.2	16.8	18.7
45.6	40.3	47.2	Long Term Debt	49.1	50.0	43.2	56.8	28.6	46.8
.3	.4	.3	Deferred Taxes	.0	.0	.0	.0	.0	1.3
8.4	11.2	7.3	All Other Non-Current	10.0	4.7	8.7	8.7	6.5	7.7
19.3	24.9	18.8	Net Worth	10.3	15.8	-1.2	12.2	48.1	25.6
100.0	100.0	100.0	Total Liabilities & Net Worth	100.0	100.0	100.0	100.0	100.0	100.0
			INCOME DATA						
100.0	100.0	100.0	Net Sales	100.0	100.0	100.0	100.0	100.0	100.0
			Gross Profit						
90.9	91.2	86.5	Operating Expenses	76.7	86.5	85.1	87.1	90.4	89.5
9.1	8.8	13.5	Operating Profit	23.3	13.5	14.9	12.9	9.6	10.5
4.9	6.3	5.7	All Other Expenses (net)	16.2	6.3	2.7	3.4	2.4	4.3
4.2	2.6	7.8	Profit Before Taxes	7.1	7.2	12.3	9.6	7.1	6.2
			RATIOS						
1.4	1.5	2.2		3.8	3.1	1.6	1.5	3.3	1.8
.6	.5	.7	Current	1.0	.5	1.1	.5	1.3	.6
.2	.3	.3		.1	.1	.1	.2	.6	.4
1.0	.9	1.6		3.7	2.7	1.4	.8	2.5	1.6
.3	.4	.5	Quick	.7	.5	1.0	.5	1.3	.5
.1	.2	.2		.1	.1	.1	.2	.4	.3
0 UND	0 UND	0 UND		0 UND	0 UND	0 UND	0 UND	0 UND	0 UND
0 UND	0 UND	0 UND	Sales/Receivables	0 UND	0 UND	0 UND	0 UND	0 UND	1 299.2
2 179.8	3 123.0	1 267.3		0 UND	1 464.0	0 UND	1 253.6	3 124.9	3 114.5
			Cost of Sales/Inventory						
			Cost of Sales/Payables						
38.0	26.0	13.6		16.1	11.2	7.4	NM	4.7	10.5
-16.1	-14.4	-24.6	Sales/Working Capital	NM	-23.5	92.0	-13.1	19.8	-18.3
-6.0	-5.8	-7.2		-2.1	-6.8	-5.8	-7.8	-27.1	-7.9
	3.9		5.5		9.5	7.0	3.4	7.5	5.3
(62) 1.5	(65) 1.7	(81) 2.5	EBIT/Interest	(18) 3.8		2.3	(13) 2.2	(10) 2.9	(24) 2.7
.7	.5	1.3		.9		1.4	1.3	2.0	1.0
		4.9	Net Profit + Depr., Dep., Amort./Cur. Mat. L/T/D						
		(17) 1.7							
		1.3							
2.0	1.4	1.8		4.8	1.2	1.5	2.5	.6	1.9
4.4	3.9	4.2	Fixed/Worth	15.8	6.5	4.0	8.1	2.6	2.9
-13.9	20.7	24.2		-8.1	-43.1	NM	-7.0	5.4	4.8
1.5	.9	1.5		4.0	.7	1.7	2.4	.1	1.7
4.4	3.5	4.3	Debt/Worth	15.6	5.5	3.3	7.9	3.1	2.9
-15.8	95.9	30.5		-10.7	-57.2	NM	-9.1	5.1	6.5
40.2	31.4	58.8			106.0		53.8	53.1	47.5
(53) 10.4	(58) 13.6	(80) 32.6	% Profit Before Taxes/Tangible Net Worth	(20) 54.6		(10) 32.3	24.8	(23) 38.0	
3.0	-6.2	8.4		8.3		10.9	4.8	3.4	
11.0	11.3	13.6		9.7	28.7	17.1	14.5	12.7	13.5
3.7	3.4	6.0	% Profit Before Taxes/Total Assets	3.4	6.3	6.7	7.8	5.9	7.2
-2.7	-3.1	1.4		-2.2	-.1	2.2	3.6	3.2	.2
3.1	3.0	3.5		8.4	5.7	12.0	5.3	3.4	2.4
1.2	1.0	1.3	Sales/Net Fixed Assets	.6	1.8	1.0	1.8	1.4	1.3
.8	.7	.8		.3	.4	.9	.9	.9	.9
1.8	1.6	1.9		1.7	2.1	1.4	2.5	1.7	1.5
1.0	.8	1.0	Sales/Total Assets	.5	1.4	.9	1.0	.9	1.0
.6	.6	.6		.3	.4	.8	.6	.7	.7
4.1	4.6	3.9		1.7	3.5		4.2	3.9	4.8
(67) 6.8	(66) 7.3	(90) 6.5	% Depr., Dep., Amort./Sales	(10) 11.9	(25) 6.5		7.2	5.6	(19) 6.6
9.6	10.8	9.9		20.9	10.9		11.0	6.3	8.0
2.9	2.4	2.4	% Officers', Directors', Owners' Comp/Sales						
(22) 5.1	(15) 3.2	(18) 3.0							
9.4	5.6	5.2							
1178865M	2042639M	2390260M	Net Sales ($)	7586M	50798M	39610M	108194M	178920M	2005152M
1392204M	2252590M	2541116M	Total Assets ($)	21700M	68753M	40654M	136262M	196384M	2077363M

Current Data Sorted By Assets | Comparative Historical Data

Type of Statement	0-500M	500M-2MM	2-10MM	10-50MM	50-100MM	100-250MM		4/1/98-3/31/99 ALL	4/1/99-3/31/00 ALL
Unqualified			6	7				11	11
Reviewed	5	3	2					3	7
Compiled	2	1	1					6	6
Tax Returns	2	3	1					1	1
Other				4				9	10
		3 (4/1-9/30/02)	8	41 (10/1/02-3/31/03)					
NUMBER OF STATEMENTS	9	7	17	11				30	35
	%	%	%	%	%	%		%	%

ASSETS	0-500M	500M-2MM	2-10MM	10-50MM	50-100MM	100-250MM		4/1/98-3/31/99 ALL	4/1/99-3/31/00 ALL
Cash & Equivalents			11.7	6.7				6.6	6.4
Trade Receivables (net)			26.5	15.9				25.1	29.3
Inventory			10.6	12.1	D	D		5.0	10.0
All Other Current			1.5	8.2	A	A		4.0	1.7
Total Current			50.4	42.9	T	T		40.7	47.5
Fixed Assets (net)			42.6	50.7	A	A		47.2	42.6
Intangibles (net)			3.4	4.4	N	N		6.7	4.5
All Other Non-Current			3.6	1.9	O	O		5.4	5.4
Total			100.0	100.0	T	T		100.0	100.0
LIABILITIES					A	A			
Notes Payable-Short Term			12.3	11.5	V	V		6.4	6.6
Cur. Mat.-L/T/D			7.4	8.9	A	A		6.2	6.3
Trade Payables			13.4	9.1	I	I		8.7	11.7
Income Taxes Payable			.3	.1	L	L		.3	.2
All Other Current			18.5	4.0	A	A		13.1	8.9
Total Current			51.8	33.7	B	B		34.8	33.9
Long Term Debt			14.1	21.3	L	L		19.3	17.9
Deferred Taxes			1.0	.4	E	E		1.6	.9
All Other Non-Current			2.6	12.8				3.0	3.0
Net Worth			30.5	31.9				41.3	44.3
Total Liabilities & Net Worth			100.0	100.0				100.0	100.0
INCOME DATA									
Net Sales			100.0	100.0				100.0	100.0
Gross Profit									
Operating Expenses			98.8	98.7				91.4	93.1
Operating Profit			1.2	1.3				8.6	6.9
All Other Expenses (net)			.2	3.8				2.2	2.0
Profit Before Taxes			1.1	-2.4				6.4	4.8

RATIOS	0-500M	500M-2MM	2-10MM	10-50MM	50-100MM	100-250MM		4/1/98-3/31/99 ALL	4/1/99-3/31/00 ALL
Current			1.4	2.0				1.8	2.8
			.9	1.2				1.3	1.3
			.7	.5				.9	.8
Quick			1.2	1.8				1.6	1.9
			.9	.6				1.1	1.1
			.6	.4				.7	.6
Sales/Receivables		38	9.7	21	17.0		40	9.1	39	9.3
		47	7.7	34	10.9		59	6.2	53	6.9
		72	5.1	59	6.1		76	4.8	74	4.9
Cost of Sales/Inventory									
Cost of Sales/Payables									
Sales/Working Capital			19.0	2.3				8.5	7.8
			-46.9	35.6				13.0	21.7
			-8.7	-5.9				-53.9	-13.0
EBIT/Interest			8.4	4.0				8.1	8.9
		(16)	2.1	1.1			(29)	3.8	(32)	3.4
			.4	-5.8				1.2	.8
Net Profit + Depr., Dep., Amort./Cur. Mat. L/T/D								4.3	4.1
							(10)	2.7	(10)	1.9
								1.9	1.0
Fixed/Worth			.9	1.1				.9	.6
			1.8	2.5				1.2	1.2
			3.6	-34.9				3.0	2.5
Debt/Worth			1.1	.7				.7	.6
			3.0	3.3				1.6	1.9
			4.9	-196.0				4.1	3.3
% Profit Before Taxes/Tangible Net Worth			33.1					45.5	55.0
		(15)	16.9				(26)	19.0	(31)	29.4
			-7.2					4.5	6.5
% Profit Before Taxes/Total Assets			10.3	13.4				19.9	15.6
			3.7	.4				6.7	8.2
			-2.2	-5.0				1.1	1.7
Sales/Net Fixed Assets			7.6	8.9				9.0	9.8
			4.9	1.9				3.1	4.5
			2.4	1.0				1.8	2.4
Sales/Total Assets			2.4	1.5				2.0	2.5
			1.8	1.0				1.5	1.7
			1.0	.6				.9	1.2
% Depr., Dep., Amort./Sales			3.7					4.2	3.9
		(15)	8.7				(22)	9.7	(31)	6.7
			17.2					13.1	10.0
% Officers', Directors', Owners' Comp/Sales									
Net Sales ($)	9234M	27064M	168459M	291504M				783600M	1043119M
Total Assets ($)	2166M	9076M	87082M	266030M				809083M	753592M

© RMA 2003

M = $ thousand   MM = $ million
See Pages 11 through 18 for Explanation of Ratios and Data

Comparative Historical Data / Current Data Sorted By Sales

	4/1/00-3/31/01 ALL	4/1/01-3/31/02 ALL	4/1/02-3/31/03 ALL	Type of Statement	0-1MM	1-3MM	3-5MM	5-10MM	10-25MM	25MM & OVER
	6	8	7	Unqualified					3	4
	9	8	6	Reviewed		1		3	2	
	13	10	10	Compiled	1		1	3	1	
	3	6	4	Tax Returns	3	4	1			
	14	16	17	Other	1	2	4	3	4	3
					\[0-1MM,1-3MM,3-5MM: 3 (4/1-9/30/02)\]			\[5-10MM,10-25MM,25MM: 41 (10/1/02-3/31/03)\]		
	45	48	44	NUMBER OF STATEMENTS	5	7	6	9	10	7
	%	%	%		%	%	%	%	%	%
				ASSETS						
	9.7	10.6	11.5	Cash & Equivalents					5.7	
	26.2	23.8	22.1	Trade Receivables (net)					22.9	
	3.9	3.6	7.6	Inventory					5.5	
	2.3	1.8	3.0	All Other Current					8.1	
	42.1	39.9	44.2	Total Current					42.2	
	45.9	49.7	46.2	Fixed Assets (net)					50.9	
	3.5	3.2	4.5	Intangibles (net)					5.7	
	8.6	7.2	5.1	All Other Non-Current					1.2	
	100.0	100.0	100.0	Total					100.0	
				LIABILITIES						
	8.2	10.8	14.2	Notes Payable-Short Term					9.9	
	5.9	8.5	7.8	Cur. Mat.-L/T/D					7.0	
	11.9	11.0	10.7	Trade Payables					14.1	
	.8	.1	.4	Income Taxes Payable					.1	
	13.5	11.6	11.2	All Other Current					8.8	
	40.3	42.0	44.4	Total Current					39.9	
	18.7	18.9	16.6	Long Term Debt					20.8	
	1.2	.8	.5	Deferred Taxes					.0	
	3.7	4.3	5.6	All Other Non-Current					8.9	
	36.2	33.9	32.9	Net Worth					30.4	
	100.0	100.0	100.0	Total Liabilities & Net Worth					100.0	
				INCOME DATA						
	100.0	100.0	100.0	Net Sales					100.0	
				Gross Profit						
	94.7	96.4	96.6	Operating Expenses					94.2	
	5.3	3.6	3.4	Operating Profit					5.8	
	2.0	1.5	1.3	All Other Expenses (net)					2.9	
	3.2	2.2	2.0	Profit Before Taxes					2.9	
				RATIOS						
	1.8	1.4	1.6	Current					2.5	
	1.1	1.0	.9						.8	
	.7	.5	.6						.4	
	1.5	1.2	1.3	Quick					1.0	
	1.0	.8	.7						.7	
	.5	.5	.5						.4	
	25 14.6	12 29.3	17 21.6	Sales/Receivables					20 18.3	
	48 7.6	37 9.8	40 9.2						40 9.1	
	64 5.7	61 6.0	58 6.3						68 5.4	
				Cost of Sales/Inventory						
				Cost of Sales/Payables						
	10.8	14.5	10.3	Sales/Working Capital					6.6	
	92.6	194.5	-46.4						-18.6	
	-15.5	-11.3	-10.1						-5.1	
	(40) 8.1	(43) 8.0	(40) 7.5	EBIT/Interest					8.6	
	1.9	2.8	2.2						2.3	
	.8	.7	.4						.8	
	(12) 4.8	(16) 3.7	(14) 3.2	Net Profit + Depr., Dep., Amort./Cur. Mat. L/T/D						
	2.5	2.0	1.7							
	1.4	1.1	.8							
	.7	.8	.9	Fixed/Worth					1.2	
	1.3	1.6	1.7						2.5	
	2.7	3.2	9.6						-27.0	
	.8	1.0	.8	Debt/Worth					.9	
	2.0	1.9	2.6						3.3	
	3.5	5.5	19.8						-148.4	
	(40) 43.4	(43) 42.7	(36) 46.5	% Profit Before Taxes/Tangible Net Worth						
	18.5	18.0	13.5							
	-.2	-6.6	-7.1							
	15.2	14.2	13.0	% Profit Before Taxes/Total Assets					19.3	
	5.2	6.2	3.6						4.7	
	-1.0	-1.9	-2.3						-.9	
	9.1	9.4	8.9	Sales/Net Fixed Assets					8.8	
	4.3	4.5	5.3						4.4	
	2.7	2.7	2.2						1.0	
	3.3	3.1	3.0	Sales/Total Assets					2.3	
	1.9	2.1	1.9						1.6	
	1.4	1.3	1.0						.8	
	(43) 4.0	(46) 3.8	(36) 4.6	% Depr., Dep., Amort./Sales						
	7.7	7.5	9.0							
	12.1	13.0	15.8							
	(24) 5.4	(18) 2.9	(14) 7.9	% Officers', Directors', Owners' Comp/Sales						
	9.1	11.2	9.9							
	15.4	13.9	16.5							
	544950M	2021142M	496261M	Net Sales ($)	2928M	11603M	25215M	64702M	143639M	248174M
	310515M	336113M	364354M	Total Assets ($)	1195M	5108M	17471M	39408M	128978M	172194M

© RMA 2003

M = $ thousand   MM = $ million
See Pages 11 through 18 for Explanation of Ratios and Data

INFORMATION—Sound Recording Studios NAICS 512240 (SIC 7389)

Current Data Sorted By Assets　　　　　　　　　　　　　　　　　　**Comparative Historical Data**

0-500M	500M-2MM	2-10MM	10-50MM	50-100MM	100-250MM	Type of Statement	4/1/98-3/31/99 ALL	4/1/99-3/31/00 ALL
	4	5	3	2		Unqualified		
	2	6	2			Reviewed		
7	8	3				Compiled		
7	4					Tax Returns		
6	11	7	6			Other		
	11 (4/1-9/30/02)		72 (10/1/02-3/31/03)					
20	29	21	11	2		NUMBER OF STATEMENTS		
%	%	%	%	%	%	**ASSETS**	%	%
16.8	11.4	13.6	11.7		D	Cash & Equivalents	D	D
31.5	34.1	35.7	24.2		A	Trade Receivables (net)	A	A
8.3	9.3	5.9	17.7		T	Inventory	T	T
.8	2.5	1.0	4.9		A	All Other Current	A	A
57.3	57.3	56.1	58.4			Total Current		
30.8	23.0	30.5	17.3		N	Fixed Assets (net)	N	N
.0	4.0	3.8	14.2		O	Intangibles (net)	O	O
11.9	15.7	9.6	10.1		T	All Other Non-Current	T	T
100.0	100.0	100.0	100.0			Total		
					A	**LIABILITIES**	A	A
39.4	15.8	9.4	16.6		V	Notes Payable-Short Term	V	V
5.1	5.5	5.4	2.0		A	Cur. Mat.-L/T/D	A	A
24.1	13.6	13.7	21.8		I	Trade Payables	I	I
.4	.0	1.3	.2		L	Income Taxes Payable	L	L
6.2	15.8	12.3	17.1		A	All Other Current	A	A
75.3	50.7	42.1	57.7		B	Total Current	B	B
14.7	12.4	15.4	11.5		L	Long Term Debt	L	L
.0	.1	2.1	.2		E	Deferred Taxes	E	E
25.6	7.1	6.3	6.5			All Other Non-Current		
-15.6	29.7	34.0	24.1			Net Worth		
100.0	100.0	100.0	100.0			Total Liabilities & Net Worth		
						INCOME DATA		
100.0	100.0	100.0	100.0			Net Sales		
						Gross Profit		
102.5	99.5	96.1	96.6			Operating Expenses		
-2.5	.5	3.9	3.4			Operating Profit		
1.6	1.2	1.4	.3			All Other Expenses (net)		
-4.1	-.7	2.5	3.1			Profit Before Taxes		
						RATIOS		
4.6	3.0	2.1	1.8					
1.2	1.2	1.4	1.0			Current		
.2	.7	.8	.8					
3.4	2.1	2.1	.9					
1.2	.9	1.3	.5			Quick		
.2	.5	.6	.5					
0　UND	25　14.4	23　15.8	13　28.1					
15　24.4	33　11.1	68　5.4	40　9.1			Sales/Receivables		
49　7.4	62　5.9	87　4.2	48　7.6					
						Cost of Sales/Inventory		
						Cost of Sales/Payables		
10.9	7.5	4.8	10.2					
51.8	30.9	11.6	-805.4			Sales/Working Capital		
-5.7	-14.8	-100.2	-22.4					
(14)　5.6	(24)　7.8	(16)　6.1	9.2					
-1.3	3.2	4.0	-.4			EBIT/Interest		
-5.2	-2.5	1.3	-3.3					
						Net Profit + Depr., Dep., Amort./Cur. Mat. L /T/D		
.3	.2	.3	.2					
1.1	.9	1.0	1.6			Fixed/Worth		
-.6	2.5	5.5	-1.2					
.3	.8	.7	1.1					
UND	2.6	1.4	4.8			Debt/Worth		
-2.1	6.7	13.4	-7.3					
88.4	38.7	34.3						
(11)　.0	(25)　15.3	(18)　20.7				% Profit Before Taxes/Tangible Net Worth		
-129.7	-5.9	4.0						
37.5	10.7	11.6	13.3					
-6.7	3.4	5.4	-4.8			% Profit Before Taxes/Total Assets		
-41.5	-5.7	-.3	-10.0					
90.8	73.9	15.7	99.2					
28.1	14.5	9.1	18.1			Sales/Net Fixed Assets		
7.6	6.6	4.4	6.5					
8.9	3.5	3.0	2.8					
4.5	2.9	2.5	2.4			Sales/Total Assets		
3.2	1.8	1.4	1.8					
.9	.8	1.8						
(12)　1.3	(24)　2.6	(15)　2.2				% Depr., Dep., Amort./Sales		
4.8	4.1	8.0						
4.3	2.6							
(12)　9.5	(16)　5.3					% Officers', Directors', Owners' Comp/Sales		
16.6	9.5							
21555M	83919M	233691M	588016M	221817M		Net Sales ($)		
2920M	31246M	102790M	207165M	140046M		Total Assets ($)		

M = $ thousand　　MM = $ million
See Pages 11 through 18 for Explanation of Ratios and Data

Comparative Historical Data   Current Data Sorted By Sales

			Type of Statement						
		14	Unqualified	1	2	2		5	4
		10	Reviewed		1	1	2	4	2
		18	Compiled	3	8	3	3	1	
		11	Tax Returns	7	2	1	1		
		30	Other	3	10	4	6	1	6
4/1/00-3/31/01 ALL	4/1/01-3/31/02 ALL	4/1/02-3/31/03 ALL 83		11 (4/1-9/30/02) 0-1MM	1-3MM	3-5MM	72 (10/1/02-3/31/03) 5-10MM	10-25MM	25MM & OVER
			NUMBER OF STATEMENTS	14	23	11	12	11	12
%	%	%	ASSETS	%	%	%	%	%	%
D	D	13.4	Cash & Equivalents	16.8	12.5	10.1	12.3	19.9	9.2
A	A	32.0	Trade Receivables (net)	25.3	28.5	40.9	47.9	32.1	22.0
T	T	10.0	Inventory	5.5	10.7	10.2	3.1	7.9	22.3
A	A	2.0	All Other Current	1.2	1.1	5.7	.1	2.2	2.7
		57.3	Total Current	48.8	52.8	66.9	63.5	62.1	56.2
N	N	26.1	Fixed Assets (net)	41.6	25.2	20.9	25.5	20.8	19.6
O	O	4.3	Intangibles (net)	.3	2.3	5.2	.9	6.3	13.5
T	T	12.4	All Other Non-Current	9.3	19.6	7.1	10.1	10.9	10.7
		100.0	Total	100.0	100.0	100.0	100.0	100.0	100.0
A	A		LIABILITIES						
V	V	19.8	Notes Payable-Short Term	42.9	20.6	10.3	16.5	5.3	16.6
A	A	4.8	Cur. Mat.-L/T/D	5.1	5.6	6.1	5.0	4.4	2.2
I	I	17.2	Trade Payables	22.2	16.2	17.1	9.6	20.0	18.5
L	L	.5	Income Taxes Payable	.0	.4	.0	2.3	.0	.2
A	A	12.6	All Other Current	6.9	12.3	8.5	16.3	15.7	16.8
B	B	54.9	Total Current	77.2	55.0	42.0	49.6	45.4	54.3
L	L	13.6	Long Term Debt	29.1	11.3	7.4	5.5	14.9	12.5
E	E	.6	Deferred Taxes	.0	1.1	.1	.8	.9	.3
		11.8	All Other Non-Current	33.8	5.8	2.8	13.4	4.9	10.5
		19.2	Net Worth	−40.0	26.8	47.7	30.7	33.8	22.4
		100.0	Total Liabilities & Net Worth	100.0	100.0	100.0	100.0	100.0	100.0
			INCOME DATA						
		100.0	Net Sales	100.0	100.0	100.0	100.0	100.0	100.0
			Gross Profit						
		98.7	Operating Expenses	100.5	97.8	98.5	102.7	94.6	98.5
		1.3	Operating Profit	−.5	2.2	1.5	−2.7	5.4	1.5
		1.2	All Other Expenses (net)	4.4	1.1	−.5	.4	−.3	1.5
		.0	Profit Before Taxes	−4.9	1.1	2.0	−3.1	5.7	.0
			RATIOS						
		2.3		3.6	2.2	4.8	2.1	2.5	1.7
		1.2	Current	.8	1.2	1.4	1.6	1.1	1.1
		.7		.1	.5	1.1	.7	.8	.8
		2.1		3.1	1.8	3.3	2.1	2.5	.9
		.9	Quick	.8	.9	1.1	1.4	1.0	.5
		.5		.1	.3	.7	.6	.5	.4
	13	29.0		0 UND	10 35.8	29 12.7	34 10.7	19 19.5	11 34.4
	34	10.8	Sales/Receivables	0 UND	31 11.8	52 7.0	69 5.3	32 11.3	37 9.9
	65	5.6		67 5.4	54 6.8	86 4.3	84 4.4	61 6.0	47 7.8
			Cost of Sales/Inventory						
			Cost of Sales/Payables						
		7.1		5.5	8.3	6.6	10.4	4.7	9.4
		30.9	Sales/Working Capital	−32.0	43.3	10.7	30.3	39.6	NM
		−17.8		−3.6	−11.8	50.0	NM	−41.9	−26.6
		6.6		1.2	8.2				8.5
	(67)	3.1	EBIT/Interest	(11) −.2	(19) 4.9				−.3
		−2.4		−2.7	−3.3				−2.9
		2.7	Net Profit + Depr., Dep.,						
	(16)	1.6	Amort./Cur. Mat. L/T/D						
		−.2							
		.2		.3	.3	.1	.2	.1	.7
		.9	Fixed/Worth	4.4	1.1	.3	.9	.6	1.3
		6.9		−.5	63.0	1.0	4.2	6.9	−3.4
		.8		2.2	.8	.3	.8	.6	1.3
		2.7	Debt/Worth	−4.6	2.4	1.4	4.7	2.1	4.6
		UND		−1.8	179.0	2.7	7.9	19.9	−12.0
		41.5	% Profit Before Taxes/Tangible		41.5	58.0	54.8		
	(63)	17.4	Net Worth	(19) 17.4	(10) 17.6	(11) 29.9			
		−4.9		−3.7	−2.7	−35.8			
		12.0	% Profit Before Taxes/Total	.9	17.4	37.5	12.5	18.3	13.0
		2.7	Assets	−6.7	7.6	6.4	5.3	2.7	−3.9
		−10.0		−38.1	−11.9	−1.7	−10.2	−.9	−9.8
		55.0		42.6	52.6	109.0	73.8	47.3	82.4
		14.5	Sales/Net Fixed Assets	8.6	17.8	19.9	13.6	15.8	10.7
		6.5		4.1	5.7	8.2	7.2	8.6	6.3
		3.7		4.2	4.3	3.4	4.9	3.0	2.8
		2.8	Sales/Total Assets	3.2	2.6	3.0	3.0	2.6	2.3
		1.9		1.0	1.9	1.8	1.6	2.4	1.9
		.9		1.3	1.4		.8		.6
	(62)	2.3	% Depr., Dep., Amort./Sales	(11) 4.6	(16) 3.0		(10) 1.7		(11) 1.4
		4.8		17.0	6.8		3.7		5.4
		2.5	% Officers', Directors',		2.4				
	(39)	6.2	Owners' Comp/Sales		(12) 4.0				
		13.2			13.0				
		1148998M	Net Sales ($)	4348M	43259M	39761M	82106M	186962M	792562M
		484167M	Total Assets ($)	3598M	27180M	15022M	32937M	68610M	336820M

M = $ thousand   MM = $ million
See Pages 11 through 18 for Explanation of Ratios and Data

Current Data Sorted By Assets   Comparative Historical Data

	0-500M	500M-2MM	2-10MM	10-50MM	50-100MM	100-250MM	Type of Statement	4/1/98-3/31/99 ALL	4/1/99-3/31/00 ALL
	2	2	11	13	2	8	Unqualified	45	34
	4	6	7	2			Reviewed	26	17
	8	13	10	1			Compiled	41	29
		3	1				Tax Returns	13	6
	2	12	10	7	5		Other	63	50
	16 (4/1-9/30/02)			113 (10/1/02-3/31/03)					
	16	36	39	23	7	8	NUMBER OF STATEMENTS	188	136
	%	%	%	%	%	%	**ASSETS**	%	%
	11.2	14.9	8.4	7.0			Cash & Equivalents	8.2	9.9
	23.2	20.4	12.9	13.6			Trade Receivables (net)	13.9	16.8
	.8	.1	.0	.0			Inventory	.2	.6
	7.7	3.2	2.0	3.4			All Other Current	1.8	3.2
	42.9	38.6	23.2	24.1			Total Current	24.1	30.5
	34.2	26.9	28.7	26.4			Fixed Assets (net)	33.0	33.7
	13.8	23.2	33.1	36.4			Intangibles (net)	31.5	27.1
	9.0	11.3	15.0	13.1			All Other Non-Current	11.4	8.7
	100.0	100.0	100.0	100.0			Total	100.0	100.0
							LIABILITIES		
	2.0	4.7	2.9	.5			Notes Payable-Short Term	4.8	2.9
	30.0	5.1	4.4	7.8			Cur. Mat.-L/T/D	5.2	5.5
	11.9	3.5	2.4	6.7			Trade Payables	3.0	4.0
	.0	.6	.1	.2			Income Taxes Payable	.2	.2
	39.3	11.5	5.8	8.6			All Other Current	7.5	9.3
	83.3	25.3	15.6	23.8			Total Current	20.6	21.9
	62.6	42.4	43.6	31.2			Long Term Debt	54.0	51.2
	.1	.0	.2	.6			Deferred Taxes	.6	.5
	17.0	9.3	11.1	11.2			All Other Non-Current	11.5	15.9
	-63.0	22.9	29.5	33.2			Net Worth	13.2	10.5
	100.0	100.0	100.0	100.0			Total Liabilities & Net Worth	100.0	100.0
							INCOME DATA		
	100.0	100.0	100.0	100.0			Net Sales	100.0	100.0
							Gross Profit		
	91.8	87.8	90.0	87.3			Operating Expenses	103.0	88.5
	8.2	12.2	10.0	12.7			Operating Profit	-3.0	11.5
	4.5	4.4	5.3	6.0			All Other Expenses (net)	8.6	5.9
	3.7	7.8	4.7	6.7			Profit Before Taxes	-11.6	5.6
							RATIOS		
	3.0 / 1.2 / .5	7.7 / 2.3 / 1.1	3.9 / 1.3 / .8	2.5 / 1.5 / .9			Current	2.9 / 1.5 / .8	3.6 / 1.9 / .9
	2.6 / 1.1 / .3	7.4 / 1.8 / .9	3.8 / 1.2 / .7	2.2 / 1.3 / .7			Quick	2.3 / 1.2 / .7	2.8 / 1.5 / .8
	0 UND / 47 7.7 / 59 6.2	42 8.7 / 53 6.9 / 65 5.7	38 9.7 / 55 6.6 / 67 5.5	49 7.4 / 66 5.6 / 75 4.9			Sales/Receivables	38 9.5 / 58 6.3 / 70 5.2	43 8.4 / 58 6.3 / 73 5.0
							Cost of Sales/Inventory		
							Cost of Sales/Payables		
	6.4 / 49.0 / -13.2	3.4 / 7.9 / 78.0	4.7 / 13.4 / -19.0	6.6 / 10.0 / -45.6			Sales/Working Capital	5.8 / 17.7 / -27.3	4.7 / 9.4 / -79.6
	(13) 15.2 / .8 / -2.0	(31) 10.4 / 3.6 / 1.2	(35) 4.7 / 1.9 / .5	(22) 7.5 / 2.5 / .5			EBIT/Interest	(154) 3.5 / 1.5 / .2	(122) 5.2 / 1.8 / .6
							Net Profit + Depr., Dep., Amort./Cur. Mat. L/T/D	(39) 5.0 / 2.1 / .9	(22) 4.3 / 1.9 / 1.0
	.6 / -2.2 / -.2	.5 / -6.6 / -.6	.7 / -2.1 / -.6	1.3 / -27.0 / -.4			Fixed/Worth	1.6 / -2.0 / -.4	.9 / -8.6 / -.6
	.5 / -3.8 / -1.6	.4 / -11.2 / -2.3	1.1 / -8.3 / -1.9	2.8 / -56.3 / -2.1			Debt/Worth	2.6 / -5.3 / -1.9	1.6 / -11.4 / -2.1
		(17) 73.8 / 33.1 / 12.7	(18) 40.5 / 19.3 / 7.1	(11) 68.2 / 12.4 / -2.1			% Profit Before Taxes/Tangible Net Worth	(79) 76.3 / 19.5 / -6.2	(62) 92.8 / 36.1 / 3.3
	9.8 / 3.1 / -8.4	21.9 / 12.9 / -.3	12.9 / 4.2 / -1.9	16.0 / 4.7 / -.9			% Profit Before Taxes/Total Assets	10.2 / .7 / -6.1	13.8 / 3.5 / -2.0
	21.8 / 10.1 / 4.1	17.6 / 5.1 / 2.7	5.4 / 3.3 / 2.0	7.3 / 3.4 / 2.4			Sales/Net Fixed Assets	5.8 / 3.2 / 1.9	5.8 / 2.9 / 1.8
	3.9 / 2.0 / 1.3	1.7 / 1.2 / .9	1.1 / .8 / .6	.9 / .7 / .5			Sales/Total Assets	1.4 / .9 / .5	1.5 / .8 / .6
	(14) 2.0 / 3.5 / 7.0	(31) 2.5 / 7.7 / 12.5	(38) 4.1 / 5.6 / 8.9	(20) 3.9 / 6.1 / 10.0			% Depr., Dep., Amort./Sales	(171) 4.2 / 8.1 / 16.1	(126) 4.6 / 7.9 / 12.6
		(15) 5.4 / 7.2 / 13.9					% Officers', Directors', Owners' Comp/Sales	(34) 7.0 / 12.9 / 16.5	(31) 6.9 / 9.8 / 16.5
	17636M	52929M	154159M	385954M	226047M	568383M	Net Sales ($)	960453M	906018M
	4823M	39507M	179632M	490049M	490587M	1240054M	Total Assets ($)	1811122M	1512280M

Comparative Historical Data | Current Data Sorted By Sales

			Type of Statement						
28	26	38	Unqualified	4	4	3	9	8	10
18	12	19	Reviewed	5	9	3	2	2	
32	23	32	Compiled	9	17	3	2	1	
8	6	4	Tax Returns	1	3				
47	36	36	Other	4	11	4	6	7	4
4/1/00- 3/31/01	4/1/01- 3/31/02	4/1/02- 3/31/03		16 (4/1-9/30/02)			113 (10/1/02-3/31/03)		
ALL	ALL	ALL		0-1MM	1-3MM	3-5MM	5-10MM	10-25MM	25MM & OVER
133	103	129	NUMBER OF STATEMENTS	23	44	10	20	18	14
%	%	%	ASSETS	%	%	%	%	%	%
8.7	8.9	10.0	Cash & Equivalents	6.5	13.8	5.7	11.0	9.0	7.1
16.5	15.2	15.8	Trade Receivables (net)	18.9	17.7	15.0	12.2	14.9	11.9
.7	.3	.2	Inventory	.0	.1	.0	.7	.0	.1
3.0	2.5	3.2	All Other Current	5.3	3.0	4.0	1.8	3.8	1.0
29.0	26.9	29.2	Total Current	30.7	34.5	24.7	25.8	27.7	20.1
31.5	29.5	27.2	Fixed Assets (net)	31.1	28.4	24.1	30.9	21.7	20.6
27.5	30.5	30.7	Intangibles (net)	24.2	27.5	27.8	27.7	38.5	48.1
12.0	13.0	12.9	All Other Non-Current	14.0	9.6	23.4	15.6	12.1	11.1
100.0	100.0	100.0	Total	100.0	100.0	100.0	100.0	100.0	100.0
			LIABILITIES						
1.7	1.8	2.6	Notes Payable-Short Term	5.1	2.3	2.8	1.8	2.5	1.2
7.7	5.3	8.2	Cur. Mat.-L/T/D	6.1	13.6	3.5	6.2	6.3	3.1
4.2	3.9	4.5	Trade Payables	5.5	3.2	2.1	6.8	4.3	5.4
.0	.1	.2	Income Taxes Payable	.0	.6	.1	.1	.1	.0
9.2	6.1	11.8	All Other Current	19.8	10.4	9.7	14.4	9.3	3.8
23.0	17.3	27.3	Total Current	36.5	30.1	18.2	29.3	22.6	13.6
50.0	44.7	43.2	Long Term Debt	67.7	41.7	41.9	27.6	34.7	41.3
.8	.7	.6	Deferred Taxes	.1	.0	.0	1.5	.7	1.9
18.9	18.5	10.5	All Other Non-Current	20.7	8.0	6.6	17.4	3.0	4.7
7.4	18.8	18.4	Net Worth	−24.9	20.2	33.3	24.1	39.0	38.6
100.0	100.0	100.0	Total Liabilities & Net Worth	100.0	100.0	100.0	100.0	100.0	100.0
			INCOME DATA						
100.0	100.0	100.0	Net Sales	100.0	100.0	100.0	100.0	100.0	100.0
			Gross Profit						
87.6	91.0	87.7	Operating Expenses	90.4	88.7	91.3	91.0	84.8	76.6
12.4	9.0	12.3	Operating Profit	9.6	11.3	8.7	9.0	15.2	23.4
6.5	7.0	5.6	All Other Expenses (net)	6.8	5.1	2.7	5.5	5.1	8.3
5.9	1.9	6.7	Profit Before Taxes	2.8	6.2	5.9	3.5	10.1	15.1
			RATIOS						
3.1	4.1	3.7		3.2	6.8	4.0	3.1	2.8	3.0
1.7	2.0	1.6	Current	1.3	1.7	1.7	1.5	1.8	1.5
.9	.9	.9		.5	1.1	.7	.8	1.0	1.1
2.9	4.1	3.4		2.6	6.5	3.8	2.5	2.4	2.9
1.6	1.8	1.5	Quick	1.2	1.6	1.7	1.2	1.7	1.4
.7	.8	.8		.4	.8	.6	.5	.7	.9
41 8.9	40 9.1	41 8.8		0 UND	45 8.0	43 8.5	50 7.3	57 6.4	
57 6.4	58 6.3	56 6.5	Sales/Receivables	50 7.3	56 6.6	52 7.0	51 7.1	61 6.0	63 5.8
68 5.4	70 5.2	67 5.4		62 5.9	67 5.5	66 5.5	73 5.0	74 4.9	69 5.3
			Cost of Sales/Inventory						
			Cost of Sales/Payables						
5.1	4.9	4.5		6.0	3.6	4.5	5.0	4.7	4.7
9.4	9.0	11.1	Sales/Working Capital	19.4	9.7	NM	15.2	8.4	13.1
−81.4	−61.3	−52.8		−5.3	89.0	−15.7	−21.0	NM	64.2
4.8	4.7	7.0		3.5	8.4		9.5	7.1	9.5
(111) 1.7	(90) 1.7	(113) 2.1	EBIT/Interest	(18) 1.1	(39) 2.5	(19) 1.9	(17) 2.4	(11) 4.4
.6	.3	.7		−.2	1.2		.3	1.3	1.9
5.6	5.6	6.1	Net Profit + Depr., Dep.,						
(21) 1.8	(15) 1.4	(19) 1.9	Amort./Cur. Mat. L/T/D						
.6	1.2	1.2							
.7	.9	.7		1.2	.6	.5	.5	1.3	1.1
−5.2	−3.5	−4.7	Fixed/Worth	−.5	NM	NM	4.6	−16.2	−4.8
−.5	−.5	−.5		−.2	−.6	−.4	−1.2	−.5	−.3
1.5	1.3	1.1		37.3	.8	1.0	.4	2.5	1.5
−10.1	−7.6	−9.1	Debt/Worth	−2.8	NM	NM	6.0	−34.4	−8.4
−2.0	−2.0	−2.1		−1.6	−2.2	−1.8	−2.8	−2.2	−2.1
57.4	37.9	61.6	% Profit Before Taxes/Tangible		86.3		47.5		
(58) 24.5	(44) 11.9	(58) 27.8	Net Worth	(22) 30.3	(11) 23.9			
3.6	−2.5	1.4			8.0		−1.4		
15.4	9.7	15.8	% Profit Before Taxes/Total	5.4	21.5	11.4	21.3	17.4	11.5
4.0	2.4	4.7	Assets	1.7	8.8	5.5	2.2	5.8	7.8
−2.1	−3.5	−1.0		−8.5	.9	−2.0	−1.6	.8	3.2
6.4	6.9	9.3		19.9	10.0	12.2	7.6	5.8	5.9
3.2	3.2	3.7	Sales/Net Fixed Assets	4.4	3.7	3.2	3.2	3.6	3.3
2.0	1.9	2.3		2.0	2.5	2.1	1.7	2.9	2.2
1.4	1.4	1.5		1.7	1.7	1.3	1.2	1.5	.8
.9	.9	.9	Sales/Total Assets	1.2	1.0	.8	.9	.8	.5
.6	.5	.6		.7	.7	.6	.5	.6	.4
3.7	3.7	3.5		3.2	4.6	2.4	2.5	3.7	4.1
(123) 7.0	(88) 8.0	(117) 5.5	% Depr., Dep., Amort./Sales	(20) 4.9	(39) 7.7	(19) 4.9	(17) 5.1	(12) 4.9
12.7	12.6	9.1		12.3	11.7	6.4	8.6	8.3	5.9
6.0	4.9	3.9	% Officers', Directors',		5.8				
(21) 11.6	(29) 10.7	(30) 7.2	Owners' Comp/Sales	(16) 7.5				
16.3	16.1	12.7			12.6				
1125885M	1170925M	1405108M	Net Sales ($)	12570M	75725M	35504M	137664M	305487M	838158M
1967011M	1796043M	2444652M	Total Assets ($)	17800M	84667M	43921M	288210M	447901M	1562153M

M = $ thousand   MM = $ million
See Pages 11 through 18 for Explanation of Ratios and Data

Current Data Sorted By Assets   Comparative Historical Data

Type of Statement	0-500M	500M-2MM	2-10MM	10-50MM	50-100MM	100-250MM		4/1/98-3/31/99 ALL	4/1/99-3/31/00 ALL
Unqualified		2	14	16	2	5		48	34
Reviewed		1	5	3				6	4
Compiled		1	2					9	4
Tax Returns	1	2	1					4	1
Other	1	2	8	6	4	1		32	17
		27 (4/1-9/30/02)		50 (10/1/02-3/31/03)					
NUMBER OF STATEMENTS	2	8	30	25	6	6		99	60
ASSETS	%	%	%	%	%	%		%	%
Cash & Equivalents			10.4	9.0				13.2	11.2
Trade Receivables (net)			15.8	8.3				13.8	14.0
Inventory			.4	.5				1.5	.3
All Other Current			8.0	4.9				4.3	4.3
Total Current			34.6	22.8				32.8	29.8
Fixed Assets (net)			45.5	52.4				34.6	37.3
Intangibles (net)			11.1	9.6				19.3	17.7
All Other Non-Current			8.8	15.2				13.3	15.2
Total			100.0	100.0				100.0	100.0
LIABILITIES									
Notes Payable-Short Term			12.2	6.8				8.7	5.4
Cur. Mat.-L/T/D			7.0	2.9				5.8	7.7
Trade Payables			6.3	5.6				6.0	6.6
Income Taxes Payable			.0	.0				.4	.1
All Other Current			12.2	4.6				9.2	12.1
Total Current			37.6	20.0				30.1	31.9
Long Term Debt			30.8	21.6				32.7	35.8
Deferred Taxes			.1	.7				.8	.3
All Other Non-Current			3.9	8.4				6.9	8.0
Net Worth			27.5	49.3				29.6	24.0
Total Liabilities & Net Worth			100.0	100.0				100.0	100.0
INCOME DATA									
Net Sales			100.0	100.0				100.0	100.0
Gross Profit									
Operating Expenses			91.3	93.7				105.0	90.3
Operating Profit			8.7	6.3				-5.0	9.7
All Other Expenses (net)			3.9	4.7				-20.3	2.6
Profit Before Taxes			4.7	1.6				15.3	7.1
RATIOS									
Current			2.4	2.3				3.4	2.0
			1.5	1.2				1.5	1.2
			.7	.6				.8	.8
Quick			1.5	1.6				2.9	1.6
			1.1	.9				1.1	1.1
			.5	.3				.6	.6
Sales/Receivables			11 34.2	20 18.2				30 12.3	34 10.9
			60 6.1	44 8.4				57 6.4	53 6.9
			66 5.5	73 5.0				73 5.0	70 5.2
Cost of Sales/Inventory									
Cost of Sales/Payables									
Sales/Working Capital			5.4	3.7				4.2	6.2
			11.0	28.2				9.8	23.4
			-13.7	-10.0				-19.4	-27.1
EBIT/Interest			(24) 6.5	(20) 4.0				(69) 7.2	(44) 5.5
			3.5	2.7				3.0	2.7
			1.4	.1				1.0	.9
Net Profit + Depr., Dep., Amort./Cur. Mat. L/T/D								(19) 3.7	(11) 3.0
								2.0	1.2
								.8	.6
Fixed/Worth			.7	.8				.7	.6
			2.3	1.0				2.2	1.8
			-5.6	3.3				-1.0	-1.2
Debt/Worth			.6	.3				.4	.4
			2.7	.7				4.5	2.4
			-9.1	2.9				-3.4	-3.8
% Profit Before Taxes/Tangible Net Worth			(19) 41.2	(21) 16.1				(59) 71.9	(37) 36.2
			7.7	2.4				16.6	17.1
			2.4	-8.2				2.8	.4
% Profit Before Taxes/Total Assets			12.4	7.8				15.8	13.6
			3.0	1.7				6.7	5.3
			.9	-4.6				-2.9	-2.4
Sales/Net Fixed Assets			4.0	2.4				4.7	4.1
			2.7	1.2				2.7	2.6
			1.6	.9				1.6	1.7
Sales/Total Assets			1.4	.8				1.4	1.3
			1.1	.6				.9	.8
			.9	.5				.5	.6
% Depr., Dep., Amort./Sales			(28) 4.6	6.4				(88) 4.7	(53) 4.1
			8.3	7.9				8.9	8.2
			14.0	12.0				14.6	11.3
% Officers', Directors', Owners' Comp/Sales								(18) 3.8	
								14.5	
								30.4	
Net Sales ($)	1626M	17068M	190562M	392145M	370388M	514669M		2098107M	1430513M
Total Assets ($)	624M	12156M	164886M	513914M	472559M	1127256M		3204109M	2174006M

M = $ thousand   MM = $ million
See Pages 11 through 18 for Explanation of Ratios and Data

Comparative Historical Data | Current Data Sorted By Sales

4/1/00-3/31/01 ALL	4/1/01-3/31/02 ALL	4/1/02-3/31/03 ALL	Type of Statement	0-1MM	1-3MM	3-5MM	5-10MM	10-25MM	25MM & OVER
37	35	39	Unqualified		4	2	14	9	10
4	8	9	Reviewed	1	1	2	4	1	
5	9	3	Compiled		2	1			
3	1	4	Tax Returns		3	1			
17	19	22	Other	1	4	4	5	3	5
					27 (4/1-9/30/02)		50 (10/1/02-3/31/03)		
66	72	77	NUMBER OF STATEMENTS	2	14	10	23	13	15
%	%	%	**ASSETS**	%	%	%	%	%	%
14.1	9.9	9.7	Cash & Equivalents		9.4	14.1	9.3	10.2	7.9
13.4	10.9	12.9	Trade Receivables (net)		13.4	12.6	13.8	14.6	11.3
1.8	1.1	1.2	Inventory		4.3	.6	.5	.5	.6
4.0	7.5	5.3	All Other Current		4.2	2.8	6.7	6.1	5.8
33.3	29.4	29.0	Total Current		31.2	30.0	30.2	31.3	25.7
40.1	41.1	44.1	Fixed Assets (net)		38.1	44.3	49.5	43.7	36.9
12.2	14.0	14.6	Intangibles (net)		14.8	19.8	6.6	13.1	26.4
14.4	15.4	12.3	All Other Non-Current		15.9	5.9	13.7	11.8	11.1
100.0	100.0	100.0	Total		100.0	100.0	100.0	100.0	100.0
			LIABILITIES						
3.7	2.7	9.5	Notes Payable-Short Term		17.2	.4	15.6	1.3	.7
5.1	6.3	6.0	Cur. Mat.-L/T/D		5.9	4.5	6.6	4.8	7.1
5.3	4.7	5.4	Trade Payables		4.1	3.9	7.5	6.0	4.3
.3	.1	.0	Income Taxes Payable		.0	.0	.0	.1	.1
9.8	9.4	8.8	All Other Current		10.2	15.7	8.2	8.2	5.2
24.2	23.3	29.6	Total Current		37.4	24.5	38.0	20.4	17.4
30.6	36.1	28.8	Long Term Debt		30.4	45.3	25.4	24.4	24.9
.4	.3	.4	Deferred Taxes		.0	.0	.8	.2	.8
10.7	10.2	5.2	All Other Non-Current		7.8	3.1	6.9	4.5	2.7
34.1	30.1	36.0	Net Worth		24.4	27.1	28.9	50.5	54.2
100.0	100.0	100.0	Total Liabilities & Net Worth		100.0	100.0	100.0	100.0	100.0
			INCOME DATA						
100.0	100.0	100.0	Net Sales		100.0	100.0	100.0	100.0	100.0
			Gross Profit						
90.0	92.6	92.6	Operating Expenses		99.4	81.4	92.1	92.1	93.0
10.0	7.4	7.4	Operating Profit		.6	18.6	7.9	7.9	7.0
.1	5.4	5.1	All Other Expenses (net)		3.4	5.0	4.3	4.5	6.8
9.9	2.0	2.4	Profit Before Taxes		-2.9	13.6	3.7	3.4	.2
			RATIOS						
3.7	2.5	2.8	Current		4.6	3.7	1.8	3.6	3.3
1.7	1.5	1.3			1.6	1.6	1.1	1.5	1.9
.9	.8	.7			.7	.9	.4	1.0	.9
3.2	2.1	1.7	Quick		2.4	3.5	1.3	2.4	2.3
1.4	1.1	1.0			1.0	1.2	.8	1.3	1.0
.7	.4	.5			.5	.8	.3	.8	.6
21 17.2	12 31.3	22 16.7	Sales/Receivables	17 21.7	4 97.9	13 27.9	25 14.7	30 12.3	
56 6.6	46 7.9	56 6.5		53 6.9	61 6.0	55 6.7	46 8.0	64 5.7	
67 5.5	71 5.2	70 5.2		64 5.7	76 4.8	69 5.3	72 5.0	74 4.9	
			Cost of Sales/Inventory						
			Cost of Sales/Payables						
3.5	4.7	4.6	Sales/Working Capital		5.0	4.9	5.3	4.4	3.3
7.8	10.9	14.1			40.3	11.0	55.3	9.9	12.5
-69.6	-11.8	-15.7			-54.1	NM	-3.6	NM	-42.0
10.9	5.2	4.6	EBIT/Interest				(22) 4.3		(12) 2.1
(46) 2.9	(51) 1.2	(60) 2.3					2.5		.9
1.0	-.7	.3					1.0		-8.4
		2.8	Net Profit + Depr., Dep., Amort./Cur. Mat. L/T/D						
	(12)	1.5							
		1.0							
.5	.6	.7	Fixed/Worth		.7	.8	.8	.6	.5
1.1	1.4	1.4			1.1	NM	2.2	1.2	1.0
NM	-2.3	-3.5			-.7	-4.7	-4.3	5.7	-.9
.3	.4	.4	Debt/Worth		.3	.8	.4	.3	.3
1.0	1.5	2.1			2.3	NM	2.0	1.5	.4
NM	-7.4	-7.0			-2.3	-7.9	-7.0	8.4	-2.5
30.9	27.7	21.1	% Profit Before Taxes/Tangible Net Worth				(16) 20.5	(11) 30.1	(10) 15.9
(50) 13.9	(48) 5.5	(53) 2.9					6.3	2.8	-4.5
1.2	-3.9	-10.4					-.2	-4.1	-13.5
17.6	10.8	9.2	% Profit Before Taxes/Total Assets		5.3	13.4	9.3	11.1	8.7
5.4	.2	2.3			-2.3	6.7	3.1	2.4	1.9
-.2	-4.9	-2.8			-11.6	2.2	-.8	-2.0	-6.3
4.6	4.7	3.7	Sales/Net Fixed Assets		5.5	3.5	3.8	4.2	2.7
2.5	2.2	2.1			2.5	1.9	2.2	2.0	1.9
1.5	1.3	1.3			1.9	1.5	.9	1.2	1.4
1.2	1.3	1.2	Sales/Total Assets		1.6	1.1	1.2	1.5	.9
.9	.8	.9			1.2	.9	.8	1.1	.6
.6	.5	.6			.9	.5	.6	.6	.5
4.6	4.0	5.2	% Depr., Dep., Amort./Sales		3.7		5.3	4.2	5.1
(56) 6.6	(67) 7.3	(68) 8.3			(11) 10.4		8.3	6.7	(10) 8.4
10.3	13.2	14.3			16.1		12.6	16.2	12.8
	2.6	1.8	% Officers', Directors', Owners' Comp/Sales						
	(13) 4.8	(11) 5.6							
	12.6	8.8							
1553205M	1436797M	1486458M	Net Sales ($)	556M	31415M	39897M	178020M	221547M	1015023M
2307154M	1906116M	2291395M	Total Assets ($)	2726M	39668M	61660M	221385M	288818M	1677138M

© RMA 2003
M = $ thousand   MM = $ million
See Pages 11 through 18 for Explanation of Ratios and Data

Current Data Sorted By Assets   Comparative Historical Data

	0-500M	500M-2MM	2-10MM	10-50MM	50-100MM	100-250MM		4/1/98-3/31/99 ALL	4/1/99-3/31/00 ALL
Type of Statement									
Unqualified			6	8	5	4		64	32
Reviewed		3	7	1		1		15	11
Compiled		3	3					17	17
Tax Returns	6	7	1			1		4	2
Other	3	4	7	4	3	2		38	17
		11 (4/1-9/30/02)		68 (10/1/02-3/31/03)					
NUMBER OF STATEMENTS	9	17	24	13	8	8		138	79
	%	%	%	%	%	%	**ASSETS**	%	%
Cash & Equivalents		10.4	9.7	7.2				8.5	11.1
Trade Receivables (net)		24.4	15.3	15.5				9.3	14.0
Inventory		2.2	4.4	5.2				2.2	2.0
All Other Current		4.5	3.9	5.5				4.9	3.8
Total Current		41.5	33.3	33.4				24.9	31.0
Fixed Assets (net)		54.2	43.7	41.2				48.6	48.9
Intangibles (net)		.3	12.2	21.5				19.8	14.7
All Other Non-Current		4.0	10.8	3.9				6.6	5.4
Total		100.0	100.0	100.0				100.0	100.0
							LIABILITIES		
Notes Payable-Short Term		7.9	1.0	14.3				7.9	8.0
Cur. Mat.-L/T/D		4.9	7.8	4.2				5.8	5.4
Trade Payables		13.2	7.8	12.2				8.3	8.3
Income Taxes Payable		.0	.5	1.1				.2	.3
All Other Current		4.6	11.8	22.2				8.5	18.6
Total Current		30.6	29.0	53.9				30.7	40.7
Long Term Debt		35.2	36.3	28.2				45.2	43.2
Deferred Taxes		.3	.2	.6				.2	.7
All Other Non-Current		26.0	7.2	6.8				10.9	8.1
Net Worth		7.9	27.2	10.5				13.0	7.2
Total Liabilities & Net Worth		100.0	100.0	100.0				100.0	100.0
							INCOME DATA		
Net Sales		100.0	100.0	100.0				100.0	100.0
Gross Profit									
Operating Expenses		98.8	92.7	96.8				96.3	90.3
Operating Profit		1.2	7.3	3.2				3.7	9.7
All Other Expenses (net)		2.4	4.7	4.1				12.0	6.1
Profit Before Taxes		-1.3	2.6	-1.0				-8.3	3.5
							RATIOS		
Current		2.1	1.4	1.6				1.4	1.5
		1.2	.6	.8				.7	.8
		.5	.3	.3				.3	.4
Quick		1.6	1.4	1.1				1.1	1.1
		1.0	.6	.5			(136)	.5	.6
		.3	.1	.2				.2	.3
Sales/Receivables		10 35.5	5 73.3	12 31.7				7 55.3	9 39.8
		28 13.0	19 19.6	39 9.4				16 22.4	24 15.4
		37 9.8	44 8.3	60 6.1				39 9.4	49 7.5
Cost of Sales/Inventory									
Cost of Sales/Payables									
Sales/Working Capital		6.8	15.1	14.2				14.7	13.1
		41.0	-8.8	-26.9				-14.8	-24.0
		-14.1	-4.3	-1.7				-4.9	-5.4
EBIT/Interest		4.3	6.8	12.0				5.2	5.5
	(16)	1.6	(21) 3.7	(12) .9			(92)	1.5	(66) 2.1
		.1	1.1	-1.7				.3	.9
Net Profit + Depr., Dep., Amort./Cur. Mat. L /T/D								2.7	4.5
							(21)	1.5	(16) 2.8
								.6	1.7
Fixed/Worth		.9	.3	2.3				1.1	.9
		2.7	4.5	-4.9				202.9	9.9
		NM	-45.0	-1.0				-1.4	-1.5
Debt/Worth		1.7	1.4	1.9				2.0	1.4
		3.3	5.0	-7.2				212.1	17.8
		NM	-69.6	-3.4				-2.9	-3.2
% Profit Before Taxes/Tangible Net Worth		74.5	43.7					52.8	57.5
	(13)	2.8	(15) 23.5				(70)	15.0	(45) 34.1
		-4.0	1.2					-33.8	6.9
% Profit Before Taxes/Total Assets		16.5	15.3	10.7				10.2	14.1
		1.3	6.2	-1.9				-.5	5.7
		-3.3	-.7	-10.5				-7.9	-1.6
Sales/Net Fixed Assets		18.5	12.8	9.3				4.7	6.5
		3.8	2.8	3.5				1.3	2.0
		1.0	1.0	1.0				.7	.9
Sales/Total Assets		3.5	2.3	1.8				1.3	1.7
		2.2	1.3	1.1				.7	.8
		.8	.5	.6				.4	.5
% Depr., Dep., Amort./Sales		1.9	4.9	7.7				5.1	3.6
	(14)	7.0	(22) 10.6	(12) 11.4			(106)	16.5	(67) 13.6
		24.3	21.9	26.1				25.7	23.2
% Officers', Directors', Owners' Comp/Sales			(11) 1.5					3.2	2.5
			4.5				(22)	4.5	(16) 4.4
			5.4					11.9	6.8
Net Sales ($)	11674M	47054M	176333M	576021M	389199M	1411737M		2993306M	1980521M
Total Assets ($)	2280M	19405M	125224M	437341M	600201M	1357896M		5410463M	2582976M

Comparative Historical Data				Type of Statement	Current Data Sorted By Sales					
19	27		23	Unqualified	1	1	1	4	5	11
12	12		12	Reviewed		3	1	4	2	2
10	10		6	Compiled		2	1	2	1	
4	6		15	Tax Returns	7	2	3	2		1
26	24		23	Other	4	2	4	3	3	7
4/1/00-	4/1/01-		4/1/02-			11 (4/1-9/30/02)		68 (10/1/02-3/31/03)		
3/31/01	3/31/02		3/31/03		0-1MM	1-3MM	3-5MM	5-10MM	10-25MM	25MM & OVER
ALL	ALL		ALL							
71	79		79	NUMBER OF STATEMENTS	12	10	10	15	11	21
%	%		%	ASSETS	%	%	%	%	%	%
10.4	11.1		10.1	Cash & Equivalents	5.7	11.3	10.0	12.0	11.9	9.8
11.8	11.1		15.9	Trade Receivables (net)	6.7	20.8	16.4	20.9	19.9	12.7
1.7	3.0		3.8	Inventory	.8	5.4	6.1	3.5	2.7	4.4
3.6	4.0		3.6	All Other Current	2.1	.2	7.3	.9	6.7	4.8
27.4	29.2		33.4	Total Current	15.3	37.7	39.8	37.4	41.2	31.7
52.3	49.3		43.7	Fixed Assets (net)	73.6	54.1	35.9	39.7	37.9	31.3
13.7	14.9		14.6	Intangibles (net)	.4	6.2	18.9	13.8	10.9	27.3
6.5	6.6		8.3	All Other Non-Current	10.8	1.9	5.5	9.1	10.0	9.6
100.0	100.0		100.0	Total	100.0	100.0	100.0	100.0	100.0	100.0
				LIABILITIES						
4.9	4.9		5.4	Notes Payable-Short Term	.7	6.5	8.3	3.9	15.1	2.2
4.8	9.7		7.3	Cur. Mat.-L/T/D	7.8	12.9	2.1	9.6	4.5	6.5
6.7	7.3		9.9	Trade Payables	13.5	3.7	10.3	14.0	6.3	9.6
.2	.1		.4	Income Taxes Payable	.1	.0	.0	.2	1.6	.4
8.7	13.1		11.9	All Other Current	8.2	6.9	20.1	8.8	10.1	15.8
25.4	35.0		34.9	Total Current	30.3	30.0	40.8	36.6	37.6	34.5
43.8	38.3		37.3	Long Term Debt	48.7	31.2	31.2	32.3	20.0	49.2
1.0	1.2		.7	Deferred Taxes	.0	.0	.0	1.7	1.8	.6
8.7	10.9		11.1	All Other Non-Current	19.4	20.8	18.9	4.0	10.6	3.3
21.1	14.6		16.0	Net Worth	1.7	18.0	9.2	25.5	30.0	12.4
100.0	100.0		100.0	Total Liabilities & Net Worth	100.0	100.0	100.0	100.0	100.0	100.0
				INCOME DATA						
100.0	100.0		100.0	Net Sales	100.0	100.0	100.0	100.0	100.0	100.0
				Gross Profit						
91.7	94.0		94.9	Operating Expenses	93.5	97.9	99.3	91.1	93.8	95.4
8.3	6.0		5.1	Operating Profit	6.5	2.1	.7	8.9	6.2	4.6
7.1	7.5		4.2	All Other Expenses (net)	4.3	4.6	3.1	3.1	4.6	5.0
1.1	−1.5		1.0	Profit Before Taxes	2.2	−2.5	−2.4	5.8	1.7	−.4
				RATIOS						
1.8	1.3		1.5		.8	1.8	3.1	1.5	2.2	1.6
.9	.8		.8	Current	.4	1.0	.6	.9	1.4	.8
.4	.3		.4		.3	.1	.4	.4	.5	.4
1.5	1.0		1.3		.8	1.8	2.4	1.5	1.7	1.2
.7	.6		.6	Quick	.3	.8	.6	.8	1.1	.8
.3	.2		.3		.2	.1	.1	.4	.4	.4
7 55.1	6 57.5	8	44.8		5 75.8	0 UND	0 UND	11 31.8	8 47.6	13 29.0
19 18.9	20 18.2	23	15.6	Sales/Receivables	14 25.8	14 26.1	13 29.0	31 11.6	38 9.5	27 13.4
37 10.0	38 9.7	43	8.6		23 15.8	51 7.2	40 9.2	43 8.5	44 8.2	54 6.7
				Cost of Sales/Inventory						
				Cost of Sales/Payables						
8.5	13.7		14.4		−36.0	16.8	6.0	14.5	8.2	8.5
−123.5	−22.5		−32.7	Sales/Working Capital	−10.5	NM	−14.9	−51.1	18.0	−36.8
−9.6	−4.6		−6.5		−5.5	−4.4	−4.5	−3.7	−7.0	−8.7
4.8	4.4		4.9		2.5			8.6		2.3
(57) 1.6	(67) 1.3	(66)	1.8	EBIT/Interest	(11) 1.7		(13)	2.4	(17)	1.2
.4	.1		.2		.2			1.5		−.1
5.5	12.6		9.5	Net Profit + Depr., Dep.,						
(15) 2.6	(17) 2.0	(13)	2.6	Amort./Cur. Mat. L/T/D						
1.2	1.0		2.1							
1.3	1.2		.9		3.4	.6	.4	1.0	.3	1.7
4.7	8.1		9.2	Fixed/Worth	NM	5.8	4.7	5.2	1.0	−2.3
−3.1	−1.8		−1.5		−8.2	−46.4	−.3	−3.0	−11.6	−.5
1.3	1.8		2.0		3.1	1.2	2.1	2.3	1.4	2.3
5.6	10.8		13.7	Debt/Worth	NM	5.3	4.9	13.7	3.0	−4.9
−4.7	−3.7		−3.9		−12.0	−50.2	−2.1	−6.3	−13.7	−2.2
59.8	45.8		48.2	% Profit Before Taxes/Tangible						
(46) 25.3	(46) 13.1	(42)	19.7	Net Worth						
−9.8	−1.0		.8							
14.7	10.4		14.3	% Profit Before Taxes/Total	19.2	22.8	9.5	26.5	12.8	7.7
2.7	.9		1.9	Assets	2.4	.4	−.2	5.2	4.3	1.5
−5.5	−6.4		−3.6		−4.9	−10.5	−4.4	.7	−2.7	−8.3
4.7	5.6		13.9		3.0	35.4	21.5	14.1	16.9	10.4
1.7	1.5		3.1	Sales/Net Fixed Assets	1.3	2.2	7.0	4.6	5.2	2.1
1.0	.8		1.0		.8	.5	2.0	2.0	.7	1.3
1.8	1.6		2.7		2.0	4.8	3.4	3.2	4.0	1.6
.9	.7		1.3	Sales/Total Assets	.8	1.4	2.0	1.8	2.0	.9
.6	.5		.5		.6	.4	.7	1.1	.5	.5
6.0	5.3		3.0		6.1			3.3	2.4	4.3
(56) 12.3	(63) 12.9	(64)	9.9	% Depr., Dep., Amort./Sales	(10) 16.2		(14)	10.6	(10) 6.8	(12) 9.2
22.6	26.0		21.6		28.4			14.7	23.2	17.3
2.6	2.5		2.8	% Officers', Directors',						
(18) 3.4	(22) 5.1	(32)	4.6	Owners' Comp/Sales						
7.0	8.5		6.9							
1305179M	1395217M		2612018M	Net Sales ($)	8015M	18609M	38903M	103394M	192278M	2250819M
2162517M	2279968M		2542347M	Total Assets ($)	10711M	26733M	36158M	171886M	344137M	1952722M

© RMA 2003   M = $ thousand   MM = $ million
See Pages 11 through 18 for Explanation of Ratios and Data

Current Data Sorted By Assets

Comparative Historical Data

							Type of Statement		
1	5	23	21	7	8		Unqualified	61	39
3	4	8	1				Reviewed	20	13
4	7	7	3				Compiled	18	16
4	2						Tax Returns	8	11
	7	22	14	3	7		Other	52	41
	15 (4/1-9/30/02)		146 (10/1/02-3/31/03)					4/1/98-3/31/99	4/1/99-3/31/00
0-500M	500M-2MM	2-10MM	10-50MM	50-100MM	100-250MM			ALL	ALL
12	25	60	39	10	15	NUMBER OF STATEMENTS		159	120
%	%	%	%	%	%	ASSETS		%	%
7.5	16.0	13.5	12.1	9.2	16.8	Cash & Equivalents		12.7	15.6
25.2	36.7	29.6	15.0	8.0	12.0	Trade Receivables (net)		22.4	25.6
9.6	10.8	7.7	4.0	1.2	1.2	Inventory		5.3	5.8
14.8	3.3	4.0	4.9	2.5	.9	All Other Current		2.6	3.1
57.2	66.7	54.8	36.0	20.9	30.8	Total Current		43.0	50.1
30.1	24.3	31.1	42.8	56.7	45.1	Fixed Assets (net)		39.9	35.9
3.0	2.5	6.8	9.0	11.1	7.3	Intangibles (net)		5.5	5.8
9.7	6.4	7.3	12.1	11.3	16.8	All Other Non-Current		11.6	8.2
100.0	100.0	100.0	100.0	100.0	100.0	Total		100.0	100.0
						LIABILITIES			
13.7	14.0	7.4	4.9	.3	.6	Notes Payable-Short Term		6.6	7.7
2.9	4.3	3.3	3.9	3.4	5.4	Cur. Mat.-L/T/D		4.5	4.0
20.6	25.1	16.8	9.7	7.8	6.3	Trade Payables		15.1	12.4
.0	.4	.4	.2	.0	.3	Income Taxes Payable		.3	.2
109.2	14.6	13.3	9.8	4.6	6.8	All Other Current		11.3	10.0
146.4	58.4	41.3	28.6	16.3	19.3	Total Current		37.8	34.3
41.8	9.8	15.2	22.9	33.2	31.9	Long Term Debt		24.6	19.0
.0	.9	1.7	1.4	1.7	2.6	Deferred Taxes		1.7	2.1
8.6	3.7	9.2	6.3	9.6	4.7	All Other Non-Current		4.7	5.2
-96.8	27.2	32.7	40.8	39.3	41.5	Net Worth		31.3	39.4
100.0	100.0	100.0	100.0	100.0	100.0	Total Liabilities & Net Worth		100.0	100.0
						INCOME DATA			
100.0	100.0	100.0	100.0	100.0	100.0	Net Sales		100.0	100.0
						Gross Profit			
91.4	95.8	90.4	85.6	87.8	87.5	Operating Expenses		127.3	88.1
8.6	4.2	9.6	14.4	12.2	12.5	Operating Profit		-27.3	11.9
2.2	1.1	2.6	4.1	10.3	5.6	All Other Expenses (net)		5.3	1.1
6.4	3.1	7.0	10.3	1.9	6.9	Profit Before Taxes		-32.6	10.8
						RATIOS			
1.3	1.6	2.4	2.6	1.9	2.5			2.1	2.9
.6	1.3	1.3	1.2	1.1	2.1	Current		1.3	1.5
.2	.9	.9	.8	.9	.7			.8	1.0

	1.2		1.4		2.2		1.8		1.8		2.2			1.6	2.2
(11)	.4		.9		1.0		.9		1.0		1.7	Quick	(158)	1.0	1.3
	.2		.5		.6		.4		.5		.6			.6	.7
0	UND	28	13.0	34	10.8	27	13.7	14	25.2	30	12.3		27	13.8	30 12.4
15	23.7	50	7.4	47	7.7	39	9.4	43	8.4	34	10.6	Sales/Receivables	43	8.4	53 6.9
38	9.6	62	5.9	58	6.3	60	6.0	49	7.5	54	6.7		67	5.4	72 5.1
												Cost of Sales/Inventory			
												Cost of Sales/Payables			
	NM		15.3		5.8		3.1		5.6		3.2			6.5	4.1
	-30.5		27.3		14.9		21.0		50.1		7.4	Sales/Working Capital		24.5	10.8
	-3.4		-47.2		-67.5		-10.3		-65.8		-11.0			-26.3	UND
	12.0		5.6		13.3		7.1		4.8		5.4			9.1	9.5
(10)	2.7	(19)	1.6	(54)	3.6	(35)	3.5		2.7	(12)	2.5	EBIT/Interest	(140)	3.4	(102) 4.3
	-2.4		-3.1		2.0		1.2		-.2		-1.0			1.5	1.9
					5.6		6.3					Net Profit + Depr., Dep.,		8.0	6.0
		(21)	2.7	(20)	3.1					Amort./Cur. Mat. L /T/D	(59)	3.2	(42) 3.6
			1.9		1.6							1.8	2.0
	.8		.3		.4		.6		1.3		.3			.7	.4
	-1.0		.7		1.0		1.6		2.4		1.3	Fixed/Worth		1.5	.9
	-.1		4.3		4.0		3.3		NM		-130.6			3.7	2.6
	7.0		1.2		.8		.6		1.2		.5			1.0	.6
	-7.1		2.1		2.6		2.1		3.4		1.7	Debt/Worth		2.3	1.3
	-1.5		21.8		11.2		6.0		NM		-145.2			9.1	4.8
			77.9		72.1		41.7				49.5	% Profit Before Taxes/Tangible		60.3	55.2
		(20)	21.7	(51)	24.2	(32)	13.7			(11)	13.0	Net Worth	(130)	25.1	(102) 19.5
			-1.5		12.6		2.3				-6.8			11.6	8.2
	74.8		16.2		17.5		11.9		8.6		8.3	% Profit Before Taxes/Total		17.5	17.3
	26.7		4.4		9.4		7.7		2.4		4.5	Assets		8.4	7.5
	-23.1		-8.1		2.6		1.4		-4.9		-3.0			1.8	1.9
	293.0		28.6		30.2		8.5		1.9		7.7			15.1	19.8
	38.6		21.4		11.6		1.6		.7		.9	Sales/Net Fixed Assets		4.1	5.8
	6.6		12.0		1.1		.8		.5		.7			.8	.9
	14.9		4.8		3.7		1.8		.8		1.6			2.9	2.7
	5.1		3.4		2.0		.6		.4		.5	Sales/Total Assets		1.6	1.7
	2.8		2.1		.5		.3		.3		.3			.4	.5
			1.1		1.4		5.5							2.3	1.5
		(19)	1.7	(56)	4.6	(38)	13.5					% Depr., Dep., Amort./Sales	(135)	6.9	(98) 6.2
			5.1		19.8		20.8							17.8	16.7
														2.3	2.8
												% Officers', Directors',	(24)	5.4	(26) 5.4
												Owners' Comp/Sales		11.5	13.7
15475M	102109M	785108M	860979M	477292M	2170127M		Net Sales ($)		4927116M	3183974M
2746M	30397M	357996M	885420M	736214M	2372923M		Total Assets ($)		4941487M	3153715M

M = $ thousand   MM = $ million
See Pages 11 through 18 for Explanation of Ratios and Data

Comparative Historical Data

Current Data Sorted By Sales

Comparative Historical Data			Type of Statement			Current Data Sorted By Sales			
42	51	64	Unqualified	1	10	5	12	17	19
12	12	14	Reviewed		1	4	4	4	1
23	22	20	Compiled	2	4	3	6	4	1
14	5	6	Tax Returns	2	2		2		
37	52	57	Other	3	7	5	9	16	17
4/1/00-3/31/01	4/1/01-3/31/02	4/1/02-3/31/03			15 (4/1-9/30/02)			146 (10/1/02-3/31/03)	
ALL	ALL	ALL		0-1MM	1-3MM	3-5MM	5-10MM	10-25MM	25MM & OVER
128	142	161	NUMBER OF STATEMENTS	8	24	17	33	41	38
%	%	%	ASSETS	%	%	%	%	%	%
12.5	11.0	13.1	Cash & Equivalents		12.4	9.7	16.6	11.8	15.4
26.0	24.3	23.8	Trade Receivables (net)		20.7	18.8	22.8	31.3	21.2
6.2	5.7	6.4	Inventory		8.4	5.3	5.4	9.5	3.8
4.0	2.7	4.5	All Other Current		8.2	1.0	5.4	4.2	4.0
48.7	43.8	47.9	Total Current		49.8	34.8	50.3	56.8	44.5
34.6	38.0	35.7	Fixed Assets (net)		31.6	50.1	33.2	26.8	39.2
7.1	7.5	6.7	Intangibles (net)		7.5	5.3	5.1	7.4	8.1
9.6	10.7	9.6	All Other Non-Current		11.0	9.8	11.4	8.9	8.2
100.0	100.0	100.0	Total		100.0	100.0	100.0	100.0	100.0
			LIABILITIES						
10.6	7.2	7.2	Notes Payable-Short Term		4.7	7.1	7.8	10.6	2.4
3.0	4.7	3.8	Cur. Mat.-L/T/D		4.1	5.2	3.1	4.5	2.8
15.3	13.8	15.1	Trade Payables		12.0	9.1	18.2	16.5	15.0
.7	.6	.3	Income Taxes Payable		.5	.3	.1	.5	.2
9.9	10.6	18.7	All Other Current		36.2	8.6	13.4	13.3	11.6
39.6	36.9	45.1	Total Current		57.5	30.3	42.6	45.4	31.9
17.9	22.8	20.9	Long Term Debt		21.6	26.9	15.5	13.4	21.7
2.2	1.9	1.4	Deferred Taxes		2.0	3.2	1.0	.9	1.4
4.9	8.9	7.2	All Other Non-Current		.6	4.0	5.2	7.8	13.0
35.5	29.4	25.4	Net Worth		18.2	35.6	35.7	32.5	32.0
100.0	100.0	100.0	Total Liabilities & Net Worth		100.0	100.0	100.0	100.0	100.0
			INCOME DATA						
100.0	100.0	100.0	Net Sales		100.0	100.0	100.0	100.0	100.0
			Gross Profit						
89.4	92.1	89.7	Operating Expenses		86.2	89.7	88.1	90.2	92.7
10.6	7.9	10.3	Operating Profit		13.8	10.3	11.8	9.8	7.3
−.6	3.6	3.4	All Other Expenses (net)		2.7	4.2	3.7	2.5	4.2
11.2	4.2	6.8	Profit Before Taxes		11.1	6.1	8.1	7.3	3.1
			RATIOS						
2.4	2.0	2.3			2.9	1.8	2.3	2.0	2.5
1.3	1.2	1.2	Current		1.2	1.4	1.3	1.2	1.3
.9	.8	.8			.9	.6	.8	.8	.9
1.8	1.6	1.8			2.7	1.7	1.9	1.7	2.0
1.0	.9 (160)	.9	Quick	(23)	1.1	1.1	1.0	.8	1.0
.5	.6	.6			.7	.5	.5	.6	.6
33 11.1	28 13.2	29 12.8		29 12.5	26 14.2	27 13.4	33 11.2	26 14.3	
49 7.4	49 7.4	42 8.6	Sales/Receivables	52 7.0	37 9.9	44 8.3	47 7.7	37 9.9	
70 5.2	69 5.3	57 6.4		64 5.7	57 6.4	61 6.0	57 6.4	48 7.6	
			Cost of Sales/Inventory						
			Cost of Sales/Payables						
4.9	6.7	5.8			3.6	6.2	2.7	7.7	5.8
18.4	29.6	23.8	Sales/Working Capital		22.6	17.5	20.9	29.2	10.5
−45.6	−17.2	−17.4			−34.7	−8.2	−20.7	−13.9	−45.0
17.8	7.2	7.1			13.0	5.1	13.6	12.3	4.7
(117) 5.4	(127) 2.7	(140) 3.5	EBIT/Interest	(21) 2.8	(16) 2.5	(29) 4.9	(34) 4.1	(33) 2.5	
1.1	.1	.6		.5	−.1	1.6	1.6	−1.4	
12.2	7.2	5.5				9.3	8.1	6.6	
(35) 5.2	(45) 2.8	(54) 2.7	Net Profit + Depr., Dep., Amort./Cur. Mat. L/T/D		(11) 2.7	(17) 3.1	(10) 4.6		
2.5	.7	1.8			1.2	1.8	2.5		
.4	.5	.4			.3	.7	.4	.4	.6
1.0	1.4	1.3	Fixed/Worth		1.2	1.5	.8	.9	1.3
2.6	15.2	5.6			8.2	4.0	3.5	11.1	NM
.7	1.0	1.0			.5	1.1	.6	1.3	1.1
2.0	2.4	2.3	Debt/Worth		2.4	1.8	2.2	2.9	1.7
5.4	61.9	18.9			30.2	5.9	6.1	20.9	NM
60.3	56.0	61.1			93.6	52.5	77.2	64.4	53.5
(108) 26.1	(110) 16.8	(126) 17.8	% Profit Before Taxes/Tangible Net Worth	(19) 14.3	(16) 11.2	(28) 23.6	(32) 29.5	(29) 6.4	
7.3	.5	4.0		4.1	2.0	12.5	12.8	−27.8	
21.4	13.9	15.3			22.0	13.6	16.3	15.9	14.4
8.6	4.1	6.5	% Profit Before Taxes/Total Assets		3.7	4.2	8.9	9.2	5.5
.6	−1.8	.7			−1.4	−3.2	2.1	2.0	−5.3
24.2	18.1	24.3			24.4	9.0	22.7	53.6	15.0
6.6	4.8	6.1	Sales/Net Fixed Assets		9.3	.8	6.8	17.4	5.6
.9	.7	.9			.7	.6	1.2	1.3	.8
3.0	2.9	3.6			3.8	2.2	3.8	3.6	3.7
1.7	1.3	1.6	Sales/Total Assets		1.3	.6	1.6	1.9	1.6
.5	.5	.5			.3	.4	.5	.5	.5
1.3	1.8	1.6			1.4	7.1	2.9	1.0	2.8
(113) 3.8	(117) 5.4	(133) 6.8	% Depr., Dep., Amort./Sales	(22) 7.4	(15) 24.1	(28) 9.3	(38) 2.0	(25) 5.1	
15.0	17.2	18.5		21.1	27.6	18.0	15.2	10.5	
3.7	2.5	2.6							
(26) 5.8	(24) 6.2	(23) 4.4	% Officers', Directors', Owners' Comp/Sales						
8.6	16.6	11.7							
3140886M	4198759M	4411090M	Net Sales ($)	4125M	45579M	68058M	235017M	707863M	3350448M
3651877M	3852025M	4385696M	Total Assets ($)	3374M	80922M	113153M	328775M	861672M	2997800M

© RMA 2003

M = $ thousand   MM = $ million

See Pages 11 through 18 for Explanation of Ratios and Data

Current Data Sorted By Assets   **Comparative Historical Data**

						Type of Statement		
2	5	3	13	7	2	Unqualified	62	30
6	7	3				Reviewed	12	12
3	2	2				Compiled	32	16
						Tax Returns	9	7
4	5	10	6	4		Other	60	56
	15 (4/1-9/30/02)		69 (10/1/02-3/31/03)				4/1/98-3/31/99	4/1/99-3/31/00
0-500M	500M-2MM	2-10MM	10-50MM	50-100MM	100-250MM		ALL	ALL
15	19	18	19	11	2	NUMBER OF STATEMENTS	175	121
%	%	%	%	%	%	**ASSETS**	%	%
23.0	11.6	9.4	8.4	14.0		Cash & Equivalents	10.7	10.2
10.7	20.4	19.6	10.2	17.0		Trade Receivables (net)	23.1	28.2
25.0	20.7	16.4	4.8	2.6		Inventory	9.7	10.1
3.5	3.3	7.4	1.7	2.8		All Other Current	2.6	2.4
62.3	55.9	52.8	25.2	36.5		Total Current	46.1	50.9
24.2	34.7	28.8	45.9	46.0		Fixed Assets (net)	36.3	32.5
3.3	4.9	1.8	14.8	1.6		Intangibles (net)	8.0	6.8
10.2	4.5	16.6	14.1	15.9		All Other Non-Current	9.7	9.8
100.0	100.0	100.0	100.0	100.0		Total	100.0	100.0
						LIABILITIES		
39.5	8.2	6.3	1.2	.3		Notes Payable-Short Term	6.6	7.0
2.7	5.6	5.1	8.2	3.3		Cur. Mat.-L/T/D	4.6	3.7
12.8	25.5	23.2	9.0	14.5		Trade Payables	13.9	17.8
.0	.6	1.0	.0	.6		Income Taxes Payable	.3	.9
15.2	22.9	10.2	6.9	8.1		All Other Current	9.4	7.6
70.3	62.9	45.8	25.3	26.9		Total Current	34.7	36.9
14.8	26.8	11.2	37.7	30.7		Long Term Debt	23.0	20.8
.0	.1	1.1	2.1	1.9		Deferred Taxes	1.5	1.8
.7	5.2	4.3	6.5	2.0		All Other Non-Current	6.6	4.2
14.2	5.0	37.5	28.3	38.4		Net Worth	34.1	36.3
100.0	100.0	100.0	100.0	100.0		Total Liabilities & Net Worth	100.0	100.0
						INCOME DATA		
100.0	100.0	100.0	100.0	100.0		Net Sales	100.0	100.0
						Gross Profit		
93.8	101.9	96.0	90.2	78.9		Operating Expenses	114.3	88.5
6.2	−1.9	4.0	9.8	21.1		Operating Profit	−14.3	11.5
−.5	.8	.7	3.6	4.5		All Other Expenses (net)	2.9	.7
6.7	−2.6	3.3	6.2	16.6		Profit Before Taxes	−17.2	10.8
						RATIOS		
3.2	1.6	1.7	2.0	2.0		Current	2.5	2.2
1.0	1.2	1.2	1.3	1.5			1.4	1.4
.5	.8	.8	.6	1.3			.8	1.0
1.7	.9	1.1	1.6	1.9		Quick	2.0	1.8
.3	.5	.7	.9	1.2			1.0	1.1
.1	.4	.4	.5	1.0			.6	.7
0 UND	14 26.9	25 14.6	33 11.1	14 26.3		Sales/Receivables	29 12.8	32 11.5
1 306.2	25 14.6	36 10.2	40 9.0	39 9.3			42 8.7	46 8.0
25 14.4	40 9.2	47 7.8	45 8.1	50 7.3			61 6.0	63 5.8
						Cost of Sales/Inventory		
						Cost of Sales/Payables		
11.7	15.1	5.3	5.3	7.6		Sales/Working Capital	5.4	6.0
342.4	53.9	25.9	15.2	9.2			13.4	16.6
−4.9	−26.7	−18.1	−8.6	15.3			−25.6	647.8
(12) 6.0	(17) 6.6	(17) 16.4	(17) 5.3	(10) 12.0		EBIT/Interest	(155) 12.3	(100) 14.4
1.7	1.3	2.5	2.5	3.1			4.9	4.7
−3.5	−5.4	.7	1.4	.7			1.6	2.1
						Net Profit + Depr., Dep., Amort./Cur. Mat. L /T/D	(53) 12.4	(38) 14.1
							5.5	3.9
							1.3	1.8
.1	.9	.2	.9	.5		Fixed/Worth	.5	.4
.6	1.6	.7	2.9	1.3			1.0	1.0
18.4	−22.9	1.5	−2.7	4.5			6.0	4.2
.3	1.9	.7	.8	.8		Debt/Worth	.8	.6
3.0	5.5	1.4	3.7	1.7			2.1	2.3
−3.2	−36.2	4.2	−6.7	4.4			12.6	10.3
(11) 225.7	(13) 89.2	(17) 44.6	(11) 38.1	(10) 61.0		% Profit Before Taxes/Tangible Net Worth	(144) 55.9	(100) 76.9
14.7	5.2	7.3	14.4	19.0			27.2	26.8
−33.3	−15.3	.4	5.5	−6.5			8.4	11.4
65.3	9.3	14.0	13.2	26.0		% Profit Before Taxes/Total Assets	18.9	22.5
7.9	1.4	2.9	3.0	6.4			9.2	9.0
−15.7	−9.7	−.9	1.5	.1			.4	2.4
62.6	25.8	18.8	5.7	4.8		Sales/Net Fixed Assets	18.0	27.8
24.1	10.1	9.9	1.4	1.5			5.4	8.1
9.0	4.3	1.5	.7	.6			1.6	1.5
7.7	4.4	2.9	1.4	2.0		Sales/Total Assets	2.9	3.2
3.5	2.4	1.9	.6	.6			2.0	2.2
1.9	1.8	.8	.4	.4			.7	.7
	(18) 1.4	(15) 1.2	(16) 6.0			% Depr., Dep., Amort./Sales	(144) 1.9	(101) 1.4
	2.2	2.5	14.7				4.8	3.5
	5.6	8.6	18.8				12.5	12.2
						% Officers', Directors', Owners' Comp/Sales	(33) 2.9	(23) 2.7
							5.1	5.9
							9.0	9.0
15954M	84292M	105168M	416102M	947449M	112725M	Net Sales ($)	3802968M	2938289M
3833M	19843M	56524M	482957M	817678M	230934M	Total Assets ($)	3252548M	2683159M

© RMA 2003   M = $ thousand   MM = $ million

See Pages 11 through 18 for Explanation of Ratios and Data

Comparative Historical Data | Current Data Sorted By Sales

	4/1/00-3/31/01 ALL	4/1/01-3/31/02 ALL	4/1/02-3/31/03 ALL	Type of Statement	0-1MM	1-3MM	3-5MM	5-10MM	10-25MM	25MM & OVER
	20	20	25	Unqualified	1		2	3	9	10
	6	7	10	Reviewed	1	5	1	2	1	
	12	20	15	Compiled	4	7	2	1		1
	10	7	5	Tax Returns	2	3				
	62	47	29	Other	2	7	3	8	4	5
						15 (4/1-9/30/02)			69 (10/1/02-3/31/03)	
NUMBER OF STATEMENTS	110	101	84		10	22	8	14	14	16
	%	%	%	**ASSETS**	%	%	%	%	%	%
	12.8	11.8	12.6	Cash & Equivalents	21.7	13.2		5.8	8.2	12.9
	25.0	22.3	15.4	Trade Receivables (net)	5.3	14.3		22.0	13.5	16.9
	11.6	13.0	14.1	Inventory	18.1	20.2		14.3	5.5	10.2
	3.1	4.9	3.8	All Other Current	.4	7.3		1.6	2.0	2.6
	52.5	51.9	45.9	Total Current	45.5	55.0		43.7	29.2	42.6
	30.8	30.6	35.9	Fixed Assets (net)	31.3	34.9		35.8	50.4	33.3
	7.6	8.5	6.5	Intangibles (net)	6.2	2.4		5.2	10.8	11.0
	9.1	9.0	11.8	All Other Non-Current	17.0	7.7		15.3	9.6	13.1
	100.0	100.0	100.0	Total	100.0	100.0		100.0	100.0	100.0
				LIABILITIES						
	3.9	7.0	10.6	Notes Payable-Short Term	41.1	13.6		5.3	2.9	1.4
	4.8	3.8	5.3	Cur. Mat.-L/T/D	2.7	3.2		7.3	10.6	3.7
	15.9	16.5	17.0	Trade Payables	12.1	17.7		22.1	12.8	19.4
	.7	.4	.5	Income Taxes Payable	.1	.0		.2	1.1	1.1
	10.0	11.7	12.9	All Other Current	4.2	26.4		7.9	7.6	7.7
	35.2	39.3	46.2	Total Current	60.1	60.9		42.8	35.0	33.3
	20.3	18.7	24.8	Long Term Debt	26.9	19.1		17.0	39.1	27.4
	1.2	1.1	1.1	Deferred Taxes	.7	.4		1.1	1.9	1.8
	7.0	10.2	4.0	All Other Non-Current	5.1	.7		7.3	2.3	1.9
	36.2	30.7	23.9	Net Worth	7.1	19.0		31.8	21.7	35.6
	100.0	100.0	100.0	Total Liabilities & Net Worth	100.0	100.0		100.0	100.0	100.0
				INCOME DATA						
	100.0	100.0	100.0	Net Sales	100.0	100.0		100.0	100.0	100.0
				Gross Profit						
	93.5	93.1	93.0	Operating Expenses	88.8	101.9		91.8	87.9	85.5
	6.5	6.9	7.0	Operating Profit	11.2	−1.9		8.2	12.1	14.5
	−1.4	2.0	1.8	All Other Expenses (net)	−.4	.7		1.3	4.5	3.7
	7.9	4.9	5.1	Profit Before Taxes	11.6	−2.5		6.8	7.6	10.8
				RATIOS						
	2.7	2.0	1.8		3.3	1.9		1.4	1.6	1.9
	1.6	1.4	1.3	Current	1.3	1.2		1.1	1.1	1.4
	1.0	.9	.7		.3	.6		.8	.5	1.0
	1.8	1.6	1.3		2.1	1.0		.9	1.4	1.7
	1.2	.9	.7	Quick	.3	.5		.6	.8	1.0
	.7	.6	.4		.1	.2		.5	.4	.7
	29 12.8	25 14.8	18 19.8		0 UND	1 294.5		26 14.1	24 15.5	25 14.5
	41 9.0	39 9.4	32 11.3	Sales/Receivables	6 58.6	25 14.6		37 10.0	39 9.4	40 9.1
	55 6.7	51 7.2	44 8.3		24 15.4	35 10.5		43 8.6	44 8.3	50 7.3
				Cost of Sales/Inventory						
				Cost of Sales/Payables						
	5.6	8.2	7.6		4.9	6.6		14.3	7.0	7.6
	12.8	17.9	27.3	Sales/Working Capital	NM	28.3		56.4	NM	10.3
	452.9	−49.3	−17.0		−4.3	−22.0		−19.7	−6.4	NM
	15.8	8.2	6.5			5.8		15.9	6.6	5.0
	(97) 3.9	(87) 3.3	(75) 2.3	EBIT/Interest	(20) .8			3.6 (13)	3.1 (15)	2.7
	.8	1.1	.4			−7.6		1.6	1.6	1.7
	21.4	16.4	10.5	Net Profit + Depr., Dep.,						
	(24) 7.1	(31) 4.0	(25) 1.6	Amort./Cur. Mat. L/T/D						
	1.8	1.7	.6							
	.4	.3	.5		.2	.5		.9	1.8	.3
	.9	.8	1.3	Fixed/Worth	.7	1.0		1.1	6.9	1.5
	NM	3.3	18.5		−2.1	6.5		2.2	−8.9	NM
	.6	.9	.8		.4	.8		1.4	1.8	.9
	1.3	2.2	2.7	Debt/Worth	11.1	2.4		3.0	9.0	2.0
	NM	18.0	NM		−2.9	36.6		5.9	−13.0	NM
	65.6	51.9	51.0	% Profit Before Taxes/Tangible		57.6		69.0		36.6
	(83) 25.7	(78) 15.1	(63) 11.4	Net Worth	(18) 4.8		(12) 19.5		(12) 12.3	
	8.7	3.1	.6			−24.5		6.0		.7
	20.1	15.3	14.6	% Profit Before Taxes/Total	65.9	9.2		22.4	15.6	19.5
	8.4	6.7	3.8	Assets	5.8	−.3		5.9	8.1	5.3
	.1	.1	−.7		−.9	−18.9		1.4	1.8	.4
	27.4	27.3	23.1		39.1	24.5		19.2	5.9	50.4
	9.2	10.0	6.2	Sales/Net Fixed Assets	9.7	9.5		9.9	1.6	3.3
	1.8	2.1	1.3		1.1	3.2		1.2	.8	.9
	3.1	3.5	3.1		3.9	3.5		3.8	1.8	2.5
	2.1	2.3	1.7	Sales/Total Assets	1.4	2.2		2.8	.9	.8
	.7	1.0	.6		.5	1.5		.4	.5	.4
	1.4	1.6	1.7			1.2		1.7	4.4	.9
	(89) 3.5	(83) 2.5	(68) 3.7	% Depr., Dep., Amort./Sales	(19) 3.2		(13) 2.7	(13) 12.7	(12) 5.5	
	9.0	7.3	13.8			6.6		19.3	18.6	19.0
	2.4	2.9	3.3	% Officers', Directors',						
	(29) 7.1	(27) 5.3	(21) 6.5	Owners' Comp/Sales						
	12.9	8.8	13.8							
	4264005M	2664564M	1681690M	Net Sales ($)	4123M	39672M	29179M	107111M	246820M	1254785M
	2555831M	2054926M	1611769M	Total Assets ($)	5647M	25881M	44647M	109220M	334172M	1092202M

© RMA 2003

M = $ thousand   MM = $ million

See Pages 11 through 18 for Explanation of Ratios and Data

Current Data Sorted By Assets | Comparative Historical Data

	0-500M	500M-2MM	2-10MM	10-50MM	50-100MM	100-250MM	Type of Statement		4/1/98-3/31/99 ALL	4/1/99-3/31/00 ALL
	3 6 5	2 5 9 2 10	10 11 5 3 12	9 1 11	5 7	3 5	Unqualified / Reviewed / Compiled / Tax Returns / Other		31 9 19 6 41	32 15 20 7 44
		24 (4/1-9/30/02)		100 (10/1/02-3/31/03)						
NUMBER OF STATEMENTS	14	28	41	21	12	8			106	118
	%	%	%	%	%	%	ASSETS		%	%
	10.9	11.5	11.8	10.4	6.8		Cash & Equivalents		10.1	10.0
	23.4	36.9	35.0	28.2	25.9		Trade Receivables (net)		26.8	33.1
	5.1	5.6	9.7	2.6	.7		Inventory		8.9	8.5
	1.4	6.7	2.5	4.2	2.5		All Other Current		2.7	3.4
	40.8	60.6	59.1	45.3	35.9		Total Current		48.4	55.0
	37.0	28.3	22.8	35.3	30.7		Fixed Assets (net)		30.1	28.8
	7.4	2.6	7.7	9.7	32.3		Intangibles (net)		12.6	8.4
	14.7	8.6	10.3	9.7	1.1		All Other Non-Current		8.9	7.8
	100.0	100.0	100.0	100.0	100.0		Total		100.0	100.0
							LIABILITIES			
	8.1	9.7	8.0	7.5	1.0		Notes Payable-Short Term		7.8	26.6
	10.6	7.7	3.3	3.5	2.0		Cur. Mat.-L/T/D		4.6	7.4
	9.6	18.6	13.8	13.2	5.8		Trade Payables		13.5	14.7
	.0	.2	.4	1.0	.4		Income Taxes Payable		.9	.3
	3.5	22.9	12.8	18.3	18.5		All Other Current		13.0	14.3
	31.9	59.1	38.3	43.4	27.7		Total Current		39.8	63.4
	43.0	15.0	11.6	31.6	31.6		Long Term Debt		34.4	19.5
	1.8	.2	.2	.3	1.3		Deferred Taxes		.7	.7
	1.2	.8	8.1	5.2	4.4		All Other Non-Current		6.7	5.1
	22.1	25.0	41.9	19.4	35.0		Net Worth		18.4	11.4
	100.0	100.0	100.0	100.0	100.0		Total Liabilities & Net Worth		100.0	100.0
							INCOME DATA			
	100.0	100.0	100.0	100.0	100.0		Net Sales		100.0	100.0
							Gross Profit			
	94.7	92.6	94.1	97.2	96.2		Operating Expenses		103.5	94.6
	5.3	7.4	5.9	2.8	3.8		Operating Profit		-3.5	5.4
	1.6	1.9	.8	3.0	2.8		All Other Expenses (net)		-1.3	1.3
	3.7	5.5	5.1	-.2	1.0		Profit Before Taxes		-2.2	4.1
							RATIOS			
	2.6	1.7	2.4	2.5	1.9				2.2	2.2
	1.0	1.1	1.4	1.2	1.4		Current		1.2	1.3
	.2	.6	1.1	.5	.8				.7	.8
	2.2	1.4	2.0	1.9	1.7				1.6	1.7
	.8	.8	1.1	1.0	1.2		Quick		1.0	.9
	.1	.4	.7	.4	.8				.5	.5
	0 UND	25 14.3	35 10.3	28 12.8	55 6.6				28 13.0	29 12.5
	21 17.6	47 7.7	57 6.4	46 7.9	74 4.9		Sales/Receivables		48 7.7	52 7.1
	61 6.0	71 5.1	69 5.3	65 5.6	78 4.7				75 4.9	77 4.7
							Cost of Sales/Inventory			
							Cost of Sales/Payables			
	7.0	8.4	6.6	7.2	8.4				6.3	7.2
	NM	29.7	15.5	30.1	13.4		Sales/Working Capital		18.6	19.9
	-12.7	-9.2	108.3	-7.5	-25.4				-12.5	-15.8
	7.8	6.7	22.3	7.7	5.2				5.7	8.1
	(12) 3.8	(21) 1.7	(36) 4.1	(20) 1.9	1.3		EBIT/Interest		(85) 1.7	(92) 2.6
	.2	-2.8	.3	-1.0	-2.2				.1	.2
							Net Profit + Depr., Dep., Amort./Cur. Mat. L /T/D		5.8 (28) 2.5 1.1	11.6 (22) 2.0 .7
	.3	.3	.2	.5	2.5				.3	.3
	1.1	1.3	.5	1.4	14.0		Fixed/Worth		2.1	.9
	-6.5	451.2	1.6	-1.4	-2.8				-1.4	4.7
	.7	.9	.6	.7	3.4				.9	.9
	2.0	5.4	1.5	6.2	41.1		Debt/Worth		4.4	2.5
	-12.2	488.7	5.9	-3.7	-9.0				-5.3	23.7
	114.5	93.5	71.2	46.5					72.8	67.9
	(10) 40.0	(22) 23.1	(37) 28.3	(12) 11.5			% Profit Before Taxes/Tangible Net Worth		(70) 22.9	(94) 23.1
	10.0	-.3	-1.5	-4.2					-3.4	-.1
	31.3	13.7	19.7	10.7	4.9				12.6	21.2
	10.6	4.3	7.1	3.9	1.7		% Profit Before Taxes/Total Assets		4.0	4.9
	-8.4	-4.8	-1.1	-6.6	-6.9				-7.0	-2.2
	29.7	37.0	28.7	17.0	8.7				18.5	27.4
	13.1	13.5	13.2	7.3	6.4		Sales/Net Fixed Assets		7.3	12.4
	8.0	3.9	5.7	3.2	2.4				2.7	3.7
	5.3	3.6	3.1	3.1	2.1				2.6	3.4
	3.0	2.6	2.4	2.0	1.2		Sales/Total Assets		1.5	2.2
	2.5	1.7	1.5	1.3	.7				.7	1.1
	2.9	1.5	1.4	3.1					1.7	1.4
	(10) 5.2	(24) 3.0	(38) 2.5	(18) 6.6			% Depr., Dep., Amort./Sales		(81) 3.5	(97) 2.3
	8.2	5.5	4.8	11.8					8.8	8.7
	6.3	3.1	2.2						3.3	5.7
	(10) 8.8	(17) 5.7	(13) 4.2				% Officers', Directors', Owners' Comp/Sales		(24) 5.5	(30) 8.5
	20.5	8.7	9.8						11.7	15.0
	12721M	89338M	421774M	1015367M	1084957M	1653180M	Net Sales ($)		2624272M	2417602M
	3466M	31523M	191657M	488781M	859104M	1277668M	Total Assets ($)		2895144M	1880549M

© RMA 2003

M = $ thousand   MM = $ million
See Pages 11 through 18 for Explanation of Ratios and Data

Comparative Historical Data | Current Data Sorted By Sales

4/1/00-3/31/01 ALL	4/1/01-3/31/02 ALL	4/1/02-3/31/03 ALL	Type of Statement	0-1MM	1-3MM	3-5MM	5-10MM	10-25MM	25MM & OVER
19	12	29	Unqualified		2		5	7	15
14	13	16	Reviewed	1	1	2	9	3	
23	30	18	Compiled	3	7	2	4	2	
9	13	11	Tax Returns	4	3	2	1	1	
58	56	50	Other	2	10	5	6	7	20
					24 (4/1-9/30/02)		100 (10/1/02-3/31/03)		
123	124	124	NUMBER OF STATEMENTS	10	23	11	25	20	35
%	%	%	**ASSETS**	%	%	%	%	%	%
10.7	10.4	10.9	Cash & Equivalents	12.7	7.1	19.0	13.3	8.6	9.9
34.4	30.5	31.1	Trade Receivables (net)	15.3	27.0	32.1	33.9	43.4	29.0
6.9	7.2	6.0	Inventory	.5	5.1	11.2	10.7	5.9	3.2
4.5	4.9	3.6	All Other Current	1.2	6.7	2.0	2.8	3.4	3.5
56.4	53.0	51.6	Total Current	29.7	45.9	64.3	60.7	61.3	45.7
31.6	30.8	28.8	Fixed Assets (net)	41.0	36.7	27.5	23.8	22.7	27.5
7.0	8.6	10.6	Intangibles (net)	10.5	5.2	.5	6.5	9.2	21.0
4.9	7.6	9.0	All Other Non-Current	18.8	12.1	7.7	9.0	6.8	5.8
100.0	100.0	100.0	Total	100.0	100.0	100.0	100.0	100.0	100.0
			LIABILITIES						
10.7	12.5	7.1	Notes Payable-Short Term	4.5	9.4	10.1	8.6	9.4	3.0
6.8	20.3	5.3	Cur. Mat.-L/T/D	10.4	10.8	1.5	3.5	3.5	3.7
13.3	14.8	13.7	Trade Payables	5.8	10.7	13.3	18.9	16.2	12.8
.5	.6	.4	Income Taxes Payable	.1	.3	.0	.1	.7	.9
11.9	11.9	15.3	All Other Current	10.5	15.0	21.1	15.1	9.2	18.4
43.3	60.1	41.7	Total Current	31.3	46.3	46.0	46.2	39.0	38.7
24.2	49.6	21.8	Long Term Debt	32.1	30.1	15.9	12.1	9.1	29.6
.6	.9	.6	Deferred Taxes	.0	1.3	.0	.3	.4	.7
7.2	8.1	4.4	All Other Non-Current	1.5	.4	4.6	5.3	10.2	3.9
24.7	−18.7	31.4	Net Worth	35.1	21.9	33.4	36.2	41.2	27.1
100.0	100.0	100.0	Total Liabilities & Net Worth	100.0	100.0	100.0	100.0	100.0	100.0
			INCOME DATA						
100.0	100.0	100.0	Net Sales	100.0	100.0	100.0	100.0	100.0	100.0
			Gross Profit						
94.4	96.0	95.1	Operating Expenses	88.4	92.2	98.3	95.5	95.2	97.6
5.5	4.0	4.9	Operating Profit	11.6	7.8	1.7	4.5	4.8	2.4
2.1	2.6	1.8	All Other Expenses (net)	4.4	1.4	.8	.7	1.3	2.6
3.4	1.4	3.1	Profit Before Taxes	7.2	6.3	.9	3.8	3.5	−.3
			RATIOS						
2.2 / 1.5 / .9	1.9 / 1.1 / .8	2.2 / 1.2 / .8	Current	3.8 / .8 / .1	2.4 / 1.0 / .4	1.7 / 1.2 / .5	2.0 / 1.3 / .9	2.7 / 1.5 / 1.1	1.9 / 1.3 / .9
1.8 / 1.1 / .8	1.4 / .9 / .6 (123)	1.7 / 1.0 / .6	Quick	3.7 / .7 / .1	1.5 / .8 / .3	1.4 / 1.1 / .4	1.6 / .8 / .7	2.3 / 1.4 / 1.0	1.6 / 1.1 / .7
29 12.7 / 51 7.2 / 74 5.0	30 12.0 / 50 7.2 / 71 5.1	29 12.7 / 53 6.9 / 71 5.1	Sales/Receivables	0 UND / 27 13.7 / 75 4.8	20 18.4 / 34 10.6 / 63 5.7	24 15.2 / 49 7.5 / 59 6.2	25 14.4 / 49 7.4 / 67 5.5	38 9.6 / 63 5.8 / 77 4.7	42 8.6 / 60 6.1 / 75 4.9
			Cost of Sales/Inventory						
			Cost of Sales/Payables						
7.0 / 16.7 / −53.3	8.0 / 50.0 / −21.7	7.8 / 18.9 / −23.7	Sales/Working Capital	4.2 / NM / −7.3	7.9 / −848.0 / −10.6	7.0 / 15.9 / −6.2	6.6 / 24.9 / −28.2	7.3 / 14.7 / 73.5	7.8 / 16.7 / −26.9
(110) 8.8 / 3.0 / 1.0	(106) 6.4 / 2.0 / −1.9	(109) 8.2 / 2.3 / −.6	EBIT/Interest		(19) 6.7 / 2.3 / −1.4		(24) 21.1 / 2.3 / −.8	(17) 22.1 / 5.6 / .8	(34) 5.2 / 2.0 / −1.4
(24) 5.3 / 2.0 / .5	(19) 4.3 / 1.4 / .6	(22) 6.8 / 2.0 / .4	Net Profit + Depr., Dep., Amort./Cur. Mat. L/T/D						
.4 / 1.3 / 7.0	.4 / 1.6 / −13.7	.3 / 1.0 / 454.5	Fixed/Worth	.2 / 2.4 / NM	.4 / 1.1 / −11.3	.2 / .4 / 1.4	.2 / .9 / 2.7	.3 / .5 / 1.5	.6 / 3.6 / −2.2
.8 / 2.8 / 33.5	1.0 / 3.9 / −39.4	.8 / 3.0 / 488.7	Debt/Worth	.7 / 2.6 / NM	.6 / 5.5 / −17.3	.5 / 2.4 / 5.9	.7 / 2.1 / 10.1	.7 / 1.1 / 15.4	1.5 / 7.2 / −9.1
(95) 72.1 / 33.6 / 2.9	(90) 82.8 / 22.5 / −12.5	(94) 67.5 / 22.6 / −5.5	% Profit Before Taxes/Tangible Net Worth		(16) 119.4 / 30.3 / −2.2	(10) 144.4 / 10.5 / −5.0	(21) 62.9 / 14.6 / −6.5	(17) 49.8 / 28.3 / 1.3	(22) 60.2 / 15.7 / −29.1
24.3 / 7.3 / −.3	15.9 / 2.8 / −7.3	14.5 / 4.8 / −4.0	% Profit Before Taxes/Total Assets	15.8 / 8.0 / −2.5	24.9 / 5.1 / −6.6	13.3 / 3.9 / −.8	17.6 / 4.8 / −3.2	14.8 / 5.0 / −2.3	8.0 / 4.1 / −7.0
24.9 / 10.8 / 3.4	27.8 / 8.9 / 3.4	25.5 / 9.9 / 4.0	Sales/Net Fixed Assets	22.7 / 5.2 / .8	22.6 / 11.3 / 3.3	47.0 / 27.1 / 2.5	32.9 / 13.2 / 4.6	30.8 / 17.3 / 7.2	9.4 / 6.8 / 4.6
3.4 / 2.5 / 1.2	3.4 / 1.9 / 1.0	3.1 / 2.2 / 1.2	Sales/Total Assets	2.9 / 1.8 / .6	3.5 / 2.3 / 1.5	3.0 / 2.2 / .6	3.8 / 2.5 / 1.4	3.6 / 2.8 / 1.6	2.6 / 1.7 / 1.1
(103) .9 / 2.5 / 7.0	(95) .9 / 2.5 / 7.7	(100) 1.6 / 3.7 / 6.8	% Depr., Dep., Amort./Sales		(19) 2.9 / 4.3 / 6.8		(22) 1.2 / 2.3 / 4.8	1.1 / 2.4 / 6.2	(22) 3.1 / 5.3 / 7.5
(38) 2.8 / 5.5 / 9.0	(37) 2.5 / 6.4 / 12.7	(46) 2.7 / 5.9 / 10.2	% Officers', Directors', Owners' Comp/Sales		(15) 4.9 / 7.3 / 12.4		(10) 2.0 / 4.1 / 11.4		
2601244M	3383617M	4277337M	Net Sales ($)	4406M	38935M	46521M	185695M	312307M	3689473M
2129182M	2991547M	2852199M	Total Assets ($)	4234M	19890M	52485M	102684M	192278M	2480628M

INFORMATION—Internet Service Providers NAICS 518111 (SIC 7375)

| Current Data Sorted By Assets | | | | | | | Comparative Historical Data | |

0-500M	500M-2MM	2-10MM	10-50MM	50-100MM	100-250MM	Type of Statement		
1	2	7	6	2	2	Unqualified	14	16
1	1	3				Reviewed	7	6
2	3					Compiled	7	3
3	3	1				Tax Returns	2	3
3	6	11	2	2	4	Other	22	15
	9 (4/1-9/30/02)			56 (10/1/02-3/31/03)			4/1/98-3/31/99 ALL	4/1/99-3/31/00 ALL
10	15	22	8	4	6	NUMBER OF STATEMENTS	52	43
%	%	%	%	%	%	**ASSETS**	%	%
10.0	20.5	11.1				Cash & Equivalents	19.4	10.5
40.3	31.8	53.2				Trade Receivables (net)	29.2	39.0
1.1	3.4	.5				Inventory	.8	1.9
1.0	6.9	4.0				All Other Current	5.2	5.3
52.4	62.7	68.8				Total Current	54.7	56.7
23.3	18.5	17.7				Fixed Assets (net)	29.1	27.7
20.1	9.2	8.2				Intangibles (net)	10.8	10.9
4.1	9.6	5.4				All Other Non-Current	5.5	4.7
100.0	100.0	100.0				Total	100.0	100.0
						LIABILITIES		
62.0	21.9	4.6				Notes Payable-Short Term	13.0	10.5
22.0	5.2	3.3				Cur. Mat.-L/T/D	5.6	6.4
15.4	17.0	16.1				Trade Payables	11.7	15.9
.0	.0	.3				Income Taxes Payable	.6	1.0
13.0	31.4	20.3				All Other Current	11.9	17.8
112.4	75.5	44.6				Total Current	42.7	51.6
25.6	12.2	5.6				Long Term Debt	15.7	16.8
.0	.0	.2				Deferred Taxes	1.4	1.0
.0	19.4	6.5				All Other Non-Current	9.7	6.8
-37.9	-7.2	43.0				Net Worth	30.5	23.9
100.0	100.0	100.0				Total Liabilities & Net Worth	100.0	100.0
						INCOME DATA		
100.0	100.0	100.0				Net Sales	100.0	100.0
						Gross Profit		
97.0	97.5	91.6				Operating Expenses	104.9	94.3
3.0	2.5	8.4				Operating Profit	-4.9	5.7
.7	1.3	1.6				All Other Expenses (net)	1.1	1.0
2.3	1.2	6.9				Profit Before Taxes	-6.1	4.7
						RATIOS		
2.2	1.6	3.0					3.1	2.5
.6	.9	1.9				Current	1.3	1.3
.2	.3	.9					.5	.6
2.2	1.6	2.8					2.9	1.9
.6	.8	1.8				Quick	1.1	1.1
.1	.3	.9					.4	.5
0 UND	12 29.3	53 6.9					26 13.9	29 12.6
35 10.3	24 14.9	59 6.2				Sales/Receivables	54 6.7	56 6.6
49 7.5	68 5.4	105 3.5					65 5.7	78 4.7
						Cost of Sales/Inventory		
						Cost of Sales/Payables		
13.5	13.7	5.7					3.7	8.3
-12.4	-20.7	10.1				Sales/Working Capital	19.3	21.5
-4.2	-4.4	-47.3					-7.5	-12.1
13.2	16.5	58.3					8.0	23.3
1.1	(10) 2.2	(15) 38.3				EBIT/Interest	(43) 2.9	(39) 2.8
-.7	-3.0	4.2					-.1	.7
						Net Profit + Depr., Dep., Amort./Cur. Mat. L./T/D	7.6 3.1 1.9 (10)	
UND	.9	.1					.3	.3
-.9	-3.0	.3				Fixed/Worth	.7	2.5
.0	-.2	2.6					54.8	-2.1
UND	2.8	.5					.8	2.0
-3.6	-5.8	1.3				Debt/Worth	2.2	6.4
-1.7	-2.6	4.6					75.8	-6.3
		52.7					63.4	85.9
	(19)	21.6				% Profit Before Taxes/Tangible Net Worth	(40) 31.6	(27) 40.5
		6.6					-.5	-9.0
33.1	48.0	24.0					17.6	22.9
-.5	.7	12.4				% Profit Before Taxes/Total Assets	4.5	5.0
-9.8	-23.5	1.4					-4.0	-2.6
166.0	50.9	84.4					23.1	25.3
52.3	20.2	22.4				Sales/Net Fixed Assets	8.4	12.6
8.0	15.4	10.9					3.0	5.3
7.2	4.0	4.2					2.9	3.5
4.8	2.3	2.5				Sales/Total Assets	2.0	2.7
3.4	1.7	1.7					.9	1.7
	.7	.7					.9	1.4
	(13) 1.9	(17) 1.7				% Depr., Dep., Amort./Sales	(36) 3.1	(37) 3.0
	2.9	2.9					5.9	4.8
						% Officers', Directors', Owners' Comp/Sales	4.7 8.2 (13) 16.9	4.5 7.2 (12) 17.2
9897M	38585M	277500M	268254M	277081M	910551M	Net Sales ($)	2146657M	1932847M
2168M	13240M	104576M	180100M	337669M	1107207M	Total Assets ($)	2017621M	1412897M

© RMA 2003

M = $ thousand   MM = $ million
See Pages 11 through 18 for Explanation of Ratios and Data

Comparative Historical Data				Current Data Sorted By Sales					
			Type of Statement						
10	13	20	Unqualified	1	2	2	2	8	7
1	4	5	Reviewed		2	2	2	1	
8	9	5	Compiled	2		3			
5	3	7	Tax Returns	2	3	2			
20	28	28	Other	2	8	3	2	5	8
4/1/00-	4/1/01-	4/1/02-			9 (4/1-9/30/02)			56 (10/1/02-3/31/03)	
3/31/01	3/31/02	3/31/03							
ALL	ALL	ALL		0-1MM	1-3MM	3-5MM	5-10MM	10-25MM	25MM & OVER
44	57	65	**NUMBER OF STATEMENTS**	7	13	10	6	14	15
%	%	%	**ASSETS**	%	%	%	%	%	%
13.4	15.0	17.3	Cash & Equivalents		8.8	30.0		11.6	26.9
38.7	31.8	37.2	Trade Receivables (net)		42.8	35.6		49.9	27.8
2.6	1.2	1.8	Inventory		3.4	.9		2.5	1.0
2.5	7.3	5.1	All Other Current		3.7	9.9		4.7	6.0
57.2	55.3	61.4	Total Current		58.7	76.4		68.7	61.6
26.8	28.8	18.9	Fixed Assets (net)		17.5	13.6		22.2	12.9
10.4	8.8	14.0	Intangibles (net)		13.0	3.7		4.8	22.1
5.6	7.1	5.7	All Other Non-Current		10.7	6.2		4.2	3.4
100.0	100.0	100.0	Total		100.0	100.0		100.0	100.0
			LIABILITIES						
8.7	12.5	17.5	Notes Payable-Short Term		23.4	6.5		7.2	3.0
5.5	7.7	6.6	Cur. Mat.-L/T/D		2.0	6.6		4.3	2.8
14.3	14.5	13.8	Trade Payables		16.1	18.8		16.9	9.2
.5	.3	.5	Income Taxes Payable		.0	.0		.6	1.4
20.7	17.6	20.9	All Other Current		25.2	36.3		21.5	17.8
49.7	52.4	59.3	Total Current		66.7	68.1		50.5	34.2
14.6	14.6	11.9	Long Term Debt		19.9	2.2		12.5	9.2
.6	.5	.6	Deferred Taxes		.0	.0		.8	2.0
4.7	5.7	7.7	All Other Non-Current		7.7	28.1		3.5	4.8
30.4	26.8	20.4	Net Worth		5.8	1.6		32.8	49.7
100.0	100.0	100.0	Total Liabilities & Net Worth		100.0	100.0		100.0	100.0
			INCOME DATA						
100.0	100.0	100.0	Net Sales		100.0	100.0		100.0	100.0
			Gross Profit						
96.1	95.6	94.3	Operating Expenses		94.5	86.7		99.1	89.0
3.9	4.4	5.7	Operating Profit		5.5	13.3		.9	11.0
.8	2.3	1.0	All Other Expenses (net)		2.9	−.6		1.0	−.2
3.1	2.1	4.7	Profit Before Taxes		2.6	13.9		−.1	11.3
			RATIOS						
2.7	2.2	2.6			3.0	2.5		2.0	3.6
1.4	1.0	1.3	Current		.9	1.3		1.5	2.0
.8	.7	.6			.4	.8		1.0	1.1
2.5	1.9	2.3			3.0	1.9		1.9	3.2
1.3	.9	1.2	Quick		.8	1.2		1.4	1.4
.7	.5	.5			.3	.6		.6	.9
25 14.4	17 21.2	30 12.3		25 14.5	10 36.4		48 7.6	48 7.5	
62 5.9	42 8.8	55 6.6	Sales/Receivables	48 7.7	38 9.7		58 6.3	56 6.5	
85 4.3	68 5.4	68 5.4		62 5.9	83 4.4		101 3.6	68 5.4	
			Cost of Sales/Inventory						
			Cost of Sales/Payables						
7.1	7.0	5.3			10.7	5.5		5.2	2.4
14.2	UND	15.3	Sales/Working Capital		−44.5	47.0		11.5	5.7
−14.2	−10.0	−9.2			−4.9	−6.8		NM	39.5
13.8	11.1	40.5			27.9	57.7		57.7	61.3
(39) 3.6	(47) 5.1	(49) 4.0	EBIT/Interest	(10) 2.2	2.5	(13) 2.5	(11) 36.0		
1.6	−.2	.0			−2.8	−2.5			2.1
25.9	13.7		Net Profit + Depr., Dep.,						
(13) 1.8	(10) 2.9		Amort./Cur. Mat. L/T/D						
.9	1.4								
.2	.3	.1			1.6	.1		.1	.3
.7	1.2	.9	Fixed/Worth		−1.3	2.2		.4	.5
NM	−30.0	−.6			−.2	−.3		5.2	.8
.9	.9	.8			1.6	.8		.9	.5
2.9	2.6	3.0	Debt/Worth		−4.9	6.9		1.5	1.6
NM	−53.7	−3.6			−2.4	−5.0		8.4	4.3
75.8	51.8	109.0						52.5	107.0
(33) 35.3	(42) 33.1	(42) 31.0	% Profit Before Taxes/Tangible Net Worth				(12) 23.9	(12) 35.5	
14.0	−3.0	2.1						−63.0	19.4
22.1	21.7	24.4			44.8	60.7		20.2	28.0
6.4	12.2	6.4	% Profit Before Taxes/Total Assets		1.5	23.7		7.1	15.7
.1	−8.2	−2.1			−23.5	1.1		−9.0	5.4
34.1	34.4	50.3			135.0	70.4		121.8	33.4
11.1	12.8	19.7	Sales/Net Fixed Assets		20.2	35.9		19.4	12.4
4.8	4.5	7.9			11.2	13.5		4.3	5.8
3.8	3.1	3.9			4.8	4.6		4.3	2.5
2.4	2.4	2.3	Sales/Total Assets		2.3	3.8		2.4	1.1
1.5	1.5	1.1			1.7	1.7		1.1	.7
1.7	1.2	.8			.5			.5	
(37) 4.3	(46) 3.4	(48) 2.4	% Depr., Dep., Amort./Sales	(10) 1.7		(12) 2.9			
7.8	7.0	6.8			3.7			10.0	
4.0	2.8	3.5							
(14) 10.6	(14) 8.4	(11) 10.6	% Officers', Directors', Owners' Comp/Sales						
16.1	22.6	17.8							
1490456M	1316018M	1781868M	Net Sales ($)	4007M	19511M	38742M	42121M	251748M	1425739M
999400M	857076M	1744960M	Total Assets ($)	4050M	14808M	20883M	19423M	147825M	1537971M

© RMA 2003

M = $ thousand   MM = $ million
See Pages 11 through 18 for Explanation of Ratios and Data

Current Data Sorted By Assets | Comparative Historical Data

0-500M	500M-2MM	2-10MM	10-50MM	50-100MM	100-250MM	Type of Statement	4/1/98-3/31/99 ALL	4/1/99-3/31/00 ALL
	1	18	19	8	4	Unqualified	48	48
2	4	14	2			Reviewed	22	26
4	11	5				Compiled	18	14
12	5	4				Tax Returns	10	9
7	22	17	9	4	1	Other	49	30
	36 (4/1-9/30/02)		137 (10/1/02-3/31/03)					
25	43	58	30	12	5	**NUMBER OF STATEMENTS**	147	127
%	%	%	%	%	%	**ASSETS**	%	%
19.9	12.2	16.3	17.5	21.3		Cash & Equivalents	16.5	13.1
38.2	46.1	36.0	29.2	23.3		Trade Receivables (net)	34.5	36.7
2.1	4.9	4.5	2.1	2.8		Inventory	2.7	2.9
6.5	2.4	3.6	4.0	7.8		All Other Current	3.9	4.0
66.7	65.6	60.4	52.7	55.2		Total Current	57.7	56.8
17.6	19.3	23.0	19.5	15.3		Fixed Assets (net)	26.4	29.1
1.1	5.6	8.4	11.2	20.5		Intangibles (net)	8.0	6.6
14.6	9.5	8.1	16.6	9.0		All Other Non-Current	7.9	7.5
100.0	100.0	100.0	100.0	100.0		Total	100.0	100.0
						LIABILITIES		
20.2	15.6	7.5	7.5	7.1		Notes Payable-Short Term	8.8	9.5
6.1	3.9	3.5	6.7	9.2		Cur. Mat.-L/T/D	4.7	4.5
23.4	16.8	12.5	8.3	8.3		Trade Payables	9.9	10.0
.4	1.4	.8	.5	.4		Income Taxes Payable	.8	.9
15.1	16.1	14.1	27.1	23.4		All Other Current	20.0	17.6
65.3	53.9	38.4	49.9	48.4		Total Current	44.3	42.5
11.7	15.1	10.9	26.3	5.1		Long Term Debt	13.0	11.8
.0	.1	1.0	1.1	.2		Deferred Taxes	1.3	.6
20.2	2.6	6.6	5.3	8.5		All Other Non-Current	5.4	4.6
2.7	28.3	43.2	17.5	37.7		Net Worth	35.9	40.5
100.0	100.0	100.0	100.0	100.0		Total Liabilities & Net Worth	100.0	100.0
						INCOME DATA		
100.0	100.0	100.0	100.0	100.0		Net Sales	100.0	100.0
						Gross Profit		
88.9	95.9	97.7	95.7	103.2		Operating Expenses	92.1	93.3
11.1	4.1	2.3	4.3	-3.2		Operating Profit	7.9	6.7
1.0	.9	.6	1.1	1.3		All Other Expenses (net)	.3	.9
10.1	3.2	1.6	3.2	-4.5		Profit Before Taxes	7.5	5.8
						RATIOS		
1.9	2.0	2.6	1.6	2.4		Current	2.3	2.3
1.4	1.4	1.5	1.2	1.3			1.5	1.5
.8	.8	1.2	.8	.8			1.0	1.0
1.9	1.7	2.2	1.3	2.4		Quick	2.2	2.1
1.2	1.2	1.4	1.0	.9			1.3	1.2
.2	.7	.9	.6	.5			.8	.8
0 UND	39 9.3	29 12.7	39 9.4	33 10.9		Sales/Receivables	32 11.4	35 10.4
30 12.3	55 6.6	43 8.6	51 7.1	66 5.5			52 7.1	56 6.6
45 8.2	72 5.1	61 6.0	80 4.6	83 4.4			73 5.0	73 5.0
						Cost of Sales/Inventory		
						Cost of Sales/Payables		
7.9	9.5	6.7	11.3	3.6		Sales/Working Capital	6.8	7.0
32.2	21.6	13.4	31.8	10.8			12.6	18.4
-26.7	-14.9	38.9	-25.9	-26.4			-306.6	-779.5
(20) 9.9	(38) 15.4	(48) 11.5	(25) 9.7	42.4		EBIT/Interest	(119) 20.2	(104) 12.6
2.6	3.4	5.4	3.0	2.2			5.6	4.8
-.4	1.4	1.1	-.3	-14.3			1.9	1.7
		(18) 16.6	(13) 7.5			Net Profit + Depr., Dep., Amort./Cur. Mat. L /T/D	(46) 8.1	(34) 7.1
		4.2	2.6				3.3	2.5
		1.2	1.3				2.2	1.3
.1	.2	.2	.4	.2		Fixed/Worth	.3	.3
.3	.8	.6	.9	.8			.7	.8
20.6	8.1	1.3	2.6	NM			2.2	2.6
1.1	1.1	.7	1.1	.9		Debt/Worth	.8	.7
2.0	2.2	1.5	2.5	2.4			1.9	1.6
NM	47.7	3.7	11.9	NM			5.8	6.1
(19) 133.3	(34) 68.1	(52) 41.5	(24) 85.7			% Profit Before Taxes/Tangible Net Worth	(126) 74.4	(108) 69.7
80.8	20.3	20.1	26.9				36.9	31.9
15.4	3.4	4.2	-14.5				13.5	10.8
45.4	20.9	16.8	15.0	8.6		% Profit Before Taxes/Total Assets	22.2	22.4
16.5	6.8	5.6	8.7	4.5			10.0	9.8
.1	.4	.4	-5.4	-7.1			2.6	2.4
295.6	42.5	31.6	20.9	21.0		Sales/Net Fixed Assets	24.0	21.3
44.8	19.9	15.6	11.8	7.4			10.9	11.0
12.6	11.7	6.9	5.8	3.6			5.9	4.9
6.8	4.1	3.7	2.5	2.2		Sales/Total Assets	3.3	3.7
3.7	2.9	2.4	1.7	.8			2.2	2.5
2.3	2.3	1.7	1.2	.7			1.4	1.4
(14) .5	(33) .6	(46) .8	(21) 2.1			% Depr., Dep., Amort./Sales	(120) 1.7	(103) 1.6
1.6	2.0	2.0	5.3				3.2	3.2
2.3	3.4	3.7	9.1				6.2	6.5
(16) 6.5	(19) 5.0	(14) 2.8				% Officers', Directors', Owners' Comp/Sales	(32) 5.3	(27) 4.8
10.5	9.3	4.3					8.6	6.9
17.2	15.9	6.4					14.6	12.2
32106M	146868M	676418M	1211344M	1245350M	968732M	Net Sales ($)	4740628M	2963259M
7215M	44854M	255376M	643171M	817203M	760336M	Total Assets ($)	3119208M	1872292M

© RMA 2003

M = $ thousand   MM = $ million
See Pages 11 through 18 for Explanation of Ratios and Data

Comparative Historical Data | **Current Data Sorted By Sales**

			Type of Statement						
32	29	50	Unqualified			2	9	13	26
19	18	22	Reviewed	1	3	4	6	6	2
24	28	20	Compiled		10	6	2	2	
10	9	21	Tax Returns	7	5	6	2	1	
32	39	60	Other	5	15	8	8		13
4/1/00-3/31/01	4/1/01-3/31/02	4/1/02-3/31/03			36 (4/1-9/30/02)		137 (10/1/02-3/31/03)		
ALL	ALL	ALL		0-1MM	1-3MM	3-5MM	5-10MM	10-25MM	25MM & OVER
117	123	173	**NUMBER OF STATEMENTS**	13	33	26	27	33	41
%	%	%	**ASSETS**	%	%	%	%	%	%
12.9	13.3	16.5	Cash & Equivalents	22.6	13.2	15.6	12.7	22.5	15.5
40.1	35.2	36.3	Trade Receivables (net)	26.0	44.5	40.9	36.3	32.6	32.9
3.7	3.0	3.6	Inventory	2.5	4.6	2.2	6.9	3.9	1.6
3.7	4.2	4.1	All Other Current	7.6	4.1	1.3	3.9	3.7	5.4
60.3	55.7	60.5	Total Current	58.6	66.4	60.0	59.8	62.7	55.3
27.7	28.6	19.9	Fixed Assets (net)	26.6	14.5	25.4	22.5	18.5	18.3
5.0	7.7	8.8	Intangibles (net)	.3	8.8	2.6	6.3	9.6	16.3
7.0	8.0	10.8	All Other Non-Current	14.5	10.3	12.0	11.4	9.1	10.0
100.0	100.0	100.0	Total	100.0	100.0	100.0	100.0	100.0	100.0
			LIABILITIES						
10.7	10.9	11.1	Notes Payable-Short Term	23.4	13.9	18.6	5.9	7.0	7.1
3.8	6.0	4.8	Cur. Mat.-L/T/D	3.9	6.7	2.9	2.9	3.4	7.3
11.0	12.3	14.3	Trade Payables	17.3	23.8	10.0	13.4	13.5	9.7
1.0	.6	.8	Income Taxes Payable	.0	1.6	1.2	.7	.6	.4
17.0	17.0	17.5	All Other Current	10.7	14.9	12.9	17.8	19.2	23.0
43.4	46.8	48.6	Total Current	55.2	60.9	45.5	40.6	43.7	47.6
11.2	15.5	14.2	Long Term Debt	16.2	13.8	16.8	9.7	7.8	20.1
.7	.6	.7	Deferred Taxes	.0	.0	.7	.6	1.0	1.3
6.7	6.6	7.6	All Other Non-Current	12.9	12.7	1.7	6.1	9.1	5.3
38.0	30.6	29.0	Net Worth	15.7	12.6	35.3	43.1	38.4	25.6
100.0	100.0	100.0	Total Liabilities & Net Worth	100.0	100.0	100.0	100.0	100.0	100.0
			INCOME DATA						
100.0	100.0	100.0	Net Sales	100.0	100.0	100.0	100.0	100.0	100.0
			Gross Profit						
95.3	95.0	95.5	Operating Expenses	81.5	98.4	95.4	92.8	101.6	94.6
4.7	5.0	4.5	Operating Profit	18.5	1.6	4.6	7.2	-1.6	5.3
.8	2.1	1.0	All Other Expenses (net)	2.3	1.4	.5	-.4	.9	1.7
4.0	2.9	3.4	Profit Before Taxes	16.1	.1	4.1	7.6	-2.5	3.6
			RATIOS						
2.1	2.2	2.0		2.0	2.0	2.0	2.6	2.1	1.9
1.4	1.2	1.4	Current	1.3	1.3	1.4	1.5	1.3	1.3
1.0	.8	.9		.3	.7	1.0	1.1	1.1	.9
1.9	1.9	1.9		2.0	1.8	1.7	2.5	1.9	1.8
1.2	1.0	1.2	Quick	.6	1.2	1.4	1.4	1.2	1.2
.8	.7	.7		.6	.6	1.0	.8	.8	.7

33	11.0	34	10.9	30	12.1	Sales/Receivables	0	UND	32	11.6	23	15.6	29	12.7	31	11.7	35	10.5
53	6.9	49	7.4	46	7.9		2	155.0	48	7.6	41	8.8	55	6.7	44	8.3	49	7.5
80	4.6	69	5.3	66	5.6		64	5.7	72	5.0	64	5.7	62	5.9	60	6.1	74	4.9

			Cost of Sales/Inventory			
			Cost of Sales/Payables			

			Sales/Working Capital						
7.9	7.5	7.1		3.3	8.4	7.4	5.2	9.4	7.3
22.2	29.2	18.8		40.3	19.8	23.7	13.3	20.3	16.4
NM	-26.2	-62.6		-2.3	-18.9	NM	117.2	111.1	-50.5

							EBIT/Interest											
	13.3		7.2		12.1					6.3		12.9		42.1		6.1		26.5
(96)	3.8	(101)	2.9	(147)	4.0			(29)	2.0	(23)	5.9	(24)	8.4	(27)	2.6	(35)	5.8
	1.1		1.0		1.0				-1.3		3.2		1.4		.5		.3

						Net Profit + Depr., Dep., Amort./Cur. Mat. L/T/D											
	6.4		4.8		8.1										13.4		12.0
(22)	3.3	(37)	2.6	(41)	2.8							(10)	5.8	(16)	3.3
	1.7		.9		1.2								2.1		1.4

			Fixed/Worth						
.3	.3	.2		.1	.2	.1	.3	.3	.4
.7	1.0	.7		2.5	.7	.7	.6	.5	.9
1.8	4.0	2.6		-3.4	6.6	1.4	4.9	1.3	4.0

			Debt/Worth						
.7	.9	1.0		.9	1.1	.7	.4	1.2	.9
1.9	2.4	1.9		1.8	2.8	1.5	1.4	1.8	2.2
5.3	28.1	13.9		-10.0	NM	3.3	9.5	5.9	23.1

						% Profit Before Taxes/Tangible Net Worth											
	71.8		57.8		63.4				70.2		55.7		42.1		68.5		63.1
(102)	27.6	(101)	28.1	(142)	22.2			(25)	16.1	(24)	26.5	(23)	14.0	(29)	22.3	(33)	24.6
	2.1		2.8		3.3				1.7		7.2		6.1		-16.0		-8.6

			% Profit Before Taxes/Total Assets						
21.8	18.6	18.0		52.2	16.7	24.3	23.9	14.7	16.6
9.2	5.2	6.9		6.9	4.0	9.8	5.6	5.5	11.0
.3	.0	.3		-.5	-6.9	4.4	2.2	-6.5	-1.3

			Sales/Net Fixed Assets						
27.8	30.1	40.8		141.2	68.1	41.1	31.1	38.7	29.4
12.2	11.6	16.2		5.6	21.6	16.4	15.5	16.7	14.6
5.5	4.3	8.0		3.5	11.9	7.7	6.9	10.1	4.9

			Sales/Total Assets						
3.9	3.5	3.7		2.4	4.0	5.0	3.6	3.8	3.1
2.6	2.3	2.4		1.9	2.9	2.9	2.8	2.7	1.9
1.6	1.5	1.6		.6	2.1	1.9	1.6	1.6	.9

						% Depr., Dep., Amort./Sales											
	1.1		.8		.9						.8		.8		1.1		1.2		.8
(91)	2.7	(100)	2.8	(126)	2.1			(23)	1.8	(21)	2.0	(22)	2.7	(25)	2.1	(28)	2.7
	5.0		6.6		4.8				2.4		4.2		5.0		5.4		6.2

						% Officers', Directors', Owners' Comp/Sales										
	3.0		3.5		4.4						5.0		2.8				
(41)	4.7	(32)	5.2	(52)	7.2		(15)	10.3	(12)	5.9	(10)	4.6				
	9.2		15.8		14.6			17.6		9.7		8.2				

			Net Sales ($)						
4686719M	2648045M	4280818M	Net Sales ($)	6654M	62268M	101597M	192857M	494803M	3422639M
1878261M	1426345M	2528155M	Total Assets ($)	6993M	27039M	41578M	119335M	269477M	2063733M

M = $ thousand   MM = $ million
See Pages 11 through 18 for Explanation of Ratios and Data

FINANCE
AND INSURANCE

Current Data Sorted By Assets   Comparative Historical Data

						Type of Statement		
1	4	13	4	1		Unqualified		
1	1	2				Reviewed		
2	1					Compiled		
3	2					Tax Returns		
	3	2		1		Other		
0-500M	6 (4/1-9/30/02) 500M-2MM	2-10MM	35 (10/1/02-3/31/03) 10-50MM	50-100MM	100-250MM		4/1/98- 3/31/99 ALL	4/1/99- 3/31/00 ALL
7	7	11	17	5	1	NUMBER OF STATEMENTS		
%	%	%	%	%	%	ASSETS	%	%
D		6.8	5.1			Cash & Equivalents	D	D
A		49.1	34.4			Trade Receivables (net)	A	A
T		1.8	.4			Inventory	T	T
A		9.0	16.7			All Other Current	A	A
		66.7	56.6			Total Current		
N		6.4	3.1			Fixed Assets (net)	N	N
O		.0	1.4			Intangibles (net)	O	O
T		26.9	38.9			All Other Non-Current	T	T
		100.0	100.0			Total		
A						LIABILITIES	A	A
V		20.2	34.8			Notes Payable-Short Term	V	V
A		6.1	10.8			Cur. Mat.-L/T/D	A	A
I		3.8	4.3			Trade Payables	I	I
L		.2	.2			Income Taxes Payable	L	L
A		2.8	6.3			All Other Current	A	A
B		33.1	56.3			Total Current	B	B
L		29.6	14.1			Long Term Debt	L	L
E		.0	.0			Deferred Taxes	E	E
		19.8	6.0			All Other Non-Current		
		17.5	23.6			Net Worth		
		100.0	100.0			Total Liabilities & Net Worth		
						INCOME DATA		
		100.0	100.0			Net Sales		
						Gross Profit		
		78.3	59.9			Operating Expenses		
		21.7	40.1			Operating Profit		
		18.1	18.1			All Other Expenses (net)		
		3.6	22.0			Profit Before Taxes		
						RATIOS		
		7.7	1.4					
		2.1	1.2			Current		
		1.1	.6					
		7.6	1.4					
		1.4	1.1			Quick		
		1.0	.0					
	10	34.8	0 UND					
	377	1.0	151 2.4			Sales/Receivables		
	763	.5	927 .4					
						Cost of Sales/Inventory		
						Cost of Sales/Payables		
		.5	1.0					
		1.3	2.3			Sales/Working Capital		
		14.8	−6.5					
						EBIT/Interest		
						Net Profit + Depr., Dep., Amort./Cur. Mat. L /T/D		
		.2	.0					
		.3	.0			Fixed/Worth		
		1.0	.1					
		3.3	1.8					
		7.2	4.5			Debt/Worth		
		100.2	11.6					
			39.3			% Profit Before Taxes/Tangible Net Worth		
			23.6					
			7.9					
		6.1	7.9			% Profit Before Taxes/Total Assets		
		1.3	3.0					
		−2.1	1.3					
		218.9	166.2			Sales/Net Fixed Assets		
		30.9	36.6					
		2.7	12.8					
		1.0	.3			Sales/Total Assets		
		.4	.2					
		.2	.2					
			.5			% Depr., Dep., Amort./Sales		
		(13)	1.3					
			3.4					
						% Officers', Directors', Owners' Comp/Sales		
	7477M	51792M	93781M	59083M	16680M	Net Sales ($)		
	9186M	61133M	408264M	344167M	227670M	Total Assets ($)		

M = $ thousand   MM = $ million
See Pages 11 through 18 for Explanation of Ratios and Data

Comparative Historical Data   ## Current Data Sorted By Sales

	4/1/00-3/31/01 ALL	4/1/01-3/31/02 ALL	4/1/02-3/31/03 ALL	Type of Statement	6 (4/1-9/30/02)		35 (10/1/02-3/31/03)			
			23	Unqualified	2	4	3	8	5	1
			4	Reviewed	2	1		1		
			3	Compiled	1		1	1		
			5	Tax Returns	3	2			1	
			6	Other		3	1	1	1	
					0-1MM	1-3MM	3-5MM	5-10MM	10-25MM	25MM & OVER
			41	NUMBER OF STATEMENTS	8	10	5	11	6	1
	%	%	%	ASSETS	%	%	%	%	%	%
	D	D	8.4	Cash & Equivalents		6.4		4.5		
	A	A	37.0	Trade Receivables (net)		36.9		35.4		
	T	T	2.4	Inventory		.1		.0		
	A	A	15.2	All Other Current		20.6		23.9		
			63.0	Total Current		64.1		63.9		
	N	N	7.7	Fixed Assets (net)		2.7		4.2		
	O	O	2.3	Intangibles (net)		7.1		.6		
	T	T	26.9	All Other Non-Current		26.1		31.3		
			100.0	Total		100.0		100.0		
	A	A		LIABILITIES						
	V	V	31.3	Notes Payable-Short Term		20.1		36.0		
	A	A	7.3	Cur. Mat.-L/T/D		10.2		10.2		
	I	I	3.9	Trade Payables		.6		7.0		
	L	L	.3	Income Taxes Payable		.0		.1		
	A	A	4.8	All Other Current		2.8		7.8		
	B	B	47.6	Total Current		33.7		61.0		
	L	L	19.2	Long Term Debt		23.5		16.0		
	E	E	.3	Deferred Taxes		.0		.0		
			11.4	All Other Non-Current		29.2		8.6		
			21.5	Net Worth		13.6		14.4		
			100.0	Total Liabilities & Net Worth		100.0		100.0		
				INCOME DATA						
			100.0	Net Sales		100.0		100.0		
				Gross Profit						
			66.7	Operating Expenses		62.9		68.9		
			33.3	Operating Profit		37.1		31.1		
			19.3	All Other Expenses (net)		25.9		12.2		
			14.0	Profit Before Taxes		11.2		18.9		
				RATIOS						
			2.1			8.3		1.5		
			1.3	Current		2.0		1.3		
			1.0			.8		.3		
			1.9			6.7		1.5		
			1.1	Quick		1.6		.2		
			.1			.1		.0		
		0	UND		0	UND		0	UND	
		151	2.4	Sales/Receivables	21	17.6		57	6.4	
		840	.4		1121	.3		800	.5	
				Cost of Sales/Inventory						
				Cost of Sales/Payables						
			.9			.4		1.1		
			1.9	Sales/Working Capital		.6		1.9		
			48.2			NM		-.6		
			5.2							
		(22)	2.8	EBIT/Interest						
			1.5							
				Net Profit + Depr., Dep., Amort./Cur. Mat. L/T/D						
			.0			.0		.1		
			.1	Fixed/Worth		.1		.1		
			.7			NM		1.0		
			2.0			2.3		2.9		
			5.1	Debt/Worth		11.2		7.7		
			19.5			NM		22.6		
			40.5					63.1		
		(38)	20.2	% Profit Before Taxes/Tangible Net Worth			(10)	26.1		
			7.6					16.1		
			6.4			3.9		8.2		
			1.9	% Profit Before Taxes/Total Assets		1.3		2.7		
			.7			-.5		.6		
			239.4			UND		51.6		
			38.9	Sales/Net Fixed Assets		39.9		30.9		
			6.6			14.6		4.8		
			.4			.4		.4		
			.2	Sales/Total Assets		.2		.2		
			.1			.1		.2		
			.6					.2		
		(29)	1.4	% Depr., Dep., Amort./Sales			(10)	.9		
			4.6					3.6		
			8.8							
		(11)	15.3	% Officers', Directors', Owners' Comp/Sales						
			33.3							
			228813M	Net Sales ($)	4403M	16448M	17699M	74457M	88374M	27432M
			1050420M	Total Assets ($)	24640M	116478M	77498M	299930M	525919M	5955M

M = $ thousand   MM = $ million
See Pages 11 through 18 for Explanation of Ratios and Data

Current Data Sorted By Assets   Comparative Historical Data

0-500M	500M-2MM	2-10MM	10-50MM	50-100MM	100-250MM	Type of Statement	4/1/98-3/31/99 ALL	4/1/99-3/31/00 ALL
2	7	19	23	6	7	Unqualified	64	51
	4	22	6			Reviewed	25	23
3	9	10	3			Compiled	40	37
3	10	2				Tax Returns	7	6
4	15	20	22	4	8	Other	62	46
	36 (4/1-9/30/02)		173 (10/1/02-3/31/03)					
12	45	73	54	10	15	**NUMBER OF STATEMENTS**	198	163
%	%	%	%	%	%	**ASSETS**	%	%
4.7	6.1	4.5	8.1	8.4	9.8	Cash & Equivalents	8.0	6.5
55.8	55.0	71.1	64.0	50.1	68.7	Trade Receivables (net)	61.6	66.9
5.8	3.7	3.1	2.0	.6	.7	Inventory	1.2	1.4
11.7	16.2	9.2	8.5	29.8	4.2	All Other Current	8.7	9.4
78.0	81.1	87.9	82.5	88.9	83.3	Total Current	79.5	84.2
9.6	5.5	2.7	5.8	5.4	4.9	Fixed Assets (net)	6.2	3.8
7.6	.7	1.3	1.6	1.2	3.2	Intangibles (net)	1.6	1.2
4.8	12.8	8.0	10.1	4.6	8.6	All Other Non-Current	12.7	10.8
100.0	100.0	100.0	100.0	100.0	100.0	Total	100.0	100.0
						LIABILITIES		
10.4	36.0	38.2	39.0	22.6	38.0	Notes Payable-Short Term	32.9	40.9
3.4	2.4	4.3	4.5	1.1	4.4	Cur. Mat.-L/T/D	2.2	2.1
.9	2.6	1.4	3.7	5.4	2.4	Trade Payables	1.5	2.6
.0	.0	.2	.3	.0	.3	Income Taxes Payable	.2	.3
19.5	14.7	7.5	12.2	7.2	11.1	All Other Current	10.8	9.5
34.0	55.8	51.5	59.8	36.2	56.2	Total Current	47.6	55.3
16.5	8.8	10.1	8.5	24.0	9.4	Long Term Debt	11.8	7.4
.0	.0	.0	.0	.0	.2	Deferred Taxes	.1	.2
11.8	10.5	9.9	8.3	7.6	8.8	All Other Non-Current	7.8	11.8
38.3	24.9	28.5	23.4	32.2	25.3	Net Worth	32.7	25.3
100.0	100.0	100.0	100.0	100.0	100.0	Total Liabilities & Net Worth	100.0	100.0
						INCOME DATA		
100.0	100.0	100.0	100.0	100.0	100.0	Net Sales	100.0	100.0
						Gross Profit		
76.3	79.5	71.1	74.4	66.7	71.1	Operating Expenses	136.3	72.3
23.7	20.5	28.8	25.6	33.3	28.9	Operating Profit	−36.3	27.7
16.0	8.4	15.1	10.8	12.7	8.9	All Other Expenses (net)	5.8	10.4
7.7	12.1	13.8	14.9	20.6	20.0	Profit Before Taxes	−42.0	17.4
						RATIOS		
5.3	3.0	2.6	1.6	10.9	2.7		3.2	2.4
3.0	1.5	1.5	1.4	2.5	1.4	Current	1.7	1.5
1.2	1.1	1.2	1.1	1.5	1.1		1.1	1.1
4.3	2.2	2.4	1.6	7.5	2.4		2.9	2.1
2.9	1.2	1.4	1.3	1.4	1.3	Quick	(197) 1.5	1.3
.8	.4	1.1	.9	.5	1.0		1.0	1.0
2 148.8	5 75.9	245 1.5	77 4.7	0 UND	147 2.5		133 2.7	145 2.5
172 2:1	418 .9	696 .5	679 .5	249 1.5	832 .4	Sales/Receivables	712 .5	879 .4
542 .7	1038 .4	1339 .3	1534 .2	1700 .2	1561 .2		1440 .3	1538 .2
						Cost of Sales/Inventory		
						Cost of Sales/Payables		
.8	.8	.5	.9	.3	.8		.5	.6
2.2	2.0	1.2	1.7	.7	2.9	Sales/Working Capital	1.2	1.3
11.2	11.6	4.0	10.0	3.7	6.2		5.3	5.9
	(36) 6.2	(45) 4.2	(34) 5.4		(13) 8.7		(91) 5.7	(78) 4.6
	2.4	2.2	2.8		5.1	EBIT/Interest	2.8	2.8
	1.5	1.2	1.8		2.2		1.6	1.8
						Net Profit + Depr., Dep.,	(17) 22.0	(19) 20.9
						Amort./Cur. Mat. L /T/D	1.2	1.6
							.1	.1
.0	.0	.0	.0	.0	.0		.0	.0
.4	.0	.1	.1	.1	.1	Fixed/Worth	.1	.1
UND	.3	.2	.4	.6	.2		.3	.3
.5	1.0	1.5	1.7	1.5	1.6		.9	1.6
8.3	3.5	3.6	5.2	3.4	3.7	Debt/Worth	2.7	3.7
UND	9.7	6.5	16.4	7.3	9.1		8.6	9.1
(10) 151.9	(40) 42.4	(69) 40.3	(51) 68.2		59.9	% Profit Before Taxes/Tangible	(184) 37.4	(152) 54.4
42.9	18.4	13.2	22.3		35.3	Net Worth	14.7	18.9
5.3	4.5	3.8	9.4		21.2		4.2	7.4
13.5	8.6	7.1	9.0	11.4	15.8	% Profit Before Taxes/Total	8.2	8.7
5.1	3.9	2.7	3.6	5.6	8.6	Assets	3.4	4.6
.6	1.1	.7	1.8	3.9	2.4		.9	1.7
UND	UND	224.3	61.6	19.8	63.8		101.7	113.8
52.4	63.7	31.8	23.5	14.3	28.6	Sales/Net Fixed Assets	26.1	26.3
14.5	13.9	13.9	6.2	11.3	10.1		7.2	11.4
3.0	1.0	.6	.7	.9	.9		.5	.6
1.0	.4	.3	.3	.3	.3	Sales/Total Assets	.3	.3
.3	.3	.2	.2	.2	.2		.2	.2
	(24) .5	(44) .4	(43) .8		(12) .7	% Depr., Dep., Amort./Sales	(120) .8	(110) .7
	.9	1.0	1.4		2.1		1.7	1.5
	3.4	1.8	3.4		3.2		3.1	2.8
	(10) 3.7	(23) 4.4	(17) 3.5			% Officers', Directors',	(49) 9.7	(31) 10.2
	11.0	10.9	6.8			Owners' Comp/Sales	18.4	13.6
	23.5	18.7	26.3				29.7	24.5
7691M	71257M	161539M	750555M	573203M	1105029M	Net Sales ($)	1347171M	2063750M
3888M	50233M	323766M	1163739M	788282M	2139038M	Total Assets ($)	3536511M	3445875M

Comparative Historical Data   Current Data Sorted By Sales

			Type of Statement			36 (4/1-9/30/02)		173 (10/1/02-3/31/03)		
40	57	64	Unqualified	15	9	14	4	10	12
16	22	32	Reviewed	12	11	5	3	1	
33	45	25	Compiled	14	7	2	2		
13	14	15	Tax Returns	10	2	2		1	
72	46	73	Other	23	12	8	10	6	14
4/1/00-3/31/01	4/1/01-3/31/02	4/1/02-3/31/03		0-1MM	1-3MM	3-5MM	5-10MM	10-25MM	25MM & OVER
ALL	ALL	ALL							
174	184	209	**NUMBER OF STATEMENTS**	74	41	31	19	18	26
%	%	%	**ASSETS**	%	%	%	%	%	%
6.6	7.1	6.3	Cash & Equivalents	4.4	3.7	4.4	5.8	13.7	13.7
65.4	64.1	63.7	Trade Receivables (net)	63.9	63.2	72.8	68.9	51.4	58.3
1.8	1.6	2.8	Inventory	1.7	2.5	5.5	7.9	1.4	.7
8.0	9.7	11.3	All Other Current	14.7	12.2	6.5	5.6	16.7	6.1
81.8	82.5	84.2	Total Current	84.7	81.5	89.2	88.2	83.1	78.8
6.3	5.6	4.8	Fixed Assets (net)	2.5	5.4	6.9	4.5	4.4	8.5
1.6	2.5	1.7	Intangibles (net)	1.3	.8	1.2	2.4	2.3	4.3
10.3	9.4	9.3	All Other Non-Current	11.5	12.4	2.8	4.9	10.2	8.4
100.0	100.0	100.0	Total	100.0	100.0	100.0	100.0	100.0	100.0
			LIABILITIES						
36.9	34.3	35.6	Notes Payable-Short Term	35.7	34.1	41.2	38.7	40.1	25.5
3.3	3.9	3.7	Cur. Mat.-L/T/D	3.3	3.0	6.9	5.4	.7	3.4
3.1	1.2	2.5	Trade Payables	.5	1.7	2.5	7.5	4.7	4.1
.1	.1	.2	Income Taxes Payable	.1	.2	.1	.1	.7	.1
10.7	11.3	11.2	All Other Current	10.4	12.3	9.3	10.1	16.9	11.0
54.1	50.9	53.2	Total Current	50.0	51.2	59.9	61.8	63.1	44.1
10.0	12.6	10.4	Long Term Debt	10.9	8.7	9.3	8.1	13.2	12.6
.0	.1	.0	Deferred Taxes	.0	.0	.0	.0	.1	.1
7.8	8.5	9.5	All Other Non-Current	9.1	10.7	9.9	16.1	3.1	8.0
28.1	27.9	26.9	Net Worth	30.1	29.3	20.8	14.0	20.4	35.1
100.0	100.0	100.0	Total Liabilities & Net Worth	100.0	100.0	100.0	100.0	100.0	100.0
			INCOME DATA						
100.0	100.0	100.0	Net Sales	100.0	100.0	100.0	100.0	100.0	100.0
			Gross Profit						
74.0	70.8	73.9	Operating Expenses	69.5	72.1	80.6	77.6	76.3	76.7
26.0	29.2	26.1	Operating Profit	30.5	27.9	19.4	22.4	23.7	23.3
10.9	15.8	12.0	All Other Expenses (net)	17.0	10.2	11.6	10.4	7.0	5.8
15.1	13.4	14.1	Profit Before Taxes	13.5	17.7	7.8	12.0	16.7	17.5
			RATIOS						
2.5	2.8	2.6	Current	3.1	2.6	2.0	2.0	2.0	4.2
1.4	1.6	1.5		1.5	1.6	1.4	1.3	1.1	1.6
1.2	1.1	1.1		1.2	1.2	1.1	1.1	1.0	1.3
2.3	2.4	2.3	Quick	2.7	2.5	1.7	1.6	1.5	2.8
1.3	1.4	1.3		1.3	1.4	1.3	1.3	1.0	1.4
1.0	1.0	1.0		1.0	1.0	1.1	1.0	.5	1.1
129 2.8	115 3.2	92 4.0	Sales/Receivables	203 1.8	28 13.3	216 1.7	129 2.8	2 164.5	85 4.3
746 .5	786 .5	633 .6		875 .4	609 .6	672 .5	633 .6	183 2.0	171 2.1
1396 .3	1382 .3	1297 .3		1598 .2	1074 .3	1305 .3	1301 .3	1069 .3	868 .4
			Cost of Sales/Inventory						
			Cost of Sales/Payables						
.7	.6	.7	Sales/Working Capital	.5	.6	1.1	.9	.7	1.5
1.3	1.2	1.5		.9	1.5	1.4	1.8	10.9	3.4
7.4	5.8	5.3		2.5	5.4	3.8	13.5	79.2	6.4
(88) 5.6	(97) 5.0	(142) 6.2	EBIT/Interest	(40) 4.3	(25) 5.9	(27) 2.9	(14) 6.4	(13) 5.6	(23) 9.7
2.8	2.6	2.6		2.3	2.6	1.8	2.1	3.9	7.8
1.5	1.5	1.7		1.7	1.5	1.2	1.5	2.3	3.3
(21) 8.7	(14) 47.1	(22) 19.0	Net Profit + Depr., Dep., Amort./Cur. Mat. L/T/D						
.8	6.8	3.6							
.1	.6	.7							
.0	.0	.0	Fixed/Worth	.0	.0	.1	.0	.0	.1
.1	.1	.1		.0	.1	.1	.2	.1	.1
.2	.3	.3		.1	.3	.8	1.4	.6	.6
1.4	1.4	1.5	Debt/Worth	1.0	1.4	2.8	2.4	1.6	1.3
3.8	4.1	4.0		4.0	3.1	5.3	6.0	6.0	2.7
9.5	11.1	10.1		10.9	6.5	12.2	17.3	12.7	5.4
(168) 43.5	(172) 44.6	(194) 48.3	% Profit Before Taxes/Tangible Net Worth	(69) 34.5	(38) 52.8	(30) 33.1	(16) 87.8	(16) 60.0	(25) 110.8
18.9	18.3	21.1		10.9	20.9	19.7	22.7	31.6	52.2
6.0	4.8	6.9		2.4	8.1	6.3	9.7	18.6	22.8
9.4	8.8	8.7	% Profit Before Taxes/Total Assets	6.9	11.3	5.0	7.1	9.5	24.3
4.1	3.5	3.8		2.5	4.1	3.0	3.4	4.7	13.7
1.1	.9	1.2		.3	.9	1.1	1.3	2.4	5.0
92.7	186.4	115.7	Sales/Net Fixed Assets	UND	382.0	58.6	110.8	66.3	60.7
23.8	26.2	30.1		50.6	30.4	24.9	26.3	21.0	17.3
9.0	10.5	11.7		14.0	13.2	9.0	6.8	11.3	10.0
.6	.6	.8	Sales/Total Assets	.4	.9	.8	1.2	1.2	1.8
.3	.3	.3		.2	.4	.4	.4	.4	.9
.2	.2	.2		.2	.2	.2	.2	.2	.3
(125) .6	(113) .8	(133) .5	% Depr., Dep., Amort./Sales	(33) .6	(27) .3	(25) .5	(14) .3	(12) 1.0	(22) 1.1
1.3	1.6	1.2		.9	.8	1.0	1.9	1.4	2.1
2.8	2.7	2.6		2.2	1.7	1.9	3.2	3.6	3.1
(39) 6.3	(41) 4.2	(53) 3.7	% Officers', Directors', Owners' Comp/Sales	(11) 9.6	(20) 3.8	(11) 6.7			
13.6	7.3	8.8		12.5	9.7	10.4			
23.2	16.1	19.4		21.5	29.5	20.1			
2876359M	2346462M	2669274M	Net Sales ($)	33653M	80462M	119454M	122065M	304105M	2009535M
4511079M	4258053M	4468946M	Total Assets ($)	160451M	260569M	332464M	391660M	946154M	2377648M

M = $ thousand   MM = $ million
See Pages 11 through 18 for Explanation of Ratios and Data

Current Data Sorted By Assets | Comparative Historical Data

						Type of Statement		
11	34	50	80	27	23	Unqualified	197	214
2	2	8	3			Reviewed	9	6
2	11	4	5		1	Compiled	11	18
10	8	6	3	1	1	Tax Returns	12	10
8	6	21	21	12	4	Other	62	66
	53 (4/1-9/30/02)		310 (10/1/02-3/31/03)				4/1/98-3/31/99	4/1/99-3/31/00
0-500M	500M-2MM	2-10MM	10-50MM	50-100MM	100-250MM		ALL	ALL
33	61	89	112	40	28	NUMBER OF STATEMENTS	291	314
%	%	%	%	%	%	ASSETS	%	%
35.8	25.9	12.4	11.4	12.8	12.2	Cash & Equivalents	17.1	19.4
10.6	20.1	28.6	25.1	27.1	23.3	Trade Receivables (net)	21.7	18.4
.0	4.2	8.6	14.5	17.5	10.0	Inventory	18.8	13.2
10.4	17.0	20.4	29.4	30.9	26.0	All Other Current	22.1	20.3
56.8	67.1	70.0	80.3	88.1	71.5	Total Current	79.7	71.4
19.5	19.8	6.7	3.7	2.6	5.1	Fixed Assets (net)	5.7	8.1
2.5	4.4	2.6	3.1	1.1	4.1	Intangibles (net)	2.7	4.8
21.2	8.7	20.8	12.8	8.2	19.3	All Other Non-Current	11.9	15.7
100.0	100.0	100.0	100.0	100.0	100.0	Total	100.0	100.0
						LIABILITIES		
15.0	26.3	47.7	50.5	58.8	57.1	Notes Payable-Short Term	45.7	39.8
5.2	3.0	2.9	4.7	2.2	2.0	Cur. Mat.-L/T/D	2.3	1.7
3.7	6.6	1.3	1.7	3.4	1.6	Trade Payables	7.7	5.3
.4	1.1	.5	.3	.2	.2	Income Taxes Payable	.3	.3
7.6	11.6	9.3	12.0	12.0	6.6	All Other Current	6.8	8.4
31.8	48.5	61.6	69.1	76.7	67.5	Total Current	62.8	55.6
17.2	8.3	8.5	8.4	4.5	16.1	Long Term Debt	7.0	8.6
.1	.2	.2	.2	.0	.4	Deferred Taxes	.3	.6
1.4	1.8	2.5	2.6	1.8	2.1	All Other Non-Current	2.0	2.1
49.4	41.1	27.2	19.7	16.9	13.9	Net Worth	27.8	33.2
100.0	100.0	100.0	100.0	100.0	100.0	Total Liabilities & Net Worth	100.0	100.0
						INCOME DATA		
100.0	100.0	100.0	100.0	100.0	100.0	Net Sales	100.0	100.0
						Gross Profit		
83.7	81.3	73.0	75.6	69.3	76.8	Operating Expenses	80.4	87.5
16.3	18.7	27.0	24.4	30.7	23.2	Operating Profit	19.6	12.5
1.8	3.3	7.1	6.6	6.4	10.2	All Other Expenses (net)	4.1	1.0
14.5	15.5	19.9	17.9	24.3	13.0	Profit Before Taxes	15.5	11.5
						RATIOS		
8.0	2.9	1.7	1.4	1.2	1.1		1.6	1.7
3.1	1.3	1.1	1.1	1.1	1.0	Current	1.1	1.2
1.3	1.0	1.0	1.0	1.0	.9		1.0	1.0
8.0	2.3	1.3	1.1	1.1	1.1		1.3	1.4
2.7	1.1	.7	.2	.2	.7	Quick	(290) .5	(313) .7
1.2	.3	.1	.1	.1	.0		.1	.1
0 UND	0 UND	0 UND	0 UND	0 UND	6 61.2		0 UND	0 UND
0 UND	11 34.6	10 38.1	23 16.0	13 27.4	31 11.8	Sales/Receivables	19 19.4	8 43.7
15 24.8	85 4.3	571 .6	675 .5	730 .5	967 .4		169 2.2	87 4.2
						Cost of Sales/Inventory		
						Cost of Sales/Payables		
5.0	2.6	1.6	1.8	1.6	2.8		2.1	2.0
11.7	7.3	6.1	4.4	4.0	9.1	Sales/Working Capital	6.0	5.7
55.5	86.0	UND	13.9	6.5	-7.6		15.8	47.6
43.2	21.5	9.9	7.1	7.1	13.3		6.7	5.5
(18) 8.5	(45) 5.7	(52) 3.0	(76) 3.6	(26) 3.7	(17) 3.2	EBIT/Interest	(180) 2.5	(196) 1.8
1.7	1.4	1.7	2.1	2.7	.8		1.5	1.0
						Net Profit + Depr., Dep.,	16.3	10.3
						Amort./Cur. Mat. L./T/D	(44) 4.1	(33) 1.9
							.9	.3
.0	.1	.0	.0	.0	.0		.0	.0
.2	.2	.1	.1	.1	.1	Fixed/Worth	.1	.1
2.0	1.3	.3	.3	.1	.7		.3	.4
.1	.5	1.4	3.2	5.6	6.7		1.8	1.2
.7	1.6	4.4	7.4	9.2	11.0	Debt/Worth	5.2	3.7
8.3	4.4	8.0	18.6	13.7	17.3		12.1	8.7
100.5	83.6	51.8	57.2	72.7	82.4	% Profit Before Taxes/Tangible	60.0	33.9
(29) 51.5	(55) 32.1	(84) 24.2	(106) 36.8	41.5	(27) 47.0	Net Worth	(279) 31.3	(291) 15.0
14.4	6.1	9.5	17.4	18.7	10.1		11.1	.2
66.0	35.1	11.6	7.8	6.3	5.8	% Profit Before Taxes/Total	9.8	8.0
23.8	8.3	4.9	4.2	4.2	2.6	Assets	4.2	3.2
3.4	2.1	1.5	1.8	2.7	.9		1.5	.1
211.0	48.4	129.2	67.6	122.1	75.4		55.0	50.3
41.6	27.3	31.8	29.8	40.3	34.7	Sales/Net Fixed Assets	26.1	23.7
20.1	7.0	14.6	13.9	23.5	15.6		13.1	12.3
10.3	2.9	.7	.4	.3	.3		.7	1.0
4.0	1.4	.4	.3	.2	.2	Sales/Total Assets	.4	.5
1.6	.7	.2	.2	.1	.1		.2	.2
.6	.7	.5	.6	.4	.7		.8	.8
(19) 1.1	(46) 1.4	(58) 1.1	(80) 1.0	(29) .8	(13) .9	% Depr., Dep., Amort./Sales	(203) 1.3	(229) 1.4
1.9	3.5	1.5	2.0	1.2	1.8		2.0	2.4
9.9	7.0	10.5	6.0			% Officers', Directors',	6.4	6.2
(13) 13.6	(25) 11.3	(21) 14.7	(24) 8.9			Owners' Comp/Sales	(85) 13.9	(72) 13.4
29.7	15.7	22.3	23.7				27.0	24.1
57244M	140875M	295793M	1718918M	825072M	1853350M	Net Sales ($)	2198613M	2409045M
8565M	65922M	455380M	2604915M	2937919M	4717380M	Total Assets ($)	7658122M	7388131M

M = $ thousand　MM = $ million
See Pages 11 through 18 for Explanation of Ratios and Data

Comparative Historical Data   ## Current Data Sorted By Sales

			Type of Statement						
167	131	225	Unqualified	23	61	39	37	37	28
5	4	15	Reviewed	7	5	1	1	1	
27	23	22	Compiled	9	8	3	1		1
13	16	29	Tax Returns	10	9	3	3	2	2
58	60	72	Other	16	16	5	11	13	11
4/1/00-3/31/01 ALL	4/1/01-3/31/02 ALL	4/1/02-3/31/03 ALL		53 (4/1-9/30/02)			310 (10/1/02-3/31/03)		
				0-1MM	1-3MM	3-5MM	5-10MM	10-25MM	25MM & OVER
270	234	363	**NUMBER OF STATEMENTS**	65	99	51	53	53	42
%	%	%	**ASSETS**	%	%	%	%	%	%
17.9	15.7	16.5	Cash & Equivalents	18.3	15.7	19.7	13.8	12.8	19.8
22.8	23.2	23.9	Trade Receivables (net)	26.1	26.4	27.1	22.7	15.9	22.0
9.2	13.5	10.0	Inventory	2.3	7.4	14.8	10.6	20.0	8.6
22.3	19.7	23.3	All Other Current	16.0	20.9	16.9	29.4	32.5	28.4
72.3	72.0	73.6	Total Current	62.7	70.4	78.5	76.6	81.1	78.9
7.7	7.4	8.6	Fixed Assets (net)	15.1	9.3	6.8	4.8	6.7	5.8
2.9	3.8	3.0	Intangibles (net)	3.6	1.5	4.5	4.6	1.7	3.5
17.1	16.7	14.8	All Other Non-Current	18.6	18.7	10.2	14.0	10.5	11.8
100.0	100.0	100.0	Total	100.0	100.0	100.0	100.0	100.0	100.0
			LIABILITIES						
44.0	47.8	43.9	Notes Payable-Short Term	31.3	39.8	47.7	44.9	53.1	55.9
1.2	4.9	3.5	Cur. Mat.-L/T/D	2.1	3.4	5.9	4.5	4.6	.5
3.7	2.9	2.8	Trade Payables	2.6	2.8	3.0	2.9	2.2	3.4
.1	.3	.5	Income Taxes Payable	.1	.1	1.2	.8	.6	.2
9.1	7.9	10.4	All Other Current	6.4	11.7	6.7	11.5	14.8	11.2
58.1	63.7	61.1	Total Current	42.5	57.8	64.6	64.7	75.3	71.3
8.3	7.5	9.4	Long Term Debt	13.4	10.8	3.8	9.1	7.1	9.9
.4	.3	.2	Deferred Taxes	.3	.1	.1	.2	.1	.4
2.7	4.0	2.2	All Other Non-Current	3.0	3.0	.8	2.0	1.1	2.4
30.5	24.6	27.1	Net Worth	40.9	28.2	30.7	24.0	16.5	16.1
100.0	100.0	100.0	Total Liabilities & Net Worth	100.0	100.0	100.0	100.0	100.0	100.0
			INCOME DATA						
100.0	100.0	100.0	Net Sales	100.0	100.0	100.0	100.0	100.0	100.0
			Gross Profit						
83.6	75.0	76.0	Operating Expenses	65.3	77.3	77.2	75.4	78.5	85.8
16.4	25.0	24.0	Operating Profit	34.7	22.7	22.7	24.6	21.5	14.2
6.1	10.0	6.0	All Other Expenses (net)	9.1	5.7	5.3	5.1	5.8	4.0
10.3	15.1	18.0	Profit Before Taxes	25.6	17.0	17.5	19.4	15.7	10.3
			RATIOS						
1.5	1.5	1.8	Current	4.7	1.8	1.6	1.6	1.2	1.2
1.1	1.1	1.1		1.6	1.1	1.1	1.2	1.1	1.1
1.0	1.0	1.0		1.0	1.0	1.0	1.0	1.0	1.0
1.2	1.1	1.4	Quick	4.5	1.6	1.3	1.2	1.0	1.1
.7	(233) .6	.8		1.5	.9	.9	.3	.2	.7
.1	.1	.1		.2	.1	.2	.1	.0	.1
0 UND	0 UND	0 UND	Sales/Receivables	0 UND	0 UND	0 UND	3 138.1	0 UND	2 217.3
16 22.8	15 24.2	14 27.0		19 19.6	10 35.7	13 28.5	24 15.5	3 145.4	23 15.7
246 1.5	256 1.4	203 1.8		589 .6	299 1.2	553 .7	151 2.4	37 10.0	214 1.7
			Cost of Sales/Inventory						
			Cost of Sales/Payables						
1.7	2.1	2.2	Sales/Working Capital	.8	2.1	2.7	1.3	2.8	4.2
5.0	7.8	5.7		4.6	5.5	7.0	3.7	6.0	8.3
39.4	−53.2	48.0		35.0	71.9	47.0	10.9	236.2	−246.2
(168) 4.0	(147) 7.3	(234) 9.6	EBIT/Interest	(33) 15.3	(62) 8.7	(34) 12.3	(34) 9.5	(36) 8.8	(35) 9.6
1.5	2.9	3.7		3.0	3.6	3.7	2.8	4.0	4.0
.9	1.4	1.9		1.4	1.7	1.8	1.8	2.6	2.1
(29) 4.9	(23) 7.5	(30) 24.2	Net Profit + Depr., Dep., Amort./Cur. Mat. L/T/D		(12) 13.8				
3.4	3.4	4.9			2.6				
.5	.3	.6			.4				
.0	.0	.0	Fixed/Worth	.0	.0	.0	.0	.0	.1
.1	.1	.1		.1	.1	.1	.1	.1	.1
.4	.4	.4		.4	.4	.4	.4	.4	.5
1.2	1.7	1.5	Debt/Worth	.6	1.1	1.1	2.7	3.7	3.3
3.8	6.3	5.5		2.0	4.6	5.1	6.1	9.0	9.2
10.6	16.5	12.9		7.2	13.1	13.7	11.0	17.2	14.1
(256) 30.8	(217) 66.4	(341) 64.7	% Profit Before Taxes/Tangible Net Worth	(61) 68.2	(91) 51.5	(48) 77.3	(49) 52.0	(52) 79.8	(40) 82.9
11.8	28.5	33.6		23.1	23.7	47.3	31.0	46.7	49.8
.5	9.3	11.6		5.8	7.2	17.1	13.2	20.9	21.2
6.0	9.3	11.9	% Profit Before Taxes/Total Assets	11.2	12.1	25.6	9.5	8.8	11.8
1.9	3.9	4.8		6.0	4.0	5.7	4.5	4.5	6.1
.1	1.3	1.7		1.6	1.3	1.7	1.9	2.0	1.7
53.3	85.1	80.3	Sales/Net Fixed Assets	UND	71.6	114.5	64.4	71.8	60.8
22.7	30.6	31.4		24.6	31.6	37.8	31.6	39.4	29.1
8.9	12.0	14.2		7.0	14.2	18.4	12.9	15.7	19.6
.7	.9	1.1	Sales/Total Assets	1.3	1.5	1.2	.6	.6	1.0
.4	.3	.3		.3	.4	.5	.3	.3	.4
.2	.2	.2		.2	.2	.2	.2	.2	.2
(188) .8	(151) .6	(245) .6	% Depr., Dep., Amort./Sales	(37) 1.1	(67) .8	(35) .4	(43) .5	(40) .5	(23) .3
1.7	1.2	1.1		1.9	1.2	.7	.8	.9	.9
2.8	1.8	1.9		4.6	1.9	1.3	1.3	1.7	1.8
(69) 5.8	(48) 6.3	(89) 7.3	% Officers', Directors', Owners' Comp/Sales	(21) 9.9	(36) 7.2		(11) 8.7		
13.0	8.2	12.4		16.2	13.7		9.9		
21.7	17.0	24.0		25.3	23.1		24.7		
1980744M	2340148M	4891252M	Net Sales ($)	36168M	191300M	197982M	386506M	791070M	3288226M
6287458M	7426573M	10790081M	Total Assets ($)	123827M	930534M	561483M	1614848M	2974157M	4585232M

M = $ thousand   MM = $ million
See Pages 11 through 18 for Explanation of Ratios and Data

FINANCE—All Other Nondepository Credit Intermediation NAICS 522298 (SIC 6019, 6153, 6159)

Current Data Sorted By Assets | **Comparative Historical Data**

	0-500M	500M-2MM	2-10MM	10-50MM	50-100MM	100-250MM	Type of Statement	4/1/98-3/31/99 ALL	4/1/99-3/31/00 ALL
	1	8	32	40	18	17	Unqualified	101	106
	1	7	18	14			Reviewed	37	38
	3	6	16	4			Compiled	23	28
	4	8	9				Tax Returns	15	15
	5	7	24	33	10	5	Other	63	48
		52 (4/1-9/30/02)			238 (10/1/02-3/31/03)				
	14	36	99	91	28	22	NUMBER OF STATEMENTS	239	235
	%	%	%	%	%	%	**ASSETS**	%	%
	15.9	12.1	8.7	5.7	6.0	2.6	Cash & Equivalents	9.5	8.6
	28.9	30.5	48.5	52.7	36.0	47.3	Trade Receivables (net)	47.9	49.5
	15.7	7.3	2.4	2.3	1.9	3.3	Inventory	1.4	1.4
	10.1	13.7	13.3	7.5	28.8	8.6	All Other Current	8.6	9.8
	70.7	63.6	73.0	68.3	72.7	61.9	Total Current	67.4	69.3
	18.0	14.3	8.1	7.4	7.8	9.7	Fixed Assets (net)	10.7	14.8
	.6	2.8	.9	1.7	3.3	3.8	Intangibles (net)	3.0	2.3
	10.7	19.3	18.1	22.6	16.2	24.6	All Other Non-Current	18.9	13.6
	100.0	100.0	100.0	100.0	100.0	100.0	Total	100.0	100.0
							LIABILITIES		
	19.6	20.6	31.9	34.3	39.2	20.0	Notes Payable-Short Term	36.1	30.6
	13.4	3.6	3.2	3.1	4.9	5.4	Cur. Mat.-L/T/D	3.9	5.3
	2.9	2.4	2.1	3.4	3.5	1.1	Trade Payables	2.6	3.1
	.1	.1	.2	.2	.3	.5	Income Taxes Payable	.1	.2
	10.5	14.6	13.3	9.2	3.3	9.7	All Other Current	10.6	10.0
	46.5	41.3	50.8	50.2	51.1	36.8	Total Current	53.3	49.1
	11.4	15.1	15.9	18.6	21.3	31.6	Long Term Debt	16.4	18.6
	.0	.0	.5	.4	.1	.3	Deferred Taxes	.8	.4
	9.0	12.4	8.2	4.0	7.7	4.9	All Other Non-Current	5.5	7.1
	33.1	31.2	24.6	26.9	19.8	26.4	Net Worth	23.9	24.8
	100.0	100.0	100.0	100.0	100.0	100.0	Total Liabilities & Net Worth	100.0	100.0
							INCOME DATA		
	100.0	100.0	100.0	100.0	100.0	100.0	Net Sales	100.0	100.0
							Gross Profit		
	81.5	78.2	67.7	65.4	64.7	59.3	Operating Expenses	78.6	68.3
	18.5	21.8	32.3	34.6	35.3	40.7	Operating Profit	21.4	31.7
	11.0	9.0	14.9	20.1	16.1	20.3	All Other Expenses (net)	15.6	14.9
	7.5	12.8	17.3	14.5	19.2	20.4	Profit Before Taxes	5.8	16.8
							RATIOS		
	2.4	3.7	2.5	1.8	1.6	5.3	Current	2.2	2.2
	1.9	1.8	1.4	1.2	1.3	1.5		1.2	1.3
	1.0	.9	1.1	1.0	1.1	1.0		1.0	1.1
	1.7	2.7	1.8	1.7	1.4	3.7	Quick	1.7	1.8
	.9	1.1	1.2	1.2	.9	1.2	(234)	1.1	1.2
	.2	.1	.4	.7	.1	.4		.6	.6
0	UND	0 UND	12 29.6	36 10.1	10 35.0	34 10.6	Sales/Receivables	16 23.4	14 27.0
26	14.2	31 11.6	312 1.2	857 .4	72 5.1	705 .5		498 .7	442 .8
813	.4	693 .5	1139 .3	1954 .2	1395 .3	2000 .1		1787 .2	1552 .2
							Cost of Sales/Inventory		
							Cost of Sales/Payables		
	2.3	.7	.6	.5	.5	.2	Sales/Working Capital	.6	.7
	3.4	2.6	1.6	1.5	1.2	.9		1.8	1.5
	NM	-41.1	12.0	-24.0	13.2	28.4		60.7	17.1
		6.4	6.8	4.2	12.3		EBIT/Interest	6.9	4.3
	(22) 3.3	(58) 2.6	(42) 2.2	(10) 2.9			(92) 3.0	(103) 2.4
	1.6	1.4	1.2	1.8				1.8	1.2
							Net Profit + Depr., Dep., Amort./Cur. Mat. L /T/D	5.0	4.0
							(24)	1.2 (28)	1.4
								.2	.3
	.0	.0	.0	.0	.0	.0	Fixed/Worth	.0	.0
	.2	.0	.1	.0	.0	.1		.0	.1
	20.6	3.0	.3	.1	1.1	.5		.6	.8
	.7	1.3	1.5	1.8	2.8	1.4	Debt/Worth	1.8	1.9
	2.4	2.4	4.9	3.7	6.2	4.9		4.4	4.3
	26.9	7.8	10.1	8.1	16.8	11.6		11.7	10.0
	(12) 61.9	(31) 50.0	(94) 55.3	(88) 29.1	(24) 40.7	(21) 25.7	% Profit Before Taxes/Tangible Net Worth	(218) 38.8	(218) 39.4
	30.2	15.9	19.6	10.4	23.7	10.3		17.8	20.2
	-3.0	4.9	6.9	3.3	11.7	6.2		6.6	6.6
	32.8	12.5	8.4	4.7	7.2	3.8	% Profit Before Taxes/Total Assets	7.3	7.5
	2.3	6.6	3.2	2.0	2.5	2.0		2.7	3.4
	-3.2	.4	1.0	.7	.9	.9		.8	1.0
	UND	UND	145.0	163.4	98.2	UND	Sales/Net Fixed Assets	960.3	94.8
	23.6	53.4	35.9	40.4	25.4	12.6		36.3	24.7
	8.7	18.2	8.8	8.4	8.7	5.2		7.8	5.2
	1.7	1.1	.5	.4	.3	.2	Sales/Total Assets	.5	.4
	.7	.4	.3	.2	.2	.1		.2	.2
	.3	.2	.1	.1	.1	.1		.1	.1
		.6	.5	.7	.7		% Depr., Dep., Amort./Sales	.6	.7
	(22) 1.5	(67) 1.2	(59) 1.4	(19) 2.4			(145) 1.8	(156) 1.7
	7.8	2.4	3.9	3.5				5.7	5.7
			4.7	2.5			% Officers', Directors', Owners' Comp/Sales	6.4	3.9
		(17) 13.4	(15) 9.0				(53) 14.0	(46) 9.3
		18.9	17.9					23.4	20.6
	5456M	66538M	358698M	956881M	1047556M	966531M	Net Sales ($)	2408891M	2206891M
	3374M	47056M	507669M	2138700M	2029423M	3446457M	Total Assets ($)	6633981M	6813628M

© RMA 2003

M = $ thousand   MM = $ million
See Pages 11 through 18 for Explanation of Ratios and Data

Comparative Historical Data			Type of Statement	Current Data Sorted By Sales					
96	90	116	Unqualified	19	29	12	18	27	11
33	33	40	Reviewed	13	16	4	5	1	1
32	37	29	Compiled	11	11	1	3	3	
11	14	21	Tax Returns	16	4		1		
57	68	84	Other	23	14	10	12	17	8
4/1/00- 3/31/01 ALL	4/1/01- 3/31/02 ALL	4/1/02- 3/31/03 ALL		52 (4/1-9/30/02)			238 (10/1/02-3/31/03)		
				0-1MM	1-3MM	3-5MM	5-10MM	10-25MM	25MM & OVER
229	242	290	**NUMBER OF STATEMENTS**	82	74	27	39	48	20
%	%	%	**ASSETS**	%	%	%	%	%	%
8.8	9.3	7.8	Cash & Equivalents	8.5	9.5	6.8	6.0	5.4	9.7
48.9	46.9	45.3	Trade Receivables (net)	37.9	54.4	61.2	39.8	40.9	42.5
.6	1.8	3.7	Inventory	3.4	2.9	1.6	7.7	.9	9.2
13.3	12.7	12.5	All Other Current	14.8	10.6	7.3	17.1	12.5	8.8
71.5	70.6	69.3	Total Current	64.5	77.3	76.8	70.6	59.7	70.2
10.9	11.0	9.2	Fixed Assets (net)	9.2	5.2	8.2	11.2	11.6	15.9
1.7	1.9	1.8	Intangibles (net)	.6	1.5	2.1	1.0	3.1	6.3
15.9	16.5	19.6	All Other Non-Current	25.7	15.9	12.8	17.1	25.7	7.7
100.0	100.0	100.0	Total	100.0	100.0	100.0	100.0	100.0	100.0
			LIABILITIES						
41.1	30.9	30.5	Notes Payable-Short Term	27.3	34.5	37.5	38.2	21.5	25.2
5.4	5.8	4.0	Cur. Mat.-L/T/D	4.0	3.8	.2	4.5	7.0	1.9
3.7	4.3	2.7	Trade Payables	2.2	2.0	1.2	3.4	2.8	7.4
.1	.1	.2	Income Taxes Payable	.0	.2	.2	.1	.2	.8
15.6	9.3	10.8	All Other Current	9.4	12.0	9.4	15.5	9.7	7.5
66.0	50.5	48.2	Total Current	43.0	52.5	48.6	61.7	41.3	42.8
17.2	18.9	18.1	Long Term Debt	19.3	13.2	18.9	15.4	27.2	13.7
.3	.2	.4	Deferred Taxes	.1	.2	.4	1.1	.4	.5
10.6	5.1	7.1	All Other Non-Current	11.3	5.9	3.7	2.4	7.6	7.1
5.9	25.2	26.2	Net Worth	26.3	28.2	28.4	19.3	23.6	35.8
100.0	100.0	100.0	Total Liabilities & Net Worth	100.0	100.0	100.0	100.0	100.0	100.0
			INCOME DATA						
100.0	100.0	100.0	Net Sales	100.0	100.0	100.0	100.0	100.0	100.0
			Gross Profit						
68.4	66.1	68.0	Operating Expenses	61.3	60.8	78.8	77.9	67.5	90.4
31.6	33.9	32.0	Operating Profit	38.7	39.2	21.2	22.1	32.5	9.6
14.1	17.8	16.1	All Other Expenses (net)	20.0	19.1	13.3	11.3	16.4	2.0
17.5	16.1	15.8	Profit Before Taxes	18.8	20.1	7.9	10.8	16.1	7.6
			RATIOS						
1.9	2.2	2.4	Current	3.1	2.1	1.9	1.5	3.3	4.2
1.3	1.3	1.3		1.5	1.4	1.3	1.2	1.3	1.4
1.0	1.0	1.0		1.0	1.1	1.1	.9	.9	1.1
1.7	1.8	1.9	Quick	2.3	1.7	1.8	1.3	2.2	2.1
1.2	1.2	1.2		1.1	1.2	1.3	.9	.9	1.3
.3	.4	.4		.2	.9	.9	.2	.3	.7
1 588.6	6 66.1	14 26.1	Sales/Receivables	0 UND	18 19.9	19 19.3	13 28.7	13 27.5	28 13.2
406 .9	300 1.2	302 1.2		218 1.7	1049 .3	857 .4	161 2.3	76 4.8	58 6.3
1456 .2	1347 .3	1418 .3		1214 .3	1755 .2	1712 .2	715 .5	1395 .3	145 2.5
			Cost of Sales/Inventory						
			Cost of Sales/Payables						
.6	.6	.6	Sales/Working Capital	.4	.5	.7	.9	.8	2.3
1.6	2.2	1.5		1.1	1.1	1.3	4.7	5.8	8.9
93.9	45.2	34.3		NM	3.1	4.8	-20.5	-58.6	41.2
(88) 3.8	(107) 4.4	(149) 5.5	EBIT/Interest	(31) 7.4	(37) 7.4	(15) 4.4	(25) 3.8	(23) 4.7	(18) 21.2
2.4	2.5	2.6		3.4	2.8	1.7	1.4	2.4	4.2
1.4	1.2	1.4		1.6	1.5	1.0	.9	1.3	1.9
(16) 3.5	(12) 3.1	(18) 12.2	Net Profit + Depr., Dep., Amort./Cur. Mat. L/T/D						
.8	.2	3.1							
.1	.0	.6							
.0	.0	.0	Fixed/Worth	.0	.0	.0	.0	.0	.0
.0	.1	.0		.0	.0	.0	.1	.2	.4
.3	.4	.4		.3	.1	.3	2.6	1.8	.9
1.9	1.8	1.5	Debt/Worth	1.3	1.5	1.9	2.2	2.4	1.5
4.4	4.4	4.2		4.8	4.8	3.3	4.3	6.1	2.8
10.6	10.5	9.4		12.3	7.8	4.4	10.6	19.9	4.0
(215) 39.4	(230) 41.0	(270) 40.8	% Profit Before Taxes/Tangible Net Worth	(76) 44.2	(71) 38.5	(26) 27.5	(35) 29.9	(42) 42.8	61.3
19.2	17.2	15.0		14.6	11.3	8.6	14.8	21.7	32.9
7.9	4.8	4.3		2.6	3.7	2.5	5.8	8.6	6.8
7.3	7.1	7.5	% Profit Before Taxes/Total Assets	7.6	7.6	5.2	4.8	7.7	16.3
3.3	3.1	2.7		2.7	3.1	2.1	2.5	2.5	8.3
.8	.6	.8		.2	1.1	.5	.4	.9	1.9
259.5	154.3	165.1	Sales/Net Fixed Assets	UND	162.5	82.6	88.0	108.0	624.1
33.3	38.7	40.1		46.5	48.4	29.1	32.8	44.9	14.8
11.7	11.5	8.4		7.6	13.9	14.7	6.9	5.2	6.2
.4	.6	.5	Sales/Total Assets	.3	.4	.5	1.2	.9	5.8
.2	.3	.2		.2	.2	.2	.4	.2	1.2
.1	.1	.1		.1	.1	.2	.1	.1	.9
(143) .8	(161) .7	(184) .6	% Depr., Dep., Amort./Sales	(45) .6	(51) .4	(17) .9	(29) .8	(30) .8	(12) .2
1.5	1.3	1.4		1.5	1.0	1.5	1.5	2.3	1.4
3.9	4.6	3.4		6.5	2.4	3.8	5.1	5.3	2.5
(51) 4.4	(50) 4.3	(47) 4.1	% Officers', Directors', Owners' Comp/Sales	(13) 7.4	(13) 5.3			(11) 2.5	
7.8	9.8	9.5		13.4	15.8			4.2	
18.1	20.2	18.4		19.4	25.9			17.9	
2070911M	3266833M	3401660M	Net Sales ($)	38014M	132998M	107402M	280963M	729907M	2112376M
6372862M	6101629M	8172679M	Total Assets ($)	294156M	890805M	473968M	1342672M	3736625M	1434453M

M = $ thousand   MM = $ million
See Pages 11 through 18 for Explanation of Ratios and Data

FINANCE—Mortgage and Nonmortgage Loan Brokers NAICS 522310 (SIC 6163)

	Current Data Sorted By Assets							Comparative Historical Data	
Type of Statement									
Unqualified	10	9	14	16	8	3		41	40
Reviewed	1	1	4	1				3	4
Compiled		3	2	1				10	3
Tax Returns	5	4	2		2			2	3
Other	4	3	4	3	2	3		12	16
	19 (4/1-9/30/02)			84 (10/1/02-3/31/03)				4/1/98-3/31/99	4/1/99-3/31/00
	0-500M	500M-2MM	2-10MM	10-50MM	50-100MM	100-250MM		ALL	ALL
NUMBER OF STATEMENTS	20	20	26	21	10	6		68	66
	%	%	%	%	%	%		%	%
ASSETS									
Cash & Equivalents	39.2	23.3	19.3	13.2	7.0			15.3	24.9
Trade Receivables (net)	13.5	30.8	22.2	26.5	35.1			33.3	25.0
Inventory	2.2	1.8	.0	11.7	9.6			10.3	7.2
All Other Current	10.7	14.5	24.6	40.5	37.3			11.6	14.2
Total Current	65.7	70.4	66.1	91.9	89.0			70.5	71.3
Fixed Assets (net)	22.4	19.7	15.9	3.1	1.5			10.3	11.5
Intangibles (net)	2.5	.4	.5	1.9	.3			3.6	2.1
All Other Non-Current	9.4	9.5	17.5	3.0	9.2			15.6	15.1
Total	100.0	100.0	100.0	100.0	100.0			100.0	100.0
LIABILITIES									
Notes Payable-Short Term	13.9	22.0	35.2	60.7	74.9			31.0	32.4
Cur. Mat.-L/T/D	1.2	5.1	6.2	.4	.1			1.9	3.6
Trade Payables	4.3	7.1	3.3	5.4	.6			5.5	5.0
Income Taxes Payable	1.0	.3	1.3	.5	.4			.2	.2
All Other Current	10.7	18.4	6.9	8.1	1.9			12.2	9.3
Total Current	31.3	52.9	52.9	75.1	77.9			50.8	50.4
Long Term Debt	7.4	9.0	13.2	4.0	.5			12.8	9.2
Deferred Taxes	.0	.3	.6	.0	.0			.3	.5
All Other Non-Current	.0	4.5	.5	4.6	4.1			1.8	3.6
Net Worth	61.3	33.4	32.7	16.4	17.5			34.3	36.3
Total Liabilities & Net Worth	100.0	100.0	100.0	100.0	100.0			100.0	100.0
INCOME DATA									
Net Sales	100.0	100.0	100.0	100.0	100.0			100.0	100.0
Gross Profit									
Operating Expenses	83.2	86.7	74.5	74.1	65.5			83.7	78.7
Operating Profit	16.8	13.3	25.5	25.9	34.5			16.3	21.3
All Other Expenses (net)	.6	.9	4.2	8.5	13.3			4.8	6.0
Profit Before Taxes	16.2	12.3	21.3	17.5	21.2			11.5	15.3
RATIOS									
Current	5.3	2.1	1.8	1.4	1.4			3.2	2.7
	2.9	1.4	1.5	1.1	1.0			1.2	1.2
	1.6	1.1	.9	1.0	1.0			1.0	1.0
Quick	5.3	1.9	1.5	1.2	1.3			2.2	2.5
	1.9	1.2	.9	.2	.4			1.1	1.1
	.9	.7	.2	.1	.0			.2	.4
Sales/Receivables	0 UND	0 UND	0 UND	2 211.7	0 UND			0 806.5	0 UND
	5 67.6	10 36.6	5 73.9	14 25.4	42 8.7			30 12.3	10 34.8
	11 31.9	118 3.1	184 2.0	803 .5	2000 .1			699 .5	157 2.3
Cost of Sales/Inventory									
Cost of Sales/Payables									
Sales/Working Capital	5.5	1.6	1.2	.9	.7			1.1	1.8
	11.2	7.9	5.3	4.6	7.1			7.3	6.6
	75.0	117.4	-9.9	12.1	NM			NM	23.7
EBIT/Interest	(11) 39.5	(12) 8.4	(19) 10.1	(17) 5.3				(35) 18.0	(39) 16.1
	16.0	4.6	5.6	3.7				3.2	4.7
	9.0	.4	2.4	1.9				1.9	1.2
Net Profit + Depr., Dep., Amort./Cur. Mat. L./T/D									(11) 2.9
									.1
									-7.6
Fixed/Worth	.1	.0	.0	.0	.0			.0	.0
	.2	.2	.1	.2	.1			.2	.1
	.8	1.5	1.0	.3	.3			.4	.3
Debt/Worth	.1	1.0	1.3	3.5	2.4			.7	.9
	.3	3.3	2.1	11.0	18.7			4.3	2.4
	1.5	5.3	6.1	16.0	39.3			9.3	5.9
% Profit Before Taxes/Tangible Net Worth	(18) 102.6	82.0	(25) 47.7	82.3				(61) 55.3	(64) 58.3
	38.4	40.9	19.7	48.8				26.5	24.4
	15.9	8.8	9.8	21.1				9.8	11.8
% Profit Before Taxes/Total Assets	87.9	26.7	11.1	8.1	7.7			12.2	21.3
	24.8	8.4	7.5	3.6	4.1			6.0	6.9
	7.2	2.0	2.3	2.0	1.9			1.0	1.2
Sales/Net Fixed Assets	57.2	UND	66.2	75.5	243.1			79.8	49.4
	28.1	44.5	22.0	28.9	41.3			20.7	24.2
	17.3	17.7	7.0	17.9	14.8			7.5	16.1
Sales/Total Assets	7.0	5.5	1.1	.6	.3			1.8	1.8
	4.6	2.3	.4	.4	.2			.4	.7
	2.1	.5	.2	.2	.1			.2	.2
% Depr., Dep., Amort./Sales	(15) .4		(18) .2	(18) .7				(47) .8	(51) .8
	.8		1.2	1.0				1.4	1.4
	1.4		1.7	1.6				2.5	2.0
% Officers', Directors', Owners' Comp/Sales								(10) 4.1	(18) 5.8
								10.2	10.8
								39.1	23.4
Net Sales ($)	20082M	65196M	131058M	222508M	168941M	182759M		942126M	379500M
Total Assets ($)	3985M	20640M	141237M	459946M	634189M	825672M		1452857M	781995M

© RMA 2003

M = $ thousand   MM = $ million
See Pages 11 through 18 for Explanation of Ratios and Data

Comparative Historical Data | Current Data Sorted By Sales

			Type of Statement						
31	36	60	Unqualified	9	15	7	11	13	5
3	7	7	Reviewed	2	2	1	2		
5	9	6	Compiled	3	2		1		
5	7	11	Tax Returns	9	2				
15	19	19	Other	4	5	2	2	3	3
4/1/00-3/31/01 ALL	4/1/01-3/31/02 ALL	4/1/02-3/31/03 ALL		19 (4/1-9/30/02)			84 (10/1/02-3/31/03)		
				0-1MM	1-3MM	3-5MM	5-10MM	10-25MM	25MM & OVER
59	78	103	**NUMBER OF STATEMENTS**	27	26	10	16	16	8
%	%	%	**ASSETS**	%	%	%	%	%	%
18.0	22.1	20.5	Cash & Equivalents	25.9	19.9	21.5	22.6	12.1	
22.4	27.2	24.2	Trade Receivables (net)	20.4	32.4	22.6	32.5	17.0	
7.1	8.0	5.0	Inventory	2.9	.0	7.9	4.8	11.8	
18.6	13.9	23.9	All Other Current	20.7	19.3	22.8	24.7	25.4	
66.1	71.2	73.6	Total Current	69.9	71.5	74.8	84.5	66.3	
16.8	13.4	13.0	Fixed Assets (net)	15.6	17.3	10.2	8.8	12.7	
2.1	1.5	1.2	Intangibles (net)	2.2	.4	.2	1.6	1.2	
15.0	13.9	12.2	All Other Non-Current	12.3	10.8	14.8	5.1	19.8	
100.0	100.0	100.0	Total	100.0	100.0	100.0	100.0	100.0	
			LIABILITIES						
41.0	32.5	37.3	Notes Payable-Short Term	25.8	33.6	45.3	41.7	47.7	
3.9	3.3	2.9	Cur. Mat.-L/T/D	6.3	2.2	2.8	1.2	1.4	
8.8	3.5	4.3	Trade Payables	1.9	3.6	2.7	4.5	8.1	
.2	.3	.8	Income Taxes Payable	.8	.2	.4	2.4	.2	
5.9	8.6	9.3	All Other Current	7.1	11.9	12.7	11.5	8.0	
59.8	48.2	54.6	Total Current	41.8	51.4	64.0	61.4	65.4	
13.8	11.9	9.6	Long Term Debt	11.1	5.3	3.3	12.9	15.9	
.1	.1	.2	Deferred Taxes	.5	.0	.5	.1	.0	
1.2	3.0	2.4	All Other Non-Current	.3	4.8	3.5	2.0	.8	
25.1	36.9	33.2	Net Worth	46.2	38.5	28.8	23.7	17.9	
100.0	100.0	100.0	Total Liabilities & Net Worth	100.0	100.0	100.0	100.0	100.0	
			INCOME DATA						
100.0	100.0	100.0	Net Sales	100.0	100.0	100.0	100.0	100.0	
			Gross Profit						
74.3	77.6	75.7	Operating Expenses	73.6	75.9	80.0	77.8	78.4	
25.7	22.4	24.3	Operating Profit	26.4	24.1	20.0	22.2	21.6	
10.7	7.9	5.2	All Other Expenses (net)	4.1	3.4	5.8	6.3	8.2	
15.0	14.5	19.1	Profit Before Taxes	22.3	20.7	14.2	15.8	13.4	
			RATIOS						
2.6	3.3	2.3		5.3	2.3	1.5	1.7	1.1	
1.4	1.5	1.3	Current	2.0	1.5	1.1	1.3	1.0	
1.1	1.0	1.0		1.2	1.1	.9	1.1	.7	
2.5	2.4	1.7		5.3	2.1	1.3	1.4	.9	
1.0 (76)	1.2	1.0	Quick	1.3	1.4	.7	1.1	.4	
.1	.2	.1		.3	.3	.1	.4	.0	
0 UND	0 UND	0 UND		0 UND	0 UND	0 UND	2 159.3	0 UND	
7 55.4	11 33.5	9 41.5	Sales/Receivables	0 UND	13 27.7	3 145.9	10 36.8	17 21.8	
108 3.4	150 2.4	97 3.7		51 7.1	219 1.7	242 1.5	338 1.1	45 8.1	
			Cost of Sales/Inventory						
			Cost of Sales/Payables						
2.8	2.4	1.5		.7	1.2	2.4	1.1	8.2	
8.2	7.1	7.4	Sales/Working Capital	6.1	4.8	4.8	6.0	14.5	
41.7	42.9	36.7		15.5	35.2	NM	55.6	−31.8	
7.0	20.0	9.8		14.4	12.9		56.6	5.4	
(40) 3.5	(55) 5.1	(69) 4.7	EBIT/Interest	(13) 4.7	(18) 6.6	(13) 4.6	(12) 3.3		
1.9	2.0	2.7		3.4	3.5	2.6	1.4		
		18.7	Net Profit + Depr., Dep.,						
	(12) 5.3		Amort./Cur. Mat. L/T/D						
		1.9							
.0	.0	.0		.0	.0	.0	.0	.0	
.1	.1	.1	Fixed/Worth	.0	.1	.1	.1	.3	
.6	.4	.4		.4	.6	.4	.6	1.2	
.9	.5	.9		.3	.7	1.3	2.2	3.6	
2.4	1.9	2.7	Debt/Worth	1.5	1.9	2.6	4.0	12.1	
6.0	8.7	10.2		5.0	6.5	9.8	9.8	22.2	
63.2	72.6	77.7		63.3	66.1	51.3	85.9	78.8	
(56) 21.7	(75) 33.5	(99) 32.7	% Profit Before Taxes/Tangible Net Worth	(24) 22.9	29.0	26.4	72.5	(15) 23.6	
6.1	17.2	15.5		9.7	15.0	17.6	25.3	3.4	
19.3	27.9	17.0		40.9	17.2	11.1	17.0	5.9	
5.7	7.8	6.9	% Profit Before Taxes/Total Assets	9.2	8.3	6.5	8.1	2.8	
1.4	2.6	2.6		2.9	3.0	2.4	4.4	.6	
60.6	85.6	107.7		587.0	64.2	70.8	106.8	UND	
26.5	35.0	30.1	Sales/Net Fixed Assets	38.0	28.3	22.8	42.5	27.0	
12.3	15.6	16.6		17.0	8.1	9.9	21.2	16.8	
2.3	3.3	2.5		4.5	2.5	1.8	4.0	1.2	
.8	.9	.6	Sales/Total Assets	1.4	.8	.4	.6	.3	
.3	.3	.2		.2	.2	.3	.4	.2	
.6	.5	.5		.3	.6		.6	.8	
(49) 1.1	(51) .9	(70) 1.0	% Depr., Dep., Amort./Sales	(15) .8	(18) 1.1	(14) 1.0	(10) 1.0		
2.3	2.1	1.6		1.3	1.7	1.3	2.1		
4.5	7.4	5.5							
(10) 8.6	(21) 13.3	(25) 14.2	% Officers', Directors', Owners' Comp/Sales						
18.9	31.2	24.3							
345572M	479686M	790544M	Net Sales ($)	13581M	48651M	40311M	112608M	231576M	343817M
684055M	1263898M	2085669M	Total Assets ($)	40151M	134508M	98693M	282773M	848178M	681366M

M = $ thousand   MM = $ million
See Pages 11 through 18 for Explanation of Ratios and Data

Current Data Sorted By Assets   Comparative Historical Data

0-500M	500M-2MM	2-10MM	10-50MM	50-100MM	100-250MM	Type of Statement	4/1/98-3/31/99 ALL	4/1/99-3/31/00 ALL
2	2	4	4	1	1	Unqualified	25	11
1	2	2				Reviewed	1	3
1	2	1				Compiled	3	5
1	1					Tax Returns	5	2
2	1	3	5	2		Other	6	8
	2 (4/1-9/30/02)		37 (10/1/02-3/31/03)					
7	9	10	9	3	1	NUMBER OF STATEMENTS	40	29
%	%	%	%	%	%	ASSETS	%	%
		51.1				Cash & Equivalents	53.1	37.7
		6.4				Trade Receivables (net)	14.4	18.2
		.5				Inventory	1.7	2.3
		3.2				All Other Current	3.2	4.5
		61.3				Total Current	72.4	62.7
		15.9				Fixed Assets (net)	13.9	18.0
		3.4				Intangibles (net)	6.3	11.2
		19.4				All Other Non-Current	7.4	8.0
		100.0				Total	100.0	100.0
						LIABILITIES		
		11.1				Notes Payable-Short Term	21.3	20.2
		1.5				Cur. Mat.-L/T/D	1.9	2.7
		8.4				Trade Payables	15.9	12.4
		.8				Income Taxes Payable	.2	.2
		3.0				All Other Current	16.9	9.8
		24.7				Total Current	56.3	45.2
		4.6				Long Term Debt	14.5	15.3
		.0				Deferred Taxes	.1	.8
		13.8				All Other Non-Current	10.8	3.4
		57.0				Net Worth	18.3	35.3
		100.0				Total Liabilities & Net Worth	100.0	100.0
						INCOME DATA		
		100.0				Net Sales	100.0	100.0
						Gross Profit		
		84.7				Operating Expenses	86.3	81.4
		15.3				Operating Profit	13.7	18.6
		3.1				All Other Expenses (net)	3.4	4.4
		12.2				Profit Before Taxes	10.3	14.2
						RATIOS		
		38.3				Current	1.8	2.2
		2.1					1.2	1.5
		1.7					1.1	1.1
		38.2				Quick	1.7	2.1
		2.1					1.2	1.2
		1.5					1.0	.9
	0	UND				Sales/Receivables	0 UND	0 UND
	0	744.2					4 81.2	16 22.3
	28	12.8					50 7.3	45 8.1
						Cost of Sales/Inventory		
						Cost of Sales/Payables		
		1.7				Sales/Working Capital	3.5	2.4
		3.6					7.9	4.6
		NM					16.1	50.0
						EBIT/Interest	(35) 11.3	(23) 20.6
							4.8	4.3
							1.1	1.1
						Net Profit + Depr., Dep., Amort./Cur. Mat. L /T/D	(10) 18.0	
							5.3	
							.7	
		.1				Fixed/Worth	.1	.1
		.3					.7	.6
		.6					2.9	NM
		.2				Debt/Worth	1.7	1.1
		.8					5.9	3.7
		2.8					18.3	NM
		31.9				% Profit Before Taxes/Tangible Net Worth	(32) 60.7	(22) 63.3
		22.7					29.1	28.6
		−1.4					.9	2.4
		18.8				% Profit Before Taxes/Total Assets	19.7	19.2
		13.3					5.2	6.9
		−1.3					.1	.5
		73.7				Sales/Net Fixed Assets	30.1	14.8
		8.3					8.7	8.3
		3.4					4.7	4.4
		1.5				Sales/Total Assets	1.5	1.7
		.8					1.0	.9
		.4					.7	.6
		.2				% Depr., Dep., Amort./Sales	(31) 2.3	(16) 1.2
		1.6					3.4	2.0
		6.4					5.3	4.4
						% Officers', Directors', Owners' Comp/Sales	(13) 3.7	(12) 2.6
							8.6	6.6
							23.5	20.6
3962M	14512M	48999M	217250M	165232M	11294M	Net Sales ($)	1857310M	657282M
1914M	9806M	40103M	206398M	206036M	191540M	Total Assets ($)	861850M	820372M

M = $ thousand   MM = $ million
See Pages 11 through 18 for Explanation of Ratios and Data

Comparative Historical Data / Current Data Sorted By Sales

			Type of Statement						
16	10	14	Unqualified	2	7	3	1	1	
3	3	5	Reviewed	2	1	1	1		
1	8	4	Compiled	1	2		1		
	2	3	Tax Returns	2	1				
6	15	13	Other	2	2		1	2	6
4/1/00-3/31/01	4/1/01-3/31/02	4/1/02-3/31/03			2 (4/1-9/30/02)		37 (10/1/02-3/31/03)		
ALL	ALL	ALL		0-1MM	1-3MM	3-5MM	5-10MM	10-25MM	25MM & OVER
26	38	39	**NUMBER OF STATEMENTS**	9	13	4	4	3	6
%	%	%	**ASSETS**	%	%	%	%	%	%
37.4	36.3	47.2	Cash & Equivalents		42.3				
31.1	22.2	16.2	Trade Receivables (net)		17.0				
1.6	2.0	.2	Inventory		.0				
2.8	4.4	9.4	All Other Current		13.3				
72.9	64.9	73.0	Total Current		72.7				
12.6	14.5	11.7	Fixed Assets (net)		12.6				
7.0	4.5	5.0	Intangibles (net)		2.5				
7.5	16.1	10.3	All Other Non-Current		12.2				
100.0	100.0	100.0	Total		100.0				
			LIABILITIES						
29.6	14.5	18.1	Notes Payable-Short Term		20.2				
1.8	1.5	3.4	Cur. Mat.-L/T/D		3.2				
11.5	17.0	8.4	Trade Payables		3.6				
.1	.0	.2	Income Taxes Payable		.0				
14.9	15.0	9.1	All Other Current		7.2				
58.0	48.0	39.2	Total Current		34.2				
13.7	12.6	8.7	Long Term Debt		15.2				
.8	.0	.0	Deferred Taxes		.0				
7.3	13.2	10.9	All Other Non-Current		14.3				
20.2	26.2	41.2	Net Worth		36.3				
100.0	100.0	100.0	Total Liabilities & Net Worth		100.0				
			INCOME DATA						
100.0	100.0	100.0	Net Sales		100.0				
			Gross Profit						
82.0	80.1	80.9	Operating Expenses		78.1				
18.0	19.9	19.1	Operating Profit		21.9				
9.8	7.4	5.9	All Other Expenses (net)		8.3				
8.2	12.6	13.3	Profit Before Taxes		13.5				
			RATIOS						
1.5	2.6	3.6			3.8				
1.2	1.3	1.9	Current		2.4				
1.0	1.0	1.2			1.5				
1.5	2.3	3.4			3.5				
1.2	1.2	1.6	Quick		1.9				
1.0	.9	1.0			.9				
0 UND	0 UND	0 UND		0 UND					
24 15.0	9 42.3	1 488.5	Sales/Receivables	9 39.2					
2000 .2	114 3.2	51 7.2		48 7.5					
			Cost of Sales/Inventory						
			Cost of Sales/Payables						
1.0	3.8	1.9			2.1				
4.3	6.4	3.6	Sales/Working Capital		2.6				
84.2	-190.1	8.8			NM				
6.7	6.8	10.3							
(15) 2.4	(22) 2.8	(27) 6.5	EBIT/Interest						
.4	.3	2.2							
			Net Profit + Depr., Dep., Amort./Cur. Mat. L/T/D						
.1	.1	.0			.1				
.5	.4	.2	Fixed/Worth		.3				
6.3	2.2	.7			.7				
3.1	1.3	.8			.8				
5.8	3.5	1.9	Debt/Worth		2.0				
46.2	13.0	4.3			14.3				
42.0	63.5	57.3			73.0				
(21) 9.4	(33) 23.5	(38) 30.4	% Profit Before Taxes/Tangible Net Worth		36.9				
-1.3	8.7	16.2			18.1				
7.9	12.4	18.2			21.1				
1.8	5.9	11.6	% Profit Before Taxes/Total Assets		11.7				
-.5	.7	2.4			1.6				
15.9	36.4	92.6			122.8				
8.4	12.8	17.6	Sales/Net Fixed Assets		17.6				
5.2	7.7	7.0			5.9				
1.2	1.6	1.6			1.7				
.7	1.1	1.1	Sales/Total Assets		1.3				
.1	.3	.5			.4				
1.6	.4	.9							
(18) 3.6	(24) 1.8	(28) 2.4	% Depr., Dep., Amort./Sales						
4.9	4.4	4.7							
10.6	3.7	10.0							
(10) 26.4	(10) 15.0	(14) 18.7	% Officers', Directors', Owners' Comp/Sales						
37.7	26.5	23.3							
474924M	846763M	461249M	Net Sales ($)	3962M	23652M	15252M	26145M	41563M	350675M
1265405M	1124649M	655797M	Total Assets ($)	5821M	44690M	35339M	75503M	214290M	280154M

M = $ thousand   MM = $ million
See Pages 11 through 18 for Explanation of Ratios and Data

Current Data Sorted By Assets | | | Comparative Historical Data

0-500M	500M-2MM	2-10MM	10-50MM	50-100MM	100-250MM	Type of Statement		
5	5	19	16	2	13	Unqualified	65	59
		3	1			Reviewed	9	10
7	2	7	3			Compiled	7	14
15	5	3			2	Tax Returns	12	14
5	9	7	2		5	Other	38	29
	28 (4/1-9/30/02)			108 (10/1/02-3/31/03)			4/1/98-3/31/99	4/1/99-3/31/00
							ALL	ALL
32	21	39	22	2	20	**NUMBER OF STATEMENTS**	131	126
%	%	%	%	%	%	**ASSETS**	%	%
33.5	25.6	32.1	34.6		29.3	Cash & Equivalents	24.8	26.1
3.6	14.1	29.2	11.6		32.6	Trade Receivables (net)	23.2	22.7
.0	1.5	6.3	11.2		4.8	Inventory	3.9	4.9
8.9	12.6	6.4	20.4		11.4	All Other Current	8.3	8.4
46.0	53.8	73.9	77.8		78.2	Total Current	60.2	62.1
39.4	23.5	8.6	11.4		5.3	Fixed Assets (net)	17.6	17.2
3.1	4.5	2.4	1.2		3.5	Intangibles (net)	4.0	3.9
11.5	18.2	15.1	9.5		13.0	All Other Non-Current	18.1	16.8
100.0	100.0	100.0	100.0		100.0	Total	100.0	100.0
						LIABILITIES		
37.1	4.1	17.8	9.0		28.9	Notes Payable-Short Term	12.5	12.5
11.5	9.2	2.1	.8		.6	Cur. Mat.-L/T/D	1.9	3.9
3.7	5.4	9.8	22.7		18.5	Trade Payables	12.0	9.8
.0	.8	.3	.0		.0	Income Taxes Payable	.3	1.1
27.5	21.4	18.8	22.5		22.3	All Other Current	14.9	25.3
79.7	41.0	48.9	55.0		70.2	Total Current	41.7	52.6
22.2	21.1	6.0	5.1		11.3	Long Term Debt	16.2	15.4
.0	.0	.3	.3		.0	Deferred Taxes	.3	.4
11.4	9.3	4.3	1.6		4.5	All Other Non-Current	3.4	3.6
−13.2	28.7	40.4	38.2		14.0	Net Worth	38.4	27.9
100.0	100.0	100.0	100.0		100.0	Total Liabilities & Net Worth	100.0	100.0
						INCOME DATA		
100.0	100.0	100.0	100.0		100.0	Net Sales	100.0	100.0
						Gross Profit		
91.0	87.6	79.6	81.5		88.4	Operating Expenses	87.5	86.6
9.0	12.4	20.4	18.5		11.6	Operating Profit	12.5	13.4
1.1	.3	2.2	2.5		1.8	All Other Expenses (net)	−45.9	2.6
7.9	12.1	18.2	16.0		9.8	Profit Before Taxes	58.4	10.8
						RATIOS		
2.5	3.4	3.3	2.0		1.3		2.6	2.6
.9	1.9	1.9	1.3		1.1	Current	1.5	1.3
.4	.4	1.1	1.1		.9		1.0	.9
2.4	2.8	2.8	1.6		1.2		2.2	1.8
(31) .9	1.3	1.3	1.0		.9	Quick	1.2	1.1
.4	.1	1.0	.1		.6		.6	.6
0 UND	0 UND	9 40.0	0 UND		16 23.5		0 UND	0 UND
0 UND	0 999.8	34 10.7	25 14.6		156 2.3	Sales/Receivables	33 11.1	30 12.3
0 UND	28 13.0	95 3.8	67 5.4		558 .7		135 2.7	70 5.2
						Cost of Sales/Inventory		
						Cost of Sales/Payables		
16.0	3.0	2.3	2.2		2.1		2.4	3.2
−187.0	16.0	5.2	4.6		4.1	Sales/Working Capital	6.8	13.9
−20.3	−33.3	87.0	11.7		−20.9		140.1	−55.5
29.6	9.5	75.0	4.7		14.4		24.8	14.2
(24) 3.5	(13) 3.3	(27) 6.2	(15) 2.9		(16) 3.7	EBIT/Interest	(84) 5.1	(83) 5.0
.5	2.2	1.5	1.5		2.3		1.8	1.0
						Net Profit + Depr., Dep., Amort./Cur. Mat. L /T/D		2.3
							(10)	.2
								−.6
.2	.0	.0	.0		.0		.0	.0
1.8	1.0	.1	.0		.1	Fixed/Worth	.1	.1
−4.1	30.0	.3	.7		.8		.7	1.0
.6	.5	.5	1.0		3.5		.5	.6
3.5	5.7	1.2	2.4		5.8	Debt/Worth	1.6	1.8
−5.1	58.6	10.0	5.1		20.2		6.5	6.0
247.3	226.4	82.5	44.3		46.2	% Profit Before Taxes/Tangible Net Worth	39.8	53.9
(21) 25.9	(17) 119.7	(33) 19.9	(21) 10.3		(17) 20.5		(118) 21.1	(111) 22.7
−48.9	2.9	2.6	1.9		13.7		6.6	.7
125.2	38.5	44.9	9.5		11.8	% Profit Before Taxes/Total Assets	17.2	18.9
11.5	10.4	6.6	2.0		3.8		5.4	6.2
−4.7	1.9	.9	.7		1.3		.8	.0
86.7	97.5	140.3	139.7		45.6	Sales/Net Fixed Assets	81.7	118.3
49.5	26.9	38.1	50.8		28.8		22.8	32.2
13.9	10.7	18.9	13.0		11.9		8.6	10.6
25.1	5.2	3.2	1.2		2.0	Sales/Total Assets	2.2	4.1
11.6	3.3	2.0	.8		.4		.6	1.4
4.7	1.1	.7	.6		.2		.2	.5
1.1	.8	.6	.4		1.2	% Depr., Dep., Amort./Sales	1.0	.6
(21) 1.5	(15) 1.7	(28) 1.0	(20) .8		(13) 2.3		(90) 1.8	(86) 1.5
3.0	3.2	1.7	2.4		3.5		4.2	3.2
10.5						% Officers', Directors', Owners' Comp/Sales	7.0	4.6
(18) 33.3							(25) 18.4	(32) 13.9
37.8							25.2	29.3
77801M	100373M	479107M	424926M	7028M	7536161M	Net Sales ($)	3136920M	4402048M
6482M	27222M	198362M	509251M	146601M	3508276M	Total Assets ($)	4123270M	3859721M

M = $ thousand   MM = $ million
See Pages 11 through 18 for Explanation of Ratios and Data

Comparative Historical Data   **Current Data Sorted By Sales**

4/1/00-3/31/01 ALL	4/1/01-3/31/02 ALL	4/1/02-3/31/03 ALL	Type of Statement	28 (4/1-9/30/02) 0-1MM	1-3MM	3-5MM	108 (10/1/02-3/31/03) 5-10MM	10-25MM	25MM & OVER
58	43	60	Unqualified	2	7	8	14	13	16
6	7	4	Reviewed		2	1			1
10	19	19	Compiled	5	6	3	1	4	
24	18	25	Tax Returns	6	5	4	2	4	4
33	41	28	Other	5	7	1	4	4	7
131	128	136	**NUMBER OF STATEMENTS**	18	27	17	21	25	28
%	%	%	**ASSETS**	%	%	%	%	%	%
28.3	32.6	31.0	Cash & Equivalents	33.1	37.4	35.6	18.8	25.3	34.8
19.3	17.4	18.1	Trade Receivables (net)	7.5	5.0	18.3	17.0	27.1	30.0
4.0	3.5	4.5	Inventory	.8	.7	6.3	10.3	3.4	6.2
11.7	11.9	11.9	All Other Current	15.5	5.9	5.3	29.0	12.4	6.0
63.3	65.3	65.5	Total Current	57.0	49.1	65.6	75.1	68.2	77.0
19.1	17.6	18.0	Fixed Assets (net)	33.6	20.4	18.6	13.0	19.4	7.7
4.0	3.9	2.8	Intangibles (net)	2.7	1.8	7.2	1.4	1.1	3.7
13.6	13.2	13.7	All Other Non-Current	6.7	28.7	8.6	10.4	11.2	11.6
100.0	100.0	100.0	Total	100.0	100.0	100.0	100.0	100.0	100.0
			LIABILITIES						
13.2	13.9	20.6	Notes Payable-Short Term	59.5	11.8	7.2	11.2	10.5	28.4
2.0	2.2	5.0	Cur. Mat.-L/T/D	6.3	6.9	3.5	6.9	5.2	1.9
9.5	10.8	10.9	Trade Payables	6.4	3.6	9.8	13.8	13.6	16.9
.4	.3	.2	Income Taxes Payable	.0	.6	.2	.3	.0	.2
19.5	25.2	22.1	All Other Current	19.9	24.1	18.0	27.6	22.5	19.8
44.6	52.4	58.9	Total Current	92.1	47.0	38.6	59.6	51.7	67.3
18.0	12.5	13.3	Long Term Debt	23.2	23.9	7.2	11.0	6.9	8.1
.1	.1	.1	Deferred Taxes	.0	.1	.4	.0	.2	.0
4.8	7.2	6.3	All Other Non-Current	18.5	6.6	4.9	6.2	3.0	2.1
32.4	27.7	21.3	Net Worth	−33.7	22.5	48.9	23.1	38.1	22.6
100.0	100.0	100.0	Total Liabilities & Net Worth	100.0	100.0	100.0	100.0	100.0	100.0
			INCOME DATA						
100.0	100.0	100.0	Net Sales	100.0	100.0	100.0	100.0	100.0	100.0
			Gross Profit						
85.0	83.4	84.4	Operating Expenses	78.3	80.1	83.1	95.1	79.3	89.9
15.0	16.6	15.6	Operating Profit	21.7	19.9	16.9	4.9	20.7	10.1
2.5	5.7	1.9	All Other Expenses (net)	3.7	3.1	2.4	.7	1.9	.4
12.5	10.9	13.6	Profit Before Taxes	18.0	16.8	14.5	4.3	18.8	9.7
			RATIOS						
2.9	3.0	2.7		3.7	2.9	4.2	3.3	2.8	1.5
1.3	1.4	1.3	Current	1.7	1.2	1.9	1.4	1.2	1.1
.9	.9	.8		.6	.3	1.0	1.0	.8	.9
2.4	2.4	1.9		2.9	2.4	3.5	2.6	2.2	1.3
(130) 1.1	(127) 1.2	(135) 1.1	Quick	1.2	1.1	1.3	(20) .8	1.1	1.0
.5	.4	.3		.1	.2	.8	.1	.3	.7
0 UND	0 UND	0 UND		0 UND	0 UND	0 UND	0 UND	0 UND	11 33.1
11 33.0	13 27.5	10 38.3	Sales/Receivables	0 UND	0 UND	9 40.0	24 15.0	50 7.3	31 11.8
69 5.3	55 6.7	65 5.6		0 UND	4 101.4	67 5.5	37 9.9	89 4.1	166 2.2
			Cost of Sales/Inventory						
			Cost of Sales/Payables						
2.7	2.5	3.1		4.6	2.3	2.1	3.7	3.0	3.1
8.0	7.7	10.7	Sales/Working Capital	23.6	96.1	9.3	5.4	9.1	16.7
−111.7	−178.0	−59.5		−25.0	−13.6	−607.1	NM	NM	−20.9
14.1	18.0	17.4		15.6	32.5		5.1	56.1	17.0
(83) 3.8	(80) 4.6	(95) 3.8	EBIT/Interest	(15) 5.7	(18) 9.2		(15) 2.0	(16) 2.7	(24) 4.2
1.3	1.2	1.5		.0	1.0		.8	1.5	2.4
31.4	7.5		Net Profit + Depr., Dep.,						
(12) 8.4	(15) 4.2		Amort./Cur. Mat. L/T/D						
−.2	.3								
.0	.0	.0		.0	.0	.0	.0	.0	.1
.2	.2	.2	Fixed/Worth	1.4	.1	.2	.2	.3	.1
1.2	1.6	2.1		NM	2.1	1.4	16.0	2.4	.8
.6	.6	.7		.6	.4	.4	.9	.3	1.7
2.0	1.9	3.0	Debt/Worth	5.2	4.7	1.2	4.0	2.5	3.8
9.2	10.2	23.8		NM	190.0	3.5	NM	15.7	10.7
70.2	59.2	83.9		324.3	70.7	136.5	34.2	166.1	47.5
(115) 26.3	(109) 27.0	(111) 23.6	% Profit Before Taxes/Tangible Net Worth	(14) 29.1	(21) 27.0	(15) 23.8	(16) 12.7	(22) 44.3	(23) 19.7
3.9	3.2	2.9		−33.7	2.5	−6.3	2.7	2.1	10.3
19.4	19.9	26.6		49.3	34.8	54.7	9.1	80.8	14.0
6.5	4.8	4.6	% Profit Before Taxes/Total Assets	10.8	7.6	10.6	4.5	4.1	4.0
.2	.5	.8		−4.1	.7	−6.5	.4	1.3	1.3
99.7	107.4	107.8		UND	136.8	68.9	117.1	141.2	96.5
34.5	33.3	36.0	Sales/Net Fixed Assets	48.1	32.2	55.4	38.1	28.8	33.3
10.2	10.4	15.0		7.9	9.6	17.7	19.9	9.4	17.7
3.7	4.0	5.7		12.5	6.1	8.2	4.2	5.7	4.8
1.5	1.6	2.0	Sales/Total Assets	3.5	1.2	2.9	2.0	1.9	1.2
.4	.6	.7		.9	.3	.9	.7	.8	.3
.6	.6	.7			.7	.7	.5	.6	.4
(103) 1.3	(83) 1.1	(98) 1.3	% Depr., Dep., Amort./Sales		(20) 1.7	(12) 1.2	(16) .9	(20) 1.6	(21) 1.3
3.9	2.6	2.5			3.0	1.5	2.4	3.0	2.0
6.9	4.6	9.7			11.1				
(32) 16.7	(37) 11.3	(44) 25.6	% Officers', Directors', Owners' Comp/Sales		(10) 33.8				
26.4	22.6	36.2			43.1				
2600797M	3604536M	8625396M	Net Sales ($)	12041M	46528M	70749M	142502M	429595M	7923981M
3703054M	3685103M	4396194M	Total Assets ($)	54918M	124428M	135010M	264498M	612739M	3204601M

M = $ thousand   MM = $ million
See Pages 11 through 18 for Explanation of Ratios and Data

Current Data Sorted By Assets   Comparative Historical Data

Type of Statement	0-500M	500M-2MM	2-10MM	10-50MM	50-100MM	100-250MM	4/1/98-3/31/99 ALL	4/1/99-3/31/00 ALL
Unqualified	2	4	6	16	4	7	24	24
Reviewed			10	4	2	1	10	13
Compiled	1	5	11	6	1		19	17
Tax Returns	7	12	7	2			19	17
Other	7	14	22	14	3	2	45	44
		22 (4/1-9/30/02)		148 (10/1/02-3/31/03)				
NUMBER OF STATEMENTS	17	35	56	42	10	10	117	115
ASSETS	%	%	%	%	%	%	%	%
Cash & Equivalents	9.2	19.2	10.1	14.5	10.3	10.7	17.0	10.7
Trade Receivables (net)	19.2	8.5	8.6	13.6	4.2	14.8	10.5	14.9
Inventory	1.4	2.5	10.9	8.6	4.1	1.8	4.6	4.6
All Other Current	6.8	5.5	4.9	7.4	5.3	4.9	4.8	5.8
Total Current	36.7	35.7	34.5	44.1	24.0	32.3	36.9	35.9
Fixed Assets (net)	46.3	48.5	47.1	22.4	29.5	25.4	31.2	33.2
Intangibles (net)	3.3	4.4	5.0	3.2	.6	18.8	4.0	5.9
All Other Non-Current	13.7	11.4	13.3	30.3	45.9	23.5	27.9	25.0
Total	100.0	100.0	100.0	100.0	100.0	100.0	100.0	100.0
LIABILITIES								
Notes Payable-Short Term	17.2	13.4	13.9	19.9	11.3	15.2	11.4	15.3
Cur. Mat.-L/T/D	11.6	1.4	2.8	1.2	2.7	2.4	3.5	5.1
Trade Payables	17.1	5.5	4.5	7.5	1.7	3.5	2.8	7.1
Income Taxes Payable	.0	.1	.2	.2	1.1	.3	.2	.1
All Other Current	12.4	8.0	7.2	7.3	2.8	2.3	8.1	8.5
Total Current	58.3	28.3	28.7	36.0	19.5	23.6	25.9	36.1
Long Term Debt	29.4	41.8	38.4	32.9	38.6	26.9	27.5	24.1
Deferred Taxes	.0	.0	.3	.0	.2	1.3	.6	.4
All Other Non-Current	7.1	8.4	5.6	4.2	1.0	.6	4.4	5.9
Net Worth	5.1	21.4	27.0	26.9	40.7	47.5	41.5	33.4
Total Liabilities & Net Worth	100.0	100.0	100.0	100.0	100.0	100.0	100.0	100.0
INCOME DATA								
Net Sales	100.0	100.0	100.0	100.0	100.0	100.0	100.0	100.0
Gross Profit								
Operating Expenses	74.4	65.9	62.2	71.7	78.9	70.6	92.8	67.2
Operating Profit	25.6	34.1	37.8	28.3	21.1	29.4	7.2	32.8
All Other Expenses (net)	10.3	18.7	16.6	13.2	1.0	14.9	−136.6	6.9
Profit Before Taxes	15.3	15.4	21.2	15.2	20.0	14.5	143.8	25.9
RATIOS								
Current	1.5	2.1	3.3	2.3	5.9	2.9	4.7	2.8
	.6	1.2	1.6	1.2	1.2	1.6	1.4	1.1
	.2	.6	.6	1.0	.6	.9	.3	.3
Quick	1.5	1.8	1.9	2.1	5.1	2.7	3.0	2.1
	.4	1.0	.9	.7	.8	1.0	.8	.7
	.1	.2	.1	.2	.2	.3	.2	.1
Sales/Receivables	0 UND	0 UND	0 UND	0 UND	0 UND	0 UND	0 UND	0 UND
	0 UND	0 UND	0 UND	10 35.1	11 34.3	19 19.3	3 118.4	2 152.7
	5 77.3	16 23.2	14 26.5	58 6.3	55 6.6	42 8.8	43 8.5	40 9.1
Cost of Sales/Inventory								
Cost of Sales/Payables								
Sales/Working Capital	69.9	7.1	1.8	1.6	1.5	2.6	1.6	2.9
	−11.9	33.1	14.2	10.5	166.4	7.0	11.4	30.2
	−2.9	−5.2	−5.6	−75.2	−1.6	NM	−3.6	−3.5
EBIT/Interest	(12) 14.4	(14) 15.8	(30) 10.5	(27) 5.9			(52) 11.2	(66) 12.8
	4.5	8.3	5.5	1.8			4.4	4.0
	−2.4	1.8	2.2	.7			1.5	1.6
Net Profit + Depr., Dep., Amort./Cur. Mat. L /T/D			(10) 5.0					
			1.2					
			−.9					
Fixed/Worth	.9	.4	.1	.0	.0	.0	.0	.0
	3.4	2.2	1.6	.1	.4	.2	.2	.5
	−1.1	124.1	25.6	4.8	1.0	25.3	3.4	8.3
Debt/Worth	.9	1.7	.9	.7	.5	.4	.2	.5
	74.5	4.3	3.1	4.6	2.0	3.6	1.7	2.7
	−5.0	999.8	−54.9	14.9	6.7	NM	7.5	50.6
% Profit Before Taxes/Tangible Net Worth		116.1	43.5	35.6			39.7	41.7
		(27) 30.1	(41) 16.9	(34) 10.6			(98) 17.5	(90) 21.6
		3.7	5.5	1.5			3.0	9.0
% Profit Before Taxes/Total Assets	34.7	12.2	12.2	6.0	7.7	4.0	14.1	14.1
	13.6	3.5	5.4	2.9	2.9	3.4	4.3	5.9
	−11.2	.4	1.7	−.1	2.0	.0	1.1	1.8
Sales/Net Fixed Assets	61.4	19.7	32.7	999.8	UND	UND	UND	114.0
	8.4	.5	.6	37.4	2.8	15.0	13.0	9.6
	.6	.2	.2	1.6	.5	.5	.5	.5
Sales/Total Assets	5.6	3.1	.7	.7	.3	.4	.8	1.4
	1.7	.3	.3	.3	.2	.2	.2	.3
	.3	.1	.2	.1	.1	.1	.1	.2
% Depr., Dep., Amort./Sales	(11) 1.8	(32) 1.9	(43) 2.6	(25) .5			(68) 1.6	(74) 1.1
	3.9	5.0	9.6	2.2			7.1	5.5
	13.1	20.1	17.4	9.9			18.6	16.8
% Officers', Directors', Owners' Comp/Sales			(10) 1.0				(13) 2.8	(13) 1.1
			1.8				7.3	3.9
			9.6				18.3	16.1
Net Sales ($)	10797M	58666M	227187M	979514M	158704M	1127849M	818652M	2353070M
Total Assets ($)	5267M	42999M	295127M	1093780M	601672M	1405939M	2468607M	2965191M

Comparative Historical Data | Current Data Sorted By Sales

31	24	33	Type of Statement						
31	24	33	Unqualified	3	4	3	4	9	10
16	19	23	Reviewed	4	9	3	5	1	1
31	33	24	Compiled	9	6	3	3	1	2
19	22	28	Tax Returns	19	4	4	1		
55	47	62	Other	24	13	5	7	9	4
4/1/00-3/31/01 ALL	4/1/01-3/31/02 ALL	4/1/02-3/31/03 ALL		22 (4/1-9/30/02)			148 (10/1/02-3/31/03)		
				0-1MM	1-3MM	3-5MM	5-10MM	10-25MM	25MM & OVER
152	145	170	**NUMBER OF STATEMENTS**	59	36	18	20	20	17
%	%	%	**ASSETS**	%	%	%	%	%	%
12.7	11.0	13.0	Cash & Equivalents	10.3	17.8	12.5	18.6	9.1	11.0
14.5	11.7	11.0	Trade Receivables (net)	7.2	6.0	24.5	13.0	11.8	16.9
5.9	4.8	6.8	Inventory	.5	7.9	11.9	10.6	11.9	10.1
5.0	7.3	5.9	All Other Current	5.9	3.2	7.6	6.6	8.0	6.1
38.1	34.8	36.6	Total Current	23.9	34.9	56.6	48.8	40.7	44.2
32.2	38.3	38.9	Fixed Assets (net)	60.1	38.5	17.1	15.5	26.3	31.5
3.9	5.1	4.8	Intangibles (net)	1.5	3.1	4.2	9.7	5.7	13.9
25.8	21.9	19.7	All Other Non-Current	14.5	23.5	22.1	26.0	27.3	10.4
100.0	100.0	100.0	Total	100.0	100.0	100.0	100.0	100.0	100.0
			LIABILITIES						
13.4	36.4	15.5	Notes Payable-Short Term	12.1	18.9	15.8	15.2	22.6	11.9
4.4	5.8	3.0	Cur. Mat.-L/T/D	2.8	4.6	4.1	2.0	1.0	2.3
4.2	4.3	6.5	Trade Payables	5.2	2.7	11.1	6.8	8.5	11.5
.1	.2	.2	Income Taxes Payable	.2	.0	.1	.6	.0	.5
8.9	10.7	7.3	All Other Current	5.7	12.1	4.1	6.7	7.4	7.0
31.1	57.4	32.6	Total Current	26.0	38.4	35.3	31.3	39.5	33.1
27.7	31.5	36.2	Long Term Debt	48.0	29.4	30.8	34.7	13.3	43.9
.6	.1	.2	Deferred Taxes	.0	.2	.0	.5	.0	.8
6.8	4.3	5.4	All Other Non-Current	6.5	5.1	2.2	3.4	9.7	3.2
33.8	6.7	25.7	Net Worth	19.5	26.8	31.7	30.1	37.5	19.0
100.0	100.0	100.0	Total Liabilities & Net Worth	100.0	100.0	100.0	100.0	100.0	100.0
			INCOME DATA						
100.0	100.0	100.0	Net Sales	100.0	100.0	100.0	100.0	100.0	100.0
63.3	65.1	68.0	Gross Profit						
63.3	65.1	68.0	Operating Expenses	49.9	70.9	72.5	84.9	79.4	86.5
36.7	34.9	32.0	Operating Profit	50.1	29.1	27.5	15.1	20.6	13.5
13.4	14.8	14.5	All Other Expenses (net)	26.1	11.1	16.6	5.7	4.1	2.3
23.3	20.0	17.5	Profit Before Taxes	24.0	18.0	11.0	9.3	16.5	11.2
			RATIOS						
2.9	2.2	2.3		2.0	2.8	5.1	2.0	2.1	2.0
1.1	1.0	1.2	Current	.9	1.1	2.2	1.3	1.1	1.2
.5	.3	.6		.3	.5	1.2	1.0	.7	.8
2.3	1.5	1.8		1.8	2.0	4.5	1.3	1.7	1.5
.7	.4	.8	Quick	.6	.8	1.2	1.0	.6	.7
.1	.1	.2		.1	.1	.7	.5	.1	.3
0 UND	0 UND	0 UND		0 UND	0 UND	1 467.4	0 UND	0 UND	6 59.3
3 131.0	0 UND	1 635.0	Sales/Receivables	0 UND	0 UND	13 29.0	8 46.2	12 30.1	24 15.1
44 8.3	30 12.3	31 11.9		0 UND	12 30.1	53 6.9	53 6.9	70 5.2	44 8.4
			Cost of Sales/Inventory						
			Cost of Sales/Payables						
2.4	2.5	2.7		1.8	2.8	1.2	2.0	7.1	6.2
23.7	254.7	22.0	Sales/Working Capital	−58.0	14.4	4.8	13.6	15.2	38.1
−4.2	−2.8	−5.5		−3.2	−3.2	16.1	NM	−29.2	NM
	16.6	10.9		9.0	10.3	21.0	6.1	18.3	12.2
(81) 6.9 2.6	(74) 3.7	(96) 3.6	EBIT/Interest	(20) 5.6	(21) 4.4	(10) 6.9	(15) 2.4	2.9	4.0
.9	1.1	1.6		.1	1.3	.3	1.4	1.7	(15) 1.7
6.5		6.9	Net Profit + Depr., Dep.,						
(14) 1.8	(19)	2.2	Amort./Cur. Mat. L/T/D						
.5		.6							
.0	.0	.0		.8	.1	.0	.0	.0	.1
.4	1.1	1.0	Fixed/Worth	4.1	.9	.2	.1	.4	.8
4.5	8.9	10.2		−162.5	3.0	.9	3.6	2.9	NM
.6	.9	1.0		.9	1.0	.7	1.2	.4	.9
2.3	3.2	3.9	Debt/Worth	11.3	2.1	3.8	3.3	4.4	5.0
12.0	394.0	NM		−24.9	−128.7	40.1	17.2	7.8	−8.3
38.1	38.8	51.5	% Profit Before Taxes/Tangible	45.6	42.9	59.0	58.0	62.2	75.6
(126) 13.4	(111) 13.3	(128) 15.7	Net Worth	(42) 16.0	(26) 16.8	(15) 18.5	(16) 12.8	(17) 14.5	(12) 20.6
2.5	2.5	3.7		3.1	2.2	.0	7.4	7.6	4.2
11.5	12.1	11.2	% Profit Before Taxes/Total	6.9	17.6	12.0	7.9	15.1	15.5
3.9	4.2	3.7	Assets	3.0	6.1	2.2	3.9	6.0	3.6
.7	.7	.4		.0	.9	.7	1.6	1.0	2.1
323.2	76.5	86.3		2.3	67.2	UND	268.2	925.2	79.1
12.5	7.7	5.5	Sales/Net Fixed Assets	.3	6.0	33.0	30.5	28.0	13.0
.5	.3	.3		.2	.5	4.6	2.6	1.5	1.9
1.6	1.1	1.0		.3	1.6	3.1	1.4	1.6	5.2
.3	.3	.3	Sales/Total Assets	.2	.4	.4	.3	.5	1.3
.1	.1	.1		.1	.2	.1	.2	.2	.5
.5	1.0	1.5		9.9	1.8	.8	.2	.4	.6
(99) 2.7	(101) 3.9	(124) 5.3	% Depr., Dep., Amort./Sales	(44) 16.0	(27) 4.0	(11) 1.6	(15) 2.6	(14) 2.2	(13) 1.5
11.9	13.5	14.5		23.3	9.9	11.0	6.5	6.1	4.4
2.7	6.2	1.5	% Officers', Directors',						
(29) 10.6	(21) 14.0	(31) 8.3	Owners' Comp/Sales						
18.9	30.8	14.0							
2906187M	2516188M	2562717M	Net Sales ($)	22641M	69717M	71436M	138454M	284168M	1976301M
3543389M	2964904M	3444784M	Total Assets ($)	186186M	294751M	369929M	553963M	848642M	1191313M

M = $ thousand   MM = $ million
See Pages 11 through 18 for Explanation of Ratios and Data

Current Data Sorted By Assets   Comparative Historical Data

0-500M	500M-2MM	2-10MM	10-50MM	50-100MM	100-250MM	Type of Statement	4/1/98-3/31/99 ALL	4/1/99-3/31/00 ALL
		6	2	1		Unqualified		
	1	2				Reviewed		
4		2				Compiled		
2	4	2	4	2		Tax Returns		
1						Other		
3 (4/1-9/30/02)			29 (10/1/02-3/31/03)					
7	5	10	7	3		NUMBER OF STATEMENTS		
%	%	%	%	%	%	**ASSETS**	%	%
		27.2				Cash & Equivalents		
		17.4				Trade Receivables (net)		
		1.1				Inventory		
		13.9				All Other Current		
		59.6				Total Current		
		20.2				Fixed Assets (net)		
		.1				Intangibles (net)		
		20.1				All Other Non-Current		
		100.0				Total		
						LIABILITIES		
		11.7				Notes Payable-Short Term		
		3.0				Cur. Mat.-L/T/D		
		3.0				Trade Payables		
		.1				Income Taxes Payable		
		15.7				All Other Current		
		33.5				Total Current		
		9.9				Long Term Debt		
		.2				Deferred Taxes		
		6.9				All Other Non-Current		
		49.5				Net Worth		
		100.0				Total Liabilities & Net Worth		
						INCOME DATA		
		100.0				Net Sales		
						Gross Profit		
		86.3				Operating Expenses		
		13.7				Operating Profit		
		2.5				All Other Expenses (net)		
		11.2				Profit Before Taxes		
						RATIOS		
		3.4				Current		
		1.9						
		1.1						
		3.1				Quick		
		1.7						
		.3						
		0 UND				Sales/Receivables		
		0 UND						
		44 8.3						
						Cost of Sales/Inventory		
						Cost of Sales/Payables		
		6.4				Sales/Working Capital		
		7.8						
		NM						
						EBIT/Interest		
						Net Profit + Depr., Dep., Amort./Cur. Mat. L /T/D		
		.0				Fixed/Worth		
		.3						
		1.0						
		.6				Debt/Worth		
		.8						
		2.3						
		92.4				% Profit Before Taxes/Tangible Net Worth		
		14.1						
		8.0						
		42.7				% Profit Before Taxes/Total Assets		
		7.9						
		2.6						
		216.4				Sales/Net Fixed Assets		
		27.9						
		6.8						
		3.3				Sales/Total Assets		
		2.6						
		.4						
						% Depr., Dep., Amort./Sales		
						% Officers', Directors', Owners' Comp/Sales		
7564M	3829M	95095M	142306M	549249M		Net Sales ($)		
2174M	6433M	48823M	184848M	228143M		Total Assets ($)		

(The columns 0-500M, 500M-2MM, 10-50MM, 50-100MM, 100-250MM and both Comparative Historical Data columns are marked "DATA NOT AVAILABLE" for the Assets, Liabilities and Income Data sections.)

M = $ thousand   MM = $ million
See Pages 11 through 18 for Explanation of Ratios and Data

Comparative Historical Data				Current Data Sorted By Sales					
			Type of Statement						
		9	Unqualified		2		2	2	3
		2	Reviewed	1	1				
		6	Compiled	3	1	1		1	
		2	Tax Returns	1	1				
		13	Other	4	3		2	3	1
4/1/00- 3/31/01 ALL	4/1/01- 3/31/02 ALL	4/1/02- 3/31/03 ALL			3 (4/1-9/30/02)		29 (10/1/02-3/31/03)		
				0-1MM	1-3MM	3-5MM	5-10MM	10-25MM	25MM & OVER
		32	**NUMBER OF STATEMENTS**	9	8	1	4	6	4
%	%	%	**ASSETS**	%	%	%	%	%	%
D	D	17.3	Cash & Equivalents						
A	A	9.7	Trade Receivables (net)						
T	T	1.1	Inventory						
A	A	5.9	All Other Current						
		34.1	Total Current						
N	N	30.2	Fixed Assets (net)						
O	O	2.5	Intangibles (net)						
T	T	33.2	All Other Non-Current						
		100.0	Total						
A	A		**LIABILITIES**						
V	V	22.1	Notes Payable-Short Term						
A	A	5.3	Cur. Mat.-L/T/D						
I	I	4.4	Trade Payables						
L	L	.1	Income Taxes Payable						
A	A	10.2	All Other Current						
B	B	42.1	Total Current						
L	L	19.8	Long Term Debt						
E	E	.1	Deferred Taxes						
		6.2	All Other Non-Current						
		31.8	Net Worth						
		100.0	Total Liabilities & Net Worth						
			INCOME DATA						
		100.0	Net Sales						
			Gross Profit						
		74.3	Operating Expenses						
		25.7	Operating Profit						
		8.2	All Other Expenses (net)						
		17.5	Profit Before Taxes						
			RATIOS						
		3.0							
		1.3	Current						
		.2							
		2.5							
		.6	Quick						
		.1							
	0	UND							
	0	UND	Sales/Receivables						
	21	17.5							
			Cost of Sales/Inventory						
			Cost of Sales/Payables						
		7.1							
		59.1	Sales/Working Capital						
		−3.0							
		21.0							
	(22)	4.6	EBIT/Interest						
		1.5							
			Net Profit + Depr., Dep., Amort./Cur. Mat. L/T/D						
		.0							
		.4	Fixed/Worth						
		3.3							
		.4							
		1.5	Debt/Worth						
		8.5							
		72.6							
	(27)	10.2	% Profit Before Taxes/Tangible Net Worth						
		2.7							
		20.2							
		4.5	% Profit Before Taxes/Total Assets						
		.1							
		310.3							
		25.4	Sales/Net Fixed Assets						
		.5							
		2.9							
		1.0	Sales/Total Assets						
		.2							
		1.1							
	(21)	5.0	% Depr., Dep., Amort./Sales						
		13.7							
			% Officers', Directors', Owners' Comp/Sales						
		798043M	Net Sales ($)	3520M	14111M	3079M	24964M	90645M	661724M
		470421M	Total Assets ($)	6770M	105169M	429M	51673M	115413M	190967M

M = $ thousand   MM = $ million
See Pages 11 through 18 for Explanation of Ratios and Data

Current Data Sorted By Assets   **Comparative Historical Data**

0-500M	500M-2MM	2-10MM	10-50MM	50-100MM	100-250MM	Type of Statement	4/1/98-3/31/99 ALL	4/1/99-3/31/00 ALL
1	5	11	8		5	Unqualified	38	44
	1	2	2			Reviewed	5	1
6	2	7	1			Compiled	10	13
8	1					Tax Returns	8	8
12	8	7	5	1	2	Other	28	29
27	14 (4/1-9/30/02) 17	27	81 (10/1/02-3/31/03) 16	1	7	**NUMBER OF STATEMENTS**	89	95
%	%	%	%	%	%	**ASSETS**	%	%
33.6	24.2	19.9	26.7			Cash & Equivalents	24.5	25.1
6.7	25.5	39.3	18.7			Trade Receivables (net)	20.4	19.8
.0	1.5	.1	3.8			Inventory	.5	2.5
6.6	4.4	3.4	2.7			All Other Current	9.9	4.9
46.9	55.5	62.7	51.9			Total Current	55.3	52.3
36.0	25.8	16.1	20.5			Fixed Assets (net)	19.4	21.7
6.9	3.8	7.8	9.2			Intangibles (net)	5.0	7.0
10.2	14.9	13.4	18.4			All Other Non-Current	20.4	19.0
100.0	100.0	100.0	100.0			Total	100.0	100.0
						LIABILITIES		
39.1	15.7	5.2	2.5			Notes Payable-Short Term	11.5	14.1
.0	8.1	4.9	4.9			Cur. Mat.-L/T/D	2.1	3.1
6.0	4.9	10.8	5.5			Trade Payables	5.7	6.9
.5	1.6	2.0	.3			Income Taxes Payable	.9	1.0
42.3	26.6	11.6	20.5			All Other Current	15.1	24.8
88.0	56.9	34.4	33.7			Total Current	35.3	49.9
5.6	12.3	10.2	10.8			Long Term Debt	15.2	11.3
.0	.9	.7	.1			Deferred Taxes	1.0	.3
8.0	1.3	9.0	4.1			All Other Non-Current	11.9	8.2
-1.5	28.6	45.7	51.2			Net Worth	36.5	30.3
100.0	100.0	100.0	100.0			Total Liabilities & Net Worth	100.0	100.0
						INCOME DATA		
100.0	100.0	100.0	100.0			Net Sales	100.0	100.0
						Gross Profit		
86.3	85.6	81.4	73.9			Operating Expenses	82.3	85.3
13.7	14.4	18.6	26.1			Operating Profit	17.7	14.7
.5	1.0	5.7	11.9			All Other Expenses (net)	-48.9	-1.2
13.1	13.4	12.9	14.1			Profit Before Taxes	66.6	15.9
						RATIOS		
2.8	2.4	3.2	9.5				3.9	2.7
.9	1.1	2.1	1.9			Current	1.7	1.3
.2	.5	1.0	.9				.7	.6
2.8	2.4	3.2	7.1				3.5	2.3
.6	1.0	2.0	1.2			Quick	1.5	1.1
.1	.3	1.0	.6				.4	.4
0 UND	2 197.1	17 21.0	2 238.2				0 UND	0 UND
0 UND	12 30.3	58 6.3	30 12.0			Sales/Receivables	15 25.0	12 30.8
3 110.2	70 5.2	91 4.0	52 7.1				66 5.5	58 6.3
						Cost of Sales/Inventory		
						Cost of Sales/Payables		
12.4	7.7	4.4	4.6				3.8	4.4
-519.0	139.8	6.6	9.2			Sales/Working Capital	10.5	22.1
-12.3	-18.3	622.8	NM				-44.5	-13.4
(19) 83.5	(11) 78.5	(22) 81.0					(49) 32.6	(56) 47.5
13.7	15.8	16.3				EBIT/Interest	7.8	5.6
-1.0	2.3	3.0					1.2	1.1
						Net Profit + Depr., Dep., Amort./Cur. Mat. L /T/D		6.9 (11) 2.1 1.4
.2	.1	.0	.1				.0	.1
1.1	.6	.2	.4			Fixed/Worth	.3	.4
-1.0	4.3	1.1	1.4				2.0	9.7
.6	.5	.3	.4				.4	.5
6.4	1.9	1.0	1.0			Debt/Worth	1.1	1.9
-2.6	6.8	6.7	3.0				15.5	148.8
(14) 131.0	(15) 138.2	(23) 91.3	(13) 126.5				(73) 87.2	(72) 90.4
68.5	50.4	58.0	66.4			% Profit Before Taxes/Tangible Net Worth	24.2	32.1
43.8	5.9	4.1	12.3				5.0	10.1
69.0	71.3	52.4	49.2				34.6	36.2
28.7	18.0	15.8	31.0			% Profit Before Taxes/Total Assets	8.8	9.5
9.7	2.1	.9	-1.3				1.3	1.5
70.7	71.0	112.5	37.6				86.1	68.8
26.1	28.3	32.0	23.0			Sales/Net Fixed Assets	25.0	27.5
12.4	6.4	11.0	6.3				11.0	9.2
15.5	5.9	3.4	2.5				3.2	3.7
6.8	2.6	2.4	2.1			Sales/Total Assets	2.2	2.1
3.5	2.0	1.5	1.3				.4	.9
(17) 1.1	(14) .6	(21) .5	(13) 1.1				(58) 1.1	(70) .7
1.7	1.2	1.2	1.4			% Depr., Dep., Amort./Sales	1.7	1.6
2.1	2.1	2.1	3.1				2.8	3.1
(12) 9.2							(17) 8.1	(12) 8.0
14.8						% Officers', Directors', Owners' Comp/Sales	15.1	20.1
26.5							26.1	37.2
37921M	82743M	386069M	914087M	162241M	649883M	Net Sales ($)	1599781M	1895824M
5475M	19918M	126287M	451652M	66602M	1116700M	Total Assets ($)	1827999M	1925660M

M = $ thousand   MM = $ million
See Pages 11 through 18 for Explanation of Ratios and Data

Comparative Historical Data | Current Data Sorted By Sales

4/1/00-3/31/01 ALL	4/1/01-3/31/02 ALL	4/1/02-3/31/03 ALL	Type of Statement	0-1MM	1-3MM	3-5MM	5-10MM	10-25MM	25MM & OVER
34	36	30	Unqualified	1	1	2	7	8	11
6	5	5	Reviewed		1	1	1	1	1
19	26	16	Compiled	2	4	3	4	1	2
8	8	9	Tax Returns	6	1	1	1		
26	31	35	Other	8	12	2	2	3	8
				14 (4/1-9/30/02)			81 (10/1/02-3/31/03)		
93	106	95	NUMBER OF STATEMENTS	17	19	9	15	13	22
%	%	%	**ASSETS**	%	%	%	%	%	%
19.0	23.8	27.8	Cash & Equivalents	37.7	26.6		20.9	21.1	36.1
22.5	20.8	22.3	Trade Receivables (net)	2.9	21.2		40.4	35.5	20.2
2.1	1.6	1.0	Inventory	.0	.0		.0	.3	2.8
7.3	8.1	4.2	All Other Current	7.4	8.7		1.8	1.3	2.3
51.0	54.3	55.2	Total Current	48.1	56.5		63.1	58.2	61.5
24.8	23.7	23.7	Fixed Assets (net)	32.7	24.2		21.3	17.3	15.4
8.3	8.2	6.8	Intangibles (net)	4.2	12.7		5.6	4.9	8.2
16.0	13.4	14.3	All Other Non-Current	15.1	6.6		10.0	19.6	14.9
100.0	100.0	100.0	Total	100.0	100.0		100.0	100.0	100.0
			LIABILITIES						
17.5	10.5	17.8	Notes Payable-Short Term	30.3	35.0		20.0	5.6	5.7
4.6	3.8	3.8	Cur. Mat.-L/T/D	5.1	.9		8.4	2.5	3.6
8.9	6.6	7.1	Trade Payables	4.1	5.8		11.7	4.8	10.5
.6	1.3	1.1	Income Taxes Payable	.0	1.8		3.3	.0	.4
15.6	21.0	25.2	All Other Current	48.8	29.1		10.6	16.6	25.6
47.2	43.2	55.1	Total Current	88.3	72.6		54.1	29.5	45.8
19.3	17.1	9.1	Long Term Debt	8.2	6.1		16.1	3.1	7.9
.7	.5	.4	Deferred Taxes	.0	.7		1.3	.0	.1
6.3	32.6	6.6	All Other Non-Current	9.0	4.3		3.1	13.9	6.5
26.5	6.5	28.9	Net Worth	−5.4	16.3		25.4	53.4	39.6
100.0	100.0	100.0	Total Liabilities & Net Worth	100.0	100.0		100.0	100.0	100.0
			INCOME DATA						
100.0	100.0	100.0	Net Sales	100.0	100.0		100.0	100.0	100.0
			Gross Profit						
84.7	80.4	82.0	Operating Expenses	77.6	90.2		85.8	71.8	82.1
15.3	19.5	18.0	Operating Profit	22.4	9.8		14.2	28.2	17.9
1.5	6.1	4.2	All Other Expenses (net)	.6	7.5		.5	1.3	4.0
13.8	13.5	13.8	Profit Before Taxes	21.8	2.3		13.7	27.0	14.0
			RATIOS						
2.8 / 1.3 / .8	3.9 / 1.7 / .9	3.0 / 1.6 / .6	Current	2.4 / .9 / .3	6.8 / 1.3 / .4		2.6 / 1.1 / .9	4.4 / 2.4 / 1.3	5.2 / 1.3 / .8
2.2 / 1.0 / .4	3.7 / 1.4 / .5	2.9 / 1.3 / .6	Quick	2.4 / .6 / .1	4.4 / 1.3 / .2		2.6 / 1.1 / .9	4.3 / 2.2 / 1.3	4.9 / 1.2 / .8
0 UND / 21 17.1 / 66 5.5	0 UND / 17 21.1 / 60 6.1	0 UND / 17 21.0 / 63 5.7	Sales/Receivables	0 UND / 0 UND / 3 141.9	0 UND / 15 24.2 / 47 7.7		7 53.1 / 64 5.7 / 91 4.0	3 114.1 / 41 8.8 / 96 3.8	3 122.4 / 30 12.0 / 59 6.2
			Cost of Sales/Inventory						
			Cost of Sales/Payables						
4.7 / 17.1 / −28.0	4.0 / 10.8 / −62.9	4.9 / 16.8 / −22.4	Sales/Working Capital	10.0 / −519.0 / −11.2	5.2 / 35.7 / −7.1		4.5 / 65.4 / −26.3	4.3 / 6.2 / NM	4.7 / 9.2 / −68.0
(59) 19.9 / 5.7 / 1.9	(65) 20.8 / 7.9 / 2.1	(65) 83.8 / 14.8 / 1.3	EBIT/Interest		(14) 43.7 / 3.7 / −3.1		(11) 84.1 / 27.4 / −6.4	(10) 609.4 / 102.2 / 21.0	(14) 153.6 / 15.2 / 1.1
(14) 11.4 / 4.3 / .5	(11) 21.5 / .6 / .2	(10) 25.3 / 7.9 / .2	Net Profit + Depr., Dep., Amort./Cur. Mat. L/T/D						
.1 / .7 / 2.3	.1 / .4 / 2.3	.1 / .5 / 4.6	Fixed/Worth	.1 / .8 / −2.6	.1 / .5 / −.6		.2 / .6 / −2.6	.1 / .2 / .4	.1 / .4 / 1.8
.5 / 1.6 / 8.0	.5 / 1.8 / 12.9	.5 / 1.5 / 15.6	Debt/Worth	.6 / 6.4 / −3.8	.5 / 2.6 / −1.9		.6 / 2.3 / −12.9	.3 / .6 / 1.5	.7 / 1.7 / 11.7
(75) 113.2 / 25.1 / 9.3	(84) 83.1 / 31.8 / 4.9	(72) 97.6 / 55.0 / 10.6	% Profit Before Taxes/Tangible Net Worth	(10) 205.8 / 86.0 / 67.0	(12) 88.2 / 37.1 / 1.8		(11) 75.8 / 50.4 / −27.2	(12) 137.2 / 79.7 / 30.8	(18) 97.4 / 50.1 / 24.2
33.5 / 10.1 / 1.7	41.5 / 10.6 / .8	52.6 / 18.0 / 2.0	% Profit Before Taxes/Total Assets	77.6 / 35.5 / 14.0	28.7 / 8.9 / −4.4		90.1 / 23.1 / −4.1	101.2 / 52.4 / 18.5	39.1 / 10.1 / 3.0
56.3 / 20.3 / 5.7	67.6 / 22.9 / 7.2	72.7 / 25.7 / 8.8	Sales/Net Fixed Assets	197.2 / 25.9 / 8.0	91.3 / 34.1 / 16.7		96.1 / 20.8 / 11.6	70.8 / 32.0 / 19.9	43.4 / 18.3 / 8.0
3.2 / 2.0 / 1.0	3.7 / 1.9 / .7	6.2 / 2.5 / 1.5	Sales/Total Assets	15.7 / 4.0 / 1.5	6.5 / 2.8 / 1.8		3.5 / 2.6 / 2.1	7.3 / 3.1 / 1.9	2.8 / 2.2 / 1.2
(70) .7 / 1.6 / 3.4	(77) .7 / 1.5 / 3.8	(71) .8 / 1.4 / 2.3	% Depr., Dep., Amort./Sales		(12) .8 / 1.7 / 2.1		(13) .8 / 1.3 / 2.3	(12) .5 / .9 / 1.6	(19) .5 / 1.4 / 2.4
(19) 6.4 / 15.4 / 31.9	(23) 4.8 / 17.1 / 34.9	(25) 6.7 / 13.6 / 26.3	% Officers', Directors', Owners' Comp/Sales						
2027289M	1937809M	2232944M	Net Sales ($)	9454M	35552M	32727M	109618M	198550M	1847043M
1164894M	1770290M	1786634M	Total Assets ($)	3339M	31715M	79850M	166647M	234451M	1270632M

M = $ thousand   MM = $ million
See Pages 11 through 18 for Explanation of Ratios and Data

Current Data Sorted By Assets   Comparative Historical Data

0-500M	500M-2MM	2-10MM	10-50MM	50-100MM	100-250MM	Type of Statement	4/1/98-3/31/99 ALL	4/1/99-3/31/00 ALL
1	2	5	5	2	1	Unqualified	15	21
		3				Reviewed	4	2
2		3	1			Compiled	4	6
	1	1	2			Tax Returns	2	4
	1	8	5		1	Other	9	13
	10 (4/1-9/30/02)		34 (10/1/02-3/31/03)					
3	4	20	13	2	2	**NUMBER OF STATEMENTS**	34	46
%	%	%	%	%	%	**ASSETS**	%	%
		20.5	22.7			Cash & Equivalents	17.8	32.7
		12.3	11.3			Trade Receivables (net)	11.8	11.7
		.3	.0			Inventory	1.2	1.8
		4.7	4.0			All Other Current	3.8	7.7
		37.7	38.0			Total Current	34.5	53.9
		36.4	35.2			Fixed Assets (net)	42.3	24.7
		2.5	4.8			Intangibles (net)	1.2	4.0
		23.3	21.9			All Other Non-Current	22.0	17.4
		100.0	100.0			Total	100.0	100.0
						LIABILITIES		
		7.2	4.7			Notes Payable-Short Term	1.5	4.4
		1.3	4.1			Cur. Mat.-L/T/D	2.2	.7
		6.2	4.9			Trade Payables	3.0	10.4
		1.1	.7			Income Taxes Payable	.1	.4
		13.1	7.9			All Other Current	7.5	13.9
		28.9	22.4			Total Current	14.4	29.8
		17.9	10.9			Long Term Debt	30.0	16.4
		.4	.0			Deferred Taxes	.8	.1
		4.3	8.2			All Other Non-Current	1.8	2.9
		48.6	58.5			Net Worth	52.9	50.8
		100.0	100.0			Total Liabilities & Net Worth	100.0	100.0
						INCOME DATA		
		100.0	100.0			Net Sales	100.0	100.0
						Gross Profit		
		67.9	72.0			Operating Expenses	60.9	79.3
		32.1	28.0			Operating Profit	39.1	20.7
		9.5	7.5			All Other Expenses (net)	−21.2	.0
		22.6	20.5			Profit Before Taxes	60.3	20.7
						RATIOS		
		7.9	5.3			Current	8.8	4.0
		1.2	1.7				1.8	2.0
		.4	1.0				.5	1.0
		5.2	4.2			Quick	7.5	3.5
		.9	1.5				1.5	1.5
		.3	.7				.3	.6
	0 UND	0 UND				Sales/Receivables	0 UND	0 UND
	15 24.1	1 696.0					0 UND	15 23.8
	38 9.7	39 9.4					41 9.0	47 7.7
						Cost of Sales/Inventory		
						Cost of Sales/Payables		
		1.9	.4			Sales/Working Capital	1.7	2.0
		23.2	11.6				8.4	5.6
		−4.9	NM				−6.0	27.7
	(11) 70.2					EBIT/Interest	(15) 34.6	(23) 79.0
	12.3						3.5	6.6
	2.6						1.5	2.7
						Net Profit + Depr., Dep., Amort./Cur. Mat. L /T/D		
		.1	.0			Fixed/Worth	.1	.0
		.6	.5				.7	.3
		2.2	1.4				3.4	1.2
		.5	.3			Debt/Worth	.1	.3
		.9	.4				1.0	1.0
		3.7	1.9				3.8	3.2
	(18) 34.2	30.6				% Profit Before Taxes/Tangible Net Worth	(31) 26.0	(43) 33.2
	18.7	6.8					14.4	15.1
	11.7	2.1					4.6	5.7
		15.7	8.9			% Profit Before Taxes/Total Assets	17.4	16.3
		8.7	3.4				7.1	8.6
		3.3	.7				2.2	2.6
		31.8	24.0			Sales/Net Fixed Assets	14.4	38.5
		11.7	8.6				1.1	15.7
		.3	.2				.3	1.1
		1.7	.9			Sales/Total Assets	1.3	1.8
		.5	.2				.3	.7
		.2	.1				.1	.2
	(18) 1.5					% Depr., Dep., Amort./Sales	(25) 1.9	(34) 1.1
	9.4						3.8	2.3
	20.4						10.8	6.1
						% Officers', Directors', Owners' Comp/Sales		
4012M	7717M	119730M	141207M	282061M	162873M	Net Sales ($)	645671M	704983M
640M	5596M	113601M	264085M	146144M	394930M	Total Assets ($)	879053M	1285380M

© RMA 2003

M = $ thousand   MM = $ million
See Pages 11 through 18 for Explanation of Ratios and Data

Comparative Historical Data / Current Data Sorted By Sales

			Type of Statement						
17	15	16	Unqualified	1	3	2	2	4	4
4	2	3	Reviewed	1			1	1	
5	9	6	Compiled	2	3			1	
2	2	4	Tax Returns	3	1				
10	14	15	Other	2	6	1	3	2	1
4/1/00- 3/31/01	4/1/01- 3/31/02	4/1/02- 3/31/03		10 (4/1-9/30/02)		34 (10/1/02-3/31/03)			
ALL	ALL	ALL		0-1MM	1-3MM	3-5MM	5-10MM	10-25MM	25MM & OVER
38	42	44	**NUMBER OF STATEMENTS**	9	13	3	6	8	5
%	%	%	**ASSETS**	%	%	%	%	%	%
22.9	20.5	21.5	Cash & Equivalents		18.9				
15.3	11.2	12.2	Trade Receivables (net)		9.2				
1.3	.9	.7	Inventory		.8				
4.8	8.2	5.3	All Other Current		9.5				
44.3	40.8	39.7	Total Current		38.5				
35.1	31.4	33.9	Fixed Assets (net)		38.8				
2.1	3.7	5.6	Intangibles (net)		6.6				
18.5	24.1	20.7	All Other Non-Current		16.1				
100.0	100.0	100.0	Total		100.0				
			LIABILITIES						
7.4	6.6	9.8	Notes Payable-Short Term		22.6				
.7	.5	2.0	Cur. Mat.-L/T/D		3.9				
9.0	6.3	5.9	Trade Payables		2.1				
.4	.5	.8	Income Taxes Payable		.1				
13.7	23.5	12.5	All Other Current		3.8				
31.2	37.3	31.0	Total Current		32.6				
28.2	19.5	14.9	Long Term Debt		21.2				
.1	.0	.2	Deferred Taxes		.0				
2.6	3.7	5.4	All Other Non-Current		.7				
37.9	39.6	48.6	Net Worth		45.5				
100.0	100.0	100.0	Total Liabilities & Net Worth		100.0				
			INCOME DATA						
100.0	100.0	100.0	Net Sales		100.0				
			Gross Profit						
69.0	71.6	76.5	Operating Expenses		62.6				
31.0	28.4	23.5	Operating Profit		37.4				
15.5	12.3	6.7	All Other Expenses (net)		11.4				
15.5	16.2	16.7	Profit Before Taxes		25.9				
			RATIOS						
4.4	3.9	5.1			3.9				
1.5	1.4	1.4	Current		1.5				
.8	.4	.7			.5				
4.1	2.8	3.1			2.8				
1.0	1.0	1.0	Quick		1.2				
.4	.3	.3			.2				
0 UND	0 UND	0 UND		0 UND					
18 20.0	6 56.6	15 25.0	Sales/Receivables	0 UND					
62 5.9	37 9.8	39 9.4		3 123.6					
			Cost of Sales/Inventory						
			Cost of Sales/Payables						
2.4	3.1	2.5			.9				
17.7	12.8	34.6	Sales/Working Capital		3.7				
−78.7	−9.8	−10.4			−17.7				
86.7	27.5	30.8							
(17) 3.5	(19) 4.7	(23) 5.4	EBIT/Interest						
1.8	1.3	2.6							
			Net Profit + Depr., Dep., Amort./Cur. Mat. L/T/D						
.0	.0	.1			.1				
.5	.4	.7	Fixed/Worth		.8				
3.6	2.7	1.7			2.7				
.6	.3	.4			.4				
2.1	1.2	.8	Debt/Worth		.8				
12.2	7.9	5.6			3.4				
42.2	24.5	32.8	% Profit Before Taxes/Tangible Net Worth		19.8				
(33) 16.4	(36) 8.1	(40) 14.3		(12) 14.1					
4.1	4.1	5.2			2.6				
17.0	8.6	11.1	% Profit Before Taxes/Total Assets		9.8				
2.9	3.9	4.8			3.9				
.7	.4	1.3			.1				
28.6	57.5	31.8	Sales/Net Fixed Assets		22.8				
12.1	14.4	12.0			.6				
.3	.3	.3			.3				
1.8	1.7	2.0	Sales/Total Assets		1.5				
.6	.6	.6			.2				
.1	.1	.2			.2				
.6	.7	1.6	% Depr., Dep., Amort./Sales						
(33) 2.1	(29) 3.9	(35) 3.1							
13.0	13.0	16.5							
			% Officers', Directors', Owners' Comp/Sales						
849655M	1004326M	717600M	Net Sales ($)	5976M	22651M	10073M	37160M	133004M	508736M
1424138M	1581777M	924996M	Total Assets ($)	54492M	125130M	28598M	54775M	252639M	409362M

M = $ thousand   MM = $ million
See Pages 11 through 18 for Explanation of Ratios and Data

Current Data Sorted By Assets — Comparative Historical Data

Type of Statement

	0-500M	500M-2MM	2-10MM	10-50MM	50-100MM	100-250MM		4/1/98-3/31/99 ALL	4/1/99-3/31/00 ALL
Unqualified	1	1	7	19	6	15		37	37
Reviewed		2						3	
Compiled		2						1	1
Tax Returns	1							2	
Other	1		3	9	5	5		31	21

Period totals: 7 (4/1-9/30/02); 72 (10/1/02-3/31/03)

Data

0-500M	500M-2MM	2-10MM	10-50MM	50-100MM	100-250MM		4/1/98-3/31/99 ALL	4/1/99-3/31/00 ALL
3	6	11	28	11	20	**NUMBER OF STATEMENTS**	74	59
%	%	%	%	%	%	**ASSETS**	%	%
		28.0	39.8	37.6	41.3	Cash & Equivalents	35.3	36.7
		23.0	19.1	23.8	9.7	Trade Receivables (net)	17.2	15.5
		8.5	.1	.0	.5	Inventory	.3	.7
		4.7	10.5	3.8	2.1	All Other Current	9.0	6.6
		64.3	69.4	65.2	53.6	Total Current	61.8	59.4
		12.4	8.3	6.7	8.3	Fixed Assets (net)	14.2	12.3
		11.0	5.8	1.2	10.1	Intangibles (net)	-1.0	8.1
		12.4	16.4	26.9	28.0	All Other Non-Current	25.1	20.2
		100.0	100.0	100.0	100.0	Total	100.0	100.0
						LIABILITIES		
		5.8	3.6	.4	.1	Notes Payable-Short Term	12.9	5.5
		1.4	1.2	.5	.6	Cur. Mat.-L/T/D	.7	1.2
		24.0	15.8	25.0	19.0	Trade Payables	16.2	14.9
		.5	.4	.6	.5	Income Taxes Payable	.1	.1
		15.9	29.1	27.0	26.7	All Other Current	20.9	36.0
		47.6	50.1	53.6	46.9	Total Current	50.8	57.7
		9.6	7.4	4.6	9.8	Long Term Debt	20.4	9.1
		1.8	.2	.2	.3	Deferred Taxes	.1	.3
		2.5	9.4	12.7	8.2	All Other Non-Current	6.1	15.5
		38.4	32.9	29.0	34.8	Net Worth	22.6	17.5
		100.0	100.0	100.0	100.0	Total Liabilities & Net Worth	100.0	100.0
						INCOME DATA		
		100.0	100.0	100.0	100.0	Net Sales	100.0	100.0
						Gross Profit		
		94.2	94.8	97.4	95.2	Operating Expenses	95.5	96.1
		5.8	5.2	2.6	4.8	Operating Profit	4.5	3.9
		.2	1.7	-.3	.7	All Other Expenses (net)	-.9	-.4
		5.6	3.5	2.9	4.1	Profit Before Taxes	5.4	4.3
						RATIOS		
		2.5	2.1	1.5	1.7		2.0	1.5
		1.4	1.4	1.2	1.2	Current	1.3	1.2
		1.1	1.0	1.0	.8		.9	.8
		1.4	1.8	1.4	1.5		1.8	1.4
		1.2	1.2	1.2	1.2	Quick	1.1	1.1
		.8	.8	.8	.8		.5	.6
		17 21.1	4 85.9	6 64.9	5 80.1		2 152.3	5 78.9
		25 14.4	19 19.4	17 21.8	9 39.7	Sales/Receivables	18 19.8	19 19.6
		47 7.8	37 9.8	81 4.5	45 8.2		38 9.6	35 10.5
						Cost of Sales/Inventory		
						Cost of Sales/Payables		
		2.2	5.3	12.3	11.6		4.5	-8.8
		13.6	12.3	21.3	25.5	Sales/Working Capital	19.8	15.6
		50.2	-163.5	96.7	-32.3		-75.8	-17.3
			12.0		8.4		17.7	9.8
			(14) 3.6		(13) 3.1	EBIT/Interest	(39) 3.6	(29) 3.2
			-1.2		-1.2		-.3	-1.4
						Net Profit + Depr., Dep., Amort./Cur. Mat. L /T/D		
		.3	.0	.0	.0		.0	.1
		.4	.1	.1	.1	Fixed/Worth	.2	.3
		1.0	1.9	.5	.7		1.0	.9
		1.9	1.0	1.6	1.2		.9	1.3
		3.4	3.5	2.8	2.4	Debt/Worth	1.6	2.8
		5.2	46.1	6.1	5.1		5.9	16.6
		106.4	35.7	39.7	43.1		33.9	44.9
		37.8	(24) 12.6	20.4	(18) 14.0	% Profit Before Taxes/Tangible Net Worth	(61) 9.1	(48) 14.7
		3.5	-12.1	.9	6.6		-4.6	2.6
		18.4	9.7	9.5	12.8		11.9	9.5
		6.7	3.3	5.6	4.5	% Profit Before Taxes/Total Assets	2.5	4.8
		2.0	-.7	.3	2.1		-4.3	.4
		48.9	544.2	454.6	294.9		127.5	99.0
		23.3	41.2	257.0	92.6	Sales/Net Fixed Assets	35.9	39.3
		4.1	24.1	17.9	13.2		14.7	14.0
		3.8	4.2	4.9	3.4		3.6	3.6
		3.3	1.9	3.7	2.2	Sales/Total Assets	2.3	2.6
		.5	1.0	.5	1.0		1.2	.9
		.4	.6		.5		.6	.5
		(10) 1.3	(17) 1.7		(10) .8	% Depr., Dep., Amort./Sales	(48) .9	(40) 1.0
		4.9	2.9		4.7		1.8	2.1
						% Officers', Directors', Owners' Comp/Sales		
3042M	29242M	199841M	2093752M	2544048M	7389778M	Net Sales ($)	7638059M	8734803M
1140M	5407M	64714M	718820M	812994M	3347359M	Total Assets ($)	3271830M	3792962M

M = $ thousand   MM = $ million
See Pages 11 through 18 for Explanation of Ratios and Data

Comparative Historical Data | Current Data Sorted By Sales

	Hist 1	Hist 2	Hist 3		0-1MM	1-3MM	3-5MM	5-10MM	10-25MM	25MM & OVER
Type of Statement										
Unqualified	38	36	49		1	1		3	7	37
Reviewed	1	2	3		1	1		1		
Compiled	3	5	2		1			1		
Tax Returns	3		2		1			1		
Other	19	35	23			4			3	16
	4/1/00- 3/31/01 ALL	4/1/01- 3/31/02 ALL	4/1/02- 3/31/03 ALL			7 (4/1-9/30/02)			72 (10/1/02-3/31/03)	
NUMBER OF STATEMENTS	64	78	79		4	6		6	10	53
ASSETS	%	%	%		%	%	%	%	%	%
Cash & Equivalents	37.9	37.9	35.9						32.3	40.9
Trade Receivables (net)	17.6	16.0	20.0						12.9	18.0
Inventory	1.8	1.7	1.4		DATA	NOT	AVAILABLE		.0	.4
All Other Current	6.2	4.2	6.0						6.2	6.0
Total Current	63.5	59.8	63.3						51.4	65.3
Fixed Assets (net)	14.4	14.0	11.1						14.7	7.4
Intangibles (net)	5.8	5.3	6.4						5.6	7.3
All Other Non-Current	16.3	20.8	19.2						28.3	20.0
Total	100.0	100.0	100.0						100.0	100.0
LIABILITIES										
Notes Payable-Short Term	3.4	3.3	4.0						.5	.8
Cur. Mat.-L/T/D	2.3	7.9	1.3						2.0	.8
Trade Payables	14.7	15.5	18.0						22.4	21.1
Income Taxes Payable	.3	.4	.5						.1	.5
All Other Current	33.7	29.2	25.1						20.3	28.1
Total Current	54.4	56.2	48.9						45.4	51.2
Long Term Debt	17.7	30.2	9.5						10.4	6.4
Deferred Taxes	.1	.3	.4						.8	.3
All Other Non-Current	4.2	6.9	7.7						20.3	6.6
Net Worth	23.7	6.3	33.4						23.1	35.4
Total Liabilities & Net Worth	100.0	100.0	100.0						100.0	100.0
INCOME DATA										
Net Sales	100.0	100.0	100.0						100.0	100.0
Gross Profit										
Operating Expenses	97.3	96.1	94.2						94.0	96.6
Operating Profit	2.7	3.9	5.8						6.0	3.4
All Other Expenses (net)	-1.2	1.6	1.1						.9	.3
Profit Before Taxes	3.9	2.3	4.7						5.2	3.0
RATIOS										
Current	2.0 / 1.3 / .7	1.7 / 1.2 / .8	1.7 / 1.3 / 1.0						1.8 / 1.4 / 1.0	1.7 / 1.2 / 1.0
Quick	1.7 / 1.1 / .6	1.5 / 1.1 / .7	1.5 / 1.2 / .8						1.6 / 1.2 / .7	1.5 / 1.1 / .8
Sales/Receivables	6 / 65.3 22 / 16.5 43 / 8.4	5 / 75.1 15 / 24.6 43 / 8.6	6 / 64.9 17 / 21.5 41 / 8.9						9 / 40.4 19 / 18.9 108 / 3.4	5 / 69.7 14 / 25.6 39 / 9.3
Cost of Sales/Inventory										
Cost of Sales/Payables										
Sales/Working Capital	5.9 / 20.7 / -14.1	7.6 / 21.7 / -29.3	7.5 / 16.9 / -103.7						6.4 / 14.2 / -61.0	9.6 / 33.0 / -82.2
EBIT/Interest	(34) 36.3 / 8.1 / 1.4	(48) 14.4 / 3.9 / .3	(43) 14.5 / 7.4 / 1.8							(25) 14.7 / 6.0 / 1.8
Net Profit + Depr., Dep., Amort./Cur. Mat. L/T/D	(10) 16.4 / 4.9 / 2.9	(14) 17.2 / 1.6 / .5	(14) 7.1 / 3.2 / 1.1							
Fixed/Worth	.1 / .3 / 1.0	.1 / .4 / 1.1	.1 / .2 / .8						.4 / 1.0 / 2.9	.0 / .1 / .6
Debt/Worth	1.2 / 2.1 / 4.7	1.4 / 2.3 / 10.9	1.3 / 2.8 / 9.0						2.1 / 4.5 / 46.2	1.2 / 2.7 / 6.7
% Profit Before Taxes/Tangible Net Worth	(56) 62.0 / 25.2 / 6.7	(66) 38.8 / 15.0 / 1.8	(72) 48.6 / 16.7 / 3.1							(48) 42.2 / 16.7 / 1.3
% Profit Before Taxes/Total Assets	15.1 / 6.5 / 1.1	12.3 / 4.6 / .0	13.0 / 5.3 / .7						15.7 / 4.5 / -.4	12.2 / 5.6 / .4
Sales/Net Fixed Assets	127.8 / 34.9 / 11.5	141.4 / 26.0 / 9.5	294.7 / 44.3 / 16.3						26.1 / 17.1 / 4.0	491.4 / 100.2 / 24.4
Sales/Total Assets	3.8 / 2.4 / 1.5	3.9 / 2.5 / 1.1	4.3 / 2.7 / .9						2.2 / 1.4 / .6	4.5 / 3.1 / 1.3
% Depr., Dep., Amort./Sales	(41) .5 / 1.2 / 3.6	(57) .5 / 1.1 / 3.2	(50) .5 / 1.2 / 3.7							(30) .4 / .7 / 2.4
% Officers', Directors', Owners' Comp/Sales			(10) 3.4 / 6.7 / 31.1							
Net Sales ($)	9350859M	10723212M	12259703M		1099M	12152M		42484M	183251M	12020717M
Total Assets ($)	3623257M	4684062M	4950434M		3851M	32142M		19250M	299166M	4596025M

© RMA 2003

M = $ thousand   MM = $ million

See Pages 11 through 18 for Explanation of Ratios and Data

Current Data Sorted By Assets   Comparative Historical Data

	0-500M	500M-2MM	2-10MM	10-50MM	50-100MM	100-250MM	Type of Statement	4/1/98-3/31/99 ALL	4/1/99-3/31/00 ALL
	1	1		6	3	5	Unqualified	11	17
	1	1	1				Reviewed	2	3
		3	2		1		Compiled	3	7
							Tax Returns		1
	1		7	7	7	4	Other	44	35
		5 (4/1-9/30/02)		45 (10/1/02-3/31/03)					
	2	5	10	13	11	9	NUMBER OF STATEMENTS	60	63
	%	%	%	%	%	%	**ASSETS**	%	%
			34.7	52.9	17.3		Cash & Equivalents	57.9	51.9
			15.5	15.7	25.2		Trade Receivables (net)	10.7	14.5
			.0	.4	.0		Inventory	.1	1.4
			8.5	9.2	14.2		All Other Current	4.1	9.0
			58.7	78.3	56.7		Total Current	72.8	76.7
			17.6	3.9	2.3		Fixed Assets (net)	4.7	4.6
			9.3	1.6	9.0		Intangibles (net)	6.9	3.3
			14.4	16.2	32.0		All Other Non-Current	15.5	15.4
			100.0	100.0	100.0		Total	100.0	100.0
							LIABILITIES		
			.8	7.4	2.8		Notes Payable-Short Term	3.8	6.3
			.3	.4	.4		Cur. Mat.-L/T/D	4.9	1.1
			25.9	19.3	32.6		Trade Payables	7.8	14.0
			.2	.5	.2		Income Taxes Payable	.2	.6
			18.2	31.4	20.5		All Other Current	34.0	31.7
			45.4	58.9	56.5		Total Current	50.7	53.6
			16.0	6.0	2.0		Long Term Debt	6.3	3.9
			.0	.0	.0		Deferred Taxes	.3	.1
			12.5	3.7	23.2		All Other Non-Current	6.3	10.1
			26.1	31.4	18.2		Net Worth	36.4	32.3
			100.0	100.0	100.0		Total Liabilities & Net Worth	100.0	100.0
							INCOME DATA		
			100.0	100.0	100.0		Net Sales	100.0	100.0
							Gross Profit		
			88.5	101.2	95.0		Operating Expenses	97.5	101.1
			11.5	-1.2	5.0		Operating Profit	2.5	-1.1
			1.3	-2.9	1.7		All Other Expenses (net)	-20.9	-7.7
			10.2	1.7	3.2		Profit Before Taxes	23.4	6.6
							RATIOS		
			3.3	1.7	2.4			2.4	2.1
			1.2	1.3	.9		Current	1.5	1.6
			.9	1.2	.5			.9	1.0
			2.4	1.5	1.1			2.4	2.0
			1.2	1.3	.7		Quick	1.3	1.4
			.7	.9	.3			.8	.9
			0 UND	24 15.2	13 27.8			5 72.4	0 UND
			33 11.1	79 4.6	59 6.2		Sales/Receivables	47 7.8	43 8.4
			97 3.8	144 2.5	439 .8			93 3.9	94 3.9
							Cost of Sales/Inventory		
							Cost of Sales/Payables		
			1.3	1.3	2.9			1.0	1.1
			28.9	4.1	-15.6		Sales/Working Capital	2.4	2.4
			NM	12.3	-3.1			-30.1	23.6
								15.4	14.4
							EBIT/Interest	(13) 2.5	(20) 8.5
								-.3	1.1
							Net Profit + Depr., Dep., Amort./Cur. Mat. L /T/D		
			.2	.0	.0			.0	.0
			.5	.0	.1		Fixed/Worth	.0	.0
			1.9	.4	.2			.1	.2
			2.8	1.5	2.1			.9	.9
			6.3	2.2	6.4		Debt/Worth	1.8	1.9
			10.6	3.4	11.3			5.9	4.8
			143.5	21.9			% Profit Before Taxes/Tangible	21.8	23.5
			33.0	(12) 11.0			Net Worth	(51) 6.5	(57) 7.1
			9.9	-6.2				-4.3	-.2
			8.0	7.3	9.4		% Profit Before Taxes/Total	8.3	10.4
			5.0	2.6	3.1		Assets	3.0	2.7
			2.1	-5.0	2.2			-.6	-.1
			26.2	UND	UND			UND	UND
			9.1	63.5	38.4		Sales/Net Fixed Assets	814.8	99.5
			6.4	11.9	14.1			16.0	22.0
			1.0	1.1	.7			.9	1.0
			.7	.7	.6		Sales/Total Assets	.5	.6
			.5	.3	.3			.3	.4
									.9
							% Depr., Dep., Amort./Sales		(22) 1.7
									3.7
									8.0
							% Officers', Directors',	(11) 16.2	(12) 18.1
							Owners' Comp/Sales	22.0	22.4
	564M	15224M	48620M	254356M	738730M	618832M	Net Sales ($)	2044525M	2052336M
	589M	7049M	56878M	352756M	853108M	1463975M	Total Assets ($)	4113393M	3745255M

	Comparative Historical Data			Type of Statement	Current Data Sorted By Sales					
	14	13	16	Unqualified	1	1	1	2	3	8
	3	2	2	Reviewed	1			1		
	8	11	6	Compiled		4		1		1
	4	3		Tax Returns						
	31	24	26	Other	1	2	3	3	4	13
	4/1/00-	4/1/01-	4/1/02-			5 (4/1-9/30/02)			45 (10/1/02-3/31/03)	
	3/31/01	3/31/02	3/31/03							
	ALL	ALL	ALL		0-1MM	1-3MM	3-5MM	5-10MM	10-25MM	25MM & OVER
	60	53	50	**NUMBER OF STATEMENTS**	3	7	4	7	7	22
	%	%	%	**ASSETS**	%	%	%	%	%	%
	41.5	33.1	38.5	Cash & Equivalents						41.0
	25.0	25.5	21.7	Trade Receivables (net)						17.1
	1.4	.9	.2	Inventory						.3
	3.9	5.0	8.3	All Other Current						11.7
	71.7	64.5	68.6	Total Current						70.2
	6.8	7.8	6.6	Fixed Assets (net)						3.2
	6.7	5.6	5.8	Intangibles (net)						1.5
	14.7	22.1	19.0	All Other Non-Current						25.1
	100.0	100.0	100.0	Total						100.0
				LIABILITIES						
	5.3	19.8	5.8	Notes Payable-Short Term						5.9
	2.7	2.6	.6	Cur. Mat.-L/T/D						.2
	18.5	20.7	21.7	Trade Payables						19.1
	.5	.4	.2	Income Taxes Payable						.4
	27.7	23.5	24.5	All Other Current						26.2
	54.7	67.0	53.0	Total Current						51.7
	6.7	7.3	6.6	Long Term Debt						1.8
	.1	.1	.0	Deferred Taxes						.0
	9.3	13.8	13.1	All Other Non-Current						17.1
	29.2	11.7	27.3	Net Worth						29.4
	100.0	100.0	100.0	Total Liabilities & Net Worth						100.0
				INCOME DATA						
	100.0	100.0	100.0	Net Sales						100.0
				Gross Profit						
	97.9	88.2	93.9	Operating Expenses						98.9
	2.1	11.8	6.1	Operating Profit						1.1
	−6.3	1.4	.1	All Other Expenses (net)						−1.7
	8.4	10.5	6.0	Profit Before Taxes						2.8
				RATIOS						
	1.9	1.7	2.2							2.4
	1.5	1.2	1.3	Current						1.3
	1.0	.8	.9							1.0
	1.7	1.6	1.6							1.6
	1.3	1.2	1.2	Quick						1.2
	.9	.7	.7							.6
25	14.6	22 16.6	20 18.1						20	18.1
55	6.6	66 5.5	58 6.3	Sales/Receivables					56	6.6
115	3.2	149 2.5	136 2.7						119	3.1
				Cost of Sales/Inventory						
				Cost of Sales/Payables						
	1.0	1.9	1.6							1.5
	2.8	11.8	7.0	Sales/Working Capital						3.7
	−96.1	−9.4	−13.7							NM
	9.5	31.7	20.2							21.6
(22)	3.8	(25) 9.1	(25) 7.1	EBIT/Interest					(12)	10.8
	1.0	3.0	2.1							5.8
				Net Profit + Depr., Dep., Amort./Cur. Mat. L/T/D						
	.0	.0	.0							.0
	.0	.1	.1	Fixed/Worth						.0
	.6	.4	.5							.2
	1.2	1.8	1.9							1.9
	2.2	2.9	3.2	Debt/Worth						2.8
	14.7	11.7	7.3							4.0
	29.9	47.4	42.7							44.8
(48)	10.9	(44) 22.4	(45) 17.9	% Profit Before Taxes/Tangible Net Worth						11.8
	−1.1	1.4	.9							−2.8
	12.8	13.9	9.0							7.8
	3.7	6.6	3.7	% Profit Before Taxes/Total Assets						3.1
	.1	1.0	.4							−1.5
	UND	264.0	313.3							946.0
	98.7	40.9	26.9	Sales/Net Fixed Assets						50.9
	15.6	14.0	11.1							18.3
	1.3	1.3	.9							.9
	.6	.7	.6	Sales/Total Assets						.6
	.4	.5	.4							.4
	.9	1.0	.6							.3
(24)	1.8	(23) 1.7	(24) 1.8	% Depr., Dep., Amort./Sales					(11)	.8
	3.7	3.6	3.0							2.7
	9.7			% Officers', Directors', Owners' Comp/Sales						
(13)	14.2									
	19.1									
	1670107M	2164607M	1676326M	Net Sales ($)	1085M	14479M	14251M	50611M	111305M	1484595M
	2839553M	2999793M	2734355M	Total Assets ($)	4737M	17443M	31837M	117231M	458275M	2104832M

© RMA 2003

M = $ thousand   MM = $ million

See Pages 11 through 18 for Explanation of Ratios and Data

Current Data Sorted By Assets   Comparative Historical Data

						Type of Statement		
7	3	16	3		3	Unqualified	14	13
	1					Reviewed	3	3
4		2				Compiled	7	10
6	3	1				Tax Returns	7	2
3	6	6	7		1	Other	34	19
	1 (4/1-9/30/02)		71 (10/1/02-3/31/03)				4/1/98-3/31/99	4/1/99-3/31/00
0-500M	500M-2MM	2-10MM	10-50MM	50-100MM	100-250MM		ALL	ALL
20	13	25	10		4	NUMBER OF STATEMENTS	65	47
%	%	%	%	%	%	ASSETS	%	%
45.2	29.7	44.2	40.2			Cash & Equivalents	44.6	32.7
12.9	1.2	5.8	4.5			Trade Receivables (net)	6.9	8.4
1.0	.0	2.4	.0			Inventory	.5	2.3
2.8	5.4	5.3	12.0			All Other Current	5.2	3.0
62.0	36.4	57.8	56.6			Total Current	57.2	46.4
19.0	33.5	23.5	18.4			Fixed Assets (net)	21.0	23.9
2.1	7.8	2.5	10.2			Intangibles (net)	4.7	10.9
16.9	22.3	16.2	14.7			All Other Non-Current	17.1	18.7
100.0	100.0	100.0	100.0			Total	100.0	100.0
						LIABILITIES		
3.1	1.3	2.2	.7			Notes Payable-Short Term	6.6	7.3
3.9	3.4	1.1	1.9			Cur. Mat.-L/T/D	1.6	3.7
13.8	8.8	8.4	6.8			Trade Payables	6.3	11.7
.7	.4	1.7	.5			Income Taxes Payable	.7	.2
27.2	10.5	17.8	26.5			All Other Current	24.4	21.4
48.8	24.3	31.1	36.3			Total Current	39.6	44.3
14.0	24.0	10.1	10.7			Long Term Debt	8.8	12.7
.0	.0	.6	1.9			Deferred Taxes	.4	.8
1.8	7.6	6.3	2.0			All Other Non-Current	5.8	4.2
35.5	44.1	52.0	49.1			Net Worth	45.4	37.9
100.0	100.0	100.0	100.0			Total Liabilities & Net Worth	100.0	100.0
						INCOME DATA		
100.0	100.0	100.0	100.0			Net Sales	100.0	100.0
						Gross Profit		
85.1	91.9	85.9	87.3			Operating Expenses	93.9	105.9
14.9	8.1	14.1	12.7			Operating Profit	6.1	−5.9
−1.0	−.3	.3	.4			All Other Expenses (net)	−86.4	−13.5
15.9	8.4	13.8	12.3			Profit Before Taxes	92.4	7.7
						RATIOS		
3.1	5.6	2.9	2.4				3.0	2.0
1.2	1.2	1.9	1.6			Current	1.7	1.3
.8	.4	1.4	1.0				1.0	.6
2.8	6.6	2.5	2.1				2.4	1.9
1.2	(12) .8	1.7	1.2			Quick	1.4	1.1
.6	.3	1.1	.6				.9	.6
0 UND	0 UND	2 148.2	0 UND				0 UND	0 999.8
8 47.0	0 999.8	5 71.6	2 216.4			Sales/Receivables	6 57.5	7 50.3
20 18.6	2 219.9	12 31.5	15 25.1				15 24.5	24 15.4
						Cost of Sales/Inventory		
						Cost of Sales/Payables		
6.9	8.7	4.6	3.6				3.9	6.6
38.0	67.7	7.3	7.4			Sales/Working Capital	9.7	29.6
−39.7	−15.4	14.0	NM				204.4	−15.6
	88.4	47.7					29.5	16.0
(11) 15.7	(14) 19.4				EBIT/Interest	(37) 10.5	(36) 6.7
	3.0	2.9					4.4	2.4
						Net Profit + Depr., Dep., Amort./Cur. Mat. L ./T/D		
.1	.3	.1	.1				.1	.2
.3	.7	.4	.4			Fixed/Worth	.3	.8
6.4	139.2	.8	.8				1.0	4.0
.4	.4	.5	.6				.8	.9
2.3	1.2	.9	1.1			Debt/Worth	1.4	1.4
10.5	333.7	2.0	2.9				3.3	−116.0
864.6	96.8	117.5				% Profit Before Taxes/Tangible Net Worth	98.5	61.4
(17) 89.7	(11) 79.5	(23) 37.1					(60) 44.6	(35) 20.0
26.6	7.1	17.9					12.4	6.3
174.9	45.9	43.7	45.8			% Profit Before Taxes/Total Assets	36.0	26.4
36.5	19.1	21.9	15.8				15.3	8.7
2.0	4.7	8.0	7.7				3.7	3.4
173.1	26.5	36.3	26.5			Sales/Net Fixed Assets	43.0	20.5
28.6	10.8	14.9	14.7				15.1	12.3
11.5	6.2	5.1	12.7				7.2	4.6
8.8	4.2	2.9	3.0			Sales/Total Assets	2.8	3.0
4.1	2.8	2.0	1.9				1.6	1.8
2.2	1.4	1.2	1.3				.7	1.0
1.1	1.0	.8	.7			% Depr., Dep., Amort./Sales	.9	1.4
(11) 1.2	(12) 1.5	(22) 1.6	1.7				(44) 1.8	(37) 2.4
1.8	2.3	2.2	2.7				2.7	3.8
						% Officers', Directors', Owners' Comp/Sales	6.1	4.6
							(21) 9.7	(21) 11.6
							13.8	19.9
21518M	43543M	269799M	551698M		761543M	Net Sales ($)	3813799M	861766M
3466M	13627M	113947M	258178M		575437M	Total Assets ($)	2144491M	618070M

© RMA 2003

M = $ thousand MM = $ million

See Pages 11 through 18 for Explanation of Ratios and Data

Comparative Historical Data | Current Data Sorted By Sales

			Type of Statement						
8	10	32	Unqualified	6	5	2	7	7	5
4	1	1	Reviewed			1			
3	8	6	Compiled	2	1	2	1		
4	9	10	Tax Returns	4	5	1			
20	12	23	Other	3	5	2	2	3	8
4/1/00-3/31/01 ALL	4/1/01-3/31/02 ALL	4/1/02-3/31/03 ALL		1 (4/1-9/30/02) 0-1MM	1-3MM	3-5MM	71 (10/1/02-3/31/03) 5-10MM	10-25MM	25MM & OVER
39	40	72	NUMBER OF STATEMENTS	15	16	7	11	10	13
%	%	%	ASSETS	%	%	%	%	%	%
33.0	32.4	41.8	Cash & Equivalents	42.1	41.7		38.7	37.2	49.7
3.5	6.8	6.8	Trade Receivables (net)	8.5	5.7		5.4	8.0	5.3
1.3	1.5	1.4	Inventory	.0	1.9		.2	2.8	1.5
6.7	9.9	6.0	All Other Current	5.5	3.4		6.6	4.4	11.6
44.6	50.5	56.0	Total Current	56.1	52.7		50.9	52.5	68.1
26.5	22.7	22.8	Fixed Assets (net)	15.3	26.0		31.4	17.6	13.9
10.1	10.0	4.5	Intangibles (net)	3.5	4.2		4.8	1.7	9.2
18.8	16.8	16.7	All Other Non-Current	25.1	17.0		13.0	28.2	8.8
100.0	100.0	100.0	Total	100.0	100.0		100.0	100.0	100.0
			LIABILITIES						
4.4	2.8	2.2	Notes Payable-Short Term	.0	3.9		1.0	.1	1.9
4.2	4.1	2.5	Cur. Mat.-L/T/D	4.6	2.4		.6	1.4	2.0
6.5	8.9	9.4	Trade Payables	7.6	11.7		6.5	6.8	6.9
.2	.3	1.1	Income Taxes Payable	.5	.3		2.2	1.9	1.0
19.6	23.4	21.1	All Other Current	26.2	17.9		13.3	18.7	28.9
35.0	39.4	36.3	Total Current	38.9	36.2		23.7	29.0	40.8
21.3	21.4	13.3	Long Term Debt	10.4	21.9		4.5	2.7	4.8
.2	.4	.5	Deferred Taxes	.0	.3		.3	1.3	.7
9.0	7.5	4.7	All Other Non-Current	5.7	.2		4.9	10.7	5.5
34.5	31.3	45.2	Net Worth	44.9	41.3		66.6	56.3	48.1
100.0	100.0	100.0	Total Liabilities & Net Worth	100.0	100.0		100.0	100.0	100.0
			INCOME DATA						
100.0	100.0	100.0	Net Sales	100.0	100.0		100.0	100.0	100.0
			Gross Profit						
101.3	91.2	87.3	Operating Expenses	83.7	86.2		86.6	90.0	89.6
–1.3	8.8	12.7	Operating Profit	16.3	13.8		13.4	10.0	10.4
–1.3	1.3	–.2	All Other Expenses (net)	–.2	.1		–.5	–.8	–.6
.0	7.5	12.9	Profit Before Taxes	16.5	13.7		13.9	10.8	11.0
			RATIOS						
2.0	1.8	2.9		3.0	3.4		3.4	4.6	2.3
1.5	1.4	1.6	Current	1.3	1.3		2.5	1.7	1.5
1.1	.9	1.0		1.1	.4		1.7	.9	1.3
1.8	1.4	2.5		2.2	3.5		3.3	3.4	2.0
(38) 1.3	(39) 1.1	(71) 1.3	Quick	1.2	(15) 1.2		1.8	1.4	1.3
.7	.7	.7		.5	.4		1.5	.8	.8
0 UND	0 UND	0 UND		0 UND	0 UND		0 999.8	4 97.9	0 UND
6 64.8	3 136.1	5 75.5	Sales/Receivables	5 76.8	0 UND		5 73.1	9 39.3	6 58.6
10 37.4	31 11.9	12 30.2		21 17.7	6 58.1		12 29.9	13 28.6	15 24.6
			Cost of Sales/Inventory						
			Cost of Sales/Payables						
5.6	4.2	5.4		6.2	2.8		5.4	8.1	3.9
14.0	29.8	12.9	Sales/Working Capital	8.0	38.0		7.3	13.4	7.4
85.5	–41.6	250.5		96.6	–20.1		44.8	–78.0	24.1
5.8	19.9	48.8			16.8				
(28) 1.0	(30) 4.0	(41) 15.7	EBIT/Interest		(11) 3.8				
–.2	.8	2.7			1.6				
3.7		16.0	Net Profit + Depr., Dep.,						
(11) 1.8		(15) 2.9	Amort./Cur. Mat. L/T/D						
–1.5		1.7							
.2	.2	.1		.0	.2		.1	.2	.1
.7	.6	.4	Fixed/Worth	.2	.6		.6	.3	.4
6.9	6.4	.9		1.0	6.7		.7	.6	.5
.8	1.0	.5		.3	.4		.4	.4	.9
1.8	1.8	1.1	Debt/Worth	1.6	1.9		.6	.9	1.1
7.4	40.9	4.3		11.0	46.1		.8	2.0	1.7
24.6	69.6	117.7	% Profit Before Taxes/Tangible	215.6	386.9		96.8	102.2	122.1
(30) 4.2	(31) 16.6	(64) 59.0	Net Worth	(13) 63.2	(14) 47.3		37.1	45.9	(12) 49.1
–18.9	.0	21.2		11.3	7.1		30.8	21.5	22.3
10.3	34.6	49.2	% Profit Before Taxes/Total	62.5	70.9		50.9	53.9	54.4
1.9	8.1	17.7	Assets	14.3	13.6		29.1	17.0	17.2
–5.3	–.4	6.0		2.5	2.8		16.0	10.2	7.5
17.2	47.8	37.1		UND	131.3		29.5	29.1	34.2
8.9	* 15.6	14.8	Sales/Net Fixed Assets	20.6	12.4		11.5	24.4	14.8
3.6	4.6	8.0		8.0	6.8		5.1	11.1	11.7
2.1	3.3	3.9		3.8	4.8		4.8	3.5	3.3
1.8	1.3	2.5	Sales/Total Assets	2.0	2.7		2.5	2.8	2.1
.8	.9	1.5		.9	1.2		1.9	2.5	1.1
2.0	.8	.9			.7		1.3		.8
(30) 3.0	(28) 2.3	(58) 1.5	% Depr., Dep., Amort./Sales		(13) 1.5	(10)	1.6		(12) 1.5
4.1	4.4	2.1			2.1		2.2		2.0
	5.2	4.7	% Officers', Directors',						
	(18) 9.9	(21) 15.1	Owners' Comp/Sales						
	34.2	33.1							
867520M	907832M	1648101M	Net Sales ($)	4859M	30309M	28394M	83113M	165152M	1336274M
595951M	844267M	964655M	Total Assets ($)	7036M	30401M	14188M	35181M	59437M	818412M

M = $ thousand   MM = $ million
See Pages 11 through 18 for Explanation of Ratios and Data

Current Data Sorted By Assets   Comparative Historical Data

						Type of Statement		
1	2	5	8	2	7	Unqualified	10	14
	1	4				Reviewed	1	1
	1					Compiled	10	6
	1					Tax Returns	1	1
2	5	7	5	4	2	Other	14	14
	5 (4/1-9/30/02)		51 (10/1/02-3/31/03)				4/1/98-3/31/99	4/1/99-3/31/00
0-500M	500M-2MM	2-10MM	10-50MM	50-100MM	100-250MM		ALL	ALL
3	9	16	13	6	9	NUMBER OF STATEMENTS	36	36
%	%	%	%	%	%	ASSETS	%	%
		35.5	32.3			Cash & Equivalents	39.8	40.8
		33.2	16.2			Trade Receivables (net)	20.3	19.3
		.0	.1			Inventory	.3	1.5
		2.0	11.7			All Other Current	3.3	6.2
		70.7	60.3			Total Current	63.8	67.8
		9.5	4.1			Fixed Assets (net)	14.3	8.0
		10.2	3.8			Intangibles (net)	7.1	6.3
		9.7	31.9			All Other Non-Current	14.8	17.8
		100.0	100.0			Total	100.0	100.0
						LIABILITIES		
		.9	1.5			Notes Payable-Short Term	33.1	7.9
		4.1	1.3			Cur. Mat.-L/T/D	1.5	1.2
		31.9	19.5			Trade Payables	16.0	20.6
		.1	.7			Income Taxes Payable	.3	1.4
		36.4	65.6			All Other Current	72.9	20.1
		73.3	88.6			Total Current	123.7	51.1
		12.5	2.7			Long Term Debt	12.5	6.6
		.0	.0			Deferred Taxes	.0	.3
		10.8	4.5			All Other Non-Current	11.1	14.6
		3.3	4.2			Net Worth	−47.4	27.3
		100.0	100.0			Total Liabilities & Net Worth	100.0	100.0
						INCOME DATA		
		100.0	100.0			Net Sales	100.0	100.0
						Gross Profit		
		81.1	92.1			Operating Expenses	100.8	90.4
		18.9	7.9			Operating Profit	−.8	9.6
		3.0	−1.8			All Other Expenses (net)	−8.8	−5.0
		15.9	9.7			Profit Before Taxes	8.0	14.6
						RATIOS		
		1.5	1.5				1.4	1.8
		1.1	.8			Current	1.0	1.1
		1.0	.3				.6	.9
		1.4	1.0				1.3	1.6
		1.0	.7			Quick	1.0	1.1
		1.0	.3				.6	.9
	43	8.6	11 32.0				1 468.3	1 439.1
	65	5.6	39 9.3			Sales/Receivables	13 27.9	19 19.6
	274	1.3	108 3.4				110 3.3	161 2.3
						Cost of Sales/Inventory		
						Cost of Sales/Payables		
		6.9	2.7				5.4	1.5
		14.6	−10.3			Sales/Working Capital	68.6	17.7
		NM	−1.1				−9.5	−27.2
							15.6	52.3
						EBIT/Interest	(17) 4.5	(18) 8.5
							−1.8	1.7
						Net Profit + Depr., Dep., Amort./Cur. Mat. L /T/D		
		.1	.0				.0	.0
		.4	.0			Fixed/Worth	.3	.2
		NM	.6				173.5	1.9
		2.2	1.2				1.8	1.6
		16.6	3.0			Debt/Worth	4.0	3.2
		−5.7	NM				−23.5	NM
		335.5	35.0				82.0	181.7
	(11)	91.2	(10) 8.2			% Profit Before Taxes/Tangible Net Worth	(26) 29.7	(27) 29.3
		69.3	.7				11.2	4.4
		26.4	15.2				13.6	33.9
		8.9	2.9			% Profit Before Taxes/Total Assets	4.3	4.6
		3.7	.8				−4.1	1.3
		85.8	UND				UND	UND
		18.5	70.5			Sales/Net Fixed Assets	32.2	33.2
		13.8	34.4				14.7	17.1
		1.8	1.2				3.1	2.5
		1.0	.6			Sales/Total Assets	1.0	.9
		.6	.4				.3	.3
							.7	.8
						% Depr., Dep., Amort./Sales	(17) 1.2	(17) 1.5
							2.0	2.9
						% Officers', Directors', Owners' Comp/Sales		
1890M	15867M	112465M	474299M	494716M	540641M	Net Sales ($)	889103M	770933M
583M	9345M	94734M	301127M	420652M	1428350M	Total Assets ($)	851293M	1408893M

M = $ thousand   MM = $ million
See Pages 11 through 18 for Explanation of Ratios and Data

Comparative Historical Data | Current Data Sorted By Sales

4/1/00-3/31/01 ALL	4/1/01-3/31/02 ALL	4/1/02-3/31/03 ALL	Type of Statement	0-1MM	1-3MM	3-5MM	5-10MM	10-25MM	25MM & OVER
11	11	25	Unqualified	1	2	2	2	8	10
2			Reviewed						
10	6	5	Compiled	2	1	1	1		
3	2	1	Tax Returns		1				
17	15	25	Other	3	5	1	7	6	3
					5 (4/1-9/30/02)		51 (10/1/02-3/31/03)		
43	**34**	**56**	**NUMBER OF STATEMENTS**	**6**	**9**	**4**	**10**	**14**	**13**
%	%	%	**ASSETS**	%	%	%	%	%	%
36.5	35.5	42.3	Cash & Equivalents				30.9	42.3	47.6
19.8	19.2	20.4	Trade Receivables (net)				21.5	20.9	17.8
.1	.6	.2	Inventory				.1	.0	.2
8.0	9.1	8.4	All Other Current				12.6	8.3	10.7
64.4	64.5	71.3	Total Current				65.1	71.5	76.4
9.9	10.1	8.8	Fixed Assets (net)				5.6	4.2	6.3
8.1	5.5	5.2	Intangibles (net)				9.7	6.2	1.9
17.6	19.8	14.7	All Other Non-Current				19.7	18.1	15.5
100.0	100.0	100.0	Total				100.0	100.0	100.0
			LIABILITIES						
3.0	3.3	2.6	Notes Payable-Short Term				.0	6.2	1.8
3.3	1.8	2.1	Cur. Mat.-L/T/D				1.1	2.4	3.1
22.1	27.8	19.1	Trade Payables				15.4	13.0	7.8
.7	1.1	.9	Income Taxes Payable				.6	.2	.1
22.7	27.9	43.4	All Other Current				26.0	60.5	49.3
51.8	61.9	68.1	Total Current				43.1	82.3	62.0
12.6	13.4	8.6	Long Term Debt				13.4	10.7	8.2
.2	.4	.2	Deferred Taxes				.0	.0	.5
12.2	7.5	6.0	All Other Non-Current				5.8	10.1	4.2
23.2	16.9	17.1	Net Worth				37.7	-3.1	25.1
100.0	100.0	100.0	Total Liabilities & Net Worth				100.0	100.0	100.0
			INCOME DATA						
100.0	100.0	100.0	Net Sales				100.0	100.0	100.0
			Gross Profit						
91.6	90.2	86.5	Operating Expenses				85.6	88.9	92.9
8.4	9.8	13.5	Operating Profit				14.4	11.1	7.1
-3.7	.1	1.8	All Other Expenses (net)				3.2	.0	1.0
12.1	9.7	11.7	Profit Before Taxes				11.2	11.1	6.1
			RATIOS						
2.0	1.7	1.8					2.9	1.6	2.0
1.1	1.1	1.1	Current				1.5	1.2	1.3
.9	.7	.8					.9	.8	1.1
1.3	1.3	1.6					2.0	1.5	1.6
1.0	.8	1.0	Quick				1.1	1.0	1.1
.7	.5	.5					.6	.6	.5
0 UND	2 181.7	0 787.0			0 UND	40 9.1		0 UND	
60 6.1	39 9.4	40 9.2	Sales/Receivables	37 10.0	64 5.7	13 28.4			
131 2.8	81 4.5	127 2.9		83 4.4	157 2.3	126 2.9			
			Cost of Sales/Inventory						
			Cost of Sales/Payables						
3.9	4.0	2.1					1.7	3.1	1.4
14.0	33.8	8.7	Sales/Working Capital				7.2	16.1	2.9
-15.1	-8.0	-8.9					NM	-8.0	70.8
7.2	14.0	24.9							
(19) 2.9	(17) 5.6	(23) 3.3	EBIT/Interest						
1.6	2.7	1.2							
			Net Profit + Depr., Dep., Amort./Cur. Mat. L/T/D						
.0	.0	.0					.0	.0	.0
.2	.3	.2	Fixed/Worth				.0	.2	.1
37.5	2.8	2.6					2.2	-.9	.2
1.3	1.2	1.3					1.0	1.8	1.6
4.7	3.4	2.9	Debt/Worth				4.3	5.3	2.4
-72.4	-6.3	116.5					58.5	-4.8	3.5
78.2	75.1	83.4							57.4
(32) 40.1	(24) 18.5	(44) 22.3	% Profit Before Taxes/Tangible Net Worth					(12) 15.3
7.1	6.5	4.4							9.3
9.5	10.7	15.2					16.1	12.6	7.7
5.0	6.4	5.6	% Profit Before Taxes/Total Assets				2.1	6.9	4.7
1.3	2.4	1.3					1.2	.7	1.2
308.0	UND	899.4					UND	UND	338.8
29.1	18.0	28.1	Sales/Net Fixed Assets				42.3	64.9	25.2
11.4	10.9	13.6					16.5	12.3	13.6
1.5	2.0	1.8					1.1	1.8	2.5
.6	.6	.6	Sales/Total Assets				.6	1.0	.6
.3	.3	.4					.3	.4	.2
.7	1.5	.6							
(26) 1.3	(20) 2.9	(29) 1.8	% Depr., Dep., Amort./Sales						
2.9	5.8	2.4							
			% Officers', Directors', Owners' Comp/Sales						
836793M	716632M	1639878M	Net Sales ($)	2843M	14448M	18176M	63541M	225624M	1315246M
1392036M	1230033M	2254791M	Total Assets ($)	9021M	11249M	38835M	161397M	514719M	1519570M

M = $ thousand   MM = $ million
See Pages 11 through 18 for Explanation of Ratios and Data

Current Data Sorted By Assets / Comparative Historical Data

	0-500M	500M-2MM	2-10MM	10-50MM	50-100MM	100-250MM	Type of Statement		4/1/98-3/31/99 ALL	4/1/99-3/31/00 ALL
	2	7	40	45	10	16	Unqualified		113	111
	11	29	51	15	1		Reviewed		137	131
	40	61	36	7	1		Compiled		162	132
	87	60	19	2		4	Tax Returns		108	104
	29	58	71	36	8	4	Other		226	169
	133 (4/1-9/30/02)			617 (10/1/02-3/31/03)						
	169	215	217	105	20	24	**NUMBER OF STATEMENTS**		746	647
	%	%	%	%	%	%	**ASSETS**		%	%
	25.1	23.9	29.3	38.6	41.5	37.8	Cash & Equivalents		26.0	27.1
	12.5	20.9	29.2	27.5	23.3	18.4	Trade Receivables (net)		24.2	24.4
	.1	.2	.4	.1	.0	.8	Inventory		.3	.3
	4.3	3.1	4.7	5.7	8.2	5.1	All Other Current		5.5	4.7
	42.0	48.0	63.6	71.8	73.0	62.1	Total Current		56.0	56.4
	20.5	14.1	13.1	8.0	6.6	7.6	Fixed Assets (net)		17.0	14.8
	17.2	19.3	10.7	8.4	7.1	11.7	Intangibles (net)		12.8	14.6
	20.3	18.5	12.6	11.8	13.3	18.6	All Other Non-Current		14.2	14.2
	100.0	100.0	100.0	100.0	100.0	100.0	Total		100.0	100.0
							LIABILITIES			
	19.2	8.9	5.1	7.7	3.7	7.4	Notes Payable-Short Term		15.5	10.1
	5.4	6.7	2.9	2.5	1.6	1.0	Cur. Mat.-L/T/D		4.2	3.7
	16.6	23.2	34.1	27.3	30.7	17.3	Trade Payables		28.8	30.0
	.2	.3	.6	.3	.5	.1	Income Taxes Payable		.3	.3
	17.8	12.6	18.5	29.3	35.3	27.1	All Other Current		19.7	17.1
	59.3	51.6	61.1	67.1	71.7	52.9	Total Current		68.5	61.1
	31.9	25.1	13.0	6.4	4.2	11.3	Long Term Debt		24.2	17.1
	.2	.1	.1	.4	.2	.3	Deferred Taxes		.4	.4
	9.3	7.0	4.2	6.8	1.2	6.6	All Other Non-Current		6.3	5.8
	-.7	16.1	21.3	19.4	22.8	28.8	Net Worth		.6	15.6
	100.0	100.0	100.0	100.0	100.0	100.0	Total Liabilities & Net Worth		100.0	100.0
							INCOME DATA			
	100.0	100.0	100.0	100.0	100.0	100.0	Net Sales		100.0	100.0
							Gross Profit			
	88.0	88.7	90.1	89.5	89.0	93.8	Operating Expenses		95.3	92.5
	12.0	11.3	9.9	10.5	11.0	6.2	Operating Profit		4.7	7.5
	2.5	2.2	1.9	-.1	-.8	.4	All Other Expenses (net)		-2.7	-.5
	9.5	9.1	8.0	10.7	11.7	5.8	Profit Before Taxes		7.4	8.0
							RATIOS			
	1.9	1.6	1.3	1.4	1.2	1.5			1.5	1.4
	.8	1.0	1.0	1.0	1.0	1.2	Current		1.0	1.0
	.3	.5	.8	.9	.8	1.0			.6	.7
	1.7	1.5	1.2	1.3	1.1	1.3			1.3	1.3
(168)	.6	1.0	1.0	1.0	.9	1.1	Quick	(741)	.9	.9
	.3	.5	.7	.8	.7	.8			.5	.6
	0 UND	0 999.8	18 20.7	24 15.2	14 25.6	1 252.4		3 105.9	8 43.5	
	1 299.0	25 14.8	63 5.8	89 4.1	53 6.9	54 6.8	Sales/Receivables	44 8.3	45 8.0	
	25 14.5	67 5.5	129 2.8	159 2.3	171 2.1	131 2.8		113 3.2	113 3.2	
							Cost of Sales/Inventory			
							Cost of Sales/Payables			
	25.4	8.0	8.7	5.0	5.7	3.9			8.1	9.4
	-34.0	123.2	66.2	14.6	NM	9.6	Sales/Working Capital		UND	999.9
	-9.1	-7.3	-11.6	-21.8	-13.7	-38.5			-7.5	-8.3
	12.5	8.6	23.7	16.4	40.2	21.2			10.1	9.2
(130)	3.9	(177) 3.6	(167) 5.3	(72) 8.1	(14) 23.3	(18) 5.9	EBIT/Interest	(579) 3.5	(488) 4.0	
	1.3	1.6	1.8	2.8	8.1	1.9			1.3	1.5
	1.9	4.4	7.4	7.4			Net Profit + Depr., Dep.,		4.5	5.3
(12)	1.1	(33) 1.9	(50) 3.0	(33) 2.9			Amort./Cur. Mat. L./T/D	(153) 1.8	(134) 2.2	
	.7	.7	.6	.8					.6	1.0
	.1	.2	.2	.1	.1	.0			.3	.3
	1.5	1.4	.7	.4	.3	.2	Fixed/Worth		1.1	1.1
	-.3	-.4	-16.8	-160.7	5.5	.5			-1.1	-1.0
	1.0	1.5	2.2	2.6	3.4	2.1			1.9	2.0
	26.3	15.5	7.9	9.3	7.6	3.9	Debt/Worth		9.0	9.8
	-2.1	-3.1	-84.1	-93.9	68.2	18.2			-4.8	-7.2
	178.0	70.4	112.7	81.0	185.0	42.7	% Profit Before Taxes/Tangible		76.5	87.8
(93)	43.4	(119) 35.0	(161) 43.3	(76) 29.6	(17) 44.4	(20) 19.3	Net Worth	(475) 23.7	(418) 27.3	
	11.0	6.8	8.7	7.2	17.5	.5			7.7	8.6
	41.5	18.3	16.6	12.6	10.4	10.1	% Profit Before Taxes/Total		15.2	14.1
	14.6	7.4	6.1	4.8	7.8	3.4	Assets		5.3	5.5
	1.4	1.8	1.6	1.6	2.7	.3			.8	1.1
	121.5	47.7	51.2	77.7	74.3	93.2			36.1	41.4
	30.6	22.4	19.9	18.9	28.1	19.7	Sales/Net Fixed Assets		16.8	18.0
	13.3	10.6	10.8	9.0	13.5	12.1			8.0	9.3
	7.1	2.5	1.9	1.3	1.1	1.4			2.6	2.4
	3.1	1.6	1.2	.8	.8	.8	Sales/Total Assets		1.3	1.3
	1.6	1.1	.8	.6	.4	.5			.8	.8
	1.3	1.3	1.0	.9	.6	.8			1.3	1.4
(88)	2.0	(147) 2.3	(174) 1.8	(77) 2.1	(15) .9	(12) 2.1	% Depr., Dep., Amort./Sales	(542) 2.4	(461) 2.5	
	3.5	3.9	3.4	3.4	1.8	2.5			3.9	4.1
	8.5	8.3	4.8	5.6			% Officers', Directors',		8.6	8.9
(103)	18.2	(140) 15.1	(80) 11.3	(18) 9.9			Owners' Comp/Sales	(349) 17.3	(284) 16.3	
	28.5	24.5	25.4	25.8					27.3	25.1
	199076M	487397M	1896726M	3465839M	2267498M	5476409M	Net Sales ($)		7875436M	9535526M
	41429M	239650M	1050447M	2207956M	1446209M	4253769M	Total Assets ($)		7574004M	7201853M

M = $ thousand   MM = $ million
See Pages 11 through 18 for Explanation of Ratios and Data

Comparative Historical Data | Current Data Sorted By Sales

4/1/00-3/31/01 ALL	4/1/01-3/31/02 ALL	4/1/02-3/31/03 ALL	Type of Statement	0-1MM	1-3MM	3-5MM	5-10MM	10-25MM	25MM & OVER
81	78	120	Unqualified	6	10	12	15	35	42
113	93	107	Reviewed	11	33	25	16	14	8
148	160	145	Compiled	39	49	25	18	10	4
117	123	172	Tax Returns	84	51	18	9	4	6
170	212	206	Other	34	57	34	35	27	19
				133 (4/1-9/30/02)		617 (10/1/02-3/31/03)			
629	666	750	NUMBER OF STATEMENTS	174	200	114	93	90	79
%	%	%	ASSETS	%	%	%	%	%	%
26.0	26.3	28.7	Cash & Equivalents	20.7	25.6	30.1	32.9	33.9	40.8
25.1	23.6	22.3	Trade Receivables (net)	15.6	21.9	27.5	25.1	27.7	21.3
.8	.4	.2	Inventory	.1	.1	.5	.5	.1	.4
4.8	4.6	4.4	All Other Current	2.8	4.4	4.0	5.0	5.5	6.4
56.6	54.9	55.6	Total Current	39.2	52.1	62.1	63.5	67.2	68.8
15.1	14.8	14.0	Fixed Assets (net)	18.3	13.7	14.6	11.8	11.9	9.4
12.5	15.6	14.3	Intangibles (net)	21.4	17.5	8.5	9.8	9.8	9.0
15.7	14.6	16.1	All Other Non-Current	21.1	16.7	14.7	15.0	11.1	12.8
100.0	100.0	100.0	Total	100.0	100.0	100.0	100.0	100.0	100.0
			LIABILITIES						
15.6	11.8	9.8	Notes Payable-Short Term	15.9	11.2	8.3	9.1	2.8	3.6
4.4	5.2	4.4	Cur. Mat.-L/T/D	3.8	6.0	3.2	6.5	3.2	2.2
26.1	26.8	25.4	Trade Payables	16.4	27.0	28.0	32.2	29.0	25.6
.4	.3	.4	Income Taxes Payable	.2	.2	.1	.7	1.2	.3
18.1	18.2	18.9	All Other Current	9.9	17.5	19.4	20.2	27.9	29.5
64.6	62.3	58.8	Total Current	46.2	61.9	58.9	68.6	64.2	61.2
19.4	21.6	19.5	Long Term Debt	30.5	27.3	13.6	9.3	9.3	7.9
.5	.4	.3	Deferred Taxes	.1	.2	.5	.2	.3	.5
9.5	7.1	6.5	All Other Non-Current	9.2	5.0	6.0	5.1	5.7	8.0
5.9	8.5	14.9	Net Worth	14.0	5.6	21.0	16.8	20.5	22.5
100.0	100.0	100.0	Total Liabilities & Net Worth	100.0	100.0	100.0	100.0	100.0	100.0
			INCOME DATA						
100.0	100.0	100.0	Net Sales	100.0	100.0	100.0	100.0	100.0	100.0
			Gross Profit						
90.9	89.9	89.2	Operating Expenses	81.9	90.2	91.6	93.5	90.8	92.7
9.1	10.1	10.8	Operating Profit	18.1	9.8	8.4	6.5	9.2	7.3
1.1	1.5	1.7	All Other Expenses (net)	4.6	2.3	.8	–.6	.2	–.3
8.0	8.5	9.0	Profit Before Taxes	13.5	7.5	7.6	7.1	9.0	7.6
			RATIOS						
1.4	1.4	1.4	Current	2.0	1.5	1.4	1.2	1.3	1.5
1.0	1.0	1.0		.9	.9	1.1	1.0	1.0	1.2
.7	.6	.7		.4	.5	.9	.6	.8	1.0
1.3	1.2	1.3	Quick	1.9	1.4	1.3	1.2	1.1	1.3
(628) .9	(628) .9	(749) 1.0		(173) .8	.9	1.0	.9	1.0	1.0
.5	.5	.5		.3	.5	.8	.5	.7	.7
3 112.0	2 185.9	1 308.0	Sales/Receivables	0 UND	1 264.7	5 71.5	9 38.8	13 28.9	8 43.2
40 9.1	33 11.0	31 11.6		7 53.7	26 14.2	55 6.7	44 8.3	57 6.4	31 11.6
113 3.2	105 3.5	99 3.7		56 6.5	75 4.9	123 3.0	115 3.2	129 2.8	114 3.2
			Cost of Sales/Inventory						
			Cost of Sales/Payables						
8.6	10.6	8.5	Sales/Working Capital	8.8	9.0	7.2	9.2	11.4	5.6
–222.0	–213.2	179.3		–81.4	–43.5	59.9	51.8	85.4	20.0
–9.7	–8.9	–10.2		–6.8	–6.0	–21.7	–11.2	–13.1	–48.5
11.8	13.6	15.6	EBIT/Interest	10.1	9.2	17.9	27.4	24.7	32.0
(482) 4.1	(525) 4.9	(578) 4.8		(122) 3.4	(168) 3.4	(90) 5.5	(73) 5.1	(68) 10.5	(57) 7.9
1.6	2.0	1.7		1.7	1.2	1.8	1.7	3.9	3.0
5.5	5.0	5.7	Net Profit + Depr., Dep., Amort./Cur. Mat. L/T/D	5.0	4.4	7.7	5.3	7.5	5.0
(111) 1.8	(112) 1.7	(139) 2.2		(16) 1.5	(29) 1.8	(23) 3.3	(18) 1.5	(31) 3.4	(22) 2.2
1.0	.9	.8		.9	.7	.6	.5	1.2	.9
.2	.2	.2	Fixed/Worth	.1	.2	.2	.2	.2	.1
.9	1.2	.8		1.6	2.0	.7	.6	.7	.3
–1.2	–.5	–1.0		–.3	–.3	2.8	–2.1	–7.4	6.9
1.8	1.9	1.8	Debt/Worth	1.2	2.3	1.7	1.9	2.5	2.1
7.5	11.1	9.3		21.8	32.7	4.8	5.1	8.7	4.6
–8.3	–4.0	–5.9		–2.3	–2.5	29.8	–17.4	–35.2	166.6
80.9	122.4	103.0	% Profit Before Taxes/Tangible Net Worth	92.5	86.2	112.8	110.6	158.5	79.4
(418) 29.3	(410) 38.1	(486) 35.8		(96) 32.7	(106) 29.8	(91) 29.4	(68) 38.3	(62) 45.8	(63) 42.3
9.4	10.9	8.3		8.7	6.7	7.1	7.2	14.0	8.6
15.9	18.4	18.6	% Profit Before Taxes/Total Assets	27.4	18.3	14.4	19.6	19.5	16.4
5.8	6.6	6.9		8.3	7.0	5.8	5.7	8.8	6.6
1.2	1.7	1.7		1.7	.5	1.9	1.6	2.5	1.7
45.3	54.0	63.4	Sales/Net Fixed Assets	103.4	57.2	58.7	44.6	68.8	89.4
19.8	21.8	22.8		16.9	27.5	19.5	27.6	18.6	28.8
9.1	10.1	11.0		7.6	12.3	11.4	14.6	10.2	12.4
2.5	2.9	2.7	Sales/Total Assets	2.8	2.8	2.2	2.4	3.1	2.4
1.3	1.4	1.4		1.3	1.6	1.2	1.5	1.2	1.2
.8	.8	.8		.6	1.1	.8	1.0	.8	.8
1.1	.9	1.0	% Depr., Dep., Amort./Sales	1.7	1.3	.9	1.0	1.0	.4
(456) 2.1	(453) 1.9	(513) 2.0		(94) 3.5	(132) 2.0	(86) 2.0	(70) 1.6	(73) 1.9	(58) 1.2
3.5	3.5	3.5		6.6	3.1	2.9	2.6	3.3	2.8
8.2	8.1	7.3	% Officers', Directors', Owners' Comp/Sales	11.2	8.0	8.1	5.7	2.9	.8
(292) 15.3	(301) 16.3	(348) 15.4		(96) 20.1	(123) 14.5	(60) 12.1	(35) 12.6	(17) 5.8	(17) 9.6
25.2	27.2	25.4		30.9	23.9	24.0	25.7	13.9	18.7
7968775M	8812942M	13792945M	Net Sales ($)	86593M	361040M	434896M	660292M	1414838M	10835286M
6699025M	7198479M	9239460M	Total Assets ($)	112187M	333009M	572799M	545253M	1273144M	6403068M

© RMA 2003

M = $ thousand   MM = $ million
See Pages 11 through 18 for Explanation of Ratios and Data

Current Data Sorted By Assets   Comparative Historical Data

0-500M	500M-2MM	2-10MM	10-50MM	50-100MM	100-250MM	Type of Statement	4/1/98-3/31/99 ALL	4/1/99-3/31/00 ALL
	3	4	4	2	3	Unqualified	13	19
		2				Reviewed		1
1	3	1	1			Compiled	5	8
3	4	2				Tax Returns	3	5
3	5	7	4	3	1	Other	12	12
	6 (4/1-9/30/02)		50 (10/1/02-3/31/03)				4/1/98-3/31/99	4/1/99-3/31/00
7	15	16	9	5	4	**NUMBER OF STATEMENTS**	33	45
%	%	%	%	%	%	**ASSETS**	%	%
	12.3	23.3				Cash & Equivalents	23.7	22.4
	9.7	4.3				Trade Receivables (net)	12.6	12.5
	.0	.0				Inventory	.0	1.4
	8.7	11.0				All Other Current	4.0	8.5
	30.8	38.6				Total Current	40.2	44.8
	51.9	32.9				Fixed Assets (net)	26.7	27.5
	.8	5.2				Intangibles (net)	4.6	1.2
	16.5	23.4				All Other Non-Current	28.4	26.6
	100.0	100.0				Total	100.0	100.0
						LIABILITIES		
	13.8	10.2				Notes Payable-Short Term	5.4	10.7
	1.6	2.2				Cur. Mat.-L/T/D	1.6	2.2
	1.5	3.7				Trade Payables	2.2	5.1
	.0	.0				Income Taxes Payable	.1	.2
	10.7	23.7				All Other Current	10.2	14.1
	27.6	39.9				Total Current	19.5	32.3
	55.1	21.7				Long Term Debt	26.9	21.6
	.0	.1				Deferred Taxes	1.1	1.8
	3.0	2.8				All Other Non-Current	8.4	4.1
	14.3	35.4				Net Worth	44.2	40.2
	100.0	100.0				Total Liabilities & Net Worth	100.0	100.0
						INCOME DATA		
	100.0	100.0				Net Sales	100.0	100.0
						Gross Profit		
	67.9	77.5				Operating Expenses	146.2	72.0
	32.1	22.5				Operating Profit	-46.2	28.0
	9.5	13.0				All Other Expenses (net)	-76.0	2.9
	22.6	9.5				Profit Before Taxes	29.8	25.0
						RATIOS		
	2.7	2.6					25.9	6.1
	.3	1.1				Current	1.9	1.5
	.1	.5					.8	.6
	1.7	2.6					25.9	3.2
	.1	.7				Quick	1.5	1.1
	.0	.2					.7	.5
0 UND	1 357.6						0 UND	0 UND
0 UND	8 45.3					Sales/Receivables	0 UND	0 UND
13 27.1	24 15.3						41 8.9	28 13.0
						Cost of Sales/Inventory		
						Cost of Sales/Payables		
	2.9	4.3					1.1	1.4
	-8.6	37.4				Sales/Working Capital	16.9	16.4
	-1.8	-5.2					-22.9	-46.6
	14.7	13.9					23.3	18.2
	(10) 4.0	(10) 2.9				EBIT/Interest	(16) 4.6	(25) 7.5
	2.1	-6.7					-3.5	.9
						Net Profit + Depr., Dep., Amort./Cur. Mat. L /T/D		
	.0	.0					.0	.1
	2.3	1.6				Fixed/Worth	.4	.3
	57.3	-16.4					7.5	6.3
	.5	.3					.1	.4
	2.3	2.8				Debt/Worth	1.7	1.1
	56.5	-22.7					10.6	6.1
	51.9	69.2					52.9	66.6
(12)	12.6	(11) 27.9				% Profit Before Taxes/Tangible Net Worth	(28) 23.6	(38) 24.4
	5.6	8.0					.5	7.8
	17.1	18.3					14.0	19.3
	6.7	4.1				% Profit Before Taxes/Total Assets	6.0	5.6
	4.0	-4.2					-1.3	.6
	16.5	34.7					42.1	46.0
	2.2	15.4				Sales/Net Fixed Assets	7.8	12.4
	.2	.4					.9	1.1
	1.3	2.0					1.9	2.4
	.6	1.1				Sales/Total Assets	.3	.7
	.2	.3					.1	.2
	2.2	1.5					1.3	.9
(12)	5.2	(13) 2.5				% Depr., Dep., Amort./Sales	(25) 3.0	(37) 1.7
	17.3	17.3					11.0	4.5
						% Officers', Directors', Owners' Comp/Sales		
8312M	18610M	93708M	39973M	74934M	847161M	Net Sales ($)	507077M	1098012M
1735M	19758M	73234M	257415M	385474M	622572M	Total Assets ($)	928636M	1514725M

	Comparative Historical Data			Current Data Sorted By Sales					
Type of Statement									
Unqualified	5	15	16	2	2	3	3	3	3
Reviewed		2	2		2				
Compiled	6	8	6	3	1	1		1	
Tax Returns	4	6	9	6	1	1	1		
Other	23	21	23	7	7	1	5	2	1
	4/1/00-3/31/01	4/1/01-3/31/02	4/1/02-3/31/03	\ 6 (4/1-9/30/02)		\ 50 (10/1/02-3/31/03)			
	ALL	ALL	ALL	0-1MM	1-3MM	3-5MM	5-10MM	10-25MM	25MM & OVER
NUMBER OF STATEMENTS	38	52	56	18	13	6	9	6	4
ASSETS	%	%	%	%	%	%	%	%	%
Cash & Equivalents	19.3	17.5	20.8	10.6	21.3				
Trade Receivables (net)	13.0	15.0	4.9	4.7	1.3				
Inventory	.1	.7	.0	.0	.0				
All Other Current	4.7	8.5	7.1	2.1	13.5				
Total Current	37.1	41.5	32.8	17.4	36.1				
Fixed Assets (net)	32.1	34.5	38.7	64.5	30.0				
Intangibles (net)	5.2	2.4	5.4	5.1	6.4				
All Other Non-Current	25.6	21.5	23.1	13.0	27.4				
Total	100.0	100.0	100.0	100.0	100.0				
LIABILITIES									
Notes Payable-Short Term	17.1	11.8	11.9	9.7	18.5				
Cur. Mat.-L/T/D	1.5	4.9	2.0	1.6	2.7				
Trade Payables	5.4	2.9	3.9	.9	5.4				
Income Taxes Payable	.3	.2	.1	.0	.0				
All Other Current	19.5	20.9	14.0	2.6	12.6				
Total Current	43.8	40.6	31.9	14.8	39.2				
Long Term Debt	22.6	15.2	35.0	71.2	26.1				
Deferred Taxes	1.5	.0	.0	.0	.0				
All Other Non-Current	6.4	11.8	3.8	6.4	4.6				
Net Worth	25.7	32.5	29.2	7.6	30.0				
Total Liabilities & Net Worth	100.0	100.0	100.0	100.0	100.0				
INCOME DATA									
Net Sales	100.0	100.0	100.0	100.0	100.0				
Gross Profit									
Operating Expenses	74.1	75.9	65.8	60.5	62.7				
Operating Profit	25.9	24.1	34.2	39.5	37.3				
All Other Expenses (net)	-1.9	4.2	10.9	20.6	8.0				
Profit Before Taxes	27.8	19.9	23.3	18.9	29.4				
RATIOS									
Current	2.8	3.8	2.7	12.7	3.7				
	1.2	1.1	1.1	.3	1.0				
	.3	.5	.2	.1	.2				
Quick	2.8	2.3	2.3	3.0	3.7				
	.9	.8	.9	.3	.2				
	.1	.1	.1	.1	.1				
Sales/Receivables	0 UND	0 UND	0 UND	0 UND	0 UND				
	0 UND	6 57.7	0 UND	0 UND	0 UND				
	47 7.7	57 6.4	15 24.2	0 UND	10 37.0				
Cost of Sales/Inventory									
Cost of Sales/Payables									
Sales/Working Capital	2.3	2.4	3.2	4.0	1.8				
	82.8	40.0	55.3	-12.8	154.9				
	-4.3	-6.8	-4.5	-1.1	-1.5				
EBIT/Interest	(25) 59.1	(31) 16.5	(35) 19.1		(11) 11.8				
	7.1	4.7	4.6		4.5				
	.7	1.4	1.0		2.6				
Net Profit + Depr., Dep., Amort./Cur. Mat. L/T/D									
Fixed/Worth	.0	.0	.0	.6	.0				
	.4	.4	1.4	8.3	1.3				
	5.0	4.5	12.3	-9.0	NM				
Debt/Worth	.5	.4	.6	.5	.5				
	1.8	1.5	1.8	7.5	2.4				
	11.7	7.8	11.6	-11.6	NM				
% Profit Before Taxes/Tangible Net Worth	(31) 71.4	(45) 53.6	(44) 50.5	(12) 70.7	(10) 42.8				
	18.5	16.6	16.5	14.6	13.9				
	2.3	5.5	4.5	5.6	7.0				
% Profit Before Taxes/Total Assets	18.6	15.8	15.4	7.6	18.1				
	4.9	5.2	5.6	4.2	8.5				
	.7	1.5	1.3	.4	2.8				
Sales/Net Fixed Assets	70.3	85.6	54.4	26.3	UND				
	12.9	16.0	13.1	.3	12.5				
	1.6	.5	.3	.2	1.9				
Sales/Total Assets	2.4	2.6	1.9	.4	1.6				
	.5	.9	.4	.2	.6				
	.1	.2	.1	.1	.2				
% Depr., Dep., Amort./Sales	(22) 1.0	(35) .8	(36) 1.7	(12) 9.8					
	2.4	2.0	4.5	17.3					
	8.7	12.4	17.3	25.4					
% Officers', Directors', Owners' Comp/Sales		(10) 5.5	(10) 5.9						
		17.6	17.5						
		38.0	27.0						
Net Sales ($)	781928M	807063M	1082698M	7112M	22327M	26055M	70336M	77041M	879827M
Total Assets ($)	1066853M	1308947M	1360188M	53041M	99519M	47257M	426252M	169139M	564980M

© RMA 2003

M = $ thousand   MM = $ million
See Pages 11 through 18 for Explanation of Ratios and Data

Current Data Sorted By Assets   Comparative Historical Data

Type of Statement

0-500M	500M-2MM	2-10MM	10-50MM	50-100MM	100-250MM		4/1/98-3/31/99 ALL	4/1/99-3/31/00 ALL
	1	1	6	5	7	Unqualified	28	16
1	3	5	4			Reviewed	8	4
1	7	11	2			Compiled	25	19
10	15	5				Tax Returns	23	15
2	8	10	3	2	5	Other	32	20
	9 (4/1-9/30/02)		105 (10/1/02-3/31/03)					
14	34	32	15	7	12	**NUMBER OF STATEMENTS**	116	74

ASSETS

0-500M %	500M-2MM %	2-10MM %	10-50MM %	50-100MM %	100-250MM %		%	%
8.8	6.7	10.3	20.0		3.3	Cash & Equivalents	6.5	6.5
.0	1.0	9.5	8.4		10.3	Trade Receivables (net)	3.1	.6
.0	4.7	4.3	.1		.0	Inventory	.3	1.6
.1	2.2	.7	1.0		1.6	All Other Current	1.5	3.1
9.0	14.5	24.8	29.4		15.2	Total Current	11.3	11.8
75.2	75.8	63.2	50.3		65.9	Fixed Assets (net)	63.5	67.6
5.8	3.8	1.5	4.2		.4	Intangibles (net)	2.0	2.7
10.1	5.8	10.6	16.1		18.6	All Other Non-Current	23.2	17.9
100.0	100.0	100.0	100.0		100.0	Total	100.0	100.0

LIABILITIES

0-500M	500M-2MM	2-10MM	10-50MM	50-100MM	100-250MM			
.2	5.4	9.7	10.1		6.9	Notes Payable-Short Term	6.7	5.4
11.2	5.9	2.3	3.1		1.2	Cur. Mat.-L/T/D	2.6	2.1
.2	1.0	4.5	.7		1.0	Trade Payables	1.1	1.1
.0	.0	.3	.0		.2	Income Taxes Payable	.1	.1
10.0	4.1	2.6	4.1		1.6	All Other Current	6.6	5.3
21.6	16.3	19.4	18.0		10.8	Total Current	17.1	14.1
70.8	63.8	43.9	42.0		44.8	Long Term Debt	47.5	54.0
.0	.0	.0	.0		1.2	Deferred Taxes	.6	1.1
4.6	6.0	3.1	7.8		4.5	All Other Non-Current	3.7	4.4
3.0	13.9	33.6	32.2		38.7	Net Worth	31.2	26.4
100.0	100.0	100.0	100.0		100.0	Total Liabilities & Net Worth	100.0	100.0

INCOME DATA

0-500M	500M-2MM	2-10MM	10-50MM	50-100MM	100-250MM			
100.0	100.0	100.0	100.0		100.0	Net Sales	100.0	100.0
						Gross Profit		
56.4	54.5	65.7	65.2		54.1	Operating Expenses	56.2	51.0
43.6	45.5	34.3	34.8		45.9	Operating Profit	43.8	49.0
23.2	32.1	18.6	27.3		21.5	All Other Expenses (net)	5.8	20.1
20.4	13.4	15.7	7.5		24.3	Profit Before Taxes	38.0	28.9

RATIOS

0-500M	500M-2MM	2-10MM	10-50MM	50-100MM	100-250MM			
5.0 / .7 / .1	3.1 / 1.2 / .1	4.2 / 1.5 / .5	14.1 / 1.4 / .7		2.2 / 1.0 / .3	Current	2.3 / .7 / .2	1.9 / .7 / .2
3.3 / .7 / .1	2.5 / .9 / .1	2.9 / 1.1 / .4	13.0 / 1.4 / .7		2.2 / .8 / .1	Quick	2.2 / .5 / .1	1.2 / .5 / .2
0 UND / 0 UND / 0 UND	0 UND / 0 UND / 0 UND	0 UND / 12 31.0 / 47 7.8	0 UND / 4 95.0 / 40 9.1		0 UND / 8 47.8 / 39 9.4	Sales/Receivables	0 UND / 0 UND / 10 37.1	0 UND / 0 UND / 9 40.4
						Cost of Sales/Inventory		
						Cost of Sales/Payables		
5.8 / UND / -3.4	3.4 / 61.6 / -5.0	2.1 / 17.3 / -4.5	1.6 / 3.9 / -3.6		7.5 / NM / -4.2	Sales/Working Capital	10.1 / -10.8 / -1.8	5.1 / -26.3 / -2.4
		(17) 8.9 / 1.9 / -1.0				EBIT/Interest	(38) 10.9 / 3.2 / 2.1	(24) 14.4 / 4.0 / 1.6
						Net Profit + Depr., Dep., Amort./Cur. Mat. L /T/D		
2.4 / NM / -4.1	3.4 / 14.9 / -34.4	.3 / 2.2 / 7.6	.0 / 1.3 / 11.5		.3 / 2.1 / 3.4	Fixed/Worth	.6 / 1.8 / 10.3	1.1 / 2.6 / 13.6
1.9 / NM / -5.9	2.5 / 14.0 / -36.9	.9 / 1.9 / 7.0	.5 / 4.1 / 16.9		.9 / 1.6 / 2.8	Debt/Worth	.8 / 1.5 / 14.3	1.0 / 2.3 / 27.0
	(22) 42.0 / 19.5 / -.1	(27) 28.0 / 18.3 / .5	16.4 / 6.6 / 1.0		14.6 / 8.0 / .7	% Profit Before Taxes/Tangible Net Worth	(95) 29.1 / 9.6 / 4.5	(60) 37.5 / 14.3 / 6.7
10.5 / 4.5 / 1.7	5.9 / 1.7 / -.3	10.1 / 3.5 / -.2	4.1 / 1.4 / .1		6.2 / 3.0 / .2	% Profit Before Taxes/Total Assets	8.1 / 3.8 / 1.3	7.8 / 4.5 / .9
.6 / .3 / .2	.6 / .2 / .1	11.4 / .3 / .2	40.5 / .3 / .1		34.5 / .2 / .1	Sales/Net Fixed Assets	1.7 / .3 / .1	1.4 / .2 / .1
.4 / .2 / .2	.3 / .2 / .1	.4 / .2 / .1	.3 / .2 / .1		.2 / .1 / .1	Sales/Total Assets	.3 / .2 / .1	.3 / .2 / .1
(13) 10.3 / 16.0 / 20.1	(32) 7.7 / 14.3 / 25.2	(25) 7.0 / 14.9 / 25.0	(12) 5.3 / 13.9 / 24.7			% Depr., Dep., Amort./Sales	(93) 9.1 / 15.1 / 19.4	(62) 9.6 / 15.4 / 20.6
						% Officers', Directors', Owners' Comp/Sales		
1237M	20339M	79918M	119254M	64075M	427994M	Net Sales ($)	664564M	557980M
4153M	39720M	141949M	378345M	486466M	2031913M	Total Assets ($)	3127397M	2987367M

Comparative Historical Data			Type of Statement	Current Data Sorted By Sales					
15	9	20	Unqualified	1	4	3	2	6	4
4	4	13	Reviewed	5	3		1	3	1
11	13	21	Compiled	16	3	1		1	
14	10	30	Tax Returns	29	1				
12	23	30	Other	14	6	1	3	5	1
4/1/00-3/31/01	4/1/01-3/31/02	4/1/02-3/31/03		9 (4/1-9/30/02)			105 (10/1/02-3/31/03)		
ALL	ALL	ALL		0-1MM	1-3MM	3-5MM	5-10MM	10-25MM	25MM & OVER
56	59	114	NUMBER OF STATEMENTS	65	17	5	6	15	6
%	%	%	**ASSETS**	%	%	%	%	%	%
4.2	5.6	10.0	Cash & Equivalents	8.0	7.5			13.6	
8.0	5.5	6.1	Trade Receivables (net)	2.1	5.4			18.9	
3.0	1.4	2.6	Inventory	1.3	.3			6.2	
2.4	2.5	1.3	All Other Current	.5	.5			1.6	
17.6	14.9	19.9	Total Current	12.0	13.8			40.4	
59.7	68.1	66.3	Fixed Assets (net)	78.2	61.2			44.7	
3.3	2.7	2.9	Intangibles (net)	3.6	.5			4.2	
19.3	14.3	10.9	All Other Non-Current	6.2	24.6			10.7	
100.0	100.0	100.0	Total	100.0	100.0			100.0	
			LIABILITIES						
11.9	3.7	6.8	Notes Payable-Short Term	5.7	8.0			9.7	
2.2	2.5	4.3	Cur. Mat.-L/T/D	6.2	2.3			1.4	
1.9	1.7	1.9	Trade Payables	.6	1.0			8.2	
.1	.2	.1	Income Taxes Payable	.0	.0			.1	
8.6	4.2	4.0	All Other Current	3.9	4.4			2.7	
24.6	12.4	17.1	Total Current	16.4	15.7			22.0	
49.3	47.8	52.6	Long Term Debt	65.4	47.4			32.1	
.6	.4	.1	Deferred Taxes	.0	.0			.0	
2.1	4.1	4.9	All Other Non-Current	3.7	4.6			3.7	
23.3	35.4	25.2	Net Worth	14.4	32.3			42.2	
100.0	100.0	100.0	Total Liabilities & Net Worth	100.0	100.0			100.0	
			INCOME DATA						
100.0	100.0	100.0	Net Sales	100.0	100.0			100.0	
			Gross Profit						
54.6	57.9	59.6	Operating Expenses	53.5	61.9			66.9	
45.4	42.1	40.4	Operating Profit	46.5	38.1			33.1	
22.4	25.1	24.4	All Other Expenses (net)	31.1	22.2			17.6	
23.0	16.9	15.9	Profit Before Taxes	15.4	16.0			15.5	
			RATIOS						
2.1	2.8	3.7		4.0	3.5			3.3	
.7	1.2	1.2	Current	1.2	1.1			1.4	
.2	.3	.3		.2	.4			.8	
1.3	2.2	2.8		2.9	3.5			2.6	
.4	1.0	1.0	Quick	1.0	1.0			1.0	
.1	.3	.3		.2	.4			.2	
0 UND	0 UND	0 UND		0 UND	0 UND			0 UND	
0 UND	0 UND	0 UND	Sales/Receivables	0 UND	0 999.8			9 38.5	
28 13.1	16 23.2	18 20.1		0 UND	8 43.1			47 7.8	
			Cost of Sales/Inventory						
			Cost of Sales/Payables						
4.1	3.9	2.4		2.6	4.2			2.1	
-62.1	14.8	26.9	Sales/Working Capital	68.2	21.0			16.4	
-2.4	-4.6	-4.8		-5.0	-3.0			-23.0	
(14) 8.7	(15) 7.4	(40) 10.1		(17) 4.8					
2.8	2.0	3.7	EBIT/Interest	1.9					
.4	.2	.8		.9					
			Net Profit + Depr., Dep., Amort./Cur. Mat. L/T/D						
.8	.8	1.1		2.5	.4			.1	
2.2	2.7	3.5	Fixed/Worth	8.5	2.1			.3	
7.7	4.9	22.8		-35.0	12.3			2.4	
1.0	1.0	1.1		2.1	.7			.8	
2.6	2.2	3.6	Debt/Worth	8.4	1.9			1.6	
9.1	9.4	30.6		-36.1	28.5			3.8	
(48) 37.0	(51) 22.7	(90) 30.4		(44) 30.8	(15) 51.6			28.0	
12.8	8.8	10.2	% Profit Before Taxes/Tangible Net Worth	16.4	6.8			12.3	
5.6	1.6	.3		.0	1.0			6.0	
8.1	6.1	6.7		6.7	8.2			6.8	
4.0	2.7	2.1	% Profit Before Taxes/Total Assets	2.0	2.0			4.5	
.8	.2	.0		.0	.0			1.4	
6.9	.6	.9		.4	10.5			133.8	
.3	.2	.3	Sales/Net Fixed Assets	.2	.3			10.5	
.2	.1	.1		.1	.2			.1	
.3	.2	.3		.2	.3			2.1	
.2	.2	.2	Sales/Total Assets	.2	.2			.1	
.1	.1	.1		.1	.1			.1	
(45) 9.0	(49) 8.8	(93) 8.6		(59) 12.0	(11) 7.9			(12) .6	
16.7	14.7	14.4	% Depr., Dep., Amort./Sales	17.1	13.8			3.0	
23.5	21.0	21.8		24.9	16.7			20.1	
			% Officers', Directors', Owners' Comp/Sales						
584982M	502483M	712817M	Net Sales ($)	19142M	29967M	19404M	41839M	227452M	375013M
2405350M	1556252M	3082546M	Total Assets ($)	139193M	258491M	106617M	323768M	1426070M	828407M

M = $ thousand   MM = $ million
See Pages 11 through 18 for Explanation of Ratios and Data

Current Data Sorted By Assets / Comparative Historical Data

0-500M	500M-2MM	2-10MM	10-50MM	50-100MM	100-250MM	Type of Statement	4/1/98-3/31/99 ALL	4/1/99-3/31/00 ALL
1	1	2	1	1	2	Unqualified	11	6
1	2	1	1			Reviewed	4	1
	2	1	1			Compiled	8	7
	5	3				Tax Returns	4	4
3	2	5		1		Other	13	11
	3 (4/1-9/30/02)		33 (10/1/02-3/31/03)					
5	12	12	3	2	2	NUMBER OF STATEMENTS	40	29
%	%	%	%	%	%	ASSETS	%	%
	13.3	20.4				Cash & Equivalents	12.1	9.8
	28.4	13.3				Trade Receivables (net)	6.4	13.6
	2.7	2.0				Inventory	1.0	3.7
	1.5	2.7				All Other Current	13.3	7.1
	46.0	38.5				Total Current	32.8	34.2
	36.9	43.7				Fixed Assets (net)	28.2	35.5
	10.8	1.6				Intangibles (net)	2.4	3.1
	6.4	16.2				All Other Non-Current	36.6	27.2
	100.0	100.0				Total	100.0	100.0
						LIABILITIES		
	24.1	18.7				Notes Payable-Short Term	15.5	29.3
	9.1	2.1				Cur. Mat.-L/T/D	1.6	2.6
	4.9	1.9				Trade Payables	9.9	1.5
	.3	.4				Income Taxes Payable	.6	.7
	15.5	16.4				All Other Current	9.6	11.0
	53.8	39.5				Total Current	37.2	45.1
	22.8	18.8				Long Term Debt	23.8	33.1
	1.6	.0				Deferred Taxes	.4	.0
	.0	1.9				All Other Non-Current	2.8	3.9
	21.8	39.8				Net Worth	35.7	17.9
	100.0	100.0				Total Liabilities & Net Worth	100.0	100.0
						INCOME DATA		
	100.0	100.0				Net Sales	100.0	100.0
						Gross Profit		
	66.1	64.2				Operating Expenses	110.6	60.3
	33.9	35.8				Operating Profit	−10.6	39.7
	20.4	12.8				All Other Expenses (net)	−191.4	8.9
	13.5	23.1				Profit Before Taxes	180.8	30.8
						RATIOS		
	7.0	2.6					5.2	2.6
	1.2	1.2				Current	1.5	.7
	.1	.3					.3	.1
	6.5	2.5					4.0	2.1
	.7	.8				Quick	.7	.4
	.1	.3					.1	.1
	0 UND	0 UND					0 UND	0 UND
	16 23.3	0 UND				Sales/Receivables	0 UND	0 UND
	90 4.1	7 54.3					14 25.8	22 16.7
						Cost of Sales/Inventory		
						Cost of Sales/Payables		
	1.3	3.8					.6	5.4
	9.7	13.7				Sales/Working Capital	11.4	−17.1
	−4.4	−3.8					−2.1	−1.3
							(15) 17.3	(13) 6.8
						EBIT/Interest	2.9	2.8
							1.9	.4
						Net Profit + Depr., Dep., Amort./Cur. Mat. L /T/D		
	.1	.1					.0	.0
	4.9	1.0				Fixed/Worth	.1	1.8
	NM	5.7					2.1	9.9
	.6	.7					.3	1.1
	6.8	1.8				Debt/Worth	1.6	3.2
	NM	9.8					4.9	28.3
		51.6					(36) 28.1	(23) 67.3
		25.4				% Profit Before Taxes/Tangible Net Worth	13.4	18.1
		17.8					−.8	6.7
	6.6	20.4					11.9	10.5
	4.1	8.8				% Profit Before Taxes/Total Assets	3.8	5.4
	.1	1.4					−.9	1.4
	51.0	52.6					UND	UND
	13.4	7.6				Sales/Net Fixed Assets	20.9	9.6
	.2	.2					.3	.9
	2.6	1.3					.3	1.5
	.7	.3				Sales/Total Assets	.2	.2
	.1	.1					.1	.1
							(26) 1.8	(19) 1.0
						% Depr., Dep., Amort./Sales	4.9	3.0
							21.3	20.0
						% Officers', Directors', Owners' Comp/Sales		
4987M	16451M	32744M	16207M	13478M	227930M	Net Sales ($)	64361M	207145M
1293M	12068M	44100M	59628M	122629M	370254M	Total Assets ($)	689949M	506508M

© RMA 2003

M = $ thousand   MM = $ million
See Pages 11 through 18 for Explanation of Ratios and Data

Comparative Historical Data | Current Data Sorted By Sales

			Type of Statement						
7	5	8	Unqualified		5		1		2
1	1	5	Reviewed	3		1		1	
10	7	4	Compiled	3	1				
9	8	8	Tax Returns	6	1	1			
11	13	11	Other	5	2	2	1	1	
4/1/00-3/31/01	4/1/01-3/31/02	4/1/02-3/31/03			3 (4/1-9/30/02)		33 (10/1/02-3/31/03)		
ALL	ALL	ALL		0-1MM	1-3MM	3-5MM	5-10MM	10-25MM	25MM & OVER
38	34	36	NUMBER OF STATEMENTS	17	9	4	2	2	2
%	%	%	ASSETS	%	%	%	%	%	%
9.6	13.3	16.8	Cash & Equivalents	13.2					
13.7	7.7	15.6	Trade Receivables (net)	16.3					
1.4	2.2	1.9	Inventory	.2					
13.6	11.9	7.4	All Other Current	8.9					
38.4	35.2	41.8	Total Current	38.6					
36.4	33.3	36.5	Fixed Assets (net)	46.8					
3.1	3.6	4.4	Intangibles (net)	.2					
22.2	28.0	17.3	All Other Non-Current	14.4					
100.0	100.0	100.0	Total	100.0					
			LIABILITIES						
17.7	14.1	21.6	Notes Payable-Short Term	24.0					
5.6	6.3	4.9	Cur. Mat.-L/T/D	9.3					
5.8	6.0	5.5	Trade Payables	2.2					
.0	.1	.2	Income Taxes Payable	.0					
4.5	7.0	14.4	All Other Current	10.5					
33.6	33.4	46.5	Total Current	46.1					
30.4	23.6	18.5	Long Term Debt	28.6					
.0	.5	.9	Deferred Taxes	.0					
6.4	9.2	1.1	All Other Non-Current	.2					
29.6	33.5	33.0	Net Worth	25.2					
100.0	100.0	100.0	Total Liabilities & Net Worth	100.0					
			INCOME DATA						
100.0	100.0	100.0	Net Sales	100.0					
			Gross Profit						
63.2	58.4	68.8	Operating Expenses	53.3					
36.8	41.6	31.2	Operating Profit	46.7					
12.9	12.8	12.9	All Other Expenses (net)	23.5					
23.8	28.8	18.3	Profit Before Taxes	23.3					
			RATIOS						
3.1	4.5	3.1		3.0					
1.3	1.6	1.3	Current	1.0					
.4	.4	.4		.2					
2.9	2.6	2.7		3.0					
(37) .7	.5	.9	Quick	.4					
.1	.1	.2		.1					
0 UND	0 UND	0 UND		0 UND					
0 UND	0 UND	2 238.2	Sales/Receivables	0 UND					
28 12.8	16 22.4	44 8.3		13 28.6					
			Cost of Sales/Inventory						
			Cost of Sales/Payables						
5.0	1.4	2.1		.6					
52.7	11.6	8.1	Sales/Working Capital	18.8					
-3.1	-8.1	-6.3		-4.6					
10.1	18.1	14.9							
(20) 3.9	(17) 4.6	(22) 5.2	EBIT/Interest						
1.1	1.6	.7							
			Net Profit + Depr., Dep., Amort./Cur. Mat. L/T/D						
.0	.0	.1		.1					
.8	.5	1.1	Fixed/Worth	1.9					
20.0	3.3	7.3		7.6					
.4	.4	.5		1.3					
3.8	1.6	2.0	Debt/Worth	5.4					
NM	22.5	10.6		10.1					
66.7	44.4	33.8	% Profit Before Taxes/Tangible Net Worth	37.9					
(29) 15.0	(28) 7.7	(32) 14.8		(16) 17.8					
1.4	4.8	.3		-2.3					
12.5	11.9	14.8	% Profit Before Taxes/Total Assets	5.0					
3.8	4.0	3.5		1.9					
.9	.8	.0		-2.7					
69.6	UND	61.0	Sales/Net Fixed Assets	253.8					
6.1	19.7	12.1		.4					
.3	.3	.2		.2					
1.5	1.1	2.3	Sales/Total Assets	.3					
.2	.2	.4		.1					
.1	.1	.1		.1					
1.0	.7	1.1	% Depr., Dep., Amort./Sales	3.1					
(28) 4.3	(22) 3.8	(22) 3.6		(11) 18.5					
16.1	16.0	18.7		27.4					
			% Officers', Directors', Owners' Comp/Sales						
425011M	178990M	311797M	Net Sales ($)	7419M	18323M	16731M	13478M	27916M	227930M
856874M	932014M	609972M	Total Assets ($)	39115M	40366M	7018M	122629M	30590M	370254M

M = $ thousand   MM = $ million
See Pages 11 through 18 for Explanation of Ratios and Data

REAL ESTATE
AND RENTAL
AND LEASING

Current Data Sorted By Assets   **Comparative Historical Data**

0-500M	500M-2MM	2-10MM	10-50MM	50-100MM	100-250MM	Type of Statement	4/1/98-3/31/99 ALL	4/1/99-3/31/00 ALL
9	39	68	29	4	5	Unqualified	139	118
8	12	15	14	3	3	Reviewed	43	51
19	47	40	11	1	1	Compiled	143	130
113	173	90	11	2	1	Tax Returns	206	177
34	80	83	30	3	4	Other	201	167
	82 (4/1-9/30/02)		869 (10/1/02-3/31/03)					
183	351	296	95	12	14	NUMBER OF STATEMENTS	732	643
%	%	%	%	%	%	**ASSETS**	%	%
13.8	6.9	5.8	5.9	16.6	9.3	Cash & Equivalents	7.2	7.9
4.1	1.4	2.6	6.5	.6	.8	Trade Receivables (net)	2.0	3.4
.4	1.6	2.4	3.2	1.0	.5	Inventory	1.7	2.1
2.0	2.3	3.4	4.8	3.7	7.0	All Other Current	2.0	2.0
20.2	12.2	14.3	20.4	22.0	17.5	Total Current	12.9	15.4
71.0	78.5	76.4	66.2	53.3	58.5	Fixed Assets (net)	75.3	72.5
2.2	2.1	1.4	1.1	11.3	1.0	Intangibles (net)	2.3	3.1
6.7	7.3	8.0	12.4	13.4	23.0	All Other Non-Current	9.5	9.0
100.0	100.0	100.0	100.0	100.0	100.0	Total	100.0	100.0
						LIABILITIES		
9.6	4.8	6.5	6.0	5.4	6.0	Notes Payable-Short Term	5.6	5.7
13.7	3.4	2.9	2.0	1.4	1.7	Cur. Mat.-L/T/D	5.1	5.1
2.9	1.3	.9	4.1	1.1	3.7	Trade Payables	2.0	1.9
.0	.2	.2	.1	.2	.0	Income Taxes Payable	.1	.1
7.9	6.9	5.0	6.0	10.1	6.1	All Other Current	8.1	7.8
34.2	16.6	15.5	18.3	18.3	17.5	Total Current	20.9	20.5
109.1	73.1	64.6	53.3	45.7	56.6	Long Term Debt	79.8	71.6
.0	.1	.1	.0	.2	.2	Deferred Taxes	.3	.2
1.9	3.4	2.4	5.4	2.6	1.6	All Other Non-Current	4.3	4.2
−45.1	6.8	17.4	23.0	33.2	24.1	Net Worth	−5.4	3.5
100.0	100.0	100.0	100.0	100.0	100.0	Total Liabilities & Net Worth	100.0	100.0
						INCOME DATA		
100.0	100.0	100.0	100.0	100.0	100.0	Net Sales	100.0	100.0
						Gross Profit		
66.9	68.5	69.1	77.3	85.6	74.1	Operating Expenses	73.8	71.1
33.1	31.5	30.9	22.7	14.4	25.9	Operating Profit	26.2	28.9
19.1	22.2	22.4	14.9	9.9	13.5	All Other Expenses (net)	19.1	18.3
13.9	9.4	8.6	7.9	4.5	12.4	Profit Before Taxes	7.1	10.6
						RATIOS		
2.0	1.5	2.2	1.8	1.5	2.7		1.9	2.0
.8	.5	.8	1.1	1.1	1.0	Current	.7	.7
.2	.2	.3	.4	.9	.6		.1	.2
1.7	1.2	1.5	1.4	1.3	1.6		1.5	1.4
.6	(350) .4	.5	.6	1.0	.8	Quick	(728) .5	.5
.2	.1	.1	.1	.5	.2		.1	.1
0 UND	0 UND	0 UND	0 UND	0 UND	0 UND		0 UND	0 UND
0 UND	0 UND	0 UND	2 241.8	0 UND	3 113.4	Sales/Receivables	0 UND	0 UND
0 UND	1 370.3	4 96.9	22 16.6	11 34.1	9 40.0		5 73.9	8 45.4
						Cost of Sales/Inventory		
						Cost of Sales/Payables		
11.5	13.8	5.0	3.8	11.3	2.4		10.2	7.3
−48.0	−12.4	−25.6	47.3	258.1	NM	Sales/Working Capital	−18.2	−19.5
−4.2	−2.8	−4.0	−3.1	−18.4	−15.4		−2.6	−3.2
(83) 5.2	(141) 4.7	(118) 5.9	(48) 6.5				(235) 6.4	(259) 4.9
2.7	2.5	2.5	2.6			EBIT/Interest	2.7	2.6
1.6	1.3	1.2	1.2				1.5	1.5
		(10) 9.9				Net Profit + Depr., Dep.,	(30) 4.9	(26) 4.9
		5.6				Amort./Cur. Mat. L /T/D	1.8	2.3
		1.1					.4	.8
1.7	2.3	1.8	1.1	.2	.8		2.1	1.7
19.6	8.0	4.1	3.2	2.8	2.4	Fixed/Worth	8.2	5.8
−1.0	−15.7	NM	−38.2	10.6	8.5		−5.3	−7.8
2.4	1.8	1.4	1.2	1.5	2.3		2.0	1.7
79.4	8.3	4.5	4.9	5.8	4.7	Debt/Worth	10.5	7.1
−2.8	−18.2	−238.1	−51.6	15.3	9.1		−6.7	−9.4
(99) 60.5	(238) 42.0	(221) 29.0	(68) 23.1	(11) 31.7	(13) 37.5	% Profit Before Taxes/Tangible	(460) 37.3	(419) 38.4
21.2	11.4	7.1	10.2	7.0	17.0	Net Worth	10.9	11.3
2.7	−.1	−2.0	−1.9	−5.0	−4.6		−1.9	−1.3
24.8	7.3	6.0	6.2	2.8	9.6	% Profit Before Taxes/Total	8.1	8.1
5.4	2.7	1.5	1.8	1.4	1.7	Assets	2.1	2.5
.0	−.5	−1.1	−1.2	−1.0	−.8		−1.4	−.8
2.4	.7	.5	.9	8.8	2.7		.9	1.0
.7	.3	.2	.3	.3	.5	Sales/Net Fixed Assets	.3	.4
.3	.2	.2	.2	.1	.2		.2	.2
1.6	.5	.4	.4	.3	.6		.5	.5
.4	.2	.2	.2	.2	.2	Sales/Total Assets	.3	.3
.2	.1	.1	.1	.1	.1		.2	.2
(156) 5.5	(311) 10.6	(258) 10.8	(81) 7.6	(11) 5.2	(10) 2.4	% Depr., Dep., Amort./Sales	(632) 10.4	(571) 8.5
11.4	18.2	17.6	16.8	17.3	11.8		16.3	15.5
19.4	24.8	24.5	25.5	23.1	22.6		23.5	23.1
(24) 4.1	(37) 2.1	(26) 4.6	(12) 3.8			% Officers', Directors',	(84) 4.3	(82) 4.7
5.5	5.0	6.6	7.8			Owners' Comp/Sales	6.7	7.2
10.1	10.0	13.9	25.2				14.1	13.4
49301M	188604M	462381M	894734M	2514092M	2159168M	Net Sales ($)	1970663M	3090134M
48154M	398326M	1284164M	1881557M	781367M	2583032M	Total Assets ($)	4165765M	4326967M

M = $ thousand   MM = $ million
See Pages 11 through 18 for Explanation of Ratios and Data

Comparative Historical Data / Current Data Sorted By Sales

			Type of Statement						
110	97	154	Unqualified	77	33	14	13	8	9
42	43	55	Reviewed	18	13	9	6	4	5
104	123	118	Compiled	85	23	4	4	1	1
249	206	390	Tax Returns	333	48	4	3		2
169	243	234	Other	143	56	11	13	6	5
4/1/00-3/31/01 ALL	4/1/01-3/31/02 ALL	4/1/02-3/31/03 ALL		0-1MM	82 (4/1-9/30/02) 1-3MM	3-5MM	869 (10/1/02-3/31/03) 5-10MM	10-25MM	25MM & OVER
674	712	951	**NUMBER OF STATEMENTS**	656	173	42	39	19	22
%	%	%	**ASSETS**	%	%	%	%	%	%
7.3	7.8	7.9	Cash & Equivalents	6.6	11.0	12.1	6.0	13.2	14.2
3.1	3.0	2.8	Trade Receivables (net)	1.4	4.2	8.2	3.6	4.9	19.1
2.2	2.2	1.8	Inventory	.9	1.9	5.9	8.4	7.6	1.8
2.8	3.1	2.9	All Other Current	1.9	3.1	8.5	6.4	4.0	12.4
15.4	16.1	15.4	Total Current	10.9	20.2	34.7	24.4	29.7	47.5
74.0	73.8	74.5	Fixed Assets (net)	81.3	65.2	54.2	62.1	44.6	31.5
2.0	1.8	1.9	Intangibles (net)	1.6	2.9	1.4	3.1	4.1	.5
8.6	8.2	8.2	All Other Non-Current	6.2	11.7	9.7	10.3	21.6	20.5
100.0	100.0	100.0	Total	100.0	100.0	100.0	100.0	100.0	100.0
			LIABILITIES						
6.1	6.8	6.4	Notes Payable-Short Term	5.6	8.8	7.6	7.0	9.4	7.6
5.5	4.8	5.0	Cur. Mat.-L/T/D	5.9	3.7	3.3	1.9	2.9	1.0
1.8	3.0	1.8	Trade Payables	1.1	2.4	2.3	3.3	2.9	14.0
.1	.1	.1	Income Taxes Payable	.1	.3	.3	.3	.1	.2
6.8	7.4	6.4	All Other Current	5.5	7.6	10.1	7.2	9.4	15.7
20.4	22.2	19.9	Total Current	18.1	22.8	23.6	19.7	24.7	38.5
71.7	75.8	74.8	Long Term Debt	81.2	67.0	54.9	55.2	65.4	26.9
.1	.1	.1	Deferred Taxes	.1	.1	.0	.2	.2	.0
4.4	3.8	3.0	All Other Non-Current	2.4	3.8	4.2	6.9	2.9	4.4
3.4	-1.9	2.3	Net Worth	-1.7	6.3	17.4	17.9	6.9	30.2
100.0	100.0	100.0	Total Liabilities & Net Worth	100.0	100.0	100.0	100.0	100.0	100.0
			INCOME DATA						
100.0	100.0	100.0	Net Sales	100.0	100.0	100.0	100.0	100.0	100.0
			Gross Profit						
71.7	71.1	69.5	Operating Expenses	66.0	74.6	77.9	81.2	88.1	83.1
28.3	28.9	30.5	Operating Profit	34.0	25.4	22.1	18.8	11.9	16.9
19.1	22.3	20.6	All Other Expenses (net)	24.6	14.6	7.0	10.4	7.9	5.5
9.2	6.6	9.8	Profit Before Taxes	9.4	10.8	15.0	8.4	4.0	11.3
			RATIOS						
2.0	1.9	1.9		1.7	2.3	2.9	2.5	2.0	1.9
.7	.7	.8	Current	.6	1.0	1.2	1.2	1.4	1.2
.1	.2	.2		.2	.3	.6	.7	1.0	.9
1.4	1.4	1.5		1.2	1.7	1.9	1.7	1.6	1.2
(673) .5	.4	(950) .5	Quick	(655) .4	.6	.5	.6	1.0	.8
.1	.1	.1		.1	.2	.2	.2	.3	.4
0 UND	0 UND	0 UND		0 UND	0 UND	0 UND	0 UND	1 484.5	0 UND
0 UND	0 UND	0 UND	Sales/Receivables	0 UND	0 UND	1 288.8	4 97.3	5 79.5	7 50.7
5 71.5	5 77.0	3 133.8		0 849.0	6 60.0	22 16.7	16 22.7	27 13.6	56 6.5
			Cost of Sales/Inventory						
			Cost of Sales/Payables						
9.3	7.6	8.3		12.5	4.6	2.2	3.8	4.4	8.4
-14.8	-18.1	-23.8	Sales/Working Capital	-12.0	-90.7	17.2	29.9	13.4	245.1
-2.9	-3.2	-3.4		-2.8	-5.2	-4.8	-10.9	-147.2	-43.4
5.4	4.7	5.6		4.1	5.7	21.8	5.6	10.9	49.3
(242) 2.7	(251) 2.5	(399) 2.6	EBIT/Interest	(226) 2.4	(98) 2.8	(27) 5.8	(23) 2.2	(14) 2.7	(11) 9.3
1.4	1.3	1.3		1.3	1.4	1.5	1.1	.7	2.3
6.8	4.4	7.7		3.9					
(24) 1.2	(19) 1.9	(31) 2.7	Net Profit + Depr., Dep., Amort./Cur. Mat. L/T/D	(14) 1.6					
.6	.5	1.1		.9					
1.8	1.9	1.8		2.3	1.1	.5	1.2	.2	.0
5.8	7.5	6.0	Fixed/Worth	7.0	6.9	1.6	7.6	1.4	.4
-13.4	-10.4	-15.4		-14.2	-8.2	16.6	-18.5	20.5	2.6
1.6	1.9	1.6		1.9	1.4	.7	1.4	1.5	1.5
6.6	8.8	6.6	Debt/Worth	7.6	8.8	2.5	7.4	2.9	3.9
-16.6	-11.7	-18.0		-16.5	-10.2	16.7	-19.6	24.8	5.2
34.9	34.2	35.7		31.4	47.2	65.7	38.5	17.4	44.5
(456) 9.8	(462) 8.9	(650) 10.0	% Profit Before Taxes/Tangible Net Worth	(444) 8.2	(111) 17.9	(33) 13.6	(26) 8.8	(15) 8.9	(21) 23.9
-1.2	-2.7	-.7		-1.8	3.4	3.1	1.6	-6.2	13.3
7.5	6.2	8.0		6.7	10.2	20.6	5.4	7.5	13.9
1.8	1.4	2.3	% Profit Before Taxes/Total Assets	1.8	3.9	6.3	1.5	2.3	8.0
-.9	-1.2	-.6		-.8	-.3	1.5	.1	-.6	2.0
.9	.9	.9		.5	2.5	5.5	1.3	8.6	168.7
.3	.3	.3	Sales/Net Fixed Assets	.2	.5	.9	.6	2.8	21.3
.2	.2	.2		.1	.2	.3	.2	.4	.5
.5	.5	.5		.4	.8	.9	.6	1.5	3.9
.2	.2	.2	Sales/Total Assets	.2	.3	.5	.4	.3	1.1
.2	.2	.1		.1	.2	.3	.2	.2	.3
8.4	8.9	9.0		11.6	6.3	4.3	2.7	1.1	.2
(600) 15.5	(621) 16.1	(827) 16.9	% Depr., Dep., Amort./Sales	(578) 18.4	(149) 12.8	(32) 10.2	(37) 9.0	(17) 6.3	(14) .5
22.9	23.7	24.1		25.0	20.0	18.5	18.2	16.7	10.3
3.7	3.7	3.7		4.0	3.5				
(83) 6.3	(86) 6.6	(101) 5.7	% Officers', Directors', Owners' Comp/Sales	(55) 5.7	(29) 5.5				
15.4	12.1	11.2		11.1	11.0				
2103171M	3874269M	6268280M	Net Sales ($)	218397M	282649M	159849M	270965M	290159M	5046261M
4747680M	5742914M	6976600M	Total Assets ($)	1086382M	953230M	433195M	1064684M	972350M	2466759M

M = $ thousand   MM = $ million
See Pages 11 through 18 for Explanation of Ratios and Data

REAL ESTATE—Lessors of Nonresidential Buildings (except Miniwarehouses)   NAICS 531120   (SIC 6512)

Current Data Sorted By Assets | **Comparative Historical Data**

	0-500M	500M-2MM	2-10MM	10-50MM	50-100MM	100-250MM	Type of Statement	4/1/98-3/31/99 ALL	4/1/99-3/31/00 ALL
	3	22	54	56	21	27	Unqualified	194	153
	10	59	98	39	6	5	Reviewed	185	170
	50	240	234	32	2	1	Compiled	479	432
	316	836	447	42	2	2	Tax Returns	818	577
	74	246	311	87	17	8	Other	520	446
		172 (4/1-9/30/02)			3175 (10/1/02-3/31/03)				
	453	1403	1144	256	48	43	NUMBER OF STATEMENTS	2196	1778
	%	%	%	%	%	%	**ASSETS**	%	%
	9.0	4.8	4.4	6.0	8.2	5.6	Cash & Equivalents	5.7	6.0
	2.4	1.2	2.1	3.2	2.2	4.3	Trade Receivables (net)	1.8	2.0
	1.2	.9	1.5	1.7	2.8	3.2	Inventory	1.7	1.8
	2.1	1.5	1.5	2.3	3.1	5.4	All Other Current	1.4	1.7
	14.7	8.4	9.5	13.3	16.4	18.5	Total Current	10.7	11.4
	79.1	85.9	83.3	75.2	69.4	59.9	Fixed Assets (net)	79.6	78.7
	1.8	1.2	1.7	2.1	1.2	2.4	Intangibles (net)	2.4	2.5
	4.4	4.6	5.5	9.5	13.0	19.3	All Other Non-Current	7.4	7.4
	100.0	100.0	100.0	100.0	100.0	100.0	Total	100.0	100.0
							LIABILITIES		
	5.6	4.4	4.8	5.5	3.4	4.1	Notes Payable-Short Term	4.9	5.8
	8.3	5.3	4.5	4.8	1.5	3.1	Cur. Mat.-L/T/D	5.0	5.1
	3.1	.9	1.1	2.4	2.2	3.7	Trade Payables	1.3	1.5
	.0	.0	.0	.1	.2	.1	Income Taxes Payable	.1	.1
	7.9	4.5	4.3	5.7	4.9	7.5	All Other Current	8.1	5.6
	24.9	15.1	14.7	18.4	12.2	18.6	Total Current	19.3	18.0
	75.0	66.1	64.4	57.5	47.8	44.2	Long Term Debt	72.5	67.9
	.1	.0	.1	.2	1.2	.4	Deferred Taxes	.2	.2
	3.0	2.7	2.8	4.0	1.7	2.3	All Other Non-Current	4.1	3.9
	-2.9	16.1	17.9	19.8	37.1	34.5	Net Worth	3.8	10.0
	100.0	100.0	100.0	100.0	100.0	100.0	Total Liabilities & Net Worth	100.0	100.0
							INCOME DATA		
	100.0	100.0	100.0	100.0	100.0	100.0	Net Sales	100.0	100.0
							Gross Profit		
	51.5	47.1	52.4	62.8	60.2	65.9	Operating Expenses	55.0	54.0
	48.5	52.9	47.6	37.2	39.8	34.1	Operating Profit	45.0	46.0
	21.5	29.0	28.3	20.9	15.3	19.1	All Other Expenses (net)	20.7	23.6
	26.9	23.9	19.3	16.3	24.5	14.9	Profit Before Taxes	24.3	22.4
							RATIOS		
	1.8	1.5	1.7	1.8	3.7	2.4	Current	3.3	1.7
	.5	.5	.6	.8	1.3	1.0		.7	.6
	.2	.1	.1	.2	.6	.3		.1	.1
	1.4	1.2	1.2	1.3	2.3	1.5	Quick	2.5	1.3
	.4	(1401) .4	.4	(255) .5	.8	.5		(2189) .5	(1777) .4
	.1	.1	.1	.1	.4	.0		.1	.1
	0 UND	0 UND	0 UND	0 UND	1 473.9	2 201.6	Sales/Receivables	0 UND	0 UND
	0 UND	0 UND	0 UND	2 186.7	9 42.9	19 19.3		0 UND	0 UND
	0 UND	0 UND	4 92.0	17 21.0	27 13.4	45 8.1		3 115.3	6 65.1
							Cost of Sales/Inventory		
							Cost of Sales/Payables		
	12.3	14.5	8.8	8.4	2.5	2.7	Sales/Working Capital	7.8	9.5
	-9.3	-7.4	-9.5	-15.3	28.3	104.1		-16.7	-10.9
	-2.2	-2.1	-2.2	-2.6	-12.6	-2.4		-2.6	-2.2
	8.4	6.5	6.0	7.7	22.7	8.1	EBIT/Interest	6.4	6.3
	(167) 4.7	(419) 4.1	(348) 3.2	(105) 3.4	(27) 5.0	(20) 2.6		(601) 3.8	(535) 3.9
	2.6	2.2	1.9	1.4	1.9	1.5		2.0	2.0
		2.3	3.3	3.1			Net Profit + Depr., Dep., Amort./Cur. Mat. L/T/D	3.2	3.8
		(48) 1.4	(64) 1.4	(47) 1.2				(138) 1.5	(120) 1.6
		.7	.6	.4				.8	1.0
	1.9	2.6	2.5	1.8	1.0	.5	Fixed/Worth	2.0	2.0
	4.9	5.5	5.9	4.7	2.5	2.4		5.4	5.5
	-20.3	55.2	92.9	277.7	7.5	9.9		-45.0	-150.6
	1.4	2.0	2.1	1.5	.3	.7	Debt/Worth	1.6	1.7
	5.1	5.2	5.7	5.1	1.9	2.5		5.5	5.6
	-21.1	60.1	101.4	302.3	12.1	14.3		-36.1	-159.3
	62.6	45.8	33.9	39.6	21.1	18.1	% Profit Before Taxes/Tangible Net Worth	47.5	46.6
	(323) 25.4	(1092) 20.9	(884) 17.6	(194) 16.5	(42) 10.1	(39) 6.5		(1574) 18.4	(1314) 20.4
	11.6	8.4	5.0	5.0	3.8	1.5		6.4	6.2
	17.0	9.2	6.8	6.9	9.6	4.8	% Profit Before Taxes/Total Assets	9.7	9.9
	7.0	4.4	3.2	3.0	3.5	2.2		4.1	4.1
	2.2	1.0	.7	.5	.4	.4		.6	.9
	.9	.3	.3	.4	.6	3.4	Sales/Net Fixed Assets	.5	.5
	.3	.2	.2	.2	.3	.4		.2	.2
	.2	.1	.1	.1	.2	.1		.2	.2
	.6	.3	.2	.3	.3	.4	Sales/Total Assets	.3	.3
	.3	.2	.2	.2	.2	.2		.2	.2
	.2	.1	.1	.1	.1	.1		.1	.1
	7.7	11.1	12.2	9.9	7.4	5.4	% Depr., Dep., Amort./Sales	10.9	10.2
	(411) 13.6	(1320) 16.3	(1081) 17.4	(240) 16.5	(42) 14.6	(32) 13.6		(2010) 16.5	(1652) 15.8
	19.5	22.4	24.2	21.8	20.1	19.3		23.0	22.0
	5.0	3.4	3.1	1.7			% Officers', Directors', Owners' Comp/Sales	2.4	3.3
	(38) 7.0	(76) 7.7	(97) 6.2	(25) 3.8				(178) 5.6	(172) 6.1
	16.7	12.6	7.1					16.1	16.3
	124685M	519757M	1663940M	2969808M	1643649M	3154036M	Net Sales ($)	5729374M	4345971M
	137031M	1580337M	4940398M	5552231M	3464073M	7145790M	Total Assets ($)	15601835M	12477215M

© RMA 2003

M = $ thousand   MM = $ million
See Pages 11 through 18 for Explanation of Ratios and Data

Comparative Historical Data / Current Data Sorted By Sales

	4/1/00-3/31/01 ALL	4/1/01-3/31/02 ALL	4/1/02-3/31/03 ALL	Type of Statement	0-1MM	1-3MM	3-5MM	5-10MM	10-25MM	25MM & OVER
	124	152	183	Unqualified	44	30	12	24	35	38
	183	178	217	Reviewed	112	43	20	18	14	10
	507	569	559	Compiled	435	90	16	8	8	2
	785	885	1645	Tax Returns	1474	130	25	8	5	3
	502	587	743	Other	520	119	36	31	17	20
					172 (4/1-9/30/02)		3175 (10/1/02-3/31/03)			
NUMBER OF STATEMENTS	2101	2371	3347		2585	412	109	89	79	73
	%	%	%	**ASSETS**	%	%	%	%	%	%
Cash & Equivalents	5.6	5.2	5.4		4.7	6.7	7.3	6.8	9.5	11.0
Trade Receivables (net)	2.3	2.2	1.9		.9	2.3	4.2	9.6	11.1	12.4
Inventory	1.7	1.6	1.2		.3	2.6	7.0	5.1	5.0	10.3
All Other Current	2.3	2.6	1.7		1.4	2.3	2.1	3.7	2.4	6.3
Total Current	11.9	11.7	10.2		7.3	13.9	20.6	25.3	28.0	40.0
Fixed Assets (net)	79.0	80.1	82.7		87.0	76.5	66.9	59.5	57.7	44.2
Intangibles (net)	2.5	2.1	1.5		1.2	2.3	2.0	4.7	3.4	1.3
All Other Non-Current	6.7	6.1	5.6		4.5	7.3	10.5	10.4	11.0	14.4
Total	100.0	100.0	100.0		100.0	100.0	100.0	100.0	100.0	100.0
				LIABILITIES						
Notes Payable-Short Term	5.2	4.3	4.7		4.1	6.2	5.9	8.0	4.6	12.3
Cur. Mat.-L/T/D	5.3	5.7	5.3		5.6	4.0	4.3	6.4	4.3	2.9
Trade Payables	1.6	1.8	1.4		.7	1.8	4.2	6.0	5.5	10.5
Income Taxes Payable	.1	.0	.0		.0	.1	.1	.2	.2	.1
All Other Current	6.0	4.8	5.0		4.5	5.6	7.7	10.6	7.8	8.2
Total Current	18.2	16.6	16.5		14.9	17.7	22.2	31.1	22.4	33.9
Long Term Debt	67.1	67.1	65.5		68.8	64.5	53.4	35.6	42.2	35.5
Deferred Taxes	.1	.1	.1		.0	.1	.0	.7	.7	.5
All Other Non-Current	3.2	2.5	2.9		2.7	3.1	4.1	5.5	2.1	3.3
Net Worth	11.4	13.6	15.0		13.5	14.5	20.3	27.2	32.7	26.7
Total Liabilities & Net Worth	100.0	100.0	100.0		100.0	100.0	100.0	100.0	100.0	100.0
				INCOME DATA						
Net Sales	100.0	100.0	100.0		100.0	100.0	100.0	100.0	100.0	100.0
Gross Profit					46.3	61.1	67.4	77.1	73.9	83.9
Operating Expenses	53.0	52.1	51.1		53.7	38.9	32.6	22.9	26.1	16.1
Operating Profit	47.0	47.9	48.9		30.0	19.3	15.5	12.0	12.4	6.5
All Other Expenses (net)	26.5	28.2	26.8							
Profit Before Taxes	20.5	19.6	22.1		23.6	19.6	17.1	10.9	13.7	9.5
				RATIOS						
Current	1.7 / .6 / .1	1.8 / .6 / .1	1.7 / .5 / .1		1.5 / .4 / .1	2.1 / .8 / .2	2.1 / .8 / .3	1.6 / .9 / .3	2.8 / 1.3 / .6	2.1 / 1.2 / .7
Quick	(2099) 1.3 / .3 / .1	(2367) 1.3 / .4 / .1	(3344) 1.3 / .4 / .1		1.2 / .3 / .1	(409) 1.4 / .5 / .1	1.6 / .4 / .1	1.3 / .6 / .1	2.0 / .8 / .4	1.3 / .6 / .3
Sales/Receivables	0 UND / 0 UND / 5 67.5	0 UND / 0 UND / 3 112.5	0 UND / 0 UND / 2 209.5		0 UND / 0 UND / 0 UND	0 UND / 0 UND / 9 41.6	0 UND / 0 UND / 8 43.4	1 676.8 / 13 28.0 / 31 11.9	3 116.5 / 20 17.8 / 39 9.4	6 60.0 / 26 14.0 / 41 9.0
Cost of Sales/Inventory										
Cost of Sales/Payables										
Sales/Working Capital	9.8 / -10.2 / -2.2	10.0 / -11.0 / -2.4	10.6 / -9.2 / -2.2		13.3 / -6.6 / -1.9	7.1 / -20.1 / -3.6	10.1 / -34.5 / -4.3	9.1 / -52.3 / -4.4	4.5 / 34.0 / -9.8	6.8 / 25.8 / -18.2
EBIT/Interest	(600) 6.5 / 3.5 / 1.6	(667) 6.2 / 3.4 / 1.8	(1086) 6.6 / 3.8 / 2.1		(688) 6.6 / 4.1 / 2.5	(184) 5.3 / 3.0 / 1.7	(51) 9.7 / 3.2 / 1.3	(60) 7.4 / 2.5 / 1.0	(49) 8.4 / 3.5 / 1.5	(54) 16.5 / 2.7 / 1.2
Net Profit + Depr., Dep., Amort./Cur. Mat. L/T/D	(112) 4.0 / 1.8 / .9	(123) 3.3 / 1.5 / .9	(181) 3.2 / 1.4 / .7		(87) 3.1 / 1.4 / .7	(34) 3.3 / 1.9 / 1.1	(12) 3.1 / 1.2 / .4	(19) 2.3 / 1.2 / .2	(11) 6.3 / 1.8 / .5	(18) 5.4 / 1.4 / .3
Fixed/Worth	2.1 / 5.2 / -115.7	2.2 / 5.6 / 254.7	2.3 / 5.4 / 81.0		2.6 / 5.9 / 81.3	1.9 / 5.2 / -32.6	1.3 / 4.3 / -26.2	1.1 / 2.7 / 87.2	.7 / 1.9 / 6.5	.4 / 1.3 / 7.2
Debt/Worth	1.7 / 5.5 / -114.7	1.9 / 5.6 / 617.0	1.9 / 5.2 / 95.0		2.0 / 5.5 / 93.5	1.7 / 5.6 / -35.3	1.8 / 4.4 / -49.4	1.1 / 4.0 / 204.2	.7 / 2.9 / 10.3	.9 / 2.8 / 13.0
% Profit Before Taxes/Tangible Net Worth	(1554) 40.9 / 19.1 / 6.2	(1788) 42.8 / 19.9 / 6.0	(2574) 41.8 / 19.2 / 6.4		(1996) 41.8 / 19.8 / 6.8	(299) 42.7 / 19.0 / 6.9	(81) 50.8 / 21.0 / 6.4	(68) 38.5 / 14.4 / 5.1	(69) 40.0 / 14.1 / 2.2	(61) 42.9 / 16.4 / 2.6
% Profit Before Taxes/Total Assets	8.9 / 3.8 / .6	8.8 / 3.8 / .6	8.7 / 4.0 / .9		8.5 / 4.0 / .9	9.6 / 4.5 / 1.2	9.2 / 4.5 / 1.2	7.7 / 3.5 / -.1	9.9 / 3.3 / .3	11.4 / 4.6 / .5
Sales/Net Fixed Assets	.5 / .2 / .2	.4 / .2 / .2	.4 / .2 / .1		.3 / .2 / .1	.7 / .3 / .2	4.1 / .4 / .2	15.3 / .6 / .2	9.5 / .5 / .2	31.4 / 3.4 / .6
Sales/Total Assets	.3 / .2 / .1	.3 / .2 / .1	.3 / .2 / .1		.2 / .2 / .1	.5 / .2 / .2	1.6 / .3 / .2	1.5 / .3 / .2	2.0 / .3 / .2	2.9 / .9 / .4
% Depr., Dep., Amort./Sales	(1976) 9.3 / 14.9 / 21.4	(2225) 9.7 / 15.1 / 21.6	(3126) 10.9 / 16.3 / 22.6		(2436) 12.3 / 17.2 / 23.7	(380) 8.5 / 13.8 / 19.8	(101) 3.7 / 10.8 / 17.6	(78) 1.6 / 11.9 / 17.9	(70) 2.8 / 8.5 / 18.7	(61) .7 / 2.9 / 8.4
% Officers', Directors', Owners' Comp/Sales	(208) 3.4 / 6.7 / 14.0	(220) 3.0 / 6.3 / 13.4	(247) 3.2 / 6.5 / 12.0		(123) 3.2 / 6.1 / 12.1	(56) 4.2 / 6.9 / 10.3	(24) 2.8 / 5.3 / 10.9	(14) 2.5 / 6.8 / 23.2	(14) 2.0 / 6.8 / 14.7	(16) 3.7 / 6.5 / 10.5
Net Sales ($)	6570280M	8030731M	10075875M		817613M	679537M	417326M	640608M	1205215M	6315576M
Total Assets ($)	15441100M	18094178M	22819860M		4778521M	2984587M	1709031M	2304132M	4624351M	6419238M

M = $ thousand   MM = $ million
See Pages 11 through 18 for Explanation of Ratios and Data

Current Data Sorted By Assets   **Comparative Historical Data**

0-500M	500M-2MM	2-10MM	10-50MM	50-100MM	100-250MM	Type of Statement	4/1/98-3/31/99 ALL	4/1/99-3/31/00 ALL
1	1	2				Unqualified		
5	7	7			1	Reviewed		
1	17	2				Compiled		
	6					Tax Returns		
						Other		
	1 (4/1-9/30/02)		49 (10/1/02-3/31/03)		1			
7	31	11			1	**NUMBER OF STATEMENTS**		
%	%	%	%	%	%	**ASSETS**	%	%
	4.5	2.8				Cash & Equivalents		
	.0	.3				Trade Receivables (net)		
	.0	.0	D	D		Inventory	D	D
	1.7	.7	A	A		All Other Current	A	A
	6.3	3.8	T	T		Total Current	T	T
	89.9	94.9	A	A		Fixed Assets (net)	A	A
	1.0	.4				Intangibles (net)		
	2.8	.8	N	N		All Other Non-Current	N	N
	100.0	100.0	O	O		Total	O	O
			T	T		**LIABILITIES**	T	T
	2.4	3.2				Notes Payable-Short Term		
	7.8	.8	A	A		Cur. Mat.-L/T/D	A	A
	.2	.4	V	V		Trade Payables	V	V
	.0	.0	A	A		Income Taxes Payable	A	A
	4.3	1.5	I	I		All Other Current	I	I
	14.7	6.0	L	L		Total Current	L	L
	79.2	79.7	A	A		Long Term Debt	A	A
	.0	.0	B	B		Deferred Taxes	B	B
	3.9	.1	L	L		All Other Non-Current	L	L
	2.2	14.2	E	E		Net Worth	E	E
	100.0	100.0				Total Liabilities & Net Worth		
						INCOME DATA		
	100.0	100.0				Net Sales		
	56.3	56.2				Gross Profit		
	43.7	43.8				Operating Expenses		
	27.8	26.1				Operating Profit		
						All Other Expenses (net)		
	16.0	17.7				Profit Before Taxes		
						RATIOS		
	1.9	32.0						
	.5	1.0				Current		
	.2	.1						
	1.2	31.5						
	.2	.5				Quick		
	.1	.1						
	0 UND	0 UND						
	0 UND	0 UND				Sales/Receivables		
	0 UND	9 39.6						
						Cost of Sales/Inventory		
						Cost of Sales/Payables		
	8.7	6.5						
	-6.4	UND				Sales/Working Capital		
	-2.8	-1.4						
	6.1							
	(12) 4.2					EBIT/Interest		
	2.0							
						Net Profit + Depr., Dep., Amort./Cur. Mat. L /T/D		
	2.9	3.2						
	10.3	9.4				Fixed/Worth		
	-22.7	-10.8						
	2.3	2.5						
	11.6	8.6				Debt/Worth		
	-26.6	-11.9						
	97.4							
	(22) 17.8					% Profit Before Taxes/Tangible Net Worth		
	6.2							
	8.8	4.4						
	3.4	2.7				% Profit Before Taxes/Total Assets		
	.2	1.1						
	.5	.3						
	.3	.2				Sales/Net Fixed Assets		
	.2	.1						
	.5	.3						
	.3	.2				Sales/Total Assets		
	.2	.1						
	11.9	12.1						
	(30) 14.3	(10) 15.8				% Depr., Dep., Amort./Sales		
	19.0	19.9						
						% Officers', Directors', Owners' Comp/Sales		
1516M	10820M	6559M			41305M	Net Sales ($)		
1703M	35164M	36816M			136844M	Total Assets ($)		

M = $ thousand   MM = $ million
See Pages 11 through 18 for Explanation of Ratios and Data

Comparative Historical Data   Current Data Sorted By Sales

4/1/00-3/31/01 ALL	4/1/01-3/31/02 ALL	4/1/02-3/31/03 ALL	Type of Statement	0-1MM	1-3MM	3-5MM	5-10MM	10-25MM	25MM & OVER
		1	Unqualified	1					
		10	Reviewed	10					
		29	Compiled	28	1				
		10	Tax Returns						1
			Other	9					
					1 (4/1-9/30/02)		49 (10/1/02-3/31/03)		
		50	NUMBER OF STATEMENTS	48	1				1
%	%	%	ASSETS	%	%	%	%	%	%
		4.4	Cash & Equivalents	4.0					
D	D	.1	Trade Receivables (net)	.1		D	D	D	
A	A	.0	Inventory	.0		A	A	A	
T	T	1.7	All Other Current	1.8		T	T	T	
A	A	6.2	Total Current	5.9		A	A	A	
		89.5	Fixed Assets (net)	89.9					
N	N	1.9	Intangibles (net)	2.0		N	N	N	
O	O	2.3	All Other Non-Current	2.2		O	O	O	
T	T	100.0	Total	100.0		T	T	T	
			LIABILITIES						
A	A	2.4	Notes Payable-Short Term	2.5		A	A	A	
V	V	5.5	Cur. Mat.-L/T/D	5.7		V	V	V	
A	A	.3	Trade Payables	.2		A	A	A	
I	I	.0	Income Taxes Payable	.0		I	I	I	
L	L	3.5	All Other Current	3.3		L	L	L	
A	A	11.7	Total Current	11.7		A	A	A	
B	B	74.7	Long Term Debt	76.6		B	B	B	
L	L	.0	Deferred Taxes	.0		L	L	L	
E	E	8.1	All Other Non-Current	8.3		E	E	E	
		5.5	Net Worth	3.3					
		100.0	Total Liabilities & Net Worth	100.0					
			INCOME DATA						
		100.0	Net Sales	100.0					
			Gross Profit						
		59.2	Operating Expenses	59.2					
		40.8	Operating Profit	40.8					
		25.5	All Other Expenses (net)	26.5					
		15.3	Profit Before Taxes	14.3					
			RATIOS						
		3.0		3.1					
		.5	Current	.5					
		.2		.2					
		1.6		1.5					
		.3	Quick	.3					
		.1		.1					
		0 UND		0 UND					
		0 UND	Sales/Receivables	0 UND					
		0 UND		0 UND					
			Cost of Sales/Inventory						
			Cost of Sales/Payables						
		8.5		8.0					
		-9.2	Sales/Working Capital	-9.2					
		-2.9		-2.8					
		(16) 6.1		(14) 4.8					
		3.7	EBIT/Interest	3.1					
		2.0		2.0					
			Net Profit + Depr., Dep., Amort./Cur. Mat. L/T/D						
		2.9		3.5					
		9.9	Fixed/Worth	11.8					
		-15.3		-12.3					
		2.3		2.9					
		10.5	Debt/Worth	12.1					
		-16.3		-13.4					
		(33) 51.7	% Profit Before Taxes/Tangible	(31) 43.2					
		16.7	Net Worth	16.7					
		7.9		6.5					
		8.9	% Profit Before Taxes/Total	8.7					
		3.5	Assets	3.4					
		.6		.5					
		.4		.4					
		.3	Sales/Net Fixed Assets	.3					
		.2		.2					
		.4		.4					
		.3	Sales/Total Assets	.3					
		.2		.2					
		(47) 10.1	% Depr., Dep., Amort./Sales	(45) 10.8					
		14.1		14.5					
		18.9		19.1					
			% Officers', Directors', Owners' Comp/Sales						
		60200M	Net Sales ($)	17576M	1319M				41305M
		210527M	Total Assets ($)	72888M	795M				136844M

© RMA 2003   M = $ thousand   MM = $ million
See Pages 11 through 18 for Explanation of Ratios and Data

Current Data Sorted By Assets   **Comparative Historical Data**

0-500M	500M-2MM	2-10MM	10-50MM	50-100MM	100-250MM	Type of Statement	4/1/98-3/31/99 ALL	4/1/99-3/31/00 ALL
4	10	33	36	6	6	Unqualified	85	87
9	27	59	14	1		Reviewed	94	92
48	101	116	27	1		Compiled	224	238
115	297	154	16			Tax Returns	384	301
41	116	170	50	6	4	Other	199	208
	86 (4/1-9/30/02)		1381 (10/1/02-3/31/03)					
217	551	532	143	14	10	NUMBER OF STATEMENTS	986	926
%	%	%	%	%	%	**ASSETS**	%	%
8.7	4.7	4.7	6.0	8.4	5.8	Cash & Equivalents	6.0	6.1
2.6	1.9	2.0	3.6	6.1	8.0	Trade Receivables (net)	1.9	2.2
1.2	1.3	2.1	1.7	3.7	11.2	Inventory	1.3	1.2
3.8	1.4	2.8	4.9	12.3	4.3	All Other Current	2.2	3.1
16.3	9.2	11.6	16.1	30.5	29.4	Total Current	11.5	12.6
76.5	84.2	79.2	71.5	58.3	42.5	Fixed Assets (net)	78.9	77.7
2.4	1.8	1.8	2.2	1.9	.1	Intangibles (net)	1.6	1.5
4.9	4.7	7.4	10.2	9.3	28.1	All Other Non-Current	8.0	8.1
100.0	100.0	100.0	100.0	100.0	100.0	Total	100.0	100.0
						LIABILITIES		
7.2	3.9	4.8	5.1	21.4	8.2	Notes Payable-Short Term	5.6	5.7
4.8	5.7	4.4	4.9	6.7	1.4	Cur. Mat.-L/T/D	5.3	4.7
1.8	.9	1.4	1.9	1.0	6.7	Trade Payables	1.3	1.5
.0	.0	.0	.1	.9	.3	Income Taxes Payable	.1	.1
12.8	6.3	5.4	5.5	6.0	7.4	All Other Current	5.1	4.9
26.6	16.8	16.1	17.5	36.1	24.0	Total Current	17.4	16.9
69.4	63.2	61.2	54.6	33.1	26.6	Long Term Debt	67.3	63.1
.0	.1	.2	.4	.3	.8	Deferred Taxes	.1	.2
5.0	2.9	3.4	2.1	1.1	11.9	All Other Non-Current	6.3	3.3
−1.0	17.1	19.0	25.4	29.4	36.7	Net Worth	8.8	16.5
100.0	100.0	100.0	100.0	100.0	100.0	Total Liabilities & Net Worth	100.0	100.0
						INCOME DATA		
100.0	100.0	100.0	100.0	100.0	100.0	Net Sales	100.0	100.0
						Gross Profit		
58.1	51.1	55.1	63.4	70.8	80.8	Operating Expenses	59.4	55.9
41.9	48.9	44.9	36.6	29.2	19.2	Operating Profit	40.6	44.1
20.0	25.5	26.0	22.2	17.9	17.3	All Other Expenses (net)	21.8	21.9
21.8	23.3	18.9	14.4	11.3	1.9	Profit Before Taxes	18.7	22.3
						RATIOS		
1.6	1.7	2.0	1.7	2.1	3.5	Current	4.2	2.1
.7	.5	.7	1.0	1.0	1.5		.8	.6
.2	.1	.2	.2	.1	1.0		.1	.2
1.2	1.3	1.4	1.4	1.1	1.7	Quick	2.9	1.5
.5	(550) .4	.4	.4	.7	.7		(982) .6	(922) .4
.1	.1	.1	.1	.1	.3		.1	.1
0 UND	0 UND	0 UND	0 UND	1 331.1	13 27.5	Sales/Receivables	0 UND	0 UND
0 UND	0 UND	0 UND	2 221.0	4 94.8	35 10.5		0 UND	0 UND
0 UND	0 UND	2 200.7	15 23.6	17 21.6	98 3.7		2 189.4	3 108.4
						Cost of Sales/Inventory		
						Cost of Sales/Payables		
22.4	12.5	7.3	4.0	3.6	1.9	Sales/Working Capital	5.8	6.5
−22.8	−9.9	−13.0	152.0	NM	10.2		−27.2	−14.9
−3.1	−2.2	−2.4	−2.1	NM	NM		−2.6	−2.7
(95) 6.0	(181) 6.5	(170) 6.4	(51) 8.8			EBIT/Interest	(287) 7.6	(345) 8.4
3.6	3.8	3.1	3.0				3.9	3.7
2.1	2.1	1.6	1.0				2.1	1.9
	(24) 3.5	(30) 3.2	(27) 2.5			Net Profit + Depr., Dep., Amort./Cur. Mat. L./T/D	(70) 4.3	(70) 3.3
	1.4	1.1	1.4				1.6	1.4
	.6	.7	.5				.8	.9
1.3	2.1	2.0	1.3	.7	.5	Fixed/Worth	1.6	1.5
4.7	4.8	5.3	3.2	1.5	1.2		4.7	3.8
−6.3	34.5	57.9	15.1	6.8	2.4		−65.0	40.4
.9	1.6	1.9	1.3	1.3	.8	Debt/Worth	1.5	1.2
6.0	4.6	5.5	3.4	2.6	1.3		4.9	3.7
−7.7	37.5	70.8	19.8	9.0	25.1		−70.5	49.7
58.0	43.2	37.6	26.7	41.7		% Profit Before Taxes/Tangible Net Worth	44.5	39.5
(146) 21.8	(428) 21.1	(411) 14.1	(115) 12.8	(12) 16.9			(725) 19.9	(720) 19.3
6.3	7.2	3.4	1.2	2.6			4.7	4.7
18.0	10.4	6.4	5.7	9.9	5.7	% Profit Before Taxes/Total Assets	10.8	11.2
6.7	4.3	2.9	2.5	2.7	1.5		4.3	4.4
1.3	1.1	.5	−.1	−.1	−2.4		.3	.7
1.9	.4	.4	.4	12.1	15.4	Sales/Net Fixed Assets	.5	.5
.4	.2	.2	.2	.5	1.4		.3	.3
.2	.1	.1	.1	.2	.3		.2	.2
.9	.3	.3	.3	.9	.9	Sales/Total Assets	.4	.4
.3	.2	.2	.2	.3	.3		.2	.2
.1	.1	.1	.1	.1	.1		.1	.1
7.7	10.6	11.6	10.4	2.0		% Depr., Dep., Amort./Sales	10.1	9.1
(189) 14.6	(520) 16.2	(493) 18.0	(133) 16.3	(11) 18.3			(903) 15.8	(870) 15.4
21.4	23.3	25.8	26.4	25.6			23.3	22.0
5.6	4.2	2.7	3.1			% Officers', Directors', Owners' Comp/Sales	5.1	3.6
(21) 10.4	(44) 7.4	(49) 6.8	(24) 9.6				(78) 8.8	(102) 7.8
18.9	20.9	15.1	13.2				17.8	18.4
69485M	255012M	797746M	1283153M	688513M	952883M	Net Sales ($)	1690812M	2153856M
65656M	621568M	2328623M	2903240M	1018934M	1583996M	Total Assets ($)	5401475M	5415098M

© RMA 2003   M = $ thousand   MM = $ million
See Pages 11 through 18 for Explanation of Ratios and Data

Comparative Historical Data / Current Data Sorted By Sales

Comparative Historical Data			Type of Statement		Current Data Sorted By Sales				
61	52	95	Unqualified	24	25	11	15	6	14
84	73	110	Reviewed	70	28	4	4	2	2
263	274	293	Compiled	215	54	10	11	2	1
348	306	582	Tax Returns	524	47	5	4	1	1
229	256	387	Other	241	74	32	19	9	12
4/1/00-3/31/01 ALL	4/1/01-3/31/02 ALL	4/1/02-3/31/03 ALL		86 (4/1-9/30/02) 0-1MM	1-3MM	3-5MM	1381 (10/1/02-3/31/03) 5-10MM	10-25MM	25MM & OVER
985	961	1467	**NUMBER OF STATEMENTS**	1074	228	62	53	20	30
%	%	%	**ASSETS**	%	%	%	%	%	%
5.8	5.8	5.4	Cash & Equivalents	4.5	7.3	6.4	10.9	4.6	12.2
2.6	2.5	2.3	Trade Receivables (net)	.8	3.0	4.4	12.9	13.6	17.9
2.1	2.2	1.7	Inventory	.3	2.8	10.4	7.3	5.2	11.4
3.8	3.9	2.7	All Other Current	1.8	4.0	5.4	6.1	10.5	9.9
14.3	14.3	12.1	Total Current	7.4	17.3	26.6	37.2	34.0	51.4
76.4	76.6	79.5	Fixed Assets (net)	85.4	71.0	62.5	49.9	53.0	36.6
1.8	1.9	1.9	Intangibles (net)	1.5	3.7	.7	4.9	2.5	1.4
7.5	7.2	6.5	All Other Non-Current	5.6	8.0	10.2	7.9	10.6	10.6
100.0	100.0	100.0	Total	100.0	100.0	100.0	100.0	100.0	100.0
			LIABILITIES						
4.9	6.1	5.0	Notes Payable-Short Term	3.9	5.7	11.5	8.1	23.6	7.8
	4.4	5.0	Cur. Mat.-L/T/D	5.3	3.9	5.2	4.1	2.5	4.7
1.6	1.5	1.4	Trade Payables	.5	1.7	3.5	6.0	8.4	11.5
.1	.1	.0	Income Taxes Payable	.0	.0	.0	.2	.0	.6
5.9	5.4	6.9	All Other Current	6.3	7.0	6.4	13.2	11.4	10.6
17.4	17.4	18.3	Total Current	16.1	18.3	26.7	31.7	45.9	35.3
65.5	62.4	62.0	Long Term Debt	65.8	59.1	49.9	42.6	43.5	20.6
.1	.2	.1	Deferred Taxes	.0	.2	1.2	.3	.3	.5
3.1	3.0	3.4	All Other Non-Current	3.0	4.9	3.0	3.9	.8	6.0
13.9	16.9	16.2	Net Worth	15.0	17.4	19.2	21.6	9.5	37.7
100.0	100.0	100.0	Total Liabilities & Net Worth	100.0	100.0	100.0	100.0	100.0	100.0
			INCOME DATA						
100.0	100.0	100.0	Net Sales	100.0	100.0	100.0	100.0	100.0	100.0
			Gross Profit						
55.6	53.6	55.2	Operating Expenses	49.8	65.4	71.3	76.1	80.0	86.3
44.4	46.4	44.8	Operating Profit	50.2	34.6	28.7	23.9	20.0	13.7
23.8	25.6	24.4	All Other Expenses (net)	27.7	18.6	14.1	9.5	14.2	7.4
20.6	20.8	20.4	Profit Before Taxes	22.6	16.1	14.6	14.5	5.8	6.2
			RATIOS						
2.1	2.1	1.9		1.7	2.3	2.0	2.0	1.4	2.1
.7	.7	.6	Current	.5	.9	1.1	1.2	1.0	1.4
.2	.2	.2		.1	.2	.3	.6	.5	1.1
1.4	1.2	1.3		1.2	1.7	1.2	1.6	.9	1.2
(984) .4	(959) .4	(1466) .4	Quick	(1073) .4	.4	.4	.6	.6	1.0
.1	.1	.1		.1	.1	.0	.6	.6	.3
0 UND	0 UND	0 UND		0 UND	0 UND	0 UND	0 999.8	3 111.1	4 86.5
0 UND	0 UND	0 UND	Sales/Receivables	0 UND	0 UND	3 108.6	8 46.8	14 25.9	19 19.1
5 78.1	3 138.8	2 165.0		0 UND	7 53.3	14 26.0	37 9.7	32 11.2	40 9.2
			Cost of Sales/Inventory						
			Cost of Sales/Payables						
6.0	5.8	9.4		13.2	5.2	6.1	7.3	15.0	4.2
-17.9	-19.7	-13.2	Sales/Working Capital	-9.9	-52.1	46.8	28.5	NM	14.1
-2.8	-2.7	-2.4		-2.1	-3.5	-2.2	-10.3	-7.1	NM
7.0	5.8	6.3		6.2	6.6	4.3	5.6	6.5	12.6
(322) 3.5	(310) 3.2	(515) 3.5	EBIT/Interest	(306) 3.8	(99) 2.9	(31) 2.1	(35) 2.5	(15) 2.7	(29) 5.1
1.6	1.7	1.8		2.1	1.5	1.0	1.1	1.0	.8
4.3	3.2	3.2		2.6	2.5		2.7		
(55) 1.5	(68) 1.3	(92) 1.5	Net Profit + Depr., Dep., Amort./Cur. Mat. L/T/D	(40) 1.2	(22) 1.1	(11) 1.3			
.8	.8	.7		.6	.5		.6		
1.8	1.8	1.9		2.2	1.3	1.1	.5	.7	.2
4.5	4.2	4.7	Fixed/Worth	5.2	4.2	4.5	1.9	3.5	.8
701.2	54.8	65.8		62.6	-44.6	-44.1	6.6	-7.7	1.6
1.6	1.6	1.5		1.6	1.4	2.2	1.2	2.5	.8
4.7	4.3	4.6	Debt/Worth	5.0	4.1	4.8	2.5	8.3	1.7
UND	74.8	85.7		82.4	-46.3	-70.8	13.2	-11.4	2.6
36.4	37.5	39.0	% Profit Before Taxes/Tangible Net Worth	37.3	45.9	44.3	39.2	50.4	50.5
(740) 17.7	(753) 18.1	(1121) 17.2		(824) 17.1	(167) 16.5	(46) 14.7	(43) 20.0	(13) 16.9	(28) 22.0
5.1	5.2	4.3		4.4	3.9	3.5	5.9	5.0	-.1
9.2	9.3	9.1	% Profit Before Taxes/Total Assets	8.8	9.6	9.0	12.5	7.3	15.4
3.8	3.8	3.8		3.8	3.7	3.3	4.1	2.1	7.4
.8	.6	.6		.6	.7	.5	1.1	-.6	-.6
.5	.5	.5		.3	1.1	4.9	23.2	56.1	21.7
.2	.2	.2	Sales/Net Fixed Assets	.2	.3	.5	1.6	.6	5.1
.2	.2	.1		.1	.2	.2	.4	.3	1.5
.4	.3	.4		.3	.5	1.0	1.9	1.3	3.0
.2	.2	.2	Sales/Total Assets	.2	.2	.4	.5	.4	1.7
.1	.1	.1		.1	.2	.2	.2	.2	.8
8.8	8.3	10.4		12.0	8.1	4.0	1.2	.9	.8
(915) 15.5	(890) 15.4	(1354) 16.5	% Depr., Dep., Amort./Sales	(1014) 17.7	(198) 14.6	(55) 12.2	(44) 6.5	(16) 9.4	(27) 2.0
22.9	22.2	24.1		25.1	21.2	21.1	13.6	24.5	4.1
3.2	2.5	4.0		4.7	5.4	4.1	1.7		
(100) 6.3	(102) 6.8	(138) 6.3	% Officers', Directors', Owners' Comp/Sales	(63) 10.4	(36) 10.3	(14) 8.6	(16) 5.2		
17.2	12.9	17.5		19.7	18.0	13.2	9.4		
2663913M	3132616M	4046792M	Net Sales ($)	352078M	390235M	235911M	361412M	273987M	2433169M
6495661M	6388840M	8522017M	Total Assets ($)	2050261M	1671566M	823773M	941091M	927475M	2107851M

© RMA 2003

M = $ thousand   MM = $ million

See Pages 11 through 18 for Explanation of Ratios and Data

Current Data Sorted By Assets   Comparative Historical Data

Type of Statement	0-500M	500M-2MM	2-10MM	10-50MM	50-100MM	100-250MM		4/1/98-3/31/99 ALL	4/1/99-3/31/00 ALL
Unqualified	3	19	31	22	13	9		137	106
Reviewed	9	22	40	15	5	2		124	93
Compiled	38	55	41	12	1	1		244	190
Tax Returns	153	107	70	6	1	5		380	290
Other	60	80	96	36	4	3		329	227
		118 (4/1-9/30/02)		841 (10/1/02-3/31/03)					
NUMBER OF STATEMENTS	263	283	278	91	24	20		1214	906
ASSETS	%	%	%	%	%	%		%	%
Cash & Equivalents	27.1	15.2	10.6	10.6	13.2	10.4		13.9	14.4
Trade Receivables (net)	7.6	5.7	8.1	10.1	5.0	2.7		6.6	6.8
Inventory	1.6	2.4	4.2	3.0	7.5	2.5		3.5	4.3
All Other Current	5.7	5.7	5.4	4.9	6.9	3.5		4.7	5.7
Total Current	42.0	29.0	28.4	28.6	32.6	19.1		28.7	31.2
Fixed Assets (net)	39.9	53.1	53.4	46.3	33.6	44.6		54.9	51.9
Intangibles (net)	5.5	5.3	4.0	4.2	2.5	3.6		3.0	3.8
All Other Non-Current	12.6	12.6	14.2	20.9	31.3	32.8		13.4	13.1
Total	100.0	100.0	100.0	100.0	100.0	100.0		100.0	100.0
LIABILITIES									
Notes Payable-Short Term	17.2	7.9	8.4	7.0	5.8	2.4		10.1	8.9
Cur. Mat.-L/T/D	5.3	4.1	3.4	3.4	1.8	1.8		4.3	4.4
Trade Payables	5.5	3.6	3.2	6.7	7.0	3.5		4.0	4.6
Income Taxes Payable	.2	.1	.3	.3	.2	.1		.2	.3
All Other Current	22.6	15.4	9.9	11.8	17.3	15.7		11.6	14.2
Total Current	50.9	31.1	25.1	29.2	32.2	23.5		30.2	32.4
Long Term Debt	28.0	37.3	42.7	32.6	31.3	32.6		44.2	40.6
Deferred Taxes	.1	.1	.2	.6	.3	1.6		.3	.3
All Other Non-Current	5.8	6.9	5.7	3.5	4.2	25.9		7.5	5.3
Net Worth	15.4	24.6	26.3	34.1	32.0	16.5		17.9	21.4
Total Liabilities & Net Worth	100.0	100.0	100.0	100.0	100.0	100.0		100.0	100.0
INCOME DATA									
Net Sales	100.0	100.0	100.0	100.0	100.0	100.0		100.0	100.0
Gross Profit									
Operating Expenses	84.0	75.9	68.9	76.3	82.9	79.4		73.4	73.9
Operating Profit	16.0	24.1	31.1	23.7	17.1	20.5		26.6	26.1
All Other Expenses (net)	5.0	12.2	15.9	9.4	6.3	14.4		11.6	11.9
Profit Before Taxes	10.9	11.8	15.2	14.3	10.8	6.1		14.9	14.1
RATIOS									
Current	2.5	1.9	2.2	1.8	1.8	2.7		2.9	2.1
	1.1	.9	.9	1.0	.9	.6		1.1	1.0
	.4	.2	.3	.4	.6	.2		.3	.3
Quick	2.1	1.5	1.7	1.3	1.1	2.0		2.1	1.5
	.8	.6	(276) .7	(89) .7	.5	.4		(1209) .7	(905) .6
	.2	.1	.1	.1	.1	.1		.1	.2
Sales/Receivables	0 UND	0 UND	0 UND	0 UND	0 UND	0 UND		0 UND	0 UND
	0 UND	0 UND	0 742.6	5 69.1	10 34.9	0 UND		0 UND	0 UND
	2 201.5	6 61.5	19 19.4	32 11.6	27 13.4	18 20.8		13 27.6	15 24.9
Cost of Sales/Inventory									
Cost of Sales/Payables									
Sales/Working Capital	17.2	12.0	5.6	9.4	2.8	7.8		7.0	8.4
	215.0	−110.7	−69.7	612.9	−151.5	−7.6		225.2	999.8
	−12.6	−4.9	−4.1	−2.7	−4.3	−1.4		−4.8	−5.8
EBIT/Interest	(143) 22.0	(157) 11.6	(152) 14.6	(58) 11.3	(17) 23.2	(11) 7.4		(602) 12.5	(499) 9.8
	5.4	4.0	4.5	3.7	5.7	2.1		3.8	3.8
	1.6	1.2	2.0	1.5	1.7	.9		1.6	1.3
Net Profit + Depr., Dep., Amort./Cur. Mat. L /T/D		(15) 8.7	(28) 8.3	(19) 8.2				(114) 5.1	(91) 4.1
		3.3	2.6	2.5				2.6	2.5
		1.0	1.3	.9				1.0	1.3
Fixed/Worth	.3	.6	.4	.3	.0	.3		.6	.5
	1.1	2.9	2.6	1.2	.9	2.4		2.2	2.2
	UND	125.2	28.8	5.2	2.8	NM		16.6	23.5
Debt/Worth	.5	1.1	1.1	.8	1.2	1.3		.9	1.1
	2.6	3.7	3.9	2.3	2.8	3.4		3.0	3.2
	−56.0	405.0	38.5	9.2	6.6	NM		30.0	45.2
% Profit Before Taxes/Tangible Net Worth	(194) 173.1	(215) 66.7	(225) 66.7	(82) 41.3	(22) 53.0	(15) 36.0		(962) 61.5	(705) 55.5
	45.2	24.2	21.4	20.1	16.6	17.4		21.6	21.3
	10.9	7.4	7.1	6.7	7.2	2.3		5.5	5.8
% Profit Before Taxes/Total Assets	56.5	13.4	12.0	12.5	16.4	11.5		15.2	14.1
	13.1	5.7	4.8	4.9	6.9	3.0		5.3	4.9
	.7	.9	.8	.9	2.1	−.7		.6	.7
Sales/Net Fixed Assets	86.8	24.5	22.4	20.7	53.4	10.0		20.7	24.1
	24.4	1.8	.6	2.9	11.1	2.8		.9	1.8
	3.7	.2	.2	.3	.6	.3		.2	.2
Sales/Total Assets	10.5	3.5	1.4	1.6	1.7	.8		2.6	2.8
	4.3	.6	.3	.4	.7	.4		.4	.6
	1.2	.2	.2	.2	.2	.2		.2	.2
% Depr., Dep., Amort./Sales	(193) .7	(237) 1.0	(239) 1.9	(73) 1.1	(16) 1.0	(15) 1.7		(1017) 1.8	(755) 1.5
	2.0	4.8	10.3	4.6	1.6	3.9		9.0	6.1
	7.9	16.0	20.4	15.5	16.9	12.5		17.6	17.0
% Officers', Directors', Owners' Comp/Sales	(108) 3.3	(68) 2.5	(51) 2.5	(18) 1.8				(259) 4.3	(213) 3.3
	8.6	5.0	7.9	5.3				8.3	8.4
	22.3	14.3	13.3	15.5				18.6	17.9
Net Sales ($)	301092M	726145M	1438695M	2193158M	2351807M	3811726M		8072363M	10097963M
Total Assets ($)	56373M	320571M	1197451M	2153162M	1684795M	3011121M		8187180M	8838917M

M = $ thousand   MM = $ million
See Pages 11 through 18 for Explanation of Ratios and Data

Comparative Historical Data   Current Data Sorted By Sales

			Type of Statement						
76	68	97	Unqualified	15	19	10	9	13	31
68	70	93	Reviewed	19	26	9	13	14	12
171	212	148	Compiled	69	42	11	14	9	3
215	250	342	Tax Returns	222	61	20	21	13	5
262	277	279	Other	110	63	24	30	31	21
4/1/00-3/31/01	4/1/01-3/31/02	4/1/02-3/31/03		118 (4/1-9/30/02)			841 (10/1/02-3/31/03)		
ALL	ALL	ALL		0-1MM	1-3MM	3-5MM	5-10MM	10-25MM	25MM & OVER
792	877	959	NUMBER OF STATEMENTS	435	211	74	87	80	72
%	%	%	ASSETS	%	%	%	%	%	%
15.3	15.3	16.5	Cash & Equivalents	12.6	19.1	22.6	22.0	17.9	18.4
7.7	7.0	7.3	Trade Receivables (net)	4.1	7.7	6.3	12.8	12.4	13.5
4.6	4.3	2.9	Inventory	1.7	3.4	5.8	2.7	2.5	6.6
6.0	6.2	5.5	All Other Current	3.6	7.4	6.1	7.2	8.1	6.0
33.5	32.7	32.2	Total Current	22.1	37.6	40.7	44.8	40.7	44.4
46.4	49.6	48.3	Fixed Assets (net)	64.5	41.5	33.3	26.7	32.6	28.5
4.1	4.5	4.8	Intangibles (net)	3.3	4.2	8.5	7.2	6.7	6.3
15.9	13.2	14.8	All Other Non-Current	10.1	16.7	17.4	21.2	19.9	20.8
100.0	100.0	100.0	Total	100.0	100.0	100.0	100.0	100.0	100.0
			LIABILITIES						
9.6	18.5	10.4	Notes Payable-Short Term	11.8	12.0	6.3	10.8	6.3	5.3
4.5	7.4	4.0	Cur. Mat.-L/T/D	5.1	3.7	1.9	4.0	2.7	2.2
5.7	4.4	4.4	Trade Payables	1.6	6.1	4.4	7.2	5.8	11.2
.1	.1	.2	Income Taxes' Payable	.1	.3	.2	.2	.2	.3
16.1	15.4	15.5	All Other Current	13.7	15.0	15.8	18.3	20.5	18.5
36.0	45.9	34.5	Total Current	32.3	37.0	28.7	40.6	35.5	37.6
34.7	38.6	35.6	Long Term Debt	47.3	31.7	24.8	21.4	23.9	17.7
.3	.3	.2	Deferred Taxes	.0	.1	.0	.4	.5	.9
5.7	6.0	6.3	All Other Non-Current	4.5	8.3	6.9	5.8	6.8	9.9
23.4	9.1	23.5	Net Worth	15.9	22.9	39.5	31.8	33.3	33.9
100.0	100.0	100.0	Total Liabilities & Net Worth	100.0	100.0	100.0	100.0	100.0	100.0
			INCOME DATA						
100.0	100.0	100.0	Net Sales	100.0	100.0	100.0	100.0	100.0	100.0
			Gross Profit						
79.0	74.3	76.4	Operating Expenses	64.7	83.1	84.5	88.9	88.3	91.1
21.0	25.7	23.6	Operating Profit	35.3	16.9	15.5	11.1	11.7	8.9
8.6	13.3	10.9	All Other Expenses (net)	18.9	6.1	5.0	1.2	4.4	2.1
12.5	12.4	12.7	Profit Before Taxes	16.4	10.9	10.6	9.9	7.3	6.8
			RATIOS						
2.2	2.1	2.1		2.1	2.0	3.0	2.3	1.9	2.3
1.0	1.0	1.0	Current	.7	1.0	1.3	1.2	1.1	1.2
.4	.3	.3		.2	.4	.7	.7	.6	.8
1.6	1.5	1.7		1.7	1.6	1.9	1.9	1.5	1.8
(791) .6	(876) .6	(955) .7	Quick	.4	(209) .7	1.0	.8	.9	(70) 1.1
.2	.1	.2		.1	.2	.2	.5	.4	.4
0 UND	0 UND	0 UND		0 UND	0 UND	0 UND	0 UND	0 936.0	0 UND
1 706.2	0 UND	0 UND	Sales/Receivables	0 UND	0 UND	0 999.8	3 106.9	6 60.7	8 43.6
15 24.3	14 26.4	10 35.9		0 832.0	11 33.0	10 37.8	29 12.7	18 19.9	34 10.8
			Cost of Sales/Inventory						
			Cost of Sales/Payables						
7.1	8.6	10.5		10.0	11.6	9.2	11.5	11.5	10.1
275.4	425.8	-245.2	Sales/Working Capital	-19.6	999.8	90.7	151.0	229.5	70.4
-6.5	-6.2	-5.5		-2.4	-8.0	-19.8	-20.5	-29.5	-18.8
9.8	8.3	14.6		8.2	9.4	23.7	21.2	20.8	32.4
(455) 3.4	(466) 3.3	(538) 4.4	EBIT/Interest	(173) 4.0	(135) 3.5	(47) 5.3	(69) 10.3	(58) 5.4	(56) 6.0
1.2	1.1	1.7		1.3	1.5	1.4	1.7	1.8	2.3
5.7	6.6	8.1	Net Profit + Depr., Dep.,	5.0	7.7			10.1	12.3
(69) 2.3	(69) 2.3	(76) 2.6	Amort./Cur. Mat. L/T/D	(15) 2.4	(14) 2.6		(16) 2.5	(16) 2.8
1.0	1.1	1.0		.9	2.1			1.0	1.2
.4	.5	.4		.9	.4	.2	.1	.2	.2
1.6	2.3	1.8	Fixed/Worth	3.7	1.3	.8	.7	1.0	.7
11.5	34.1	32.0		104.6	132.7	4.7	7.4	4.6	2.4
.9	1.0	.9		1.1	.8	.6	.7	.7	.8
3.1	3.9	3.2	Debt/Worth	5.3	2.9	1.9	1.9	3.2	2.0
28.3	563.2	80.4		999.8	267.0	10.6	14.6	11.2	5.4
56.6	62.3	76.4	% Profit Before Taxes/Tangible	69.6	70.9	99.7	98.4	83.7	70.8
(629) 19.7	(664) 19.1	(753) 25.2	Net Worth	(332) 21.5	(161) 25.2	(59) 18.6	(71) 34.9	(67) 41.0	(63) 42.5
4.4	4.6	7.5		4.4	7.5	5.6	12.2	11.9	23.7
14.2	13.7	18.7	% Profit Before Taxes/Total	11.4	24.2	29.5	29.2	25.8	27.2
5.1	5.0	6.2	Assets	4.1	6.3	7.1	13.9	8.5	12.3
.5	.4	.9		.2	.9	.7	3.2	2.1	5.0
30.6	28.4	34.4		8.8	37.9	66.8	75.9	54.2	34.4
5.4	3.5	5.3	Sales/Net Fixed Assets	.3	11.2	28.1	24.0	23.8	17.7
.3	.2	.3		.2	.5	3.2	10.0	4.2	5.9
3.5	3.4	4.0		1.2	4.9	6.5	6.9	7.6	4.3
.7	.7	.8	Sales/Total Assets	.2	1.7	2.5	2.7	2.9	2.5
.2	.2	.2		.1	.4	.5	1.3	.6	.8
1.1	1.1	1.1		4.8	1.1	.4	.5	.5	.8
(640) 3.8	(706) 4.2	(773) 4.4	% Depr., Dep., Amort./Sales	(358) 13.1	(169) 2.6	(61) 1.1	(65) 1.2	(65) 1.0	(55) 1.2
14.3	15.0	15.9		22.0	11.4	4.9	2.2	2.4	2.8
3.6	3.0	2.7		8.0	2.7	1.7	2.0	1.2	1.9
(220) 8.2	(209) 7.6	(249) 7.2	% Officers', Directors',	(76) 16.9	(65) 8.3	(33) 5.0	(33) 3.2	(25) 2.3	(17) 7.4
15.7	14.0	16.9	Owners' Comp/Sales	24.6	14.8	10.4	6.2	4.2	15.0
9560377M	13104698M	10822623M	Net Sales ($)	166323M	378415M	292022M	595641M	1225827M	8164395M
7757795M	7612258M	8423473M	Total Assets ($)	669589M	642911M	487248M	608539M	1718757M	4296429M

M = $ thousand   MM = $ million
See Pages 11 through 18 for Explanation of Ratios and Data

Current Data Sorted By Assets   Comparative Historical Data

Type of Statement

							4/1/98-3/31/99 ALL	4/1/99-3/31/00 ALL
1	1		3			Unqualified		
		2	1			Reviewed		
2	2	2	1			Compiled		
8	5	3				Tax Returns		
4	3	2	1			Other		
0-500M	6 (4/1-9/30/02) 500M-2MM	2-10MM	35 (10/1/02-3/31/03) 10-50MM	50-100MM	100-250MM			
15	11	9	6			NUMBER OF STATEMENTS		
%	%	%	%	%	%	ASSETS	%	%
39.3	6.5			D	D	Cash & Equivalents	D	D
1.5	4.3			A	A	Trade Receivables (net)	A	A
8.0	5.5			T	T	Inventory	T	T
6.5	13.4			A	A	All Other Current	A	A
55.3	29.7					Total Current		
34.0	51.6			N	N	Fixed Assets (net)	N	N
1.3	14.1			O	O	Intangibles (net)	O	O
9.4	4.5			T	T	All Other Non-Current	T	T
100.0	100.0					Total		
				A	A	LIABILITIES	A	A
10.5	17.2			V	V	Notes Payable-Short Term	V	V
4.4	1.7			A	A	Cur. Mat.-L/T/D	A	A
2.2	2.8			I	I	Trade Payables	I	I
.0	.0			L	L	Income Taxes Payable	L	L
29.0	1.9			A	A	All Other Current	A	A
46.1	23.5			B	B	Total Current	B	B
32.0	54.6			L	L	Long Term Debt	L	L
.0	.0			E	E	Deferred Taxes	E	E
2.2	2.4					All Other Non-Current		
19.7	19.4					Net Worth		
100.0	100.0					Total Liabilities & Net Worth		
						INCOME DATA		
100.0	100.0					Net Sales		
						Gross Profit		
82.3	84.3					Operating Expenses		
17.7	15.7					Operating Profit		
8.8	8.2					All Other Expenses (net)		
8.9	7.5					Profit Before Taxes		
						RATIOS		
10.1	2.9							
2.5	1.3					Current		
.5	.3							
2.7	2.5							
1.1	.4					Quick		
.1	.2							
0 UND	0 UND							
0 UND	0 UND					Sales/Receivables		
0 UND	21 17.0							
						Cost of Sales/Inventory		
						Cost of Sales/Payables		
3.6	3.6							
52.4	25.0					Sales/Working Capital		
−19.5	−3.6							
						EBIT/Interest		
						Net Profit + Depr., Dep., Amort./Cur. Mat. L /T/D		
.0	1.3							
.6	48.0					Fixed/Worth		
6.5	−1.6							
.4	1.1							
1.1	376.5					Debt/Worth		
−7.7	−3.0							
246.8						% Profit Before Taxes/Tangible Net Worth		
(11) 90.3								
7.1								
160.9	9.8					% Profit Before Taxes/Total Assets		
51.4	1.9							
.0	−2.8							
999.8	40.3					Sales/Net Fixed Assets		
34.4	.4							
5.0	.2							
10.5	2.2					Sales/Total Assets		
4.5	.3							
.9	.2							
						% Depr., Dep., Amort./Sales		
						% Officers', Directors', Owners' Comp/Sales		
15065M	11228M	67313M	33998M			Net Sales ($)		
2730M	12925M	37939M	159023M			Total Assets ($)		

M = $ thousand   MM = $ million
See Pages 11 through 18 for Explanation of Ratios and Data

Comparative Historical Data   **Current Data Sorted By Sales**

4/1/00-3/31/01 ALL	4/1/01-3/31/02 ALL	4/1/02-3/31/03 ALL	Type of Statement	0-1MM	1-3MM	3-5MM	5-10MM	10-25MM	25MM & OVER
		5	Unqualified	2			3		
		3	Reviewed				2	1	
		7	Compiled	4	2				1
		16	Tax Returns	8	6	2			
		10	Other	3	6	1			
		41	NUMBER OF STATEMENTS	17	14	3	5	1	1
				6 (4/1-9/30/02)			35 (10/1/02-3/31/03)		
%	%	%	**ASSETS**	%	%	%	%	%	%
		18.7	Cash & Equivalents	19.3	23.0				
D	D	6.1	Trade Receivables (net)	1.7	3.0				
A	A	10.1	Inventory	.0	25.0				
T	T	11.2	All Other Current	7.0	10.3				
A	A	46.1	Total Current	27.9	61.2				
		43.4	Fixed Assets (net)	65.1	20.1				
N	N	4.4	Intangibles (net)	1.1	11.2				
O	O	6.1	All Other Non-Current	5.9	7.5				
T	T	100.0	Total	100.0	100.0				
			LIABILITIES						
A	A	12.1	Notes Payable-Short Term	3.9	23.1				
V	V	4.1	Cur. Mat.-L/T/D	6.2	3.4				
A	A	2.6	Trade Payables	1.9	2.2				
I	I	.0	Income Taxes Payable	.0	.0				
L	L	13.4	All Other Current	18.0	12.5				
A	A	32.2	Total Current	30.0	41.2				
B	B	38.5	Long Term Debt	51.2	30.5				
L	L	.0	Deferred Taxes	.0	.0				
E	E	2.0	All Other Non-Current	2.9	.4				
		27.3	Net Worth	15.9	27.9				
		100.0	Total Liabilities & Net Worth	100.0	100.0				
			INCOME DATA						
		100.0	Net Sales	100.0	100.0				
			Gross Profit						
		80.2	Operating Expenses	74.1	90.3				
		19.7	Operating Profit	25.9	9.7				
		8.3	All Other Expenses (net)	18.0	1.3				
		11.5	Profit Before Taxes	7.9	8.4				
			RATIOS						
		4.2		3.8	2.8				
		1.8	Current	1.2	2.0				
		.7		.2	1.0				
		2.9		2.8	2.6				
		.6	Quick	.5	.2				
		.1		.1	.1				
	0	UND		0	UND	0	UND		
	0	UND	Sales/Receivables	0	UND	0	UND		
	15	23.6		15	23.6	0	UND		
			Cost of Sales/Inventory						
			Cost of Sales/Payables						
		3.1		2.4	3.6				
		17.4	Sales/Working Capital	39.7	21.4				
		−27.8		−4.2	NM				
		22.2							
	(21)	3.7	EBIT/Interest						
		1.5							
			Net Profit + Depr., Dep., Amort./Cur. Mat. L/T/D						
		.1		1.0	.1				
		1.3	Fixed/Worth	4.9	.6				
		8.2		−131.3	NM				
		.6		1.0	.5				
		3.2	Debt/Worth	4.2	2.5				
		193.9		−137.2	−2.3				
		89.5		16.9	137.9				
	(32)	18.9	% Profit Before Taxes/Tangible Net Worth	(12) 11.4	(10) 61.1				
		4.4		−.5	22.0				
		46.2		13.2	54.9				
		7.0	% Profit Before Taxes/Total Assets	1.9	16.6				
		.0		−2.8	.2				
		45.3		21.7	183.9				
		18.3	Sales/Net Fixed Assets	.3	39.1				
		.2		.2	20.8				
		4.0		2.0	12.3				
		.8	Sales/Total Assets	.3	3.3				
		.2		.1	.7				
		1.0		15.4					
	(29)	4.8	% Depr., Dep., Amort./Sales	(12) 21.2					
		20.4		25.6					
		2.9							
	(12)	9.4	% Officers', Directors', Owners' Comp/Sales						
		14.9							
		127604M	Net Sales ($)	5404M	25964M	12917M	36523M	19121M	27675M
		212617M	Total Assets ($)	20733M	27242M	14206M	135814M	7237M	7385M

© RMA 2003   M = $ thousand   MM = $ million
See Pages 11 through 18 for Explanation of Ratios and Data

Current Data Sorted By Assets							Comparative Historical Data	
						Type of Statement		
2		1	3	1		Unqualified		
	2	2	1			Reviewed		
	5	3	1			Compiled		
10	15	13	3			Tax Returns		
3	9	3	3	2	2	Other		
7 (4/1-9/30/02)			77 (10/1/02-3/31/03)				4/1/98-3/31/99	4/1/99-3/31/00
0-500M	**500M-2MM**	**2-10MM**	**10-50MM**	**50-100MM**	**100-250MM**		**ALL**	**ALL**
15	31	22	11	3	2	**NUMBER OF STATEMENTS**		
%	%	%	%	%	%	**ASSETS**	%	%
23.7	7.8	5.1	10.4			Cash & Equivalents	DATA NOT AVAILABLE	DATA NOT AVAILABLE
3.9	12.5	4.3	6.7			Trade Receivables (net)		
6.3	14.1	24.0	14.4			Inventory		
10.3	5.2	4.2	24.1			All Other Current		
44.2	39.5	37.5	55.7			Total Current		
37.5	46.4	44.2	35.7			Fixed Assets (net)		
.1	2.9	1.3	.2			Intangibles (net)		
18.3	11.1	17.0	8.5			All Other Non-Current		
100.0	100.0	100.0	100.0			Total		
						LIABILITIES		
30.3	16.8	14.3	29.2			Notes Payable-Short Term		
6.6	2.9	4.2	1.3			Cur. Mat.-L/T/D		
1.2	5.2	2.0	.9			Trade Payables		
.0	.0	.0	.1			Income Taxes Payable		
14.1	6.5	3.9	8.5			All Other Current		
52.2	31.3	24.5	39.9			Total Current		
13.0	41.7	44.4	31.0			Long Term Debt		
.5	.0	.1	.3			Deferred Taxes		
9.8	4.8	4.4	.0			All Other Non-Current		
24.5	22.2	26.6	28.7			Net Worth		
100.0	100.0	100.0	100.0			Total Liabilities & Net Worth		
						INCOME DATA		
100.0	100.0	100.0	100.0			Net Sales		
						Gross Profit		
89.1	73.6	64.0	76.7			Operating Expenses		
10.9	26.4	36.0	23.3			Operating Profit		
4.2	12.1	16.6	14.5			All Other Expenses (net)		
6.8	14.3	19.4	8.8			Profit Before Taxes		
						RATIOS		
4.6	3.1	6.1	3.9					
1.2	1.4	1.3	1.1			Current		
.2	.7	.3	.9					
2.2	1.5	1.7	.9					
.7	.7	.4	.5			Quick		
.0	.1	.1	.1					
0 UND	0 UND	0 UND	0 UND					
0 UND	0 UND	0 UND	0 UND			Sales/Receivables		
0 UND	70 5.2	7 52.4	9 41.4					
						Cost of Sales/Inventory		
						Cost of Sales/Payables		
3.8	4.2	1.8	.9					
21.0	33.5	23.9	3.7			Sales/Working Capital		
-.9	-6.9	-1.6	-138.1					
	10.8	36.0						
	(17) 2.6	(10) 4.2				EBIT/Interest		
	.7	2.0						
						Net Profit + Depr., Dep., Amort./Cur. Mat. L /T/D		
.0	.1	.2	.0					
.7	2.1	2.5	1.5			Fixed/Worth		
19.9	6.1	32.7	2.8					
.5	1.6	1.7	1.6					
2.6	5.4	3.9	3.5			Debt/Worth		
UND	27.1	50.3	4.2					
60.3	99.4	82.7	70.5					
(12) 12.1	(25) 22.5	(18) 27.2	5.7			% Profit Before Taxes/Tangible Net Worth		
-30.0	2.0	3.4	.0					
13.2	16.5	16.5	10.4					
5.0	3.6	2.4	1.2			% Profit Before Taxes/Total Assets		
-1.9	-.4	.9	.0					
363.2	44.8	19.3	183.8					
24.5	2.7	.5	5.0			Sales/Net Fixed Assets		
3.9	.3	.2	.3					
3.7	2.3	.6	1.0					
1.5	.8	.2	.3			Sales/Total Assets		
.7	.2	.1	.2					
	1.3	1.6						
	(19) 7.5	(18) 5.6				% Depr., Dep., Amort./Sales		
	12.0	17.3						
						% Officers', Directors', Owners' Comp/Sales		
9188M	53924M	60439M	301949M	203062M	561164M	Net Sales ($)		
4142M	36022M	96381M	226114M	248409M	296501M	Total Assets ($)		

M = $ thousand MM = $ million

See Pages 11 through 18 for Explanation of Ratios and Data

Comparative Historical Data | Current Data Sorted By Sales

			Type of Statement	0-1MM	1-3MM	3-5MM	5-10MM	10-25MM	25MM & OVER
		7	Unqualified	1	2		1		3
		5	Reviewed	1	2		2		
		9	Compiled	5	2	2			
		41	Tax Returns	27	9	3	2		
		22	Other	9	3	2	1	2	5
4/1/00-3/31/01 ALL	4/1/01-3/31/02 ALL	4/1/02-3/31/03 ALL		7 (4/1-9/30/02)			77 (10/1/02-3/31/03)		
		84	NUMBER OF STATEMENTS	43	18	7	6	2	8
%	%	%	ASSETS	%	%	%	%	%	%
D	D	11.3	Cash & Equivalents	8.2	15.3				
A	A	7.8	Trade Receivables (net)	4.1	7.1				
T	T	14.6	Inventory	11.7	21.1				
A	A	8.7	All Other Current	4.4	3.4				
		42.4	Total Current	28.5	46.8				
N	N	42.8	Fixed Assets (net)	52.9	46.5				
O	O	1.5	Intangibles (net)	.3	1.3				
T	T	13.4	All Other Non-Current	18.3	5.4				
		100.0	Total	100.0	100.0				
A	A		LIABILITIES						
V	V	19.9	Notes Payable-Short Term	15.1	19.9				
A	A	3.8	Cur. Mat.-L/T/D	5.8	.9				
I	I	3.0	Trade Payables	.7	7.1				
L	L	.1	Income Taxes Payable	.0	.0				
A	A	7.5	All Other Current	6.5	5.3				
B	B	34.2	Total Current	28.1	33.2				
L	L	35.1	Long Term Debt	42.4	41.1				
E	E	.1	Deferred Taxes	.1	.4				
		5.3	All Other Non-Current	6.0	3.3				
		25.3	Net Worth	23.5	22.0				
		100.0	Total Liabilities & Net Worth	100.0	100.0				
			INCOME DATA						
		100.0	Net Sales	100.0	100.0				
			Gross Profit						
		75.1	Operating Expenses	65.1	82.9				
		24.9	Operating Profit	34.9	17.1				
		11.5	All Other Expenses (net)	17.4	10.0				
		13.4	Profit Before Taxes	17.5	7.1				
			RATIOS						
		3.6		2.8	4.9				
		1.3	Current	1.2	1.7				
		.5		.2	.6				
		1.6		1.5	2.1				
		.6	Quick	.5	.6				
		.1		.1	.1				
	0 UND	0 UND		0 UND	0 UND				
	0 UND	0 UND	Sales/Receivables	0 UND	1 341.3				
	18 20.6			0 UND	9 39.5				
			Cost of Sales/Inventory						
			Cost of Sales/Payables						
		2.7		2.4	2.5				
		21.0	Sales/Working Capital	21.0	23.7				
		-10.0		-2.8	-104.3				
		15.0		22.7	10.0				
	(43) 3.3		EBIT/Interest	(13) 2.1	(13) 3.3				
	1.1			.5	1.6				
			Net Profit + Depr., Dep., Amort./Cur. Mat. L/T/D						
		.1		.1	.1				
		1.6	Fixed/Worth	2.4	1.6				
		4.7		11.3	6.1				
		1.5		1.6	1.7				
		3.7	Debt/Worth	3.8	5.0				
		18.2		77.3	14.5				
		72.4	% Profit Before Taxes/Tangible Net Worth	63.5	61.2				
	(71) 17.1			(35) 9.0	(15) 15.1				
	1.1			1.1	.0				
		15.3	% Profit Before Taxes/Total Assets	8.1	14.4				
		3.4		1.7	3.5				
		.2		.0	.0				
		36.8	Sales/Net Fixed Assets	24.8	157.9				
		6.0		.4	3.3				
		.3		.2	.5				
		1.7	Sales/Total Assets	.7	2.7				
		.5		.2	1.2				
		.2		.2	.3				
		1.2	% Depr., Dep., Amort./Sales	3.1	.9				
	(57) 4.1			(30) 10.8	(13) 5.4				
	13.0			17.4	21.2				
		3.7	% Officers', Directors', Owners' Comp/Sales						
	(20) 5.7								
	19.5								
	1189726M		Net Sales ($)	15575M	35424M	25972M	46336M	26420M	1039999M
	907569M		Total Assets ($)	81245M	84466M	23103M	58602M	38053M	622100M

M = $ thousand   MM = $ million
See Pages 11 through 18 for Explanation of Ratios and Data

1118

Current Data Sorted By Assets   **Comparative Historical Data**

Type of Statement	0-500M	500M-2MM	2-10MM	10-50MM	50-100MM	100-250MM		4/1/98-3/31/99 ALL	4/1/99-3/31/00 ALL
		15 (4/1-9/30/02)		125 (10/1/02-3/31/03)					
Unqualified	1	5	4	6	1	2		35	20
Reviewed	3	7	23	7	2	1		29	32
Compiled	8	6	11	5				41	38
Tax Returns	3	10	2	8	1	3		16	15
Other			21					26	30
NUMBER OF STATEMENTS	15	28	61	26	4	6		147	135
	%	%	%	%	%	%		%	%
ASSETS									
Cash & Equivalents	21.0	10.6	6.0	4.6				8.9	7.7
Trade Receivables (net)	3.7	4.0	4.6	4.6				5.4	4.8
Inventory	8.7	14.1	16.7	26.2				13.4	16.1
All Other Current	.6	2.1	5.8	6.8				4.1	3.9
Total Current	34.1	30.7	33.1	42.2				31.9	32.5
Fixed Assets (net)	58.3	55.6	61.4	53.7				58.7	57.7
Intangibles (net)	1.4	7.9	1.8	1.9				2.5	3.3
All Other Non-Current	6.1	5.8	3.7	2.2				6.9	6.4
Total	100.0	100.0	100.0	100.0				100.0	100.0
LIABILITIES									
Notes Payable-Short Term	30.9	18.4	35.3	37.0				27.5	35.8
Cur. Mat.-L/T/D	6.9	8.6	9.6	7.4				11.3	8.1
Trade Payables	13.3	6.7	3.1	1.7				4.1	4.2
Income Taxes Payable	.0	.0	.4	.0				.2	.1
All Other Current	2.8	10.5	8.1	3.1				6.0	5.7
Total Current	53.8	44.2	56.5	49.2				49.2	53.9
Long Term Debt	37.0	27.3	23.3	29.1				30.4	28.5
Deferred Taxes	.0	.0	.5	1.4				.7	.5
All Other Non-Current	9.7	3.7	2.6	.7				4.0	2.0
Net Worth	-.7	24.8	17.1	19.6				15.8	15.1
Total Liabilities & Net Worth	100.0	100.0	100.0	100.0				100.0	100.0
INCOME DATA									
Net Sales	100.0	100.0	100.0	100.0				100.0	100.0
Gross Profit									
Operating Expenses	102.7	99.7	96.2	92.9				92.9	92.4
Operating Profit	-2.7	.3	3.8	7.1				7.1	7.6
All Other Expenses (net)	1.7	-.8	1.6	3.1				2.5	3.5
Profit Before Taxes	-4.4	1.1	2.2	4.0				4.6	4.1
RATIOS									
Current	11.0	1.7	1.1	1.3				1.5	1.3
	1.0	.6	.5	1.0				.6	.5
	.2	.3	.2	.2				.1	.1
Quick	10.0	.8	.3	.5				.8	.7
	.4	.4	(59) .1	.2				.3	.2
	.2	.1	.1	.1				.1	.1
Sales/Receivables	0 UND	2 157.3	5 76.2	10 37.0				4 97.0	3 124.4
	10 35.4	7 54.4	10 35.5	18 20.1				11 32.6	11 34.6
	18 20.1	16 22.3	23 15.7	28 12.9				25 14.5	20 18.0
Cost of Sales/Inventory									
Cost of Sales/Payables									
Sales/Working Capital	6.3	14.3	18.1	6.3				11.0	10.6
	-60.5	-10.5	-4.9	NM				-10.1	-9.5
	-2.3	-2.7	-1.7	-2.6				-1.7	-1.5
EBIT/Interest	(12) 1.0	(23) 4.3	(54) 3.3	(24) 2.3				(139) 2.6	(120) 2.3
	.5	2.4	1.7	1.6				1.6	1.6
	-1.0	.6	1.0	1.3				1.1	1.1
Net Profit + Depr., Dep., Amort./Cur. Mat. L/T/D								(20) 1.6	(17) 1.6
								1.1	1.2
								.8	.8
Fixed/Worth	.5	1.3	1.9	.2				1.0	.7
	26.2	3.7	4.9	2.9				4.0	4.4
	-2.6	NM	14.7	7.7				10.0	21.7
Debt/Worth	1.8	1.5	3.2	4.0				2.7	3.1
	147.0	3.9	5.5	5.4				5.9	7.2
	-3.6	NM	14.6	10.7				16.5	37.4
% Profit Before Taxes/Tangible Net Worth		(21) 28.7	(50) 37.8	42.6				(128) 43.5	(113) 51.4
		12.7	15.5	14.6				23.1	26.0
		1.1	3.7	4.1				5.6	7.7
% Profit Before Taxes/Total Assets	1.7	8.0	6.0	4.8				7.2	8.2
	-1.3	3.1	2.4	2.0				3.1	3.0
	-7.7	-2.3	-.5	.8				.4	.6
Sales/Net Fixed Assets	28.4	9.3	3.9	34.8				11.7	17.5
	1.6	2.4	1.3	1.1				1.2	1.6
	1.0	.8	.8	.6				.7	.8
Sales/Total Assets	2.4	1.8	1.4	.9				1.3	1.6
	1.2	1.0	.7	.6				.7	.8
	.7	.6	.5	.5				.5	.6
% Depr., Dep., Amort./Sales	(11) 30.7	(24) 7.4	(50) 12.2	(16) 15.7				(109) 9.3	(96) 9.6
	39.3	20.9	27.5	32.3				26.0	27.1
	63.2	34.4	42.7	40.5				38.4	37.3
% Officers', Directors', Owners' Comp/Sales			(25) 2.1					(46) 2.8	(45) 2.0
			3.3					4.8	5.0
			5.1					9.3	10.3
Net Sales ($)	7482M	44554M	340824M	370743M	242182M	734855M		1354365M	1402044M
Total Assets ($)	3908M	35125M	287925M	514953M	277766M	668880M		1851757M	1779255M

M = $ thousand   MM = $ million
See Pages 11 through 18 for Explanation of Ratios and Data

Comparative Historical Data

Current Data Sorted By Sales

Type of Statement	4/1/00-3/31/01 ALL	4/1/01-3/31/02 ALL	4/1/02-3/31/03 ALL	0-1MM	1-3MM	3-5MM	5-10MM	10-25MM	25MM & OVER
Unqualified	16	19	13		2	2	3	2	4
Reviewed	21	27	38	2	9	8	12	4	3
Compiled	29	25	27	8	10	2	2	4	1
Tax Returns	12	10	16	9	5	1	1		
Other	29	44	46	8	11	7	8		6
				15 (4/1-9/30/02)		125 (10/1/02-3/31/03)			
NUMBER OF STATEMENTS	107	125	140	27	37	20	26	16	14
ASSETS	%	%	%	%	%	%	%	%	%
Cash & Equivalents	6.9	6.7	8.1	11.1	9.2	8.1	4.6	7.8	6.4
Trade Receivables (net)	6.3	4.8	4.5	3.2	3.5	4.1	5.1	6.6	6.5
Inventory	8.0	11.4	19.3	10.8	19.1	14.7	15.8	29.0	38.3
All Other Current	4.2	5.4	4.4	1.3	4.6	6.8	3.4	9.0	3.0
Total Current	25.4	28.4	36.3	26.4	36.4	33.7	28.9	52.4	54.3
Fixed Assets (net)	65.2	64.9	56.7	61.6	55.4	63.1	66.3	43.5	38.5
Intangibles (net)	1.8	1.2	3.0	5.5	3.9	.8	2.0	.8	3.3
All Other Non-Current	7.7	5.5	4.0	6.4	4.3	2.5	2.7	3.3	3.9
Total	100.0	100.0	100.0	100.0	100.0	100.0	100.0	100.0	100.0
LIABILITIES									
Notes Payable-Short Term	31.3	36.4	32.0	26.2	32.5	40.9	27.9	34.5	34.0
Cur. Mat.-L/T/D	10.1	7.8	8.4	4.6	11.2	9.5	9.2	8.0	5.4
Trade Payables	4.6	3.4	4.6	5.8	7.1	4.6	2.4	2.0	2.4
Income Taxes Payable	.1	.2	.2	.0	.1	.3	.6	.1	.0
All Other Current	4.8	5.0	6.8	12.6	5.4	2.9	3.6	4.8	12.7
Total Current	50.8	52.8	51.9	49.3	56.3	58.3	43.6	49.4	54.4
Long Term Debt	29.3	26.4	26.8	35.7	23.1	11.6	35.2	28.6	23.5
Deferred Taxes	.4	.5	.5	.0	.3	.7	.4	1.7	.3
All Other Non-Current	3.7	2.1	3.3	6.4	4.3	2.0	1.5	.4	3.6
Net Worth	15.8	18.2	17.4	8.6	15.9	27.4	19.2	19.9	18.1
Total Liabilities & Net Worth	100.0	100.0	100.0	100.0	100.0	100.0	100.0	100.0	100.0
INCOME DATA									
Net Sales	100.0	100.0	100.0	100.0	100.0	100.0	100.0	100.0	100.0
Gross Profit									
Operating Expenses	91.7	94.8	96.6	100.2	97.7	97.2	95.0	94.7	91.7
Operating Profit	8.3	5.2	3.4	−.2	2.3	2.8	5.0	5.3	8.3
All Other Expenses (net)	3.9	4.9	1.5	1.2	.9	1.1	2.1	1.9	2.8
Profit Before Taxes	4.4	.3	1.8	−1.3	1.4	1.7	3.0	3.4	5.5
RATIOS									
Current	1.1 / .4 / .2	1.1 / .4 / .2	1.2 / .7 / .2	4.7 / .5 / .1	1.2 / .5 / .3	1.1 / .4 / .1	1.1 / .5 / .3	2.0 / 1.1 / .5	1.7 / 1.1 / .4
Quick	.9 / .2 / .1	.5 / .2 / .1	(138) .5 / .2 / .1	4.5 / .2 / .1	(36) .5 / .2 / .1	.4 / .1 / .0	(25) .5 / .2 / .1	.7 / .2 / .1	.5 / .3 / .1
Sales/Receivables	6 59.3 / 13 28.2 / 27 13.5	6 61.7 / 11 33.4 / 24 15.4	5 80.5 / 11 32.6 / 23 15.8	0 UND / 12 29.5 / 20 18.1	3 121.8 / 8 45.0 / 15 24.5	6 61.1 / 9 41.5 / 21 17.1	6 58.2 / 14 25.9 / 23 16.0	7 55.2 / 19 19.1 / 28 12.9	11 33.8 / 21 17.7 / 33 11.1
Cost of Sales/Inventory									
Cost of Sales/Payables									
Sales/Working Capital	25.8 / −6.0 / −1.6	25.9 / −6.9 / −1.5	10.5 / −12.4 / −2.3	6.7 / −3.5 / −1.4	12.4 / −6.2 / −2.0	23.7 / −5.4 / −1.1	18.3 / −11.5 / −2.8	7.0 / 12.6 / −5.9	8.0 / 36.7 / −4.0
EBIT/Interest	(100) 2.2 / 1.3 / 1.0	(120) 1.8 / 1.3 / .7	(122) 3.2 / 1.6 / .7	(19) 1.6 / .9 / −1.0	(35) 2.6 / 1.7 / .7	(17) 3.8 / 1.5 / .7	(25) 3.6 / 2.0 / 1.4	(13) 2.2 / 1.5 / 1.1	(13) 5.8 / 2.4 / 1.3
Net Profit + Depr., Dep., Amort./Cur. Mat. L/T/D	(13) 4.3 / 1.5 / 1.0	(13) 5.4 / 1.5 / 1.1	(13) 11.3 / 1.2 / .9						
Fixed/Worth	1.8 / 4.7 / 21.2	1.7 / 4.3 / 10.7	.9 / 4.2 / 13.5	2.1 / 26.2 / −6.1	1.7 / 4.2 / NM	1.0 / 3.3 / 7.1	2.0 / 4.8 / 6.6	.1 / 1.1 / 11.3	.4 / 2.0 / 17.5
Debt/Worth	3.6 / 6.4 / 25.5	2.7 / 4.9 / 12.2	2.7 / 5.5 / 19.0	2.8 / 147.0 / −10.4	2.4 / 4.3 / NM	1.7 / 4.3 / 10.5	3.7 / 5.4 / 6.9	3.8 / 5.8 / 11.4	3.7 / 7.6 / 32.5
% Profit Before Taxes/Tangible Net Worth	(93) 46.4 / 18.3 / 3.3	(105) 25.5 / 9.1 / −2.0	(115) 36.9 / 14.7 / 2.2	(15) 18.0 / 1.5 / −8.3	(28) 29.3 / 12.7 / 2.7	(19) 36.1 / 14.7 / −.2	(24) 43.5 / 21.7 / 6.0	(15) 42.4 / 17.3 / 4.3	59.9 / 26.7 / 8.5
% Profit Before Taxes/Total Assets	6.3 / 2.0 / .2	4.6 / 1.3 / −1.8	6.0 / 2.2 / −.8	3.3 / .1 / −7.7	5.1 / 2.4 / −1.3	7.4 / 1.9 / −1.4	6.4 / 3.4 / 1.3	5.1 / 2.0 / .7	6.8 / 4.3 / 2.1
Sales/Net Fixed Assets	4.0 / 1.1 / .7	3.6 / 1.1 / .8	11.0 / 1.6 / .7	3.1 / 1.0 / .6	6.5 / 1.3 / .8	11.0 / 1.2 / .8	4.3 / 1.6 / .7	102.7 / 10.0 / .7	51.2 / 8.2 / 1.9
Sales/Total Assets	1.3 / .8 / .6	1.2 / .8 / .6	1.4 / .8 / .5	1.2 / .7 / .5	1.2 / .7 / .6	1.3 / .9 / .5	1.5 / .9 / .5	1.9 / .8 / .6	2.1 / 1.0 / .6
% Depr., Dep., Amort./Sales	(81) 15.0 / 30.2 / 38.9	(104) 14.2 / 28.5 / 39.0	(101) 10.6 / 29.6 / 42.7	(23) 19.5 / 39.3 / 62.7	(28) 11.7 / 27.4 / 39.4	(16) 12.9 / 27.9 / 41.3	(22) 10.6 / 23.0 / 36.0		
% Officers', Directors', Owners' Comp/Sales	(38) 2.1 / 3.9 / 8.6	(46) 1.8 / 4.2 / 9.8	(47) 2.2 / 3.8 / 5.9		(12) 3.0 / 4.1 / 7.6		(12) 1.1 / 2.6 / 3.8		
Net Sales ($)	1244978M	1095438M	1740640M	13137M	73653M	83352M	185298M	273610M	1111590M
Total Assets ($)	1473006M	1235842M	1788557M	22309M	98294M	102520M	242359M	293605M	1029470M

© RMA 2003

M = $ thousand   MM = $ million

See Pages 11 through 18 for Explanation of Ratios and Data

Current Data Sorted By Assets   Comparative Historical Data

		4	8	2	2	Type of Statement		
	3	3	8			Unqualified	29	34
3	5	12	3			Reviewed	30	25
6	2	2	1			Compiled	37	39
2	4	11	12	1	4	Tax Returns	12	17
						Other	37	29
		26 (4/1-9/30/02)		72 (10/1/02-3/31/03)			4/1/98-	4/1/99-
							3/31/99	3/31/00
0-500M	500M-2MM	2-10MM	10-50MM	50-100MM	100-250MM		ALL	ALL
11	14	32	32	3	6	NUMBER OF STATEMENTS	145	144
%	%	%	%	%	%	**ASSETS**	%	%
10.8	8.7	5.4	2.2			Cash & Equivalents	5.3	5.5
.6	10.4	6.8	8.9			Trade Receivables (net)	8.9	10.5
3.3	9.7	6.8	12.4			Inventory	7.7	4.2
.2	3.1	.7	11.7			All Other Current	3.9	5.2
14.9	31.8	19.7	35.3			Total Current	25.8	25.5
73.2	59.5	55.9	31.9			Fixed Assets (net)	58.1	59.9
.8	.8	.3	.6			Intangibles (net)	.8	1.0
11.1	7.8	24.2	32.2			All Other Non-Current	15.4	13.7
100.0	100.0	100.0	100.0			Total	100.0	100.0
						LIABILITIES		
33.9	25.0	12.4	8.1			Notes Payable-Short Term	19.0	20.2
11.2	5.2	8.6	13.7			Cur. Mat.-L/T/D	16.4	10.5
2.1	5.6	4.2	4.6			Trade Payables	3.3	4.7
.0	.0	.0	.4			Income Taxes Payable	.3	.3
11.1	8.3	6.0	6.5			All Other Current	6.0	4.7
58.3	44.0	31.2	33.3			Total Current	45.0	40.4
50.8	21.1	45.0	43.6			Long Term Debt	40.1	38.8
.1	.0	.1	1.7			Deferred Taxes	1.1	1.1
1.5	2.6	6.3	7.2			All Other Non-Current	10.0	3.5
−10.7	32.3	17.4	14.2			Net Worth	3.9	16.2
100.0	100.0	100.0	100.0			Total Liabilities & Net Worth	100.0	100.0
						INCOME DATA		
100.0	100.0	100.0	100.0			Net Sales	100.0	100.0
						Gross Profit		
84.7	94.7	87.5	90.4			Operating Expenses	89.1	88.7
15.3	5.3	12.5	9.6			Operating Profit	10.9	11.3
5.8	1.2	9.4	5.3			All Other Expenses (net)	7.3	6.6
9.5	4.1	3.1	4.3			Profit Before Taxes	3.6	4.7
						RATIOS		
.6	1.7	1.5	2.4				1.6	1.5
.2	.5	1.1	1.1			Current	.8	.7
.1	.4	.2	.6				.2	.2
.6	.8	1.2	1.3				1.0	1.1
.2	.5	.4	.3			Quick	.3	.3
.0	.2	.2	.1				.1	.1
0 UND	6 60.5	2 178.4	12 30.9				2 161.0	5 79.6
0 UND	12 29.7	19 19.2	19 19.1			Sales/Receivables	12 30.4	15 24.2
3 112.0	66 5.5	32 11.3	52 7.0				28 12.9	33 10.9
						Cost of Sales/Inventory		
						Cost of Sales/Payables		
−12.2	7.8	13.3	6.1				9.5	13.3
−1.6	−13.3	186.3	27.2			Sales/Working Capital	−33.8	−17.9
−1.3	−2.0	−1.6	−2.8				−2.1	−1.6
6.3	10.7	2.7	2.2				2.1	2.3
(10) 1.9	(10) 1.8	(24) 1.2	(25) 1.6			EBIT/Interest	(114) 1.3	(107) 1.4
.5	−.4	.9	1.2				1.0	1.1
						Net Profit + Depr., Dep.,	1.9	2.7
						Amort./Cur. Mat. L /T/D	(24) 1.1	(22) 1.5
							.7	.9
2.7	.8	.3	.1				.9	1.4
20.5	1.9	3.7	1.5			Fixed/Worth	4.5	4.5
−5.2	7.2	16.2	4.0				13.4	13.5
3.0	.9	1.9	4.1				3.5	3.3
20.7	1.9	5.2	7.9			Debt/Worth	7.7	7.1
−9.8	11.6	30.6	15.7				32.4	23.7
	34.2	30.6	31.3			% Profit Before Taxes/Tangible	33.7	40.0
(12)	15.4 (27)	7.4 (30)	11.7			Net Worth	(122) 13.7	(121) 14.1
	−6.2	.0	5.8				3.7	4.8
18.5	11.8	3.3	2.7			% Profit Before Taxes/Total	5.3	6.0
4.0	3.1	1.0	1.7			Assets	1.6	1.8
−3.1	−7.0	−.3	.6				.2	.3
2.1	5.9	36.2	50.7				8.5	5.9
1.5	1.4	.9	6.7			Sales/Net Fixed Assets	.8	.8
.5	.5	.5	.6				.5	.5
1.5	2.1	.7	.7				.9	.8
.9	.9	.5	.4			Sales/Total Assets	.5	.5
.4	.4	.3	.3				.4	.3
24.5	16.1	13.5	.8				10.4	14.9
29.5 (12)	45.7 (24)	51.6 (19)	28.6			% Depr., Dep., Amort./Sales	(114) 38.4	(115) 38.3
52.9	88.9	65.3	61.5				63.6	58.3
			1.3				1.2	1.3
		(11)	4.1			% Officers', Directors',	(41) 3.3	(43) 3.3
			4.8			Owners' Comp/Sales	6.6	7.2
4440M	26512M	124293M	568155M	70882M	779983M	Net Sales ($)	2716610M	1937008M
2729M	15180M	157244M	742749M	225375M	1006221M	Total Assets ($)	2277614M	2744537M

© RMA 2003

M = $ thousand   MM = $ million
See Pages 11 through 18 for Explanation of Ratios and Data

Comparative Historical Data			Type of Statement	Current Data Sorted By Sales					
22	21	16	Unqualified	1	3	2	1	5	4
13	16	14	Reviewed	2	3	3	2	3	1
29	27	23	Compiled	5	11	3	3	1	
10	9	11	Tax Returns	8	2			1	
34	40	34	Other	7	5	4	4	8	6
4/1/00- 3/31/01 ALL	4/1/01- 3/31/02 ALL	4/1/02- 3/31/03 ALL		26 (4/1-9/30/02)			72 (10/1/02-3/31/03)		
				0-1MM	1-3MM	3-5MM	5-10MM	10-25MM	25MM & OVER
108	113	98	NUMBER OF STATEMENTS	23	24	12	10	18	11
%	%	%	ASSETS	%	%	%	%	%	%
5.3	4.6	5.3	Cash & Equivalents	6.8	8.3	2.9	2.7	3.5	3.4
10.1	9.4	7.6	Trade Receivables (net)	5.9	4.4	3.9	11.7	8.4	16.7
7.9	10.9	8.2	Inventory	5.8	7.2	2.3	12.6	11.3	12.9
4.6	6.5	5.7	All Other Current	1.8	3.1	5.2	13.7	12.3	1.5
27.8	31.4	26.7	Total Current	20.3	23.0	14.2	40.7	35.6	34.5
57.9	54.4	51.6	Fixed Assets (net)	67.8	62.7	31.0	37.4	35.9	54.2
.6	.9	.5	Intangibles (net)	.6	.4	.4	.1	1.3	.1
13.7	13.3	21.2	All Other Non-Current	11.3	13.9	54.4	21.7	27.2	11.2
100.0	100.0	100.0	Total	100.0	100.0	100.0	100.0	100.0	100.0
			LIABILITIES						
21.9	24.2	17.6	Notes Payable-Short Term	28.0	19.1	.4	24.4	7.9	20.5
10.1	11.0	9.4	Cur. Mat.-L/T/D	9.0	12.4	9.6	10.3	9.1	3.2
3.8	5.3	4.1	Trade Payables	1.9	1.8	1.1	1.7	8.8	11.2
.3	.2	.4	Income Taxes Payable	.0	.1	.1	.0	1.3	.8
7.0	4.2	6.9	All Other Current	8.4	3.0	13.8	6.4	3.3	10.6
43.1	45.0	38.3	Total Current	47.3	36.4	25.0	42.9	30.4	46.2
35.5	35.3	39.8	Long Term Debt	38.7	44.7	40.3	34.7	45.8	25.8
1.1	1.5	.7	Deferred Taxes	.0	.5	.5	.0	2.1	1.5
2.3	1.8	5.1	All Other Non-Current	2.4	2.5	15.2	6.0	6.7	2.1
17.9	16.5	16.1	Net Worth	11.4	15.9	19.0	16.3	15.0	24.4
100.0	100.0	100.0	Total Liabilities & Net Worth	100.0	100.0	100.0	100.0	100.0	100.0
			INCOME DATA						
100.0	100.0	100.0	Net Sales	100.0	100.0	100.0	100.0	100.0	100.0
			Gross Profit						
86.7	87.8	88.5	Operating Expenses	84.6	88.0	94.2	88.6	86.7	94.6
13.3	12.2	11.5	Operating Profit	15.4	12.0	5.8	11.4	13.3	5.4
6.6	8.0	6.3	All Other Expenses (net)	9.3	7.5	1.0	6.3	7.5	1.4
6.6	4.3	5.1	Profit Before Taxes	6.1	4.5	4.8	5.1	5.8	3.9
			RATIOS						
1.2	1.5	1.5		1.2	1.6	2.9	1.3	4.0	1.3
.7	.9	.9	Current	.4	.5	1.1	1.1	1.2	1.0
.2	.3	.2		.1	.2	.4	.5	.7	.2
.7	1.0	1.1		1.0	.6	1.2	.8	1.9	1.2
.3	.3	.3	Quick	.3	.3	.4	.1	.5	.3
.1	.1	.1		.1	.2	.2	.1	.1	.1
6 59.1	5 67.3	6 60.5		0 UND	4 97.1	2 178.4	15 25.0	9 42.5	13 29.1
14 26.4	16 22.4	16 23.0	Sales/Receivables	9 42.0	17 21.3	10 34.9	18 20.6	14 26.4	18 20.3
45 8.1	43 8.5	35 10.3		61 6.0	35 10.6	37 9.8	32 11.4	38 9.6	33 11.0
			Cost of Sales/Inventory						
			Cost of Sales/Payables						
21.6	8.8	8.8		16.4	9.2	9.5	6.7	5.9	26.7
-8.4	-55.4	-24.7	Sales/Working Capital	-1.9	-8.3	58.7	136.3	34.0	181.7
-1.5	-2.1	-1.6		-1.1	-1.7	-17.2	-1.5	-5.0	-2.1
2.4	2.0	2.8		5.1	2.8	25.2		1.9	6.2
(83) 1.5	(90) 1.3	(77) 1.6	EBIT/Interest	(16) 2.0	(18) 1.5	(10) 1.3		(14) 1.5	2.4
1.1	.9	1.1		.6	.8	1.0		1.1	1.7
1.6	1.3		Net Profit + Depr., Dep.,						
(17) 1.1	(15) .9		Amort./Cur. Mat. L/T/D						
.5	.2								
1.3	.8	.3		1.0	1.4	.0	.1	.0	1.9
3.6	3.2	2.4	Fixed/Worth	2.7	3.9	.4	2.4	.8	2.3
14.5	13.1	8.5		-62.0	30.7	3.7	5.3	6.6	4.2
3.0	2.3	2.1		1.4	2.0	2.4	3.0	4.0	1.6
6.0	6.4	5.7	Debt/Worth	4.3	7.1	5.2	6.0	8.3	3.8
27.2	21.1	19.6		-78.8	50.7	12.6	16.5	17.9	8.6
40.8	32.0	31.5		43.4	31.7	30.6		21.0	41.1
(97) 12.0	(101) 11.1	(84) 11.9	% Profit Before Taxes/Tangible Net Worth	(17) 6.3	(20) 14.3	(11) 7.4		(16) 13.0	13.6
4.9	.8	3.7		-1.8	8.5	-5.5		5.2	3.9
5.1	4.0	4.0		5.8	5.8	3.1	2.8	3.1	5.4
2.2	1.5	2.0	% Profit Before Taxes/Total Assets	2.0	1.8	1.4	2.1	1.5	4.0
.5	-.8	.2		-3.1	.6	-.4	.9	.4	1.7
8.7	17.7	23.4		1.6	3.5	359.4	63.5	162.5	34.4
1.0	1.2	1.4	Sales/Net Fixed Assets	.5	.9	25.4	3.8	14.8	1.2
.5	.5	.5		.4	.5	1.3	.5	.6	.9
1.0	1.0	.9		.8	1.1	.9	.8	.8	3.2
.5	.5	.5	Sales/Total Assets	.4	.5	.4	.4	.4	1.1
.3	.4	.3		.2	.3	.4	.3	.4	.8
6.6	6.9	11.6		27.9	18.7			.6	
(85) 34.9	(87) 32.4	(69) 36.0	% Depr., Dep., Amort./Sales	(21) 52.9	(21) 46.2		(10) 19.5		
59.8	64.8	59.2		63.5	64.7			43.9	
1.0	1.1	1.3							
(33) 3.8	(38) 3.7	(30) 3.1	% Officers', Directors', Owners' Comp/Sales						
5.0	7.6	5.2							
1723350M	1565195M	1574265M	Net Sales ($)	8720M	48223M	48775M	72470M	258761M	1137316M
2390473M	2315637M	2149498M	Total Assets ($)	31059M	135894M	113104M	178853M	629789M	1060799M

© RMA 2003

M = $ thousand   MM = $ million
See Pages 11 through 18 for Explanation of Ratios and Data

Current Data Sorted By Assets — **Comparative Historical Data**

						Type of Statement		
1	2	12	21	6	7	Unqualified	42	50
1	4	29	26	3		Reviewed	59	50
11	12	9	2			Compiled	52	43
6	2	2				Tax Returns	25	17
10	12	24	15	5	4	Other	56	42
	40 (4/1-9/30/02)		186 (10/1/02-3/31/03)				4/1/98-3/31/99 ALL	4/1/99-3/31/00 ALL
0-500M	500M-2MM	2-10MM	10-50MM	50-100MM	100-250MM			
29	32	76	64	14	11	NUMBER OF STATEMENTS	234	202
%	%	%	%	%	%	ASSETS	%	%
10.9	10.4	6.6	5.3	2.4	4.3	Cash & Equivalents	7.7	7.1
10.0	16.3	9.9	13.5	9.1	8.5	Trade Receivables (net)	9.3	10.2
8.0	8.4	8.7	8.8	6.9	4.0	Inventory	4.8	6.5
2.7	3.1	5.0	2.2	5.0	10.2	All Other Current	3.0	2.5
31.6	38.2	30.1	29.8	23.4	26.9	Total Current	24.8	26.3
59.1	49.2	60.3	58.8	61.8	61.4	Fixed Assets (net)	65.0	64.0
1.9	.2	.6	.6	.3	1.1	Intangibles (net)	2.2	.8
7.4	12.3	9.0	10.9	14.5	10.6	All Other Non-Current	8.0	8.9
100.0	100.0	100.0	100.0	100.0	100.0	Total	100.0	100.0
						LIABILITIES		
14.5	11.4	7.2	8.6	7.0	9.3	Notes Payable-Short Term	9.4	8.7
15.2	11.2	13.7	11.8	12.8	14.5	Cur. Mat.-L/T/D	13.0	12.1
2.1	4.5	3.5	5.9	3.3	3.3	Trade Payables	4.9	4.2
.0	.4	.2	.4	.1	.8	Income Taxes Payable	.2	.2
14.1	7.4	6.2	5.2	5.3	4.8	All Other Current	6.8	4.6
45.9	34.9	30.8	31.9	28.4	32.7	Total Current	34.3	29.8
39.7	21.3	36.2	35.3	41.7	34.1	Long Term Debt	38.5	38.6
.2	.5	.9	2.6	3.2	7.2	Deferred Taxes	1.8	1.9
2.1	1.9	4.2	2.9	8.7	.3	All Other Non-Current	5.1	3.8
12.1	41.4	27.9	27.2	18.0	25.8	Net Worth	20.2	25.9
100.0	100.0	100.0	100.0	100.0	100.0	Total Liabilities & Net Worth	100.0	100.0
						INCOME DATA		
100.0	100.0	100.0	100.0	100.0	100.0	Net Sales	100.0	100.0
						Gross Profit		
83.5	85.1	88.4	89.7	88.1	84.8	Operating Expenses	87.2	88.2
16.5	14.9	11.6	10.3	11.9	15.2	Operating Profit	12.8	11.8
6.1	4.4	5.2	5.1	9.7	10.3	All Other Expenses (net)	4.7	3.3
10.3	10.4	6.4	5.2	2.2	4.9	Profit Before Taxes	8.1	8.4
						RATIOS		
1.5	1.9	1.6	1.3	1.3	1.4		1.5	1.6
.8	1.1	.9	.9	.9	.6	Current	.7	.8
.2	.6	.4	.6	.6	.5		.3	.4
.7	1.7	1.0	1.1	.8	.7		1.1	1.3
.4	.6	.5	.4	.4	.5	Quick	(233) .5	.5
.2	.3	.2	.3	.2	.4		.2	.2
0 UND	1 572.1	1 254.9	24 15.2	26 13.8	27 13.4		3 121.1	2 231.0
5 77.1	21 17.4	24 15.0	35 10.4	38 9.5	46 8.0	Sales/Receivables	25 14.4	28 12.9
19 19.2	75 4.9	49 7.4	51 7.2	45 8.1	55 6.6		45 8.1	44 8.4
						Cost of Sales/Inventory		
						Cost of Sales/Payables		
22.4	7.3	7.6	17.1	28.4	5.0		11.2	10.7
-18.9	319.7	-26.7	-38.4	-54.9	-26.0	Sales/Working Capital	-15.9	-21.3
-3.1	-5.9	-3.5	-5.8	-7.4	-6.8		-2.9	-3.3
(22) 5.4	(27) 9.4	(63) 3.2	(57) 3.1	(12) 2.3	(10) 4.4		(196) 3.4	(174) 2.8
3.9	2.5	1.4	1.7	1.3	1.6	EBIT/Interest	1.9	1.8
1.2	.8	.8	1.0	1.1	1.3		1.1	1.2
		(18) 2.3	(30) 1.7			Net Profit + Depr., Dep.,	(71) 2.2	(57) 2.6
		1.2	1.4			Amort./Cur. Mat. L /T/D	1.3	1.3
		.7	.9				.9	.9
.9	.5	1.1	1.3	1.9	.5		1.3	1.3
3.2	1.4	2.4	2.5	3.8	5.1	Fixed/Worth	3.6	3.5
-56.2	2.5	5.0	4.7	6.9	6.0		12.1	7.9
1.8	.4	1.3	1.8	3.2	2.4		1.7	1.5
5.1	1.7	2.7	3.3	5.7	5.2	Debt/Worth	4.2	4.2
-59.4	6.1	10.6	6.7	7.1	6.7		16.4	10.3
(21) 71.9	(30) 39.3	(64) 25.8	(63) 22.5	11.5	17.5	% Profit Before Taxes/Tangible	(197) 34.9	(177) 32.6
40.4	7.9	9.1	10.5	4.6	12.1	Net Worth	17.9	18.3
11.0	-3.5	.6	.9	2.8	6.9		6.1	7.6
20.9	14.2	6.9	5.5	1.9	3.5	% Profit Before Taxes/Total	8.6	7.7
7.0	5.1	1.6	2.3	1.1	2.3	Assets	3.5	3.3
1.1	-1.4	-1.4	.2	.3	2.0		.7	1.0
8.4	6.2	5.0	4.7	3.5	5.1		2.8	3.1
2.4	2.1	1.0	1.3	.9	.9	Sales/Net Fixed Assets	1.1	.9
1.1	.9	.6	.7	.6	.8		.6	.6
3.4	1.8	1.5	1.9	.9	.9		1.4	1.5
1.3	.9	.6	.8	.5	.7	Sales/Total Assets	.7	.7
.6	.6	.3	.5	.4	.6		.4	.4
(22) 8.9	(27) 10.2	(71) 7.5	(61) 5.3	(11) 5.5		% Depr., Dep., Amort./Sales	(212) 10.9	(181) 9.5
26.7	26.7	31.0	18.3	14.8			26.5	25.2
56.2	45.4	52.5	33.7	26.2			50.3	43.6
		(21) .7	(14) .8			% Officers', Directors',	(55) 2.7	(41) 1.1
		3.1	1.7			Owners' Comp/Sales	4.8	2.8
		8.2	5.3				10.6	7.9
16970M	59439M	390053M	1751558M	692250M	1444598M	Net Sales ($)	2607022M	2863321M
8295M	37436M	368044M	1293679M	934578M	1614488M	Total Assets ($)	3013931M	3341609M

© RMA 2003

M = $ thousand   MM = $ million
See Pages 11 through 18 for Explanation of Ratios and Data

Comparative Historical Data — Current Data Sorted By Sales

4/1/00-3/31/01 ALL	4/1/01-3/31/02 ALL	4/1/02-3/31/03 ALL	Type of Statement	0-1MM	1-3MM	3-5MM	5-10MM	10-25MM	25MM & OVER
28	32	49	Unqualified	3	3		10	12	21
46	41	63	Reviewed	11	15	5	10	11	11
50	39	34	Compiled	21	7	3	2	1	
17	15	10	Tax Returns	4	4	1	1		
41	64	70	Other	16	12	6	16	8	12
				40 (4/1-9/30/02)		186 (10/1/02-3/31/03)			
182	191	226	**NUMBER OF STATEMENTS**	55	41	15	39	32	44
%	%	%	**ASSETS**	%	%	%	%	%	%
6.6	6.8	6.9	Cash & Equivalents	8.7	11.0	1.8	4.6	7.9	4.1
9.5	11.6	11.7	Trade Receivables (net)	9.1	10.3	9.0	13.1	13.2	15.0
8.0	5.6	8.3	Inventory	4.9	4.8	13.2	8.5	7.8	14.1
2.6	2.8	3.9	All Other Current	3.9	5.4	1.9	2.7	5.5	2.9
26.7	26.8	30.8	Total Current	26.6	31.5	26.0	28.9	34.4	36.1
61.5	61.5	58.3	Fixed Assets (net)	60.3	59.3	65.7	61.3	54.4	52.5
1.2	1.6	.7	Intangibles (net)	.8	1.0	.6	.3	.7	.5
10.6	10.2	10.2	All Other Non-Current	12.3	8.2	7.7	9.5	10.5	10.9
100.0	100.0	100.0	Total	100.0	100.0	100.0	100.0	100.0	100.0
			LIABILITIES						
10.5	9.5	9.2	Notes Payable-Short Term	11.1	6.5	9.0	4.1	10.3	13.1
13.7	12.9	13.0	Cur. Mat.-L/T/D	13.3	14.5	11.9	14.1	10.6	12.3
4.8	5.4	4.1	Trade Payables	1.8	3.1	3.7	4.2	5.6	7.1
.1	.3	.3	Income Taxes Payable	.0	.4	.1	.6	.4	.3
5.4	6.3	7.0	All Other Current	10.5	6.0	2.0	6.7	4.1	7.6
34.4	34.4	33.6	Total Current	36.8	30.5	26.6	29.7	31.0	40.3
36.1	35.5	34.5	Long Term Debt	32.8	35.6	47.4	39.3	27.9	31.7
1.6	1.8	1.7	Deferred Taxes	.5	.8	1.5	1.7	2.4	3.5
5.2	3.4	3.4	All Other Non-Current	2.2	2.6	4.8	5.4	6.6	.9
22.7	24.8	26.9	Net Worth	27.7	30.4	19.7	23.9	32.2	23.6
100.0	100.0	100.0	Total Liabilities & Net Worth	100.0	100.0	100.0	100.0	100.0	100.0
			INCOME DATA						
100.0	100.0	100.0	Net Sales	100.0	100.0	100.0	100.0	100.0	100.0
			Gross Profit						
91.5	89.0	87.5	Operating Expenses	78.5	83.4	91.0	91.5	91.5	94.9
8.5	11.0	12.5	Operating Profit	21.5	16.6	9.0	8.5	8.5	5.1
4.1	5.7	5.7	All Other Expenses (net)	9.1	4.2	8.0	5.9	4.2	3.0
4.4	5.3	6.8	Profit Before Taxes	12.5	12.4	1.0	2.5	4.2	2.1
			RATIOS						
1.4	1.3	1.5	Current	1.8	1.6	2.7	1.3	2.1	1.1
.8	.8	.9		.7	1.0	.8	.9	1.0	.9
.3	.4	.5		.2	.4	.3	.6	.6	.6
.9	1.1	1.0	Quick	1.2	1.2	1.4	1.0	1.9	.7
.4	.5	.5		.4	.6	.6	.5	.7	.5
.2	.2	.2		.2	.1	.2	.3	.3	.2
0 UND	1 271.0	6 60.8	Sales/Receivables	0 UND	0 UND	0 UND	22 16.8	20 17.8	26 13.9
26 13.8	33 11.1	29 12.5		9 39.5	12 29.7	32 11.3	36 10.0	31 11.7	37 9.8
43 8.4	53 6.9	49 7.4		53 6.9	47 7.8	52 7.0	53 6.9	47 7.8	45 8.1
			Cost of Sales/Inventory						
			Cost of Sales/Payables						
17.3	13.8	10.2	Sales/Working Capital	4.7	7.7	6.0	10.4	8.6	62.4
-16.3	-16.6	-30.8		-10.1	575.0	-82.4	-28.6	375.6	-38.4
-2.8	-3.7	-5.1		-2.4	-3.4	-2.6	-6.3	-7.5	-8.8
(158) 2.4	(163) 2.6	(191) 3.8	EBIT/Interest	(38) 10.0	(36) 3.8	(13) 2.4	(35) 2.6	(26) 3.6	(43) 3.1
1.5	1.5	1.6		2.8	1.6	1.2	1.4	1.9	1.5
1.0	.9	1.0		1.1	1.1	.1	.8	.9	1.1
(44) 2.7	(55) 1.8	(56) 1.8	Net Profit + Depr., Dep., Amort./Cur. Mat. L/T/D				(14) 2.3	(14) 1.7	(16) 5.7
1.1	1.2	1.3					1.3	1.4	1.3
.6	.6	.9					1.0	1.0	.7
1.3	1.1	.9	Fixed/Worth	.7	1.2	1.2	1.4	.8	1.0
2.4	3.0	2.4		1.7	2.5	2.0	3.4	2.0	2.7
7.8	10.7	5.7		6.9	4.1	14.4	7.0	4.8	5.8
1.5	1.5	1.4	Debt/Worth	1.0	1.1	1.3	1.6	1.4	2.4
4.2	3.8	3.3		3.0	3.0	3.7	3.8	2.4	4.4
11.9	13.9	7.2		9.2	6.2	14.4	24.1	5.1	6.4
(156) 24.9	(165) 28.9	(203) 28.4	% Profit Before Taxes/Tangible Net Worth	(45) 47.1	(39) 49.8	(12) 14.1	(33) 20.3	(30) 20.2	17.5
11.9	9.7	10.5		14.0	18.4	8.1	5.2	12.0	8.0
4.0	.0	1.4		1.8	1.4	-10.9	-3.2	4.3	2.7
6.4	6.4	7.5	% Profit Before Taxes/Total Assets	14.4	10.1	3.7	4.4	6.7	4.8
2.1	1.7	2.4		5.3	2.5	1.1	1.1	3.1	1.9
-.2	-.5	.1		.4	.3	-5.6	-1.3	-.3	.4
3.4	3.5	5.1	Sales/Net Fixed Assets	3.5	3.4	2.1	5.6	8.9	6.9
1.2	1.3	1.3		1.1	1.0	.9	.9	1.9	3.8
.6	.6	.7		.6	.5	.6	.7	.9	.9
1.4	1.4	1.7	Sales/Total Assets	1.1	1.3	1.1	2.1	2.2	2.5
.7	.7	.8		.6	.6	.6	.7	1.0	1.6
.5	.5	.5		.3	.3	.5	.5	.5	.7
(163) 6.3	(168) 7.6	(194) 7.4	% Depr., Dep., Amort./Sales	(46) 21.5	(36) 22.7	(14) 9.0	(37) 6.3	(28) 4.4	(33) 2.6
23.0	23.0	24.0		45.6	35.8	25.6	25.8	18.4	4.7
52.1	44.4	41.3		66.5	48.3	51.4	37.2	25.7	14.4
(38) .8	(46) 1.4	(51) 1.4	% Officers', Directors', Owners' Comp/Sales		(14) 2.0		(10) .9		
3.0	2.4	4.0			4.3		1.8		
6.2	5.3	7.6			10.7		4.4		
2373537M	2663487M	4354868M	Net Sales ($)	30641M	77710M	55615M	294973M	530309M	3365620M
2814550M	3073489M	4256520M	Total Assets ($)	76804M	148732M	102188M	421831M	801375M	2705590M

M = $ thousand   MM = $ million
See Pages 11 through 18 for Explanation of Ratios and Data

Current Data Sorted By Assets　　　　　　　　　　**Comparative Historical Data**

						Type of Statement		
			1	6		Unqualified		
2	1		8	1		Reviewed		
8	6		5			Compiled		
7	7		3			Tax Returns		
3	11		6	2	1	Other		
	10 (4/1-9/30/02)			68 (10/1/02-3/31/03)			4/1/98-3/31/99 ALL	4/1/99-3/31/00 ALL
0-500M	500M-2MM	2-10MM	10-50MM	50-100MM	100-250MM			
20	25	23	9		1	NUMBER OF STATEMENTS		
%	%	%	%	%	%	ASSETS	%	%
6.2	6.9	6.3				Cash & Equivalents		
15.9	9.2	9.6		D		Trade Receivables (net)	D	D
9.7	7.8	13.9		A		Inventory	A	A
1.3	.7	5.5		T		All Other Current	T	T
33.1	24.6	35.4		A		Total Current	A	A
54.6	64.4	53.7				Fixed Assets (net)		
.5	2.5	1.4		N		Intangibles (net)	N	N
11.8	8.5	9.5		O		All Other Non-Current	O	O
100.0	100.0	100.0		T		Total	T	T
						LIABILITIES		
17.6	16.7	13.4		A		Notes Payable-Short Term	A	A
13.2	12.6	13.4		V		Cur. Mat.-L/T/D	V	V
6.3	2.3	3.6		A		Trade Payables	A	A
.1	.0	.6		I		Income Taxes Payable	I	I
9.8	5.1	2.4		L		All Other Current	L	L
47.0	36.8	33.4		A		Total Current	A	A
51.4	37.0	31.5		B		Long Term Debt	B	B
.7	.2	.7		L		Deferred Taxes	L	L
3.1	7.4	2.5		E		All Other Non-Current	E	E
-2.2	18.7	31.8				Net Worth		
100.0	100.0	100.0				Total Liabilities & Net Worth		
						INCOME DATA		
100.0	100.0	100.0				Net Sales		
						Gross Profit		
88.8	86.6	85.7				Operating Expenses		
11.2	13.4	14.3				Operating Profit		
4.9	7.5	6.0				All Other Expenses (net)		
6.3	5.9	8.3				Profit Before Taxes		
						RATIOS		
1.4	1.3	2.5						
.7	.5	1.1				Current		
.1	.2	.3						
.8	.7	1.8						
.3	.4	.4				Quick		
.1	.1	.1						
0 UND	0 UND	1 427.6						
3 117.8	0 999.8	15 24.3				Sales/Receivables		
18 20.3	31 11.8	54 6.8						
						Cost of Sales/Inventory		
						Cost of Sales/Payables		
15.2	11.1	3.5						
-23.3	-11.9	21.8				Sales/Working Capital		
-4.3	-2.4	-5.9						
12.4	2.6	4.8						
(16) 2.8	(23) .7	(19) 2.6				EBIT/Interest		
.6	.2	1.3						
						Net Profit + Depr., Dep., Amort./Cur. Mat. L /T/D		
.9	1.7	.5						
3.4	5.3	2.0				Fixed/Worth		
17.6	-16.3	4.7						
1.9	1.4	1.5						
5.3	6.4	2.5				Debt/Worth		
NM	-23.3	8.9						
156.6	50.0	40.3						
(15) 17.9	(17) 10.1	(19) 16.8				% Profit Before Taxes/Tangible Net Worth		
.0	-11.3	3.8						
23.5	5.4	8.4						
4.2	-.6	3.8				% Profit Before Taxes/Total Assets		
-4.4	-4.0	.3						
9.2	4.7	4.9						
4.1	1.2	1.9				Sales/Net Fixed Assets		
1.4	.6	.5						
3.0	2.1	1.8						
2.2	.9	1.1				Sales/Total Assets		
.7	.4	.3						
4.7	11.3	9.7						
(16) 12.8	(20) 22.2	(21) 21.8				% Depr., Dep., Amort./Sales		
37.7	46.3	53.3						
						% Officers', Directors', Owners' Comp/Sales		
10222M	30378M	130544M	134997M		96800M	Net Sales ($)		
4979M	24309M	113509M	222661M		197106M	Total Assets ($)		

© RMA 2003　　　　　　　　　　M = $ thousand　　MM = $ million
See Pages 11 through 18 for Explanation of Ratios and Data

Comparative Historical Data — Current Data Sorted By Sales

	4/1/00-3/31/01 ALL	4/1/01-3/31/02 ALL	4/1/02-3/31/03 ALL	Type of Statement	0-1MM	1-3MM	3-5MM	5-10MM	10-25MM	25MM & OVER
	7			Unqualified		1		4	1	1
	11			Reviewed	3	3		3	2	
	20			Compiled	11	5	1	1	2	
	17			Tax Returns	11	4	1		1	
	23			Other	9	8		1	3	2
					10 (4/1-9/30/02)			68 (10/1/02-3/31/03)		
NUMBER OF STATEMENTS			78		34	21	2	9	9	3
	%	%	%	ASSETS	%	%	%	%	%	%
			6.5	Cash & Equivalents	4.6	9.8				
			10.7	Trade Receivables (net)	11.0	8.5				
			11.7	Inventory	4.7	11.1				
			3.6	All Other Current	.8	7.9				
			32.5	Total Current	21.0	37.3				
			54.6	Fixed Assets (net)	64.7	52.2				
			1.5	Intangibles (net)	1.1	2.1				
			11.4	All Other Non-Current	13.1	8.5				
			100.0	Total	100.0	100.0				
				LIABILITIES						
			17.1	Notes Payable-Short Term	14.6	20.5				
			13.3	Cur. Mat.-L/T/D	12.3	15.6				
			3.9	Trade Payables	3.8	3.6				
			.2	Income Taxes Payable	.0	.0				
			5.2	All Other Current	7.7	3.2				
			39.8	Total Current	38.4	42.9				
			37.4	Long Term Debt	50.2	34.4				
			.7	Deferred Taxes	.4	.2				
			5.0	All Other Non-Current	5.3	3.6				
			17.2	Net Worth	5.7	18.9				
			100.0	Total Liabilities & Net Worth	100.0	100.0				
				INCOME DATA						
			100.0	Net Sales	100.0	100.0				
				Gross Profit						
			86.6	Operating Expenses	80.6	90.3				
			13.4	Operating Profit	19.4	9.7				
			7.1	All Other Expenses (net)	9.0	6.2				
			6.3	Profit Before Taxes	10.3	3.5				
				RATIOS						
			1.5		1.1	1.4				
			.7	Current	.4	1.0				
			.3		.1	.5				
			.8		.7	.8				
			.3	Quick	.3	.4				
			.1		.1	.1				
		0	UND		0 UND	0 UND				
		10	38.1	Sales/Receivables	0 UND	9 42.9				
		34	10.8		25 14.6	30 12.1				
				Cost of Sales/Inventory						
				Cost of Sales/Payables						
			6.9		151.2	6.8				
			−19.2	Sales/Working Capital	−7.0	−79.9				
			−3.4		−1.8	−12.4				
			4.4		3.7	9.4				
		(66)	2.0	EBIT/Interest	(28) 2.0	(17) .8				
			.5		.6	−1.7				
			2.2	Net Profit + Depr., Dep.,						
		(10)	1.5	Amort./Cur. Mat. L/T/D						
			.2							
			1.0		1.7	1.0				
			2.6	Fixed/Worth	5.6	2.1				
			59.9		−66.1	NM				
			1.5		2.7	1.3				
			4.5	Debt/Worth	6.0	2.7				
			114.1		−36.2	NM				
			42.7	% Profit Before Taxes/Tangible	41.8	79.9				
		(60)	13.8	Net Worth	(24) 16.7	(16) 13.4				
			−1.9		−4.5	−8.6				
			8.6	% Profit Before Taxes/Total	6.2	23.9				
			2.2	Assets	3.2	1.0				
			−2.1		−2.1	−5.7				
			6.2		3.6	9.2				
			2.5	Sales/Net Fixed Assets	.9	4.5				
			.7		.4	2.0				
			2.1		1.5	3.1				
			1.1	Sales/Total Assets	.5	1.8				
			.4		.3	.4				
			8.9	% Depr., Dep., Amort./Sales	15.3	4.8				
		(63)	17.5		(31) 31.4	(15) 11.3				
			38.8		57.8	41.9				
			4.4	% Officers', Directors',						
		(24)	6.2	Owners' Comp/Sales						
			12.7							
			402941M	Net Sales ($)	14969M	36879M	7128M	62270M	123142M	158553M
			562564M	Total Assets ($)	30985M	58799M	5012M	107235M	123274M	237259M

M = $ thousand   MM = $ million
See Pages 11 through 18 for Explanation of Ratios and Data

(Comparative Historical Data for 4/1/00-3/31/01 ALL and 4/1/01-3/31/02 ALL columns: DATA NOT AVAILABLE)

Current Data Sorted By Assets   **Comparative Historical Data**

Type of Statement	0-500M	500M-2MM	2-10MM	10-50MM	50-100MM	100-250MM	4/1/98-3/31/99 ALL	4/1/99-3/31/00 ALL
Unqualified	6	1	1			1	6	4
Reviewed			2				2	4
Compiled			3				13	9
Tax Returns	10	1					11	8
Other	3	4	3	1	1	2	17	11
		0 (4/1-9/30/02)		39 (10/1/02-3/31/03)				
NUMBER OF STATEMENTS	19	6	9	1	1	3	49	36
ASSETS	%	%	%	%	%	%	%	%
Cash & Equivalents	17.3						9.5	12.2
Trade Receivables (net)	.5						3.2	3.6
Inventory	8.9						14.5	13.8
All Other Current	2.3						1.8	3.7
Total Current	29.1						29.0	33.2
Fixed Assets (net)	48.8						54.7	48.1
Intangibles (net)	14.3						10.6	13.9
All Other Non-Current	7.8						5.7	4.8
Total	100.0						100.0	100.0
LIABILITIES								
Notes Payable-Short Term	5.0						5.4	6.8
Cur. Mat.-L/T/D	4.5						9.3	4.5
Trade Payables	8.2						14.0	23.7
Income Taxes Payable	.0						.3	.2
All Other Current	12.6						12.1	12.2
Total Current	30.3						41.0	47.5
Long Term Debt	42.7						46.9	26.6
Deferred Taxes	.0						.1	.0
All Other Non-Current	16.4						8.0	3.0
Net Worth	10.7						4.0	22.9
Total Liabilities & Net Worth	100.0						100.0	100.0
INCOME DATA								
Net Sales	100.0						100.0	100.0
Gross Profit								
Operating Expenses	98.5						95.6	96.5
Operating Profit	1.5						4.4	3.5
All Other Expenses (net)	−.3						3.3	3.1
Profit Before Taxes	1.8						1.1	.4
RATIOS								
Current	5.2 / 1.0 / .6						1.7 / .8 / .3	1.9 / .8 / .5
Quick	3.2 / .4 / .2						(48) .9 / .3 / .1	.9 / .4 / .1
Sales/Receivables	0 UND / 0 UND / 0 UND						0 UND / 0 999.8 / 6 62.1	0 UND / 0 UND / 5 66.4
Cost of Sales/Inventory								
Cost of Sales/Payables								
Sales/Working Capital	10.4 / −200.4 / −15.0						20.0 / −34.7 / −11.1	25.6 / −60.0 / −9.8
EBIT/Interest	(10) 10.6 / 4.0 / .2						(42) 6.8 / 1.8 / .5	(33) 9.0 / 3.2 / .0
Net Profit + Depr., Dep., Amort./Cur. Mat. L./T/D								
Fixed/Worth	.5 / 9.7 / −2.6						1.1 / 2.4 / NM	1.0 / 2.6 / −1.6
Debt/Worth	.6 / 10.1 / −4.9						1.4 / 3.9 / NM	1.0 / 3.1 / −6.9
% Profit Before Taxes/Tangible Net Worth	(10) 96.1 / 46.1 / 20.9						(37) 109.4 / 27.1 / 4.4	(25) 61.8 / 28.8 / .3
% Profit Before Taxes/Total Assets	32.6 / 14.8 / 1.2						18.5 / 4.4 / −5.1	13.9 / 6.0 / −4.8
Sales/Net Fixed Assets	12.7 / 5.7 / 1.5						10.5 / 4.5 / 2.8	9.1 / 6.2 / 3.5
Sales/Total Assets	3.4 / 2.3 / 1.1						3.2 / 2.4 / 1.7	4.2 / 2.2 / 1.6
% Depr., Dep., Amort./Sales	(12) 1.3 / 11.3 / 28.6						(28) 2.5 / 7.2 / 13.9	(24) 1.4 / 3.1 / 7.3
% Officers', Directors', Owners' Comp/Sales	(11) 3.1 / 10.1 / 26.6						(21) 2.4 / 5.5 / 11.6	(14) 2.0 / 3.9 / 9.3
Net Sales ($)	8945M	17029M	109063M	21480M	681369M	943559M	1076686M	1993831M
Total Assets ($)	3998M	5971M	40377M	24204M	79205M	524148M	825032M	1145933M

© RMA 2003

M = $ thousand   MM = $ million
See Pages 11 through 18 for Explanation of Ratios and Data

Comparative Historical Data | Current Data Sorted By Sales

4/1/00-3/31/01 ALL	4/1/01-3/31/02 ALL	4/1/02-3/31/03 ALL	Type of Statement	0-1MM	1-3MM	3-5MM	5-10MM	10-25MM	25MM & OVER
4	3	3	Unqualified					2	1
8	5	2	Reviewed						2
8	9	9	Compiled	6	1	1	2		1
7	10	11	Tax Returns	9	2		2	2	
12	13	14	Other	3	2	2	2	2	3
					0 (4/1-9/30/02)		39 (10/1/02-3/31/03)		
39	40	39	**NUMBER OF STATEMENTS**	18	5	3	4	5	4
%	%	%	**ASSETS**	%	%	%	%	%	%
9.8	14.0	14.5	Cash & Equivalents	19.1					
6.0	3.2	2.5	Trade Receivables (net)	.5					
18.5	10.8	16.7	Inventory	7.3					
1.1	.5	2.1	All Other Current	2.5					
35.5	28.6	35.8	Total Current	29.5					
49.7	53.2	44.3	Fixed Assets (net)	48.4					
7.2	8.9	13.3	Intangibles (net)	18.8					
7.6	9.4	6.6	All Other Non-Current	3.4					
100.0	100.0	100.0	Total	100.0					
			LIABILITIES						
6.5	3.7	5.0	Notes Payable-Short Term	6.1					
8.9	9.3	6.5	Cur. Mat.-L/T/D	5.3					
17.9	12.4	15.6	Trade Payables	5.6					
.1	.0	.0	Income Taxes Payable	.0					
12.4	11.1	10.6	All Other Current	13.0					
45.9	36.5	37.6	Total Current	30.0					
27.6	25.9	31.4	Long Term Debt	40.7					
.1	.0	.0	Deferred Taxes	.0					
6.7	10.9	8.5	All Other Non-Current	17.3					
19.6	26.8	22.6	Net Worth	12.1					
100.0	100.0	100.0	Total Liabilities & Net Worth	100.0					
			INCOME DATA						
100.0	100.0	100.0	Net Sales	100.0					
			Gross Profit						
94.2	88.1	95.1	Operating Expenses	98.8					
5.8	11.9	4.9	Operating Profit	1.2					
2.5	2.5	.4	All Other Expenses (net)	−.2					
3.3	9.4	4.5	Profit Before Taxes	1.4					
			RATIOS						
1.2 / .8 / .3	1.7 / .6 / .3	1.9 / 1.0 / .5	Current	5.5 / .9 / .6					
.7 / .2 / .1	1.3 / .3 / .1	.7 / .4 / .2	Quick	3.5 / .6 / .3					
0 UND / 4 103.1 / 12 31.5	0 UND / 0 UND / 5 72.5	0 UND / 0 UND / 4 83.6	Sales/Receivables	0 UND / 0 UND / 0 UND					
			Cost of Sales/Inventory						
			Cost of Sales/Payables						
48.6 / -32.5 / -8.1	18.4 / -18.4 / -6.8	13.1 / -200.4 / -13.1	Sales/Working Capital	10.3 / UND / -13.0					
(36) 7.3 / 2.1 / 1.0	(34) 7.5 / 3.9 / .9	(26) 14.5 / 5.4 / 2.9	EBIT/Interest	(10) 7.0 / 4.0 / .2					
			Net Profit + Depr., Dep., Amort./Cur. Mat. L/T/D						
1.1 / 3.0 / -4.1	1.1 / 2.0 / 25.3	.5 / 1.9 / -3.1	Fixed/Worth	.4 / NM / -2.4					
1.6 / 3.4 / -16.6	.9 / 2.7 / 574.7	.9 / 3.6 / -6.9	Debt/Worth	.5 / NM / -4.6					
(27) 60.0 / 33.5 / 10.3	(31) 94.9 / 49.5 / 17.0	(25) 97.4 / 44.8 / 20.9	% Profit Before Taxes/Tangible Net Worth						
15.1 / 5.2 / -.3	24.3 / 10.7 / .8	26.5 / 12.5 / 4.3	% Profit Before Taxes/Total Assets	29.0 / 13.9 / -1.5					
12.3 / 5.2 / 1.8	14.7 / 7.1 / 2.2	14.6 / 7.4 / 3.2	Sales/Net Fixed Assets	13.9 / 6.6 / 1.4					
3.7 / 1.9 / 1.1	4.0 / 2.4 / 1.2	3.4 / 2.5 / 1.2	Sales/Total Assets	2.9 / 2.2 / 1.1					
(23) 2.2 / 6.7 / 24.0	(26) 2.1 / 7.0 / 15.6	(22) 1.2 / 3.1 / 18.8	% Depr., Dep., Amort./Sales	(10) 1.3 / 14.8 / 30.6					
(11) 1.9 / 4.3 / 8.9	(14) 2.6 / 6.3 / 16.0	(16) 3.1 / 6.5 / 23.3	% Officers', Directors', Owners' Comp/Sales						
998401M	443763M	1781445M	Net Sales ($)	7306M	7276M	13671M	28139M	100125M	1624928M
750197M	290989M	677903M	Total Assets ($)	3925M	2988M	8580M	12296M	46761M	603353M

© RMA 2003

M = $ thousand   MM = $ million
See Pages 11 through 18 for Explanation of Ratios and Data

Current Data Sorted By Assets   Comparative Historical Data

		1		2	4	3	1	Type of Statement			
	2	4		7	2			Unqualified		11	11
	1	6		1	1			Reviewed		17	17
	7	5		2				Compiled		17	19
	3	9		9	2		1	Tax Returns		16	6
		16 (4/1-9/30/02)			57 (10/1/02-3/31/03)			Other		18	18
	0-500M	500M-2MM		2-10MM	10-50MM	50-100MM	100-250MM			4/1/98-3/31/99 ALL	4/1/99-3/31/00 ALL
	13	25		21	9	3	2	NUMBER OF STATEMENTS		79	71
	%	%		%	%	%	%	ASSETS		%	%
	5.3	9.9		10.7				Cash & Equivalents		6.2	7.7
	16.2	28.7		30.6				Trade Receivables (net)		26.8	34.8
	24.5	5.3		13.4				Inventory		13.4	14.6
	5.3	3.2		2.1				All Other Current		3.3	2.2
	51.2	47.2		56.7				Total Current		49.7	59.4
	45.8	45.1		34.8				Fixed Assets (net)		38.2	30.8
	2.2	1.8		1.9				Intangibles (net)		4.5	5.2
	.8	5.9		6.6				All Other Non-Current		7.6	4.5
	100.0	100.0		100.0				Total		100.0	100.0
								LIABILITIES			
	11.1	17.4		4.7				Notes Payable-Short Term		10.5	12.9
	9.4	9.9		8.3				Cur. Mat.-L/T/D		7.2	7.6
	9.2	10.3		11.4				Trade Payables		9.7	12.2
	.0	1.0		2.1				Income Taxes Payable		.3	.4
	1.8	5.3		8.6				All Other Current		5.6	10.3
	31.4	44.0		35.0				Total Current		33.4	43.4
	24.9	24.3		20.5				Long Term Debt		32.3	20.9
	.0	.9		.3				Deferred Taxes		.9	.9
	5.8	7.5		.9				All Other Non-Current		3.6	2.9
	37.9	23.4		43.3				Net Worth		29.8	31.9
	100.0	100.0		100.0				Total Liabilities & Net Worth		100.0	100.0
								INCOME DATA			
	100.0	100.0		100.0				Net Sales		100.0	100.0
								Gross Profit			
	87.2	94.3		92.7				Operating Expenses		87.3	92.1
	12.7	5.7		7.3				Operating Profit		12.7	7.9
	3.1	4.6		2.4				All Other Expenses (net)		4.1	2.5
	9.6	1.1		4.9				Profit Before Taxes		8.6	5.4
								RATIOS			
	4.1	2.0		2.8						2.9	2.5
	2.6	1.1		1.5				Current		1.5	1.5
	.6	.3		1.3						.9	1.0
	1.9	1.8		2.0						1.9	1.7
	.7	.9		1.1				Quick		1.0	1.0
	.2	.3		.8						.4	.6
0	UND	0 UND	42	8.8					0	UND	41	8.9
11	34.0	49 7.5	62	5.9				Sales/Receivables	56	6.5	70	5.2
52	7.0	86 4.2	86	4.2					93	3.9	101	3.6
								Cost of Sales/Inventory			
								Cost of Sales/Payables			
	5.9	6.9		3.4						4.1	4.5
	8.7	85.8		8.4				Sales/Working Capital		10.3	8.7
	-18.2	-4.0		17.4						-26.6	UND
	14.7	2.7		8.0						8.5	6.1
(11)	5.6	(20) 1.4	(18)	4.2				EBIT/Interest	(63)	2.9	(63)	2.6
	1.7	-.7		.2						1.4	.9
								Net Profit + Depr., Dep.,		4.3	4.5
								Amort./Cur. Mat. L /T/D	(25)	1.5	(19)	2.5
										.9	1.3
	.3	.9		.3						.4	.3
	.9	1.9		.6				Fixed/Worth		1.1	.9
	-23.8	NM		1.4						2.9	4.8
	.3	1.4		.9						.7	.9
	1.0	2.8		1.5				Debt/Worth		2.2	2.3
	-27.5	NM		2.9						5.2	9.1
		28.4		36.2						44.7	46.3
		(19) 13.6		9.5				% Profit Before Taxes/Tangible	(69)	20.6	(59)	22.5
		1.2		-15.3				Net Worth		4.9	7.5
	25.6	8.5		14.7						14.5	11.6
	16.9	2.7		4.2				% Profit Before Taxes/Total		6.0	6.4
	4.0	-4.7		-5.7				Assets		1.3	.0
	21.4	12.3		16.7						14.2	18.8
	4.8	4.2		5.6				Sales/Net Fixed Assets		5.7	6.5
	1.6	1.9		2.3						1.6	3.5
	4.0	2.1		1.9						2.2	2.4
	2.2	1.7		1.6				Sales/Total Assets		1.5	1.8
	1.3	1.0		1.2						.7	1.2
	3.1	4.5		2.3						2.1	1.7
(12)	10.3	(23) 9.0	(19)	6.4				% Depr., Dep., Amort./Sales	(69)	7.1	(63)	5.5
	25.4	14.9		14.6						15.1	11.3
		4.0								3.4	2.8
		(11) 7.5						% Officers', Directors',	(24)	6.1	(19)	5.9
		21.1						Owners' Comp/Sales		21.9	17.1
	9418M	40163M		111889M	256997M	38151M	758208M	Net Sales ($)		1329483M	649451M
	3452M	26690M		63510M	264208M	233774M	311648M	Total Assets ($)		818409M	589631M

M = $ thousand   MM = $ million
See Pages 11 through 18 for Explanation of Ratios and Data

Comparative Historical Data | Current Data Sorted By Sales

			Type of Statement	0-1MM	1-3MM	3-5MM	5-10MM	10-25MM	25MM & OVER
9	11	11	Unqualified	1		2	2	3	3
21	26	15	Reviewed	3	3	4	3	2	
19	22	9	Compiled	1	6	1		1	
5	12	14	Tax Returns	6	7		1		
23	43	24	Other	9	8	1	2	1	3
4/1/00-3/31/01 ALL	4/1/01-3/31/02 ALL	4/1/02-3/31/03 ALL		16 (4/1-9/30/02)		57 (10/1/02-3/31/03)			
77	114	73	NUMBER OF STATEMENTS	20	24	8	8	7	6
%	%	%	ASSETS	%	%	%	%	%	%
6.7	7.9	8.1	Cash & Equivalents	3.1	13.9				
28.7	24.6	30.0	Trade Receivables (net)	12.1	31.6				
10.1	9.3	11.4	Inventory	9.6	11.0				
3.2	1.5	2.8	All Other Current	5.8	1.5				
48.8	43.3	52.4	Total Current	30.6	58.0				
41.0	46.5	40.4	Fixed Assets (net)	59.1	37.0				
3.9	3.4	2.2	Intangibles (net)	1.5	2.1				
6.3	6.7	5.1	All Other Non-Current	8.8	2.9				
100.0	100.0	100.0	Total	100.0	100.0				
			LIABILITIES						
13.0	10.9	10.2	Notes Payable-Short Term	10.8	16.0				
7.1	10.0	9.2	Cur. Mat.-L/T/D	11.4	8.2				
11.8	9.3	10.4	Trade Payables	6.4	11.7				
.5	.8	1.2	Income Taxes Payable	.0	1.0				
7.6	5.7	7.7	All Other Current	2.2	4.7				
40.1	36.6	38.7	Total Current	30.9	41.7				
27.0	27.4	24.1	Long Term Debt	32.2	22.0				
1.4	.8	.7	Deferred Taxes	.0	.9				
3.5	5.0	5.3	All Other Non-Current	9.0	3.4				
28.1	30.2	31.1	Net Worth	27.9	32.0				
100.0	100.0	100.0	Total Liabilities & Net Worth	100.0	100.0				
			INCOME DATA						
100.0	100.0	100.0	Net Sales	100.0	100.0				
			Gross Profit						
88.6	85.0	90.2	Operating Expenses	82.2	95.9				
11.4	15.0	9.8	Operating Profit	17.8	4.1				
5.4	6.1	4.2	All Other Expenses (net)	6.6	2.6				
6.0	8.9	5.5	Profit Before Taxes	11.3	1.4				
			RATIOS						
2.2	2.1	2.6		3.0	2.9				
1.4	1.3	1.5	Current	1.2	1.2				
.6	.6	1.0		.1	1.0				
1.7	1.6	1.8		1.7	2.1				
.9	.9	1.0	Quick	.3	1.0				
.4	.4	.5		.1	.7				
18 20.5	8 43.8	14 25.5		0 UND	7 51.5				
61 6.0	46 7.9	57 6.4	Sales/Receivables	14 25.5	49 7.4				
91 4.0	83 4.4	91 4.0		55 6.7	80 4.6				
			Cost of Sales/Inventory						
			Cost of Sales/Payables						
5.7	6.8	5.3		5.3	6.4				
14.1	18.1	10.1	Sales/Working Capital	NM	19.4				
-14.9	-9.1	NM		-1.7	213.1				
5.4	5.8	7.4		5.2	9.6				
(63) 2.4	(95) 2.3	(61) 2.6	EBIT/Interest	(16) 1.9	(20) 2.0				
1.0	1.3	1.0		1.2	.4				
4.8	3.2	6.5	Net Profit + Depr., Dep.,						
(19) 1.8	(21) 1.4	(16) 1.6	Amort./Cur. Mat. L/T/D						
1.0	.4	1.1							
.6	.6	.4		.9	.4				
1.4	1.6	1.2	Fixed/Worth	2.3	1.2				
8.3	4.9	4.3		-5.9	4.2				
1.1	1.2	1.0		.8	1.2				
2.6	2.4	2.2	Debt/Worth	2.1	3.0				
11.8	7.3	7.4		-8.8	6.0				
46.2	64.3	35.0	% Profit Before Taxes/Tangible	87.3	32.3				
(66) 17.4	(100) 24.2	(61) 17.8	Net Worth	(13) 23.9	(21) 6.4				
.4	4.7	1.7		10.6	-17.6				
14.0	14.9	14.0	% Profit Before Taxes/Total	15.4	13.6				
4.8	6.5	5.0	Assets	5.0	3.2				
.0	1.2	-.3		.8	-4.9				
11.5	12.5	14.2		4.7	14.2				
4.6	4.3	5.0	Sales/Net Fixed Assets	1.5	9.2				
1.4	1.0	1.5		.6	2.9				
2.3	2.3	2.2		2.0	2.9				
1.5	1.4	1.6	Sales/Total Assets	1.0	1.9				
.7	.6	.8		.5	1.4				
1.7	2.6	3.3		12.5	3.3				
(70) 5.9	(106) 8.6	(65) 7.6	% Depr., Dep., Amort./Sales	(18) 23.1	(23) 6.3				
12.0	22.4	23.1		81.2	11.2				
1.5	3.9	3.5	% Officers', Directors',		3.7				
(25) 5.1	(29) 6.9	(25) 7.5	Owners' Comp/Sales		(13) 5.1				
15.0	15.9	18.1			18.1				
933214M	1774345M	1214826M	Net Sales ($)	10603M	48226M	34711M	56124M	138371M	926791M
933701M	1401578M	903282M	Total Assets ($)	16835M	28364M	48579M	87970M	302385M	419149M

© RMA 2003   M = $ thousand   MM = $ million
See Pages 11 through 18 for Explanation of Ratios and Data

Current Data Sorted By Assets | **Comparative Historical Data**

	0-500M	500M-2MM	2-10MM	10-50MM	50-100MM	100-250MM	Type of Statement	4/1/98-3/31/99 ALL	4/1/99-3/31/00 ALL
		1	7	17	3	9	Unqualified	45	60
		11	29	12		2	Reviewed	83	74
	6	11	27	10			Compiled	46	36
	9	11	4				Tax Returns	31	16
	3	12	28	19	5	2	Other	72	61
		47 (4/1-9/30/02)		191 (10/1/02-3/31/03)					
NUMBER OF STATEMENTS	18	46	95	58	8	13		277	247
	%	%	%	%	%	%	ASSETS	%	%
	20.3	6.8	5.7	4.4		2.5	Cash & Equivalents	7.7	7.0
	7.2	21.6	16.5	17.3		9.0	Trade Receivables (net)	15.5	15.8
	2.8	3.5	10.0	14.5		11.1	Inventory	10.4	10.8
	2.4	2.3	3.2	2.3		1.8	All Other Current	2.1	2.9
	32.7	34.2	35.3	38.5		24.4	Total Current	35.7	36.5
	57.6	60.5	56.9	54.5		62.3	Fixed Assets (net)	56.8	53.4
	2.7	1.4	1.1	1.2		10.0	Intangibles (net)	2.1	2.5
	7.1	3.9	6.6	5.8		3.3	All Other Non-Current	5.3	7.7
	100.0	100.0	100.0	100.0		100.0	Total	100.0	100.0
							LIABILITIES		
	21.6	11.0	7.3	10.4		26.3	Notes Payable-Short Term	8.7	12.7
	9.6	14.8	12.5	10.1		5.4	Cur. Mat.-L/T/D	10.6	8.7
	4.3	6.4	5.6	6.6		5.2	Trade Payables	6.9	6.1
	.0	.3	.4	.2		.2	Income Taxes Payable	.3	.3
	2.5	7.6	5.5	5.5		1.8	All Other Current	6.8	5.9
	38.0	40.0	31.2	32.7		39.0	Total Current	33.2	33.7
	28.0	31.0	30.4	30.7		32.3	Long Term Debt	31.1	28.1
	.3	.4	1.8	1.4		.3	Deferred Taxes	1.0	.8
	7.4	5.7	2.5	3.3		1.3	All Other Non-Current	5.5	5.0
	26.4	22.9	34.1	31.8		27.1	Net Worth	29.1	32.3
	100.0	100.0	100.0	100.0		100.0	Total Liabilities & Net Worth	100.0	100.0
							INCOME DATA		
	100.0	100.0	100.0	100.0		100.0	Net Sales	100.0	100.0
							Gross Profit		
	86.4	89.1	90.7	91.7		85.0	Operating Expenses	88.6	86.4
	13.6	10.9	9.3	8.3		15.0	Operating Profit	11.4	13.6
	2.3	4.2	4.1	3.6		10.7	All Other Expenses (net)	3.3	3.2
	11.4	6.7	5.2	4.8		4.3	Profit Before Taxes	8.1	10.4
							RATIOS		
	2.7	1.6	1.8	1.9		1.6		1.9	1.9
	1.1	.9	1.1	1.2		1.0	Current	1.1	1.1
	.1	.4	.6	.7		.2		.6	.6
	2.1	1.4	1.3	1.1		.9		1.4	1.4
	1.1	.7	.7	.8		.5	Quick	.6	.7
	.1	.3	.4	.4		.2		.3	.3
	0 UND	0 UND	28 13.1	37 9.9		46 7.9		10 36.6	21 17.7
	0 UND	45 8.0	48 7.7	53 6.8		50 7.3	Sales/Receivables	43 8.4	44 8.2
	26 13.9	78 4.7	73 5.0	79 4.6		62 5.8		65 5.6	69 5.3
							Cost of Sales/Inventory		
							Cost of Sales/Payables		
	6.6	8.7	6.0	5.7		8.4		6.5	6.0
	46.9	-23.9	48.0	19.0		48.9	Sales/Working Capital	70.7	51.1
	-1.2	-3.8	-8.1	-11.4		-1.3		-5.8	-5.6
	(12) 8.5	(45) 4.1	(88) 3.5	(55) 2.9				(238) 4.6	(209) 4.7
	2.2	2.0	1.9	1.9			EBIT/Interest	2.4	2.3
	.2	-.6	.5	1.4				1.4	1.4
			(39) 2.6	(17) 1.9			Net Profit + Depr., Dep.,	(90) 3.5	(69) 3.0
			1.6	1.4			Amort./Cur. Mat. L/T/D	1.5	1.7
			.8	1.0				.8	1.2
	.7	1.2	1.0	.8		1.4		.9	.9
	1.7	3.0	1.9	1.7		6.0	Fixed/Worth	2.1	1.8
	6.7	UND	5.0	4.2		NM		4.8	4.2
	.4	1.2	.9	1.5		2.2		1.3	1.1
	1.5	3.8	2.4	3.0		5.7	Debt/Worth	2.9	2.3
	8.3	UND	7.4	5.3		NM		6.8	5.8
	(16) 53.7	(36) 44.8	(90) 28.7	(57) 23.3		(10) 24.5	% Profit Before Taxes/Tangible	(252) 44.9	(223) 41.0
	26.3	14.7	9.1	13.0		10.4	Net Worth	20.8	21.7
	-4.0	-23.2	-3.1	5.9		3.2		7.7	7.9
	22.5	9.9	7.8	6.0		3.2	% Profit Before Taxes/Total	11.5	12.2
	7.8	2.2	2.9	3.3		1.6	Assets	5.6	5.1
	-2.8	-7.4	-1.6	1.7		-.4		1.5	1.4
	5.2	4.0	4.0	4.6		1.6		4.8	5.2
	1.9	1.9	1.8	2.0		.8	Sales/Net Fixed Assets	1.7	1.7
	1.0	.8	1.0	.8		.5		.9	.9
	2.6	2.0	1.6	1.5		.8		1.5	1.5
	1.2	1.1	1.1	1.0		.6	Sales/Total Assets	1.0	.9
	.6	.5	.7	.6		.4		.5	.6
	(16) 9.3	(43) 6.5	(92) 7.5	(53) 7.1			% Depr., Dep., Amort./Sales	(250) 5.2	(218) 5.1
	33.0	14.9	13.7	13.0				12.6	12.8
	51.0	35.1	26.8	19.3				29.2	28.5
		(19) 4.0	(32) 2.8	(11) 1.1			% Officers', Directors',	(82) 2.6	(64) 2.3
		5.6	4.3	3.6			Owners' Comp/Sales	4.9	5.3
		12.6	9.4					9.2	9.6
	9718M	70284M	587293M	1310767M	487838M	1174783M	Net Sales ($)	2904998M	3931927M
	4993M	53119M	477345M	1218408M	562204M	1900676M	Total Assets ($)	2947427M	4009100M

© RMA 2003

M = $ thousand   MM = $ million
See Pages 11 through 18 for Explanation of Ratios and Data

Comparative Historical Data

Current Data Sorted By Sales

			Type of Statement						
26	34	37	Unqualified		3	5	1	10	18
51	46	54	Reviewed	5	9	10	12	11	7
55	62	54	Compiled	13	11	10	9	8	3
21	19	24	Tax Returns	12	9	1	1	1	
68	72	69	Other	9	15	5	15	12	13
4/1/00-3/31/01 ALL	4/1/01-3/31/02 ALL	4/1/02-3/31/03 ALL		47 (4/1-9/30/02)			191 (10/1/02-3/31/03)		
				0-1MM	1-3MM	3-5MM	5-10MM	10-25MM	25MM & OVER
221	233	238	**NUMBER OF STATEMENTS**	39	47	31	38	42	41
%	%	%	**ASSETS**	%	%	%	%	%	%
7.8	6.7	6.5	Cash & Equivalents	12.0	6.8	4.8	6.6	4.4	4.1
15.5	16.4	16.4	Trade Receivables (net)	8.3	14.2	18.9	19.9	21.2	16.5
8.3	9.8	9.1	Inventory	1.7	3.9	8.6	9.3	12.0	19.6
3.2	2.9	2.9	All Other Current	2.0	3.7	1.8	2.4	3.0	4.3
34.7	35.8	35.0	Total Current	24.1	28.7	34.1	38.3	40.5	44.4
57.1	56.1	57.4	Fixed Assets (net)	68.1	65.3	55.6	54.4	52.1	47.6
1.9	1.9	1.9	Intangibles (net)	1.3	1.2	1.6	2.3	.8	4.2
6.3	6.2	5.8	All Other Non-Current	6.6	4.8	8.7	5.0	6.6	3.8
100.0	100.0	100.0	Total	100.0	100.0	100.0	100.0	100.0	100.0
			LIABILITIES						
11.7	11.2	10.9	Notes Payable-Short Term	11.6	9.4	5.9	7.5	13.4	16.2
9.9	12.0	11.6	Cur. Mat.-L/T/D	13.4	14.4	13.9	11.2	9.1	7.7
5.3	6.4	5.9	Trade Payables	2.6	5.5	6.1	6.3	6.3	8.5
.2	.3	.3	Income Taxes Payable	.0	.4	.9	.0	.2	.4
5.9	6.3	5.5	All Other Current	2.9	5.5	7.7	5.9	5.7	5.8
33.0	36.2	34.2	Total Current	30.5	35.2	34.5	30.9	34.7	38.6
30.9	34.0	30.6	Long Term Debt	35.7	32.6	30.7	28.1	27.5	28.8
1.2	1.0	1.2	Deferred Taxes	.1	1.2	1.6	1.3	1.9	1.0
7.2	3.1	3.9	All Other Non-Current	7.6	2.5	2.2	3.2	3.8	3.8
27.7	25.7	30.2	Net Worth	26.1	28.5	31.1	36.5	32.0	27.8
100.0	100.0	100.0	Total Liabilities & Net Worth	100.0	100.0	100.0	100.0	100.0	100.0
			INCOME DATA						
100.0	100.0	100.0	Net Sales	100.0	100.0	100.0	100.0	100.0	100.0
			Gross Profit						
89.0	88.4	89.9	Operating Expenses	78.6	91.7	90.1	91.6	94.8	91.8
11.0	11.6	10.1	Operating Profit	21.4	8.3	9.9	8.4	5.2	8.2
2.5	5.3	4.3	All Other Expenses (net)	7.2	4.5	3.8	2.0	3.0	5.1
8.4	6.3	5.8	Profit Before Taxes	14.1	3.8	6.1	6.4	2.3	3.1
			RATIOS						
2.1	1.7	1.8		1.8	1.6	1.7	1.9	2.1	1.8
1.1	1.0	1.1	Current	.4	.8	.9	1.2	1.2	1.2
.5	.5	.5		.2	.4	.5	.8	.9	.6
1.7	1.4	1.3		1.4	1.3	1.5	1.4	1.7	.9
.8	.7	.7	Quick	.4	.6	.6	.8	1.0	.6
.3	.3	.3		.1	.3	.3	.5	.5	.3
14 25.8	13 27.9	25 14.7		0 UND	25 14.4	18 19.7	42 8.7	43 8.6	37 9.9
42 8.7	45 8.1	48 7.6	Sales/Receivables	0 UND	46 7.9	51 7.2	51 7.1	63 5.8	50 7.3
67 5.4	68 5.4	72 5.1		41 8.9	75 4.9	73 5.0	78 4.7	80 4.6	62 5.8
			Cost of Sales/Inventory						
			Cost of Sales/Payables						
6.5	8.1	6.7		3.2	8.2	8.4	6.6	5.6	6.1
34.8	UND	51.1	Sales/Working Capital	-7.1	-17.2	-34.6	37.4	19.0	16.9
-7.2	-5.1	-6.6		-1.9	-4.1	-6.4	-20.4	-30.3	-8.1
4.6	4.4	3.5		6.8	3.3	4.8	3.2	2.8	2.9
(193) 2.2	(206) 1.8	(216) 2.0	EBIT/Interest	(30) 3.1	(44) 1.2	(29) 2.7	(36) 1.7	(41) 2.0	(36) 1.6
1.2	1.0	.6		.4	.0	.8	.4	.8	1.3
3.6	2.8	2.0	Net Profit + Depr., Dep.,		14.2	2.6	2.0	2.0	1.9
(57) 2.0	(60) 1.9	(67) 1.4	Amort./Cur. Mat. L/T/D	(11) 1.7	(14) 1.0	(14) 1.4	(13) 1.4	(12) 1.6
1.0	1.0	.8		.7	.7	.8	1.1	1.0
.9	1.0	1.0		1.1	1.2	.9	1.0	.8	.8
1.9	2.2	2.0	Fixed/Worth	2.4	2.3	2.1	1.8	1.7	1.9
5.5	5.5	5.5		8.1	8.7	10.9	2.7	4.9	6.0
1.0	1.2	1.2		1.0	.8	.8	1.2	1.2	1.7
2.2	3.1	2.6	Debt/Worth	2.4	3.2	2.8	1.9	3.0	2.8
6.7	6.8	7.4		9.3	11.3	15.3	3.7	5.9	5.8
34.7	33.1	32.4	% Profit Before Taxes/Tangible	49.7	31.0	38.0	32.4	22.5	20.7
(194) 16.9	(204) 14.3	(216) 11.8	Net Worth	(33) 20.0	(41) 2.9	(29) 16.1	(35) 13.3	11.6	(36) 11.2
3.1	2.9	-1.5		-6.5	-16.9	-1.1	-3.1	-2.5	5.8
13.0	11.6	7.5	% Profit Before Taxes/Total	20.8	7.8	9.7	9.0	5.2	5.6
4.1	2.9	3.1	Assets	6.4	.9	5.1	3.1	3.3	2.4
.2	.3	-1.5		-3.7	-5.3	-.7	-1.6	-.7	.8
4.2	4.4	4.0		2.1	2.8	6.2	3.6	5.7	10.1
1.6	1.8	1.7	Sales/Net Fixed Assets	.9	1.4	1.5	2.2	2.5	3.0
.8	.8	.8		.4	.8	.6	1.4	1.2	.9
1.6	1.7	1.5		1.1	1.4	2.1	1.5	1.6	1.7
1.0	1.0	1.0	Sales/Total Assets	.5	.8	1.0	1.2	1.2	1.0
.6	.6	.6		.3	.6	.5	.9	.8	.6
5.9	4.7	7.2	% Depr., Dep., Amort./Sales	15.9	11.0	4.4	8.5	6.5	2.2
(197) 15.2	(205) 13.8	(215) 13.8		(36) 35.2	(46) 18.1	(30) 14.3	(36) 13.1	(39) 11.7	(28) 6.3
26.3	28.6	28.7		59.8	33.8	38.3	21.1	16.5	14.1
2.6	2.3	2.4	% Officers', Directors',		4.3	2.3	2.7		
(59) 4.9	(63) 5.0	(69) 4.4	Owners' Comp/Sales	(20) 6.6	(13) 4.1	(15) 5.0		
12.6	11.0	10.1		13.2	9.0	7.7		
3309875M	2991172M	3640683M	Net Sales ($)	16756M	83057M	120945M	271035M	682220M	2466670M
3487775M	3270932M	4216745M	Total Assets ($)	40162M	127749M	151961M	255210M	711429M	2930234M

M = $ thousand   MM = $ million
See Pages 11 through 18 for Explanation of Ratios and Data

Current Data Sorted By Assets   Comparative Historical Data

						Type of Statement		
		2	4	5	1	Unqualified	23	16
		6	3			Reviewed	15	9
	1	3				Compiled	6	4
1	3	1				Tax Returns	5	
3	6	6	3			Other	21	13
	8 (4/1-9/30/02)		40 (10/1/02-3/31/03)				4/1/98-3/31/99	4/1/99-3/31/00
0-500M	500M-2MM	2-10MM	10-50MM	50-100MM	100-250MM		ALL	ALL
4	10	18	10	5	1	NUMBER OF STATEMENTS	70	42
%	%	%	%	%	%	ASSETS	%	%
	17.5	5.6	5.6			Cash & Equivalents	6.8	7.2
	13.2	14.5	42.8			Trade Receivables (net)	23.4	18.8
	16.7	2.6	1.1			Inventory	7.0	3.8
	.4	5.4	2.8			All Other Current	6.6	6.7
	47.8	28.1	52.4			Total Current	43.7	36.4
	46.1	51.0	41.2			Fixed Assets (net)	39.1	40.1
	.0	3.5	.5			Intangibles (net)	3.5	1.3
	6.0	17.3	6.0			All Other Non-Current	13.6	22.2
	100.0	100.0	100.0			Total	100.0	100.0
						LIABILITIES		
	6.9	15.1	23.3			Notes Payable-Short Term	7.7	15.0
	7.4	17.6	15.8			Cur. Mat.-L/T/D	16.3	11.9
	10.2	6.2	9.1			Trade Payables	10.4	8.3
	.2	.3	.1			Income Taxes Payable	.3	1.0
	10.4	4.3	4.6			All Other Current	8.4	9.1
	35.0	43.5	52.9			Total Current	43.1	45.3
	37.4	28.2	20.6			Long Term Debt	22.2	25.6
	.0	.4	.9			Deferred Taxes	1.3	.7
	7.6	9.2	4.6			All Other Non-Current	8.8	4.4
	20.0	18.7	21.0			Net Worth	24.6	23.9
	100.0	100.0	100.0			Total Liabilities & Net Worth	100.0	100.0
						INCOME DATA		
	100.0	100.0	100.0			Net Sales	100.0	100.0
						Gross Profit		
	88.0	91.7	84.7			Operating Expenses	84.5	87.0
	12.0	8.3	15.3			Operating Profit	15.5	13.0
	5.7	9.8	11.5			All Other Expenses (net)	7.4	8.0
	6.3	-1.5	3.7			Profit Before Taxes	8.1	5.0
						RATIOS		
	3.3	1.0	1.6				1.5	1.4
	1.8	.5	.8			Current	.9	.7
	.8	.3	.1				.4	.3
	3.1	.6	1.4				1.3	1.0
	.8	.3	.7			Quick	.5	.5
	.6	.2	.1				.2	.2
0 UND	4 103.6	5 70.8					11 33.2	14 27.0
21 17.0	32 11.5	60 6.0				Sales/Receivables	39 9.4	42 8.7
52 7.0	60 6.1	1686 .2					71 5.1	55 6.6
						Cost of Sales/Inventory		
						Cost of Sales/Payables		
	5.1	NM	1.0				10.0	17.0
	11.2	-4.3	NM			Sales/Working Capital	-48.8	-11.0
	-5.6	-3.0	-1.6				-3.0	-2.8
		3.6					4.2	5.2
	(16)	1.2				EBIT/Interest	(52) 2.2	(37) 1.8
		-1.3					1.5	1.3
						Net Profit + Depr., Dep.,	1.3	
						Amort./Cur. Mat. L/T/D	(18) .8	
							.4	
	1.0	1.1	.0				.3	.3
	2.8	2.3	.7			Fixed/Worth	1.6	1.2
	UND	7.9	6.6				5.9	5.3
	1.8	1.9	2.2				1.8	1.4
	2.8	3.4	4.4			Debt/Worth	4.1	3.6
	UND	9.2	10.6				9.0	12.9
		38.7	18.0			% Profit Before Taxes/Tangible	47.2	43.5
	(15)	9.6	10.2			Net Worth	(63) 28.9	(37) 23.9
		-21.9	5.7				12.4	11.2
	8.5	4.6	3.0			% Profit Before Taxes/Total	11.7	9.6
	-1.1	1.2	1.6			Assets	4.5	3.7
	-8.3	-10.7	.5				2.2	.8
	28.1	8.1	96.6				29.9	17.7
	3.9	2.7	3.9			Sales/Net Fixed Assets	6.7	4.0
	.8	.7	.8				.9	1.4
	3.1	1.3	1.3				2.6	2.4
	1.3	.9	.6			Sales/Total Assets	.9	.9
	.5	.5	.2				.5	.5
		13.4					1.2	1.2
	(14)	24.0				% Depr., Dep., Amort./Sales	(50) 10.0	(27) 9.5
		57.5					37.5	28.8
						% Officers', Directors',	3.1	2.4
						Owners' Comp/Sales	(16) 7.7	(11) 3.2
							13.4	21.8
3712M	17405M	137021M	190504M	151452M	332710M	Net Sales ($)	3528700M	3408564M
902M	10084M	107972M	194832M	359940M	191477M	Total Assets ($)	1238463M	1399922M

Comparative Historical Data | Current Data Sorted By Sales

			Type of Statement						
17	11	12	Unqualified				3	4	5
9	6	9	Reviewed		2	1	2	3	1
2	3	4	Compiled	1		3			
4	2	5	Tax Returns	5					
15	10	18	Other	2	7	3	4	1	1
4/1/00- 3/31/01	4/1/01- 3/31/02	4/1/02- 3/31/03				8 (4/1-9/30/02)	40 (10/1/02-3/31/03)		
ALL	ALL	ALL		0-1MM	1-3MM	3-5MM	5-10MM	10-25MM	25MM & OVER
47	32	48	**NUMBER OF STATEMENTS**	8	9	7	9	8	7
%	%	%	**ASSETS**	%	%	%	%	%	%
10.2	5.7	9.4	Cash & Equivalents						
16.3	17.3	21.8	Trade Receivables (net)						
8.3	4.9	5.1	Inventory						
5.7	9.4	3.1	All Other Current						
40.5	37.3	39.4	Total Current						
39.7	40.7	43.3	Fixed Assets (net)						
2.9	.9	1.5	Intangibles (net)						
16.9	21.1	15.8	All Other Non-Current						
100.0	100.0	100.0	Total						
			LIABILITIES						
10.4	26.9	13.6	Notes Payable-Short Term						
19.4	8.3	15.1	Cur. Mat.-L/T/D						
7.9	7.9	7.9	Trade Payables						
.6	.1	.2	Income Taxes Payable						
6.2	7.0	6.8	All Other Current						
44.6	50.1	43.7	Total Current						
19.9	26.2	27.4	Long Term Debt						
.2	.2	.4	Deferred Taxes						
5.4	13.6	7.0	All Other Non-Current						
29.9	9.9	21.5	Net Worth						
100.0	100.0	100.0	Total Liabilities & Net Worth						
			INCOME DATA						
100.0	100.0	100.0	Net Sales						
			Gross Profit						
88.5	89.0	87.0	Operating Expenses						
11.5	11.0	13.0	Operating Profit						
4.8	8.9	10.0	All Other Expenses (net)						
6.8	2.1	3.1	Profit Before Taxes						
			RATIOS						
1.8	1.1	1.7							
1.0	.7	.7	Current						
.3	.3	.3							
1.4	.9	1.2							
.6	.3	.6	Quick						
.2	.1	.3							
5 73.6	11 34.4	5 74.7							
34 10.6	32 11.5	29 12.6	Sales/Receivables						
53 6.9	46 7.9	67 5.5							
			Cost of Sales/Inventory						
			Cost of Sales/Payables						
9.9	16.2	6.3							
275.6	−11.8	−15.1	Sales/Working Capital						
−2.5	−1.8	−3.1							
4.3	2.0	2.8							
(40) 1.8	(25) 1.2	(40) 1.3	EBIT/Interest						
1.4	−1.3	−1.4							
			Net Profit + Depr., Dep., Amort./Cur. Mat. L/T/D						
.2	.3	.4							
1.4	1.8	1.8	Fixed/Worth						
3.7	7.1	5.3							
1.6	2.1	1.9							
3.2	5.8	3.2	Debt/Worth						
7.4	20.5	10.9							
52.9	30.7	39.4							
(42) 18.6	(27) 4.7	(42) 10.3	% Profit Before Taxes/Tangible Net Worth						
7.3	−12.2	−7.2							
13.3	4.1	4.4							
4.0	.9	1.4	% Profit Before Taxes/Total Assets						
2.1	−6.4	−6.0							
27.3	31.1	15.9							
6.5	4.6	3.8	Sales/Net Fixed Assets						
1.2	1.1	.8							
2.8	2.6	2.2							
.9	.8	.9	Sales/Total Assets						
.6	.4	.5							
3.0	3.2	4.3							
(29) 14.0	(18) 16.5	(36) 16.8	% Depr., Dep., Amort./Sales						
27.4	49.0	60.0							
		3.0							
	(15) 7.8	% Officers', Directors', Owners' Comp/Sales							
		16.1							
1058081M	2171665M	832804M	Net Sales ($)	3703M	17057M	24704M	61227M	116703M	609410M
1009956M	896221M	865207M	Total Assets ($)	9160M	38189M	55370M	78156M	294068M	390264M

© RMA 2003

M = $ thousand   MM = $ million
See Pages 11 through 18 for Explanation of Ratios and Data

Current Data Sorted By Assets | **Comparative Historical Data**

0-500M	500M-2MM	2-10MM	10-50MM	50-100MM	100-250MM		ALL 4/1/98-3/31/99	ALL 4/1/99-3/31/00
	94 (4/1-9/30/02)		457 (10/1/02-3/31/03)			**Type of Statement**		
2	4	22	24	17	7	Unqualified	118	94
8	23	50	13	1		Reviewed	128	114
28	54	31	8			Compiled	208	199
42	37	8	1		1	Tax Returns	121	92
30	44	54	31	5	6	Other	210	201
110	162	165	77	23	14	**NUMBER OF STATEMENTS**	785	700
%	%	%	%	%	%	**ASSETS**	%	%
10.2	7.8	7.6	6.6	3.4	6.6	Cash & Equivalents	7.5	7.5
8.5	9.2	15.6	23.5	9.9	15.5	Trade Receivables (net)	14.0	14.0
8.9	6.9	9.8	7.2	4.3	2.3	Inventory	8.3	8.0
1.3	2.4	4.1	12.7	14.4	10.1	All Other Current	3.5	4.4
28.9	26.2	37.2	50.0	32.0	34.5	Total Current	33.3	33.9
63.9	65.0	49.3	36.5	46.2	49.9	Fixed Assets (net)	54.2	53.4
2.6	3.1	1.8	2.8	3.3	2.7	Intangibles (net)	1.9	2.4
4.6	5.6	11.8	10.7	18.5	12.9	All Other Non-Current	10.6	10.4
100.0	100.0	100.0	100.0	100.0	100.0	Total	100.0	100.0
						LIABILITIES		
13.5	9.3	10.8	16.1	23.7	17.2	Notes Payable-Short Term	10.8	11.6
12.0	11.9	10.0	10.1	5.2	8.2	Cur. Mat.-L/T/D	9.1	9.3
5.2	4.7	6.2	5.2	4.8	2.4	Trade Payables	6.0	5.8
.2	.1	.5	.5	1.4	.4	Income Taxes Payable	.3	.2
11.0	7.9	7.9	5.9	5.0	8.5	All Other Current	7.1	7.1
42.0	33.9	35.4	37.8	40.1	36.7	Total Current	33.3	34.1
40.3	33.4	28.9	29.9	27.2	37.8	Long Term Debt	34.3	30.8
.1	.3	.9	1.0	1.9	1.8	Deferred Taxes	.7	.6
7.4	3.4	5.7	9.1	6.7	25.9	All Other Non-Current	6.3	4.8
10.2	28.9	29.1	22.3	24.1	-2.1	Net Worth	25.5	29.7
100.0	100.0	100.0	100.0	100.0	100.0	Total Liabilities & Net Worth	100.0	100.0
						INCOME DATA		
100.0	100.0	100.0	100.0	100.0	100.0	Net Sales	100.0	100.0
						Gross Profit		
87.1	87.5	84.0	79.3	80.3	92.3	Operating Expenses	85.1	83.0
12.9	12.5	16.0	20.7	19.7	7.7	Operating Profit	14.9	17.0
3.8	6.5	6.8	11.6	15.9	7.3	All Other Expenses (net)	5.0	5.4
9.0	6.0	9.2	9.1	3.8	.4	Profit Before Taxes	9.9	11.6
						RATIOS		
1.7	1.5	1.9	2.3	1.5	1.9	Current	2.1	1.9
.6	.7	1.0	1.2	1.1	1.0		1.1	1.0
.2	.3	.6	.9	.3	.3		.4	.4
1.2	1.0	1.1	1.5	.8	1.0	Quick	1.5	1.2
.4	(161) .5	.6	.7	.4	.5		(784) .7	(699) .6
.1	.1	.3	.3	.1	.2		.2	.2
0 UND	0 UND	7 55.3	24 15.2	24 14.9	0 UND	Sales/Receivables	0 UND	0 999.8
0 UND	10 36.6	28 12.9	53 6.9	44 8.3	46 8.0		23 16.2	23 15.5
18 20.5	36 10.2	61 5.9	78 4.7	58 6.3	82 4.4		53 6.9	50 7.2
						Cost of Sales/Inventory		
						Cost of Sales/Payables		
19.0	13.1	5.6	3.2	6.7	1.2	Sales/Working Capital	6.2	7.3
-19.0	-18.8	97.0	9.5	22.0	NM		57.1	221.9
-4.4	-2.7	-4.5	-12.3	-1.6	-6.6		-5.3	-4.6
8.1	4.5	6.0	3.9	2.8	2.5	EBIT/Interest	5.7	6.4
(88) 2.3	(144) 2.0	(134) 2.4	(52) 2.3	(14) 2.0	(10) 1.3		(603) 2.6	(560) 2.8
.3	.4	1.2	1.5	1.2	.8		1.3	1.4
	3.1	2.6	2.5			Net Profit + Depr., Dep., Amort./Cur. Mat. L /T/D	3.6	3.7
	(30) 2.2	(33) 1.9	(16) 1.7				(184) 1.7	(140) 1.8
	1.4	1.1	.3				1.0	.9
1.2	1.1	.6	.2	1.2	.3	Fixed/Worth	.8	.7
4.0	2.4	1.6	1.4	2.3	2.1		1.8	1.7
-9.0	9.0	4.4	4.3	5.2	8.2		6.0	5.7
1.2	1.0	1.1	1.6	1.6	2.3	Debt/Worth	1.0	1.0
4.1	2.9	2.6	4.3	4.6	4.2		2.9	2.8
-11.5	10.4	8.2	7.5	12.5	9.5		10.8	10.2
91.3	31.1	32.0	32.0	24.6	11.6	% Profit Before Taxes/Tangible Net Worth	47.8	47.4
(74) 29.7	(137) 12.9	(148) 15.5	(71) 17.9	(21) 9.1	(12) 4.0		(675) 23.3	(599) 22.3
.1	-4.5	3.3	7.7	-1.3	-4.0		7.4	7.4
26.3	9.1	8.8	6.6	4.2	2.6	% Profit Before Taxes/Total Assets	13.7	13.9
6.0	3.8	3.4	3.5	2.2	1.2		5.6	5.5
-3.7	-2.0	.8	1.2	-.1	-1.5		1.0	1.0
8.0	3.5	11.5	26.6	7.1	7.5	Sales/Net Fixed Assets	6.5	6.6
3.0	1.6	2.0	3.2	2.1	1.7		2.1	2.3
1.0	.6	.7	1.2	.6	.5		.7	.8
3.1	1.8	1.6	1.3	1.3	.8	Sales/Total Assets	1.7	1.9
1.8	.9	.7	.6	.4	.4		.9	1.0
.8	.5	.3	.2	.1	.3		.4	.4
6.2	10.1	5.2	1.9	3.3		% Depr., Dep., Amort./Sales	6.0	4.6
(100) 12.0	(154) 16.4	(145) 16.0	(64) 6.9	(13) 7.4			(671) 14.0	(610) 13.4
37.2	52.5	38.6	18.8	29.6			32.8	34.7
5.7	2.8	1.8	2.0			% Officers', Directors', Owners' Comp/Sales	3.4	3.5
(41) 9.3	(54) 5.5	(38) 4.8	(18) 4.4				(232) 7.0	(215) 6.6
14.5	8.3	9.8	11.4				12.5	11.8
64735M	228892M	1017758M	1479688M	1171035M	1801885M	Net Sales ($)	5663430M	6445712M
28652M	174410M	786821M	1556156M	1643344M	2234884M	Total Assets ($)	7956784M	7813370M

M = $ thousand   MM = $ million
See Pages 11 through 18 for Explanation of Ratios and Data

Comparative Historical Data | Current Data Sorted By Sales

			Type of Statement						
75	64	76	Unqualified	9	12	5	14	15	21
100	87	95	Reviewed	25	26	14	15	12	3
173	159	121	Compiled	64	29	13	9	5	1
99	91	89	Tax Returns	56	22	7	2		2
185	198	170	Other	60	35	22	16	16	21
4/1/00-3/31/01 ALL	4/1/01-3/31/02 ALL	4/1/02-3/31/03 ALL		94 (4/1-9/30/02) 0-1MM	1-3MM	3-5MM	457 (10/1/02-3/31/03) 5-10MM	10-25MM	25MM & OVER
632	599	551	NUMBER OF STATEMENTS	214	124	61	56	48	48
%	%	%	ASSETS	%	%	%	%	%	%
7.2	7.7	7.8	Cash & Equivalents	8.2	9.2	7.7	5.9	6.1	6.8
13.8	12.4	13.2	Trade Receivables (net)	7.0	15.9	14.1	16.7	21.7	19.5
9.4	7.9	8.0	Inventory	5.8	5.8	8.8	11.3	14.9	11.6
3.5	4.4	4.8	All Other Current	2.3	5.4	7.9	8.0	4.9	7.1
33.9	32.3	33.8	Total Current	23.3	36.3	38.5	42.0	47.6	45.0
52.8	53.5	54.9	Fixed Assets (net)	66.9	52.8	45.9	48.9	38.3	42.2
2.8	3.1	2.6	Intangibles (net)	2.4	1.9	2.7	3.6	2.1	4.2
10.4	11.1	8.7	All Other Non-Current	7.4	9.0	12.9	5.5	12.1	8.6
100.0	100.0	100.0	Total	100.0	100.0	100.0	100.0	100.0	100.0
			LIABILITIES						
14.0	12.8	12.3	Notes Payable-Short Term	11.0	11.2	9.4	16.2	19.0	13.6
10.5	10.4	10.7	Cur. Mat.-L/T/D	12.0	11.7	10.7	9.8	7.2	7.4
5.9	5.2	5.3	Trade Payables	3.2	5.6	4.6	7.3	8.8	8.6
.2	.3	.4	Income Taxes Payable	.2	.4	.4	1.1	.3	.2
7.6	7.9	8.1	All Other Current	8.3	7.5	6.6	6.7	10.9	9.9
38.2	36.6	36.8	Total Current	34.7	36.3	31.7	41.2	46.2	39.7
29.3	31.4	32.8	Long Term Debt	39.9	32.6	26.3	27.6	24.8	24.2
.5	.5	.6	Deferred Taxes	.2	.7	.9	.7	1.3	1.5
5.7	5.8	6.4	All Other Non-Current	4.5	6.4	3.4	3.7	8.8	19.3
26.3	25.6	23.3	Net Worth	20.7	24.1	37.7	26.7	18.9	15.2
100.0	100.0	100.0	Total Liabilities & Net Worth	100.0	100.0	100.0	100.0	100.0	100.0
			INCOME DATA						
100.0	100.0	100.0	Net Sales	100.0	100.0	100.0	100.0	100.0	100.0
			Gross Profit						
83.4	83.3	85.0	Operating Expenses	80.2	86.0	89.3	85.9	89.1	93.6
16.6	16.7	15.0	Operating Profit	19.8	14.0	10.7	14.1	10.9	6.4
6.6	8.4	7.2	All Other Expenses (net)	8.9	7.1	4.0	7.3	8.0	3.1
10.1	8.2	7.8	Profit Before Taxes	10.9	6.9	6.7	6.8	3.0	3.3
			RATIOS						
1.9	1.6	1.7		1.4	2.1	2.0	1.4	2.1	1.6
.9	.9	.9	Current	.6	1.0	1.1	1.0	1.3	1.1
.4	.3	.4		.2	.5	.6	.7	.8	.8
1.3	1.1	1.1		1.1	1.3	1.1	.8	1.3	.9
(629) .5	(598) .5	(550) .5	Quick	(213) .4	.7	.6	.5	.8	.5
.2	.2	.2		.1	.3	.2	.2	.4	.3
0 UND	0 UND	0 UND		0 UND	4 91.0	4 97.4	12 29.6	26 13.9	21 17.0
23 15.8	18 19.8	21 17.2	Sales/Receivables	0 UND	23 15.9	28 13.2	30 12.3	42 8.7	41 9.0
54 6.8	50 7.4	51 7.1		30 12.1	47 7.7	56 6.5	66 5.5	66 5.6	61 5.9
			Cost of Sales/Inventory						
			Cost of Sales/Payables						
7.1	8.0	7.6		13.3	6.5	5.5	9.4	4.9	8.0
-90.2	-54.0	-124.2	Sales/Working Capital	-6.4	174.3	46.2	-161.2	12.8	43.3
-4.8	-4.4	-4.2		-1.8	-7.1	-12.5	-7.0	-18.1	-17.5
5.6	5.4	5.3		4.8	5.3	6.7	5.4	6.0	2.8
(499) 2.6	(470) 2.1	(442) 2.2	EBIT/Interest	(163) 2.2	(103) 2.1	(49) 2.7	(46) 2.5	(38) 1.8	(43) 2.1
1.1	.9	.9		.6	.4	1.1	1.5	1.1	.9
3.6	3.9	2.8		3.6	2.7		2.3	2.8	3.6
(119) 1.8	(93) 1.9	(93) 1.9	Net Profit + Depr., Dep., Amort./Cur. Mat. L/T/D	(27) 1.9	(20) 2.3	(13) 1.7	(10) 2.1	(15) 2.0	
1.1	.9	1.2		1.3	.6		1.0	1.5	1.4
.6	.7	.8		1.2	.7	.6	.5	.4	.8
1.8	1.9	2.0	Fixed/Worth	3.2	2.2	1.1	2.0	1.4	1.5
7.0	10.2	8.2		32.7	7.6	3.4	4.1	4.1	6.9
1.0	1.1	1.2		.9	1.3	.9	1.6	1.3	1.5
2.7	3.3	3.2	Debt/Worth	3.7	3.2	1.5	3.1	3.5	3.3
12.1	18.2	11.9		44.2	11.4	5.3	7.4	8.1	10.4
42.7	41.4	34.7		42.6	40.8	29.1	32.5	31.7	28.4
(544) 20.3	(502) 16.6	(463) 14.7	% Profit Before Taxes/Tangible Net Worth	(169) 16.0	(103) 13.6	(55) 8.0	(51) 20.9	(43) 13.0	(42) 11.8
4.3	1.5	2.1		.2	.0	1.1	7.7	3.3	3.2
14.4	10.3	10.0		10.0	10.8	10.4	8.6	6.6	8.3
5.0	3.6	3.6	% Profit Before Taxes/Total Assets	3.7	3.1	3.8	4.6	2.3	3.5
.6	.0	-.3		-1.2	-1.5	.1	1.9	.2	.6
8.2	7.4	7.2		3.0	9.9	15.3	10.8	28.8	15.7
2.4	2.3	2.2	Sales/Net Fixed Assets	1.0	2.8	3.5	2.2	4.2	3.7
.9	.8	.7		.5	1.0	1.6	.9	1.7	1.7
2.0	1.9	1.9		1.3	2.2	2.1	2.1	2.6	2.9
1.1	1.0	.9	Sales/Total Assets	.6	1.1	1.2	1.0	1.3	1.6
.4	.4	.4		.3	.4	.5	.4	.6	.7
4.3	5.0	6.1		11.4	5.8	3.3	5.6	1.6	1.4
(549) 11.3	(511) 13.0	(480) 14.6	% Depr., Dep., Amort./Sales	(194) 30.7	(115) 11.8	(56) 12.6	(48) 14.5	(37) 6.2	(30) 4.4
29.7	33.9	38.9		60.8	21.0	21.5	26.6	16.5	7.7
3.6	3.6	2.6		4.1	2.5	2.5	3.6	1.7	
(203) 6.5	(170) 6.7	(154) 6.2	% Officers', Directors', Owners' Comp/Sales	(47) 9.3	(50) 5.6	(22) 5.1	(19) 6.9	(11) 2.9	
12.0	12.0	10.8		15.5	8.3	9.8	23.7	6.9	
6222206M	5228546M	5763993M	Net Sales ($)	102482M	224409M	235433M	397861M	776566M	4027242M
6985457M	6484760M	6424267M	Total Assets ($)	231058M	455651M	390186M	785220M	1356596M	3205556M

© RMA 2003   **M = $ thousand   MM = $ million**
See Pages 11 through 18 for Explanation of Ratios and Data

Current Data Sorted By Assets   **Comparative Historical Data**

0-500M	500M-2MM	2-10MM	10-50MM	50-100MM	100-250MM	Type of Statement	4/1/98-3/31/99 ALL	4/1/99-3/31/00 ALL
						Type of Statement		
4	5		12		1	Unqualified		10
			1			Reviewed		1
	1					Compiled		
	3		4			Tax Returns		1
	1	3	4		1	Other		8
	8 (4/1-9/30/02)		28 (10/1/02-3/31/03)					
	9	8	17		2	NUMBER OF STATEMENTS		20
%	%	%	%	%	%	ASSETS	%	%
D	D	D	20.3	D	D	Cash & Equivalents	D	16.2
A	A	A	15.3	A	A	Trade Receivables (net)	A	27.2
T	T	T	3.7	T	T	Inventory	T	8.8
A	A	A	7.4	A	A	All Other Current	A	5.1
			46.7			Total Current		57.2
N	N	N	22.6	N	N	Fixed Assets (net)	N	17.8
O	O	O	19.9	O	O	Intangibles (net)	O	11.0
T	T	T	10.8	T	T	All Other Non-Current	T	14.0
			100.0			Total		100.0
A	A	A		A	A	LIABILITIES	A	
V	V	V	3.5	V	V	Notes Payable-Short Term	V	8.9
A	A	A	3.5	A	A	Cur. Mat.-L/T/D	A	4.5
I	I	I	16.7	I	I	Trade Payables	I	14.8
L	L	L	.2	L	L	Income Taxes Payable	L	.5
A	A	A	13.2	A	A	All Other Current	A	16.2
B	B	B	37.1	B	B	Total Current	B	44.9
L	L	L	23.9	L	L	Long Term Debt	L	10.0
E	E	E	.9	E	E	Deferred Taxes	E	.4
			16.4			All Other Non-Current		4.5
			21.7			Net Worth		40.2
			100.0			Total Liabilities & Net Worth		100.0
						INCOME DATA		
			100.0			Net Sales		100.0
						Gross Profit		
			90.5			Operating Expenses		92.6
			9.5			Operating Profit		7.4
			1.2			All Other Expenses (net)		.9
			8.3			Profit Before Taxes		6.5
						RATIOS		
			2.5					2.1
			1.3			Current		1.2
			.6					.9
			1.9					1.4
			1.1			Quick		1.0
			.5					.5
		20	18.6				16	23.4
		28	12.9			Sales/Receivables	29	12.7
		78	4.7				72	5.1
						Cost of Sales/Inventory		
						Cost of Sales/Payables		
			3.3					6.4
			11.2			Sales/Working Capital		16.5
			−11.6					−53.3
			28.4					17.0
		(15)	4.8			EBIT/Interest	(18)	7.0
			1.5					2.0
						Net Profit + Depr., Dep., Amort./Cur. Mat. L /T/D		
			.2					.3
			3.1			Fixed/Worth		.7
			−.2					1.8
			1.4					.8
			5.0			Debt/Worth		2.3
			−3.1					9.4
			72.6					59.0
		(10)	23.2			% Profit Before Taxes/Tangible Net Worth	(17)	40.4
			9.5					16.7
			16.2					20.5
			6.6			% Profit Before Taxes/Total Assets		11.4
			3.3					.2
			33.4					49.0
			10.8			Sales/Net Fixed Assets		16.0
			6.4					6.5
			2.4					3.3
			1.0			Sales/Total Assets		2.0
			.6					1.3
			1.8					.7
		(13)	2.8			% Depr., Dep., Amort./Sales	(17)	2.7
			4.8					4.9
						% Officers', Directors', Owners' Comp/Sales		
	25770M	102365M	669197M		360791M	Net Sales ($)		531328M
	9049M	48038M	448395M		266368M	Total Assets ($)		379345M

M = $ thousand   MM = $ million
See Pages 11 through 18 for Explanation of Ratios and Data

Comparative Historical Data   Current Data Sorted By Sales

			Type of Statement						
10	9	22	Unqualified	1		4	2	8	7
1	1	1	Reviewed					1	
1	6	1	Compiled			1			
	1	3	Tax Returns	3					
6	29	9	Other		1	2	1	1	4
4/1/00-3/31/01 ALL	4/1/01-3/31/02 ALL	4/1/02-3/31/03 ALL		8 (4/1-9/30/02)			28 (10/1/02-3/31/03)		
				0-1MM	1-3MM	3-5MM	5-10MM	10-25MM	25MM & OVER
18	46	36	NUMBER OF STATEMENTS	4	1	7	3	10	11
%	%	%	**ASSETS**	%	%	%	%	%	%
24.6	10.7	22.1	Cash & Equivalents					16.0	20.9
17.2	7.0	13.8	Trade Receivables (net)					17.6	17.3
8.1	4.0	4.9	Inventory					3.6	3.2
7.4	6.6	6.5	All Other Current					8.5	9.2
57.3	28.4	47.2	Total Current					45.6	50.6
19.6	48.9	28.1	Fixed Assets (net)					31.6	20.1
10.6	13.3	12.0	Intangibles (net)					13.4	18.1
12.5	9.4	12.6	All Other Non-Current					9.4	11.2
100.0	100.0	100.0	Total					100.0	100.0
			LIABILITIES						
12.1	1.2	4.2	Notes Payable-Short Term					2.7	8.3
5.2	12.6	2.9	Cur. Mat.-L/T/D					3.2	3.8
15.8	10.9	12.4	Trade Payables					10.4	22.5
.9	.6	2.7	Income Taxes Payable					.1	7.7
35.8	11.6	11.4	All Other Current					8.2	17.1
69.8	36.9	33.7	Total Current					24.7	59.4
15.4	50.2	22.5	Long Term Debt					29.5	14.8
.1	.2	.8	Deferred Taxes					1.5	.2
5.6	8.6	10.1	All Other Non-Current					10.1	16.9
9.2	4.1	32.9	Net Worth					34.2	8.6
100.0	100.0	100.0	Total Liabilities & Net Worth					100.0	100.0
			INCOME DATA						
100.0	100.0	100.0	Net Sales					100.0	100.0
			Gross Profit						
89.3	89.4	85.7	Operating Expenses					81.7	91.7
10.7	10.6	14.3	Operating Profit					18.3	8.3
−.3	4.1	2.9	All Other Expenses (net)					1.4	2.7
11.0	6.5	11.4	Profit Before Taxes					16.9	5.6
			RATIOS						
1.9	1.2	3.0						4.5	1.9
1.3	.6	1.6	Current					1.6	.7
.8	.4	.7						1.0	.5
1.6	.6	2.7						3.0	1.9
1.0	.3	1.3	Quick					1.3	.5
.6	.1	.5						.8	.2
13 28.2	0 UND	6 63.8						22 16.5	4 84.2
24 15.5	1 280.6	23 16.0	Sales/Receivables					33 11.2	19 19.5
35 10.4	14 25.9	44 8.4						114 3.2	46 8.0
			Cost of Sales/Inventory						
			Cost of Sales/Payables						
4.4	36.2	4.1						1.7	5.8
12.3	−27.6	9.8	Sales/Working Capital					9.6	−13.8
−56.8	−14.9	−15.2						NM	−9.0
(15) 10.4	(44) 6.0	(28) 32.9							
6.5	2.3	6.8	EBIT/Interest						
2.3	1.3	2.8							
			Net Profit + Depr., Dep., Amort./Cur. Mat. L/T/D						
.2	1.4	.2						.1	.3
.5	26.8	1.0	Fixed/Worth					1.0	−2.2
1.2	−3.9	NM						4.8	−.1
.9	2.5	.6						.4	2.7
1.7	39.8	2.3	Debt/Worth					1.8	−5.9
11.6	−5.7	NM						6.0	−2.5
43.1	172.7	61.7							
(15) 30.4	(27) 29.0	(27) 24.6	% Profit Before Taxes/Tangible Net Worth						
19.1	10.5	10.5							
20.0	15.2	20.6						34.7	21.0
7.6	5.7	6.7	% Profit Before Taxes/Total Assets					9.6	6.6
1.0	1.8	3.0						5.7	2.0
32.2	12.0	30.9						19.3	65.6
18.8	6.5	14.7	Sales/Net Fixed Assets					9.2	26.9
6.1	2.2	1.6						1.5	7.9
4.6	4.4	2.9						1.5	4.2
2.2	2.4	1.1	Sales/Total Assets					.7	2.0
1.0	1.5	.6						.6	1.0
(14) .5	2.1	1.4							
1.3	(39) 3.1	(27) 2.9	% Depr., Dep., Amort./Sales						
2.4	4.5	4.6							
			% Officers', Directors', Owners' Comp/Sales						
500608M	2310662M	1158123M	Net Sales ($)	1622M	1049M	27062M	24239M	167369M	936782M
356609M	1242298M	771850M	Total Assets ($)	2922M	3318M	27458M	26111M	210770M	501271M

    M = $ thousand   MM = $ million
See Pages 11 through 18 for Explanation of Ratios and Data

PROFESSIONAL, SCIENTIFIC, AND TECHNICAL SERVICES

Current Data Sorted By Assets   Comparative Historical Data

						Type of Statement		
4	7	23	33	11	4	Unqualified	79	66
4	34	98	42	3		Reviewed	163	171
98	92	74	8	1	2	Compiled	320	290
228	75	31	10	1	3	Tax Returns	265	218
158	171	167	84	13	11	Other	487	448
	94 (4/1-9/30/02)			1396 (10/1/02-3/31/03)			4/1/98-3/31/99	4/1/99-3/31/00
0-500M	500M-2MM	2-10MM	10-50MM	50-100MM	100-250MM		ALL	ALL
492	379	393	177	29	20	NUMBER OF STATEMENTS	1314	1193
%	%	%	%	%	%	ASSETS	%	%
33.3	28.7	26.2	32.1	33.8	27.4	Cash & Equivalents	26.0	25.6
9.0	18.1	25.2	21.8	14.5	14.6	Trade Receivables (net)	18.6	19.7
.4	2.2	2.1	2.4	.0	.0	Inventory	1.0	1.5
10.7	14.6	13.6	9.5	9.2	18.5	All Other Current	9.7	10.2
53.3	63.6	67.1	65.9	57.5	60.5	Total Current	55.2	57.1
30.2	22.9	20.3	23.9	29.0	29.0	Fixed Assets (net)	29.1	28.2
2.6	1.5	1.3	1.1	1.8	1.5	Intangibles (net)	2.6	2.8
13.9	12.0	11.3	9.1	11.8	9.1	All Other Non-Current	13.1	11.9
100.0	100.0	100.0	100.0	100.0	100.0	Total	100.0	100.0
						LIABILITIES		
44.6	21.7	12.8	5.3	9.3	13.9	Notes Payable-Short Term	25.7	22.5
9.5	4.7	3.5	3.4	2.9	1.7	Cur. Mat.-L/T/D	5.3	5.8
2.5	2.9	2.9	4.3	.7	.7	Trade Payables	2.3	3.0
.1	.2	1.0	.6	.0	1.1	Income Taxes Payable	.5	.4
44.2	27.7	25.5	17.0	11.6	20.1	All Other Current	27.2	25.8
101.0	57.2	45.7	30.6	25.3	37.5	Total Current	61.1	57.5
18.5	10.7	9.4	10.8	7.3	11.3	Long Term Debt	14.4	13.6
.0	.2	1.1	.7	.7	.0	Deferred Taxes	.7	.5
7.4	6.5	5.2	6.4	5.3	2.7	All Other Non-Current	5.5	6.1
-26.9	25.5	38.6	51.5	61.4	48.5	Net Worth	18.3	22.2
100.0	100.0	100.0	100.0	100.0	100.0	Total Liabilities & Net Worth	100.0	100.0
						INCOME DATA		
100.0	100.0	100.0	100.0	100.0	100.0	Net Sales	100.0	100.0
						Gross Profit		
86.3	84.9	78.8	72.3	68.2	71.3	Operating Expenses	85.3	81.5
13.7	15.1	21.2	27.7	31.8	28.7	Operating Profit	14.7	18.5
.5	1.0	1.4	2.6	1.3	-.1	All Other Expenses (net)	1.3	1.2
13.1	14.1	19.8	25.2	30.5	28.8	Profit Before Taxes	13.4	17.3
						RATIOS		
1.4	2.4	3.5	5.2	11.5	7.6		3.2	3.0
.6	1.1	1.6	2.5	3.6	3.4	Current	1.1	1.2
.3	.7	.9	1.3	2.0	.7		.5	.6
1.1	1.8	2.9	4.4	9.5	4.7		2.6	2.5
(491) .5	(378) .9	1.2	2.0	3.4	2.6	Quick	(1311) 1.0	(1188) 1.0
.1	.4	.7	1.0	1.7	.5		.3	.4
0 UND	0 UND	0 UND	0 999.8	0 UND	0 UND		0 UND	0 UND
0 UND	0 UND	9 39.4	9 40.2	8 47.7	0 UND	Sales/Receivables	0 UND	1 251.9
0 UND	29 12.5	76 4.8	66 5.5	47 7.7	54 6.7		31 11.9	41 8.8
						Cost of Sales/Inventory		
						Cost of Sales/Payables		
52.7	11.0	4.8	3.9	6.0	4.0		9.4	8.2
-54.6	80.4	16.7	8.4	8.1	7.1	Sales/Working Capital	80.9	54.0
-14.6	-26.0	-182.3	39.1	15.1	-91.9		-25.5	-28.8
48.4	68.0	130.7	150.5	107.1	130.8		53.7	55.6
(380) 7.9	(327) 9.6	(336) 20.8	(158) 59.0	(23) 72.8	(16) 53.8	EBIT/Interest	(1083) 8.9	(1026) 10.9
1.0	1.0	2.6	7.9	28.4	8.9		1.3	1.6
	3.7	7.2	9.5			Net Profit + Depr., Dep.,	3.4	3.5
	(30) 2.0	(56) 3.0	(14) 1.4			Amort./Cur. Mat. L/T/D	(80) 1.6	(79) 1.7
	.9	1.5	.6				.6	.5
.4	.2	.1	.2	.3	.2		.3	.3
7.9	.8	.4	.5	.4	.4	Fixed/Worth	.8	.8
-.5	242.0	1.4	1.0	.6	1.6		57.7	7.8
1.8	.7	.5	.3	.2	.3		.6	.6
UND	2.6	1.5	.7	.5	.5	Debt/Worth	2.3	2.0
-2.8	-299.0	6.8	3.1	.8	13.2		UND	52.8
725.3	274.8	269.2	271.5	199.5	199.0	% Profit Before Taxes/Tangible	316.4	273.0
(246) 139.5	(283) 61.2	(342) 85.0	(166) 151.5	(28) 149.5	(17) 117.8	Net Worth	(986) 95.8	(921) 94.6
16.4	10.8	9.0	26.0	91.3	87.7		10.2	8.9
193.3	88.2	117.1	145.2	139.5	129.8	% Profit Before Taxes/Total	138.1	127.1
28.0	15.2	30.1	85.9	116.0	70.5	Assets	21.7	25.6
-.6	-.1	2.9	6.0	47.6	50.7		.9	1.4
133.0	67.6	45.1	24.5	17.1	38.0		48.2	44.7
53.7	33.2	25.9	16.0	13.5	14.8	Sales/Net Fixed Assets	23.5	23.3
23.2	16.1	14.5	10.4	9.6	8.7		13.3	12.5
17.9	7.6	5.5	4.3	4.2	5.9		8.7	8.0
9.7	4.4	3.1	3.0	3.2	3.3	Sales/Total Assets	4.8	4.6
5.2	2.5	1.9	1.9	2.2	2.1		2.6	2.6
.5	.8	.9	1.1	1.4	1.0		.9	.9
(294) 1.0	(285) 1.2	(335) 1.4	(163) 1.8	(26) 2.0	(11) 1.6	% Depr., Dep., Amort./Sales	(1047) 1.5	(947) 1.6
1.7	1.9	2.0	2.3	2.5	2.0		2.2	2.2
15.3	13.5	9.8	5.9			% Officers', Directors',	16.8	15.6
(284) 24.9	(188) 24.9	(159) 24.8	(53) 20.4			Owners' Comp/Sales	(578) 29.0	(519) 27.5
37.8	35.2	35.1	32.6				38.1	37.0
1074616M	2161509M	7417148M	13374962M	7259474M	16189574M	Net Sales ($)	28729411M	27710357M
96079M	407360M	1790325M	3965628M	2164656M	3080424M	Total Assets ($)	7754436M	7621898M

© RMA 2003

M = $ thousand   MM = $ million
See Pages 11 through 18 for Explanation of Ratios and Data

Comparative Historical Data | | | | ## Current Data Sorted By Sales

4/1/00-3/31/01 ALL	4/1/01-3/31/02 ALL	4/1/02-3/31/03 ALL	Type of Statement	0-1MM	1-3MM	3-5MM	5-10MM	10-25MM	25MM & OVER
56	52	82	Unqualified	3	4	2	3	12	58
155	148	181	Reviewed	2	3	19	38	59	60
325	305	275	Compiled	38	66	56	52	45	18
245	283	348	Tax Returns	100	119	48	41	21	19
448	535	604	Other	60	122	77	113	100	132
				94 (4/1-9/30/02)			1396 (10/1/02-3/31/03)		
1229	1323	1490	NUMBER OF STATEMENTS	203	314	202	247	237	287
%	%	%	**ASSETS**	%	%	%	%	%	%
27.2	28.7	30.0	Cash & Equivalents	35.9	32.8	24.8	26.5	26.3	32.6
18.0	17.1	17.3	Trade Receivables (net)	11.2	12.5	21.2	20.9	23.2	16.0
1.4	1.4	1.5	Inventory	.5	1.1	2.7	1.2	2.8	1.2
11.2	12.7	12.4	All Other Current	8.9	13.3	15.3	13.3	13.1	10.5
57.7	59.9	61.2	Total Current	56.5	59.8	64.0	61.9	65.4	60.3
26.3	25.9	24.9	Fixed Assets (net)	27.2	24.2	22.1	24.6	22.6	28.4
2.8	2.7	1.8	Intangibles (net)	1.7	2.2	2.6	1.4	1.5	1.2
13.2	11.5	12.1	All Other Non-Current	14.6	13.8	11.2	12.1	10.5	10.1
100.0	100.0	100.0	Total	100.0	100.0	100.0	100.0	100.0	100.0
			LIABILITIES						
24.8	30.6	24.6	Notes Payable-Short Term	36.6	41.5	30.6	20.3	11.7	7.8
6.0	5.5	5.8	Cur. Mat.-L/T/D	7.4	8.0	6.3	4.9	4.1	3.9
3.0	2.9	2.9	Trade Payables	2.6	4.2	2.8	2.4	3.2	1.9
.5	.5	.4	Income Taxes Payable	.1	.0	.8	.3	1.0	.5
27.0	31.6	30.9	All Other Current	37.6	36.2	31.0	32.7	28.1	20.9
61.3	71.1	64.6	Total Current	84.3	90.0	71.4	60.7	48.0	34.9
16.2	14.5	12.9	Long Term Debt	18.9	16.6	14.6	8.5	9.3	10.0
.5	.4	.4	Deferred Taxes	.0	.1	.2	.9	1.0	.4
5.5	6.7	6.4	All Other Non-Current	11.9	5.8	6.5	6.3	4.7	4.5
16.6	7.2	15.8	Net Worth	−15.2	−12.5	7.2	23.7	37.0	50.2
100.0	100.0	100.0	Total Liabilities & Net Worth	100.0	100.0	100.0	100.0	100.0	100.0
			INCOME DATA						
100.0	100.0	100.0	Net Sales	100.0	100.0	100.0	100.0	100.0	100.0
			Gross Profit						
81.1	82.2	81.8	Operating Expenses	84.3	84.1	87.4	85.8	79.2	72.0
18.9	17.8	18.2	Operating Profit	15.7	15.9	12.6	14.2	20.8	28.0
.9	1.1	1.1	All Other Expenses (net)	2.0	.6	.7	.3	.9	2.2
18.0	16.6	17.1	Profit Before Taxes	13.7	15.3	11.9	13.8	19.9	25.7
			RATIOS						
3.0	2.9	2.8	Current	1.7	1.7	2.4	2.8	3.6	4.8
1.2	1.1	1.2		.8	.9	1.2	1.2	1.5	2.3
.6	.6	.6		.4	.4	.6	.6	.9	1.0
(1226) 2.4	(1319) 2.2	(1488) 2.3	Quick	(202) 1.4	1.4	(201) 1.7	2.6	2.5	4.2
1.0	.9	.9		.7	.6	.8	.9	1.1	1.8
.3	.3	.4		.2	.2	.2	.4	.6	.8
0 UND	0 UND	0 UND	Sales/Receivables	0 UND	0 UND	0 UND	0 UND	0 UND	0 UND
0 UND	0 UND	0 UND		0 UND	0 UND	0 999.8	0 999.8	7 54.3	6 60.7
31 11.9	29 12.7	26 13.8		5 74.1	8 44.9	49 7.5	53 6.9	61 6.0	15 23.8
			Cost of Sales/Inventory						
			Cost of Sales/Payables						
8.7	8.9	8.1	Sales/Working Capital	15.0	18.2	8.5	7.1	6.2	6.2
78.4	101.1	63.3		−53.6	−92.5	68.3	71.7	27.2	16.2
−26.9	−27.2	−27.8		−10.7	−12.9	−28.8	−30.8	−118.0	432.3
(1050) 62.7	(1095) 58.1	(1240) 92.9	EBIT/Interest	(139) 32.0	(264) 55.1	(177) 43.8	(212) 73.5	(244) 166.5	164.5
12.3	9.8	15.9		6.9	11.4	6.4	9.6	34.9	63.5
1.3	1.3	1.6		1.0	1.0	.6	1.0	3.8	7.9
(81) 5.7	(85) 3.3	(110) 5.9	Net Profit + Depr., Dep., Amort./Cur. Mat. L/T/D		(11) 5.0	(12) 2.1	(21) 10.2	(36) 5.4	(28) 19.8
1.6	1.3	2.1			1.4	1.3	3.0	1.7	3.5
.5	.4	1.1			.6	.5	1.0	1.2	1.9
.2	.2	.2	Fixed/Worth	.1	.3	.2	.2	.2	.3
.8	.9	.8		2.3	2.4	.9	.7	.5	.5
UND	404.0	−29.8		−1.2	−.5	−2.2	−18.6	1.9	1.0
.6	.6	.6	Debt/Worth	1.4	1.5	1.0	.6	.5	.3
2.3	2.5	2.5		54.0	20.8	4.4	2.0	1.5	.7
−48.1	−72.5	−28.1		−4.1	−3.7	−13.3	−38.8	10.0	2.4
(905) 324.8	(979) 312.9	(1082) 319.3	% Profit Before Taxes/Tangible Net Worth	(110) 351.6	(179) 370.9	(137) 205.4	(181) 254.4	(269) 365.4	297.5
108.3	111.3	100.8		86.4	95.0	45.6	78.1	103.4	161.3
14.6	11.8	13.5		16.9	10.8	4.0	7.8	15.3	24.5
139.8	129.4	135.6	% Profit Before Taxes/Total Assets	96.1	140.6	78.5	87.5	146.9	178.0
31.6	28.0	29.0		23.3	22.0	13.1	16.8	45.8	100.8
1.2	.8	.9		−.5	−.1	−1.2	.0	3.4	7.9
59.8	62.3	65.8	Sales/Net Fixed Assets	211.0	99.2	84.0	60.9	53.2	27.9
26.7	28.0	29.8		33.6	37.5	42.0	33.5	28.9	17.8
14.6	14.7	14.9		10.7	19.3	19.2	18.9	17.3	11.7
8.4	9.3	9.0	Sales/Total Assets	9.0	12.1	10.3	10.4	7.5	6.4
4.6	4.7	4.6		4.4	5.5	4.7	5.1	4.1	4.2
2.6	2.6	2.5		2.0	2.6	2.4	2.6	2.4	2.9
(956) .7	(996) .6	(1114) .8	% Depr., Dep., Amort./Sales	(110) .8	(196) .5	(148) .7	(207) .8	(201) .8	(252) 1.1
1.3	1.1	1.3		1.8	1.0	1.1	1.3	1.3	1.6
2.0	1.8	2.0		3.9	1.7	1.6	2.0	1.9	2.2
(553) 15.4	(643) 13.5	(702) 13.5	% Officers', Directors', Owners' Comp/Sales	(112) 15.8	(186) 14.6	(100) 14.4	(120) 16.9	(94) 9.7	(90) 10.2
28.2	27.0	24.8		25.3	22.9	27.4	27.4	23.0	25.3
36.5	36.9	35.7		35.2	37.4	34.4	36.2	35.3	33.6
32970034M	40990770M	47477283M	Net Sales ($)	111522M	588596M	789584M	1780173M	3633189M	40574219M
8933538M	10528285M	11504472M	Total Assets ($)	57638M	218622M	270663M	528826M	1131649M	9297074M

M = $ thousand   MM = $ million
See Pages 11 through 18 for Explanation of Ratios and Data

Current Data Sorted By Assets | Comparative Historical Data

0-500M	500M-2MM	2-10MM	10-50MM	50-100MM	100-250MM	Type of Statement	4/1/98-3/31/99 ALL	4/1/99-3/31/00 ALL
1		1		3	1	Unqualified	3	7
	3	4	1			Reviewed	2	6
1	9	1		1		Compiled	11	5
5	2	3			1	Tax Returns	9	5
7	5	7	1	1		Other	10	5
7 (4/1-9/30/02)			51 (10/1/02-3/31/03)					
14	19	16	5	3	1	NUMBER OF STATEMENTS	35	28
%	%	%	%	%	%	**ASSETS**	%	%
33.7	27.2	38.7				Cash & Equivalents	30.8	27.8
10.5	7.7	15.0				Trade Receivables (net)	12.2	17.8
.0	.0	.0				Inventory	.0	.0
10.7	13.5	5.1				All Other Current	4.9	9.0
54.9	48.4	58.8				Total Current	47.9	54.7
31.0	21.0	24.0				Fixed Assets (net)	27.5	25.1
5.9	11.9	13.9				Intangibles (net)	6.7	9.9
8.2	18.6	3.2				All Other Non-Current	17.9	10.3
100.0	100.0	100.0				Total	100.0	100.0
						LIABILITIES		
3.4	8.7	11.9				Notes Payable-Short Term	3.6	9.2
1.6	8.4	4.1				Cur. Mat.-L/T/D	4.0	2.6
8.0	8.8	16.3				Trade Payables	9.3	10.7
.0	.0	.2				Income Taxes Payable	.7	.2
65.0	20.2	13.4				All Other Current	18.3	26.8
78.0	46.0	46.0				Total Current	35.8	49.4
21.4	19.8	10.5				Long Term Debt	29.9	10.4
.0	.0	.0				Deferred Taxes	.2	.2
1.9	1.4	8.2				All Other Non-Current	7.2	7.8
-1.2	32.7	35.3				Net Worth	26.9	32.2
100.0	100.0	100.0				Total Liabilities & Net Worth	100.0	100.0
						INCOME DATA		
100.0	100.0	100.0				Net Sales	100.0	100.0
						Gross Profit		
88.6	86.5	85.7				Operating Expenses	87.3	92.2
11.4	13.5	14.3				Operating Profit	12.7	7.8
.4	5.4	1.7				All Other Expenses (net)	-.5	-1.8
10.9	8.0	12.6				Profit Before Taxes	13.2	9.6
						RATIOS		
6.1 / 2.5 / .2	2.7 / 1.0 / .9	2.9 / 1.2 / .7				Current	5.0 / 1.2 / .8	1.9 / 1.1 / .8
3.9 / 1.4 / .2	1.8 / .9 / .2	2.1 / 1.1 / .7				Quick	4.1 / 1.0 / .7	1.8 / 1.0 / .6
0 UND / 0 UND / 0 UND	0 UND / 0 UND / 26 14.1	3 133.2 / 5 76.7 / 51 7.2				Sales/Receivables	0 UND / 6 61.9 / 36 10.2	0 UND / 12 30.6 / 36 10.2
						Cost of Sales/Inventory		
						Cost of Sales/Payables		
9.3 / 30.7 / -21.4	5.7 / 999.8 / -35.2	5.7 / 19.2 / -17.7				Sales/Working Capital	8.5 / 64.6 / -20.6	11.1 / 45.4 / -18.8
	(16) 41.7 / 13.5 / 3.7	(10) 40.8 / 5.0 / 2.2				EBIT/Interest	(28) 23.9 / 10.1 / 2.8	(20) 21.0 / 8.0 / -.2
						Net Profit + Depr., Dep., Amort./Cur. Mat. L./T/D		
.2 / .7 / NM	.3 / .7 / -4.3	.3 / .9 / -12.4				Fixed/Worth	.4 / .8 / 1.6	.6 / 1.2 / -6.4
.4 / 1.3 / NM	.6 / 6.7 / -59.0	.7 / 2.6 / -40.5				Debt/Worth	.5 / 2.3 / 10.5	.9 / 4.9 / -53.1
(11) 567.2 / 197.7 / 10.3	(14) 85.8 / 35.5 / 12.0	(11) 129.8 / 62.3 / 26.1				% Profit Before Taxes/Tangible Net Worth	(30) 158.6 / 76.4 / 23.7	(19) 118.9 / 42.6 / -23.7
173.7 / 13.3 / -24.4	26.8 / 12.4 / 4.1	41.1 / 23.0 / 4.4				% Profit Before Taxes/Total Assets	45.4 / 20.3 / 10.1	28.2 / 10.2 / -3.4
72.8 / 19.0 / 9.2	45.0 / 13.3 / 6.7	55.2 / 16.3 / 4.9				Sales/Net Fixed Assets	28.3 / 14.6 / 6.9	28.9 / 16.9 / 6.4
9.2 / 6.5 / 3.0	3.0 / 2.1 / 1.3	3.8 / 2.2 / .8				Sales/Total Assets	4.5 / 3.6 / 1.3	3.0 / 2.6 / 1.7
(10) .6 / 1.3 / 2.7	(13) 1.2 / 2.2 / 4.7	(11) 1.2 / 1.9 / 4.1				% Depr., Dep., Amort./Sales	(29) 1.0 / 1.9 / 3.2	(27) 1.5 / 2.7 / 4.0
(10) 10.7 / 13.2 / 19.1	(11) 6.6 / 19.1 / 31.1					% Officers', Directors', Owners' Comp/Sales	(17) 8.1 / 14.8 / 18.8	(15) 6.2 / 16.3 / 25.8
13814M	47032M	174932M	167019M	877368M	352420M	Net Sales ($)	158041M	246314M
2991M	19003M	72820M	89408M	214996M	133406M	Total Assets ($)	81494M	108345M

M = $ thousand   MM = $ million
See Pages 11 through 18 for Explanation of Ratios and Data

	Comparative Historical Data			Current Data Sorted By Sales					
Type of Statement					7 (4/1-9/30/02)		51 (10/1/02-3/31/03)		
	4/1/00-3/31/01	4/1/01-3/31/02	4/1/02-3/31/03						
	ALL	ALL	ALL	0-1MM	1-3MM	3-5MM	5-10MM	10-25MM	25MM & OVER
Unqualified	6	3	6		1			1	4
Reviewed	2	4	8		3		2	2	
Compiled	13	13	12	3	5	1	2		1
Tax Returns	10	14	11	3	5	2	1		1
Other	3	13	21	5	7	1	3	2	3
NUMBER OF STATEMENTS	34	47	58	11	21	4	8	5	9
ASSETS	%	%	%	%	%	%	%	%	%
Cash & Equivalents	30.8	35.7	35.0	20.8	36.2				
Trade Receivables (net)	7.0	13.6	11.2	3.4	15.5				
Inventory	.1	.1	.0	.0	.0				
All Other Current	5.4	8.0	9.4	19.4	7.1				
Total Current	43.3	57.4	55.6	43.5	58.9				
Fixed Assets (net)	28.8	21.8	23.3	33.0	22.1				
Intangibles (net)	12.3	8.6	10.1	13.4	7.8				
All Other Non-Current	15.5	12.2	11.0	10.1	11.2				
Total	100.0	100.0	100.0	100.0	100.0				
LIABILITIES									
Notes Payable-Short Term	17.0	10.9	8.4	9.8	4.1				
Cur. Mat.-L/T/D	4.9	2.7	4.3	8.7	3.4				
Trade Payables	8.3	12.8	10.7	5.6	10.4				
Income Taxes Payable	.1	.1	.1	.0	.1				
All Other Current	25.3	21.2	30.3	73.0	26.2				
Total Current	55.5	47.7	53.9	97.1	44.2				
Long Term Debt	22.5	12.8	15.2	29.3	18.1				
Deferred Taxes	.4	.1	.0	.0	.0				
All Other Non-Current	10.0	6.5	4.2	.0	2.6				
Net Worth	11.6	32.9	26.6	−26.5	35.1				
Total Liabilities & Net Worth	100.0	100.0	100.0	100.0	100.0				
INCOME DATA									
Net Sales	100.0	100.0	100.0	100.0	100.0				
Gross Profit									
Operating Expenses	96.3	88.2	86.7	84.8	86.8				
Operating Profit	3.7	11.8	13.3	15.2	13.2				
All Other Expenses (net)	−2.8	−1.0	2.3	12.6	−.2				
Profit Before Taxes	6.5	12.8	11.0	2.6	13.4				
RATIOS									
Current	1.9	3.0	2.9	2.6	3.2				
	.9	1.1	1.3	1.1	1.4				
	.3	.7	.9	.1	.9				
Quick	1.6	2.8	2.4	1.6	3.2				
	.9	1.0	1.1	.9	1.4				
	.3	.6	.7	.1	.9				
Sales/Receivables	0 UND	0 UND	0 UND	0 UND	0 UND				
	0 UND	5 71.6	1 356.1	0 UND	0 UND				
	21 17.0	28 13.0	23 15.8	4 83.1	24 15.2				
Cost of Sales/Inventory									
Cost of Sales/Payables									
Sales/Working Capital	9.6	8.3	9.3	7.6	7.3				
	−44.1	34.3	22.8	46.1	20.4				
	−9.4	−24.1	−33.3	−7.5	−39.5				
EBIT/Interest	(31) 10.0	(38) 35.4	(40) 47.3		(18) 28.5				
	2.5	12.2	16.5		12.0				
	−1.6	3.6	2.3		3.1				
Net Profit + Depr., Dep., Amort./Cur. Mat. L/T/D									
Fixed/Worth	.4	.3	.3	.2	.3				
	1.6	.9	.7	6.0	.7				
	−1.2	9.4	16.1	−.3	NM				
Debt/Worth	1.0	.9	.6	.5	.7				
	4.5	4.9	2.4	15.5	2.2				
	−7.2	46.0	161.2	−1.5	NM				
% Profit Before Taxes/Tangible Net Worth	(23) 93.5	(39) 213.2	(45) 208.6		(16) 237.8				
	16.2	108.6	66.1		54.4				
	−5.6	40.6	18.9		11.3				
% Profit Before Taxes/Total Assets	18.9	42.2	53.3	15.4	50.8				
	3.9	16.3	18.8	4.3	18.6				
	−6.4	3.2	4.2	−5.1	5.3				
Sales/Net Fixed Assets	22.6	34.5	40.0	107.7	47.4				
	12.5	16.5	17.2	12.4	13.3				
	6.6	8.2	9.7	9.7	7.9				
Sales/Total Assets	3.8	4.1	4.1	10.8	4.2				
	2.4	2.6	2.6	2.5	2.6				
	1.4	1.6	1.4	.1	1.8				
% Depr., Dep., Amort./Sales	(31) 1.3	(36) .8	(42) 1.1		(11) .9				
	2.0	1.5	1.9		2.1				
	4.6	2.6	2.8		2.5				
% Officers', Directors', Owners' Comp/Sales	(19) 6.8	(16) 4.4	(28) 7.1		(11) 5.4				
	14.7	12.8	13.0		13.1				
	21.8	27.1	24.0		28.5				
Net Sales ($)	272891M	418955M	1632585M	5047M	37746M	14130M	59348M	86840M	1429474M
Total Assets ($)	139338M	190860M	532624M	9306M	18980M	11264M	33314M	38454M	421306M

© RMA 2003   M = $ thousand   MM = $ million
See Pages 11 through 18 for Explanation of Ratios and Data

Current Data Sorted By Assets

Comparative Historical Data

	0-500M	500M-2MM	2-10MM	10-50MM	50-100MM	100-250MM	Type of Statement	4/1/98-3/31/99 ALL	4/1/99-3/31/00 ALL
	2	3	6	4	3	4	Unqualified	30	17
	1	4	6				Reviewed	14	11
	32	43	27	7		3	Compiled	122	122
	67	13	2	2	1		Tax Returns	67	65
	109	137	113	17	3	3	Other	408	351
	169 (4/1-9/30/02)			443 (10/1/02-3/31/03)					
	211	200	154	30	7	10	**NUMBER OF STATEMENTS**	641	566
	%	%	%	%	%	%	**ASSETS**	%	%
	19.4	9.1	10.0	10.0		6.1	Cash & Equivalents	11.5	11.7
	24.9	43.3	44.3	34.1		39.2	Trade Receivables (net)	37.0	38.4
	2.2	5.9	5.9	2.7		8.5	Inventory	4.0	3.6
	5.3	5.7	7.7	15.2		5.1	All Other Current	6.2	6.9
	51.8	64.0	67.8	62.0		58.9	Total Current	58.8	60.6
	25.1	16.1	15.8	17.4		17.6	Fixed Assets (net)	20.6	19.9
	9.1	9.5	6.1	11.9		11.9	Intangibles (net)	7.7	7.8
	14.0	10.4	10.2	8.7		11.6	All Other Non-Current	12.9	11.7
	100.0	100.0	100.0	100.0		100.0	Total	100.0	100.0
							LIABILITIES		
	30.2	13.1	10.4	14.7		14.2	Notes Payable-Short Term	20.7	15.3
	7.9	3.9	3.3	4.3		5.9	Cur. Mat.-L/T/D	5.9	7.1
	2.9	2.6	3.8	4.8		6.7	Trade Payables	4.1	3.5
	.6	.6	.6	.1		.1	Income Taxes Payable	.3	.4
	25.8	13.7	15.8	12.1		35.4	All Other Current	16.9	16.2
	67.5	33.9	33.9	36.0		62.4	Total Current	47.9	42.5
	23.1	13.2	13.4	13.7		10.2	Long Term Debt	19.0	17.7
	.0	.2	1.0	.4		.2	Deferred Taxes	.6	.5
	8.7	6.7	6.1	6.0		5.5	All Other Non-Current	6.1	5.1
	.7	46.0	45.6	43.9		21.7	Net Worth	26.5	34.2
	100.0	100.0	100.0	100.0		100.0	Total Liabilities & Net Worth	100.0	100.0
							INCOME DATA		
	100.0	100.0	100.0	100.0		100.0	Net Sales	100.0	100.0
							Gross Profit		
	87.7	85.5	86.9	85.3		89.2	Operating Expenses	86.4	85.6
	12.3	14.5	13.1	14.7		10.8	Operating Profit	13.6	14.4
	2.0	1.9	3.4	.7		1.5	All Other Expenses (net)	3.4	1.8
	10.3	12.6	9.7	14.0		9.4	Profit Before Taxes	10.2	12.6
							RATIOS		
	2.3	4.0	3.3	4.7		2.7		3.9	3.6
	1.0	2.2	2.2	2.4		1.5	Current	1.9	1.9
	.4	1.2	1.3	1.0		.7		1.0	1.0
	2.0	3.4	2.7	3.6		2.1		(637) 2.9	2.9
	.9	1.7	1.6	2.1		1.0	Quick	1.6	1.5
	.3	1.0	1.0	.8		.6		.7	.8
	0 UND	38 9.5	43 8.6	29 12.7		42 8.8		23 15.5	27 13.7
	10 36.6	67 5.4	66 5.5	61 6.0		66 5.5	Sales/Receivables	54 6.8	56 6.5
	47 7.8	93 3.9	92 3.9	82 4.4		76 4.8		85 4.3	87 4.2
							Cost of Sales/Inventory		
							Cost of Sales/Payables		
	11.5	4.6	4.4	3.9		5.1		4.6	4.9
	327.9	7.6	7.0	5.7		NM	Sales/Working Capital	9.3	9.6
	-18.3	24.7	14.3	76.8		-12.3		-276.6	233.7
	(163) 20.6	(169) 40.5	(132) 40.1	(27) 32.6				(552) 18.5	(485) 24.6
	4.4	10.2	9.0	11.6			EBIT/Interest	5.0	6.0
	.8	2.5	1.9	3.7				1.7	1.4
		(12) 9.1	(19) 4.7					(44) 4.4	(38) 7.5
		2.6	1.4				Net Profit + Depr., Dep., Amort./Cur. Mat. L/T/D	1.4	2.3
		.7	.8					.7	.7
	.2	.1	.1	.2		.2		.2	.2
	1.2	.3	.3	.5		.7	Fixed/Worth	.4	.4
	-1.3	.9	1.0	1.2		NM		2.5	2.0
	.9	.4	.5	.6		.9		.6	.5
	7.4	1.3	1.3	1.4		2.7	Debt/Worth	1.4	1.2
	-4.4	4.1	4.7	24.3		NM		11.4	6.7
	(131) 252.9	(171) 115.8	(137) 91.0	(26) 115.8			% Profit Before Taxes/Tangible Net Worth	(511) 115.0	(458) 112.5
	91.2	30.3	27.9	76.9				33.3	37.5
	12.3	6.3	5.1	42.2				7.6	7.6
	59.8	44.5	38.5	58.3		44.3	% Profit Before Taxes/Total Assets	50.5	55.5
	17.9	13.4	9.0	21.6		13.4		12.7	14.1
	.0	2.3	1.7	2.6		2.5		1.8	1.6
	130.9	49.4	36.2	23.1		27.8	Sales/Net Fixed Assets	36.5	36.4
	30.5	26.7	21.4	14.2		20.5		20.0	20.7
	15.7	14.5	13.9	10.6		9.2		12.2	12.1
	9.2	3.3	3.0	2.7		3.5	Sales/Total Assets	3.8	4.0
	4.7	2.5	2.4	1.9		2.2		2.6	2.7
	3.0	1.7	1.8	1.5		1.6		1.9	1.9
	(120) 1.2	(147) 1.1	(122) 1.3	(24) 2.2			% Depr., Dep., Amort./Sales	(484) 1.3	(434) 1.4
	1.9	1.8	1.9	2.5				2.0	2.1
	2.8	2.7	2.7	3.2				2.9	2.9
	(131) 16.9	(103) 15.8	(71) 9.6	(10) 12.6			% Officers', Directors', Owners' Comp/Sales	(314) 16.9	(295) 15.4
	27.0	23.5	23.3	25.7				25.9	25.8
	33.4	33.1	30.2	31.7				34.5	33.7
	236915M	668422M	1780502M	4490461M	1568296M	4448053M	Net Sales ($)	10080551M	10211485M
	43479M	204617M	623124M	656275M	525291M	1561260M	Total Assets ($)	3107669M	3039839M

M = $ thousand   MM = $ million
See Pages 11 through 18 for Explanation of Ratios and Data

Comparative Historical Data				Current Data Sorted By Sales					
			Type of Statement						
16	20	22	Unqualified	2	3	1	1	3	12
14	12	11	Reviewed	3	2	1	2	3	
101	111	112	Compiled	20	38	14	23	7	10
74	91	85	Tax Returns	54	19	7	1	1	3
340	352	382	Other	86	112	54	64	48	18
4/1/00-	4/1/01-	4/1/02-			169 (4/1-9/30/02)			443 (10/1/02-3/31/03)	
3/31/01	3/31/02	3/31/03		0-1MM	1-3MM	3-5MM	5-10MM	10-25MM	25MM & OVER
ALL	ALL	ALL							
545	586	612	**NUMBER OF STATEMENTS**	165	174	77	91	62	43
%	%	%	**ASSETS**	%	%	%	%	%	%
12.1	13.0	13.1	Cash & Equivalents	15.0	12.9	14.2	8.6	11.8	16.3
39.6	36.8	36.4	Trade Receivables (net)	24.4	38.4	42.5	45.1	45.1	32.9
3.7	3.9	4.5	Inventory	2.2	5.2	5.1	5.2	6.9	4.1
6.8	5.5	6.7	All Other Current	6.2	5.4	5.0	8.7	7.4	11.6
62.2	59.2	60.7	Total Current	47.8	61.9	66.9	67.6	71.0	64.8
18.8	20.7	19.2	Fixed Assets (net)	27.2	15.2	17.7	17.3	14.6	17.4
8.4	8.6	8.6	Intangibles (net)	11.7	10.0	4.9	4.8	6.5	9.1
10.7	11.5	11.5	All Other Non-Current	13.3	12.9	10.4	10.2	7.9	8.6
100.0	100.0	100.0	Total	100.0	100.0	100.0	100.0	100.0	100.0
			LIABILITIES						
18.0	24.9	18.3	Notes Payable-Short Term	27.1	18.4	15.7	12.3	10.8	12.1
5.0	4.4	5.2	Cur. Mat.-L/T/D	8.0	4.9	3.1	3.3	2.9	6.0
3.5	4.1	3.2	Trade Payables	3.1	2.4	3.4	2.9	4.2	5.6
.2	.3	.6	Income Taxes Payable	.2	.7	1.0	.8	.7	.1
18.6	20.8	19.2	All Other Current	24.0	14.6	18.2	16.7	18.8	26.6
45.2	54.5	46.4	Total Current	62.3	41.1	41.4	36.0	37.4	50.4
16.8	19.1	16.5	Long Term Debt	26.8	14.8	17.3	8.6	8.9	10.3
1.0	.6	.4	Deferred Taxes	.0	.2	.8	1.2	.2	.1
5.3	6.5	7.2	All Other Non-Current	10.0	7.1	3.8	5.9	8.1	4.2
31.6	19.3	29.6	Net Worth	.9	36.8	36.7	48.3	45.4	35.0
100.0	100.0	100.0	Total Liabilities & Net Worth	100.0	100.0	100.0	100.0	100.0	100.0
			INCOME DATA						
100.0	100.0	100.0	Net Sales	100.0	100.0	100.0	100.0	100.0	100.0
			Gross Profit						
86.8	86.3	86.7	Operating Expenses	82.8	88.5	89.4	88.0	85.9	88.0
13.2	13.7	13.3	Operating Profit	17.2	11.5	10.6	12.0	14.1	12.0
1.7	2.2	2.2	All Other Expenses (net)	3.7	2.1	1.4	1.6	1.6	.8
11.5	11.5	11.1	Profit Before Taxes	13.5	9.4	9.2	10.4	12.5	11.2
			RATIOS						
3.7	3.4	3.3		2.4	3.7	3.4	3.7	4.0	3.1
1.8	1.8	1.7	Current	1.1	1.8	2.1	2.2	2.4	1.9
1.0	.9	1.0		.5	1.0	1.2	1.4	1.3	.9
2.9	2.8	2.8		2.0	3.0	2.8	2.9	3.6	2.8
1.5	1.4	1.4	Quick	.9	1.4	1.7	1.6	1.7	1.3
.8	.8	.7		.3	.8	1.0	1.2	1.0	.6
28 13.1	8 45.6	18 20.1		0 UND	25 14.5	30 12.4	43 8.5	37 9.9	27 13.7
56 6.5	51 7.1	50 7.3	Sales/Receivables	26 14.2	52 7.0	59 6.2	63 5.8	63 5.8	45 8.1
82 4.4	80 4.6	80 4.6		55 6.6	85 4.3	89 4.1	94 3.9	81 4.5	78 4.7
			Cost of Sales/Inventory						
			Cost of Sales/Payables						
5.1	5.5	5.3		9.5	5.4	5.0	4.4	4.1	5.0
9.6	11.8	10.9	Sales/Working Capital	133.2	10.7	7.4	7.0	6.9	9.1
172.3	-115.5	-172.1		-14.9	UND	32.4	14.7	16.4	-241.9
	21.3		21.1		29.0		25.5		20.9		30.1		52.4		60.9		28.1
(476) 5.6	(503) 5.0	(507) 7.2	EBIT/Interest	(120) 7.3	(151) 5.0	(68) 6.5	(76) 10.8	(55) 13.4	(37) 8.5
1.5	1.5	1.8		1.9	1.1	1.6	1.7	2.4	2.6
4.9	2.3	4.7			7.1		4.7		
(32) 1.5	(43) 1.3	(42) 1.8	Net Profit + Depr., Dep., Amort./Cur. Mat. L/T/D		(13) 1.9		(10) 1.7		
.8	.5	.8			.7		.8		
.2	.1	.1		.2	.1	.2	.1	.2	.2
.4	.5	.4	Fixed/Worth	1.5	.3	.3	.3	.3	.5
2.1	5.0	4.3		-2.5	4.6	1.7	.9	.8	3.2
.5	.6	.6		1.0	.4	.6	.4	.5	.6
1.6	1.6	1.7	Debt/Worth	7.9	1.5	1.4	.9	1.3	2.0
9.0	24.1	37.3		-4.4	17.3	4.2	4.1	3.3	18.8
115.3	131.9	121.4		306.9	111.3	104.6	93.4	109.9	116.7
(446) 39.9	(458) 40.5	(478) 42.9	% Profit Before Taxes/Tangible Net Worth	(103) 95.1	(136) 26.3	(64) 29.4	(84) 24.7	(56) 36.3	(35) 78.6
7.5	8.9	6.8		20.0	2.9	8.2	2.9	12.7	33.6
55.5	53.5	49.7		62.4	36.0	43.5	49.6	53.4	54.9
12.2	13.5	13.0	% Profit Before Taxes/Total Assets	21.2	9.8	10.0	9.7	18.4	23.5
1.4	1.8	1.3		2.2	.7	1.5	.5	2.6	1.9
41.3	49.2	49.6		91.0	71.0	52.1	38.4	32.7	42.1
22.2	23.4	24.6	Sales/Net Fixed Assets	23.0	28.8	28.7	24.3	20.6	20.7
13.4	12.1	14.1		9.3	16.2	18.5	13.8	16.9	11.4
4.1	4.7	4.2		6.7	4.0	4.2	3.4	3.3	3.8
2.8	2.9	2.8	Sales/Total Assets	3.3	2.7	3.0	2.6	2.7	2.2
2.0	2.1	1.9		1.6	1.9	2.1	2.0	2.2	1.8
1.2	1.1	1.2		1.3	1.1	1.1	1.3	1.4	.8
(396) 1.9	(430) 1.8	(424) 1.9	% Depr., Dep., Amort./Sales	(97) 2.4	(117) 1.8	(60) 1.6	(70) 1.9	(50) 2.0	(30) 2.3
2.7	2.6	2.8		4.8	2.6	2.4	2.4	2.6	2.9
17.1	14.8	14.8		13.9	16.4	19.6	16.1	8.6	2.6
(285) 25.3	(320) 25.0	(322) 24.4	% Officers', Directors', Owners' Comp/Sales	(91) 21.8	(97) 25.7	(45) 27.6	(45) 26.0	(29) 25.2	(15) 21.4
32.9	32.3	32.9		32.0	34.0	33.4	34.8	31.1	30.7
10553101M	6769069M	13192649M	Net Sales ($)	90893M	313758M	308580M	650344M	931907M	10897167M
2802408M	2956309M	3614046M	Total Assets ($)	61609M	151903M	108089M	303752M	348816M	2639877M

M = $ thousand   MM = $ million
See Pages 11 through 18 for Explanation of Ratios and Data

Current Data Sorted By Assets   Comparative Historical Data

						Type of Statement		
1	3	7	16	3	4	Unqualified	41	31
3	15	45	11			Reviewed	85	65
17	40	25	2			Compiled	86	72
38	8	2		1	2	Tax Returns	40	32
18	44	39	10	3	1	Other	89	96
	40 (4/1-9/30/02)			318 (10/1/02-3/31/03)			4/1/98-3/31/99	4/1/99-3/31/00
0-500M	500M-2MM	2-10MM	10-50MM	50-100MM	100-250MM		ALL	ALL
77	110	118	39	7	7	NUMBER OF STATEMENTS	341	296
%	%	%	%	%	%	ASSETS	%	%
21.9	6.3	6.4	9.6			Cash & Equivalents	10.9	10.6
21.0	56.4	61.8	50.2			Trade Receivables (net)	46.8	47.8
.1	2.9	1.9	.9			Inventory	1.6	1.9
1.6	4.5	8.5	15.1			All Other Current	5.5	7.0
44.7	70.1	78.6	75.9			Total Current	64.8	67.2
37.0	18.3	13.2	14.6			Fixed Assets (net)	23.4	22.3
3.4	2.5	.9	1.3			Intangibles (net)	2.9	2.2
14.9	9.1	7.3	8.2			All Other Non-Current	8.8	8.3
100.0	100.0	100.0	100.0			Total	100.0	100.0
						LIABILITIES		
49.4	11.4	9.1	10.3			Notes Payable-Short Term	15.2	18.0
5.5	4.1	3.0	1.9			Cur. Mat.-L/T/D	3.6	3.5
8.4	20.3	22.2	15.2			Trade Payables	14.2	15.6
.6	1.1	2.8	2.8			Income Taxes Payable	1.0	1.1
37.4	11.3	17.1	19.9			All Other Current	18.7	18.3
101.2	48.3	54.2	50.1			Total Current	52.7	56.5
22.0	13.8	5.3	7.7			Long Term Debt	11.4	13.8
.2	1.8	3.0	2.3			Deferred Taxes	3.2	2.2
5.4	3.5	3.4	3.8			All Other Non-Current	3.8	3.9
-28.8	32.7	34.1	36.2			Net Worth	28.9	23.6
100.0	100.0	100.0	100.0			Total Liabilities & Net Worth	100.0	100.0
						INCOME DATA		
100.0	100.0	100.0	100.0			Net Sales	100.0	100.0
						Gross Profit		
96.9	97.1	97.2	96.1			Operating Expenses	93.8	94.4
3.1	2.9	2.8	3.9			Operating Profit	6.2	5.6
.3	2.0	.9	1.0			All Other Expenses (net)	1.2	1.2
2.8	.9	1.9	2.9			Profit Before Taxes	5.0	4.4
						RATIOS		
1.8	2.9	2.0	2.5			Current	2.3	2.0
.6	1.5	1.5	1.4				1.4	1.4
.2	1.0	1.2	1.1				1.0	1.0
1.7	2.4	1.7	1.8			Quick	(340) 2.0	1.9
.6	1.3	1.3	1.1				1.3	1.2
.1	.9	1.0	.9				.8	.8
0 UND	44 8.3	72 5.1	63 5.8			Sales/Receivables	28 13.1	33 10.9
0 UND	67 5.4	90 4.0	85 4.3				69 5.3	73 5.0
49 7.5	103 3.5	114 3.2	98 3.7				102 3.6	104 3.5
						Cost of Sales/Inventory		
						Cost of Sales/Payables		
21.4	5.4	5.3	6.1			Sales/Working Capital	6.7	7.0
-46.3	13.9	9.6	10.9				14.0	14.9
-15.0	NM	20.9	32.0				UND	-184.5
(62) 22.0	(84) 7.5	(99) 21.9	(34) 22.1			EBIT/Interest	(275) 16.0	(252) 16.6
3.5	2.3	6.0	6.1				4.7	5.6
-2.7	-2.5	1.2	2.1				1.2	1.6
	(24) 3.4	(38) 4.8	(19) 6.2			Net Profit + Depr., Dep., Amort./Cur. Mat. L /T/D	(81) 5.1	(70) 6.3
	2.0	1.5	3.2				2.7	2.7
	.0	.1	.8				1.2	1.4
.4	.2	.2	.2			Fixed/Worth	.3	.2
10.0	.4	.4	.3				.6	.5
-.8	1.9	.7	.9				1.9	1.6
1.0	.7	1.1	1.2			Debt/Worth	.9	1.0
17.9	1.7	1.9	2.1				2.1	2.2
-3.0	9.6	3.6	4.0				6.9	6.6
(42) 133.8	(93) 44.1	(110) 37.0	33.0			% Profit Before Taxes/Tangible Net Worth	(291) 72.6	(264) 63.7
58.8	9.3	11.6	18.2				31.0	28.9
-17.5	-8.7	1.1	6.4				7.2	9.0
50.2	14.1	11.7	12.1			% Profit Before Taxes/Total Assets	26.7	22.3
5.1	2.3	3.5	5.4				9.0	8.0
-20.2	-9.2	-.1	1.8				1.1	.9
69.5	46.9	37.1	32.7			Sales/Net Fixed Assets	36.2	31.9
27.2	25.9	25.6	19.9				21.9	20.0
17.3	13.0	14.8	10.5				13.3	13.0
17.1	3.8	3.0	2.6			Sales/Total Assets	4.3	4.0
7.2	2.8	2.5	2.2				2.9	2.7
3.6	2.1	2.0	1.7				2.1	2.1
(58) .8	(91) .9	(105) 1.0	(36) 1.2			% Depr., Dep., Amort./Sales	(298) 1.0	(262) 1.1
1.4	1.4	1.5	1.8				1.6	1.7
2.5	2.5	2.1	2.3				2.4	2.4
(48) 9.7	(48) 5.7	(33) 4.0				% Officers', Directors', Owners' Comp/Sales	(124) 6.5	(110) 5.9
15.5	9.6	9.7					11.8	12.2
28.1	13.2	19.3					20.4	21.5
127611M	376299M	1411630M	1604045M	1936822M	6611196M	Net Sales ($)	4177098M	4866897M
15920M	124111M	564559M	689315M	483996M	1147504M	Total Assets ($)	1726258M	1814324M

© RMA 2003

M = $ thousand   MM = $ million

See Pages 11 through 18 for Explanation of Ratios and Data

Comparative Historical Data | Current Data Sorted By Sales

			Type of Statement						
22	21	34	Unqualified	1	3		2	6	22
64	59	74	Reviewed		9	6	16	35	8
100	79	84	Compiled	10	22	14	26	10	2
34	37	51	Tax Returns	19	21	3	4	1	3
90	97	115	Other	12	34	16	21	21	11
4/1/00-3/31/01 ALL	4/1/01-3/31/02 ALL	4/1/02-3/31/03 ALL		40 (4/1-9/30/02)			318 (10/1/02-3/31/03)		
				0-1MM	1-3MM	3-5MM	5-10MM	10-25MM	25MM & OVER
310	293	358	**NUMBER OF STATEMENTS**	42	89	39	69	73	46
%	%	%	**ASSETS**	%	%	%	%	%	%
10.1	10.5	10.3	Cash & Equivalents	16.3	13.5	7.2	7.7	7.1	10.7
50.7	51.0	49.2	Trade Receivables (net)	27.0	41.2	54.5	59.0	60.7	47.2
1.8	2.0	1.7	Inventory	.6	1.3	4.7	2.1	1.2	1.0
6.6	6.5	6.5	All Other Current	1.1	3.5	6.9	6.3	9.7	11.9
69.2	70.0	67.7	Total Current	45.0	59.5	73.3	75.0	78.7	70.9
19.7	19.3	20.1	Fixed Assets (net)	31.9	28.5	17.3	13.8	13.7	15.4
1.8	1.7	2.2	Intangibles (net)	6.2	2.4	.1	1.7	.8	2.7
9.3	9.1	10.0	All Other Non-Current	16.8	9.6	9.4	9.5	6.8	11.0
100.0	100.0	100.0	Total	100.0	100.0	100.0	100.0	100.0	100.0
			LIABILITIES						
15.3	17.3	19.0	Notes Payable-Short Term	48.3	27.9	11.5	8.9	9.9	10.7
4.3	3.8	3.9	Cur. Mat.-L/T/D	4.2	5.4	4.7	2.9	2.3	3.9
15.4	16.0	17.4	Trade Payables	9.6	16.9	18.2	23.6	18.5	14.0
1.4	1.3	1.8	Income Taxes Payable	.3	.6	1.6	1.7	3.5	3.2
18.0	17.4	20.3	All Other Current	29.0	20.7	14.4	14.9	20.8	23.7
54.4	55.8	62.4	Total Current	91.4	71.6	50.3	52.1	55.0	55.5
10.3	12.2	11.8	Long Term Debt	37.8	11.6	7.9	8.1	5.9	7.0
1.9	3.0	1.8	Deferred Taxes	.3	.8	3.4	1.7	3.0	2.0
2.9	3.5	4.1	All Other Non-Current	1.6	7.7	2.5	2.0	3.7	4.1
30.5	25.5	19.9	Net Worth	−31.2	8.3	35.9	36.1	32.3	31.4
100.0	100.0	100.0	Total Liabilities & Net Worth	100.0	100.0	100.0	100.0	100.0	100.0
			INCOME DATA						
100.0	100.0	100.0	Net Sales	100.0	100.0	100.0	100.0	100.0	100.0
			Gross Profit						
94.3	94.7	97.0	Operating Expenses	91.8	98.3	99.5	96.7	97.7	96.0
5.7	5.3	3.0	Operating Profit	8.2	1.7	.5	3.3	2.3	3.9
1.2	1.3	1.1	All Other Expenses (net)	3.4	.8	.9	.9	.6	.7
4.6	4.0	2.0	Profit Before Taxes	4.8	.9	−.5	2.4	1.7	3.2
			RATIOS						
2.2	2.2	2.1		1.9	2.1	2.8	2.5	1.9	1.9
1.4	1.4	1.4	Current	.8	1.2	1.5	1.5	1.5	1.2
1.0	1.0	1.0		.3	.5	1.1	1.1	1.2	1.1
2.0	1.9	1.8		1.9	1.9	1.8	2.0	1.7	1.7
1.2	(292) 1.3	1.2	Quick	.8	1.1	1.2	1.4	1.2	1.1
.8	.9	.8		.4	.4	.9	1.0	1.0	.9
39 9.3	46 7.9	39 9.2		0 UND	0 UND	43 8.5	58 6.3	64 5.7	56 6.5
75 4.9	70 5.2	72 5.1	Sales/Receivables	25 14.9	56 6.5	73 5.0	82 4.4	86 4.2	75 4.9
106 3.4	100 3.6	103 3.6		69 5.3	99 3.7	111 3.3	107 3.4	110 3.3	93 3.9
			Cost of Sales/Inventory						
			Cost of Sales/Payables						
6.3	6.9	6.6		9.1	6.6	6.4	5.4	6.1	8.8
13.9	16.2	14.4	Sales/Working Capital	−126.1	28.8	9.5	10.7	10.2	17.6
UND	510.5	−527.3		−6.1	−26.1	72.8	49.4	29.4	32.1
20.2	25.5	17.3		15.0	14.5	17.3	16.9	21.9	20.0
(270) 5.6	(257) 6.0	(291) 4.0	EBIT/Interest	(32) 2.6	(74) 3.3	(33) 1.0	(51) 4.7	(63) 4.2	(38) 9.4
1.1	1.3	−.7		−.3	−4.5	−8.2	.8	−.9	2.7
9.8	5.1	3.9			2.5	4.8	8.6		5.3
(65) 2.7	(65) 2.1	(89) 1.8	Net Profit + Depr., Dep., Amort./Cur. Mat. L/T/D		(15) .2	(21) 2.6	(24) 1.7	(20) 3.2	
1.0	.6	.2			−.9	1.4	−.4		1.0
.2	.2	.2		.3	.2	.2	.1	.2	.3
.5	.5	.5	Fixed/Worth	2.1	.7	.3	.3	.4	.4
1.2	1.3	1.8		−.5	−2.7	1.3	.8	.8	.9
.8	1.0	1.0		.9	.8	.5	.7	1.2	1.4
2.3	2.2	2.1	Debt/Worth	11.8	2.1	2.0	1.7	2.3	2.2
6.0	7.0	9.9		−2.6	−10.3	4.8	4.2	5.0	4.0
57.0	61.1	46.0		76.0	97.9	35.8	44.1	27.7	55.1
(276) 27.3	(251) 25.6	(295) 14.9	% Profit Before Taxes/Tangible Net Worth	(24) 27.5	(62) 16.4	(33) 6.0	(61) 16.4	(72) 10.2	(43) 26.6
5.8	3.5	−1.4		−3.3	−1.7	−30.1	−.2	−10.0	6.6
21.9	23.2	15.7		33.1	24.7	11.4	14.4	7.5	19.5
7.9	7.7	3.5	% Profit Before Taxes/Total Assets	5.9	3.3	.0	4.6	2.8	7.5
.4	.6	−4.6		−6.3	−17.4	−12.4	−.7	−3.5	1.8
36.5	42.5	44.7		76.2	47.9	44.4	48.5	38.9	34.5
23.1	22.6	25.0	Sales/Net Fixed Assets	23.6	22.7	23.4	28.0	26.3	20.1
13.6	14.0	13.7		7.5	14.0	12.0	15.8	17.5	10.8
3.9	3.8	4.0		7.1	7.3	4.1	3.5	3.1	3.1
2.8	2.9	2.7	Sales/Total Assets	3.0	3.5	2.7	2.8	2.5	2.6
2.1	2.1	2.1		1.7	2.4	2.0	2.3	2.0	2.2
.9	.9	.9		.3	1.0	1.1	.9	1.0	1.0
(270) 1.5	(250) 1.5	(297) 1.5	% Depr., Dep., Amort./Sales	(31) 1.1	(67) 1.7	(36) 1.4	(60) 1.4	(65) 1.4	(38) 1.7
2.2	2.2	2.2		2.7	2.7	2.2	2.1	2.0	2.1
6.4	4.9	6.6		8.0	8.4	5.9	4.3	3.8	14.5
(135) 11.2	(118) 10.6	(142) 11.1	% Officers', Directors', Owners' Comp/Sales	(24) 12.1	(45) 12.4	(14) 8.9	(24) 10.1	(25) 9.0	(10) 21.4
17.9	18.3	19.7		28.1	19.8	11.7	18.4	16.7	24.2
3751432M	7786079M	12067603M	Net Sales ($)	23965M	182094M	155063M	486950M	1170121M	10049410M
1668038M	2153484M	3025405M	Total Assets ($)	12666M	58117M	61108M	179275M	489103M	2225136M

© RMA 2003

M = $ thousand   MM = $ million
See Pages 11 through 18 for Explanation of Ratios and Data

Current Data Sorted By Assets　　　　　　　　　　　　Comparative Historical Data

						Type of Statement		
1	2 18	2 33	2 3		2	Unqualified	13	13
13	22	5			1	Reviewed	55	46
31	16	1				Compiled	84	56
20	17	17	1	1	1	Tax Returns	39	32
						Other	52	34
	26 (4/1-9/30/02)		183 (10/1/02-3/31/03)				4/1/98-3/31/99	4/1/99-3/31/00
0-500M	500M-2MM	2-10MM	10-50MM	50-100MM	100-250MM		ALL	ALL
65	75	58	6	1	4	NUMBER OF STATEMENTS	243	181
%	%	%	%	%	%	ASSETS	%	%
15.8	8.0	8.5				Cash & Equivalents	12.1	11.6
20.2	33.4	41.4				Trade Receivables (net)	26.3	26.8
5.6	10.6	6.7				Inventory	10.1	9.3
5.5	3.5	5.1				All Other Current	2.7	2.9
47.1	55.5	61.7				Total Current	51.3	50.5
46.7	37.2	28.9				Fixed Assets (net)	40.6	41.3
.6	1.7	3.4				Intangibles (net)	2.4	2.4
5.6	5.6	6.0				All Other Non-Current	5.8	5.8
100.0	100.0	100.0				Total	100.0	100.0
						LIABILITIES		
19.2	10.5	9.2				Notes Payable-Short Term	12.4	9.5
6.2	6.6	6.2				Cur. Mat.-L/T/D	6.1	7.2
10.9	11.6	11.7				Trade Payables	11.0	10.8
.4	.8	2.0				Income Taxes Payable	.6	1.0
8.4	6.8	10.2				All Other Current	9.8	12.3
45.0	36.4	39.2				Total Current	39.8	40.7
31.9	22.4	14.4				Long Term Debt	23.9	25.0
.3	.5	2.0				Deferred Taxes	.9	1.5
7.1	2.9	3.9				All Other Non-Current	4.7	3.1
15.6	37.9	40.5				Net Worth	30.7	29.6
100.0	100.0	100.0				Total Liabilities & Net Worth	100.0	100.0
						INCOME DATA		
100.0	100.0	100.0				Net Sales	100.0	100.0
						Gross Profit		
94.7	96.1	94.9				Operating Expenses	95.1	95.8
5.3	3.9	5.1				Operating Profit	4.9	4.2
1.6	1.2	1.0				All Other Expenses (net)	.1	.7
3.7	2.7	4.1				Profit Before Taxes	4.8	3.5
						RATIOS		
3.1	2.3	2.4					2.7	2.1
1.2	1.5	1.7				Current	1.5	1.4
.6	1.0	1.1					.9	1.0
(64) 2.5	1.9	2.0					(242) 2.0	1.6
.9	1.1	1.3				Quick	1.1	1.0
.2	.6	.9					.5	.6
0 UND	23 15.8	42 8.7					9 41.6	11 34.2
8 48.1	43 8.5	57 6.4				Sales/Receivables	31 11.9	31 11.8
31 11.8	65 5.6	81 4.5					58 6.3	57 6.4
						Cost of Sales/Inventory		
						Cost of Sales/Payables		
15.7	7.4	6.3					8.4	9.9
60.9	18.0	11.1				Sales/Working Capital	19.9	22.6
-17.6	999.8	72.7					-113.5	-321.7
6.7	11.1	16.0					9.2	7.3
(53) 2.7	(70) 3.1	(52) 4.9				EBIT/Interest	(224) 3.6	(170) 3.5
1.0	1.1	1.5					1.5	1.3
	3.3	5.0				Net Profit + Depr., Dep.,	3.2	3.6
(17)	1.5	(23) 2.5				Amort./Cur. Mat. L./T/D	(64) 2.0	(58) 2.3
	.8	1.1					1.2	1.3
.7	.5	.4					.5	.6
1.9	.9	.6				Fixed/Worth	1.0	1.3
UND	2.2	1.4					3.2	3.2
.7	.8	.8					.8	1.0
3.6	1.7	1.7				Debt/Worth	1.7	2.0
UND	3.7	3.1					7.4	5.3
141.9	54.7	47.6				% Profit Before Taxes/Tangible	61.7	55.3
(49) 31.9	(71) 14.1	(55) 19.9				Net Worth	(211) 29.4	(157) 23.8
10.8	1.2	3.4					8.5	7.2
37.0	17.8	16.9				% Profit Before Taxes/Total	23.4	18.7
11.4	4.8	7.2				Assets	8.9	7.3
-.5	.0	1.2					1.8	1.1
19.6	15.1	18.3					14.4	14.9
9.9	8.1	8.7				Sales/Net Fixed Assets	8.2	7.9
5.7	5.2	6.0					5.0	4.2
6.3	3.7	3.0					4.1	4.0
4.0	2.9	2.6				Sales/Total Assets	2.9	2.8
2.8	2.1	1.9					2.0	2.0
2.5	2.1	1.6					2.3	1.9
(50) 3.7	(68) 3.6	(53) 3.0				% Depr., Dep., Amort./Sales	(214) 3.3	(164) 3.4
5.9	5.6	4.8					5.4	4.8
5.7	2.7	2.0				% Officers', Directors',	2.9	2.5
(39) 10.3	(44) 4.8	(21) 3.0				Owners' Comp/Sales	(124) 5.2	(97) 4.8
16.6	8.4	5.3					8.8	7.8
69585M	243985M	548767M	155591M	316441M	1455981M	Net Sales ($)	1910129M	1706668M
16179M	83996M	230509M	90113M	59972M	662164M	Total Assets ($)	637935M	674841M

M = $ thousand   MM = $ million
See Pages 11 through 18 for Explanation of Ratios and Data

Comparative Historical Data | Current Data Sorted By Sales

			Type of Statement						
10	5	8	Unqualified		1	1	2	1	3
50	39	55	Reviewed	1	9	7	18	17	3
59	50	41	Compiled	8	19	6	6	1	1
38	27	48	Tax Returns	19	22	4	2	1	
40	41	57	Other	10	21	10	8	6	2
4/1/00-3/31/01 ALL	4/1/01-3/31/02 ALL	4/1/02-3/31/03 ALL		26 (4/1-9/30/02) 0-1MM	1-3MM	3-5MM	183 (10/1/02-3/31/03) 5-10MM	10-25MM	25MM & OVER
197	162	209	NUMBER OF STATEMENTS	38	72	28	36	26	9
%	%	%	**ASSETS**	%	%	%	%	%	%
10.0	9.0	10.3	Cash & Equivalents	17.9	10.3	4.3	10.0	8.6	
28.6	30.1	31.1	Trade Receivables (net)	13.5	27.7	38.1	39.5	48.6	
9.8	9.1	8.2	Inventory	10.2	7.0	8.2	9.0	6.1	
4.5	4.0	4.6	All Other Current	4.8	4.5	5.7	4.7	3.6	
52.9	52.3	54.1	Total Current	46.4	49.4	56.2	63.2	66.9	
39.3	39.4	38.2	Fixed Assets (net)	49.7	42.3	33.3	29.5	25.6	
1.9	2.4	2.1	Intangibles (net)	.2	1.4	3.1	1.5	4.3	
5.9	5.9	5.6	All Other Non-Current	3.8	6.9	7.3	5.8	3.3	
100.0	100.0	100.0	Total	100.0	100.0	100.0	100.0	100.0	
			LIABILITIES						
10.5	14.3	12.9	Notes Payable-Short Term	18.0	13.0	15.3	7.6	10.3	
7.5	5.7	6.2	Cur. Mat.-L/T/D	2.4	8.9	5.8	6.6	5.6	
9.8	10.8	11.4	Trade Payables	11.0	10.7	11.3	10.1	15.8	
.5	.5	1.0	Income Taxes Payable	.0	.9	1.0	2.8	.4	
11.5	12.7	8.5	All Other Current	9.4	5.8	8.1	8.8	13.0	
39.8	44.0	40.1	Total Current	40.8	39.3	41.5	36.0	45.1	
23.5	24.2	22.9	Long Term Debt	35.5	27.6	18.0	14.3	10.8	
1.4	1.7	1.0	Deferred Taxes	.0	.4	.4	2.1	2.6	
2.7	3.6	4.7	All Other Non-Current	4.7	6.8	1.3	1.6	5.5	
32.5	26.5	31.3	Net Worth	19.1	25.9	38.8	45.9	36.0	
100.0	100.0	100.0	Total Liabilities & Net Worth	100.0	100.0	100.0	100.0	100.0	
			INCOME DATA						
100.0	100.0	100.0	Net Sales	100.0	100.0	100.0	100.0	100.0	
			Gross Profit						
94.5	94.6	95.4	Operating Expenses	92.7	96.6	95.2	94.7	96.7	
5.5	5.4	4.6	Operating Profit	7.3	3.4	4.8	5.3	3.3	
.9	1.5	1.2	All Other Expenses (net)	2.7	1.1	1.8	.6	.2	
4.6	3.9	3.4	Profit Before Taxes	4.6	2.3	3.0	4.7	3.1	
			RATIOS						
2.1	2.3	2.4		2.8	2.9	2.2	2.5	2.2	
1.4	1.3	1.5	Current	1.4	1.3	1.5	2.1	1.6	
.9	.9	1.0		.6	.8	1.0	1.3	1.0	
1.8	1.7	2.0		2.2	1.9	2.2	2.0	1.8	
1.0 (161)	.9 (208)	1.1	Quick	(37) .6	1.0	.9	1.6	1.3	
.5	.5	.6		.2	.5	.6	1.0	.8	
14 25.5	12 31.4	10 35.9		0 UND	8 48.0	33 11.2	29 12.8	42 8.7	
40 9.2	40 9.2	39 9.3	Sales/Receivables	5 76.2	29 12.7	56 6.5	43 8.5	56 6.5	
61 6.0	63 5.8	64 5.7		28 13.2	64 5.7	69 5.3	77 4.7	70 5.2	
			Cost of Sales/Inventory						
			Cost of Sales/Payables						
8.7	8.5	7.9		10.7	9.6	8.3	6.2	7.8	
19.2	20.2	20.4	Sales/Working Capital	42.2	28.8	17.5	11.0	13.7	
-86.0	-58.8	-472.0		-15.3	-55.4	NM	19.3	NM	
8.1	8.4	9.6		8.3	8.2	11.0	22.3	16.0	
(185) 3.8	(149) 3.1	(185) 3.2	EBIT/Interest	(31) 2.7	(64) 2.5	(25) 2.0	(33) 7.1	(24) 5.9	
1.6	1.2	1.2		1.5	.9	.7	2.0	1.8	
5.2	4.5	3.5			3.2		4.0	5.0	
(54) 2.4	(37) 1.9	(46) 2.1	Net Profit + Depr., Dep., Amort./Cur. Mat. L/T/D		(14) 1.5		(12) 2.9	(11) 3.1	
1.6	1.2	1.0			.9		1.1	1.5	
.5	.6	.5		.6	.7	.2	.4	.4	
1.1	1.1	1.0	Fixed/Worth	1.7	1.3	.8	.6	.6	
2.3	3.3	3.1		NM	4.7	2.4	1.0	1.5	
1.0	1.0	.8		.8	.8	.7	.7	.9	
1.9	2.1	2.0	Debt/Worth	3.6	2.4	2.3	1.2	2.0	
4.4	4.9	5.3		-15.5	7.0	5.5	2.1	3.5	
63.9	52.1	60.0		109.9	70.7	45.2	58.5	39.4	
(179) 25.3	(140) 22.8	(185) 19.9	% Profit Before Taxes/Tangible Net Worth	(28) 16.9	(64) 19.3	(26) 18.9	22.5	(23) 19.6	
7.1	5.1	2.9		.5	.9	-2.3	4.1	8.1	
20.3	17.6	18.8		25.5	18.3	15.4	27.2	10.5	
8.1	7.3	6.7	% Profit Before Taxes/Total Assets	6.3	7.2	5.0	10.8	7.1	
2.5	1.0	.5		-.3	-.3	-2.0	1.4	1.4	
16.0	14.6	16.1		16.3	15.7	17.7	18.5	21.5	
7.9	7.9	8.5	Sales/Net Fixed Assets	5.8	8.7	8.7	8.9	12.0	
4.7	4.8	5.4		3.1	5.4	5.9	7.2	6.6	
3.9	3.9	3.9		4.6	4.6	3.3	3.6	3.3	
2.8	2.7	2.9	Sales/Total Assets	2.8	3.3	2.6	3.0	2.8	
1.9	1.8	2.1		1.9	2.2	1.9	2.3	2.2	
1.9	1.8	2.1		2.3	2.6	2.1	1.4	1.6	
(171) 3.8	(146) 3.5	(177) 3.6	% Depr., Dep., Amort./Sales	(30) 4.4	(61) 3.9	(24) 3.9	(34) 2.6	(24) 3.0	
5.4	5.3	5.2		7.5	5.8	6.1	3.8	3.8	
3.0	3.0	2.8		6.1	3.3	2.7	1.3		
(115) 5.4	(91) 6.4	(109) 5.5	% Officers', Directors', Owners' Comp/Sales	(22) 11.5	(45) 5.7	(15) 6.6	(16) 2.3		
8.6	10.2	11.5		20.8	11.0	10.7	5.3		
2018452M	1182525M	2790350M	Net Sales ($)	20541M	138817M	106149M	245475M	380565M	1898803M
814861M	514159M	1142933M	Total Assets ($)	10658M	54572M	49567M	93668M	143801M	790667M

© RMA 2003   M = $ thousand   MM = $ million
See Pages 11 through 18 for Explanation of Ratios and Data

Current Data Sorted By Assets   Comparative Historical Data

						Type of Statement		
7	14	92	76	19	18	Unqualified	198	189
13	102	174	37	1		Reviewed	307	314
47	114	74	5	1	1	Compiled	293	257
94	33	8	1	2	1	Tax Returns	83	82
47	135	104	64	9	5	Other	326	311
	197 (4/1-9/30/02)		1101 (10/1/02-3/31/03)				4/1/98-3/31/99	4/1/99-3/31/00
0-500M	500M-2MM	2-10MM	10-50MM	50-100MM	100-250MM		ALL	ALL
208	398	452	183	32	25	NUMBER OF STATEMENTS	1207	1153
%	%	%	%	%	%	**ASSETS**	%	%
22.5	10.0	9.0	9.1	9.6	9.7	Cash & Equivalents	10.1	9.6
26.7	51.7	51.7	48.1	37.6	39.8	Trade Receivables (net)	48.4	49.4
2.2	4.1	4.6	3.0	2.1	2.6	Inventory	3.7	3.8
3.1	5.7	8.3	12.3	12.7	15.5	All Other Current	6.8	7.0
54.5	71.5	73.5	72.4	61.9	67.6	Total Current	68.9	69.8
32.2	17.9	17.0	17.3	18.4	12.8	Fixed Assets (net)	20.5	19.5
2.6	2.6	2.3	1.9	7.1	9.4	Intangibles (net)	2.4	2.9
10.8	8.1	7.1	8.4	12.5	10.2	All Other Non-Current	8.1	7.8
100.0	100.0	100.0	100.0	100.0	100.0	Total	100.0	100.0
						LIABILITIES		
27.7	13.7	11.8	9.3	5.3	1.4	Notes Payable-Short Term	13.7	13.4
5.8	3.1	2.9	3.4	3.6	1.3	Cur. Mat.-L/T/D	3.5	3.5
9.8	9.8	12.3	11.7	9.9	14.5	Trade Payables	10.4	11.2
.3	1.4	2.7	3.6	2.8	1.6	Income Taxes Payable	1.2	1.4
22.6	13.8	15.9	19.7	19.7	25.8	All Other Current	16.7	15.8
66.3	41.9	45.6	47.5	41.4	44.6	Total Current	45.5	45.2
19.8	10.1	8.6	11.0	14.2	13.4	Long Term Debt	10.3	10.9
.1	1.8	1.8	2.2	1.2	1.0	Deferred Taxes	2.8	3.0
10.5	4.2	3.1	4.0	6.5	6.8	All Other Non-Current	5.2	4.0
3.4	42.1	40.9	35.2	36.8	34.2	Net Worth	36.2	36.9
100.0	100.0	100.0	100.0	100.0	100.0	Total Liabilities & Net Worth	100.0	100.0
						INCOME DATA		
100.0	100.0	100.0	100.0	100.0	100.0	Net Sales	100.0	100.0
						Gross Profit		
96.8	96.1	95.9	95.9	94.1	96.1	Operating Expenses	94.7	94.7
3.2	3.9	4.1	4.1	5.9	3.9	Operating Profit	5.3	5.3
.7	.8	.7	1.1	1.3	.2	All Other Expenses (net)	.8	.7
2.5	3.1	3.3	3.0	4.6	3.7	Profit Before Taxes	4.5	4.6
						RATIOS		
2.2	3.5	2.4	2.1	1.9	2.1		2.7	2.6
1.2	1.8	1.6	1.5	1.4	1.6	Current	1.7	1.6
.4	1.2	1.2	1.2	1.2	1.3		1.2	1.2
2.1	3.1	2.1	1.7	1.5	1.5		2.3	2.2
1.0	1.5	1.3	1.2	1.1	1.1	Quick	(1205) 1.4	1.4
.3	1.0	1.0	.9	.8	1.0		.9	1.0
0 UND	44 8.2	53 6.9	58 6.3	57 6.4	43 8.4		46 7.9	49 7.5
0 UND	72 5.0	72 5.1	82 4.4	71 5.1	61 6.0	Sales/Receivables	73 5.0	75 4.9
56 6.5	101 3.6	98 3.7	106 3.4	85 4.3	91 4.0		98 3.7	102 3.6
						Cost of Sales/Inventory		
						Cost of Sales/Payables		
12.0	4.9	5.4	5.3	6.2	5.6		5.3	5.0
90.7	8.6	9.2	9.2	9.2	7.3	Sales/Working Capital	9.5	9.4
-23.3	33.2	21.4	16.6	34.1	20.5		30.4	29.5
(149) 12.3	(342) 13.5	(419) 17.2	(168) 20.2	(29) 15.9	(20) 22.0		(1039) 11.7	(1015) 15.4
3.2	3.5	5.2	7.4	3.6	8.0	EBIT/Interest	4.6	5.1
-2.1	-.2	1.4	2.3	1.6	3.4		1.6	1.5
(15) 5.6	(82) 3.9	(169) 7.1	(83) 5.7	(16) 15.0	(13) 25.2	Net Profit + Depr., Dep.,	(397) 6.2	(362) 6.0
2.2	1.7	2.6	2.5	4.3	4.1	Amort./Cur. Mat. L/T/D	2.7	2.6
.3	.2	1.0	1.0	2.1	1.7		1.2	1.2
.3	.1	.2	.2	.2	.2		.2	.2
1.0	.3	.4	.4	.6	.5	Fixed/Worth	.4	.4
-4.1	.8	.8	.9	1.2	.8		1.0	1.0
.7	.5	.8	1.1	1.0	1.3		.7	.8
2.5	1.3	1.5	1.9	2.7	1.8	Debt/Worth	1.6	1.6
-9.9	3.5	3.1	3.3	6.1	5.5		3.9	3.6
(146) 131.8	(358) 46.8	(434) 39.1	(170) 31.8	(31) 35.1	(22) 33.8	% Profit Before Taxes/Tangible	(1092) 49.3	(1059) 47.2
41.4	16.1	17.5	17.4	21.7	23.6	Net Worth	24.9	23.3
-2.1	-2.4	2.2	7.3	7.5	3.7		8.4	6.8
39.9	18.7	15.8	11.2	12.4	9.9	% Profit Before Taxes/Total	19.0	17.5
11.0	5.2	6.1	6.2	6.3	6.4	Assets	8.8	7.4
-9.4	-2.9	.4	2.0	2.4	2.0		2.0	1.5
55.7	43.2	40.0	41.1	47.7	47.9		39.4	36.6
26.5	20.5	18.9	18.9	20.5	22.8	Sales/Net Fixed Assets	18.9	18.9
13.5	12.0	10.5	9.1	8.9	12.1		10.6	10.5
10.4	3.5	3.1	2.6	3.0	2.7		3.5	3.4
5.2	2.6	2.5	2.2	2.0	2.1	Sales/Total Assets	2.6	2.5
3.3	2.1	2.0	1.6	1.1	1.3		2.0	1.9
(150) 1.1	(331) 1.1	(418) 1.0	(166) 1.0	(24) .6	(20) .6		(1055) 1.0	(998) 1.1
2.0	1.8	1.8	1.9	2.0	1.5	% Depr., Dep., Amort./Sales	1.9	1.9
3.7	3.0	2.8	2.9	2.9	2.1		2.9	2.9
(133) 7.9	(185) 5.0	(132) 2.8	(24) 1.9			% Officers', Directors',	(410) 4.3	(381) 4.1
12.8	9.4	5.3	4.3			Owners' Comp/Sales	8.5	8.2
18.6	15.4	11.9	8.6				16.0	14.1
322426M	1344315M	5408517M	8455047M	6021241M	10451195M	Net Sales ($)	21436386M	27380423M
49928M	463146M	2063140M	3912029M	2216828M	4257165M	Total Assets ($)	9631793M	10840319M

M = $ thousand   MM = $ million
See Pages 11 through 18 for Explanation of Ratios and Data

Comparative Historical Data | | **Current Data Sorted By Sales**

						Type of Statement						
	153		180		226	Unqualified	5	5	11	38	62	105
	260		232		327	Reviewed	7	52	55	83	93	37
	277		285		242	Compiled	26	83	53	50	24	6
	103		90		139	Tax Returns	35	67	18	11	5	3
	379		360		364	Other	28	94	46	61	64	71
	4/1/00-3/31/01 ALL		4/1/01-3/31/02 ALL		4/1/02-3/31/03 ALL		197 (4/1-9/30/02)			1101 (10/1/02-3/31/03)		
							0-1MM	1-3MM	3-5MM	5-10MM	10-25MM	25MM & OVER
	1172		1147		1298	**NUMBER OF STATEMENTS**	101	301	183	243	248	222
	%		%		%	**ASSETS**	%	%	%	%	%	%
	9.7		10.4		11.5	Cash & Equivalents	19.4	14.1	11.3	10.6	8.5	8.8
	51.1		49.6		46.6	Trade Receivables (net)	30.0	42.8	49.3	50.2	49.7	49.6
	3.6		4.0		3.7	Inventory	1.6	4.3	2.7	5.0	4.5	2.6
	6.6		6.5		7.5	All Other Current	3.4	4.5	6.3	7.3	9.0	12.8
	71.0		70.5		69.3	Total Current	54.4	65.7	69.6	73.2	71.7	73.7
	18.3		18.8		19.7	Fixed Assets (net)	30.9	23.1	18.3	17.6	18.8	14.5
	2.5		3.1		2.6	Intangibles (net)	2.9	2.8	2.8	2.1	1.7	3.8
	8.2		7.6		8.4	All Other Non-Current	11.9	8.5	9.3	7.1	7.8	8.0
	100.0		100.0		100.0	Total	100.0	100.0	100.0	100.0	100.0	100.0
						LIABILITIES						
	12.7		14.5		14.2	Notes Payable-Short Term	21.6	19.5	14.4	12.3	11.8	8.3
	3.9		3.4		3.5	Cur. Mat.-L/T/D	3.0	4.5	3.7	3.2	3.4	2.7
	11.5		11.8		11.0	Trade Payables	10.3	10.1	8.5	11.1	12.3	13.1
	1.5		1.7		2.0	Income Taxes Payable	.4	.8	2.3	1.7	3.1	3.4
	16.6		16.9		17.1	All Other Current	20.7	16.5	14.7	14.3	17.3	21.3
	46.2		48.2		47.9	Total Current	56.1	51.4	43.6	42.7	47.9	48.8
	10.0		10.4		11.4	Long Term Debt	14.3	16.1	9.4	9.1	9.9	9.7
	2.8		2.3		1.6	Deferred Taxes	.5	1.4	2.4	1.1	1.9	1.7
	4.4		5.2		4.9	All Other Non-Current	11.2	4.7	6.4	3.4	2.8	4.9
	36.7		33.9		34.2	Net Worth	17.8	26.5	38.2	43.8	37.4	34.9
	100.0		100.0		100.0	Total Liabilities & Net Worth	100.0	100.0	100.0	100.0	100.0	100.0
						INCOME DATA						
	100.0		100.0		100.0	Net Sales	100.0	100.0	100.0	100.0	100.0	100.0
						Gross Profit						
	94.6		95.6		96.1	Operating Expenses	95.1	96.6	95.7	96.2	96.2	95.7
	5.4		4.4		3.9	Operating Profit	4.9	3.4	4.3	3.8	3.8	4.3
	.9		1.0		.8	All Other Expenses (net)	1.3	.8	.6	.7	.9	.8
	4.5		3.3		3.1	Profit Before Taxes	3.5	2.6	3.7	3.2	2.9	3.5
						RATIOS						
	2.6		2.5		2.6		3.1	3.0	3.4	2.7	2.2	2.0
	1.6		1.6		1.6	Current	1.4	1.6	1.7	1.8	1.5	1.5
	1.2		1.1		1.1		.6	1.0	1.1	1.3	1.2	1.3
	2.2		2.2		2.2		3.1	2.7	3.1	2.4	1.7	1.5
	1.4	(1146)	1.3		1.3	Quick	1.3	1.3	1.5	1.4	1.2	1.2
	1.0		.9		.9		.4	.7	.9	1.0	.9	.9
52	7.1	48	7.5	42	8.7	Sales/Receivables	0 UND	22 16.3	46 7.9	47 7.8	52 7.1	54 6.7
76	4.8	71	5.1	69	5.3		33 11.1	64 5.7	74 4.9	70 5.2	70 5.2	72 5.1
103	3.6	97	3.8	96	3.8		83 4.4	102 3.6	100 3.6	94 3.9	92 4.0	95 3.8
						Cost of Sales/Inventory						
						Cost of Sales/Payables						
	5.1		5.4		5.5	Sales/Working Capital	4.9	5.1	4.7	5.5	5.6	6.4
	9.5		10.1		10.5		24.0	13.2	8.9	8.8	11.3	9.7
	29.4		39.1		42.0		-23.1	-157.5	76.9	20.4	28.1	17.8
	15.6		15.1		15.8	EBIT/Interest	9.2	11.2	17.0	20.8	15.4	20.5
(1036)	4.9	(997)	4.3	(1127)	4.7		(63) 3.2	(258) 2.7	(154) 4.4	(221) 5.7	(231) 4.9	(200) 7.5
	1.5		1.1		.242		-2.0	-1.2	.1	.2	1.5	2.5
	6.5		6.7		5.8	Net Profit + Depr., Dep., Amort./Cur. Mat. L/T/D		4.0	5.1	9.2	4.8	8.1
(334)	2.8	(301)	2.9	(378)	2.2			(46) 1.6	(53) 2.0	(69) 2.2	(98) 2.1	(106) 3.1
	1.3		1.1		1.0			.1	.4	.9	.9	1.5
	.2		.2		.2	Fixed/Worth	.2	.2	.2	.2	.2	.2
	.4		.4		.4		.8	.5	.3	.3	.4	.4
	.9		1.0		1.1		-8.1	3.2	.9	.7	1.0	.8
	.8		.8		.7	Debt/Worth	.7	.6	.6	.6	1.0	1.2
	1.7		1.7		1.6		1.7	1.7	1.2	1.3	1.8	1.9
	3.8		4.0		4.3		-14.9	8.0	4.0	2.8	3.7	4.0
	52.1		46.7		45.6	% Profit Before Taxes/Tangible Net Worth	121.4	53.4	49.4	47.3	36.7	35.1
(1073)	25.6	(1030)	21.6	(1161)	19.0		(73) 21.6	(249) 16.0	(164) 20.0	(233) 17.5	(235) 16.9	(207) 21.0
	6.6		4.0		2.5		-1.1	-4.6	-.8	.8	4.0	6.4
	18.8		17.5		17.2	% Profit Before Taxes/Total Assets	28.4	20.7	21.5	17.5	14.5	12.7
	8.8		7.1		6.2		7.8	5.2	6.2	6.2	5.9	6.7
	1.6		.3		-.1		-9.7	-5.3	-3.0	-.8	.9	2.1
	41.5		42.0		43.8	Sales/Net Fixed Assets	40.0	42.5	43.1	44.8	41.0	45.6
	21.4		20.6		20.4		17.3	19.7	19.8	22.0	18.8	23.3
	10.9		10.8		11.4		8.0	11.0	13.0	12.0	10.0	12.8
	3.4		3.5		3.6	Sales/Total Assets	5.4	4.3	3.4	3.6	3.2	3.1
	2.5		2.6		2.6		2.9	2.7	2.6	2.6	2.5	2.4
	1.9		2.0		2.0		1.4	2.1	2.1	2.1	2.0	1.9
	1.0		.9		1.0	% Depr., Dep., Amort./Sales	1.2	1.1	1.2	1.1	.9	.8
(994)	1.7	(987)	1.8	(1109)	1.8		(74) 2.3	(235) 2.1	(157) 1.9	(220) 1.8	(230) 1.8	(193) 1.6
	2.6		2.8		2.9		4.3	3.5	2.8	2.6	2.8	2.4
	4.9		4.2		4.5	% Officers', Directors', Owners' Comp/Sales	8.7	7.3	4.6	2.8	2.4	1.7
(395)	8.9	(386)	8.7	(480)	8.7		(53) 16.7	(166) 11.1	(78) 9.0	(93) 5.6	(64) 5.0	(26) 5.6
	16.1		15.3		15.7		22.5	17.4	14.5	10.9	10.8	10.1
	22650419M		27095055M		32002741M	Net Sales ($)	57843M	597511M	721481M	1758647M	3903373M	24963886M
	9777165M		11072024M		12962236M	Total Assets ($)	30755M	236016M	304096M	748024M	1738805M	9904540M

M = $ thousand   MM = $ million
See Pages 11 through 18 for Explanation of Ratios and Data

Current Data Sorted By Assets   Comparative Historical Data

						Type of Statement		
			2	3		Unqualified	5	6
3			9			Reviewed	9	11
5	9		2			Compiled	29	18
17	3					Tax Returns	12	12
7	9	7	2			Other	21	24
	6 (4/1-9/30/02)		72 (10/1/02-3/31/03)				4/1/98-3/31/99	4/1/99-3/31/00
0-500M	500M-2MM	2-10MM	10-50MM	50-100MM	100-250MM		ALL	ALL
32	21	18	7			NUMBER OF STATEMENTS	76	71
%	%	%	%	%	%	**ASSETS**	%	%
22.3	6.8	11.2				Cash & Equivalents	11.6	10.4
21.0	43.0	42.2	D	D		Trade Receivables (net)	35.5	38.5
2.0	3.5	1.6	A	A		Inventory	3.5	3.6
1.0	3.1	7.9	T	T		All Other Current	5.7	4.0
46.2	56.3	62.9	A	A		Total Current	56.3	56.6
40.2	38.9	29.3	N	N		Fixed Assets (net)	35.6	35.2
2.9	1.1	.8	O	O		Intangibles (net)	2.4	2.6
10.9	3.7	7.0	T	T		All Other Non-Current	5.7	5.7
100.0	100.0	100.0				Total	100.0	100.0
			A	A		**LIABILITIES**		
11.2	12.1	10.8	V	V		Notes Payable-Short Term	13.5	9.9
4.6	7.4	4.8	A	A		Cur. Mat.-L/T/D	4.2	4.4
2.4	8.1	5.0	I	I		Trade Payables	7.3	6.6
1.3	.3	3.7	L	L		Income Taxes Payable	.9	.6
10.2	7.6	12.1	A	A		All Other Current	13.0	12.7
29.7	35.4	36.4	B	B		Total Current	39.0	34.2
29.9	23.9	14.0	L	L		Long Term Debt	22.9	22.5
.5	.1	.7	E	E		Deferred Taxes	1.5	1.7
5.7	7.9	3.2				All Other Non-Current	5.4	3.5
34.3	32.7	45.7				Net Worth	31.2	38.2
100.0	100.0	100.0				Total Liabilities & Net Worth	100.0	100.0
						INCOME DATA		
100.0	100.0	100.0				Net Sales	100.0	100.0
						Gross Profit		
90.6	95.3	93.9				Operating Expenses	91.8	93.9
9.4	4.7	6.1				Operating Profit	8.2	6.1
.8	1.2	.8				All Other Expenses (net)	1.3	1.2
8.6	3.5	5.3				Profit Before Taxes	7.0	5.0
						RATIOS		
5.5	2.7	4.5					3.3	3.4
2.5	1.9	1.6				Current	1.7	1.9
.6	1.1	1.1					.9	1.2
5.5	2.6	4.3					3.0	2.9
2.5	1.4	1.2				Quick	1.4	1.6
.6	.9	.8					.7	.9
0 UND	30 12.3	61 6.0					0 UND	38 9.5
0 UND	65 5.7	69 5.3				Sales/Receivables	59 6.2	72 5.0
64 5.7	99 3.7	97 3.8					97 3.8	106 3.5
						Cost of Sales/Inventory		
						Cost of Sales/Payables		
6.3	6.1	4.8					4.6	4.6
19.4	9.1	9.5				Sales/Working Capital	9.3	7.2
-42.5	NM	NM					-57.4	55.1
20.7	5.1	22.5					15.7	12.1
(28) 8.7	2.3	(17) 7.7				EBIT/Interest	(66) 5.4	(62) 3.7
.4	-1.3	2.3					1.0	1.3
		6.2					5.1	3.1
	(10)	4.6				Net Profit + Depr., Dep., Amort./Cur. Mat. L /T/D	(18) 2.9	(22) 2.0
		1.2					1.2	1.4
.4	.4	.3					.3	.3
1.2	1.2	.8				Fixed/Worth	.7	.7
2.7	4.2	1.4					4.2	1.9
.4	.6	.6					.6	.7
1.9	2.1	1.4				Debt/Worth	1.6	1.4
8.6	5.5	4.2					8.9	3.5
160.6	71.3	40.1					73.4	47.1
(28) 75.2	(18) 18.2	20.8				% Profit Before Taxes/Tangible Net Worth	(60) 39.3	(61) 22.4
2.2	-4.3	5.7					9.9	4.0
64.6	27.4	16.5					32.9	19.6
25.6	5.1	6.5				% Profit Before Taxes/Total Assets	17.1	6.6
-.9	-2.6	2.6					.5	.1
16.1	16.1	23.2					19.5	15.1
10.6	7.7	11.8				Sales/Net Fixed Assets	10.4	9.7
5.7	3.7	5.8					5.8	5.8
5.8	3.5	3.0					3.6	3.6
3.4	2.5	2.3				Sales/Total Assets	2.3	2.2
2.0	1.8	1.6					1.6	1.8
2.3	3.5	2.1					2.2	1.9
(28) 3.7	(17) 4.6	2.8				% Depr., Dep., Amort./Sales	(64) 3.4	(65) 3.3
5.8	7.1	5.3					5.2	5.0
8.4							6.2	5.5
(22) 14.0						% Officers', Directors', Owners' Comp/Sales	(33) 9.6	(35) 12.8
16.2							18.0	16.0
28340M	55310M	223964M	201757M			Net Sales ($)	318575M	1215506M
8251M	21017M	86839M	132414M			Total Assets ($)	195447M	510682M

© RMA 2003

M = $ thousand   MM = $ million
See Pages 11 through 18 for Explanation of Ratios and Data

Comparative Historical Data				Current Data Sorted By Sales					
			Type of Statement						
5	5	5	Unqualified				1	3	1
7	6	12	Reviewed	1	2	1	2	6	
11	20	16	Compiled	3	8	2	1	1	1
10	13	20	Tax Returns	11	7	2			
18	24	25	Other	5	9	5	1	2	3
4/1/00-3/31/01	4/1/01-3/31/02	4/1/02-3/31/03		6 (4/1-9/30/02)			72 (10/1/02-3/31/03)		
ALL	ALL	ALL		0-1MM	1-3MM	3-5MM	5-10MM	10-25MM	25MM & OVER
51	68	78	**NUMBER OF STATEMENTS**	20	26	10	5	12	5
%	%	%	**ASSETS**	%	%	%	%	%	%
13.3	10.3	14.3	Cash & Equivalents	24.4	10.8	9.9		9.6	
34.9	32.7	33.2	Trade Receivables (net)	20.2	34.0	45.9		42.3	
3.1	4.9	2.3	Inventory	1.3	2.6	4.7		1.5	
4.9	5.2	4.5	All Other Current	.6	3.0	2.3		11.2	
56.2	53.1	54.4	Total Current	46.6	50.4	62.7		64.6	
30.3	34.4	35.5	Fixed Assets (net)	38.7	42.0	33.3		21.0	
3.6	3.5	2.8	Intangibles (net)	3.8	.8	.4		6.5	
9.9	9.0	7.4	All Other Non-Current	11.1	6.7	3.6		7.8	
100.0	100.0	100.0	Total	100.0	100.0	100.0		100.0	
			LIABILITIES						
9.1	10.9	10.7	Notes Payable-Short Term	11.1	12.8	10.4		6.7	
7.7	8.6	5.5	Cur. Mat.-L/T/D	4.2	5.7	8.2		5.3	
8.6	10.9	5.1	Trade Payables	2.2	4.0	11.0		6.5	
.9	.7	1.5	Income Taxes Payable	.0	1.8	.0		5.6	
11.3	12.0	9.9	All Other Current	10.0	8.2	9.8		14.5	
37.6	43.0	32.7	Total Current	27.5	32.6	39.4		38.5	
21.2	29.8	22.8	Long Term Debt	31.6	26.9	14.7		15.3	
1.1	.6	.4	Deferred Taxes	.0	.7	.0		.6	
3.8	2.9	6.0	All Other Non-Current	2.6	11.1	1.0		3.4	
36.3	23.7	38.1	Net Worth	38.3	28.7	44.8		42.2	
100.0	100.0	100.0	Total Liabilities & Net Worth	100.0	100.0	100.0		100.0	
			INCOME DATA						
100.0	100.0	100.0	Net Sales	100.0	100.0	100.0		100.0	
			Gross Profit						
92.7	95.2	93.2	Operating Expenses	87.5	97.1	91.9		95.1	
7.3	4.8	6.8	Operating Profit	12.5	2.9	8.1		4.9	
1.5	2.0	.9	All Other Expenses (net)	1.2	.8	.8		.9	
5.8	2.8	5.9	Profit Before Taxes	11.3	2.2	7.3		4.0	
			RATIOS						
3.3	2.9	4.5		12.9	2.7	3.8		2.8	
1.9	1.3	1.9	Current	3.6	1.8	1.8		1.6	
1.0	.9	1.0		.8	.8	.9		1.1	
2.5	2.1	4.4		12.9	2.6	3.6		1.8	
1.4	1.1	1.5	Quick	3.6	1.3	1.4		1.1	
.9	.7	.8		.7	.6	.8		1.0	
23 15.8	9 40.4	0 UND		0 UND	0 UND	31 11.7		50 7.3	
68 5.3	57 6.4	62 5.9	Sales/Receivables	0 UND	60 6.0	61 5.9		66 5.5	
94 3.9	86 4.3	85 4.3		77 4.7	89 4.1	115 3.2		76 4.8	
			Cost of Sales/Inventory						
			Cost of Sales/Payables						
4.8	6.7	5.4		6.2	6.0	4.9		5.1	
11.4	22.6	10.6	Sales/Working Capital	16.4	10.9	11.4		9.5	
-614.2	-140.1	-87.9		-47.4	-57.6	-35.4		77.2	
(47) 15.1	(64) 6.0	(73) 16.5		(16) 28.9	14.8			13.9	
4.7	2.4	4.4	EBIT/Interest	6.7	2.1			9.1	
1.7	.0	.6		.4	-2.1			4.0	
(13) 8.0	(12) 3.8	(19) 5.9	Net Profit + Depr., Dep.,						
1.6	1.8	2.8	Amort./Cur. Mat. L/T/D						
.6	.2	1.1							
.3	.4	.3		.5	.3	.1		.2	
.8	1.3	.9	Fixed/Worth	1.4	1.3	.8		.7	
2.4	-12.2	2.2		2.7	7.7	2.0		1.5	
.5	.8	.6		.4	.7	.3		.8	
1.6	2.3	1.6	Debt/Worth	2.8	1.3	1.3		1.5	
5.3	-52.1	5.2		6.7	17.7	2.4		5.8	
(43) 82.1	(50) 73.1	(70) 77.4	% Profit Before Taxes/Tangible	(18) 170.1	(22) 74.8		(11)	48.2	
28.9	15.8	21.4	Net Worth	96.7	18.5			27.2	
11.6	-2.0	4.7		-3.5	-6.7			6.7	
24.6	20.3	33.8	% Profit Before Taxes/Total	76.9	28.6	39.1		17.2	
8.4	4.7	9.7	Assets	25.6	5.8	17.2		9.9	
2.6	-1.8	-.1		-.9	-10.6	4.0		3.0	
19.6	17.5	17.4		14.3	17.5	31.1		23.9	
10.6	11.3	10.6	Sales/Net Fixed Assets	9.4	12.2	11.1		16.8	
6.4	5.1	4.8		4.3	3.7	5.5		9.8	
4.1	3.6	4.0		4.1	4.4	4.4		3.1	
2.1	2.3	2.5	Sales/Total Assets	2.4	2.9	3.0		2.6	
1.4	1.8	1.6		1.6	1.8	1.7		1.5	
(47) 2.1	(54) 1.9	(68) 2.5	% Depr., Dep., Amort./Sales	(19) 2.6	(20) 3.1		(10)	2.2	
3.3	3.0	3.8		4.3	4.2			3.1	
6.7	4.9	6.2		7.1	7.3			4.1	
(27) 6.5	(36) 5.3	(33) 7.7	% Officers', Directors',	(13) 9.1	(13) 8.7				
11.7	12.1	13.1	Owners' Comp/Sales	15.2	13.1				
20.8	14.2	16.1		23.7	15.7				
1197469M	1617520M	509371M	Net Sales ($)	10387M	44639M	39603M	39417M	192800M	182525M
565988M	791060M	248521M	Total Assets ($)	4342M	18307M	15601M	21253M	92541M	96477M

© RMA 2003   M = $ thousand   MM = $ million
See Pages 11 through 18 for Explanation of Ratios and Data

Current Data Sorted By Assets   Comparative Historical Data

Current period totals: **27 (4/1-9/30/02)**   **140 (10/1/02-3/31/03)**

	0-500M	500M-2MM	2-10MM	10-50MM	50-100MM	100-250MM	Type of Statement	4/1/98-3/31/99 ALL	4/1/99-3/31/00 ALL
		1	10	11	3	1	Unqualified	24	23
		15	27	3			Reviewed	52	44
	5	12	11				Compiled	44	37
	8	8					Tax Returns	11	8
	4	24	11	9	3	1	Other	42	36
NUMBER OF STATEMENTS	17	60	59	23	6	2		173	148
	%	%	%	%	%	%	**ASSETS**	%	%
	18.2	8.3	9.4	10.7			Cash & Equivalents	9.3	8.6
	21.9	39.4	40.0	37.0			Trade Receivables (net)	39.4	37.2
	2.6	1.9	3.1	2.4			Inventory	1.8	3.1
	6.0	2.6	4.2	6.4			All Other Current	2.9	2.6
	48.7	52.2	56.8	56.4			Total Current	53.3	51.4
	36.5	40.3	36.0	33.7			Fixed Assets (net)	37.6	38.8
	6.0	3.0	2.5	3.0			Intangibles (net)	3.2	3.3
	8.7	4.5	4.7	6.8			All Other Non-Current	5.9	6.4
	100.0	100.0	100.0	100.0			Total	100.0	100.0
							LIABILITIES		
	18.8	8.4	10.6	4.4			Notes Payable-Short Term	7.6	9.2
	7.2	6.0	5.9	5.9			Cur. Mat.-L/T/D	6.4	5.1
	10.7	9.0	8.1	7.9			Trade Payables	10.4	9.1
	.8	.4	.6	1.2			Income Taxes Payable	.5	1.1
	9.3	10.0	7.5	16.5			All Other Current	11.7	11.0
	46.9	33.6	32.7	36.0			Total Current	36.5	35.6
	32.2	23.1	18.2	18.6			Long Term Debt	21.8	18.4
	.5	1.5	.8	1.2			Deferred Taxes	1.4	1.7
	8.3	5.1	2.8	3.4			All Other Non-Current	7.4	4.7
	12.1	36.6	45.5	40.8			Net Worth	32.9	39.5
	100.0	100.0	100.0	100.0			Total Liabilities & Net Worth	100.0	100.0
							INCOME DATA		
	100.0	100.0	100.0	100.0			Net Sales	100.0	100.0
							Gross Profit		
	95.4	93.8	90.6	92.5			Operating Expenses	97.6	92.5
	4.6	6.2	9.4	7.5			Operating Profit	2.4	7.5
	1.7	2.4	1.2	.7			All Other Expenses (net)	1.9	1.2
	2.9	3.8	8.2	6.8			Profit Before Taxes	.5	6.3
							RATIOS		
	2.1	2.5	3.1	2.6			Current	2.6	2.4
	1.4	1.4	1.7	1.7				1.6	1.5
	.8	1.1	1.2	1.2				1.2	1.1
	1.7	2.2	2.5	2.4			Quick	2.4	2.1
	1.2	1.3	1.5	1.5				1.4	1.3
	.6	.9	1.0	.9				1.0	.9
	0 UND	46 8.0	58 6.3	44 8.2			Sales/Receivables	44 8.4	45 8.2
	11 32.9	67 5.5	77 4.7	73 5.0				66 5.6	64 5.7
	46 7.9	84 4.4	100 3.7	88 4.1				91 4.0	85 4.3
							Cost of Sales/Inventory		
							Cost of Sales/Payables		
	18.7	6.2	4.4	4.3			Sales/Working Capital	6.3	6.6
	37.9	15.0	8.6	9.5				11.8	13.1
	-23.1	62.8	24.9	36.3				40.1	91.8
	(15) 23.3	(56) 10.3	(55) 14.0	(22) 13.9			EBIT/Interest	(152) 8.1	(135) 13.4
	4.0	4.0	4.0	7.3				3.2	3.9
	.7	1.1	1.5	2.6				1.2	1.6
		(15) 3.3	(30) 12.5				Net Profit + Depr., Dep., Amort./Cur. Mat. L./T/D	(57) 5.4	(53) 4.5
		2.1	2.7					2.3	2.2
		1.0	1.6					1.3	1.5
	.2	.6	.5	.3			Fixed/Worth	.5	.6
	1.9	1.0	.9	.9				1.0	1.0
	NM	3.2	1.7	1.8				3.1	2.2
	1.1	.7	.5	.9			Debt/Worth	.8	.8
	4.1	1.4	1.4	1.6				1.7	1.8
	NM	5.5	2.9	2.9				5.5	3.8
	(13) 187.2	(50) 35.4	(58) 47.4	(21) 49.7			% Profit Before Taxes/Tangible Net Worth	(146) 44.9	(134) 58.9
	100.0	16.7	20.1	21.5				19.7	28.1
	20.9	1.8	5.3	5.7				4.4	9.5
	45.8	16.8	19.7	20.7			% Profit Before Taxes/Total Assets	17.0	21.1
	12.7	6.3	6.9	11.3				7.3	8.6
	3.2	.1	1.7	1.9				.3	2.2
	48.7	9.6	10.7	10.7			Sales/Net Fixed Assets	12.9	11.1
	19.2	6.8	5.8	5.7				5.9	6.4
	8.0	3.3	3.4	3.3				3.3	3.5
	7.7	2.9	2.3	2.4			Sales/Total Assets	3.0	2.6
	4.9	2.4	1.8	1.7				2.1	2.0
	2.8	1.5	1.5	1.3				1.4	1.5
	(14) .8	(55) 2.5	(56) 2.5	(21) 2.7			% Depr., Dep., Amort./Sales	(156) 2.8	(138) 2.8
	2.3	4.6	4.4	3.4				4.7	4.8
	3.1	7.5	7.5	5.2				7.0	7.1
	(11) 4.0	(23) 3.3	(18) 2.9				% Officers', Directors', Owners' Comp/Sales	(66) 4.4	(48) 4.3
	6.7	7.4	4.8					8.8	8.5
	12.3	11.5	7.9					16.3	15.9
	20203M	171940M	534278M	783534M	556530M	303363M	Net Sales ($)	1773392M	1089428M
	4327M	75672M	287556M	456027M	381654M	349061M	Total Assets ($)	1249129M	662585M

M = $ thousand   MM = $ million
See Pages 11 through 18 for Explanation of Ratios and Data

Comparative Historical Data   **Current Data Sorted By Sales**

	4/1/00-3/31/01 ALL	4/1/01-3/31/02 ALL	4/1/02-3/31/03 ALL		0-1MM	1-3MM	3-5MM	5-10MM	10-25MM	25MM & OVER
Type of Statement					27 (4/1-9/30/02)			140 (10/1/02-3/31/03)		
Unqualified	15	20	26			1	2	2	11	10
Reviewed	42	36	45		2	6	12	14	9	2
Compiled	53	54	28		4	5	9	6	4	
Tax Returns	15	14	16		3	13				
Other	31	55	52		4	18	8	3	8	11
NUMBER OF STATEMENTS	156	179	167		13	43	31	25	32	23
ASSETS	%	%	%		%	%	%	%	%	%
Cash & Equivalents	10.1	7.8	10.2		13.7	10.4	9.9	11.4	7.2	11.2
Trade Receivables (net)	38.5	36.5	36.7		16.3	31.8	42.1	40.7	46.7	32.1
Inventory	2.9	3.9	2.4		.7	2.6	2.6	4.4	1.0	2.5
All Other Current	3.1	2.8	4.1		6.7	2.8	3.4	2.5	6.0	5.0
Total Current	54.6	51.0	53.4		37.4	47.6	57.9	59.1	61.0	50.7
Fixed Assets (net)	35.7	37.8	36.9		49.3	43.3	35.0	33.0	32.7	30.4
Intangibles (net)	3.9	5.2	4.2		7.9	3.3	1.6	4.6	1.1	11.5
All Other Non-Current	5.9	5.9	5.5		5.3	5.8	5.5	3.3	5.3	7.4
Total	100.0	100.0	100.0		100.0	100.0	100.0	100.0	100.0	100.0
LIABILITIES										
Notes Payable-Short Term	9.7	10.3	9.4		7.1	11.0	10.4	9.4	11.7	3.3
Cur. Mat.-L/T/D	5.3	6.2	6.0		5.8	6.3	6.5	6.2	5.3	5.6
Trade Payables	9.4	9.4	8.5		8.0	7.7	8.4	11.0	9.0	6.8
Income Taxes Payable	.8	.6	.6		.9	.4	.3	.1	.9	1.4
All Other Current	13.1	11.0	10.1		7.6	9.0	9.6	7.6	11.9	14.7
Total Current	38.2	37.4	34.7		29.4	34.4	35.3	34.4	38.8	31.9
Long Term Debt	19.5	21.6	21.3		59.0	22.2	17.3	18.9	13.5	17.3
Deferred Taxes	1.3	1.2	1.1		2.0	1.3	.8	.9	.6	1.4
All Other Non-Current	4.1	3.8	4.3		2.3	5.7	6.6	2.7	2.8	3.7
Net Worth	36.9	36.0	38.6		7.4	36.3	39.9	43.1	44.3	45.7
Total Liabilities & Net Worth	100.0	100.0	100.0		100.0	100.0	100.0	100.0	100.0	100.0
INCOME DATA										
Net Sales	100.0	100.0	100.0		100.0	100.0	100.0	100.0	100.0	100.0
Gross Profit										
Operating Expenses	94.7	93.6	92.4		86.5	93.8	91.8	93.3	94.4	90.3
Operating Profit	5.3	6.4	7.6		13.5	6.2	8.2	6.7	5.6	9.7
All Other Expenses (net)	1.3	1.9	1.6		8.1	1.4	1.4	.5	.8	1.0
Profit Before Taxes	4.0	4.4	5.9		5.4	4.8	6.8	6.1	4.7	8.7
RATIOS										
Current	2.3 / 1.5 / 1.1	2.4 / 1.5 / 1.0	2.7 / 1.6 / 1.1		2.8 / 1.5 / .6	3.6 / 1.4 / .9	2.6 / 1.6 / 1.3	3.6 / 1.4 / 1.2	2.5 / 1.6 / 1.1	2.9 / 1.6 / 1.2
Quick	2.1 / 1.3 / .9	2.2 / 1.3 / .8	2.3 / 1.4 / .9		1.9 / .7 / .5	2.8 / 1.2 / .8	2.4 / 1.5 / 1.0	2.9 / 1.3 / 1.0	2.1 / 1.5 / .9	2.5 / 1.5 / .9
Sales/Receivables	45 8.2 / 62 5.9 / 82 4.4	43 8.4 / 60 6.1 / 81 4.5	44 8.3 / 68 5.4 / 87 4.2		0 UND / 36 10.0 / 58 6.3	38 9.7 / 58 6.3 / 83 4.4	49 7.4 / 67 5.5 / 83 4.4	45 8.1 / 68 5.4 / 100 3.6	70 5.2 / 85 4.3 / 103 3.5	44 8.3 / 66 5.6 / 80 4.5
Cost of Sales/Inventory										
Cost of Sales/Payables										
Sales/Working Capital	6.1 / 13.3 / 75.5	6.7 / 15.6 / -143.9	5.3 / 12.1 / 55.6		10.3 / 63.0 / -7.0	5.9 / 14.9 / -46.4	5.4 / 12.1 / 22.3	4.9 / 11.5 / 24.2	4.5 / 9.0 / 51.2	4.4 / 9.5 / 35.7
EBIT/Interest	(143) 8.1 / 3.0 / .8	(168) 6.2 / 2.9 / 1.2	(153) 11.9 / 4.0 / 1.5			(41) 8.8 / 4.0 / .8	(29) 13.9 / 4.0 / 1.5	(24) 11.8 / 5.4 / 1.1	(30) 13.8 / 4.0 / 1.8	(20) 15.3 / 3.8 / 2.2
Net Profit + Depr., Dep., Amort./Cur. Mat. L/T/D	(44) 4.6 / 2.3 / 1.5	(57) 3.6 / 2.2 / 1.2	(61) 6.2 / 2.5 / 1.4			(10) 7.3 / 2.2 / 1.0			(19) 9.2 / 2.3 / 1.5	(11) 6.2 / 1.6 / .9
Fixed/Worth	.5 / .9 / 2.1	.5 / 1.0 / 2.7	.4 / 1.0 / 2.0		.8 / 9.4 / -24.6	.5 / 1.3 / 3.2	.4 / .8 / 1.4	.5 / .9 / 1.7	.4 / .7 / 1.7	.3 / .9 / 2.4
Debt/Worth	.8 / 1.6 / 3.7	.9 / 1.8 / 5.1	.7 / 1.6 / 4.4		1.1 / 9.0 / -39.5	.7 / 1.7 / 5.6	.6 / 1.3 / 2.7	.8 / 2.1 / 4.0	.7 / 1.3 / 3.0	.6 / 1.6 / 4.4
% Profit Before Taxes/Tangible Net Worth	(137) 42.7 / 19.8 / .8	(155) 44.1 / 19.0 / 4.6	(149) 51.1 / 21.4 / 5.8			(36) 45.4 / 19.9 / 1.7	(28) 44.6 / 22.0 / 5.8	(24) 58.3 / 16.3 / -7.5	40.4 / 13.1 / 3.3	(20) 51.9 / 31.7 / 14.0
% Profit Before Taxes/Total Assets	16.1 / 7.0 / -.2	15.0 / 6.8 / .6	19.7 / 7.4 / 1.3		42.9 / 6.8 / .0	18.9 / 7.2 / -1.8	20.1 / 9.3 / 2.2	27.4 / 6.9 / .9	17.6 / 6.4 / 1.2	20.3 / 9.6 / 2.5
Sales/Net Fixed Assets	15.3 / 7.1 / 4.3	12.4 / 6.9 / 3.5	11.0 / 6.6 / 3.3		23.8 / 5.4 / .6	9.5 / 6.8 / 2.8	15.2 / 6.0 / 5.2	10.8 / 7.6 / 4.5	11.3 / 6.4 / 3.4	13.0 / 6.7 / 3.3
Sales/Total Assets	3.0 / 2.2 / 1.6	2.9 / 2.1 / 1.5	2.8 / 2.0 / 1.5		4.9 / 2.3 / .4	3.4 / 2.0 / 1.1	2.8 / 2.4 / 1.6	2.9 / 2.2 / 1.6	2.3 / 1.9 / 1.5	2.5 / 1.9 / 1.1
% Depr., Dep., Amort./Sales	(143) 1.7 / 4.0 / 6.3	(162) 2.2 / 4.1 / 6.2	(153) 2.4 / 3.8 / 7.2		(11) 2.4 / 3.3 / 10.2	(40) 2.1 / 4.0 / 7.5	(27) 2.2 / 4.9 / 7.4	(23) 2.7 / 3.4 / 5.3	(30) 2.1 / 3.8 / 6.7	(22) 2.4 / 3.3 / 5.9
% Officers', Directors', Owners' Comp/Sales	(63) 3.9 / 7.8 / 12.7	(74) 3.2 / 7.7 / 12.6	(56) 3.2 / 6.3 / 10.2			(20) 4.1 / 5.9 / 9.7	(11) 2.4 / / 10.1		(10) 2.0 / 3.6 / 5.5	
Net Sales ($)	1993565M	1911441M	2369848M		6983M	84146M	123471M	177493M	487272M	1490483M
Total Assets ($)	1198663M	1356049M	1554297M		5759M	50482M	57783M	94551M	292916M	1052806M

M = $ thousand   MM = $ million
See Pages 11 through 18 for Explanation of Ratios and Data

Current Data Sorted By Assets   Comparative Historical Data

						Type of Statement		
	1	11	6		1	Unqualified	12	10
	9	16	1			Reviewed	38	30
11	17	9	1			Compiled	56	35
6	9	1				Tax Returns	36	27
14	28	12	5		2	Other	54	54
	43 (4/1-9/30/02)		117 (10/1/02-3/31/03)				4/1/98-3/31/99	4/1/99-3/31/00
0-500M	500M-2MM	2-10MM	10-50MM	50-100MM	100-250MM		ALL	ALL
31	64	49	13		3	NUMBER OF STATEMENTS	196	156
%	%	%	%	%	%	ASSETS	%	%
12.1	13.4	10.9	11.4			Cash & Equivalents	9.9	11.4
35.9	36.7	35.6	21.8			Trade Receivables (net)	33.1	34.6
4.5	7.3	7.2	9.6	D		Inventory	9.3	9.7
3.0	2.6	4.6	1.8	A		All Other Current	3.0	2.6
55.6	60.0	58.3	44.7	T		Total Current	55.3	58.4
28.5	28.6	30.7	22.2	A		Fixed Assets (net)	34.8	31.5
2.2	5.0	5.2	21.8			Intangibles (net)	3.5	4.8
13.7	6.4	5.8	11.3	N		All Other Non-Current	6.4	5.3
100.0	100.0	100.0	100.0	O		Total	100.0	100.0
				T		LIABILITIES		
27.9	13.2	10.6	6.0			Notes Payable-Short Term	11.8	13.4
3.4	8.9	4.3	6.5	A		Cur. Mat.-L/T/D	5.0	5.7
16.6	16.2	12.4	12.4	V		Trade Payables	14.6	14.0
.0	.4	1.0	.3	A		Income Taxes Payable	.8	.8
18.2	17.3	10.0	10.0	I		All Other Current	12.7	12.0
66.2	56.0	38.3	35.2	L		Total Current	44.8	46.0
14.4	18.4	19.6	21.3	A		Long Term Debt	20.6	15.0
.0	.2	1.0	.2	B		Deferred Taxes	.9	.5
2.8	1.6	4.5	13.1	L		All Other Non-Current	2.8	2.9
16.7	23.8	36.6	30.2	E		Net Worth	30.9	35.7
100.0	100.0	100.0	100.0			Total Liabilities & Net Worth	100.0	100.0
						INCOME DATA		
100.0	100.0	100.0	100.0			Net Sales	100.0	100.0
						Gross Profit		
95.8	98.0	94.0	93.4			Operating Expenses	95.1	95.1
4.2	2.0	6.0	6.6			Operating Profit	4.9	4.9
.8	.8	2.4	3.2			All Other Expenses (net)	1.1	1.1
3.3	1.2	3.6	3.4			Profit Before Taxes	3.8	3.8
						RATIOS		
2.6	2.3	2.5	1.8				2.2	2.3
.9	1.3	1.5	1.1			Current	1.4	1.4
.5	.8	1.1	.9				.9	.9
2.2	2.1	2.1	1.4				1.7	1.9
.6	1.0	1.2	1.0			Quick	1.1	1.1
.2	.6	.9	.6				.6	.7

0	UND	30	12.2	38	9.6	25	14.8			Sales/Receivables	30	12.2	33	11.0

(Sales/Receivables block)

0	UND	30	12.2	38	9.6	25	14.8	Sales/Receivables	30	12.2	33	11.0
36	10.2	47	7.8	55	6.6	49	7.5		44	8.3	50	7.3
45	8.1	69	5.3	70	5.2	88	4.1		62	5.9	68	5.4

Cost of Sales/Inventory

Cost of Sales/Payables

0-500M	500M-2MM	2-10MM	10-50MM		Ratio	ALL	ALL
11.9	8.4	5.7	6.9		Sales/Working Capital	8.1	7.5
-43.9	23.9	13.8	32.2			17.8	15.7
-9.2	-18.6	89.2	NM			-82.6	-86.2
19.6	6.6	6.2			EBIT/Interest	11.2	14.2
(24) 3.9	(56) 1.8	(39) 2.1				(170) 3.1	(145) 3.9
-1.0	-4.1	.4				1.3	1.3
	3.7	5.9			Net Profit + Depr., Dep., Amort./Cur. Mat. L /T/D	5.6	4.7
	(11) 1.5	(16) 1.9				(58) 2.5	(28) 2.0
	.8	.9				1.3	.8
.3	.3	.4	.2		Fixed/Worth	.4	.3
1.1	.9	.8	1.4			1.1	.8
-.8	2.5	2.3	NM			3.8	2.9
.6	.8	.9	1.1		Debt/Worth	.9	.8
2.1	2.4	2.0	1.7			2.3	1.9
-3.6	8.1	4.9	NM			9.0	5.6
165.2	44.2	41.6	76.6		% Profit Before Taxes/Tangible Net Worth	79.5	64.3
(19) 44.4	(54) 12.8	(45) 5.8	(10) 25.4			(167) 30.6	(137) 26.6
7.7	-21.8	-7.4	10.2			7.3	8.2
55.2	18.0	9.6	12.9		% Profit Before Taxes/Total Assets	22.7	18.5
5.5	2.7	3.0	5.4			9.0	8.9
-14.5	-10.1	-2.2	1.0			.6	1.1
85.0	24.5	19.5	65.0		Sales/Net Fixed Assets	21.2	23.3
18.2	11.1	7.9	7.8			9.6	10.4
9.4	5.7	3.8	3.9			4.7	4.5
5.9	3.6	3.0	2.1		Sales/Total Assets	3.9	3.7
4.3	2.7	2.3	1.4			2.6	2.7
2.8	1.9	1.5	.8			1.8	1.9
.7	1.1	1.4	.6		% Depr., Dep., Amort./Sales	1.5	1.6
(19) 2.7	(54) 3.1	(45) 2.6	(11) 3.0			(175) 3.1	(135) 2.8
3.5	6.2	6.0	4.9			5.3	5.2
4.8	6.5	2.6			% Officers', Directors', Owners' Comp/Sales	5.2	5.5
(18) 13.1	(32) 8.1	(13) 5.5				(95) 9.6	(81) 8.4
19.9	12.2	12.7				17.0	14.4
34441M	190456M	465727M	492059M	916843M	Net Sales ($)	2374472M	1898520M
7172M	62956M	203928M	307107M	506420M	Total Assets ($)	1155911M	989948M

M = $ thousand   MM = $ million
See Pages 11 through 18 for Explanation of Ratios and Data

Comparative Historical Data　　　　　　　　　　　　　　Current Data Sorted By Sales

Hist 1	Hist 2	Hist 3	Type of Statement	0-1MM	1-3MM	3-5MM	5-10MM	10-25MM	25MM & OVER
9	8	19	Unqualified		1		8	6	4
30	21	26	Reviewed	1	6	1	10	8	
40	34	38	Compiled	8	18	5	4	2	1
34	23	16	Tax Returns	5	5	3	3		
37	56	61	Other	11	21	8	10	7	4
4/1/00-3/31/01 ALL	4/1/01-3/31/02 ALL	4/1/02-3/31/03 ALL		43 (4/1-9/30/02)			117 (10/1/02-3/31/03)		
150	142	160	NUMBER OF STATEMENTS	25	51	17	35	23	9
%	%	%	ASSETS	%	%	%	%	%	%
9.9	10.0	12.2	Cash & Equivalents	11.4	12.6	14.1	12.3	9.7	
35.1	35.4	34.9	Trade Receivables (net)	27.7	37.5	34.0	36.4	37.4	
9.9	9.9	6.8	Inventory	4.5	6.4	5.5	8.6	8.5	
3.4	2.6	3.2	All Other Current	2.4	2.4	2.2	3.4	6.7	
58.4	57.8	57.2	Total Current	46.1	58.9	55.9	60.7	62.3	
32.4	29.9	28.7	Fixed Assets (net)	36.9	28.5	35.3	25.3	20.8	
3.0	4.7	6.0	Intangibles (net)	7.0	2.6	4.5	9.2	7.1	
6.2	7.5	8.1	All Other Non-Current	9.9	10.1	4.3	4.7	9.8	
100.0	100.0	100.0	Total	100.0	100.0	100.0	100.0	100.0	
			LIABILITIES						
12.7	13.0	14.6	Notes Payable-Short Term	22.4	17.3	12.3	9.9	12.2	
6.6	5.1	6.1	Cur. Mat.-L/T/D	5.4	5.3	15.7	3.7	5.3	
16.6	15.3	14.6	Trade Payables	13.5	17.1	12.9	12.4	14.2	
.4	.3	.5	Income Taxes Payable	.2	.5	.1	.3	1.4	
12.8	11.5	14.4	All Other Current	18.3	12.6	18.7	11.8	16.7	
49.1	45.3	50.2	Total Current	59.8	52.7	59.7	38.2	49.8	
20.5	17.7	18.1	Long Term Debt	35.7	16.1	15.3	12.7	15.2	
.6	.7	.4	Deferred Taxes	.0	.1	1.4	.6	.8	
4.8	3.5	3.7	All Other Non-Current	1.1	1.6	2.3	5.1	10.8	
25.0	32.9	27.6	Net Worth	3.4	29.5	21.2	43.4	23.4	
100.0	100.0	100.0	Total Liabilities & Net Worth	100.0	100.0	100.0	100.0	100.0	
			INCOME DATA						
100.0	100.0	100.0	Net Sales	100.0	100.0	100.0	100.0	100.0	
			Gross Profit						
94.8	96.8	95.7	Operating Expenses	94.4	95.4	99.1	96.3	97.3	
5.2	3.2	4.3	Operating Profit	5.6	4.6	.9	3.7	2.7	
1.4	1.4	1.5	All Other Expenses (net)	1.2	1.6	1.4	1.5	1.6	
3.8	1.8	2.8	Profit Before Taxes	4.4	3.0	−.6	2.3	1.0	
			RATIOS						
2.3	2.5	2.3		2.7	2.3	3.1	2.5	1.7	
1.4	1.5	1.3	Current	.9	1.2	1.6	1.6	1.2	
1.0	.9	.8		.4	.7	1.0	1.1	1.0	
1.9	2.1	1.9		2.3	2.1	2.7	2.4	1.3	
(149) 1.0	(141) 1.1	1.0	Quick	.6	1.0	1.5	1.2	1.0	
.7	.7	.6		.2	.5	.8	.8	.7	
30 12.3	29 12.6	30 12.2		0 UND	29 12.8	38 9.7	40 9.2	31 11.7	
50 7.3	46 7.9	46 8.0	Sales/Receivables	38 9.6	43 8.6	49 7.4	52 7.0	53 6.9	
65 5.6	62 5.9	68 5.3		50 7.4	72 5.1	60 6.1	73 5.0	67 5.5	
			Cost of Sales/Inventory						
			Cost of Sales/Payables						
7.9	7.2	7.7		6.5	9.3	6.3	5.9	11.0	
18.3	21.6	20.2	Sales/Working Capital	−43.9	24.6	13.7	13.6	29.0	
−136.1	−55.4	−29.4		−7.2	−14.3	NM	64.4	−277.1	
8.0	11.8	6.7		8.6	6.0	15.8	7.0	9.1	
(133) 2.9	(121) 1.7	(131) 2.3	EBIT/Interest	(18) 1.8	(44) 1.5	(16) 2.0	(25) 2.3	(21) 3.6	
.7	−1.0	−1.1		−3.1	−3.8	−4.1	.8	−.3	
5.1	5.4	4.2	Net Profit + Depr., Dep.,						
(38) 1.8	(31) 2.0	(30) 1.5	Amort./Cur. Mat. L/T/D						
.7	.7	.8							
.4	.3	.3		.5	.3	.3	.3	.2	
1.0	.8	.9	Fixed/Worth	9.4	.9	.7	.7	.7	
5.1	3.7	4.0		−.5	5.1	4.4	1.5	2.4	
.9	.5	.8		.5	.8	.5	.8	1.4	
2.4	2.4	2.1	Debt/Worth	UND	2.5	1.7	1.9	2.8	
13.9	13.7	10.9		−2.8	11.5	7.0	4.1	12.9	
62.3	47.4	56.2	% Profit Before Taxes/Tangible	62.6	71.6	33.5	43.2	43.0	
(126) 22.6	(115) 12.9	(131) 14.5	Net Worth	(13) 15.6	(42) 12.8	(15) 7.4	(32) 7.6	(20) 9.6	
4.9	−14.2	−6.9		−5.3	−23.5	−31.7	1.3	−12.3	
18.4	13.1	15.3	% Profit Before Taxes/Total	21.8	17.7	15.2	8.7	15.6	
6.5	2.7	3.9	Assets	.0	3.5	4.4	3.0	3.9	
.1	−7.8	−5.4		−16.1	−11.1	−10.1	−.3	−4.4	
25.8	29.0	27.5		21.1	27.9	28.2	20.9	66.2	
11.5	11.5	11.3	Sales/Net Fixed Assets	9.9	11.9	8.2	11.4	19.4	
5.0	5.4	5.5		2.9	5.6	4.5	5.6	7.5	
3.5	3.8	3.9		4.5	3.7	4.0	3.4	4.2	
2.6	2.8	2.6	Sales/Total Assets	2.6	2.7	3.1	2.4	2.9	
1.8	1.9	1.7		1.0	2.1	1.6	1.9	1.7	
1.2	1.2	1.1		1.1	1.7	.9	1.2	1.4	
(131) 2.7	(114) 2.8	(129) 2.8	% Depr., Dep., Amort./Sales	(16) 3.0	(40) 3.6	(15) 2.4	(33) 2.4	(19) 1.8	
5.1	5.3	5.4		9.9	6.2	6.2	6.0	3.1	
3.5	3.9	5.0	% Officers', Directors',		6.5			4.4	
(79) 6.6	(62) 7.9	(65) 8.3	Owners' Comp/Sales	(31)	8.7		(10)	7.1	
13.3	11.9	14.9			13.3			17.2	
1020759M	1159796M	2099526M	Net Sales ($)	13418M	100977M	62688M	250646M	377080M	1294717M
462595M	477362M	1087583M	Total Assets ($)	10129M	45500M	28199M	124305M	198986M	680464M

Current Data Sorted By Assets　　　　　　　　　　　　　　　Comparative Historical Data

Type of Statement	0-500M	500M-2MM	2-10MM	10-50MM	50-100MM	100-250MM	ALL 4/1/98-3/31/99	ALL 4/1/99-3/31/00
Unqualified		6	27	26	2	3	105	95
Reviewed	4	27	35				36	36
Compiled	16	32	6			1	56	53
Tax Returns	16	12	6	1			38	28
Other	19	42	33	12	4	3	150	131
		48 (4/1-9/30/02)		285 (10/1/02-3/31/03)				
NUMBER OF STATEMENTS	55	119	107	39	6	7	385	343
	%	%	%	%	%	%	%	%
ASSETS								
Cash & Equivalents	20.2	14.3	15.7	19.6			17.3	18.5
Trade Receivables (net)	36.7	45.8	46.3	35.8			43.6	45.5
Inventory	1.9	2.6	2.5	3.2			2.4	2.3
All Other Current	3.3	3.5	6.5	5.7			4.4	4.4
Total Current	62.0	66.3	71.0	64.2			67.8	70.7
Fixed Assets (net)	22.2	14.6	12.9	14.0			19.0	15.8
Intangibles (net)	3.8	8.8	7.5	12.8			6.4	6.5
All Other Non-Current	11.9	10.2	8.6	9.1			6.8	7.0
Total	100.0	100.0	100.0	100.0			100.0	100.0
LIABILITIES								
Notes Payable-Short Term	22.6	13.8	11.1	22.8			18.0	15.1
Cur. Mat.-L/T/D	16.8	3.9	3.7	3.9			9.5	2.8
Trade Payables	20.6	14.0	11.5	10.8			13.6	11.5
Income Taxes Payable	.5	.5	.8	1.6			.6	.5
All Other Current	27.2	17.8	20.6	23.4			28.9	21.0
Total Current	87.8	50.0	47.8	62.5			70.5	50.8
Long Term Debt	22.9	10.7	8.1	10.3			10.8	11.1
Deferred Taxes	.1	1.0	1.1	1.3			1.2	.9
All Other Non-Current	7.5	9.0	5.6	10.1			11.3	7.1
Net Worth	−18.3	29.3	37.4	15.8			6.2	30.2
Total Liabilities & Net Worth	100.0	100.0	100.0	100.0			100.0	100.0
INCOME DATA								
Net Sales	100.0	100.0	100.0	100.0			100.0	100.0
Gross Profit								
Operating Expenses	96.5	96.3	94.8	98.6			140.4	94.4
Operating Profit	3.5	3.7	5.2	1.4			−40.4	5.6
All Other Expenses (net)	1.4	.8	.5	1.4			.7	.5
Profit Before Taxes	2.1	2.9	4.7	.0			−41.1	5.1
RATIOS								
Current	3.0	2.5	2.9	2.8			2.8	2.7
	1.1	1.4	1.6	1.5			1.6	1.6
	.3	.9	1.1	1.1			1.0	1.1
Quick	2.9	2.3	2.9	2.1			2.5	2.4
	.9	1.3	1.5	1.3			1.4	1.4
	.3	.8	1.0	.9			.9	1.0
Sales/Receivables	0 UND	34 10.7	40 9.0	38 9.6			42 8.6	38 9.7
	25 14.5	47 7.7	57 6.4	70 5.2			62 5.8	58 6.2
	52 7.1	70 5.2	75 4.8	87 4.2			88 4.1	84 4.3
Cost of Sales/Inventory								
Cost of Sales/Payables								
Sales/Working Capital	9.9	7.5	5.8	4.5			4.9	6.0
	123.2	14.7	11.3	11.0			11.7	12.7
	−16.6	−89.2	68.3	87.9			UND	63.7
EBIT/Interest	(41) 24.2	(102) 14.0	(80) 47.7	(32) 28.0			(292) 18.0	(276) 26.2
	5.5	3.3	7.4	6.8			4.6	6.0
	−.4	−.8	1.6	.7			.9	1.1
Net Profit + Depr., Dep., Amort./Cur. Mat. L/T/D		(14) 5.5	(14) 7.3	(14) 28.7			(60) 12.7	(43) 13.0
		1.1	2.2	6.8			4.9	4.0
		.6	.0	3.0			1.2	.7
Fixed/Worth	.1	.1	.1	.1			.2	.1
	.7	.3	.3	.5			.5	.3
	−2.7	27.4	1.2	−5.6			4.8	1.5
Debt/Worth	.9	.6	.6	.9			.7	.6
	4.2	1.9	1.5	2.7			2.0	1.7
	−3.0	124.6	6.0	−9.9			15.3	7.1
% Profit Before Taxes/Tangible Net Worth	(36) 175.5	(90) 62.4	(93) 69.1	(28) 46.0			(305) 66.7	(289) 76.1
	58.4	20.4	36.7	31.5			37.1	35.8
	7.9	−.9	9.6	−17.7			6.4	10.8
% Profit Before Taxes/Total Assets	38.0	23.5	25.9	18.1			24.6	30.6
	17.9	7.1	8.8	6.5			9.4	12.0
	−21.3	−4.4	1.3	−6.3			−1.1	1.0
Sales/Net Fixed Assets	143.6	71.3	65.4	61.3			45.0	59.5
	38.2	29.5	35.1	20.2			19.4	24.7
	18.3	15.5	15.8	12.9			9.0	11.7
Sales/Total Assets	8.9	4.2	3.8	2.9			4.0	4.3
	5.5	3.1	2.5	1.7			2.5	2.8
	3.4	2.4	1.7	1.4			1.5	1.8
% Depr., Dep., Amort./Sales	(30) .5	(87) .7	(76) .7	(27) .9			(273) .8	(239) .8
	1.2	1.5	1.3	2.1			1.9	1.7
	3.2	2.4	2.7	3.7			3.6	3.6
% Officers', Directors', Owners' Comp/Sales	(29) 5.7	(47) 3.2	(27) 3.1				(98) 3.6	(85) 3.0
	12.2	6.3	4.4				8.4	7.6
	25.2	9.8	9.1				13.7	15.9
Net Sales ($)	79365M	481453M	1269681M	3848638M	672982M	1418445M	8558952M	9569781M
Total Assets ($)	12271M	139296M	464948M	806265M	482590M	1188306M	5262843M	4905172M

M = $ thousand　　MM = $ million
See Pages 11 through 18 for Explanation of Ratios and Data

Comparative Historical Data | | | | Current Data Sorted By Sales

			Type of Statement						
67	53	64	Unqualified		3	6	14	16	25
40	45	66	Reviewed	1	11	13	22	17	2
59	73	55	Compiled	7	22	14	10	1	1
26	29	35	Tax Returns	8	10	7	5	4	1
134	109	113	Other	13	22	16	27	18	17
4/1/00-	4/1/01-	4/1/02-			48 (4/1-9/30/02)			285 (10/1/02-3/31/03)	
3/31/01	3/31/02	3/31/03							
ALL	ALL	ALL		0-1MM	1-3MM	3-5MM	5-10MM	10-25MM	25MM & OVER
326	309	333	**NUMBER OF STATEMENTS**	29	68	56	78	56	46
%	%	%	**ASSETS**	%	%	%	%	%	%
14.8	15.0	17.0	Cash & Equivalents	21.9	15.9	15.8	14.9	18.5	18.8
47.8	44.6	42.5	Trade Receivables (net)	34.0	40.2	39.4	46.6	49.1	39.9
3.0	3.6	2.6	Inventory	1.8	2.8	2.5	2.6	2.2	3.5
5.3	4.3	4.7	All Other Current	3.7	3.1	3.5	6.7	4.5	6.4
71.0	67.5	66.8	Total Current	61.3	61.9	61.1	70.8	74.2	68.6
14.1	14.9	15.1	Fixed Assets (net)	19.0	17.2	17.6	13.8	11.2	13.5
8.0	8.0	8.4	Intangibles (net)	5.5	11.0	7.8	6.4	7.9	10.9
6.9	9.5	9.7	All Other Non-Current	14.1	9.9	13.4	9.1	6.7	7.0
100.0	100.0	100.0	Total	100.0	100.0	100.0	100.0	100.0	100.0
			LIABILITIES						
19.4	16.8	14.9	Notes Payable-Short Term	22.8	13.6	13.3	15.2	8.4	21.4
2.9	3.6	5.9	Cur. Mat.-L/T/D	24.6	3.8	4.7	3.6	2.6	2.6
13.7	10.5	13.6	Trade Payables	19.2	15.0	12.7	12.5	11.8	13.5
.7	.7	.7	Income Taxes Payable	.0	.5	.6	1.0	.9	1.0
22.3	25.2	21.2	All Other Current	29.9	21.8	19.9	16.8	21.2	24.3
58.9	56.8	56.5	Total Current	96.4	54.7	51.2	49.1	48.4	62.8
15.0	13.9	11.7	Long Term Debt	34.1	11.2	11.4	9.8	5.9	8.8
.9	1.1	.9	Deferred Taxes	.0	.6	.2	2.0	.7	1.3
5.3	13.4	7.7	All Other Non-Current	7.9	5.2	8.6	9.8	6.9	7.8
19.8	14.8	23.2	Net Worth	-38.4	28.3	28.5	29.4	38.1	19.4
100.0	100.0	100.0	Total Liabilities & Net Worth	100.0	100.0	100.0	100.0	100.0	100.0
			INCOME DATA						
100.0	100.0	100.0	Net Sales	100.0	100.0	100.0	100.0	100.0	100.0
			Gross Profit						
95.2	95.8	95.8	Operating Expenses	94.0	96.1	96.0	96.0	98.7	92.6
4.8	4.2	4.2	Operating Profit	6.0	3.9	4.0	4.0	1.3	7.4
.8	.9	.9	All Other Expenses (net)	3.1	.3	.6	1.1	.4	.9
4.0	3.3	3.3	Profit Before Taxes	2.9	3.6	3.4	2.9	.9	6.5
			RATIOS						
2.4	2.6	2.8		3.7	3.0	2.5	2.6	2.9	2.8
1.5	1.5	1.5	Current	1.0	1.5	1.4	1.5	1.7	1.4
1.0	.9	.9		.4	.6	.9	1.0	1.2	1.1
2.3	2.3	2.6		3.7	3.0	2.4	2.3	2.8	2.4
1.3	1.3	1.3	Quick	.9	1.2	1.4	1.3	1.5	1.2
.8	.8	.8		.4	.6	.8	.8	1.2	.8
39 9.2	35 10.4	32 11.5		6 65.7	17 22.1	32 11.5	38 9.7	34 10.7	40 9.2
60 6.1	53 6.9	51 7.2	Sales/Receivables	30 12.1	47 7.8	45 8.0	55 6.6	58 6.3	61 5.9
80 4.6	75 4.9	73 5.0		65 5.6	69 5.3	69 5.3	72 5.1	75 4.9	84 4.3
			Cost of Sales/Inventory						
			Cost of Sales/Payables						
6.4	6.8	6.0		6.7	5.4	6.6	6.9	6.0	4.5
15.0	16.6	14.7	Sales/Working Capital	-188.5	14.5	20.9	13.7	13.2	12.2
114.0	-103.2	-63.9		-11.9	-17.8	-70.0	102.1	28.5	276.3
18.6	13.2	21.2		10.1	23.7	20.4	20.1	36.7	32.1
(258) 5.6	(258) 2.7	(265) 5.2	EBIT/Interest	(22) 2.3	(55) 6.0	(44) 3.8	(64) 4.0	(41) 7.3	(39) 7.3
.8	-2.3	.5		-2.5	-.4	-.5	.7	.0	3.5
17.3	13.2	8.2					7.5		18.9
(38) 3.7	(45) 6.0	(48) 3.8	Net Profit + Depr., Dep., Amort./Cur. Mat. L/T/D			(12) 1.6		(15) 6.9	
.8	.4	.8					.3		3.1
.1	.1	.1		.0	.1	.1	.1	.1	.2
.4	.4	.3	Fixed/Worth	.3	.8	.5	.3	.2	.3
1.5	2.6	4.0		9.0	-5.6	5.1	1.3	1.1	-11.9
.8	.7	.6		.6	.5	.8	.6	.6	.5
2.1	2.2	2.0	Debt/Worth	4.2	2.7	1.7	1.8	1.2	2.6
12.0	21.6	81.9		-2.0	-17.9	81.7	6.5	6.6	-48.2
76.7	77.2	67.1		105.3	132.3	63.4	51.8	68.0	45.3
(263) 40.5	(237) 30.9	(256) 31.1	% Profit Before Taxes/Tangible Net Worth	(19) 41.2	(49) 50.9	(43) 22.4	(64) 21.7	(48) 33.8	(33) 36.7
10.0	-3.1	3.9		.5	14.3	-4.6	-1.5	4.7	17.2
28.6	23.7	25.3		40.8	28.0	30.5	19.2	22.5	19.0
10.6	6.4	8.1	% Profit Before Taxes/Total Assets	4.5	9.3	8.0	6.1	8.6	10.4
.4	-7.2	-3.7		-22.3	-5.0	-7.2	-1.5	-6.6	3.6
75.4	66.8	69.5		227.6	57.3	58.8	96.0	82.0	61.7
30.2	29.6	29.1	Sales/Net Fixed Assets	35.1	27.2	24.3	41.0	33.4	23.5
13.3	13.7	14.8		13.1	15.3	13.1	17.2	19.5	10.8
4.3	4.6	4.4		5.7	4.4	4.2	4.2	4.8	3.5
3.1	3.2	3.0	Sales/Total Assets	3.4	3.0	3.0	3.1	3.4	2.1
1.9	2.0	1.9		1.8	2.2	2.2	1.8	1.9	1.2
.5	.6	.7		.6	1.0	.9	.5	.6	.8
(230) 1.4	(223) 1.5	(228) 1.5	% Depr., Dep., Amort./Sales	(11) 3.5	(49) 1.6	(38) 1.4	(55) 1.3	(40) 1.1	(35) 1.9
2.5	2.8	2.9		6.3	2.7	2.4	2.7	2.5	3.8
3.5	2.7	3.5		12.2	4.2	3.4	3.1	2.7	
(98) 5.0	(101) 5.7	(109) 6.6	% Officers', Directors', Owners' Comp/Sales	(14) 20.2	(29) 7.2	(20) 7.4	(27) 4.4	(13) 3.9	
9.8	11.6	13.4		31.8	17.0	9.8	9.6	7.0	
9072755M	6299587M	7770564M	Net Sales ($)	15066M	132836M	216464M	569583M	850243M	5986372M
4661605M	2959181M	3093676M	Total Assets ($)	7517M	54526M	85291M	261827M	324188M	2360327M

© RMA 2003   M = $ thousand   MM = $ million
See Pages 11 through 18 for Explanation of Ratios and Data

Current Data Sorted By Assets   Comparative Historical Data

Type of Statement	0-500M	500M-2MM	2-10MM	10-50MM	50-100MM	100-250MM	4/1/98-3/31/99 ALL	4/1/99-3/31/00 ALL
Unqualified	1	10	54	46	11	7	110	119
Reviewed	3	29	34	4			68	78
Compiled	8	23	9	1			54	54
Tax Returns	17	12	3			1	24	20
Other	28	42	48	31	5	4	143	140
		65 (4/1-9/30/02)			366 (10/1/02-3/31/03)			
NUMBER OF STATEMENTS	57	116	148	82	16	12	399	411
ASSETS	%	%	%	%	%	%	%	%
Cash & Equivalents	22.0	15.3	16.4	18.7	20.3	17.1	13.2	14.7
Trade Receivables (net)	36.8	50.6	44.5	42.3	28.2	33.3	47.5	47.7
Inventory	7.1	6.9	7.0	5.1	4.4	2.6	6.5	7.0
All Other Current	1.2	3.5	7.5	5.8	3.7	8.0	4.1	4.0
Total Current	67.0	76.4	75.5	71.9	56.6	60.9	71.3	73.4
Fixed Assets (net)	23.5	13.1	11.7	12.4	14.5	16.1	15.6	15.1
Intangibles (net)	2.7	3.6	5.8	8.6	23.7	19.5	6.6	5.4
All Other Non-Current	6.8	6.9	7.1	7.1	5.2	3.4	6.5	6.0
Total	100.0	100.0	100.0	100.0	100.0	100.0	100.0	100.0
LIABILITIES								
Notes Payable-Short Term	38.6	17.0	10.4	11.4	8.5	3.1	5.2	12.8
Cur. Mat.-L/T/D	8.9	2.5	1.7	2.3	2.5	3.0	3.4	2.5
Trade Payables	19.0	17.2	17.6	13.8	10.4	9.7	19.4	19.1
Income Taxes Payable	.3	.4	.6	.6	.1	.5	.6	.5
All Other Current	18.3	17.4	22.7	24.2	16.0	14.0	17.0	18.8
Total Current	85.1	54.5	53.0	52.4	37.5	30.3	45.6	53.7
Long Term Debt	13.0	7.4	4.7	5.4	9.8	23.0	9.5	9.3
Deferred Taxes	.1	.8	.4	.6	.8	.8	.8	.9
All Other Non-Current	16.8	5.6	5.7	4.4	6.1	10.9	5.2	6.0
Net Worth	−14.9	31.7	36.2	37.2	45.7	35.0	38.9	30.0
Total Liabilities & Net Worth	100.0	100.0	100.0	100.0	100.0	100.0	100.0	100.0
INCOME DATA								
Net Sales	100.0	100.0	100.0	100.0	100.0	100.0	100.0	100.0
Gross Profit								
Operating Expenses	96.7	95.3	95.5	95.6	96.9	95.6	102.8	95.6
Operating Profit	3.3	4.7	4.5	4.4	3.1	4.4	−2.8	4.4
All Other Expenses (net)	.9	.5	.1	1.3	.2	.2	.7	.7
Profit Before Taxes	2.3	4.2	4.3	3.0	2.8	4.2	−3.4	3.7
RATIOS								
Current	2.0	2.4	2.2	1.9	3.1	3.1	2.2	2.3
	1.2	1.6	1.4	1.3	1.6	2.4	1.4	1.5
	.5	.9	1.0	1.1	.8	1.2	1.0	1.0
Quick	1.8	2.2	1.8	1.8	3.0	2.9	1.9	2.0
	1.0	1.3	1.2	1.1	1.0	2.2	1.2	1.2
	.4	.7	.7	.8	.8	.8	.8	.8
Sales/Receivables	8 45.9	32 11.4	40 9.1	55 6.6	50 7.3	58 6.3	43 8.6	41 8.9
	30 12.1	51 7.2	55 6.7	69 5.3	76 4.8	78 4.7	62 5.9	62 5.9
	48 7.6	76 4.8	73 5.0	88 4.2	112 3.3	101 3.6	87 4.2	86 4.2
Cost of Sales/Inventory								
Cost of Sales/Payables								
Sales/Working Capital	11.2	7.3	6.6	5.6	4.6	2.2	5.6	5.9
	51.9	14.9	13.1	12.5	6.1	5.7	14.4	14.9
	−16.7	−47.7	380.4	47.8	−32.2	18.9	332.2	549.5
EBIT/Interest	(44) 9.5	(99) 19.2	(129) 31.8	(67) 25.2	(14) 16.8		(342) 17.9	(333) 19.6
	2.9	4.5	9.0	6.0	3.3		4.1	4.7
	−3.0	1.2	1.6	1.5	1.1		.5	1.1
Net Profit + Depr., Dep., Amort./Cur. Mat. L /T/D		(13) 15.7	(26) 33.8	(20) 39.5			(82) 8.3	(73) 14.6
		1.9	7.2	7.3			4.0	6.0
		.9	2.6	1.8			1.0	1.4
Fixed/Worth	.2	.1	.1	.1	.1	.2	.2	.1
	.9	.4	.3	.3	1.2	.9	.5	.4
	−.7	2.8	1.4	.8	NM	4.1	2.2	1.5
Debt/Worth	1.0	.8	.9	1.0	.6	.5	.9	.9
	3.5	2.2	2.0	2.0	2.2	5.2	2.2	2.2
	−3.6	25.4	7.9	7.5	NM	33.3	10.2	7.8
% Profit Before Taxes/Tangible Net Worth	(37) 108.7	(89) 64.1	(129) 60.3	(72) 60.2	(12) 55.4	(10) 132.4	(327) 72.5	(345) 69.7
	25.8	32.7	37.0	35.9	11.0	21.8	33.3	34.3
	−37.4	2.1	7.0	3.9	2.2	2.6	5.5	5.6
% Profit Before Taxes/Total Assets	48.8	25.1	21.5	19.4	7.9	16.9	20.3	21.0
	5.0	6.6	10.8	7.7	4.2	7.9	8.3	8.8
	−19.7	.2	2.2	.6	1.4	−.6	−.9	.6
Sales/Net Fixed Assets	117.9	99.2	83.3	60.5	51.3	31.7	53.4	64.7
	35.4	39.7	33.5	22.8	17.6	13.5	24.3	27.4
	16.4	19.5	18.0	12.4	5.8	6.6	12.5	14.0
Sales/Total Assets	7.4	4.6	3.7	2.9	1.6	1.8	4.0	4.1
	5.2	3.3	2.9	2.1	1.4	1.5	2.6	2.9
	3.7	2.5	2.1	1.3	.9	1.0	1.7	1.7
% Depr., Dep., Amort./Sales	(35) .6	(86) .5	(121) .5	(57) .6		(10) 1.2	(327) .7	(315) .6
	1.2	1.0	1.2	2.2		1.6	1.5	1.3
	3.3	2.3	2.2	4.5		3.4	3.0	2.9
% Officers', Directors', Owners' Comp/Sales	(27) 6.6	(42) 3.6	(38) 2.5				(90) 2.6	(117) 2.7
	10.8	5.7	5.2				6.2	5.7
	17.9	13.9	8.0				11.8	11.9
Net Sales ($)	75785M	502442M	2008901M	4062941M	1661274M	2894987M	13628954M	11393839M
Total Assets ($)	14056M	140286M	689449M	1911493M	1249163M	1917137M	6442614M	6590067M

M = $ thousand   MM = $ million
See Pages 11 through 18 for Explanation of Ratios and Data

Comparative Historical Data | Current Data Sorted By Sales

Hist 1	Hist 2	Hist 3			Type of Statement	0-1MM	1-3MM	3-5MM	5-10MM	10-25MM	25MM & OVER
83	66	129			Unqualified	1	4	5	15	38	66
57	52	70			Reviewed		12	15	22	15	6
89	85	41			Compiled	3	13	9	11	4	1
21	18	33			Tax Returns	9	12	6	3	2	1
115	126	158			Other	12	29	21	27	35	34
4/1/00-3/31/01 ALL	4/1/01-3/31/02 ALL	4/1/02-3/31/03 ALL				65 (4/1-9/30/02)			366 (10/1/02-3/31/03)		
365	347	431			**NUMBER OF STATEMENTS**	25	70	56	78	94	108
%	%	%			**ASSETS**	%	%	%	%	%	%
15.6	15.5	17.5			Cash & Equivalents	17.6	18.7	17.6	14.5	20.6	16.0
46.8	43.5	43.8			Trade Receivables (net)	25.0	43.7	45.4	49.2	41.0	45.8
6.3	6.9	6.4			Inventory	9.5	6.9	5.6	7.9	6.0	5.0
5.9	6.5	5.2			All Other Current	1.7	3.8	4.4	6.0	7.2	4.9
74.6	72.4	72.8			Total Current	53.9	73.1	73.0	77.5	74.9	71.7
14.3	14.3	14.0			Fixed Assets (net)	31.3	16.5	13.5	10.3	13.1	12.1
5.4	6.2	6.4			Intangibles (net)	6.4	4.0	4.2	5.8	5.8	10.0
5.7	7.1	6.8			All Other Non-Current	8.4	6.4	9.2	6.5	6.2	6.3
100.0	100.0	100.0			Total	100.0	100.0	100.0	100.0	100.0	100.0
					LIABILITIES						
12.8	15.5	15.8			Notes Payable-Short Term	45.6	20.5	15.5	16.2	9.0	11.8
3.1	3.4	3.1			Cur. Mat.-L/T/D	8.2	5.0	2.9	2.3	1.6	2.6
17.5	16.7	16.5			Trade Payables	22.9	16.0	14.5	14.8	18.4	15.9
.6	.7	.5			Income Taxes Payable	.5	.4	.2	.5	.5	.6
17.4	19.2	20.5			All Other Current	14.8	18.0	24.5	16.1	24.2	21.3
51.5	55.5	56.3			Total Current	92.0	59.8	57.6	49.8	53.7	52.2
8.4	7.4	7.3			Long Term Debt	5.4	16.2	5.7	5.5	4.9	6.4
.7	.5	.5			Deferred Taxes	.1	.4	.6	.5	.5	.7
5.2	8.9	7.1			All Other Non-Current	13.3	12.6	4.2	8.0	5.0	4.6
34.3	27.8	28.7			Net Worth	−10.9	10.9	32.0	36.3	35.8	36.1
100.0	100.0	100.0			Total Liabilities & Net Worth	100.0	100.0	100.0	100.0	100.0	100.0
					INCOME DATA						
100.0	100.0	100.0			Net Sales	100.0	100.0	100.0	100.0	100.0	100.0
					Gross Profit						
97.9	96.9	95.7			Operating Expenses	95.3	95.3	94.6	96.9	96.3	95.3
2.1	3.1	4.3			Operating Profit	4.7	4.7	5.4	3.1	3.7	4.7
.0	1.0	.6			All Other Expenses (net)	1.8	.5	.1	.2	.7	.7
2.1	2.1	3.7			Profit Before Taxes	2.9	4.2	5.3	2.9	3.1	4.0
					RATIOS						
2.6	2.1	2.3			Current	1.7	2.2	2.3	2.6	2.3	2.0
1.4	1.4	1.4				.7	1.5	1.5	1.6	1.4	1.3
1.1	1.0	1.0				.4	.9	.9	1.1	1.0	1.1
2.2	1.8	2.0			Quick	1.6	1.9	2.2	2.0	1.9	1.9
1.2	1.1	1.2				.6	1.3	1.3	1.4	1.1	1.1
.9	.7	.7				.2	.6	.8	.8	.7	.8
43 8.5	33 11.0	36 10.2			Sales/Receivables	8 45.9	28 13.1	31 11.8	36 10.0	38 9.6	53 6.9
62 5.9	52 7.0	57 6.5				32 11.5	46 7.9	58 6.3	55 6.7	55 6.6	66 5.5
85 4.3	74 4.9	78 4.7				42 8.6	74 5.0	83 4.4	71 5.1	71 5.1	87 4.2
					Cost of Sales/Inventory						
					Cost of Sales/Payables						
5.4	7.1	6.7			Sales/Working Capital	13.8	7.7	5.3	7.1	6.5	6.0
12.9	16.8	14.4				−18.2	16.0	9.5	12.7	14.1	15.3
51.1	137.2	−130.1				−6.1	−49.7	−35.7	45.8	282.3	69.3
(293) 16.0	(286) 11.7	(362) 23.5			EBIT/Interest	(19) 6.2	(56) 24.7	(44) 20.2	(68) 21.0	(83) 28.6	(92) 29.9
3.3	3.1	5.6				1.8	4.3	4.6	6.8	7.8	6.1
−.5	.2	1.2				−3.3	.5	1.2	1.1	.1	2.1
(66) 9.6	(63) 15.0	(64) 29.6			Net Profit + Depr., Dep., Amort./Cur. Mat. L/T/D				(19) 47.4	(25) 38.2	
3.5	3.2	6.6							12.2	8.0	
1.5	.9	1.8							2.1	2.3	
.1	.2	.1			Fixed/Worth	.4	.1	.1	.1	.1	.1
.3	.4	.4				3.7	.6	.3	.2	.4	.3
1.2	2.1	1.9				−.5	NM	1.6	1.6	1.5	1.5
.8	.8	.9			Debt/Worth	1.0	1.1	.8	.6	.9	.9
2.3	2.5	2.2				5.4	2.5	1.8	2.0	1.7	2.4
7.3	12.2	10.6				−2.8	−45.8	14.2	8.9	7.7	8.6
(321) 67.7	(281) 56.7	(349) 65.8			% Profit Before Taxes/Tangible Net Worth	(15) 91.0	(52) 93.8	(45) 60.9	(64) 61.1	(81) 57.9	(92) 65.8
25.1	29.4	33.5				8.9	34.3	23.5	39.5	35.1	39.8
1.0	2.0	4.5				−34.1	1.4	3.8	3.4	−1.5	12.5
20.6	19.3	22.0			% Profit Before Taxes/Total Assets	46.9	31.9	20.1	24.4	20.7	20.6
6.3	5.9	8.0				2.0	7.7	6.0	8.3	9.4	8.1
−1.9	−2.1	.3				−25.5	−2.7	.6	.2	−.7	2.5
68.1	71.3	75.2			Sales/Net Fixed Assets	46.7	85.8	73.8	87.9	83.6	64.7
29.4	31.9	32.3				16.0	31.3	30.4	44.0	28.9	32.4
12.8	13.8	15.9				6.8	16.5	17.7	21.5	15.7	14.3
3.9	4.6	4.1			Sales/Total Assets	7.0	5.2	4.1	4.3	3.8	3.3
2.8	3.0	3.0				4.2	3.4	3.0	3.2	3.0	2.3
1.7	1.9	1.9				1.6	1.9	2.1	2.7	1.6	1.6
(278) .4	(256) .3	(318) .6			% Depr., Dep., Amort./Sales	(15) .5	(47) .7	(42) .5	(59) .1	(74) .5	(81) .6
1.1	.9	1.3				3.0	1.5	1.1	1.1	1.1	1.3
2.5	2.2	2.5				4.9	3.2	2.3	2.1	3.0	2.6
(87) 2.7	(86) 2.5	(118) 3.2			% Officers', Directors', Owners' Comp/Sales	(10) 12.4	(30) 4.5	(22) 3.4	(23) 3.5	(23) 1.6	(10) .7
6.7	6.7	5.9				18.7	16.5	5.4	5.2	2.6	1.5
11.9	11.9	13.7				28.8		7.2	6.9	9.9	8.5
9717149M	9228982M	11206330M			Net Sales ($)	13391M	132875M	219492M	551823M	1436696M	8852053M
5944273M	4871726M	5921584M			Total Assets ($)	7335M	58687M	109648M	195743M	743983M	4806188M

M = $ thousand   MM = $ million
See Pages 11 through 18 for Explanation of Ratios and Data

Current Data Sorted By Assets   Comparative Historical Data

0-500M	500M-2MM	2-10MM	10-50MM	50-100MM	100-250MM	Type of Statement	4/1/98-3/31/99	4/1/99-3/31/00
2	7	24	24	3	5	Unqualified	71	62
1	16	24	1			Reviewed	45	42
16	26	2	2	1		Compiled	55	55
23	16	6	1	1	1	Tax Returns	37	37
19	41	40	14	2	2	Other	120	142
42 (4/1-9/30/02)			**278 (10/1/02-3/31/03)**				**ALL**	**ALL**
61	106	96	42	7	8	**NUMBER OF STATEMENTS**	328	338
%	%	%	%	%	%	**ASSETS**	%	%
20.4	9.1	11.8	13.1			Cash & Equivalents	13.4	14.7
32.8	52.6	50.8	44.5			Trade Receivables (net)	46.5	46.8
4.4	3.9	3.2	3.2			Inventory	4.7	3.6
1.9	3.1	5.2	4.8			All Other Current	3.4	3.8
59.6	68.7	71.0	65.6			Total Current	68.0	69.0
26.0	19.7	13.6	16.4			Fixed Assets (net)	19.7	18.4
5.6	4.6	6.8	11.8			Intangibles (net)	5.7	5.8
8.8	7.0	8.6	6.2			All Other Non-Current	6.5	6.8
100.0	100.0	100.0	100.0			Total	100.0	100.0
						LIABILITIES		
37.6	18.2	14.0	9.9			Notes Payable-Short Term	13.4	14.3
6.4	4.9	3.3	3.4			Cur. Mat.-L/T/D	2.4	2.4
14.6	17.4	17.8	13.9			Trade Payables	16.5	17.9
.1	.6	.9	.4			Income Taxes Payable	.6	.7
25.0	17.9	21.5	21.0			All Other Current	19.1	18.3
83.6	59.1	57.5	48.7			Total Current	54.5	53.7
19.4	12.7	7.0	7.0			Long Term Debt	12.0	10.7
.0	.8	1.2	.6			Deferred Taxes	1.0	.7
18.6	8.1	3.5	6.2			All Other Non-Current	6.9	7.1
-21.6	19.3	30.7	37.5			Net Worth	25.6	27.8
100.0	100.0	100.0	100.0			Total Liabilities & Net Worth	100.0	100.0
						INCOME DATA		
100.0	100.0	100.0	100.0			Net Sales	100.0	100.0
						Gross Profit		
94.9	96.6	95.8	94.9			Operating Expenses	100.7	95.3
5.1	3.4	4.2	5.1			Operating Profit	-.7	4.7
1.1	1.1	1.4	1.9			All Other Expenses (net)	.7	.7
4.0	2.3	2.9	3.2			Profit Before Taxes	-1.4	4.1
						RATIOS		
1.9	2.1	1.7	2.2			Current	2.4	2.4
.8	1.5	1.3	1.4				1.5	1.4
.5	1.0	1.0	1.0				1.0	1.0
1.8	2.0	1.5	1.9			Quick	2.2	2.2
.8	1.2	1.2	1.2				1.3	1.2
.3	.8	1.0	.8				.9	.8
0 UND	35 10.5	40 9.0	47 7.8			Sales/Receivables	33 11.1	33 11.1
23 16.1	47 7.8	55 6.7	65 5.6				54 6.8	55 6.7
42 8.7	61 6.0	79 4.6	79 4.6				77 4.7	75 4.9
						Cost of Sales/Inventory		
						Cost of Sales/Payables		
19.4	9.9	10.3	4.2			Sales/Working Capital	7.3	7.6
-83.3	19.5	23.2	16.2				16.1	18.6
-12.4	-421.4	260.9	297.2				218.7	999.8
(44) 9.2	(88) 14.1	(88) 21.5	(34) 11.4			EBIT/Interest	(260) 16.9	(276) 23.0
3.3	3.3	4.3	4.7				5.5	4.8
-.7	1.0	-.8	2.0				1.1	.4
	(18) 4.0	(26) 14.4				Net Profit + Depr., Dep., Amort./Cur. Mat. L /T/D	(58) 9.6	(43) 11.2
	2.4	2.8					4.4	4.3
	.6	.0					.6	1.1
.4	.2	.1	.1			Fixed/Worth	.2	.2
16.3	.6	.4	.4				.4	.6
-.4	3.6	1.3	1.8				3.2	2.4
1.5	.8	1.2	.7			Debt/Worth	.8	.8
-36.5	2.5	2.3	2.8				2.1	2.3
-3.6	14.2	9.5	13.4				10.9	13.0
(30) 118.6	(83) 65.3	(82) 61.0	(35) 72.9			% Profit Before Taxes/Tangible Net Worth	(261) 84.4	(277) 89.3
62.1	24.5	30.6	25.2				46.5	43.2
28.2	3.7	1.5	8.6				15.9	11.3
43.3	18.1	19.6	17.4			% Profit Before Taxes/Total Assets	27.0	27.3
16.5	7.4	6.9	7.4				12.2	9.8
-9.5	-1.3	-4.0	1.1				.1	-1.8
81.6	75.3	79.7	57.5			Sales/Net Fixed Assets	66.2	56.1
37.0	32.3	40.1	28.1				24.7	24.6
14.3	13.3	17.4	6.9				10.6	13.4
8.5	4.8	4.0	3.2			Sales/Total Assets	5.0	4.7
5.3	3.8	3.3	2.5				3.3	3.4
3.5	3.0	2.3	1.1				2.1	2.2
(42) .9	(87) .6	(71) .7	(34) .7			% Depr., Dep., Amort./Sales	(255) .6	(250) .7
1.3	1.3	1.2	1.7				1.4	1.4
2.4	3.1	2.7	5.0				3.0	2.9
(30) 6.7	(46) 4.3	(21) 2.6				% Officers', Directors', Owners' Comp/Sales	(97) 3.4	(86) 3.2
8.8	7.1	4.0					7.2	7.1
11.7	11.3	8.5					11.6	12.3
79528M	447262M	1398061M	2473652M	1480307M	7440283M	Net Sales ($)	6569085M	6760444M
13659M	111983M	432662M	998265M	506825M	1311811M	Total Assets ($)	3665811M	3697478M

© RMA 2003

M = $ thousand   MM = $ million
See Pages 11 through 18 for Explanation of Ratios and Data

Comparative Historical Data						Current Data Sorted By Sales					

				Type of Statement							
53		45		65	Unqualified		3	4	8	17	33
43		29		42	Reviewed		3	8	14	17	
70		59		47	Compiled	10	13	12	8	1	3
36		38		48	Tax Returns	15	15	4	9	1	4
136		135		118	Other	8	25	14	26	25	20
4/1/00-3/31/01 ALL		4/1/01-3/31/02 ALL		4/1/02-3/31/03 ALL		42 (4/1-9/30/02)			278 (10/1/02-3/31/03)		
						0-1MM	1-3MM	3-5MM	5-10MM	10-25MM	25MM & OVER
338		306		320	NUMBER OF STATEMENTS	33	59	42	65	61	60
%		%		%	ASSETS	%	%	%	%	%	%
12.8		12.5		12.9	Cash & Equivalents	16.2	16.6	8.5	12.5	10.5	13.5
50.3		47.5		46.0	Trade Receivables (net)	31.3	37.7	50.0	52.4	51.3	47.2
3.8		3.4		3.6	Inventory	1.7	6.0	4.6	2.3	3.8	3.0
3.7		4.3		3.8	All Other Current	1.5	3.4	3.3	2.8	5.9	4.8
70.6		67.7		66.4	Total Current	50.8	63.8	66.4	69.9	71.5	68.5
16.8		18.0		18.8	Fixed Assets (net)	37.0	20.6	19.9	16.7	11.6	15.6
6.0		8.0		6.8	Intangibles (net)	3.3	6.3	9.0	5.0	6.3	10.0
6.6		6.2		8.1	All Other Non-Current	8.9	9.3	4.7	8.4	10.6	5.9
100.0		100.0		100.0	Total	100.0	100.0	100.0	100.0	100.0	100.0
					LIABILITIES						
18.2		22.2		19.1	Notes Payable-Short Term	28.1	25.1	21.7	19.9	15.3	9.5
4.4		4.2		4.3	Cur. Mat.-L/T/D	4.4	6.8	5.5	4.1	2.9	2.9
14.9		17.7		16.0	Trade Payables	16.2	10.7	17.5	17.8	19.1	15.0
.6		.5		.6	Income Taxes Payable	.0	.2	.6	1.1	.8	.8
15.5		18.7		20.6	All Other Current	33.6	17.9	19.9	18.2	17.2	22.4
53.6		63.4		60.7	Total Current	82.3	60.7	65.2	61.1	55.3	50.6
11.1		9.3		11.6	Long Term Debt	31.5	11.8	18.1	7.5	5.4	6.9
1.0		.7		.7	Deferred Taxes	.0	.6	.4	1.0	1.4	.4
4.7		8.3		8.2	All Other Non-Current	5.9	8.7	9.9	15.1	5.1	3.6
29.5		18.2		18.8	Net Worth	−19.8	18.2	6.4	15.3	32.8	38.5
100.0		100.0		100.0	Total Liabilities & Net Worth	100.0	100.0	100.0	100.0	100.0	100.0
					INCOME DATA						
100.0		100.0		100.0	Net Sales	100.0	100.0	100.0	100.0	100.0	100.0
					Gross Profit						
96.9		97.2		95.5	Operating Expenses	93.8	94.1	95.8	96.5	96.9	94.9
3.1		2.8		4.5	Operating Profit	6.2	5.9	4.2	3.5	3.1	5.1
.9		1.6		1.3	All Other Expenses (net)	3.2	.7	1.9	.6	1.3	1.4
2.3		1.2		3.2	Profit Before Taxes	2.9	5.2	2.3	2.9	1.8	3.7
					RATIOS						
2.4		2.3		1.9		2.0	2.3	1.9	2.0	1.8	1.8
1.4		1.3		1.3	Current	.8	1.2	1.3	1.4	1.3	1.4
1.0		.9		.8		.3	.7	1.0	1.0	1.0	1.0
2.2		1.9		1.8		2.0	2.2	1.6	1.9	1.6	1.7
1.2		1.1		1.1	Quick	.8	.9	1.1	1.2	1.2	1.2
.8		.8		.7		.2	.5	.7	.8	.8	.9
39	9.3	35	10.4	29	12.4	0	UND	14	25.4	37	9.9	28	13.1	41	8.9	40	9.0
56	6.5	51	7.1	48	7.6	Sales/Receivables	28	12.9	35	10.5	48	7.6	48	7.5	53	6.8	58	6.3
77	4.7	69	5.3	66	5.5		47	7.7	59	6.2	67	5.4	65	5.6	73	5.0	74	4.9
					Cost of Sales/Inventory						
					Cost of Sales/Payables						
7.3		9.0		9.7		12.2	10.2	12.8	9.7	7.8	7.4
20.5		23.8		24.8	Sales/Working Capital	−83.3	70.6	30.5	20.0	18.8	22.8
−842.9		−49.6		−36.1		−8.2	−20.0	−421.4	261.3	119.1	483.5
	11.6		8.7		15.7			5.4		19.4		10.8		20.4		20.0		17.7
(283)	3.1	(258)	2.3	(266)	3.6	EBIT/Interest	(21)	2.3	(46)	5.2	(38)	2.6	(54)	3.3	(54)	3.0	(53)	4.7
	−.3		−1.8		.7			−6.7		1.6		−1.6		.1		−.1		2.1
	7.6		8.9		9.8	Net Profit + Depr., Dep.,					20.1		8.9		37.3
(43)	2.7	(46)	2.3	(59)	3.0	Amort./Cur. Mat. L/T/D					(20)	2.3	(13)	3.7	(10)	7.3
	.1		.5		1.1							.3		.6		3.0
.2		.2		.2		.3	.2	.4	.2	.1	.1
.5		.5		.6	Fixed/Worth	3.5	1.4	.9	.5	.3	.3
2.7		6.9		13.2		−1.1	−.7	−75.2	2.0	1.1	1.1
.8		1.0		1.1		1.8	.8	1.4	.8	1.0	1.0
2.3		2.8		2.8	Debt/Worth	15.0	3.4	3.8	2.2	2.0	2.1
17.2		36.9		71.5		−3.6	−6.2	−155.7	19.1	9.0	5.3
	75.0		80.1		73.1	% Profit Before Taxes/Tangible		94.2		109.7		82.4		61.6		42.0		85.6
(271)	32.9	(237)	24.8	(244)	28.9	Net Worth	(19)	57.1	(36)	38.5	(31)	39.7	(53)	25.3	(51)	12.9	(54)	29.0
	−1.1		.3		7.2			25.0		16.8		1.9		3.0		−2.5		13.4
20.3		20.6		21.2		27.4	38.8	22.6	15.1	15.2	18.2
6.7		4.7		7.5	% Profit Before Taxes/Total Assets	7.1	20.2	7.6	7.5	5.2	10.2
−4.5		−9.2		−1.7		−34.3	2.8	−12.1	−2.3	−4.0	3.0
74.2		74.5		71.3		60.2	88.2	41.1	73.1	90.4	81.1
29.1		31.4		34.8	Sales/Net Fixed Assets	20.0	35.9	24.0	37.2	46.5	39.9
13.1		13.4		13.6		3.6	12.7	13.5	12.8	21.3	20.7
4.8		5.2		4.7		5.5	5.4	4.4	5.2	4.2	4.2
3.3		3.6		3.5	Sales/Total Assets	3.6	3.7	3.8	3.6	3.5	2.8
2.3		2.2		2.4		1.5	2.7	2.9	2.5	2.6	2.0
	.4		.5		.7			1.0		1.1		.7		.6		.6		.5
(244)	1.1	(228)	1.3	(241)	1.3	% Depr., Dep., Amort./Sales	(26)	1.8	(38)	1.6	(33)	1.9	(57)	1.2	(46)	1.2	(41)	1.2
	2.3		3.0		2.9			8.2		3.6		4.3		2.5		2.6		2.4
	3.3		3.5		4.0	% Officers', Directors',		6.6		6.7		1.9		3.0		2.6		.8
(105)	7.2	(89)	6.4	(103)	7.3	Owners' Comp/Sales	(13)	8.6	(30)	9.7	(16)	5.3	(23)	6.9	(10)	5.4	(11)	6.7
	14.9		13.2		11.0			18.8		11.7		9.8		8.7		9.3		10.5
7689152M		6819270M		13319093M	Net Sales ($)	18835M	110176M	157390M	428468M	969920M	11634304M
3772035M		3231937M		3375205M	Total Assets ($)	12873M	31272M	53651M	145250M	562029M	2570130M

© RMA 2003   M = $ thousand   MM = $ million
See Pages 11 through 18 for Explanation of Ratios and Data

Current Data Sorted By Assets

Comparative Historical Data

						Type of Statement		
3	15	48	25	6	10	Unqualified	117	102
12	24	33	3		1	Reviewed	91	88
20	14	15	3		1	Compiled	85	74
28	16	4	1		1	Tax Returns	46	48
26	39	46	19	5	9	Other	142	136
	65 (4/1-9/30/02)			362 (10/1/02-3/31/03)			4/1/98-3/31/99	4/1/99-3/31/00
0-500M	500M-2MM	2-10MM	10-50MM	50-100MM	100-250MM		ALL	ALL
89	108	146	51	11	22	**NUMBER OF STATEMENTS**	481	448
%	%	%	%	%	%	**ASSETS**	%	%
27.7	13.5	16.8	13.7	13.2	13.5	Cash & Equivalents	17.4	15.7
26.5	47.0	42.7	38.0	36.0	29.4	Trade Receivables (net)	39.4	41.7
3.0	1.6	2.2	2.7	1.4	3.6	Inventory	2.2	2.2
7.7	7.0	7.2	7.6	13.8	5.0	All Other Current	5.0	5.8
65.0	69.1	69.0	62.0	64.4	51.6	Total Current	64.0	65.3
21.8	14.6	16.7	16.9	14.3	17.2	Fixed Assets (net)	17.5	17.9
1.6	4.3	4.6	7.6	10.8	20.1	Intangibles (net)	6.0	6.0
11.6	12.0	9.8	13.5	10.5	11.0	All Other Non-Current	12.6	10.8
100.0	100.0	100.0	100.0	100.0	100.0	Total	100.0	100.0
						LIABILITIES		
29.4	16.1	9.0	7.0	14.5	4.2	Notes Payable-Short Term	12.1	19.8
6.9	3.7	2.8	3.4	2.5	3.1	Cur. Mat.-L/T/D	2.7	3.5
15.1	11.7	13.1	10.8	7.6	15.8	Trade Payables	12.0	13.3
.4	.4	1.2	.7	2.7	.3	Income Taxes Payable	.7	.5
28.5	14.8	18.2	22.0	22.4	16.8	All Other Current	22.1	19.3
80.3	46.8	44.3	43.9	49.7	40.1	Total Current	49.6	56.5
9.4	13.3	10.2	20.7	5.7	23.5	Long Term Debt	10.4	13.8
.2	1.0	1.0	.8	.0	.4	Deferred Taxes	1.3	1.3
7.6	12.6	6.5	6.0	6.3	7.0	All Other Non-Current	8.5	6.2
2.5	26.3	38.0	28.5	38.3	28.9	Net Worth	30.3	22.3
100.0	100.0	100.0	100.0	100.0	100.0	Total Liabilities & Net Worth	100.0	100.0
						INCOME DATA		
100.0	100.0	100.0	100.0	100.0	100.0	Net Sales	100.0	100.0
						Gross Profit		
94.7	94.8	93.1	87.9	101.2	89.6	Operating Expenses	97.9	95.9
5.3	5.2	6.9	12.1	-1.2	10.4	Operating Profit	2.1	4.1
1.1	.8	2.1	6.6	1.0	14.5	All Other Expenses (net)	.5	-.7
4.2	4.4	4.8	5.4	-2.2	-4.2	Profit Before Taxes	1.6	4.9
						RATIOS		
2.4	4.0	2.6	2.3	2.5	2.0		2.6	2.5
1.1	1.7	1.6	1.4	1.3	1.3	Current	1.5	1.5
.6	1.0	1.1	1.0	.9	.9		1.0	1.0
2.0	2.8	2.2	2.0	1.5	1.4		2.4	2.2
(88) 1.0	1.4	1.4	1.2	1.2	1.0	Quick	1.3	1.2
.3	.9	.9	.7	.8	.6		.8	.8

0	UND	25	14.4	36	10.0	40	9.0	59	6.2	47	7.8		15	24.0	23	16.1
6	59.8	54	6.7	54	6.8	61	6.0	74	5.0	56	6.6	Sales/Receivables	56	6.5	54	6.8
45	8.1	95	3.9	77	4.7	87	4.2	100	3.6	79	4.6		81	4.5	81	4.5

						Cost of Sales/Inventory		
						Cost of Sales/Payables		
11.0	5.9	5.0	5.6	4.9	6.7		6.7	6.6
98.0	11.6	9.3	12.7	12.2	13.6	Sales/Working Capital	15.0	15.0
-24.0	629.7	62.2	-232.1	-62.6	-165.7		UND	-352.4
17.0	20.7	18.7	61.2	13.8	6.5		26.0	15.4
(59) 4.2	(87) 4.3	(112) 6.9	(38) 8.3	(10) 2.7	(19) 1.7	EBIT/Interest	(379) 5.7	(360) 4.7
-1.1	-.6	.7	4.1	-.4	-.3		1.4	.8
	2.2	11.7	7.5				7.2	7.4
	(13) .9	(35) 3.5	(19) 2.6			Net Profit + Depr., Dep.,	(104) 2.9	(81) 2.9
	-.1	1.0	1.1			Amort./Cur. Mat. L /T/D	.5	1.0
.1	.1	.1	.1	.2	.7		.1	.1
.6	.3	.3	.5	.6	4.3	Fixed/Worth	.4	.5
-7.1	3.4	2.5	2.8	1.0	-.4		1.7	1.7
.7	.5	.7	1.1	.8	2.2		.7	.8
2.8	1.8	1.6	4.9	3.0	20.1	Debt/Worth	1.9	2.2
-5.1	11.2	5.0	26.6	20.7	-5.2		9.5	9.8
100.5	67.7	54.7	62.5		32.8		68.6	76.2
(61) 43.8	(86) 24.3	(120) 25.7	(42) 29.1		(13) 11.6	% Profit Before Taxes/Tangible	(389) 30.1	(373) 33.3
1.8	-.4	2.9	5.9		-22.0	Net Worth	5.9	5.1
37.2	23.1	21.2	21.6	9.1	4.9		23.8	24.7
15.5	7.1	7.7	6.7	2.9	1.8	% Profit Before Taxes/Total	9.2	8.6
-4.3	-3.0	-.3	1.2	-9.8	-2.7	Assets	.6	.0
186.2	94.6	67.9	55.3	23.8	43.9		60.2	63.9
48.5	35.9	31.3	20.1	12.1	14.6	Sales/Net Fixed Assets	26.7	26.7
16.7	12.9	13.7	10.3	6.7	3.6		12.5	12.7
7.7	4.6	3.5	2.8	2.3	1.8		4.3	4.3
5.1	2.9	2.7	2.1	1.6	1.4	Sales/Total Assets	2.8	2.9
3.6	2.0	1.6	1.3	1.4	.9		1.8	1.8
.5	.6	.6	.9	1.6	2.3		.7	.8
(48) 1.2	(78) 1.2	(116) 1.6	(45) 1.8	(10) 3.4	(11) 3.0	% Depr., Dep., Amort./Sales	(400) 1.5	(349) 1.5
2.7	2.4	2.8	4.1	7.7	5.1		2.7	2.5
4.3	3.1	3.3					4.3	5.6
(40) 11.5	(51) 6.3	(25) 5.4				% Officers', Directors',	(145) 11.8	(137) 11.3
21.5	13.0	16.6				Owners' Comp/Sales	22.1	21.1

139164M	530963M	1951289M	2563919M	1362712M	8131530M	Net Sales ($)	8692997M	8071438M
22418M	124039M	678885M	1112815M	790828M	3315221M	Total Assets ($)	5362217M	4309724M

M = $ thousand   MM = $ million
See Pages 11 through 18 for Explanation of Ratios and Data

Comparative Historical Data				Type of Statement	Current Data Sorted By Sales					
85	78		107	Unqualified	2	10	11	18	21	45
68	59		73	Reviewed	4	19	12	20	12	6
80	86		53	Compiled	8	16	8	13	2	6
40	29		50	Tax Returns	20	18	4	6		2
144	130		144	Other	20	33	15	19	23	34
4/1/00-3/31/01	4/1/01-3/31/02		4/1/02-3/31/03		65 (4/1-9/30/02)			362 (10/1/02-3/31/03)		
ALL	ALL		ALL		0-1MM	1-3MM	3-5MM	5-10MM	10-25MM	25MM & OVER
417	382		427	NUMBER OF STATEMENTS	54	96	50	76	58	93
%	%		%	ASSETS	%	%	%	%	%	%
15.8	16.6		17.6	Cash & Equivalents	22.5	18.5	16.3	19.4	17.5	13.1
44.2	43.5		39.0	Trade Receivables (net)	16.0	40.7	39.3	43.7	45.6	42.4
1.9	1.6		2.3	Inventory	2.1	2.6	1.8	2.0	2.1	2.9
5.2	5.5		7.4	All Other Current	8.8	5.7	6.8	7.8	7.6	8.1
67.2	67.2		66.3	Total Current	49.4	67.6	64.2	72.9	72.8	66.5
16.8	18.4		17.2	Fixed Assets (net)	30.1	18.6	14.4	13.9	15.4	13.6
5.3	5.2		5.2	Intangibles (net)	.8	3.8	5.6	3.6	4.2	10.9
10.7	9.2		11.2	All Other Non-Current	19.6	10.0	15.7	9.6	7.6	8.9
100.0	100.0		100.0	Total	100.0	100.0	100.0	100.0	100.0	100.0
				LIABILITIES						
14.2	14.5		14.7	Notes Payable-Short Term	28.1	20.7	13.4	11.9	7.9	8.0
2.5	3.9		4.0	Cur. Mat.-L/T/D	7.8	4.6	2.7	2.1	3.4	3.7
12.3	13.0		12.9	Trade Payables	10.6	12.6	8.0	14.3	13.3	15.7
.8	.9		.8	Income Taxes Payable	.3	.3	1.9	.8	.8	.9
19.0	20.3		20.0	All Other Current	25.0	16.1	16.2	17.8	22.2	23.5
48.8	52.6		52.3	Total Current	71.7	54.3	42.1	46.9	47.6	51.8
10.9	11.3		12.6	Long Term Debt	23.3	12.6	8.4	12.2	5.4	13.6
1.3	1.4		.8	Deferred Taxes	.0	1.1	1.1	.8	.8	.6
7.1	14.0		8.2	All Other Non-Current	19.4	6.7	6.6	5.0	10.2	5.6
31.9	20.7		26.0	Net Worth	-14.5	25.2	41.8	35.0	36.0	28.4
100.0	100.0		100.0	Total Liabilities & Net Worth	100.0	100.0	100.0	100.0	100.0	100.0
				INCOME DATA						
100.0	100.0		100.0	Net Sales	100.0	100.0	100.0	100.0	100.0	100.0
				Gross Profit						
94.4	96.0		93.3	Operating Expenses	88.5	94.7	93.2	91.1	95.1	95.1
5.6	4.0		6.7	Operating Profit	11.5	5.2	6.8	8.9	4.9	4.9
.4	1.1		2.7	All Other Expenses (net)	3.9	3.2	.4	3.9	.9	3.0
5.2	2.9		4.0	Profit Before Taxes	7.6	2.1	6.4	4.9	4.0	1.9
				RATIOS						
2.7	2.4		2.6		3.1	2.6	3.3	2.8	2.7	2.1
1.5	1.4		1.5	Current	1.0	1.6	1.7	1.7	1.5	1.3
1.0	.9		.9		.3	1.0	1.0	1.2	1.1	1.0
2.4	2.2		2.2		1.9	2.5	2.8	2.5	2.3	1.7
1.4	1.3	(426)	1.3	Quick	(53) 1.9 .8	1.5	1.4	1.5	1.3	1.1
.9	.8		.8		.2	.7	.8	.9	.9	.8
28 13.3	28 12.8	20 18.5			0 UND	14 25.8	4 82.6	30 12.1	40 9.0	41 8.9
57 6.5	53 6.9	50 7.3		Sales/Receivables	0 UND	51 7.1	48 7.5	49 7.5	55 6.7	58 6.3
82 4.5	77 4.7	78 4.7			51 7.2	93 3.9	85 4.3	77 4.7	76 4.8	76 4.8
				Cost of Sales/Inventory						
				Cost of Sales/Payables						
6.6	6.9		5.9		5.5	5.0	6.6	5.3	6.6	7.1
13.0	17.0		13.5	Sales/Working Capital	UND	14.0	12.1	8.7	11.5	17.6
399.0	-96.6		-169.6		-5.9	NM	-240.3	36.7	311.9	-147.1
21.7	20.4		19.5		12.3	27.7	20.3	25.3	22.6	19.3
(315) 5.2	(310) 3.1	(325) 5.4		EBIT/Interest	(36) 3.4	(70) 2.0	(40) 7.9	(56) 5.1	(44) 7.3	(79) 6.4
1.4	-1.1		.6		.0	-4.2	1.2	-3.3	1.4	1.3
8.2	5.7		6.9					3.5	15.9	7.8
(67) 3.8	(72) 1.9	(82) 2.1		Net Profit + Depr., Dep., Amort./Cur. Mat. L/T/D			(13) 2.0	(17) 5.2	(34) 2.2
1.2	.3		.9					-.1	.6	1.6
.1	.1		.1		.1	.1	.1	.1	.1	.2
.4	.5		.4	Fixed/Worth	.9	.4	.3	.2	.1	.7
1.8	3.6		4.1		-3.4	2.1	1.4	2.2	1.8	-3.0
.7	.8		.7		.7	.6	.6	.5	.6	1.1
2.0	2.4		2.1	Debt/Worth	3.2	2.0	1.5	1.6	1.7	4.5
11.0	12.8		32.9		-5.3	28.0	4.3	10.1	9.1	-28.4
66.0	64.3		63.0		103.6	66.7	54.4	70.8	50.4	60.6
(341) 32.0	(308) 26.8	(331) 27.8		% Profit Before Taxes/Tangible Net Worth	(34) 43.8	(76) 13.4	(45) 33.5	(62) 17.2	(46) 29.6	(68) 27.3
10.6	-.1		1.0		16.6	-6.4	1.8	-11.2	8.4	1.9
25.7	24.6		22.1		27.5	26.2	19.8	23.3	24.9	18.4
9.2	5.1		7.5	% Profit Before Taxes/Total Assets	14.6	3.4	11.1	7.8	7.9	6.7
1.2	-4.3		-1.5		-2.1	-5.9	.0	-6.4	.1	.1
69.6	71.0		86.8		96.9	94.3	67.4	120.6	80.1	55.0
30.1	26.3		32.4	Sales/Net Fixed Assets	13.5	42.4	30.5	38.1	33.1	24.7
13.8	12.6		13.0		3.9	12.9	19.3	18.7	13.7	12.4
4.5	4.6		4.6		5.0	5.7	4.6	4.2	3.9	3.9
3.1	3.1		2.8	Sales/Total Assets	2.6	3.2	2.8	2.8	3.2	2.6
2.0	2.0		1.7		.8	1.7	1.9	1.8	2.3	1.6
.7	.6		.7		1.2	.7	1.1	.5	.6	.8
(303) 1.3	(291) 1.4	(308) 1.6		% Depr., Dep., Amort./Sales	(30) 2.8	(66) 1.4	(35) 1.5	(58) 1.1	(46) 1.5	(73) 1.6
2.3	2.6		2.8		5.6	3.0	2.4	2.1	2.8	3.4
5.9	3.8		3.4		8.4	4.1	4.0	2.5		.4
(126) 10.9	(102) 8.6	(124) 7.2		% Officers', Directors', Owners' Comp/Sales	(23) 16.0	(42) 8.1	(18) 5.6	(23) 4.7	(15) 1.9
20.2	18.8		17.3		25.9	17.7	10.2	10.9		13.0
13715231M	10003431M		14679577M	Net Sales ($)	27816M	192074M	194407M	573613M	889960M	12801707M
4712385M	3995771M		6044206M	Total Assets ($)	31398M	136687M	78517M	403474M	480012M	4914118M

M = $ thousand   MM = $ million
See Pages 11 through 18 for Explanation of Ratios and Data

Current Data Sorted By Assets   **Comparative Historical Data**

						Type of Statement		
	1	5	1		2	Unqualified		
	2	2				Reviewed		
3	6	3				Compiled		
6	2	2				Tax Returns		
11	13	10	1	2	2	Other	4/1/98-3/31/99 ALL	4/1/99-3/31/00 ALL
	10 (4/1-9/30/02)		62 (10/1/02-3/31/03)					
0-500M	500M-2MM	2-10MM	10-50MM	50-100MM	100-250MM			
20	24	22	2	2	2	NUMBER OF STATEMENTS		
%	%	%	%	%	%	**ASSETS**	%	%
17.7	13.4	10.0				Cash & Equivalents	D	D
40.1	52.8	55.8				Trade Receivables (net)	A	A
.0	.0	.0				Inventory	T	T
7.1	5.2	6.5				All Other Current	A	A
64.9	71.4	72.3				Total Current		
10.7	9.6	12.1				Fixed Assets (net)	N	N
5.8	5.2	3.8				Intangibles (net)	O	O
18.6	13.8	11.9				All Other Non-Current	T	T
100.0	100.0	100.0				Total		
						LIABILITIES	A	A
23.0	26.9	14.8				Notes Payable-Short Term	V	V
4.7	4.6	5.8				Cur. Mat.-L/T/D	A	A
3.1	7.7	11.9				Trade Payables	I	I
.0	.0	.0				Income Taxes Payable	L	L
19.3	23.5	19.9				All Other Current	A	A
50.1	62.7	52.4				Total Current	B	B
6.1	9.4	4.3				Long Term Debt	L	L
1.8	.6	.0				Deferred Taxes	E	E
17.6	12.5	5.6				All Other Non-Current		
24.4	14.8	37.8				Net Worth		
100.0	100.0	100.0				Total Liabilities & Net Worth		
						INCOME DATA		
100.0	100.0	100.0				Net Sales		
						Gross Profit		
99.7	97.2	95.2				Operating Expenses		
.3	2.8	4.8				Operating Profit		
.7	1.7	.5				All Other Expenses (net)		
-.4	1.1	4.3				Profit Before Taxes		
						RATIOS		
4.0	2.4	2.8						
1.6	1.4	1.4				Current		
.8	.9	1.0						
3.5	2.4	2.3						
1.5	1.4	1.2				Quick		
.3	.8	1.0						
0 UND	35 10.4	35 10.6						
19 18.9	51 7.2	52 7.0				Sales/Receivables		
44 8.3	58 6.2	68 5.4						
						Cost of Sales/Inventory		
						Cost of Sales/Payables		
11.2	8.9	8.1						
36.8	16.1	28.3				Sales/Working Capital		
-167.1	NM	NM						
(13) 8.1	(20) 15.1	(17) 40.2						
2.4	2.8	6.9				EBIT/Interest		
-.1	-4.4	3.5						
						Net Profit + Depr., Dep., Amort./Cur. Mat. L /T/D		
.0	.1	.2						
.1	.3	.3				Fixed/Worth		
-18.0	-1.2	.9						
.4	.8	.7						
1.1	2.8	1.6				Debt/Worth		
-20.0	-17.2	5.2						
(13) 69.6	(17) 34.2	(20) 61.6				% Profit Before Taxes/Tangible		
20.2	16.2	38.6				Net Worth		
3.7	-.8	14.3						
29.6	11.2	26.1				% Profit Before Taxes/Total		
6.6	4.5	12.1				Assets		
-21.5	-4.5	5.2						
209.7	188.3	70.2						
83.8	54.4	43.6				Sales/Net Fixed Assets		
29.8	37.7	23.8						
7.8	6.0	5.3						
5.2	4.5	4.1				Sales/Total Assets		
3.3	2.5	3.0						
(11) .4	(15) .3	(17) .4				% Depr., Dep., Amort./Sales		
.6	.8	1.0						
3.0	1.4	1.6						
	1.5					% Officers', Directors',		
	(11) 4.6					Owners' Comp/Sales		
	5.5							
33170M	133973M	390940M	278615M	602963M	527150M	Net Sales ($)		
4866M	27060M	91053M	45726M	165898M	363760M	Total Assets ($)		

M = $ thousand   MM = $ million
See Pages 11 through 18 for Explanation of Ratios and Data

Comparative Historical Data | Current Data Sorted By Sales

4/1/00-3/31/01 ALL	4/1/01-3/31/02 ALL	4/1/02-3/31/03 ALL	Type of Statement						
		9	Unqualified		2			2	5
		4	Reviewed		1	1		1	1
		12	Compiled		5	1	3	3	
		10	Tax Returns	5	2			1	2
		37	Other	5	8	5	9	7	3
				10 (4/1-9/30/02)			62 (10/1/02-3/31/03)		
				0-1MM	1-3MM	3-5MM	5-10MM	10-25MM	25MM & OVER
		72	NUMBER OF STATEMENTS	10	18	7	12	14	11
%	%	%	ASSETS	%	%	%	%	%	%
D	D	13.6	Cash & Equivalents	20.3	14.5		15.9	7.4	12.8
A	A	48.6	Trade Receivables (net)	24.6	35.6		63.7	63.2	43.5
T	T	.0	Inventory	.0	.0		.1	.0	.0
A	A	6.4	All Other Current	5.0	11.3		2.3	5.1	6.8
		68.6	Total Current	49.9	61.4		82.0	75.7	63.2
N	N	11.1	Fixed Assets (net)	16.9	7.8		6.6	13.5	15.8
O	O	6.3	Intangibles (net)	11.5	6.0		4.7	2.9	11.9
T	T	14.0	All Other Non-Current	21.7	24.8		6.8	7.9	9.1
		100.0	Total	100.0	100.0		100.0	100.0	100.0
A	A		LIABILITIES						
V	V	20.5	Notes Payable-Short Term	23.0	23.0		17.7	22.6	15.9
A	A	4.7	Cur. Mat.-L/T/D	8.2	3.8		6.7	3.5	.7
I	I	7.6	Trade Payables	2.1	8.4		5.5	15.6	7.0
L	L	.0	Income Taxes Payable	.0	.0		.0	.0	.1
A	A	21.3	All Other Current	14.5	12.6		46.8	16.4	24.6
B	B	54.1	Total Current	47.8	47.7		76.7	58.1	48.2
L	L	6.2	Long Term Debt	15.6	7.0		7.7	4.5	.6
E	E	.7	Deferred Taxes	.0	.1		2.9	.0	.0
		11.1	All Other Non-Current	35.2	14.2		7.0	5.6	2.7
		27.8	Net Worth	1.4	31.0		5.7	31.8	48.5
		100.0	Total Liabilities & Net Worth	100.0	100.0		100.0	100.0	100.0
			INCOME DATA						
		100.0	Net Sales	100.0	100.0		100.0	100.0	100.0
			Gross Profit						
		97.5	Operating Expenses	96.1	99.1		96.2	95.9	98.8
		2.5	Operating Profit	3.9	.9		3.8	4.1	1.2
		.9	All Other Expenses (net)	4.0	.4		.6	.5	.1
		1.6	Profit Before Taxes	−.1	.5		3.3	3.6	1.1
			RATIOS						
		2.5		3.9	4.0		1.9	2.5	1.6
		1.5	Current	1.7	1.8		1.3	1.2	1.3
		1.0		.6	.9		.9	.9	1.0
		2.2		3.9	2.8		1.9	2.3	1.4
		1.3	Quick	1.7	1.2		1.3	1.2	1.3
		.8		.2	.3		.9	.8	.7
18	46	19.8		0 UND	0 UND		31 11.8	37 9.9	24 15.2
46		8.0	Sales/Receivables	0 UND	39 9.2		51 7.2	48 7.6	54 6.8
60		6.1		33 11.1	56 6.6		61 5.9	69 5.3	65 5.6
			Cost of Sales/Inventory						
			Cost of Sales/Payables						
		9.7		5.0	10.2		12.1	8.1	11.1
		20.3	Sales/Working Capital	88.1	16.3		48.4	30.7	29.5
		NM		−6.7	−441.9		NM	−199.2	795.3
		19.6			4.0			25.5	116.5
	(55)	4.0	EBIT/Interest	(11) 2.2			(11) 6.3	(10) 2.3	
		−1.3		−10.0			2.1	−5.4	
			Net Profit + Depr., Dep., Amort./Cur. Mat. L/T/D						
		.1		.1	.0		.2	.2	.2
		.3	Fixed/Worth	1.1	.1		1.5	.4	.4
		1.2		−.2	NM		−.5	1.0	.6
		.8		.4	.3		1.4	.8	1.1
		1.7	Debt/Worth	2.7	1.4		21.7	2.6	1.5
		11.4		−1.8	−143.9		−8.8	6.0	2.1
		56.1			32.5			61.6	38.6
	(56)	21.2	% Profit Before Taxes/Tangible Net Worth	(13) 10.5			(12) 42.9	3.4	
		−3.1		−5.0			16.4	−20.9	
		18.6		16.0	17.3		23.8	26.7	16.1
		5.9	% Profit Before Taxes/Total Assets	5.3	2.9		12.1	9.1	1.6
		−5.1		−35.5	−5.9		−.4	1.4	−5.1
		136.3		81.7	UND		211.3	97.3	67.4
		54.4	Sales/Net Fixed Assets	41.0	49.3		135.4	40.4	52.0
		26.2		7.4	16.2		55.2	26.2	7.9
		6.0		4.3	5.9		10.4	5.6	7.7
		4.4	Sales/Total Assets	2.9	2.7		5.8	4.8	4.9
		2.5		1.4	1.9		3.3	3.7	1.5
		.4			.4			.5	.6
	(49)	1.0	% Depr., Dep., Amort./Sales	(10) .7			(13) 1.2	1.0	
		1.6		1.5			1.6	3.6	
		1.6							
	(28)	4.3	% Officers', Directors', Owners' Comp/Sales						
		11.3							
		1966811M	Net Sales ($)	4771M	34838M	26881M	84759M	202051M	1613511M
		698363M	Total Assets ($)	3384M	16318M	5633M	20094M	45551M	607383M

M = $ thousand   MM = $ million
See Pages 11 through 18 for Explanation of Ratios and Data

Current Data Sorted By Assets   **Comparative Historical Data**

						Type of Statement		
		2	1			Unqualified		
1	4	8	3			Reviewed		
	6	3				Compiled		
1						Tax Returns		
	1	3	3		1	Other	4/1/98-3/31/99	4/1/99-3/31/00
	8 (4/1-9/30/02)		29 (10/1/02-3/31/03)				ALL	ALL
0-500M	500M-2MM	2-10MM	10-50MM	50-100MM	100-250MM			
2	11	16	7		1	NUMBER OF STATEMENTS		
%	%	%	%	%	%	ASSETS	%	%
	6.8	7.7		D		Cash & Equivalents	D	D
	60.0	49.0		A		Trade Receivables (net)	A	A
	.0	.5		T		Inventory	T	T
	2.5	5.1		A		All Other Current	A	A
	69.3	62.3				Total Current		
	24.0	22.4		N		Fixed Assets (net)	N	N
	.0	4.6		O		Intangibles (net)	O	O
	6.7	10.7		T		All Other Non-Current	T	T
	100.0	100.0				Total		
				A		LIABILITIES	A	A
	14.9	11.4		V		Notes Payable-Short Term	V	V
	5.2	3.2		A		Cur. Mat.-L/T/D	A	A
	30.0	33.9		I		Trade Payables	I	I
	.0	.6		L		Income Taxes Payable	L	L
	6.7	12.6		A		All Other Current	A	A
	56.8	61.7		B		Total Current	B	B
	12.4	9.0		L		Long Term Debt	L	L
	.3	1.0		E		Deferred Taxes	E	E
	.9	2.8				All Other Non-Current		
	29.6	25.4				Net Worth		
	100.0	100.0				Total Liabilities & Net Worth		
						INCOME DATA		
	100.0	100.0				Net Sales		
						Gross Profit		
	92.7	96.4				Operating Expenses		
	7.3	3.6				Operating Profit		
	.9	.7				All Other Expenses (net)		
	6.4	2.8				Profit Before Taxes		
						RATIOS		
	1.5	1.2						
	1.2	1.0				Current		
	.9	.8						
	1.5	1.1						
	1.1	1.0				Quick		
	.8	.6						
	29 12.5	27 13.7						
	43 8.5	35 10.5				Sales/Receivables		
	73 5.0	56 6.5						
						Cost of Sales/Inventory		
						Cost of Sales/Payables		
	8.4	34.4						
	47.7	-676.8				Sales/Working Capital		
	-69.9	-44.6						
		53.5						
	(15)	7.3				EBIT/Interest		
		1.2						
						Net Profit + Depr., Dep., Amort./Cur. Mat. L /T/D		
	.0	.2						
	.1	1.0				Fixed/Worth		
	1.6	4.0						
	.9	2.0						
	3.7	4.6				Debt/Worth		
	13.3	11.2						
		74.0				% Profit Before Taxes/Tangible Net Worth		
	(14)	32.3						
		-6.9						
	30.0	12.2				% Profit Before Taxes/Total Assets		
	22.9	4.3						
	2.4	-.7						
	UND	82.4						
	53.1	56.3				Sales/Net Fixed Assets		
	7.7	12.0						
	5.0	6.8						
	4.8	4.5				Sales/Total Assets		
	1.5	2.8						
		.2				% Depr., Dep., Amort./Sales		
		.5						
		1.9						
						% Officers', Directors', Owners' Comp/Sales		
2927M	60787M	383924M	394794M		155675M	Net Sales ($)		
491M	13789M	74504M	168225M		216636M	Total Assets ($)		

M = $ thousand   MM = $ million
See Pages 11 through 18 for Explanation of Ratios and Data

Comparative Historical Data | **Current Data Sorted By Sales**

4/1/00-3/31/01 ALL	4/1/01-3/31/02 ALL	4/1/02-3/31/03 ALL	Type of Statement	0-1MM	1-3MM	3-5MM	5-10MM	10-25MM	25MM & OVER
					8 (4/1-9/30/02)			29 (10/1/02-3/31/03)	
		3	Unqualified						3
		16	Reviewed	2		1	3	4	6
		9	Compiled	1	2	2	2	2	
		1	Tax Returns		1				
		8	Other				1	2	5
		37	**NUMBER OF STATEMENTS**	3	3	3	6	8	14
%	%	%	**ASSETS**	%	%	%	%	%	%
D	D	8.1	Cash & Equivalents						12.9
A	A	48.5	Trade Receivables (net)						43.1
T	T	.2	Inventory						.6
A	A	6.2	All Other Current						11.2
		63.0	Total Current						67.8
N	N	23.3	Fixed Assets (net)						17.7
O	O	3.0	Intangibles (net)						4.4
T	T	10.7	All Other Non-Current						10.1
		100.0	Total						100.0
A	A		**LIABILITIES**						
V	V	11.8	Notes Payable-Short Term						9.1
A	A	3.3	Cur. Mat.-L/T/D						1.2
I	I	29.3	Trade Payables						31.3
L	L	.3	Income Taxes Payable						.4
A	A	12.6	All Other Current						16.1
B	B	57.3	Total Current						58.1
L	L	9.2	Long Term Debt						6.2
E	E	.9	Deferred Taxes						.4
		1.9	All Other Non-Current						1.3
		30.6	Net Worth						33.9
		100.0	Total Liabilities & Net Worth						100.0
			INCOME DATA						
		100.0	Net Sales						100.0
			Gross Profit						
		93.9	Operating Expenses						93.4
		6.1	Operating Profit						6.6
		.9	All Other Expenses (net)						.8
		5.2	Profit Before Taxes						5.8
			RATIOS						
		1.3	Current						1.5
		1.1							1.1
		.8							.9
		1.3	Quick						1.3
		1.0							1.0
		.6							.5
	27	13.3	Sales/Receivables					11	32.1
	35	10.3						32	11.3
	61	6.0						44	8.3
			Cost of Sales/Inventory						
			Cost of Sales/Payables						
		17.2	Sales/Working Capital						12.0
		87.3							53.7
		-61.3							-119.0
		36.8	EBIT/Interest						60.3
	(32)	8.0					(13)	8.0
		1.6							5.3
		15.2	Net Profit + Depr., Dep., Amort./Cur. Mat. L/T/D						
	(11)	9.8							
		2.1							
		.1	Fixed/Worth						.1
		.7							.7
		1.6							1.0
		1.4	Debt/Worth						1.5
		3.3							2.2
		6.0							7.1
		76.0	% Profit Before Taxes/Tangible Net Worth						80.7
	(33)	34.9							47.4
		13.9							29.7
		25.6	% Profit Before Taxes/Total Assets						25.6
		9.4							10.7
		2.4							5.4
		127.2	Sales/Net Fixed Assets						166.2
		54.6							63.0
		7.5							10.7
		5.5	Sales/Total Assets						6.9
		4.0							4.1
		2.4							3.3
		.4	% Depr., Dep., Amort./Sales						.2
	(31)	1.0					(13)	.8
		2.4							1.4
		2.8	% Officers', Directors', Owners' Comp/Sales						
	(13)	4.1							
		8.9							
		998107M	Net Sales ($)	1988M	6620M	11964M	42268M	128843M	806424M
		473645M	Total Assets ($)	2119M	2541M	7081M	9930M	52746M	399228M

© RMA 2003

M = $ thousand   MM = $ million
See Pages 11 through 18 for Explanation of Ratios and Data

Current Data Sorted By Assets   Comparative Historical Data

						Type of Statement		
1	8	29	16	1	3	Unqualified	56	41
1	18	18	3			Reviewed	38	39
15	14	7	2			Compiled	52	47
23	4	1				Tax Returns	52	28
23	36	27	11	3	2	Other	82	81
	41 (4/1-9/30/02)		225 (10/1/02-3/31/03)				4/1/98-3/31/99	4/1/99-3/31/00
0-500M	500M-2MM	2-10MM	10-50MM	50-100MM	100-250MM		ALL	ALL
63	80	82	32	4	5	NUMBER OF STATEMENTS	280	236
%	%	%	%	%	%	ASSETS	%	%
24.3	11.8	15.6	12.1			Cash & Equivalents	14.6	13.8
31.8	51.1	47.3	39.6			Trade Receivables (net)	41.8	44.2
.4	3.0	1.4	4.3			Inventory	2.5	3.4
3.2	4.6	7.0	5.0			All Other Current	5.4	6.2
59.7	70.6	71.3	61.1			Total Current	64.3	67.6
27.1	19.6	15.3	18.7			Fixed Assets (net)	20.0	20.0
4.2	4.2	5.7	9.5			Intangibles (net)	4.5	3.4
8.9	5.6	7.7	10.7			All Other Non-Current	11.2	9.0
100.0	100.0	100.0	100.0			Total	100.0	100.0
						LIABILITIES		
29.5	18.3	9.4	5.6			Notes Payable-Short Term	14.2	28.2
7.9	1.9	3.1	2.6			Cur. Mat.-L/T/D	4.3	3.6
9.1	13.3	13.6	14.3			Trade Payables	11.9	15.3
.0	.8	1.0	.5			Income Taxes Payable	.8	.8
38.5	17.8	18.0	23.4			All Other Current	18.4	20.5
85.0	52.0	45.1	46.4			Total Current	49.6	68.4
11.9	15.5	7.2	15.1			Long Term Debt	23.0	12.6
.0	.9	.7	.9			Deferred Taxes	1.0	1.5
13.8	4.1	4.8	2.6			All Other Non-Current	4.6	4.4
−10.8	27.4	42.2	34.9			Net Worth	21.7	13.0
100.0	100.0	100.0	100.0			Total Liabilities & Net Worth	100.0	100.0
						INCOME DATA		
100.0	100.0	100.0	100.0			Net Sales	100.0	100.0
						Gross Profit		
97.2	94.5	93.2	91.6			Operating Expenses	104.0	94.9
2.8	5.5	6.8	8.4			Operating Profit	−4.0	5.1
.5	1.2	.9	2.3			All Other Expenses (net)	−3.1	−.6
2.4	4.3	5.9	6.1			Profit Before Taxes	−.9	5.7
						RATIOS		
2.6	2.5	2.5	2.0				2.8	2.4
.9	1.5	1.4	1.3			Current	1.6	1.4
.3	1.1	1.0	1.1				1.0	1.0
2.6	2.3	2.0	1.7				2.6	2.0
.9	1.3	1.3	1.1			Quick	(279) 1.4	(235) 1.2
.3	1.0	.8	.7				.8	.7
0 UND	40 9.1	42 8.6	32 11.6				25 14.7	28 13.1
23 16.1	59 6.2	70 5.2	53 6.9			Sales/Receivables	61 6.0	60 6.1
53 6.8	94 3.9	88 4.2	88 4.2				92 4.0	89 4.1
						Cost of Sales/Inventory		
						Cost of Sales/Payables		
13.4	5.5	5.7	7.0				6.0	6.2
−70.1	11.3	13.3	11.6			Sales/Working Capital	13.9	14.0
−13.9	61.6	124.1	72.2				UND	UND
15.0	19.9	24.3	61.1				14.7	16.3
(39) 4.5	(68) 3.6	(66) 8.2	(30) 5.1			EBIT/Interest	(226) 4.5	(184) 4.9
.2	1.5	3.1	3.1				1.3	1.7
	13.3	10.4	8.1			Net Profit + Depr., Dep.,	7.3	5.4
	(11) 3.8	(19) 4.4	(11) 4.5			Amort./Cur. Mat. L /T/D	(45) 2.7	(47) 2.8
	1.8	1.3	.9				.8	1.2
.2	.2	.1	.2				.1	.2
1.1	.4	.4	.6			Fixed/Worth	.4	.4
−4.2	1.3	1.1	1.6				1.5	1.7
.9	.8	.7	1.1				.6	.7
4.6	1.6	1.6	2.9			Debt/Worth	1.9	1.9
−3.5	7.1	5.2	8.3				5.4	9.2
200.0	71.0	59.9	62.0			% Profit Before Taxes/Tangible	79.6	73.0
(39) 49.6	(69) 25.2	(73) 26.3	(26) 16.0			Net Worth	(234) 31.8	(196) 35.3
18.7	6.5	4.8	5.6				10.7	9.6
39.0	21.1	20.2	16.6			% Profit Before Taxes/Total	30.3	26.2
8.4	5.7	10.6	6.1			Assets	9.5	9.3
−5.0	.4	1.6	2.3				1.1	1.4
110.3	75.7	54.9	32.4				63.4	54.5
35.3	29.6	29.3	23.5			Sales/Net Fixed Assets	26.3	24.4
14.9	7.8	16.0	7.8				10.8	11.8
10.4	4.2	3.2	3.6				4.2	3.9
5.0	2.8	2.5	2.0			Sales/Total Assets	2.9	2.9
3.5	1.8	2.0	1.3				1.8	1.9
1.2	.8	.7	1.0				.7	.7
(33) 2.5	(59) 1.6	(70) 1.4	(30) 1.7			% Depr., Dep., Amort./Sales	(217) 1.6	(182) 1.6
4.0	4.0	2.3	2.9				2.9	3.0
6.5	6.1	2.4				% Officers', Directors',	4.3	5.7
(32) 13.3	(24) 10.5	(19) 6.0				Owners' Comp/Sales	(89) 10.2	(66) 9.8
23.1	16.5	19.3					20.1	19.0
82412M	290965M	946341M	1725990M	588856M	1196720M	Net Sales ($)	3728007M	5411430M
12417M	89133M	358358M	686585M	275397M	797798M	Total Assets ($)	2224368M	2061608M

M = $ thousand   MM = $ million
See Pages 11 through 18 for Explanation of Ratios and Data

Comparative Historical Data | Current Data Sorted By Sales

	Hist 1	Hist 2	Hist 3	Type of Statement	0-1MM	1-3MM	3-5MM	5-10MM	10-25MM	25MM & OVER
	37	44	58	Unqualified	2	3	7	9	23	14
	41	47	40	Reviewed	2	7	9	8	12	2
	53	60	38	Compiled	11	9	4	11	1	2
	38	38	28	Tax Returns	19	6	1	1	1	
	81	107	102	Other	16	27	10	17	16	16
	4/1/00-3/31/01 ALL	4/1/01-3/31/02 ALL	4/1/02-3/31/03 ALL		41 (4/1-9/30/02)			225 (10/1/02-3/31/03)		
	250	296	266	**NUMBER OF STATEMENTS**	50	52	31	46	53	34
	%	%	%	**ASSETS**	%	%	%	%	%	%
	14.5	14.4	16.3	Cash & Equivalents	26.0	10.9	19.3	17.5	11.5	13.4
	44.1	44.7	43.6	Trade Receivables (net)	30.9	43.3	45.3	49.6	47.6	46.5
	3.3	3.1	2.0	Inventory	1.1	3.6	1.1	.9	1.0	4.6
	4.8	5.2	5.0	All Other Current	4.8	2.4	5.2	4.7	7.7	5.1
	66.6	67.5	66.9	Total Current	62.8	60.2	71.0	72.8	67.8	69.6
	20.2	19.4	20.1	Fixed Assets (net)	27.8	24.1	18.1	15.2	18.0	14.3
	3.9	4.1	5.5	Intangibles (net)	2.0	7.1	5.6	5.3	4.5	9.7
	9.2	9.0	7.6	All Other Non-Current	7.3	8.6	5.3	6.7	9.6	6.4
	100.0	100.0	100.0	Total	100.0	100.0	100.0	100.0	100.0	100.0
				LIABILITIES						
	16.0	17.3	16.1	Notes Payable-Short Term	28.4	24.6	7.9	13.9	9.5	5.5
	4.6	7.2	3.8	Cur. Mat.-L/T/D	6.5	3.8	4.1	3.4	2.0	3.3
	12.7	12.1	12.3	Trade Payables	7.8	11.1	13.9	9.0	17.7	15.1
	1.1	.7	.7	Income Taxes Payable	.0	.1	1.4	1.8	.3	1.1
	17.0	18.1	23.4	All Other Current	39.6	11.8	24.4	18.8	22.6	23.4
	51.4	55.4	56.3	Total Current	82.4	51.5	51.8	46.9	52.1	48.5
	12.2	13.3	11.9	Long Term Debt	16.9	12.5	9.7	13.3	7.9	9.7
	.7	1.0	.6	Deferred Taxes	.0	.8	1.1	.5	.5	1.0
	15.4	7.9	6.5	All Other Non-Current	14.4	8.0	1.9	4.5	4.0	3.0
	20.3	22.4	24.8	Net Worth	−13.7	27.1	35.5	34.9	35.6	37.7
	100.0	100.0	100.0	Total Liabilities & Net Worth	100.0	100.0	100.0	100.0	100.0	100.0
				INCOME DATA						
	100.0	100.0	100.0	Net Sales	100.0	100.0	100.0	100.0	100.0	100.0
				Gross Profit						
	92.8	94.0	94.3	Operating Expenses	95.8	94.8	95.3	94.4	92.4	93.1
	7.2	6.0	5.7	Operating Profit	4.2	5.2	4.7	5.6	7.6	6.9
	1.3	2.1	1.0	All Other Expenses (net)	.7	1.0	1.0	1.3	1.3	.7
	5.9	3.9	4.7	Profit Before Taxes	3.5	4.1	3.7	4.3	6.3	6.2
				RATIOS						
	2.4	2.2	2.5	Current	4.1	2.5	2.8	3.1	1.9	2.4
	1.4	1.4	1.4		1.5	1.3	1.6	1.4	1.4	1.4
	.9	1.0	1.0		.4	.8	1.1	1.0	1.1	1.1
	2.2	2.0	2.2	Quick	3.4	2.1	2.3	3.1	1.8	2.2
	1.2	1.3	1.2		1.2	1.2	1.3	1.3	1.2	1.1
	.8	.8	.8		.3	.6	1.1	.9	.8	.8
	23 15.7	30 12.1	29 12.8	Sales/Receivables	0 UND	29 12.6	41 9.0	35 10.4	30 12.3	41 8.8
	62 5.8	58 6.3	53 6.8		32 11.3	51 7.2	51 7.1	59 6.1	54 6.8	62 5.9
	91 4.0	88 4.2	86 4.2		75 4.8	88 4.2	85 4.3	88 4.2	87 4.2	89 4.1
				Cost of Sales/Inventory						
				Cost of Sales/Payables						
	6.2	7.2	6.4	Sales/Working Capital	4.3	9.1	5.5	4.6	7.5	7.0
	17.3	15.9	14.8		18.7	24.6	9.9	11.3	16.2	12.8
	−103.0	UND	−142.2		−13.8	−44.7	68.9	125.1	63.8	56.5
	(200) 13.8	(244) 11.6	(211) 22.0	EBIT/Interest	(32) 7.4	(38) 12.9	(26) 9.9	(37) 30.1	(45) 27.5	(33) 34.2
	4.4	3.5	5.1		2.3	3.2	3.7	4.4	12.8	7.4
	1.4	.9	1.6		−.1	1.1	1.7	1.2	5.5	3.8
	(40) 6.9	(50) 8.4	(45) 9.9	Net Profit + Depr., Dep., Amort./Cur. Mat. L/T/D				(10) 22.2	(13) 7.7	
	2.1	3.0	4.4					7.8	3.9	
	.8	.8	1.3					3.9	1.4	
	.2	.2	.2	Fixed/Worth	.1	.2	.1	.1	.1	.2
	.4	.5	.4		.6	.7	.3	.3	.5	.4
	2.4	2.3	2.2		−4.6	10.1	1.0	1.3	1.3	1.1
	.8	.8	.8	Debt/Worth	.8	.8	.6	.6	.9	1.1
	2.1	2.4	1.9		3.3	2.7	1.4	1.9	1.6	2.4
	9.7	11.3	10.2		−5.0	28.8	2.6	5.5	7.9	4.4
	(205) 75.3	(246) 70.3	(216) 71.5	% Profit Before Taxes/Tangible Net Worth	(33) 75.0	(41) 116.6	(27) 47.8	(41) 73.3	(45) 85.4	(29) 75.8
	30.8	24.1	29.3		27.7	42.1	14.4	30.7	32.3	26.7
	6.5	2.6	6.3		.5	2.1	6.2	2.8	16.0	9.1
	29.3	19.9	21.9	% Profit Before Taxes/Total Assets	17.9	28.7	15.2	23.2	21.9	22.3
	10.3	7.0	8.3		1.2	8.2	4.1	6.7	14.5	8.1
	.9	−.9	.8		−6.9	.4	1.2	.1	6.8	3.6
	56.5	68.4	63.4	Sales/Net Fixed Assets	117.2	57.4	68.7	74.0	53.3	34.6
	26.5	26.5	27.3		23.8	28.2	19.5	35.2	29.7	24.9
	13.0	11.1	12.2		5.2	7.5	8.8	19.4	14.0	15.4
	4.4	4.7	4.3	Sales/Total Assets	6.6	4.9	4.3	3.9	4.4	3.8
	2.8	2.9	2.8		3.5	3.2	2.7	2.9	2.9	2.5
	2.0	1.9	1.9		1.3	2.0	1.8	2.4	1.4	1.7
	(196) .7	(228) .5	(197) .8	% Depr., Dep., Amort./Sales	(26) 1.9	(35) .8	(23) .8	(36) .8	(49) .6	(28) .7
	1.3	1.4	1.6		3.6	1.7	1.8	1.4	1.4	1.4
	2.6	2.9	3.3		5.3	4.2	3.8	2.3	2.6	2.2
	(95) 5.7	(93) 5.1	(79) 3.7	% Officers', Directors', Owners' Comp/Sales	(26) 8.4	(19) 6.2	(10) 3.0	(10) 3.2	(10) 3.0	
	9.7	8.3	9.4		13.3	11.8	9.4	4.9	7.4	
	18.6	16.4	20.2		21.7	22.3	17.7	7.9	24.2	
	7829114M	5708356M	4831284M	Net Sales ($)	30015M	99741M	118904M	321261M	805515M	3455848M
	2100805M	2678111M	2219688M	Total Assets ($)	15235M	45305M	55174M	135917M	495773M	1472284M

M = $ thousand   MM = $ million
See Pages 11 through 18 for Explanation of Ratios and Data

Current Data Sorted By Assets   Comparative Historical Data

						Type of Statement		
1	2	18	29	12	8	Unqualified	80	86
2	11	11	3			Reviewed	14	21
5	7	4				Compiled	12	14
5	2	5				Tax Returns	8	5
5	12	19	5	3	4	Other	56	51
	37 (4/1-9/30/02)			136 (10/1/02-3/31/03)			4/1/98-3/31/99	4/1/99-3/31/00
0-500M	500M-2MM	2-10MM	10-50MM	50-100MM	100-250MM		ALL	ALL
18	34	57	37	15	12	NUMBER OF STATEMENTS	170	177
%	%	%	%	%	%	ASSETS	%	%
24.7	14.2	16.6	12.5	18.3	12.6	Cash & Equivalents	20.6	15.0
16.6	46.8	32.1	28.7	20.6	18.2	Trade Receivables (net)	30.1	33.7
.6	5.5	3.1	3.4	4.6	2.7	Inventory	3.8	3.5
6.5	2.7	10.1	9.0	5.9	7.1	All Other Current	3.4	4.7
48.5	69.2	61.8	53.7	49.5	40.7	Total Current	57.8	56.9
26.6	27.0	23.4	26.3	26.7	37.5	Fixed Assets (net)	25.7	27.6
11.1	1.3	3.8	5.4	9.6	7.1	Intangibles (net)	4.0	3.8
13.6	2.6	11.0	14.6	14.2	14.7	All Other Non-Current	12.6	11.6
100.0	100.0	100.0	100.0	100.0	100.0	Total	100.0	100.0
						LIABILITIES		
29.5	7.0	6.9	2.6	6.4	1.9	Notes Payable-Short Term	5.2	6.5
6.3	1.6	2.6	2.9	1.0	1.2	Cur. Mat.-L/T/D	2.2	2.5
8.4	11.9	10.1	7.9	6.9	5.4	Trade Payables	9.8	10.8
.0	.0	.5	.8	.1	.4	Income Taxes Payable	.3	.7
25.4	15.5	15.6	17.6	13.0	11.5	All Other Current	14.5	14.4
69.6	36.1	35.6	31.8	27.3	20.3	Total Current	32.0	34.9
21.5	14.9	9.8	8.6	16.7	13.3	Long Term Debt	14.4	11.4
.0	1.0	.6	1.7	.5	.4	Deferred Taxes	.8	.6
22.6	3.5	5.2	5.1	7.2	3.7	All Other Non-Current	5.2	3.6
-13.8	44.5	48.7	52.8	48.3	62.3	Net Worth	47.6	49.4
100.0	100.0	100.0	100.0	100.0	100.0	Total Liabilities & Net Worth	100.0	100.0
						INCOME DATA		
100.0	100.0	100.0	100.0	100.0	100.0	Net Sales	100.0	100.0
						Gross Profit		
90.8	95.3	95.8	93.6	94.6	93.6	Operating Expenses	136.6	95.3
9.2	4.7	4.2	6.4	5.4	6.4	Operating Profit	-36.6	4.7
6.4	.7	.6	1.3	9.8	.1	All Other Expenses (net)	-4.4	-1.5
2.8	4.1	3.6	5.1	-4.4	6.3	Profit Before Taxes	-32.3	6.2
						RATIOS		
1.4	3.0	2.9	3.5	2.2	3.5	Current	3.6	3.0
.7	2.1	1.7	1.6	1.8	1.7		1.9	1.7
.4	1.4	1.2	1.2	1.6	1.2		1.1	1.2
1.4	2.7	2.4	1.8	2.0	2.6	Quick	3.1	2.7
.6	1.7	1.4	1.3	1.7	1.4		1.6	1.5
.4	1.2	.9	.9	.9	.9		.9	.9
0 UND	42 8.8	29 12.5	41 8.8	32 11.5	36 10.2	Sales/Receivables	32 11.3	41 8.9
0 UND	59 6.2	54 6.7	54 6.7	65 5.6	59 6.2		57 6.4	61 6.0
78 4.7	86 4.2	69 5.3	98 3.7	82 4.4	80 4.6		88 4.1	80 4.6
						Cost of Sales/Inventory		
						Cost of Sales/Payables		
30.8	5.8	4.7	3.0	2.4	2.2	Sales/Working Capital	3.1	4.6
-41.8	7.8	10.6	7.0	6.9	7.9		7.4	8.8
-3.6	15.4	26.7	21.4	9.6	29.7		39.1	30.2
(11) 11.0	(28) 15.9	(43) 18.2	(31) 24.7	(12) 8.7		EBIT/Interest	(124) 15.5	(140) 15.2
1.0	4.8	7.8	6.3	1.9			5.7	5.9
-2.6	1.9	.2	1.3	.2			.7	.3
		(15) 10.5	(10) 18.5			Net Profit + Depr., Dep., Amort./Cur. Mat. L /T/D	(35) 8.7	(43) 9.4
		5.3	5.5				3.9	3.4
		3.1	1.8				1.7	1.0
.0	.3	.2	.2	.3	.5	Fixed/Worth	.2	.3
6.2	.4	.4	.5	.7	.7		.5	.6
-4.4	1.1	.9	.9	1.5	1.1		1.2	1.0
4.0	.5	.5	.4	.8	.3	Debt/Worth	.4	.4
UND	1.2	1.4	.8	1.4	.8		1.0	1.0
-2.8	2.9	2.5	1.9	4.0	2.2		2.5	2.8
	46.9	42.7	26.2	20.7	18.3	% Profit Before Taxes/Tangible Net Worth	(158) 40.0	(165) 43.8
	(31) 24.2	(53) 27.5	(34) 10.0	(13) 4.1	4.1		15.5	15.1
	10.7	3.4	-2.1	-2.3	-1.2		2.6	2.2
26.1	24.5	20.1	14.8	7.3	5.8	% Profit Before Taxes/Total Assets	17.0	17.7
9.2	8.1	9.8	3.8	1.8	2.7		6.5	7.0
-5.5	2.6	-1.5	-.9	.9	-.9		-.4	.5
UND	29.9	28.8	21.3	25.9	7.2	Sales/Net Fixed Assets	23.3	20.9
14.8	11.0	15.1	6.9	4.4	2.4		7.8	9.0
5.5	5.8	4.5	2.9	1.6	1.1		2.9	3.2
3.5	3.7	3.1	2.5	1.4	1.4	Sales/Total Assets	2.7	3.0
2.4	2.7	2.3	1.5	.9	.8		1.6	1.7
1.3	1.9	1.2	.7	.5	.6		.8	1.0
(10) 1.4	(30) 1.5	(51) 1.2	(35) 1.4	1.7		% Depr., Dep., Amort./Sales	(134) 1.7	(147) 1.5
4.5	2.1	1.9	2.6	3.9			3.2	2.7
9.1	5.1	3.4	4.0	12.9			5.3	5.2
(12) 11.5	(11) 8.2					% Officers', Directors', Owners' Comp/Sales	(27) 4.4	(26) 3.5
22.6	11.1						7.6	5.0
41.3	17.4						14.0	9.3
10352M	124499M	569199M	1720680M	1202264M	1851223M	Net Sales ($)	6009052M	5137134M
3581M	41130M	266329M	987642M	1010034M	1816186M	Total Assets ($)	5562686M	4311841M

© RMA 2003

M = $ thousand   MM = $ million
See Pages 11 through 18 for Explanation of Ratios and Data

Comparative Historical Data | Current Data Sorted By Sales

Type of Statement	4/1/00-3/31/01 ALL	4/1/01-3/31/02 ALL	4/1/02-3/31/03 ALL	0-1MM	1-3MM	3-5MM	5-10MM	10-25MM	25MM & OVER
					37 (4/1-9/30/02)			136 (10/1/02-3/31/03)	
Unqualified	66	44	70	2	2	7	6	17	36
Reviewed	15	13	27	2	3	5	10	7	
Compiled	22	30	16	4	4	3	3	2	
Tax Returns	5	2	12	5	3	1	3		
Other	48	40	48	5	9	5	10	8	11
NUMBER OF STATEMENTS	156	129	173	18	21	21	32	34	47
ASSETS	%	%	%	%	%	%	%	%	%
Cash & Equivalents	17.0	16.1	16.0	20.9	13.8	18.1	14.0	15.8	15.6
Trade Receivables (net)	32.4	32.9	30.7	21.7	28.9	29.6	38.7	31.8	29.1
Inventory	3.3	3.8	3.5	1.8	6.5	1.9	3.8	3.7	3.1
All Other Current	5.7	6.2	7.5	6.5	3.2	7.2	7.7	8.9	8.6
Total Current	58.3	59.0	57.6	50.9	52.4	56.9	64.3	60.2	56.4
Fixed Assets (net)	26.1	24.1	26.3	27.0	38.6	27.0	20.7	25.8	24.5
Intangibles (net)	4.1	5.1	5.1	11.0	2.0	3.5	2.4	3.8	7.8
All Other Non-Current	11.4	11.9	10.9	11.0	7.1	12.6	12.6	10.1	11.3
Total	100.0	100.0	100.0	100.0	100.0	100.0	100.0	100.0	100.0
LIABILITIES									
Notes Payable-Short Term	6.6	8.2	8.0	28.8	5.5	4.2	7.0	6.5	4.5
Cur. Mat.-L/T/D	3.3	2.4	2.6	5.2	2.3	2.6	2.4	2.2	2.2
Trade Payables	10.0	12.1	9.2	10.4	8.2	9.8	9.2	9.4	8.7
Income Taxes Payable	.7	.8	.4	.0	.0	.0	.6	.5	.6
All Other Current	17.3	15.7	16.5	19.6	12.0	14.3	14.3	18.9	18.2
Total Current	37.9	39.2	36.7	64.1	28.0	30.9	33.5	37.4	34.2
Long Term Debt	10.8	11.4	12.6	13.8	29.6	11.9	5.3	12.2	10.2
Deferred Taxes	.6	.8	.8	.0	.0	1.9	.5	.7	1.4
All Other Non-Current	3.7	4.3	6.7	24.8	5.1	6.3	3.0	4.0	5.1
Net Worth	47.0	44.4	43.2	-2.7	37.3	48.9	57.7	45.7	49.1
Total Liabilities & Net Worth	100.0	100.0	100.0	100.0	100.0	100.0	100.0	100.0	100.0
INCOME DATA									
Net Sales	100.0	100.0	100.0	100.0	100.0	100.0	100.0	100.0	100.0
Gross Profit									
Operating Expenses	96.7	94.8	94.4	92.4	95.1	97.7	93.6	94.5	94.0
Operating Profit	3.3	5.2	5.6	7.6	4.9	2.3	6.4	5.5	6.0
All Other Expenses (net)	-1.9	1.5	2.1	7.1	1.6	.2	1.1	1.9	2.2
Profit Before Taxes	5.2	3.7	3.4	.5	3.3	2.1	5.3	3.6	3.8
RATIOS									
Current	2.9	2.6	2.8	1.6	4.6	3.5	3.0	3.8	2.2
	1.7	1.7	1.6	.8	2.5	1.7	1.8	1.7	1.6
	1.2	1.1	1.2	.4	1.2	1.2	1.3	1.2	1.3
Quick	2.5	2.2	2.4	1.5	3.2	2.7	2.5	2.3	1.9
	1.4	1.3	1.4	.7	1.8	1.5	1.4	1.3	1.5
	.9	.9	.9	.4	.7	.9	1.1	.9	.9
Sales/Receivables	37 9.9	38 9.6	32 11.4	0 UND	18 19.9	24 15.3	32 11.3	42 8.6	35 10.5
	59 6.1	53 6.8	56 6.6	33 10.9	59 6.2	54 6.8	54 6.7	62 5.9	52 7.0
	83 4.4	82 4.4	81 4.5	89 4.1	76 4.8	70 5.2	83 4.4	83 4.4	80 4.5
Cost of Sales/Inventory									
Cost of Sales/Payables									
Sales/Working Capital	4.3	4.5	4.7	11.8	4.8	5.2	4.8	2.8	4.9
	9.4	9.1	9.0	-39.4	8.5	10.7	7.9	9.8	8.5
	26.8	89.2	29.9	-3.3	70.8	19.8	27.1	61.7	14.9
EBIT/Interest	18.3	16.7	16.6	13.6	9.7	9.3	20.6	22.5	20.3
	(113) 5.9	(95) 5.5	(134) 4.9	(13) 1.1	(13) 3.0	(17) 1.8	(28) 8.7	(26) 8.6	(37) 5.8
	1.0	.6	1.1	-2.4	-1.5	-5.0	3.9	-.2	1.7
Net Profit + Depr., Dep., Amort./Cur. Mat. L/T/D	12.5	9.4	10.7					13.0	16.9
	(29) 3.2	(30) 3.4	(38) 3.9					(13) 6.0	(11) 6.0
	1.8	1.6	2.6					2.3	3.3
Fixed/Worth	.2	.2	.2	.0	.4	.2	.2	.2	.3
	.5	.5	.5	4.1	.9	.5	.3	.5	.6
	1.1	1.1	1.2	-5.0	4.2	1.0	.5	1.2	1.0
Debt/Worth	.5	.5	.5	.6	.3	.4	.4	.6	.5
	1.0	1.2	1.2	UND	2.6	1.2	.8	1.4	1.2
	2.1	3.6	3.4	-7.7	10.9	2.8	1.6	3.0	2.6
% Profit Before Taxes/Tangible Net Worth	36.3	45.5	37.4		44.1	47.2	38.9	42.9	22.0
	(143) 12.8	(115) 13.0	(152) 18.7		(17) 20.1	(20) 11.7	24.5	(31) 28.0	(43) 13.1
	2.3	.6	2.5		4.1	-6.2	4.0	-3.7	2.2
% Profit Before Taxes/Total Assets	16.7	18.7	18.3	20.0	23.1	19.6	19.8	19.8	13.0
	7.0	6.8	5.4	6.5	7.5	4.0	10.3	7.4	3.8
	.5	-1.6	-.4	-5.5	-.8	-2.0	2.1	-2.3	1.0
Sales/Net Fixed Assets	27.3	27.6	26.7	UND	17.3	21.2	35.7	29.8	24.1
	8.9	13.2	11.0	12.6	6.8	7.6	18.7	12.9	9.1
	3.1	3.3	3.8	3.3	3.5	4.1	6.9	3.7	2.8
Sales/Total Assets	2.8	3.1	3.0	2.7	3.3	2.8	3.2	3.3	2.6
	1.8	2.0	2.0	1.7	2.0	2.0	2.5	1.9	1.6
	.9	.8	1.0	1.1	1.2	.9	1.3	1.1	.9
% Depr., Dep., Amort./Sales	1.3	1.2	1.5	.8	1.8	2.0	1.2	1.1	1.5
	(131) 2.1	(111) 2.1	(150) 2.5	(10) 4.5	(18) 2.3	(19) 2.7	(30) 1.8	(30) 2.7	(43) 2.6
	4.8	4.3	5.1	11.5	6.1	5.0	4.3	3.6	5.1
% Officers', Directors', Owners' Comp/Sales	2.6	2.6	6.2	11.0					
	(34) 5.3	(24) 6.2	(33) 10.8	(10) 19.3					
	11.1	15.7	22.6	34.7					
Net Sales ($)	4863771M	3592086M	5478217M	8068M	42749M	82601M	230127M	548678M	4565994M
Total Assets ($)	4253708M	2981389M	4124902M	15909M	26638M	92301M	167017M	592095M	3230942M

M = $ thousand   MM = $ million
See Pages 11 through 18 for Explanation of Ratios and Data

Current Data Sorted By Assets   Comparative Historical Data

Type of Statement	0-500M	500M-2MM	2-10MM	10-50MM	50-100MM	100-250MM			
Unqualified		2	7	6	1	1		39	37
Reviewed	2	23	45	4	1	1		80	72
Compiled	16	19	25	1		1		106	86
Tax Returns	26	19	8			1		48	49
Other	15	33	47	7	2			114	102
	48 (4/1-9/30/02)			265 (10/1/02-3/31/03)				4/1/98-3/31/99 ALL	4/1/99-3/31/00 ALL
	0-500M	500M-2MM	2-10MM	10-50MM	50-100MM	100-250MM			
NUMBER OF STATEMENTS	59	96	132	18	4	4		387	346
ASSETS	%	%	%	%	%	%		%	%
Cash & Equivalents	15.8	14.9	16.4	25.2				15.1	15.1
Trade Receivables (net)	33.1	50.8	49.0	46.4				48.5	48.3
Inventory	2.4	3.1	3.0	3.1				3.2	3.5
All Other Current	5.8	4.9	3.9	2.4				3.6	4.0
Total Current	57.2	73.7	72.4	77.1				70.4	70.9
Fixed Assets (net)	29.5	16.8	15.3	10.3				17.8	16.1
Intangibles (net)	4.8	2.4	3.7	4.1				4.2	5.5
All Other Non-Current	8.5	7.1	8.6	8.5				7.6	7.5
Total	100.0	100.0	100.0	100.0				100.0	100.0
LIABILITIES									
Notes Payable-Short Term	29.5	12.4	6.8	3.4				9.9	9.2
Cur. Mat.-L/T/D	12.5	2.4	3.0	2.2				3.5	3.3
Trade Payables	27.1	33.6	34.2	35.3				32.8	32.0
Income Taxes Payable	.0	1.0	.3	.6				.5	.4
All Other Current	34.3	15.6	21.3	25.4				16.2	18.0
Total Current	103.5	64.9	65.7	67.0				62.8	62.9
Long Term Debt	27.8	6.5	8.3	2.7				12.4	8.8
Deferred Taxes	1.9	.4	.3	.3				.7	.5
All Other Non-Current	3.9	3.2	3.4	7.3				3.4	4.9
Net Worth	−37.1	25.0	22.4	22.7				20.7	22.9
Total Liabilities & Net Worth	100.0	100.0	100.0	100.0				100.0	100.0
INCOME DATA									
Net Sales	100.0	100.0	100.0	100.0				100.0	100.0
Gross Profit									
Operating Expenses	97.9	96.3	96.8	92.6				95.7	95.6
Operating Profit	2.1	3.7	3.2	7.3				4.3	4.4
All Other Expenses (net)	1.6	.8	.6	.3				−1.1	.8
Profit Before Taxes	.6	3.0	2.6	7.0				5.3	3.5
RATIOS									
Current	1.7	1.8	1.5	1.7				1.5	1.6
	.8	1.1	1.1	1.1				1.1	1.1
	.4	.9	.9	1.0				.9	.9
Quick	1.3	1.7	1.3	1.6				1.4	1.5
	.7	1.0	1.0	1.0				1.0	1.0
	.3	.8	.8	.9				.8	.8
Sales/Receivables	0 UND	27 13.6	37 9.8	32 11.5				32 11.4	33 11.1
	27 13.3	47 7.7	57 6.5	53 6.9				50 7.3	55 6.7
	42 8.6	64 5.7	85 4.3	73 5.0				74 4.9	83 4.4
Cost of Sales/Inventory									
Cost of Sales/Payables									
Sales/Working Capital	33.5	11.8	13.7	10.1				13.1	12.0
	−64.7	54.3	53.0	42.6				44.6	40.2
	−7.0	−44.3	−61.9	−46.6				−92.0	−46.4
EBIT/Interest	(40) 8.1	(84) 17.4	(112) 16.0	(14) 78.4				(321) 15.7	(278) 20.6
	2.1	4.5	4.3	13.5				5.0	4.8
	−5.7	1.2	.6	4.6				1.5	1.4
Net Profit + Depr., Dep., Amort./Cur. Mat. L /T/D		(10) 14.8	(30) 5.7					(100) 8.7	(82) 8.2
		3.4	1.9					2.8	3.3
		−1.2	.7					1.4	1.2
Fixed/Worth	.7	.2	.3	.1				.3	.2
	5.0	.7	.6	.7				.7	.6
	−1.0	38.8	5.0	NM				2.8	5.8
Debt/Worth	2.0	1.2	1.7	2.2				1.6	1.3
	71.0	3.8	3.9	7.7				4.2	4.2
	−3.1	364.2	35.7	NM				16.9	53.7
% Profit Before Taxes/Tangible Net Worth	(32) 214.9	(73) 67.4	(103) 64.7	(14) 154.0				(318) 84.9	(266) 90.5
	31.3	28.4	23.5	59.9				32.6	38.1
	−58.7	1.1	2.8	29.4				8.3	9.6
% Profit Before Taxes/Total Assets	23.8	21.2	14.5	22.1				19.4	18.9
	5.8	4.4	4.1	7.5				5.9	6.4
	−23.5	−.4	−.2	3.7				1.1	1.0
Sales/Net Fixed Assets	81.5	84.1	69.7	88.0				70.5	77.0
	31.1	40.5	32.3	43.0				31.3	30.8
	12.1	17.2	13.5	12.1				14.7	14.4
Sales/Total Assets	8.1	5.2	4.4	3.8				5.2	5.0
	5.1	3.9	3.3	3.3				3.7	3.4
	3.2	3.2	1.9	1.3				2.5	2.2
% Depr., Dep., Amort./Sales	(40) .9	(78) .6	(122) .6	(15) .7				(324) .6	(288) .6
	1.9	1.1	1.1	.8				1.1	1.2
	3.0	1.8	2.4	2.2				2.1	2.1
% Officers', Directors', Owners' Comp/Sales	(38) 9.1	(44) 4.0	(55) 2.1					(182) 3.5	(138) 3.4
	10.5	5.7	3.4					6.4	5.9
	13.8	9.5	6.8					11.5	11.4
Net Sales ($)	79563M	504656M	2061373M	1084826M	723504M	2843446M		5899823M	5142105M
Total Assets ($)	12395M	106457M	587628M	347535M	305486M	555420M		1931390M	2167001M

© RMA 2003

M = $ thousand   MM = $ million
See Pages 11 through 18 for Explanation of Ratios and Data

Comparative Historical Data   Current Data Sorted By Sales

4/1/00-3/31/01 ALL	4/1/01-3/31/02 ALL	4/1/02-3/31/03 ALL	Type of Statement	48 (4/1-9/30/02) 0-1MM	1-3MM	265 (10/1/02-3/31/03) 3-5MM	5-10MM	10-25MM	25MM & OVER
23	17	17	Unqualified			3	1	6	7
82	65	76	Reviewed	2	7	11	18	27	11
95	91	62	Compiled	11	12	10	8	16	5
52	36	54	Tax Returns	11	21	9	7	3	3
131	142	104	Other	10	14	15	26	25	14
383	**351**	**313**	**NUMBER OF STATEMENTS**	**34**	**54**	**48**	**60**	**77**	**40**
%	%	%	**ASSETS**	%	%	%	%	%	%
12.8	15.3	16.7	Cash & Equivalents	12.6	19.4	16.3	14.0	16.0	22.3
47.6	45.9	45.5	Trade Receivables (net)	34.9	43.8	41.0	45.2	53.6	47.4
3.1	2.1	2.9	Inventory	1.7	2.4	4.4	3.2	3.4	1.5
4.1	4.0	4.4	All Other Current	5.6	3.2	7.0	4.9	3.8	2.4
67.6	67.2	69.6	Total Current	54.9	68.7	68.7	67.5	76.8	73.6
18.7	18.8	18.1	Fixed Assets (net)	31.3	20.2	18.9	18.6	14.0	10.3
5.4	6.3	3.9	Intangibles (net)	4.8	4.3	1.9	4.7	3.0	5.5
8.3	7.7	8.4	All Other Non-Current	9.1	6.8	10.6	9.2	6.2	10.6
100.0	100.0	100.0	Total	100.0	100.0	100.0	100.0	100.0	100.0
			LIABILITIES						
14.2	10.1	12.6	Notes Payable-Short Term	40.6	12.1	9.3	10.5	9.0	3.3
2.5	3.2	4.5	Cur. Mat.-L/T/D	5.6	11.2	3.4	3.0	2.6	2.0
31.2	32.9	32.5	Trade Payables	24.7	30.4	28.5	32.9	35.1	41.2
.5	.4	.5	Income Taxes Payable	.1	.2	1.6	.5	.3	.4
17.4	18.8	22.2	All Other Current	41.3	17.8	19.9	16.6	24.7	17.9
65.7	65.3	72.3	Total Current	112.3	71.7	62.8	63.5	71.7	64.9
10.6	11.0	11.2	Long Term Debt	29.7	14.5	10.8	11.0	3.8	5.6
.6	.3	.6	Deferred Taxes	3.3	.3	.6	.2	.1	.3
4.4	4.3	3.8	All Other Non-Current	7.5	3.9	2.2	3.0	1.9	7.2
18.7	19.2	12.1	Net Worth	-52.8	9.5	23.6	22.2	22.4	21.9
100.0	100.0	100.0	Total Liabilities & Net Worth	100.0	100.0	100.0	100.0	100.0	100.0
			INCOME DATA						
100.0	100.0	100.0	Net Sales	100.0	100.0	100.0	100.0	100.0	100.0
			Gross Profit						
95.6	97.7	96.6	Operating Expenses	94.1	98.5	97.7	95.4	96.8	96.0
4.4	2.3	3.4	Operating Profit	5.9	1.5	2.3	4.6	3.2	4.0
1.2	1.2	.9	All Other Expenses (net)	2.8	.7	.6	1.2	.2	.5
3.2	1.1	2.6	Profit Before Taxes	3.2	.8	1.6	3.4	3.0	3.5
			RATIOS						
1.6	1.5	1.6	Current	1.7	2.0	1.7	1.5	1.5	1.3
1.1	1.0	1.1		.8	1.2	1.1	1.0	1.0	1.1
.9	.8	.8		.4	.8	.9	.8	.9	1.0
1.5	1.3	1.4	Quick	1.7	1.9	1.6	1.3	1.3	1.2
1.0	1.0	1.0		.7	1.1	.9	.9	1.0	1.0
.8	.7	.7		.3	.7	.7	.7	.8	.9
32 11.4	28 12.8	28 13.0	Sales/Receivables	17 21.3	20 18.1	26 14.0	34 10.8	31 11.9	24 15.3
51 7.2	49 7.4	47 7.8		40 9.1	39 9.4	51 7.2	50 7.3	43 8.5	53 6.9
78 4.7	74 4.9	71 5.2		60 6.1	79 4.6	69 5.3	73 5.0	69 5.3	72 5.1
			Cost of Sales/Inventory						
			Cost of Sales/Payables						
12.5	17.3	14.1	Sales/Working Capital	16.3	10.3	12.4	16.0	14.7	21.1
57.2	167.7	88.8		-13.3	78.9	58.5	128.0	130.6	74.6
-41.4	-27.7	-32.1		-5.1	-17.7	-53.0	-27.6	-60.3	749.8
(316) 13.3	(281) 8.5	(257) 16.8	EBIT/Interest	(21) 6.0	(45) 17.1	(43) 17.5	(54) 16.6	(64) 30.8	(30) 34.9
4.2	2.1	4.3		2.0	3.2	4.0	4.8	4.3	10.7
1.2	-2.2	.3		-5.7	-2.4	-1.5	.1	1.0	4.4
(73) 11.0	(57) 6.8	(50) 7.7	Net Profit + Depr., Dep., Amort./Cur. Mat. L/T/D				(11) 5.2	(15) 10.5	
3.2	2.2	2.0					1.2	4.5	
1.7	.3	.4					-.5	1.3	
.3	.3	.3	Fixed/Worth	.8	.2	.2	.3	.3	.1
.8	1.1	.8		-7.7	.7	.8	1.0	.6	.6
7.0	-3.9	-11.8		-.3	UND	33.8	-4.0	23.7	3.7
1.3	1.7	1.6	Debt/Worth	2.0	1.2	1.2	2.1	1.3	2.7
4.0	5.0	4.6		-12.6	4.9	3.4	4.4	4.0	5.4
83.5	-18.3	-57.4		-2.6	-23.1	360.1	-62.1	290.1	33.4
77.3	65.4	77.6	% Profit Before Taxes/Tangible Net Worth	(15) 100.0	(39) 68.0	(38) 56.8	(44) 77.0	(59) 73.4	(33) 114.4
(291) 32.2	(243) 19.0	(228) 27.7		20.8	27.9	17.1	27.2	27.6	58.5
8.3	-1.6	3.6		-70.0	-8.6	-2.4	3.6	4.4	16.1
17.9	12.3	17.0	% Profit Before Taxes/Total Assets	23.5	15.7	11.6	18.0	17.8	21.2
6.0	2.3	5.2		4.0	5.4	3.3	5.5	5.2	6.7
.7	-3.8	-.5		-25.5	-7.8	-5.2	-.1	.7	2.9
66.3	68.0	74.7	Sales/Net Fixed Assets	38.1	62.8	86.0	58.6	102.4	167.8
29.3	29.5	34.0		14.4	25.1	36.7	28.5	34.7	54.7
13.2	12.8	13.7		6.2	11.0	13.3	12.7	18.6	22.8
5.3	5.2	5.1	Sales/Total Assets	4.0	6.3	4.9	4.7	5.9	5.1
3.5	3.5	3.7		3.1	3.5	3.7	3.5	4.1	3.9
2.3	2.2	2.4		1.9	1.9	2.2	2.0	3.1	3.2
.6	.6	.6	% Depr., Dep., Amort./Sales	(24) 1.6	(43) 1.0	(39) .6	(52) .8	(69) .4	(33) .4
(308) 1.2	(281) 1.3	(260) 1.2		2.6	1.5	1.1	1.5	.9	.7
2.2	2.7	2.4		8.8	2.7	2.7	2.7	1.4	1.2
3.6	3.9	3.1	% Officers', Directors', Owners' Comp/Sales	(15) 10.5	(31) 5.4	(22) 4.5	(30) 2.4	(29) 1.6	(14) 2.2
(172) 6.3	(149) 7.5	(141) 6.1		12.0	9.5	8.7	3.9	4.1	3.9
11.6	13.6	10.9		18.5	13.4	11.4	8.1	5.4	14.8
6296183M	6422059M	7297368M	Net Sales ($)	17810M	108937M	189467M	423897M	1154741M	5402516M
2730871M	2571225M	1914921M	Total Assets ($)	7921M	49007M	75385M	171540M	343142M	1267926M

M = $ thousand   MM = $ million
See Pages 11 through 18 for Explanation of Ratios and Data

Current Data Sorted By Assets   Comparative Historical Data

						Type of Statement		
	1	6	3		1	Unqualified	10	11
	3	4	1			Reviewed	13	13
5	7	6				Compiled	11	12
4	3	1				Tax Returns	3	6
5	11	6	1	2		Other	24	26
	15 (4/1-9/30/02)			55 (10/1/02-3/31/03)			4/1/98-3/31/99	4/1/99-3/31/00
0-500M	500M-2MM	2-10MM	10-50MM	50-100MM	100-250MM		ALL	ALL
14	25	23	5	2	1	**NUMBER OF STATEMENTS**	61	68
%	%	%	%	%	%	**ASSETS**	%	%
25.4	11.7	12.3				Cash & Equivalents	16.2	15.1
23.4	58.3	50.4				Trade Receivables (net)	39.0	41.0
.3	1.0	6.1				Inventory	4.3	3.9
5.2	5.8	4.0				All Other Current	5.0	6.6
54.3	76.8	72.8				Total Current	64.5	66.7
33.2	12.1	13.8				Fixed Assets (net)	16.5	20.2
3.8	2.3	3.5				Intangibles (net)	4.2	2.8
8.6	8.8	9.9				All Other Non-Current	14.8	10.3
100.0	100.0	100.0				Total	100.0	100.0
						LIABILITIES		
6.9	15.5	11.5				Notes Payable-Short Term	10.9	13.4
4.6	3.8	2.4				Cur. Mat.-L/T/D	3.7	3.0
23.7	16.1	23.0				Trade Payables	14.4	13.2
.0	.4	1.7				Income Taxes Payable	1.2	.8
49.8	15.4	20.3				All Other Current	17.9	19.3
85.0	51.3	59.0				Total Current	48.0	49.7
12.5	4.9	9.1				Long Term Debt	8.9	12.7
.1	.8	.6				Deferred Taxes	1.1	1.0
7.4	7.6	8.0				All Other Non-Current	11.1	2.3
−5.0	35.4	23.3				Net Worth	30.8	34.3
100.0	100.0	100.0				Total Liabilities & Net Worth	100.0	100.0
						INCOME DATA		
100.0	100.0	100.0				Net Sales	100.0	100.0
						Gross Profit		
99.7	95.8	96.3				Operating Expenses	92.4	91.7
.3	4.2	3.7				Operating Profit	7.6	8.3
−.2	1.3	1.4				All Other Expenses (net)	.4	.5
.4	2.9	2.3				Profit Before Taxes	7.3	7.8
						RATIOS		
1.7	3.2	2.3				Current	2.7	2.5
1.1	1.5	1.4					1.5	1.4
.4	1.0	.9					1.1	.9
1.7	3.2	1.9				Quick	1.8	2.1
.9	1.4	1.1					1.2	1.1
.4	.8	.7					.7	.8
0 UND	38 9.5	28 12.8				Sales/Receivables	25 14.5	25 14.7
18 20.1	54 6.8	61 6.0					55 6.6	54 6.8
36 10.2	82 4.5	79 4.6					75 4.9	81 4.5
						Cost of Sales/Inventory		
						Cost of Sales/Payables		
16.4	6.9	6.4				Sales/Working Capital	7.5	5.6
NM	16.8	16.7					20.5	19.3
−45.7	NM	−23.9					81.4	−137.5
	16.3	15.2				EBIT/Interest	24.3	43.9
(19) 1.6	(19) 1.6	5.0					(49) 7.3	(57) 7.3
	−5.8	1.3					3.8	1.9
						Net Profit + Depr., Dep., Amort./Cur. Mat. L./T/D	17.5	4.2
						(14)	(14) 3.9	2.7
							.8	1.7
.5	.1	.1				Fixed/Worth	.2	.1
6.4	.3	.3					.3	.4
UND	.9	3.1					1.0	1.6
1.3	1.0	1.3				Debt/Worth	.8	.7
15.8	2.5	2.3					1.9	1.4
UND	6.7	21.9					6.1	5.0
79.5	134.4	58.9				% Profit Before Taxes/Tangible Net Worth	94.5	86.2
(12) 9.9	(22) 14.4	(18) 18.5					(53) 29.3	(59) 31.1
−18.2	−17.6	−.3					11.9	11.8
19.9	38.1	23.6				% Profit Before Taxes/Total Assets	28.3	34.5
.4	3.8	2.6					8.5	13.4
−12.3	−5.8	−1.1					2.9	2.2
45.0	111.9	76.6				Sales/Net Fixed Assets	48.3	49.6
19.2	40.8	34.4					23.5	25.9
13.5	22.8	11.1					13.7	8.8
14.3	4.3	3.6				Sales/Total Assets	5.2	4.0
5.4	3.4	2.8					3.1	2.7
3.2	3.0	1.7					2.2	2.0
.5	.7	.7				% Depr., Dep., Amort./Sales	.6	.6
(12) 1.1	(17) 1.4	(20) 1.2					(49) 1.5	(52) 1.5
2.2	2.1	2.2					2.1	3.3
	7.4					% Officers', Directors', Owners' Comp/Sales	8.0	4.7
	(16) 15.4						(20) 11.8	(28) 10.8
	34.2						21.3	16.5
17457M	93008M	289909M	140006M	236631M	221338M	Net Sales ($)	733112M	1057251M
3287M	24191M	96808M	75820M	121806M	102461M	Total Assets ($)	543269M	354392M

M = $ thousand   MM = $ million
See Pages 11 through 18 for Explanation of Ratios and Data

Comparative Historical Data   Current Data Sorted By Sales

H1	H2	H3	Type of Statement	0-1MM	1-3MM	3-5MM	5-10MM	10-25MM	25MM & OVER
6	6	3	Unqualified			1	2		
4	6	10	Reviewed		3	2	3	1	1
8	11	15	Compiled	7	6		2		
6	6	5	Tax Returns	4	1				
17	12	14	Other	5	1	1	2	4	1
4/1/00-3/31/01	4/1/01-3/31/02	4/1/02-3/31/03			4 (4/1-9/30/02)		43 (10/1/02-3/31/03)		
ALL	ALL	ALL		0-1MM	1-3MM	3-5MM	5-10MM	10-25MM	25MM & OVER
41	41	47	**NUMBER OF STATEMENTS**	16	11	4	9	5	2
%	%	%	**ASSETS**	%	%	%	%	%	%
8.6	6.9	7.8	Cash & Equivalents	5.7	16.7				
24.2	19.2	21.8	Trade Receivables (net)	5.7	23.5				
6.2	4.1	5.1	Inventory	1.1	1.5				
2.4	2.9	3.4	All Other Current	2.6	6.0				
41.4	33.0	38.0	Total Current	15.2	47.7				
50.0	58.3	48.2	Fixed Assets (net)	72.1	39.5				
2.0	1.9	4.4	Intangibles (net)	1.4	7.2				
6.5	6.7	9.4	All Other Non-Current	11.4	5.5				
100.0	100.0	100.0	Total	100.0	100.0				
			LIABILITIES						
3.9	7.1	5.3	Notes Payable-Short Term	1.3	7.0				
8.2	6.3	6.9	Cur. Mat.-L/T/D	7.8	3.1				
13.0	8.9	11.9	Trade Payables	1.6	12.3				
.3	.1	.0	Income Taxes Payable	.0	.0				
6.2	8.2	10.9	All Other Current	7.1	7.6				
31.5	30.5	35.0	Total Current	17.9	30.1				
38.6	40.5	31.4	Long Term Debt	43.7	21.1				
.2	.2	.0	Deferred Taxes	.0	.1				
1.8	2.1	5.1	All Other Non-Current	8.1	2.4				
27.8	26.7	28.4	Net Worth	30.3	46.3				
100.0	100.0	100.0	Total Liabilities & Net Worth	100.0	100.0				
			INCOME DATA						
100.0	100.0	100.0	Net Sales	100.0	100.0				
			Gross Profit						
84.6	84.2	86.3	Operating Expenses	70.3	97.7				
15.4	15.8	13.7	Operating Profit	29.7	2.3				
5.5	7.4	4.3	All Other Expenses (net)	8.3	1.4				
9.9	8.3	9.4	Profit Before Taxes	21.4	.9				
			RATIOS						
3.0	2.0	2.0	Current	3.6	2.7				
1.6	1.2	1.0		.7	1.7				
.8	.5	.5		.2	.9				
2.7	1.5	1.6	Quick	2.7	2.6				
1.0	.8	.8		.5	1.6				
.4	.4	.5		.2	.7				
23 15.8	3 129.3	21 17.1	Sales/Receivables	0 UND	18 20.6				
43 8.5	30 12.2	41 9.0		25 14.8	42 8.6				
57 6.4	62 5.9	53 6.9		47 7.8	55 6.7				
			Cost of Sales/Inventory						
			Cost of Sales/Payables						
4.3	8.3	8.0	Sales/Working Capital	8.0	5.2				
11.1	28.8	227.7		-186.8	8.0				
-22.2	-7.2	-15.2		-5.3	-23.0				
4.8	4.1	6.8	EBIT/Interest	8.9					
(31) 2.9	(34) 2.1	(40) 2.9		(12) 3.4					
1.1	.6	1.1		.5					
			Net Profit + Depr., Dep., Amort./Cur. Mat. L/T/D						
.5	1.1	.4	Fixed/Worth	1.0	.4				
1.5	2.5	1.3		2.0	1.0				
6.3	15.0	23.1		101.6	-999.8				
.7	1.0	.9	Debt/Worth	.6	.1				
1.8	4.1	2.1		2.2	.9				
8.7	42.0	254.0		192.6	-999.8				
73.2	67.4	32.3	% Profit Before Taxes/Tangible Net Worth	70.4					
(36) 22.4	(33) 14.8	(36) 14.3		(13) 12.3					
.9	-4.2	-.4		1.0					
19.7	12.5	15.3	% Profit Before Taxes/Total Assets	24.5	13.5				
6.6	4.4	6.4		11.2	2.0				
-.2	-.7	.0		1.2	-16.4				
12.5	7.5	14.3	Sales/Net Fixed Assets	4.1	34.6				
3.7	1.6	2.6		1.1	4.1				
.5	.5	.9		.3	1.1				
3.1	1.7	3.4	Sales/Total Assets	1.6	3.4				
1.5	1.0	1.2		.6	1.3				
.4	.4	.6		.3	1.0				
1.9	2.1	2.3	% Depr., Dep., Amort./Sales	5.2	1.5				
(39) 6.3	(36) 7.0	(40) 5.1		(13) 13.6	(10) 3.2				
13.4	13.4	14.7		17.5	6.9				
4.4	4.4	3.7	% Officers', Directors', Owners' Comp/Sales						
(13) 7.3	(14) 7.2	(16) 9.6							
14.0	12.0	12.5							
541626M	347457M	320380M	Net Sales ($)	7498M	19069M	16003M	72712M	66710M	138388M
417233M	290525M	344187M	Total Assets ($)	18022M	31593M	20650M	28774M	44339M	200809M

© RMA 2003   M = $ thousand   MM = $ million
See Pages 11 through 18 for Explanation of Ratios and Data

Current Data Sorted By Assets   Comparative Historical Data

Type of Statement	0-500M	500M-2MM	2-10MM	10-50MM	50-100MM	100-250MM	4/1/98-3/31/99 ALL	4/1/99-3/31/00 ALL
Unqualified		1	8	16		1	39	27
Reviewed	1	8	15	7			43	36
Compiled	2	11	7				37	33
Tax Returns	5	8	1				14	12
Other	4	20	16	4	2	1	38	41
		25 (4/1-9/30/02)		113 (10/1/02-3/31/03)				
NUMBER OF STATEMENTS	12	48	47	27	2	2	171	149
ASSETS	%	%	%	%	%	%	%	%
Cash & Equivalents	29.2	19.1	17.3	15.8			14.2	12.1
Trade Receivables (net)	39.5	38.4	34.9	30.8			35.1	41.2
Inventory	.5	2.7	4.0	5.8			4.0	3.8
All Other Current	.3	2.3	1.9	3.2			2.8	3.0
Total Current	69.6	62.5	58.1	55.5			56.1	60.1
Fixed Assets (net)	21.9	24.8	31.8	25.1			28.7	27.0
Intangibles (net)	6.5	3.8	3.5	7.8			7.7	5.4
All Other Non-Current	2.0	8.9	6.6	11.6			7.5	7.5
Total	100.0	100.0	100.0	100.0			100.0	100.0
LIABILITIES								
Notes Payable-Short Term	19.2	6.6	9.6	5.8			8.5	9.0
Cur. Mat.-L/T/D	3.3	5.0	8.2	6.3			5.0	4.4
Trade Payables	41.7	19.6	15.8	17.2			13.6	17.1
Income Taxes Payable	.0	.5	.1	.0			.3	.4
All Other Current	12.8	16.1	22.2	22.7			18.5	22.5
Total Current	77.0	47.8	55.9	52.0			46.0	53.4
Long Term Debt	31.8	14.8	11.2	17.2			18.5	16.7
Deferred Taxes	.0	.1	.4	.1			.6	.5
All Other Non-Current	20.3	9.4	2.3	3.7			11.8	4.1
Net Worth	-29.2	27.9	30.2	27.0			23.2	25.3
Total Liabilities & Net Worth	100.0	100.0	100.0	100.0			100.0	100.0
INCOME DATA								
Net Sales	100.0	100.0	100.0	100.0			100.0	100.0
Gross Profit								
Operating Expenses	103.4	96.8	97.1	92.3			94.5	94.9
Operating Profit	-3.4	3.1	2.9	7.7			5.5	5.1
All Other Expenses (net)	.6	1.0	1.2	4.5			.8	1.5
Profit Before Taxes	-4.0	2.2	1.6	3.2			4.7	3.6
RATIOS								
Current	1.7	2.3	2.0	1.6			1.9	1.9
	1.1	1.4	1.0	1.0			1.2	1.2
	.7	1.0	.7	.8			.9	.8
Quick	1.7	2.1	1.6	1.5			1.7	1.7
	1.1	1.3	1.0	.8			(170) 1.1	1.0
	.7	.9	.6	.6			.7	.7
Sales/Receivables	12 30.5	28 13.0	38 9.6	40 9.2			28 13.1	32 11.3
	33 10.9	42 8.7	52 7.0	48 7.7			55 6.6	56 6.5
	46 7.9	61 6.0	62 5.8	58 6.3			71 5.1	77 4.8
Cost of Sales/Inventory								
Cost of Sales/Payables								
Sales/Working Capital	20.4	9.2	8.1	8.9			9.4	9.1
	66.6	23.5	-999.8	-313.8			33.2	25.0
	-33.0	-98.1	-12.3	-18.5			-43.4	-26.6
EBIT/Interest		16.9	8.2	18.1			7.9	8.3
	(41) 5.4	(44) 3.0	(25) 5.2				(145) 4.1	(126) 3.9
	1.2	-2.3	.5				1.4	1.5
Net Profit + Depr., Dep., Amort./Cur. Mat. L /T/D			3.8	15.3			4.9	4.9
		(18) 1.4	(10) 3.3				(45) 2.5	(39) 2.3
		.4	1.2				1.5	1.3
Fixed/Worth	.3	.3	.4	.4			.5	.4
	4.5	.8	1.2	1.1			1.3	1.1
	-.1	5.2	2.5	-4.8			3.5	4.2
Debt/Worth	2.8	1.0	1.0	1.3			1.1	1.2
	-24.7	2.8	3.0	3.2			3.0	3.3
	-1.8	19.0	6.2	-10.9			10.8	21.4
% Profit Before Taxes/Tangible Net Worth		67.6	51.4	96.0			69.7	72.3
	(39) 19.7	(43) 18.9	(20) 52.4				(142) 33.6	(117) 32.1
	2.4	-7.6	12.3				9.3	10.3
% Profit Before Taxes/Total Assets	1.8	17.8	12.4	22.7			17.7	15.4
	-20.8	4.9	3.8	5.6			8.8	6.9
	-80.7	-2.8	-4.0	.0			1.6	1.9
Sales/Net Fixed Assets	463.5	45.1	16.2	15.3			20.4	25.5
	17.3	13.0	9.2	10.5			9.8	11.2
	11.1	6.4	5.1	5.4			5.7	5.9
Sales/Total Assets	7.0	5.0	2.8	2.5			3.4	3.8
	4.1	3.0	2.3	2.0			2.4	2.6
	3.8	2.1	1.9	1.6			1.7	1.8
% Depr., Dep., Amort./Sales		1.2	1.6	1.4			1.5	1.1
	(42) 2.9	(43) 3.6	(25) 3.8				(157) 3.1	(135) 2.8
	6.0	5.8	5.2				4.6	4.9
% Officers', Directors', Owners' Comp/Sales		3.5	2.1				3.8	2.8
	(28) 5.2	(23) 3.7					(74) 6.7	(63) 5.5
	8.7	10.7					10.8	9.0
Net Sales ($)	13321M	191413M	530735M	1301468M	126099M	422989M	3921654M	2997483M
Total Assets ($)	2680M	52788M	218468M	608674M	123476M	237595M	1664493M	1195406M

M = $ thousand   MM = $ million
See Pages 11 through 18 for Explanation of Ratios and Data

	Comparative Historical Data			Type of Statement		Current Data Sorted By Sales				
	22	24	26	Unqualified		1		2	8	15
	35	26	31	Reviewed		3	2	12	8	6
	44	42	20	Compiled	1	7	4	7	1	
	14	12	14	Tax Returns	3	7	1	2	1	
	33	39	47	Other	6	10	7	9	8	7
	4/1/00-3/31/01 ALL	4/1/01-3/31/02 ALL	4/1/02-3/31/03 ALL			25 (4/1-9/30/02)		113 (10/1/02-3/31/03)		
					0-1MM	1-3MM	3-5MM	5-10MM	10-25MM	25MM & OVER
	148	143	138	NUMBER OF STATEMENTS	10	28	14	32	26	28
	%	%	%	ASSETS	%	%	%	%	%	%
	14.6	14.6	18.6	Cash & Equivalents	24.9	21.4	15.2	19.9	18.3	14.0
	37.4	34.0	35.2	Trade Receivables (net)	24.2	36.2	44.5	35.4	35.8	32.6
	4.7	3.9	3.6	Inventory	.7	2.2	1.2	4.6	3.5	6.0
	2.7	3.2	2.2	All Other Current	.4	2.4	2.1	1.6	2.6	3.0
	59.4	55.7	59.5	Total Current	50.2	62.3	62.9	61.5	60.1	55.7
	27.6	29.5	27.4	Fixed Assets (net)	30.4	28.5	24.2	26.9	29.2	26.0
	5.4	7.1	5.0	Intangibles (net)	11.4	1.1	8.8	1.7	5.1	8.5
	7.6	7.6	8.0	All Other Non-Current	8.0	8.1	4.0	9.9	5.6	9.8
	100.0	100.0	100.0	Total	100.0	100.0	100.0	100.0	100.0	100.0
				LIABILITIES						
	9.4	7.3	8.6	Notes Payable-Short Term	20.9	6.0	2.8	10.5	9.8	6.2
	5.0	5.4	6.1	Cur. Mat.-L/T/D	5.2	8.1	6.4	6.4	4.2	5.8
	16.5	17.1	19.6	Trade Payables	13.4	23.6	19.2	19.5	16.3	21.1
	.4	.1	.2	Income Taxes Payable	.0	.2	1.0	.2	.1	.1
	23.1	20.4	19.3	All Other Current	15.3	12.7	28.1	17.2	24.3	20.6
	54.4	50.4	53.7	Total Current	54.9	50.5	57.4	53.7	54.7	53.8
	16.1	17.1	16.2	Long Term Debt	48.0	15.0	7.7	10.7	12.3	20.2
	.4	.2	.2	Deferred Taxes	.0	.1	.3	.5	.2	.0
	5.5	4.4	6.8	All Other Non-Current	22.1	5.7	14.2	6.3	1.0	4.8
	23.6	27.9	23.1	Net Worth	−25.1	28.8	20.4	28.8	31.9	21.2
	100.0	100.0	100.0	Total Liabilities & Net Worth	100.0	100.0	100.0	100.0	100.0	100.0
				INCOME DATA						
	100.0	100.0	100.0	Net Sales	100.0	100.0	100.0	100.0	100.0	100.0
				Gross Profit						
	95.2	96.1	96.5	Operating Expenses	90.9	99.1	98.9	97.5	95.2	94.8
	4.8	3.9	3.5	Operating Profit	9.1	.9	1.1	2.5	4.8	5.2
	1.0	2.0	1.8	All Other Expenses (net)	10.9	.6	.4	.9	1.2	2.0
	3.8	1.9	1.7	Profit Before Taxes	−1.8	.3	.7	1.6	3.6	3.2
				RATIOS						
	1.6	1.6	1.9		1.3	2.8	2.0	1.8	2.2	1.5
	1.2	1.1	1.1	Current	1.0	1.7	1.3	1.3	1.1	.9
	.9	.8	.8		.6	.9	.7	.9	.7	.8
	1.5	1.5	1.7		1.2	2.6	1.9	1.6	2.0	1.0
	1.1	1.0	1.0	Quick	1.0	1.4	1.1	1.1	1.0	.8
	.7	.6	.7		.6	.8	.7	.8	.6	.6
33	11.1	29 / 12.6	31 / 11.9		0 UND	37 / 9.9	39 / 9.4	37 / 10.0	28 / 13.2	29 / 12.4
53	6.9	49 / 7.5	47 / 7.8	Sales/Receivables	12 / 29.8	47 / 7.8	65 / 5.6	52 / 7.0	47 / 7.8	46 / 8.0
69	5.3	66 / 5.5	61 / 5.9		33 / 11.2	71 / 5.2	76 / 4.8	59 / 6.2	56 / 6.5	57 / 6.4
				Cost of Sales/Inventory						
				Cost of Sales/Payables						
	9.8	10.0	8.8		26.9	5.6	13.0	8.3	7.6	15.8
	29.4	42.6	45.2	Sales/Working Capital	NM	10.8	21.1	35.1	90.8	−77.9
	−42.5	−19.3	−22.7		−12.9	−55.6	−19.6	−28.2	−21.6	−14.6
	10.2	9.1	14.7			14.9	16.8	19.0	10.7	16.4
(133)	3.1	(125) / 2.5	(121) / 3.5	EBIT/Interest	(26) / 2.3	(11) / 5.4	(28) / 3.0	(23) / 4.8	(27) / 3.3	
	.8	.4	1.1		−1.7	1.1	1.5	−1.9	1.5	
	2.9	2.7	4.0	Net Profit + Depr., Dep.,						6.6
(39)	1.4	(30) / 1.5	(35) / 1.4	Amort./Cur. Mat. L/T/D					(12) / 3.3	
	.9	.8	.5						1.3	
	.5	.4	.4		1.0	.4	.5	.2	.4	.5
	1.1	1.5	1.0	Fixed/Worth	NM	.7	2.7	.8	.9	2.0
	3.5	10.5	5.5		−.2	2.4	−6.0	2.7	2.2	NM
	1.3	1.2	1.1		2.8	.8	.8	1.1	.9	1.8
	2.8	3.6	3.5	Debt/Worth	−24.6	2.0	4.8	3.1	1.7	5.2
	10.6	51.0	20.3		−1.9	8.2	−48.1	7.1	5.3	NM
	68.8	56.8	63.0	% Profit Before Taxes/Tangible		28.6		77.8	45.0	110.0
(123)	26.4	(115) / 15.8	(110) / 20.5	Net Worth	(26) / 15.4		(28) / 40.3	(22) / 19.4	(21) / 53.1	
	5.5	−6.8	2.3		−15.6		4.0	7.6	15.5	
	15.7	12.4	16.0	% Profit Before Taxes/Total	2.3	10.3	12.2	19.5	18.6	21.9
	6.1	3.7	4.1	Assets	−2.3	2.2	4.4	4.6	5.8	5.6
	−.6	−2.5	−4.1		−56.5	−8.0	−6.1	1.0	−4.4	2.0
	24.8	23.1	20.1		104.0	13.4	39.1	39.9	26.1	16.7
	12.1	10.3	10.9	Sales/Net Fixed Assets	13.8	8.9	14.3	12.6	11.6	10.1
	5.8	4.9	6.0		7.0	5.4	6.3	8.7	5.6	5.6
	4.1	3.5	4.0		5.0	3.1	4.0	4.7	4.6	3.1
	2.5	2.3	2.4	Sales/Total Assets	3.8	2.2	2.7	2.4	2.5	2.2
	1.8	1.7	1.9		.8	1.8	2.1	2.0	2.0	1.6
	.9	1.1	1.4			2.1	1.6	.9	1.5	1.1
(128)	2.5	(124) / 2.9	(122) / 3.4	% Depr., Dep., Amort./Sales	(27) / 5.6	(11) / 2.4	(27) / 2.8	(24) / 3.5	(26) / 3.2	
	4.3	4.8	5.8		6.8	4.1	5.6	5.5	5.2	
	2.2	2.5	2.7	% Officers', Directors',		3.3		1.5	3.4	
(64)	4.6	(56) / 4.9	(62) / 4.8	Owners' Comp/Sales	(20) / 6.8		(18) / 5.6	(11) / 3.8		
	8.9	7.8	8.6		8.7		11.5	9.2		
	2791194M	3359130M	2586025M	Net Sales ($)	5862M	56110M	52947M	227894M	393636M	1849576M
	1558301M	1702765M	1243681M	Total Assets ($)	25818M	30398M	20791M	96342M	157600M	912732M

© RMA 2003

M = $ thousand   MM = $ million
See Pages 11 through 18 for Explanation of Ratios and Data

Current Data Sorted By Assets   Comparative Historical Data

	0-500M	500M-2MM	2-10MM	10-50MM	50-100MM	100-250MM	Type of Statement	4/1/98-3/31/99 ALL	4/1/99-3/31/00 ALL
	1	2	3	5		4	Unqualified	11	16
	4	3	5				Reviewed	9	10
	9	3	2				Compiled	17	17
	4	2	1				Tax Returns	4	4
		3	4	6	2	1	Other	17	16
		11 (4/1-9/30/02)			53 (10/1/02-3/31/03)				
NUMBER OF STATEMENTS	18	13	15	11	2	5		58	63
ASSETS	%	%	%	%	%	%		%	%
Cash & Equivalents	11.8	11.8	15.2	23.1				10.8	12.6
Trade Receivables (net)	29.7	36.2	39.2	25.0				33.4	38.0
Inventory	2.7	7.3	5.7	5.4				5.3	5.8
All Other Current	4.7	19.0	6.5	9.8				4.0	4.6
Total Current	48.9	74.2	66.6	63.3				53.6	61.0
Fixed Assets (net)	34.3	21.2	22.2	17.6				23.2	22.3
Intangibles (net)	1.3	1.1	1.4	17.8				14.3	6.3
All Other Non-Current	15.4	3.6	9.8	1.3				8.9	10.4
Total	100.0	100.0	100.0	100.0				100.0	100.0
LIABILITIES									
Notes Payable-Short Term	57.0	13.6	13.6	5.3				17.9	19.3
Cur. Mat.-L/T/D	14.5	12.9	3.8	7.0				5.4	4.2
Trade Payables	22.1	12.4	17.5	12.6				20.1	22.8
Income Taxes Payable	.0	.1	.4	.3				.5	.4
All Other Current	10.5	17.4	20.1	25.9				21.4	13.4
Total Current	104.1	56.4	55.2	51.2				65.4	60.1
Long Term Debt	28.5	4.0	11.5	12.3				13.7	14.5
Deferred Taxes	.0	.1	.3	.0				.7	1.6
All Other Non-Current	11.3	.7	6.7	3.4				13.8	7.0
Net Worth	-44.0	38.8	26.3	33.1				6.3	16.7
Total Liabilities & Net Worth	100.0	100.0	100.0	100.0				100.0	100.0
INCOME DATA									
Net Sales	100.0	100.0	100.0	100.0				100.0	100.0
Gross Profit									
Operating Expenses	98.2	95.5	98.5	88.5				93.0	93.4
Operating Profit	1.8	4.5	1.5	11.5				7.0	6.6
All Other Expenses (net)	2.3	1.6	.4	2.2				1.4	2.0
Profit Before Taxes	-.5	2.9	1.1	9.3				5.6	4.6
RATIOS									
Current	1.1 / .6 / .1	2.0 / 1.3 / .9	2.0 / 1.3 / .9	2.3 / 1.0 / .8				2.0 / 1.2 / .6	1.9 / 1.2 / .9
Quick	1.0 / .5 / .1	1.3 / .8 / .4	1.5 / 1.2 / .6	2.2 / .9 / .5				1.6 / 1.0 / .5	1.6 / 1.0 / .7
Sales/Receivables	0 UND / 19 19.5 / 43 8.4	0 UND / 31 11.9 / 63 5.8	37 9.8 / 49 7.5 / 62 5.9	25 14.6 / 50 7.3 / 76 4.8				8 48.1 / 47 7.8 / 65 5.6	32 11.5 / 52 7.0 / 82 4.5
Cost of Sales/Inventory									
Cost of Sales/Payables									
Sales/Working Capital	59.3 / -13.4 / -6.4	9.3 / 19.4 / NM	9.2 / 20.4 / -29.8	7.9 / 132.8 / -23.7				11.3 / 190.5 / -14.7	7.9 / 19.2 / -43.9
EBIT/Interest	(16) 5.2 / 3.0 / -1.1	(10) 20.5 / 7.1 / 1.3	24.5 / 4.4 / 1.4	(10) 43.5 / 16.9 / 4.2				(49) 7.9 / 2.5 / 1.2	(51) 12.1 / 3.4 / .4
Net Profit + Depr., Dep., Amort./Cur. Mat. L /T/D								(15) 5.1 / 1.3 / .4	(16) 3.6 / 2.0 / .1
Fixed/Worth	1.2 / -2.7 / -.6	.1 / .3 / 3.0	.3 / .5 / 2.0	.2 / 1.3 / -.7				.2 / 1.0 / 12.7	.3 / .8 / 14.2
Debt/Worth	8.5 / -7.4 / -3.1	.5 / 1.7 / 8.2	.8 / 2.1 / 7.7	.6 / 11.1 / -4.4				1.5 / 4.2 / -5.9	1.4 / 3.2 / -20.5
% Profit Before Taxes/Tangible Net Worth		122.9 / 11.3 / -.1	(14) 61.1 / 44.5 / 1.5					(41) 71.9 / 39.8 / 8.0	(46) 76.1 / 32.8 / 6.9
% Profit Before Taxes/Total Assets	20.1 / 7.1 / -16.7	50.8 / 7.0 / -.1	20.1 / 7.7 / 2.5	19.4 / 14.5 / 7.9				17.4 / 7.0 / 1.1	17.9 / 8.3 / .3
Sales/Net Fixed Assets	41.4 / 27.3 / 9.5	135.5 / 35.7 / 7.7	39.3 / 14.2 / 10.5	42.5 / 27.3 / 4.2				81.3 / 19.6 / 6.2	52.0 / 15.6 / 7.7
Sales/Total Assets	9.2 / 5.5 / 2.5	6.0 / 3.8 / 1.7	4.3 / 3.5 / 2.2	4.3 / 1.8 / 1.3				4.0 / 2.7 / 1.6	4.2 / 2.8 / 1.6
% Depr., Dep., Amort./Sales	(14) .9 / 2.3 / 4.3	(10) .2 / 1.1 / 3.3	.5 / 2.6 / 4.0	(10) .9 / 3.2 / 6.8				(49) .6 / 1.4 / 3.9	(49) .6 / 1.7 / 3.7
% Officers', Directors', Owners' Comp/Sales	(13) 4.3 / 6.4 / 13.9							(17) 3.5 / 6.6 / 13.6	(25) 3.3 / 5.9 / 8.6
Net Sales ($)	19965M	68748M	255403M	536113M	654561M	1423709M		2247816M	2710883M
Total Assets ($)	4027M	15241M	73412M	204170M	112440M	727361M		869064M	1675732M

M = $ thousand   MM = $ million
See Pages 11 through 18 for Explanation of Ratios and Data

Comparative Historical Data | Current Data Sorted By Sales

Type of Statement	4/1/00-3/31/01	4/1/01-3/31/02	4/1/02-3/31/03	0-1MM	1-3MM	3-5MM	5-10MM	10-25MM	25MM & OVER
Unqualified	7	8	14			1	2	4	7
Reviewed	7	8	9	1		2	2	3	1
Compiled	16	15	9	2	5	1	1		1
Tax Returns	13	9	12	6	4		1	1	
Other	16	22	20	1	2	2	3	4	8
	ALL	ALL	ALL	11 (4/1-9/30/02)			53 (10/1/02-3/31/03)		
	59	62	64						
NUMBER OF STATEMENTS	59	62	64	10	11	5	9	12	17
ASSETS	%	%	%	%	%	%	%	%	%
Cash & Equivalents	15.0	11.2	14.2	6.2	13.5			23.1	15.2
Trade Receivables (net)	40.9	47.7	33.3	18.9	34.0			37.8	32.0
Inventory	5.7	5.7	6.2	.8	4.9			1.1	11.5
All Other Current	5.1	3.9	9.2	6.4	14.1			11.5	9.1
Total Current	66.7	68.5	62.9	32.3	66.6			73.5	67.9
Fixed Assets (net)	19.5	17.3	23.0	43.6	26.1			19.2	15.3
Intangibles (net)	4.9	6.3	5.8	.5	1.9			3.6	11.7
All Other Non-Current	8.9	7.8	8.2	23.5	5.5			3.7	5.1
Total	100.0	100.0	100.0	100.0	100.0			100.0	100.0
LIABILITIES									
Notes Payable-Short Term	16.1	13.0	24.1	75.6	20.4			4.2	9.4
Cur. Mat.-L/T/D	3.8	5.3	9.0	28.5	6.0			9.0	4.9
Trade Payables	23.7	23.4	17.7	21.2	22.1			15.3	19.0
Income Taxes Payable	.8	.4	.3	.0	.0			.0	.9
All Other Current	23.1	13.5	16.7	5.1	10.8			18.5	18.4
Total Current	67.6	55.6	67.9	130.5	59.3			47.1	52.7
Long Term Debt	15.6	16.2	15.3	25.7	21.1			12.3	11.5
Deferred Taxes	.8	.3	.1	.0	.0			.0	.3
All Other Non-Current	5.5	5.0	6.5	12.6	7.0			8.5	5.9
Net Worth	10.5	23.0	10.3	-68.9	12.6			32.1	29.6
Total Liabilities & Net Worth	100.0	100.0	100.0	100.0	100.0			100.0	100.0
INCOME DATA									
Net Sales	100.0	100.0	100.0	100.0	100.0			100.0	100.0
Gross Profit									
Operating Expenses	89.6	92.7	95.4	96.3	99.1			92.9	93.3
Operating Profit	10.4	7.3	4.6	3.7	.9			7.1	6.7
All Other Expenses (net)	1.0	1.2	1.7	5.6	.3			.1	2.4
Profit Before Taxes	9.4	6.1	2.8	-2.0	.6			7.0	4.2
RATIOS									
Current	2.0	2.1	1.7	.5	1.7			2.5	2.1
Current	1.2	1.3	1.1	.2	1.1			1.6	1.1
Current	.8	1.0	.7	.1	.8			1.3	.9
Quick	1.7	1.9	1.3	.5	1.1			2.3	1.5
Quick	.9	1.1	.8	.2	.8			1.4	.8
Quick	.6	.7	.5	.0	.6			1.1	.6
Sales/Receivables	23 · 16.0	35 · 10.4	17 · 22.0	0 · UND	0 · UND			27 · 13.4	21 · 17.5
Sales/Receivables	50 · 7.3	50 · 7.3	44 · 8.2	12 · 30.4	42 · 8.6			54 · 6.7	50 · 7.3
Sales/Receivables	91 · 4.0	81 · 4.5	65 · 5.6	36 · 10.1	62 · 5.9			68 · 5.3	78 · 4.7
Cost of Sales/Inventory									
Cost of Sales/Payables									
Sales/Working Capital	7.2	8.3	11.9	-14.6	6.2			4.4	8.7
Sales/Working Capital	46.3	16.9	49.8	-6.1	39.3			12.6	32.2
Sales/Working Capital	-32.3	282.7	-19.6	-2.4	-52.6			20.3	-71.9
EBIT/Interest	(48) 27.2	(53) 15.2	(58) 18.2		(10) 7.2			(11) 28.9	(16) 31.4
EBIT/Interest	4.7	5.2	5.1		4.2			18.3	9.9
EBIT/Interest	2.5	1.8	1.5		.7			1.4	2.7
Net Profit + Depr., Dep., Amort./Cur. Mat. L/T/D	(13) 6.7	(13) 10.5	(13) 10.0						
Net Profit + Depr., Dep., Amort./Cur. Mat. L/T/D	2.8	3.6	2.0						
Net Profit + Depr., Dep., Amort./Cur. Mat. L/T/D	1.0	.6	.7						
Fixed/Worth	.1	.2	.3	6.8	.3			.3	.2
Fixed/Worth	.7	.5	1.2	-2.1	1.2			.5	1.2
Fixed/Worth	3.7	-11.7	-4.4	-.5	-3.0			1.2	NM
Debt/Worth	1.1	1.2	1.1	6.8	1.0			.5	1.0
Debt/Worth	3.2	3.2	7.8	-3.7	8.8			1.2	7.8
Debt/Worth	-28.7	-27.8	-13.4	-2.8	-11.1			10.2	NM
% Profit Before Taxes/Tangible Net Worth	(44) 110.6	(43) 72.7	(47) 90.6					(11) 90.6	(13) 190.8
% Profit Before Taxes/Tangible Net Worth	54.1	31.9	43.6					43.6	48.8
% Profit Before Taxes/Tangible Net Worth	28.1	5.4	9.6					3.2	32.9
% Profit Before Taxes/Total Assets	30.2	20.6	19.9	10.2	18.9			42.7	21.0
% Profit Before Taxes/Total Assets	17.9	7.2	9.6	-7.2	8.1			15.5	14.2
% Profit Before Taxes/Total Assets	7.4	.6	1.4	-20.2	-9.1			3.6	6.1
Sales/Net Fixed Assets	79.5	63.8	46.1	30.6	41.6			55.9	61.6
Sales/Net Fixed Assets	31.5	27.4	23.3	18.9	35.0			14.4	34.7
Sales/Net Fixed Assets	12.1	11.4	9.6	2.8	9.5			10.7	8.8
Sales/Total Assets	4.7	4.6	5.5	8.2	8.4			4.4	5.3
Sales/Total Assets	2.9	3.2	3.4	3.1	4.9			2.2	2.6
Sales/Total Assets	1.7	1.6	1.8	1.5	2.4			1.8	1.3
% Depr., Dep., Amort./Sales	(45) .4	(49) .4	(54) .6					(11) 1.6	(14) .4
% Depr., Dep., Amort./Sales	1.1	1.4	2.1					3.6	1.2
% Depr., Dep., Amort./Sales	2.3	2.4	4.2					4.8	3.7
% Officers', Directors', Owners' Comp/Sales	(27) 5.6	(27) 3.8	(25) 3.2						
% Officers', Directors', Owners' Comp/Sales	10.2	7.4	5.1						
% Officers', Directors', Owners' Comp/Sales	18.6	14.8	9.3						
Net Sales ($)	617258M	1249413M	2958499M	4376M	18188M	18914M	62908M	198530M	2655583M
Total Assets ($)	407742M	840915M	1136651M	2262M	5841M	5007M	29289M	76650M	1017602M

Current Data Sorted By Assets   **Comparative Historical Data**

0-500M	500M-2MM	2-10MM	10-50MM	50-100MM	100-250MM	Type of Statement	4/1/98-3/31/99 ALL	4/1/99-3/31/00 ALL
	1	3		1	1	Unqualified		
			1			Reviewed		
6	8	8	1			Compiled		
4	4	2	1			Tax Returns		
2	5	6				Other		
	10 (4/1-9/30/02)		43 (10/1/02-3/31/03)					
12	18	19	2	1	1	NUMBER OF STATEMENTS		
%	%	%	%	%	%	**ASSETS**	%	%
19.3	12.3	12.5				Cash & Equivalents	D	D
45.7	34.9	32.2				Trade Receivables (net)	A	A
10.7	26.8	28.1				Inventory	T	T
1.0	.6	3.9				All Other Current	A	A
76.7	74.6	76.7				Total Current		
14.1	19.7	13.1				Fixed Assets (net)	N	N
2.1	.5	1.2				Intangibles (net)	O	O
7.0	5.2	9.0				All Other Non-Current	T	T
100.0	100.0	100.0				Total		
						LIABILITIES	A	A
23.4	8.1	20.8				Notes Payable-Short Term	V	V
1.4	7.5	1.6				Cur. Mat.-L/T/D	A	A
26.1	19.2	15.9				Trade Payables	I	I
.0	.0	1.0				Income Taxes Payable	L	L
12.0	8.8	11.8				All Other Current	A	A
63.0	43.6	51.1				Total Current	B	B
7.2	17.1	5.6				Long Term Debt	L	L
.0	.0	.0				Deferred Taxes	E	E
10.5	12.3	6.0				All Other Non-Current		
19.4	26.9	37.3				Net Worth		
100.0	100.0	100.0				Total Liabilities & Net Worth		
						INCOME DATA		
100.0	100.0	100.0				Net Sales		
						Gross Profit		
94.3	98.1	92.3				Operating Expenses		
5.7	1.9	7.7				Operating Profit		
.7	.3	2.3				All Other Expenses (net)		
5.0	1.6	5.4				Profit Before Taxes		
						RATIOS		
3.6	5.3	2.7				Current		
1.4	1.9	1.3						
.8	.9	1.1						
3.0	2.2	1.8				Quick		
1.2	1.3	.8						
.7	.7	.5						
27 13.6	19 18.8	28 13.0				Sales/Receivables		
33 11.0	33 11.1	40 9.0						
62 5.9	48 7.5	57 6.4						
						Cost of Sales/Inventory		
						Cost of Sales/Payables		
5.4	4.3	5.1				Sales/Working Capital		
37.2	9.2	8.4						
-28.1	-111.8	62.2						
138.5	15.8	8.3				EBIT/Interest		
3.0	(16) 1.9	(15) 1.7						
-4.0	-1.8	1.0						
						Net Profit + Depr., Dep., Amort./Cur. Mat. L /T/D		
.0	.0	.1				Fixed/Worth		
.3	.5	.2						
-2.4	NM	1.6						
.7	.9	.5				Debt/Worth		
4.4	1.7	2.6						
-5.9	NM	4.3						
	48.2	46.1				% Profit Before Taxes/Tangible Net Worth		
	(14) 15.6	(17) 20.1						
	2.4	3.1						
55.5	19.1	20.4				% Profit Before Taxes/Total Assets		
2.0	4.3	8.3						
-4.3	-4.5	.2						
523.2	266.2	76.8				Sales/Net Fixed Assets		
137.6	31.4	41.9						
20.1	8.4	26.9						
7.6	4.7	3.6				Sales/Total Assets		
5.0	3.4	2.7						
2.8	1.9	1.8						
	.5	.4				% Depr., Dep., Amort./Sales		
	(14) 1.3	(18) .5						
	2.9	1.2						
	1.9					% Officers', Directors', Owners' Comp/Sales		
	(12) 4.7							
	7.6							
14833M	82462M	239883M	68731M	53409M	159312M	Net Sales ($)		
3432M	21401M	88614M	21199M	60799M	112862M	Total Assets ($)		

© RMA 2003

M = $ thousand   MM = $ million
See Pages 11 through 18 for Explanation of Ratios and Data

Comparative Historical Data | **Current Data Sorted By Sales**

Type of Statement

	4/1/02-3/31/03 ALL		0-1MM	1-3MM	3-5MM	5-10MM	10-25MM	25MM & OVER
Unqualified	6				1	1	2	3
Reviewed	9					4	2	2
Compiled	16		4	6	1	3	2	
Tax Returns	8		1	5	1	1	2	
Other	14			5	3	2	4	

Statement date ranges for current data: **10 (4/1-9/30/02)** covers 0-1MM and 1-3MM groups; **43 (10/1/02-3/31/03)** covers 5-10MM, 10-25MM, 25MM & OVER groups.

Historical columns 4/1/00-3/31/01 ALL and 4/1/01-3/31/02 ALL: DATA NOT AVAILABLE.

		4/1/02-3/31/03 ALL		0-1MM	1-3MM	3-5MM	5-10MM	10-25MM	25MM & OVER
		53	**NUMBER OF STATEMENTS**	5	16	6	11	10	5
		%	**ASSETS**	%	%	%	%	%	%
		15.3	Cash & Equivalents		20.8		13.1	10.9	
		35.6	Trade Receivables (net)		34.4		40.2	34.4	
		23.0	Inventory		12.8		22.9	31.2	
		1.9	All Other Current		.8		2.0	5.2	
		75.8	Total Current		68.8		78.2	81.6	
		15.5	Fixed Assets (net)		26.0		16.6	7.6	
		1.1	Intangibles (net)		2.0		.5	1.0	
		7.6	All Other Non-Current		3.1		4.7	9.8	
		100.0	Total		100.0		100.0	100.0	
			LIABILITIES						
		15.5	Notes Payable-Short Term		8.9		15.5	8.6	
		3.5	Cur. Mat.-L/T/D		5.9		5.7	1.7	
		19.1	Trade Payables		20.8		20.3	15.8	
		.6	Income Taxes Payable		.0		.0	2.7	
		10.4	All Other Current		9.2		9.7	12.3	
		49.1	Total Current		44.8		51.2	41.1	
		10.0	Long Term Debt		18.7		8.1	4.6	
		.1	Deferred Taxes		.0		.0	.0	
		9.4	All Other Non-Current		1.2		17.2	5.3	
		31.5	Net Worth		35.3		23.5	49.0	
		100.0	Total Liabilities & Net Worth		100.0		100.0	100.0	
			INCOME DATA						
		100.0	Net Sales		100.0		100.0	100.0	
			Gross Profit						
		94.3	Operating Expenses		94.9		95.8	90.9	
		5.7	Operating Profit		5.1		4.2	9.1	
		1.1	All Other Expenses (net)		.4		1.7	2.6	
		4.6	Profit Before Taxes		4.7		2.5	6.5	
			RATIOS						
		3.7 / 1.8 / 1.1	Current		3.9 / 1.9 / .9		6.8 / 1.3 / .9	4.4 / 2.3 / 1.1	
		2.0 / 1.2 / .6	Quick		3.3 / 1.3 / .7		3.8 / 1.0 / .6	1.9 / 1.6 / .6	
	28 / 34 / 53	13.3 / 10.6 / 6.9	Sales/Receivables		8 / 33 / 48 — 43.6 / 11.2 / 7.6		28 / 37 / 81 — 13.2 / 9.9 / 4.5	18 / 50 / 53 — 20.0 / 7.4 / 6.9	
			Cost of Sales/Inventory						
			Cost of Sales/Payables						
		4.5 / 8.7 / 92.7	Sales/Working Capital		4.5 / 19.9 / −55.2		4.3 / 8.7 / −79.0	5.1 / 9.1 / 58.5	
		(46) 15.2 / 2.5 / −.3	EBIT/Interest		31.1 / 5.3 / .5				
			Net Profit + Depr., Dep., Amort./Cur. Mat. L/T/D						
		.1 / .2 / 2.0	Fixed/Worth		.1 / .5 / 2.0		.1 / .2 / 3.9	.1 / .1 / .4	
		.5 / 2.1 / 11.8	Debt/Worth		.4 / 2.0 / NM		.9 / 4.0 / 7.4	.5 / 1.0 / 2.6	
		(42) 48.9 / 19.4 / 2.5	% Profit Before Taxes/Tangible Net Worth		(12) 69.5 / 9.2 / 3.3			87.8 / 39.7 / 11.0	
		20.2 / 6.3 / −.9	% Profit Before Taxes/Total Assets		18.1 / 3.1 / −2.0		19.2 / 1.7 / −4.1	37.1 / 10.0 / 6.6	
		177.7 / 44.9 / 14.3	Sales/Net Fixed Assets		161.0 / 33.4 / 7.2		136.9 / 48.1 / 17.7	161.3 / 58.3 / 37.2	
		4.3 / 3.1 / 1.9	Sales/Total Assets		5.1 / 3.2 / 2.0		4.5 / 3.1 / 1.5	4.0 / 3.2 / 2.6	
		(42) .4 / .9 / 2.6	% Depr., Dep., Amort./Sales		(11) .9 / 2.8 / 4.6				
		(27) 1.7 / 4.4 / 7.4	% Officers', Directors', Owners' Comp/Sales		(10) 3.6 / 4.7 / 10.9				
		618630M	Net Sales ($)	2707M	30269M	24487M	82972M	165766M	312429M
		308307M	Total Assets ($)	1603M	10836M	9683M	35035M	52162M	198988M

M = $ thousand   MM = $ million
See Pages 11 through 18 for Explanation of Ratios and Data

Current Data Sorted By Assets   **Comparative Historical Data**

Type of Statement	0-500M	500M-2MM	2-10MM	10-50MM	50-100MM	100-250MM		4/1/98-3/31/99 ALL	4/1/99-3/31/00 ALL
Unqualified		1	6	11	1	3		37	28
Reviewed	2	5	4					15	23
Compiled	1	3	4					21	23
Tax Returns	2	2						7	7
Other	6	6	8	6	2	1		24	27
		18 (4/1-9/30/02)		56 (10/1/02-3/31/03)					
NUMBER OF STATEMENTS	11	17	22	17	3	4		104	108
ASSETS	%	%	%	%	%	%		%	%
Cash & Equivalents	17.7	18.5	20.6	13.3				15.3	13.1
Trade Receivables (net)	27.7	47.8	40.7	45.6				39.3	42.3
Inventory	.2	.6	4.2	1.4				1.8	1.7
All Other Current	1.1	3.7	2.8	5.5				4.6	5.9
Total Current	46.6	70.5	68.3	65.7				61.0	63.0
Fixed Assets (net)	35.6	18.0	19.0	19.9				24.9	21.2
Intangibles (net)	11.1	7.0	2.4	7.0				6.6	5.6
All Other Non-Current	6.4	4.4	10.3	7.3				7.5	10.1
Total	100.0	100.0	100.0	100.0				100.0	100.0
LIABILITIES									
Notes Payable-Short Term	21.9	15.4	5.5	4.7				9.8	11.2
Cur. Mat.-L/T/D	6.6	1.7	3.0	3.0				2.6	2.5
Trade Payables	14.3	14.0	10.3	14.9				12.6	13.1
Income Taxes Payable	.1	1.2	.7	.9				.5	.8
All Other Current	19.2	12.2	25.9	24.4				17.0	16.4
Total Current	62.0	44.4	45.5	47.9				42.4	44.0
Long Term Debt	11.7	16.5	5.7	11.2				14.8	13.8
Deferred Taxes	.5	1.4	.0	.1				.9	.9
All Other Non-Current	1.0	8.8	8.8	10.0				6.2	5.4
Net Worth	24.6	28.9	40.0	30.9				35.7	35.9
Total Liabilities & Net Worth	100.0	100.0	100.0	100.0				100.0	100.0
INCOME DATA									
Net Sales	100.0	100.0	100.0	100.0				100.0	100.0
Gross Profit									
Operating Expenses	94.4	94.5	96.5	98.6				96.5	94.9
Operating Profit	5.6	5.5	3.5	1.4				3.5	5.1
All Other Expenses (net)	.8	.1	1.0	1.2				.5	.4
Profit Before Taxes	4.8	5.5	2.5	.2				3.0	4.6
RATIOS									
Current	1.5	4.6	1.8	1.7				2.5	2.2
	.8	1.7	1.5	1.2				1.5	1.4
	.3	1.2	1.2	1.1				1.0	1.1
Quick	1.5	4.6	1.7	1.5				2.1	2.0
	.8	1.5	1.5	1.1				1.3	1.3
	.3	1.0	1.0	1.0				.9	.9
Sales/Receivables	0 UND	39 9.3	42 8.6	60 6.1				40 9.2	41 9.0
	34 10.7	50 7.3	56 6.5	87 4.2				63 5.8	57 6.4
	59 6.2	74 4.9	100 3.6	99 3.7				83 4.4	80 4.6
Cost of Sales/Inventory									
Cost of Sales/Payables									
Sales/Working Capital	15.4	6.5	6.0	8.5				5.9	5.9
	-30.5	14.7	9.5	17.5				18.5	15.9
	-9.8	19.6	35.3	35.7				797.8	83.2
EBIT/Interest		16.7	29.1	23.7				19.4	15.3
		(14) 4.2	(21) 9.9	(14) 5.3				(88) 4.2	(84) 2.7
		1.8	1.1	1.7				1.7	1.1
Net Profit + Depr., Dep., Amort./Cur. Mat. L/T/D								9.7	5.2
								(24) 3.1	(32) 2.5
								1.8	.9
Fixed/Worth	.4	.3	.2	.2				.2	.2
	1.6	.6	.4	.7				.8	.6
	-1.8	4.8	.5	122.1				3.5	2.4
Debt/Worth	1.6	.5	1.0	1.0				.7	.8
	2.8	2.0	1.6	1.7				1.6	1.6
	-3.8	27.9	2.8	259.6				14.7	5.7
% Profit Before Taxes/Tangible Net Worth		83.2	49.7	35.0				61.0	47.0
		(14) 27.8	(21) 6.5	(14) 16.9				(87) 24.9	(86) 18.7
		6.7	-4.2	10.4				8.8	5.1
% Profit Before Taxes/Total Assets	31.1	29.2	13.1	11.6				17.9	16.0
	2.0	11.3	4.3	6.6				9.0	5.8
	-4.6	2.4	-.1	3.0				1.5	.1
Sales/Net Fixed Assets	38.4	66.1	44.4	49.5				26.0	30.0
	10.8	21.4	24.1	17.3				15.1	18.1
	6.6	11.4	8.5	6.3				7.1	10.1
Sales/Total Assets	8.3	4.1	3.1	2.9				3.8	3.9
	3.7	3.3	2.5	2.1				2.5	2.9
	2.3	2.3	1.6	1.5				1.6	1.8
% Depr., Dep., Amort./Sales		1.0	.8	.8				1.5	1.1
		(13) 1.5	(20) 1.5	(14) 1.8				(93) 2.5	(89) 2.1
		1.8	4.2	2.7				3.8	3.3
% Officers', Directors', Owners' Comp/Sales								4.1	3.8
								(27) 9.5	(25) 6.5
								17.2	17.8
Net Sales ($)	20883M	79105M	368451M	898971M	461648M	996174M		2169969M	2148586M
Total Assets ($)	3209M	19206M	113142M	418405M	194760M	574622M		1393156M	1481789M

Comparative Historical Data / Current Data Sorted By Sales

4/1/00-3/31/01 ALL	4/1/01-3/31/02 ALL	4/1/02-3/31/03 ALL		0-1MM	1-3MM	3-5MM	5-10MM	10-25MM	25MM & OVER
			Type of Statement		18 (4/1-9/30/02)			56 (10/1/02-3/31/03)	
24	20	22	Unqualified		1		2	4	15
17	10	11	Reviewed	1	2	3	3	2	
22	20	8	Compiled		1	1	3	2	1
7	9	4	Tax Returns	1	1	1	1		
33	37	29	Other	2	7	2	6	4	8
103	96	74	**NUMBER OF STATEMENTS**	4	12	7	15	12	24
%	%	%	**ASSETS**	%	%	%	%	%	%
14.7	11.5	17.1	Cash & Equivalents		10.8		19.9	22.1	13.6
40.1	44.2	41.2	Trade Receivables (net)		47.6		41.2	38.6	42.2
1.2	.8	2.2	Inventory		.0		3.7	3.1	2.4
6.3	6.4	3.6	All Other Current		.8		2.8	4.2	5.5
62.4	63.0	64.1	Total Current		59.2		67.6	67.9	63.8
19.9	18.8	21.5	Fixed Assets (net)		24.6		23.1	18.1	19.1
5.2	7.4	7.0	Intangibles (net)		10.2		4.5	2.4	10.1
12.5	10.8	7.3	All Other Non-Current		6.1		4.8	11.5	7.1
100.0	100.0	100.0	Total		100.0		100.0	100.0	100.0
			LIABILITIES						
9.9	12.4	9.7	Notes Payable-Short Term		18.5		11.1	6.5	3.5
2.7	3.5	3.5	Cur. Mat.-L/T/D		5.6		3.2	4.1	3.4
14.5	14.9	13.2	Trade Payables		13.9		10.3	16.5	14.6
1.1	.3	1.0	Income Taxes Payable		.0		1.4	.0	1.5
16.9	21.5	21.2	All Other Current		8.2		27.2	22.1	25.9
45.1	52.5	48.7	Total Current		46.2		53.2	49.3	48.9
11.4	13.1	12.1	Long Term Debt		14.9		12.8	11.1	13.5
1.0	.7	.4	Deferred Taxes		.7		.0	.1	.1
4.6	4.4	8.1	All Other Non-Current		3.1		7.3	17.0	9.9
38.0	29.2	30.7	Net Worth		35.0		26.6	22.6	27.6
100.0	100.0	100.0	Total Liabilities & Net Worth		100.0		100.0	100.0	100.0
			INCOME DATA						
100.0	100.0	100.0	Net Sales		100.0		100.0	100.0	100.0
			Gross Profit						
91.1	94.8	95.6	Operating Expenses		92.7		96.1	96.2	96.6
8.9	5.2	4.4	Operating Profit		7.3		3.9	3.8	3.4
.8	1.7	.8	All Other Expenses (net)		.6		.8	1.2	1.1
8.1	3.5	3.5	Profit Before Taxes		6.7		3.1	2.7	2.3
			RATIOS						
2.0	1.7	2.0			4.8		2.1	1.7	1.8
1.4	1.3	1.4	Current		1.7		1.5	1.3	1.3
1.1	1.0	1.1			.6		1.0	1.1	1.1
1.9	1.5	1.8			4.8		1.9	1.6	1.5
1.3	1.1	1.1	Quick		1.7		1.4	1.1	1.0
.9	.8	.9			.6		.9	.9	.9
37 9.8	37 9.9	38 9.5			36 10.2		39 9.4	36 10.1	39 9.4
63 5.8	64 5.7	58 6.3	Sales/Receivables		58 6.3		52 7.1	49 7.4	71 5.1
86 4.3	79 4.6	91 4.0			84 4.3		74 4.9	96 3.8	98 3.7
			Cost of Sales/Inventory						
			Cost of Sales/Payables						
6.7	7.3	7.0			5.2		4.8	8.3	6.1
13.0	23.1	16.1	Sales/Working Capital		12.8		10.2	16.1	17.8
45.4	-293.0	60.4			-25.2		-200.3	38.9	46.7
(72) 22.7	(79) 17.3	(64) 22.3			22.8		20.4	21.8	28.0
7.0	4.1	5.3	EBIT/Interest	(10) 6.5		(13) 4.8	(11) 9.9	(21) 9.1	
2.3	1.0	1.4			2.1		1.1	.3	1.6
(20) 7.7	(14) 4.2	(14) 11.2	Net Profit + Depr., Dep.,						
4.0	2.4	3.1	Amort./Cur. Mat. L/T/D						
1.0	.6	.9							
.2	.2	.3			.2		.3	.2	.3
.5	.6	.6	Fixed/Worth		.6		.4	.4	.8
1.5	3.0	2.4			-1.6		8.4	1.8	182.9
.8	.9	1.0			.6		1.0	1.3	1.0
1.6	2.6	1.9	Debt/Worth		1.7		3.9	1.7	2.6
6.7	8.2	7.2			-5.7		20.8	2.4	387.1
(88) 73.4	(78) 51.4	(61) 51.9					68.8	41.0	51.9
29.2	22.4	18.6	% Profit Before Taxes/Tangible Net Worth			(13) 12.6	(10) 18.0	(19) 18.6	
9.6	3.4	2.7					1.4	-8.6	9.4
19.1	16.3	16.9			28.2		12.8	20.1	15.7
9.7	6.9	7.3	% Profit Before Taxes/Total Assets		13.3		2.6	11.0	8.7
2.9	.3	.7			.1		.3	-1.3	2.7
35.1	39.1	42.0			33.6		48.8	57.6	39.7
20.4	20.3	18.6	Sales/Net Fixed Assets		13.0		26.6	24.1	17.7
10.0	9.3	8.1			8.6		6.1	9.2	10.1
3.5	3.7	3.3			3.7		3.6	3.5	2.9
2.4	2.6	2.5	Sales/Total Assets		3.1		2.5	2.6	2.2
1.5	1.7	1.8			2.0		1.7	1.5	1.6
(81) .8	(75) .9	(62) 1.0					1.0	.9	.9
1.6	1.7	1.7	% Depr., Dep., Amort./Sales			(14)	1.6	(11) 1.4	(20) 1.7
2.8	3.3	3.0					4.2	3.7	2.6
(24) 4.2	(29) 4.2	(21) 3.5	% Officers', Directors',						
8.8	8.5	5.8	Owners' Comp/Sales						
20.9	13.6	19.7							
2971590M	2821343M	2825232M	Net Sales ($)	1622M	21794M	27382M	110155M	188458M	2475821M
1990773M	1983942M	1323344M	Total Assets ($)	661M	7524M	9381M	49387M	85984M	1170407M

Current Data Sorted By Assets   **Comparative Historical Data**

			2			Type of Statement		4	4
1	2	4				Unqualified			
8	2	2			1	Reviewed		9	8
15	1	1				Compiled		25	18
7	2	2	1		1	Tax Returns		12	6
						Other		8	14
	11 (4/1-9/30/02)			41 (10/1/02-3/31/03)				4/1/98-3/31/99	4/1/99-3/31/00
0-500M	500M-2MM	2-10MM	10-50MM	50-100MM	100-250MM			ALL	ALL
31	7	9	3		2	**NUMBER OF STATEMENTS**		58	50
%	%	%	%	%	%	**ASSETS**		%	%
20.1				D		Cash & Equivalents		10.2	16.6
4.9				A		Trade Receivables (net)		11.2	8.7
6.3				T		Inventory		7.8	7.7
2.9				A		All Other Current		3.1	2.1
34.2						Total Current		32.3	35.1
53.6				N		Fixed Assets (net)		52.1	40.5
7.8				O		Intangibles (net)		6.2	12.5
4.4				T		All Other Non-Current		9.3	11.9
100.0						Total		100.0	100.0
				A		**LIABILITIES**			
11.4				V		Notes Payable-Short Term		12.8	11.8
4.9				A		Cur. Mat.-L/T/D		5.8	8.9
8.5				I		Trade Payables		11.0	14.4
.0				L		Income Taxes Payable		.6	.4
13.7				A		All Other Current		16.8	14.9
38.5				B		Total Current		47.1	50.4
51.4				L		Long Term Debt		31.6	25.2
.0				E		Deferred Taxes		.3	.2
13.6						All Other Non-Current		7.1	9.3
-3.5						Net Worth		13.9	14.9
100.0						Total Liabilities & Net Worth		100.0	100.0
						INCOME DATA			
100.0						Net Sales		100.0	100.0
						Gross Profit			
95.0						Operating Expenses		94.9	94.8
5.0						Operating Profit		5.1	5.2
1.8						All Other Expenses (net)		1.8	1.7
3.2						Profit Before Taxes		3.3	3.5
						RATIOS			
1.9								2.0	1.4
.9						Current		.8	.7
.5								.3	.4
1.4								1.6	1.1
.6						Quick	(55)	.4	.4
.3								.1	.1
0 UND							0 UND	0 UND	
0 UND						Sales/Receivables	3 144.1	2 148.5	
6 62.8							18 19.9	12 31.6	
						Cost of Sales/Inventory			
						Cost of Sales/Payables			
28.3								24.1	21.0
-227.5						Sales/Working Capital		-37.7	-30.1
-25.7								-8.4	-11.0
7.1								5.9	6.4
(25) 1.2						EBIT/Interest	(52)	2.0	(46) 3.0
-.1								.5	.8
						Net Profit + Depr., Dep., Amort./Cur. Mat. L /T/D			
1.2								.9	1.0
5.7						Fixed/Worth		2.4	2.6
-3.7								-4.7	-1.3
1.1								1.0	1.2
6.4						Debt/Worth		2.8	4.8
-5.1								-7.6	-3.2
85.5						% Profit Before Taxes/Tangible		64.2	71.4
(20) 52.9						Net Worth	(40)	25.8	(32) 41.5
-1.3								.7	4.2
25.4						% Profit Before Taxes/Total		19.0	22.0
1.6						Assets		6.3	10.5
-8.2								-1.8	-.1
17.9								11.8	26.9
7.3						Sales/Net Fixed Assets		7.7	10.4
4.2								3.5	5.8
5.6								5.3	5.8
3.4						Sales/Total Assets		3.3	3.4
2.6								2.3	2.5
1.8								2.0	1.7
(27) 4.1						% Depr., Dep., Amort./Sales	(46)	3.6	(41) 2.9
5.8								5.4	4.4
3.6						% Officers', Directors',		5.9	8.2
(23) 11.1						Owners' Comp/Sales	(26)	9.1	(25) 10.9
20.4								13.1	15.3
27760M	35548M	101834M	117542M		1268230M	Net Sales ($)		883016M	766031M
7320M	9384M	33388M	71793M		279367M	Total Assets ($)		413357M	403612M

© RMA 2003

M = $ thousand   MM = $ million
See Pages 11 through 18 for Explanation of Ratios and Data

Comparative Historical Data | Current Data Sorted By Sales

			Type of Statement	0-1MM	1-3MM	3-5MM	5-10MM	10-25MM	25MM & OVER
2	1	2	Unqualified					1	1
8	6	7	Reviewed		3	1		3	
17	16	13	Compiled	6	3	1	1	1	1
11	11	17	Tax Returns	12	2	1	2		
13	11	13	Other	4	4	1	1	1	2
4/1/00-3/31/01	4/1/01-3/31/02	4/1/02-3/31/03		11 (4/1-9/30/02)		41 (10/1/02-3/31/03)			
ALL	ALL	ALL							
51	45	52	NUMBER OF STATEMENTS	22	12	4	4	6	4
%	%	%	ASSETS	%	%	%	%	%	%
13.9	11.7	18.8	Cash & Equivalents	18.0	20.4				
11.2	9.7	6.6	Trade Receivables (net)	6.4	4.7				
8.5	7.9	6.4	Inventory	5.9	6.8				
7.1	.9	2.8	All Other Current	2.4	3.0				
40.7	30.2	34.6	Total Current	32.8	34.8				
42.0	47.0	49.8	Fixed Assets (net)	53.5	54.4				
8.1	13.8	8.6	Intangibles (net)	8.3	5.9				
9.1	9.0	6.9	All Other Non-Current	5.3	4.9				
100.0	100.0	100.0	Total	100.0	100.0				
			LIABILITIES						
7.9	7.8	11.3	Notes Payable-Short Term	15.9	2.9				
7.7	3.9	4.6	Cur. Mat.-L/T/D	5.4	3.3				
13.6	11.5	9.0	Trade Payables	9.9	5.1				
.5	.3	.1	Income Taxes Payable	.0	.0				
14.2	21.1	12.0	All Other Current	13.8	9.7				
43.8	44.5	37.0	Total Current	45.1	21.1				
30.5	31.2	44.0	Long Term Debt	56.5	35.1				
.4	.5	.2	Deferred Taxes	.0	.0				
15.4	6.5	11.5	All Other Non-Current	19.2	3.1				
9.9	17.4	7.3	Net Worth	-20.8	40.8				
100.0	100.0	100.0	Total Liabilities & Net Worth	100.0	100.0				
			INCOME DATA						
100.0	100.0	100.0	Net Sales	100.0	100.0				
			Gross Profit						
94.9	92.7	95.3	Operating Expenses	94.1	97.5				
5.1	7.3	4.7	Operating Profit	5.9	2.5				
.8	2.8	1.7	All Other Expenses (net)	2.3	1.1				
4.2	4.5	3.0	Profit Before Taxes	3.6	1.4				
			RATIOS						
2.0 / 1.0 / .6	1.3 / .6 / .3	1.8 / .9 / .6	Current	1.3 / .7 / .5	2.6 / 1.8 / 1.0				
(50) 1.4 / .6 / .2	(44) 1.1 / .4 / .2	1.5 / .7 / .3	Quick	1.2 / .5 / .2	2.1 / 1.0 / .5				
0 UND / 4 94.8 / 17 21.5	0 UND / 3 124.0 / 14 26.1	0 UND / 1 708.9 / 7 53.0	Sales/Receivables	0 UND / 0 UND / 10 35.5	0 UND / 1 511.3 / 5 74.3				
			Cost of Sales/Inventory						
			Cost of Sales/Payables						
18.5 / -87.4 / -24.8	42.1 / -28.7 / -11.6	25.8 / -428.7 / -27.6	Sales/Working Capital	87.0 / -56.8 / -15.4	7.0 / 28.0 / NM				
(43) 10.5 / 3.5 / 1.0	(37) 6.0 / 2.7 / .8	(44) 7.5 / 1.8 / .5	EBIT/Interest	(18) 7.3 / 1.6 / -.7	(11) 7.8 / 1.2 / .6				
(10) 14.7 / 2.1 / .8			Net Profit + Depr., Dep., Amort./Cur. Mat. L/T/D						
.8 / 1.9 / -1.2	1.2 / 3.7 / -1.3	1.2 / 2.1 / -3.8	Fixed/Worth	1.3 / 6.9 / -.6	.8 / 1.2 / 78.8				
.8 / 2.9 / -2.9	1.0 / 4.2 / -3.4	.9 / 5.0 / -6.5	Debt/Worth	2.6 / 18.5 / -1.8	.7 / 1.2 / 84.9				
(35) 96.6 / 35.2 / 5.1	(28) 69.8 / 34.3 / 6.8	(36) 72.0 / 32.2 / .4	% Profit Before Taxes/Tangible Net Worth	(13) 81.1 / 50.0 / -45.0	(10) 97.4 / 13.1 / -4.1				
19.7 / 10.0 / .0	25.3 / 5.9 / -1.4	16.4 / 3.1 / -2.9	% Profit Before Taxes/Total Assets	25.8 / 1.3 / -13.5	14.3 / 1.4 / -2.9				
16.8 / 10.5 / 6.3	23.4 / 10.3 / 2.5	17.5 / 6.7 / 4.0	Sales/Net Fixed Assets	30.6 / 6.9 / 3.9	10.9 / 5.0 / 3.7				
5.7 / 3.3 / 2.2	5.1 / 2.7 / 1.3	4.3 / 3.2 / 2.3	Sales/Total Assets	6.9 / 3.3 / 2.5	3.9 / 3.3 / 2.0				
(45) 1.6 / 2.9 / 4.8	(35) 1.7 / 4.4 / 7.6	(44) 1.6 / 3.7 / 5.6	% Depr., Dep., Amort./Sales	(18) 3.0 / 4.7 / 7.1	1.1 / 3.7 / 4.9				
(28) 4.5 / 9.2 / 12.4	(24) 4.2 / 8.4 / 13.4	(36) 2.1 / 6.4 / 17.1	% Officers', Directors', Owners' Comp/Sales	(16) 3.3 / 15.3 / 20.6					
779088M	515930M	1550914M	Net Sales ($)	10239M	22714M	16798M	28270M	98694M	1374199M
417760M	219001M	401252M	Total Assets ($)	3280M	9976M	4565M	11176M	32315M	339940M

M = $ thousand   MM = $ million
See Pages 11 through 18 for Explanation of Ratios and Data

PROFESSIONAL SERVICES—Commercial Photography   NAICS 541922   (SIC 7335)

Current Data Sorted By Assets   **Comparative Historical Data**

	0-500M	500M-2MM	2-10MM	10-50MM	50-100MM	100-250MM		4/1/98-3/31/99 ALL	4/1/99-3/31/00 ALL
Type of Statement									
Unqualified								1	1
Reviewed		1	3					12	7
Compiled	3	4						11	12
Tax Returns	3							5	7
Other	4	7	1	1				10	15
		12 (4/1-9/30/02)		15 (10/1/02-3/31/03)					
NUMBER OF STATEMENTS	10	12	4	1				39	42
ASSETS	%	%	%	%	%	%		%	%
Cash & Equivalents	20.7	10.8						11.5	11.0
Trade Receivables (net)	18.7	17.0						26.6	29.9
Inventory	2.1	3.2			D	D		5.0	7.0
All Other Current	2.3	5.5			A	A		1.2	2.6
Total Current	43.7	36.5			T	T		44.3	50.6
Fixed Assets (net)	40.9	46.9			A	A		43.9	39.1
Intangibles (net)	10.4	5.8						6.3	3.0
All Other Non-Current	5.0	10.8			N	N		5.5	7.3
Total	100.0	100.0			O	O		100.0	100.0
LIABILITIES					T	T			
Notes Payable-Short Term	11.1	10.8						9.0	12.4
Cur. Mat.-L/T/D	4.8	5.7			A	A		5.9	4.4
Trade Payables	15.1	8.2			V	V		8.6	11.3
Income Taxes Payable	.1	1.5			A	A		1.1	.4
All Other Current	15.5	15.8			I	I		34.7	12.6
Total Current	46.6	42.0			L	L		59.2	41.2
Long Term Debt	21.3	20.3			A	A		33.3	28.6
Deferred Taxes	1.5	.2			B	B		1.2	1.0
All Other Non-Current	15.7	8.4			L	L		7.7	9.1
Net Worth	14.8	29.1			E	E		-1.5	20.1
Total Liabilities & Net Worth	100.0	100.0						100.0	100.0
INCOME DATA									
Net Sales	100.0	100.0						100.0	100.0
Gross Profit									
Operating Expenses	93.0	97.7						92.1	96.1
Operating Profit	7.0	2.3						7.9	3.9
All Other Expenses (net)	.8	.4						1.5	2.0
Profit Before Taxes	6.2	1.9						6.4	1.9
RATIOS									
Current	5.1	2.1						5.1	1.9
	1.5	.8						1.3	1.3
	.4	.4						.8	.9
Quick	5.1	2.0						2.9	1.6
	.7	.7					(37)	1.2	1.0
	.3	.3						.7	.6
Sales/Receivables	0 UND	0 756.5					17	21.3	25 14.4
	0 UND	29 12.4					48	7.7	45 8.1
	85 4.3	47 7.8					72	5.1	66 5.5
Cost of Sales/Inventory									
Cost of Sales/Payables									
Sales/Working Capital	3.0	8.7						6.8	10.9
	NM	NM						26.1	29.9
	-17.3	-5.8						-36.5	-142.1
EBIT/Interest		11.5					(35)	13.5	(40) 8.5
	(10)	2.3						3.0	3.0
		.3						.1	1.2
Net Profit + Depr., Dep., Amort./Cur. Mat. L /T/D							(13)	12.7	
								1.8	
								.8	
Fixed/Worth	.6	.7						.6	.5
	1.6	1.9						1.1	.9
	-2.7	NM						3.3	4.9
Debt/Worth	.3	.8						.6	1.0
	1.4	2.2						1.5	1.9
	-6.2	NM						3.2	11.5
% Profit Before Taxes/Tangible Net Worth							(33)	59.0	(34) 39.8
								27.0	17.8
								.1	2.9
% Profit Before Taxes/Total Assets	35.0	10.6						37.9	12.9
	16.9	6.2						8.8	7.4
	-9.5	-1.8						-2.6	.6
Sales/Net Fixed Assets	50.2	7.5						14.6	19.5
	6.1	4.9						8.6	9.6
	3.5	2.9						3.2	2.5
Sales/Total Assets	4.3	2.9						4.3	5.1
	2.8	2.1						2.5	2.6
	1.3	1.3						1.7	1.4
% Depr., Dep., Amort./Sales		2.3					(36)	1.9	(31) 2.3
	(10)	5.5						3.6	3.9
		8.8						6.3	7.7
% Officers', Directors', Owners' Comp/Sales							(22)	6.8	(25) 2.7
								7.8	7.8
								15.2	19.8
Net Sales ($)	5095M	30737M	66093M	11641M				117597M	377970M
Total Assets ($)	1945M	14122M	16637M	12955M				58906M	229813M

M = $ thousand   MM = $ million
See Pages 11 through 18 for Explanation of Ratios and Data

Comparative Historical Data / Current Data Sorted By Sales

					Type of Statement						
	2		1		Unqualified						
	4		5	4	Reviewed			1	1	1	1
	16		12	7	Compiled	4	2	1			
	8		5	3	Tax Returns	2	1				
	6		12	13	Other	5	5	2		1	
	4/1/00-3/31/01 ALL		4/1/01-3/31/02 ALL	4/1/02-3/31/03 ALL		0-1MM	12 (4/1-9/30/02) 1-3MM	3-5MM	15 (10/1/02-3/31/03) 5-10MM	10-25MM	25MM & OVER
	36		35	27	NUMBER OF STATEMENTS	11	8	4	1	2	1
	%		%	%	ASSETS	%	%	%	%	%	%
	12.2		6.8	14.1	Cash & Equivalents	21.9					
	33.4		26.0	17.5	Trade Receivables (net)	20.3					
	4.1		2.0	3.8	Inventory	.1					
	1.4		4.3	3.6	All Other Current	2.1					
	51.1		39.0	38.9	Total Current	44.4					
	40.2		44.2	44.0	Fixed Assets (net)	45.3					
	2.0		6.5	8.2	Intangibles (net)	6.9					
	6.7		10.3	8.8	All Other Non-Current	3.4					
	100.0		100.0	100.0	Total	100.0					
					LIABILITIES						
	11.3		15.7	9.4	Notes Payable-Short Term	9.8					
	8.0		6.0	5.4	Cur. Mat.-L/T/D	5.2					
	10.0		11.4	11.8	Trade Payables	14.4					
	.6		.7	.8	Income Taxes Payable	.1					
	10.5		12.8	20.2	All Other Current	13.9					
	40.4		46.6	47.8	Total Current	43.4					
	43.9		29.2	19.8	Long Term Debt	26.6					
	.8		.8	1.3	Deferred Taxes	1.4					
	9.9		4.6	10.3	All Other Non-Current	14.3					
	5.0		18.9	20.8	Net Worth	14.3					
	100.0		100.0	100.0	Total Liabilities & Net Worth	100.0					
					INCOME DATA						
	100.0		100.0	100.0	Net Sales	100.0					
					Gross Profit						
	97.2		95.5	96.1	Operating Expenses	93.8					
	2.8		4.5	3.9	Operating Profit	6.2					
	.1		1.4	1.2	All Other Expenses (net)	.9					
	2.7		3.1	2.7	Profit Before Taxes	5.4					
					RATIOS						
	2.3		2.3	2.2		6.1					
	1.2		1.0	.8	Current	2.2					
	.8		.5	.4		.4					
	2.3		1.8	2.2		6.0					
	1.0		1.0	.6	Quick	2.2					
	.7		.4	.3		.4					
26	14.2	10	35.5	0 UND		0 UND					
51	7.2	43	8.4	29 12.7	Sales/Receivables	34 10.7					
73	5.0	66	5.5	53 6.8		97 3.7					
					Cost of Sales/Inventory						
					Cost of Sales/Payables						
	7.8		7.1	9.6		2.9					
	34.9		577.7	-19.8	Sales/Working Capital	12.8					
	-45.1		-12.2	-8.0		-18.7					
	8.3		4.9	5.6							
(29)	2.7	(29)	2.2	(21) 2.1	EBIT/Interest						
	.0		-.2	-.9							
					Net Profit + Depr., Dep., Amort./Cur. Mat. L/T/D						
	.4		.8	.7		.9					
	1.5		1.7	2.1	Fixed/Worth	2.1					
	NM		-2.5	-3.5		-3.5					
	1.2		.8	.8		.3					
	2.3		2.9	2.8	Debt/Worth	2.0					
	NM		-5.1	-7.8		-7.8					
	36.9		41.2	29.8		31.1					
(27)	13.4	(25)	9.5	(19) 11.6	% Profit Before Taxes/Tangible Net Worth	8.7					
	.0		-4.1	-7.6		-6.8					
	20.2		17.4	16.7		31.1					
	4.5		6.1	6.5	% Profit Before Taxes/Total Assets	8.7					
	-4.8		-1.9	-4.5		-6.8					
	18.8		12.4	10.8		37.7					
	7.9		6.4	4.9	Sales/Net Fixed Assets	4.2					
	3.4		3.1	2.8		1.6					
	3.8		3.7	3.2		2.9					
	2.8		2.6	2.2	Sales/Total Assets	2.2					
	1.8		1.5	1.3		1.0					
	1.5		1.6	2.0							
(31)	4.3	(27)	5.2	(20) 4.5	% Depr., Dep., Amort./Sales						
	6.3		9.1	9.6							
	5.7		5.6	4.4							
(27)	9.6	(20)	10.4	(13) 8.0	% Officers', Directors', Owners' Comp/Sales						
	16.0		15.8	16.3							
	130989M		104772M	113566M	Net Sales ($)	5639M	15786M	17702M	6047M	24732M	43660M
	55150M		52431M	45659M	Total Assets ($)	3153M	8508M	7850M	1727M	15776M	8645M

© RMA 2003

M = $ thousand   MM = $ million
See Pages 11 through 18 for Explanation of Ratios and Data

Current Data Sorted By Assets | Comparative Historical Data

0-500M	500M-2MM	2-10MM	10-50MM	50-100MM	100-250MM	Type of Statement	4/1/98-3/31/99 ALL	4/1/99-3/31/00 ALL
2	2	1	2	1		Unqualified	2	3
3	3	5	1			Reviewed	7	4
46	22	2				Compiled	56	44
75	15	2	1		4	Tax Returns	69	52
34	13	4	2	1		Other	29	42
	20 (4/1-9/30/02)		221 (10/1/02-3/31/03)					
160	55	14	6	2	4	NUMBER OF STATEMENTS	163	145
%	%	%	%	%	%	**ASSETS**	%	%
23.7	11.1	8.6				Cash & Equivalents	19.1	18.3
7.2	12.9	25.7				Trade Receivables (net)	6.2	7.9
13.6	6.1	8.6				Inventory	11.2	14.3
2.0	2.6	3.2				All Other Current	2.1	1.3
46.5	32.7	46.1				Total Current	38.6	41.9
36.6	51.0	44.4				Fixed Assets (net)	42.1	38.4
9.6	8.5	3.3				Intangibles (net)	9.8	9.7
7.4	7.8	6.2				All Other Non-Current	9.5	9.9
100.0	100.0	100.0				Total	100.0	100.0
						LIABILITIES		
8.9	7.4	15.2				Notes Payable-Short Term	8.3	10.4
5.4	5.7	2.6				Cur. Mat.-L/T/D	5.4	3.6
8.9	8.7	10.1				Trade Payables	8.0	9.0
.3	.0	1.3				Income Taxes Payable	.6	.1
18.1	8.1	8.6				All Other Current	18.8	10.1
41.6	29.9	37.9				Total Current	41.1	33.1
25.4	37.4	21.8				Long Term Debt	47.0	29.3
.1	.5	.5				Deferred Taxes	.1	.1
7.5	4.3	.5				All Other Non-Current	14.8	2.2
25.5	27.9	39.4				Net Worth	-2.9	35.3
100.0	100.0	100.0				Total Liabilities & Net Worth	100.0	100.0
						INCOME DATA		
100.0	100.0	100.0				Net Sales	100.0	100.0
						Gross Profit		
91.7	91.4	91.6				Operating Expenses	91.5	90.0
8.3	8.6	8.4				Operating Profit	8.5	10.0
1.4	3.5	5.5				All Other Expenses (net)	2.2	1.7
6.9	5.1	2.9				Profit Before Taxes	6.2	8.3
						RATIOS		
3.7	2.1	1.7					3.5	2.8
1.4	1.3	1.3				Current	1.3	1.4
.7	.5	.4					.5	.6
(159) 2.2	1.3	1.5					(161) 2.1	2.0
.9	.9	.8				Quick	.9	.8
.3	.3	.3					.3	.2
0 UND	0 UND	2 227.9					0 UND	0 UND
0 UND	4 82.9	45 8.2				Sales/Receivables	0 UND	2 189.0
6 57.8	20 18.4	74 5.0					7 51.6	9 42.4
						Cost of Sales/Inventory		
						Cost of Sales/Payables		
14.8	13.4	5.8					17.4	13.2
62.6	53.5	19.8				Sales/Working Capital	58.1	36.6
-42.5	-18.6	-11.4					-34.5	-42.4
(114) 14.5	(46) 6.8	(13) 27.1					(119) 13.6	(113) 13.8
5.6	2.6	2.8				EBIT/Interest	4.0	5.0
2.2	1.0	.5					1.3	1.3
						Net Profit + Depr., Dep., Amort./Cur. Mat. L /T/D	(10) 2.0
							1.4	
							.8	
.4	1.0	.6					.5	.4
1.4	3.7	1.1				Fixed/Worth	1.7	1.1
-5.2	-6.2	2.1					-13.8	30.8
.5	.8	1.0					.5	.6
2.3	4.7	1.7				Debt/Worth	2.6	1.9
-11.0	-13.4	3.8					-22.7	34.5
(112) 183.6	(38) 86.8	(13) 40.5				% Profit Before Taxes/Tangible Net Worth	(116) 168.0	(113) 127.7
80.2	23.2	9.4					55.4	51.9
24.1	9.3	-2.7					9.9	17.5
60.4	19.7	13.0				% Profit Before Taxes/Total Assets	54.9	41.4
25.1	7.1	1.9					17.1	14.9
5.4	.6	-.8					.5	2.4
45.8	14.4	27.1				Sales/Net Fixed Assets	39.2	35.9
19.8	7.2	6.2					19.0	16.5
10.1	1.9	1.4					5.7	5.6
9.5	4.2	3.3				Sales/Total Assets	7.8	6.6
5.8	2.2	1.7					5.1	4.3
3.4	1.5	.9					2.9	2.1
(119) 1.1	(49) 1.7	(11) 1.5				% Depr., Dep., Amort./Sales	(126) .9	(100) 1.3
2.1	2.8	4.3					1.9	2.2
3.2	5.3	10.0					3.2	4.1
(117) 8.8	(28) 3.8					% Officers', Directors', Owners' Comp/Sales	(107) 8.7	(91) 8.9
12.8	7.8						13.3	14.8
17.9	16.1						18.2	20.1
180550M	147843M	118199M	1629298M	904673M	4333259M	Net Sales ($)	3546071M	188687M
32335M	50354M	58951M	158047M	112406M	500356M	Total Assets ($)	522307M	102991M

M = $ thousand   MM = $ million
See Pages 11 through 18 for Explanation of Ratios and Data

Comparative Historical Data | Current Data Sorted By Sales

Type of Statement									
	2	4	8	Unqualified		4			1	3

Type of Statement	Hist 4/1/00-3/31/01 ALL	Hist 4/1/01-3/31/02 ALL	Hist 4/1/02-3/31/03 ALL	0-1MM	1-3MM	3-5MM	5-10MM	10-25MM	25MM & OVER
Unqualified	2	4	8		4			1	3
Reviewed	4	6	12		4	1	5	2	
Compiled	43	52	70	29	34	5		2	
Tax Returns	61	51	97	44	41	4	2	1	5
Other	30	53	54	19	23	5	3	1	3
				20 (4/1-9/30/02)		221 (10/1/02-3/31/03)			
NUMBER OF STATEMENTS	140	166	241	92	106	15	10	7	11
ASSETS	%	%	%	%	%	%	%	%	%
Cash & Equivalents	17.1	17.5	20.0	17.6	22.7	19.1	10.6		24.6
Trade Receivables (net)	5.8	9.8	9.8	5.1	11.0	14.1	26.5		9.4
Inventory	12.8	11.4	11.2	11.2	12.0	11.8	8.7		5.7
All Other Current	2.5	2.2	2.3	.9	2.9	5.0	4.3		4.1
Total Current	38.2	40.8	43.3	34.9	48.6	50.1	50.1		43.8
Fixed Assets (net)	40.7	41.3	40.8	45.8	36.5	36.7	46.4		49.6
Intangibles (net)	12.1	10.0	8.6	12.2	7.6	4.4	.1		2.6
All Other Non-Current	9.0	7.9	7.2	7.1	7.3	8.8	3.4		4.0
Total	100.0	100.0	100.0	100.0	100.0	100.0	100.0		100.0
LIABILITIES									
Notes Payable-Short Term	9.2	7.0	8.9	11.5	6.6	7.5	13.6		7.8
Cur. Mat.-L/T/D	6.6	5.7	5.1	4.3	6.3	3.4	5.5		2.4
Trade Payables	7.5	11.3	8.7	6.7	9.2	17.0	8.7		4.2
Income Taxes Payable	.2	.2	.3	.3	.2	1.3	.0		1.8
All Other Current	13.3	12.8	14.7	17.5	14.3	10.2	9.2		7.6
Total Current	36.7	37.1	37.7	40.2	36.6	39.4	37.1		23.8
Long Term Debt	26.5	38.4	27.7	33.2	25.7	18.7	30.2		22.7
Deferred Taxes	.2	.5	.2	.0	.4	.0	.6		.7
All Other Non-Current	5.8	4.7	6.7	11.6	2.3	3.8	6.7		16.9
Net Worth	30.8	19.3	27.6	15.0	35.1	38.1	25.5		36.0
Total Liabilities & Net Worth	100.0	100.0	100.0	100.0	100.0	100.0	100.0		100.0
INCOME DATA									
Net Sales	100.0	100.0	100.0	100.0	100.0	100.0	100.0		100.0
Gross Profit									
Operating Expenses	90.4	91.0	91.5	89.1	92.7	95.3	95.9		88.4
Operating Profit	9.6	9.0	8.5	10.9	7.3	4.7	4.1		11.6
All Other Expenses (net)	1.6	2.8	2.1	3.0	1.7	1.1	2.2		1.4
Profit Before Taxes	7.9	6.3	6.4	7.9	5.6	3.6	1.9		10.2
RATIOS									
Current	2.3	2.5	3.1	3.2	3.2	2.5	1.8		3.4
	1.3	1.4	1.4	1.4	1.4	1.4	1.3		2.4
	.5	.6	.7	.5	.6	.9	.9		1.5
Quick	1.5	1.9	2.1	2.1	1.7	1.5	1.3		2.8
	.7 (165)	.9 (240)	.9	.8 (91)	.9	.8	.9		1.5
	.2	.3	.4	.3	.3	.5	.7		1.2
Sales/Receivables	0 UND	0 UND	0 UND	0 UND	0 UND	0 UND	2 180.0		0 UND
	0 UND	2 231.2	1 246.9	0 UND	2 166.8	6 58.2	16 22.5		4 81.6
	6 60.4	10 37.9	11 32.2	6 57.1	11 34.4	17 21.0	74 5.0		61 6.0
Cost of Sales/Inventory									
Cost of Sales/Payables									
Sales/Working Capital	20.3	14.8	14.3	14.0	14.8	8.8	15.7		7.9
	83.9	54.8	53.5	82.3	55.0	53.5	43.3		30.2
	-28.8	-38.7	-35.2	-25.2	-35.5	-154.9	-105.8		227.2
EBIT/Interest	(110) 11.0	(133) 11.3	(182) 12.0	(65) 10.5	(79) 12.5	(13) 27.9	8.9		
	4.6	4.4	4.8	3.5	5.4	6.9	2.7		
	1.1	1.4	1.7	1.6	1.7	1.6	.8		
Net Profit + Depr., Dep., Amort./Cur. Mat. L/T/D	(11) 5.8	(14) 6.3	(16) 5.9						
	1.0	1.4	3.9						
	.4	-.5	1.9						
Fixed/Worth	.5	.6	.5	.8	.4	.2	1.1		.7
	2.1	2.0	1.5	5.5	1.1	1.0	1.6		1.1
	-7.9	-4.3	-12.5	-1.6	79.5	-9.4	-16.9		2.1
Debt/Worth	.6	.6	.5	.7	.5	.4	1.0		.3
	3.4	3.3	2.3	5.4	1.7	1.6	1.8		1.4
	-12.3	-8.6	-18.4	-3.9	265.0	-17.6	-113.9		3.4
% Profit Before Taxes/Tangible Net Worth	(96) 154.7	(113) 130.6	(174) 148.8	(59) 179.5	(81) 164.3	(11) 91.6			(10) 224.7
	70.9	52.9	55.0	78.8	54.1	45.5			65.8
	9.1	15.1	15.8	19.7	16.7	9.8			5.9
% Profit Before Taxes/Total Assets	60.7	43.9	44.1	51.8	50.0	39.2	16.7		58.4
	16.0	15.0	18.1	18.0	19.9	11.2	5.1		22.8
	.0	2.1	2.4	2.9	2.3	4.3	-.8		2.5
Sales/Net Fixed Assets	43.5	32.5	34.3	35.3	40.1	44.8	30.5		23.7
	17.4	15.9	15.8	10.6	19.6	13.3	9.0		17.2
	7.7	6.3	6.8	4.4	10.7	9.8	3.6		3.0
Sales/Total Assets	8.1	8.4	7.5	7.9	7.6	7.2	6.0		15.3
	5.0	4.6	4.6	3.6	5.3	5.0	4.0		4.3
	2.7	2.1	2.2	1.8	2.9	2.9	1.6		1.4
% Depr., Dep., Amort./Sales	(112) .9	(132) 1.0	(187) 1.2	(67) 1.4	(87) 1.1	(11) 1.5			
	1.8	1.8	2.3	2.7	2.1	2.3			
	3.0	3.3	4.2	5.9	3.4	3.1			
% Officers', Directors', Owners' Comp/Sales	(104) 7.0	(108) 8.1	(154) 7.4	(57) 8.7	(76) 6.8				
	13.3	13.9	12.3	12.3	11.7				
	20.6	20.8	17.4	17.1	19.3				
Net Sales ($)	205097M	1350608M	7313822M	55027M	177280M	52693M	73094M	112553M	6843175M
Total Assets ($)	61336M	633741M	912449M	22378M	49456M	13761M	28051M	38049M	760754M

M = $ thousand   MM = $ million
See Pages 11 through 18 for Explanation of Ratios and Data

Current Data Sorted By Assets   **Comparative Historical Data**

Type of Statement	0-500M	500M-2MM	2-10MM	10-50MM	50-100MM	100-250MM	4/1/98-3/31/99 ALL	4/1/99-3/31/00 ALL
Unqualified	6	7	28	22	4	4	88	90
Reviewed	4	11	25	5			37	44
Compiled	24	26	16	2		1	85	86
Tax Returns	45	20	7		1	2	53	60
Other	26	36	33	17	4	5	105	116
	78 (4/1-9/30/02)			303 (10/1/02-3/31/03)				
NUMBER OF STATEMENTS	105	100	109	46	9	12	368	396
ASSETS	%	%	%	%	%	%	%	%
Cash & Equivalents	20.2	15.6	11.5	13.6		16.1	12.1	16.0
Trade Receivables (net)	20.9	30.8	27.6	20.0		19.3	26.8	25.2
Inventory	6.4	7.3	5.9	7.6		1.3	6.9	6.3
All Other Current	4.4	3.5	4.9	3.1		2.9	4.5	4.1
Total Current	51.9	57.1	49.9	44.4		39.6	50.3	51.6
Fixed Assets (net)	32.6	30.5	35.9	36.6		40.8	34.5	34.9
Intangibles (net)	6.7	4.0	5.1	7.9		13.9	4.3	5.0
All Other Non-Current	8.8	8.3	9.1	11.1		5.6	10.9	8.5
Total	100.0	100.0	100.0	100.0		100.0	100.0	100.0
LIABILITIES								
Notes Payable-Short Term	12.8	8.9	10.8	5.5		5.8	11.7	10.0
Cur. Mat.-L/T/D	11.5	5.5	4.0	3.2		2.1	5.1	4.4
Trade Payables	10.3	12.0	12.5	7.8		7.7	11.8	13.2
Income Taxes Payable	.3	.6	.6	.4		.1	.4	.2
All Other Current	20.7	10.7	10.6	10.4		20.1	13.2	13.3
Total Current	55.6	37.8	38.5	27.4		35.8	42.2	41.1
Long Term Debt	30.0	23.0	18.9	20.4		22.2	22.0	21.4
Deferred Taxes	.3	.6	.4	.2		1.2	.4	.5
All Other Non-Current	5.8	5.9	3.8	4.7		7.9	5.7	19.7
Net Worth	8.3	32.7	38.4	47.4		32.8	29.7	17.4
Total Liabilities & Net Worth	100.0	100.0	100.0	100.0		100.0	100.0	100.0
INCOME DATA								
Net Sales	100.0	100.0	100.0	100.0		100.0	100.0	100.0
Gross Profit								
Operating Expenses	92.5	91.6	91.7	92.6		89.7	93.4	89.9
Operating Profit	7.5	8.4	8.3	7.4		10.3	6.6	10.1
All Other Expenses (net)	2.2	2.0	1.6	1.2		1.1	.0	1.1
Profit Before Taxes	5.4	6.3	6.7	6.2		9.2	6.6	9.0
RATIOS								
Current	2.8	2.7	2.2	3.1		2.9	2.5	2.6
	1.1	1.5	1.2	1.5		1.4	1.3	1.4
	.4	.9	.9	1.0		1.0	.8	.8
Quick	(104) 2.1	2.3	1.6	2.3		1.9	(367) 2.0	2.4
	.9	1.1	1.0	1.1		1.4	1.0	1.1
	.3	.7	.6	.7		1.4 / .7	.4	.5
Sales/Receivables	0 UND	10 37.0	12 30.7	24 15.1		0 UND	2 153.1	4 92.4
	3 113.4	34 10.7	36 10.0	45 8.2		22 16.5	33 11.1	32 11.5
	33 11.2	61 6.0	63 5.8	71 5.1		64 5.7	58 6.3	59 6.2
Cost of Sales/Inventory								
Cost of Sales/Payables								
Sales/Working Capital	9.0	6.4	6.8	4.0		5.7	7.0	6.5
	195.0	20.3	26.4	8.4		24.5	19.1	18.1
	−15.7	−51.5	−45.9	−79.6		NM	−35.0	−58.4
EBIT/Interest	(72) 7.6	(75) 7.6	(96) 8.2	(33) 8.8		(11) 8.3	(270) 8.4	(297) 12.7
	3.5	2.3	3.5	2.9		2.9	2.9	4.9
	−.7	.9	1.4	1.6		−1.2	1.1	1.4
Net Profit + Depr., Dep., Amort./Cur. Mat. L /T/D		(20) 4.2	(23) 4.2				(60) 4.9	(67) 4.4
		1.9	1.6				2.0	2.5
		.7	.8				1.0	1.7
Fixed/Worth	.2	.1	.5	.3		.5	.2	.2
	1.2	.8	.8	.8		1.4	1.0	.9
	−1.6	20.6	2.5	2.3		3.2	5.6	3.4
Debt/Worth	.7	.6	.6	.5		.6	.7	.6
	4.0	1.8	1.9	1.5		2.1	2.4	1.8
	−4.8	44.9	5.8	4.5		8.2	21.6	9.5
% Profit Before Taxes/Tangible Net Worth	(72) 128.7	(77) 63.0	(97) 43.5	(40) 21.9		(10) 109.1	(291) 51.1	(325) 64.1
	43.5	22.4	17.1	8.1		23.8	21.7	23.2
	4.2	1.5	2.5	1.3		7.0	2.8	5.9
% Profit Before Taxes/Total Assets	35.6	20.6	12.4	12.3		32.6	17.0	22.5
	9.5	5.7	5.8	3.5		8.6	6.5	7.8
	−1.3	−.1	1.0	.8		−3.1	.3	.9
Sales/Net Fixed Assets	108.9	48.9	22.2	25.2		28.2	43.5	34.5
	27.6	12.3	8.0	5.4		3.3	10.0	9.9
	8.4	4.5	1.5	1.0		1.1	2.9	3.0
Sales/Total Assets	6.9	3.7	3.2	1.9		4.3	4.2	3.8
	4.0	2.6	2.1	1.0		1.1	2.2	2.3
	2.5	1.5	.8	.4		.9	.8	1.0
% Depr., Dep., Amort./Sales	(75) 1.0	(85) .8	(96) 1.3	(40) 1.5			(289) 1.0	(326) 1.2
	2.3	2.3	3.2	4.2			2.9	2.7
	5.1	4.4	5.2	7.6			7.3	5.9
% Officers', Directors', Owners' Comp/Sales	(46) 4.8	(38) 4.0	(24) 1.5				(103) 4.7	(117) 3.0
	12.7	6.9	3.3				8.5	6.6
	18.8	10.8	5.3				15.2	13.8
Net Sales ($)	125594M	344287M	1066969M	1265174M	705396M	8805519M	4804977M	8203747M
Total Assets ($)	24476M	109357M	491992M	996430M	679057M	1931573M	3711436M	4460312M

M = $ thousand   MM = $ million
See Pages 11 through 18 for Explanation of Ratios and Data

Comparative Historical Data   **Current Data Sorted By Sales**

			Type of Statement						
70	63	71	Unqualified	9	14	8	11	13	16
43	31	45	Reviewed	3	8	9	7	13	5
115	83	69	Compiled	17	22	10	13	4	3
56	49	75	Tax Returns	35	26	7		4	3
132	114	121	Other	23	27	15	17	22	17
4/1/00-3/31/01 ALL	4/1/01-3/31/02 ALL	4/1/02-3/31/03 ALL		78 (4/1-9/30/02)			303 (10/1/02-3/31/03)		
				0-1MM	1-3MM	3-5MM	5-10MM	10-25MM	25MM & OVER
416	340	381	NUMBER OF STATEMENTS	87	97	49	48	56	44
%	%	%	ASSETS	%	%	%	%	%	%
16.0	14.7	15.6	Cash & Equivalents	19.2	18.9	10.4	12.7	12.3	13.9
26.0	26.8	25.2	Trade Receivables (net)	13.4	24.4	29.9	30.6	33.7	28.1
5.8	5.2	6.3	Inventory	4.4	5.7	5.9	10.2	6.0	8.2
4.4	5.5	4.1	All Other Current	4.0	4.6	2.9	2.6	6.1	3.8
52.1	52.2	51.2	Total Current	41.0	53.6	49.1	56.1	58.2	54.0
35.3	32.4	33.8	Fixed Assets (net)	40.0	34.2	39.1	25.8	29.8	28.7
4.5	5.4	5.9	Intangibles (net)	9.0	2.5	2.3	10.2	2.8	10.8
8.1	10.1	9.1	All Other Non-Current	10.0	9.6	9.6	7.9	9.3	6.5
100.0	100.0	100.0	Total	100.0	100.0	100.0	100.0	100.0	100.0
			LIABILITIES						
8.9	10.4	9.9	Notes Payable-Short Term	11.6	6.1	13.8	8.7	14.9	5.7
4.1	4.5	6.3	Cur. Mat.-L/T/D	11.4	5.8	7.5	3.5	3.3	*2.7
11.4	15.8	11.3	Trade Payables	5.6	10.4	10.5	15.5	14.2	17.6
.4	.5	.5	Income Taxes Payable	.1	.9	.1	.7	.5	.5
15.6	12.9	13.6	All Other Current	11.6	15.6	12.6	11.8	14.7	15.1
40.3	44.2	41.7	Total Current	40.2	38.8	44.6	40.2	47.7	41.7
20.6	28.5	23.4	Long Term Debt	38.8	20.9	25.7	18.5	10.6	17.3
.5	.6	.4	Deferred Taxes	.2	.6	1.1	.2	.0	.6
5.9	7.0	5.1	All Other Non-Current	5.2	6.9	2.8	4.4	4.8	4.8
32.7	19.8	29.4	Net Worth	15.7	32.8	25.8	36.8	36.9	35.5
100.0	100.0	100.0	Total Liabilities & Net Worth	100.0	100.0	100.0	100.0	100.0	100.0
			INCOME DATA						
100.0	100.0	100.0	Net Sales	100.0	100.0	100.0	100.0	100.0	100.0
			Gross Profit						
92.5	92.8	92.1	Operating Expenses	83.3	92.6	97.2	94.0	97.1	93.9
7.5	7.2	7.9	Operating Profit	16.7	7.4	2.8	6.0	2.9	6.1
.6	2.5	1.9	All Other Expenses (net)	5.4	.8	1.0	1.5	.3	.7
6.9	4.7	6.0	Profit Before Taxes	11.3	6.6	1.8	4.4	2.5	5.3
			RATIOS						
2.5	2.9	2.5		4.2	3.0	2.1	2.3	1.9	2.5
1.4	1.4	1.3	Current	1.0	1.7	1.3	1.3	1.2	1.3
.9	.9	.8		.4	.9	.8	1.0	.9	.9
2.2	2.1	2.0		3.6	2.6	1.9	2.0	1.5	1.8
1.1	1.1	(380) 1.0	Quick	(86) .8	1.3	1.0	1.0	1.0	1.1
.6	.6	.5		.3	.6	.5	.7	.6	.7
4 101.4	2 161.3	2 174.8		0 UND	0 UND	13 29.0	13 28.7	22 16.4	22 16.8
32 11.4	32 11.3	30 12.0	Sales/Receivables	4 102.0	25 14.6	38 9.7	35 10.4	47 7.8	41 8.9
62 5.9	59 6.2	55 6.6		33 11.1	55 6.6	65 5.6	62 5.9	68 5.4	56 6.6
			Cost of Sales/Inventory						
			Cost of Sales/Payables						
6.0	5.6	6.9		5.9	5.4	9.4	7.1	11.7	6.7
18.2	17.4	26.4	Sales/Working Capital	67.4	15.1	29.5	27.6	31.3	19.4
-84.8	-65.3	-33.2		-8.4	-52.1	-24.5	-156.9	-59.2	-73.9
	10.5	11.0	8.2		7.4	10.8	5.4	8.1	17.9	20.4
(322) 3.6	(259) 3.1	(293) 3.4	EBIT/Interest	(62) 3.4	(64) 2.5	(44) 1.4	(39) 3.4	(48) 4.3	(36) 5.3
1.0	.8	1.0		-.2	.6	.2	1.9	1.1	1.9
5.9	4.9	5.2			6.7		4.6		9.8
(58) 2.2	(45) 2.5	(58) 2.3	Net Profit + Depr., Dep., Amort./Cur. Mat. L/T/D		(14) 1.4		(10) 2.8		(13) 3.3
1.0	1.4	1.1			.7		1.4		1.9
.3	.2	.3		.1	.2	.5	.3	.2	.3
.9	.7	.9	Fixed/Worth	1.2	.9	1.1	.8	.8	.8
3.3	3.5	5.0		-4.9	5.8	NM	3.3	1.4	2.7
.7	.6	.6		.5	.5	.9	.6	.7	.6
2.0	2.1	2.2	Debt/Worth	3.6	1.6	2.9	2.5	2.0	2.7
8.6	10.8	16.7		-5.6	20.3	NM	19.2	5.0	10.6
57.1	56.6	56.8		100.0	64.5	25.4	52.3	51.3	38.0
(349) 21.0	(277) 17.8	(305) 18.2	% Profit Before Taxes/Tangible Net Worth	(61) 21.9	(77) 26.8	(37) 6.9	(39) 11.7	(54) 20.5	(37) 17.9
4.0	1.0	1.9		1.8	1.8	-11.3	4.9	2.6	3.1
20.0	17.3	16.9		30.9	25.6	10.0	16.4	13.9	14.5
6.8	5.4	5.5	% Profit Before Taxes/Total Assets	7.0	7.4	.9	6.2	5.7	5.1
.0	-.4	.0		-.5	-.1	-5.6	2.0	.4	.6
34.6	40.3	43.2		56.2	54.2	32.8	54.2	43.6	36.9
9.8	11.4	12.2	Sales/Net Fixed Assets	9.2	15.1	8.9	14.1	12.4	16.1
2.6	3.6	3.3		1.3	3.3	3.0	4.7	3.3	3.4
4.0	4.0	4.0		3.3	5.3	3.6	4.4	3.9	3.7
2.1	2.3	2.5	Sales/Total Assets	1.8	2.9	2.5	2.7	2.7	1.9
1.0	1.2	1.1		.5	1.2	1.3	1.9	1.5	1.1
.8	.7	1.1		2.3	.9	1.1	.9	.9	.8
(337) 2.4	(270) 2.2	(313) 2.7	% Depr., Dep., Amort./Sales	(63) 4.3	(78) 2.5	(46) 2.3	(45) 2.6	(44) 2.9	(37) 2.0
5.3	4.5	5.3		12.7	5.4	4.8	4.5	4.6	4.6
3.3	3.1	3.6		6.2	3.9	4.1	1.7	1.3	
(140) 6.5	(116) 6.3	(118) 6.9	% Officers', Directors', Owners' Comp/Sales	(29) 13.9	(41) 6.1	(16) 8.0	(12) 5.3	(12) 2.7	
11.7	13.3	14.5		19.9	13.8	10.9	12.1	5.8	
6923313M	6693167M	12312939M	Net Sales ($)	44436M	180824M	187469M	368091M	896926M	10635193M
4974049M	3485632M	4232885M	Total Assets ($)	61166M	189909M	154737M	281742M	655404M	2889927M

M = $ thousand   MM = $ million
See Pages 11 through 18 for Explanation of Ratios and Data

MANAGEMENT
OF COMPANIES
AND ENTERPRISES

Current Data Sorted By Assets   Comparative Historical Data

						Type of Statement		
	1		1	1	6	Unqualified	7	8
		2				Reviewed	5	1
1	2	3	1		1	Compiled	16	17
		2				Tax Returns	4	2
	3	9	2	2	3	Other	27	20
	4 (4/1-9/30/02)		36 (10/1/02-3/31/03)				4/1/98-3/31/99	4/1/99-3/31/00
0-500M	500M-2MM	2-10MM	10-50MM	50-100MM	100-250MM		ALL	ALL
1	6	16	4	3	10	NUMBER OF STATEMENTS	59	48
%	%	%	%	%	%	ASSETS	%	%
		11.7			16.1	Cash & Equivalents	3.8	8.8
		.9			21.2	Trade Receivables (net)	5.2	7.3
		7.8			4.0	Inventory	4.6	3.4
		2.4			8.7	All Other Current	1.2	4.0
		22.8			49.9	Total Current	14.8	23.4
		50.5			6.5	Fixed Assets (net)	22.5	24.8
		.6			.4	Intangibles (net)	1.4	3.2
		26.0			43.3	All Other Non-Current	61.4	48.6
		100.0			100.0	Total	100.0	100.0
						LIABILITIES		
		20.8			20.3	Notes Payable-Short Term	9.5	12.8
		2.1			2.8	Cur. Mat.-L/T/D	1.1	5.7
		1.3			2.8	Trade Payables	1.3	2.4
		.0			.0	Income Taxes Payable	.0	.2
		2.4			43.7	All Other Current	3.8	5.8
		26.7			69.6	Total Current	15.7	26.8
		37.3			9.2	Long Term Debt	25.7	24.3
		.6			.0	Deferred Taxes	.1	.7
		.1			.6	All Other Non-Current	1.0	1.4
		35.3			20.6	Net Worth	57.3	46.8
		100.0			100.0	Total Liabilities & Net Worth	100.0	100.0
						INCOME DATA		
		100.0			100.0	Net Sales	100.0	100.0
						Gross Profit		
		51.0			63.3	Operating Expenses	28.4	46.2
		49.0			36.7	Operating Profit	71.6	53.8
		20.3			11.9	All Other Expenses (net)	10.4	8.3
		28.6			24.8	Profit Before Taxes	61.3	45.5
						RATIOS		
		3.0			1.3		2.3	2.7
		.9			1.0	Current	.9	1.0
		.3			.3		.1	.1
		1.7			1.1		2.0	2.5
		.5			.3	Quick	.4	.3
		.2			.2		.1	.1
	0 UND			0 UND			0 UND	0 UND
	0 UND			9 40.7		Sales/Receivables	0 UND	0 UND
	1 381.9			1772 .2			0 UND	7 54.0
						Cost of Sales/Inventory		
						Cost of Sales/Payables		
		3.4			1.0		5.8	5.9
		−179.3			8.2	Sales/Working Capital	−73.6	UND
		−6.4			−.1		−2.2	−.8
							14.5	21.8
						EBIT/Interest	(26) 6.9	(23) 10.2
							3.2	4.2
						Net Profit + Depr., Dep., Amort./Cur. Mat. L /T/D		
		.0			.0		.0	.0
		2.5			.2	Fixed/Worth	.0	.0
		21.9			.4		1.6	1.4
		.5			5.7		.1	.2
		1.6			11.5	Debt/Worth	.5	.6
		34.2			13.6		2.8	5.7
		46.9			25.4	% Profit Before Taxes/Tangible Net Worth	16.5	16.9
	(13) 8.6			17.7		(56) 10.9	(43) 11.6
		6.1			7.7		6.1	5.8
		10.4			2.4	% Profit Before Taxes/Total Assets	9.8	8.8
		3.1			1.5		6.4	5.5
		2.1			.7		3.7	2.1
		79.4			UND	Sales/Net Fixed Assets	UND	UND
		1.2			2.9		UND	10.4
		.2			2.4		1.9	2.2
		.8			.2	Sales/Total Assets	.2	.2
		.2			.1		.1	.1
		.1			.1		.1	.1
		2.2				% Depr., Dep., Amort./Sales	3.2	1.4
	(11) 11.6					(19) 12.7	(21) 8.5
		15.7					17.7	17.7
						% Officers', Directors', Owners' Comp/Sales		
53M	2974M	71127M	63240M	18215M	217253M	Net Sales ($)	424235M	609453M
442M	6513M	88850M	66766M	190217M	1594929M	Total Assets ($)	1438239M	1084217M

M = $ thousand   MM = $ million
See Pages 11 through 18 for Explanation of Ratios and Data

Comparative Historical Data | Current Data Sorted By Sales

			Type of Statement		1		1	4	3
6	7	9	Unqualified		1		1	4	3
1	1	2	Reviewed	1	1				
14	8	8	Compiled	6		1	1		
4	3	2	Tax Returns	2					
16	21	19	Other	7	5	1	2	3	1
4/1/00-3/31/01	4/1/01-3/31/02	4/1/02-3/31/03			4 (4/1-9/30/02)		36 (10/1/02-3/31/03)		
ALL	ALL	ALL		0-1MM	1-3MM	3-5MM	5-10MM	10-25MM	25MM & OVER
41	40	40	**NUMBER OF STATEMENTS**	16	7	2	4	7	4
%	%	%	**ASSETS**	%	%	%	%	%	%
6.6	10.9	14.9	Cash & Equivalents	7.1					
3.2	8.0	7.0	Trade Receivables (net)	.3					
.0	1.2	4.1	Inventory	.0					
2.4	6.6	3.2	All Other Current	.4					
12.3	26.7	29.2	Total Current	7.8					
28.5	35.5	36.1	Fixed Assets (net)	67.9					
5.2	1.4	.6	Intangibles (net)	.5					
53.9	36.4	34.1	All Other Non-Current	23.7					
100.0	100.0	100.0	Total	100.0					
			LIABILITIES						
15.5	8.9	14.0	Notes Payable-Short Term	12.5					
2.6	4.3	2.2	Cur. Mat.-L/T/D	1.9					
2.7	5.5	1.3	Trade Payables	.2					
.8	.1	.0	Income Taxes Payable	.0					
3.7	11.4	16.2	All Other Current	1.9					
25.3	30.2	33.7	Total Current	16.5					
32.5	31.3	37.7	Long Term Debt	66.7					
-.0	.0	.2	Deferred Taxes	.0					
2.2	3.2	.6	All Other Non-Current	1.1					
40.0	35.2	27.7	Net Worth	15.7					
100.0	100.0	100.0	Total Liabilities & Net Worth	100.0					
			INCOME DATA						
100.0	100.0	100.0	Net Sales	100.0					
			Gross Profit						
47.0	52.2	51.7	Operating Expenses	37.4					
53.0	47.8	48.3	Operating Profit	62.6					
5.5	17.4	18.3	All Other Expenses (net)	30.2					
47.5	30.4	30.0	Profit Before Taxes	32.4					
			RATIOS						
1.3	2.1	1.9		1.8					
.4	1.0	1.0	Current	.9					
.1	.2	.2		.1					
1.1	1.3	1.6		1.6					
.3	.4	.5	Quick	.6					
.0	.1	.1		.1					
0 UND	0 UND	0 UND		0 UND					
0 UND	0 UND	0 UND	Sales/Receivables	0 UND					
0 UND	9 42.0	11 32.4		0 UND					
			Cost of Sales/Inventory						
			Cost of Sales/Payables						
7.1	2.9	3.2		8.5					
-2.9	NM	NM	Sales/Working Capital	-24.0					
-.5	-1.6	-2.6		-2.6					
17.7	12.8	14.6							
(13) 9.1	(13) 6.6	(18) 5.8	EBIT/Interest						
4.3	2.5	1.1							
			Net Profit + Depr., Dep., Amort./Cur. Mat. L/T/D						
.0	.0	.0		.7					
.0	.4	.3	Fixed/Worth	6.0					
2.8	6.1	9.8		64.9					
.1	.3	.5		.8					
.6	4.1	5.2	Debt/Worth	5.2					
6.3	14.8	14.6		68.2					
19.0	23.5	23.6		44.0					
(37) 8.2	(36) 14.0	(35) 10.9	% Profit Before Taxes/Tangible Net Worth	(13) 8.6					
3.1	6.6	5.9		6.4					
9.8	7.9	5.8		5.3					
4.4	2.9	2.3	% Profit Before Taxes/Total Assets	2.7					
.7	.9	1.2		1.5					
UND	67.7	99.3		1.1					
16.0	3.2	2.6	Sales/Net Fixed Assets	.2					
.2	.2	.3		.1					
.2	.2	.3		.2					
.1	.1	.1	Sales/Total Assets	.1					
.1	.1	.1		.1					
9.6	2.1	2.4		7.0					
(17) 13.7	(28) 5.7	(21) 7.4	% Depr., Dep., Amort./Sales	(10) 18.2					
23.6	13.9	18.2		25.5					
			% Officers', Directors', Owners' Comp/Sales						
67102M	259265M	372862M	Net Sales ($)	7123M	12017M	8291M	29951M	91941M	223539M
509713M	1335854M	1947717M	Total Assets ($)	64116M	114770M	61913M	412069M	996644M	298205M

© RMA 2003

M = $ thousand   MM = $ million
See Pages 11 through 18 for Explanation of Ratios and Data

Current Data Sorted By Assets   Comparative Historical Data

						Type of Statement		
3	10	29	36	19	16	Unqualified	198	153
7	24	52	25	3	1	Reviewed	152	126
24	95	96	25	2		Compiled	391	335
45	144	89	6	1		Tax Returns	380	351
26	88	115	50	18	11	Other	401	331
	109 (4/1-9/30/02)		951 (10/1/02-3/31/03)				4/1/98-3/31/99	4/1/99-3/31/00
0-500M	500M-2MM	2-10MM	10-50MM	50-100MM	100-250MM		ALL	ALL
105	361	381	142	43	28	**NUMBER OF STATEMENTS**	1522	1296
%	%	%	%	%	%	**ASSETS**	%	%
9.0	5.6	5.2	8.5	10.1	6.7	Cash & Equivalents	6.1	5.8
5.3	1.5	5.6	9.2	9.3	16.5	Trade Receivables (net)	3.8	3.9
3.0	1.1	3.5	10.1	11.5	7.7	Inventory	3.4	3.5
3.4	2.7	3.4	4.0	8.9	7.8	All Other Current	2.4	2.5
20.6	10.9	17.6	31.7	39.9	38.7	Total Current	15.6	15.8
72.3	80.2	71.2	52.4	38.5	33.3	Fixed Assets (net)	72.2	73.2
1.1	1.3	1.6	3.7	2.4	4.8	Intangibles (net)	2.5	2.5
6.1	7.6	9.5	12.2	19.3	23.2	All Other Non-Current	9.7	8.5
100.0	100.0	100.0	100.0	100.0	100.0	Total	100.0	100.0
						LIABILITIES		
5.8	3.9	5.1	7.6	11.9	10.9	Notes Payable-Short Term	6.2	6.5
7.2	6.4	5.1	4.3	4.7	3.6	Cur. Mat.-L/T/D	4.9	5.8
3.6	1.3	3.4	5.9	5.7	7.6	Trade Payables	2.6	3.0
.2	.1	.1	.3	.3	.2	Income Taxes Payable	.1	.1
13.9	5.1	6.8	7.9	8.8	13.3	All Other Current	7.3	6.0
30.8	16.8	20.5	25.9	31.4	35.5	Total Current	21.1	21.4
68.6	58.5	50.0	37.4	22.0	19.4	Long Term Debt	57.0	56.3
.0	.0	.2	.9	1.4	1.7	Deferred Taxes	.3	.3
4.7	5.1	3.8	4.5	7.4	6.2	All Other Non-Current	6.7	4.1
-4.1	19.6	25.6	31.3	37.8	37.1	Net Worth	14.8	17.9
100.0	100.0	100.0	100.0	100.0	100.0	Total Liabilities & Net Worth	100.0	100.0
						INCOME DATA		
100.0	100.0	100.0	100.0	100.0	100.0	Net Sales	100.0	100.0
						Gross Profit		
61.0	48.8	59.1	72.1	77.6	84.8	Operating Expenses	59.3	55.9
39.0	51.2	40.9	27.9	22.4	15.2	Operating Profit	40.7	44.1
16.4	24.8	20.3	11.5	6.6	7.0	All Other Expenses (net)	17.4	21.8
22.5	26.4	20.7	16.5	15.8	8.2	Profit Before Taxes	23.3	22.3
						RATIOS		
1.6	1.4	1.5	1.9	2.6	1.6		2.2	1.4
.5	.4	.6	1.1	1.3	1.2	Current	.7	.5
.1	.1	.2	.5	.7	.7		.1	.1
1.3	.9	1.0	1.4	1.3	1.0		1.6	1.0
.3	.3	.3	.5	.5	.8	Quick	(1515) .4 (1293) .4	
.1	.1	.1	.2	.2	.3		.1	.1
0 UND	0 UND	0 UND	0 UND	1 284.0	7 51.6		0 UND	0 UND
0 UND	0 UND	0 UND	12 30.7	15 24.9	40 9.1	Sales/Receivables	0 UND	0 UND
3 138.4	0 UND	12 31.3	47 7.8	50 7.3	70 5.2		8 48.1	9 39.2
						Cost of Sales/Inventory		
						Cost of Sales/Payables		
13.4	27.4	11.7	4.7	3.8	5.5		7.3	12.0
-9.4	-5.8	-7.9	60.5	10.2	12.6	Sales/Working Capital	-15.2	-8.0
-2.2	-2.1	-2.0	-6.0	-7.6	-4.9		-2.3	-2.1
7.1	6.7	7.9	5.7	6.6	4.3		6.9	6.9
(51) 4.4	(134) 4.2	(173) 4.1	(88) 2.1	(33) 3.3	(21) 2.4	EBIT/Interest	(499) 3.6 (449) 3.5	
1.8	2.0	1.4	.5	1.1	1.6		1.7	1.6
	4.2	3.1	2.8	4.0	3.2	Net Profit + Depr., Dep.,	3.6	3.5
(17) 1.7	(39) 1.7	(34) 1.4	(15) 1.9	(10) 1.9		Amort./Cur. Mat. L/T/D	(172) 1.5 (135) 1.5	
1.2	.6	.9	.3	.6			.9	.8
1.3	1.6	1.3	.5	.3	.2		1.5	1.5
4.1	4.2	3.4	1.8	1.0	1.0	Fixed/Worth	3.9	4.1
-20.2	21.4	12.5	5.8	3.1	2.3		30.1	37.7
1.3	1.3	1.3	1.2	.8	1.2		1.5	1.4
3.7	3.7	3.7	2.8	2.4	2.2	Debt/Worth	4.1	4.2
-17.7	22.6	13.0	11.8	5.7	4.3		40.3	43.9
53.4	38.8	40.4	26.8	33.5	24.1	% Profit Before Taxes/Tangible	40.6	41.9
(71) 20.8	(295) 19.1	(327) 18.2	(121) 12.8	(41) 11.4	(27) 6.4	Net Worth	(1196) 19.1 (1020) 18.2	
8.4	7.8	5.6	.9	2.0	3.5		5.3	5.9
18.7	9.7	9.1	6.4	8.8	4.9	% Profit Before Taxes/Total	9.3	9.2
6.8	4.5	4.0	3.3	2.6	2.3	Assets	4.2	4.4
1.4	1.2	.8	.3	.4	.5		.7	1.2
2.2	.4	.8	9.5	18.0	19.1		.8	.7
.4	.2	.2	1.6	2.5	4.3	Sales/Net Fixed Assets	.2	.3
.2	.2	.1	.2	.4	.8		.2	.2
1.4	.3	.4	1.3	1.3	1.6		.4	.4
.4	.2	.2	.4	.6	.6	Sales/Total Assets	.2	.2
.2	.1	.1	.2	.2	.2		.1	.1
4.5	11.3	7.0	3.1	1.4	1.1		9.3	8.9
(92) 13.1	(339) 16.8	(344) 16.3	(124) 10.2	(35) 4.5	(20) 4.1	% Depr., Dep., Amort./Sales	(1366) 16.3 (1192) 15.0	
22.4	23.7	25.3	18.5	14.8	15.4		23.3	22.0
4.0	2.4	2.0	1.6			% Officers', Directors',	2.6	2.9
(13) 12.1	(26) 5.9	(49) 4.8	(17) 3.6			Owners' Comp/Sales	(139) 6.5 (137) 6.0	
18.0	18.3	10.0	10.5				14.4	12.7
33378M	186431M	1225088M	2907012M	2851778M	3760061M	Net Sales ($)	12582891M	10144347M
31341M	423223M	1671480M	2964072M	3060042M	4441524M	Total Assets ($)	15591594M	11971758M

M = $ thousand   MM = $ million
See Pages 11 through 18 for Explanation of Ratios and Data

Comparative Historical Data | Current Data Sorted By Sales

			Type of Statement						
123	97	113	Unqualified	25	11	7	13	26	31
100	89	112	Reviewed	48	20	10	8	15	11
297	284	242	Compiled	177	39	7	9	7	3
240	227	285	Tax Returns	252	24	2	3	2	2
299	339	308	Other	172	46	13	10	22	45
4/1/00-3/31/01 ALL	4/1/01-3/31/02 ALL	4/1/02-3/31/03 ALL		0-1MM	1-3MM	3-5MM	5-10MM	10-25MM	25MM & OVER
				109 (4/1-9/30/02)		951 (10/1/02-3/31/03)			
1059	1036	1060	**NUMBER OF STATEMENTS**	674	140	39	43	72	92
%	%	%	**ASSETS**	%	%	%	%	%	%
5.8	6.3	6.4	Cash & Equivalents	5.2	5.4	9.3	12.3	11.5	8.3
5.2	4.8	5.1	Trade Receivables (net)	1.3	3.4	9.4	5.6	23.2	19.1
4.0	4.6	3.9	Inventory	.5	5.7	6.7	5.8	11.1	18.5
3.8	4.3	3.6	All Other Current	2.1	5.7	5.2	6.8	5.9	7.4
18.8	20.0	19.0	Total Current	9.1	20.2	30.6	30.5	51.7	53.3
68.6	69.0	69.5	Fixed Assets (net)	82.8	64.8	50.7	37.4	36.6	28.3
3.0	2.8	1.8	Intangibles (net)	1.2	1.0	3.6	5.5	2.8	4.4
9.5	8.2	9.6	All Other Non-Current	6.9	13.9	15.2	26.5	8.8	14.0
100.0	100.0	100.0	Total	100.0	100.0	100.0	100.0	100.0	100.0
			LIABILITIES						
5.7	6.3	5.5	Notes Payable-Short Term	3.6	6.8	5.9	6.3	14.7	9.7
6.2	5.3	5.6	Cur. Mat.-L/T/D	5.9	5.6	4.5	3.5	4.5	5.6
2.6	2.9	3.2	Trade Payables	.7	2.4	7.1	5.8	12.9	12.5
.1	.1	.1	Income Taxes Payable	.1	.1	.4	.3	.3	.4
6.3	6.0	7.4	All Other Current	5.3	12.0	6.0	7.9	9.9	13.8
21.0	20.7	21.8	Total Current	15.6	26.9	23.8	23.8	42.3	42.0
52.6	54.0	51.1	Long Term Debt	61.4	48.8	39.7	31.3	15.9	20.8
.3	.3	.3	Deferred Taxes	.1	.2	.0	.4	1.3	1.3
3.9	5.6	4.6	All Other Non-Current	4.1	6.1	6.0	5.0	5.8	4.3
22.3	19.5	22.2	Net Worth	18.9	17.9	30.5	39.4	34.7	31.6
100.0	100.0	100.0	Total Liabilities & Net Worth	100.0	100.0	100.0	100.0	100.0	100.0
			INCOME DATA						
100.0	100.0	100.0	Net Sales	100.0	100.0	100.0	100.0	100.0	100.0
			Gross Profit						
56.6	57.2	58.9	Operating Expenses	48.4	60.9	75.5	73.1	89.7	95.6
43.4	42.8	41.1	Operating Profit	51.6	39.1	24.5	26.9	10.3	4.4
21.6	23.1	19.4	All Other Expenses (net)	25.8	14.1	12.4	7.6	3.8	1.1
21.8	19.8	21.7	Profit Before Taxes	25.9	25.0	12.1	19.3	6.6	3.3
			RATIOS						
1.7	2.1	1.6	Current	1.3	1.7	2.3	2.4	2.2	1.8
.7	.8	.6		.4	.7	1.0	1.1	1.4	1.3
.2	.2	.2		.1	.2	.6	.4	.8	1.0
1.0	1.3	1.1	Quick	.9	1.3	1.3	1.5	1.7	1.0
(1058) .4	.4	.4		.3	.3	.8	.5	.9	.7
.1	.1	.1		.1	.1	.1	.1	.4	.4
0 UND	0 UND	0 UND	Sales/Receivables	0 UND	0 UND	0 UND	0 UND	13 27.9	14 26.9
0 UND	0 UND	0 UND		0 UND	0 UND	1 273.6	7 54.3	39 9.5	31 11.6
10 36.2	13 29.0	13 27.6		0 UND	10 38.4	40 9.2	35 10.3	62 5.9	54 6.7
			Cost of Sales/Inventory						
			Cost of Sales/Payables						
7.9	5.4	8.5	Sales/Working Capital	25.0	5.5	5.2	3.2	4.8	7.5
-15.2	-23.9	-10.6		-4.9	-15.0	240.5	81.9	16.8	13.4
-2.6	-2.6	-2.3		-1.8	-2.4	-7.2	-5.3	-16.2	NM
(395) 5.7	(391) 6.2	(500) 6.9	EBIT/Interest	(218) 7.1	(85) 6.5	(23) 6.8	(31) 10.0	(60) 9.7	(83) 5.7
3.5	3.3	3.6		4.4	3.9	1.7	1.7	3.0	2.3
1.8	1.4	1.5		2.2	1.5	.7	.4	.5	1.2
(98) 3.8	(81) 4.1	(121) 3.1	Net Profit + Depr., Dep., Amort./Cur. Mat. L/T/D	(32) 3.5	(10) 2.4	(11) 2.1	(10) 3.2	(26) 2.6	(32) 3.7
1.5	1.3	1.7		1.5	1.7	1.7	1.8	1.3	1.8
.7	.6	.8		.9	1.2	.4	.5	.6	.8
1.4	1.3	1.2	Fixed/Worth	1.9	1.0	.4	.2	.3	.3
3.6	3.3	3.1		4.5	3.3	1.7	.9	1.1	1.0
14.1	23.8	14.0		26.3	13.0	4.7	2.2	3.1	2.3
1.4	1.4	1.2	Debt/Worth	1.3	1.6	.8	.7	.8	1.4
3.8	3.6	3.4		3.9	3.9	2.6	1.8	2.3	2.4
22.2	33.6	19.2		27.7	13.4	5.8	3.3	10.3	6.9
(868) 40.6	(819) 38.9	(882) 37.5	% Profit Before Taxes/Tangible Net Worth	(549) 36.5	(117) 58.4	(32) 25.3	(38) 40.9	(63) 26.8	(83) 27.7
19.3	17.2	17.8		18.6	21.1	8.5	10.5	13.7	10.5
5.6	5.4	5.1		6.2	11.1	.9	-.4	1.1	1.4
9.8	8.8	9.4	% Profit Before Taxes/Total Assets	9.3	11.2	5.3	15.3	10.2	7.3
4.4	4.0	4.1		4.2	4.9	2.3	3.4	2.9	2.7
.9	.8	.9		1.1	1.7	-.1	-.2	-1.0	.3
1.3	1.3	1.6	Sales/Net Fixed Assets	.3	3.6	17.5	21.7	15.8	34.2
.3	.3	.3		.2	.4	1.8	2.5	7.0	7.7
.2	.2	.2		.1	.2	.2	.5	1.8	2.8
.5	.4	.5	Sales/Total Assets	.3	.5	1.6	1.2	2.8	2.8
.2	.2	.2		.2	.2	.5	.5	1.4	1.5
.1	.1	.1		.1	.2	.2	.2	.5	1.0
(969) 5.7	(927) 6.4	(954) 6.8	% Depr., Dep., Amort./Sales	(626) 12.3	(119) 5.3	(32) 1.8	(35) 4.1	(67) 1.3	(75) .8
14.4	14.8	15.1		18.1	13.4	11.5	7.8	2.8	1.9
22.0	21.8	23.2		25.7	23.1	15.2	15.1	7.0	4.0
(105) 2.7	(108) 2.2	(110) 2.1	% Officers', Directors', Owners' Comp/Sales	(42) 2.6	(21) 3.0		(10) 2.5	(15) .8	(13) .3
5.6	5.1	4.9		6.5	7.1		3.4	2.0	1.6
11.8	11.2	12.2		16.3	18.2		7.3	3.9	6.2
10148214M	9322781M	10963748M	Net Sales ($)	233067M	239242M	149503M	316228M	1159132M	8866576M
11717285M	11499468M	12591682M	Total Assets ($)	1396614M	1009474M	594052M	1052676M	2015288M	6523578M

© RMA 2003   M = $ thousand   MM = $ million
See Pages 11 through 18 for Explanation of Ratios and Data

ADMINISTRATIVE AND SUPPORT AND WASTE MANAGEMENT AND REMEDIATION

Current Data Sorted By Assets

Comparative Historical Data

						Type of Statement		
2	6	17	21	6	12	Unqualified	97	71
4	13	17	3			Reviewed	26	30
8	12	4	2			Compiled	50	39
16	11	5				Tax Returns	26	31
18	15	24	20	6	4	Other	97	97
	29 (4/1-9/30/02)		217 (10/1/02-3/31/03)				4/1/98-3/31/99	4/1/99-3/31/00
0-500M	500M-2MM	2-10MM	10-50MM	50-100MM	100-250MM		ALL	ALL
48	57	67	46	12	16	NUMBER OF STATEMENTS	296	268
%	%	%	%	%	%	ASSETS	%	%
21.5	14.1	17.3	18.5	20.8	9.9	Cash & Equivalents	17.7	17.4
16.3	30.4	26.7	23.5	25.6	17.6	Trade Receivables (net)	23.5	26.1
1.5	2.9	1.9	3.7	2.2	6.3	Inventory	3.7	3.0
9.7	6.3	8.7	6.3	3.6	5.3	All Other Current	5.8	7.1
49.0	53.7	54.6	52.0	52.2	39.1	Total Current	50.7	53.6
29.7	22.3	24.9	26.4	31.8	31.9	Fixed Assets (net)	27.0	23.9
3.0	5.3	7.1	9.2	8.3	15.2	Intangibles (net)	7.1	7.5
18.3	18.7	13.5	12.4	7.6	13.8	All Other Non-Current	15.2	14.9
100.0	100.0	100.0	100.0	100.0	100.0	Total	100.0	100.0
						LIABILITIES		
17.1	10.2	8.9	6.4	5.6	5.1	Notes Payable-Short Term	11.7	9.8
3.0	2.8	3.5	4.9	1.5	3.6	Cur. Mat.-L/T/D	3.3	3.1
10.9	12.1	10.7	14.3	7.7	8.1	Trade Payables	15.5	15.5
.1	1.0	.9	.2	.2	.7	Income Taxes Payable	.3	.4
33.0	15.8	15.2	12.2	15.4	14.2	All Other Current	14.1	18.9
64.1	41.8	39.3	38.0	30.5	31.7	Total Current	44.9	47.6
14.0	22.2	16.9	18.3	24.8	27.2	Long Term Debt	21.2	20.2
.0	.0	.3	.3	1.9	.4	Deferred Taxes	.8	.7
8.1	8.0	5.0	6.9	4.9	8.7	All Other Non-Current	8.3	9.0
13.8	27.9	38.5	36.5	37.8	32.0	Net Worth	24.8	22.5
100.0	100.0	100.0	100.0	100.0	100.0	Total Liabilities & Net Worth	100.0	100.0
						INCOME DATA		
100.0	100.0	100.0	100.0	100.0	100.0	Net Sales	100.0	100.0
						Gross Profit		
94.4	87.6	91.5	91.2	90.2	94.9	Operating Expenses	105.6	91.8
5.6	12.4	8.5	8.8	9.8	5.1	Operating Profit	−5.6	8.2
−.4	1.2	1.2	2.6	4.8	3.0	All Other Expenses (net)	−.8	.7
6.0	11.2	7.3	6.2	5.0	2.1	Profit Before Taxes	−4.8	7.4
						RATIOS		
3.3	2.5	2.7	2.3	2.8	2.1		2.5	2.0
1.3	1.2	1.3	1.3	1.7	1.3	Current	1.3	1.2
.6	.7	.9	1.0	1.2	1.0		.8	.8
2.7	2.2	1.9	2.3	2.6	1.6		1.9	1.7
.9	1.0	1.1	1.2	1.6	1.1	Quick	1.0 (267)	1.0
.2	.4	.7	.5	.9	.6		.5	.5
0 UND	0 UND	0 999.8	20 18.0	6 61.9	25 14.5		0 UND	0 UND
0 UND	24 15.1	33 11.2	47 7.7	33 11.1	44 8.3	Sales/Receivables	31 11.7	34 10.8
25 14.5	50 7.3	60 6.0	71 5.2	70 5.2	56 6.5		60 6.1	64 5.7
						Cost of Sales/Inventory		
						Cost of Sales/Payables		
16.7	9.3	5.5	4.7	2.4	6.5		5.7	6.9
84.0	59.5	14.5	15.7	9.5	36.5	Sales/Working Capital	29.1	20.7
−19.1	−30.1	−235.3	NM	41.5	176.1		−27.3	−35.2
26.7	26.1	17.4	13.3		7.3		10.7	12.1
(28) 7.7	(42) 5.3	(52) 5.4	(40) 2.8		(13) 1.9	EBIT/Interest	(201) 4.0	(197) 3.9
1.0	2.2	1.4	1.0		−.2		1.7	1.2
		11.2				Net Profit + Depr., Dep.,	9.2	5.8
	(14)	5.3				Amort./Cur. Mat. L /T/D	(63) 3.0	(43) 2.5
		2.2					1.3	1.0
.1	.1	.2	.4	.2	.7		.2	.1
.6	.4	.7	1.0	.9	1.2	Fixed/Worth	.8	.7
6.1	3.5	2.0	6.5	14.4	26.5		7.0	7.1
.4	.7	.7	.8	.5	1.4		.9	1.0
1.6	2.8	2.2	2.6	2.9	1.8	Debt/Worth	2.7	3.0
34.0	11.1	8.9	19.7	16.4	31.7		94.6	110.4
217.3	118.1	53.6	54.0	60.5	41.3	% Profit Before Taxes/Tangible	71.5	72.0
(38) 56.3	(48) 53.7	(60) 15.1	(37) 21.6	(10) 35.6	(13) 9.1	Net Worth	(230) 26.9	(206) 23.5
14.5	20.7	6.3	−1.0	2.2	−12.4		9.2	5.3
43.5	28.7	18.8	16.8	18.0	5.8	% Profit Before Taxes/Total	19.9	20.7
16.7	10.9	7.0	7.1	4.8	2.0	Assets	6.9	6.5
.0	4.0	2.2	−1.0	.6	−3.0		1.2	.1
133.2	93.3	57.9	26.5	32.8	19.3		63.2	85.4
30.3	30.6	11.1	9.1	10.7	8.3	Sales/Net Fixed Assets	15.5	17.9
10.8	8.0	4.8	3.8	1.0	2.3		3.9	5.2
9.3	5.0	3.1	2.6	3.6	1.8		3.5	4.4
5.1	2.8	2.0	1.6	2.1	1.1	Sales/Total Assets	1.9	2.2
2.7	1.4	1.1	.8	.4	1.0		.8	1.0
.6	.6	.7	.7	1.2	1.1		.9	.7
(32) 1.6	(39) 1.4	(60) 1.9	(40) 2.4	(10) 2.3		% Depr., Dep., Amort./Sales	(225) 2.2	(202) 2.1
4.9	3.3	5.1	5.1	13.3			5.1	4.3
5.0	4.6	3.2				% Officers', Directors',	5.8	4.3
(19) 16.7	(24) 10.2	(15) 4.9				Owners' Comp/Sales	(57) 11.5	(65) 11.7
24.0	17.5	11.3					20.3	22.9
69350M	267856M	841013M	1828696M	1671721M	4958701M	Net Sales ($)	11519731M	11112696M
11327M	64163M	299596M	1012231M	900153M	2710822M	Total Assets ($)	5556701M	4958999M

M = $ thousand   MM = $ million
See Pages 11 through 18 for Explanation of Ratios and Data

Comparative Historical Data   **Current Data Sorted By Sales**

4/1/00-3/31/01 ALL	4/1/01-3/31/02 ALL	4/1/02-3/31/03 ALL	Type of Statement	0-1MM	1-3MM	3-5MM	5-10MM	10-25MM	25MM & OVER
66	58	64	Unqualified	3	3	5	7	15	31
27	27	37	Reviewed	2	7	9	12	2	5
46	46	26	Compiled	7	4	7	5	2	1
27	20	32	Tax Returns	17	7	3	5	5	
95	86	87	Other	13	16	12	9	13	24
				29 (4/1-9/30/02)			217 (10/1/02-3/31/03)		
261	237	246	NUMBER OF STATEMENTS	42	37	36	38	32	61
%	%	%	ASSETS	%	%	%	%	%	%
14.7	15.7	17.3	Cash & Equivalents	13.7	26.4	17.8	12.5	17.5	16.8
27.6	23.5	24.3	Trade Receivables (net)	17.0	13.1	17.8	36.3	32.1	28.4
2.8	2.5	2.7	Inventory	1.0	3.1	1.6	1.8	2.5	4.8
6.5	5.9	7.4	All Other Current	3.7	13.3	11.5	6.3	7.0	5.0
51.6	47.6	51.7	Total Current	35.5	55.9	48.7	57.0	59.1	55.0
24.2	23.1	26.3	Fixed Assets (net)	35.4	25.9	24.7	20.4	25.7	25.1
9.9	8.9	6.9	Intangibles (net)	1.9	3.8	7.5	7.9	6.7	11.1
14.4	20.5	15.2	All Other Non-Current	27.2	14.5	19.0	14.7	8.5	8.8
100.0	100.0	100.0	Total	100.0	100.0	100.0	100.0	100.0	100.0
			LIABILITIES						
10.3	9.4	9.9	Notes Payable-Short Term	13.3	9.6	11.9	13.2	7.2	6.0
2.9	3.2	3.4	Cur. Mat.-L/T/D	1.7	2.5	5.3	3.8	1.8	4.8
15.4	12.3	11.4	Trade Payables	7.5	11.4	9.8	11.3	11.2	15.3
.6	.2	.6	Income Taxes Payable	.1	.3	1.1	.2	.5	1.1
20.1	18.5	18.2	All Other Current	25.7	22.2	18.2	11.8	13.6	17.0
49.3	43.6	43.5	Total Current	48.3	45.9	46.4	40.3	34.3	44.0
16.4	19.1	18.9	Long Term Debt	26.6	19.2	15.4	18.6	9.4	20.7
.4	.2	.3	Deferred Taxes	.0	.0	.1	.1	.7	.4
7.4	7.6	6.9	All Other Non-Current	5.6	18.1	1.0	5.4	5.5	6.0
26.6	29.6	30.4	Net Worth	19.5	16.8	37.1	35.3	50.2	28.8
100.0	100.0	100.0	Total Liabilities & Net Worth	100.0	100.0	100.0	100.0	100.0	100.0
			INCOME DATA						
100.0	100.0	100.0	Net Sales	100.0	100.0	100.0	100.0	100.0	100.0
			Gross Profit						
91.4	91.2	91.3	Operating Expenses	84.8	90.0	92.2	91.7	93.2	94.7
8.6	8.8	8.7	Operating Profit	15.2	9.9	7.8	8.3	6.8	5.3
.6	1.9	1.4	All Other Expenses (net)	2.1	1.2	1.0	1.6	.4	1.8
8.0	6.9	7.3	Profit Before Taxes	13.1	8.8	6.8	6.8	6.4	3.5
			RATIOS						
2.1	2.0	2.4	Current	2.1	3.1	2.7	2.9	3.5	1.9
1.2	1.2	1.3		.9	1.5	1.2	1.5	1.7	1.2
.7	.6	.8		.4	.9	.6	1.0	1.1	1.0
1.7	1.6	2.0	Quick	1.7	2.7	2.2	2.5	3.4	1.6
1.0	(236) 1.0	1.1		.7	1.0	.8	1.4	1.4	1.1
.5	.4	.5		.1	.3	.4	.8	.8	.6
2 190.1	1 493.9	0 UND	Sales/Receivables	0 UND	0 UND	0 UND	12 29.6	18 20.7	18 20.3
38 9.5	29 12.6	26 13.8		0 UND	1 333.9	18 20.4	46 8.0	49 7.4	39 9.5
64 5.7	64 5.7	55 6.6		36 10.1	27 13.3	38 9.5	71 5.2	74 5.0	55 6.6
			Cost of Sales/Inventory						
			Cost of Sales/Payables						
6.7	8.1	7.7	Sales/Working Capital	23.8	5.8	4.7	5.6	4.7	11.0
30.9	50.1	29.8		-50.9	39.5	26.7	19.6	10.1	31.9
-22.9	-17.1	-39.4		-4.6	-175.7	-16.3	-393.7	117.5	NM
(203) 12.0	(173) 12.5	(183) 17.3	EBIT/Interest	(22) 7.5	(26) 33.7	(23) 10.0	(34) 28.9	(26) 17.3	(52) 13.6
3.1	3.3	4.9		2.2	15.5	2.8	5.9	5.4	3.4
1.1	.9	1.4		.1	5.1	.8	1.7	2.0	1.4
(47) 6.8	(39) 7.5	(38) 14.3	Net Profit + Depr., Dep., Amort./Cur. Mat. L/T/D					(14) 22.2	
3.0	4.1	4.4						5.0	
.9	1.9	1.3						2.1	
.2	.2	.2	Fixed/Worth	.1	.1	.2	.1	.2	.4
.8	.7	.7		1.3	.6	.4	.9	.7	1.0
30.0	6.3	3.3		66.9	1.9	3.4	4.1	1.5	5.3
.9	.9	.8	Debt/Worth	.9	.3	.6	.7	.4	1.5
3.5	3.4	2.4		3.0	2.0	1.4	3.3	1.0	3.1
UND	42.0	14.8		91.8	12.3	6.6	12.9	3.2	22.6
(197) 79.5	(186) 68.1	(206) 75.0	% Profit Before Taxes/Tangible Net Worth	(35) 99.7	(30) 102.8	(31) 50.3	(31) 158.8	(29) 36.0	(50) 61.0
30.0	25.4	30.5		30.2	57.7	21.4	49.6	15.4	31.1
7.7	2.8	6.4		2.3	19.1	1.9	8.7	4.6	6.5
18.7	20.0	20.5	% Profit Before Taxes/Total Assets	22.9	42.1	23.2	27.7	17.2	15.2
7.3	6.2	8.0		6.1	17.4	4.2	9.1	8.7	6.4
.6	-.1	.7		-.5	6.7	.1	2.4	2.7	.5
51.0	65.9	56.4	Sales/Net Fixed Assets	53.0	168.5	54.1	77.1	60.2	38.3
18.1	18.3	15.4		11.8	16.3	20.4	20.3	10.2	16.4
5.9	6.3	5.0		2.7	5.1	5.2	7.8	4.9	5.8
3.8	3.8	4.1	Sales/Total Assets	3.2	5.4	5.1	4.0	3.2	4.0
2.4	2.1	2.3		1.6	3.0	2.1	2.4	1.9	2.4
1.2	1.1	1.1		.6	1.2	1.1	1.5	1.1	1.3
(212) .8	(183) .9	(189) .8	% Depr., Dep., Amort./Sales	(28) 1.5	(22) .5	(30) .7	(34) .7	(28) .9	(47) .8
1.8	1.9	1.8		4.8	1.0	2.1	1.3	2.4	1.7
3.6	4.1	4.8		10.6	2.9	5.7	4.2	5.2	3.5
(63) 3.7	(70) 2.5	(64) 4.2	% Officers', Directors', Owners' Comp/Sales	(15) 6.2	(13) 4.8	(15) 4.6	(10) 1.7		
9.3	8.2	8.6		15.3	9.9	8.6	4.6		
18.3	24.0	17.5		33.3	21.3	13.7	12.1		
10036108M	6008062M	9637337M	Net Sales ($)	22456M	69663M	133973M	262118M	511011M	8638116M
5077409M	4004019M	4998292M	Total Assets ($)	28918M	59706M	142569M	282702M	332537M	4151860M

© RMA 2003

M = $ thousand   MM = $ million
See Pages 11 through 18 for Explanation of Ratios and Data

Current Data Sorted By Assets | **Comparative Historical Data**

0-500M	500M-2MM	2-10MM	10-50MM	50-100MM	100-250MM		4/1/98-3/31/99 ALL	4/1/99-3/31/00 ALL
						Type of Statement		
	2	6	6	3	1	Unqualified	13	8
	5	2	2			Reviewed	4	7
	2	2	1			Compiled	3	6
						Tax Returns		2
	7	5	9	1		Other	12	10
	7 (4/1-9/30/02)		47 (10/1/02-3/31/03)					
	16	15	18	4	1	**NUMBER OF STATEMENTS**	32	33
%	%	%	%	%	%	**ASSETS**	%	%
DATA NOT AVAILABLE	11.6	12.4	3.5			Cash & Equivalents	9.7	10.0
	49.0	51.1	42.0			Trade Receivables (net)	51.9	47.5
	1.1	2.1	3.0			Inventory	.9	1.0
	7.6	5.0	9.3			All Other Current	3.2	8.2
	69.4	70.6	57.8			Total Current	65.7	66.7
	23.5	20.1	22.9			Fixed Assets (net)	20.8	18.7
	.1	.8	16.2			Intangibles (net)	4.1	3.2
	7.0	8.6	3.1			All Other Non-Current	9.3	11.4
	100.0	100.0	100.0			Total	100.0	100.0
						LIABILITIES		
	31.5	10.2	18.5			Notes Payable-Short Term	13.2	15.4
	3.6	3.5	5.5			Cur. Mat.-L/T/D	2.1	4.4
	9.3	14.4	16.7			Trade Payables	13.4	17.4
	.1	.3	.1			Income Taxes Payable	.4	.0
	18.4	15.2	15.1			All Other Current	17.5	17.8
	62.8	43.6	55.9			Total Current	46.6	55.0
	10.9	9.8	19.8			Long Term Debt	11.1	6.7
	.0	1.2	.5			Deferred Taxes	.3	.2
	1.5	5.8	4.2			All Other Non-Current	4.9	9.7
	24.9	39.7	19.5			Net Worth	37.1	28.5
	100.0	100.0	100.0			Total Liabilities & Net Worth	100.0	100.0
						INCOME DATA		
	100.0	100.0	100.0			Net Sales	100.0	100.0
						Gross Profit		
	94.3	94.4	94.1			Operating Expenses	91.1	93.5
	5.7	5.6	5.9			Operating Profit	8.9	6.5
	.8	2.3	4.0			All Other Expenses (net)	1.9	1.7
	4.9	3.3	1.9			Profit Before Taxes	6.9	4.8
						RATIOS		
	3.1	3.2	1.3				3.2	1.8
	1.6	1.6	1.1			Current	1.4	1.1
	1.0	1.2	.9				1.1	1.0
	2.5	3.2	1.1				2.7	1.8
	1.6	1.5	.8			Quick	1.4	1.0
	.9	1.1	.7				1.0	.8
	29 12.4	**47** 7.7	**44** 8.2				**44** 8.2	**29** 12.7
	42 8.7	**59** 6.2	**63** 5.8			Sales/Receivables	**67** 5.4	**45** 8.2
	56 6.5	**79** 4.6	**71** 5.1				**92** 4.0	**71** 5.1
						Cost of Sales/Inventory		
						Cost of Sales/Payables		
	9.6	6.6	14.3				6.3	10.6
	18.5	14.6	76.0			Sales/Working Capital	13.2	99.7
	NM	48.2	-54.6				67.2	-194.9
	60.5	28.0	14.6				15.2	14.9
	(15) 6.4	(12) 6.9	(17) 3.9			EBIT/Interest	(27) 5.8	(30) 3.6
	2.1	1.6	2.6				1.6	.8
							34.2	
						Net Profit + Depr., Dep., Amort./Cur. Mat. L /T/D	(10) 9.9	
							2.4	
	.1	.1	.3				.1	.1
	.3	.2	2.1			Fixed/Worth	.7	.4
	2.5	1.1	-4.8				1.6	1.4
	.3	.8	4.5				.7	1.0
	1.0	1.5	13.1			Debt/Worth	1.9	2.5
	17.7	6.3	-7.3				8.9	9.9
	143.0	66.0	98.2				111.2	75.2
	(14) 66.3	(14) 30.2	(13) 69.2			% Profit Before Taxes/Tangible Net Worth	(30) 38.3	(28) 27.8
	6.6	4.3	18.8				5.6	4.1
	43.3	29.9	9.1				20.3	21.4
	21.6	16.2	6.2			% Profit Before Taxes/Total Assets	7.7	9.6
	1.4	.4	3.7				2.8	.6
	139.0	72.2	136.5				81.0	187.1
	35.4	38.4	34.2			Sales/Net Fixed Assets	27.7	41.5
	16.5	10.0	6.9				7.3	11.6
	5.4	4.7	2.9				3.8	5.3
	4.4	3.4	2.5			Sales/Total Assets	2.4	3.9
	2.8	1.9	1.2				1.5	1.9
	.3	.4	.2				.5	.3
	(14) .8	1.4	(15) .6			% Depr., Dep., Amort./Sales	(26) 1.8	(23) 1.1
	3.6	3.7	4.9				3.6	2.4
						% Officers', Directors', Owners' Comp/Sales		
	88058M	**247645M**	**824244M**	**573743M**	**318739M**	Net Sales ($)	**711015M**	**1050033M**
	18977M	**79189M**	**378356M**	**325390M**	**142012M**	Total Assets ($)	**434718M**	**452397M**

M = $ thousand MM = $ million

See Pages 11 through 18 for Explanation of Ratios and Data

Comparative Historical Data / Current Data Sorted By Sales

Hist 4/1/00-3/31/01 ALL	Hist 4/1/01-3/31/02 ALL	Hist 4/1/02-3/31/03 ALL	Type of Statement	0-1MM	1-3MM	3-5MM	5-10MM	10-25MM	25MM & OVER
14	11	18	Unqualified	1		1	3	2	11
5	7	9	Reviewed		1	3	2	1	2
3	4	5	Compiled	1			1	2	1
2	1		Tax Returns						
11	10	22	Other		2		5	8	7
					7 (4/1-9/30/02)		47 (10/1/02-3/31/03)		
35	33	54	NUMBER OF STATEMENTS	2	3	4	11	13	21
%	%	%	ASSETS	%	%	%	%	%	%
8.4	6.4	9.2	Cash & Equivalents				10.0	13.8	5.8
41.5	51.2	45.2	Trade Receivables (net)				62.9	40.0	46.8
1.7	1.9	1.9	Inventory				1.0	2.5	2.6
8.8	4.8	8.7	All Other Current				3.6	7.5	13.5
60.4	64.4	65.0	Total Current				77.5	63.8	68.7
22.3	19.3	21.5	Fixed Assets (net)				15.1	17.7	17.1
9.0	7.3	7.4	Intangibles (net)				.0	10.7	11.4
8.3	9.0	6.1	All Other Non-Current				7.4	7.9	2.8
100.0	100.0	100.0	Total				100.0	100.0	100.0
			LIABILITIES						
17.7	26.0	18.5	Notes Payable-Short Term				41.3	12.4	12.5
3.8	3.4	4.2	Cur. Mat.-L/T/D				2.5	2.5	5.3
14.4	12.1	12.7	Trade Payables				12.3	11.1	16.5
.2	.6	.3	Income Taxes Payable				.5	.0	.6
16.8	15.8	17.4	All Other Current				22.0	14.1	19.8
53.0	57.9	53.1	Total Current				78.7	40.2	54.7
16.6	17.0	14.2	Long Term Debt				5.8	18.8	12.6
.2	.3	.6	Deferred Taxes				.0	.4	1.4
3.0	6.0	4.1	All Other Non-Current				3.8	6.0	2.1
27.2	18.8	28.0	Net Worth				11.7	34.5	29.3
100.0	100.0	100.0	Total Liabilities & Net Worth				100.0	100.0	100.0
			INCOME DATA						
100.0	100.0	100.0	Net Sales				100.0	100.0	100.0
			Gross Profit						
93.4	95.5	94.5	Operating Expenses				93.6	92.4	96.3
6.6	4.5	5.5	Operating Profit				6.4	7.6	3.7
1.4	2.0	2.1	All Other Expenses (net)				.5	2.6	.5
5.2	2.5	3.4	Profit Before Taxes				5.9	5.0	3.2
			RATIOS						
2.0 1.4 1.0	1.9 1.3 1.0	2.0 1.4 1.0	Current				3.1 1.6 1.0	5.2 1.6 1.1	1.6 1.2 1.0
1.8 1.2 .7	1.7 1.1 .8	1.8 1.1 .7	Quick				3.1 1.5 .9	4.0 1.2 .7	1.4 .8 .7
34 10.6 53 6.8 74 4.9	39 9.4 52 7.1 72 5.1	34 10.7 56 6.5 68 5.3	Sales/Receivables				32 11.5 54 6.8 66 5.5	7 54.7 50 7.3 74 4.9	49 7.5 62 5.8 72 5.0
			Cost of Sales/Inventory						
			Cost of Sales/Payables						
9.9 14.2 453.9	11.1 30.5 −149.8	9.1 18.9 NM	Sales/Working Capital				6.6 14.3 −243.0	8.2 20.9 NM	10.6 16.8 235.8
(28) 9.2 3.4 1.8	(32) 8.7 3.1 1.3	(48) 19.1 5.4 1.9	EBIT/Interest				(10) 33.7 6.8 1.1	(11) 16.4 3.5 1.7	(20) 25.4 4.9 2.2
		(13) 4.9 1.3 .3	Net Profit + Depr., Dep., Amort./Cur. Mat. L/T/D						
.2 .6 5.2	.2 .4 2.5	.1 .7 2.5	Fixed/Worth				.1 .2 .9	.1 1.0 NM	.2 .8 2.5
.8 2.3 12.7	1.1 4.2 −15.4	.9 3.1 18.0	Debt/Worth				.9 1.1 8.7	.8 2.7 NM	2.0 4.9 13.1
(28) 73.5 19.9 12.0	(24) 88.2 29.3 9.2	(45) 101.9 46.5 8.1	% Profit Before Taxes/Tangible Net Worth					(10) 121.9 44.2 6.2	(19) 87.3 46.0 12.8
14.2 6.1 .9	16.7 7.9 1.4	22.4 7.9 1.4	% Profit Before Taxes/Total Assets				46.5 23.6 .4	27.6 11.2 1.2	13.0 6.2 3.6
63.9 34.8 5.8	76.6 32.3 10.7	118.8 37.8 8.7	Sales/Net Fixed Assets				89.1 28.1 15.5	101.4 49.2 9.9	140.4 44.4 7.7
4.3 2.8 1.4	5.1 3.6 2.3	4.4 2.7 1.8	Sales/Total Assets				5.5 4.5 2.0	4.8 2.8 1.4	3.4 2.7 2.0
(25) .3 1.6 3.9	(28) .4 1.0 2.6	(46) .3 1.2 3.8	% Depr., Dep., Amort./Sales				(10) .4 1.2 1.8	(11) .3 1.5 4.9	(16) .2 .8 2.5
		(13) .8 3.0 4.6	% Officers', Directors', Owners' Comp/Sales						
1476403M 700152M	3729224M 609790M	2052429M 943924M	Net Sales ($) Total Assets ($)	1264M 5918M	6083M 3575M	15068M 27833M	78135M 24319M	211855M 106547M	1740024M 775732M

© RMA 2003

M = $ thousand   MM = $ million

See Pages 11 through 18 for Explanation of Ratios and Data

Current Data Sorted By Assets | **Comparative Historical Data**

						Type of Statement		
1	7	14	24	2	2	Unqualified	43	43
1	21	31	2			Reviewed	63	58
21	24	10			1	Compiled	76	75
28	11	5	1		1	Tax Returns	34	28
24	41	40	10	5	1	Other	98	128
	35 (4/1-9/30/02)		293 (10/1/02-3/31/03)				4/1/98-3/31/99	4/1/99-3/31/00
0-500M	500M-2MM	2-10MM	10-50MM	50-100MM	100-250MM		ALL	ALL
75	104	100	37	7	5	NUMBER OF STATEMENTS	314	332
%	%	%	%	%	%	ASSETS	%	%
25.5	10.0	11.5	15.4			Cash & Equivalents	12.5	12.8
30.0	56.5	52.1	51.8			Trade Receivables (net)	56.5	54.4
.0	.5	.3	.0			Inventory	.6	.3
7.2	5.6	5.3	5.8			All Other Current	3.9	3.9
62.6	72.7	69.2	73.0			Total Current	73.5	71.5
18.2	12.5	16.2	8.5			Fixed Assets (net)	13.6	13.8
3.5	4.0	6.3	11.3			Intangibles (net)	5.0	5.5
15.6	10.8	8.3	7.2			All Other Non-Current	7.9	9.2
100.0	100.0	100.0	100.0			Total	100.0	100.0
						LIABILITIES		
24.4	21.2	16.9	13.4			Notes Payable-Short Term	22.3	22.4
4.7	1.7	2.0	1.2			Cur. Mat.-L/T/D	2.4	5.6
9.8	6.1	6.3	8.3			Trade Payables	6.4	7.5
1.4	.8	.6	.8			Income Taxes Payable	1.2	.8
21.6	24.3	21.2	24.5			All Other Current	22.5	21.1
61.8	54.0	47.1	48.2			Total Current	54.8	57.4
12.3	7.7	6.4	5.6			Long Term Debt	9.9	8.9
.5	.5	.5	.9			Deferred Taxes	.7	.5
11.5	5.0	4.9	13.5			All Other Non-Current	4.2	5.7
13.9	32.8	41.0	31.8			Net Worth	30.3	27.5
100.0	100.0	100.0	100.0			Total Liabilities & Net Worth	100.0	100.0
						INCOME DATA		
100.0	100.0	100.0	100.0			Net Sales	100.0	100.0
						Gross Profit		
96.1	99.1	97.9	99.0			Operating Expenses	96.0	96.2
3.9	.9	2.1	1.0			Operating Profit	4.0	3.8
1.7	.6	.7	.3			All Other Expenses (net)	.3	.3
2.2	.3	1.4	.6			Profit Before Taxes	3.7	3.5
						RATIOS		
2.3	2.4	2.3	2.6				2.8	2.5
1.3	1.6	1.3	1.3			Current	1.6	1.6
.6	1.0	1.0	1.0				1.1	1.1
2.3	2.3	2.2	2.4				2.5	2.4
(74) 1.2	1.4	1.2	1.2			Quick (313)	1.5	1.5
.4	.9	.8	.9				1.0	1.0
0 UND	26 13.8	26 13.9	31 11.7				28 13.0	26 14.2
16 23.2	38 9.6	40 9.1	47 7.8			Sales/Receivables 41 ... 43	41 8.9	43 8.6
35 10.5	49 7.5	53 6.9	62 5.9				54 6.7	54 6.8
						Cost of Sales/Inventory		
						Cost of Sales/Payables		
19.9	11.2	10.5	8.0				9.5	10.9
74.1	20.5	29.4	27.8			Sales/Working Capital	19.4	22.1
−31.1	−363.6	−418.5	289.1				122.7	176.8
12.2	18.0	18.9	7.5				19.0	18.7
(49) 4.0	(86) 2.3	(85) 3.8	(27) 2.3			EBIT/Interest (254) ... (280)	5.6	5.7
−1.6	−2.5	.5	.7				1.4	1.3
			3.8				21.2	15.0
		(11) 2.3				Net Profit + Depr., Dep., Amort./Cur. Mat. L./T/D (50) ... (49)	6.5	5.6
			.3				1.0	1.1
.1	.1	.1	.1				.1	.1
.4	.2	.3	.6			Fixed/Worth	.2	.3
8.0	2.0	1.2	NM				.9	1.0
.6	.6	.7	.7				.6	.7
2.2	1.2	2.1	4.9			Debt/Worth	1.6	1.7
66.3	21.2	5.1	NM				5.2	5.3
107.8	66.0	40.7	94.3				83.1	73.3
(58) 36.4	(83) 14.9	(90) 23.2	(28) 24.4			% Profit Before Taxes/Tangible Net Worth (278) ... (286)	39.8	38.2
−1.5	−11.8	.4	.5				11.0	12.6
35.9	19.4	14.0	10.0				28.4	28.3
15.6	3.1	5.5	2.8			% Profit Before Taxes/Total Assets	13.5	12.6
−12.8	−10.2	−.6	−1.6				1.8	1.4
275.8	190.0	216.4	115.8				156.0	163.2
85.5	81.9	66.4	62.9			Sales/Net Fixed Assets	72.4	63.9
30.4	39.5	29.0	39.3				34.5	29.0
14.3	7.2	6.8	5.6				7.6	7.5
7.1	5.8	4.8	4.0			Sales/Total Assets	5.6	5.5
4.5	4.1	3.4	3.1				3.8	3.8
.2	.2	.3	.3				.3	.3
(46) .5	(81) .5	(79) .6	(30) .6			% Depr., Dep., Amort./Sales (254) ... (261)	.5	.6
1.4	1.3	1.4	1.0				1.0	1.2
2.4	2.4	1.0					2.6	2.4
(44) 5.9	(46) 4.1	(35) 2.3				% Officers', Directors', Owners' Comp/Sales (131) ... (125)	5.8	5.1
10.3	7.9	4.9					10.4	10.0
159431M	803633M	2473830M	4097738M	1927857M	8976581M	Net Sales ($)	13287177M	10560654M
17878M	109568M	422203M	712161M	494664M	914585M	Total Assets ($)	2429292M	2281854M

© RMA 2003

M = $ thousand   MM = $ million
See Pages 11 through 18 for Explanation of Ratios and Data

Comparative Historical Data / Current Data Sorted By Sales

4/1/00-3/31/01 ALL	4/1/01-3/31/02 ALL	4/1/02-3/31/03 ALL	Type of Statement	0-1MM	1-3MM	3-5MM	5-10MM	10-25MM	25MM & OVER
					35 (4/1-9/30/02)		293 (10/1/02-3/31/03)		
33	33	50	Unqualified	1		2	6	7	34
71	62	55	Reviewed	1	5	3	17	14	15
87	92	56	Compiled	5	14	13	12	10	2
42	41	46	Tax Returns	10	19	7	5	3	2
118	125	121	Other	12	17	14	23	20	35
351	353	328	**NUMBER OF STATEMENTS**	29	55	39	63	54	88
%	%	%	**ASSETS**	%	%	%	%	%	%
13.7	14.6	14.9	Cash & Equivalents	21.0	20.8	18.8	6.2	11.6	15.6
56.5	49.6	47.8	Trade Receivables (net)	22.2	32.0	46.9	61.9	59.3	49.5
.3	.2	.3	Inventory	.4	.1	1.0	.2	.1	.2
2.8	5.2	5.8	All Other Current	3.9	4.9	8.3	5.2	6.0	6.3
73.3	69.7	68.8	Total Current	47.4	57.9	75.0	73.5	77.1	71.6
13.4	13.5	14.4	Fixed Assets (net)	37.8	17.5	13.5	11.3	11.3	9.2
4.4	6.0	6.0	Intangibles (net)	3.9	6.8	1.2	5.8	4.1	9.6
8.9	10.9	10.8	All Other Non-Current	10.8	17.8	10.3	9.4	7.5	9.6
100.0	100.0	100.0	Total	100.0	100.0	100.0	100.0	100.0	100.0
			LIABILITIES						
22.5	27.7	19.7	Notes Payable-Short Term	17.1	25.1	23.1	21.6	20.7	13.6
3.7	3.1	2.4	Cur. Mat.-L/T/D	5.1	2.9	1.7	3.2	.9	1.9
6.5	7.0	7.3	Trade Payables	15.2	5.1	5.9	6.3	7.4	7.3
.7	.9	.9	Income Taxes Payable	.0	.4	.7	1.6	.3	1.3
30.4	21.4	22.4	All Other Current	14.4	18.7	22.1	24.4	21.4	26.7
63.9	60.2	52.7	Total Current	51.8	52.2	53.4	57.2	50.8	50.8
10.5	10.9	8.1	Long Term Debt	27.1	10.8	4.6	8.6	2.3	5.0
.5	.7	.6	Deferred Taxes	.0	.8	.5	.6	.2	.7
8.9	6.5	7.3	All Other Non-Current	13.5	11.8	6.0	3.8	4.5	7.2
16.2	21.7	31.4	Net Worth	7.6	24.4	35.4	29.8	42.1	36.2
100.0	100.0	100.0	Total Liabilities & Net Worth	100.0	100.0	100.0	100.0	100.0	100.0
			INCOME DATA						
100.0	100.0	100.0	Net Sales	100.0	100.0	100.0	100.0	100.0	100.0
			Gross Profit						
96.4	98.8	98.0	Operating Expenses	90.3	99.7	97.4	98.6	99.2	98.5
3.6	1.2	2.0	Operating Profit	9.6	.3	2.6	1.4	.8	1.5
-.6	.6	.9	All Other Expenses (net)	7.0	.6	.0	.3	.0	.3
4.2	.6	1.2	Profit Before Taxes	2.7	-.3	2.7	1.1	.8	1.1
			RATIOS						
2.6 1.6 1.1	2.7 1.4 .9	2.3 1.4 .9	Current	2.1 .9 .2	2.3 1.3 .8	3.0 1.5 .9	2.3 1.7 .9	2.4 1.5 1.1	2.2 1.3 1.0
2.5 1.5 1.0	2.6 1.3 .8	2.2 (327) 1.3 .8	Quick	(28) 1.9 .7 .2	2.3 1.3 .8	3.0 1.4 .7	2.3 1.4 .9	2.4 1.4 1.1	1.8 1.2 .9
28 12.9 42 8.7 55 6.6	21 17.6 34 10.8 51 7.1	18 20.3 37 9.9 50 7.2	Sales/Receivables	0 UND 21 17.1 47 7.7	0 UND 28 13.0 42 8.7	18 20.3 28 13.0 49 7.4	32 11.5 41 8.8 58 6.3	32 11.6 42 8.6 52 7.1	10 35.6 39 9.3 51 7.1
			Cost of Sales/Inventory						
			Cost of Sales/Payables						
11.5 21.9 118.3	11.6 29.9 -162.3	11.3 30.0 -251.9	Sales/Working Capital	20.8 -61.5 -5.4	13.7 40.9 -37.2	9.1 20.7 -285.5	11.3 27.6 -213.2	9.4 19.6 61.8	11.3 30.8 506.2
(305) 18.0 5.8 1.6	(300) 10.2 2.0 -2.2	(259) 14.6 3.3 -.8	EBIT/Interest	(15) 7.2 .2 -2.5	(43) 10.2 2.4 -1.2	(26) 29.5 2.5 -3.0	(55) 17.3 2.1 -2.7	(46) 16.4 6.0 -.6	(74) 28.7 3.7 .9
(44) 13.8 3.7 1.6	(40) 14.9 1.9 -1.8	(26) 5.3 2.4 .5	Net Profit + Depr., Dep., Amort./Cur. Mat. L/T/D					(10) 5.0 2.6 1.5	
.1 .3 1.1	.1 .3 1.9	.1 .3 2.0	Fixed/Worth	.3 2.1 -2.3	.1 .4 6.5	.1 .2 1.6	.1 .2 2.2	.1 .2 .8	.1 .3 1.3
.7 1.9 7.5	.7 2.2 14.4	.6 1.7 13.9	Debt/Worth	1.2 3.6 -4.2	.5 1.7 45.5	.5 1.2 4.9	.6 1.0 23.5	.6 1.5 4.1	.9 2.2 11.1
(294) 76.2 41.4 16.4	(282) 57.2 18.0 -15.8	(269) 60.6 22.1 -1.7	% Profit Before Taxes/Tangible Net Worth	(20) 334.5 1.2 -25.0	(43) 60.7 16.7 -2.8	(33) 83.3 15.6 2.8	(50) 59.9 22.8 -27.0	(50) 37.0 23.4 -1.2	(73) 62.9 25.6 2.3
33.0 14.3 2.5	21.3 4.8 -10.6	19.4 5.3 -3.8	% Profit Before Taxes/Total Assets	15.9 .0 -17.3	27.2 4.1 -10.5	48.3 8.7 .2	29.0 2.8 -9.0	14.5 6.9 -2.3	13.1 5.8 .1
157.3 65.3 30.8	185.3 69.2 30.2	193.3 71.7 33.2	Sales/Net Fixed Assets	113.1 24.7 2.4	161.7 62.9 25.6	231.1 76.9 43.4	193.6 95.2 46.8	132.7 72.7 32.9	247.1 74.2 42.6
7.7 5.4 4.0	8.0 5.3 3.9	7.4 5.3 3.5	Sales/Total Assets	5.5 2.4 .6	9.6 5.5 3.4	9.4 5.9 4.4	7.4 5.0 4.0	6.7 5.0 3.9	9.5 5.6 3.7
(262) .3 .6 1.2	(249) .2 .6 1.2	(246) .2 .5 1.2	% Depr., Dep., Amort./Sales	(18) 1.8 4.0 15.0	(39) .2 .6 1.9	(28) .3 .8 1.2	(49) .2 .4 .9	(41) .4 .6 1.0	(71) .2 .4 .8
(143) 2.3 5.0 10.0	(143) 2.0 4.8 9.1	(130) 2.0 3.8 7.9	% Officers', Directors', Owners' Comp/Sales	(12) 4.6 14.1 21.8	(36) 3.4 6.3 10.3	(20) 1.3 3.7 6.0	(25) 2.7 3.8 7.4	(22) 1.1 2.4 5.0	(15) .8 1.3 2.3
10598039M 2294685M	8571913M 1875023M	18439070M 2671059M	Net Sales ($) Total Assets ($)	16311M 18651M	107109M 32460M	157952M 34766M	458883M 98589M	859427M 189313M	16839388M 2297280M

M = $ thousand   MM = $ million
See Pages 11 through 18 for Explanation of Ratios and Data

Current Data Sorted By Assets — Comparative Historical Data

						Type of Statement		
4	9	22	10	4	3	Unqualified	46	46
10	17	21	3			Reviewed	58	51
12	33	11	1			Compiled	47	52
8	3	2	1			Tax Returns	17	21
8	25	22	14	11	8	Other	69	68
	30 (4/1-9/30/02)			232 (10/1/02-3/31/03)			4/1/98-3/31/99	4/1/99-3/31/00
0-500M	500M-2MM	2-10MM	10-50MM	50-100MM	100-250MM		ALL	ALL
42	87	78	29	15	11	NUMBER OF STATEMENTS	237	238
%	%	%	%	%	%	ASSETS	%	%
20.7	9.3	11.4	9.1	8.6	8.6	Cash & Equivalents	11.3	9.9
45.3	62.2	60.2	46.8	32.4	44.8	Trade Receivables (net)	56.9	58.5
.5	.6	1.0	1.0	.1	.0	Inventory	.5	.9
7.2	5.8	6.1	6.3	8.1	7.4	All Other Current	4.0	3.1
73.7	78.0	78.9	63.2	49.3	60.7	Total Current	72.7	72.4
12.2	8.7	9.7	9.5	9.8	6.4	Fixed Assets (net)	11.1	11.9
2.8	5.3	4.5	17.6	30.6	24.5	Intangibles (net)	8.8	8.4
11.3	8.0	6.9	9.7	10.3	8.4	All Other Non-Current	7.4	7.3
100.0	100.0	100.0	100.0	100.0	100.0	Total	100.0	100.0
						LIABILITIES		
43.5	21.7	18.8	12.3	7.3	10.0	Notes Payable-Short Term	18.4	22.4
14.0	4.2	3.1	3.8	3.7	1.5	Cur. Mat.-L/T/D	2.3	2.6
6.8	7.5	5.1	7.1	8.0	8.5	Trade Payables	5.7	6.0
.2	.9	.3	.1	.5	.6	Income Taxes Payable	.6	.6
26.2	17.9	26.1	23.0	16.9	16.8	All Other Current	20.9	21.3
90.7	52.2	53.3	46.2	36.3	37.4	Total Current	47.8	52.9
13.4	7.5	4.3	16.5	12.1	14.2	Long Term Debt	8.4	7.9
.0	.2	.2	.3	.0	.3	Deferred Taxes	.5	.4
12.4	7.8	4.8	4.7	15.1	9.5	All Other Non-Current	7.7	4.7
−16.5	32.2	37.4	32.3	36.4	38.6	Net Worth	35.5	34.0
100.0	100.0	100.0	100.0	100.0	100.0	Total Liabilities & Net Worth	100.0	100.0
						INCOME DATA		
100.0	100.0	100.0	100.0	100.0	100.0	Net Sales	100.0	100.0
						Gross Profit		
99.8	98.4	98.1	98.9	97.1	98.9	Operating Expenses	96.1	96.9
.2	1.6	1.9	1.1	2.9	1.1	Operating Profit	3.9	3.1
.5	.5	.6	.5	.2	1.3	All Other Expenses (net)	.5	.0
−.3	1.1	1.3	.5	2.7	−.3	Profit Before Taxes	3.4	3.1
						RATIOS		
2.5	2.3	2.3	2.3	1.6	2.8		2.7	2.6
1.2	1.5	1.5	1.4	1.4	2.2	Current	1.6	1.5
.6	1.1	1.1	1.0	1.1	1.1		1.1	1.0
2.2	2.1	2.0	1.9	1.6	2.5		2.6	2.5
1.0	1.5	1.3	1.2	1.1	1.7	Quick (235)	1.5	1.4
.4	1.1	1.0	.9	1.0	1.1		1.0	1.0

0	UND	25	14.4	29	12.6	32	11.2	13	27.1	44	8.3	Sales/Receivables	26	14.3	29	12.4
31	11.9	37	9.8	38	9.5	42	8.8	46	7.9	48	7.5		40	9.1	41	8.8
43	8.5	56	6.5	50	7.4	49	7.5	70	5.2	62	5.9		53	6.8	55	6.6

0-500M	500M-2MM	2-10MM	10-50MM	50-100MM	100-250MM		ALL	ALL
						Cost of Sales/Inventory		
						Cost of Sales/Payables		
11.7	12.3	10.8	13.1	10.5	5.0	Sales/Working Capital	10.7	10.6
68.5	24.2	22.0	28.4	19.3	12.5		21.0	23.0
−59.3	52.1	313.5	NM	107.5	92.2		111.0	318.7
8.6	10.9	13.4	5.8	29.4	25.7	EBIT/Interest	16.7	14.4
(30) 1.8	(74) 2.7	(71) 2.6	(26) 2.7	4.2	(10) 1.6		(206) 5.0	(211) 5.3
−1.1	−.2	.2	−.2	−.7	−3.0		1.7	1.3
		6.3				Net Profit + Depr., Dep., Amort./Cur. Mat. L /T/D	25.5	15.0
		(13) 1.3					(49) 4.5	(39) 3.0
		.2					1.7	.9
.0	.1	.1	.2	.2	.1	Fixed/Worth	.1	.1
.3	.2	.2	.5	.9	.2		.3	.3
NM	.5	.8	NM	−.3	.6		1.5	1.4
.7	.7	.6	1.2	1.4	.5	Debt/Worth	.7	.8
4.5	1.9	2.1	3.5	6.2	1.8		2.1	2.0
−4.9	4.7	6.2	NM	−2.5	11.8		11.6	8.4
33.3	49.3	37.6	59.3			% Profit Before Taxes/Tangible Net Worth	72.4	67.1
(27) 11.1	(75) 18.8	(66) 16.3	(22) 14.2				(194) 43.4	(191) 39.4
−15.4	−2.9	−1.1	5.7				20.4	12.1
16.1	16.4	10.7	10.0	18.2	9.1	% Profit Before Taxes/Total Assets	26.4	25.3
3.9	6.2	3.7	6.2	5.2	1.7		12.1	12.7
−14.7	−1.7	−1.4	−1.6	−4.5	−14.4		3.7	1.7
999.8	204.7	218.9	130.4	82.1	71.5	Sales/Net Fixed Assets	209.8	175.9
129.9	110.8	90.0	51.6	41.1	42.2		78.6	78.0
43.5	49.4	40.2	25.7	29.8	32.7		40.5	41.9
11.1	8.0	7.5	6.1	3.7	4.2	Sales/Total Assets	8.2	7.5
7.3	5.7	5.6	4.2	2.7	3.2		6.0	5.5
4.9	3.8	4.3	3.3	1.3	2.3		4.2	4.0
.2	.2	.1	.5	.6		% Depr., Dep., Amort./Sales	.3	.3
(25) .4	(64) .5	(69) .5	(25) 1.0	(11) 1.3			(190) .5	(188) .5
1.0	.9	.8	1.7	2.0			1.0	1.0
1.9	2.3	1.1				% Officers', Directors', Owners' Comp/Sales	1.7	1.3
(13) 3.4	(33) 3.0	(29) 2.1					(95) 3.1	(81) 3.3
5.8	6.2	3.2					6.7	7.1
118113M	647890M	2513569M	3670758M	3627362M	5289791M	Net Sales ($)	18034175M	15412801M
11217M	98692M	298863M	707323M	1045474M	1777685M	Total Assets ($)	3813816M	3039327M

M = $ thousand   MM = $ million
See Pages 11 through 18 for Explanation of Ratios and Data

Comparative Historical Data | | | | **Current Data Sorted By Sales** | | | | | |

			Type of Statement						
34	39	52	Unqualified		4	3	6	8	31
39	39	51	Reviewed	1	9	9	6	19	7
59	61	57	Compiled	6	9	10	14	16	2
21	18	14	Tax Returns	2	7	1	1	2	1
108	87	88	Other	5	6	6	12	18	41
4/1/00-3/31/01 ALL	4/1/01-3/31/02 ALL	4/1/02-3/31/03 ALL		30 (4/1-9/30/02) 0-1MM	1-3MM	3-5MM	232 (10/1/02-3/31/03) 5-10MM	10-25MM	25MM & OVER
261	244	262	**NUMBER OF STATEMENTS**	14	35	29	39	63	82
%	%	%	**ASSETS**	%	%	%	%	%	%
9.8	11.5	11.7	Cash & Equivalents	7.4	18.8	8.2	12.0	11.5	10.5
58.9	53.4	54.8	Trade Receivables (net)	43.3	49.8	57.6	65.3	60.9	48.1
.6	.7	.7	Inventory	.1	.2	1.2	.9	1.1	.4
3.9	5.2	6.4	All Other Current	16.9	3.1	8.7	2.4	6.1	7.3
73.3	70.8	73.6	Total Current	67.7	72.0	75.7	80.7	79.7	66.4
10.2	11.5	9.6	Fixed Assets (net)	22.2	7.0	9.6	9.1	10.1	8.5
7.6	8.5	8.3	Intangibles (net)	4.7	6.1	9.3	1.0	3.9	16.3
9.1	9.1	8.5	All Other Non-Current	5.4	15.0	5.3	9.2	6.3	8.9
100.0	100.0	100.0	Total	100.0	100.0	100.0	100.0	100.0	100.0
			LIABILITIES						
19.7	17.8	22.0	Notes Payable-Short Term	65.6	32.2	24.0	23.8	19.3	10.6
3.0	4.3	5.3	Cur. Mat.-L/T/D	.0	16.2	2.5	3.6	5.4	3.1
8.1	6.8	6.7	Trade Payables	4.2	5.3	9.3	6.0	7.4	6.6
.5	.5	.5	Income Taxes Payable	.1	.2	.5	.7	.5	.5
26.1	22.0	22.1	All Other Current	12.8	23.8	21.8	19.3	18.9	27.0
57.4	51.3	56.5	Total Current	82.6	77.7	58.1	53.3	51.5	47.8
8.9	8.9	9.1	Long Term Debt	21.5	14.5	7.9	3.4	4.7	11.1
.4	.3	.2	Deferred Taxes	.0	.0	.1	.2	.3	.2
5.9	5.5	7.8	All Other Non-Current	7.1	12.8	1.1	7.6	8.5	7.7
27.4	34.0	26.5	Net Worth	−11.3	−5.0	32.8	35.6	34.9	33.2
100.0	100.0	100.0	Total Liabilities & Net Worth	100.0	100.0	100.0	100.0	100.0	100.0
			INCOME DATA						
100.0	100.0	100.0	Net Sales	100.0	100.0	100.0	100.0	100.0	100.0
			Gross Profit						
97.5	98.4	98.5	Operating Expenses	93.5	100.3	97.9	98.5	98.8	98.7
2.5	1.6	1.4	Operating Profit	6.5	−.3	2.1	1.5	1.2	1.3
.2	.4	.6	All Other Expenses (net)	5.3	.3	.7	.3	.0	.4
2.3	1.1	.9	Profit Before Taxes	1.2	−.6	1.3	1.2	1.2	.9
			RATIOS						
2.4	2.7	2.3	Current	6.0	2.8	2.3	2.1	2.8	2.2
1.4	1.5	1.5		1.7	1.2	1.2	1.5	1.5	1.4
1.1	1.0	1.0		.8	.6	1.0	1.1	1.1	1.1
2.2	2.5	2.0	Quick	2.1	2.3	1.9	2.0	2.5	1.9
1.3	1.4	1.4		1.5	1.1	1.1	1.5	1.5	1.2
1.0	.9	.9		.8	.6	.7	1.1	1.1	.9
28 13.1	24 15.3	25 14.3	Sales/Receivables	0 UND	21 17.4	30 12.1	25 14.8	28 13.1	25 14.8
40 9.1	38 9.6	38 9.5		33 11.1	42 8.7	47 7.7	37 9.9	37 9.8	40 9.1
56 6.6	50 7.3	52 7.0		66 5.6	67 5.4	70 5.2	56 6.5	45 8.1	50 7.3
			Cost of Sales/Inventory						
			Cost of Sales/Payables						
11.6	11.5	11.1	Sales/Working Capital	6.3	7.5	10.5	14.3	11.9	12.2
26.7	25.2	22.8		11.6	28.1	27.6	22.5	22.1	29.6
186.9	226.2	271.7		−229.6	−32.7	NM	60.7	64.8	229.4
(219) 12.2	(211) 7.5	(226) 10.9	EBIT/Interest	(26) 10.0	(25) 6.1	(34) 8.9	(55) 12.0		(77) 16.6
3.7	2.3	2.6		1.0	1.9	2.8	3.0		3.1
1.3	−.7	−.3		−2.1	−.3	−2.2	.2		−.2
(34) 7.6	(32) 4.6	(37) 3.8	Net Profit + Depr., Dep., Amort./Cur. Mat. L/T/D					(22) 5.2	
2.4	1.2	1.4						1.2	
1.3	.0	.1						−.4	
.1	.1	.1	Fixed/Worth	.0	.0	.1	.1	.1	.1
.3	.3	.2		.2	.2	.1	.2	.2	.4
1.2	2.0	1.0		NM	7.0	1.0	.4	1.0	7.3
.8	.6	.8	Debt/Worth	.9	.6	.9	.6	.6	1.2
2.1	2.0	2.2		1.4	3.9	2.2	1.8	1.6	2.9
7.8	15.1	11.4		−12.6	−4.2	10.2	3.4	5.8	86.5
(211) 59.8	(188) 49.8	(208) 44.9	% Profit Before Taxes/Tangible Net Worth	(10) 25.3	(24) 32.6	(23) 53.5	(35) 48.9	(51) 44.9	(65) 51.7
32.6	15.7	15.9		8.3	2.0	15.7	21.5	17.8	17.8
12.9	−9.7	−3.2		−29.3	−21.5	−2.9	2.6	−1.0	2.8
20.5	15.5	14.4	% Profit Before Taxes/Total Assets	15.2	11.6	14.5	15.9	15.2	11.0
9.3	3.8	4.5		2.7	.3	3.1	5.4	4.1	5.3
1.6	−7.0	−3.2		−10.0	−12.8	−1.4	−3.4	−1.4	−1.9
178.0	164.8	218.9	Sales/Net Fixed Assets	UND	994.7	291.7	174.2	169.4	202.3
81.3	63.1	85.9		64.8	171.2	80.2	98.4	96.9	58.8
41.3	35.9	38.9		16.7	40.2	43.2	52.9	40.3	32.3
8.0	8.0	7.7	Sales/Total Assets	5.3	7.6	6.7	9.1	7.5	8.0
5.7	5.3	5.3		3.3	4.8	4.4	6.3	6.4	4.7
4.0	3.7	3.6		.7	3.3	3.5	4.6	5.0	3.2
(193) .2	(181) .3	(202) .2	% Depr., Dep., Amort./Sales	(21) .3	(21) .2	(28) .3	(55) .2		(70) .2
.4	.5	.5		.4	.5	.5	.4		.7
.8	.9	1.0		1.2	1.0	.8	.7		1.3
(88) 1.3	(81) 1.3	(78) 1.5	% Officers', Directors', Owners' Comp/Sales	(11) 2.4	(12) 1.2	(16) 2.6	(23) 1.1		(11) .4
2.7	2.4	2.8		4.7	2.8	3.2	2.8		1.3
5.8	4.3	4.7		9.2	3.9	6.2	3.6		1.6
17375546M	16311238M	15867483M	Net Sales ($)	7612M	68138M	114818M	285520M	993824M	14397571M
3263274M	3626169M	3939254M	Total Assets ($)	7776M	16092M	32724M	48688M	167604M	3666370M

M = $ thousand   MM = $ million
See Pages 11 through 18 for Explanation of Ratios and Data

Current Data Sorted By Assets   Comparative Historical Data

							Type of Statement		
	1	2	3		1		Unqualified	5	4
	2	6	1				Reviewed	18	15
7	8	2					Compiled	32	31
4	3	3			1		Tax Returns	13	15
5	10	10	2	1			Other	38	27
	19 (4/1-9/30/02)		53 (10/1/02-3/31/03)					4/1/98-3/31/99	4/1/99-3/31/00
0-500M	500M-2MM	2-10MM	10-50MM	50-100MM	100-250MM			ALL	ALL
16	24	23	6	1	2	NUMBER OF STATEMENTS		106	92
%	%	%	%	%	%	ASSETS		%	%
16.4	11.5	8.9				Cash & Equivalents		9.5	10.7
28.8	27.0	28.5				Trade Receivables (net)		29.3	30.9
5.0	11.3	9.9				Inventory		10.2	9.5
1.1	2.1	2.2				All Other Current		2.0	2.0
51.3	51.8	49.4				Total Current		51.0	53.1
29.3	36.9	37.6				Fixed Assets (net)		38.1	37.4
9.3	1.5	3.3				Intangibles (net)		3.5	5.1
10.0	9.8	9.7				All Other Non-Current		7.3	4.4
100.0	100.0	100.0				Total		100.0	100.0
						LIABILITIES			
26.2	7.9	7.1				Notes Payable-Short Term		9.4	9.1
3.1	7.8	6.5				Cur. Mat.-L/T/D		7.8	6.1
25.9	14.8	10.3				Trade Payables		14.6	13.4
.2	.3	.2				Income Taxes Payable		.3	.4
6.1	12.5	8.4				All Other Current		11.0	9.7
61.5	43.4	32.4				Total Current		43.1	38.8
18.6	30.1	24.2				Long Term Debt		28.2	23.9
.0	.2	.5				Deferred Taxes		.4	.4
12.4	3.4	3.4				All Other Non-Current		7.3	3.1
7.4	23.0	39.5				Net Worth		21.0	33.8
100.0	100.0	100.0				Total Liabilities & Net Worth		100.0	100.0
						INCOME DATA			
100.0	100.0	100.0				Net Sales		100.0	100.0
						Gross Profit			
95.3	99.4	94.6				Operating Expenses		97.5	94.5
4.7	.6	5.4				Operating Profit		2.5	5.5
1.4	2.2	.9				All Other Expenses (net)		1.9	1.3
3.3	−1.6	4.5				Profit Before Taxes		.6	4.3
						RATIOS			
2.0	2.0	2.8						2.3	2.8
1.1	1.3	1.5				Current		1.4	1.4
.6	.9	1.0						.9	.9
1.7	1.4	2.2						1.7	2.1
1.0	.9	1.3				Quick		1.0	1.0
.5	.5	.7						.6	.7
0 UND	27 13.6	41 8.9						26 14.3	28 12.8
28 13.2	41 9.0	47 7.7				Sales/Receivables		41 8.9	43 8.5
53 6.9	57 6.4	53 6.8						54 6.7	55 6.7
						Cost of Sales/Inventory			
						Cost of Sales/Payables			
21.4	10.6	7.4						8.4	6.3
NM	24.4	17.1				Sales/Working Capital		20.5	16.4
−12.0	−90.4	−370.2						−46.1	−83.3
12.5	8.2	12.4						9.2	5.5
(14) 3.2	(23) 1.5	(21) 3.0				EBIT/Interest		(95) 3.3	(83) 2.8
−2.4	−2.8	1.3						1.2	.9
						Net Profit + Depr., Dep., Amort./Cur. Mat. L /T/D		3.0 (25) 1.5 1.1	4.0 (24) 1.4 .9
.6	.4	.6						.5	.5
2.6	1.1	1.3				Fixed/Worth		1.2	1.3
−.5	NM	2.5						6.4	3.9
1.1	1.1	.9						.9	.9
4.1	2.5	2.0				Debt/Worth		2.5	2.2
−2.4	NM	3.6						9.4	7.4
	45.3	71.3						64.1	54.1
	(18) 17.0	(21) 16.8				% Profit Before Taxes/Tangible Net Worth		(84) 28.0	(77) 21.8
	−15.4	1.1						7.8	−.8
33.3	13.3	16.5						19.5	19.5
7.5	2.2	4.4				% Profit Before Taxes/Total Assets		8.7	5.9
−5.9	−10.7	.4						1.4	−.3
29.0	13.6	9.3						14.1	14.0
9.9	8.0	5.7				Sales/Net Fixed Assets		7.0	7.0
7.6	3.7	3.9						4.3	4.3
6.9	3.1	2.6						3.9	3.3
3.3	2.5	1.9				Sales/Total Assets		2.8	2.6
2.4	1.7	1.5						1.9	1.9
2.1	2.6	1.9						2.7	2.2
(14) 5.4	(20) 5.4	(21) 5.5				% Depr., Dep., Amort./Sales		(94) 4.1	(81) 3.9
7.0	8.4	6.9						6.7	6.6
	3.5							4.4	3.6
	(15) 4.6					% Officers', Directors', Owners' Comp/Sales		(49) 7.3	(39) 6.6
	9.3							10.9	10.9
14348M	65675M	219013M	265203M	70552M	288016M	Net Sales ($)		635410M	1027034M
3853M	27531M	106183M	156622M	80573M	208653M	Total Assets ($)		405063M	541053M

M = $ thousand   MM = $ million
See Pages 11 through 18 for Explanation of Ratios and Data

Comparative Historical Data | | Current Data Sorted By Sales

			Type of Statement						
3	8	7	Unqualified	1			1	2	3
14	12	9	Reviewed			1	5	3	
26	26	17	Compiled	5	7	3	2		
8	8	11	Tax Returns	4	2	2	2		1
23	36	28	Other	3	9	5		5	3
4/1/00- 3/31/01 ALL	4/1/01- 3/31/02 ALL	4/1/02- 3/31/03 ALL		0-1MM	19 (4/1-9/30/02) 1-3MM	3-5MM	53 (10/1/02-3/31/03) 5-10MM	10-25MM	25MM & OVER
74	90	72	NUMBER OF STATEMENTS	13	18	11	13	10	7
%	%	%	ASSETS	%	%	%	%	%	%
7.8	9.4	10.8	Cash & Equivalents	19.1	11.8	9.7	9.0	6.2	
32.7	29.3	26.5	Trade Receivables (net)	28.1	23.4	29.1	26.3	33.9	
11.0	10.4	9.5	Inventory	5.9	8.6	12.9	9.7	11.7	
1.7	1.9	1.8	All Other Current	1.9	1.7	1.6	2.8	1.3	
53.2	51.0	48.6	Total Current	55.0	45.5	53.4	47.8	53.1	
34.9	35.6	35.8	Fixed Assets (net)	22.2	42.5	35.1	40.4	37.5	
4.0	7.6	5.2	Intangibles (net)	10.3	1.4	2.9	4.1	1.7	
7.9	5.8	10.4	All Other Non-Current	12.5	10.6	8.7	7.8	7.7	
100.0	100.0	100.0	Total	100.0	100.0	100.0	100.0	100.0	
			LIABILITIES						
10.4	9.0	11.9	Notes Payable-Short Term	20.6	15.7	7.0	6.5	8.9	
8.0	7.4	5.9	Cur. Mat.-L/T/D	3.2	7.8	5.3	6.0	7.7	
15.6	15.6	14.8	Trade Payables	28.7	13.6	12.7	10.4	12.6	
.3	.5	.2	Income Taxes Payable	.3	.0	.5	.2	.4	
8.2	10.3	8.9	All Other Current	6.0	14.1	6.3	8.0	9.8	
42.5	42.8	41.8	Total Current	58.7	51.2	31.8	31.0	39.4	
29.3	24.5	24.7	Long Term Debt	22.7	32.3	21.7	25.7	21.6	
.2	.6	.5	Deferred Taxes	.0	.0	.2	1.2	.9	
5.9	8.0	6.1	All Other Non-Current	15.6	3.7	1.1	2.2	4.7	
22.1	24.2	26.8	Net Worth	2.9	12.9	45.2	39.9	33.4	
100.0	100.0	100.0	Total Liabilities & Net Worth	100.0	100.0	100.0	100.0	100.0	
			INCOME DATA						
100.0	100.0	100.0	Net Sales	100.0	100.0	100.0	100.0	100.0	
			Gross Profit						
95.4	97.5	96.3	Operating Expenses	96.4	99.3	97.1	92.4	96.3	
4.6	2.5	3.7	Operating Profit	3.6	.7	2.9	7.6	3.7	
2.2	1.0	1.6	All Other Expenses (net)	1.1	2.9	.6	1.2	1.3	
2.4	1.6	2.1	Profit Before Taxes	2.5	-2.2	2.3	6.3	2.4	
			RATIOS						
1.9	2.0	2.1		2.6	1.6	2.4	2.8	2.1	
1.3	1.3	1.3	Current	1.2	1.0	1.6	1.4	1.2	
.9	.8	.9		.8	.5	1.3	1.1	1.0	
1.4	1.9	1.9		2.4	1.2	2.2	2.2	1.9	
.9	.9	1.0	Quick	1.1	.7	1.2	1.3	.9	
.6	.6	.6		.6	.4	.7	.6	.7	
31 11.7	30 12.1	29 12.8		0 UND	26 13.9	27 13.6	37 9.9	40 9.1	
45 8.1	41 8.9	41 8.9	Sales/Receivables	31 11.8	35 10.3	45 8.1	47 7.7	48 7.6	
61 6.0	53 6.9	53 6.9		64 5.7	59 6.2	51 7.2	54 6.8	54 6.8	
			Cost of Sales/Inventory						
			Cost of Sales/Payables						
9.2	8.8	11.2		16.3	18.9	8.7	8.6	10.6	
17.8	22.6	22.4	Sales/Working Capital	53.2	-102.8	11.6	17.9	27.9	
-40.0	-31.1	-90.4		-33.1	-6.6	26.1	NM	-303.7	
4.4	5.3	8.2		7.0	16.5	8.0	13.1	29.4	
(65) 1.6	(80) 1.6	(67) 2.5	EBIT/Interest	(11) 1.7	(17) 1.5	(10) 1.9	(12) 6.0	2.1	
.4	-.2	-.1		-1.2	-2.9	-.4	1.7	-.1	
2.5	3.2	3.5	Net Profit + Depr., Dep.,						
(19) 1.2	(19) 1.4	(20) 2.3	Amort./Cur. Mat. L/T/D						
.6	.3	1.0							
.7	.5	.6		.3	.9	.6	.6	.7	
1.5	1.5	1.3	Fixed/Worth	1.2	2.5	.9	2.0	1.3	
5.8	10.7	6.1		-.5	-2.7	1.3	2.5	5.5	
1.0	.9	1.1		.9	1.2	.8	.8	1.0	
2.9	2.6	2.2	Debt/Worth	2.1	5.1	1.1	2.6	1.7	
15.2	20.6	13.0		-2.3	-7.6	3.1	4.1	10.6	
46.3	43.3	60.8	% Profit Before Taxes/Tangible		66.0	21.3	94.9		
(60) 18.3	(69) 11.6	(56) 14.8	Net Worth		(11) 17.7	14.1	(12) 36.2		
-6.5	-8.9	.9			-29.0	1.5	6.1		
11.8	13.1	16.4	% Profit Before Taxes/Total	38.3	15.3	10.4	21.2	33.7	
3.7	3.0	3.6	Assets	3.7	.5	3.4	10.2	2.4	
-3.1	-4.2	-5.4		-6.9	-12.1	.8	1.2	-5.8	
16.8	17.3	13.6		112.9	12.2	22.4	11.8	9.1	
6.2	7.8	7.8	Sales/Net Fixed Assets	12.5	5.6	8.2	5.7	7.4	
4.2	4.3	4.1		8.0	3.1	4.6	3.5	3.8	
3.1	3.4	3.1		5.9	3.0	3.2	2.8	3.3	
2.3	2.4	2.3	Sales/Total Assets	2.9	2.4	2.7	2.0	2.2	
1.8	1.6	1.5		2.0	1.5	1.6	1.4	1.8	
1.9	2.0	2.2		1.8	2.6		4.5	1.6	
(67) 4.2	(81) 3.9	(63) 5.5	% Depr., Dep., Amort./Sales	(10) 5.1	(16) 5.9	(12) 5.5	2.9		
6.4	6.1	7.3		7.0	10.1		8.6	5.7	
4.8	4.2	3.7	% Officers', Directors',		3.5				
(37) 5.8	(48) 5.9	(32) 6.5	Owners' Comp/Sales		(12) 5.6				
13.7	7.5	11.9			15.4				
823896M	630504M	922807M	Net Sales ($)	7354M	33385M	42365M	91517M	146969M	601217M
485930M	275784M	583415M	Total Assets ($)	3008M	16168M	19151M	58512M	66705M	419871M

M = $ thousand   MM = $ million
See Pages 11 through 18 for Explanation of Ratios and Data

ADMIN & WASTE MANAGEMENT SERVICES—Collection Agencies NAICS 561440 (SIC 7322, 7389)

Current Data Sorted By Assets							Comparative Historical Data	
1	3	14	17	4	1	**Type of Statement**		
4	4	11	2			Unqualified	23	25
4	4	3		4		Reviewed	16	14
10	4	2				Compiled	26	18
5	4	12	4	2		Tax Returns	13	8
						Other	27	23
		10 (4/1-9/30/02)		105 (10/1/02-3/31/03)			4/1/98-3/31/99	4/1/99-3/31/00
0-500M	500M-2MM	2-10MM	10-50MM	50-100MM	100-250MM		ALL	ALL
24	19	42	23	6	1	**NUMBER OF STATEMENTS**	105	88
%	%	%	%	%	%	**ASSETS**	%	%
34.6	18.7	24.8	18.2			Cash & Equivalents	17.7	23.6
18.2	18.4	27.4	20.7			Trade Receivables (net)	27.1	23.2
.5	.3	2.1	3.6			Inventory	.1	2.6
12.5	9.9	6.2	23.0			All Other Current	6.5	7.8
65.7	47.4	60.5	65.5			Total Current	51.5	57.2
24.4	30.3	18.1	15.3			Fixed Assets (net)	25.0	23.5
2.8	10.2	7.5	14.1			Intangibles (net)	13.8	9.7
7.0	12.1	13.8	5.2			All Other Non-Current	9.7	9.6
100.0	100.0	100.0	100.0			Total	100.0	100.0
						LIABILITIES		
20.4	15.6	8.9	12.9			Notes Payable-Short Term	12.4	13.3
10.7	3.2	6.3	7.6			Cur. Mat.-L/T/D	7.5	4.1
10.1	14.4	10.0	6.2			Trade Payables	11.5	11.1
.1	.3	2.1	.2			Income Taxes Payable	.2	.2
28.5	18.3	20.5	10.8			All Other Current	18.2	25.9
69.7	51.8	47.7	37.8			Total Current	49.8	54.6
31.4	26.4	10.4	14.7			Long Term Debt	21.7	13.8
.6	.0	.9	.2			Deferred Taxes	.3	.4
26.1	3.8	4.2	8.1			All Other Non-Current	3.9	4.9
-27.9	17.9	36.8	39.3			Net Worth	24.3	26.3
100.0	100.0	100.0	100.0			Total Liabilities & Net Worth	100.0	100.0
						INCOME DATA		
100.0	100.0	100.0	100.0			Net Sales	100.0	100.0
						Gross Profit		
94.5	98.6	89.9	84.1			Operating Expenses	89.6	90.0
5.5	1.4	10.1	15.9			Operating Profit	10.4	10.0
.8	1.2	1.2	3.3			All Other Expenses (net)	3.1	1.1
4.7	.2	8.9	12.6			Profit Before Taxes	7.4	8.9
						RATIOS		
4.1	1.7	2.0	4.6				2.4	1.7
1.2	1.0	1.2	1.6			Current	1.1	1.2
.5	.6	.9	1.2				.7	.8
3.2	1.5	1.8	1.9				2.2	1.5
.9	.8	1.2	.9			Quick	1.0	1.0
.3	.5	.8	.3				.6	.6
0 UND	6 58.9	6 62.8	7 50.8				7 51.0	3 145.9
0 UND	20 18.3	27 13.4	28 13.1			Sales/Receivables	26 13.9	26 13.9
19 19.0	27 13.4	61 6.0	49 7.4				50 7.2	42 8.7
						Cost of Sales/Inventory		
						Cost of Sales/Payables		
12.5	14.2	8.3	2.5				9.5	11.2
568.7	-999.8	37.3	4.3			Sales/Working Capital	70.3	38.7
-18.0	-23.5	-68.3	25.0				-19.3	-28.4
8.5	9.0	57.7	16.2				11.0	15.5
(17) 2.8	(16) 1.5	(35) 10.8	(20) 7.5			EBIT/Interest	(87) 4.3	(72) 5.0
.3	-.2	3.2	4.6				1.3	1.4
						Net Profit + Depr., Dep.,	10.6	4.4
						Amort./Cur. Mat. L /T/D	(22) 2.5	(16) 1.8
							1.3	.8
.3	.7	.2	.1				.3	.3
1.4	1.7	.6	.4			Fixed/Worth	1.0	1.1
-.4	-11.4	1.4	1.4				-5.0	11.3
.7	1.2	1.0	.6				.7	1.1
7.1	6.8	2.1	2.9			Debt/Worth	3.0	4.0
-2.7	-25.8	9.1	19.5				-8.6	29.5
224.0	79.5	104.8	81.8				77.0	108.2
(13) 4.5	(13) 18.3	(38) 64.5	(19) 64.2			% Profit Before Taxes/Tangible	(71) 42.3	(69) 38.7
-88.5	-3.3	21.4	28.2			Net Worth	13.7	6.6
44.3	47.9	36.7	25.1				30.0	29.7
16.2	2.0	15.8	11.8			% Profit Before Taxes/Total	10.4	9.2
-27.4	-2.0	4.6	4.6			Assets	.9	1.2
122.1	27.1	43.4	26.0				30.3	33.9
54.3	13.2	18.1	13.0			Sales/Net Fixed Assets	15.6	15.1
25.5	6.4	9.5	7.7				8.5	8.2
13.8	4.3	4.2	2.9				4.7	4.4
10.2	3.6	2.5	1.0			Sales/Total Assets	2.7	2.6
5.7	1.1	1.3	.5				1.2	1.6
.6	1.5	1.0	1.5				1.2	1.3
(17) 1.3	(15) 2.1	(34) 1.8	(22) 2.8			% Depr., Dep., Amort./Sales	(87) 2.3	(72) 2.2
2.1	3.8	2.7	3.5				3.7	3.4
7.6	3.6	2.3					5.7	6.0
(10) 10.2	(10) 7.5	(16) 7.0				% Officers', Directors',	(45) 11.2	(29) 10.6
17.2	13.8	12.1				Owners' Comp/Sales	18.0	19.9
40409M	63856M	619616M	699862M	884836M	326852M	Net Sales ($)	1662682M	1060216M
4795M	19656M	205319M	409404M	409219M	180531M	Total Assets ($)	1116584M	893022M

M = $ thousand   MM = $ million
See Pages 11 through 18 for Explanation of Ratios and Data

Comparative Historical Data   **Current Data Sorted By Sales**

			Type of Statement						
25	18	40	Unqualified	1	4	2	6	10	17
12	10	21	Reviewed	4	1	4	5	3	4
18	20	11	Compiled	2	3	2	4		
12	14	16	Tax Returns	8	3	4		1	
19	25	27	Other	1	6	2	8	5	5
4/1/00-3/31/01 ALL	4/1/01-3/31/02 ALL	4/1/02-3/31/03 ALL		10 (4/1-9/30/02)			105 (10/1/02-3/31/03)		
				0-1MM	1-3MM	3-5MM	5-10MM	10-25MM	25MM & OVER
86	87	115	**NUMBER OF STATEMENTS**	16	17	14	23	19	26
%	%	%	**ASSETS**	%	%	%	%	%	%
19.4	21.8	24.6	Cash & Equivalents	33.6	20.2	32.9	15.2	23.2	27.0
26.2	22.8	22.1	Trade Receivables (net)	22.8	21.0	15.7	21.7	19.0	28.6
1.6	2.7	1.6	Inventory	.7	.3	.1	4.2	3.8	.1
5.5	8.2	11.8	All Other Current	14.3	10.9	13.8	16.0	11.7	5.9
52.7	55.5	60.2	Total Current	71.4	52.4	62.5	57.1	57.7	61.7
24.2	21.0	20.5	Fixed Assets (net)	20.2	28.0	22.2	15.9	17.9	20.7
10.0	8.8	8.1	Intangibles (net)	1.7	7.7	4.0	18.3	8.1	5.5
13.0	14.7	11.2	All Other Non-Current	6.7	11.8	11.3	8.7	16.3	12.1
100.0	100.0	100.0	Total	100.0	100.0	100.0	100.0	100.0	100.0
			LIABILITIES						
17.8	11.8	13.1	Notes Payable-Short Term	14.8	33.3	10.7	16.3	2.4	5.1
6.5	13.2	7.7	Cur. Mat.-L/T/D	11.6	2.9	10.1	6.5	9.2	7.3
8.7	11.2	10.2	Trade Payables	4.4	12.0	16.4	10.7	6.7	11.2
.1	1.5	.9	Income Taxes Payable		.4	.0	.4	.3	3.0
20.0	19.0	19.3	All Other Current	26.7	22.6	11.9	15.6	19.6	19.6
53.1	56.6	51.2	Total Current	57.6	71.3	49.1	49.5	38.2	46.2
23.7	15.0	17.9	Long Term Debt	49.3	20.5	21.4	10.3	9.7	7.6
.3	.0	.5	Deferred Taxes	.0	.8	.2	1.5	.2	.1
5.0	6.9	9.4	All Other Non-Current	24.1	7.9	14.4	1.3	10.8	4.7
18.0	21.3	21.1	Net Worth	−31.0	−.6	15.0	37.3	41.2	41.5
100.0	100.0	100.0	Total Liabilities & Net Worth	100.0	100.0	100.0	100.0	100.0	100.0
			INCOME DATA						
100.0	100.0	100.0	Net Sales	100.0	100.0	100.0	100.0	100.0	100.0
			Gross Profit						
87.1	85.6	90.1	Operating Expenses	99.5	92.8	90.4	88.2	91.2	83.2
12.9	14.4	9.9	Operating Profit	.5	7.2	9.6	11.8	8.8	16.8
3.7	1.6	2.1	All Other Expenses (net)	1.8	1.6	2.4	1.3	1.9	3.2
9.2	12.7	7.8	Profit Before Taxes	−1.3	5.6	7.2	10.5	6.8	13.5
			RATIOS						
1.6	2.1	2.2		4.8	2.0	5.0	1.3	3.8	1.9
1.1	1.2	1.2	Current	1.7	1.0	1.4	1.2	1.3	1.4
.6	.7	.8		.8	.4	.7	.8	.9	1.0
1.6	1.6	1.9		3.9	1.8	3.7	1.2	2.3	1.7
.9	(86) 1.0	1.0	Quick	1.2	1.0	1.2	.7	1.0	1.3
.4	.4	.5		.4	.2	.5	.4	.8	.8
4 94.4	0 UND	2 208.1		0 UND	0 UND	0 UND	14 27.0	3 145.1	7 52.7
23 15.8	16 22.4	20 18.3	Sales/Receivables	16 22.8	16 22.7	0 UND	27 13.4	25 14.4	27 13.4
44 8.3	44 8.2	46 8.0		30 12.0	36 10.1	24 15.4	40 9.1	60 6.1	52 7.1
			Cost of Sales/Inventory						
			Cost of Sales/Payables						
12.2	6.6	6.9		4.7	12.9	3.9	3.4	4.1	13.8
85.5	51.1	35.8	Sales/Working Capital	35.0	999.8	80.4	66.3	16.7	26.5
−31.2	−25.0	−35.7		−27.0	−14.0	−46.3	−32.2	−57.2	NM
(72) 14.3	(70) 29.9	(95) 24.8		(12) 7.7	(14) 8.7	(10) 7.4	(21) 19.5	(14) 185.5	(24) 65.5
4.5	8.2	5.6	EBIT/Interest	1.0	3.6	1.8	5.6	15.2	18.0
1.6	1.9	1.8		−6.2	.3	1.2	2.5	5.3	4.9
(13) 13.8	(12) 24.7	(12) 6.5	Net Profit + Depr., Dep.,						
5.6	9.7	3.5	Amort./Cur. Mat. L/T/D						
2.9	3.3	1.7							
.4	.2	.2		.2	.5	.3	.1	.1	.1
1.0	.9	.8	Fixed/Worth	.7	4.7	1.2	1.1	.6	.8
6.0	19.3	2.8		NM	−.3	−12.2	4.9	.8	1.1
1.5	.9	.8		1.3	.7	.6	1.2	.4	.7
4.5	3.1	3.6	Debt/Worth	6.2	9.5	4.9	4.6	1.8	1.1
25.6	−99.9	19.5		−7.3	−2.5	−13.9	17.4	8.5	5.8
(67) 178.1	(65) 163.0	(89) 99.1	% Profit Before Taxes/Tangible	(11) 181.4			(19) 248.7	(17) 96.8	(24) 185.2
49.1	72.4	56.3	Net Worth	−5.4			75.7	56.3	71.9
11.3	21.6	9.9		−40.1			6.3	39.9	34.0
34.0	40.9	37.3	% Profit Before Taxes/Total	44.2	29.4	35.9	23.2	27.4	55.8
11.3	20.2	12.7	Assets	−1.0	15.4	3.0	10.6	14.0	34.5
2.5	3.2	1.9		−22.3	−12.0	1.0	1.9	9.8	7.4
26.5	54.4	50.6		122.1	73.0	48.7	24.3	101.7	47.2
15.3	19.7	21.1	Sales/Net Fixed Assets	46.8	21.5	26.3	18.7	15.7	17.6
9.4	11.0	9.9		14.6	8.2	8.3	9.9	11.1	9.5
4.4	5.6	5.6		11.7	10.0	10.1	3.4	4.1	5.5
3.3	2.9	2.8	Sales/Total Assets	4.8	3.6	3.9	1.4	2.2	3.4
2.0	1.6	1.3		.8	2.3	1.3	.9	1.4	2.0
(75) 1.6	(68) .9	(93) 1.2	% Depr., Dep., Amort./Sales	(10) .9	(14) 1.2	(12) .6	(21) 1.5	(15) 1.5	(21) .7
2.2	1.8	1.9		1.9	1.9	1.5	2.2	2.0	1.8
3.1	2.6	3.1		4.6	2.8	2.9	2.9	4.2	2.7
(25) 5.5	(37) 4.3	(44) 4.5	% Officers', Directors',				(12) 6.7		
9.6	8.0	7.9	Owners' Comp/Sales				10.4		
19.9	21.1	13.7					13.2		
1239227M	1492362M	2635431M	Net Sales ($)	10144M	33626M	52212M	169390M	314628M	2055431M
877082M	729063M	1228924M	Total Assets ($)	7430M	14265M	40199M	138700M	178983M	849347M

M = $ thousand   MM = $ million

See Pages 11 through 18 for Explanation of Ratios and Data

Current Data Sorted By Assets   Comparative Historical Data

<!-- Type of Statement -->

0-500M	500M-2MM	2-10MM	10-50MM	50-100MM	100-250MM	Type of Statement	4/1/98-3/31/99 ALL	4/1/99-3/31/00 ALL
4	9	43	39	20	20	Unqualified	152	190
13	42	56	14			Reviewed	167	196
35	70	41	4			Compiled	234	212
63	40	11	2			Tax Returns	164	163
49	88	85	33	17	14	Other	290	377
150 (4/1-9/30/02)			662 (10/1/02-3/31/03)					
164	249	236	92	37	34	NUMBER OF STATEMENTS	1007	1138

ASSETS (%)

0-500M	500M-2MM	2-10MM	10-50MM	50-100MM	100-250MM		ALL	ALL
19.1	14.6	13.4	11.4	12.5	13.4	Cash & Equivalents	15.0	13.9
29.8	35.1	33.8	35.1	25.9	25.3	Trade Receivables (net)	30.8	31.5
5.4	7.9	8.1	7.7	5.5	3.3	Inventory	6.9	8.8
3.8	5.2	4.7	4.0	9.0	6.2	All Other Current	4.2	4.4
58.1	62.8	60.0	58.2	53.0	48.2	Total Current	56.9	58.6
26.0	25.3	26.7	21.9	25.6	16.8	Fixed Assets (net)	28.6	27.7
4.6	4.6	5.4	11.5	16.2	21.5	Intangibles (net)	5.3	5.2
11.3	7.2	8.0	8.4	5.2	13.5	All Other Non-Current	9.2	8.5
100.0	100.0	100.0	100.0	100.0	100.0	Total	100.0	100.0

LIABILITIES

0-500M	500M-2MM	2-10MM	10-50MM	50-100MM	100-250MM		ALL	ALL
18.9	11.3	12.7	8.8	10.1	5.3	Notes Payable-Short Term	13.0	13.1
6.2	4.8	4.0	4.5	5.0	7.4	Cur. Mat.-L/T/D	4.8	4.5
14.0	16.2	14.6	17.6	11.9	14.6	Trade Payables	12.7	14.2
.1	.6	.7	.5	.5	1.0	Income Taxes Payable	.5	.4
25.6	17.2	15.3	15.6	13.3	16.0	All Other Current	17.5	18.1
64.8	50.0	47.3	47.0	40.8	44.3	Total Current	48.5	50.2
18.4	14.6	16.6	14.6	15.3	12.7	Long Term Debt	25.0	17.3
.1	.4	.6	1.0	.2	.4	Deferred Taxes	.5	.4
11.9	4.8	4.3	7.4	8.4	6.8	All Other Non-Current	7.9	6.4
4.9	30.2	31.2	30.0	35.2	35.8	Net Worth	18.1	25.6
100.0	100.0	100.0	100.0	100.0	100.0	Total Liabilities & Net Worth	100.0	100.0

INCOME DATA

0-500M	500M-2MM	2-10MM	10-50MM	50-100MM	100-250MM		ALL	ALL
100.0	100.0	100.0	100.0	100.0	100.0	Net Sales	100.0	100.0
						Gross Profit		
94.1	94.3	93.8	90.7	93.7	88.5	Operating Expenses	142.7	92.0
5.9	5.7	6.2	9.3	6.3	11.5	Operating Profit	−42.7	8.0
1.7	.9	2.2	4.1	3.8	5.2	All Other Expenses (net)	.6	1.6
4.2	4.8	4.0	5.2	2.5	6.3	Profit Before Taxes	−43.3	6.4

RATIOS

0-500M	500M-2MM	2-10MM	10-50MM	50-100MM	100-250MM		ALL	ALL
2.1	2.1	2.0	1.6	1.9	1.4	Current	2.5	2.3
1.0	1.2	1.2	1.3	1.3	1.0		1.3	1.4
.5	.9	.9	.9	.9	.7		.9	.9
(162) 1.8	1.6	1.7	1.3	1.6	1.1	Quick	(1003) 2.1	(1137) 1.8
.9	1.0	1.0	1.0	.9	.8		1.1	1.0
.5	.6	.6	.7	.7	.6		.6	.6
0 UND	16 22.9	26 14.2	32 11.3	39 9.4	29 12.5	Sales/Receivables	14 27.0	18 20.3
22 16.8	36 10.0	47 7.8	52 7.0	53 6.9	63 5.8		38 9.7	41 8.9
45 8.1	64 5.7	66 5.6	89 4.1	81 4.5	76 4.8		61 6.0	64 5.7
						Cost of Sales/Inventory		
						Cost of Sales/Payables		
13.3	8.9	7.6	8.3	5.7	8.6	Sales/Working Capital	7.3	6.9
325.1	31.3	19.5	19.9	16.8	129.5		20.2	20.2
−22.1	−61.9	−35.2	−53.5	−41.7	−14.2		−39.8	−51.4
8.9	15.9	11.9	16.7	9.7	22.4	EBIT/Interest	12.7	11.9
(115) 3.2	(216) 4.2	(199) 3.5	(79) 4.7	(32) 2.3	(31) 4.5		(813) 3.7	(930) 3.8
.2	1.3	1.1	1.4	−2.4	1.2		1.3	1.3
	5.2	8.4	8.1	4.2	11.0	Net Profit + Depr., Dep., Amort./Cur. Mat. L /T/D	5.4	7.8
	(37) 1.7	(51) 2.6	(32) 2.3	(10) 1.2	(10) 2.2		(208) 2.4	(195) 2.8
	.6	1.2	1.1	.2	−.2		1.2	1.2
.1	.3	.2	.2	.4	.4	Fixed/Worth	.2	.3
1.1	.8	.9	1.2	1.7	1.2		.8	.9
−4.2	3.5	2.9	2.7	−2.7	−2.4		4.0	4.0
1.1	.9	1.0	1.6	1.2	2.3	Debt/Worth	.8	.9
4.1	2.4	2.4	2.7	3.3	9.7		2.3	2.4
−7.9	17.5	11.0	15.1	−20.2	−5.8		10.4	14.5
130.1	61.8	53.6	55.2	68.4	108.4	% Profit Before Taxes/Tangible Net Worth	76.5	74.5
(109) 40.0	(198) 23.1	(193) 23.7	(76) 27.9	(26) 23.3	(24) 42.7		(821) 33.2	(926) 33.3
5.7	2.2	3.9	11.3	−1.2	2.0		8.3	8.2
31.9	20.1	15.1	13.1	10.1	14.8	% Profit Before Taxes/Total Assets	25.1	22.4
10.6	7.6	5.1	8.0	3.1	6.5		8.8	8.9
.0	.5	.2	1.0	−4.0	−.1		1.1	1.2
114.1	50.4	39.9	48.6	28.6	28.4	Sales/Net Fixed Assets	41.2	40.0
30.6	16.8	12.6	14.4	8.8	10.0		14.6	14.1
12.4	8.4	5.0	5.8	4.2	5.3		5.6	5.4
7.3	4.4	3.4	3.0	2.5	2.0	Sales/Total Assets	4.3	4.0
4.5	2.9	2.4	1.8	1.4	1.4		2.7	2.6
2.9	1.9	1.3	.9	.7	.6		1.5	1.5
1.0	.7	1.0	.9	2.2	1.1	% Depr., Dep., Amort./Sales	.9	.9
(104) 1.8	(212) 1.6	(195) 2.7	(71) 2.2	(25) 3.5	(22) 2.7		(812) 2.2	(935) 2.2
3.6	3.9	5.4	3.8	6.1	4.1		4.7	4.6
5.8	3.2	1.9	1.9			% Officers', Directors', Owners' Comp/Sales	3.5	3.2
(91) 10.3	(105) 6.9	(72) 3.7	(14) 3.5				(399) 7.2	(400) 6.0
17.6	11.3	7.2	6.9				12.9	11.5
210040M	1119473M	2677292M	4404251M	4392533M	6957234M	Net Sales ($)	16724116M	26925460M
38775M	280888M	1117845M	2148364M	2653611M	5171598M	Total Assets ($)	9080943M	13881862M

M = $ thousand   MM = $ million
See Pages 11 through 18 for Explanation of Ratios and Data

Comparative Historical Data   **Current Data Sorted By Sales**

	4/1/00-3/31/01 ALL	4/1/01-3/31/02 ALL	4/1/02-3/31/03 ALL	Type of Statement	150 (4/1-9/30/02) 0-1MM	1-3MM	3-5MM	662 (10/1/02-3/31/03) 5-10MM	10-25MM	25MM & OVER
	166	146	135	Unqualified	4	12	8	10	29	72
	177	147	125	Reviewed	11	29	18	29	26	12
	256	241	150	Compiled	21	42	38	22	20	7
	138	138	116	Tax Returns	50	40	11	10	3	2
	353	317	286	Other	32	70	37	42	41	64
NUMBER OF STATEMENTS	1090	989	812		118	193	112	113	119	157
	%	%	%	**ASSETS**	%	%	%	%	%	%
	14.0	14.0	14.7	Cash & Equivalents	20.2	14.7	12.7	13.0	13.8	13.8
	32.4	32.2	32.8	Trade Receivables (net)	21.4	31.1	35.3	37.4	39.0	33.9
	7.9	6.9	7.1	Inventory	4.4	6.9	9.4	8.9	6.4	7.0
	4.1	4.7	4.8	All Other Current	4.3	5.9	4.1	3.5	4.4	5.8
	58.4	57.8	59.5	Total Current	50.2	58.6	61.6	62.7	63.5	60.4
	26.7	27.0	25.1	Fixed Assets (net)	32.0	27.1	23.5	25.3	23.1	20.0
	5.7	6.6	6.9	Intangibles (net)	6.0	4.4	5.7	5.3	7.3	12.2
	9.2	8.6	8.6	All Other Non-Current	11.7	9.9	9.2	6.6	6.0	7.4
	100.0	100.0	100.0	Total	100.0	100.0	100.0	100.0	100.0	100.0
				LIABILITIES						
	14.2	15.8	12.6	Notes Payable-Short Term	18.1	13.9	13.4	13.3	11.3	7.1
	6.1	4.9	4.9	Cur. Mat.-L/T/D	6.1	4.5	5.5	4.5	4.7	4.7
	14.9	13.7	15.2	Trade Payables	11.2	15.7	15.1	16.4	14.8	17.0
	.5	.5	.5	Income Taxes Payable	.1	.6	.2	.5	.9	.7
	16.7	17.0	17.9	All Other Current	26.7	13.9	15.6	17.9	17.3	18.3
	52.6	51.8	51.2	Total Current	62.2	48.6	49.8	52.5	49.1	47.8
	17.4	17.5	15.9	Long Term Debt	24.2	16.5	19.4	13.6	11.6	11.3
	.6	.5	.4	Deferred Taxes	.1	.4	.5	.4	.8	.6
	8.6	6.6	6.6	All Other Non-Current	7.6	8.0	4.3	6.4	5.6	6.9
	20.9	23.6	25.8	Net Worth	6.0	26.6	25.9	27.1	32.9	33.4
	100.0	100.0	100.0	Total Liabilities & Net Worth	100.0	100.0	100.0	100.0	100.0	100.0
				INCOME DATA						
	100.0	100.0	100.0	Net Sales	100.0	100.0	100.0	100.0	100.0	100.0
				Gross Profit						
	93.6	93.6	93.4	Operating Expenses	88.9	91.9	95.8	95.9	94.8	94.1
	6.4	6.4	6.6	Operating Profit	11.1	8.1	4.2	4.1	5.2	5.8
	1.6	1.9	2.1	All Other Expenses (net)	3.4	3.1	1.1	1.0	2.2	1.5
	4.8	4.5	4.4	Profit Before Taxes	7.7	5.0	3.1	3.1	3.0	4.4
				RATIOS						
	2.2	2.3	1.9		2.6	2.4	2.1	1.8	1.9	1.7
	1.3	1.3	1.2	Current	1.0	1.2	1.2	1.2	1.2	1.3
	.9	.8	.8		.5	.8	.9	.8	.9	.9
	(1089) 1.8	1.7	(810) 1.6		(117) 1.8	(192) 1.7	1.7	1.6	1.7	1.4
	1.0	1.0	1.0	Quick	.8	.9	1.0	1.0	1.0	1.0
	.6	.6	.6		.3	.6	.6	.6	.7	.7
	18 20.5	17 21.9	17 21.6		0 UND	8 44.0	21 17.7	21 17.7	29 12.7	31 12.0
	43 8.6	40 9.0	40 9.1	Sales/Receivables	21 17.6	37 9.8	41 8.8	40 9.2	46 8.0	50 7.3
	68 5.4	64 5.7	65 5.6		56 6.5	65 5.6	65 5.6	66 5.5	64 5.7	66 5.5
				Cost of Sales/Inventory						
				Cost of Sales/Payables						
	7.5	7.9	8.8		8.4	7.3	8.8	9.2	9.6	8.9
	23.3	25.0	30.4	Sales/Working Capital	UND	44.3	28.5	27.9	26.9	21.1
	-45.0	-31.9	-33.8		-9.2	-30.7	-62.0	-56.6	-64.8	-63.4
	(898) 10.7	(842) 10.3	(672) 12.9		(79) 8.5	(149) 13.2	(102) 7.3	(103) 17.4	(99) 13.8	(140) 19.7
	3.4	3.2	3.7	EBIT/Interest	2.6	3.5	2.3	3.5	4.2	6.2
	1.1	.8	1.1		.0	1.1	.6	1.1	1.8	1.5
	(200) 6.0	(184) 5.9	(149) 5.9			(18) 7.1	(24) 2.9	(24) 5.3	(29) 21.5	(48) 5.3
	2.1	2.2	2.2	Net Profit + Depr., Dep., Amort./Cur. Mat. L/T/D		2.5	1.5	1.4	3.4	2.2
	1.0	.8	.9			-.3	.6	.0	1.9	1.1
	.3	.2	.2		.1	.2	.3	.3	.2	.3
	.9	.9	.9	Fixed/Worth	1.5	.9	.8	.9	.8	1.0
	5.1	4.6	5.5		-26.0	5.4	NM	3.3	2.6	2.8
	.9	.9	1.1		.9	.9	.9	1.2	1.0	1.4
	2.6	2.6	2.7	Debt/Worth	4.5	2.4	3.0	2.4	2.5	2.8
	16.5	17.4	38.9		-7.9	61.0	-108.4	15.2	10.2	16.6
	(873) 68.6	(782) 64.8	(626) 66.0		(79) 93.6	(147) 66.0	(83) 47.9	(93) 54.4	(98) 65.9	(126) 74.4
	31.2	26.1	25.3	% Profit Before Taxes/Tangible Net Worth	22.0	24.2	15.5	16.0	34.1	31.0
	6.6	4.4	4.2		.0	4.2	-.7	2.0	14.3	12.3
	21.0	19.2	19.0		20.5	21.4	15.6	19.6	20.7	15.9
	7.2	6.4	6.9	% Profit Before Taxes/Total Assets	4.6	6.1	3.4	6.2	8.8	8.0
	.6	-.4	.1		-1.6	.3	-.9	.4	1.6	1.3
	41.8	44.8	52.4		69.6	51.6	47.4	45.4	67.0	48.3
	15.3	16.4	16.5	Sales/Net Fixed Assets	16.0	16.9	17.5	16.8	18.4	14.5
	6.1	6.3	6.7		4.1	7.0	8.6	8.0	6.8	6.5
	4.0	4.1	4.2		4.3	4.3	4.4	4.8	4.3	3.5
	2.6	2.7	2.7	Sales/Total Assets	2.5	2.6	2.9	3.2	2.8	2.3
	1.4	1.6	1.6		1.0	1.4	1.9	1.9	1.8	1.4
	(876) .7	(764) .9	(629) .9		(80) 1.3	(142) 1.2	(94) .9	(95) .7	(102) .7	(116) .9
	2.6	2.1	2.1	% Depr., Dep., Amort./Sales	3.4	2.2	1.7	1.9	2.4	2.0
	4.5	4.5	4.6		7.6	4.0	4.4	4.6	4.9	3.7
	(409) 3.1	(371) 3.5	(285) 3.2		(52) 7.9	(81) 5.1	(51) 3.6	(43) 2.1	(38) 1.8	(20) 1.7
	6.3	6.7	6.7	% Officers', Directors', Owners' Comp/Sales	13.1	8.5	5.8	3.8	2.6	3.0
	12.6	12.4	12.1		19.5	16.1	9.5			4.4
	25049185M	23008467M	19760823M	Net Sales ($)	65704M	369024M	440611M	848251M	1801483M	16235750M
	15472240M	12198216M	11411081M	Total Assets ($)	86234M	351555M	233301M	368830M	1208488M	9162673M

M = $ thousand   MM = $ million
See Pages 11 through 18 for Explanation of Ratios and Data

Current Data Sorted By Assets   Comparative Historical Data

0-500M	500M-2MM	2-10MM	10-50MM	50-100MM	100-250MM	Type of Statement	4/1/98-3/31/99 ALL	4/1/99-3/31/00 ALL
1		3	7	4	1	1	Unqualified	18	6
1		3	10	3	1		Reviewed	17	18
18	6	6	2			Compiled	54	39
15	4	1				Tax Returns	29	17
9	15	15	10	5	1	1	Other	47	36
	24 (4/1-9/30/02)		101 (10/1/02-3/31/03)					
44	28	34	14	3	2	**NUMBER OF STATEMENTS**	165	116

0-500M %	500M-2MM %	2-10MM %	10-50MM %	50-100MM %	100-250MM %	ASSETS	%	%
35.8	21.4	28.5	32.0			Cash & Equivalents	26.1	27.2
17.5	22.0	26.9	24.8			Trade Receivables (net)	24.6	23.6
.8	.9	.9	.0			Inventory	.9	.5
4.6	5.0	3.5	3.6			All Other Current	3.2	4.2
58.7	49.4	59.7	60.4			Total Current	54.9	55.4
21.2	20.7	20.8	7.2			Fixed Assets (net)	20.1	19.1
3.3	11.3	5.7	11.2			Intangibles (net)	10.4	10.2
16.9	18.7	13.8	21.2			All Other Non-Current	14.5	15.3
100.0	100.0	100.0	100.0			Total	100.0	100.0

						LIABILITIES		
23.5	7.7	2.1	2.3			Notes Payable-Short Term	14.2	9.4
2.0	7.6	3.0	.4			Cur. Mat.-L/T/D	6.4	3.7
32.8	19.5	18.3	27.5			Trade Payables	18.0	20.9
.3	.2	.2	3.0			Income Taxes Payable	.4	.3
22.2	27.7	30.1	40.4			All Other Current	31.0	28.1
80.7	62.8	53.7	73.6			Total Current	70.1	62.3
10.3	11.3	7.2	5.1			Long Term Debt	13.9	13.3
.0	.0	.4	.1			Deferred Taxes	.4	.6
57.8	16.3	3.0	.9			All Other Non-Current	9.4	3.4
-48.8	9.5	35.6	20.4			Net Worth	6.3	20.3
100.0	100.0	100.0	100.0			Total Liabilities & Net Worth	100.0	100.0

						INCOME DATA		
100.0	100.0	100.0	100.0			Net Sales	100.0	100.0
						Gross Profit		
101.1	102.6	96.8	98.3			Operating Expenses	98.2	97.3
-1.1	-2.6	3.2	1.7			Operating Profit	1.8	2.7
.1	.8	-1.0	-.4			All Other Expenses (net)	68.4	.1
-1.2	-3.5	4.2	2.1			Profit Before Taxes	-66.6	2.6

						RATIOS		
2.0	1.9	1.7	1.1			Current	1.9	1.7
1.0	.8	1.0	.9				1.1	1.0
.5	.4	.7	.5				.6	.6
2.0	1.5	1.6	1.1			Quick	1.7	1.5
.8	.7	1.0	.9			(164)	.9	.9
.4	.4	.6	.4				.5	.6
0 UND	2 147.8	4 81.8	1 252.0			Sales/Receivables	2 235.5	2 203.8
2 165.8	10 37.4	24 15.3	21 17.0				10 34.8	7 54.2
13 27.5	21 17.5	51 7.2	55 6.6				36 10.0	23 16.0
						Cost of Sales/Inventory		
						Cost of Sales/Payables		
71.5	25.3	12.0	30.4			Sales/Working Capital	22.6	48.0
806.4	-98.6	557.0	-173.1				363.7	588.1
-28.3	-7.7	-30.8	-6.0				-28.3	-37.4
(27) 5.8	(19) 5.8	(26) 99.2				EBIT/Interest	8.1	14.8
.9	-.1	9.3					(117) 3.0	(80) 3.8
-6.3	-6.5	1.7					-.5	1.0
		(11) 9.5				Net Profit + Depr., Dep., Amort./Cur. Mat. L /T/D	9.4	5.9
		5.6					(31) 4.2	(15) 2.6
		-.8					1.2	1.4
.1	.3	.2	.3			Fixed/Worth	.2	.3
.9	16.2	.5	.8				.8	.9
-.3	-.7	1.7	-.7				-3.2	-5.5
.9	1.3	1.0	2.6			Debt/Worth	1.1	1.2
3.7	45.8	3.1	20.4				4.5	3.5
-2.8	-4.6	7.8	-45.8				-7.8	-43.8
(25) 17.5	(15) 141.9	(30) 56.6				% Profit Before Taxes/Tangible Net Worth	74.2	86.4
1.9	24.2	24.3					(114) 22.9	(84) 33.7
-26.7	-9.1	6.3					.1	7.5
13.6	12.3	16.4	6.9			% Profit Before Taxes/Total Assets	15.8	18.1
.6	.0	6.9	4.6				6.2	8.6
-21.4	-12.8	1.9	1.6				-4.0	.8
841.3	232.2	81.2	189.1			Sales/Net Fixed Assets	278.0	165.8
121.8	74.0	36.1	60.2				50.1	55.4
25.5	14.2	12.5	28.5				16.1	15.7
29.6	22.3	5.9	4.3			Sales/Total Assets	18.3	19.9
10.5	5.3	3.5	2.8				5.4	6.7
4.1	2.1	1.4	1.7				2.2	2.2
(25) .1	(21) .2	(29) .3	(11) .3			% Depr., Dep., Amort./Sales	(127) .2	(88) .2
.4	.8	.7	.6				.8	.7
1.5	2.4	2.8	1.4				2.1	2.5
(24) 1.2	(13) 2.3					% Officers', Directors', Owners' Comp/Sales	1.3	1.1
3.0	3.0						(61) 2.7	(43) 4.6
7.5	3.5						9.6	10.1
118851M	547572M	813228M	1001075M	383804M	758897M	Net Sales ($)	5669837M	6646143M
6663M	33919M	173204M	280161M	263846M	389244M	Total Assets ($)	1805474M	904162M

M = $ thousand   MM = $ million
See Pages 11 through 18 for Explanation of Ratios and Data

Comparative Historical Data				Current Data Sorted By Sales					
			Type of Statement	2	2	2		2	8
11	10	14	Unqualified		2	2		2	8
19	10	18	Reviewed	1	1	1	4	6	5
32	27	32	Compiled	9	6	3	5	1	8
20	12	20	Tax Returns	10	4	2	2	1	1
38	26	41	Other	3	2	12	4	7	13
4/1/00-3/31/01 ALL	4/1/01-3/31/02 ALL	4/1/02-3/31/03 ALL		24 (4/1-9/30/02)			101 (10/1/02-3/31/03)		
				0-1MM	1-3MM	3-5MM	5-10MM	10-25MM	25MM & OVER
120	85	125	NUMBER OF STATEMENTS	23	15	20	15	17	35
%	%	%	ASSETS	%	%	%	%	%	%
25.5	28.7	29.1	Cash & Equivalents	32.6	32.5	24.5	28.7	26.8	29.0
25.2	22.3	21.9	Trade Receivables (net)	16.2	9.8	16.1	28.8	30.9	26.9
.9	.9	.7	Inventory	1.4	.0	.3	.1	1.2	.8
4.2	6.9	4.3	All Other Current	4.5	4.4	3.1	1.6	5.6	5.4
55.7	58.9	56.0	Total Current	54.8	46.8	44.0	59.1	64.6	62.1
19.2	15.6	19.0	Fixed Assets (net)	25.6	24.1	27.6	10.9	14.6	13.1
11.3	11.6	8.0	Intangibles (net)	4.3	1.6	14.5	12.5	.9	11.1
13.9	14.0	17.0	All Other Non-Current	15.3	27.7	14.0	17.5	19.8	13.7
100.0	100.0	100.0	Total	100.0	100.0	100.0	100.0	100.0	100.0
			LIABILITIES						
11.6	15.1	11.1	Notes Payable-Short Term	29.6	24.4	4.6	.9	8.8	2.3
6.0	3.5	3.4	Cur. Mat.-L/T/D	3.9	.9	4.0	4.1	.5	4.8
18.9	15.2	24.6	Trade Payables	28.2	24.3	20.2	22.2	23.6	26.5
.8	.5	.5	Income Taxes Payable	.0	.0	.2	.0	.9	1.3
27.3	35.5	27.9	All Other Current	23.5	21.1	23.6	37.3	25.6	33.5
64.6	69.8	67.5	Total Current	85.2	70.7	52.7	64.6	59.4	68.4
19.8	12.6	9.7	Long Term Debt	13.8	3.4	14.4	11.2	6.5	7.7
.3	.0	.1	Deferred Taxes	.0	.7	.0	.0	.2	.1
10.4	5.4	25.2	All Other Non-Current	43.7	98.6	13.9	9.5	3.5	5.4
4.8	12.2	-2.6	Net Worth	-42.7	-73.4	19.0	14.7	30.4	18.4
100.0	100.0	100.0	Total Liabilities & Net Worth	100.0	100.0	100.0	100.0	100.0	100.0
			INCOME DATA						
100.0	100.0	100.0	Net Sales	100.0	100.0	100.0	100.0	100.0	100.0
			Gross Profit						
97.0	98.7	99.5	Operating Expenses	101.3	100.4	101.6	100.1	95.3	98.4
2.9	1.3	.5	Operating Profit	-1.3	-.4	-1.6	-.1	4.7	1.6
-.3	.2	.0	All Other Expenses (net)	1.2	-1.5	.3	-.5	.5	-.1
3.2	1.1	.5	Profit Before Taxes	-2.4	1.1	-1.9	.4	4.2	1.8
			RATIOS						
1.7	1.5	1.7		1.6	2.3	1.9	1.9	2.8	1.2
1.0	1.0	1.0	Current	1.0	.7	.7	1.0	1.1	.9
.6	.6	.5		.2	.4	.4	.6	.7	.6
1.6	1.3	1.5		1.6	1.8	1.8	1.9	1.9	1.1
(119) .9	.9	.9	Quick	.8	.7	.7	1.0	1.0	.9
.6	.5	.5		.2	.4	.3	.6	.7	.5
2 223.5	1 243.4	1 362.9		1 454.0	0 UND	2 229.5	0 UND	2 149.5	3 121.5
10 36.1	12 29.5	8 43.1	Sales/Receivables	12 30.6	0 UND	6 65.8	21 17.3	30 12.1	6 63.8
32 11.3	32 11.4	30 12.1		26 13.9	23 15.8	19 19.6	32 11.4	63 5.8	30 12.0
			Cost of Sales/Inventory						
			Cost of Sales/Payables						
27.7	23.2	24.0		14.0	12.4	17.5	70.5	15.8	46.2
507.7	999.8	-315.5	Sales/Working Capital	-88.0	-133.2	-37.4	-872.7	999.8	-325.2
-23.7	-16.1	-18.0		-13.1	-7.7	-9.4	-49.9	-14.6	-28.5
14.0	24.8	10.2		3.0		4.6	12.1	110.0	26.7
(78) 3.6	(63) 3.1	(82) 3.4	EBIT/Interest	(15) -1.7		(14) -.1	(10) 7.9	(13) 10.3	(22) 5.6
1.1	-1.1	-2.0		-6.3		-3.1	-5.3	.6	2.4
11.8	4.8	21.0							
(14) 3.8	(10) 1.2	(17) 6.1	Net Profit + Depr., Dep., Amort./Cur. Mat. L/T/D						
1.9	-4.5	.7							
.2	.3	.2		.1	.3	.3	.1	.1	.3
.7	.7	.7	Fixed/Worth	.8	1.2	1.9	.5	.3	.5
-14.3	-2.7	-1.6		-1.5	-.1	-1.1	-.2	NM	-3.5
1.1	1.8	1.2		.9	.7	.9	.7	.4	2.9
4.2	3.9	4.9	Debt/Worth	4.6	2.9	3.6	7.2	2.5	11.1
-11.5	-14.5	-7.0		-3.0	-2.3	-5.4	-3.5	-51.3	-23.6
74.6	64.1	39.9		9.2		53.6		40.1	390.0
(82) 31.8	(57) 19.1	(80) 17.8	% Profit Before Taxes/Tangible Net Worth	(14) 1.0		(14) 14.3		(12) 27.2	(23) 24.2
4.1	-6.0	.0		-62.5		-9.6		9.7	13.1
18.0	11.2	12.4		3.5	22.4	10.6	13.9	13.3	15.6
8.0	2.9	4.0	% Profit Before Taxes/Total Assets	-.6	2.0	.6	7.7	6.8	5.9
.5	-5.4	-5.1		-34.8	-15.9	-9.9	-25.8	-1.2	1.8
193.3	126.8	240.1		172.5	280.6	109.5	610.0	185.9	242.6
60.4	47.2	55.7	Sales/Net Fixed Assets	38.3	21.0	19.0	211.1	47.8	65.7
12.9	19.9	15.0		7.7	13.3	7.9	49.0	21.2	36.1
18.3	7.8	13.7		9.5	23.1	6.9	37.0	18.8	17.6
5.0	4.7	4.4	Sales/Total Assets	3.8	5.5	3.1	8.4	3.6	5.9
1.9	2.0	2.0		1.9	1.8	1.9	2.3	1.9	2.9
.2	.2	.2		.6	.3	.8		.2	.2
(87) .8	(65) .7	(89) .7	% Depr., Dep., Amort./Sales	(14) 1.2	(11) 1.5	(13) 2.7		(13) .5	(29) .4
2.6	2.2	2.1		3.1	3.3	8.1		1.1	.9
1.2	1.5	1.1		2.7					.4
(55) 4.2	(31) 5.9	(50) 2.8	% Officers', Directors', Owners' Comp/Sales	(14) 5.4				(10) .7	
10.0	11.2	5.9		16.4					2.6
5111736M	3261409M	3623427M	Net Sales ($)	10966M	28989M	73731M	105278M	282683M	3121780M
1062804M	754305M	1147037M	Total Assets ($)	4202M	13096M	31028M	31448M	156332M	910931M

M = $ thousand   MM = $ million
See Pages 11 through 18 for Explanation of Ratios and Data

ADMIN & WASTE MANAGEMENT SERVICES—Tour Operators   NAICS 561520   (SIC 4725)

| Current Data Sorted By Assets | | | | | | | Comparative Historical Data | |

0-500M	500M-2MM	2-10MM	10-50MM	50-100MM	100-250MM	Type of Statement	4/1/98-3/31/99 ALL	4/1/99-3/31/00 ALL
		1	5	1		Unqualified	2	2
	1	5				Reviewed	4	
3	3	7				Compiled	10	6
1	1	1				Tax Returns	5	2
	4	4	2	2		Other	11	7
	3 (4/1-9/30/02)		38 (10/1/02-3/31/03)					
4	9	18	7	3		NUMBER OF STATEMENTS	32	17
%	%	%	%	%	%		%	%
						ASSETS		
		25.6				Cash & Equivalents	22.1	33.7
		14.6			D	Trade Receivables (net)	11.2	9.4
		2.5			A	Inventory	1.8	1.5
		7.5			T	All Other Current	5.4	5.2
		50.1			A	Total Current	40.4	49.8
		35.7				Fixed Assets (net)	41.5	32.1
		3.2			N	Intangibles (net)	4.5	7.8
		10.9			O	All Other Non-Current	13.6	10.3
		100.0			T	Total	100.0	100.0
						LIABILITIES		
		1.0			A	Notes Payable-Short Term	13.7	5.5
		7.6			V	Cur. Mat.-L/T/D	2.8	1.8
		16.1			A	Trade Payables	9.9	11.6
		.4			I	Income Taxes Payable	.1	.2
		33.2			L	All Other Current	21.9	33.4
		58.4			A	Total Current	48.4	52.5
		26.0			B	Long Term Debt	30.1	22.7
		.6			L	Deferred Taxes	.4	.0
		1.9			E	All Other Non-Current	6.9	19.0
		13.1				Net Worth	14.2	5.8
		100.0				Total Liabilities & Net Worth	100.0	100.0
						INCOME DATA		
		100.0				Net Sales	100.0	100.0
						Gross Profit		
		97.0				Operating Expenses	96.7	97.7
		3.0				Operating Profit	3.3	2.3
		2.0				All Other Expenses (net)	.9	1.0
		1.1				Profit Before Taxes	2.4	1.3
						RATIOS		
		1.5				Current	1.6	2.0
		1.0					.8	1.0
		.7					.4	.6
		1.4				Quick	1.2	1.8
		.8					.7	.8
		.6					.2	.5
		2 233.9				Sales/Receivables	0 UND	0 UND
		10 36.2					1 442.7	3 128.2
		46 7.9					16 23.1	31 11.8
						Cost of Sales/Inventory		
						Cost of Sales/Payables		
		17.8				Sales/Working Capital	28.3	18.7
		93.8					−29.8	283.9
		−24.5					−8.8	−16.0
		(12) 7.4				EBIT/Interest	(23) 4.7	(13) 12.5
		.8					3.0	1.7
		−.1					.0	−.7
						Net Profit + Depr., Dep., Amort./Cur. Mat. L /T/D		
		.7				Fixed/Worth	.3	.6
		1.4					1.7	1.6
		7.4					−24.2	−.3
		1.3				Debt/Worth	1.1	.8
		4.8					4.3	3.9
		25.8					−27.3	−3.8
		(15) 46.0				% Profit Before Taxes/Tangible Net Worth	(23) 82.9	(11) 66.6
		24.2					45.2	60.1
		−6.4					9.5	8.2
		16.6				% Profit Before Taxes/Total Assets	17.6	37.7
		2.7					7.4	4.1
		−4.7					.8	−3.5
		79.2				Sales/Net Fixed Assets	80.4	161.5
		10.5					6.2	18.6
		2.4					1.6	2.5
		5.4				Sales/Total Assets	4.3	8.2
		1.8					2.3	2.6
		1.3					1.0	1.2
		(17) .4				% Depr., Dep., Amort./Sales	(23) .4	(14) .1
		3.3					2.0	3.6
		8.3					6.8	6.0
						% Officers', Directors', Owners' Comp/Sales	(12) 1.1	
							3.6	
							13.7	
7016M	30483M	288813M	383812M	203075M		Net Sales ($)	192713M	689459M
1185M	10125M	74099M	163189M	192651M		Total Assets ($)	104354M	568658M

© RMA 2003

M = $ thousand   MM = $ million
See Pages 11 through 18 for Explanation of Ratios and Data

Comparative Historical Data				Current Data Sorted By Sales					

Type of Statement

				Type of Statement						
4	9	7	Unqualified			1	1	5		
	4	6	Reviewed		1	2	2	1		
7	13	13	Compiled	3	5	3	2			
5	4	3	Tax Returns	1	1		1			
9	20	12	Other		2	3		4	3	
4/1/00- 3/31/01 ALL	4/1/01- 3/31/02 ALL	4/1/02- 3/31/03 ALL			3 (4/1-9/30/02)			38 (10/1/02-3/31/03)		
				0-1MM	1-3MM	3-5MM	5-10MM	10-25MM	25MM & OVER
25	50	41	NUMBER OF STATEMENTS	4	8	7	6	7	9

%	%	%	ASSETS	%	%	%	%	%	%
35.1	22.8	27.7	Cash & Equivalents						
7.7	6.7	11.2	Trade Receivables (net)						
1.9	1.4	2.1	Inventory						
3.9	8.4	7.4	All Other Current						
48.6	39.3	48.5	Total Current						
36.8	43.7	38.4	Fixed Assets (net)						
6.9	4.5	2.6	Intangibles (net)						
7.7	12.5	10.5	All Other Non-Current						
100.0	100.0	100.0	Total						

			LIABILITIES						
14.8	11.7	2.2	Notes Payable-Short Term						
3.4	7.3	4.8	Cur. Mat.-L/T/D						
7.1	10.0	11.1	Trade Payables						
.4	.1	.2	Income Taxes Payable						
25.8	21.4	30.2	All Other Current						
51.5	50.4	48.6	Total Current						
24.2	28.8	30.8	Long Term Debt						
.1	.7	.4	Deferred Taxes						
3.3	14.2	3.0	All Other Non-Current						
21.0	6.0	17.2	Net Worth						
100.0	100.0	100.0	Total Liabilities & Net Worth						

			INCOME DATA						
100.0	100.0	100.0	Net Sales						
			Gross Profit						
97.0	98.2	92.8	Operating Expenses						
3.0	1.8	7.2	Operating Profit						
3.3	1.0	2.9	All Other Expenses (net)						
-.3	.8	4.3	Profit Before Taxes						

			RATIOS						
1.4	1.6	1.7							
1.2	1.1	1.1	Current						
.9	.4	.8							
1.3	1.2	1.4							
1.1	.7	1.0	Quick						
.7	.2	.7							
0 UND	0 UND	1 402.4							
2 243.1	3 110.5	8 47.6	Sales/Receivables						
35 10.5	21 17.5	29 12.4							
			Cost of Sales/Inventory						
			Cost of Sales/Payables						
19.5	17.6	11.1							
36.4	141.6	36.3	Sales/Working Capital						
-77.5	-7.2	-46.8							
14.7	3.3	6.6							
(21) 1.6	(38) 1.1	(29) 1.9	EBIT/Interest						
-.2	-2.0	.2							
			Net Profit + Depr., Dep., Amort./Cur. Mat. L/T/D						
.2	.4	.5							
1.7	1.7	1.4	Fixed/Worth						
NM	-6.4	9.2							
.9	1.3	1.4							
1.9	3.4	3.7	Debt/Worth						
NM	-19.5	35.4							
48.2	43.1	68.6							
(19) 27.9	(35) 12.3	(33) 24.2	% Profit Before Taxes/Tangible Net Worth						
.5	-6.6	-1.9							
14.5	14.6	15.8							
1.7	2.3	3.4	% Profit Before Taxes/Total Assets						
-2.4	-9.4	-1.8							
72.1	46.0	38.1							
21.8	4.2	4.7	Sales/Net Fixed Assets						
2.2	2.0	2.0							
3.9	3.9	4.3							
2.7	2.2	2.0	Sales/Total Assets						
1.5	1.3	1.3							
.4	.9	.5							
(20) 2.9	(43) 4.3	(40) 3.7	% Depr., Dep., Amort./Sales						
7.8	7.0	7.1							
	.9	2.3							
(16) 4.0	(10) 3.6	% Officers', Directors', Owners' Comp/Sales							
	10.4	4.4							

934572M	1643478M	913199M	Net Sales ($)	2401M	17914M	28540M	49430M	120097M	694817M
454184M	859006M	441249M	Total Assets ($)	2784M	19533M	41684M	38981M	28833M	309434M

© RMA 2003   M = $ thousand   MM = $ million
See Pages 11 through 18 for Explanation of Ratios and Data

Current Data Sorted By Assets

Comparative Historical Data

	2 4 4	2 5 1 3	3 1 1 8	2	3	2	Type of Statement Unqualified Reviewed Compiled Tax Returns Other		4/1/98- 3/31/99 ALL	4/1/99- 3/31/00 ALL
		9 (4/1-9/30/02)			33 (10/1/02-3/31/03)					
	0-500M	500M-2MM	2-10MM	10-50MM	50-100MM	100-250MM				
	10	11	13	2	3	3	NUMBER OF STATEMENTS			
	%	%	%	%	%	%	ASSETS		%	%
	28.3	9.3	14.2				Cash & Equivalents		D	D
	2.1	3.6	5.0				Trade Receivables (net)		A	A
	11.4	7.6	6.6				Inventory		T	T
	4.5	6.4	3.0				All Other Current		A	A
	46.4	26.8	28.8				Total Current			
	52.6	58.9	61.8				Fixed Assets (net)		N	N
	.0	6.6	4.2				Intangibles (net)		O	O
	1.0	7.7	5.2				All Other Non-Current		T	T
	100.0	100.0	100.0				Total		A	A
							LIABILITIES		V	V
	.0	4.7	.9				Notes Payable-Short Term		A	A
	8.9	4.1	5.4				Cur. Mat.-L/T/D		I	I
	5.7	4.5	3.9				Trade Payables		L	L
	.0	.0	1.2				Income Taxes Payable		A	A
	8.7	3.8	6.5				All Other Current		B	B
	23.4	17.2	17.9				Total Current		L	L
	72.7	36.2	36.7				Long Term Debt		E	E
	.0	.0	.0				Deferred Taxes			
	.2	7.1	5.6				All Other Non-Current			
	3.8	39.5	39.9				Net Worth			
	100.0	100.0	100.0				Total Liabilities & Net Worth			
							INCOME DATA			
	100.0	100.0	100.0				Net Sales			
							Gross Profit			
	75.0	88.8	83.8				Operating Expenses			
	25.0	11.2	16.2				Operating Profit			
	8.2	7.7	7.6				All Other Expenses (net)			
	16.9	3.5	8.6				Profit Before Taxes			
							RATIOS			
	22.2	4.5	11.5							
	3.9	1.7	2.7				Current			
	1.4	1.0	.6							
	13.5	1.5	7.5							
	3.8	1.0	.9				Quick			
	.6	.1	.3							
	0 UND	0 UND	0 UND							
	0 UND	0 UND	5 79.2				Sales/Receivables			
	3 142.6	4 101.3	8 43.4							
							Cost of Sales/Inventory			
							Cost of Sales/Payables			
	4.0	6.6	2.5							
	9.6	9.8	9.1				Sales/Working Capital			
	NM	128.2	−18.9							
			21.5							
		(11)	2.6				EBIT/Interest			
			1.2							
							Net Profit + Depr., Dep., Amort./Cur. Mat. L./T/D			
	.4	.8	.8							
	3.0	1.7	1.9				Fixed/Worth			
	−3.1	−3.9	3.6							
	.2	.4	.7							
	5.1	1.5	2.0				Debt/Worth			
	−4.9	−5.5	8.0							
			50.9				% Profit Before Taxes/Tangible Net Worth			
		(11)	15.4							
			1.6							
	73.1	6.0	22.9				% Profit Before Taxes/Total Assets			
	20.7	1.0	5.5							
	−5.5	−6.7	.7							
	19.8	2.9	8.1							
	7.7	2.0	1.0				Sales/Net Fixed Assets			
	3.3	.5	.4							
	5.2	1.4	2.7							
	3.9	1.0	.7				Sales/Total Assets			
	1.4	.4	.4							
		2.1	3.0							
	(10)	7.8	8.1				% Depr., Dep., Amort./Sales			
		13.5	14.3							
							% Officers', Directors', Owners' Comp/Sales			
	7914M	19032M	91237M	90337M	255945M	385371M	Net Sales ($)			
	2447M	16139M	58544M	62644M	186716M	448830M	Total Assets ($)			

© RMA 2003

M = $ thousand   MM = $ million
See Pages 11 through 18 for Explanation of Ratios and Data

Comparative Historical Data   Current Data Sorted By Sales

4/1/00-3/31/01 ALL	4/1/01-3/31/02 ALL	4/1/02-3/31/03 ALL	Type of Statement	9 (4/1-9/30/02) 0-1MM	1-3MM	33 (10/1/02-3/31/03) 3-5MM	5-10MM	10-25MM	25MM & OVER
		10	Unqualified		1	1	1	2	5
		3	Reviewed	1	2				
		8	Compiled	4	2	1	1		
		5	Tax Returns	3	2				
		16	Other	7	4			4	1
		42	**NUMBER OF STATEMENTS**	15	11	2	2	6	6
%	%	%	**ASSETS**	%	%	%	%	%	%
D	D	16.6	Cash & Equivalents	21.4	13.3				
A	A	4.4	Trade Receivables (net)	.4	3.3				
T	T	6.9	Inventory	4.8	8.0				
A	A	4.2	All Other Current	3.1	6.6				
		32.2	Total Current	29.7	31.2				
N	N	58.8	Fixed Assets (net)	69.7	54.6				
O	O	3.3	Intangibles (net)	.0	6.7				
T	T	5.7	All Other Non-Current	.6	7.4				
		100.0	Total	100.0	100.0				
A	A		**LIABILITIES**						
V	V	2.0	Notes Payable-Short Term	.0	3.7				
A	A	6.3	Cur. Mat.-L/T/D	6.1	7.3				
I	I	5.0	Trade Payables	1.1	8.7				
L	L	1.0	Income Taxes Payable	.0	.0				
A	A	7.8	All Other Current	5.5	2.5				
B	B	22.1	Total Current	12.7	22.3				
L	L	42.1	Long Term Debt	57.5	58.4				
E	E	.0	Deferred Taxes	.0	.0				
		4.9	All Other Non-Current	1.7	4.9				
		30.9	Net Worth	28.1	14.5				
		100.0	Total Liabilities & Net Worth	100.0	100.0				
			INCOME DATA						
		100.0	Net Sales	100.0	100.0				
			Gross Profit						
		83.7	Operating Expenses	68.1	95.1				
		16.3	Operating Profit	31.9	4.9				
		7.7	All Other Expenses (net)	15.3	3.1				
		8.7	Profit Before Taxes	16.6	1.8				
			RATIOS						
		6.0		9.1	23.8				
		1.7	Current	3.2	1.7				
		.7		1.6	.4				
		4.1		9.1	15.4				
		.9	Quick	1.5	1.4				
		.4		.2	.3				
	0	UND		0 UND	0 UND				
	2	161.9	Sales/Receivables	0 UND	2 155.8				
	9	40.3		1 641.0	5 79.2				
			Cost of Sales/Inventory						
			Cost of Sales/Payables						
		3.8		1.6	3.5				
		10.3	Sales/Working Capital	9.8	8.3				
		−21.2		28.8	−14.4				
		6.9			2.5				
	(31)	2.2	EBIT/Interest	(10) 1.6	1.6				
		.7			−1.8				
			Net Profit + Depr., Dep., Amort./Cur. Mat. L/T/D						
		.8		1.0	.8				
		1.8	Fixed/Worth	2.3	2.0				
		11.1		7.0	−2.4				
		.5		.5	.4				
		2.3	Debt/Worth	2.8	2.6				
		16.0		12.7	−4.7				
		57.1	% Profit Before Taxes/Tangible	148.3					
	(34)	11.7	Net Worth	(12) 14.1					
		.5		1.8					
		20.2	% Profit Before Taxes/Total	21.5	17.2				
		5.0	Assets	3.6	6.0				
		.2		.6	−6.6				
		8.3		6.8	19.0				
		2.1	Sales/Net Fixed Assets	.6	2.2				
		.6		.3	1.0				
		2.8		4.0	1.4				
		1.2	Sales/Total Assets	.5	1.1				
		.5		.2	.7				
		2.7		4.9	1.8				
	(36)	6.4	% Depr., Dep., Amort./Sales	(12) 7.8	(10) 5.6				
		10.5		14.5	16.7				
		4.5	% Officers', Directors',						
	(13)	11.8	Owners' Comp/Sales						
		17.2							
		849836M	Net Sales ($)	7336M	22563M	8228M	15225M	92631M	703853M
		775320M	Total Assets ($)	15413M	23450M	9903M	67164M	55372M	604018M

M = $ thousand   MM = $ million
See Pages 11 through 18 for Explanation of Ratios and Data

Current Data Sorted By Assets   **Comparative Historical Data**

						Type of Statement		
		5	4	1	3	Unqualified	15	18
2	4	8	1			Reviewed	18	16
2	6	4		1		Compiled	18	18
4	1	1				Tax Returns	8	11
3	8	5	6	1	1	Other	23	27
	13 (4/1-9/30/02)		58 (10/1/02-3/31/03)				4/1/98-3/31/99	4/1/99-3/31/00
0-500M	500M-2MM	2-10MM	10-50MM	50-100MM	100-250MM		ALL	ALL
11	19	23	11	3	4	**NUMBER OF STATEMENTS**	82	90
%	%	%	%	%	%	**ASSETS**	%	%
17.5	5.4	10.5	5.8			Cash & Equivalents	10.3	10.0
33.7	58.1	53.9	53.3			Trade Receivables (net)	45.9	49.2
2.0	1.5	.8	1.1			Inventory	1.9	2.7
6.1	6.8	5.5	11.3			All Other Current	3.9	3.9
59.3	71.9	70.7	71.5			Total Current	62.0	65.6
22.6	12.2	13.7	13.6			Fixed Assets (net)	21.1	17.1
6.2	5.8	8.1	7.4			Intangibles (net)	6.3	7.0
11.9	10.2	7.5	7.5			All Other Non-Current	10.7	10.2
100.0	100.0	100.0	100.0			Total	100.0	100.0
						LIABILITIES		
20.6	17.1	24.9	20.8			Notes Payable-Short Term	17.7	18.2
7.8	6.8	4.7	9.2			Cur. Mat.-L/T/D	3.9	5.5
4.1	4.5	8.4	7.7			Trade Payables	6.7	7.4
.3	1.8	.4	.3			Income Taxes Payable	1.0	.4
20.6	21.8	18.1	32.0			All Other Current	18.0	22.0
53.3	52.0	56.4	70.1			Total Current	47.2	53.6
43.1	8.6	11.5	9.5			Long Term Debt	13.4	11.5
.0	.1	1.1	.1			Deferred Taxes	.5	.5
12.0	8.0	2.8	2.6			All Other Non-Current	5.2	4.5
-8.4	31.3	28.2	17.7			Net Worth	33.7	30.0
100.0	100.0	100.0	100.0			Total Liabilities & Net Worth	100.0	100.0
						INCOME DATA		
100.0	100.0	100.0	100.0			Net Sales	100.0	100.0
						Gross Profit		
100.6	94.0	96.0	96.0			Operating Expenses	95.3	96.7
-.6	6.0	4.0	4.0			Operating Profit	4.7	3.3
.0	1.6	.2	1.3			All Other Expenses (net)	1.6	.2
-.7	4.3	3.8	2.7			Profit Before Taxes	3.1	3.1
						RATIOS		
4.4	1.7	1.5	1.2				2.2	2.0
1.4	1.4	1.2	1.1			Current	1.3	1.2
.8	1.1	1.0	.9				1.0	.9
4.4	1.7	1.5	1.1				2.0	1.9
1.1	1.3	1.0	.9			Quick	1.2 (89)	1.1
.6	.9	.7	.6				.9	.8
0 UND	38 9.6	40 9.2	38 9.5				33 11.1	34 10.9
19 19.3	49 7.5	48 7.6	48 7.6			Sales/Receivables	43 8.6	41 8.9
47 7.7	60 6.1	61 6.0	80 4.6				52 7.0	54 6.7
						Cost of Sales/Inventory		
						Cost of Sales/Payables		
11.4	10.9	18.7	15.3				10.7	13.7
51.7	28.3	35.8	84.2			Sales/Working Capital	28.3	37.1
-24.2	92.3	-206.0	-93.4				-256.9	-68.3
	8.6	8.8	16.4				9.3	7.5
(18)	3.1 (21)	3.5	9.0			EBIT/Interest	(76) 4.6	(81) 3.3
	.3	.2	1.8				1.7	1.6
							8.5	3.5
						Net Profit + Depr., Dep.,	(19) 1.8	(26) 1.7
						Amort./Cur. Mat. L /T/D	1.7	.8
.1	.1	.1	.2				.2	.2
.3	.5	.8	.6			Fixed/Worth	.6	.7
39.0	4.1	-.9	-26.6				2.6	2.1
.9	1.4	1.9	2.2				.8	1.1
6.6	1.9	3.7	10.6			Debt/Worth	2.5	2.7
141.7	107.9	-7.2	-54.4				8.7	8.3
	83.9	77.9					48.9	58.6
(15)	27.0 (16)	38.7				% Profit Before Taxes/Tangible	(70) 30.3	(75) 25.8
	.7	15.2				Net Worth	13.6	13.7
9.0	24.5	17.7	10.4				18.2	15.0
6.1	5.0	4.3	6.2			% Profit Before Taxes/Total	8.5	7.4
-6.0	-4.5	-.7	3.2			Assets	2.2	2.3
999.8	92.2	94.3	131.1				95.3	86.6
45.0	68.2	37.3	77.8			Sales/Net Fixed Assets	37.7	33.5
11.8	22.3	21.2	14.5				10.9	14.7
8.8	5.4	4.9	5.7				5.4	5.5
7.5	4.4	4.3	3.7			Sales/Total Assets	4.4	4.3
5.7	3.5	2.9	2.6				2.6	2.8
	.4	.6	.2				.5	.3
(15)	1.1 (20)	1.2 (10)	.7			% Depr., Dep., Amort./Sales	(67) .9	(73) 1.0
	1.8	2.2	2.0				2.1	2.0
							1.8	1.6
						% Officers', Directors',	(30) 4.2	(38) 3.4
						Owners' Comp/Sales	7.4	6.1
21935M	101815M	427028M	1064775M	1259067M	1239797M	Net Sales ($)	4027683M	4280024M
2942M	22615M	107091M	250037M	212055M	590823M	Total Assets ($)	1336522M	1409260M

M = $ thousand   MM = $ million
See Pages 11 through 18 for Explanation of Ratios and Data

Comparative Historical Data | Current Data Sorted By Sales

			Type of Statement						
10	10	13	Unqualified					2	11
19	17	15	Reviewed		2	2	5	3	3
13	17	13	Compiled	2	1	2	5	2	1
7	9	6	Tax Returns	1	3	2			
25	22	24	Other	1	4	1	5	4	9
4/1/00-3/31/01 ALL	4/1/01-3/31/02 ALL	4/1/02-3/31/03 ALL			13 (4/1-9/30/02)			58 (10/1/02-3/31/03)	
				0-1MM	1-3MM	3-5MM	5-10MM	10-25MM	25MM & OVER
74	75	71	NUMBER OF STATEMENTS	4	10	7	15	11	24
%	%	%	ASSETS	%	%	%	%	%	%
9.7	10.0	9.7	Cash & Equivalents		9.6		6.2	9.2	7.0
48.2	48.5	49.2	Trade Receivables (net)		50.1		54.3	59.2	49.3
2.4	1.6	1.4	Inventory		2.2		1.2	.0	1.6
3.9	3.4	7.0	All Other Current		10.1		3.7	11.1	6.9
64.2	63.6	67.2	Total Current		72.0		65.4	79.5	64.8
19.5	21.4	16.0	Fixed Assets (net)		8.7		11.6	12.2	18.3
8.3	8.3	7.8	Intangibles (net)		9.0		13.0	1.8	9.3
8.0	6.8	8.9	All Other Non-Current		10.3		9.9	6.5	7.6
100.0	100.0	100.0	Total		100.0		100.0	100.0	100.0
			LIABILITIES						
17.4	17.7	19.1	Notes Payable-Short Term		19.3		11.9	30.0	17.1
4.4	4.4	6.2	Cur. Mat.-L/T/D		8.9		5.6	5.1	5.9
8.3	7.9	6.2	Trade Payables		3.3		4.1	8.7	8.3
.7	1.2	1.0	Income Taxes Payable		3.1		.4	.6	1.1
19.3	18.4	22.7	All Other Current		13.5		22.7	19.1	30.0
50.1	49.6	55.2	Total Current		48.1		44.8	63.5	62.4
13.6	17.5	17.0	Long Term Debt		24.2		8.1	6.4	17.0
.6	.8	.5	Deferred Taxes		.0		.0	2.0	.5
5.6	8.6	6.5	All Other Non-Current		7.0		7.4	2.4	4.1
30.2	23.5	20.8	Net Worth		20.7		39.7	25.8	16.1
100.0	100.0	100.0	Total Liabilities & Net Worth		100.0		100.0	100.0	100.0
			INCOME DATA						
100.0	100.0	100.0	Net Sales		100.0		100.0	100.0	100.0
			Gross Profit						
96.3	95.4	96.3	Operating Expenses		97.8		97.0	97.2	97.3
3.7	4.6	3.7	Operating Profit		2.2		3.0	2.8	2.7
.5	1.1	.8	All Other Expenses (net)		1.2		.3	.7	1.1
3.2	3.5	2.9	Profit Before Taxes		1.0		2.7	2.1	1.6
			RATIOS						
1.9	1.9	1.7			3.7		2.1	1.7	1.3
1.3	1.2	1.2	Current		1.5		1.4	1.2	1.1
1.0	1.0	1.0			1.1		1.1	1.0	.9
1.7	1.8	1.5			2.9		1.7	1.6	1.2
1.2	1.1	1.1	Quick		1.2		1.4	1.0	1.0
.9	.8	.8			.9		.9	.7	.7
33 10.9	28 13.2	37 9.9		7 55.9		38 9.6	40 9.2	38 9.5	
44 8.2	44 8.4	42 8.7	Sales/Receivables	50 7.2		42 8.8	51 7.2	41 8.9	
57 6.4	58 6.3	55 6.6		64 5.7		54 6.8	61 6.0	54 6.8	
			Cost of Sales/Inventory						
			Cost of Sales/Payables						
10.2	12.0	13.9			8.0		10.9	12.8	18.1
41.7	41.6	35.8	Sales/Working Capital		29.9		26.1	35.8	46.3
-201.0	633.2	261.2			88.7		98.9	218.8	-151.7
7.2	8.6	9.1			8.6		11.4	8.7	9.2
(67) 3.0	(69) 4.0	(65) 3.5	EBIT/Interest		(13) 2.5	(10) 3.4	(10) 3.5	(23) 4.4	
1.2	1.6	1.1			-1.0		1.1	.4	1.8
5.7	7.2	4.6	Net Profit + Depr., Dep.,						8.9
(17) 3.5	(19) 2.8	(24) 1.5	Amort./Cur. Mat. L/T/D					(13) 2.2	
1.5	2.0	.9							1.0
.2	.1	.2			.2		.1	.2	.3
.6	.7	.7	Fixed/Worth		.3		.6	.6	.9
2.8	9.9	39.0			2.0		-.9	2.5	-8.7
1.4	1.3	1.6			1.6		.8	1.6	2.4
2.7	3.9	3.9	Debt/Worth		4.1		1.7	4.5	5.5
NM	-33.6	141.7			54.4		-36.6	31.8	-20.5
69.2	55.9	83.9					73.4		56.0
(56) 30.1	(56) 34.6	(54) 28.5	% Profit Before Taxes/Tangible Net Worth		(11) 14.4				(17) 31.6
9.2	18.1	12.5			.9				15.2
15.7	15.6	13.5			21.6		17.7	24.2	11.9
6.7	10.3	5.0	% Profit Before Taxes/Total Assets		5.5		8.7	3.9	4.6
1.1	2.2	.2			-8.6		.2	.5	2.1
71.8	81.5	94.3			428.5		124.2	120.5	110.3
33.3	37.9	45.1	Sales/Net Fixed Assets		68.5		57.3	50.3	34.6
15.5	19.5	18.1			32.8		13.3	34.8	13.2
5.5	6.2	5.8			7.5		5.9	5.0	5.6
4.4	4.3	4.3	Sales/Total Assets		5.3		4.9	4.3	4.4
2.7	3.0	2.9			3.4		2.8	3.3	2.9
.5	.5	.5					.3	.5	.3
(60) 1.1	(60) .9	(53) 1.1	% Depr., Dep., Amort./Sales			(12)	.9	(10) .7	(20) 1.1
2.2	2.4	2.2					2.7	1.2	2.0
2.1	1.5	1.6							
(30) 4.7	(34) 4.0	(18) 4.8	% Officers', Directors', Owners' Comp/Sales						
8.3	7.8	8.6							
4459378M	3696706M	4114417M	Net Sales ($)	1285M	21866M	29338M	108887M	185761M	3767280M
1807564M	1195896M	1185563M	Total Assets ($)	1058M	4953M	6876M	32399M	59770M	1080507M

Current Data Sorted By Assets   **Comparative Historical Data**

						Type of Statement		
1		9	10	1	3	Unqualified	28	34
1	20	17	3			Reviewed	26	32
5	14	9				Compiled	35	33
12	11	1				Tax Returns	6	15
7	13	10	4	2	3	Other	43	44
	30 (4/1-9/30/02)		126 (10/1/02-3/31/03)				4/1/98-3/31/99	4/1/99-3/31/00
0-500M	500M-2MM	2-10MM	10-50MM	50-100MM	100-250MM		ALL	ALL
26	58	46	17	3	6	NUMBER OF STATEMENTS	138	158
%	%	%	%	%	%	ASSETS	%	%
15.2	10.4	7.7	10.5			Cash & Equivalents	8.8	7.8
31.8	36.7	41.1	27.3			Trade Receivables (net)	35.1	37.8
9.8	10.6	9.0	9.1			Inventory	10.5	9.3
3.2	3.7	4.3	9.1			All Other Current	4.1	4.0
60.0	61.4	62.0	55.9			Total Current	58.5	58.9
22.2	17.1	15.7	19.3			Fixed Assets (net)	20.1	19.5
7.6	12.9	14.8	8.6			Intangibles (net)	11.4	13.9
10.3	8.6	7.4	16.3			All Other Non-Current	10.0	7.8
100.0	100.0	100.0	100.0			Total	100.0	100.0
						LIABILITIES		
40.5	12.3	13.8	11.1			Notes Payable-Short Term	19.1	12.7
4.5	7.9	7.9	7.1			Cur. Mat.-L/T/D	4.2	4.6
16.5	14.2	14.2	8.7			Trade Payables	14.5	13.5
.2	.4	.7	.1			Income Taxes Payable	.6	.6
18.1	17.2	18.0	13.7			All Other Current	14.0	17.4
79.9	52.0	54.6	40.7			Total Current	52.4	48.9
14.4	26.2	15.9	19.1			Long Term Debt	24.1	21.6
.0	.2	.6	1.0			Deferred Taxes	.9	.6
14.6	5.9	1.6	7.7			All Other Non-Current	7.3	6.0
-8.9	15.7	27.3	31.4			Net Worth	15.3	23.0
100.0	100.0	100.0	100.0			Total Liabilities & Net Worth	100.0	100.0
						INCOME DATA		
100.0	100.0	100.0	100.0			Net Sales	100.0	100.0
						Gross Profit		
94.8	95.6	91.6	98.1			Operating Expenses	96.2	95.0
5.2	4.4	8.4	1.9			Operating Profit	3.7	5.0
2.4	1.5	2.5	3.7			All Other Expenses (net)	2.6	2.4
2.8	2.9	5.8	-1.9			Profit Before Taxes	1.2	2.6
						RATIOS		
2.7	1.9	1.7	2.3				2.1	2.0
1.2	1.3	1.2	1.1			Current	1.3	1.3
.5	.8	.9	1.0				.9	.9
2.2	1.5	1.4	1.4				1.6	1.5
.8	.9	.9	1.0			Quick	(136) 1.1	1.0
.3	.5	.6	.6				.6	.7
0 UND	24 15.2	37 9.8	34 10.8				29 12.5	33 10.9
26 14.0	36 10.3	55 6.7	52 7.0			Sales/Receivables	42 8.7	51 7.2
49 7.5	65 5.6	70 5.2	68 5.3				63 5.8	68 5.4
						Cost of Sales/Inventory		
						Cost of Sales/Payables		
8.0	8.8	7.5	4.8				9.0	8.1
50.6	17.6	32.9	22.9			Sales/Working Capital	19.4	20.7
-8.0	-28.6	-73.6	152.7				-38.1	-38.4
5.0	10.0	14.8	21.0				6.3	7.4
(19) 2.7	(53) 4.4	(42) 5.0	(16) 2.5			EBIT/Interest	(122) 2.4	(143) 2.6
-2.3	1.6	1.9	.1				1.0	1.2
	3.2	6.4					4.5	7.0
	(16) 1.9	(12) 2.1				Net Profit + Depr., Dep.,	(39) 2.3	(48) 2.8
	1.5	.7				Amort./Cur. Mat. L /T/D	1.1	1.1
.1	.2	.2	.1				.3	.3
.9	.5	.7	.6			Fixed/Worth	.9	1.0
-4.3	NM	4.5	2.0				-3.0	-4.6
1.1	.9	1.7	1.7				1.1	1.4
7.7	2.9	3.8	2.9			Debt/Worth	3.2	3.7
-3.5	-24.7	NM	6.4				-11.9	-17.8
240.7	69.0	101.5	64.7			% Profit Before Taxes/Tangible	41.7	63.6
(16) 34.1	(43) 26.3	(35) 40.6	(15) 31.1			Net Worth	(95) 24.3	(110) 29.6
4.2	5.2	17.3	5.0				4.7	10.4
24.1	15.3	21.9	12.6			% Profit Before Taxes/Total	14.6	15.8
10.6	6.3	9.1	4.7			Assets	4.7	6.5
-9.6	1.3	2.2	-4.8				-.1	.5
278.4	43.5	46.8	49.8				39.4	36.6
27.7	21.7	21.7	13.5			Sales/Net Fixed Assets	17.0	18.7
18.3	14.3	13.1	6.1				8.2	9.0
7.8	3.8	3.5	3.3				4.4	3.7
3.6	3.1	2.4	1.6			Sales/Total Assets	2.8	2.7
2.7	2.1	1.4	.5				1.6	1.7
1.8	.6	.6	.6				.7	.8
(13) 2.2	(45) 1.7	(38) 1.4	(12) 1.9			% Depr., Dep., Amort./Sales	(107) 2.1	(128) 2.0
3.7	3.0	2.6	7.1				3.5	3.3
4.8	4.4	2.7				% Officers', Directors',	3.9	3.8
(18) 10.3	(29) 7.0	(16) 5.0				Owners' Comp/Sales	(58) 6.9	(67) 5.6
16.1	12.3	7.8					12.5	11.8
27872M	211762M	532296M	603158M	172699M	542585M	Net Sales ($)	1773368M	2106016M
6221M	64874M	215351M	390670M	186475M	858785M	Total Assets ($)	1250446M	1597855M

M = $ thousand   MM = $ million
See Pages 11 through 18 for Explanation of Ratios and Data

Comparative Historical Data / Current Data Sorted By Sales

			Type of Statement						
18	16	24	Unqualified	1			3	10	10
28	26	41	Reviewed	1	5	10	15	8	2
27	24	28	Compiled	2	14	5	2	3	2
10	12	24	Tax Returns	9	11	2	1	1	
32	29	39	Other	6	10	6	4	6	7
4/1/00-3/31/01 ALL	4/1/01-3/31/02 ALL	4/1/02-3/31/03 ALL		30 (4/1-9/30/02)			126 (10/1/02-3/31/03)		
				0-1MM	1-3MM	3-5MM	5-10MM	10-25MM	25MM & OVER
115	107	156	**NUMBER OF STATEMENTS**	19	40	23	25	28	21
%	%	%	**ASSETS**	%	%	%	%	%	%
10.4	7.7	10.2	Cash & Equivalents	10.6	13.8	9.9	9.8	6.8	8.3
36.7	34.6	35.5	Trade Receivables (net)	21.1	32.6	36.9	39.5	41.8	39.2
11.1	11.6	9.8	Inventory	11.4	10.5	10.1	7.8	8.5	10.7
3.1	4.3	4.4	All Other Current	3.1	1.8	5.9	5.4	5.9	5.5
61.3	58.2	59.8	Total Current	46.3	58.7	62.7	62.5	62.9	63.7
19.2	19.5	17.2	Fixed Assets (net)	19.3	20.7	17.2	21.6	12.6	9.7
10.5	14.9	12.9	Intangibles (net)	20.3	13.1	10.8	10.1	10.6	15.0
8.9	7.5	10.0	All Other Non-Current	14.0	7.6	9.3	5.8	13.9	11.6
100.0	100.0	100.0	Total	100.0	100.0	100.0	100.0	100.0	100.0
			LIABILITIES						
14.9	11.6	17.1	Notes Payable-Short Term	45.7	13.7	12.4	11.9	16.0	10.5
5.8	4.8	7.3	Cur. Mat.-L/T/D	5.5	4.7	11.9	7.4	9.6	5.7
14.4	13.3	13.5	Trade Payables	16.3	12.0	14.5	13.1	13.8	13.1
.4	.7	.4	Income Taxes Payable	.1	.3	.1	.9	.6	.1
23.9	14.3	16.8	All Other Current	22.1	14.3	16.6	17.3	16.7	16.9
59.4	44.6	55.2	Total Current	89.8	45.1	55.4	50.8	56.7	46.3
21.3	18.2	20.1	Long Term Debt	18.5	15.1	45.8	16.5	17.0	10.9
.4	.8	.4	Deferred Taxes	.0	.2	.2	.0	1.6	.2
5.1	7.6	6.1	All Other Non-Current	13.4	6.0	8.0	2.4	3.2	6.2
13.8	28.7	18.2	Net Worth	−21.6	33.6	−9.5	30.3	21.5	36.3
100.0	100.0	100.0	Total Liabilities & Net Worth	100.0	100.0	100.0	100.0	100.0	100.0
			INCOME DATA						
100.0	100.0	100.0	Net Sales	100.0	100.0	100.0	100.0	100.0	100.0
			Gross Profit						
95.5	93.9	94.4	Operating Expenses	92.4	93.5	94.5	95.6	94.6	96.1
4.5	6.1	5.6	Operating Profit	7.6	6.5	5.5	4.4	5.4	3.9
2.4	3.0	2.8	All Other Expenses (net)	5.2	2.0	2.1	1.6	4.5	2.5
2.1	3.1	2.8	Profit Before Taxes	2.4	4.5	3.4	2.8	.9	1.4
			RATIOS						
1.7	2.0	1.9		2.4	2.3	1.9	2.1	1.4	2.1
1.2	1.4	1.3	Current	.6	1.3	1.4	1.3	1.1	1.5
.9	.9	.8		.1	.8	.8	.9	.9	1.0
1.4	1.6	1.5		1.2	2.1	1.5	1.7	1.3	1.6
.9	1.0	.9	Quick	.4	1.1	.9	1.0	.9	1.0
.6	.6	.5		.1	.5	.6	.7	.5	.8
28 13.3	28 13.0	26 13.8		0 UND	24 15.1	23 15.5	26 14.0	38 9.7	35 10.6
44 8.2	43 8.6	43 8.4	Sales/Receivables	24 15.1	38 9.6	35 10.5	50 7.2	52 7.0	53 6.9
62 5.9	65 5.6	66 5.5		44 8.3	61 6.0	67 5.4	65 5.6	68 5.4	76 4.8
			Cost of Sales/Inventory						
			Cost of Sales/Payables						
9.4	7.0	7.6		8.0	7.3	7.4	7.2	10.5	4.9
24.0	14.3	24.3	Sales/Working Capital	−19.5	22.3	14.6	20.0	43.3	14.3
−57.5	−67.2	−36.8		−2.8	−51.6	−29.7	−105.3	−122.1	254.6
	6.7		11.4		10.7		6.5		8.2		13.7		8.5		9.9		22.0
(106) 2.2	(96) 3.7	(136) 3.7	EBIT/Interest	(14) 2.1	(35) 4.4	(20) 4.6	(24) 4.2	(24) 3.1	(19) 3.4
1.2	1.4	1.4		−2.6	1.4	1.5	.0	1.8	1.4
8.7	4.5	4.2					4.6		5.2
(34) 3.3	(26) 2.9	(42) 2.1	Net Profit + Depr., Dep., Amort./Cur. Mat. L/T/D			(11) 2.1		(10) 2.0
1.5	.9	1.2					1.3		.7
.3	.2	.2		.2	.2	.3	.2	.2	.1
1.0	.7	.6	Fixed/Worth	1.1	.7	.5	.7	.6	.4
8.7	−5.7	10.9		−.2	−3.9	3.0	4.2	4.6	1.5
1.4	1.2	1.2		1.2	.9	1.1	1.4	2.1	1.1
4.4	3.2	3.9	Debt/Worth	−4.0	2.9	3.5	3.0	5.0	4.2
−23.0	−13.9	−13.5		−1.7	−21.6	39.4	27.8	11.8	10.5
56.5	63.9	79.9			87.9	79.0	71.0	75.1	73.9
(85) 30.6	(77) 27.3	(115) 30.7	% Profit Before Taxes/Tangible Net Worth	(29) 39.9	(19) 22.8	(20) 22.5	(22) 38.8	(18) 23.9
12.4	11.7	5.4			4.5	6.4	2.1	15.5	5.5
13.2	17.4	18.1		16.5	20.2	12.4	15.9	22.8	13.3
4.8	7.5	6.0	% Profit Before Taxes/Total Assets	2.5	11.8	5.4	5.7	6.5	4.7
.6	1.5	.3		−16.9	1.7	−.7	−.9	1.5	−.5
40.5	46.1	43.3		36.3	37.5	26.0	43.9	48.2	81.0
19.7	21.1	20.8	Sales/Net Fixed Assets	26.0	19.9	18.5	20.7	21.7	17.9
9.3	9.7	11.9		14.4	11.5	15.2	9.7	10.9	10.3
4.0	4.0	3.7		3.5	4.1	3.5	3.6	4.2	4.5
2.7	2.7	2.7	Sales/Total Assets	2.7	2.7	3.1	2.9	2.4	2.0
1.8	1.5	1.5		1.3	1.6	1.7	1.8	1.2	.9
.9	.6	.7			1.1	1.3	1.1	.5	.5
(92) 1.9	(78) 1.7	(113) 1.8	% Depr., Dep., Amort./Sales	(27) 2.2	(19) 1.8	(21) 1.6	(22) .9	(16) 1.2
4.4	3.8	3.5			3.9	2.4	3.3	3.4	3.3
4.1	3.4	3.8		7.6	4.6	3.3			
(49) 6.2	(43) 6.9	(66) 7.0	% Officers', Directors', Owners' Comp/Sales	(13) 14.4	(20) 9.0	(12) 4.7			
9.2	11.4	11.1		19.3	13.0	5.9			
1731539M	1089162M	2090372M	Net Sales ($)	11210M	76900M	88817M	171570M	439043M	1302832M
1061486M	969380M	1722376M	Total Assets ($)	10029M	42406M	35729M	106990M	453236M	1073986M

© RMA 2003

M = $ thousand   MM = $ million

See Pages 11 through 18 for Explanation of Ratios and Data

Current Data Sorted By Assets   **Comparative Historical Data**

Type of Statement								
1		1	4		Unqualified		6	5
	1	3	3		Reviewed		8	18
4	4		1		Compiled		21	18
9	2	2			Tax Returns		6	10
4	2	4	2		Other		20	8

0-500M	500M-2MM	2-10MM	10-50MM	50-100MM	100-250MM		4/1/98-3/31/99 ALL	4/1/99-3/31/00 ALL
	7 (4/1-9/30/02)		42 (10/1/02-3/31/03)					
18	11	10	10			**NUMBER OF STATEMENTS**	61	59
%	%	%	%	%	%	**ASSETS**	%	%
12.7	11.3	15.6	17.2	D	D	Cash & Equivalents	14.3	15.5
22.5	19.9	18.6	19.5	A	A	Trade Receivables (net)	23.4	26.2
1.6	3.1	2.6	9.2	T	T	Inventory	3.1	3.5
2.0	1.4	3.7	3.5	A	A	All Other Current	2.3	2.5
38.9	35.8	40.6	49.4			Total Current	43.1	47.7
53.0	39.7	35.7	35.4	N	N	Fixed Assets (net)	36.1	34.9
2.5	10.0	14.7	7.7	O	O	Intangibles (net)	9.4	8.0
5.7	14.5	9.0	7.5	T	T	All Other Non-Current	11.3	9.4
100.0	100.0	100.0	100.0			Total	100.0	100.0
				A	A	**LIABILITIES**		
10.5	8.7	2.9	2.7	V	V	Notes Payable-Short Term	6.6	7.3
8.3	4.0	8.6	4.0	A	A	Cur. Mat.-L/T/D	5.7	5.4
7.4	7.6	5.0	13.8	I	I	Trade Payables	7.5	6.7
.0	.1	.2	.4	L	L	Income Taxes Payable	.2	.6
17.6	6.1	14.4	23.3	A	A	All Other Current	17.0	19.1
43.8	26.5	31.0	44.2	B	B	Total Current	36.9	39.1
48.1	13.7	18.7	13.8	L	L	Long Term Debt	26.1	20.0
.0	1.5	.6	.1	E	E	Deferred Taxes	.4	.5
1.7	8.1	.6	2.6			All Other Non-Current	8.0	2.7
6.3	50.3	49.2	39.3			Net Worth	28.6	37.7
100.0	100.0	100.0	100.0			Total Liabilities & Net Worth	100.0	100.0
						INCOME DATA		
100.0	100.0	100.0	100.0			Net Sales	100.0	100.0
						Gross Profit		
93.8	93.3	88.5	95.5			Operating Expenses	92.8	94.3
6.2	6.7	11.5	4.5			Operating Profit	7.1	5.7
2.0	.7	4.5	-.2			All Other Expenses (net)	1.6	.7
4.2	5.9	7.0	4.7			Profit Before Taxes	5.6	5.0
						RATIOS		
2.0	2.1	2.7	1.3				2.1	2.1
1.1	1.4	1.1	1.1			Current	1.3	1.4
.3	1.1	.8	.9				.7	.9
1.7	2.0	2.2	1.1				1.8	1.7
1.0	1.4	1.0	.6			Quick	1.1	1.3
.2	.7	.6	.6				.6	.7
0 UND	14 25.4	0 UND	16 23.3				18 20.7	18 20.4
18 20.4	26 14.1	18 19.8	19 18.8			Sales/Receivables	25 14.6	27 13.6
34 10.8	29 12.6	31 11.7	28 13.0				37 9.8	42 8.7
						Cost of Sales/Inventory		
						Cost of Sales/Payables		
17.2	15.3	21.1	32.4				11.1	10.7
NM	29.2	NM	92.1			Sales/Working Capital	35.8	26.4
-14.1	75.4	-61.7	-754.4				-17.7	-87.1
(15) 21.0	(10) 13.8		23.8				(50) 12.5	(55) 11.5
3.6	8.4		10.8			EBIT/Interest	5.5	6.7
1.2	3.2		4.3				2.6	2.4
						Net Profit + Depr., Dep.,	(19) 12.0	(15) 5.3
						Amort./Cur. Mat. L /T/D	3.0	3.6
							1.6	2.1
.7	.7	.4	.6				.6	.5
74.0	1.1	1.1	1.1			Fixed/Worth	1.0	1.0
-1.8	1.5	2.2	2.4				20.3	2.8
.9	.5	.8	.8				.9	.9
83.7	1.3	1.7	1.8			Debt/Worth	2.2	2.0
-3.7	2.9	4.0	7.2				77.3	4.3
(10) 118.1	(10) 52.6	97.4	84.5			% Profit Before Taxes/Tangible	(47) 61.9	(51) 80.3
93.5	21.9	50.4	37.2			Net Worth	31.4	33.9
32.7	-1.1	19.4	22.9				19.4	10.0
22.6	23.7	30.9	25.9			% Profit Before Taxes/Total	23.2	22.0
10.6	14.3	16.9	10.9			Assets	13.0	11.7
.7	.7	7.8	7.0				5.3	3.5
16.0	22.5	25.8	18.5				17.1	18.4
10.7	7.2	8.9	10.6			Sales/Net Fixed Assets	8.5	10.8
4.9	5.5	5.5	3.8				6.3	6.8
7.3	4.5	4.0	4.2				3.9	3.9
4.8	3.0	3.1	3.2			Sales/Total Assets	3.2	3.1
2.8	1.8	1.9	2.1				2.5	2.0
(16) 3.8			2.0			% Depr., Dep., Amort./Sales	(55) 2.1	(56) 1.9
5.0			3.2				3.3	3.1
7.8			4.7				4.5	4.9
(10) 6.5						% Officers', Directors',	(29) 5.2	(35) 3.9
8.9						Owners' Comp/Sales	8.6	6.1
13.4							16.9	13.3
18592M	37237M	130669M	612024M			Net Sales ($)	730553M	798236M
3914M	11952M	46772M	202051M			Total Assets ($)	223169M	286961M

M = $ thousand   MM = $ million
See Pages 11 through 18 for Explanation of Ratios and Data

Comparative Historical Data | Current Data Sorted By Sales

			Type of Statement						
4	4	6	Unqualified		1			1	4
5	6	7	Reviewed	1			1	1	4
22	19	9	Compiled	2	2	3	1		1
12	8	13	Tax Returns	6	3	1	2	1	
19	10	14	Other	4	4	1	1	2	2
4/1/00-3/31/01 ALL	4/1/01-3/31/02 ALL	4/1/02-3/31/03 ALL		7 (4/1-9/30/02) 0-1MM	1-3MM	3-5MM	42 (10/1/02-3/31/03) 5-10MM	10-25MM	25MM & OVER
62	47	49	**NUMBER OF STATEMENTS**	13	10	5	5	5	11
%	%	%	**ASSETS**	%	%	%	%	%	%
14.4	12.6	13.9	Cash & Equivalents	7.4	18.4				16.6
23.7	24.4	20.5	Trade Receivables (net)	17.5	21.2				20.6
4.0	7.1	3.7	Inventory	.6	2.1				8.6
2.5	2.7	2.5	All Other Current	1.7	1.4				3.6
44.7	46.8	40.7	Total Current	27.2	43.0				49.4
33.0	35.6	42.9	Fixed Assets (net)	64.9	41.4				33.9
9.0	5.7	7.7	Intangibles (net)	4.4	3.1				9.4
13.3	11.9	8.7	All Other Non-Current	3.6	12.5				7.4
100.0	100.0	100.0	Total	100.0	100.0				100.0
			LIABILITIES						
16.1	8.7	6.9	Notes Payable-Short Term	8.8	14.2				2.5
5.1	6.3	6.5	Cur. Mat.-L/T/D	6.8	8.3				4.4
9.8	12.1	8.3	Trade Payables	6.5	6.7				13.6
.2	.7	.2	Income Taxes Payable	.0	.0				.4
16.3	11.8	15.5	All Other Current	13.9	14.7				23.8
47.5	39.7	37.4	Total Current	36.0	43.9				44.7
17.9	20.6	27.4	Long Term Debt	45.8	42.1				13.1
.6	.5	.5	Deferred Taxes	1.2	.0				.1
6.2	3.5	3.1	All Other Non-Current	1.2	1.7				2.3
27.8	35.8	31.7	Net Worth	15.7	12.3				39.7
100.0	100.0	100.0	Total Liabilities & Net Worth	100.0	100.0				100.0
			INCOME DATA						
100.0	100.0	100.0	Net Sales	100.0	100.0				100.0
			Gross Profit						
93.4	92.8	92.9	Operating Expenses	88.0	96.5				95.6
6.6	7.2	7.1	Operating Profit	12.0	3.5				4.3
1.7	1.0	1.8	All Other Expenses (net)	6.6	.4				−.1
5.0	6.2	5.3	Profit Before Taxes	5.5	3.1				4.5
			RATIOS						
1.7	1.5	1.9		1.5	2.2				1.3
1.1	1.2	1.1	Current	.5	1.1				1.1
.7	.9	.6		.2	.5				1.0
1.4	1.4	1.6		1.4	1.9				1.1
.9	1.0	1.0	Quick	.5	1.0				.7
.6	.6	.6		.2	.5				.6
16 22.5	11 32.2	11 32.1		0 UND	0 UND				16 23.1
27 13.3	26 13.8	22 16.9	Sales/Receivables	25 14.7	13 27.5				21 17.5
40 9.2	37 9.9	29 12.4		31 11.8	33 10.9				28 13.2
			Cost of Sales/Inventory						
			Cost of Sales/Payables						
17.6	18.2	18.0		19.8	17.2				34.4
102.1	66.9	69.7	Sales/Working Capital	−14.7	NM				92.3
−28.8	−72.4	−19.7		−8.6	−20.3				−410.8
11.7	10.3	18.8							18.8
(55) 4.5	(44) 4.3	(43) 7.9	EBIT/Interest						9.2
2.0	1.6	3.2							5.0
7.2	6.4	9.8	Net Profit + Depr., Dep.,						
(14) 2.3	(12) 2.3	(13) 2.7	Amort./Cur. Mat. L/T/D						
1.5	.6	2.3							
.5	.5	.7		1.2	.6				.6
1.2	1.1	1.2	Fixed/Worth	44.3	1.4				1.1
5.0	1.8	8.1		−6.2	NM				2.1
1.0	1.0	.9		.9	.9				.9
1.8	1.8	2.1	Debt/Worth	43.4	3.9				2.1
NM	4.9	16.4		−8.1	NM				6.6
62.1	50.7	97.6	% Profit Before Taxes/Tangible						82.5
(47) 26.6	(41) 23.9	(40) 41.5	Net Worth						46.2
7.1	9.1	16.9							25.2
20.5	20.5	24.1	% Profit Before Taxes/Total	18.1	37.5				24.5
9.1	9.1	14.1	Assets	6.5	14.1				9.4
2.0	2.0	4.4		−3.2	4.3				7.3
28.4	24.0	16.9		11.4	26.3				22.5
11.5	10.1	9.1	Sales/Net Fixed Assets	4.7	14.0				12.9
6.7	6.3	5.4		.6	8.9				3.8
4.7	5.5	4.7		4.6	8.7				4.3
3.6	3.7	3.6	Sales/Total Assets	2.7	5.2				3.6
2.3	1.9	2.6		.5	4.2				2.2
1.0	1.1	2.3		4.5					2.0
(55) 2.7	(41) 3.2	(44) 4.4	% Depr., Dep., Amort./Sales	(11) 6.0					3.1
4.2	4.0	5.4		17.2					4.7
3.7	2.9	3.5	% Officers', Directors',						
(34) 7.6	(21) 5.9	(25) 6.9	Owners' Comp/Sales						
13.8	16.0	13.3							
979209M	585193M	798522M	Net Sales ($)	6976M	16457M	19530M	35224M	76270M	644065M
345611M	207935M	264689M	Total Assets ($)	7485M	2941M	6186M	13802M	24766M	209509M

Current Data Sorted By Assets   Comparative Historical Data

	0-500M	500M-2MM	2-10MM	10-50MM	50-100MM	100-250MM	Type of Statement	4/1/98-3/31/99 ALL	4/1/99-3/31/00 ALL
		3	17	5	5		Unqualified	33	37
	6	11	25	3	1		Reviewed	59	53
	18	23	6	1			Compiled	73	71
	24	14	1			1	Tax Returns	31	43
	17	25	15	11	1	1	Other	63	68
		38 (4/1-9/30/02)		195 (10/1/02-3/31/03)					
	65	76	64	20	6	2	**NUMBER OF STATEMENTS**	259	272
	%	%	%	%	%	%	**ASSETS**	%	%
	14.2	12.1	9.4	8.9			Cash & Equivalents	11.6	10.3
	31.9	38.5	45.1	46.8			Trade Receivables (net)	39.0	41.1
	4.0	3.7	1.1	3.0			Inventory	3.3	2.6
	2.7	5.6	6.6	6.1			All Other Current	4.9	4.5
	52.8	59.9	62.2	64.9			Total Current	58.8	58.5
	31.0	24.1	23.2	16.2			Fixed Assets (net)	25.6	26.3
	7.8	5.6	3.6	10.5			Intangibles (net)	4.9	5.4
	8.5	10.5	11.0	8.4			All Other Non-Current	10.7	9.7
	100.0	100.0	100.0	100.0			Total	100.0	100.0
							LIABILITIES		
	21.8	11.1	13.3	15.8			Notes Payable-Short Term	12.0	11.8
	5.5	4.1	2.9	4.3			Cur. Mat.-L/T/D	5.2	4.6
	7.9	14.2	12.6	15.3			Trade Payables	11.2	10.7
	.0	.8	.5	.1			Income Taxes Payable	.5	.5
	20.9	14.4	16.8	15.4			All Other Current	15.9	14.4
	56.1	44.7	46.0	50.8			Total Current	44.8	42.0
	24.0	13.3	9.0	11.9			Long Term Debt	17.7	15.4
	.1	.5	.4	.1			Deferred Taxes	.5	.6
	4.1	6.3	6.7	2.8			All Other Non-Current	4.8	5.5
	15.6	35.1	37.8	34.3			Net Worth	32.2	36.6
	100.0	100.0	100.0	100.0			Total Liabilities & Net Worth	100.0	100.0
							INCOME DATA		
	100.0	100.0	100.0	100.0			Net Sales	100.0	100.0
							Gross Profit		
	96.5	96.1	94.7	96.0			Operating Expenses	95.6	94.7
	3.5	3.9	5.3	4.0			Operating Profit	4.4	5.3
	1.7	1.1	1.5	.4			All Other Expenses (net)	.4	.8
	1.8	2.8	3.8	3.5			Profit Before Taxes	4.0	4.5
							RATIOS		
	2.6	2.1	2.1	1.6				2.0	2.4
	1.4	1.3	1.2	1.2			Current	1.3	1.3
	.6	.9	1.0	.9				.9	1.0
	2.5	1.8	1.9	1.4				1.7	2.1
(64)	1.3	1.1	1.0	1.0			Quick	1.1	1.2
	.5	.7	.9	.9				.7	.8
0	UND	18 20.1	29 12.4	35 10.5				21 17.1	24 15.4
21	17.3	30 12.1	40 9.2	53 6.9			Sales/Receivables	36 10.1	37 10.0
34	10.8	44 8.3	58 6.3	73 5.0				55 6.7	56 6.5
							Cost of Sales/Inventory		
							Cost of Sales/Payables		
	15.3	12.9	12.7	11.7				11.3	11.2
	48.9	37.1	40.0	31.8			Sales/Working Capital	30.3	27.9
	-22.6	-171.7	-825.0	-47.9				-87.6	-363.6
(54)	8.1	(70) 9.4	(51) 21.9	(17) 11.3				(223) 8.5	(244) 13.1
	2.1	3.4	6.4	3.8			EBIT/Interest	4.0	4.5
	-.6	1.5	1.8	2.7				2.0	1.9
		(23) 6.0	(13) 4.8				Net Profit + Depr., Dep.,	(66) 5.0	(68) 5.9
		2.2	3.3				Amort./Cur. Mat. L./T/D	2.6	3.0
		1.1	1.3					1.2	1.7
	.4	.3	.2	.2				.3	.3
	.8	.5	.5	.5			Fixed/Worth	.7	.7
	-1.9	2.0	1.1	3.2				2.5	2.1
	.8	1.0	.6	1.3				.9	.9
	3.8	2.0	2.1	3.2			Debt/Worth	1.9	1.9
	-4.7	4.6	5.0	9.5				7.0	5.3
	141.0	46.2	59.1	78.8			% Profit Before Taxes/Tangible	61.4	68.4
(44)	40.7	(62) 18.8	(58) 33.4	(17) 38.3			Net Worth	(220) 32.2	(233) 27.4
	4.1	8.0	12.9	19.1				8.9	8.9
	35.1	17.5	23.6	14.3			% Profit Before Taxes/Total	22.3	24.6
	5.1	7.8	10.3	6.9			Assets	10.6	9.4
	-7.1	2.4	3.3	5.2				2.9	2.9
	57.7	57.1	58.0	59.8				45.6	41.2
	27.6	24.0	25.0	32.9			Sales/Net Fixed Assets	24.6	20.9
	11.9	11.8	12.6	13.2				9.6	8.9
	9.3	5.7	5.5	4.2				5.8	5.7
	5.9	4.2	4.7	3.8			Sales/Total Assets	4.2	3.7
	3.8	3.0	2.0	1.8				2.6	2.5
	.7	.8	.8	.6				.7	.8
(49)	1.7	(69) 1.4	(59) 1.2	(16) 1.0			% Depr., Dep., Amort./Sales	(220) 1.4	(232) 1.5
	3.2	2.5	2.3	2.5				3.3	3.2
	5.3	2.8	2.1				% Officers', Directors',	3.0	3.0
(37)	7.5	(48) 4.3	(18) 2.7				Owners' Comp/Sales	(119) 5.7	(142) 5.6
	12.8	8.1	7.0					9.2	8.7
	92155M	385302M	1246697M	1475558M	991188M	1947746M	Net Sales ($)	3904914M	5616474M
	15425M	79897M	312088M	432464M	439898M	357426M	Total Assets ($)	1012599M	1724345M

Comparative Historical Data / Current Data Sorted By Sales

			Type of Statement	0-1MM	1-3MM	3-5MM	5-10MM	10-25MM	25MM & OVER
29	18	30	Unqualified		2	1	1	11	15
40	41	45	Reviewed	1	7	9	5	14	9
64	74	48	Compiled	10	16	7	9	3	3
39	34	40	Tax Returns	13	17	3	5	1	1
58	69	70	Other	6	15	12	10	11	16
4/1/00-3/31/01 ALL	4/1/01-3/31/02 ALL	4/1/02-3/31/03 ALL		38 (4/1-9/30/02)			195 (10/1/02-3/31/03)		
230	236	233	NUMBER OF STATEMENTS	30	57	32	30	40	44
%	%	%	**ASSETS**	%	%	%	%	%	%
10.6	10.3	11.5	Cash & Equivalents	15.3	11.5	10.7	12.8	10.2	9.8
41.8	37.8	39.0	Trade Receivables (net)	23.3	33.3	38.1	43.7	45.3	48.7
3.4	3.9	2.9	Inventory	6.1	2.3	3.4	4.0	1.2	2.1
4.1	4.5	5.1	All Other Current	3.3	3.8	7.8	4.6	6.5	5.3
60.0	56.4	58.6	Total Current	48.0	50.9	60.0	65.0	63.2	66.0
27.2	27.8	24.7	Fixed Assets (net)	33.1	34.0	26.6	19.9	19.2	13.7
4.7	6.9	6.9	Intangibles (net)	11.5	6.3	2.6	5.1	4.0	11.4
8.1	8.9	9.9	All Other Non-Current	7.4	8.7	10.7	9.9	13.6	8.9
100.0	100.0	100.0	Total	100.0	100.0	100.0	100.0	100.0	100.0
			LIABILITIES						
13.5	14.5	15.0	Notes Payable-Short Term	16.9	20.0	14.9	10.1	13.0	12.3
4.6	5.4	4.2	Cur. Mat.-L/T/D	6.1	4.7	4.5	3.7	3.1	3.1
11.9	11.2	12.2	Trade Payables	5.4	9.6	11.8	17.5	12.7	16.4
.5	.4	.4	Income Taxes Payable	.0	.5	1.1	.6	.1	.4
15.1	14.7	17.1	All Other Current	13.3	18.2	13.3	17.7	19.6	18.1
45.6	46.2	48.8	Total Current	41.7	52.9	45.6	49.8	48.5	50.3
13.2	16.7	15.2	Long Term Debt	26.0	23.5	11.8	11.2	7.0	9.7
.7	.5	.4	Deferred Taxes	.1	.3	.9	.3	.4	.2
6.8	5.0	5.8	All Other Non-Current	4.2	6.0	6.4	5.3	8.4	4.0
33.6	31.6	29.9	Net Worth	28.0	17.3	35.2	33.5	35.7	35.8
100.0	100.0	100.0	Total Liabilities & Net Worth	100.0	100.0	100.0	100.0	100.0	100.0
			INCOME DATA						
100.0	100.0	100.0	Net Sales	100.0	100.0	100.0	100.0	100.0	100.0
			Gross Profit						
95.2	95.7	95.9	Operating Expenses	95.0	95.5	96.1	96.8	95.3	96.7
4.8	4.3	4.1	Operating Profit	5.0	4.5	3.9	3.2	4.7	3.3
.8	1.4	1.3	All Other Expenses (net)	2.4	2.3	.8	1.0	.7	.5
4.0	2.9	2.8	Profit Before Taxes	2.6	2.2	3.1	2.2	4.0	2.8
			RATIOS						
2.0	1.9	2.1		3.9	1.9	2.8	2.1	2.1	1.7
1.4	1.3	1.3	Current	1.6	1.2	1.2	1.3	1.3	1.2
1.0	.9	.9		.6	.5	.9	1.0	1.0	1.0
1.8	1.6	1.9		3.1	1.8	1.8	1.9	1.9	1.6
1.2	1.1	(232) 1.1	Quick	1.4	(56) 1.1	1.0	1.2	1.0	1.0
.8	.7	.7		.4	.4	.7	.8	.8	.9
22 16.3	21 17.8	19 19.1		0 UND	14 25.4	19 19.6	19 19.3	24 15.5	29 12.6
37 9.8	34 10.8	32 11.5	Sales/Receivables	19 18.9	29 12.7	31 11.8	37 9.8	37 9.9	38 9.5
57 6.4	51 7.2	47 7.8		42 8.6	42 8.6	61 6.0	47 7.8	52 7.1	47 7.8
			Cost of Sales/Inventory						
			Cost of Sales/Payables						
11.6	12.5	13.0		9.4	16.0	12.8	13.5	11.9	13.9
28.1	32.2	40.9	Sales/Working Capital	33.4	59.2	40.2	27.3	37.8	48.8
-270.6	-74.5	-80.1		-60.0	-21.8	-70.1	NM	-620.4	-484.1
(209) 13.1	(210) 12.4	(200) 12.6		(22) 6.2	(50) 6.5	(31) 6.9	(28) 13.0	(31) 24.9	(38) 17.2
3.9	3.5	3.4	EBIT/Interest	1.5	2.5	3.0	4.0	6.0	5.4
1.4	1.3	1.3		.4	-.2	1.2	.9	2.6	2.0
(53) 6.9	(50) 5.0	(47) 4.9	Net Profit + Depr., Dep.,			(10) 3.6			(11) 4.8
2.9	2.0	2.1	Amort./Cur. Mat. L/T/D			1.1			1.9
1.4	1.2	1.1				.7			.4
.3	.4	.3		.3	.4	.3	.2	.2	.2
.7	.8	.7	Fixed/Worth	1.6	.8	.8	.5	.5	.6
1.6	2.9	4.4		-1.5	-3.9	2.0	1.7	1.1	1.7
.9	.9	.9		.5	.9	1.0	1.1	.7	1.4
1.9	2.1	2.3	Debt/Worth	3.4	2.1	1.9	2.3	2.4	2.5
6.2	7.9	13.5		-5.3	-7.7	4.0	6.7	5.2	7.4
(206) 69.3	(193) 62.1	(184) 68.0	% Profit Before Taxes/Tangible	(21) 73.0	(38) 103.0	(28) 39.7	(25) 48.9	(35) 83.2	(37) 82.8
26.6	22.2	25.5	Net Worth	15.2	23.8	13.0	23.2	38.3	38.1
6.4	8.9	8.3		2.8	6.2	2.3	13.5	13.5	17.4
21.5	18.0	19.9	% Profit Before Taxes/Total	11.7	22.3	14.8	18.1	26.5	17.7
9.0	8.5	7.1	Assets	3.1	7.2	5.1	8.5	12.4	7.4
1.3	.9	1.6		-3.1	-3.2	1.1	2.0	4.1	3.8
47.6	47.8	58.4		37.7	41.8	38.2	92.3	71.3	67.6
20.6	20.5	25.3	Sales/Net Fixed Assets	18.8	20.4	19.7	27.7	34.4	31.4
9.5	8.8	12.5		7.9	-7.4	10.2	17.4	14.6	23.7
5.5	5.8	6.1		6.4	7.6	6.4	5.8	6.1	5.6
4.1	4.1	4.6	Sales/Total Assets	3.8	4.5	4.1	5.1	4.7	4.7
2.7	2.5	2.9		2.0	2.7	2.6	3.6	2.8	3.5
(202) .8	(204) .7	(199) .8		(22) .9	(46) .8	(30) 1.0	(28) .6	(37) .7	(36) .6
1.4	1.5	1.3	% Depr., Dep., Amort./Sales	2.5	1.8	1.4	1.5	1.1	.9
3.0	3.3	2.4		6.6	3.9	2.6	2.0	2.2	1.2
(125) 2.9	(130) 2.2	(105) 2.9	% Officers', Directors',	(17) 6.3	(34) 4.2	(22) 2.9	(16) 3.4	(11) .8	
5.7	4.4	5.5	Owners' Comp/Sales	8.5	6.1	5.1	4.3	1.9	
9.5	8.0	8.0		15.3	9.8			2.6	
4128240M	4813308M	6138646M	Net Sales ($)	16605M	105322M	126366M	217124M	622505M	5050724M
1456195M	1499028M	1637198M	Total Assets ($)	6408M	34182M	40626M	60451M	184779M	1310752M

Current Data Sorted By Assets   Comparative Historical Data

	0-500M	500M-2MM	2-10MM	10-50MM	50-100MM	100-250MM	Type of Statement	4/1/98-3/31/99 ALL	4/1/99-3/31/00 ALL
		2	9	3	1	2	Unqualified	23	12
	6	21	18	1			Reviewed	49	51
	39	22	9	1		2	Compiled	68	72
	71	23	1			3	Tax Returns	38	40
	35	23	13	2	1	1	Other	50	64
		42 (4/1-9/30/02)		267 (10/1/02-3/31/03)					
NUMBER OF STATEMENTS	151	91	50	7	2	8		228	239
	%	%	%	%	%	%	ASSETS	%	%
	11.9	9.5	8.3				Cash & Equivalents	11.9	9.0
	14.7	30.7	30.7				Trade Receivables (net)	24.9	25.2
	7.6	8.8	9.1				Inventory	8.0	7.3
	1.8	3.0	4.3				All Other Current	2.3	2.4
	36.0	51.9	52.4				Total Current	47.1	43.8
	55.9	39.2	39.4				Fixed Assets (net)	44.3	46.6
	1.9	3.0	.9				Intangibles (net)	2.4	3.4
	6.3	5.9	7.3				All Other Non-Current	6.2	6.2
	100.0	100.0	100.0				Total	100.0	100.0
							LIABILITIES		
	12.1	12.6	9.8				Notes Payable-Short Term	9.8	9.8
	8.2	6.6	7.6				Cur. Mat.-L/T/D	7.5	8.6
	8.6	11.3	11.9				Trade Payables	11.0	10.8
	.2	.4	.5				Income Taxes Payable	.2	.4
	10.7	7.7	9.5				All Other Current	9.3	16.8
	39.9	38.6	39.2				Total Current	37.8	46.5
	36.9	19.3	18.6				Long Term Debt	23.0	27.5
	.1	.6	1.9				Deferred Taxes	.8	.8
	6.0	4.2	2.6				All Other Non-Current	4.5	2.5
	17.1	37.3	37.7				Net Worth	34.0	22.6
	100.0	100.0	100.0				Total Liabilities & Net Worth	100.0	100.0
							INCOME DATA		
	100.0	100.0	100.0				Net Sales	100.0	100.0
							Gross Profit		
	95.3	95.8	94.3				Operating Expenses	93.8	94.7
	4.7	4.2	5.7				Operating Profit	6.2	5.3
	1.0	1.1	1.5				All Other Expenses (net)	1.2	1.2
	3.6	3.2	4.2				Profit Before Taxes	4.9	4.0
							RATIOS		
	2.0	2.3	1.6					2.4	1.9
	.9	1.4	1.4				Current	1.3	1.2
	.4	.9	1.1					.8	.7
	1.6	1.8	1.3					1.8	1.5
	.6	1.1	1.0				Quick	(226) 1.0	.9
	.2	.6	.7					.5	.4
	0 UND	19 19.4	28 12.9					9 39.7	7 48.7
	6 57.8	36 10.2	40 9.1				Sales/Receivables	29 12.8	31 11.8
	24 15.2	53 6.8	61 6.0					56 6.5	51 7.1
							Cost of Sales/Inventory		
							Cost of Sales/Payables		
	19.6	8.1	10.5					9.6	12.5
	-170.5	21.6	20.8				Sales/Working Capital	30.0	41.3
	-16.4	-116.6	127.2					-43.0	-28.8
	(130) 7.0	(87) 9.5	(46) 7.8					(205) 9.0	(228) 7.7
	2.3	2.8	4.0				EBIT/Interest	4.2	3.2
	.3	1.4	1.7					1.7	1.4
		(28) 4.7	(21) 2.5				Net Profit + Depr., Dep.,	(56) 3.3	(55) 2.9
		2.1	1.6				Amort./Cur. Mat. L /T/D	2.0	1.8
		1.1	1.1					1.2	1.3
	.9	.6	.6					.6	.7
	2.7	1.1	1.0				Fixed/Worth	1.3	1.4
	UND	2.7	1.8					3.3	3.7
	1.2	.8	1.0					.8	1.0
	3.8	1.6	1.8				Debt/Worth	1.9	2.0
	-105.0	5.3	3.1					5.1	5.6
	117.7	59.0	39.1				% Profit Before Taxes/Tangible	72.2	54.7
	(113) 24.6	(84) 19.6	(48) 14.1				Net Worth	(203) 30.9	(207) 27.5
	-2.4	4.8	4.4					10.8	8.9
	29.4	14.7	11.7				% Profit Before Taxes/Total	23.5	20.7
	6.1	5.4	6.5				Assets	10.9	9.0
	-2.7	1.7	1.3					2.9	1.9
	14.3	13.7	11.4					12.7	13.8
	7.4	8.5	7.9				Sales/Net Fixed Assets	7.2	7.7
	4.5	5.6	4.2					4.6	4.1
	5.6	3.9	3.4					4.0	4.3
	3.8	3.0	2.5				Sales/Total Assets	2.8	2.9
	2.7	2.1	1.8					2.1	1.9
	2.9	2.6	2.5					2.5	2.4
	(127) 5.3	3.7	(45) 3.3				% Depr., Dep., Amort./Sales	(200) 4.0	(220) 4.0
	8.4	6.1	5.7					5.9	6.7
	4.1	2.2	1.6				% Officers', Directors',	3.4	3.3
	(93) 6.6	(54) 3.9	(19) 3.1				Owners' Comp/Sales	(113) 5.7	(134) 6.0
	11.5	5.9	6.3					9.2	9.5
	135675M	316185M	517015M	403784M	159005M	8889558M	Net Sales ($)	3141085M	3461787M
	34678M	102234M	206463M	162427M	126422M	1300870M	Total Assets ($)	1258989M	1060042M

M = $ thousand   MM = $ million

See Pages 11 through 18 for Explanation of Ratios and Data

Comparative Historical Data   Current Data Sorted By Sales

				Type of Statement						
14		16		17	Unqualified		1	2	2	4	8
43		42		46	Reviewed	4	16	4	14	8	
73		74		73	Compiled	25	26	7	8	4	3
41		56		98	Tax Returns	54	24	12	4	1	3
68		88		75	Other	21	26	6	14	3	5
4/1/00-3/31/01 ALL		4/1/01-3/31/02 ALL		4/1/02-3/31/03 ALL		42 (4/1-9/30/02)			267 (10/1/02-3/31/03)		
						0-1MM	1-3MM	3-5MM	5-10MM	10-25MM	25MM & OVER
239		276		309	NUMBER OF STATEMENTS	104	93	31	42	20	19
%		%		%	ASSETS	%	%	%	%	%	%
10.1		9.1		10.5	Cash & Equivalents	11.5	9.5	11.9	8.0	14.1	9.4
28.0		24.0		22.0	Trade Receivables (net)	12.2	23.8	27.4	34.1	33.7	19.1
9.3		9.3		8.5	Inventory	7.1	9.1	6.5	11.5	7.4	10.9
2.4		3.3		2.8	All Other Current	1.8	2.1	4.1	3.8	3.0	6.6
49.8		45.8		43.8	Total Current	32.5	44.5	50.0	57.4	58.2	46.0
43.5		46.0		47.6	Fixed Assets (net)	59.0	46.7	42.3	34.3	34.5	41.1
2.1		2.6		2.3	Intangibles (net)	1.3	3.6	1.7	1.4	.6	6.8
4.6		5.6		6.3	All Other Non-Current	7.2	5.2	6.0	6.9	6.7	6.1
100.0		100.0		100.0	Total	100.0	100.0	100.0	100.0	100.0	100.0
					LIABILITIES						
9.7		13.8		11.9	Notes Payable-Short Term	8.4	16.4	13.5	10.6	10.6	11.6
7.8		9.7		7.5	Cur. Mat.-L/T/D	8.2	7.1	8.0	8.3	5.3	5.4
12.2		12.6		9.9	Trade Payables	7.5	9.9	13.7	12.6	12.2	9.1
.2		.2		.3	Income Taxes Payable	.2	.2	.4	.8	.3	.4
12.2		20.1		9.6	All Other Current	10.6	8.0	8.2	8.7	13.8	11.3
42.2		56.4		39.3	Total Current	34.9	41.5	43.7	41.0	42.3	37.8
25.4		30.6		28.4	Long Term Debt	40.7	26.2	19.9	15.8	15.1	27.0
.7		.7		.6	Deferred Taxes	.1	.2	1.1	2.0	1.5	.6
3.3		5.5		4.7	All Other Non-Current	6.8	4.4	3.1	3.3	1.9	3.9
28.4		6.8		27.0	Net Worth	17.5	27.7	32.1	37.9	39.3	30.6
100.0		100.0		100.0	Total Liabilities & Net Worth	100.0	100.0	100.0	100.0	100.0	100.0
					INCOME DATA						
100.0		100.0		100.0	Net Sales	100.0	100.0	100.0	100.0	100.0	100.0
					Gross Profit						
95.3		95.7		95.2	Operating Expenses	94.5	95.7	95.2	96.6	94.7	93.8
4.7		4.3		4.8	Operating Profit	5.5	4.3	4.8	3.4	5.3	6.2
1.0		1.3		1.1	All Other Expenses (net)	1.6	1.0	.8	.8	.7	1.3
3.7		3.1		3.7	Profit Before Taxes	3.9	3.4	4.1	2.6	4.6	4.9
					RATIOS						
2.0		1.9		2.0		2.0	2.3	2.0	1.9	1.8	1.8
1.2		1.1		1.2	Current	.9	1.3	1.2	1.4	1.2	1.3
.8		.7		.7		.4	.6	.8	1.1	.9	1.0

	1.4		1.4		1.5	Quick		1.7		1.6		1.5		1.4		1.3		1.5
(238)	.9	(274)	.8		.9			.5		.9		1.0		1.0		1.0		.9
	.5		.4		.4			.2		.4		.6		.7		.7		.6

							Sales/Receivables										
14	25.4	6	59.6	4	96.0		0	UND	7	54.7	14	25.3	27	13.3	25	14.9	11	33.5
32	11.3	25	14.5	24	15.5		5	66.4	26	14.1	34	10.8	40	9.2	39	9.4	30	12.0
54	6.7	50	7.3	43	8.4		24	15.4	47	7.8	53	6.8	58	6.3	54	6.7	45	8.1

					Cost of Sales/Inventory						

					Cost of Sales/Payables						

					Sales/Working Capital						
11.5		12.7		12.5		20.8	10.1	10.9	10.8	10.2	18.3
42.3		56.3		49.6		-190.7	42.6	34.0	22.5	21.5	45.4
-47.6		-27.9		-26.1		-17.3	-18.9	-65.9	128.1	-66.1	999.8

								EBIT/Interest									
	8.0		7.1		8.2			5.7		8.8		24.9		8.2		13.2		8.9
(223)	2.8	(265)	2.3	(279)	2.8		(86)	1.4	(88)	2.4	(29)	5.4	(40)	2.7	(18)	4.7	(18)	4.8
	1.2		.9		1.0			-.7		1.0		1.9		1.4		2.7		2.1

							Net Profit + Depr., Dep., Amort./Cur. Mat. L/T/D								
	3.1		2.7		4.2				5.4		3.2		2.9		
(51)	1.6	(57)	2.0	(62)	2.1		(19)	2.0	(10)	2.2	(17)	1.4		
	.8		1.1		1.1			1.1		1.4		.9		

					Fixed/Worth						
.7		.8		.7		1.0	.7	.7	.5	.5	.8
1.2		1.5		1.6		2.6	1.5	1.4	.9	.9	1.4
3.0		6.4		5.1		UND	5.0	3.2	2.1	1.9	4.3

					Debt/Worth						
1.0		1.2		1.0		.9	1.1	.9	.8	.9	1.4
2.2		2.7		2.2		3.1	2.5	1.7	1.6	2.1	2.2
5.2		11.6		8.2		UND	9.0	6.2	4.2	2.6	4.3

							% Profit Before Taxes/Tangible Net Worth								
	53.2		50.0		69.3			95.7		86.3		77.7		40.4		41.7		159.0
(200)	23.1	(226)	20.6	(260)	19.8		(79)	14.8	(78)	16.7	(28)	29.4	(39)	12.3	(19)	33.7	(17)	25.6
	5.8		2.1		3.3			-12.2		4.2		12.0		3.8		13.8		12.7

					% Profit Before Taxes/Total Assets						
20.0		17.3		20.7		29.8	17.3	29.6	11.6	19.2	29.8
7.5		6.1		6.0		2.3	5.4	7.7	5.3	10.9	8.6
.9		-1.0		.0		-6.2	.6	2.1	1.8	5.0	2.9

					Sales/Net Fixed Assets						
13.2		13.4		13.6		11.5	14.1	18.8	14.5	15.0	12.3
7.8		7.6		7.7		6.4	8.5	7.8	9.3	8.6	9.0
4.4		4.5		4.6		3.9	4.4	6.4	6.3	7.1	4.8

					Sales/Total Assets						
4.3		4.4		4.4		5.3	4.4	5.3	3.8	3.8	4.0
3.0		3.0		3.2		3.4	3.1	3.6	3.2	2.8	3.2
2.2		2.1		2.2		2.2	2.3	2.5	2.2	2.1	1.8

							% Depr., Dep., Amort./Sales								
	2.2		2.2		2.7			3.1		3.0		2.4		2.3		1.6		2.3
(211)	3.7	(246)	3.9	(273)	4.2		(89)	5.9	(83)	4.6	(41)	3.3	(18)	2.8	(11)	5.2
	5.3		6.4		7.3			9.6		7.3		6.6		4.6		3.9		6.6

							% Officers', Directors', Owners' Comp/Sales								
	3.0		3.1		2.6			5.1		2.9		1.8		1.6		1.5		
(125)	5.3	(138)	5.3	(173)	5.0		(56)	8.0	(64)	4.5	(15)	2.5	(21)	4.8	(11)	2.8		
	9.4		8.1		8.8			12.1		8.5		4.9		7.3		5.0		

					Net Sales ($)						
2245962M		3138307M		10421222M		54607M	161898M	121925M	276134M	291496M	9515162M
923373M		1283730M		1933094M	Total Assets ($)	21502M	63670M	38585M	99545M	109454M	1600338M

© RMA 2003   M = $ thousand   MM = $ million
See Pages 11 through 18 for Explanation of Ratios and Data

Current Data Sorted By Assets   Comparative Historical Data

			1			Type of Statement		
	2		1			Unqualified	3	3
6	2				1	Reviewed	1	2
5	1	1			1	Compiled	6	11
3		1	1			Tax Returns	5	7
			1			Other	4	5

0-500M	500M-2MM	2-10MM	10-50MM	50-100MM	100-250MM		4/1/98-3/31/99 ALL	4/1/99-3/31/00 ALL
	3 (4/1-9/30/02)			23 (10/1/02-3/31/03)				
14	5	2	3		2	**NUMBER OF STATEMENTS**	19	28
%	%	%	%	%	%	**ASSETS**	%	%
14.3				D		Cash & Equivalents	11.9	15.8
26.8				A		Trade Receivables (net)	19.3	14.4
6.4				T		Inventory	4.9	5.7
9.2				A		All Other Current	5.6	4.9
56.6						Total Current	41.7	40.8
30.2				N		Fixed Assets (net)	43.5	44.5
8.2				O		Intangibles (net)	6.4	8.4
4.9				T		All Other Non-Current	8.4	6.2
100.0						Total	100.0	100.0
				A		**LIABILITIES**		
32.9				V		Notes Payable-Short Term	10.3	10.0
10.8				A		Cur. Mat.-L/T/D	6.7	12.2
8.6				I		Trade Payables	6.3	5.6
.1				L		Income Taxes Payable	.6	.2
10.9				A		All Other Current	9.6	7.3
63.2				B		Total Current	33.6	35.3
25.6				L		Long Term Debt	30.4	23.7
.0				E		Deferred Taxes	.0	.2
1.4						All Other Non-Current	2.4	8.9
9.7						Net Worth	33.6	32.0
100.0						Total Liabilities & Net Worth	100.0	100.0
						INCOME DATA		
100.0						Net Sales	100.0	100.0
						Gross Profit		
92.5						Operating Expenses	91.0	94.5
7.5						Operating Profit	9.0	5.5
1.4						All Other Expenses (net)	1.4	-3.3
6.1						Profit Before Taxes	7.6	8.8
						RATIOS		
4.8							2.0	2.1
1.0						Current	1.1	1.3
.5							.5	.6
4.3							1.3	1.8
.7						Quick	.8	.7
.1							.3	.5
0 UND							0 UND	0 UND
12 29.7						Sales/Receivables	14 26.5	12 29.2
54 6.7							49 7.4	29 12.4
						Cost of Sales/Inventory		
						Cost of Sales/Payables		
5.2							8.4	14.5
NM						Sales/Working Capital	191.0	42.0
-18.0							-19.2	-22.6
46.7							16.3	12.5
6.5						EBIT/Interest	(18) 3.3	(26) 3.8
1.9							.7	.9
						Net Profit + Depr., Dep., Amort./Cur. Mat. L /T/D		
.4							.7	.6
15.3						Fixed/Worth	1.4	1.4
-1.1							5.7	25.7
.9							.9	.5
40.5						Debt/Worth	2.2	1.8
-5.7							8.1	57.1
						% Profit Before Taxes/Tangible Net Worth	(16) 99.5 / 63.3 / 10.2	(22) 106.9 / 31.5 / 5.2
67.8							35.8	71.7
25.8						% Profit Before Taxes/Total Assets	22.0	17.4
2.7							-.6	-.3
54.5							17.3	17.8
13.4						Sales/Net Fixed Assets	5.8	10.0
8.8							4.7	5.1
6.3							3.6	5.3
5.2						Sales/Total Assets	2.5	3.1
2.9							2.0	2.2
2.6							3.0	2.1
(10) 3.3						% Depr., Dep., Amort./Sales	(18) 4.3	(23) 3.7
8.2							6.7	5.5
						% Officers', Directors', Owners' Comp/Sales		(11) 8.5 / 11.3 / 15.0
11628M	17890M	14435M	157254M		2763015M	Net Sales ($)	498289M	251984M
2583M	4401M	5573M	62976M		268965M	Total Assets ($)	233683M	88742M

Note in 50-100MM column: **DATA NOT AVAILABLE**

M = $ thousand   MM = $ million
See Pages 11 through 18 for Explanation of Ratios and Data

Comparative Historical Data   Current Data Sorted By Sales

1	1	1	Type of Statement						
									1
1	2	3	Unqualified						
9	4	9	Reviewed			1	2		1
4	13	8	Compiled	5	3				1
4	8	5	Tax Returns	3	2	2			1
			Other	1	2			1	1
4/1/00-3/31/01 ALL	4/1/01-3/31/02 ALL	4/1/02-3/31/03 ALL		**3 (4/1-9/30/02)**			**23 (10/1/02-3/31/03)**		
				0-1MM	1-3MM	3-5MM	5-10MM	10-25MM	25MM & OVER
19	28	26	**NUMBER OF STATEMENTS**	9	7	3	2	1	4
%	%	%	**ASSETS**	%	%	%	%	%	%
19.0	16.7	12.6	Cash & Equivalents						
24.5	16.7	26.0	Trade Receivables (net)						
1.9	5.2	4.4	Inventory						
4.1	2.1	7.7	All Other Current						
49.5	40.7	50.8	Total Current						
35.2	30.4	30.7	Fixed Assets (net)						
9.0	21.9	13.4	Intangibles (net)						
6.4	7.0	5.1	All Other Non-Current						
100.0	100.0	100.0	Total						
			LIABILITIES						
15.7	6.2	20.5	Notes Payable-Short Term						
7.0	8.1	7.4	Cur. Mat.-L/T/D						
10.0	6.4	8.2	Trade Payables						
.1	.6	.1	Income Taxes Payable						
9.2	10.8	11.5	All Other Current						
41.9	32.1	47.6	Total Current						
22.5	16.5	22.4	Long Term Debt						
.0	.7	.1	Deferred Taxes						
3.3	1.2	6.9	All Other Non-Current						
32.3	49.5	23.0	Net Worth						
100.0	100.0	100.0	Total Liabilities & Net Worth						
			INCOME DATA						
100.0	100.0	100.0	Net Sales						
			Gross Profit						
94.6	89.2	92.5	Operating Expenses						
5.4	10.8	7.5	Operating Profit						
–1.1	1.4	1.3	All Other Expenses (net)						
6.5	9.4	6.2	Profit Before Taxes						
			RATIOS						
2.9	2.9	3.5	Current						
1.2	1.4	1.1							
.7	.5	.6							
2.6	2.8	3.3	Quick						
1.1	.7	.7							
.6	.2	.3							
4 101.2	0 UND	0 UND	Sales/Receivables						
25 14.9	9 39.2	15 23.7							
44 8.2	32 11.5	54 6.7							
			Cost of Sales/Inventory						
			Cost of Sales/Payables						
10.2	10.8	6.8	Sales/Working Capital						
48.2	40.5	118.6							
–25.8	–31.8	–31.4							
(18) 34.0	(24) 18.1	(25) 46.7	EBIT/Interest						
7.6	6.2	6.3							
2.2	1.9	1.6							
			Net Profit + Depr., Dep., Amort./Cur. Mat. L/T/D						
.6	.5	.4	Fixed/Worth						
1.1	1.5	1.4							
3.6	NM	–4.4							
.7	.6	.6	Debt/Worth						
2.0	1.6	1.8							
13.1	NM	–10.5							
(15) 84.9	(21) 107.5	(17) 103.3	% Profit Before Taxes/Tangible Net Worth						
41.2	80.0	46.9							
12.2	5.6	22.1							
30.7	50.4	57.3	% Profit Before Taxes/Total Assets						
19.0	20.8	19.6							
5.6	2.6	2.3							
23.5	31.7	24.4	Sales/Net Fixed Assets						
14.6	16.1	13.5							
7.2	7.7	9.4							
5.2	7.5	6.3	Sales/Total Assets						
3.9	3.2	3.9							
2.9	2.2	2.9							
(16) 1.2	(17) 1.4	(19) 1.6	% Depr., Dep., Amort./Sales						
3.4	2.8	3.1							
5.3	4.7	4.3							
(12) 5.8	(16) 2.7	(13) 4.4	% Officers', Directors', Owners' Comp/Sales						
8.9	7.5	8.9							
14.5	14.5	11.7							
2386073M	1459520M	2964222M	Net Sales ($)	4103M	11601M	11923M	12121M	10661M	2913813M
287980M	333029M	344498M	Total Assets ($)	1267M	2547M	4191M	14334M	2664M	319495M

© RMA 2003

M = $ thousand   MM = $ million
See Pages 11 through 18 for Explanation of Ratios and Data

Current Data Sorted By Assets | Comparative Historical Data

0-500M	500M-2MM	2-10MM	10-50MM	50-100MM	100-250MM		4/1/98-3/31/99 ALL	4/1/99-3/31/00 ALL
		2 4	1			Type of Statement Unqualified		
2 2 2	2 7 5 8	1	3	1		Reviewed / Compiled / Tax Returns / Other		
	8 (4/1-9/30/02)		32 (10/1/02-3/31/03)					
6	22	7	4	1		**NUMBER OF STATEMENTS**		
%	%	%	%	%	%	**ASSETS**	%	%
	8.6				D	Cash & Equivalents	D	D
	40.2				A	Trade Receivables (net)	A	A
	3.9				T	Inventory	T	T
	5.0				A	All Other Current	A	A
	57.7					Total Current		
	21.7				N	Fixed Assets (net)	N	N
	6.0				O	Intangibles (net)	O	O
	14.6				T	All Other Non-Current	T	T
	100.0					Total		
					A	**LIABILITIES**	A	A
	14.8				V	Notes Payable-Short Term	V	V
	6.7				A	Cur. Mat.-L/T/D	A	A
	12.7				I	Trade Payables	I	I
	.0				L	Income Taxes Payable	L	L
	11.8				A	All Other Current	A	A
	46.0				B	Total Current	B	B
	13.0				L	Long Term Debt	L	L
	.1				E	Deferred Taxes	E	E
	.4					All Other Non-Current		
	40.5					Net Worth		
	100.0					Total Liabilities & Net Worth		
	100.0					**INCOME DATA** Net Sales		
						Gross Profit		
	98.0					Operating Expenses		
	2.0					Operating Profit		
	.8					All Other Expenses (net)		
	1.2					Profit Before Taxes		
	1.9					**RATIOS**		
	1.3					Current		
	.9							
	1.7							
	1.0					Quick		
	.7							
20	18.4							
31	11.6					Sales/Receivables		
50	7.3							
						Cost of Sales/Inventory		
						Cost of Sales/Payables		
	11.9							
	41.5					Sales/Working Capital		
	−131.8							
	7.6							
	2.4					EBIT/Interest		
	.3							
						Net Profit + Depr., Dep., Amort./Cur. Mat. L /T/D		
	.3							
	.7					Fixed/Worth		
	1.2							
	.8							
	1.8					Debt/Worth		
	4.4							
	38.9					% Profit Before Taxes/Tangible		
(20)	13.8					Net Worth		
	−1.2							
	19.0					% Profit Before Taxes/Total		
	2.9					Assets		
	−1.2							
	44.3							
	27.9					Sales/Net Fixed Assets		
	11.3							
	6.0							
	3.7					Sales/Total Assets		
	2.7							
	.8							
(17)	1.5					% Depr., Dep., Amort./Sales		
	3.4							
	3.8					% Officers', Directors',		
(15)	6.3					Owners' Comp/Sales		
	8.2							
9676M	94294M	85539M	289836M	151414M		Net Sales ($)		
1610M	22774M	34333M	78894M	95755M		Total Assets ($)		

M = $ thousand   MM = $ million
See Pages 11 through 18 for Explanation of Ratios and Data

Comparative Historical Data   Current Data Sorted By Sales

Type of Statement

		4/1/02-3/31/03 ALL		0-1MM	1-3MM	3-5MM	5-10MM	10-25MM	25MM & OVER
4/1/00-3/31/01 ALL	4/1/01-3/31/02 ALL								
		2	Unqualified					2	
		7	Reviewed			1	3	1	2
		9	Compiled		4	2	2	1	
		7	Tax Returns	1	5	1			
		15	Other	1	4	4	2		4
				8 (4/1-9/30/02)		32 (10/1/02-3/31/03)			
		40	**NUMBER OF STATEMENTS**	2	13	8	7	4	6

(Columns 4/1/00-3/31/01 ALL and 4/1/01-3/31/02 ALL: **DATA NOT AVAILABLE**)

%	%	%		%	%	%	%	%	%
			ASSETS						
		9.2	Cash & Equivalents		7.2				
		40.0	Trade Receivables (net)		38.6				
		4.6	Inventory		2.9				
		4.0	All Other Current		4.2				
		57.8	Total Current		52.8				
		24.7	Fixed Assets (net)		23.8				
		5.6	Intangibles (net)		9.0				
		11.8	All Other Non-Current		14.4				
		100.0	Total		100.0				
			LIABILITIES						
		18.5	Notes Payable-Short Term		11.7				
		5.6	Cur. Mat.-L/T/D		5.1				
		14.1	Trade Payables		13.1				
		.0	Income Taxes Payable		.0				
		10.6	All Other Current		8.4				
		48.7	Total Current		38.3				
		19.0	Long Term Debt		23.5				
		.1	Deferred Taxes		.0				
		2.6	All Other Non-Current		1.4				
		29.6	Net Worth		36.7				
		100.0	Total Liabilities & Net Worth		100.0				
			INCOME DATA						
		100.0	Net Sales		100.0				
			Gross Profit						
		97.9	Operating Expenses		96.3				
		2.1	Operating Profit		3.7				
		.9	All Other Expenses (net)		.8				
		1.2	Profit Before Taxes		2.9				
			RATIOS						
		1.8			2.2				
		1.3	Current		1.4				
		.9			.8				
		1.4			1.8				
		1.0	Quick		1.1				
		.8			.7				
		25 14.4			0 UND				
		40 9.1	Sales/Receivables		31 11.8				
		56 6.5			60 6.1				
			Cost of Sales/Inventory						
			Cost of Sales/Payables						
		13.0			11.6				
		34.1	Sales/Working Capital		15.5				
		−118.8			−81.7				
		7.5			22.0				
		2.2	EBIT/Interest		6.1				
		.2			1.0				
			Net Profit + Depr., Dep., Amort./Cur. Mat. L/T/D						
		.3			.3				
		.8	Fixed/Worth		.7				
		21.7			NM				
		1.2			.9				
		2.2	Debt/Worth		1.6				
		30.2			NM				
		37.6			56.5				
		(32) 13.8	% Profit Before Taxes/Tangible Net Worth		(10) 38.5				
		−4.2			15.2				
		16.1			28.7				
		2.4	% Profit Before Taxes/Total Assets		12.1				
		−1.4			.0				
		43.5			35.8				
		23.8	Sales/Net Fixed Assets		24.2				
		9.4			8.2				
		5.7			5.4				
		3.5	Sales/Total Assets		3.4				
		2.6			2.4				
		1.1			1.4				
		(33) 1.6	% Depr., Dep., Amort./Sales		(10) 2.0				
		3.8			7.5				
		3.3							
		(24) 5.6	% Officers', Directors', Owners' Comp/Sales						
		8.4							
		630759M	Net Sales ($)	643M	29643M	32203M	46941M	48519M	472810M
		233366M	Total Assets ($)	137M	9354M	9143M	11208M	21774M	181750M

M = $ thousand   MM = $ million
See Pages 11 through 18 for Explanation of Ratios and Data

Current Data Sorted By Assets　　　　　　　　　　　　　　　　　**Comparative Historical Data**

						Type of Statement		
		5	1		2	Unqualified		
	1	1				Reviewed		
2	3	2				Compiled		
1	2	1				Tax Returns		
2	4	6	6	1	2	Other		
	5 (4/1-9/30/02)		37 (10/1/02-3/31/03)				4/1/98-3/31/99 ALL	4/1/99-3/31/00 ALL
0-500M	500M-2MM	2-10MM	10-50MM	50-100MM	100-250MM			
5	10	15	7	1	4	NUMBER OF STATEMENTS		
%	%	%	%	%	%	ASSETS	%	%
	12.0	17.2				Cash & Equivalents	D	D
	30.8	33.2				Trade Receivables (net)	A	A
	22.1	4.5				Inventory	T	T
	2.4	3.3				All Other Current	A	A
	67.3	58.2				Total Current		
	18.9	32.4				Fixed Assets (net)	N	N
	10.7	6.6				Intangibles (net)	O	O
	3.1	2.8				All Other Non-Current	T	T
	100.0	100.0				Total		
						LIABILITIES	A	A
	11.1	7.5				Notes Payable-Short Term	V	V
	3.4	5.0				Cur. Mat.-L/T/D	A	A
	15.9	8.6				Trade Payables	I	I
	.0	.9				Income Taxes Payable	L	L
	18.8	13.4				All Other Current	A	A
	49.2	35.4				Total Current	B	B
	11.6	19.7				Long Term Debt	L	L
	.0	.1				Deferred Taxes	E	E
	9.4	5.9				All Other Non-Current		
	29.7	39.0				Net Worth		
	100.0	100.0				Total Liabilities & Net Worth		
						INCOME DATA		
	100.0	100.0				Net Sales		
						Gross Profit		
	93.6	89.1				Operating Expenses		
	6.4	10.9				Operating Profit		
	1.7	6.9				All Other Expenses (net)		
	4.8	4.0				Profit Before Taxes		
						RATIOS		
	2.9	1.7						
	1.1	1.4				Current		
	1.0	1.0						
	1.1	1.5						
	.8	1.0				Quick		
	.1	.8						
	0　UND	14　25.6						
	32　11.3	49　7.4				Sales/Receivables		
	77　4.7	81　4.5						
						Cost of Sales/Inventory		
						Cost of Sales/Payables		
	10.5	5.0						
	28.9	14.3				Sales/Working Capital		
	-178.7	150.5						
		22.5						
	(12)	3.0				EBIT/Interest		
		1.3						
						Net Profit + Depr., Dep., Amort./Cur. Mat. L./T/D		
	.3	.2						
	.6	.7				Fixed/Worth		
	-1.2	2.4						
	1.2	1.0						
	4.8	2.0				Debt/Worth		
	-5.2	3.2						
		53.2				% Profit Before Taxes/Tangible Net Worth		
	(13)	11.4						
		4.2						
	13.0	24.3				% Profit Before Taxes/Total Assets		
	4.0	2.5						
	-8.6	1.3						
	49.5	34.9						
	25.8	12.4				Sales/Net Fixed Assets		
	11.8	1.9						
	5.4	3.6						
	3.2	1.7				Sales/Total Assets		
	1.5	1.0						
		1.4				% Depr., Dep., Amort./Sales		
		3.4						
		7.9						
						% Officers', Directors', Owners' Comp/Sales		
4474M	32373M	190197M	382763M	24940M	681105M	Net Sales ($)		
699M	9222M	77009M	157321M	90966M	636196M	Total Assets ($)		

© RMA 2003

M = $ thousand　　MM = $ million
See Pages 11 through 18 for Explanation of Ratios and Data

Comparative Historical Data | **Current Data Sorted By Sales**

Type of Statement

	4/1/00-3/31/01 ALL	4/1/01-3/31/02 ALL	4/1/02-3/31/03 ALL		0-1MM	1-3MM	3-5MM	5-10MM	10-25MM	25MM & OVER
Unqualified			8					4	1	3
Reviewed			2			1				
Compiled			7		2	2		2	1	
Tax Returns			4		2		1	1		
Other			21		2	5	1	3	4	6
						5 (4/1-9/30/02)		37 (10/1/02-3/31/03)		
NUMBER OF STATEMENTS			42		6	7	3	10	6	10

(Historical columns 4/1/00-3/31/01 ALL and 4/1/01-3/31/02 ALL: DATA NOT AVAILABLE)

Financial Data

	4/1/00-3/31/01 ALL	4/1/01-3/31/02 ALL	4/1/02-3/31/03 ALL		0-1MM	1-3MM	3-5MM	5-10MM	10-25MM	25MM & OVER
	%	%	%	**ASSETS**	%	%	%	%	%	%
Cash & Equivalents			13.2					26.4		7.3
Trade Receivables (net)			31.8					28.3		38.2
Inventory			7.8					.2		3.9
All Other Current			4.5					2.6		7.7
Total Current			57.3					57.5		57.1
Fixed Assets (net)			28.0					34.9		17.0
Intangibles (net)			9.7					4.0		19.0
All Other Non-Current			4.9					3.6		7.0
Total			100.0					100.0		100.0
				LIABILITIES						
Notes Payable-Short Term			12.1					12.5		12.3
Cur. Mat.-L/T/D			6.0					3.0		4.3
Trade Payables			11.9					6.5		12.5
Income Taxes Payable			1.2					.8		.9
All Other Current			17.0					24.7		21.4
Total Current			48.3					47.5		51.4
Long Term Debt			19.8					9.4		20.3
Deferred Taxes			.2					.0		.8
All Other Non-Current			7.0					3.3		2.7
Net Worth			24.6					39.8		24.8
Total Liabilities & Net Worth			100.0					100.0		100.0
				INCOME DATA						
Net Sales			100.0					100.0		100.0
Gross Profit										
Operating Expenses			91.9					93.0		93.7
Operating Profit			8.1					7.0		6.3
All Other Expenses (net)			3.6					2.1		1.7
Profit Before Taxes			4.5					5.0		4.6

Ratios

	4/1/02-3/31/03 ALL		5-10MM	25MM & OVER
Current	1.6 / 1.2 / .8		1.8 / 1.2 / .8	1.4 / 1.0 / .8
Quick	1.3 / .9 / .5		1.6 / 1.2 / .7	1.1 / .9 / .6
Sales/Receivables	10 38.1 / 46 8.0 / 80 4.5		5 67.1 / 45 8.2 / 73 5.0	19 19.4 / 53 6.8 / 87 4.2
Cost of Sales/Inventory				
Cost of Sales/Payables				
Sales/Working Capital	10.5 / 73.7 / -23.9		4.9 / 30.0 / -91.8	15.2 / 258.9 / -26.8
EBIT/Interest	(37) 7.0 / 2.8 / .8			
Net Profit + Depr., Dep., Amort./Cur. Mat. L/T/D	(10) 6.4 / 2.9 / .7			
Fixed/Worth	.3 / .9 / -16.0		.2 / .7 / 2.6	.4 / 1.0 / -.5
Debt/Worth	1.4 / 3.3 / -24.6		1.1 / 2.5 / 3.6	1.9 / 5.2 / -2.9
% Profit Before Taxes/Tangible Net Worth	(30) 57.5 / 15.9 / 4.5		17.7 / 10.0 / -5.0	
% Profit Before Taxes/Total Assets	23.5 / 3.4 / -.2		5.4 / 2.9 / -.6	25.0 / 4.1 / 1.5
Sales/Net Fixed Assets	46.9 / 17.2 / 6.4		51.1 / 23.5 / 1.6	44.2 / 20.2 / 10.7
Sales/Total Assets	4.3 / 2.3 / 1.0		4.8 / 1.5 / .9	4.3 / 2.6 / 1.0
% Depr., Dep., Amort./Sales	(33) 1.0 / 2.1 / 4.8		.9 / 2.0 / 11.4	
% Officers', Directors', Owners' Comp/Sales	(10) 2.0 / 4.7 / 9.7			

	4/1/02-3/31/03 ALL		0-1MM	1-3MM	3-5MM	5-10MM	10-25MM	25MM & OVER
Net Sales ($)	1315852M		3780M	11966M	10610M	77224M	111188M	1101084M
Total Assets ($)	971413M		4212M	8101M	4917M	80995M	126849M	746339M

M = $ thousand   MM = $ million
See Pages 11 through 18 for Explanation of Ratios and Data

Current Data Sorted By Assets   **Comparative Historical Data**

							Type of Statement	4/1/98-3/31/99 ALL	4/1/99-3/31/00 ALL
		3	7	5	2	1	Unqualified		
3		10	6	2			Reviewed		
3		9	2	1			Compiled		
7		3				1	Tax Returns		
4		7	7		1	1	Other		
	15 (4/1-9/30/02)			70 (10/1/02-3/31/03)					
0-500M	500M-2MM	2-10MM	10-50MM	50-100MM	100-250MM				
17	32	22	8	4	2		NUMBER OF STATEMENTS		
%	%	%	%	%	%		ASSETS	%	%
19.6	7.8	9.6					Cash & Equivalents	D	D
16.6	26.3	21.9					Trade Receivables (net)	A	A
1.6	.4	.7					Inventory	T	T
8.2	3.7	4.5					All Other Current	A	A
46.0	38.3	36.8					Total Current		
48.0	46.6	51.2					Fixed Assets (net)	N	N
.2	3.8	3.1					Intangibles (net)	O	O
5.9	11.3	8.9					All Other Non-Current	T	T
100.0	100.0	100.0					Total		
							LIABILITIES	A	A
20.1	13.6	7.2					Notes Payable-Short Term	V	V
12.5	12.4	6.3					Cur. Mat.-L/T/D	A	A
5.9	10.7	10.2					Trade Payables	I	I
.0	.6	.1					Income Taxes Payable	L	L
14.7	9.0	9.5					All Other Current	A	A
53.3	46.4	33.3					Total Current	B	B
38.8	35.3	27.3					Long Term Debt	L	L
.1	.5	1.9					Deferred Taxes	E	E
13.7	2.8	5.7					All Other Non-Current		
-5.8	15.1	31.9					Net Worth		
100.0	100.0	100.0					Total Liabilities & Net Worth		
							INCOME DATA		
100.0	100.0	100.0					Net Sales		
							Gross Profit		
92.3	95.4	92.4					Operating Expenses		
7.7	4.6	7.6					Operating Profit		
3.3	1.8	3.0					All Other Expenses (net)		
4.4	2.8	4.6					Profit Before Taxes		
							RATIOS		
1.6	1.9	1.8							
.8	.9	1.0					Current		
.5	.4	.8							
1.6	1.9	1.8							
.7	.8	.8					Quick		
.4	.4	.6							
0 UND	24 15.5	26 14.0							
8 44.3	35 10.4	37 10.0					Sales/Receivables		
31 11.9	42 8.7	47 7.8							
							Cost of Sales/Inventory		
							Cost of Sales/Payables		
23.5	20.1	9.6							
-77.1	-62.2	NM					Sales/Working Capital		
-20.5	-6.0	-22.6							
9.0	5.5	6.1							
(13) 2.3	(29) 2.3	(20) 2.2					EBIT/Interest		
-.1	.3	.3							
							Net Profit + Depr., Dep., Amort./Cur. Mat. L /T/D		
1.1	.5	.7							
3.3	2.4	1.1					Fixed/Worth		
-4.0	-7.7	4.1							
1.4	1.2	.9							
14.0	2.9	1.8					Debt/Worth		
-7.9	-10.9	6.7							
60.0	42.1	42.1							
(11) 46.4	(23) 23.3	(18) 17.2					% Profit Before Taxes/Tangible Net Worth		
.0	-.4	5.3							
14.0	15.6	9.5							
8.4	3.2	4.0					% Profit Before Taxes/Total Assets		
-.3	-4.4	-.9							
28.6	9.9	9.0							
7.7	5.8	3.7					Sales/Net Fixed Assets		
5.2	3.4	1.9							
10.0	3.7	2.5							
3.5	2.7	2.2					Sales/Total Assets		
2.9	1.9	1.4							
2.1	2.3	4.6							
(11) 4.7	(31) 5.6	(21) 6.4					% Depr., Dep., Amort./Sales		
9.1	10.9	8.8							
	4.5	2.1							
	(13) 5.5	(10) 4.1					% Officers', Directors', Owners' Comp/Sales		
	9.3	6.9							
20087M	99736M	179725M	185064M	565400M	85408M		Net Sales ($)		
3810M	35337M	87072M	177527M	280043M	331589M		Total Assets ($)		

© RMA 2003

M = $ thousand   MM = $ million
See Pages 11 through 18 for Explanation of Ratios and Data

Comparative Historical Data | **Current Data Sorted By Sales**

4/1/00-3/31/01 ALL	4/1/01-3/31/02 ALL	4/1/02-3/31/03 ALL		0-1MM	1-3MM	3-5MM	5-10MM	10-25MM	25MM & OVER
			Type of Statement						
		18	Unqualified	1		5	3	5	4
		21	Reviewed	4	4	6	2	4	1
		15	Compiled		6	4	3	2	
		11	Tax Returns	4	5	1			1
		20	Other	3	4	6	3	3	1
				15 (4/1-9/30/02)			70 (10/1/02-3/31/03)		
		85	**NUMBER OF STATEMENTS**	12	19	22	11	14	7
%	%	%	**ASSETS**	%	%	%	%	%	%
DATA NOT AVAILABLE	DATA NOT AVAILABLE	10.4	Cash & Equivalents	14.6	11.0	8.4	11.7	9.1	
		22.7	Trade Receivables (net)	17.5	16.9	27.4	26.1	25.8	
		.8	Inventory	.0	2.0	.1	.9	1.0	
		4.5	All Other Current	2.3	3.0	6.9	6.6	4.0	
		38.4	Total Current	34.4	33.0	42.9	45.3	39.8	
		48.7	Fixed Assets (net)	56.5	52.3	47.2	39.9	45.0	
		3.9	Intangibles (net)	1.1	4.6	1.6	3.6	6.5	
		9.0	All Other Non-Current	8.0	10.1	8.3	11.2	8.7	
		100.0	Total	100.0	100.0	100.0	100.0	100.0	
			LIABILITIES						
		11.5	Notes Payable-Short Term	19.2	14.0	7.4	17.9	7.3	
		10.0	Cur. Mat.-L/T/D	13.4	15.8	7.9	5.3	9.0	
		9.1	Trade Payables	5.7	6.8	8.8	16.1	9.1	
		.3	Income Taxes Payable	.0	.1	.8	.5	.2	
		9.6	All Other Current	6.6	5.7	13.2	17.2	8.1	
		40.5	Total Current	44.8	42.4	38.1	57.0	33.7	
		36.2	Long Term Debt	35.9	48.8	29.1	24.7	33.0	
		.8	Deferred Taxes	.0	.2	1.4	1.4	1.1	
		6.2	All Other Non-Current	7.1	10.5	4.1	5.9	3.1	
		16.3	Net Worth	12.2	–1.9	27.2	11.0	29.1	
		100.0	Total Liabilities & Net Worth	100.0	100.0	100.0	100.0	100.0	
			INCOME DATA						
		100.0	Net Sales	100.0	100.0	100.0	100.0	100.0	
			Gross Profit						
		92.4	Operating Expenses	80.2	95.9	97.0	97.7	88.8	
		7.6	Operating Profit	19.8	4.1	3.0	2.3	11.2	
		3.9	All Other Expenses (net)	8.3	1.5	1.3	.8	7.5	
		3.8	Profit Before Taxes	11.4	2.6	1.7	1.5	3.7	
			RATIOS						
		1.9		1.5	2.9	2.0	2.3	2.9	
		1.0	Current	.5	.8	1.1	1.3	1.0	
		.6		.2	.4	.8	.9	.6	
		1.8		1.5	2.8	1.9	2.3	2.7	
		.8	Quick	.5	.7	.9	.8	.8	
		.5		.2	.3	.7	.6	.6	
		21 17.6		0 UND	0 UND	28 12.8	14 25.6	27 13.3	
		35 10.5	Sales/Receivables	0 UND	27 13.6	34 10.6	35 10.4	36 10.1	
		47 7.8		49 7.4	39 9.4	47 7.8	54 6.7	46 7.9	
			Cost of Sales/Inventory						
			Cost of Sales/Payables						
		11.8		9.8	38.5	17.3	8.0	6.2	
		–328.0	Sales/Working Capital	–50.8	–29.9	127.0	31.3	–149.3	
		–17.0		–2.8	–7.1	–39.5	–23.9	–12.3	
		4.4			3.6	7.0		4.7	
		(74) 2.2	EBIT/Interest		1.2	(19) 2.6		(13) 1.8	
		.6			–.9	.6		1.0	
		3.1							
		(22) 1.7	Net Profit + Depr., Dep., Amort./Cur. Mat. L/T/D						
		1.1							
		.8		1.0	1.2	.6	.5	.6	
		2.2	Fixed/Worth	2.5	10.2	1.9	.8	1.6	
		–12.4		23.9	–2.9	NM	2.2	NM	
		1.2		1.2	1.9	1.1	.5	1.1	
		3.1	Debt/Worth	3.5	14.0	2.2	1.2	2.7	
		–16.9		NM	–6.2	NM	4.5	NM	
		43.3			45.3	43.3		36.7	
		(60) 20.6	% Profit Before Taxes/Tangible Net Worth		(11) 3.8	(17) 25.8		(11) 10.3	
		–.3			–58.1	6.9		–.8	
		11.1		14.4	11.4	12.5	17.9	5.9	
		3.1	% Profit Before Taxes/Total Assets	4.3	1.2	6.6	1.4	2.3	
		–.5		.6	–9.5	–2.6	–4.7	.4	
		10.0		9.3	8.2	15.5	24.0	18.4	
		4.8	Sales/Net Fixed Assets	2.5	5.6	6.1	7.3	4.1	
		2.4		.6	3.8	3.0	3.3	1.7	
		3.5		3.3	3.9	4.5	3.9	2.5	
		2.3	Sales/Total Assets	1.7	2.8	3.0	2.4	2.1	
		1.4		.4	1.9	1.7	2.2	1.0	
		4.2			2.5	3.2		3.0	
		(74) 6.3	% Depr., Dep., Amort./Sales		(17) 5.8	(20) 6.5		(13) 5.1	
		9.4			11.2	9.2		7.2	
		3.6							
		(34) 5.4	% Officers', Directors', Owners' Comp/Sales						
		10.1							
		1135420M	Net Sales ($)	**4870M**	**35009M**	**84502M**	**82026M**	**208179M**	**720834M**
		915378M	Total Assets ($)	**6910M**	**13915M**	**36454M**	**63561M**	**327741M**	**466797M**

M = $ thousand MM = $ million

See Pages 11 through 18 for Explanation of Ratios and Data

Current Data Sorted By Assets   Comparative Historical Data

Type of Statement	0-500M	500M-2MM	2-10MM	10-50MM	50-100MM	100-250MM	4/1/98-3/31/99 ALL	4/1/99-3/31/00 ALL
Unqualified		3	11	21	8	5	79	54
Reviewed	1	9	32	6	1		48	55
Compiled	9	15	9	4			53	41
Tax Returns	12	12	8				24	16
Other	5	12	24	10		1	74	78
		42 (4/1-9/30/02)		176 (10/1/02-3/31/03)				
NUMBER OF STATEMENTS	27	51	84	41	9	6	278	244
ASSETS	%	%	%	%	%	%	%	%
Cash & Equivalents	8.8	10.3	10.1	6.6			8.4	8.3
Trade Receivables (net)	15.9	22.3	20.7	20.0			17.1	19.6
Inventory	2.2	1.7	1.3	1.6			2.5	2.9
All Other Current	2.4	1.7	1.6	2.8			3.7	4.6
Total Current	29.2	36.0	33.6	30.9			31.7	35.3
Fixed Assets (net)	62.6	49.6	54.0	53.5			51.4	48.4
Intangibles (net)	1.3	5.1	4.7	5.1			7.0	6.8
All Other Non-Current	6.8	9.2	7.7	10.5			9.9	9.4
Total	100.0	100.0	100.0	100.0			100.0	100.0
LIABILITIES								
Notes Payable-Short Term	11.6	9.6	5.2	5.9			6.5	6.7
Cur. Mat.-L/T/D	12.8	5.7	7.6	7.3			7.0	7.3
Trade Payables	16.0	15.5	11.5	8.4			9.1	10.0
Income Taxes Payable	.2	.1	.2	.1			.2	.4
All Other Current	7.8	10.1	9.2	9.5			9.5	9.1
Total Current	48.4	41.0	33.7	31.2			32.4	33.6
Long Term Debt	30.7	28.4	28.3	27.6			31.4	28.1
Deferred Taxes	.0	.4	.7	1.5			1.1	.8
All Other Non-Current	5.3	5.1	6.5	4.9			6.6	7.8
Net Worth	15.6	25.2	30.8	34.8			28.5	29.8
Total Liabilities & Net Worth	100.0	100.0	100.0	100.0			100.0	100.0
INCOME DATA								
Net Sales	100.0	100.0	100.0	100.0			100.0	100.0
Gross Profit								
Operating Expenses	92.7	92.4	94.1	91.2			91.9	92.6
Operating Profit	7.3	7.6	5.9	8.8			8.1	7.4
All Other Expenses (net)	1.9	3.0	2.9	1.5			3.3	2.4
Profit Before Taxes	5.5	4.6	3.0	7.3			4.8	5.0
RATIOS								
Current	1.1	1.6	1.5	1.3			1.7	1.6
	.6	1.0	1.1	1.1			1.0	1.1
	.2	.5	.6	.8			.6	.7
Quick	(26) 1.0	1.6	1.4	1.1			1.4	1.4
	.5	1.0	.9	.9			.8	.8
	.2	.4	.5	.6			.5	.5
Sales/Receivables	0 UND	5 78.0	30 12.0	37 10.0			24 15.5	30 12.1
	18 20.5	38 9.5	40 9.1	54 6.7			41 8.8	42 8.8
	29 12.6	57 6.3	58 6.3	72 5.0			61 6.0	60 6.1
Cost of Sales/Inventory								
Cost of Sales/Payables								
Sales/Working Capital	99.2	12.4	13.5	12.8			9.7	11.3
	-20.0	-165.6	88.0	51.2			NM	56.5
	-8.8	-10.5	-10.3	-19.3			-10.5	-12.3
EBIT/Interest	(22) 5.3	(47) 12.5	(82) 6.3	(39) 7.2			(242) 6.5	(223) 7.1
	2.0	2.4	2.8	2.8			2.5	2.7
	.4	1.0	.9	1.3			1.1	1.3
Net Profit + Depr., Dep., Amort./Cur. Mat. L/T/D			(21) 8.9	(13) 3.0			(90) 4.2	(85) 4.2
			1.6	1.5			2.1	2.2
			1.2	1.2			1.1	1.2
Fixed/Worth	.9	.7	.8	1.2			.9	.8
	6.2	1.7	2.2	1.7			2.3	2.0
	-7.9	-20.7	6.7	2.8			8.1	12.9
Debt/Worth	.8	.9	1.3	1.3			1.1	1.1
	5.7	2.4	2.2	2.3			2.8	2.5
	-13.8	-30.8	12.0	4.1			12.2	23.2
% Profit Before Taxes/Tangible Net Worth	(19) 48.8	(37) 51.1	(72) 48.9	(39) 44.4			(227) 57.0	(192) 46.9
	20.2	19.2	22.3	20.2			23.6	25.1
	-8.2	5.1	6.1	3.6			5.4	10.2
% Profit Before Taxes/Total Assets	25.0	12.0	12.1	12.8			14.1	14.4
	6.5	4.9	5.6	4.0			5.3	6.2
	-2.7	.3	-.3	.2			.4	.4
Sales/Net Fixed Assets	7.6	13.5	5.5	3.4			5.8	6.7
	5.0	4.2	2.8	2.0			2.6	3.2
	3.4	2.1	1.8	1.4			1.5	1.7
Sales/Total Assets	3.8	2.9	2.2	1.6			2.1	2.4
	3.2	2.2	1.7	1.2			1.4	1.5
	2.3	1.4	1.1	.8			.8	.9
% Depr., Dep., Amort./Sales	(23) 5.3	(48) 2.7	(76) 4.1	(40) 4.6			(254) 3.8	(228) 3.5
	8.5	6.7	7.0	8.0			7.5	6.4
	14.1	10.0	10.2	10.9			12.3	11.3
% Officers', Directors', Owners' Comp/Sales	(15) 1.5	(22) 2.9	(32) 2.3				(95) 2.6	(75) 2.5
	8.1	5.5	3.4				5.5	5.5
	7.6	10.0	4.9				9.5	8.7
Net Sales ($)	20629M	142756M	697116M	1026735M	550342M	678337M	4832956M	3475821M
Total Assets ($)	7138M	59862M	418660M	820968M	641883M	883679M	4940932M	3685043M

© RMA 2003

M = $ thousand   MM = $ million
See Pages 11 through 18 for Explanation of Ratios and Data

Comparative Historical Data | Current Data Sorted By Sales

4/1/00-3/31/01 ALL	4/1/01-3/31/02 ALL	4/1/02-3/31/03 ALL	Type of Statement	0-1MM	1-3MM	3-5MM	5-10MM	10-25MM	25MM & OVER
54	40	48	Unqualified	2	1	4	4	16	21
41	38	49	Reviewed	4	9	6	14	13	3
38	52	37	Compiled	8	14	5	4	5	1
20	20	32	Tax Returns	10	13	1	5	3	
94	82	52	Other	4	12	9	10	11	6
				42 (4/1-9/30/02)			176 (10/1/02-3/31/03)		
247	232	218	**NUMBER OF STATEMENTS**	28	49	25	37	48	31
%	%	%	**ASSETS**	%	%	%	%	%	%
8.9	8.6	8.9	Cash & Equivalents	8.3	10.7	5.5	10.8	9.8	5.8
19.5	20.3	19.6	Trade Receivables (net)	12.2	14.3	21.1	23.5	25.2	19.9
2.4	1.9	1.5	Inventory	2.3	.7	.5	2.6	1.2	2.0
2.2	2.9	2.0	All Other Current	.9	2.2	2.0	1.5	2.1	3.2
33.0	33.6	32.0	Total Current	23.8	28.0	29.0	38.5	38.3	31.0
50.3	51.0	53.8	Fixed Assets (net)	66.6	56.8	54.7	49.9	49.6	48.3
6.6	7.2	5.5	Intangibles (net)	1.1	5.1	8.2	2.0	4.9	13.2
10.1	8.2	8.6	All Other Non-Current	8.5	10.1	8.1	9.6	7.2	7.6
100.0	100.0	100.0	Total	100.0	100.0	100.0	100.0	100.0	100.0
			LIABILITIES						
7.5	5.6	7.1	Notes Payable-Short Term	10.0	8.7	4.7	5.5	7.7	4.6
7.5	8.5	7.5	Cur. Mat.-L/T/D	10.7	7.6	10.2	5.9	6.7	5.3
10.5	11.5	11.9	Trade Payables	15.4	9.1	10.8	16.4	12.1	8.5
.4	.2	.1	Income Taxes Payable	.2	.2	.0	.2	.1	.1
8.3	8.2	9.2	All Other Current	6.1	8.7	10.4	11.4	8.3	10.5
34.2	34.0	35.8	Total Current	42.3	34.2	36.1	39.4	35.0	28.9
31.0	31.4	29.1	Long Term Debt	36.2	34.6	36.3	21.6	20.6	30.3
.5	.6	.7	Deferred Taxes	.4	.5	1.1	.3	1.0	1.3
9.8	8.2	5.7	All Other Non-Current	6.1	8.6	3.9	6.6	3.4	4.9
24.5	25.8	28.7	Net Worth	15.1	22.1	22.6	32.0	40.1	34.6
100.0	100.0	100.0	Total Liabilities & Net Worth	100.0	100.0	100.0	100.0	100.0	100.0
			INCOME DATA						
100.0	100.0	100.0	Net Sales	100.0	100.0	100.0	100.0	100.0	100.0
			Gross Profit						
93.1	93.0	92.7	Operating Expenses	91.8	91.7	92.3	95.5	92.2	92.9
6.9	7.0	7.3	Operating Profit	8.2	8.3	7.7	4.5	7.8	7.1
1.4	3.1	2.8	All Other Expenses (net)	3.0	3.9	5.2	1.6	.6	3.7
5.4	4.0	4.5	Profit Before Taxes	5.2	4.4	2.5	2.9	7.2	3.4
			RATIOS						
1.8	1.6	1.4	Current	1.3	1.5	1.1	1.5	1.5	1.4
1.1	1.0	1.0		.5	.8	.8	1.2	1.2	1.1
.6	.5	.5		.2	.4	.4	.6	.8	.8
1.7	1.5	1.3	Quick	1.3	1.4	1.1	1.4	1.5	1.2
.9	.9	(217) .9		(27) .5	.6	.6	1.1	1.0	1.0
.5	.4	.4		.1	.4	.4	.6	.7	.7
23 15.6	28 13.0	25 14.4	Sales/Receivables	0 UND	0 UND	32 11.4	29 12.7	31 11.8	36 10.1
37 9.8	39 9.3	38 9.5		22 16.8	31 11.8	47 7.7	38 9.7	50 7.4	52 7.1
58 6.3	55 6.6	59 6.1		40 9.2	57 6.4	60 6.1	49 7.5	64 5.7	66 5.5
			Cost of Sales/Inventory						
			Cost of Sales/Payables						
11.5	11.7	14.1	Sales/Working Capital	22.7	13.9	32.2	14.3	12.0	10.7
84.2	-508.8	528.4		-18.9	-21.8	-11.3	43.1	26.0	28.5
-10.0	-8.7	-10.6		-7.5	-7.4	-6.5	-13.1	-22.4	-37.5
(228) 7.4	(210) 6.3	(205) 6.3	EBIT/Interest	(24) 5.7	(46) 4.5	7.5	(35) 7.1	(44) 15.6	3.7
2.8	2.3	2.6		2.0	1.9	2.1	3.1	4.7	1.9
1.1	.8	1.0		.5	-.5	.8	1.0	2.6	1.1
(77) 4.4	(60) 3.4	(52) 4.4	Net Profit + Depr., Dep., Amort./Cur. Mat. L/T/D					(17) 5.5	(15) 8.5
2.2	1.6	1.8						1.8	2.5
1.3	1.1	1.1						1.3	1.4
.8	.9	.9	Fixed/Worth	1.2	1.2	1.1	.7	.7	1.2
1.7	2.4	2.2		4.1	2.6	2.9	1.7	1.6	2.4
29.0	72.0	8.1		-8.2	-29.3	NM	4.4	2.5	4.6
.9	1.0	1.2	Debt/Worth	.9	1.0	1.7	1.1	.9	1.3
2.4	3.1	2.4		4.4	3.2	3.7	1.8	1.7	3.5
61.6	99.0	13.1		-12.9	-54.9	NM	6.9	3.5	7.0
(191) 52.9	(176) 51.9	(178) 46.7	% Profit Before Taxes/Tangible Net Worth	(19) 33.6	(36) 80.8	(19) 46.9	(34) 42.8	(44) 49.9	(26) 32.5
28.2	22.8	20.2		20.2	20.5	18.7	24.3	23.0	14.6
7.4	1.2	4.4		5.4	-1.4	.8	.5	6.7	1.2
15.6	15.1	12.2	% Profit Before Taxes/Total Assets	20.1	11.4	6.8	13.1	17.3	6.8
6.6	4.7	4.6		5.7	4.1	4.4	4.1	8.9	3.4
.2	-.8	.1		-1.9	-5.6	-.7	-.7	2.7	.5
6.9	6.6	5.9	Sales/Net Fixed Assets	5.6	5.8	5.5	8.3	7.1	3.8
3.3	3.1	3.1		3.5	2.9	2.1	3.4	3.3	2.3
1.7	1.6	1.8		1.4	1.4	1.0	2.0	2.0	1.7
2.4	2.4	2.4	Sales/Total Assets	3.3	2.8	2.5	2.5	2.2	1.6
1.6	1.6	1.7		2.3	1.8	1.3	1.9	1.8	1.1
.9	.9	1.1		.7	.9	.8	1.3	1.3	.8
(229) 3.3	(211) 3.4	(199) 4.1	% Depr., Dep., Amort./Sales	(24) 6.3	(43) 5.5	(34) 6.4	(45) 3.6	(28) 3.7	4.1
6.2	6.2	7.6		9.5	8.7	9.7	6.5	5.3	6.9
10.9	10.5	11.1		14.0	13.9	12.7	8.7	8.7	10.1
(83) 2.6	(68) 1.8	(78) 2.1	% Officers', Directors', Owners' Comp/Sales	(12) .9	(19) 3.6	(11) 2.2	(18) 2.2	(13) 1.4	
4.4	3.5	3.9		8.2	7.1	3.4	3.8	2.4	
8.6	7.5	7.5		11.9	11.7	4.9	7.2	4.3	
3581526M	3909359M	3115915M	Net Sales ($)	15909M	91297M	95368M	259118M	733467M	1920756M
3142929M	3664238M	2832190M	Total Assets ($)	16410M	79825M	130849M	213253M	473313M	1918540M

M = $ thousand   MM = $ million
See Pages 11 through 18 for Explanation of Ratios and Data

Current Data Sorted By Assets   **Comparative Historical Data**

0-500M	500M-2MM	2-10MM	10-50MM	50-100MM	100-250MM	Type of Statement	4/1/98-3/31/99 ALL	4/1/99-3/31/00 ALL
		1	6	2	2	Unqualified		
1	2	3				Reviewed		
1	1	3				Compiled		
1						Tax Returns		
1	2	4	1			Other		
	11 (4/1-9/30/02)			20 (10/1/02-3/31/03)				
4	5	11	7	2	2	**NUMBER OF STATEMENTS**		
%	%	%	%	%	%	**ASSETS**	%	%
		4.8				Cash & Equivalents		
		24.9				Trade Receivables (net)	D	D
		.0				Inventory	A	A
		1.3				All Other Current	T	T
		31.0				Total Current	A	A
		58.3				Fixed Assets (net)		
		6.8				Intangibles (net)	N	N
		3.9				All Other Non-Current	O	O
		100.0				Total	T	T
						LIABILITIES	A	A
		4.9				Notes Payable-Short Term	V	V
		8.0				Cur. Mat.-L/T/D	A	A
		9.2				Trade Payables	I	I
		.0				Income Taxes Payable	L	L
		6.9				All Other Current	A	A
		29.0				Total Current	B	B
		37.4				Long Term Debt	L	L
		.1				Deferred Taxes	E	E
		2.4				All Other Non-Current		
		31.0				Net Worth		
		100.0				Total Liabilities & Net Worth		
						INCOME DATA		
		100.0				Net Sales		
						Gross Profit		
		86.7				Operating Expenses		
		13.3				Operating Profit		
		3.1				All Other Expenses (net)		
		10.1				Profit Before Taxes		
						RATIOS		
		1.5				Current		
		1.1						
		.5						
		1.4				Quick		
		1.0						
		.5						
	34	10.8				Sales/Receivables		
	49	7.5						
	68	5.4						
						Cost of Sales/Inventory		
						Cost of Sales/Payables		
		16.7				Sales/Working Capital		
		41.7						
		−6.6						
		8.8				EBIT/Interest		
		3.3						
		1.2						
						Net Profit + Depr., Dep., Amort./Cur. Mat. L /T/D		
		1.1				Fixed/Worth		
		2.4						
		7.4						
		.7				Debt/Worth		
		5.6						
		7.4						
		138.5				% Profit Before Taxes/Tangible Net Worth		
	(10)	22.1						
		3.1						
		13.4				% Profit Before Taxes/Total Assets		
		8.0						
		.6						
		8.1				Sales/Net Fixed Assets		
		2.4						
		1.2						
		2.3				Sales/Total Assets		
		1.6						
		.6						
		4.1				% Depr., Dep., Amort./Sales		
	(10)	6.9						
		11.3						
						% Officers', Directors', Owners' Comp/Sales		
3231M	9515M	62163M	115919M	5545103M	189285M	Net Sales ($)		
1139M	6071M	41471M	129538M	145538M	282512M	Total Assets ($)		

M = $ thousand   MM = $ million
See Pages 11 through 18 for Explanation of Ratios and Data

Comparative Historical Data				Current Data Sorted By Sales					

			Type of Statement						
		11	Unqualified		1		1	4	5
		6	Reviewed	1	1	2	1	1	
		5	Compiled		2		3		
		1	Tax Returns	1					
		8	Other		5	1	1	1	
4/1/00- 3/31/01 ALL	4/1/01- 3/31/02 ALL	4/1/02- 3/31/03 ALL		11 (4/1-9/30/02)			20 (10/1/02-3/31/03)		
		31	NUMBER OF STATEMENTS	0-1MM	1-3MM	3-5MM	5-10MM	10-25MM	25MM & OVER
				2	9	3	6	6	5
%	%	%	ASSETS	%	%	%	%	%	%
D	D	7.5	Cash & Equivalents						
A	A	18.5	Trade Receivables (net)						
T	T	2.4	Inventory						
A	A	3.1	All Other Current						
		31.5	Total Current						
N	N	53.7	Fixed Assets (net)						
O	O	7.3	Intangibles (net)						
T	T	7.6	All Other Non-Current						
		100.0	Total						
A	A		LIABILITIES						
V	V	4.4	Notes Payable-Short Term						
A	A	7.3	Cur. Mat.-L/T/D						
I	I	8.8	Trade Payables						
L	L	.0	Income Taxes Payable						
A	A	7.0	All Other Current						
B	B	27.5	Total Current						
L	L	39.0	Long Term Debt						
E	E	.8	Deferred Taxes						
		5.2	All Other Non-Current						
		27.4	Net Worth						
		100.0	Total Liabilities & Net Worth						
			INCOME DATA						
		100.0	Net Sales						
			Gross Profit						
		91.9	Operating Expenses						
		8.1	Operating Profit						
		2.5	All Other Expenses (net)						
		5.6	Profit Before Taxes						
			RATIOS						
		1.7							
		1.0	Current						
		.5							
		1.4							
		1.0	Quick						
		.5							
	31	11.7							
	37	9.9	Sales/Receivables						
	61	6.0							
			Cost of Sales/Inventory						
			Cost of Sales/Payables						
		16.7							
		95.5	Sales/Working Capital						
		−7.3							
		8.4							
	(30)	2.8	EBIT/Interest						
		1.2							
		2.6	Net Profit + Depr., Dep.,						
	(13)	1.3	Amort./Cur. Mat. L/T/D						
		1.0							
		1.5							
		3.8	Fixed/Worth						
		33.0							
		1.3							
		5.6	Debt/Worth						
		39.3							
		87.3	% Profit Before Taxes/Tangible						
	(24)	28.0	Net Worth						
		9.0							
		12.5							
		6.1	% Profit Before Taxes/Total						
		.6	Assets						
		8.1							
		2.2	Sales/Net Fixed Assets						
		1.2							
		2.4							
		1.3	Sales/Total Assets						
		.8							
		4.7							
	(28)	8.2	% Depr., Dep., Amort./Sales						
		10.1							
			% Officers', Directors', Owners' Comp/Sales						
		5925216M	Net Sales ($)	750M	13658M	10719M	46091M	90771M	5763227M
		606269M	Total Assets ($)	210M	14385M	7485M	30022M	98271M	455896M

M = $ thousand   MM = $ million
See Pages 11 through 18 for Explanation of Ratios and Data

Current Data Sorted By Assets   **Comparative Historical Data**

0-500M	500M-2MM	2-10MM	10-50MM	50-100MM	100-250MM	Type of Statement	4/1/98-3/31/99 ALL	4/1/99-3/31/00 ALL
4	1	9	1	1	2	Unqualified	11	9
2	8	7				Reviewed	5	8
3	8	4				Compiled	14	14
	3					Tax Returns	9	7
2	7	4	1	1	2	Other	11	12
	11 (4/1-9/30/02)			59 (10/1/02-3/31/03)				
11	27	24	2	2	4	**NUMBER OF STATEMENTS**	50	50
%	%	%	%	%	%	**ASSETS**	%	%
20.5	10.3	4.8				Cash & Equivalents	10.8	10.7
12.4	22.6	25.5				Trade Receivables (net)	25.3	20.9
1.6	.5	1.1				Inventory	2.0	2.9
.1	3.3	2.4				All Other Current	2.5	2.5
34.5	36.7	33.9				Total Current	40.5	36.9
55.2	55.2	43.3				Fixed Assets (net)	47.2	52.3
3.1	1.1	8.9				Intangibles (net)	5.4	4.6
7.2	7.0	13.9				All Other Non-Current	6.8	6.2
100.0	100.0	100.0				Total	100.0	100.0
						LIABILITIES		
1.5	3.7	7.2				Notes Payable-Short Term	4.8	4.8
20.1	10.8	9.6				Cur. Mat.-L/T/D	8.7	6.9
4.8	10.0	14.9				Trade Payables	11.0	9.7
.7	.5	.0				Income Taxes Payable	.2	.5
13.4	4.1	7.4				All Other Current	5.9	8.2
40.4	29.1	39.2				Total Current	30.6	30.1
59.1	31.7	26.2				Long Term Debt	30.5	31.5
.0	.1	.4				Deferred Taxes	.7	.7
6.6	2.5	6.0				All Other Non-Current	5.0	5.3
-6.1	36.6	28.2				Net Worth	33.2	32.4
100.0	100.0	100.0				Total Liabilities & Net Worth	100.0	100.0
						INCOME DATA		
100.0	100.0	100.0				Net Sales	100.0	100.0
						Gross Profit		
92.8	88.8	95.5				Operating Expenses	95.7	93.7
7.2	11.2	4.5				Operating Profit	4.3	6.3
2.6	3.2	2.6				All Other Expenses (net)	.1	1.9
4.7	7.9	1.9				Profit Before Taxes	4.2	4.4
						RATIOS		
2.2	2.4	1.4				Current	3.2	3.2
.9	1.4	.9					1.5	1.1
.4	.5	.6					1.0	.7
2.2	2.3	1.4				Quick	(49) 3.1	2.3
.8	1.2	.8					1.3	.9
.4	.4	.4					.8	.6
0 UND	17 20.9	34 10.7				Sales/Receivables	23 15.6	18 20.3
15 24.9	33 11.1	41 8.9					38 9.6	41 8.9
37 9.9	45 8.1	67 5.4					58 6.3	62 5.9
						Cost of Sales/Inventory		
						Cost of Sales/Payables		
18.1	6.3	14.8				Sales/Working Capital	6.8	7.7
-116.0	23.7	-118.2					12.5	41.0
-8.5	-18.9	-7.5					-650.6	-15.2
11.6	16.4	6.2				EBIT/Interest	5.6	8.1
(10) 2.3	(26) 3.6	(21) 1.5					(44) 2.3	(44) 3.9
.7	1.6	.5					1.3	1.3
						Net Profit + Depr., Dep., Amort./Cur. Mat. L /T/D	2.9	6.0
							(14) 2.0	(10) 2.8
							1.6	.8
1.2	.5	.7				Fixed/Worth	.5	.8
2.9	1.3	1.5					2.1	2.0
-3.3	3.4	NM					20.8	3.9
1.0	.8	1.1				Debt/Worth	.7	.9
2.5	1.4	2.4					2.2	2.7
-6.0	4.7	NM					27.8	6.7
	70.4	33.2				% Profit Before Taxes/Tangible Net Worth	65.9	63.9
	(24) 27.8	(18) 15.2					(41) 18.6	(42) 29.6
	5.4	-3.2					1.6	4.9
84.1	21.1	11.7				% Profit Before Taxes/Total Assets	15.0	15.8
11.6	4.4	2.4					5.3	7.4
.0	.5	-1.8					.7	1.3
9.0	11.4	6.4				Sales/Net Fixed Assets	11.6	6.9
6.1	2.5	4.5					4.5	3.3
1.3	1.5	2.3					1.9	1.9
3.8	2.8	2.2				Sales/Total Assets	2.9	2.6
2.8	1.7	1.8					2.1	1.9
.8	1.2	1.2					1.1	1.1
5.6	5.3	4.1				% Depr., Dep., Amort./Sales	2.8	3.9
(10) 10.2	(23) 8.4	7.5					(46) 5.9	(47) 7.1
21.2	16.3	9.8					9.2	13.8
		2.6				% Officers', Directors', Owners' Comp/Sales	3.6	3.0
	(12)	5.2					(16) 6.9	(15) 4.8
		7.3					19.6	10.0
6321M	51036M	226181M	86892M	56507M	386425M	Net Sales ($)	613439M	420726M
2645M	28071M	122346M	29341M	159291M	643270M	Total Assets ($)	666431M	467800M

© RMA 2003

M = $ thousand   MM = $ million
See Pages 11 through 18 for Explanation of Ratios and Data

Comparative Historical Data | Current Data Sorted By Sales

11	10	14	Type of Statement						
11	7	19	Unqualified	1	1	1	5	4	2
15	20	14	Reviewed	3	7	3	3	2	1
12	8	6	Compiled	4	4	3	2	1	
23	25	17	Tax Returns	4	2				
			Other	4	6	2		1	4

4/1/00-3/31/01 ALL	4/1/01-3/31/02 ALL	4/1/02-3/31/03 ALL		11 (4/1-9/30/02)			59 (10/1/02-3/31/03)		
				0-1MM	1-3MM	3-5MM	5-10MM	10-25MM	25MM & OVER
72	70	70	**NUMBER OF STATEMENTS**	16	20	9	10	8	7
%	%	%	**ASSETS**	%	%	%	%	%	%
12.3	12.0	9.2	Cash & Equivalents	19.3	8.8		4.6		
20.6	21.7	20.9	Trade Receivables (net)	7.0	21.0		27.6		
1.5	2.1	1.0	Inventory	.9	.3		.2		
3.0	3.3	3.2	All Other Current	1.3	3.2		.7		
37.4	39.0	34.3	Total Current	28.6	33.2		33.1		
46.8	49.8	50.4	Fixed Assets (net)	64.4	53.8		48.2		
7.7	4.9	5.7	Intangibles (net)	.8	7.1		1.0		
8.1	6.2	9.6	All Other Non-Current	6.3	5.9		17.7		
100.0	100.0	100.0	Total	100.0	100.0		100.0		
			LIABILITIES						
11.6	7.0	4.3	Notes Payable-Short Term	.3	3.6		4.2		
6.5	6.8	11.1	Cur. Mat.-L/T/D	15.0	9.1		8.0		
9.3	9.1	10.3	Trade Payables	1.6	9.5		12.6		
4.6	.2	.3	Income Taxes Payable	.5	.1		1.2		
7.2	10.8	7.4	All Other Current	8.8	5.3		9.9		
39.2	33.9	33.4	Total Current	26.2	27.6		36.0		
29.3	26.5	33.9	Long Term Debt	50.7	38.5		22.8		
.4	.4	.2	Deferred Taxes	.0	.0		.2		
5.2	6.6	5.8	All Other Non-Current	1.0	6.4		11.3		
25.9	32.7	26.7	Net Worth	22.1	27.5		29.7		
100.0	100.0	100.0	Total Liabilities & Net Worth	100.0	100.0		100.0		
			INCOME DATA						
100.0	100.0	100.0	Net Sales	100.0	100.0		100.0		
			Gross Profit						
94.0	90.4	91.5	Operating Expenses	85.3	92.2		92.1		
6.0	9.6	8.5	Operating Profit	14.7	7.8		7.9		
2.4	2.9	3.6	All Other Expenses (net)	6.5	2.5		2.2		
3.5	6.7	4.9	Profit Before Taxes	8.2	5.2		5.7		
			RATIOS						
1.9 / 1.1 / .7	2.2 / 1.3 / .7	2.0 / 1.0 / .6	Current	3.6 / 1.0 / .5	2.3 / 1.2 / .5		1.8 / 1.3 / .4		
1.8 / 1.0 / .6	1.9 / 1.1 / .6	1.7 / .9 / .4	Quick	2.1 / 1.0 / .4	2.3 / 1.0 / .5		1.7 / 1.3 / .4		
20 18.4 / 41 8.8 / 56 6.5	21 17.1 / 39 9.3 / 51 7.1	25 14.4 / 37 9.8 / 53 6.9	Sales/Receivables	0 UND / 27 13.8 / 36 10.2	16 22.7 / 40 9.1 / 56 6.5		36 10.2 / 41 8.9 / 69 5.3		
			Cost of Sales/Inventory						
			Cost of Sales/Payables						
9.8 / 66.3 / -18.2	11.6 / 35.3 / -17.7	9.4 / NM / -15.4	Sales/Working Capital	3.4 / -211.6 / -16.9	9.8 / NM / -19.4		13.3 / 20.4 / -6.1		
(65) 5.5 / 2.5 / .7	(68) 12.6 / 3.5 / 1.0	(65) 7.4 / 1.9 / .8	EBIT/Interest	(13) 10.5 / 3.1 / 1.6	16.8 / 2.6 / .1				
(18) 3.3 / 2.2 / 1.3	(16) 3.2 / 1.9 / 1.1	(19) 3.8 / 2.0 / 1.1	Net Profit + Depr., Dep., Amort./Cur. Mat. L/T/D						
.7 / 2.0 / 129.7	.9 / 1.4 / 6.4	.9 / 1.7 / 7.9	Fixed/Worth	1.0 / 1.7 / 3.0	.7 / 2.3 / NM		.4 / 1.3 / 3.6		
.9 / 2.2 / NM	1.0 / 1.8 / 9.1	.9 / 2.1 / 11.5	Debt/Worth	.4 / 1.2 / 2.4	.8 / 1.8 / NM		.9 / 1.3 / 4.2		
(54) 76.5 / 23.2 / 3.1	(56) 56.8 / 29.9 / 8.6	(55) 44.9 / 21.1 / 1.1	% Profit Before Taxes/Tangible Net Worth	(14) 54.5 / 10.8 / .8	(15) 75.3 / 29.3 / 6.7				
17.2 / 5.3 / -1.1	22.6 / 8.2 / .3	16.1 / 3.6 / -1.0	% Profit Before Taxes/Total Assets	16.3 / 3.8 / .2	29.6 / 3.7 / -4.0		15.1 / 3.2 / .8		
10.2 / 3.9 / 1.5	7.9 / 4.0 / 2.4	8.5 / 3.5 / 1.6	Sales/Net Fixed Assets	4.6 / 1.0 / .3	7.9 / 2.9 / 2.0		11.7 / 5.1 / 2.1		
3.3 / 1.9 / .8	3.0 / 2.1 / 1.3	2.7 / 1.7 / .8	Sales/Total Assets	2.1 / .7 / .2	2.8 / 2.0 / 1.4		2.7 / 2.0 / 1.1		
(66) 2.7 / 6.7 / 11.3	(64) 3.1 / 6.8 / 10.3	(64) 5.3 / 8.6 / 14.5	% Depr., Dep., Amort./Sales	(14) 8.1 / 13.1 / 27.3	(18) 5.4 / 8.4 / 16.7		2.9 / 6.0 / 7.7		
(29) 3.5 / 7.0 / 11.1	(30) 3.5 / 4.4 / 9.6	(26) 3.9 / 6.0 / 9.8	% Officers', Directors', Owners' Comp/Sales						
854116M	1239153M	813362M	Net Sales ($)	6864M	32864M	35355M	79450M	113213M	545616M
919816M	888591M	984964M	Total Assets ($)	16677M	23024M	19943M	132580M	57137M	735603M

M = $ thousand   MM = $ million
See Pages 11 through 18 for Explanation of Ratios and Data

EDUCATIONAL
SERVICES

Current Data Sorted By Assets | **Comparative Historical Data**

						Type of Statement		
19	59	183	276	55	33	Unqualified	391	440
	16	24	10	1		Reviewed	40	32
7	11	21	4	1	1	Compiled	44	47
6	10	6				Tax Returns	9	13
26	46	61	65	12	6	Other	155	120
	784 (4/1-9/30/02)			175 (10/1/02-3/31/03)			4/1/98-3/31/99	4/1/99-3/31/00
0-500M	500M-2MM	2-10MM	10-50MM	50-100MM	100-250MM		ALL	ALL
58	142	295	355	69	40	NUMBER OF STATEMENTS	639	652
%	%	%	%	%	%	**ASSETS**	%	%
42.9	29.8	21.3	19.3	12.3	17.0	Cash & Equivalents	23.1	22.4
7.5	10.0	6.3	4.5	3.8	3.3	Trade Receivables (net)	6.8	6.8
.2	.1	.2	.2	.6	.2	Inventory	.4	.3
6.2	3.2	3.8	4.1	3.4	2.5	All Other Current	3.3	3.3
56.7	43.1	31.6	28.1	20.1	23.1	Total Current	33.5	32.8
32.9	48.6	58.8	54.1	48.7	45.7	Fixed Assets (net)	50.7	49.5
1.8	1.0	.3	.4	1.0	1.2	Intangibles (net)	.8	1.0
8.5	7.3	9.2	17.5	30.1	30.0	All Other Non-Current	15.0	16.7
100.0	100.0	100.0	100.0	100.0	100.0	Total	100.0	100.0
						LIABILITIES		
15.0	4.4	2.7	2.0	1.8	.6	Notes Payable-Short Term	3.1	4.2
2.2	2.4	1.5	1.0	1.0	1.0	Cur. Mat.-L/T/D	1.5	3.0
10.2	4.5	2.6	2.6	1.8	2.0	Trade Payables	3.1	3.0
.2	.2	.0	.0	.0	.0	Income Taxes Payable	.0	.0
27.1	18.9	12.8	8.5	4.5	4.8	All Other Current	12.3	10.9
54.6	30.4	19.7	14.1	9.2	8.4	Total Current	20.0	21.1
16.6	20.1	25.1	20.6	23.1	25.3	Long Term Debt	17.1	16.5
.0	.0	.0	.0	.0	.0	Deferred Taxes	.2	.0
11.2	7.6	6.3	5.1	6.5	3.1	All Other Non-Current	5.0	5.0
17.5	41.8	48.9	60.1	61.1	63.3	Net Worth	57.7	57.4
100.0	100.0	100.0	100.0	100.0	100.0	Total Liabilities & Net Worth	100.0	100.0
						INCOME DATA		
100.0	100.0	100.0	100.0	100.0	100.0	Net Sales	100.0	100.0
						Gross Profit		
95.9	94.8	93.8	94.3	97.8	98.8	Operating Expenses	93.1	94.8
4.1	5.2	6.2	5.7	2.2	1.2	Operating Profit	6.9	5.2
1.5	1.2	2.7	2.6	8.5	7.0	All Other Expenses (net)	−4.4	−6.1
2.6	4.1	3.5	3.1	−6.3	−5.8	Profit Before Taxes	11.3	11.2
						RATIOS		
3.1	3.6	4.3	4.7	4.2	4.1	Current	4.4	4.2
1.5	1.4	1.7	2.1	2.3	2.5		1.9	1.8
.6	.8	.8	1.0	1.1	1.4		1.0	1.0
2.7	3.2	3.7	3.8	3.7	3.8	Quick	3.8	3.6
1.1	1.4	1.5	1.7	1.3	2.1		1.6	1.5
.6	.7	.6	.8	.6	1.0		.8	.8
0 UND	1 377.3	1 441.7	2 204.2	2 156.4	2 208.3	Sales/Receivables	1 253.7	2 205.7
0 999.8	6 60.1	5 73.9	6 58.1	9 42.8	11 33.2		7 56.1	7 49.6
7 53.9	19 19.0	23 15.8	29 12.5	24 15.3	20 18.3		28 13.0	24 14.9
						Cost of Sales/Inventory		
						Cost of Sales/Payables		
7.3	5.7	3.5	2.3	2.9	2.5	Sales/Working Capital	3.4	3.3
25.9	18.2	10.2	5.5	4.7	5.4		8.4	9.0
−27.5	−29.8	−21.9	150.0	249.3	11.4		−219.2	−88.2
9.0	8.0	4.0	8.3	2.2	2.8	EBIT/Interest	14.6	12.9
(23) 1.7	(97) 2.5	(209) 1.6	(240) 2.3	(44) .4	(22) −.2		(398) 3.6	(395) 3.7
−1.2	.9	−.2	.2	−3.4	−2.5		1.3	1.4
						Net Profit + Depr., Dep.,	19.1	
						Amort./Cur. Mat. L /T/D	(11) 4.3	
							2.7	
.2	.5	.8	.6	.5	.5	Fixed/Worth	.5	.5
1.0	1.3	1.2	.9	.8	.8		.8	.8
4.5	2.8	2.2	1.3	.9	1.0		1.4	1.4
.5	.6	.5	.3	.2	.2	Debt/Worth	.2	.2
1.2	1.1	1.0	.6	.6	.6		.6	.6
17.4	2.9	2.3	1.2	1.0	1.0		1.4	1.3
66.4	26.4	13.1	9.1	1.8	1.2	% Profit Before Taxes/Tangible	22.4	20.2
(45) 15.7	(125) 7.6	(285) 3.3	(350) 2.6	(66) −1.2	−1.6	Net Worth	(614) 11.3	(634) 9.3
−.1	−6.2	−4.4	−2.9	−5.2	−5.9		1.9	2.0
29.6	9.9	5.0	5.0	1.5	.9	% Profit Before Taxes/Total	13.0	10.8
7.2	3.2	1.7	1.4	−.6	−.9	Assets	6.3	5.4
−1.3	−3.2	−2.1	−1.7	−4.0	−4.2		.8	.9
54.4	17.1	2.1	1.2	.9	1.4	Sales/Net Fixed Assets	3.5	2.5
25.1	2.6	1.1	.8	.7	.8		1.3	1.2
6.8	1.4	.7	.6	.5	.5		.8	.8
7.4	2.6	1.1	.7	.5	.7	Sales/Total Assets	1.2	1.2
4.0	1.5	.7	.5	.3	.3		.8	.7
2.3	1.0	.5	.3	.2	.2		.5	.4
.7	1.7	3.2	4.3	5.1	1.7	% Depr., Dep., Amort./Sales	2.7	2.8
(33) 1.7	(100) 2.8	(230) 4.9	(287) 5.8	(44) 7.4	(18) 4.3		(444) 4.1	(469) 4.4
3.4	4.0	6.5	7.7	9.8	10.1		5.8	6.1
2.3	3.0	2.3	4.1	2.7		% Officers', Directors',	4.7	3.5
(12) 3.6	(27) 5.8	(34) 7.7	(33) 7.7	(12) 6.5		Owners' Comp/Sales	(66) 6.4	(69) 7.6
10.9	13.6	18.8	17.7	15.3			12.1	13.7
71584M	385483M	1754622M	5975086M	2128523M	4144346M	Net Sales ($)	7832421M	8716275M
14957M	173384M	1570158M	7936193M	4837356M	6486470M	Total Assets ($)	11593001M	14062301M

M = $ thousand   MM = $ million
See Pages 11 through 18 for Explanation of Ratios and Data

Comparative Historical Data   **Current Data Sorted By Sales**

			Type of Statement	0-1MM	1-3MM	3-5MM	5-10MM	10-25MM	25MM & OVER
442	365	625	Unqualified	19	106	85	184	138	93
31	36	51	Reviewed	4	26	9	9	3	
126	151	45	Compiled	9	19	8	7		2
19	23	22	Tax Returns	11	9			2	
154	161	216	Other	25	66	31	41	29	24
4/1/00- 3/31/01 ALL	4/1/01- 3/31/02 ALL	4/1/02- 3/31/03 ALL		784 (4/1-9/30/02)			175 (10/1/02-3/31/03)		
772	736	959	**NUMBER OF STATEMENTS**	68	226	133	241	172	119
%	%	%	**ASSETS**	%	%	%	%	%	%
22.2	20.7	22.3	Cash & Equivalents	31.1	23.3	21.4	19.5	17.6	28.8
6.9	6.3	5.9	Trade Receivables (net)	4.0	6.7	4.1	6.1	4.0	10.1
.3	.4	.2	Inventory	.2	.1	.1	.2	.2	.7
5.0	5.9	3.9	All Other Current	2.9	2.6	3.5	4.3	4.0	6.2
34.4	33.3	32.3	Total Current	38.2	32.7	29.2	30.1	25.8	45.9
48.7	51.2	52.7	Fixed Assets (net)	54.2	57.4	59.0	55.8	49.0	35.2
.8	.9	.6	Intangibles (net)	.9	1.0	.4	.3	.5	1.0
16.0	14.6	14.3	All Other Non-Current	6.8	9.0	11.5	13.8	24.7	17.9
100.0	100.0	100.0	Total	100.0	100.0	100.0	100.0	100.0	100.0
			LIABILITIES						
3.6	2.8	3.3	Notes Payable-Short Term	9.8	3.9	3.7	2.6	1.5	1.8
1.3	1.2	1.4	Cur. Mat.-L/T/D	3.3	1.8	1.7	1.0	.6	1.4
3.6	3.2	3.3	Trade Payables	3.0	3.9	2.7	2.6	2.5	5.3
.0	.1	.1	Income Taxes Payable	.0	.2	.0	.0	.0	.0
11.5	11.1	12.1	All Other Current	12.7	15.1	12.4	10.5	7.7	15.1
20.1	18.4	20.1	Total Current	28.9	24.8	20.5	16.8	12.3	23.8
18.9	20.6	22.0	Long Term Debt	30.3	27.4	21.5	17.3	19.1	21.5
.1	.0	.0	Deferred Taxes	.0	.0	.0	.0	.0	.0
5.8	5.9	6.2	All Other Non-Current	7.1	7.5	4.8	5.6	5.4	7.5
55.2	55.1	51.6	Net Worth	33.7	40.3	53.3	60.3	63.2	47.1
100.0	100.0	100.0	Total Liabilities & Net Worth	100.0	100.0	100.0	100.0	100.0	100.0
			INCOME DATA						
100.0	100.0	100.0	Net Sales	100.0	100.0	100.0	100.0	100.0	100.0
			Gross Profit						
93.8	94.5	94.8	Operating Expenses	88.7	94.8	97.3	94.1	94.4	97.2
6.2	5.5	5.2	Operating Profit	11.3	5.2	2.7	5.9	5.6	2.8
-4.6	1.8	2.9	All Other Expenses (net)	4.8	2.4	2.1	2.0	5.2	2.4
10.8	3.7	2.3	Profit Before Taxes	6.4	2.8	.7	3.9	.3	.4
			RATIOS						
4.2	4.9	4.2	Current	6.7	4.3	3.6	4.4	4.5	3.7
1.9	2.0	1.9		2.5	1.5	1.5	2.0	2.2	2.3
1.0	1.0	.9		1.0	.7	.7	1.1	1.0	1.1
3.3	3.7	3.6	Quick	6.1	3.7	3.1	3.6	4.1	3.3
(771) 1.5	1.4	1.6		2.4	1.3	1.2	1.6	1.6	2.0
.8	.7	.7		.8	.6	.5	.9	.9	.9
2 226.7	1 287.8	1 327.9	Sales/Receivables	0 UND	0 999.8	1 687.2	2 202.0	2 192.6	1 316.8
7 49.9	6 63.4	6 62.0		3 129.4	6 60.8	4 97.2	6 62.8	7 53.8	13 28.2
27 13.7	23 15.6	24 15.4		12 31.0	18 20.7	18 20.4	29 12.6	24 15.2	27 13.7
			Cost of Sales/Inventory						
			Cost of Sales/Payables						
3.0	2.8	3.1	Sales/Working Capital	4.0	4.5	2.9	2.4	2.8	3.6
7.4	7.8	8.5		9.9	17.3	9.6	6.6	6.2	7.8
999.8	-632.2	-50.7		-67.2	-21.4	-14.9	98.6	-97.2	84.5
11.1	4.9	5.6	EBIT/Interest	6.5	4.0	3.8	13.7	5.8	3.5
(456) 3.6	(481) 2.1	(635) 1.8		(38) 1.9	(158) 1.7	(89) 1.3	(177) 3.1	(111) 1.5	(62) 1.2
1.2	.3	-.3		.6	.2	-1.8	.3	-1.4	.0
		6.5	Net Profit + Depr., Dep.,						
		(13) 2.2	Amort./Cur. Mat. L/T/D						
		2.1							
.4	.5	.6	Fixed/Worth	.6	.9	.7	.6	.5	.0
.9	.9	1.0		1.4	1.4	1.1	.9	.8	.8
1.4	1.6	1.8		3.4	2.9	1.8	1.4	1.1	1.0
.3	.3	.4	Debt/Worth	.5	.6	.3	.2	.2	.5
.6	.7	.8		1.1	1.4	.8	.5	.5	.9
1.6	1.7	1.8		3.2	3.2	1.6	1.2	1.0	2.8
19.0	14.3	12.4	% Profit Before Taxes/Tangible	28.1	16.0	7.6	12.8	6.0	15.5
(743) 7.5	(704) 4.5	(911) 2.8	Net Worth	(61) 8.0	(208) 5.3	(126) 2.0	(234) 2.8	1.3	(110) .8
.7	-2.5	-3.9		-1.7	-4.7	-5.9	-3.4	-3.7	-5.7
10.4	7.0	5.7	% Profit Before Taxes/Total	12.3	7.0	4.0	6.4	3.5	6.3
4.2	2.4	1.5	Assets	3.9	1.9	1.3	1.6	.6	.5
.3	-1.6	-2.1		-.9	-1.9	-2.7	-1.9	-2.7	-2.9
3.3	2.8	2.6	Sales/Net Fixed Assets	11.8	4.3	1.7	1.5	1.2	UND
1.2	1.1	1.1		1.7	1.4	1.0	.9	.9	2.5
.7	.7	.7		.7	.7	.7	.6	.6	.9
1.2	1.2	1.2	Sales/Total Assets	2.4	1.8	.9	.8	.7	3.6
.6	.6	.6		.9	.9	.6	.5	.5	1.2
.4	.4	.4		.5	.5	.4	.4	.3	.5
2.0	2.2	3.0	% Depr., Dep., Amort./Sales	1.9	2.5	3.5	3.8	4.1	2.1
(550) 4.0	(544) 4.3	(712) 4.9		(49) 3.6	(167) 3.7	(110) 5.4	(211) 5.8	(136) 5.6	(39) 3.2
6.0	6.5	7.0		5.4	5.7	7.3	7.7	7.6	5.3
4.0	4.8	2.9	% Officers', Directors',	1.7	3.0	2.4	4.0	4.1	2.4
(96) 7.8	(93) 8.6	(123) 8.6	Owners' Comp/Sales	(12) 8.3	(31) 5.8	(18) 4.2	(19) 9.4	(23) 7.1	(20) 18.3
14.3	23.5	16.4		12.1	14.0	11.9	20.5	15.1	32.3
10807584M	8983384M	14459644M	Net Sales ($)	46135M	431104M	528622M	1760139M	2586304M	9107340M
18336245M	15552237M	21018518M	Total Assets ($)	71911M	676459M	1025145M	3764905M	6636204M	8843894M

Current Data Sorted By Assets   Comparative Historical Data

0-500M	500M-2MM	2-10MM	10-50MM	50-100MM	100-250MM	Type of Statement	4/1/98-3/31/99 ALL	4/1/99-3/31/00 ALL
	3	6	16	2	5	Unqualified	35	32
1			1			Reviewed	1	1
		1				Compiled		
						Tax Returns		
		6	3		2	Other	7	7
	31 (4/1-9/30/02)		15 (10/1/02-3/31/03)					
1	3	13	20	2	7	NUMBER OF STATEMENTS	43	40
%	%	%	%	%	%		%	%
						ASSETS		
		22.2	19.2			Cash & Equivalents	23.2	23.1
		18.6	9.7			Trade Receivables (net)	9.9	12.8
		.9	1.2			Inventory	1.3	1.3
		1.8	4.5			All Other Current	3.4	4.7
		43.5	34.6			Total Current	37.8	42.0
		40.1	46.2			Fixed Assets (net)	39.1	42.9
		10.5	2.7			Intangibles (net)	3.0	2.4
		5.9	16.5			All Other Non-Current	20.1	12.7
		100.0	100.0			Total	100.0	100.0
						LIABILITIES		
		.2	1.3			Notes Payable-Short Term	2.2	1.4
		3.1	2.2			Cur. Mat.-L/T/D	1.7	1.1
		2.6	5.4			Trade Payables	4.9	4.6
		.1	.0			Income Taxes Payable	.2	.1
		22.6	13.1			All Other Current	9.1	17.3
		28.6	22.0			Total Current	18.1	24.6
		14.9	17.4			Long Term Debt	13.1	13.6
		.0	.1			Deferred Taxes	.2	.1
		6.9	2.7			All Other Non-Current	9.1	9.3
		49.6	57.7			Net Worth	59.5	52.4
		100.0	100.0			Total Liabilities & Net Worth	100.0	100.0
						INCOME DATA		
		100.0	100.0			Net Sales	100.0	100.0
						Gross Profit		
		85.5	92.7			Operating Expenses	87.8	93.2
		14.5	7.3			Operating Profit	12.2	6.8
		6.3	.7			All Other Expenses (net)	.2	-.8
		8.2	6.7			Profit Before Taxes	12.0	7.5
						RATIOS		
		8.6	2.5			Current	4.1	5.6
		1.7	1.6				1.9	1.8
		.9	1.1				1.2	1.1
		7.1	2.4			Quick	3.6	4.7
		1.6	1.2				1.6	1.6
		.8	.7				1.0	.9
		7 54.3	5 79.8			Sales/Receivables	8 46.4	4 103.0
		19 19.7	17 21.3				15 24.6	15 24.6
		67 5.4	36 10.2				27 13.3	33 11.0
						Cost of Sales/Inventory		
						Cost of Sales/Payables		
		2.6	4.5			Sales/Working Capital	4.5	3.5
		6.7	10.3				8.8	8.7
		NM	36.8				27.7	36.5
		(10) 20.4	(14) 15.1			EBIT/Interest	(23) 15.8	(25) 42.5
		7.4	5.9				9.6	11.9
		3.2	2.3				3.7	3.8
						Net Profit + Depr., Dep., Amort./Cur. Mat. L /T/D		
		.5	.7			Fixed/Worth	.4	.4
		1.0	.9				.8	.8
		4.2	1.0				1.0	1.3
		.2	.4			Debt/Worth	.3	.4
		2.2	.7				.5	.8
		5.8	1.9				1.4	2.0
		(12) 49.8	54.0			% Profit Before Taxes/Tangible Net Worth	(42) 24.0	(38) 30.9
		25.8	14.4				10.0	10.7
		3.6	5.3				5.2	2.7
		13.0	20.2			% Profit Before Taxes/Total Assets	14.3	13.6
		4.4	8.0				6.1	5.5
		2.9	2.8				2.9	1.2
		9.4	7.3			Sales/Net Fixed Assets	16.5	19.0
		4.6	1.8				2.1	1.8
		.9	1.0				.9	.9
		1.2	1.7			Sales/Total Assets	2.1	2.6
		.9	1.1				.8	.8
		.5	.5				.5	.5
		(11) 2.6	(16) 3.0			% Depr., Dep., Amort./Sales	(24) 2.5	(20) 2.0
		4.3	4.0				3.4	3.3
		14.0	5.0				6.4	5.5
						% Officers', Directors', Owners' Comp/Sales		
575M	7636M	96384M	539321M	85990M	621926M	Net Sales ($)	1402432M	1729628M
286M	4929M	86078M	441213M	135741M	1062976M	Total Assets ($)	1706611M	2123622M

M = $ thousand   MM = $ million
See Pages 11 through 18 for Explanation of Ratios and Data

Comparative Historical Data | Current Data Sorted By Sales

			Type of Statement						
40	28	32	Unqualified	3	2	2	3	11	11
		1	Reviewed				1		1
2	1	2	Compiled	1					
			Tax Returns						
13	13	11	Other			2	3	2	4
4/1/00-3/31/01	4/1/01-3/31/02	4/1/02-3/31/03		31 (4/1-9/30/02)			15 (10/1/02-3/31/03)		
ALL	ALL	ALL		0-1MM	1-3MM	3-5MM	5-10MM	10-25MM	25MM & OVER
55	42	46	**NUMBER OF STATEMENTS**	4	2	4	7	13	16
%	%	%	**ASSETS**	%	%	%	%	%	%
16.9	19.9	19.0	Cash & Equivalents					25.0	14.7
12.9	7.1	12.3	Trade Receivables (net)					5.6	14.8
1.5	1.4	1.0	Inventory					.7	1.3
4.5	5.6	4.2	All Other Current					4.9	6.7
35.8	34.0	36.5	Total Current					36.1	37.4
47.7	46.8	46.4	Fixed Assets (net)					49.1	45.5
2.1	4.1	5.6	Intangibles (net)					2.2	5.7
14.4	15.1	11.5	All Other Non-Current					12.6	11.4
100.0	100.0	100.0	Total					100.0	100.0
			LIABILITIES						
2.3	.7	.7	Notes Payable-Short Term					.6	.3
1.4	2.0	2.6	Cur. Mat.-L/T/D					1.9	2.0
4.5	4.2	3.7	Trade Payables					4.2	4.5
.2	.1	.4	Income Taxes Payable					.0	1.2
18.6	12.9	15.7	All Other Current					8.4	18.2
27.0	20.0	23.1	Total Current					15.0	26.2
13.3	14.6	15.7	Long Term Debt					18.2	13.0
.1	.5	.1	Deferred Taxes					.0	.3
6.0	6.3	4.7	All Other Non-Current					5.3	5.5
53.6	58.7	56.4	Net Worth					61.6	55.0
100.0	100.0	100.0	Total Liabilities & Net Worth					100.0	100.0
			INCOME DATA						
100.0	100.0	100.0	Net Sales					100.0	100.0
			Gross Profit						
95.2	93.7	90.4	Operating Expenses					88.5	91.7
4.8	6.3	9.6	Operating Profit					11.5	8.3
-1.3	2.5	2.5	All Other Expenses (net)					4.1	.2
6.0	3.8	7.1	Profit Before Taxes					7.4	8.1
			RATIOS						
2.9	3.4	3.7						5.8	3.4
1.5	1.9	1.8	Current					2.1	1.7
.9	1.1	1.0						1.6	.9
2.2	2.7	2.7						5.5	2.3
1.3	1.4	1.4	Quick					1.7	1.0
.8	.7	.7						.7	.7
6 59.6	4 87.0	5 75.1						5 77.6	5 77.5
14 25.5	14 26.3	16 23.4	Sales/Receivables					17 21.6	17 20.9
37 9.9	25 14.3	35 10.5						39 9.3	33 11.0
			Cost of Sales/Inventory						
			Cost of Sales/Payables						
4.2	3.3	3.3						3.2	4.4
14.7	6.3	9.0	Sales/Working Capital					9.1	14.9
-215.8	37.9	NM						11.1	NM
(35) 21.9	(23) 6.9	(33) 13.7						15.3	34.9
6.1	3.0	6.3	EBIT/Interest				(10)	6.8	(11) 6.8
2.9	.2	3.2						1.4	5.1
			Net Profit + Depr., Dep., Amort./Cur. Mat. L/T/D						
.6	.6	.7						.6	.8
.9	.8	.9	Fixed/Worth					.9	.9
1.2	1.1	1.2						1.2	1.3
.3	.2	.4						.4	.2
.6	.7	.9	Debt/Worth					.6	.8
2.4	2.0	2.3						1.3	2.6
(53) 18.2	(40) 12.9	(44) 40.1	% Profit Before Taxes/Tangible					45.0	49.3
6.3	2.8	12.7	Net Worth					15.4	(15) 13.3
.3	-1.1	3.4						1.9	5.0
8.3	9.1	13.3	% Profit Before Taxes/Total					22.4	13.2
3.6	1.7	5.6	Assets					9.2	7.4
.2	-.3	2.7						1.4	3.0
10.0	5.6	6.2						5.5	8.0
1.6	1.3	1.6	Sales/Net Fixed Assets					2.1	1.5
.8	.7	.9						1.0	1.1
2.1	1.6	1.4						1.3	2.3
.8	.7	.9	Sales/Total Assets					1.1	.9
.5	.4	.5						.6	.6
(27) 2.0	(22) 3.3	(38) 3.3	% Depr., Dep., Amort./Sales						2.9
4.7	4.5	4.5							(14) 4.6
6.4	6.9	5.4							5.1
			% Officers', Directors', Owners' Comp/Sales						
2328712M	1641608M	1351832M	Net Sales ($)	3497M	3519M	16366M	56958M	204431M	1067061M
2679610M	2180617M	1731223M	Total Assets ($)	15621M	3244M	15164M	102295M	261833M	1333066M

M = $ thousand   MM = $ million
See Pages 11 through 18 for Explanation of Ratios and Data

EDUCATION—Colleges, Universities, and Professional Schools NAICS 611310 (SIC 8221)

Current Data Sorted By Assets — **Comparative Historical Data**

0-500M	500M-2MM	2-10MM	10-50MM	50-100MM	100-250MM	Type of Statement	4/1/98-3/31/99 ALL	4/1/99-3/31/00 ALL
1	15	37	179	130	132	Unqualified	356	434
	1		1	1	3	Reviewed	5	2
1			3			Compiled	5	13
1			1			Tax Returns		
1	2	10	34	23	21	Other	67	55
	455 (4/1-9/30/02)			142 (10/1/02-3/31/03)				
4	18	48	218	153	156	**NUMBER OF STATEMENTS**	433	504
%	%	%	%	%	%	**ASSETS**	%	%
	40.0	19.6	12.2	12.1	15.0	Cash & Equivalents	16.6	16.3
	12.8	7.3	6.0	3.6	3.7	Trade Receivables (net)	5.9	5.5
	1.8	1.0	.5	.3	.2	Inventory	1.0	.6
	2.1	6.2	4.6	3.9	4.0	All Other Current	3.0	3.4
	56.7	34.2	23.2	20.0	23.0	Total Current	26.5	25.8
	28.6	51.0	52.8	49.7	42.1	Fixed Assets (net)	40.8	42.3
	1.5	.4	1.0	.5	.5	Intangibles (net)	.9	.6
	13.2	14.4	23.0	29.8	34.4	All Other Non-Current	31.8	31.3
	100.0	100.0	100.0	100.0	100.0	Total	100.0	100.0
						LIABILITIES		
	4.0	3.0	1.8	1.5	.5	Notes Payable-Short Term	1.6	1.5
	2.8	1.9	1.6	.8	.7	Cur. Mat.-L/T/D	.8	1.1
	3.7	4.4	3.6	2.3	2.5	Trade Payables	3.1	2.9
	.6	.0	.1	.0	.1	Income Taxes Payable	.1	.1
	19.8	10.8	6.0	5.2	4.6	All Other Current	7.0	6.8
	30.8	20.1	13.1	9.8	8.3	Total Current	12.5	12.4
	10.3	19.1	24.4	21.8	22.4	Long Term Debt	17.4	19.1
	.0	.3	.1	.1	.1	Deferred Taxes	.0	.1
	6.3	3.5	4.7	3.6	3.4	All Other Non-Current	4.4	4.1
	52.6	57.0	57.7	64.8	65.9	Net Worth	65.7	64.3
	100.0	100.0	100.0	100.0	100.0	Total Liabilities & Net Worth	100.0	100.0
						INCOME DATA		
	100.0	100.0	100.0	100.0	100.0	Net Sales	100.0	100.0
						Gross Profit		
	98.7	95.7	96.4	98.1	97.3	Operating Expenses	90.5	92.6
	1.3	4.3	3.6	1.9	2.7	Operating Profit	9.5	7.4
	.9	3.8	3.9	4.1	6.9	All Other Expenses (net)	-9.9	-5.3
	.3	.5	-.3	-2.2	-4.2	Profit Before Taxes	19.3	12.7
						RATIOS		
	3.7	6.2	3.4	4.0	3.8		4.3	4.4
	2.3	1.5	1.7	1.8	2.4	Current	1.9	2.0
	1.0	.7	1.0	1.0	1.4		1.0	1.1
	3.1	4.1	2.8	3.3	3.3		3.6	3.6
	2.3	1.4	1.3	1.3	1.6	Quick	1.5	1.5
	1.0	.5	.6	.6	.8		.7	.8
	4 102.7	3 123.1	9 39.9	8 46.4	9 42.1		7 49.9	8 48.4
	10 36.2	8 45.6	20 18.5	20 18.2	18 19.8	Sales/Receivables	19 19.6	17 21.1
	33 11.0	24 15.2	41 8.9	37 9.8	48 7.6		45 8.2	41 8.8
						Cost of Sales/Inventory		
						Cost of Sales/Payables		
	3.5	2.6	3.6	2.2	1.7		3.0	2.5
	7.0	9.6	9.8	8.0	5.3	Sales/Working Capital	7.4	7.3
	-310.6	-21.1	-750.7	-554.5	16.7		-495.6	96.8
	21.0	(34) 6.7	(163) 5.0	(107) 4.2	(121) 3.5		(281) 18.6	(331) 13.2
	(10) 4.7	.7	1.6	.7	.8	EBIT/Interest	7.2	5.3
	.2	-1.9	-.1	-3.7	-2.1		3.1	2.2
								11.2
						Net Profit + Depr., Dep., Amort./Cur. Mat. L /T/D	(15) 2.9	
								.7
	.2	.4	.6	.6	.4		.4	.4
	.5	.8	.9	.7	.6	Fixed/Worth	.6	.6
	1.1	1.5	1.4	1.0	.9		.9	1.0
	.4	.2	.4	.3	.3		.2	.2
	.6	.6	.6	.5	.5	Debt/Worth	.4	.5
	1.5	1.9	1.4	.8	.8		.8	.9
	29.5	13.0	7.0	4.4	3.4		17.5	12.5
	(17) 4.0	(46) 1.3	(216) .9	-.4	-1.2	% Profit Before Taxes/Tangible Net Worth	(428) 11.2	(501) 7.1
	-13.3	-6.8	-4.0	-5.8	-4.8		5.8	2.7
	14.0	5.2	3.7	2.5	2.2		11.2	8.2
	3.7	.7	.7	-.3	-.6	% Profit Before Taxes/Total Assets	7.2	4.7
	-8.2	-3.2	-2.5	-3.7	-3.0		3.4	1.6
	158.9	4.0	1.6	1.1	1.1		1.9	1.6
	10.4	1.4	1.0	.8	.8	Sales/Net Fixed Assets	1.2	1.1
	1.8	.8	.8	.7	.6		.9	.8
	3.0	1.2	.8	.5	.5		.8	.7
	1.9	.8	.6	.4	.3	Sales/Total Assets	.5	.5
	.8	.8	.4	.3	.3		.3	.3
	.7	2.9	4.3	4.7	4.7		3.4	3.8
	(16) 2.5	(45) 5.7	(198) 5.7	(136) 6.4	(140) 6.3	% Depr., Dep., Amort./Sales	(342) 4.9	(417) 4.9
	3.3	8.9	7.6	7.7	8.1		6.3	6.3
			6.3	5.0	3.1		4.3	6.4
		(28)	14.6	(19) 7.9	(22) 10.6	% Officers', Directors', Owners' Comp/Sales	(49) 9.9	(60) 9.6
			32.1	16.8	15.1		16.5	18.5
2887M	75593M	337273M	4157783M	5048747M	9649463M	Net Sales ($)	14570552M	16807641M
906M	22464M	292722M	6359481M	11289422M	24783023M	Total Assets ($)	26289062M	34091805M

© RMA 2003

M = $ thousand   MM = $ million
See Pages 11 through 18 for Explanation of Ratios and Data

Comparative Historical Data | **Current Data Sorted By Sales**

390	395	494	Type of Statement	9	22	13	46	161	243
	1	6	Unqualified / Reviewed				2	1	3
42	62	4	Compiled	1	1				1
	1	1	Tax Returns	1				2	
83	91	91	Other	4	1	2	8	30	46
4/1/00-3/31/01	4/1/01-3/31/02	4/1/02-3/31/03		455 (4/1-9/30/02)			142 (10/1/02-3/31/03)		
ALL	ALL	ALL		0-1MM	1-3MM	3-5MM	5-10MM	10-25MM	25MM & OVER
515	550	597	**NUMBER OF STATEMENTS**	15	24	15	56	194	293
%	%	%	**ASSETS**	%	%	%	%	%	%
14.6	15.1	14.4	Cash & Equivalents	19.4	20.3	29.5	13.1	11.9	14.7
5.4	5.0	5.1	Trade Receivables (net)	5.6	3.6	8.9	6.2	5.0	4.9
.6	.5	.5	Inventory	1.5	.7	.6	1.0	.4	.4
3.8	5.1	4.3	All Other Current	1.5	6.4	2.9	4.1	4.5	4.2
24.4	25.7	24.3	Total Current	27.9	30.9	41.9	24.5	21.8	24.3
41.3	44.6	48.1	Fixed Assets (net)	53.3	48.2	41.5	51.7	50.2	46.2
.7	.8	.7	Intangibles (net)	.1	.9	.5	1.2	.8	.6
33.7	28.8	26.8	All Other Non-Current	18.6	20.0	16.1	22.6	27.1	29.0
100.0	100.0	100.0	Total	100.0	100.0	100.0	100.0	100.0	100.0
			LIABILITIES						
1.6	1.7	1.6	Notes Payable-Short Term	1.4	4.5	3.1	3.7	1.9	.7
.9	1.1	1.2	Cur. Mat.-L/T/D	2.8	.9	1.6	1.6	1.5	.9
2.9	3.2	3.0	Trade Payables	1.1	1.7	2.1	4.3	2.9	3.1
.1	.1	.1	Income Taxes Payable	.1	.0	.1	.0	.1	.1
6.2	6.2	6.3	All Other Current	4.4	9.4	16.3	7.5	5.8	5.7
11.7	12.2	12.2	Total Current	9.9	16.5	23.1	17.2	12.2	10.5
18.2	21.4	22.3	Long Term Debt	27.4	20.5	17.4	20.6	22.8	22.4
.1	.1	.1	Deferred Taxes	.0	.0	.7	.0	.1	.1
3.8	4.2	4.1	All Other Non-Current	3.9	1.2	7.4	2.9	3.8	4.6
66.1	62.0	61.3	Net Worth	58.8	61.8	51.4	59.4	61.2	62.4
100.0	100.0	100.0	Total Liabilities & Net Worth	100.0	100.0	100.0	100.0	100.0	100.0
			INCOME DATA						
100.0	100.0	100.0	Net Sales	100.0	100.0	100.0	100.0	100.0	100.0
			Gross Profit						
95.2	95.3	97.1	Operating Expenses	92.1	96.9	97.2	100.0	97.8	96.4
4.8	4.7	2.9	Operating Profit	7.9	3.1	2.8	.0	2.2	3.6
-6.1	3.6	4.6	All Other Expenses (net)	10.4	5.0	4.2	2.3	4.7	4.7
10.9	1.1	-1.7	Profit Before Taxes	-2.4	-1.9	-1.4	-2.3	-2.5	-1.1
			RATIOS						
4.0 2.0 1.0	3.9 2.0 1.0	3.7 1.9 1.0	Current	11.2 3.3 .8	8.9 1.9 1.3	8.7 1.7 .9	3.9 1.3 .9	3.6 1.9 1.0	3.5 2.0 1.2
3.3 1.4 .7	3.0 1.4 .7	3.1 1.4 .7	Quick	9.0 2.6 .8	4.9 1.9 .9	7.3 1.7 .8	2.7 1.0 .5	2.9 1.3 .6	3.1 1.4 .8
8 46.4 19 18.9 43 8.4	7 50.4 18 20.2 41 9.0	8 47.1 18 20.1 41 8.9	Sales/Receivables	0 UND 5 78.1 29 12.4	1 260.1 5 76.8 21 17.6	8 43.2 11 33.9 32 11.5	6 59.7 16 23.1 32 11.6	9 40.2 18 20.6 42 8.6	8 43.2 22 16.9 42 8.7
			Cost of Sales/Inventory						
			Cost of Sales/Payables						
2.6 7.4 148.0	2.5 7.1 191.9	2.5 7.6 110.3	Sales/Working Capital	1.4 3.4 -16.6	.7 8.3 13.3	1.9 6.0 -51.0	3.4 12.8 -31.2	2.6 7.2 -106.5	2.4 7.4 35.6
(339) 9.5 4.3 1.4	(395) 4.2 1.6 -.7	(437) 4.2 1.3 -1.5	EBIT/Interest		(18) 2.8 1.0 -1.0		(38) 4.4 .6 -3.9	(149) 4.4 1.4 -1.3	(216) 4.0 1.3 -1.5
(10) 79.8 3.8 2.6		(13) 64.1 7.6 3.0	Net Profit + Depr., Dep., Amort./Cur. Mat. L/T/D						
.4 .6 .9	.5 .7 1.0	.5 .8 1.1	Fixed/Worth	.3 .8 1.8	.4 .8 1.4	.4 .8 1.5	.5 .9 1.4	.6 .8 1.1	.5 .7 1.0
.2 .4 .8	.3 .5 1.0	.3 .5 1.0	Debt/Worth	.2 .4 1.2	.2 .5 1.3	.1 .6 1.9	.2 .6 1.4	.3 .5 1.0	.4 .5 .9
(514) 11.1 6.1 1.3	(543) 7.2 1.5 -2.8	(591) 5.5 .3 -4.8	% Profit Before Taxes/Tangible Net Worth	4.0 .0 -3.2	(23) 4.8 .6 -6.6	(14) 27.3 -.9 -9.3	(54) 6.4 -1.4 -6.3	(193) 5.5 .1 -5.3	(292) 5.2 .5 -4.4
7.4 4.0 .7	4.3 .9 -1.8	3.2 .2 -3.0	% Profit Before Taxes/Total Assets	2.9 .0 -1.2	1.6 .5 -3.9	12.0 .4 -3.7	3.9 -.6 -3.9	3.2 .1 -3.4	3.3 .3 -2.5
1.6 1.0 .8	1.5 1.0 .8	1.4 .9 .7	Sales/Net Fixed Assets	1.9 .6 .3	1.7 1.0 .5	10.0 1.1 .8	1.8 1.0 .7	1.2 .9 .7	1.4 1.0 .7
.6 .4 .3	.7 .5 .3	.7 .5 .3	Sales/Total Assets	.7 .4 .1	1.2 .5 .2	1.9 .6 .4	.9 .6 .3	.7 .5 .3	.7 .5 .3
(408) 3.5 5.0 6.5	(486) 3.5 5.1 7.0	(539) 4.4 6.0 7.8	% Depr., Dep., Amort./Sales	2.5 8.9 27.0	(23) 3.5 6.7 11.7	2.7 4.4 6.1	(49) 3.7 5.4 7.7	(177) 4.9 6.3 8.0	(260) 4.4 5.8 7.3
(51) 6.4 11.7 19.6	(70) 4.5 11.0 18.7	(74) 5.0 11.7 24.2	% Officers', Directors', Owners' Comp/Sales					(21) 7.7 15.8 31.0	(40) 3.5 10.4 15.4
18341080M 38822302M	18327979M 39666592M	19271746M 42748018M	Net Sales ($) Total Assets ($)	8799M 39671M	47751M 239489M	63137M 125844M	427705M 923608M	3372807M 8526215M	15351547M 32893191M

M = $ thousand   MM = $ million
See Pages 11 through 18 for Explanation of Ratios and Data

Current Data Sorted By Assets   Comparative Historical Data

0-500M	500M-2MM	2-10MM	10-50MM	50-100MM	100-250MM	Type of Statement	4/1/98-3/31/99 ALL	4/1/99-3/31/00 ALL
2	8	12	10	1	2	Unqualified	41	43
1	1	1				Reviewed	1	4
2	1	1				Compiled	5	7
2						Tax Returns	5	4
	4	9	3			Other	15	17
	32 (4/1-9/30/02)		28 (10/1/02-3/31/03)					
7	14	23	13	1	2	NUMBER OF STATEMENTS	67	75
%	%	%	%	%	%	ASSETS	%	%
	18.6	16.7	14.5			Cash & Equivalents	16.6	18.4
	34.9	22.8	26.0			Trade Receivables (net)	27.5	23.4
	4.3	1.2	1.0			Inventory	2.8	3.9
	.8	4.5	4.7			All Other Current	2.8	2.8
	58.7	45.2	46.3			Total Current	49.7	48.5
	24.2	41.0	22.5			Fixed Assets (net)	33.6	35.9
	2.5	2.7	11.7			Intangibles (net)	4.8	3.4
	14.6	11.0	19.5			All Other Non-Current	12.0	12.2
	100.0	100.0	100.0			Total	100.0	100.0
						LIABILITIES		
	17.0	6.5	2.5			Notes Payable-Short Term	3.6	4.8
	2.3	2.6	2.5			Cur. Mat.-L/T/D	2.4	1.7
	16.2	6.8	3.9			Trade Payables	5.3	6.8
	.4	.8	.0			Income Taxes Payable	.4	.4
	35.3	13.2	18.3			All Other Current	22.4	18.7
	71.2	29.9	27.2			Total Current	34.3	32.5
	17.0	16.5	12.4			Long Term Debt	13.7	13.3
	.0	.1	.1			Deferred Taxes	.1	.2
	10.1	8.3	10.9			All Other Non-Current	7.1	7.2
	1.7	45.2	49.5			Net Worth	44.8	46.8
	100.0	100.0	100.0			Total Liabilities & Net Worth	100.0	100.0
						INCOME DATA		
	100.0	100.0	100.0			Net Sales	100.0	100.0
						Gross Profit		
	99.8	93.1	84.1			Operating Expenses	96.9	98.9
	.2	6.9	15.9			Operating Profit	3.1	1.1
	1.1	1.7	10.1			All Other Expenses (net)	-2.3	-1.6
	-.9	5.2	5.8			Profit Before Taxes	5.4	2.7
						RATIOS		
	2.4	2.7	2.7			Current	3.5	2.9
	.8	1.5	1.7				1.4	1.5
	.5	1.0	1.0				1.0	1.0
	2.3	2.5	2.5			Quick	2.5	2.2
	.8	1.2	1.3				1.3	1.2
	.5	.9	.8				.8	.9
	16 23.3	24 15.5	19 18.7			Sales/Receivables	11 34.7	6 56.9
	41 9.0	31 11.6	34 10.9				47 7.8	36 10.0
	99 3.7	87 4.2	101 3.6				119 3.1	74 4.9
						Cost of Sales/Inventory		
						Cost of Sales/Payables		
	6.2	5.0	4.7			Sales/Working Capital	4.5	4.4
	-98.8	8.4	8.2				13.6	13.7
	-4.8	-239.3	NM				UND	108.5
	6.9	12.6				EBIT/Interest	13.6	19.4
	(11) -.1	(20) 4.9					(46) 3.8	(55) 5.8
	-4.5	1.3					1.0	.9
						Net Profit + Depr., Dep.,	12.3	8.2
						Amort./Cur. Mat. L /T/D	(14) 4.6 (17) 3.6	
							2.1	2.1
	.4	.4	.2			Fixed/Worth	.4	.4
	4.5	1.1	.5				.8	.8
	-2.0	1.8	1.2				1.7	1.6
	2.1	.7	.4			Debt/Worth	.3	.4
	18.5	1.4	1.9				1.5	1.1
	-6.9	2.6	13.4				3.8	2.7
		36.8	41.2			% Profit Before Taxes/Tangible	62.6	41.9
	(22) 8.2	(11) 15.4				Net Worth	(62) 18.1	(70) 17.3
	-3.4	.0					3.6	-5.4
	9.5	14.8	29.1			% Profit Before Taxes/Total	13.8	17.9
	2.6	5.3	9.2			Assets	6.5	4.4
	-13.2	-1.9	.6				1.2	-4.1
	28.2	15.3	29.3			Sales/Net Fixed Assets	20.0	16.5
	14.1	4.4	11.4				5.0	5.4
	7.5	1.6	2.2				2.1	2.1
	3.0	2.2	2.0			Sales/Total Assets	2.1	2.6
	2.2	1.3	1.1				1.4	1.4
	1.6	.9	.5				.8	.8
	1.2	1.7	1.3			% Depr., Dep., Amort./Sales	1.8	1.2
	(11) 1.8	(21) 3.4	(12) 1.8				(57) 3.2	(64) 2.7
	2.5	4.5	5.7				6.0	4.3
						% Officers', Directors',	4.0	4.3
						Owners' Comp/Sales	(18) 9.3	(16) 9.9
							25.4	20.4
6896M	132007M	184744M	357913M	70585M	610574M	Net Sales ($)	1237734M	1139922M
1947M	19633M	122696M	273240M	70708M	438735M	Total Assets ($)	1216095M	1071867M

M = $thousand   MM = $million
See Pages 11 through 18 for Explanation of Ratios and Data

Comparative Historical Data / Current Data Sorted By Sales

			Type of Statement						
36	32	35	Unqualified	2	5	6	7	7	8
5	2	3	Reviewed		2		1		
12	10	4	Compiled	1	2	1			
2	1	2	Tax Returns	2					
16	19	16	Other	1	2	4	3	5	1
4/1/00-3/31/01	4/1/01-3/31/02	4/1/02-3/31/03			32 (4/1-9/30/02)			28 (10/1/02-3/31/03)	
ALL	ALL	ALL		0-1MM	1-3MM	3-5MM	5-10MM	10-25MM	25MM & OVER
71	64	60	NUMBER OF STATEMENTS	6	11	11	11	12	9
%	%	%	ASSETS	%	%	%	%	%	%
16.5	16.4	17.8	Cash & Equivalents		11.5	15.0	19.7	16.2	
25.8	27.8	27.6	Trade Receivables (net)		30.9	24.5	16.6	38.9	
2.7	1.2	2.4	Inventory		2.6	4.8	1.2	1.5	
4.5	3.4	3.4	All Other Current		1.0	1.7	3.6	5.0	
49.6	48.7	51.1	Total Current		45.9	46.1	41.1	61.6	
34.8	35.8	31.6	Fixed Assets (net)		32.6	36.7	39.3	21.0	
2.4	5.3	4.5	Intangibles (net)		1.8	.4	6.6	5.3	
13.2	10.2	12.9	All Other Non-Current		19.7	16.8	13.1	12.1	
100.0	100.0	100.0	Total		100.0	100.0	100.0	100.0	
			LIABILITIES						
3.5	5.0	8.1	Notes Payable-Short Term		20.2	2.3	8.8	9.2	
2.1	1.8	2.9	Cur. Mat.-L/T/D		3.1	1.7	2.7	3.4	
4.9	6.3	9.6	Trade Payables		9.1	6.6	5.6	11.3	
.2	.3	.4	Income Taxes Payable		.0	.5	1.6	.0	
17.5	19.7	22.6	All Other Current		19.4	15.2	12.3	30.0	
28.1	33.0	43.7	Total Current		51.8	26.4	31.1	53.9	
15.1	17.7	17.6	Long Term Debt		24.2	15.9	13.6	9.9	
.7	.7	.1	Deferred Taxes		.0	.0	.1	.2	
9.4	7.1	10.7	All Other Non-Current		8.0	4.5	11.8	11.7	
46.7	41.5	27.9	Net Worth		16.0	53.3	43.5	24.4	
100.0	100.0	100.0	Total Liabilities & Net Worth		100.0	100.0	100.0	100.0	
			INCOME DATA						
100.0	100.0	100.0	Net Sales		100.0	100.0	100.0	100.0	
			Gross Profit						
92.1	92.0	92.1	Operating Expenses		89.7	93.1	93.3	95.6	
7.9	8.0	7.9	Operating Profit		10.3	6.9	6.7	4.4	
−1.7	2.4	3.2	All Other Expenses (net)		10.8	1.1	.4	3.4	
9.6	5.6	4.7	Profit Before Taxes		−.5	5.7	6.3	1.0	
			RATIOS						
4.5	2.6	2.2			2.8	2.7	3.5	2.0	
2.0	1.6	1.3	Current		.9	1.9	1.4	1.6	
1.0	1.1	.8			.6	1.2	.7	1.0	
3.3	2.0	2.0			2.8	2.5	3.5	1.9	
1.4	1.3	1.1	Quick		.7	1.2	1.0	1.5	
.8	.9	.7			.5	1.1	.6	.8	
6 58.7	8 45.2	19 19.4	Sales/Receivables	8 47.7	25 14.3	21 17.4	28 13.1		
46 7.9	45 8.1	32 11.4		35 10.5	39 9.3	24 15.4	54 6.7		
111 3.3	123 3.0	93 3.9		105 3.5	67 5.5	87 4.2	107 3.4		
			Cost of Sales/Inventory						
			Cost of Sales/Payables						
2.9	4.2	5.6	Sales/Working Capital		4.4	5.2	5.6	4.8	
7.7	9.8	14.3			−56.0	6.7	8.4	8.0	
57.4	52.7	−28.6			−6.6	18.9	−20.6	NM	
19.0	10.3	13.9	EBIT/Interest				16.8	52.4	
(42) 9.6	(44) 4.1	(45) 4.6				(10) 6.3	(10) 6.3		
3.4	1.6	.8					2.4	−.1	
12.3	8.0	9.0	Net Profit + Depr., Dep., Amort./Cur. Mat. L/T/D						
(11) 4.3	(16) 4.1	(12) 3.1							
2.4	2.5	1.8							
.3	.4	.4	Fixed/Worth		.9	.1	.3	.1	
.7	.9	1.0			1.8	.8	1.1	.5	
1.9	2.2	2.8			7.8	1.8	1.5	1.2	
.3	.6	1.0	Debt/Worth		2.5	.1	.5	.7	
1.5	1.9	2.4			6.7	1.2	1.3	2.3	
3.5	4.4	12.2			33.1	1.9	2.8	11.9	
42.7	38.0	47.6	% Profit Before Taxes/Tangible Net Worth			46.7	39.3	40.3	
(66) 15.9	(55) 20.1	(49) 16.4				11.7	(10) 11.5	(10) 13.5	
3.7	2.1	2.4				−5.0	2.5	−15.2	
14.8	14.5	15.9	% Profit Before Taxes/Total Assets		10.3	18.2	12.7	13.5	
5.6	6.4	6.5			3.2	6.1	6.6	4.1	
1.8	−.1	−.6			−2.3	−4.6	1.1	−7.9	
19.8	15.3	22.7	Sales/Net Fixed Assets		18.6	18.3	28.7	33.0	
5.3	5.4	7.5			7.8	6.7	3.3	11.4	
1.2	1.7	3.1			4.8	1.6	1.6	2.8	
1.8	2.3	2.5	Sales/Total Assets		2.7	2.3	2.4	3.6	
1.1	1.2	1.6			1.8	1.0	1.4	1.7	
.5	.8	.9			.4	.8	.9	1.0	
1.4	1.6	1.4	% Depr., Dep., Amort./Sales				1.6	1.8	
(56) 3.2	(53) 2.7	(52) 2.3				(10) 3.6	(11) 2.2		
5.4	3.9	4.6					4.2	6.0	
6.4	3.4	2.9	% Officers', Officers', Owners' Compensation/Sales						
(14) 12.2	(14) 6.6	(12) 7.7							
16.9	19.0	13.2							
741645M	1441900M	1362719M	Net Sales	3834M	20373M	42852M	71811M	199441M	1024408M
858221M	1130897M	926959M	Total Assets	2817M	33981M	40056M	65842M	165295M	618968M

Current Data Sorted By Assets

Comparative Historical Data

2	4	5	3				Type of Statement		
1							Unqualified		
2							Reviewed		
3							Compiled		
	3					1	Tax Returns		
	15 (4/1-9/30/02)			9 (10/1/02-3/31/03)			Other	4/1/98-3/31/99 ALL	4/1/99-3/31/00 ALL
0-500M	500M-2MM	2-10MM	10-50MM	50-100MM		100-250MM			
8	7	5	3			1	NUMBER OF STATEMENTS		
%	%	%	%	%		%	ASSETS	%	%
				D			Cash & Equivalents	D	D
				A			Trade Receivables (net)	A	A
				T			Inventory	T	T
				A			All Other Current	A	A
							Total Current		
				N			Fixed Assets (net)	N	N
				O			Intangibles (net)	O	O
				T			All Other Non-Current	T	T
							Total		
				A			LIABILITIES	A	A
				V			Notes Payable-Short Term	V	V
				A			Cur. Mat.-L/T/D	A	A
				I			Trade Payables	I	I
				L			Income Taxes Payable	L	L
				A			All Other Current	A	A
				B			Total Current	B	B
				L			Long Term Debt	L	L
				E			Deferred Taxes	E	E
							All Other Non-Current		
							Net Worth		
							Total Liabilities & Net Worth		

INCOME DATA
Net Sales
Gross Profit
Operating Expenses
Operating Profit
All Other Expenses (net)
Profit Before Taxes

RATIOS

Current

Quick

Sales/Receivables

Cost of Sales/Inventory

Cost of Sales/Payables

Sales/Working Capital

EBIT/Interest

Net Profit + Depr., Dep.,
Amort./Cur. Mat. L /T/D

Fixed/Worth

Debt/Worth

% Profit Before Taxes/Tangible
Net Worth

% Profit Before Taxes/Total
Assets

Sales/Net Fixed Assets

Sales/Total Assets

% Depr., Dep., Amort./Sales

% Officers', Directors',
Owners' Comp/Sales

| 4893M | 15948M | 17508M | 32652M | | 8363M | | Sales ($) | | |
| 1377M | 8197M | 24386M | 63152M | | 107274M | | Assets ($) | | |

M = $ thousand   MM = $ million
See Pages 11 through 15 for Explanation of Ratios and Data

Comparative Historical Data				Current Data Sorted By Sales					
			Type of Statement						
12	7	14	Unqualified	2	5	1	5	1	
1	4		Reviewed						
6	8	1	Compiled	1					
5	6	2	Tax Returns	2					
6	7	7	Other	5		1		1	
4/1/00-3/31/01 ALL	4/1/01-3/31/02 ALL	4/1/02-3/31/03 ALL			15 (4/1-9/30/02)		9 (10/1/02-3/31/03)		
				0-1MM	1-3MM	3-5MM	5-10MM	10-25MM	25MM & OVER
30	32	24	**NUMBER OF STATEMENTS**	10	5	2	6	1	
%	%	%	**ASSETS**	%	%	%	%	%	%
19.6	16.8	14.2	Cash & Equivalents	18.9					D
3.6	4.9	6.5	Trade Receivables (net)	8.2					A
2.9	7.4	3.8	Inventory	8.4					T
3.3	3.8	3.5	All Other Current	.9					A
29.4	32.8	27.9	Total Current	36.5					
54.3	54.0	53.1	Fixed Assets (net)	54.5					N
2.6	2.0	1.0	Intangibles (net)	2.4					O
13.7	11.2	18.0	All Other Non-Current	6.6					T
100.0	100.0	100.0	Total	100.0					
			LIABILITIES						A
1.2	4.0	7.1	Notes Payable-Short Term	9.9					V
4.6	4.2	2.7	Cur. Mat.-L/T/D	4.4					A
9.1	5.4	5.0	Trade Payables	6.5					I
.1	.0	.0	Income Taxes Payable	.0					L
20.1	9.7	15.5	All Other Current	21.7					A
35.0	23.3	30.3	Total Current	42.5					B
24.4	31.7	15.7	Long Term Debt	21.7					L
.1	.4	.0	Deferred Taxes	.0					E
2.5	6.4	4.9	All Other Non-Current	6.9					
38.0	38.3	49.1	Net Worth	28.9					
100.0	100.0	100.0	Total Liabilities & Net Worth	100.0					
			INCOME DATA						
100.0	100.0	100.0	Net Sales	100.0					
			Gross Profit						
90.3	84.9	91.0	Operating Expenses	92.7					
9.7	15.1	9.0	Operating Profit	7.3					
.9	3.8	2.2	All Other Expenses (net)	1.7					
8.7	11.3	6.8	Profit Before Taxes	5.7					
			RATIOS						
4.2	5.3	2.0		1.9					
1.3	1.7	.9	Current	.7					
.5	.7	.4		.2					
3.6	4.5	1.3		1.1					
1.0	.9	.6	Quick	.6					
.2	.5	.2		.1					
0 UND	0 UND	0 UND		0 UND					
2 150.6	1 243.8	5 80.1	Sales/Receivables	1 506.2					
16 23.3	25 14.7	22 16.9		26 14.3					
			Cost of Sales/Inventory						
			Cost of Sales/Payables						
6.8	3.2	6.4		24.9					
36.6	18.9	-74.8	Sales/Working Capital	-19.9					
-21.1	-25.2	-10.0		-8.8					
6.2	8.5	19.3							
(19) 2.8	(22) 2.8	(17) 1.5	EBIT/Interest						
-2.2	1.6	-2.5							
			Net Profit + Depr., Dep., Amort./Cur. Mat. L/T/D						
.4	.6	.6		1.0					
1.0	1.1	1.1	Fixed/Worth	2.0					
1.9	4.3	2.3		3.4					
.3	.2	.3		1.6					
.7	.8	1.0	Debt/Worth	2.5					
2.3	4.1	2.7		8.3					
44.6	46.4	39.5		78.3					
(26) 20.0	(28) 11.2	(23) 18.1	% Profit Before Taxes/Tangible Net Worth	27.5					
5.7	1.7	-5.0		-3.8					
24.2	15.0	16.0		14.5					
9.8	5.3	6.9	% Profit Before Taxes/Total Assets	4.6					
-.6	.7	-1.8		-1.6					
18.5	12.1	13.7		25.7					
1.9	2.3	2.5	Sales/Net Fixed Assets	5.4					
.9	.6	1.3		1.5					
3.1	2.8	3.1		3.5					
1.1	1.2	1.5	Sales/Total Assets	2.7					
.6	.5	.7		1.2					
1.7	1.5	1.6							
(21) 5.0	(24) 3.4	(18) 3.1	% Depr., Dep., Amort./Sales						
12.6	10.9	5.2							
		3.7							
	(11) 5.1		% Officers', Directors', Owners' Comp/Sales						
	7.2								
182598M	123670M	79364M	Net Sales ($)	5718M	8775M	6635M	43175M	15061M	
160270M	306184M	204386M	Total Assets ($)	4078M	12771M	2672M	162829M	22036M	

M = $ thousand   MM = $ million
                  See Pages 11 through 18 for Explanation of Ratios and Data

Current Data Sorted By Assets   Comparative Historical Data

						Type of Statement		
10	28	66	43	12	8	Unqualified	145	143
1	1	7	1			Reviewed	13	5
2	6	12	1			Compiled	25	18
10	4	3				Tax Returns	22	9
19	20	32	12	2	3	Other	61	70
	198 (4/1-9/30/02)			105 (10/1/02-3/31/03)			4/1/98-3/31/99	4/1/99-3/31/00
0-500M	500M-2MM	2-10MM	10-50MM	50-100MM	100-250MM		ALL	ALL
42	59	120	57	14	11	NUMBER OF STATEMENTS	266	245
%	%	%	%	%	%	ASSETS	%	%
34.0	23.4	18.4	17.4	14.5	15.2	Cash & Equivalents	21.2	20.1
18.4	21.1	15.2	8.8	9.0	6.8	Trade Receivables (net)	13.6	12.1
1.2	1.9	1.1	1.9	.4	.2	Inventory	1.1	1.0
5.9	2.8	5.0	3.4	5.9	2.2	All Other Current	3.8	4.1
59.4	49.2	39.6	31.6	29.8	24.5	Total Current	39.6	37.3
25.3	44.9	49.4	45.1	40.2	38.2	Fixed Assets (net)	42.0	41.5
2.7	.5	1.1	1.4	6.6	7.3	Intangibles (net)	4.4	3.2
12.5	5.4	9.8	21.9	23.4	30.0	All Other Non-Current	13.9	18.0
100.0	100.0	100.0	100.0	100.0	100.0	Total	100.0	100.0
						LIABILITIES		
19.6	8.3	4.5	3.0	1.4	1.0	Notes Payable-Short Term	5.9	4.4
1.2	2.6	1.6	1.6	2.1	.7	Cur. Mat.-L/T/D	2.1	2.0
6.0	8.4	6.1	5.1	1.6	3.3	Trade Payables	5.7	5.7
.2	.3	.2	.1	.0	.5	Income Taxes Payable	.2	.1
22.5	15.1	12.1	8.8	11.7	5.8	All Other Current	13.1	11.7
49.6	34.7	24.6	18.5	16.9	11.3	Total Current	26.9	23.8
18.3	17.8	25.8	23.0	15.7	26.5	Long Term Debt	17.9	18.8
.0	.3	.3	.1	.5	.8	Deferred Taxes	.1	.1
3.7	3.7	5.3	3.5	7.6	10.3	All Other Non-Current	7.2	5.5
28.4	43.5	44.1	54.8	59.4	51.1	Net Worth	47.9	51.8
100.0	100.0	100.0	100.0	100.0	100.0	Total Liabilities & Net Worth	100.0	100.0
						INCOME DATA		
100.0	100.0	100.0	100.0	100.0	100.0	Net Sales	100.0	100.0
						Gross Profit		
97.4	93.2	92.0	96.9	99.3	93.6	Operating Expenses	97.8	93.6
2.6	6.8	8.0	3.1	.7	6.4	Operating Profit	2.2	6.4
.4	3.1	2.2	.8	1.3	4.8	All Other Expenses (net)	−5.4	−3.8
2.3	3.7	5.8	2.2	−.6	1.7	Profit Before Taxes	7.6	10.2
						RATIOS		
3.9	2.7	3.2	3.9	4.0	3.9	Current	3.6	4.1
1.9	1.4	1.7	1.9	1.6	1.3		1.6	1.8
.6	.8	1.0	1.0	1.1	.9		.9	.9
3.8	2.3	2.6	3.3	2.5	3.9	Quick	(265) 2.9	3.7
1.6	1.1	1.5	1.4	1.3	1.1		1.4	1.4
.3	.6	.8	.7	.9	.8		.7	.7
0 UND	0 UND	3 113.6	2 196.5	0 UND	11 32.8	Sales/Receivables	2 209.9	3 132.9
3 117.8	19 19.7	21 17.5	14 27.0	19 18.9	24 15.1		16 22.6	16 23.3
30 12.1	53 6.9	50 7.3	42 8.7	52 7.1	50 7.3		49 7.4	45 8.1
						Cost of Sales/Inventory		
						Cost of Sales/Payables		
6.8	6.0	3.7	2.9	4.4	2.9	Sales/Working Capital	4.1	3.7
13.2	20.7	10.8	6.9	7.7	13.1		11.8	10.4
−45.6	−24.2	173.8	−516.3	NM	−130.6		−67.8	−69.1
(22) 20.1	(41) 6.4	(83) 9.2	(41) 9.0	(11) 7.1		EBIT/Interest	(176) 7.4	(159) 12.9
1.0	1.8	3.3	1.5	2.0			3.6	4.0
−5.5	−.4	1.0	−2.1	−2.3			1.6	1.3
						Net Profit + Depr., Dep., Amort./Cur. Mat. L /T/D	(22) 4.2	(12) 10.9
							2.4	4.7
							1.4	.8
.1	.3	.5	.5	.5	.2	Fixed/Worth	.4	.3
.4	1.0	1.1	.8	.8	1.0		.8	.8
6.9	2.2	2.4	1.0	1.4	2.1		1.6	1.6
.3	.6	.5	.3	.4	.3	Debt/Worth	.4	.3
.8	1.2	1.4	.6	.7	1.2		.9	.9
NM	3.1	3.3	1.5	2.0	3.5		2.4	2.2
(32) 58.4	(55) 36.1	(112) 19.2	(55) 9.5	15.6		% Profit Before Taxes/Tangible Net Worth	(244) 28.7	(223) 23.5
19.6	10.8	7.3	2.5	5.6			12.9	11.6
−14.2	−3.1	−.4	−7.2	−6.0			4.6	2.7
30.7	17.5	8.1	4.9	6.4	8.0	% Profit Before Taxes/Total Assets	13.6	11.6
7.5	2.8	2.7	1.7	2.6	2.5		6.0	5.3
−11.3	−2.1	−.2	−3.2	−4.6	−7.1		1.6	1.6
81.7	29.4	6.6	5.7	6.0	5.2	Sales/Net Fixed Assets	11.8	10.9
22.4	5.2	2.4	1.0	1.7	3.8		3.4	3.1
14.4	1.7	.7	.7	.9	.6		1.1	1.0
7.3	2.8	1.9	1.4	1.4	1.4	Sales/Total Assets	2.3	2.2
3.8	1.8	1.0	.5	.7	.7		1.1	1.0
2.5	1.2	.5	.4	.5	.4		.6	.5
(24) 1.0	(44) 1.0	(106) 2.2	(47) 1.9	(12) 3.5		% Depr., Dep., Amort./Sales	(219) 2.0	(187) 1.8
1.4	2.4	3.8	3.8	4.2			3.4	3.5
2.7	4.5	6.4	7.1	5.9			6.3	6.8
(14) 4.9	(17) 3.5	(16) 5.0				% Officers', Directors', Owners' Comp/Sales	(41) 5.7	(46) 3.0
7.6	6.0	9.0					11.2	10.6
18.8	11.0	14.6					21.7	21.4
45963M	149066M	765724M	1069022M	929913M	1629680M	Net Sales ($)	5837689M	5414297M
10457M	68596M	615382M	1192258M	950819M	2063916M	Total Assets ($)	4664355M	5320118M

© RMA 2003   M = $ thousand   MM = $ million
See Pages 11 through 18 for Explanation of Ratios and Data

Comparative Historical Data				Current Data Sorted By Sales					
			Type of Statement						
131	108	167	Unqualified	9	45	24	33	31	25
8	5	10	Reviewed		4	2	2	2	
51	48	21	Compiled	6	8	2	2	1	2
20	15	17	Tax Returns	8	7		2		
60	65	88	Other	14	25	14	15	9	11
4/1/00- 3/31/01 ALL	4/1/01- 3/31/02 ALL	4/1/02- 3/31/03 ALL		198 (4/1-9/30/02)			105 (10/1/02-3/31/03)		
				0-1MM	1-3MM	3-5MM	5-10MM	10-25MM	25MM & OVER
270	241	303	**NUMBER OF STATEMENTS**	37	89	42	54	43	38
%	%	%	**ASSETS**	%	%	%	%	%	%
19.5	20.7	21.1	Cash & Equivalents	24.6	21.2	23.5	19.5	19.9	18.0
13.3	12.5	15.0	Trade Receivables (net)	11.9	12.6	15.0	17.7	20.0	14.2
2.3	1.3	1.3	Inventory	.7	1.5	.5	.9	2.2	2.1
6.5	4.8	4.3	All Other Current	4.8	4.7	2.8	6.0	2.2	4.9
41.5	39.3	41.7	Total Current	42.0	40.0	41.8	44.0	44.3	39.2
37.8	41.9	43.6	Fixed Assets (net)	49.6	47.2	48.0	41.1	37.8	34.1
2.3	3.4	1.8	Intangibles (net)	3.3	.5	1.2	.8	.9	6.0
18.3	15.4	13.0	All Other Non-Current	5.1	12.2	9.0	14.1	17.0	20.7
100.0	100.0	100.0	Total	100.0	100.0	100.0	100.0	100.0	100.0
			LIABILITIES						
4.6	4.6	6.8	Notes Payable-Short Term	14.1	7.6	4.6	4.1	8.0	2.7
1.6	2.7	1.7	Cur. Mat.-L/T/D	1.1	2.2	2.3	1.3	1.1	1.8
6.2	5.5	6.1	Trade Payables	2.2	5.7	7.6	7.1	7.1	6.1
.1	.1	.2	Income Taxes Payable	.2	.1	.3	.2	.1	.3
13.8	12.1	13.3	All Other Current	14.9	12.3	14.4	13.3	12.2	13.9
26.3	25.1	28.0	Total Current	32.5	27.9	29.3	26.0	28.5	24.9
15.8	21.9	22.2	Long Term Debt	22.3	29.4	13.0	18.6	18.8	24.7
.3	.1	.2	Deferred Taxes	.0	.2	.1	.1	.6	.6
6.3	4.2	4.7	All Other Non-Current	1.9	2.5	4.9	6.5	6.2	7.9
51.3	48.7	44.8	Net Worth	43.3	40.0	52.6	48.7	45.8	41.9
100.0	100.0	100.0	Total Liabilities & Net Worth	100.0	100.0	100.0	100.0	100.0	100.0
			INCOME DATA						
100.0	100.0	100.0	Net Sales	100.0	100.0	100.0	100.0	100.0	100.0
			Gross Profit						
93.7	91.1	94.3	Operating Expenses	89.1	89.5	98.1	97.8	99.0	96.1
6.3	8.9	5.7	Operating Profit	10.9	10.5	1.9	2.2	1.0	3.9
−1.7	1.9	1.9	All Other Expenses (net)	5.2	1.6	.6	2.1	.9	1.9
7.9	7.0	3.8	Profit Before Taxes	5.7	8.9	1.4	.0	.2	2.0
			RATIOS						
5.0	4.3	3.4		4.9	3.6	4.1	3.1	3.1	3.2
1.9	1.9	1.7	Current	1.5	1.7	1.5	1.7	1.8	1.5
.9	1.0	.9		.6	.9	1.0	1.1	1.0	1.0
		3.0		4.9	2.7	3.1	3.0	3.1	2.7
(269) 4.3	3.7	1.4	Quick	1.1	1.4	1.4	1.7	1.4	1.2
1.5	1.5	.7		.5	.6	.9	.8	.7	.8
.7	.7								
4 91.6	1 398.1	2 206.4		0 UND	1 662.0	1 429.4	6 56.7	11 33.6	12 31.0
18 19.8	12 30.6	14 27.0	Sales/Receivables	0 UND	9 40.3	13 27.4	23 15.7	28 13.0	31 11.6
47 7.7	46 7.9	48 7.5		33 11.0	29 12.7	56 6.5	52 7.1	50 7.3	50 7.3
			Cost of Sales/Inventory						
			Cost of Sales/Payables						
2.9	3.2	4.1		4.3	4.0	3.6	3.2	4.5	4.4
8.7	9.2	12.1	Sales/Working Capital	13.7	15.9	11.3	8.7	9.5	15.5
−81.2	−448.7	−130.6		−7.7	−53.5	−68.5	52.7	−751.8	NM
12.7	7.0	9.1		17.0	6.7	7.9	12.9	8.2	19.7
(179) 3.3	(153) 3.0	(206) 2.0	EBIT/Interest	(20) 2.4	(62) 2.7	(29) 2.1	(37) 1.9	(29) .6	(29) 2.0
1.1	1.0	−.5		−.4	.8	−2.3	.6	−1.7	−1.6
	7.4	9.9							
	(10) 3.4	(16) 3.8	Net Profit + Depr., Dep.,						
	1.0	1.4	Amort./Cur. Mat. L/T/D						
.3	.4	.4		.3	.3	.5	.4	.4	.3
.8	.8	.9	Fixed/Worth	1.2	1.0	.9	.8	.8	.8
1.5	2.1	1.8		3.0	2.4	1.3	1.5	1.4	1.8
.3	.3	.4		.4	.5	.2	.3	.4	.5
.8	1.0	1.0	Debt/Worth	.7	1.2	.6	.9	1.5	1.2
2.4	3.2	2.9		5.3	3.7	2.6	2.5	3.2	2.6
27.3	27.3	21.7	% Profit Before Taxes/Tangible	23.9	30.7	21.6	26.9	10.8	21.8
(249) 9.0	(220) 9.3	(277) 7.1	Net Worth	(31) 10.2	(80) 8.1	(40) 7.1	(51) 5.0	(40) 3.0	(35) 9.7
.3	−.1	−2.5		−7.9	−.1	−2.2	−2.3	−12.0	−8.2
12.5	11.1	9.3	% Profit Before Taxes/Total	17.1	13.1	8.3	9.6	5.4	9.2
4.3	3.8	2.6	Assets	3.5	3.5	2.1	2.1	1.7	2.8
−.5	−.1	−2.1		−5.8	−.4	−2.1	−.7	−4.9	−5.0
15.2	10.7	17.3		22.4	18.8	8.7	13.4	22.3	10.6
3.6	2.8	3.2	Sales/Net Fixed Assets	2.3	3.7	1.9	3.0	4.3	5.2
1.1	1.0	.9		.4	.7	.7	1.3	.9	1.9
2.3	2.5	2.5		2.9	2.7	2.0	2.1	2.7	2.0
1.1	1.0	1.3	Sales/Total Assets	1.2	1.4	1.0	1.3	1.2	1.5
.5	.5	.5		.4	.5	.5	.7	.5	.7
.9	1.0	1.6		2.5	1.3	2.1	1.3	1.9	1.5
(209) 2.7	(185) 3.0	(241) 3.3	% Depr., Dep., Amort./Sales	(24) 4.1	(74) 2.8	(33) 3.8	(46) 2.7	(34) 3.7	(30) 2.7
5.2	5.5	5.9		17.4	6.0	5.9	5.4	6.0	3.8
4.9	4.5	4.8			3.9		2.9		
(43) 9.6	(45) 8.9	(59) 9.0	% Officers', Directors',		(19) 6.0		(10) 8.1		
19.7	17.2	13.6	Owners' Comp/Sales		11.1		13.6		
5630070M	3401231M	4589368M	Net Sales ($)	20401M	163229M	163796M	410437M	649885M	3181620M
5062029M	3770022M	4901428M	Total Assets ($)	37687M	263559M	224576M	476217M	738918M	3160471M

HEALTH CARE AND
SOCIAL ASSISTANCE

Current Data Sorted By Assets　　　　　　　　　Comparative Historical Data

						Type of Statement		
11	18	56	54	13	11	Unqualified	155	172
23	41	56	16			Reviewed	82	86
290	185	65	7	3	1	Compiled	460	428
490	125	34	9	4	8	Tax Returns	438	356
207	144	126	46	12	3	Other	475	395
	295 (4/1-9/30/02)			1763 (10/1/02-3/31/03)			4/1/98-3/31/99	4/1/99-3/31/00
0-500M	500M-2MM	2-10MM	10-50MM	50-100MM	100-250MM		ALL	ALL
1021	513	337	132	32	23	**NUMBER OF STATEMENTS**	1610	1437
%	%	%	%	%	%	**ASSETS**	%	%
33.1	20.0	13.5	14.7	14.2	27.1	Cash & Equivalents	19.0	21.2
4.0	15.1	23.9	25.3	16.4	12.1	Trade Receivables (net)	14.3	15.2
.6	.9	1.0	1.3	1.8	.5	Inventory	.9	1.1
4.2	3.6	3.6	4.3	6.3	1.9	All Other Current	2.4	3.3
42.0	39.6	42.0	45.6	38.7	41.5	Total Current	36.6	40.8
42.7	46.6	44.8	40.0	37.8	35.2	Fixed Assets (net)	45.3	44.4
3.6	4.3	3.6	3.6	8.0	11.0	Intangibles (net)	4.8	4.9
11.8	9.5	9.7	10.8	15.5	12.2	All Other Non-Current	13.2	9.9
100.0	100.0	100.0	100.0	100.0	100.0	Total	100.0	100.0
						LIABILITIES		
35.1	14.7	7.1	6.8	29.9	34.9	Notes Payable-Short Term	24.6	19.6
9.6	7.7	6.2	5.6	5.3	.9	Cur. Mat.-L/T/D	7.9	7.9
2.0	2.8	4.4	10.5	3.5	5.6	Trade Payables	2.8	3.7
.2	.4	.7	.9	1.3	.0	Income Taxes Payable	.6	.5
37.8	19.3	18.2	21.3	23.9	27.5	All Other Current	34.7	30.4
84.7	44.8	36.7	45.2	66.3	68.9	Total Current	70.7	62.2
32.4	31.8	33.6	26.5	23.9	30.2	Long Term Debt	31.3	31.5
.2	.1	.6	.7	.9	.1	Deferred Taxes	.6	.8
7.1	4.0	3.8	6.5	5.1	4.4	All Other Non-Current	5.5	6.1
-24.3	19.2	25.3	21.0	3.8	-3.7	Net Worth	-8.0	-.5
100.0	100.0	100.0	100.0	100.0	100.0	Total Liabilities & Net Worth	100.0	100.0
						INCOME DATA		
100.0	100.0	100.0	100.0	100.0	100.0	Net Sales	100.0	100.0
						Gross Profit		
92.9	88.9	88.0	90.9	94.9	94.1	Operating Expenses	103.8	92.2
7.1	11.1	12.0	9.1	5.1	5.9	Operating Profit	-3.8	7.8
.8	2.5	3.8	4.1	1.9	.3	All Other Expenses (net)	-1.8	1.8
6.3	8.7	8.3	5.0	3.2	5.6	Profit Before Taxes	-2.0	6.1
						RATIOS		
1.3	2.3	2.4	1.8	2.1	2.0		2.1	2.0
.6	.9	1.3	1.2	1.2	1.0	Current	.8	.8
.2	.4	.6	.8	.6	.4		.2	.3

	1.1		2.0		2.1		1.7		1.8		1.9			2.0		1.7

												Quick				
(1018)	.5		.8	(336)	1.1		1.1		1.0		1.0	(1594)	.7	(1433)	.7
	.1		.3		.5		.6		.4		.4		.1		.2

												Sales/Receivables				
0	UND	0	UND	0	UND	9	39.8	0	UND	0	UND	0	UND	0	UND
0	UND	0	UND	30	12.0	42	8.7	49	7.4	4	100.2	0	UND	0	UND
0	UND	32	11.4	54	6.8	64	5.7	62	5.9	57	6.4	37	10.0	44	8.2

Cost of Sales/Inventory

Cost of Sales/Payables

												Sales/Working Capital				
	120.1		16.8		7.7		10.3		7.0		4.9		20.1		17.8
	-63.8		-184.6		29.6		29.5		32.9		382.5		-105.5		-110.3
	-20.8		-20.7		-31.3		-42.6		-34.1		-39.0		-17.1		-20.6

												EBIT/Interest				
	12.2		14.9		15.4		8.3		3.9		18.2		8.0		8.7
(753)	2.5	(435)	3.0	(274)	3.7	(109)	2.3	(25)	1.7	(17)	2.1	(1215)	2.0	(1141)	2.2
	-.7		.4		1.0		.6		-2.0		1.2		.1		.1

												Net Profit + Depr., Dep., Amort./Cur. Mat. L /T/D				
	3.3		3.0		2.6		4.3		4.1				3.7		3.2
(39)	1.7	(40)	1.8	(44)	1.5	(23)	1.8	(12)	2.3			(125)	1.3	(105)	1.6
	.9		.9		.8		1.3		1.2				.3		.8

												Fixed/Worth				
	.8		.7		.6		.6		.6		.8		.6		.7
	13.9		3.1		1.9		1.7		3.1		2.2		2.6		2.9
	-1.1		-14.5		18.1		13.1		NM		-3.3		-3.7		-3.5

												Debt/Worth				
	2.0		1.1		1.0		1.4		1.1		1.0		1.1		1.1
	UND		5.9		3.4		2.5		4.1		11.1		5.7		6.0
	-3.1		-20.5		31.9		29.4		NM		-6.2		-6.6		-7.0

												% Profit Before Taxes/Tangible Net Worth				
	309.3		145.0		88.4		48.4		148.9		118.1		101.2		105.0
(512)	88.1	(344)	29.5	(266)	23.5	(110)	15.3	(24)	10.6	(15)	14.2	(1023)	20.8	(900)	24.8
	1.0		.8		1.6		-1.1		-.6		1.3		-1.0		.0

												% Profit Before Taxes/Total Assets				
	61.6		31.4		23.1		12.0		14.0		19.4		24.6		25.6
	7.3		5.7		5.4		3.1		3.5		5.4		3.8		4.1
	-6.5		-1.4		-.2		-.4		-2.7		.0		-3.4		-2.9

												Sales/Net Fixed Assets				
	108.6		32.4		22.4		22.5		32.6		55.4		48.1		42.7
	36.1		15.1		9.1		7.9		8.5		20.2		18.7		18.4
	16.3		7.0		2.7		2.6		2.9		2.8		6.6		6.8

												Sales/Total Assets				
	22.6		9.7		4.9		3.6		10.2		12.2		14.2		13.6
	12.7		5.0		2.8		2.2		1.8		3.2		5.7		5.7
	6.4		2.3		1.4		1.2		1.3		1.2		2.1		2.2

												% Depr., Dep., Amort./Sales				
	.6		1.2		1.6		1.3		1.9		.5		1.0		1.0
(734)	1.3	(441)	2.4	(301)	2.9	(118)	2.6	(22)	2.7	(11)	1.9	(1296)	1.8	(1162)	1.8
	2.6		4.4		6.0		4.6		4.4		6.1		3.6		3.3

												% Officers', Directors', Owners' Comp/Sales				
	16.6		14.2		12.7		18.0				18.6		19.6		17.5
(681)	26.5	(262)	25.7	(103)	26.8	(31)	29.0			(11)	29.5	(810)	30.4	(685)	29.9
	36.4		37.5		37.8		37.7				36.4		39.9		39.3

2759480M	3301263M	5851032M	13155790M	17769339M	23443452M	Net Sales ($)	23007641M	25900297M
198348M	530468M	1508408M	2600161M	2342719M	3519842M	Total Assets ($)	8507225M	9221791M

M = $ thousand　　MM = $ million
See Pages 11 through 18 for Explanation of Ratios and Data

Comparative Historical Data | Current Data Sorted By Sales

				Type of Statement						
111	120	163		Unqualified	8	16	15	21	35	68
79	94	136		Reviewed	9	18	16	25	37	31
448	533	551		Compiled	110	169	98	89	65	20
403	429	670		Tax Returns	174	228	99	102	39	28
390	515	538		Other	74	132	72	92	95	73
4/1/00- 3/31/01	4/1/01- 3/31/02	4/1/02- 3/31/03			295 (4/1-9/30/02)			1763 (10/1/02-3/31/03)		
ALL	ALL	ALL			0-1MM	1-3MM	3-5MM	5-10MM	10-25MM	25MM & OVER
1431	1691	2058		NUMBER OF STATEMENTS	375	563	300	329	271	220
%	%	%		ASSETS	%	%	%	%	%	%
22.1	23.8	25.1		Cash & Equivalents	25.2	29.1	26.2	23.9	22.0	18.8
14.2	12.6	11.6		Trade Receivables (net)	6.3	8.4	11.6	11.5	16.4	23.4
.9	1.2	.8		Inventory	.6	.8	.9	.9	1.0	1.1
3.6	3.7	4.0		All Other Current	2.8	4.9	3.4	4.2	3.9	4.3
40.8	41.3	41.5		Total Current	34.9	43.1	42.1	40.5	43.2	47.6
44.2	43.7	43.7		Fixed Assets (net)	47.2	43.4	45.2	44.8	42.7	35.7
4.8	4.1	3.9		Intangibles (net)	4.2	3.7	3.8	3.9	3.6	4.7
10.1	10.8	10.9		All Other Non-Current	13.7	9.8	8.9	10.8	10.5	11.9
100.0	100.0	100.0		Total	100.0	100.0	100.0	100.0	100.0	100.0
				LIABILITIES						
21.4	23.4	23.5		Notes Payable-Short Term	30.8	30.8	17.2	21.9	14.3	14.7
8.3	8.4	8.1		Cur. Mat.-L/T/D	8.5	9.7	7.3	8.1	7.2	5.9
3.0	3.6	3.3		Trade Payables	1.4	2.6	2.2	2.6	4.4	9.2
.5	.4	.4		Income Taxes Payable	.5	.1	.3	.1	.8	.9
29.9	32.3	28.6		All Other Current	24.4	30.1	29.5	32.1	26.1	28.5
63.2	68.1	63.9		Total Current	65.6	73.2	56.5	65.0	52.8	59.2
30.6	32.0	31.9		Long Term Debt	42.6	31.8	35.0	25.5	26.8	25.4
.6	.5	.3		Deferred Taxes	.1	.2	.3	.1	.7	.5
6.2	5.6	5.7		All Other Non-Current	7.8	6.9	6.6	1.5	3.7	6.3
−.6	−6.2	−1.8		Net Worth	−16.1	−12.2	1.7	7.9	15.9	8.6
100.0	100.0	100.0		Total Liabilities & Net Worth	100.0	100.0	100.0	100.0	100.0	100.0
				INCOME DATA						
100.0	100.0	100.0		Net Sales	100.0	100.0	100.0	100.0	100.0	100.0
				Gross Profit						
91.7	91.5	91.0		Operating Expenses	83.7	91.1	92.2	93.1	94.1	94.5
8.3	8.5	9.0		Operating Profit	16.3	8.9	7.8	6.9	5.9	5.5
2.0	1.8	1.9		All Other Expenses (net)	5.9	1.6	.7	.8	.4	1.3
6.3	6.6	7.1		Profit Before Taxes	10.3	7.2	7.1	6.1	5.5	4.2
				RATIOS						
1.8	1.8	1.8			1.8	1.8	2.1	1.7	1.9	1.7
.8	.9	.8		Current	.7	.7	.9	.8	1.0	1.1
.3	.3	.3			.2	.3	.3	.3	.5	.6
1.6	1.6	1.6			1.7	1.5	1.9	1.5	1.7	1.6
(1426) .7	(1687) .7	(2054) .7		Quick	(374) .5	(561) .6	(299) .8	.7	.9	1.0
.2	.2	.2			.1	.2	.3	.2	.3	.5
0 UND	0 UND	0 UND			0 UND	0 UND	0 UND	0 UND	0 UND	0 UND
0 UND	0 UND	0 UND		Sales/Receivables	0 UND	0 UND	0 UND	0 UND	0 UND	29 12.7
36 10.2	28 12.9	20 18.2			0 UND	0 UND	5 67.8	18 20.5	43 8.4	56 6.6
				Cost of Sales/Inventory						
				Cost of Sales/Payables						
20.8	23.9	25.2			26.8	41.5	27.0	28.7	20.5	14.9
−138.0	−164.6	−134.9		Sales/Working Capital	−40.5	−74.7	−279.4	−125.8	−999.8	188.9
−22.3	−20.9	−21.8			−8.6	−20.6	−25.2	−25.3	−37.9	−36.9
8.7	10.6	12.0			10.5	14.4	12.3	11.7	12.5	9.7
(1127) 2.2	(1332) 2.7	(1613) 2.7		EBIT/Interest	(244) 3.5	(426) 3.0	(243) 2.7	(277) 2.3	(236) 2.5	(187) 2.0
.4	.6	.2			−.3	.2	.4	−.6	.4	.6
3.0	3.5	3.1				3.8	3.3	2.7	2.6	3.7
(112) 1.6	(114) 1.7	(159) 1.7		Net Profit + Depr., Dep., Amort./Cur. Mat. L/T/D	(295)	(21) 1.7	(22) 2.0	(24) 1.8	(40) 1.5	(44) 1.8
.8	.8	1.0				1.1	1.1	1.0	.9	1.1
.7	.7	.7			.7	.8	.7	.8	.7	.5
3.5	3.1	4.0		Fixed/Worth	5.7	5.6	4.1	4.0	2.6	2.4
−2.7	−3.4	−3.1			−1.5	−1.4	−3.6	−5.1	−21.6	UND
1.3	1.4	1.4			1.5	1.4	1.2	1.3	1.2	1.8
7.8	7.1	9.2		Debt/Worth	35.0	15.1	8.3	8.8	4.4	6.2
−6.1	−6.1	−6.4			−3.2	−4.3	−7.4	−12.7	−26.9	−40.1
105.2	146.3	160.4			185.2	282.4	160.3	135.5	99.8	93.2
(863) 25.2	(1063) 36.4	(1271) 36.1		% Profit Before Taxes/Tangible Net Worth	(200) 57.7	(327) 74.3	(179) 37.5	(213) 31.8	(190) 18.0	(162) 19.8
.4	2.2	.8			16.0	1.6	.8	.0	−1.6	−.7
26.2	33.5	38.3			54.9	54.2	38.0	29.2	27.5	15.8
4.1	6.2	5.7		% Profit Before Taxes/Total Assets	10.6	7.1	5.6	4.2	3.5	2.8
−2.5	−1.6	−2.6			−2.1	−4.7	−2.4	−3.1	−1.4	−1.0
48.4	56.9	59.0			50.4	77.2	54.1	55.6	45.8	50.7
19.2	20.0	20.8		Sales/Net Fixed Assets	13.9	27.1	25.4	24.2	18.1	16.1
7.2	7.8	8.2			2.8	9.7	9.2	11.4	9.1	6.3
14.4	14.1	14.3			10.5	17.3	17.1	17.2	12.6	9.9
6.0	6.5	6.8		Sales/Total Assets	4.3	8.4	8.2	9.6	6.7	4.0
2.4	2.7	2.9			1.3	3.8	3.3	3.9	2.8	2.2
.8	.7	.9			1.4	.7	.9	.8	.9	.9
(1186) 1.6	(1339) 1.6	(1627) 1.9		% Depr., Dep., Amort./Sales	(266) 3.3	(430) 1.7	(250) 1.7	(269) 1.7	(241) 1.9	(171) 1.9
3.3	3.0	3.7			12.3	3.8	3.5	3.1	3.0	3.0
17.1	16.4	15.4			14.8	16.2	15.4	15.9	13.8	15.4
(726) 28.6	(874) 28.5	(1097) 26.5		% Officers', Directors', Owners' Comp/Sales	(206) 22.7	(349) 26.3	(184) 29.3	(168) 27.3	(114) 28.9	(76) 29.3
39.1	38.1	37.0			32.8	36.3	39.2	38.1	39.8	36.7
17814452M	42359798M	66280356M		Net Sales ($)	216751M	1070026M	1167541M	2273484M	4274455M	57278099M
7062784M	9516407M	10699946M		Total Assets ($)	181411M	358818M	356623M	489959M	1094845M	8218290M

M = $ thousand   MM = $ million
See Pages 11 through 18 for Explanation of Ratios and Data

Current Data Sorted By Assets   Comparative Historical Data

0-500M	500M-2MM	2-10MM	10-50MM	50-100MM	100-250MM	Type of Statement	4/1/98-3/31/99 ALL	4/1/99-3/31/00 ALL
3	1	2	4	2	1	Unqualified	13	9
3	3	3	1			Reviewed	6	7
103	41	5			4	Compiled	168	147
236	40	3	2	5	9	Tax Returns	176	140
84	24	4	2		2	Other	95	89
	69 (4/1-9/30/02)			518 (10/1/02-3/31/03)				
429	109	17	9	7	16	**NUMBER OF STATEMENTS**	458	392
%	%	%	%	%	%	**ASSETS**	%	%
22.1	15.0	5.9			20.3	Cash & Equivalents	14.9	19.6
5.0	11.3	28.5			1.1	Trade Receivables (net)	9.2	11.1
.4	.2	1.5			3.4	Inventory	.7	1.0
2.1	3.0	2.1			6.5	All Other Current	1.8	2.7
29.7	29.5	38.1			31.3	Total Current	26.5	34.4
49.1	47.8	30.6			34.8	Fixed Assets (net)	50.6	44.2
13.6	11.6	10.4			21.7	Intangibles (net)	11.9	11.7
7.7	11.1	20.9			12.1	All Other Non-Current	11.0	9.7
100.0	100.0	100.0			100.0	Total	100.0	100.0
						LIABILITIES		
17.4	9.1	2.2			1.9	Notes Payable-Short Term	21.5	13.9
10.9	6.1	5.9			14.5	Cur. Mat.-L/T/D	11.2	10.2
2.4	2.9	5.7			5.1	Trade Payables	4.0	1.9
.7	.7	.2			.0	Income Taxes Payable	.2	.5
21.5	11.8	26.1			16.6	All Other Current	22.8	19.1
52.8	30.7	40.1			38.1	Total Current	59.7	45.5
42.7	41.9	35.2			49.1	Long Term Debt	45.1	41.9
.0	.5	1.1			.5	Deferred Taxes	.1	.3
6.2	5.2	5.0			3.3	All Other Non-Current	4.7	5.9
-1.7	21.7	18.6			9.1	Net Worth	-9.6	6.3
100.0	100.0	100.0			100.0	Total Liabilities & Net Worth	100.0	100.0
						INCOME DATA		
100.0	100.0	100.0			100.0	Net Sales	100.0	100.0
						Gross Profit		
89.7	87.1	86.7			87.3	Operating Expenses	88.7	89.5
10.3	12.9	13.3			12.7	Operating Profit	11.3	10.5
1.6	4.3	6.2			2.1	All Other Expenses (net)	1.7	1.8
8.7	8.6	7.1			10.6	Profit Before Taxes	9.6	8.8
						RATIOS		
1.5	2.6	1.6			2.2	Current	2.1	2.4
.6	.9	1.2			1.0		.6	.7
.2	.3	.8			.3		.1	.2
(426) 1.4	2.3	1.5			2.2	Quick	(449) 1.9	2.2
.5	.8	1.1			.7		.5	.7
.1	.2	.5			.1		.1	.2
0 UND	0 UND	0 UND			0 UND	Sales/Receivables	0 UND	0 UND
0 UND	0 UND	38 9.5			0 UND		0 UND	0 UND
0 UND	30 12.1	58 6.3			0 UND		0 999.8	20 17.9
						Cost of Sales/Inventory		
						Cost of Sales/Payables		
47.7	10.2	17.9			34.5	Sales/Working Capital	28.4	17.6
-56.8	-128.6	45.4			NM		-57.7	-97.2
-15.7	-19.2	-30.2			-20.4		-13.7	-16.7
(347) 13.2	(91) 7.5	(15) 11.4		(15) 7.4		EBIT/Interest	(381) 10.2	(312) 12.0
3.9	2.5	5.0		3.6			3.2	2.9
.9	1.0	1.9		1.3			1.0	1.0
(13) 13.9						Net Profit + Depr., Dep., Amort./Cur. Mat. L /T/D	(27) 5.4	(30) 6.5
3.7							3.0	2.2
1.0							.9	1.0
1.4	1.1	.7			1.6	Fixed/Worth	.9	.7
UND	6.6	3.0			-2.6		5.7	5.3
-1.1	-3.7	NM			-.4		-1.5	-2.2
1.8	1.7	2.7			2.1	Debt/Worth	1.2	1.3
-106.3	9.6	7.1			-6.3		8.3	8.7
-2.6	-8.9	-65.3			-2.8		-3.3	-4.7
(212) 315.7	119.5	(12) 86.6				% Profit Before Taxes/Tangible Net Worth	(269) 218.4	(231) 180.1
95.5	(68) 39.5	58.8					62.5	51.4
23.6	4.8	22.4					8.3	4.2
65.3	26.8	14.0			91.5	% Profit Before Taxes/Total Assets	56.7	44.5
20.7	6.3	9.0			11.9		13.0	9.7
.0	.0	3.9			3.5		.0	.0
33.2	19.5	53.6			31.0	Sales/Net Fixed Assets	30.7	31.4
14.8	6.6	9.1			16.0		12.7	14.2
6.9	3.0	3.7			11.0		5.9	6.9
10.9	4.1	4.3			9.6	Sales/Total Assets	10.8	8.8
5.9	2.5	2.2			4.9		5.0	4.7
3.1	1.4	1.3			3.5		2.4	2.6
(325) 1.3	(87) 2.1	(13) .8				% Depr., Dep., Amort./Sales	(364) 1.4	(314) 1.2
2.7	3.8	2.7					2.5	2.7
5.1	6.2	3.4					4.4	4.3
(312) 15.2	(68) 11.8			(11) 8.3		% Officers', Directors', Owners' Comp/Sales	(301) 16.7	(252) 16.1
20.6	18.6			18.2			23.0	24.0
28.2	26.3			23.2			31.7	33.0
531933M	323698M	158056M	3418967M	3467813M	17016499M	Net Sales ($)	5285342M	3899969M
90922M	98007M	61850M	272944M	523029M	2717432M	Total Assets ($)	1447149M	1595517M

M = $ thousand   MM = $ million
See Pages 11 through 18 for Explanation of Ratios and Data

Comparative Historical Data				Current Data Sorted By Sales					
10	11	13	**Type of Statement** Unqualified	3			1	2	7
6	8	10	Reviewed		5	2		2	1
119	110	153	Compiled	58	64	16	6	5	4
148	177	295	Tax Returns	144	117	10	5	3	16
88	115	116	Other	50	46	9	6	1	4
4/1/00-3/31/01 ALL	4/1/01-3/31/02 ALL	4/1/02-3/31/03 ALL		69 (4/1-9/30/02)			518 (10/1/02-3/31/03)		
				0-1MM	1-3MM	3-5MM	5-10MM	10-25MM	25MM & OVER
371	421	587	**NUMBER OF STATEMENTS**	255	232	37	18	13	32
%	%	%	**ASSETS**	%	%	%	%	%	%
20.7	19.8	20.4	Cash & Equivalents	21.1	19.9	20.9	21.5	5.8	24.0
8.1	8.0	6.8	Trade Receivables (net)	5.2	6.5	11.5	14.6	26.6	4.0
.7	.7	.5	Inventory	.5	.1	.4	.4	1.8	3.6
3.4	2.8	2.4	All Other Current	2.6	1.9	.9	.5	10.9	4.4
33.0	31.4	30.2	Total Current	29.4	28.4	33.7	37.0	45.0	36.0
46.3	46.7	47.4	Fixed Assets (net)	47.6	49.4	52.3	46.2	32.4	32.1
12.5	12.2	13.4	Intangibles (net)	16.2	12.0	3.5	4.5	11.2	18.7
8.2	9.8	9.0	All Other Non-Current	6.9	10.2	10.5	12.3	11.4	13.3
100.0	100.0	100.0	Total	100.0	100.0	100.0	100.0	100.0	100.0
			LIABILITIES						
12.9	15.6	14.6	Notes Payable-Short Term	15.3	15.6	16.5	12.4	10.7	2.6
8.7	11.9	9.9	Cur. Mat.-L/T/D	7.6	12.3	12.7	6.5	4.6	11.7
2.3	2.8	2.7	Trade Payables	2.4	2.1	1.9	9.1	6.1	4.5
1.3	.4	.7	Income Taxes Payable	1.0	.1	.2	4.1	.2	.5
19.9	22.5	19.8	All Other Current	15.1	23.0	28.3	15.0	34.7	20.5
45.1	53.3	47.6	Total Current	41.5	53.1	59.7	47.2	56.4	39.8
36.5	46.4	42.7	Long Term Debt	48.4	39.1	29.7	33.2	29.5	48.1
.1	.2	.1	Deferred Taxes	.0	.0	.9	1.9	.1	.2
13.6	9.3	5.8	All Other Non-Current	7.0	5.3	5.9	1.8	3.6	3.3
4.7	-9.2	3.8	Net Worth	3.1	2.5	3.8	15.9	10.4	8.6
100.0	100.0	100.0	Total Liabilities & Net Worth	100.0	100.0	100.0	100.0	100.0	100.0
			INCOME DATA						
100.0	100.0	100.0	Net Sales	100.0	100.0	100.0	100.0	100.0	100.0
			Gross Profit						
89.2	89.0	89.1	Operating Expenses	86.8	90.8	91.3	94.7	88.6	90.4
10.8	11.0	10.9	Operating Profit	13.2	9.2	8.7	5.3	11.4	9.6
1.9	1.9	2.3	All Other Expenses (net)	3.1	1.4	1.8	.6	5.8	2.9
8.9	9.1	8.6	Profit Before Taxes	10.1	7.8	6.9	4.6	5.6	6.7
			RATIOS						
1.9	1.8	1.7	Current	2.5	1.4	1.6	2.1	1.5	2.8
.9	.6	.7		.9	.5	.7	.9	.8	1.0
.2	.2	.2		.2	.2	.7	.3	.4	.5
1.7	1.6	1.6	Quick	2.3	1.1	1.5	2.1	1.1	2.6
(370) .7	(417) .5	(584) .6		(252) .7	.5	.6	.9	.7	.7
.2	.2	.2		.2	.1	.2	.3	.3	.1
0 UND	0 UND	0 UND	Sales/Receivables	0 UND	0 UND	0 UND	0 UND	0 UND	0 UND
0 UND	0 UND	0 UND		0 UND	0 UND	0 UND	0 UND	34 10.7	0 UND
0 UND	0 UND	0 UND		0 UND	0 UND	1 539.2	21 17.4	48 7.6	6 64.0
			Cost of Sales/Inventory						
			Cost of Sales/Payables						
29.8	32.9	28.0	Sales/Working Capital	18.7	87.5	67.2	19.6	28.3	27.6
-117.1	-65.9	-71.1		-135.6	-44.3	-91.2	NM	-33.5	NM
-17.9	-14.4	-16.5		-13.2	-16.0	-18.9	-25.0	-23.9	-20.1
10.7	12.6	12.3	EBIT/Interest	9.9	15.7	19.8	15.8	16.9	10.9
(299) 3.1	(353) 3.1	(483) 3.5		(196) 3.6	(196) 3.4	(35) 2.3	(16) 2.8	(10) 3.7	(30) 3.3
.9	1.0	1.0		.7	1.0	.7	-.6	2.1	1.3
4.2	7.4	8.4	Net Profit + Depr., Dep., Amort./Cur. Mat. L/T/D		4.9				
(24) 1.8	(19) 2.5	(27) 2.4			(10) 1.8				
1.1	.6	1.3			.9				
1.0	1.1	1.3	Fixed/Worth	1.2	1.5	1.3	.6	1.2	1.1
7.0	16.0	17.1		19.5	UND	7.4	6.2	28.7	14.0
-1.7	-1.3	-1.3		-.8	-1.8	-2.6	38.1	-1.6	-.5
1.5	1.7	1.8	Debt/Worth	1.5	2.4	1.9	4.2	3.4	2.1
12.9	34.2	59.0		66.0	UND	11.0	12.6	301.9	33.2
-3.9	-3.0	-3.3		-2.4	-3.6	-9.2	53.5	-9.8	-3.6
190.0	252.2	266.5	% Profit Before Taxes/Tangible Net Worth	195.2	320.4	267.6	130.4		207.4
(206) 59.0	(226) 74.4	(309) 75.2		(131) 74.1	(116) 100.0	(23) 34.0	(15) 38.3		(17) 53.1
2.1	8.8	13.2		14.1	26.1	.0	-8.4		8.0
49.2	58.4	56.9	% Profit Before Taxes/Total Assets	60.2	59.2	53.5	24.5	22.6	50.8
10.6	12.3	13.5		19.8	13.2	5.9	3.1	12.1	9.4
-.2	.0	.0		.6	.0	-.5	-4.5	7.1	3.4
26.9	30.3	33.0	Sales/Net Fixed Assets	22.9	33.2	36.1	39.5	133.6	45.5
12.6	13.5	12.8		9.2	14.5	16.6	21.3	20.7	18.9
5.8	5.8	5.9		3.6	7.7	9.9	8.4	10.6	10.1
8.7	9.0	9.4	Sales/Total Assets	7.2	10.3	13.3	12.5	10.0	9.6
4.4	5.0	4.5		3.2	5.6	8.0	5.1	4.9	4.5
2.3	2.7	2.4		1.7	3.3	3.9	3.5	3.2	2.5
1.1	1.1	1.4	% Depr., Dep., Amort./Sales	1.6	1.4	1.1	.8		.4
(288) 2.5	(333) 2.4	(439) 2.8		(190) 4.1	(177) 2.7	(32) 1.6	2.0		(14) 1.7
4.7	4.5	5.1		7.5	4.2	2.8	3.6		3.7
15.4	15.7	14.2	% Officers', Directors', Owners' Comp/Sales	14.4	15.1	12.2	5.4		10.6
(244) 23.1	(298) 22.6	(406) 20.0		(176) 19.0	(171) 22.0	(26) 20.0	(10) 23.3		(18) 16.1
30.9	30.9	27.9		26.6	30.0	36.2	31.4		23.5
5062927M	9027610M	24916966M	Net Sales ($)	157259M	397118M	142702M	124126M	192482M	23903279M
1924013M	2506276M	3764184M	Total Assets ($)	63289M	91959M	28509M	25239M	41783M	3513405M

M = $ thousand   MM = $ million
See Pages 11 through 18 for Explanation of Ratios and Data

Current Data Sorted By Assets   Comparative Historical Data

	0-500M	500M-2MM	2-10MM	10-50MM	50-100MM	100-250MM	Type of Statement		3	2
		1			1		Unqualified		3	
							Reviewed		1	
	13	3		1			Compiled		19	11
	41	2			1		Tax Returns		21	22
	15	1	3	1			Other		13	15
		2 (4/1-9/30/02)		81 (10/1/02-3/31/03)					4/1/98-3/31/99	4/1/99-3/31/00
									ALL	ALL
	69	7	3	2	2		NUMBER OF STATEMENTS		57	50
	%	%	%	%	%	%	ASSETS		%	%
	26.6						Cash & Equivalents		17.5	26.0
	11.3						Trade Receivables (net)		9.8	10.3
	.7						Inventory		.1	.3
	2.8						All Other Current		4.9	4.1
	41.4						Total Current		32.2	40.7
	43.4						Fixed Assets (net)		48.1	33.1
	6.2						Intangibles (net)		5.6	12.6
	9.0						All Other Non-Current		14.0	13.6
	100.0						Total		100.0	100.0
							LIABILITIES			
	39.2						Notes Payable-Short Term		15.0	18.1
	6.3						Cur. Mat.-L/T/D		7.0	10.3
	6.3						Trade Payables		.9	1.1
	.9						Income Taxes Payable		.5	.7
	22.4						All Other Current		18.6	16.2
	75.1						Total Current		42.0	46.4
	31.0						Long Term Debt		39.9	48.5
	.0						Deferred Taxes		.3	.3
	7.6						All Other Non-Current		7.0	7.8
	-13.5						Net Worth		10.8	-3.0
	100.0						Total Liabilities & Net Worth		100.0	100.0
							INCOME DATA			
	100.0						Net Sales		100.0	100.0
							Gross Profit			
	86.6						Operating Expenses		86.6	82.5
	13.4						Operating Profit		13.4	17.5
	2.0						All Other Expenses (net)		1.6	2.1
	11.4						Profit Before Taxes		11.8	15.4
							RATIOS			
	3.6								12.5	2.9
	1.1						Current		1.4	.8
	.2								.1	.4
	3.0								5.5	2.7
	1.0						Quick		.8	.7
	.2								.1	.3
	0 UND							0 UND	0 UND	
	0 UND						Sales/Receivables	0 UND	0 UND	
	2 211.5							1 424.5	4 100.0	
							Cost of Sales/Inventory			
							Cost of Sales/Payables			
	13.1								9.6	10.3
	390.5						Sales/Working Capital		UND	-144.5
	-9.4								-25.5	-11.9
	12.0								10.0	17.5
(51)	4.0						EBIT/Interest	(39) 3.1	(42) 2.4	
	.7								1.3	.7
							Net Profit + Depr., Dep., Amort./Cur. Mat. L /T/D			
	.6								.4	.7
	2.4						Fixed/Worth		1.6	7.2
	-1.1								-14.1	-.5
	.7								.4	1.4
	8.0						Debt/Worth		2.0	38.0
	-2.3								-8.0	-2.0
	292.4						% Profit Before Taxes/Tangible		194.4	825.9
(44)	121.4						Net Worth	(41) 64.2	(27) 100.0	
	30.0								3.7	11.1
	111.9						% Profit Before Taxes/Total		80.5	72.1
	32.3						Assets		20.0	12.8
	1.6								.4	-2.1
	50.1								40.5	72.6
	15.1						Sales/Net Fixed Assets		16.6	15.0
	7.3								5.1	6.5
	9.3								15.1	8.2
	5.5						Sales/Total Assets		6.3	3.5
	2.9								1.8	1.8
	1.4								1.1	.9
(44)	2.8						% Depr., Dep., Amort./Sales	(39) 1.8	(34) 2.3	
	4.8								4.1	5.6
	8.1						% Officers', Directors',		12.7	12.7
(44)	14.7						Owners' Comp/Sales	(31) 23.4	(20) 20.6	
	24.8								28.0	33.0
	44012M	10941M	29370M	172072M	450039M		Net Sales ($)		280769M	81343M
	9026M	6288M	17293M	70227M	104851M		Total Assets ($)		224568M	37664M

M = $ thousand   MM = $ million
See Pages 11 through 18 for Explanation of Ratios and Data

Comparative Historical Data   Current Data Sorted By Sales

			Type of Statement						
		1	Unqualified						1
		1	Reviewed	1					1
19	24	17	Compiled	13	3				1
22	15	44	Tax Returns	35	5	3			1
9	11	20	Other	11	5	1	1	1	1
4/1/00-	4/1/01-	4/1/02-			2 (4/1-9/30/02)			81 (10/1/02-3/31/03)	
3/31/01	3/31/02	3/31/03		0-1MM	1-3MM	3-5MM	5-10MM	10-25MM	25MM & OVER
ALL	ALL	ALL							
50	50	83	**NUMBER OF STATEMENTS**	60	13	4	1	1	4
%	%	%	**ASSETS**	%	%	%	%	%	%
19.2	22.1	24.0	Cash & Equivalents	24.8	22.6				
7.8	12.5	15.2	Trade Receivables (net)	11.9	18.0				
.5	.7	.6	Inventory	.8	.0				
6.1	2.6	2.7	All Other Current	2.6	.4				
33.6	37.9	42.6	Total Current	40.2	41.0				
39.1	40.7	42.1	Fixed Assets (net)	42.9	48.9				
13.5	12.2	7.2	Intangibles (net)	9.2	.9				
13.8	9.3	8.2	All Other Non-Current	7.7	9.2				
100.0	100.0	100.0	Total	100.0	100.0				
			LIABILITIES						
18.8	16.5	36.1	Notes Payable-Short Term	25.3	36.1				
13.9	6.4	6.7	Cur. Mat.-L/T/D	6.4	1.4				
5.1	1.3	5.7	Trade Payables	1.8	25.2				
.2	.3	.8	Income Taxes Payable	1.0	.4				
17.7	78.0	20.9	All Other Current	16.3	49.4				
55.7	102.6	70.2	Total Current	50.9	112.4				
26.7	39.8	29.3	Long Term Debt	34.7	20.0				
.4	.5	.3	Deferred Taxes	.0	.0				
14.5	3.2	7.0	All Other Non-Current	7.3	8.6				
2.7	−46.1	−6.8	Net Worth	7.2	−40.8				
100.0	100.0	100.0	Total Liabilities & Net Worth	100.0	100.0				
			INCOME DATA						
100.0	100.0	100.0	Net Sales	100.0	100.0				
			Gross Profit						
91.5	85.2	85.1	Operating Expenses	81.5	95.6				
8.5	14.8	14.9	Operating Profit	18.5	4.4				
.5	2.0	2.7	All Other Expenses (net)	3.8	.5				
8.0	12.8	12.1	Profit Before Taxes	14.7	3.9				
			RATIOS						
2.1	2.5	5.2		5.2	1.8				
.7	.9	1.2	Current	1.2	1.0				
.1	.3	.2		.3	.1				
1.8	2.5	3.6		5.2	1.8				
(49) .6	(49) .8	1.2	Quick	1.2	.9				
.1	.2	.2		.2	.1				
0 UND	0 UND	0 UND		0 UND	0 UND				
0 UND	0 UND	0 UND	Sales/Receivables	0 UND	0 UND				
0 UND	0 UND	18 20.3		9 39.3	3 128.9				
			Cost of Sales/Inventory						
			Cost of Sales/Payables						
37.5	16.3	9.5		9.8	22.6				
−44.7	UND	112.0	Sales/Working Capital	80.5	−74.6				
−8.0	−11.8	−8.8		−18.6	−7.2				
14.6	16.1	28.2		13.5					
(36) 2.0	(36) 4.8	(62) 4.5	EBIT/Interest	(43) 4.8					
.7	1.2	.7		1.0					
			Net Profit + Depr., Dep., Amort./Cur. Mat. L/T/D						
.4	.5	.4		.5	1.6				
2.3	2.5	2.0	Fixed/Worth	1.4	15.0				
−1.5	−1.6	−1.5		−1.4	−.9				
1.2	1.3	.7		.5	2.2				
9.1	7.1	5.2	Debt/Worth	3.5	238.0				
−2.5	−3.4	−2.7		−2.3	−2.7				
268.6	243.9	295.4	% Profit Before Taxes/Tangible Net Worth	394.2					
(29) 44.8	(33) 85.7	(53) 121.0		(40) 137.7					
−.6	28.4	25.4		39.9					
41.0	49.8	104.2	% Profit Before Taxes/Total Assets	113.8	41.1				
6.4	19.3	28.5		36.8	6.0				
−2.6	.8	2.3		4.4	−30.8				
63.0	54.0	35.3	Sales/Net Fixed Assets	35.3	51.4				
16.4	10.4	14.7		13.9	16.9				
7.1	5.3	6.5		6.2	6.4				
7.6	5.4	8.8	Sales/Total Assets	9.0	7.6				
4.6	2.9	4.0		3.7	4.8				
2.9	1.6	1.9		1.8	3.6				
.9	1.1	1.4	% Depr., Dep., Amort./Sales	1.5					
(34) 2.2	(36) 2.2	(52) 2.8		(39) 2.8					
4.7	4.4	4.9		5.0					
13.4	14.0	7.9	% Officers', Directors', Owners' Comp/Sales	9.1					
(31) 23.0	(26) 26.4	(50) 13.7		(36) 16.6					
30.7	34.2	25.7		27.6					
60801M	65934M	706434M	Net Sales ($)	23981M	18087M	15521M	8699M	18035M	622111M
97513M	46758M	207685M	Total Assets ($)	9031M	5197M	3378M	5015M	9986M	175078M

M = $ thousand   MM = $ million
See Pages 11 through 18 for Explanation of Ratios and Data

Current Data Sorted By Assets   **Comparative Historical Data**

0-500M	500M-2MM	2-10MM	10-50MM	50-100MM	100-250MM	Type of Statement	4/1/98-3/31/99 ALL	4/1/99-3/31/00 ALL
2	2	1	3		1	Unqualified	3	5
3	5	2				Reviewed	6	6
28	18	2				Compiled	27	33
48	14	3				Tax Returns	43	36
21	12	5		1	1	Other	23	28
	25 (4/1-9/30/02)			147 (10/1/02-3/31/03)				
102	51	13	3	1	2	**NUMBER OF STATEMENTS**	102	108
%	%	%	%	%	%	**ASSETS**	%	%
19.2	13.2	9.1				Cash & Equivalents	14.3	13.6
8.1	10.7	19.1				Trade Receivables (net)	9.5	11.7
13.8	8.5	5.7				Inventory	13.1	13.1
2.6	2.4	1.3				All Other Current	.7	2.0
43.7	34.8	35.1				Total Current	37.5	40.5
42.2	52.6	42.0				Fixed Assets (net)	47.7	45.7
9.0	6.2	1.8				Intangibles (net)	6.1	6.6
5.1	6.4	21.1				All Other Non-Current	8.7	7.2
100.0	100.0	100.0				Total	100.0	100.0
						LIABILITIES		
19.9	10.2	9.3				Notes Payable-Short Term	8.6	14.4
10.0	8.1	7.8				Cur. Mat.-L/T/D	7.3	7.2
6.5	4.1	8.6				Trade Payables	8.2	6.5
.2	1.0	.5				Income Taxes Payable	.0	.5
12.9	13.3	11.2				All Other Current	18.7	16.0
49.6	36.7	37.4				Total Current	42.9	44.5
31.2	43.9	31.4				Long Term Debt	53.5	32.0
.0	.4	.2				Deferred Taxes	.0	.0
5.0	1.7	10.3				All Other Non-Current	6.1	2.8
14.1	17.3	20.8				Net Worth	-2.5	20.7
100.0	100.0	100.0				Total Liabilities & Net Worth	100.0	100.0
						INCOME DATA		
100.0	100.0	100.0				Net Sales	100.0	100.0
						Gross Profit		
92.7	90.6	86.6				Operating Expenses	91.9	88.7
7.3	9.4	13.4				Operating Profit	8.1	11.3
.8	2.3	.9				All Other Expenses (net)	1.0	1.8
6.5	7.1	12.5				Profit Before Taxes	7.1	9.5
						RATIOS		
2.4	2.3	2.1				Current	2.6	2.3
1.0	.9	1.1					1.1	1.2
.4	.2	.6					.5	.5
1.4	1.3	1.8				Quick	1.5	1.8
.5	(50) .6	.6					(106) .6	.6
.2	.2	.4					.2	.3
0 UND	0 UND	0 UND				Sales/Receivables	0 UND	0 UND
0 UND	1 374.3	25 14.6					0 UND	0 UND
12 30.4	25 14.8	40 9.1					19 19.5	24 15.3
						Cost of Sales/Inventory		
						Cost of Sales/Payables		
20.5	19.2	19.6				Sales/Working Capital	16.6	16.3
-529.6	-122.6	53.1					110.8	86.1
-18.4	-14.8	-13.0					-28.0	-25.9
11.4	9.2	7.0				EBIT/Interest	7.7	10.0
(83) 4.1	(46) 3.2	(12) 3.1					(85) 2.5	(82) 3.3
1.0	.8	1.1					.4	.8
						Net Profit + Depr., Dep., Amort./Cur. Mat. L/T/D		
.7	.8	.7				Fixed/Worth	.8	.7
2.4	6.5	1.4					3.5	2.2
-2.5	-3.5	-2.5					-6.0	-21.1
1.0	1.7	.9				Debt/Worth	.8	.8
5.5	8.1	5.1					3.9	3.6
-6.1	-7.1	-7.3					-9.1	-21.2
116.8	149.9					% Profit Before Taxes/Tangible Net Worth	126.0	189.5
(66) 49.3	(33) 31.4						(69) 30.3	(79) 51.7
5.5	2.9						-2.3	12.1
50.4	21.9	30.3				% Profit Before Taxes/Total Assets	32.4	32.1
9.7	7.7	8.2					7.2	10.7
-.7	-1.2	.4					-2.1	.0
29.6	13.8	13.0				Sales/Net Fixed Assets	19.4	21.3
15.2	8.6	7.5					11.3	10.8
8.1	4.7	4.6					5.4	5.5
9.9	6.5	4.4				Sales/Total Assets	7.4	6.6
5.5	3.9	3.0					4.5	4.2
3.5	2.4	1.5					2.7	2.6
2.0	2.1	1.7				% Depr., Dep., Amort./Sales	1.7	1.7
(74) 2.9	(45) 3.8	(11) 4.1					(88) 2.8	(98) 2.8
4.7	6.6	4.8					3.8	4.2
9.6	13.9					% Officers', Directors', Owners' Comp/Sales	10.0	12.6
(67) 17.2	(34) 21.9						(65) 16.9	(58) 21.0
28.0	29.4						27.0	29.9
147687M	210326M	114133M	96435M	53773M	1967900M	Net Sales ($)	632796M	430981M
22904M	46072M	43338M	58966M	64128M	414904M	Total Assets ($)	368205M	161177M

© RMA 2003

M = $ thousand   MM = $ million
See Pages 11 through 18 for Explanation of Ratios and Data

Comparative Historical Data			Type of Statement	Current Data Sorted By Sales					
2	3	9	Unqualified	1	2			3	3
4	8	10	Reviewed	1	2	3	3	1	
33	48	48	Compiled	16	19	7	5	1	
41	37	65	Tax Returns	24	26	7	6	2	
26	34	40	Other	8	18	4	7	1	2
4/1/00-3/31/01 ALL	4/1/01-3/31/02 ALL	4/1/02-3/31/03 ALL		25 (4/1-9/30/02)		147 (10/1/02-3/31/03)			
				0-1MM	1-3MM	3-5MM	5-10MM	10-25MM	25MM & OVER
106	130	172	NUMBER OF STATEMENTS	50	67	21	21	8	5
%	%	%	ASSETS	%	%	%	%	%	%
14.3	13.2	16.6	Cash & Equivalents	17.9	14.2	22.7	15.7		
13.7	11.8	10.2	Trade Receivables (net)	9.2	9.4	9.6	10.3		
14.4	14.1	11.4	Inventory	13.8	13.8	5.7	5.9		
2.2	2.6	2.6	All Other Current	3.0	1.8	1.8	.5		
44.7	41.8	40.7	Total Current	43.9	39.3	39.8	32.3		
44.1	43.3	44.5	Fixed Assets (net)	38.7	49.8	48.2	50.4		
4.2	9.5	7.6	Intangibles (net)	11.8	5.9	7.4	5.0		
6.9	5.4	7.2	All Other Non-Current	5.6	5.0	4.6	12.2		
100.0	100.0	100.0	Total	100.0	100.0	100.0	100.0		
			LIABILITIES						
10.7	11.4	15.6	Notes Payable-Short Term	19.9	17.2	7.1	11.5		
7.2	8.8	9.1	Cur. Mat.-L/T/D	8.9	9.8	8.9	11.0		
9.1	6.6	6.0	Trade Payables	7.2	6.5	2.9	4.7		
.8	.1	.5	Income Taxes Payable	.0	.4	2.0	.4		
15.4	20.9	12.9	All Other Current	7.1	11.8	18.1	19.8		
43.3	47.7	44.0	Total Current	43.0	45.8	39.0	47.4		
37.5	31.8	34.3	Long Term Debt	38.2	28.7	50.5	37.9		
.4	.2	.2	Deferred Taxes	.0	.1	.7	.0		
3.4	7.1	4.6	All Other Non-Current	3.1	5.9	.0	8.3		
15.4	13.0	16.8	Net Worth	15.6	19.5	9.8	6.3		
100.0	100.0	100.0	Total Liabilities & Net Worth	100.0	100.0	100.0	100.0		
			INCOME DATA						
100.0	100.0	100.0	Net Sales	100.0	100.0	100.0	100.0		
			Gross Profit						
92.0	90.9	91.7	Operating Expenses	89.7	91.8	90.7	94.2		
8.0	9.1	8.3	Operating Profit	10.3	8.2	9.3	5.7		
1.5	1.8	1.2	All Other Expenses (net)	2.3	.9	.7	1.0		
6.5	7.2	7.1	Profit Before Taxes	8.0	7.3	8.6	4.7		
			RATIOS						
2.4	2.1	2.4		3.6	2.1	3.0	1.5		
1.1	1.2	1.0	Current	1.6	.8	1.2	.6		
.5	.6	.4		.5	.4	.4	.2		
1.7	1.3	1.4		2.5	.8	2.3	1.2		
(105) .6	(128) .6	(171) .5	Quick	.6	.5	(20) 1.0	.4		
.2	.3	.2		.1	.2	.3	.2		
0 UND	0 UND	0 UND		0 UND	0 UND	0 UND	0 UND		
1 341.8	4 85.7	0 UND	Sales/Receivables	0 UND	0 UND	0 UND	0 UND		
28 13.0	22 16.7	21 17.1		24 15.1	18 20.5	3 143.8	25 14.8		
			Cost of Sales/Inventory						
			Cost of Sales/Payables						
14.0	15.6	19.3		10.3	31.6	24.5	28.0		
124.3	61.8	-612.7	Sales/Working Capital	47.4	-81.2	86.8	-30.1		
-22.7	-30.1	-18.2		-15.3	-18.1	-29.1	-13.2		
7.6	14.9	10.3		11.4	9.1	8.4	17.5		
(93) 3.1	(114) 3.1	(145) 3.7	EBIT/Interest	(39) 4.5	(59) 3.9	(18) 4.5	(18) 3.5		
.9	.7	.9		1.5	.3	.8	.3		
		2.5	Net Profit + Depr., Dep.,						
	(15) 1.4		Amort./Cur. Mat. L/T/D						
		.8							
.7	.5	.7		.5	.8	.7	1.1		
3.6	2.5	2.5	Fixed/Worth	3.5	2.4	2.6	16.1		
-3.0	-7.8	-2.8		-2.7	-3.0	-3.7	-1.7		
1.7	1.0	1.0		.9	1.0	1.3	1.9		
7.2	3.2	5.2	Debt/Worth	5.5	5.8	4.0	30.8		
-6.7	-11.8	-6.5		-5.9	-7.6	-5.3	-3.9		
124.1	137.7	113.2	% Profit Before Taxes/Tangible	95.2	254.0	72.7	261.8		
(65) 37.2	(84) 53.7	(112) 44.0	Net Worth	(33) 47.1	(44) 65.8	(14) 24.9	(11) 38.3		
3.8	14.8	4.3		17.4	-2.4	-.1	17.5		
24.9	36.3	39.7	% Profit Before Taxes/Total	40.6	52.0	100.6	23.9		
8.6	9.5	8.6	Assets	9.0	10.9	8.5	7.7		
-.4	-.9	-.9		4.3	-1.9	-1.2	-2.7		
28.9	28.5	23.5		27.8	18.8	26.8	21.2		
12.6	14.1	11.5	Sales/Net Fixed Assets	11.1	10.2	17.1	11.8		
4.9	6.6	6.5		5.4	5.7	8.3	7.6		
7.8	7.0	7.6		6.5	7.7	9.9	8.3		
4.6	4.7	4.7	Sales/Total Assets	3.2	4.6	6.5	6.1		
2.4	2.7	2.7		1.8	3.2	4.4	3.5		
1.5	1.4	1.9		1.3	2.4	1.8	2.0		
(92) 2.4	(105) 2.6	(135) 3.2	% Depr., Dep., Amort./Sales	(34) 2.5	(55) 3.8	(17) 2.6	(17) 3.7		
3.9	4.1	5.3		4.4	6.4	4.7	5.0		
9.4	11.6	9.9	% Officers', Directors',	9.7	8.9	19.0	9.3		
(76) 18.5	(86) 19.9	(108) 19.0	Owners' Comp/Sales	(32) 11.9	(42) 21.7	(14) 24.2	(16) 16.3		
27.9	28.9	28.9		21.0	28.3	32.3	32.0		
381088M	1311675M	2590254M	Net Sales ($)	26291M	118964M	82776M	141289M	120707M	2100227M
134737M	374327M	650312M	Total Assets ($)	10145M	31259M	15934M	36540M	29592M	526842M

M = $ thousand   MM = $ million
See Pages 11 through 18 for Explanation of Ratios and Data

Current Data Sorted By Assets   **Comparative Historical Data**

0-500M	500M-2MM	2-10MM	10-50MM	50-100MM	100-250MM	Type of Statement	4/1/98-3/31/99 ALL	4/1/99-3/31/00 ALL
	1	5				Unqualified		
	1	1				Reviewed		
8	1	2				Compiled		
9	3					Tax Returns		
2	1	2				Other		
	4 (4/1-9/30/02)		32 (10/1/02-3/31/03)					
19	7	10				**NUMBER OF STATEMENTS**		
%	%	%	%	%	%	**ASSETS**	%	%
36.3		11.2				Cash & Equivalents		
8.2		44.4	D	D	D	Trade Receivables (net)	D	D
.1		.0	A	A	A	Inventory	A	A
1.3		3.5	T	T	T	All Other Current	T	T
46.0		59.1	A	A	A	Total Current	A	A
28.1		35.2				Fixed Assets (net)		
4.0		.9	N	N	N	Intangibles (net)	N	N
21.9		4.9	O	O	O	All Other Non-Current	O	O
100.0		100.0	T	T	T	Total	T	T
						LIABILITIES		
36.5		3.2	A	A	A	Notes Payable-Short Term	A	A
13.2		7.4	V	V	V	Cur. Mat.-L/T/D	V	V
.7		8.8	A	A	A	Trade Payables	A	A
.0		.0	I	I	I	Income Taxes Payable	I	I
32.2		19.8	L	L	L	All Other Current	L	L
82.7		39.2	A	A	A	Total Current	A	A
67.3		11.0	B	B	B	Long Term Debt	B	B
.0		.0	L	L	L	Deferred Taxes	L	L
21.0		7.9	E	E	E	All Other Non-Current	E	E
−71.0		42.0				Net Worth		
100.0		100.0				Total Liabilities & Net Worth		
						INCOME DATA		
100.0		100.0				Net Sales		
						Gross Profit		
92.6		91.6				Operating Expenses		
7.4		8.4				Operating Profit		
−.7		.7				All Other Expenses (net)		
8.1		7.6				Profit Before Taxes		
						RATIOS		
2.3		3.8						
.8		2.1				Current		
.2		1.3						
2.3		3.7						
.8		2.0				Quick		
.2		1.1						
0 UND		42 8.8						
0 UND		65 5.6				Sales/Receivables		
0 UND		89 4.1						
						Cost of Sales/Inventory		
						Cost of Sales/Payables		
15.6		4.4						
−170.5		8.3				Sales/Working Capital		
−20.3		NM						
13.6								
(13) 1.2						EBIT/Interest		
.1								
						Net Profit + Depr., Dep., Amort./Cur. Mat. L /T/D		
.3		.2						
1.9		.5				Fixed/Worth		
−.4		1.6						
1.0		.3						
408.0		.8				Debt/Worth		
−1.8		1.9						
327.4								
(10) 66.2						% Profit Before Taxes/Tangible Net Worth		
−47.3								
238.0		21.7						
4.8		3.9				% Profit Before Taxes/Total Assets		
−1.7		−.1						
151.6		17.5						
53.7		8.9				Sales/Net Fixed Assets		
10.7		4.2						
28.4		3.7						
10.9		2.5				Sales/Total Assets		
2.5		1.9						
.6		1.4						
(15) 1.0		2.1				% Depr., Dep., Amort./Sales		
1.9		3.5						
						% Officers', Directors', Owners' Comp/Sales		
30527M	33015M	96570M				Net Sales ($)		
3285M	7925M	37095M				Total Assets ($)		

M = $ thousand   MM = $ million
See Pages 11 through 18 for Explanation of Ratios and Data

Comparative Historical Data / Current Data Sorted By Sales

			Type of Statement						
		6	Unqualified		1		3	2	
		2	Reviewed			1		1	
		11	Compiled	2	4	5			
		12	Tax Returns	5	4	1	1	1	
		5	Other	2	1			2	
4/1/00- 3/31/01 ALL	4/1/01- 3/31/02 ALL	4/1/02- 3/31/03 ALL		0-1MM	4 (4/1-9/30/02) 1-3MM	3-5MM	32 (10/1/02-3/31/03) 5-10MM	10-25MM	25MM & OVER
		36	**NUMBER OF STATEMENTS**	9	10	7	4	6	
%	%	%	**ASSETS**	%	%	%	%	%	%
D	D	24.9	Cash & Equivalents		30.6				D
A	A	20.1	Trade Receivables (net)		2.9				A
T	T	.9	Inventory		.1				T
A	A	4.5	All Other Current		11.3				A
		50.4	Total Current		44.8				
N	N	32.3	Fixed Assets (net)		32.6				N
O	O	3.3	Intangibles (net)		4.8				O
T	T	13.9	All Other Non-Current		17.8				T
		100.0	Total		100.0				
A	A		**LIABILITIES**						A
V	V	24.2	Notes Payable-Short Term		62.7				V
A	A	9.7	Cur. Mat.-L/T/D		3.6				A
I	I	3.8	Trade Payables		.5				I
L	L	.0	Income Taxes Payable		.0				L
A	A	25.2	All Other Current		23.0				A
B	B	62.9	Total Current		89.8				B
L	L	40.3	Long Term Debt		21.8				L
E	E	.0	Deferred Taxes		.0				E
		14.7	All Other Non-Current		44.7				
		−17.9	Net Worth		−56.3				
		100.0	Total Liabilities & Net Worth		100.0				
			INCOME DATA						
		100.0	Net Sales		100.0				
			Gross Profit						
		92.6	Operating Expenses		93.6				
		7.4	Operating Profit		6.4				
		−.3	All Other Expenses (net)		−1.4				
		7.7	Profit Before Taxes		7.8				
			RATIOS						
		2.8			2.8				
		1.3	Current		.4				
		.4			.2				
		2.3			1.5				
		1.1	Quick		.4				
		.3			.2				
	0	UND			0	UND			
	0	UND	Sales/Receivables		0	UND			
	65	5.6			0	UND			
			Cost of Sales/Inventory						
			Cost of Sales/Payables						
		7.3			12.7				
		455.5	Sales/Working Capital		−95.4				
		−22.9			−12.2				
		15.4							
	(28)	1.4	EBIT/Interest						
		.8							
			Net Profit + Depr., Dep., Amort./Cur. Mat. L/T/D						
		.3			.3				
		.9	Fixed/Worth		NM				
		−4.3			−.3				
		.4			.9				
		2.9	Debt/Worth		NM				
		−5.9			−1.6				
		96.1	% Profit Before Taxes/Tangible						
	(24)	25.3	Net Worth						
		−2.7							
		40.5	% Profit Before Taxes/Total		39.2				
		5.2	Assets		8.4				
		−.9			−6.3				
		74.0			115.7				
		17.3	Sales/Net Fixed Assets		66.3				
		6.4			5.9				
		13.5			22.0				
		4.3	Sales/Total Assets		8.1				
		2.2			2.3				
		.9							
	(32)	1.8	% Depr., Dep., Amort./Sales						
		2.4							
		10.8	% Officers', Directors',						
	(17)	17.2	Owners' Comp/Sales						
		31.4							
		160112M	Net Sales ($)	4637M	20904M	28399M	26368M	79804M	
		48305M	Total Assets ($)	1213M	5039M	8356M	9559M	24138M	

M = $ thousand   MM = $ million
See Pages 11 through 18 for Explanation of Ratios and Data

Current Data Sorted By Assets   **Comparative Historical Data**

						Type of Statement		
1	5	7	4			Unqualified	15	10
1	4	2				Reviewed	3	3
15	9	5	1			Compiled	37	38
45	3	1			1	Tax Returns	32	26
23	8	5	2	1	1	Other	43	26
	18 (4/1-9/30/02)			126 (10/1/02-3/31/03)			4/1/98-3/31/99	4/1/99-3/31/00
0-500M	500M-2MM	2-10MM	10-50MM	50-100MM	100-250MM		ALL	ALL
85	29	20	7	1	2	**NUMBER OF STATEMENTS**	130	103
%	%	%	%	%	%	**ASSETS**	%	%
27.1	17.8	6.5				Cash & Equivalents	20.2	19.5
7.5	29.1	38.8				Trade Receivables (net)	22.8	28.1
1.2	.9	1.7				Inventory	.7	.9
7.1	.6	3.7				All Other Current	4.4	2.8
42.9	48.5	50.8				Total Current	48.1	51.3
44.2	38.0	38.1				Fixed Assets (net)	38.7	34.2
3.6	2.7	2.5				Intangibles (net)	3.6	4.2
9.4	10.9	8.6				All Other Non-Current	9.6	10.3
100.0	100.0	100.0				Total	100.0	100.0
						LIABILITIES		
30.6	16.8	6.7				Notes Payable-Short Term	17.2	23.3
6.7	3.0	3.0				Cur. Mat.-L/T/D	7.5	14.4
3.1	5.5	8.6				Trade Payables	4.9	5.0
.2	.2	1.3				Income Taxes Payable	.5	.1
35.0	19.3	10.1				All Other Current	21.5	22.4
75.7	44.7	29.9				Total Current	51.7	65.1
26.1	23.2	25.2				Long Term Debt	28.0	29.6
.0	.0	.2				Deferred Taxes	.4	.7
10.2	3.3	1.4				All Other Non-Current	4.5	6.4
-12.1	28.7	43.3				Net Worth	15.4	-1.8
100.0	100.0	100.0				Total Liabilities & Net Worth	100.0	100.0
						INCOME DATA		
100.0	100.0	100.0				Net Sales	100.0	100.0
						Gross Profit		
92.8	89.8	92.6				Operating Expenses	92.4	94.1
7.2	10.2	7.4				Operating Profit	7.6	5.8
.4	1.5	1.9				All Other Expenses (net)	1.8	1.9
6.8	8.8	5.4				Profit Before Taxes	5.7	3.9
						RATIOS		
1.9	4.0	2.4				Current	3.3	2.3
.8	1.3	1.6					1.4	1.1
.2	.6	1.2					.4	.5
1.7	4.0	2.3				Quick	3.2	2.2
.6	1.3	1.4				(127)	1.4	1.0
.1	.5	1.0					.4	.5
0 UND	0 UND	40 9.2				Sales/Receivables	0 UND	0 UND
0 UND	27 13.7	51 7.1					0 UND	2 151.0
0 UND	57 6.4	87 4.2					63 5.8	71 5.1
						Cost of Sales/Inventory		
						Cost of Sales/Payables		
39.5	5.0	6.5				Sales/Working Capital	7.8	9.0
-95.5	64.4	12.6					42.2	92.0
-17.7	-19.8	46.7					-34.1	-28.3
(67) 15.2	(25) 16.6	(16) 15.6				EBIT/Interest	(96) 12.7	(83) 8.4
1.9	7.5	2.9					2.9	2.7
-1.3	1.5	-.1					.2	.6
						Net Profit + Depr., Dep., Amort./Cur. Mat. L /T/D	(10) 9.7	
							1.6	
							.9	
.6	.3	.3				Fixed/Worth	.3	.3
2.5	1.2	.9					1.1	1.5
-2.4	NM	4.3					49.0	-3.0
1.4	.6	.5				Debt/Worth	.6	1.0
9.2	2.6	1.3					2.2	3.1
-4.1	NM	4.9					-28.8	-11.1
(56) 304.4	(22) 134.3	(18) 28.6				% Profit Before Taxes/Tangible Net Worth	(96) 87.3	(72) 97.3
78.8	46.1	6.7					40.9	19.1
.0	6.3	-7.8					6.2	-1.6
63.0	31.7	15.3				% Profit Before Taxes/Total Assets	32.4	34.7
15.9	11.8	3.7					10.0	5.8
-5.4	.9	-1.9					-2.8	-2.5
91.4	41.6	33.2				Sales/Net Fixed Assets	53.7	66.1
19.2	7.9	8.4					17.6	24.3
9.5	4.4	1.5					6.3	9.0
12.2	6.3	3.3				Sales/Total Assets	10.0	10.8
6.8	2.9	2.3					4.1	4.0
3.4	1.3	.9					2.4	2.1
(52) 1.0	(24) .8	(17) .9				% Depr., Dep., Amort./Sales	(104) .9	(80) .9
1.9	3.4	1.7					2.1	1.7
3.2	5.5	6.9					3.6	3.0
(55) 12.2						% Officers', Directors', Owners' Comp/Sales	(60) 8.7	(54) 7.4
18.2							15.4	18.5
29.9							27.8	
122683M	114249M	228255M	147664M	152144M	2708359M	Net Sales ($)	1157193M	1256264M
15229M	29542M	103468M	93632M	62996M	477210M	Total Assets ($)	362689M	417387M

M = $ thousand   MM = $ million
See Pages 11 through 18 for Explanation of Ratios and Data

Comparative Historical Data				Current Data Sorted By Sales					
			Type of Statement						
14	15	17	Unqualified	2	3	1	5	6	
8	7	7	Reviewed		2	1	2	2	
47	46	30	Compiled	9	8	1	8	3	1
33	45	50	Tax Returns	27	15	2	4		2
31	40	40	Other	17	14	2	1	2	4
4/1/00-3/31/01 ALL	4/1/01-3/31/02 ALL	4/1/02-3/31/03 ALL		0-1MM	1-3MM	3-5MM	5-10MM	10-25MM	25MM & OVER
				18 (4/1-9/30/02)			126 (10/1/02-3/31/03)		
133	153	144	**NUMBER OF STATEMENTS**	55	42	7	20	13	7
%	%	%	**ASSETS**	%	%	%	%	%	%
18.7	25.8	21.6	Cash & Equivalents	25.0	21.8		24.0	10.8	
20.2	20.6	17.7	Trade Receivables (net)	8.8	15.9		22.2	35.3	
.7	.7	1.1	Inventory	1.4	.6		.0	.9	
4.8	3.5	5.1	All Other Current	6.5	6.0		2.8	2.4	
44.4	50.6	45.4	Total Current	41.7	44.2		49.0	49.4	
43.6	37.7	41.7	Fixed Assets (net)	41.1	46.5		43.1	37.4	
4.8	4.8	3.4	Intangibles (net)	4.3	3.3		1.8	1.6	
7.2	6.9	9.5	All Other Non-Current	12.9	5.9		6.1	11.6	
100.0	100.0	100.0	Total	100.0	100.0		100.0	100.0	
			LIABILITIES						
28.9	20.5	22.5	Notes Payable-Short Term	32.5	17.5		25.0	11.4	
11.6	6.3	5.3	Cur. Mat.-L/T/D	5.9	6.8		4.0	1.2	
5.0	3.6	4.5	Trade Payables	3.5	3.2		5.4	7.8	
.3	.9	.5	Income Taxes Payable	.1	.2		.5	2.2	
32.9	18.0	26.8	All Other Current	18.4	42.0		36.1	13.3	
78.6	49.3	59.6	Total Current	60.2	69.7		70.9	35.8	
43.0	26.4	25.2	Long Term Debt	26.6	26.3		28.1	16.5	
.8	.3	.0	Deferred Taxes	.0	.0		.0	.2	
2.9	3.6	7.0	All Other Non-Current	9.0	8.9		.5	1.4	
−25.3	20.3	8.2	Net Worth	4.2	−4.9		.4	46.0	
100.0	100.0	100.0	Total Liabilities & Net Worth	100.0	100.0		100.0	100.0	
			INCOME DATA						
100.0	100.0	100.0	Net Sales	100.0	100.0		100.0	100.0	
			Gross Profit						
90.7	88.5	92.3	Operating Expenses	88.9	94.4		96.3	96.4	
9.3	11.5	7.7	Operating Profit	11.1	5.6		3.7	3.6	
2.0	2.7	.9	All Other Expenses (net)	1.5	.2		−.2	1.9	
7.3	8.8	6.8	Profit Before Taxes	9.5	5.4		3.9	1.7	
			RATIOS						
2.4	2.5	2.4		2.4	3.2		1.6	2.0	
1.0	1.3	1.2	Current	.9	1.0		.7	1.2	
.3	.6	.4		.3	.4		.4	1.1	
2.1	2.4	2.1		1.8	3.2		1.6	1.8	
.9	1.2	1.0	Quick	.7	.9		.7	1.2	
.2	.4	.3		.2	.2		.3	1.0	
0 UND	0 UND	0 UND		0 UND	0 UND		0 UND	37 9.9	
0 UND	0 UND	0 UND	Sales/Receivables	0 UND	0 UND		8 45.8	50 7.3	
53 6.8	58 6.3	44 8.3		17 21.2	33 11.0		47 7.7	85 4.3	
			Cost of Sales/Inventory						
			Cost of Sales/Payables						
8.0	9.5	12.7		26.5	12.2		14.5	8.2	
692.7	60.6	138.0	Sales/Working Capital	−154.0	NM		−147.6	22.3	
−24.4	−33.9	−26.8		−10.5	−19.0		−31.4	55.8	
	10.7		12.6		15.1		12.6		23.4			15.4		19.6	
(113) 3.3	(124) 5.6	(117) 3.2	EBIT/Interest	(42) 3.1	(34) 1.8		(18) 3.6	(10) 3.9	
.9	1.0	−.2		−.2	−1.5		−.1	−.3	
7.7	10.1		Net Profit + Depr., Dep.,						
(10) 1.1	(10) 2.1		Amort./Cur. Mat. L/T/D						
−9.7	.3								
.4	.3	.5		.6	.4		.9	.3	
1.8	1.3	1.6	Fixed/Worth	1.9	1.9		5.6	.7	
−20.6	22.1	60.1		21.8	−2.4		−1.8	1.5	
.7	.8	1.0		1.6	.6		1.2	.8	
3.4	2.8	3.3	Debt/Worth	5.8	3.1		6.7	1.3	
−21.9	NM	−59.5		−15.7	−4.4		−9.0	2.2	
112.7	124.0	145.5	% Profit Before Taxes/Tangible	240.3	192.9		106.2	14.4	
(94) 29.5	(115) 46.2	(106) 42.3	Net Worth	(40) 64.9	(28) 51.6		(14) 41.9	(12) 8.5	
.7	10.6	−.4		1.4	1.4		−19.9	−9.4	
32.2	48.3	43.2	% Profit Before Taxes/Total	48.1	72.7		27.8	8.4	
7.6	14.0	10.7	Assets	11.4	16.7		8.0	3.0	
−.4	1.1	−3.5		−5.1	−4.9		−1.8	−2.9	
37.2	50.5	44.5		68.4	37.6		108.0	44.4	
13.1	18.5	15.1	Sales/Net Fixed Assets	14.0	14.1		26.3	6.2	
6.1	6.8	6.0		6.0	6.9		5.3	3.3	
9.7	9.4	8.9		7.2	11.3		16.8	4.0	
4.6	3.8	4.2	Sales/Total Assets	3.8	5.9		6.1	2.3	
2.1	2.2	2.3		1.5	3.1		2.5	1.5	
.8	.7	1.0		1.1	1.3		.7	1.1	
(116) 1.6	(121) 1.5	(102) 2.0	% Depr., Dep., Amort./Sales	(33) 2.5	(27) 2.0		(18) 1.3	(11) 1.3	
3.2	3.0	4.0		5.1	3.7		4.5	2.5	
8.3	8.6	8.9	% Officers', Directors',	11.9	7.1		3.5		
(62) 15.8	(72) 18.8	(73) 16.1	Owners' Comp/Sales	(34) 18.2	(23) 15.7		(10) 13.0		
27.8	26.1	26.4		30.0	25.9		21.4		
3301296M	1792683M	3473354M	Net Sales ($)	28545M	83373M	27303M	138624M	220899M	2974610M
655687M	497817M	782077M	Total Assets ($)	15196M	28636M	7531M	41965M	98812M	589937M

M = $ thousand   MM = $ million
See Pages 11 through 18 for Explanation of Ratios and Data

Current Data Sorted By Assets

Comparative Historical Data

		1				Type of Statement		
						Unqualified		
2	2	1				Reviewed		
10	1	1				Compiled		
2	7	3	4			Tax Returns		
						Other	4/1/98- 3/31/99	4/1/99- 3/31/00
	3 (4/1-9/30/02)		31 (10/1/02-3/31/03)					
0-500M	500M-2MM	2-10MM	10-50MM	50-100MM	100-250MM		ALL	ALL
14	10	6	4			NUMBER OF STATEMENTS		
%	%	%	%	%	%	ASSETS	%	%
37.6	13.0			D	D	Cash & Equivalents	D	D
5.0	34.6			A	A	Trade Receivables (net)	A	A
1.1	1.5			T	T	Inventory	T	T
6.0	1.0			A	A	All Other Current	A	A
49.7	50.1					Total Current		
41.9	32.5			N	N	Fixed Assets (net)	N	N
2.5	.3			O	O	Intangibles (net)	O	O
5.9	17.1			T	T	All Other Non-Current	T	T
100.0	100.0					Total		
				A	A	LIABILITIES	A	A
9.7	12.1			V	V	Notes Payable-Short Term	V	V
22.0	5.6			A	A	Cur. Mat.-L/T/D	A	A
.7	6.5			I	I	Trade Payables	I	I
.0	.2			L	L	Income Taxes Payable	L	L
23.6	17.6			A	A	All Other Current	A	A
55.9	42.0			B	B	Total Current	B	B
17.2	31.2			L	L	Long Term Debt	L	L
.0	.0			E	E	Deferred Taxes	E	E
9.8	5.8					All Other Non-Current		
17.1	21.0					Net Worth		
100.0	100.0					Total Liabilities & Net Worth		
						INCOME DATA		
100.0	100.0					Net Sales		
						Gross Profit		
95.0	83.0					Operating Expenses		
5.0	17.0					Operating Profit		
.3	1.7					All Other Expenses (net)		
4.7	15.3					Profit Before Taxes		
						RATIOS		
4.7	3.2							
1.2	1.2					Current		
.4	.2							
3.0	3.1							
(13) 1.2	1.2					Quick		
.5	.2							
0 UND	0 UND							
0 UND	0 UND					Sales/Receivables		
0 UND	77 4.7							
						Cost of Sales/Inventory		
						Cost of Sales/Payables		
49.9	6.2							
193.6	NM					Sales/Working Capital		
−39.2	−12.0							
						EBIT/Interest		
						Net Profit + Depr., Dep., Amort./Cur. Mat. L /T/D		
.4	.1							
1.4	.2					Fixed/Worth		
−2.1	−9.4							
.7	.6							
2.3	2.5					Debt/Worth		
−6.6	−27.7							
						% Profit Before Taxes/Tangible Net Worth		
89.2	40.8							
20.2	20.4					% Profit Before Taxes/Total Assets		
−1.6	5.8							
74.5	229.3							
30.6	29.8					Sales/Net Fixed Assets		
15.7	7.3							
21.7	5.1							
11.2	4.5					Sales/Total Assets		
6.9	2.6							
						% Depr., Dep., Amort./Sales		
						% Officers', Directors', Owners' Comp/Sales		
41632M	35621M	49203M	307257M			Net Sales ($)		
2419M	9426M	30089M	104345M			Total Assets ($)		

M = $ thousand   MM = $ million
See Pages 11 through 18 for Explanation of Ratios and Data

Comparative Historical Data   **Current Data Sorted By Sales**

4/1/00-3/31/01 ALL	4/1/01-3/31/02 ALL	4/1/02-3/31/03 ALL	Type of Statement	0-1MM	1-3MM	3-5MM	5-10MM	10-25MM	25MM & OVER
		1	Unqualified					1	
			Reviewed						
		5	Compiled	1	1	2	1		
		12	Tax Returns	5	4	1	1	1	
		16	Other	1	2	5	3		4
					3 (4/1-9/30/02)		31 (10/1/02-3/31/03)		
		34	**NUMBER OF STATEMENTS**	7	7	8	5	3	4
%	%	%	**ASSETS**	%	%	%	%	%	%
D	D	22.5	Cash & Equivalents						
A	A	22.3	Trade Receivables (net)						
T	T	1.3	Inventory						
A	A	3.3	All Other Current						
		49.4	Total Current						
N	N	35.2	Fixed Assets (net)						
O	O	4.5	Intangibles (net)						
T	T	10.9	All Other Non-Current						
		100.0	Total						
A	A		**LIABILITIES**						
V	V	8.2	Notes Payable-Short Term						
A	A	11.8	Cur. Mat.-L/T/D						
I	I	5.0	Trade Payables						
L	L	.2	Income Taxes Payable						
A	A	20.0	All Other Current						
B	B	45.2	Total Current						
L	L	21.3	Long Term Debt						
E	E	.0	Deferred Taxes						
		10.8	All Other Non-Current						
		22.7	Net Worth						
		100.0	Total Liabilities & Net Worth						
			INCOME DATA						
		100.0	Net Sales						
			Gross Profit						
		92.6	Operating Expenses						
		7.4	Operating Profit						
		.8	All Other Expenses (net)						
		6.6	Profit Before Taxes						
			RATIOS						
		3.0							
		1.2	Current						
		.4							
		2.5							
	(33)	1.2	Quick						
		.4							
0	UND								
0	UND		Sales/Receivables						
	52	7.0							
			Cost of Sales/Inventory						
			Cost of Sales/Payables						
		15.8							
		77.2	Sales/Working Capital						
		−30.3							
		11.8							
	(26)	2.9	EBIT/Interest						
		−1.3							
			Net Profit + Depr., Dep., Amort./Cur. Mat. L/T/D						
		.2							
		1.1	Fixed/Worth						
		−15.2							
		.7							
		2.5	Debt/Worth						
		−88.6							
		110.6							
	(24)	33.7	% Profit Before Taxes/Tangible Net Worth						
		6.8							
		38.7							
		8.1	% Profit Before Taxes/Total Assets						
		−2.3							
		56.3							
		26.4	Sales/Net Fixed Assets						
		8.1							
		9.3							
		4.5	Sales/Total Assets						
		2.1							
		1.0							
	(22)	1.5	% Depr., Dep., Amort./Sales						
		5.0							
		7.4							
	(11)	18.3	% Officers', Directors', Owners' Comp/Sales						
		29.5							
		433713M	Net Sales ($)	3068M	13741M	31739M	31502M	46406M	307257M
		146279M	Total Assets ($)	1800M	7414M	10003M	7583M	15134M	104345M

M = $ thousand   MM = $ million
See Pages 11 through 18 for Explanation of Ratios and Data

Current Data Sorted By Assets

Comparative Historical Data

						Type of Statement	4/1/98-3/31/99 ALL	4/1/99-3/31/00 ALL
1	2	10	1			Unqualified		
	1					Reviewed		
1		3				Compiled		
3	2	1				Tax Returns		
1	4	3	1			Other		
	15 (4/1-9/30/02)			**19 (10/1/02-3/31/03)**				
0-500M	500M-2MM	2-10MM	10-50MM	50-100MM	100-250MM	NUMBER OF STATEMENTS		
6	9	17	2					
%	%	%	%	%	%	ASSETS	%	%
		16.4				Cash & Equivalents		
		29.8		D	D	Trade Receivables (net)	D	D
		1.6		A	A	Inventory	A	A
		3.1		T	T	All Other Current	T	T
		50.9		A	A	Total Current	A	A
		41.3				Fixed Assets (net)		
		.8		N	N	Intangibles (net)	N	N
		7.0		O	O	All Other Non-Current	O	O
		100.0		T	T	Total	T	T
						LIABILITIES		
		9.9		A	A	Notes Payable-Short Term	A	A
		4.4		V	V	Cur. Mat.-L/T/D	V	V
		16.4		A	A	Trade Payables	A	A
		.0		I	I	Income Taxes Payable	I	I
		19.6		L	L	All Other Current	L	L
		50.4		A	A	Total Current	A	A
		28.4		B	B	Long Term Debt	B	B
		.0		L	L	Deferred Taxes	L	L
		3.7		E	E	All Other Non-Current	E	E
		17.5				Net Worth		
		100.0				Total Liabilities & Net Worth		
						INCOME DATA		
		100.0				Net Sales		
						Gross Profit		
		91.1				Operating Expenses		
		8.9				Operating Profit		
		.3				All Other Expenses (net)		
		8.6				Profit Before Taxes		
						RATIOS		
		3.3						
		1.5				Current		
		1.1						
		2.8						
		1.5				Quick		
		.9						
		15 24.0						
		42 8.7				Sales/Receivables		
		61 6.0						
						Cost of Sales/Inventory		
						Cost of Sales/Payables		
		5.7						
		12.8				Sales/Working Capital		
		121.6						
		16.1						
		(13) 2.1				EBIT/Interest		
		.3						
						Net Profit + Depr., Dep., Amort./Cur. Mat. L /T/D		
		.6						
		1.2				Fixed/Worth		
		22.4						
		.8						
		1.6				Debt/Worth		
		35.0						
		26.7				% Profit Before Taxes/Tangible		
		(14) 4.7				Net Worth		
		-1.1						
		16.9				% Profit Before Taxes/Total		
		2.2				Assets		
		-.8						
		14.7						
		5.2				Sales/Net Fixed Assets		
		3.0						
		3.8						
		2.0				Sales/Total Assets		
		1.7						
		1.1						
		(16) 2.2				% Depr., Dep., Amort./Sales		
		3.9						
						% Officers', Directors', Owners' Comp/Sales		
14753M	34315M	356280M	63170M			Net Sales ($)		
1413M	10935M	68192M	39566M			Total Assets ($)		

M = $ thousand   MM = $ million
See Pages 11 through 18 for Explanation of Ratios and Data

Comparative Historical Data | Current Data Sorted By Sales

			Type of Statement						
		14	Unqualified		5	1	5	1	2
		1	Reviewed					1	
		4	Compiled		1		2	1	
		6	Tax Returns		3	1	1	1	
		9	Other	2	1	1	2		1
4/1/00- 3/31/01 ALL	4/1/01- 3/31/02 ALL	4/1/02- 3/31/03 ALL			15 (4/1-9/30/02)		19 (10/1/02-3/31/03)		
				0-1MM	1-3MM	3-5MM	5-10MM	10-25MM	25MM & OVER
		34	**NUMBER OF STATEMENTS**	2	10	3	10	6	3
%	%	%	**ASSETS**	%	%	%	%	%	%
D	D	13.0	Cash & Equivalents		10.1		9.5		
A	A	24.8	Trade Receivables (net)		25.9		19.8		
T	T	1.2	Inventory		.8		.1		
A	A	4.3	All Other Current		4.5		4.3		
		43.4	Total Current		41.3		33.7		
N	N	45.3	Fixed Assets (net)		49.5		51.1		
O	O	2.4	Intangibles (net)		.8		6.1		
T	T	8.8	All Other Non-Current		8.4		9.1		
		100.0	Total		100.0		100.0		
A	A		**LIABILITIES**						
V	V	11.7	Notes Payable-Short Term		13.7		5.9		
A	A	5.3	Cur. Mat.-L/T/D		5.5		5.1		
I	I	9.8	Trade Payables		4.7		6.2		
L	L	.0	Income Taxes Payable		.0		.0		
A	A	15.5	All Other Current		4.9		20.7		
B	B	42.4	Total Current		28.8		37.9		
L	L	26.2	Long Term Debt		33.3		28.6		
E	E	.0	Deferred Taxes		.0		.0		
		2.2	All Other Non-Current		1.1		.2		
		29.2	Net Worth		36.8		33.3		
		100.0	Total Liabilities & Net Worth		100.0		100.0		
			INCOME DATA						
		100.0	Net Sales		100.0		100.0		
			Gross Profit						
		93.4	Operating Expenses		93.8		93.2		
		6.6	Operating Profit		6.2		6.8		
		.5	All Other Expenses (net)		.8		−.8		
		6.1	Profit Before Taxes		5.3		7.7		
			RATIOS						
		2.9			5.7		1.8		
		1.5	Current		2.5		1.2		
		.9			.2		.7		
		2.7			5.4		1.6		
		1.3	Quick		2.2		1.1		
		.5			.2		.2		
	5	75.8		0 UND		0 UND			
	30	12.3	Sales/Receivables	49 7.4		21 17.4			
	61	6.0		67 5.4		49 7.5			
			Cost of Sales/Inventory						
			Cost of Sales/Payables						
		6.0			4.5		11.2		
		24.4	Sales/Working Capital		8.0		71.0		
		−122.4			−12.8		−119.1		
		16.1							
	(25)	3.2	EBIT/Interest						
		.9							
			Net Profit + Depr., Dep., Amort./Cur. Mat. L/T/D						
		.5			.3		.6		
		1.1	Fixed/Worth		1.1		1.1		
		NM			NM		NM		
		.5			.4		.8		
		1.5	Debt/Worth		1.1		1.8		
		NM			NM		NM		
		31.6	% Profit Before Taxes/Tangible Net Worth						
	(26)	8.3							
		−1.1							
		25.5	% Profit Before Taxes/Total Assets		37.3		33.9		
		5.8			5.6		1.6		
		−.7			−5.2		−1.5		
		29.0			43.6		19.2		
		6.0	Sales/Net Fixed Assets		4.7		6.0		
		2.9			2.3		3.1		
		4.0			4.0		5.6		
		2.8	Sales/Total Assets		2.5		2.4		
		1.6			1.3		1.8		
		1.1					1.3		
	(30)	2.2	% Depr., Dep., Amort./Sales				2.4		
		4.0					3.4		
		9.2	% Officers', Directors', Owners' Comp/Sales						
	(10)	12.5							
		29.3							
		468518M	Net Sales ($)	977M	20589M	10966M	72214M	77011M	286761M
		120106M	Total Assets ($)	1610M	13514M	4712M	27349M	43575M	29346M

M = $ thousand   MM = $ million
See Pages 11 through 18 for Explanation of Ratios and Data

Current Data Sorted By Assets   **Comparative Historical Data**

						Type of Statement		
		2				Unqualified	5	5
2	3	2				Reviewed	2	2
1						Compiled	3	3
						Tax Returns	4	4
2	6	10	4			Other	5	13
	0 (4/1-9/30/02)		32 (10/1/02-3/31/03)				4/1/98-3/31/99	4/1/99-3/31/00
0-500M	500M-2MM	2-10MM	10-50MM	50-100MM	100-250MM		ALL	ALL
5	9	14	4			NUMBER OF STATEMENTS	19	27
%	%	%	%	%	%	**ASSETS**	%	%
		6.0		D	D	Cash & Equivalents	16.1	8.4
		33.4		A	A	Trade Receivables (net)	16.3	24.9
		3.4		T	T	Inventory	1.6	3.4
		1.2		A	A	All Other Current	4.2	2.8
		44.0				Total Current	38.2	39.5
		44.5		N	N	Fixed Assets (net)	46.2	41.9
		7.5		O	O	Intangibles (net)	7.2	10.6
		4.0		T	T	All Other Non-Current	8.4	8.0
		100.0				Total	100.0	100.0
				A	A	**LIABILITIES**		
		16.2		V	V	Notes Payable-Short Term	18.0	4.3
		3.8		A	A	Cur. Mat.-L/T/D	8.4	6.2
		6.8		I	I	Trade Payables	6.9	14.4
		.0		L	L	Income Taxes Payable	.0	.5
		21.3		A	A	All Other Current	21.9	19.0
		48.1		B	B	Total Current	55.2	44.4
		17.3		L	L	Long Term Debt	20.0	33.4
		.0		E	E	Deferred Taxes	.0	.1
		.7				All Other Non-Current	1.4	5.4
		33.9				Net Worth	23.3	16.7
		100.0				Total Liabilities & Net Worth	100.0	100.0
						INCOME DATA		
		100.0				Net Sales	100.0	100.0
						Gross Profit		
		85.2				Operating Expenses	111.4	91.5
		14.8				Operating Profit	−11.4	8.5
		3.6				All Other Expenses (net)	3.7	6.3
		11.2				Profit Before Taxes	−15.2	2.2
						RATIOS		
		2.7					2.2	2.3
		1.4				Current	.6	1.3
		.6					.5	.4
		2.4					2.0	1.6
		1.2				Quick	.6	1.2
		.6					.4	.4
	52	7.1					0 UND	35 10.4
	60	6.1				Sales/Receivables	44 8.3	62 5.9
	76	4.8					86 4.2	83 4.4
						Cost of Sales/Inventory		
						Cost of Sales/Payables		
		6.9					4.2	5.4
		16.2				Sales/Working Capital	−45.8	15.5
		−7.2					−3.0	−8.1
		50.4					7.3	17.0
	(13)	10.0				EBIT/Interest	(13) 3.7	(24) 2.8
		3.9					.4	.5
						Net Profit + Depr., Dep., Amort./Cur. Mat. L /T/D		
		.6					.8	.7
		1.2				Fixed/Worth	3.6	1.7
		5.3					−3.3	−1.0
		.9					.7	1.3
		1.7				Debt/Worth	6.2	3.9
		8.1					−6.7	−2.9
		147.4					76.6	130.4
	(12)	89.9				% Profit Before Taxes/Tangible Net Worth	(13) 56.4	(17) 32.1
		51.3					8.2	4.0
		53.9					23.0	21.6
		19.8				% Profit Before Taxes/Total Assets	7.0	4.3
		5.6					−1.3	.0
		11.2					24.4	8.4
		4.7				Sales/Net Fixed Assets	3.6	5.2
		2.0					1.9	3.2
		2.6					4.9	2.5
		1.8				Sales/Total Assets	1.2	1.5
		1.4					1.0	1.0
		1.7					2.3	2.1
	(13)	3.0				% Depr., Dep., Amort./Sales	(16) 2.8	(24) 4.2
		4.7					5.6	7.5
						% Officers', Directors', Owners' Comp/Sales		
13923M	33603M	136180M	114989M			Net Sales ($)	332325M	720595M
945M	11055M	68401M	61189M			Total Assets ($)	342825M	712820M

M = $ thousand   MM = $ million
See Pages 11 through 18 for Explanation of Ratios and Data

Comparative Historical Data | Current Data Sorted By Sales

			Type of Statement						
1	2	2	Unqualified			2			
2			Reviewed						
2	4	7	Compiled	1	1	3	1	1	
4		1	Tax Returns			1			
16	16	22	Other	1	3	5	6	6	1
4/1/00-3/31/01 ALL	4/1/01-3/31/02 ALL	4/1/02-3/31/03 ALL		0-1MM	0 (4/1-9/30/02) 1-3MM	3-5MM	32 (10/1/02-3/31/03) 5-10MM	10-25MM	25MM & OVER
25	22	32	NUMBER OF STATEMENTS	2	4	11	7	7	1
%	%	%	ASSETS	%	%	%	%	%	%
12.4	14.2	15.5	Cash & Equivalents			12.4			
25.3	25.6	27.1	Trade Receivables (net)			33.2			
2.4	5.7	2.4	Inventory			1.9			
1.5	1.8	2.3	All Other Current			1.7			
41.5	47.4	47.3	Total Current			49.2			
39.3	33.5	40.6	Fixed Assets (net)			38.2			
12.0	10.8	6.3	Intangibles (net)			3.4			
7.1	8.3	5.8	All Other Non-Current			9.2			
100.0	100.0	100.0	Total			100.0			
			LIABILITIES						
6.2	6.1	13.3	Notes Payable-Short Term			10.0			
5.3	33.2	3.6	Cur. Mat.-L/T/D			3.7			
23.3	5.1	6.4	Trade Payables			3.4			
.0	.1	.5	Income Taxes Payable			1.5			
8.1	14.7	17.2	All Other Current			26.3			
42.9	59.2	41.0	Total Current			44.9			
31.0	21.8	19.3	Long Term Debt			27.3			
.0	.0	.0	Deferred Taxes			.0			
7.5	9.0	2.3	All Other Non-Current			2.2			
18.6	10.0	37.4	Net Worth			25.6			
100.0	100.0	100.0	Total Liabilities & Net Worth			100.0			
			INCOME DATA						
100.0	100.0	100.0	Net Sales			100.0			
			Gross Profit						
90.7	85.4	88.2	Operating Expenses			87.5			
9.3	14.6	11.8	Operating Profit			12.5			
4.7	4.7	1.4	All Other Expenses (net)			1.5			
4.6	9.9	10.4	Profit Before Taxes			11.0			
			RATIOS						
2.3	3.9	3.4				3.7			
1.2	2.6	1.9	Current			1.7			
.5	.4	1.0				.6			
2.1	3.8	3.1				3.4			
.7	1.9	1.8	Quick			1.7			
.5	.4	.8				.5			
3 116.9	0 UND	0 UND				0 UND			
49 7.4	63 5.8	54 6.8	Sales/Receivables			67 5.5			
72 5.1	78 4.7	67 5.5				79 4.6			
			Cost of Sales/Inventory						
			Cost of Sales/Payables						
8.9	4.0	6.5				5.9			
15.2	5.7	14.9	Sales/Working Capital			68.0			
−8.5	−13.3	NM				−8.9			
11.4	71.0	42.0				42.0			
(20) 1.4	(18) 5.8	(27) 10.0	EBIT/Interest			10.0			
−.2	3.2	4.0				3.9			
			Net Profit + Depr., Dep., Amort./Cur. Mat. L/T/D						
.7	.3	.4				.4			
1.3	.8	.9	Fixed/Worth			.7			
−.9	9.8	6.3				−2.4			
1.1	.4	.4				.3			
4.3	1.7	1.2	Debt/Worth			1.1			
−3.3	NM	8.4				−8.8			
116.6	81.4	128.5							
(15) 56.9	(17) 37.4	(26) 59.8	% Profit Before Taxes/Tangible Net Worth						
10.5	16.7	38.0							
42.3	34.5	43.9				45.3			
3.1	14.4	21.7	% Profit Before Taxes/Total Assets			23.3			
−8.2	2.4	6.3				14.7			
13.4	15.3	19.1				18.2			
5.5	5.0	7.9	Sales/Net Fixed Assets			8.6			
2.4	2.9	3.5				6.8			
3.4	3.2	3.8				6.3			
1.8	1.7	2.5	Sales/Total Assets			2.7			
1.1	1.0	1.6				1.9			
2.1	1.4	1.4				1.7			
(20) 4.3	(17) 3.4	(30) 2.1	% Depr., Dep., Amort./Sales			2.1			
6.0	5.2	4.4				4.6			
		5.3							
	(10)	7.9	% Officers', Directors', Owners' Comp/Sales						
		46.7							
314771M	155230M	298695M	Net Sales ($)	1406M	9166M	42909M	52385M	131295M	61534M
363631M	111044M	141590M	Total Assets ($)	2117M	2504M	16639M	29882M	75064M	15384M

M = $ thousand   MM = $ million
See Pages 11 through 18 for Explanation of Ratios and Data

Current Data Sorted By Assets   **Comparative Historical Data**

0-500M	500M-2MM	2-10MM	10-50MM	50-100MM	100-250MM	Type of Statement	4/1/98-3/31/99 ALL	4/1/99-3/31/00 ALL
		1	5		2	Unqualified		
2	2		1			Reviewed		
24	12	3	1			Compiled		
22	4	4	1			Tax Returns		
8	11	5	4			Other		
	21 (4/1-9/30/02)		90 (10/1/02-3/31/03)					
56	29	13	11		2	NUMBER OF STATEMENTS		
%	%	%	%	%	%	**ASSETS**	%	%
28.8	20.6	14.8	20.1	D		Cash & Equivalents	D	D
2.9	18.2	25.6	17.6	A		Trade Receivables (net)	A	A
.1	1.8	1.4	1.6	T		Inventory	T	T
3.7	.2	3.3	8.6	A		All Other Current	A	A
35.4	40.8	45.2	47.9			Total Current		
45.6	48.8	46.5	43.8	N		Fixed Assets (net)	N	N
6.8	5.0	2.4	.1	O		Intangibles (net)	O	O
12.1	5.4	5.9	8.2	T		All Other Non-Current	T	T
100.0	100.0	100.0	100.0			Total		
				A		**LIABILITIES**	A	A
34.7	12.9	4.9	2.4	V		Notes Payable-Short Term	V	V
10.0	5.9	3.6	6.8	A		Cur. Mat.-L/T/D	A	A
1.2	6.0	4.1	5.8	I		Trade Payables	I	I
.2	1.2	.0	.7	L		Income Taxes Payable	L	L
48.7	20.2	22.8	25.8	A		All Other Current	A	A
94.9	46.3	35.4	41.5	B		Total Current	B	B
36.8	27.0	29.6	16.5	L		Long Term Debt	L	L
.0	.0	.0	.8	E		Deferred Taxes	E	E
18.4	3.5	4.3	2.6			All Other Non-Current		
-50.1	23.2	30.7	38.7			Net Worth		
100.0	100.0	100.0	100.0			Total Liabilities & Net Worth		
						INCOME DATA		
100.0	100.0	100.0	100.0			Net Sales		
						Gross Profit		
97.6	90.1	89.0	95.5			Operating Expenses		
2.4	9.9	11.0	4.5			Operating Profit		
-.3	1.7	1.2	.8			All Other Expenses (net)		
2.7	8.2	9.8	3.8			Profit Before Taxes		
						RATIOS		
.8	1.4	3.4	1.6			Current		
.3	.8	1.6	1.4					
.1	.5	.7	.9					
.8	1.3	3.2	1.4			Quick		
.3	.8	1.3	1.2					
.1	.4	.5	.7					
0 UND	0 UND	1 257.9	0 UND			Sales/Receivables		
0 UND	0 999.8	34 10.8	40 9.1					
0 UND	61 6.0	42 8.6	75 4.9					
						Cost of Sales/Inventory		
						Cost of Sales/Payables		
-94.7	51.6	6.4	7.7			Sales/Working Capital		
-32.3	-128.6	19.0	18.4					
-12.3	-13.2	-89.4	-18.6					
(42) 10.8	(25) 15.7	105.5				EBIT/Interest		
3.2	4.4	3.4						
-1.0	1.0	1.7						
						Net Profit + Depr., Dep., Amort./Cur. Mat. L./T/D		
4.0	.9	.7	.4			Fixed/Worth		
-5.0	3.1	2.0	1.2					
-.6	-5.3	14.7	2.4					
5.8	1.3	.5	.8			Debt/Worth		
-11.4	3.8	1.8	1.7					
-2.1	-9.6	34.7	3.5					
(23) 400.0	(20) 88.5	(11) 204.5	22.7			% Profit Before Taxes/Tangible Net Worth		
170.3	49.1	56.5	8.0					
31.0	1.3	13.6	-1.8					
43.0	25.3	49.4	11.1			% Profit Before Taxes/Total Assets		
7.7	6.4	6.3	4.7					
-7.8	.1	1.9	-.5					
75.6	31.6	13.1	7.2			Sales/Net Fixed Assets		
36.8	12.8	7.6	3.0					
11.8	6.3	4.2	1.7					
27.3	10.0	5.3	2.7			Sales/Total Assets		
11.9	5.0	3.8	1.4					
5.9	1.9	2.3	1.2					
(38) .8	(19) .9	(12) 2.1	(10) 1.7			% Depr., Dep., Amort./Sales		
1.1	1.8	3.1	3.0					
2.8	5.8	6.6	9.0					
(43) 13.7	(20) .9					% Officers', Directors', Owners' Comp/Sales		
27.9	5.3							
40.5	28.2							
142601M	198785M	182468M	479533M		192386M	Net Sales ($)		
11194M	34779M	52085M	244357M		208624M	Total Assets ($)		

Comparative Historical Data / **Current Data Sorted By Sales**

			Type of Statement	0-1MM	1-3MM	3-5MM	5-10MM	10-25MM	25MM & OVER
		8	Unqualified					1	7
		5	Reviewed	1	1	1		1	1
		39	Compiled	8	17	6	4	4	
		31	Tax Returns	5	12	2	6	5	1
		28	Other	4	3	6	5	7	3
4/1/00-3/31/01 ALL	4/1/01-3/31/02 ALL	4/1/02-3/31/03 ALL		21 (4/1-9/30/02)			90 (10/1/02-3/31/03)		
		111	**NUMBER OF STATEMENTS**	18	33	15	15	18	12
%	%	%	**ASSETS**	%	%	%	%	%	%
D	D	24.1	Cash & Equivalents	19.5	33.9	17.9	13.9	26.5	20.6
A	A	11.1	Trade Receivables (net)	8.8	5.7	16.8	8.6	12.1	23.8
T	T	.9	Inventory	.3	.0	2.3	.5	2.3	.7
A	A	3.2	All Other Current	.9	2.4	4.6	5.4	4.0	2.9
		39.2	Total Current	29.4	41.9	41.7	28.4	44.9	48.1
N	N	46.2	Fixed Assets (net)	46.4	44.4	41.5	58.4	48.1	38.8
O	O	5.0	Intangibles (net)	12.2	4.4	10.5	2.2	.3	.1
T	T	9.5	All Other Non-Current	12.1	9.3	6.3	11.0	6.7	13.0
		100.0	Total	100.0	100.0	100.0	100.0	100.0	100.0
A	A		**LIABILITIES**						
V	V	21.7	Notes Payable-Short Term	45.0	25.8	23.3	8.3	13.3	2.8
A	A	7.7	Cur. Mat.-L/T/D	6.7	13.9	2.4	5.0	5.0	6.2
I	I	3.3	Trade Payables	.3	2.3	4.8	1.7	6.4	6.1
L	L	.5	Income Taxes Payable	.3	.4	2.0	.0	.0	.6
A	A	35.2	All Other Current	19.4	51.4	28.9	42.2	21.5	34.3
B	B	68.5	Total Current	71.7	93.8	61.4	57.2	46.2	50.1
L	L	31.1	Long Term Debt	29.3	39.9	13.7	51.9	21.3	20.3
E	E	.1	Deferred Taxes	.0	.0	.0	.0	.0	.7
		11.0	All Other Non-Current	12.2	23.8	4.7	1.2	3.6	5.3
		−10.6	Net Worth	−13.2	−57.4	20.2	−10.3	28.9	23.5
		100.0	Total Liabilities & Net Worth	100.0	100.0	100.0	100.0	100.0	100.0
			INCOME DATA						
		100.0	Net Sales	100.0	100.0	100.0	100.0	100.0	100.0
			Gross Profit						
		94.4	Operating Expenses	87.5	96.4	94.9	96.1	94.4	96.5
		5.6	Operating Profit	12.5	3.6	5.1	3.9	5.6	3.5
		.5	All Other Expenses (net)	3.1	−.5	.2	.4	.0	.8
		5.1	Profit Before Taxes	9.4	4.1	4.9	3.5	5.6	2.6
			RATIOS						
		1.5		2.4	.9	1.2	1.6	2.1	1.5
		.7	Current	.3	.6	.7	.6	1.1	1.2
		.3		.1	.3	.3	.1	.6	.8
		1.3		2.4	.9	1.0	1.1	2.0	1.3
		.6	Quick	.3	.5	.5	.5	.8	1.1
		.2		.1	.3	.0	.1	.5	.7
	0	UND		0 UND	0 UND	0 UND	0 UND	0 UND	26 14.1
	0	UND	Sales/Receivables	0 UND	0 UND	0 926.6	0 UND	0 UND	39 9.4
	26	13.9		13 27.5	0 UND	61 5.9	18 20.3	12 30.7	47 7.8
			Cost of Sales/Inventory						
			Cost of Sales/Payables						
		46.3		105.0	−613.5	22.9	19.0	12.0	14.3
		−52.4	Sales/Working Capital	−23.5	−32.4	−83.3	−58.2	293.5	33.5
		−17.9		−6.1	−11.5	−10.9	−30.6	−46.2	−15.2
		10.8		(15) 9.7	(25) 12.7	(11) 12.0	(13) 10.8	(17) 75.9	(10) 4.1
	(91)	3.3	EBIT/Interest	5.8	2.6	4.4	3.8	3.5	3.1
		1.0		−.9	−2.9	1.0	2.1	1.0	1.1
		5.6	Net Profit + Depr., Dep.,						
	(11)	1.5	Amort./Cur. Mat. L/T/D						
		.1							
		1.2		1.3	4.2	1.1	1.8	.6	.6
		5.8	Fixed/Worth	9.2	−3.2	6.7	2.8	1.3	1.2
		−1.3		−.8	−.5	−3.8	−4.2	NM	11.4
		1.8		2.7	5.4	1.8	1.8	.5	.7
		8.9	Debt/Worth	28.5	−8.3	8.9	3.7	1.6	2.6
		−5.6		−2.0	−2.6	−6.6	−6.6	NM	17.1
		203.0	% Profit Before Taxes/Tangible	(10) 439.0	(13) 538.1		(11) 204.5	(14) 81.5	(11) 69.6
	(67)	50.9	Net Worth	87.5	203.0		59.9	26.1	5.0
		6.6		12.5	24.8		13.6	1.4	3.5
		33.9	% Profit Before Taxes/Total	45.5	43.0	20.5	38.0	23.0	9.7
		6.1	Assets	11.1	10.1	6.4	6.1	4.8	2.3
		.0		−10.6	−13.0	.0	4.5	.1	−.1
		59.5		68.3	92.3	67.9	57.7	31.5	39.8
		15.9	Sales/Net Fixed Assets	10.9	27.5	25.9	16.7	16.3	3.9
		6.1		3.5	10.2	10.9	4.9	8.9	2.0
		14.8		15.4	21.8	17.5	20.5	13.7	4.0
		5.9	Sales/Total Assets	3.6	8.3	6.4	9.5	7.6	1.7
		2.6		1.6	4.7	2.7	2.6	4.9	1.1
		.9		(13) 1.0	(21) .9	(10) .7	(13) .8	(13) .8	(11) 1.1
	(81)	1.9	% Depr., Dep., Amort./Sales	5.6	1.3	1.7	1.6	2.2	3.6
		5.0		10.2	5.2	4.0	4.8	3.0	8.5
		4.8		(10) 7.3	(25) 14.8	(12) 3.8		(11) .8	
	(67)	22.7	% Officers', Directors',	13.1	30.9	18.2		6.1	
		39.3	Owners' Comp/Sales	23.9	40.5	41.5		39.2	
		1195773M	Net Sales ($)	10550M	57995M	55344M	110996M	268607M	692281M
		551039M	Total Assets ($)	6416M	10984M	15967M	28985M	61278M	427409M

© RMA 2003
M = $ thousand   MM = $ million
See Pages 11 through 18 for Explanation of Ratios and Data

Current Data Sorted By Assets   Comparative Historical Data

							Type of Statement		
2	10	58	18	6	6		Unqualified	92	98
3	6	7			1		Reviewed	8	12
11	13	7	2				Compiled	21	26
11	2	1			1		Tax Returns	10	10
8	19	23	9	3	2		Other	41	33
	95 (4/1-9/30/02)			134 (10/1/02-3/31/03)				4/1/98-3/31/99	4/1/99-3/31/00
0-500M	500M-2MM	2-10MM	10-50MM	50-100MM	100-250MM			ALL	ALL
35	50	96	29	9	10		NUMBER OF STATEMENTS	172	179
%	%	%	%	%	%		**ASSETS**	%	%
23.3	14.5	17.3	15.2		12.2		Cash & Equivalents	14.2	16.0
9.5	27.0	23.7	20.2		14.9		Trade Receivables (net)	21.6	24.5
2.5	1.2	1.1	1.2		.3		Inventory	1.4	1.1
12.2	6.1	2.7	2.9		3.2		All Other Current	3.2	2.6
47.4	48.8	44.8	39.5		30.5		Total Current	40.3	44.2
39.2	41.8	46.7	40.6		20.9		Fixed Assets (net)	45.7	41.8
3.8	2.6	1.3	7.2		23.1		Intangibles (net)	5.3	5.5
9.6	6.9	7.2	12.7		25.5		All Other Non-Current	8.6	8.4
100.0	100.0	100.0	100.0		100.0		Total	100.0	100.0
							LIABILITIES		
18.3	10.0	2.5	2.9		12.0		Notes Payable-Short Term	8.9	7.4
30.3	6.3	3.3	4.1		2.5		Cur. Mat.-L/T/D	3.7	4.0
8.7	8.2	7.0	5.5		4.0		Trade Payables	7.2	7.1
.7	.0	.2	.1		1.0		Income Taxes Payable	.1	.1
29.2	18.6	10.9	12.5		7.9		All Other Current	13.6	13.6
87.3	43.0	23.9	25.0		27.4		Total Current	33.4	32.2
48.0	29.3	27.1	23.1		27.6		Long Term Debt	27.4	19.5
.0	.6	.0	.1		.8		Deferred Taxes	.2	.2
2.1	1.9	1.9	4.8		15.3		All Other Non-Current	15.3	3.0
−37.4	25.2	47.1	47.0		28.9		Net Worth	23.6	45.0
100.0	100.0	100.0	100.0		100.0		Total Liabilities & Net Worth	100.0	100.0
							INCOME DATA		
100.0	100.0	100.0	100.0		100.0		Net Sales	100.0	100.0
							Gross Profit		
93.8	91.4	91.5	92.1		93.7		Operating Expenses	93.5	95.1
6.2	8.6	8.5	7.9		6.3		Operating Profit	6.5	4.9
.7	2.0	.8	.2		1.2		All Other Expenses (net)	1.2	−1.1
5.4	6.6	7.7	7.7		5.1		Profit Before Taxes	5.3	5.9
							RATIOS		
1.1	2.0	3.0	2.9		2.4			2.8	2.8
.7	1.1	2.0	1.8		2.2		Current	1.6	1.6
.3	.7	1.2	1.1		1.1			.9	1.0
.9	1.9	2.7	2.3		2.3			2.6	2.5
.5	1.0	1.9	1.4		1.7		Quick	(171) 1.5	1.5
.0	.4	1.1	.9		.8			.8	.8
0 UND	0 UND	27 13.6	34 10.7		0 UND			21 17.5	23 15.8
0 UND	32 11.3	46 7.9	45 8.1		60 6.1		Sales/Receivables	44 8.4	45 8.1
4 88.6	60 6.1	63 5.8	67 5.4		68 5.4			66 5.5	72 5.1
							Cost of Sales/Inventory		
							Cost of Sales/Payables		
312.8	8.4	4.7	5.2		4.0			5.6	5.3
−52.7	78.6	8.8	10.2		9.3		Sales/Working Capital	13.1	12.0
−11.7	−21.4	31.8	126.1		NM			−53.9	−116.6
23.5	20.9	10.0	16.7					8.1	10.3
(28) 2.4	(37) 3.0	(70) 2.8	(28) 4.6				EBIT/Interest	(132) 2.3	(140) 3.4
−2.3	−3.8	.8	1.2					1.1	.7
							Net Profit + Depr., Dep., Amort./Cur. Mat. L /T/D		
.7	.6	.6	.6		.5			.6	.6
32.0	1.5	1.0	1.0		UND		Fixed/Worth	1.3	1.0
−.8	−6.6	2.0	2.8		−.6			9.2	2.5
2.4	.8	.5	.5		1.0			.6	.5
−31.6	2.4	1.0	.9		UND		Debt/Worth	1.5	1.1
−2.7	−13.2	2.1	4.6		−2.6			13.2	4.3
524.5	99.1	39.8	31.6				% Profit Before Taxes/Tangible Net Worth	41.0	37.4
(17) 70.7	(34) 22.0	(87) 13.0	(27) 10.9					(144) 12.2	(155) 12.3
15.8	−.3	2.4	.5					1.9	.2
50.0	42.8	17.5	13.3		8.2		% Profit Before Taxes/Total Assets	15.2	16.6
10.5	8.6	5.9	5.7		2.7			3.4	5.1
−7.4	−7.6	.5	.4		.0			.2	−.7
65.4	22.9	7.4	6.0		29.7		Sales/Net Fixed Assets	11.0	13.4
32.4	8.9	4.0	3.0		10.3			3.9	4.7
9.2	2.2	1.9	2.0		2.3			1.8	2.3
14.7	4.7	2.4	2.1		1.6		Sales/Total Assets	3.0	2.7
8.3	2.8	1.8	1.4		1.0			1.6	1.9
3.3	1.5	1.1	.8		.7			1.0	1.2
.8	1.1	1.8	2.1				% Depr., Dep., Amort./Sales	1.7	1.6
(25) 1.8	(46) 2.7	(92) 2.6	(27) 3.0					(149) 2.8	(162) 2.7
3.5	5.2	4.6	5.8					6.3	4.4
8.3	3.1						% Officers', Directors', Owners' Comp/Sales	5.2	7.3
(15) 18.4	(14) 8.4							(28) 15.3	(22) 15.8
37.6	26.6							33.2	33.8
58101M	232511M	843139M	998059M	859332M	3562480M		Net Sales ($)	2339328M	2299454M
7474M	58585M	480733M	680360M	598161M	1664723M		Total Assets ($)	1716339M	1741805M

M = $ thousand   MM = $ million
See Pages 11 through 18 for Explanation of Ratios and Data

	Comparative Historical Data			Type of Statement	Current Data Sorted By Sales					
	80	87	100	Unqualified	2	9	8	31	31	19
	10	14	17	Reviewed	3	2	3	7	1	1
	22	45	33	Compiled	7	12	3	7	2	2
	9	17	15	Tax Returns	2	5	6	1	1	1
	44	59	64	Other	5	13	11	16	8	11
	4/1/00- 3/31/01	4/1/01- 3/31/02	4/1/02- 3/31/03		95 (4/1-9/30/02)			134 (10/1/02-3/31/03)		
	ALL	ALL	ALL		0-1MM	1-3MM	3-5MM	5-10MM	10-25MM	25MM & OVER
	165	222	229	NUMBER OF STATEMENTS	19	41	31	61	43	34
	%	%	%	ASSETS	%	%	%	%	%	%
	16.6	17.7	17.1	Cash & Equivalents	11.7	24.0	15.5	15.2	16.8	17.1
	20.9	21.2	21.0	Trade Receivables (net)	7.6	18.0	17.0	29.5	22.7	18.2
	1.1	.7	1.3	Inventory	3.3	.7	1.9	1.6	.4	1.0
	3.5	5.2	5.0	All Other Current	11.9	8.1	7.3	1.7	2.9	3.6
	42.2	44.8	44.3	Total Current	34.5	50.8	41.7	48.0	42.7	39.9
	44.6	41.8	42.6	Fixed Assets (net)	55.0	41.0	44.6	42.0	45.0	34.1
	4.1	5.0	3.9	Intangibles (net)	1.2	2.4	3.9	1.7	3.9	11.4
	9.1	8.5	9.1	All Other Non-Current	9.3	5.8	9.8	8.3	8.4	14.7
	100.0	100.0	100.0	Total	100.0	100.0	100.0	100.0	100.0	100.0
				LIABILITIES						
	5.3	6.4	7.1	Notes Payable-Short Term	14.8	10.7	8.9	3.6	3.8	7.4
	5.2	3.8	8.1	Cur. Mat.-L/T/D	12.4	14.8	18.2	3.1	2.9	3.7
	7.7	7.5	7.2	Trade Payables	6.9	6.8	6.5	7.4	8.8	6.0
	.6	.1	.3	Income Taxes Payable	.0	.6	.0	.2	.2	.3
	12.8	11.5	15.5	All Other Current	31.1	13.3	17.3	11.2	14.9	16.2
	31.7	29.4	38.1	Total Current	65.2	46.1	51.0	25.5	30.6	33.5
	31.1	25.4	30.4	Long Term Debt	56.9	40.4	33.0	24.2	20.8	24.3
	.3	.1	.2	Deferred Taxes	.0	.0	.0	.5	.1	.4
	4.0	3.0	2.9	All Other Non-Current	3.8	1.0	1.2	3.1	2.2	6.8
	33.0	42.2	28.4	Net Worth	−25.9	12.5	14.8	46.7	46.3	35.0
	100.0	100.0	100.0	Total Liabilities & Net Worth	100.0	100.0	100.0	100.0	100.0	100.0
				INCOME DATA						
	100.0	100.0	100.0	Net Sales	100.0	100.0	100.0	100.0	100.0	100.0
				Gross Profit						
	92.4	90.6	91.9	Operating Expenses	97.1	91.6	87.1	90.8	94.4	92.7
	7.6	9.4	8.1	Operating Profit	2.9	8.4	12.8	9.2	5.6	7.3
	.9	2.6	1.0	All Other Expenses (net)	5.0	2.2	1.2	−.1	−.1	.7
	6.7	6.8	7.1	Profit Before Taxes	−2.2	6.2	11.7	9.4	5.7	6.6
				RATIOS						
	2.8	3.5	2.7		1.5	3.9	2.8	3.0	2.4	2.4
	1.6	1.8	1.6	Current	.7	1.3	1.2	2.0	1.6	1.4
	1.0	1.0	.8		.3	.7	.5	1.2	1.1	1.0
	2.5	3.0	2.4		.6	3.2	2.3	2.6	2.1	2.2
	1.4	1.6	1.4	Quick	.4	1.3	.8	1.8	1.4	1.4
	.8	.9	.7		.0	.6	.3	1.1	1.0	.8
15	24.3	5	76.4	10	38.2	Sales/Receivables	0 UND	0 UND	0 UND	27 13.4	24 15.3	30 12.1
41	8.8	40	9.2	39	9.4		2 184.0	28 13.0	18 20.5	51 7.2	41 8.8	48 7.5
63	5.8	63	5.8	59	6.1		28 13.0	57 6.4	49 7.4	67 5.4	54 6.8	60 6.1
				Cost of Sales/Inventory						
				Cost of Sales/Payables						
	5.6	4.9	5.5	Sales/Working Capital	65.1	4.6	4.7	4.7	7.8	5.2
	15.2	10.6	17.6		−48.2	36.5	31.4	9.0	18.3	11.4
	−671.9	483.9	−61.2		−5.3	−21.2	−17.0	35.3	81.2	−176.5
	8.4	11.5	14.5	EBIT/Interest	4.5	22.3	20.9	11.9	17.2	8.7
(129)	3.5	(174) 4.3	(179) 3.2		(12) −.3	(32) 5.1	(25) 2.9	(45) 2.6	(34) 5.8	(31) 3.9
	1.2	1.5	.6		−4.9	−.7	.7	.7	−.7	1.3
	11.1		8.3	Net Profit + Depr., Dep., Amort./Cur. Mat. L/T/D						
(11)	7.1	(22) 2.5							
	4.8	1.3							
	.6	.5	.6	Fixed/Worth	1.0	.5	.7	.5	.4	.6
	1.2	1.0	1.3		−9.5	1.5	1.6	.9	1.0	1.6
	3.6	3.1	5.7		−.8	−1.6	−10.9	2.0	2.0	UND
	.6	.5	.6	Debt/Worth	1.6	.4	.6	.5	.6	.8
	1.5	1.2	1.8		−31.6	2.4	3.1	1.0	1.1	2.5
	8.4	4.5	17.0		−2.5	−6.1	−15.3	2.6	2.5	UND
	43.7	49.5	60.4	% Profit Before Taxes/Tangible Net Worth		85.8	99.3	58.5	37.6	52.7
(136)	14.3	(195) 15.3	(179) 14.1		(27) 24.7	(21) 42.7	(55) 13.2	(41) 8.7	(26) 14.1
	3.2	2.9	2.4			.2	5.0	1.8	−6.9	3.4
	14.3	19.5	19.8	% Profit Before Taxes/Total Assets	10.0	39.4	49.5	21.0	17.4	9.9
	4.5	6.0	6.4		−.4	11.4	14.9	5.1	5.7	4.2
	.6	.8	−1.1		−17.6	−8.2	.1	−.3	−1.7	.4
	12.7	16.1	17.0	Sales/Net Fixed Assets	27.2	44.1	25.9	11.9	11.6	16.2
	4.0	5.0	5.2		5.3	5.6	8.3	4.4	4.6	4.0
	2.0	2.2	2.3		1.7	1.7	1.8	2.3	2.6	2.5
	2.8	3.1	3.5	Sales/Total Assets	5.8	5.1	8.3	2.7	2.9	2.4
	1.8	1.8	2.0		2.7	1.8	2.8	1.9	2.3	1.3
	1.1	1.1	1.1		1.0	1.2	1.0	1.1	1.7	1.0
	1.4	1.3	1.4	% Depr., Dep., Amort./Sales	1.8	.9	1.7	1.6	1.3	1.4
(149)	2.8	(198) 2.4	(204) 2.6		(15) 4.0	(36) 3.3	(27) 3.4	(58) 2.6	(40) 2.4	(28) 3.3
	4.8	3.9	4.9		16.0	7.6	5.3	4.0	3.6	4.6
	4.9	5.3	4.8	% Officers', Directors', Owners' Comp/Sales		6.2	5.4			
(22)	9.5	(38) 9.3	(40) 14.6		(14) 13.3	(11) 14.6			
	13.3	19.0	30.4			30.5	36.1			
	2626520M	3068203M	6553622M	Net Sales ($)	12916M	76803M	118077M	445664M	653624M	5246538M
	1905945M	2277980M	3490036M	Total Assets ($)	8037M	51138M	60241M	348182M	405188M	2617250M

M = $ thousand   MM = $ million
See Pages 11 through 18 for Explanation of Ratios and Data

HEALTH CARE—Medical Laboratories NAICS 621511 (SIC 8071)

	Current Data Sorted By Assets							Comparative Historical Data	
Type of Statement									
Unqualified		1	7	17	2	2		58	50
Reviewed	1	2	8	4				19	18
Compiled	3	11	7	1				32	21
Tax Returns	10	6	5	1				21	19
Other	2	20	21	15	2	6		70	52
		24 (4/1-9/30/02)		130 (10/1/02-3/31/03)				4/1/98-3/31/99	4/1/99-3/31/00
	0-500M	500M-2MM	2-10MM	10-50MM	50-100MM	100-250MM		ALL	ALL
NUMBER OF STATEMENTS	16	40	48	37	5	8		200	160
	%	%	%	%	%	%	**ASSETS**	%	%
Cash & Equivalents	33.1	9.2	13.9	11.8				14.3	13.2
Trade Receivables (net)	13.1	28.9	30.0	26.7				26.6	26.3
Inventory	.0	4.8	1.3	4.4				2.9	3.9
All Other Current	5.2	2.0	2.8	2.3				3.2	2.2
Total Current	51.4	44.9	48.0	45.2				47.0	45.6
Fixed Assets (net)	36.9	41.5	40.8	36.4				36.7	37.3
Intangibles (net)	6.9	3.7	5.2	6.4				7.4	7.8
All Other Non-Current	4.8	9.8	6.0	12.1				8.9	9.3
Total	100.0	100.0	100.0	100.0				100.0	100.0
							LIABILITIES		
Notes Payable-Short Term	36.9	13.3	5.5	4.0				10.5	8.7
Cur. Mat.-L/T/D	30.3	4.2	8.4	5.1				5.1	6.1
Trade Payables	2.4	8.9	7.0	9.9				7.6	7.5
Income Taxes Payable	.0	.2	1.5	1.0				.2	.2
All Other Current	19.1	10.2	14.2	9.2				13.5	10.9
Total Current	88.8	36.8	36.6	29.3				36.9	33.4
Long Term Debt	31.6	36.6	23.3	22.6				22.4	22.2
Deferred Taxes	.0	.7	.2	.2				1.0	.7
All Other Non-Current	4.4	5.7	2.2	2.0				5.2	3.5
Net Worth	−24.9	20.2	37.7	46.0				34.6	40.2
Total Liabilities & Net Worth	100.0	100.0	100.0	100.0				100.0	100.0
							INCOME DATA		
Net Sales	100.0	100.0	100.0	100.0				100.0	100.0
Gross Profit									
Operating Expenses	93.6	88.9	90.6	89.2				97.8	88.7
Operating Profit	6.4	11.1	9.4	10.8				2.2	11.3
All Other Expenses (net)	3.6	3.3	1.1	2.7				−.2	1.2
Profit Before Taxes	2.8	7.8	8.3	8.2				2.5	10.1
							RATIOS		
Current	3.0	3.1	2.4	2.1				3.3	3.0
	.9	1.2	1.6	1.6				1.7	1.6
	.4	.7	.8	1.1				.9	1.0
Quick	3.0	3.0	2.3	1.9				3.1	2.9
	.8	1.1	1.4	1.2			(198)	1.4	1.5
	.2	.4	.7	.9				.8	.7
Sales/Receivables	0 UND	0 UND	24 15.2	33 11.1				19 19.4	25 14.4
	0 UND	45 8.1	48 7.7	53 6.9				53 6.8	52 7.0
	1 263.3	72 5.0	72 5.1	72 5.1				78 4.7	78 4.7
Cost of Sales/Inventory									
Cost of Sales/Payables									
Sales/Working Capital	159.1	6.5	7.0	6.2				4.9	5.6
	−535.1	18.9	18.5	10.9				13.1	11.0
	−12.6	−22.4	−50.0	44.7				−92.0	−138.8
EBIT/Interest	8.1	10.6	16.9	21.4				14.8	19.1
	(11) 1.1	(37) 4.1	(42) 5.6	(34) 7.9			(162)	4.3	(135) 5.1
	−11.7	.5	1.5	2.5				1.0	1.9
Net Profit + Depr., Dep., Amort./Cur. Mat. L./T/D			9.1	34.6				6.0	5.2
		(11) 1.9	(10) 5.4				(43)	2.2	(34) 2.1
			1.3	1.7				1.2	1.0
Fixed/Worth	.7	.4	.4	.4				.4	.4
	3.9	1.4	1.0	.8				.9	.9
	−1.0	NM	3.0	1.7				6.2	6.7
Debt/Worth	.9	1.4	.7	.5				.6	.5
	NM	2.5	1.5	1.1				1.7	1.6
	−3.2	NM	9.8	3.6				17.8	10.6
% Profit Before Taxes/Tangible Net Worth		86.2	60.3	82.7				81.2	61.1
	(30) 51.1	(42) 28.0	(33) 24.4				(158)	30.1	(129) 27.3
		13.4	2.3	14.5				8.2	6.0
% Profit Before Taxes/Total Assets	75.2	28.0	21.8	20.3				21.0	24.5
	7.5	11.1	11.2	8.4				9.3	10.4
	−38.5	−1.2	1.2	2.2				.6	1.8
Sales/Net Fixed Assets	69.6	29.9	15.4	9.6				15.7	15.8
	48.4	6.6	6.9	5.7				6.7	7.0
	12.5	2.6	2.9	2.8				2.6	2.5
Sales/Total Assets	17.4	3.1	3.6	2.2				2.9	3.2
	7.4	2.5	2.3	1.7				1.9	1.8
	3.6	1.5	1.4	1.1				1.1	1.0
% Depr., Dep., Amort./Sales	1.0	1.5	1.9	2.7				1.8	1.9
	(13) 2.7	(31) 4.3	(46) 2.7	(35) 3.8			(169)	3.7	(142) 3.3
	4.4	15.8	7.9	7.0				6.9	6.9
% Officers', Directors', Owners' Comp/Sales		5.0	3.8					4.9	5.5
		(13) 12.9	(14) 11.6				(41)	9.0	(41) 10.0
		33.9	26.2					16.7	26.0
Net Sales ($)	48783M	157474M	553359M	1462321M	788341M	1314948M		5191334M	4419018M
Total Assets ($)	4040M	47665M	212840M	840880M	378012M	1294000M		3556171M	2821186M

M = $ thousand   MM = $ million
See Pages 11 through 18 for Explanation of Ratios and Data

Comparative Historical Data

Current Data Sorted By Sales

						Type of Statement						
	37		27		29	Unqualified		1		6	6	16
	14		15		15	Reviewed		2		4	6	3
	35		23		22	Compiled	2	4	7	5	3	1
	17		19		22	Tax Returns	6	5	3	3	4	1
	55		61		66	Other	2	11	7	12	12	22
	4/1/00-		4/1/01-		4/1/02-			24 (4/1-9/30/02)		130 (10/1/02-3/31/03)		
	3/31/01		3/31/02		3/31/03							
	ALL		ALL		ALL		0-1MM	1-3MM	3-5MM	5-10MM	10-25MM	25MM & OVER
	158		145		154	**NUMBER OF STATEMENTS**	10	23	17	30	31	43
	%		%		%	**ASSETS**	%	%	%	%	%	%
	12.4		16.0		14.2	Cash & Equivalents	25.1	16.6	5.9	19.7	12.6	11.1
	28.6		28.8		26.1	Trade Receivables (net)	18.1	15.4	34.6	27.2	31.8	25.4
	4.2		4.1		2.9	Inventory	1.1	1.3	8.8	1.1	1.2	4.3
	2.3		2.4		2.7	All Other Current	.0	3.7	3.0	1.9	4.5	2.1
	47.5		51.3		45.9	Total Current	44.3	37.1	52.4	49.8	50.1	42.8
	38.2		36.1		38.7	Fixed Assets (net)	42.6	51.8	32.8	40.5	35.2	34.4
	4.7		4.6		6.6	Intangibles (net)	3.3	4.2	6.2	3.0	7.8	10.6
	9.6		8.0		8.7	All Other Non-Current	9.8	6.9	8.6	6.7	6.9	12.2
	100.0		100.0		100.0	Total	100.0	100.0	100.0	100.0	100.0	100.0
						LIABILITIES						
	8.9		6.8		10.0	Notes Payable-Short Term	52.0	7.5	19.7	6.0	6.4	3.0
	5.7		5.4		8.3	Cur. Mat.-L/T/D	26.3	15.5	2.4	9.4	5.2	4.0
	7.7		7.7		7.6	Trade Payables	3.4	5.2	11.3	6.8	7.5	9.0
	.7		.6		.8	Income Taxes Payable	.0	.0	.4	.1	1.8	1.3
	15.7		15.3		12.3	All Other Current	4.2	5.3	6.9	15.5	19.1	13.0
	38.7		35.8		38.9	Total Current	85.8	33.6	40.7	37.8	39.9	30.3
	18.4		24.0		26.9	Long Term Debt	38.2	55.2	25.3	20.7	16.9	21.4
	.9		.7		.4	Deferred Taxes	.0	.1	.9	.4	.3	.4
	3.4		6.8		4.0	All Other Non-Current	7.3	2.7	8.3	1.5	3.1	4.6
	38.7		32.7		29.8	Net Worth	−31.2	8.3	24.8	39.7	39.8	43.3
	100.0		100.0		100.0	Total Liabilities & Net Worth	100.0	100.0	100.0	100.0	100.0	100.0
						INCOME DATA						
	100.0		100.0		100.0	Net Sales	100.0	100.0	100.0	100.0	100.0	100.0
						Gross Profit						
	87.7		88.5		89.8	Operating Expenses	79.8	88.5	93.0	90.1	93.1	89.1
	12.3		11.5		10.2	Operating Profit	20.2	11.5	7.0	9.8	6.9	10.9
	1.4		1.2		2.4	All Other Expenses (net)	7.7	2.9	1.1	3.0	.4	2.4
	10.9		10.3		7.8	Profit Before Taxes	12.4	8.6	6.0	6.9	6.5	8.5
						RATIOS						
	2.6		3.4		2.5		5.8	5.0	1.9	3.6	2.0	2.2
	1.4		1.8		1.5	Current	1.3	1.0	1.0	1.4	1.6	1.6
	.9		1.1		.9		.2	.4	.7	1.0	1.0	1.0
	2.1		2.9		2.3		5.8	5.0	1.7	2.8	1.6	2.0
	1.2		1.5		1.1	Quick	1.0	1.0	.8	1.3	1.4	1.2
	.7		.9		.7		.2	.4	.4	.9	.7	.9
29	12.6	32	11.6	10	35.5		0 UND	0 UND	0 UND	25 14.9	20 17.9	34 10.7
55	6.6	53	6.9	47	7.7	Sales/Receivables	0 UND	34 10.8	44 8.2	52 7.1	48 7.6	52 7.0
74	4.9	69	5.3	68	5.4		35 10.5	66 5.5	74 4.9	63 5.8	73 5.0	68 5.4
						Cost of Sales/Inventory						
						Cost of Sales/Payables						
	5.8		5.1		6.9		4.9	5.7	9.0	5.1	7.1	6.9
	17.0		9.6		17.0	Sales/Working Capital	NM	423.7	286.6	18.5	13.6	12.2
	−50.0		94.1		−105.1		−6.6	−9.6	−11.8	NM	−322.3	999.8
	15.5		21.3		15.7			9.9	9.5	16.9	26.2	21.7
(128)	4.6	(123)	5.8	(135)	5.1	EBIT/Interest	(22) 3.2	(15) 4.1	(26) 5.9	(29) 8.0	(37) 6.1
	1.5		1.5		1.4			−1.1	.5	1.5	1.6	2.0
	14.1		6.4		14.0	Net Profit + Depr., Dep.,					12.4	
(25)	2.3	(23)	2.9	(29)	4.2	Amort./Cur. Mat. L/T/D				(12) 1.9	
	1.1		1.0		1.6						1.4	
	.4		.4		.4		.3	1.4	.4	.4	.4	.5
	.9		.9		1.1	Fixed/Worth	1.2	3.7	.5	1.0	.7	.8
	2.2		2.1		7.2		−1.2	−1.6	18.1	2.1	2.5	4.3
	.6		.5		.7		.2	1.6	1.6	.6	.6	.5
	1.6		1.3		2.0	Debt/Worth	1.1	4.7	2.1	1.6	1.2	1.5
	4.2		4.8		22.6		−3.2	−5.9	NM	9.4	7.4	5.6
	68.4		90.1		86.2	% Profit Before Taxes/Tangible		96.2	77.3	69.1	66.0	94.4
(141)	30.1	(122)	32.4	(122)	29.8	Net Worth	(15) 45.5	(13) 39.5	(26) 40.4	(28) 19.2	(34) 23.2
	5.4		7.9		9.2			11.1	−19.9	4.3	9.1	8.5
	29.0		37.3		22.2	% Profit Before Taxes/Total	63.4	28.7	28.7	21.0	21.1	19.9
	11.9		11.3		8.5	Assets	15.0	9.6	5.5	13.3	8.4	8.1
	1.4		2.0		1.0		−38.4	−7.1	−2.3	1.3	1.9	1.7
	16.9		18.6		17.2		61.8	11.0	31.3	14.0	17.3	16.3
	6.9		8.1		6.3	Sales/Net Fixed Assets	12.4	2.9	14.2	4.9	8.2	5.8
	2.6		2.9		2.8		1.2	2.1	6.6	2.2	4.7	2.8
	3.2		3.4		3.2		11.6	2.6	4.3	3.1	4.3	2.4
	1.9		2.2		2.2	Sales/Total Assets	2.2	1.9	2.9	2.1	2.8	1.7
	1.3		1.4		1.4		.7	1.3	2.0	1.3	1.6	1.2
	1.7		1.5		2.1			4.0	1.1	2.2	1.6	2.3
(140)	3.3	(131)	3.3	(133)	3.7	% Depr., Dep., Amort./Sales	(18) 8.5	(13) 2.7	(28) 5.6	(29) 2.6	(36) 3.6
	7.0		6.3		7.3			16.7	7.9	8.0	5.4	4.7
	5.6		5.1		5.0	% Officers', Directors',				3.4	7.4	
(33)	9.9	(48)	11.5	(41)	11.6	Owners' Comp/Sales			(10) 8.9	(11) 14.9	
	21.2		24.2		27.0					13.7	28.9	
	3167893M		2888220M		4325226M	Net Sales ($)	5946M	37028M	63845M	225224M	441543M	3551640M
	2183347M		1932658M		2777437M	Total Assets ($)	5405M	22865M	25577M	140161M	216486M	2366943M

M = $ thousand   MM = $ million
See Pages 11 through 18 for Explanation of Ratios and Data

Current Data Sorted By Assets · **Comparative Historical Data**

						Type of Statement		
3	13	38	23	4	7	Unqualified	96	90
4	11	10		1		Reviewed	15	15
8	16	5		1	1	Compiled	28	24
7	8	2	2			Tax Returns	14	12
4	15	29	19	3		Other	98	86

0-500M	500M-2MM	2-10MM	10-50MM	50-100MM	100-250MM		4/1/98-3/31/99 ALL	4/1/99-3/31/00 ALL
	74 (4/1-9/30/02)		160 (10/1/02-3/31/03)					
26	63	84	44	9	8	NUMBER OF STATEMENTS	251	227
%	%	%	%	%	%	ASSETS	%	%
19.9	13.5	19.2	13.7			Cash & Equivalents	14.5	13.8
47.2	48.8	42.8	34.1			Trade Receivables (net)	41.7	42.4
1.7	5.3	3.2	1.5			Inventory	1.7	2.5
2.6	4.5	4.4	5.5			All Other Current	4.0	4.5
71.3	72.0	69.6	54.7			Total Current	61.9	63.2
17.1	17.9	16.9	24.2			Fixed Assets (net)	23.6	20.0
4.6	3.4	1.4	5.6			Intangibles (net)	5.0	4.8
7.0	6.7	12.1	15.5			All Other Non-Current	9.5	11.9
100.0	100.0	100.0	100.0			Total	100.0	100.0
						LIABILITIES		
22.6	12.3	8.1	6.8			Notes Payable-Short Term	15.1	12.8
9.4	4.4	2.0	4.0			Cur. Mat.-L/T/D	3.7	3.6
8.0	9.8	11.9	8.6			Trade Payables	10.4	11.5
.2	.2	.6	.4			Income Taxes Payable	.3	.2
30.2	25.7	23.7	19.9			All Other Current	19.3	19.5
70.4	52.4	46.4	39.7			Total Current	48.7	47.6
9.7	11.2	7.4	18.0			Long Term Debt	17.9	13.7
.0	.1	.3	.7			Deferred Taxes	.3	.3
5.1	5.1	2.4	2.9			All Other Non-Current	3.7	32.3
14.8	31.1	43.5	38.7			Net Worth	29.3	6.2
100.0	100.0	100.0	100.0			Total Liabilities & Net Worth	100.0	100.0
						INCOME DATA		
100.0	100.0	100.0	100.0			Net Sales	100.0	100.0
						Gross Profit		
96.0	96.9	94.5	94.8			Operating Expenses	99.9	97.8
4.0	3.1	5.5	5.2			Operating Profit	.1	2.2
.8	.7	−.1	1.5			All Other Expenses (net)	−.5	−.7
3.2	2.4	5.6	3.7			Profit Before Taxes	.6	2.9
						RATIOS		
3.9	3.1	2.8	2.1				2.5	2.2
1.2	1.6	1.6	1.4			Current	1.5	1.4
.7	1.0	1.2	.9				.9	1.0
3.9	2.6	2.5	2.1				2.2	1.9
1.2	1.4	1.5	1.3			Quick	1.3	1.2
.6	.8	1.0	.8				.8	.8
0 UND	31 11.9	44 8.4	34 10.6				32 11.5	33 10.9
31 11.8	52 7.0	50 7.2	53 6.9			Sales/Receivables	55 6.7	54 6.8
56 6.5	74 4.9	72 5.1	83 4.4				83 4.4	78 4.7
						Cost of Sales/Inventory		
						Cost of Sales/Payables		
9.3	6.8	5.2	6.3				5.7	6.5
87.2	12.7	10.6	15.3			Sales/Working Capital	14.9	17.8
−31.4	−346.0	42.3	−70.4				−36.6	−222.3
24.6	13.9	44.4	18.7				6.2	9.4
(19) 9.1	(50) 3.4	(66) 13.6	(33) 4.0			EBIT/Interest	(205) 1.8	(182) 3.0
−.1	.0	4.1	1.5				−1.4	.8
		16.8				Net Profit + Depr., Dep.,	4.4	3.1
	(10) 5.7					Amort./Cur. Mat. L /T/D	(28) 1.4	(12) 1.8
		2.6					.1	.6
.1	.1	.1	.2				.2	.2
.6	.5	.2	.8			Fixed/Worth	.6	.4
−1.2	3.4	.7	2.1				16.2	2.3
.6	.6	.4	.7				.7	.6
7.4	3.1	1.0	1.5			Debt/Worth	1.8	1.7
−5.0	13.8	2.8	10.8				43.6	10.5
499.3	74.9	39.3	46.9			% Profit Before Taxes/Tangible	36.1	38.5
(18) 148.3	(51) 19.4	(77) 27.0	(38) 20.1			Net Worth	(194) 8.4	(184) 11.5
39.6	−1.6	13.1	2.1				−5.7	.4
47.8	21.7	23.0	19.9			% Profit Before Taxes/Total	12.5	13.7
26.5	7.5	10.8	5.0			Assets	2.3	4.5
4.3	−1.9	3.5	.3				−4.7	−2.3
179.4	98.5	71.6	53.7				69.3	70.2
73.3	45.0	22.5	11.3			Sales/Net Fixed Assets	19.0	25.0
31.6	13.4	7.8	5.9				4.8	7.6
7.5	4.5	3.6	2.9				3.9	4.1
5.1	3.5	2.5	2.0			Sales/Total Assets	2.5	2.6
4.2	2.2	1.7	1.3				1.5	1.6
.3	.4	.6	1.2				.6	.6
(18) .6	(52) .9	(74) 1.2	(38) 1.8			% Depr., Dep., Amort./Sales	(204) 1.3	(189) 1.1
1.4	2.3	2.0	2.2				3.3	2.6
1.8	2.7	2.4					1.9	3.7
(12) 4.8	(22) 4.7	(12) 3.7				% Officers', Directors',	(46) 6.4	(43) 7.5
14.4	8.5	4.7				Owners' Comp/Sales	14.2	11.7
52005M	236672M	1021279M	3345135M	737120M	2324874M	Net Sales ($)	4726219M	3609884M
7695M	69283M	385373M	994281M	602030M	1128743M	Total Assets ($)	3230943M	2308116M

M = $ thousand   MM = $ million
See Pages 11 through 18 for Explanation of Ratios and Data

Comparative Historical Data | Current Data Sorted By Sales

			Type of Statement						
78	64	88	Unqualified	1	9	13	15	24	26
14	12	26	Reviewed		5	3	9	7	2
36	28	31	Compiled	3	12	5	7	2	2
13	13	19	Tax Returns	5	9	2	1		2
67	76	70	Other	3	8	7	13	20	19
4/1/00-3/31/01	4/1/01-3/31/02	4/1/02-3/31/03		74 (4/1-9/30/02)			160 (10/1/02-3/31/03)		
ALL	ALL	ALL		0-1MM	1-3MM	3-5MM	5-10MM	10-25MM	25MM & OVER
208	193	234	NUMBER OF STATEMENTS	12	43	30	45	53	51
%	%	%	ASSETS	%	%	%	%	%	%
14.1	17.0	15.9	Cash & Equivalents	15.6	13.6	20.9	17.8	18.1	11.0
42.6	38.3	41.6	Trade Receivables (net)	31.3	46.9	38.9	44.1	40.4	40.4
1.7	2.5	3.1	Inventory	7.0	6.2	2.8	1.8	2.5	1.5
3.4	3.3	4.3	All Other Current	4.9	3.2	5.6	3.3	5.0	4.5
61.8	61.1	64.9	Total Current	58.8	69.8	68.2	66.9	65.9	57.4
22.5	22.6	19.6	Fixed Assets (net)	27.6	20.0	16.8	19.8	19.3	19.3
4.7	5.7	4.4	Intangibles (net)	8.4	2.9	2.6	2.6	1.9	9.9
11.0	10.6	11.1	All Other Non-Current	5.2	7.2	12.5	10.7	12.9	13.4
100.0	100.0	100.0	Total	100.0	100.0	100.0	100.0	100.0	100.0
			LIABILITIES						
11.0	12.1	10.3	Notes Payable-Short Term	15.4	15.7	10.3	10.2	7.9	7.2
4.0	4.8	3.9	Cur. Mat.-L/T/D	7.0	4.0	2.9	5.5	2.1	4.0
10.6	10.1	9.8	Trade Payables	4.3	10.1	9.0	8.8	12.0	9.9
.3	.2	.4	Income Taxes Payable	.0	.3	.0	.9	.3	.4
24.8	18.5	23.3	All Other Current	34.8	22.2	25.1	19.2	27.7	19.3
50.7	45.7	47.6	Total Current	61.5	52.4	47.3	44.5	49.9	40.7
13.1	15.0	12.2	Long Term Debt	22.2	14.2	7.2	8.9	9.5	16.9
.1	.1	.3	Deferred Taxes	.0	.0	.0	.2	.3	.8
7.1	3.8	4.1	All Other Non-Current	12.4	4.2	2.1	3.6	2.7	5.5
28.9	35.4	35.7	Net Worth	3.9	29.2	43.4	42.9	37.6	36.1
100.0	100.0	100.0	Total Liabilities & Net Worth	100.0	100.0	100.0	100.0	100.0	100.0
			INCOME DATA						
100.0	100.0	100.0	Net Sales	100.0	100.0	100.0	100.0	100.0	100.0
			Gross Profit						
96.9	94.0	95.3	Operating Expenses	102.8	94.2	95.8	94.7	95.6	94.5
3.1	6.0	4.7	Operating Profit	−2.8	5.8	4.2	5.3	4.4	5.5
−.1	.4	.7	All Other Expenses (net)	3.4	1.4	.2	−.2	.2	1.0
3.1	5.6	4.0	Profit Before Taxes	−6.2	4.4	4.0	5.5	4.2	4.5
			RATIOS						
2.3	2.5	2.7		7.1	4.3	2.9	2.7	2.6	2.0
1.4	1.5	1.6	Current	1.2	1.8	1.6	1.7	1.6	1.4
.9	1.0	1.0		.5	1.0	.9	1.1	1.0	1.0
2.1	2.3	2.5		2.7	3.5	2.5	2.5	2.2	1.9
(207) 1.3	1.4	1.3	Quick	.8	1.8	1.3	1.5	1.3	1.3
.9	.9	.9		.4	.8	.9	.9	.9	.9
37 10.0	31 11.8	33 11.1		0 UND	30 12.1	28 13.0	33 10.9	35 10.4	41 9.0
56 6.6	52 7.1	50 7.3	Sales/Receivables	0 UND	54 6.8	48 7.6	49 7.5	49 7.4	60 6.1
74 4.9	75 4.9	73 5.0		65 5.7	70 5.2	69 5.3	79 4.6	59 6.2	83 4.4
			Cost of Sales/Inventory						
			Cost of Sales/Payables						
7.5	6.1	6.3		4.0	5.8	6.3	5.3	6.6	6.6
15.0	14.6	13.8	Sales/Working Capital	104.9	10.3	13.0	10.9	14.6	18.4
−79.6	721.4	216.2		−7.5	−222.7	−75.0	106.5	102.0	137.0
11.3	14.0	24.6			19.7	64.2	35.0	30.4	22.0
(175) 3.5	(164) 4.8	(183) 6.6	EBIT/Interest	(32) 5.3	(23) 13.7	(36) 7.4	(42) 8.3	(41) 5.8	
.0	1.4	1.2		.5	1.2	1.9	1.8	1.5	
21.5	12.7	18.3							20.8
(14) 6.2	(14) 2.3	(25) 8.1	Net Profit + Depr., Dep.,					(14) 9.0	
3.1	.2	2.8	Amort./Cur. Mat. L/T/D					3.0	
.2	.1	.1		.1	.1	.1	.1	.1	.3
.5	.4	.5	Fixed/Worth	5.5	.6	.3	.3	.3	.8
2.7	1.9	2.2		−.5	4.8	2.2	1.3	.9	2.6
.5	.5	.5		3.8	.5	.4	.4	.5	.7
1.7	1.4	1.6	Debt/Worth	14.7	1.7	1.3	1.0	1.3	2.2
12.5	7.5	9.3		−3.0	147.0	6.7	4.2	2.7	14.3
50.0	58.6	65.5	% Profit Before Taxes/Tangible		102.5	63.9	48.4	47.2	72.8
(165) 16.3	(158) 23.6	(196) 27.1	Net Worth	(34) 31.7	(26) 24.8	(38) 28.2	(49) 22.3	(42) 27.9	
.7	4.6	4.7		3.9	.5	12.4	6.0	2.5	
17.1	24.2	23.6	% Profit Before Taxes/Total	25.1	30.2	25.7	23.4	24.7	19.9
5.9	9.1	10.3	Assets	−2.3	13.5	9.3	10.7	9.2	10.1
−1.6	1.0	1.4		−20.7	−.2	.1	3.0	2.3	2.0
66.2	57.9	79.5		199.2	89.4	75.1	97.8	53.0	65.4
19.9	21.9	26.6	Sales/Net Fixed Assets	10.2	31.6	49.2	29.3	22.7	19.6
6.8	7.7	7.4		1.5	7.8	9.2	11.7	7.5	6.7
3.8	4.1	4.2		4.1	5.0	4.5	4.6	3.9	3.6
2.6	2.5	2.6	Sales/Total Assets	1.7	3.6	2.6	3.0	2.4	2.3
1.7	1.7	1.7		.6	1.6	1.7	2.1	1.5	1.7
.5	.5	.5			.4	.5	.4	.7	.7
(180) 1.2	(160) 1.2	(197) 1.3	% Depr., Dep., Amort./Sales	(33) 1.1	(28) 1.2	(39) .9	(47) 1.3	(43) 1.8	
2.3	2.3	2.2		3.3	1.6	2.1	2.3	2.2	
3.2	2.1	2.7			3.3		2.0		
(31) 4.1	(32) 5.7	(53) 4.4	% Officers', Directors',	(20) 5.8		(11) 3.2			
9.7	8.4	9.2	Owners' Comp/Sales	14.4		3.8			
4441846M	4000051M	7717085M	Net Sales ($)	7126M	86069M	120101M	314139M	883173M	6306477M
2160465M	1693659M	3187405M	Total Assets ($)	7473M	44920M	56260M	131918M	665982M	2280852M

M = $ thousand   MM = $ million
See Pages 11 through 18 for Explanation of Ratios and Data

HEALTH CARE—Blood and Organ Banks NAICS 621991 (SIC 8099)

Current Data Sorted By Assets   Comparative Historical Data

0-500M	500M-2MM	2-10MM	10-50MM	50-100MM	100-250MM	Type of Statement	4/1/98-3/31/99 ALL	4/1/99-3/31/00 ALL
		6	5	1	1	Unqualified		
		1				Reviewed		
1	2	2	1			Compiled		
						Tax Returns		
1	1	3	4		1	Other		
	14 (4/1-9/30/02)		16 (10/1/02-3/31/03)					
2	3	12	10	1	2	NUMBER OF STATEMENTS		
%	%	%	%	%	%	**ASSETS**	%	%
		17.3	14.2			Cash & Equivalents	D	D
		24.8	26.7			Trade Receivables (net)	A	A
		1.6	3.6			Inventory	T	T
		13.9	2.0			All Other Current	A	A
		57.7	46.5			Total Current		
		38.9	42.5			Fixed Assets (net)	N	N
		.2	.4			Intangibles (net)	O	O
		3.2	10.6			All Other Non-Current	T	T
		100.0	100.0			Total		
						LIABILITIES	A	A
		.9	4.1			Notes Payable-Short Term	V	V
		1.2	1.5			Cur. Mat.-L/T/D	A	A
		8.5	7.0			Trade Payables	I	I
		.0	.0			Income Taxes Payable	L	L
		9.1	11.7			All Other Current	A	A
		19.7	24.3			Total Current	B	B
		14.8	21.1			Long Term Debt	L	L
		.1	.0			Deferred Taxes	E	E
		3.6	1.7			All Other Non-Current		
		61.9	52.9			Net Worth		
		100.0	100.0			Total Liabilities & Net Worth		
						INCOME DATA		
		100.0	100.0			Net Sales		
						Gross Profit		
		91.1	92.5			Operating Expenses		
		8.9	7.5			Operating Profit		
		1.7	.6			All Other Expenses (net)		
		7.2	6.8			Profit Before Taxes		
						RATIOS		
		8.0	3.1					
		4.6	2.1			Current		
		1.2	1.2					
		4.8	2.7					
		1.7	1.8			Quick		
		.9	.9					
		22 16.9	35 10.5					
		47 7.8	52 7.1			Sales/Receivables		
		60 6.1	59 6.1					
						Cost of Sales/Inventory		
						Cost of Sales/Payables		
		1.6	3.6					
		3.2	6.3			Sales/Working Capital		
		18.7	48.8					
						EBIT/Interest		
						Net Profit + Depr., Dep., Amort./Cur. Mat. L /T/D		
		.3	.4					
		.5	.8			Fixed/Worth		
		1.5	1.9					
		.2	.2					
		.5	1.3			Debt/Worth		
		1.5	2.3					
		31.5	26.0			% Profit Before Taxes/Tangible		
		12.4	9.5			Net Worth		
		.2	2.3					
		14.7	16.7			% Profit Before Taxes/Total		
		9.0	5.4			Assets		
		.0	.4					
		13.5	7.3					
		3.9	4.7			Sales/Net Fixed Assets		
		3.0	2.1					
		2.4	2.2					
		1.3	1.5			Sales/Total Assets		
		.8	.9					
		1.8						
		(10) 2.8				% Depr., Dep., Amort./Sales		
		4.9						
						% Officers', Directors', Owners' Comp/Sales		
1520M	12592M	96194M	275001M	137124M	696444M	Net Sales ($)		
553M	3482M	60764M	171350M	61676M	405464M	Total Assets ($)		

© RMA 2003

M = $ thousand   MM = $ million
See Pages 11 through 18 for Explanation of Ratios and Data

Comparative Historical Data | Current Data Sorted By Sales

4/1/00-3/31/01 ALL	4/1/01-3/31/02 ALL	4/1/02-3/31/03 ALL		0-1MM	1-3MM	3-5MM	5-10MM	10-25MM	25MM & OVER
			Type of Statement		14 (4/1-9/30/02)			16 (10/1/02-3/31/03)	
		13	Unqualified		1	1	2	3	6
		1	Reviewed				1		
		6	Compiled	1	1		2	2	
			Tax Returns						
		10	Other		1	2	2	4	1
		30	**NUMBER OF STATEMENTS**	1	3	3	7	9	7
%	%	%	**ASSETS**	%	%	%	%	%	%
D	D	15.9	Cash & Equivalents						
A	A	25.2	Trade Receivables (net)						
T	T	2.0	Inventory						
A	A	7.6	All Other Current						
		50.6	Total Current						
N	N	38.4	Fixed Assets (net)						
O	O	3.3	Intangibles (net)						
T	T	7.6	All Other Non-Current						
		100.0	Total						
A	A		**LIABILITIES**						
V	V	3.4	Notes Payable-Short Term						
A	A	1.2	Cur. Mat.-L/T/D						
I	I	7.3	Trade Payables						
L	L	.1	Income Taxes Payable						
A	A	10.2	All Other Current						
B	B	22.1	Total Current						
L	L	17.8	Long Term Debt						
E	E	.1	Deferred Taxes						
		2.8	All Other Non-Current						
		57.2	Net Worth						
		100.0	Total Liabilities & Net Worth						
			INCOME DATA						
		100.0	Net Sales						
			Gross Profit						
		92.2	Operating Expenses						
		7.8	Operating Profit						
		1.0	All Other Expenses (net)						
		6.8	Profit Before Taxes						
			RATIOS						
		4.6							
		2.7	Current						
		1.3							
		3.5							
		2.0	Quick						
		.9							
	29	12.8							
	47	7.8	Sales/Receivables						
	58	6.3							
			Cost of Sales/Inventory						
			Cost of Sales/Payables						
		2.8							
		6.8	Sales/Working Capital						
		31.1							
		37.5							
	(21)	5.5	EBIT/Interest						
		1.6							
			Net Profit + Depr., Dep., Amort./Cur. Mat. L/T/D						
		.3							
		.6	Fixed/Worth						
		1.8							
		.2							
		.6	Debt/Worth						
		1.8							
		32.1							
	(28)	10.1	% Profit Before Taxes/Tangible Net Worth						
		3.3							
		16.1							
		8.0	% Profit Before Taxes/Total Assets						
		2.1							
		11.1							
		5.7	Sales/Net Fixed Assets						
		3.1							
		2.7							
		1.7	Sales/Total Assets						
		1.0							
		1.9							
	(24)	2.7	% Depr., Dep., Amort./Sales						
		3.9							
			% Officers', Directors', Owners' Comp/Sales						
		1218875M	Net Sales ($)	426M	4542M	12413M	46202M	148345M	1006947M
		703289M	Total Assets ($)	79M	6217M	15007M	29343M	98143M	554500M

M = $ thousand   MM = $ million
See Pages 11 through 18 for Explanation of Ratios and Data

Current Data Sorted By Assets   **Comparative Historical Data**

						Type of Statement		
5	19	72	39	8	15	Unqualified	160	144
1	8	13	1			Reviewed	20	18
7	14	4	1			Compiled	47	41
22	9	4				Tax Returns	47	27
14	27	40	22	4	5	Other	106	106
	138 (4/1-9/30/02)		216 (10/1/02-3/31/03)				4/1/98-3/31/99	4/1/99-3/31/00
0-500M	500M-2MM	2-10MM	10-50MM	50-100MM	100-250MM		ALL	ALL
49	77	133	63	12	20	NUMBER OF STATEMENTS	380	336
%	%	%	%	%	%	**ASSETS**	%	%
32.9	14.5	17.4	18.4	18.2	17.5	Cash & Equivalents	18.4	16.6
14.6	33.3	24.2	22.1	20.8	21.2	Trade Receivables (net)	25.2	27.6
1.9	2.1	1.3	1.9	4.8	5.3	Inventory	3.1	3.2
3.8	6.0	4.1	4.3	1.0	3.8	All Other Current	5.0	4.6
53.3	55.9	47.0	46.7	44.8	47.8	Total Current	51.8	52.0
30.8	31.3	42.2	39.2	32.6	26.0	Fixed Assets (net)	32.8	32.0
5.0	4.5	2.0	2.5	4.2	13.1	Intangibles (net)	4.6	5.3
10.9	8.3	8.8	11.6	18.5	13.1	All Other Non-Current	10.9	10.7
100.0	100.0	100.0	100.0	100.0	100.0	Total	100.0	100.0
						LIABILITIES		
28.1	9.3	4.7	2.8	2.4	4.6	Notes Payable-Short Term	12.9	9.2
6.5	3.6	3.6	2.0	1.7	2.3	Cur. Mat.-L/T/D	4.9	4.3
9.9	11.9	7.6	8.8	11.5	12.9	Trade Payables	7.9	10.1
.0	.8	.4	.4	.0	.2	Income Taxes Payable	.1	.2
31.8	20.6	12.1	15.1	9.4	15.1	All Other Current	16.8	14.9
76.3	46.1	28.4	29.2	25.0	35.0	Total Current	42.7	38.6
18.1	19.1	22.5	23.3	24.5	18.1	Long Term Debt	18.4	18.3
.0	.3	.1	.2	.0	.2	Deferred Taxes	.3	.4
2.6	6.8	7.9	4.0	.7	5.8	All Other Non-Current	5.3	4.6
2.9	27.6	41.1	43.3	49.7	40.9	Net Worth	33.3	38.1
100.0	100.0	100.0	100.0	100.0	100.0	Total Liabilities & Net Worth	100.0	100.0
						INCOME DATA		
100.0	100.0	100.0	100.0	100.0	100.0	Net Sales	100.0	100.0
						Gross Profit		
90.4	94.8	94.0	93.8	94.7	93.0	Operating Expenses	94.4	93.1
9.6	5.2	6.0	6.2	5.3	7.0	Operating Profit	5.6	6.9
.4	1.0	2.6	.8	2.1	1.0	All Other Expenses (net)	−1.2	1.1
9.2	4.1	3.4	5.4	3.1	5.9	Profit Before Taxes	6.8	5.8
						RATIOS		
3.4	2.7	3.7	3.0	2.9	2.6		3.5	3.1
1.0	1.4	1.6	1.7	2.0	1.8	Current	1.7	1.6
.3	.8	1.0	1.1	1.2	1.1		1.0	.9
2.8	2.3	3.1	2.5	2.9	2.4		3.0	2.6
1.0	1.3	1.5	1.4	1.8	1.4	Quick	(379) 1.4	1.3
.3	.7	.8	1.0	1.0	.8		.7	.8
0 UND	7 49.7	22 16.2	27 13.4	51 7.2	34 10.9		6 58.0	21 17.5
0 UND	28 13.2	40 9.1	46 7.9	62 5.9	47 7.7	Sales/Receivables	41 8.9	47 7.8
12 31.5	53 6.9	60 6.1	62 5.9	70 5.2	57 6.4		65 5.6	67 5.4
						Cost of Sales/Inventory		
						Cost of Sales/Payables		
19.2	7.7	5.1	4.4	3.1	5.2		4.8	5.4
974.5	25.5	10.9	9.7	6.7	8.4	Sales/Working Capital	12.8	15.7
−22.6	−87.0	−89.8	34.8	31.8	39.1		UND	−62.8
12.4	16.9	8.2	13.7	9.7	13.2		11.0	13.8
(32) 4.2	(54) 4.5	(103) 2.9	(52) 3.0	(11) 4.8	(18) 4.5	EBIT/Interest	(267) 3.4	(254) 3.2
1.3	.8	1.0	1.0	.3	2.2		1.0	.8
	3.4	4.8				Net Profit + Depr., Dep.,	10.4	16.3
	(10) 2.1	(10) 3.2				Amort./Cur. Mat. L/T/D	(32) 2.8	(41) 5.7
	1.0	1.1					1.6	1.5
.2	.2	.4	.5	.5	.5		.2	.3
2.5	1.0	.9	.9	.6	.9	Fixed/Worth	.7	.8
−1.4	7.7	2.4	1.9	1.6	−3.6		2.6	2.3
.4	.7	.4	.5	.5	.7		.4	.5
4.2	2.3	1.1	1.1	1.4	1.1	Debt/Worth	1.3	1.6
−4.8	NM	3.7	3.6	1.7	−27.0		6.6	6.0
330.3	71.9	23.4	28.2	65.7	39.1		48.7	48.2
(34) 53.9	(58) 21.0	(117) 7.8	(60) 12.1	9.9	(14) 17.6	% Profit Before Taxes/Tangible Net Worth	(311) 16.3	(292) 12.2
1.5	4.9	.2	1.1	−1.2	7.6		1.9	−1.9
55.9	25.4	10.1	12.0	10.9	11.4		18.6	16.0
17.6	7.6	3.6	3.5	4.3	6.2	% Profit Before Taxes/Total Assets	5.7	4.9
.9	−.6	−.3	.3	−.8	2.7		−.2	−1.7
226.8	71.7	10.1	10.8	16.4	80.0		35.0	34.0
43.8	19.5	4.3	3.6	3.1	4.9	Sales/Net Fixed Assets	9.7	8.3
12.1	4.9	2.1	2.2	2.4	2.4		2.9	2.8
15.4	5.4	2.5	2.1	1.8	3.2		3.7	3.7
7.4	3.2	1.7	1.5	1.2	1.5	Sales/Total Assets	2.1	1.9
3.0	1.9	1.1	1.0	.9	.9		1.1	1.0
.4	.9	1.8	1.7	1.6	1.4		1.2	1.1
(30) 1.2	(59) 1.7	(125) 3.2	(60) 2.7	2.9	(18) 3.2	% Depr., Dep., Amort./Sales	(310) 2.4	(284) 2.5
3.6	3.2	4.8	3.9	5.1	5.3		4.7	5.1
11.3	5.3	5.5					4.1	3.4
(22) 17.6	(19) 8.9	(19) 6.8				% Officers', Directors', Owners' Comp/Sales	(72) 9.6	(58) 8.1
30.4	15.3	22.2					25.0	19.3
139096M	485431M	1334849M	2394162M	1267342M	6024901M	Net Sales ($)	8832380M	8576917M
10232M	88157M	668898M	1276049M	863152M	3055522M	Total Assets ($)	5382090M	6301935M

M = $ thousand   MM = $ million
See Pages 11 through 18 for Explanation of Ratios and Data

	Comparative Historical Data			Type of Statement	Current Data Sorted By Sales					
	152	148	158	Unqualified	10	16	15	26	46	45
	20	15	23	Reviewed	1	6	4	4	7	1
	73	68	26	Compiled	4	8	4	7	2	1
	35	26	35	Tax Returns	12	11	5	5	2	
	92	115	112	Other	12	14	11	21	26	28
	4/1/00-3/31/01 ALL	4/1/01-3/31/02 ALL	4/1/02-3/31/03 ALL		138 (4/1-9/30/02) 0-1MM	1-3MM	3-5MM	216 (10/1/02-3/31/03) 5-10MM	10-25MM	25MM & OVER
	372	372	354	NUMBER OF STATEMENTS	39	55	39	63	83	75
	%	%	%	ASSETS	%	%	%	%	%	%
	16.4	17.7	19.1	Cash & Equivalents	24.2	20.7	17.0	15.9	19.1	19.2
	25.4	27.4	24.2	Trade Receivables (net)	13.4	23.1	19.3	27.7	28.6	25.3
	2.2	2.2	2.0	Inventory	2.2	1.2	1.9	1.5	1.7	3.4
	4.8	5.3	4.4	All Other Current	5.3	4.3	4.0	3.7	4.2	5.1
	48.7	52.6	49.7	Total Current	45.1	49.2	42.1	48.8	53.6	52.9
	33.7	31.7	36.5	Fixed Assets (net)	41.0	37.2	46.1	38.3	35.4	28.2
	4.4	4.1	3.8	Intangibles (net)	2.5	5.7	3.7	2.9	1.7	6.0
	13.1	11.7	10.1	All Other Non-Current	11.4	7.8	8.1	10.0	9.3	12.9
	100.0	100.0	100.0	Total	100.0	100.0	100.0	100.0	100.0	100.0
				LIABILITIES						
	11.9	10.9	8.5	Notes Payable-Short Term	10.9	10.6	2.6	7.1	13.7	4.4
	3.9	3.5	3.6	Cur. Mat.-L/T/D	2.3	6.5	5.3	3.8	2.9	1.8
	9.5	10.0	9.5	Trade Payables	11.5	6.2	6.5	9.7	10.8	10.7
	.2	.1	.4	Income Taxes Payable	.0	.9	.2	.4	.2	.6
	15.8	14.0	17.3	All Other Current	14.7	18.8	17.2	12.5	17.7	21.1
	41.3	38.6	39.3	Total Current	39.4	43.1	31.8	33.5	45.2	38.7
	21.8	23.6	21.1	Long Term Debt	27.6	23.4	29.9	17.7	17.4	18.5
	.4	.4	.1	Deferred Taxes	.0	.3	.0	.1	.1	.2
	5.5	4.2	5.9	All Other Non-Current	3.7	3.1	1.6	7.6	3.9	12.1
	31.0	33.2	33.5	Net Worth	29.3	30.0	36.7	41.2	33.4	30.4
	100.0	100.0	100.0	Total Liabilities & Net Worth	100.0	100.0	100.0	100.0	100.0	100.0
				INCOME DATA						
	100.0	100.0	100.0	Net Sales	100.0	100.0	100.0	100.0	100.0	100.0
				Gross Profit						
	93.7	92.2	93.6	Operating Expenses	89.5	94.2	94.5	93.3	94.4	94.3
	6.3	7.8	6.4	Operating Profit	10.5	5.8	5.5	6.7	5.6	5.7
	1.5	2.7	1.5	All Other Expenses (net)	5.9	1.0	1.9	.7	.7	1.1
	4.8	5.2	4.8	Profit Before Taxes	4.6	4.8	3.6	5.9	4.9	4.6
				RATIOS						
	2.8	3.3	3.0		5.1	5.3	2.7	3.6	2.9	2.6
	1.6	1.7	1.5	Current	.9	1.6	1.5	1.5	1.7	1.6
	.9	1.0	.9		.4	.8	.9	1.0	1.1	1.0
	2.3	2.8	2.7		3.2	4.5	2.6	3.3	2.6	2.3
	1.3	1.4	1.3	Quick	.9	1.5	1.3	1.3	1.5	1.3
	.8	.8	.7		.3	.7	.6	.8	.9	.8
13	28.2	20	18.1	11	32.4	Sales/Receivables	0	UND	0	UND	8	43.6	20	18.2	24	15.1	22	16.9

Sales/Receivables detail									
13 28.2	20 18.1	11 32.4	0 UND / 3 111.0 / 20 18.3	0 UND / 29 12.4 / 53 6.9	8 43.6 / 33 11.1 / 58 6.3	20 18.2 / 37 9.8 / 57 6.4	24 15.1 / 41 8.8 / 58 6.2	22 16.9 / 47 7.7 / 62 5.9
44 8.3	44 8.2	37 9.7						
66 5.5	66 5.6	57 6.4						

	Comparative				Current					
				Cost of Sales/Inventory						
				Cost of Sales/Payables						
	5.6	4.5	5.8	Sales/Working Capital	5.0	5.7	7.5	5.0	5.3	6.0
	13.7	12.3	15.2		-117.6	16.0	11.3	16.8	12.8	12.5
	-92.9	163.4	-98.0		-14.2	-103.9	-55.2	-97.4	88.0	-999.8
	8.6	10.8	10.6	EBIT/Interest	6.8	10.6	9.5	14.9	12.9	11.0
(267)	2.7	(275) 3.4	(270) 3.4		(23) 1.8	(34) 3.5	(34) 2.5	(50) 3.7	(65) 4.3	(64) 3.0
	.5	1.0	1.0		.2	.6	1.0	.9	1.6	.4
	14.6	11.0	5.0	Net Profit + Depr., Dep., Amort./Cur. Mat. L/T/D						15.0
(31)	3.3	(28) 3.1	(32) 2.7						(10)	5.2
	1.5	1.0	1.2							1.7
	.3	.2	.4	Fixed/Worth	.1	.3	.7	.3	.4	.5
	.8	.7	.9		1.1	1.2	1.4	.9	.8	.8
	2.8	2.8	3.6		6.6	-8.1	3.5	2.5	2.3	2.6
	.5	.5	.5	Debt/Worth	.6	.4	.6	.4	.5	.8
	1.2	1.4	1.4		3.3	1.3	2.3	1.0	1.1	1.5
	7.0	5.5	7.7		21.9	-207.2	4.3	4.1	5.0	17.8
	42.5	45.5	39.4	% Profit Before Taxes/Tangible Net Worth	70.3	80.8	28.3	71.9	30.8	34.0
(313)	12.6	(315) 14.0	(295) 13.4		(32) 17.1	(41) 13.6	(34) 10.7	(54) 17.1	(72) 14.5	(62) 12.2
	-1.0	.4	1.0		-6.4	.3	.3	-.4	4.4	.4
	14.8	16.5	15.0	% Profit Before Taxes/Total Assets	23.8	21.7	10.6	22.6	13.7	11.4
	3.6	5.4	4.9		4.0	6.8	3.7	4.7	5.7	3.8
	-1.6	-.4	.1		-3.6	.3	-.3	-.7	1.8	-.7
	34.4	30.3	29.7	Sales/Net Fixed Assets	53.4	46.9	19.2	23.3	25.2	50.9
	7.3	7.7	6.3		9.4	9.3	3.6	5.0	6.1	6.1
	2.6	3.0	2.7		1.3	3.0	1.8	2.6	3.3	3.0
	3.3	3.5	3.8	Sales/Total Assets	5.1	4.0	2.8	4.4	3.6	3.6
	1.8	2.0	2.0		1.9	2.6	1.6	1.9	2.3	2.0
	1.1	1.1	1.2		.5	1.2	1.1	1.2	1.5	1.1
	.9	.9	1.2	% Depr., Dep., Amort./Sales	1.3	.9	1.4	1.8	1.0	.9
(316)	2.5	(306) 2.2	(304) 2.6		(25) 4.0	(44) 2.7	(36) 2.9	(54) 3.0	(77) 2.6	(68) 2.1
	4.7	4.2	4.4		11.9	5.4	5.6	4.6	3.8	3.5
	3.8	5.6	4.9	% Officers', Directors', Owners' Comp/Sales	10.0	3.8		5.8	4.6	
(74)	7.5	(75) 9.5	(67) 9.3		(12) 16.6	(18) 16.6	(12)	(12) 9.7	(11) 6.7	
	21.9	18.2	20.9		23.2	25.9		29.1	11.4	
	6734699M	8611782M	11645781M	Net Sales ($)	20640M	109134M	149680M	452169M	1303916M	9610242M
	5610946M	5674295M	5962010M	Total Assets ($)	34007M	74781M	113121M	271349M	677713M	4791039M

© RMA 2003

M = $ thousand   MM = $ million
See Pages 11 through 18 for Explanation of Ratios and Data

1294

Current Data Sorted By Assets   **Comparative Historical Data**

Type of Statement	0-500M	500M-2MM	2-10MM	10-50MM	50-100MM	100-250MM	4/1/98-3/31/99 ALL	4/1/99-3/31/00 ALL
Unqualified	3	5	50	144	102	123	379	424
Reviewed		7		1	1	2	4	10
Compiled	1	5	6	1			13	17
Tax Returns	6	1	4				12	5
Other	9	7	37	55	46	52	174	132
	355 (4/1-9/30/02)			313 (10/1/02-3/31/03)				
NUMBER OF STATEMENTS	19	18	104	201	149	177	582	588

ASSETS	%	%	%	%	%	%	%	%
Cash & Equivalents	28.0	20.4	12.6	10.4	10.8	9.1	9.9	8.9
Trade Receivables (net)	7.3	15.6	23.4	17.6	15.5	14.3	16.9	18.1
Inventory	.6	2.0	2.8	2.2	1.6	1.4	1.7	1.9
All Other Current	6.5	6.1	2.3	4.2	3.8	2.8	2.5	3.1
Total Current	42.3	44.1	41.1	34.3	31.7	27.6	31.1	32.0
Fixed Assets (net)	47.7	41.0	45.6	47.9	45.0	44.6	45.1	45.2
Intangibles (net)	.7	5.4	2.7	.8	.6	1.6	2.0	1.3
All Other Non-Current	9.4	9.5	10.7	17.0	22.7	26.2	21.7	21.5
Total	100.0	100.0	100.0	100.0	100.0	100.0	100.0	100.0

LIABILITIES								
Notes Payable-Short Term	5.6	16.6	4.3	1.0	1.2	.7	1.3	1.5
Cur. Mat.-L/T/D	6.4	2.7	3.2	2.5	2.9	1.6	2.7	2.0
Trade Payables	3.5	5.4	5.7	6.0	5.3	5.0	5.4	5.8
Income Taxes Payable	.0	.9	.1	.0	.3	.0	.1	.0
All Other Current	30.0	38.0	14.7	11.7	8.7	8.4	15.9	9.7
Total Current	45.5	63.6	28.0	21.2	18.4	15.8	25.4	19.0
Long Term Debt	50.2	28.2	29.6	24.9	24.4	29.9	29.0	25.1
Deferred Taxes	.0	.2	.3	.0	.0	.0	.1	.1
All Other Non-Current	.1	4.3	2.9	2.7	4.1	5.2	3.6	4.2
Net Worth	4.1	3.8	39.2	51.2	53.1	49.1	41.9	51.6
Total Liabilities & Net Worth	100.0	100.0	100.0	100.0	100.0	100.0	100.0	100.0

INCOME DATA								
Net Sales	100.0	100.0	100.0	100.0	100.0	100.0	100.0	100.0
Gross Profit								
Operating Expenses	91.2	84.7	85.6	96.9	96.1	96.2	99.8	95.8
Operating Profit	8.8	15.3	14.4	3.1	3.9	3.8	.2	4.2
All Other Expenses (net)	.2	2.7	3.3	.7	.9	2.5	.2	.8
Profit Before Taxes	8.6	12.5	11.2	2.4	2.9	1.2	.0	3.4

RATIOS								
Current	2.0	2.8	3.2	2.8	2.8	2.5	2.7	2.6
	1.1	.8	1.7	2.0	2.1	1.8	1.9	1.9
	.2	.4	1.0	1.2	1.4	1.3	1.3	1.4
Quick	1.6	2.1	2.7	2.3	2.3	2.1	2.3	2.2
	1.0	.7	1.4	1.7	1.6	1.5	1.6 (580)	1.6
	.2	.3	.8	1.0	1.2	1.1	1.1	1.1
Sales/Receivables	0 UND	0 UND	34 / 10.7	41 / 8.8	46 / 7.9	46 / 7.9	48 / 7.6	51 / 7.1
	0 UND	6 / 61.8	49 / 7.4	54 / 6.7	55 / 6.6	55 / 6.6	62 / 5.9	63 / 5.8
	39 / 9.5	33 / 10.9	67 / 5.5	63 / 5.8	67 / 5.5	63 / 5.8	74 / 4.9	77 / 4.8
Cost of Sales/Inventory								
Cost of Sales/Payables								
Sales/Working Capital	17.3	6.6	4.5	4.7	4.2	5.2	5.0	4.9
	213.1	−110.0	9.0	7.4	6.7	8.2	7.8	7.7
	−27.6	−7.6	NM	27.6	14.0	17.8	18.5	16.2
EBIT/Interest	(14) 65.0	(10) 36.8	(88) 17.3	(184) 5.2	(132) 5.9	(166) 3.7	(527) 7.1	(516) 6.4
	2.5	9.2	4.6	1.8	2.7	1.9	3.3	2.7
	.0	3.2	1.0	.1	.9	.5	1.3	.9
Net Profit + Depr., Dep., Amort./Cur. Mat. L/T/D						(34)	10.2	(16) 7.7
							2.9	3.8
							.9	1.3
Fixed/Worth	.4	.8	.5	.6	.6	.7	.6	.6
	1.1	1.5	1.0	.8	.8	.9	.9	.8
	−19.0	−1.0	2.2	1.4	1.2	1.2	1.4	1.3
Debt/Worth	.6	1.0	.5	.5	.4	.7	.5	.4
	6.0	2.3	1.2	.7	.7	1.1	.8	.8
	−7.3	−4.0	4.5	1.5	1.5	1.7	1.6	1.7
% Profit Before Taxes/Tangible Net Worth	(13) 138.5	(12) 113.6	(93) 59.8	(191) 9.0	(145) 7.9	(176) 8.8	(552) 12.7	(565) 10.1
	18.0	54.8	17.1	4.0	3.6	2.9	7.3	5.1
	−18.1	.3	1.9	−2.1	.1	−1.4	2.3	−.2
% Profit Before Taxes/Total Assets	62.5	43.6	21.6	5.0	4.7	3.7	7.0	5.7
	7.4	25.2	5.7	1.8	2.1	1.6	4.0	2.8
	−2.9	3.1	.5	−1.2	.0	−.7	.6	−.3
Sales/Net Fixed Assets	127.1	66.2	7.9	3.2	2.7	2.5	2.9	2.8
	15.4	14.3	3.5	2.3	2.1	2.1	2.1	2.1
	2.3	2.3	1.8	1.8	1.7	1.7	1.6	1.6
Sales/Total Assets	23.1	6.3	2.1	1.4	1.2	1.1	1.2	1.2
	5.1	2.7	1.4	1.1	1.0	.9	.9	.9
	1.2	1.3	.8	.9	.8	.8	.7	.7
% Depr., Dep., Amort./Sales	(15) 1.0	(15) 1.1	(94) 2.8	(194) 4.1	(148) 4.2	(123) 4.5	(529) 4.4	(532) 4.4
	3.5	3.6	4.2	5.1	5.4	5.4	5.6	5.8
	6.2	7.2	6.6	6.0	6.3	6.4	6.7	6.9
% Officers', Directors', Owners' Comp/Sales	(10) 10.5			(27) 3.5	(20) 8.2	(18) 6.4	(63) 6.4	(68) 6.2
	23.7			9.4	28.3	13.5	12.7	20.6
	30.9			35.8	40.8	41.0	36.9	40.1
Net Sales ($)	41934M	80747M	963045M	6621678M	10997063M	28107723M	33770481M	37245795M
Total Assets ($)	4082M	17967M	598167M	5421005M	10874305M	29283176M	38898090M	41272178M

M = $ thousand   MM = $ million
See Pages 11 through 18 for Explanation of Ratios and Data

Comparative Historical Data | Current Data Sorted By Sales

			Type of Statement						
309	311	427	Unqualified	5	9	8	27	65	313
9	9	11	Reviewed		2		1	3	5
45	40	13	Compiled	2	2	2	3	3	1
5	3	11	Tax Returns	3	4		2	2	
189	148	206	Other	9	14	10	14	31	128
4/1/00-3/31/01	4/1/01-3/31/02	4/1/02-3/31/03		355 (4/1-9/30/02)			313 (10/1/02-3/31/03)		
ALL	ALL	ALL		0-1MM	1-3MM	3-5MM	5-10MM	10-25MM	25MM & OVER
557	511	668	**NUMBER OF STATEMENTS**	19	31	20	47	104	447
%	%	%	**ASSETS**	%	%	%	%	%	%
8.7	9.4	11.3	Cash & Equivalents	13.8	16.0	13.8	13.9	13.0	10.0
16.6	17.0	16.8	Trade Receivables (net)	9.0	6.3	18.7	22.2	19.6	16.5
2.1	1.9	1.9	Inventory	.7	1.0	2.2	3.4	2.3	1.7
3.1	3.5	3.6	All Other Current	5.1	5.7	2.5	2.8	3.5	3.5
30.4	31.8	33.5	Total Current	28.5	29.1	37.4	42.3	38.5	31.8
45.2	45.4	45.8	Fixed Assets (net)	58.3	55.2	43.6	44.6	45.2	45.0
2.4	1.7	1.4	Intangibles (net)	.7	3.6	6.1	1.3	1.3	1.1
22.0	21.1	19.3	All Other Non-Current	12.5	12.1	13.0	11.9	15.0	22.2
100.0	100.0	100.0	Total	100.0	100.0	100.0	100.0	100.0	100.0
			LIABILITIES						
2.0	2.3	2.0	Notes Payable-Short Term	5.7	15.0	3.5	1.0	2.1	1.0
2.8	2.2	2.6	Cur. Mat.-L/T/D	6.8	3.0	2.4	2.6	2.7	2.3
5.6	5.8	5.5	Trade Payables	6.0	2.1	3.6	5.6	5.3	5.8
.1	.0	.1	Income Taxes Payable	.0	.0	.8	.2	.0	.1
9.2	9.5	11.9	All Other Current	19.7	21.6	12.6	12.4	14.3	10.2
19.7	19.8	22.1	Total Current	38.2	41.7	22.9	21.8	24.3	19.5
27.0	27.8	27.6	Long Term Debt	59.9	40.2	24.4	32.8	23.8	25.9
.1	.1	.1	Deferred Taxes	.2	.0	.2	.0	.3	.0
3.7	2.7	3.7	All Other Non-Current	3.3	.7	1.1	5.0	1.8	4.3
49.5	49.7	46.6	Net Worth	−1.5	17.3	51.4	40.4	49.8	50.3
100.0	100.0	100.0	Total Liabilities & Net Worth	100.0	100.0	100.0	100.0	100.0	100.0
			INCOME DATA						
100.0	100.0	100.0	Net Sales	100.0	100.0	100.0	100.0	100.0	100.0
			Gross Profit						
95.6	95.8	94.3	Operating Expenses	75.6	73.9	82.9	88.8	96.6	97.0
4.4	4.2	5.7	Operating Profit	24.4	26.1	17.1	11.2	3.4	3.0
.5	1.3	1.7	All Other Expenses (net)	5.0	8.8	5.9	1.5	.3	1.2
3.9	2.9	4.0	Profit Before Taxes	19.5	17.3	11.2	9.7	3.0	1.8
			RATIOS						
2.6	2.6	2.7		2.3	1.9	4.2	3.7	3.1	2.6
1.8	1.9	1.9	Current	1.3	.7	1.8	2.6	2.0	1.9
1.3	1.4	1.2		.3	.2	.8	1.4	1.2	1.3
2.2	2.2	2.3		2.0	1.1	3.3	3.3	2.6	2.2
1.5	1.6	1.6	Quick	1.0	.5	1.3	1.9	1.7	1.6
1.0	1.1	1.0		.1	.2	.8	1.2	1.0	1.1
49 7.4	49 7.5	42 8.7		0 UND	0 UND	0 UND	36 10.1	40 9.1	45 8.0
62 5.9	61 6.0	53 6.9	Sales/Receivables	16 22.3	0 UND	44 8.3	52 7.0	52 7.1	55 6.6
74 4.9	71 5.1	64 5.7		45 8.1	24 15.3	68 5.3	67 5.4	63 5.8	64 5.7
			Cost of Sales/Inventory						
			Cost of Sales/Payables						
4.6	5.0	4.8		6.2	10.2	4.6	3.9	4.4	5.0
8.0	7.7	7.9	Sales/Working Capital	26.2	−16.9	9.0	5.6	7.6	7.7
20.1	15.5	26.6		−3.5	−3.2	UND	17.4	37.4	18.4
(503) 5.6	(455) 5.0	(594) 5.6			(21) 38.5	(17) 17.3	(42) 26.6	(95) 7.9	(411) 4.3
2.6	2.2	2.3	EBIT/Interest		2.7	3.5	5.0	1.9	2.0
.8	.5	.5			.9	1.2	2.0	.4	.2
(18) 10.5	(18) 18.5	(27) 8.7	Net Profit + Depr., Dep.,						(19) 8.7
4.9	5.8	5.3	Amort./Cur. Mat. L/T/D						4.4
1.0	2.7	2.0							.3
.6	.6	.6		.7	.7	.7	.5	.6	.6
.8	.8	.9	Fixed/Worth	1.6	1.7	1.1	1.0	.8	.9
1.4	1.3	1.4		9.2	53.8	2.3	2.0	1.3	1.3
.5	.5	.5		1.0	.7	.3	.4	.5	.5
.9	.9	.9	Debt/Worth	3.0	1.7	1.0	.9	.8	.9
1.8	1.6	1.8		32.1	−7.3	4.2	2.9	1.6	1.6
(527) 10.8	(494) 10.4	(630) 11.3	% Profit Before Taxes/Tangible	(15) 71.2	(22) 80.1	(18) 60.1	(44) 62.2	(98) 9.5	(433) 8.9
5.4	4.7	4.5	Net Worth	27.9	11.5	24.2	17.1	3.8	3.8
.5	−.6	−.6		5.0	.2	−.4	2.8	−1.4	−1.5
5.8	5.2	5.7	% Profit Before Taxes/Total	22.1	22.1	27.7	20.3	6.0	4.5
2.6	2.3	2.3	Assets	7.4	4.5	9.5	4.3	1.7	1.8
−.2	−.6	−.5		2.8	.3	.2	1.2	−.8	−.9
2.8	3.0	3.2		9.8	18.8	7.0	7.5	4.4	2.8
2.1	2.2	2.3	Sales/Net Fixed Assets	2.0	3.0	2.6	2.4	2.5	2.3
1.6	1.7	1.7		1.1	.3	1.4	1.5	1.8	1.8
1.2	1.2	1.4		1.3	3.8	2.2	1.9	1.6	1.2
.9	1.0	1.0	Sales/Total Assets	1.0	.8	1.4	1.3	1.2	1.0
.7	.8	.7		.2	.2	.7	.9	.9	.8
(494) 4.2	(448) 4.2	(589) 3.9		(13) 5.1	(28) 2.5	(17) 4.5	(45) 2.8	(101) 3.4	(385) 4.2
5.6	5.4	5.2	% Depr., Dep., Amort./Sales	6.2	6.9	6.5	4.0	4.6	5.3
6.9	6.4	6.3		11.7	18.7	9.5	6.0	5.8	6.2
(71) 4.5	(78) 6.4	(90) 5.9	% Officers', Directors',					(13) 5.5	(58) 5.3
13.3	17.2	14.9	Owners' Comp/Sales					14.5	14.9
35.4	40.3	36.2						34.3	40.7
38765091M	37950772M	46812190M	Net Sales ($)	10174M	62106M	80494M	351846M	1812128M	44495442M
42817213M	39122642M	46198702M	Total Assets ($)	48405M	142465M	248092M	482797M	1624824M	43652119M

M = $ thousand   MM = $ million

See Pages 11 through 18 for Explanation of Ratios and Data

	Current Data Sorted By Assets							Comparative Historical Data	
							Type of Statement		
1	1	2	33	12	48		Unqualified		
							Reviewed		
							Compiled		
							Tax Returns		
		1	5	5	6		Other	4/1/98-3/31/99 ALL	4/1/99-3/31/00 ALL
	83 (4/1-9/30/02)		31 (10/1/02-3/31/03)						
0-500M	500M-2MM	2-10MM	10-50MM	50-100MM	100-250MM				
1	1	3	38	17	54		NUMBER OF STATEMENTS		
%	%	%	%	%	%		**ASSETS**	%	%
			10.1	11.0	7.7		Cash & Equivalents	D	D
			17.7	16.0	14.9		Trade Receivables (net)	A	A
			1.8	1.4	1.4		Inventory	T	T
			2.9	2.3	5.9		All Other Current	A	A
			32.4	30.6	29.9		Total Current		
			47.7	48.1	42.9		Fixed Assets (net)	N	N
			.6	.4	1.0		Intangibles (net)	O	O
			19.3	20.8	26.2		All Other Non-Current	T	T
			100.0	100.0	100.0		Total		
							LIABILITIES	A	A
			1.0	.5	.4		Notes Payable-Short Term	V	V
			2.0	1.3	1.6		Cur. Mat.-L/T/D	A	A
			7.7	4.9	5.7		Trade Payables	I	I
			.0	.0	.0		Income Taxes Payable	L	L
			8.9	7.4	7.9		All Other Current	A	A
			19.6	14.2	15.7		Total Current	B	B
			22.5	25.8	33.1		Long Term Debt	L	L
			.0	.0	.0		Deferred Taxes	E	E
			1.6	5.8	3.0		All Other Non-Current		
			56.3	54.2	48.2		Net Worth		
			100.0	100.0	100.0		Total Liabilities & Net Worth		
							INCOME DATA		
			100.0	100.0	100.0		Net Sales		
							Gross Profit		
			98.2	99.6	96.5		Operating Expenses		
			1.8	.4	3.5		Operating Profit		
			.9	.3	2.1		All Other Expenses (net)		
			.8	.1	1.4		Profit Before Taxes		
							RATIOS		
			2.7	3.2	2.6				
			1.9	2.1	2.0		Current		
			1.4	1.6	1.4				
			2.2	2.6	2.1				
			1.7	1.9	1.5		Quick		
			1.1	1.3	1.1				
		47	7.7	48 7.6	51 7.1				
		60	6.1	57 6.4	58 6.3		Sales/Receivables		
		70	5.2	70 5.2	67 5.4				
							Cost of Sales/Inventory		
							Cost of Sales/Payables		
			5.3	4.0	4.6				
			7.3	5.9	6.4		Sales/Working Capital		
			13.4	10.8	11.7				
			3.7	3.7	3.8				
			(35) 2.1	(15) 1.6	(53) 2.0		EBIT/Interest		
			–.4	–.6	.5				
							Net Profit + Depr., Dep., Amort./Cur. Mat. L /T/D		
			.6	.7	.7				
			.8	.9	.9		Fixed/Worth		
			1.2	1.3	1.4				
			.5	.5	.7				
			.6	.8	1.0		Debt/Worth		
			1.2	1.5	1.8				
			7.1	3.3	7.6				
			2.7	1.5	(53) 3.1		% Profit Before Taxes/Tangible Net Worth		
			–2.7	–4.9	–1.4				
			3.7	2.2	4.0				
			1.7	.8	1.4		% Profit Before Taxes/Total Assets		
			–1.4	–2.2	–.8				
			3.3	2.3	2.6				
			2.3	1.9	2.0		Sales/Net Fixed Assets		
			1.8	1.7	1.6				
			1.4	1.1	1.1				
			1.1	1.0	.8		Sales/Total Assets		
			.8	.8	.7				
			4.2	4.7	4.9				
			(37) 5.3	4.9	(34) 6.2		% Depr., Dep., Amort./Sales		
			6.1	6.2	7.1				
							% Officers', Directors', Owners' Comp/Sales		
31M	2105M	23517M	1484151M	1198338M	8540316M		Net Sales ($)		
26M	1899M	16512M	1215939M	1250630M	9423429M		Total Assets ($)		

© RMA 2003

M = $ thousand   MM = $ million
See Pages 11 through 18 for Explanation of Ratios and Data

Comparative Historical Data				Current Data Sorted By Sales					
	11	97	Type of Statement Unqualified	1	1	2	1	7	85
			Reviewed						
			Compiled						
			Tax Returns						
	23	17	Other				1	1	15
4/1/00- 3/31/01 ALL	4/1/01- 3/31/02 ALL	4/1/02- 3/31/03 ALL			83 (4/1-9/30/02)			31 (10/1/02-3/31/03)	
				0-1MM	1-3MM	3-5MM	5-10MM	10-25MM	25MM & OVER
	34	114	NUMBER OF STATEMENTS	1	1	2	2	8	100
%	%	%	ASSETS	%	%	%	%	%	%
	8.4	9.2	Cash & Equivalents						9.0
	19.4	16.1	Trade Receivables (net)						16.2
	2.0	1.6	Inventory						1.5
	1.9	4.2	All Other Current						4.4
	31.7	31.2	Total Current						31.1
	46.9	45.1	Fixed Assets (net)						44.5
	.6	.7	Intangibles (net)						.8
	20.8	23.1	All Other Non-Current						23.6
	100.0	100.0	Total						100.0
			LIABILITIES						
	1.0	.6	Notes Payable-Short Term						.6
	2.7	1.8	Cur. Mat.-L/T/D						1.7
	8.4	6.4	Trade Payables						6.5
	.0	.0	Income Taxes Payable						.0
	12.6	8.3	All Other Current						8.0
	24.8	17.0	Total Current						16.9
	28.8	27.8	Long Term Debt						28.6
	.0	.0	Deferred Taxes						.0
	6.3	3.1	All Other Non-Current						3.2
	40.1	52.1	Net Worth						51.3
	100.0	100.0	Total Liabilities & Net Worth						100.0
			INCOME DATA						
	100.0	100.0	Net Sales						100.0
			Gross Profit						
	95.6	97.4	Operating Expenses						97.9
	4.4	2.6	Operating Profit						2.1
	2.8	1.2	All Other Expenses (net)						1.4
	1.6	1.3	Profit Before Taxes						.7
			RATIOS						
	1.8	2.6							2.6
	1.4	1.9	Current						1.9
	1.0	1.4							1.4
	1.5	2.2							2.2
	1.3	1.6	Quick						1.6
	1.0	1.1							1.1
	52 7.0	50 7.3							50 7.2
	59 6.1	57 6.4	Sales/Receivables						58 6.3
	68 5.3	68 5.4							68 5.3
			Cost of Sales/Inventory						
			Cost of Sales/Payables						
	8.0	5.0							5.0
	13.0	7.1	Sales/Working Capital						7.1
	177.1	13.1							13.0
	5.5	3.8							3.7
	(33) 2.2	(106) 2.0	EBIT/Interest						(95) 2.0
	1.1	.4							.4
			Net Profit + Depr., Dep., Amort./Cur. Mat. L/T/D						
	.7	.7							.7
	1.0	.8	Fixed/Worth						.8
	2.2	1.2							1.3
	.6	.5							.5
	1.0	.9	Debt/Worth						.9
	3.0	1.5							1.5
	9.1	6.9							6.3
	(30) 4.5	(113) 2.8	% Profit Before Taxes/Tangible Net Worth						(99) 2.5
	-.5	-2.6							-2.8
	5.4	3.7							3.7
	1.8	1.4	% Profit Before Taxes/Total Assets						1.2
	-.3	-1.3							-1.3
	3.2	2.7							2.7
	2.4	2.1	Sales/Net Fixed Assets						2.1
	1.7	1.7							1.7
	1.4	1.1							1.1
	1.1	.9	Sales/Total Assets						.9
	.8	.8							.8
	4.1	4.4							4.5
	(31) 5.0	(93) 5.5	% Depr., Dep., Amort./Sales						(79) 5.5
	5.9	6.6							6.6
			% Officers', Directors', Owners' Comp/Sales						
	2349403M	11248458M	Net Sales ($)	31M	2105M	8317M	18758M	144969M	11074278M
	2362695M	11908435M	Total Assets ($)	26M	1899M	18341M	13417M	165819M	11708933M

M = $ thousand   MM = $ million
See Pages 11 through 18 for Explanation of Ratios and Data

Current Data Sorted By Assets   **Comparative Historical Data**

0-500M	500M-2MM	2-10MM	10-50MM	50-100MM	100-250MM		4/1/98-3/31/99 ALL	4/1/99-3/31/00 ALL
						Type of Statement		
2	2	26	14	3	3	Unqualified	44	46
						Reviewed		1
1						Compiled	4	
						Tax Returns		1
2		8	9		1	Other	13	13
	37 (4/1-9/30/02)		34 (10/1/02-3/31/03)					
5	2	34	23	3	4	**NUMBER OF STATEMENTS**	61	61
%	%	%	%	%	%	**ASSETS**	%	%
		12.4	15.0			Cash & Equivalents	17.4	13.9
		24.4	17.0			Trade Receivables (net)	24.9	27.4
		.4	.2			Inventory	.3	.4
		4.5	5.9			All Other Current	2.7	5.1
		41.7	38.2			Total Current	45.4	46.8
		49.7	48.8			Fixed Assets (net)	39.7	37.1
		1.5	1.1			Intangibles (net)	1.5	4.2
		7.0	11.9			All Other Non-Current	13.4	11.9
		100.0	100.0			Total	100.0	100.0
						LIABILITIES		
		4.9	2.4			Notes Payable-Short Term	5.0	4.9
		2.8	2.2			Cur. Mat.-L/T/D	2.0	3.5
		5.8	5.5			Trade Payables	6.9	9.0
		.0	.0			Income Taxes Payable	.2	.0
		16.4	9.1			All Other Current	14.6	14.1
		29.8	19.2			Total Current	28.8	31.5
		23.3	32.7			Long Term Debt	20.1	22.7
		.0	.0			Deferred Taxes	.1	.3
		5.4	1.0			All Other Non-Current	3.1	2.3
		41.6	47.2			Net Worth	47.9	43.2
		100.0	100.0			Total Liabilities & Net Worth	100.0	100.0
						INCOME DATA		
		100.0	100.0			Net Sales	100.0	100.0
						Gross Profit		
		93.2	98.2			Operating Expenses	96.6	100.1
		6.8	1.8			Operating Profit	3.4	−.1
		1.4	1.3			All Other Expenses (net)	−1.3	−1.5
		5.4	.4			Profit Before Taxes	4.7	1.4
						RATIOS		
		2.7	3.3			Current	3.1	2.4
		2.0	2.2				1.7	1.6
		1.1	1.6				1.1	1.2
		2.3	3.3			Quick	2.9	2.2
		1.7	2.0				1.6	1.5
		.9	1.0				1.1	.9
		33 10.9	24 15.5			Sales/Receivables	25 14.8	33 10.9
		44 8.3	47 7.7				44 8.3	51 7.1
		58 6.3	69 5.3				68 5.4	82 4.5
						Cost of Sales/Inventory		
						Cost of Sales/Payables		
		4.6	4.0			Sales/Working Capital	5.2	5.4
		11.9	7.0				12.4	11.9
		67.0	15.8				57.6	43.1
		5.0	4.9			EBIT/Interest	6.7	4.2
		(28) 3.6	(21) 1.0				(50) 2.8	(55) 1.7
		1.0	−1.5				.8	−.7
						Net Profit + Depr., Dep., Amort./Cur. Mat. L /T/D		
		.7	.5			Fixed/Worth	.4	.4
		1.0	1.2				.9	.9
		2.0	2.4				1.9	2.0
		.5	.4			Debt/Worth	.4	.5
		1.0	1.3				1.0	1.1
		2.0	3.0				3.4	3.9
		26.1	11.8			% Profit Before Taxes/Tangible Net Worth	16.9	14.9
		(30) 9.3	(22) 2.0				(57) 8.2	(53) 5.3
		.3	−5.7				.0	−3.5
		8.8	4.8			% Profit Before Taxes/Total Assets	9.5	6.7
		6.4	1.2				3.5	2.7
		.0	−2.3				−.2	−3.2
		5.3	3.9			Sales/Net Fixed Assets	8.8	17.7
		2.7	3.0				3.7	3.2
		1.8	2.5				2.1	2.2
		2.5	1.6			Sales/Total Assets	2.5	2.9
		1.4	1.5				1.5	1.4
		1.0	1.2				1.0	1.0
		1.8	2.1			% Depr., Dep., Amort./Sales	1.6	1.5
		(32) 2.6	3.1				(56) 2.8	(49) 3.0
		3.7	3.6				4.2	4.0
						% Officers', Directors', Owners' Comp/Sales		
5586M	8918M	326684M	593357M	318473M	643771M	Net Sales ($)	1140178M	1588515M
1306M	3309M	183004M	419133M	240563M	648183M	Total Assets ($)	1211683M	1451227M

M = $ thousand   MM = $ million
See Pages 11 through 18 for Explanation of Ratios and Data

Comparative Historical Data / Current Data Sorted By Sales

	31	32	50	Type of Statement	2	4	4	10	16	14
		1		Unqualified						
				Reviewed						
	3	4	1	Compiled		1				
	1			Tax Returns						
	19	20	20	Other	2	1		3	9	5
	4/1/00-3/31/01 ALL	4/1/01-3/31/02 ALL	4/1/02-3/31/03 ALL		37 (4/1-9/30/02) 0-1MM	1-3MM	3-5MM	34 (10/1/02-3/31/03) 5-10MM	10-25MM	25MM & OVER
NUMBER OF STATEMENTS	54	57	71		4	6	4	13	25	19
	%	%	%	**ASSETS**	%	%	%	%	%	%
Cash & Equivalents	14.2	14.0	13.1					10.0	14.0	8.8
Trade Receivables (net)	23.9	24.2	22.2					18.9	24.6	21.2
Inventory	.4	.3	.3					.6	.2	.5
All Other Current	3.1	4.1	4.8					3.6	4.6	6.2
Total Current	41.6	42.6	40.4					33.1	43.4	36.7
Fixed Assets (net)	45.1	43.8	46.9					61.1	45.8	40.2
Intangibles (net)	1.9	3.2	3.1					.5	1.7	8.3
All Other Non-Current	11.4	10.4	9.5					5.3	9.0	14.8
Total	100.0	100.0	100.0					100.0	100.0	100.0
				LIABILITIES						
Notes Payable-Short Term	3.1	7.4	3.7					3.6	5.3	2.5
Cur. Mat.-L/T/D	2.5	2.3	3.4					2.5	2.2	4.2
Trade Payables	5.5	8.0	6.0					5.3	7.0	6.1
Income Taxes Payable	.0	.1	.0					.0	.0	.0
All Other Current	12.3	13.2	17.6					8.6	13.4	18.6
Total Current	23.5	31.0	30.8					20.0	27.9	31.5
Long Term Debt	21.5	28.9	25.9					27.6	23.5	26.7
Deferred Taxes	.0	.1	.0					.0	.0	.1
All Other Non-Current	2.9	3.4	3.5					2.0	.6	3.5
Net Worth	52.1	36.7	39.8					50.4	48.0	38.2
Total Liabilities & Net Worth	100.0	100.0	100.0					100.0	100.0	100.0
				INCOME DATA						
Net Sales	100.0	100.0	100.0					100.0	100.0	100.0
Gross Profit										
Operating Expenses	97.3	98.4	95.3					95.1	98.3	96.6
Operating Profit	2.7	1.6	4.7					4.9	1.7	3.4
All Other Expenses (net)	−.2	.6	1.7					.1	.2	3.2
Profit Before Taxes	2.9	1.0	3.0					4.8	1.5	.2
				RATIOS						
Current	3.5	2.8	2.7					2.4	3.0	2.2
	1.9	1.5	1.9					1.9	2.0	1.7
	1.3	.9	1.1					1.1	1.1	1.0
Quick	3.2	2.3	2.4					2.2	2.6	2.0
	1.6	1.2	1.5					1.8	1.9	1.1
	1.2	.8	.9					1.0	.8	.9
Sales/Receivables	28 13.2	27 13.4	32 11.6					35 10.3	33 11.0	34 10.7
	51 7.1	46 7.8	44 8.3					44 8.2	49 7.4	45 8.1
	66 5.6	59 6.2	58 6.3					50 7.3	60 6.1	69 5.3
Cost of Sales/Inventory										
Cost of Sales/Payables										
Sales/Working Capital	5.4	5.7	4.7					6.2	4.4	6.7
	10.5	13.3	10.7					10.7	13.1	10.7
	21.9	−76.2	69.7					43.4	302.0	161.0
EBIT/Interest	(45) 6.9	(51) 6.0	(60) 5.0					(11) 5.4	(22) 6.1	(16) 5.8
	3.7	1.6	1.8					3.7	2.2	1.4
	1.1	−.3	.3					1.1	−1.9	−.9
Net Profit + Depr., Dep., Amort./Cur. Mat. L/T/D										
Fixed/Worth	.5	.6	.6					.9	.5	.6
	.9	1.1	1.2					1.2	.9	1.5
	1.8	2.8	2.6					2.1	1.8	19.4
Debt/Worth	.5	.5	.5					.4	.4	.5
	.8	1.1	1.3					.8	1.1	2.1
	2.0	4.1	4.0					2.2	1.8	34.5
% Profit Before Taxes/Tangible Net Worth	17.5	21.2	22.9					31.5	16.3	22.9
	(51) 5.9	(50) 3.4	(63) 8.6					9.4	(24) 2.0	(15) 8.6
	.1	−3.3	−2.1					1.2	−8.1	−1.7
% Profit Before Taxes/Total Assets	10.7	11.6	8.5					11.4	7.6	6.2
	3.3	1.7	2.8					4.1	1.9	2.8
	.0	−2.5	−1.3					.9	−1.5	−2.3
Sales/Net Fixed Assets	6.9	8.0	4.4					3.0	6.7	4.2
	3.0	3.7	3.0					2.4	3.5	3.3
	2.3	2.3	2.2					1.7	2.5	2.7
Sales/Total Assets	2.3	2.3	2.2					2.0	2.5	1.6
	1.6	1.7	1.5					1.3	1.6	1.5
	1.2	1.2	1.1					1.0	1.3	1.2
% Depr., Dep., Amort./Sales	1.6	1.3	2.0					2.4	1.5	1.7
	(51) 2.6	(55) 2.4	(64) 2.7					3.5	(24) 2.5	(16) 3.0
	3.5	3.1	3.7					3.8	3.2	4.7
% Officers', Directors', Owners' Comp/Sales										
Net Sales ($)	1287719M	1218292M	1896789M		3065M	11910M	17514M	90960M	405623M	1367717M
Total Assets ($)	1015968M	802957M	1495498M		11406M	9260M	11345M	70545M	258244M	1134698M

M = $ thousand   MM = $ million
See Pages 11 through 18 for Explanation of Ratios and Data

Current Data Sorted By Assets

Comparative Historical Data

1	1	16	21	12	10	Type of Statement		
	1	1	1			Unqualified	49	60
2	5	4				Reviewed	6	6
4	2	2	2			Compiled	12	8
6	6	14	9	2	8	Tax Returns	2	6
						Other	28	32
	47 (4/1-9/30/02)			83 (10/1/02-3/31/03)			4/1/98-3/31/99	4/1/99-3/31/00
0-500M	500M-2MM	2-10MM	10-50MM	50-100MM	100-250MM		ALL	ALL
13	15	37	33	14	18	NUMBER OF STATEMENTS	97	112
%	%	%	%	%	%	ASSETS	%	%
53.2	13.3	11.9	9.0	12.3	8.1	Cash & Equivalents	11.7	13.7
3.6	21.5	27.0	20.1	13.4	21.5	Trade Receivables (net)	20.8	20.1
4.9	.6	1.4	1.3	.6	1.4	Inventory	.8	.6
.4	7.3	5.7	5.1	3.1	2.3	All Other Current	4.5	3.6
62.0	42.6	46.0	35.5	29.5	33.2	Total Current	37.8	38.0
29.3	42.3	39.6	43.3	41.4	36.3	Fixed Assets (net)	42.3	42.1
2.0	11.6	1.3	6.8	5.1	8.2	Intangibles (net)	3.0	3.1
6.7	3.5	13.1	14.4	24.1	22.3	All Other Non-Current	17.0	16.9
100.0	100.0	100.0	100.0	100.0	100.0	Total	100.0	100.0
						LIABILITIES		
9.3	8.7	8.6	4.7	1.6	1.9	Notes Payable-Short Term	7.1	11.0
7.4	5.5	4.4	4.0	1.9	1.1	Cur. Mat.-L/T/D	2.1	2.3
5.9	12.9	6.7	5.7	3.3	5.2	Trade Payables	7.0	8.1
1.8	.2	.0	.0	.0	.1	Income Taxes Payable	.0	.1
53.0	63.0	15.9	15.2	8.8	12.8	All Other Current	21.5	15.7
77.5	90.2	35.6	29.7	15.6	21.1	Total Current	37.7	37.2
12.1	34.1	23.2	28.9	27.4	15.5	Long Term Debt	21.2	22.8
.4	.0	.4	.0	.2	.1	Deferred Taxes	.3	.3
3.0	2.7	4.4	1.8	5.7	4.1	All Other Non-Current	2.7	2.4
7.2	−27.1	36.4	39.6	51.1	59.2	Net Worth	38.2	37.3
100.0	100.0	100.0	100.0	100.0	100.0	Total Liabilities & Net Worth	100.0	100.0
						INCOME DATA		
100.0	100.0	100.0	100.0	100.0	100.0	Net Sales	100.0	100.0
						Gross Profit		
89.7	81.5	93.2	91.1	96.3	94.1	Operating Expenses	94.7	93.3
10.3	18.5	6.8	8.9	3.7	5.9	Operating Profit	5.3	6.7
.3	8.5	1.7	2.1	3.3	1.6	All Other Expenses (net)	−3.0	−1.1
10.0	10.0	5.0	6.8	.4	4.4	Profit Before Taxes	8.2	7.8
						RATIOS		
1.2	2.9	2.6	2.4	3.0	2.4		2.9	2.5
1.0	.7	2.0	1.3	2.1	1.8	Current	1.7	1.6
.5	.4	1.3	.8	1.3	1.2		1.0	1.0
1.2	2.2	2.5	1.9	2.8	2.1		2.4	2.4
1.0	.4	1.5	1.2	1.7	1.5	Quick	1.5	1.4
.3	.3	1.0	.7	.9	1.0		.7	.9
0 UND	0 UND	22 16.4	44 8.2	30 12.2	54 6.7		20 18.2	29 12.5
0 UND	6 63.1	47 7.7	58 6.3	58 6.3	68 5.4	Sales/Receivables	58 6.3	59 6.2
0 UND	56 6.5	69 5.3	77 4.7	76 4.8	73 5.0		83 4.4	75 4.9
						Cost of Sales/Inventory		
						Cost of Sales/Payables		
58.3	15.7	5.2	4.7	3.5	4.5		5.0	5.4
−289.3	−17.5	9.3	11.0	6.7	7.1	Sales/Working Capital	9.7	10.0
−30.5	−4.4	21.9	−23.4	18.9	42.3		418.2	802.4
(10) 64.0	(11) 23.8	(33) 8.4	(29) 11.3	(12) 3.4	21.2		(73) 8.9	(93) 12.5
8.1	2.2	3.3	3.4	1.4	4.7	EBIT/Interest	3.5	3.2
.6	.2	.0	.9	−3.9	.6		1.0	1.2
						Net Profit + Depr., Dep., Amort./Cur. Mat. L /T/D		
.1	1.1	.4	.5	.5	.4		.5	.5
.9	3.4	1.1	1.3	.9	.8	Fixed/Worth	1.0	1.0
−1.8	−.8	NM	4.0	2.9	1.1		2.4	2.4
.9	1.2	.6	.5	.5	.4		.4	.5
2.3	5.6	1.1	1.6	.9	.7	Debt/Worth	1.1	1.4
−3.3	−2.4	NM	7.7	4.7	1.5		3.8	3.7
		(28) 26.5	(27) 26.0	(13) 9.8	(16) 16.9	% Profit Before Taxes/Tangible	(86) 30.3	(97) 57.3
		12.3	11.8	.0	7.3	Net Worth	12.4	11.3
		−.1	−1.2	−9.6	−4.3		1.9	1.0
139.5	50.1	13.1	11.8	6.1	9.8	% Profit Before Taxes/Total	10.5	13.5
35.3	7.9	6.7	4.3	.1	4.7	Assets	5.0	5.0
−2.1	−1.9	−2.3	−1.4	−4.7	−1.0		.0	−.1
UND	131.8	17.9	6.1	3.4	5.2		9.2	7.9
32.5	8.1	6.0	2.3	1.9	2.5	Sales/Net Fixed Assets	2.6	2.5
12.2	1.3	2.2	1.5	1.1	1.8		1.5	1.6
23.0	6.0	2.9	1.5	1.2	1.5		2.2	2.1
7.1	1.7	1.7	1.2	.7	1.1	Sales/Total Assets	1.2	1.2
4.8	.7	.9	.6	.4	.7		.7	.7
	(10) 2.2	(34) 1.0	(31) 2.5	(12) 3.6	(13) 2.5	% Depr., Dep., Amort./Sales	(85) 2.0	(95) 2.5
	8.2	3.1	4.5	5.6	3.7		4.0	4.0
	18.4	5.4	6.2	7.6	5.6		5.9	6.7
						% Officers', Directors', Owners' Comp/Sales	(12) 2.2	
							9.2	
							22.0	
28401M	50344M	363044M	882998M	754691M	3456475M	Net Sales ($)	2793931M	3776829M
2913M	17544M	196611M	812027M	978828M	2937375M	Total Assets ($)	3048471M	5088065M

Comparative Historical Data | **Current Data Sorted By Sales**

		Comparative Historical Data		Type of Statement		Current Data Sorted By Sales				
	46	69	61	Unqualified	1	1	5	8	14	32
	2	6	3	Reviewed		1		1	1	
	20	14	11	Compiled	2	4		4	1	
	4		10	Tax Returns	4	3	2		1	
	34	56	45	Other	3	7	2	8	9	16
	4/1/00-3/31/01 ALL	4/1/01-3/31/02 ALL	4/1/02-3/31/03 ALL		47 (4/1-9/30/02)			83 (10/1/02-3/31/03)		
					0-1MM	1-3MM	3-5MM	5-10MM	10-25MM	25MM & OVER
NUMBER OF STATEMENTS	106	145	130		10	16	9	21	26	48
	%	%	%	**ASSETS**	%	%	%	%	%	%
Cash & Equivalents	11.5	13.1	15.0		18.2	27.2		16.2	13.1	7.3
Trade Receivables (net)	17.8	20.1	20.0		4.7	6.6		23.2	25.5	23.4
Inventory	1.1	1.6	1.5		1.6	3.5		.7	1.2	1.6
All Other Current	4.4	4.0	4.4		.8	7.8		3.1	9.2	2.7
Total Current	34.8	38.8	41.0		25.4	45.1		43.2	49.0	35.0
Fixed Assets (net)	46.7	41.9	39.6		59.9	41.2		36.3	33.6	41.2
Intangibles (net)	3.9	3.2	5.3		1.4	4.7		6.9	2.9	6.8
All Other Non-Current	14.6	16.1	14.1		13.3	9.0		13.6	14.4	17.0
Total	100.0	100.0	100.0		100.0	100.0		100.0	100.0	100.0
				LIABILITIES						
Notes Payable-Short Term	7.4	4.0	6.0		3.8	7.3		7.9	8.6	3.2
Cur. Mat.-L/T/D	4.1	2.6	4.0		7.8	6.6		5.3	2.7	2.8
Trade Payables	6.5	8.4	6.5		2.5	5.9		7.3	5.1	7.1
Income Taxes Payable	.0	.0	.2		.1	1.6		.0	.0	.0
All Other Current	10.8	13.6	23.7		18.7	23.5		58.5	13.3	13.4
Total Current	28.8	28.7	40.4		32.8	44.8		78.9	29.7	26.5
Long Term Debt	34.2	29.8	24.2		34.4	23.1		26.7	19.8	23.8
Deferred Taxes	.0	.2	.2		.5	.0		.7	.0	.1
All Other Non-Current	2.1	3.7	3.5		1.0	8.9		.8	2.0	4.4
Net Worth	35.0	37.6	31.7		31.4	23.2		-7.1	48.5	45.2
Total Liabilities & Net Worth	100.0	100.0	100.0		100.0	100.0		100.0	100.0	100.0
				INCOME DATA						
Net Sales	100.0	100.0	100.0		100.0	100.0		100.0	100.0	100.0
Gross Profit										
Operating Expenses	94.2	92.1	91.4		80.3	81.0		92.1	95.1	93.7
Operating Profit	5.8	7.9	8.6		19.7	19.0		7.9	4.9	6.3
All Other Expenses (net)	1.0	4.2	2.6		7.8	3.8		3.8	-.4	2.1
Profit Before Taxes	4.8	3.7	6.0		11.8	15.2		4.1	5.3	4.1
				RATIOS						
Current	2.9	2.9	2.4		3.9	3.1		2.3	2.7	2.2
	1.8	1.9	1.5		.7	1.4		1.3	2.0	1.6
	1.0	1.1	.8		.3	.7		.3	1.3	1.1
Quick	2.6	2.6	2.2		3.6	3.0		2.3	2.1	1.9
	1.4	1.5	1.3		.5	1.0		1.0	1.6	1.3
	.7	.9	.6		.3	.2		.2	1.2	.9
Sales/Receivables	25 14.7	42 8.7	14 26.0		0 UND	0 UND		0 UND	40 9.2	49 7.5
	54 6.8	55 6.6	50 7.3		0 UND	0 UND		36 10.1	53 6.9	66 5.5
	77 4.8	69 5.3	71 5.1		36 10.0	14 26.0		58 6.3	80 4.6	74 4.9
Cost of Sales/Inventory										
Cost of Sales/Payables										
Sales/Working Capital	4.8	4.5	5.1		32.2	4.1		8.6	4.6	5.3
	9.2	8.2	12.9		-51.2	18.6		95.6	8.0	12.2
	435.6	45.7	-52.4		-3.1	-30.1		-6.1	16.1	62.8
EBIT/Interest	(90) 8.4	(127) 7.7	(113) 12.3			31.8		9.7	13.6	12.5
	2.9	2.4	3.3			(12) 5.5		(17) 1.8	(24) 4.4	(46) 3.0
	.5	.8	.3			-2.2		-3.5	1.3	.7
Net Profit + Depr., Dep., Amort./Cur. Mat. L/T/D		(10) 27.5								
		3.8								
		2.1								
Fixed/Worth	.5	.5	.5		.4	.6		.4	.3	.6
	1.3	.9	1.0		1.8	1.4		1.2	.7	.9
	6.0	2.3	4.4		-5.6	NM		-3.9	1.5	2.5
Debt/Worth	.5	.5	.6		.4	.9		.6	.4	.5
	1.2	.9	1.2		1.8	1.9		1.2	1.2	1.0
	8.1	6.2	12.5		-6.7	-10.0		-4.0	2.2	2.5
% Profit Before Taxes/Tangible Net Worth	(84) 30.9	(123) 20.7	(101) 32.1			(11) 195.8		(13) 33.4	(25) 44.2	(40) 24.7
	7.0	5.8	8.2			26.8		7.0	12.3	7.3
	-3.0	-.6	-.4			4.7		-4.7	.8	-6.1
% Profit Before Taxes/Total Assets	11.8	7.8	15.0		31.1	48.7		13.8	11.4	11.3
	5.2	2.7	4.2		7.3	10.3		2.0	7.8	3.5
	-2.0	-.5	-1.6		.3	-2.9		-6.6	.7	-2.4
Sales/Net Fixed Assets	5.9	5.2	14.1		48.1	28.3		101.7	8.2	5.8
	2.3	2.3	3.3		3.6	7.1		7.1	3.4	2.4
	1.4	1.6	1.6		.2	1.1		2.7	1.6	1.7
Sales/Total Assets	1.9	1.8	2.7		6.4	5.0		5.0	2.1	1.6
	1.1	1.1	1.4		.5	1.7		2.0	1.4	1.2
	.6	.7	.7		.2	.6		1.2	.7	.8
% Depr., Dep., Amort./Sales	(97) 1.8	(131) 2.3	(108) 2.1			5.2		.9	1.4	2.5
	3.2	4.5	3.7			(12) 8.0		(17) 3.1	(24) 3.2	(41) 3.7
	6.3	5.9	6.5			22.3		4.2	5.6	5.8
% Officers', Directors', Owners' Comp/Sales		(12) 2.1	(14) 9.6							
		11.4	19.1							
		26.2	33.4							
Net Sales ($)	2858112M	8775809M	5535953M		5586M	29293M	36088M	151840M	445216M	4867930M
Total Assets ($)	3763928M	7904781M	4945298M		11762M	34623M	38632M	119438M	479797M	4261046M

M = $ thousand   MM = $ million
See Pages 11 through 18 for Explanation of Ratios and Data

HEALTH CARE—Nursing Care Facilities NAICS 623110 (SIC 8051, 8052, 8059)

		Current Data Sorted By Assets						Comparative Historical Data		
							Type of Statement			
3	32	173	190	52	40		Unqualified		470	491
6	32	50	15				Reviewed		109	99
21	56	60	11				Compiled		161	136
26	27	23	1				Tax Returns		61	61
41	108	213	87	19	11		Other		397	403
	354 (4/1-9/30/02)		943 (10/1/02-3/31/03)						4/1/98-3/31/99	4/1/99-3/31/00
0-500M	500M-2MM	2-10MM	10-50MM	50-100MM	100-250MM				ALL	ALL
97	255	519	304	71	51		NUMBER OF STATEMENTS		1198	1190
%	%	%	%	%	%		ASSETS		%	%
23.1	11.1	9.1	9.0	10.3	6.3		Cash & Equivalents		9.4	9.9
19.3	31.0	16.3	11.5	6.0	9.3		Trade Receivables (net)		16.3	16.1
.4	.4	.2	.2	.2	.3		Inventory		.4	.6
6.8	4.7	2.6	2.2	1.6	4.3		All Other Current		3.2	3.0
49.6	47.3	28.2	22.9	18.0	20.2		Total Current		29.4	29.6
38.7	39.0	55.7	55.8	60.7	53.1		Fixed Assets (net)		54.0	52.7
3.9	3.6	5.7	3.7	2.9	6.0		Intangibles (net)		3.6	4.2
7.8	10.1	10.4	17.6	18.4	20.7		All Other Non-Current		13.0	13.5
100.0	100.0	100.0	100.0	100.0	100.0		Total		100.0	100.0
							LIABILITIES			
18.2	7.3	4.1	3.1	1.1	3.2		Notes Payable-Short Term		4.5	4.2
1.2	3.6	3.5	3.7	4.4	2.6		Cur. Mat.-L/T/D		3.2	3.0
16.7	11.4	6.1	4.7	3.0	4.5		Trade Payables		7.4	7.6
.6	.1	.1	.1	.2	.1		Income Taxes Payable		.1	.1
50.8	27.3	15.2	9.7	4.9	5.9		All Other Current		16.8	18.9
87.5	49.7	29.1	21.3	13.6	16.4		Total Current		32.0	33.7
23.1	40.0	51.4	45.3	50.2	49.0		Long Term Debt		44.2	45.7
.1	.2	.1	.1	.1	.2		Deferred Taxes		.3	.4
29.1	9.3	4.7	7.6	20.2	20.5		All Other Non-Current		7.3	8.0
-39.7	.8	14.7	25.8	15.8	13.9		Net Worth		16.3	12.3
100.0	100.0	100.0	100.0	100.0	100.0		Total Liabilities & Net Worth		100.0	100.0
							INCOME DATA			
100.0	100.0	100.0	100.0	100.0	100.0		Net Sales		100.0	100.0
							Gross Profit			
94.9	90.3	88.0	92.4	95.3	96.3		Operating Expenses		92.7	91.8
5.1	9.7	12.0	7.6	4.7	3.7		Operating Profit		7.3	8.2
1.9	4.3	7.1	5.1	6.5	6.0		All Other Expenses (net)		3.1	4.0
3.3	5.3	4.9	2.5	-1.8	-2.2		Profit Before Taxes		4.2	4.2
							RATIOS			
1.8	1.8	2.0	2.2	3.3	1.8				2.0	2.0
.8	1.1	1.1	1.3	1.6	1.2		Current		1.2	1.2
.3	.7	.5	.8	.9	.9				.7	.7
1.8	1.5	1.8	1.9	3.2	1.4				1.7	1.8
.7	1.0	1.0	1.1	1.2	1.1		Quick	(1192)	1.0	(1186) 1.1
.2	.5	.5	.6	.7	.6				.6	.6
0 UND	7 51.4	13 28.4	23 15.7	17 21.1	10 36.5			13	29.1	12 29.3
1 264.6	30 12.3	32 11.3	34 10.6	28 12.9	29 12.5		Sales/Receivables	32	11.3	31 11.8
25 14.8	45 8.1	49 7.4	48 7.6	38 9.6	43 8.4			48	7.6	48 7.6
							Cost of Sales/Inventory			
							Cost of Sales/Payables			
26.8	14.1	10.2	6.7	3.3	6.4				9.0	8.5
-54.5	103.0	60.8	21.1	11.7	25.6		Sales/Working Capital		41.8	35.7
-7.5	-17.3	-10.2	-20.3	-33.3	-64.9				-14.7	-21.2
8.9	8.6	4.5	3.1	1.8	1.9				4.1	3.8
(48) 2.9	(196) 2.5	(410) 2.1	(267) 1.4	(64) .9	(44) 1.1		EBIT/Interest	(943)	1.9	(976) 1.7
-1.7	.6	1.0	.4	.1	.4				1.0	.7
	11.5	5.6	4.8				Net Profit + Depr., Dep.,		4.4	7.2
	(13) 5.4	(37) 2.6	(31) 2.8				Amort./Cur. Mat. L./T/D	(99)	2.2	(95) 2.7
	1.9	.8	.9						.9	1.0
.5	.5	1.2	1.1	2.0	2.5				1.1	1.1
2.8	3.8	5.7	2.2	6.1	7.4		Fixed/Worth		3.5	3.5
-.4	-1.9	-5.0	31.4	-39.5	-6.8				-54.9	-11.2
.9	1.4	1.6	1.1	2.5	3.0				1.3	1.4
7.4	7.1	7.4	2.9	6.9	8.2		Debt/Worth		4.9	5.0
-2.3	-4.2	-8.4	43.3	-60.0	-10.1				-52.0	-18.3
111.7	87.7	46.6	24.1	15.6	27.9		% Profit Before Taxes/Tangible		47.4	36.0
(52) 40.2	(154) 38.5	(321) 16.9	(235) 4.6	(50) .3	(32) 5.0		Net Worth	(881)	14.6	(828) 11.3
10.0	5.2	1.8	-2.3	-10.5	-4.1				2.2	-.3
31.1	21.0	9.9	5.0	2.0	2.4		% Profit Before Taxes/Total		9.7	8.0
8.3	5.5	3.9	1.3	-.3	.3		Assets		3.4	2.5
-11.1	-1.3	-.5	-1.6	-2.1	-2.5				-.2	-1.3
62.6	40.4	5.2	2.4	1.5	2.8				6.7	8.1
22.5	10.9	2.1	1.3	.6	1.2		Sales/Net Fixed Assets		1.9	1.8
5.6	2.6	1.0	.8	.4	.5				.8	.8
7.9	4.6	1.9	1.1	.8	1.4				2.2	2.2
5.3	2.8	1.1	.8	.4	.6		Sales/Total Assets		1.1	1.0
2.9	1.4	.7	.5	.2	.3				.5	.5
.6	.7	1.9	3.3	4.7	3.6				2.2	1.9
(74) 1.2	(229) 1.6	(503) 3.3	(296) 5.2	8.9	(44) 6.5		% Depr., Dep., Amort./Sales	(1099)	3.9	(1125) 4.0
2.8	4.1	6.0	7.9	13.1	10.1				7.0	7.2
2.5	1.7	1.8	2.8				% Officers', Directors',		2.0	2.0
(38) 5.5	(59) 3.9	(66) 4.1	(31) 7.8				Owners' Comp/Sales	(192)	5.3	(186) 4.5
10.6	5.6	9.3	29.8						12.0	9.6
122376M	894784M	3330345M	6378637M	3004143M	6621929M		Net Sales ($)		15581217M	16911435M
22186M	307601M	2522463M	6917153M	4909706M	8106727M		Total Assets ($)		19003048M	23241890M

M = $ thousand   MM = $ million
See Pages 11 through 18 for Explanation of Ratios and Data

Comparative Historical Data / Current Data Sorted By Sales

			Type of Statement						
438	465	490	Unqualified	14	34	51	136	151	104
113	113	103	Reviewed	9	19	14	39	17	5
238	262	148	Compiled	15	46	36	30	18	3
65	63	77	Tax Returns	35	29	5	5	3	
409	505	479	Other	66	97	87	117	70	42
4/1/00-3/31/01 ALL	4/1/01-3/31/02 ALL	4/1/02-3/31/03 ALL		354 (4/1-9/30/02) 0-1MM	1-3MM	3-5MM	943 (10/1/02-3/31/03) 5-10MM	10-25MM	25MM & OVER
1263	1408	1297	NUMBER OF STATEMENTS	139	225	193	327	259	154
%	%	%	ASSETS	%	%	%	%	%	%
8.5	9.0	10.5	Cash & Equivalents	13.2	12.6	9.5	10.0	9.2	9.2
17.4	17.4	17.4	Trade Receivables (net)	2.8	13.2	26.3	21.0	17.5	18.0
.4	.3	.3	Inventory	.1	.3	.3	.3	.3	.4
3.0	3.4	3.2	All Other Current	4.0	4.1	3.4	2.6	2.4	3.8
29.3	30.1	31.4	Total Current	20.1	30.2	39.5	33.9	29.4	31.4
53.3	51.8	51.3	Fixed Assets (net)	65.7	53.2	44.0	49.5	50.6	50.1
4.7	4.8	4.6	Intangibles (net)	4.4	5.9	5.9	3.6	3.8	4.2
12.8	13.4	12.7	All Other Non-Current	9.8	10.7	10.6	12.9	16.3	14.3
100.0	100.0	100.0	Total	100.0	100.0	100.0	100.0	100.0	100.0
			LIABILITIES						
4.4	6.6	5.3	Notes Payable-Short Term	5.0	8.8	8.7	3.3	2.8	5.0
3.2	3.6	3.4	Cur. Mat.-L/T/D	1.8	2.2	5.1	2.8	4.5	4.2
7.4	7.7	7.4	Trade Payables	5.7	6.7	9.5	7.4	7.1	7.5
.1	.2	.1	Income Taxes Payable	.0	.3	.2	.0	.1	.1
14.7	16.0	18.0	All Other Current	22.2	22.6	18.6	19.2	12.7	13.5
29.7	34.1	34.3	Total Current	34.8	40.6	42.2	32.7	27.2	30.3
48.0	48.2	45.5	Long Term Debt	59.1	54.8	37.6	43.1	40.0	43.5
.3	.1	.1	Deferred Taxes	.0	.1	.1	.2	.1	.1
7.4	9.3	9.6	All Other Non-Current	11.2	14.2	7.2	7.4	9.0	10.1
14.6	8.3	10.5	Net Worth	−5.1	−9.7	13.0	16.6	23.7	16.0
100.0	100.0	100.0	Total Liabilities & Net Worth	100.0	100.0	100.0	100.0	100.0	100.0
			INCOME DATA						
100.0	100.0	100.0	Net Sales	100.0	100.0	100.0	100.0	100.0	100.0
			Gross Profit						
91.8	90.5	90.7	Operating Expenses	69.9	88.2	92.7	94.6	95.0	95.2
8.2	9.5	9.3	Operating Profit	30.1	11.8	7.3	5.3	5.0	4.8
4.9	6.0	5.6	All Other Expenses (net)	18.1	7.7	3.1	3.5	2.8	3.8
3.3	3.4	3.7	Profit Before Taxes	12.0	4.1	4.2	1.9	2.2	1.0
			RATIOS						
1.9	2.0	2.0	Current	2.3	2.0	1.8	2.1	2.5	1.8
1.1	1.1	1.1		.7	.9	1.2	1.2	1.3	1.2
.7	.6	.6		.2	.4	.7	.8	.8	.9
1.7	1.7	1.8	Quick	1.6	1.7	1.7	1.9	2.2	1.5
1.0	.9	1.0		.4	.8	1.0	1.1	1.1	1.1
.6	.5	.5		.1	.3	.5	.6	.7	.7
15 24.7	14 25.5	12 29.6	Sales/Receivables	0 UND	1 580.6	21 17.2	24 15.4	25 14.4	27 13.4
32 11.3	31 11.9	31 11.9		0 UND	14 25.5	35 10.5	35 10.4	35 10.4	37 9.8
49 7.4	47 7.8	46 7.9		5 70.5	34 10.6	53 6.9	47 7.8	51 7.2	50 7.4
			Cost of Sales/Inventory						
			Cost of Sales/Payables						
9.6	9.1	9.0	Sales/Working Capital	8.1	12.2	11.4	8.6	6.2	10.6
47.2	58.4	55.5		−23.3	−94.2	54.2	36.5	24.4	25.3
−16.8	−15.0	−14.8		−4.0	−9.0	−18.3	−22.1	−23.5	−32.9
3.4	3.5	4.1	EBIT/Interest	4.1	4.7	5.4	4.1	4.7	2.8
(1029) 1.5	(1134) 1.6	(1029) 1.8		(54) 1.9	(161) 1.9	(155) 2.3	(289) 1.9	(225) 1.6	(145) 1.3
.6	.6	.6		.8	.6	.7	.6	.5	.5
3.9	4.1	5.5	Net Profit + Depr., Dep.,			6.1	4.3	6.4	5.2
(87) 2.1	(80) 2.1	(97) 2.6	Amort./Cur. Mat. L/T/D		(12) 2.3	(21) 2.4	(29) 1.8	(25) 2.6
.6	1.1	1.2				1.1	1.1	.4	.8
1.1	1.2	1.0	Fixed/Worth	1.5	1.3	.8	.9	.9	1.8
4.6	4.1	3.7		71.4	13.7	2.7	2.6	2.4	4.1
−7.4	−6.2	−5.6		−2.4	−1.9	−4.9	−11.0	−24.5	−159.2
1.6	1.6	1.4	Debt/Worth	2.2	2.3	1.1	1.3	1.2	2.4
6.9	6.8	5.9		191.9	21.6	3.9	4.0	3.4	6.6
−11.6	−9.4	−9.2		−3.6	−4.2	−7.1	−17.0	−61.7	−225.1
40.8	50.7	47.0	% Profit Before Taxes/Tangible	72.5	72.0	55.0	48.2	28.2	42.6
(838) 9.4	(918) 13.0	(844) 12.5	Net Worth	(70) 28.7	(116) 29.4	(127) 21.1	(227) 8.3	(189) 4.8	(115) 15.5
−.5	−1.1	−.1		1.3	4.1	4.6	−.8	−4.2	−.6
7.9	9.4	9.8	% Profit Before Taxes/Total	12.8	13.8	13.6	8.7	7.0	6.1
2.0	2.5	2.6	Assets	3.9	3.7	4.0	2.3	1.5	1.8
−1.8	−1.5	−1.3		−1.4	−2.0	−.8	−1.4	−1.5	−1.3
7.2	8.4	9.2	Sales/Net Fixed Assets	4.3	18.5	19.4	8.0	4.9	4.9
1.8	2.0	2.2		.6	2.5	4.4	2.3	1.7	2.3
.8	.8	.9		.3	.7	1.6	1.2	.9	1.1
2.2	2.4	2.4	Sales/Total Assets	1.4	3.0	3.2	2.4	1.9	2.1
1.1	1.1	1.1		.5	1.1	1.7	1.3	1.0	1.3
.5	.5	.6		.2	.5	.9	.7	.5	.7
1.7	1.5	1.7	% Depr., Dep., Amort./Sales	4.8	1.5	1.1	1.7	2.1	2.1
(1189) 3.9	(1308) 3.7	(1217) 3.6		(119) 10.8	(201) 3.8	(184) 2.5	(313) 3.3	(255) 4.1	(145) 3.6
7.1	7.1	7.1		22.5	7.8	4.2	5.5	7.0	6.3
1.6	1.9	2.0	% Officers', Directors',	5.6	2.4	1.6	1.1	1.8	.0
(213) 4.5	(198) 4.8	(200) 4.7	Owners' Comp/Sales	(28) 11.0	(53) 4.5	(31) 3.6	(41) 3.5	(36) 3.2	(11) 11.1
9.3		9.4	10.0		36.3	8.5	5.5	10.2	7.9	18.5
19338070M	21458484M	20352214M	Net Sales ($)	74007M	456649M	756090M	2371102M	3955493M	12738873M
22585247M	26301731M	22785836M	Total Assets ($)	266302M	630636M	726269M	2991072M	6509423M	11662134M

M = $ thousand   MM = $ million
See Pages 11 through 18 for Explanation of Ratios and Data

HEALTH CARE—Residential Mental Health and Substance Abuse Facilities   NAICS 623220   (SIC 8361)

Current Data Sorted By Assets   **Comparative Historical Data**

0-500M	500M-2MM	2-10MM	10-50MM	50-100MM	100-250MM	Type of Statement	4/1/98-3/31/99 ALL	4/1/99-3/31/00 ALL
6	26	104	67	10	5	Unqualified	204	219
	5	6	1	2		Reviewed	10	11
4	1	4				Compiled	22	17
6	5	1	1			Tax Returns	7	9
7	5	30	16	4	1	Other	66	70
	176 (4/1-9/30/02)		141 (10/1/02-3/31/03)					
23	42	145	85	16	6	NUMBER OF STATEMENTS	309	326
%	%	%	%	%	%	ASSETS	%	%
18.4	11.9	13.6	11.2	13.7		Cash & Equivalents	14.0	15.2
25.6	20.3	17.6	13.6	5.9		Trade Receivables (net)	15.4	16.5
2.5	.2	.2	.4	.1		Inventory	.3	.4
4.9	4.0	2.5	2.8	1.0		All Other Current	2.5	2.8
51.5	36.4	34.0	27.9	20.7		Total Current	32.3	35.0
37.3	54.6	54.2	54.3	55.1		Fixed Assets (net)	53.1	50.1
2.8	1.2	2.8	1.5	1.4		Intangibles (net)	1.9	1.9
8.6	7.9	9.1	16.3	22.7		All Other Non-Current	12.7	13.1
100.0	100.0	100.0	100.0	100.0		Total	100.0	100.0
						LIABILITIES		
19.2	3.4	4.0	3.8	1.4		Notes Payable-Short Term	4.3	3.4
1.9	3.0	2.5	1.8	1.3		Cur. Mat.-L/T/D	2.5	2.8
14.7	8.3	5.2	4.4	3.2		Trade Payables	5.2	6.3
.0	.0	.0	.0	.0		Income Taxes Payable	.1	.0
54.3	20.5	12.2	10.1	11.3		All Other Current	15.5	11.6
90.1	35.1	23.9	20.1	17.3		Total Current	27.6	24.2
14.7	50.1	34.9	30.9	32.6		Long Term Debt	29.9	31.4
.0	.0	.8	.0	.0		Deferred Taxes	.0	.2
.8	1.9	2.2	2.1	12.6		All Other Non-Current	4.8	6.0
−5.9	12.8	38.2	46.9	37.5		Net Worth	37.6	38.2
100.0	100.0	100.0	100.0	100.0		Total Liabilities & Net Worth	100.0	100.0
						INCOME DATA		
100.0	100.0	100.0	100.0	100.0		Net Sales	100.0	100.0
						Gross Profit		
95.6	96.4	94.8	98.2	93.4		Operating Expenses	94.5	95.3
4.4	3.6	5.2	1.8	6.6		Operating Profit	5.5	4.7
2.1	4.0	3.8	3.4	12.3		All Other Expenses (net)	.0	−.9
2.3	−.4	1.4	−1.6	−5.7		Profit Before Taxes	5.6	5.6
						RATIOS		
1.4	2.2	2.5	2.4	5.2		Current	2.7	3.0
.8	1.3	1.4	1.4	1.4			1.5	1.6
.3	.7	.9	.9	.4			.9	1.0
1.4	2.1	2.2	2.1	4.7		Quick	2.4	2.6
.6	1.1	1.4	1.3	1.3		(307)	1.3	1.4
.2	.5	.7	.8	.4			.8	.8
0 UND	7 53.5	11 33.6	29 12.5	7 52.9		Sales/Receivables	9 40.0	11 33.3
10 35.3	29 12.5	33 11.0	47 7.8	18 20.3			31 11.7	31 11.8
34 10.7	40 9.1	47 7.7	62 5.9	61 6.0			47 7.7	51 7.2
						Cost of Sales/Inventory		
						Cost of Sales/Payables		
25.4	8.8	6.8	4.5	1.4		Sales/Working Capital	6.3	5.5
−24.4	38.1	15.2	15.4	10.5			17.5	15.3
−6.0	−17.2	−93.9	−60.7	−24.0			−44.0	−118.8
(10) 9.1	(33) 4.0	(116) 4.0	(68) 3.3	(14) 1.7		EBIT/Interest	(229) 6.7	(234) 5.2
3.3	1.3	1.5	1.1	.4			2.9	2.0
−1.8	.2	.8	−.3	−.7			1.4	1.0
						Net Profit + Depr., Dep., Amort./Cur. Mat. L /T/D	(11) 4.6	(13) 6.2
							2.6	3.3
							1.4	1.1
.3	.9	.8	.7	.6		Fixed/Worth	.7	.6
1.2	2.5	1.4	1.1	1.7			1.3	1.2
−1.3	9.6	3.8	2.6	11.0			3.3	4.2
1.1	1.2	.6	.5	.6		Debt/Worth	.6	.6
4.7	3.8	1.5	1.0	1.9			1.5	1.5
−5.3	18.2	5.7	3.0	12.8			5.2	6.7
(17) 98.0	(35) 8.3	(122) 20.0	(81) 10.2	(15) 1.8		% Profit Before Taxes/Tangible Net Worth	(273) 24.0	(283) 22.1
42.9	.4	5.3	1.5	−4.5			10.4	8.6
14.3	−20.9	−1.8	−4.8	−15.3			3.3	1.5
18.3	5.3	6.5	3.6	1.0		% Profit Before Taxes/Total Assets	8.7	7.2
3.9	−.8	1.4	.4	−1.2			3.8	3.0
−3.9	−4.7	−1.1	−2.6	−2.7			.9	.0
128.7	11.0	4.8	2.8	1.6		Sales/Net Fixed Assets	5.2	6.1
18.5	4.0	2.5	1.9	.7			2.2	2.6
6.0	1.4	1.2	1.1	.6			.9	1.2
7.2	3.3	2.2	1.5	.8		Sales/Total Assets	2.2	2.2
4.3	2.1	1.5	1.0	.4			1.2	1.3
2.1	1.1	.8	.6	.2			.5	.6
(17) .3	(40) 1.5	(141) 1.9	(80) 2.8	4.4		% Depr., Dep., Amort./Sales	(276) 2.2	(291) 1.9
1.4	2.3	3.0	3.9	7.8			3.7	3.4
2.7	3.9	5.3	5.3	11.3			7.0	5.8
(10) 5.8	(14) 4.3					% Officers', Directors', Owners' Comp/Sales	(29) 4.3	(39) 3.9
7.2	10.8						14.1	8.2
11.5	28.4						28.2	14.0
21778M	119108M	1111796M	1815028M	546482M	589972M	Net Sales ($)	3337419M	3534722M
4876M	48667M	725413M	1722638M	1109149M	1132460M	Total Assets ($)	4040070M	4226987M

© RMA 2003

M = $ thousand   MM = $ million
See Pages 11 through 18 for Explanation of Ratios and Data

Comparative Historical Data			Type of Statement	Current Data Sorted By Sales					
179	165	218	Unqualified	12	32	23	47	74	30
20	9	14	Reviewed	4	3	2		3	2
21	36	9	Compiled	2	5	1	1		
14	16	13	Tax Returns	7	6				
63	81	63	Other	8	10	9	16	13	7
4/1/00-3/31/01 ALL	4/1/01-3/31/02 ALL	4/1/02-3/31/03 ALL		176 (4/1-9/30/02)			141 (10/1/02-3/31/03)		
				0-1MM	1-3MM	3-5MM	5-10MM	10-25MM	25MM & OVER
297	307	317	**NUMBER OF STATEMENTS**	33	56	35	64	90	39
%	%	%	**ASSETS**	%	%	%	%	%	%
13.9	12.3	13.0	Cash & Equivalents	14.3	8.4	13.0	14.2	14.9	11.7
14.6	15.8	16.7	Trade Receivables (net)	9.4	13.1	13.7	19.9	20.1	17.3
.4	.5	.4	Inventory	1.8	.1	.2	.3	.3	.4
2.5	3.5	2.9	All Other Current	1.0	4.5	2.8	1.7	3.4	3.4
31.4	32.0	33.0	Total Current	26.5	26.1	29.7	36.2	38.7	32.8
52.0	53.1	53.0	Fixed Assets (net)	57.1	63.6	52.7	51.4	46.3	52.3
2.3	2.5	2.1	Intangibles (net)	5.7	1.7	2.0	1.7	1.7	1.5
14.3	12.3	12.0	All Other Non-Current	10.9	8.7	15.6	10.7	13.3	13.4
100.0	100.0	100.0	Total	100.0	100.0	100.0	100.0	100.0	100.0
			LIABILITIES						
3.2	4.0	4.8	Notes Payable-Short Term	13.7	3.2	2.4	4.2	4.1	4.2
3.0	2.8	2.3	Cur. Mat.-L/T/D	1.7	1.9	2.1	2.6	2.7	2.2
5.5	5.3	5.9	Trade Payables	5.6	5.6	5.3	4.8	7.3	5.8
.2	.1	.0	Income Taxes Payable	.0	.0	.0	.0	.0	.0
11.4	11.0	15.6	All Other Current	24.1	16.5	11.0	12.9	16.3	14.1
23.3	23.1	28.6	Total Current	45.1	27.2	20.8	24.5	30.4	26.3
32.3	34.6	34.2	Long Term Debt	42.1	48.4	32.3	27.5	29.1	31.4
.1	.1	.4	Deferred Taxes	.0	2.0	.0	.0	.1	.0
5.4	5.7	2.7	All Other Non-Current	2.5	1.6	2.1	1.4	4.4	3.6
38.8	36.4	34.1	Net Worth	10.0	20.8	44.9	46.6	36.1	38.7
100.0	100.0	100.0	Total Liabilities & Net Worth	100.0	100.0	100.0	100.0	100.0	100.0
			INCOME DATA						
100.0	100.0	100.0	Net Sales	100.0	100.0	100.0	100.0	100.0	100.0
			Gross Profit						
96.0	94.2	96.0	Operating Expenses	91.1	92.6	98.4	96.4	97.7	98.5
4.0	5.8	4.0	Operating Profit	8.9	7.4	1.6	3.6	2.3	1.5
.5	2.6	4.0	All Other Expenses (net)	12.8	7.3	2.3	1.8	1.9	1.7
3.6	3.2	.0	Profit Before Taxes	-4.0	.0	-.7	1.8	.4	-.3
			RATIOS						
2.6	2.8	2.3		1.2	2.3	3.2	2.6	2.7	1.7
1.4	1.5	1.4	Current	.6	1.4	1.9	1.6	1.4	1.3
.8	.9	.9		.2	.5	1.0	1.0	1.0	.8
2.4	2.4	2.2		1.2	2.2	3.1	2.5	2.7	1.5
1.3	1.3	1.3	Quick	.5	1.2	1.5	1.5	1.3	1.1
.7	.8	.7		.1	.3	.6	.9	.9	.7
8 45.5	10 35.2	13 27.8		0 UND	2 157.8	18 20.2	27 13.3	27 13.4	26 14.1
30 12.1	31 11.9	34 10.8	Sales/Receivables	3 143.8	13 27.9	34 10.8	38 9.7	40 9.1	40 9.1
46 8.0	49 7.5	51 7.1		13 27.2	38 9.6	51 7.1	53 6.9	60 6.1	56 6.5
			Cost of Sales/Inventory						
			Cost of Sales/Payables						
6.4	6.3	6.7		36.6	6.8	4.3	6.7	6.0	11.0
20.8	19.0	19.3	Sales/Working Capital	-13.9	25.9	13.7	17.9	14.6	23.5
-42.4	-53.8	-43.6		-3.0	-13.9	UND	207.5	168.1	-47.4
(226) 4.6	(223) 4.0	(247) 3.7		(15) 4.0	(41) 2.5	(27) 3.8	(55) 4.5	(76) 4.0	(33) 2.8
1.5	1.7	1.4	EBIT/Interest	.8	1.0	1.6	1.8	1.3	1.2
.6	.8	.3		-.1	.4	.9	.5	-.2	.2
			Net Profit + Depr., Dep., Amort./Cur. Mat. L/T/D						
.6	.7	.8		1.0	.9	.6	.8	.7	.7
1.4	1.4	1.4	Fixed/Worth	3.6	3.1	1.2	1.1	1.0	1.5
4.8	4.7	4.5		-17.2	-41.8	7.6	2.1	2.5	2.5
.6	.6	.6		1.0	.8	.2	.5	.6	.8
1.4	1.6	1.5	Debt/Worth	6.3	4.3	1.2	1.1	1.4	1.7
6.4	7.4	5.9		-20.5	-44.0	7.1	2.8	3.1	2.8
(261) 18.9	(263) 19.3	(276) 15.0		(24) 54.5	(40) 21.1	(30) 24.7	(60) 13.7	(85) 12.6	(37) 9.7
6.1	5.3	2.8	% Profit Before Taxes/Tangible Net Worth	7.0	-2.7	1.7	6.1	2.7	1.5
-1.0	-1.4	-4.9		-6.5	-16.0	-3.9	-1.0	-4.6	-4.0
7.3	6.7	5.2		3.8	5.1	5.3	6.2	6.0	3.0
1.8	1.8	.8	% Profit Before Taxes/Total Assets	-1.1	-.7	1.1	2.4	1.0	.4
-.7	-.8	-2.1		-4.8	-3.1	-.8	-.8	-2.1	-1.5
5.3	5.2	4.9		10.6	6.6	3.9	5.9	4.5	3.9
2.6	2.5	2.4	Sales/Net Fixed Assets	1.0	1.4	2.5	2.5	2.7	2.4
1.2	1.1	1.1		.2	.5	1.1	1.4	1.8	1.6
2.1	2.3	2.2		2.7	2.3	2.2	2.4	2.1	2.0
1.2	1.4	1.3	Sales/Total Assets	.8	1.0	1.3	1.4	1.4	1.4
.7	.6	.6		.2	.4	.6	.7	.9	.8
(277) 1.9	(280) 1.6	(299) 2.0		(26) 3.7	(54) 2.1	(62) 1.4	(86) 1.7	2.0	(36) 2.1
3.4	3.0	3.2	% Depr., Dep., Amort./Sales	8.1	4.2	2.9	3.1	2.9	3.1
5.5	5.8	5.6		20.6	10.5	5.0	4.1	4.5	5.8
(31) 5.1	(38) 3.7	(40) 4.4			(12) 6.0				
6.8	6.8	8.0	% Officers', Directors', Owners' Comp/Sales		9.1				
13.2	12.7	15.6			15.7				
2920910M	4356707M	4204164M	Net Sales ($)	16941M	106688M	146309M	462259M	1355164M	2116803M
3404129M	3964943M	4743203M	Total Assets ($)	59018M	174966M	252803M	462362M	1419224M	2374830M

M = $ thousand   MM = $ million
See Pages 11 through 18 for Explanation of Ratios and Data

Current Data Sorted By Assets   Comparative Historical Data

	0-500M	500M-2MM	2-10MM	10-50MM	50-100MM	100-250MM	Type of Statement	4/1/98-3/31/99 ALL	4/1/99-3/31/00 ALL
	1	7	34	50	12	10	Unqualified	54	61
	2	7	10	3			Reviewed	15	9
	6	17	13	2			Compiled	21	22
	6	2	8	1			Tax Returns	17	7
	7	9	39	20	11	5	Other	37	37
		80 (4/1-9/30/02)			202 (10/1/02-3/31/03)				
NUMBER OF STATEMENTS	22	42	104	76	23	15		144	136
ASSETS	%	%	%	%	%	%		%	%
Cash & Equivalents	22.9	9.1	6.7	10.1	10.7	6.1		7.9	11.3
Trade Receivables (net)	25.5	28.2	11.0	7.3	3.1	3.1		17.2	17.5
Inventory	1.0	.2	.2	1.4	.1	.1		.4	.8
All Other Current	2.8	4.8	2.0	2.1	1.6	1.7		3.7	4.6
Total Current	52.2	42.2	20.0	20.8	15.5	11.1		29.3	34.2
Fixed Assets (net)	39.6	44.6	69.7	60.7	64.0	59.7		55.5	51.1
Intangibles (net)	2.3	1.2	1.4	2.4	1.7	.6		3.3	2.5
All Other Non-Current	5.9	11.9	8.9	16.1	18.8	28.7		11.8	12.2
Total	100.0	100.0	100.0	100.0	100.0	100.0		100.0	100.0
LIABILITIES									
Notes Payable-Short Term	23.1	6.1	3.3	2.6	3.3	3.2		5.3	4.4
Cur. Mat.-L/T/D	3.4	4.5	2.9	1.9	4.4	2.6		2.5	2.2
Trade Payables	13.6	11.1	5.8	2.9	2.1	2.1		6.0	8.2
Income Taxes Payable	.0	.0	.1	.0	.0	.1		.1	.2
All Other Current	74.3	16.9	6.8	8.2	3.6	5.4		16.6	33.5
Total Current	114.4	38.6	19.0	15.7	13.5	13.4		30.5	48.6
Long Term Debt	36.0	35.9	59.2	47.2	47.0	47.7		41.1	46.0
Deferred Taxes	.0	.1	.2	.5	.2	.3		.5	1.0
All Other Non-Current	24.9	7.4	6.3	12.5	25.5	20.5		6.9	8.2
Net Worth	-75.4	18.0	15.2	24.2	13.9	18.1		21.0	-3.8
Total Liabilities & Net Worth	100.0	100.0	100.0	100.0	100.0	100.0		100.0	100.0
INCOME DATA									
Net Sales	100.0	100.0	100.0	100.0	100.0	100.0		100.0	100.0
Gross Profit									
Operating Expenses	99.0	89.3	84.6	93.0	96.9	90.3		93.1	91.8
Operating Profit	1.0	10.7	15.4	7.0	3.1	9.7		6.9	8.2
All Other Expenses (net)	.2	4.7	10.5	5.5	8.9	8.4		5.1	4.7
Profit Before Taxes	.9	6.0	4.9	1.5	-5.8	1.4		1.8	3.5
RATIOS									
Current	1.4	1.8	2.0	2.3	3.8	1.6		2.2	2.7
	.9	1.1	1.0	1.6	1.7	.9		1.2	1.4
	.4	.6	.4	.9	1.1	.4		.6	.9
Quick	1.4	1.5	1.6	2.2	3.6	1.4		2.0	2.1
	.8	1.0	.9	1.3	1.5	.7	(141)	1.1	(135) 1.1
	.3	.4	.3	.7	.7	.3		.5	.6
Sales/Receivables	0 UND	8 43.7	1 324.2	11 32.5	7 51.5	4 82.2		4 88.5	6 60.4
	15 24.2	27 13.4	13 27.6	24 15.0	20 17.8	21 17.7		28 13.1	31 11.7
	36 10.0	48 7.6	37 9.7	40 9.1	32 11.3	27 13.3		43 8.4	54 6.7
Cost of Sales/Inventory									
Cost of Sales/Payables									
Sales/Working Capital	29.4	21.8	11.0	5.6	1.6	7.0		9.4	5.9
	-108.8	85.2	148.0	11.3	9.9	-46.8		42.8	15.5
	-10.0	-19.6	-8.5	-47.8	38.7	-5.3		-16.9	-58.2
EBIT/Interest	(17) 19.5	(34) 17.5	(81) 3.3	(69) 3.5	(18) 1.7	(14) 2.8	(99)	3.4	(97) 3.6
	2.5	2.5	1.5	1.6	.7	1.6		2.1	2.0
	-8.5	.0	.9	.7	-1.0	-.6		.9	.9
Net Profit + Depr., Dep., Amort./Cur. Mat. L/T/D							(10)	3.2	(14) 4.6
								2.1	2.2
								.7	1.5
Fixed/Worth	.7	.5	1.8	1.4	2.0	1.2		.9	.8
	9.1	1.4	5.4	3.0	8.5	2.4		2.1	3.4
	-.5	-2.8	-22.3	-16.7	554.3	-7.2		31.0	-22.3
Debt/Worth	2.6	.6	1.8	1.3	2.4	1.2		1.3	1.1
	NM	3.2	6.3	3.8	10.5	2.9		3.9	5.1
	-2.2	-5.9	-28.1	-28.1	687.9	-9.9		NM	-26.4
% Profit Before Taxes/Tangible Net Worth	(11) 187.5	(27) 72.2	(73) 37.4	(56) 20.8	(18) 4.9	(10) 22.8	(108)	49.7	(99) 35.9
	20.0	26.8	12.4	7.8	-1.5	3.7		13.9	13.9
	-4.2	15.1	-.4	-.6	-28.4	-1.0		-2.4	2.2
% Profit Before Taxes/Total Assets	27.0	20.3	5.2	4.3	.9	3.5		8.8	9.4
	2.3	6.4	2.1	1.3	-.8	.7		2.3	3.1
	-20.7	-1.7	-.7	-.7	-2.4	-4.9		-2.1	-1.2
Sales/Net Fixed Assets	37.6	17.3	2.7	2.0	1.3	.9		6.4	7.5
	18.6	6.3	1.1	.8	.4	.5		2.4	2.2
	13.2	3.3	.4	.5	.3	.3		.9	.6
Sales/Total Assets	10.9	4.1	1.4	1.0	.4	.5		2.5	1.9
	6.1	2.6	.9	.5	.3	.3		1.3	1.2
	3.7	1.1	.4	.3	.2	.2		.5	.5
% Depr., Dep., Amort./Sales	(17) .8	(38) 1.1	(103) 2.9	(73) 3.6	(22) 5.6	(14) 4.5	(127)	2.2	(126) 1.8
	1.4	1.9	4.9	6.5	10.8	8.8		3.5	3.3
	2.8	5.3	11.3	10.4	15.3	10.3		7.9	7.4
% Officers', Directors', Owners' Comp/Sales		(13) 2.3	(16) 1.2	(11) 8.7			(23)	2.7	(23) 2.6
		4.1	3.8	14.2				9.4	8.3
		9.8	9.6	37.0				20.3	21.4
Net Sales ($)	23794M	134392M	475285M	1395339M	696827M	977349M		2026180M	1665797M
Total Assets ($)	4347M	47923M	484556M	1819660M	1612668M	2202188M		1857382M	2178659M

Comparative Historical Data / Current Data Sorted By Sales

			Type of Statement						
32	44	114	Unqualified	4	11	13	26	39	21
7	8	22	Reviewed	2	10	4	5		1
23	31	38	Compiled	9	12	9	8		
9	9	17	Tax Returns	5	10	1		1	
40	46	91	Other	8	23	15	15	16	14
4/1/00-3/31/01 ALL	4/1/01-3/31/02 ALL	4/1/02-3/31/03 ALL		0-1MM	80 (4/1-9/30/02) 1-3MM	3-5MM	5-10MM	202 (10/1/02-3/31/03) 10-25MM	25MM & OVER
111	138	282	NUMBER OF STATEMENTS	28	66	42	54	56	36
%	%	%	ASSETS	%	%	%	%	%	%
10.3	11.0	9.5	Cash & Equivalents	12.8	7.5	9.3	7.9	11.1	11.0
14.6	15.4	12.6	Trade Receivables (net)	5.6	9.5	19.7	16.0	11.7	12.1
.4	.3	.6	Inventory	.1	.4	2.6	.2	.2	.1
4.2	3.6	2.5	All Other Current	3.3	2.1	1.8	2.7	2.6	2.7
29.5	30.2	25.2	Total Current	21.7	19.6	33.3	26.8	25.5	25.9
57.9	57.6	60.2	Fixed Assets (net)	68.3	68.6	59.0	55.5	54.9	55.4
1.9	2.7	1.7	Intangibles (net)	1.7	1.7	1.0	1.6	2.0	2.0
10.7	9.5	12.9	All Other Non-Current	8.3	10.2	6.8	16.1	17.5	16.6
100.0	100.0	100.0	Total	100.0	100.0	100.0	100.0	100.0	100.0
			LIABILITIES						
5.3	5.4	5.1	Notes Payable-Short Term	14.1	5.9	5.9	2.7	1.9	4.1
4.9	2.6	3.0	Cur. Mat.-L/T/D	2.9	3.9	3.1	2.3	1.5	4.9
7.6	5.5	5.9	Trade Payables	4.8	6.2	5.3	8.4	4.8	5.2
.2	.1	.0	Income Taxes Payable	.0	.0	.0	.1	.0	.0
10.8	12.0	13.6	All Other Current	24.0	23.1	10.6	6.9	7.9	10.9
28.7	25.5	27.7	Total Current	45.8	39.1	24.9	20.4	16.1	25.2
43.5	47.5	49.1	Long Term Debt	58.9	66.2	47.0	40.5	36.6	44.9
.1	.2	.3	Deferred Taxes	.0	.1	.1	.3	.8	.3
8.3	13.9	11.9	All Other Non-Current	14.0	8.8	4.3	12.7	18.8	12.9
19.4	13.0	11.0	Net Worth	−18.6	−14.2	23.6	26.2	27.8	16.7
100.0	100.0	100.0	Total Liabilities & Net Worth	100.0	100.0	100.0	100.0	100.0	100.0
			INCOME DATA						
100.0	100.0	100.0	Net Sales	100.0	100.0	100.0	100.0	100.0	100.0
			Gross Profit						
91.5	91.5	90.0	Operating Expenses	75.6	84.5	91.0	95.9	94.3	94.5
8.5	8.5	10.0	Operating Profit	24.4	15.5	9.0	4.1	5.7	5.5
3.3	6.1	7.3	All Other Expenses (net)	19.1	9.4	5.4	4.2	4.6	5.1
5.2	2.4	2.8	Profit Before Taxes	5.4	6.1	3.6	−.1	1.1	.4
			RATIOS						
2.6	2.8	2.0		2.3	1.3	2.1	2.4	2.9	1.9
1.4	1.3	1.2	Current	.8	.6	1.3	1.5	1.6	1.3
.7	.7	.6		.3	.2	.8	.9	1.1	.8
2.2	2.3	1.8		1.4	1.3	1.8	2.3	2.7	1.7
1.2	1.2	1.0	Quick	.4	.5	1.1	1.2	1.3	1.0
.4	.5	.4		.2	.1	.7	.7	.9	.7
5 73.4	6 56.5	4 88.3		0 UND	0 UND	15 23.9	15 24.8	13 28.3	14 25.4
26 14.3	29 12.7	21 17.6	Sales/Receivables	0 UND	4 97.2	35 10.3	32 11.5	23 16.1	31 11.9
45 8.1	46 7.9	38 9.6		16 23.5	18 20.8	47 7.8	48 7.6	37 10.0	48 7.6
			Cost of Sales/Inventory						
			Cost of Sales/Payables						
7.4	5.9	8.6		10.0	33.8	9.7	6.6	4.5	9.8
24.3	21.1	37.6	Sales/Working Capital	−60.6	−23.1	42.1	16.9	13.6	16.6
−24.9	−27.6	−14.7		−3.8	−4.1	−25.6	−77.0	64.1	−33.3
4.0	2.9	3.4		9.5	3.4	3.4	2.8	4.4	3.4
(96) 2.0	(111) 1.7	(233) 1.6	EBIT/Interest	(17) 1.6	(51) 1.6	(39) 1.2	(43) 1.6	(48) 1.7	(35) 1.8
1.1	1.0	.6		−2.3	.6	.9	.5	.5	.5
	4.7	5.0	Net Profit + Depr., Dep.,						
	(10) 1.6	(15) 1.5	Amort./Cur. Mat. L/T/D						
	.7	.7							
1.1	1.2	1.3		2.1	2.0	.8	1.3	1.0	1.5
3.0	3.9	4.0	Fixed/Worth	5.0	40.0	4.0	3.6	1.8	3.0
163.7	−137.9	−12.8		−3.7	−3.7	−35.4	−24.0	98.2	10.9
1.0	1.3	1.5		2.6	2.9	1.2	.7	1.3	1.7
4.5	4.6	5.6	Debt/Worth	8.0	147.8	3.9	6.1	2.1	5.0
363.1	−52.1	−14.8		−7.5	−5.4	−71.5	−41.6	246.4	12.7
54.1	36.5	30.9	% Profit Before Taxes/Tangible	45.2	105.7	33.6	26.8	16.1	29.7
(84) 9.2	(100) 9.3	(195) 10.0	Net Worth	(17) 15.1	(35) 17.5	(31) 12.8	(39) 6.5	(45) 4.6	(28) 8.0
2.3	.2	−.9		.5	−3.6	.0	−2.9	−4.1	.0
7.7	6.5	6.3	% Profit Before Taxes/Total	13.8	8.5	8.3	5.6	4.6	6.3
3.2	2.3	1.3	Assets	2.6	1.4	2.4	.6	.9	1.4
−.5	−1.2	−1.4		−.9	−2.4	−.4	−1.9	−1.4	−2.5
4.9	4.8	4.8		13.2	7.6	6.1	4.2	2.3	3.3
1.8	1.8	1.2	Sales/Net Fixed Assets	.5	.6	1.9	1.4	.8	1.9
.6	.6	.5		.2	.3	.9	.7	.4	.8
1.9	2.0	1.9		3.7	2.6	2.4	1.7	1.3	1.7
1.1	1.0	.8	Sales/Total Assets	.4	.5	1.2	.9	.5	1.0
.4	.4	.3		.2	.3	.6	.4	.3	.5
1.3	1.7	2.2		2.7	2.2	1.9	1.8	2.7	2.2
(104) 3.5	(125) 4.0	(267) 5.2	% Depr., Dep., Amort./Sales	(27) 11.2	(59) 8.6	(40) 3.5	3.8	(52) 6.9	(35) 4.1
8.1	8.4	10.5		22.2	12.8	6.3	7.7	10.5	5.9
2.7	2.4	2.5	% Officers', Directors',		3.3	1.0			
(15) 5.9	(17) 5.7	(52) 6.0	Owners' Comp/Sales		(16) 5.7	(11) 3.6			
18.4	16.3	12.5			14.1	7.9			
1393646M	1819050M	3702986M	Net Sales ($)	14043M	125215M	165028M	387816M	834951M	2175933M
1675008M	2195648M	6171342M	Total Assets ($)	37647M	272929M	190831M	843593M	2170217M	2656125M

M = $ thousand   MM = $ million
See Pages 11 through 18 for Explanation of Ratios and Data

Current Data Sorted By Assets

Comparative Historical Data

	0-500M	500M-2MM	2-10MM	10-50MM	50-100MM	100-250MM	Type of Statement	4/1/98-3/31/99 ALL	4/1/99-3/31/00 ALL
		1	11	5	3	2	Unqualified		
	1		2				Reviewed		
	3	1	1	1			Compiled		
	3	2	1				Tax Returns		
	1	1	4	4	1		Other		
17 (4/1-9/30/02)				30 (10/1/02-3/31/03)					
NUMBER OF STATEMENTS	8	5	18	10	4	2			
	%	%	%	%	%	%	**ASSETS**	%	%
			6.7	6.5			Cash & Equivalents	D	D
			7.4	6.6			Trade Receivables (net)	A	A
			.1	.1			Inventory	T	T
			.6	7.3			All Other Current	A	A
			14.8	20.4			Total Current		
			65.8	71.2			Fixed Assets (net)	N	N
			1.5	.0			Intangibles (net)	O	O
			17.9	8.3			All Other Non-Current	T	T
			100.0	100.0			Total		
							LIABILITIES	A	A
			2.1	.1			Notes Payable-Short Term	V	V
			8.5	3.3			Cur. Mat.-L/T/D	A	A
			2.3	2.8			Trade Payables	I	I
			.0	.0			Income Taxes Payable	L	L
			4.3	3.9			All Other Current	A	A
			17.3	10.1			Total Current	B	B
			43.2	33.0			Long Term Debt	L	L
			.0	.0			Deferred Taxes	E	E
			8.5	19.8			All Other Non-Current		
			31.0	37.2			Net Worth		
			100.0	100.0			Total Liabilities & Net Worth		
							INCOME DATA		
			100.0	100.0			Net Sales		
							Gross Profit		
			88.3	94.1			Operating Expenses		
			11.7	5.9			Operating Profit		
			7.3	5.8			All Other Expenses (net)		
			4.4	.0			Profit Before Taxes		
							RATIOS		
			2.2	2.9			Current		
			1.2	1.2					
			.5	1.2					
			2.2	2.1			Quick		
			1.2	1.2					
			.4	.8					
			3 144.1	10 35.1			Sales/Receivables		
			16 23.5	22 16.7					
			38 9.6	55 6.6					
							Cost of Sales/Inventory		
							Cost of Sales/Payables		
			7.3	4.7			Sales/Working Capital		
			38.2	13.2					
			-9.8	42.8					
			2.8				EBIT/Interest		
		(16)	1.7						
			1.0						
							Net Profit + Depr., Dep., Amort./Cur. Mat. L /T/D		
			1.4	1.0			Fixed/Worth		
			3.2	2.4					
			15.3	NM					
			1.0	.5			Debt/Worth		
			3.6	1.8					
			17.5	NM					
			16.5				% Profit Before Taxes/Tangible Net Worth		
		(15)	7.3						
			3.1						
			6.6	7.0			% Profit Before Taxes/Total Assets		
			2.5	1.3					
			.0	-2.7					
			2.9	1.3			Sales/Net Fixed Assets		
			.8	.6					
			.6	.5					
			1.5	1.0			Sales/Total Assets		
			.6	.4					
			.3	.3					
			2.7				% Depr., Dep., Amort./Sales		
		(17)	6.6						
			11.0						
							% Officers', Directors', Owners' Comp/Sales		
	12451M	10458M	103643M	104671M	98020M	75850M	Net Sales ($)		
	2004M	5032M	117137M	218822M	315086M	229888M	Total Assets ($)		

M = $ thousand   MM = $ million
See Pages 11 through 18 for Explanation of Ratios and Data

Comparative Historical Data				Current Data Sorted By Sales					
4/1/00-3/31/01 ALL	4/1/01-3/31/02 ALL	4/1/02-3/31/03 ALL	**Type of Statement**	0-1MM	1-3MM	3-5MM	5-10MM	10-25MM	25MM & OVER
22			Unqualified	1	3	1	7	8	2
3			Reviewed		2	1			
5			Compiled	2	1	1		1	
6			Tax Returns	2	3	1			
11			Other	2	2	1	2	3	1
					17 (4/1-9/30/02)		30 (10/1/02-3/31/03)		
		47	**NUMBER OF STATEMENTS**	7	11	5	10	11	3
%	%	%	**ASSETS**	%	%	%	%	%	%
D	D	11.7	Cash & Equivalents		19.6		9.9	4.6	
A	A	9.1	Trade Receivables (net)		3.0		4.8	13.9	
T	T	.1	Inventory		.0		.1	.2	
A	A	2.0	All Other Current		.4		7.2	1.5	
		22.9	Total Current		22.9		21.8	20.2	
N	N	61.4	Fixed Assets (net)		52.3		71.7	63.1	
O	O	2.7	Intangibles (net)		.7		.1	1.9	
T	T	13.0	All Other Non-Current		24.1		6.3	14.9	
		100.0	Total		100.0		100.0	100.0	
A	A		**LIABILITIES**						
V	V	3.7	Notes Payable-Short Term		9.1		.3	4.9	
A	A	6.2	Cur. Mat.-L/T/D		14.9		5.6	2.5	
I	I	3.9	Trade Payables		3.4		3.4	4.5	
L	L	.6	Income Taxes Payable		1.6		.0	.1	
A	A	4.9	All Other Current		3.2		5.0	6.5	
B	B	19.4	Total Current		32.3		14.3	18.4	
L	L	37.4	Long Term Debt		40.7		28.9	40.6	
E	E	.0	Deferred Taxes		.0		.0	.0	
		10.4	All Other Non-Current		.3		21.1	11.1	
		32.8	Net Worth		26.6		35.6	29.8	
		100.0	Total Liabilities & Net Worth		100.0		100.0	100.0	
			INCOME DATA						
		100.0	Net Sales		100.0		100.0	100.0	
			Gross Profit						
		90.2	Operating Expenses		81.4		94.1	94.5	
		9.8	Operating Profit		18.6		5.9	5.5	
		6.0	All Other Expenses (net)		9.4		6.6	3.7	
		3.9	Profit Before Taxes		9.2		-.7	1.9	
			RATIOS						
		3.1	Current		2.6		3.0	2.4	
		1.2			.8		1.2	1.2	
		.7			.2		.9	.8	
		2.5	Quick		2.5		2.0	2.1	
		1.2			.8		1.2	1.1	
		.5			.2		.7	.3	
	3	135.0	Sales/Receivables	0	UND	15	25.1	27 13.6	
	16	22.9		0	UND	18	20.5	43 8.4	
	32	11.4		5	78.9	29	12.6	53 6.9	
			Cost of Sales/Inventory						
			Cost of Sales/Payables						
		6.9	Sales/Working Capital		7.6		5.1	8.0	
		26.9			-188.4		13.0	28.8	
		-16.6			-7.1		NM	-27.2	
	(38)	3.2	EBIT/Interest		23.4			3.6	
		1.6		(10)	1.6			1.6	
		.9			.9			.8	
			Net Profit + Depr., Dep., Amort./Cur. Mat. L/T/D						
		1.1	Fixed/Worth		.4		1.1	1.2	
		1.8			4.9		2.1	2.1	
		16.4			-14.5		21.7	5.4	
		.9	Debt/Worth		.9		.8	1.2	
		3.6			6.5		1.3	2.0	
		22.1			-18.5		26.8	6.5	
	(37)	19.8	% Profit Before Taxes/Tangible Net Worth						
		7.3							
		3.0							
		7.6	% Profit Before Taxes/Total Assets		30.8		6.8	6.7	
		2.3			2.9		1.1	2.4	
		-.4			-.4		-1.3	-.6	
		3.3	Sales/Net Fixed Assets		27.0		1.5	3.0	
		.9			.7		.6	1.4	
		.5			.5		.5	.4	
		1.9	Sales/Total Assets		5.8		1.0	1.9	
		.6			.6		.5	1.1	
		.3			.3		.3	.2	
	(39)	2.6	% Depr., Dep., Amort./Sales					(10) 2.5	
		6.6						3.4	
		10.3						8.6	
	(10)	4.4	% Officers', Directors', Owners' Comp/Sales						
		6.6							
		12.4							
		405093M	Net Sales ($)	3343M	22957M	17697M	66009M	186750M	108337M
		887969M	Total Assets ($)	9157M	44711M	16489M	162267M	394096M	261249M

© RMA 2003
M = $ thousand   MM = $ million
See Pages 11 through 18 for Explanation of Ratios and Data

Current Data Sorted By Assets   **Comparative Historical Data**

0-500M	500M-2MM	2-10MM	10-50MM	50-100MM	100-250MM	Type of Statement	4/1/98-3/31/99 ALL	4/1/99-3/31/00 ALL
		3	12	8		Unqualified		
		1				Reviewed		
1		1				Compiled		
1	1	1		1	1	Tax Returns		
						Other		
	14 (4/1-9/30/02)		16 (10/1/02-3/31/03)					
2	4	14	8	1	1	**NUMBER OF STATEMENTS**		
%	%	%	%	%	%	**ASSETS**	%	%
		12.7				Cash & Equivalents	D	D
		12.6				Trade Receivables (net)	A	A
		.1				Inventory	T	T
		8.1				All Other Current	A	A
		33.5				Total Current		
		56.2				Fixed Assets (net)	N	N
		2.0				Intangibles (net)	O	O
		8.3				All Other Non-Current	T	T
		100.0				Total		
						LIABILITIES	A	A
		3.3				Notes Payable-Short Term	V	V
		2.9				Cur. Mat.-L/T/D	A	A
		3.1				Trade Payables	I	I
		.0				Income Taxes Payable	L	L
		8.4				All Other Current	A	A
		17.7				Total Current	B	B
		41.9				Long Term Debt	L	L
		.1				Deferred Taxes	E	E
		6.5				All Other Non-Current		
		33.8				Net Worth		
		100.0				Total Liabilities & Net Worth		
						INCOME DATA		
		100.0				Net Sales		
						Gross Profit		
		95.4				Operating Expenses		
		4.6				Operating Profit		
		1.1				All Other Expenses (net)		
		3.5				Profit Before Taxes		
						RATIOS		
		4.2						
		1.7				Current		
		.9						
		2.5						
		1.2				Quick		
		.5						
	0	UND						
	23	16.1				Sales/Receivables		
	44	8.3						
						Cost of Sales/Inventory		
						Cost of Sales/Payables		
		3.9						
		24.9				Sales/Working Capital		
		−57.4						
		2.4						
	(11)	1.8				EBIT/Interest		
		−.7						
						Net Profit + Depr., Dep., Amort./Cur. Mat. L./T/D		
		.6						
		2.0				Fixed/Worth		
		10.2						
		.4						
		3.0				Debt/Worth		
		14.4						
		29.3				% Profit Before Taxes/Tangible Net Worth		
	(12)	5.1						
		−1.2						
		7.2				% Profit Before Taxes/Total Assets		
		2.8						
		−.2						
		4.7						
		2.8				Sales/Net Fixed Assets		
		1.6						
		2.2						
		1.5				Sales/Total Assets		
		.9						
		2.8						
		2.9				% Depr., Dep., Amort./Sales		
		4.8						
						% Officers', Directors', Owners' Comp/Sales		
711M	17401M	95412M	291783M	53695M	28320M	Net Sales ($)		
93M	5806M	61199M	169229M	70263M	119178M	Total Assets ($)		

© RMA 2003

M = $ thousand   MM = $ million
See Pages 11 through 18 for Explanation of Ratios and Data

Comparative Historical Data — **Current Data Sorted By Sales**

Type of Statement	4/1/00-3/31/01 ALL	4/1/01-3/31/02 ALL	4/1/02-3/31/03 ALL	0-1MM	1-3MM	3-5MM	5-10MM	10-25MM	25MM & OVER
					14 (4/1-9/30/02)		16 (10/1/02-3/31/03)		
Unqualified			23	2	3	5	4	3	6
Reviewed									
Compiled			1		1				
Tax Returns			1	1					
Other			5	1	1		1		2
NUMBER OF STATEMENTS			30	4	4	6	5	3	8
ASSETS	%	%	%	%	%	%	%	%	%
Cash & Equivalents	D	D	14.2						
Trade Receivables (net)	A	A	13.5						
Inventory	T	T	.1						
All Other Current	A	A	7.3						
Total Current			35.1						
Fixed Assets (net)	N	N	51.6						
Intangibles (net)	O	O	1.5						
All Other Non-Current	T	T	11.8						
Total			100.0						
LIABILITIES	A	A							
Notes Payable-Short Term	V	V	3.3						
Cur. Mat.-L/T/D	A	A	3.5						
Trade Payables	I	I	5.3						
Income Taxes Payable	L	L	.0						
All Other Current	A	A	13.3						
Total Current	B	B	25.4						
Long Term Debt	L	L	36.4						
Deferred Taxes	E	E	.0						
All Other Non-Current			14.5						
Net Worth			23.7						
Total Liabilities & Net Worth			100.0						
INCOME DATA									
Net Sales			100.0						
Gross Profit									
Operating Expenses			92.3						
Operating Profit			7.7						
All Other Expenses (net)			4.9						
Profit Before Taxes			2.8						
RATIOS									
Current			4.2 / 1.9 / .9						
Quick			2.4 / 1.5 / .7						
Sales/Receivables			0 UND / 24 15.5 / 43 8.5						
Cost of Sales/Inventory									
Cost of Sales/Payables									
Sales/Working Capital			4.7 / 20.9 / -244.9						
EBIT/Interest			(21) 2.9 / 1.8 / .6						
Net Profit + Depr., Dep., Amort./Cur. Mat. L/T/D									
Fixed/Worth			.6 / 1.3 / 10.6						
Debt/Worth			.4 / 2.1 / 17.9						
% Profit Before Taxes/Tangible Net Worth			(25) 38.1 / 6.9 / -.6						
% Profit Before Taxes/Total Assets			6.4 / 2.5 / -.2						
Sales/Net Fixed Assets			7.3 / 3.4 / 1.3						
Sales/Total Assets			2.9 / 1.6 / .7						
% Depr., Dep., Amort./Sales			(27) 2.5 / 2.9 / 5.0						
% Officers', Directors', Owners' Comp/Sales									
Net Sales ($)			487322M	2140M	7888M	25140M	35742M	46292M	370120M
Total Assets ($)			425768M	13897M	28042M	23315M	14661M	18888M	326965M

© RMA 2003   M = $ thousand   MM = $ million
See Pages 11 through 18 for Explanation of Ratios and Data

Current Data Sorted By Assets						Type of Statement	Comparative Historical Data	
3	25	30	13	1	4	Unqualified		
	1	1				Reviewed		
2	2					Compiled		
2	9	6	3			Tax Returns		
						Other		
	75 (4/1-9/30/02)		27 (10/1/02-3/31/03)				4/1/98-3/31/99 ALL	4/1/99-3/31/00 ALL
0-500M	500M-2MM	2-10MM	10-50MM	50-100MM	100-250MM			
7	37	37	16	1	4	NUMBER OF STATEMENTS		
%	%	%	%	%	%	ASSETS	%	%
	21.3	15.2	25.8			Cash & Equivalents	D	D
	15.9	14.4	13.6			Trade Receivables (net)	A	A
	.2	.3	1.1			Inventory	T	T
	11.2	11.0	5.1			All Other Current	A	A
	48.6	40.9	45.7			Total Current		
	46.4	47.8	41.1			Fixed Assets (net)	N	N
	.1	.2	.0			Intangibles (net)	O	O
	4.9	11.2	13.2			All Other Non-Current	T	T
	100.0	100.0	100.0			Total		
						LIABILITIES	A	A
	3.1	5.7	2.8			Notes Payable-Short Term	V	V
	1.6	1.0	.9			Cur. Mat.-L/T/D	A	A
	7.7	11.2	7.0			Trade Payables	I	I
	.0	.0	.0			Income Taxes Payable	L	L
	10.3	8.7	9.5			All Other Current	A	A
	22.7	26.6	20.2			Total Current	B	B
	20.3	18.3	13.5			Long Term Debt	L	L
	.4	.0	.1			Deferred Taxes	E	E
	3.7	4.8	3.2			All Other Non-Current		
	52.9	50.2	63.0			Net Worth		
	100.0	100.0	100.0			Total Liabilities & Net Worth		
						INCOME DATA		
	100.0	100.0	100.0			Net Sales		
						Gross Profit		
	92.4	93.9	91.6			Operating Expenses		
	7.6	6.1	8.4			Operating Profit		
	2.9	2.5	.8			All Other Expenses (net)		
	4.7	3.5	7.6			Profit Before Taxes		
						RATIOS		
	6.1	3.3	4.0					
	2.0	1.5	2.7			Current		
	1.0	1.1	2.3					
	4.6	2.2	2.8					
	1.5	1.3	2.4			Quick		
	.9	.8	1.9					

								Sales/Receivables		
0	UND	3	141.4	13	27.6					
20	18.1	30	12.2	33	11.1					
50	7.3	47	7.7	50	7.4					

Cost of Sales/Inventory

Cost of Sales/Payables

					Sales/Working Capital
	4.2	4.5	2.7		
	11.9	20.6	6.3		
	NM	54.3	8.4		

						EBIT/Interest
	6.6		8.7			
(20)	1.8	(20)	2.3			
	-1.3		-.4			

Net Profit + Depr., Dep., Amort./Cur. Mat. L/T/D

					Fixed/Worth
	.4	.4	.4		
	.9	1.1	.6		
	1.7	1.9	1.1		

					Debt/Worth
	.4	.2	.1		
	.8	1.3	.5		
	2.2	2.2	1.0		

							% Profit Before Taxes/Tangible Net Worth
	18.0		16.3		15.8		
(36)	6.0	(35)	10.3	(15)	8.4		
	-4.8		-4.8		1.3		

					% Profit Before Taxes/Total Assets
	9.7	7.7	12.4		
	2.8	2.4	6.0		
	-4.0	-3.2	1.4		

					Sales/Net Fixed Assets
	14.8	9.6	5.8		
	4.6	3.8	2.9		
	1.3	1.1	1.6		

					Sales/Total Assets
	2.7	2.5	2.4		
	1.8	1.5	1.1		
	.9	.7	.5		

							% Depr., Dep., Amort./Sales
	1.4		1.2		1.3		
(32)	2.3	(30)	2.4	(15)	2.1		
	3.4		4.7		3.1		

% Officers', Directors', Owners' Comp/Sales

						Net Sales ($) / Total Assets ($)
9729M	86105M	343772M	516135M	65363M	540481M	Net Sales ($)
2262M	44808M	188237M	355178M	73304M	590129M	Total Assets ($)

M = $ thousand   MM = $ million
See Pages 11 through 18 for Explanation of Ratios and Data

Comparative Historical Data / Current Data Sorted By Sales

4/1/00-3/31/01 ALL	4/1/01-3/31/02 ALL	4/1/02-3/31/03 ALL	Type of Statement	0-1MM	1-3MM	3-5MM	5-10MM	10-25MM	25MM & OVER
		76	Unqualified	6	20	10	15	14	11
			Reviewed						
		2	Compiled	1	1				
		4	Tax Returns	2	2				
		20	Other	3	6	3	4	1	3
				75 (4/1-9/30/02)			27 (10/1/02-3/31/03)		
4/1/00-3/31/01 ALL	4/1/01-3/31/02 ALL	4/1/02-3/31/03 ALL	NUMBER OF STATEMENTS	0-1MM	1-3MM	3-5MM	5-10MM	10-25MM	25MM & OVER
		102		12	29	13	19	15	14
%	%	%	ASSETS	%	%	%	%	%	%
D	D	18.8	Cash & Equivalents	15.7	17.3	31.7	8.5	20.2	25.4
A	A	15.4	Trade Receivables (net)	13.8	11.4	19.3	15.7	15.7	20.8
T	T	.7	Inventory	.0	1.2	.4	.4	.5	.9
A	A	9.0	All Other Current	1.8	7.3	10.1	15.5	13.7	3.9
		43.9	Total Current	31.3	37.2	61.4	40.1	50.1	50.9
N	N	45.6	Fixed Assets (net)	64.0	51.4	33.9	48.8	40.7	29.8
O	O	.2	Intangibles (net)	.1	.1	.1	.2	.3	.6
T	T	10.2	All Other Non-Current	4.6	11.3	4.7	10.8	8.8	18.7
		100.0	Total	100.0	100.0	100.0	100.0	100.0	100.0
A	A		LIABILITIES						
V	V	3.7	Notes Payable-Short Term	.8	3.5	2.2	5.8	3.0	5.8
A	A	1.9	Cur. Mat.-L/T/D	1.3	3.5	1.0	1.3	.9	1.7
I	I	8.3	Trade Payables	.4	4.5	8.8	10.3	12.1	15.7
L	L	.0	Income Taxes Payable	.0	.0	.0	.0	.0	.0
A	A	10.0	All Other Current	4.3	9.5	9.1	10.0	12.5	14.1
B	B	23.9	Total Current	6.8	21.0	21.2	27.4	28.5	37.3
L	L	19.0	Long Term Debt	39.6	17.8	10.4	17.9	11.2	21.4
E	E	.2	Deferred Taxes	.0	.0	.0	.0	.0	.1
		4.7	All Other Non-Current	5.0	3.6	6.5	3.6	2.0	9.2
		52.3	Net Worth	48.5	57.6	61.9	50.3	58.3	32.0
		100.0	Total Liabilities & Net Worth	100.0	100.0	100.0	100.0	100.0	100.0
			INCOME DATA						
		100.0	Net Sales	100.0	100.0	100.0	100.0	100.0	100.0
			Gross Profit						
		92.8	Operating Expenses	65.3	99.5	92.5	96.0	93.3	97.8
		7.2	Operating Profit	34.7	.5	7.5	4.0	6.7	2.2
		2.7	All Other Expenses (net)	15.5	.6	1.1	1.5	1.0	.9
		4.6	Profit Before Taxes	19.2	.0	6.3	2.6	5.7	1.3
			RATIOS						
		4.2		8.1	5.1	5.6	2.6	4.3	2.2
		1.9	Current	5.3	2.0	2.7	1.5	2.8	1.3
		1.1		.9	.9	1.4	1.0	1.3	.9
		2.6		8.0	2.4	4.6	1.6	4.3	2.2
		1.5	Quick	4.0	1.2	1.7	1.0	2.3	1.2
		.8		.9	.6	1.3	.6	1.3	.8
	3	118.6		0 UND	2 229.6	2 205.3	12 31.5	13 28.9	16 22.3
	28	13.2	Sales/Receivables	0 UND	20 18.1	30 12.2	42 8.6	32 11.4	27 13.6
	48	7.5		54 6.7	37 9.8	56 6.5	51 7.2	49 7.4	54 6.8
			Cost of Sales/Inventory						
			Cost of Sales/Payables						
		4.3		1.8	5.0	4.5	4.6	4.1	8.1
		12.2	Sales/Working Capital	3.4	12.1	9.8	16.6	6.6	20.2
		67.0		-33.2	-67.1	23.1	97.3	25.7	-37.6
		9.8			10.3		11.3		9.4
	(57)	2.0	EBIT/Interest	(20) 3.5		(11) 3.8		(11) 1.8
		-.7			-.8		-.3		1.4
			Net Profit + Depr., Dep., Amort./Cur. Mat. L/T/D						
		.4		.5	.5	.1	.5	.4	.3
		1.0	Fixed/Worth	1.4	1.0	.3	1.2	.7	1.1
		1.8		4.5	1.5	1.2	1.8	1.1	3.5
		.2		.2	.3	.2	.3	.1	.7
		.9	Debt/Worth	.9	.6	.4	1.2	.5	2.1
		2.2		3.7	1.8	2.2	1.6	1.9	12.3
		18.6		31.5	18.5	12.9	19.8	14.7	19.7
	(97)	8.9	% Profit Before Taxes/Tangible Net Worth	(11) 12.4	4.6	4.2	(18) 13.2	(14) 7.3	(12) 12.8
		-1.9		4.5	-6.1	-.4	-7.1	-.9	2.1
		10.1		15.1	10.2	7.5	14.3	7.8	9.6
		2.9	% Profit Before Taxes/Total Assets	3.8	3.7	2.6	2.4	4.0	3.7
		-2.2		1.2	-4.0	-.1	-4.4	-3.1	.5
		11.9		1.7	8.5	58.0	6.3	6.3	48.8
		3.7	Sales/Net Fixed Assets	.6	2.6	7.7	3.0	3.8	5.2
		1.3		.1	1.3	3.2	1.4	1.8	3.5
		2.6		.8	2.6	4.3	2.6	2.3	4.0
		1.6	Sales/Total Assets	.5	1.6	2.2	1.6	1.7	2.3
		.7		.1	.8	1.4	.8	.6	1.1
		1.3		4.6	1.4		1.1	1.7	.9
	(87)	2.3	% Depr., Dep., Amort./Sales	(10) 13.7	(28) 2.3		(14) 1.7	2.5	(11) 1.4
		4.1		29.7	3.1		4.1	3.0	4.1
		3.4							
	(10)	7.4	% Officers', Directors', Owners' Comp/Sales						
		10.9							
	1561585M		Net Sales ($)	5497M	53508M	51970M	132973M	225181M	1092456M
	1253918M		Total Assets ($)	18211M	46535M	28849M	140667M	198390M	821266M

Current Data Sorted By Assets   Comparative Historical Data

0-500M	500M-2MM	2-10MM	10-50MM	50-100MM	100-250MM	Type of Statement	4/1/98-3/31/99 ALL	4/1/99-3/31/00 ALL
31	92	227	105	16	5	Unqualified	377	420
1	4	3				Reviewed	10	14
8	2	3				Compiled	19	18
4	3	5				Tax Returns	9	8
20	30	52	25	2	2	Other	142	117
	445 (4/1-9/30/02)		195 (10/1/02-3/31/03)					
64	131	290	130	18	7	NUMBER OF STATEMENTS	557	577
%	%	%	%	%	%	ASSETS	%	%
22.9	19.0	16.7	17.9	14.8		Cash & Equivalents	19.9	19.4
20.6	20.3	19.7	13.6	10.1		Trade Receivables (net)	19.5	20.9
.2	.9	.8	.5	.7		Inventory	1.1	.9
8.7	7.9	4.0	4.1	1.1		All Other Current	4.5	4.3
52.3	48.0	41.2	36.1	26.7		Total Current	45.0	45.6
35.7	41.0	47.7	44.4	40.4		Fixed Assets (net)	42.3	39.4
1.6	.3	.6	1.5	3.2		Intangibles (net)	1.3	.9
10.3	10.7	10.5	18.0	29.7		All Other Non-Current	11.3	14.2
100.0	100.0	100.0	100.0	100.0		Total	100.0	100.0
						LIABILITIES		
20.2	3.7	3.5	3.0	1.2		Notes Payable-Short Term	4.4	4.4
1.4	2.0	2.2	1.9	2.1		Cur. Mat.-L/T/D	2.3	1.8
9.4	7.0	6.9	5.9	5.3		Trade Payables	7.9	8.4
.1	.1	.1	.0	.0		Income Taxes Payable	.0	.1
18.4	13.1	12.1	10.5	5.3		All Other Current	12.6	12.6
49.6	25.9	24.9	21.4	13.8		Total Current	27.2	27.3
15.7	18.8	19.4	21.0	24.3		Long Term Debt	17.0	16.7
.0	.1	.0	.0	.0		Deferred Taxes	.1	.1
17.3	1.2	2.0	2.3	7.8		All Other Non-Current	2.9	3.6
17.4	53.9	53.8	55.3	54.1		Net Worth	52.8	52.4
100.0	100.0	100.0	100.0	100.0		Total Liabilities & Net Worth	100.0	100.0
						INCOME DATA		
100.0	100.0	100.0	100.0	100.0		Net Sales	100.0	100.0
						Gross Profit		
99.8	95.6	97.1	96.7	104.1		Operating Expenses	96.0	94.7
.2	4.4	2.9	3.3	-4.1		Operating Profit	4.0	5.3
.4	1.5	.8	1.9	7.2		All Other Expenses (net)	-4.0	-1.5
-.2	2.9	2.1	1.5	-11.3		Profit Before Taxes	8.0	6.8
						RATIOS		
4.0	3.7	3.2	3.2	3.0		Current	3.5	3.4
1.7	2.1	1.7	1.7	1.6			1.6	1.8
.7	1.2	1.1	1.2	1.3			1.1	1.1
3.1	3.3	2.7	2.8	2.8		Quick	2.9	2.9
1.1	1.7	1.5	1.5	1.5			1.4	1.6
.4	1.0	.9	1.0	1.1			.9	.9
0 UND	8 43.9	20 18.2	15 23.9	26 13.9		Sales/Receivables	10 35.9	15 24.8
21 17.8	32 11.6	34 10.8	35 10.4	44 8.2			32 11.4	33 11.0
35 10.4	45 8.1	51 7.1	56 6.5	62 5.9			49 7.5	53 6.9
						Cost of Sales/Inventory		
						Cost of Sales/Payables		
6.3	4.6	5.3	4.2	4.4		Sales/Working Capital	4.8	5.0
18.3	10.0	11.0	10.5	10.3			13.7	11.7
-31.2	41.6	98.3	42.5	22.4			117.7	70.1
(35) 13.2	(77) 9.5	(202) 6.7	(93) 5.0	(14) 1.0		EBIT/Interest	(365) 9.8	(379) 12.7
4.6	2.3	2.3	1.4	-2.3			3.2	3.6
-1.5	-1.0	.2	-.4	-11.8			1.1	1.1
						Net Profit + Depr., Dep., Amort./Cur. Mat. L /T/D	(10) 6.9	
							4.1	
							1.4	
.3	.2	.5	.5	.4		Fixed/Worth	.3	.3
.9	.7	.9	.9	.8			.8	.8
UND	1.7	1.5	1.6	1.6			1.4	1.3
.3	.2	.4	.3	.3		Debt/Worth	.3	.3
1.0	.7	.9	.9	.9			.8	.8
UND	1.9	1.8	1.8	2.5			1.9	2.0
(48) 19.4	(123) 28.4	(286) 16.6	(129) 10.9	-2.0		% Profit Before Taxes/Tangible Net Worth	(532) 23.2	(558) 22.2
4.9	5.3	3.9	2.4	-8.5			11.2	9.1
-12.2	-5.9	-2.9	-4.4	-20.7			1.4	.8
13.9	15.4	7.5	5.6	-1.5		% Profit Before Taxes/Total Assets	11.4	11.7
1.4	2.7	1.9	.9	-3.7			5.1	4.9
-12.0	-3.4	-1.2	-2.2	-7.6			.3	.1
61.1	19.6	8.0	4.8	3.6		Sales/Net Fixed Assets	14.2	13.9
16.9	6.5	3.4	2.9	1.9			4.1	4.7
3.3	2.1	1.8	1.6	1.4			1.8	2.2
5.6	3.3	2.3	1.8	1.3		Sales/Total Assets	3.1	3.0
2.9	2.1	1.6	1.2	.7			1.7	1.8
1.5	1.2	.9	.6	.5			.8	.9
(43) .9	(115) 1.3	(262) 1.4	(121) 1.6	(17) 2.8		% Depr., Dep., Amort./Sales	(483) 1.3	(497) 1.2
1.9	2.0	2.3	2.6	3.9			2.4	2.1
3.2	3.5	3.6	3.7	6.3			4.0	3.4
(16) 2.3		(29) 3.8	(11) 2.4			% Officers', Directors', Owners' Comp/Sales	(52) 3.4	(43) 4.1
7.3		8.3	4.9				8.0	7.3
15.1		17.2	8.7				25.4	15.0
54682M	394225M	2674002M	3450387M	1058257M	1704505M	Net Sales ($)	4627437M	8677346M
14934M	164115M	1465335M	2599861M	1239944M	1340392M	Total Assets ($)	3526576M	5321663M

© RMA 2003

M = $ thousand   MM = $ million
See Pages 11 through 18 for Explanation of Ratios and Data

Comparative Historical Data | Current Data Sorted By Sales

				Type of Statement						
376		417		476	Unqualified	47	94	72	75	123	65
11		8		8	Reviewed	3	3			2	
40		43		13	Compiled	4	7	1	1		
13		11		12	Tax Returns	3	4	3	1	1	
133		155		131	Other	22	21	17	20	35	16
4/1/00-		4/1/01-		4/1/02-			445 (4/1-9/30/02)			195 (10/1/02-3/31/03)	
3/31/01		3/31/02		3/31/03		0-1MM	1-3MM	3-5MM	5-10MM	10-25MM	25MM & OVER
ALL		ALL		ALL							
573		634		640	**NUMBER OF STATEMENTS**	79	129	93	97	161	81
%		%		%	**ASSETS**	%	%	%	%	%	%
18.4		17.6		18.1	Cash & Equivalents	17.9	19.0	16.1	17.0	18.1	20.2
19.6		19.6		18.3	Trade Receivables (net)	9.4	16.5	15.6	21.9	22.5	20.5
.8		.8		.7	Inventory	.1	1.3	.4	.5	.4	1.2
4.8		5.6		5.2	All Other Current	4.4	7.0	8.1	5.4	3.5	2.7
43.6		43.6		42.2	Total Current	31.8	43.8	40.1	44.8	44.5	44.5
41.1		43.1		44.1	Fixed Assets (net)	52.6	44.3	46.3	43.5	41.9	38.2
1.2		.9		.9	Intangibles (net)	1.1	.2	.3	.6	.8	3.0
14.1		12.4		12.8	All Other Non-Current	14.5	11.7	13.3	11.1	12.8	14.3
100.0		100.0		100.0	Total	100.0	100.0	100.0	100.0	100.0	100.0
				LIABILITIES						
4.9		4.5		5.0	Notes Payable-Short Term	10.2	7.0	3.3	2.5	4.3	3.3
2.0		2.0		2.0	Cur. Mat.-L/T/D	1.8	2.0	2.4	2.0	1.8	2.1
8.4		7.6		6.9	Trade Payables	4.4	6.0	5.9	6.9	8.1	9.5
.0		.0		.1	Income Taxes Payable	.1	.0	.1	.1	.1	.0
11.1		11.5		12.4	All Other Current	12.4	8.9	9.2	17.1	13.6	13.6
26.5		25.6		26.4	Total Current	28.9	23.9	21.0	28.6	28.0	28.5
17.8		19.6		19.5	Long Term Debt	25.7	17.7	18.2	20.6	17.3	20.8
.1		.1		.0	Deferred Taxes	.0	.0	.0	.1	.0	.0
4.8		4.6		3.7	All Other Non-Current	6.3	6.0	2.0	1.8	2.4	3.9
50.7		50.1		50.4	Net Worth	39.1	52.3	58.8	48.9	52.3	46.8
100.0		100.0		100.0	Total Liabilities & Net Worth	100.0	100.0	100.0	100.0	100.0	100.0
				INCOME DATA						
100.0		100.0		100.0	Net Sales	100.0	100.0	100.0	100.0	100.0	100.0
				Gross Profit						
95.0		96.0		97.2	Operating Expenses	96.5	94.8	96.6	97.2	98.6	99.6
5.0		4.0		2.8	Operating Profit	3.5	5.2	3.4	2.8	1.4	.4
-.9		1.3		1.3	All Other Expenses (net)	4.4	.9	1.0	.6	.7	1.3
5.9		2.6		1.5	Profit Before Taxes	-.9	4.3	2.4	2.2	.7	-.9
				RATIOS						
3.3		3.4		3.3		5.0	5.0	3.8	3.3	2.6	2.5
1.8		1.9		1.8	Current	1.9	2.1	2.1	1.8	1.7	1.5
1.1		1.1		1.1		.8	1.2	1.2	1.0	1.1	1.2
2.8		3.0		2.8		4.2	4.3	3.1	2.6	2.3	2.0
1.6		1.6		1.5	Quick	1.6	1.6	1.7	1.5	1.5	1.4
.9		.9		.9		.5	.8	.8	.9	1.0	1.0
13	27.6	11	33.0	15	23.9		0	UND	11	32.2	10	36.3	25	14.6	25	14.4	21	17.6

Sales/Receivables:											
13	27.6	11	33.0	15	23.9	0 UND	11 32.2	10 36.3	25 14.6	25 14.4	21 17.6
33	11.0	32	11.5	33	11.1	8 43.9	28 13.1	30 12.2	37 9.8	36 10.0	36 10.2
52	7.0	51	7.2	49	7.4	36 10.1	43 8.5	50 7.3	54 6.8	55 6.6	52 7.0

Cost of Sales/Inventory

Cost of Sales/Payables

					Sales/Working Capital						
	4.6		5.1		5.0	4.2	3.5	4.3	5.4	6.2	7.3
	10.1		10.7		10.9	10.9	7.2	9.5	9.9	11.8	16.1
	71.1		46.2		84.7	-34.0	40.3	47.8	226.4	94.2	43.4

						EBIT/Interest						
		9.8		6.9		6.8		5.0		11.7		9.5		6.4		4.8
(376)	2.9	(434)	2.1	(425)	1.9	(45)	.8	(77)	2.8	(57) 1.5	(69) 2.3	(118) 2.2	(59) 1.4
	.7		.1		-.5		-2.7		-.1	-2.1	-1.1	.4	-.2

Detailed EBIT/Interest:
	9.8		6.9		6.8	5.0	11.7	4.9	9.5	6.4	4.8
(376) 2.9		(434) 2.1		(425) 1.9		(45) .8	(77) 2.8	(57) 1.5	(69) 2.3	(118) 2.2	(59) 1.4
.7		.1		-.5		-2.7	-.1	-2.1	-1.1	.4	-.2

Net Profit + Depr., Dep., Amort./Cur. Mat. L/T/D

					Fixed/Worth						
	.4		.4		.4	.4	.4	.3	.5	.5	.4
	.8		.8		.9	1.2	.7	.8	.9	.8	1.0
	1.5		1.5		1.6	3.0	1.6	1.4	1.7	1.4	1.8

					Debt/Worth						
	.3		.3		.3	.2	.2	.2	.3	.5	.6
	.8		.9		.8	.7	.5	.7	1.0	1.0	1.2
	1.9		1.9		1.9	3.9	1.7	1.4	2.5	1.7	2.5

						% Profit Before Taxes/Tangible Net Worth						
	19.3		16.5		16.5		8.8	20.0	15.7	22.3	15.5	12.8
(551) 7.1		(604) 5.1		(611) 3.5		(64) -.1	(123) 4.2	(92) 3.1	(92) 5.3	(160) 4.0	(80) 2.1
.0			-3.0		-5.0		-12.9	-4.5	-4.7	-5.1	-4.0	-6.8

					% Profit Before Taxes/Total Assets						
	11.0		8.5		7.6	6.4	12.2	7.5	9.4	6.9	5.6
	3.3		2.5		1.6	-.3	2.2	1.5	2.6	2.3	.8
	-.4		-1.6		-2.7	-9.6	-2.6	-2.7	-2.3	-2.2	-3.0

					Sales/Net Fixed Assets						
	11.9		12.9		10.8	13.2	17.9	8.4	9.3	9.5	11.9
	4.1		3.9		3.6	2.4	3.0	3.5	3.6	4.1	4.0
	1.9		1.9		1.8	.6	1.2	1.4	2.2	2.7	2.3

					Sales/Total Assets						
	2.7		2.9		2.6	2.1	2.9	2.3	2.7	2.8	2.8
	1.6		1.6		1.6	1.0	1.3	1.6	1.7	1.9	1.8
	.8		.9		.9	.4	.7	.8	1.0	1.2	1.0

						% Depr., Dep., Amort./Sales						
	1.3		1.2		1.4		1.8	1.5	1.3	1.4	1.4	.9
(503) 2.1		(560) 2.2		(563) 2.3		(63) 4.7	(105) 2.5	(85) 2.2	(88) 2.2	(148) 2.1	(74) 2.1
3.6		3.7		3.6		9.9	4.5	3.9	3.4	3.2	3.4

						% Officers', Directors', Owners' Comp/Sales						
	3.2		3.4		3.2		3.9	2.3	2.8		4.8	3.7
(55) 6.0		(62) 7.1		(68) 7.2		(11) 13.3	(13) 6.9	(10) 4.3		(15) 6.7	(10) 8.0
18.9		14.4		13.8		19.9	9.2	13.2		13.9	12.2

6136629M	7656954M	9336058M	Net Sales ($)	38812M	260191M	359593M	704018M	2537668M	5435776M
5060948M	6391190M	6824581M	Total Assets ($)	83121M	339653M	379015M	534553M	1774771M	3713468M

© RMA 2003

M = $ thousand   MM = $ million
See Pages 11 through 18 for Explanation of Ratios and Data

Current Data Sorted By Assets							Comparative Historical Data	
5	28	78	36	5	1	**Type of Statement** Unqualified	125	137
	4	1				Reviewed	2	2
		3				Compiled	6	3
4	3					Tax Returns	1	2
2	11	26	11	1	1	Other	37	33
	125 (4/1-9/30/02)		95 (10/1/02-3/31/03)				4/1/98- 3/31/99	4/1/99- 3/31/00
0-500M	500M-2MM	2-10MM	10-50MM	50-100MM	100-250MM		ALL	ALL
11	46	108	47	6	2	**NUMBER OF STATEMENTS**	171	177
%	%	%	%	%	%	**ASSETS**	%	%
29.6	20.0	14.9	16.3			Cash & Equivalents	15.9	14.8
27.6	23.5	19.2	16.7			Trade Receivables (net)	21.8	20.2
.2	1.1	2.9	3.0			Inventory	2.6	2.4
3.7	2.7	3.8	4.1			All Other Current	3.9	3.6
61.1	47.3	40.8	40.0			Total Current	44.2	41.0
26.5	44.3	50.1	42.0			Fixed Assets (net)	46.1	45.7
3.0	.7	1.1	.4			Intangibles (net)	1.1	1.4
9.5	7.7	8.0	17.6			All Other Non-Current	8.5	11.9
100.0	100.0	100.0	100.0			Total	100.0	100.0
						LIABILITIES		
11.7	5.9	4.1	1.2			Notes Payable-Short Term	4.4	5.1
33.7	2.6	2.5	1.8			Cur. Mat.-L/T/D	2.5	2.1
21.6	6.5	6.7	9.6			Trade Payables	8.3	6.7
.0	.2	.0	.0			Income Taxes Payable	.0	.1
17.8	11.0	11.4	10.4			All Other Current	12.3	12.6
84.8	26.2	24.7	22.9			Total Current	27.5	26.6
43.7	26.1	19.3	19.7			Long Term Debt	20.1	20.5
.0	.0	.0	.2			Deferred Taxes	.1	.0
17.0	1.9	1.4	2.2			All Other Non-Current	2.2	4.2
−45.5	45.8	54.5	55.0			Net Worth	50.2	48.6
100.0	100.0	100.0	100.0			Total Liabilities & Net Worth	100.0	100.0
						INCOME DATA		
100.0	100.0	100.0	100.0			Net Sales	100.0	100.0
						Gross Profit		
101.5	100.3	94.1	97.2			Operating Expenses	96.1	98.4
−1.5	−.3	5.9	2.8			Operating Profit	3.9	1.6
.3	.7	2.7	2.1			All Other Expenses (net)	−1.0	−1.1
−1.8	−1.0	3.1	.7			Profit Before Taxes	5.0	2.6
						RATIOS		
2.2	4.0	2.9	3.6			Current	2.9	2.7
1.1	2.4	1.8	2.1				1.7	1.8
.5	1.4	1.1	1.2				1.1	1.1
2.1	3.7	2.4	3.2			Quick	2.5	2.5
1.1	2.3	1.5	1.8				1.4	1.5
.3	1.1	1.0	.9				1.0	1.0
0 UND	19 19.2	18 19.8	20 18.0			Sales/Receivables	22 16.4	23 15.6
28 13.0	30 12.0	34 10.6	33 11.2				35 10.4	39 9.4
54 6.8	51 7.1	50 7.2	44 8.4				51 7.2	52 7.0
						Cost of Sales/Inventory		
						Cost of Sales/Payables		
6.5	4.5	6.1	4.0			Sales/Working Capital	5.8	5.6
156.8	10.0	12.3	8.2				14.3	12.0
−25.5	27.7	47.3	29.7				51.4	66.8
	(35) 4.4	(87) 9.5	(38) 4.2			EBIT/Interest	(127) 8.0	(139) 6.6
	.8	3.0	1.7				3.3	2.2
	−3.7	1.0	−.1				1.1	1.0
						Net Profit + Depr., Dep., Amort./Cur. Mat. L /T/D		
.3	.4	.6	.4			Fixed/Worth	.6	.5
1.3	.9	1.0	.8				1.0	.9
−.5	1.4	1.5	1.4				1.6	1.5
.9	.3	.4	.4			Debt/Worth	.4	.4
4.4	.7	.7	.9				1.0	.9
−2.1	2.5	1.8	1.4				1.9	1.9
	(42) 12.4	(107) 16.7	(46) 9.3			% Profit Before Taxes/Tangible Net Worth	(163) 20.7	(171) 14.4
	−.8	8.2	2.6				8.4	6.9
	−17.5	.1	−2.1				1.6	−.1
10.5	4.8	9.7	4.3			% Profit Before Taxes/Total Assets	9.9	8.4
1.4	−.9	4.2	1.6				4.4	3.3
−22.3	−11.2	.1	−1.1				.5	−.2
197.7	12.0	7.0	6.4			Sales/Net Fixed Assets	9.4	9.3
24.1	5.5	3.4	3.3				3.9	3.1
10.5	3.4	1.8	2.2				2.1	1.9
8.7	2.9	2.3	1.9			Sales/Total Assets	2.9	2.4
3.3	2.1	1.6	1.5				1.7	1.6
2.4	1.6	1.0	.7				1.1	1.0
	(44) 1.7	(98) 1.9	(44) 1.9			% Depr., Dep., Amort./Sales	(148) 2.0	(161) 1.8
	2.5	3.0	2.6				3.1	3.0
	4.1	5.0	3.4				4.4	4.5
						% Officers', Directors', Owners' Comp/Sales	(14) 1.7	(19) 5.9
							5.1	13.5
							12.9	34.2
14566M	135843M	1019417M	1250475M	966684M	1623851M	Net Sales ($)	2669335M	2168667M
2703M	56296M	578688M	879437M	486029M	337208M	Total Assets ($)	1120701M	1639219M

M = $ thousand   MM = $ million
See Pages 11 through 18 for Explanation of Ratios and Data

Comparative Historical Data | Current Data Sorted By Sales

			Type of Statement						
114	112	153	Unqualified	7	24	29	29	39	25
4	4	1	Reviewed					1	
15	25	7	Compiled		4	3			
3	4	7	Tax Returns	1	4	2			
42	45	52	Other	1	12	5	9	19	6
4/1/00-3/31/01 ALL	4/1/01-3/31/02 ALL	4/1/02-3/31/03 ALL		125 (4/1-9/30/02)			95 (10/1/02-3/31/03)		
				0-1MM	1-3MM	3-5MM	5-10MM	10-25MM	25MM & OVER
178	190	220	NUMBER OF STATEMENTS	9	44	36	41	59	31
%	%	%	**ASSETS**	%	%	%	%	%	%
14.6	15.6	17.1	Cash & Equivalents		20.5	15.8	17.3	13.2	18.4
26.6	21.8	20.2	Trade Receivables (net)		20.2	17.9	19.7	22.2	22.6
2.0	2.5	2.3	Inventory		.7	1.8	3.0	3.2	3.4
3.3	4.6	3.6	All Other Current		3.5	1.2	3.4	4.8	4.2
46.5	44.5	43.3	Total Current		44.8	36.7	43.5	43.4	48.7
43.4	41.8	45.4	Fixed Assets (net)		47.4	50.2	46.9	43.4	37.4
1.4	1.3	1.1	Intangibles (net)		1.3	1.5	.6	.9	1.7
8.7	12.3	10.3	All Other Non-Current		6.5	11.6	9.0	12.3	12.2
100.0	100.0	100.0	Total		100.0	100.0	100.0	100.0	100.0
			LIABILITIES						
5.8	5.8	4.3	Notes Payable-Short Term		5.9	3.3	2.9	3.2	2.6
3.8	2.4	3.9	Cur. Mat.-L/T/D		3.1	10.3	2.7	1.9	1.4
8.9	7.8	8.2	Trade Payables		8.3	7.0	5.3	9.1	11.7
.1	.1	.0	Income Taxes Payable		.0	.3	.0	.0	.0
12.5	11.7	11.4	All Other Current		8.6	12.0	12.2	10.8	17.3
31.1	27.7	27.9	Total Current		25.9	32.8	23.2	25.0	33.0
20.0	19.4	21.9	Long Term Debt		27.0	29.5	18.8	19.7	17.6
.0	.0	.0	Deferred Taxes		.0	.0	.0	.1	.0
3.4	3.6	2.7	All Other Non-Current		4.7	1.0	1.3	1.4	4.4
45.4	49.3	47.5	Net Worth		42.3	36.8	56.7	53.8	45.0
100.0	100.0	100.0	Total Liabilities & Net Worth		100.0	100.0	100.0	100.0	100.0
			INCOME DATA						
100.0	100.0	100.0	Net Sales		100.0	100.0	100.0	100.0	100.0
			Gross Profit						
97.1	96.6	96.5	Operating Expenses		96.3	93.1	96.9	97.5	98.0
2.9	3.4	3.5	Operating Profit		3.7	6.9	3.1	2.5	2.0
−.3	.6	2.0	All Other Expenses (net)		6.0	.9	1.2	1.1	.7
3.2	2.8	1.5	Profit Before Taxes		−2.3	5.9	1.9	1.4	1.2
			RATIOS						
2.7	3.5	3.3	Current		3.6	3.1	3.2	3.4	2.2
1.7	1.9	1.8			1.9	1.9	1.9	1.8	1.7
1.2	1.2	1.1			1.1	1.1	1.1	1.2	1.1
2.5	2.7	2.8	Quick		3.1	2.7	2.7	3.0	1.9
1.4	1.6	1.6			1.7	1.6	1.6	1.6	1.6
1.0	.9	1.0			.8	1.1	.8	1.1	.8
27 13.7	19 19.4	19 18.8	Sales/Receivables		13 27.9	16 22.7	15 23.6	22 16.8	21 17.7
39 9.3	36 10.3	34 10.8			34 10.8	33 11.0	31 11.9	38 9.5	35 10.5
53 6.9	50 7.3	51 7.1			51 7.1	53 6.9	50 7.3	52 7.0	55 6.6
			Cost of Sales/Inventory						
			Cost of Sales/Payables						
6.3	4.5	5.3	Sales/Working Capital		4.4	4.5	6.1	5.4	7.2
12.9	11.7	11.3			10.9	12.2	9.6	10.2	13.2
53.3	33.3	39.7			149.1	64.0	27.0	31.3	114.3
(142) 7.4	(146) 6.1	(174) 6.2	EBIT/Interest		(31) 3.4	(28) 13.6	(36) 5.1	(47) 7.8	(27) 4.0
2.9	2.3	2.2			.1	5.4	2.7	2.7	2.0
.9	.7	−.3			−3.7	.0	.6	1.2	−.4
			Net Profit + Depr., Dep., Amort./Cur. Mat. L/T/D						
.4	.5	.5	Fixed/Worth		.5	.5	.5	.5	.5
1.0	.8	1.0			1.1	1.0	1.0	.9	.9
1.6	1.4	1.5			2.0	1.6	1.4	1.4	1.9
.5	.4	.4	Debt/Worth		.4	.4	.3	.4	.5
1.1	.8	.8			.8	.8	.7	.7	1.2
2.2	1.8	1.9			3.3	1.5	1.8	2.0	2.7
(168) 19.3	(175) 17.2	(210) 14.8	% Profit Before Taxes/Tangible Net Worth		(39) 5.1	(34) 25.1	16.5	14.8	(29) 11.4
7.5	5.1	4.7			−.8	12.3	6.1	7.8	4.8
−.1	−.9	−3.8			−17.6	−4.7	−2.2	.0	−.5
9.3	7.8	7.4	% Profit Before Taxes/Total Assets		3.5	13.7	8.8	6.9	5.2
3.8	2.5	2.4			−.8	5.3	4.0	3.5	2.0
−.4	−.8	−2.5			−10.4	−2.8	−1.5	.0	−.4
12.9	11.4	8.9	Sales/Net Fixed Assets		8.5	7.3	7.6	8.0	12.9
4.2	4.2	3.9			4.7	2.9	3.7	3.9	4.2
2.2	2.2	2.3			1.6	1.6	2.0	2.7	3.1
2.9	2.5	2.4	Sales/Total Assets		2.5	2.3	2.4	2.4	3.0
1.8	1.7	1.8			1.7	1.6	1.8	1.8	2.0
1.1	1.1	1.1			.9	.9	1.0	1.4	1.4
(162) 1.3	(174) 1.4	(201) 1.9	% Depr., Dep., Amort./Sales		(38) 2.1	(35) 1.7	(38) 1.9	(54) 1.7	(27) 1.1
2.6	2.8	2.7			3.4	3.3	2.9	2.7	2.3
3.8	4.0	4.1			5.5	4.7	5.1	3.5	2.9
(18) 2.6	(23) 5.6	(25) 2.8	% Officers', Directors', Owners' Comp/Sales						
5.2	11.0	9.0							
17.4	19.9	29.3							
2875199M	5318253M	5010836M	Net Sales ($)	5643M	81823M	148510M	299332M	955627M	3519901M
1857754M	1886883M	2340361M	Total Assets ($)	8802M	80636M	139101M	210065M	669626M	1232131M

M = $ thousand   MM = $ million
See Pages 11 through 18 for Explanation of Ratios and Data

Current Data Sorted By Assets — Comparative Historical Data

	0-500M	500M-2MM	2-10MM	10-50MM	50-100MM	100-250MM		4/1/98-3/31/99 ALL	4/1/99-3/31/00 ALL
Type of Statement									
Unqualified	4	15	23	5	2	2		41	43
Reviewed	2	2	4		2			14	8
Compiled	23	17	9	1	1			66	41
Tax Returns	63	22	3			1		55	45
Other	22	18	16	5				54	45
		70 (4/1-9/30/02)			192 (10/1/02-3/31/03)				
NUMBER OF STATEMENTS	114	74	55	11	5	3		230	182
	%	%	%	%	%	%		%	%
ASSETS									
Cash & Equivalents	23.1	15.1	11.6	15.7				18.0	18.9
Trade Receivables (net)	7.0	9.2	11.3	16.4				10.1	12.2
Inventory	.2	.1	.0	.2				.1	.4
All Other Current	5.1	2.8	2.7	.3				2.6	3.2
Total Current	35.3	27.2	25.7	32.7				30.9	34.7
Fixed Assets (net)	46.0	61.2	67.2	55.0				57.0	52.9
Intangibles (net)	8.5	3.9	1.9	5.9				5.0	4.5
All Other Non-Current	10.1	7.6	5.1	6.4				7.1	7.9
Total	100.0	100.0	100.0	100.0				100.0	100.0
LIABILITIES									
Notes Payable-Short Term	13.8	4.5	3.8	1.3				5.5	6.1
Cur. Mat.-L/T/D	10.0	5.1	2.3	2.7				3.8	3.8
Trade Payables	4.7	3.9	6.1	10.4				5.9	7.1
Income Taxes Payable	.1	.2	.0	.1				.4	.5
All Other Current	35.1	9.1	9.3	12.8				16.1	15.8
Total Current	63.7	22.9	21.6	27.3				31.8	33.2
Long Term Debt	28.6	40.4	37.2	34.3				34.4	30.2
Deferred Taxes	.0	.2	.2	.9				.1	.1
All Other Non-Current	29.3	3.6	3.5	13.2				8.8	6.9
Net Worth	−21.6	33.0	37.6	24.4				24.9	29.5
Total Liabilities & Net Worth	100.0	100.0	100.0	100.0				100.0	100.0
INCOME DATA									
Net Sales	100.0	100.0	100.0	100.0				100.0	100.0
Gross Profit									
Operating Expenses	94.6	89.4	89.5	93.8				93.4	92.8
Operating Profit	5.4	10.6	10.5	6.2				6.6	7.2
All Other Expenses (net)	1.9	4.6	5.8	1.4				2.8	1.7
Profit Before Taxes	3.6	6.1	4.7	4.8				3.8	5.4
RATIOS									
Current	2.3	2.8	2.0	1.8				2.5	2.6
	.7	1.1	1.1	1.2				1.2	1.1
	.1	.3	.4	.4				.5	.4
Quick	1.8	2.7	1.9	1.8				2.3	2.0
	(113) .6	(73) 1.0	.8	1.2				(225) 1.1	1.1
	.1	.3	.4	.4				.4	.4
Sales/Receivables	0 UND	0 UND	0 999.8	13 28.0				0 UND	0 UND
	0 UND	3 135.9	8 48.2	21 17.0				4 97.9	4 102.4
	5 76.4	19 18.8	29 12.6	44 8.3				18 20.1	18 19.9
Cost of Sales/Inventory									
Cost of Sales/Payables									
Sales/Working Capital	39.4	9.2	14.9	7.6				12.3	12.3
	−59.0	121.7	68.8	51.1				132.0	102.5
	−13.2	−16.1	−10.4	−13.7				−19.8	−28.1
EBIT/Interest	9.8	8.1	4.0					7.9	12.3
	(76) 2.3	(56) 3.5	(39) 2.4					(184) 3.0	(127) 3.7
	.8	1.2	1.2					1.0	1.4
Net Profit + Depr., Dep., Amort./Cur. Mat. L /T/D								4.9	8.9
								(23) 3.2	(17) 2.4
								2.2	1.5
Fixed/Worth	.7	.8	.9	.7				.8	.7
	4.6	1.9	1.7	3.1				1.9	1.4
	−1.1	UND	6.2	−34.9				54.1	24.4
Debt/Worth	1.0	.6	.7	2.4				.7	.7
	9.2	1.8	2.1	3.3				2.5	1.8
	−2.6	UND	7.1	−45.2				242.0	32.8
% Profit Before Taxes/Tangible Net Worth	148.9	46.2	29.6					79.5	67.7
	(69) 53.4	(58) 25.8	(50) 7.8					(176) 29.7	(146) 27.7
	5.8	7.1	1.0					9.8	7.1
% Profit Before Taxes/Total Assets	41.5	16.0	8.0	7.6				21.0	22.0
	11.0	8.1	2.9	4.7				7.2	7.8
	−.7	.5	.2	−.3				.0	.8
Sales/Net Fixed Assets	38.6	10.7	5.8	4.5				15.3	20.6
	17.3	2.4	1.4	3.3				6.2	7.2
	5.6	1.0	.7	1.4				1.8	1.9
Sales/Total Assets	11.1	3.0	2.4	3.4				5.8	6.2
	5.7	1.5	1.0	1.5				2.8	2.8
	2.8	.9	.6	1.3				1.2	1.2
% Depr., Dep., Amort./Sales	1.0	1.8	1.6					1.5	1.2
	(83) 2.2	(66) 2.6	(49) 3.5					(202) 2.8	(152) 2.3
	3.8	5.2	7.2					4.8	4.4
% Officers', Directors', Owners' Comp/Sales	3.1	3.1	2.6					3.6	4.6
	(57) 6.4	(29) 5.4	(13) 4.4					(85) 6.3	(65) 7.3
	13.2	10.9	14.3					11.1	11.4
Net Sales ($)	94521M	150110M	401334M	391594M	1327409M	1137324M		2587485M	2083379M
Total Assets ($)	20554M	77052M	235392M	183614M	405569M	488323M		1212647M	999352M

M = $ thousand   MM = $ million
See Pages 11 through 18 for Explanation of Ratios and Data

Comparative Historical Data			Type of Statement	Current Data Sorted By Sales					
36	32	51	Unqualified	12	7	7	11	7	7
8	6	10	Reviewed	1	5		1	1	2
39	55	51	Compiled	25	16	5	2	2	1
57	41	89	Tax Returns	57	27	3	1		1
47	43	61	Other	22	23	5	2	4	5
4/1/00-3/31/01	4/1/01-3/31/02	4/1/02-3/31/03		70 (4/1-9/30/02)			192 (10/1/02-3/31/03)		
ALL	ALL	ALL		0-1MM	1-3MM	3-5MM	5-10MM	10-25MM	25MM & OVER
187	177	262	NUMBER OF STATEMENTS	117	78	20	17	14	16
%	%	%	**ASSETS**	%	%	%	%	%	%
16.1	18.2	17.6	Cash & Equivalents	18.7	16.0	19.1	16.4	21.5	12.1
9.1	9.8	8.9	Trade Receivables (net)	5.5	6.9	15.3	18.3	22.5	13.6
.4	.8	.1	Inventory	.2	.1	.3	.0	.1	.1
3.6	4.1	4.0	All Other Current	3.5	3.2	7.8	2.2	2.4	9.7
29.3	32.9	30.6	Total Current	28.0	26.3	42.5	36.9	46.4	35.4
57.5	51.4	55.4	Fixed Assets (net)	57.8	57.5	49.2	55.1	39.8	49.7
4.9	7.3	5.9	Intangibles (net)	5.9	7.5	.4	.8	5.9	10.6
8.3	8.3	8.0	All Other Non-Current	8.3	8.7	7.9	7.2	7.8	4.2
100.0	100.0	100.0	Total	100.0	100.0	100.0	100.0	100.0	100.0
			LIABILITIES						
6.7	8.1	8.2	Notes Payable-Short Term	10.1	9.2	1.5	5.5	6.9	1.0
3.7	4.4	6.5	Cur. Mat.-L/T/D	9.9	3.9	5.1	3.6	1.8	3.3
5.6	6.3	5.0	Trade Payables	3.8	3.5	5.8	8.8	7.4	14.7
.1	.2	.1	Income Taxes Payable	.1	.3	.1	.1	.1	.1
24.9	17.1	20.7	All Other Current	24.6	15.1	33.3	11.1	21.6	12.9
41.0	36.1	40.5	Total Current	48.5	31.9	45.8	29.2	37.8	32.1
33.0	32.3	34.5	Long Term Debt	38.9	36.6	26.5	18.1	22.1	30.5
.1	.1	.1	Deferred Taxes	.0	.0	.6	.1	.1	1.2
17.4	12.4	15.4	All Other Non-Current	19.4	14.4	15.2	2.2	6.7	12.7
8.5	19.1	9.5	Net Worth	-6.8	17.1	11.9	50.5	33.3	23.5
100.0	100.0	100.0	Total Liabilities & Net Worth	100.0	100.0	100.0	100.0	100.0	100.0
			INCOME DATA						
100.0	100.0	100.0	Net Sales	100.0	100.0	100.0	100.0	100.0	100.0
			Gross Profit						
93.7	92.5	91.8	Operating Expenses	89.7	91.1	97.7	93.6	96.8	97.3
6.3	7.5	8.2	Operating Profit	10.3	8.9	2.3	6.4	3.2	2.7
2.8	3.5	3.6	All Other Expenses (net)	5.7	2.5	-.6	3.1	.9	1.7
3.5	4.0	4.6	Profit Before Taxes	4.6	6.5	2.9	3.3	2.3	1.0
			RATIOS						
2.5	2.5	2.2		2.3	2.7	3.8	1.9	1.9	1.7
.9	1.1	.9	Current	.6	.8	2.2	1.2	1.2	1.0
.2	.3	.3		.1	.4	1.0	1.0	.7	.6
2.2	2.1	2.0		1.7	2.3	3.6	1.7	1.9	1.4
.7 (176)	.8 (260)	.8	Quick (115)	.5	.8	1.7	1.2	1.1	.7
.2	.2	.2		.1	.3	.8	1.0	.5	.4
0 UND	0 UND	0 UND		0 UND	0 UND	2 203.1	8 47.5	2 186.1	8 48.6
3 132.5	3 108.8	2 187.0	Sales/Receivables	0 UND	1 279.0	12 30.7	19 19.7	22 16.3	13 27.2
17 22.0	18 20.5	17 21.8		4 83.0	13 28.2	51 7.2	43 8.4	39 9.3	21 17.3
			Cost of Sales/Inventory						
			Cost of Sales/Payables						
14.4	12.4	16.9		35.1	19.7	5.7	12.9	14.9	14.3
-234.3	234.4	-243.4	Sales/Working Capital	-38.4	-86.4	11.1	48.6	43.7	NM
-14.2	-20.7	-13.5		-8.2	-14.5	NM	NM	-22.9	-20.2
6.7	6.9	6.5		6.2	9.1	11.1	4.4	25.8	5.9
(136) 2.1	(122) 2.1	(184) 2.6	EBIT/Interest (75)	2.3	(62) 2.6	(13) 2.0	(12) 3.9	(10) 3.4	(12) 1.9
.8	1.2	1.1		.7	1.2	-6.6	.9	1.7	.8
8.5	12.1	5.0	Net Profit + Depr., Dep.,						
(15) 3.2	(19) 2.0	(22) 2.0	Amort./Cur. Mat. L/T/D						
1.7	.6	1.4							
.8	.5	.8		.8	1.1	.4	.5	.3	1.0
2.0	1.5	2.6	Fixed/Worth	4.5	3.8	1.3	.9	1.7	3.8
21.5	-41.4	-32.5		-3.8	-32.5	4.3	1.9	5.1	NM
.6	.5	.8		.9	.8	.5	.3	.9	2.6
2.8	2.6	3.7	Debt/Worth	5.7	4.7	.9	1.2	3.0	6.2
44.5	-29.9	-35.1		-4.7	-66.6	4.2	2.6	9.4	NM
52.6	52.8	64.2	% Profit Before Taxes/Tangible	83.3	88.2	26.2	23.9	68.6	33.4
(146) 18.0	(128) 21.7	(191) 21.1	Net Worth (75) 20.0		(57) 41.6	(18) 16.5	7.6	(12) 11.3	(12) 14.7
3.0	5.5	4.4		2.2	14.5	3.1	-1.3	3.2	-16.3
16.5	19.2	19.6	% Profit Before Taxes/Total	25.2	23.1	13.7	8.9	10.9	9.0
5.0	5.4	6.1	Assets	5.6	9.0	6.5	3.7	3.7	3.1
-.6	.2	.1		-1.3	1.2	-4.1	-.4	.7	-3.8
15.8	19.6	25.3		30.0	25.2	15.8	11.8	121.7	23.8
5.3	7.1	5.6	Sales/Net Fixed Assets	5.7	5.3	7.4	2.8	7.8	4.7
1.4	2.0	1.4		1.2	1.2	1.6	1.4	3.3	3.4
5.2	5.4	5.6		7.4	5.7	3.9	3.1	5.0	3.8
2.4	2.7	2.4	Sales/Total Assets	2.5	2.6	2.2	2.1	3.9	2.6
1.0	1.1	1.1		1.0	1.0	1.3	1.1	1.6	1.8
1.3	.7	1.3		1.7	1.6	.7	1.4	.7	.5
(156) 2.5	(150) 2.0	(212) 2.5	% Depr., Dep., Amort./Sales (89) 3.1		(66) 2.4	(17) 1.8	(15) 2.0	(12) 1.9	(13) 2.1
4.1	3.6	5.2		6.4	5.0	4.1	4.6	2.3	4.7
4.9	3.8	3.1	% Officers', Directors',	3.6	3.0				
(69) 7.5	(67) 7.8	(101) 5.8	Owners' Comp/Sales (49) 7.2		(35) 4.8				
16.6	16.0	12.7		13.2	9.7				
1633386M	1855695M	3502292M	Net Sales ($)	65946M	139245M	77082M	120875M	209919M	2889225M
1045107M	1106025M	1410504M	Total Assets ($)	71443M	104492M	45587M	148749M	82408M	957825M

© RMA 2003

M = $ thousand   MM = $ million
See Pages 11 through 18 for Explanation of Ratios and Data

ARTS, ENTERTAINMENT,
AND RECREATION

Current Data Sorted By Assets | Comparative Historical Data

						Type of Statement		
6	5	16	20	2	8	Unqualified	50	60
2	5	6	3			Reviewed	12	15
9	10	10	2			Compiled	13	15
24	9	5				Tax Returns	5	7
17	22	15	7	1	1	Other	41	40
	76 (4/1-9/30/02)			129 (10/1/02-3/31/03)			4/1/98-3/31/99	4/1/99-3/31/00
0-500M	500M-2MM	2-10MM	10-50MM	50-100MM	100-250MM		ALL	ALL
58	51	52	32	3	9	**NUMBER OF STATEMENTS**	121	137
%	%	%	%	%	%	**ASSETS**	%	%
22.4	10.5	13.9	20.6			Cash & Equivalents	16.0	17.8
4.6	9.8	4.0	7.6			Trade Receivables (net)	11.6	13.5
6.2	2.8	4.4	1.5			Inventory	1.4	3.3
3.6	5.3	5.7	7.7			All Other Current	5.0	4.9
36.8	28.4	28.0	37.3			Total Current	33.9	39.5
43.9	55.0	52.1	34.0			Fixed Assets (net)	43.8	39.2
9.8	5.8	4.9	4.6			Intangibles (net)	4.0	4.2
9.5	10.9	15.0	24.2			All Other Non-Current	18.4	17.0
100.0	100.0	100.0	100.0			Total	100.0	100.0
						LIABILITIES		
43.9	11.6	4.9	15.0			Notes Payable-Short Term	8.3	12.0
7.2	8.7	4.8	4.8			Cur. Mat.-L/T/D	3.3	5.0
13.0	6.7	8.4	7.3			Trade Payables	9.7	11.2
.0	.1	.7	.7			Income Taxes Payable	.1	.1
34.7	12.3	12.1	9.2			All Other Current	25.7	19.5
98.9	39.5	30.8	36.9			Total Current	47.1	47.8
19.9	34.4	21.3	12.2			Long Term Debt	17.2	18.9
.0	.0	.1	.0			Deferred Taxes	1.0	.2
6.9	8.9	6.0	10.5			All Other Non-Current	10.0	8.1
-25.8	17.2	41.7	40.4			Net Worth	24.7	25.0
100.0	100.0	100.0	100.0			Total Liabilities & Net Worth	100.0	100.0
						INCOME DATA		
100.0	100.0	100.0	100.0			Net Sales	100.0	100.0
						Gross Profit		
98.8	95.3	91.8	94.0			Operating Expenses	141.0	122.2
1.2	4.7	8.2	6.0			Operating Profit	-41.0	-22.2
1.3	1.1	1.4	2.0			All Other Expenses (net)	-50.1	-31.5
-.1	3.6	6.8	4.0			Profit Before Taxes	9.0	9.3
						RATIOS		
1.3	1.4	1.3	3.9				3.3	2.7
.6	.5	.7	2.1			Current	1.1	1.2
.2	.2	.4	.6				.5	.6
.9	1.0	1.1	3.6				2.7	2.2
.3	.3	.4	1.2			Quick	.8	.9
.1	.1	.2	.2					.4
0 UND	0 UND	0 UND	2 191.2				4 90.5	1 251.6
0 UND	1 412.4	1 471.0	15 23.6			Sales/Receivables	16 22.9	16 23.0
1 274.5	14 26.1	7 53.2	67 5.4				48 7.5	51 7.2
						Cost of Sales/Inventory		
						Cost of Sales/Payables		
48.5	21.5	29.8	1.8				5.4	3.7
-27.3	-21.1	-30.4	4.3			Sales/Working Capital	66.5	34.9
-9.0	-11.4	-15.3	-12.7				-8.6	-10.8
(37) 10.6	(43) 4.7	(38) 7.1	(22) 14.0				(84) 19.2	(95) 13.9
2.9	2.3	2.6	-1.1			EBIT/Interest	4.4	4.0
.3	.8	1.1	-15.0				1.0	-.2
						Net Profit + Depr., Dep.,		11.8
						Amort./Cur. Mat. L /T/D	(10)	3.2
								1.5
.7	.9	.4	.1				.3	.3
2.7	2.3	1.6	.5			Fixed/Worth	.9	.8
-.5	-5.3	5.2	1.1				2.7	2.7
.8	.7	.4	.2				.3	.3
13.3	1.8	1.5	.4			Debt/Worth	1.0	1.2
-2.6	-9.2	7.2	1.0				4.3	6.1
(32) 92.9	(33) 40.9	(45) 72.8	(27) 7.3			% Profit Before Taxes/Tangible	(99) 31.7	(113) 47.7
24.2	14.6	12.0	1.1			Net Worth	12.7	8.3
-7.5	-.3	-.2	-6.3				1.4	-.9
19.7	17.5	12.7	11.4			% Profit Before Taxes/Total	16.8	17.4
5.5	6.0	4.9	.2			Assets	6.0	4.2
-9.5	-1.0	-2.4	-5.1				-.6	-1.8
66.9	11.3	8.6	14.0				16.8	18.6
13.8	5.6	3.8	4.2			Sales/Net Fixed Assets	2.8	3.9
7.2	2.9	1.5	.6				1.0	1.3
7.9	4.5	3.1	1.6				2.7	2.6
5.4	2.8	1.4	.5			Sales/Total Assets	1.2	1.3
3.1	1.4	.8	.3				.5	.4
(47) 1.0	(45) 1.8	(47) 1.8	(28) 1.2			% Depr., Dep., Amort./Sales	(101) 1.7	(109) 1.6
2.3	3.2	3.2	2.4				4.2	3.6
3.5	5.8	5.1	6.7				8.6	7.4
(21) 2.7	(15) 2.4	(13) 1.6				% Officers', Directors',	(27) 3.5	(25) 5.3
4.4	7.3	3.1				Owners' Comp/Sales	4.8	9.2
8.1	13.0	5.5					10.2	18.8
77982M	157057M	366475M	1382071M	167433M	1279223M	Net Sales ($)	1286273M	1591063M
13622M	54415M	198335M	562940M	226255M	1475913M	Total Assets ($)	1732554M	2161178M

M = $ thousand   MM = $ million
See Pages 11 through 18 for Explanation of Ratios and Data

Comparative Historical Data | | Current Data Sorted By Sales

Comparative Historical Data			Type of Statement	Current Data Sorted By Sales					
58	47	57	Unqualified	5	11	6	12	11	12
6	9	16	Reviewed	1	2	1	8	1	3
13	12	31	Compiled	6	14	3	5	1	2
11	10	38	Tax Returns	12	19	5	2		
28	27	63	Other	12	21	13	10	6	1
4/1/00- 3/31/01 ALL	4/1/01- 3/31/02 ALL	4/1/02- 3/31/03 ALL		76 (4/1-9/30/02)			129 (10/1/02-3/31/03)		
				0-1MM	1-3MM	3-5MM	5-10MM	10-25MM	25MM & OVER
116	105	205	NUMBER OF STATEMENTS	36	67	28	37	19	18
%	%	%	ASSETS	%	%	%	%	%	%
18.6	16.1	16.4	Cash & Equivalents	17.0	15.1	17.9	14.7	22.8	14.1
11.4	11.5	6.2	Trade Receivables (net)	4.2	5.4	4.9	9.1	10.4	4.7
2.9	3.3	3.8	Inventory	3.9	4.4	4.1	3.2	3.2	3.4
5.0	6.7	5.4	All Other Current	4.7	4.2	9.7	5.9	3.7	5.9
38.0	37.6	31.9	Total Current	29.8	29.1	36.6	32.9	40.1	28.0
39.7	40.2	48.1	Fixed Assets (net)	54.7	50.0	49.2	42.1	41.7	44.8
5.5	5.6	6.3	Intangibles (net)	10.6	4.8	5.4	5.9	6.0	6.2
16.8	16.6	13.7	All Other Non-Current	5.0	16.1	8.7	19.1	12.3	20.9
100.0	100.0	100.0	Total	100.0	100.0	100.0	100.0	100.0	100.0
			LIABILITIES						
9.3	15.1	18.9	Notes Payable-Short Term	45.7	16.5	9.6	10.8	2.5	22.6
2.4	3.9	6.4	Cur. Mat.-L/T/D	6.1	7.9	5.5	7.0	2.7	5.6
8.4	8.1	8.9	Trade Payables	10.9	7.1	9.1	5.0	15.9	12.3
.2	.6	.4	Income Taxes Payable	.0	.0	.1	.1	1.9	1.5
16.2	17.3	17.8	All Other Current	42.2	12.2	14.5	11.9	11.4	13.8
36.5	45.0	52.4	Total Current	105.0	43.8	38.8	34.8	34.4	55.8
13.5	14.2	23.1	Long Term Debt	31.7	22.4	27.7	16.6	13.6	25.1
.4	.0	.0	Deferred Taxes	.0	.0	.0	.2	.0	.0
6.0	7.3	7.6	All Other Non-Current	7.7	4.0	14.4	6.3	6.3	14.2
43.6	33.4	16.8	Net Worth	−44.5	29.9	19.1	42.1	45.7	4.9
100.0	100.0	100.0	Total Liabilities & Net Worth	100.0	100.0	100.0	100.0	100.0	100.0
			INCOME DATA						
100.0	100.0	100.0	Net Sales	100.0	100.0	100.0	100.0	100.0	100.0
			Gross Profit						
105.4	97.0	95.5	Operating Expenses	96.9	93.3	97.6	97.4	96.2	92.6
−5.4	3.0	4.5	Operating Profit	3.1	6.7	2.4	2.6	3.8	7.4
−15.3	2.6	1.4	All Other Expenses (net)	3.6	2.3	−.9	.5	.1	1.1
9.9	.4	3.1	Profit Before Taxes	−.5	4.4	3.3	2.2	3.8	6.3
			RATIOS						
4.6	2.5	1.7		1.2	2.1	1.8	1.7	3.2	1.6
1.3	1.1	.7	Current	.4	.7	.9	.8	1.2	.7
.6	.5	.4		.1	.3	.5	.4	.6	.2
3.3	1.7	1.3		.8	1.2	1.2	1.3	2.9	1.1
1.1	.7	.4	Quick	.2	.4	.5	.4	1.1	.6
.3	.3	.2		.1	.2	.3	.2	.4	.2
1 403.7	0 UND	0 UND		0 UND	0 UND	0 955.7	0 UND	2 163.3	0 999.8
12 30.5	10 37.8	1 412.4	Sales/Receivables	0 UND	0 UND	3 120.4	2 210.8	7 50.7	7 49.6
45 8.0	35 10.5	12 29.9		0 UND	9 40.1	46 7.9	13 28.5	44 8.3	40 9.1
			Cost of Sales/Inventory						
			Cost of Sales/Payables						
3.1	5.4	12.8		47.0	11.3	16.1	11.3	2.2	11.0
19.4	30.8	−32.4	Sales/Working Capital	−16.5	−38.2	−26.9	−48.3	58.6	−38.9
−16.6	−9.4	−11.4		−3.2	−11.3	−11.5	−17.6	−18.8	−8.6
13.3	7.5	7.1		2.2	8.6	12.3	6.8	5.8	48.1
(74) 3.8	(75) 1.0	(150) 2.2	EBIT/Interest	(23) .8	(50) 3.2	(21) 1.8	(28) 2.5	(13) 1.7	(15) 4.8
.2	−5.3	.2		−1.8	1.1	−.4	−4.6	−6.3	.7
		4.3	Net Profit + Depr., Dep.,						
	(19)	1.5	Amort./Cur. Mat. L/T/D						
		.3							
.3	.4	.5		.9	.6	.6	.3	.4	.4
.8	.9	1.5	Fixed/Worth	2.1	1.6	1.3	.9	.9	1.3
2.5	3.6	−12.2		−.5	−7.2	7.4	4.9	5.3	−7.1
.2	.4	.5		.8	.5	.4	.4	.4	.3
.9	1.0	1.6	Debt/Worth	15.1	1.6	1.7	1.5	.8	1.7
3.3	6.0	−11.2		−2.1	−11.5	NM	5.9	9.3	−3.5
39.3	31.6	47.8		64.8	43.1	54.0	75.1	51.0	43.5
(97) 13.6	(84) 7.5	(147) 8.1	% Profit Before Taxes/Tangible Net Worth	(19) .0	(48) 11.1	(21) 3.1	(31) 3.4	(16) 4.3	(12) 20.5
2.7	−11.1	−4.1		−12.6	−.6	−17.7	−5.2	−3.6	−1.8
15.5	14.6	14.5		9.6	15.7	18.8	18.2	10.9	35.6
7.4	1.7	4.0	% Profit Before Taxes/Total Assets	−.6	7.2	.5	5.6	1.4	10.6
.2	−10.8	−3.7		−13.4	−.9	−7.5	−2.6	−3.1	−1.9
19.5	23.2	14.6		20.9	18.3	11.2	12.5	15.8	27.8
3.9	6.9	6.4	Sales/Net Fixed Assets	4.0	8.4	4.3	6.4	8.1	4.8
1.2	1.3	1.9		1.5	1.3	1.3	3.3	2.1	1.1
2.7	3.0	4.7		4.1	6.4	4.2	4.2	4.4	3.8
1.3	1.4	2.3	Sales/Total Assets	2.4	3.0	2.1	2.3	1.9	1.6
.5	.6	.9		1.1	1.1	.6	.7	.6	.7
1.3	.9	1.4		1.9	1.8	1.9	1.0	1.1	.7
(97) 3.2	(88) 2.6	(174) 3.0	% Depr., Dep., Amort./Sales	(30) 3.8	(56) 2.8	(24) 3.3	(33) 2.8	2.1	(12) 3.9
6.7	5.2	5.5		6.7	4.0	5.9	4.1	5.1	9.5
6.8	3.4	2.3			2.4	3.0			
(24) 8.1	(21) 9.1	(56) 3.7	% Officers', Directors', Owners' Comp/Sales	(19) 3.3	(11) 5.9				
13.0	14.1	4.1			6.5	13.0			
1196931M	1100073M	3430241M	Net Sales ($)	20842M	129296M	112484M	250337M	277000M	2640282M
1741134M	1301663M	2531480M	Total Assets ($)	18245M	120695M	121384M	324838M	278073M	1668245M

M = $ thousand   MM = $ million
See Pages 11 through 18 for Explanation of Ratios and Data

Current Data Sorted By Assets | Comparative Historical Data

0-500M	500M-2MM	2-10MM	10-50MM	50-100MM	100-250MM	Type of Statement	4/1/98-3/31/99 ALL	4/1/99-3/31/00 ALL
4	5	8	7	3	3	Unqualified	23	28
						Reviewed		3
8	2	2				Compiled	8	3
4		1				Tax Returns	3	1
9	3	7	3	3	1	Other	11	9
	32 (4/1-9/30/02)		41 (10/1/02-3/31/03)					
25	10	18	10	6	4	**NUMBER OF STATEMENTS**	45	44
%	%	%	%	%	%	**ASSETS**	%	%
38.3	15.0	17.7	20.6			Cash & Equivalents	16.6	24.3
20.3	20.6	5.5	13.0			Trade Receivables (net)	10.5	11.2
2.4	.2	1.6	2.8			Inventory	3.8	1.0
2.9	7.7	4.8	7.7			All Other Current	8.6	7.5
63.9	43.6	29.7	44.0			Total Current	39.5	44.0
20.1	41.5	25.5	23.1			Fixed Assets (net)	27.1	28.2
1.9	.0	9.8	1.9			Intangibles (net)	3.8	1.7
14.1	14.9	35.0	30.9			All Other Non-Current	29.7	26.1
100.0	100.0	100.0	100.0			Total	100.0	100.0
						LIABILITIES		
42.3	11.0	10.1	8.8			Notes Payable-Short Term	6.6	13.7
2.2	8.8	4.2	1.0			Cur. Mat.-L/T/D	2.8	1.9
19.6	5.8	2.8	6.9			Trade Payables	5.7	6.5
.0	5.8	.1	.8			Income Taxes Payable	.1	.1
27.4	20.6	11.7	6.9			All Other Current	11.5	14.1
91.4	52.1	28.9	24.3			Total Current	26.7	36.3
7.9	9.1	10.8	5.1			Long Term Debt	20.5	12.0
.0	.0	.0	.1			Deferred Taxes	1.2	1.7
11.0	4.4	6.8	1.7			All Other Non-Current	12.3	13.0
-10.4	34.4	53.5	68.7			Net Worth	39.4	37.0
100.0	100.0	100.0	100.0			Total Liabilities & Net Worth	100.0	100.0
						INCOME DATA		
100.0	100.0	100.0	100.0			Net Sales	100.0	100.0
						Gross Profit		
93.2	100.6	83.3	84.2			Operating Expenses	123.1	104.1
6.8	-.6	16.7	15.8			Operating Profit	-23.1	-4.1
.0	4.9	1.9	1.3			All Other Expenses (net)	-26.8	-18.6
6.7	-5.5	14.7	14.5			Profit Before Taxes	3.7	14.6
						RATIOS		
5.4	2.0	2.2	8.7			Current	3.8	3.1
1.7	1.3	.9	1.6				1.4	1.5
.5	.4	.4	1.0				.8	.7
4.6		1.6	5.5			Quick	3.3	2.9
1.6		.6	1.1				.9	1.0
.5		.3	.7				.3	.4
0 UND	0 UND	2 233.2	6 58.3			Sales/Receivables	0 UND	0 915.8
4 93.3	7 51.3	8 48.3	35 10.5				18 19.8	15 24.7
26 14.0	53 6.9	30 12.3	98 3.7				68 5.3	78 4.7
						Cost of Sales/Inventory		
						Cost of Sales/Payables		
9.0	8.4	6.4	1.5			Sales/Working Capital	4.6	3.7
90.1	19.4	-98.9	9.6				35.9	14.7
-49.9	-6.3	-7.7	-409.1				-14.3	-25.1
		(12) 19.5				EBIT/Interest	(31) 25.6	(26) 27.8
		3.3					6.5	5.1
		-5.5					.9	.3
						Net Profit + Depr., Dep., Amort./Cur. Mat. L /T/D		
.0	.2	.0	.1			Fixed/Worth	.1	.1
.2	1.6	.4	.3				.4	.4
UND	3.8	1.9	.5				2.5	2.7
.3	1.0	.2	.2			Debt/Worth	.3	.3
.8	1.4	1.0	.5				.8	.9
-5.1	12.2	4.6	.7				8.0	4.6
305.6		84.2	42.7			% Profit Before Taxes/Tangible Net Worth	66.6	38.8
(18) 73.6		(16) 1.2	16.1				(37) 18.4	(35) 14.3
28.3		-12.6	-3.5				.9	1.8
124.7	10.8	25.9	24.7			% Profit Before Taxes/Total Assets	20.8	22.7
15.2	-6.0	6.3	11.5				9.2	10.9
1.4	-17.5	-4.0	-2.2				-.1	.2
UND	86.6	75.0	19.4			Sales/Net Fixed Assets	40.0	55.2
162.7	16.7	11.8	8.9				7.3	10.6
14.7	1.5	1.8	1.4				1.8	1.9
13.6	3.7	1.7	1.0			Sales/Total Assets	3.0	3.4
5.6	1.6	.9	.7				1.2	1.4
2.5	.9	.4	.5				.4	.5
.3		.7				% Depr., Dep., Amort./Sales	.6	.6
(12) .7		(15) 1.1					(36) 1.9	(35) 1.2
4.3		4.7					6.1	4.8
						% Officers', Directors', Owners' Comp/Sales	6.0	
							(13) 12.3	
							21.7	
28493M	22831M	115851M	266135M	158512M	129647M	Net Sales ($)	345209M	1167442M
4899M	10498M	87463M	267600M	389444M	581586M	Total Assets ($)	961036M	1067321M

M = $ thousand   MM = $ million
See Pages 11 through 18 for Explanation of Ratios and Data

Comparative Historical Data — **Current Data Sorted By Sales**

Type of Statement					32 (4/1-9/30/02)		41 (10/1/02-3/31/03)			
					0-1MM	1-3MM	3-5MM	5-10MM	10-25MM	25MM & OVER
Unqualified	20	14	30		4	6	4	5	6	5
Reviewed	1									
Compiled	9	9	12		2	8	2			
Tax Returns	2	4	5		2	2	1			
Other	11	8	26		8	5	1	4	3	5
	4/1/00-3/31/01 ALL	4/1/01-3/31/02 ALL	4/1/02-3/31/03 ALL							
NUMBER OF STATEMENTS	43	35	73		16	21	8	9	9	10
ASSETS	%	%	%		%	%	%	%	%	%
Cash & Equivalents	18.2	16.8	23.5		35.4	29.0				20.0
Trade Receivables (net)	13.1	9.2	13.3		13.8	16.8				8.6
Inventory	5.3	1.2	1.6		.0	2.9				4.9
All Other Current	4.1	8.1	4.7		5.5	2.4				4.0
Total Current	40.7	35.3	43.1		54.7	51.2				37.4
Fixed Assets (net)	29.5	28.9	27.1		27.9	26.1				21.2
Intangibles (net)	1.4	7.8	3.4		2.9	.2				11.7
All Other Non-Current	28.4	28.1	26.4		14.5	22.5				29.6
Total	100.0	100.0	100.0		100.0	100.0				100.0
LIABILITIES										
Notes Payable-Short Term	16.0	7.1	19.8		66.2	2.2				6.6
Cur. Mat.-L/T/D	1.2	4.0	3.3		3.5	2.4				3.3
Trade Payables	14.3	15.8	9.5		20.7	8.6				7.1
Income Taxes Payable	.2	.0	.9		.0	2.8				.9
All Other Current	15.2	10.1	16.7		21.9	22.0				8.4
Total Current	46.9	37.0	50.2		112.4	37.9				26.2
Long Term Debt	15.6	18.8	9.7		13.5	9.2				9.3
Deferred Taxes	1.5	1.7	.0		.0	.0				.1
All Other Non-Current	4.8	20.8	7.3		15.9	6.6				6.5
Net Worth	31.2	21.7	32.8		−41.9	46.2				58.0
Total Liabilities & Net Worth	100.0	100.0	100.0		100.0	100.0				100.0
INCOME DATA										
Net Sales	100.0	100.0	100.0		100.0	100.0				100.0
Gross Profit										
Operating Expenses	102.7	88.4	92.4		97.5	89.4				81.9
Operating Profit	−2.7	11.5	7.6		2.5	10.6				18.1
All Other Expenses (net)	−17.4	2.3	2.4		4.1	.1				3.5
Profit Before Taxes	14.7	9.2	5.2		−1.6	10.6				14.6
RATIOS										
Current	2.6	2.1	2.9		5.7	4.7				10.4
	1.3	1.2	1.3		1.3	1.7				1.9
	.8	.4	.6		.3	.9				.9
Quick	2.1	1.9	2.8		4.4	4.0				9.5
	.9	.9	(72) 1.0		1.0	1.4				1.5
	.3	.3	.5		.3	.8				.7
Sales/Receivables	3 120.8	0 UND	1 328.2		0 UND	0 UND				7 51.6
	24 15.0	8 47.3	11 32.5		6 63.6	4 93.3				27 13.4
	77 4.7	26 14.1	38 9.6		22 16.3	30 12.0				36 10.3
Cost of Sales/Inventory										
Cost of Sales/Payables										
Sales/Working Capital	4.5	8.4	5.7		3.9	10.2				2.5
	8.7	32.6	41.1		86.9	37.9				11.7
	−12.2	−10.2	−16.2		−5.9	NM				−126.0
EBIT/Interest	(23) 14.7	(18) 6.8	(37) 15.8							
	4.7	−.1	1.9							
	1.7	−10.0	−8.9							
Net Profit + Depr., Dep., Amort./Cur. Mat. L/T/D										
Fixed/Worth	.1	.1	.0		.0	.0				.1
	.4	.8	.4		1.2	.2				.4
	1.5	−1.4	1.4		−1.8	1.6				.7
Debt/Worth	.1	.2	.2		.5	.2				.2
	.4	.9	.8		7.6	.8				.8
	6.1	−3.3	4.9		−1.9	3.9				NM
% Profit Before Taxes/Tangible Net Worth	(39) 74.3	(24) 36.5	(63) 70.1		(10) 368.8	(19) 100.0				
	16.3	10.6	16.2		16.7	40.0				
	2.3	−2.4	−7.6		−9.4	1.9				
% Profit Before Taxes/Total Assets	17.9	13.7	25.9		38.4	40.6				24.7
	10.2	3.7	6.0		1.4	19.3				12.3
	1.2	−6.5	−4.9		−18.2	.3				.3
Sales/Net Fixed Assets	40.0	82.8	93.9		279.2	UND				94.0
	5.9	29.6	14.5		28.6	29.5				6.2
	1.6	2.6	1.8		2.1	2.7				1.5
Sales/Total Assets	2.7	4.8	4.3		7.8	8.0				3.2
	1.0	1.3	1.4		2.2	3.5				1.1
	.4	.5	.5		.7	.7				.5
% Depr., Dep., Amort./Sales	(37) .4	(28) .4	(51) .7		(10) .3	(11) .7				
	1.5	.8	1.7		1.4	1.1				
	5.0	2.2	4.7		10.6	7.6				
% Officers', Directors', Owners' Comp/Sales	(11) 2.7		(15) 4.7							
	6.3		11.9							
	9.4		24.0							
Net Sales ($)	637858M	369029M	721469M		8379M	33059M	31709M	61807M	149812M	436703M
Total Assets ($)	1183431M	708052M	1341490M		30077M	26766M	22262M	111730M	568106M	582549M

M = $ thousand   MM = $ million
See Pages 11 through 18 for Explanation of Ratios and Data

Current Data Sorted By Assets   Comparative Historical Data

Type of Statement	0-500M	500M-2MM	2-10MM	10-50MM	50-100MM	100-250MM		4/1/98-3/31/99 ALL	4/1/99-3/31/00 ALL
Unqualified	1	3	4	8	9	14		27	32
Reviewed		3	1	2				7	7
Compiled	1	5	2					13	10
Tax Returns	3	1						6	5
Other	2	3	6	5	4	15		40	24
		31 (4/1-9/30/02)		61 (10/1/02-3/31/03)					
NUMBER OF STATEMENTS	7	15	13	15	13	29		93	78
ASSETS	%	%	%	%	%	%		%	%
Cash & Equivalents		17.7	15.7	15.6	16.2	9.3		15.8	15.6
Trade Receivables (net)		5.9	4.2	22.2	10.3	6.6		7.5	10.9
Inventory		5.1	1.6	.6	.2	.1		1.6	2.2
All Other Current		10.1	1.2	6.7	5.2	5.4		3.5	3.3
Total Current		38.9	22.7	45.1	31.9	21.4		28.3	32.0
Fixed Assets (net)		24.2	39.7	25.5	34.3	26.8		32.1	21.2
Intangibles (net)		12.8	21.6	16.0	18.9	33.2		21.5	27.6
All Other Non-Current		24.2	16.1	13.4	15.0	18.6		18.0	19.3
Total		100.0	100.0	100.0	100.0	100.0		100.0	100.0
LIABILITIES									
Notes Payable-Short Term		3.9	6.3	8.7	5.8	7.7		7.6	9.5
Cur. Mat.-L/T/D		4.5	5.7	6.8	9.3	2.0		3.8	3.0
Trade Payables		14.5	4.6	11.7	3.8	4.2		8.0	9.5
Income Taxes Payable		.0	.4	4.2	.0	.5		.1	.3
All Other Current		16.1	9.3	34.6	25.5	21.4		21.4	36.0
Total Current		39.0	26.4	66.0	44.6	35.7		40.8	58.2
Long Term Debt		31.6	16.8	33.6	56.4	46.1		30.1	38.1
Deferred Taxes		2.2	.0	.0	.0	.4		.4	.2
All Other Non-Current		30.4	31.3	36.0	38.7	23.4		21.6	16.2
Net Worth		-3.2	25.5	-35.5	-39.7	-5.7		7.1	-12.8
Total Liabilities & Net Worth		100.0	100.0	100.0	100.0	100.0		100.0	100.0
INCOME DATA									
Net Sales		100.0	100.0	100.0	100.0	100.0		100.0	100.0
Gross Profit									
Operating Expenses		99.6	98.1	91.1	104.6	92.6		104.5	98.4
Operating Profit		.4	1.9	8.9	-4.6	7.4		-4.5	1.6
All Other Expenses (net)		3.8	7.1	3.1	4.2	6.4		2.9	3.0
Profit Before Taxes		-3.3	-5.2	5.7	-8.7	1.0		-7.4	-1.5
RATIOS									
Current		2.4	3.8	1.3	1.8	1.2		1.5	1.4
		.7	.8	.7	1.0	.7		.7	.5
		.5	.3	.4	.5	.4		.3	.3
Quick		1.5	3.4	1.3	1.8	.9		1.2	1.2
		.7	.5	.7	.7	.6		.5	.4
		.2	.2	.3	.3	.2		.2	.2
Sales/Receivables		1 369.1	2 174.6	5 69.8	14 25.2	10 35.3		3 108.2	8 48.3
		8 44.1	18 20.3	31 11.7	41 8.9	20 18.0		12 30.8	22 16.5
		16 23.5	41 9.0	93 3.9	48 7.5	51 7.2		37 9.8	43 8.5
Cost of Sales/Inventory									
Cost of Sales/Payables									
Sales/Working Capital		9.0	3.3	15.2	15.2	40.2		16.4	21.0
		-10.9	-42.5	-12.2	999.8	-8.2		-19.3	-6.9
		-7.5	-4.6	-4.2	-3.3	-3.5		-4.4	-2.6
EBIT/Interest		(10) 5.5		(14) 8.4		(21) 7.8		(71) 6.6	(64) 3.8
		2.0		1.8		1.0		1.4	1.1
		-1.2		-1.4		-1.1		.1	-1.3
Net Profit + Depr., Dep., Amort./Cur. Mat. L /T/D									
Fixed/Worth		.3	.1	2.0	1.9	NM		.8	.6
		3.6	.8	-.3	-.4	-.8		5.6	-1.0
		.0	NM	-.1	-.1	-.1		-.1	-.1
Debt/Worth		1.6	.2	1.2	2.0	NM		2.4	2.6
		5.7	1.5	-4.2	-3.7	-3.5		34.8	-3.6
		-2.9	-44.2	-1.7	-1.6	-1.6		-2.6	-1.8
% Profit Before Taxes/Tangible Net Worth		(10) 55.6						(49) 53.5	(31) 61.9
		18.9						15.8	13.8
		-3.5						-3.0	6.5
% Profit Before Taxes/Total Assets		7.0	4.0	12.9	9.3	7.6		14.9	8.6
		-.3	.5	1.0	-6.4	.0		.9	2.2
		-37.3	-4.8	-7.9	-17.5	-7.1		-4.1	-11.4
Sales/Net Fixed Assets		88.7	41.4	72.8	34.1	33.7		41.9	47.1
		35.8	2.2	10.5	4.1	5.3		10.5	15.6
		5.3	.5	2.4	1.2	1.2		1.4	4.9
Sales/Total Assets		3.2	1.1	2.7	1.3	1.0		1.8	2.0
		2.2	.5	1.3	1.1	.7		1.0	1.1
		1.0	.3	.5	.6	.6		.5	.6
% Depr., Dep., Amort./Sales		(10) .4		(13) .4	(10) 1.4	(14) 1.0		(62) 1.8	(52) 1.0
		1.5		1.7	4.3	2.7		5.3	2.1
		2.6		8.7	8.2	4.8		10.1	5.8
% Officers', Directors', Owners' Comp/Sales								(20) 2.1	(15) 3.9
								6.1	7.1
								22.4	35.8
Net Sales ($)	2408M	38558M	37683M	796244M	988575M	3298885M		2881783M	3175740M
Total Assets ($)	1223M	18771M	63615M	502810M	934577M	4769685M		3476437M	3607330M

© RMA 2003   M = $ thousand   MM = $ million
See Pages 11 through 18 for Explanation of Ratios and Data

Comparative Historical Data | | | | Current Data Sorted By Sales

			Type of Statement						
31	36	39	Unqualified	2	4	1	2	4	26
4	7	6	Reviewed	1	3		1		1
12	14	8	Compiled	1	5	2			
4	3	4	Tax Returns	3		1			
30	20	35	Other	4	4	2	3	2	20
4/1/00-3/31/01	4/1/01-3/31/02	4/1/02-3/31/03		**31 (4/1-9/30/02)**		**61 (10/1/02-3/31/03)**			
ALL	ALL	ALL		0-1MM	1-3MM	3-5MM	5-10MM	10-25MM	25MM & OVER
81	80	92	**NUMBER OF STATEMENTS**	11	16	6	6	6	47
%	%	%	**ASSETS**	%	%	%	%	%	%
13.9	10.8	15.9	Cash & Equivalents	26.4	18.6				12.8
12.0	10.6	9.1	Trade Receivables (net)	3.4	5.4				11.4
1.6	1.1	1.3	Inventory	.5	3.5				.3
4.2	4.0	5.3	All Other Current	.0	4.6				5.5
31.8	26.4	31.6	Total Current	30.3	32.1				29.9
21.5	30.1	30.9	Fixed Assets (net)	59.1	26.3				22.9
27.4	24.4	21.0	Intangibles (net)	.6	19.5				28.1
19.3	19.1	16.5	All Other Non-Current	10.0	22.1				19.1
100.0	100.0	100.0	Total	100.0	100.0				100.0
			LIABILITIES						
13.9	10.9	6.5	Notes Payable-Short Term	2.5	6.4				7.6
4.4	4.7	4.6	Cur. Mat.-L/T/D	5.3	4.1				5.7
8.4	7.2	8.2	Trade Payables	12.8	10.7				6.2
1.2	1.2	.9	Income Taxes Payable	.0	.3				1.7
25.0	17.8	22.1	All Other Current	18.3	9.1				28.5
52.9	41.8	42.3	Total Current	39.0	30.7				49.6
32.7	38.7	36.4	Long Term Debt	25.9	20.1				50.0
.1	.3	.5	Deferred Taxes	.0	.2				.3
22.3	21.3	28.3	All Other Non-Current	9.5	16.9				34.3
-8.1	-2.2	-7.5	Net Worth	25.6	32.1				-34.2
100.0	100.0	100.0	Total Liabilities & Net Worth	100.0	100.0				100.0
			INCOME DATA						
100.0	100.0	100.0	Net Sales	100.0	100.0				100.0
			Gross Profit						
97.8	95.8	94.9	Operating Expenses	80.9	100.6				95.0
2.2	4.2	5.1	Operating Profit	19.1	-.6				5.0
3.9	6.1	4.9	All Other Expenses (net)	8.1	3.7				5.3
-1.6	-1.9	.2	Profit Before Taxes	11.0	-4.3				-.3
			RATIOS						
1.4	1.3	1.8		2.4	2.3				1.2
.5	.6	.8	Current	1.4	.8				.7
.3	.3	.4		.1	.5				.4
1.1	1.0	1.4		2.3	1.5				1.0
.4	.4	.7	Quick	1.3	.6				.6
.2	.2	.3		.1	.3				.3
8 48.0	5 73.0	5 77.5		0 UND	4 88.8				16 23.0
23 15.7	17 22.1	18 20.4	Sales/Receivables	0 UND	14 26.8				31 11.7
50 7.3	46 7.9	42 8.6		7 51.5	29 12.8				49 7.4
			Cost of Sales/Inventory						
			Cost of Sales/Payables						
27.5	19.4	10.8		10.0	6.3				25.1
-5.7	-10.4	-14.0	Sales/Working Capital	58.5	-27.2				-10.1
-2.9	-3.3	-4.4		-3.9	-8.8				-3.8
(64) 3.7	(62) 2.0	(65) 7.1			(12) 3.5				(35) 4.8
.3	.1	1.0	EBIT/Interest		.2				.0
-1.9	-3.6	-1.9			-5.0				-2.3
			Net Profit + Depr., Dep., Amort./Cur. Mat. L/T/D						
.9	.7	1.0		.8	.1				-3.2
-1.4	5.6	-2.9	Fixed/Worth	1.3	.8				-.3
-.1	-.1	-.1		17.4	NM				-.1
2.3	2.0	1.6		.4	.4				-6.2
-3.2	-12.3	-6.0	Debt/Worth	2.7	2.5				-2.5
-1.6	-1.6	-1.7		-6.3	NM				-1.6
(32) 68.7	(39) 52.1	(40) 65.4	% Profit Before Taxes/Tangible		(12) 19.0				(10) 145.6
16.6	10.6	18.3	Net Worth		3.1				55.6
.0	-10.0	-.5			-2.5				8.4
7.8	5.1	9.1	% Profit Before Taxes/Total	96.7	4.5				9.3
-.3	-3.6	.1	Assets	12.9	-.1				-1.3
-10.5	-15.1	-7.4		.2	-12.3				-9.1
39.5	33.9	42.1		54.4	86.7				40.1
13.9	10.9	8.3	Sales/Net Fixed Assets	14.0	16.4				10.0
4.3	1.9	1.4		.3	1.8				1.9
1.8	1.9	1.9		7.1	2.4				1.3
1.1	.9	1.0	Sales/Total Assets	.6	1.0				1.0
.5	.5	.5		.3	.5				.7
(46) 1.1	(52) .5	(55) .9							(27) .8
2.4	2.3	3.0	% Depr., Dep., Amort./Sales						1.7
5.9	9.9	5.7							3.8
(15) 4.8	(10) 1.1	(11) 1.3							
9.9	4.7	8.5	% Officers', Directors', Owners' Comp/Sales						
21.8	7.1	16.1							
3762115M	3515934M	5162353M	Net Sales ($)	5257M	34212M	23017M	40468M	115611M	4943788M
4102455M	4256737M	6290681M	Total Assets ($)	16461M	44175M	37711M	87912M	360322M	5744100M

M = $ thousand   MM = $ million
See Pages 11 through 18 for Explanation of Ratios and Data

Current Data Sorted By Assets   **Comparative Historical Data**

						Type of Statement		
	2	7	16	2	2	Unqualified	20	26
1	2	2				Reviewed	4	4
1	2	2				Compiled	9	8
3						Tax Returns	5	5
3	3	9	7	4	1	Other	17	17
	6 (4/1-9/30/02)		61 (10/1/02-3/31/03)				4/1/98-3/31/99	4/1/99-3/31/00
0-500M	500M-2MM	2-10MM	10-50MM	50-100MM	100-250MM		ALL	ALL
8	7	20	23	6	3	**NUMBER OF STATEMENTS**	55	60
%	%	%	%	%	%	**ASSETS**	%	%
		12.8	12.9			Cash & Equivalents	15.2	14.2
		6.9	10.4			Trade Receivables (net)	3.0	5.3
		.9	3.0			Inventory	4.4	2.5
		2.4	5.0			All Other Current	1.2	1.7
		23.1	31.2			Total Current	23.8	23.7
		66.0	50.2			Fixed Assets (net)	62.9	60.0
		2.0	4.7			Intangibles (net)	3.9	4.6
		9.0	13.9			All Other Non-Current	9.4	11.6
		100.0	100.0			Total	100.0	100.0
						LIABILITIES		
		3.4	7.6			Notes Payable-Short Term	7.3	3.7
		2.8	2.2			Cur. Mat.-L/T/D	4.6	3.5
		7.2	8.4			Trade Payables	10.4	7.7
		.1	1.4			Income Taxes Payable	.4	.6
		19.5	14.5			All Other Current	13.7	16.5
		33.0	34.1			Total Current	36.4	31.9
		27.7	22.7			Long Term Debt	44.0	30.5
		.4	.1			Deferred Taxes	1.1	1.7
		5.6	10.6			All Other Non-Current	24.1	9.4
		33.4	32.5			Net Worth	-5.6	26.5
		100.0	100.0			Total Liabilities & Net Worth	100.0	100.0
						INCOME DATA		
		100.0	100.0			Net Sales	100.0	100.0
						Gross Profit		
		97.9	90.9			Operating Expenses	90.6	93.9
		2.1	9.1			Operating Profit	9.4	6.1
		.7	1.5			All Other Expenses (net)	4.7	1.4
		1.4	7.5			Profit Before Taxes	4.7	4.8
						RATIOS		
		1.3	1.5			Current	1.8	1.6
		.6	1.0				1.0	.9
		.4	.5				.6	.4
		.7	1.2			Quick	1.6	1.2
		.5	1.0				.9	.6
		.3	.3				.3	.3
		1 558.5	5 71.3			Sales/Receivables	0 UND	1 490.1
		6 61.1	10 35.0				6 59.4	9 41.4
		23 15.7	33 11.0				12 31.4	24 15.5
						Cost of Sales/Inventory		
						Cost of Sales/Payables		
		UND	17.7			Sales/Working Capital	13.3	19.0
		-17.6	105.0				UND	-33.0
		-7.2	-13.1				-15.7	-14.1
		(17) 11.3	(21) 147.0			EBIT/Interest	(44) 14.5	(55) 12.0
		2.3	4.0				1.7	2.5
		-.8	.6				.0	.9
						Net Profit + Depr., Dep., Amort./Cur. Mat. L /T/D	(13) 42.3	(12) 7.8
							2.5	3.0
							1.4	1.2
		1.3	.8			Fixed/Worth	1.0	.8
		2.0	1.5				1.9	2.1
		9.7	6.2				-6.7	13.2
		1.0	.6			Debt/Worth	.5	.7
		1.6	1.8				1.7	1.9
		12.9	8.8				-11.7	15.9
		(17) 37.8	(19) 89.3			% Profit Before Taxes/Tangible Net Worth	(40) 34.0	(50) 45.0
		11.0	45.0				12.3	15.9
		-6.9	5.7				4.4	-2.8
		10.5	30.2			% Profit Before Taxes/Total Assets	15.9	20.2
		1.3	12.7				3.6	5.2
		-3.3	-.3				-2.4	-1.2
		3.7	4.9			Sales/Net Fixed Assets	4.1	5.0
		2.8	2.9				2.2	2.7
		1.4	2.6				1.1	1.2
		2.2	2.2			Sales/Total Assets	2.7	2.3
		1.8	1.6				1.3	1.3
		.9	1.2				.8	.8
		2.9	(21) 2.3			% Depr., Dep., Amort./Sales	(53) 2.1	(56) 2.6
		5.1	3.5				3.8	4.2
		8.9	4.1				7.5	6.6
						% Officers', Directors', Owners' Comp/Sales		(11) 4.5
								6.2
								31.1
6112M	62364M	192752M	937409M	500403M	389983M	Net Sales ($)	4366785M	2063222M
1833M	8813M	108975M	562090M	402690M	528527M	Total Assets ($)	1598708M	1921954M

M = $ thousand   MM = $ million
See Pages 11 through 18 for Explanation of Ratios and Data

Comparative Historical Data | Current Data Sorted By Sales

	4/1/00-3/31/01 ALL	4/1/01-3/31/02 ALL	4/1/02-3/31/03 ALL		0-1MM	6 (4/1-9/30/02) 1-3MM	3-5MM	5-10MM	61 (10/1/02-3/31/03) 10-25MM	25MM & OVER
Type of Statement										
Unqualified	16	17	29			1	2	2	8	16
Reviewed	4	2	3			1		1	1	
Compiled	11	15	5		1	2		1	1	
Tax Returns	3	5	3		2	1	1			
Other	13	13	27		4	4	1	4	4	9
NUMBER OF STATEMENTS	47	52	67		7	9	4	8	14	25
	%	%	%		%	%	%	%	%	%
ASSETS										
Cash & Equivalents	14.4	13.0	14.1						12.5	11.8
Trade Receivables (net)	7.5	8.0	6.8						7.3	9.2
Inventory	5.2	2.5	3.7						2.5	3.4
All Other Current	4.9	5.8	3.6						3.4	5.7
Total Current	32.0	29.3	28.1						25.7	30.1
Fixed Assets (net)	52.6	56.6	57.3						55.5	55.1
Intangibles (net)	2.3	4.4	2.8						2.9	3.0
All Other Non-Current	13.2	9.7	11.8						16.0	11.9
Total	100.0	100.0	100.0						100.0	100.0
LIABILITIES										
Notes Payable-Short Term	6.4	5.8	4.7						3.6	3.7
Cur. Mat.-L/T/D	4.3	5.9	3.0						4.8	2.6
Trade Payables	9.6	8.4	7.3						16.3	6.8
Income Taxes Payable	.9	.6	.6						.4	1.2
All Other Current	17.4	15.3	19.1						27.5	14.2
Total Current	38.5	36.1	34.8						52.6	28.5
Long Term Debt	23.2	31.2	26.9						34.3	23.5
Deferred Taxes	1.0	.2	.2						.6	.2
All Other Non-Current	4.7	3.7	8.2						4.8	9.2
Net Worth	32.6	28.8	29.9						7.8	38.6
Total Liabilities & Net Worth	100.0	100.0	100.0						100.0	100.0
INCOME DATA										
Net Sales	100.0	100.0	100.0						100.0	100.0
Gross Profit										
Operating Expenses	93.4	93.1	94.3						101.6	91.4
Operating Profit	6.6	6.9	5.7						-1.6	8.6
All Other Expenses (net)	1.3	2.5	1.5						3.8	.0
Profit Before Taxes	5.2	4.4	4.2						-5.4	8.6
RATIOS										
Current	1.6 / .9 / .4	1.7 / .9 / .5	1.5 / .9 / .5						1.4 / .6 / .3	1.5 / 1.1 / .8
Quick	1.4 / .6 / .2	1.5 / .7 / .4	1.3 / .6 / .3						1.3 / .6 / .3	1.2 / 1.0 / .5
Sales/Receivables	3 111.3 / 8 43.3 / 25 14.8	2 189.7 / 11 34.4 / 23 15.7	1 491.5 / 6 57.7 / 26 14.2						5 79.2 / 10 35.8 / 37 9.9	4 82.9 / 8 43.7 / 26 14.1
Cost of Sales/Inventory										
Cost of Sales/Payables										
Sales/Working Capital	11.5 / -82.6 / -6.5	19.1 / -148.0 / -15.6	20.6 / -204.0 / -9.2						19.4 / -10.5 / -5.1	19.1 / 202.9 / -33.5
EBIT/Interest	(40) 12.0 / 3.3 / .5	(47) 13.2 / 3.1 / 1.0	(60) 20.3 / 2.8 / -.3						27.8 / .2 / -1.4	(22) 103.1 / 6.3 / 1.0
Net Profit + Depr., Dep., Amort./Cur. Mat. L/T/D										
Fixed/Worth	.8 / 1.5 / 7.6	1.0 / 2.3 / 38.4	.9 / 1.8 / 5.9						1.0 / 4.9 / -18.1	.8 / 1.4 / 3.7
Debt/Worth	.7 / 2.1 / 11.1	1.0 / 3.2 / 84.8	.7 / 1.8 / 8.8						.5 / 4.4 / -30.3	.3 / 1.5 / 4.7
% Profit Before Taxes/Tangible Net Worth	(39) 56.8 / 15.8 / -.6	(40) 66.5 / 27.4 / 6.5	(57) 63.4 / 20.5 / -4.8						(10) 23.5 / 4.3 / -29.7	(22) 88.3 / 40.2 / 4.3
% Profit Before Taxes/Total Assets	15.7 / 4.0 / -1.5	23.7 / 7.8 / -.5	22.8 / 5.9 / -2.8						12.6 / -2.9 / -7.0	32.7 / 12.8 / -.1
Sales/Net Fixed Assets	6.6 / 3.5 / 1.5	6.0 / 3.5 / 1.4	5.5 / 2.9 / 2.1						4.9 / 2.8 / 1.8	5.5 / 3.9 / 2.6
Sales/Total Assets	2.5 / 1.5 / .9	2.8 / 1.7 / .9	2.4 / 1.7 / 1.0						2.2 / 1.6 / .8	2.8 / 2.0 / 1.2
% Depr., Dep., Amort./Sales	(43) .8 / 3.3 / 6.4	(49) .2 / 3.9 / 9.0	(61) 2.1 / 3.7 / 7.1						2.1 / 4.0 / 9.5	(22) 2.4 / 3.3 / 4.0
% Officers', Directors', Owners' Comp/Sales	(10) 2.2 / 4.4 / 11.2	(10) 2.3 / 7.1 / 16.8	(15) 2.4 / 8.3 / 17.6							
Net Sales ($)	1370989M	1642326M	2089023M		3960M	18692M	17429M	56325M	234152M	1758465M
Total Assets ($)	1119054M	1112030M	1612928M		2858M	21041M	11039M	68216M	346182M	1163592M

© RMA 2003

M = $ thousand   MM = $ million
See Pages 11 through 18 for Explanation of Ratios and Data

Current Data Sorted By Assets   **Comparative Historical Data**

						Type of Statement	4/1/98-3/31/99 ALL	4/1/99-3/31/00 ALL
	1	1	6	4	3	Unqualified		
	5	4	1	1		Reviewed		
11	14	11	11		1	Compiled		
20	22	12	1			Tax Returns		
2	11	9	3	5		Other		
0-500M	16 (4/1-9/30/02) 500M-2MM	2-10MM	133 (10/1/02-3/31/03) 10-50MM	50-100MM	100-250MM			
33	53	37	12	10	4	**NUMBER OF STATEMENTS**		
%	%	%	%	%	%	**ASSETS**	%	%
10.7	4.6	6.6	8.5	7.5		Cash & Equivalents		
3.6	4.9	3.1	1.5	4.5		Trade Receivables (net)	D	D
1.1	.6	.2	.0	8.3		Inventory	A	A
1.4	.7	.1	1.1	9.2		All Other Current	T	T
16.8	10.7	10.0	11.1	29.4		Total Current	A	A
68.7	83.3	84.7	78.6	47.4		Fixed Assets (net)		
3.0	.3	.5	.4	6.6		Intangibles (net)	N	N
11.4	5.7	4.7	9.9	16.6		All Other Non-Current	O	O
100.0	100.0	100.0	100.0	100.0		Total	T	T
						LIABILITIES	A	A
1.8	4.6	2.9	4.6	3.8		Notes Payable-Short Term	V	V
5.4	6.4	3.2	2.3	3.0		Cur. Mat.-L/T/D	A	A
.6	2.0	.9	.6	4.4		Trade Payables	I	I
.0	.1	.1	.0	.7		Income Taxes Payable	L	L
7.1	2.6	1.4	1.8	3.9		All Other Current	A	A
14.9	15.6	8.5	9.2	15.9		Total Current	B	B
71.7	59.1	58.4	59.2	58.8		Long Term Debt	L	L
.0	.1	.0	.0	.3		Deferred Taxes	E	E
12.3	6.0	4.0	.7	13.7		All Other Non-Current		
1.1	19.3	29.1	30.8	11.3		Net Worth		
100.0	100.0	100.0	100.0	100.0		Total Liabilities & Net Worth		
						INCOME DATA		
100.0	100.0	100.0	100.0	100.0		Net Sales		
						Gross Profit		
47.4	51.9	50.0	57.2	73.9		Operating Expenses		
52.6	48.1	50.0	42.8	26.0		Operating Profit		
24.9	27.9	27.3	31.0	14.0		All Other Expenses (net)		
27.8	20.2	22.7	11.8	12.1		Profit Before Taxes		
						RATIOS		
7.1	1.5	3.3	2.4	3.7				
.6	.5	.8	1.4	2.5		Current		
.1	.1	.2	.4	.8				
6.4	1.4	2.9	2.4	1.9				
.5	.4	.5	1.0	1.3		Quick		
.1	.1	.2	.2	.4				
0 UND	0 UND	0 UND	2 223.5	0 UND				
0 UND	0 UND	0 UND	10 35.2	24 15.0		Sales/Receivables		
0 UND	0 UND	2 159.5	45 8.0	54 6.7				
						Cost of Sales/Inventory		
						Cost of Sales/Payables		
3.8	14.1	2.7	3.5	2.6				
-10.3	-11.0	-202.5	20.1	4.0		Sales/Working Capital		
-2.0	-2.4	-4.0	-3.9	-35.7				
15.0	12.6							
(12) 5.0	(17) 2.9					EBIT/Interest		
3.7	2.0							
						Net Profit + Depr., Dep., Amort./Cur. Mat. L/T/D		
.9	2.5	1.8	1.3	.5				
4.9	5.3	3.7	3.8	2.7		Fixed/Worth		
NM	39.7	9.2	100.2	NM				
1.5	1.9	1.0	1.2	.3				
5.6	4.7	2.8	3.2	4.0		Debt/Worth		
NM	40.1	9.1	106.8	NM				
64.2	44.9	27.5	20.3					
(25) 35.8	(42) 19.0	(33) 15.8	(10) 7.7			% Profit Before Taxes/Tangible Net Worth		
12.2	6.3	4.4	1.4					
16.9	7.1	6.8	3.8	11.5				
9.4	4.4	3.6	1.8	1.3		% Profit Before Taxes/Total Assets		
2.1	1.4	1.5	.2	-.6				
1.3	.4	.3	.3	3.2				
.3	.2	.2	.2	1.2		Sales/Net Fixed Assets		
.2	.2	.1	.1	.3				
.5	.4	.2	.2	.6				
.2	.2	.2	.2	.3		Sales/Total Assets		
.1	.1	.1	.1	.2				
6.3	9.0	12.4	15.6					
(29) 14.6	(50) 15.2	(36) 18.3	(10) 21.6			% Depr., Dep., Amort./Sales		
27.5	23.8	24.0	26.7					
						% Officers', Directors', Owners' Comp/Sales		
4803M	26674M	32088M	46415M	281508M	241931M	Net Sales ($)		
10346M	59861M	158462M	272623M	676985M	755214M	Total Assets ($)		

M = $ thousand   MM = $ million
See Pages 11 through 18 for Explanation of Ratios and Data

Comparative Historical Data | | | | **Current Data Sorted By Sales**

			Type of Statement						
		15	Unqualified	1	5	1	1	2	5
		11	Reviewed	6	3	1	1		1
		38	Compiled	30	6	1			
		55	Tax Returns	53	1		1	2	
		30	Other	17	4	3	3	2	1
4/1/00-3/31/01 ALL	4/1/01-3/31/02 ALL	4/1/02-3/31/03 ALL		16 (4/1-9/30/02)			133 (10/1/02-3/31/03)		
				0-1MM	1-3MM	3-5MM	5-10MM	10-25MM	25MM & OVER
		149	**NUMBER OF STATEMENTS**	107	19	6	6	4	7
%	%	%	**ASSETS**	%	%	%	%	%	%
		7.0	Cash & Equivalents	6.0	10.1				
		3.8	Trade Receivables (net)	2.3	7.3				
D	D	1.0	Inventory	.1	1.9				
A	A	1.3	All Other Current	.6	1.4				
T	T	13.1	Total Current	9.0	20.7				
A	A	77.6	Fixed Assets (net)	82.3	75.5				
		1.4	Intangibles (net)	1.3	.3				
N	N	7.8	All Other Non-Current	7.4	3.5				
O	O	100.0	Total	100.0	100.0				
T	T		**LIABILITIES**						
		3.4	Notes Payable-Short Term	2.9	7.2				
A	A	4.7	Cur. Mat.-L/T/D	5.1	4.8				
V	V	1.4	Trade Payables	.4	2.2				
A	A	.1	Income Taxes Payable	.0	.0				
I	I	3.4	All Other Current	3.1	4.7				
L	L	13.0	Total Current	11.6	18.9				
A	A	62.1	Long Term Debt	65.8	47.3				
B	B	.1	Deferred Taxes	.0	.0				
L	L	7.2	All Other Non-Current	7.6	3.4				
E	E	17.6	Net Worth	15.0	30.5				
		100.0	Total Liabilities & Net Worth	100.0	100.0				
			INCOME DATA						
		100.0	Net Sales	100.0	100.0				
			Gross Profit						
		52.9	Operating Expenses	46.6	64.1				
		47.1	Operating Profit	53.4	35.9				
		26.1	All Other Expenses (net)	28.9	23.5				
		21.0	Profit Before Taxes	24.5	12.3				
			RATIOS						
		2.9	Current	2.7	1.7				
		.8		.5	1.2				
		.2		.1	.3				
		2.4	Quick	2.4	1.5				
		.5		.4	1.1				
		.1		.1	.2				
		0 UND	Sales/Receivables	0 UND	0 999.8				
		0 UND		0 UND	6 62.1				
		17 22.1		0 UND	86 4.2				
			Cost of Sales/Inventory						
			Cost of Sales/Payables						
		5.3	Sales/Working Capital	6.9	2.8				
		-46.7		-10.3	22.4				
		-2.8		-2.5	-3.8				
		11.0	EBIT/Interest	9.1					
	(44)	3.3		(26) 3.6					
		2.1		2.0					
			Net Profit + Depr., Dep., Amort./Cur. Mat. L/T/D						
		1.8	Fixed/Worth	2.1	1.6				
		4.7		4.9	3.9				
		39.7		46.2	8.7				
		1.4	Debt/Worth	1.6	.9				
		4.5		4.7	3.0				
		41.3		46.3	8.3				
		41.9	% Profit Before Taxes/Tangible Net Worth	47.2	30.7				
	(120)	16.8		(86) 19.7	(16) 9.4				
		5.1		6.3	1.3				
		8.1	% Profit Before Taxes/Total Assets	8.8	5.3				
		4.0		4.2	2.9				
		1.4		1.5	.1				
		.6	Sales/Net Fixed Assets	.4	1.0				
		.2		.2	.3				
		.2		.1	.1				
		.3	Sales/Total Assets	.3	.8				
		.2		.2	.2				
		.2		.1	.1				
		8.8	% Depr., Dep., Amort./Sales	11.7	6.2				
	(137)	16.5		(100) 17.4	(18) 15.4				
		23.8		24.1	24.2				
		3.0	% Officers', Directors', Owners' Comp/Sales						
	(19)	8.7							
		13.6							
		633419M	Net Sales ($)	30503M	33919M	25971M	42080M	71477M	429469M
		1933491M	Total Assets ($)	160867M	163875M	88266M	265468M	266556M	988459M

M = $ thousand   MM = $ million
See Pages 11 through 18 for Explanation of Ratios and Data

Current Data Sorted By Assets   Comparative Historical Data

0-500M	500M-2MM	2-10MM	10-50MM	50-100MM	100-250MM	Type of Statement	4/1/98-3/31/99 ALL	4/1/99-3/31/00 ALL
5	3	28	33	14	6	Unqualified	59	71
	4		1		1	Reviewed	7	4
2		5	1			Compiled	3	6
1	1	1	1			Tax Returns	3	4
1	6	9	20	1	2	Other	22	23
	69 (4/1-9/30/02)		75 (10/1/02-3/31/03)					
9	10	47	54	15	9	**NUMBER OF STATEMENTS**	94	108
%	%	%	%	%	%	**ASSETS**	%	%
	17.3	8.1	9.2	19.4		Cash & Equivalents	14.0	14.4
	10.3	5.0	5.1	2.7		Trade Receivables (net)	4.3	7.0
	16.4	9.4	5.0	1.6		Inventory	7.7	5.9
	7.6	3.3	4.9	6.0		All Other Current	3.4	3.7
	51.6	25.8	24.2	29.7		Total Current	29.4	31.1
	29.3	56.0	52.5	36.4		Fixed Assets (net)	44.9	44.4
	5.6	.9	.3	.1		Intangibles (net)	.6	1.8
	13.4	17.4	23.0	33.8		All Other Non-Current	25.1	22.7
	100.0	100.0	100.0	100.0		Total	100.0	100.0
						LIABILITIES		
	10.8	4.9	2.3	1.5		Notes Payable-Short Term	5.4	4.9
	2.7	2.8	.8	.2		Cur. Mat.-L/T/D	1.3	2.1
	18.9	5.3	4.1	3.1		Trade Payables	3.7	5.5
	.0	.0	.0	.0		Income Taxes Payable	.2	.0
	9.9	4.3	2.0	1.8		All Other Current	4.7	3.4
	42.4	17.4	9.3	6.6		Total Current	15.3	15.9
	21.4	11.5	12.2	8.2		Long Term Debt	10.1	12.3
	.0	.0	.0	.0		Deferred Taxes	.0	.0
	5.2	1.7	1.9	1.1		All Other Non-Current	4.1	1.4
	30.9	69.5	76.7	84.1		Net Worth	70.5	70.4
	100.0	100.0	100.0	100.0		Total Liabilities & Net Worth	100.0	100.0
						INCOME DATA		
	100.0	100.0	100.0	100.0		Net Sales	100.0	100.0
						Gross Profit		
	94.1	97.1	90.1	78.1		Operating Expenses	92.8	87.3
	5.9	2.9	9.9	21.9		Operating Profit	7.2	12.7
	.5	4.0	5.5	4.2		All Other Expenses (net)	-11.7	-8.2
	5.4	-1.2	4.4	17.7		Profit Before Taxes	19.0	20.9
						RATIOS		
	2.4	3.1	13.2	11.1		Current	4.4	6.8
	1.5	1.5	3.0	2.7			2.6	2.3
	.8	.6	1.3	1.0			1.0	1.0
	1.5	2.0	6.3	7.7		Quick	3.8	5.5
	.8	.7	2.0	1.6			1.6 (107)	1.5
	.2	.4	.5	.4			.4	.5
7	54.2	2 174.8	0 762.7	2 162.3		Sales/Receivables	0 UND	1 260.5
19	19.7	9 40.7	13 28.8	10 36.5			10 38.1	16 23.5
41	8.8	32 11.2	92 4.0	35 10.5			45 8.1	62 5.9
						Cost of Sales/Inventory		
						Cost of Sales/Payables		
	3.0	3.1	1.2	1.2		Sales/Working Capital	2.2	1.6
	5.6	9.3	3.0	2.9			3.8	4.3
	-24.3	-13.9	16.2	136.5			-282.5	179.6
		4.9	7.0			EBIT/Interest	15.9	25.0
	(30)	3.7	(25) .3				(51) 3.7	(58) 4.8
		-3.5	-3.7				.5	1.5
						Net Profit + Depr., Dep., Amort./Cur. Mat. L /T/D		
	.6	.4	.4	.2		Fixed/Worth	.2	.3
	.9	.8	.7	.3			.6	.7
	-1.0	1.1	.9	.6			1.0	1.0
	.6	.1	.1	.1		Debt/Worth	.1	.1
	1.1	.3	.2	.1			.2	.2
	-4.5	1.0	.5	.3			.7	.7
		9.8	5.7	12.4		% Profit Before Taxes/Tangible Net Worth	12.7	26.8
		.3	.5	1.9			(91) 5.6	(104) 6.9
		-6.5	-6.1	-1.5			-1.5	1.0
	14.4	4.5	4.6	11.6		% Profit Before Taxes/Total Assets	11.3	13.0
	2.8	.2	.4	1.8			2.5	5.0
	-12.4	-6.3	-4.9	-1.3			-1.4	.8
	20.4	3.4	.8	4.6		Sales/Net Fixed Assets	3.7	4.5
	4.3	.8	.5	.9			.8	.9
	1.8	.4	.3	.5			.5	.4
	2.1	.9	.4	.5		Sales/Total Assets	.7	.8
	1.5	.4	.3	.3			.4	.4
	.6	.2	.2	.2			.2	.2
		4.1	4.4	3.1		% Depr., Dep., Amort./Sales	2.3	1.9
	(38)	8.8	(46) 8.7	(14) 7.3			(87) 6.4	(92) 4.8
		15.3	13.8	11.3			11.6	10.1
	(12) 6.2					% Officers', Directors', Owners' Comp/Sales	(15) 5.7	(14) 2.4
	13.8						15.0	4.9
	32.4						25.2	15.4
4845M	21163M	159697M	411143M	434759M	479668M	Net Sales ($)	770037M	796966M
2246M	12409M	264621M	1362523M	1124084M	1284760M	Total Assets ($)	3029994M	2772355M

M = $ thousand   MM = $ million
See Pages 11 through 18 for Explanation of Ratios and Data

Comparative Historical Data			Type of Statement	Current Data Sorted By Sales					
53	52	89	Unqualified	9	29	7	14	22	8
3	4	6	Reviewed		2		2	1	1
6	14	7	Compiled	3	1	2	1		
3	4	3	Tax Returns	1	1	1			
32	29	39	Other	3	9	6	15	4	2
4/1/00-3/31/01 ALL	4/1/01-3/31/02 ALL	4/1/02-3/31/03 ALL		69 (4/1-9/30/02)			75 (10/1/02-3/31/03)		
				0-1MM	1-3MM	3-5MM	5-10MM	10-25MM	25MM & OVER
97	103	144	NUMBER OF STATEMENTS	16	42	16	32	27	11
%	%	%	ASSETS	%	%	%	%	%	%
13.1	13.1	12.5	Cash & Equivalents	16.4	12.9	8.6	10.0	11.5	20.2
5.6	5.3	4.9	Trade Receivables (net)	2.8	3.2	5.1	7.1	6.4	4.5
6.4	9.5	7.8	Inventory	9.7	3.0	13.8	14.3	1.3	11.5
3.9	4.3	4.4	All Other Current	3.4	3.9	4.5	5.4	3.8	5.6
29.0	32.1	29.5	Total Current	32.3	23.0	32.0	36.8	23.0	41.8
43.9	47.2	47.6	Fixed Assets (net)	55.5	58.3	40.8	42.1	47.3	22.4
4.2	1.1	1.0	Intangibles (net)	2.8	.3	.3	.2	1.8	2.6
23.0	19.6	21.8	All Other Non-Current	8.8	18.4	27.0	20.9	28.0	33.2
100.0	100.0	100.0	Total	100.0	100.0	100.0	100.0	100.0	100.0
			LIABILITIES						
5.0	4.2	3.7	Notes Payable-Short Term	4.5	4.9	2.6	4.0	2.8	.4
2.8	3.8	1.6	Cur. Mat.-L/T/D	2.7	1.5	1.9	2.1	.8	.2
5.1	5.7	5.8	Trade Payables	8.5	3.4	6.3	7.9	6.0	3.3
.0	.0	.0	Income Taxes Payable	.0	.0	.1	.0	.0	.0
3.9	3.3	3.4	All Other Current	3.0	2.9	1.8	4.8	3.2	4.7
16.9	17.0	14.4	Total Current	18.7	12.7	12.7	18.7	12.7	8.5
14.0	13.8	12.9	Long Term Debt	24.1	11.6	13.3	9.7	12.9	10.7
.0	.1	.0	Deferred Taxes	.0	.0	.0	.0	.0	.0
2.0	6.4	1.9	All Other Non-Current	2.7	1.1	.9	3.6	1.5	.9
67.1	62.8	70.8	Net Worth	54.4	74.6	73.0	68.0	72.9	79.9
100.0	100.0	100.0	Total Liabilities & Net Worth	100.0	100.0	100.0	100.0	100.0	100.0
			INCOME DATA						
100.0	100.0	100.0	Net Sales	100.0	100.0	100.0	100.0	100.0	100.0
			Gross Profit						
88.9	87.2	92.7	Operating Expenses	103.3	97.0	83.1	90.1	93.1	81.4
11.1	12.8	7.3	Operating Profit	-3.3	3.0	16.9	9.9	6.9	18.6
-4.5	4.5	5.7	All Other Expenses (net)	2.1	5.1	4.7	6.2	9.7	3.7
15.6	8.3	1.6	Profit Before Taxes	-5.4	-2.1	12.1	3.7	-2.8	15.0
			RATIOS						
6.6	6.6	6.5		2.8	6.9	6.7	5.6	4.1	18.0
2.0	2.2	2.2	Current	1.2	2.7	3.1	1.7	1.3	7.1
.9	1.2	.9		.4	.9	1.4	1.1	.9	1.9
4.0	4.2	4.1		2.0	5.0	6.0	3.1	3.4	7.7
1.4	1.3	1.2	Quick	.8	1.8	1.3	1.4	.9	6.3
.4	.4	.4		.2	.5	.5	.6	.4	.9
2 195.2	1 273.7	1 436.2		0 UND	0 999.8	1 582.5	1 261.6	4 91.9	8 43.6
13 28.8	15 24.0	11 34.2	Sales/Receivables	3 144.9	7 51.2	32 11.2	19 19.6	12 29.7	10 36.3
43 8.5	59 6.2	45 8.1		26 14.3	35 10.5	62 5.9	68 5.3	54 6.7	45 8.1
			Cost of Sales/Inventory						
			Cost of Sales/Payables						
1.7	1.8	1.8		2.8	2.2	1.8	1.3	2.3	1.2
5.5	4.0	4.7	Sales/Working Capital	UND	4.7	3.4	4.6	10.6	2.7
-35.3	35.2	-55.6		-6.7	-28.6	14.8	89.6	-51.7	5.8
(57) 20.0	(59) 8.1	(79) 6.5			(22) 7.2	(12) 4.3	(16) 7.5	(15) 13.5	
4.1	2.6	1.4	EBIT/Interest		3.1	3.9	-.9	-1.1	
.5	-2.3	-5.3			-.6	-1.4	-19.2	-6.4	
			Net Profit + Depr., Dep., Amort./Cur. Mat. L/T/D						
.3	.3	.3		.6	.5	.1	.3	.3	.0
.6	.7	.7	Fixed/Worth	1.0	.8	.6	.5	.6	.2
1.1	1.0	1.0		1.4	1.1	.8	.9	1.2	.6
.1	.1	.1		.2	.1	.1	.1	.1	.1
.3	.3	.2	Debt/Worth	.3	.2	.2	.3	.2	.2
.8	1.1	.8		2.2	.6	.8	.9	.8	.3
(92) 15.2	(98) 17.7	(139) 8.9	% Profit Before Taxes/Tangible	(14) 12.5	(40) 3.3	20.6	(31) 11.4	5.2	30.5
5.0	2.0	.5	Net Worth	-.1	.3	4.1	.7	-.6	1.9
-.8	-3.5	-5.9		-8.1	-5.3	-1.5	-7.3	-7.6	-5.5
10.2	12.0	4.5	% Profit Before Taxes/Total	4.1	2.9	7.9	7.3	3.2	24.8
4.1	1.5	.3	Assets	.0	-.1	3.1	.3	-.5	1.8
-.5	-2.5	-5.3		-6.3	-5.4	-1.3	-6.7	-5.0	-4.4
4.0	5.1	3.6		4.0	1.7	6.8	5.6	1.8	124.7
.9	.8	.8	Sales/Net Fixed Assets	1.1	.5	1.0	.8	.7	5.8
.5	.4	.4		.2	.3	.5	.5	.5	.8
.8	1.0	.7		1.2	.6	.8	1.1	.4	.9
.4	.4	.3	Sales/Total Assets	.4	.3	.4	.3	.3	.5
.2	.2	.2		.1	.2	.1	.2	.2	.3
(81) 1.9	(91) .9	(116) 3.4	% Depr., Dep., Amort./Sales	(12) 2.6	(30) 5.9	(13) 1.8	(29) 1.0	(23) 4.3	
4.8	4.8	6.8		10.1	10.1	6.8	5.2	6.7	
10.2	9.9	12.6		23.9	15.4	10.8	10.8	11.0	
(12) 1.3	(17) 4.7	(25) 4.0	% Officers', Directors',						
4.7	9.5	12.4	Owners' Comp/Sales						
14.2	24.7	27.9							
1331292M	1175501M	1511275M	Net Sales ($)	7450M	86144M	58037M	231296M	433426M	694922M
3134446M	2758919M	4050643M	Total Assets ($)	25677M	305558M	203474M	693391M	1581901M	1240642M

M = $ thousand   MM = $ million
See Pages 11 through 18 for Explanation of Ratios and Data

Current Data Sorted By Assets   Comparative Historical Data

	0-500M	500M-2MM	2-10MM	10-50MM	50-100MM	100-250MM	Type of Statement	4/1/98-3/31/99 ALL	4/1/99-3/31/00 ALL
			2	8	1	3	Unqualified	18	16
	1	1	12	5	1		Reviewed	23	21
	7	12	2	1			Compiled	35	18
	9	1	5	2			Tax Returns	8	17
	5	4	7	3		1	Other	27	25
		12 (4/1-9/30/02)		81 (10/1/02-3/31/03)					
NUMBER OF STATEMENTS	22	18	28	19	3	3		111	97
	%	%	%	%	%	%	**ASSETS**	%	%
Cash & Equivalents	12.9	6.9	7.8	6.8				9.0	11.4
Trade Receivables (net)	.3	.2	.4	1.0				1.1	1.4
Inventory	1.8	3.4	1.5	2.2				3.8	3.7
All Other Current	12.0	.7	2.9	1.1				1.7	1.8
Total Current	26.9	11.1	12.6	11.1				15.6	18.3
Fixed Assets (net)	65.5	79.0	73.9	76.1				72.5	68.6
Intangibles (net)	2.6	.8	3.1	2.8				2.4	3.2
All Other Non-Current	4.9	9.1	10.3	9.9				9.5	9.9
Total	100.0	100.0	100.0	100.0				100.0	100.0
							LIABILITIES		
Notes Payable-Short Term	19.6	12.9	.3	6.0				5.1	5.8
Cur. Mat.-L/T/D	4.7	4.9	10.4	5.1				6.2	7.4
Trade Payables	3.6	1.4	2.2	2.2				3.5	3.8
Income Taxes Payable	1.1	.0	.1	.3				.5	.5
All Other Current	27.6	8.7	6.2	4.2				12.0	17.0
Total Current	56.7	27.9	19.3	17.7				27.3	34.4
Long Term Debt	25.8	42.5	43.7	41.4				36.5	40.3
Deferred Taxes	.0	.0	.8	1.2				.7	.5
All Other Non-Current	25.6	8.4	15.6	1.4				6.2	4.2
Net Worth	-8.1	21.2	20.6	38.3				29.2	20.6
Total Liabilities & Net Worth	100.0	100.0	100.0	100.0				100.0	100.0
							INCOME DATA		
Net Sales	100.0	100.0	100.0	100.0				100.0	100.0
Gross Profit									
Operating Expenses	91.9	86.4	87.7	86.9				90.1	89.1
Operating Profit	8.1	13.6	12.3	13.1				9.9	10.9
All Other Expenses (net)	5.4	6.3	8.1	3.7				7.4	6.0
Profit Before Taxes	2.6	7.2	4.2	9.5				2.6	5.0
							RATIOS		
Current	2.6	1.0	1.3	1.0				1.4	1.8
	1.0	.2	.7	.6				.6	.7
	.3	.1	.3	.2				.2	.2
Quick	(21) 1.7	.8	1.0	1.0				(110) 1.2	(96) 1.3
	.2	.2	.5	.4				.5	.5
	.1	.1	.2	.2				.1	.1
Sales/Receivables	0 UND	0 UND	0 UND	0 999.8				0 UND	0 UND
	0 UND	0 UND	0 854.1	3 113.4				0 UND	0 999.8
	0 UND	0 UND	3 114.7	11 32.6				4 89.0	4 95.4
Cost of Sales/Inventory									
Cost of Sales/Payables									
Sales/Working Capital	31.9	NM	26.1	171.3				25.8	13.4
	UND	-12.5	-20.7	-18.1				-18.0	-26.9
	-32.2	-4.2	-8.4	-5.2				-4.8	-5.0
EBIT/Interest	(10) 4.7	(17) 5.9	(24) 2.9	(18) 4.1				(97) 4.5	(84) 4.8
	1.4	2.9	1.6	2.5				2.0	2.2
	-2.5	.0	.4	1.5				.6	1.0
Net Profit + Depr., Dep., Amort./Cur. Mat. L /T/D								(29) 6.6	(22) 5.7
								3.1	2.8
								1.5	1.0
Fixed/Worth	.9	1.5	1.5	1.2				1.3	1.1
	1.2	3.4	2.3	1.8				2.6	2.5
	-1.6	-151.9	21.9	5.7				12.0	11.9
Debt/Worth	.3	1.3	.8	.8				.7	.7
	1.4	2.9	2.4	1.2				2.5	2.2
	-2.7	-157.5	25.1	5.6				14.0	15.2
% Profit Before Taxes/Tangible Net Worth	(14) 135.3	(13) 46.5	(22) 31.4	(17) 27.7				(91) 38.2	(79) 25.6
	25.7	32.1	8.6	13.3				17.3	14.4
	-18.1	16.3	.7	2.0				.0	.0
% Profit Before Taxes/Total Assets	21.2	17.3	5.8	9.8				12.5	11.1
	4.2	11.1	3.5	5.5				4.9	5.0
	-16.3	-2.0	-2.0	1.4				-2.2	-1.1
Sales/Net Fixed Assets	16.2	6.1	1.5	1.4				2.8	3.1
	3.5	.9	1.0	.9				1.3	1.6
	2.0	.5	.7	.5				.7	.8
Sales/Total Assets	6.7	2.8	1.1	1.0				1.5	1.8
	3.0	.8	.8	.8				1.0	1.0
	1.3	.4	.5	.4				.6	.6
% Depr., Dep., Amort./Sales	(18) 4.9	(17) 2.9	(27) 7.2	5.4				(106) 5.6	(91) 5.7
	8.7	7.0	12.8	10.3				9.8	9.8
	13.3	15.8	16.2	16.2				17.6	13.7
% Officers', Directors', Owners' Comp/Sales	(12) 6.2							(23) 3.6	(29) 3.6
	9.3							7.8	5.6
	16.0							14.6	10.8
Net Sales ($)	13222M	38272M	116720M	327751M	180649M	348653M		1306785M	1133133M
Total Assets ($)	4916M	18231M	139529M	449944M	223588M	411649M		1520748M	1271982M

Comparative Historical Data | Current Data Sorted By Sales

			Type of Statement						
10	12	14	Unqualified		1		1	4	8
15	14	20	Reviewed	1	5	4	5	3	2
14	17	22	Compiled	11	6	2	1	2	
13	13	17	Tax Returns	10	4		2	1	
25	27	20	Other	9	5	1	3		2
4/1/00-3/31/01	4/1/01-3/31/02	4/1/02-3/31/03		12 (4/1-9/30/02)			81 (10/1/02-3/31/03)		
ALL	ALL	ALL		0-1MM	1-3MM	3-5MM	5-10MM	10-25MM	25MM & OVER
77	83	93	NUMBER OF STATEMENTS	31	21	7	12	10	12
%	%	%	ASSETS	%	%	%	%	%	%
8.7	8.8	8.8	Cash & Equivalents	9.8	6.4		12.5	10.6	8.0
2.4	.5	.5	Trade Receivables (net)	.1	.4		.5	.7	1.7
2.6	2.9	2.1	Inventory	.6	2.7		2.1	1.2	3.6
2.1	2.5	4.1	All Other Current	8.6	1.9		1.1	4.2	.6
15.9	14.7	15.5	Total Current	19.2	11.4		16.3	16.6	14.0
70.4	72.3	73.2	Fixed Assets (net)	75.0	71.7		71.9	73.1	68.8
5.0	4.1	2.7	Intangibles (net)	2.2	3.5		.9	4.5	4.0
8.7	8.9	8.6	All Other Non-Current	3.6	13.3		10.9	5.7	13.2
100.0	100.0	100.0	Total	100.0	100.0		100.0	100.0	100.0
			LIABILITIES						
8.1	8.0	9.1	Notes Payable-Short Term	14.1	3.4		3.8	11.1	10.5
5.3	4.8	6.8	Cur. Mat.-L/T/D	5.6	9.4		5.7	5.3	6.1
4.0	2.1	2.3	Trade Payables	2.3	1.7		2.8	3.3	1.9
.2	.1	.3	Income Taxes Payable	.8	.1		.0	.0	.2
15.9	18.8	11.5	All Other Current	19.9	4.4		9.6	7.8	7.5
33.4	33.8	30.1	Total Current	42.6	19.0		21.9	27.5	26.2
42.8	43.5	36.6	Long Term Debt	42.4	32.9		52.9	42.9	18.5
.4	.2	.5	Deferred Taxes	.0	.4		1.2	.0	2.0
6.2	8.9	13.2	All Other Non-Current	19.9	22.8		.1	1.4	5.4
17.2	13.7	19.6	Net Worth	-4.9	24.9		23.8	28.2	47.9
100.0	100.0	100.0	Total Liabilities & Net Worth	100.0	100.0		100.0	100.0	100.0
			INCOME DATA						
100.0	100.0	100.0	Net Sales	100.0	100.0		100.0	100.0	100.0
			Gross Profit						
93.2	90.7	87.5	Operating Expenses	85.8	89.7		90.1	87.7	82.2
6.8	9.2	12.5	Operating Profit	14.2	10.3		9.8	12.3	17.8
3.2	5.7	5.9	All Other Expenses (net)	8.4	4.7		5.2	7.5	2.7
3.6	3.6	6.6	Profit Before Taxes	5.8	5.7		4.6	4.8	15.1
			RATIOS						
1.5	1.2	1.2	Current	1.5	4.2		1.2	1.9	1.0
.6	.6	.7		.9	.7		.7	.8	.4
.1	.2	.2		.1	.2		.3	.2	.2
1.0	1.0	1.0	Quick	(30) 1.1	2.5		.7	1.0	.8
.3	.3	(92) .3		.2	.4		.5	.5	.2
.0	.1	.1		.1	.2		.2	.2	.1
0 UND	0 UND	0 UND	Sales/Receivables	0 UND	0 UND		0 UND	0 UND	4 100.5
0 999.8	0 UND	0 UND		0 UND	0 UND		0 UND	1 486.5	5 70.6
6 65.5	3 126.2	3 108.3		0 UND	1 278.1		4 100.9	5 69.4	10 36.4
			Cost of Sales/Inventory						
			Cost of Sales/Payables						
39.0	76.5	37.5	Sales/Working Capital	31.9	14.8		33.9	16.0	NM
-14.7	-36.9	-27.0		-81.8	-31.7		-9.2	-94.4	-8.1
-3.9	-5.2	-7.0		-5.3	-9.1		-4.5	-15.0	-2.6
(67) 3.3	(70) 4.4	(74) 4.1	EBIT/Interest	(19) 6.7	(16) 2.9		3.8		(11) 7.2
1.6	1.9	2.4		2.6	1.9		1.7		5.0
.0	.7	.7		-.7	-2.0		.9		2.8
(15) 7.4	(10) 2.9	(16) 3.3	Net Profit + Depr., Dep., Amort./Cur. Mat. L/T/D						
1.0	.9	2.2							
.2	.1	1.1							
1.4	1.2	1.2	Fixed/Worth	1.2	1.1		1.1	1.2	.9
2.5	2.1	2.2		4.1	2.2		2.5	2.0	1.5
NM	-47.3	52.1		-2.3	NM		27.6	-5.0	3.3
1.0	.7	.7	Debt/Worth	.5	.5		.9	.7	.6
2.1	1.5	2.1		3.5	2.1		4.0	1.4	1.1
-9.8	-69.6	61.1		-3.6	NM		34.7	-7.3	2.6
(56) 21.5	(62) 33.6	(71) 37.8	% Profit Before Taxes/Tangible Net Worth	(20) 51.0	(16) 40.1		(10) 24.1		(11) 41.1
9.6	12.8	18.9		26.3	12.7		11.7		28.2
.6	-1.6	2.4		-4.1	-12.1		7.6		13.3
8.5	14.0	13.5	% Profit Before Taxes/Total Assets	21.1	11.9		9.9	10.8	23.3
2.8	3.6	5.3		6.8	4.1		2.8	3.6	10.7
-6.2	-4.6	-2.4		-12.5	-7.7		-1.6	-1.8	5.3
2.2	2.6	3.2	Sales/Net Fixed Assets	3.6	4.5		2.5	2.8	2.1
1.3	1.2	1.2		1.0	1.4		1.1	1.4	1.0
.7	.8	.8		.5	.7		.6	.9	.9
1.4	1.9	1.7	Sales/Total Assets	2.7	2.5		1.3	1.9	1.0
.9	.9	.9		.8	1.0		.9	1.0	.8
.5	.6	.6		.4	.5		.5	.8	.7
(72) 6.2	(80) 5.1	(85) 5.4	% Depr., Dep., Amort./Sales	(27) 7.0	(19) 3.3		7.6	4.0	(10) 5.4
10.6	10.2	10.2		11.8	8.2		13.2	7.5	9.1
16.1	15.6	15.3		19.2	15.4		16.0	13.8	12.5
(24) 3.1	(30) 3.8	(30) 3.7	% Officers', Directors', Owners' Comp/Sales	(14) 4.4					
6.6	5.8	7.7		9.4					
10.3	11.2	12.8		19.1					
981045M	903013M	1025267M	Net Sales ($)	14706M	39697M	29889M	74546M	148648M	717781M
1654981M	1309511M	1247857M	Total Assets ($)	46096M	56103M	39643M	99580M	166881M	839554M

© RMA 2003

M = $ thousand   MM = $ million
See Pages 11 through 18 for Explanation of Ratios and Data

Current Data Sorted By Assets   Comparative Historical Data

						Type of Statement		
2		3	7	2	13	Unqualified	18	10
3	2	3				Reviewed	12	5
3	8	6	1			Compiled	26	19
6	6	1				Tax Returns	16	5
4	3		9	7 1	3	Other	25	15
	29 (4/1-9/30/02)		64 (10/1/02-3/31/03)				4/1/98-3/31/99	4/1/99-3/31/00
0-500M	500M-2MM	2-10MM	10-50MM	50-100MM	100-250MM		ALL	ALL
18	19	22	15	3	16	NUMBER OF STATEMENTS	97	54
%	%	%	%	%	%	ASSETS	%	%
23.0	9.0	17.3	16.5		10.6	Cash & Equivalents	13.6	12.1
.3	1.6	5.3	4.0		1.6	Trade Receivables (net)	3.3	4.9
7.6	4.1	5.3	4.5		.9	Inventory	5.9	4.0
3.9	2.8	5.7	1.2		2.2	All Other Current	1.9	1.3
34.9	17.6	33.6	26.1		15.3	Total Current	24.7	22.3
51.2	72.0	59.5	59.9		70.1	Fixed Assets (net)	60.1	65.3
7.2	3.7	2.1	6.7		4.3	Intangibles (net)	5.6	5.7
6.7	6.7	4.8	7.3		10.3	All Other Non-Current	9.6	6.7
100.0	100.0	100.0	100.0		100.0	Total	100.0	100.0
						LIABILITIES		
9.9	5.5	4.0	.6		1.4	Notes Payable-Short Term	3.1	4.8
13.5	6.1	9.3	6.3		4.5	Cur. Mat.-L/T/D	8.4	9.9
4.7	4.5	5.5	4.3		3.1	Trade Payables	5.1	5.4
.6	.0	.5	.0		.0	Income Taxes Payable	.3	.0
12.5	6.9	10.0	5.8		7.5	All Other Current	6.2	7.7
41.2	23.0	29.2	16.9		16.6	Total Current	23.1	27.8
39.2	33.0	25.2	22.2		33.4	Long Term Debt	29.9	34.8
.1	.0	.0	.6		1.8	Deferred Taxes	.1	.1
7.6	15.6	1.1	1.5		11.8	All Other Non-Current	6.6	4.4
12.0	28.4	44.5	58.7		36.3	Net Worth	40.2	32.9
100.0	100.0	100.0	100.0		100.0	Total Liabilities & Net Worth	100.0	100.0
						INCOME DATA		
100.0	100.0	100.0	100.0		100.0	Net Sales	100.0	100.0
						Gross Profit		
91.0	96.8	93.2	71.0		77.1	Operating Expenses	87.6	88.9
9.0	3.2	6.8	29.0		22.9	Operating Profit	12.4	11.1
4.6	3.0	1.5	5.2		5.7	All Other Expenses (net)	4.0	3.1
4.3	.2	5.3	23.9		17.2	Profit Before Taxes	8.4	8.0
						RATIOS		
1.6	1.8	2.3	1.8		1.8		2.9	1.8
.7	.7	1.4	1.2		.8	Current	1.1	.8
.2	.2	.5	.9		.5		.4	.3
.9	1.1	1.5	1.7		1.5		2.0	1.4
.5	.4	.8	1.0		.8	Quick	(96) .7	.5
.1	.2	.3			.4		.2	.1
0 UND	0 UND	0 UND	0 999.8		0 UND		0 UND	0 UND
0 UND	0 UND	2 201.3	1 247.5		2 206.0	Sales/Receivables	0 UND	1 331.4
0 UND	1 350.0	8 45.6	4 92.3		8 48.5		3 134.6	6 60.1
						Cost of Sales/Inventory		
						Cost of Sales/Payables		
81.3	22.8	14.5	10.6		28.9		13.7	24.6
-23.1	-35.2	40.9	84.9		-33.0	Sales/Working Capital	241.5	-48.0
-7.8	-8.9	-11.3	-35.9		-11.4		-9.9	-8.7
(14) 11.9	(18) 5.1	(18) 13.4	(12) 15.4		(14) 18.9		(83) 13.2	(49) 10.4
1.2	2.3	4.3	8.0		3.8	EBIT/Interest	2.8	3.0
-.5	-1.2	1.5	4.8		1.0		1.0	1.2
						Net Profit + Depr., Dep., Amort./Cur. Mat. L /T/D	(17) 14.0	
							2.0	
							.9	
.4	1.2	.6	.9		1.1		.8	1.0
1.6	2.2	1.5	1.2		2.3	Fixed/Worth	1.9	2.2
-7.7	-27.5	3.6	2.1		6.8		5.8	27.2
.8	.7	.5	.2		.6		.5	.6
1.6	2.0	1.6	.7		2.1	Debt/Worth	1.6	2.3
-4.1	-32.4	4.2	1.8		7.2		8.0	30.5
(11) 107.3	(14) 33.1	(19) 63.6	(13) 92.0		(14) 101.6	% Profit Before Taxes/Tangible Net Worth	(81) 87.7	(43) 62.1
50.7	10.3	31.7	47.5		75.9		40.5	24.6
-3.1	-4.1	.8	9.6		10.2		8.0	8.8
25.5	10.5	22.3	33.0		47.1	% Profit Before Taxes/Total Assets	36.5	18.2
.2	3.8	7.0	24.7		15.2		11.1	8.0
-10.8	-1.8	1.7	6.2		.9		-.4	1.1
18.4	4.6	17.3	4.3		2.3	Sales/Net Fixed Assets	6.4	4.7
4.3	2.8	3.1	2.0		1.7		2.7	2.6
3.0	1.3	1.9	1.3		1.1		1.7	1.3
4.1	3.5	3.9	1.8		1.5	Sales/Total Assets	2.6	2.7
2.0	1.7	2.1	1.4		1.0		1.6	1.3
1.3	1.1	1.4	.9		.8		.9	.9
(15) 1.5	(16) 4.2	(21) 2.6	(14) 2.8			% Depr., Dep., Amort./Sales	(87) 4.7	(51) 4.2
11.2	11.6	7.3	4.4				10.0	8.1
16.2	17.8	11.4	7.1				19.0	16.0
(10) 3.1						% Officers', Directors', Owners' Comp/Sales	(35) 2.2	(19) 2.0
8.0							4.7	3.6
11.8							7.8	5.8
18809M	44723M	275012M	593507M	274091M	3043830M	Net Sales ($)	1673310M	882450M
4788M	20424M	99982M	398106M	206547M	2608695M	Total Assets ($)	1520044M	694540M

M = $ thousand   MM = $ million
See Pages 11 through 18 for Explanation of Ratios and Data

Comparative Historical Data				Current Data Sorted By Sales					

Type of Statement

4/1/00-3/31/01 ALL	4/1/01-3/31/02 ALL	4/1/02-3/31/03 ALL		0-1MM	1-3MM	3-5MM	5-10MM	10-25MM	25MM & OVER
					29 (4/1-9/30/02)			64 (10/1/02-3/31/03)	
7	19	27	Unqualified	2	2	2	1	2	22
5	3	8	Reviewed	3	2		1		
16	14	18	Compiled	2	9	2	5		
10	9	13	Tax Returns	7	2	1	3		
25	36	27	Other	4	2	1	3	7	10
63	81	93	**NUMBER OF STATEMENTS**	18	15	6	13	9	32
%	%	%	**ASSETS**	%	%	%	%	%	%
15.8	14.4	15.2	Cash & Equivalents	19.4	7.9		15.3		15.0
2.0	3.6	2.6	Trade Receivables (net)	.3	2.0		1.4		2.8
6.8	2.8	4.5	Inventory	7.3	5.4		1.7		3.2
1.7	2.8	3.3	All Other Current	3.7	4.2		3.8		2.2
26.3	23.6	25.6	Total Current	30.7	19.5		22.2		23.2
60.0	63.6	63.0	Fixed Assets (net)	56.1	74.5		68.0		64.4
7.5	6.9	4.5	Intangibles (net)	6.2	2.3		6.3		3.8
6.2	5.9	6.9	All Other Non-Current	6.8	3.8		3.4		8.6
100.0	100.0	100.0	Total	100.0	100.0		100.0		100.0
			LIABILITIES						
3.1	2.8	4.3	Notes Payable-Short Term	7.7	8.4		3.0		.9
7.3	7.9	8.2	Cur. Mat.-L/T/D	12.8	7.5		12.9		6.0
6.4	5.5	4.4	Trade Payables	3.7	3.8		6.0		4.1
.2	.1	.2	Income Taxes Payable	.6	.0		.8		.0
8.8	11.7	8.7	All Other Current	10.1	7.5		10.4		9.0
25.7	28.0	25.9	Total Current	34.9	27.3		33.2		20.1
32.2	29.8	30.2	Long Term Debt	42.8	31.3		28.3		26.7
.1	.1	.4	Deferred Taxes	.1	.0		.0		1.2
5.1	5.3	7.2	All Other Non-Current	10.0	14.7		1.8		6.1
36.9	36.7	36.2	Net Worth	12.2	26.7		36.7		45.9
100.0	100.0	100.0	Total Liabilities & Net Worth	100.0	100.0		100.0		100.0
			INCOME DATA						
100.0	100.0	100.0	Net Sales	100.0	100.0		100.0		100.0
			Gross Profit						
87.4	84.5	86.3	Operating Expenses	89.6	100.0		94.9		75.5
12.6	15.5	13.7	Operating Profit	10.4	.0		5.1		24.5
.9	3.5	3.6	All Other Expenses (net)	7.5	2.1		.8		4.0
11.7	12.0	10.1	Profit Before Taxes	2.9	-2.1		4.3		20.5
			RATIOS						
1.9	1.5	1.8		1.9	1.8		1.5		1.7
1.0	.9	.9	Current	.7	.7		.7		.7
.5	.4	.5		.2	.4		.3		.7
1.4	1.1	1.2		.8	1.0		1.3		1.4
(62) .6	(80) .7	.7	Quick	.3	.4		.5		.9
.3	.3	.2		.1	.1		.2		.5
0 UND	0 UND	0 UND		0 UND	0 UND		0 UND		1 527.1
1 570.9	1 294.1	1 704.2	Sales/Receivables	0 UND	0 UND		0 999.8		2 204.8
4 87.2	5 72.9	4 97.5		0 UND	4 94.9		2 154.1		5 68.3
			Cost of Sales/Inventory						
			Cost of Sales/Payables						
20.8	31.8	21.3		17.8	16.5		76.0		38.3
-170.2	-70.1	-82.8	Sales/Working Capital	-19.3	-35.2		-20.1		-83.1
-13.7	-11.3	-10.1		-5.2	-8.9		-4.4		-16.6
11.0	12.6	11.4		8.2	4.9		6.8		19.7
(54) 2.5	(72) 3.7	(79) 4.2	EBIT/Interest	(14) 1.2	(14) 1.5		(12) 5.0		(27) 8.7
1.1	1.7	1.1		-1.0	-1.6		1.4		3.3
		10.5	Net Profit + Depr., Dep.,						
	(11)	4.5	Amort./Cur. Mat. L/T/D						
		1.7							
.9	1.0	.9		.4	1.1		1.3		.9
1.9	2.1	1.6	Fixed/Worth	1.7	2.0		2.4		1.4
9.4	5.8	6.2		NM	-9.5		-17.0		2.5
.6	.7	.6		.8	.7		.8		.5
2.1	2.1	1.5	Debt/Worth	1.8	1.5		2.9		.9
16.0	7.6	8.7		-5.4	-13.4		-19.7		3.9
111.3	127.6	87.2	% Profit Before Taxes/Tangible	54.3	48.4				101.9
(50) 35.9	(68) 45.5	(74) 32.4	Net Worth	(12) .2	(11) 9.6				(29) 80.2
11.7	13.3	6.8		-10.4	-2.2				13.4
39.9	44.0	28.5	% Profit Before Taxes/Total	15.7	7.1		16.9		48.9
8.9	9.7	7.9	Assets	-1.1	2.4		7.5		27.5
.9	2.3	.5		-7.1	-7.7		2.9		6.7
7.0	5.7	5.2		9.9	4.1		6.6		5.0
3.7	2.3	2.5	Sales/Net Fixed Assets	3.4	3.1		3.1		2.0
1.6	1.4	1.4		1.5	1.3		1.9		1.2
3.8	3.0	2.4		2.3	3.1		4.7		1.9
2.0	1.5	1.5	Sales/Total Assets	1.4	1.8		2.2		1.4
1.1	1.0	1.1		1.1	1.1		1.4		.9
3.1	3.3	2.9		7.1	7.7		2.6		2.7
(55) 5.1	(60) 5.3	(74) 6.7	% Depr., Dep., Amort./Sales	(14) 12.5	(14) 13.3		6.6		(21) 4.2
12.9	11.3	12.9		18.4	18.8		13.9		5.0
1.3	1.1	3.4	% Officers', Directors',						
(23) 2.2	(17) 3.8	(24) 6.2	Owners' Comp/Sales						
6.1	10.9	11.2							
1544464M	4998468M	4249972M	Net Sales ($)	8152M	27300M	23249M	93540M	127834M	3969897M
1093987M	3793874M	3338542M	Total Assets ($)	6431M	19814M	34694M	44653M	113060M	3119890M

M = $ thousand   MM = $ million
See Pages 11 through 18 for Explanation of Ratios and Data

Current Data Sorted By Assets   Comparative Historical Data

						Type of Statement		
	1	1	9	1	5	Unqualified		
1						Reviewed		
3						Compiled		
2		1	6	2	1	Tax Returns		
	1 (4/1-9/30/02)		32 (10/1/02-3/31/03)			Other	4/1/98-3/31/99	4/1/99-3/31/00
0-500M	500M-2MM	2-10MM	10-50MM	50-100MM	100-250MM		ALL	ALL
6	1	2	15	3	6	NUMBER OF STATEMENTS		
%	%	%	%	%	%	ASSETS	%	%
			17.7			Cash & Equivalents	D	D
			.7			Trade Receivables (net)	A	A
			.6			Inventory	T	T
			1.5			All Other Current	A	A
			20.5			Total Current		
			77.2			Fixed Assets (net)	N	N
			.9			Intangibles (net)	O	O
			1.4			All Other Non-Current	T	T
			100.0			Total		
						LIABILITIES	A	A
			5.3			Notes Payable-Short Term	V	V
			9.1			Cur. Mat.-L/T/D	A	A
			4.3			Trade Payables	I	I
			.0			Income Taxes Payable	L	L
			10.3			All Other Current	A	A
			29.0			Total Current	B	B
			43.9			Long Term Debt	L	L
			.0			Deferred Taxes	E	E
			3.3			All Other Non-Current		
			23.7			Net Worth		
			100.0			Total Liabilities & Net Worth		
						INCOME DATA		
			100.0			Net Sales		
						Gross Profit		
			69.3			Operating Expenses		
			30.7			Operating Profit		
			8.4			All Other Expenses (net)		
			22.3			Profit Before Taxes		
						RATIOS		
			1.1					
			.9			Current		
			.5					
			1.1					
			.8			Quick		
			.5					
			1 509.2					
			1 319.9			Sales/Receivables		
			2 149.2					
						Cost of Sales/Inventory		
						Cost of Sales/Payables		
			68.1					
			−64.6			Sales/Working Capital		
			−14.0					
			18.9					
			(14) 10.2			EBIT/Interest		
			3.1					
						Net Profit + Depr., Dep., Amort./Cur. Mat. L /T/D		
			1.6					
			2.3			Fixed/Worth		
			−419.0					
			1.0					
			2.0			Debt/Worth		
			−574.3					
			143.2					
			(11) 55.6			% Profit Before Taxes/Tangible Net Worth		
			42.3					
			46.5					
			31.6			% Profit Before Taxes/Total Assets		
			8.6					
			3.7					
			1.9			Sales/Net Fixed Assets		
			1.4					
			2.5					
			1.5			Sales/Total Assets		
			1.1					
			4.1					
			5.1			% Depr., Dep., Amort./Sales		
			7.4					
						% Officers', Directors', Owners' Comp/Sales		
7333M	24387M	19004M	558722M	531660M	1100682M	Net Sales ($)		
912M	1189M	11553M	371121M	174241M	712429M	Total Assets ($)		

© RMA 2003

M = $ thousand   MM = $ million
See Pages 11 through 18 for Explanation of Ratios and Data

Comparative Historical Data				Current Data Sorted By Sales					
		17	**Type of Statement** Unqualified					4	13
			Reviewed						
		1	Compiled	1					
		3	Tax Returns	2	1				
		12	Other	1	1		1	1	8
4/1/00-3/31/01 ALL	4/1/01-3/31/02 ALL	4/1/02-3/31/03 ALL		0-1MM	1 (4/1-9/30/02) 1-3MM	3-5MM	32 (10/1/02-3/31/03) 5-10MM	10-25MM	25MM & OVER
		33	**NUMBER OF STATEMENTS**	4	2		1	5	21
%	%	%	**ASSETS**	%	%	%	%	%	%
D	D	21.3	Cash & Equivalents			D			18.8
A	A	.6	Trade Receivables (net)			A			.7
T	T	1.1	Inventory			T			.7
A	A	1.9	All Other Current			A			1.6
		25.0	Total Current						21.8
N	N	62.8	Fixed Assets (net)			N			75.6
O	O	9.7	Intangibles (net)			O			.5
T	T	2.6	All Other Non-Current			T			2.0
		100.0	Total						100.0
A	A		**LIABILITIES**			A			
V	V	2.9	Notes Payable-Short Term			V			4.2
A	A	5.6	Cur. Mat.-L/T/D			A			5.8
I	I	4.3	Trade Payables			I			4.3
L	L	.0	Income Taxes Payable			L			.0
A	A	10.6	All Other Current			A			11.1
B	B	23.5	Total Current			B			25.4
L	L	36.0	Long Term Debt			L			33.9
E	E	.0	Deferred Taxes			E			.0
		1.7	All Other Non-Current						1.8
		38.7	Net Worth						38.9
		100.0	Total Liabilities & Net Worth						100.0
			INCOME DATA						
		100.0	Net Sales						100.0
			Gross Profit						
		69.5	Operating Expenses						62.7
		30.5	Operating Profit						37.3
		4.1	All Other Expenses (net)						4.9
		26.4	Profit Before Taxes						32.4
			RATIOS						
		1.7							1.5
		1.0	Current						1.0
		.7							.7
		1.5							1.3
		.9	Quick						.9
		.6							.6
	0	UND						0	845.8
	1	497.5	Sales/Receivables					1	414.9
	2	176.1						2	154.5
			Cost of Sales/Inventory						
			Cost of Sales/Payables						
		21.7							21.7
		164.0	Sales/Working Capital						999.8
		−42.6							−27.6
		32.1							41.8
	(28)	13.0	EBIT/Interest					(18)	16.4
		3.6							3.6
			Net Profit + Depr., Dep., Amort./Cur. Mat. L/T/D						
		.9							1.0
		1.8	Fixed/Worth						1.9
		NM							22.8
		.4							.4
		1.4	Debt/Worth						1.4
		−340.8							33.5
		228.9	% Profit Before Taxes/Tangible Net Worth						224.9
	(24)	92.5						(17)	99.6
		43.2							49.4
		75.9	% Profit Before Taxes/Total Assets						77.8
		43.5							48.6
		19.2							29.6
		5.0							3.9
		2.5	Sales/Net Fixed Assets						2.5
		1.5							1.5
		3.6							2.6
		1.8	Sales/Total Assets						1.8
		1.2							1.2
		3.4	% Depr., Dep., Amort./Sales						3.8
	(26)	4.7						(19)	4.6
		6.8							6.6
			% Officers', Directors', Owners' Comp/Sales						
		2241788M	Net Sales ($)	2450M	4883M		7539M	85386M	2141530M
		1271445M	Total Assets ($)	490M	422M		4495M	57500M	1208538M

M = $ thousand   MM = $ million
See Pages 11 through 18 for Explanation of Ratios and Data

Current Data Sorted By Assets   Comparative Historical Data

						Type of Statement		
4	19	151	95	10	4	Unqualified	284	284
6	29	89	17			Reviewed	138	119
18	71	62	4			Compiled	223	217
41	28	28	2	1	1	Tax Returns	91	67
26	64	144	63	3	3	Other	269	240
	201 (4/1-9/30/02)		782 (10/1/02-3/31/03)				4/1/98- 3/31/99	4/1/99- 3/31/00
0-500M	500M-2MM	2-10MM	10-50MM	50-100MM	100-250MM		ALL	ALL
95	211	474	181	14	8	NUMBER OF STATEMENTS	1005	927
%	%	%	%	%	%	ASSETS	%	%
21.1	6.7	5.6	6.0	14.2		Cash & Equivalents	7.2	7.8
5.3	6.0	5.4	3.7	7.5		Trade Receivables (net)	5.1	5.2
8.0	3.4	1.5	1.8	3.0		Inventory	2.5	2.8
1.9	1.4	1.4	1.3	2.1		All Other Current	1.5	1.6
36.3	17.5	13.9	12.9	26.8		Total Current	16.3	17.4
57.0	76.7	81.6	78.3	53.0		Fixed Assets (net)	76.0	74.4
1.8	1.9	.7	2.2	7.6		Intangibles (net)	1.8	2.0
4.8	3.9	3.7	6.6	12.7		All Other Non-Current	5.9	6.2
100.0	100.0	100.0	100.0	100.0		Total	100.0	100.0
						LIABILITIES		
9.4	6.3	2.3	1.1	.2		Notes Payable-Short Term	3.8	3.8
9.5	4.1	3.5	2.2	9.9		Cur. Mat.-L/T/D	4.2	3.5
6.8	3.9	2.5	2.0	4.3		Trade Payables	3.4	3.8
.0	.1	.1	.1	.0		Income Taxes Payable	.1	.1
18.3	10.2	7.7	7.7	17.2		All Other Current	8.4	12.7
44.0	24.5	16.1	13.2	31.7		Total Current	19.9	23.9
31.4	47.1	40.3	28.0	21.7		Long Term Debt	37.1	35.8
.0	.1	.2	.2	.0		Deferred Taxes	.1	.2
28.9	13.9	4.8	5.0	30.8		All Other Non-Current	6.9	7.5
−4.4	14.5	38.6	53.6	15.8		Net Worth	35.9	32.6
100.0	100.0	100.0	100.0	100.0		Total Liabilities & Net Worth	100.0	100.0
						INCOME DATA		
100.0	100.0	100.0	100.0	100.0		Net Sales	100.0	100.0
						Gross Profit		
99.5	94.9	98.1	100.3	100.9		Operating Expenses	96.1	96.1
.5	5.1	1.9	−.3	−.9		Operating Profit	3.9	3.9
.9	5.3	4.4	2.7	3.3		All Other Expenses (net)	3.2	1.3
−.4	−.2	−2.5	−3.0	−4.2		Profit Before Taxes	.7	2.5
						RATIOS		
3.2	1.7	1.6	1.8	5.0			1.9	1.8
.8	.8	1.0	1.0	1.1	Current	1.1	1.0
.3	.4	.5	.5	.6		.5	.5
2.2	1.4	1.3	1.4	2.5		1.6	1.5
.5	.5 (472)	.8	.7	1.0	Quick (997)	.8 (926)	.8
.2	.2	.4	.4	.4		.3	.3
0 UND	0 UND	3 109.0	14 26.4	8 43.4		1 564.7	1 362.0
0 UND	5 69.6	24 15.4	26 14.1	15 24.4	Sales/Receivables	19 19.6	19 19.0
3 107.8	29 12.4	39 9.3	42 8.7	56 6.5		38 9.5	38 9.5
						Cost of Sales/Inventory		
						Cost of Sales/Payables		
13.5	13.8	11.6	7.4	4.3		9.3	9.7
−40.4	−34.8	−238.7	−102.5	NM	Sales/Working Capital	86.7	186.3
−9.6	−7.9	−7.8	−5.7	−9.4		−8.6	−9.4
2.7	2.4	1.8	1.9			3.6	3.5
(67) 1.0	(179) 1.0	(404) .8	(142) .6		EBIT/Interest (785)	1.5 (746)	1.5
−1.6	.1	−.3	−1.2			.5	.3
	2.9	3.1	3.9		Net Profit + Depr., Dep.,	3.8	4.8
(23) 1.2	(48) 1.6	(25) 2.6		Amort./Cur. Mat. L /T/D (94)	2.3 (83)	2.3
.9	.5	1.5			1.3	1.3
.9	1.6	1.2	1.1	.8		1.1	1.1
2.3	2.8	2.0	1.5	1.3	Fixed/Worth	1.9	1.8
−3.1	−47.5	4.4	2.4	3.6		6.5	4.6
.8	.9	.5	.3	.6		.5	.5
3.7	2.5	1.4	.7	1.1	Debt/Worth	1.5	1.3
−4.7	−54.2	4.4	2.1	NM		7.8	5.2
30.0	14.2	4.9	4.9	21.4	% Profit Before Taxes/Tangible	14.4	14.7
(62) 4.3	(157) .9	(411) −.4	(170) −.3	(11) .3	Net Worth (842)	3.6 (785)	3.6
−8.8	−8.8	−7.9	−7.4	−7.6		−2.8	−3.4
10.3	4.6	2.0	2.3	2.2	% Profit Before Taxes/Total	5.8	5.8
1.0	.2	−.5	−.2	−2.0	Assets	1.5	1.3
−12.0	−4.1	−4.1	−3.6	−6.3		−2.1	−2.4
20.2	2.0	1.0	.8	6.0		1.4	1.5
4.6	1.1	.7	.5	.9	Sales/Net Fixed Assets	.8	.9
2.3	.7	.5	.3	.4		.5	.5
4.6	1.3	.8	.5	1.1		.9	1.0
2.5	.9	.6	.4	.5	Sales/Total Assets	.6	.7
1.4	.7	.4	.3	.3		.4	.5
2.7	5.9	8.1	8.1	3.2		6.5	5.9
(81) 5.1	(189) 8.9	(445) 10.4	(168) 11.8	(13) 7.1	% Depr., Dep., Amort./Sales (914)	9.2 (856)	8.9
8.1	12.5	13.3	14.9	15.6		12.4	12.0
4.4	3.7	4.9	1.6		% Officers', Directors',	4.5	4.1
(29) 6.9	(60) 8.2	(59) 8.2	(18) 4.1		Owners' Comp/Sales (163)	7.9 (154)	7.7
12.9	17.1	18.8	15.8			18.4	15.0
66811M	271486M	1455085M	1304434M	1563951M	1678896M	Net Sales ($)	4901522M	4946504M
22775M	263033M	2394120M	3289527M	981059M	1221458M	Total Assets ($)	6497196M	7449797M

© RMA 2003

M = $ thousand   MM = $ million
See Pages 11 through 18 for Explanation of Ratios and Data

	Comparative Historical Data			Type of Statement	Current Data Sorted By Sales					
	241	196	283	Unqualified	5	75	81	86	26	10
	115	101	141	Reviewed	22	71	36	11	1	
	220	239	155	Compiled	56	87	9	2	1	
	62	77	101	Tax Returns	63	28	6	2		2
	234	253	303	Other	63	118	64	38	15	5
	4/1/00-3/31/01 ALL	4/1/01-3/31/02 ALL	4/1/02-3/31/03 ALL		201 (4/1-9/30/02)			782 (10/1/02-3/31/03)		
					0-1MM	1-3MM	3-5MM	5-10MM	10-25MM	25MM & OVER
NUMBER OF STATEMENTS	872	866	983		209	379	196	139	43	17
ASSETS	%	%	%		%	%	%	%	%	%
Cash & Equivalents	7.6	7.5	7.6		11.0	6.6	6.3	6.4	7.9	13.0
Trade Receivables (net)	5.4	5.1	5.2		2.8	5.1	6.9	6.3	5.5	7.9
Inventory	2.8	2.6	2.6		3.3	2.6	1.9	1.5	7.1	2.9
All Other Current	2.5	3.8	1.4		1.8	1.3	1.2	1.4	1.9	1.5
Total Current	18.4	19.1	16.9		18.8	15.6	16.3	15.6	22.3	25.3
Fixed Assets (net)	73.8	74.3	76.9		75.5	79.1	79.7	75.5	67.0	48.2
Intangibles (net)	1.8	1.4	1.5		1.9	1.2	.5	2.2	3.0	6.9
All Other Non-Current	6.0	5.2	4.7		3.7	4.1	3.5	6.8	7.7	19.6
Total	100.0	100.0	100.0		100.0	100.0	100.0	100.0	100.0	100.0
LIABILITIES										
Notes Payable-Short Term	3.8	4.4	3.6		4.8	4.6	2.3	1.4	2.5	.2
Cur. Mat.-L/T/D	3.5	3.5	4.0		5.9	3.9	3.5	2.2	3.2	5.7
Trade Payables	3.9	4.1	3.2		2.8	3.3	3.4	2.6	4.0	5.1
Income Taxes Payable	.1	.1	.1		.1	.1	.1	.1	.1	.0
All Other Current	8.8	8.5	9.5		11.2	8.0	10.0	9.1	8.9	20.3
Total Current	20.0	20.7	20.3		24.8	19.9	19.3	15.5	18.7	31.3
Long Term Debt	35.6	38.1	38.3		45.9	42.1	35.3	26.4	24.5	27.6
Deferred Taxes	.1	.1	.1		.3	.1	.1	.0	.8	.2
All Other Non-Current	7.0	6.5	9.6		17.0	7.2	7.7	6.7	4.3	29.6
Net Worth	37.3	34.6	31.6		12.1	30.7	37.6	51.4	51.8	11.3
Total Liabilities & Net Worth	100.0	100.0	100.0		100.0	100.0	100.0	100.0	100.0	100.0
INCOME DATA										
Net Sales	100.0	100.0	100.0		100.0	100.0	100.0	100.0	100.0	100.0
Gross Profit										
Operating Expenses	96.7	96.1	97.9		95.5	97.8	100.4	99.3	97.7	92.7
Operating Profit	3.3	3.9	2.1		4.5	2.2	-.4	.7	2.3	7.3
All Other Expenses (net)	2.4	4.5	4.0		6.9	4.2	2.5	.8	3.9	4.6
Profit Before Taxes	.9	-.5	-1.9		-2.4	-2.0	-2.9	-.1	-1.6	2.8
RATIOS										
Current	1.9	2.0	1.7		2.5	1.6	1.6	1.7	1.6	1.9
	1.1	1.1	.9		.7	.9	1.0	1.1	1.1	1.3
	.5	.6	.5		.3	.4	.6	.7	.5	.7
Quick	1.5	1.5	1.4		1.6	1.3	1.4	1.4	1.1	1.9
	(871) .8	(865) .8	(981) .7		.5	(377) .6	.8	.9	.7	1.2
	.3	.3	.3		.1	.3	.4	.5	.3	.5
Sales/Receivables	1 282.5	1 398.1	1 378.2		0 UND	1 354.3	18 19.8	18 19.8	7 49.4	9 42.3
	19 19.1	19 19.2	18 19.7		0 UND	16 22.7	31 11.8	28 13.2	23 15.7	14 26.9
	38 9.6	38 9.7	37 10.0		7 54.3	35 10.3	44 8.4	41 9.0	49 7.5	36 10.2
Cost of Sales/Inventory										
Cost of Sales/Payables										
Sales/Working Capital	9.3	8.2	11.3		8.1	15.5	10.7	8.6	8.9	7.3
	94.5	69.3	-102.5		-29.9	-45.1	-126.6	82.1	82.9	16.7
	-10.6	-10.8	-7.8		-5.0	-7.7	-8.8	-11.6	-7.8	-13.2
EBIT/Interest	2.8	2.3	2.1		1.9	1.8	1.7	3.2	3.5	28.3
	(689) 1.2	(705) 1.0	(807) .9		(155) 1.0	(327) .8	(169) .6	(107) 1.2	(36) 1.3	(13) 1.8
	.2	-.2	-.4		.0	-.6	-.4	-.1	-.6	-.4
Net Profit + Depr., Dep., Amort./Cur. Mat. L/T/D	4.4	4.1	3.4		3.0	2.6	3.3	3.9		
	(82) 2.6	(82) 1.8	(98) 1.7		(11) 1.6	(40) 1.5	(18) 1.6	(19) 2.3		
	.9	1.0	1.0		.9	.7	.7	1.2		
Fixed/Worth	1.1	1.1	1.2		1.4	1.3	1.2	1.0	1.0	1.0
	1.7	1.8	2.0		2.9	2.2	1.8	1.5	1.3	1.4
	4.2	5.6	5.3		-12.3	5.4	3.4	2.8	2.1	-1.9
Debt/Worth	.5	.5	.5		.8	.7	.5	.3	.3	.7
	1.3	1.4	1.5		2.9	1.8	1.2	.8	.6	3.1
	4.5	6.0	6.0		-13.6	7.3	3.3	2.4	2.6	-5.7
% Profit Before Taxes/Tangible Net Worth	11.4	8.8	6.2		9.4	6.7	5.0	6.2	6.1	31.1
	(748) 2.2	(737) .3	(816) .2		(150) .6	(313) .2	(174) -.9	(127) .5	(41) 1.2	(11) -.5
	-5.9	-7.8	-7.9		-8.6	-9.2	-7.7	-4.8	-8.3	-3.2
% Profit Before Taxes/Total Assets	5.2	3.7	2.6		3.0	2.3	2.1	3.6	5.2	9.5
	.7	-.1	-.2		-.1	-.4	-1.0	.3	.6	-.4
	-3.1	-3.9	-4.2		-4.4	-4.3	-4.2	-2.9	-3.5	-3.4
Sales/Net Fixed Assets	1.5	1.4	1.3		2.3	1.4	1.0	1.0	1.3	15.5
	.9	.9	.8		.8	.8	.7	.8	.8	1.1
	.6	.5	.5		.4	.5	.5	.6	.5	.8
Sales/Total Assets	1.0	1.0	1.0		1.4	1.0	.8	.8	.8	1.4
	.7	.6	.6		.7	.7	.6	.6	.5	.8
	.5	.4	.4		.3	.4	.4	.4	.4	.5
% Depr., Dep., Amort./Sales	5.7	5.4	7.1		6.0	7.0	8.2	7.4	5.7	2.0
	(799) 8.8	(798) 8.8	(901) 9.9		(188) 10.5	(355) 9.9	(175) 10.5	(133) 9.3	(37) 8.5	(13) 6.7
	11.9	11.8	13.0		15.4	12.8	12.8	12.6	12.3	9.3
% Officers', Directors', Owners' Comp/Sales	4.5	4.4	3.9		5.5	3.7	3.2	1.7		
	(160) 8.6	(170) 7.7	(171) 8.0		(52) 8.5	(71) 6.3	(22) 10.1	(19) 3.8		
	18.9	15.7	16.4		18.3	15.5	26.6	13.9		
Net Sales ($)	4026247M	4081368M	6340663M		121682M	727250M	778473M	925309M	618366M	3169583M
Total Assets ($)	6385857M	5885675M	8171972M		265405M	1394540M	1593437M	1768255M	1315349M	1834986M

© RMA 2003

M = $ thousand   MM = $ million

See Pages 11 through 18 for Explanation of Ratios and Data

Current Data Sorted By Assets | **Comparative Historical Data**

Type of Statement	0-500M	500M-2MM	2-10MM	10-50MM	50-100MM	100-250MM		4/1/98-3/31/99 ALL	4/1/99-3/31/00 ALL
Unqualified			1					13	9
Reviewed	1	7	10	1				20	29
Compiled	5	10	16					51	40
Tax Returns	12	18	10	1				25	14
Other	1	11	20	6	1			36	42
	12 (4/1-9/30/02)			119 (10/1/02-3/31/03)					
NUMBER OF STATEMENTS	19	46	57	8	1			145	134

	0-500M %	500M-2MM %	2-10MM %	10-50MM %	50-100MM %	100-250MM %		ALL %	ALL %
ASSETS									
Cash & Equivalents	18.8	8.3	8.0					8.4	7.9
Trade Receivables (net)	10.0	8.7	4.7					4.9	6.8
Inventory	8.6	15.2	22.0					13.3	15.4
All Other Current	7.2	3.2	1.6					1.9	1.8
Total Current	44.6	35.4	36.4					28.5	31.9
Fixed Assets (net)	44.3	57.6	55.5					59.1	58.1
Intangibles (net)	1.7	4.7	4.2					4.0	2.6
All Other Non-Current	9.4	2.2	3.9					8.3	7.4
Total	100.0	100.0	100.0					100.0	100.0
LIABILITIES									
Notes Payable-Short Term	9.5	8.1	10.5					9.5	7.9
Cur. Mat.-L/T/D	6.2	5.1	7.2					4.2	3.9
Trade Payables	5.1	6.3	3.1					4.2	3.8
Income Taxes Payable	.5	.1	.3					.1	.4
All Other Current	22.7	13.6	12.0					13.3	11.6
Total Current	44.0	33.1	33.2					31.3	27.6
Long Term Debt	40.7	45.3	44.5					47.8	49.3
Deferred Taxes	.0	.1	.0					.6	.1
All Other Non-Current	14.3	7.8	6.7					8.9	8.9
Net Worth	1.0	13.7	15.5					11.5	14.1
Total Liabilities & Net Worth	100.0	100.0	100.0					100.0	100.0
INCOME DATA									
Net Sales	100.0	100.0	100.0					100.0	100.0
Gross Profit									
Operating Expenses	92.9	88.9	89.7					90.4	90.0
Operating Profit	7.1	11.1	10.3					9.6	10.0
All Other Expenses (net)	7.9	6.6	5.3					7.1	3.9
Profit Before Taxes	–.8	4.4	5.1					2.5	6.1

(Columns 10-50MM, 50-100MM, 100-250MM marked "DATA NOT AVAILABLE")

RATIOS	0-500M	500M-2MM	2-10MM					ALL 145	ALL 134
Current	2.0	2.6	2.6					2.3	2.3
	1.1	1.2	1.2					1.1	1.2
	.5	.5	.8					.6	.7
Quick	1.1	1.2	1.5					1.3	1.4
	.4	.6	.4					.5	.6
	.3	.2	.1					.1	.2
Sales/Receivables	0 UND	2 173.9	3 105.2					0 909.5	2 159.4
	5 66.5	16 22.2	12 29.6					7 55.0	12 30.2
	19 19.4	36 10.2	28 12.8					24 15.3	29 12.6
Cost of Sales/Inventory									
Cost of Sales/Payables									
Sales/Working Capital	14.6	8.2	6.2					8.7	7.7
	51.8	23.1	21.0					27.7	28.6
	–12.2	–5.5	–19.4					–11.4	–12.8
EBIT/Interest	(15) 8.0	(39) 4.5	(52) 2.8					(109) 3.2	(112) 4.1
	2.0	2.2	1.6					1.9	1.9
	.1	1.3	1.1					1.1	1.1
Net Profit + Depr., Dep., Amort./Cur. Mat. L/T/D		(10) 5.2						(17) 2.7	(16) 7.1
		2.0						1.4	2.6
		.8						.6	1.1
Fixed/Worth	.8	1.4	1.3					1.2	1.1
	7.3	7.9	3.7					3.5	3.1
	–3.8	–4.5	–8.2					–15.1	–13.5
Debt/Worth	1.7	1.6	1.9					1.2	1.2
	10.5	7.7	6.5					5.3	6.3
	–6.4	–7.7	–16.0					–22.0	–19.1
% Profit Before Taxes/Tangible Net Worth	(12) 82.5	(30) 73.1	(38) 32.8					(101) 38.4	(91) 37.0
	21.0	25.6	15.3					12.7	16.8
	3.9	11.3	2.5					1.8	3.7
% Profit Before Taxes/Total Assets	11.9	8.1	7.0					10.1	9.9
	5.8	4.3	2.7					3.6	3.2
	–4.6	1.0	.0					.1	.4
Sales/Net Fixed Assets	39.6	8.2	4.9					4.9	5.0
	4.4	1.7	1.3					1.5	1.4
	1.5	.8	.8					.5	.7
Sales/Total Assets	5.7	2.1	1.6					1.9	2.0
	2.0	1.0	.8					.8	.9
	.9	.6	.5					.4	.5
% Depr., Dep., Amort./Sales	(15) 1.6	(42) 2.4	(55) 2.1					(138) 2.4	(122) 2.6
	4.3	5.6	7.5					6.3	7.7
	10.2	12.3	12.3					12.9	13.0
% Officers', Directors', Owners' Comp/Sales		(17) 3.0	(19) 1.4					(54) 2.9	(50) 3.1
		5.9	3.9					6.3	6.8
		9.6	6.7					10.7	12.6

	0-500M	500M-2MM	2-10MM	10-50MM	50-100MM			ALL	ALL
Net Sales ($)	17127M	67835M	316435M	103708M	66346M			529145M	477116M
Total Assets ($)	4846M	49524M	283060M	108786M	98090M			449748M	399391M

© RMA 2003

M = $ thousand   MM = $ million
See Pages 11 through 18 for Explanation of Ratios and Data

Comparative Historical Data | Current Data Sorted By Sales

			Type of Statement						
7	3	1	Unqualified				1		
24	17	19	Reviewed	1	6	4	5	2	1
28	38	31	Compiled	9	11	6	2	3	
28	30	41	Tax Returns	20	12	6	1	1	1
45	42	39	Other	11	14	5	3	5	1
4/1/00-3/31/01 ALL	4/1/01-3/31/02 ALL	4/1/02-3/31/03 ALL		0-1MM	12 (4/1-9/30/02) 1-3MM	3-5MM	5-10MM	119 (10/1/02-3/31/03) 10-25MM	25MM & OVER
132	130	131	**NUMBER OF STATEMENTS**	41	43	21	12	11	3
%	%	%	**ASSETS**	%	%	%	%	%	%
8.6	7.1	9.8	Cash & Equivalents	8.8	12.0	12.1	4.6	4.6	
6.5	6.6	6.9	Trade Receivables (net)	7.1	6.9	6.8	8.9	5.0	
16.3	18.3	16.9	Inventory	4.9	9.9	26.5	42.6	47.4	
1.5	2.2	3.4	All Other Current	4.2	2.9	3.1	4.8	2.2	
32.8	34.3	37.0	Total Current	25.0	31.7	48.4	60.9	59.3	
55.5	57.8	54.9	Fixed Assets (net)	65.3	58.6	48.6	31.7	34.1	
3.7	2.6	3.9	Intangibles (net)	4.1	6.4	.5	2.2	2.1	
8.0	5.3	4.1	All Other Non-Current	5.6	3.3	2.5	5.2	4.5	
100.0	100.0	100.0	Total	100.0	100.0	100.0	100.0	100.0	
			LIABILITIES						
9.9	9.4	9.4	Notes Payable-Short Term	6.3	5.5	11.5	13.5	30.7	
2.9	5.1	6.0	Cur. Mat.-L/T/D	5.0	4.8	5.1	20.4	1.1	
5.0	4.1	4.5	Trade Payables	2.7	4.3	7.6	5.9	4.6	
.0	.1	.3	Income Taxes Payable	.3	.1	.7	.1	.2	
14.4	12.2	14.4	All Other Current	15.1	11.3	13.0	20.5	21.3	
32.3	30.8	34.5	Total Current	29.3	26.0	37.8	60.4	57.9	
43.5	40.9	44.0	Long Term Debt	54.1	48.2	34.0	29.1	21.8	
.1	.2	.1	Deferred Taxes	.1	.1	.0	.0	.0	
9.5	10.0	7.9	All Other Non-Current	6.8	5.9	16.6	8.0	4.2	
14.6	18.1	13.6	Net Worth	9.7	19.7	11.6	2.4	16.1	
100.0	100.0	100.0	Total Liabilities & Net Worth	100.0	100.0	100.0	100.0	100.0	
			INCOME DATA						
100.0	100.0	100.0	Net Sales	100.0	100.0	100.0	100.0	100.0	
			Gross Profit						
90.4	87.2	89.5	Operating Expenses	85.8	87.4	94.4	94.6	96.3	
9.6	12.8	10.5	Operating Profit	14.2	12.6	5.6	5.4	3.7	
5.1	6.5	6.2	All Other Expenses (net)	10.9	6.1	2.0	4.5	.5	
4.5	6.3	4.3	Profit Before Taxes	3.2	6.6	3.6	.9	3.2	
			RATIOS						
2.2	2.8	2.3		2.3	3.2	3.2	1.4	1.3	
1.2	1.3	1.2	Current	.9	1.4	1.6	1.0	1.0	
.6	.7	.7		.4	.8	1.1	.8	.7	
1.3	1.5	1.2		1.0	2.4	2.0	.5	.3	
.5	(129) .5	.4	Quick	.5	.7	.8	.2	.1	
.2	.2	.2		.2	.2	.2	.1	.0	
4 90.0	2 226.4	2 195.0		0 UND	2 207.6	6 59.2	6 57.5	2 195.0	
11 32.5	12 29.9	12 30.9	Sales/Receivables	12 31.1	14 25.5	11 34.6	17 21.4	8 46.1	
31 11.6	33 11.1	29 12.4		36 10.0	32 11.3	25 14.7	28 12.9	13 28.2	
			Cost of Sales/Inventory						
			Cost of Sales/Payables						
8.8	6.6	7.4		10.4	5.2	5.2	13.0	9.0	
25.4	21.9	27.0	Sales/Working Capital	−62.1	23.7	10.6	327.7	65.7	
−12.1	−12.7	−13.7		−3.7	−13.7	21.0	−47.2	−15.8	
3.7	4.3	4.4		4.5	4.9	8.7	1.7	2.5	
(111) 1.7	(115) 2.1	(114) 2.0	EBIT/Interest	(30) 2.0	(38) 2.4	(20) 2.6	1.4	1.6	
1.0	1.1	1.2		.1	1.5	1.2	1.3	1.0	
4.6	2.8	5.1	Net Profit + Depr., Dep.,						
(18) 3.0	(14) 1.4	(20) 2.0	Amort./Cur. Mat. L/T/D						
1.2	.1	.9							
1.2	1.3	1.3		2.0	1.3	1.3	1.1	.9	
3.3	3.2	5.0	Fixed/Worth	22.1	3.2	5.2	3.5	1.4	
−13.1	14.7	−8.8		−4.1	−8.8	NM	−2.2	14.3	
1.5	1.3	1.7		1.7	1.1	1.8	2.4	1.8	
4.9	5.2	7.4	Debt/Worth	25.8	4.1	5.9	33.7	6.5	
−22.9	115.9	−11.2		−6.4	−10.9	NM	−6.9	41.0	
43.2	44.1	38.8	% Profit Before Taxes/Tangible	45.8	37.2	61.2			
(91) 16.7	(99) 19.0	(87) 21.1	Net Worth	(24) 21.8	(29) 21.1	(16) 27.1			
2.9	3.0	8.2		8.7	9.3	3.3			
7.7	13.1	8.5	% Profit Before Taxes/Total	8.0	10.2	11.5	6.1	4.9	
3.0	3.5	3.4	Assets	3.1	4.4	3.1	2.6	2.4	
−.3	.3	.3		−3.3	.8	.5	.4	.0	
6.7	6.5	6.7		3.2	4.3	8.2	38.8	13.8	
1.7	1.6	1.7	Sales/Net Fixed Assets	1.0	1.2	3.1	7.4	6.3	
.7	.7	.8		.5	.8	.8	1.9	3.3	
2.0	2.0	1.9		1.4	1.5	2.4	3.2	2.7	
1.0	1.0	1.0	Sales/Total Assets	.8	.8	1.5	1.6	1.7	
.5	.5	.6		.3	.6	.5	1.2	1.3	
2.0	2.0	2.1		3.2	3.1	2.0	.5	1.0	
(124) 5.6	(120) 5.2	(121) 5.5	% Depr., Dep., Amort./Sales	(35) 8.6	(41) 7.7	(20) 2.8	(11) 1.5	2.1	
11.9	11.3	11.8		18.0	12.3	13.4	7.5	3.4	
2.8	3.2	2.6	% Officers', Directors',	3.3	3.3				
(46) 5.5	(44) 6.6	(50) 4.0	Owners' Comp/Sales	(12) 6.6	(18) 4.9				
13.0	14.2	8.1		13.1	9.0				
408858M	1417814M	571451M	Net Sales ($)	21395M	85851M	79148M	85922M	166804M	132331M
424109M	1076128M	544306M	Total Assets ($)	41488M	137755M	88166M	54087M	100000M	122810M

© RMA 2003

M = $ thousand   MM = $ million

See Pages 11 through 18 for Explanation of Ratios and Data

Current Data Sorted By Assets   Comparative Historical Data

						Type of Statement		
1	2	20	20	2	1	Unqualified	29	36
3	6	16	5			Reviewed	20	9
16	21	17	3	1		Compiled	63	31
47	26	6				Tax Returns	37	33
28	22	33	16	1	1	Other	50	68
	42 (4/1-9/30/02)		272 (10/1/02-3/31/03)				4/1/98-3/31/99	4/1/99-3/31/00
0-500M	500M-2MM	2-10MM	10-50MM	50-100MM	100-250MM		ALL	ALL
95	77	92	44	4	2	NUMBER OF STATEMENTS	199	177
%	%	%	%	%	%	ASSETS	%	%
20.4	9.9	8.8	7.7			Cash & Equivalents	11.5	10.8
4.0	3.8	3.6	5.1			Trade Receivables (net)	2.9	5.5
3.0	2.8	.5	2.1			Inventory	1.7	1.8
1.3	3.3	2.2	2.2			All Other Current	1.9	1.7
28.7	19.8	15.1	17.1			Total Current	18.1	19.8
55.6	66.1	73.5	69.1			Fixed Assets (net)	69.2	66.4
7.5	4.5	1.9	4.3			Intangibles (net)	5.0	5.6
8.1	9.6	9.4	9.5			All Other Non-Current	7.7	8.3
100.0	100.0	100.0	100.0			Total	100.0	100.0
						LIABILITIES		
12.3	5.0	1.6	2.0			Notes Payable-Short Term	5.6	3.0
4.8	5.8	2.8	3.0			Cur. Mat.-L/T/D	5.1	5.6
7.7	5.3	3.4	3.7			Trade Payables	3.9	4.2
.1	.2	.1	.8			Income Taxes Payable	.2	.3
19.2	12.8	5.9	5.8			All Other Current	14.4	10.2
44.1	29.2	13.8	15.3			Total Current	29.1	23.4
42.6	37.8	41.2	41.1			Long Term Debt	39.1	39.7
.0	.0	.1	.3			Deferred Taxes	.4	.0
12.5	8.9	7.0	6.9			All Other Non-Current	10.1	10.0
.8	24.1	37.9	36.5			Net Worth	21.3	26.8
100.0	100.0	100.0	100.0			Total Liabilities & Net Worth	100.0	100.0
						INCOME DATA		
100.0	100.0	100.0	100.0			Net Sales	100.0	100.0
						Gross Profit		
94.1	90.7	88.5	92.2			Operating Expenses	92.9	90.7
5.9	9.3	11.5	7.8			Operating Profit	7.1	9.3
3.2	3.7	6.4	3.8			All Other Expenses (net)	−.7	4.1
2.8	5.6	5.1	4.0			Profit Before Taxes	7.7	5.2
						RATIOS		
3.3	1.9	2.8	1.7				1.3	1.7
1.0	.7	1.1	.9			Current	.5	.7
.2	.2	.5	.4				.2	.4
2.4	1.2	2.4	1.4				1.1	1.4
.7	(75) .4	.8	.7			Quick	(195) .4	(175) .6
.1	.1	.4	.3				.1	.2
0 UND	0 UND	0 UND	6 65.4				0 UND	0 UND
0 UND	0 UND	3 134.0	11 32.1			Sales/Receivables	0 UND	3 111.3
0 UND	7 53.0	18 20.7	28 13.0				5 69.2	17 21.7
						Cost of Sales/Inventory		
						Cost of Sales/Payables		
14.7	16.5	8.1	6.3				48.8	14.8
−496.5	−23.8	NM	−58.5			Sales/Working Capital	−18.5	−27.4
−8.2	−7.2	−10.9	−8.8				−6.6	−8.9
11.8	7.1	5.6	5.8				6.2	5.2
(74) 3.0	(66) 1.8	(77) 2.4	(41) 1.8			EBIT/Interest	(158) 2.6	(150) 2.4
.0	.8	.9	.6				1.2	.9
						Net Profit + Depr., Dep.,	5.7	5.4
						Amort./Cur. Mat. L /T/D	(24) 1.8 (16)	2.8
							1.1	1.5
.9	1.2	1.2	1.1				1.2	1.1
12.1	3.3	2.2	2.1			Fixed/Worth	3.0	2.8
−1.5	238.7	5.6	4.5				58.2	15.2
.9	1.0	.6	.7				.9	.8
17.0	3.1	2.0	1.9			Debt/Worth	3.1	2.5
−3.3	405.2	5.7	5.6				79.0	22.1
87.3	73.5	31.6	11.3			% Profit Before Taxes/Tangible	73.2	58.1
(51) 23.5	(60) 29.9	(83) 12.1	(37) 4.0			Net Worth	(153) 20.2	(140) 18.5
5.4	1.8	−2.7	−2.1				5.9	3.7
25.7	18.5	10.7	5.4			% Profit Before Taxes/Total	16.9	16.9
6.5	4.6	3.4	1.7			Assets	6.1	4.2
−7.8	−.3	−1.0	−.7				1.0	−.5
11.5	4.7	1.7	1.7				4.2	4.4
5.9	2.6	.9	.9			Sales/Net Fixed Assets	1.8	1.4
2.6	1.5	.6	.5				.8	.6
4.7	2.5	1.1	1.0				2.5	2.1
2.8	1.5	.6	.6			Sales/Total Assets	1.2	.9
1.8	.9	.4	.4				.6	.5
3.4	3.9	5.3	5.3				4.2	5.2
(78) 5.5	(70) 6.0	(86) 8.0	(43) 8.0			% Depr., Dep., Amort./Sales	(172) 6.1	(160) 7.6
9.1	12.0	13.0	9.4				8.8	10.4
4.8	3.6	2.7					4.0	3.4
(40) 9.0	(34) 5.9	(21) 5.6				% Officers', Directors',	(45) 8.6	(41) 5.4
17.3	10.9	7.8				Owners' Comp/Sales	17.7	10.0
71400M	184621M	375101M	704672M	171661M	432904M	Net Sales ($)	1099085M	1188506M
21170M	83091M	440003M	879814M	270069M	270357M	Total Assets ($)	1169769M	1290738M

M = $ thousand   MM = $ million
See Pages 11 through 18 for Explanation of Ratios and Data

Comparative Historical Data — **Current Data Sorted By Sales**

32	30	46	Type of Statement						
32	30	46	Unqualified	1	10	9	9	12	5
29	19	30	Reviewed	5	9	6	8	2	
33	51	58	Compiled	23	17	7	7	1	3
35	50	79	Tax Returns	51	24	2	2		
48	63	101	Other	29	27	19	11	9	6
4/1/00-3/31/01 ALL	4/1/01-3/31/02 ALL	4/1/02-3/31/03 ALL		42 (4/1-9/30/02)		272 (10/1/02-3/31/03)			
				0-1MM	1-3MM	3-5MM	5-10MM	10-25MM	25MM & OVER
177	213	314	**NUMBER OF STATEMENTS**	109	87	43	37	24	14
%	%	%	**ASSETS**	%	%	%	%	%	%
10.7	10.7	12.4	Cash & Equivalents	12.9	15.0	9.3	11.1	11.0	7.7
4.9	3.3	3.9	Trade Receivables (net)	3.6	3.5	4.1	3.0	7.4	5.1
1.5	1.1	2.0	Inventory	1.9	1.6	2.1	3.0	1.4	4.5
3.5	2.5	2.2	All Other Current	1.8	2.2	1.6	1.8	6.4	1.8
20.7	17.5	20.6	Total Current	20.2	22.3	17.1	19.0	26.2	19.0
65.1	67.8	65.5	Fixed Assets (net)	64.2	65.4	72.6	65.3	64.4	56.5
6.1	6.5	4.6	Intangibles (net)	7.3	2.8	1.6	4.5	2.0	9.0
8.1	8.1	9.3	All Other Non-Current	8.4	9.5	8.7	11.2	7.4	15.5
100.0	100.0	100.0	Total	100.0	100.0	100.0	100.0	100.0	100.0
			LIABILITIES						
2.5	4.4	5.8	Notes Payable-Short Term	9.6	5.7	2.4	1.6	2.8	3.2
4.8	4.6	4.2	Cur. Mat.-L/T/D	5.4	4.0	3.2	2.8	3.6	3.6
4.9	3.9	5.2	Trade Payables	4.3	6.0	4.2	5.1	7.4	7.6
.1	.4	.2	Income Taxes Payable	.0	.1	.4	.2	.8	.9
10.1	11.5	11.6	All Other Current	17.7	8.5	5.5	11.3	6.8	10.1
22.6	24.8	27.0	Total Current	37.0	24.3	15.7	21.0	21.4	25.3
39.3	40.5	40.8	Long Term Debt	49.9	35.8	41.4	35.1	22.3	46.5
.0	.1	.1	Deferred Taxes	.0	.1	.2	.0	.1	.8
10.4	6.9	9.2	All Other Non-Current	13.1	7.3	5.6	7.4	5.2	13.8
27.7	27.7	22.9	Net Worth	.0	32.5	37.0	36.6	51.0	13.6
100.0	100.0	100.0	Total Liabilities & Net Worth	100.0	100.0	100.0	100.0	100.0	100.0
			INCOME DATA						
100.0	100.0	100.0	Net Sales	100.0	100.0	100.0	100.0	100.0	100.0
			Gross Profit						
88.6	90.3	91.1	Operating Expenses	90.7	91.4	93.2	90.0	90.8	89.2
11.4	9.7	8.9	Operating Profit	9.3	8.6	6.8	10.0	9.2	10.8
4.5	4.6	4.4	All Other Expenses (net)	6.3	3.6	3.5	3.7	1.3	4.2
6.9	5.1	4.5	Profit Before Taxes	3.0	5.1	3.3	6.4	7.9	6.6
			RATIOS						
1.8 / .8 / .4	1.7 / .7 / .2	2.4 / .9 / .3	Current	2.9 / .8 / .1	2.6 / 1.0 / .3	2.1 / .8 / .5	2.1 / .9 / .4	1.6 / 1.2 / .8	1.5 / .7 / .3
(176) 1.4 / .7 / .3	1.4 / .5 / .1	(312) 1.9 / .7 / .2	Quick	(107) 2.4 / .6 / .1	2.3 / .8 / .2	1.7 / .6 / .4	1.4 / .6 / .3	1.5 / .9 / .4	1.0 / .5 / .2
0 UND / 3 142.2 / 16 23.1	0 UND / 0 UND / 8 44.5	0 UND / 1 503.2 / 11 33.3	Sales/Receivables	0 UND / 0 UND / 1 727.5	0 UND / 0 UND / 8 46.8	0 UND / 5 70.1 / 23 16.1	1 576.6 / 4 81.1 / 18 20.6	8 44.4 / 11 34.0 / 20 18.4	3 118.5 / 6 56.5 / 19 19.0
			Cost of Sales/Inventory						
			Cost of Sales/Payables						
15.3 / -60.7 / -9.9	21.4 / -37.8 / -8.3	12.8 / -108.4 / -9.2	Sales/Working Capital	13.9 / -48.9 / -4.8	13.1 / UND / -11.3	10.0 / -41.0 / -11.7	12.3 / -58.5 / -10.8	5.4 / 62.5 / -28.5	31.7 / -18.0 / -7.6
(140) 6.6 / 2.6 / 1.2	(178) 6.3 / 2.3 / 1.0	(264) 6.7 / 2.2 / .8	EBIT/Interest	(86) 4.8 / 1.7 / -.1	(70) 8.7 / 2.5 / .9	(38) 4.7 / 1.9 / .6	(34) 7.6 / 2.4 / 1.7	(22) 14.3 / 4.8 / 1.3	12.2 / 2.9 / .6
(15) 5.7 / 3.4 / 2.3	(15) 4.7 / 2.2 / .9	(25) 4.5 / 2.9 / 2.0	Net Profit + Depr., Dep., Amort./Cur. Mat. L/T/D						
1.1 / 2.6 / 14.5	1.1 / 2.8 / 12.8	1.1 / 2.7 / 295.5	Fixed/Worth	1.5 / 12.1 / -2.5	.9 / 2.2 / 9.9	1.4 / 2.0 / 4.2	1.2 / 2.4 / 6.2	.8 / 1.2 / 2.7	1.0 / 2.7 / -6.3
.8 / 2.5 / 30.3	.8 / 2.8 / 29.1	.9 / 2.9 / NM	Debt/Worth	1.2 / 31.1 / -4.2	.6 / 1.9 / 9.5	1.1 / 1.9 / 4.7	.7 / 2.9 / 5.6	.4 / 1.2 / 2.6	1.6 / 8.2 / -7.1
(139) 66.7 / 19.9 / 4.0	(166) 58.1 / 21.2 / 2.2	(236) 62.4 / 15.0 / .6	% Profit Before Taxes/Tangible Net Worth	(61) 61.4 / 12.4 / -2.1	(71) 74.0 / 19.0 / .5	(39) 31.6 / 9.1 / -3.5	(34) 71.6 / 20.6 / 2.5	(23) 69.2 / 8.4 / 2.2	
15.6 / 4.5 / .4	17.3 / 5.0 / -.1	15.4 / 3.9 / -1.4	% Profit Before Taxes/Total Assets	15.1 / 3.4 / -7.9	17.9 / 4.6 / -.3	11.1 / 3.0 / -1.0	12.0 / 5.0 / .8	17.9 / 3.9 / .9	12.8 / 4.9 / -1.5
5.0 / 1.5 / .7	4.8 / 1.9 / .8	5.4 / 2.0 / .8	Sales/Net Fixed Assets	7.1 / 2.9 / .9	5.4 / 2.2 / .8	2.5 / 1.2 / .6	5.7 / 1.3 / .7	2.4 / 1.6 / 1.1	11.4 / 2.7 / 1.0
2.5 / 1.0 / .5	2.6 / 1.2 / .6	2.5 / 1.3 / .6	Sales/Total Assets	2.9 / 1.5 / .7	2.8 / 1.5 / .6	1.5 / .9 / .5	1.9 / 1.0 / .5	1.7 / 1.0 / .8	2.2 / 1.6 / .7
(158) 3.5 / 6.3 / 9.6	(194) 3.7 / 6.4 / 9.0	(281) 4.2 / 7.1 / 10.6	% Depr., Dep., Amort./Sales	(98) 4.3 / 8.4 / 14.2	(73) 4.0 / 6.9 / 10.3	(39) 4.6 / 6.9 / 8.8	(36) 5.0 / 7.7 / 9.3	3.8 / 5.5 / 8.1	(11) 1.8 / 5.3 / 6.7
(51) 3.7 / 6.4 / 9.9	(72) 4.2 / 6.6 / 13.0	(102) 3.5 / 7.1 / 13.2	% Officers', Directors', Owners' Comp/Sales	(38) 5.9 / 11.4 / 17.0	(36) 3.9 / 8.9	(11) 2.3 / 5.6 / 10.9	(12) .9 / 3.4 / 5.7		
1890227M	1145759M	1940359M	Net Sales ($)	55220M	147691M	166319M	258948M	368758M	943423M
1719439M	1447255M	1964504M	Total Assets ($)	73087M	174487M	243372M	350438M	380568M	742552M

M = $ thousand   MM = $ million
See Pages 11 through 18 for Explanation of Ratios and Data

Current Data Sorted By Assets | Comparative Historical Data

Type of Statement	0-500M	500M-2MM	2-10MM	10-50MM	50-100MM	100-250MM		4/1/98-3/31/99 ALL	4/1/99-3/31/00 ALL
Unqualified			1	1	1	1		9	2
Reviewed	3	10	7	1				11	15
Compiled	17	18	15					68	62
Tax Returns	11	16	7		1			35	32
Other	10	8	6	1				31	22
		30 (4/1-9/30/02)		103 (10/1/02-3/31/03)					
NUMBER OF STATEMENTS	41	52	36	3	1			154	133
ASSETS	%	%	%	%	%	%		%	%
Cash & Equivalents	20.7	9.7	6.8					11.7	10.2
Trade Receivables (net)	2.5	.5	1.0					1.9	1.1
Inventory	5.5	2.2	2.7					4.0	4.2
All Other Current	2.3	1.5	1.5					1.6	2.9
Total Current	31.1	14.0	12.0					19.2	18.4
Fixed Assets (net)	55.7	73.3	81.9					68.2	66.7
Intangibles (net)	6.2	4.9	3.0					4.0	7.1
All Other Non-Current	7.1	7.8	3.2					8.6	7.8
Total	100.0	100.0	100.0					100.0	100.0
LIABILITIES									
Notes Payable-Short Term	13.2	3.0	3.5					7.6	7.6
Cur. Mat.-L/T/D	8.0	7.1	5.3					8.5	6.3
Trade Payables	9.5	2.6	3.8					4.6	5.4
Income Taxes Payable	.3	.0	.0					.6	.3
All Other Current	33.3	19.9	8.5					10.1	13.4
Total Current	64.3	32.6	21.2					31.4	33.0
Long Term Debt	85.0	76.5	67.6					59.7	69.7
Deferred Taxes	.2	.1	.3					.5	.2
All Other Non-Current	29.3	4.2	5.5					13.6	11.0
Net Worth	-78.6	-13.4	5.4					-5.1	-14.0
Total Liabilities & Net Worth	100.0	100.0	100.0					100.0	100.0
INCOME DATA									
Net Sales	100.0	100.0	100.0					100.0	100.0
Gross Profit									
Operating Expenses	95.2	91.9	88.5					92.7	90.8
Operating Profit	4.8	8.1	11.5					7.3	9.2
All Other Expenses (net)	3.4	5.7	8.5					4.3	5.3
Profit Before Taxes	1.4	2.4	3.0					3.0	3.9
RATIOS									
Current	2.4	1.1	1.2					1.7	1.5
	.5	.5	.5					.6	.6
	.2	.1	.3					.2	.2
Quick	2.0	.9	.9					1.3	1.1
	(40) .3	(51) .3	.4					(151) .4	(131) .4
	.1	.1	.1					.1	.1
Sales/Receivables	0 UND	0 UND	0 UND					0 UND	0 UND
	0 UND	0 UND	0 UND					0 UND	0 UND
	1 255.7	1 350.1	2 200.8					1 299.2	1 337.8
Cost of Sales/Inventory									
Cost of Sales/Payables									
Sales/Working Capital	13.3	80.3	44.4					24.9	21.3
	-22.8	-15.9	-13.7					-21.8	-22.0
	-6.7	-5.0	-4.6					-5.5	-6.0
EBIT/Interest	2.4	3.0	2.6					3.2	3.5
	(29) 1.3	(47) 1.3	(31) 1.4					(132) 1.6	(115) 1.6
	-.4	.6	.9					1.0	.9
Net Profit + Depr., Dep., Amort./Cur. Mat. L/T/D								3.2	10.2
								(23) 1.4	(11) 3.3
								1.0	2.5
Fixed/Worth	.9	3.8	3.5					1.6	3.1
	-6.1	-7.0	18.0					9.5	31.1
	-.5	-2.0	-6.9					-2.9	-1.5
Debt/Worth	1.6	4.1	3.2					1.6	2.8
	-5.8	-9.7	21.2					10.4	30.9
	-1.7	-3.4	-9.5					-4.7	-3.2
% Profit Before Taxes/Tangible Net Worth	35.3	64.3	68.3					38.0	86.6
	(18) 14.0	(22) 20.4	(22) 13.7					(85) 19.2	(70) 29.1
	-1.5	1.7	-.4					2.5	6.2
% Profit Before Taxes/Total Assets	14.0	9.8	8.2					10.8	12.2
	4.8	.9	2.4					3.3	4.6
	-9.2	-3.8	-1.1					-2.5	-1.2
Sales/Net Fixed Assets	12.2	3.0	1.6					4.0	4.4
	4.7	1.5	.9					1.9	1.8
	2.3	1.1	.5					1.0	1.1
Sales/Total Assets	4.4	1.9	1.1					2.1	2.1
	2.3	1.2	.7					1.3	1.2
	1.7	.8	.5					.8	.9
% Depr., Dep., Amort./Sales	2.6	4.4	7.7					4.7	4.9
	(35) 5.2	(51) 8.0	(34) 10.6					(148) 7.8	(127) 7.7
	7.5	11.7	13.7					11.6	11.7
% Officers', Directors', Owners' Comp/Sales	3.1	4.9	3.4					4.4	5.1
	(16) 6.1	(19) 6.8	(11) 5.4					(66) 7.2	(53) 7.5
	14.6	12.5	8.9					10.6	10.5
Net Sales ($)	27874M	81409M	119333M	35444M	160727M			644605M	534348M
Total Assets ($)	10167M	62193M	131490M	59703M	86138M			447555M	325356M

M = $ thousand MM = $ million
See Pages 11 through 18 for Explanation of Ratios and Data

Comparative Historical Data | Current Data Sorted By Sales

			Type of Statement						
3	1	3	Unqualified					2	1
15	18	21	Reviewed	4	10	5	2	2	
53	44	50	Compiled	19	25	3	3		
33	24	34	Tax Returns	20	10	4			
15	28	25	Other	10	12	1		2	
4/1/00- 3/31/01	4/1/01- 3/31/02	4/1/02- 3/31/03		30 (4/1-9/30/02)			103 (10/1/02-3/31/03)		
ALL	ALL	ALL		0-1MM	1-3MM	3-5MM	5-10MM	10-25MM	25MM & OVER
119	115	133	**NUMBER OF STATEMENTS**	53	57	13	5	4	1
%	%	%	**ASSETS**	%	%	%	%	%	%
12.2	10.9	12.3	Cash & Equivalents	16.4	9.8	6.6			
2.2	2.7	1.3	Trade Receivables (net)	1.9	.6	.6			
3.6	4.3	3.4	Inventory	3.7	2.7	1.5			
2.3	1.5	2.0	All Other Current	1.9	1.9	.2			
20.1	19.3	19.0	Total Current	23.9	15.1	8.9			
64.3	63.3	70.3	Fixed Assets (net)	64.6	74.0	80.5			
5.1	4.6	4.6	Intangibles (net)	5.7	3.9	5.7			
10.4	12.8	6.1	All Other Non-Current	5.7	7.0	4.9			
100.0	100.0	100.0	Total	100.0	100.0	100.0			
			LIABILITIES						
8.7	9.5	6.2	Notes Payable-Short Term	9.7	3.6	8.1			
4.7	4.7	6.8	Cur. Mat.-L/T/D	7.9	6.6	4.2			
6.8	6.8	5.0	Trade Payables	6.3	3.9	4.0			
.1	.0	.1	Income Taxes Payable	.2	.0	.0			
16.9	13.1	20.6	All Other Current	24.2	17.2	23.9			
37.3	34.1	38.7	Total Current	48.2	31.4	40.2			
65.2	54.3	75.8	Long Term Debt	82.3	79.8	42.0			
.2	.3	.2	Deferred Taxes	.2	.1	.2			
11.3	20.0	12.4	All Other Non-Current	24.1	3.3	11.6			
−14.0	−8.7	−27.1	Net Worth	−54.8	−14.6	6.1			
100.0	100.0	100.0	Total Liabilities & Net Worth	100.0	100.0	100.0			
			INCOME DATA						
100.0	100.0	100.0	Net Sales	100.0	100.0	100.0			
			Gross Profit						
92.0	93.7	91.9	Operating Expenses	92.6	91.2	93.8			
8.0	6.3	8.1	Operating Profit	7.4	8.8	6.2			
4.2	3.5	5.7	All Other Expenses (net)	6.4	5.7	4.8			
3.8	2.8	2.4	Profit Before Taxes	1.0	3.1	1.4			
			RATIOS						
1.5	1.4	1.4		2.3	1.1	.7			
.7	.6	.5	Current	.5	.5	.3			
.2	.2	.2		.2	.2	.1			
1.1	1.0	.9		1.6	.9	.6			
(118) .5	(114) .3	(131) .3	Quick	.3	(55) .3	.2			
.1	.1	.1		.1	.1	.0			
0 UND	0 UND	0 UND		0 UND	0 UND	0 UND			
0 UND	0 UND	0 UND	Sales/Receivables	0 UND	0 999.8	0 854.5			
1 257.8	1 290.5	1 265.5		0 762.0	1 261.3	2 193.4			
			Cost of Sales/Inventory						
			Cost of Sales/Payables						
23.8	29.0	30.0		10.6	54.4	−30.1			
−29.2	−15.1	−20.6	Sales/Working Capital	−19.7	−23.8	−7.5			
−6.1	−5.7	−5.5		−3.8	−5.6	−2.8			
3.2	2.9	2.6		1.6	3.0	1.4			
(108) 1.5	(104) 1.6	(111) 1.3	EBIT/Interest	(34) .9	(55) 1.6	(12) 1.0			
.7	.6	.6		.1	.6	.7			
5.2	3.1	3.7	Net Profit + Depr., Dep.,						
(16) 2.5	(17) 1.7	(16) 1.8	Amort./Cur. Mat. L/T/D						
1.7	1.0	1.2							
2.0	1.8	2.6		2.2	2.5	4.9			
−155.6	999.8	62.7	Fixed/Worth	−8.5	62.7	−42.6			
−1.8	−2.2	−2.1		−1.2	−2.5	−9.7			
2.1	2.0	2.7		2.4	1.9	5.0			
−104.7	−170.0	−66.0	Debt/Worth	−7.5	66.3	−46.5			
−3.1	−4.0	−3.2		−2.2	−4.2	−12.9			
58.6	52.7	60.7	% Profit Before Taxes/Tangible	38.4	69.8				
(58) 13.0	(57) 11.4	(66) 14.4	Net Worth	(23) 14.1	(29) 20.0				
−3.4	−.1	.6		−.6	4.4				
11.8	10.2	10.7	% Profit Before Taxes/Total	11.5	10.2	3.3			
3.7	3.7	2.2	Assets	2.0	2.8	.1			
−1.9	−2.8	−2.1		−4.9	−3.8	−1.6			
6.5	5.5	4.1		5.4	3.2	2.0			
2.2	2.6	1.8	Sales/Net Fixed Assets	2.1	1.5	1.5			
1.2	1.1	.9		.9	.9	1.0			
2.6	2.4	2.1		2.5	2.0	1.7			
1.4	1.4	1.3	Sales/Total Assets	1.5	1.2	1.1			
.9	.8	.8		.7	.8	.8			
3.9	3.3	4.4		5.2	4.3	5.9			
(115) 6.6	(110) 6.9	(124) 7.6	% Depr., Dep., Amort./Sales	(47) 7.6	(54) 7.6	8.1			
9.9	9.9	11.8		13.5	11.8	11.4			
4.3	3.9	4.6	% Officers', Directors',	5.2	2.6				
(48) 8.3	(49) 6.1	(48) 6.1	Owners' Comp/Sales	(18) 7.7	(18) 6.3				
12.1	9.8	11.6		15.6	12.0				
210654M	348449M	424787M	Net Sales ($)	29847M	95845M	48797M	32530M	57041M	160727M
186674M	247844M	349691M	Total Assets ($)	35798M	92825M	49980M	25418M	59532M	86138M

© RMA 2003
M = $ thousand MM = $ million
See Pages 11 through 18 for Explanation of Ratios and Data

Current Data Sorted By Assets							Comparative Historical Data		

Type of Statement

							Type of Statement		
2	8	26	17	5	9		Unqualified	73	55
3	6	15	5				Reviewed	35	25
10	20	9			1		Compiled	40	38
44	14	3		1			Tax Returns	27	29
18	18	25	10	4	3		Other	90	73
	54 (4/1-9/30/02)		222 (10/1/02-3/31/03)					4/1/98- 3/31/99	4/1/99- 3/31/00
0-500M	500M-2MM	2-10MM	10-50MM	50-100MM	100-250MM			ALL	ALL
77	66	78	32	10	13		NUMBER OF STATEMENTS	265	220
%	%	%	%	%	%		ASSETS	%	%
20.0	11.2	9.2	12.2	8.0	8.3		Cash & Equivalents	11.6	10.7
5.0	2.9	5.2	6.8	6.4	2.0		Trade Receivables (net)	3.6	4.6
6.5	6.0	5.2	6.4	2.0	1.2		Inventory	4.3	4.9
3.5	1.2	2.3	4.6	3.0	2.9		All Other Current	2.3	2.2
35.0	21.3	21.9	30.0	19.5	14.5		Total Current	21.8	22.5
48.8	64.5	71.6	57.7	55.4	68.1		Fixed Assets (net)	62.5	65.8
5.2	2.8	1.4	2.5	1.4	1.4		Intangibles (net)	4.3	2.5
10.9	11.4	5.1	9.8	23.8	16.0		All Other Non-Current	11.4	9.2
100.0	100.0	100.0	100.0	100.0	100.0		Total	100.0	100.0
							LIABILITIES		
20.2	4.9	3.8	2.4	40.4	1.4		Notes Payable-Short Term	5.8	11.2
5.4	3.6	4.3	2.7	.4	5.0		Cur. Mat.-L/T/D	4.3	5.0
9.6	6.0	3.8	5.4	7.4	4.2		Trade Payables	5.9	5.8
.1	.1	.0	.6	1.0	.2		Income Taxes Payable	.2	.5
21.3	8.0	8.2	8.3	21.7	12.4		All Other Current	13.0	11.2
56.7	22.5	20.1	19.4	70.9	23.2		Total Current	29.1	33.7
36.6	39.3	40.1	17.9	25.6	31.0		Long Term Debt	30.1	29.7
.1	.0	.3	.6	.4	.2		Deferred Taxes	.8	.3
29.3	14.6	6.2	3.3	2.0	9.5		All Other Non-Current	12.7	9.0
-22.7	23.5	33.2	58.7	1.2	36.0		Net Worth	27.2	27.2
100.0	100.0	100.0	100.0	100.0	100.0		Total Liabilities & Net Worth	100.0	100.0
							INCOME DATA		
100.0	100.0	100.0	100.0	100.0	100.0		Net Sales	100.0	100.0
							Gross Profit		
95.2	91.3	90.6	89.4	87.6	78.5		Operating Expenses	94.6	92.0
4.8	8.7	9.4	10.6	12.4	21.5		Operating Profit	5.4	8.0
1.9	3.8	7.7	2.9	3.1	4.9		All Other Expenses (net)	5.3	3.9
2.9	5.0	1.8	7.7	9.3	16.6		Profit Before Taxes	.1	4.1
							RATIOS		
2.0	3.5	1.9	2.8	1.8	1.3			2.1	1.8
.6	.8	1.0	1.1	1.0	.7	Current	.9	.8
.2	.3	.4	.6	.4	.4		.4	.3
1.4	2.5	1.1	1.9	1.6	1.0			1.5	1.3
.4	(65) .5	.6	.8	.4	.5	Quick	.6	.5
.2	.2	.2	.4	.1	.2		.2	.1
0 UND	0 UND	0 999.8	1 386.3	2 197.7	1 316.4			0 UND	0 UND
0 UND	0 999.8	5 73.0	4 99.4	8 43.2	3 142.2	Sales/Receivables	1 244.8	2 161.8
1 420.2	7 53.5	19 18.7	27 13.5	37 10.0	15 24.6		10 37.7	12 29.7
							Cost of Sales/Inventory		
							Cost of Sales/Payables		
23.1	10.3	7.9	5.1	6.5	39.3			9.0	15.6
-35.7	-28.5	-531.4	48.1	NM	-18.1	Sales/Working Capital	-87.0	-31.2
-7.3	-11.0	-6.5	-17.4	-5.5	-5.9		-8.2	-5.5
12.7	9.9	3.3	10.2		19.2		9.3	5.7
(47) 2.2	(57) 2.2	(62) 1.4	(29) 3.8		7.0	EBIT/Interest	(210) 2.8	(172) 1.7
-1.1	.6	.2	1.3		1.1		.9	.4
						Net Profit + Depr., Dep., Amort./Cur. Mat. L /T/D		11.2	3.9
							(34) 3.1	(20) 1.9
							1.2	.8
.5	1.2	1.1	.7	.9	1.3			1.0	1.0
4.0	3.1	2.2	1.1	1.3	1.7	Fixed/Worth	2.0	2.2
-3.5	267.6	14.2	1.8	NM	5.0		6.0	7.0
.9	.7	.9	.3	.1	.8			.5	.7
11.0	2.9	1.7	.7	2.6	1.7	Debt/Worth	1.9	1.9
-2.1	269.0	15.8	1.4	NM	6.2		14.2	9.5
108.4	73.2	18.2	23.8		101.2		42.2	30.8
(43) 38.2	(51) 17.8	(64) 3.6	(30) 10.0		(11) 65.9	% Profit Before Taxes/Tangible Net Worth	(204) 14.7	(177) 9.1
7.9	-.4	-4.7	1.2		35.4		1.3	-2.5
32.7	13.3	5.1	12.7	9.8	42.5			16.7	11.2
7.4	3.2	.9	5.7	1.3	15.3	% Profit Before Taxes/Total Assets	4.2	2.8
-10.9	-1.8	-3.2	.6	-2.5	.7		-2.1	-2.6
32.7	4.3	2.4	3.2	5.0	2.2			4.4	5.0
8.7	1.6	.7	1.5	1.1	1.7	Sales/Net Fixed Assets	1.5	1.5
2.3	.9	.3	.9	.3	1.1		.7	.7
6.3	1.8	1.3	1.2	1.2	1.5			1.9	2.2
2.7	1.1	.6	.8	.6	1.2	Sales/Total Assets	1.0	1.1
1.5	.6	.3	.7	.2	.8		.5	.6
2.1	2.8	5.4	4.4				3.7	3.8
(54) 5.4	(59) 6.6	(74) 8.8	(28) 7.3			% Depr., Dep., Amort./Sales	(233) 7.4	(198) 7.7
13.7	11.0	13.3	9.8				13.3	10.7
4.5	2.0	2.5					3.6	2.9
(28) 7.8	(26) 5.9	(13) 6.0				% Officers', Directors', Owners' Comp/Sales	(53) 5.5	(51) 5.0
17.7	11.9	12.2					11.8	9.3
49861M	111613M	389070M	968808M	1046560M	2355795M		Net Sales ($)	4371308M	4407784M
15289M	72772M	362105M	799470M	726497M	1926248M		Total Assets ($)	4564834M	2918401M

M = $ thousand   MM = $ million
See Pages 11 through 18 for Explanation of Ratios and Data

Comparative Historical Data   **Current Data Sorted By Sales**

Hist 1	Hist 2	Hist 3	Type of Statement	0-1MM	1-3MM	3-5MM	5-10MM	10-25MM	25MM & OVER
58	58	67	Unqualified	7	10	9	7	14	20
28	29	29	Reviewed	7	6	5	5	5	1
57	68	40	Compiled	17	17	5			1
39	40	62	Tax Returns	48	13				1
68	108	78	Other	30	18	8	5	11	6
4/1/00-3/31/01 ALL	4/1/01-3/31/02 ALL	4/1/02-3/31/03 ALL		54 (4/1-9/30/02)		222 (10/1/02-3/31/03)			
250	303	276	**NUMBER OF STATEMENTS**	109	64	27	17	30	29
%	%	%	**ASSETS**	%	%	%	%	%	%
12.9	12.4	13.0	Cash & Equivalents	13.6	12.0	13.5	11.9	12.6	13.3
4.0	4.5	4.7	Trade Receivables (net)	3.3	3.6	1.5	10.7	9.6	6.7
4.9	4.7	5.6	Inventory	4.3	5.9	3.2	11.4	9.3	4.7
3.8	2.6	2.7	All Other Current	1.9	2.3	2.8	2.8	6.0	2.9
25.5	24.1	25.9	Total Current	23.0	23.8	21.1	36.7	37.4	27.6
63.0	63.7	61.2	Fixed Assets (net)	62.7	64.2	67.2	51.2	54.3	56.2
3.3	3.1	2.9	Intangibles (net)	4.9	.9	2.5	2.5	1.3	2.4
8.2	9.1	10.0	All Other Non-Current	9.4	11.2	9.2	9.6	6.9	13.8
100.0	100.0	100.0	Total	100.0	100.0	100.0	100.0	100.0	100.0
			LIABILITIES						
6.7	4.7	9.7	Notes Payable-Short Term	13.2	4.5	9.7	11.2	2.1	14.6
4.3	4.4	4.2	Cur. Mat.-L/T/D	5.2	4.0	3.4	1.4	4.2	2.6
5.9	6.0	6.3	Trade Payables	6.2	4.4	5.1	12.3	6.0	8.4
.3	.1	.2	Income Taxes Payable	.1	.1	.2	.4	.3	.5
13.7	10.7	12.5	All Other Current	13.1	11.5	8.9	11.0	13.4	15.9
30.9	25.8	32.8	Total Current	37.9	24.5	27.3	36.3	26.1	42.0
31.3	33.2	35.4	Long Term Debt	44.8	38.1	36.7	16.9	16.9	23.0
.5	.5	.2	Deferred Taxes	.1	.0	.6	.0	.8	.4
7.6	21.2	14.3	All Other Non-Current	19.9	16.3	13.4	7.7	3.1	5.7
29.7	19.2	17.2	Net Worth	−2.6	21.0	22.1	39.1	53.1	28.9
100.0	100.0	100.0	Total Liabilities & Net Worth	100.0	100.0	100.0	100.0	100.0	100.0
			INCOME DATA						
100.0	100.0	100.0	Net Sales	100.0	100.0	100.0	100.0	100.0	100.0
			Gross Profit						
88.2	88.7	91.2	Operating Expenses	91.6	91.9	93.4	98.0	91.9	81.6
11.8	11.3	8.8	Operating Profit	8.4	8.1	6.6	2.0	8.1	18.4
4.5	5.7	4.3	All Other Expenses (net)	6.1	3.4	3.5	−1.0	3.2	4.3
7.4	5.6	4.5	Profit Before Taxes	2.3	4.7	3.1	3.0	4.9	14.1
			RATIOS						
2.3 / 1.0 / .4	1.9 / .9 / .4	2.0 / .9 / .3	Current	2.3 / .7 / .2	3.4 / .7 / .3	1.8 / 1.0 / .5	1.8 / 1.4 / .7	2.5 / 1.1 / .6	1.4 / .9 / .5
1.4 / .6 / .2	(302) 1.3 / .6 / .2	(275) 1.5 / .5 / .2	Quick	(108) 1.9 / .4 / .2	1.9 / .4 / .2	1.4 / .6 / .3	1.2 / .7 / .3	2.0 / .7 / .3	1.3 / .7 / .3
0 UND / 2 213.6 / 12 30.2	0 UND / 2 232.0 / 9 41.9	0 UND / 1 322.5 / 11 33.3	Sales/Receivables	0 UND / 0 UND / 3 109.1	0 UND / 1 610.1 / 11 32.9	0 UND / 1 276.1 / 10 36.5	1 598.1 / 14 26.4 / 28 13.1	1 375.8 / 7 53.5 / 36 10.1	2 233.1 / 3 134.8 / 18 20.4
			Cost of Sales/Inventory						
			Cost of Sales/Payables						
8.3 / −199.2 / −6.3	11.8 / −57.4 / −9.8	12.6 / −60.5 / −8.4	Sales/Working Capital	24.0 / −25.7 / −6.4	11.2 / −26.7 / −6.5	8.7 / −999.8 / −14.6	6.1 / 31.4 / −19.4	6.1 / 31.9 / −22.2	23.3 / −45.0 / −8.5
(197) 6.2 / 2.0 / .7	(248) 8.0 / 2.7 / .5	(215) 7.3 / 2.2 / .3	EBIT/Interest	(65) 3.6 / 1.3 / −1.1	(57) 10.5 / 2.2 / .7	(25) 5.6 / 1.4 / .3	(15) 3.6 / 2.4 / .6	(24) 6.7 / 3.6 / 1.7	35.8 / 6.9 / 1.8
(37) 8.0 / 2.6 / 1.5	(36) 5.4 / 2.8 / 1.0	(26) 7.5 / 3.7 / 1.8	Net Profit + Depr., Dep., Amort./Cur. Mat. L/T/D						
.9 / 1.9 / 9.7	.9 / 2.0 / 7.7	1.0 / 2.0 / 24.2	Fixed/Worth	.9 / 4.5 / −13.3	1.0 / 2.3 / 22.8	1.1 / 2.1 / 4.7	.9 / 1.3 / −63.5	.6 / 1.2 / 2.0	1.0 / 1.4 / 2.3
.6 / 1.8 / 10.2	.6 / 1.8 / 14.6	.7 / 1.9 / NM	Debt/Worth	.9 / 6.6 / −10.1	.5 / 3.1 / −19.2	1.0 / 1.7 / 17.4	.4 / 1.6 / −244.5	.3 / 1.0 / 1.6	.6 / 1.2 / 4.6
(202) 44.0 / 10.9 / −1.3	(247) 44.9 / 15.7 / −1.3	(207) 45.2 / 15.2 / .3	% Profit Before Taxes/Tangible Net Worth	(73) 57.9 / 17.8 / −.2	(47) 35.2 / 15.7 / −.4	(22) 32.5 / 9.3 / −3.5	(12) 8.4 / 3.1 / −.3	(29) 27.6 / 11.2 / −2.7	(24) 95.1 / 38.3 / 15.1
15.9 / 3.5 / −1.3	15.7 / 4.8 / −1.6	14.4 / 3.0 / −2.6	% Profit Before Taxes/Total Assets	12.2 / 2.2 / −4.4	15.1 / 2.4 / −3.1	12.4 / 1.5 / −2.7	6.7 / 2.3 / −.7	14.9 / 4.5 / −.6	35.2 / 12.9 / 1.6
4.2 / 1.6 / .7	4.3 / 1.6 / .8	7.2 / 1.7 / .8	Sales/Net Fixed Assets	9.8 / 1.7 / .5	4.6 / 1.6 / .7	4.1 / 1.0 / .8	17.1 / 4.5 / 1.2	8.3 / 1.7 / .9	5.2 / 2.1 / 1.4
1.9 / 1.0 / .5	2.0 / 1.0 / .6	2.4 / 1.1 / .6	Sales/Total Assets	3.0 / 1.1 / .5	2.4 / 1.2 / .5	1.7 / .8 / .6	3.5 / 1.5 / .7	2.3 / .9 / .7	2.2 / 1.3 / .8
(225) 3.3 / 7.1 / 11.9	(267) 3.2 / 6.3 / 9.8	(231) 3.1 / 7.4 / 11.6	% Depr., Dep., Amort./Sales	(85) 4.1 / 10.6 / 16.2	(58) 3.2 / 7.5 / 11.4	(25) 4.1 / 7.5 / 10.0	(15) 1.9 / 3.0 / 10.7	(28) 2.7 / 7.0 / 9.6	(20) 2.6 / 3.8 / 7.4
(66) 4.5 / 7.2 / 19.4	(78) 2.9 / 5.8 / 14.5	(72) 2.9 / 6.6 / 19.4	% Officers', Directors', Owners' Comp/Sales	(35) 4.7 / 7.0 / 11.4	(19) 4.1 / 7.1 / 11.4				
4563643M	5070878M	4921707M	Net Sales ($)	52941M	109717M	107554M	132006M	504444M	4015045M
4551662M	5323556M	3902381M	Total Assets ($)	89646M	224584M	124260M	158090M	614179M	2691622M

M = $ thousand   MM = $ million
See Pages 11 through 18 for Explanation of Ratios and Data

ACCOMMODATION AND FOOD SERVICES

Current Data Sorted By Assets   Comparative Historical Data

						Type of Statement		
3	7	65	56	22	17	Unqualified	208	170
7	31	98	35	1		Reviewed	158	143
42	138	137	19	1		Compiled	404	292
117	165	137	8	1	1	Tax Returns	261	236
38	115	210	63	15	5	Other	415	358
	127 (4/1-9/30/02)		1427 (10/1/02-3/31/03)				4/1/98-3/31/99	4/1/99-3/31/00
0-500M	500M-2MM	2-10MM	10-50MM	50-100MM	100-250MM		ALL	ALL
207	456	647	181	40	23	NUMBER OF STATEMENTS	1446	1199
%	%	%	%	%	%	**ASSETS**	%	%
21.8	7.9	5.3	7.0	8.5	7.8	Cash & Equivalents	8.4	8.6
5.8	2.9	1.7	3.0	3.3	5.4	Trade Receivables (net)	2.8	2.9
3.0	.9	.7	1.4	1.0	1.9	Inventory	1.4	1.3
4.3	2.2	1.5	2.1	2.3	3.8	All Other Current	1.5	1.8
34.9	13.9	9.2	13.6	15.1	18.9	Total Current	14.0	14.6
49.9	76.0	81.6	74.1	72.2	65.6	Fixed Assets (net)	74.8	74.4
7.8	3.9	3.4	2.0	3.6	2.2	Intangibles (net)	3.7	3.5
7.4	6.1	5.8	10.3	9.2	13.3	All Other Non-Current	7.5	7.6
100.0	100.0	100.0	100.0	100.0	100.0	Total	100.0	100.0
						LIABILITIES		
10.7	3.9	2.6	2.9	5.0	2.9	Notes Payable-Short Term	4.4	4.9
2.8	4.2	3.9	4.3	5.1	9.0	Cur. Mat.-L/T/D	3.9	3.7
11.8	2.5	2.0	2.9	2.8	3.3	Trade Payables	3.3	3.4
.1	.1	.0	.1	.1	.5	Income Taxes Payable	.2	.1
38.4	10.1	5.7	9.9	6.4	9.6	All Other Current	8.7	8.9
63.8	20.8	14.2	20.2	19.4	25.2	Total Current	20.5	21.0
33.9	63.8	72.7	56.0	50.5	35.6	Long Term Debt	60.7	61.7
.0	.1	.1	.3	.4	.6	Deferred Taxes	.2	.2
17.7	7.7	5.2	6.2	8.7	4.3	All Other Non-Current	8.2	9.2
-15.3	7.7	7.7	17.3	21.1	34.2	Net Worth	10.4	7.9
100.0	100.0	100.0	100.0	100.0	100.0	Total Liabilities & Net Worth	100.0	100.0
						INCOME DATA		
100.0	100.0	100.0	100.0	100.0	100.0	Net Sales	100.0	100.0
						Gross Profit		
93.6	84.5	83.4	85.6	90.0	89.6	Operating Expenses	84.2	83.6
6.4	15.5	16.6	14.4	10.0	10.4	Operating Profit	15.7	16.4
4.4	9.7	12.9	11.0	7.6	9.3	All Other Expenses (net)	11.3	10.2
2.0	5.8	3.7	3.4	2.3	1.1	Profit Before Taxes	4.4	6.2
						RATIOS		
2.3	2.0	1.7	1.5	1.1	1.7	Current	1.8	1.6
.7	.7	.7	.8	.8	.8		.7	.7
.2	.2	.2	.3	.4	.2		.2	.3
2.1	1.6	1.3	1.2	1.0	1.0	Quick	1.5	1.4
.5 (455)	.5 (646)	.5 (180)	.5	.4	.5		.6 (1434)	.6 (1196)
.2	.1	.2	.2	.2	.1		.2	.2
0 UND	0 UND	1 534.5	4 89.3	8 44.7	7 51.0	Sales/Receivables	0 UND	0 879.0
0 UND	2 220.4	5 73.7	9 39.2	13 27.8	10 35.1		4 82.7	5 75.3
4 103.2	8 48.4	10 38.3	16 22.8	18 20.2	23 15.8		10 35.4	11 33.9
						Cost of Sales/Inventory		
						Cost of Sales/Payables		
23.0	17.1	19.7	15.3	45.1	23.3	Sales/Working Capital	17.1	18.0
-54.0	-38.1	-21.0	-26.1	-18.8	-18.8		-36.9	-33.1
-6.9	-5.6	-5.9	-6.0	-5.3	-5.5		-6.6	-6.9
4.5	3.1	2.6	2.8	2.6	7.7	EBIT/Interest	3.1	3.2
1.4 (116)	1.7 (351)	1.5 (499)	1.5 (156)	1.2 (38)	1.4 (19)		1.8 (1046)	1.7 (902)
-.3	1.0	.9	.7	.2	.5		1.0	1.1
	7.7	3.5	4.9			Net Profit + Depr., Dep., Amort./Cur. Mat. L /T/D	5.8	5.5
	4.7 (23)	2.1 (54)	2.6 (26)				3.0 (150)	2.3 (101)
	1.6	1.1	.7				1.4	1.4
.6	2.3	3.4	1.8	2.0	1.1	Fixed/Worth	2.0	2.2
4.4	8.2	11.0	3.7	4.0	2.0		5.7	6.7
-1.1	-6.9	-8.1	-173.8	35.1	5.1		-15.1	-13.0
.8	2.3	3.1	1.5	1.7	1.3	Debt/Worth	1.8	2.2
15.0	9.3	12.1	4.4	3.9	2.3		6.3	7.4
-2.7	-8.9	-9.9	-199.8	42.2	4.9		-16.7	-14.8
79.9	43.2	43.6	21.2	20.8	24.5	% Profit Before Taxes/Tangible Net Worth	43.7	57.2
22.8 (121)	16.5 (280)	16.3 (405)	9.2 (133)	4.7 (32)	6.4 (21)		16.9 (972)	20.9 (802)
.5	2.2	.4	-2.8	-6.9	-12.9		1.9	2.9
16.0	9.1	6.5	6.3	4.9	7.0	% Profit Before Taxes/Total Assets	9.5	10.2
3.3	2.8	1.9	1.9	.4	-.6		3.7	3.4
-7.9	-1.1	-1.7	-1.8	-3.5	-2.6		-1.0	-.8
36.0	1.6	.9	1.2	1.0	1.4	Sales/Net Fixed Assets	1.7	1.6
7.7	.7	.6	.7	.6	.8		.8	.7
2.3	.4	.4	.4	.5	.5		.5	.5
6.6	1.1	.7	.8	.7	.7	Sales/Total Assets	1.1	1.1
3.4	.6	.5	.5	.5	.5		.6	.6
1.2	.4	.3	.3	.4	.4		.4	.4
1.9	6.0	7.7	7.3	7.1	7.3	% Depr., Dep., Amort./Sales	6.1	6.2
4.8 (164)	9.2 (425)	10.6 (613)	9.9 (170)	9.8 (38)	10.3 (14)		9.3 (1329)	9.2 (1103)
9.9	13.3	15.0	14.6	13.6	12.1		13.4	13.3
3.4	2.3	2.3	1.3			% Officers', Directors', Owners' Comp/Sales	2.8	2.6
7.4 (103)	5.2 (147)	4.0 (135)	3.1 (24)				5.6 (370)	5.0 (273)
12.1	13.3	6.6	6.1				11.3	9.0
157296M	479177M	1743975M	2486138M	2958978M	3212289M	Net Sales ($)	9483625M	8394689M
47089M	539162M	2874575M	3797658M	2931042M	3397702M	Total Assets ($)	13850664M	11571810M

Comparative Historical Data   **Current Data Sorted By Sales**

4/1/00-3/31/01 ALL	4/1/01-3/31/02 ALL	4/1/02-3/31/03 ALL	Type of Statement	0-1MM	1-3MM	3-5MM	5-10MM	10-25MM	25MM & OVER
147	149	170	Unqualified	8	31	28	28	35	40
133	142	172	Reviewed	17	79	26	18	29	3
297	309	337	Compiled	136	143	33	15	9	1
287	275	429	Tax Returns	267	134	17	7	1	3
348	428	446	Other	149	157	47	41	28	24
					127 (4/1-9/30/02)		1427 (10/1/02-3/31/03)		
1212	1303	1554	NUMBER OF STATEMENTS	577	544	151	109	102	71
%	%	%	ASSETS	%	%	%	%	%	%
8.3	8.9	8.6	Cash & Equivalents	8.8	8.6	5.9	9.5	9.6	9.2
2.7	2.4	2.9	Trade Receivables (net)	1.8	3.2	3.0	3.2	4.4	5.7
1.5	1.3	1.2	Inventory	.8	.9	2.2	1.4	2.4	2.4
2.0	1.6	2.2	All Other Current	2.1	2.3	2.5	1.6	2.2	2.8
14.5	14.2	14.8	Total Current	13.4	15.1	13.5	15.7	18.7	20.0
74.4	75.1	74.4	Fixed Assets (net)	75.3	74.6	76.1	74.8	68.8	68.9
4.1	3.8	4.0	Intangibles (net)	5.3	3.7	2.8	2.6	2.2	2.9
7.0	7.0	6.8	All Other Non-Current	6.0	6.6	7.5	6.9	10.3	8.2
100.0	100.0	100.0	Total	100.0	100.0	100.0	100.0	100.0	100.0
			LIABILITIES						
3.2	3.5	4.2	Notes Payable-Short Term	5.6	3.4	3.5	3.7	2.5	3.1
4.3	3.5	4.0	Cur. Mat.-L/T/D	3.7	3.7	4.3	3.5	5.3	6.8
3.7	3.4	3.6	Trade Payables	2.7	3.9	4.8	4.1	4.3	3.9
.1	.1	.1	Income Taxes Payable	.1	.1	.0	.1	.1	.4
8.6	10.0	11.9	All Other Current	13.0	11.5	7.3	11.7	15.6	11.0
19.9	20.5	23.8	Total Current	25.1	22.6	20.0	23.0	27.8	25.1
62.3	61.2	61.8	Long Term Debt	61.8	63.6	65.8	64.2	57.9	41.7
.3	.2	.1	Deferred Taxes	.0	.1	.2	.5	.3	.4
6.4	7.8	7.8	All Other Non-Current	7.8	7.5	10.3	6.3	6.1	9.6
11.1	10.4	6.5	Net Worth	5.3	6.3	3.6	6.0	7.9	23.1
100.0	100.0	100.0	Total Liabilities & Net Worth	100.0	100.0	100.0	100.0	100.0	100.0
			INCOME DATA						
100.0	100.0	100.0	Net Sales	100.0	100.0	100.0	100.0	100.0	100.0
			Gross Profit						
83.9	85.4	85.6	Operating Expenses	83.3	85.5	86.3	90.0	90.6	89.9
16.1	14.6	14.4	Operating Profit	16.7	14.5	13.7	10.0	9.4	10.1
10.5	10.8	10.4	All Other Expenses (net)	12.9	10.1	8.9	7.1	6.4	6.3
5.6	3.8	4.0	Profit Before Taxes	3.8	4.3	4.7	2.9	2.9	3.8
			RATIOS						
1.7	1.7	1.8	Current	2.0	1.9	1.4	1.5	1.4	1.2
.8	.7	.7		.6	.7	.6	.7	.8	.8
.3	.3	.2		.2	.2	.3	.3	.4	.4
1.4	1.4	1.4	Quick	1.7	1.6	1.0	1.3	1.1	.9
(1210) .6	(1299) .5	(1551) .5		(576) .5	(542) .5	.4	.5	.5	.5
.2	.2	.2		.1	.2	.2	.2	.2	.2
0 UND	0 UND	0 UND	Sales/Receivables	0 UND	0 999.8	3 109.5	4 88.9	4 83.4	6 61.8
5 73.9	4 84.3	4 94.9		0 UND	4 82.1	7 52.5	9 39.2	9 39.3	10 34.8
11 32.9	10 35.9	10 37.3		4 81.4	9 40.0	13 29.0	16 23.4	15 24.2	18 19.9
			Cost of Sales/Inventory						
			Cost of Sales/Payables						
15.9	18.6	18.9	Sales/Working Capital	19.2	14.5	24.5	20.1	21.4	40.6
−41.1	−30.7	−28.0		−27.5	−32.1	−27.9	−20.1	−35.1	−27.5
−7.7	−6.7	−6.0		−5.1	−6.4	−6.4	−6.9	−6.4	−7.2
3.0	2.8	2.9	EBIT/Interest	2.7	3.1	2.6	2.6	2.6	5.0
(878) 1.8	(973) 1.5	(1179) 1.6		(361) 1.6	(421) 1.6	(139) 1.5	(99) 1.4	(95) 1.5	(64) 2.0
1.0	.8	.8		1.0	1.0	.8	.6	.7	.7
5.0	4.3	4.7	Net Profit + Depr., Dep., Amort./Cur. Mat. L/T/D	5.5	4.8	6.5	3.5	6.1	4.7
(99) 2.2	(84) 2.2	(121) 2.4		(10) 2.8	(32) 2.6	(23) 2.1	(19) 2.4	(18) 2.6	(19) 2.2
1.2	.9	1.1		1.2	1.5	.8	.9	.9	.9
2.2	2.2	2.3	Fixed/Worth	2.5	2.7	2.7	1.6	1.9	1.4
6.0	6.5	7.5		10.5	7.9	7.5	6.2	3.6	3.5
−14.6	−13.1	−8.2		−7.1	−8.4	−8.6	−3.6	−7.8	40.6
2.0	2.0	2.2	Debt/Worth	2.5	2.6	2.7	1.2	1.8	1.4
6.6	6.9	8.5		12.3	9.4	8.0	6.6	4.6	3.2
−16.6	−15.1	−9.9		−9.0	−10.1	−10.0	−6.5	−10.9	50.1
45.5	44.5	42.2	% Profit Before Taxes/Tangible Net Worth	42.2	48.4	44.9	26.1	28.3	30.1
(817) 18.2	(866) 15.5	(992) 15.1		(358) 13.4	(341) 19.4	(99) 15.5	(69) 9.1	(69) 9.8	(56) 11.7
1.7	−.3	.0		−1.1	2.7	−.5	−1.0	−3.2	−5.0
9.2	8.4	7.7	% Profit Before Taxes/Total Assets	7.5	8.3	7.3	6.9	8.6	8.0
3.4	2.1	2.2		1.5	2.6	2.0	2.1	2.0	3.7
−.8	−2.4	−1.8		−2.1	−1.3	−1.4	−2.1	−1.9	−2.1
1.9	1.7	1.6	Sales/Net Fixed Assets	1.5	1.5	1.5	1.9	1.9	1.9
.7	.7	.7		.6	.7	.8	1.0	1.1	1.0
.5	.4	.4		.3	.4	.6	.7	.6	.6
1.2	1.1	1.0	Sales/Total Assets	.9	1.1	1.0	1.4	1.1	1.0
.6	.6	.6		.5	.6	.6	.8	.7	.7
.4	.4	.4		.3	.4	.4	.5	.5	.5
5.5	5.7	6.3	% Depr., Dep., Amort./Sales	6.8	6.2	6.0	6.4	5.4	5.2
(1102) 9.2	(1212) 9.4	(1424) 9.7		(525) 10.9	(498) 9.5	(142) 9.5	(101) 8.8	(99) 8.8	(59) 8.7
13.4	13.7	13.9		15.9	13.6	12.9	12.4	12.1	11.3
2.8	2.3	2.5	% Officers', Directors', Owners' Comp/Sales	3.1	2.0	2.0	2.1	.8	
(309) 5.0	(333) 4.5	(417) 4.8		(205) 6.6	(141) 4.0	(26) 3.9	(21) 4.0	(16) 3.0	
				10.9	7.6	10.0	9.3	4.9	
10096362M	9441419M	11037853M	Net Sales ($)	312297M	937945M	583305M	780692M	1559122M	6864492M
11783919M	13794660M	13587228M	Total Assets ($)	741047M	1872645M	1065336M	1225190M	2617168M	6065842M

M = $ thousand   MM = $ million
See Pages 11 through 18 for Explanation of Ratios and Data

Current Data Sorted By Assets   Comparative Historical Data

						Type of Statement		
		2	2	2		Unqualified	2	2
	3					Reviewed	5	5
6	9	5				Compiled	18	9
15	19	2				Tax Returns	16	9
4	6	1		1		Other	8	7
	7 (4/1-9/30/02)		70 (10/1/02-3/31/03)				4/1/98-3/31/99	4/1/99-3/31/00
0-500M	500M-2MM	2-10MM	10-50MM	50-100MM	100-250MM		ALL	ALL
25	37	10	2	3		**NUMBER OF STATEMENTS**	49	32
%	%	%	%	%	%	**ASSETS**	%	%
12.0	6.3	2.9				Cash & Equivalents	9.4	6.2
1.7	.9	1.8				Trade Receivables (net)	1.3	1.3
3.0	3.4	8.5				Inventory	3.9	6.6
2.8	.5	1.7				All Other Current	.5	5.9
19.4	11.2	15.0				Total Current	15.0	20.0
75.9	75.8	70.8				Fixed Assets (net)	75.7	65.8
2.2	5.3	.9				Intangibles (net)	3.3	3.0
2.5	7.7	13.3				All Other Non-Current	6.0	11.2
100.0	100.0	100.0				Total	100.0	100.0
						LIABILITIES		
8.7	5.9	2.8				Notes Payable-Short Term	6.6	9.0
3.8	3.1	3.1				Cur. Mat.-L/T/D	6.5	4.5
.4	.7	1.2				Trade Payables	2.9	2.3
.1	.0	.0				Income Taxes Payable	.0	.0
11.2	11.4	5.6				All Other Current	9.2	13.3
24.2	21.1	12.8				Total Current	25.2	29.1
44.5	70.5	54.4				Long Term Debt	54.4	48.9
.0	.0	.0				Deferred Taxes	.4	.1
14.3	4.6	17.0				All Other Non-Current	9.0	5.7
17.1	3.8	15.8				Net Worth	11.0	16.1
100.0	100.0	100.0				Total Liabilities & Net Worth	100.0	100.0
						INCOME DATA		
100.0	100.0	100.0				Net Sales	100.0	100.0
						Gross Profit		
92.4	76.5	83.9				Operating Expenses	87.3	83.3
7.6	23.5	16.1				Operating Profit	12.7	16.7
5.6	15.1	7.9				All Other Expenses (net)	13.2	10.1
2.0	8.3	8.2				Profit Before Taxes	-.5	6.6
						RATIOS		
1.7	2.9	3.6					2.4	1.6
1.0	.7	.4				Current	.6	.8
.2	.2	.1					.3	.4
1.1	2.2	.8					1.9	1.0
.4	.5	.2				Quick	.3 (31)	.3
.1	.1	.0					.1	.1
0 UND	0 UND	0 UND					0 UND	0 UND
0 UND	0 UND	0 UND				Sales/Receivables	0 UND	0 UND
0 UND	4 93.3	13 27.5					6 59.9	3 118.9
						Cost of Sales/Inventory		
						Cost of Sales/Payables		
28.0	9.7	3.0					11.5	16.8
UND	-20.9	-20.4				Sales/Working Capital	-16.1	-18.5
-3.7	-5.3	-6.9					-4.5	-5.2
4.1	5.0						7.2	6.6
(21) 1.7	(24) 1.8					EBIT/Interest	(37) 2.4	(27) 2.2
-1.2	1.0						1.0	1.0
						Net Profit + Depr., Dep., Amort./Cur. Mat. L /T/D		
1.4	2.3	1.8					1.2	1.1
3.3	16.2	3.3				Fixed/Worth	23.0	32.7
-24.1	-2.7	-11.9					-3.7	-10.1
1.1	1.9	2.4					.9	1.2
3.6	17.4	5.0				Debt/Worth	22.5	33.2
-26.0	-5.8	-15.3					-5.3	-12.2
66.1	48.1					% Profit Before Taxes/Tangible	57.8	96.0
(17) 4.1	(22) 18.5					Net Worth	(30) 19.5	(18) 22.0
-20.9	5.8						7.2	11.2
11.2	6.6	11.7				% Profit Before Taxes/Total	14.0	15.3
1.9	3.3	5.7				Assets	1.9	5.3
-5.6	-.5	1.5					-2.0	-.9
4.0	2.0	1.6					1.3	3.2
1.3	.6	1.2				Sales/Net Fixed Assets	.8	1.0
.6	.4	.8					.5	.5
2.4	1.0	1.1					.9	2.0
1.1	.4	.8				Sales/Total Assets	.6	.6
.5	.3	.6					.4	.4
4.5	5.5	3.5					6.0	3.9
(21) 7.6	(36) 10.0	10.2				% Depr., Dep., Amort./Sales	(47) 10.1	(28) 8.8
15.8	17.3	14.5					15.8	18.7
7.4	2.4					% Officers', Directors',	3.1	3.1
(11) 11.0	(11) 4.1					Owners' Comp/Sales	(18) 7.8	(15) 10.5
16.2	13.7						12.1	14.7
8293M	29296M	31453M	56418M	175231M		Net Sales ($)	120655M	91324M
6812M	42889M	38567M	70335M	231851M		Total Assets ($)	190688M	133744M

M = $ thousand   MM = $ million
See Pages 11 through 18 for Explanation of Ratios and Data

Comparative Historical Data | Current Data Sorted By Sales

			Type of Statement						
5	3	6	Unqualified		1		1	1	3
4	2	3	Reviewed	2	1				
18	18	20	Compiled	11	7	1	1		
15	19	36	Tax Returns	33	2	1			
8	13	12	Other	7	3	1			1
4/1/00- 3/31/01 ALL	4/1/01- 3/31/02 ALL	4/1/02- 3/31/03 ALL		0-1MM	7 (4/1-9/30/02) 1-3MM	3-5MM	70 (10/1/02-3/31/03) 5-10MM	10-25MM	25MM & OVER
50	55	77	**NUMBER OF STATEMENTS**	53	14	3	2	1	4
%	%	%	**ASSETS**	%	%	%	%	%	%
6.1	7.6	7.7	Cash & Equivalents	8.9	4.9				
1.5	2.4	1.4	Trade Receivables (net)	1.3	1.1				
6.4	6.1	3.8	Inventory	2.3	11.0				
4.7	2.2	1.6	All Other Current	1.4	1.1				
18.6	18.4	14.5	Total Current	14.0	18.1				
68.9	69.7	74.3	Fixed Assets (net)	76.9	70.6				
3.1	4.1	3.7	Intangibles (net)	3.7	4.7				
9.3	7.7	7.4	All Other Non-Current	5.4	6.6				
100.0	100.0	100.0	Total	100.0	100.0				
			LIABILITIES						
6.0	7.6	6.0	Notes Payable-Short Term	6.7	6.6				
3.8	4.0	3.2	Cur. Mat.-L/T/D	3.2	4.0				
2.6	2.4	.9	Trade Payables	.4	1.6				
.1	.1	.1	Income Taxes Payable	.1	.0				
6.9	11.3	10.8	All Other Current	9.5	15.6				
19.4	25.4	21.0	Total Current	19.8	27.8				
57.7	51.5	56.3	Long Term Debt	58.3	70.8				
.1	.1	.1	Deferred Taxes	.0	.0				
5.6	11.9	10.2	All Other Non-Current	8.0	9.8				
17.3	11.1	12.5	Net Worth	13.8	−8.4				
100.0	100.0	100.0	Total Liabilities & Net Worth	100.0	100.0				
			INCOME DATA						
100.0	100.0	100.0	Net Sales	100.0	100.0				
			Gross Profit						
81.9	83.1	83.0	Operating Expenses	82.2	86.8				
18.1	16.9	17.0	Operating Profit	17.8	13.2				
12.2	11.0	10.2	All Other Expenses (net)	13.0	6.0				
5.9	5.9	6.8	Profit Before Taxes	4.8	7.1				
			RATIOS						
1.6	2.1	1.7		2.0	1.2				
.7	.5	.7	Current	.9	.6				
.3	.3	.2		.2	.2				
1.1	1.0	1.2		1.6	.6				
(49) .3	.4	.4	Quick	.5	.2				
.1	.2	.1		.1	.1				
0 UND	0 UND	0 UND		0 UND	0 UND				
0 UND	0 UND	0 UND	Sales/Receivables	0 UND	1 704.4				
3 108.3	3 121.7	5 75.7		2 158.8	7 51.3				
			Cost of Sales/Inventory						
			Cost of Sales/Payables						
14.9	8.4	16.3		10.1	32.3				
−29.0	−15.2	−26.0	Sales/Working Capital	−33.8	−17.6				
−5.0	−5.6	−5.0		−3.7	−4.8				
5.6	3.8	5.4		4.1	4.2				
(32) 2.7	(42) 1.5	(59) 1.9	EBIT/Interest	(37) 1.7	(13) 2.0				
1.2	1.0	1.0		.6	1.1				
			Net Profit + Depr., Dep., Amort./Cur. Mat. L/T/D						
1.1	1.4	1.7		1.7	2.0				
4.3	14.2	4.5	Fixed/Worth	5.9	8.7				
−24.4	−6.4	−10.8		−9.1	−2.2				
1.1	1.4	1.4		1.3	1.9				
4.4	18.9	5.2	Debt/Worth	5.6	11.3				
−60.4	−8.8	−14.7		−11.1	−4.0				
40.9	96.5	50.3	% Profit Before Taxes/Tangible	48.0					
(35) 24.1	(33) 30.9	(51) 18.9	Net Worth	(34) 10.6					
4.0	5.2	−1.8		−6.7					
12.1	10.3	12.5	% Profit Before Taxes/Total	7.3	8.4				
5.5	3.2	3.3	Assets	2.2	4.5				
−.8	.0	−1.7		−4.1	1.2				
2.2	2.3	2.0		1.5	2.8				
.8	1.1	.9	Sales/Net Fixed Assets	.6	1.5				
.4	.5	.5		.4	.8				
1.6	1.3	1.2		1.1	1.6				
.6	.7	.6	Sales/Total Assets	.5	.8				
.3	.4	.4		.3	.6				
4.3	4.5	4.7		5.7	4.5				
(47) 7.7	(51) 7.4	(72) 8.4	% Depr., Dep., Amort./Sales	(48) 10.8	6.8				
14.7	14.8	15.6		18.5	10.9				
2.8	4.1	3.8	% Officers', Directors',	4.4					
(20) 6.2	(17) 7.7	(26) 7.7	Owners' Comp/Sales	(20) 8.5					
8.6	11.5	13.4		14.1					
209037M	220824M	300691M	Net Sales ($)	20051M	24175M	10964M	13852M	21631M	210018M
272363M	341621M	390454M	Total Assets ($)	39761M	26449M	8302M	13756M	32975M	269211M

M = $ thousand   MM = $ million
See Pages 11 through 18 for Explanation of Ratios and Data

Current Data Sorted By Assets   Comparative Historical Data

	0-500M	500M-2MM	2-10MM	10-50MM	50-100MM	100-250MM	Type of Statement	4/1/98-3/31/99 ALL	4/1/99-3/31/00 ALL
	2	1	5				Unqualified	4	6
		4	4				Reviewed	7	8
	1	7	3				Compiled	7	9
	6	4	2				Tax Returns	6	7
		4	4				Other	9	8
	12 (4/1-9/30/02)			35 (10/1/02-3/31/03)					
NUMBER OF STATEMENTS	9	20	18					33	38
ASSETS	%	%	%	%	%	%		%	%
Cash & Equivalents		9.9	7.7	D	D	D		9.0	10.3
Trade Receivables (net)		.6	.6	A	A	A		3.0	1.8
Inventory		.7	2.0	T	T	T		2.0	2.5
All Other Current		7.4	2.3	A	A	A		1.0	1.0
Total Current		18.6	12.5					15.0	15.5
Fixed Assets (net)		68.4	78.0	N	N	N		74.4	75.0
Intangibles (net)		3.6	1.3	O	O	O		1.9	2.5
All Other Non-Current		9.3	8.2	T	T	T		8.7	7.0
Total		100.0	100.0					100.0	100.0
LIABILITIES				A	A	A			
Notes Payable-Short Term		15.2	1.6	V	V	V		4.8	4.1
Cur. Mat.-L/T/D		2.7	4.8	A	A	A		3.3	3.7
Trade Payables		3.2	1.8	I	I	I		3.3	3.7
Income Taxes Payable		.1	.0	L	L	L		.6	.1
All Other Current		11.4	8.0	A	A	A		19.7	15.3
Total Current		32.6	16.2	B	B	B		31.7	26.9
Long Term Debt		31.8	33.4	L	L	L		40.9	35.5
Deferred Taxes		.1	.0	E	E	E		.1	.1
All Other Non-Current		11.1	2.0					2.1	5.1
Net Worth		24.4	48.4					25.2	32.4
Total Liabilities & Net Worth		100.0	100.0					100.0	100.0
INCOME DATA									
Net Sales		100.0	100.0					100.0	100.0
Gross Profit									
Operating Expenses		96.2	89.4					87.7	88.9
Operating Profit		3.8	10.6					12.3	11.1
All Other Expenses (net)		3.7	3.7					5.9	4.1
Profit Before Taxes		.1	6.8					6.4	7.0
RATIOS									
Current		1.4	1.9					1.2	1.3
		.4	.9					.5	.6
		.1	.4					.1	.3
Quick		1.4	1.7					1.0	1.1
		.2	.7					.4	.5
		.0	.2					.1	.2
Sales/Receivables		0 UND	0 UND					0 UND	0 UND
		0 UND	0 UND					2 175.8	1 606.5
		0 999.8	3 118.8					7 52.5	5 68.0
Cost of Sales/Inventory									
Cost of Sales/Payables									
Sales/Working Capital		33.0	15.4					42.5	18.9
		-13.9	NM					-10.7	-14.9
		-3.3	-7.1					-3.9	-5.6
EBIT/Interest	(18)	8.8	(17) 4.7					(29) 9.7	(31) 5.0
		1.9	1.7					2.4	3.5
		-1.9	.9					1.1	1.2
Net Profit + Depr., Dep., Amort./Cur. Mat. L /T/D									
Fixed/Worth		1.2	1.2					1.2	1.5
		5.1	1.6					3.2	2.5
		-4.8	2.5					NM	7.8
Debt/Worth		.6	.4					1.2	.9
		20.3	1.4					2.7	2.3
		-6.4	2.9					NM	8.0
% Profit Before Taxes/Tangible Net Worth	(11)	129.9	15.4					(25) 41.8	(31) 46.5
		24.0	4.2					15.0	9.6
		-11.0	-1.2					2.6	.9
% Profit Before Taxes/Total Assets		15.1	7.7					11.0	12.7
		2.8	1.7					5.6	6.3
		-5.8	-.7					.8	.6
Sales/Net Fixed Assets		6.2	1.4					3.2	3.0
		1.9	.8					1.2	1.3
		1.0	.3					.6	.7
Sales/Total Assets		2.2	.9					1.7	1.8
		1.1	.5					1.0	1.0
		.6	.3					.5	.6
% Depr., Dep., Amort./Sales	(17)	3.0	(15) 5.8					(29) 3.2	(32) 3.7
		4.6	7.8					5.6	5.1
		10.1	9.3					9.8	8.2
% Officers', Directors', Owners' Comp/Sales								(10) 4.1	(11) 6.2
								6.0	7.6
								13.8	11.1
Net Sales ($)	6825M	36543M	42247M					96118M	82440M
Total Assets ($)	2191M	21648M	75570M					130644M	94764M

© RMA 2003

M = $ thousand   MM = $ million

See Pages 11 through 18 for Explanation of Ratios and Data

Comparative Historical Data | | | **Current Data Sorted By Sales**

			Type of Statement						
3	4	8	Unqualified	3	4	1			
9	8	8	Reviewed		7	1			
9	7	11	Compiled	5	4	1	1		
7	6	12	Tax Returns	6	5	1			
6	7	8	Other	3	3	2			
4/1/00-3/31/01	4/1/01-3/31/02	4/1/02-3/31/03		12 (4/1-9/30/02)			35 (10/1/02-3/31/03)		
ALL	ALL	ALL		0-1MM	1-3MM	3-5MM	5-10MM	10-25MM	25MM & OVER
34	32	47	**NUMBER OF STATEMENTS**	17	23	6	1		
%	%	%	**ASSETS**	%	%	%	%	%	%
7.7	12.3	8.8	Cash & Equivalents	5.2	12.6			D	D
2.5	2.0	1.0	Trade Receivables (net)	.5	1.3			A	A
2.7	1.7	1.3	Inventory	.8	1.9			T	T
3.0	3.1	5.1	All Other Current	8.2	4.3			A	A
15.9	19.1	16.2	Total Current	14.6	20.1				
72.0	68.5	72.3	Fixed Assets (net)	73.5	70.8			N	N
2.6	3.8	3.3	Intangibles (net)	5.9	2.0			O	O
9.5	8.6	8.3	All Other Non-Current	6.0	7.1			T	T
100.0	100.0	100.0	Total	100.0	100.0				
			LIABILITIES					A	A
8.1	3.7	13.5	Notes Payable-Short Term	26.6	7.1			V	V
4.5	3.1	4.3	Cur. Mat.-L/T/D	5.4	3.9			A	A
3.3	2.5	2.3	Trade Payables	1.2	3.5			I	I
.0	.1	.0	Income Taxes Payable	.0	.0			L	L
14.1	11.3	11.5	All Other Current	7.9	13.9			A	A
30.0	20.6	31.6	Total Current	41.1	28.5			B	B
32.0	33.4	35.5	Long Term Debt	53.3	24.1			L	L
.2	.4	.0	Deferred Taxes	.0	.1			E	E
10.5	10.9	5.5	All Other Non-Current	7.4	5.0				
27.4	34.8	27.3	Net Worth	−1.8	42.4				
100.0	100.0	100.0	Total Liabilities & Net Worth	100.0	100.0				
			INCOME DATA						
100.0	100.0	100.0	Net Sales	100.0	100.0				
			Gross Profit						
90.7	90.5	91.9	Operating Expenses	93.6	90.3				
9.2	9.5	8.1	Operating Profit	6.4	9.7				
3.6	5.3	4.8	All Other Expenses (net)	9.7	1.8				
5.6	4.1	3.3	Profit Before Taxes	−3.2	7.9				
			RATIOS						
1.6	1.5	1.4		2.9	1.4				
.7	.8	.6	Current	.5	.8				
.2	.3	.2		.1	.3				
1.1	1.3	1.3		2.5	1.4				
.3	.6	.3	Quick	.1	.6				
.1	.1	.1		.0	.2				
0 UND	0 UND	0 UND		0 UND	0 UND				
1 342.0	0 999.8	0 UND	Sales/Receivables	0 UND	0 UND				
11 33.8	3 107.2	2 199.2		0 UND	2 199.2				
			Cost of Sales/Inventory						
			Cost of Sales/Payables						
19.8	16.3	28.0		11.9	28.0				
−17.1	−21.2	−16.0	Sales/Working Capital	−11.8	−20.7				
−3.8	−7.5	−3.8		−2.3	−6.8				
4.3	3.9	5.2		2.9	8.5				
(29) 2.0	(25) 2.4	(40) 2.0	EBIT/Interest	(13) 1.2	(20) 2.8				
.6	1.5	.6		−.8	.6				
			Net Profit + Depr., Dep., Amort./Cur. Mat. L/T/D						
1.1	.9	1.2		1.5	1.1				
3.4	2.1	2.3	Fixed/Worth	−43.4	1.6				
−150.9	5.1	−43.4		−1.3	5.9				
.8	.6	.6		.8	.2				
3.1	2.0	1.9	Debt/Worth	−49.7	1.9				
−261.1	8.7	−49.7		−3.0	5.1				
32.3	34.7	33.6			35.4				
(25) 10.3	(28) 12.0	(35) 10.0	% Profit Before Taxes/Tangible Net Worth		(20) 11.5				
1.1	3.7	−3.1			−2.4				
13.2	9.1	12.7		7.3	17.4				
3.2	4.5	1.8	% Profit Before Taxes/Total Assets	.7	3.7				
−1.1	1.4	−2.0		−4.5	−1.9				
3.1	3.8	4.0		2.2	5.2				
1.6	1.3	1.4	Sales/Net Fixed Assets	.7	1.7				
.8	.8	.6		.3	.8				
2.0	1.4	2.2		1.0	2.3				
1.1	1.0	1.0	Sales/Total Assets	.6	1.1				
.7	.5	.5		.3	.6				
4.9	3.7	3.5		5.3	3.1				
(29) 7.3	(29) 6.7	(40) 6.2	% Depr., Dep., Amort./Sales	(15) 11.5	(19) 6.0				
10.9	9.9	10.1		23.5	8.4				
1.5	3.7	2.7			2.7				
(10) 4.7	(10) 8.8	(16) 7.3	% Officers', Directors', Owners' Comp/Sales		(10) 10.3				
6.2	11.0	13.6			15.7				
75654M	153014M	85615M	Net Sales ($)	7954M	45229M	24040M	8392M		
79415M	142789M	99409M	Total Assets ($)	19299M	53627M	25526M	957M		

© RMA 2003

M = $ thousand   MM = $ million
See Pages 11 through 18 for Explanation of Ratios and Data

Current Data Sorted By Assets   Comparative Historical Data

								4/1/98- 3/31/99	4/1/99- 3/31/00
							Type of Statement	215	188
4	24	31	77	22	32		Unqualified	215	188
26	66	92	36	4			Reviewed	208	179
276	227	111	11		4		Compiled	621	543
476	219	58	2	4	10		Tax Returns	420	413
211	241	199	95	11	18		Other	641	578
	289 (4/1-9/30/02)		2298 (10/1/02-3/31/03)					ALL	ALL
0-500M	500M-2MM	2-10MM	10-50MM	50-100MM	100-250MM			2105	1901
993	777	491	221	41	64		NUMBER OF STATEMENTS		
%	%	%	%	%	%		ASSETS	%	%
15.7	13.1	11.4	8.9	9.1	7.0		Cash & Equivalents	13.0	13.8
2.5	2.9	2.7	2.3	2.2	2.8		Trade Receivables (net)	2.9	3.4
8.9	4.6	3.9	2.7	4.8	4.4		Inventory	6.9	6.9
3.2	3.6	3.0	3.0	3.1	3.2		All Other Current	2.5	2.4
30.3	24.2	21.0	17.0	19.2	17.3		Total Current	25.4	26.5
48.9	56.4	60.7	61.9	56.9	57.3		Fixed Assets (net)	54.8	53.7
9.5	9.5	8.3	12.3	15.5	18.8		Intangibles (net)	9.2	10.0
11.4	9.8	10.1	8.7	8.4	6.6		All Other Non-Current	10.5	9.8
100.0	100.0	100.0	100.0	100.0	100.0		Total	100.0	100.0
							LIABILITIES		
9.3	4.0	2.7	2.5	2.0	3.0		Notes Payable-Short Term	6.2	6.6
5.4	5.4	6.3	6.3	4.0	7.7		Cur. Mat.-L/T/D	5.2	5.6
14.6	9.3	8.4	7.3	5.6	7.4		Trade Payables	12.3	11.9
.3	.2	.1	.1	.1	.5		Income Taxes Payable	.3	.3
24.6	14.9	12.7	9.8	12.3	12.2		All Other Current	19.2	22.0
54.1	33.8	30.1	26.1	24.0	30.7		Total Current	43.2	46.4
33.1	39.2	41.8	45.2	40.6	40.5		Long Term Debt	35.6	36.4
.1	.0	.2	.3	.7	.8		Deferred Taxes	.2	.1
17.3	7.6	4.1	3.1	5.2	9.2		All Other Non-Current	10.8	8.8
-4.6	19.4	23.8	25.3	29.4	18.8		Net Worth	10.3	8.3
100.0	100.0	100.0	100.0	100.0	100.0		Total Liabilities & Net Worth	100.0	100.0
							INCOME DATA		
100.0	100.0	100.0	100.0	100.0	100.0		Net Sales	100.0	100.0
59.2	60.9	60.9	58.3	53.8	53.0		Gross Profit	58.2	57.9
55.7	56.5	55.5	52.9	47.2	48.2		Operating Expenses	54.3	53.8
3.5	4.4	5.4	5.4	6.6	4.8		Operating Profit	3.9	4.1
.9	1.7	1.9	2.1	3.4	2.1		All Other Expenses (net)	1.3	1.1
2.6	2.7	3.6	3.3	3.2	2.7		Profit Before Taxes	2.6	3.0
							RATIOS		
1.6	1.5	1.3	1.0	1.1	.8			1.3	1.4
.7	.7	.6	.6	.7	.5		Current	.6	.7
.3	.3	.3	.3	.4	.2			.3	.3
1.0	1.0	.9	.7	.7	.4			.9	1.0
(973) .3	(772) .4	.4	.4	.4	(62) .2		Quick	(2061) .4	(1876) .4
.1	.1	.1	.1	.2	.1			.1	.1
0 UND	0 UND	0 UND	0 UND	0 999.8	0 UND			0 UND	0 UND
0 UND	0 999.8	1 688.4	1 469.1	2 234.6	2 174.2		Sales/Receivables	0 999.8	0 999.8
1 592.8	2 229.0	3 139.4	3 107.7	6 55.3	5 68.2			2 148.4	3 138.2
6 64.7	7 55.5	7 51.8	6 65.8	6 60.7	5 72.2			7 55.9	6 57.0
10 37.3	10 37.3	11 34.0	10 37.3	10 35.2	10 36.5		Cost of Sales/Inventory	11 33.7	11 34.0
17 21.7	16 22.8	16 22.8	15 25.0	21 17.5	19 19.6			18 20.0	19 19.7
0 UND	7 48.7	14 26.4	15 24.1	14 26.4	12 31.0			7 55.5	6 58.4
13 27.3	22 16.6	27 13.7	26 13.9	24 15.5	22 16.6		Cost of Sales/Payables	21 17.2	20 18.6
30 12.3	40 9.0	46 7.9	47 7.8	43 8.5	40 9.1			40 9.1	38 9.6
54.4	38.4	50.2	-312.8	96.9	-57.6			57.3	43.4
-57.0	-52.7	-28.8	-22.8	-22.4	-15.0		Sales/Working Capital	-35.7	-44.5
-15.8	-12.9	-11.4	-11.7	-13.9	-10.2			-12.2	-13.1
9.0	9.0	7.3	5.2	9.4	3.5			6.4	7.4
(680) 3.1	(694) 2.8	(458) 2.5	(215) 2.7	(37) 2.4	(56) 1.8		EBIT/Interest	(1732) 2.6	(1597) 2.5
.1	.8	1.0	1.2	1.4	1.1			.9	.9
5.6	5.3	4.2	3.5	5.3	3.6		Net Profit + Depr., Dep.,	4.8	5.0
(24) 2.5	(50) 2.7	(79) 1.8	(59) 2.1	(20) 2.9	(13) 2.3		Amort./Cur. Mat. L /T/D	(268) 2.2	(210) 2.5
1.2	1.3	1.1	1.3	1.9	1.7			1.2	1.2
.8	1.2	1.4	1.6	1.2	2.0			1.1	1.0
3.9	4.1	3.3	3.8	4.2	21.5		Fixed/Worth	3.4	3.3
-1.4	-5.3	-9.2	-2.9	-33.2	-1.9			-5.0	-4.3
.9	1.3	1.4	1.4	.8	1.7			1.1	1.0
8.3	4.9	4.5	4.0	5.7	24.4		Debt/Worth	4.8	4.4
-3.1	-9.1	-13.4	-6.6	-10.1	-3.8			-7.1	-7.1
120.9	88.2	63.0	51.3	62.9	64.9		% Profit Before Taxes/Tangible	92.3	77.7
(571) 44.4	(510) 35.9	(338) 30.3	(148) 25.5	(29) 26.5	(34) 21.0		Net Worth	(1378) 36.3	(1244) 35.0
9.7	9.0	8.0	8.3	12.6	8.9			10.0	9.9
32.4	21.8	16.3	11.2	12.5	10.6		% Profit Before Taxes/Total	21.8	21.8
11.2	7.7	6.4	6.7	6.2	6.1		Assets	7.6	8.5
-2.1	-1.1	.4	1.2	1.0	1.3			-.3	-.1
30.0	10.3	7.3	5.1	5.6	5.7			15.9	15.2
12.0	5.6	4.0	2.9	2.8	3.1		Sales/Net Fixed Assets	6.3	6.4
6.3	2.6	2.2	2.1	1.9	2.3			2.8	3.0
8.6	4.4	3.4	2.6	2.3	2.7			5.4	5.3
5.4	2.8	2.2	1.9	1.5	1.9		Sales/Total Assets	3.3	3.3
3.4	1.7	1.5	1.4	1.2	1.5			1.9	1.9
1.1	1.8	2.2	2.8	3.5	2.6			1.5	1.5
(843) 2.1	(720) 2.9	(476) 3.2	(214) 3.6	(35) 4.4	(22) 3.2		% Depr., Dep., Amort./Sales	(1861) 2.6	(1711) 2.7
3.6	4.6	4.4	4.7	5.1	3.9			4.0	4.2
3.1	2.0	1.3	.8		3.7		% Officers', Directors',	2.5	2.5
(535) 5.6	(319) 3.8	(192) 2.7	(42) 1.9		(13) 5.8		Owners' Comp/Sales	(808) 4.5	(820) 4.5
8.8	6.7	5.4	4.9		8.8			7.9	7.8
1198443M	2487606M	5437907M	10495912M	7361930M	29986056M		Net Sales ($)	27744431M	33145245M
226048M	800062M	2168580M	4827364M	3012935M	10332650M		Total Assets ($)	12411646M	13714943M

M = $ thousand   MM = $ million
See Pages 11 through 18 for Explanation of Ratios and Data

Comparative Historical Data | Current Data Sorted By Sales

4/1/00-3/31/01 ALL	4/1/01-3/31/02 ALL	4/1/02-3/31/03 ALL	Type of Statement	0-1MM	1-3MM	3-5MM	5-10MM	10-25MM	25MM & OVER
124	142	190	Unqualified	6	7	11	15	23	128
143	156	224	Reviewed	17	37	31	50	56	33
536	530	629	Compiled	129	288	71	74	52	15
466	489	769	Tax Returns	284	342	73	37	17	16
564	606	775	Other	128	224	98	119	105	101
				289 (4/1-9/30/02)		2298 (10/1/02-3/31/03)			
1833	1923	2587	NUMBER OF STATEMENTS	564	898	284	295	253	293
%	%	%	ASSETS	%	%	%	%	%	%
12.8	13.1	13.2	Cash & Equivalents	13.3	14.2	14.0	12.7	13.4	9.4
3.5	3.4	2.6	Trade Receivables (net)	1.6	2.5	3.1	4.2	2.5	3.0
6.4	6.9	6.0	Inventory	7.7	6.5	4.8	5.3	4.5	4.0
3.0	3.2	3.3	All Other Current	1.6	4.3	3.6	3.8	2.7	3.1
25.7	26.6	25.1	Total Current	24.2	27.5	25.6	26.0	23.2	19.5
54.4	53.5	54.8	Fixed Assets (net)	55.5	52.4	54.8	54.5	58.3	58.4
10.3	9.7	9.8	Intangibles (net)	9.5	9.7	7.7	9.1	9.5	14.0
9.6	10.2	10.3	All Other Non-Current	10.9	10.4	12.0	10.3	9.0	8.1
100.0	100.0	100.0	Total	100.0	100.0	100.0	100.0	100.0	100.0
			LIABILITIES						
6.9	6.1	5.6	Notes Payable-Short Term	12.2	4.2	3.7	4.9	2.1	2.8
6.0	5.3	5.7	Cur. Mat.-L/T/D	5.3	5.2	5.0	6.6	6.9	6.4
11.4	11.6	10.9	Trade Payables	9.1	12.9	10.6	11.0	10.4	8.3
.3	.3	.2	Income Taxes Payable	.4	.2	.2	.1	.1	.2
20.1	18.2	17.7	All Other Current	20.7	19.0	16.0	18.0	13.7	12.3
44.7	41.5	40.0	Total Current	47.6	41.6	35.6	40.7	33.3	30.0
36.0	36.8	37.9	Long Term Debt	42.0	35.9	35.4	37.1	37.8	39.9
.1	.1	.1	Deferred Taxes	.1	.0	.1	.2	.2	.5
11.7	11.4	10.3	All Other Non-Current	17.8	11.4	6.8	6.6	3.9	4.7
7.5	10.2	11.7	Net Worth	−7.6	11.1	22.2	15.5	24.9	24.9
100.0	100.0	100.0	Total Liabilities & Net Worth	100.0	100.0	100.0	100.0	100.0	100.0
			INCOME DATA						
100.0	100.0	100.0	Net Sales	100.0	100.0	100.0	100.0	100.0	100.0
59.1	58.1	59.7	Gross Profit	59.8	59.9	61.9	61.3	58.2	56.5
55.0	54.2	55.3	Operating Expenses	56.4	55.6	56.4	57.3	53.5	50.9
4.1	3.9	4.4	Operating Profit	3.4	4.3	5.5	4.0	4.6	5.6
1.3	1.6	1.5	All Other Expenses (net)	2.0	1.4	.9	1.0	1.5	2.0
2.8	2.3	2.9	Profit Before Taxes	1.4	2.9	4.6	3.1	3.2	3.6
			RATIOS						
1.4	1.4	1.4	Current	1.5	1.6	1.4	1.2	1.2	.9
.6	.7	.7		.7	.7	.7	.6	.6	.6
.3	.3	.3		.2	.3	.4	.3	.3	.3
(1803) .9	(1908) .9	(2560) .9	Quick	(553) .9	(887) 1.1	(282) 1.0	.8	(252) .8	(291) .7
.4	.4	.4		.3	.4	.4	.4	.4	.4
.1	.1	.1		.1	.1	.1	.1	.1	.1
0 UND	0 UND	0 UND	Sales/Receivables	0 UND	0 UND	0 UND	0 UND	0 UND	0 999.8
0 999.8	0 999.8	0 999.8		0 UND	0 UND	0 999.8	0 768.7	1 688.4	1 305.9
3 130.5	3 127.2	2 213.4		0 UND	1 292.5	2 172.6	3 132.1	2 147.0	5 80.6
7 54.7	6 59.7	6 58.8	Cost of Sales/Inventory	6 63.2	6 58.9	6 57.7	7 51.6	6 60.6	6 65.0
11 34.4	11 34.1	10 36.4		11 33.3	10 38.0	9 39.0	11 33.7	10 36.6	10 37.3
18 20.9	19 19.4	16 22.4		20 18.1	15 23.8	15 24.1	18 20.2	13 27.4	16 23.2
7 55.2	7 49.7	7 55.5	Cost of Sales/Payables	0 UND	6 64.7	8 45.2	13 27.7	15 25.1	14 26.5
21 17.5	22 16.8	21 17.6		10 38.0	19 18.8	23 15.6	25 14.6	26 14.0	25 14.8
40 9.0	40 9.1	38 9.6		30 12.2	36 10.0	40 9.1	42 8.7	45 8.1	43 8.5
44.8	49.5	53.6	Sales/Working Capital	51.9	39.3	62.5	63.6	57.8	−237.8
−36.6	−44.3	−39.2		−48.4	−58.1	−50.0	−30.5	−28.5	−21.5
−11.3	−13.6	−13.1		−10.6	−14.8	−14.5	−11.8	−12.9	−12.2
(1527) 6.9	(1588) 6.4	(2140) 8.1	EBIT/Interest	(410) 5.6	(690) 8.5	(255) 12.5	(277) 8.1	(235) 8.6	(273) 7.1
2.3	2.3	2.8		2.0	2.7	3.8	2.7	2.6	3.0
.8	.7	.9		−.2	.7	1.2	.9	1.1	1.5
(179) 5.9	(179) 4.2	(245) 4.3	Net Profit + Depr., Dep., Amort./Cur. Mat. L/T/D	(10) 4.8	(39) 4.6	(22) 4.5	(40) 6.8	(49) 3.9	(85) 4.3
2.2	2.0	2.2		2.9	2.4	2.1	2.1	1.9	2.7
1.1	.9	1.3		.8	1.2	1.3	1.1	1.2	1.4
1.2	1.1	1.1	Fixed/Worth	1.2	.9	1.1	1.2	1.3	1.6
4.8	4.8	3.9		10.1	3.7	2.9	3.5	3.7	3.7
−3.1	−3.1	−3.2		−1.4	−3.4	−15.5	−4.4	−8.0	−3.0
1.3	1.2	1.1	Debt/Worth	1.1	.9	1.0	1.2	1.3	1.4
6.7	6.7	5.6		27.9	5.3	3.7	4.9	4.7	4.5
−5.2	−5.6	−5.4		−3.1	−5.5	−19.5	−6.5	−12.7	−5.6
(1138) 86.6	(1189) 81.4	(1630) 86.4	% Profit Before Taxes/Tangible Net Worth	(297) 81.8	(574) 99.5	(205) 117.7	(189) 77.3	(170) 68.8	(195) 59.6
34.5	30.6	34.4		30.3	37.5	45.0	28.4	31.1	29.8
8.4	6.6	8.8		3.4	9.1	16.4	7.6	7.4	12.8
19.7	20.0	22.2	% Profit Before Taxes/Total Assets	23.2	24.4	26.6	18.4	19.4	14.7
7.2	6.1	7.7		5.0	8.8	11.0	7.4	7.1	7.5
−.6	−1.2	−.3		−5.6	−.7	1.2	−.2	.6	2.4
13.8	14.8	14.2	Sales/Net Fixed Assets	18.5	19.4	12.4	11.3	8.2	7.5
6.2	6.5	6.5		7.2	8.1	6.3	5.8	4.7	3.7
3.0	3.1	2.9		2.5	3.7	3.3	3.0	2.5	2.5
5.3	5.3	5.4	Sales/Total Assets	6.1	6.6	4.9	5.0	4.0	3.2
3.2	3.2	3.2		3.5	3.8	3.2	3.1	2.7	2.1
1.9	1.9	1.9		1.7	2.2	2.1	1.9	1.7	1.6
(1634) 1.4	(1725) 1.3	(2310) 1.6	% Depr., Dep., Amort./Sales	(479) 1.5	(800) 1.4	(266) 1.7	(277) 1.9	(248) 2.2	(240) 2.4
2.6	2.5	2.8		3.0	2.5	2.5	2.9	3.2	3.3
4.1	4.1	4.3		5.2	4.1	3.5	4.2	4.4	4.3
(802) 2.4	(851) 2.4	(1109) 2.2	% Officers', Directors', Owners' Comp/Sales	(282) 3.6	(444) 2.4	(115) 1.8	(121) 1.7	(90) 1.1	(57) 1.0
4.5	4.5	4.3		6.4	4.5	2.8	3.2	2.4	2.9
7.6	7.4	7.9		9.6	6.2	6.0	6.2	4.4	6.0
32684125M	36509895M	56967854M	Net Sales ($)	350639M	1618788M	1090866M	2125526M	4041468M	47740567M
12668553M	14947577M	21367639M	Total Assets ($)	168036M	595511M	442565M	843493M	1878366M	17439668M

© RMA 2003   M = $ thousand   MM = $ million
See Pages 11 through 18 for Explanation of Ratios and Data

Current Data Sorted By Assets — Comparative Historical Data

1		3	9	1	2	Type of Statement	64	58
	3	4	1			Unqualified	91	80
15	8	13	2			Reviewed	221	222
47	13	5		1		Compiled	82	77
13	12	13	3	1	1	Tax Returns	201	140
						Other		
	16 (4/1-9/30/02)			155 (10/1/02-3/31/03)			4/1/98- 3/31/99	4/1/99- 3/31/00
0-500M	500M-2MM	2-10MM	10-50MM	50-100MM	100-250MM		ALL	ALL
76	36	38	15	3	3	NUMBER OF STATEMENTS	659	577
%	%	%	%	%	%	ASSETS	%	%
15.0	12.3	10.4	7.0			Cash & Equivalents	14.5	13.9
.5	1.2	.9	1.0			Trade Receivables (net)	1.9	1.4
4.7	2.3	2.3	1.8			Inventory	4.4	4.0
2.3	1.9	3.6	2.9			All Other Current	2.5	3.1
22.5	17.8	17.1	12.7			Total Current	23.4	22.4
52.5	58.7	61.9	66.0			Fixed Assets (net)	54.2	53.8
14.8	14.7	12.2	13.7			Intangibles (net)	12.6	14.2
10.1	8.8	8.8	7.5			All Other Non-Current	9.8	9.6
100.0	100.0	100.0	100.0			Total	100.0	100.0
						LIABILITIES		
8.4	3.5	4.4	1.0			Notes Payable-Short Term	10.0	4.7
5.9	6.3	6.2	6.6			Cur. Mat.-L/T/D	7.0	7.8
7.4	7.0	7.4	5.8			Trade Payables	9.1	9.5
.3	.3	.1	.0			Income Taxes Payable	.2	.2
27.6	8.1	7.5	11.2			All Other Current	12.8	13.0
49.6	25.1	25.6	24.6			Total Current	39.1	35.0
44.8	46.1	42.4	50.4			Long Term Debt	40.9	40.7
.0	.0	.1	1.2			Deferred Taxes	.1	.2
10.7	9.3	4.5	4.9			All Other Non-Current	6.4	5.3
-5.1	19.4	27.3	18.9			Net Worth	13.5	18.8
100.0	100.0	100.0	100.0			Total Liabilities & Net Worth	100.0	100.0
						INCOME DATA		
100.0	100.0	100.0	100.0			Net Sales	100.0	100.0
63.3	63.4	54.3	57.8			Gross Profit	62.3	63.4
59.1	58.5	49.5	52.1			Operating Expenses	56.3	57.2
4.2	4.9	4.8	5.7			Operating Profit	6.0	6.3
1.9	1.1	1.4	2.4			All Other Expenses (net)	1.9	2.1
2.3	3.9	3.4	3.3			Profit Before Taxes	4.1	4.2

RATIOS

0-500M	500M-2MM	2-10MM	10-50MM	50-100MM	100-250MM		Hist 1	Hist 2
2.0	1.4	1.2	.6			Current	1.3	1.3
.6	.9	.8	.4				.6	.7
.2	.3	.3	.3				.3	.3
1.6	1.2	.9	.4			Quick	1.0	1.0
.4	.6	.6	.3				(648) .4	(574) .4
.1	.1	.1	.2				.1	.1
0 UND	0 UND	0 UND	0 UND			Sales/Receivables	0 UND	0 UND
0 UND	0 UND	0 999.8	1 529.0				0 UND	0 UND
0 UND	1 320.0	1 306.9	2 234.6				1 393.8	1 417.1
5 73.9	6 56.5	4 83.6	4 93.7			Cost of Sales/Inventory	6 60.6	7 54.8
7 51.3	7 49.3	7 52.8	9 41.7				9 40.3	10 38.4
14 26.3	12 29.6	11 32.3	12 29.4				13 28.5	13 27.6
0 UND	6 65.7	14 26.3	17 21.6			Cost of Sales/Payables	8 46.0	9 39.1
9 42.8	16 22.4	19 19.1	23 16.2				20 18.1	22 16.9
24 15.5	35 10.4	32 11.5	41 9.0				36 10.1	40 9.2
34.7	48.3	77.5	-25.1			Sales/Working Capital	72.5	55.9
-48.4	-106.3	-51.2	-15.8				-38.8	-38.4
-13.0	-18.8	-20.6	-10.9				-13.0	-13.3
8.9	6.7	5.0	3.2			EBIT/Interest	7.1	6.3
(63) 2.7	(31) 2.3	(36) 2.2	(14) 1.5				(582) 2.8	(510) 2.7
.7	1.1	.9	.8				1.4	1.3
						Net Profit + Depr., Dep., Amort./Cur. Mat. L /T/D	4.2	4.2
							(73) 2.2	(63) 2.5
							1.3	1.2
1.3	1.9	1.2	1.9			Fixed/Worth	1.2	1.3
29.0	UND	4.1	24.0				4.4	4.9
-1.6	-2.9	-6.3	-2.9				-3.7	-3.9
2.0	1.7	1.1	1.5			Debt/Worth	1.2	1.2
-110.0	UND	5.5	25.6				6.4	7.3
-3.1	-5.6	-8.4	-5.0				-6.6	-6.1
151.6	183.0	76.6				% Profit Before Taxes/Tangible Net Worth	112.8	103.0
(37) 58.7	(19) 85.8	(28) 24.7					(421) 48.1	(362) 40.0
2.8	37.2	6.7					16.9	12.9
39.4	25.6	14.0	13.7			% Profit Before Taxes/Total Assets	23.9	20.6
8.9	6.4	4.8	3.0				10.5	8.7
-1.7	.2	-.3	-.5				2.4	1.9
18.1	10.1	7.3	5.1			Sales/Net Fixed Assets	12.9	12.0
8.4	4.7	4.6	2.0				6.3	6.1
4.0	2.6	2.9	1.8				2.7	3.1
6.1	4.3	3.6	2.7			Sales/Total Assets	5.1	4.8
3.8	2.7	2.5	1.5				3.1	3.0
2.5	2.0	1.7	1.3				1.7	1.9
1.8	2.5	2.6	3.3			% Depr., Dep., Amort./Sales	1.9	2.1
(68) 2.9	(33) 3.8	3.6	(14) 4.8				(584) 3.0	(505) 3.1
5.1	4.9	4.7	5.9				4.5	4.5
1.8	1.8	1.1				% Officers', Directors', Owners' Comp/Sales	2.0	1.9
(35) 4.8	(13) 4.2	(14) 1.7					(265) 3.5	(224) 3.0
7.2	7.5	4.5					6.5	5.3
60700M	142345M	523375M	699415M	964627M	551354M	Net Sales ($)	9750246M	11488039M
15376M	42518M	186625M	391591M	271905M	417334M	Total Assets ($)	5130384M	5679772M

M = $ thousand MM = $ million
See Pages 11 through 18 for Explanation of Ratios and Data

Comparative Historical Data | Current Data Sorted By Sales

Type of Statement	4/1/00-3/31/01 ALL	4/1/01-3/31/02 ALL	4/1/02-3/31/03 ALL	16 (4/1-9/30/02) 0-1MM	1-3MM	3-5MM	155 (10/1/02-3/31/03) 5-10MM	10-25MM	25MM & OVER
Unqualified	46	35	16	1				2	13
Reviewed	68	59	8		1	2	2	2	1
Compiled	147	101	38	9	8	5	9	5	2
Tax Returns	94	77	66	36	19	4	2	4	1
Other	189	151	43	12	6	5	9	6	5
NUMBER OF STATEMENTS	544	423	171	58	34	16	22	19	22
ASSETS	%	%	%	%	%	%	%	%	%
Cash & Equivalents	13.4	12.8	12.4	12.3	17.6	8.4	13.2	9.9	9.0
Trade Receivables (net)	1.6	1.6	.9	.5	.9	1.4	.4	1.2	1.6
Inventory	4.3	4.0	3.3	4.5	3.5	2.3	2.2	2.6	2.1
All Other Current	1.9	2.6	2.6	.6	4.8	5.1	1.2	3.1	3.5
Total Current	21.3	21.0	19.2	17.9	26.9	17.2	17.0	16.7	16.2
Fixed Assets (net)	55.9	54.7	57.0	53.7	55.7	55.0	64.9	62.4	56.8
Intangibles (net)	13.6	13.3	14.2	18.7	8.6	13.8	10.3	12.8	16.1
All Other Non-Current	9.2	11.0	9.6	9.7	8.8	13.9	7.8	8.1	10.9
Total	100.0	100.0	100.0	100.0	100.0	100.0	100.0	100.0	100.0
LIABILITIES									
Notes Payable-Short Term	9.8	4.7	5.6	9.0	3.9	12.0	2.9	1.1	.9
Cur. Mat.-L/T/D	6.3	6.1	6.0	5.6	5.3	6.1	8.8	6.4	4.9
Trade Payables	9.5	9.2	7.4	6.5	7.4	6.9	7.9	7.1	9.8
Income Taxes Payable	.2	.2	.2	.1	.6	.3	.1	.0	.0
All Other Current	15.2	13.9	16.9	29.7	12.4	9.0	7.6	12.1	9.3
Total Current	41.0	34.1	36.1	51.0	29.5	34.4	27.4	26.7	24.9
Long Term Debt	41.1	40.2	45.6	49.6	40.0	36.7	50.5	39.6	50.8
Deferred Taxes	.1	.1	.2	.0	.1	.0	.0	.2	.9
All Other Non-Current	5.3	4.7	8.3	14.1	6.1	7.4	3.3	4.1	5.2
Net Worth	12.4	20.9	9.9	−14.7	24.3	21.5	18.8	29.4	18.2
Total Liabilities & Net Worth	100.0	100.0	100.0	100.0	100.0	100.0	100.0	100.0	100.0
INCOME DATA									
Net Sales	100.0	100.0	100.0	100.0	100.0	100.0	100.0	100.0	100.0
Gross Profit	62.4	60.3	60.3	61.3	66.7	60.2	59.4	56.4	51.9
Operating Expenses	57.9	56.3	55.6	58.3	60.1	56.5	53.0	52.7	45.8
Operating Profit	4.5	4.0	4.7	3.0	6.6	3.7	6.4	3.6	6.1
All Other Expenses (net)	1.5	1.3	1.6	2.5	1.0	.0	2.4	.2	2.1
Profit Before Taxes	3.0	2.7	3.0	.5	5.6	3.7	4.0	3.4	4.0

RATIOS

Ratio	4/1/00-3/31/01	4/1/01-3/31/02	4/1/02-3/31/03	0-1MM	1-3MM	3-5MM	5-10MM	10-25MM	25MM & OVER
Current	1.2 / .5 / .3	1.4 / .6 / .3	1.5 / .6 / .3	1.8 / .5 / .2	2.3 / 1.0 / .5	1.3 / .5 / .2	1.2 / .7 / .3	1.0 / .6 / .3	1.0 / .4 / .3
Quick	(541) .9 / .4 / .1	(418) 1.0 / .4 / .1	(170) 1.2 / .4 / .1	1.5 / .3 / .0	1.7 / .6 / .4	1.2 / .3 / .1	1.0 / .6 / .1	.9 / .5 / .1	(21) .7 / .3 / .2
Sales/Receivables	0 UND / 0 UND / 1 336.7	0 UND / 0 UND / 1 267.3	0 UND / 0 UND / 1 599.0	0 UND / 0 UND / 0 UND	0 UND / 0 UND / 0 999.8	0 UND / 1 467.3 / 3 123.6	0 UND / 0 UND / 0 848.2	0 UND / 1 582.7 / 2 205.8	0 UND / 0 887.2 / 1 303.1
Cost of Sales/Inventory	6 58.8 / 10 37.0 / 14 26.7	5 66.4 / 9 41.7 / 12 29.7	5 78.5 / 7 49.6 / 12 31.3	5 79.0 / 7 53.2 / 16 22.6	6 62.2 / 7 49.3 / 13 28.2	7 54.9 / 7 48.9 / 12 30.9	4 82.1 / 7 51.3 / 11 33.9	2 98.2 / 8 45.2 / 12 29.4	3 114.5 / 6 59.0 / 10 36.5
Cost of Sales/Payables	10 36.3 / 22 16.3 / 38 9.6	7 54.1 / 20 18.3 / 34 10.7	5 75.0 / 16 22.2 / 30 12.3	0 UND / 5 71.0 / 28 13.2	5 72.4 / 13 27.2 / 26 14.2	10 38.4 / 17 21.2 / 40 9.2	10 36.8 / 23 15.7 / 33 11.1	14 26.4 / 19 19.6 / 21 17.6	17 21.5 / 27 13.7 / 44 8.2
Sales/Working Capital	56.7 / −29.5 / −13.7	69.4 / −35.1 / −14.5	50.9 / −46.5 / −14.1	35.5 / −37.6 / −12.0	26.9 / 675.0 / −40.5	271.8 / −16.4 / −13.0	121.8 / −40.2 / −19.3	409.1 / −47.7 / −15.8	−346.0 / −19.8 / −14.0
EBIT/Interest	(490) 5.6 / 2.3 / .9	(376) 6.2 / 2.2 / .9	(149) 6.2 / 2.2 / 1.0	(48) 4.2 / 1.9 / −.4	(27) 17.4 / 4.0 / 1.2	(15) 6.4 / 1.8 / .2	9.2 / 2.5 / 1.2	(18) 10.7 / 2.4 / .9	(19) 4.5 / 1.8 / 1.0
Net Profit + Depr., Dep., Amort./Cur. Mat. L/T/D	(59) 5.0 / 2.2 / 1.2	(45) 4.4 / 2.0 / 1.1	(18) 4.7 / 2.1 / 1.5						
Fixed/Worth	1.4 / 5.8 / −2.9	1.3 / 3.7 / −4.8	1.5 / 16.2 / −2.6	1.8 / −10.7 / −1.3	1.0 / 11.1 / −4.4	1.1 / 4.4 / −2.3	1.6 / 7.6 / −2.1	1.5 / 4.1 / −12.5	1.3 / NM / −2.9
Debt/Worth	1.3 / 7.8 / −5.1	1.3 / 4.7 / −7.7	1.6 / 26.7 / −4.4	3.2 / −7.8 / −2.4	.9 / 16.8 / −8.9	1.3 / 6.4 / −4.0	1.5 / 8.9 / −3.6	1.4 / 4.2 / −15.9	1.4 / NM / −4.7
% Profit Before Taxes/Tangible Net Worth	(330) 87.2 / 33.7 / 8.5	(276) 86.6 / 28.6 / 7.5	(95) 118.8 / 52.6 / 8.1	(25) 190.1 / 52.6 / 1.6	(21) 155.2 / 65.8 / 20.6		(15) 154.1 / 29.9 / 4.9	(14) 70.4 / 27.3 / 13.2	(11) 118.3 / 59.1 / 4.9
% Profit Before Taxes/Total Assets	18.7 / 6.7 / −.4	18.4 / 6.2 / .1	20.6 / 5.9 / −.2	23.0 / 6.0 / −6.1	53.3 / 12.6 / 2.7	23.0 / 2.3 / −4.6	16.0 / 6.5 / .2	17.8 / 4.6 / −.5	20.8 / 4.3 / .4
Sales/Net Fixed Assets	11.7 / 5.8 / 2.8	12.4 / 6.4 / 2.8	10.8 / 5.5 / 2.8	17.1 / 6.3 / 2.8	15.8 / 8.4 / 3.9	7.7 / 4.7 / 2.8	6.9 / 4.8 / 1.9	8.0 / 4.7 / 2.6	9.6 / 4.3 / 2.8
Sales/Total Assets	5.0 / 3.1 / 1.8	5.1 / 3.1 / 1.8	4.6 / 3.0 / 1.9	4.6 / 3.4 / 1.8	6.6 / 3.9 / 2.4	3.5 / 2.5 / 2.0	3.9 / 3.3 / 1.5	3.9 / 2.6 / 1.7	3.5 / 2.1 / 1.4
% Depr., Dep., Amort./Sales	(508) 2.0 / 3.1 / 4.6	(377) 1.9 / 2.8 / 4.4	(156) 2.2 / 3.5 / 5.0	(51) 2.2 / 3.5 / 6.9	(31) 1.8 / 2.7 / 4.5	(15) 3.2 / 3.7 / 4.9	2.9 / 3.9 / 4.8	(18) 2.1 / 3.0 / 4.1	(19) 2.6 / 4.5 / 5.1
% Officers', Directors', Owners' Comp/Sales	(205) 1.9 / 3.3 / 5.6	(171) 1.7 / 3.2 / 5.8	(64) 1.5 / 4.0 / 5.6	(26) 2.5 / 5.8 / 8.7	(15) 1.2 / 3.4 / 5.4				
Net Sales ($)	10211746M	8891875M	2941816M	29864M	55940M	66042M	169262M	306546M	2314162M
Total Assets ($)	4958094M	4384163M	1325349M	12140M	17889M	28943M	77454M	131931M	1056992M

M = $ thousand   MM = $ million
See Pages 11 through 18 for Explanation of Ratios and Data

Current Data Sorted By Assets   Comparative Historical Data

Type of Statement	0-500M	500M-2MM	2-10MM	10-50MM	50-100MM	100-250MM		4/1/98-3/31/99 ALL	4/1/99-3/31/00 ALL
Unqualified	1		2	3				6	4
Reviewed		1	1	1				7	7
Compiled	23	10	3	1				46	41
Tax Returns	68	11	1					43	36
Other	22	13	3	6				49	44
	17 (4/1-9/30/02)		152 (10/1/02-3/31/03)						
NUMBER OF STATEMENTS	114	35	10	10				151	132
ASSETS	%	%	%	%	%	%		%	%
Cash & Equivalents	16.5	14.2	16.0	15.8	D A T A N O T A V A I L A B L E	D A T A N O T A V A I L A B L E		12.1	13.0
Trade Receivables (net)	1.6	.8	6.8	.9				1.8	2.5
Inventory	11.5	6.2	5.1	5.6				9.5	10.2
All Other Current	3.4	3.2	2.0	16.0				2.9	2.1
Total Current	33.0	24.4	30.0	38.4				26.3	27.9
Fixed Assets (net)	44.2	63.8	51.5	40.0				57.2	51.1
Intangibles (net)	11.4	4.9	7.9	7.7				9.6	10.9
All Other Non-Current	11.4	7.0	10.6	14.0				6.8	10.1
Total	100.0	100.0	100.0	100.0				100.0	100.0
LIABILITIES									
Notes Payable-Short Term	6.8	5.3	3.3	5.7				4.4	6.1
Cur. Mat.-L/T/D	2.5	3.5	6.2	1.2				4.7	4.4
Trade Payables	6.9	7.8	9.3	3.6				8.1	7.6
Income Taxes Payable	.4	.1	.7	.2				.3	.1
All Other Current	17.2	6.4	14.8	8.6				20.7	18.6
Total Current	33.9	23.1	34.3	19.3				38.3	36.8
Long Term Debt	31.3	39.6	32.8	24.2				35.5	32.5
Deferred Taxes	.0	.0	.0	.2				.0	.0
All Other Non-Current	16.9	16.5	1.8	10.3				11.3	13.7
Net Worth	18.0	20.8	31.1	46.1				14.8	17.0
Total Liabilities & Net Worth	100.0	100.0	100.0	100.0				100.0	100.0
INCOME DATA									
Net Sales	100.0	100.0	100.0	100.0				100.0	100.0
Gross Profit	57.9	62.9	57.1	54.0				59.6	56.3
Operating Expenses	54.2	56.0	50.3	46.4				55.6	51.4
Operating Profit	3.7	7.0	6.8	7.5				4.0	4.9
All Other Expenses (net)	1.1	1.7	2.1	.2				.5	1.1
Profit Before Taxes	2.6	5.3	4.7	7.3				3.5	3.8

RATIOS

Ratio	0-500M	500M-2MM	2-10MM	10-50MM		Comparative (4/1/98-3/31/99)		Comparative (4/1/99-3/31/00)
Current	3.9 / 1.3 / .3	3.0 / .9 / .5	1.3 / .9 / .4	4.8 / 2.3 / .7		2.0 / .9 / .3		2.6 / 1.0 / .4
Quick	1.9 / .7 / .1	2.5 / .4 / .2	1.0 / .7 / .3	3.0 / .6 / .4		(147) 1.1 / .3 / .1		1.6 / .5 / .1
Sales/Receivables	0 UND / 0 UND / 0 UND	0 UND / 0 UND / 1 289.7	0 UND / 2 205.7 / 6 65.3	0 UND / 0 917.4 / 1 263.3		0 UND / 0 UND / 1 492.5		0 UND / 0 UND / 1 258.1
Cost of Sales/Inventory	8 48.4 / 19 19.0 / 30 12.0	12 30.3 / 17 21.8 / 28 13.2	10 38.0 / 17 21.4 / 31 11.6	6 62.3 / 17 21.2 / 30 12.1		11 34.2 / 18 20.0 / 31 11.6		12 29.6 / 21 17.1 / 37 9.8
Cost of Sales/Payables	0 UND / 2 171.2 / 25 14.8	10 35.2 / 24 15.3 / 51 7.2	6 62.5 / 40 9.0 / 89 4.1	3 105.6 / 9 39.1 / 30 12.2		0 UND / 11 34.4 / 34 10.8		0 UND / 17 21.7 / 38 9.6
Sales/Working Capital	17.1 / 70.2 / -18.1	16.3 / -188.3 / -26.3	39.5 / NM / -7.0	7.2 / 12.9 / -74.5		22.8 / -208.0 / -11.2		16.9 / -578.5 / -18.2
EBIT/Interest	(69) 5.2 / 1.9 / .4	(31) 17.1 / 2.9 / .2				(121) 5.0 / 2.2 / .8		(103) 7.0 / 2.8 / .8
Net Profit + Depr., Dep., Amort./Cur. Mat. L./T/D								
Fixed/Worth	.4 / 2.0 / -2.5	.9 / 2.8 / -9.2	1.1 / 1.9 / 5.4	.1 / .9 / 3.8		1.2 / 3.2 / -4.1		.8 / 2.1 / -6.0
Debt/Worth	.4 / 3.3 / -4.6	.5 / 3.6 / -11.6	1.3 / 3.4 / 9.7	.6 / 1.6 / NM		1.0 / 3.6 / -5.6		.8 / 2.4 / -10.4
% Profit Before Taxes/Tangible Net Worth	(72) 67.4 / 26.6 / 3.0	(22) 66.8 / 44.5 / 3.9				(99) 83.1 / 32.8 / 11.8		(89) 59.0 / 33.7 / 7.7
% Profit Before Taxes/Total Assets	24.4 / 4.9 / -3.7	34.5 / 9.0 / -3.8	22.4 / 5.2 / -.7	22.4 / 15.0 / 8.7		19.3 / 7.0 / .0		20.6 / 7.5 / -.6
Sales/Net Fixed Assets	29.6 / 10.4 / 5.3	6.9 / 3.4 / 2.5	24.3 / 3.9 / 1.5	UND / 4.4 / 2.1		11.9 / 5.3 / 2.2		13.9 / 6.3 / 2.8
Sales/Total Assets	5.7 / 3.8 / 2.4	3.1 / 2.5 / 1.9	6.4 / 2.0 / 1.0	4.0 / 1.9 / .9		5.1 / 2.9 / 1.6		4.7 / 2.8 / 1.7
% Depr., Dep., Amort./Sales	(92) 1.2 / 2.3 / 5.2	(33) 2.1 / 3.1 / 4.9	1.6 / 2.7 / 5.7			(130) 1.5 / 3.0 / 5.6		(112) 1.5 / 2.9 / 4.2
% Officers', Directors', Owners' Comp/Sales	(52) 3.2 / 7.0 / 10.9	(15) 2.1 / 2.6 / 6.5				(71) 3.2 / 5.7 / 10.6		(55) 2.4 / 5.4 / 9.8
Net Sales ($)	92902M	89543M	244945M	378188M		942076M		274007M
Total Assets ($)	24851M	33931M	59491M	132289M		454551M		163215M

© RMA 2003

M = $ thousand   MM = $ million
See Pages 11 through 18 for Explanation of Ratios and Data

Comparative Historical Data				Current Data Sorted By Sales					
			Type of Statement						
4	7	6	Unqualified		1			1	4
3	2	2	Reviewed			1		1	
51	33	37	Compiled	13	18	3	1	2	
50	56	80	Tax Returns	50	26	4	2	5	3
38	44	44	Other	16	15	3			
4/1/00-3/31/01 ALL	4/1/01-3/31/02 ALL	4/1/02-3/31/03 ALL		17 (4/1-9/30/02) 0-1MM	1-3MM	3-5MM	152 (10/1/02-3/31/03) 5-10MM	10-25MM	25MM & OVER
146	142	169	**NUMBER OF STATEMENTS**	79	60	11	3	9	7
%	%	%	**ASSETS**	%	%	%	%	%	%
12.9	13.8	16.0	Cash & Equivalents	15.8	16.5	10.8			
1.2	1.5	1.7	Trade Receivables (net)	.3	3.0	2.4			
9.7	9.2	9.7	Inventory	9.9	10.5	6.4			
2.7	2.9	4.0	All Other Current	3.1	3.0	5.9			
26.5	27.5	31.4	Total Current	29.1	33.1	25.5			
48.4	48.5	48.4	Fixed Assets (net)	47.7	49.7	61.1			
13.2	11.7	9.6	Intangibles (net)	12.0	7.9	3.8			
11.9	12.2	10.6	All Other Non-Current	11.1	9.4	9.6			
100.0	100.0	100.0	Total	100.0	100.0	100.0			
			LIABILITIES						
5.9	3.2	6.2	Notes Payable-Short Term	7.7	5.4	3.5			
4.5	3.8	2.8	Cur. Mat.-L/T/D	3.4	1.6	5.4			
6.3	11.1	7.1	Trade Payables	4.7	9.8	6.2			
.2	.2	.4	Income Taxes Payable	.5	.2	.0			
26.5	22.8	14.3	All Other Current	18.2	11.2	7.4			
43.4	41.1	30.8	Total Current	34.4	28.4	22.5			
31.9	38.3	32.7	Long Term Debt	37.2	28.5	37.9			
.1	.0	.0	Deferred Taxes	.1	.0	.0			
14.4	13.8	15.5	All Other Non-Current	22.9	9.7	8.2			
10.2	6.7	21.0	Net Worth	5.4	33.5	31.3			
100.0	100.0	100.0	Total Liabilities & Net Worth	100.0	100.0	100.0			
			INCOME DATA						
100.0	100.0	100.0	Net Sales	100.0	100.0	100.0			
59.3	58.2	58.7	Gross Profit	59.4	58.6	59.4			
54.2	53.5	53.9	Operating Expenses	55.5	53.3	55.6			
5.1	4.7	4.8	Operating Profit	3.9	5.3	3.9			
.8	1.6	1.2	All Other Expenses (net)	1.9	.8	.9			
4.3	3.1	3.5	Profit Before Taxes	2.0	4.5	2.9			
			RATIOS						
2.2	2.3	3.5	Current	3.9	3.3	5.2			
.9	.8	1.2		1.2	1.2	.9			
.3	.3	.5		.3	.6	.7			
1.2	1.1	1.8	Quick	2.3	1.6	3.1			
(144) .4	(140) .4	.6		.5	.8	.6			
.1	.1	.1		.1	.2	.1			
0 UND	0 UND	0 UND	Sales/Receivables	0 UND	0 UND	0 UND			
0 UND	0 UND	0 UND		0 UND	0 UND	0 836.7			
1 534.4	1 488.2	0 978.9		0 UND	1 245.6	2 185.8			
10 36.6	9 39.4	8 43.4	Cost of Sales/Inventory	8 48.0	9 41.6	8 45.0			
15 24.7	16 22.3	18 20.4		20 18.0	15 24.5	17 22.1			
24 14.9	29 12.5	29 12.6		32 11.5	26 14.1	25 14.5			
0 UND	0 UND	0 UND	Cost of Sales/Payables	0 UND	2 195.0	0 UND			
7 53.2	14 26.5	8 43.7		0 UND	20 18.1	24 15.3			
34 10.7	38 9.5	31 11.6		17 21.8	43 8.5	36 10.0			
25.7	28.0	15.6	Sales/Working Capital	17.4	17.0	9.9			
-153.6	-93.3	94.0		158.7	95.0	-188.3			
-18.3	-14.2	-19.1		-14.8	-35.6	-26.3			
6.4	7.2	7.6	EBIT/Interest	2.7	11.7	9.6			
(110) 2.7	(110) 2.0	(117) 2.1		(48) 1.4	(43) 3.0	(10) 1.3			
1.2	.7	.6		-.2	1.4	.0			
			Net Profit + Depr., Dep., Amort./Cur. Mat. L/T/D						
.7	.9	.5	Fixed/Worth	.5	.5	.9			
3.0	2.6	2.2		4.5	1.6	2.5			
-3.4	-4.1	-5.0		-1.3	-21.0	4.7			
.7	.8	.5	Debt/Worth	.5	.4	.5			
3.4	3.5	3.1		10.2	2.0	2.2			
-5.3	-7.4	-8.2		-2.7	-14.3	5.9			
73.8	91.3	67.4	% Profit Before Taxes/Tangible Net Worth	78.7	58.8				
(93) 39.0	(92) 40.1	(111) 30.2		(44) 30.5	(42) 26.9				
14.8	11.1	4.7		-.8	4.6				
23.6	25.5	28.8	% Profit Before Taxes/Total Assets	24.2	33.9	33.2			
8.3	6.6	6.5		3.4	8.7	2.9			
1.6	-2.1	-2.3		-7.1	1.1	-3.3			
17.2	21.5	21.6	Sales/Net Fixed Assets	26.1	21.8	7.3			
8.4	8.3	7.3		7.6	7.8	4.8			
3.9	3.5	3.2		3.1	3.9	2.6			
5.4	5.9	4.9	Sales/Total Assets	5.2	4.7	3.4			
3.2	3.2	3.2		3.0	3.8	2.5			
2.0	1.9	2.0		1.8	2.6	2.1			
1.2	1.3	1.5	% Depr., Dep., Amort./Sales	1.4	1.5	1.9			
(124) 2.4	(116) 2.5	(143) 2.6		(61) 3.3	(54) 2.3	2.6			
3.8	4.1	5.1		8.0	3.7	5.5			
3.1	3.7	2.6	% Officers', Directors', Owners' Comp/Sales	3.0	3.0				
(64) 6.9	(64) 6.0	(74) 6.0		(33) 6.5	(30) 6.9				
9.5	9.3	10.5		11.0	10.7				
4042806M	483670M	805578M	Net Sales ($)	38734M	99914M	40848M	20428M	128638M	477016M
634727M	222806M	250562M	Total Assets ($)	15085M	32011M	23134M	6236M	86906M	87190M

© RMA 2003

M = $ thousand   MM = $ million
See Pages 11 through 18 for Explanation of Ratios and Data

OTHER SERVICES
(EXCEPT PUBLIC
ADMINISTRATION)

Current Data Sorted By Assets   **Comparative Historical Data**

0-500M	500M-2MM	2-10MM	10-50MM	50-100MM	100-250MM	Type of Statement	4/1/98-3/31/99 ALL	4/1/99-3/31/00 ALL
3		2	2	2	1	Unqualified	10	16
5	10	14				Reviewed	27	28
51	36	12			1	Compiled	137	117
112	28	4		1	2	Tax Returns	104	97
50	20	7	4	1	2	Other	94	87
	63 (4/1-9/30/02)		307 (10/1/02-3/31/03)					
221	94	39	6	4	6	NUMBER OF STATEMENTS	372	345
%	%	%	%	%	%	ASSETS	%	%
17.6	10.0	7.2				Cash & Equivalents	12.9	11.7
10.0	12.5	14.0				Trade Receivables (net)	13.7	16.0
19.6	21.2	22.1				Inventory	21.2	21.9
2.1	1.8	3.4				All Other Current	1.8	2.0
49.2	45.5	46.7				Total Current	49.6	51.7
37.4	43.1	38.4				Fixed Assets (net)	39.6	35.8
5.0	3.2	4.6				Intangibles (net)	4.1	4.5
8.5	8.2	10.3				All Other Non-Current	6.7	8.1
100.0	100.0	100.0				Total	100.0	100.0
						LIABILITIES		
10.4	7.7	10.3				Notes Payable-Short Term	8.5	9.1
5.5	4.5	3.6				Cur. Mat.-L/T/D	6.0	5.4
13.0	11.8	12.7				Trade Payables	14.7	17.3
.2	.1	.2				Income Taxes Payable	.3	.4
14.6	6.7	6.9				All Other Current	10.5	11.9
43.7	30.9	33.8				Total Current	40.1	44.1
28.8	30.6	24.0				Long Term Debt	28.2	25.2
.0	.2	.3				Deferred Taxes	.2	.4
7.8	4.7	5.8				All Other Non-Current	5.4	10.9
19.7	33.7	36.1				Net Worth	26.0	19.4
100.0	100.0	100.0				Total Liabilities & Net Worth	100.0	100.0
						INCOME DATA		
100.0	100.0	100.0				Net Sales	100.0	100.0
						Gross Profit		
95.9	95.9	96.8				Operating Expenses	95.2	94.3
4.1	4.1	3.2				Operating Profit	4.8	5.7
1.1	1.9	.7				All Other Expenses (net)	1.1	1.3
3.0	2.2	2.5				Profit Before Taxes	3.7	4.3
						RATIOS		
2.9	2.9	2.8				Current	2.4	2.2
1.3	1.4	1.4					1.4	1.4
.7	.7	.9					.9	.8
2.0	1.6	1.2				Quick	1.3	1.4
(219) .7	.7	.6					(369) .7	(340) .7
.3	.3	.3					.3	.3
0 UND	2 228.5	4 90.7				Sales/Receivables	2 184.6	2 180.4
3 118.3	11 32.8	17 20.9					9 39.9	11 34.7
11 33.6	28 13.0	36 10.2					24 15.2	30 12.0
						Cost of Sales/Inventory		
						Cost of Sales/Payables		
13.8	6.7	7.7				Sales/Working Capital	11.4	11.0
65.0	26.9	23.8					29.0	31.9
-50.1	-22.0	-146.3					-80.5	-47.1
10.4	5.1	9.8				EBIT/Interest	8.0	7.0
(162) 3.7	(89) 1.8	(38) 3.3					(322) 3.0	(282) 2.9
1.0	.7	1.4					1.1	1.0
	5.2					Net Profit + Depr., Dep., Amort./Cur. Mat. L /T/D	5.1	5.2
	(15) 2.5						(48) 2.2	(48) 2.0
	.6						.9	.8
.4	.4	.4				Fixed/Worth	.5	.4
1.5	1.7	1.0					1.3	1.2
-10.4	5.4	2.6					11.4	UND
.7	.7	1.1				Debt/Worth	.8	.9
2.9	2.5	1.8					2.3	2.5
-15.4	9.7	4.8					30.2	-131.2
99.2	32.7	39.2				% Profit Before Taxes/Tangible Net Worth	59.4	66.3
(160) 23.4	(77) 9.8	(35) 13.0					(289) 22.8	(257) 22.7
.1	1.3	3.2					7.1	7.6
29.7	8.9	10.7				% Profit Before Taxes/Total Assets	21.4	19.3
8.7	2.9	3.8					6.9	6.8
-.2	-1.1	.9					.6	.0
49.0	16.4	17.2				Sales/Net Fixed Assets	29.1	29.7
18.9	8.5	12.0					11.6	13.6
8.1	2.3	3.2					4.7	6.2
8.4	3.4	3.8				Sales/Total Assets	5.8	5.4
4.9	2.5	2.3					3.5	3.6
3.1	1.6	1.7					2.1	2.1
.9	1.5	1.2				% Depr., Dep., Amort./Sales	1.2	1.1
(157) 1.9	(88) 2.8	(38) 1.7					(310) 2.2	(288) 2.2
3.3	4.4	3.0					3.5	3.4
4.6	2.7	2.4				% Officers', Directors', Owners' Comp/Sales	3.8	4.1
(154) 7.4	(61) 4.8	(16) 3.6					(203) 6.6	(195) 6.8
11.2	8.1	4.6					10.3	10.1
200143M	248549M	403280M	234529M	1833261M	4889478M	Net Sales ($)	3569107M	4055766M
43040M	91678M	143934M	182478M	311084M	899698M	Total Assets ($)	774427M	1348584M

M = $ thousand   MM = $ million
See Pages 11 through 18 for Explanation of Ratios and Data

Comparative Historical Data | Current Data Sorted By Sales

Type of Statement									
	4	9	10	2	2			2	4
Unqualified	23	19	29	4	7	5	3	9	1
Reviewed	91	95	100	31	48	10	6	4	1
Compiled	99	103	147	92	39	8	5		3
Tax Returns	66	71	84	37	30	4	5		6
Other	4/1/00-3/31/01	4/1/01-3/31/02	4/1/02-3/31/03	63 (4/1-9/30/02)			307 (10/1/02-3/31/03)		
	ALL	ALL	ALL	0-1MM	1-3MM	3-5MM	5-10MM	10-25MM	25MM & OVER
NUMBER OF STATEMENTS	283	297	370	166	126	27	19	17	15
ASSETS	%	%	%	%	%	%	%	%	%
Cash & Equivalents	10.4	10.7	14.0	15.1	15.9	10.3	9.7	8.3	5.3
Trade Receivables (net)	15.0	13.7	11.1	7.6	12.9	15.5	13.5	21.1	13.3
Inventory	23.5	21.7	20.0	18.4	20.4	24.5	20.8	28.7	14.9
All Other Current	1.5	3.0	2.3	1.8	2.3	1.5	2.1	2.7	8.8
Total Current	50.5	49.0	47.4	42.8	51.6	51.7	46.1	60.7	42.3
Fixed Assets (net)	35.6	37.2	39.7	44.3	36.0	33.5	36.5	27.0	50.4
Intangibles (net)	5.9	6.0	4.4	4.3	4.5	6.1	4.6	2.8	2.1
All Other Non-Current	8.0	7.8	8.5	8.6	7.9	8.7	12.7	9.6	5.2
Total	100.0	100.0	100.0	100.0	100.0	100.0	100.0	100.0	100.0
LIABILITIES									
Notes Payable-Short Term	12.8	11.1	9.7	9.6	9.5	11.4	6.2	11.5	12.4
Cur. Mat.-L/T/D	5.0	5.4	5.1	6.2	4.2	4.0	3.8	4.7	5.5
Trade Payables	16.4	14.7	12.8	9.9	15.4	10.7	14.3	19.2	17.0
Income Taxes Payable	.2	.3	.3	.2	.2	.0	.1	.3	2.5
All Other Current	9.9	11.6	11.8	14.7	9.3	7.2	7.0	10.6	18.0
Total Current	44.3	43.1	39.7	40.5	38.6	33.3	31.4	46.3	55.3
Long Term Debt	25.6	29.6	28.9	35.4	26.0	16.4	23.6	13.1	27.3
Deferred Taxes	.2	.2	.1	.0	.1	.0	.3	.6	.0
All Other Non-Current	5.8	7.0	7.1	7.3	7.5	4.8	4.1	2.9	14.0
Net Worth	24.1	20.1	24.2	16.8	27.8	45.5	40.6	37.2	3.4
Total Liabilities & Net Worth	100.0	100.0	100.0	100.0	100.0	100.0	100.0	100.0	100.0
INCOME DATA									
Net Sales	100.0	100.0	100.0	100.0	100.0	100.0	100.0	100.0	100.0
Gross Profit									
Operating Expenses	95.8	95.9	95.8	94.5	96.6	97.6	97.1	98.0	95.2
Operating Profit	4.2	4.1	4.2	5.4	3.4	2.4	2.9	2.0	4.8
All Other Expenses (net)	1.4	1.9	1.5	2.1	1.3	.4	.1	.4	1.1
Profit Before Taxes	2.8	2.2	2.7	3.4	2.0	2.0	2.8	1.6	3.7
RATIOS									
Current	2.4	2.2	2.8	3.1	2.9	3.1	2.2	1.7	1.8
	1.4	1.2	1.3	1.2	1.4	1.5	1.3	1.2	.8
	.8	.7	.7	.6	.8	1.0	1.0	.9	.4
Quick	(281) 1.3	(294) 1.2	(368) 1.7	(165) 1.9	(125) 2.1	1.8	1.1	.9	.7
	.6	.5	.7	.6	.7	.9	.7	.7	.2
	.2	.3	.3	.2	.3	.5	.4	.3	.1
Sales/Receivables	2 236.6	2 187.2	0 999.8	0 UND	1 648.2	8 43.0	3 121.9	5 66.7	2 214.0
	9 38.8	10 36.6	5 66.8	3 141.5	8 44.8	17 21.5	11 34.7	21 17.4	7 52.8
	27 13.4	24 15.0	19 19.2	10 35.3	24 15.5	29 12.8	30 12.0	33 11.2	21 17.5
Cost of Sales/Inventory									
Cost of Sales/Payables									
Sales/Working Capital	11.2	12.4	10.9	11.1	10.6	8.8	12.0	8.3	11.4
	31.6	46.4	47.9	85.4	32.0	13.3	42.5	61.3	-40.5
	-45.3	-28.6	-42.9	-21.4	-121.6	972.2	489.2	-92.8	-9.3
EBIT/Interest	(243) 6.3	(254) 7.2	(303) 8.3	(126) 7.4	(101) 10.0	(26) 11.6	(16) 7.6	19.2	6.2
	2.5	2.1	2.6	2.3	2.3	3.1	3.9	3.1	3.4
	1.0	.9	1.0	1.0	1.0	1.0	1.6	1.5	.7
Net Profit + Depr., Dep., Amort./Cur. Mat. L/T/D	(32) 4.7	(40) 3.0	(36) 4.9		(16) 4.8				
	2.1	1.8	2.5		1.6				
	1.3	.7	.7		.1				
Fixed/Worth	.4	.5	.4	.5	.4	.3	.3	.4	1.7
	1.4	1.5	1.6	2.3	1.2	.8	1.0	.7	5.3
	-20.0	-21.5	59.0	-63.7	-145.0	2.2	2.3	1.8	-1.7
Debt/Worth	1.0	1.1	.8	.9	.6	.5	.7	.9	2.5
	2.7	3.4	2.6	3.4	2.6	1.2	1.9	1.5	10.4
	-44.1	-41.2	UND	-41.4	-498.1	4.8	3.9	6.4	-6.2
% Profit Before Taxes/Tangible Net Worth	(208) 62.8	(218) 70.2	(282) 60.5	(122) 85.6	(94) 42.0	(24) 32.6	(18) 45.0	(15) 37.4	
	20.6	22.8	19.1	21.8	11.7	12.5	18.7	13.0	
	5.8	2.8	1.6	.0	.2	1.6	2.0	7.1	
% Profit Before Taxes/Total Assets	16.8	17.8	19.3	23.8	15.7	12.5	9.4	11.1	14.2
	5.7	5.6	5.4	8.0	3.2	2.9	6.3	5.0	7.5
	.0	-.7	.0	-.1	-1.6	.0	.7	1.9	-4.3
Sales/Net Fixed Assets	33.5	29.4	32.0	30.8	43.2	31.2	29.0	18.2	22.8
	13.7	13.5	13.7	12.8	15.5	14.0	13.4	14.2	8.6
	6.0	5.7	5.0	4.3	6.0	6.2	5.7	11.8	2.5
Sales/Total Assets	5.5	5.3	6.2	6.8	6.6	4.9	4.1	5.3	6.6
	3.5	3.5	3.7	4.0	3.9	3.2	3.2	4.1	3.5
	2.2	2.2	2.2	2.0	2.2	1.9	2.3	2.5	1.5
% Depr., Dep., Amort./Sales	(247) .9	(255) 1.0	(294) 1.1	(119) 1.5	(105) .9	(24) 1.2	1.1	1.1	(10) .8
	1.8	1.9	2.1	2.5	2.0	1.9	1.8	1.4	1.6
	3.4	3.5	3.6	4.4	3.1	3.8	3.4	1.9	5.5
% Officers', Directors', Owners' Comp/Sales	(181) 3.5	(175) 3.1	(236) 3.9	(108) 5.7	(90) 3.5	(19) 2.7	(11) 1.9		
	5.9	5.9	6.5	8.7	5.2	4.7	3.0		
	10.0	9.7	10.3	12.0	8.4	7.0	4.3		
Net Sales ($)	2358044M	2748927M	7809240M	91012M	225132M	102048M	134233M	271917M	6984898M
Total Assets ($)	727736M	882719M	1671912M	38642M	116732M	37930M	43710M	76191M	1358707M

M = $ thousand   MM = $ million
See Pages 11 through 18 for Explanation of Ratios and Data

Current Data Sorted By Assets   Comparative Historical Data

Type of Statement	0-500M	500M-2MM	2-10MM	10-50MM	50-100MM	100-250MM		4/1/98-3/31/99 ALL	4/1/99-3/31/00 ALL
Unqualified	1	1						1	1
Reviewed		1						3	5
Compiled	1	4	3					20	27
Tax Returns	4	5	1					10	11
Other	3	3	4	2				19	13
		3 (4/1-9/30/02)		30 (10/1/02-3/31/03)					
NUMBER OF STATEMENTS	9	14	8	2				53	57
	%	%	%	%	%	%	**ASSETS**	%	%
Cash & Equivalents		15.2			D	D		11.6	13.7
Trade Receivables (net)		6.2			A	A		5.7	3.6
Inventory		22.2			T	T		21.4	23.9
All Other Current		4.1			A	A		1.7	3.5
Total Current		47.6						40.3	44.8
Fixed Assets (net)		36.1			N	N		40.8	35.1
Intangibles (net)		9.3			O	O		9.0	10.5
All Other Non-Current		6.9			T	T		9.8	9.7
Total		100.0						100.0	100.0
					A	A	**LIABILITIES**		
Notes Payable-Short Term		5.5			V	V		6.6	8.0
Cur. Mat.-L/T/D		9.7			A	A		3.2	5.5
Trade Payables		17.8			I	I		11.3	13.6
Income Taxes Payable		.0			L	L		.5	.5
All Other Current		8.7			A	A		10.7	12.4
Total Current		41.7			B	B		32.3	40.1
Long Term Debt		24.5			L	L		35.2	24.6
Deferred Taxes		.0			E	E		.1	.2
All Other Non-Current		1.1						7.2	10.7
Net Worth		32.7						25.1	24.4
Total Liabilities & Net Worth		100.0						100.0	100.0
							INCOME DATA		
Net Sales		100.0						100.0	100.0
Gross Profit									
Operating Expenses		98.5						93.5	94.9
Operating Profit		1.5						6.5	5.1
All Other Expenses (net)		.9						1.3	1.2
Profit Before Taxes		.6						5.3	3.8
							RATIOS		
Current		3.3						2.5	2.1
		1.3						1.3	1.3
		.4						.7	.8
Quick		1.5						.9	.7
		.4					(52)	.4	.4
		.1						.2	.2
Sales/Receivables		2 206.0					1	245.7	0 802.4
		3 135.0					2	149.9	2 227.7
		6 64.9					5	71.6	3 124.8
Cost of Sales/Inventory									
Cost of Sales/Payables									
Sales/Working Capital		9.4						14.5	14.6
		30.0						29.2	37.3
		-9.8						-27.2	-50.1
EBIT/Interest		2.5						8.0	8.2
	(11)	1.8					(46)	2.8	(49) 4.8
		-2.2						.9	1.3
Net Profit + Depr., Dep., Amort./Cur. Mat. L /T/D									
Fixed/Worth		.3						.4	.5
		2.7						1.8	1.7
		NM						-3.9	40.5
Debt/Worth		.7						.9	1.1
		3.8						2.3	2.7
		NM						-13.5	NM
% Profit Before Taxes/Tangible Net Worth		51.0						80.0	140.1
	(11)	43.3					(35)	41.9	(43) 41.5
		2.1						11.6	7.8
% Profit Before Taxes/Total Assets		27.6						23.6	21.9
		4.0						8.4	8.6
		-.3						1.0	1.6
Sales/Net Fixed Assets		23.3						26.1	32.8
		11.2						9.7	12.8
		7.8						3.3	5.7
Sales/Total Assets		5.0						4.1	4.8
		4.1						2.7	3.6
		2.1						1.7	2.1
% Depr., Dep., Amort./Sales		1.4						1.1	1.6
		2.2					(42)	1.8	(42) 2.4
		3.5						3.7	3.7
% Officers', Directors', Owners' Comp/Sales		2.9						4.0	3.1
	(10)	3.5					(38)	7.0	(35) 5.3
		7.8						10.7	8.6
Net Sales ($)	3996M	55993M	83599M	127274M				1014063M	727783M
Total Assets ($)	1260M	15227M	28211M	54141M				728881M	531619M

© RMA 2003

M = $ thousand   MM = $ million
See Pages 11 through 18 for Explanation of Ratios and Data

Comparative Historical Data | Current Data Sorted By Sales

			Type of Statement		3 (4/1-9/30/02)		30 (10/1/02-3/31/03)		
1	1	2	Unqualified	1			1		
3	7	1	Reviewed				1		
19	12	8	Compiled		4	1	3		
6	9	10	Tax Returns	4	2	1	3		
16	10	12	Other	4		3		3	2
4/1/00-3/31/01	4/1/01-3/31/02	4/1/02-3/31/03		0-1MM	1-3MM	3-5MM	5-10MM	10-25MM	25MM & OVER
ALL	ALL	ALL							
45	**39**	**33**	**NUMBER OF STATEMENTS**	**9**	**6**	**5**	**8**	**3**	**2**
%	%	%	**ASSETS**	%	%	%	%	%	%
9.9	10.2	14.0	Cash & Equivalents						
6.5	5.6	5.8	Trade Receivables (net)						
25.3	29.5	21.7	Inventory						
3.1	2.8	2.2	All Other Current						
44.9	48.1	43.6	Total Current						
30.5	33.1	41.0	Fixed Assets (net)						
13.7	8.5	8.6	Intangibles (net)						
10.9	10.3	6.8	All Other Non-Current						
100.0	100.0	100.0	Total						
			LIABILITIES						
6.3	6.6	5.1	Notes Payable-Short Term						
4.9	5.2	6.8	Cur. Mat.-L/T/D						
14.9	19.1	22.3	Trade Payables						
.9	.6	.1	Income Taxes Payable						
7.8	19.1	33.2	All Other Current						
34.7	50.6	67.4	Total Current						
33.6	29.4	34.8	Long Term Debt						
.0	.1	.0	Deferred Taxes						
6.1	5.6	.7	All Other Non-Current						
25.5	14.3	-3.0	Net Worth						
100.0	100.0	100.0	Total Liabilities & Net Worth						
			INCOME DATA						
100.0	100.0	100.0	Net Sales						
			Gross Profit						
94.2	97.1	95.1	Operating Expenses						
5.8	2.9	4.9	Operating Profit						
1.6	2.7	1.9	All Other Expenses (net)						
4.2	.2	3.0	Profit Before Taxes						
			RATIOS						
1.9	1.6	1.7	Current						
1.3	1.0	.8							
.9	.6	.4							
.7	.5	.7	Quick						
(44) .3	.2	.3							
.1	.1	.1							
1 297.8	1 289.6	1 377.3	Sales/Receivables						
3 131.3	2 149.4	2 149.1							
5 73.9	5 77.7	4 91.4							
			Cost of Sales/Inventory						
			Cost of Sales/Payables						
15.9	17.1	22.8	Sales/Working Capital						
41.9	999.8	-44.4							
-82.8	-15.6	-11.5							
5.8	3.6	6.6	EBIT/Interest						
(37) 2.1	(33) 1.2	(24) 1.7							
.5	-2.0	1.2							
			Net Profit + Depr., Dep., Amort./Cur. Mat. L/T/D						
.3	.6	.6	Fixed/Worth						
1.5	3.6	4.3							
-3.0	-1.4	-16.4							
.8	.8	1.3	Debt/Worth						
7.1	3.8	6.9							
-6.3	-3.9	-6.1							
77.6	60.2	52.4	% Profit Before Taxes/Tangible Net Worth						
(29) 33.6	(23) 40.3	(21) 37.2							
6.1	5.4	17.1							
21.5	20.6	22.9	% Profit Before Taxes/Total Assets						
6.7	1.5	4.4							
-1.9	-13.2	-1.6							
27.9	36.3	21.4	Sales/Net Fixed Assets						
15.5	13.1	10.8							
6.5	6.7	3.6							
5.1	5.8	5.1	Sales/Total Assets						
3.4	4.0	3.6							
2.1	2.2	2.0							
1.2	.4	1.5	% Depr., Dep., Amort./Sales						
(37) 1.9	(34) 1.2	(29) 2.4							
3.1	2.9	3.9							
2.4	3.3	2.9	% Officers', Directors', Owners' Comp/Sales						
(25) 5.1	(24) 4.6	(17) 3.8							
8.1	8.3	7.8							
242091M	121494M	270862M	Net Sales ($)	3421M	13253M	20412M	65794M	40708M	127274M
110551M	42761M	98839M	Total Assets ($)	2102M	5222M	4411M	22375M	10588M	54141M

© RMA 2003

M = $ thousand   MM = $ million
See Pages 11 through 18 for Explanation of Ratios and Data

Current Data Sorted By Assets   **Comparative Historical Data**

Type of Statement	0-500M	500M-2MM	2-10MM	10-50MM	50-100MM	100-250MM		4/1/98-3/31/99 ALL	4/1/99-3/31/00 ALL
Unqualified				2		1			
Reviewed	9	2	3	1					
Compiled	14	4	2	1					
Tax Returns	3	1	1						
Other		1	1						
NUMBER OF STATEMENTS	26	8	8	4		1			
ASSETS	%	%	%	%	%	%		%	%
Cash & Equivalents	12.4				D	D		D	D
Trade Receivables (net)	21.4				A	A		A	A
Inventory	22.8				T	T		T	T
All Other Current	2.4				A	A		A	A
Total Current	59.0								
Fixed Assets (net)	26.8				N	N		N	N
Intangibles (net)	4.1				O	O		O	O
All Other Non-Current	10.2				T	T		T	T
Total	100.0								
LIABILITIES					A	A		A	A
Notes Payable-Short Term	18.6				V	V		V	V
Cur. Mat.-L/T/D	6.2				A	A		A	A
Trade Payables	21.9				I	I		I	I
Income Taxes Payable	.0				L	L		L	L
All Other Current	46.5				A	A		A	A
Total Current	93.2				B	B		B	B
Long Term Debt	14.9				L	L		L	L
Deferred Taxes	.0				E	E		E	E
All Other Non-Current	15.7								
Net Worth	-23.8								
Total Liabilities & Net Worth	100.0								
INCOME DATA									
Net Sales	100.0								
Gross Profit									
Operating Expenses	94.8								
Operating Profit	5.2								
All Other Expenses (net)	2.1								
Profit Before Taxes	3.1								
RATIOS									
Current	2.1 / 1.1 / .5								
Quick	1.2 / .5 / .1								
Sales/Receivables	0 UND / 5 80.4 / 42 8.8								
Cost of Sales/Inventory									
Cost of Sales/Payables									
Sales/Working Capital	9.2 / 130.0 / -9.4								
EBIT/Interest	(21) 11.0 / 2.2 / .2								
Net Profit + Depr., Dep., Amort./Cur. Mat. L/T/D									
Fixed/Worth	.2 / 1.1 / -5.9								
Debt/Worth	.6 / 12.9 / -3.5								
% Profit Before Taxes/Tangible Net Worth	(15) 64.1 / 15.4 / -5.5								
% Profit Before Taxes/Total Assets	28.0 / 6.8 / .6								
Sales/Net Fixed Assets	80.3 / 26.8 / 7.3								
Sales/Total Assets	6.3 / 4.0 / 2.6								
% Depr., Dep., Amort./Sales	(15) .9 / 2.4 / 2.9								
% Officers', Directors', Owners' Comp/Sales	(16) 5.4 / 7.1 / 9.8								
Net Sales ($)	21051M	23610M	55496M	125375M		258026M			
Total Assets ($)	4858M	7977M	29405M	75150M		208007M			

© RMA 2003

M = $ thousand   MM = $ million
See Pages 11 through 18 for Explanation of Ratios and Data

Comparative Historical Data | Current Data Sorted By Sales

4/1/00-3/31/01 ALL	4/1/01-3/31/02 ALL	4/1/02-3/31/03 ALL	Type of Statement	0-1MM	1-3MM	3-5MM	5-10MM	10-25MM	25MM & OVER
		3	Unqualified					1	2
		6	Reviewed		1		2	2	
		15	Compiled	7	5	1	1	1	
		16	Tax Returns	12	3	1	1		
		7	Other	1	3		1		
				6 (4/1-9/30/02)		**41 (10/1/02-3/31/03)**			
D A T A N O T A V A I L A B L E	D A T A N O T A V A I L A B L E	47	**NUMBER OF STATEMENTS**	20	12	4	4	5	2
%	%	%	**ASSETS**	%	%	%	%	%	%
		9.3	Cash & Equivalents	11.7	9.2				
		17.9	Trade Receivables (net)	23.2	17.0				
		24.0	Inventory	17.8	24.6				
		3.0	All Other Current	.0	5.2				
		54.2	Total Current	52.7	56.0				
		33.9	Fixed Assets (net)	32.8	34.4				
		4.4	Intangibles (net)	4.6	3.0				
		7.6	All Other Non-Current	10.0	6.6				
		100.0	Total	100.0	100.0				
			LIABILITIES						
		13.4	Notes Payable-Short Term	24.5	7.4				
		5.6	Cur. Mat.-L/T/D	5.6	6.2				
		16.1	Trade Payables	18.8	17.8				
		.6	Income Taxes Payable	.0	.0				
		30.8	All Other Current	55.8	12.6				
		66.4	Total Current	104.7	44.1				
		19.6	Long Term Debt	21.0	13.6				
		.5	Deferred Taxes	.0	2.0				
		10.4	All Other Non-Current	18.9	4.7				
		3.1	Net Worth	-44.6	35.7				
		100.0	Total Liabilities & Net Worth	100.0	100.0				
			INCOME DATA						
		100.0	Net Sales	100.0	100.0				
			Gross Profit						
		95.2	Operating Expenses	93.0	98.6				
		4.8	Operating Profit	7.0	1.4				
		2.1	All Other Expenses (net)	4.0	.8				
		2.7	Profit Before Taxes	3.0	.6				
			RATIOS						
		2.0	Current	1.7	11.3				
		1.3		.9	1.4				
		.6		.3	.5				
		1.2	Quick	1.1	5.0				
		.6		.5	.5				
		.1		.1	.1				
	0	999.8	Sales/Receivables	0 UND	0 UND				
	7	52.7		5 80.4	6 64.5				
	41	8.8		50 7.3	33 11.0				
			Cost of Sales/Inventory						
			Cost of Sales/Payables						
		8.2	Sales/Working Capital	10.8	7.9				
		50.5		NM	89.6				
		-14.3		-3.8	-9.3				
		9.0	EBIT/Interest	10.0	4.3				
	(40)	2.3		(15) 1.9	(11) 1.7				
		.8		-.4	1.0				
			Net Profit + Depr., Dep., Amort./Cur. Mat. L/T/D						
		.3	Fixed/Worth	.3	.3				
		1.2		2.4	.6				
		-30.9		-3.5	-26.2				
		.7	Debt/Worth	1.7	.4				
		3.1		58.0	2.9				
		-20.1		-2.6	-30.7				
		58.7	% Profit Before Taxes/Tangible Net Worth	83.1					
	(32)	13.5		(11) 7.9					
		-1.7		-5.5					
		21.3	% Profit Before Taxes/Total Assets	27.8	8.7				
		4.8		6.8	1.3				
		.0		.2	-4.4				
		33.4	Sales/Net Fixed Assets	49.8	53.8				
		13.0		17.6	10.9				
		4.9		4.3	5.6				
		5.0	Sales/Total Assets	5.6	6.6				
		2.7		2.7	3.8				
		1.9		2.3	2.4				
		1.2	% Depr., Dep., Amort./Sales	1.1					
	(35)	2.5		(12) 2.7					
		3.8		7.5					
		4.5	% Officers', Directors', Owners' Comp/Sales	4.7					
	(25)	7.2		(10) 7.5					
		10.0		11.5					
		483558M	Net Sales ($)	10491M	17460M	16174M	29973M	76377M	333083M
		325397M	Total Assets ($)	5422M	6407M	7870M	11533M	44807M	249358M

M = $ thousand   MM = $ million
See Pages 11 through 18 for Explanation of Ratios and Data

Current Data Sorted By Assets   Comparative Historical Data

0-500M	500M-2MM	2-10MM	10-50MM	50-100MM	100-250MM	Type of Statement	4/1/98-3/31/99 ALL	4/1/99-3/31/00 ALL
8	5	2	3		2	Unqualified	3	9
48	29	4	1		1	Reviewed	20	13
60	18	4		2	1	Compiled	84	93
23	18	5	3	2	1	Tax Returns	63	59
						Other	76	59
	56 (4/1-9/30/02)		186 (10/1/02-3/31/03)					
139	70	17	7	4	5	**NUMBER OF STATEMENTS**	246	233
%	%	%	%	%	%	**ASSETS**	%	%
16.7	11.9	9.9				Cash & Equivalents	12.9	15.5
13.3	17.1	14.6				Trade Receivables (net)	13.6	16.4
10.3	11.8	17.9				Inventory	13.7	14.7
2.7	1.8	2.9				All Other Current	2.2	1.9
43.0	42.6	45.3				Total Current	42.4	48.4
43.1	41.0	35.5				Fixed Assets (net)	44.3	39.4
4.5	6.9	13.4				Intangibles (net)	5.5	5.2
9.4	9.5	5.8				All Other Non-Current	7.7	7.0
100.0	100.0	100.0				Total	100.0	100.0
						LIABILITIES		
9.9	8.0	12.7				Notes Payable-Short Term	8.6	8.9
7.5	3.4	3.7				Cur. Mat.-L/T/D	4.5	4.9
16.0	14.5	10.8				Trade Payables	16.2	15.6
.1	.1	.7				Income Taxes Payable	.3	.7
13.2	8.0	6.9				All Other Current	10.2	10.4
46.7	34.0	34.8				Total Current	39.7	40.4
29.5	32.7	30.2				Long Term Debt	29.0	30.8
.3	.1	.0				Deferred Taxes	.1	.2
8.1	5.6	1.6				All Other Non-Current	4.1	3.7
15.4	27.5	33.4				Net Worth	27.1	24.9
100.0	100.0	100.0				Total Liabilities & Net Worth	100.0	100.0
						INCOME DATA		
100.0	100.0	100.0				Net Sales	100.0	100.0
						Gross Profit		
96.3	95.3	94.7				Operating Expenses	95.6	95.1
3.7	4.7	5.3				Operating Profit	4.4	4.9
1.5	2.0	.4				All Other Expenses (net)	1.5	1.2
2.3	2.7	4.9				Profit Before Taxes	2.9	3.7
						RATIOS		
1.8	2.0	2.5					2.2	2.2
.9	1.2	1.7				Current	1.2	1.2
.6	.7	1.0					.7	.8
1.6	1.4	2.2					1.5	1.8
(138) .7	.9	(16) .8				Quick	(243) .8	.9
.3	.4	.3					.4	.4
0 UND	5 79.3	8 47.3					1 310.5	3 126.9
8 45.9	14 27.0	13 29.2				Sales/Receivables	9 38.5	12 30.8
16 22.6	25 14.7	27 13.5					17 21.2	22 16.8
						Cost of Sales/Inventory		
						Cost of Sales/Payables		
22.2	13.3	9.3					17.4	16.3
-196.5	38.8	15.8				Sales/Working Capital	80.4	61.8
-27.8	-40.6	NM					-55.1	-42.3
11.4	5.6	13.0					8.4	9.5
(109) 2.4	(64) 2.2	(14) 3.7				EBIT/Interest	(207) 3.2	(198) 3.3
.6	.7	2.6					1.1	1.0
3.9						Net Profit + Depr., Dep.,	5.3	8.5
(17) 1.4						Amort./Cur. Mat. L /T/D	(35) 2.3	(35) 3.2
.2							.9	1.1
.5	.5	.6					.7	.6
1.5	2.0	1.0				Fixed/Worth	1.5	1.6
-6.3	-31.7	-9.6					9.0	10.2
.7	1.2	.9					1.0	.9
2.1	4.0	4.2				Debt/Worth	2.5	3.0
-11.2	-81.0	-19.4					12.7	17.0
51.2	52.6	71.2				% Profit Before Taxes/Tangible	65.5	99.9
(93) 24.0	(51) 16.8	(12) 49.2				Net Worth	(193) 22.9	(184) 37.5
3.4	-4.0	10.7					7.0	11.8
24.9	16.2	17.5				% Profit Before Taxes/Total	20.8	31.7
6.0	5.5	10.5				Assets	8.5	10.9
-1.9	-.9	3.1					.9	.6
29.8	26.8	29.1					24.4	31.9
15.3	9.2	10.9				Sales/Net Fixed Assets	12.3	12.4
7.2	4.5	4.2					6.0	6.6
7.6	4.3	4.3					6.4	6.5
5.0	3.2	2.3				Sales/Total Assets	4.0	4.2
2.9	2.3	1.6					2.5	2.5
1.1	1.0	1.1					1.3	1.0
(122) 1.9	(68) 1.8	(15) 1.8				% Depr., Dep., Amort./Sales	(217) 1.9	(204) 2.0
3.3	3.6	3.2					2.9	3.3
4.4	2.7						3.1	3.0
(95) 6.4	(50) 4.0					% Officers', Directors',	(162) 5.5	(133) 5.3
9.9	6.2					Owners' Comp/Sales	9.3	8.0
170619M	221361M	195004M	348252M	2691248M	2969049M	Net Sales ($)	1804986M	1892962M
35680M	63715M	64134M	172561M	278057M	810439M	Total Assets ($)	533917M	624302M

© RMA 2003   M = $ thousand   MM = $ million
See Pages 11 through 18 for Explanation of Ratios and Data

Comparative Historical Data | Current Data Sorted By Sales

			Type of Statement						
2	2	7	Unqualified			1		1	5
19	17	16	Reviewed	4	5	1	3	1	2
84	77	82	Compiled	26	36	13	4	2	1
66	81	85	Tax Returns	23	44	11	1	3	3
49	58	52	Other	13	28	1	3	1	6
4/1/00-3/31/01	4/1/01-3/31/02	4/1/02-3/31/03		56 (4/1-9/30/02)			186 (10/1/02-3/31/03)		
ALL	ALL	ALL		0-1MM	1-3MM	3-5MM	5-10MM	10-25MM	25MM & OVER
220	235	242	**NUMBER OF STATEMENTS**	66	113	27	11	8	17
%	%	%	**ASSETS**	%	%	%	%	%	%
15.9	14.6	14.0	Cash & Equivalents	14.5	15.5	11.8	22.7		4.3
16.4	15.0	14.4	Trade Receivables (net)	9.7	15.9	14.8	23.1		13.4
14.4	13.5	11.1	Inventory	9.7	9.5	18.4	14.2		11.8
2.6	2.4	2.4	All Other Current	3.5	1.7	3.0	1.9		1.9
49.3	45.4	42.0	Total Current	37.5	42.7	48.0	62.0		31.5
39.2	42.2	42.0	Fixed Assets (net)	50.6	40.3	34.0	30.3		44.1
4.6	5.0	6.6	Intangibles (net)	4.9	5.3	10.0	1.7		15.6
6.9	7.4	9.5	All Other Non-Current	6.9	11.8	8.0	6.0		8.8
100.0	100.0	100.0	Total	100.0	100.0	100.0	100.0		100.0
			LIABILITIES						
9.4	9.7	9.3	Notes Payable-Short Term	9.2	8.8	11.1	7.6		7.4
4.8	5.3	5.9	Cur. Mat.-L/T/D	7.4	5.7	5.4	3.2		6.2
17.2	13.1	15.2	Trade Payables	11.1	17.8	11.6	20.3		16.8
.4	.4	.2	Income Taxes Payable	.1	.1	.2	.3		.6
12.3	9.9	10.7	All Other Current	9.8	12.6	9.0	8.4		6.3
44.1	38.4	41.3	Total Current	37.6	45.0	37.3	39.8		37.3
25.3	42.8	30.8	Long Term Debt	39.5	28.9	23.2	24.0		32.4
.2	.2	.2	Deferred Taxes	.1	.4	.3	.0		.0
7.4	5.5	7.0	All Other Non-Current	6.6	8.6	2.5	1.7		7.6
23.1	13.0	20.7	Net Worth	16.2	17.0	36.7	34.5		22.7
100.0	100.0	100.0	Total Liabilities & Net Worth	100.0	100.0	100.0	100.0		100.0
			INCOME DATA						
100.0	100.0	100.0	Net Sales	100.0	100.0	100.0	100.0		100.0
			Gross Profit						
95.2	95.7	95.8	Operating Expenses	94.2	96.2	96.0	96.4		97.4
4.8	4.3	4.2	Operating Profit	5.7	3.8	4.0	3.6		2.6
1.1	1.1	1.6	All Other Expenses (net)	3.8	.9	1.1	.2		.7
3.8	3.2	2.6	Profit Before Taxes	2.0	2.9	3.0	3.3		2.0
			RATIOS						
2.1	2.0	1.9	Current	2.2	1.7	2.4	2.4		1.9
1.2	1.2	1.1		.9	1.0	1.4	1.7		.8
.7	.7	.6		.6	.6	1.0	1.1		.4
1.5	1.5	1.6	Quick	1.7	1.5	1.9	2.0		1.1
(219) .7	(233) .7	(240) .7		(65) .6	(112) .8	.8	1.4		.4
.4	.4	.3		.2	.4	.4	.7		.3
3 142.9	2 159.3	2 205.7	Sales/Receivables	0 UND	2 200.2	6 66.3	9 40.3		5 74.2
13 28.7	10 36.2	11 33.6		6 56.8	11 32.9	11 32.7	16 23.1		15 24.0
20 18.4	20 18.3	19 18.8		19 19.5	19 19.3	18 19.9	28 13.3		20 18.2
			Cost of Sales/Inventory						
			Cost of Sales/Payables						
15.5	16.4	17.1	Sales/Working Capital	15.5	23.4	10.9	11.5		23.9
73.4	82.0	216.6		-94.0	562.0	23.0	18.0		-46.0
-40.3	-41.1	-28.2		-21.3	-28.7	999.8	45.7		-21.9
11.7	7.2	9.2	EBIT/Interest	6.4	11.4	11.0			3.9
(181) 3.6	(192) 3.0	(202) 2.6		(49) 1.3	(97) 2.4	(25) 3.2			3.1
1.5	1.2	.8		.0	.9	1.2			1.2
3.8	3.3	4.6	Net Profit + Depr., Dep., Amort./Cur. Mat. L/T/D		4.0				
(27) 2.5	(22) 1.7	(33) 1.9			(13) 1.4				
1.4	1.2	.9			.2				
.6	.6	.5	Fixed/Worth	.6	.5	.5	.3		1.2
1.4	1.6	1.8		2.2	1.9	1.3	.8		2.3
13.1	12.0	-10.2		-4.3	-10.1	4.8	3.5		-7.0
.9	.9	1.0	Debt/Worth	.6	1.0	.8	.6		1.6
3.2	2.6	3.4		2.1	4.0	1.7	2.3		4.2
50.1	39.9	-20.4		-9.0	-18.3	6.9	4.7		-16.9
103.4	69.5	52.6	% Profit Before Taxes/Tangible Net Worth	41.8	61.8	55.8	46.5		79.3
(172) 36.3	(183) 30.5	(167) 25.5		(41) 15.4	(78) 26.0	(21) 27.0	(10) 16.3	(11) 29.3	
8.7	6.7	1.3		-3.1	3.1	.8	-1.5		8.3
32.5	20.5	20.8	% Profit Before Taxes/Total Assets	15.2	23.4	14.6	28.3		16.3
8.5	7.5	6.3		1.5	8.3	7.4	6.2		10.2
.8	.5	-1.0		-7.3	.0	.3	-.6		1.3
31.9	25.3	27.7	Sales/Net Fixed Assets	26.0	26.7	41.8	41.9		32.5
14.6	12.2	12.0		8.7	13.4	18.2	26.2		6.3
6.9	5.2	5.1		2.2	7.5	4.9	6.4		3.8
7.2	6.3	6.1	Sales/Total Assets	4.8	6.5	5.8	6.5		6.1
4.2	4.2	4.0		2.6	4.8	4.1	3.8		2.5
2.7	2.6	2.4		1.4	3.0	2.4	2.8		2.0
.8	1.1	1.1	% Depr., Dep., Amort./Sales	1.3	1.0	1.2	.9		1.2
(195) 1.7	(208) 1.8	(216) 1.9		(59) 2.6	(100) 1.7	(26) 1.7	1.3	(12) 2.6	
3.2	3.0	3.4		5.0	3.1	3.5	3.2		3.5
3.1	3.2	3.3	% Officers', Directors', Owners' Comp/Sales	4.8	3.4	2.4			
(140) 5.5	(144) 5.6	(158) 5.5		(38) 7.4	(83) 5.7	(20) 3.2			
8.9	8.5	8.4		14.7	14.0	4.9			
1153981M	4382565M	6595533M	Net Sales ($)	40064M	195528M	106132M	69098M	117648M	6067063M
499504M	904297M	1424586M	Total Assets ($)	19837M	62016M	32910M	17244M	33806M	1258773M

M = $ thousand   MM = $ million
See Pages 11 through 18 for Explanation of Ratios and Data

| Current Data Sorted By Assets | | | | | | | Comparative Historical Data | |

0-500M	500M-2MM	2-10MM	10-50MM	50-100MM	100-250MM	Type of Statement	4/1/98-3/31/99 ALL	4/1/99-3/31/00 ALL
1	1	4		1	1	Unqualified	2	1
	1					Reviewed	5	4
2	2	1				Compiled	5	5
5	3	2				Tax Returns	4	4
1	3	6	2			Other	11	11
	7 (4/1-9/30/02)		29 (10/1/02-3/31/03)					
9	10	13	2	1	1	NUMBER OF STATEMENTS	27	25
%	%	%	%	%	%	ASSETS	%	%
	6.5	10.8				Cash & Equivalents	10.7	10.9
	32.0	29.9				Trade Receivables (net)	29.1	35.3
	13.4	15.4				Inventory	19.5	17.4
	4.7	2.2				All Other Current	.6	2.0
	56.5	58.3				Total Current	59.9	65.6
	26.7	22.3				Fixed Assets (net)	28.7	26.7
	2.2	3.9				Intangibles (net)	3.5	4.3
	14.6	15.5				All Other Non-Current	7.9	3.4
	100.0	100.0				Total	100.0	100.0
						LIABILITIES		
	7.9	14.2				Notes Payable-Short Term	8.7	5.8
	8.0	3.0				Cur. Mat.-L/T/D	4.3	3.9
	20.8	24.2				Trade Payables	16.2	23.5
	.2	.0				Income Taxes Payable	.1	.2
	7.2	12.9				All Other Current	10.5	12.9
	44.0	54.4				Total Current	39.7	46.3
	16.0	12.8				Long Term Debt	18.4	10.0
	.3	.0				Deferred Taxes	.1	.2
	2.3	7.6				All Other Non-Current	3.0	5.4
	37.3	25.3				Net Worth	38.7	38.1
	100.0	100.0				Total Liabilities & Net Worth	100.0	100.0
						INCOME DATA		
	100.0	100.0				Net Sales	100.0	100.0
						Gross Profit		
	98.0	96.3				Operating Expenses	93.6	97.6
	2.0	3.7				Operating Profit	6.4	2.4
	-.6	1.7				All Other Expenses (net)	.4	-.2
	2.6	1.9				Profit Before Taxes	6.0	2.5
						RATIOS		
	3.2	1.7					2.7	2.8
	1.5	1.3				Current	1.6	1.6
	.8	.7					1.2	1.1
	2.2	1.1					1.6	1.5
	1.1	.8				Quick	(26) 1.1	1.2
	.5	.4					.7	.8
	24 15.2	18 20.3					20 18.5	24 15.2
	31 11.9	24 15.3				Sales/Receivables	26 13.9	28 13.2
	56 6.5	74 4.9					35 10.3	45 8.2
						Cost of Sales/Inventory		
						Cost of Sales/Payables		
	4.6	10.8					8.7	7.7
	23.9	21.3				Sales/Working Capital	16.4	21.3
	-19.8	-14.6					76.9	144.7
	19.9	34.3					(22) 23.3	(20) 11.3
	3.1	2.4				EBIT/Interest	6.4	2.7
	.2	.6					3.2	-4.5
						Net Profit + Depr., Dep., Amort./Cur. Mat. L./T/D		
	.3	.4					.4	.3
	.8	.9				Fixed/Worth	.9	.7
	2.2	1.4					1.8	3.7
	.8	1.6					.8	.6
	1.4	2.3				Debt/Worth	1.6	1.0
	8.8	5.3					6.8	20.0
		66.7					(22) 91.2	(22) 50.4
	(12)	16.0				% Profit Before Taxes/Tangible Net Worth	37.7	20.9
		-8.3					10.1	1.2
	16.6	14.8					42.0	32.4
	4.2	4.8				% Profit Before Taxes/Total Assets	13.0	5.5
	-.4	-1.1					7.1	-6.7
	28.8	30.7					32.4	25.2
	16.6	13.3				Sales/Net Fixed Assets	16.3	16.7
	5.8	8.7					11.6	9.1
	4.4	4.9					5.6	4.8
	3.0	2.7				Sales/Total Assets	4.1	4.0
	1.6	2.0					2.3	2.6
	1.4	.9					(21) 1.0	(22) 1.0
	1.8	1.9				% Depr., Dep., Amort./Sales	2.0	1.6
	5.1	2.3					2.8	2.9
							(11) 3.1	
						% Officers', Directors', Owners' Comp/Sales	7.2	
							10.9	
12418M	33938M	291259M	109637M	248695M	64610M	Net Sales ($)	446333M	756014M
2390M	10486M	91749M	51371M	97767M	100002M	Total Assets ($)	116434M	315875M

M = $ thousand   MM = $ million
See Pages 11 through 18 for Explanation of Ratios and Data

Comparative Historical Data | Current Data Sorted By Sales

				Type of Statement						
1		1		8	Unqualified			1	2	1	4
7		8		1	Reviewed		1				
5		4		5	Compiled	1	1	2		1	
5		4		10	Tax Returns	3	4	2	2		1
10		8		12	Other	2	1	1		4	4
4/1/00- 3/31/01 ALL		4/1/01- 3/31/02 ALL		4/1/02- 3/31/03 ALL			7 (4/1-9/30/02)		29 (10/1/02-3/31/03)		
						0-1MM	1-3MM	3-5MM	5-10MM	10-25MM	25MM & OVER
28		25		36	NUMBER OF STATEMENTS	6	7	4	4	6	9
%		%		%	ASSETS	%	%	%	%	%	%
7.1		11.9		9.2	Cash & Equivalents						
32.7		34.7		30.9	Trade Receivables (net)						
24.5		18.6		14.0	Inventory						
2.4		2.4		2.8	All Other Current						
66.8		67.6		56.9	Total Current						
19.2		19.8		28.5	Fixed Assets (net)						
6.3		1.8		2.4	Intangibles (net)						
7.6		10.8		12.2	All Other Non-Current						
100.0		100.0		100.0	Total						
					LIABILITIES						
14.2		5.0		9.9	Notes Payable-Short Term						
3.2		3.3		4.2	Cur. Mat.-L/T/D						
24.4		25.4		21.1	Trade Payables						
.4		.1		.2	Income Taxes Payable						
8.5		10.3		10.7	All Other Current						
50.7		44.2		46.1	Total Current						
16.7		9.9		16.4	Long Term Debt						
.2		.2		.1	Deferred Taxes						
4.8		1.0		10.3	All Other Non-Current						
27.6		44.7		27.1	Net Worth						
100.0		100.0		100.0	Total Liabilities & Net Worth						
					INCOME DATA						
100.0		100.0		100.0	Net Sales						
					Gross Profit						
97.9		94.7		97.8	Operating Expenses						
2.1		5.3		2.2	Operating Profit						
.3		.2		.6	All Other Expenses (net)						
1.8		5.1		1.6	Profit Before Taxes						
					RATIOS						
3.1		2.2		1.8							
1.7		1.6		1.4	Current						
1.0		1.2		.8							
1.7		1.6		1.5							
1.0		1.2		1.1	Quick						
.6		.7		.5							
23	16.2	20	17.8	19	19.7						
27	13.4	29	12.7	25	14.6	Sales/Receivables					
43	8.5	40	9.2	65	5.7						
					Cost of Sales/Inventory						
					Cost of Sales/Payables						
7.1		10.0		8.4							
11.5		14.9		22.1	Sales/Working Capital						
NM		87.0		-32.5							
	28.7		46.0		13.1						
(26)	4.4	(21)	6.6	(34)	2.0	EBIT/Interest					
	.5		1.6		.3						
					Net Profit + Depr., Dep., Amort./Cur. Mat. L/T/D						
.2		.1		.4							
.5		.3		1.1	Fixed/Worth						
2.9		1.1		2.2							
.5		.5		1.1							
1.6		1.2		2.1	Debt/Worth						
11.8		2.4		7.3							
	39.4		87.5		69.9	% Profit Before Taxes/Tangible Net Worth					
(22)	15.0	(23)	21.5	(30)	9.9						
	1.4		5.5		-5.7						
22.2		49.8		17.2	% Profit Before Taxes/Total Assets						
5.0		11.5		3.8							
-1.9		1.0		-2.2							
43.6		63.6		28.5							
25.2		25.6		14.7	Sales/Net Fixed Assets						
13.9		11.7		6.1							
5.1		5.3		5.0							
3.2		4.4		2.9	Sales/Total Assets						
2.1		2.6		2.1							
	.6		.5		1.0	% Depr., Dep., Amort./Sales					
(27)	1.2	(21)	1.1	(34)	1.9						
	1.8		1.8		3.2						
			2.4		1.3	% Officers', Directors', Owners' Comp/Sales					
		(10)	5.3	(11)	2.7						
			10.0		4.8						
421992M		305606M		760557M	Net Sales ($)	3325M	13695M	14944M	27304M	108813M	592476M
196225M		98309M		353765M	Total Assets ($)	1343M	4850M	4293M	9117M	48829M	285333M

M = $ thousand   MM = $ million
See Pages 11 through 18 for Explanation of Ratios and Data

OTHER SERVICES—Car Washes NAICS 811192 (SIC 7542)

	Current Data Sorted By Assets						Comparative Historical Data	
Type of Statement								
Unqualified	3	1	1	1	1		8	6
Reviewed	1	6	4	2			10	10
Compiled	27	27	15			1	78	64
Tax Returns	43	26	7				42	45
Other	35	25	17	5	1		78	56
		26 (4/1-9/30/02)		223 (10/1/02-3/31/03)			4/1/98-3/31/99	4/1/99-3/31/00
	0-500M	500M-2MM	2-10MM	10-50MM	50-100MM	100-250MM	ALL	ALL
NUMBER OF STATEMENTS	109	85	44	8	2	1	216	181
	%	%	%	%	%	%	%	%
ASSETS								
Cash & Equivalents	13.9	8.8	8.2				12.0	13.7
Trade Receivables (net)	4.6	1.6	1.4				3.1	3.4
Inventory	5.2	2.3	2.8				2.7	5.4
All Other Current	2.4	2.1	2.1				1.4	2.5
Total Current	26.1	14.9	14.6				19.2	25.1
Fixed Assets (net)	61.7	77.4	68.6				71.0	61.5
Intangibles (net)	6.2	2.8	12.3				3.8	7.4
All Other Non-Current	6.0	4.9	4.5				6.0	6.0
Total	100.0	100.0	100.0				100.0	100.0
LIABILITIES								
Notes Payable-Short Term	9.6	2.3	.8				9.4	6.9
Cur. Mat.-L/T/D	6.1	4.8	4.3				4.2	6.2
Trade Payables	8.3	2.4	3.1				4.2	4.8
Income Taxes Payable	.0	.0	.0				.2	.1
All Other Current	16.2	5.0	7.2				7.6	16.0
Total Current	40.3	14.6	15.5				25.5	34.1
Long Term Debt	41.6	68.2	62.0				45.2	48.9
Deferred Taxes	.0	.1	.0				.0	.0
All Other Non-Current	9.1	4.1	5.5				6.3	9.9
Net Worth	9.1	13.0	17.0				22.9	7.1
Total Liabilities & Net Worth	100.0	100.0	100.0				100.0	100.0
INCOME DATA								
Net Sales	100.0	100.0	100.0				100.0	100.0
Gross Profit								
Operating Expenses	86.7	84.4	88.8				89.7	88.6
Operating Profit	13.3	15.6	11.2				10.3	11.4
All Other Expenses (net)	6.1	12.1	8.7				7.8	6.9
Profit Before Taxes	7.2	3.5	2.5				2.5	4.5
RATIOS								
	3.0	2.0	1.8				2.4	2.4
Current	.7	.9	.7				.8	.9
	.2	.3	.4				.2	.3
	2.6	1.6	1.2				1.6	1.4
Quick	.4	.6	.5			(214) .5	(180) .5
	.1	.2	.2				.1	.2
	0 UND	0 UND	0 UND				0 UND	0 UND
Sales/Receivables	0 UND	0 UND	1 261.7				0 UND	0 UND
	0 979.9	1 291.5	5 68.1				3 124.2	4 98.6
Cost of Sales/Inventory								
Cost of Sales/Payables								
	16.9	19.9	21.1				21.1	14.2
Sales/Working Capital	−43.7	−217.2	−57.7				−59.9	−159.8
	−4.8	−7.6	−6.1				−5.5	−7.5
	5.5	3.7	2.9				6.0	5.1
EBIT/Interest	(80) 2.1	(57) 2.0	(38) 1.6			(149) 2.0	(123) 2.1
	.3	1.0	.8				1.2	.9
			10.5				4.5	4.7
Net Profit + Depr., Dep., Amort./Cur.Mat. L./T/D		(10) 2.0				(26) 2.3	(15) 2.3
			1.2				1.7	1.3
	.9	2.3	2.2				1.2	1.0
Fixed/Worth	10.7	8.0	26.6				4.5	6.4
	−3.7	−14.7	−7.0				−10.0	−6.4
	.6	2.3	2.2				.9	1.3
Debt/Worth	10.1	8.8	28.0				4.7	11.5
	−6.8	−17.3	−8.4				−11.8	−7.8
	100.3	59.7	53.1				64.0	59.7
% Profit Before Taxes/Tangible Net Worth	(65) 40.6	(55) 13.4	(24) 9.8			(151) 28.8	(113) 28.7
	7.5	3.2	−17.4				.3	10.1
	20.6	8.8	5.7				18.4	16.7
% Profit Before Taxes/Total Assets	6.9	2.4	3.1				4.5	4.7
	−2.1	−1.9	−3.1				−1.1	−.9
	12.9	2.5	2.7				5.7	10.0
Sales/Net Fixed Assets	3.2	.8	1.1				1.3	1.6
	.7	.4	.5				.6	.6
	3.5	1.3	1.7				2.8	3.2
Sales/Total Assets	1.6	.7	.9				1.0	1.2
	.7	.3	.4				.5	.5
	2.9	3.4	3.5				3.2	2.7
% Depr., Dep., Amort./Sales	(91) 8.3	(75) 8.7	(42) 7.4			(194) 7.0	(162) 6.7
	18.8	23.6	14.7				18.5	13.8
	5.6	2.2	1.9				3.6	3.0
% Officers', Directors', Owners' Comp/Sales	(38) 9.2	(26) 4.9	(20) 4.2			(80) 8.0	(63) 7.0
	17.0	8.4	8.5				18.5	15.5
Net Sales ($)	59780M	116920M	211768M	196182M	194143M	71743M	1118155M	1119974M
Total Assets ($)	26510M	89220M	173450M	175291M	161600M	212344M	502220M	618884M

M = $ thousand   MM = $ million
See Pages 11 through 18 for Explanation of Ratios and Data

Comparative Historical Data				Current Data Sorted By Sales					
			Type of Statement						
4	3	7	Unqualified	4			1	1	1
13	10	13	Reviewed	1	3	2	3	4	
67	52	70	Compiled	42	17	5	5		1
43	60	76	Tax Returns	58	11	4	3		
47	63	83	Other	53	13	5	5	5	3
4/1/00- 3/31/01	4/1/01- 3/31/02	4/1/02- 3/31/03		26 (4/1-9/30/02)			223 (10/1/02-3/31/03)		
ALL	ALL	ALL		0-1MM	1-3MM	3-5MM	5-10MM	10-25MM	25MM & OVER
174	188	249	**NUMBER OF STATEMENTS**	158	44	16	16	10	5
%	%	%	**ASSETS**	%	%	%	%	%	%
11.8	10.4	10.8	Cash & Equivalents	9.9	13.7	13.5	9.7	14.7	
2.5	4.2	3.0	Trade Receivables (net)	1.9	5.1	6.7	2.9	7.0	
3.7	4.0	4.0	Inventory	2.3	7.1	6.1	4.0	13.7	
1.4	2.3	2.4	All Other Current	1.4	4.0	5.7	1.2	7.5	
19.3	20.9	20.1	Total Current	15.4	29.9	32.0	17.8	42.9	
66.9	69.2	68.3	Fixed Assets (net)	73.5	59.7	62.2	61.1	39.6	
7.4	4.3	6.1	Intangibles (net)	5.9	4.2	3.5	14.4	9.5	
6.3	5.6	5.4	All Other Non-Current	5.2	6.2	2.2	6.7	8.0	
100.0	100.0	100.0	Total	100.0	100.0	100.0	100.0	100.0	
			LIABILITIES						
3.0	4.5	5.8	Notes Payable-Short Term	7.0	2.9	1.3	.9	12.8	
5.9	5.1	5.2	Cur. Mat.-L/T/D	5.3	5.9	3.6	6.0	3.1	
3.7	4.3	5.2	Trade Payables	4.3	7.4	5.1	7.4	6.3	
.2	.2	.0	Income Taxes Payable	.0	.1	.0	.0	.0	
15.7	10.7	10.3	All Other Current	12.6	4.9	7.2	7.3	9.5	
28.4	24.6	26.5	Total Current	29.3	21.2	17.2	21.6	31.8	
49.2	55.4	54.3	Long Term Debt	56.1	53.2	54.7	57.5	25.0	
.1	.0	.0	Deferred Taxes	.0	.0	.2	.0	.0	
9.3	21.1	6.5	All Other Non-Current	5.8	11.2	2.9	3.4	10.6	
12.9	−1.2	12.7	Net Worth	8.8	14.4	24.9	17.4	32.6	
100.0	100.0	100.0	Total Liabilities & Net Worth	100.0	100.0	100.0	100.0	100.0	
			INCOME DATA						
100.0	100.0	100.0	Net Sales	100.0	100.0	100.0	100.0	100.0	
			Gross Profit						
86.8	88.1	86.5	Operating Expenses	83.4	89.8	92.8	93.4	95.4	
13.2	11.9	13.5	Operating Profit	16.6	10.2	7.2	6.6	4.6	
6.8	8.3	8.4	All Other Expenses (net)	11.4	4.3	2.5	2.9	.9	
6.4	3.5	5.0	Profit Before Taxes	5.2	5.9	4.7	3.7	3.7	
			RATIOS						
1.9	2.0	2.1		2.1	3.3	3.8	1.6	2.2	
.7	.9	.8	Current	.5	1.6	1.5	1.1	1.7	
.2	.3	.2		.1	.6	.7	.4	.7	
1.3	1.3	1.5		1.5	2.4	2.0	1.1	1.8	
.5	.5	(248) .5	Quick	.4	.6	.7	.7	.7	
.1	.2	.1		.1	.3	.4	.3	.2	
0 UND	0 UND	0 UND		0 UND	0 UND	0 999.7	1 580.7	0 UND	
0 UND	0 UND	0 UND	Sales/Receivables	0 UND	0 979.9	1 309.4	2 177.4	3 140.7	
4 102.8	4 96.3	2 213.7		0 UND	6 64.2	6 58.9	5 80.1	22 16.6	
			Cost of Sales/Inventory						
			Cost of Sales/Payables						
18.8	18.4	18.6		22.3	14.9	13.2	40.2	6.8	
−34.5	−156.2	−70.4	Sales/Working Capital	−16.6	28.7	45.9	141.6	19.6	
−6.4	−10.4	−5.9		−4.1	−43.6	−41.3	−13.6	−12.9	
4.9	3.9	4.6		4.0	4.4	5.1	8.2	6.8	
(131) 2.1	(146) 1.7	(186) 1.9	EBIT/Interest	(102) 1.8	(41) 1.6	(12) 2.3	2.4	4.0	
.9	.6	.6		.5	.3	1.1	1.5	1.4	
3.8	4.6	7.4	Net Profit + Depr., Dep.,						
(18) 2.4	(17) 1.9	(21) 1.3	Amort./Cur. Mat. L/T/D						
.7	.9	.8							
1.3	1.6	1.4		1.7	1.9	.8	1.5	.6	
5.0	7.8	9.8	Fixed/Worth	11.6	10.2	3.6	19.6	1.2	
−6.6	−8.7	−7.0		−6.7	−5.4	NM	−2.8	NM	
1.4	1.7	1.2		1.4	1.7	1.0	1.1	1.1	
6.6	12.1	10.1	Debt/Worth	12.4	15.4	3.0	20.1	1.5	
−7.8	−9.6	−8.8		−8.5	−8.2	NM	−4.2	NM	
78.1	71.2	70.2	% Profit Before Taxes/Tangible	83.2	66.2	68.8			
(107) 25.2	(116) 18.2	(152) 19.8	Net Worth	(93) 19.8	(27) 9.1	(12) 41.6			
7.7	−.7	4.0		4.3	−2.7	7.6			
14.5	11.3	11.4	% Profit Before Taxes/Total	10.4	14.1	21.7	18.6	9.5	
5.3	3.3	3.9	Assets	3.1	3.3	4.4	5.7	5.5	
−1.1	−2.8	−1.9		−2.9	−2.0	.9	2.9	2.2	
5.2	6.0	5.0		4.1	13.4	11.8	9.1	22.8	
1.4	1.4	1.5	Sales/Net Fixed Assets	.9	2.1	3.9	3.5	6.1	
.7	.6	.5		.4	1.0	2.0	1.7	2.0	
2.3	2.7	2.4		1.7	3.2	3.9	3.8	3.3	
1.0	1.0	1.0	Sales/Total Assets	.7	1.3	2.6	2.2	1.7	
.5	.5	.5		.3	.7	1.1	1.1	1.0	
2.9	2.5	3.3		6.1	2.4	1.7	2.1		
(154) 7.4	(174) 6.8	(217) 7.8	% Depr., Dep., Amort./Sales	(135) 13.2	(37) 5.2	3.3	3.5		
16.4	15.6	18.7		24.3	10.7	4.9	6.0		
3.5	3.1	3.4	% Officers', Directors',	5.1	3.8				
(66) 6.6	(78) 5.9	(86) 6.8	Owners' Comp/Sales	(48) 8.5	(20) 6.8				
9.2	10.2	11.4		16.3	8.7				
740650M	736924M	850536M	Net Sales ($)	61043M	76872M	64208M	114301M	164033M	370079M
699316M	454698M	838415M	Total Assets ($)	99932M	65566M	40911M	72388M	114778M	444840M

M = $ thousand   MM = $ million
See Pages 11 through 18 for Explanation of Ratios and Data

Current Data Sorted By Assets   **Comparative Historical Data**

Type of Statement	0-500M	500M-2MM	2-10MM	10-50MM	50-100MM	100-250MM		4/1/98-3/31/99 ALL	4/1/99-3/31/00 ALL
Unqualified	1		3	2	1			8	2
Reviewed	2	2	2					11	11
Compiled	16	8	1	1				28	31
Tax Returns	14	9	1	1				29	23
Other	11	7	3	1	1	1		17	23
	16 (4/1-9/30/02)			72 (10/1/02-3/31/03)					
NUMBER OF STATEMENTS	44	26	10	5	2	1		93	90
ASSETS	%	%	%	%	%	%		%	%
Cash & Equivalents	12.5	12.8	6.1					10.5	11.0
Trade Receivables (net)	13.7	18.4	9.5					15.0	17.0
Inventory	23.1	30.4	28.6					24.9	24.6
All Other Current	2.5	1.9	.7					1.4	1.4
Total Current	51.9	63.5	44.9					51.9	54.0
Fixed Assets (net)	37.5	23.8	38.3					36.4	32.6
Intangibles (net)	2.3	4.9	4.4					4.8	4.0
All Other Non-Current	8.3	7.8	12.4					6.9	9.4
Total	100.0	100.0	100.0					100.0	100.0
LIABILITIES									
Notes Payable-Short Term	8.0	11.1	13.7					8.0	12.0
Cur. Mat.-L/T/D	6.7	4.3	6.9					2.9	5.1
Trade Payables	15.3	25.6	10.9					13.0	16.6
Income Taxes Payable	.0	.0	.1					.4	.2
All Other Current	20.4	5.4	5.4					11.9	12.3
Total Current	50.4	46.4	36.9					36.1	46.1
Long Term Debt	40.1	20.2	25.8					21.4	28.6
Deferred Taxes	.0	.0	.0					1.2	.3
All Other Non-Current	13.5	7.1	11.2					2.5	3.2
Net Worth	-4.0	26.2	26.1					38.9	21.8
Total Liabilities & Net Worth	100.0	100.0	100.0					100.0	100.0
INCOME DATA									
Net Sales	100.0	100.0	100.0					100.0	100.0
Gross Profit									
Operating Expenses	96.5	97.5	93.9					93.4	93.9
Operating Profit	3.5	2.5	6.1					6.6	6.1
All Other Expenses (net)	1.0	1.3	2.1					1.1	1.5
Profit Before Taxes	2.5	1.2	4.0					5.4	4.6
RATIOS									
Current	2.7	2.6	1.6					2.7	2.6
	1.1	1.4	1.0					1.5	1.2
	.6	.9	.5					.9	.8
Quick	1.5	1.6	.5					1.7	1.2
	.5	.6	.3					.6	.6
	.2	.3	.1					.3	.3
Sales/Receivables	0 UND	4 87.9	2 217.5					2 205.5	3 110.0
	4 89.3	20 18.1	4 81.5					10 35.7	14 26.1
	20 18.7	32 11.3	23 15.9					27 13.6	27 13.4
Cost of Sales/Inventory									
Cost of Sales/Payables									
Sales/Working Capital	14.9	8.1	7.0					7.7	9.4
	108.4	18.4	NM					20.3	41.9
	-17.9	-91.6	-10.9					-67.5	-48.6
EBIT/Interest	(36) 8.1	(25) 4.0						(74) 9.3	(77) 7.3
	2.6	2.0						3.9	2.8
	-2.3	.3						1.8	1.4
Net Profit + Depr., Dep., Amort./Cur. Mat. L /T/D								(15) 10.5	(11) 2.3
								3.2	1.5
								1.0	.5
Fixed/Worth	.6	.3	.4					.2	.3
	2.6	.7	.7					.9	1.1
	-2.3	3.0	3.4					3.9	5.9
Debt/Worth	1.3	1.5	1.6					.6	.8
	7.4	3.1	2.5					1.5	2.7
	-5.1	8.7	3.8					10.3	10.9
% Profit Before Taxes/Tangible Net Worth	(28) 124.5	(23) 40.1						(78) 61.0	(72) 85.2
	29.6	8.7						24.0	26.7
	2.8	-9.8						10.5	4.5
% Profit Before Taxes/Total Assets	37.3	8.0	8.9					20.6	21.3
	4.8	2.4	6.9					10.5	7.3
	-11.4	-1.5	3.0					3.1	1.3
Sales/Net Fixed Assets	63.7	42.4	33.3					38.0	31.5
	16.2	19.6	16.3					14.3	14.4
	5.1	11.3	1.8					3.6	6.8
Sales/Total Assets	7.3	4.7	3.5					4.5	5.0
	4.5	3.3	1.6					2.6	3.4
	2.4	1.8	1.4					1.7	2.1
% Depr., Dep., Amort./Sales	(32) 1.3	(21) 1.0	1.1					(80) .8	(77) 1.1
	2.5	1.9	1.5					1.7	1.9
	4.2	2.9	3.5					3.3	3.0
% Officers', Directors', Owners' Comp/Sales	(24) 1.5	(12) 1.5						(49) 2.4	(49) 3.8
	5.2	3.1						5.1	6.4
	10.7	6.4						10.1	9.8
Net Sales ($)	40962M	78893M	115034M	816661M	172756M	389111M		2379977M	1891232M
Total Assets ($)	8787M	22314M	43833M	121828M	150788M	109153M		794883M	770305M

M = $ thousand   MM = $ million
See Pages 11 through 18 for Explanation of Ratios and Data

Comparative Historical Data | Current Data Sorted By Sales

4/1/00-3/31/01 ALL	4/1/01-3/31/02 ALL	4/1/02-3/31/03 ALL	Type of Statement	16 (4/1-9/30/02) 0-1MM	1-3MM	3-5MM	72 (10/1/02-3/31/03) 5-10MM	10-25MM	25MM & OVER
4	3	7	Unqualified	1			1	1	4
11	6	6	Reviewed		2	2	1	1	1
33	36	26	Compiled	14	8	3	3		1
28	32	25	Tax Returns	12	8	1		1	3
15	25	24	Other	10	5	4	1		3
91	102	88	**NUMBER OF STATEMENTS**	37	23	10	6	3	9
%	%	%	**ASSETS**	%	%	%	%	%	%
11.2	10.4	11.8	Cash & Equivalents	13.0	9.4	6.7			
17.2	14.5	14.8	Trade Receivables (net)	11.9	16.6	20.2			
28.1	27.9	24.7	Inventory	21.2	27.9	41.0			
1.7	1.5	2.2	All Other Current	3.3	.8	1.4			
58.2	54.3	53.5	Total Current	49.4	54.7	69.3			
31.4	35.5	33.5	Fixed Assets (net)	36.3	34.8	17.9			
2.6	2.8	4.2	Intangibles (net)	3.4	3.5	2.4			
7.9	7.4	8.8	All Other Non-Current	10.7	7.0	10.4			
100.0	100.0	100.0	Total	100.0	100.0	100.0			
			LIABILITIES						
9.5	54.3	8.9	Notes Payable-Short Term	9.2	8.4	10.8			
4.3	5.8	5.7	Cur. Mat.-L/T/D	8.1	3.5	6.9			
16.1	14.8	21.1	Trade Payables	11.7	23.0	26.7			
.2	.5	.0	Income Taxes Payable	.0	.1	.0			
83.6	16.5	14.0	All Other Current	19.6	9.2	5.2			
113.6	91.9	49.7	Total Current	48.6	44.2	49.7			
119.2	49.2	32.1	Long Term Debt	45.5	21.8	17.4			
.0	.0	.0	Deferred Taxes	.0	.0	.0			
72.5	12.3	18.4	All Other Non-Current	15.6	3.9	7.2			
−205.4	−53.4	−.2	Net Worth	−9.7	30.0	25.8			
100.0	100.0	100.0	Total Liabilities & Net Worth	100.0	100.0	100.0			
			INCOME DATA						
100.0	100.0	100.0	Net Sales	100.0	100.0	100.0			
			Gross Profit						
97.0	95.4	96.6	Operating Expenses	96.5	95.7	96.8			
3.0	4.6	3.4	Operating Profit	3.5	4.3	3.2			
.6	1.5	1.3	All Other Expenses (net)	2.2	.5	.3			
2.4	3.1	2.0	Profit Before Taxes	1.3	3.7	3.0			
			RATIOS						
2.3 1.3 .8	2.3 1.3 .7	2.6 1.2 .6	Current	2.7 1.3 .4	2.6 1.3 .7	2.1 1.5 .9			
(90) 1.3 .6 .2	(101) 1.1 .5 .2	1.3 .5 .2	Quick	1.7 .5 .1	1.1 .6 .2	1.6 .3 .2			
2 167.5 15 24.9 31 11.9	1 628.0 12 31.7 29 12.6	1 272.0 10 35.0 27 13.4	Sales/Receivables	0 UND 4 86.6 20 18.4	1 245.4 18 20.9 35 10.3	6 57.8 19 19.4 30 12.1			
			Cost of Sales/Inventory						
			Cost of Sales/Payables						
10.6 26.8 −102.3	8.9 33.1 −29.1	9.7 40.8 −24.9	Sales/Working Capital	11.1 106.0 −8.1	8.7 30.2 −28.1	7.1 17.6 −91.6			
(74) 6.7 2.0 1.0	(85) 4.9 2.6 1.1	(77) 4.8 2.4 .1	EBIT/Interest	(30) 3.5 1.8 −2.8	(22) 10.1 2.8 .4				
(17) 5.6 1.9 .6	(12) 4.2 .9 .5		Net Profit + Depr., Dep., Amort./Cur. Mat. L/T/D						
.3 .9 7.4	.4 1.6 −9.9	.3 1.5 −10.0	Fixed/Worth	.1 4.9 −1.7	.3 1.2 3.1	.3 .6 1.8			
.8 2.3 46.0	.9 2.5 −21.9	1.6 3.8 −11.3	Debt/Worth	1.5 10.8 −3.9	1.0 2.0 7.1	1.6 2.8 6.7			
(70) 46.9 18.8 5.2	(75) 35.7 18.5 4.4	(62) 57.2 16.8 1.8	% Profit Before Taxes/Tangible Net Worth	(22) 141.3 25.2 1.6	(20) 65.1 20.8 −3.6				
15.2 5.0 .0	16.5 5.7 .3	12.2 3.4 −3.5	% Profit Before Taxes/Total Assets	12.7 1.7 −13.4	22.7 4.3 −2.4	18.5 5.6 1.9			
31.5 14.2 7.6	37.9 13.9 5.9	52.1 16.8 5.1	Sales/Net Fixed Assets	87.3 16.1 3.7	40.9 15.9 7.3	51.5 26.0 14.4			
4.7 3.0 2.2	5.1 3.3 2.1	5.9 3.3 1.8	Sales/Total Assets	5.6 2.9 1.8	6.2 3.7 2.2	6.5 4.0 1.5			
(78) 1.1 1.8 3.2	(86) .9 1.9 3.8	(70) 1.2 2.3 3.5	% Depr., Dep., Amort./Sales	(25) 1.7 2.9 5.6	(19) 1.0 2.4 3.1				
(54) 2.7 5.0 11.0	(59) 2.7 5.2 10.9	(41) 1.5 4.9 9.9	% Officers', Directors', Owners' Comp/Sales	(18) 2.3 5.0 11.6	(11) 2.5 4.9 7.0				
786913M	619115M	1613417M	Net Sales ($)	19233M	40701M	41178M	43800M	41196M	1427309M
472103M	364491M	456703M	Total Assets ($)	10553M	13191M	15010M	13356M	40896M	363697M

© RMA 2003

M = $ thousand   MM = $ million
See Pages 11 through 18 for Explanation of Ratios and Data

Current Data Sorted By Assets   Comparative Historical Data

Type of Statement	0-500M	500M-2MM	2-10MM	10-50MM	50-100MM	100-250MM		4/1/98-3/31/99 ALL	4/1/99-3/31/00 ALL
Unqualified			2	1				9	6
Reviewed	2	3	1					8	11
Compiled	2		1	2				13	11
Tax Returns	3	1	2					8	2
Other	3	2	3	1				11	16
		4 (4/1-9/30/02)		22 (10/1/02-3/31/03)					
NUMBER OF STATEMENTS	10	6	8	2				49	46
	%	%	%	%	%	%		%	%
ASSETS									
Cash & Equivalents	15.7				D	D		12.3	13.4
Trade Receivables (net)	34.4				A	A		41.1	41.6
Inventory	14.1				T	T		16.7	15.5
All Other Current	.6				A	A		2.5	4.6
Total Current	64.8							72.6	75.0
Fixed Assets (net)	23.6				N	N		16.9	15.3
Intangibles (net)	.0				O	O		5.3	3.3
All Other Non-Current	11.6				T	T		5.3	6.4
Total	100.0							100.0	100.0
LIABILITIES					A	A			
Notes Payable-Short Term	27.2				V	V		10.1	13.9
Cur. Mat.-L/T/D	1.5				A	A		2.4	2.4
Trade Payables	17.8				I	I		20.0	18.6
Income Taxes Payable	.0				L	L		.6	.7
All Other Current	17.3				A	A		16.6	14.8
Total Current	63.8				B	B		49.7	50.4
Long Term Debt	12.0				L	L		8.3	11.9
Deferred Taxes	.0				E	E		.4	.3
All Other Non-Current	17.9							5.2	4.0
Net Worth	6.3							36.4	33.4
Total Liabilities & Net Worth	100.0							100.0	100.0
INCOME DATA									
Net Sales	100.0							100.0	100.0
Gross Profit									
Operating Expenses	94.2							98.1	97.7
Operating Profit	5.8							1.9	2.3
All Other Expenses (net)	.7							.8	.6
Profit Before Taxes	5.1							1.1	1.7
RATIOS									
Current	1.8							2.4	2.7
	1.5							1.5	1.5
	.8							1.1	1.1
Quick	1.6							1.7	1.8
	1.3							1.1	1.1
	.5							.8	.8
Sales/Receivables	15 23.8							25 14.7	27 13.5
	27 13.5							43 8.4	43 8.5
	37 9.9							56 6.5	58 6.3
Cost of Sales/Inventory									
Cost of Sales/Payables									
Sales/Working Capital	11.8							8.5	7.1
	15.7							15.4	15.2
	−50.9							58.7	59.7
EBIT/Interest							(42)	10.6	9.0 (39)
								4.5	3.0
								.8	1.0
Net Profit + Depr., Dep., Amort./Cur. Mat. L/T/D							(15)	6.5	3.9 (15)
								2.3	1.1
								.4	−2.7
Fixed/Worth	.1							.2	.2
	2.3							.4	.4
	NM							1.0	1.5
Debt/Worth	1.3							1.0	.7
	8.3							1.8	2.4
	NM							3.9	7.9
% Profit Before Taxes/Tangible Net Worth							(42)	42.6	59.5 (38)
								22.3	22.1
								9.0	3.7
% Profit Before Taxes/Total Assets	30.0							14.9	14.2
	6.6							7.0	7.0
	−1.3							−.4	−.5
Sales/Net Fixed Assets	131.6							65.0	61.4
	55.4							25.5	29.7
	5.2							13.1	16.9
Sales/Total Assets	7.6							4.6	4.9
	4.9							3.6	3.6
	2.3							2.9	2.6
% Depr., Dep., Amort./Sales							(43)	.6	.6 (37)
								1.5	1.0
								3.0	2.1
% Officers', Directors', Owners' Comp/Sales							(25)	3.5	2.8 (17)
								5.0	4.9
								10.1	6.7
Net Sales ($)	14266M	24970M	133481M	132705M				541035M	440201M
Total Assets ($)	2456M	5845M	39712M	31448M				180710M	165297M

© RMA 2003

M = $ thousand   MM = $ million
See Pages 11 through 18 for Explanation of Ratios and Data

Comparative Historical Data   Current Data Sorted By Sales

			Type of Statement						
3	2	3	Unqualified			1	1		2
6	3	6	Reviewed		1	4	1		
11	12	4	Compiled	2			1	1	
6	5	4	Tax Returns	3			1		
10	13	9	Other	2		2		2	2
4/1/00-3/31/01	4/1/01-3/31/02	4/1/02-3/31/03			4 (4/1-9/30/02)		22 (10/1/02-3/31/03)		
ALL	ALL	ALL		0-1MM	1-3MM	3-5MM	5-10MM	10-25MM	25MM & OVER
36	35	26	NUMBER OF STATEMENTS	7	1	6	5	3	4
%	%	%	ASSETS	%	%	%	%	%	%
14.2	9.3	12.6	Cash & Equivalents						
41.2	39.4	43.8	Trade Receivables (net)						
13.5	20.2	14.6	Inventory						
3.5	3.1	2.4	All Other Current						
72.4	72.0	73.5	Total Current						
18.3	15.0	17.1	Fixed Assets (net)						
3.3	6.8	3.0	Intangibles (net)						
6.0	6.2	6.5	All Other Non-Current						
100.0	100.0	100.0	Total						
			LIABILITIES						
19.3	13.1	18.6	Notes Payable-Short Term						
4.2	3.7	4.5	Cur. Mat.-L/T/D						
23.4	21.1	19.5	Trade Payables						
.8	.6	.4	Income Taxes Payable						
21.2	14.9	17.3	All Other Current						
68.8	53.4	60.4	Total Current						
11.6	8.9	10.2	Long Term Debt						
.2	.2	.0	Deferred Taxes						
6.0	35.1	10.0	All Other Non-Current						
13.4	2.4	19.4	Net Worth						
100.0	100.0	100.0	Total Liabilities & Net Worth						
			INCOME DATA						
100.0	100.0	100.0	Net Sales						
			Gross Profit						
98.7	93.8	95.2	Operating Expenses						
1.3	6.2	4.8	Operating Profit						
.4	.6	.9	All Other Expenses (net)						
.9	5.6	3.8	Profit Before Taxes						
			RATIOS						
2.2	2.5	1.7	Current						
1.3	1.4	1.4							
.9	1.0	1.1							
1.8	1.8	1.4	Quick						
1.1	1.0	1.1							
.6	.6	.7							
26 14.3	25 14.4	25 14.9	Sales/Receivables						
41 9.0	41 8.8	37 9.8							
52 7.0	55 6.7	58 6.3							
			Cost of Sales/Inventory						
			Cost of Sales/Payables						
7.3	8.8	11.8	Sales/Working Capital						
23.3	17.3	17.5							
−215.1	−96.0	43.8							
6.6	18.8	17.2	EBIT/Interest						
(30) 1.7	(31) 5.0	(24) 3.0							
.0	1.7	1.2							
3.9			Net Profit + Depr., Dep., Amort./Cur. Mat. L/T/D						
(11) 1.5									
.1									
.2	.2	.2	Fixed/Worth						
.5	.5	.5							
1.2	3.2	2.6							
1.1	.9	1.9	Debt/Worth						
2.5	2.7	3.7							
7.9	23.0	16.9							
87.2	73.0	56.2	% Profit Before Taxes/Tangible Net Worth						
(31) 7.0	(27) 38.1	(22) 32.1							
−9.8	4.8	7.6							
18.7	28.9	23.4	% Profit Before Taxes/Total Assets						
2.2	10.3	6.9							
−6.5	2.8	2.4							
58.0	64.7	97.0	Sales/Net Fixed Assets						
28.7	34.6	44.7							
15.6	16.4	17.1							
4.8	5.7	5.6	Sales/Total Assets						
3.9	4.0	3.9							
3.1	2.4	3.0							
.6	.7	.5	% Depr., Dep., Amort./Sales						
(31) 1.1	(25) 1.3	(22) 1.0							
2.5	2.2	1.6							
4.0	2.2	3.8	% Officers', Directors', Owners' Comp/Sales						
(16) 5.6	(15) 4.4	(15) 6.4							
10.2	9.9	12.2							
320279M	473270M	305422M	Net Sales ($)	3760M	1345M	22472M	33270M	41854M	202721M
96119M	256354M	79461M	Total Assets ($)	1508M	279M	5016M	13954M	11304M	47400M

© RMA 2003

M = $ thousand   MM = $ million
See Pages 11 through 18 for Explanation of Ratios and Data

Current Data Sorted By Assets   **Comparative Historical Data**

						Type of Statement		
1	2	7	7	2	3	Unqualified	25	25
6	27	20	5			Reviewed	61	78
21	27	12		1	2	Compiled	85	97
23	15	1				Tax Returns	47	37
15	16	10	3		1	Other	61	62
	44 (4/1-9/30/02)		183 (10/1/02-3/31/03)				4/1/98-3/31/99	4/1/99-3/31/00
0-500M	500M-2MM	2-10MM	10-50MM	50-100MM	100-250MM		ALL	ALL
66	87	50	15	3	6	NUMBER OF STATEMENTS	279	299
%	%	%	%	%	%	ASSETS	%	%
12.2	8.6	10.6	7.5			Cash & Equivalents	9.7	8.9
28.4	34.3	32.8	30.7			Trade Receivables (net)	29.5	31.5
20.8	22.8	17.5	13.6			Inventory	18.2	18.9
1.2	2.5	4.6	3.5			All Other Current	2.9	2.7
62.6	68.1	65.6	55.3			Total Current	60.4	62.0
30.7	23.8	25.8	32.3			Fixed Assets (net)	30.3	28.1
1.0	2.1	1.7	7.1			Intangibles (net)	3.2	3.7
5.7	5.9	6.9	5.3			All Other Non-Current	6.1	6.3
100.0	100.0	100.0	100.0			Total	100.0	100.0
						LIABILITIES		
15.7	13.5	13.4	11.5			Notes Payable-Short Term	10.5	10.5
7.8	5.2	5.4	5.0			Cur. Mat.-L/T/D	4.6	5.1
17.2	15.5	14.0	9.5			Trade Payables	14.5	15.4
.1	.5	.2	.2			Income Taxes Payable	.4	.3
8.6	9.9	14.7	11.4			All Other Current	15.3	11.9
49.4	44.5	47.7	37.6			Total Current	45.3	43.2
20.7	18.7	13.7	15.2			Long Term Debt	20.8	18.3
.1	.4	.5	1.1			Deferred Taxes	.4	.4
6.4	3.0	3.4	2.7			All Other Non-Current	4.5	4.3
23.4	33.3	34.7	43.3			Net Worth	29.0	33.9
100.0	100.0	100.0	100.0			Total Liabilities & Net Worth	100.0	100.0
						INCOME DATA		
100.0	100.0	100.0	100.0			Net Sales	100.0	100.0
						Gross Profit		
94.3	95.1	95.4	93.6			Operating Expenses	95.3	94.8
5.7	4.9	4.6	6.3			Operating Profit	4.7	5.2
1.2	1.1	.7	.7			All Other Expenses (net)	.5	1.0
4.5	3.8	3.9	5.6			Profit Before Taxes	4.2	4.2
						RATIOS		
2.6	3.1	2.0	2.2				2.6	2.6
1.6	1.5	1.4	1.3			Current	1.5	1.5
.7	1.0	1.1	1.0				1.0	1.0
1.8	1.7	1.3	1.3				1.6	1.7
.8	1.0	.9	1.0			Quick	1.0	1.0
.5	.6	.6	.6			(278)	.6	.5
12 29.6	25 14.3	33 11.2	42 8.6				28 13.0	27 13.7
26 14.1	41 8.8	49 7.5	53 6.9			Sales/Receivables	42 8.7	43 8.6
45 8.0	56 6.5	64 5.7	58 6.3				57 6.5	58 6.3
						Cost of Sales/Inventory		
						Cost of Sales/Payables		
7.9	5.7	6.1	8.5				6.9	6.4
17.4	14.6	12.9	14.2			Sales/Working Capital	14.0	13.3
-46.8	84.8	130.6	191.2				878.0	272.6
12.7	10.7	6.8	12.5				11.0	8.7
(56) 3.0	(80) 4.1	(43) 2.5	(14) 5.6			EBIT/Interest	(254) 3.7	(264) 3.3
1.1	1.1	.8	2.8				1.5	1.2
	5.6	9.3					4.8	4.4
	(22) 2.8	(13) 2.6				Net Profit + Depr., Dep., Amort./Cur. Mat. L /T/D	(69) 2.0	(77) 2.2
	1.3	.9					.9	1.1
.2	.2	.3	.3				.4	.3
1.2	.7	.7	.9			Fixed/Worth	.9	.8
NM	3.0	2.1	2.1				3.0	2.2
.5	.7	1.1	.6				.8	.8
2.7	2.3	2.1	1.8			Debt/Worth	2.2	2.0
NM	9.0	5.1	4.4				6.9	6.8
93.7	66.3	30.9	53.4				54.6	53.0
(50) 29.4	(75) 17.6	(46) 13.9	(14) 33.5			% Profit Before Taxes/Tangible Net Worth	(235) 25.7	(252) 22.3
3.5	.7	3.7	17.1				8.3	6.2
29.1	14.2	12.6	18.9				17.4	17.4
6.3	6.4	3.9	9.6			% Profit Before Taxes/Total Assets	8.2	6.8
-1.3	.0	.8	5.0				1.6	.8
42.0	39.6	27.0	19.2				24.3	27.1
16.3	15.8	11.8	8.5			Sales/Net Fixed Assets	11.6	12.9
7.5	7.7	6.9	2.2				5.1	6.1
5.4	3.6	3.2	2.5				3.6	3.6
3.8	2.7	2.5	2.0			Sales/Total Assets	2.6	2.6
2.4	2.3	1.8	1.4				1.9	1.8
.9	.8	1.2	2.0				1.2	1.1
(49) 2.8	(78) 1.8	(47) 2.1	(14) 3.1			% Depr., Dep., Amort./Sales	(243) 2.2	(269) 2.2
4.4	3.9	3.1	6.1				4.0	3.8
	3.5	2.4					4.0	3.9
(40) 8.3	(47) 5.8	(19) 3.7				% Officers', Directors', Owners' Comp/Sales	(140) 6.8	(155) 6.6
12.3	7.9	6.8					11.4	11.2
70154M	276668M	504548M	541118M	327749M	1820656M	Net Sales ($)	2826277M	2528704M
18358M	95090M	197558M	289418M	203084M	852164M	Total Assets ($)	1388984M	1208813M

© RMA 2003

M = $ thousand   MM = $ million
See Pages 11 through 18 for Explanation of Ratios and Data

Comparative Historical Data — Current Data Sorted By Sales

4/1/00-3/31/01 ALL	4/1/01-3/31/02 ALL	4/1/02-3/31/03 ALL		0-1MM	1-3MM	3-5MM	5-10MM	10-25MM	25MM & OVER
			Type of Statement		44 (4/1-9/30/02)			183 (10/1/02-3/31/03)	
22	20	22	Unqualified	2	1	2	1	7	11
62	51	58	Reviewed		16	14	13	12	1
101	89	63	Compiled	14	23	11	9	3	3
48	45	39	Tax Returns	14	21	3	1		
67	67	45	Other	10	13	7	5	7	3
300	272	227	**NUMBER OF STATEMENTS**	40	74	37	29	29	18
%	%	%	**ASSETS**	%	%	%	%	%	%
8.9	10.2	9.9	Cash & Equivalents	13.3	8.0	11.9	11.7	5.9	9.7
33.3	31.1	31.9	Trade Receivables (net)	20.5	30.7	41.1	31.4	38.1	33.8
18.9	18.4	20.4	Inventory	17.3	25.3	19.1	19.7	17.5	15.5
2.6	2.9	2.6	All Other Current	1.1	2.4	3.4	3.0	4.3	2.2
63.5	62.5	64.8	Total Current	52.3	66.5	75.4	65.9	65.8	61.2
27.0	29.3	26.8	Fixed Assets (net)	40.6	24.9	19.1	23.3	27.0	25.5
3.7	2.3	2.1	Intangibles (net)	1.3	1.8	1.0	2.7	2.4	5.9
5.7	5.8	6.2	All Other Non-Current	5.7	6.8	4.5	8.2	4.8	7.3
100.0	100.0	100.0	Total	100.0	100.0	100.0	100.0	100.0	100.0
			LIABILITIES						
12.4	9.9	13.9	Notes Payable-Short Term	16.9	12.7	12.4	12.6	18.9	9.2
4.8	5.6	6.0	Cur. Mat.-L/T/D	7.5	6.6	3.3	4.4	8.1	5.0
16.1	15.0	15.2	Trade Payables	13.7	15.1	16.3	18.1	13.9	13.9
.3	.4	.3	Income Taxes Payable	.1	.2	.7	.2	.2	.2
11.1	9.2	10.7	All Other Current	12.4	6.9	14.3	13.0	10.8	11.1
44.8	40.1	46.1	Total Current	50.7	41.6	47.0	48.5	51.9	39.3
18.8	18.2	18.4	Long Term Debt	24.3	21.5	15.8	11.6	10.8	20.3
.7	.6	.4	Deferred Taxes	.0	.2	.8	.8	.4	.7
5.0	5.5	4.3	All Other Non-Current	6.5	4.9	3.6	2.6	1.1	6.2
30.7	35.5	30.9	Net Worth	18.7	31.8	32.8	36.5	35.8	33.5
100.0	100.0	100.0	Total Liabilities & Net Worth	100.0	100.0	100.0	100.0	100.0	100.0
			INCOME DATA						
100.0	100.0	100.0	Net Sales	100.0	100.0	100.0	100.0	100.0	100.0
			Gross Profit						
95.5	95.4	94.8	Operating Expenses	89.8	96.7	95.0	97.0	95.1	93.9
4.5	4.6	5.2	Operating Profit	10.2	3.3	5.0	3.0	4.9	6.1
1.2	1.3	1.0	All Other Expenses (net)	2.5	1.0	.4	.4	.6	.9
3.3	3.3	4.2	Profit Before Taxes	7.7	2.3	4.6	2.6	4.3	5.2
			RATIOS						
2.5	2.7	2.6	Current	2.6	3.3	3.1	2.0	1.5	2.9
1.4	1.5	1.4		1.4	1.7	1.7	1.4	1.2	1.5
1.0	1.1	1.0		.5	1.0	1.2	1.1	1.0	1.1
1.7	1.7	1.6	Quick	1.8	1.9	1.7	1.4	1.1	1.5
.9	1.0	.9		.5	.9	1.1	1.1	.8	1.0
.5	.6	.6		.3	.5	.9	.7	.6	.7
30 12.2	25 14.7	24 15.1	Sales/Receivables	11 33.2	22 16.3	35 10.4	23 15.9	33 10.9	42 8.7
45 8.2	39 9.4	41 9.0		24 14.9	36 10.1	49 7.5	41 8.8	51 7.2	53 6.9
59 6.1	56 6.6	56 6.5		39 9.4	54 6.7	61 6.0	60 6.1	65 5.6	74 4.9
			Cost of Sales/Inventory						
			Cost of Sales/Payables						
6.5	5.8	6.0	Sales/Working Capital	7.6	5.5	5.2	6.6	11.5	4.6
13.3	13.8	14.2		30.4	12.1	10.4	15.4	18.4	10.7
300.1	73.7	-839.0		-10.9	-236.4	47.3	39.6	NM	142.7
(261) 6.9	(238) 8.7	(201) 9.5	EBIT/Interest	(31) 13.8	(67) 8.5	(33) 9.2	(27) 11.1	(28) 10.4	(15) 9.5
2.3	2.8	3.7		3.0	2.9	4.2	3.5	3.6	5.0
1.0	1.0	1.1		1.2	.1	1.2	1.9	.5	1.4
(64) 4.4	(53) 3.6	(47) 5.6	Net Profit + Depr., Dep., Amort./Cur. Mat. L/T/D		(11) 5.5		(12) 7.8		
2.1	1.8	2.3			2.7		2.7		
1.2	.6	.4			.4		1.3		
.3	.3	.3	Fixed/Worth	.6	.2	.2	.3	.3	.3
.8	.7	.8		1.7	.8	.7	.6	.7	.8
4.1	2.5	3.9		-110.2	7.2	4.6	1.5	1.5	2.7
.8	.7	.8	Debt/Worth	.5	.7		.9	1.2	.8
2.3	2.0	2.2		3.3	2.3	2.1	2.0	2.1	1.7
15.5	5.0	8.8		-135.0	13.3	15.1	4.1	3.9	6.4
(249) 51.7	(240) 44.5	(193) 61.8	% Profit Before Taxes/Tangible Net Worth	(29) 78.3	(60) 67.6	(32) 87.4	(27) 37.5	47.6	(16) 53.3
21.2	17.5	20.0		22.2	14.4	30.1	17.6	19.2	26.7
3.6	1.3	2.4		6.8	-.2	2.7	4.1	-3.2	-2.4
13.6	15.9	17.0	% Profit Before Taxes/Total Assets	25.4	17.6	20.3	9.8	14.5	20.4
4.9	5.8	6.0		6.6	3.3	9.5	5.8	5.0	8.9
.0	.0	.4		.6	-2.7	.8	2.2	-1.4	.5
29.4	29.2	34.2	Sales/Net Fixed Assets	22.0	39.7	85.6	38.1	25.1	19.8
12.6	12.8	13.4		10.3	16.1	27.7	16.4	11.2	10.3
6.0	5.6	6.9		2.9	7.1	11.2	7.8	7.0	5.9
3.7	3.6	3.7	Sales/Total Assets	4.4	4.4	3.8	3.4	3.3	3.0
2.6	2.7	2.8		2.5	2.8	3.0	2.8	3.0	2.3
1.7	1.9	2.0		1.1	2.3	2.2	2.2	1.8	1.6
(259) 1.0	(237) .9	(194) 1.1	% Depr., Dep., Amort./Sales	(30) 1.3	(62) 1.0	(32) .7	(28) 1.2	(28) .9	(14) 1.8
2.0	1.9	2.2		3.5	2.4	1.5	1.7	2.4	2.6
4.1	3.7	4.2		6.3	4.7	2.5	2.7	4.4	4.2
(149) 2.9	(128) 3.3	(110) 3.5	% Officers', Directors', Owners' Comp/Sales	(21) 4.3	(47) 5.2	(18) 3.0	(13) 2.8		
5.5	6.4	5.9		10.1	7.0	4.3	3.7		
10.5	9.4	9.0		16.1	9.3	6.9	8.8		
2926404M	3043916M	3540893M	Net Sales ($)	21588M	134945M	142135M	189838M	473926M	2578461M
1523988M	1522814M	1655672M	Total Assets ($)	9473M	55292M	56424M	75452M	223246M	1235785M

M = $ thousand   MM = $ million
See Pages 11 through 18 for Explanation of Ratios and Data

Current Data Sorted By Assets   Comparative Historical Data

0-500M	500M-2MM	2-10MM	10-50MM	50-100MM	100-250MM	Type of Statement	4/1/98-3/31/99 ALL	4/1/99-3/31/00 ALL
						Unqualified		
2	4	16	3			Reviewed	21	27
15	15	7	2			Compiled	34	36
17	8	1				Tax Returns	11	10
11	14	4	2			Other	24	19
	30 (4/1-9/30/02)		91 (10/1/02-3/31/03)					
45	41	28	7			**NUMBER OF STATEMENTS**	90	92
%	%	%	%	%	%	**ASSETS**	%	%
12.7	6.0	11.9				Cash & Equivalents	9.5	7.7
26.1	32.9	34.2				Trade Receivables (net)	30.1	30.3
14.2	20.2	13.8	D	D		Inventory	17.5	16.6
3.9	2.5	2.6	A	A		All Other Current	3.2	1.2
57.0	61.6	62.4	T	T		Total Current	60.3	55.9
35.0	30.1	30.3	A	A		Fixed Assets (net)	32.7	36.2
2.5	.8	3.3				Intangibles (net)	2.6	2.3
5.5	7.4	4.0	N	N		All Other Non-Current	4.4	5.6
100.0	100.0	100.0	O	O		Total	100.0	100.0
			T	T		**LIABILITIES**		
9.0	11.8	11.9				Notes Payable-Short Term	10.2	9.9
8.7	6.0	4.6	A	A		Cur. Mat.-L/T/D	5.9	6.0
10.9	15.3	11.2	V	V		Trade Payables	16.9	12.3
.1	.4	.4	A	A		Income Taxes Payable	.4	.2
6.2	7.9	8.1	I	I		All Other Current	8.3	8.7
34.9	41.4	36.2	L	L		Total Current	41.7	37.0
36.1	22.1	16.2	A	A		Long Term Debt	19.8	22.4
.0	.0	.3	B	B		Deferred Taxes	.4	.4
4.4	11.0	4.2	L	L		All Other Non-Current	6.0	6.2
24.5	25.5	43.1	E	E		Net Worth	32.0	34.1
100.0	100.0	100.0				Total Liabilities & Net Worth	100.0	100.0
						INCOME DATA		
100.0	100.0	100.0				Net Sales	100.0	100.0
						Gross Profit		
96.9	98.2	95.8				Operating Expenses	94.2	96.0
3.1	1.8	4.2				Operating Profit	5.8	4.0
.7	1.5	1.4				All Other Expenses (net)	1.6	.5
2.4	.3	2.8				Profit Before Taxes	4.2	3.5
						RATIOS		
3.6	2.3	2.8					2.5	2.6
1.9	1.4	1.8				Current	1.6	1.5
1.1	1.1	1.1					.9	1.1
2.8	1.2	1.9					1.7	1.5
(44) 1.3	.8	1.3				Quick (88)	1.1	1.0
.7	.7	.8					.7	.7
4 98.4	33 11.1	49 7.4					28 13.2	30 12.2
34 10.8	54 6.7	59 6.2				Sales/Receivables	40 9.0	47 7.7
48 7.6	69 5.3	78 4.7					58 6.3	58 6.3
						Cost of Sales/Inventory		
						Cost of Sales/Payables		
7.1	6.5	5.5					6.3	6.7
11.8	14.6	8.9				Sales/Working Capital	13.5	11.3
116.6	96.1	49.9					−204.7	40.4
8.1	2.8	8.5					7.4	7.3
(36) 2.5	(39) 1.0	(27) 3.1				EBIT/Interest (85) (88)	2.9	2.3
−.6	−2.4	1.6					1.1	1.0
						Net Profit + Depr., Dep.,	5.8	4.7
						Amort./Cur. Mat. L/T/D (20) (28)	2.4	2.7
							.9	1.4
.2	.4	.3					.5	.5
1.6	1.1	.8				Fixed/Worth	1.1	1.0
−5.3	4.7	1.4					4.1	2.3
.7	1.3	.7					.8	.9
2.7	2.2	1.2				Debt/Worth	2.6	1.8
−8.5	11.4	3.9					9.3	4.4
73.2	19.0	29.2				% Profit Before Taxes/Tangible	60.4	45.6
(30) 22.3	(35) 2.9	(26) 11.9				Net Worth (75) (82)	20.4	17.4
−1.3	−13.9	3.6					7.3	1.1
16.8	4.3	11.3				% Profit Before Taxes/Total	21.9	14.9
5.8	.4	4.2				Assets	7.1	5.4
−10.0	−7.2	2.0					1.0	.0
34.2	16.4	18.2					20.0	15.4
11.0	10.6	8.2				Sales/Net Fixed Assets	10.0	8.5
4.6	5.1	3.2					5.1	3.5
3.9	3.4	2.6					3.5	3.4
2.9	2.3	2.2				Sales/Total Assets	2.6	2.6
2.1	1.9	1.4					1.9	1.7
1.4	1.4	1.3					1.3	1.4
(30) 2.6	(35) 2.8	2.5				% Depr., Dep., Amort./Sales (83) (88)	2.2	2.4
5.2	4.4	5.4					3.9	4.6
5.3	3.6						2.8	3.4
(30) 8.0	(25) 6.4					% Officers', Directors', Owners' Comp/Sales (53) (53)	6.0	6.2
15.7	10.8						11.7	10.7
42060M	118179M	270571M	244057M			Net Sales ($)	826261M	511956M
13950M	47549M	113584M	131403M			Total Assets ($)	311995M	230641M

M = $ thousand   MM = $ million
See Pages 11 through 18 for Explanation of Ratios and Data

Comparative Historical Data | Current Data Sorted By Sales

				Type of Statement						
4	3	3		Unqualified						3
17	19	24		Reviewed	1	4	5	6	5	3
25	20	37		Compiled	11	11	8	6	1	
6	16	26		Tax Returns	14	10	2			
24	20	31		Other	8	11	6	2	3	1
4/1/00- 3/31/01	4/1/01- 3/31/02	4/1/02- 3/31/03				30 (4/1-9/30/02)			91 (10/1/02-3/31/03)	
ALL	ALL	ALL			0-1MM	1-3MM	3-5MM	5-10MM	10-25MM	25MM & OVER
76	78	121		NUMBER OF STATEMENTS	34	36	21	14	9	7
%	%	%		ASSETS	%	%	%	%	%	%
9.3	7.7	10.0		Cash & Equivalents	10.1	9.2	8.4	9.8		
31.6	35.9	30.5		Trade Receivables (net)	23.1	30.0	33.3	36.7		
14.2	12.8	16.1		Inventory	15.9	15.4	23.6	14.5		
2.4	1.8	3.0		All Other Current	4.2	2.7	3.0	1.7		
57.5	58.1	59.7		Total Current	53.3	57.3	68.3	62.7		
35.2	34.4	32.3		Fixed Assets (net)	36.4	34.6	24.6	31.0		
2.1	1.7	2.2		Intangibles (net)	2.7	2.8	1.0	1.4		
5.3	5.8	5.8		All Other Non-Current	7.6	5.3	6.0	4.9		
100.0	100.0	100.0		Total	100.0	100.0	100.0	100.0		
				LIABILITIES						
11.7	14.4	10.9		Notes Payable-Short Term	11.4	8.6	10.7	13.4		
5.2	9.6	6.5		Cur. Mat.-L/T/D	8.0	8.1	4.8	4.6		
13.2	14.0	12.4		Trade Payables	8.0	14.1	15.9	17.6		
.2	.8	.3		Income Taxes Payable	.0	.6	.1	.5		
8.0	9.8	7.3		All Other Current	6.0	5.4	8.2	10.2		
38.2	48.5	37.3		Total Current	33.3	36.8	39.6	46.3		
23.1	20.0	25.4		Long Term Debt	38.7	29.6	12.9	16.3		
.4	.2	.2		Deferred Taxes	.0	.1	.2	.1		
5.0	5.2	6.4		All Other Non-Current	6.6	8.3	10.9	.3		
33.3	26.1	30.6		Net Worth	21.4	25.2	36.5	37.0		
100.0	100.0	100.0		Total Liabilities & Net Worth	100.0	100.0	100.0	100.0		
				INCOME DATA						
100.0	100.0	100.0		Net Sales	100.0	100.0	100.0	100.0		
				Gross Profit						
95.2	96.4	96.8		Operating Expenses	96.5	97.6	100.0	96.1		
4.8	3.6	3.2		Operating Profit	3.5	2.4	.0	3.9		
1.0	2.0	1.2		All Other Expenses (net)	.7	1.6	.4	.9		
3.8	1.6	2.0		Profit Before Taxes	2.8	.7	−.4	2.9		
				RATIOS						
2.9	1.8	2.8			4.2	2.7	2.8	2.2		
1.4	1.3	1.7		Current	1.7	1.8	1.7	1.2		
1.1	.9	1.1			1.0	1.1	1.1	.9		
1.8	1.5	1.9			2.3	2.1	1.6	1.4		
1.0	1.0 (120)	1.2		Quick	(33) 1.2	1.1	.8	1.0		
.6	.6	.7			.6	.7	.8	.7		
33 10.9	41 8.9	31 11.9			1 378.2	30 12.2	35 10.3	35 10.3		
46 7.9	50 7.2	50 7.4		Sales/Receivables	34 10.6	46 7.9	54 6.7	54 6.7		
62 5.9	64 5.7	66 5.6			57 6.4	58 6.3	75 4.9	63 5.8		
				Cost of Sales/Inventory						
				Cost of Sales/Payables						
6.3	7.0	6.3			6.1	6.5	5.1	5.6		
16.1	17.5	11.0		Sales/Working Capital	12.4	11.2	9.1	28.1		
124.9	−87.7	99.6			NM	97.3	46.4	−71.6		
6.3	5.4	5.6			3.9	5.5	3.4	7.6		
(68) 2.3	(77) 2.9	(108) 2.2		EBIT/Interest	(25) 2.2	(34) 1.7	(20) .6	2.7		
.8	.1	−.4			−.4	−3.0	−2.7	1.6		
4.2	3.8	3.5		Net Profit + Depr., Dep.,						
(19) 1.7	(16) 1.5	(20) 1.7		Amort./Cur. Mat. L/T/D						
.8	−.2	.4								
.5	.5	.3			.2	.5	.2	.3		
.9	1.2	1.0		Fixed/Worth	2.7	1.1	.9	.8		
2.3	4.0	5.1			−5.6	20.0	1.9	3.6		
.9	1.3	.8			1.0	.9	.9	.7		
1.9	2.8	2.0		Debt/Worth	3.7	2.0	1.7	1.9		
4.0	8.7	13.2			−7.9	30.1	4.9	6.8		
41.1	50.8	28.5			73.2	27.6	17.2	42.2		
(67) 20.8	(67) 15.0	(98) 10.8		% Profit Before Taxes/Tangible Net Worth	(22) 12.8	(28) 8.9	(18) 1.5	10.7		
.2	3.3	−1.3			−1.3	−16.1	−17.7	3.2		
15.7	15.6	11.4			12.1	15.2	4.8	10.8		
6.3	3.3	3.0		% Profit Before Taxes/Total Assets	1.6	2.9	.1	3.0		
−.8	−6.4	−4.6			−6.4	−10.0	−8.9	1.7		
17.4	16.9	19.4			33.9	14.4	28.7	16.1		
9.8	8.7	9.4		Sales/Net Fixed Assets	7.7	8.9	16.4	12.9		
5.8	4.7	4.5			3.3	4.6	5.0	6.7		
3.7	3.3	3.4			3.4	3.6	3.5	3.1		
2.7	2.6	2.4		Sales/Total Assets	2.2	2.5	2.3	2.4		
1.6	1.8	1.8			1.5	2.0	1.7	2.0		
1.4	1.6	1.4			1.9	1.5	1.0	1.3		
(69) 2.2	(72) 2.6	(99) 2.7		% Depr., Dep., Amort./Sales	(23) 4.0	(30) 3.2	(17) 1.6	1.6		
4.1	4.4	4.8			6.4	4.9	4.3	2.6		
3.0	3.4	3.8			6.5	3.9	1.8			
(38) 4.2	(37) 6.2	(65) 6.8		% Officers', Directors', Owners' Comp/Sales	(18) 8.8	(27) 6.2	(12) 6.5			
6.9	9.7	12.7			16.3	10.8	11.4			
509629M	575457M	674867M		Net Sales ($)	21540M	68998M	77880M	93145M	140382M	272922M
238739M	254140M	306486M		Total Assets ($)	11077M	30255M	38677M	41026M	68188M	117263M

M = $ thousand   MM = $ million
See Pages 11 through 18 for Explanation of Ratios and Data

Current Data Sorted By Assets   **Comparative Historical Data**

		14 (4/1-9/30/02)		32 (10/1/02-3/31/03)			Type of Statement		4/1/98-3/31/99 ALL	4/1/99-3/31/00 ALL
	0-500M	500M-2MM	2-10MM	10-50MM	50-100MM	100-250MM				
1		1	2				Unqualified		9	2
2	4	2					Reviewed		20	15
4	4	1					Compiled		26	12
1	4						Tax Returns		10	11
5	8	4	3				Other		20	17
	13	20	8	5			NUMBER OF STATEMENTS		85	57
	%	%	%	%	%	%	**ASSETS**		%	%
	14.7	13.9			D	D	Cash & Equivalents		11.2	10.6
	40.1	37.0			A	A	Trade Receivables (net)		37.7	38.4
	9.1	14.2			T	T	Inventory		15.8	16.2
	1.9	7.6			A	A	All Other Current		3.4	4.9
	65.7	72.7					Total Current		68.1	70.0
	28.5	18.3			N	N	Fixed Assets (net)		21.2	20.6
	1.4	.5			O	O	Intangibles (net)		1.6	2.5
	4.4	8.5			T	T	All Other Non-Current		9.1	6.8
	100.0	100.0					Total		100.0	100.0
					A	A	**LIABILITIES**			
	6.3	8.6			V	V	Notes Payable-Short Term		6.2	7.5
	3.5	4.2			A	A	Cur. Mat.-L/T/D		3.8	4.3
	20.1	24.9			I	I	Trade Payables		17.4	16.7
	.1	1.7			L	L	Income Taxes Payable		.4	.5
	21.3	11.0			A	A	All Other Current		11.6	12.1
	51.2	50.4			B	B	Total Current		39.4	41.1
	8.9	10.0			L	L	Long Term Debt		13.8	14.0
	.0	.6			E	E	Deferred Taxes		.3	.2
	5.7	3.1					All Other Non-Current		2.5	1.5
	34.1	35.8					Net Worth		44.1	43.3
	100.0	100.0					Total Liabilities & Net Worth		100.0	100.0
							INCOME DATA			
	100.0	100.0					Net Sales		100.0	100.0
							Gross Profit			
	97.3	95.6					Operating Expenses		95.7	96.2
	2.7	4.4					Operating Profit		4.3	3.8
	.5	1.2					All Other Expenses (net)		-.3	-.7
	2.1	3.3					Profit Before Taxes		4.6	4.5
							RATIOS			
	3.4	2.6					Current		2.8	3.2
	1.2	1.4							1.8	1.9
	1.1	1.0							1.2	1.3
	3.3	1.7					Quick		2.2	2.1
	1.0	.8							1.3	(56) 1.3
	.9	.7							.8	1.0
1	346.8	24 15.4					Sales/Receivables	27	13.6	29 12.5
42	8.6	35 10.3						42	8.7	42 8.8
47	7.8	56 6.5						63	5.8	59 6.2
							Cost of Sales/Inventory			
							Cost of Sales/Payables			
	9.6	8.7					Sales/Working Capital		6.2	5.6
	34.0	16.6							11.4	10.9
	184.6	NM							26.6	25.6
		(16) 9.3					EBIT/Interest	(74)	25.7	(45) 14.1
		2.5							6.2	3.7
		1.4							2.5	1.9
							Net Profit + Depr., Dep., Amort./Cur. Mat. L /T/D	(21)	5.4	
									2.3	
									1.5	
	.3	.2					Fixed/Worth		.2	.2
	.5	.5							.5	.5
	2.2	1.4							1.0	.8
	.8	.7					Debt/Worth		.5	.5
	1.9	1.3							1.3	1.2
	5.0	8.4							3.2	2.8
	49.7	82.5					% Profit Before Taxes/Tangible Net Worth		65.3	54.1
(11)	11.1	(18) 15.3						(81)	30.2	(53) 26.8
	-2.0	5.4							10.7	10.8
	18.1	14.3					% Profit Before Taxes/Total Assets		25.1	22.2
	4.5	5.7							9.4	10.4
	-1.6	1.5							3.5	2.3
	37.3	35.4					Sales/Net Fixed Assets		36.8	40.8
	25.2	23.6							21.0	22.8
	13.4	16.4							9.6	11.9
	5.4	4.3					Sales/Total Assets		4.2	4.6
	4.3	3.5							3.3	3.0
	3.5	2.6							2.3	2.2
	1.2	.8					% Depr., Dep., Amort./Sales		1.0	.9
(12)	2.2	(19) 1.5						(69)	1.7	(47) 1.7
	3.9	2.4							2.7	2.4
	5.4	3.8					% Officers', Directors', Owners' Comp/Sales		2.4	2.7
(10)	8.0	(12) 6.9						(48)	4.3	(31) 5.0
	11.6	9.8							7.6	10.6
	17962M	72629M	69603M	243614M			Net Sales ($)		387100M	432821M
	3986M	21042M	27213M	84936M			Total Assets ($)		277299M	251022M

M = $ thousand   MM = $ million
See Pages 11 through 18 for Explanation of Ratios and Data

Comparative Historical Data				Current Data Sorted By Sales					
			Type of Statement					1	2
2		4	Unqualified	1			1	1	
23	12	8	Reviewed		2	4	1	1	
20	23	9	Compiled		5	2	2		
12	12	5	Tax Returns		4	1			
13	24	20	Other	3	6	3	3	1	3
4/1/00-3/31/01	4/1/01-3/31/02	4/1/02-3/31/03			14 (4/1-9/30/02)		32 (10/1/02-3/31/03)		
ALL	ALL	ALL		0-1MM	1-3MM	3-5MM	5-10MM	10-25MM	25MM & OVER
70	71	46	**NUMBER OF STATEMENTS**	4	17	10	7	3	5
%	%	%	**ASSETS**	%	%	%	%	%	%
13.8	9.0	12.5	Cash & Equivalents		13.7	14.9			
35.0	35.3	38.8	Trade Receivables (net)		37.6	39.0			
16.4	16.2	12.1	Inventory		15.0	9.0			
3.6	4.8	6.2	All Other Current		2.5	13.5			
68.8	65.2	69.6	Total Current		68.7	76.3			
22.7	26.0	21.5	Fixed Assets (net)		20.7	17.7			
2.2	2.2	2.2	Intangibles (net)		.0	.9			
6.3	6.6	6.7	All Other Non-Current		10.6	5.0			
100.0	100.0	100.0	Total		100.0	100.0			
			LIABILITIES						
8.4	24.2	10.5	Notes Payable-Short Term		7.9	15.7			
5.6	5.1	3.4	Cur. Mat.-L/T/D		4.0	2.1			
16.9	16.0	21.5	Trade Payables		21.0	27.5			
.4	.2	.8	Income Taxes Payable		1.8	.6			
8.2	10.0	16.8	All Other Current		16.5	8.6			
39.5	55.5	53.1	Total Current		51.2	54.4			
14.2	13.8	8.1	Long Term Debt		14.2	4.8			
.4	.6	.3	Deferred Taxes		.0	1.2			
2.3	9.8	4.5	All Other Non-Current		.6	4.5			
43.7	20.3	34.0	Net Worth		34.0	35.2			
100.0	100.0	100.0	Total Liabilities & Net Worth		100.0	100.0			
			INCOME DATA						
100.0	100.0	100.0	Net Sales		100.0	100.0			
			Gross Profit						
95.8	97.1	96.7	Operating Expenses		95.4	97.6			
4.2	2.9	3.3	Operating Profit		4.6	2.4			
.0	.9	.8	All Other Expenses (net)		1.8	−.6			
4.2	2.0	2.5	Profit Before Taxes		2.8	3.0			
			RATIOS						
2.8	2.1	2.2	Current		2.4	2.0			
1.6	1.5	1.3			1.4	1.4			
1.2	1.1	1.0			1.1	1.1			
2.1	1.6	1.7	Quick		1.8	1.7			
1.3	1.1	1.0			1.0	.9			
.7	.6	.7			.7	.7			
23 15.7	26 14.0	26 13.8	Sales/Receivables		25 14.7	26 14.1			
43 8.4	48 7.7	43 8.6			35 10.3	38 9.7			
57 6.4	70 5.2	56 6.5			48 7.6	52 7.0			
			Cost of Sales/Inventory						
			Cost of Sales/Payables						
6.2	8.4	9.3	Sales/Working Capital		7.7	10.0			
11.2	13.4	22.4			25.7	17.7			
31.9	84.7	189.8			184.6	126.2			
(62) 17.4	(68) 8.7	(38) 13.0	EBIT/Interest		(13) 26.3				
4.0	2.8	3.5			2.2				
1.9	−.1	.9			1.0				
(20) 5.2	(14) 4.0	(12) 7.9	Net Profit + Depr., Dep., Amort./Cur. Mat. L/T/D						
2.4	2.2	3.0							
1.7	.7	.8							
.2	.4	.3	Fixed/Worth		.2	.3			
.5	.7	.6			.4	.5			
1.0	1.9	1.5			2.1	1.0			
.7	1.2	.8	Debt/Worth		.7	.7			
1.5	1.7	1.9			1.2	2.0			
3.2	6.8	7.6			6.3	9.1			
(65) 42.0	(61) 36.1	(40) 54.5	% Profit Before Taxes/Tangible Net Worth		(14) 39.4				
18.6	21.8	14.0			11.9				
8.3	−4.6	2.2			1.9				
16.7	15.3	8.7	% Profit Before Taxes/Total Assets		18.2	18.3			
6.0	5.4	5.0			3.4	3.8			
2.2	−4.1	.6			.5	−3.9			
30.6	27.6	34.5	Sales/Net Fixed Assets		34.1	50.7			
17.5	18.0	24.0			24.9	34.5			
8.8	8.5	15.4			18.0	18.9			
3.8	4.1	4.3	Sales/Total Assets		4.9	5.0			
2.9	3.2	3.5			3.9	3.6			
2.1	2.0	2.5			2.6	3.1			
(64) 1.2	(63) 1.2	(43) 1.1	% Depr., Dep., Amort./Sales		(16) .8				
2.4	2.0	1.7			2.1				
3.6	3.1	2.6			3.3				
(49) 2.7	(43) 4.6	(27) 3.2	% Officers', Directors', Owners' Comp/Sales		(12) 4.7				
5.1	6.2	6.2			6.6				
9.4	11.2	10.3			11.4				
476383M	444999M	403808M	Net Sales ($)	2352M	32932M	40547M	39254M	45109M	243614M
258330M	185893M	137177M	Total Assets ($)	1020M	10091M	12153M	13900M	15077M	84936M

© RMA 2003

M = $ thousand   MM = $ million
See Pages 11 through 18 for Explanation of Ratios and Data

Current Data Sorted By Assets **Comparative Historical Data**

0-500M	500M-2MM	2-10MM	10-50MM	50-100MM	100-250MM	Type of Statement	4/1/98-3/31/99 ALL	4/1/99-3/31/00 ALL
	1		1			Unqualified	6	10
1	2	2				Reviewed	8	7
9	7					Compiled	26	30
36	12	5	1		1	Tax Returns	33	17
17	12	5	1		1	Other	41	36
	13 (4/1-9/30/02)			101 (10/1/02-3/31/03)				
63	34	12	3		2	**NUMBER OF STATEMENTS**	114	100
%	%	%	%	%	%	**ASSETS**	%	%
27.3	14.8	10.6				Cash & Equivalents	17.0	18.9
.8	7.1	3.2				Trade Receivables (net)	3.0	3.5
11.3	11.1	10.9				Inventory	10.8	11.0
.6	.8	2.0				All Other Current	2.4	1.9
39.9	33.8	26.6				Total Current	33.2	35.3
45.3	51.3	61.3				Fixed Assets (net)	46.7	45.7
7.4	6.2	4.7				Intangibles (net)	12.8	12.9
7.4	8.8	7.3				All Other Non-Current	7.3	6.2
100.0	100.0	100.0				Total	100.0	100.0
						LIABILITIES		
9.1	5.5	4.5				Notes Payable-Short Term	20.7	5.8
7.2	6.6	3.8				Cur. Mat.-L/T/D	4.6	6.3
6.4	8.3	9.0				Trade Payables	7.1	6.9
.2	.5	.0				Income Taxes Payable	1.0	.3
29.1	15.7	17.6				All Other Current	17.2	16.1
51.9	36.5	34.8				Total Current	50.6	35.3
25.0	35.8	33.7				Long Term Debt	33.6	28.4
.0	.0	.0				Deferred Taxes	.7	.1
26.9	7.4	8.7				All Other Non-Current	16.9	6.5
-3.9	20.3	22.8				Net Worth	-1.7	29.7
100.0	100.0	100.0				Total Liabilities & Net Worth	100.0	100.0
						INCOME DATA		
100.0	100.0	100.0				Net Sales	100.0	100.0
						Gross Profit		
94.6	96.4	95.8				Operating Expenses	98.7	94.4
5.4	3.6	4.2				Operating Profit	1.3	5.6
1.0	1.6	.5				All Other Expenses (net)	.7	.3
4.4	1.9	3.7				Profit Before Taxes	.6	5.3
						RATIOS		
2.4	1.4	1.3					2.6	2.3
.9	1.0	.6				Current	.9	1.1
.3	.4	.4					.4	.5
1.5	1.2	.7					1.6	1.5
(61) .5	1.2 .5	.3				Quick (113)	.5	.6
.1	.1	.2					.1	.2
0 UND	0 UND	0 UND					0 UND	0 UND
0 UND	0 999.8	0 UND				Sales/Receivables	0 UND	0 UND
0 UND	2 165.5	4 93.7					0 999.8	0 999.8
						Cost of Sales/Inventory		
						Cost of Sales/Payables		
20.0	31.3	26.6					23.6	25.5
-307.0	NM	-32.1				Sales/Working Capital	-241.3	229.8
-13.8	-16.9	-12.4					-16.6	-28.6
(39) 5.7	(30) 5.8	(10) 11.6				EBIT/Interest (87) (82)	10.0 13.8	
2.1	2.3	3.2					4.6	5.7
.0	.2	1.9					1.2	2.0
						Net Profit + Depr., Dep., Amort./Cur. Mat. L/T/D (10)		9.9
								2.9
								1.6
.5	1.3	1.3					1.1	.9
10.2	3.6	5.6				Fixed/Worth	3.4	1.7
-2.0	-26.5	NM					-1.7	-24.3
.9	1.7	1.1					1.1	.9
75.0	3.5	7.0				Debt/Worth	5.2	2.2
-3.8	-31.7	NM					-4.3	-17.8
(33) 77.2	(24) 80.0					% Profit Before Taxes/Tangible Net Worth (71) (72)	174.2 129.8	
19.2	22.0						54.1	62.5
.0	-5.3						10.0	25.4
37.6	16.5	31.4					35.4	35.2
7.3	5.1	9.5				% Profit Before Taxes/Total Assets	17.3	20.9
-1.5	-2.5	2.0					1.8	4.3
51.0	13.9	7.0					21.3	24.2
14.2	7.6	5.8				Sales/Net Fixed Assets	9.1	11.3
6.8	2.8	2.1					5.8	6.5
10.2	4.1	4.2					6.4	6.9
5.3	2.9	3.0				Sales/Total Assets	4.3	4.7
3.2	1.7	1.3					2.5	3.0
.8	1.6	1.7					1.2	1.1
(43) 1.5	(32) 2.3	4.1				% Depr., Dep., Amort./Sales (96) (87)	2.1 1.9	
3.5	6.2	6.9					3.3	3.0
4.6	1.3						3.8	4.9
(37) 7.7	(20) 3.5					% Officers', Directors', Owners' Comp/Sales (61) (46)	6.5 6.8	
14.6	9.2						13.1	12.0
46590M	106865M	140893M	167352M		949492M	Net Sales ($)	876959M	780273M
9343M	35359M	48631M	67853M		317093M	Total Assets ($)	219563M	245701M

(Columns 10-50MM, 50-100MM, and 100-250MM marked "DATA NOT AVAILABLE" for ratio sections.)

M = $ thousand   MM = $ million
See Pages 11 through 18 for Explanation of Ratios and Data

Comparative Historical Data | | | | Current Data Sorted By Sales

			Type of Statement						
8	7	2	Unqualified	1					1
9	7	5	Reviewed	1		2		2	
22	20	16	Compiled	5	7	3	1	1	2
28	39	55	Tax Returns	29	17	5	1	6	2
23	43	36	Other	15	6	3	4		
4/1/00-3/31/01 ALL	4/1/01-3/31/02 ALL	4/1/02-3/31/03 ALL		13 (4/1-9/30/02)			101 (10/1/02-3/31/03)		
				0-1MM	1-3MM	3-5MM	5-10MM	10-25MM	25MM & OVER
90	116	114	NUMBER OF STATEMENTS	51	30	13	6	9	5
%	%	%	ASSETS	%	%	%	%	%	%
19.8	17.5	21.8	Cash & Equivalents	24.9	23.6	12.9			
3.1	3.6	3.1	Trade Receivables (net)	2.2	.9	11.0			
9.2	11.1	10.9	Inventory	9.9	10.8	14.1			
1.3	1.9	1.0	All Other Current	.6	.8	.3			
33.5	34.1	36.7	Total Current	37.6	36.0	38.3			
47.0	48.5	48.7	Fixed Assets (net)	48.1	53.8	42.2			
12.2	9.6	6.9	Intangibles (net)	7.3	4.6	7.7			
7.4	7.9	7.6	All Other Non-Current	7.0	5.6	11.8			
100.0	100.0	100.0	Total	100.0	100.0	100.0			
			LIABILITIES						
5.6	9.2	7.1	Notes Payable-Short Term	9.9	6.1	6.3			
5.6	6.0	6.6	Cur. Mat.-L/T/D	7.2	6.0	9.7			
10.4	7.0	7.1	Trade Payables	2.5	13.8	6.7			
.3	.2	.3	Income Taxes Payable	.0	.5	1.4			
18.9	18.6	23.6	All Other Current	30.2	16.5	15.9			
40.8	41.1	44.7	Total Current	49.7	42.9	39.9			
28.9	25.1	29.4	Long Term Debt	24.3	40.0	31.1			
.1	.0	.0	Deferred Taxes	.0	.0	.0			
10.4	8.0	20.6	All Other Non-Current	23.5	21.2	7.2			
19.8	25.9	5.3	Net Worth	2.4	-4.1	21.8			
100.0	100.0	100.0	Total Liabilities & Net Worth	100.0	100.0	100.0			
			INCOME DATA						
100.0	100.0	100.0	Net Sales	100.0	100.0	100.0			
			Gross Profit						
93.9	94.8	95.3	Operating Expenses	93.8	97.6	95.5			
6.1	5.2	4.7	Operating Profit	6.2	2.4	4.5			
.9	1.0	1.2	All Other Expenses (net)	1.9	.8	-.2			
5.2	4.2	3.6	Profit Before Taxes	4.3	1.6	4.7			
			RATIOS						
1.9	1.4	1.8	Current	2.0	1.8	1.5			
1.1	.9	.9		1.1	.8	.9			
.5	.4	.4		.3	.4	.4			
1.1	1.0	1.3	Quick	1.4	1.4	.8			
(89) .7	(115) .3	(112) .5		(49) .5	.5	.6			
.2	.2	.2		.1	.1	.2			
0 UND	0 UND	0 UND	Sales/Receivables	0 UND	0 UND	0 UND			
0 UND	0 UND	0 UND		0 UND	0 UND	0 999.8			
0 UND	2 230.7	0 999.8		0 UND	0 999.8	18 20.5			
			Cost of Sales/Inventory						
			Cost of Sales/Payables						
24.5	27.2	22.1	Sales/Working Capital	18.6	32.2	14.6			
258.5	-106.9	-290.8		172.8	-184.7	-311.7			
-22.4	-12.2	-13.7		-12.2	-18.2	-12.6			
9.0	9.0	6.4	EBIT/Interest	5.5	3.7	6.0			
(75) 3.8	(94) 3.3	(84) 2.3		(29) 2.1	(26) 1.9	(11) 3.3			
1.8	1.3	.8		.5	-.2	1.3			
5.1	6.7		Net Profit + Depr., Dep., Amort./Cur. Mat. L/T/D						
(15) 3.7	(12) 3.3								
2.0	1.3								
.9	.9	1.0	Fixed/Worth	.5	1.9	.6			
3.0	2.2	5.5		3.4	NM	5.3			
-3.1	-9.8	-2.9		-2.5	-2.5	-2.2			
.9	1.0	1.4	Debt/Worth	.6	2.1	1.2			
4.7	3.4	7.3		3.3	NM	7.1			
-6.4	-13.7	-5.1		-4.2	-4.4	-4.4			
100.0	83.5	78.0	% Profit Before Taxes/Tangible Net Worth	32.9	84.0				
(61) 48.6	(80) 47.1	(68) 21.4		(30) 16.9	(15) 24.5				
16.6	10.2	4.7		.0	-72.7				
39.1	28.6	30.3	% Profit Before Taxes/Total Assets	31.6	35.6	26.0			
13.0	10.4	6.9		6.0	5.1	8.1			
4.0	.3	-.4		-2.4	-2.2	-1.7			
22.4	20.9	22.6	Sales/Net Fixed Assets	51.0	24.5	25.4			
10.5	9.2	9.4		11.0	8.8	9.1			
5.7	4.7	4.4		4.0	3.6	4.5			
6.2	6.0	6.6	Sales/Total Assets	8.5	8.0	4.4			
4.3	3.5	3.9		3.9	4.1	3.6			
2.5	2.4	2.5		2.3	2.6	2.1			
1.1	1.0	1.2	% Depr., Dep., Amort./Sales	.9	.9	1.4			
(78) 2.1	(96) 2.0	(91) 2.0		(36) 1.8	(24) 2.1	(12) 2.3			
3.1	3.1	4.8		5.3	4.9	4.3			
3.0	3.5	3.4	% Officers', Directors', Owners' Comp/Sales	5.5	1.4				
(45) 5.5	(54) 5.3	(61) 5.8		(30) 9.7	(19) 3.6				
13.6	11.4	11.6		15.3	6.1				
762042M	1440241M	1411192M	Net Sales ($)	24969M	50899M	51617M	33387M	133476M	1116844M
227041M	610369M	478279M	Total Assets ($)	10657M	14712M	21616M	9402M	36946M	384946M

© RMA 2003

M = $ thousand   MM = $ million
See Pages 11 through 18 for Explanation of Ratios and Data

Current Data Sorted By Assets   Comparative Historical Data

						Type of Statement		
2	3	5	3		1	Unqualified	13	11
5	7	12				Reviewed	30	30
33	46	24	1			Compiled	107	122
27	29	12			1	Tax Returns	65	60
11	31	13	2	1	1	Other	73	66
	73 (4/1-9/30/02)			197 (10/1/02-3/31/03)			4/1/98-3/31/99	4/1/99-3/31/00
0-500M	500M-2MM	2-10MM	10-50MM	50-100MM	100-250MM		ALL	ALL
78	116	66	6	1	3	NUMBER OF STATEMENTS	288	289
%	%	%	%	%	%	ASSETS	%	%
14.2	9.4	8.8				Cash & Equivalents	11.3	10.8
22.0	14.9	8.9				Trade Receivables (net)	15.4	15.7
6.9	4.4	4.4				Inventory	5.5	6.3
1.2	3.3	2.5				All Other Current	2.6	2.5
44.3	32.0	24.6				Total Current	34.8	35.3
35.4	45.5	49.2				Fixed Assets (net)	44.8	46.2
10.3	8.1	6.7				Intangibles (net)	7.7	6.5
10.0	14.4	19.5				All Other Non-Current	12.7	12.0
100.0	100.0	100.0				Total	100.0	100.0
						LIABILITIES		
13.0	3.7	3.9				Notes Payable-Short Term	4.7	5.3
4.8	3.7	3.8				Cur. Mat.-L/T/D	3.4	3.6
6.6	4.0	3.1				Trade Payables	4.7	4.8
.3	.2	.2				Income Taxes Payable	.2	.3
10.4	7.3	4.4				All Other Current	8.3	8.5
35.2	18.9	15.5				Total Current	21.2	22.4
31.8	38.1	38.5				Long Term Debt	33.2	33.3
.0	.0	.1				Deferred Taxes	.1	.2
12.0	9.0	13.2				All Other Non-Current	10.5	8.6
21.0	34.1	32.7				Net Worth	34.9	35.5
100.0	100.0	100.0				Total Liabilities & Net Worth	100.0	100.0
						INCOME DATA		
100.0	100.0	100.0				Net Sales	100.0	100.0
						Gross Profit		
96.7	94.2	89.9				Operating Expenses	92.1	90.7
3.3	5.8	10.1				Operating Profit	7.9	9.3
.9	1.5	5.2				All Other Expenses (net)	2.0	1.4
2.4	4.3	4.9				Profit Before Taxes	6.0	7.9
						RATIOS		
4.9	3.4	2.8					3.7	3.8
1.6	1.8	1.5				Current	1.8	1.9
.7	1.0	.9					1.0	1.0
4.0	2.8	1.9					2.9	2.8
1.4	1.4	1.2				Quick	1.3 (286)	1.4
.6	.7	.6					.7	.7
15 24.9	24 15.5	23 16.1					20 18.7	21 17.4
34 10.8	37 9.9	34 10.8				Sales/Receivables	36 10.1	38 9.7
46 8.0	52 7.0	47 7.7					51 7.1	50 7.4
						Cost of Sales/Inventory		
						Cost of Sales/Payables		
7.1	5.0	5.5					4.9	4.6
17.5	12.0	13.2				Sales/Working Capital	11.7	10.5
−17.1	−200.2	−48.9					UND	−547.5
10.7	4.5	4.0					6.7	7.8
(62) 2.0	(95) 2.1	(57) 2.6				EBIT/Interest	(238) 3.1	(241) 2.9
.6	1.2	1.0					1.2	1.4
	2.6	6.3				Net Profit + Depr., Dep.,	4.5	4.2
	(23) 1.8	(19) 2.1				Amort./Cur. Mat. L /T/D	(60) 2.8	(63) 2.0
	.8	1.3					1.4	1.2
.5	.6	.8					.6	.6
1.4	1.5	1.8				Fixed/Worth	1.2	1.4
−2.9	19.4	5.3					6.8	5.5
.5	.7	1.3					.6	.5
1.5	1.8	2.8				Debt/Worth	1.8	1.9
−9.8	61.1	10.8					12.2	8.9
45.5	34.4	27.0				% Profit Before Taxes/Tangible	40.2	37.8
(54) 14.4	(90) 9.9	(56) 9.8				Net Worth	(228) 17.6	(236) 18.2
−2.6	3.0	1.4					4.1	5.1
17.7	10.0	6.7				% Profit Before Taxes/Total	14.4	13.9
5.0	4.3	2.3				Assets	5.8	6.6
−3.9	.8	.1					.5	1.3
12.4	5.7	3.4					7.4	7.5
7.0	3.2	1.9				Sales/Net Fixed Assets	3.3	2.9
4.3	2.0	1.0					1.3	1.4
3.6	1.9	1.4					2.1	2.1
2.4	1.3	.8				Sales/Total Assets	1.2	1.3
1.7	.8	.5					.6	.7
1.6	2.7	3.0					2.7	2.7
(68) 3.3	(111) 4.5	(65) 4.6				% Depr., Dep., Amort./Sales	(263) 4.3	(271) 4.6
5.3	7.7	7.5					6.8	7.1
7.8	8.6	7.1					7.4	7.8
(62) 11.6	(74) 11.1	(39) 11.0				% Officers', Directors', Owners' Comp/Sales	(169) 11.3	(162) 12.8
17.7	16.0	17.4					15.5	18.3
53208M	168502M	225574M	75198M	14017M	716087M	Net Sales ($)	1519928M	1217103M
21357M	125475M	264726M	97822M	64555M	366847M	Total Assets ($)	1511516M	1262876M

M = $ thousand   MM = $ million
See Pages 11 through 18 for Explanation of Ratios and Data

Comparative Historical Data				**Current Data Sorted By Sales**					
			Type of Statement						
7	11	14	Unqualified	4	5	1	2	2	
35	22	24	Reviewed	7	8	5	4		
107	99	104	Compiled	41	50	11	1	1	
46	59	69	Tax Returns	39	25	4			1
54	61	59	Other	25	21	5	5	2	1
4/1/00-3/31/01 ALL	4/1/01-3/31/02 ALL	4/1/02-3/31/03 ALL		**73 (4/1-9/30/02)**			**197 (10/1/02-3/31/03)**		
			0-1MM	1-3MM	3-5MM	5-10MM	10-25MM	25MM & OVER
249	252	270	**NUMBER OF STATEMENTS**	116	109	26	12	5	2
%	%	%	**ASSETS**	%	%	%	%	%	%
10.7	9.2	10.9	Cash & Equivalents	11.7	9.8	8.3	9.8		
14.3	15.7	15.3	Trade Receivables (net)	15.6	15.9	13.8	11.0		
4.6	4.8	5.1	Inventory	6.0	4.7	3.0	4.2		
3.1	2.6	2.5	All Other Current	2.0	3.0	2.6	3.6		
32.7	32.3	33.8	Total Current	35.3	33.3	27.8	28.6		
45.6	46.9	42.8	Fixed Assets (net)	41.3	43.4	47.0	56.6		
8.1	8.2	8.2	Intangibles (net)	10.1	6.8	9.4	3.6		
13.6	12.6	15.2	All Other Non-Current	13.4	16.5	15.8	11.2		
100.0	100.0	100.0	Total	100.0	100.0	100.0	100.0		
			LIABILITIES						
5.0	5.7	6.6	Notes Payable-Short Term	8.8	3.8	9.4	1.8		
3.5	4.0	4.0	Cur. Mat.-L/T/D	4.3	3.3	4.9	5.9		
5.0	6.0	4.5	Trade Payables	4.0	5.1	3.6	6.4		
.2	.2	.2	Income Taxes Payable	.1	.3	.3	.9		
7.5	6.8	7.6	All Other Current	9.1	7.0	4.6	6.0		
21.2	22.6	23.0	Total Current	26.3	19.5	22.7	21.0		
33.0	37.6	35.7	Long Term Debt	36.4	37.2	29.8	39.1		
.2	.1	.1	Deferred Taxes	.0	.0	.0	.7		
7.7	7.8	11.1	All Other Non-Current	14.6	9.1	7.8	5.5		
37.9	31.9	30.1	Net Worth	22.7	34.3	39.6	33.8		
100.0	100.0	100.0	Total Liabilities & Net Worth	100.0	100.0	100.0	100.0		
			INCOME DATA						
100.0	100.0	100.0	Net Sales	100.0	100.0	100.0	100.0		
			Gross Profit						
92.8	91.5	93.8	Operating Expenses	93.0	94.5	94.6	94.3		
7.2	8.5	6.2	Operating Profit	7.0	5.5	5.4	5.7		
1.0	3.2	2.7	All Other Expenses (net)	3.5	1.3	3.5	3.6		
6.1	5.4	3.4	Profit Before Taxes	3.5	4.1	1.9	2.1		
			RATIOS						
3.1	3.0	3.2	Current	4.8	3.1	2.7	2.3		
1.6	1.6	1.7		1.7	1.8	1.4	1.4		
.9	.9	.9		.7	1.0	.8	.9		
2.7	2.5	2.7	Quick	3.3	2.7	1.7	1.6		
1.2	1.2	1.3		1.3	1.4	1.1	.9		
.6	.6	.6		.5	.7	.5	.5		
20 18.0	18 20.0	22 16.7	Sales/Receivables	16 23.4	24 15.1	25 14.7	21 17.6		
37 9.8	36 10.2	36 10.2		36 10.2	36 10.2	35 10.4	23 15.8		
54 6.8	49 7.4	50 7.3		54 6.8	44 8.2	51 7.1	45 8.0		
			Cost of Sales/Inventory						
			Cost of Sales/Payables						
4.9	6.2	5.5	Sales/Working Capital	4.6	6.0	8.6	5.7		
12.5	14.8	12.4		12.1	12.6	18.6	21.2		
-50.1	-66.4	-58.1		-15.9	377.3	-15.9	-60.7		
(205) 5.8	(213) 5.3	(221) 4.8	EBIT/Interest	(90) 4.3	(90) 6.1	(23) 2.9	7.5		
2.4	2.2	2.2		2.0	2.6	2.5	1.7		
1.2	1.0	1.0		.9	1.2	1.0	.1		
(67) 4.3	(42) 4.0	(51) 3.0	Net Profit + Depr., Dep., Amort./Cur. Mat. L/T/D	(13) 5.0	(26) 2.9				
2.2	1.9	1.9		1.9	2.0				
1.1	1.2	1.2		1.1	1.4				
.6	.7	.6	Fixed/Worth	.6	.6	.9	1.0		
1.4	1.6	1.6		2.3	1.2	1.9	1.9		
7.0	9.4	17.5		-3.5	2.6	5.3	7.9		
.5	.7	.7	Debt/Worth	.6	.7	.8	.8		
1.7	2.3	2.2		3.9	1.6	2.8	2.5		
11.6	13.3	33.2		-13.3	5.4	8.6	9.0		
(205) 32.6	(195) 43.5	(209) 31.9	% Profit Before Taxes/Tangible Net Worth	(79) 44.7	(90) 29.2	(23) 27.8	(10) 27.5		
13.2	16.6	10.5		10.6	13.9	9.4	11.9		
2.9	2.0	.7		1.9	1.7	-4.7	-9.7		
10.4	13.9	9.6	% Profit Before Taxes/Total Assets	11.1	9.4	7.0	14.6		
5.1	5.3	3.8		3.6	4.0	4.0	2.1		
.8	.0	-.2		-.6	.5	-.2	-3.6		
6.8	7.2	7.6	Sales/Net Fixed Assets	10.2	7.2	5.4	3.2		
2.9	3.6	3.6		4.3	3.5	2.9	1.8		
1.4	1.6	2.0		2.0	2.1	1.2	1.6		
2.0	2.3	2.2	Sales/Total Assets	2.3	2.5	1.7	2.0		
1.2	1.5	1.4		1.3	1.4	1.4	1.0		
.7	.8	.8		.7	.9	.8	.8		
(227) 2.7	(234) 2.2	(251) 2.4	% Depr., Dep., Amort./Sales	(102) 2.6	(107) 2.3	(25) 2.4	3.0		
4.5	3.6	4.3		5.1	4.0	3.8	3.7		
6.9	6.1	7.0		8.8	6.4	5.9	4.6		
(155) 6.8	(154) 7.5	(179) 7.8	% Officers', Directors', Owners' Comp/Sales	(78) 7.8	(74) 8.1	(18) 5.2			
11.2	10.9	11.1		10.8	11.5	11.1			
16.9	16.6	16.4		16.1	17.1	16.2			
1105969M	486911M	1252586M	Net Sales ($)	69338M	190918M	102476M	86188M	70747M	732919M
1132167M	621343M	940782M	Total Assets ($)	78352M	193224M	111469M	76094M	299690M	181953M

© RMA 2003   M = $ thousand   MM = $ million
See Pages 11 through 18 for Explanation of Ratios and Data

Current Data Sorted By Assets / Comparative Historical Data

0-500M	500M-2MM	2-10MM	10-50MM	50-100MM	100-250MM	Type of Statement	4/1/98-3/31/99 ALL	4/1/99-3/31/00 ALL
						Unqualified		
	2	3	1	1	1	Reviewed		
1	7	5	2			Compiled		
1	1	1				Tax Returns		
1	7	3	1		1	Other		
	6 (4/1-9/30/02)		33 (10/1/02-3/31/03)					
3	17	11	5	1	2	**NUMBER OF STATEMENTS**		
%	%	%	%	%	%	**ASSETS**	%	%
	8.0	10.0				Cash & Equivalents	D	D
	16.2	11.7				Trade Receivables (net)	A	A
	11.5	3.8				Inventory	T	T
	1.0	.5				All Other Current	A	A
	36.7	26.0				Total Current		
	42.5	49.8				Fixed Assets (net)	N	N
	8.7	4.4				Intangibles (net)	O	O
	12.1	19.8				All Other Non-Current	T	T
	100.0	100.0				Total		
						LIABILITIES	A	A
	5.5	3.0				Notes Payable-Short Term	V	V
	3.0	3.1				Cur. Mat.-L/T/D	A	A
	4.1	4.3				Trade Payables	I	I
	.0	.1				Income Taxes Payable	L	L
	8.2	6.0				All Other Current	A	A
	20.9	16.5				Total Current	B	B
	47.5	37.6				Long Term Debt	L	L
	.0	.9				Deferred Taxes	E	E
	11.6	7.9				All Other Non-Current		
	20.0	37.2				Net Worth		
	100.0	100.0				Total Liabilities & Net Worth		
						INCOME DATA		
	100.0	100.0				Net Sales		
						Gross Profit		
	90.0	79.1				Operating Expenses		
	10.0	20.9				Operating Profit		
	2.5	7.5				All Other Expenses (net)		
	7.5	13.4				Profit Before Taxes		
						RATIOS		
	3.7	3.9				Current		
	1.8	1.1						
	.8	.6						
	2.5	3.2				Quick		
	1.3	1.0						
	.5	.4						
	12 29.3	20 18.2				Sales/Receivables		
	29 12.8	31 11.8						
	69 5.3	53 6.8						
						Cost of Sales/Inventory		
						Cost of Sales/Payables		
	2.4	2.8				Sales/Working Capital		
	8.9	45.4						
	-13.1	-9.2						
	6.7					EBIT/Interest		
	(15) 1.6							
	1.1							
						Net Profit + Depr., Dep., Amort./Cur. Mat. L./T/D		
	.6	.5				Fixed/Worth		
	2.3	1.2						
	-1.3	2.8						
	.8	.6				Debt/Worth		
	7.0	2.4						
	-13.0	10.2						
	16.0	36.2				% Profit Before Taxes/Tangible Net Worth		
	(11) 6.7	(10) 21.9						
	-.5	9.9						
	7.3	10.4				% Profit Before Taxes/Total Assets		
	2.9	7.5						
	.0	4.0						
	10.1	4.1				Sales/Net Fixed Assets		
	3.3	1.9						
	.7	.6						
	1.3	1.3				Sales/Total Assets		
	.7	.9						
	.4	.3						
	2.6	1.4				% Depr., Dep., Amort./Sales		
	(12) 3.3	(10) 4.1						
	4.9	9.3						
						% Officers', Directors', Owners' Comp/Sales		
2966M	23819M	37392M	51745M	15577M	106639M	Net Sales ($)		
992M	21551M	40170M	117015M	57640M	270510M	Total Assets ($)		

© RMA 2003

M = $ thousand   MM = $ million
See Pages 11 through 18 for Explanation of Ratios and Data

Comparative Historical Data   ## Current Data Sorted By Sales

4/1/00-3/31/01 ALL	4/1/01-3/31/02 ALL	4/1/02-3/31/03 ALL	Type of Statement	6 (4/1-9/30/02)			33 (10/1/02-3/31/03)		
				0-1MM	1-3MM	3-5MM	5-10MM	10-25MM	25MM & OVER
		3	Unqualified		1			2	
		6	Reviewed	2	1	1	1	1	
		15	Compiled	9	2	2	1	1	
		2	Tax Returns	1	1				
		13	Other	5	2	2	2	1	1
		39	**NUMBER OF STATEMENTS**	17	7	5	4	5	1
%	%	%	**ASSETS**	%	%	%	%	%	%
D	D	10.4	Cash & Equivalents	9.0					
A	A	14.3	Trade Receivables (net)	12.9					
T	T	10.2	Inventory	11.3					
A	A	1.5	All Other Current	.7					
		36.5	Total Current	33.9					
N	N	42.2	Fixed Assets (net)	44.0					
O	O	6.3	Intangibles (net)	4.8					
T	T	15.0	All Other Non-Current	17.3					
		100.0	Total	100.0					
A	A		**LIABILITIES**						
V	V	5.4	Notes Payable-Short Term	3.6					
A	A	3.2	Cur. Mat.-L/T/D	2.3					
I	I	3.8	Trade Payables	3.0					
L	L	.3	Income Taxes Payable	.3					
A	A	7.7	All Other Current	7.8					
B	B	20.4	Total Current	16.9					
L	L	35.6	Long Term Debt	36.4					
E	E	.3	Deferred Taxes	.0					
		9.6	All Other Non-Current	9.7					
		34.0	Net Worth	36.9					
		100.0	Total Liabilities & Net Worth	100.0					
			INCOME DATA						
		100.0	Net Sales	100.0					
			Gross Profit						
		87.4	Operating Expenses	82.1					
		12.6	Operating Profit	17.9					
		3.5	All Other Expenses (net)	7.0					
		9.1	Profit Before Taxes	11.0					
			RATIOS						
		3.6		4.5					
		1.8	Current	1.8					
		.8		.8					
		2.4		3.3					
		1.2	Quick	1.6					
		.4		.5					
	19	19.1		0 UND					
	35	10.4	Sales/Receivables	35 10.4					
	79	4.6		65 5.7					
			Cost of Sales/Inventory						
			Cost of Sales/Payables						
		2.3		2.1					
		8.1	Sales/Working Capital	8.6					
		−20.2		−10.8					
		8.0		5.6					
	(33)	2.6	EBIT/Interest	(13) 2.0					
		1.4		1.3					
			Net Profit + Depr., Dep., Amort./Cur. Mat. L/T/D						
		.4		.2					
		1.5	Fixed/Worth	1.5					
		24.2		5.1					
		.6		.8					
		2.0	Debt/Worth	1.7					
		45.5		27.8					
		27.9	% Profit Before Taxes/Tangible	33.9					
	(31)	12.2	Net Worth	(14) 9.8					
		2.3		.2					
		8.4	% Profit Before Taxes/Total	7.3					
		4.0	Assets	4.1					
		.9		.0					
		6.6		11.8					
		2.1	Sales/Net Fixed Assets	1.9					
		1.0		.5					
		1.2		.7					
		.7	Sales/Total Assets	.5					
		.4		.4					
		2.6		1.8					
	(32)	3.7	% Depr., Dep., Amort./Sales	(13) 3.0					
		5.5		6.9					
		3.8	% Officers', Directors',						
	(16)	9.2	Owners' Comp/Sales						
		16.5							
		238138M	Net Sales ($)	11262M	14268M	18561M	31113M	67074M	95860M
		507878M	Total Assets ($)	24277M	30725M	21711M	17279M	269531M	144355M

M = $ thousand   MM = $ million
                                  See Pages 11 through 18 for Explanation of Ratios and Data

		Current Data Sorted By Assets						Comparative Historical Data	

0-500M	500M-2MM	2-10MM	10-50MM	50-100MM	100-250MM	Type of Statement		4/1/98-3/31/99 ALL	4/1/99-3/31/00 ALL
1	2	5	3		1	Unqualified		4	4
13	3	1				Reviewed		5	4
10	7				1	Compiled		15	7
3	3	7		1		Tax Returns		14	8
						Other		2	10
	5 (4/1-9/30/02)		56 (10/1/02-3/31/03)						
27	15	13	3	1	2	**NUMBER OF STATEMENTS**		40	33
%	%	%	%	%	%	**ASSETS**		%	%
18.8	3.9	11.0				Cash & Equivalents		7.5	8.5
.5	1.5	4.4				Trade Receivables (net)		6.7	2.8
1.1	.3	2.6				Inventory		1.9	6.2
3.6	7.1	.7				All Other Current		2.8	1.0
24.1	12.8	18.7				Total Current		19.0	18.5
63.7	76.9	64.2				Fixed Assets (net)		63.7	65.9
5.7	6.6	10.2				Intangibles (net)		8.4	11.1
6.4	3.7	6.9				All Other Non-Current		8.9	4.4
100.0	100.0	100.0				Total		100.0	100.0
						LIABILITIES			
8.1	11.7	1.8				Notes Payable-Short Term		4.0	7.4
16.3	7.3	12.4				Cur. Mat.-L/T/D		6.7	7.8
2.4	2.3	3.9				Trade Payables		5.1	6.6
.0	.0	.4				Income Taxes Payable		2.4	.3
8.8	9.1	6.9				All Other Current		23.4	6.0
35.6	30.3	25.5				Total Current		41.6	28.1
54.6	43.6	25.5				Long Term Debt		63.7	39.4
.0	.0	.4				Deferred Taxes		.1	.3
15.3	3.4	4.1				All Other Non-Current		5.0	8.5
-5.5	22.7	44.6				Net Worth		-10.5	23.7
100.0	100.0	100.0				Total Liabilities & Net Worth		100.0	100.0
						INCOME DATA			
100.0	100.0	100.0				Net Sales		100.0	100.0
						Gross Profit			
90.9	95.7	95.1				Operating Expenses		105.2	91.7
9.1	4.3	4.9				Operating Profit		-5.2	8.3
3.2	7.1	1.4				All Other Expenses (net)		3.6	2.7
5.9	-2.8	3.5				Profit Before Taxes		-8.8	5.5
						RATIOS			
1.5	1.0	1.5						1.7	1.0
.7	.4	.4				Current		.8	.7
.4	.1	.3						.1	.3
1.3	.7	1.0						1.3	.7
.7	.3	.3				Quick		.4	.4
.2	.1	.1						.1	.1
0 UND	0 UND	0 UND						0 UND	0 UND
0 UND	0 UND	1 432.0				Sales/Receivables		0 811.4	1 410.0
0 UND	7 54.2	6 61.7						8 46.9	7 51.0
						Cost of Sales/Inventory			
						Cost of Sales/Payables			
52.6	-97.5	18.2						24.0	585.5
-87.0	-15.3	-19.4				Sales/Working Capital		-34.2	-23.6
-11.9	-4.0	-6.1						-3.1	-8.0
(24) 7.9	(12) 1.6	3.8						(28) 6.5	(27) 3.1
3.3	.6	1.8				EBIT/Interest		3.7	1.9
1.6	-1.9	1.0						1.1	1.3
						Net Profit + Depr., Dep., Amort./Cur. Mat. L/T/D			
.9	1.7	1.2						1.1	1.8
17.7	4.4	2.3				Fixed/Worth		5.1	5.5
-1.3	-7.9	NM						-19.9	UND
.8	1.5	.6						.9	1.7
21.2	3.9	2.2				Debt/Worth		10.5	6.9
-2.5	-9.3	NM						-7.9	UND
(15) 114.9		35.7				% Profit Before Taxes/Tangible Net Worth		(25) 30.9	(25) 83.9
40.8	(10) 9.6							12.6	21.1
8.7	.3							2.3	4.1
29.3	3.9	13.3				% Profit Before Taxes/Total Assets		12.0	12.8
14.9	.0	2.5						4.4	5.4
8.0	-6.5	.1						-4.3	1.3
13.0	2.9	3.2				Sales/Net Fixed Assets		6.5	4.7
5.3	1.5	1.9						2.3	2.0
1.9	.6	1.4						.7	1.3
7.1	1.9	1.7				Sales/Total Assets		2.9	2.3
3.6	1.2	1.4						1.4	1.3
1.7	.5	1.1						.6	.8
(22) 3.8	4.9	6.9				% Depr., Dep., Amort./Sales		(34) 4.5	(25) 6.3
7.3	13.9	(12) 10.8						9.1	12.2
13.0	17.5	16.0						16.0	15.9
(15) 4.7						% Officers', Directors', Owners' Comp/Sales		(14) 6.0	(12) 2.6
9.2								9.4	6.3
12.4								16.5	16.3
11700M	18022M	86549M	179953M	55278M	295995M	Net Sales ($)		336065M	420743M
3901M	15353M	56758M	100898M	57700M	269557M	Total Assets ($)		430956M	436014M

M = $ thousand   MM = $ million
See Pages 11 through 18 for Explanation of Ratios and Data

Comparative Historical Data				Current Data Sorted By Sales					
			Type of Statement						
2	1	4	Unqualified						4
6	6	8	Reviewed	1	3	1	3		
8	9	17	Compiled	12	4	1			
7	10	18	Tax Returns	14	3		1	2	1
15	13	14	Other	6	2	2	1		1
4/1/00-	4/1/01-	4/1/02-			5 (4/1-9/30/02)			56 (10/1/02-3/31/03)	
3/31/01	3/31/02	3/31/03		0-1MM	1-3MM	3-5MM	5-10MM	10-25MM	25MM & OVER
ALL	ALL	ALL							
38	39	61	**NUMBER OF STATEMENTS**	33	12	4	4	2	6
%	%	%	**ASSETS**	%	%	%	%	%	%
5.9	8.6	12.3	Cash & Equivalents	14.7	7.5				
4.3	4.9	1.7	Trade Receivables (net)	.4	1.9				
5.0	3.8	1.3	Inventory	1.0	1.1				
1.5	1.4	5.1	All Other Current	5.9	1.0				
16.7	18.8	20.4	Total Current	22.1	11.6				
62.8	64.7	65.0	Fixed Assets (net)	66.6	73.6				
15.2	11.5	8.6	Intangibles (net)	6.0	10.2				
5.3	5.1	5.9	All Other Non-Current	5.3	4.6				
100.0	100.0	100.0	Total	100.0	100.0				
			LIABILITIES						
6.7	4.9	6.9	Notes Payable-Short Term	10.3	4.8				
6.8	8.5	12.1	Cur. Mat.-L/T/D	13.0	11.0				
4.5	6.4	2.8	Trade Payables	2.0	3.4				
.1	.5	.1	Income Taxes Payable	.0	.1				
4.0	3.8	8.3	All Other Current	10.5	2.3				
22.2	24.1	30.2	Total Current	35.9	21.6				
50.3	53.4	45.0	Long Term Debt	52.6	42.3				
.6	.2	.3	Deferred Taxes	.0	.0				
6.5	7.2	8.9	All Other Non-Current	12.8	3.5				
20.4	15.0	15.7	Net Worth	−1.3	32.7				
100.0	100.0	100.0	Total Liabilities & Net Worth	100.0	100.0				
			INCOME DATA						
100.0	100.0	100.0	Net Sales	100.0	100.0				
			Gross Profit						
93.3	92.8	93.0	Operating Expenses	92.3	93.7				
6.7	7.2	7.0	Operating Profit	7.7	6.3				
4.8	5.0	3.8	All Other Expenses (net)	5.5	1.4				
1.9	2.2	3.2	Profit Before Taxes	2.2	4.9				
			RATIOS						
1.6	1.7	1.3		1.3	1.2				
.7	.5	.6	Current	.7	.4				
.4	.2	.3		.3	.2				
.8	1.3	1.1		1.2	.9				
.5	.3	.4	Quick	.4	.4				
.1	.2	.1		.1	.1				
0 UND	0 UND	0 UND		0 UND	0 UND				
0 999.8	0 UND	0 UND	Sales/Receivables	0 UND	1 616.3				
8 47.6	6 58.1	2 160.0		0 UND	5 71.3				
			Cost of Sales/Inventory						
			Cost of Sales/Payables						
20.6	37.3	61.8		61.8	115.6				
−44.6	−14.2	−25.9	Sales/Working Capital	−39.9	−28.8				
−10.1	−7.2	−9.9		−10.3	−9.0				
2.2	2.3	3.9		3.9	6.7				
(35) 1.5	(34) 1.6	(55) 1.8	EBIT/Interest	(27) 2.3	1.7				
.3	1.0	.5		.2	−1.7				
			Net Profit + Depr., Dep., Amort./Cur. Mat. L/T/D						
2.1	2.1	1.2		1.0	1.6				
8.0	6.4	4.2	Fixed/Worth	10.3	2.3				
−9.8	−6.9	−7.2		−1.6	−27.1				
2.1	2.4	.9		.9	1.0				
9.8	8.5	5.5	Debt/Worth	21.2	2.0				
−12.1	−8.4	−9.0		−3.0	−29.7				
47.8	54.2	60.4	% Profit Before Taxes/Tangible	93.7					
(25) 22.0	(24) 16.6	(38) 18.6	Net Worth	(19) 21.3					
−8.0	3.3	.0		.0					
7.4	10.0	18.4	% Profit Before Taxes/Total	19.5	21.1				
2.3	3.1	4.9	Assets	12.1	3.2				
−2.9	−3.1	−.9		−2.9	−5.0				
4.8	3.4	7.1		12.6	3.4				
2.0	2.4	2.8	Sales/Net Fixed Assets	3.8	2.5				
.9	1.1	1.4		1.0	1.4				
1.8	2.1	3.4		5.4	2.5				
1.4	1.6	1.7	Sales/Total Assets	2.8	1.8				
.8	.9	1.1		.7	1.2				
5.4	5.1	4.7		2.6	4.6				
(31) 12.8	(35) 10.4	(52) 9.1	% Depr., Dep., Amort./Sales	(28) 7.8	(11) 8.9				
15.2	15.9	16.4		17.3	13.9				
1.9	4.2	4.6	% Officers', Directors',	8.5					
(12) 6.5	(20) 7.1	(29) 9.2	Owners' Comp/Sales	(17) 9.6					
10.9	10.3	12.6		14.5					
527425M	245272M	647497M	Net Sales ($)	14001M	22499M	18030M	27965M	33776M	531226M
540824M	233951M	504167M	Total Assets ($)	11377M	15633M	11794M	21408M	15800M	428155M

M = $ thousand   MM = $ million
See Pages 11 through 18 for Explanation of Ratios and Data

Current Data Sorted By Assets   **Comparative Historical Data**

Type of Statement	0-500M	500M-2MM	2-10MM	10-50MM	50-100MM	100-250MM		4/1/98-3/31/99 ALL	4/1/99-3/31/00 ALL
Unqualified	2		5	3				9	8
Reviewed	1	11	13	1				13	14
Compiled	20	23	8	2		1		52	44
Tax Returns	28	9	2		1			28	20
Other	7	16	14	5	1	2		33	38
		33 (4/1-9/30/02)		141 (10/1/02-3/31/03)					
NUMBER OF STATEMENTS	58	59	42	10	2	3		135	124
ASSETS	%	%	%	%	%	%		%	%
Cash & Equivalents	10.1	9.9	11.9	3.1				9.5	9.9
Trade Receivables (net)	7.7	13.5	7.9	4.5				9.0	9.0
Inventory	3.9	5.2	4.9	1.8				4.3	4.6
All Other Current	2.4	2.6	3.6	3.6				1.7	1.1
Total Current	24.1	31.3	28.3	12.9				24.5	24.7
Fixed Assets (net)	55.9	54.1	55.5	68.9				59.3	58.7
Intangibles (net)	7.7	6.0	7.1	7.4				6.3	7.7
All Other Non-Current	12.3	8.6	9.0	10.7				9.9	8.9
Total	100.0	100.0	100.0	100.0				100.0	100.0
LIABILITIES									
Notes Payable-Short Term	11.6	8.6	3.0	2.1				7.2	5.7
Cur. Mat.-L/T/D	8.5	6.6	4.9	9.3				8.0	8.5
Trade Payables	5.6	7.4	5.8	2.8				5.0	7.6
Income Taxes Payable	1.9	.7	.5	.6				.4	.4
All Other Current	11.9	10.7	6.5	4.1				8.8	9.1
Total Current	39.4	33.9	20.6	19.0				29.5	31.4
Long Term Debt	70.5	37.0	49.0	44.7				47.6	57.0
Deferred Taxes	.2	.2	.5	.0				.3	.3
All Other Non-Current	10.3	4.3	2.9	2.3				6.2	7.8
Net Worth	-20.4	24.7	26.9	34.0				16.3	3.6
Total Liabilities & Net Worth	100.0	100.0	100.0	100.0				100.0	100.0
INCOME DATA									
Net Sales	100.0	100.0	100.0	100.0				100.0	100.0
Gross Profit									
Operating Expenses	94.4	90.9	91.2	95.6				92.0	94.6
Operating Profit	5.6	9.1	8.8	4.4				8.0	5.4
All Other Expenses (net)	1.5	3.9	4.3	7.3				2.8	2.7
Profit Before Taxes	4.1	5.2	4.5	-3.0				5.2	2.7
RATIOS									
Current	1.7	1.9	3.0	2.3				2.0	1.7
	.8	.8	1.4	.8				.9	.7
	.3	.3	.9	.3				.3	.3
Quick	(57) 1.2	1.4	1.4	.9			(134)	1.6	1.3
	.6	.7	.8	.4				.6	.5
	.1	.2	.4	.2				.2	.2
Sales/Receivables	0 UND	0 UND	3 132.0	4 91.0			0	UND	0 UND
	3 139.7	11 33.3	10 35.1	13 27.1			5	79.5	8 46.8
	12 30.2	28 13.3	31 11.8	35 10.4			18	20.2	22 16.3
Cost of Sales/Inventory									
Cost of Sales/Payables									
Sales/Working Capital	32.3	13.5	7.3	11.4				16.5	15.9
	-63.0	-53.2	29.6	-23.0				-83.5	-45.6
	-11.0	-11.1	-54.0	-5.8				-14.6	-14.2
EBIT/Interest	(54) 4.0	(56) 8.0	(36) 3.8				(121)	3.8	(114) 4.9
	1.9	3.1	2.1					1.9	1.9
	.6	1.2	1.2					.8	.6
Net Profit + Depr., Dep., Amort./Cur. Mat. L /T/D		(12) 5.9	(10) 2.4				(22)	2.5	(21) 3.9
		2.4	1.8					1.9	1.9
		1.2	1.5					1.2	1.0
Fixed/Worth	1.1	.8	1.0	1.5				1.2	1.1
	UND	1.7	2.1	2.3				2.5	2.9
	-1.2	-39.1	NM	NM				-10.6	-6.5
Debt/Worth	2.0	1.0	1.0	1.1				1.1	1.1
	-22.3	3.2	2.1	1.8				4.0	3.9
	-2.7	-22.1	NM	NM				-14.2	-8.4
% Profit Before Taxes/Tangible Net Worth	(28) 71.9	(43) 39.9	(32) 36.2				(94)	44.8	(82) 59.9
	23.3	23.9	16.6					18.9	23.7
	-2.7	2.9	3.9					-.2	4.0
% Profit Before Taxes/Total Assets	18.0	18.7	10.4	6.7				14.7	16.3
	7.3	7.0	5.3	1.4				7.0	5.0
	-3.7	.2	1.6	-6.1				-.8	-3.5
Sales/Net Fixed Assets	12.7	12.6	5.4	2.7				8.6	7.4
	6.4	4.7	3.5	1.1				4.5	4.5
	4.4	1.3	1.5	.4				2.4	2.5
Sales/Total Assets	5.3	3.9	2.3	1.2				3.7	3.7
	3.5	2.2	1.8	.7				2.6	2.4
	2.3	1.0	1.0	.3				1.5	1.5
% Depr., Dep., Amort./Sales	(51) 3.0	(53) 2.9	(38) 4.2	5.8			(125)	3.4	(117) 3.3
	4.6	4.3	5.4	8.6				5.0	4.6
	8.1	10.1	8.3	14.1				7.6	8.4
% Officers', Directors', Owners' Comp/Sales	(38) 5.2	(24) 3.1	(18) 1.9				(68)	5.1	(61) 5.1
	9.1	4.6	4.6					6.7	7.6
	12.3	6.4	5.4					10.5	11.0
Net Sales ($)	47851M	162274M	291692M	140043M	257255M	779832M		912123M	708524M
Total Assets ($)	13058M	67267M	169809M	185384M	155365M	391613M		324261M	463830M

M = $ thousand   MM = $ million
See Pages 11 through 18 for Explanation of Ratios and Data

Comparative Historical Data   **Current Data Sorted By Sales**

4	3	10	Type of Statement	2	1	4	9	2	1
16	19	26	Unqualified	1	6	7	8	3	
42	33	53	Reviewed	20	16	6	2	2	1
27	22	40	Compiled	22	12	3	6		1
24	34	45	Tax Returns	7	17	5	6	6	4
4/1/00-	4/1/01-	4/1/02-	Other						
3/31/01	3/31/02	3/31/03		33 (4/1-9/30/02)		141 (10/1/02-3/31/03)			
ALL	ALL	ALL		0-1MM	1-3MM	3-5MM	5-10MM	10-25MM	25MM & OVER
113	111	174	**NUMBER OF STATEMENTS**	52	52	25	25	13	7
%	%	%	**ASSETS**	%	%	%	%	%	%
12.4	12.7	9.9	Cash & Equivalents	10.9	6.4	12.9	13.1	11.2	
11.1	11.3	9.6	Trade Receivables (net)	5.5	7.5	16.3	17.6	5.9	
4.0	4.4	4.6	Inventory	3.6	4.0	5.6	6.4	4.3	
1.4	1.7	2.8	All Other Current	2.8	3.1	1.6	4.2	1.5	
29.0	30.0	26.8	Total Current	22.9	21.1	36.4	41.2	22.8	
54.5	50.9	56.3	Fixed Assets (net)	61.8	57.8	51.6	45.1	51.6	
7.4	9.6	6.9	Intangibles (net)	4.5	12.5	.9	4.9	10.4	
9.2	9.5	10.0	All Other Non-Current	10.8	8.7	11.1	8.7	15.2	
100.0	100.0	100.0	Total	100.0	100.0	100.0	100.0	100.0	
			LIABILITIES						
6.9	5.0	8.1	Notes Payable-Short Term	8.4	8.7	11.5	4.3	2.7	
6.8	8.5	7.5	Cur. Mat.-L/T/D	5.4	7.9	5.9	8.3	9.0	
10.8	16.0	6.0	Trade Payables	3.6	5.3	7.7	11.7	5.4	
.3	.1	1.0	Income Taxes Payable	.2	2.4	1.4	.1	.5	
10.8	7.5	9.6	All Other Current	10.0	8.3	7.3	14.7	9.1	
35.5	37.2	32.2	Total Current	27.6	32.6	33.8	39.1	26.6	
44.4	61.4	51.3	Long Term Debt	68.8	63.1	26.8	33.8	22.8	
.3	.4	.2	Deferred Taxes	.2	.0	.6	.0	.6	
8.8	5.5	6.1	All Other Non-Current	7.8	6.6	6.1	3.6	.1	
11.0	−4.5	10.2	Net Worth	−4.3	−2.4	32.7	23.1	49.9	
100.0	100.0	100.0	Total Liabilities & Net Worth	100.0	100.0	100.0	100.0	100.0	
			INCOME DATA						
100.0	100.0	100.0	Net Sales	100.0	100.0	100.0	100.0	100.0	
			Gross Profit						
95.9	94.0	92.5	Operating Expenses	89.7	92.3	94.3	94.8	95.4	
4.1	6.0	7.5	Operating Profit	10.3	7.7	5.7	5.2	4.6	
2.2	2.8	3.4	All Other Expenses (net)	4.3	4.6	2.1	1.0	2.0	
1.9	3.2	4.2	Profit Before Taxes	6.0	3.2	3.7	4.2	2.6	
			RATIOS						
1.7	2.0	2.0		1.9	3.1	2.5	1.7	1.8	
.8	1.2	1.0	Current	.9	.7	1.0	1.2	.9	
.4	.5	.4		.3	.3	.7	.7	.7	
1.2	1.8	.6		1.4	1.2	2.0	1.4	1.2	
.5	.9 (173)	.6	Quick	.6 (51)	.4	.8	.8	.6	
.3	.3	.3		.2	.2	.3	.5	.4	
0 UND	0 999.8	0 UND		0 UND	0 UND	4 89.4	5 79.9	1 264.5	
11 34.3	12 31.6	8 47.6	Sales/Receivables	0 UND	7 53.2	26 14.2	17 21.4	8 45.1	
23 16.0	28 12.9	27 13.5		11 33.8	17 21.1	35 10.3	33 10.9	29 12.6	
			Cost of Sales/Inventory						
			Cost of Sales/Payables						
20.7	13.6	14.3		23.8	10.4	8.8	9.6	28.8	
−62.2	100.6	−612.0	Sales/Working Capital	−103.4	−43.7	234.6	66.0	−54.7	
−11.4	−16.8	−14.4		−10.4	−11.3	−25.9	−48.2	−16.6	
3.8	4.3	5.0		4.5	4.8	7.2	10.0	4.0	
1.6 (102)	2.1 (96)	2.1 (157)	EBIT/Interest	2.2 (47)	1.7 (48)	1.7 (24)	3.9 (21)	3.0 (12)	
.4	.8	1.0		.9	1.1	1.0	1.8	.8	
3.3	4.1	3.3	Net Profit + Depr., Dep.,						
1.3 (19)	1.8 (15)	1.8 (31)	Amort./Cur. Mat. L/T/D						
.6	.8	1.4							
1.1	.9	1.1		1.0	1.9	.6	.6	.5	
2.9	2.4	2.9	Fixed/Worth	3.5	76.0	1.5	1.4	1.4	
−3.0	−4.5	−5.1		−3.2	−1.5	NM	2.6	2.5	
1.0	1.0	1.1		1.4	4.1	.7	1.0	.5	
4.1	2.5	3.6	Debt/Worth	4.1	NM	1.3	1.8	1.0	
−5.9	−7.7	−6.6		−4.4	−2.9	NM	4.6	2.7	
42.9	43.4	39.6	% Profit Before Taxes/Tangible	37.7	57.5	45.0	40.9	28.7	
15.8 (73)	22.1 (74)	18.9 (113)	Net Worth	23.2 (31)	19.0 (26)	13.3 (19)	20.9 (21)	15.8 (12)	
1.4	7.0	2.0		−4.3	2.5	−.3	11.3	−1.4	
12.8	14.5	14.2	% Profit Before Taxes/Total	16.2	13.5	8.9	19.1	9.7	
2.9	5.2	5.6	Assets	7.0	4.1	2.6	9.7	6.2	
−2.0	−.6	.1		−1.8	.3	.1	3.8	.2	
10.0	11.1	.9.3		9.6	6.7	12.5	15.1	8.0	
5.2	5.3	4.5	Sales/Net Fixed Assets	4.5	4.6	4.6	5.5	4.5	
2.9	2.4	1.7		1.3	1.3	1.8	3.5	2.7	
4.1	3.7	3.6		4.3	3.4	4.4	4.1	2.8	
2.4	2.3	2.2	Sales/Total Assets	2.5	1.8	2.4	2.3	2.2	
1.6	1.6	1.1		.9	1.0	1.0	1.8	1.3	
3.0	2.8	3.4		3.9	3.5	2.4	3.4	3.1	
4.2 (110)	4.6 (97)	4.8 (154)	% Depr., Dep., Amort./Sales	7.1 (46)	4.6 (46)	4.7 (21)	4.4 (12)	4.1	
6.5	6.3	9.0		13.8	8.7	10.0	6.0	6.6	
3.5	3.3	3.4	% Officers', Directors',	6.1	3.4	2.1	1.7		
5.7 (58)	5.7 (58)	5.7 (82)	Owners' Comp/Sales	10.4 (28)	5.0 (25)	3.2 (12)	4.4 (15)		
8.3	8.8	10.1		12.6	7.8	4.8	8.1		
740483M	540157M	1678947M	Net Sales ($)	25508M	95466M	103219M	172181M	192786M	1089787M
514157M	275189M	982496M	Total Assets ($)	17191M	77532M	81791M	71923M	145127M	588932M

M = $ thousand   MM = $ million
See Pages 11 through 18 for Explanation of Ratios and Data

Current Data Sorted By Assets   Comparative Historical Data

	0-500M	500M-2MM	2-10MM	10-50MM	50-100MM	100-250MM	Type of Statement	4/1/98-3/31/99 ALL	4/1/99-3/31/00 ALL
		1	7	7	1	1	Unqualified	20	17
		3	14	3			Reviewed	16	16
	2	7	3	3			Compiled	7	6
	1	4					Tax Returns	4	5
	2	4	7	5		1	Other	19	19
		24 (4/1-9/30/02)		52 (10/1/02-3/31/03)					
NUMBER OF STATEMENTS	5	19	31	18	1	2		66	63

ASSETS

0-500M	500M-2MM	2-10MM	10-50MM	50-100MM	100-250MM		99 ALL	00 ALL
%	%	%	%	%	%		%	%
	11.2	8.0	6.5			Cash & Equivalents	7.0	7.3
	21.2	20.6	18.3			Trade Receivables (net)	17.8	21.7
	14.1	9.0	14.3			Inventory	14.4	13.0
	3.5	1.9	2.9			All Other Current	2.1	2.9
	49.9	39.6	42.1			Total Current	41.3	45.0
	45.1	44.9	37.2			Fixed Assets (net)	47.0	42.5
	1.0	4.3	6.5			Intangibles (net)	5.7	6.0
	4.0	11.3	14.2			All Other Non-Current	6.1	6.6
	100.0	100.0	100.0			Total	100.0	100.0

LIABILITIES

0-500M	500M-2MM	2-10MM	10-50MM	50-100MM	100-250MM		99 ALL	00 ALL
	19.9	4.4	5.2			Notes Payable-Short Term	5.5	6.4
	6.5	6.2	4.1			Cur. Mat.-L/T/D	5.0	4.7
	8.8	9.8	10.5			Trade Payables	11.0	12.3
	.1	.6	.4			Income Taxes Payable	.1	.1
	10.6	11.0	7.0			All Other Current	6.3	7.8
	45.9	31.9	27.2			Total Current	28.0	31.4
	36.9	20.4	23.2			Long Term Debt	26.5	24.3
	.4	.7	1.0			Deferred Taxes	1.5	1.7
	2.4	9.4	5.8			All Other Non-Current	5.8	5.9
	14.3	37.6	42.9			Net Worth	38.3	36.7
	100.0	100.0	100.0			Total Liabilities & Net Worth	100.0	100.0

INCOME DATA

0-500M	500M-2MM	2-10MM	10-50MM	50-100MM	100-250MM		99 ALL	00 ALL
	100.0	100.0	100.0			Net Sales	100.0	100.0
						Gross Profit		
	97.1	94.8	94.7			Operating Expenses	94.4	95.4
	2.9	5.2	5.3			Operating Profit	5.6	4.6
	1.0	1.6	.7			All Other Expenses (net)	2.6	1.6
	1.9	3.6	4.6			Profit Before Taxes	3.0	3.0

RATIOS

0-500M	500M-2MM	2-10MM	10-50MM	50-100MM	100-250MM		99 ALL	00 ALL
	1.6	1.9	2.0			Current	2.4	2.3
	1.3	1.2	1.5				1.8	1.5
	.7	.9	1.2				1.1	1.0
	1.3	1.3	1.3			Quick	1.2	1.4
	.9	.8	1.0				.9	.9
	.4	.6	.6				.6	.6
	24 15.0	30 12.2	32 11.3			Sales/Receivables	33 11.2	32 11.3
	30 12.3	35 10.5	40 9.1				38 9.7	38 9.5
	38 9.6	43 8.5	47 7.8				44 8.3	44 8.3
						Cost of Sales/Inventory		
						Cost of Sales/Payables		
	15.1	8.2	8.0			Sales/Working Capital	5.9	6.0
	28.4	27.7	10.6				10.0	13.4
	-28.0	-49.8	31.5				48.5	999.8
	5.6	7.4	8.6			EBIT/Interest	4.7	7.5
	(18) 3.3	(29) 3.2	(17) 4.2				(62) 2.2	(58) 2.2
	.7	1.6	1.2				.5	1.1
		3.3	7.9			Net Profit + Depr., Dep.,	2.7	7.2
		(11) 2.2	(10) 3.7			Amort./Cur. Mat. L /T/D	(26) 1.7	(19) 2.0
		1.5	.6				1.0	1.4
	.9	.7	.6			Fixed/Worth	.7	.6
	1.3	1.1	1.1				1.5	1.3
	6.1	2.1	1.8				3.6	7.5
	.8	.9	.6			Debt/Worth	.8	.7
	3.1	1.4	1.6				1.8	1.8
	20.2	3.2	3.6				10.5	13.6
	92.9	40.1	31.3			% Profit Before Taxes/Tangible	28.6	28.1
	(16) 16.0	(29) 18.1	(16) 18.0			Net Worth	(58) 14.4	(51) 10.9
	5.1	7.7	9.8				-1.5	3.7
	15.1	13.1	10.7			% Profit Before Taxes/Total	10.9	11.5
	6.0	6.5	7.3			Assets	4.5	4.2
	.2	2.0	1.1				-1.0	.2
	15.6	10.1	7.0			Sales/Net Fixed Assets	5.7	8.3
	6.3	5.1	4.7				3.8	5.1
	3.5	2.6	2.9				2.3	3.0
	3.4	2.4	2.1			Sales/Total Assets	2.1	2.7
	2.5	2.0	1.6				1.5	1.8
	1.6	1.4	1.1				1.2	1.2
	2.0	2.6	2.2			% Depr., Dep., Amort./Sales	2.8	2.2
	4.9	(30) 4.0	(16) 3.5				(63) 3.8	(58) 3.6
	11.7	6.0	4.5				7.8	5.9
	4.2	2.0				% Officers', Directors',	2.6	2.7
	(14) 6.2	(15) 6.9				Owners' Comp/Sales	(27) 4.8	(29) 5.4
	10.8	10.1					6.3	8.2

0-500M	500M-2MM	2-10MM	10-50MM	50-100MM	100-250MM		99 ALL	00 ALL
6260M	48710M	300634M	566630M	86564M	504227M	Net Sales ($)	1453788M	1202634M
1826M	18980M	150341M	334400M	91906M	329922M	Total Assets ($)	1104588M	909215M

M = $ thousand   MM = $ million
See Pages 11 through 18 for Explanation of Ratios and Data

Comparative Historical Data | Current Data Sorted By Sales

4/1/00-3/31/01 ALL	4/1/01-3/31/02 ALL	4/1/02-3/31/03 ALL	Type of Statement	0-1MM	1-3MM	3-5MM	5-10MM	10-25MM	25MM & OVER
11	8	17	Unqualified		1	3	2	4	7
16	18	20	Reviewed		2	3	7	6	2
19	17	15	Compiled	1	7	2	3	2	
4	1	5	Tax Returns	1	2		2	3	
13	23	19	Other		5	2	2	5	4
				24 (4/1-9/30/02)		52 (10/1/02-3/31/03)			
63	67	76	NUMBER OF STATEMENTS	2	17	10	14	18	15
%	%	%	**ASSETS**	%	%	%	%	%	%
6.0	8.4	8.1	Cash & Equivalents		6.3	18.9	6.9	7.4	5.2
21.1	20.1	19.4	Trade Receivables (net)		20.3	16.5	20.2	21.0	19.4
10.4	11.5	13.5	Inventory		17.7	13.1	8.7	8.4	16.7
3.5	3.8	2.5	All Other Current		2.0	5.2	1.3	2.7	2.5
40.9	43.8	43.5	Total Current		46.3	53.7	37.1	39.5	43.9
45.5	44.6	42.0	Fixed Assets (net)		45.5	36.4	50.3	39.4	36.2
7.2	4.9	4.6	Intangibles (net)		2.9	3.5	3.2	4.6	8.3
6.4	6.5	10.0	All Other Non-Current		5.3	6.4	9.5	16.5	11.6
100.0	100.0	100.0	Total		100.0	100.0	100.0	100.0	100.0
			LIABILITIES						
6.4	9.0	8.0	Notes Payable-Short Term		14.4	13.3	6.1	3.9	4.9
5.7	4.7	5.7	Cur. Mat.-L/T/D		7.1	8.1	6.3	4.5	2.9
10.9	10.1	9.5	Trade Payables		8.7	8.5	9.7	10.2	10.7
.7	.7	.4	Income Taxes Payable		.5	1.1	.4	.3	.3
6.7	9.0	9.5	All Other Current		6.1	17.1	11.8	8.9	8.1
30.5	33.5	33.2	Total Current		36.8	48.2	34.2	27.8	26.9
27.8	23.0	25.9	Long Term Debt		45.4	10.5	30.2	18.9	19.9
1.2	.7	.7	Deferred Taxes		.6	1.0	.7	1.0	.2
6.3	5.2	7.9	All Other Non-Current		4.7	.2	14.4	5.1	10.8
34.3	37.4	32.3	Net Worth		12.5	40.1	20.5	47.3	42.2
100.0	100.0	100.0	Total Liabilities & Net Worth		100.0	100.0	100.0	100.0	100.0
			INCOME DATA						
100.0	100.0	100.0	Net Sales		100.0	100.0	100.0	100.0	100.0
			Gross Profit						
93.6	94.7	95.5	Operating Expenses		97.5	93.5	95.9	94.6	95.5
6.4	5.3	4.5	Operating Profit		2.5	6.5	4.1	5.4	4.5
2.2	2.0	1.3	All Other Expenses (net)		1.4	.9	2.0	1.4	.7
4.3	3.3	3.1	Profit Before Taxes		1.1	5.7	2.1	3.9	3.8
			RATIOS						
2.2	2.2	1.9			1.9	2.2	1.7	1.8	2.5
1.4	1.5	1.4	Current		1.4	1.3	.9	1.4	1.9
.8	1.0	1.0			.9	1.0	.7	1.1	1.1
1.4	1.6	1.3			1.3	1.5	1.3	1.3	1.1
(62) .9	.9	1.0	Quick		.9	1.0	.7	1.0	1.0
.5	.5	.6			.5	.4	.4	.8	.8
31 11.9	28 13.0	27 13.7		21 17.6	18 19.8	27 13.6	32 11.4	35 10.5	
37 9.9	35 10.5	35 10.5	Sales/Receivables	29 12.6	27 13.4	35 10.5	38 9.5	40 9.1	
46 7.9	41 8.8	43 8.5		38 9.7	34 10.8	47 7.8	47 7.8	43 8.4	
			Cost of Sales/Inventory						
			Cost of Sales/Payables						
7.8	7.6	8.6			11.1	8.0	11.0	9.1	7.5
17.7	13.7	17.6	Sales/Working Capital		18.9	19.0	-46.5	15.9	8.7
-49.1	-142.1	-366.4			-238.2	NM	-21.7	97.8	43.8
6.7	7.1	6.8			5.9		6.5	7.4	8.3
(61) 2.1	(61) 2.7	(72) 3.4	EBIT/Interest		3.0		(13) 2.8	(16) 3.2	4.6
.8	.9	1.2			-1.2		1.5	1.2	2.2
4.9	3.7	5.4	Net Profit + Depr., Dep.,						
(16) 2.3	(17) 1.6	(24) 2.1	Amort./Cur. Mat. L/T/D						
.8	.6	1.2							
.9	.7	.7			1.0	.4	.9	.5	.7
1.4	1.1	1.2	Fixed/Worth		1.9	.8	1.6	1.0	1.0
5.7	3.4	2.9			-7.7	1.7	7.0	1.6	1.8
.9	.8	.7			.6	.9	.9	.6	.6
2.3	1.5	1.8	Debt/Worth		3.1	2.0	2.3	1.5	1.9
7.0	6.6	4.7			-12.6	3.7	15.6	2.4	4.7
50.3	40.7	40.1	% Profit Before Taxes/Tangible		54.0	82.2	47.2	34.3	29.6
(51) 18.9	(57) 11.8	(65) 18.1	Net Worth	(12)	12.3	34.2	(12) 21.2	(17) 15.8	(13) 20.1
2.2	2.6	7.9			5.1	8.7	8.1	3.5	8.4
14.1	13.2	13.0	% Profit Before Taxes/Total		14.1	20.9	10.3	12.8	8.0
4.3	3.3	6.2	Assets		4.8	7.9	4.7	7.4	5.4
-.8	-.5	.8			-4.2	4.6	2.0	.5	3.8
7.8	7.1	9.7			14.3	17.8	8.3	10.2	7.0
4.9	4.5	5.4	Sales/Net Fixed Assets		6.3	7.7	4.5	5.2	5.0
2.6	3.0	3.1			2.3	1.9	2.8	3.5	3.6
2.6	2.6	2.5			3.2	3.3	3.1	2.4	2.3
2.0	2.0	2.1	Sales/Total Assets		2.4	1.9	1.9	2.1	1.8
1.3	1.3	1.4			1.6	1.3	1.4	1.2	1.4
2.6	2.3	2.4			2.4	3.0	2.4	2.9	2.2
(57) 4.4	(63) 4.0	(70) 4.1	% Depr., Dep., Amort./Sales	(15)	8.0	5.1	3.6	(16) 4.1	(13) 2.6
6.5	5.2	6.3			22.4	6.0	6.7	5.9	4.4
2.3	2.0	3.0	% Officers', Directors',		3.8				
(30) 4.8	(25) 5.3	(37) 6.1	Owners' Comp/Sales	(11)	6.0				
8.5	8.2	10.3			7.0				
1442957M	1440652M	1513025M	Net Sales ($)	1628M	30597M	36148M	108428M	267628M	1068596M
766045M	982851M	927375M	Total Assets ($)	944M	14939M	20705M	58263M	154009M	678515M

© RMA 2003

M = $ thousand   MM = $ million

See Pages 11 through 18 for Explanation of Ratios and Data

Current Data Sorted By Assets   Comparative Historical Data

0-500M	500M-2MM	2-10MM	10-50MM	50-100MM	100-250MM	Type of Statement	4/1/98-3/31/99 ALL	4/1/99-3/31/00 ALL
1	2	1	1			Unqualified	4	6
2	2	2				Reviewed	17	11
	10	4				Compiled	24	19
2	2					Tax Returns	7	7
7	4	8				Other	20	17
	10 (4/1-9/30/02)			38 (10/1/02-3/31/03)				
12	20	15	1			NUMBER OF STATEMENTS	72	60
%	%	%	%	%	%	ASSETS	%	%
10.6	12.0	8.0		D	D	Cash & Equivalents	10.4	9.4
19.5	27.6	23.8		A	A	Trade Receivables (net)	22.0	23.9
8.8	7.7	12.4		T	T	Inventory	9.4	9.2
5.1	.6	2.5		A	A	All Other Current	2.0	2.3
43.9	47.8	46.6				Total Current	43.9	44.8
49.6	37.3	44.8		N	N	Fixed Assets (net)	46.7	44.9
1.7	4.9	2.1		O	O	Intangibles (net)	3.8	4.8
4.8	10.0	6.5		T	T	All Other Non-Current	5.6	5.4
100.0	100.0	100.0				Total	100.0	100.0
				A	A	LIABILITIES		
11.2	9.8	13.4		V	V	Notes Payable-Short Term	6.1	4.5
10.8	5.7	6.2		A	A	Cur. Mat.-L/T/D	8.9	8.1
8.8	11.6	9.0		I	I	Trade Payables	12.0	12.4
.2	.0	.0		L	L	Income Taxes Payable	.5	.3
5.7	7.6	12.8		A	A	All Other Current	6.6	14.0
36.6	34.7	41.5		B	B	Total Current	34.2	39.2
38.8	25.3	14.0		L	L	Long Term Debt	29.0	23.8
.0	.3	.5		E	E	Deferred Taxes	.6	.8
9.2	.8	3.0				All Other Non-Current	2.2	4.5
15.4	38.9	41.0				Net Worth	34.0	31.7
100.0	100.0	100.0				Total Liabilities & Net Worth	100.0	100.0
						INCOME DATA		
100.0	100.0	100.0				Net Sales	100.0	100.0
						Gross Profit		
96.3	98.6	96.7				Operating Expenses	96.8	96.9
3.7	1.4	3.3				Operating Profit	3.2	3.1
1.5	1.0	1.1				All Other Expenses (net)	2.2	2.0
2.2	.4	2.2				Profit Before Taxes	1.0	1.1
						RATIOS		
3.3	3.4	1.9					2.2	1.9
1.4	1.3	1.0				Current	1.4	1.3
.7	.8	.8					.8	.9
2.7	2.8	1.4					1.8	1.6
.7	1.0	.7				Quick	.9	.9
.4	.7	.4					.5	.5
0 UND	20 18.0	22 16.9					20 18.5	22 16.6
18 20.4	37 10.0	30 12.0				Sales/Receivables	32 11.4	32 11.3
46 7.9	62 5.9	53 6.8					50 7.3	54 6.8
						Cost of Sales/Inventory		
						Cost of Sales/Payables		
14.1	6.8	10.7					6.9	9.5
47.4	29.7	-79.5				Sales/Working Capital	20.7	26.8
-18.1	-25.1	-12.1					-32.8	-43.3
	(18) 6.1	18.9					(66) 5.2	(56) 4.0
	1.9	3.1				EBIT/Interest	1.9	1.8
	-.2	.7					.4	.6
						Net Profit + Depr., Dep.,	(27) 2.5	(18) 3.7
						Amort./Cur. Mat. L /T/D	1.5	1.7
							1.0	1.2
1.1	.4	.7					.6	.7
8.1	.9	1.3				Fixed/Worth	1.4	1.3
-12.0	5.1	2.6					6.8	4.4
1.3	.6	.9					.6	.9
58.3	1.3	1.6				Debt/Worth	2.1	1.9
-23.9	6.4	5.2					9.1	9.3
	(17) 30.8	30.1				% Profit Before Taxes/Tangible	(60) 35.7	(50) 36.9
	13.2	22.7				Net Worth	13.4	14.0
	4.5	-2.4					-4.8	3.0
18.2	11.0	17.5				% Profit Before Taxes/Total	10.5	9.5
3.5	3.3	4.9				Assets	4.2	3.2
-2.6	-1.8	-.8					-2.5	-1.4
10.0	27.2	7.0					8.7	9.6
5.2	5.5	4.8				Sales/Net Fixed Assets	5.0	5.0
2.7	3.0	4.1					3.0	2.8
3.0	2.9	2.8					2.7	2.9
1.9	2.3	2.4				Sales/Total Assets	2.2	2.1
1.5	1.7	2.1					1.7	1.5
(11) 2.7	(18) 2.5	(14) 3.0				% Depr., Dep., Amort./Sales	(65) 4.2	(53) 3.4
6.5	5.1	5.0					5.6	5.2
10.6	6.8	6.4					9.1	8.6
	(10) 2.3					% Officers', Directors',	(39) 4.6	(32) 3.2
	4.3					Owners' Comp/Sales	6.6	6.2
	8.6						12.2	10.8
7099M	62320M	148325M	24316M			Net Sales ($)	424699M	334983M
3114M	26453M	58319M	11839M			Total Assets ($)	286313M	163714M

© RMA 2003

M = $ thousand   MM = $ million
See Pages 11 through 18 for Explanation of Ratios and Data

Comparative Historical Data   Current Data Sorted By Sales

			Type of Statement						
7	5	5	Unqualified	1			1	1	2
13	8	6	Reviewed	2	1		1	1	1
19	15	14	Compiled		6	3	4		1
22	1	4	Tax Returns	2	1	1			
33	24	19	Other	6	5		5		3
4/1/00-3/31/01	4/1/01-3/31/02	4/1/02-3/31/03			10 (4/1-9/30/02)		38 (10/1/02-3/31/03)		
ALL	ALL	ALL		0-1MM	1-3MM	3-5MM	5-10MM	10-25MM	25MM & OVER
94	53	48	**NUMBER OF STATEMENTS**	11	13	6	11	7	
%	%	%	**ASSETS**	%	%	%	%	%	%
14.3	12.1	10.8	Cash & Equivalents	11.1	9.6		10.7		D
16.8	21.3	24.4	Trade Receivables (net)	19.7	19.8		26.5		A
13.9	10.7	9.5	Inventory	3.1	13.6		10.4		T
2.4	2.0	2.4	All Other Current	5.5	1.0		1.9		A
47.4	46.1	47.1	Total Current	39.4	44.1		49.5		
44.5	41.8	42.3	Fixed Assets (net)	53.5	36.7		44.4		N
2.3	5.7	3.1	Intangibles (net)	1.9	6.4		1.6		O
5.8	6.3	7.5	All Other Non-Current	5.2	12.8		4.5		T
100.0	100.0	100.0	Total	100.0	100.0		100.0		
			LIABILITIES						A
3.7	9.6	11.1	Notes Payable-Short Term	12.2	8.8		14.6		V
8.3	7.6	7.0	Cur. Mat.-L/T/D	9.8	6.5		8.7		A
11.1	13.1	10.2	Trade Payables	7.4	13.1		10.1		I
.3	.3	.1	Income Taxes Payable	.2	.0		.0		L
7.2	11.8	9.0	All Other Current	5.5	7.2		9.2		A
30.7	42.4	37.3	Total Current	35.1	35.6		42.5		B
29.4	21.2	24.7	Long Term Debt	38.2	33.5		15.2		L
.5	.6	.3	Deferred Taxes	.0	.0		.9		E
9.8	3.8	3.6	All Other Non-Current	10.1	1.6		.0		
29.5	32.0	34.2	Net Worth	16.7	29.4		41.4		
100.0	100.0	100.0	Total Liabilities & Net Worth	100.0	100.0		100.0		
			INCOME DATA						
100.0	100.0	100.0	Net Sales	100.0	100.0		100.0		
			Gross Profit						
96.3	98.9	97.2	Operating Expenses	95.6	101.0		97.6		
3.7	1.1	2.8	Operating Profit	4.4	-1.0		2.4		
1.4	1.8	1.1	All Other Expenses (net)	1.5	1.3		.8		
2.3	-.7	1.6	Profit Before Taxes	2.8	-2.3		1.6		
			RATIOS						
3.4	1.8	2.9		3.3	2.4		2.1		
1.6	1.1	1.3	Current	1.1	1.3		1.0		
1.0	.7	.8		.6	.8		.8		
2.1	1.4	2.3		3.1	1.9		1.9		
1.1	(52) .9	.9	Quick	.9	.8		.7		
.5	.4	.5		.3	.3		.4		
6 64.5	9 42.4	18 20.3		0 UND	13 28.1		23 16.1		
20 18.4	28 13.1	30 12.0	Sales/Receivables	18 20.1	30 12.3		31 11.9		
40 9.1	47 7.8	55 6.6		56 6.6	64 5.7		45 8.1		
			Cost of Sales/Inventory						
			Cost of Sales/Payables						
7.7	11.4	7.7		13.6	11.3		8.2		
16.1	112.9	29.7	Sales/Working Capital	73.6	36.8		-79.5		
514.2	-14.0	-22.1		-15.8	-12.9		-24.5		
(82) 4.8	(48) 3.4	(42) 8.5			2.6		7.7		
2.0	1.2	2.4	EBIT/Interest	(11) 1.3		2.1			
.6	-.9	.6			-3.4		.7		
(21) 3.7	(15) 7.9		Net Profit + Depr., Dep.,						
1.3	2.7		Amort./Cur. Mat. L/T/D						
.8	1.0								
.6	.7	.6		1.1	.3		.8		
1.3	1.7	1.3	Fixed/Worth	11.6	2.4		1.3		
3.8	7.2	5.1		-6.3	5.3		1.9		
.7	.9	.8		1.3	.7		.8		
1.7	2.2	1.6	Debt/Worth	44.2	2.1		1.6		
5.8	10.0	8.2		-10.5	39.6		2.0		
41.2	21.4	35.3			18.0		30.1		
(78) 8.2	(42) 7.4	(40) 16.5	% Profit Before Taxes/Tangible Net Worth	(11) 7.6		(10) 10.6			
-.5	-29.1	-1.4			-8.6		-6.6		
15.6	8.9	16.8		19.6	5.8		15.8		
3.3	1.3	4.2	% Profit Before Taxes/Total Assets	6.3	1.0		3.3		
-2.0	-9.6	-1.4		-1.6	-20.0		-.8		
10.1	11.2	10.8		5.9	45.3		7.0		
5.3	6.9	5.3	Sales/Net Fixed Assets	4.9	3.0		6.0		
3.2	3.1	3.1		2.7	2.5		4.1		
3.0	3.3	2.8		2.5	2.5		3.0		
2.3	2.5	2.2	Sales/Total Assets	1.8	1.8		2.7		
1.8	1.6	1.8		1.5	1.4		2.1		
3.3	3.4	2.7		3.9	.8		3.2		
(84) 4.9	(48) 4.9	(43) 5.3	% Depr., Dep., Amort./Sales	(10) 7.3	(11) 5.0		5.3		
7.0	7.3	7.3		10.7	8.5		7.3		
4.6	4.2	2.8							
(64) 8.2	(20) 4.8	(25) 5.3	% Officers', Directors', Owners' Comp/Sales						
13.3	7.6	10.8							
505183M	344808M	242060M	Net Sales ($)	5706M	27037M	23295M	81485M	104537M	
225228M	165174M	99725M	Total Assets ($)	2894M	15419M	8827M	33263M	39322M	

© RMA 2003   M = $ thousand   MM = $ million
See Pages 11 through 18 for Explanation of Ratios and Data

Current Data Sorted By Assets   Comparative Historical Data

1	1	4	5	1	2	Type of Statement		
		4	1			Unqualified	10	8
	3	3				Reviewed	5	1
1						Compiled	6	5
2	6	4	4	2	1	Tax Returns		3
	7 (4/1-9/30/02)		38 (10/1/02-3/31/03)			Other	10	13
							4/1/98-	4/1/99-
							3/31/99	3/31/00
0-500M	500M-2MM	2-10MM	10-50MM	50-100MM	100-250MM		ALL	ALL
4	10	15	10	3	3	NUMBER OF STATEMENTS	31	30
%	%	%	%	%	%	ASSETS	%	%
	25.3	5.9	11.6			Cash & Equivalents	13.3	13.7
	20.4	8.0	12.2			Trade Receivables (net)	13.8	10.3
	.0	.0	.0			Inventory	2.2	.6
	3.8	1.2	4.4			All Other Current	4.2	3.3
	49.5	15.1	28.2			Total Current	33.4	27.9
	31.8	69.8	59.7			Fixed Assets (net)	51.4	55.0
	7.9	5.4	3.7			Intangibles (net)	5.0	6.6
	10.8	9.7	8.4			All Other Non-Current	10.1	10.5
	100.0	100.0	100.0			Total	100.0	100.0
						LIABILITIES		
	3.6	1.8	2.7			Notes Payable-Short Term	8.1	7.7
	4.2	5.6	1.9			Cur. Mat.-L/T/D	2.2	2.1
	8.4	3.9	8.3			Trade Payables	6.4	7.9
	.4	.4	.4			Income Taxes Payable	.4	.8
	28.6	16.3	13.5			All Other Current	15.0	10.2
	45.2	28.0	26.9			Total Current	32.2	28.7
	13.8	52.9	42.1			Long Term Debt	35.5	38.0
	.0	.5	.0			Deferred Taxes	.1	.2
	.7	13.8	4.6			All Other Non-Current	5.9	6.8
	40.3	4.8	26.4			Net Worth	26.4	26.4
	100.0	100.0	100.0			Total Liabilities & Net Worth	100.0	100.0
						INCOME DATA		
	100.0	100.0	100.0			Net Sales	100.0	100.0
						Gross Profit		
	92.9	82.1	85.7			Operating Expenses	86.3	77.3
	7.1	17.9	14.3			Operating Profit	13.6	22.7
	1.4	15.3	8.8			All Other Expenses (net)	19.5	9.7
	5.7	2.7	5.6			Profit Before Taxes	−5.9	13.0
						RATIOS		
	2.2	1.0	1.9				1.5	1.9
	1.0	.7	1.0			Current	1.2	.8
	.6	.3	.8				.4	.3
	2.0	.9	1.2				1.4	1.6
	.9	.6	.9			Quick	.8	.7
	.5	.2	.5				.2	.3
	0 UND	1 724.0	2 220.6				0 UND	1 460.3
	21 17.7	7 52.3	18 20.3			Sales/Receivables	5 67.7	10 34.8
	32 11.5	19 18.8	39 9.3				24 15.3	35 10.4
						Cost of Sales/Inventory		
						Cost of Sales/Payables		
	18.4	−128.3	14.4				13.0	11.3
	−616.9	−18.6	−567.8			Sales/Working Capital	48.3	−54.4
	−5.9	−5.6	−29.8				−6.4	−7.5
	37.2	5.0					5.6	6.2
	4.5	(10) 1.4				EBIT/Interest	(20) 3.4	(19) 3.5
	1.6	.3					1.9	1.1
						Net Profit + Depr., Dep., Amort./Cur. Mat. L /T/D		
	.4	2.1	1.0				.5	.7
	.8	−32.5	2.6			Fixed/Worth	2.1	2.8
	5.0	−2.7	6.2				25.9	23.3
	.7	3.8	3.1				.9	1.4
	1.7	−85.5	4.3			Debt/Worth	2.7	3.2
	8.8	−5.0	6.1				70.8	25.4
						% Profit Before Taxes/Tangible Net Worth	63.6	92.9
							(24) 25.3	(25) 28.1
							5.6	8.9
	29.6	9.7	22.2			% Profit Before Taxes/Total Assets	12.8	21.6
	10.0	1.2	2.5				6.7	4.8
	.0	−2.3	−.2				−.2	−.1
	77.9	1.6	14.2				23.7	31.8
	16.9	.6	.7			Sales/Net Fixed Assets	2.9	1.5
	1.5	.2	.2				.2	.4
	7.5	.9	3.3				3.6	2.8
	3.5	.5	.6			Sales/Total Assets	.9	.8
	1.0	.2	.2				.2	.2
		6.2	1.6				.9	1.1
		(14) 12.2	10.1			% Depr., Dep., Amort./Sales	(29) 4.2	(27) 4.2
		19.4	20.3				14.6	16.9
						% Officers', Directors', Owners' Comp/Sales		
2433M	60500M	94105M	268969M	235068M	467823M	Net Sales ($)	1106354M	490376M
822M	13289M	75793M	157190M	222348M	553481M	Total Assets ($)	691536M	549416M

M = $ thousand   MM = $ million
See Pages 11 through 18 for Explanation of Ratios and Data

Comparative Historical Data | Current Data Sorted By Sales

			Type of Statement	0-1MM	1-3MM	3-5MM	5-10MM	10-25MM	25MM & OVER
10	8	14	Unqualified	2	1	2		2	7
3	2	5	Reviewed		2	1	1		1
6	10	6	Compiled	1	3	2	2		
4	4	1	Tax Returns	1					
6	7	19	Other	6	4	2	3	1	3
4/1/00-3/31/01 ALL	4/1/01-3/31/02 ALL	4/1/02-3/31/03 ALL		7 (4/1-9/30/02)		38 (10/1/02-3/31/03)			
29	31	45	NUMBER OF STATEMENTS	10	10	5	6	3	11
%	%	%	ASSETS	%	%	%	%	%	%
13.3	18.3	12.9	Cash & Equivalents	7.7	8.1				16.5
11.5	8.1	11.5	Trade Receivables (net)	5.1	2.5				19.0
.3	.8	.0	Inventory	.0	.0				.1
4.0	6.2	4.1	All Other Current	7.8	2.8				3.8
29.1	33.5	28.4	Total Current	20.6	13.4				39.5
56.1	47.9	53.7	Fixed Assets (net)	68.7	79.1				31.8
4.3	6.2	7.7	Intangibles (net)	1.0	2.6				16.3
10.6	12.4	10.2	All Other Non-Current	9.7	4.8				12.5
100.0	100.0	100.0	Total	100.0	100.0				100.0
			LIABILITIES						
3.5	2.7	3.4	Notes Payable-Short Term	6.3	3.0				2.9
3.8	5.9	4.0	Cur. Mat.-L/T/D	1.1	5.3				4.0
5.1	8.5	6.9	Trade Payables	6.4	1.4				10.6
.1	.0	.3	Income Taxes Payable	.0	.6				.4
17.5	15.0	17.9	All Other Current	19.1	14.7				23.3
30.1	32.1	32.5	Total Current	32.9	25.0				41.2
38.4	35.9	36.6	Long Term Debt	31.2	52.4				28.8
.2	.2	.4	Deferred Taxes	.0	.0				1.6
12.6	10.1	8.8	All Other Non-Current	10.0	10.8				13.6
18.8	21.7	21.7	Net Worth	25.9	11.9				14.8
100.0	100.0	100.0	Total Liabilities & Net Worth	100.0	100.0				100.0
			INCOME DATA						
100.0	100.0	100.0	Net Sales	100.0	100.0				100.0
			Gross Profit						
86.0	83.4	86.2	Operating Expenses	80.5	79.0				92.8
14.0	16.6	13.8	Operating Profit	19.5	21.0				7.2
2.9	11.2	7.9	All Other Expenses (net)	12.2	14.5				1.5
11.1	5.4	5.9	Profit Before Taxes	7.3	6.5				5.7
			RATIOS						
1.7	1.7	1.7		9.5	1.2				1.1
.9	.8	.9	Current	1.3	.6				1.0
.6	.4	.6		.1	.3				.8
1.6	1.7	1.4		5.4	.9				1.0
.9	.5	.9	Quick	1.2	.6				.9
.5	.3	.5		.1	.2				.7
2 153.5	0 UND	1 376.0		0 UND	0 UND			10	35.6
11 34.2	4 84.6	10 35.6	Sales/Receivables	8 45.9	4 101.8			25	14.6
27 13.6	17 22.0	33 11.2		45 8.1	17 20.9			47	7.7
			Cost of Sales/Inventory						
			Cost of Sales/Payables						
9.4	16.5	25.7		3.6	63.7				25.9
-86.9	-52.9	-86.4	Sales/Working Capital	NM	-10.1				-87.8
-18.0	-8.5	-10.4		-11.8	-4.7				-24.3
(22) 7.1	(15) 30.8	(31) 6.0							
3.8	4.9	2.9	EBIT/Interest						
2.0	1.5	.8							
			Net Profit + Depr., Dep., Amort./Cur. Mat. L/T/D						
1.0	.7	1.0		.9	3.4				1.0
2.0	3.5	4.0	Fixed/Worth	5.1	5.0				2.4
10.9	8.2	-9.3		-14.7	-9.4				-8.4
1.3	2.1	1.7		.5	3.7				2.3
2.5	3.6	5.4	Debt/Worth	4.2	5.5				5.4
12.7	28.9	-16.7		-18.0	-10.8				-20.4
(24) 72.1	(26) 67.0	(31) 84.2							
15.5	34.2	18.7	% Profit Before Taxes/Tangible Net Worth						
10.1	1.9	-1.0							
13.4	26.6	16.4		16.2	7.7				19.9
5.7	4.7	2.7	% Profit Before Taxes/Total Assets	.7	.1				4.9
2.0	.1	-.4		-.8	-2.3				1.2
19.7	27.0	17.5		19.0	1.3				15.2
1.4	9.7	1.2	Sales/Net Fixed Assets	.4	.5				11.1
.4	.6	.3		.2	.2				1.2
4.5	6.1	3.5		5.0	1.0				3.6
.9	2.4	.9	Sales/Total Assets	.3	.4				1.5
.3	.2	.3		.2	.2				.7
(25) 1.1	(26) .6	(43) 1.2		5.0				(10)	1.5
3.5	3.4	4.2	% Depr., Dep., Amort./Sales	11.9					2.7
16.5	8.9	14.7		19.7					4.0
(13) 3.0	(11) 3.4	(14) 2.6							
4.2	4.9	8.2	% Officers', Directors', Owners' Comp/Sales						
6.8	6.9	17.1							
604925M	746926M	1128898M	Net Sales ($)	6664M	18859M	19405M	47000M	53884M	983086M
542155M	572381M	1022923M	Total Assets ($)	21805M	52319M	66331M	17029M	19049M	846390M

© RMA 2003

M = $ thousand   MM = $ million
See Pages 11 through 18 for Explanation of Ratios and Data

Current Data Sorted By Assets   Comparative Historical Data

Type of Statement	0-500M	500M-2MM	2-10MM	10-50MM	50-100MM	100-250MM	4/1/98-3/31/99 ALL	4/1/99-3/31/00 ALL
Unqualified	3	4	5	4		2	9	9
Reviewed			6				9	11
Compiled	10	15	5				25	31
Tax Returns	34	12	2				20	19
Other	9	12	5	2		2	26	29
	18 (4/1-9/30/02)			114 (10/1/02-3/31/03)				
NUMBER OF STATEMENTS	56	43	23	6		4	89	99
	%	%	%	%	%	%	%	%
ASSETS								
Cash & Equivalents	17.1	12.3	12.2				15.9	15.0
Trade Receivables (net)	12.8	16.6	25.1				12.4	15.4
Inventory	3.7	2.8	2.8	D			6.9	4.6
All Other Current	4.9	4.1	2.1	A			2.5	2.1
Total Current	38.6	35.9	42.2	T			37.6	37.1
Fixed Assets (net)	43.0	50.9	41.2	A			44.6	45.1
Intangibles (net)	4.0	3.5	5.8				5.0	8.3
All Other Non-Current	14.4	9.6	10.9	N			12.8	9.5
Total	100.0	100.0	100.0	O			100.0	100.0
LIABILITIES				T				
Notes Payable-Short Term	17.0	9.5	8.2				11.3	9.5
Cur. Mat.-L/T/D	10.2	5.5	5.7	A			4.9	4.3
Trade Payables	12.3	5.5	9.0	V			11.6	8.3
Income Taxes Payable	.1	1.2	.8	A			.3	.4
All Other Current	24.7	10.3	13.9	I			16.2	15.2
Total Current	64.3	32.0	37.6	L			44.3	37.6
Long Term Debt	24.9	33.9	17.6	A			22.9	24.9
Deferred Taxes	.2	.1	.4	B			.2	.2
All Other Non-Current	7.1	7.1	2.0	L			11.1	8.9
Net Worth	3.5	26.9	42.4	E			21.5	28.4
Total Liabilities & Net Worth	100.0	100.0	100.0				100.0	100.0
INCOME DATA								
Net Sales	100.0	100.0	100.0				100.0	100.0
Gross Profit								
Operating Expenses	94.3	87.9	88.7				91.9	91.7
Operating Profit	5.7	12.1	11.3				8.1	8.3
All Other Expenses (net)	1.9	8.5	2.4				3.1	1.9
Profit Before Taxes	3.8	3.7	8.9				4.9	6.3
RATIOS								
Current	1.5	2.1	2.6				1.8	2.5
	.7	1.2	1.5				.9	1.1
	.3	.2	.7				.4	.5
Quick	1.5	1.6	2.4				1.3	2.2
	.4	.9	1.2				.7	.9
	.1	.1	.7				.3	.4
Sales/Receivables	0 UND	0 UND	4 100.0				0 UND	0 UND
	0 UND	5 68.9	33 10.9				6 65.6	4 86.6
	15 24.8	44 8.2	52 7.1				22 16.3	31 11.7
Cost of Sales/Inventory								
Cost of Sales/Payables								
Sales/Working Capital	28.1	6.5	6.3				13.9	10.9
	-34.8	66.0	16.6				-122.0	89.5
	-9.4	-6.1	-13.1				-9.9	-10.1
EBIT/Interest	(43) 9.5	(31) 8.8	(20) 15.9				(67) 9.8	(65) 16.8
	3.3	2.1	3.6				2.9	3.5
	.2	-.3	1.5				1.6	.8
Net Profit + Depr., Dep., Amort./Cur. Mat. L/T/D							(13) 11.3	
							2.2	
							1.1	
Fixed/Worth	.7	.6	.5				.4	.4
	2.8	2.8	1.0				1.7	1.3
	-5.2	19.7	2.1				12.6	-43.0
Debt/Worth	1.6	1.2	.6				.9	.6
	5.4	3.1	1.8				2.2	1.6
	-8.0	33.8	4.2				39.7	-32.2
% Profit Before Taxes/Tangible Net Worth	(36) 140.0	(36) 83.3	(22) 46.8				(70) 58.1	(71) 100.8
	41.4	21.6	19.8				31.1	34.8
	.8	1.3	4.3				7.6	6.2
% Profit Before Taxes/Total Assets	34.4	13.1	17.3				20.0	29.3
	5.2	4.4	9.1				8.3	8.3
	-5.4	-1.5	1.2				1.8	-.3
Sales/Net Fixed Assets	41.9	14.3	32.3				25.7	29.4
	11.9	3.9	5.7				7.6	6.3
	4.2	1.1	2.5				2.3	1.9
Sales/Total Assets	7.7	3.1	2.9				5.0	3.8
	3.9	1.5	2.0				2.1	2.1
	2.2	.6	1.3				1.1	1.0
% Depr., Dep., Amort./Sales	(41) 1.2	(37) 2.1	(20) .9				(70) 2.0	(73) 1.3
	3.5	4.7	3.3				3.4	3.9
	9.3	9.8	6.4				7.2	8.0
% Officers', Directors', Owners' Comp/Sales	(35) 5.5	(15) 1.6					(34) 3.6	(32) 4.6
	7.6	4.3					9.5	7.8
	14.0	7.5					13.5	17.8
Net Sales ($)	55874M	119897M	307846M	216808M		763611M	3081345M	1410727M
Total Assets ($)	11372M	43518M	89573M	136817M		646624M	759971M	470537M

M = $ thousand   MM = $ million
See Pages 11 through 18 for Explanation of Ratios and Data

Comparative Historical Data			Type of Statement	Current Data Sorted By Sales					
12	8	14	Unqualified	2	2		3		7
8	10	10	Reviewed		1	1	6	1	1
28	34	30	Compiled	10	9	3	7		1
31	31	48	Tax Returns	31	13	3	1	1	
41	46	30	Other	13	6	6		3	2
4/1/00-3/31/01	4/1/01-3/31/02	4/1/02-3/31/03		18 (4/1-9/30/02)			114 (10/1/02-3/31/03)		
ALL	ALL	ALL		0-1MM	1-3MM	3-5MM	5-10MM	10-25MM	25MM & OVER
120	129	132	NUMBER OF STATEMENTS	56	31	13	17	5	10
%	%	%	ASSETS	%	%	%	%	%	%
14.8	19.0	14.5	Cash & Equivalents	13.7	14.7	17.7	13.3		18.7
18.9	15.5	15.6	Trade Receivables (net)	9.3	15.5	12.2	30.3		21.8
4.3	5.5	3.2	Inventory	2.5	4.7	1.5	2.5		2.6
5.1	4.3	3.9	All Other Current	2.7	5.1	2.0	8.5		2.8
43.2	44.2	37.3	Total Current	28.2	40.0	33.5	54.7		45.9
40.9	37.1	44.4	Fixed Assets (net)	53.6	47.8	41.9	28.1		17.7
6.9	6.7	5.0	Intangibles (net)	3.7	2.6	5.0	9.5		13.3
9.0	11.9	13.3	All Other Non-Current	14.4	9.6	19.6	7.7		23.1
100.0	100.0	100.0	Total	100.0	100.0	100.0	100.0		100.0
			LIABILITIES						
10.3	8.3	11.8	Notes Payable-Short Term	9.1	22.8	5.9	11.0		5.3
4.2	6.3	7.5	Cur. Mat.-L/T/D	10.1	7.6	7.8	3.9		1.5
8.9	10.4	9.5	Trade Payables	9.3	8.8	5.8	5.6		15.4
2.0	.4	.6	Income Taxes Payable	.1	.3	2.0	.1		1.8
20.4	16.9	17.6	All Other Current	18.4	13.0	26.9	14.5		22.8
45.9	42.2	46.9	Total Current	47.1	52.4	48.6	35.1		46.9
26.9	23.5	27.0	Long Term Debt	32.2	30.2	20.9	16.8		23.3
.5	.3	.2	Deferred Taxes	.1	.2	.2	.6		.0
6.9	5.9	7.0	All Other Non-Current	7.0	7.0	7.0	7.0		9.5
19.9	28.0	18.9	Net Worth	13.6	10.3	23.4	40.4		20.3
100.0	100.0	100.0	Total Liabilities & Net Worth	100.0	100.0	100.0	100.0		100.0
			INCOME DATA						
100.0	100.0	100.0	Net Sales	100.0	100.0	100.0	100.0		100.0
			Gross Profit						
91.7	91.9	91.5	Operating Expenses	84.9	97.3	93.2	96.1		97.0
8.3	8.1	8.5	Operating Profit	15.1	2.7	6.8	3.9		3.0
3.1	3.3	4.4	All Other Expenses (net)	8.1	1.3	2.5	1.5		3.1
5.2	4.8	4.1	Profit Before Taxes	7.1	1.4	4.2	2.4		-.1
			RATIOS						
2.3	2.1	2.0		2.3	1.8	1.7	3.1		1.7
1.2	1.2	.9	Current	.7	.8	.6	1.6		1.0
.6	.5	.4		.1	.4	.3	.9		.6
1.9	1.8	1.6		2.0	1.5	1.5	2.6		1.5
(119) .9	(128) .8	.7	Quick	.4	.6	.5	1.3		1.0
.4	.3	.2		.1	.2	.2	.6		.4
0 UND	0 UND	0 UND		0 UND	0 UND	0 UND	8 44.1		8 43.0
10 35.9	7 51.5	5 78.8	Sales/Receivables	0 UND	5 80.3	4 100.0	37 9.8		21 17.5
38 9.5	35 10.4	31 11.8		14 25.8	40 9.2	29 12.8	56 6.5		41 9.0
			Cost of Sales/Inventory						
			Cost of Sales/Payables						
11.7	10.7	12.1		9.0	19.0	16.4	6.2		9.3
57.0	36.7	-219.2	Sales/Working Capital	-27.9	-42.6	-25.4	16.7		NM
-18.0	-16.9	-9.3		-3.1	-14.2	-9.3	NM		-11.5
(87) 8.9	(95) 10.1	(102) 9.5		(38) 9.8	(27) 8.0	(12) 15.4	(14) 15.2		
2.8	3.2	2.9	EBIT/Interest	3.0	1.9	3.9	2.0		
1.4	.8	.2		1.1	-2.1	1.6	.4		
		8.6	Net Profit + Depr., Dep.,						
	(12) 1.7		Amort./Cur. Mat. L/T/D						
		1.5							
.4	.4	.6		1.1	.6	.5	.2		.2
1.5	1.3	2.2	Fixed/Worth	2.8	3.2	7.5	.6		.6
-12.6	UND	24.1		NM	UND	52.8	3.3		-1.3
1.0	.9	1.3		1.6	1.4	1.3	.5		1.0
3.0	2.8	3.6	Debt/Worth	4.0	5.5	7.6	2.6		3.2
-67.9	UND	182.2		-50.0	-63.9	158.3	5.4		-5.2
(88) 78.9	(97) 78.2	(101) 79.3	% Profit Before Taxes/Tangible	(41) 89.7	(23) 67.1	(11) 476.4	(14) 81.6		
32.2	26.4	24.0	Net Worth	16.0	37.7	35.0	7.7		
8.4	7.4	1.5		.5	6.2	9.8	-.9		
22.0	18.1	17.6	% Profit Before Taxes/Total	14.9	17.3	44.4	14.9		17.7
9.2	6.1	5.0	Assets	3.4	5.7	10.0	2.7		3.2
1.9	-.5	-2.4		-1.1	-9.2	2.7	-1.7		-7.3
49.8	36.6	24.7		15.3	27.8	29.0	56.0		114.2
10.0	10.1	7.0	Sales/Net Fixed Assets	3.4	7.2	13.1	12.9		13.9
3.1	3.1	2.2		1.1	2.8	2.9	4.2		4.0
5.3	4.8	5.2		3.9	6.4	6.7	4.1		5.1
2.7	2.3	2.4	Sales/Total Assets	1.5	3.1	3.8	2.4		1.5
1.5	1.3	1.1		.5	1.7	1.6	1.6		.9
1.0	.8	1.6		2.7	1.7	1.6	1.1		
(92) 3.4	(101) 3.0	(105) 4.1	% Depr., Dep., Amort./Sales	(43) 6.9	(25) 4.7	(11) 2.2	(14) 2.6		
7.6	7.3	8.6		12.7	7.9	7.3	4.2		
5.0	2.5	3.6		7.1	4.1				
(51) 7.5	(48) 7.4	(59) 7.0	% Officers', Directors',	(24) 9.3	(17) 5.8				
16.2	13.9	11.3	Owners' Comp/Sales	19.9	8.4				
6171189M	4762969M	1464036M	Net Sales ($)	22659M	55701M	44991M	111441M	83206M	1146038M
1232265M	1831151M	927904M	Total Assets ($)	30090M	25402M	32611M	59549M	15088M	765164M

© RMA 2003

M = $ thousand   MM = $ million
See Pages 11 through 18 for Explanation of Ratios and Data

Current Data Sorted By Assets   Comparative Historical Data

0-500M	500M-2MM	2-10MM	10-50MM	50-100MM	100-250MM	Type of Statement	4/1/98-3/31/99 ALL	4/1/99-3/31/00 ALL
8	19	93	123	31	28	Unqualified	214	209
1	9	58	28	5		Reviewed	70	78
14	49	74	20		4	Compiled	127	117
1		1				Tax Returns	5	1
80	172	383	101	14	11	Other	503	418
	418 (4/1-9/30/02)			909 (10/1/02-3/31/03)				
104	249	609	272	50	43	**NUMBER OF STATEMENTS**	919	823
%	%	%	%	%	%	**ASSETS**	%	%
55.8	15.5	10.1	14.5	24.5	27.2	Cash & Equivalents	19.7	18.9
3.4	1.4	1.4	2.6	4.0	5.9	Trade Receivables (net)	2.1	2.2
.4	.6	.3	.5	.4	.3	Inventory	.4	.6
2.9	1.2	1.4	2.6	3.6	4.3	All Other Current	1.9	1.9
62.5	18.7	13.3	20.2	32.5	37.6	Total Current	24.0	23.7
29.6	77.1	82.2	66.9	37.2	27.6	Fixed Assets (net)	66.7	66.6
.1	.2	.2	.4	1.0	.7	Intangibles (net)	.3	.4
7.8	4.0	4.4	12.4	29.3	34.1	All Other Non-Current	9.0	9.3
100.0	100.0	100.0	100.0	100.0	100.0	Total	100.0	100.0
						LIABILITIES		
3.0	3.0	1.5	3.3	2.9	4.4	Notes Payable-Short Term	3.2	2.5
1.0	2.1	2.0	1.6	.9	.5	Cur. Mat.-L/T/D	2.6	2.3
3.2	1.0	.8	1.4	2.3	2.9	Trade Payables	1.8	1.9
.0	.0	.0	.1	.0	.0	Income Taxes Payable	.0	.1
13.0	3.7	2.1	3.9	7.6	14.5	All Other Current	4.0	4.3
20.2	9.8	6.4	10.3	13.6	22.3	Total Current	11.7	11.1
19.5	30.6	28.3	23.0	15.1	21.3	Long Term Debt	36.6	21.9
.0	.0	.0	.0	.0	.0	Deferred Taxes	-.4	.0
2.1	1.1	.9	3.5	5.5	8.5	All Other Non-Current	2.1	2.3
58.1	58.5	64.4	63.2	65.7	47.8	Net Worth	49.9	64.7
100.0	100.0	100.0	100.0	100.0	100.0	Total Liabilities & Net Worth	100.0	100.0
						INCOME DATA		
100.0	100.0	100.0	100.0	100.0	100.0	Net Sales	100.0	100.0
						Gross Profit		
92.3	85.3	86.9	88.7	89.2	102.3	Operating Expenses	85.3	86.5
7.7	14.7	13.1	11.3	10.8	-2.3	Operating Profit	14.7	13.5
2.5	6.0	5.6	5.3	7.3	4.7	All Other Expenses (net)	-1.8	-.1
5.2	8.7	7.5	6.0	3.5	-7.0	Profit Before Taxes	16.5	13.6
						RATIOS		
25.4	8.3	9.2	8.3	6.1	5.1		34.1	9.5
4.8	3.0	2.7	2.5	2.2	1.5	Current	3.4	2.7
1.8	1.1	.8	1.0	1.0	.8		1.2	1.0
22.9	7.4	8.5	7.0	5.3	3.6		31.8	8.8
4.6	2.8	2.4	2.1	1.8	1.2	Quick	3.2	(822) 2.3
1.6	.9	.7	.8	.7	.5		1.0	.9
0 UND	0 UND	0 UND	0 UND	2 174.2	2 164.0		0 UND	0 UND
0 UND	0 UND	0 UND	1 UND	15 24.7	26 14.1	Sales/Receivables	0 UND	0 UND
0 UND	0 UND	1 375.5	18 20.5	47 7.8	63 5.8		5 77.3	5 79.6
						Cost of Sales/Inventory		
						Cost of Sales/Payables		
2.5	3.0	3.0	2.2	.9	.9		2.7	2.8
5.9	9.1	9.6	6.1	4.7	4.3	Sales/Working Capital	7.2	7.6
18.8	609.9	-44.6	-152.3	NM	-12.6		53.0	164.4
11.7	3.3	3.9	4.2	5.9	2.6		7.3	8.8
(29) 2.7	(147) 1.6	(359) 1.8	(175) 1.8	(33) 1.5	(29) -1.2	EBIT/Interest	(467) 2.9	(444) 3.5
.0	.7	1.0	-.3	-1.3	-5.1		1.3	1.7
						Net Profit + Depr., Dep., Amort./Cur. Mat. L /T/D		
.0	.9	1.0	.7	.2	.1		.6	.6
.1	1.4	1.3	1.1	.5	.4	Fixed/Worth	1.1	1.0
.9	2.1	1.8	1.6	1.1	.8		1.6	1.5
.1	.2	.2	.2	.3	.3		.1	.2
.3	.7	.5	.5	.6	.9	Debt/Worth	.4	.5
1.4	1.3	1.0	1.0	.9	1.9		1.0	1.0
40.3	14.1	8.2	7.8	5.3	1.7		15.6	14.6
(98) 12.2	(245) 3.5	(603) 2.4	(269) 1.5	(49) .3	(42) -7.1	% Profit Before Taxes/Tangible Net Worth	(899) 6.4	(811) 6.4
.0	-.9	-.2	-1.8	-2.8	-15.8		1.0	1.4
25.4	7.8	4.8	5.0	3.5	1.5		9.7	9.1
8.8	2.0	1.5	.8	.1	-3.2	% Profit Before Taxes/Total Assets	3.8	3.9
-.2	-.6	-.2	-1.1	-2.0	-5.8		.6	.9
UND	.9	.6	1.1	3.4	3.9		1.5	1.3
34.6	.5	.4	.4	1.0	1.2	Sales/Net Fixed Assets	.6	.6
1.4	.3	.2	.3	.6	.7		.3	.3
4.1	.7	.5	.5	.5	.4		.7	.6
1.7	.4	.3	.3	.3	.3	Sales/Total Assets	.4	.4
.8	.3	.2	.2	.2	.2		.2	.2
.7	3.5	3.7	3.6	1.4	1.7		2.6	3.0
(26) 2.7	(98) 7.3	(249) 6.5	(194) 6.0	(41) 4.3	(30) 3.0	% Depr., Dep., Amort./Sales	(380) 4.9	(383) 5.1
9.3	11.5	10.0	9.2	8.0	5.0		7.9	8.2
8.3	9.0	5.9	4.9				5.0	7.0
(27) 17.1	(57) 18.4	(115) 12.6	(29) 9.7			% Officers', Directors', Owners' Comp/Sales	(141) 12.1	(105) 18.2
27.8	30.0	24.3	28.2				23.8	28.4
57787M	165834M	1259399M	2615850M	1547418M	3073940M	Net Sales ($)	4883371M	4588655M
26611M	309115M	3029133M	5768719M	3711379M	6502799M	Total Assets ($)	10519359M	10834302M

M = $ thousand   MM = $ million
See Pages 11 through 18 for Explanation of Ratios and Data

Comparative Historical Data				Current Data Sorted By Sales					

			Type of Statement						
211	197	302	Unqualified	29	59	46	56	64	48
55	51	101	Reviewed	16	44	14	14	10	3
135	186	161	Compiled	85	42	18	11	2	3
5	1	2	Tax Returns	1	1				
445	520	761	Other	369	247	62	38	29	16
4/1/00-3/31/01	4/1/01-3/31/02	4/1/02-3/31/03		418 (4/1-9/30/02)			909 (10/1/02-3/31/03)		
ALL	ALL	ALL		0-1MM	1-3MM	3-5MM	5-10MM	10-25MM	25MM & OVER
851	955	1327	**NUMBER OF STATEMENTS**	500	393	140	119	105	70
%	%	%	**ASSETS**	%	%	%	%	%	%
19.0	17.6	16.7	Cash & Equivalents	17.3	14.4	13.7	17.6	20.2	24.2
2.4	2.4	2.0	Trade Receivables (net)	.9	2.0	1.7	2.3	5.8	5.3
.5	.3	.4	Inventory	.4	.3	.4	.6	.8	.8
3.1	3.9	1.9	All Other Current	.9	1.8	1.8	3.6	3.8	4.4
25.0	24.2	21.1	Total Current	19.5	18.5	17.6	24.0	30.6	34.7
64.0	67.4	70.5	Fixed Assets (net)	76.0	76.8	73.7	65.1	44.5	37.1
.4	.2	.3	Intangibles (net)	.2	.1	.2	.4	.9	1.0
10.6	8.1	8.1	All Other Non-Current	4.3	4.5	8.5	10.5	24.0	27.2
100.0	100.0	100.0	Total	100.0	100.0	100.0	100.0	100.0	100.0
			LIABILITIES						
3.1	2.4	2.4	Notes Payable-Short Term	2.5	1.7	2.0	3.0	4.1	3.1
2.6	2.2	1.8	Cur. Mat.-L/T/D	1.6	1.8	3.1	2.5	.6	1.0
2.0	1.7	1.3	Trade Payables	.7	1.3	1.1	1.4	2.5	3.8
.0	.0	.0	Income Taxes Payable	.0	.0	.0	.0	.0	.0
4.9	4.9	4.2	All Other Current	3.1	3.7	3.5	4.6	8.7	9.3
12.6	11.1	9.7	Total Current	7.9	8.5	9.7	11.6	15.9	17.3
40.1	24.1	26.2	Long Term Debt	27.3	29.9	27.5	21.8	16.6	16.8
.0	.0	.0	Deferred Taxes	.0	.0	.0	.0	.0	.0
3.1	2.8	2.0	All Other Non-Current	.7	1.3	1.1	2.8	7.8	6.7
44.1	62.0	62.1	Net Worth	64.0	60.2	61.7	63.9	59.7	59.2
100.0	100.0	100.0	Total Liabilities & Net Worth	100.0	100.0	100.0	100.0	100.0	100.0
			INCOME DATA						
100.0	100.0	100.0	Net Sales	100.0	100.0	100.0	100.0	100.0	100.0
			Gross Profit						
87.0	87.6	88.0	Operating Expenses	85.8	88.3	85.9	88.8	92.6	97.1
13.0	12.4	12.0	Operating Profit	14.2	11.7	14.1	11.2	7.4	2.9
.3	4.7	5.4	All Other Expenses (net)	6.7	5.3	4.8	3.8	4.8	2.2
12.6	7.6	6.6	Profit Before Taxes	7.6	6.4	9.2	7.3	2.6	.6
			RATIOS						
8.7	10.6	8.9	Current	10.8	9.1	8.2	9.6	6.3	3.6
2.7	2.8	2.7		3.3	3.1	2.4	2.1	2.1	1.8
1.0	1.1	.9		.9	1.1	.9	.9	.9	1.1
7.6	8.4	8.2	Quick	10.0	8.5	7.9	7.3	4.7	3.2
2.3	(954) 2.2	2.4		3.2	2.8	2.1	1.7	1.7	1.6
.8	.8	.8		.8	.9	.6	.5	.6	.7
0 UND	0 UND	0 UND	Sales/Receivables	0 UND	0 UND	0 UND	0 UND	0 UND	2 174.2
0 UND	0 UND	0 UND		0 UND	0 UND	0 UND	1 604.2	11 33.5	16 22.3
7 49.7	7 50.7	4 101.3		0 UND	1 270.2	8 47.4	14 26.9	43 8.6	53 6.9
			Cost of Sales/Inventory						
			Cost of Sales/Payables						
2.3	2.6	2.7	Sales/Working Capital	2.6	2.8	3.1	3.0	1.6	2.9
7.2	6.7	8.0		7.8	8.4	9.1	8.7	4.9	7.6
742.8	107.0	−128.5		−140.7	91.0	−45.0	−35.8	−77.0	79.0
6.7	4.5	3.9	EBIT/Interest	3.6	3.4	4.4	6.2	5.0	3.8
(458) 2.7	(516) 1.9	(772) 1.8		(243) 1.8	(237) 1.6	(93) 2.1	(84) 2.2	(69) 1.2	(46) −.1
1.2	.9	.6		.8	.9	1.0	.0	−1.2	−11.0
			Net Profit + Depr., Dep., Amort./Cur. Mat. L/T/D						
.5	.7	.7	Fixed/Worth	.9	.9	.9	.6	.3	.3
1.0	1.1	1.2		1.2	1.3	1.3	1.2	.7	.5
1.5	1.6	1.7		1.8	1.8	1.7	1.5	1.1	1.0
.2	.2	.2	Debt/Worth	.2	.2	.3	.3	.2	.2
.5	.5	.5		.5	.6	.6	.5	.6	.6
1.1	1.1	1.1		1.1	1.2	1.4	1.0	1.4	.9
15.0	11.1	9.8	% Profit Before Taxes/Tangible Net Worth	9.9	10.4	11.6	11.1	6.2	5.4
(830) 6.0	(933) 2.9	(1306) 2.4		(494) 2.2	(385) 2.9	(139) 5.2	(118) 2.5	(102) .2	(68) −.3
.6	−.5	−.9		−.4	−.4	.0	−1.5	−4.5	−8.4
8.8	6.3	5.7	% Profit Before Taxes/Total Assets	5.8	5.7	6.2	6.3	4.1	3.3
3.2	1.7	1.4		1.4	1.6	3.1	1.7	.1	−.3
.3	−.4	−.6		−.3	−.3	.0	−1.0	−2.9	−5.8
1.5	1.1	1.0	Sales/Net Fixed Assets	.7	.7	.8	1.2	3.1	5.9
.6	.5	.5		.3	.4	.5	.7	1.0	2.5
.3	.3	.3		.2	.3	.4	.4	.5	.9
.6	.6	.6	Sales/Total Assets	.5	.6	.5	.7	.7	1.3
.4	.4	.3		.3	.4	.4	.4	.3	.6
.2	.2	.2		.2	.2	.3	.3	.2	.4
2.3	1.7	3.0	% Depr., Dep., Amort./Sales	3.7	3.7	4.9	3.4	2.2	1.4
(439) 5.1	(447) 5.0	(638) 6.1		(147) 8.9	(170) 6.7	(92) 6.4	(86) 5.3	(89) 4.2	(54) 2.7
8.7	8.4	9.5		14.2	10.0	8.4	8.9	7.0	4.6
6.2	8.0	6.6	% Officers', Directors', Owners' Comp/Sales	8.1	6.6	2.0	4.3		
(132) 13.6	(155) 14.9	(237) 14.7		(126) 16.3	(60) 12.6	(18) 14.8	(17) 7.0		
25.1	27.2	27.9		29.2	25.5	29.2	25.5		
5665033M	6665701M	8720228M	Net Sales ($)	265413M	676784M	541192M	814078M	1665960M	4756801M
13933699M	15367161M	19347756M	Total Assets ($)	1035289M	2142563M	1503317M	2311446M	5782452M	6572689M

© RMA 2003

M = $ thousand   MM = $ million
See Pages 11 through 18 for Explanation of Ratios and Data

Current Data Sorted By Assets							Comparative Historical Data	
						Type of Statement		
3	4	13	8	1	1	Unqualified		
		1				Reviewed		
						Compiled		
1	2	4	5	1	1	Tax Returns		
2						Other		
27 (4/1-9/30/02)			20 (10/1/02-3/31/03)				4/1/98-3/31/99 ALL	4/1/99-3/31/00 ALL
0-500M	500M-2MM	2-10MM	10-50MM	50-100MM	100-250MM			
6	6	18	13	2	2	**NUMBER OF STATEMENTS**		
%	%	%	%	%	%	**ASSETS**	%	%
		13.2	21.0			Cash & Equivalents	D	D
		16.0	19.8			Trade Receivables (net)	A	A
		1.2	1.1			Inventory	T	T
		3.8	8.1			All Other Current	A	A
		34.2	50.0			Total Current		
		56.7	29.0			Fixed Assets (net)	N	N
		.2	.3			Intangibles (net)	O	O
		8.9	20.7			All Other Non-Current	T	T
		100.0	100.0			Total		
						LIABILITIES	A	A
		.8	4.5			Notes Payable-Short Term	V	V
		2.9	.5			Cur. Mat.-L/T/D	A	A
		4.4	5.4			Trade Payables	I	I
		.1	.0			Income Taxes Payable	L	L
		9.0	15.9			All Other Current	A	A
		17.2	26.2			Total Current	B	B
		21.3	7.4			Long Term Debt	L	L
		.0	.0			Deferred Taxes	E	E
		1.2	5.5			All Other Non-Current		
		60.3	60.8			Net Worth		
		100.0	100.0			Total Liabilities & Net Worth		
						INCOME DATA		
		100.0	100.0			Net Sales		
						Gross Profit		
		95.9	93.4			Operating Expenses		
		4.1	6.6			Operating Profit		
		1.3	3.2			All Other Expenses (net)		
		2.9	3.4			Profit Before Taxes		
						RATIOS		
		5.4	3.5					
		2.0	1.6			Current		
		1.2	1.2					
		3.0	3.1					
		1.8	1.4			Quick		
		1.1	1.1					
		16 22.6	3 130.2					
		35 10.5	32 11.6			Sales/Receivables		
		44 8.2	73 5.0					
						Cost of Sales/Inventory		
						Cost of Sales/Payables		
		3.4	3.8					
		12.8	6.0			Sales/Working Capital		
		NM	28.6					
		9.8						
	(16)	1.5				EBIT/Interest		
		-.7						
						Net Profit + Depr., Dep., Amort./Cur. Mat. L /T/D		
		.5	.1					
		1.0	.4			Fixed/Worth		
		1.5	.7					
		.3	.3					
		.6	.6			Debt/Worth		
		1.2	1.2					
		23.9	8.1					
		5.2	4.2			% Profit Before Taxes/Tangible Net Worth		
		-3.5	-4.0					
		12.9	4.7					
		2.6	3.5			% Profit Before Taxes/Total Assets		
		-2.2	-3.0					
		4.7	45.7					
		2.7	4.8			Sales/Net Fixed Assets		
		1.1	2.5					
		2.2	2.3					
		1.2	1.0			Sales/Total Assets		
		.8	.6					
		1.4						
	(17)	3.1				% Depr., Dep., Amort./Sales		
		4.4						
						% Officers', Directors', Owners' Comp/Sales		
6062M	10508M	123841M	272325M	113104M	422058M	Net Sales ($)		
1292M	6189M	69636M	241802M	150552M	254062M	Total Assets ($)		

© RMA 2003

M = $ thousand   MM = $ million
See Pages 11 through 18 for Explanation of Ratios and Data

Comparative Historical Data | **Current Data Sorted By Sales**

4/1/00-3/31/01 ALL	4/1/01-3/31/02 ALL	4/1/02-3/31/03 ALL	Type of Statement	0-1MM	1-3MM	3-5MM	5-10MM	10-25MM	25MM & OVER
		30	Unqualified	3	12	1	4	5	5
			Reviewed					1	
		1	Compiled						
		1	Tax Returns	1					
		15	Other		4	2	1	5	3
					27 (4/1-9/30/02)		20 (10/1/02-3/31/03)		
		47	NUMBER OF STATEMENTS	4	16	3	5	11	8
%	%	%	**ASSETS**	%	%	%	%	%	%
D	D	19.8	Cash & Equivalents		20.7			18.5	
A	A	20.0	Trade Receivables (net)		16.2			17.7	
T	T	1.0	Inventory		1.5			1.7	
A	A	4.6	All Other Current		4.4			8.5	
		45.4	Total Current		42.9			46.4	
N	N	38.9	Fixed Assets (net)		41.6			38.2	
O	O	1.0	Intangibles (net)		.0			.3	
T	T	14.6	All Other Non-Current		15.4			15.2	
		100.0	Total		100.0			100.0	
A	A		**LIABILITIES**						
V	V	3.6	Notes Payable-Short Term		2.1			.0	
A	A	1.7	Cur. Mat.-L/T/D		2.5			1.1	
I	I	7.0	Trade Payables		8.4			6.2	
L	L	.0	Income Taxes Payable		.0			.2	
A	A	14.5	All Other Current		16.2			18.0	
B	B	26.9	Total Current		29.2			25.6	
L	L	16.0	Long Term Debt		12.4			16.4	
E	E	.0	Deferred Taxes		.0			.0	
		3.4	All Other Non-Current		.9			5.8	
		53.7	Net Worth		57.5			52.3	
		100.0	Total Liabilities & Net Worth		100.0			100.0	
			INCOME DATA						
		100.0	Net Sales		100.0			100.0	
			Gross Profit						
		93.3	Operating Expenses		92.7			96.7	
		6.7	Operating Profit		7.3			3.3	
		2.3	All Other Expenses (net)		2.3			3.2	
		4.4	Profit Before Taxes		5.1			.1	
			RATIOS						
		3.1	Current		3.2			2.7	
		1.7			1.7			2.0	
		1.1			1.0			1.5	
		2.5	Quick		2.4			2.4	
		1.4			1.3			1.7	
		.9			.9			1.0	
	8	44.5	Sales/Receivables		13	28.6		4	103.3
	32	11.6			30	12.3		25	14.5
	47	7.8			44	8.3		46	7.9
			Cost of Sales/Inventory						
			Cost of Sales/Payables						
		4.1	Sales/Working Capital		3.2			6.0	
		11.7			16.5			10.2	
		55.8			-250.8			15.0	
		6.7	EBIT/Interest		10.8				
	(30)	1.2			(12)	2.6			
		-.9			-.7				
			Net Profit + Depr., Dep., Amort./Cur. Mat. L/T/D						
		.2	Fixed/Worth		.2			.3	
		.6			.7			.6	
		1.4			1.3			1.6	
		.3	Debt/Worth		.3			.4	
		.6			.6			.6	
		1.4			1.2			1.4	
		16.5	% Profit Before Taxes/Tangible Net Worth		14.9			30.9	
	(43)	4.9			2.9			7.5	
		-5.1			-16.4			-1.4	
		5.5	% Profit Before Taxes/Total Assets		5.9			13.9	
		1.3			2.0			3.8	
		-3.2			-4.2			-.8	
		38.6	Sales/Net Fixed Assets		49.1			10.1	
		4.5			2.1			4.9	
		1.6			1.0			2.7	
		2.4	Sales/Total Assets		2.6			3.4	
		1.3			.9			1.6	
		.8			.7			1.0	
		.9	% Depr., Dep., Amort./Sales		.8				
	(38)	2.3			(14)	2.0			
		4.3			4.5				
			% Officers', Directors', Owners' Comp/Sales						
		947898M	Net Sales ($)	1041M	32385M	12317M	33558M	173796M	694801M
		723533M	Total Assets ($)	1168M	59358M	21456M	26616M	130954M	483981M

© RMA 2003

M = $ thousand   MM = $ million
See Pages 11 through 18 for Explanation of Ratios and Data

Current Data Sorted By Assets | Comparative Historical Data

0-500M	500M-2MM	2-10MM	10-50MM	50-100MM	100-250MM	Type of Statement	4/1/98-3/31/99 ALL	4/1/99-3/31/00 ALL
13	36	120	77	17	7	Unqualified	216	232
1	4	4	2			Reviewed	7	2
4	5	2	2			Compiled	13	10
2	4	2			1	Tax Returns	2	5
10	25	33	15	3	3	Other	59	72
272 (4/1-9/30/02)			120 (10/1/02-3/31/03)					
30	74	161	96	20	11	NUMBER OF STATEMENTS	297	321
%	%	%	%	%	%	ASSETS	%	%
29.2	18.9	17.7	17.7	26.0	25.0	Cash & Equivalents	21.4	21.6
18.5	23.8	19.8	15.4	11.5	16.3	Trade Receivables (net)	15.7	16.5
.6	1.4	1.7	1.2	.0	.6	Inventory	1.8	1.6
2.7	6.4	5.4	4.4	6.4	5.1	All Other Current	4.0	4.6
51.1	50.5	44.6	38.8	43.8	46.9	Total Current	42.9	44.3
31.4	40.0	42.0	41.3	36.7	24.2	Fixed Assets (net)	40.2	39.2
1.8	1.4	.6	.7	2.0	.9	Intangibles (net)	1.7	.7
15.9	8.1	12.7	19.2	17.5	28.1	All Other Non-Current	15.2	15.8
100.0	100.0	100.0	100.0	100.0	100.0	Total	100.0	100.0
						LIABILITIES		
14.3	3.5	3.3	2.8	.7	5.0	Notes Payable-Short Term	3.3	3.1
3.4	2.3	1.5	1.4	.8	.5	Cur. Mat.-L/T/D	2.4	1.4
12.9	8.7	7.3	5.4	4.7	6.2	Trade Payables	7.8	6.5
.1	.2	.2	.0	.0	.0	Income Taxes Payable	.1	.0
17.4	12.5	11.3	9.9	12.4	8.0	All Other Current	14.4	10.0
48.1	27.2	23.7	19.6	18.6	19.7	Total Current	28.0	21.1
27.4	15.8	19.8	19.1	20.8	14.3	Long Term Debt	18.7	20.2
.0	.0	.0	.0	.0	.2	Deferred Taxes	.0	.2
5.7	3.7	2.6	3.7	4.0	9.0	All Other Non-Current	3.7	3.6
18.8	53.4	53.9	57.6	56.6	56.8	Net Worth	49.7	54.9
100.0	100.0	100.0	100.0	100.0	100.0	Total Liabilities & Net Worth	100.0	100.0
						INCOME DATA		
100.0	100.0	100.0	100.0	100.0	100.0	Net Sales	100.0	100.0
						Gross Profit		
95.5	96.1	95.4	95.0	99.0	101.5	Operating Expenses	101.6	92.3
4.5	3.9	4.6	5.0	1.0	-1.5	Operating Profit	-1.6	7.7
1.2	.2	2.0	2.6	2.9	9.6	All Other Expenses (net)	-8.3	-1.6
3.3	3.7	2.5	2.4	-1.8	-11.2	Profit Before Taxes	6.7	9.3
						RATIOS		
4.9	4.1	4.2	4.3	5.0	4.4	Current	4.2	5.0
1.1	2.4	2.1	2.3	2.5	2.2		1.9	2.3
.4	1.2	1.3	1.1	1.5	1.2		1.1	1.2
4.9	3.6	3.3	3.8	4.5	3.6	Quick	3.7	4.5
1.1	1.9	1.7	1.7	1.7	2.1		1.6	1.7
.4	.8	1.0	1.0	1.3	1.0		.9	1.0
0 UND	5 75.4	11 33.0	11 34.2	28 12.9	33 11.1	Sales/Receivables	6 57.2	7 51.4
10 37.8	30 12.0	36 10.2	38 9.7	47 7.7	56 6.5		31 11.9	35 10.6
30 12.2	59 6.2	55 6.6	59 6.1	82 4.4	80 4.6		49 7.5	59 6.2
						Cost of Sales/Inventory		
						Cost of Sales/Payables		
8.3	5.0	3.7	2.9	1.6	.3	Sales/Working Capital	4.0	2.8
UND	10.1	8.2	6.4	5.6	8.8		9.8	6.7
-14.5	41.9	25.9	30.7	10.9	23.3		71.4	28.1
(15) 3.6	(41) 6.5	(112) 8.1	(59) 6.4	(13) 4.3		EBIT/Interest	(176) 11.4	(174) 11.5
-.2	2.9	2.6	1.5	.5			3.8	3.6
-5.1	-.9	-1.2	-3.2	-.8			1.0	.9
						Net Profit + Depr., Dep., Amort./Cur. Mat. L /T/D		
.1	.2	.3	.3	.3	.1	Fixed/Worth	.3	.2
1.0	.8	.8	.7	.6	.3		.7	.7
UND	1.5	1.2	1.1	1.8	1.2		1.3	1.5
.8	.3	.4	.2	.2	.4	Debt/Worth	.3	.3
2.0	.8	.7	.8	.8	.6		.7	.7
UND	2.0	1.9	1.6	2.3	1.5		2.0	1.8
(24) 90.7	(71) 27.1	(158) 15.6	(95) 10.1	(19) 7.0	(10) 2.0	% Profit Before Taxes/Tangible Net Worth	(283) 21.8	(305) 20.2
17.5	13.3	5.3	2.3	-.7	-3.1		9.2	8.4
-29.6	-4.6	-6.9	-3.6	-9.6	-10.6		.9	1.6
26.4	13.3	6.9	4.8	2.8	6.6	% Profit Before Taxes/Total Assets	10.7	10.5
.9	5.7	2.2	.7	-.4	-1.1		4.5	4.2
-19.9	-3.1	-2.9	-2.3	-2.7	-4.0		.1	.1
42.9	32.4	17.0	6.2	4.2	10.9	Sales/Net Fixed Assets	13.3	14.7
23.8	5.6	3.6	2.6	2.4	2.5		3.7	3.4
7.5	2.5	1.5	1.2	1.2	1.2		1.6	1.3
5.3	3.2	2.4	1.7	1.1	2.2	Sales/Total Assets	2.5	2.1
4.2	2.0	1.4	.9	.6	.3		1.3	1.1
2.9	1.1	.7	.5	.5	.2		.6	.5
(20) .8	(63) .8	(152) 1.1	(82) 1.7	(19) 1.5		% Depr., Dep., Amort./Sales	(253) 1.2	(265) 1.1
1.4	2.1	2.6	3.0	3.4			2.5	2.5
2.2	3.1	4.5	5.0	4.6			4.4	5.0
		(17) 1.7				% Officers', Directors', Owners' Comp/Sales	4.3	(19) 3.9
		6.7					(22) 9.3	7.0
		13.8					26.7	16.1
32594M	205239M	1371027M	2408250M	1113718M	2062203M	Net Sales ($)	3982470M	4247977M
8016M	89931M	787979M	1902003M	1489814M	1903286M	Total Assets ($)	2917699M	3805265M

M = $ thousand   MM = $ million
See Pages 11 through 18 for Explanation of Ratios and Data

Comparative Historical Data | Current Data Sorted By Sales

				Type of Statement						
	244	214	270	Unqualified	22	41	34	65	60	48
	4	6	11	Reviewed	3	1	2	3		2
	34	51	13	Compiled	4	6		1	1	1
	3	5	9	Tax Returns	3	3	1	1	1	1
	76	102	89	Other	11	24	13	17	13	11
	4/1/00-3/31/01	4/1/01-3/31/02	4/1/02-3/31/03		272 (4/1-9/30/02)			120 (10/1/02-3/31/03)		
	ALL	ALL	ALL		0-1MM	1-3MM	3-5MM	5-10MM	10-25MM	25MM & OVER
	361	378	392	NUMBER OF STATEMENTS	43	75	50	87	74	63
	%	%	%	ASSETS	%	%	%	%	%	%
	20.0	18.3	19.5	Cash & Equivalents	19.6	18.9	21.2	16.3	22.4	19.6
	18.3	18.6	18.9	Trade Receivables (net)	8.1	16.2	16.5	23.7	22.6	20.1
	1.4	1.4	1.3	Inventory	.5	1.5	.1	1.8	.9	2.5
	5.3	6.5	5.2	All Other Current	6.2	4.7	7.1	3.3	5.1	6.2
	44.9	44.8	44.8	Total Current	34.4	41.3	45.0	45.2	51.0	48.4
	40.7	39.7	39.9	Fixed Assets (net)	49.2	41.8	42.6	39.9	36.7	32.7
	.8	.9	1.0	Intangibles (net)	.3	1.5	.6	1.3	.4	1.4
	13.5	14.6	14.4	All Other Non-Current	16.3	15.4	11.9	13.7	12.0	17.5
	100.0	100.0	100.0	Total	100.0	100.0	100.0	100.0	100.0	100.0
				LIABILITIES						
	4.4	3.8	4.0	Notes Payable-Short Term	9.5	2.9	2.3	3.7	3.3	4.0
	1.6	2.0	1.7	Cur. Mat.-L/T/D	2.0	2.4	2.2	1.9	1.2	.9
	7.1	7.3	7.4	Trade Payables	7.6	5.9	4.1	8.5	8.6	8.3
	.0	.1	.1	Income Taxes Payable	.0	.2	.0	.4	.0	.0
	11.4	11.1	11.6	All Other Current	10.8	9.7	10.8	11.4	15.2	11.5
	24.5	24.3	24.8	Total Current	29.8	21.0	19.4	25.9	28.3	24.7
	18.7	18.2	19.3	Long Term Debt	29.8	18.6	25.8	15.1	15.5	18.4
	.1	.0	.0	Deferred Taxes	.0	.0	.0	.0	.0	.0
	2.8	3.3	3.6	All Other Non-Current	5.3	2.0	2.2	2.7	4.5	5.4
	53.9	54.0	52.3	Net Worth	35.1	58.4	52.6	56.3	51.7	51.5
	100.0	100.0	100.0	Total Liabilities & Net Worth	100.0	100.0	100.0	100.0	100.0	100.0
				INCOME DATA						
	100.0	100.0	100.0	Net Sales	100.0	100.0	100.0	100.0	100.0	100.0
				Gross Profit						
	94.6	95.0	95.8	Operating Expenses	90.8	94.2	92.9	95.7	98.9	99.9
	5.4	5.0	4.2	Operating Profit	9.2	5.8	7.1	4.3	1.1	.1
	-2.3	1.8	2.0	All Other Expenses (net)	4.5	3.7	.9	.6	1.2	2.1
	7.7	3.2	2.2	Profit Before Taxes	4.7	2.1	6.2	3.7	-.2	-2.0
				RATIOS						
	4.9	3.9	4.3		5.4	5.6	5.5	3.7	4.0	3.8
	2.1	2.0	2.2	Current	1.7	2.4	3.4	2.0	1.8	1.9
	1.2	1.1	1.2		.7	1.0	1.4	1.1	1.3	1.4
	4.2	3.3	3.6		4.7	4.7	5.1	3.3	3.3	2.8
	1.7	1.6	1.7	Quick	1.3	2.1	2.7	1.7	1.6	1.7
	1.0	.9	1.0		.5	.8	1.2	.9	1.2	1.1
	9 38.6	6 61.7	9 41.0		0 UND	1 256.0	6 61.7	21 17.3	17 21.1	22 16.5
	35 10.6	32 11.6	32 11.2	Sales/Receivables	8 47.5	28 13.1	29 12.8	42 8.8	40 9.0	35 10.3
	55 6.6	52 7.0	56 6.5		32 11.5	50 7.3	68 5.3	64 5.7	57 6.3	56 6.5
				Cost of Sales/Inventory						
				Cost of Sales/Payables						
	3.2	4.1	3.7		3.3	2.9	2.6	3.8	4.4	4.5
	7.7	9.1	8.6	Sales/Working Capital	9.1	7.3	5.4	8.4	10.3	10.2
	36.2	42.3	34.5		-11.9	-700.7	15.1	49.8	27.8	24.5
	(221) 8.2	(228) 6.0	(249) 6.6		(18) 7.8	(43) 4.0	(33) 7.0	(60) 10.7	(53) 6.4	(42) 4.8
	3.0	2.0	2.2	EBIT/Interest	3.3	.6	3.6	2.8	2.1	1.2
	.8	.0	-1.8		-.5	-2.9	1.0	-2.9	-6.0	-1.6
				Net Profit + Depr., Dep., Amort./Cur. Mat. L/T/D						
	.3	.3	.3		.3	.2	.2	.4	.3	.3
	.7	.7	.7	Fixed/Worth	1.3	.7	.8	.7	.7	.5
	1.5	1.5	1.4		2.9	1.5	1.3	1.2	1.1	1.7
	.3	.3	.3		.5	.2	.4	.2	.5	.3
	.8	.7	.8	Debt/Worth	1.7	.7	.7	.7	.8	.9
	1.7	1.9	2.0		4.8	1.6	1.6	1.9	1.8	2.6
	(344) 16.6	(363) 15.9	(377) 16.5	% Profit Before Taxes/Tangible	(38) 28.4	(73) 21.7	(48) 22.3	(85) 16.5	(73) 11.9	(60) 8.1
	8.0	4.1	4.7	Net Worth	13.1	3.6	11.3	4.8	2.3	.8
	.0	-3.3	-6.4		-6.2	-9.3	2.7	-6.5	-8.1	-7.2
	9.3	7.0	7.8	% Profit Before Taxes/Total	10.4	9.0	14.0	8.0	6.7	3.4
	4.3	1.5	2.1	Assets	2.6	2.1	5.4	2.2	1.4	.2
	.0	-1.7	-3.4		-3.0	-4.8	1.8	-4.0	-3.7	-2.9
	14.4	17.8	16.2		23.9	15.8	20.8	11.5	18.8	13.4
	3.4	4.4	3.8	Sales/Net Fixed Assets	2.1	3.5	3.7	4.0	3.7	4.4
	1.4	1.5	1.6		.4	1.2	1.3	1.5	2.4	1.9
	2.4	2.6	2.6		3.0	2.7	2.8	2.4	2.8	2.2
	1.2	1.4	1.4	Sales/Total Assets	.6	1.4	1.4	1.4	1.8	1.3
	.6	.6	.7		.2	.4	.7	.7	1.2	.7
	(298) 1.0	(311) .9	(343) 1.1		(32) 1.6	(68) 1.5	(45) 1.4	(76) 1.2	(69) .9	(53) .8
	2.2	2.3	2.4	% Depr., Dep., Amort./Sales	3.9	2.5	2.2	2.8	1.8	1.8
	4.2	4.4	4.3		7.4	6.0	4.3	4.3	3.5	3.7
	(21) 1.7	(45) 1.8	(35) 1.8	% Officers', Directors',						
	9.3	9.4	9.2	Owners' Comp/Sales						
	34.6	21.5	14.6							
	5212878M	7285091M	7193031M	Net Sales ($)	26004M	135107M	200116M	631823M	1209334M	4990647M
	4788233M	5254868M	6181029M	Total Assets ($)	72370M	218980M	272492M	616676M	1119681M	3880830M

M = $ thousand   MM = $ million
See Pages 11 through 18 for Explanation of Ratios and Data

Current Data Sorted By Assets | **Comparative Historical Data**

							Type of Statement			
	14	18	75	49	9	7	Unqualified		169	154
	4	5	2				Reviewed		15	10
	3	10	3	1			Compiled		22	20
	12	9	1				Tax Returns		7	11
	19	18	31	24	4	2	Other		73	68
		143 (4/1-9/30/02)			177 (10/1/02-3/31/03)				4/1/98-3/31/99	4/1/99-3/31/00
	0-500M	500M-2MM	2-10MM	10-50MM	50-100MM	100-250MM			ALL	ALL
	52	60	112	74	13	9	NUMBER OF STATEMENTS		286	263
	%	%	%	%	%	%	ASSETS		%	%
	40.2	18.6	21.4	20.0	16.0		Cash & Equivalents		24.2	21.8
	7.5	7.6	6.6	5.1	4.9		Trade Receivables (net)		6.0	7.1
	1.2	1.5	1.3	1.3	.2		Inventory		1.6	1.7
	2.5	3.4	3.1	3.7	3.6		All Other Current		3.7	3.6
	51.4	31.1	32.4	30.0	24.8		Total Current		35.6	34.1
	42.3	57.7	54.7	54.0	52.4		Fixed Assets (net)		47.5	48.9
	.1	.8	.5	.6	.2		Intangibles (net)		.9	.9
	6.0	10.4	12.4	15.4	22.5		All Other Non-Current		16.0	16.0
	100.0	100.0	100.0	100.0	100.0		Total		100.0	100.0
							LIABILITIES			
	8.7	3.5	2.0	1.1	.5		Notes Payable-Short Term		3.5	3.6
	7.2	2.7	1.0	1.6	.4		Cur. Mat.-L/T/D		1.8	1.3
	20.2	4.9	3.8	2.6	2.3		Trade Payables		4.4	4.8
	.5	.0	.0	.0	.0		Income Taxes Payable		.0	.1
	8.6	6.6	7.0	8.2	3.3		All Other Current		7.6	7.2
	45.1	17.7	14.0	13.6	6.5		Total Current		17.3	16.9
	45.9	18.0	18.6	14.9	25.3		Long Term Debt		20.7	16.7
	.0	.0	.1	.0	.0		Deferred Taxes		.0	.0
	10.6	3.9	3.5	2.5	3.4		All Other Non-Current		4.7	8.0
	−1.7	60.3	63.8	69.0	64.8		Net Worth		57.4	58.3
	100.0	100.0	100.0	100.0	100.0		Total Liabilities & Net Worth		100.0	100.0
							INCOME DATA			
	100.0	100.0	100.0	100.0	100.0		Net Sales		100.0	100.0
							Gross Profit			
	92.2	91.7	96.6	93.8	102.8		Operating Expenses		95.0	92.6
	7.8	8.3	3.3	6.2	−2.8		Operating Profit		5.0	7.4
	3.5	1.7	1.7	3.1	2.9		All Other Expenses (net)		−4.6	−2.0
	4.2	6.6	1.7	3.1	−5.6		Profit Before Taxes		9.7	9.3
							RATIOS			
	4.2	5.0	5.0	5.7	10.6				6.5	5.7
	1.9	1.9	2.6	2.2	3.6		Current		2.1	2.1
	.5	1.1	1.1	1.1	1.6				1.0	1.0
	4.2	4.0	4.4	4.1	9.0				5.5	4.7
	1.4	1.6	2.2	1.4	3.3		Quick		1.8	1.6
	.5	1.0	.8	.7	1.0				.7	.8

0	UND	0	UND	1	296.2	2	187.4	8	44.3			Sales/Receivables	1	330.5	1	401.0

0	UND	5	79.9	15	25.0	10	35.7	22	16.4		Sales/Receivables	9	39.2	12	31.5
9	42.8	29	12.6	44	8.2	33	11.1	55	6.6			40	9.2	39	9.3

							Cost of Sales/Inventory			

							Cost of Sales/Payables			

	4.2	3.9	2.8	2.2	1.5		Sales/Working Capital		1.8	2.4
	10.0	8.4	5.8	4.8	3.0				6.3	6.8
	−11.9	60.2	28.9	32.9	21.9				−159.7	208.2

	4.1		7.4		9.4		4.1		4.4		EBIT/Interest		
(30)	1.7	(36)	1.9	(74)	1.8	(44)	1.7	(10)	−2.1		(169) 2.2	(160) 3.4
	−.4		.7		−1.5		−1.5		−9.6		7.9 / .7	9.1 / .9

							Net Profit + Depr., Dep., Amort./Cur. Mat. L /T/D			

	.0	.5	.4	.4	.4		Fixed/Worth		.2	.2
	1.1	.9	.9	.8	.9				.8	.8
	7.3	1.5	1.4	1.4	1.3				1.5	1.4
	.5	.2	.2	.1	.2		Debt/Worth		.2	.2
	1.6	.6	.4	.3	.5				.5	.4
	NM	1.4	1.0	.9	1.0				1.4	1.2

	34.8		21.5		8.6		6.2		5.1		% Profit Before Taxes/Tangible Net Worth	14.6	15.2
(39)	7.1	(58)	5.2	(109)	2.2		.6		−1.1		(271) 5.6	(250) 6.3
	−1.8		−2.0		−4.8		−4.2		−5.2		.1	.0

	19.9	10.0	5.4	3.2	2.4		% Profit Before Taxes/Total Assets		10.1	9.3
	4.2	2.7	1.0	.5	−1.0				3.2	3.7
	−2.5	−1.1	−4.2	−2.5	−2.9				.0	−.1
	UND	7.1	2.9	2.6	1.1		Sales/Net Fixed Assets		7.4	5.8
	8.9	1.6	1.1	.9	.9				1.3	1.4
	1.2	.5	.8	.5	.7				.8	.8
	3.9	1.6	1.0	.8	.6		Sales/Total Assets		1.1	1.2
	1.8	1.0	.6	.5	.5				.7	.7
	.9	.4	.5	.3	.3				.4	.4

	2.0		1.8		2.6		2.7		4.2		% Depr., Dep., Amort./Sales	3.1	2.6
(22)	3.3	(45)	3.9	(97)	5.0	(64)	6.3	(11)	5.8		(212) 5.2	(208) 4.9
	6.9		8.8		7.7		7.8		8.0		8.3	8.1

							% Officers', Directors', Owners' Comp/Sales		4.2	5.6
								(24)	11.6	(26) 15.4
									25.3	27.2

	20241M	98964M	487332M	876405M	409063M	1471157M	Net Sales ($)		1900681M	1741473M
	10393M	65624M	590846M	1425831M	915379M	1258241M	Total Assets ($)		3742942M	2992542M

M = $ thousand　　MM = $ million
See Pages 11 through 18 for Explanation of Ratios and Data

Comparative Historical Data | Current Data Sorted By Sales

						Type of Statement						
	146		117		172	Unqualified	17	47	36	31	21	20
	4		10		11	Reviewed	7	4				
	37		44		17	Compiled	12	4		1		
	15		15		22	Tax Returns	18	2	1		1	
	67		93		98	Other	28	23	13	20	7	7
	4/1/00-3/31/01		4/1/01-3/31/02		4/1/02-3/31/03		143 (4/1-9/30/02)			177 (10/1/02-3/31/03)		
	ALL		ALL		ALL		0-1MM	1-3MM	3-5MM	5-10MM	10-25MM	25MM & OVER
	269		279		320	NUMBER OF STATEMENTS	82	80	50	52	29	27
	%		%		%	ASSETS	%	%	%	%	%	%
	21.9		22.8		23.3	Cash & Equivalents	31.4	17.4	25.1	19.0	23.9	20.9
	6.3		6.6		6.5	Trade Receivables (net)	3.6	6.9	6.8	8.2	8.6	8.4
	1.7		1.5		1.3	Inventory	1.1	1.4	1.0	1.4	.8	2.3
	4.1		4.2		3.4	All Other Current	3.1	2.7	1.9	4.6	5.3	4.8
	34.0		35.3		34.5	Total Current	39.1	28.4	34.7	33.2	38.6	36.5
	48.8		51.0		52.4	Fixed Assets (net)	54.5	54.5	52.5	54.9	42.0	45.8
	.8		.8		.6	Intangibles (net)	.1	1.2	.6	.1	.5	1.2
	16.3		12.9		12.5	All Other Non-Current	6.1	15.9	12.2	11.8	18.8	16.5
	100.0		100.0		100.0	Total	100.0	100.0	100.0	100.0	100.0	100.0
						LIABILITIES						
	2.7		2.8		3.4	Notes Payable-Short Term	4.4	4.9	1.1	1.3	3.2	4.7
	2.7		2.1		2.5	Cur. Mat.-L/T/D	4.9	2.3	1.0	1.6	1.5	1.1
	3.8		3.9		6.4	Trade Payables	11.2	5.6	3.7	5.1	4.3	3.8
	.0		.1		.1	Income Taxes Payable	.3	.0	.1	.0	.0	.1
	6.3		6.4		7.6	All Other Current	4.5	7.7	7.9	9.0	12.4	8.6
	15.6		15.4		20.0	Total Current	25.3	20.5	13.8	17.1	21.4	18.2
	16.0		17.5		22.1	Long Term Debt	37.6	18.0	16.9	16.4	14.2	16.0
	.0		.0		.0	Deferred Taxes	.0	.0	.2	.0	.0	.1
	2.8		2.9		4.5	All Other Non-Current	7.0	3.7	4.0	2.9	2.9	4.9
	65.6		64.3		53.4	Net Worth	30.1	57.9	65.1	63.5	61.5	60.9
	100.0		100.0		100.0	Total Liabilities & Net Worth	100.0	100.0	100.0	100.0	100.0	100.0
						INCOME DATA						
	100.0		100.0		100.0	Net Sales	100.0	100.0	100.0	100.0	100.0	100.0
						Gross Profit						
	96.0		94.1		94.9	Operating Expenses	89.2	97.9	94.6	93.8	100.9	99.2
	4.0		5.9		5.1	Operating Profit	10.8	2.1	5.4	6.1	-.9	.8
	-3.5		3.3		2.3	All Other Expenses (net)	3.8	1.0	2.9	2.0	1.2	2.0
	7.5		2.6		2.8	Profit Before Taxes	7.0	1.0	2.5	4.1	-2.1	-1.2
						RATIOS						
	5.8		6.7		5.0		6.0	5.4	5.5	4.1	4.6	6.2
	2.4		2.6		2.2	Current	2.5	1.9	2.8	2.2	1.9	1.9
	1.1		1.2		1.0		1.0	.9	1.2	1.2	.8	.9
	4.3		5.6		4.3		5.4	3.9	5.4	2.7	4.6	3.5
	1.8		2.1		1.7	Quick	1.7	1.5	2.2	1.5	1.4	1.6
	.8		.9		.7		.7	.6	.8	1.0	.6	.6
2	238.9	0	UND	0	UND		0 UND	0 917.9	3 122.2	3 138.8	5 79.7	8 47.5
13	28.4	10	37.1	9	42.4	Sales/Receivables	0 UND	11 33.5	21 17.6	20 18.7	12 30.1	17 20.9
36	10.2	35	10.5	34	10.8		6 62.6	36 10.0	48 7.7	36 10.1	41 9.0	39 9.3
						Cost of Sales/Inventory						
						Cost of Sales/Payables						
	2.0		2.2		2.8		2.1	4.1	1.9	2.8	3.2	3.0
	5.8		5.8		7.0	Sales/Working Capital	7.1	9.3	4.0	6.9	6.1	11.4
	78.6		31.7		160.7		UND	-39.5	46.9	30.1	-42.4	-42.7
	9.5		6.3		5.2		3.8	8.5	5.3	9.7	4.1	5.3
(175)	2.1	(160)	2.0	(199)	1.7	EBIT/Interest	(48) 1.9	(55) 1.4	(25) 1.9	(35) 1.7	(19) 1.5	(17) 1.0
	.4		-.9		-1.5		.8	-3.1	.8	-4.5	-10.3	-7.2
					11.0	Net Profit + Depr., Dep.,						
				(13)	3.5	Amort./Cur. Mat. L/T/D						
					.6							
	.3		.3		.4		.2	.4	.3	.5	.3	.4
	.8		.8		.9	Fixed/Worth	1.0	.9	.9	.9	.6	.8
	1.3		1.4		1.5		1.9	1.7	1.4	1.4	1.3	1.3
	.1		.1		.2		.3	.1	.2	.2	.2	.2
	.4		.4		.5	Debt/Worth	.6	.5	.4	.5	.8	.5
	1.0		1.2		1.4		2.4	1.6	1.1	1.0	1.2	1.3
	11.3		10.2		9.4		11.9	13.9	6.0	10.9	5.2	6.1
(266)	3.2	(270)	2.7	(301)	2.2	% Profit Before Taxes/Tangible Net Worth	(70) 3.8	(75) 4.7	1.8	(51) 5.4	.5	(26) .4
	-2.5		-3.8		-3.7		-1.5	-5.9	-2.4	-5.1	-7.5	-3.4
	8.4		6.1		6.0		9.1	7.1	3.3	8.6	2.6	3.6
	1.9		1.6		1.4	% Profit Before Taxes/Total Assets	2.0	2.0	.8	2.2	.3	.1
	-1.4		-2.8		-2.7		-1.5	-4.6	-1.3	-4.5	-4.2	-3.6
	4.5		4.1		5.7		18.7	3.6	2.7	3.1	9.2	5.7
	1.5		1.4		1.3	Sales/Net Fixed Assets	1.3	1.2	1.1	1.1	1.9	1.9
	.7		.7		.7		.5	.7	.6	.7	.9	.9
	1.1		1.2		1.3		1.9	1.3	.9	1.3	1.5	1.8
	.6		.7		.7	Sales/Total Assets	.7	.7	.6	.6	.9	.8
	.4		.4		.4		.3	.5	.4	.4	.5	.6
	2.0		1.7		2.5		3.3	2.1	3.1	2.1	1.8	2.9
(217)	4.8	(215)	4.6	(246)	4.8	% Depr., Dep., Amort./Sales	(42) 5.3	(69) 4.8	(40) 5.7	(49) 4.4	(24) 3.9	(22) 4.6
	7.1		7.7		7.8		13.9	9.2	8.4	7.2	7.2	6.6
	5.1		2.4		3.7	% Officers', Directors',						
(30)	9.2	(40)	5.3	(31)	10.2	Owners' Comp/Sales						
	19.1		20.1		21.4							
	2548849M		2244130M		3363162M	Net Sales ($)	30463M	155998M	192431M	362312M	454386M	2167572M
	4119979M		3470403M		4266314M	Total Assets ($)	84122M	357876M	462444M	653190M	716393M	1992289M

© RMA 2003

M = $ thousand   MM = $ million
See Pages 11 through 18 for Explanation of Ratios and Data

OTHER SERVICES—Business Associations NAICS 813910 (SIC 8611, 8699)

Current Data Sorted By Assets | **Comparative Historical Data**

						Type of Statement		
4	24	33	31	4	4	Unqualified	107	115
5	4	2				Reviewed	6	11
	6	2	1		1	Compiled	7	8
2	1	3				Tax Returns	3	3
9	8	13	11	2		Other	41	43
	76 (4/1-9/30/02)			94 (10/1/02-3/31/03)			4/1/98-3/31/99	4/1/99-3/31/00
0-500M	500M-2MM	2-10MM	10-50MM	50-100MM	100-250MM		ALL	ALL
20	43	53	43	6	5	NUMBER OF STATEMENTS	164	180
%	%	%	%	%	%	ASSETS	%	%
35.2	31.2	31.0	32.3			Cash & Equivalents	38.2	36.6
22.6	16.9	14.0	12.6			Trade Receivables (net)	11.8	11.7
.8	1.4	2.1	1.9			Inventory	1.0	1.8
2.3	4.2	8.8	4.2			All Other Current	4.7	3.2
60.9	53.7	55.9	50.9			Total Current	55.7	53.4
33.0	32.7	27.2	31.2			Fixed Assets (net)	27.2	28.8
.8	.5	.4	1.4			Intangibles (net)	1.4	1.9
5.1	13.1	16.6	16.5			All Other Non-Current	15.7	16.0
100.0	100.0	100.0	100.0			Total	100.0	100.0
						LIABILITIES		
10.2	4.5	4.0	1.1			Notes Payable-Short Term	1.8	3.2
1.7	2.3	3.7	1.2			Cur. Mat.-L/T/D	1.2	1.3
15.5	12.5	14.9	13.8			Trade Payables	10.1	10.4
.2	.2	.0	.0			Income Taxes Payable	.1	.2
22.3	11.6	13.0	13.2			All Other Current	15.9	20.0
49.9	31.1	35.5	29.3			Total Current	29.0	35.0
13.4	11.8	9.8	13.6			Long Term Debt	12.5	10.7
.2	.0	.0	.0			Deferred Taxes	.6	.0
10.3	2.8	7.2	8.5			All Other Non-Current	8.2	7.7
26.1	54.2	47.4	48.6			Net Worth	49.6	46.6
100.0	100.0	100.0	100.0			Total Liabilities & Net Worth	100.0	100.0
						INCOME DATA		
100.0	100.0	100.0	100.0			Net Sales	100.0	100.0
						Gross Profit		
97.4	99.1	99.0	99.4			Operating Expenses	96.1	98.7
2.6	.9	1.0	.6			Operating Profit	3.9	1.3
.9	.5	.9	2.4			All Other Expenses (net)	−1.1	−3.0
1.7	.3	.1	−1.8			Profit Before Taxes	5.0	4.3
						RATIOS		
6.2	5.2	3.9	3.0				4.3	3.8
1.1	2.0	1.8	1.8			Current	2.0	1.8
.7	1.0	1.1	1.2				1.2	1.1
6.2	4.6	3.0	2.9				3.6	3.4
1.1	1.6	1.5	1.5			Quick	2.0	1.7
.7	.9	.8	1.0				.9	.9
0 UND	2 171.7	9 41.5	7 49.3				4 91.3	6 59.7
12 30.0	26 14.0	16 23.0	24 14.9			Sales/Receivables	19 19.6	17 21.6
50 7.4	50 7.4	29 12.6	53 6.8				40 9.0	34 10.6
						Cost of Sales/Inventory		
						Cost of Sales/Payables		
6.6	2.3	3.0	2.2				2.2	2.3
34.6	5.8	6.4	4.6			Sales/Working Capital	4.8	5.1
−42.8	68.2	65.2	12.7				45.4	41.4
12.7	11.3	5.4	7.4				21.1	10.6
(13) 7.7	(20) 1.5	(27) 2.0	(24) .6			EBIT/Interest	(83) 4.9	(86) 3.5
1.6	−.8	−4.0	−6.5				.7	1.3
						Net Profit + Depr., Dep., Amort./Cur. Mat. L /T/D		
.1	.1	.2	.2				.1	.1
.7	.4	.4	.5			Fixed/Worth	.5	.4
3.6	1.2	1.0	1.4				1.0	1.0
.2	.3	.3	.5				.4	.4
2.5	.9	1.1	.9			Debt/Worth	.9	.8
UND	2.0	3.6	2.6				2.4	2.0
45.9	12.2	12.7	10.2				24.0	16.4
(16) 16.4	(42) 1.1	(49) 1.5	(41) −1.4			% Profit Before Taxes/Tangible Net Worth	(156) 9.9	(174) 6.2
−.7	−15.2	−9.8	−7.5				.1	−.5
18.6	5.8	4.8	4.0				12.5	8.1
4.7	.6	1.0	−.6			% Profit Before Taxes/Total Assets	5.0	2.4
−10.3	−6.1	−5.9	−4.6				−.1	−.5
755.8	48.1	19.1	11.0				30.9	23.2
12.6	13.7	5.3	3.8			Sales/Net Fixed Assets	6.4	7.0
3.9	1.6	1.9	1.3				2.0	1.8
5.5	2.2	2.1	1.3				2.0	1.8
3.3	1.4	1.1	.8			Sales/Total Assets	1.0	1.0
1.4	.6	.6	.4				.6	.6
1.0	1.0	1.3	2.4				1.2	1.6
(11) 2.3	(29) 2.9	(46) 2.5	(39) 3.6			% Depr., Dep., Amort./Sales	(130) 2.4	(149) 2.7
3.7	3.9	4.5	4.8				3.4	4.3
								.9
						% Officers', Directors', Owners' Comp/Sales	2.6	2.1
							(17) 16.2	(14) 35.3	28.6
14800M	85225M	487115M	808450M	149999M	1155246M	Net Sales ($)	1748984M	2293504M
4290M	50056M	262848M	959857M	381332M	766654M	Total Assets ($)	2035026M	2571909M

M = $ thousand   MM = $ million
See Pages 11 through 18 for Explanation of Ratios and Data

Comparative Historical Data   Current Data Sorted By Sales

			Type of Statement						
100	72	100	Unqualified	8	30	12	12	20	18
6	10	11	Reviewed	7	4			1	
19	25	10	Compiled	5	1	1	1		1
4	1	6	Tax Returns	2	1	1		2	
37	37	43	Other	11	8	1	9	9	5
4/1/00-3/31/01	4/1/01-3/31/02	4/1/02-3/31/03		76 (4/1-9/30/02)			94 (10/1/02-3/31/03)		
ALL	ALL	ALL		0-1MM	1-3MM	3-5MM	5-10MM	10-25MM	25MM & OVER
166	145	170	**NUMBER OF STATEMENTS**	33	44	15	22	32	24
%	%	%	**ASSETS**	%	%	%	%	%	%
37.5	33.5	32.0	Cash & Equivalents	28.1	33.5	18.0	36.1	36.9	32.9
13.0	13.1	15.1	Trade Receivables (net)	13.1	17.6	2.5	14.5	18.8	16.8
1.6	1.3	1.8	Inventory	.6	1.2	1.2	1.3	2.0	4.9
3.4	4.4	5.2	All Other Current	3.4	6.3	11.4	2.6	5.8	3.6
55.4	52.3	54.1	Total Current	45.2	58.6	33.0	54.6	63.5	58.1
27.4	31.2	30.6	Fixed Assets (net)	45.6	27.0	40.4	24.9	21.7	27.3
1.3	1.3	.8	Intangibles (net)	.1	.5	.5	1.9	.8	1.3
15.7	15.2	14.5	All Other Non-Current	9.0	13.9	26.1	18.5	14.0	13.3
100.0	100.0	100.0	Total	100.0	100.0	100.0	100.0	100.0	100.0
			LIABILITIES						
2.4	4.2	3.9	Notes Payable-Short Term	9.0	2.5	6.7	1.3	1.9	2.8
3.3	2.2	2.2	Cur. Mat.-L/T/D	2.2	3.6	.8	4.0	1.0	1.0
11.3	12.9	13.7	Trade Payables	10.7	13.0	3.6	10.6	19.5	20.4
.1	.1	.3	Income Taxes Payable	.1	.2	.0	.1	.0	1.8
19.3	17.8	14.0	All Other Current	8.6	17.3	12.1	14.2	15.4	14.3
36.4	37.3	34.2	Total Current	30.6	36.7	23.4	30.2	37.5	40.3
17.9	23.4	12.2	Long Term Debt	18.8	10.6	14.2	7.8	7.7	14.9
.3	.0	.0	Deferred Taxes	.1	.0	.0	.1	.0	.0
7.8	6.9	6.9	All Other Non-Current	7.4	3.6	10.9	1.9	9.8	10.6
37.5	32.3	46.7	Net Worth	43.1	49.1	51.6	60.0	45.0	34.1
100.0	100.0	100.0	Total Liabilities & Net Worth	100.0	100.0	100.0	100.0	100.0	100.0
			INCOME DATA						
100.0	100.0	100.0	Net Sales	100.0	100.0	100.0	100.0	100.0	100.0
			Gross Profit						
98.6	95.9	98.8	Operating Expenses	102.2	95.5	102.2	98.9	98.7	98.0
1.4	4.1	1.2	Operating Profit	-2.2	4.5	-2.2	1.1	1.3	2.0
-2.8	3.1	1.8	All Other Expenses (net)	3.3	.2	-.2	2.6	.1	5.5
4.2	1.0	-.6	Profit Before Taxes	-5.5	4.3	-2.0	-1.4	1.2	-3.4
			RATIOS						
4.1	2.9	4.2		5.4	6.2	2.7	3.4	4.1	2.3
1.9	1.5	1.8	Current	1.6	2.0	1.8	2.0	1.8	1.5
1.0	1.0	1.1		.8	1.1	.8	1.5	1.1	1.1
3.5	2.8	3.5		4.6	5.1	2.3	3.1	3.4	2.3
1.7	1.3	1.5	Quick	1.4	1.5	1.4	1.9	1.5	1.2
.8	.8	.9		.7	.9	.6	1.2	.9	.8
6 62.1	7 53.8	6 61.3		0 UND	5 74.7	9 42.2	4 102.9	11 32.6	14 25.9
17 21.3	18 20.8	19 19.1	Sales/Receivables	13 28.6	17 21.1	13 27.6	18 20.0	25 14.4	29 12.5
44 8.3	36 10.3	45 8.1		48 7.7	45 8.0	16 23.1	50 7.3	53 6.9	55 6.6
			Cost of Sales/Inventory						
			Cost of Sales/Payables						
2.1	2.9	2.5		2.0	2.7	3.7	2.0	2.4	3.9
6.3	7.9	6.3	Sales/Working Capital	7.3	6.0	5.9	5.9	5.7	11.5
-82.2	UND	69.6		-55.7	50.4	-13.4	15.7	49.2	69.4
(82) 14.0	(74) 5.7	(90) 9.1		(17) 4.3	(22) 13.9		(14) 9.4	(15) 17.1	(14) 4.6
3.3	2.1	1.7	EBIT/Interest	1.6	5.3		-1.4	1.3	-.9
1.3	-1.7	-2.8		.2	.4		-23.7	-6.0	-6.6
			Net Profit + Depr., Dep., Amort./Cur. Mat. L/T/D						
.1	.1	.1		.4	.1	.3	.1	.1	.3
.5	.6	.5	Fixed/Worth	1.1	.4	.8	.3	.2	.7
1.6	1.4	1.2		3.1	.9	1.3	.8	.9	1.5
.4	.4	.4		.2	.3	.4	.2	.4	1.2
1.0	1.1	1.1	Debt/Worth	1.4	.9	.7	.7	1.1	1.8
2.8	2.9	2.9		4.6	3.1	1.6	1.1	4.1	3.1
(150) 18.9	(135) 12.6	(159) 14.1	% Profit Before Taxes/Tangible	(31) 10.8	(41) 18.1	(14) 6.9	(21) 5.7	(30) 29.4	(22) 14.4
7.1	2.7	1.0	Net Worth	-.4	9.3	-2.3	-2.0	-.9	2.8
.1	-11.1	-10.4		-15.0	-1.7	-7.6	-20.5	-9.5	-17.8
7.4	5.3	5.8	% Profit Before Taxes/Total	1.6	10.9	3.3	3.8	8.2	4.8
2.6	.6	.2	Assets	-.4	4.8	-1.0	-1.5	-.3	-.8
.0	-5.6	-6.0		-9.7	-.9	-5.4	-12.5	-5.8	-10.7
39.1	32.8	20.5		13.5	47.2	7.2	20.6	47.5	14.9
7.4	5.7	5.4	Sales/Net Fixed Assets	2.4	8.7	1.8	7.0	12.5	5.2
2.1	1.8	1.9		.7	2.3	.7	2.8	2.8	2.6
1.8	2.2	2.0		1.7	2.3	1.0	2.8	1.9	2.8
1.1	1.1	1.1	Sales/Total Assets	.7	1.4	.6	1.0	1.3	1.2
.7	.6	.6		.4	.7	.5	.5	.8	.7
(138) 1.1	(117) .9	(133) 1.3	% Depr., Dep., Amort./Sales	(19) 2.9	(34) 1.0	(18) 1.8	(28) 1.2	(19) .7	(19) 1.0
2.4	2.8	3.1		3.7	2.2	4.8	3.1	3.4	2.7
4.0	5.0	4.7		6.5	3.8	6.4	4.4	4.4	4.1
(11) 6.1	(12) 5.8	(14) 5.8	% Officers', Directors',						
10.2	12.5	11.7	Owners' Comp/Sales						
14.9	17.3	14.9							
2767123M	2124706M	2700835M	Net Sales ($)	17222M	79993M	56613M	161642M	485881M	1899484M
2649640M	1911949M	2425037M	Total Assets ($)	40281M	97272M	124495M	265649M	531896M	1365444M

© RMA 2003

M = $ thousand   MM = $ million
See Pages 11 through 18 for Explanation of Ratios and Data

OTHER SERVICES—Professional Organizations NAICS 813920 (SIC 8621)

Current Data Sorted By Assets | Comparative Historical Data

						Type of Statement		
3	4	30	30	3	5	Unqualified	85	87
	1	1				Reviewed	2	2
4	2	1				Compiled	2	7
1						Tax Returns	3	1
4	5	8	14		4	Other	27	25
	54 (4/1-9/30/02)		66 (10/1/02-3/31/03)				4/1/98-3/31/99	4/1/99-3/31/00
0-500M	500M-2MM	2-10MM	10-50MM	50-100MM	100-250MM		ALL	ALL
12	12	40	44	3	9	NUMBER OF STATEMENTS	119	122
%	%	%	%	%	%	ASSETS	%	%
42.5	25.1	34.0	28.4			Cash & Equivalents	32.6	39.2
1.9	19.9	11.4	5.8			Trade Receivables (net)	11.5	10.4
2.9	6.3	.8	1.8			Inventory	1.9	1.2
1.5	4.9	2.3	3.7			All Other Current	3.8	2.3
48.8	56.2	48.5	39.7			Total Current	49.9	53.0
32.2	30.4	31.4	29.7			Fixed Assets (net)	25.5	27.2
4.3	2.4	.1	1.1			Intangibles (net)	4.1	1.7
14.2	11.0	20.0	29.5			All Other Non-Current	20.5	18.1
100.0	100.0	100.0	100.0			Total	100.0	100.0
						LIABILITIES		
7.8	5.4	.7	1.0			Notes Payable-Short Term	3.3	2.7
20.7	1.2	1.5	1.4			Cur. Mat.-L/T/D	1.3	1.3
8.2	5.4	5.4	6.7			Trade Payables	7.6	7.2
4.8	.0	.1	.0			Income Taxes Payable	.3	.2
8.8	15.0	19.4	15.3			All Other Current	18.3	18.8
50.3	27.0	27.1	24.4			Total Current	30.6	30.1
52.6	16.7	11.9	10.8			Long Term Debt	12.0	10.8
.0	.0	.2	.8			Deferred Taxes	.6	.6
7.3	.5	7.9	12.5			All Other Non-Current	7.7	8.5
-10.2	55.8	52.9	51.5			Net Worth	49.1	50.0
100.0	100.0	100.0	100.0			Total Liabilities & Net Worth	100.0	100.0
						INCOME DATA		
100.0	100.0	100.0	100.0			Net Sales	100.0	100.0
						Gross Profit		
92.5	96.7	97.5	100.5			Operating Expenses	101.8	98.8
7.5	3.3	2.5	-.5			Operating Profit	-1.8	1.2
-1.4	1.5	1.5	5.7			All Other Expenses (net)	-4.4	-3.8
8.9	1.7	1.0	-6.1			Profit Before Taxes	2.6	5.0
						RATIOS		
4.3	4.6	3.8	2.4				3.5	4.2
1.3	1.9	1.7	1.5			Current	1.7	1.7
1.0	1.4	1.0	.8				1.1	1.1
4.3	4.5	3.8	2.0				3.1	3.8
1.3	1.6	1.6	1.3			Quick	1.5	1.7
.8	.8	.9	.8				.9	.8

0	UND	0	UND	6	57.6	10	35.1	Sales/Receivables	9	42.3	6	61.1
0	UND	11	34.3	22	16.7	19	19.2		20	18.2	17	21.8
1	273.8	45	8.1	40	9.2	33	11.2		49	7.4	31	11.7

						Cost of Sales/Inventory		

						Cost of Sales/Payables		

4.5	3.4	2.7	2.6			Sales/Working Capital	2.7	2.1
26.6	7.9	7.2	11.4				7.1	6.4
NM	19.5	276.8	-15.6				67.5	80.8

				16.2		4.1			9.1		11.3	
		(21)	1.3	(26)	.2		EBIT/Interest	(64)	4.2	(72)	3.0	
			-1.0		-11.6			1.7		-1.1		

						Net Profit + Depr., Dep.,		18.4	
						Amort./Cur. Mat. L /T/D	(12)	3.8	
								2.6	

.1	.1	.2	.3			Fixed/Worth	.1	.1
1.1	.5	.6	.5				.5	.5
NM	1.0	1.0	1.0				.9	1.1

.4	.4	.5	.5			Debt/Worth	.4	.4
2.1	1.0	.8	1.0				.9	.8
NM	1.7	1.6	1.6				2.2	2.0

		28.0		16.1		5.4		% Profit Before Taxes/Tangible		18.4		20.9
		8.7		.6	(42)	-4.1		Net Worth	(110)	7.4	(117)	7.6
		.3		-10.8		-13.3				1.9		-.4

20.4	14.1	8.2	3.0			% Profit Before Taxes/Total	9.0	8.2
9.4	5.7	.3	-2.0			Assets	4.5	2.8
-16.8	.1	-4.6	-9.4				.7	-1.5

51.5	47.0	21.2	7.3			Sales/Net Fixed Assets	18.6	20.0
14.3	10.6	4.2	3.2				6.3	5.0
2.8	2.8	2.0	1.9				2.7	2.4

10.2	3.6	1.6	1.2			Sales/Total Assets	1.7	1.6
1.8	1.7	1.1	.8				1.1	1.0
1.1	.8	.7	.5				.6	.7

				1.6		2.5		% Depr., Dep., Amort./Sales		1.6		1.7
		(36)	2.6	(41)	3.3			(95)	2.4	(106)	2.8	
			3.6		4.3				3.7		3.9	

						% Officers', Directors',			2.7
						Owners' Comp/Sales		(10)	9.3
									32.3

11904M	28421M	299374M	765827M	209136M	1739050M	Net Sales ($)	1927715M	1833910M
3178M	12321M	225119M	901675M	230450M	1521797M	Total Assets ($)	2113098M	2180395M

© RMA 2003

M = $ thousand   MM = $ million
See Pages 11 through 18 for Explanation of Ratios and Data

	Comparative Historical Data			Type of Statement	Current Data Sorted By Sales					
	68	59	75	Unqualified	5	7	9	22	22	10
	7	4	2	Reviewed	1			1		
	16	22	7	Compiled	4			3		
		2	1	Tax Returns		1				
	29	32	35	Other	4	4	3	8	5	11
	4/1/00-	4/1/01-	4/1/02-		54 (4/1-9/30/02)			66 (10/1/02-3/31/03)		
	3/31/01	3/31/02	3/31/03							
	ALL	ALL	ALL		0-1MM	1-3MM	3-5MM	5-10MM	10-25MM	25MM & OVER
	120	119	120	NUMBER OF STATEMENTS	14	12	12	34	27	21
	%	%	%	ASSETS	%	%	%	%	%	%
	35.0	29.9	31.7	Cash & Equivalents	38.4	34.7	27.4	31.2	28.4	33.2
	9.7	10.0	9.0	Trade Receivables (net)	2.4	7.6	11.1	9.5	11.3	9.2
	1.6	1.5	2.0	Inventory	.4	6.2	3.5	.8	1.1	2.9
	5.6	4.3	3.0	All Other Current	1.8	2.8	2.4	3.3	4.0	2.5
	51.8	45.7	45.7	Total Current	43.0	51.3	44.5	44.7	44.8	47.7
	24.0	29.2	30.3	Fixed Assets (net)	39.5	32.3	40.0	26.7	26.6	28.0
	1.9	1.6	1.3	Intangibles (net)	2.9	.9	.5	1.1	1.3	1.4
	22.4	23.5	22.6	All Other Non-Current	14.2	15.5	15.0	27.5	27.2	22.9
	100.0	100.0	100.0	Total	100.0	100.0	100.0	100.0	100.0	100.0
				LIABILITIES						
	4.2	1.8	2.0	Notes Payable-Short Term	2.5	5.6	2.5	1.9	1.2	.5
	1.1	1.4	3.4	Cur. Mat.-L/T/D	1.8	20.2	2.4	1.4	1.2	1.2
	6.9	6.1	6.3	Trade Payables	1.6	10.7	5.1	5.1	7.8	7.5
	.4	.3	.5	Income Taxes Payable	4.1	.0	.1	.0	.1	.0
	34.6	16.2	16.1	All Other Current	4.0	5.8	17.6	21.0	17.4	19.7
	47.2	25.8	28.3	Total Current	14.0	42.2	27.7	29.5	27.7	29.0
	9.4	13.0	16.4	Long Term Debt	52.4	16.1	13.1	10.6	8.9	13.6
	.4	.0	.4	Deferred Taxes	.0	.0	.0	.8	.7	.1
	8.1	8.8	8.6	All Other Non-Current	5.9	4.6	8.8	6.8	10.9	12.7
	34.8	52.4	46.3	Net Worth	27.7	37.1	50.4	52.3	51.8	44.7
	100.0	100.0	100.0	Total Liabilities & Net Worth	100.0	100.0	100.0	100.0	100.0	100.0
				INCOME DATA						
	100.0	100.0	100.0	Net Sales	100.0	100.0	100.0	100.0	100.0	100.0
				Gross Profit						
	98.0	99.2	97.7	Operating Expenses	94.9	97.1	98.9	98.9	98.0	96.8
	2.0	.8	2.3	Operating Profit	5.1	2.9	1.1	1.1	2.0	3.2
	-1.1	1.1	3.2	All Other Expenses (net)	-.2	2.3	.2	4.6	4.6	3.4
	3.1	-.3	-.9	Profit Before Taxes	5.3	.6	1.0	-3.6	-2.6	-.1
				RATIOS						
	4.1	3.7	3.1		4.6	10.8	2.4	2.5	2.7	2.3
	1.8	1.9	1.6	Current	2.7	3.6	1.3	1.4	1.7	1.4
	1.0	1.0	.9		1.3	1.1	1.1	.8	1.0	.9
	3.6	2.9	2.8		4.6	9.8	2.4	2.5	2.3	2.1
	1.6	1.5	1.4	Quick	2.5	3.2	1.1	1.4	1.4	1.2
	.8	.8	.8		1.2	.8	.8	.7	.9	.8
6 63.9	8 46.9	6 57.6		Sales/Receivables	0 UND	2 169.3	5 76.5	6 60.3	14 26.0	13 28.9
18 19.9	23 15.7	19 19.0			0 UND	8 46.2	13 27.6	21 17.3	21 17.6	26 14.1
36 10.1	40 9.2	34 10.7			3 134.4	42 8.6	34 10.8	39 9.3	42 8.8	36 10.2
				Cost of Sales/Inventory						
				Cost of Sales/Payables						
	2.5	2.8	3.0		2.7	2.4	6.0	2.3	3.4	3.6
	5.2	6.3	9.3	Sales/Working Capital	7.4	3.7	18.6	11.7	9.1	9.7
	117.4	-999.8	-89.9		30.3	NM	53.3	-11.8	-41.0	NM
	10.1	4.9	5.1					12.3	29.3	7.2
(64) 2.3	(57) 1.0	(67) 1.0	EBIT/Interest			(18) 1.0	(15) .2	(12) .9	
	-1.6	-2.8	-4.7					-2.8	-9.2	-5.8
				Net Profit + Depr., Dep., Amort./Cur. Mat. L/T/D						
	.1	.2	.2		.1	.3	.2	.1	.3	.4
	.3	.5	.6	Fixed/Worth	.9	.9	.7	.4	.5	.7
	.8	.9	1.1		1.9	1.1	1.0	1.3	.8	1.1
	.4	.5	.5		.2	.3	.5	.5	.5	.7
	.8	.8	.9	Debt/Worth	1.0	.7	.9	.8	.8	1.1
	1.7	1.8	1.8		2.1	1.4	1.8	1.7	1.6	2.8
	10.7	11.0	14.4		34.9	19.7	18.6	10.1	8.6	14.8
(116) 4.0	(117) .1	(115) -.2	% Profit Before Taxes/Tangible Net Worth	(13) 10.3	(11) 2.7	.1	(33) .0	(26) -7.1	(20) -1.4
	-1.3	-10.5	-12.0		-17.1	-.2	-9.9	-11.6	-18.1	-12.4
	6.8	5.9	7.3		18.3	10.4	9.7	7.2	3.9	3.7
	2.2	.0	-.1	% Profit Before Taxes/Total Assets	8.1	1.2	.1	-.1	-3.5	-1.0
	-.6	-4.6	-6.3		-5.7	-.1	-6.5	-6.5	-6.5	-7.0
	22.9	13.6	15.1		22.1	84.8	25.1	22.8	11.4	6.9
	6.0	3.4	3.9	Sales/Net Fixed Assets	8.3	4.4	3.1	4.1	3.9	3.2
	2.5	2.4	2.1		1.7	1.3	1.4	1.9	2.5	2.3
	1.5	1.4	1.5		1.7	2.4	2.0	1.3	1.5	1.4
	1.0	1.0	1.0	Sales/Total Assets	1.3	.8	1.0	.8	1.1	1.0
	.6	.6	.6		.6	.6	.7	.5	.7	.7
	1.3	.6	1.8				2.0	1.6	1.8	1.8
(106) 2.2	(104) 2.6	(103) 2.9	% Depr., Dep., Amort./Sales		(11) 2.9	(32) 2.6	(24) 3.1	(18) 2.8	
	3.3	4.2	4.1				5.1	3.5	3.9	4.2
		9.9	5.3		% Officers', Directors', Owners' Comp/Sales					
	(19) 16.7	(16) 14.8								
	22.4	28.6								
	1940248M	2442889M	3053712M	Net Sales ($)	7230M	21587M	46301M	262240M	421694M	2294660M
	2655715M	3177079M	2894540M	Total Assets ($)	7710M	29903M	65916M	351108M	436539M	2003364M

© RMA 2003

M = $ thousand   MM = $ million
See Pages 11 through 18 for Explanation of Ratios and Data

Current Data Sorted By Assets   Comparative Historical Data

0-500M	500M-2MM	2-10MM	10-50MM	50-100MM	100-250MM	Type of Statement	4/1/98-3/31/99 ALL	4/1/99-3/31/00 ALL
1	9	16	4	3	1	Unqualified	17	22
	3	2				Reviewed		2
1	1	1				Compiled	4	1
						Tax Returns	1	
1	7	10	2	2		Other	12	18
	30 (4/1-9/30/02)		34 (10/1/02-3/31/03)					
3	20	29	6	5	1	NUMBER OF STATEMENTS	34	43
%	%	%	%	%	%	**ASSETS**	%	%
	36.2	38.7				Cash & Equivalents	31.4	32.0
	5.3	2.7				Trade Receivables (net)	7.9	14.4
	.0	.4				Inventory	1.4	.3
	.7	.4				All Other Current	4.4	4.0
	42.2	42.2				Total Current	45.1	50.7
	48.6	40.2				Fixed Assets (net)	37.8	30.7
	.0	1.4				Intangibles (net)	4.9	7.1
	9.2	16.2				All Other Non-Current	12.1	11.5
	100.0	100.0				Total	100.0	100.0
						LIABILITIES		
	2.4	1.5				Notes Payable-Short Term	1.5	8.5
	5.1	2.4				Cur. Mat.-L/T/D	3.1	1.5
	2.5	2.9				Trade Payables	30.8	11.4
	.0	.1				Income Taxes Payable	.0	.1
	2.3	5.8				All Other Current	12.5	35.3
	12.4	12.6				Total Current	48.0	56.7
	22.3	21.4				Long Term Debt	11.9	8.8
	.0	.0				Deferred Taxes	.0	.2
	.0	1.7				All Other Non-Current	4.7	3.3
	65.3	64.3				Net Worth	35.4	30.9
	100.0	100.0				Total Liabilities & Net Worth	100.0	100.0
						INCOME DATA		
	100.0	100.0				Net Sales	100.0	100.0
						Gross Profit		
	90.4	84.6				Operating Expenses	92.2	99.4
	9.6	15.4				Operating Profit	7.8	.6
	2.0	10.0				All Other Expenses (net)	−2.3	−8.8
	7.5	5.3				Profit Before Taxes	10.2	9.4
						RATIOS		
	11.4	37.0					22.5	5.2
	2.0	3.7				Current	2.6	1.5
	1.1	1.5					1.3	.9
	11.4	37.0					21.6	3.2
	1.9	3.7				Quick	1.8	1.4
	1.1	1.5					.9	.8
	0 UND	0 UND					0 UND	0 UND
	0 UND	0 UND				Sales/Receivables	0 UND	7 51.4
	27 13.5	26 14.1					29 12.6	38 9.5
						Cost of Sales/Inventory		
						Cost of Sales/Payables		
	1.6	1.4					1.5	2.2
	7.1	5.4				Sales/Working Capital	6.2	7.0
	49.9	18.6					UND	−86.8
	3.3	18.6					12.9	12.2
	(12) 1.1	(15) 2.1				EBIT/Interest	(21) 2.8	(26) 2.9
	−.3	−.7					1.1	.0
						Net Profit + Depr., Dep., Amort./Cur. Mat. L /T/D		
	.1	.2					.2	.1
	.9	.5				Fixed/Worth	.7	.5
	1.7	1.4					1.3	1.5
	.1	.0					.3	.2
	.5	.4				Debt/Worth	.4	.9
	1.4	1.8					2.0	4.4
	15.7	14.1					26.2	21.9
	7.8	(27) 5.9				% Profit Before Taxes/Tangible Net Worth	(31) 14.3	(35) 11.7
	−3.8	−2.9					2.9	1.7
	14.7	11.1					14.0	12.5
	4.4	3.0				% Profit Before Taxes/Total Assets	7.1	3.2
	−2.3	−2.1					.3	.1
	50.4	12.1					12.2	26.8
	1.9	3.0				Sales/Net Fixed Assets	3.5	5.7
	1.0	1.0					1.4	1.4
	1.4	1.3					2.4	2.9
	.9	.7				Sales/Total Assets	1.1	1.2
	.6	.4					.7	.5
	1.5	1.4					1.8	1.5
	(12) 4.2	(22) 2.0				% Depr., Dep., Amort./Sales	(24) 2.6	(31) 2.5
	5.8	3.9					4.5	4.2
		7.0						6.4
		(10) 30.6				% Officers', Directors', Owners' Comp/Sales		(10) 14.3
		41.0						24.1
2397M	20958M	126777M	149683M	270797M	552114M	Net Sales ($)	689118M	1007241M
1037M	19678M	145204M	121958M	372971M	174706M	Total Assets ($)	538287M	730886M

M = $ thousand   MM = $ million
See Pages 11 through 18 for Explanation of Ratios and Data

Comparative Historical Data   Current Data Sorted By Sales

			Type of Statement						
18	18	34	Unqualified	6	8	6	6	4	4
3			Reviewed						
4	12	5	Compiled	1	4				
1	3	3	Tax Returns	3					
13	12	22	Other	7	8	1	1	2	3
4/1/00-3/31/01 ALL	4/1/01-3/31/02 ALL	4/1/02-3/31/03 ALL		30 (4/1-9/30/02)		34 (10/1/02-3/31/03)			
				0-1MM	1-3MM	3-5MM	5-10MM	10-25MM	25MM & OVER
39	45	64	**NUMBER OF STATEMENTS**	17	20	7	7	6	7
%	%	%	**ASSETS**	%	%	%	%	%	%
36.6	38.2	37.5	Cash & Equivalents	35.3	31.4				
10.7	6.3	4.9	Trade Receivables (net)	3.1	5.2				
.3	.6	.4	Inventory	.0	.1				
3.5	5.8	1.7	All Other Current	.7	.6				
51.2	50.9	44.5	Total Current	39.1	37.3				
30.3	36.2	39.0	Fixed Assets (net)	52.5	43.0				
6.4	1.0	1.2	Intangibles (net)	.0	.1				
12.1	11.9	15.3	All Other Non-Current	8.4	19.6				
100.0	100.0	100.0	Total	100.0	100.0				
			LIABILITIES						
2.1	.3	1.7	Notes Payable-Short Term	.6	2.9				
2.0	2.8	2.9	Cur. Mat.-L/T/D	3.6	5.6				
7.4	4.7	4.1	Trade Payables	2.7	2.4				
.1	.0	.1	Income Taxes Payable	.0	.0				
62.8	10.2	7.1	All Other Current	1.6	3.1				
74.4	18.0	16.0	Total Current	8.6	14.0				
12.1	13.8	19.6	Long Term Debt	31.2	20.1				
.0	.0	.0	Deferred Taxes	.0	.0				
5.1	2.4	1.6	All Other Non-Current	2.2	.0				
8.5	65.7	62.9	Net Worth	58.0	65.8				
100.0	100.0	100.0	Total Liabilities & Net Worth	100.0	100.0				
			INCOME DATA						
100.0	100.0	100.0	Net Sales	100.0	100.0				
			Gross Profit						
98.8	94.4	89.2	Operating Expenses	88.6	87.8				
1.2	5.6	10.8	Operating Profit	11.4	12.2				
−6.1	−.8	5.1	All Other Expenses (net)	8.7	6.7				
7.2	6.4	5.6	Profit Before Taxes	2.8	5.5				
			RATIOS						
22.2	26.2	11.5		9.4	30.4				
2.4	3.6	3.1	Current	3.6	3.8				
1.5	1.5	1.3		1.4	1.2				
20.4	21.9	11.5		9.4	30.3				
2.4	2.6	3.0	Quick	3.4	2.8				
.9	1.3	1.3		1.4	1.2				
0 UND	0 UND	0 UND		0 UND	0 UND				
1 266.6	3 144.0	0 UND	Sales/Receivables	0 UND	0 UND				
37 10.0	27 13.7	27 13.7		23 15.7	32 11.4				
			Cost of Sales/Inventory						
			Cost of Sales/Payables						
1.4	1.9	1.5		1.4	1.6				
5.1	4.2	6.0	Sales/Working Capital	5.5	6.8				
20.0	13.0	25.9		29.3	24.4				
3.7	13.4	13.1			25.8				
(20) 1.4	(26) 3.8	(33) 2.1	EBIT/Interest		(12) 2.3				
−3.3	1.9	.3			−.3				
			Net Profit + Depr., Dep., Amort./Cur. Mat. L/T/D						
.0	.2	.1		.2	.0				
.4	.6	.5	Fixed/Worth	1.3	.5				
1.5	1.1	1.4		2.1	1.4				
.0	.1	.1		.0	.1				
.7	.4	.5	Debt/Worth	.7	.4				
2.4	1.1	1.5		2.0	1.2				
13.3	26.5	13.8		13.7	15.3				
(33) 6.0	(44) 6.4	(61) 5.8	% Profit Before Taxes/Tangible Net Worth	(16) 5.6	6.1				
−.6	−1.4	−4.8		−5.4	−4.4				
7.6	14.8	11.3		6.7	12.0				
2.2	4.3	2.9	% Profit Before Taxes/Total Assets	2.7	4.6				
−1.5	−.8	−2.5		−2.7	−3.0				
52.0	10.3	13.0		12.6	54.0				
5.4	4.3	3.5	Sales/Net Fixed Assets	1.5	2.3				
2.1	1.2	1.2		.5	.9				
1.5	1.5	1.4		1.0	1.4				
1.0	1.3	1.0	Sales/Total Assets	.7	.9				
.4	.7	.5		.3	.5				
1.2	1.1	1.4		1.8	1.2				
(28) 2.1	(41) 1.7	(45) 2.9	% Depr., Dep., Amort./Sales	(10) 4.7	(12) 3.0				
4.9	3.9	4.2		9.9	5.7				
	14.0	6.6			6.5				
	(13) 26.0	(21) 23.3	% Officers', Directors', Owners' Comp/Sales		(11) 17.8				
	29.7	31.5			40.0				
859125M	837791M	1122726M	Net Sales ($)	10207M	38782M	25587M	45101M	93379M	909670M
801147M	600245M	835554M	Total Assets ($)	29280M	58546M	30290M	121694M	80896M	514848M

Current Data Sorted By Assets   Comparative Historical Data

0-500M	500M-2MM	2-10MM	10-50MM	50-100MM	100-250MM		4/1/98-3/31/99 ALL	4/1/99-3/31/00 ALL
						Type of Statement		
4	14	39	47	8	3	Unqualified	105	85
3	3					Reviewed	3	2
2	2	5	1			Compiled	8	11
4	2					Tax Returns	7	9
9	8	24	21	6	4	Other	39	42
	78 (4/1-9/30/02)		131 (10/1/02-3/31/03)					
22	29	68	69	14	7	**NUMBER OF STATEMENTS**	162	149
%	%	%	%	%	%	**ASSETS**	%	%
36.0	24.6	19.4	19.3	38.0		Cash & Equivalents	24.1	23.0
10.7	6.8	7.5	5.3	7.2		Trade Receivables (net)	8.3	9.4
.8	.6	1.9	3.5	.5		Inventory	2.6	2.3
2.6	5.8	3.9	3.2	3.2		All Other Current	3.2	3.0
50.2	37.8	32.7	31.4	48.9		Total Current	38.2	37.7
39.4	47.4	54.0	51.3	32.0		Fixed Assets (net)	39.2	39.8
.6	.7	.4	1.5	1.5		Intangibles (net)	1.4	1.5
9.9	14.1	12.9	15.8	17.6		All Other Non-Current	21.2	21.0
100.0	100.0	100.0	100.0	100.0		Total	100.0	100.0
						LIABILITIES		
32.9	4.0	3.9	1.8	1.1		Notes Payable-Short Term	2.2	3.2
7.8	2.2	2.8	1.2	.8		Cur. Mat.-L/T/D	2.0	1.6
10.5	6.9	4.9	4.4	6.8		Trade Payables	7.1	5.5
.0	.1	.1	.1	.0		Income Taxes Payable	.1	.0
10.1	9.7	7.0	8.7	15.2		All Other Current	9.3	13.9
61.3	22.8	18.7	16.2	23.9		Total Current	20.6	24.3
45.3	15.7	11.4	20.4	18.7		Long Term Debt	19.8	19.7
.1	.1	.0	.1	.1		Deferred Taxes	.6	.3
14.7	6.3	5.1	5.3	8.1		All Other Non-Current	8.2	7.4
-21.5	55.1	64.7	58.0	49.1		Net Worth	50.9	48.3
100.0	100.0	100.0	100.0	100.0		Total Liabilities & Net Worth	100.0	100.0
						INCOME DATA		
100.0	100.0	100.0	100.0	100.0		Net Sales	100.0	100.0
						Gross Profit		
90.7	94.4	94.7	94.3	100.9		Operating Expenses	93.0	92.6
9.3	5.6	5.3	5.7	-.9		Operating Profit	7.0	7.4
.7	3.2	.8	4.0	9.5		All Other Expenses (net)	-2.4	-2.7
8.6	2.3	4.5	1.7	-10.5		Profit Before Taxes	9.3	10.1
						RATIOS		
7.8	6.0	4.4	3.6	4.7			4.4	4.3
1.2	1.8	1.8	1.9	1.9		Current	2.1	1.7
.3	1.3	.8	1.1	1.3			.9	1.0
7.8	5.2	3.6	3.1	3.2			3.8	3.3
1.1	1.8	1.5	1.4	1.6		Quick	1.7	1.4
.2	.9	.7	.7	1.2			.7	.7
0 UND	0 UND	3 127.5	4 82.9	7 55.8			1 306.4	2 170.9
5 79.9	3 120.0	13 28.1	14 26.2	19 19.0		Sales/Receivables	11 34.5	16 22.5
17 22.0	23 15.8	36 10.1	44 8.3	129 2.8			30 12.1	40 9.0
						Cost of Sales/Inventory		
						Cost of Sales/Payables		
3.1	4.0	3.3	2.4	1.0			3.1	2.8
21.7	8.9	6.0	7.1	3.2		Sales/Working Capital	8.2	11.1
-9.6	97.0	-27.7	40.6	11.4			-74.5	145.1
(12) 7.8	(16) 7.9	(41) 3.8	(43) 10.5				(88) 15.7	(76) 6.8
1.7	4.2	1.1	1.0			EBIT/Interest	3.2	3.0
-5.7	1.5	-2.1	-3.0				.9	.7
							(11) 7.7	(10) 7.2
						Net Profit + Depr., Dep., Amort./Cur. Mat. L /T/D	3.7	4.7
							1.2	.5
.0	.2	.5	.4	.4			.2	.2
.8	.8	.9	1.0	.4		Fixed/Worth	.7	.7
2.2	1.1	1.4	1.6	.8			1.5	1.3
.1	.2	.1	.3	.5			.2	.2
1.2	.7	.4	.7	.8		Debt/Worth	.8	.8
-11.0	3.3	1.2	1.7	2.2			1.7	2.5
(16) 49.2	19.3	(67) 8.7	(68) 5.3	(13) -3.8		% Profit Before Taxes/Tangible Net Worth	(148) 20.5	(134) 20.9
22.7	2.0	1.8	.5	-6.2			9.4	7.5
-1.1	-3.4	-5.1	-5.2	-13.7			.4	.8
46.7	8.5	4.8	4.0	-2.4		% Profit Before Taxes/Total Assets	10.8	11.3
8.3	1.4	.4	.1	-3.8			4.0	4.2
-6.4	-1.4	-4.0	-3.4	-5.3			-.1	.2
UND	23.3	3.7	4.8	5.8		Sales/Net Fixed Assets	15.8	10.5
6.7	1.5	1.4	.8	2.2			3.6	3.1
1.5	.5	.8	.5	.7			1.1	.9
3.7	3.5	1.2	1.0	1.0		Sales/Total Assets	1.6	1.6
1.4	.9	.7	.5	.5			1.0	.7
1.1	.4	.5	.3	.2			.5	.4
(12) 1.4	(23) .8	(55) 2.1	(60) 2.1	(12) 2.1		% Depr., Dep., Amort./Sales	(131) 1.8	(113) 2.0
6.0	2.4	4.0	5.9	3.2			3.4	3.9
8.0	9.6	8.2	9.8	8.4			6.2	7.4
							(14) 1.4	(15) 1.5
						% Officers', Directors', Owners' Comp/Sales	3.2	9.4
							14.8	31.6
11665M	96918M	370488M	1137723M	606890M	666585M	Net Sales ($)	2729138M	2068139M
5191M	33847M	363604M	1520118M	996392M	1114211M	Total Assets ($)	3081542M	2708097M

Comparative Historical Data | | | Current Data Sorted By Sales

			Type of Statement						
82	59	115	Unqualified	8	20	22	22	24	19
3	2	6	Reviewed	3	2	1			
32	29	10	Compiled	6	2	2			
8	8	6	Tax Returns	5	1				
31	39	72	Other	14	16	10	11	8	13
4/1/00- 3/31/01 ALL	4/1/01- 3/31/02 ALL	4/1/02- 3/31/03 ALL		0-1MM	78 (4/1-9/30/02) 1-3MM	3-5MM	131 (10/1/02-3/31/03) 5-10MM	10-25MM	25MM & OVER
156	137	209	**NUMBER OF STATEMENTS**	36	41	35	33	32	32
%	%	%	**ASSETS**	%	%	%	%	%	%
23.0	24.7	23.5	Cash & Equivalents	26.2	17.7	20.4	23.1	25.6	29.6
7.3	7.9	7.1	Trade Receivables (net)	4.7	5.3	7.8	7.4	7.7	10.4
2.8	1.7	2.0	Inventory	.8	2.4	1.1	2.2	1.6	4.0
5.1	5.7	3.7	All Other Current	2.0	4.0	5.9	2.3	4.3	3.8
38.2	39.9	36.3	Total Current	33.7	29.3	35.3	35.0	39.2	47.8
37.8	44.4	48.1	Fixed Assets (net)	55.0	51.5	48.8	53.3	47.3	30.8
1.1	.4	1.2	Intangibles (net)	.6	.4	.2	.6	.8	5.3
22.9	15.3	14.3	All Other Non-Current	10.7	18.8	15.7	11.0	12.6	16.2
100.0	100.0	100.0	Total	100.0	100.0	100.0	100.0	100.0	100.0
			LIABILITIES						
2.7	3.0	6.0	Notes Payable-Short Term	17.8	5.3	7.0	1.7	.9	2.1
1.4	2.2	2.5	Cur. Mat.-L/T/D	5.4	1.5	4.8	1.3	.9	.9
4.4	7.4	5.7	Trade Payables	6.4	2.1	5.1	4.9	8.6	8.1
.0	.0	.1	Income Taxes Payable	.1	.1	.0	.0	.1	.1
8.4	6.9	9.0	All Other Current	7.8	4.1	7.4	9.7	11.4	15.3
17.0	19.6	23.3	Total Current	37.4	13.1	24.3	17.6	21.9	26.4
14.4	19.0	19.4	Long Term Debt	34.7	17.7	12.5	24.6	12.4	13.5
.3	.1	.1	Deferred Taxes	.1	.1	.0	.0	.0	.4
6.9	4.5	7.2	All Other Non-Current	5.1	2.7	8.9	7.6	6.8	13.0
61.4	56.8	50.1	Net Worth	22.7	66.4	54.2	50.1	58.8	46.6
100.0	100.0	100.0	Total Liabilities & Net Worth	100.0	100.0	100.0	100.0	100.0	100.0
			INCOME DATA						
100.0	100.0	100.0	Net Sales	100.0	100.0	100.0	100.0	100.0	100.0
			Gross Profit						
96.9	94.6	94.2	Operating Expenses	90.9	90.0	94.5	98.6	98.6	94.4
3.1	5.4	5.8	Operating Profit	9.1	10.0	5.5	1.4	1.4	5.6
-4.3	2.3	3.0	All Other Expenses (net)	2.4	5.2	-1.3	3.7	4.4	3.4
7.4	3.1	2.8	Profit Before Taxes	6.7	4.8	6.7	-2.2	-2.9	2.3
			RATIOS						
5.6	5.7	4.4		8.5	5.0	5.9	3.0	3.6	2.9
2.4	2.4	1.8	Current	1.8	1.8	1.4	2.2	2.2	1.6
1.2	1.1	1.0		.5	1.2	.8	1.1	.9	1.1
3.6	5.0	3.5		8.3	3.7	5.6	2.7	2.7	2.7
1.8	1.7	1.5	Quick	1.8	1.6	1.1	1.9	1.4	1.4
.9	.7	.7		.4	.7	.6	1.0	.8	.8
1 250.3	1 435.5	3 136.1		0 UND	0 UND	4 84.9	9 42.0	5 72.7	7 50.0
12 30.6	14 25.7	12 29.4	Sales/Receivables	4 82.3	5 71.7	13 27.7	21 17.2	11 31.8	18 20.6
33 10.9	34 10.9	36 10.1		23 15.7	33 11.0	36 10.0	52 7.0	52 7.0	46 8.0
			Cost of Sales/Inventory						
			Cost of Sales/Payables						
2.3	2.1	2.7		2.2	2.0	2.7	3.6	2.7	3.1
7.2	6.4	7.1	Sales/Working Capital	8.1	5.2	10.2	7.1	6.4	12.0
44.9	46.8	666.9		-6.7	111.7	-26.7	62.5	-58.4	39.4
15.0	4.5	5.3		5.3	12.3	6.1	1.1	10.4	8.6
(83) 2.6	(84) 1.4	(126) 1.1	EBIT/Interest	(22) 2.0	(22) 3.2	(22) 1.9	(22) -1.0	(17) .8	(21) .5
-.2	-1.1	-3.0		-.4	-2.8	-1.9	-2.3	-9.8	-6.4
		3.3	Net Profit + Depr., Dep.,						
	(11)	2.4	Amort./Cur. Mat. L/T/D						
		.2							
.2	.3	.4		.2	.2	.3	.5	.4	.4
.5	.7	.9	Fixed/Worth	.9	.9	.8	1.1	1.0	.7
1.1	1.3	1.4		1.9	1.1	1.4	2.0	1.4	1.4
.1	.2	.2		.2	.1	.1	.4	.2	.6
.5	.5	.7	Debt/Worth	.7	.3	.5	1.1	.6	1.5
1.2	1.3	1.8		1.9	1.1	1.4	1.9	2.3	2.3
15.7	11.4	11.7	% Profit Before Taxes/Tangible	22.8	16.2	17.4	6.0	4.6	7.6
(146) 6.9	(129) 2.8	(198) 1.2	Net Worth	(32) 7.2	(40) 1.8	(33) 2.6	(31) -.1	-2.8	(29) -4.5
.1	-3.7	-5.5		-1.0	-4.2	-4.5	-7.2	-14.4	-10.4
9.2	6.6	5.4	% Profit Before Taxes/Total	11.4	10.1	7.4	2.4	3.7	4.6
3.9	1.3	.3	Assets	2.7	.4	.7	-.1	-1.8	-1.8
-.4	-2.9	-3.8		-.8	-4.1	-4.2	-3.1	-5.6	-5.0
10.1	10.9	7.3		7.1	5.3	11.5	5.0	4.6	13.6
2.6	2.0	1.5	Sales/Net Fixed Assets	.9	1.1	1.1	.9	2.7	5.2
1.0	.8	.7		.3	.6	.7	.5	.7	2.0
1.4	1.5	1.3		1.4	.9	1.6	1.3	1.3	1.5
.8	.8	.7	Sales/Total Assets	.6	.6	.6	.7	.7	1.0
.4	.5	.4		.2	.2	.3	.4	.5	.7
.7	.6	1.9		2.2	2.5	.9	2.6	2.0	.7
(130) 2.9	(112) 2.7	(165) 4.4	% Depr., Dep., Amort./Sales	(21) 8.1	(28) 5.9	(34) 4.2	(26) 5.8	(29) 4.0	(27) 2.6
5.5	6.8	8.9		10.3	11.4	8.7	9.8	7.8	4.0
1.6	2.4	4.7	% Officers', Directors',						
(26) 8.4	(15) 10.5	(18) 8.4	Owners' Comp/Sales						
19.4	19.5	17.2							
2771895M	2125356M	2890269M	Net Sales ($)	14087M	77276M	135920M	231123M	488981M	1942882M
3427450M	2736204M	4033363M	Total Assets ($)	33040M	248071M	254791M	498538M	922019M	2076904M

M = $ thousand   MM = $ million
See Pages 11 through 18 for Explanation of Ratios and Data

Current Data Sorted By Assets   Comparative Historical Data

Type of Statement	0-500M	500M-2MM	2-10MM	10-50MM	50-100MM	100-250MM		4/1/98-3/31/99 ALL	4/1/99-3/31/00 ALL
Unqualified		3	5	9	2			14	8
Reviewed	1	6	9	2	1			3	7
Compiled	12	8	10	3				8	7
Tax Returns	5	3	3	2				7	5
Other	9	13	10	13				16	21
	21 (4/1-9/30/02)			108 (10/1/02-3/31/03)					
NUMBER OF STATEMENTS	27	33	37	29	3			48	48
	%	%	%	%	%	%		%	%
ASSETS									
Cash & Equivalents	21.8	12.0	7.4	11.2			D	18.5	16.3
Trade Receivables (net)	19.8	21.8	14.2	22.6			A	18.9	19.7
Inventory	11.7	13.2	22.8	6.6			T	8.9	7.6
All Other Current	4.2	2.4	5.6	3.9			A	2.0	8.4
Total Current	57.6	49.3	50.0	44.2				48.3	52.1
Fixed Assets (net)	30.4	42.8	36.2	41.1			N	34.5	37.5
Intangibles (net)	7.2	.2	3.1	5.0			O	2.9	2.7
All Other Non-Current	4.8	7.6	10.7	9.7			T	14.2	7.7
Total	100.0	100.0	100.0	100.0				100.0	100.0
LIABILITIES							A		
Notes Payable-Short Term	17.0	10.4	14.9	7.2			V	14.0	9.1
Cur. Mat.-L/T/D	6.7	4.2	5.3	2.9			A	3.4	3.7
Trade Payables	8.5	8.1	7.6	8.3			I	9.2	9.8
Income Taxes Payable	.8	.3	.2	.1			L	.2	.0
All Other Current	26.7	12.5	5.6	11.3			A	5.2	12.6
Total Current	59.7	35.5	33.7	29.8			B	32.0	35.2
Long Term Debt	37.4	21.6	21.1	22.1			L	19.3	25.8
Deferred Taxes	.3	.4	.0	.7			E	.4	.7
All Other Non-Current	14.7	4.7	5.4	2.0				5.1	5.2
Net Worth	−12.1	37.8	39.8	45.3				43.2	33.1
Total Liabilities & Net Worth	100.0	100.0	100.0	100.0				100.0	100.0
INCOME DATA									
Net Sales	100.0	100.0	100.0	100.0				100.0	100.0
Gross Profit									
Operating Expenses	89.9	87.1	88.2	86.2				130.8	89.3
Operating Profit	10.1	12.9	11.8	13.8				−30.8	10.7
All Other Expenses (net)	3.5	7.8	6.8	4.8				8.8	3.2
Profit Before Taxes	6.6	5.1	5.0	9.0				−39.7	7.5
RATIOS									
Current	1.9	2.6	2.6	2.7				5.1	2.9
	1.1	1.2	1.4	1.3				1.5	1.7
	.5	.5	.7	.9				.9	1.0
Quick	1.6	1.9	1.3	2.1				4.9	2.0
	.7	.8	.7	1.0				1.3	1.1
	.2	.4	.2	.7				.4	.5
Sales/Receivables	0 UND	0 UND	4 99.4	10 38.0				0 UND	0 UND
	0 UND	8 48.2	20 18.7	35 10.5				29 12.4	32 11.5
	30 12.0	50 7.3	45 8.1	56 6.5				54 6.7	57 6.4
Cost of Sales/Inventory									
Cost of Sales/Payables									
Sales/Working Capital	13.2	7.1	5.9	5.0				5.2	3.9
	179.6	23.3	20.6	12.3				15.1	9.6
	−26.7	−9.7	−10.5	−101.5				−50.1	300.6
EBIT/Interest	(21) 10.2	(22) 10.4	(34) 10.8	(20) 35.8				(32) 12.3	(37) 18.3
	3.3	2.0	3.3	5.7				3.8	3.5
	1.9	.9	−.4	1.4				1.3	2.2
Net Profit + Depr., Dep., Amort./Cur. Mat. L /T/D									
Fixed/Worth	.1	.2	.1	.4				.2	.3
	3.8	1.2	1.0	.9				.6	.9
	−.6	3.3	2.4	2.0				3.0	3.3
Debt/Worth	2.9	.6	.7	.5				.3	.7
	75.0	1.2	1.7	1.2				1.3	2.5
	−3.2	4.3	2.7	4.6				7.9	5.8
% Profit Before Taxes/Tangible Net Worth	(14) 163.7	(29) 23.3	(34) 51.8	(28) 37.4				(43) 65.7	(42) 62.7
	55.3	12.4	17.0	18.3				20.4	23.4
	−1.9	−.7	−2.3	4.1				−1.1	4.6
% Profit Before Taxes/Total Assets	58.6	15.9	17.5	12.1				21.0	18.7
	13.9	3.0	3.8	4.8				6.6	9.0
	.0	−.3	−1.4	.9				−2.1	1.8
Sales/Net Fixed Assets	190.0	35.3	81.2	12.0				36.5	27.1
	33.0	11.1	8.9	3.6				7.8	7.7
	13.3	.3	1.5	.8				.5	1.9
Sales/Total Assets	7.5	4.4	2.7	2.9				2.9	3.5
	4.6	2.3	1.8	1.8				1.4	2.2
	3.0	.3	.6	.4				.2	1.0
% Depr., Dep., Amort./Sales	(17) .6	(25) 1.4	(31) .9	(26) 1.5				(40) .9	(39) 1.9
	1.4	4.2	3.6	3.2				2.5	3.4
	7.5	13.3	13.1	7.5				13.1	8.8
% Officers', Directors', Owners' Comp/Sales	(10) 5.5							(14) 3.0	(16) 3.1
	14.4							6.8	5.9
	28.9							16.4	19.1
Net Sales ($)	43492M	116439M	348921M	1434406M	258258M			946399M	960677M
Total Assets ($)	6950M	38086M	199379M	583493M	201280M			779105M	570652M

© RMA 2003

M = $ thousand   MM = $ million
See Pages 11 through 18 for Explanation of Ratios and Data

Comparative Historical Data | Current Data Sorted By Sales

Hist 1	Hist 2	Hist 3	Type of Statement	0-1MM	1-3MM	3-5MM	5-10MM	10-25MM	25MM & OVER
9	14	19	Unqualified		4	1		3	11
9	10	19	Reviewed	1	6	3	2	5	2
15	14	33	Compiled	9	7	4	7	5	1
27	6	13	Tax Returns	6	6	1	1		
26	26	45	Other	12	11	2	6	6	8
4/1/00-3/31/01 ALL	4/1/01-3/31/02 ALL	4/1/02-3/31/03 ALL		21 (4/1-9/30/02)			108 (10/1/02-3/31/03)		
86	70	129	NUMBER OF STATEMENTS	28	34	11	15	19	22
%	%	%	ASSETS	%	%	%	%	%	%
13.1	13.3	12.4	Cash & Equivalents	12.8	15.6	14.4	8.4	15.2	6.1
16.8	20.4	19.0	Trade Receivables (net)	8.9	19.9	16.7	21.8	20.4	28.7
12.5	16.6	13.9	Inventory	12.0	9.5	6.5	19.5	22.5	15.7
3.8	3.2	4.5	All Other Current	2.4	2.6	9.1	4.5	4.4	8.1
46.2	53.6	49.9	Total Current	36.2	47.8	46.7	54.3	62.4	58.6
40.4	37.0	38.2	Fixed Assets (net)	51.4	39.2	42.9	35.7	26.3	29.3
2.4	2.1	3.6	Intangibles (net)	1.9	3.2	5.0	5.2	2.7	5.2
11.0	7.4	8.3	All Other Non-Current	10.5	9.9	5.4	4.8	8.5	6.9
100.0	100.0	100.0	Total	100.0	100.0	100.0	100.0	100.0	100.0
			LIABILITIES						
12.1	11.2	12.3	Notes Payable-Short Term	10.3	13.6	13.8	15.1	15.9	6.9
4.8	4.2	4.9	Cur. Mat.-L/T/D	3.9	3.3	10.1	7.9	4.7	3.9
8.4	11.3	8.0	Trade Payables	3.6	6.5	5.8	8.2	13.7	12.1
.3	.2	.3	Income Taxes Payable	.7	.1	.0	.5	.4	.2
7.2	7.9	13.2	All Other Current	17.3	11.1	8.7	10.9	18.5	10.3
32.8	34.9	38.6	Total Current	35.8	34.6	38.3	42.5	53.2	33.4
25.2	20.9	25.0	Long Term Debt	39.0	28.1	27.6	22.1	10.2	15.8
.4	.2	.3	Deferred Taxes	.3	.3	.3	.0	.1	.9
9.2	4.1	6.4	All Other Non-Current	6.2	9.9	2.6	13.5	2.1	2.0
32.3	39.9	29.6	Net Worth	18.8	27.1	31.1	21.8	34.4	47.8
100.0	100.0	100.0	Total Liabilities & Net Worth	100.0	100.0	100.0	100.0	100.0	100.0
			INCOME DATA						
100.0	100.0	100.0	Net Sales	100.0	100.0	100.0	100.0	100.0	100.0
			Gross Profit						
85.8	87.1	87.8	Operating Expenses	76.6	86.5	98.6	90.7	93.1	92.2
14.2	12.9	12.2	Operating Profit	23.4	13.5	1.4	9.3	6.9	7.8
5.4	5.3	5.8	All Other Expenses (net)	17.4	5.7	1.5	.9	.9	1.1
8.8	7.6	6.4	Profit Before Taxes	6.0	7.8	.0	8.4	6.0	6.6
			RATIOS						
3.8 / 1.8 / .9	3.1 / 1.3 / .9	2.5 / 1.3 / .7	Current	1.2 / .9 / .2	3.5 / 1.6 / .9	3.1 / 1.3 / .5	2.6 / 1.6 / .6	2.1 / 1.2 / .8	2.6 / 1.7 / 1.0
2.2 / 1.1 / .4	2.1 / 1.0 / .4	1.6 / .8 / .3	Quick	1.1 / .4 / .1	2.9 / 1.0 / .4	1.9 / 1.0 / .3	1.5 / .7 / .2	1.2 / .8 / .4	1.6 / .8 / .5
0 UND / 9 42.4 / 53 6.9	2 150.4 / 28 12.9 / 50 7.2	0 UND / 15 24.0 / 46 8.0	Sales/Receivables	0 UND / 0 UND / 0 UND	0 UND / 14 25.4 / 52 7.1	9 39.6 / 20 18.7 / 63 5.8	8 45.5 / 14 25.3 / 31 11.9	3 125.4 / 39 9.3 / 46 8.0	19 18.9 / 35 10.5 / 57 6.4
			Cost of Sales/Inventory						
			Cost of Sales/Payables						
5.0 / 14.4 / -60.6	5.0 / 17.3 / -28.9	6.4 / 30.2 / -19.1	Sales/Working Capital	19.6 / -147.2 / -2.6	4.2 / 22.5 / -270.9	4.8 / 9.6 / -10.2	7.4 / 9.0 / -20.2	8.4 / 22.9 / -32.8	6.3 / 9.1 / -109.5
(63) 12.4 / 3.0 / 1.2	(59) 17.5 / 5.8 / 1.5	(100) 12.7 / 3.7 / 1.1	EBIT/Interest	(14) 8.9 / 2.6 / .9	(28) 9.1 / 2.2 / .6	8.2 / 2.1 / .2	(13) 12.6 / 2.2 / -.3	(16) 30.7 / 9.0 / 1.9	(18) 26.0 / 7.0 / 1.7
	(12) 14.8 / 2.4 / 1.5	(20) 6.0 / 2.7 / 1.2	Net Profit + Depr., Dep., Amort./Cur. Mat. L/T/D						
.3 / 1.0 / 5.9	.2 / .9 / 2.2	.2 / 1.0 / 3.8	Fixed/Worth	.1 / 1.5 / 4.4	.2 / 1.6 / UND	.1 / 1.7 / 2.4	.3 / 1.1 / 117.0	.3 / .9 / 4.0	.2 / .5 / 1.8
.7 / 2.1 / 8.7	.5 / 1.4 / 6.6	.8 / 1.9 / 7.7	Debt/Worth	.8 / 2.8 / 61.9	.8 / 2.0 / UND	.8 / 1.9 / 3.9	1.2 / 2.1 / 999.8	.8 / 2.2 / 6.4	.5 / 1.1 / 2.5
(69) 63.0 / 22.4 / 2.2	(61) 53.4 / 23.7 / 6.0	(108) 53.3 / 16.0 / .0	% Profit Before Taxes/Tangible Net Worth	(22) 30.4 / 2.1 / -3.8	(27) 78.6 / 11.7 / -2.2	(10) 25.3 / 13.3 / -11.1	(12) 117.6 / 47.4 / -.1	(16) 47.0 / 26.8 / 6.9	(21) 38.2 / 19.7 / 7.9
20.9 / 6.1 / .3	20.5 / 6.5 / 2.0	18.5 / 4.8 / .0	% Profit Before Taxes/Total Assets	15.8 / .7 / -1.6	19.0 / 5.8 / -.1	12.6 / 3.8 / -1.9	22.2 / 2.7 / -.1	23.6 / 7.8 / .6	19.8 / 8.6 / 2.1
26.8 / 8.5 / 1.6	32.0 / 10.1 / 2.4	51.3 / 9.9 / 1.7	Sales/Net Fixed Assets	189.7 / .6 / .2	37.6 / 15.5 / 2.0	190.7 / 5.9 / .9	48.6 / 9.7 / 3.4	51.1 / 12.5 / 3.6	43.6 / 9.7 / 5.4
3.9 / 2.2 / 1.0	3.6 / 2.1 / 1.1	3.8 / 2.2 / .7	Sales/Total Assets	2.8 / .6 / .1	4.6 / 2.4 / .4	3.0 / 1.3 / .6	4.3 / 2.0 / 1.7	3.7 / 2.4 / 1.9	3.6 / 2.4 / 1.7
(71) 1.1 / 3.2 / 8.2	(56) .9 / 3.2 / 6.5	(100) 1.0 / 2.8 / 11.4	% Depr., Dep., Amort./Sales	(19) 9.6 / 17.6 / 26.1	(26) 1.4 / 2.5 / 7.9		(11) .7 / 4.4 / 7.4	(16) .6 / 1.9 / 3.0	(19) .8 / 1.6 / 3.4
(39) 1.9 / 5.6 / 10.6	(20) 1.3 / 4.1 / 11.4	(31) 2.5 / 7.7 / 17.3	% Officers', Directors', Owners' Comp/Sales		(10) 3.7 / 8.1 / 14.2				
1640856M / 800320M	1292890M / 630686M	2201516M / 1029188M	Net Sales ($) / Total Assets ($)	11318M / 35347M	67032M / 109826M	42197M / 46038M	104587M / 45553M	319671M / 171426M	1656711M / 620998M

M = $ thousand   MM = $ million
See Pages 11 through 18 for Explanation of Ratios and Data

PUBLIC
ADMINISTRATION

Current Data Sorted By Assets | Comparative Historical Data

2	1	6	9	1	7	Type of Statement		
						Unqualified	27	16
						Reviewed		
						Compiled	1	
						Tax Returns		
		1	4		1	Other	9	7
	21 (4/1-9/30/02)		11 (10/1/02-3/31/03)				4/1/98-3/31/99	4/1/99-3/31/00
0-500M	500M-2MM	2-10MM	10-50MM	50-100MM	100-250MM		ALL	ALL
2	1	7	13	1	8	NUMBER OF STATEMENTS	37	23
%	%	%	%	%	%	ASSETS	%	%
			23.3			Cash & Equivalents	30.5	31.4
			10.0			Trade Receivables (net)	6.7	4.2
			.1			Inventory	.3	.3
			3.0			All Other Current	5.0	7.1
			36.4			Total Current	42.4	43.1
			55.0			Fixed Assets (net)	40.5	42.9
			.1			Intangibles (net)	.7	.8
			8.4			All Other Non-Current	16.4	13.2
			100.0			Total	100.0	100.0
						LIABILITIES		
			.1			Notes Payable-Short Term	.3	.2
			1.1			Cur. Mat.-L/T/D	1.0	1.0
			1.7			Trade Payables	3.2	3.2
			.0			Income Taxes Payable	.8	.0
			8.3			All Other Current	7.8	6.0
			11.2			Total Current	13.0	10.5
			18.4			Long Term Debt	15.1	16.3
			.0			Deferred Taxes	.0	1.5
			4.6			All Other Non-Current	3.3	4.3
			65.8			Net Worth	68.6	67.5
			100.0			Total Liabilities & Net Worth	100.0	100.0
						INCOME DATA		
			100.0			Net Sales	100.0	100.0
						Gross Profit		
			98.9			Operating Expenses	92.1	100.1
			1.1			Operating Profit	7.9	-.1
			4.5			All Other Expenses (net)	-1.3	-5.2
			-3.4			Profit Before Taxes	9.3	5.1
						RATIOS		
			7.4				6.6	6.4
			5.8			Current	3.7	4.1
			2.8				2.0	2.3
			6.9				6.4	5.0
			5.2			Quick	3.4	3.6
			2.6				1.7	1.6
		14 25.6					11 31.8	1 289.2
		28 13.1				Sales/Receivables	27 13.5	28 13.1
		42 8.6					46 8.0	41 9.0
						Cost of Sales/Inventory		
						Cost of Sales/Payables		
			1.3				1.0	1.0
			1.8			Sales/Working Capital	2.4	2.4
			3.8				4.9	6.2
							(22) 4.2	(14) 3.7
						EBIT/Interest	3.1	2.3
							1.3	.4
						Net Profit + Depr., Dep., Amort./Cur. Mat. L /T/D		
			.5				.0	.0
			.8			Fixed/Worth	.7	.7
			1.2				.9	1.0
			.2				.2	.1
			.3			Debt/Worth	.5	.5
			1.2				.7	.8
			4.0				(36) 11.1	6.6
			.8			% Profit Before Taxes/Tangible Net Worth	3.4	2.6
			-9.4				.5	.4
			3.1				8.0	4.6
			.7			% Profit Before Taxes/Total Assets	1.8	1.7
			-3.7				.2	.2
			1.1				UND	UND
			.5			Sales/Net Fixed Assets	.7	.7
			.4				.3	.3
			.5				.8	1.0
			.4			Sales/Total Assets	.4	.4
			.2				.2	.2
							(17) 4.3	(12) 4.9
						% Depr., Dep., Amort./Sales	6.0	6.1
							11.3	12.5
						% Officers', Directors', Owners' Comp/Sales		
183M	318M	32994M	126298M	34358M	893275M	Net Sales ($)	886795M	475517M
53M	1276M	44851M	212680M	97385M	1260019M	Total Assets ($)	1997772M	1001337M

M = $ thousand   MM = $ million
See Pages 11 through 18 for Explanation of Ratios and Data

Comparative Historical Data   ## Current Data Sorted By Sales

			Type of Statement						
12	10	26	Unqualified	4	2	2	5	6	7
	1		Reviewed						
1	1		Compiled						
			Tax Returns						
1	7	6	Other		4			1	1
4/1/00-	4/1/01-	4/1/02-			21 (4/1-9/30/02)		11 (10/1/02-3/31/03)		
3/31/01	3/31/02	3/31/03		0-1MM	1-3MM	3-5MM	5-10MM	10-25MM	25MM & OVER
ALL	ALL	ALL							
14	19	32	NUMBER OF STATEMENTS	4	6	2	5	7	8
%	%	%	ASSETS	%	%	%	%	%	%
20.8	41.2	22.5	Cash & Equivalents						
2.4	6.6	8.9	Trade Receivables (net)						
.3	.6	.4	Inventory						
1.1	4.7	8.2	All Other Current						
24.6	53.1	40.0	Total Current						
50.0	31.1	49.5	Fixed Assets (net)						
.8	.3	.1	Intangibles (net)						
24.6	15.6	10.5	All Other Non-Current						
100.0	100.0	100.0	Total						
			LIABILITIES						
.3	.0	.5	Notes Payable-Short Term						
1.3	.9	1.0	Cur. Mat.-L/T/D						
1.5	7.1	2.0	Trade Payables						
.0	.6	.0	Income Taxes Payable						
3.9	20.0	6.9	All Other Current						
7.0	28.6	10.4	Total Current						
22.2	17.5	14.8	Long Term Debt						
.4	.0	.9	Deferred Taxes						
2.5	4.7	6.4	All Other Non-Current						
67.9	49.1	67.5	Net Worth						
100.0	100.0	100.0	Total Liabilities & Net Worth						
			INCOME DATA						
100.0	100.0	100.0	Net Sales						
			Gross Profit						
100.0	96.8	93.7	Operating Expenses						
.0	3.2	6.3	Operating Profit						
−3.4	−.9	5.0	All Other Expenses (net)						
3.4	4.1	1.3	Profit Before Taxes						
			RATIOS						
6.2	6.5	8.7							
3.6	3.5	4.4	Current						
1.8	1.0	2.6							
5.9	5.4	7.0							
3.3	3.3	4.1	Quick						
1.2	1.0	2.1							
6 60.6	2 165.4	11 32.5							
24 15.2	22 16.3	27 13.7	Sales/Receivables						
35 10.5	59 6.2	48 7.7							
			Cost of Sales/Inventory						
			Cost of Sales/Payables						
1.0	1.2	1.2							
2.5	2.8	2.0	Sales/Working Capital						
8.5	−129.9	5.6							
6.7	4.8	6.2							
(11) 1.8	(11) 3.0	(20) 2.6	EBIT/Interest						
−.8	−.5	.9							
			Net Profit + Depr., Dep., Amort./Cur. Mat. L/T/D						
.7	.0	.5							
.8	.5	.7	Fixed/Worth						
.9	.7	1.0							
.2	.4	.2							
.6	.7	.3	Debt/Worth						
.7	4.3	1.0							
4.0	7.0	7.9							
.6	(17) 2.0	1.4	% Profit Before Taxes/Tangible Net Worth						
−2.1	−3.5	−5.9							
2.5	4.0	4.7							
.4	1.0	1.1	% Profit Before Taxes/Total Assets						
−1.3	−3.2	−3.9							
.9	UND	1.9							
.6	1.4	.5	Sales/Net Fixed Assets						
.4	.4	.3							
.5	4.1	.8							
.3	.5	.3	Sales/Total Assets						
.2	.2	.2							
		2.9							
	(15) 6.3	6.3	% Depr., Dep., Amort./Sales						
		13.3							
			% Officers', Directors', Owners' Comp/Sales						
206740M	456688M	1087426M	Net Sales ($)	1283M	12236M	8529M	31331M	102377M	931670M
940397M	1393770M	1616264M	Total Assets ($)	4753M	56917M	19638M	93796M	314386M	1126774M

© RMA 2003   M = $ thousand   MM = $ million
See Pages 11 through 18 for Explanation of Ratios and Data

PUBLIC ADMINISTRATION—Other General Government Support   NAICS 921190 (SIC 9199)

	Current Data Sorted By Assets						Type of Statement	Comparative Historical Data	
4	8	37	73	31	41		Unqualified	114	113
	1	2					Reviewed	3	
1		1	3				Compiled	2	3
	1						Tax Returns	1	1
4	3	17	18	3	2		Other	29	33
	177 (4/1-9/30/02)		73 (10/1/02-3/31/03)					4/1/98-3/31/99	4/1/99-3/31/00
0-500M	500M-2MM	2-10MM	10-50MM	50-100MM	100-250MM			ALL	ALL
9	13	57	94	34	43		NUMBER OF STATEMENTS	149	150
%	%	%	%	%	%		ASSETS	%	%
	26.5	31.3	22.1	25.8	17.4		Cash & Equivalents	26.1	28.4
	14.2	7.4	6.2	4.1	2.8		Trade Receivables (net)	8.2	6.7
	5.4	.2	.4	.3	.6		Inventory	.3	.4
	10.3	5.2	4.9	5.8	3.2		All Other Current	3.3	5.2
	56.4	44.0	33.6	36.0	24.0		Total Current	38.0	40.6
	40.9	43.4	53.4	50.2	54.6		Fixed Assets (net)	45.1	42.1
	.1	.5	.5	.4	.4		Intangibles (net)	.7	.9
	2.6	12.1	12.5	13.4	21.0		All Other Non-Current	16.2	16.3
	100.0	100.0	100.0	100.0	100.0		Total	100.0	100.0
							LIABILITIES		
	16.0	2.0	1.5	.3	.4		Notes Payable-Short Term	2.7	1.6
	1.1	.6	1.4	.5	1.3		Cur. Mat.-L/T/D	1.2	1.0
	7.8	4.1	3.6	2.9	2.3		Trade Payables	3.4	3.8
	.1	.2	.0	.0	.0		Income Taxes Payable	.1	.1
	13.1	5.9	6.0	4.2	2.7		All Other Current	5.2	6.6
	38.1	12.8	12.6	7.9	6.8		Total Current	12.6	13.0
	14.2	18.6	20.8	15.9	28.6		Long Term Debt	20.3	17.7
	.0	.2	.1	.0	.2		Deferred Taxes	.5	.1
	1.0	3.8	3.9	5.3	4.8		All Other Non-Current	3.5	8.0
	46.7	64.5	62.7	70.9	59.7		Net Worth	63.1	61.1
	100.0	100.0	100.0	100.0	100.0		Total Liabilities & Net Worth	100.0	100.0
							INCOME DATA		
	100.0	100.0	100.0	100.0	100.0		Net Sales	100.0	100.0
							Gross Profit		
	96.7	92.3	88.4	93.5	92.4		Operating Expenses	98.0	95.2
	3.3	7.7	11.6	6.5	7.5		Operating Profit	2.0	4.8
	2.8	4.0	4.9	1.7	4.9		All Other Expenses (net)	-3.2	-3.4
	.5	3.8	6.7	4.9	2.6		Profit Before Taxes	5.1	8.1
							RATIOS		
	2.7	16.4	6.9	6.4	5.2			6.9	7.2
	1.6	4.9	3.2	5.3	3.7		Current	4.0	4.1
	.8	1.6	1.6	2.3	2.2			1.9	2.0
	2.6	14.7	5.7	5.5	4.4			6.5	6.4
	1.1	4.4	2.5	4.3	2.7		Quick	3.5	3.4
	.5	1.6	1.3	1.8	1.7			1.5	1.5
0 UND	0 UND	10 36.4	6 64.0	11 34.2			Sales/Receivables	5 72.0	8 44.3
0 UND	12 29.4	25 14.7	20 17.8	23 16.1				22 16.9	23 16.1
22 16.4	35 10.5	43 8.4	44 8.3	45 8.1				46 8.0	38 9.7
							Cost of Sales/Inventory		
							Cost of Sales/Payables		
	1.7	1.2	1.0	1.2	1.2			1.4	1.2
	13.5	2.6	2.5	2.0	2.9		Sales/Working Capital	2.7	2.3
	NM	9.7	6.4	4.3	6.2			6.8	7.1
		7.1	7.3	5.7	2.9			8.7	8.9
	(37)	1.9	(66) 2.6	(26) 2.6	(36) 1.7		EBIT/Interest	(98) 2.4	(101) 3.1
		.1	-.3	-1.5	.8			.7	.9
							Net Profit + Depr., Dep., Amort./Cur. Mat. L /T/D		
	.0	.0	.6	.6	.7			.4	.3
	.9	.8	.9	.8	.9		Fixed/Worth	.8	.8
	2.1	1.2	1.2	1.0	1.1			1.0	1.0
	.5	.1	.2	.2	.3			.3	.2
	1.1	.6	.5	.4	.6		Debt/Worth	.5	.5
	11.9	.9	.9	.6	1.2			1.0	1.0
	72.1	11.8	6.4	4.4	3.8			12.3	8.3
(12)	6.1	(56) 1.7	(93) 2.6	2.3	(42) 1.0		% Profit Before Taxes/Tangible Net Worth	(148) 3.1	(146) 3.5
	-5.5	-3.4	-1.2	-1.4	-1.9			-.8	.0
	18.1	7.3	3.6	3.1	2.1			6.0	5.3
	1.9	1.5	1.5	1.6	.7		% Profit Before Taxes/Total Assets	2.0	2.0
	-6.0	-2.3	-.9	-.8	-.8			-.5	-.1
	UND	UND	1.6	1.3	.9			17.9	19.7
	30.0	.8	.5	.5	.6		Sales/Net Fixed Assets	.7	.7
	.4	.3	.3	.3	.4			.3	.4
	10.6	1.5	.7	.6	.4			1.1	1.1
	3.8	.5	.3	.3	.4		Sales/Total Assets	.3	.4
	.4	.2	.2	.2	.2			.2	.2
		3.7	3.6	.5	2.5			1.8	2.0
	(29)	8.1	(58) 6.4	(22) 6.0	(25) 5.6		% Depr., Dep., Amort./Sales	(85) 5.2	(76) 4.8
		18.1	11.7	9.4	9.0			10.4	7.5
								5.4	4.5
							% Officers', Directors', Owners' Comp/Sales	(14) 12.0	(21) 9.0
								20.1	18.5
6124M	101810M	268784M	1598967M	2029029M	2630597M		Net Sales ($)	3106265M	2646076M
2139M	17142M	298338M	2192271M	2376573M	6588274M		Total Assets ($)	6938544M	7059583M

M = $ thousand   MM = $ million
See Pages 11 through 18 for Explanation of Ratios and Data

Comparative Historical Data | **Current Data Sorted By Sales**

Type of Statement									
	116	78	194	Unqualified	21	26	24	20	42	61
	1		3	Reviewed		1			2	
	5	11	5	Compiled	1	1			2	1
		1	1	Tax Returns					1	
	27	50	47	Other	4	15	5	11	7	5
	4/1/00-3/31/01 ALL	4/1/01-3/31/02 ALL	4/1/02-3/31/03 ALL		0-1MM	1-3MM	3-5MM	5-10MM	10-25MM	25MM & OVER
					177 (4/1-9/30/02)			73 (10/1/02-3/31/03)		
NUMBER OF STATEMENTS	149	140	250		26	42	29	32	54	67

	%	%	%	ASSETS	%	%	%	%	%	%
	30.3	25.2	25.6	Cash & Equivalents	23.1	30.1	21.1	20.7	29.2	25.0
	5.0	3.8	6.0	Trade Receivables (net)	2.4	1.8	4.2	8.3	7.9	8.2
	.6	.4	.6	Inventory	.2	.4	.1	.2	1.7	.6
	5.9	8.1	5.6	All Other Current	9.3	3.3	4.2	5.0	4.4	7.3
	41.8	37.5	37.8	Total Current	35.0	35.6	29.6	34.2	43.2	41.1
	38.3	42.6	48.3	Fixed Assets (net)	57.2	50.3	57.2	54.3	42.8	41.3
	1.4	.9	.4	Intangibles (net)	1.6	.1	.1	.1	.7	.3
	18.5	19.0	13.5	All Other Non-Current	6.2	14.0	13.1	11.4	13.2	17.4
	100.0	100.0	100.0	Total	100.0	100.0	100.0	100.0	100.0	100.0

				LIABILITIES						
	2.0	.9	2.1	Notes Payable-Short Term	3.9	1.0	1.5	.7	3.0	2.2
	.7	1.7	1.0	Cur. Mat.-L/T/D	1.0	.6	1.5	1.7	.6	1.1
	3.5	2.9	3.6	Trade Payables	2.1	.9	2.2	2.7	4.7	5.8
	.0	.4	.1	Income Taxes Payable	.0	.0	.0	.0	.3	.0
	5.9	5.1	6.0	All Other Current	5.7	3.1	7.1	5.7	6.6	7.1
	12.1	11.0	12.7	Total Current	12.7	5.7	12.2	10.8	15.3	16.2
	17.1	20.1	20.0	Long Term Debt	19.5	19.8	20.9	16.4	18.8	22.7
	.0	.2	.1	Deferred Taxes	.0	.0	.0	.4	.1	.1
	6.3	4.9	4.0	All Other Non-Current	.4	4.2	2.5	5.0	3.0	6.4
	64.3	63.8	63.1	Net Worth	67.3	70.3	64.4	67.5	62.9	54.5
	100.0	100.0	100.0	Total Liabilities & Net Worth	100.0	100.0	100.0	100.0	100.0	100.0

				INCOME DATA						
	100.0	100.0	100.0	Net Sales	100.0	100.0	100.0	100.0	100.0	100.0
				Gross Profit						
	98.5	92.9	91.7	Operating Expenses	87.8	87.6	93.8	92.7	93.1	93.4
	1.4	7.1	8.3	Operating Profit	12.2	12.4	6.2	7.3	6.9	6.6
	−4.3	3.7	4.0	All Other Expenses (net)	6.9	4.0	4.7	2.6	1.5	5.2
	5.7	3.4	4.3	Profit Before Taxes	5.3	8.4	1.5	4.7	5.4	1.4

				RATIOS						
	8.0	9.4	8.0	Current	15.4	15.5	7.2	8.2	6.9	5.5
	4.1	4.2	3.8		2.0	5.8	3.2	4.6	3.4	3.5
	2.1	1.9	1.7		1.5	2.7	1.6	1.9	1.6	1.7
	6.5	7.0	6.0	Quick	13.7	15.5	6.2	6.9	5.8	4.4
	3.4	3.1	2.9		1.8	5.0	2.2	3.0	2.9	2.5
	1.7	1.5	1.4		.9	2.2	1.2	1.6	1.6	1.4
	1 243.7	0 810.3	4 84.3	Sales/Receivables	0 UND	0 UND	10 36.9	9 40.3	8 48.1	5 68.0
	16 22.6	12 30.8	21 17.6		8 45.2	13 29.1	24 15.5	24 15.4	23 15.9	19 18.9
	38 9.5	40 9.1	41 8.8		37 9.8	33 11.0	41 8.8	52 7.0	48 7.5	39 9.3
				Cost of Sales/Inventory						
				Cost of Sales/Payables						
	1.4	1.1	1.2	Sales/Working Capital	.9	1.0	1.0	.9	1.0	1.9
	2.5	2.9	2.6		1.9	1.9	2.0	1.9	3.0	3.7
	6.8	7.2	7.9		13.3	4.2	6.6	8.2	7.9	10.3
	(93) 5.9	(81) 4.6	(177) 5.7	EBIT/Interest	(17) 7.0	(28) 7.2	(25) 7.5	(23) 7.2	(34) 5.7	(50) 3.1
	2.0	1.4	2.1		1.6	2.3	2.2	2.9	3.4	1.5
	.6	−.8	−.1		−.2	−.8	−1.5	.1	1.9	−.4
				Net Profit + Depr., Dep., Amort./Cur. Mat. L/T/D						
	.0	.0	.4	Fixed/Worth	.0	.0	.7	.6	.3	.4
	.7	.7	.8		.9	.9	.9	.9	.7	.8
	1.0	1.0	1.1		1.5	1.2	1.2	1.1	1.0	1.1
	.2	.2	.2	Debt/Worth	.1	.1	.3	.2	.2	.4
	.5	.5	.5		.6	.4	.5	.5	.5	.7
	.9	1.0	.9		.9	.8	.9	.8	.9	1.6
	(146) 7.4	(137) 7.5	(246) 6.4	% Profit Before Taxes/Tangible Net Worth	5.1	7.7	(28) 5.2	6.4	(53) 11.2	(65) 5.2
	1.5	1.6	2.0		1.1	1.6	1.3	2.0	3.5	1.1
	−1.2	−2.4	−1.9		−4.3	−3.7	−2.9	−1.3	1.1	−4.1
	4.6	5.1	3.8	% Profit Before Taxes/Total Assets	3.8	3.9	3.4	4.7	7.9	3.1
	.9	.9	1.1		.6	.9	.8	1.4	2.7	.4
	−.8	−1.5	−1.3		−2.1	−2.9	−2.8	−.8	.8	−1.8
	UND	142.6	11.9	Sales/Net Fixed Assets	UND	UND	.8	1.3	17.9	290.6
	.9	.8	.6		.3	.4	.4	.4	.4	1.2
	.4	.4	.3		.1	.2	.3	.2	.4	.6
	1.0	.9	.9	Sales/Total Assets	.9	.6	.4	.5	1.3	1.4
	.4	.4	.4		.3	.3	.3	.3	.4	.6
	.2	.2	.2		.1	.2	.2	.2	.2	.4
	(66) 1.1	(63) 1.6	(139) 2.3	% Depr., Dep., Amort./Sales	(13) 10.9	(25) 5.5	(19) 3.1	(19) 2.9	(30) .7	(33) .5
	4.7	6.2	6.1		18.1	9.3	6.2	5.7	5.8	2.8
	9.9	11.8	10.7		30.1	20.9	8.3	10.3	7.9	6.4
	(22) 6.4	(24) 7.5	(24) 3.1	% Officers', Directors', Owners' Comp/Sales						
	14.6	16.0	7.5							
	21.5	27.9	19.5							
	3727064M	3638455M	6635311M	Net Sales ($)	14913M	85593M	112999M	242991M	841041M	5337774M
	7408753M	5969670M	11474737M	Total Assets ($)	77705M	356322M	466421M	982540M	2644963M	6946786M

M = $ thousand   MM = $ million
See Pages 11 through 18 for Explanation of Ratios and Data

Current Data Sorted By Assets   **Comparative Historical Data**

0-500M	500M-2MM	2-10MM	10-50MM	50-100MM	100-250MM	Type of Statement	4/1/98-3/31/99 ALL	4/1/99-3/31/00 ALL
	2	7	2			Unqualified	15	14
	4	2				Reviewed	6	2
2	4	2				Compiled	12	10
4	5					Tax Returns	7	4
3	2	4	1			Other	16	8
	18 (4/1-9/30/02)		26 (10/1/02-3/31/03)					
9	17	15	3			NUMBER OF STATEMENTS	56	38
%	%	%	%	%	%	**ASSETS**	%	%
	14.1	16.9				Cash & Equivalents	24.4	21.7
	18.0	12.0	D	D		Trade Receivables (net)	4.5	10.6
	9.7	3.4	A	A		Inventory	2.3	2.9
	1.6	2.5	T	T		All Other Current	3.2	1.0
	43.3	34.9	A	A		Total Current	34.5	36.2
	52.7	59.3				Fixed Assets (net)	58.2	56.6
	2.1	1.7	N	N		Intangibles (net)	.8	1.1
	1.8	4.2	O	O		All Other Non-Current	6.5	6.0
	100.0	100.0	T	T		Total	100.0	100.0
						LIABILITIES		
	2.6	5.0	A	A		Notes Payable-Short Term	2.4	6.8
	3.5	2.9	V	V		Cur. Mat.-L/T/D	1.7	2.0
	6.8	3.7	A	A		Trade Payables	1.8	4.0
	.4	.0	I	I		Income Taxes Payable	.0	.0
	5.7	3.8	L	L		All Other Current	1.5	2.4
	19.0	15.4	A	A		Total Current	7.5	15.3
	18.8	20.2	B	B		Long Term Debt	19.0	14.8
	.0	.0	L	L		Deferred Taxes	.0	.1
	4.9	4.3	E	E		All Other Non-Current	1.1	2.0
	57.3	60.1				Net Worth	72.4	67.8
	100.0	100.0				Total Liabilities & Net Worth	100.0	100.0
						INCOME DATA		
	100.0	100.0				Net Sales	100.0	100.0
						Gross Profit		
	92.2	88.1				Operating Expenses	83.2	89.4
	7.8	11.9				Operating Profit	16.8	10.6
	1.4	6.1				All Other Expenses (net)	1.1	-5.4
	6.4	5.8				Profit Before Taxes	15.7	16.0
						RATIOS		
	5.6	8.4					UND	15.9
	2.5	4.3				Current	8.6	4.6
	1.6	2.0					1.6	1.9
	4.0	8.4					UND	15.9
	2.0	4.0				Quick	8.4	4.6
	.9	1.7					1.4	1.6
0	UND	0 UND					0 UND	0 UND
19	18.8	11 34.3				Sales/Receivables	0 UND	1 283.9
59	6.2	41 8.9					6 57.4	39 9.4
						Cost of Sales/Inventory		
						Cost of Sales/Payables		
	2.3	2.0					.8	.9
	5.8	3.1				Sales/Working Capital	1.5	1.5
	9.2	4.7					10.6	6.8
	7.5	29.5					8.7	9.1
(13)	4.3	(12) 2.8				EBIT/Interest	(43) 4.8	(25) 3.2
	1.3	-.3					.3	1.4
						Net Profit + Depr., Dep., Amort./Cur. Mat. L./T/D		
	.4	.7					.5	.6
	.9	1.0				Fixed/Worth	.9	.8
	2.1	2.2					1.1	1.1
	.3	.2					.1	.1
	.5	.5				Debt/Worth	.3	.4
	1.9	1.4					.9	1.0
	12.6	10.3				% Profit Before Taxes/Tangible Net Worth	12.3	11.7
	6.8	(14) 2.8					6.9	7.8
	-.7	-3.6					-.2	2.1
	7.4	5.4				% Profit Before Taxes/Total Assets	9.2	8.8
	5.0	.9					4.9	5.5
	-.2	-3.6					-.1	1.1
	15.1	4.5				Sales/Net Fixed Assets	1.0	1.7
	.8	.7					.5	.5
	.3	.3					.3	.3
	2.3	1.6				Sales/Total Assets	.5	.9
	.7	.5					.3	.3
	.3	.2					.2	.2
	3.2	2.0				% Depr., Dep., Amort./Sales	8.9	3.0
(13)	10.5	(10) 9.2					(31) 19.9	(24) 17.8
	26.4	29.6					27.2	25.7
						% Officers', Directors', Owners' Comp/Sales		
4542M	26195M	50030M	9814M			Net Sales ($)	108149M	62816M
1765M	20125M	58206M	32922M			Total Assets ($)	242360M	104180M

M = $ thousand   MM = $ million
See Pages 11 through 18 for Explanation of Ratios and Data

Comparative Historical Data			Type of Statement	Current Data Sorted By Sales					
17	9	11	Unqualified	4	4	3			
5	3	6	Reviewed	3	2	3	1		
4	12	8	Compiled	5	3				
1	6	9	Tax Returns	8	1				
2	7	10	Other	4	2	2	1	1	
					18 (4/1-9/30/02)			26 (10/1/02-3/31/03)	
4/1/00-3/31/01 ALL	4/1/01-3/31/02 ALL	4/1/02-3/31/03 ALL		0-1MM	1-3MM	3-5MM	5-10MM	10-25MM	25MM & OVER
29	37	44	NUMBER OF STATEMENTS	21	12	8	2	1	
%	%	%	ASSETS	%	%	%	%	%	%
18.1	20.1	17.8	Cash & Equivalents	17.9	18.6				D
4.7	9.0	12.7	Trade Receivables (net)	3.8	13.3				A
2.2	4.0	6.0	Inventory	2.3	9.2				T
1.0	3.0	2.7	All Other Current	.3	4.9				A
26.0	36.1	39.3	Total Current	24.4	46.1				
65.0	55.4	51.2	Fixed Assets (net)	66.1	43.1				N
1.1	2.2	3.6	Intangibles (net)	4.8	3.0				O
7.9	6.3	5.9	All Other Non-Current	4.8	7.8				T
100.0	100.0	100.0	Total	100.0	100.0				
			LIABILITIES						A
1.3	3.2	4.9	Notes Payable-Short Term	5.2	2.2				V
2.2	2.0	9.2	Cur. Mat.-L/T/D	15.9	3.9				A
2.4	3.9	4.9	Trade Payables	2.2	4.5				I
.0	.4	.1	Income Taxes Payable	.0	.5				L
1.7	4.0	7.0	All Other Current	8.5	4.2				A
7.6	13.4	26.2	Total Current	31.8	15.3				B
18.6	21.5	21.9	Long Term Debt	31.0	20.5				L
.1	.0	.0	Deferred Taxes	.0	.0				E
1.6	1.2	3.4	All Other Non-Current	.0	6.9				
72.2	63.8	48.5	Net Worth	37.2	57.2				
100.0	100.0	100.0	Total Liabilities & Net Worth	100.0	100.0				
			INCOME DATA						
100.0	100.0	100.0	Net Sales	100.0	100.0				
			Gross Profit						
94.2	93.1	91.2	Operating Expenses	87.0	94.5				
5.8	6.9	8.8	Operating Profit	13.0	5.5				
−3.2	3.3	4.3	All Other Expenses (net)	3.7	5.6				
9.0	3.6	4.4	Profit Before Taxes	9.3	−.1				
			RATIOS						
12.8	8.0	7.3		7.1	8.1				
5.1	5.1	3.1	Current	2.7	3.9				
2.8	1.7	1.2		.6	1.6				
12.7	7.5	7.2		7.1	8.1				
4.8	3.8	2.7	Quick	2.6	2.9				
2.8	1.2	.8		.4	.8				
0 UND	0 UND	0 UND		0 UND	0 UND				
0 UND	0 UND	0 UND	Sales/Receivables	0 UND	12 31.6				
17 21.9	35 10.6	38 9.7		13 27.5	44 8.3				
			Cost of Sales/Inventory						
			Cost of Sales/Payables						
.8	1.1	2.1		1.9	2.5				
2.3	2.1	− 4.8	Sales/Working Capital	3.1	5.0				
4.5	8.8	33.1		−21.4	13.8				
8.0	6.5	7.6		6.9	13.1				
(23) 5.0	(27) 3.8	(33) 3.6	EBIT/Interest	(15) 2.0	(10) 2.9				
.5	1.4	.3		.6	.5				
			Net Profit + Depr., Dep., Amort./Cur. Mat. L/T/D						
.7	.6	.7		.9	.4				
.9	.9	1.0	Fixed/Worth	1.4	1.0				
1.1	1.1	2.3		3.7	2.0				
.1	.2	.3		.2	.2				
.3	.3	.5	Debt/Worth	.4	.7				
.5	1.2	2.2		5.9	2.2				
10.1	9.7	14.4	% Profit Before Taxes/Tangible Net Worth	14.2	23.3				
(28) 5.2	(35) 2.3	(40) 6.5		(18) 6.7	3.6				
−2.8	−1.7	−2.8		1.6	−3.6				
7.6	5.9	9.5	% Profit Before Taxes/Total Assets	9.2	11.9				
4.1	1.8	2.3		5.0	1.8				
−3.4	−1.3	−3.5		−.8	−3.4				
.7	6.7	12.9		6.7	17.5				
.4	.6	.8	Sales/Net Fixed Assets	.6	2.4				
.3	.3	.4		.2	.4				
.4	1.4	2.5		2.3	2.3				
.3	.4	.6	Sales/Total Assets	.4	1.0				
.2	.2	.3		.2	.4				
10.8	5.3	2.8		6.7					
(14) 17.7	(22) 14.7	(27) 7.5	% Depr., Dep., Amort./Sales	(14) 20.2					
23.3	34.3	25.2		40.9					
		3.1	% Officers', Directors', Owners' Comp/Sales						
		(14) 5.1							
		20.5							
66551M	69757M	90581M	Net Sales ($)	8531M	22033M	32502M	13859M	13656M	
180740M	113711M	113018M	Total Assets ($)	26287M	36399M	41895M	4873M	3564M	

M = $ thousand   MM = $ million
See Pages 11 through 18 for Explanation of Ratios and Data

Current Data Sorted By Assets   Comparative Historical Data

						Type of Statement	4/1/98-3/31/99 ALL	4/1/99-3/31/00 ALL
4	4	9	11	5	7	Unqualified		23
		1				Reviewed		1
						Compiled		
						Tax Returns		
	1	3	6	1		Other		7
	45 (4/1-9/30/02)		7 (10/1/02-3/31/03)					
0-500M	500M-2MM	2-10MM	10-50MM	50-100MM	100-250MM			
4	5	13	17	6	7	NUMBER OF STATEMENTS		31
%	%	%	%	%	%	**ASSETS**	%	%
		34.4	21.9			Cash & Equivalents	D	36.1
		12.0	19.6			Trade Receivables (net)	A	5.3
		.4	.3			Inventory	T	.1
		13.0	7.3			All Other Current	A	4.6
		59.8	49.1			Total Current		46.2
		33.5	30.1			Fixed Assets (net)	N	33.8
		.1	.1			Intangibles (net)	O	.6
		6.6	20.7			All Other Non-Current	T	19.5
		100.0	100.0			Total		100.0
						LIABILITIES	A	
		.7	3.6			Notes Payable-Short Term	V	3.6
		2.7	.4			Cur. Mat.-L/T/D	A	1.5
		5.4	4.2			Trade Payables	I	2.5
		.0	.1			Income Taxes Payable	L	.0
		15.3	15.9			All Other Current	A	13.2
		24.0	24.1			Total Current	B	20.8
		12.4	6.7			Long Term Debt	L	13.8
		.0	.0			Deferred Taxes	E	.0
		14.8	3.3			All Other Non-Current		3.0
		48.8	65.9			Net Worth		62.4
		100.0	100.0			Total Liabilities & Net Worth		100.0
						INCOME DATA		
		100.0	100.0			Net Sales		100.0
						Gross Profit		
		92.2	92.5			Operating Expenses		90.6
		7.8	7.5			Operating Profit		9.4
		.5	4.9			All Other Expenses (net)		−2.3
		7.3	2.7			Profit Before Taxes		11.7
						RATIOS		
		3.3	4.4					6.3
		3.0	1.8			Current		2.9
		1.6	1.4					1.5
		3.1	4.3					5.9
		3.0	1.7			Quick		2.5
		1.3	1.3					1.2
		1 466.2	3 124.9				0 UND	
		19 19.0	31 11.9			Sales/Receivables	4 96.7	
		41 9.0	74 4.9				19 19.1	
						Cost of Sales/Inventory		
						Cost of Sales/Payables		
		2.0	4.3					1.6
		9.8	10.6			Sales/Working Capital		2.6
		19.3	20.5					28.2
						EBIT/Interest		
						Net Profit + Depr., Dep., Amort./Cur. Mat. L /T/D		
		.0	.0					.1
		.6	.5			Fixed/Worth		.6
		1.4	.9					.9
		.4	.2					.1
		1.4	.4			Debt/Worth		.6
		1.7	.7					1.3
		23.5	9.5					26.9
	(12)	16.9	.5			% Profit Before Taxes/Tangible Net Worth		8.6
		6.4	−3.1					3.4
		14.6	4.8					15.9
		9.7	.3			% Profit Before Taxes/Total Assets		5.1
		3.4	−2.5					1.5
		103.5	UND					21.5
		5.6	5.8			Sales/Net Fixed Assets		2.4
		1.8	1.1					.9
		2.6	3.9					1.0
		1.6	.9			Sales/Total Assets		.6
		.9	.5					.4
								.3
						% Depr., Dep., Amort./Sales	(16)	.8
								3.9
						% Officers', Directors', Owners' Comp/Sales		
9198M	20495M	136177M	844322M	259739M	505987M	Net Sales ($)		812408M
1309M	5140M	63748M	404901M	425914M	1006629M	Total Assets ($)		1690887M

Comparative Historical Data / Current Data Sorted By Sales

				Type of Statement						
	26	28	40	Unqualified	2	3	6	3	11	15
	1			Reviewed					1	
	2	3	1	Compiled						
				Tax Returns						
	7	9	11	Other	1	2		3	1	4
	4/1/00- 3/31/01	4/1/01- 3/31/02	4/1/02- 3/31/03		45 (4/1-9/30/02)			7 (10/1/02-3/31/03)		
	ALL	ALL	ALL		0-1MM	1-3MM	3-5MM	5-10MM	10-25MM	25MM & OVER
NUMBER OF STATEMENTS	36	40	52		3	5	6	6	13	19
	%	%	%	**ASSETS**	%	%	%	%	%	%
	31.3	22.8	24.0	Cash & Equivalents					19.1	21.2
	11.7	13.2	13.1	Trade Receivables (net)					9.1	12.2
	.1	.3	.2	Inventory					.2	.3
	8.4	6.8	8.7	All Other Current					7.6	12.7
	51.5	43.1	46.0	Total Current					35.9	46.3
	33.3	39.0	34.8	Fixed Assets (net)					43.3	34.2
	.4	1.3	1.0	Intangibles (net)					.2	2.5
	14.8	16.6	18.1	All Other Non-Current					20.7	17.0
	100.0	100.0	100.0	Total					100.0	100.0
				LIABILITIES						
	.7	2.9	1.6	Notes Payable-Short Term					.9	.8
	.5	.9	1.3	Cur. Mat.-L/T/D					1.8	.9
	6.3	5.7	4.0	Trade Payables					2.0	4.7
	.0	.0	.0	Income Taxes Payable					.1	.0
	14.5	11.2	13.0	All Other Current					8.1	16.7
	21.9	20.8	20.1	Total Current					12.8	23.2
	11.9	14.8	16.9	Long Term Debt					23.9	21.9
	.0	.0	.0	Deferred Taxes					.0	.0
	9.7	6.0	6.0	All Other Non-Current					5.4	2.4
	56.4	58.4	57.1	Net Worth					57.8	52.5
	100.0	100.0	100.0	Total Liabilities & Net Worth					100.0	100.0
				INCOME DATA						
	100.0	100.0	100.0	Net Sales					100.0	100.0
				Gross Profit						
	97.3	96.9	94.0	Operating Expenses					97.7	96.1
	2.7	3.1	6.0	Operating Profit					2.3	3.9
	-4.4	3.5	2.4	All Other Expenses (net)					1.2	2.7
	7.1	-.3	3.6	Profit Before Taxes					1.1	1.2
				RATIOS						
	4.7	6.1	4.9	Current					7.3	3.0
	2.5	2.2	2.6						3.4	1.7
	1.6	1.3	1.4						1.8	1.1
	4.1	5.2	4.6	Quick					6.6	2.9
	1.7	1.8	2.1						2.8	1.5
	1.1	1.0	1.3						1.5	.7
	2 231.2	0 803.1	1 395.6	Sales/Receivables					2 182.2	1 694.1
	19 19.1	18 20.2	12 30.3						10 36.1	4 99.4
	54 6.7	36 10.2	36 10.2						30 12.3	31 11.8
				Cost of Sales/Inventory						
				Cost of Sales/Payables						
	2.3	2.5	2.8	Sales/Working Capital					2.8	8.4
	5.3	8.6	10.1						9.5	11.3
	11.3	43.1	23.0						14.5	60.6
	42.9	11.8	5.6	EBIT/Interest						
	(13) 3.1	(12) 1.9	(19) 2.7							
	1.6	.1	1.0							
				Net Profit + Depr., Dep., Amort./Cur. Mat. L/T/D						
	.1	.2	.0	Fixed/Worth					.6	.0
	.6	.8	.6						.7	.8
	.9	1.0	.9						.9	1.7
	.3	.2	.3	Debt/Worth					.4	.3
	.6	.6	.6						.5	.9
	1.6	1.5	1.7						1.6	2.5
	(34) 21.7	(39) 6.7	(49) 23.1	% Profit Before Taxes/Tangible Net Worth					(12) 18.5	(18) 19.5
	6.0	.3	4.0						4.6	-4.6
	.8	-3.6	-2.5						-4.3	
	15.8	3.0	11.7	% Profit Before Taxes/Total Assets					9.4	5.3
	2.2	.0	2.3						2.4	.2
	.5	-2.4	-1.3						-1.8	-2.8
	43.5	47.8	112.9	Sales/Net Fixed Assets					17.3	UND
	2.5	2.8	3.0						1.1	2.3
	.9	.9	1.1						.8	.9
	2.3	2.7	2.7	Sales/Total Assets					2.6	4.2
	.9	.9	1.0						.7	1.2
	.6	.4	.6						.4	.7
	.5	.9	.3	% Depr., Dep., Amort./Sales						
	(19) 1.2	(15) 3.0	(20) 1.9							
	5.2	4.9	4.6							
				% Officers', Directors', Owners' Comp/Sales						
	936419M	848232M	1775918M	Net Sales ($)	2157M	7822M	22006M	45904M	205318M	1492711M
	1478189M	1666965M	1907641M	Total Assets ($)	1931M	32147M	26090M	112838M	452162M	1282473M

M = $ thousand   MM = $ million
See Pages 11 through 18 for Explanation of Ratios and Data

Current Data Sorted By Assets | Comparative Historical Data

Type of Statement	0-500M	500M-2MM	2-10MM	10-50MM	50-100MM	100-250MM		4/1/98-3/31/99 ALL	4/1/99-3/31/00 ALL
Unqualified		1	15	11	8	5		28	40
Reviewed		4	5					5	5
Compiled	3	1	2	1				9	8
Tax Returns	1	1	1		1				2
Other	4		6	4	3	2		18	16
	34 (4/1-9/30/02)			49 (10/1/02-3/31/03)					
NUMBER OF STATEMENTS	8	11	29	16	12	7		60	71

	0-500M %	500M-2MM %	2-10MM %	10-50MM %	50-100MM %	100-250MM %		%	%
ASSETS									
Cash & Equivalents		14.6	16.6	6.7	8.1			18.2	10.4
Trade Receivables (net)		24.9	17.9	11.6	5.2			20.5	16.1
Inventory		1.7	1.8	2.9	.5			1.9	1.0
All Other Current		2.6	4.1	1.5	1.2			4.4	3.8
Total Current		43.8	40.3	22.6	15.0			45.1	31.2
Fixed Assets (net)		45.4	50.9	61.7	59.6			42.8	52.0
Intangibles (net)		.0	5.7	1.1	9.7			3.3	4.2
All Other Non-Current		10.8	3.0	14.6	15.6			8.8	12.6
Total		100.0	100.0	100.0	100.0			100.0	100.0
LIABILITIES									
Notes Payable-Short Term		15.4	4.0	1.4	.1			8.0	3.3
Cur. Mat.-L/T/D		5.5	5.1	4.6	7.2			2.9	3.5
Trade Payables		14.9	8.6	4.6	2.3			9.2	6.7
Income Taxes Payable		.0	.1	.0	.0			.4	.1
All Other Current		12.8	5.8	5.2	3.4			6.9	6.1
Total Current		48.5	23.6	15.8	13.0			27.3	19.7
Long Term Debt		15.0	19.9	23.3	37.9			21.9	30.7
Deferred Taxes		.1	.7	.3	.0			.5	.4
All Other Non-Current		.8	9.4	9.8	1.8			4.7	4.9
Net Worth		35.6	46.3	50.8	47.3			45.5	44.2
Total Liabilities & Net Worth		100.0	100.0	100.0	100.0			100.0	100.0
INCOME DATA									
Net Sales		100.0	100.0	100.0	100.0			100.0	100.0
Gross Profit									
Operating Expenses		94.8	91.3	91.5	85.2			91.5	88.0
Operating Profit		5.2	8.7	8.5	14.8			8.5	12.0
All Other Expenses (net)		5.2	2.5	-.5	5.9			1.6	3.2
Profit Before Taxes		.0	6.2	9.1	8.8			6.9	8.8
RATIOS									
Current		1.5	6.1	3.1	4.7			4.1	5.0
		1.0	2.2	1.1	2.7			1.8	2.0
		.4	1.0	.6	.4			1.2	1.2
Quick		1.5	5.1	2.7	4.1			3.9	4.3
		.9	2.0	.9	2.2			1.5	1.8
		.4	.8	.5	.3			.9	.8
Sales/Receivables	15	24.5	17 21.9	30 12.0	25 14.4			31 11.7	25 14.5
	55	6.6	43 8.6	44 8.2	38 9.7			47 7.8	44 8.3
	87	4.2	69 5.3	67 5.5	53 6.9			74 4.9	68 5.3
Cost of Sales/Inventory									
Cost of Sales/Payables									
Sales/Working Capital		3.4	1.3	4.8	1.2			1.4	1.4
		151.8	4.1	46.7	2.6			5.7	4.6
		-3.6	126.2	-8.1	-11.0			39.2	44.8
EBIT/Interest			(23) 6.6	10.2			(47) 9.6	(57) 5.9
			2.4	2.4			2.9	2.7
			1.0	1.3			1.0	1.4
Net Profit + Depr., Dep., Amort./Cur. Mat. L /T/D									
Fixed/Worth		.2	.7	.9	.6			.4	.7
		1.4	1.3	1.1	1.4			1.0	1.0
		3.1	4.1	2.3	3.0			2.0	2.9
Debt/Worth		.6	.3	.4	.5			.4	.4
		2.1	1.4	.8	.8			1.1	.9
		3.3	4.8	2.2	12.5			4.5	5.1
% Profit Before Taxes/Tangible Net Worth			(24) 25.6	17.9	(10) 5.9			(54) 36.3	(61) 24.2
			11.2	7.2	4.0			11.4	5.4
			.3	.4	.7			1.2	1.7
% Profit Before Taxes/Total Assets		12.1	9.8	6.3	3.5			11.7	6.9
		.2	2.5	2.4	1.8			3.7	2.4
		-1.8	.3	.3	.2			.4	.4
Sales/Net Fixed Assets		15.2	12.0	1.6	3.4			10.2	5.0
		6.7	1.4	.5	.4			3.9	.7
		.7	.3	.2	.1			.5	.2
Sales/Total Assets		2.2	2.2	1.1	.8			1.9	1.8
		1.3	.5	.3	.2			1.0	.3
		.6	.2	.2	.1			.2	.1
% Depr., Dep., Amort./Sales	(10) 3.1		(24) 3.1	7.6	(10) 7.0			(50) 3.5	(60) 4.9
	6.3		7.3	13.7	15.1			6.1	9.6
	10.7		16.1	18.0	19.4			12.1	18.4
% Officers', Directors', Owners' Comp/Sales								(14) 5.7	(14) 4.1
								8.9	6.2
								14.7	14.5
Net Sales ($)	11090M	14221M	179651M	405512M	447729M	306467M		714908M	1016533M
Total Assets ($)	2110M	11603M	155094M	451192M	914838M	1051676M		1724323M	2831483M

M = $ thousand   MM = $ million
See Pages 11 through 18 for Explanation of Ratios and Data

Comparative Historical Data / Current Data Sorted By Sales

				Type of Statement						
35	24		40	Unqualified	5	7	3	8	12	5
2	4		9	Reviewed	1	3	1	1	3	
9	9		7	Compiled	3	3				1
6	2		4	Tax Returns		1	1	1		1
12	19		23	Other	2	11	1	1	3	5
4/1/00-	4/1/01-		4/1/02-			34 (4/1-9/30/02)			49 (10/1/02-3/31/03)	
3/31/01	3/31/02		3/31/03		0-1MM	1-3MM	3-5MM	5-10MM	10-25MM	25MM & OVER
ALL	ALL		ALL							
64	58		83	NUMBER OF STATEMENTS	11	25	6	11	18	12
%	%		%	ASSETS	%	%	%	%	%	%
13.2	12.3		13.4	Cash & Equivalents	15.6	14.5		8.5	10.1	9.2
20.8	21.8		15.2	Trade Receivables (net)	4.2	17.1		18.0	19.6	15.6
1.6	1.8		1.7	Inventory	1.4	1.6		2.8	.7	3.2
2.7	2.9		2.3	All Other Current	.1	1.6		4.7	3.9	1.0
38.4	38.8		32.6	Total Current	21.4	34.8		34.1	34.3	29.0
49.2	47.2		53.7	Fixed Assets (net)	71.2	52.5		53.7	53.1	50.8
2.1	4.4		4.3	Intangibles (net)	2.4	4.5		1.8	2.3	8.9
10.2	9.6		9.3	All Other Non-Current	5.1	8.2		10.4	10.3	11.3
100.0	100.0		100.0	Total	100.0	100.0		100.0	100.0	100.0
				LIABILITIES						
5.1	3.5		5.6	Notes Payable-Short Term	13.7	5.6		3.5	4.5	1.2
5.6	4.7		5.7	Cur. Mat.-L/T/D	7.4	3.6		2.8	8.1	8.6
10.2	11.2		7.7	Trade Payables	5.5	8.1		8.4	7.7	9.1
.1	.1		.1	Income Taxes Payable	.0	.4		.0	.1	.0
5.9	5.9		6.9	All Other Current	9.7	7.4		8.2	3.9	3.6
26.8	25.4		26.0	Total Current	36.3	25.1		22.9	24.3	22.5
31.4	23.8		25.0	Long Term Debt	28.8	23.6		13.2	26.4	33.8
.0	.2		.3	Deferred Taxes	.0	.5		.0	.6	.2
6.4	2.9		6.3	All Other Non-Current	3.5	8.1		13.3	4.8	3.8
35.4	47.6		42.4	Net Worth	31.4	42.7		50.6	43.8	39.7
100.0	100.0		100.0	Total Liabilities & Net Worth	100.0	100.0		100.0	100.0	100.0
				INCOME DATA						
100.0	100.0		100.0	Net Sales	100.0	100.0		100.0	100.0	100.0
				Gross Profit						
90.7	88.6		90.1	Operating Expenses	90.3	92.2		89.3	86.9	88.8
9.3	11.4		9.9	Operating Profit	9.7	7.8		10.7	13.1	11.2
2.5	3.6		3.2	All Other Expenses (net)	11.2	1.2		.2	2.6	4.3
6.8	7.8		6.7	Profit Before Taxes	-1.5	6.6		10.5	10.5	6.8
				RATIOS						
3.6	4.0		4.0		3.5	6.6		2.3	4.2	3.8
1.8	1.7		1.5	Current	1.3	1.4		1.0	2.6	1.9
.9	1.0		.8		.1	.8		.6	1.0	.6
3.0	3.7		3.4		3.5	5.9		2.2	3.6	2.9
1.4	1.4		1.3	Quick	1.3	1.2		.7	1.5	1.8
.7	1.0		.6		.1	.6		.4	.8	.6
31 11.8	26 13.8		25 14.7		1 436.5	15 25.1		43 8.5	39 9.5	28 13.2
48 7.5	46 7.9		43 8.5	Sales/Receivables	18 20.6	33 11.1		56 6.5	47 7.8	37 9.9
73 5.0	77 4.7		64 5.7		49 7.5	82 4.4		89 4.1	71 5.1	61 6.0
				Cost of Sales/Inventory						
				Cost of Sales/Payables						
1.8	2.4		1.5		1.0	1.9		4.1	1.3	3.0
9.8	7.5		10.4	Sales/Working Capital	3.4	10.4		108.9	5.4	7.8
-40.7	113.8		-13.9		-3.5	-16.9		-6.9	182.7	NM
	2.9			4.3			4.3			5.3		5.9	10.8
(49) 1.7	(50) 2.6	(70) 2.4	EBIT/Interest	(22) 2.6	(10) 2.5	(15) 2.7	2.6
.7	1.5		1.2			1.1		1.4	2.1	1.7
			15.9	Net Profit + Depr., Dep.,						
		(11)	2.1	Amort./Cur. Mat. L/T/D						
			1.1							
.7	.6		.8		.9	.8		.5	.8	.8
1.4	1.3		1.4	Fixed/Worth	2.0	1.5		1.1	1.2	1.5
5.2	2.2		3.1		-2.5	4.4		3.5	2.4	10.7
.4	.4		.4		.5	.3		.3	.7	.7
1.4	1.3		1.4	Debt/Worth	1.5	1.4		.4	1.5	1.7
8.0	3.9		4.0		-3.8	6.1		4.0	3.1	13.4
31.0	45.2		23.3	% Profit Before Taxes/Tangible		30.4		22.5	77.2
(53) 5.6	(55) 13.6	(71) 7.4	Net Worth	(20) 9.7		9.8	(10) 11.0
.5	1.4		.6			.6			4.7	3.9
6.9	13.5		7.6	% Profit Before Taxes/Total	4.0	8.4		5.4	8.7	11.0
2.2	4.4		2.7	Assets	.0	2.5		1.9	3.9	4.3
-.1	.8		.2		-1.8	.4		.4	1.5	1.6
10.8	8.5		8.2		4.4	12.4		7.5	4.4	4.2
1.9	2.0		1.2	Sales/Net Fixed Assets	.4	1.4		.4	1.3	2.0
.3	.4		.3		.1	.3		.2	.3	.4
2.5	2.2		2.0		1.6	2.1		2.3	2.0	2.1
.8	1.0		.5	Sales/Total Assets	.2	.5		.3	.6	.9
.2	.2		.2		.1	.2		.2	.2	.2
2.8	3.4		4.6			4.6		4.9	2.2	2.2
(56) 8.8	(50) 6.5	(71) 9.4	% Depr., Dep., Amort./Sales	(23) 8.9	(10) 12.3	10.0	(10) 8.1
17.1	13.7		17.7			17.4		15.1	16.6	13.8
3.7	2.7		2.9	% Officers', Directors',						
(13) 7.0	(15) 3.9	(18) 6.9	Owners' Comp/Sales						
11.9	8.0		12.8							
567691M	578997M		1364670M	Net Sales ($)	5110M	40935M	19600M	75613M	279785M	943627M
2004689M	1201531M		2586513M	Total Assets ($)	24139M	133498M	153439M	319654M	816437M	1139346M

© RMA 2003

M = $ thousand   MM = $ million
See Pages 11 through 18 for Explanation of Ratios and Data

Current Data Sorted By Assets   Comparative Historical Data

						Type of Statement		
1	13	24	20	3	5	Unqualified	42	47
						Reviewed		
		1	2			Compiled	3	3
1	1	2				Tax Returns		
	4	9	12	1		Other	10	15
	53 (4/1-9/30/02)		44 (10/1/02-3/31/03)				4/1/98-3/31/99	4/1/99-3/31/00
0-500M	500M-2MM	2-10MM	10-50MM	50-100MM	100-250MM		ALL	ALL
2	18	36	32	4	5	NUMBER OF STATEMENTS	55	65
%	%	%	%	%	%	**ASSETS**	%	%
	13.3	16.7	12.4			Cash & Equivalents	12.0	14.3
	11.2	7.8	12.0			Trade Receivables (net)	6.7	9.8
	5.1	1.4	2.1			Inventory	3.9	2.6
	8.7	4.5	3.2			All Other Current	5.1	5.7
	38.3	30.4	29.7			Total Current	27.6	32.5
	36.9	55.4	45.8			Fixed Assets (net)	52.0	47.8
	.0	.1	1.5			Intangibles (net)	1.6	1.6
	24.8	14.1	23.0			All Other Non-Current	18.8	18.2
	100.0	100.0	100.0			Total	100.0	100.0
						LIABILITIES		
	2.6	8.1	2.9			Notes Payable-Short Term	6.1	3.3
	2.4	1.8	2.1			Cur. Mat.-L/T/D	1.3	1.4
	5.4	2.1	3.3			Trade Payables	5.9	5.4
	.1	.0	.0			Income Taxes Payable	.0	.0
	10.9	6.7	7.7			All Other Current	7.6	5.0
	21.4	18.7	16.0			Total Current	20.9	15.1
	22.8	26.9	30.4			Long Term Debt	37.5	38.3
	2.1	.0	.0			Deferred Taxes	.0	.0
	3.5	6.5	3.5			All Other Non-Current	2.1	3.1
	50.1	47.8	50.1			Net Worth	39.5	43.5
	100.0	100.0	100.0			Total Liabilities & Net Worth	100.0	100.0
						INCOME DATA		
	100.0	100.0	100.0			Net Sales	100.0	100.0
						Gross Profit		
	91.0	85.8	83.1			Operating Expenses	148.2	91.0
	9.0	14.2	16.9			Operating Profit	-48.2	9.0
	5.7	4.9	6.7			All Other Expenses (net)	-9.9	-3.7
	3.4	9.4	10.1			Profit Before Taxes	-38.4	12.7
						RATIOS		
	6.3	5.5	5.6				3.3	6.2
	2.2	2.2	2.5			Current	1.9	1.9
	.3	.7	1.0				.7	1.0
	2.5	4.5	4.0				3.2	4.0
	.8	1.6	1.5			Quick	(54) 1.0	1.4
	.2	.6	.7				.5	.7
0 UND	2 241.0	5 71.6					2 221.0	4 103.9
2 176.7	13 27.6	19 18.8				Sales/Receivables	14 25.2	16 22.7
61 6.0	39 9.2	77 4.8					51 7.1	39 9.4
						Cost of Sales/Inventory		
						Cost of Sales/Payables		
	4.6	1.7	1.5				1.8	1.7
	9.4	6.2	5.6			Sales/Working Capital	5.6	5.6
	-2.8	-21.0	NM				-7.5	-188.1
		1.8	11.0				5.4	10.0
	(19) 1.2	(23) 2.4				EBIT/Interest	(27) 1.6	(39) 4.6
	-.4	1.4					-2.3	1.6
						Net Profit + Depr., Dep., Amort./Cur. Mat. L /T/D		
	.1	.8	.2				.3	.1
	.6	1.3	1.0			Fixed/Worth	1.4	1.1
	3.0	2.3	1.5				3.5	2.6
	.2	.5	.3				.4	.4
	.6	1.3	1.1			Debt/Worth	2.0	1.8
	9.2	2.4	3.6				6.2	4.4
	17.4	15.3	11.4			% Profit Before Taxes/Tangible Net Worth	10.1	27.5
(16)	3.6 (35)	.9	5.8				(50) 2.1 (63)	9.4
	-6.6	-3.8	.9				-10.8	.5
	11.8	7.5	4.1			% Profit Before Taxes/Total Assets	3.1	9.1
	2.4	.7	1.7				.3	2.1
	-2.9	-1.6	.3				-4.9	.0
	22.3	2.6	18.6			Sales/Net Fixed Assets	4.0	23.3
	4.9	1.0	1.0				.6	.6
	1.7	.4	.6				.2	.2
	2.9	1.0	.7			Sales/Total Assets	.8	1.0
	.9	.4	.4				.2	.3
	.3	.3	.2				.1	.1
	.4	1.8	1.3			% Depr., Dep., Amort./Sales	1.5	1.2
(13)	1.7 (27)	3.4 (26)	4.6				(39) 4.2 (47)	7.8
	8.1	9.2	6.0				14.2	15.1
						% Officers', Directors', Owners' Comp/Sales		
1068M	29353M	129489M	491942M	79563M	232510M	Net Sales ($)	179413M	490377M
293M	20251M	188316M	750200M	298200M	723503M	Total Assets ($)	694061M	1319830M

M = $ thousand   MM = $ million
See Pages 11 through 18 for Explanation of Ratios and Data

Comparative Historical Data
Current Data Sorted By Sales

			Type of Statement						
42	39	66	Unqualified	10	13	11	15	9	8
2			Reviewed						
6	2	1	Compiled		1				
2		4	Tax Returns	1	3				
11	14	26	Other	5	8	4	3	4	2
4/1/00-3/31/01	4/1/01-3/31/02	4/1/02-3/31/03		53 (4/1-9/30/02)			44 (10/1/02-3/31/03)		
ALL	ALL	ALL		0-1MM	1-3MM	3-5MM	5-10MM	10-25MM	25MM & OVER
63	55	97	**NUMBER OF STATEMENTS**	16	25	15	18	13	10
%	%	%	**ASSETS**	%	%	%	%	%	%
15.5	17.0	14.0	Cash & Equivalents	9.3	13.5	11.7	17.1	19.7	13.1
8.5	9.8	9.0	Trade Receivables (net)	4.3	11.6	3.1	11.1	7.9	17.0
2.9	2.4	2.2	Inventory	4.7	1.6	2.5	3.0	.2	.1
4.9	3.3	5.0	All Other Current	6.8	1.1	11.0	6.5	4.3	.6
31.8	32.5	30.2	Total Current	25.2	27.8	28.2	37.6	32.1	30.8
50.3	49.0	49.9	Fixed Assets (net)	49.4	46.7	57.0	39.6	59.9	54.0
1.8	2.4	.5	Intangibles (net)	1.5	.7	.0	.1	.2	.8
16.1	16.1	19.4	All Other Non-Current	24.0	24.8	14.7	22.7	7.8	14.4
100.0	100.0	100.0	Total	100.0	100.0	100.0	100.0	100.0	100.0
			LIABILITIES						
4.1	4.7	4.5	Notes Payable-Short Term	9.1	6.9	1.4	3.5	.6	3.1
1.3	2.2	1.9	Cur. Mat.-L/T/D	4.0	.7	1.9	1.5	2.1	2.0
4.3	3.2	3.4	Trade Payables	3.7	3.8	3.0	2.5	2.3	5.9
.0	.0	.0	Income Taxes Payable	.0	.1	.0	.0	.0	.0
7.1	5.0	7.4	All Other Current	4.5	5.9	8.3	9.2	5.3	13.7
16.8	15.2	17.3	Total Current	21.2	17.4	14.6	16.7	10.2	24.7
33.1	34.5	27.4	Long Term Debt	27.3	31.8	27.7	26.3	24.4	22.4
.0	.5	.4	Deferred Taxes	2.4	.0	.0	.0	.0	.0
3.0	3.0	5.4	All Other Non-Current	.4	2.4	4.3	4.2	13.0	15.4
47.1	46.8	49.5	Net Worth	48.8	48.4	53.4	52.8	52.4	37.5
100.0	100.0	100.0	Total Liabilities & Net Worth	100.0	100.0	100.0	100.0	100.0	100.0
			INCOME DATA						
100.0	100.0	100.0	Net Sales	100.0	100.0	100.0	100.0	100.0	100.0
			Gross Profit						
101.1	90.4	86.8	Operating Expenses	79.5	81.2	86.1	90.8	94.4	96.0
-1.1	9.6	13.2	Operating Profit	20.5	18.8	13.9	9.2	5.6	4.0
-10.3	5.2	6.1	All Other Expenses (net)	13.5	8.8	2.5	4.4	.6	3.0
9.2	4.5	7.2	Profit Before Taxes	7.1	10.0	11.4	4.8	5.0	1.0
			RATIOS						
5.4	3.8	5.4	Current	7.3	5.4	4.7	6.3	4.9	4.2
1.8	1.9	2.4		1.5	2.4	2.7	2.2	3.7	.9
1.0	1.0	.8		.3	.8	.7	1.4	1.3	.7
4.3	2.4	3.9	Quick	3.9	4.4	2.1	4.0	4.6	3.5
1.4	1.5	1.2		.7	1.3	1.0	1.9	3.0	.9
.7	1.0	.6		.2	.6	.5	.8	.9	.5
1 243.4	1 302.0	1 625.4	Sales/Receivables	0 UND	2 180.5	0 UND	0 UND	1 575.0	6 62.7
11 34.7	12 29.9	12 31.5		2 231.0	16 22.5	9 41.3	18 19.8	9 38.9	16 23.5
41 9.0	52 7.0	45 8.1		14 25.6	66 5.5	35 10.5	63 5.8	25 14.7	36 10.2
			Cost of Sales/Inventory						
			Cost of Sales/Payables						
1.9	3.0	1.9	Sales/Working Capital	.8	1.6	4.0	1.5	2.5	5.9
6.5	9.2	7.0		NM	4.9	7.1	2.2	5.4	-142.1
UND	-488.1	-22.2		-1.2	-26.8	-23.3	18.8	24.3	-34.1
6.9	3.6	5.3	EBIT/Interest	(17) 12.0		(11) 5.6			4.7
(33) 2.0	(26) 1.7	(57) 1.7		1.5		2.7			1.0
.5	-.1	.6		.7		.0			.7
			Net Profit + Depr., Dep., Amort./Cur. Mat. L/T/D						
.5	.3	.2	Fixed/Worth	.1	.2	.8	.2	.5	.9
1.1	.9	1.0		1.0	.9	.9	.8	1.1	1.2
2.1	2.1	1.7		9.7	2.1	3.1	1.4	1.7	7.5
.3	.3	.3	Debt/Worth	.2	.3	.2	.5	.3	.6
1.2	1.0	1.0		.6	1.7	1.2	.9	.9	2.8
3.5	8.3	3.0		36.3	4.0	2.8	2.0	2.4	8.5
15.2	21.3	11.1	% Profit Before Taxes/Tangible Net Worth	(13) 6.2	17.1	28.4	11.1	18.1	6.3
(61) 6.7	(49) 4.3	(94) 3.2		-1.5	5.4	5.7	1.7	3.8	.3
-.4	-1.2	-3.2		-7.1	-2.0	-8.3	-4.8	1.7	-17.3
7.9	5.7	4.3	% Profit Before Taxes/Total Assets	4.0	6.7	9.8	6.0	3.9	3.3
1.9	1.1	1.3		.5	1.6	3.2	.8	2.0	.1
-.4	-1.3	-1.3		-3.8	-.7	-3.2	-2.5	1.3	-1.5
9.2	13.4	5.1	Sales/Net Fixed Assets	12.9	6.0	4.9	5.4	15.9	13.7
.7	1.0	1.1		1.0	1.0	1.0	2.2	1.0	1.0
.3	.5	.5		.3	.4	.4	.6	.6	.5
1.3	1.2	1.0	Sales/Total Assets	.4	.9	1.8	1.4	1.1	2.6
.3	.5	.4		.2	.3	.6	.6	.6	.7
.2	.2	.3		.1	.2	.4	.2	.5	.4
1.5	2.3	1.4	% Depr., Dep., Amort./Sales	(14) .9	(19) .4	(11) 1.1	(12) 1.5		1.6
(50) 6.1	(43) 6.4	(75) 3.8		4.4	3.8	2.4	2.2		6.0
16.3	13.4	8.9		15.8	8.7	11.5	4.8		7.7
			% Officers', Directors', Owners' Comp/Sales						
565979M	352234M	963925M	Net Sales ($)	8700M	45023M	57272M	128162M	223460M	501308M
1076389M	634484M	1980763M	Total Assets ($)	42678M	213730M	124693M	443452M	363658M	792552M

M = $ thousand   MM = $ million
See Pages 11 through 18 for Explanation of Ratios and Data

Current Data Sorted By Assets   Comparative Historical Data

						Type of Statement		
	4	17	9	3	5	Unqualified	27	36
		1				Reviewed	1	
1			1			Compiled	3	3
						Tax Returns		1
4	3	6	7			Other	15	5
	41 (4/1-9/30/02)		20 (10/1/02-3/31/03)				4/1/98-3/31/99	4/1/99-3/31/00
0-500M	500M-2MM	2-10MM	10-50MM	50-100MM	100-250MM		ALL	ALL
5	7	24	17	3	5	NUMBER OF STATEMENTS	46	45
%	%	%	%	%	%	**ASSETS**	%	%
		12.9	11.5			Cash & Equivalents	17.5	15.5
		12.3	5.8			Trade Receivables (net)	8.9	10.6
		1.3	.0			Inventory	1.9	4.3
		6.5	.9			All Other Current	7.9	6.5
		32.9	18.2			Total Current	36.1	36.9
		43.8	49.8			Fixed Assets (net)	44.1	40.3
		.1	4.7			Intangibles (net)	.6	.8
		23.2	27.3			All Other Non-Current	19.2	22.0
		100.0	100.0			Total	100.0	100.0
						LIABILITIES		
		9.3	.9			Notes Payable-Short Term	5.7	6.1
		3.9	1.9			Cur. Mat.-L/T/D	3.1	2.2
		4.8	2.5			Trade Payables	3.5	4.4
		.0	.0			Income Taxes Payable	.0	.0
		8.0	3.0			All Other Current	5.2	6.9
		26.0	8.3			Total Current	17.6	19.7
		27.5	27.0			Long Term Debt	82.9	28.0
		.0	.0			Deferred Taxes	.0	.5
		5.7	8.1			All Other Non-Current	2.8	4.4
		40.8	56.5			Net Worth	-3.2	47.3
		100.0	100.0			Total Liabilities & Net Worth	100.0	100.0
						INCOME DATA		
		100.0	100.0			Net Sales	100.0	100.0
						Gross Profit		
		90.4	85.0			Operating Expenses	169.2	80.2
		9.6	15.0			Operating Profit	-69.2	19.8
		5.2	9.3			All Other Expenses (net)	-125.4	6.2
		4.3	5.7			Profit Before Taxes	56.2	13.6
						RATIOS		
		3.9	6.4			Current	5.7	3.1
		1.5	1.7				1.9	2.0
		.8	.7				1.1	1.1
		3.7	6.4			Quick	4.0	2.4
		1.4	1.7				1.2	1.1
		.4	.5				.5	.5
		5 71.2	6 64.0			Sales/Receivables	0 UND	0 UND
		29 12.5	21 17.6				20 18.5	17 21.9
		66 5.5	54 6.7				80 4.6	65 5.6
						Cost of Sales/Inventory		
						Cost of Sales/Payables		
		2.0	1.0			Sales/Working Capital	.9	1.5
		5.1	9.2				3.9	5.3
		-34.8	-31.3				25.4	135.9
		4.0	1.9			EBIT/Interest	4.6	8.7
		(17) 1.5	(12) 1.4				(26) 2.6	(27) 3.1
		-2.5	-5.9				-.6	1.1
						Net Profit + Depr., Dep., Amort./Cur. Mat. L /T/D		
		.3	.4			Fixed/Worth	.3	.1
		1.3	.8				.9	.6
		2.3	1.6				2.7	1.7
		.7	.4			Debt/Worth	.2	.3
		1.1	.8				1.2	1.1
		4.3	1.7				3.7	3.2
		13.7	3.4			% Profit Before Taxes/Tangible Net Worth	16.4	18.6
		(22) 2.5	(16) 1.1				(43) 3.6	(41) 9.1
		-7.1	-7.0				-5.5	1.4
		5.2	1.9			% Profit Before Taxes/Total Assets	5.8	9.1
		1.6	.9				1.3	3.7
		-3.7	-2.6				-3.8	-1.8
		7.6	2.2			Sales/Net Fixed Assets	6.5	17.4
		1.8	.5				.5	1.3
		.7	.2				.2	.3
		1.4	.3			Sales/Total Assets	.5	.9
		.6	.1				.2	.3
		.3	.1				.1	.1
		1.9	4.5			% Depr., Dep., Amort./Sales	2.0	1.2
		(21) 4.9	(14) 8.0				(34) 6.6	(35) 3.7
		6.6	13.8				14.1	8.5
						% Officers', Directors', Owners' Comp/Sales		
2645M	5717M	133713M	114525M	23842M	535908M	Net Sales ($)	153884M	270557M
1630M	9027M	127717M	338811M	218543M	732689M	Total Assets ($)	977465M	916593M

Comparative Historical Data · **Current Data Sorted By Sales**

			Type of Statement						
30	19	38	Unqualified	6	12	3	8	4	5
1	1	1	Reviewed					1	
5	6	2	Compiled	1		1			
2	3		Tax Returns						
5	8	20	Other	6	9		3	2	
4/1/00-	4/1/01-	4/1/02-			41 (4/1-9/30/02)		20 (10/1/02-3/31/03)		
3/31/01	3/31/02	3/31/03							
ALL	ALL	ALL		0-1MM	1-3MM	3-5MM	5-10MM	10-25MM	25MM & OVER
43	37	61	**NUMBER OF STATEMENTS**	13	21	4	11	7	5
%	%	%	**ASSETS**	%	%	%	%	%	%
20.7	16.0	18.2	Cash & Equivalents	25.7	14.8		17.2		
9.6	8.4	10.1	Trade Receivables (net)	13.0	9.6		4.2		
5.0	10.9	.5	Inventory	.0	1.3		.1		
4.5	8.5	4.5	All Other Current	.4	4.2		7.1		
39.9	43.8	33.3	Total Current	39.2	29.9		28.6		
42.0	40.6	41.0	Fixed Assets (net)	38.8	44.4		41.0		
.4	.6	2.3	Intangibles (net)	.2	2.8		2.0		
17.7	15.0	23.3	All Other Non-Current	21.8	22.9		28.5		
100.0	100.0	100.0	Total	100.0	100.0		100.0		
			LIABILITIES						
8.7	8.3	5.5	Notes Payable-Short Term	5.6	6.4		9.9		
1.5	1.3	3.1	Cur. Mat.-L/T/D	2.4	2.6		2.3		
3.0	6.0	3.8	Trade Payables	4.7	1.8		1.8		
.0	.0	.0	Income Taxes Payable	.0	.0		.0		
3.9	6.8	6.5	All Other Current	4.8	8.7		3.5		
17.1	22.4	18.9	Total Current	17.5	19.5		17.6		
32.4	30.1	28.3	Long Term Debt	33.7	27.9		19.7		
.0	.0	.0	Deferred Taxes	.0	.0		.0		
5.1	7.0	5.2	All Other Non-Current	6.7	4.2		7.2		
45.4	40.5	47.7	Net Worth	42.2	48.4		55.5		
100.0	100.0	100.0	Total Liabilities & Net Worth	100.0	100.0		100.0		
			INCOME DATA						
100.0	100.0	100.0	Net Sales	100.0	100.0		100.0		
			Gross Profit						
75.9	84.4	88.6	Operating Expenses	75.2	90.9		97.4		
24.1	15.6	11.4	Operating Profit	24.8	9.1		2.6		
5.4	9.1	7.2	All Other Expenses (net)	12.7	5.0		.9		
18.7	6.6	4.2	Profit Before Taxes	12.1	4.1		1.7		
			RATIOS						
6.3	3.9	4.3		5.4	4.1		5.5		
2.2	1.6	1.9	Current	2.0	1.5		2.6		
1.1	1.2	.9		1.0	.7		1.4		
3.9	2.2	4.2		5.4	4.1		4.4		
1.9	1.1	1.7	Quick	1.8	1.0		2.3		
1.0	.4	.4		1.0	.2		1.4		
0 UND	0 UND	5 71.0		0 UND	0 UND		5 71.6		
23 16.2	12 30.1	21 17.3	Sales/Receivables	27 13.5	9 39.6		34 10.7		
65 5.6	48 7.5	61 6.0		106 3.4	67 5.5		81 4.5		
			Cost of Sales/Inventory						
			Cost of Sales/Payables						
1.1	1.8	1.4		1.1	1.4		1.1		
2.8	3.0	4.7	Sales/Working Capital	2.7	3.9		5.3		
14.8	21.7	−70.5		NM	−5.9		15.9		
	6.3		9.1		3.5			2.1			
(25) 3.4	(22) 2.4	(40) 1.5	EBIT/Interest		(13) 1.4				
.9	.4	−1.7			−1.9				
			Net Profit + Depr., Dep., Amort./Cur. Mat. L/T/D						
.2	.1	.1		.0	.2		.0		
.7	.9	.8	Fixed/Worth	1.3	.8		.6		
2.1	2.3	1.6		3.3	2.0		1.6		
.5	.6	.5		.2	.5		.2		
1.0	1.7	.9	Debt/Worth	1.9	.8		.9		
3.4	4.8	2.7		7.4	4.2		1.7		
25.4	24.6	10.9		41.4	9.8		5.3		
(40) 11.5	(34) 8.8	(56) 1.7	% Profit Before Taxes/Tangible Net Worth	21.5	(18) 2.0		(10) −.4		
.6	−1.2	−4.0		−3.0	−4.2		−7.4		
11.7	7.9	3.6		17.3	2.1		2.8		
3.1	2.5	1.0	% Profit Before Taxes/Total Assets	3.1	.9		1.2		
−.4	−1.5	−2.8		−1.5	−2.6		−3.4		
19.4	30.5	9.3		UND	7.7		54.2		
1.0	1.2	1.1	Sales/Net Fixed Assets	1.4	.8		2.2		
.3	.3	.5		.4	.4		.9		
.9	.9	1.1		.9	.7		1.0		
.3	.6	.4	Sales/Total Assets	.4	.3		.4		
.1	.2	.1		.2	.1		.2		
1.8	.6	2.3			1.4				
(29) 3.8	(31) 2.4	(46) 5.4	% Depr., Dep., Amort./Sales		(18) 5.4				
12.7	10.3	9.6			9.1				
			% Officers', Directors', Owners' Comp/Sales						
137442M	237107M	816350M	Net Sales ($)	6016M	36708M	13324M	83403M	102254M	574645M
661580M	567788M	1428417M	Total Assets ($)	25413M	177376M	102941M	327782M	162224M	632681M

© RMA 2003

M = $ thousand   MM = $ million
See Pages 11 through 18 for Explanation of Ratios and Data

Current Data Sorted By Assets   Comparative Historical Data

						Type of Statement		
3	8	19	19	3	4	Unqualified	18	23
	1	6	1			Reviewed		2
	7	1				Compiled	4	2
	3					Tax Returns	1	1
	6	13	18	2	4	Other	6	4
	47 (4/1-9/30/02)		71 (10/1/02-3/31/03)				4/1/98-3/31/99	4/1/99-3/31/00
0-500M	500M-2MM	2-10MM	10-50MM	50-100MM	100-250MM		ALL	ALL
3	25	39	38	5	8	NUMBER OF STATEMENTS	29	32
%	%	%	%	%	%	ASSETS	%	%
	19.2	17.4	9.6			Cash & Equivalents	18.8	19.0
	15.7	14.2	5.8			Trade Receivables (net)	11.7	15.8
	5.8	4.6	4.6			Inventory	3.5	1.4
	2.3	5.9	4.9			All Other Current	10.4	8.2
	43.0	42.1	24.9			Total Current	44.4	44.4
	41.0	28.4	53.1			Fixed Assets (net)	37.6	26.9
	1.8	4.7	1.4			Intangibles (net)	.4	.5
	14.2	24.8	20.5			All Other Non-Current	17.6	28.2
	100.0	100.0	100.0			Total	100.0	100.0
						LIABILITIES		
	5.4	3.0	4.7			Notes Payable-Short Term	3.2	3.7
	6.7	3.4	2.1			Cur. Mat.-L/T/D	1.8	2.6
	10.7	5.3	3.6			Trade Payables	4.5	5.4
	.0	.6	.0			Income Taxes Payable	.0	.0
	4.8	8.6	5.0			All Other Current	10.7	8.1
	27.6	20.8	15.5			Total Current	20.3	19.8
	28.4	29.6	31.6			Long Term Debt	28.3	32.6
	.1	.0	.1			Deferred Taxes	.0	.3
	1.0	6.9	1.5			All Other Non-Current	2.7	2.5
	42.9	42.6	51.3			Net Worth	48.7	44.8
	100.0	100.0	100.0			Total Liabilities & Net Worth	100.0	100.0
						INCOME DATA		
	100.0	100.0	100.0			Net Sales	100.0	100.0
						Gross Profit		
	76.0	82.3	68.8			Operating Expenses	72.3	83.7
	24.0	17.7	31.2			Operating Profit	27.7	16.3
	11.0	4.7	10.6			All Other Expenses (net)	33.4	2.7
	13.0	13.0	20.6			Profit Before Taxes	−5.8	13.6
						RATIOS		
	4.7	5.4	3.5				5.7	5.9
	1.6	2.3	1.8			Current	2.1	3.2
	.8	1.5	.6				1.0	1.1
	4.0	5.4	2.2				3.0	3.9
	1.3	1.9	(37) 1.0			Quick	1.6	1.7
	.2	1.0	.3				.4	.8
0 UND	0 UND	3 112.5	0 UND				0 UND	0 UND
	6 62.1	31 11.9	18 20.2			Sales/Receivables	4 82.7	19 19.0
	41 8.9	65 5.6	70 5.2				43 8.5	82 4.5
						Cost of Sales/Inventory		
						Cost of Sales/Payables		
	2.0	1.1	1.4				.9	.6
	8.7	5.0	5.0			Sales/Working Capital	4.0	1.6
	−40.2	10.5	−5.5				NM	5.2
	4.9	7.9	5.7				8.5	10.4
	(11) 1.6	(18) 3.3	(21) 3.8			EBIT/Interest	(14) 3.0	(16) 5.1
	.9	1.0	.5				1.6	2.0
						Net Profit + Depr., Dep., Amort./Cur. Mat. L /T/D		
	.2	.1	.7				.1	.2
	.9	.5	1.1			Fixed/Worth	.7	.5
	4.4	1.5	1.4				2.0	1.0
	.4	.7	.3				.4	.6
	1.3	1.1	.9			Debt/Worth	.9	1.4
	8.6	2.8	3.4				4.7	2.9
	31.0	33.6	15.5			% Profit Before Taxes/Tangible Net Worth	19.8	17.7
	(23) 11.9	(36) 10.7	(37) 4.5				(27) 6.2	7.5
	−.2	−4.1	−.4				2.2	.8
	8.3	13.7	5.3			% Profit Before Taxes/Total Assets	6.1	6.1
	3.4	4.1	2.5				2.5	2.1
	.0	−1.6	−.6				.7	.4
	36.3	28.6	1.8			Sales/Net Fixed Assets	38.7	30.6
	5.4	8.3	.5				1.8	3.6
	.2	.8	.1				.2	.4
	2.5	1.8	.7			Sales/Total Assets	.7	1.2
	.4	.4	.2				.2	.3
	.2	.2	.1				.1	.1
	.6	1.0	2.8			% Depr., Dep., Amort./Sales	.7	.8
	(20) 2.3	(26) 1.8	(28) 5.8				(17) 3.4	(24) 1.9
	20.1	3.7	15.4				13.2	6.6
						% Officers', Directors', Owners' Comp/Sales		
2249M	47688M	183795M	359226M	331324M	652463M	Net Sales ($)	1113965M	114252M
687M	35830M	196331M	826088M	375586M	1438044M	Total Assets ($)	514982M	642880M

© RMA 2003   M = $ thousand   MM = $ million
See Pages 11 through 18 for Explanation of Ratios and Data

Comparative Historical Data | Current Data Sorted By Sales

			Type of Statement						
26	24	56	Unqualified	10	17	7	9	9	4
	2	8	Reviewed	2			2	4	
2	10	8	Compiled	7		1			
1	4	3	Tax Returns	2		1			
7	12	43	Other	13	8	6	4	5	7
4/1/00-3/31/01 ALL	4/1/01-3/31/02 ALL	4/1/02-3/31/03 ALL		47 (4/1-9/30/02)			71 (10/1/02-3/31/03)		
				0-1MM	1-3MM	3-5MM	5-10MM	10-25MM	25MM & OVER
36	52	118	**NUMBER OF STATEMENTS**	34	25	15	15	18	11
%	%	%	**ASSETS**	%	%	%	%	%	%
23.9	23.6	15.6	Cash & Equivalents	15.1	17.9	10.9	17.4	14.8	16.9
16.9	10.0	10.7	Trade Receivables (net)	6.0	5.3	13.8	23.0	14.4	11.0
.1	5.1	4.9	Inventory	5.2	.3	5.9	10.0	3.6	8.5
4.2	5.0	4.8	All Other Current	2.2	2.5	8.5	6.1	7.5	8.5
45.2	43.7	36.0	Total Current	28.5	26.1	39.2	56.5	40.3	42.6
30.2	34.2	42.1	Fixed Assets (net)	55.7	37.0	29.6	25.6	48.2	41.1
.6	2.5	2.7	Intangibles (net)	1.4	4.3	.1	7.7	.4	4.1
24.0	19.6	19.1	All Other Non-Current	14.4	32.6	31.2	10.2	11.1	12.1
100.0	100.0	100.0	Total	100.0	100.0	100.0	100.0	100.0	100.0
			LIABILITIES						
3.4	3.4	5.1	Notes Payable-Short Term	4.7	4.7	11.5	3.1	1.3	6.9
1.4	2.7	3.4	Cur. Mat.-L/T/D	4.9	2.6	4.2	1.7	3.8	1.3
5.1	4.7	6.5	Trade Payables	2.9	3.7	7.7	11.2	9.6	11.0
.0	.0	.3	Income Taxes Payable	.0	.1	.0	.0	1.1	1.0
6.5	6.0	6.3	All Other Current	1.5	6.4	4.8	14.6	6.0	12.3
16.4	16.7	21.6	Total Current	14.0	17.6	28.3	30.5	21.7	32.5
32.4	24.8	28.6	Long Term Debt	34.6	37.9	27.7	18.0	20.7	17.7
.0	.0	.2	Deferred Taxes	.0	.1	.0	.0	.3	1.9
2.7	4.6	3.1	All Other Non-Current	1.1	5.0	2.8	6.5	3.2	.7
48.5	53.9	46.4	Net Worth	50.3	39.4	41.2	44.9	54.1	47.3
100.0	100.0	100.0	Total Liabilities & Net Worth	100.0	100.0	100.0	100.0	100.0	100.0
			INCOME DATA						
100.0	100.0	100.0	Net Sales	100.0	100.0	100.0	100.0	100.0	100.0
			Gross Profit						
80.6	76.6	78.1	Operating Expenses	62.6	76.6	77.9	91.0	89.1	93.6
19.4	23.4	21.9	Operating Profit	37.4	23.4	22.1	9.0	10.9	6.4
5.0	4.9	7.6	All Other Expenses (net)	14.2	8.9	5.9	1.7	4.1	.6
14.4	18.5	14.3	Profit Before Taxes	23.2	14.5	16.2	7.3	6.7	5.8
			RATIOS						
9.5	7.6	3.8	Current	8.5	6.3	2.5	2.5	3.0	2.6
2.4	2.9	1.9		3.0	2.4	1.9	1.9	2.0	1.1
1.0	1.5	1.1		.5	.9	.6	1.5	1.3	1.0
8.1	5.1	3.2	Quick	5.5	6.8	2.5	2.3	2.3	1.4
1.9	2.2	(117) 1.4		1.6	(24) 2.3	1.2	1.6	1.3	.9
.9	1.4	.6		.1	.8	.5	1.1	.7	.4
6 59.1	0 UND	1 592.9	Sales/Receivables	0 UND	0 UND	0 999.8	20 18.3	17 21.1	5 75.9
34 10.7	11 34.4	21 17.3		0 UND	29 12.4	34 10.8	27 13.7	46 8.0	12 31.0
86 4.2	54 6.7	60 6.1		31 11.8	83 4.4	58 6.3	59 6.2	79 4.6	54 6.7
			Cost of Sales/Inventory						
			Cost of Sales/Payables						
.6	1.0	1.6	Sales/Working Capital	.8	.9	3.6	2.7	3.6	3.6
2.8	2.6	6.5		4.7	2.9	8.7	6.5	7.5	15.5
83.9	10.2	58.8		-3.7	-17.0	-5.9	12.5	12.4	807.8
(16) 9.4	(24) 10.1	(62) 6.0	EBIT/Interest	(12) 4.9	(12) 6.8			(11) 6.2	(10) 11.7
4.9	4.7	3.3		2.5	3.2			3.6	4.2
1.2	2.2	.9		1.0	.0			.5	-.6
			Net Profit + Depr., Dep., Amort./Cur. Mat. L/T/D						
.1	.1	.3	Fixed/Worth	.2	.0	.2	.3	.6	.4
.5	.5	.9		1.1	1.0	.7	.9	.8	1.0
1.4	1.2	1.8		2.8	2.1	1.4	1.5	1.2	1.1
.4	.3	.5	Debt/Worth	.3	.6	.7	.7	.2	.6
1.4	.8	1.0		.8	2.1	1.4	1.2	.8	1.5
2.6	2.2	3.9		5.4	4.3	3.3	4.8	2.7	3.5
(35) 14.6	(50) 25.4	(111) 21.1	% Profit Before Taxes/Tangible Net Worth	(32) 21.5	(22) 13.8	(14) 32.1	(14) 87.4	17.0	21.8
6.9	9.1	7.0		5.1	6.5	9.0	17.5	5.0	10.3
1.2	1.2	-.7		-.1	-3.4	-1.3	-10.0	-5.1	-5.9
7.3	10.2	7.9	% Profit Before Taxes/Total Assets	6.7	8.0	11.7	12.8	10.2	6.0
1.7	4.6	3.0		2.0	3.3	4.8	4.4	2.1	5.0
.3	.6	-.6		-.1	-1.4	.0	-3.5	-1.5	-1.3
35.2	24.3	18.1	Sales/Net Fixed Assets	17.1	19.0	22.6	36.4	9.9	16.0
4.3	3.5	1.5		.3	.8	5.4	8.8	1.6	1.5
.4	.4	.2		.1	.2	.5	2.3	.3	1.3
.9	1.1	1.2	Sales/Total Assets	.3	.5	1.8	3.7	2.1	1.5
.4	.3	.3		.1	.2	.4	1.9	.8	.9
.2	.1	.1		.1	.1	.1	.7	.2	.5
(22) 1.0	(33) .7	(85) 1.3	% Depr., Dep., Amort./Sales	(22) 1.3	(20) 1.0	(12) .7	(13) 1.1	(12) 2.7	
2.8	2.1	3.2		5.7	2.4	2.9	2.8	5.6	
6.5	9.2	12.4		25.5	10.5	14.8	4.3	18.6	
		(12) 2.7	% Officers', Directors', Owners' Comp/Sales						
		3.9							
		19.8							
259186M	348066M	1576745M	Net Sales ($)	15623M	45526M	59848M	102383M	315640M	1037725M
803537M	911636M	2872566M	Total Assets ($)	178359M	230039M	193015M	163960M	974663M	1132530M

CONSTRUCTION—
PERCENTAGE OF COMPLETION
BASIS OF ACCOUNTING*

Current Data Sorted By Revenue   **Comparative Historical Data**

	0-1MM	1-10MM	10-50MM	50 & OVER	ALL	Type of Statement	4/1/98-3/31/99 ALL	4/1/99-3/31/00 ALL	4/1/00-3/31/01 ALL	4/1/01-3/31/02 ALL	4/1/02-3/31/03 ALL
		3	2	13	18	Unqualified	3	8	11	14	18
		7	1		8	Reviewed	5	5	4	3	8
	8	20	1		29	Compiled	12	15	12	18	29
	2	2	1		5	Tax Returns	2	3	4	5	5
	1	18	4	7	30	Other	18	14	18	31	30
	16 (4/1-9/30/02)			74 (10/1/02-3/31/03)							
NUMBER OF STATEMENTS	11	50	9	20	90		40	45	49	71	90

ASSETS

ASSETS	0-1MM %	1-10MM %	10-50MM %	50 & OVER %	ALL %		98/99 %	99/00 %	00/01 %	01/02 %	02/03 %
Cash & Equivalents	8.9	9.2		4.6	8.8		13.0	8.7	6.9	10.8	8.8
A/R - Progress Billings	40.3	35.8		17.6	30.7		30.3	27.0	32.3	27.9	30.7
A/R - Current Retention	.0	.9		.0	.5		.0	.2	.2	.4	.5
Inventory	.0	3.3		11.7	4.7		3.4	10.4	11.2	7.6	4.7
Cost & Est. Earnings In Excess of Billings	.0	.2		.5	.2		.6	.2	.6	.1	.2
All Other Current	7.8	2.5		5.4	4.2		3.2	4.6	3.2	4.1	4.2
Total Current	56.9	51.9		39.8	49.2		50.4	51.1	54.3	50.9	49.2
Fixed Assets (net)	39.2	37.3		41.6	39.7		40.3	37.3	38.5	41.4	39.7
Joint Ventures & Investments	2.9	4.2		3.6	3.5		2.5	1.4	1.3	.8	3.5
Intangibles (net)	.4	1.8		8.8	3.1		1.5	1.6	1.3	2.2	3.1
All Other Non-Current	.6	4.7		6.3	4.5		5.2	8.6	4.5	4.7	4.5
Total	100.0	100.0		100.0	100.0		100.0	100.0	100.0	100.0	100.0

LIABILITIES

LIABILITIES	0-1MM	1-10MM	10-50MM	50 & OVER	ALL		98/99	99/00	00/01	01/02	02/03
Notes Payable - Short Term	18.5	12.2		3.2	10.3		6.0	10.1	15.8	9.1	10.3
A/P - Trade	13.6	9.6		10.8	11.3		12.5	16.7	9.9	10.8	11.3
A/P - Retention	.0	.0		.0	.0		.1	.0	.0	.1	.0
Billings in Excess of Costs & Est. Earnings	.0	.2		.3	.2		.7	.2	.6	.2	.2
Income Taxes Payable	.0	.8		.3	.5		.4	.6	.8	.8	.5
Cur. Mat.-L/T/D	6.0	4.6		1.8	4.2		5.4	19.5	3.5	4.0	4.2
All Other Current	1.4	7.0		6.9	6.3		7.4	17.9	8.1	6.8	6.3
Total Current	39.4	34.4		23.2	32.8		32.4	65.1	38.4	31.9	32.8
Long Term Debt	24.8	17.9		18.9	19.3		18.0	17.2	19.8	17.7	19.3
Deferred Taxes	.0	.2		2.3	.8		.9	1.0	.6	.4	.8
All Other Non-Current	17.7	3.9		4.4	5.5		1.1	2.7	6.3	6.6	5.5
Net Worth	18.1	43.6		51.2	41.6		47.6	14.0	34.9	43.4	41.6
Total Liabilities & Net Worth	100.0	100.0		100.0	100.0		100.0	100.0	100.0	100.0	100.0

INCOME DATA

INCOME DATA	0-1MM	1-10MM	10-50MM	50 & OVER	ALL		98/99	99/00	00/01	01/02	02/03
Contract Revenues	100.0	100.0		100.0	100.0		100.0	100.0	100.0	100.0	100.0
Gross Profit											
Operating Expenses	93.1	90.3		89.1	91.2		91.8	98.6	92.2	86.7	91.2
Operating Profit	6.9	9.7		10.9	8.8		8.2	1.4	7.8	13.3	8.8
All Other Expenses (net)	1.5	1.7		5.1	2.4		-2.7	-.3	2.3	3.3	2.4
Profit Before Taxes	5.4	8.0		5.8	6.4		10.9	1.7	5.5	9.9	6.4

RATIOS

RATIOS	0-1MM	1-10MM	10-50MM	50 & OVER	ALL		98/99	99/00	00/01	01/02	02/03
Current	2.4	2.2		2.3	2.2		2.6	2.5	2.1	2.4	2.2
	1.6	1.7		1.6	1.6		1.6	1.5	1.3	1.6	1.6
	1.1	1.1		1.2	1.1		1.1	1.2	1.0	1.1	1.1
Receivables/Payables	13.1	12.3		2.8	7.3		19.3	7.7	6.0	6.0	7.3
	3.6	(47) 4.5		(19) 1.8	(86) 2.9		(38) 3.7	(43) 3.0	(45) 3.3	(66) 3.1	(86) 2.9
	.9	1.7		1.3	1.4		1.7	1.8	1.8	1.4	1.4
Revenues/Receivables	44 8.3	43 8.5		44 8.3	42 8.6		40 9.0	49 7.4	52 7.1	30 12.1	42 8.6
	75 4.8	67 5.4		63 5.8	65 5.6		57 6.4	68 5.4	70 5.2	59 6.2	65 5.6
	112 3.2	95 3.9		87 4.2	93 3.9		75 4.9	89 4.1	96 3.8	95 3.8	93 3.9
Cost of Revenues/Payables											
Revenues/Working Capital	5.9	5.9		3.3	5.8		5.7	4.0	4.6	4.5	5.8
	11.7	12.8		7.7	11.4		10.5	8.3	10.2	9.6	11.4
	45.5	79.2		30.8	58.8		38.5	20.3	NM	36.6	58.8
EBIT/Interest	(10) 20.3	(45) 18.0		(83) 8.3	11.3		(36) 17.7	(43) 10.3	(45) 7.3	(60) 17.7	(83) 11.3
	4.0	4.3		1.9	3.6		10.0	2.8	2.8	6.5	3.6
	-5.6	1.6		.8	1.2		4.1	.0	1.1	2.4	1.2
Net Profit + Depr., Dep., Amort./Cur. Mat. L /T/D				(14)	6.4		(15) 3.8	(15) 3.5	(12) 25.2	(18) 12.6	(14) 6.4
					4.5		2.3	1.3	3.3	4.2	4.5
					2.0		1.6	.4	.8	1.9	2.0
Fixed/Worth	.6	.3		.5	.4		.5	.3	.4	.4	.4
	2.8	.9		1.1	1.0		.7	.7	.8	.8	1.0
	-2.5	2.1		2.3	2.3		1.6	2.0	2.3	1.6	2.3
Debt/Worth	1.1	.6		.6	.6		.4	.5	.7	.6	.6
	6.3	1.2		1.3	1.5		1.1	1.0	1.8	1.3	1.5
	-8.4	3.3		1.9	3.1		3.0	3.5	4.8	2.9	3.1
% Profit Before Taxes/Tangible Net Worth		(44) 34.6		(79) 20.0	26.5		(36) 55.2	(42) 33.6	(45) 42.4	(66) 48.6	(79) 26.5
		11.9		7.7	11.5		38.0	11.0	19.5	29.1	11.5
		3.7		-1.7	3.7		9.0	-8.4	2.2	11.4	3.7
% Profit Before Taxes/Total Assets	62.6	16.5		8.6	12.8		26.3	20.1	16.9	25.1	12.8
	14.5	7.6		2.4	4.7		12.0	4.5	7.2	11.0	4.7
	-14.4	1.2		-.2	.3		6.3	-3.3	.4	3.0	.3
% Depr., Dep., Amort./Revenues	(10) 2.1	(41) 2.2		(67) 2.3		(34) 1.9	(35) 1.3	(41) 1.8	(61) 2.1	(67) 2.3
	7.0	4.8			5.7		3.4	5.0	5.0	5.0	5.7
	17.0	10.6			9.0		5.5	11.5	11.5	8.6	9.0
% Officers', Directors', Owners' Comp/Revenues		(22) 3.8		(31) 3.4		(15) 1.4	(14) 2.6	(17) 2.3	(20) 2.8	(31) 3.4
		7.3			6.0		3.5	5.4	7.1	4.4	6.0
		10.6			10.0		7.4	18.9	22.3	13.5	10.0
Contract Revenues ($)	7177M	183435M	183998M	15521115M	15895725M		500213M	4307288M	3267187M	3631218M	15895725M
Total Assets ($)	6024M	186171M	134166M	15899692M	16226053M		367573M	5373048M	7028888M	4966533M	16226053M

M = $ thousand   MM = $ million
See Pages 11 through 18 for Explanation of Ratios and Data

Current Data Sorted By Revenue

Comparative Historical Data

					Type of Statement		58	52	51	53	54
1	8	17	28	54	Unqualified		58	52	51	53	54
6	61	40	5	112	Reviewed		164	139	130	124	112
27	119	26	9	181	Compiled		261	234	226	211	181
84	194	16	8	302	Tax Returns		245	234	230	295	302
30	107	38	18	193	Other		213	189	169	169	193

							4/1/98- 3/31/99	4/1/99- 3/31/00	4/1/00- 3/31/01	4/1/01- 3/31/02	4/1/02- 3/31/03
147 (4/1-9/30/02)			695 (10/1/02-3/31/03)								
0-1MM	1-10MM	10-50MM	50 & OVER	ALL	NUMBER OF STATEMENTS		ALL	ALL	ALL	ALL	ALL
148	489	137	68	842			941	848	806	852	842

%	%	%	%	%	ASSETS		%	%	%	%	%
14.9	10.0	8.5	7.5	10.4	Cash & Equivalents		9.8	10.8	9.9	10.7	10.4
4.9	9.5	8.4	5.7	8.2	A/R - Progress Billings		12.2	11.9	11.2	10.0	8.2
.0	.4	1.9	.6	.6	A/R - Current Retention		1.1	.8	.9	.6	.6
42.1	47.7	55.8	60.6	49.1	Inventory		40.1	40.6	42.6	45.0	49.1
1.4	3.0	2.8	1.3	2.5	Cost & Est. Earnings In Excess of Billings		4.8	4.5	4.6	3.7	2.5
5.7	5.4	5.0	3.4	5.3	All Other Current		6.3	6.3	7.2	6.1	5.3
68.9	76.0	82.5	79.2	76.1	Total Current		74.3	74.9	76.4	76.2	76.1
20.4	14.4	8.1	10.3	14.1	Fixed Assets (net)		14.9	15.2	13.2	13.8	14.1
2.2	1.5	4.0	2.6	2.1	Joint Ventures & Investments		3.2	3.0	3.1	2.3	2.1
.3	.6	.4	.7	.5	Intangibles (net)		1.6	1.5	1.1	1.3	.5
8.3	7.5	5.0	7.2	7.2	All Other Non-Current		5.9	5.3	6.2	6.4	7.2
100.0	100.0	100.0	100.0	100.0	Total		100.0	100.0	100.0	100.0	100.0

					LIABILITIES						
31.4	31.5	31.1	25.7	30.9	Notes Payable - Short Term		32.3	32.2	32.6	32.5	30.9
6.9	10.3	12.7	11.6	10.2	A/P - Trade		11.8	12.5	12.8	10.6	10.2
.2	.2	1.4	.4	.4	A/P - Retention		.5	.5	.3	.5	.4
.6	2.6	2.4	.7	2.1	Billings in Excess of Costs & Est. Earnings		2.2	2.4	2.5	2.3	2.1
.0	.2	.1	.1	.1	Income Taxes Payable		.4	.3	.2	.3	.1
4.6	5.4	3.8	2.5	4.8	Cur. Mat.-L/T/D		4.3	4.6	3.9	5.1	4.8
6.5	9.8	8.4	11.7	9.2	All Other Current		9.0	8.9	9.3	11.9	9.2
50.3	60.0	60.0	52.8	57.7	Total Current		60.6	61.4	61.6	63.1	57.7
16.0	12.8	9.1	13.7	12.8	Long Term Debt		13.1	12.2	12.3	12.2	12.8
.1	.2	.1	.1	.2	Deferred Taxes		.3	.3	.2	.2	.2
11.0	5.7	4.6	6.5	6.5	All Other Non-Current		4.1	4.3	4.2	5.0	6.5
22.6	21.3	26.2	26.9	22.8	Net Worth		21.9	21.8	21.6	19.4	22.8
100.0	100.0	100.0	100.0	100.0	Total Liabilities & Net Worth		100.0	100.0	100.0	100.0	100.0

					INCOME DATA						
100.0	100.0	100.0	100.0	100.0	Contract Revenues		100.0	100.0	100.0	100.0	100.0
29.1	18.2	15.7	20.2	19.9	Gross Profit		16.9	18.2	18.3	19.1	19.9
25.2	14.1	10.3	13.1	15.4	Operating Expenses		15.5	14.8	14.5	15.0	15.4
3.9	4.1	5.4	7.1	4.5	Operating Profit		1.4	3.4	3.8	4.1	4.5
1.5	.4	.1	.5	.6	All Other Expenses (net)		−.9	.0	.5	.7	.6
2.4	3.6	5.3	6.6	3.9	Profit Before Taxes		2.3	3.4	3.3	3.4	3.9

					RATIOS						
3.5	2.0	1.7	2.5	2.1	Current		1.8	1.7	1.7	1.9	2.1
1.4	1.2	1.3	1.4	1.3			1.2	1.2	1.2	1.2	1.3
.9	1.0	1.1	1.2	1.0			1.0	1.0	1.0	1.0	1.0

												Receivables/Payables											

	1.0		1.6		1.2		.6		1.3	Receivables/Payables			1.7		1.5		1.4		1.6		1.3
(87)	.0	(375)	.2	(129)	.0	(62)	.2	(653)	.1		(729)	.4	(685)	.2	(655)	.2	(680)	.2	(653)	.1
	.0		.0		.0		.0		.0			.0		.0		.0		.0		.0

0	UND	0	UND	0	UND	0	UND	0	UND	Revenues/Receivables	0	UND	0	UND	0	UND	0	UND	0	UND
0	UND	0	UND	0	999.8	2	158.8	0	UND		1	659.8	1	555.7	0	838.6	0	999.8	0	UND
2	174.7	13	28.4	9	39.8	8	44.4	10	37.4		21	17.7	19	18.7	18	20.0	11	31.8	10	37.4

0	UND	0	UND	6	56.4	11	34.5	0	UND	Cost of Revenues/Payables	0	UND	1	656.8	0	867.5	0	UND	0	UND
2	174.6	11	32.5	21	17.7	20	17.8	13	27.3		12	31.3	16	23.3	13	27.6	12	29.5	13	27.3
36	10.2	27	13.3	32	11.3	41	8.8	31	11.7		30	12.1	32	11.2	31	11.8	29	12.6	31	11.7

3.1	7.2	6.3	3.5	5.9	Revenues/Working Capital		8.0	7.7	7.7	7.3	5.9
11.0	19.6	12.3	9.2	15.0			21.6	20.7	22.5	20.2	15.0
−56.4	−999.8	34.4	25.2	UND			−552.4	−318.1	−99.2	−264.2	UND

	10.2		15.5		36.2		32.1		17.6	EBIT/Interest			9.8		11.4		12.0		12.7		17.6
(104)	2.5	(385)	4.1	(113)	10.3	(59)	7.0	(661)	5.2		(745)	3.1	(680)	3.5	(655)	3.6	(687)	3.6	(661)	5.2
	.2		1.3		4.0		3.7		1.4			1.4		1.5		1.3		1.3		1.4

			7.2		17.7				7.3	Net Profit + Depr., Dep., Amort./Cur. Mat. L /T/D			5.9		5.0		9.1		8.0		7.3
		(51)	2.8	(20)	5.0			(76)	3.2			(127)	2.8	(110)	2.2	(91)	3.5	(76)	2.2	(76)	3.2
			.4		2.4				.9				.7		.9		1.1		.7		.9

.0	.1	.0	.0	.0	Fixed/Worth		.1	.1	.1	.1	.0
.5	.4	.1	.1	.3			.4	.4	.3	.3	.3
5.3	2.3	.7	.3	1.9			1.9	1.7	1.5	1.9	1.9

1.3	1.6	1.8	1.9	1.6	Debt/Worth		1.7	1.7	1.6	1.7	1.6
4.1	4.9	3.9	2.6	4.3			4.6	4.3	4.5	4.8	4.3
UND	33.2	7.6	5.1	21.6			18.8	18.5	20.1	21.2	21.6

	86.1		90.1		82.4		64.4		83.1	% Profit Before Taxes/ Tangible Net Worth			78.8		73.5		74.4		82.3		83.1
(115)	27.5	(416)	36.0	(131)	45.9	(64)	41.7	(726)	37.9		(806)	30.6	(733)	32.7	(687)	31.2	(723)	34.5	(726)	37.9
	1.3		9.8		25.2		29.0		11.4			10.0		9.9		7.9		9.3		11.4

12.8	15.0	17.4	17.6	15.3	% Profit Before Taxes/ Total Assets		13.6	13.7	14.1	17.0	15.3
2.7	5.9	9.3	10.9	6.7			5.6	5.6	5.3	5.4	6.7
−2.2	.6	4.4	5.2	.8			1.0	1.1	.5	.7	.8

	1.0		.3		.2		.1		.3	% Depr., Dep., Amort./ Revenues			.3		.3		.2		.2		.3
(79)	1.9	(339)	.6	(103)	.4	(23)	.3	(544)	.6		(668)	.6	(636)	.6	(598)	.5	(593)	.6	(544)	.6
	4.2		1.4		.5		.7		1.4			1.4		1.4		1.3		1.4		1.4

	3.5		1.8		1.1		1.8		1.8	% Officers', Directors', Owners' Comp/Revenues			1.6		1.7		1.7		1.7		1.8
(86)	7.0	(289)	3.4	(65)	2.1	(16)	2.6	(456)	3.5		(475)	3.2	(449)	3.2	(446)	3.2	(464)	3.4	(456)	3.5
	10.5		4.9		4.0		5.1		7.0			5.9		5.9		5.9		5.9		7.0

83198M	1900772M	3096809M	79911871M	84992650M	Contract Revenues ($)		30622812M	63634361M	146145845M	28308103M	84992650M
106151M	1167874M	1573300M	39138532M	41985857M	Total Assets ($)		17854586M	19888785M	50957860M	18803027M	41985857M

M = $ thousand   MM = $ million
See Pages 11 through 18 for Explanation of Ratios and Data

Current Data Sorted By Revenue

Comparative Historical Data

					Type of Statement					
	2	6	4	12	Unqualified	25	19	27	36	12
	23	8	1	32	Reviewed	41	32	51	73	32
1	19			20	Compiled	31	38	26	38	20
10	22		1	33	Tax Returns	47	30	36	46	33
5	12	5	1	23	Other	37	29	26	37	23
	18 (4/1-9/30/02)		102 (10/1/02-3/31/03)			4/1/98-3/31/99	4/1/99-3/31/00	4/1/00-3/31/01	4/1/01-3/31/02	4/1/02-3/31/03
0-1MM	1-10MM	10-50MM	50 & OVER	ALL		ALL	ALL	ALL	ALL	ALL
16	78	19	7	120	NUMBER OF STATEMENTS	181	148	166	230	120
%	%	%	%	%	ASSETS	%	%	%	%	%
10.3	15.7	17.4		14.8	Cash & Equivalents	13.6	13.9	14.6	16.9	14.8
11.2	20.3	32.0		20.6	A/R - Progress Billings	18.6	19.7	21.6	25.0	20.6
.0	.6	4.1		1.2	A/R - Current Retention	1.8	2.2	3.1	2.8	1.2
31.9	28.6	18.6		28.9	Inventory	22.3	26.4	20.6	16.1	28.9
.1	1.7	3.0		1.7	Cost & Est. Earnings In Excess of Billings	2.8	3.6	3.8	3.2	1.7
17.5	7.6	7.0		8.4	All Other Current	7.3	7.4	8.3	8.7	8.4
71.1	74.6	82.2		75.5	Total Current	66.5	73.3	72.0	72.8	75.5
21.1	17.4	7.2		15.4	Fixed Assets (net)	22.2	15.3	17.5	16.8	15.4
.1	.5	2.6		1.6	Joint Ventures & Investments	3.1	2.9	2.2	1.7	1.6
2.3	.4	.7		.8	Intangibles (net)	.8	1.4	1.9	.9	.8
5.4	7.1	7.4		6.7	All Other Non-Current	7.5	7.1	6.5	7.7	6.7
100.0	100.0	100.0		100.0	Total	100.0	100.0	100.0	100.0	100.0
					LIABILITIES					
31.1	19.9	12.3		20.7	Notes Payable - Short Term	16.8	18.0	13.6	11.5	20.7
5.7	16.0	24.6		15.9	A/P - Trade	20.3	18.6	20.4	22.1	15.9
.0	.5	3.5		1.0	A/P - Retention	.5	.7	1.7	1.4	1.0
.0	2.7	9.5		3.3	Billings in Excess of Costs & Est. Earnings	3.0	3.7	4.9	5.6	3.3
.0	.5	.4		.4	Income Taxes Payable	.3	.5	.5	.2	.4
7.5	4.6	1.3		4.6	Cur. Mat.-L/T/D	3.3	3.6	4.3	4.4	4.6
11.3	11.7	14.0		11.9	All Other Current	8.4	12.5	11.3	11.1	11.9
55.6	55.9	65.6		57.9	Total Current	52.5	57.6	56.6	56.3	57.9
18.6	11.0	3.1		10.2	Long Term Debt	16.4	10.0	10.8	10.7	10.2
.1	.1	.3		.2	Deferred Taxes	.4	.3	.2	.5	.2
7.1	2.7	.5		3.2	All Other Non-Current	4.0	4.2	4.1	4.4	3.2
18.6	30.3	30.5		28.5	Net Worth	26.8	27.8	28.3	28.1	28.5
100.0	100.0	100.0		100.0	Total Liabilities & Net Worth	100.0	100.0	100.0	100.0	100.0
					INCOME DATA					
100.0	100.0	100.0		100.0	Contract Revenues	100.0	100.0	100.0	100.0	100.0
27.7	21.5	13.6		20.9	Gross Profit	20.8	19.6	17.8	19.0	20.9
20.0	16.8	8.8		15.7	Operating Expenses	16.9	14.8	14.4	14.6	15.7
7.6	4.7	4.7		5.2	Operating Profit	3.9	4.7	3.4	4.4	5.2
3.4	.4	-.3		.7	All Other Expenses (net)	-1.1	-.4	.3	.6	.7
4.2	4.3	5.0		4.5	Profit Before Taxes	5.0	5.1	3.2	3.8	4.5
					RATIOS					
2.2	2.3	1.5		1.9	Current	2.0	1.9	1.8	1.8	1.9
1.4	1.4	1.3		1.3		1.3	1.3	1.3	1.3	1.3
1.0	1.0	1.0		1.0		1.0	1.1	1.1	1.1	1.0
(10) 6.4	(64) 3.1	1.5	(99) 2.4		Receivables/Payables	(147) 1.8	(125) 1.8	(154) 1.9	(198) 2.0	(99) 2.4
.1	1.2	1.2	1.1			1.0	.9	1.1	1.1	1.1
.0	.0	.8	.0			.0	.0	.1	.5	.0
0 UND	0 UND	6 65.9	0 UND		Revenues/Receivables	0 UND	0 UND	0 999.8	0 UND	0 UND
0 UND	4 100.9	34 10.7	5 71.5			5 76.9	6 63.0	15 24.0	22 16.9	5 71.5
34 10.7	32 11.3	54 6.7	39 9.3			45 8.0	38 9.5	50 7.2	51 7.1	39 9.3
0 UND	0 999.8	16 23.2	0 751.2		Cost of Revenues/Payables	0 UND	2 155.5	6 60.2	7 55.8	0 751.2
4 81.5	16 22.7	32 11.3	20 18.5			21 17.3	21 17.3	25 14.8	25 14.7	20 18.5
30 12.0	36 10.2	56 6.6	38 9.7			46 7.9	39 9.3	46 7.9	50 7.3	38 9.7
5.8	7.1	9.5		7.4	Revenues/Working Capital	7.1	9.3	10.1	9.1	7.4
15.9	14.1	19.1		14.3		17.8	19.2	25.0	22.3	14.3
-45.9	420.9	685.3		570.9		195.7	145.8	87.6	100.2	570.9
(11) 7.0	(64) 34.0	(14) 134.6	(94) 36.2		EBIT/Interest	(137) 12.7	(115) 11.6	(136) 21.7	(184) 26.9	(94) 36.2
4.8	7.5	35.9	7.3			3.4	5.2	5.9	6.7	7.3
2.0	2.3	5.7	2.5			1.2	1.8	1.3	2.0	2.5
	(11) 2.5		(20) 7.3		Net Profit + Depr., Dep., Amort./Cur. Mat. L/T/D	(23) 10.3	(18) 24.8	(21) 6.3	(40) 7.8	(20) 7.3
	1.7		2.2			5.2	4.5	2.5	2.5	2.2
	.6		1.1			.7	2.0	1.4	1.2	1.1
.0	.1	.1		.1	Fixed/Worth	.1	.1	.1	.1	.1
.7	.3	.2		.3		.5	.4	.4	.3	.3
2.8	1.6	.6		1.4		1.5	.9	1.1	1.1	1.4
2.4	1.1	1.6		1.3	Debt/Worth	1.4	1.3	1.3	1.3	1.3
9.0	2.2	2.0		2.4		2.8	2.8	2.8	2.9	2.4
40.2	12.1	2.8		12.1		8.6	8.5	8.8	7.7	12.1
(14) 124.3	(71) 68.0	(18) 59.8	(110) 66.4		% Profit Before Taxes/Tangible Net Worth	(160) 60.2	(133) 64.5	(151) 58.7	(207) 72.0	(110) 66.4
42.0	28.5	28.5	31.3			25.7	37.2	28.1	29.9	31.3
4.6	12.2	7.4	12.2			5.7	14.4	9.6	9.4	12.2
11.0	22.4	23.2		21.1	% Profit Before Taxes/Total Assets	13.6	18.5	16.6	17.2	21.1
5.4	7.6	9.9		7.4		6.2	8.3	6.0	7.1	7.4
-3.3	2.1	2.4		2.4		1.4	2.2	1.0	1.6	2.4
	(62) .3	(15) .2	(87) .3		% Depr., Dep., Amort./Revenues	(141) .3	(101) .3	(126) .2	(184) .3	(87) .3
	.6	.3	.5			.8	.7	.7	.6	.5
	1.3	.5	1.3			2.5	1.3	1.7	1.6	1.3
	(42) 1.9	(12) .5	(60) 1.5		% Officers', Directors', Owners' Comp/Revenues	(79) 1.7	(66) 1.6	(85) 1.3	(112) 1.1	(60) 1.5
	3.4	1.2	2.9			2.8	3.8	3.0	2.4	2.9
	6.8	2.7	6.1			6.9	7.2	6.1	6.3	6.1
9803M	281633M	408920M	10867420M	11567776M	Contract Revenues ($)	62109052M	38630195M	35874627M	39722064M	11567776M
12844M	138940M	125587M	10958679M	11236050M	Total Assets ($)	22217000M	23171196M	12797396M	17353390M	11236050M

M = $ thousand   MM = $ million
See Pages 11 through 18 for Explanation of Ratios and Data

Current Data Sorted By Revenue   **Comparative Historical Data**

0-1MM	1-10MM	10-50MM	50 & OVER	ALL	Type of Statement	4/1/98-3/31/99 ALL	4/1/99-3/31/00 ALL	4/1/00-3/31/01 ALL	4/1/01-3/31/02 ALL	4/1/02-3/31/03 ALL
1	13	32	17	63	Unqualified	255	199	165	96	63
6	71	24	4	105 *	Reviewed	274	239	211	158	105
	5			5	Compiled	47	32	39	23	5
2	12	2		16	Tax Returns	22	21	17	13	16
	10	12	3	25	Other	75	75	60	31	25
59 (4/1-9/30/02)			155 (10/1/02-3/31/03)							
9	111	70	24	214	**NUMBER OF STATEMENTS**	673	566	492	321	214
%	%	%	%	%	**ASSETS**	%	%	%	%	%
	20.5	22.5	20.1	20.8	Cash & Equivalents	18.8	18.9	19.3	19.3	20.8
	33.9	45.2	42.6	38.8	A/R - Progress Billings	40.6	41.0	39.9	39.3	38.8
	3.5	5.0	4.1	3.9	A/R - Current Retention	6.1	5.0	5.1	4.9	3.9
	3.0	.6	1.2	2.1	Inventory	2.7	2.0	2.0	1.6	2.1
	4.8	4.7	3.8	4.8	Cost & Est. Earnings In Excess of Billings	5.3	5.0	5.2	4.5	4.8
	5.3	5.9	8.3	5.9	All Other Current	3.9	4.8	4.2	5.3	5.9
	71.0	84.0	80.2	76.4	Total Current	77.5	76.8	75.7	75.0	76.4
	19.6	9.6	8.7	15.0	Fixed Assets (net)	14.7	14.9	14.7	15.5	15.0
	.8	1.6	.8	1.1	Joint Ventures & Investments	1.8	1.9	1.9	1.8	1.1
	.2	.3	2.3	.5	Intangibles (net)	1.1	1.5	1.7	1.6	.5
	8.4	4.6	7.9	7.1	All Other Non-Current	4.9	5.0	5.9	6.2	7.1
	100.0	100.0	100.0	100.0	Total	100.0	100.0	100.0	100.0	100.0
					LIABILITIES					
	9.6	3.8	3.4	7.6	Notes Payable - Short Term	6.2	5.0	5.6	6.4	7.6
	27.1	35.5	28.3	30.1	A/P - Trade	32.7	31.2	30.9	30.1	30.1
	1.3	2.7	1.8	1.8	A/P - Retention	3.0	2.9	2.8	2.5	1.8
	5.7	10.0	13.0	8.0	Billings in Excess of Costs & Est. Earnings	7.3	7.5	7.7	7.1	8.0
	.6	.3	.2	.4	Income Taxes Payable	.5	.4	.5	.4	.4
	3.0	1.2	.8	2.2	Cur. Mat.-L/T/D	2.5	2.0	2.4	2.2	2.2
	7.0	9.8	16.0	8.9	All Other Current	6.5	7.5	7.2	7.8	8.9
	54.3	63.2	63.5	59.0	Total Current	58.7	56.4	57.0	56.5	59.0
	8.6	3.0	10.5	7.1	Long Term Debt	6.0	5.9	6.4	6.8	7.1
	.2	.3	.1	.2	Deferred Taxes	1.0	1.0	.8	.5	.2
	1.8	.7	3.1	2.2	All Other Non-Current	1.5	1.6	3.2	3.1	2.2
	35.1	32.8	22.7	31.5	Net Worth	32.8	35.2	32.6	33.0	31.5
	100.0	100.0	100.0	100.0	Total Liabilities & Net Worth	100.0	100.0	100.0	100.0	100.0
					INCOME DATA					
	100.0	100.0	100.0	100.0	Contract Revenues	100.0	100.0	100.0	100.0	100.0
	17.5	10.6	11.0	15.4	Gross Profit	13.2	13.9	13.9	15.0	15.4
	16.1	8.2	9.6	13.9	Operating Expenses	10.8	11.5	12.0	12.7	13.9
	1.3	2.5	1.4	1.5	Operating Profit	2.4	2.4	1.9	2.3	1.5
	.3	.1	.2	.3	All Other Expenses (net)	.0	−.3	−.1	.0	.3
	1.0	2.4	1.1	1.2	Profit Before Taxes	2.4	2.7	2.0	2.4	1.2
					RATIOS					
	1.8	1.6	1.3	1.7	Current	1.7	1.7	1.8	1.8	1.7
	1.5	1.3	1.2	1.3		1.3	1.3	1.3	1.3	1.3
	1.1	1.1	1.1	1.1		1.1	1.1	1.1	1.1	1.1
	2.4	1.7	2.4	2.2	Receivables/Payables	2.0	1.9	2.0	2.1	2.2
(105)	1.4	(23) 1.3	(207) 1.5	1.3		(660) 1.3	(557) 1.3	(478) 1.3	(312) 1.4	(207) 1.3
	1.0	1.1	1.0	1.0		1.0	1.0	1.0	1.0	1.0
31	11.7	35 10.3	33 11.0	33 11.1	Revenues/Receivables	33 10.9	35 10.3	34 10.8	29 12.6	33 11.1
40	9.1	55 6.6	57 6.4	45 8.1		53 6.8	50 7.3	50 7.3	48 7.6	45 8.1
60	6.1	66 5.5	78 4.7	66 5.5		70 5.2	68 5.4	69 5.3	67 5.5	66 5.5
16	22.4	27 13.4	19 19.5	22 16.3	Cost of Revenues/Payables	25 14.6	24 15.2	25 14.6	23 16.1	22 16.3
32	11.6	47 7.7	36 10.2	38 9.6		42 8.6	41 9.0	42 8.7	38 9.7	38 9.6
54	6.7	62 5.9	50 7.3	55 6.6		60 6.1	57 6.4	58 6.3	57 6.4	55 6.6
	8.9	10.4	13.9	9.4	Revenues/Working Capital	10.2	9.6	9.4	9.5	9.4
	14.4	18.7	24.2	17.5		19.3	19.1	18.9	20.2	17.5
	45.2	48.5	31.2	47.5		45.0	48.2	44.4	59.9	47.5
	10.8	52.7	34.3	17.3	EBIT/Interest	25.3	26.0	22.9	19.5	17.3
(88)	5.1	(52) 13.0	(20) 10.3	(167) 6.6		(566) 7.8	(466) 8.5	(405) 5.5	(261) 6.3	(167) 6.6
	−.9	3.4	3.8	1.3		2.1	2.4	1.3	1.9	1.3
	3.7	12.5	23.7	10.8	Net Profit + Depr., Dep., Amort./Cur. Mat. L /T/D	9.4	7.5	7.8	8.3	10.8
(30)	2.1	(27) 6.1	(11) 5.4	(70) 3.3		(230) 3.2	(188) 3.6	(150) 3.4	(95) 3.1	(70) 3.3
	.2	1.8	1.3	1.0		1.1	1.3	1.6	.3	1.0
	.2	.1	.1	.1	Fixed/Worth	.1	.2	.2	.2	.1
	.4	.3	.2	.3		.3	.3	.3	.3	.3
	.8	.4	.7	.6		.8	.6	.6	.8	.6
	.8	1.4	2.3	1.0	Debt/Worth	1.1	1.1	1.0	1.1	1.0
	1.4	2.4	3.3	2.0		2.4	2.2	2.3	2.3	2.0
	2.8	4.1	7.6	3.8		4.4	3.9	4.1	4.4	3.8
	26.4	42.9	38.1	35.4	% Profit Before Taxes/Tangible Net Worth	42.9	44.2	40.9	40.3	35.4
(101)	10.7	(68) 18.0	(21) 17.6	(196) 13.7		(646) 22.1	(546) 20.9	(463) 17.5	(301) 19.5	(196) 13.7
	−3.9	7.2	8.2	1.9		6.8	4.7	4.8	4.8	1.9
	9.6	10.6	9.8	9.9	% Profit Before Taxes/Total Assets	13.3	12.9	11.1	13.3	9.9
	4.0	5.3	2.9	4.1		5.9	6.5	5.1	5.0	4.1
	−2.8	2.4	1.1	.5		1.6	2.0	1.0	.9	.5
	.5	.2	.1	.3	% Depr., Dep., Amort./Revenues	.3	.3	.4	.3	.3
(98)	1.1	(66) .5	(21) .2	(191) .7		(603) .6	(515) .6	(435) .7	(292) .7	(191) .7
	2.2	.8	.7	1.4		1.4	1.4	1.6	1.4	1.4
	1.6	.8		1.2	% Officers', Directors', Owners' Comp/Revenues	1.3	1.0	1.1	1.1	1.2
(65)	2.9	(34) 1.3		(112) 2.0		(301) 2.2	(281) 2.0	(232) 1.9	(169) 2.3	(112) 2.0
	4.8	2.0		4.4		4.2	3.9	3.9	4.2	4.4
5069M	498993M	1537750M	3707888M	5749700M	Contract Revenues ($)	50802799M	31779189M	52677626M	21846236M	5749700M
2378M	200982M	481282M	1488479M	2173121M	Total Assets ($)	22260574M	10311025M	18762339M	7538701M	2173121M

M = $ thousand   MM = $ million
See Pages 11 through 18 for Explanation of Ratios and Data

Current Data Sorted By Revenue   **Comparative Historical Data**

					Type of Statement					
1	18	56	49	124	Unqualified	147	160	130	100	124
12	131	75	7	225	Reviewed	143	173	147	135	225
8	31	8	1	48	Compiled	26	43	35	22	48
11	34	1	3	49	Tax Returns	22	19	22	19	49
6	38	20	11	75	Other	43	51	41	44	75
118 (4/1-9/30/02)			403 (10/1/02-3/31/03)			4/1/98-3/31/99	4/1/99-3/31/00	4/1/00-3/31/01	4/1/01-3/31/02	4/1/02-3/31/03
0-1MM	1-10MM	10-50MM	50 & OVER	ALL	**NUMBER OF STATEMENTS**	ALL	ALL	ALL	ALL	ALL
38	252	160	71	521		381	446	375	320	521
%	%	%	%	%	**ASSETS**	%	%	%	%	%
16.0	18.9	18.9	22.0	19.1	Cash & Equivalents	19.3	18.2	18.8	19.6	19.1
23.2	33.6	45.1	34.7	36.6	A/R - Progress Billings	39.7	39.6	40.7	39.8	36.6
2.4	1.1	4.5	5.1	2.8	A/R - Current Retention	5.7	5.5	5.1	3.5	2.8
9.6	6.2	1.7	3.4	4.7	Inventory	2.3	2.2	1.3	1.3	4.7
4.4	5.5	5.2	2.9	5.0	Cost & Est. Earnings In Excess of Billings	5.2	5.9	4.8	4.5	5.0
9.3	7.9	7.0	12.4	8.3	All Other Current	3.7	6.5	6.1	8.2	8.3
64.9	73.2	82.5	80.5	76.4	Total Current	76.0	77.9	76.9	77.0	76.4
26.1	17.2	9.9	11.9	14.9	Fixed Assets (net)	15.9	14.4	14.0	14.9	14.9
4.1	.9	1.3	1.9	1.4	Joint Ventures & Investments	1.5	1.4	1.8	1.1	1.4
.3	.5	.4	1.4	.6	Intangibles (net)	1.0	1.1	1.7	2.0	.6
4.5	8.2	5.9	4.3	6.7	All Other Non-Current	5.6	5.2	5.6	5.0	6.7
100.0	100.0	100.0	100.0	100.0	Total	100.0	100.0	100.0	100.0	100.0
					LIABILITIES					
18.3	12.7	4.2	3.3	9.2	Notes Payable - Short Term	5.8	5.6	6.7	6.1	9.2
15.5	24.5	37.6	35.1	29.3	A/P - Trade	32.2	31.9	32.9	31.6	29.3
.3	.5	2.8	3.1	1.6	A/P - Retention	2.9	3.0	3.5	1.8	1.6
2.1	4.4	10.0	11.7	7.0	Billings in Excess of Costs & Est. Earnings	6.5	7.3	8.6	7.4	7.0
.1	.5	.2	.1	.3	Income Taxes Payable	.5	.6	.4	.4	.3
3.1	3.4	1.3	.6	2.4	Cur. Mat.-L/T/D	2.2	2.2	2.3	3.3	2.4
7.0	10.7	8.6	12.2	10.0	All Other Current	6.4	8.2	6.7	9.1	10.0
46.5	56.8	64.7	66.2	59.7	Total Current	56.5	58.8	61.1	60.0	59.7
20.1	11.4	4.7	7.1	9.4	Long Term Debt	8.2	6.8	7.3	7.3	9.4
.0	1.0	.3	.4	.6	Deferred Taxes	.9	.7	.7	.7	.6
6.9	3.8	2.3	3.2	3.5	All Other Non-Current	1.4	1.2	1.7	1.8	3.5
26.4	27.0	28.0	23.1	26.8	Net Worth	32.9	32.5	29.2	30.2	26.8
100.0	100.0	100.0	100.0	100.0	Total Liabilities & Net Worth	100.0	100.0	100.0	100.0	100.0
					INCOME DATA					
100.0	100.0	100.0	100.0	100.0	Contract Revenues	100.0	100.0	100.0	100.0	100.0
28.6	18.5	11.2	10.2	15.9	Gross Profit	14.8	13.6	13.9	14.4	15.9
24.6	16.4	9.1	8.3	13.6	Operating Expenses	12.0	11.3	12.0	12.2	13.6
4.0	2.1	2.1	2.0	2.2	Operating Profit	2.8	2.3	1.9	2.1	2.2
.9	.2	.4	.1	.3	All Other Expenses (net)	−.2	−.5	−.2	.1	.3
3.1	2.0	1.8	1.9	2.0	Profit Before Taxes	2.9	2.8	2.1	2.0	2.0
					RATIOS					
3.5	2.0	1.5	1.4	1.8	Current	1.7	1.7	1.6	1.7	1.8
1.3	1.3	1.3	1.2	1.3		1.3	1.3	1.3	1.3	1.3
.9	1.1	1.1	1.1	1.1		1.1	1.1	1.1	1.1	1.1
(31) 7.9	(239) 2.5	(159) 1.7	(70) 1.4	1.9	Receivables/Payables	(370) 1.9	(441) 1.9	(363) 1.9	(311) 2.0	(499) 1.9
2.0	1.3	1.3	1.1	1.3		1.3	1.3	1.2	1.3	1.3
.4	.8	1.0	.8	.8		1.0	.9	.9	.9	.8
0 UND	14 25.2	36 10.1	37 9.9	21 17.6	Revenues/Receivables	34 10.6	33 11.1	34 10.8	27 13.4	21 17.6
18 20.1	40 9.1	52 7.0	52 7.0	45 8.1		52 7.0	50 7.4	50 7.3	48 7.5	45 8.1
58 6.3	65 5.6	68 5.4	62 5.9	65 5.6		69 5.3	67 5.6	71 5.6	65 5.6	65 5.6
0 UND	14 26.2	30 12.0	39 9.4	20 18.0	Cost of Revenues/Payables	26 14.3	23 15.7	26 14.1	22 16.5	20 18.0
23 16.0	29 12.5	44 8.3	50 7.3	38 9.5		43 8.4	44 8.4	44 8.4	42 8.8	38 9.5
51 7.1	51 7.2	63 5.8	66 5.5	57 6.4		64 5.7	60 6.1	65 5.6	58 6.3	57 6.4
5.3	7.8	12.4	13.8	9.4	Revenues/Working Capital	10.2	10.5	10.4	10.4	9.4
34.1	16.8	20.8	22.9	19.5		18.7	18.3	21.4	21.3	19.5
−18.8	99.8	46.2	73.9	72.1		45.5	41.6	57.1	61.8	72.1
11.4	11.3	25.1	29.9	15.8	EBIT/Interest	26.3	28.6	26.3	20.0	15.8
(26) 2.7	(205) 3.2	(126) 7.7	(52) 7.3	(409) 5.5		(314) 7.7	(372) 8.2	(306) 7.6	(251) 6.4	(409) 5.5
1.2	.5	1.9	2.3	1.2		2.0	2.3	2.0	2.0	1.2
	7.4	8.0	9.7	7.9	Net Profit + Depr., Dep., Amort./Cur. Mat. L /T/D	8.7	8.7	10.1	8.9	7.9
(73)	−1.8 (57)	4.3 (14)	4.2 (146)	3.3		(135) 3.1	(134) 3.7	(113) 3.6	(96) 4.0	(146) 3.3
	−.3	1.6	2.5	.9		1.5	1.5	1.0	1.6	.9
.3	.1	.1	.1	.1	Fixed/Worth	.1	.1	.1	.1	.1
1.9	.4	.3	.2	.3		.3	.3	.3	.3	.3
UND	1.0	.6	.7	.8		.8	.7	.7	.9	.8
1.0	.8	1.6	2.1	1.2	Debt/Worth	1.2	1.2	1.4	1.2	1.2
4.0	1.9	2.7	4.2	2.6		2.3	2.5	2.6	2.6	2.6
UND	4.9	5.3	7.0	5.9		4.3	4.1	5.3	4.9	5.9
87.3	45.3	37.3	35.8	41.0	% Profit Before Taxes/ Tangible Net Worth	44.4	46.7	49.2	38.7	41.0
(29) 21.1	(227) 13.1	(157) 15.4	(69) 26.7	(482) 15.9		(362) 22.1	(428) 22.4	(344) 25.8	(291) 18.7	(482) 15.9
1.6	.3	3.2	5.7	2.0		7.8	7.7	7.7	6.7	2.0
12.6	17.2	9.0	8.1	11.3	% Profit Before Taxes/ Total Assets	15.0	14.1	13.8	11.9	11.3
3.7	4.1	4.1	4.9	4.1		6.3	6.3	6.0	5.5	4.1
−.3	−.1	.9	1.0	.4		1.7	2.1	1.9	1.3	.4
.7	.4	.2	.1	.3	% Depr., Dep., Amort./ Revenues	.3	.3	.3	.3	.3
(30) 1.4	(217) .8	(142) .4	(55) .3	(444) .6		(334) .6	(396) .7	(329) .5	(289) .6	(444) .6
3.4	1.8	.8	.4	1.4		1.4	1.4	1.2	1.4	1.4
4.7	1.9	.8	.6	1.3	% Officers', Directors', Owners' Comp/Revenues	1.4	1.6	1.2	1.2	1.3
(16) 8.8	(140) 3.2	(91) 1.5	(18) 1.2	(265) 2.5		(164) 2.5	(194) 2.6	(167) 2.7	(157) 2.7	(265) 2.5
12.0	5.5	2.8	2.7	4.7		4.7	4.7	4.7	4.9	4.7
23344M	1107279M	3360421M	31459789M	35950833M	Contract Revenues ($)	52838146M	109842168M	73625045M	10857941M	35950833M
22232M	396650M	1142312M	11675263M	13236457M	Total Assets ($)	24684147M	27323617M	22296859M	3526496M	13236457M

M = $ thousand   MM = $ million
See Pages 11 through 18 for Explanation of Ratios and Data

Current Data Sorted By Revenue   **Comparative Historical Data**

					Type of Statement					
	24	18	6	48	Unqualified	91	72	74	45	48
6	46	18	1	71	Reviewed	101	92	94	71	71
5	12	2		19	Compiled	23	26	24	18	19
8	13			21	Tax Returns	10	12	11	15	21
1	11	5	3	20	Other	31	29	21	33	20
46 (4/1-9/30/02)			133 (10/1/02-3/31/03)			4/1/98-3/31/99	4/1/99-3/31/00	4/1/00-3/31/01	4/1/01-3/31/02	4/1/02-3/31/03
0-1MM	1-10MM	10-50MM	50 & OVER	ALL		ALL	ALL	ALL	ALL	ALL
20	106	43	10	179	NUMBER OF STATEMENTS	256	231	224	182	179
%	%	%	%	%	ASSETS	%	%	%	%	%
10.9	15.1	12.4	8.0	13.6	Cash & Equivalents	14.3	13.4	13.2	14.4	13.6
21.1	30.4	34.6	25.3	30.1	A/R - Progress Billings	28.8	30.5	30.5	28.0	30.1
.0	1.5	2.3	1.5	1.5	A/R - Current Retention	3.7	2.5	2.7	1.9	1.5
2.8	2.7	1.0	3.0	2.3	Inventory	1.6	2.5	1.5	2.3	2.3
.6	2.9	4.5	4.3	3.1	Cost & Est. Earnings In Excess of Billings	4.3	3.3	4.3	3.7	3.1
.1	4.7	7.5	8.6	5.1	All Other Current	3.8	3.9	3.8	4.9	5.1
35.5	57.3	62.4	50.7	55.7	Total Current	56.5	56.1	56.0	55.2	55.7
52.3	34.8	30.3	32.9	35.6	Fixed Assets (net)	35.4	36.5	34.5	36.3	35.6
.0	1.8	2.4	1.4	1.7	Joint Ventures & Investments	1.7	1.6	2.3	1.0	1.7
4.3	.6	.5	7.3	1.4	Intangibles (net)	.9	1.2	1.7	1.9	1.4
7.9	5.5	4.3	7.7	5.6	All Other Non-Current	5.4	4.7	5.5	5.6	5.6
100.0	100.0	100.0	100.0	100.0	Total	100.0	100.0	100.0	100.0	100.0
					LIABILITIES					
7.6	8.7	7.5	2.6	7.9	Notes Payable - Short Term	5.7	6.7	7.3	7.3	7.9
11.9	13.6	20.1	12.0	14.9	A/P - Trade	14.0	13.8	14.0	14.0	14.9
.0	.1	.2	.5	.1	A/P - Retention	.4	.3	.6	.2	.1
.0	2.1	6.2	2.9	2.9	Billings in Excess of Costs & Est. Earnings	3.2	2.7	3.1	3.0	2.9
.0	.3	.3	.3	.3	Income Taxes Payable	.6	.5	.8	.4	.3
16.4	6.5	4.9	2.3	7.0	Cur. Mat.-L/T/D	5.8	6.8	5.9	6.3	7.0
8.4	4.9	6.4	12.3	6.1	All Other Current	5.5	6.8	5.1	5.5	6.1
44.3	36.2	45.6	32.9	39.2	Total Current	35.3	37.7	36.8	36.8	39.2
45.0	16.8	13.2	19.3	19.2	Long Term Debt	13.5	14.7	13.4	15.6	19.2
.0	1.8	.8	1.3	1.3	Deferred Taxes	2.0	1.6	1.8	1.4	1.3
7.2	2.5	3.9	3.4	3.4	All Other Non-Current	1.3	1.9	3.0	2.7	3.4
3.6	42.7	36.5	43.1	36.9	Net Worth	47.9	44.1	45.1	43.5	36.9
100.0	100.0	100.0	100.0	100.0	Total Liabilities & Net Worth	100.0	100.0	100.0	100.0	100.0
					INCOME DATA					
100.0	100.0	100.0	100.0	100.0	Contract Revenues	100.0	100.0	100.0	100.0	100.0
45.3	30.5	19.7	16.4	28.8	Gross Profit	22.0	24.0	25.4	28.8	28.8
43.8	27.1	15.7	13.0	25.4	Operating Expenses	17.1	19.5	19.8	23.6	25.4
1.5	3.4	4.0	3.4	3.3	Operating Profit	4.9	4.5	5.6	5.1	3.3
1.4	.4	.4	.9	.5	All Other Expenses (net)	−.9	.1	.1	.5	.5
.1	3.0	3.6	2.5	2.8	Profit Before Taxes	5.8	4.5	5.5	4.6	2.8
					RATIOS					
2.8	2.8	1.7	2.3	2.5		2.3	2.5	2.5	2.6	2.5
.9	1.7	1.4	1.5	1.5	Current	1.5	1.5	1.6	1.4	1.5
.4	1.1	1.1	1.2	1.1		1.2	1.1	1.1	1.1	1.1
8.6	5.4	3.0	5.4	4.4		4.2	4.6	4.3	4.7	4.4
(16) 2.1	(104) 2.5	(42) 1.7	1.9	(172) 2.1	Receivables/Payables	(250) 2.5	(222) 2.6	(217) 2.6	(173) 2.3	(172) 2.1
.9	1.4	1.2	1.1	1.3		1.5	1.6	1.5	1.3	1.3
9 40.9	26 13.9	35 10.3	46 7.9	27 13.7		38 9.5	35 10.3	35 10.3	30 12.2	27 13.7
26 13.9	51 7.2	60 6.1	54 6.8	51 7.2	Revenues/Receivables	57 6.4	57 6.5	53 6.9	49 7.5	51 7.2
45 8.1	69 5.3	81 4.5	63 6.8	70 5.2		75 4.9	79 4.6	77 4.8	71 5.1	70 5.2
1 599.0	12 31.7	23 15.7	15 24.9	12 30.3		15 24.8	11 32.2	12 30.0	14 26.5	12 30.3
13 28.7	28 13.0	36 10.1	32 11.6	30 12.3	Cost of Revenues/Payables	27 13.7	25 14.5	25 14.5	28 13.0	30 12.3
91 4.0	44 8.4	51 7.2	44 8.3	48 7.6		43 8.4	44 8.4	44 8.3	50 7.3	48 7.6
9.4	5.6	8.5	6.1	6.2		6.4	6.0	5.6	6.0	6.2
−70.1	10.0	14.4	10.0	12.2	Revenues/Working Capital	11.3	11.8	10.6	12.4	12.2
−14.1	52.2	92.2	26.6	67.6		32.2	53.8	51.6	66.1	67.6
3.4	9.8	13.7		9.9		12.7	14.6	12.7	13.4	9.9
(18) 1.8	(93) 3.6	(39) 5.1	(159) 3.3		EBIT/Interest	(232) 5.0	(211) 5.4	(204) 5.3	(161) 4.1	(159) 3.3
−1.0	1.0	2.3		.6		1.9	1.5	2.1	1.1	.6
	6.1	4.1		6.0		4.5	4.3	4.8	5.3	6.0
(42) 2.2	(23) 1.9	(71) 1.9		Net Profit + Depr., Dep., Amort./Cur. Mat. L /T/D	(117) 2.4	(90) 2.0	(80) 2.6	(61) 2.0	(71) 1.9
.9	1.2		1.0			1.3	1.2	1.5	1.0	1.0
1.0	.4	.5	.7	.5		.4	.5	.5	.5	.5
6.2	.7	.9	.9	.9	Fixed/Worth	.8	.9	.7	.8	.9
−1.2	1.5	1.3	1.4	1.7		1.3	1.4	1.3	1.6	1.7
.9	.7	1.4	.5	.7		.6	.6	.6	.6	.7
7.9	1.2	2.0	1.6	1.6	Debt/Worth	1.2	1.4	1.2	1.3	1.6
−3.5	2.5	3.2	3.9	3.6		2.1	2.6	2.6	3.1	3.6
55.0	30.6	52.1		37.6		36.9	45.7	40.6	39.9	37.6
(13) 29.8	(101) 10.6	17.2	(166) 13.6		% Profit Before Taxes/ Tangible Net Worth	(254) 17.4	(221) 20.0	(214) 18.9	(173) 17.1	(166) 13.6
−19.0	.8	5.8		2.1		5.2	5.4	6.3	1.2	2.1
13.7	11.5	15.8	13.5	12.2		15.8	18.1	18.1	17.4	12.2
5.0	5.2	7.0	4.5	5.4	% Profit Before Taxes/ Total Assets	7.8	7.0	9.1	6.6	5.4
−15.8	.3	1.4	−2.6	.4		1.9	1.9	2.7	.3	.4
5.0	2.3	1.1		2.0		2.3	2.4	2.0	2.6	2.0
(15) 7.5	(94) 4.7	(42) 2.5	(158) 3.8		% Depr., Dep., Amort./ Revenues	(242) 4.0	(206) 4.2	(200) 3.8	(165) 4.0	(158) 3.8
9.5	7.9	4.2		6.7		6.2	7.1	6.1	6.4	6.7
5.5	1.9	1.2		1.8		1.9	1.7	1.8	1.8	1.8
(11) 7.1	(56) 3.9	(20) 1.8	(89) 3.4		% Officers', Directors', Owners' Comp/Revenues	(126) 4.3	(101) 4.1	(93) 4.0	(94) 3.6	(89) 3.4
13.9	7.1	7.1		7.0		6.5	7.2	6.9	7.0	7.0
12983M	473467M	905831M	1145952M	2538233M	Contract Revenues ($)	4700393M	29682222M	35114503M	2994279M	2538233M
5487M	219256M	510894M	736382M	1472019M	Total Assets ($)	2593931M	13847328M	18785966M	1734394M	1472019M

M = $ thousand   MM = $ million
See Pages 11 through 18 for Explanation of Ratios and Data

Current Data Sorted By Revenue　　　　　　　　　　　　　**Comparative Historical Data**

					Type of Statement					
	2	3	9	14	Unqualified					14
5	15	3	3	26	Reviewed					26
7	15	2		24	Compiled					24
28	23	1	1	53	Tax Returns					53
12	30	6	11	59	Other					59

28 (4/1-9/30/02)　　　　　　　　**148 (10/1/02-3/31/03)**

						4/1/98-3/31/99	4/1/99-3/31/00	4/1/00-3/31/01	4/1/01-3/31/02	4/1/02-3/31/03
0-1MM	1-10MM	10-50MM	50 & OVER	ALL		ALL	ALL	ALL	ALL	ALL
52	85	15	24	176	NUMBER OF STATEMENTS					176
%	%	%	%	%	ASSETS	%	%	%	%	%
10.5	7.1	5.1	6.9	7.9	Cash & Equivalents					7.9
2.3	5.5	1.6	9.8	4.8	A/R - Progress Billings	D	D	D	D	4.8
.1	.1	1.2	.3	.2	A/R - Current Retention	A	A	A	A	.2
33.2	33.6	43.2	31.6	34.0	Inventory	T	T	T	T	34.0
.0	.3	.0	.7	.3	Cost & Est. Earnings In Excess of Billings	A	A	A	A	.3
.6	5.6	9.5	8.5	4.8	All Other Current	N	N	N	N	4.8
46.7	52.2	60.6	58.0	52.1	Total Current	O	O	O	O	52.1
41.1	31.9	14.8	27.5	32.5	Fixed Assets (net)	T	T	T	T	32.5
4.2	3.6	18.0	8.0	5.6	Joint Ventures & Investments					5.6
.7	.4	.0	.6	.5	Intangibles (net)	A	A	A	A	.5
7.3	11.9	6.5	5.9	9.3	All Other Non-Current	V	V	V	V	9.3
100.0	100.0	100.0	100.0	100.0	Total	A	A	A	A	100.0
					LIABILITIES	I	I	I	I	
14.0	18.0	16.2	13.8	16.1	Notes Payable - Short Term	L	L	L	L	16.1
9.4	5.7	8.4	15.3	8.3	A/P - Trade	B	B	B	B	8.3
.0	2.2	.0	.1	1.1	A/P - Retention	L	L	L	L	1.1
.0	.6	.0	1.9	.5	Billings in Excess of Costs & Est. Earnings	E	E	E	E	.5
.0	.1	.0	.2	.1	Income Taxes Payable					.1
2.9	1.0	12.3	1.7	2.7	Cur. Mat.-L/T/D					2.7
9.1	10.0	4.7	4.7	8.6	All Other Current					8.6
35.5	37.6	41.6	37.7	37.3	Total Current					37.3
49.7	31.9	30.1	25.3	36.1	Long Term Debt					36.1
.0	.0	.0	1.0	.2	Deferred Taxes					.2
7.4	8.4	4.1	5.8	7.4	All Other Non-Current					7.4
7.3	22.0	24.2	30.1	19.0	Net Worth					19.0
100.0	100.0	100.0	100.0	100.0	Total Liabilities & Net Worth					100.0
					INCOME DATA					
100.0	100.0	100.0	100.0	100.0	Contract Revenues					100.0
					Gross Profit					
74.9	84.1	94.8	86.6	82.6	Operating Expenses					82.6
25.1	15.9	5.2	13.4	17.4	Operating Profit					17.4
10.5	4.3	2.2	4.8	6.0	All Other Expenses (net)					6.0
14.6	11.5	3.0	8.7	11.3	Profit Before Taxes					11.3
					RATIOS					
4.1	4.0	2.7	1.8	3.4	Current					3.4
1.3	1.4	1.4	1.4	1.4						1.4
.4	.8	1.0	.9	.8						.8

							Receivables/Payables					
	1.9		1.6		.7		.7	1.3				1.3
(34)	.0	(69)	.2		.3	(23)	.2	(141)	.2	(141)		.2
	.0		.0		.0		.0	.0				.0

								Revenues/Receivables					
0	UND	0	UND	0	999.8	1	520.9	0	UND	0	UND		UND
0	UND	1	340.6	5	78.1	9	40.2	1	580.5	1	580.5		
7	49.5	13	28.0	23	16.2	24	15.2	16	22.9	16	22.9		

					Cost of Revenues/Payables					

					Revenues/Working Capital					
1.5	1.6	2.9	3.5	1.8						1.8
12.1	10.8	6.7	8.1	8.5						8.5
-9.6	-14.5	270.4	-257.7	-11.5						-11.5

							EBIT/Interest					
	6.6		24.0				16.8	13.9				13.9
(30)	3.9	(62)	3.9			(18)	6.4	(119)	4.1	(119)		4.1
	1.2		.6				1.9	1.4				1.4

					Net Profit + Depr., Dep., Amort./Cur. Mat. L /T/D					

					Fixed/Worth					
.0	.0	.0	.0	.0						.0
1.6	.7	.1	.2	.6						.6
10.1	8.6	1.0	2.0	5.2						5.2

					Debt/Worth					
1.6	1.1	1.6	1.6	1.3						1.3
6.4	5.2	5.5	2.5	4.5						4.5
-41.0	31.0	11.0	3.5	18.5						18.5

							% Profit Before Taxes/ Tangible Net Worth					
	52.9		82.1		88.3		39.3	61.6				61.6
(38)	19.9	(71)	22.0		29.5	(23)	27.9	(147)	24.2	(147)		24.2
	5.0		6.0		.1		9.5	7.3				7.3

					% Profit Before Taxes/ Total Assets					
12.8	13.3	13.0	13.5	13.0						13.0
4.7	5.1	2.8	8.1	5.3						5.3
.4	.6	.1	2.5	.9						.9

							% Depr., Dep., Amort./ Revenues					
	1.2		.5					.5				.5
(27)	7.9	(55)	1.6					(97)	1.8	(97)		1.8
	12.7		6.5					8.0				8.0

							% Officers', Directors', Owners' Comp/Revenues					
			1.4					1.9				1.9
	(34)		4.5				(44)	4.6	(44)			4.6
			8.0					8.3				8.3

26635M	298353M	388922M	25320847M	26034757M	Contract Revenues ($)				26034757M
76345M	757177M	646777M	28902400M	30382699M	Total Assets ($)				30382699M

M = $ thousand   MM = $ million

See Pages 11 through 18 for Explanation of Ratios and Data

Current Data Sorted By Revenue   **Comparative Historical Data**

0-1MM	1-10MM	10-50MM	50 & OVER	ALL	Type of Statement	4/1/98-3/31/99 ALL	4/1/99-3/31/00 ALL	4/1/00-3/31/01 ALL	4/1/01-3/31/02 ALL	4/1/02-3/31/03 ALL
3	41	70	23	137	Unqualified	222	209	182	147	137
5	46	16	1	68	Reviewed	102	109	95	72	68
3	11	3	2	19	Compiled	29	37	29	24	19
5	7	2	1	15	Tax Returns	13	13	15	13	15
2	13	7	5	27	Other	66	53	54	39	27
50 (4/1-9/30/02)			216 (10/1/02-3/31/03)							
18	118	98	32	266	NUMBER OF STATEMENTS	432	421	375	295	266
%	%	%	%	%	ASSETS	%	%	%	%	%
17.4	14.3	18.9	13.6	16.1	Cash & Equivalents	16.0	16.9	15.7	15.6	16.1
23.2	25.7	26.8	24.5	25.8	A/R - Progress Billings	26.8	26.5	26.6	26.3	25.8
.0	2.4	2.7	4.8	2.6	A/R - Current Retention	3.8	3.1	3.5	3.0	2.6
2.7	2.9	2.7	4.6	3.0	Inventory	3.2	2.3	2.6	2.5	3.0
2.7	2.3	3.5	3.6	3.0	Cost & Est. Earnings In Excess of Billings	2.8	2.8	3.4	3.1	3.0
4.1	4.4	6.4	8.8	5.6	All Other Current	3.5	3.6	4.2	5.5	5.6
50.2	52.0	61.0	59.9	56.1	Total Current	56.0	55.1	55.9	55.9	56.1
46.6	39.1	32.6	32.7	36.4	Fixed Assets (net)	36.2	36.4	36.0	35.6	36.4
.0	1.7	1.8	1.2	1.5	Joint Ventures & Investments	1.4	1.6	1.4	1.1	1.5
.6	.3	.4	.5	.4	Intangibles (net)	1.6	1.6	1.4	1.6	.4
2.6	7.0	4.2	5.7	5.5	All Other Non-Current	4.7	5.3	5.4	5.8	5.5
100.0	100.0	100.0	100.0	100.0	Total	100.0	100.0	100.0	100.0	100.0
					LIABILITIES					
11.9	8.8	4.7	5.3	7.1	Notes Payable - Short Term	5.6	6.0	6.8	6.2	7.1
10.8	13.8	16.2	19.9	15.2	A/P - Trade	16.1	15.2	17.1	15.4	15.2
.0	.3	.7	1.5	.6	A/P - Retention	1.0	.8	.8	.8	.6
1.1	2.2	4.2	5.7	3.3	Billings in Excess of Costs & Est. Earnings	3.1	3.2	3.6	3.7	3.3
.1	.2	.3	.2	.2	Income Taxes Payable	.5	.7	.4	.3	.2
9.1	7.0	5.3	5.2	6.3	Cur. Mat.-L/T/D	5.4	6.2	5.8	5.6	6.3
32.9	5.9	5.8	7.0	7.8	All Other Current	5.3	5.4	4.5	6.6	7.8
66.0	38.3	37.1	44.8	40.5	Total Current	37.0	37.5	39.0	38.6	40.5
25.8	16.4	13.1	16.4	15.8	Long Term Debt	15.3	15.1	13.8	16.4	15.8
.3	1.5	1.3	1.8	1.4	Deferred Taxes	1.8	1.8	1.7	1.2	1.4
7.5	2.9	2.8	.9	3.0	All Other Non-Current	1.8	2.1	1.9	2.9	3.0
.5	40.8	45.7	36.1	39.3	Net Worth	44.2	43.5	43.5	40.8	39.3
100.0	100.0	100.0	100.0	100.0	Total Liabilities & Net Worth	100.0	100.0	100.0	100.0	100.0
					INCOME DATA					
100.0	100.0	100.0	100.0	100.0	Contract Revenues	100.0	100.0	100.0	100.0	100.0
39.8	23.8	16.4	11.8	20.7	Gross Profit	19.0	20.1	18.0	21.3	20.7
38.0	22.1	12.9	9.4	18.3	Operating Expenses	14.8	15.3	14.7	17.8	18.3
1.7	1.7	3.5	2.4	2.4	Operating Profit	4.2	4.8	3.3	3.4	2.4
1.5	.3	.3	.6	.4	All Other Expenses (net)	−.3	.0	.0	.6	.4
.2	1.3	3.2	1.8	2.0	Profit Before Taxes	4.5	4.8	3.3	2.8	2.0
					RATIOS					
2.9	2.2	2.4	1.6	2.2	Current	2.2	2.1	2.1	2.1	2.2
1.2	1.4	1.6	1.3	1.4		1.5	1.5	1.4	1.4	1.4
.3	1.0	1.2	1.1	1.1		1.2	1.1	1.1	1.1	1.1
(16) 9.8	(116) 4.2	(97) 2.7	2.0	(261) 3.5	Receivables/Payables	(424) 3.0	(415) 3.1	(371) 2.7	(290) 3.3	(261) 3.5
3.5	2.2	1.9	1.4	1.9		1.9	2.0	1.8	1.9	1.9
1.2	1.2	1.2	1.0	1.2		1.3	1.2	1.2	1.2	1.2
10 35.0	22 16.5	32 11.3	30 12.3	24 15.0	Revenues/Receivables	29 12.4	30 12.3	28 13.0	27 13.6	24 15.0
24 15.0	41 8.8	45 8.1	38 9.5	43 8.5		49 7.5	47 7.8	49 7.5	48 7.7	43 8.5
76 4.8	72 5.0	58 6.3	60 6.0	67 5.5		70 5.2	68 5.3	68 5.4	67 5.5	67 5.5
0 UND	9 39.6	18 20.3	19 19.0	13 28.1	Cost of Revenues/Payables	16 23.3	14 25.4	15 24.1	13 27.7	13 28.1
11 33.2	27 13.5	29 12.7	31 11.8	28 13.2		30 12.1	28 13.2	33 11.1	30 12.2	28 13.2
29 12.5	50 7.3	42 8.6	51 7.2	45 8.0		46 7.9	48 7.6	51 7.2	51 7.2	45 8.0
6.8	7.0	6.4	9.2	6.8	Revenues/Working Capital	6.6	7.1	7.4	7.6	6.8
33.7	14.7	10.5	15.2	13.5		12.5	13.5	13.8	14.1	13.5
−16.4	−117.5	27.3	32.2	58.4		31.5	42.2	47.1	55.2	58.4
(13) 4.2	(105) 6.5	(92) 19.5	(30) 14.8	(240) 10.7	EBIT/Interest	(399) 12.7	(373) 12.8	(343) 10.6	(271) 9.9	(240) 10.7
1.3	2.6	5.1	3.4	3.1		5.1	5.1	3.4	3.7	3.1
−3.0	.0	2.0	.6	1.1		2.1	2.1	1.3	1.4	1.1
	2.6	4.7	3.0	3.2	Net Profit + Depr., Dep., Amort./Cur. Mat. L /T/D	(204) 4.3	(172) 4.7	(151) 4.7	(112) 4.3	(101) 3.2
	(43) 1.3	(47) 2.3	(10) 1.6	(101) 1.7		2.3	2.4	2.2	1.9	1.7
	.3	1.1	1.2	.8		1.4	1.4	1.1	1.1	.8
.5	.5	.5	.6	.5	Fixed/Worth	.5	.5	.5	.5	.5
1.2	1.0	.7	.8	.8		.8	.8	.8	.8	.8
17.5	1.9	1.2	1.2	1.5		1.4	1.3	1.4	1.5	1.5
.5	.7	.6	1.0	.7	Debt/Worth	.6	.7	.7	.8	.7
2.3	1.6	1.3	2.0	1.6		1.3	1.4	1.3	1.5	1.6
NM	3.4	2.2	3.2	3.1		2.5	2.4	2.7	3.1	3.1
(14) 37.9	(115) 25.6	25.6	23.7	(259) 25.6	% Profit Before Taxes/ Tangible Net Worth	(419) 38.1	(404) 35.5	(361) 30.7	(282) 29.2	(259) 25.6
18.1	7.6	14.2	11.0	11.9		21.2	19.3	13.1	13.4	11.9
7.5	−3.0	4.2	1.9	1.9		8.9	7.8	2.5	3.3	1.9
18.9	8.5	11.6	8.8	9.7	% Profit Before Taxes/ Total Assets	15.2	14.2	11.7	11.5	9.7
5.8	3.1	6.1	4.4	4.0		8.4	7.9	4.8	4.8	4.0
−17.1	−2.9	1.9	.8	.3		2.8	2.9	.7	1.2	.3
	1.7	2.0	1.3	1.9	% Depr., Dep., Amort./ Revenues	(389) 2.3	(378) 2.2	(332) 2.2	(261) 2.5	(222) 1.9
	(99) 4.2	(92) 3.2	(22) 2.5	(222) 3.6		3.6	3.6	3.5	4.0	3.6
	6.3	4.4	4.5	5.4		5.3	5.5	5.6	6.0	5.4
	2.0	1.2		1.5	% Officers', Directors', Owners' Comp/Revenues	(184) 1.4	(190) 1.4	(161) 1.2	(131) 1.2	(122) 1.5
	(66) 3.1	(42) 1.9		(122) 2.6		2.4	2.6	2.5	2.5	2.6
	6.6	2.6		5.4		4.3	4.3	5.6	5.4	5.4
9926M	557953M	2249663M	19863796M	22681338M	Contract Revenues ($)	30484894M	9047636M	25140493M	8637730M	22681338M
4426M	298467M	1086652M	6670244M	8059789M	Total Assets ($)	21314841M	4648511M	11876667M	4195980M	8059789M

M = $ thousand   MM = $ million
See Pages 11 through 18 for Explanation of Ratios and Data

Current Data Sorted By Revenue **Comparative Historical Data**

0-1MM	1-10MM	10-50MM	50 & OVER	ALL	Type of Statement	4/1/98-3/31/99 ALL	4/1/99-3/31/00 ALL	4/1/00-3/31/01 ALL	4/1/01-3/31/02 ALL	4/1/02-3/31/03 ALL
	3	15	12	30	Unqualified	32	48	47	36	30
1	13	5	2	21	Reviewed	27	28	36	33	21
4	7			11	Compiled	8	10	6	8	11
7				7	Tax Returns	10	6	6	9	7
2	3	2	3	10	Other	8	20	13	13	10
17 (4/1-9/30/02)			62 (10/1/02-3/31/03)							
14	26	22	17	79	**NUMBER OF STATEMENTS**	85	112	108	99	79
%	%	%	%	%	**ASSETS**	%	%	%	%	%
5.8	14.7	15.7	7.7	11.9	Cash & Equivalents	15.4	13.3	15.2	11.6	11.9
32.1	25.2	24.0	29.8	27.1	A/R - Progress Billings	33.1	30.1	31.8	32.1	27.1
.0	1.7	3.3	2.1	1.9	A/R - Current Retention	3.3	2.8	1.6	1.6	1.9
1.6	5.7	6.3	1.2	4.2	Inventory	2.6	3.2	2.2	3.8	4.2
.0	3.6	2.8	7.9	3.7	Cost & Est. Earnings In Excess of Billings	3.4	3.9	3.9	3.4	3.7
5.8	6.0	13.3	7.8	8.4	All Other Current	3.2	5.6	5.3	5.7	8.4
45.3	56.9	65.5	56.5	57.1	Total Current	61.0	58.8	60.1	58.2	57.1
49.9	36.3	24.7	30.7	34.3	Fixed Assets (net)	31.1	31.9	33.1	33.8	34.3
.0	2.2	2.7	.5	1.6	Joint Ventures & Investments	.5	1.4	1.0	.8	1.6
1.4	.1	.0	8.9	2.2	Intangibles (net)	.9	1.0	.8	.9	2.2
3.4	4.5	7.0	3.3	4.8	All Other Non-Current	6.5	7.0	5.1	6.4	4.8
100.0	100.0	100.0	100.0	100.0	Total	100.0	100.0	100.0	100.0	100.0
					LIABILITIES					
20.1	8.0	7.6	2.2	8.8	Notes Payable - Short Term	8.6	6.3	7.2	6.9	8.8
10.6	18.4	19.0	17.3	16.9	A/P - Trade	18.0	19.3	18.2	18.4	16.9
.0	.3	1.5	1.0	.7	A/P - Retention	.6	1.0	.8	1.6	.7
.0	2.9	4.9	9.1	4.3	Billings in Excess of Costs & Est. Earnings	3.0	3.4	3.8	4.1	4.3
.1	.5	.2	.5	.3	Income Taxes Payable	.6	.5	.9	.2	.3
6.2	4.9	5.3	3.5	4.9	Cur. Mat.-L/T/D	4.9	5.6	4.7	4.9	4.9
13.3	3.6	6.5	9.7	7.4	All Other Current	8.3	7.3	6.4	8.2	7.4
50.3	38.6	45.0	43.3	43.4	Total Current	44.0	43.4	42.0	44.1	43.4
28.8	21.2	19.8	20.5	22.0	Long Term Debt	15.2	16.2	14.5	16.8	22.0
.0	.7	1.5	2.7	1.2	Deferred Taxes	1.8	1.5	1.8	1.2	1.2
5.0	.7	.9	1.4	1.7	All Other Non-Current	1.7	1.6	4.0	4.0	1.7
15.9	38.7	32.9	32.1	31.7	Net Worth	37.2	37.3	37.6	33.9	31.7
100.0	100.0	100.0	100.0	100.0	Total Liabilities & Net Worth	100.0	100.0	100.0	100.0	100.0
					INCOME DATA					
100.0	100.0	100.0	100.0	100.0	Contract Revenues	100.0	100.0	100.0	100.0	100.0
45.6	28.9	15.9	17.6	25.8	Gross Profit	23.5	21.5	21.0	24.6	25.8
42.8	26.6	13.0	11.7	22.5	Operating Expenses	17.8	17.5	20.4	20.8	22.5
2.8	2.3	2.9	5.9	3.3	Operating Profit	5.7	4.0	.6	3.8	3.3
2.2	.8	.4	2.1	1.2	All Other Expenses (net)	.5	.1	-2.2	1.3	1.2
.6	1.5	2.5	3.9	2.1	Profit Before Taxes	5.2	3.9	2.7	2.5	2.1
					RATIOS					
1.2	2.4	1.9	1.7	1.9	Current	2.5	1.9	2.1	1.8	1.9
.9	1.7	1.3	1.3	1.3		1.5	1.3	1.4	1.3	1.3
.7	.8	1.1	1.1	1.0		1.1	1.0	1.1	1.0	1.0
7.5	5.4	2.4	3.8	3.9	Receivables/Payables	3.9	3.5	3.1	3.3	3.9
(12) 4.1	(25) 1.5	1.6	1.8	(76) 1.8		(82) 2.2	(109) 1.9	(103) 2.0	(95) 1.8	(76) 1.8
1.7	1.0	1.1	1.1	1.0		1.3	1.1	1.3	1.2	1.0
9 42.4	36 10.1	25 14.3	38 9.5	31 11.8	Revenues/Receivables	37 9.9	31 11.7	34 10.7	34 10.7	31 11.8
48 7.7	42 8.7	39 9.3	51 7.1	45 8.2		67 5.4	52 7.1	54 6.8	51 7.2	45 8.2
99 3.7	60 6.1	57 6.4	83 4.4	63 5.8		87 4.2	74 5.0	72 5.1	68 5.3	63 5.8
0 UND	11 33.0	17 21.9	19 19.5	15 24.9	Cost of Revenues/Payables	18 20.7	20 18.3	15 24.0	18 20.6	15 24.9
18 20.4	35 10.4	32 11.3	30 12.1	32 11.5		33 11.0	32 11.4	29 12.6	32 11.5	32 11.5
50 7.3	60 6.1	53 6.9	47 7.7	51 7.2		54 6.8	54 6.7	51 7.2	49 7.5	51 7.2
24.9	5.1	9.7	9.4	8.7	Revenues/Working Capital	5.8	7.0	5.9	7.1	8.7
-45.0	9.5	15.6	21.0	19.6		13.3	19.2	14.9	18.3	19.6
-7.1	-45.1	41.3	51.4	300.5		37.2	210.2	53.7	-566.8	300.5
8.5	10.8	13.5	14.1	11.1	EBIT/Interest	12.5	14.1	15.2	12.7	11.1
(13) 2.0	(23) 5.0	(20) 2.8	(16) 8.1	(72) 3.6		(77) 4.6	(101) 3.7	(97) 3.6	(92) 4.2	(72) 3.6
.5	.7	.3	2.5	1.0		1.9	1.5	1.8	1.2	1.0
				3.8	Net Profit + Depr., Dep., Amort./Cur. Mat. L /T/D	5.7	5.2	10.6	5.7	3.8
			(22)	1.4		(41) 2.5	(44) 2.4	(42) 2.5	(39) 2.3	(22) 1.4
				.1		1.2	1.0	1.1	1.1	.1
1.2	.4	.1	.5	.4	Fixed/Worth	.3	.4	.4	.5	.4
6.6	.9	.8	1.0	1.0		.7	.8	.8	.8	1.0
-6.2	2.1	1.1	2.4	2.6		1.5	1.7	1.3	1.6	2.6
1.3	1.0	1.0	1.7	1.1	Debt/Worth	.6	.8	.8	.9	1.1
7.4	1.5	2.4	2.8	2.6		1.7	1.7	1.7	1.9	2.6
-16.6	4.2	4.7	10.0	6.8		3.1	3.6	3.9	3.8	6.8
33.6	45.6	35.3	47.5	36.3	% Profit Before Taxes/Tangible Net Worth	44.7	40.3	35.4	49.5	36.3
(10) 9.7	(25) 12.9	(21) 16.1	(15) 28.3	(71) 20.3		(81) 18.1	(104) 18.9	(102) 19.8	(89) 18.3	(71) 20.3
-11.0	-3.3	-1.8	20.3	1.6		6.9	3.2	5.2	5.1	1.6
14.4	13.8	9.8	12.6	12.6	% Profit Before Taxes/Total Assets	16.3	14.8	12.8	13.8	12.6
2.9	4.8	3.0	7.7	4.6		7.0	7.0	6.2	6.6	4.6
-2.7	-3.3	-.1	2.4	.6		2.4	1.2	1.9	1.5	.6
3.3	2.8	.2	.5	.7	% Depr., Dep., Amort./Revenues	1.2	1.3	1.1	1.2	.7
(12) 10.6	(23) 4.5	(18) 1.2	(10) 1.1	(63) 3.0		(80) 2.7	(97) 2.6	(97) 2.5	(95) 2.7	(63) 3.0
19.5	9.2	3.1	2.1	9.2		5.6	4.5	6.4	5.3	9.2
	1.1			1.3	% Officers', Directors', Owners' Comp/Revenues	1.4	1.6	1.8	1.7	1.3
	(14) 3.3			(31) 3.5		(37) 3.6	(50) 3.3	(43) 3.6	(52) 2.6	(31) 3.5
	4.5			4.8		6.4	5.4	6.1	5.0	4.8
9072M	103802M	525584M	6916569M	7555027M	Contract Revenues ($)	2334556M	4948051M	3810583M	3699689M	7555027M
6805M	53583M	455878M	4691451M	5207717M	Total Assets ($)	1082463M	2737613M	2322859M	1710678M	5207717M

M = $ thousand   MM = $ million
See Pages 11 through 18 for Explanation of Ratios and Data

Current Data Sorted By Revenue | **Comparative Historical Data**

Type of Statement	0-1MM	1-10MM	10-50MM	50 & OVER	ALL		4/1/98-3/31/99	4/1/99-3/31/00	4/1/00-3/31/01	4/1/01-3/31/02	4/1/02-3/31/03
Unqualified		5	4	2	11		33	32	26	14	11
Reviewed	2	27	8		37		70	67	66	47	37
Compiled	4	7			11		42	42	33	23	11
Tax Returns	6	13	1		20		19	22	24	27	20
Other		14	8	1	23		21	27	32	36	23
	23 (4/1-9/30/02)			79 (10/1/02-3/31/03)			ALL	ALL	ALL	ALL	ALL
NUMBER OF STATEMENTS	12	66	21	3	102		185	190	181	147	102
ASSETS	%	%	%	%	%		%	%	%	%	%
Cash & Equivalents	11.1	10.7	12.5		11.0		13.4	14.5	12.1	14.1	11.0
A/R - Progress Billings	14.2	36.1	35.4		33.7		37.5	35.9	36.9	33.2	33.7
A/R - Current Retention	.2	1.5	3.6		2.0		2.9	2.1	2.4	1.4	2.0
Inventory	8.3	.6	1.9		1.7		2.2	1.6	1.3	2.0	1.7
Cost & Est. Earnings In Excess of Billings	1.1	1.8	3.0		2.0		1.8	1.9	2.2	2.1	2.0
All Other Current	.3	4.7	4.5		4.4		2.5	2.6	3.7	3.8	4.4
Total Current	35.2	55.2	60.8		54.8		60.4	58.6	58.4	56.6	54.8
Fixed Assets (net)	54.7	38.6	32.5		38.5		32.2	34.5	33.5	34.8	38.5
Joint Ventures & Investments	.0	.3	1.6		.5		.9	.5	1.0	.6	.5
Intangibles (net)	.0	.9	.1		.6		.7	1.1	1.6	1.1	.6
All Other Non-Current	10.2	5.0	5.0		5.5		5.7	5.2	5.4	6.8	5.5
Total	100.0	100.0	100.0		100.0		100.0	100.0	100.0	100.0	100.0
LIABILITIES											
Notes Payable - Short Term	9.3	7.3	5.4		7.3		7.9	9.6	8.3	6.5	7.3
A/P - Trade	4.4	16.8	21.6		16.9		17.7	16.8	16.0	16.4	16.9
A/P - Retention	.0	.0	.4		.1		.1	.3	.2	.1	.1
Billings in Excess of Costs & Est. Earnings	.0	1.3	4.1		2.3		2.9	3.4	3.5	1.9	2.3
Income Taxes Payable	.0	.5	.5		.4		.6	.4	.4	.2	.4
Cur. Mat.-L/T/D	9.9	4.9	4.3		5.3		7.3	6.5	5.4	5.4	5.3
All Other Current	2.0	5.3	7.8		5.4		5.7	5.1	6.1	5.1	5.4
Total Current	25.6	36.2	44.1		37.7		42.4	42.0	39.8	35.6	37.7
Long Term Debt	28.4	21.3	14.3		20.2		13.2	15.5	14.8	18.6	20.2
Deferred Taxes	.0	1.2	1.1		1.0		.9	1.2	.9	.9	1.0
All Other Non-Current	7.8	3.2	1.6		3.4		4.3	2.4	2.0	5.7	3.4
Net Worth	38.2	38.2	38.9		37.8		39.2	39.0	42.6	39.1	37.8
Total Liabilities & Net Worth	100.0	100.0	100.0		100.0		100.0	100.0	100.0	100.0	100.0
INCOME DATA											
Contract Revenues	100.0	100.0	100.0		100.0		100.0	100.0	100.0	100.0	100.0
Gross Profit	46.7	29.2	19.5		28.7		28.2	25.5	25.5	28.7	28.7
Operating Expenses	40.6	25.3	15.2		24.5		23.2	21.2	20.1	24.1	24.5
Operating Profit	6.1	4.0	4.2		4.3		5.0	4.3	5.3	4.6	4.3
All Other Expenses (net)	.9	.7	-.2		.5		.6	.8	.5	.6	.5
Profit Before Taxes	5.2	3.3	4.4		3.7		4.4	3.4	4.8	4.0	3.7
RATIOS											
Current	5.9	2.6	2.0		2.3		2.4	2.2	2.5	2.6	2.3
	1.1	1.8	1.3		1.7		1.5	1.4	1.5	1.7	1.7
	.5	1.0	1.1		1.0		1.1	1.0	1.1	1.1	1.0
Receivables/Payables		4.4	2.8		4.1		(169) 4.9	(177) 3.8	(164) 5.7	(137) 4.8	(91) 4.1
		(60) 2.4	2.0		(91) 2.2		2.4	2.3	2.7	2.5	2.2
		1.6	1.4		1.5		1.6	1.7	1.6	1.4	1.5
Revenues/Receivables	0 UND	31 11.8	39 9.3		28 12.8		28 12.8	24 15.0	31 11.9	23 15.9	28 12.8
	0 UND	52 7.0	56 6.5		51 7.2		56 6.5	50 7.3	52 7.1	47 7.8	51 7.2
	24 15.2	78 4.7	67 5.4		72 5.1		81 4.5	72 5.1	74 4.9	67 5.4	72 5.1
Cost of Revenues/Payables	0 UND	9 39.9	25 14.4		11 32.9		12 30.0	10 36.9	7 48.7	9 40.1	11 32.9
	0 UND	26 14.1	32 11.6		27 13.7		29 12.7	27 13.7	23 15.7	24 15.3	27 13.7
	16 23.2	50 7.2	47 7.7		48 7.7		46 7.9	41 8.9	40 9.1	50 7.3	48 7.7
Revenues/Working Capital	22.5	6.8	8.3		7.5		7.2	8.9	7.6	6.8	7.5
	NM	13.0	13.3		18.0		14.1	18.5	15.4	14.6	18.0
	-24.2	134.3	36.5		NM		72.6	594.0	89.3	72.5	NM
EBIT/Interest	7.0	10.6	17.5		10.5		(165) 14.0	(167) 11.5	(159) 15.4	(130) 10.8	(93) 10.5
	(11) 3.0	(62) 4.6	(18) 2.5	(93)	4.4		5.2	4.7	5.1	3.4	4.4
	.8	1.2	.7		1.1		2.0	1.7	1.7	1.4	1.1
Net Profit + Depr., Dep., Amort./Cur. Mat. L /T/D		4.6			4.3		(68) 5.2	(68) 3.2	(55) 8.8	(36) 3.9	(31) 4.3
		(21) 2.5		(31)	1.7		2.4	1.9	2.2	2.1	1.7
		1.3			1.0		1.3	1.3	1.3	.7	1.0
Fixed/Worth	.5	.5	.3		.4		.3	.3	.3	.4	.4
	1.6	1.1	.9		1.0		.7	.9	.7	.8	1.0
	3.6	2.1	1.7		1.9		1.6	1.9	1.5	2.2	1.9
Debt/Worth	.6	.8	.8		.8		.7	.9	.6	.6	.8
	2.2	1.4	1.4		1.4		1.4	1.7	1.5	1.3	1.4
	14.8	5.1	3.8		4.4		3.1	3.8	3.1	3.5	4.4
% Profit Before Taxes/ Tangible Net Worth	97.7	51.5	62.6		59.4		(174) 54.1	(182) 49.0	(174) 47.5	(133) 53.2	(96) 59.4
	(10) 41.9	(62) 17.4	20.2	(96)	21.0		26.5	22.5	20.7	22.3	21.0
	14.5	6.5	.3		6.8		9.9	8.1	8.7	6.2	6.8
% Profit Before Taxes/ Total Assets	48.9	15.5	16.0		17.4		21.4	18.6	22.0	19.8	17.4
	16.0	6.1	4.8		6.4		9.4	7.9	10.4	7.8	6.4
	.6	1.3	.0		1.3		3.3	1.8	3.0	1.2	1.3
% Depr., Dep., Amort./ Revenues	.9	1.7	.6		1.3		(171) 1.3	(177) 1.4	(168) 1.2	(130) 1.5	(92) 1.3
	(11) 3.8	(59) 3.0	(19) 2.3	(92)	2.9		2.7	2.8	2.2	3.0	2.9
	4.8	5.6	4.4		4.7		4.4	4.7	4.6	4.8	4.7
% Officers', Directors', Owners' Comp/Revenues	7.4	2.4			2.5		(116) 2.4	(116) 2.7	(107) 2.1	(92) 2.5	(71) 2.5
	(10) 10.2	(51) 3.7		(71)	3.9		4.8	5.3	3.2	4.2	3.9
	15.7	6.0			7.5		8.5	8.6	7.4	7.7	7.5
Contract Revenues ($)	7555M	300712M	442319M	333496M	1084082M		23453125M	3610577M	17912948M	2958870M	1084082M
Total Assets ($)	2305M	125218M	193388M	99113M	420024M		7456579M	888422M	11247191M	1076984M	420024M

M = $ thousand   MM = $ million
See Pages 11 through 18 for Explanation of Ratios and Data

Current Data Sorted By Revenue   Comparative Historical Data

0-1MM	1-10MM	10-50MM	50 & OVER	ALL	Type of Statement	4/1/98-3/31/99 ALL	4/1/99-3/31/00 ALL	4/1/00-3/31/01 ALL	4/1/01-3/31/02 ALL	4/1/02-3/31/03 ALL
	2	6	3	11	Unqualified	9	11	9	15	11
	23	7		30	Reviewed	30	23	20	23	30
2	11			13	Compiled	13	18	15	10	13
1	5			5	Tax Returns	4	5	3	6	5
	10		1	12	Other	8	10	9	10	12
15 (4/1-9/30/02)			56 (10/1/02-3/31/03)							
3	51	13	4	71	**NUMBER OF STATEMENTS**	64	67	56	64	71
%	%	%	%	%	**ASSETS**	%	%	%	%	%
	11.9	19.3		12.7	Cash & Equivalents	10.0	10.0	6.5	11.1	12.7
	46.0	41.1		43.7	A/R - Progress Billings	43.0	44.6	43.9	44.1	43.7
	2.1	.7		1.6	A/R - Current Retention	2.4	2.2	3.0	1.7	1.6
	3.3	2.0		2.8	Inventory	2.4	2.0	3.7	1.8	2.8
	4.7	6.3		4.9	Cost & Est. Earnings In Excess of Billings	5.3	5.1	7.2	4.6	4.9
	3.1	5.7		4.2	All Other Current	4.9	6.7	6.3	4.0	4.2
	71.1	75.1		69.9	Total Current	68.0	70.6	70.5	67.3	69.9
	23.1	15.6		22.2	Fixed Assets (net)	25.4	23.4	23.6	27.0	22.2
	1.4	.7		1.1	Joint Ventures & Investments	.7	1.0	1.2	1.1	1.1
	.2	2.4		.8	Intangibles (net)	1.1	1.4	.6	.3	.8
	4.2	6.1		6.0	All Other Non-Current	4.8	3.6	4.1	4.3	6.0
	100.0	100.0		100.0	Total	100.0	100.0	100.0	100.0	100.0
					LIABILITIES					
	13.0	2.8		10.8	Notes Payable - Short Term	11.8	10.4	9.8	9.4	10.8
	13.5	15.3		13.7	A/P - Trade	18.3	18.4	21.0	15.2	13.7
	.9	.2		1.0	A/P - Retention	.2	.3	.0	.0	1.0
	3.6	7.5		4.2	Billings in Excess of Costs & Est. Earnings	4.7	4.6	6.5	6.2	4.2
	.0	1.2		.3	Income Taxes Payable	.9	.6	.7	.6	.3
	2.7	1.5		2.5	Cur. Mat.-L/T/D	3.7	3.2	1.6	3.1	2.5
	9.7	8.9		9.5	All Other Current	10.1	8.9	7.1	9.9	9.5
	43.4	37.4		42.1	Total Current	49.8	46.4	46.7	44.4	42.1
	10.1	1.8		8.7	Long Term Debt	11.0	8.6	7.7	12.2	8.7
	.4	.8		.5	Deferred Taxes	1.1	.9	1.6	1.0	.5
	4.6	3.5		4.5	All Other Non-Current	4.0	3.1	1.5	5.3	4.5
	41.5	56.4		44.3	Net Worth	34.1	41.0	42.5	37.1	44.3
	100.0	100.0		100.0	Total Liabilities & Net Worth	100.0	100.0	100.0	100.0	100.0
					INCOME DATA					
	100.0	100.0		100.0	Contract Revenues	100.0	100.0	100.0	100.0	100.0
	22.9	18.4		22.0	Gross Profit	-53.6	24.8	19.8	22.6	22.0
	21.0	14.1		20.0	Operating Expenses	28.3	19.0	16.5	18.3	20.0
	1.9	4.2		2.0	Operating Profit	-81.8	5.7	3.3	4.2	2.0
	.4	-.5		.3	All Other Expenses (net)	-85.7	-.7	-1.0	.3	.3
	1.5	4.8		1.7	Profit Before Taxes	3.8	6.4	4.3	3.9	1.7
					RATIOS					
	2.2	4.5		2.6	Current	2.3	2.0	2.2	2.3	2.6
	1.6	2.1		1.6		1.4	1.5	1.7	1.7	1.6
	1.2	1.3		1.2		1.0	1.1	1.2	1.3	1.2
	(50) 10.2	6.9		(70) 8.7	Receivables/Payables	(63) 5.6	(65) 6.3	5.4	7.3	(70) 8.7
	3.9	2.8		3.9		2.6	2.4	2.5	3.8	3.9
	2.0	1.8		2.1		1.5	1.7	1.5	1.8	2.1
	49 · 7.4	37 · 9.9		46 · 7.9	Revenues/Receivables	42 · 8.7	39 · 9.5	40 · 9.0	46 · 7.9	46 · 7.9
	76 · 4.8	52 · 7.0		71 · 5.1		56 · 6.5	63 · 5.8	65 · 5.6	65 · 5.6	71 · 5.1
	88 · 4.1	67 · 5.5		88 · 4.2		79 · 4.6	81 · 4.5	85 · 4.3	87 · 4.2	88 · 4.2
	10 · 35.4	9 · 40.3		10 · 35.4	Cost of Revenues/Payables	11 · 32.4	12 · 30.6	13 · 27.1	11 · 33.5	10 · 35.4
	22 · 16.7	20 · 18.4		21 · 17.4		29 · 12.7	26 · 13.9	33 · 11.1	23 · 15.9	21 · 17.4
	36 · 10.0	31 · 11.8		36 · 10.2		52 · 7.0	56 · 6.5	44 · 8.4	36 · 10.1	36 · 10.2
	5.9	3.9		5.2	Revenues/Working Capital	7.2	7.0	6.3	5.9	5.2
	8.1	9.5		8.3		13.5	13.0	10.0	10.1	8.3
	28.0	17.4		27.0		-178.0	31.5	27.2	21.4	27.0
	(48) 6.9	(11) 208.7		(66) 8.0	EBIT/Interest	(57) 15.4	(63) 16.6	(51) 15.1	(57) 14.3	(66) 8.0
	2.3	10.1		3.1		4.4	4.9	5.6	3.8	3.1
	-1.7	3.2		-.3		1.8	2.6	2.7	1.8	-.3
	(12) 10.0			(19) 7.8	Net Profit + Depr., Dep., Amort./Cur. Mat. L /T/D	(18) 4.7	(21) 5.7	(16) 15.6	(17) 7.3	(19) 7.8
	3.3			3.4		3.2	3.2	3.3	3.1	3.4
	1.1			1.6		.8	1.9	2.1	1.4	1.6
	.2	.1		.2	Fixed/Worth	.2	.3	.2	.2	.2
	.5	.2		.5		.8	.6	.5	.6	.5
	1.3	.5		1.0		1.7	1.1	.8	1.0	1.0
	.8	.2		.6	Debt/Worth	.8	.8	.7	.7	.6
	1.3	1.1		1.3		2.3	1.5	1.4	1.2	1.3
	2.6	2.2		2.6		4.2	3.7	2.9	2.9	2.6
	(46) 26.4	38.1		(66) 27.3	% Profit Before Taxes/ Tangible Net Worth	(57) 55.2	(64) 55.1	(53) 43.0	(59) 32.0	(66) 27.3
	9.1	27.0		11.5		25.3	31.1	22.9	18.1	11.5
	-5.1	5.0		-2.9		6.3	15.3	4.4	4.8	-2.9
	10.4	26.9		11.5	% Profit Before Taxes/ Total Assets	21.6	21.5	18.1	15.1	11.5
	3.5	9.6		3.5		8.7	9.0	8.2	7.5	3.5
	-2.1	1.9		-1.9		1.2	5.2	2.1	2.1	-1.9
	(47) .5	(12) .2		(65) .5	% Depr., Dep., Amort./ Revenues	(57) .9	(59) .8	(50) .8	(60) .8	(65) .5
	1.2	1.2		1.2		1.9	1.6	1.6	1.8	1.2
	2.6	2.8		2.7		3.2	2.9	3.0	3.5	2.7
	(28) 1.7			(39) 2.5	% Officers', Directors', Owners' Comp/Revenues	(34) 1.8	(32) 1.9	(29) 1.9	(33) 2.8	(39) 2.5
	4.0			4.0		4.6	4.5	4.1	4.6	4.0
	7.0			7.2		8.2	7.9	7.4	7.7	7.2
1334M	207093M	264949M	590301M	1063677M	Contract Revenues ($)	613082M	842380M	612372M	618216M	1063677M
1347M	93613M	95619M	303725M	494304M	Total Assets ($)	321825M	389514M	273428M	267802M	494304M

M = $ thousand   MM = $ million
See Pages 11 through 18 for Explanation of Ratios and Data

Current Data Sorted By Revenue   **Comparative Historical Data**

Type of Statement										
			6		6	Unqualified	10	8	4	5	6
5	19	8		32		Reviewed	37	46	45	32	32
5	14			19		Compiled	16	13	19	9	19
3	13	2		18		Tax Returns	3	6	7	18	18
2	6	2		10		Other	19	19	15	12	10

21 (4/1-9/30/02)			64 (10/1/02-3/31/03)				4/1/98-3/31/99	4/1/99-3/31/00	4/1/00-3/31/01	4/1/01-3/31/02	4/1/02-3/31/03
0-1MM	1-10MM	10-50MM	50 & OVER	ALL			ALL	ALL	ALL	ALL	ALL
15	52	18		85		**NUMBER OF STATEMENTS**	85	92	90	76	85
%	%	%	%	%		**ASSETS**	%	%	%	%	%
24.9	11.0	15.4		14.4		Cash & Equivalents	15.3	13.4	14.7	14.1	14.4
23.0	41.0	38.9	D	37.4		A/R - Progress Billings	39.1	41.6	39.1	38.9	37.4
.0	1.7	3.1	A	1.7		A/R - Current Retention	6.3	5.4	4.5	2.7	1.7
3.7	3.4	3.0	T	3.4		Inventory	2.0	3.4	1.8	3.3	3.4
.2	2.4	4.3	A	2.4		Cost & Est. Earnings In Excess of Billings	4.3	3.3	2.7	2.2	2.4
3.0	6.5	12.2	N	7.1		All Other Current	3.8	3.1	4.6	5.8	7.1
54.8	66.0	76.8	O	66.3		Total Current	70.9	70.2	67.4	67.0	66.3
32.6	26.1	15.0	T	24.9		Fixed Assets (net)	23.2	22.6	25.2	25.4	24.9
.1	.5	.7		.5		Joint Ventures & Investments	.8	2.3	2.2	.8	.5
3.0	1.0	.0	A	1.2		Intangibles (net)	.7	1.1	1.2	.9	1.2
9.5	6.4	7.4	V	7.2		All Other Non-Current	4.5	3.9	4.0	5.9	7.2
100.0	100.0	100.0	A	100.0		Total	100.0	100.0	100.0	100.0	100.0
			I			**LIABILITIES**					
7.2	11.5	5.5	L	9.5		Notes Payable - Short Term	9.6	7.7	10.4	9.1	9.5
10.6	14.9	17.5	A	14.7		A/P - Trade	12.9	13.7	15.3	14.9	14.7
.0	.0	.0	B	.0		A/P - Retention	.0	.2	.1	.3	.0
3.8	4.4	8.3	L	5.1		Billings in Excess of Costs & Est. Earnings	6.0	6.0	4.7	3.5	5.1
.4	.7	.5	E	.6		Income Taxes Payable	.3	.9	.2	.4	.6
2.6	3.3	3.1		3.1		Cur. Mat.-L/T/D	2.3	3.6	3.9	4.3	3.1
8.5	10.6	11.3		10.4		All Other Current	10.4	9.2	8.1	10.3	10.4
33.2	45.4	46.2		43.4		Total Current	41.5	41.2	42.8	43.0	43.4
10.3	15.7	7.5		13.0		Long Term Debt	8.3	9.9	10.8	12.1	13.0
.1	.9	2.1		1.0		Deferred Taxes	1.5	1.1	1.1	.6	1.0
13.2	4.4	2.2		5.5		All Other Non-Current	2.3	2.9	2.9	9.0	5.5
43.2	33.7	42.0		37.1		Net Worth	46.4	44.9	42.4	35.4	37.1
100.0	100.0	100.0		100.0		Total Liabilities & Net Worth	100.0	100.0	100.0	100.0	100.0
						INCOME DATA					
100.0	100.0	100.0		100.0		Contract Revenues	100.0	100.0	100.0	100.0	100.0
37.4	24.8	20.5		26.1		Gross Profit	25.2	22.1	23.7	27.4	26.1
32.2	22.2	16.9		22.9		Operating Expenses	19.8	18.5	20.5	23.9	22.9
5.1	2.6	3.6		3.3		Operating Profit	5.3	3.7	3.2	3.6	3.3
.3	.2	.1		.2		All Other Expenses (net)	.7	.4	.4	.6	.2
4.9	2.3	3.5		3.0		Profit Before Taxes	4.6	3.2	2.8	3.0	3.0
						RATIOS					
5.4	2.9	2.0		2.9			2.7	3.1	2.8	2.8	2.9
1.8	1.7	1.7		1.7		Current	1.9	1.9	1.7	1.7	1.7
.6	.9	1.4		1.1			1.3	1.2	1.1	1.1	1.1

	0-1MM		1-10MM		10-50MM		50 & OVER	ALL			4/1/98-3/31/99		4/1/99-3/31/00		4/1/00-3/31/01		4/1/01-3/31/02		4/1/02-3/31/03
	11.9		6.4		4.1			6.1			7.1		6.6		7.3		6.6		6.1
(13)	4.2	(49)	3.4		2.4	(80)		3.1	Receivables/Payables	(80)	3.7	(88)	3.9	(86)	3.9	(72)	3.5	(80)	3.1
	.8		1.7		1.2			1.6			2.3		2.4		1.8		1.8		1.6
8	45.3	30	12.3	40	9.2	26		14.1		42	8.7	45	8.0	38	9.6	31	11.9	26	14.1
40	9.0	51	7.1	55	6.6	51		7.1	Revenues/Receivables	61	5.9	58	6.3	59	6.2	50	7.3	51	7.1
75	4.8	73	5.0	77	4.7	73		5.0		82	4.4	84	4.3	73	5.0	70	5.2	73	5.0
3	126.0	7	52.4	20	17.9	8		45.7		11	32.1	11	33.4	10	37.4	10	36.3	8	45.7
15	24.8	18	20.4	28	13.2	20		18.1	Cost of Revenues/Payables	22	16.2	18	20.7	19	19.7	19	19.6	20	18.1
38	9.7	32	11.4	32	11.2	32		11.3		33	11.2	34	10.8	32	11.3	35	10.6	32	11.3
	3.4		6.4		6.6			5.8			5.0		5.3		6.0		6.3		5.8
	11.5		12.0		9.3			11.4	Revenues/Working Capital		8.6		8.7		11.0		13.5		11.4
	-246.0		NM		16.3			81.5			22.6		29.4		54.6		34.3		81.5
	14.3		16.7		33.8			17.2			21.3		19.0		18.3		14.8		17.2
(11)	11.0	(47)	4.5	(15)	10.9	(73)		6.0	EBIT/Interest	(74)	7.2	(81)	7.6	(83)	5.3	(70)	4.6	(73)	6.0
	4.7		1.2		2.0			2.1			2.8		2.8		1.8		1.9		2.1
								16.8			10.5		6.2		9.4		19.1		16.8
						(18)		5.7	Net Profit + Depr., Dep., Amort./Cur. Mat. L /T/D	(23)	3.9	(29)	3.6	(23)	3.7	(13)	4.6	(18)	5.7
								1.3			1.2		1.9		2.1		1.8		1.3
	.1		.2		.1			.2			.2		.2		.2		.2		.2
	.8		.7		.3			.6	Fixed/Worth		.4		.4		.5		.6		.6
	5.0		2.2		.7			1.6			.8		.9		1.2		1.6		1.6
	.3		.7		.8			.6			.5		.5		.6		.6		.6
	.6		1.3		1.3			1.2	Debt/Worth		1.1		1.1		1.3		1.5		1.2
	4.5		6.3		2.8			4.6			2.1		3.2		4.3		5.5		4.6
	76.8		40.1		36.9			42.5			44.8		54.5		45.6		54.0		42.5
(12)	30.0	(42)	15.5		15.4	(72)		16.9	% Profit Before Taxes/ Tangible Net Worth	(79)	19.0	(87)	28.6	(83)	23.6	(69)	24.2	(72)	16.9
	10.8		2.1		4.9			5.2			3.2		11.3		4.8		9.2		5.2
	34.8		17.6		16.6			18.3			21.0		21.0		20.1		18.2		18.3
	16.1		8.5		6.5			8.5	% Profit Before Taxes/ Total Assets		8.1		13.1		8.2		7.0		8.5
	6.6		.5		1.5			.9			1.8		3.8		1.4		2.4		.9
	.9		1.1		1.0			1.0			.9		1.3		1.1		1.1		1.0
.(11)	3.7	(44)	2.2	(15)	1.6	(70)		2.1	% Depr., Dep., Amort./ Revenues	(73)	1.7	(83)	2.1	(87)	2.3	(68)	2.1	(70)	2.1
	7.2		4.0		2.4			3.7			2.7		3.0		3.0		3.1		3.7
	5.2		2.9		1.4			3.0			2.3		2.4		2.3		2.7		3.0
(10)	8.7	(36)	3.7	(10)	4.2	(56)		4.3	% Officers', Directors', Owners' Comp/Revenues	(44)	4.0	(58)	4.8	(61)	4.3	(44)	3.8	(56)	4.3
	13.8		8.1		6.9			8.3			7.1		8.5		8.4		6.7		8.3

7611M	190472M	299082M		497165M		Contract Revenues ($)	412054M	467382M	467651M	394426M	497165M
4222M	65036M	118268M		187526M		Total Assets ($)	156325M	173078M	168993M	151720M	187526M

M = $ thousand   MM = $ million
See Pages 11 through 18 for Explanation of Ratios and Data

Current Data Sorted By Revenue — **Comparative Historical Data**

0-1MM	1-10MM	10-50MM	50 & OVER	ALL	Type of Statement	4/1/98-3/31/99 ALL	4/1/99-3/31/00 ALL	4/1/00-3/31/01 ALL	4/1/01-3/31/02 ALL	4/1/02-3/31/03 ALL
	1	3	1	5	Unqualified	3	4	3	4	5
	12	6		18	Reviewed	21	15	16	19	18
2	5	2		9	Compiled	15	14	8	8	9
4	6		2	12	Tax Returns	9	7	11	9	12
	5	1	1	7	Other	3	6	6	8	7
14 (4/1-9/30/02)			37 (10/1/02-3/31/03)							
6	29	12	4	51	**NUMBER OF STATEMENTS**	51	46	44	48	51
%	%	%	%	%	**ASSETS**	%	%	%	%	%
	11.0	8.3		12.1	Cash & Equivalents	9.2	10.8	9.6	10.8	12.1
	52.2	48.3		45.8	A/R - Progress Billings	47.0	46.7	50.7	47.8	45.8
	.6	6.6		1.9	A/R - Current Retention	3.9	4.1	3.9	1.9	1.9
	7.5	2.1		7.0	Inventory	7.6	8.2	8.6	6.5	7.0
	4.9	5.3		4.1	Cost & Est. Earnings In Excess of Billings	2.7	3.0	2.3	2.6	4.1
	1.9	11.4		3.8	All Other Current	3.0	1.9	2.5	4.3	3.8
	78.2	82.0		74.7	Total Current	73.3	74.7	77.7	73.8	74.7
	15.8	14.1		18.9	Fixed Assets (net)	21.0	18.1	13.6	17.4	18.9
	.2	1.3		.7	Joint Ventures & Investments	.1	.4	1.2	.7	.7
	1.9	.0		1.9	Intangibles (net)	1.3	2.8	1.8	1.5	1.9
	3.9	2.7		3.8	All Other Non-Current	4.2	3.9	5.7	6.7	3.8
	100.0	100.0		100.0	Total	100.0	100.0	100.0	100.0	100.0
					LIABILITIES					
	12.7	5.1		9.0	Notes Payable - Short Term	8.6	8.0	7.5	10.9	9.0
	22.1	18.6		20.0	A/P - Trade	25.5	25.1	25.8	22.0	20.0
	.4	.2		.2	A/P - Retention	.0	.0	.1	.5	.2
	1.4	9.4		3.3	Billings in Excess of Costs & Est. Earnings	2.7	5.3	4.7	5.5	3.3
	.1	.0		.1	Income Taxes Payable	.2	.3	.3	.3	.1
	4.9	1.0		3.3	Cur. Mat.-L/T/D	4.1	3.1	3.2	3.2	3.3
	8.1	14.5		9.4	All Other Current	7.1	6.4	7.1	9.3	9.4
	49.6	48.8		45.3	Total Current	48.3	48.3	48.7	51.7	45.3
	12.3	3.6		17.8	Long Term Debt	11.8	9.0	10.2	11.4	17.8
	.7	1.5		.7	Deferred Taxes	1.4	1.5	1.3	.5	.7
	4.9	1.9		8.5	All Other Non-Current	5.3	4.8	5.9	6.6	8.5
	32.4	44.2		27.7	Net Worth	33.2	36.5	33.8	29.8	27.7
	100.0	100.0		100.0	Total Liabilities & Net Worth	100.0	100.0	100.0	100.0	100.0
					INCOME DATA					
	100.0	100.0		100.0	Contract Revenues	100.0	100.0	100.0	100.0	100.0
	32.6	28.6		35.3	Gross Profit	30.0	30.7	30.5	33.2	35.3
	28.9	21.3		29.4	Operating Expenses	25.9	25.6	25.1	29.4	29.4
	3.7	7.3		5.9	Operating Profit	4.1	5.2	5.5	3.8	5.9
	.7	.2		.7	All Other Expenses (net)	.3	1.0	.2	.3	.7
	3.0	7.1		5.2	Profit Before Taxes	3.8	4.2	5.3	3.5	5.2
					RATIOS					
	2.4	2.7		2.5	Current	2.2	2.5	2.5	2.1	2.5
	1.7	1.7		1.8		1.6	1.5	1.5	1.5	1.8
	1.3	1.3		1.3		1.2	1.1	1.2	1.1	1.3
	3.7	8.3		4.0	Receivables/Payables	(49) 2.7	(45) 4.2	4.2	(46) 5.0	(50) 4.0
	2.7	3.7	(50)	2.8		2.1	2.1	2.4	2.5	2.8
	1.7	1.3		1.5		1.6	1.5	1.6	1.7	1.5
39 9.3	72 5.0			31 11.6	Revenues/Receivables	27 13.5	46 7.9	41 8.9	38 9.5	31 11.6
65 5.7	86 4.2			66 5.5		63 5.8	64 5.7	65 5.6	63 5.8	66 5.5
78 4.7	99 3.7			87 4.2		80 4.6	84 4.4	89 4.1	86 4.2	87 4.2
20 18.0	14 26.8			20 18.0	Cost of Revenues/Payables	24 15.3	19 18.9	18 19.8	13 28.9	20 18.0
28 12.9	27 13.4			30 12.3		36 10.0	43 8.5	44 8.2	31 11.7	30 12.3
52 7.0	42 8.6			49 7.4		50 7.3	65 5.6	64 5.7	57 6.4	49 7.4
	5.9	5.1		6.2	Revenues/Working Capital	7.3	6.8	6.7	8.5	6.2
	8.7	8.3		8.7		12.6	12.3	11.2	12.2	8.7
	21.8	11.7		14.9		36.3	81.4	21.5	80.5	14.9
	10.4	163.6		27.8	EBIT/Interest	(46) 30.2	11.7	18.5	16.7	27.8
	(26) 5.5	(11) 28.5	(45)	6.9		5.5	(40) 5.0	(41) 6.8	(42) 5.1	(45) 6.9
	2.6	12.4		3.0		2.3	1.5	2.7	-.7	3.0
			(12)	12.8	Net Profit + Depr., Dep., Amort./Cur. Mat. L /T/D	(23) 9.6	10.3	15.7	24.6	12.8
				3.1		3.0	(11) 6.0	(12) 3.7	(11) 4.2	(12) 3.1
				1.0		1.5	1.9	1.3	.6	1.0
	.2	.2		.2	Fixed/Worth	.2	.2	.2	.2	.2
	.3	.3		.4		.5	.5	.4	.4	.4
	1.9	.6		1.2		1.4	1.4	.7	2.3	1.2
	.7	.6		.7	Debt/Worth	.9	.9	1.0	1.2	.7
	1.5	1.2		1.3		1.9	2.3	2.0	2.3	1.3
	6.1	3.5		4.2		4.0	5.5	5.1	6.4	4.2
	44.8	61.3		51.6	% Profit Before Taxes/Tangible Net Worth	(47) 39.6	(42) 56.1	(39) 72.9	(38) 62.1	(44) 51.6
	(25) 16.6	42.2	(44)	30.7		22.9	24.0	34.4	17.0	30.7
	6.6	30.0		10.3		8.6	4.1	21.1	-5.4	10.3
	11.8	29.7		22.1	% Profit Before Taxes/Total Assets	20.6	16.7	21.5	17.8	22.1
	5.9	20.6		8.8		6.9	7.4	11.4	4.5	8.8
	3.2	12.9		4.6		2.4	1.1	6.5	-6.1	4.6
	.8	.4		.7	% Depr., Dep., Amort./Revenues	(47) .7	(39) .6	(42) .5	(38) .7	(44) .7
	(27) 1.1	(11) .8	(44)	1.1		1.0	1.1	.9	1.2	1.1
	1.9	1.2		1.9		1.6	1.8	1.4	1.7	1.9
	2.5			2.7	% Officers', Directors', Owners' Comp/Revenues	(34) 2.7	(27) 3.1	(37) 1.4	(31) 3.5	(30) 2.7
	(15) 5.6		(30)	5.7		4.4	6.5	6.1	6.0	5.7
	10.8			12.4		7.6	9.6	9.9	8.5	12.4
3063M	116184M	205339M	4599405M	4923991M	Contract Revenues ($)	2219883M	212423M	382300M	632271M	4923991M
1382M	39088M	81390M	871110M	992970M	Total Assets ($)	945845M	77562M	159371M	261414M	992970M

M = $ thousand   MM = $ million
See Pages 11 through 18 for Explanation of Ratios and Data

Current Data Sorted By Revenue					Type of Statement	Comparative Historical Data				
	2	6	1	9	Unqualified	22	25	27	15	9
4	44	12	1	61	Reviewed	103	106	98	73	61
4	22	1		27	Compiled	31	32	32	34	27
8	12	1	1	21	Tax Returns	14	17	16	17	21
2	27	3	1	33	Other	36	32	34	31	33
31 (4/1-9/30/02)			120 (10/1/02-3/31/03)			4/1/98-3/31/99	4/1/99-3/31/00	4/1/00-3/31/01	4/1/01-3/31/02	4/1/02-3/31/03
0-1MM	1-10MM	10-50MM	50 & OVER	ALL		ALL	ALL	ALL	ALL	ALL
18	107	22	4	151	NUMBER OF STATEMENTS	206	212	207	170	151
%	%	%	%	%	ASSETS	%	%	%	%	%
18.4	15.3	6.5		14.1	Cash & Equivalents	12.7	11.0	12.2	12.0	14.1
28.8	36.4	43.8		37.2	A/R - Progress Billings	43.2	41.9	39.9	39.8	37.2
.0	1.0	2.5		1.1	A/R - Current Retention	3.0	2.2	2.3	.9	1.1
4.9	6.3	4.9		5.9	Inventory	6.5	7.5	6.2	7.4	5.9
2.2	3.8	6.2		3.9	Cost & Est. Earnings In Excess of Billings	5.0	5.7	5.7	3.4	3.9
3.2	5.7	12.8		6.5	All Other Current	2.5	3.5	2.7	4.6	6.5
57.5	68.6	76.7		68.7	Total Current	73.0	71.8	69.0	68.1	68.7
30.7	23.6	13.6		22.7	Fixed Assets (net)	20.4	20.1	21.9	22.7	22.7
.0	.6	.1		.5	Joint Ventures & Investments	.7	.4	.7	.3	.5
5.1	1.2	2.4		1.8	Intangibles (net)	1.5	2.0	2.1	3.1	1.8
6.7	6.0	7.3		6.3	All Other Non-Current	4.4	5.7	6.2	5.9	6.3
100.0	100.0	100.0		100.0	Total	100.0	100.0	100.0	100.0	100.0
					LIABILITIES					
18.9	11.2	12.8		12.4	Notes Payable - Short Term	9.1	11.3	13.1	11.1	12.4
16.2	18.2	19.8		18.6	A/P - Trade	20.5	21.5	19.5	20.0	18.6
.0	.2	.6		.2	A/P - Retention	.1	.1	.1	.1	.2
.0	2.7	8.4		3.4	Billings in Excess of Costs & Est. Earnings	4.1	3.5	4.2	3.4	3.4
4.9	.3	.2		.8	Income Taxes Payable	.8	.4	.4	.7	.8
9.7	3.9	2.0		4.4	Cur. Mat.-L/T/D	3.5	3.5	2.8	5.5	4.4
20.6	9.4	11.9		11.2	All Other Current	10.0	9.9	8.0	8.6	11.2
70.2	46.0	55.8		51.1	Total Current	48.0	50.2	48.1	49.0	51.1
22.4	10.7	4.6		11.1	Long Term Debt	11.6	10.2	10.7	13.2	11.1
.0	.8	.2		.6	Deferred Taxes	1.4	1.3	1.5	.6	.6
4.9	3.0	4.2		3.4	All Other Non-Current	2.2	1.9	2.4	3.1	3.4
2.4	39.5	35.1		33.9	Net Worth	36.8	36.5	37.3	34.1	33.9
100.0	100.0	100.0		100.0	Total Liabilities & Net Worth	100.0	100.0	100.0	100.0	100.0
					INCOME DATA					
100.0	100.0	100.0		100.0	Contract Revenues	100.0	100.0	100.0	100.0	100.0
46.0	30.3	19.3		30.3	Gross Profit	25.9	27.1	26.2	30.5	30.3
44.2	27.5	17.2		27.7	Operating Expenses	22.6	23.4	23.1	26.6	27.7
1.8	2.9	2.2		2.6	Operating Profit	3.3	3.7	3.1	3.9	2.6
1.4	.6	.4		.7	All Other Expenses (net)	.2	.3	.2	.7	.7
.4	2.2	1.7		1.9	Profit Before Taxes	3.2	3.3	2.9	3.2	1.9
					RATIOS					
2.2	2.3	1.6		2.1		2.4	2.3	2.2	2.1	2.1
1.1	1.4	1.4		1.4	Current	1.6	1.6	1.5	1.5	1.4
.4	1.1	1.1		1.1		1.1	1.2	1.2	1.1	1.1
10.1	5.0	4.6		4.6		3.9	4.2	4.2	4.1	4.6
(14) 2.5	(100) 2.2	(21) 2.8	(139)	2.2	Receivables/Payables	(202) 2.6	(205) 2.3	(202) 2.4	(168) 2.2	(139) 2.2
1.0	1.1	1.5		1.2		1.6	1.5	1.5	1.4	1.2
0 UND	19 19.4	46 7.9	19	19.4		34 10.6	35 10.4	31 11.9	27 13.4	19 19.4
23 15.7	46 8.0	67 5.4	46	7.9	Revenues/Receivables	56 6.5	57 6.4	50 7.3	47 7.8	46 7.9
76 4.8	66 5.6	88 4.2	73	5.0		74 4.9	74 4.9	74 4.9	68 5.3	73 5.0
0 UND	12 30.5	21 17.7	12	29.5		16 22.7	16 22.9	16 22.7	17 21.8	12 29.5
22 16.7	26 14.0	29 12.5	27	13.6	Cost of Revenues/Payables	29 12.7	30 12.3	27 13.6	29 12.4	27 13.6
47 7.8	48 7.6	52 7.1	48	7.5		44 8.2	47 7.7	43 8.5	51 7.2	48 7.5
5.0	7.8	8.3		8.2		7.4	6.7	7.0	7.7	8.2
229.6	17.2	12.8		17.2	Revenues/Working Capital	12.7	13.2	14.3	14.3	17.2
-13.1	67.4	48.3		76.9		39.8	34.7	41.1	53.9	76.9
11.6	17.7	9.7		14.9		12.4	11.9	11.3	14.4	14.9
(14) 2.7	(95) 3.9	(20) 4.6	(133)	4.1	EBIT/Interest	(181) 4.8	(197) 4.5	(189) 4.4	(150) 4.6	(133) 4.1
-.9	.2	1.6		.4		1.7	1.9	1.5	1.4	.4
	3.8	10.1		5.3		7.2	6.5	7.7	6.9	5.3
(30) 1.6	(10) 3.5	(42)	2.2	Net Profit + Depr., Dep., Amort./Cur. Mat. L /T/D	(66) 3.5	(74) 2.6	(64) 3.9	(43) 2.9	(42) 2.2
	-.6	1.7		.1		1.9	1.2	1.4	1.5	.1
.2	.3	.2		.3		.2	.3	.3	.2	.3
1.5	.5	.4		.5	Fixed/Worth	.5	.5	.5	.5	.5
-1.6	1.1	.9		1.2		1.0	1.2	1.1	1.3	1.2
1.1	.7	1.0		.8		.8	.7	.8	.9	.8
3.4	1.5	2.6		1.8	Debt/Worth	1.6	1.6	1.5	1.5	1.8
-7.1	3.5	3.7		4.1		4.1	4.5	3.4	4.2	4.1
88.7	40.9	23.4		38.2		55.5	45.4	48.5	48.1	38.2
(12) 9.2	(97) 13.1	(21) 20.1	(134)	14.0	% Profit Before Taxes/ Tangible Net Worth	(191) 28.5	(195) 21.2	(192) 21.7	(152) 19.3	(134) 14.0
-2.1	-1.1	6.9		-.1		8.9	7.7	4.4	4.9	-.1
24.5	17.2	8.4		14.6		20.3	17.4	16.4	16.2	14.6
1.4	5.8	4.8		5.0	% Profit Before Taxes/ Total Assets	9.0	6.6	6.6	6.9	5.0
-10.9	-2.3	1.7		-1.7		2.5	2.3	1.5	.8	-1.7
.8	1.0	1.0		.9		.9	.9	.9	.9	.9
(15) 1.9	(95) 1.9	(21) 1.3	(133)	1.7	% Depr., Dep., Amort./ Revenues	(185) 1.4	(197) 1.4	(185) 1.6	(150) 1.6	(133) 1.7
4.0	2.9	1.8		2.8		2.1	2.2	2.5	2.5	2.8
7.9	2.2	1.6		2.2		2.4	2.6	2.4	2.6	2.2
(11) 10.9	(69) 3.6	(12) 2.9	(95)	4.4	% Officers', Directors', Owners' Comp/Revenues	(115) 3.9	(120) 4.2	(114) 4.3	(97) 4.3	(95) 4.4
14.4	7.0	7.0		7.9		7.7	7.4	7.4	7.8	7.9
10130M	404646M	339252M	9984426M	10738454M	Contract Revenues ($)	9545497M	6509105M	30584784M	8295579M	10738454M
4584M	143805M	133327M	3251267M	3532983M	Total Assets ($)	4353304M	1694007M	14366245M	3126227M	3532983M

© RMA 2003

M = $ thousand   MM = $ million
See Pages 11 through 18 for Explanation of Ratios and Data

Current Data Sorted By Revenue | Comparative Historical Data

Type of Statement

	0-1MM	1-10MM	10-50MM	50 & OVER	ALL	Type of Statement	4/1/98-3/31/99	4/1/99-3/31/00	4/1/00-3/31/01	4/1/01-3/31/02	4/1/02-3/31/03
		20	16	6	42	Unqualified	76	78	61	47	42
	5	103	45	1	154	Reviewed	203	226	198	168	154
	17	41	1		59	Compiled	87	81	88	76	59
	14	31		1	46	Tax Returns	29	31	31	34	46
	7	45	8	4	64	Other	75	70	63	66	64

88 (4/1-9/30/02) 277 (10/1/02-3/31/03)

	0-1MM	1-10MM	10-50MM	50 & OVER	ALL		ALL	ALL	ALL	ALL	ALL
NUMBER OF STATEMENTS	43	240	70	12	365		470	486	441	391	365
	%	%	%	%	%	**ASSETS**	%	%	%	%	%
	11.8	13.4	13.5	16.3	13.3	Cash & Equivalents	11.2	12.1	11.8	13.4	13.3
	33.0	44.2	50.7	45.8	44.2	A/R - Progress Billings	46.1	46.7	46.0	42.7	44.2
	.0	1.6	2.3	3.0	1.6	A/R - Current Retention	3.4	3.3	2.5	1.9	1.6
	9.9	5.8	2.3	2.7	5.5	Inventory	6.3	5.6	5.5	5.6	5.5
	2.5	4.2	7.4	4.5	4.6	Cost & Est. Earnings In Excess of Billings	5.1	5.2	5.2	4.6	4.6
	.9	4.4	8.7	6.6	4.9	All Other Current	3.1	4.6	3.9	5.3	4.9
	58.1	73.5	84.9	78.9	74.1	Total Current	75.2	77.6	75.0	73.5	74.1
	31.4	18.6	9.2	6.7	17.9	Fixed Assets (net)	17.9	15.6	17.4	18.2	17.9
	.1	.7	.3	.8	.5	Joint Ventures & Investments	.9	.8	1.1	.6	.5
	.9	1.0	1.4	3.9	1.2	Intangibles (net)	1.5	1.9	1.6	2.4	1.2
	9.5	6.2	4.0	9.8	6.3	All Other Non-Current	4.5	4.1	4.9	5.3	6.3
	100.0	100.0	100.0	100.0	100.0	Total	100.0	100.0	100.0	100.0	100.0
						LIABILITIES					
	33.2	12.5	8.3	5.7	13.9	Notes Payable - Short Term	10.8	11.1	10.7	9.9	13.9
	20.3	18.2	20.5	15.5	18.8	A/P - Trade	19.6	18.9	19.3	18.5	18.8
	.0	.1	.1	.0	.1	A/P - Retention	.3	.1	.3	.2	.1
	.5	3.8	11.5	10.8	5.1	Billings in Excess of Costs & Est. Earnings	5.1	6.2	6.0	5.5	5.1
	.1	.3	.4	.3	.3	Income Taxes Payable	.7	.5	.6	.5	.3
	6.8	4.5	3.0	1.6	4.4	Cur. Mat.-L/T/D	3.2	2.8	3.5	3.5	4.4
	7.9	7.9	10.2	10.7	8.4	All Other Current	8.6	9.8	8.9	10.2	8.4
	68.8	47.4	54.0	44.7	51.1	Total Current	48.4	49.4	49.3	48.4	51.1
	20.2	8.8	3.8	4.9	9.0	Long Term Debt	8.9	8.2	9.3	10.3	9.0
	.0	.8	.8	.9	.7	Deferred Taxes	1.0	.8	1.1	.6	.7
	21.9	3.2	2.1	1.0	5.1	All Other Non-Current	2.7	1.8	2.3	2.4	5.1
	-10.8	39.8	39.2	48.5	34.0	Net Worth	39.0	39.8	38.1	38.3	34.0
	100.0	100.0	100.0	100.0	100.0	Total Liabilities & Net Worth	100.0	100.0	100.0	100.0	100.0
						INCOME DATA					
	100.0	100.0	100.0	100.0	100.0	Contract Revenues	100.0	100.0	100.0	100.0	100.0
	44.7	28.1	17.9	21.5	27.9	Gross Profit	25.6	25.5	27.1	28.6	27.9
	44.6	26.5	15.2	17.9	26.2	Operating Expenses	22.4	21.3	23.5	24.8	26.2
	.1	1.6	2.7	3.5	1.7	Operating Profit	3.2	4.2	3.6	3.7	1.7
	.8	.4	.1	1.6	.5	All Other Expenses (net)	.4	.3	.5	.6	.5
	-.6	1.2	2.6	1.9	1.2	Profit Before Taxes	2.8	3.9	3.1	3.1	1.2
						RATIOS					
	2.6	2.3	2.0	2.2	2.3	Current	2.1	2.2	2.2	2.3	2.3
	1.2	1.6	1.6	1.6	1.5		1.6	1.6	1.6	1.6	1.5
	.7	1.2	1.3	1.4	1.2		1.2	1.2	1.2	1.2	1.2
	4.6	4.8	3.8	6.5	4.6	Receivables/Payables	4.4	4.8	4.5	4.9	4.6
	(37) 2.8	(233) 2.9	2.7	3.3	(352) 2.8		(454) 2.8	(473) 3.0	(425) 2.7	(371) 2.8	(352) 2.8
	1.3	1.9	1.9	2.1	1.9		1.7	1.9	1.8	1.9	1.9
	11 33.7	38 9.6	47 7.7	50 7.2	40 9.2	Revenues/Receivables	44 8.2	44 8.3	42 8.7	33 11.1	40 9.2
	44 8.2	55 6.7	64 5.7	81 4.5	56 6.5		61 6.0	61 6.0	60 6.1	56 6.6	56 6.5
	69 5.3	76 4.8	82 4.5	89 4.1	78 4.7		79 4.6	81 4.5	79 4.6	76 4.8	78 4.7
	0 UND	16 23.3	20 18.2	18 20.4	16 23.0	Cost of Revenues/Payables	17 21.9	17 22.0	16 22.5	14 25.6	16 23.0
	27 13.5	25 14.5	29 12.4	27 13.3	25 14.3		27 13.4	26 13.8	29 12.7	25 14.5	25 14.3
	53 6.9	43 8.4	41 8.8	42 8.8	44 8.3		44 8.3	42 8.7	44 8.3	42 8.7	44 8.3
	7.3	6.3	6.9	6.5	6.5	Revenues/Working Capital	7.3	6.7	6.9	6.6	6.5
	20.3	12.0	10.0	8.2	11.6		11.8	10.6	10.9	10.9	11.6
	-25.4	30.5	15.8	12.1	29.4		26.8	22.2	25.9	27.2	29.4
	6.0	16.5	13.3		13.5	EBIT/Interest	14.7	14.5	14.5	16.6	13.5
	(34) 1.7	(212) 2.7	(60) 5.3		(315) 3.2		(413) 5.1	(419) 5.6	(391) 4.3	(348) 5.4	(315) 3.2
	-1.9	-1.3	2.6		-.5		1.7	1.8	1.4	2.1	-.5
		8.9	12.7		9.0	Net Profit + Depr., Dep., Amort./Cur. Mat. L /T/D	7.8	10.0	5.6	7.9	9.0
	(68) 3.0	(29) 3.2		(102) 3.0			(173) 3.7	(141) 3.8	(140) 2.7	(104) 3.1	(102) 3.0
	.7	.9		.7			1.5	1.8	1.3	1.4	.7
	.3	.2	.1	.0	.2	Fixed/Worth	.2	.2	.2	.2	.2
	1.4	.4	.2	.2	.4		.4	.3	.4	.4	.4
	-4.3	.9	.4	.3	.9		.8	.7	.8	.8	.9
	.8	.7	1.1	.7	.8	Debt/Worth	.8	.8	.8	.7	.8
	2.3	1.4	1.7	1.5	1.5		1.7	1.6	1.7	1.5	1.5
	-7.7	3.5	3.1	2.5	3.7		3.2	3.5	3.6	3.2	3.7
	65.8	33.1	28.4	30.0	33.1	% Profit Before Taxes/ Tangible Net Worth	43.7	49.7	52.4	51.7	33.1
	(31) 10.0	(214) 11.9	(69) 14.1	5.8	(326) 11.9		(443) 21.5	(458) 23.5	(412) 22.0	(352) 23.0	(326) 11.9
	-16.0	-2.7	4.5	-3.8	.3		7.4	8.2	5.4	7.8	.3
	14.5	13.3	11.5	7.4	12.6	% Profit Before Taxes/ Total Assets	16.1	18.5	18.1	18.4	12.6
	1.7	3.5	4.0	2.6	3.4		7.1	8.0	7.1	8.7	3.4
	-12.1	-4.5	2.2	-1.1	-2.6		2.1	2.2	1.0	2.3	-2.6
	1.6	.8	.4		.6	% Depr., Dep., Amort./ Revenues	.7	.7	.7	.7	.6
	(37) 2.6	(223) 1.4	(66) .8		(334) 1.3		(424) 1.2	(433) 1.2	(390) 1.3	(345) 1.2	(334) 1.3
	4.2	2.2	1.2		2.3		1.9	1.9	2.1	2.3	2.3
	4.6	3.0	1.3		2.8	% Officers', Directors', Owners' Comp/Revenues	2.7	2.7	2.7	2.7	2.8
	(31) 9.3	(167) 5.3	(35) 1.9		(238) 5.3		(260) 4.7	(274) 4.4	(246) 4.7	(230) 4.5	(238) 5.3
	16.7	8.4	5.4		8.5		7.7	7.5	8.3	8.3	8.5
	24340M	955570M	1404805M	28646510M	31031225M	Contract Revenues ($)	93911575M	40078203M	55857686M	17843272M	31031225M
	9969M	347731M	499417M	11015740M	11872857M	Total Assets ($)	32048397M	14472541M	21567310M	8818003M	11872857M

M = $ thousand MM = $ million
See Pages 11 through 18 for Explanation of Ratios and Data

Current Data Sorted By Revenue | **Comparative Historical Data**

0-1MM	1-10MM	10-50MM	50 & OVER	ALL	Type of Statement	4/1/98-3/31/99 ALL	4/1/99-3/31/00 ALL	4/1/00-3/31/01 ALL	4/1/01-3/31/02 ALL	4/1/02-3/31/03 ALL
	7	29	7	43	Unqualified	94	69	58	46	43
7	107	46	2	162	Reviewed	228	222	210	189	162
20	76	5		101	Compiled	125	114	83	79	101
27	46		2	75	Tax Returns	42	46	65	60	75
13	47	18	4	82	Other	73	74	70	72	82

149 (4/1-9/30/02)   314 (10/1/02-3/31/03)

0-1MM	1-10MM	10-50MM	50 & OVER	ALL	NUMBER OF STATEMENTS	562	525	486	446	463
67	283	98	15	463						
%	%	%	%	%	**ASSETS**	%	%	%	%	%
13.7	11.7	11.8	11.4	12.0	Cash & Equivalents	12.1	12.2	11.5	11.4	12.0
27.5	40.0	48.0	41.0	39.9	A/R - Progress Billings	43.9	44.2	43.9	41.4	39.9
.8	2.0	3.8	2.7	2.2	A/R - Current Retention	4.1	3.2	2.9	3.0	2.2
12.8	10.4	5.1	3.2	9.4	Inventory	7.3	7.5	7.8	8.9	9.4
.4	3.3	5.7	6.0	3.5	Cost & Est. Earnings In Excess of Billings	4.0	4.1	3.7	3.4	3.5
4.4	4.1	6.4	7.8	4.8	All Other Current	3.6	3.9	4.0	4.5	4.8
59.5	71.4	80.9	72.0	71.7	Total Current	75.1	75.1	73.8	72.6	71.7
29.8	20.3	12.4	21.2	20.0	Fixed Assets (net)	17.7	18.4	19.1	19.6	20.0
.7	1.0	.5	1.0	.8	Joint Ventures & Investments	.5	.9	.7	.6	.8
1.9	.9	1.0	3.0	1.1	Intangibles (net)	2.0	1.5	1.8	1.8	1.1
8.1	6.4	5.1	2.8	6.3	All Other Non-Current	4.7	4.0	4.6	5.3	6.3
100.0	100.0	100.0	100.0	100.0	Total	100.0	100.0	100.0	100.0	100.0
					LIABILITIES					
22.9	8.7	7.7	5.9	10.5	Notes Payable - Short Term	8.5	9.2	8.8	11.4	10.5
17.0	22.4	25.9	21.2	22.3	A/P - Trade	23.5	25.3	23.5	23.2	22.3
.6	.3	.6	.4	.4	A/P - Retention	.6	.6	.5	1.6	.4
.6	3.6	10.3	11.4	4.8	Billings in Excess of Costs & Est. Earnings	5.3	5.4	5.0	5.4	4.8
.2	.4	.5	.7	.4	Income Taxes Payable	.6	.6	.6	.4	.4
8.0	4.3	1.7	1.4	4.2	Cur. Mat.-L/T/D	3.7	3.9	3.9	4.1	4.2
7.7	7.5	11.1	8.8	8.3	All Other Current	9.4	9.7	7.6	7.9	8.3
57.2	47.3	57.8	49.8	51.0	Total Current	51.6	54.7	49.9	54.0	51.0
24.6	13.0	5.4	10.9	13.0	Long Term Debt	9.4	10.3	11.2	11.1	13.0
.3	.6	.5	.8	.5	Deferred Taxes	.8	.7	.6	.5	.5
3.5	4.2	1.7	6.0	3.6	All Other Non-Current	2.7	2.1	2.4	4.1	3.6
14.4	35.0	34.5	32.5	31.8	Net Worth	35.6	32.3	35.9	30.3	31.8
100.0	100.0	100.0	100.0	100.0	Total Liabilities & Net Worth	100.0	100.0	100.0	100.0	100.0
					INCOME DATA					
100.0	100.0	100.0	100.0	100.0	Contract Revenues	100.0	100.0	100.0	100.0	100.0
44.5	31.2	18.5	20.0	30.0	Gross Profit	25.3	26.5	26.5	28.2	30.0
41.2	29.3	15.9	16.9	27.8	Operating Expenses	22.1	22.9	23.4	25.2	27.8
3.3	1.9	2.6	3.2	2.3	Operating Profit	3.3	3.6	3.2	3.0	2.3
1.8	.3	.3	.0	.5	All Other Expenses (net)	.2	.3	.3	.6	.5
1.5	1.6	2.3	3.1	1.8	Profit Before Taxes	3.1	3.3	2.8	2.4	1.8
					RATIOS					
2.9	2.5	1.9	1.5	2.3	Current	2.1	2.0	2.2	2.1	2.3
1.3	1.6	1.3	1.3	1.5		1.5	1.5	1.5	1.4	1.5
.7	1.1	1.1	1.2	1.1		1.1	1.2	1.1	1.1	1.1
(58) 5.7	(273) 3.5	(97) 3.1	(14) 2.7	(442) 3.4	Receivables/Payables	(543) 3.4	(514) 3.4	(477) 3.4	(439) 3.4	(442) 3.4
1.9	2.1	2.1	2.1	2.1		2.1	2.2	2.2	2.1	2.1
.8	1.3	1.5	1.5	1.3		1.5	1.5	1.4	1.4	1.3
9 42.3	28 13.0	44 8.3	33 11.1	28 13.0	Revenues/Receivables	37 9.8	36 10.1	35 10.4	33 11.2	28 13.0
31 11.7	50 7.4	60 6.1	58 6.3	50 7.3		56 6.5	55 6.7	52 7.1	51 7.2	50 7.3
49 7.5	74 5.0	80 4.6	77 4.7	74 5.0		74 5.0	74 5.0	74 4.9	71 5.1	74 5.0
4 94.2	19 19.7	21 17.0	15 23.9	18 20.6	Cost of Revenues/Payables	20 18.3	20 18.5	20 18.4	19 19.0	18 20.6
23 15.6	32 11.4	31 11.7	36 10.2	31 11.9		32 11.5	33 11.2	32 11.5	32 11.3	31 11.9
59 6.2	51 7.1	50 7.3	45 8.1	51 7.2		49 7.5	48 7.6	49 7.5	50 7.3	51 7.2
8.6	6.7	8.7	8.6	7.1	Revenues/Working Capital	7.1	7.6	7.2	7.9	7.1
32.0	12.7	16.8	17.4	14.7		13.3	13.5	13.5	15.2	14.7
-27.7	41.2	32.0	28.7	43.6		35.6	29.8	43.6	49.8	43.6
(59) 11.0	(246) 12.0	(85) 25.9	(14) 26.4	(404) 14.5	EBIT/Interest	(495) 16.2	(460) 13.6	(431) 13.0	(398) 12.1	(404) 14.5
2.4	3.6	8.2	3.8	4.2		4.8	5.2	4.6	3.8	4.2
-.4	.5	2.7	1.0	.8		1.9	1.6	1.5	1.1	.8
	3.6	10.8		5.7	Net Profit + Depr., Dep., Amort./Cur. Mat. L /T/D	(198) 6.9	(190) 5.7	(152) 5.8	(116) 6.2	(146) 5.7
	(96) 1.8	(46) 3.8		(146) 2.1		2.9	2.4	3.1	2.8	2.1
	.7	.8		.7		1.5	1.2	1.5	1.2	.7
.4	.2	.1	.2	.2	Fixed/Worth	.2	.2	.2	.2	.2
1.0	.5	.3	.5	.5		.4	.4	.4	.5	.5
28.7	1.4	.6	2.4	1.3		.9	1.0	1.1	1.2	1.3
.7	.7	1.1	1.1	.8	Debt/Worth	.9	.9	.8	.9	.8
2.4	2.0	2.0	2.5	2.0		1.8	1.9	1.7	2.2	2.0
-64.0	4.9	3.7	5.5	5.0		4.1	3.9	3.9	5.1	5.0
(50) 72.9	(254) 39.5	(95) 43.4	(14) 40.0	(413) 43.5	% Profit Before Taxes/Tangible Net Worth	(526) 44.9	(483) 47.9	(442) 46.5	(396) 46.5	(413) 43.5
19.5	10.8	19.9	20.1	14.8		24.1	22.6	18.0	18.9	14.8
-1.3	-1.9	4.9	3.0	.2		8.6	7.1	4.8	3.1	.2
16.6	14.3	13.2	15.1	14.4	% Profit Before Taxes/Total Assets	16.1	16.9	16.0	13.8	14.4
6.0	4.6	5.9	4.5	5.0		7.6	7.4	6.2	5.4	5.0
-9.3	-1.1	1.8	.7	-.8		2.4	2.1	1.2	.2	-.8
(53) 1.7	(256) 1.0	(90) .3	(10) .3	(409) .8	% Depr., Dep., Amort./Revenues	(517) .7	(475) .8	(437) .7	(399) .8	(409) .8
3.1	1.6	.9	.5	1.5		1.2	1.3	1.3	1.4	1.5
5.0	2.6	1.2	1.0	2.5		2.0	2.1	2.2	2.3	2.5
(38) 6.2	(193) 2.8	(50) 1.3		(288) 2.5	% Officers', Directors', Owners' Comp/Revenues	(328) 2.0	(309) 2.4	(287) 2.4	(261) 2.1	(288) 2.5
9.8	4.6	2.4		4.5		4.1	4.2	4.3	4.2	4.5
14.8	7.3	3.5		7.7		7.5	7.7	7.7	7.7	7.7
43499M	1080419M	1928349M	15957949M	19010216M	Contract Revenues ($)	28418881M	44637742M	35398122M	25827947M	19010216M
16699M	388893M	644262M	9818322M	10868176M	Total Assets ($)	9227900M	14247985M	13533233M	10433513M	10868176M

M = $ thousand   MM = $ million
See Pages 11 through 18 for Explanation of Ratios and Data

Current Data Sorted By Revenue — **Comparative Historical Data**

0-1MM	1-10MM	10-50MM	50 & OVER	ALL		4/1/98-3/31/99 ALL	4/1/99-3/31/00 ALL	4/1/00-3/31/01 ALL	4/1/01-3/31/02 ALL	4/1/02-3/31/03 ALL
					Type of Statement					
		1		1	Unqualified	6	6	4	2	1
	8	2		10	Reviewed	14	14	15	14	10
2	4			6	Compiled	3	6	3	5	6
2	3			5	Tax Returns	3	5	2	3	5
1	3			4	Other		4	8	5	4
5 (4/1-9/30/02)		21 (10/1/02-3/31/03)								
5	18	3		26	**NUMBER OF STATEMENTS**	26	35	32	29	26
%	%	%	%	%	**ASSETS**	%	%	%	%	%
	13.0		DATA NOT AVAILABLE	16.6	Cash & Equivalents	8.1	15.1	11.9	9.5	16.6
	37.9			39.4	A/R - Progress Billings	46.2	44.7	44.6	44.8	39.4
	.5			.4	A/R - Current Retention	1.7	1.9	2.0	1.4	.4
	15.0			12.7	Inventory	6.9	4.7	6.1	6.8	12.7
	5.2			5.4	Cost & Est. Earnings In Excess of Billings	4.1	4.3	6.6	3.5	5.4
	1.5			1.9	All Other Current	4.4	2.8	1.7	2.4	1.9
	73.1			76.3	Total Current	71.4	73.6	72.9	68.4	76.3
	18.5			16.5	Fixed Assets (net)	21.4	19.2	16.9	22.0	16.5
	.8			.9	Joint Ventures & Investments	1.7	.3	1.0	.7	.9
	.2			.1	Intangibles (net)	2.3	1.1	3.3	2.2	.1
	7.4			6.1	All Other Non-Current	3.3	5.8	5.9	6.7	6.1
	100.0			100.0	Total	100.0	100.0	100.0	100.0	100.0
					LIABILITIES					
	16.2			12.7	Notes Payable - Short Term	9.7	12.0	12.9	10.8	12.7
	23.4			24.9	A/P - Trade	14.8	17.4	16.7	15.8	24.9
	.0			.0	A/P - Retention	.0	.1	.2	.0	.0
	2.3			2.5	Billings in Excess of Costs & Est. Earnings	3.4	5.6	5.4	1.7	2.5
	.3			.2	Income Taxes Payable	1.4	.6	.4	.8	.2
	4.3			3.4	Cur. Mat.-L/T/D	4.6	4.1	3.6	4.8	3.4
	12.4			11.0	All Other Current	12.4	11.2	8.6	11.5	11.0
	58.8			54.7	Total Current	46.4	51.0	47.7	45.4	54.7
	12.2			8.7	Long Term Debt	15.4	12.7	10.4	10.0	8.7
	.4			.3	Deferred Taxes	.5	.5	.6	.8	.3
	4.2			5.6	All Other Non-Current	6.8	1.9	2.0	3.3	5.6
	24.4			30.8	Net Worth	30.9	33.9	39.2	40.6	30.8
	100.0			100.0	Total Liabilities & Net Worth	100.0	100.0	100.0	100.0	100.0
					INCOME DATA					
	100.0			100.0	Contract Revenues	100.0	100.0	100.0	100.0	100.0
	26.4			30.9	Gross Profit	24.5	30.1	27.3	23.5	30.9
	26.0			28.3	Operating Expenses	21.7	26.0	23.6	21.3	28.3
	.4			2.6	Operating Profit	2.8	4.0	3.7	2.2	2.6
	1.3			1.1	All Other Expenses (net)	.4	.2	.8	.8	1.1
	-.8			1.5	Profit Before Taxes	2.4	3.8	2.9	1.4	1.5
					RATIOS					
	1.7			1.9		2.0	2.1	2.1	2.5	1.9
	1.3			1.4	Current	1.5	1.5	1.5	1.6	1.4
	.9			1.0		1.2	1.1	1.0	1.0	1.0
	3.5			3.4		7.3	6.5	4.8	5.8	3.4
	(17) 2.4			(25) 2.4	Receivables/Payables	(25) 4.3	(32) 2.8	2.7	(28) 3.2	(25) 2.4
	1.3			1.3		2.1	1.5	2.2	2.4	1.3
	29 12.8			**34** 10.6		**41** 8.9	**33** 10.9	**38** 9.5	**42** 8.8	**34** 10.6
	49 7.4			**52** 7.0	Revenues/Receivables	**55** 6.7	**67** 5.4	**53** 6.9	**59** 6.2	**52** 7.0
	71 5.1			**71** 5.1		**82** 4.4	**101** 3.6	**66** 5.5	**76** 4.8	**71** 5.1
	17 21.0			**19** 19.0		**13** 28.9	**12** 30.5	**17** 21.2	**10** 35.4	**19** 19.0
	38 9.7			**38** 9.6	Cost of Revenues/Payables	**19** 19.6	**25** 14.8	**24** 15.4	**26** 13.9	**38** 9.6
	48 7.6			**47** 7.7		**32** 11.3	**54** 6.8	**35** 10.5	**36** 10.1	**47** 7.7
	7.5			6.7		7.3	5.5	6.1	6.6	6.7
	15.8			11.7	Revenues/Working Capital	15.5	10.7	14.7	12.9	11.7
	-125.0			-193.1		27.9	45.8	165.0	NM	-193.1
	17.8			6.2		14.2	33.3	11.5	9.2	6.2
	3.1			(23) 2.0	EBIT/Interest	(25) 3.1	6.6	(30) 4.7	(28) 2.3	(23) 2.0
	.5			-.8		1.2	1.1	1.6	-.5	-.8
						7.1		2.8	12.3	
					Net Profit + Depr., Dep., Amort./Cur. Mat. L/T/D	(10) 2.0		(10) 1.3	(13) 1.4	
						1.5		-.2	.1	
	.2			.2		.3	.1	.1	.2	.2
	.5			.5	Fixed/Worth	.7	.4	.4	.4	.5
	2.8			2.0		2.0	1.1	1.9	1.3	2.0
	2.2			1.1		.9	1.1	.8	.7	1.1
	3.4			2.8	Debt/Worth	2.1	2.0	1.9	1.2	2.8
	15.0			9.8		14.4	4.4	4.2	3.0	9.8
	66.6			39.5		49.7	93.9	56.1	16.0	39.5
	(16) 25.9			(23) 23.5	% Profit Before Taxes/Tangible Net Worth	(22) 24.6	(33) 25.8	(29) 26.0	(28) 5.9	(23) 23.5
	9.2			1.2		3.1	6.6	8.8	-9.7	1.2
	15.7			15.7		15.1	25.1	19.4	8.6	15.7
	5.2			4.6	% Profit Before Taxes/Total Assets	4.6	10.4	10.2	3.3	4.6
	-1.1			-1.9		.8	.5	2.8	-4.4	-1.9
	.4			.4		.6	.7	.6	1.1	.4
	(17) 1.1			(24) 1.0	% Depr., Dep., Amort./Revenues	(25) 1.5	(31) 1.2	(29) 1.2	(27) 1.6	(24) 1.0
	2.2			2.0		3.1	2.2	2.1	2.3	2.0
	3.6			3.6		2.0	3.9	3.1	2.9	3.6
	(11) 5.2			(15) 7.0	% Officers', Directors', Owners' Comp/Revenues	(13) 5.5	(21) 5.9	(21) 4.9	(17) 6.8	(15) 7.0
	8.9			13.4		8.0	8.7	8.8	8.6	13.4
3641M	**91856M**	**80663M**		**176160M**	Contract Revenues ($)	**393235M**	**417300M**	**372333M**	**219010M**	**176160M**
1837M	**30293M**	**51074M**		**83204M**	Total Assets ($)	**161443M**	**185227M**	**182736M**	**97739M**	**83204M**

M = $ thousand MM = $ million

See Pages 11 through 18 for Explanation of Ratios and Data

Current Data Sorted By Revenue   **Comparative Historical Data**

					Type of Statement					
	6	8	2	16	Unqualified	26	17	17	11	16
2	47	10	1	60	Reviewed	62	62	71	55	60
3	23			26	Compiled	22	27	20	25	26
4	12		1	17	Tax Returns	7	14	14	19	17
1	16	4	1	22	Other	24	12	17	19	22

	33 (4/1-9/30/02)		108 (10/1/02-3/31/03)							
0-1MM	1-10MM	10-50MM	50 & OVER	ALL		4/1/98-3/31/99	4/1/99-3/31/00	4/1/00-3/31/01	4/1/01-3/31/02	4/1/02-3/31/03
						ALL	ALL	ALL	ALL	ALL
10	104	23	4	141	**NUMBER OF STATEMENTS**	141	132	139	129	141
%	%	%	%	%	**ASSETS**	%	%	%	%	%
11.7	13.4	5.8		11.8	Cash & Equivalents	12.7	11.0	11.2	11.8	11.8
39.1	47.6	48.0		47.1	A/R - Progress Billings	47.5	51.5	51.8	50.2	47.1
.0	1.4	2.7		1.5	A/R - Current Retention	4.5	4.0	4.6	2.2	1.5
6.5	4.6	1.7		4.2	Inventory	4.9	5.3	4.4	4.6	4.2
.0	3.6	4.8		4.0	Cost & Est. Earnings In Excess of Billings	3.6	3.5	3.6	3.0	4.0
8.5	3.4	11.5		5.1	All Other Current	3.6	3.5	2.5	4.6	5.1
65.9	73.9	74.5		73.6	Total Current	77.0	78.8	78.1	76.4	73.6
22.5	19.0	20.0		19.3	Fixed Assets (net)	15.2	14.2	14.5	15.3	19.3
.0	.4	.9		.5	Joint Ventures & Investments	.9	.6	.9	2.0	.5
.2	.6	.3		.5	Intangibles (net)	2.0	1.1	1.1	.6	.5
11.4	6.0	4.3		6.1	All Other Non-Current	4.9	5.4	5.4	5.6	6.1
100.0	100.0	100.0		100.0	Total	100.0	100.0	100.0	100.0	100.0
					LIABILITIES					
12.4	9.3	16.7		10.7	Notes Payable - Short Term	10.9	10.4	11.5	11.4	10.7
22.4	14.4	13.2		15.1	A/P - Trade	15.5	16.3	16.0	15.0	15.1
6.7	.3	.0		.7	A/P - Retention	.4	.3	.2	.4	.7
2.5	2.7	9.5		4.0	Billings in Excess of Costs & Est. Earnings	7.0	6.4	7.0	6.3	4.0
.0	.2	.1		.2	Income Taxes Payable	.7	.6	.4	.3	.2
3.8	2.7	4.3		3.0	Cur. Mat.-L/T/D	2.7	2.4	2.4	3.3	3.0
4.6	10.6	10.5		10.3	All Other Current	10.6	8.8	9.4	9.8	10.3
52.4	40.2	54.4		43.9	Total Current	47.7	45.3	46.9	46.4	43.9
8.6	11.0	8.0		10.2	Long Term Debt	7.1	6.5	7.5	8.8	10.2
.4	.9	.9		.8	Deferred Taxes	1.3	1.2	1.2	1.0	.8
2.1	4.8	2.7		4.2	All Other Non-Current	2.8	3.1	1.7	3.4	4.2
36.5	43.2	34.0		40.9	Net Worth	41.0	43.9	42.7	40.4	40.9
100.0	100.0	100.0		100.0	Total Liabilities & Net Worth	100.0	100.0	100.0	100.0	100.0
					INCOME DATA					
100.0	100.0	100.0		100.0	Contract Revenues	100.0	100.0	100.0	100.0	100.0
27.8	26.6	14.5		24.3	Gross Profit	25.3	23.8	23.9	26.2	24.3
30.1	23.0	11.2		21.3	Operating Expenses	20.5	18.9	19.3	21.2	21.3
-2.3	3.5	3.2		3.1	Operating Profit	4.8	4.9	4.6	5.1	3.1
-.7	.1	.0		.1	All Other Expenses (net)	.4	-.2	.2	.4	.1
-1.6	3.4	3.2		3.0	Profit Before Taxes	4.4	5.1	4.4	4.7	3.0
					RATIOS					
2.7	3.3	2.1		2.9	Current	2.3	2.8	2.4	2.4	2.9
1.5	2.0	1.6		1.9		1.7	1.7	1.7	1.7	1.9
.7	1.3	1.2		1.2		1.3	1.4	1.3	1.2	1.2
	(102) 7.7	(21) 6.1		(136) 7.3	Receivables/Payables	(136) 6.3	(130) 6.5	(135) 6.7	(123) 7.4	(136) 7.3
	4.0	4.4		3.9		3.8	4.0	4.4	4.5	3.9
	2.3	2.9		2.2		2.2	2.3	2.5	2.5	2.2
30 12.3	36 10.0	43 8.5		37 9.8	Revenues/Receivables	41 9.0	43 8.6	46 8.0	40 9.1	37 9.8
56 6.5	53 6.9	70 5.2		54 6.8		67 5.4	64 5.7	66 5.6	62 5.9	54 6.8
108 3.4	75 4.9	92 4.0		79 4.6		81 4.3	85 4.3	86 4.3	79 4.5	79 4.6
24 15.0	8 45.2	12 29.4		10 36.7	Cost of Revenues/Payables	13 29.1	11 32.2	11 33.6	9 39.1	10 36.7
39 9.3	18 20.8	17 21.5		19 19.1		20 18.1	19 19.6	18 20.3	18 20.4	19 19.1
89 4.1	33 11.1	25 14.6		33 11.0		30 12.4	32 11.6	31 11.6	32 11.4	33 11.0
5.1	6.2	7.7		6.2	Revenues/Working Capital	5.9	5.7	6.6	6.1	6.2
NM	9.5	13.4		9.8		10.6	9.9	10.9	10.7	9.8
-11.4	22.2	32.0		30.2		20.4	20.5	18.8	25.3	30.2
	(87) 25.8	(22) 23.8		(119) 20.3	EBIT/Interest	(121) 21.7	(113) 29.9	(120) 31.6	(112) 22.2	(119) 20.3
	5.7	7.5		5.6		8.8	8.8	6.2	8.7	5.6
	1.7	2.0		1.7		3.0	2.4	2.4	2.5	1.7
	(32) 5.4			(43) 4.6	Net Profit + Depr., Dep., Amort./Cur. Mat. L /T/D	(33) 10.5	(40) 15.5	(47) 16.2	(23) 9.7	(43) 4.6
	2.3			2.0		3.2	4.0	6.6	3.5	2.0
	.5			.5		1.3	1.5	1.9	2.3	.5
.0	.1	.1		.1	Fixed/Worth	.1	.1	.1	.1	.1
.9	.3	.3		.3		.3	.3	.3	.3	.3
1.9	1.0	1.0		1.0		.6	.5	.5	.7	1.0
.9	.6	1.0		.6	Debt/Worth	.7	.6	.7	.6	.6
2.1	1.2	1.8		1.3		1.3	1.4	1.3	1.6	1.3
5.4	2.6	3.9		3.0		2.6	3.0	3.0	3.0	3.0
159.1	45.6	37.6		43.9	% Profit Before Taxes/Tangible Net Worth	55.7	65.6	55.2	71.1	43.9
16.3	(97) 17.4	(22) 23.7		(133) 19.8		(134) 28.0	(130) 34.0	(134) 31.4	(124) 30.1	(133) 19.8
-26.2	5.5	5.7		5.5		12.3	12.0	9.9	7.9	5.5
28.2	16.7	14.8		16.3	% Profit Before Taxes/Total Assets	22.6	27.0	24.2	24.4	16.3
2.7	8.8	5.2		7.0		10.9	12.2	9.9	11.6	7.0
-10.2	1.7	2.1		1.8		4.2	3.4	3.3	2.5	1.8
	(91) .5	(21) .5		(123) .5	% Depr., Dep., Amort./Revenues	(129) .6	(115) .5	(125) .4	(115) .4	(123) .5
	1.1	.7		1.0		1.0	.9	.9	.7	1.0
	2.1	1.5		2.1		1.7	1.4	1.4	1.4	2.1
	(67) 2.5	(12) .9		(85) 2.2	% Officers', Directors', Owners' Comp/Revenues	(68) 2.4	(83) 1.9	(86) 2.8	(82) 2.1	(85) 2.2
	4.2	1.9		4.2		3.7	4.3	4.3	4.4	4.2
	9.2	3.7		8.9		6.7	7.7	8.6	8.6	8.9
5034M	445267M	430727M	358162M	1239190M	Contract Revenues ($)	7014291M	20631881M	1570925M	1163613M	1239190M
2854M	154880M	149804M	131908M	439446M	Total Assets ($)	2203788M	9987205M	518044M	386837M	439446M

M = $ thousand   MM = $ million
See Pages 11 through 18 for Explanation of Ratios and Data

Current Data Sorted By Revenue　　　　　　　　　　　　　**Comparative Historical Data**

Type of Statement	0-1MM	1-10MM	10-50MM	50 & OVER	ALL		4/1/98-3/31/99 ALL	4/1/99-3/31/00 ALL	4/1/00-3/31/01 ALL	4/1/01-3/31/02 ALL	4/1/02-3/31/03 ALL
Unqualified		8	8	2	18		9	12	14	8	18
Reviewed	3	42	7	1	53		42	25	35	35	53
Compiled	7	27	3		37		23	20	20	18	37
Tax Returns	8	18		1	27		10	13	13	15	27
Other	12	14	2	1	29		14	15	10	15	29

43 (4/1-9/30/02)　　　121 (10/1/02-3/31/03)

	0-1MM	1-10MM	10-50MM	50 & OVER	ALL		4/1/98-3/31/99	4/1/99-3/31/00	4/1/00-3/31/01	4/1/01-3/31/02	4/1/02-3/31/03
NUMBER OF STATEMENTS	30	109	20	5	164		98	85	92	91	164
	%	%	%	%	%		%	%	%	%	%
ASSETS											
Cash & Equivalents	18.3	13.9	9.9		13.9		13.4	13.6	13.0	11.7	13.9
A/R - Progress Billings	24.1	38.8	49.2		37.0		41.2	43.6	45.6	43.8	37.0
A/R - Current Retention	.0	1.3	.6		.9		1.7	1.6	1.3	.7	.9
Inventory	7.7	3.9	3.1		4.5		2.8	3.4	1.9	3.0	4.5
Cost & Est. Earnings In Excess of Billings	1.2	5.1	6.0		4.4		4.1	4.4	5.1	4.4	4.4
All Other Current	4.9	3.5	6.3		4.4		4.0	2.3	2.8	3.2	4.4
Total Current	56.1	66.4	75.1		65.1		67.1	68.9	69.6	66.8	65.1
Fixed Assets (net)	31.7	24.8	15.8		25.4		21.8	19.5	19.8	23.3	25.4
Joint Ventures & Investments	.1	.5	.7		.5		1.9	1.6	1.8	.4	.5
Intangibles (net)	.1	.6	1.7		.6		2.2	1.2	.9	.7	.6
All Other Non-Current	12.0	7.7	6.7		8.3		7.0	8.8	8.0	8.7	8.3
Total	100.0	100.0	100.0		100.0		100.0	100.0	100.0	100.0	100.0
LIABILITIES											
Notes Payable - Short Term	13.4	16.4	10.6		15.0		11.0	16.7	11.5	21.0	15.0
A/P - Trade	10.6	12.9	22.7		13.9		13.8	13.3	13.1	14.9	13.9
A/P - Retention	.0	.2	.1		.2		.7	.3	1.2	.3	.2
Billings in Excess of Costs & Est. Earnings	.2	2.6	4.1		2.4		2.0	2.5	2.1	2.5	2.4
Income Taxes Payable	.2	.7	1.0		.6		1.3	1.3	1.0	.7	.6
Cur. Mat.-L/T/D	5.8	7.2	1.6		6.2		2.6	2.6	4.7	3.5	6.2
All Other Current	9.7	12.1	12.1		11.4		9.9	11.9	10.5	13.2	11.4
Total Current	40.0	52.0	52.3		49.7		41.4	48.5	44.1	56.1	49.7
Long Term Debt	21.9	12.5	7.2		13.8		10.8	9.8	10.7	14.7	13.8
Deferred Taxes	.2	1.0	.3		.8		1.0	.8	1.2	.9	.8
All Other Non-Current	7.1	6.6	2.0		6.0		6.7	12.6	7.8	16.6	6.0
Net Worth	30.7	27.9	38.3		29.7		40.1	28.3	36.2	11.7	29.7
Total Liabilities & Net Worth	100.0	100.0	100.0		100.0		100.0	100.0	100.0	100.0	100.0
INCOME DATA											
Contract Revenues	100.0	100.0	100.0		100.0		100.0	100.0	100.0	100.0	100.0
Gross Profit	41.5	30.2	20.9		31.2		31.0	29.7	29.6	31.6	31.2
Operating Expenses	41.4	27.9	16.0		29.0		27.8	25.9	26.8	27.7	29.0
Operating Profit	.2	2.3	4.9		2.2		3.2	3.8	2.8	3.9	2.2
All Other Expenses (net)	.3	.7	.4		.6		.1	.3	.4	.6	.6
Profit Before Taxes	-.1	1.6	4.5		1.5		3.1	3.5	2.4	3.3	1.5
RATIOS											
Current	5.4	2.2	2.0		2.3		2.7	3.2	2.8	2.5	2.3
	1.7	1.6	1.5		1.5		1.7	1.7	1.7	1.4	1.5
	.7	1.1	1.2		1.1		1.2	1.1	1.1	1.0	1.1
Receivables/Payables	UND	6.4	4.5		6.3		7.9	8.4	6.8	7.3	6.3
	(24) 3.4	(100) 4.0	2.5		(149) 3.8		(95) 3.4	(81) 3.8	(86) 3.8	(84) 3.6	(149) 3.8
	.8	1.8	1.4		1.5		1.7	2.3	2.3	1.9	1.5
Revenues/Receivables	6 66.2	23 15.6	53 6.9		22 16.2		33 11.0	29 12.6	44 8.3	27 13.3	22 16.2
	25 14.8	52 7.0	65 5.6		52 7.0		54 6.7	63 5.8	64 5.7	58 6.3	52 7.0
	68 5.4	77 4.7	77 4.7		76 4.8		76 4.8	79 4.6	84 4.3	80 4.6	76 4.8
Cost of Revenues/Payables	0 UND	9 41.3	16 22.1		8 44.7		7 49.5	7 49.7	9 38.5	9 39.6	8 44.7
	9 42.8	19 19.0	29 12.7		20 18.1		20 18.6	19 19.3	19 19.1	18 19.9	20 18.1
	54 6.8	32 11.4	55 6.6		38 9.7		36 10.1	36 10.3	35 10.4	43 8.5	38 9.7
Revenues/Working Capital	7.0	7.3	9.1		7.6		7.2	6.5	6.0	7.8	7.6
	14.5	14.1	11.6		13.9		10.9	11.2	8.9	17.2	13.9
	-26.5	51.2	23.7		51.5		35.8	40.5	51.5	303.0	51.5
EBIT/Interest	(23) 4.4	(98) 8.6	18.0		(145) 8.2		(81) 10.0	(70) 14.9	(76) 8.6	(82) 9.0	(145) 8.2
	-.2	2.9	(19) 5.4		2.8		3.6	3.4	3.3	3.2	2.8
	-4.9	.0	2.5		-.5		1.3	1.1	-.9	1.2	-.5
Net Profit + Depr., Dep., Amort./Cur. Mat. L /T/D		(34) 2.8	27.3		4.2		(27) 9.7	7.6	5.3	3.6	(49) 4.2
		1.3	(11) 6.9		(49) 1.9		2.3	(14) 2.3	(17) 1.0	(25) 2.3	1.9
		.7	2.4		.8		1.2	.6	-.2	1.2	.8
Fixed/Worth	.4	.2	.2		.3		.2	.2	.2	.2	.3
	.8	.5	.5		.5		.4	.3	.3	.5	.5
	12.0	1.5	1.0		1.6		.8	.9	.9	1.7	1.6
Debt/Worth	.3	.8	.8		.8		.6	.6	.6	.9	.8
	2.0	1.5	1.2		1.6		1.4	1.5	1.2	1.9	1.6
	44.1	3.9	4.5		4.7		2.8	3.5	3.1	6.0	4.7
% Profit Before Taxes/ Tangible Net Worth	(25) 46.0	(99) 38.4	52.3		(147) 41.5		(90) 49.7	(78) 43.8	(85) 40.3	(80) 48.1	(147) 41.5
	1.3	12.9	(18) 25.0		12.9		19.8	19.2	12.1	17.4	12.9
	-15.2	-1.9	8.6		-2.9		2.8	3.2	-.6	2.3	-2.9
% Profit Before Taxes/ Total Assets	15.1	12.5	23.6		13.2		18.1	23.1	15.6	20.6	13.2
	.9	4.8	8.4		4.7		7.3	5.4	5.6	5.6	4.7
	-8.7	-2.9	4.1		-3.5		.8	.5	-2.3	.3	-3.5
% Depr., Dep., Amort./ Revenues	(22) 1.6	(103) .8	.4		(145) .8		(81) .9	(68) .9	(74) .9	(82) .7	(145) .8
	3.3	1.6	(18) 1.0		1.6		1.7	1.5	1.6	1.6	1.6
	4.3	2.7	1.4		2.8		3.3	2.3	2.5	2.8	2.8
% Officers', Directors', Owners' Comp/Revenues	(18) 6.0	(70) 2.8	1.8		(104) 2.9		(59) 4.5	(44) 3.6	(54) 2.6	(58) 2.7	(104) 2.9
	10.8	5.6	(12) 3.4		5.6		6.8	5.6	4.5	4.7	5.6
	16.5	8.4	6.8		9.2		11.2	10.0	8.7	9.4	9.2
Contract Revenues ($)	19724M	425504M	343979M	10684736M	11473943M		7939915M	352014M	10134428M	334104M	11473943M
Total Assets ($)	11189M	157378M	119637M	5445997M	5734201M		2712498M	133954M	3127768M	123814M	5734201M

© RMA 2003　　　　M = $ thousand　　MM = $ million
See Pages 11 through 18 for Explanation of Ratios and Data

Current Data Sorted By Revenue | **Comparative Historical Data**

0-1MM	1-10MM	10-50MM	50 & OVER	ALL		4/1/98-3/31/99	4/1/99-3/31/00	4/1/00-3/31/01	4/1/01-3/31/02	4/1/02-3/31/03
					Type of Statement					
					Unqualified		1			
2	9	8		19	Reviewed	23	22	25	23	19
1	11	1		13	Compiled	10	14	13	16	13
1	4			5	Tax Returns	5	6	5	8	5
1	10	2	1	14	Other	7	11	10	12	14
	13 (4/1-9/30/02)		38 (10/1/02-3/31/03)			ALL	ALL	ALL	ALL	ALL
5	34	11	1	51	**NUMBER OF STATEMENTS**	45	54	53	59	51
%	%	%	%	%	**ASSETS**	%	%	%	%	%
	9.8	7.8		9.9	Cash & Equivalents	7.8	7.5	7.7	8.7	9.9
	49.7	60.0		50.5	A/R - Progress Billings	51.8	52.1	49.2	44.4	50.5
	1.3	.0		.8	A/R - Current Retention	3.5	2.2	1.1	1.0	.8
	8.4	9.0		8.7	Inventory	10.0	13.6	14.1	10.8	8.7
	4.2	1.4		3.2	Cost & Est. Earnings In Excess of Billings	3.5	2.5	3.0	3.8	3.2
	4.6	4.9		5.6	All Other Current	3.3	4.4	4.1	6.2	5.6
	78.0	83.1		78.8	Total Current	79.9	82.3	79.2	74.8	78.8
	13.3	9.2		12.8	Fixed Assets (net)	15.3	11.6	13.0	19.1	12.8
	.0	.0		.0	Joint Ventures & Investments	.4	.1	1.6	.3	.0
	1.3	3.2		2.1	Intangibles (net)	.8	1.8	1.7	1.0	2.1
	7.3	4.5		6.4	All Other Non-Current	3.8	4.2	4.6	4.8	6.4
	100.0	100.0		100.0	Total	100.0	100.0	100.0	100.0	100.0
					LIABILITIES					
	23.2	17.5		20.9	Notes Payable - Short Term	16.7	15.5	17.9	14.6	20.9
	26.6	16.6		22.9	A/P - Trade	20.4	22.2	22.9	18.7	22.9
	1.4	.0		.9	A/P - Retention	.0	.0	.1	1.0	.9
	1.2	1.7		1.3	Billings in Excess of Costs & Est. Earnings	1.7	1.9	3.2	1.2	1.3
	1.5	.1		1.3	Income Taxes Payable	.8	.4	.2	.7	1.3
	5.0	1.6		3.9	Cur. Mat.-L/T/D	2.3	2.7	2.6	5.0	3.9
	8.9	9.3		9.3	All Other Current	7.2	8.4	8.5	11.9	9.3
	67.8	46.8		60.6	Total Current	49.1	51.1	55.4	53.0	60.6
	7.5	6.6		7.0	Long Term Debt	6.7	3.7	7.5	10.7	7.0
	.5	.5		.6	Deferred Taxes	.4	.3	.4	.8	.6
	2.4	6.5		3.2	All Other Non-Current	1.7	2.4	2.9	3.6	3.2
	21.7	39.5		28.7	Net Worth	42.0	42.5	33.8	31.9	28.7
	100.0	100.0		100.0	Total Liabilities & Net Worth	100.0	100.0	100.0	100.0	100.0
					INCOME DATA					
	100.0	100.0		100.0	Contract Revenues	100.0	100.0	100.0	100.0	100.0
	27.1	22.1		26.7	Gross Profit	25.0	26.3	23.7	29.6	26.7
	25.5	19.1		24.7	Operating Expenses	20.8	23.2	20.7	25.8	24.7
	1.6	3.0		2.1	Operating Profit	4.2	3.1	3.1	3.8	2.1
	.6	.1		.3	All Other Expenses (net)	.3	.4	.5	.0	.3
	1.0	2.9		1.8	Profit Before Taxes	3.9	2.7	2.5	3.9	1.8
					RATIOS					
	2.1	3.1		2.3		2.1	2.3	2.2	2.2	2.3
	1.3	1.6		1.4	Current	1.6	1.6	1.4	1.4	1.4
	1.1	1.4		1.1		1.2	1.2	1.1	1.0	1.1
	3.6	6.2		4.8		5.7	6.1	4.2	5.0	4.8
	(32) 2.1	4.5	(49)	2.4	Receivables/Payables	(43) 2.9	(53) 2.4	(50) 2.9	(56) 2.5	(49) 2.4
	1.2	2.3		1.7		2.1	1.5	1.5	1.4	1.7
	29 12.7	57 6.5		32 11.4		42 8.8	39 9.2	30 12.3	23 15.8	32 11.4
	54 6.8	65 5.6		58 6.3	Revenues/Receivables	56 6.5	56 6.5	55 6.6	46 8.0	58 6.3
	78 4.7	88 4.1		77 4.7		73 5.0	85 4.3	75 4.9	67 5.5	77 4.7
	17 21.7	12 31.0		14 26.5		12 29.3	12 29.6	14 25.7	12 31.5	14 26.5
	30 12.0	23 15.8		27 13.7	Cost of Revenues/Payables	25 14.8	28 13.0	25 14.8	28 13.2	27 13.7
	50 7.4	39 9.4		41 8.8		37 9.8	42 8.7	41 8.9	39 9.3	41 8.8
	8.1	7.6		8.0		8.7	6.7	8.3	8.1	8.0
	19.3	9.0		14.4	Revenues/Working Capital	12.9	12.2	14.2	14.7	14.4
	76.9	14.4		46.4		26.1	28.6	61.0	-999.8	46.4
	10.2	27.7		12.9		13.7	14.4	10.0	12.9	12.9
	(30) 2.9	6.9	(46)	3.7	EBIT/Interest	(42) 5.9	(48) 4.8	(48) 3.5	(54) 5.3	(46) 3.7
	-.1	1.3		1.0		3.2	2.0	1.5	2.0	1.0
	5.8			8.0		8.6	6.9	11.3	9.3	8.0
	(10) 2.9		(18)	4.1	Net Profit + Depr., Dep., Amort./Cur. Mat. L./T/D	(10) 4.5	(13) 4.0	(14) 3.5	(20) 3.1	(18) 4.1
	.8			1.4		2.5	1.6	1.6	1.3	1.4
	.2	.2		.2		.2	.1	.1	.1	.2
	.3	.2		.3	Fixed/Worth	.3	.2	.3	.4	.3
	NM	.5		1.0		.7	.5	.7	1.9	1.0
	1.0	.6		.7		.8	.7	.9	.8	.7
	3.2	1.5		3.0	Debt/Worth	1.6	1.3	2.1	2.3	3.0
	-37.9	7.2		8.0		3.3	3.2	5.3	11.3	8.0
	34.7	64.8		49.1		64.2	48.7	43.6	52.5	49.1
	(25) 18.7	20.7	(41)	19.9	% Profit Before Taxes/Tangible Net Worth	(44) 34.9	(52) 26.5	(49) 22.8	(50) 31.1	(41) 19.9
	5.2	5.1		5.4		17.3	7.1	8.2	14.5	5.4
	12.8	14.2		13.6		26.4	18.5	14.9	23.5	13.6
	4.3	8.8		5.4	% Profit Before Taxes/Total Assets	11.2	7.9	6.3	8.5	5.4
	-2.7	1.2		.2		6.3	2.6	2.5	3.3	.2
	.5	.5		.5		.5	.3	.5	.5	.5
	(30) 1.0	(10) .7	(46)	1.0	% Depr., Dep., Amort./Revenues	(34) .8	(48) .8	(47) .8	(54) .8	(46) 1.0
	1.3	1.1		1.3		1.6	1.3	1.5	1.5	1.3
	2.5			2.6		3.0	3.4	2.7	2.6	2.6
	(25) 5.1		(38)	4.2	% Officers', Directors', Owners' Comp/Revenues	(29) 5.2	(40) 4.9	(36) 5.2	(41) 4.6	(38) 4.2
	7.2			6.5		8.3	7.7	9.0	6.6	6.5
2836M	148237M	200415M	60005M	411493M	Contract Revenues ($)	213727M	250788M	8231863M	423707M	411493M
784M	42476M	64074M	22105M	129439M	Total Assets ($)	56576M	73951M	1855703M	121118M	129439M

M = $ thousand   MM = $ million
See Pages 11 through 18 for Explanation of Ratios and Data

Current Data Sorted By Revenue   **Comparative Historical Data**

					Type of Statement					
1	13	15	2	31	Unqualified	70	63	53	42	31
10	84	23	2	119	Reviewed	132	116	133	99	119
13	25	4		42	Compiled	57	50	48	54	42
11	20	1	1	33	Tax Returns	34	22	36	28	33
5	33	8	3	49	Other	45	42	34	40	49
53 (4/1-9/30/02)			221 (10/1/02-3/31/03)			4/1/98-3/31/99	4/1/99-3/31/00	4/1/00-3/31/01	4/1/01-3/31/02	4/1/02-3/31/03
0-1MM	1-10MM	10-50MM	50 & OVER	ALL		ALL	ALL	ALL	ALL	ALL
40	175	51	8	274	**NUMBER OF STATEMENTS**	338	293	304	263	274
%	%	%	%	%	**ASSETS**	%	%	%	%	%
7.0	8.3	6.7		8.0	Cash & Equivalents	8.9	10.3	8.5	8.2	8.0
13.6	29.3	32.3		27.6	A/R - Progress Billings	28.1	27.2	28.8	26.8	27.6
.2	1.0	2.5		1.2	A/R - Current Retention	2.6	2.5	2.3	1.3	1.2
3.1	1.9	1.1		1.8	Inventory	1.4	1.6	1.7	2.3	1.8
.0	2.5	4.5		2.5	Cost & Est. Earnings In Excess of Billings	2.3	2.5	2.8	2.7	2.5
3.3	4.6	6.8		4.9	All Other Current	3.2	3.2	2.6	4.4	4.9
27.1	47.6	53.8		46.0	Total Current	46.7	47.3	46.7	45.7	46.0
62.7	45.7	38.9		46.3	Fixed Assets (net)	46.8	47.3	47.1	48.6	46.3
2.8	1.3	.2		1.8	Joint Ventures & Investments	.7	.6	.7	.7	1.8
.0	.5	.9		.5	Intangibles (net)	1.3	.6	.9	.9	.5
7.4	4.9	6.2		5.4	All Other Non-Current	4.6	4.1	4.6	4.1	5.4
100.0	100.0	100.0		100.0	Total	100.0	100.0	100.0	100.0	100.0
					LIABILITIES					
14.5	7.2	7.0		8.1	Notes Payable - Short Term	5.7	5.3	6.0	7.2	8.1
9.1	12.6	17.2		13.1	A/P - Trade	14.2	14.0	14.0	13.4	13.1
.3	.2	1.2		.4	A/P - Retention	.5	.2	.2	.2	.4
.0	2.4	4.3		2.4	Billings in Excess of Costs & Est. Earnings	1.9	2.7	2.5	2.4	2.4
.3	.3	.1		.2	Income Taxes Payable	.4	.4	.4	.2	.2
11.7	9.1	7.4		9.0	Cur. Mat.-L/T/D	8.8	8.9	9.4	9.5	9.0
4.8	4.2	6.2		4.8	All Other Current	4.5	4.3	4.8	4.3	4.8
40.7	36.0	43.4		38.1	Total Current	36.0	36.0	37.2	37.1	38.1
31.8	19.6	16.6		20.7	Long Term Debt	21.1	21.7	21.7	22.9	20.7
.5	1.6	1.4		1.4	Deferred Taxes	1.8	1.4	1.3	1.4	1.4
8.6	2.7	1.5		3.5	All Other Non-Current	2.6	3.0	3.3	2.6	3.5
18.3	40.0	37.1		36.3	Net Worth	38.6	37.8	36.5	36.0	36.3
100.0	100.0	100.0		100.0	Total Liabilities & Net Worth	100.0	100.0	100.0	100.0	100.0
					INCOME DATA					
100.0	100.0	100.0		100.0	Contract Revenues	100.0	100.0	100.0	100.0	100.0
49.8	31.8	19.1		31.9	Gross Profit	30.4	29.7	28.6	35.2	31.9
46.8	29.3	16.6		29.2	Operating Expenses	24.5	23.1	24.6	29.3	29.2
3.0	2.5	2.5		2.7	Operating Profit	5.8	6.6	4.1	5.9	2.7
3.1	1.0	.6		1.2	All Other Expenses (net)	.7	1.2	1.2	1.3	1.2
–.1	1.6	1.9		1.5	Profit Before Taxes	5.1	5.4	2.9	4.6	1.5
					RATIOS					
1.3	2.0	1.6		1.8		2.0	1.8	1.9	1.7	1.8
.6	1.3	1.2		1.2	Current	1.3	1.3	1.3	1.2	1.2
.3	1.0	1.0		.8		.9	.9	.9	.9	.8
	33.7	4.9	3.4	4.3		4.4	3.7	4.6	4.1	4.3
(29) 2.5	(166) 2.7	(50) 1.8	(252) 2.4		Receivables/Payables	(308) 2.3	(273) 2.1	(286) 2.4	(244) 2.1	(252) 2.4
.6	1.5	1.2		1.4		1.4	1.5	1.4	1.3	1.4
0 UND	29 12.5	42 8.6	28 13.1			33 11.1	30 12.0	32 11.4	29 12.6	28 13.1
13 27.5	48 7.7	53 6.9	46 7.9		Revenues/Receivables	55 6.7	55 6.6	54 6.8	49 7.5	46 7.9
53 6.8	74 4.9	75 4.9	73 5.0			80 4.6	76 4.8	75 4.9	71 5.2	73 5.0
0 UND	12 29.6	22 16.6	12 31.2			12 30.6	15 25.1	13 28.6	14 25.7	12 31.2
9 38.7	25 14.5	35 10.5	26 14.0		Cost of Revenues/Payables	28 12.9	30 12.3	28 12.9	29 12.5	26 14.0
28 12.9	50 7.3	46 7.9	48 7.6			53 6.9	50 7.3	47 7.7	50 7.3	48 7.6
15.8	8.1	10.0		8.8		8.1	8.9	9.1	11.4	8.8
–13.4	21.1	22.3		24.7	Revenues/Working Capital	19.1	20.4	22.0	28.9	24.7
–7.3	–217.3	–147.2		–44.1		–74.7	–99.2	–89.0	–40.3	–44.1
3.1	8.4	6.4		7.4		7.7	8.8	6.4	7.7	7.4
(39) .9	(165) 2.7	(46) 2.8	(257) 2.5		EBIT/Interest	(320) 3.5	(280) 4.0	(288) 3.0	(250) 2.9	(257) 2.5
–.6	.3	1.3		.3		1.7	1.7	1.1	1.4	.3
	3.1	2.4		3.0		2.8	3.0	2.9	3.2	3.0
(70) 1.7	(16) 1.6	(88) 1.6			Net Profit + Depr., Dep., Amort./Cur. Mat. L /T/D	(131) 1.9	(95) 1.9	(106) 1.6	(74) 1.9	(88) 1.6
.9	1.0			.9		1.2	1.3	1.1	1.4	.9
1.1	.6	.7		.7		.7	.7	.7	.8	.7
6.1	1.2	1.0		1.2	Fixed/Worth	1.2	1.2	1.3	1.4	1.2
–11.5	2.0	2.1		2.3		2.0	2.2	2.3	2.3	2.3
1.1	.7	1.1		.9		.9	.9	.9	.9	.9
9.1	1.6	1.7		1.7	Debt/Worth	1.6	1.6	1.8	2.0	1.7
–19.9	3.2	4.0		4.0		3.3	3.3	3.8	3.8	4.0
25.3	30.9	23.8		30.0		41.7	43.7	36.5	36.8	30.0
(28) 1.9	(165) 12.1	11.4	(252) 11.3		% Profit Before Taxes/ Tangible Net Worth	(320) 19.2	(279) 22.9	(280) 17.3	(244) 19.8	(252) 11.3
–20.7	–5.4	1.6		–3.9		6.3	5.8	3.7	5.3	–3.9
7.4	13.0	6.3		10.4		14.9	16.7	11.7	13.3	10.4
–1.0	4.0	4.1		3.7	% Profit Before Taxes/ Total Assets	7.0	7.6	5.8	5.8	3.7
–7.1	–3.0	.5		–2.5		1.9	2.3	.7	1.2	–2.5
5.6	3.7	1.8		3.4		3.2	3.5	3.3	3.6	3.4
(37) 12.1	(157) 6.3	(48) 4.5	(246) 5.8		% Depr., Dep., Amort./ Revenues	(308) 5.6	(274) 5.4	(285) 5.6	(246) 6.5	(246) 5.8
16.2	9.0	6.1		9.2		8.6	8.4	8.7	9.5	9.2
5.5	2.2	.8		2.1		2.0	2.3	2.1	2.3	2.1
(26) 7.3	(106) 4.3	(27) 1.7	(159) 4.4		% Officers', Directors', Owners' Comp/Revenues	(197) 3.6	(167) 4.1	(169) 4.3	(141) 4.4	(159) 4.4
8.6	6.4	3.6		6.6		7.1	7.8	8.4	7.1	6.6
22882M	658307M	907244M	8845879M	10434312M	Contract Revenues ($)	13893816M	2153884M	34465773M	7043658M	10434312M
19395M	379113M	453119M	2546620M	3398247M	Total Assets ($)	7467005M	1129185M	13804354M	4719638M	3398247M

M = $ thousand   MM = $ million
See Pages 11 through 18 for Explanation of Ratios and Data

Current Data Sorted By Revenue | **Comparative Historical Data**

0-1MM	1-10MM	10-50MM	50 & OVER	ALL	Type of Statement	4/1/98-3/31/99	4/1/99-3/31/00	4/1/00-3/31/01	4/1/01-3/31/02	4/1/02-3/31/03
	4	3	1	8	Unqualified	17	16	17	14	8
5	47	10	2	64	Reviewed	62	76	68	69	64
8	20	2	2	32	Compiled	36	41	40	51	32
16	21	2		37	Tax Returns	25	33	25	42	37
5	14	3		22	Other	27	36	39	44	22
36 (4/1-9/30/02)			127 (10/1/02-3/31/03)							
						ALL	ALL	ALL	ALL	ALL
34	106	18	5	163	NUMBER OF STATEMENTS	167	202	189	220	163
%	%	%	%	%	ASSETS	%	%	%	%	%
17.4	10.4	12.6		12.0	Cash & Equivalents	8.4	9.8	9.7	11.0	12.0
22.1	37.6	45.0		35.5	A/R - Progress Billings	37.4	36.1	36.1	34.7	35.5
.1	.5	1.7		.6	A/R - Current Retention	2.3	1.6	1.3	.7	.6
5.9	8.2	6.3		7.5	Inventory	8.1	7.7	9.5	9.5	7.5
.8	3.3	4.4		2.9	Cost & Est. Earnings In Excess of Billings	3.6	4.4	3.8	2.4	2.9
5.1	4.3	4.6		4.9	All Other Current	4.2	3.3	3.6	3.7	4.9
51.4	64.3	74.6		63.4	Total Current	63.9	62.9	64.0	61.9	63.4
41.6	24.6	19.6		27.2	Fixed Assets (net)	27.6	28.5	27.8	27.7	27.2
.0	.1	.0		.1	Joint Ventures & Investments	.5	.7	.7	.4	.1
.0	2.3	2.5		1.8	Intangibles (net)	1.7	1.6	2.0	2.2	1.8
6.9	8.6	3.3		7.5	All Other Non-Current	6.3	6.3	5.4	7.8	7.5
100.0	100.0	100.0		100.0	Total	100.0	100.0	100.0	100.0	100.0
					LIABILITIES					
13.6	10.5	11.9		11.4	Notes Payable - Short Term	12.3	10.8	10.5	11.5	11.4
12.2	17.9	25.0		17.7	A/P - Trade	19.4	18.1	17.5	17.4	17.7
.0	.1	1.9		.3	A/P - Retention	.4	.3	.4	.0	.3
.1	4.2	6.4		3.5	Billings in Excess of Costs & Est. Earnings	3.0	3.2	2.5	2.2	3.5
.0	.3	.3		.3	Income Taxes Payable	.5	.6	.5	.4	.3
6.3	5.4	2.9		5.2	Cur. Mat.-L/T/D	4.3	4.4	4.8	4.9	5.2
11.0	6.1	5.3		7.3	All Other Current	9.6	8.1	7.8	9.0	7.3
43.1	44.5	53.9		45.7	Total Current	49.6	45.4	44.0	45.4	45.7
24.6	14.1	7.1		15.6	Long Term Debt	16.7	16.6	13.0	15.6	15.6
.2	.9	1.1		.8	Deferred Taxes	1.3	1.0	1.1	.8	.8
4.2	4.8	.2		4.1	All Other Non-Current	5.9	3.3	2.6	3.7	4.1
27.9	35.7	37.7		33.9	Net Worth	26.5	33.7	39.3	34.5	33.9
100.0	100.0	100.0		100.0	Total Liabilities & Net Worth	100.0	100.0	100.0	100.0	100.0
					INCOME DATA					
100.0	100.0	100.0		100.0	Contract Revenues	100.0	100.0	100.0	100.0	100.0
47.7	31.2	20.8		33.3	Gross Profit	30.7	29.6	31.9	34.1	33.3
43.4	27.2	18.9		29.5	Operating Expenses	26.8	25.9	26.8	29.1	29.5
4.4	4.0	1.9		3.8	Operating Profit	3.9	3.7	5.1	5.0	3.8
3.0	.7	-.3		1.1	All Other Expenses (net)	.8	.6	.7	.7	1.1
1.4	3.3	2.2		2.8	Profit Before Taxes	3.1	3.1	4.4	4.3	2.8
					RATIOS					
3.4	2.1	1.9		2.1	Current	2.2	2.2	2.2	2.3	2.1
1.4	1.4	1.3		1.4		1.4	1.4	1.4	1.5	1.4
.8	1.1	1.1		1.0		1.0	1.0	1.0	1.0	1.0
13.8	4.6	3.3		4.8	Receivables/Payables	4.5	4.2	4.5	5.7	4.8
(25) 3.3	(101) 2.5	1.5	(149) 2.4			(155) 2.1	(196) 2.4	(183) 2.4	(207) 2.5	(149) 2.4
1.1	1.2	1.1		1.2		1.2	1.3	1.2	1.2	1.2
0 UND	24 15.1	41 8.9	23 16.1		Revenues/Receivables	21 17.8	24 15.1	23 16.1	23 15.9	23 16.1
24 15.1	51 7.2	53 6.8	47 7.8			48 7.6	47 7.8	50 7.3	41 8.9	47 7.8
45 8.1	69 5.3	67 5.5	67 5.5			73 5.0	69 5.3	73 5.0	68 5.4	67 5.5
0 UND	15 25.1	16 23.5	13 28.0		Cost of Revenues/Payables	13 28.1	15 24.5	13 28.0	10 38.0	13 28.0
6 56.9	28 12.9	36 10.0	27 13.4			27 13.5	27 13.7	29 12.4	23 15.7	27 13.4
39 9.3	43 8.4	63 5.7	45 8.2			52 7.0	45 8.1	48 7.7	44 8.3	45 8.2
4.6	7.2	9.9		7.2	Revenues/Working Capital	8.5	7.8	7.9	6.8	7.2
29.7	16.2	16.4		17.5		20.3	20.2	14.5	17.1	17.5
-35.1	101.6	55.4		232.9		-947.8	384.1	173.2	847.6	232.9
7.3	11.1	24.6		11.1	EBIT/Interest	13.2	10.2	11.1	12.0	11.1
(28) 2.4	(98) 4.0	(15) 5.4	(146) 3.5			(146) 3.7	(181) 4.0	(172) 3.6	(199) 4.5	(146) 3.5
-2.1	1.3	-2.8		1.1		1.0	1.5	1.5	1.7	1.1
	7.2			7.6	Net Profit + Depr., Dep., Amort./Cur. Mat. L /T/D	6.1	4.7	5.5	5.5	7.6
	(32) 2.9		(46) 2.6			(46) 2.2	(48) 2.4	(50) 3.4	(52) 3.0	(46) 2.6
	1.4			1.2		.9	1.2	1.7	1.1	1.2
.4	.2	.1		.2	Fixed/Worth	.2	.3	.3	.3	.2
1.0	.6	.5		.7		.8	.7	.7	.8	.7
NM	1.5	1.0		1.6		1.8	2.0	1.6	1.7	1.6
.5	.7	1.1		.7	Debt/Worth	.9	.9	.7	.7	.7
1.8	1.7	1.8		1.8		2.3	2.0	1.8	1.7	1.8
NM	5.4	2.9		5.7		5.6	5.1	4.1	5.9	5.7
50.9	56.2	35.0		53.4	% Profit Before Taxes/Tangible Net Worth	54.5	52.6	46.5	61.0	53.4
(26) 16.9	(97) 21.5	(17) 22.0	(145) 21.1			(149) 29.5	(178) 23.5	(179) 24.7	(193) 24.6	(145) 21.1
-6.2	2.0	6.7		2.0		6.1	8.5	6.3	7.4	2.0
24.1	18.0	19.0		19.3	% Profit Before Taxes/Total Assets	18.4	17.3	17.4	22.9	19.3
5.8	7.1	6.3		6.2		8.3	7.1	8.2	8.3	6.2
-6.0	.4	-.2		.0		.4	1.5	2.0	1.6	.0
1.4	.6	.3		.6	% Depr., Dep., Amort./Revenues	.7	1.0	.8	.8	.6
(30) 4.1	(88) 1.8	.9	(137) 1.9			(142) 1.8	(178) 1.9	(165) 1.8	(193) 1.9	(137) 1.9
7.4	3.5	2.0		4.1		3.1	3.3	3.4	3.4	4.1
7.5	2.5	.9		2.5	% Officers', Directors', Owners' Comp/Revenues	2.7	2.6	2.7	2.9	2.5
(25) 11.7	(72) 4.6	(11) 1.8	(110) 5.5			(92) 4.7	(120) 4.7	(99) 4.4	(120) 5.1	(110) 5.5
14.0	7.5	3.7		10.3		7.2	7.7	7.8	8.5	10.3
21060M	384080M	368806M	15110558M	15884504M	Contract Revenues ($)	12861978M	12117672M	9681453M	8120118M	15884504M
11299M	143090M	117932M	5894647M	6166968M	Total Assets ($)	3158954M	3941144M	2867026M	3624007M	6166968M

M = $ thousand   MM = $ million
See Pages 11 through 18 for Explanation of Ratios and Data

CONSTRUCTION
FINANCIAL MANAGEMENT
ASSOCIATION DATA

Interpretation of the
Construction Financial Management Association (CFMA) Data

CFMA's data should only be regarded as general information. It cannot be used to establish industry norms for a number of reasons, including the following:

(1) The financial statements used in the composite are not selected by any random or statistically reliable method. CFMA members voluntarily submitted financial data pertaining to themselves. Note that contractors' statements have no upper asset/sales limit.

(2) Many companies provide varied services; CFMA includes a contractor in a classification if at least one-half (1/2) of its annual contract revenue was completed within that classification.

(3) Some of the NAIC/SIC group samples may be rather small in relation to the total number of firms in a given industry category. A relatively small sample can increase the chances that some of our composites do not fully represent an industry group.

(4) There is the chance that an extreme statement can be present in a sample, causing a disproportionate influence on the industry composite. This is particularly true in a relatively small sample.

(5) Companies within the same industry may differ in their method of operations, which in turn can directly influence their financial statements. Since such differences affect financial data included in our sample, our composite calculations could be significantly affected.

(6) Other considerations that can result in variation among different companies engaged in the same general line of business are: different labor markets; geographical location; different accounting methods; quality of service rendered; sources and methods of financing; and terms of sale.

The use of CFMA's data may be helpful when considered with other methods of financial analysis. Nevertheless, RMA and CFMA do not recommend the use of CFMA's data to establish norms or parameters for a given industry or grouping, or the industry as a whole. Although CFMA believes that its data is accurate and representative within the confines of the aforementioned reasons, RMA and CFMA specifically make no representations regarding the accuracy of representativeness of the figures printed in this supplement of the RMA Annual Statement Studies.

ABOUT THE CONSTRUCTION FINANCIAL MANAGEMENT ASSOCIATION (CFMA) DATA
Web site: www.cfma.org

Once again, we are delighted to include excerpts from *CFMA's 2003 Construction Industry Annual Financial Survey.* CFMA is **The Source and Resource for Construction Financial Professionals** and has more than 7,000 members in 86 chapters throughout the U.S.

The data presented are based on a survey sent to approximately 4,100 general members employed within U.S. construction firms, plus a small number of other U.S. contractors. Of the 794 total survey participants, 63% or 503 companies participated in the CFMA survey in 2002 and 73% or 577 companies provided detailed financial statement information. The data submitted were compiled and analyzed by Moss Adams LLP in cooperation with CFMA. Almost all companies (87%) included in the survey recognize contract revenue and profit in accordance with the percentage of completion method of accounting. Likewise, our *Statement Studies* contractor data primarily reflects only this method of accounting. It is entirely possible that some of the same contractor companies are included in both the CFMA and *Statement Studies* data presentations. The inclusion of the CFMA data has not affected our *Statement Studies* contractor composite data.

Fiscal year-end closing dates reflected in the CFMA survey data range from 3/31/02 through 3/31/03. The CFMA data are most comparable to the RMA contractor data from 4/1/02 through 3/31/03 appearing in this edition.

The survey respondents were classified into three categories of construction based on the type of work performed. Classification was based on the level of contract volume reported for various NAIC/SIC codes. A contractor was included in a classification if at least one half of its annual contract revenue was attributable to that classification. CFMA categorized certain NAIC/SIC codes together. The classifications and NAIC/SIC codes included in each are as follows:

NAIC Codes		SIC Codes	
INDUSTRIAL AND NONRESIDENTIAL CONTRACTORS:			
23332	Commercial and Institutional Building Construction *(incl. Warehouse, Hotel and Motel Construction)*	1541	General Contractors-Industrial Buildings and Warehouses
23331	Manufacturing and Light Industrial Building Construction *(Except Warehouse Construction)*	1542	General Contractors-Nonresidential Buildings *(Other than Industrial Buildings and Warehouses)*
HEAVY AND HIGHWAY CONTRACTORS:			
23411	Highway and Street Construction	1611	Highway and Street Construction, *(Except Elevated Highways)*
23412	Bridge and Tunnel Construction		
23491	Water, Sewer and Pipeline Construction	1622	Bridge, Tunnel, and Elevated Highway Construction
		1623	Water, Sewer, Pipeline, and Communications, Power Line Construction
23492	Power and Communication Transmission Line Construction		
23493	Industrial Non-building Structure Construction		
23499	All Other Heavy Construction	1629	Heavy Construction, NEC
SPECIALTY TRADES CONTRACTORS:			
23511	Plumbing, Heating and Air-Conditioning	1711	Plumbing, Heating, and Air-Conditioning Contractors
23521	Painting and Wall Covering Contractors	1721	Painting and Paper Hanging
23531	Electrical Contractors	1731	Electrical Work
23541	Masonry and Stone Contractors	1741	Masonry, Stone Setting and Other Stone Work
23542	Drywall, Plastering, Acoustical and Insulation Contractors	1742	Plastering, Drywall, Acoustical and Insulation Work
23543	Tile, Marble, Terrazzo and Mosaic Contractors	1743	Terrazzo, Tile, Marble, and Mosaic Work Contractors
23551	Carpentry Contractors	1751	Carpentry Work
23552	Floor Laying and Other Floor Contractors	1752	Floor Laying and Other Floor Work, NEC
23561	Roofing, Siding, and Sheet Metal Contractors	1761	Roofing, Siding, and Sheet Metal Work
23571	Concrete Contractors	1771	Concrete Work Stucco Construction
23581	Water Well Drilling Contractors	1781	Water Well Drilling
23591	Structural Steel Erection Contractors	1791	Structural Steel Erection
23592	Glass and Glazing Contractors	1793	Glass and Glazing Work
23593	Excavation Contractors	1794	Excavation Work
23594	Wrecking and Demolition Contractors	1795	Wrecking and Demolition Work
23595	Building Equipment and Other Machinery Installation Contractors	1796	Installation or Erection of Building Equipment
23599	All Other Special Trade Contractors	1799	Special Trade Contractors, NEC
56162	Security Systems Services		
56291	Environmental Remediation Services		

The CFMA financial data includes balance sheets, statements of earnings, and financial ratios. The balance sheets and statements of earning represent a weighted average of all companies included in each classification. Percentages are presented for each dollar amount in the financial statements. Due to rounding, the totals may not agree to the sum of various accounts. Such variations are few and insignificant.

The financial ratios are calculated from the composite balance sheets and statements of earning data. They are not averages of ratios for all companies included in the classification.

If you wish to purchase **CFMA's 2003 Construction Industry Annual Financial Survey** or have questions regarding the data, contact Brian Summers, Associate Director; Construction Financial Management Association, 29 Emmons Drive #F50, Princeton, NJ 08540; Phone 609-452-8000; Fax 609-452-0474; E-mail bsummers@cfma.org.

All Companies
Composite

Balance Sheet

	2003 Participants		2002 Participants	
Current Assets:	Amount	Percent	Amount	Percent
Cash and cash equivalents	$ 4,195,264	14.7 %	$ 3,649,119	12.5 %
Marketable securities & short-term investments	1,696,467	5.9	1,241,498	4.3
Receivables:				
Contract receivables currently due	10,948,304	38.4	10,647,367	36.6
Retainages on contracts	3,317,786	11.6	3,112,677	10.7
Unbilled work	169,837	0.6	375,277	1.3
Other receivables	454,299	1.6	386,562	1.3
Less allowance for doubtful accounts	(67,701)	(0.2)	(69,581)	(0.2)
Total receivables, net:	14,822,526	52.0	14,452,302	49.7
Inventories	341,077	1.2	32,552	0.1
Costs and recognized earnings in excess of billings on uncompleted contracts	1,226,244	4.3	1,367,957	4.7
Investments in and advances to construction joint ventures	169,692	0.6	407,252	1.4
Income taxes:				
Current/refundable	38,773	0.1	47,684	0.2
Deferred	100,833	0.4	147,558	0.5
Other current assets	641,791	2.2	1,596,639	5.5
Total current assets	23,232,667	81.4	23,232,561	79.8
Property, plant and equipment	8,308,797	29.1	8,167,403	28.1
Less accumulated depreciation	(4,976,227)	(17.4)	(4,651,087)	(16.0)
Property, plant and equipment, net	3,332,570	11.7	3,516,316	12.1
Noncurrent assets:				
Long-term investments	349,784	1.2	67,991	0.2
Deferred income taxes	103,366	0.4	98,721	0.3
Other assets	1,512,003	5.3	2,190,565	7.5
Total noncurrent assets	1,965,152	6.9	2,357,277	8.1
Total assets	$ 28,530,389	100.0 %	$ 29,106,154	100.0 %

	2003 Participants		2002 Participants	
Current liabilities:	Amount	Percent	Amount	Percent
Current maturity on long-term debt	$ 381,728	1.3 %	$ 338,945	1.2 %
Notes payable and lines of credit	428,737	1.5	702,664	2.4
Accounts payable:				
Trade, including currently due to subcontractors	8,159,017	28.6	7,765,123	26.7
Subcontracts retainages	2,633,816	9.2	2,411,910	8.3
Other	379,761	1.3	166,528	0.6
Total accounts payable	11,172,593	39.2	10,343,560	35.5
Accrued expenses	1,640,998	5.8	1,596,218	5.5
Billings in excess of costs and recognized earnings on uncompleted contracts	3,441,742	12.1	3,349,830	11.5
Income taxes:				
Current	50,230	0.2	76,019	0.3
Deferred	26,416	0.1	24,623	0.1
Other current liabilities	228,642	0.8	803,752	2.8
Total current liabilities	17,371,086	60.9	17,235,611	59.2
Noncurrent liabilities				
Long-term debt, excluding current maturities	2,147,492	7.5	2,203,127	7.6
Deferred income taxes	92,696	0.3	78,036	0.3
Other	267,088	0.9	738,946	2.5
Total liabilities	19,878,363	69.7	20,279,935	69.7
Minority interests	52,319	0.2	24,215	0.1
Net worth:				
Common stock, par value	249,248	0.9	261,238	0.9
Preferred stock, stated value	51,364	0.2	245,455	0.8
Additional paid-in capital	1,710,667	6.0	2,316,797	8.0
Retained earnings	6,301,571	22.1	6,110,659	21.0
Treasury stock	(308,553)	(1.1)	(306,205)	(1.1)
Excess value of marketable securities	(2,350)	(0.0)	(192,324)	(0.7)
Other equity	597,761	2.1	390,601	1.3
Total net worth	8,599,707	30.1	8,826,220	30.3
Total liabilities and net worth	$ 28,530,389	100.0 %	$ 29,106,155	100.0 %

All Companies

Composite

Statement of Earnings

	2003 Participants		2002 Participants	
	Amount	Percent	Amount	Percent
Contract revenue	$ 83,780,270	98.3 %	$ 82,388,449	98.2 %
Other revenue	1,457,696	1.7	1,521,069	1.8
Total Revenue	85,237,965	100.0	83,909,519	100.0
Contract cost	(76,869,320)	(90.2)	(75,376,650)	(89.8)
Other cost	(1,094,886)	(1.3)	(811,272)	(1.0)
Total cost	(77,964,206)	(91.5)	(76,187,922)	(90.8)
Gross Profit	7,273,759	8.5	7,721,596	9.2
Selling, general & adminstrative expenses:				
Payroll	(2,726,107)	(3.2)	(2,472,939)	(2.9)
Professional fees	(161,957)	(0.2)	(173,871)	(0.2)
Sales & marketing costs	(192,417)	(0.2)	(208,859)	(0.2)
Technology costs	(138,340)	(0.2)	(122,952)	(0.1)
Administrative bonuses	(425,232)	(0.5)	(427,221)	(0.5)
Other	(1,840,797)	(2.2)	(1,935,062)	(2.3)
Total SG&A expenses	(5,484,849)	(6.4)	(5,340,904)	(6.4)
Income from operations	1,788,910	2.1	2,380,693	2.8
Interest income	142,767	0.2	199,484	0.2
Interest expense	(156,372)	(0.2)	(198,333)	(0.2)
Other income / (expense), net	(38,740)	(0.0)	86,625	0.1
Net earnings / (loss) before income taxes	1,736,565	2.0	2,468,470	2.9
Income tax (expense) / benefit	(272,990)	(0.3)	(292,516)	(0.3)
Net earnings	$ 1,463,575	1.7	$ 2,175,954	2.6

Number of Participants

	Number
2003	575
2002	546

Financial Ratios

	2003 Participants		2002 Participants
	Average	Median	Average
Liquidity Ratios			
Current Ratio	1.3	1.4	1.3
Quick Ratio	1.2	1.2	1.1
Days of Cash	17.7	12.2	15.7
Working Capital Turnover	14.5	13.4	14.0
Profitability Ratios			
Return on Assets	5.1	4.4 %	7.5 %
Return on Equity	17.0	14.4 %	24.7 %
Times Interest Earned	12.1	6.3	13.4
Leverage Ratios			
Debt to Equity	2.3	2.0	2.3
Revenue to Equity	9.9	9.6	9.5
Asset Turnover	3.0	3.2	2.9
Fixed Asset Ratio	38.8	29.0 %	39.8 %
Equity to SG&A Expense	1.6	1.2	1.7
Underbillings to Equity	16.2	11.6 %	19.8 %
Backlog to Equity	5.6	3.4	6.5
Efficiency Ratios			
Backlog to Working Capital	8.2	4.9	9.5
Months in Backlog	6.8	4.8	8.2
Days in Accounts Receivable	47.9	49.7	47.0
Days in Inventory	1.6	0.0	1.5
Days in Accounts Payable	39.4	32.9	37.5
Operating Cycle	27.7	32.3	26.7

Industrial & Nonresidential Contractors
Composite

Balance Sheet

	2003 Participants		2002 Participants	
	Amount	Percent	Amount	Percent
Current Assets:				
Cash and cash equivalents	$ 6,340,661	18.1 %	$ 5,203,779	15.3 %
Marketable securities & short-term investments	3,320,405	9.5	2,441,134	7.2
Receivables:				
Contract receivables currently due	14,166,796	40.4	14,324,015	42.2
Retainages on contracts	5,047,057	14.4	4,775,322	14.1
Unbilled work	254,958	0.7	711,045	2.1
Other receivables	303,281	0.9	471,169	1.4
Less allowance for doubtful accounts	(39,884)	(0.1)	(39,939)	(0.1)
Total receivables, net:	19,732,206	56.3	20,241,611	59.6
Inventories	152,009	0.4	136,675	0.4
Costs and recognized earnings in excess of billings on uncompleted contracts	1,076,475	3.1	1,398,149	4.1
Investments in and advances to construction joint ventures	123,413	0.4	524,699	1.5
Income taxes:				
Current/refundable	51,930	0.1	62,019	0.2
Deferred	114,336	0.3	195,373	0.6
Other current assets	673,115	1.9	871,358	2.6
Total current assets	31,584,550	90.1	31,074,797	91.5
Property, plant and equipment	4,552,810	13.0	4,549,906	13.4
Less accumulated depreciation	(2,607,852)	(7.4)	(2,672,696)	(7.9)
Property, plant and equipment, net	1,944,958	5.5	1,877,210	5.5
Noncurrent assets:				
Long-term investments	565,716	1.6	68,447	0.2
Deferred income taxes	51,451	0.1	137,014	0.4
Other assets	919,091	2.6	795,093	2.3
Total noncurrent assets	1,536,258	4.4	1,000,554	2.9
Total assets	$ 35,065,766	100.0 %	$ 33,952,561	100.0 %

	2003 Participants		2002 Participants	
	Amount	Percent	Amount	Percent
Current liabilities:				
Current maturity on long-term debt	$ 157,171	0.4 %	$ 181,700	0.5 %
Notes payable and lines of credit	241,176	0.7	225,668	0.7
Accounts payable:				
Trade, including currently due to subcontractors	13,773,907	39.3	13,085,639	38.5
Subcontracts retainages	5,348,142	15.3	4,770,830	14.1
Other	331,129	0.9	229,011	0.7
Total accounts payable	19,453,178	55.5	18,085,481	53.3
Accrued expenses	1,406,905	4.0	1,622,723	4.8
Billings in excess of costs and recognized earnings on uncompleted contracts	4,498,450	12.8	4,327,196	12.7
Income taxes:				
Current	42,896	0.1	91,351	0.3
Deferred	10,276	0.0	15,006	0.0
Other current liabilities	214,579	0.6	795,119	2.3
Total current liabilities	26,024,632	74.2	25,344,244	74.6
Noncurrent liabilities:				
Long-term debt, excluding current maturities	1,009,347	2.9	618,222	1.8
Deferred income taxes	36,047	0.1	16,727	0.0
Other	178,114	0.5	498,988	1.5
Total liabilities	27,248,139	77.7	26,529,986	78.1
Minority interests	87,853	0.3	51,805	0.2
Net worth:				
Common stock, par value	278,706	0.8	410,722	1.2
Preferred stock, stated value	66,873	0.2	161,603	0.5
Additional paid-in capital	807,330	2.3	1,140,568	3.4
Retained earnings	6,161,714	17.6	5,476,485	16.1
Treasury stock	(194,700)	(0.6)	(229,307)	(0.7)
Excess value of marketable securities	(11,824)	(0.0)	(32,360)	(0.1)
Other equity	621,674	1.8	494,865	1.5
Total net worth	7,729,774	22.0	7,422,575	21.9
Total liabilities and net worth	$ 35,065,766	100.0 %	$ 33,952,561	100.0 %

Industrial & Nonresidential Contractors

Composite

Statement of Earnings

	2003 Participants		2002 Participants	
	Amount	Percent	Amount	Percent
Contract revenue	$ 118,497,807	99.7 %	$ 117,896,663	98.6 %
Other revenue	415,660	0.3	1,698,060	1.4
Total Revenue	118,913,467	100.0	119,594,723	100.0
Contract cost	(111,882,899)	(94.1)	(112,071,842)	(93.7)
Other cost	(241,639)	(0.2)	(480,980)	(0.4)
Total cost	(112,124,538)	(94.3)	(112,552,822)	(94.1)
Gross Profit	6,788,929	5.7	7,041,901	5.9
Selling, general & adminstrative expenses:				
Payroll	(2,452,779)	(2.1)	(2,453,741)	(2.1)
Professional fees	(150,337)	(0.1)	(177,334)	(0.1)
Sales & marketing costs	(230,437)	(0.2)	(208,551)	(0.2)
Technology costs	(147,531)	(0.1)	(121,213)	(0.1)
Administrative bonuses	(439,973)	(0.4)	(484,083)	(0.4)
Other	(1,710,143)	(1.4)	(1,878,183)	(1.6)
Total SG&A expenses	(5,131,199)	(4.3)	(5,323,105)	(4.5)
Income from operations	1,657,730	1.4	1,718,796	1.4
Interest income	228,460	0.2	321,357	0.3
Interest expense	(75,885)	(0.1)	(52,267)	(0.0)
Other income / (expense), net	70,668	0.1	202,773	0.2
Net earnings / (loss) before income taxes	1,880,973	1.6	2,190,660	1.8
Income tax (expense) / benefit	(256,027)	(0.2)	(352,446)	(0.3)
Net earnings	$ 1,624,945	1.4	$ 1,838,214	1.5

Number of Participants

	Number
2003	256
2002	238

Financial Ratios

	2003 Participants		2002 Participants
	Average	Median	Average
Liquidity Ratios			
Current Ratio	1.2	1.3	1.2
Quick Ratio	1.1	1.2	1.1
Days of Cash	19.2	17.6	15.7
Working Capital Turnover	21.4	18.1	20.9
Profitability Ratios			
Return on Assets	4.6	4.0 %	5.4 %
Return on Equity	21.0	17.0 %	24.8 %
Times Interest Earned	25.8	11.8	42.9
Leverage Ratios			
Debt to Equity	3.5	2.9	3.6
Revenue to Equity	15.4	14.6	16.1
Asset Turnover	3.4	3.7	3.5
Fixed Asset Ratio	25.2	22.0 %	25.3 %
Equity to SG&A Expense	1.5	1.2	1.4
Underbillings to Equity	17.2	10.7 %	28.4 %
Backlog to Equity	3.4	6.6	11.9
Efficiency Ratios			
Backlog to Working Capital	4.8	8.6	15.4
Months in Backlog	2.7	5.8	8.9
Days in Accounts Receivable	43.7	43.2	44.4
Days in Inventory	0.5	0.0	0.4
Days in Accounts Payable	45.3	40.0	42.6
Operating Cycle	18.1	22.8	17.9

Heavy & Highway Contractors
Composite

Balance Sheet

	2003 Participants		2002 Participants	
	Amount	Percent	Amount	Percent
Current Assets:				
Cash and cash equivalents	$ 4,161,121	14.0 %	$ 4,921,301	14.8 %
Marketable securities & short-term investments	518,660	1.7	593,351	1.8
Receivables:				
Contract receivables currently due	7,541,852	25.4	8,195,953	24.7
Retainages on contracts	1,900,855	6.4	2,166,257	6.5
Unbilled work	124,085	0.4	309,768	0.9
Other receivables	773,509	2.6	706,202	2.1
Less allowance for doubtful accounts	(60,898)	(0.2)	(51,557)	(0.2)
Total receivables, net	10,279,405	34.6	11,326,622	34.1
Inventories	699,170	2.4	802,907	2.4
Costs and recognized earnings in excess of billings on uncompleted contracts	1,082,610	3.6	1,619,453	4.9
Investments in and advances to construction joint ventures	457,252	1.5	762,803	2.3
Income taxes:				
Current/refundable	20,721	0.1	31,388	0.1
Deferred	116,412	0.4	130,008	0.4
Other current assets	894,039	3.0	1,035,362	3.1
Total current assets	18,229,390	61.4	21,223,195	63.8
Property, plant and equipment	21,889,759	73.8	22,470,309	67.6
Less accumulated depreciation	(13,198,956)	(44.5)	(12,805,048)	(38.5)
Property, plant and equipment, net	8,690,802	29.3	9,665,261	29.1
Noncurrent assets:				
Long-term investments	347,481	1.2	88,944	0.3
Deferred income taxes	324,651	1.1	171,591	0.5
Other assets	2,087,726	7.0	2,095,331	6.3
Total noncurrent assets	2,759,857	9.3	2,355,865	7.1
Total assets	$ 29,680,050	100.0 %	$ 33,244,322	100.0 %

	2003 Participants		2002 Participants	
	Amount	Percent	Amount	Percent
Current liabilities:				
Current maturity on long-term debt	$ 1,059,386	3.6 %	$ 890,081	2.7 %
Notes payable and lines of credit	242,391	0.8	542,374	1.6
Accounts payable:				
Trade, including currently due to subcontractors	4,108,098	13.8	4,862,889	14.6
Subcontracts retainages	737,521	2.5	846,167	2.5
Other	200,559	0.7	176,765	0.5
Total accounts payable	5,046,177	17.0	5,885,820	17.7
Accrued expenses	1,837,501	6.2	2,047,789	6.2
Billings in excess of costs and recognized earnings on uncompleted contracts	3,080,050	10.4	3,903,316	11.7
Income taxes:				
Current	185,808	0.6	101,843	0.3
Deferred	60,686	0.2	45,325	0.1
Other current liabilities	217,776	0.7	392,267	1.2
Total current liabilities	11,729,775	39.5	13,808,815	41.5
Noncurrent liabilities				
Long-term debt, excluding current maturities	4,086,380	13.8	4,636,037	13.9
Deferred income taxes	251,135	0.8	271,927	0.8
Other	753,345	2.5	775,975	2.3
Total liabilities	16,820,636	56.7	19,493,231	58.6
Minority interests	1,594	0.0	476	0.0
Net worth:				
Common stock, par value	216,812	0.7	224,252	0.7
Preferred stock, stated value	21,791	0.1	183,257	0.6
Additional paid-in capital	2,607,183	8.8	2,161,109	6.5
Retained earnings	9,729,729	32.8	11,270,221	33.9
Treasury stock	(445,208)	(1.5)	(640,186)	(1.9)
Excess value of marketable securities	(7,747)	(0.0)	(22,822)	(0.1)
Other equity	735,259	2.5	575,259	1.7
Total net worth	12,857,819	43.3	13,751,091	41.4
Total liabilities and net worth	$ 29,680,050	100.0 %	$ 33,244,322	100.0 %

Heavy & Highway Contractors
Composite

Statement of Earnings

	2003 Participants		2002 Participants	
	Amount	Percent	Amount	Percent
Contract revenue	$ 66,386,501	95.5 %	$ 74,629,131	97.3 %
Other revenue	3,153,627	4.5	2,108,002	2.7
Total Revenue	69,540,128	100.0	76,737,133	100.0
Contract cost	(59,253,894)	(85.2)	(64,953,654)	(84.6)
Other cost	(2,682,179)	(3.9)	(1,493,818)	(1.9)
Total cost	(61,936,072)	(89.1)	(66,447,471)	(86.6)
Gross Profit	7,604,056	10.9	10,289,661	13.4
Selling, general & administrative expenses:				
Payroll	(2,399,420)	(3.5)	(2,437,441)	(3.2)
Professional fees	(164,045)	(0.2)	(208,568)	(0.3)
Sales & marketing costs	(67,251)	(0.1)	(141,244)	(0.2)
Technology costs	(109,756)	(0.2)	(141,482)	(0.2)
Administrative bonuses	(378,171)	(0.5)	(373,557)	(0.5)
Other	(1,711,825)	(2.5)	(1,479,709)	(1.9)
Total SG&A expenses	(4,830,467)	(6.9)	(4,782,000)	(6.2)
Income from operations	2,773,589	4.0	5,507,662	7.2
Interest income	122,920	0.2	201,831	0.3
Interest expense	(263,474)	(0.4)	(397,556)	(0.5)
Other income / (expense), net	93,053	0.1	88,939	0.1
Net earnings / (loss) before income taxes	2,726,089	3.9	5,400,876	7.0
Income tax (expense) / benefit	(505,747)	(0.7)	(305,567)	(0.4)
Net earnings	$ 2,220,342	3.2	$ 5,095,309	6.6

Number of Participants

	Number
2003	123
2002	105

Financial Ratios

	2003 Participants		2002 Participants
	Average	Median	Average
Liquidity Ratios			
Current Ratio	1.6	1.5	1.5
Quick Ratio	1.3	1.3	1.2
Days of Cash	21.5	13.1	23.1
Working Capital Turnover	10.7	10.5	10.3
Profitability Ratios			
Return on Assets	7.5	5.1 %	15.3 %
Return on Equity	17.3	11.7 %	37.1 %
Times Interest Earned	11.3	5.9	14.6
Leverage Ratios			
Debt to Equity	1.3	1.5	1.4
Revenue to Equity	5.4	6.0	5.6
Asset Turnover	2.3	2.4	2.3
Fixed Asset Ratio	67.6	66.1 %	70.3 %
Equity to SG&A Expense	2.7	2.0	2.9
Underbillings to Equity	9.4	8.2 %	14.0 %
Backlog to Equity	4.0	1.8	4.2
Efficiency Ratios			
Backlog to Working Capital	7.9	4.4	7.7
Months in Backlog	8.9	4.5	9.0
Days in Accounts Receivable	42.7	42.9	41.5
Days in Inventory	4.1	0.0	4.4
Days in Accounts Payable	25.0	25.2	27.3
Operating Cycle	43.3	39.8	41.7

Specialty Trade Contractors
Composite

Balance Sheet

	2003 Participants		2002 Participants	
	Amount	Percent	Amount	Percent
Current Assets:				
Cash and cash equivalents	$ 1,447,267	7.2 %	$ 1,103,125	4.9 %
Marketable securities & short-term investments	312,857	1.6	152,763	0.7
Receivables:				
Contract receivables currently due	9,461,199	47.1	8,095,287	36.0
Retainages on contracts	2,067,227	10.3	1,750,309	7.8
Unbilled work	65,841	0.3	10,128	0.0
Other receivables	437,063	2.2	118,045	0.5
Less allowance for doubtful accounts	(117,974)	(0.6)	(123,778)	(0.5)
Total receivables, net	11,913,357	59.4	9,849,991	43.8
Inventories	327,110	1.6	292,540	1.3
Costs and recognized earnings in excess of billings on uncompleted contracts	1,587,963	7.9	1,370,220	6.1
Investments in and advances to construction joint ventures	54,397	0.3	31,362	0.1
Income taxes:				
Current/refundable	31,757	0.2	20,807	0.1
Deferred	79,970	0.4	106,349	0.5
Other current assets	460,935	2.3	3,272,052	14.5
Total current assets	16,215,613	80.8	16,199,209	72.0
Property, plant and equipment	4,609,720	23.0	4,351,925	19.3
Less accumulated depreciation	(2,891,416)	(14.4)	(2,674,289)	(11.9)
Property, plant and equipment, net	1,718,304	8.6	1,677,636	7.5
Noncurrent assets:				
Long-term investments	75,766	0.4	41,709	0.2
Deferred income taxes	32,686	0.2	9,987	0.0
Other assets	2,025,992	10.1	4,579,889	20.3
Total noncurrent assets	2,134,445	10.6	4,631,585	20.6
Total assets	$ 20,068,362	100.0 %	$ 22,508,430	100.0 %

	2003 Participants		2002 Participants	
	Amount	Percent	Amount	Percent
Current liabilities:				
Current maturity on long-term debt	$ 241,590	1.2 %	$ 214,359	1.0 %
Notes payable and lines of credit	790,683	3.9	1,581,233	7.0
Accounts payable:				
Trade, including currently due to subcontractors	3,428,748	17.1	3,011,071	13.4
Subcontracts retainages	247,834	1.2	384,639	1.7
Other	599,510	3.0	91,102	0.4
Total accounts payable	4,276,092	21.3	3,486,813	15.5
Accrued expenses	1,933,589	9.6	1,415,991	6.3
Billings in excess of costs and recognized earnings on uncompleted contracts	2,449,146	12.2	2,069,733	9.2
Income taxes:				
Current	(31,762)	(0.2)	49,016	0.2
Deferred	25,276	0.1	16,874	0.1
Other current liabilities	277,857	1.4	1,256,831	5.6
Total current liabilities	9,962,472	49.6	10,090,850	44.8
Noncurrent liabilities:				
Long-term debt, excluding current maturities	2,540,856	12.7	2,951,514	13.1
Deferred income taxes	53,732	0.3	47,955	0.2
Other	74,974	0.4	524,799	2.3
Total liabilities	12,632,034	62.9	13,620,221	60.5
Minority interests	17,190	0.1	5,102	0.0
Net worth:				
Common stock, par value	212,501	1.1	82,108	0.4
Preferred stock, stated value	54,382	0.3	79,266	0.4
Additional paid-in capital	2,491,870	12.4	4,265,414	19.0
Retained earnings	4,526,655	22.6	4,505,554	20.0
Treasury stock	(398,316)	(2.0)	(260,769)	(1.2)
Excess value of marketable securities	14,863	0.1	10,413	0.0
Other equity	517,181	2.6	206,224	0.9
Total net worth	7,419,137	37.0	8,888,210	39.5
Total liabilities and net worth	$ 20,068,362	100.0 %	$ 22,508,430	100.0 %

Specialty Trade Contractors

Statement of Earnings

	2003 Participants Amount	Percent	2002 Participants Amount	Percent
Contract revenue	$ 51,508,539	97.5 %	$ 46,416,316	97.5 %
Other revenue	1,326,467	2.5	1,198,944	2.5
Total Revenue	52,835,006	100.0	47,615,260	100.0
Contract cost	(43,951,220)	(83.2)	(39,036,583)	(82.0)
Other cost	(842,768)	(1.6)	(952,285)	(2.0)
Total cost	(44,793,988)	(84.8)	(39,988,868)	(84.0)
Gross Profit	8,041,018	15.2	7,626,392	16.0
Selling, general & adminstrative expenses:				
Payroll	(3,441,205)	(6.5)	(2,652,793)	(5.6)
Professional fees	(180,477)	(0.3)	(159,090)	(0.3)
Sales & marketing costs	(219,490)	(0.4)	(221,411)	(0.5)
Technology costs	(150,760)	(0.3)	(123,550)	(0.3)
Administrative bonuses	(462,964)	(0.9)	(443,960)	(0.9)
Other	(2,218,107)	(4.2)	(2,375,925)	(5.0)
Total SG&A expenses	(6,673,003)	(12.6)	(5,976,729)	(12.6)
Income from operations	1,368,014	2.6	1,649,663	3.5
Interest income	42,716	0.1	56,481	0.1
Interest expense	(197,239)	(0.4)	(234,446)	(0.5)
Other income / (expense), net	(292,782)	(0.6)	(65,447)	(0.1)
Net earnings / (loss) before income taxes	920,709	1.7	1,406,251	3.0
Income tax (expense) / benefit	(151,135)	(0.3)	(229,292)	(0.5)
Net earnings	$ 769,574	1.5	$ 1,176,959	2.5

Number of Participants	Number
2003	179
2002	165

Financial Ratios

	2003 Participants Average	Median	2002 Participants Average
Liquidity Ratios			
Current Ratio	1.6	1.6	1.6
Quick Ratio	1.4	1.3	1.1
Days of Cash	9.9	4.5	8.3
Working Capital Turnover	8.4	9.3	7.8
Profitability Ratios			
Return on Assets	3.8	4.5 %	5.2 %
Return on Equity	10.4	13.9 %	13.2 %
Times Interest Earned	5.7	4.5	7.0
Leverage Ratios			
Debt to Equity	1.7	1.5	1.5
Revenue to Equity	7.1	7.5	5.4
Asset Turnover	2.6	3.0	2.1
Fixed Asset Ratio	23.2	27.8 %	18.9 %
Equity to SG&A Expense	1.1	0.9	1.5
Underbillings to Equity	22.3	17.4 %	15.5 %
Backlog to Equity	8.2	2.2	2.3
Efficiency Ratios			
Backlog to Working Capital	9.7	2.8	3.4
Months in Backlog	13.8	3.8	5.2
Days in Accounts Receivable	66.6	61.6	61.2
Days in Inventory	2.6	1.8	2.6
Days in Accounts Payable	32.4	26.0	27.9
Operating Cycle	46.8	43.5	44.2

CFMA Comparative Financial Data

Balance Sheet
Most Recent Year End

	All Companies		Industrial & Nonresidential		Heavy & Highway		Specialty Trades	
	Amount	Percent	Amount	Percent	Amount	Percent	Amount	Percent
Current Assets:								
Cash and cash equivalents	$ 4,195,264	14.7 %	$ 6,340,661	18.1 %	$ 4,161,121	14.0 %	$ 1,447,267	7.2 %
Marketable securities & short-term investments	1,696,467	5.9	3,320,405	9.5	518,660	1.7	312,857	1.6
Receivables:								
Contract receivables currently due	10,948,304	38.4	14,166,796	40.4	7,541,852	25.4	9,461,199	47.1
Retainages on contracts	3,317,786	11.6	5,047,057	14.4	1,900,855	6.4	2,067,227	10.3
Unbilled work	169,837	0.6	254,958	0.7	124,085	0.4	65,841	0.3
Other receivables	454,299	1.6	303,281	0.9	773,509	2.6	437,063	2.2
Less allowance for doubtful accounts	(67,701)	(0.2)	(39,884)	(0.1)	(60,898)	(0.2)	(117,974)	(0.6)
Total receivables, net:	14,822,526	52.0	19,732,206	56.3	10,279,405	34.6	11,913,357	59.4
Inventories	341,077	1.2	152,009	0.4	699,170	2.4	327,110	1.6
Costs and recognized earnings in excess of billings on uncompleted contracts	1,226,244	4.3	1,076,475	3.1	1,082,610	3.6	1,587,963	7.9
Investments in and advances to construction joint ventures	169,692	0.6	123,413	0.4	457,252	1.5	54,397	0.3
Income taxes:								
Current/refundable	38,773	0.1	51,930	0.1	20,721	0.1	31,757	0.2
Deferred	100,833	0.4	114,336	0.3	116,412	0.4	79,970	0.4
Other current assets	641,791	2.2	673,115	1.9	894,039	3.0	460,935	2.3
Total current assets	23,232,667	81.4	31,584,550	90.1	18,229,390	61.4	16,215,613	80.8
Property, plant and equipment	8,308,797	29.1	4,552,810	13.0	21,889,759	73.8	4,609,720	23.0
Less accumulated depreciation	(4,976,227)	(17.4)	(2,607,852)	(7.4)	(13,198,956)	(44.5)	(2,891,416)	(14.4)
Property, plant and equipment, net	3,332,570	11.7	1,944,958	5.5	8,690,802	29.3	1,718,304	8.6
Noncurrent assets:								
Long-term investments	349,784	1.2	565,716	1.6	347,481	1.2	75,766	0.4
Deferred income taxes	103,366	0.4	51,451	0.1	324,651	1.1	32,686	0.2
Other assets	1,512,003	5.3	919,091	2.6	2,087,726	7.0	2,025,992	10.1
Total noncurrent assets	1,965,152	6.9	1,536,258	4.4	2,759,857	9.3	2,134,445	10.6
Total assets	$ 28,530,389	100.0 %	$ 35,065,766	100.0 %	$ 29,680,050	100.0 %	$ 20,068,362	100.0 %

CFMA Comparative Financial Data

	All Companies		Industrial & Nonresidential		Heavy & Highway		Specialty Trades	
	Amount	Percent	Amount	Percent	Amount	Percent	Amount	Percent
Current liabilities:								
Current maturity on long-term debt	$ 381,728	1.3 %	$ 157,171	0.4 %	$ 1,059,386	3.6 %	$ 241,590	1.2 %
Notes payable and lines of credit	428,737	1.5	241,176	0.7	242,391	0.8	790,683	3.9
Accounts payable:								
Trade, including currently due to subcontractors	8,159,017	28.6	13,773,907	39.3	4,108,098	13.8	3,428,748	17.1
Subcontracts retainages	2,633,816	9.2	5,348,142	15.3	737,521	2.5	247,834	1.2
Other	379,761	1.3	331,129	0.9	200,559	0.7	599,510	3.0
Total accounts payable	11,172,593	39.2	19,453,178	55.5	5,046,177	17.0	4,276,092	21.3
Accrued expenses	1,640,998	5.8	1,406,905	4.0	1,837,501	6.2	1,933,589	9.6
Billings in excess of costs and recognized earnings on uncompleted contracts	3,441,742	12.1	4,498,450	12.8	3,080,050	10.4	2,449,146	12.2
Income taxes:								
Current	50,230	0.2	42,896	0.1	185,808	0.6	(31,762)	(0.2)
Deferred	26,416	0.1	10,276	0.0	60,686	0.2	25,276	0.1
Other current liabilities	228,642	0.8	214,579	0.6	217,776	0.7	277,857	1.4
Total current liabilities	17,371,086	60.9	26,024,632	74.2	11,729,775	39.5	9,962,472	49.6
Noncurrent liabilities								
Long-term debt, excluding current maturities	2,147,492	7.5	1,009,347	2.9	4,086,380	13.8	2,540,856	12.7
Deferred income taxes	92,696	0.3	36,047	0.1	251,135	0.8	53,732	0.3
Other	267,088	0.9	178,114	0.5	753,345	2.5	74,974	0.4
Total liabilities	19,878,363	69.7	27,248,139	77.7	16,820,636	56.7	12,632,034	62.9
Minority interests	52,319	0.2	87,853	0.3	1,594	0.0	17,190	0.1
Net worth:								
Common stock, par value	249,248	0.9	278,706	0.8	216,812	0.7	212,501	1.1
Preferred stock, stated value	51,364	0.2	66,873	0.2	21,791	0.1	54,382	0.3
Additional paid-in capital	1,710,667	6.0	807,330	2.3	2,607,183	8.8	2,491,870	12.4
Retained earnings	6,301,571	22.1	6,161,714	17.6	9,729,729	32.8	4,526,655	22.6
Treasury stock	(308,553)	(1.1)	(194,700)	(0.6)	(445,208)	(1.5)	(398,316)	(2.0)
Excess value of marketable securities	(2,350)	(0.0)	(11,824)	(0.0)	(7,747)	(0.0)	14,863	0.1
Other equity	597,761	2.1	621,674	1.8	735,259	2.5	517,181	2.6
Total net worth	8,599,707	30.1	7,729,774	22.0	12,857,819	43.3	7,419,137	37.0
Total liabilities and net worth	$ 28,530,389	100.0 %	$ 35,065,766	100.0 %	$ 29,680,050	100.0 %	$ 20,068,362	100.0 %

CFMA Comparative Financial Data

Statement of Earnings
Most Recent Year End

	All Companies		Industrial & Nonresidential		Heavy & Highway		Specialty Trades	
	Amount	Percent	Amount	Percent	Amount	Percent	Amount	Percent
Contract revenue	$ 83,780,270	98.3 %	$ 118,497,807	99.7 %	$ 66,386,501	95.5 %	$ 51,508,539	97.5 %
Other revenue	1,457,696	1.7	415,660	0.3	3,153,627	4.5	1,326,467	2.5
Total Revenue	85,237,965	100.0	118,913,467	100.0	69,540,128	100.0	52,835,006	100.0
Contract cost	(76,869,320)	(90.2)	(111,882,899)	(94.1)	(59,253,894)	(85.2)	(43,951,220)	(83.2)
Other cost	(1,094,886)	(1.3)	(241,639)	(0.2)	(2,682,179)	(3.9)	(842,768)	(1.6)
Total cost	(77,964,206)	(91.5)	(112,124,538)	(94.3)	(61,936,072)	(89.1)	(44,793,988)	(84.8)
Gross Profit	7,273,759	8.5	6,788,929	5.7	7,604,056	10.9	8,041,018	15.2
Selling, general & administrative expenses:								
Payroll	(2,726,107)	(3.2)	(2,452,779)	(2.1)	(2,399,420)	(3.5)	(3,441,205)	(6.5)
Professional fees	(161,957)	(0.2)	(150,337)	(0.1)	(164,045)	(0.2)	(180,477)	(0.3)
Sales & marketing costs	(192,417)	(0.2)	(230,437)	(0.2)	(67,251)	(0.1)	(219,490)	(0.4)
Technology costs	(138,340)	(0.2)	(147,531)	(0.1)	(109,756)	(0.2)	(150,760)	(0.3)
Administrative bonuses	(425,232)	(0.5)	(439,973)	(0.4)	(378,171)	(0.5)	(462,964)	(0.9)
Other	(1,840,797)	(2.2)	(1,710,143)	(1.4)	(1,711,825)	(2.5)	(2,218,107)	(4.2)
Total SG&A expenses	(5,484,849)	(6.4)	(5,131,199)	(4.3)	(4,830,467)	(6.9)	(6,673,003)	(12.6)
Income from operations	1,788,910	2.1	1,657,730	1.4	2,773,589	4.0	1,368,014	2.6
Interest income	142,767	0.2	228,460	0.2	122,920	0.2	42,716	0.1
Interest expense	(156,372)	(0.2)	(75,885)	(0.1)	(263,474)	(0.4)	(197,239)	(0.4)
Other income / (expense), net	(38,740)	(0.0)	70,668	0.1	93,053	0.1	(292,782)	(0.6)
Net earnings / (loss) before income taxes	1,736,565	2.0	1,880,973	1.6	2,726,089	3.9	920,709	1.7
Income tax (expense) / benefit	(272,990)	(0.3)	(256,027)	(0.2)	(505,747)	(0.7)	(151,135)	(0.3)
Net earnings	$ 1,463,575	1.7	$ 1,624,945	1.4	$ 2,220,342	3.2	$ 769,574	1.5

Number of Participants

	All Companies	Industrial & Nonresidential	Heavy & Highway	Specialty Trades
	Number	Number	Number	Number
2003	575	256	123	179
2002	546	238	105	165

CFMA Comparative Financial Data

Financial Ratios
Most Recent Year End

	All Companies		Industrial & Nonresidential		Heavy & Highway		Specialty Trades	
	Average	Median	Average	Median	Average	Median	Average	Median
Liquidity Ratios								
Current Ratio	1.3	1.4	1.2	1.3	1.6	1.5	1.6	1.6
Quick Ratio	1.2	1.2	1.1	1.2	1.3	1.3	1.4	1.3
Days of Cash	17.7	12.2	19.2	17.6	21.5	13.1	9.9	4.5
Working Capital Turnover	14.5	13.4	21.4	18.1	10.7	10.5	8.4	9.3
Profitability Ratios								
Return on Assets	5.1 %	4.4 %	4.6 %	4.0 %	7.5 %	5.1 %	3.8 %	4.5 %
Return on Equity	17.0 %	14.4 %	21.0 %	17.0 %	17.3 %	11.7 %	10.4 %	13.9 %
Times Interest Earned	12.1	6.3	25.8	11.8	11.3	5.9	5.7	4.5
Leverage Ratios								
Debt to Equity	2.3	2.0	3.5	2.9	1.3	1.5	1.7	1.5
Revenue to Equity	9.9	9.6	15.4	14.6	5.4	6.0	7.1	7.5
Asset Turnover	3.0	3.2	3.4	3.7	2.3	2.4	2.6	3.0
Fixed Asset Ratio	38.8 %	29.0 %	25.2 %	22.0 %	67.6 %	66.1 %	23.2 %	27.8 %
Equity to SG&A Expense	1.6	1.2	1.5	1.2	2.7	2.0	1.1	0.9
Underbillings to Equity	16.2 %	11.6 %	17.2 %	10.7 %	9.4 %	8.2 %	22.3 %	17.4 %
Backlog to Equity	5.6	3.4	3.4	6.6	4.0	1.8	8.2	2.2
Efficiency Ratios								
Backlog to Working Capital	8.2	4.9	4.8	8.6	7.9	4.4	9.7	2.8
Months in Backlog	6.8	4.8	2.7	5.8	8.9	4.5	13.8	3.8
Days in Accounts Receivable	47.9	49.7	43.7	43.2	42.7	42.9	66.6	61.6
Days in Inventory	1.6	0.0	0.5	0.0	4.1	0.0	2.6	1.8
Days in Accounts Payable	39.4	32.9	45.3	40.0	25.0	25.2	32.4	26.0
Operating Cycle	27.7	32.3	18.1	22.8	43.3	39.8	46.8	43.5

THE BANK ONE CONSUMER AND DIVERSIFIED FINANCE COMPANY RATIOS

Bank One Consumer and Diversified Finance Company Ratios	Consumer Sector		Diversified Sector	
	2002	2001	2002	2001
Assets				
Average Owned Receivables	25,074	26,059	56,654	42,254
Average Managed Receivables	31,845	26,458	84,073	55,748
Average Managed Assets	34,602	27,908	110,106	78,652
Consumer Real Estate Receivables / Total Receivables	45.9%	44.0%	4.8%	3.9%
Other Consumer Receivables / Total Receivables	40.1%	37.9%	11.3%	10.5%
Retail Contract Receivables / Total Receivables	13.2%	13.3%	35.6%	38.5%
Commercial Receivables / Total Receivables	8.8%	4.8%	43.8%	47.1%
Asset Quality				
Consumer Delinquencies (60+ Days) / Total Receivables	4.10%	3.75%	2.57%	2.86%
Commercial Delinquencies (60+ Days) / Total Receivables	5.40%	6.70%	1.83%	2.57%
Reserve for Losses / Total Receivables	5.35%	4.74%	2.08%	1.78%
Loss Provision / Average Receivables	4.27%	3.70%	1.14%	0.96%
Net Charge-Offs / Average Receivables	4.60%	4.15%	0.83%	0.74%
Reserve for Losses / Net Charge-Offs	1.22	1.28	1.79	2.08
Recoveries / Gross Charge-Offs	10.43%	12.45%	10.55%	14.05%
Leverage				
Short-term Debt / Total Senior Debt	41.52%	43.66%	35.72%	45.74%
Total Debt / Net Worth + Loss Reserves	4.36	4.48	6.09	5.92
Managed Debt / Net Worth + Loss Reserves	5.88	5.46	8.61	7.57
Subordinated Term Debt / Capital Funds	0.37%	0.39%	1.00%	5.11%
Owned Receivables Net of Reserves / Senior Debt	0.96	1.00	0.88	1.01
Managed Receivables Net of Reserves / Managed Debt	0.99	1.01	0.91	1.00
Managed Assets / Managed Debt	1.19	1.23	1.24	1.35
Earnings				
Gross Finance Revenue / Average Managed Receivables	14.14%	15.43%	9.95%	10.81%
Gross Revenue / Average Managed Assets	13.10%	14.40%	9.27%	10.96%
Operating Expenses / Total Revenues	36.04%	34.24%	19.68%	18.10%
Operating Expenses / Average Managed Assets	4.26%	4.60%	1.93%	2.07%
Interest Expense / Average Owned Receivables	3.31%	5.49%	4.57%	5.50%
Int. and Depreciation Exp. / Avg. Owned Rec. + Operating Leases	na	na	7.13%	8.27%
Interest Expense / Avg. Total Consolidated Debt	4.85%	5.90%	3.99%	5.23%
Consolidated Net Income / Average Managed Assets	1.34%	1.02%	1.08%	1.30%
Consolidated Net Income / Average Net Worth	12.25%	9.31%	10.07%	12.39%
Dividends / Consolidated Net Income	24.26%	59.66%	42.75%	37.29%
Interest Coverage Ratio (EBIT / Interest Expense)	1.46	1.35	1.65	1.64

TEXT—KEY WORD INDEX
OF INDUSTRIES APPEARING
IN THE STATEMENT STUDIES

STATEMENT STUDIES KEY WORD INDEX

A complete description of each industry category listed below begins on page 29.

STATEMENT STUDIES KEY WORD INDEX

A complete description of each industry category listed below begins on page 29.

STATEMENT STUDIES KEY WORD INDEX

A complete description of each industry category listed below begins on page 29.

STATEMENT STUDIES KEY WORD INDEX

A complete description of each industry category listed below begins on page 29.

STATEMENT STUDIES KEY WORD INDEX

A complete description of each industry category listed below begins on page 29.

Radio Stations, 1046, 1047, info

Radio, Television, and Other Electronics Stores, 876, 877, rtl

Railroad Rolling Stock Manufacturing, 656, 657, mfg

Ready-Mix Concrete Manufacturing, 424, 425, mfg

Real Estate Credit, 1068, 1069, fin

Real Estate Investment Trusts, 1098, 1099, fin

Recreational and Vacation Camps (except Campgrounds), 1356, 1357, rest/lodg

Recreational Vehicle Dealers, 856, 857, rtl

Recyclable Material Merchant Wholesalers, 780, 781, wsle

Refrigerated Warehousing and Storage, 1018, 1019, trans

Refrigeration Equipment and Supplies Merchant Wholesalers, 762, 763, wsle

Relay and Industrial Control Manufacturing, 632, 633, mfg

Religious Organizations, 1406, 1407, other

Rendering and Meat Byproduct Processing, 236, 237, mfg

Research and Development in the Physical, Engineering, and Life Sciences, 1172, 1173, prof serv

Residential Electric Lighting Fixture Manufacturing, 620, 621, mfg

Residential Mental Health and Substance Abuse Facilities, 1304, 1305, HC

Residential Property Managers, 1114, 1115, R/E

Retail Bakeries, 242, 243, mfg

Rolled Steel Shape Manufacturing, 438, 439, mfg

Roofing Contractors, 188, 189, cons-g

Roofing Contractors, 1457, cons-%

Roofing, Siding, and Insulation Material Merchant Wholesalers, 728, 729, wsle

Rubber and Plastics Hoses and Belting Manufacturing, 414, 415, mfg

Rubber Product Manufacturing for Mechanical Use, 416, 417, mfg

RV (Recreational Vehicle) Parks and Campgrounds, 1354, 1355, rest/lodg

S

Sales Financing, 1064, 1065, fin

Sawmills, 306, 307, mfg

Scenic and Sightseeing Transportation, Water, 994, 995, trans

Scheduled Passenger Air Transportation, 968, 969, trans

School and Employee Bus Transportation, 988, 989, trans

Search, Detection, Navigation, Guidance, Aeronautical, and Nautical System and Instrument Manufacturing, 606, 607, mfg

Secondary Smelting, Refining, and Alloying of Nonferrous Metal (except Copper and Aluminum), 448, 449, mfg

Securities Brokerage, 1076, 1077, fin

Security Guards and Patrol Services, 1224, 1225, Admin

Security Systems Services (except Locksmiths), 1226, 1227, Admin

Semiconductor and Related Device Manufacturing, 596, 597, mfg

Service Establishment Equipment and Supplies Merchant Wholesalers, 772, 773, wsle

Setup Paperboard Box Manufacturing, 336, 337, mfg

Sheet Metal Work Manufacturing, 478, 479, mfg

Shellfish Fishing, 126, 127, ag

Ship Building and Repairing, 658, 659, mfg

Shoe Stores, 926, 927, rtl

Showcase, Partition, Shelving, and Locker Manufacturing, 676, 677, mfg

Sign Manufacturing, 700, 701, mfg

Site Preparation Contractors, 206, 207, cons-g

Site Preparation Contractors, 1464, cons-%

Soap and Other Detergent Manufacturing, 392, 393, mfg

Soft Drink Manufacturing, 258, 259, mfg

Software Publishers, 1036, 1037, info

Soil Preparation, Planting, and Cultivating, 130, 131, ag

Solid Waste Collection, 1240, 1241, Admin

Solid Waste Landfill, 1242, 1243, Admin

Sound Recording Studios, 1044, 1045, info

Special Die and Tool, Die Set, Jig, and Fixture Manufacturing, 554, 555, mfg

Specialized Freight (except Used Goods) Trucking, Local, 982, 983, trans

Specialized Freight (except Used Goods) Trucking, Long-Distance, 984, 985, trans

Specialty (except Psychiatric and Substance Abuse) Hospitals, 1300, 1301, HC

Speed Changer, Industrial High-Speed Drive, and Gear Manufacturing, 560, 561, mfg

Sporting and Athletic Goods Manufacturing, 696, 697, mfg

Sporting and Recreational Goods and Supplies Merchant Wholesalers, 776, 777, wsle

Sporting Goods Stores, 930, 931, rtl

Sports Teams and Clubs, 1326, 1327, ent

Spring (Light Gauge) Manufacturing, 484, 485, mfg

Stationery and Office Supplies Merchant Wholesalers, 788, 789, wsle

Steel Foundries (except Investment), 452, 453, mfg

Steel Wire Drawing, 440, 441, mfg

Structural Steel and Precast Concrete Contractors, 182, 183, cons-g

Structural Steel and Precast Concrete Contractors, 1454, cons-%

Supermarkets and Other Grocery (except Convenience) Stores, 892, 893, rtl

Support Activities for Animal Production, 134, 135, ag

Support Activities for Oil and Gas Operations, 150, 151, mng

Support Activities for Oil and Gas Operations, 1444, cons-%

Surgical and Medical Instrument Manufacturing, 682, 683, mfg

Surgical Appliance and Supplies Manufacturing, 684, 685, mfg

Surveying and Mapping (except Geophysical) Services, 1152, 1153, prof serv

Switchgear and Switchboard Apparatus Manufacturing, 630, 631, mfg

T

Taxi Service, 986, 987, trans

Telephone Apparatus Manufacturing, 584, 585, mfg

Television Broadcasting, 1048, 1049, info

Temporary Help Services, 1210, 1211, Admin

Testing Laboratories, 1154, 1155, prof serv

Textile Machinery Manufacturing, 528, 529, mfg

Theater Companies and Dinner Theaters, 1322, 1323, ent

Tile and Terrazzo Contractors, 202, 203, cons-g

Timber Tract Operations, 120, 121, ag

Tire and Tube Merchant Wholesalers, 716, 717, wsle

Tire Dealers, 866, 867, rtl

Tire Retreading, 412, 413, mfg

Title Abstract and Settlement Offices, 1142, 1143, prof serv

Tobacco and Tobacco Product Merchant Wholesalers, 844, 845, wsle

Tobacco Stores, 952, 953, rtl

Toilet Preparation Manufacturing, 396, 397, mfg

Totalizing Fluid Meter and Counting Device Manufacturing, 612, 613, mfg

Tour Operators, 1220, 1221, Admin

Toy and Hobby Goods and Supplies Merchant Wholesalers, 778, 779, wsle

Tradebinding and Related Work, 360, 361, mfg

Transportation Equipment and Supplies (except Motor Vehicle) Merchant Wholesalers, 774, 775, wsle

Travel Agencies, 1218, 1219, Admin

Travel Trailer and Camper Manufacturing, 644, 645, mfg

Tree Nut Farming, 102, 103, ag

Truck Trailer Manufacturing, 642, 643, mfg

Truck, Utility Trailer, and RV (Recreational Vehicle) Rental and Leasing, 1122, 1123, R/E

Truss Manufacturing, 312, 313, mfg

Trust, Fiduciary, and Custody Activities, 1084, 1085, fin

U

Unsupported Plastics Film and Sheet (except Packaging) Manufacturing, 400, 401, mfg

Unsupported Plastics Profile Shape Manufacturing, 402, 403, mfg

Upholstered Household Furniture Manufacturing, 666, 667, mfg

Used Car Dealers, 854, 855, rtl

Used Merchandise Stores, 948, 949, rtl

V

Vending Machine Operators, 958, 959, rtl

Veterinary Services, 1192, 1193, prof serv

Video Tape and Disc Rental, 1126, 1127, R/E

Vocational Rehabilitation Services, 1316, 1317, HC

Voluntary Health Organizations, 1408, 1409, other

W

Warm Air Heating and Air-Conditioning Equipment and Supplies Merchant Wholesalers, 760, 761, wsle

Water and Sewer Line and Related Structures Construction, 172, 173, cons-g

Water and Sewer Line and Related Structures Construction, 1449, cons-%

Water Supply and Irrigation Systems, 158, 159, util

Welding and Soldering Equipment Manufacturing, 572, 573, mfg

Wheat Farming, 86, 87, ag

Wine and Distilled Alcoholic Beverage Merchant Wholesalers, 836, 837, wsle

Wineries, 264, 265, mfg

Wired Telecommunications Carriers, 1052, 1053, info

Women's Clothing Stores, 918, 919, rtl

Women's, Children's, and Infants' Clothing and Accessories Merchant Wholesalers, 798, 799, wsle

Women's and Girls' Cut and Sew Blouse and Shirt Manufacturing, 292, 293, mfg

Women's and Girls' Cut and Sew Dress Manufacturing, 294, 295, mfg

Women's and Girls' Cut and Sew Other Outerwear Manufacturing, 298, 299, mfg

Women's and Girls' Cut and Sew Suit, Coat, Tailored Jacket, and Skirt Manufacturing, 296, 297, mfg

Wood Container and Pallet Manufacturing, 320, 321, mfg

Wood Kitchen Cabinet and Countertop Manufacturing, 664, 665, mfg

Wood Office Furniture Manufacturing, 672, 673, mfg

Wood Preservation, 308, 309, mfg

Wood Window and Door Manufacturing, 314, 315, mfg

Y

Yarn Spinning Mills, 266, 267, mfg

NOTES

NOTES

NOTES

NOTES

NOTES

NOTES

NOTES

NOTES

NOTES

NOTES

NOTES

NOTES

NOTES